masculino	**m**	mascul
Márketing	**Marketing**	Market
Matemáticas	**Mat, Math**	Mather
Mecánica	**Mec, Mech Eng**	Mechar Engin
Medicina	**Med**	Medicin
Metalurgia	**Metal, Metall**	Metallurgy
Meteorología	**Meteo**	Meteorology
México	**Méx**	Mexico
masculino y femenino	**mf**	masculine and feminine
masculino, femenino	**m, f**	masculine, feminine
Militar	**Mil**	Military
Minería	**Min**	Mining
Mitología	**Mit**	Mythology
masculino plural	**mpl**	masculine plural
Música	**Mús, Mus**	Music
Mitología	**Myth**	Mythology
nombre, sustantivo	**n**	noun
Náutica	**Náut, Naut**	Nautical
negativo	**neg**	negative
Nicaragua	**Nic**	Nicaragua
Física nuclear	**Nucl Phys**	Nuclear Physics
obsoleto	**obs**	obsolete
Ocultismo	**Occult**	Occult
Ocio	**Ocio**	Leisure
Odontología	**Odont**	Dentistry
Óptica	**Ópt, Opt**	Optics
Panamá	**Pan**	Panama
Paraguay	**Par**	Paraguay
participio pasado	**past p**	past participle
peyorativo	**pej**	pejorative
Perú	**Per**	Peru
lenguaje periodístico	**period**	journalese
Periodismo	**Period**	Journalism
peyorativo	**pey**	pejorative
Farmacología	**Pharm**	Pharmacology
Filosofía	**Phil**	Philosophy
Fotografía	**Phot**	Photography
Física	**Phys**	Physics
Fisiología	**Physiol**	Physiology
plural	**pl**	plural
sustantivo plural	**pl n**	plural noun
poético	**poet**	poetic
Política	**Pol**	Politics
Correo	**Post**	Post
participio pasado	**pp**	past participle
Puerto Rico	**PR**	Puerto Rico
prefijo	**pref**	prefix
preposición	**prep**	preposition
participio presente	**pres p**	present participle
Imprenta	**Print**	Printing
pronombre	**pron**	pronoun
pronombre demostrativo	**pron dem**	demonstrative pronoun
pronombre personal	**pron pers**	personal pronoun
pronombre relativo	**pron rel**	relative pronoun
Psicología	**Psic, Psych**	Psychology
Industria editorial	**Publ**	Publishing
Química	**Quím**	Chemistry
marca registrada	**®**	registered trade mark
Radio	**Rad**	Radio
Ferrocarriles	**Rail**	Railways
República Dominicana	**RD**	Dominican Republic
recíproco	**recípr**	reciprocal
reflexivo	**refl**	reflexive
El Salvador	**Sal**	El Salvador
alguien	**sb**	somebody
inglés de Escocia	**Scot**	Scottish English
Servicios Sociales	**Servs Socs**	Social Administration
singular	**sing**	singular
argot	**sl**	slang
Servicios Sociales	**Soc Adm**	Social Administration
Sociología	**Sociol**	Sociology
Deporte	**Sport**	Sport
algo	**sth**	something
sufijo	**suf, suff**	suffix
Tauromaquia	**Taur**	Bullfighting
Fisco	**Tax**	Tax
también	**tb**	also
Teatro	**Teatr**	Theater
Tecnología	**Tec, Tech**	Technology
lenguaje técnico	**téc, tech**	technical language
Telecomunicaciones	**Telec**	Tele-communications
Textiles	**Tex**	Textiles
Teatro	**Theat**	Theater
Turismo	**Tourism**	Tourism
Transporte	**Transp**	Transport
Televisión	**TV**	Television
no numerable	**U**	uncountable
Unión Europea	**UE**	European Union
no numerable	**uncount**	uncountable
Uruguay	**Ur**	Uruguay
verbo	**v**	verb
verbo auxiliar	**v aux**	auxiliary verb
verbo	**vb**	verb
Venezuela	**Ven**	Venezuela
Veterinaria	**Vet, Vet Sci**	Veterinary Science
verbo intransitivo	**vi**	intransitive verb
Vídeo	**Vídeo, Video**	Video
verbo impersonal	**v impers**	impersonal verb
Vinicultura	**Vin**	Wine
verbo modal	**v mod**	modal verb
verbo pronominal	**v pron**	pronominal verb
verbo reflexivo	**v refl**	reflexive verb
verbo transitivo	**vt**	transitive verb
vulgar	**vulg**	vulgar
Zoología	**Zool**	Zoology

The Concise Oxford Spanish Dictionary

Spanish → English
English → Spanish

Chief editors
Carol Styles Carvajal · Jane Horwood

Fourth edition
Nicholas Rollin

OXFORD
UNIVERSITY PRESS

Great Clarendon Street, Oxford OX2 6DP

Oxford University Press is a department of the University of Oxford.
It furthers the University's objective of excellence in research, scholarship,
and education by publishing worldwide in

Oxford New York

Auckland Cape Town Dar es Salaam Hong Kong Karachi
Kuala Lumpur Madrid Melbourne Mexico City Nairobi
New Delhi Shanghai Taipei Toronto

With offices in

Argentina Austria Brazil Chile Czech Republic France Greece
Guatemala Hungary Italy Japan Poland Portugal Singapore
South Korea Switzerland Thailand Turkey Ukraine Vietnam

Published in the United States
by Oxford University Press Inc., New York

First edition published 1996
Second edition published 1998
Third edition published 2004
Fourth edition published 2009

British Library Cataloguing in Publication Data
Data available

Library of Congress Cataloging in Publication Data
Data available

ISBN 9780199560943 (UK and US English cover edition)
ISBN 9780199560936 (Latin American Spanish cover edition)

10 9 8 7 6 5 4 3 2 1

Typeset in Swift, Arial and Meta
by Interactive Sciences Ltd
Printed in Great Britain by
Clays Ltd, St Ives plc

Preface
Prólogo

This new edition of the *Concise Oxford Spanish Dictionary* draws on the major revision of the highly acclaimed *Oxford Spanish Dictionary*, 2008. The principle sources for the updating of the Oxford Spanish dictionary range are the continuing research into language development carried out at Oxford University Press and the use of sophisticated electronic search techniques to identify new terminology appearing in Internet sources in both Spanish and English. These, together with valuable readers' comments and observations from around the world, have enabled the editors to update and enrich the text in many ways.

The new edition also sees the introduction of some popular features of the *Oxford Spanish Dictionary*. These include a *Guide to effective communication* in Spanish and English. Notes on the life and culture of the Spanish and English-speaking countries of the world are listed alphabetically in the Spanish–English and English–Spanish sides of the dictionary respectively.

We are confident that these improvements will continue to make the *Concise Oxford Spanish Dictionary* an essential tool for all those who need an authoritative, concise, and up-to-date guide to Spanish and English.

The Editors

Para esta nueva edición del *Diccionario Oxford Esencial* se ha hecho uso de la edición completamente revisada del muy elogiado *Diccionario Oxford*, 2008. Las fuentes principales que se utilizan para actualizar toda la gama de diccionarios Oxford en español, son: la continua investigación del desarrollo del idioma que se lleva a cabo en Oxford University Press y el uso de técnicas electrónicas altamente desarrolladas para la identificación de la nueva terminología que aparece en Internet tanto en inglés como en español. Esto, conjuntamente con los valiosos comentarios y observaciones que se reciben de los lectores de todo el mundo, ha permitido a los editores actualizar y enriquecer el texto en muchos sentidos.

La nueva edición también incluye algunas características de mucho éxito del *Diccionario Oxford*, como una *Guía para la communicación eficaz* tanto en inglés como en español. Las notas sobre la vida y cultura de los países del mundo anglosajón e hispanohablante se incluyen alfabéticamente a través del texto del diccionario, en la sección español–inglés e inglés–español respectivamente.

Estamos seguros de que todas estas mejoras al texto seguirán haciendo del *Diccionario Oxford Esencial* una herramienta esencial para todos aquellos que requieran de una guía seria, concisa y actual en el empleo del español y del inglés.

Los Editores

List of contributors
Lista de colaboradores

Fourth edition/Cuarta Edición

Chief Editor/Dirección editorial
Nicholas Rollin

First Edition/Primera Edición

Project direction/Dirección
Michael Clark

Chief Editors/Dirección editorial
Carol Styles Carvajal · Jane Horwood

Senior Editor/Editor
Michael Britton

Editors/Redactores
Ana Cristina Llompart
Haydn Kirnon
Malihe Forghani-Nowbari
Julie Watkins
Victoria Zaragoza
Sarah Gray
Ximena Castillo
Alison Sadler
Enrique González
Margaret Jull Costa
Dileri Borunda Johnston
Jeremy Munday
Carmen Fernández-Marsden
Bernadette Mohan
Stephanie Parker

Contents — Índice

Structure of a Spanish–English entry

1 Headword and Sense Divisions/Vocablo cabeza de artículo y sus distintas acepciones

Headword
Vocablo cabeza de artículo

abreviatura *f* abbreviation

All entries are listed in strict alphabetical order except for compounds
Todos los artículos aparecen en riguroso orden alfabético con la excepción de los sustantivos compuestos

Variant form of headword
Variante del vocablo cabeza de artículo

abrigada *f*, **abrigadero** *m* shelter

Words which, though spelled the same, have different parts of speech
Homógrafos con diferente función gramatical

abstemio[1] **-mia** *adj* teetotal
abstemio[2] **-mia** *m,f* teetotaler*

Abbreviations and acronyms follow the same strict alphabetical order as other headwords
Las abreviaturas y las siglas siguen el mismo orden alfabético que los demás vocablos cabeza de artículo

ACNUR /ak'nur/ *m* (= **Alto Comisionado de las Naciones Unidas para los Refugiados**) UNHCR

a. de C. (= **antes de Cristo**) BC, before Christ

Sense divisions. Letters are used for major divisions, numbers for subdivisions or lesser divisions. Roman numerals (I, II etc) are used for even broader divisions
Divisiones correspondientes a las distintas acepciones. Se utilizan letras para indicar las divisiones principales, números para las subdivisiones de éstas. Los números romanos indican divisiones semánticas aún más amplias

acusación *f*
A 1 (imputación) accusation 2 (Der) charge; **negó la ~** he denied the charges; **formular una ~ contra algn** to bring charges against sb
B (parte): **la ~** the prosecution

A change of part of speech of a verb is marked by a box ■
Todo cambio de categoría gramatical dentro de un verbo se indica con el símbolo ■

adelgazar [A4] *vt* ‹*caderas/cintura*› to reduce; ‹*kilos*› to lose
■ **adelgazar** *vi* to lose weight

afear [A1] *vt* 1 ‹*persona*› to make … look ugly; ‹*paisaje*› to spoil 2 ‹*conducta*› to criticize
■ **afearse** *v pron* to lose one's looks

Compounds appear under the headword which forms their first element. Where there are sense divisions, they appear at the end of the division to which they relate semantically
Los sustantivos compuestos aparecen bajo el vocablo cabeza de artículo que constituye su primer elemento. Cuando existen distintas acepciones aparecen al final de la división a la cual corresponden semánticamente

agente *mf*
A (Com, Fin) agent
(Compuestos)
- **agente artístico/de publicidad** artistic/advertising agent
- **agente de seguros** insurance broker
- **agente de viajes** travel agent

B (frml) (funcionario) employee
(Compuestos)
- **agente de policía** *or* (period) **del orden** police officer
- **agente de tráfico** *or* (Arg, Méx) **de tránsito** ≈ traffic policeman (*in US*), ≈ traffic warden (*in UK*)
- **agente secreto** secret agent

C **agente** *m* (Med, Tec, Ling) agent

agregado -da *m,f*
A (de embajada) attaché
B (Educ) **1** (en Ur) *assistant head of department* **2** (en Esp) senior teacher *o* lecturer
(Compuesto) **agregado -da comercial/cultural** commercial/cultural attaché
C (Col) (arrendatario) sharecropper
D **agregado** *m* (añadido) addition

agujeta *f*
A (Méx) (de zapato) (shoe) lace
B **agujetas** *fpl* (Esp) stiffness; **tengo ~s en las piernas** my legs are stiff

Senses restricted to a particular form of a noun appear in a separate division
Las acepciones limitadas a una de las formas de un sustantivo aparecen bajo una división aparte

2 Grammatical information/Información gramatical

Part of Speech
Función gramatical

abadesa *f* abbess

abalear [A1] *vt* (Andes fam) to shoot

abrebotellas *m* (*pl* ~) bottle opener

Irregular plural form
Plurales irregulares

Every verb has a reference to the verb tables on p. 1473
Cada verbo se remite a la tabla de conjugaciones en la página 1473

absolver [E11] *vt* **1** (Relig) to absolve; **~ a algn DE algo** to absolve sb OF sth **2** (Der) ‹*acusado*› to acquit, find ... not guilty

aburrido[1] **-da** *adj*
A ‹*persona*› **1** [ESTAR] (sin entretenimiento) bored; **estoy muy ~** I'm bored stiff **2** [ESTAR] (harto) fed up; **~ DE algo** tired OF sth, fed up WITH sth; **~ DE + INF** tired of -ING
B [SER] ‹*película/persona*› boring; ‹*trabajo*› boring, tedious

The use of *ser* or *estar* with adjectives is marked when necessary
El uso de *ser* o *estar* con adjetivos se indica donde es necesario

The part of speech *f*‡ indicates a feminine noun that takes the masculine article in the singular
La función gramatical *f*‡ indica un sustantivo femenino usado con el artículo masculino en el singular

alba *f*‡
A (del día) dawn, daybreak; **al rayar** *or* **romper el ~** (liter) at the break of day (liter); **al** *or* **con el ~** at the crack of dawn
B (Relig) alb

aprestar [A1] *vt* **1** (preparar) to prepare **2** ‹*tela*› to size
▪ **aprestarse** *v pron* (*refl*) (frml) **~se PARA algo** to prepare FOR sth; **~se A + INF** to prepare to + INF

Grammatical constructions in which the headword commonly occurs are indicated with the use of small capitals
Las construcciones gramaticales en las que suele aparecer el vocablo cabeza de artículo se destacan mediante versalitas

Syntactical information about the translation is given in parentheses after the translation
La información sintáctica relativa a la traducción aparece en paréntesis después de la traducción

aprovisionamiento *m* (acción) provisioning; (provisiones) supplies (*pl*), provisions (*pl*)

ausentista *adj* absentee (*before n*)

Spanish verbs (or senses of them) which are typically used with the indirect object pronouns me, te, le, nos, os and les
El indicador (+ me/te/le/ etc) señala las acepciones de los verbos españoles en las que éstos se emplean con los pronombres personales de objeto indirecto me, te, le, nos, os y les

antojarse [A1] *v pron (en 3ª pers)*
A (apetecer) (+ *me/te/le etc*): **se me antojó una cerveza** I felt like (having) a beer; **de embarazada se me antojaban las uvas** when I was pregnant, I had a craving for grapes; **hace lo que se le antoja** he does as he pleases; **porque no se me antoja** because I don't feel like it

Pronominal verbs are labeled to indicate whether they are reflexive (refl), reciprocal (recípr), emphatic (enf) or causative (caus)
Los verbos pronominales llevan indicadores que denotan su uso reflexivo (refl), recíproco (recípr), enfático (enf) o causativo (caus)

anudar [A1] *vt* ‹*cordón/corbata*› to tie
■ **anudarse** *v pron* (*refl*) ‹*corbata/pañuelo*› to tie; **con la camisa anudada a la cintura** with her shirt knotted at the waist

■ **anularse** *v pron* (*recípr*): **las dos fuerzas se anulan** the two forces cancel each other out

3 Labels/Indicadores

Sense indicators
Indicadores semánticos

cabezal *m*
A (de un torno) headstock
B 1 (almohada) bolster 2 (de sillón) headrest
C (AmL) (de cama) headboard/footboard
D (AmL) (terminal) terminal
E (Audio, Video) head

Field labels
Indicadores de campo semántico

cápsula *f*
A (Farm) capsule
B (Audio) cartridge
C (Espac) capsule

Regional labels
Indicadores de uso regional

carcacha *f* (Andes, Méx fam) (auto viejo) wreck (colloq), old heap (colloq); (otro aparato) contraption (colloq)

carcamal[1], (Méx, RPl) **carcamán -mana** *adj* (fam & pey) decrepit

Stylistic labels
Indicadores de estilo

cascarrabias[1] *adj inv* (fam) cantankerous, grumpy

casitas *fpl* (Chi fam & euf) (cuarto de baño) bathroom (euph)

casorio *m* (fam & hum): **están de ~** they're at a wedding (colloq)

Regional and stylistic labels of translations
Indicadores de uso regional y de estilo de la traducción

castañuela *f* castanet; ***como unas ~s*** as happy as a clam (AmE) *o* (BrE) a sandboy

cataplasma *f* poultice, cataplasm (tech)

4 Phrases/Ejemplos de uso

Examples (with a swung dash representing the headword)
Ejemplos (la tilde representa el vocablo cabeza de artículo)

desgaste *m* 1 (de ropa, suelas) wear; (de rocas) erosion, wearing away 2 (debilitamiento): **~ físico** debilitation; **indicios del ~ de la dictadura** signs that the dictatorship is weakening

Structure of a Spanish–English entry

Idioms
Modismos

desierto² *m* desert; ***predicar*** *or* ***clamar en el ~*** to preach in the wilderness

diablo² *m*
A (demonio) devil; **este niño es el mismo ~** this child is a real devil; ***como (el*** *or* ***un) ~*** like crazy *o* mad (colloq); ***del ~*** *or* ***de todos los ~s*** *or* ***de mil ~s*** (fam) devilish (colloq); **está de un humor de mil ~s** she's in a devil of a mood (colloq); ***donde el ~ perdió el poncho*** (AmS fam) (en un lugar — aislado) in the back of beyond; (— lejano) miles away (colloq); ***irse al ~*** (fam): **¡vete al ~!** go to hell! (colloq); ***mandar a algn al ~*** (fam) to tell sb to go to hell (colloq); ***mandar algo al ~*** (fam) to pack sth in (colloq); ***tener el ~ en el cuerpo*** to be a devil; ***el ~ las carga*** don't play with guns; ***más sabe el ~ por viejo que por ~*** there's no substitute for experience; ***más vale ~ conocido que ciento*** (Chi) *or* (Arg) ***santo por conocer*** better the devil you know than the devil you don't

Proverbs
Proverbios

Idioms and proverbs appear in bold italics after examples. They are entered at the article corresponding to the first noun in the idiom; where there is no noun, the idiom or proverb appears at the article for the first verb, adjective or adverb.

Los modismos y los proverbios aparecen en negritas redondas después de los ejemplos. Se encuentran en el artículo correspondiente al primer sustantivo del modismo o proverbio respectivo. Cuando el modismo o el proverbio no contiene un sustantivo, aparece en el artículo correspondiente a su primer verbo, adjetivo o adverbio

Ⓢ indicates the use of the headword in signs, notices, warnings, etc
El símbolo Ⓢ indica el uso del vocablo cabeza de artículo en letreros, anuncios, advertencias, etc

duelo *m*
A **1** (dolor) sorrow, grief; (luto) mourning; **estar de ~** to be in mourning; Ⓢ **cerrado por duelo** (AmL) closed owing to bereavement; **~ nacional** national mourning **2** (Esp frml): **el ~** (el cortejo) the cortege; (los deudos) the mourners (*pl*)

5 Translations/Traducciones

Translation
Traducción

ancestro *m* ancestor

andén *m*
A (en estación) platform
B (AmC, Col) (acera) sidewalk (AmE), pavement (BrE)

Regional translations
Traducciones de uso regional

basurero -ra *m,f*
A (persona) garbage collector (AmE), dustman (BrE)

Universally valid translation(s) followed by regional alternative(s)
Traducción universalmente válida seguida de alternativas regionales

batatazo *m* **1** (Andes fam) (golpe de suerte) stroke of luck **2** (Chi) (triunfo inesperado) shock *o* surprise win **3** (Col) (idea genial) stroke of genius, brainstorm (AmE), brainwave (BrE)

Words often used with the headword, shown to help select the correct translation for each context
Palabras que suelen acompañar al vocablo cabeza de artículo y que ayudan a elegir la traducción que corresponde a cada contexto

brusco -ca *adj* **1** ‹*movimiento/cambio*› abrupt, sudden; ‹*subida/descenso*› sharp, sudden, abrupt; **el ~ giro de los acontecimientos** the sudden turn of events **2** ‹*carácter/modales*› rough; ‹*tono/gesto*› brusque, abrupt

Nouns modified by an adjective
Sustantivos calificados por un adjetivo

comunitariamente *adv* ‹*vivir/trabajar*› communally; ‹*luchar*› as a community

Verbs or adjectives modified by an adverb
Verbos o adjetivos modificados por un adverbio

ejecutar [A1] *vt*
A ‹*condenado/reo*› to execute
B ‹*plan*› to implement, carry out; ‹*orden/trabajo*› to carry out; ‹*sentencia*› to execute, enforce; ‹*ejercicio/salto*› to perform; ‹*sinfonía/himno nacional*› to play, perform

Objects of a verb
Complementos de un verbo

emanar [A1] *vi* (frml) **~ DE algo** «*radiación/olor/gas*» to emanate FROM sth (frml), to come FROM sth; «*poder/decisión*» to emanate *o* derive FROM sth (frml)
■ **emanar** *vt* to exude

Subjects of a verb appear in double angled parentheses
Los posibles sujetos de un verbo aparecen entre paréntesis angulares dobles

Where a general translation is not possible, contextualized examples are given, preceded by a colon
Cuando resulta imposible dar una traducción general se dan ejemplos contextualizados precedidos de dos puntos

escucha *f*
A (acción): **los servicios de ~ de la marina** the navy's monitoring services; **permanezcan a la ~** stay tuned
(Compuesto) **escucha telefónica** wire tap (AmE), phone tap (BrE)
B **escucha** *mf* **1** (Mil) scout **2** (AmL) (oyente) listener

españolada *f: movie, etc which presents a clichéd image of Spain*

A definition is provided where no equivalent exists in English
Se da una definición cuando no existe una palabra equivalente en inglés

Additional information to clarify a translation
Acotación que aclara el significado de una traducción

estoque *m* sword (*used for killing bull*)

fiscal[2] **-cala** *m,f*, **fiscal** *mf* ≈ district attorney (*in US*), ≈ public prosecutor (*in UK*)
(Compuesto) **Fiscal General del Estado** ≈ Attorney General (*in US*), ≈ Director of Public Prosecutions (*in UK*)

The sign ≈ is used to indicate approximate equivalence
El símbolo ≈ indica un equivalente aproximado en la lengua de destino

Expansion of an acronym or abbreviation
Expansión de una sigla o abreviatura

FSE *m* (= **Fondo Social Europeo**) ESF

6 Cross-references/Remisiones a otros artículos

An arrow directs the user to another entry with the same meaning or to where a compound or idiomatic expression is to be found
Se utiliza una flecha para remitir al usuario a una variante sinónima o a otro artículo donde aparece un compuesto o un modismo

aburridor -dora *adj* (AmL) ▸ **aburrido**[1] **B**

adosado -da *adj* ~ **A algo**: **estaba ~ a la pared** it was against the wall; **un invernadero ~ a la casa** a greenhouse built onto the house; ▸ **casa**

brujo[2] **-ja** (*m*) warlock; (*f*) witch; *ver tb* **bruja**

'ver tb' directs the user to a headword where additional information is to be found
'ver tb' remite al usuario a otro artículo donde se hallará información complementaria

Estructura del artículo Inglés–Español

1 Vocablo cabeza de artículo, pronunciación y distintas acepciones/Headword, pronunciation, and sense divisions

Vocablo cabeza de artículo. Todos los artículos aparecen en riguroso orden alfabético, a excepción de los verbos con partícula. Los nombres compuestos aparecen agrupados en una sección
Headword. All entries are listed in strict alphabetical order, except for phrasal verbs. Two or more compounds are grouped together

baboon /bæ'buːn || bə'buːn/ *n* babuino *m*

baby: **~-blue** /'beɪbi'bluː/ *adj* (*pred* ~ **blue**) azul celeste *or* claro *adj inv*, celeste (AmL); **~ boom** *n* boom *m* de la natalidad

babyish /'beɪbiɪʃ/ *adj* infantil

La transcripción fonética aparece inmediatamente después del vocablo cabeza de artículo respectivo [ver página xxi]
Pronunciation is shown immediately after the headword [see p. xxi]

Cuando la pronunciación británica difiere de la norteamericana, la variante británica aparece precedida por barras verticales
Vertical lines indicate British English pronunciation, always shown if different from the American pronunciation

backless /'bækləs || 'bæklɪs/ *adj* sin espalda

bait¹ /beɪt/ *n* [u] cebo *m*, carnada *f*; ***to rise to the*** ~ picar*, morder* el anzuelo

bait² *vt*

A ‹*hook/trap*› cebar

B (persecute, torment) acosar

Homógrafos con diferente función gramatical
Words which, though spelled the same, have different parts of speech

Variante del vocablo cabeza de artículo
Variant form of a headword

bandanna, bandana /'bæn'dænə/ *n* pañuelo *m* (*de colores*)

B & B /'biːən'biː/ *n* = **bed and breakfast**

Las abreviaturas y las siglas siguen el mismo orden alfabético que los demás vocablos cabeza de artículo
Abbreviations and acronyms follow the same strict alphabetical order as other headwords

Divisiones correspondientes a las distintas acepciones. Se utilizan letras para indicar las divisiones principales y números para las subdivisiones de éstas. Los números romanos indican divisiones semánticas aún más amplias
Sense divisions. Numbers are used for major divisions, letters for subdivisions or lesser divisions. Roman numerals [I, II etc] are used for broader divisions

beauty /'bju:ti/ *n* (*pl* **-ties**)
A **1** [u] (quality) belleza *f*, hermosura *f*; **~ *is in the eye of the beholder*** todo es según el color del cristal con que se mira; (*before n*) **~ contest** *o* (esp AmE) **pageant** concurso *m* de belleza; **~ queen** reina *f* de la belleza **2** [c] (advantage) (colloq): **the ~ of the plan is that ...** lo bueno del plan es que ...
B [c] **1** (woman) belleza *f*, beldad *f*; **B~ and the Beast** la Bella y la Bestia **2** (fine specimen) (colloq) preciosidad *f*, preciosura *f* (AmL), maravilla *f*

bend[1] /bend/ *n* **1** (in road, river) curva *f*; **to take a ~** tomar *or* (esp Esp) coger* una curva; ***to be round the ~*** (esp BrE colloq) estar* chiflado (fam); **I'm going round the ~** me estoy volviendo loco; **that noise is driving me round the ~** ese ruido me está volviendo loco **2** **bends** *pl* **the ~s** la enfermedad del buzo

Si el plural de un sustantivo tiene un significado especial, éste aparece bajo una división aparte
A plural form with a different meaning appears in a division of its own

(before n) señala el uso de un sustantivo con función adjetival
(before n) introduces uses of a noun as a modifier of other nouns

Bermuda /bər'mju:də ‖ bə'mju:də/ *n* las (islas) Bermudas; (*before n*) **~ shorts** bermudas *fpl*; **the ~ Triangle** el triángulo de las Bermudas

blast[2] *vt*
A **1** (blow) ‹*rock*› volar*; **they used dynamite to ~ the safe open** usaron dinamita para volar *or* hacer saltar la caja fuerte **2** (shoot) (journ) acribillar **3** (attack) (journ) atacar*, arremeter contra
B (expressing annoyance) (esp BrE colloq): **~ it!** ¡maldición! (fam); **~ the exam!** ¡al diablo con el examen!

Phrasal verbs
• **blast off** [v ▸ adv] despegar*
• **blast out** [v ▸ prep ▸ o] ‹*message*› emitir a todo volumen; ‹*music*› tocar* a todo lo que da (fam)

Los verbos con partícula aparecen al final del artículo correspondiente, precedidos por el símbolo •
Phrasal verbs appear at the end of the root word entry and are marked by the symbol •

Todo cambio de categoría gramatical de un verbo se indica con el símbolo ■
A change of part of speech of a verb is marked by a box ■

blink[2] *vi* «*eye/person*» pestañear, parpadear; «*light*» parpadear; **if you ~, you'll miss it!** (colloq & hum) si te descuidas, te lo pierdes
■ **blink** *vt* ‹*eye*› guiñar, picar* (Col); **to ~ back tears** contener* las lágrimas

2 Información gramatical/Grammatical information

Función gramatical
Part of speech

abbot /'æbət/ *n* abad *m*

abbreviate /ə'bri:vieɪt/ *vt* abreviar

baby[3] *vt* **-bies, -bying, -bied** mimar, malcriar*

Inflexiones irregulares
Irregular inflections

baddie, baddy /'bædi/ *n* (*pl* **-dies**) (BrE colloq) malo, -la *m,f* (de la película) (fam)

El comparativo y el superlativo del adjetivo
Comparative and superlative forms of an adjective

baggy /'bægi/ *adj* **-gier, -giest** ancho, suelto, guango (Méx)

bass[1] *n*
A /beɪs/ (*pl* **~es**) (Mus) **1** [u c] (voice, singer) bajo *m* **2** [c] (double bass or bass guitar) (contra)bajo *m*; (*before n*) **~ player** (contra)bajo *mf*, (contra)bajista *mf* **3** [u] (Audio) graves *mpl*

Acepciones numerables [C] y no numerables [U] de un sustantivo
Countable [C] or uncountable [U] senses of a noun

Estructura del artículo Inglés–Español

Las construcciones gramaticales en las que suele aparecer el vocablo cabeza de artículo se destacan mediante versalitas
Grammatical constructions in which the headword commonly occurs are indicated with the use of small capitals

benefit[2] **-t-** *or* (AmE also) **-tt-** *vt* beneficiar
■ **benefit** *vi* beneficiarse; **to ~ FROM sth**: **he didn't ~ much from the experience** no sacó mucho (provecho) de la experiencia; **you will all ~ from the change** todos se van a beneficiar con el cambio

- **block in** [v ▸ o ▸ adv, v ▸ adv ▸ o] (hem in) cerrarle* el paso a
- **block off** [v ▸ o ▸ adv, v ▸ adv ▸ o] ‹*street*› cortar
- **block out** [v ▸ o ▸ adv, v ▸ adv ▸ o] 1 (shut out) ‹*thought*› ahuyentar, borrar de la mente 2 (obstruct) ‹*light*› tapar
- **block up**
A [v ▸ o ▸ adv, v ▸ adv ▸ o] 1 (seal) ‹*entrance/window*› tapiar, cerrar* 2 (cause obstruction in) ‹*drain/sink*› atascar*, tapar (AmL); **my nose is ~ed up** tengo la nariz tapada
B [v ▸ adv] (become obstructed) atascarse*, taparse (AmL)

Fórmulas que demuestran el comportamiento sintáctico de cada verbo con partícula. Señalan las posibles combinaciones de verbo [v], adverbio [adv], preposición [prep] y complemento [o]
Syntactical pattern of phrasal verbs, showing the possible combinations of verb [v], adverb [adv], preposition [prep] and object [o]

Un asterisco señala los verbos de conjugación irregular en la traducción al español
An asterisk indicates an irregular verb in the translation

bloom[2] *vi* ‹‹*plant/garden*›› florecer*; ‹‹*flower*›› abrirse*

3 Indicadores/Labels

Indicadores semánticos
Sense indicators

banger /ˈbæŋər ‖ ˈbæŋə(r)/ *n* (BrE colloq) 1 (sausage) salchicha *f* 2 (firework) petardo *m* 3 (car) (*old* ~) cacharro *m* (fam)

blight[1] /blaɪt/ *n* [u] 1 (Agr, Hort) añublo *m*; (loosely) peste *f* 2 (curse) plaga *f*, cáncer *m*

Indicadores de campo semántico
Field labels

bobby /ˈbɑːbi ‖ ˈbɒbi/ *n* (*pl* **-bies**) (BrE colloq) bobby *m* (*policía británico*)

Indicadores de uso regional
Regional labels

bobbysoxer /ˈbɑːbiˌsɑːksər ‖ ˈbɒbiˌsɒksə(r)/ *n* (AmE colloq) quinceañera *f* (fam), calcetinera *f* (Chi)

Indicadores de estilo
Stylistic labels

Indicadores de uso regional de la traducción
Regional labels of translation

bozo /ˈbəʊzəʊ/ *n* (*pl* **bozos**) (AmE sl & pej) sujeto *m* (pey)

Indicadores de estilo de la traducción
Stylistic labels of translation

brimstone /ˈbrɪmstəʊn/ *n* [u] (arch) azufre *m*; *see also* **fire**[1] **A1**

4 Ejemplos de uso/Phrases

Ejemplos (la tilde representa el vocablo cabeza de artículo)
Examples (with a swung dash representing the headword)

meaning /ˈmiːnɪŋ/ *n* [c u] (of word) significado *m*, acepción *f*; (of symbol, act) significado *m*; **literal/figurative ~** sentido *m* literal/figurado; **work? you don't know the ~ of the word** ¿trabajar? ¡tú no sabes qué significa trabajar!; **if you take** *o* **get my ~** si me entiendes

meat /miːt/ *n* 1 [u c] carne *f*; **cold** *o* **cooked ~s** fiambres *mpl*, carnes *fpl* frías (Méx); ***the ~ and potatoes*** (AmE) lo básico; ***one man's ~ is another man's poison*** lo que a uno cura a otro mata; (*before n*) ‹*product*› cárnico 2 [u] (substance) sustancia *f*, enjundia *f*

Los modismos y los proverbios aparecen en negritas cursivas después de los ejemplos. Se encuentran en el artículo correspondiente al primer sustantivo del modismo o proverbio respectivo. Cuando el modismo o el proverbio no contiene un sustantivo, aparece en el artículo correspondiente a su primer verbo, adjetivo o adverbio
Idioms and proverbs appear in bold italics after examples. They are entered at the article corresponding to the first noun in the idiom; where there is no noun, the idiom or proverb appears at the article for the first verb, adjective or adverb

El símbolo Ⓢ indica el uso del vocablo cabeza de artículo en letreros, anuncios, advertencias, etc
Ⓢ indicates the use of the headword in signs, notices, warnings, etc

menu /ˈmenjuː/ *n* 1 (in restaurant) carta *f*, menú *m* (esp AmL); Ⓢ **set menu** menú de la casa 2 (Comput) menú *m*

5 Traducciones/Translations

Traducción
Translation

amnesty /ˈæmnəsti/ *n* (*pl* **-ties**) amnistía *f*

Traducción universalmente válida seguida de alternativas regionales
Universal Spanish translation followed by regional alternatives

automobile /ˈɔːtəməbiːl/ *n* (esp AmE) coche *m*, carro *m* (AmL exc CS), auto *m* (esp CS), automóvil *m* (frml); (*before n*) **~ industry** industria *f* automotriz *or* del automóvil

Traducción de uso extendido excepto en las regiones que se especifican
Translation used in all areas except those specified

bean[1] /biːn/ *n*
A 1 (fresh, in pod) ▸ **green bean** 2 (dried) frijol *m* *or* (Esp) alubia *f* *or* judía *f* *or* (CS) poroto *m* *or* (Ven) caraota *f*; ***to be full of ~s*** (colloq) estar* lleno de vida; ***to spill the ~s*** descubrir* el pastel, levantar la liebre *or* (RPl) la perdiz 3 (*coffee ~*) grano *m* (de café)

Complementos de un verbo
Objects of a verb

fake[3] *vt* 1 (forge) ‹*document/signature*› falsificar*; ‹*results/evidence*› falsear, amañar 2 (AmE Sport) amagar* 3 (feign) ‹*illness/enthusiasm*› fingir*

Los posibles sujetos de un verbo aparecen entre paréntesis angulares dobles
Subjects of a verb appear in double angled brackets

Palabras que suelen acompañar al vocablo cabeza de artículo y que ayudan a elegir la traducción que corresponde a cada contexto
Words often used with the headword, shown to help select the correct translation for each context

gurgle[1] /ˈgɜːrgəl ‖ ˈgɜːgəl/ *vi* «*water/brook*» borbotar, gorgotear; «*baby*» gorjear

Sustantivos calificados por un adjetivo
Nouns modified by an adjective

grumbling /ˈgrʌmblɪŋ/ *adj* ‹*voice*› quejoso; ‹*person*› gruñón, refunfuñón

Verbos o adjetivos modificados por un adverbio
Verbs or adjectives modified by an adverb

handsomely /ˈhænsəmli/ *adv*
A ‹*illustrated/bound*› magníficamente
B ‹*contribute/reward*› con generosidad *or* esplendidez; ‹*profit*› enormemente
C (with skill) (AmE) ‹*perform*› hábilmente

Estructura del artículo Inglés–Español

Cuando resulta imposible dar una traducción general se dan ejemplos contextualizados, precedidos de dos puntos
Where a general translation is not possible, contextualized examples are given, preceded by a colon

handle[2] *vt*
A [1] (touch): **please do not ~ the goods** se ruega no tocar la mercancía; ⊖ **handle with care** frágil

hp (= **horsepower**) CV, HP

HQ *n* = **headquarters**

Expansión de una sigla o abreviatura
Expansion of an acronym or abbreviation

Se da una definición cuando no existe una palabra equivalente en español
A definition is provided where no equivalent exists in Spanish

impeachment /ɪm'pi:tʃmənt/ *n*: *acusación formulada contra un alto cargo por delitos cometidos en el desempeño de sus funciones*

inch[1] /ɪntʃ/ *n* pulgada *f* (*2,54 centímetros*); **two ~es of rain** dos pulgadas *or* (fam) cuatro dedos de lluvia; **I was within an ~ of getting that job** estuve a un paso *or* en un tris de que me dieran el trabajo; **I've searched every ~ of the house** he buscado hasta en el último rincón de la casa; **he looked every ~ the English aristocrat** de pies a cabeza parecía el típico aristócrata inglés; **she wouldn't budge** *o* **give an ~** no cedió ni un ápice; ***give them an ~ and they'll take a mile*** les das la mano y te toman *or* (esp Esp) te cogen el brazo

Acotación que aclara el significado de una traducción
Additional information to clarify a translation

El símbolo ≈ indica un equivalente aproximado en la lengua de destino
The sign ≈ is used to indicate approximate equivalence

Indian: **~ file** *n* (BrE) **in ~ file** en fila india; **~ giver** *n* (AmE) *niño que regala algo y luego quiere que se lo devuelvan*; **~ ink**, **i~ ink** *n* [u] (esp BrE) ▸ **India ink**; **~ Ocean** *n* **the ~ Ocean** el (Océano) Índico; **~ summer** *n* (in northern hemisphere) ≈ veranillo *m* de San Martín *or* de San Miguel; (in southern hemisphere) ≈ veranillo *m* de San Juan

6 Remisiones a otros artículos/Cross-references

Se utiliza una flecha para remitir al usuario a una variante sinónima o a otro artículo donde aparece un compuesto o un modismo
An arrow directs the user to another entry with the same meaning or to where a compound or idiomatic expression is to be found

inmost /'ɪnməʊst/ *adj* ▸ **innermost**

lark /lɑ:rk ‖ lɑ:k/ *n*
A (Zool) alondra *f*; ***to be up*** *o* ***rise with the ~*** levantarse al cantar el gallo; ▸ **happy A1**

July /dʒʊ'laɪ/ *n* julio *m*; *see also* **January**

'see also' remite al usuario a otro artículo donde se hallará información complementaria
'see also' directs the user to a headword where additional information is to be found

The pronunciation of Spanish

Symbols used in this dictionary

The pronunciation of Spanish words is directly represented by their written form and therefore phonetic transcriptions have only been supplied for loan words which retain their original spelling.

The phonetic symbols used in Spanish pronunciations given in the dictionary are listed below. Each symbol is followed by an example and a brief description of the sound, where possible by approximating it to an English sound. These approximations are intended only as a guide and should not be taken as strict phonetic equivalents.

1 Consonants and semi-vowels

Symbol	Example	Approximation
/b/	**boca** /'boka/ **vaso** /'baso/	English *b* in *bin* but without the aspiration that follows it.
/β/	**cabo** /'kaβo/ **ave** /'aβe/	Very soft *b*, produced with the lips hardly meeting.
/d/	**dolor** /do'lor/	English *d* in *den*. There is no aspiration.
/ð/	**cada** /'kaða/ **arde** /'arðe/	English *th* in *rather.*
/f/	**fino** /'fino/	English *f* in *feat.*
/g/	**gota** /'gota/	English g in *goat.*
/ɣ/	**pago** /'paɣo/ **largo** /'larɣo/	Very soft continuous sound, like /g/ but without the sudden release of air.
/ɹ/	**mayo** /'maɹo/ **llave** /'ɹaβe/	English *y* in *yet.* For regional variants see points 7 and 14 of **General Rules of Spanish Pronunciation**, page xix.
/j/	**tiene** /'tjene/	English *y* in *yet.*
/k/	**cama** /'kama/ **copa** /'kopa/ **cuna** /'kuna/ **que** /ke/ **quiso** /'kiso/ **kilo** /'kilo/	English *c* in *cap* but without the aspiration that follows it.
/l/	**lago** /'laɣo/	English l in lid.
/m/	**mono** /'mono/	English *m* in *most.*
/n/	**no** /no/	English *n* in *nib.*
/ŋ/	**banco** /'baŋko/	English *ng* in *song.*
/ɲ/	**año** /'aɲo/	Like *gn* in French *soigné,* similar to the *ni* in *onion.*
/p/	**peso** /'peso/	English *p* in *spin.*
/r/	**aro** /'aro/ **árbol** /'arβol/	A single flap with a curved tongue against the palate.
/rr/	**rato** /'rrato/ **parra** /'parra/	A rolled 'r' as found in some Scottish accents.
/s/	**asa** /'asa/ **celo** /'selo/ **cinco** /'siŋko/ **azote** /a'sote/	(celo, cinco, azote: Latin-American Spanish) English *s* in *stop.*
/θ/	**celo** /'θelo/ **cinco** /'θiŋko/ **azote** /a'θote/	European Spanish: English *th* in *thin.*
/t/	**todo** /'toðo/	English *t* in *step.*
/tʃ/	**chapa** /'tʃapa/	English *ch* in *church* but without the aspiration that follows it.
/w/	**cuatro** /'kwatro/	English *w.*
/x/	**jota** /'xota/ **general** /xene'ral/ **gigante** /xi'ɣante/	*ch* in Scottish *loch* or German *auch.*
/z/	**desde** /'dezðe/	English *s* in *is.*

2 Vowels

The five Spanish vowels are uniformly pronounced throughout the Spanish-speaking world but none of them corresponds exactly to an English vowel.

Symbol	Example	Approximation
/a/	**casa** /'kasa/	Shorter than *a* in *father.*
/e/	**seco** /'seko/	English *e* in *pen.*
/i/	**fin** /fin/	Between English *ee* in *seen* and *i* in *sin.*
/o/	**oro** /'oro/	Shorter than English *o* in *rose.*
/u/	**uña** /'uɲa/	Between English *oo* in *boot* and *oo* in *foot.*

3 Diphthongs and triphthongs

These are combinations of the above vowels and the semi-vowels /j/ and /w/:

cuando /ˈkwando/
tiene /ˈtjene/
indio /ˈindjo/
fui /fwi/
actuáis /akˈtwajs/

4 The stress mark

When phonetic transcriptions of Spanish headwords are given in the dictionary, the symbol ˈ precedes the syllable that carries the stress:

footing /ˈfutin/

For information about where other words should be stressed, see section **2 Stress** on the next page.

General rules of Spanish pronunciation

1 Consonants

1 The letters *b* and *v* are pronounced in exactly the same way: /b/ when at the beginning of an utterance or after *m* or *n* (**barco** /ˈbarko/, **vaca** /ˈbaka/, **ambos** /ˈambos/, **en vano** /emˈbano/) and /β/ in all other contexts (**rabo** /ˈrraβo/, **ave** /ˈaβe/, **árbol** /ˈarβol/, **Elvira** /elˈβira/).

2 *C* is pronounced /k/ when followed by a consonant other than *h* or by *a*, *o* or *u* (**acto** /ˈakto/, **casa** /ˈkasa/, **coma** /ˈkoma/, **cupo** /ˈkupo/). When it is followed by *e* or *i*, it is pronounced /s/ in Latin America and parts of southern Spain and /θ/ in the rest of Spain (**cero** /ˈsero/, /ˈθero/; **cinco** /ˈsiŋko/, /ˈθiŋko/).

3 *D* is pronounced /d/ when it occurs at the beginning of an utterance or after *n* or *l* (**digo** /ˈdiɣo/, **anda** /ˈanda/, **el dueño** /elˈdweɲo/) and /ð/ in all other contexts (**hada** /ˈaða/, **arde** /ˈarðe/, **los dados** /lozˈðaðos/). It is often not pronounced at all at the end of a word (**libertad** /liβerˈta(ð)/, **Madrid** /maˈðri(ð)/).

4 *G* is pronounced /x/ when followed by *e* or *i* (**gitano** /xiˈtano/, **auge** /ˈawxe/). When followed by *a*, *o*, *u*, *ue* or *ui* it is pronounced /g/ if at the beginning of an utterance or after *n* (**gato** /ˈgato/, **gula** /ˈgula/, **tango** /ˈtaŋgo/, **guiso** /ˈgiso/) and /ɣ/ in all other contexts (**hago** /ˈaɣo/, **trague** /ˈtraɣe/, **alga** /ˈalɣa/, **águila** /ˈaɣila/). Note that the *u* is not pronounced in the combinations *gue* and *gui*, unless it is written with a diaeresis (**paragüero** /paraˈɣwero/, **agüita** /aˈɣwita/).

5 *H* is mute in Spanish, (**huevo** /ˈweβo/, **almohada** /almoˈaða/) except in the combination *ch*, which is pronounced /tʃ/ (**chico** /ˈtʃiko/, **leche** /ˈletʃe/).

6 *J* is always pronounced /x/ (**jamón** /xaˈmon/, **jefe** /ˈxefe/).

7 The pronunciation of *ll* varies greatly throughout the Spanish-speaking world.
(*a*) It is pronounced rather like the *y* in English *yes* by the majority of speakers, who do not distinguish between the pronunciation of *ll* and that of *y* (e.g. between *haya* and *halla*). The sound is pronounced slightly more emphatically when at the beginning of an utterance.
(*b*) In some areas, particularly Bolivia, parts of Peru and Castile in Spain, the distinction between *ll* and *y* has been preserved. In these areas *ll* is pronounced with the tongue against the palate, the air escaping through narrow channels on either side. (The nearest sound in English would be that of *lli* in *million*).
(*c*) In the River Plate area *ll* is pronounced /ʒ/ (as in English *measure*), with some speakers using a sound which tends toward /ʃ/ (as in *shop*).
When phonetic transcriptions of Spanish headwords containing *ll* are given in the dictionary, the symbol /ɹ/ is used to represent the range of pronunciations described above.

8 *Ñ* is always pronounced /ɲ/.

9 *Q* is always followed by *ue* or *ui*. It is pronounced /k/, and the *u* is silent (**quema** /ˈkema/, **quiso** /ˈkiso/).

10 *R* is pronounced /r/ when it occurs between vowels or in syllable-final position (**aro** /ˈaro/, **horma** /ˈorma/, **barco** /ˈbarko/, **cantar** /kanˈtar/). It is pronounced /rr/ when in initial position (**rama** /ˈrrama/, **romper** /rromˈper/). The double consonant *rr* is always pronounced /rr/.

11 *S* is pronounced /s/ but it is aspirated in many dialects of Spanish when it occurs in syllable-final position (**hasta** /ˈahta/, **los cuatro** /lohˈkwatro/). In other dialects it is voiced when followed by a voiced consonant (**mismo** /ˈmɪzmo/, **los dos** /lozˈðos/).

12 *V* see 1 above.

13 *X* is pronounced /ks/, although there is a marked tendency to render it as /s/ before consonants, especially in less careful speech (**extra** /ˈekstra/, /ˈestra/, or in some dialects /ˈehtra/, see 11 above).
In some words derived from Nahuatl and other Indian languages it is pronounced /x/ (**México** /ˈmexiko/) and in others it is pronounced /s/ (**Xochimilco** /sotʃiˈmilko/).

14 (*a*) When followed by a vowel within the same syllable *y* is pronounced rather like the *y* in English *yes* (slightly more emphatically when at the beginning of an utterance). In the River Plate area it is pronounced /ʒ/ (as in English *measure*), with some speakers using a sound which tends toward /ʃ/ (as in *shop*).

When phonetic transcriptions of Spanish headwords containing *y* are given in the dictionary, the symbol /ɟ/ is used to represent both pronunciations described above.
(*b*) As the conjunction *y* and in syllable-final position, *y* is pronounced /i/.

15 *Z* is pronounced /s/ in Latin America and parts of southern Spain and /θ/ in the rest of Spain.

2 Stress

When no phonetic transcription is given for a Spanish headword, the following rules determine where it should be stressed:

1 If there is no written accent:
(*a*) a word is stressed on the penultimate syllable if it ends in a vowel, or in *n* or *s*:
arma /ˈarma/
mariposas /mariˈposas/
ponen /ˈponen/

(*b*) words which end in a consonant other than *n* or *s* are stressed on the last syllable:
cantar /kanˈtar/
delantal /delanˈtal/
libertad /liβerˈta(ð)/
maguey /maˈɣei/
perdiz /perˈdis/ (in Latin America)
/perˈdiθ/ (in Spain)

2 If a word is not stressed in accordance with the above rules, the written accent indicates the syllable where the emphasis is to be placed:
balcón /balˈkon/
salí /saˈli/
carácter /kaˈrakter/
hágase /ˈaɣase/

It should be noted that unstressed vowels have the same quality as stressed vowels and are not noticeably weakened as they are in English. For example, there is no perceptible difference between any of the e's in *entenderé* or between the a's in *Panamá*.

3 Combinations of vowels

A combination of a strong vowel (*a*, *e* or *o*) and a weak vowel (*i* or *u*) or of two weak vowels forms a diphthong and is therefore pronounced as one syllable. The stress falls on the strong vowel if there is one. In a combination of two weak vowels, it falls on the second element:
cuando /ˈkwando/ (stressed on the /a/)
aula /ˈawla/ (stressed on the /a/)
viudo /ˈbjuðo/ (stressed on the /u/)

A combination of two strong vowels does not form a diphthong and the vowels retain their separate values. They count as two separate syllables for the purposes of applying the above rules on stress:
faena /faˈena/ (stressed on the /e/)
polea /poˈlea/ (stressed on the /e/)

La pronunciación del inglés

La transcripción fonética que sigue a cada palabra cabeza de artículo corresponde a la pronunciación norteamericana de uso más extendido en los Estados Unidos. Se ha incluido la pronunciación británica (precedida por el símbolo ||) únicamente en aquellos casos en que ésta difiere sustancialmente de la pronunciación norteamericana. Ejemplo:

address[1] /'ædres || ə'dres/
induce /ɪn'duːs || ɪn'djuːs/

Se reconoce la validez de muchas variantes regionales, tanto norteamericanas como británicas, pero éstas no se han incluido por razones de espacio.

Los símbolos empleados en las transcripciones son los del Alfabeto Fonético Internacional (AFI). Éstos se enumeran a continuación, seguidos de un ejemplo y una breve aproximación o descripción del sonido que representan. Estas descripciones no siguen criterios fonéticos estrictos.

1 Consonantes y semivocales

Símbolo	Ejemplo		Aproximación
/b/	**bat**	/bæt/	Sonido más explosivo que el de una *b* inicial española.
/d/	**dig**	/dɪg/	Sonido más explosivo que el de una *d* inicial española.
/dʒ/	**jam**	/dʒæm/	Como una *ch* pero mas cercano al sonido inicial de *Giuseppe* en italiano.
/f/	**fit**	/fɪt/	Como la *f* española.
/g/	**good**	/gʊd/	Sonido más explosivo que el de una *g* inicial española.
/h/	**hat**	/hæt/	Sonido de aspiración más suave que la *j* española, articulado como si se estuviera intentando empañar un espejo con el aliento.
/hw/	**wheel**	/hwiːl/	Una /w/ con la aspiración de la /h/ (muchos hablantes no distinguen entre /hw/ y /w/ y pronuncian *whale* de la misma manera que *wail*).
/j/	**yes**	/jes/	Como la *y* española en *yema* y *yo* (excepto en el español rioplatense).
/k/	**cat**	/kæt/	Sonido más explosivo que el de una *c* española en *cama* o *acto*.
/l/	**lid**	/lɪd/	Como la *l* española.
/m/	**mat**	/mæt/	Como la *m* española.
/n/	**nib**	/nɪb/	Como la *n* española.
/n̩/	**threaten**	/'θretn̩/	*n* alargada y resonante.
/ŋ/	**sing**	/sɪŋ/	Como la *n* española en *banco* o *anca*.
/p/	**pet**	/pet/	Sonido más explosivo que el de una *p* española.
/r/	**rat**	/ræt/	Entre la *r* y la *rr* españolas, pronunciado con la punta de la lengua curvada hacia atrás y sin llegar a tocar el paladar.
/s/	**sip**	/sɪp/	Como la *s* española.
/ʃ/	**ship**	/ʃɪp/	Sonido similar al de la interjección *¡sh!*, utilizada para pedir silencio (ver también tʃ).
/t/	**tip**	/tɪp/	Sonido más explosivo que el de una *t* española.
/tʃ/	**chin**	/tʃɪn/	Como la *ch* española.
/θ/	**thin**	/θɪn/	Como la *c* o la *z* del español europeo en *cinco* o *zapato*.
/ð/	**the**	/ðə/	Sonido similar a una *d* intervocálica española como la de *cada* o *modo*.
/v/	**van**	/væn/	Sonido sonoro que se produce con los incisivos superiores sobre el labio inferior.

Símbolo	Ejemplo		Aproximación
/w/	**win**	/wɪn/	Similar al sonido inicial de *huevo*.
/x/	**loch**	/lɑːx/	Como la *j* española.
/z/	**zip**	/zɪp/	s sonora (con zumbido), similar a la del español europeo en *desde*.
/ʒ/	**vision**	/ˈvɪʒən/	Sonido similar al de la *y* o la *ll* del español rioplatense en *yo* o *llave*, o al de la *j* francesa en *je* (ver también /dʒ/).

2 Vocales y diptongos

(El símbolo **:** indica que la vocal precedente es larga)

Símbolo	Ejemplo		Aproximación
/ɑː/	**father**	/ˈfɑːðər/	Sonido más largo que el de una *a* española.
/æ/	**fat**	/fæt/	Sonido que se obtiene al pronunciar una *a* española con los labios en la posición de pronunciar la *e*.
/ʌ/	**cup**	/kʌp/	Sonido más breve que la *a* española y que se pronuncia en la parte posterior de la boca.
/e/	**met**	/met/	Sonido parecido a la *e* española en *mesa*.
/ə/	**ago**	/əˈgəʊ/	Sonido similar al de la *e* francesa en *je* (ver también /əʊ/).
/ɜː/	**fur**	/fɜːr/	Sonido que se obtiene al pronunciar una *e* española con los labios en la posición de pronunciar la *o*.
/ɪ/	**bit**	/bɪt/	Sonido más breve que el de la *i* española.
/iː/	**beat**	/biːt/	Sonido más largo que el de la *i* española.
/i/	**very**	/ˈveri/	Sonido similar al de la *i* española en *papi*.
/ɔː/	**paw**	/pɔː/	Sonido más largo que el de la *o* española.
/uː/	**boot**	/buːt/	Sonido más largo que el de una *u* española.
/ʊ/	**book**	/bʊk/	Sonido más breve que el de la *u* española.

Símbolo	Ejemplo		Aproximación
/aɪ/	**fine**	/faɪn/	Como *ai* en las palabras españolas *aire, baile*.
/aʊ/	**now**	/naʊ/	Como *au* en las palabras españolas *pausa, flauta*.
/eɪ/	**fate**	/feɪt/	Como *ei* en las palabras españolas *peine, aceite*.
/əʊ/	**goat**	/gəʊt/	Como una *o* pronunciada sin redondear demasiado los labios.
/ɔɪ/	**boil**	/bɔɪl/	Como *oy* en *voy, coypu*.
/uə/	**sexual**	/ˈsekʃuəl/	Como una *u* pronunciada sin redondear demasido los labios y seguida de una /ə/.

3 Símbolos adicionales utilizados en la transcripción de sonidos vocálicos británicos

Símbolo	Ejemplo		Aproximación
/ɒ/	**dog**	/dɒg/	Similar a una *o* española.
/eə/	**fair**	/feə(r)/	Como una *e* española seguida de /ə/.
/ɪə/	**near**	/nɪə(r)/	Como una *i* española seguida de /ə/.
/ʊə/	**tour**	/tʊə(r)/	Como una *u* española pronunciada sin redondear demasiado los labios y seguida de /ə/.

4 Acentuación

El símbolo ˈ precede a la sílaba sobre la cual recae el acento tónico primario:

ago /əˈgəʊ/
dinosaur /ˈdaɪnəsɔːr/

El símbolo ˌ precede a la sílaba sobre la cual recae el acento tónico secundario:

blackmailer /ˈblækˌmeɪlər/

A no ser que se indique lo contrario, las palabras cabeza de artículo y palabras compuestas que aparecen con dos acentos primarios se pronuncian con acento inicial secundario en inglés británico.

	Pronunciación norteamericana	Pronunciación británica
fundamental	/ˈfʌndəˈmentl̩/	/ˌfʌndəˈmentl̩/
high-pitched	/ˈhaɪˈpɪtʃt/	/ˌhaɪˈpɪtʃt/

Aa

A, **a** *f* (*pl* **aes**) *(read as /a/) the letter* **A, a**

a *prep*

A [1] (indicando dirección) to; **voy a México/la tienda** I'm going to Mexico/to the shop; **voy a casa** I'm going home; **dobla a la derecha** turn right; **se cayó al río** she fell into the river; **al norte de Toledo** (to the) north of Toledo [2] (indicando posición) at; **estaban sentados a la mesa** they were sitting at the table; **a orillas del Ebro** on the banks of the Ebro; **se sentó al sol** he sat in the sun; **se sentó a mi derecha** he sat down on my right [3] (indicando distancia): **a diez kilómetros de aquí** ten kilometers from here

B [1] (señalando hora, momento, fecha) at; **a las ocho** at eight o'clock; **a los tres años de edad** at the age of three; **¿a qué hora vengo?** what time shall I come?; **a mediados de abril** in mid-April; **hoy estamos a 20** it's the 20th today; **al día siguiente** the next *o* following day; **a la mañana/noche** (RPl) in the morning/at night [2] **al + INF**: **se cayó al bajar del tren** she fell as she was getting off the train; **al enterarse de la noticia** when he learnt *o* on learning the news [3] (indicando distancia en el tiempo): **a escasos minutos de su llegada** (después) a few minutes after she arrived; (antes) a few minutes before she arrived; **de lunes a viernes** (from) Monday to Friday

C (en relaciones de proporción, equivalencia): **tres veces al día** three times a day; **sale a 100 pesos cada uno** it works out at 100 pesos each; **a 100 kilómetros por hora** (at) 100 kilometers per hour; **nos ganaron cinco a tres** they beat us five three *o* (AmE) five to three

D (indicando modo, medio, estilo): **a pie/a caballo** on foot/on horseback; **pollo al horno** roast chicken; **a crédito** on credit; **funciona a pilas** it runs on batteries; **a mano** by hand; **ilustraciones a todo color** full-color illustrations; **a rayas** striped

E [1] (introduciendo el complemento directo de persona): **¿viste a José?** did you see José?; **buscan al asesino** they are looking for the murderer; **no he leído a Freud** I haven't read (any) Freud; [*the personal* **a** *is only used when a specific person or persons are involved*: **necesita una secretaria** he needs a secretary] [2] (introduciendo el complemento indirecto): **le escribió una carta a su padre** he wrote a letter to his father, he wrote his father a letter; **dáselo/dáselos a ella** give it/them to her; **les enseña inglés a mis hijos** she teaches my children English; **le echó (la) llave a la puerta** she locked the door; **suave al tacto** soft to the touch [3] (indicando procedencia): **se lo compré a una gitana** I bought it from *o* (colloq) off a gipsy

F [1] (en complementos de finalidad) to; **fue a preguntar** he went to ask; **a que + SUBJ** to + INF; **los instó a que participaran** he urged them to take part; **voy a que me hagan un chequeo** I'm going to have a checkup [2] (fam) (para): **¿a qué tanto escándalo?** what's all the fuss about?; **¿a qué le fuiste a decir eso?** what did you go and tell him that for?; **a por** (Esp fam): **bajo a por pan** I'm going down for some bread; **¡a por ello!** go for it!

G (señalando una acción que ha de realizarse) **a + INF**: **los puntos a tratar** the points to be discussed; **una idea a tener en cuenta** an idea to bear in mind; **total a pagar** total payable

H [1] (en órdenes): **¡a la cama, niños!** off to bed, children!; **¡a callar!** shut up! (colloq) [2] (con valor condicional) **a + INF**: **a decir verdad** to tell you the truth; **a juzgar por lo que dices** judging from what you say [3] (indicando causa): **a petición del interesado** (frml) at the request of the interested party; **al + INF**: **al no saber idiomas está en desventaja** he's at a disadvantage, not speaking any languages [4] (expresando desafío): **¿a que no sabes qué?** you'll never guess what!; **tú no te atreverías — ¿a que sí?** you wouldn't dare — do you want to *o* a bet? (colloq); **¡a que no puedes!** bet you can't! (colloq)

AA.EE *mpl* = **Asuntos Exteriores**

ábaco *m* abacus

abad *m* abbot

abadesa *f* abbess

abadía *f* (monasterio) abbey; (dignidad) abbacy

abajeño -ña *adj* (Per) from the coastal area

abajo *adv*

A [1] (lugar, parte): **ahí/aquí ~** down there/down here; **en el estante de ~** (el siguiente) on the shelf below; (el último) on the bottom shelf; **la sábana de ~** the bottom sheet; **más ~** further down; **por ~** underneath; **Ⓢ ver el cuadro más abajo** see table below; **la parte de ~** the bottom (part); **~ llevaba un vestido** (esp AmL) underneath she was wearing a dress [2] (en un edificio) downstairs; **los vecinos de ~** the people downstairs [3] (en una escala, jerarquía): **del jefe para ~** from the boss down *o* downward(s); **de 20 años para ~** 20 or under; **de $1.000 para ~** $1,000 or less

(Compuesto) **abajo firmante** *mf*: **el ~ ~/los ~ ~s** the undersigned

B (expresando dirección, movimiento) down; **calle/escaleras ~** down the street/stairs; **tire hacia ~** pull down *o* downward(s)

C **abajo de** (AmL) under; **~ de la cama** under the bed; **no cuesta ~ de un millón** it costs at least a million

D (en interjecciones) down with; **¡~ la dictadura!** down with the dictatorship!

abalanzarse [A4] *v pron*: **se abalanzaron hacia las salidas** they rushed toward(s) the exits; **~ SOBRE algn/algo** to leap ON sb/sth

abalear [A1] *vt* (Andes fam) to shoot

abalorio *m* glass bead

abanderado -da *m,f* [1] (deportista, soldado) standard-bearer; (defensor) champion [2] (Méx) (Dep) linesman

abanderizarse [A4] *v pron* (Chi) to declare one's support

abandonado -da *adj*

A [ESTAR] (deshabitado) deserted

B [ESTAR] ‹*niño/perro/coche*› abandoned

C [ESTAR] (desatendido, descuidado) ‹*jardín/parque*› neglected; **nos tienes muy ~s** you've forgotten us; **tiene a su familia muy abandonada** he hardly spends any time with his family

abandonar [A1] *vt*

A [1] (frml) ‹*lugar*› to leave; **las tropas ~on el área** the troops pulled out of *o* left the area; **abandonó la reunión en señal de protesta** he walked out of the meeting in protest [2] ‹*familia/bebé*› to leave, abandon; ‹*marido/amante*› to leave; ‹*coche/barco*› to abandon; **~ a algn A algo** to abandon sb TO sth; **los abandonó a su suerte** he abandoned them to their fate

B ‹‹*fuerzas*›› to desert; **la suerte me ha abandonado** my luck has run out; **nunca lo abandona el buen humor** his

good humor never deserts him
C 1 ‹*actividad/propósito/esperanza*› to give up; **abandonó la lucha** he gave up the fight, he abandoned the struggle; **~ los estudios** to drop out of school/college 2 (Dep) ‹*carrera/partido*› to retire from, pull out of
■ **abandonar** *vi* (Dep) 1 (antes de la carrera, competición) to withdraw, pull out 2 (iniciada la carrera, competición) to retire, pull out; (en ajedrez) to resign; (en boxeo, lucha) to concede defeat
■ **abandonarse** *v pron*
A (entregarse) **~se A algo** ‹*a vicios/placeres*› to abandon oneself TO sth; **se abandonó al sueño** he succumbed to sleep
B (en el aspecto personal) to let oneself go

abandono *m*
A 1 (frml) (de un lugar): **hicieron ~ del recinto** they vacated the premises; **el capitán ordenó el ~ del barco** the captain gave the order to abandon ship 2 (de una persona) abandonment
(Compuesto) **abandono del hogar** desertion
B (Dep) (antes de la carrera, competición) withdrawal; (iniciada la carrera, competición) retirement; (en ajedrez) resignation
C (descuido, desatención) neglect; **estado de ~** state of neglect; **la dejó en el más completo ~** he left her utterly destitute

abanicar [A2] *vt/vi* to fan
■ **abanicarse** *v pron* to fan oneself

abanico *m*
A (utensilio) fan; **se desplegaron en ~** they fanned out; **puso las cartas en ~** he fanned out his cards
(Compuesto) **abanico de salida** (Inf) fan-out
B (gama) range; **~ salarial** *or* **de salarios** wage scale

abaratamiento *m* (de precios) reduction; **el ~ del petróleo** the fall *o* reduction in the price of oil

abaratar [A1] *vt* ‹*precios/costos*› to reduce; ‹*producto*› to make ... cheaper, reduce the price of
■ **abaratarse** *v pron* «*costos*» to drop, come down; «*producto*» to become cheaper, come down in price

abarca *f* sandal

abarcar [A2] *vt* 1 ‹*temas/materias*› to cover; ‹*superficie/territorio*› to span, cover; ‹*siglos/generaciones*› to span; **la conversación abarcó varios temas** the conversation ranged over many topics; **su reinado abarcó 8 décadas** her reign spanned 8 decades; **el libro abarca desde el siglo XVII hasta nuestros días** the book covers *o* spans from the 17th century to the present day; **desde allí se abarca toda la bahía** all the bay can be seen from there 2 (dar abasto con) ‹*trabajos/actividades*› to cope with; ***quien mucho abarca poco aprieta*** you shouldn't bite off more than you can chew 3 (con los brazos, la mano) to encircle; **abarcó la habitación con una mirada** he took in the whole room at a glance

abarrotado -da *adj* crammed, packed; **~ DE algo** ‹*de gente*› packed *o* crammed WITH sth

abarrotar [A1] *vt* ‹*sala/teatro*› to pack

abarrotería *f* (Méx) grocery store (AmE), grocer's (shop) (BrE)

abarrotero -ra *m,f* 1 (Chi, Méx) (tendero) storekeeper (AmE), shopkeeper (BrE) 2 (Méx pey) (inmigrante) ignorant (Spanish) immigrant

abarrotes *mpl* (AmC, Andes, Méx) (comestibles) groceries (*pl*); (tienda) grocery store (AmE), grocer's (shop) (BrE)

abastecedor -dora *m,f* supplier

abastecer [E3] *vt* to supply; **una zona bien abastecida de agua** an area with a plentiful water supply; **~ a algn DE algo** to supply sb WITH sth
■ **abastecerse** *v pron* **~se DE algo** (obtener) to obtain sth; (almacenar) to stock up WITH sth

abastecimiento *m* supply; **~ de agua** water supply

abasto *m* 1 (aprovisionamiento) supply; ***no dar ~***: **no dan ~ con el trabajo** they can't cope with all the work 2 (provisiones) *tb* **~s** *mpl* basic provisions (*pl*) (*esp foodstuffs*)

abatible *adj* ‹*respaldo*› reclining (*before n*); (hacia adelante) folding (*before n*); **mesa de alas ~s** drop-leaf table

abatido -da *adj* 1 [ESTAR] (deprimido, triste) depressed; **está muy ~ por su muerte** her death has left him very depressed 2 [ESTAR] (desanimado) downhearted, dispirited

abatimiento *m*
A (depresión) depression; (desánimo) despondency, dejection
B (destrucción) destruction

abatir [I1] *vt*
A (derribar) ‹*pájaro/avión*› to bring down; ‹*muro/edificio*› to knock down; ‹*árbol*› to fell; **fue abatido a tiros** he was gunned down
B (deprimir, entristecer): **la enfermedad lo abatió mucho** his illness made him feel very low; **no te dejes ~ por las preocupaciones** don't let your worries get you down
C ‹*asiento*› to recline
■ **abatirse** *v pron*
A (deprimirse) to get depressed
B (frml) **~se SOBRE algo/algn** «*pájaro/avión*» to swoop down ON sth/sb; «*desgracia*» to befall sth/sb (frml); **el caos se abatió sobre el país** the country was plunged into chaos

abdicación *f* abdication

abdicar [A2] *vi* 1 «*soberano*» to abdicate; **~ EN algn** to abdicate IN FAVOR OF sb 2 (frml) (renunciar) **~ DE algo** to abdicate sth (frml); **abdicó de sus derechos** she abdicated her rights
■ **abdicar** *vt* 1 ‹*trono/corona*› to give up, abdicate 2 (frml) ‹*creencias/ideales*› to renounce

abdomen *m* abdomen

abdominal[1] *adj* abdominal

abdominal[2] *m* sit-up

abecé *m*
A (abecedario) alphabet; **¿ya te sabes el ~?** do you know your ABCs (AmE) *o* (BrE) your ABC yet?
B (fundamento, base): **el ~ de algo** the basics of sth

abecedario *m* alphabet

abedul *m* birch

abeja *f* bee
(Compuesto) **abeja obrera/reina** worker/queen bee

abejorro *m* bumblebee

aberración *f* 1 (disparate, extravío) outrage; **robarle a un ciego es una ~** stealing from sb who's blind is outrageous; **es una ~ decir eso** that's an absurd thing to say 2 (Biol, Fís) aberration

aberrante *adj* ‹*conducta*› aberrant

abertura *f* (en general) opening; (agujero) hole; (rendija) gap; (corte, tajo) slit; **queda una ~ entre los dos postigos** there's a gap between the two shutters

abeto *m* fir, fir tree
(Compuestos)
• **abeto blanco** silver fir
• **abeto falso** *or* **rojo** spruce

abiertamente *adv* openly; **se mostró ~ hostil** he was openly hostile.

abierto[1] **-ta** *adj*
A 1 ‹*ventana/boca*› open; **está ~** it's open; **con los ojos muy ~s** with eyes wide open; **no dejes la botella abierta** don't leave the top off the bottle; **un sobre ~** an unsealed envelope; **la carta venía abierta** the letter was already open when it arrived; **los espacios ~s de la ciudad** the city's open spaces 2 [ESTAR] ‹*válvula*› open; **dejaste la llave ~** you left the faucet (AmE) *o* (BrE) tap running *o* on 3 (desabrochado) undone; **llevas la blusa abierta** your blouse is undone 4 ‹*herida*› open; ‹*madera/costura*› split
B ‹*comercio/museo*› open; **estar ~ al público** to be open to the public
C (Ling) ‹*vocal*› open
D 1 [SER] (espontáneo) open; **tiene un carácter muy ~** she has a very open nature 2 (receptivo) open-minded; **~ A algo** open TO sth; **es muy abierta al diálogo** she's very open to dialogue; **estoy ~ a toda sugerencia** I'm open to suggestions
E (manifiesto, directo) open

abierto[2] *m*
A (Dep) open (tournament)
B (Col) (claro) clearing

abigarrado -da *adj* (multicolor) multicolored*, rainbow-colored*; (mezclado, heterogéneo) motley

abismado -da *adj* [1] (absorto) engrossed, lost in thought; **miraban ~s tanta belleza** they were lost in contemplation of so much beauty [2] (sorprendido) amazed, astonished

abismal *adj* enormous, vast

abismante *adj* (Andes) ‹*valentía*› extraordinary; ‹*belleza*› breathtaking ‹*cifra/cantidad*› staggering

abismar [A1] *vt* (Andes) to amaze

■ **abismar** *vi* (Andes): **tiene un desparpajo que abisma** she has an incredible *o* extraordinary nerve (colloq)

abismo *m* abyss; **al borde del ~** on the edge of the abyss; **hay un profundo ~ entre ellos** there's a deep rift between them; **salvar el ~** to bridge the gulf

abjurar [A1] *vi* (frml) **~ DE algo** ‹*de la fé*› to abjure sth; **abjuró de su herejía** he recanted his heresy

ablandamiento *m* [1] (de cera, cuero, agua) softening [2] (de persona) softening [3] (CS) (Auto) running in

ablandar [A1] *vt* [1] ‹*cera/cuero*› to soften; ‹*carne*› to tenderize [2] ‹*persona*› to soften; ‹*corazón*› to melt [3] (CS) (Auto) to run … in

■ **ablandarse** *v pron* [1] «*cera/cuero*» to soften [2] «*persona*» to soften up; «*mirada*» to soften

ablativo *m* ablative

ablución *f* (frml) ablution (frml); **hacer sus abluciones** (frml *o* hum) to perform one's ablutions (frml *or* hum)

ablusado -da *adj* bloused, in the shape/style of a blouse

abnegación *f* self-denial, abnegation (frml); **con ~** selflessly

abnegado -da *adj* self-sacrificing, selfless

abocado -da *adj* [1] (encaminado) **~ A algo**: **un plan ~ al fracaso** a plan doomed to fail *o* to failure; **están ~s a un desastre** they are heading for disaster [2] (AmL frml) [ESTAR] (dedicado) **~ A algo**: ‹*a una campaña/causa*› devoted TO sth

abocarse *v pron* [1] (dirigirse) **~ HACIA algo** to head TOWARD(S) *o* FOR sth [2] (AmL frml) (dedicarse) **~ A algo** to address oneself TO sth; **hemos de abocarnos a esta tarea** we must address ourselves to this task (frml); **se encuentran abocados a la búsqueda de una solución** they are channeling their efforts into seeking a solution

abochornado -da *adj* [1] (avergonzado) embarrassed; **sonrió ~** he smiled uncomfortably [2] (Chi) (Meteo) muggy and overcast

abochornar [A1] *vt* to embarrass

■ **abochornarse** *v pron* [1] (avergonzarse) to feel embarrassed [2] (Chi) (Meteo) to become muggy and overcast

abofetear [A1] *vt* to slap

abogacía *f* law; **ejercer la ~** to practice law

abogado -da *m,f* (en general) lawyer, solicitor (*in UK*); (ante un tribunal superior) attorney (*in US*), barrister (*in UK*)

(Compuestos)

- **abogado -da criminalista** *m,f* criminal lawyer
- **abogado defensor -da defensora** *m,f* defense lawyer (AmE), defence counsel (BrE)
- **abogado del diablo** *m* devil's advocate
- **abogado -da de oficio** *m,f*: *lawyer provided under the legal aid scheme*, public defender (*in US*)

abogar [A3] *vi* (frml) **~ POR** *or* **EN FAVOR DE algn/algo** to defend sb/sth, to champion sb/sth

abolengo *m* ancestry; **de rancio ~** of noble ancestry *o* descent

abolición *f* abolition

abolicionismo *m* abolitionism

abolicionista *mf* abolitionist

abolir [I32] *vt* to abolish

abolladura *f* dent

abollar [A1] *vt* ‹*coche/cacerola*› to dent

■ **abollarse** *v pron* to get dented

abombado -da *adj*

[A] (AmL fam) (atontado) dopey (colloq), dozy (colloq)

[B] (AmS) (en mal estado) ‹*alimento*›: **esta carne está abombada** this meat has gone bad *o* (BrE) is off

[C] ‹*superficie*› convex; ‹*techo*› domed

abombarse [A1] *v pron* (AmS) to go bad, go off

abominable *adj* abominable

abominar [A1] *vt* to detest, abominate (frml)

■ **abominar** *vi* **~ DE algo/algn** (frml) to loathe sth/sb

abonado -da *m,f* (del teléfono, a revista) subscriber; (del gas) consumer, customer; (a espectáculo, transporte) season-ticket holder

abonar [A1] *vt*

[A] ‹*tierra/campo*› to fertilize

[B] [1] (frml) (pagar) ‹*cantidad/honorarios*› to pay; **¿cómo lo quiere ~?** how would you like to pay?; **el cheque se lo ~án en caja** you can cash the check at the cash desk [2] (depositar) to credit; **hemos abonado la cantidad en su cuenta** we have credited your account with the amount [3] (Andes, Méx) (dar a cuenta) to give … on account

[C] (avalar) ‹*hipótesis*› to lend weight to

■ **abonarse** *v pron* **~se A algo** ‹*a espectáculo*› to buy a season ticket FOR sth; ‹*a revista*› to subscribe TO sth

abono *m*

[A] (Agr) fertilizer

(Compuesto) **abono orgánico/químico** organic/chemical fertilizer

[B] (para espectáculos, transporte) season ticket; **sacar un ~** to buy *o* get a season ticket

[C] (frml) [1] (pago) payment [2] (en una cuenta) credit [3] (Andes, Méx) (cuota) installment*

abordaje *m* (Náut) (ataque) boarding

abordar [A1] *vt*

[A] [1] (encarar) ‹*problema*› to tackle, deal with; **el libro aborda temas difíciles** the book deals with *o* tackles difficult subjects [2] (plantear) ‹*tema/asunto*› to raise; **no se abordó el tema del presupuesto** the question of the budget was not raised

[B] ‹*persona*› to approach

[C] (Náut) [1] (chocar con) to collide with; (embestir) to ram [2] «*guardacostas/piratas*» to board

[D] (Méx) «*pasajero*» ‹*barco/avión*› to board; ‹*automóvil*› to get into

■ **abordar** *vi* (Méx) (subir a bordo) to board

aborigen¹ *adj* aboriginal, indigenous

aborigen² *mf* aborigine, aboriginal; **los aborígenes de Australia** (Australian) Aborigines

aborrascarse [A2] *v pron* to become stormy

aborrecer [E3] *vt*

[A] ‹*persona/actividad*› to detest, loathe

[B] ‹*crías*› to reject

aborrecible *adj* ‹*persona*› loathsome, detestable; ‹*objeto*› hideous

aborrecimiento *m* loathing

abortar [A1] *vi*

[A] (Med) (de forma espontánea) to have a miscarriage, miscarry, abort; (de forma provocada) to have an abortion, abort

[B] «*plan/conspiración*» to miscarry

■ **abortar** *vt* ‹*maniobra/aterrizaje*› to abort

abortero -ra *m,f* abortionist

abortista *mf* [1] (partidario) pro-abortionist, pro-choicer (AmE euph) [2] (ilegal) abortionist **~ clandestino** backstreet abortionist

abortivo¹ -va *adj* [1] ‹*método*› abortion (*before n*) [2] ‹*droga*› abortion-inducing

abortivo² *m* abortion-inducing drug

aborto *m*

[A] (Med) (espontáneo) miscarriage; (provocado) abortion

(Compuesto) **aborto terapéutico** therapeutic abortion

[B] [1] (de plan) failure [2] (fam) (persona fea) dog (colloq)

abotagado -da *adj* ‹*cara*› swollen; ‹*cuerpo*› bloated

abotagarse [A3] *v pron* «*cara*» to swell up; «*cuerpo*» to become bloated

abotonadura *f*: **una chaqueta con ~ simple/doble** a single-breasted/double-breasted jacket; **un vestido con ~ atrás** a dress which buttons down the back

abotonar [A1] *vt* to button up, do up

■ **abotonarse** *v pron* ‹*chaqueta/camisa*› to button up, do up

abovedado -da *adj* vaulted

abr. (= **abril**) Apr

abra *f‡* [1] (ensenada) cove, inlet [2] (RPl, Méx) (claro) clearing

a

abracadabra *m* abracadabra

abrasador -dora *adj* burning (*before n*)

abrasar [A1] *vt* 1 (quemar) to burn; **murieron abrasados** they were burned to death 2 «*bebida*» to scald, burn; «*comida*» to burn 3 (liter) «*pasión*» to consume (liter)
■ **abrasar** *vi* «*sol*» to burn, scorch
■ **abrasarse** *v pron* «*bosque*» to be burned (down); «*planta*» to get scorched; **nos abrasábamos bajo el sol** we were sweltering under the sun; **se abrasaba en deseo** (liter) he was aflame with desire (liter)

abrasivo -va *adj/m* abrasive

abrazadera *f* clamp; (redonda) hose clamp, hose clip (BrE)

abrazar [A4] *vt*
A 1 ‹*persona*› to hug; (con más sentimiento) to embrace; **abrázame fuerte** hold me tight 2 ‹*tronco/columna*› to encircle
B (liter) ‹*religión/causa*› to embrace
■ **abrazarse** *v pron* 1 (*recípr*) to hug each other; (con más sentimiento) to embrace each other 2 **~se A algn/algo** to hold on *o* cling TO sb/sth

abrazo *m* hug; (con más sentimiento) embrace; **me dio un ~** he gave me a hug, he hugged/embraced me; **dale un ~ de mi parte** give my love to her; **se fundieron en un cálido ~** (liter) they held each other in a warm embrace; **un ~, Miguel** (en cartas) best wishes, Miguel, regards, Miguel; (más íntimo) love, Miguel

abrebotellas *m* (*pl* ~) bottle opener

abrecartas *m* (*pl* ~) letter opener

abrelatas *m* (*pl* ~) can opener, tin opener (BrE)

abrevadero *m* (pila) (water) trough; (natural) watering hole

abrevar [A1] *vt* to water

abreviación *f* (acción) abbreviation; (texto) abridgment; (Ling) shortening

abreviar [A1] *vt* ‹*permanencia/visita*› to cut short; ‹*plazo*› to shorten; ‹*texto/artículo*› to abridge; ‹*palabra*› to abbreviate
■ **abreviar** *vi*: **abrevia, que se hace tarde** cut it short, it's getting late; **abreviando ...** in short ...

abreviatura *f* abbreviation

abridor¹ -dora *adj* (Dep) starting (*before n*)

abridor² *m* (de botellas) bottle opener; (de latas) can opener, tin opener (BrE)

abrigada *f*, **abrigadero** *m* shelter

abrigado -da *adj* 1 [ESTAR] ‹*lugar*› sheltered; **~ DE algo** sheltered *o* protected FROM sth 2 [ESTAR] ‹*persona*›: **¿estás bien ~ con esas mantas?** are you warm enough with those blankets?; **está demasiado ~** he has too many clothes on; **iba bien ~** he was wrapped up warm 3 [SER] (RPl, Ven) ‹*ropa*› warm

abrigador -dora *adj* [SER] (Andes, Méx) ‹*ropa*› warm

abrigar [A3] *vt*
A (con ropa) to wrap ... up warm; **el pañuelo me abriga el cuello** the scarf keeps my neck warm
B ‹*idea/esperanza*› to cherish; ‹*sospecha/duda*› to harbor*, entertain
■ **abrigar** *vi* «*ropa*» to be warm
■ **abrigarse** *v pron* (*refl*) to wrap up warm; **abrígate el pecho** keep your chest warm

abrigo *m*
A 1 (prenda) coat; **~ de invierno** winter coat 2 (calor que brinda la ropa): **necesita más ~** she needs to be wrapped up more warmly; **con una manta no tengo suficiente ~** I'm not warm enough with one blanket; **ropa de ~** warm clothes; **un raído vestido era todo su ~** (liter) all she was wearing was a threadbare dress
B (refugio, protección) shelter; ***al ~ de algo/algn***: **al ~ de los árboles** sheltered under the trees; **al ~ de la lumbre** by the fireside; **corrió al ~ de su madre** she ran to her mother for protection

abril *m* April; *para ejemplos ver* **enero**; **tenía quince ~es** (liter) she was a girl of fifteen summers (liter)

abrillantar [A1] *vt* to polish

abrir [I33] *vt*
A (en general) to open; ‹*paraguas*› to open, put up; ‹*mapa*› to open out, unfold; ‹*cortinas*› to open, draw back; ‹*persianas*› to raise, pull up; ‹*cremallera*› to undo
B ‹*llave/gas*› to turn on; ‹*válvula*› to open; ‹*cerradura*› to unlock
C 1 ‹*zanja/túnel*› to dig; ‹*agujero*› to make; **le abrió la cabeza de una pedrada** he hit her with a stone and gashed her head 2 ‹*absceso*› to open ... up; ‹*paciente*› (fam) to open ... up (colloq)
D 1 ‹*comercio/museo*› (para el quehacer diario) to open; (inaugurar) to open (up); **¿a qué hora abren la taquilla?** what time does the box office open?; **~ algo al público** to open sth to the public 2 ‹*carretera/aeropuerto*› to open; ‹*frontera*› to open (up) 3 (Com) to open up
E 1 (iniciar) ‹*cuenta bancaria*› to open; ‹*negocio*› to start, set up; ‹*suscripción*› to take out; ‹*caso*› to open; ‹*investigación*› to begin, set up; **el plazo para la presentación de solicitudes se ~á el 2 de junio** applications will be accepted from June 2; **no han abierto la matrícula aún** registration hasn't begun yet 2 ‹*acto/debate/baile*› to open 3 ‹*desfile/cortejo*› to head, lead 4 ‹*paréntesis/comillas*› to open 5 **~ fuego** to open fire
F ‹*apetito*› to whet
G ‹*perspectivas*› to open up; ‹*etapa*› to mark the beginning of; **el acuerdo abre un panorama desolador** the agreement points to a bleak future
H (hacer más receptivo): **le abrió la mente** it made her more open-minded; **~ algo A algo** to open sth up TO sth; **para ~ nuestro país a nuevas tendencias** to open our country up to new trends
■ **abrir** *vi*
A «*persona*» to open up; **¡abre! soy yo** open the door *o* open up! it's me
B «*puerta/cajón*» to open; **esta ventana no abre (bien)** this window doesn't open (properly)
C «*comercio/museo*» to open; **abre de nueve a tres** it opens from nine till three
D «*acto/ceremonia*» to open; (Jueg) to open
■ **abrir** *v impers* (fam) (Meteo): **parece que quiere ~** it looks as if it's going to clear up
■ **abrirse** *v pron*
A 1 «*puerta/ventana*» to open; **~se A algo** ‹*a jardín/corredor*› to open ONTO sth 2 «*flor/almeja*» to open; «*paracaídas*» to open
B 1 (*refl*) ‹*chaqueta/cremallera*› to undo 2 (rajarse) «*madera/costura*» to split; **se cayó y se abrió la cabeza** she fell and split her head open
C 1 (liter) (ofrecerse a la vista) to appear, unfold; **un espléndido panorama se abrió ante sus ojos** the most wonderful view unfolded before their eyes (liter) 2 «*porvenir*» to lie ahead; «*perspectivas*» to open up; **con este descubrimiento se abren nuevos horizontes** this discovery opens up new horizons
D «*período/era*» to begin; **con este tratado se abre una nueva etapa** this treaty marks *o* heralds a new era
E 1 (confiarse) **~se A algn** to open up TO sb 2 (hacerse más receptivo) **~se A algo** to open up TO sth 3 (hacerse más accesible) **~se A algn/algo** to open up TO sb/sth; **China se ha abierto a los extranjeros** China has opened up to foreigners
F (AmL fam) (echarse atrás) to back out, get cold feet

abrochar [A1] *vt* 1 ‹*chaqueta/botón*› to fasten, do up; ‹*collar/cinturón de seguridad*› to fasten 2 (AmL) ‹*papeles*› to staple
■ **abrocharse** *v pron* ‹*chaqueta/botón*› to fasten, do up; ‹*collar*› to fasten; Ⓢ **abróchense los cinturones de seguridad** fasten your seatbelts

abrojo *m* (Bot) burr

abrumador -dora *adj* 1 ‹*victoria/mayoría*› overwhelming 2 ‹*trabajo/tarea*› exhausting; ‹*responsabilidad/carga*› onerous, heavy

abrumar [A1] *vt* to overwhelm; **~ a algn CON algo** ‹*con problemas/quejas*› to wear sb out WITH sth; **la ~on con sus atenciones** she was overwhelmed by their kindness; **estar abrumado de trabajo** to be snowed under with work; **abrumado por las preocupaciones** weighed down with worry

abrupto -ta *adj* 1 ‹*camino/pendiente*› steep; ‹*terreno*› rough 2 ‹*tono*› abrupt 3 ‹*cambio/descenso*› abrupt, sudden

absceso *m* abscess

absentismo *m* (Esp) ▸ **ausentismo**

absolución *f* 1 (Relig) absolution; **dar la ~** to give absolution 2 (Der) acquittal

absolutamente *adv* totally, absolutely; **no se ve ~ nada** you can't see a thing; **~ nadie** not a soul; **es ~ falso** it is utterly untrue; **¿estás segura? — absolutamente** are you sure? — absolutely *o* I'm positive

absolutismo *m* absolutism

absolutista *adj/mf* absolutist

absoluto -ta *adj*
A ‹*monarca/poder*› absolute
B [1] (total) total, absolute; complete; **en la ruina más absoluta** utterly destitute; **tengo la absoluta certeza** I am absolutely convinced [2] **en absoluto** (*loc adv*): **¿te gustó? — en ~** did you like it? — no, not at all; **no lo consentiré en ~** there is absolutely no way I will agree to it; **es un caso en ~ aislado** it is by no means an isolated case

absolutorio -ria *adj*: **un fallo ~** ≈ a verdict of not guilty

absolver [E11] *vt* [1] (Relig) to absolve; **~ a algn DE algo** to absolve sb OF sth [2] (Der) ‹*acusado*› to acquit, find … not guilty

absorbencia *f* absorbency

absorbente *adj*
A ‹*esponja/papel*› absorbent
B ‹*persona*› demanding; ‹*hobby/tarea*› time-consuming; ‹*profesión*› demanding

absorber [E1] *vt*
A [1] ‹*líquido/ruido/calor*› to absorb [2] ‹*tiempo*› to occupy, take up; ‹*recursos/energía*› to absorb; **una actividad que te absorbe totalmente** an activity that takes up all your time and energy
B ‹*empresa*› to take over

absorción *f*
A (de líquido, calor, ruido) absorption
B (Fin) takeover

absorto -ta *adj* engrossed, absorbed; **quedarse ~** to become engrossed in one's thoughts

abstemio[1] **-mia** *adj* teetotal

abstemio[2] **-mia** *m,f* teetotaler•

abstención *f* abstention

abstencionismo *m* abstentionism

abstencionista[1] *adj* pro-abstention (*before n*)

abstencionista[2] *mf* (que se abstiene) *person who abstains*; (que propugna la abstención) pro-abstentionist

abstenerse [E27] *v pron* [1] (en votación) to abstain [2] (frml) (no hacer): **en la duda lo mejor es ~** (fr hecha) if in doubt, don't; **~ DE + INF** to refrain FROM -ING [3] (privarse de) **~ DE algo**: **~ del alcohol** to avoid alcohol

abstinencia *f* abstinence

abstracción *f* (acción) abstraction; (idea abstracta) abstraction (frml), abstract idea; **hacer ~ de algo** ‹*de caso/factor*› to leave sth aside; ‹*del ruido*› to block … out

abstracto -ta *adj* abstract

abstraer [E23] *vt* to abstract
■ **abstraerse** *v pron* **~se DE algo** ‹*de pensamiento/preocupación*› to block out FROM sth

abstraído -da *adj*: **estar ~ en algo** to be absorbed in sth; **lo noté como ~** he seemed rather preoccupied

abstruso -sa *adj* abstruse

absuelto -ta *pp*: *see* **absolver**

absurdo[1] **-da** *adj* absurd, ridiculous; **es ~ que te comportes así** it's absurd of you to behave like this; **lo más ~ de todo es …** the ridiculous thing about it all is …

absurdo[2] *m* (absurdez): **es un ~ que trates de ocultarlo** it's absurd (of you) to try to hide it

abuchear [A1] *vt* to boo

abucheo *m* booing; **fue recibido con un ~** he was booed when he came on

abuelito -ta (*m*) grandpa (colloq), granddad (colloq); (*f*) grandma (colloq), granny (colloq)

abuelo -la *m,f*
A (pariente) (*m*) grandfather; (*f*) grandmother; **mis ~s** my grandparents; **~ paterno/materno** paternal/maternal grandfather; ***como éramos pocos, parió la abuela*** (fam & hum) that is/was all we needed (colloq); ***¡cuéntaselo a tu abuela!*** (fam) pull the other one! (colloq); ***no tener abuela*** (Méx fam) (ser muy bueno) to be incredible; (ser muy malo) to be terrible; ***¡tu abuela!*** (fam): **¿los lavas tú? — sí, tu abuelita** will you wash them? — like hell I will! (colloq)
B (fam) (persona mayor) (*m*) old man, old guy (colloq); (*f*) old woman, old lady; **¡oiga ~!** hey, granddad! (colloq)

abulia *f* extreme apathy, abulia (tech)

abúlico -ca *adj* apathetic

abultado -da *adj* [1] ‹*ojos/vientre*› bulging; ‹*labios*› thick; ‹*cartera*› bulging [2] (abundante) ‹*deuda/suma*› enormous, huge; ‹*porción*› generous; **su abultada ficha personal** his extensive record; **una derrota abultada** (period) a crushing defeat [3] (exagerado) ‹*cifra/cantidad*› inflated

abultar [A1] *vi* [1] (formar un bulto) to make a bulge; **la pistola le abultaba debajo de la chaqueta** the gun made a bulge under his jacket [2] (ocupar lugar) to be bulky; **dóblalo bien para que no abulte** fold it neatly so that it lies flat
■ **abultar** *vt* ‹*cifras/resultados*› to inflate

abundancia *f*
A (gran cantidad) abundance; **la ~ de peces** the abundance of fish; **hay ~ de aves en la región** the area abounds in *o* with bird life; **hay comida en ~** there's an abundance of food; **aquí existen datos en ~** there's a wealth of information here; **darse en ~** to be plentiful
B (riqueza): **tiempos de ~** times of plenty; **viven en la ~** they're well-off; ***nadar en la ~*** to be rolling in money (colloq)

abundante *adj* [1] ‹*reservas/cosecha*› plentiful, abundant; **la pesca es ~** the fishing is good; **~ EN algo**: **aguas ~s en especies marinas** waters which abound in marine life; **un informe ~ en datos estadísticos** a report containing ample statistical data [2] (*en pl*) (numerosos) plenty of, abundant

abundar [A1] *vi*
A [1] (existir en gran número o cantidad) «*especie/mineral*» to be abundant; **aquí lo que abunda son los problemas** there's certainly no shortage of problems here [2] (tener mucho) **~ EN algo** to abound *o* be rich IN sth; **el país abunda en recursos naturales** the country abounds *o* is rich in natural resources
B (extenderse al hablar) **~ EN algo** to go into great detail ABOUT sth; **abundó en el tema** he talked about the subject at great length
C (en una opinión, creencia) (frml) **~ EN algo** to share sth; **los dos partidos abundan en esa opinión** both parties share that view; **abundo en la opinión de mi colega de que …** I share my colleague's opinion that …

aburguesado -da *adj* bourgeois

aburguesamiento *m*: *adoption of bourgeois ways*

aburguesarse [A1] *v pron* to become bourgeois

aburrición *f* (Col, Méx) ▸ **aburrimiento**

aburrido[1] **-da** *adj*
A ‹*persona*› [1] [ESTAR] (sin entretenimiento) bored; **estoy muy ~** I'm bored stiff [2] [ESTAR] (harto) fed up; **~ DE algo** tired OF sth, fed up WITH sth; **~ DE + INF** tired of -ING
B [SER] ‹*película/persona*› boring; ‹*trabajo*› boring, tedious

aburrido[2] **-da** *m,f* bore

aburridor -dora *adj* (AmL) ▸ **aburrido**[1] **B**

aburrimiento *m* [1] (estado) boredom [2] (cosa aburrida): **¡qué ~!** what a bore!

aburrir [I1] *vt* to bore
■ **aburrirse** *v pron* [1] (por falta de entretenimiento) to get bored; **nunca me había aburrido tanto** I'd never been so bored [2] (hartarse) **~se DE algo/algn** to get tired OF *o* fed up WITH sth/sb; **~se DE + INF** to get tired OF -ING

abusado[1] **-da** *adj* (Méx fam) bright (colloq), smart; **es muy ~ para las ciencias** he's very hot on science (colloq); **(ponte) ~ con la bolsa** be careful with *o* watch your bag

abusado[2] *interj* (Méx fam) watch out!, look out!

abusador[1] **-dora** *adj* (aprovechado) ‹*comerciante*› opportunist; **¡qué ~ eres!** you really take advantage of the situation!; **no seas ~, ya ha trabajado diez horas** don't be so demanding, she's already done ten hours' work

abusador[2] **-dora** *m,f* (aprovechado): **estos comerciantes son unos ~es** these shopkeepers really take advantage; **es un ~ con sus padres** he takes advantage of his parents

abusar [A1] *vi*
A [1] (aprovecharse): **es muy hospitalaria pero no abuses**

she's very hospitable but don't take advantage of her; **~ DE algo** ‹*de autoridad/posición*› to abuse sth; ‹*de hospitalidad/generosidad*› to abuse sth, take unfair advantage OF sth; **no quisiera ~ de su amabilidad** I don't want to impose (on you); **~ DE algn** ‹*de padres/amigo*› to take advantage OF sb 2 (sexualmente) **~ DE algn** to sexually abuse sb

B (usar en exceso): **~ DE algo: abusa de tranquilizantes** he takes too many tranquilizers; **no se debe ~ del alcohol** alcohol should be drunk in moderation

abusivo -va *adj* ‹*precio/interés*› outrageous; **dos cláusulas francamente abusivas** two clauses which are blatantly unfair

abuso *m* 1 (uso excesivo) abuse; **el ~ en la bebida** alcohol abuse 2 (de hospitalidad, generosidad): **espero no lo considere un ~** I hope you don't think it an imposition 3 (injusticia) outrage; **prestarse a ~s** to lend itself to abuse

Compuestos
- **abuso de autoridad** *m* abuse of authority
- **abuso de confianza** *m* (Der) breach of trust *o* confidence; **¡qué ~ de ~!** (fam) what a nerve! (colloq)
- **abusos deshonestos** *mpl* indecent assault
- **abuso sexual infantil** *m* child abuse

abusón -sona *adj* (Esp, Méx fam) ▸ **abusador**

abyección *f* 1 (acto abyecto) despicable act 2 (cualidad): **caer en la ~** to debase oneself

abyecto -ta *adj* ‹*persona/conducta*› contemptible, despicable; **un crimen ~** a heinous crime

a/c = a cuenta

acá *adv*

A (en el espacio) here; [*where the location is more precise and no comparison is involved European Spanish prefers* **aquí**] **¡ven ~!** come here!; **viven por ~** they live around *o* near here; **ya viene para ~** he's on his way over; **se vino hasta ~ caminando** he came here on foot; **~ y allá** here and there; **nos pasamos el día de ~ para allá** we spent the whole day going to and fro; **un poquito más ~** a little closer *o* nearer (to me)

B (en el tiempo): **del verano (para) ~ han pasado muchas cosas** a lot has happened since the summer; **¿de cuándo ~?** since when?

acabado¹ -da *adj* 1 [ESTAR] ‹*trabajo*› finished; **son todos productos muy bien ~s** they are all well-finished products 2 [ESTAR] ‹*persona*› finished

acabado² *m* finish

acabar [A1] *vi*

Sentido I 1 «*reunión/película*» to finish, end; «*persona*» to finish; «*novios*» to split up; **ya casi acabo** I've nearly finished; **¡acabáramos!** (fam) now I get it! (colloq) 2 (en un estado, situación) to end up; **¿cómo acabó lo de anoche?** how did things end up last night?; **acabó en la cárcel** he ended up in jail; (+ *compl*) **acabamos cansadísimos** by the end we were exhausted; **tanta historia para ~ en nada** all that fuss for nothing; **ese chico va a ~ mal** that boy will come to no good; **esto puede ~ mal** things could turn nasty *o* get ugly; **la película acabó bien** the movie had a happy ending; **~ + GER** *o* **~ POR + INF** to end up -ING; **~án aceptándolo** *o* **por aceptarlo** they'll end up accepting it; **acabé por convencerme de que ...** in the end I became convinced that ...; **~ DE algo** to end up AS sth; **acabó de camarero** he ended up (working) as a waiter 3 (rematar) **~ EN algo** to end IN sth; **la palabra acaba en vocal** the word ends in a vowel

Sentido II **acabar con** 1 **~ CON algo** (terminar) ‹*con libro/tarea*› to finish WITH sth; ‹*con bombones/bebidas*› to finish off sth; ‹*con salud/carrera*› to ruin sth; ‹*con sueldo/herencia*› to fritter AWAY sth; ‹*con abuso/problema*› to put an end TO sth; **estás acabando con mi paciencia** you're trying my patience 2 (fam) **~ CON algn** (pelearse) to finish WITH sb; (matar) to do away WITH sb (colloq); **este niño va a ~ conmigo** this child will be the death of me

Sentido III **acabar de** 1 (terminar) **~ DE + INF** to finish -ING; **cuando acabes de leerlo** when you've finished reading it; **para ~ de arreglarlo se puso a llover** to top *o* cap it all it started to rain 2 (para referirse a acción reciente) **~ DE + INF: acaba de salir** she's just gone out; **acababa de meterme en la cama cuando ...** I had just got into bed when ... 3 (llegar a) **~ DE + INF: no acabo de entenderlo** I just don't understand; **no acababa de gustarle/convencerla** she wasn't totally happy about it/totally convinced

■ **acabar** *vt*

A ‹*trabajo/libro*› to finish; ‹*curso/carrera*› to finish, complete

B (destrozar): **el esfuerzo lo acabó** he was exhausted by the effort; **la tragedia la acabó** the tragedy destroyed her

■ **acabarse** *v pron*

A (terminarse) «*provisiones/comida*» to run out; «*problema*» to be over; «*reunión/fiesta*» to end; **se nos acabó el café** we ran out of coffee; **se le ~on las fuerzas** he ran out of energy; **se me está acabando la paciencia** I'm running out of patience; **es un trabajo que no se acaba nunca** it's a never-ending *o* an endless task; **¡esto se acabó!** that's it!; ***y (san) se acabó*** (fam) and that's that

B 1 (liter) (morir): **se fue acabando poco a poco** her life's breath slowly ebbed away (liter) 2 (Méx) (quedar destrozado): **se acabó en ese trabajo** that job finished him off (colloq)

C (*enf*) (comer) to finish (up)

acabóse *m* (fam): **¡esto es el ~!** this is the end *o* limit! (colloq); **el ~ de feo** incredibly ugly; **como administrador es el ~** as an administrator he's a complete disaster; **la fiesta fue el ~** (fue muy mala) the party was terrible *o* the pits (colloq); (fue muy buena) the party was fantastic *o* incredible

acacia *f* acacia

academia *f* 1 (sociedad) academy 2 (Educ) school 3 (RPl) (mundo académico): **la ~** academia, the academic world

Compuestos
- **academia de conductores** *or* (AmL) **choferes** driving school
- **academia de idiomas** language school
- **academia militar** military academy

académico¹ -ca *adj* 1 ‹*estudios/año*› academic (*before n*) 2 ‹*sillón/normas*› Academy (*before n*) (*esp of the Royal Academy of the Spanish language*) 3 ‹*estilo/lenguaje*› academic

académico² -ca *m,f* academician

Compuesto **académico -ca de número** *m,f* permanent member (*esp of the Royal Academy of the Spanish language*)

acaecer [E3] *vi* (*en 3ª pers*) (frml) to occur (frml), take place

acalambrarse [A1] *v pron* to get (a) cramp

acallar [A1] *vt* ‹*voces/gritos*› to silence, to quiet (AmE), to quieten (BrE); ‹*rumor/clamor*› to quieten down; ‹*críticas/protestas*› to silence

acalorado -da *adj*

A [SER] ‹*discusión/riña*› heated

B [ESTAR] ‹*persona*› (enfadado) worked up; (con calor) hot

acaloramiento *m* heatedness, heat

acalorarse [A1] *v pron* (enfadarse) to get worked up; (sofocarse) to get hot

acampada *f* camp; **ir de ~** to go camping

acampanado -da *adj* ‹*falda/pantalones*› bell-bottomed (AmE), flared (BrE)

acampante *mf* camper

acampar [A1] *vi* to camp

acanalado -da *adj* ‹*columna*› fluted; ‹*techo/cartón*› corrugated

acanalar [A1] *vt* (rebajar) to groove, flute; (doblar) to corrugate

acantilado *m* cliff

acanto *m* acanthus

acantonar [A1] *vt* to station

acaparador¹ -dora *adj* (egoísta) selfish, greedy; (posesivo) possessive

acaparador² -dora *m,f* 1 (de productos) hoarder 2 (persona egoísta) selfish person

acaparamiento *m* hoarding, stockpiling

acaparar [A1] *vt* 1 ‹*productos/existencias*› to hoard, stockpile 2 ‹*interés/atención*› to capture; **el trabajo acapara todo su tiempo** work takes up all his time; **acaparó todas las miradas** all eyes were on her 3 (fam) (monopolizar) to hog (colloq)

a capella /a ka'pela/ (*loc adv*) ‹*cantar*› a capella, unaccompanied

acápite *m* (AmL) (sección) section; (encabezamiento) heading; (párrafo) paragraph

acaramelado -da *adj* 1 ‹*pareja*›: **estaban ~s** they were hugging and kissing 2 ‹*voz*› sugary 3 (Coc) toffee-coated

acaramelar [A1] *vt* to coat … with caramel

acariciador -dora *adj* 1 ‹*voz/mirada*› tender 2 ‹*brisa*› (liter) caressing (*before n*) (liter)

acariciar [A1] *vt*
A 1 ‹*persona*› to caress; ‹*mejilla/pelo*› to stroke, caress; ‹*perro/gato*› to stroke 2 (liter) «*sol/brisa*» to caress (liter)
B ‹*idea/plan*› to nurture
■ **acariciarse** *v pron* (*refl*): **~se la barba** to stroke one's beard

ácaro *m* mite

acarraladura *f* (Per) run (AmE), ladder (BrE)

acarrear [A1] *vt* 1 ‹*problema*› to give rise to, lead to; **esto le acarreó problemas** this caused her problems 2 ‹*materiales/paquetes*› to carry 3 (Chi fam) ‹*persona*› to take 4 (Méx) (Pol): *to transport people to a political meeting or polling place*

acarreo *m* 1 (en vehículo) haulage, transport; (con esfuerzo físico) carrying 2 (Dep) carry

acartonado -da *adj* 1 ‹*piel*› wizened 2 ‹*estilo*› stilted; ‹*actuación*› wooden; ‹*modales*› stuffy, stilted; ‹*sociedad*› stultified

acartonarse *v pron* «*piel*» to become wizened

acaserarse [A1] *v pron* (Chi, Per fam) to become a regular customer

acaso *adv*
A (en preguntas): **¿~ no te lo dije?** I told you, didn't I?; **¿cómo lo sabes? ¿~ estabas allí?** how do you know? were you there or something?; **¿~ tengo yo la culpa?** is it *my* fault?; **¿~ no sabes que …?** don't you know that …?
B (*en locs*) **por si acaso** just in case; **por si ~ no te lo han dicho** (just) in case nobody's told you; **si acaso**: **si ~ me necesitaras** if you need me; **no fue tan horrible, si ~ un poco largo** it wasn't that bad, a bit long maybe *o* perhaps
C (liter) (quizás) **~ + SUBJ** maybe, perhaps; **~ sea cierto lo que dijo** maybe *o* perhaps what she said is true

acatamiento *m* (de orden) observance; **el ~ de las leyes** compliance with the laws

acatar [A1] *vt* ‹*leyes/orden*› to obey, comply with; **~ la voluntad de la mayoría** to comply with the wishes of the majority

acatarrado -da *adj*: **estar ~** to have a cold

acatarrar [A1] *vt* (Méx fam) to hassle (colloq)
■ **acatarrarse** *v pron* (resfriarse) to catch a cold

acaudalado -da *adj* wealthy, rich, affluent

acaudillar [A1] *vt* to lead

acceder [E1] *vi*
A **~ A algo** ‹*a lugar*› to gain access TO sth; ‹*a premio*› to be eligible FOR sth; ‹*a cargo*› obtain sth; **accedió al trono** he came *o* succeeded to the throne
B (ceder): **accedió a regañadientes** he agreed with great reluctance, he reluctantly gave in; **~ A algo** to agree TO sth, to accede TO sth (frml); **~ A + INF** to agree TO + INF; **accedió a contestar las preguntas** she agreed to answer the questions

accesibilidad *f* accessibility

accesible *adj* 1 ‹*lugar*› accessible; ‹*persona*› approachable; ‹*precio*› affordable; **~ a todos los bolsillos** within everyone's price range 2 ‹*novela/lenguaje*› accessible; ‹*explicación*› easily comprehensible

accésit *m* second prize, consolation prize

acceso *m*
A 1 (a un lugar) access; **rutas de ~** approach roads; **los ~s a la ciudad** roads into *o* approaches to the city; **es el único ~ al jardín** it's the only means of access to the garden 2 (a persona, documento) access 3 (Inf) access; **~ aleatorio/secuencial** random/sequential access
B 1 (a puesto, cargo) accession (frml); **desde su ~ al poder** since coming to *o* assuming power 2 (a curso) entrance; **pruebas de ~** entrance examinations; **curso de ~** preparatory course
(Compuesto) **acceso directo** direct entry
C (Med) attack; **~ de tos** coughing fit; **en un ~ de ira/celos** in a fit of rage/jealousy

accesorio¹ -ria *adj* incidental

accesorio² *m* accessory; **~s del vestir** accessories; **~s de baño** bathroom fittings

accidentado¹ -da *adj*
A 1 ‹*viaje*› eventful; ‹*historia*› turbulent; ‹*carrera/pasado*› checkered* (*before n*); ‹*vida*› troubled 2 ‹*terreno*› rough, rugged; ‹*costa*› broken
B ‹*persona*› hurt, injured

accidentado² -da *m,f*: **llevaron a los ~s al hospital** those injured *o* hurt in the accident were taken to hospital

accidental *adj* ‹*encuentro*› chance (*before n*), accidental; ‹*circunstancias*› coincidental

accidentalmente *adv* (sin querer) accidentally, unintentionally; (de casualidad) by chance

accidentarse [A1] *v pron* to have an accident

accidente *m*
A (percance) accident; **tuvo** *or* **sufrió un ~** he had an accident
(Compuestos)
• **accidente aéreo** plane crash, air accident (frml)
• **accidente de circulación/tráfico** traffic *o* road accident
• **accidente de trabajo** industrial accident
B (hecho fortuito) coincidence; **por ~** by chance *o* coincidence
C (del terreno) unevenness
(Compuesto) **accidente geográfico** geographical feature

acción *f*
A (acto, hecho) act; **hacer una buena ~** to do a good deed; **acciones dignas de elogio** praiseworthy acts *o* actions
(Compuesto) **acción de gracias** thanksgiving
B (actividad) action; **poner algo en ~** to put sth into action; **novela de ~** adventure story; **¡luces, cámara, ~!** lights, camera, action!
C (Mil) action; **entrar en ~** to go into action; **~ defensiva/ofensiva** defensive/offensive action; **muerto en ~** killed in action
D (influencia, efecto) action; **está bajo la ~ de un sedante** she is under sedation
E (Cin, Lit) (trama) action, plot
F (Der) action, lawsuit
G (Fin) share; **acciones** shares *o* stock; **emitir acciones** to issue shares *o* stock
(Compuesto) **acciones nominales/ordinarias** *fpl* registered/ordinary stock, registered/ordinary shares (*pl*)
H (Per) (de una rifa) ticket

accionar [A1] *vt* ‹*palanca*› to pull; ‹*mecanismo/dispositivo*› activate, trigger

accionista *mf* stockholder, shareholder

acebo *m* holly; (árbol) holly tree

acebuche *m* wild olive

acechar [A1] *vt* ‹*enemigo/presa*› to lie in wait for; **el peligro que nos acecha** the danger that lies ahead of us

acecho *m*: **al ~** lying in wait

acéfalo -la *adj* (sin cabeza) headless, acephalous (tech); (sin líder) leaderless

aceitar [A1] *vt* ‹*máquina/gozne*› to oil; ‹*molde*› to grease

aceite *m* oil; **~ lubricante** lubricating oil
(Compuestos)
• **aceite de colza/oliva/girasol** rapeseed/olive/sunflower oil
• **aceite solar** suntan oil
• **aceite de ricino** castor oil

aceitera *f* (Tec) oilcan; (Coc) cruet

aceitero -ra *adj* oil (*before n*)

aceitoso -sa *adj* oily

aceituna *f* olive; **~s rellenas/sin hueso** stuffed/pitted olives
(Compuesto) **aceituna negra/verde** black/green olive

aceitunado -da *adj* olive (*before n*), olive-colored*

aceitunero -ra *m,f* olive-picker

aceituno[1] -na *adj* olive, olive-colored*

aceituno[2] *m* (Bot) olive tree

aceleración *f* acceleration

acelerada *f* (esp AmL) burst of acceleration

acelerado -da *adj*
A ‹*curso*› intensive, crash (*before n*); **a paso ~** at a brisk pace
B (fam) ‹*persona*› nervous

acelerador *m* (Auto) accelerator; **pisar** *or* **apretar el ~** to put one's foot on *o* press the accelerator

acelerar [A1] *vt* 1 ‹*coche/motor*›: **aceleró el coche** (en marcha) he accelerated; (sin desplazarse) he revved the engine *o* car (up) 2 ‹*proceso/cambio*› to speed up; ‹*paso*› to quicken
■ **acelerar** *vi* 1 (Auto) to accelerate 2 (fam) (darse prisa) to hurry (up)
■ **acelerarse** *v pron* (AmL fam) to get overexcited, lose one's cool (colloq)

acelerón *m* burst of acceleration

acelgas *fpl* Swiss chard

acendrado -da *adj* (liter) ‹*cariño*› pure; ‹*honradez*› unblemished; ‹*vocación*› true

acendrar [A1] *vt* (liter) to refine

acento *m*
A 1 (Ling) accent; **el ~ recae en la última sílaba** the stress falls on the last syllable; **no lleva ~** it doesn't have an accent on it 2 (énfasis) emphasis
(Compuesto) **acento agudo/circunflejo/ortográfico** acute/circumflex/written accent
B 1 (dejo, pronunciación) accent; **tiene ~ francés** he has a French accent; **un ~ raro** a funny accent 2 (tono) tone; **de marcado ~ europeo** markedly European in tone

acentuación *f* accentuation

acentuado -da *adj* 1 ‹*palabra/sílaba*› accented 2 ‹*diferencia/cambio*› marked, distinct

acentuar [A18] *vt* 1 (Ling) (al hablar) to stress, accent; (al escribir) to accent 2 (intensificar, hacer resaltar) to accentuate, emphasize; **maquillaje que acentúa los ojos** make up which accentuates the eyes
■ **acentuarse** *v pron* to become accentuated

acepción *f* sense, meaning

aceptabilidad *f* acceptability

aceptable *adj* acceptable, passable

aceptación *f* 1 (éxito) success; **de gran ~ entre los jóvenes** very popular *o* successful with young people 2 (acción) acceptance

aceptar [A1] *vt* ‹*excusas/invitación/cargo*› to accept; ‹*términos/condiciones*› to agree to; **¿acepta a Luis como** *or* **por legítimo esposo?** (frml) do you take Luis to be your lawful wedded husband? (frml); **aceptan cheques** they take checks; ⊗ **no aceptamos devoluciones** no refunds; **~ + INF** to agree to + INF; **aceptó venir** she agreed to come; **no acepto que me digas eso** I won't have you saying that to me; **¿por qué aceptas que te trate así?** why do you allow her to treat you like that?

acequia *f* irrigation ditch *o* channel

acera *f* 1 (para peatones) sidewalk (AmE), pavement (BrE) 2 (lado de la calle): **viven en la misma ~** they live on the same side of the street; ***ser de la ~ de enfrente*** (fam) to be gay

acerado -da *adj* 1 ‹*navaja/hoja*› steel (*before n*) 2 ‹*cielo*› steely

acerar [A1] *vt* (recubrir) to coat ... in steel; ‹*persona*› to toughen, harden

acerbidad *f* harshness, acerbity

acerbo -ba *adj* ‹*tono/crítica*› harsh, caustic; ‹*sabor*› sharp

acerca de *loc prep* about

acercamiento *m* (entre posturas, países) rapprochement; (entre personas): **ese incidente produjo un ~ entre ellos** that incident brought them closer together

acercar [A2] *vt*
A 1 (aproximar) to bring ... closer *o* nearer; **~on la mesa a la puerta** they moved the table closer *o* nearer to the door; **acercó la silla a la mesa** she drew her chair up to the table; **acercó las manos al fuego** he held his hands closer to the fire; **¿puedes ~me ese libro?** can you pass *o* give me that book? 2 (unir) ‹*posturas/países*› to bring ... closer; **su primer hijo los acercó mucho** their first child brought them much closer together
B (llevar): **me acercó a la parada** she gave me a ride (AmE) *o* (BrE) lift to the bus stop
■ **acercarse** *v pron*
A 1 (aproximarse) to approach, to get closer *o* nearer; **acércate más** (acercándose al hablante) come *o* get closer *o* nearer; (alejándose del hablante) go *o* get closer *o* nearer; **¡no te acerques!** keep away!; **~se A algo/algn** to approach sth/sb; **se le ~on dos policías** two policemen came up to *o* approached him 2 «*amigos/países*» to draw *o* come closer together 3 «*hora/momento*» to draw near, approach; **ahora que se acercan las Navidades** now that Christmas is coming 4 «*postura/ideas*» (asemejarse) **~se A algo** to lean *o* tend TOWARD(S) sth
B (ir, pasar): **acércate una tarde a tomar café** come around for coffee some afternoon; **me acerqué a la oficina a saludarlo** I dropped by his office to say hello

acerería, acería *f* steelworks (*sing or pl*)

acerero -ra *adj* steel (*before n*)

acerico *m* pincushion

acero *m* (Metal) steel; (arma) (liter) blade (liter)
(Compuesto) **acero inoxidable** stainless steel

acérrimo -ma *adj* ‹*partidario/defensor*› staunch; ‹*enemigo*› bitter

acertado -da *adj* ‹*comentario*› pertinent; ‹*solución/elección*› good; **no estuviste muy ~ en decirle eso** it wasn't very clever *o* smart of you to tell her that

acertante[1] *adj* winning (*before n*)

acertante[2] *mf* winner; **los máximos ~s** the big *o* major prize winners

acertar [A5] *vt* ‹*respuesta/resultado*› to get ... right; **a ver si aciertas quién es** see if you can guess who it is
■ **acertar** *vi*
A 1 (dar, pegar): **~le A algo** to hit sth; **acertó en el medio** he hit it (right) in the middle; **tiró pero no le acertó** he shot at it but (he) missed 2 (atinar) to be right; **acertaste al no comprarlo** you did the right thing not buying it; **~ CON algo** ‹*con solución*› to hit ON sth; **acertaste con el regalo** your present was perfect; **no acerté con la casa** I couldn't find the house
B (lograr, atinar) **~ A + INF** to manage to + INF; **no acertó a decir palabra** she didn't manage to say a single word; **no acierto a comprenderlo** I just can't understand it
C (liter) (suceder casualmente) **~ A + INF** to happen to + INF; **acertó a pasar por allí** he happened to pass that way

acertijo *m* riddle, puzzle

acervo *m*: **el ~ cultural de su país** the cultural heritage of their country; **el ~ familiar** the family fortune

acetato *m* 1 (Tex) acetate rayon 2 (Quím) acetate 3 (period) (disco) acetate

acetileno *m* acetylene

acetona *f* (Quím) acetone; (quitaesmaltes) nail-polish remover

acezante *adj* puffing and panting, out of breath

acezar [A4] *vi* to puff and pant

achacar [A2] *vt*: **~le la culpa a algn** to lay *o* put the blame on sb; **le ~on la responsabilidad del accidente** he was held responsible for the accident

achacoso -sa *adj*: **un viejo ~** an old man suffering from all sorts of (minor) ailments; **estaba tan ~** he had so many aches and pains *o* so many ailments

achantar [A1] *vt* (fam) to intimidate
■ **achantarse** *v pron* (fam) to back down

achaparrado -da *adj* (fam) ‹*persona*› squat; ‹*árbol*› stunted

achaques *mpl* ailments (*pl*); **los ~s de la vejez** the ailments *o* the aches and pains of old age

acharolado -da *adj* lacquered; **de piel acharolada** with jet-black skin

achatar [A1] *vt* to flatten

achicar [A2] *vt*
A 1 ‹*chaqueta/vestido*› to take in 2 ‹*persona*› to intimidate, daunt; **nada lo achica** he's not daunted by anything

B ‹*agua*› to bail out
■ **achicarse** *v pron* **1** (de tamaño) to shrink **2** (amilanarse) to be intimidated, be daunted

achicharrante *adj* (fam) ‹*sol*› scorching; **ayer hizo un calor ~** it was scorching yesterday

achicharrar [A1] *vt* **1** (fam) (quemar) ‹*carne/comida*› (Coc) to burn … to a cinder (colloq); «*sol*» ‹*planta*› to scorch; **hace un sol que achicharra** the sun is scorching hot **2** (Chi fam) (aplastar) to crush; (deformar) to buckle
■ **achicharrarse** *v pron* (fam) **1** «*persona*» to fry (colloq); «*planta*» to get scorched **2** (fam) «*carne/comida*» to be burned to a crisp (colloq)

achichincle, achichinque *mf* (Méx fam & pey) hanger-on (colloq & pej)

achicopalar [A1] *vt* (Col, Méx fam) to intimidate
■ **achicopalarse** *v pron* (Col, Méx fam) to feel intimidated

achicoria *f* chicory
(Compuesto) **achicoria roja** radicchio

achinado -da *adj* ‹*ojos*› slanting; ‹*cara*› oriental-looking

achiote *m* (AmL) annatto

achiquillado -da *adj* (Méx, RPl) childish

achís *interj* achoo!, atishoo! (BrE)

achispado -da *adj* (fam) tipsy (colloq)

achisparse [A1] *v pron* (fam) to get tipsy (colloq)

achoclonar [A1] *vt* (AmS fam) to group … together
■ **achoclonarse** *v pron* (*refl*) (AmS fam) «*personas*» to crowd together; **se ~on a su alrededor** they crowded around him

achocolatado -da *adj* chocolate-brown

acholado -da *adj* (Andes) (mestizo) mestizo (*of mixed European and Amerindian ancestry*)

acholarse *v pron*
A (Andes) (hacerse cholo) to go native *o* local (*adopting* **cholo** *ways*)
B (Chi fam) (avergonzarse) to get embarrassed

achote *m* (AmL) annatto

achuchado -da *adj* **1** (Esp fam) (difícil) hard, tough **2** (RPl fam) ‹*persona*› feverish

achuchar [A1] *vt*: **nos achuchó los perros** he set the dogs on us
■ **achucharse** *v pron* (RPl fam) to get scared

achulado -da, achulapado -da *adj* (Esp) cocky

achunchar [A1] *vt* (Chi, Per fam) (turbar) to embarrass
■ **achuncharse** *v pron* (Chi, Per fam) (turbarse) to get embarrassed; (por algo reprensible) to feel ashamed

achuntar [A1] *vi*
A (Chi fam) (dar, pegar) **~le A/EN algo**: **lo tiró y le achuntó a la caja** he threw it and it landed right in the box; **tiró a la canasta pero no le achuntó** he shot at the basket but he missed (it)
B (Chi fam) (acertar); **~(le) A algo** to get sth right; **le achuntó al número premiado** she got the winning number; **le achuntaste con el regalo** your present was perfect

achurar [A1] *vt* (RPl fam) ‹*animal*› to gut; ‹*persona*› to kill

achuras *fpl* (RPl) offal

achús *interj* achoo!, atishoo! (BrE)

aciago -ga *adj* tragic; **aquel ~ día** that tragic *o* fateful day

aciano *m* cornflower

acíbar *m* (planta) aloe; (jugo) bitter aloes

acicalado -da *adj* dressed up

acicalarse [A1] *v pron* to dress up, get dressed up

acicate *m* **1** (estímulo) incentive; **el ~ de su existencia** his reason for living **2** (espuela) spur

acicatear [A1] *vt* to spur … on

acidez *f* (Quím) acidity; (Med) (en el estómago) acidity; (en el esófago) heartburn

acidificar [A2] *vt* to acidify
■ **acidificarse** *v pron* to acidify

ácido[1] -da *adj* **1** ‹*sabor*› acid; ‹*fruta*› acid, tart, sharp; ‹*vino*› sharp **2** ‹*carácter/tono*› acid, caustic

ácido[2] *m* **1** (Quím) acid **2** (arg) (droga) acid (sl)
(Compuestos)
• **ácido acético/cítrico/nítrico** acetic/citric/nitric acid
• **ácido desoxirribonucleico** deoxyribonucleic acid, DNA
• **ácido ribonucleico** ribonucleic acid, RNA

acidular [A1] *vt* to acidulate, make … taste sharp

acierta, aciertas, etc *see* **acertar**

acierto *m*
A (decisión correcta) good decision, good *o* wise move; **su mayor ~ fue …** her best decision *o* move was …
B (tino, habilidad) skill; **con gran ~** with great skill
C (respuesta correcta) correct answer

ácimo -ma *adj* ▸**pan**

acinturado -da *adj* (Chi) ‹*persona*› with a slim waist; ‹*ropa*› tight-fitting

acitronar [A1] *vt* (Méx) to fry … until golden brown

aclamación *f* acclaim; **por ~ popular** by popular acclaim; **salió al escenario entre las aclamaciones del público** she came on stage to great applause *o* acclaim from the audience

aclamar [A1] *vt* to acclaim, applaud

aclaración *f* explanation; **esto requiere una ~** this needs some explanation *o* clarification; **una ~ al margen** an explanation in the margin; **quisiera hacer una ~** I'd like to make one thing clear *o* I'd like to clarify one thing; **pedir aclaraciones** to ask for an explanation of *o* for clarification

aclarado *m* (Esp) rinse

aclarar [A1] *v impers* **1** (amanecer): **aclara temprano** it gets light early; **cuando nos levantamos estaba aclarando** dawn *o* day was breaking when we got up **2** (escampar) to clear up
■ **aclarar** *vi* **1** «*día*» (empezar) to break, dawn **2** «*tiempo/día*» (escampar) to clear up
■ **aclarar** *vt*
A (quitar color a) to lighten
B ‹*ideas*› to get … straight; ‹*duda*› to clear up, clarify; **no pudo ~me nada sobre el tema** she couldn't throw any light on the subject; **quiero ~ que yo no sabía nada** I want to make it clear that I didn't know anything
C **1** ‹*salsa*› to thin **2** ‹*vegetación/bosque*› to clear
D (Esp) ‹*ropa/vajilla*› to rinse
■ **aclararse** *v pron*
A **~se la voz** to clear one's throat
B (Esp fam) **1** (entender) to understand; **sigo sin ~me** I still don't understand; **~se CON algo** to work sth out; **no me aclaro con esta máquina** I can't work out how to use this machine; ***a ver si nos aclaramos*** let's see if we can sort things out *o* get things straight **2** (decidirse) to make up one's mind

aclaratorio -ria *adj* explanatory

aclimatación *f* acclimatization

aclimatarse [A1] *v pron* to acclimatize, get *o* become acclimatized

acné *m or f* acne

ACNUR /ak'nur/ *m* (= **Alto Comisionado de las Naciones Unidas para los Refugiados**) UNHCR

acobardar [A1] *vt* ‹*persona*› to unnerve, intimidate
■ **acobardarse** *v pron* to lose one's nerve; **~se ANTE algo** to be daunted by sth; **~se ante el peligro** to lose one's nerve in the face of danger; **no se acobarda ante nada** nothing daunts her

acocote *m* (Méx) bottle gourd, calabash

acodar [A1] *vt* **1** ‹*tubería*› to bend … into an elbow **2** (Agr) to layer
■ **acodarse** *v pron* **~se SOBRE algo** to lean (one's elbows) on sth; **estaba acodado sobre el mostrador** he was leaning on the counter

acogedor -dora *adj* **1** ‹*casa/habitación*› cozy*, welcoming; ‹*ambiente*› warm, friendly **2** ‹*persona/actitud*› friendly, warm

acoger [E6] *vt*
A ‹*huérfano/anciano*› to take in; ‹*refugiado*› to accept, admit; **nos acogió en su casa** he took us in; **que el Señor lo acoja en su seno** may the Lord receive his Spirit
B (+ *compl*) ‹*propuesta/persona*› to receive; **acogieron la noticia con satisfacción** the news was well received
■ **acogerse** *v pron* **~se A algo**: ‹*a la ley*› to have recourse TO sth; ‹*a un régimen*› to opt FOR sth; **me acogí a su protección** I turned to them for protection; **se acogió al**

derecho de asilo he claimed asylum; **~se a la jubilación anticipada** to take early retirement

acogida *f*
A (de persona) welcome; (de noticia, propuesta) reception; **tuvo una ~ favorable** it was favorably received *o* got a favorable reception
B (de huérfano) taking in; (de refugiado) acceptance

acogimiento familiar *m* fostering

acogotar [A1] *vt* **1** ‹*animal*› to kill (*with a blow to the back of the neck*); ‹*persona*› (fam): **si lo encuentro, lo acogoto** if I find him, I'll break his neck (colloq) **2** (CS fam) (estrangular) to choke (colloq) **3** (CS fam) (abrumar): **está acogotado de deudas/trabajo** he's up to his eyes in debt/work (colloq)

acojonar [A1] *vt* (Esp) **1** (fam) (asustar) to frighten the life out of (colloq) **2** (arg) (asombrar) to knock … dead (colloq)
■ **acojonarse** *v pron* (Esp fam) to get scared

acolchado¹ -da *adj* ‹*bata/tela*› quilted; ‹*pared*› padded

acolchado² *m* **1** (de puerta, pared) padding **2** (RPl) (colcha) eiderdown

acolchar [A1], **acolchonar** *vt* ‹*bata/tela*› to quilt; ‹*pared/puerta*› to pad

acolitar [A1] *vi* (Col) to serve (*as an altar boy*)
■ **acolitar** *vt* (Col fam) to cover for

acólito *m* **1** (Relig) (eclesiástico) server; (monaguillo) altar boy **2** (ayudante) helper

acomedido -da *adj* (Chi, Méx, Per) obliging, helpful; ***estar de ~ con algn*** (Méx fam & pey) to suck up to sb (colloq)

acomedirse [I14] *v pron* (Méx) to offer to help

acometer [E1] *vt*
A (atacar) to attack
B ‹*empresa/proyecto*› to undertake, tackle; ‹*reforma*› to undertake
C (asaltar) «*temor/deseo*» to take hold of; **me acometió el sueño** I was overcome by sleep; **me acometió la duda** I was assailed by doubt
■ **acometer** *vi* to attack; **~ CONTRA algo/algn** to attack sth/sb

acometida *f* attack

acomodadizo -za *adj* ▸ **acomodaticio**

acomodado¹ -da *adj*
A ‹*familia/gente*› well-off, well-to-do; **de posición acomodada** well-off, well-to-do
B (CS, Méx fam) (que tiene palanca): **estar ~** to have contacts *o* connections

acomodado² -da *m,f* (CS, Méx fam): **está lleno de ~s** it's full of people who got their jobs by pulling strings

acomodador -dora (*m*) usher; (*f*) usherette

acomodar [A1] *vt*
A (adaptar, amoldar) to adapt; **no puedes ~ las reglas a tu antojo** you can't bend the rules just to suit you
B ‹*huésped*› to put … up
C **1** (AmL) (arreglar) to arrange; (poner) to put; **acomodó la cabeza en la almohada** he settled his head on the pillow **2** (fam) ‹*persona*› (en puesto): **su tío lo acomodó en su sección** his uncle fixed him up with a job in his department
■ **acomodarse** *v pron* **1** (ponerse cómodo) to make oneself comfortable; **se acomodó en el sillón** he settled himself (comfortably) in the armchair **2** (adaptarse, amoldarse) **~se A algo** to adapt TO sth **3** (AmL) (arreglarse) ‹*ropa/anteojos*› to adjust

acomodaticio -cia *adj* **1** ‹*persona/actitud*› easygoing; (pey) pliable (pej) **2** (pey) ‹*acuerdo/arreglo*› cozy* (pej)

acomodo *m* **1** (amiguismo) (AmL fam) string-pulling **2** (Esp) (trabajo) job (*obtained through string-pulling*)

acompañado -da *adj* accompanied; **bien/mal ~** in good/bad company; **~ DE algn** accompanied by sb; **aparece en la foto ~ de un amigo** he appears in the photo with a friend; **todos los platos vienen ~s de guarnición** all dishes are served with vegetables

acompañamiento *m* **1** (Mús) accompaniment; **canta sin ~** she sings unaccompanied **2** (Coc) accompaniment; **¿con qué ~ lo quiere?** what would you like it served with?

acompañante *mf* **1** (compañero): **los ~s por favor esperen aquí** would all those accompanying the children (*o* patients *etc*) please wait here?; **la actriz y su asiduo ~** the actress and her constant companion **2** (Mús) accompanist

acompañar [A1] *vt*
A **1** (a un lugar) to go with, accompany (frml); **lo acompañé al doctor** I went with him to the doctor; **acompáñalo hasta la puerta** see him to the door, see him out; **la acompañé a su casa** I walked her home; **¿me acompañas a hablar con él?** will you come with me to talk to him? **2** (hacer compañía) to keep … company; **lo acompañó la buena suerte** luck was with him; **el tiempo no nos acompañó** we didn't have very good weather **3** (en el dolor, la desgracia) **~ a algn EN algo**: **la/lo/los acompaño en el sentimiento** (fr hecha) my deepest sympathy; **la acompañó en su dolor** he comforted her in her grief **4** (Mús) to accompany
B ‹*comida*› to accompany, go with
C (frml) (adjuntar) to enclose; **debe ir acompañado de un certificado médico** it must be accompanied by a medical certificate
■ **acompañarse** *v pron* **1** (Mús) to accompany oneself **2** (*recípr*) to be company for each other

acompasado -da *adj* ‹*ritmo/paso*› measured, regular; ‹*movimiento*› rhythmic

acompasar [A1] *vt*: **~ el paso** to keep in step; **~ los movimientos a la música** to keep one's movements in time to the music

acomplejado¹ -da *adj*: **es muy ~** he's full of complexes; **está ~ por su gordura** he has a complex about being fat

acomplejado² -da *m,f*: **es un ~** he's a mass of complexes

acomplejante *adj* (AmL fam): **su eficiencia es ~** she's so efficient she makes you feel inferior

acomplejar [A1] *vt* to give … a complex
■ **acomplejarse** *v pron* to get a complex

aconcharse [A1] *v pron* (Chi) to clear

acondicionador *m*: *tb* **~ de pelo** (hair) conditioner
(Compuesto) **acondicionador de aire** air conditioner

acondicionamiento *m* fitting-out

acondicionar [A1] *vt*
A **1** ‹*vivienda/local*› to equip, fit out; **un hospital debidamente acondicionado** a properly-equipped hospital **2** (Col) ‹*carro*› to soup up
B ‹*pelo*› to condition

acongojado -da *adj* upset, distressed

acongojar [A1] *vt* (liter) to grieve (liter), to distress
■ **acongojarse** *v pron* (liter) to become distressed (liter)

aconsejable *adj* advisable

aconsejar [A1] *vt* to advise; **¿qué me aconsejas?** what do you suggest?; **has sido bien/mal aconsejado** you've been given good/bad advice; **necesito que alguien me aconseje** I need some advice; **le aconsejó reposo** he advised her to rest; **~le a algn + INF/QUE + SUBJ** to advise sb to + INF; **te aconsejo ir/que vayas** I advise you to go; **se aconseja utilizar cadenas** snowchains are advisable
■ **aconsejarse** *v pron* **~se (CON** *or* **DE algn)** to seek advice (FROM sb)

acontecer¹ [E3] *vi* (*en 3ª pers*) (frml) to take place, occur (frml); **los sucesos acontecidos ayer** the events which took place *o* occurred yesterday

acontecer² *m*: **el diario ~** everyday events *o* occurrences

acontecimiento *m* event; **una fiesta para celebrar el ~** a party to celebrate the occasion *o* event; **fue todo un ~** it was quite an event; **adelantarse** *or* **anticiparse a los ~s** to jump the gun

acopio *m*: **haciendo ~ de todas sus fuerzas** gathering all his strength; **hizo ~ de todo su valor** he mustered all his courage

acoplado *m* (CS) (remolque) trailer

acoplador *m* coupler
(Compuesto) **acoplador acústico** acoustic coupler

acoplamiento *m* **1** (de piezas) fitting together **2** (Elec) connection **3** (Ferr) coupling **4** (Espac) docking

acoplar [A1] *vt* **1** ‹*piezas*› to fit *o* put together **2** (Elec) to connect **3** (Ferr) to couple
■ **acoplarse** *v pron*

A 1 (adaptarse) to adapt 2 (CS) (a una huelga) to join; **hubo una excursión y se ~on** there was an excursion and they went along
B (Audio) to produce feedback
C (Aviac, Espac) to dock

acoquinar [A1] *vt* to intimidate, cow
■ **acoquinarse** *v pron* to be *o* feel intimidated *o* cowed

acorazado *m* battleship

acorazar [A4] *vt* (Mil) to armor-plate*
■ **acorazarse** *v pron* (defenderse) to protect oneself

acordar [A10] *vt*
A ‹*términos*› to agree; ‹*precio/fecha*› to agree (on)
B (esp AmL fml) ‹*premio*› to award
C (recordar) **~le a algn DE + INF/QUE + SUBJ** (Andes) to remind sb to + INF; **háganme ~ de llamarlo** (RPl) remind me to phone him
■ **acordarse** *v pron* to remember; **si mal no me acuerdo** if I remember right; **~se DE algn/algo** to remember sb/sth; **no quiero ni ~me** I don't even want to think about it; **~se DE + INF** (de una acción que hay/había que realizar) to remember to + INF; (de una acción que ya se realizó) to remember *o* recall -ING; **acuérdate de dárselo** remember *o* don't forget to give it to him; **se acordó de haberlo visto allí** she remembered *o* recalled seeing him there; **~se (DE) QUE ...** to remember THAT ...

acorde[1] *adj* 1 (en armonía): **tienen posturas ~s** they hold the same views; **estamos todos ~s** we are all agreed *o* in agreement; **colores ~s** colors that go *o* blend well together; **con un salario ~** with a salary to match; **~ CON** *or* **A algo** appropriate TO sth, in keeping WITH sth 2 ‹*sonidos*› harmonious

acorde[2] *m* chord; **a los ~s de un vals** to the strains of a waltz

acordeón *m*
A (Mús) accordion
B (Méx fam) (para un examen) crib

acordeonista *mf* accordionist

acordonado -da *adj* [ESTAR] ‹*lugar/calle*› cordoned off; **zapatos ~s** lace-up shoes

acordonar [A1] *vt* 1 ‹*lugar*› to cordon off 2 ‹*zapatos*› to lace (up)

acorralar [A1] *vt* 1 ‹*animal/fugitivo*› to corner 2 ‹*ganado*› to round up

acortamiento *m* (de vestido, texto) shortening; (de distancia) reduction

acortar [A1] *vt* ‹*falda/vestido*› to shorten; ‹*texto/artículo*› to cut, shorten; ‹*vacaciones/permanencia*› to cut short; ‹*película/carrera*› to reduce the length of; **~ camino** to take a short cut
■ **acortarse** *v pron* to get shorter

acosador -dora *m,f*
A (de famoso) stalker
B (en el colegio, trabajo) bully
C (perseguidor) tormentor, persecutor

acosar [A1] *vt* 1 ‹*persona*› to hound; **~ sexualmente a algn** to sexually harass sb; **acosados por el hambre** beset by hunger; **me ~on con preguntas** they plagued *o* bombarded me with questions 2 ‹*presa*› to hound

acosijar [A1] *vt* (Méx) to badger, pester

acoso *m* 1 (de persona) hounding, harassment; **~ sexual** sexual harassment 2 (en el colegio) bullying; **~ escolar** school bullying 3 (de presa) hounding, relentless pursuit

acostar [A10] *vt*
A ‹*persona*› to put ... to bed
B ‹*nave*› to moor
■ **acostar** *vi* (Náut) to moor
■ **acostarse** *v pron* 1 (irse a dormir) to go to bed; **es hora de ~se** it's time for bed; ***nunca te ~ás sin saber una cosa más*** you learn something new every day 2 (tenderse, tumbarse) to lie down; **~se boca abajo** to lie face down 3 (tener relaciones sexuales) to go to bed together, sleep together; **~se CON algn** to go to bed WITH sb, sleep WITH sb 4 (liter) «*sol*» to set

acostumbrado -da *adj* 1 (habituado): **está mal ~** he's got into bad habits; **~ A algo** used TO sth; **estoy ~ al frío** I'm used to the cold; **~ A + INF** used TO -ING; **estamos ~s a cenar temprano** we're used to having dinner early; **~ A QUE + SUBJ**: **está ~ a que le sirvan** he's used to being served; **no estoy ~ a que me traten así** I am not accustomed *o* used to being treated like that 2 (habitual) customary, usual

acostumbramiento *m* (CS): **puede producir ~** it can be habit-forming

acostumbrar [A1] *vt* **~ a algn A algo/+ INF** to get sb used TO sth/-ING
■ **acostumbrar** *vi*: **~ A + INF** to be accustomed TO -ING, be in the habit OF -ING; **acostumbraba a dar un paseo después de comer** I used to go for a walk after lunch, I was accustomed to *o* in the habit of going for a walk after lunch
■ **acostumbrarse** *v pron* **~se A algo/algn** to get used TO sth/sb; **~se A + INF** to get used TO -ING

acotación *f* (de texto) marginal note, annotation; (al hablar) comment; **hacer una ~** to make a comment

acotado *adj* ‹*terreno*› fenced, fenced-in; ‹*mapa/plano*› contour (*before n*)

acotamiento *m* (Méx) shoulder (AmE), hard shoulder (BrE)

acotar [A1] *vt* 1 ‹*terreno*› to fence in 2 ‹*texto*› to annotate; ‹*plano/mapa*› to mark the contour lines on

acre[1] *adj* ‹*olor*› acrid; ‹*humor/tono*› caustic; ‹*crítica*› harsh, biting

acre[2] *m* acre

acrecentamiento *m* growth, increase

acrecentar [A5] *vt* to increase
■ **acrecentarse** *v pron* to increase, grow

acrecer [E3] *vi* to accrue

acreditación *f* (acción) accreditation; (documento) credentials (*pl*)

acreditado -da *adj* 1 (de renombre) ‹*establecimiento/marca*› reputable, well-known 2 ‹*diplomático/periodista*› accredited; ‹*agente/representante*› authorized, official; **~ ante la Santa Sede** accredited to the Holy See

acreditar [A1] *vt*
A ‹*diplomático/periodista*› to accredit; ‹*representante*› to authorize
B (frml) 1 (probar, avalar) ‹*pago*› to prove; **este libro lo acredita como un gran pensador** this book confirms him as a great thinker; **una empresa acreditada como líder en su campo** a firm recognized as the leader in its field 2 (dar renombre): **con la calidad qué lo acredita** with the quality for which it's renowned
C (Fin) to credit
■ **acreditarse** *v pron* 1 ‹*victoria/logro*› to achieve 2 (lograr renombre) to get *o* gain a good reputation

acreditativo -va *adj* (frml) supporting (*before n*); **~ DE algo**: **los documentos ~s de la propiedad** the documents which certify ownership; **recibo ~ de pago** receipt (*that proves payment*)

acreedor[1] -dora *adj* **~ A algo** worthy *o* deserving OF sth; **se hizo ~ al primer premio** he won first prize

acreedor[2] -dora *m,f* creditor

acribillar [A1] *vt* 1 (llenar de agujeros): **lo ~on a balazos** they riddled him with bullets; **los mosquitos me han acribillado** I've been bitten all over by mosquitos 2 (asediar): **me ~on a preguntas** they fired a barrage of questions at me

acrílico[1] -ca *adj* acrylic

acrílico[2] *m* 1 (Tex, Art) acrylic 2 (plástico) acrylic 3 (AmL) (para techos) Plexiglas® (AmE), Perspex® (BrE)

acriminar [A1] *vt* 1 (Der) to incriminate 2 (fam) (comprometer) to get ... into trouble
■ **acriminarse** *v pron* 1 (Der) to incriminate oneself 2 (fam) (comprometerse) to get into trouble

acrimonia *f* bitterness, acrimony

acrimonioso -sa *adj* acrimonious

acriollarse [A1] *v pron* to go native

acrisolar [A1] *vt* 1 ‹*metal*› to refine 2 (liter) ‹*virtud/amor*› to purify

acristalar [A1] *vt* to glaze

acritud *f* (frml) asperity (frml), harshness

acrobacia *f* (arte) acrobatics; **hacer ~s** to perform acrobatics; **~s financieras** financial juggling
(Compuesto) **acrobacia aérea** aerobatics

acróbata *mf* acrobat

a

acrobático -ca *adj* acrobatic
acromático -ca *adj* achromatic
acrónimo *m* acronym
acta *f*‡ 1 (de reunión) minutes (*pl*); **consta en (el) ~** it appears in the minutes; **levantar (el) ~** to take (the) minutes 2 (acuerdo) agreement, accord (frml) 3 (de exámenes) certificate

Compuestos
- **acta de defunción** (Col, Méx, Ven) entry in the register of deaths
- **acta de diputado** certificate of election
- **acta de matrimonio/nacimiento** (Méx) marriage/ birth certificate
- **acta notarial** notarial deed

actitud *f* 1 (disposición) attitude; **su ~ lo hace parecer más joven** his attitude to life makes him seem younger (than his years); **adoptar una ~ firme (con algn)** to be firm (with sb); **¿cuál fue su ~?** what was his reaction? 2 (postura): **estaban todos en ~ de estudiar** they were all bent over their work; **pasaba horas en ~ pensativa** he would spend hours apparently deep in thought; **una ~ de amenaza** a threatening stance
activación *f* 1 (agilización): **la ~ de los procesos es una prioridad** speeding up proceedings is a priority; **medidas para la ~ de la economía** measures to stimulate *o* revitalize the economy 2 (de dispositivo) activation
activar [A1] *vt* 1 (agilizar) ‹*proceso/crecimiento*› to speed up; ‹*economía/producción*› to stimulate; ‹*circulación*› to stimulate; **~ las negociaciones** to give fresh impetus to the negotiations 2 (avivar): **una ráfaga activó las llamas** a gust of wind fanned the flames 3 (poner en funcionamiento) ‹*alarma*› to activate, trigger; ‹*dispositivo*› to activate; ‹*máquina*› to set … in motion
■ **activarse** *v pron* 1 «*alarma*» to go off; «*dispositivo*» to start working 2 (Méx) «*obreros/disidentes*» to take active steps
actividad *f* 1 (ocupación) activity; **~es extraescolares** extracurricular activities 2 (vida, movimiento) activity; **el lugar bullía de ~** the place was buzzing with activity; **un volcán en ~** an active volcano
activista *mf* activist
activo¹ -va *adj* 1 ‹*persona/población*› active; **tomar parte activa en algo** to take an active part in sth 2 (Ling) active 3 ‹*volcán*› active
activo² *m* 1 (bien, derecho) asset; **~s líquidos** liquid assets 2 (conjunto) assets (*pl*); **el ~ y el pasivo** the assets and liabilities

Compuesto **activo neto** net assets (*pl*), net worth

acto *m*
A 1 (acción) act 2 (*en locs*) **acto seguido** immediately after; **en el acto**: **murió en el ~** he died instantly; **lo despidieron en el ~** he was fired on the spot; **acudieron en el ~** they arrived immediately; Ⓢ **fotocopias en el acto** photocopies while you wait

Compuestos
- **acto bélico** *or* **de guerra** act of war
- **acto carnal** (frml) **el ~ ~** the sexual act (frml)
- **acto de presencia**: **hacer ~ de ~** to put in an appearance
- **acto de servicio**: **morir en ~ de ~** «*soldado*» to die on active service; «*policía/bombero*» to die in the course of one's duty
- **acto sexual** sexual act (frml); **durante el ~ ~** during sexual intercourse *o* the sexual act

B (ceremonia): **~ de clausura** closing ceremony; **los ~s conmemorativos de ...** the celebrations to commemorate …; **~s oficiales** official functions
C (Teatr) act
actor *m* actor

Compuesto **actor de reparto** supporting actor

actriz *f* actress

Compuesto **actriz de reparto** supporting actress

actuación *f* 1 (acción) action; **la rápida ~ del médico lo salvó** the doctor's prompt action saved him 2 (Cin, Dep, Teatr) performance; **la ~ es pésima** the acting is appalling; **la brillante ~ del equipo** the team's brilliant performance 3 (conducta) conduct; **criticó la ~ de la policía** he criticized the conduct of the police 4 (recital, sesión) performance, concert
actual *adj* present, current; **el ~ campeón** the current *o* reigning champion; **en las circunstancias ~es** in the present circumstances; **en el Chile ~** in present-day Chile; **en el mundo ~** in the modern world, in today's world; **una moda ~** an up-to-the-minute style; **su carta del 20 del ~** (Corresp) your letter of the 20th of this month
actualidad *f* 1 (tiempo presente): **en la ~** currently, at present; **no se hace así en la ~** it's not done that way nowadays *o* today 2 (situación actual) current situation; **la ~ cubana** the current situation in Cuba; **con toda la ~ informativa** (period) with the latest news 3 (de tema, noticia) topicality; **las noticias de ~** today's (*o* this week's *etc*) news; **un tema de palpitante** *or* **candente ~** (period) a highly topical subject 4 **actualidades** *fpl* (Period) current affairs (*pl*)
actualización *f* updating; **curso de ~** refresher course
actualizar [A4] *vt* ‹*salarios/pensiones/legislación*› to bring … up to date; ‹*información/manual*› to update
actualmente *adv*: **era un lujo pero ~ es una necesidad** it used to be a luxury but nowadays it is a necessity; **se encuentra ~ en Suecia** she is currently in Sweden, she is in Sweden at present; **~ la situación es mucho más grave** the situation is now much more serious
actuar [A18] *vi* 1 «*persona*» (obrar) to act; **forma de ~** behavior* 2 «*medicamento*» to work, act; **dejar ~ a la naturaleza** let nature take its course 3 «*actor*» to act; «*torero*» to perform; **¿quién actúa en esa película?** who's in the movie? 4 (Der) to act
actuario -ria *m,f* 1 (en tribunal) clerk of the court 2 *tb* **~ de seguros** actuary
acualón *m* (Méx) aqualung
acuarela *f* watercolor*; **pintar a la ~** to paint in watercolor(s)
acuarelista *mf* watercolorist*
acuario *m* aquarium
Acuario¹ *m* (signo) Aquarius; **es (de) ~** he's an Aquarius *o* Aquarian
Acuario², acuario *mf* (persona) Aquarian, Aquarius
acuartelamiento *m*
A 1 (alojamiento) billeting, quartering 2 (en previsión de disturbios) confining to barracks
B (cuartel) barracks (*sing or pl*)
acuartelar [A1] *vt* 1 (alojar) to billet, quarter 2 (en previsión de disturbios) to confine … to barracks
■ **acuartelarse** *v pron* to withdraw to barracks
acuático -ca *adj* aquatic
acuatizaje *m*: *landing on water*
acuatizar [A4] *vi* to land on water
acuchillar [A1] *vt* 1 ‹*persona*› to stab 2 (pulir) to sand (down); (raspar) to scrape
acuciante *adj* ‹*necesidad/problema*› urgent, pressing; ‹*deseo*› burning (*before n*), ardent; **una sed/un hambre ~** a raging thirst/a gnawing hunger
acuciar [A1] *vt* 1 «*problema*» to plague, beset; **acuciado por el hambre** driven by hunger 2 «*persona*» to pester, hassle (colloq)
acuclillarse [A1] *v pron* to squat (down)
acudir [I1] *vi*
A (frml) (a lugar): **acudió a la hora prevista** she came *o* arrived at the arranged time; **nadie acudió en su ayuda** nobody came to his aid; **deberá ~ en ayunas** you should not eat anything before attending; **~ A algo** ‹*cita*› to turn up for sth; ‹*reunión*› to attend sth; **~ a las urnas** to go to the polls; **la policía acudió al lugar de los hechos** the police arrived at the scene (of the incident); **los recuerdos acuden a mi mente** (liter) memories come flooding back to me; **señorita Fernández, acuda al teléfono** telephone call for Miss Fernández
B (recurrir) **~ A algn** to turn TO sb; **no tenía a quien ~** he had nobody to turn to; **acudieron a un árbitro** they went to arbitration
acueducto *m* aqueduct
acuerdo *m*
A 1 (arreglo) agreement; **llegar a** *or* **alcanzar un ~** to reach

an agreement; **de común ~** by mutual agreement **2** (pacto) agreement; **~ de paz** peace agreement *o* (frml) accord

B (*en locs*) **1 de acuerdo**: **estar de ~** to agree; **ponerse de ~** to come to *o* reach an agreement; **estar de ~ EN algo** to agree ON something; **estamos de ~ en que ...** we all agree *o* we're all agreed that ...; **estar de ~ CON algn/algo** to agree WITH sb/sth; **no estoy de ~ con pagarle tanto** I don't think we should pay him so much; **¿mañana a las ocho? — de ~** (*indep*) tomorrow at eight? — OK *o* all right **2 de acuerdo con** *or* **a** in accordance with

acuesta, acuestas, etc *see* **acostar**

acullá *adv* (arc) yonder (arch); **aquí, allá y ~** here, there and everywhere

acumulación *f* accumulation

acumulador *m* storage battery, accumulator (BrE)

(Compuesto) **acumulador de calor** storage heater

acumular [A1] *vt* ‹*riquezas/poder*› to accumulate; ‹*experiencia*› to gain

■ **acumularse** *v pron* «*trabajo*» to pile up, mount up; «*intereses*» to accumulate; «*deudas*» to mount up; **se me ~on las deudas** my debts mounted (up); **se acumula mucho polvo aquí** a lot of dust accumulates here

acumulativo -va *adj* cumulative

acunar [A1] *vt* to rock

acuñación *f* (de monedas) minting; (de palabras, frases) coining

acuñar [A1] *vt* ‹*moneda*› to mint; ‹*frase/palabra*› to coin

acuoso -sa *adj* watery

acupuntura *f* acupuncture

acupunturista *mf* acupuncturist

acurrucarse [A2] *v pron* to curl up

acusación *f*

A 1 (imputación) accusation **2** (Der) charge; **negó la ~** he denied the charges; **formular una ~ contra algn** to bring charges against sb

B (parte): **la ~** the prosecution

acusado¹ -da *adj* **1** ‹*persona*›: **las personas acusadas de ...** the people accused of ... **2** ‹*tendencia*› marked, pronounced; ‹*semejanza/contraste*› marked, striking; **un ~ rasgo de su personalidad** a prominent feature of his personality; **un ~ sentido del humor/olfato** a sharp *o* an acute sense of humor/smell

acusado² -da *m,f*: **el ~** the accused, the defendant; **los ~s** the accused, the defendants

acusador¹ -dora *adj* accusing, accusatory (frml); **una mirada ~a** an accusing look

acusador² -dora *m,f* prosecuting attorney (AmE), prosecuting counsel (BrE)

acusar [A1] *vt*

A 1 (culpar) to accuse; **~ a algn DE algo** to accuse sb OF sth; **me acusan de haber mentido** they accuse me of lying **2** (Der) **~ a algn DE algo** to charge sb WITH sth; **está acusado de espionaje** he is charged with spying **3** (fam) (delatar) to tell on (colloq); **lo acusó a** *or* **con la maestra** she went to the teacher and told on him (colloq)

B 1 (mostrar, revelar) to show signs of **2** (advertir) to pick up, register; **acusa el menor movimiento** it picks up the slightest movement

C (reconocer): **~ recibo de algo** (Corresp) to acknowledge receipt of sth

■ **acusarse** *v pron* (*refl*) **~se DE algo** to confess TO sth

acusativo *adj/m* accusative

acusatorio -ria *adj* accusatory

acuse de recibo *m* acknowledgment of receipt

acusetas *mf* (*pl* ~), **acusete -ta** *m,f* (fam) tattletale (AmE colloq), telltale (BrE colloq)

acústica *f* (ciencia) acoustics; (de local) acoustics (*pl*)

acústico -ca *adj* acoustic

adagio *m* (Mús) adagio; (máxima) adage, saying

adalid *m* champion

adamascado -da *adj* damask

adán *m*: **ir hecho un ~** to look a sight *o* mess (colloq)

adaptabilidad *f* adaptability

adaptable *adj* adaptable

adaptación *f* **1** (proceso) adaptation, adjustment; **capacidad de ~** ability to adapt **2** (cosa adaptada) adaptation; **la ~ cinematográfica** the screen version

adaptador *m* adaptor

adaptar [A1] *vt* ‹*cortinas/vestido*› to alter; ‹*habitación*› to convert; ‹*pieza/motor*› to adapt; (Inf) to convert; **adaptó la obra al** *or* **para el cine** he adapted the play for the screen

■ **adaptarse** *v pron* to adapt; **~se A algo/+ INF** to adapt TO sth/-ING; **un coche que se adapta a cualquier terreno** a car which is well suited to any terrain

a. de C. (= **antes de Cristo**) BC, before Christ

adecentar [A1] *vt* ‹*habitación*› to tidy up

adecuación *f* adaptation

adecuado -da *adj* **1** (apropiado): **un vestido ~ para una boda** a suitable dress for a wedding; **la persona adecuada para el cargo** the right person for the job; **el momento ~** the right moment; **no disponemos de los medios ~s** we do not have adequate *o* the necessary resources **2** (aceptable) adequate

adecuar [A1] *or* [A18] *vt* **~ algo A algo** to adapt sth TO sth; **el sistema puede ~se a las necesidades de cada cliente** the system can be adapted to (meet) the needs of each client

■ **adecuarse** *v pron* **~se A algo** to fit in WITH sth

adefesio *m* (cosa) eyesore; (persona): **es un ~** he's so ugly; **estar/ir hecho un ~** to look a sight *o* fright; **un ~ de sombrero** a hideous hat

adelantado¹ -da *adj*

A 1 (desarrollado) ‹*país*› advanced; **una filosofía muy adelantada para su época** a philosophy well ahead of its time **2** (aventajado): **está** *or* **va muy ~ en sus estudios** he is doing very well in his studies; **va ~ para su edad** he's advanced for his age

B (antes de tiempo) **1** ‹*cosecha*› early; **llegar ~** (Chi) to arrive early **2** ‹*reloj*› fast; **estar** *or* **ir ~** to be (running) fast

C (Com, Fin): **pago ~** payment in advance; **por ~** in advance; **pagar/cobrar por ~** to pay/be paid in advance

D (avanzado): **las obras están muy adelantadas** construction is already well underway; **llevo muy ~ el libro** I'm quite far into the book; **vamos bastante ~s** we're quite far ahead with it

E (Dep) (pase) forward

adelantado² *m* governor (*of a border province under Spanish colonial rule*)

adelantamiento *m* passing maneuver (AmE), overtaking manoeuvre (BrE)

adelantar [A1] *vt*

A 1 ‹*fecha/viaje*› to bring forward **2** ‹*pieza/ficha*› to move ... forward

B (pasar) **1** (Auto) to pass, overtake **2** ‹*corredor*› to overtake, pass

C 1 ‹*información*› to disclose; ‹*noticia*› to break; **te adelanto que no es ninguna maravilla** I warn you, it's nothing special; **les adelantamos la programación de mañana** here is a rundown of tomorrow's programs **2** ‹*dinero*›: **le adelantó una parte del sueldo** she gave him an advance on his salary; **la empresa te adelanta el dinero para comprarlo** the company lends you the money to buy it

D ‹*reloj*› to put ... forward

E ‹*balón*› to pass ... forward

F ‹*trabajo*› to get on with

G 1 (conseguir) to gain; **con llorar no adelantas nada** crying won't get you anywhere **2** (en una clasificación) ‹*puestos*› to go up, move up

■ **adelantar** *vi*

A 1 (avanzar) to make progress **2** «*reloj*» to gain

B (Auto) to pass, overtake (BrE); ⊗ **prohibido adelantar** no passing (AmE), no overtaking (BrE)

■ **adelantarse** *v pron*

A 1 (avanzar) to move forward **2** (ir delante) to go ahead; **se adelantó para comprar las entradas** she went (on) ahead to buy the tickets

B (respecto de lo esperado) «*cosecha*» to be early; «*verano/frío*» to arrive early

C (anticiparse): **se adelantó a su época** he was ahead of his time; **~se a los acontecimientos** to jump the gun; (+ *me/te/le etc*) **yo iba a pagar, pero él se me adelantó** I was

a

going to pay, but he beat me to it; **alguien se me había adelantado** someone had beaten me to it
D «*reloj*» to gain

adelante *adv*
A (en el espacio) **1** (expresando dirección, movimiento) forward; **para/hacia ~** forward; **seguir ~** to go on; ***llevar algo ~*** to carry on with sth **2** (lugar, posición): **se sentó ~** (en coche) she sat in front; (en clase, cine) she sat at the front; **más ~ la calle se bifurca** further on, the road forks; ❸ **ver explicación más adelante** see explanation below; **la fila dos es muy ~** the second row is too near the front; **la parte de ~** the front; **tiene un bolsillo ~** (esp AmL) it has a pocket at the front
B (en el tiempo): **más ~** later; **trataremos ese tema más ~** we will deal with that subject later (on); **(de ahora) en ~** from now on; **de hoy en ~** as of *o* from today
C **adelante de** (*loc prep*) (AmL) **1** (en lugar anterior a) in front of; **~ de mí/ti/él** in front of me/you/him; **la colocó ~ de la mía** she put it in front of mine **2** (en presencia de) in front of
D **¡~!** (*como interj*) (autorizando la entrada) come in!; (ordenando marchar) forward!; (invitando a continuar) go on!, carry on!

adelanto *m*
A (avance) step forward; **supone un gran ~** it represents a great step forward; **los ~s de la ciencia** the advances of science
B (del sueldo) advance; (depósito) deposit
C (en el tiempo): **lleva un ~ de tres minutos con respecto a los otros corredores** he has a three minute lead over the rest of the field; **llegó con un poco de ~** he/she/it arrived slightly early

adelgazamiento *m* slimming

adelgazante *adj* weight-reducing (*before n*), slimming (*before n*) (BrE)

adelgazar [A4] *vt* ‹*caderas/cintura*› to reduce; ‹*kilos*› to lose
■ **adelgazar** *vi* to lose weight

ademán *m* **1** (expresión) expression; **con un ~ compungido** with a sad expression **2** (movimiento, gesto) gesture; **me hizo un ~ para que me callara** he motioned me to be quiet; **hacer ~ DE + INF** to make as if TO + INF; **hizo ~ de levantarse** he made as if to get up; **levantó los hombros en ~ de indiferencia** she shrugged indifferently **3** **ademanes** (*pl*): **sus ademanes dejan mucho que desear** his manners leave a lot to be desired

además *adv*
A : **estudia y ~ trabaja** she's working as well as studying; **~ ¿a mí qué me importa?** anyway, what do I care?; **y es que ~, la insultó** on top of everything else he insulted her; **señaló, ~, que su objetivo era ...** he indicated, furthermore *o* moreover, that his aim was to ... (frml)
B **además de** besides, apart from; **~ de eso, está la cuestión del dinero** apart from that there is the question of money; **~ de nuestro pedido anterior** in addition to our previous order; **~ de hacerte mal, engorda** besides *o* apart from *o* as well as being bad for you, it's also fattening; **~ de hacerlos, los diseña** he designs them as well as making them

adenoides *fpl* adenoids (*pl*)

adentrarse [A1] *v pron* **~ EN algo** ‹*en el mar/túnel*› to go deep INTO sth; ‹*en tema/materia*› to go INTO sth in more depth; **según nos adentrábamos en la selva** as we went deeper into the jungle

adentro *adv*
A **1** (expresando dirección, movimiento): **vamos para ~** let's go in *o* inside; **ven aquí ~** come in here; **mar ~** out to sea; **tierra ~** inland **2** (lugar, parte) inside; [*European Spanish prefers* **dentro** *in many of these examples*] **¡qué calor hace aquí ~!** it's so hot in here!; **¿comemos ~?** shall we eat indoors *o* inside?; **por ~** on the inside; **la parte de ~** the inside; ***ser bien*** *o* ***bueno de ~*** (Chi, Per fam) to be a good sort
B **adentro de** (AmL) in, inside; **~ del edificio** inside *o* in the building; **~ del zapato** in my (*o* his *etc*) shoe; **~ de los límites territoriales** inside *o* within our boundaries

adentros *mpl*: **dije para mis ~** I said to myself; **se rió para sus ~s** he chuckled to himself

adepto¹ -ta *adj*: **ser ~ A algo** ‹*a secta*› to be a follower OF sth; ‹*a partido*› to be a supporter OF sth; **un político ~ al monetarismo** a politicain who espouses monetarism

adepto² -ta *m,f* (de secta) follower; (de partido) supporter; **una idea que tiene muchos ~s** an idea which has a lot of supporters; **es una gran adepta de la disciplina** she is a great advocate of *o* believer in discipline

aderezar [A4] *vt* **1** ‹*guiso*› to season; ‹*ensalada*› to dress **2** ‹*pieles*› to cure

aderezo *m* **1** (de guiso) seasoning; (de ensalada) dressing **2** (de pieles) curing **3** (joyas) matching set of jewelry*

adeudar [A1] *vt* **1** (deber) to owe **2** (frml) ‹*cuenta*› to debit (frml); **hemos adeudado su cuenta en la suma de ...** we have debited your account with the sum of ...

adeudo *m* **1** (frml) (débito) debit (frml); **el ~ efectuado en su cuenta** the sum debited to *o* from your account **2** (Méx) (deuda) debt

adherencia *f* **1** (acción) adherence **2** (Auto) grip, road-holding **3** (Med) adhesion

adherente *adj* adhesive

adherir [I11] *vi* to stick, adhere (frml)
■ **adherir** *vt* to stick
■ **adherirse** *v pron* **1** (a superficie) to stick, adhere (frml); **~se A algo** to stick *o* adhere TO sth **2** (dar apoyo) **~se A algo** ‹*a propuesta/causa*› to give one's support TO sth; **quisiera ~me a lo expresado** I would like to express my support for what was said **3** (a movimiento, partido) to join; **~se A algo** to join sth

adhesión *f* **1** (a una superficie) adhesion **2** (apoyo) support; **muestras de ~** demonstration of support; **su ~ al proceso democrático** his support of *o* adherence to the democratic process **3** (a una organización) joining; (a un tratado) accession (frml); **con la ~ de Turquía a la organización** when Turkey joins (*o* joined *etc*) the organization **4** (contribución) donation

adhesivo¹ -va *adj* adhesive, sticky

adhesivo² *m* adhesive

adicción *f* addiction; **~ a la heroína** heroin addiction

adición *f* **1** (acción) addition; (parte añadida) addition **2** (Mat) addition **3** (RPl) (cuenta) check (AmE), bill (BrE)

adicional *adj* additional; **una cantidad ~** a supplement

adicionar [A1] *vt* (frml) to add

adicto¹ -ta *adj*
A (a la bebida, la droga) addicted; **~ A algo** addicted TO sth; **es ~ al juego** he is addicted to gambling
B ▸ **adepto¹**

adicto² -ta *m,f* addict; **los ~s a la cocaína** cocaine addicts

adiestrar [A1] *vt* ‹*animal/persona*› to train; **~ a algn EN algo** to train sb IN sth

adinerado -da *adj* wealthy, moneyed

adiós *m/interj* (al despedirse) goodbye, bye (colloq); (al pasar) hello; ▸ **decir²** *vt* **C2**

adiposidad *f* adiposity

adiposo -sa *adj* adipose

aditamento *m* (de aparato) accessory; (de informe) appendix

aditivo *m* additive

adivinación *f* (por conjeturas, al azar) guessing, guesswork; (por magia) prediction; **la ~ del futuro** fortune-telling

adivinanza *f* riddle; **jugar a las ~s** to play at guessing riddles

adivinar [A1] *vt* **1** (por conjeturas, al azar) to guess; **¿a que no adivinas quién?** you'll never guess who; **~le el pensamiento a algn** to read sb's mind **2** (por magia) to foretell, predict **3** (entrever): **el gesto dejó ~ sus sentimientos** the gesture suggested *o* betrayed his feelings
■ **adivinar** *vi* to guess

adivino -na *m,f* fortune-teller

adj. (Corresp) (= **adjunto**) enc.

adjetivar [A1] *vt* to use ... adjectivally *o* attributively

adjetivo¹ -va *adj* adjectival

adjetivo² *m* adjective
(Compuesto) **adjetivo calificativo/demostrativo/posesivo** qualifying/demonstrative/possessive adjective

adjudicación *f* **1** (de premio, contrato) awarding; (de viviendas) allocation **2** (en subasta) sale

adjudicar [A2] *vt* 1 ‹*premio/contrato*› to award; ‹*vivienda*› to allot, allocate 2 (en subasta): **le ~on la alfombra al anticuario** the carpet was sold to *o* went to the antique dealer; **¡adjudicado!** sold!

■ **adjudicarse** *v pron* (period) ‹*trofeo/premio*› to win; **nuestro equipo se adjudicó la victoria** our team won

adjuntar [A1] *vt* to enclose; **le adjunto una copia del contrato** I enclose *o* attach a copy of the contract

adjunto¹ -ta *adj* 1 ‹*director*› deputy (*before n*); **profesor ~** associate professor (AmE), senior lecturer (BrE) 2 ‹*lista/copia*› enclosed, attached

adjunto² *adv* enclosed; **~ les envío el recibo** please find enclosed the receipt

adjunto³ -ta *m,f* (en cargo): **~ a la cátedra de filosofía** associate philosophy professor (AmE), senior philosophy lecturer (BrE); el cargo de ~ del director the post of deputy director

adminículo *m* (frml) accessory

administración *f*

A (de empresa, organización) management, running; (de bienes) management, administration

B 1 (conjunto de personas) management 2 (oficina, departamento) administration 3 (Esp) (de lotería) *office or kiosk where lottery tickets are sold*

(Compuesto) **administración pública** civil service

C (Pol) administration

D (Med): **está desaconsejada la ~ de este fármaco durante el embarazo** the use of this drug during pregnancy is not advised; Ⓢ **administración por vía oral** to be taken orally

administrador -dora *m,f* (de empresa) manager, administrator; (de bienes) administrator; **es buen ~** (fam) he's good with money

administrar [A1] *vt* 1 ‹*empresa*› to manage, run; ‹*bienes*› to manage, administer (frml) 2 (frml) (dar) ‹*sacramentos/medicamento*› to give, administer (frml)

■ **administrarse** *v pron*: **debes aprender a ~te** you have to learn to budget; **~se bien/mal** to manage one's money well/badly

administrativo¹ -va *adj* administrative

administrativo² -va *m,f* administrative assistant (*o* officer *etc*); (con funciones más rutinarias) clerk

admirable *adj* admirable

admiración *f* 1 (respeto) admiration; **siento gran ~ por usted** I have great admiration for you; **es digno de ~** he's/it's admirable 2 (sorpresa) amazement

admirado -da *adj* 1 (reconocido) admired; **fue muy ~ en su época** he was much admired in his time 2 (sorprendido) amazed; **me quedé admirada** I was amazed

admirador -dora *m,f* 1 (de persona) admirer, fan 2 (hum) (pretendiente) admirer (hum)

admirar [A1] *vt* 1 (respetar) ‹*persona/cualidad*› to admire 2 (contemplar) to admire 3 (sorprender) to amaze; **me admira la tolerancia de esta gente** I'm amazed at the tolerance of these people

■ **admirarse** *v pron* **~se DE algo** to be amazed AT *o* ABOUT sth

admirativo -va *adj* admiring

admisibilidad *f* admissibility

admisible *adj* ‹*comportamiento*› admissible, acceptable; ‹*excusa*› acceptable

admisión *f* 1 (aceptación) admission; **examen** *or* **prueba de ~** entrance examination *o* test; Ⓢ **reservado el derecho de admisión** the management reserves the right to refuse admission 2 (de error) admission

admitir [I1] *vt*

A 1 (aceptar) to accept; **no lo admitieron en el colegio** he wasn't accepted by the school; Ⓢ **se admiten tarjetas de crédito** we take *o* accept credit cards 2 (permitir) to allow; Ⓢ **no se admiten perros** no dogs allowed; **admite varias interpretaciones** it allows of *o* admits of several different interpretations (frml); **eso no admite discusión** you can't argue with that; **el asunto no admite demora** the matter must be dealt with immediately

B (confesar, reconocer) to admit

C (dar cabida a) ‹‹*local*›› to hold; **el estadio admite 4.000 personas** the stadium holds 4,000 people

admonición *f* (frml) admonishment (frml); **recibir una ~** to be admonished (frml)

admonitorio -ria *adj* (frml) admonitory (frml)

ADN *m* (= **ácido desoxirribonucleico**) DNA

adobar [A1] *vt* 1 ‹*carne/pescado*› (condimentar) to marinade; (para conservar) to pickle; (para curar) to cure 2 ‹*pieles*› to tan

adobe *m* adobe; **una casa de ~** an adobe (house)

adobo *m* 1 (Coc) (condimento) marinade; (para conservar) pickle 2 (de pieles) tanning

adocenado -da *adj* (pey) run-of-the-mill (pej)

adoctrinamiento *m* indoctrination

adoctrinar [A1] *vt* to indoctrinate

adolecer [E3] *vi* (de enfermedad, defecto) **~ DE algo** to suffer FROM sth; **adolece de muchos errores** it contains many mistakes

adolescencia *f*: **un comportamiento típico de la ~** typical adolescent behavior; **durante su ~** (when he was) in his teens, in adolescence (frml)

adolescente¹ *adj* adolescent; **tiene dos hijos ~s** she has two teenage *o* adolescent children

adolescente² *mf* (en contextos no técnicos) teenager; (Med, Psic) adolescent

adolorido -da *adj* (esp AmL) ▸**dolorido**

adonde *adv* where; **el lugar ~ se dirigían** the place where *o* to which they were going; **la ciudad ~ habíamos llegado** the city we had arrived in; ***~ fueres haz lo que vieres*** when in Rome, do as the Romans do

adónde *adv* where

adondequiera *adv*: **~ QUE** wherever; **~ que vayas** wherever you go

Adonis Adonis; **no es ningún ~** he's no Adonis

adopción *f* adoption

adoptado -da *m,f* adopted child

adoptar [A1] *vt* 1 ‹*actitud/costumbre*› to adopt; ‹*decisión/medida/posición*› to take; **la decisión fue adoptada por unanimidad** the decision was unanimous 2 ‹*niño/nacionalidad*› to adopt

adoptivo -va *adj* 1 ‹*hijo*› adopted; ‹*padres*› adoptive; **lo declararon hijo ~ de la ciudad** he was given the freedom of the city 2 ‹*patria/país*› adopted

adoquín *m* 1 (de piedra) paving stone; (ovalado) cobblestone 2 (fam) (tonto) blockhead (colloq) 3 (Per) (helado) popsicle® (AmE), ice lolly (BrE)

adoquinado *m* paving

adoquinar [A1] *vt* to pave

adorable *adj* adorable

adoración *f* 1 (de persona) adoration; **siente ~ por su padre** she worships *o* adores her father; **una mirada de ~** an adoring look 2 (de deidad) adoration, worship

adorador -dora *m,f* (de deidad) worshipper

adorar [A1] *vt* 1 ‹*persona/cosa*› to adore 2 ‹*deidad*› to worship, adore

adormecedor -dora *adj* soporific; **tiene un efecto ~** it has a soporific effect *o* sends you to sleep

adormecer [E3] *vt* 1 ‹*persona*› to make ... sleepy *o* drowsy; **adormece los sentidos** it numbs *o* dulls the senses 2 ‹*pierna/mano*› to numb

■ **adormecerse** *v pron* to fall asleep, doze off

adormecimiento *m* 1 (somnolencia) sleepiness, drowsiness 2 (de un miembro) numbness

adormidera *f* poppy

adormilarse [A1] *v pron* to doze; **estás adormilado** you're half asleep

adornar [A1] *vt* 1 ‹*habitación/sombrero/comida*› to decorate 2 ‹*relato/discurso*› to embellish 3 ‹‹*flores/banderas*›› to adorn

■ **adornarse** *v pron* (*refl*) ‹*cabeza/pelo*› to adorn; **se adornó los brazos con pulseras** she adorned her arms with bracelets

adorno *m* 1 (objeto) ornament; **los ~s de Navidad** the Christmas decorations 2 (decoración) adornment; **eso era su único ~** that was her only adornment; **una falda con ~ de pasamanería** a skirt trimmed with frills; **de ~** for decoration; **lo tenemos de ~** (hum) it's just for show

adosado -da *adj* ~ **A algo**: **estaba ~ a la pared** it was against the wall; **un invernadero ~ a la casa** a greenhouse built onto the house; ▸**casa**

adosar [A1] *vt* 1 ‹*armario/escritorio*› ~ **algo A algo** to put *o* place sth AGAINST sth 2 (Méx) ‹*documento*› to enclose, attach

adquiera, adquirió, etc *see* **adquirir**

adquirir [I13] *vt* to acquire, obtain; **adquiera su nuevo coche antes del día 30** purchase *o* buy your new car before the 30th; **adquirió renombre internacional** he attained *o* achieved international renown; **ha adquirido experiencia** he has gained experience; ~ **malas costumbres** to get into bad habits

adquisición *f* 1 (objeto, cosa) acquisition; **fue una buena ~** it was a good buy 2 (acción) acquisition; **es de reciente ~** it is a recent acquisition *o* purchase; **la ~ de la casa** the purchase of the house

adquisitivo -va *adj* purchasing

adrede *adv* on purpose, deliberately

adrenalina *f* adrenaline

Adriático *m*: **el (mar) ~** the Adriatic (Sea)

adscribir [I34] *vt* ~ **a algn A algo** to assign *o* attach sb TO sth; **los oficiales adscritos a la dirección** the officials attached to head office

■ **adscribirse** *v pron* to join, become a member of

adscrito -ta *pp ver* **adscribir**

ADSL *m* = **Asymmetric Digital Subscriber Line** ADSL

aduana *f* customs; **libre de derechos de ~** duty free; **pasar por la ~** to go through customs

aduanero[1] -ra *adj* customs (*before n*)

aduanero[2] -ra *m,f* customs officer

aducir [I6] *vt* ‹*razones/argumentos*› to put forward, adduce (frml); ‹*pruebas*› to provide, furnish; **adujo no haber sido informado** he claimed that he had not been informed

adueñarse [A1] *v pron* 1 «*persona*» ~ **DE algo** to take over sth; **se adueñó de su corazón** she won his heart 2 (liter) «*miedo/pánico*» ~ **DE algn**: **el miedo/pánico se adueñó de ellos** they were seized by panic

adulación *f* flattery

adulador[1] -dora *adj* flattering, sycophantic

adulador[2] -dora *m,f* flatterer, sycophant

adular [A1] *vt* to flatter

adulón[1] -lona *adj* (fam) fawning

adulón[2] -lona *m,f* (fam) bootlicker (colloq)

adulteración *f* (de producto) adulteration; (de información) falsification

adulterar [A1] *vt* ‹*alimento/vino*› to adulterate; ‹*información*› to falsify

adulterio *m* adultery

adúltero[1] -ra *adj* adulterous

adúltero[2] -ra *m,f* adulterer

adultez *f* adulthood

adulto[1] -ta *adj* 1 ‹*persona/animal*› adult (*before n*) 2 ‹*reacción/opinión*› adult

adulto[2] -ta *m,f* adult

adustez *f* harshness

adusto -ta *adj* ‹*persona/expresión*› austere, severe; ‹*paisaje*› bleak, harsh

advenedizo[1] -za *adj* upstart (*before n*)

advenedizo[2] -za *m,f* social climber

advenimiento *m* advent; ~ **al trono** accession to the throne

adverbial *adj* adverbial

adverbio *m* adverb

adversario[1] -ria *adj* opposing (*before n*)

adversario[2] -ria *m,f* opponent, adversary

adversidad *f* 1 (hecho) adversity; **sufrió todo tipo de ~es** he suffered all sorts of setbacks *o* adversities 2 (situación): **en la ~** in adversity 3 (cualidad) harshness, severity

adverso -sa *adj* ‹*circunstancias/resultado*› adverse; **la suerte le fue adversa** (liter) fortune did not favor him (liter)

advertencia *f* warning; **que les sirva de ~** let it be a warning to them

advertir [I11] *vt* 1 (avisar) to warn; **¡te lo advierto!** I'm warning you!; **quedas/estás advertido** you've been warned; ~**le A algn DE algo** to warn sb ABOUT sth; **te advierto que no me sorprendió nada** I must say I wasn't at all surprised; ~**le A algn QUE + SUBJ**: **le advertí que tuviera cuidado** I warned him to be careful 2 (notar) to notice

adviento *m* Advent

advierta, advirtió, etc *see* **advertir**

adyacencias *fpl* (CS) vicinity

adyacente *adj* adjacent

aéreo -rea *adj* ‹*vista*› aerial; ‹*tráfico*› air (*before n*)

aerobic /e'roβik/ *m*, (Méx) **aerobics** *mpl* aerobics

aeróbico -ca *adj* aerobic

aerobismo *m* (CS) aerobics

aerobús *m* airbus

aeroclub *m* flying club

aerodeslizador *m*
A (Náut) hovercraft
B (Chi) (Dep) hang glider

aerodinámica *f* aerodynamics

aerodinámico -ca *adj* aerodynamic

aeródromo *m* aerodrome, airfield

aeroespacial *adj* aerospace (*before n*)

aerofumigación *f* crop-dusting

aerogenerador *m* wind turbine

aerograma *m* aerogram, air (mail) letter

aerolínea *f* airline

aerolito *m* (meteorito) meteorite; (estrella fugaz) shooting star

aeromodelismo *m* model airplane making

aeromodelista *mf* model airplane enthusiast

aeromotor *m* aero-engine

aeromozo -za *m,f* (AmL) flight attendant

aeronáutica *f* 1 (ciencia) aeronautics 2 (RPl) (aviación militar) air force

aeronáutico -ca *adj* aeronautic, aeronautical

aeronaval *adj* air and sea (*before n*)

aeronave *f* 1 (globo dirigible) airship 2 (frml) (avión) airliner, aircraft

aeropirata *mf* hijacker, skyjacker (journ)

aeroplano *m* (ant) airplane, aeroplane (BrE)

aeropuerto *m* airport

aerosol *m* aerosol, spray can; **desodorante en ~** spray deodorant

aerostato, aeróstato *m* aerostat

aerotransportado -da *adj* airborne

aerotransportar [A1] *vt* to airlift

afabilidad *f* affability

afable *adj* affable

afamado -da *adj* famous

afán *m*
A 1 (anhelo) eagerness; **su ~ de aventuras** his thirst for adventure; ~ **DE + INF** eagerness TO + INF; **su ~ de agradar** their eagerness to please; **tiene ~ de aprender** she's eager to learn; **su ~ por alcanzar la fama** his desire to become famous 2 (empeño) effort; **pone mucho ~ en** he puts a lot (of effort) into
B (Col fam) (prisa) hurry

afanado -da *adj*
A [ESTAR] ‹*persona*› busy
B [ESTAR] (Col, Per fam) (con prisa) in a hurry

afanador -dora *m,f*
A (arg) (ladrón) thief
B (Méx) (limpiador) cleaner

afanar [A1] *vt*
A (arg) (robar) to pinch (colloq)
B (Col fam) 1 (apurar) to rush 2 (preocupar) to worry
C (Per fam) ‹*chica*› to hit on, to try to get off with (BrE colloq)

■ **afanarse** *v pron*
A (esforzarse) to work, toil; ~**se EN** *or* **POR + INF** to strive TO + INF
B (*enf*) (arg) (robar) to pinch (colloq)

afano *m* (RPl arg) rip-off

afanoso -sa *adj* **1** ‹*búsqueda/tarea*› painstaking; ‹*empeño/dedicación*› unflagging **2** ‹*persona*› industrious

afasia *f* aphasia

afear [A1] *vt* **1** ‹*persona*› to make … look ugly; ‹*paisaje*› to spoil **2** ‹*conducta*› to criticize

■ **afearse** *v pron* to lose one's looks

afección *f* (frml) complaint; **una ~ cardíaca** a heart condition

afectación *f* affectation

afectado -da *adj* **1** ‹*gestos/acento*› affected **2** ‹*área/órgano*› affected; **está afectado de una grave enfermedad** (frml) he is suffering from a serious disease

afectar [A1] *vt*

A **1** (tener efecto en) to affect; **esto nos afecta a todos** this affects us all; **le afectó el cerebro** it affected her brain **2** (afligir) to affect (frml); **la noticia lo afectó mucho** the news upset him terribly

B (fingir) ‹*admiración/indiferencia*› to affect, feign

afectísimo -ma *adj* (Corresp) (frml): **suyo ~** yours truly

afectivo -va *adj* emotional

afecto[1] -ta *adj*

A **1** [SER] (simpatizante) **~ A algo** ‹*a ideas/un régimen*› sympathetic TO sth **2** [SER] (aficionado) **~ A algo** keen ON sth; **~ A + INF** given TO -ING

B (frml) (sujeto, ligado) **~ A algo**: **los empleados ~s a esa sucursal** those employed at that branch

C (frml) (afectado) **~ DE algo** afflicted WITH sth (frml)

afecto[2] *m* (cariño) affection; **tenerle ~ a** *or* **sentir ~ por algn** to be fond of sb; **tomarle ~ a algn** to grow fond of sb

afectuoso -sa *adj* ‹*persona*› affectionate; **recibe un ~ saludo** (Corresp) with warm *o* kind regards

afeitado *m* **1** (de la barba) shave **2** (Taur) shaving

afeitadora *f* shaver, electric razor

afeitar [A1] *vt* **1** ‹*persona/cabeza*› to shave; ‹*barba*› to shave off; ‹*crines/cola*› to trim **2** (Taur) ‹*cuernos*› to shave **3** (fam) (rozar) to scrape

■ **afeitarse** *v pron* (*refl*) to shave; **se afeitó la barba** he shaved off his beard

afeite *m* (ant *o* hum) make-up

afelpado -da *adj* velvety

afeminado -da *adj* effeminate

aferrar [A1] *vt* **1** (apretar con fuerza) to clutch; **llevaba al bebé aferrado contra su pecho** she was clutching the baby to her bosom **2** (con el ancla) to anchor

■ **aferrarse** *v pron*: **aférrate bien** hold (on) tight; **~se A algo/algn** to cling (ON) TO sth/sb

affidávit *m* (*pl* **~s**) affidavit

affmo. affma. (Corresp) (frml) = **afectísimo, -ma**

Afganistán *m* Afghanistan

afgano -na *adj/m,f* Afghan

afianzamiento *m* consolidation

afianzar [A4] *vt* ‹*posición/postura*› to consolidate; **afianzó un pie en la cornisa** he got a firm foothold on the ledge

■ **afianzarse** *v pron* «*prestigio/sistema*» to become consolidated; **se fue afianzando en esa convicción** he became more and more convinced of it

afiche *m* (esp AmL) poster

afición *f* **1** (inclinación, gusto) love, liking; **~ a la lectura/música** love of reading/music; **¿cuáles son tus aficiones?** what are your interests?; **escribe por ~** she writes as a hobby **2** (Dep, Taur): **la ~** the fans (*pl*); **agradecer a la ~** to thank one's supporters

aficionado[1] -da *adj* [SER] **1** (entusiasta) **~ A algo** fond OF *o* keen ON sth; **las personas aficionadas al teatro** keen theatergoers **2** (no profesional) amateur

aficionado[2] -da *m,f* **1** (entusiasta) enthusiast; **~ A algo**: **para los ~s al bricolaje** for do-it-yourself enthusiasts; **un ~ a la música** a music lover; **los ~s al tenis/fútbol** tennis/football fans; **los ~s a los toros** bullfighting aficionados **2** (no profesional) amateur

aficionar [A1] *vt* **~ a algn A algo** to get sb interested IN sth

■ **aficionarse** *v pron* **~se A algo** to become interested IN sth; **se aficionó a correr** he took up running

afiebrado -da *adj* [ESTAR] feverish

afilado -da *adj*

A **1** ‹*borde/cuchillo*› sharp **2** ‹*nariz*› pointed; ‹*rasgos*› sharp; ‹*dedos*› long; **de rostro ~** with a long, thin face

B (mordaz) ‹*lengua*› sharp; ‹*pluma*› biting

afilador -dora *m,f* **1** (persona) knife grinder **2** **afilador** *m* (utensilio) sharpener

afilalápices *m* (*pl* **~**) pencil sharpener

afilar [A1] *vt* ‹*navaja/cuchillo*› to sharpen, hone

afiliación *f* affiliation

afiliado -da *m,f* member

afiliar [A1] *vt* **~ a algn A algo** to make sb a member of sth

■ **afiliarse** *v pron* **~se A algo** «*persona*» ‹*a partido/sindicato*› to become a member OF sth, to join sth; ‹*a sistema*› to join sth; **los trabajadores afiliados al sindicato** workers who are affiliated to the union

afín *adj* ‹*temas/lenguas*› related; ‹*culturas/ideologías*› similar; **intereses afines** common interests; **~ A algo**: **ideas afines a las nuestras** ideas which have a lot in common with our own

afinación *f* tuning

afinador -dora *m,f* tuner

afinar [A1] *vt*

A **1** ‹*instrumento*› to tune **2** ‹*coche*› to tune up; ‹*motor*› to tune

B ‹*punta*› to sharpen

■ **afinarse** *v pron* to become thinner

afincarse [A2] *v pron* «*persona*» to settle; «*creencias/valores*» to become established

afinidad *f* (entre personas, caracteres) affinity; **no tengo ninguna ~ con él** I have nothing in common with him

afirmación *f* (declaración) statement, assertion; (respuesta positiva) affirmation

afirmar [A1] *vt*

A (aseverar) to state, declare, assert (frml); **no lo afirmó ni lo negó** she neither confirmed nor denied it

B ‹*escalera*› to steady

■ **afirmar** *vi*: **afirmó con la cabeza** he nodded

■ **afirmarse** *v pron* **1** (físicamente) to steady oneself; **~se EN algo/algn** to hold ON to sth/sb **2** (ratificarse, consolidarse): **se fue afirmando en su convicción** she was more and more convinced of it; **se afirmó en su posición/en lo que había dicho** she reaffirmed her stance/her previous statement

afirmativo -va *adj* ‹*respuesta/frase*› affirmative; **en caso ~** (frml) if that is the case (frml)

aflautado -da *adj* high-pitched, fluty

aflicción *f* (liter) grief, sorrow

afligido -da *adj* [ESTAR] upset; **su afligida viuda** his grief-stricken widow

afligir [I7] *vt* **1** (afectar) to afflict **2** (apenar) to upset

■ **afligirse** *v pron* to get upset

aflojar [A1] *vt*

A ‹*cinturón/tornillo*› to loosen; ‹*cuerda/riendas*› to slacken; ‹*presión/tensión*› to ease; ‹*marcha/paso*› to slow down

B (fam) ‹*dinero*› to hand over; **no aflojó ni un centavo** he didn't part with a cent

C (AmL) ‹*motor*› to run in

■ **aflojar** *vi*

A «*tormenta*» to ease off; «*fiebre/viento*» to drop; «*calor*» to let up; «*tensión/presión*» to ease off

B (ceder) to budge, give way; **no les aflojes** don't give in to them; **aflójale un poco al pobre chico** ease up on the poor boy a little

■ **aflojarse** *v pron*

A **1** (*refl*) ‹*cinturón*› to loosen **2** «*tornillo/tuerca*» to come *o* work loose

B (Méx) «*estómago*»: **se me aflojó el estómago** I got diarrhea

aflorar [A1] *vi* **1** «*filón/mineral*» to surface; «*agua*» to rise **2** «*sentimientos*» to come to the surface; «*tensiones*» to erupt

afluencia *f* **1** (de personas, dinero) influx; **contó con una gran ~ de público** it attracted large crowds **2** (de agua, sangre) flow

afluente *m* tributary, affluent

afluir [I20] *vi* **1** «*gente/público*» to flock; **2** «*agua/sangre*» to flow

a

aflujo *m* afflux
afonía *f* loss of voice, aphonia (tech)
afónico -ca *adj*: **estar/quedarse** ~ to loose one's voice
aforar [A1] *vt* (valorar) to assess, value
aforismo *m* aphorism
aforo *m* capacity; **el estadio tiene un ~ de ...** the stadium has a capacity of *o* the stadium holds ...
afortunadamente *adv* fortunately, luckily
afortunado *adj* ‹*persona*› lucky, fortunate; ‹*encuentro/coincidencia*› happy, fortunate; **una elección poco afortunada** a rather unfortunate choice
afrancesado[1] **-da** *adj* 1 (pey) ‹*modas/costumbres*› Frenchified (pej) 2 (pey) (Hist) ‹*persona*›: *who supported the French during the Peninsular War*
afrancesado[2] **-da** *m,f* (pey) (Hist) *supporter of the French during the Peninsular War*
afrancesarse [A1] *v pron* (pey) to become Frenchified (pej)
afrecho *m* bran
afrenta *f* (frml) affront (frml), insult
afrentar [A1] *vt* (frml) to affront (frml), to insult
África *f*‡: *tb* **el** ~ Africa
África del Sur *f*‡ South Africa
africano -na *adj/m,f* African
afrikaans *m* Afrikaans
afrikaner *adj/mf* (*pl* **-ners**) Afrikaner
afro *adj inv* Afro
afrodisíaco[1] **-ca** *adj* aphrodisiac
afrodisíaco[2] *m* aphrodisiac
afrontar [A1] *vt* ‹*problema/responsabilidad*› to face up to; ‹*desafío/peligro*› to face
afrutado -da *adj* fruity
aftosa *f* foot-and-mouth disease
afuera *adv*
A 1 (expresando dirección, movimiento) outside; **ven aquí ~** come out here; **¡~!** get out of here! 2 (lugar, parte) outside; [*European Spanish prefers* **fuera** *in many of these examples*] **aquí ~ se está muy bien** it's really nice out here; **comimos ~** (en el jardín) we ate outside *o* outdoors; (en un restaurante) we ate out; **por ~ es rojo** it's red on the outside; **de** *o* **desde ~** from the outside; **los de ~** outsiders; **lavar para ~** to take in washing
B **afuera de** (AmL): **¿qué haces ~ de la cama?** what are you doing out of bed?; **~ del edificio** outside the building
afuerano -na *m,f* outsider
afueras *fpl*: **las ~** the outskirts; **un barrio de las ~s** an outlying district
afuerino -na *m,f* (Chi) outsider
agachar [A1] *vt* ‹*cabeza*› to lower
■ **agacharse** *v pron* 1 (ponerse en cuclillas) to crouch down; (inclinarse) to bend down; **tiró la piedra y me agaché** he threw the stone and I ducked 2 (AmL fam) (rebajarse) to eat humble pie *o* (AmE) crow (colloq)
agalla *f*
A (Zool) gill
B (Bot) gall, oak apple
C **agallas** *fpl* (fam) (valor) guts (*pl*) (colloq); **con ~s** gutsy (colloq); **hay que tener ~s** it takes guts (colloq)
agalludo -da *adj*
A (AmL fam) (valiente) gutsy (colloq)
B (Col fam) (codicioso) grasping
ágape *m* (frml *or* hum) banquet (*in sb's honor*)
agarrada *f* (fam) set-to (colloq), fight (colloq)
agarradera *f* 1 (en autobús, tren) strap, handgrip 2 (AmL) (de taza, olla) handle; (paño) pot holder; (guante) oven glove
agarrado[1] **-da** *adj* 1 [SER] (fam) (tacaño) tightfisted (colloq) 2 [ESTAR] (CS fam) (enamorado) in love; **está muy ~ de ella** he's crazy about her (colloq)
agarrado[2] **-da** *m,f* (fam) (tacaño) skinflint (colloq), tightwad (AmE colloq)
agarrado[3] *adv*: **bailar ~** to dance closely
agarrador *m* (paño) pot holder; (guante) oven glove
agarrar [A1] *vt*
A (sujetar) to grab, get hold of; **lo agarró de las solapas** he grabbed him by the lapels; **me agarró del brazo** (para apoyar) she took hold of my arm; (con violencia, rapidez) she grabbed me by the arm
B (esp AmL) ‹*objeto*› (tomar) to take; (atajar) to catch; **agarra un papel y toma nota** get a piece of paper and take this down; **te lo tiro ¡agárralo!** I'll throw it to you, catch!; ***no hay por dónde ~lo*** (fam) ‹*tema/asunto*› you can't make head nor tail of it (colloq); ‹*persona*› you don't know how to take him
C (AmL) (pescar, atrapar) to catch; **me agarró desprevenido** she caught me off guard; **si lo agarro, lo mato** if I get *o* lay my hands on him, I'll kill him; ***~la con algn*** (AmL fam) to take it out on sb
D (esp AmL) (adquirir) ‹*resfriado/pulmonía*› to catch; ‹*costumbre/vicio*› to pick up; ‹*ritmo*› to get into; ‹*velocidad*› to gather, pick up; (+ *me/te/le etc*) **~le cariño a algn** to grow fond of sb; **le agarró asco** he got sick of it; **le he agarrado odio** I've come to hate him
E (AmL) (entender) ‹*indirecta/chiste*› to get
■ **agarrar** *vi*
A (asir, sujetar) to take hold of, hold; **toma, agarra** here, hold this
B «*planta/injerto*» to take; «*tornillo*» to grip, catch; «*ruedas*» to grip; «*tinte*» to take
C (esp AmL) (ir): **~on por esa calle** they went up that street; **mañana agarramos para Medellín** we're off to Medellín tomorrow; **no sabe para dónde ~** he doesn't know which way to turn
D (esp AmL fam) **~ y ...**: **un buen día agarró y lo dejó todo** one fine day she upped and left everything; **así que agarré y presenté la renuncia** so I gave in my notice there and then
■ **agarrarse** *v pron*
A (asirse) to hold on; **agárrate bien** *or* **fuerte** hold on tight; **¿sabes a quién vi? ¡agárrate!** (fam) do you know who I saw? wait for it! (colloq); **~se A** *or* **DE algo** to hold on TO sth; **iban agarrados del brazo** they were walking along arm in arm; **se agarró de eso para no venir** he latched on to that as an excuse not to come; **se ha agarrado a esa esperanza** she's clinging to that hope
B (pillarse): **me agarré el dedo en el cajón** I caught my finger in the drawer
C (esp AmL) ‹*resfriado/pulmonía*› to catch; **~se una borrachera** to get drunk; **~se un disgusto** to get upset; **~se una rabieta** to get into a temper
D (AmL fam) (pelearse) to get into a fight; **se ~on a patadas** they started kicking each other; **por poco se agarran de los pelos** they almost came to blows; **~se CON algn** to have a set-to WITH sb (colloq); ***agarrársela(s) con algn*** (AmL fam) to take it out on sb (colloq)
agarre *m* (de neumático) grip; (de coche) roadholding
agarrón *m* 1 (en fútbol): **hubo ~ de Ramírez a García** Ramírez grabbed García's shirt *o* was holding García 2 (AmL fam) (discusión, pelea) set-to (colloq)
agarrotamiento *m* (de músculos) stiffness, tightness
agarrotar [A1] *vt* ‹*piernas/músculos*› to make ... stiff
■ **agarrotarse** *v pron* 1 «*manos/músculos*» to stiffen up; **tengo las manos agarrotadas** my hands are stiff 2 «*motor/máquina*» to seize up
agasajado -da *m,f* (frml) guest of honor
agasajar [A1] *vt* (frml) to fête (frml); **la ~on con una magnífica fiesta** a splendid party was given in her honor
agasajo *m* (frml) 1 (acción): **los ~s con motivo de su boda** the celebrations in honor of her wedding; **una cena en su ~** a dinner in her honor 2 (atención): **nos recibieron con todo tipo de ~s** they lavished attention on us
ágata *f*‡ agate
agazaparse [A1] *v pron* «*animal*» to crouch; «*persona*» to crouch (down)
agencia *f* (oficina) office; (sucursal) branch
Compuestos
- **agencia de colocaciones** employment agency *o* bureau (*generally for domestic staff*)
- **agencia de contactos/publicidad** dating/advertising agency
- **agencia de prensa** *or* **de noticias** press *o* news agency
- **agencia de viajes** travel agent's, travel agency
- **agencia matrimonial** marriage bureau

agenciar [A1] *vt* (fam) (conseguir) to wangle (colloq)
■ **agenciarse** *v pron* 1 (fam) (robar) to swipe (colloq), to pinch (BrE colloq) 2 (fam) (conseguir) to get hold of; ***agenciárselas*** (fam): **se las agenció para que lo invitaran** he fixed it so that they invited him; **agénciatelas como puedas** you'll have to get by as best you can (colloq)

agenda *f* (libreta) appointment book (AmE), diary (BrE); (programa) agenda; **establecer una ~** to draw up an agenda

(Compuestos)
- **agenda de bolsillo** pocket diary
- **agenda de trabajo** engagement book

agente *mf*
A (Com, Fin) agent
(Compuestos)
- **agente artístico/de publicidad** artistic/advertising agent
- **agente de seguros** insurance broker
- **agente de viajes** travel agent

B (frml) (funcionario) employee
(Compuestos)
- **agente de policía** *or* (period) **del orden** police officer
- **agente de tráfico** *or* (Arg, Méx) **de tránsito** ≈ traffic policeman (*in US*), ≈ traffic warden (*in UK*)
- **agente secreto** secret agent

C **agente** *m* (Med, Tec, Ling) agent

agigantado -da *adj* ‹*proporciones/figura*› gigantic

agigantar [A1] *vt* 1 ‹*ritmo/rendimiento*› to increase … considerably; **agigantados por su público** boosted by their supporters 2 (exagerar) to exaggerate
■ **agigantarse** *v pron* 1 «*rendimiento*» to increase considerably 2 «*problema*» to take on huge proportions

ágil *adj* ‹*persona/movimiento*› agile; ‹*estilo/programa*› lively

agilidad *f* (de persona) agility; (de estilo) liveliness

agilización *f* speeding up

agilizar [A4] *vt* ‹*gestiones/proceso*› to speed up; ‹*pensamiento*› to sharpen; ‹*ritmo/presentación*› to make … livelier *o* more dynamic

agiotaje *m* speculation

agiotista *mf* 1 (ant) (cambista) moneychanger 2 (AmL) (usurero, especulador) shark (colloq)

agitación *f* 1 (Pol) agitation; **la ~ reinante** the prevailing state of unrest 2 (nerviosismo) agitation 3 (de calle, ciudad) bustle

agitado -da *adj* 1 ‹*mar*› rough, choppy 2 ‹*día/vida*› hectic, busy 3 (Pol): **una época agitada** a period of unrest 4 ‹*persona*› worked up, agitated

agitador -dora *m,f* (persona) agitator

agitanado -da *adj* gypsy-like

agitar [A1] *vt* 1 ‹*líquido/botella*› to shake; Ⓢ **agítese antes de usar** shake well before use 2 ‹*brazo/pañuelo*› to wave; ‹*alas*› to flap; **el viento agitaba las hojas** the leaves rustled in the wind 3 ‹*sociedad/país*› to cause unrest in
■ **agitarse** *v pron* 1 «*mar*» to get rough; «*barca*» to toss; «*toldo*» to flap 2 (inquietarse) to get worked up

aglomeración *f* 1 (de gente): **se produjo una ~ a la entrada** people crowded at the entrance; **para evitar las aglomeraciones** to avoid crowding; **las aglomeraciones urbanas** the built-up urban areas 2 (de tráfico) buildup

aglomerar [A1] *vt* to pile up
■ **aglomerarse** *v pron* to crowd (together)

aglutinación *f* agglutination

aglutinador -dora *adj* agglutinative, agglutinating (*before n*)

aglutinar [A1] *vt* ‹*grupos/organizaciones*› to draw together, bring together
■ **aglutinarse** *v pron* «*partidos/grupos*» to get together, to unite

agnosticismo *m* agnosticism

agnóstico -ca *adj/m,f* agnostic

ago. (= **agosto**) Aug, August

agobiado -da *adj* 1 (abrumado): **estar ~ de trabajo** to be snowed under with work; **estar ~ de deudas** to be overwhelmed with debts; **estaba agobiada con tantos problemas** she was weighed down by all those problems 2 (esp Esp) (angustiado): **estar ~** to be in a real state (colloq)

agobiante *adj*, **agobiador -dora** *adj* ‹*trabajo/día*› exhausting; ‹*calor*› stifling; **es una carga ~ para él** it's/he's/she's a terrible burden on him

agobiar [A1] *vt* (abrumar) «*problemas/responsabilidad*» to weigh *o* get … down; «*calor*» to oppress, get … down; **te agobia con tanta amabilidad** she smothers you with kindness; **este niño me agobia** this child is too much for me
■ **agobiarse** *v pron* (esp Esp fam) to get uptight (colloq)

agobio *m*: **una sensación de ~** a sense of oppression; **el ~ que produce el calor** the stifling sensation brought on by the heat; **el ~ de vivir en una gran ciudad** the pressure(s) of living in a big city

agolpamiento *m* (de gente) crowd; (de ideas, problemas) rush

agolparse [A1] *v pron* «*personas*» to crowd; **las ideas se me agolpaban en la cabeza** ideas crowded into my head

agonía *f* 1 (de moribundo) death throes (*pl*) 2 (sufrimiento) suffering

agónico -ca *adj* dying (*before n*); **estar en estado ~** to be dying; **estertores ~s** death rattle

agonizante *adj* ‹*persona*› dying (*before n*); ‹*imperio/régimen*› crumbling (*before n*); **la luz ~ del crepúsculo** (liter) the fading light of dusk

agonizar [A4] *vi* «*persona*» to be dying, be in the throes of death; «*imperio/régimen*» be in its death throes; «*luz*» (liter) to fade

agorafobia *f* agoraphobia

agorar [A12] *vt* to prophesy, predict

agorero -ra *adj* ominous; **ave agorera** bird of ill omen

agostar [A1] *vt* ‹*campos/plantas*› to parch
■ **agostarse** *v pron* to become parched; **su imaginación no se agosta** (liter) his imagination is inexhaustible

agosto *m* August; *para ejemplos ver* **enero**; ***hacer su ~*** to make a fortune, to make a killing (colloq)

agotado -da *adj* 1 [ESTAR] ‹*recursos*› exhausted; ‹*edición*› sold out; ‹*pila*› dead, flat; Ⓢ **agotadas todas las localidades** sold out 2 [ESTAR] ‹*persona*› exhausted

agotador -dora *adj* exhausting

agotamiento *m* 1 (cansancio) exhaustion 2 (de recursos, mina) exhaustion

agotar [A1] *vt* 1 ‹*recursos*› to exhaust, use up; ‹*pila*› to wear out, run down; ‹*mina/tierra*› to exhaust; **el público agotó la edición** the edition sold out; **agotó sus fuerzas** he used up all his strength; **~on todos los temas de conversación** they exhausted all topics of conversation 2 (cansar) ‹*persona*› to tire … out, wear … out
■ **agotarse** *v pron* 1 «*existencias/reservas*» to run out, be used up; «*pila*» to run down; «*mina/tierra*» to become exhausted; «*edición*» to sell out; **se me está agotando la paciencia** my patience is running out 2 «*persona*» to wear *o* tire oneself out

agraciado¹ -da *adj* 1 ‹*persona/figura*› attractive; **es muy poco ~** he's not very attractive 2 (frml) (en sorteo): **resultó ~ con el primer premio** he was the lucky winner of the first prize

agraciado² -da *m,f* winner, prizewinner

agradable *adj* ‹*persona*› pleasant, nice; ‹*carácter*› pleasant; ‹*día/velada*› enjoyable, nice; ‹*sensación/efecto*› pleasant, pleasing; ‹*sabor/olor*› pleasant, nice; **su secretaria es una persona muy ~** her secretary is a very agreeable person; **trata de ser más ~ con ellos** try to be (a bit) nicer to them; **pasamos un día muy ~** we had a very nice *o* enjoyable day; **~ a la vista** pleasing to the eye; **no fue un espectáculo ~** it wasn't a pretty sight

agradar [A1] *vi* (frml): **aquí su presencia siempre agrada** it's always a pleasure to see you here; (+ *me/te/le etc*) **¿le agrada éste, señora?** is this one to your liking, madam? (frml); **la idea no me agrada** the idea doesn't appeal to me; **nos agrada complacer a la gente** we enjoy making people happy; **le agrada verlo contento** it gives her pleasure to see him happy; **me ~ía mucho verlos allí** I would be very pleased to see you there
■ **agradar** *vt* to please

agradecer [E3] *vt* 1 (sentir gratitud por) ‹*ayuda/amabilidad*› to appreciate, to be grateful for; **~le algo A algn** to be grateful to sb for sth; **se lo agradezco de veras** I'm very grateful to you; **le ~ía (que) me llamara** (frml) I would appreciate it if you would call me (frml) 2 (dar las gracias por) to thank; **ni siquiera me lo agradeció** she didn't even thank me *o* say thank you; **¡y así es como me lo agradece!** and this is all the thanks I get!

agradecido -da *adj* ‹*persona*› grateful; **estar/quedar ~** to be grateful; **¡qué poco ~ eres!** you're so ungrateful!; **sonrió agradecida** she smiled gratefully

agradecimiento *m* gratitude; **con nuestro más sincero ~** with our most sincere thanks; **en ~ por todo lo que ha hecho** in appreciation of all you have done

agradezca, agradezcas, etc *see* **agradecer**

agrado *m* (frml): **no veo con ~ su relación con él** I'm not pleased about her relationship with him; **espero que sea de su ~** I hope this is to your liking; **con sumo ~** gladly; **tener el ~ de + INF** to have the pleasure of -ING; **tuve el ~ de verla** I had the pleasure of seeing her; **tengo el ~ de dirigirme a Ud. para informarle que ...** (Corresp) (frml) I'm pleased to inform you that ... (frml)

agrandar [A1] *vt* 1 ‹*casa*› to extend; ‹*agujero/pozo*› to make ... larger *o* bigger; ‹*fotocopia*› to enlarge, blow up; ‹*vestido*› to let out 2 (exagerar) to exaggerate

■ **agrandarse** *v pron* «*agujero/bulto*» to grow larger, get bigger; **el equipo se agrandó con el triunfo** the team grew in stature after the victory

agrario -ria *adj* ‹*sector/política*› agricultural (*before n*); ‹*sociedad*› agrarian

agrarismo *m* agrarian reform movement (*in Mexico*)

agrarista *mf* advocate of agrarian reform (*in Mexico*)

agravación *f*, **agravamiento** *m* worsening

agravante¹ *adj* aggravating

agravante² *f or m* (Der) aggravating factor *o* circumstance; **con la ~ de que estaba borracho** what makes it even worse is that he was drunk

agravar [A1] *vt* to make ... worse, aggravate

■ **agravarse** *v pron* «*problema/situación*» to become worse, worsen; «*enfermo*» to deteriorate, get worse

agraviar [A1] *vt* (frml) ‹*persona*› to offend, affront (frml); **se sintió agraviado** he felt offended *o* insulted; **eso agravia mi dignidad** that is an affront to my dignity

agravio *m* (frml) (ofensa) affront (frml), insult; **lo considero un ~ a mi persona** I take that as a personal insult

agredir [I32] *vt* (frml) to attack, assault; **lo agredió de palabra** she attacked him verbally

agregado -da *m,f*

A (de embajada) attaché

B (Educ) 1 (en Ur) *assistant head of department* 2 (en Esp) senior teacher *o* lecturer

(Compuesto) **agregado -da comercial/cultural** commercial/cultural attaché

C (Col) (arrendatario) sharecropper

D **agregado** *m* (añadido) addition

agregar [A3] *vt*

A (añadir) to add; **~ algo A algo** to add sth TO sth

B ‹*empleado*› **~ a algn A algo** to attach *o* appoint sb TO sth

■ **agregarse** *v pron* (*refl*) **~se A algo** to join sth

agremiarse [A1] *v pron* (AmL) to form a union

agresión *f* aggression; **una ~ brutal** a brutal attack; **se lo acusa de ~** (Der) he's charged with assault

(Compuesto) **agresión sexual** sexual assault

agresividad *f* aggressiveness

agresivo -va *adj* aggressive

agresor¹ -sora *adj* ‹*ejército*› attacking (*before n*); ‹*país*› aggressor (*before n*)

agresor² -sora *m,f* (país, ejército) aggressor; (persona) attacker, assailant (frml)

agreste *adj* ‹*terreno/camino*› rough; ‹*paisaje*› rugged; ‹*vegetación/animal*› wild

agriar [A1 *or* A17] *vt* ‹*leche/vino*› to sour; ‹*carácter/persona*› to make ... bitter

■ **agriarse** *v pron* «*leche/vino*» to turn *o* go sour; «*carácter/persona*» to become bitter *o* embittered

agrícola *adj* ‹*técnicas*› agricultural, farming (*before n*)

agricultor -tora *m,f* farmer

agricultura *f* agriculture

(Compuesto) **agricultura biológica** *or* **ecológica** *or* **orgánica** organic farming

agridulce *adj* bittersweet; (Coc) sweet-and-sour

agrietar [A1] *vt* ‹*tierra/pintura*› to crack; **labios agrietados** chapped lips

■ **agrietarse** *v pron* «*tierra/pared*» to crack; «*piel*» to chap, become chapped

agrimensor -sora *m,f* surveyor

agrimensura *f* surveying

agringado -da *adj* (AmL fam & pey) ‹*persona*› Americanized; ‹*acento/costumbres*› (norteamericanizado) Americanized; (extranjero) foreign

agringarse [A3] *v pron* (AmL fam & pey) (norteamericanizarse) to become Americanized; (extranjerizarse) to become like a **gringo² 1**

agrio, agria *adj* 1 ‹*manzana*› sour, tart; ‹*naranja/limón*› sour, sharp; **este vino está ~/es muy ~** this wine has gone sour/is very vinegary 2 ‹*tono/persona*› sour, sharp; ‹*disputa*› bitter

agriparse [A1] *v pron* (Andes) to get the flu (AmE), to get flu (BrE); **está agripado** he has (the) flu

agro *m*: **el ~** the farming world

agroindustria *f* agribusiness (*agriculture and related industries*)

agronomía *f* agronomy

agrónomo¹ -ma *adj* agronomic

agrónomo² -ma *m,f* agronomist

agropecuario -ria *adj* ‹*producción*› agricultural and livestock; ‹*política*› agricultural, farming (*before n*)

agroturismo *m* rural tourism

agrumarse [A1] *v pron* to go lumpy

agrupación *f*

A (grupo) group; (asociación) association

(Compuesto) **agrupación coral** choral group, choir

B (acción) grouping (together)

agrupar [A1] *vt* 1 (formar grupos) to put ... into groups, to group; **agrupa esos libros por autores** group those books by author 2 (reunir) ‹*organizaciones/partidos*› to bring together

■ **agruparse** *v pron* 1 (formar un grupo) «*niños/policías*» to gather; «*partidos*» to come together 2 (dividirse en grupos) to get into groups

agua *f*‡

A water; **~ de lluvia/mar** rainwater/seawater; ***bailarle el ~ a algn*** (adularlo) (Esp fam) to suck up to sb (colloq); ***cambiarle el ~ a las aceitunas*** *or* ***al canario*** (fam & hum) to take *o* have a leak (colloq & hum); ***como ~ para chocolate*** (Méx fam) furious; ***estar con el ~ al cuello*** to be up to one's neck; ***estar más claro que el ~*** to be (patently) obvious; ***hacer ~*** «*embarcación*» to take in water; «*negocio/institución*» to founder; ***hacérsele ~ la boca a algn*** (AmL): **se me hizo ~ la boca** it made my mouth water; ***ha corrido*** *or* ***pasado mucha ~ bajo el puente*** a lot of water has flowed under the bridge since then; ***llevar el ~ a su molino*** to turn things to one's advantage; ***lo que por ~ viene, por ~ se va*** (Col) easy come, easy go; ***más claro, échale*** *or* ***echarle ~*** it's obvious; ***quedar en ~ de borrajas*** to come to nothing; ***ser ~ pasada*** to be a thing of the past; ***sin decir ~ va*** without so much as a by-your-leave; ***venirle a algn como ~ de mayo*** (Esp) to come just at the right moment; ***~ pasada no mueve molino*** it's no use crying over spilt milk; ***~ que no has de beber déjala correr*** if you're not interested, don't spoil things for me/for other people; ***nunca digas de esta ~ no beberé*** you never know when the same thing might happen to you

(Compuestos)

- **agua bendita** holy water
- **agua corriente/destilada** running/distilled water
- **agua de colonia** eau de cologne
- **agua de rosas** rosewater
- **agua dulce** fresh water; **un pescado de ~ ~** a freshwater fish
- **agua mineral** mineral water; **~ ~ con gas/sin gas** sparkling/still mineral water
- **agua oxigenada** peroxide, hydrogen peroxide (tech)
- **agua potable/salada** drinking/salt water

- **aguas negras** *fpl* sewage
- **agua tónica** *or* (Méx, Ven) **quina** tonic water

B (lluvia) rain

(Compuesto) **agua nieve** sleet

C (AmC, Andes) **1** (fam) (bebida gaseosa) soda (AmE), fizzy drink (BrE) **2** (infusión) herb tea (AmE), herbal tea (BrE); **~ de menta** mint tea

D **aguas** *fpl* **1** (de mar, río) waters (*pl*); ***estar*** *or* ***nadar entre dos ~s*** to sit on the fence; **los votantes que están entre dos ~s** the undecided voters; ***volver las ~s a su cauce***: **una vez que las ~s vuelvan a su cauce** once things settle down *o* return to normal **2** (de balneario, manantial) waters (*pl*); **tomar las ~s** to take the waters

(Compuestos)
- **aguas jurisdiccionales/territoriales** *fpl* territorial waters (*pl*)
- **aguas termales** *fpl* thermal waters (*pl*)

E **aguas** *fpl* (Fisiol) *tb* **~s amnióticas** amniotic fluid; **rompió ~s** her waters broke

(Compuestos)
- **aguas mayores** *fpl* (euf): **hacer ~ ~** to move one's bowels (euph)
- **aguas menores** *fpl* (euf): **hacer ~ ~** to pass water (euph)

F **aguas** *fpl* (vertientes) slope; **tejado a dos ~s** gable *o* apex *o* saddle roof

aguacate *m* (árbol) avocado; (fruto) avocado (pear)

aguacero *m* downpour

aguachento -ta *adj* (CS) ‹*sopa/bebida*› watery

aguachirle *f or m* (Esp fam) dishwater (colloq) (*watery drink or soup*)

aguada *f*

A (Art) (técnica) wash; (dibujo) wash drawing

B (bebedero) watering hole, spring

aguadilla *f* (Esp fam) ducking (colloq); **le hicieron una ~** they gave him a ducking

aguado -da *adj*

A ‹*leche/vino*› watered-down; ‹*sopa*› watery, thin; ‹*café*› weak; ‹*salsa*› thin

B (AmC, Méx fam) (aburrido) [**ESTAR**] ‹*fiesta/película*› boring, dull; [**SER**] ‹*persona*› boring, dull

aguafiestas *mf* (*pl* ~) (fam) wet blanket (colloq), party pooper (AmE colloq)

aguafuerte *m* (grabado) etching

aguaitar [A1] *vt* (AmS fam) (espiar) to spy on; (vigilar) to keep an eye on

■ **aguaitar** *vi* (AmS fam) (espiar) to snoop (colloq); (mirar) to have a look

aguaje *m* drinking trough

aguamala *f* (Col, Méx, Ven) jellyfish

aguamanil *m* **1** (jarra) pitcher, jug; (palangana) basin, bowl; (mueble) washstand **2** (para la mesa) finger bowl

aguamar *m* jellyfish

aguamarina *f* aquamarine

aguanieve *f* sleet

aguantaderas *fpl* (fam): **tener ~** to be patient; **¡hay que tener ~s!** you need the patience of a saint! (colloq)

aguantador -dora *adj* (AmL)

A (fam) (resistente) ‹*tela/ropa*› hard-wearing; ‹*coche*› sturdy; ‹*zapatos*› hard-wearing, sturdy

B (fam) ‹*persona*› **1** (paciente, tolerante): **es muy ~** he puts up with a lot (colloq) **2** (del dolor, sufrimiento) tough (colloq)

aguantar [A1] *vt*

A ‹*dolor/sufrimiento*› to bear, endure; **aguanto bien el calor** I can take the heat; **tuvieron que ~ temperaturas altísimas** they had to endure extremely high temperatures; **no tengo por qué ~ esto** I don't have to put up with this; **su madre le aguanta todo** his mother lets him get away with murder; **aguantó su mirada un momento** he held her stare for a moment; **este calor no hay quien lo aguante** this heat is unbearable; **no sabes ~ una broma** you can't take a joke; **no los aguanto** I can't stand them; **no puedo ~ este dolor de muelas** this toothache's unbearable

B **1** ‹*peso/carga*› to support, bear; ‹*presión*› to withstand; **ella aguanta el doble que yo bebiendo** she can take twice as much drink as I can **2** (durar): **estas botas ~án otro invierno** these boots will last (me/you/him) another winter; **han aguantado el paso del tiempo** they have survived the passing of time

C (sostener) to hold; **aguántame los paquetes** hold (on to) the parcels for me

D (contener, reprimir) ‹*risa/lágrimas*› to hold back; **~ la respiración** to hold one's breath; **ya no aguanto las ganas de decírselo** I can't resist the temptation to tell him any longer

■ **aguantar** *vi*: **¡ya no aguanto más!** I can't take any more!; **con ese tren de vida no hay salud que aguante** that sort of lifestyle would be enough to destroy anyone's health; **¿puedes ~ hasta que lleguemos?** can you hang *o* hold on until we arrive?; **no creo que este clavo aguante** I don't think this nail will hold

■ **aguantarse** *v pron*

A (conformarse, resignarse): **me tendré que ~** I'll just have to put up with it; **si no le gusta, que se aguante** if he doesn't like it, he can lump it (colloq)

B (euf) (reprimirse, contenerse): **no me pude ~ y me puse a llorar** I couldn't contain myself and burst into tears; **aguántate un poquito que ya llegamos** just hold *o* hang on a minute, we'll soon be there; **no se aguanta las ganas de abrirlos** he can't resist opening them

C (AmL fam) (esperarse) to hang on (colloq)

aguante *m*

A (de un pueblo) powers of endurance; (paciencia) patience

B (resistencia física de una persona) stamina; **es una máquina de mucho ~** it is a very sturdy machine

aguar [A16] *vt* **1** ‹*leche/vino*› to water down **2** (fam) (estropear) to put a damper on (colloq)

■ **aguarse** *v pron* (fam) to be spoiled

aguardar [A1] *vt* ‹*persona*› to wait for; ‹*acontecimiento*› to await; **~ (A) QUE + SUBJ**: **aguardó (a) que le respondiera** she waited for him to reply

■ **aguardar** *vi* «*noticia/destino*» to await; **nos aguardan tiempos duros** hard times lie ahead of us; **les aguardaba una sorpresa** there was a surprise in store for them

aguardentoso -sa *adj*: ‹*aliento*› smelling *o* reeking of alcohol; ‹*voz*› drunken

aguardiente *m* eau-de-vie (*clear brandy distilled from fermented fruit juice*)

aguarrás *m* turpentine, turps (colloq)

aguate *m* (Méx) prickle

aguatero -ra *m,f* (CS, Per) water carrier

aguatinta *m* aquatint

aguaviva *f* (RPl) jellyfish

aguayo *m* (Bol) *multicolored cloth*

agudeza *f*

A **1** (de voz, sonido) high pitch **2** (de dolor — duradero) intensity; (— momentáneo) sharpness

B (perspicacia) sharpness; (de sentido, instinto) keenness, sharpness

C (comentario ingenioso) witty comment

agudización *f* (de sentidos) sharpening; (de sensación) heightening; (de crisis) worsening

agudizar [A4] *vt* ‹*sensación*› to heighten; ‹*crisis/conflicto*› make worse; ‹*instinto*› to heighten; ‹*sentido*› to sharpen

■ **agudizarse** *v pron* «*sensación*» to heighten; «*dolor*» to get worse; «*crisis*» to worsen; «*instinto*» to become heightened; «*sentido*» to become sharper; **se le ha agudizado el ingenio** he's become sharper

agudo -da *adj*

A **1** ‹*filo/punta*› sharp **2** ‹*ángulo*› acute

B **1** ‹*voz/sonido*› high-pitched; ‹*nota*› high **2** ‹*dolor*› (duradero) intense, acute; (momentáneo) sharp **3** ‹*crisis*› severe **4** ‹*aumento/descenso*› sharp

C **1** (perspicaz) ‹*persona*› quick-witted, sharp; ‹*comentario*› shrewd **2** (gracioso) ‹*comentario/persona*› witty **3** ‹*sentido/instinto*› sharp

D ‹*palabra*› stressed on the last syllable; ‹*acento*› acute

agudos *mpl* treble

agüero *m*: **ser de mal/buen ~** (presagio) to be a bad/good omen; (causa) to bring bad/good luck

aguerrido -da *adj* ‹*soldado*› (valiente) brave, valiant; (experimentado) battle-hardened

agüevado -da *adj* [**ESTAR**] (AmC fam) upset

aguijón *m* **1** (vara) goad **2** (Zool) sting; **sintió el ~ de los celos** (liter) he felt a sharp stab of jealousy (liter)

a

aguijonear [A1] *vt* 1 ‹*animal*› to goad 2 (apremiar) «*sospecha/incertidumbre*» to gnaw at; **lo aguijoneaba el remordimiento** he felt stabs of remorse

águila *f‡* 1 (ave) eagle; ***ser un*** ~ to be very sharp 2 (Méx) (de moneda) ≈ heads (*pl*); **¿~ o sol?** heads or tails?

(Compuestos)
- **águila blanca/real** white-headed/golden eagle
- **águila ratonera** buzzard

aguileña *f* columbine

aguileño -ña *adj* ‹*nariz*› aquiline

aguilera *f* aerie (AmE), eyrie (BrE)

aguilucho *m* 1 (cría de águila) eaglet 2 (AmL) (halcón) ornate hawk-eagle

aguinaldo *m*
A 1 (propina) *money given to postmen, caretakers, etc, around Christmas*, Christmas box (BrE) 2 (de un niño) pocket money 3 (paga extra) *extra month's salary paid at Christmas*, Christmas bonus (AmE)
B (Col, Ven) (canción) ≈ Christmas carol

agüita *f* (Chi) ▸**agua C2**

aguja *f* 1 (de coser, tejer) needle; (para inyecciones) needle; (de tocadiscos) stylus, needle; (de instrumento) needle; (de balanza) pointer, needle; **las ~s del reloj** the hands of the clock; ***buscar una ~ en un pajar*** to look for a needle in a haystack 2 (Inf) pin 3 (Arquit) spire, steeple

(Compuestos)
- **aguja de crochet** crochet hook
- **aguja de punto** *or* (AmL) **de tejer** knitting needle
- **aguja hipodérmica** hypodermic needle
- **aguja de bitácora** ship's compass

B **agujas** *fpl* (Ferr) switches (*pl*) (AmE), points (*pl*) (BrE)

agujereado -da *adj*: **está ~** it has holes in it; **está todo ~** it's full of *o* riddled with holes

agujerear [A1] *vt* (hacer agujeros en) to make holes in; (atravesar) to pierce

agujero *m* 1 (en prenda, pared) hole; **hacerse ~s en las orejas** to have one's ears pierced; **tiene más ~s que un colador** it's riddled with holes 2 (Fin) shortfall, hole; ***tapar ~s*** (fam) to pay off one's debts

(Compuesto) **agujero negro** black hole

agujeta *f*
A (Méx) (de zapato) (shoe) lace
B **agujetas** *fpl* (Esp)stiffness; **tengo ~s en las piernas** my legs are stiff

agustino -na, **agustiniano -na** *adj/m,f* Augustinian

aguzar [A4] *vt* to sharpen; **aguzó el oído** he pricked up his ears

ah *interj* 1 (expresando sorpresa, lástima, asentimiento) oh! 2 (Andes, Ven) ▸**eh 2,3**

ahí *adv*
A 1 (en el espacio) there; **~ está/viene** there he is/here he comes; **~ arriba/abajo** up/down there; **~ mismo** *or* (AmL) **nomás** *o* (Méx) **mero** right *o* just there 2 (*en locs*) **por ahí** somewhere; **debe estar como a 200 pesos — sí, por ~ anda** it must be about 200 pesos — yes, that's about right; **tendrá unos 35 años o por ~** he must be 35 or thereabouts; **ahí sí que** (AmL): **~ sí que me pillaste** you've really got me there! (colloq); **de ahí a que: de ~ a que venga es otra cosa** whether or not he actually comes is another matter
B 1 (refiriéndose a un lugar figurado): **~ está el truco** that's the secret; **de ~ a la drogadicción sólo hay un paso** from there it's just a short step to becoming a drug addict; **de ~ a decir que es excelente hay un buen trecho** there's a big difference between that and saying it's excellent; ***hasta ~ llego yo*** that's as far as I'm prepared to go 2 **de ahí** hence; **de ~ que** (+ *subj*); **de ~ que hayan fracasado** that is why they failed
C (en el tiempo) then; **de ~ en adelante** from then on; **~ es cuando...** that's when...; **~ mismo** there and then
D (AmL) (más o menos): **¿cómo sigue tu abuelo? — ~ anda** how's your grandfather getting on? — oh, so-so

ahijado -da
A (por bautizo) (*m*) godson; (*f*) goddaughter; **mis ~s** my godchildren
B (protegido) (*m*) protegé; (*f*) protegée

ahijar [A1] *vt* to adopt

ahijuna *interj* (RPl fam) damn it! (colloq)

ahínco *m* 1 (empeño): **con ~** diligently, hard 2 (resolución) determination

ahíto -ta *adj* (liter) sated (liter)

ahogado -da *adj*
A (en agua): **dos niños resultaron ~s** two children were drowned; **morir ~** (en agua) to drown; (asfixiarse) to suffocate; (atragantarse) to choke to death
B ‹*llanto/grito*› stifled; **una voz ahogada en llanto** a voice choked by sobs
C (Méx fam) (borracho) blind *o* rolling drunk (colloq)

ahogador *m* (Chi, Méx) (Auto) choke

ahogar [A3] *vt*
A 1 ‹*persona/animal*› (en agua) to drown; (asfixiar) to suffocate 2 ‹*motor*› to flood
B 1 ‹*palabras/voz*› to drown (out); ‹*llanto/grito*› to stifle 2 ‹*penas*› to drown 3 (en ajedrez): **~ el rey** to stalemate
■ **ahogarse** *v pron* 1 «*persona/animal*» (en agua) to drown; (asfixiarse) to suffocate; (atragantarse) to choke; **me ahogo con este humo** the smoke's making me choke 2 «*motor*» to flood

ahogo *m* breathlessness; **tiene ~s** he gets out of breath

ahondar [A1] *vi* to go into (greater) detail; **~ EN algo** ‹*en tema*› to look at sth in (greater) detail *o* in depth; ‹*en problema*› to examine sth in (greater) detail
■ **ahondar** *vt* ‹*pozo*› to make ... deeper

ahora *adv*
A 1 (en el momento presente) now; **¡~ me lo dices!** now you tell me!; **la juventud de ~** young people today; **~ que lo pienso** now I come to think of it; **problemas hasta ~ insolubles** hitherto insoluble problems; **hasta ~** so far *o* up to now; **de ~ en adelante** *or* **desde ~** from now on; **por ~ va todo bien** everything's going all right so far; **por ~** for the time being 2 (inmediatamente, pronto): **~ mismo** right now *o* away; **~ te lo muestro** I'll show it to you in a minute *o* second *o* moment; **¡~ voy!** I'm coming!; **¡hasta ~!** (esp Esp) see you soon! 3 (hace un momento) a moment ago; **~ último** (Chi) recently
B 1 (*indep*) (con sentido adversativo): **ésta es mi sugerencia. A~, si tú tienes una idea mejor ...** that's my advice. Of course, if you have a better idea ... 2 **ahora bien** (*indep*) however

ahorcado -da *m,f* 1 (persona) hanged person 2 **el ahorcado** *m* (Jueg) hangman

ahorcajarse [A1] *v pron* **~ EN algo** to sit astride sth

ahorcamiento *m* hanging

ahorcar [A2] *vt* to hang; **este cuello me ahorca** this collar's choking me
■ **ahorcarse** *v pron* (*refl*) to hang oneself

ahorita *adv* (esp AmL fam) 1 (en este momento) just *o* right now; **~ mismo** right now *o* away 2 (inmediatamente, pronto): **~ te lo doy** I'll give it to you in a second *o* moment *o* minute 3 (hace un momento) a moment ago

ahoritica *adv* (AmC, Col, Ven) ▸**ahorita**

ahorquillado -da *adj* forked

ahorrador[1] **-dora** *adj* thrifty; **no soy muy ~a** I'm not very good at saving (money)

ahorrador[2] **-dora** *m,f* saver, investor

ahorrante *mf* (Chi) saver, investor

ahorrar [A1] *vt*
A ‹*dinero/energía/agua*› to save; ‹*tiempo*› to save
B (evitar) ‹*molestia/viaje*› (+ *me/te/le etc*) to save, spare
■ **ahorrar** *vi* to save
■ **ahorrarse** *v pron* (*enf*) 1 ‹*dinero*› to save (oneself) 2 (evitarse) ‹*molestia/viaje*› to save oneself

ahorrativo -va *adj* thrifty

ahorrista *mf* (RPl) saver, investor

ahorro *m* 1 (acción) saving; **supone un gran ~ de tiempo** it saves a lot of time 2 **ahorros** *mpl* (cantidad) savings (*pl*)

ahuchar [A1] *vt* (Col) to urge on

ahuecar [A2] *vt*
A 1 ‹*tronco/calabaza*› to hollow out; ‹*mano*› to cup 2 ‹*almohadón*› to plump up; ‹*pelo*› to give volume to
B ‹*voz*› to deepen

ahuesarse [A1] *v pron* (Per fam) ⟨⟨*persona*⟩⟩ to get into a rut; **ese modelo se ha ahuesado en las tiendas** that model just hasn't sold

ahuizote *m* (Méx fam) scourge

ahumado *adj* 1 (Coc) smoked 2 ⟨*cristal*⟩ smoked; ⟨*gafas*⟩ tinted

ahumar [A23] *vt* 1 ⟨*jamón/pescado*⟩ to smoke 2 ⟨*colmena*⟩ to smoke out; ⟨*habitación*⟩ to fill … with smoke 3 ⟨*paredes/techo*⟩ to blacken

■ **ahumarse** *v pron* 1 ⟨⟨*paredes/techo*⟩⟩ to become blackened 2 ⟨⟨*casa/habitación*⟩⟩ to fill with smoke

ahusado -da *adj* tapering

ahuyentar [A1] *vt* 1 (hacer huir) ⟨*ladrón/animal*⟩ to frighten off *or* away 2 (mantener a distancia) ⟨*fiera/mosquitos*⟩ to keep … away 3 ⟨*dudas*⟩ to dispel; **~ los malos pensamientos** to banish evil thoughts from one's mind

aimará¹ *adj* Aymara

aimará² *mf* Aymara Indian

> **aimará**
>
> A large Indian ethnic group living on the harsh Titicaca plateau in the Andes in southern Peru and northern Bolivia, who speak Aymara. They were conquered by the Incas, then by the Spaniards. Inca influence remains in religious beliefs, folklore, food, and art. The Aymara are mostly farmers and keep herds of llamas

aindiado -da *adj* (AmL) Indian-like, Indian-looking

airado -da *adj* angry, irate; **—es injusto —protestó ~** it's not fair, he complained angrily

airar [A19] *vt* to anger

aire *m*

A air; **sintió que le faltaba el ~** she felt as if she was going to suffocate; **para que entre un poco de ~** to let some (fresh) air in; **salir a tomar el ~** to go outside for a breath of fresh air; **ponerles ~ a las ruedas** to put some air in the tires; **se elevó por los ~s** it rose up into the air; **al ~ libre** outdoors, in the open air; **un vestido con la espalda al ~** a backless dress; **deja la herida al ~** leave the wound uncovered; **disparar un tiro al ~** to fire a shot into the air; ***a mi/tu/su ~***: **ellos salen en grupo, yo prefiero ir a mi ~** they go out in a group, I prefer doing my own thing (colloq); ***cambiar*** *or* ***mudar de ~(s)***: **necesito cambiar de ~s** I need a change of scene *o* air; ***dejar a algn en el ~*** to leave sb in suspense; ***quedar en el ~***: **todo quedó en el ~** everything was left up in the air; **su futuro quedó en el ~** his future hung in the balance; ***saltar*** *or* ***volar por los ~s*** to explode, blow up; ***vivir del ~*** to live on air

(Compuestos)

- **aire acondicionado** air-conditioning; **con ~ ~** air-conditioned
- **aire comprimido** compressed air; **una escopeta de ~ ~** an air rifle

B (viento) wind; (corriente) draft (AmE), draught (BrE); **no corre nada de ~** there's not a breath of wind

C (Rad, TV): **estar en el ~** to be on the air; ⓢ **en el aire** on air; ***salir al ~*** to go out

D 1 (aspecto) air; **tiene un ~ aristocrático** she has an aristocratic air; **un rostro con un ~ infantil** a face with a childish look to it; **sus composiciones tienen un ~ melancólico** her compositions have a melancholy feel to them; **esto tiene todo el ~ de tratarse de una broma** this looks for all the world like a joke; **la protesta tomó ~s de revuelta** the protest began to look like a revolt; ***darse ~s (de grandeza)*** to put on *o* give oneself airs 2 (parecido) resemblance; **le encuentro un ~ a Alberto** I think he looks (a little) like Alberto; **tienen un ~** they look a bit alike

(Compuesto) **aire de familia** family resemblance

E (Mús) tune; **~s populares** traditional tunes *o* airs

aireación *f* aeration

airear [A1] *vt* 1 (ventilar) to air 2 (hacer público) ⟨*asunto*⟩ to air; **una revista que airea las intimidades de los famosos** a magazine that publishes details about the private lives of famous people 3 ⟨*masa/tierra*⟩ to aerate

■ **airearse** *v pron* 1 ⟨⟨*persona*⟩⟩ to get some (fresh) air 2 ⟨⟨*manta/abrigo*⟩⟩ to air; **abre la ventana para que se airee el cuarto** open the window to let some air into the room

airoso -sa *adj* graceful; ***salir ~ de algo*** to acquit oneself well (in sth)

aislacionismo *m* isolationism

aislacionista *adj/mf* isolationist

aislado -da *adj*

A 1 (alejado) remote, isolated 2 (sin comunicación) cut off; **quedar ~** to be cut off; **se siente muy ~** he feels very isolated; **~ DE algo** cut off *o* isolated FROM sth; **vive ~ del mundo** he's cut himself off from the world 3 ⟨*caso*⟩ isolated

B (Elec) insulated

aislador -dora *adj* ▸**aislante¹**

aislamiento *m*

A (en general) isolation

B (Elec) insulation

(Compuesto) **aislamiento acústico** soundproofing

aislante¹ *adj* insulating, insulation (*before n*)

aislante² *m* insulator

aislar [A19] *vt*

A 1 (apartar, separar) ⟨*enfermo*⟩ to isolate, keep in isolation; ⟨*preso*⟩ to place … in solitary confinement; ⟨*virus*⟩ to isolate; **sus amigos los han aislado** their friends have turned their backs on them 2 (dejar sin communicación) ⟨*lugar*⟩ to cut off

B (Elec) to insulate

■ **aislarse** *v pron* (*refl*) to cut oneself off

ajá *interj* (expresando — asentimiento) uh-huh; (— satisfacción) aha!

ajado -da *adj* ⟨*ropa*⟩ worn; ⟨*manos*⟩ wrinkly; ⟨*piel*⟩ wrinkled; **el sofá está muy ~** the sofa's very shabby; **las flores están ajadas** the flowers have wilted

ajamonarse [A1] *v pron* (fam) to get porky (colloq)

ajar [A1] *vt* (estropear) ⟨*flor*⟩ to wilt; **el tiempo había ajado la pintura** time had taken its toll on the paintwork; **esto aja las manos** this makes your hands wrinkly

■ **ajarse** *v pron* (estropearse) ⟨⟨*flor*⟩⟩ to wilt; **la chaqueta se había ajado** the jacket had become worn; **se le ~on las manos** his hands became rough

ajardinar [A1] *vt* to landscape; **zonas ajardinadas** areas of parks and gardens

ajedrecista *mf* chess player

ajedrez *m* (juego) chess; (tablero y fichas) chess set

ajenjo *m* (planta) wormwood, absinthe; (licor) absinthe

ajeno -na *adj*

A [SER] 1 (que no corresponde, pertenece): **mis ideales le son totalmente ~s** my ideals are completely alien to him; **aquel ambiente me era ~** that environment was alien *o* foreign to me; **un asunto que le era ~** a matter that was *o* had nothing to do with him; **~ A algo**: **por razones ajenas a nuestra voluntad** for reasons beyond our control; ⓢ **prohibido el paso a toda persona ajena a la empresa** staff only; **intereses ~s a los de la empresa** interests not in accord with those of the company 2 (que pertenece, corresponde a otro): **una tarjeta de crédito ajena** someone else's credit card; **por el bien ~** for the good of others; **las desgracias ajenas** other people's misfortunes

B 1 [ESTAR] (ignorante) **~ A algo** unaware OF sth, oblivious TO sth 2 [ESTAR] (indiferente) **~ A algo**: **permaneció ~ a sus problemas** he remained indifferent to her problems 3 [SER] (no involucrado) **~ A algo**: **irregularidades a las que han sido ~s** irregularities in which they have not been involved

ajetreado -da *adj* hectic, busy

ajetreo *m* hustle and bustle; **un día de mucho ~** a hectic day

ají *m* 1 (chile) chili*; ***ponerse como un ~ (picante)*** (AmS fam) to get furious 2 (Andes) (salsa) chili* sauce 3 (RPl) (pimiento) pepper

ajiaco *m*: *spicy potato dish*

ajilimójili *m* (Esp) piquant sauce

ajillo *m*: **al ~** with garlic; **champiñones al ~** garlic mushrooms

ajo *m* (Coc) garlic; **un diente de ~** a clove of garlic; **esto tiene mucho ~** there's a lot of garlic in this; ***echar*** *or* ***soltar ~s (y cebollas)*** (AmL fam) to swear; ***estar (metido) en el ~*** (fam) to be involved

ajonjolí *m* sesame

ajotado -da *adj* (Méx fam) camp (colloq)

ajuar *m* (de novia) trousseau; (de bebé) layette

ajustado -da *adj*

A 1 (ceñido) tight; **este me queda muy ~** it's too tight (for me) 2 ‹*presupuesto*› tight

B (en correspondencia con) **~ A algo** in accordance WITH sth

ajustar [A1] *vt*

A 1 (apretar) to tighten (up) 2 (regular) to adjust; **~ la entrada de agua** to regulate the flow of water 3 ‹*retrovisor/asiento/cinturón de seguridad*› to adjust 4 (encajar) ‹*piezas*› to fit

B (en costura) to take in

C 1 ‹*gastos/horarios*› **~ algo A algo** to adapt sth TO sth 2 ‹*sueldo/jubilación*› to adjust; **les ajustan el sueldo con la inflación** their wages are adjusted in line with inflation

D ‹*precio/alquiler/sueldo*› to fix, set

E ‹*cuentas*› (sacar el resultado de) to balance; (saldar) to settle

■ **ajustar** *vi* to fit

■ **ajustarse** *v pron*

A (*refl*) ‹*cinturón de seguridad*› to adjust

B «*piezas*» to fit

C (ceñirse, atenerse) **~se A algo**: **su declaración no se ajusta a la verdad** his statement is not strictly true; **deberá ~se a estas condiciones** it will have to comply with these conditions; **una sentencia que no se ajusta a derecho** a legally flawed verdict

ajuste *m*

A 1 (apretamiento) tightening (up) 2 (regulación) adjustment

B (de gastos, horarios) readjustment; (de sueldos) adjustment

C (de precio) fixing; **sólo falta el ~ del precio** all that remains is to fix the price

(Compuesto) **ajuste de cuentas** settling of scores

ajusticiado -da *m,f* (*m*) executed man; (*f*) executed woman

ajusticiamiento *m* execution

ajusticiar [A1] *vt* to execute

al: *contraction of* **a** *and* **el**

ala[1] *f*‡

A (de ave, de avión) wing; ***ahuecar el ~*** (fam) to beat it (colloq); ***cobrar ~s*** to spread one's wings; ***cortarle las ~s a algn*** to clip sb's wings; ***darle ~s a algn***: **si le das ~s, luego no podrás controlarlo** if you let him have his own way, you won't be able to control him later; ***estar tocado del ~*** (fam) to be nutty *o* crazy (colloq)

(Compuesto) **ala delta** (deporte) hang gliding; (aparato) hang glider

B (de sombrero) brim

C 1 (de edificio) wing 2 (facción) wing 3 (flanco) flank, wing 4 (Dep) (posición) wing

ala[2] *mf* (jugador) wing, winger

(Compuestos)

- **ala abierta** wide receiver
- **ala cerrada** tight end

Alá Allah

alabanza *f* praise; **digno de ~** praiseworthy

alabar [A1] *vt* to praise; **¡alabado sea Dios!** praise the Lord; **siempre la está alabando** he's always singing her praises

alabarda *f* halberd

alabardero *m* (Mil) halberdier

alabastro *m* alabaster

alacena *f* larder

alacrán *m* scorpion

ALADI /a'laði/ *f* = **Asociación Latinoamericana de Integración**

alado -da *adj* 1 (con alas) winged 2 (liter) (veloz) swift

ALALC /a'lalk/ *f* (= **Asociación Latinoamericana de Libre Comercio**) LAFTA

alambicado -da *adj* ‹*lenguaje/estilo*› complicated; ‹*personaje*› complex

alambicar [A2] *vt*

A ‹*líquido*› to distill•

B ‹*estilo*› to complicate

alambique *m* still

alambrada *f* (valla) wire fence; (material) wire fencing

alambrado *m* (AmL) 1 (acción) fencing in/off 2 (valla) wire fence

alambrar [A1] *vt* to fence in/off

alambre *m*

A (hilo metálico) wire; **barreras de ~ electrificado** electrified *o* electric fences

(Compuestos)

- **alambre de púas** barbed wire, barbwire (AmE)
- **alambre de tierra** ground wire (AmE), earth wire (BrE)

B (Chi) (cable) cable

alambrera *f* (Col) wire screen

alambrista *mf* (en el circo) tightrope walker

alameda *f* (avenida) tree-lined avenue; (terreno con álamos) poplar grove

álamo *m* poplar

alano *mf* mastiff

alarde *m* show, display; **hacer ~ de fuerza/riqueza** to show off strength/wealth

alardear [A1] *vi* **~ DE algo** to boast ABOUT sth; **alardea de tener dinero** she boasts about being well-off

alargado -da *adj* ‹*forma*› elongated; ‹*hoja*› elongate

alargador *m* extension cord (AmE), extension lead (BrE)

alargamiento *m* (de cable) lengthening; (de período) extension

alargar [A3] *vt*

A 1 ‹*vestido/pantalón*› to let down, lengthen; ‹*manguera/cable*› to lengthen, extend; ‹*riendas/soga*› to let out; ‹*paso*› to lengthen 2 ‹*cuento/discurso*› to drag out; ‹*vacaciones/plazo*› to extend; **puede ~le la vida** it could prolong her life

B 1 (extender) ‹*mano/brazo*› to hold out 2 (alcanzar) **~le algo A algn** to hand *o* give *o* pass sth TO sb

■ **alargarse** *v pron* 1 «*cara/sombra*» to get longer; «*días*» to grow longer; «*reunión/fiesta*» to go on 2 (Méx) «*bola*» to go too far; **se alargó por la tercera base** it went past third base

alarido *m* (de miedo) shriek; (de dolor) scream; **daba ~s de miedo** she was shrieking with fear

alarma *f*

A (ante peligro) alarm; **sembró la ~ en** *or* **entre la población** it caused alarm among the population; **dar la voz de ~** to sound *o* raise the alarm

B (dispositivo) alarm; **el timbre de la ~** the alarm bell;

(Compuestos)

- **alarma amarilla/roja** red/yellow alert
- **alarma contra robos/incendios** burglar/fire alarm

alarmante *adj* alarming

alarmar [A1] *vt* to alarm

■ **alarmarse** *v pron* to be alarmed

alarmismo *m* alarmism

alarmista *adj/mf* alarmist

alazán -zana *adj/m,f* sorrel

alba *f*‡

A (del día) dawn, daybreak; **al rayar** *or* **romper el ~** (liter) at the break of day (liter); **al** *or* **con el ~** at the crack of dawn

B (Relig) alb

albacea *mf* executor

albacora *f* (atún) albacore; (pez espada) (Chi) swordfish

albahaca *f* basil

albanés[1] **-nesa** *adj/m,f* Albanian

albanés[2] *m* (idioma) Albanian

Albania *f* Albania

albañal *m* (Col) sewer, drain

albañil *m* (constructor) builder; (que coloca ladrillos) bricklayer

albañilería *f* 1 (profesión) building; (de colocar ladrillos) bricklaying 2 (obra) brickwork; **trabajo de ~** building work

albarán *m* delivery note

albarda *f* packsaddle

albaricoque *m* (Esp) apricot

albaricoquero *m* (Esp) apricot tree

albatros *m* (*pl* ~) albatross

albedrío *m* (free) will; **lo hizo a su ~** he did it of his own free will; **lo dejo a tu libre ~** I leave it entirely up to you

alberca *f* 1 (embalse) reservoir 2 (Méx) (piscina) swimming pool 3 (Col) (lavadero) sink (*for washing clothes*) 4 (Bol, Per) (comedero) trough

albergar [A3] *vt*
A ‹*personas*› to house, accommodate; ‹*biblioteca/exposición*› to house; **el hotel alberga a 2.000 turistas** the hotel accommodates 2,000 tourists; **el parque alberga una fauna muy variada** the park is home to many different species of wildlife
B (liter) ‹*duda/odio*› to harbor*; ‹*esperanzas*› to cherish
■ **albergarse** *v pron* 1 (hospedarse) to lodge 2 (refugiarse) to shelter, take refuge

albergue *m* 1 (alojamiento) lodging, accommodations (*pl*) (AmE); **darle ~ a algn** to take sb in 2 (hostal) hostel; (en la montaña) refuge, shelter; (para vagabundos, mendigos) shelter
(Compuesto) **albergue juvenil** *or* **de la juventud** youth hostel

alberguista *mf* youth hosteler*; **carné de ~ internacional** international youth hostel card

albino -na *adj/m,f* albino

albo -ba *adj* (liter) white

albóndiga *f* meatball

albor *m* 1 (comienzo): **los ~es de la civilización** the dawn of civilization (liter); **está en el ~ de la vida** she is in the springtime of her life 2 (liter) (alba) dawn; (blancura) whiteness

alborada *f* 1 (liter) (alba) dawn 2 (Lit, Mús) aubade

alborear [A1] *v impers* (liter): **alboreaba cuando salieron** day was breaking *o* (liter) dawning when they set off
■ **alborear** *vi* (liter) to dawn (liter); **alborea una nueva época** a new age is dawning

albornoz *m* bathrobe

alborotado -da *adj*
A 1 (nervioso) agitated; (animado, excitado) excited 2 (ruidoso) noisy, rowdy; (amotinado) riotous
B ‹*mar*› rough; ‹*pelo*› untidy, disheveled*
C (precipitado) hasty, rash

alborotador¹ -dora *adj* rowdy, noisy

alborotador² -dora *m,f* troublemaker

alborotar [A1] *vi* to make a racket
■ **alborotar** *vt* 1 (agitar) to agitate, get ... agitated; (excitar) to get ... excited 2 ‹*muchedumbre*› to stir up
■ **alborotarse** *v pron*
A 1 (agitarse) to get agitated *o* upset; (excitarse) to get excited 2 (amotinarse) to riot
B «*mar*» to get rough

alboroto *m* 1 (agitación, nerviosismo) agitation; (excitación) excitement 2 (ruido) racket 3 (disturbio, jaleo) disturbance, commotion; (motín) riot

alborozado -da *adj* (liter) jubilant

alborozar [A4] *vt* (liter) to rejoice (liter); **la noticia alborozó a toda la familia** the whole family rejoiced at the news (liter)
■ **alborozarse** *v pron* to rejoice (liter)

alborozo *m* (liter) rejoicing (liter); **con ~** with joy

albricias *interj* (arc) (enhorabuena) congratulations!; (exclamación de júbilo) hooray!

álbum *m*
A (de fotos, sellos) album; (libro de historietas) comic book
B (disco) album

albúmina *f* albumin

albur *m*
A (liter) (azar) chance; (riesgo) risk
B (Méx) (doble sentido) double meaning; (juego de palabras) play on words, pun

albura *f* (liter) whiteness

alburero -ra *m,f* (Méx fam) *person fond of making puns or using double entendres*

alca *f*‡ auk

alcachofa *f* 1 (Bot, Coc) artichoke 2 (de ducha) shower head; (de regadera) sprinkler (AmE), rose (BrE)

alcahuete -ta *m,f* 1 (ant) (mediador) procurer (arch) 2 (CS fam) (chismoso) gossip (colloq); (soplón) tattletale (AmE colloq), telltale (BrE colloq)

alcahuetear [A1] *vi* 1 (hacer de mediador) to act as a go-between 2 (CS fam) (chismear) to gossip (colloq)
■ **alcahuetear** *vt* 1 (fam) (delatar) to tell *o* snitch on (colloq) 2 (Andes fam) (tapar): **les alcahuetea las travesuras** he lets them get away with all kinds of things; **les alcahuetea las mentiras** she covers up for him when he lies

alcaide *m* (ant) (carcelero) jailer; (director) keeper (arch)

alcalde -desa *m,f*
A (Gob) mayor
B **alcaldesa** *f* (mujer del alcalde) mayoress

alcaldía *f* (cargo) mayoralty; (oficina) mayor's office; (ayuntamiento) city hall (AmE), town hall (BrE)

álcali *m* alkali

alcalino -na *adj* alkaline

alcaloide *m* (Quím) alkaloid; (cocaína) (period) cocaine

alcance *m*
A 1 (de persona) reach; ⓢ **mantenga los medicamentos fuera del ~ de los niños** keep all medicines out of reach of children; **está fuera de mi ~** it is beyond my means 2 (de arma, emisora) range; **misiles de corto/largo ~** short-range/long-range missiles 3 (de ley, proyecto) scope; (de declaración, noticia) implications; **una política educativa de largo ~** a far-reaching education policy 4 (*en locs*) **al alcance de** within reach of; **poner la cultura al ~ de todos** to make culture accessible to everyone; **precios al ~ de su bolsillo** prices to suit your pocket; **un lujo que no está a mi ~** a luxury I can't afford; **tiene mucha ayuda a su ~** he has a lot of help at his disposal; **no está al ~ de su inteligencia** it's beyond their grasp; ***al ~ de la mano*** (literal) at hand; (fácil de conseguir) within reach; ***hacer un ~*** (Chi) to add/clarify sth
B (Fin) deficit

alcancía *f* (AmL) (de niño) piggy bank; (para colectas) collection box

alcanfor *m* camphor

alcantarilla *f* (cloaca) sewer; (sumidero) drain

alcantarillado *m* sewer system, drains (*pl*)

alcantarillar [A1] *vt* to lay sewers in

alcantarillero -ra *m,f* (CS) sewer worker

alcanzado -da *adj* (Col) short of money

alcanzar [A4] *vt*
A 1 ‹*persona*› (llegar a la altura de) to catch up with, to catch ... up (BrE); (pillar, agarrar) to catch; **lo alcancé en la curva** I caught up with him on the bend; **¡a que no me alcanzas!** I bet you can't catch me! (colloq) 2 (en tarea, estatura) to catch up with
B (llegar a) ‹*lugar*› to reach, get to; ‹*temperatura/nivel/edad*› to reach; **a pesar del tráfico alcancé el avión** despite the traffic I managed to catch the plane; **casi no alcanzo el tren** I almost missed the train; **lo alcancé con un palo** I used a pole to get at it *o* reach it; **estos árboles alcanzan una gran altura** these trees can reach *o* grow to a great height; **alcanza una velocidad de ...** it reaches a speed of ...; **alcanza enormes distancias** it covers vast distances; **~ la mayoría de edad** to come of age
C (conseguir, obtener) ‹*objetivo/éxito*› to achieve; ‹*acuerdo*› to reach; **se pretende ~ los 100 millones de pesos** they are hoping to reach a target of 100 million pesos
D (acercar, pasar) **~le algo A algn** to pass sb sth, to pass sth TO sb; **¿me alcanzas el libro?** could you pass me the book?
E 1 «*bala/misil*» to hit; **fue alcanzado por un misil** it was hit by a missile 2 (afectar) to affect; **la medida ha alcanzado a la clase trabajadora** the measure has affected the working classes
■ **alcanzar** *vi*
A (llegar): **está muy alto, no alcanzo** it's too high, I can't reach it; **hasta donde alcanzaba la vista** as far as the eye could see; **~ A + INF** to manage to + INF; **no alcanzó a terminar** she didn't manage to finish; **hasta donde alcanzo a ver** as far as I can see
B (ser suficiente) «*comida/provisones*» to be enough; **el sueldo no le alcanza** he can't manage on his salary; **me ~á hasta final de mes** it will see me through to the end of the month; **con una limpiadita, alcanza** just a quick clean will do

alcaparra *f* caper

alcatraz *m* (Zool) gannet; (Bot) arum

alcaucil *m* (RPl) artichoke

alcazaba *f* citadel, castle

alcázar *m* 1 (fortaleza) fortress; (palacio) palace 2 (Náut) quarterdeck

alce *m* elk, moose

alcista *adj* ‹*tendencia*› upward; ‹*mercado*› bull (*before n*)

alcoba *f* bedroom, bedchamber (liter)

alcohol *m*

A (Quím) alcohol; (Farm) *tb* **~ de 90 (grados)** rubbing alcohol (AmE), surgical spirit (BrE)

(Compuestos)

- **alcohol desnaturalizado** *or* **de quemar** methyl alcohol (AmE), methylated spirits (BrE)
- **alcohol etílico/metílico** ethyl/methyl alcohol

B (bebida) alcohol, drink

alcoholemia *f*: **hacerle la prueba de la ~ a algn** to breathalyze sb; **tasa de ~** blood alcohol level, level of alcohol in the blood

alcohólico[1] -ca *adj* alcoholic; **bebida no alcohólica** nonalcoholic drink

alcohólico[2] -ca *m,f* alcoholic

alcoholímetro *m* Breathalyzer®, drunkometer (AmE)

alcoholismo *m* alcoholism

alcoholizado -da *adj* alcoholic **está totalmente ~** he has become an alcoholic

alcoholizarse [A4] *v pron* to become an alcoholic

alcornoque *m* 1 (árbol) cork oak 2 (fam) (persona) idiot

alcurnia *f* ancestry, lineage (liter); **de alta ~** of noble birth; **una familia de ~** an old family

alcuza *f* (Chi) cruet (stand)

aldaba *f* (llamador) doorknocker; (cerrojo) latch

aldea *f* small village, hamlet

aldeano[1] -na *adj* village (*before n*)

aldeano[2] -na *m,f* villager

aleación *f* alloy

alear [A1] *vt* to alloy

aleatorio -ria *adj* ‹*suceso/resultado*› fortuitous; ‹*muestreo*› random

aleatorizar [A4] *vt* to randomize

alebrestar [A1] *vt* 1 (Col) (poner nervioso) to startle 2 (Méx) ‹*emoción*› to awaken, arouse 3 (Ven fam) (animar) to get … excited; (excesivamente) to get … overexcited

■ **alebrestarse** *v pron* 1 (Col, Méx) (alterarse, agitarse) to get worked up, agitated 2 (Ven fam) (animarse) to get excited; (excesivamente) to get overexcited

aleccionador -dora *adj* ‹*palabras/discurso*› instructive; **fue una experiencia ~a** the experience taught me a lesson

aleccionar [A1] *vt* 1 (dar instrucciones) to instruct; **lo aleccionó sobre cómo comportarse** she instructed him how to behave 2 (sermonear) to lecture

aledaño -ña *adj* ‹*países/pueblos*› neighboring* (*before n*); **tierras aledañas al río** land bordering the river

aledaños *mpl*: **los ~ de la ciudad** the outskirts of the town; **vive en los ~ del castillo** she lives near the castle; **la capital y sus ~** the capital and its environs (frml)

alegación *f* declaration, statement

alegador *adj* (Andes fam) argumentative

alegar [A3] *vt* ‹*motivos/causas*› to cite; ‹*razones*› to put forward; ‹*ignorancia/defensa propia*›to plead; **~ inmunidad diplomática** to claim diplomatic immunity; **alegó que no lo sabía** she claimed not to know

■ **alegar** *vi* 1 (AmL) (discutir) to argue; **~ DE algo** to argue ABOUT sth; **~ CON algn** to argue *o* quarrel WITH sb 2 (AmL) (protestar) to complain; **alega por ~** he complains for the sake of it; **~ POR algo** to complain ABOUT sth

alegata *f* (Méx) argument

alegato *m* 1 (exposición) statement, declaration; **el discurso fue un ~ contra el racismo** the speech denounced racism; **un ~ a favor de algn/algo** a plea on behalf of sb/sth 2 (Der) (escrito) submission; (en primera instancia) (Méx) summing-up; (en segunda instancia) (Chi) speech (*in appeal court*) 3 (Andes) (discusión) argument

alegoría *f* allegory

alegórico -ca *adj* allegorical

alegrar [A1] *vt* 1 (hacer feliz) ‹*persona*› to make … happy; **los nietos ~on su vejez** his grandchildren brought happiness to his old age; **me alegra saberlo** I'm glad *o* pleased to hear it 2 (animar) ‹*persona*› to cheer up; ‹*fiesta*› to liven up; **¡alegra esa cara!** cheer up!; **unas flores ~ían la habitación** some flowers would brighten up the room 3 (Taur) to excite

■ **alegrarse** *v pron* 1 (ponerse feliz, contento): **me alegro mucho por ti** I'm really happy for you; **se alegró muchísimo cuando lo vio** she was really happy when she saw him; **¡cuánto me alegro!** I'm so happy *o* pleased!; **está mucho mejor — me alegro** she's much better — I'm glad (to hear that); **~se CON algo** to be glad *o* pleased ABOUT sth; **se alegró mucho con la noticia** she was very pleased to hear the news; **~se DE + INF** to be pleased to + INF; **me alegro de verte** it's good *o* nice to see you; **¿no te alegras de haber venido?** aren't you glad *o* pleased you came?; **me alegro de que todo haya salido bien** I'm glad *o* pleased that everything went well 2 (animarse) to cheer up 3 (por el alcohol) to get tipsy (colloq)

alegre *adj* 1 ‹*persona/carácter*› happy, cheerful; ‹*color*› bright; ‹*fiesta/música*› lively; **su habitación es muy ~** her room is nice and bright; **es muy ~** she's very cheerful, she's a very happy girl; **se puso muy ~ con la noticia** the news made him very happy 2 [ESTAR] (por el alcohol) tipsy (colloq)

alegremente *adv* 1 (con alegría) cheerfully, happily 2 (con ligereza) blithely, gaily

alegría *f* (dicha, felicidad) happiness, joy; **¡qué ~ verte!** it's great to see you!; **qué ~ me das con esa noticia** that news has really made my day; **para gran ~ nuestra** to our great delight; **saltar de ~** to jump for joy

(Compuesto) **alegría de vivir** joie de vivre

alegrón *m* (fam) thrill (colloq)

alejado -da *adj* 1 ‹*lugar*› remote; **su casa está algo alejada** her house is a little out of the way *o* remote 2 (distanciado) ‹*persona*› **~ DE algo/algn**: **hace tiempo que está ~ de la política** he's been away from *o* out of politics for some time; **está ~ de su familia** he's estranged from his family

alejamiento *m* 1 (de lugar, cargo): **su ~ del cargo** his removal from the post; **un ~ temporal** a short absence 2 (entre personas — físico) separation; (— emocional) rift; **el ~ entre los dos se profundizó** the rift between them deepened

alejandrino *m* alexandrine

alejar [A1] *vt* 1 (poner lejos, más lejos) to move … (further) away from; **~ algo/a algn DE algo/algn** to move sth/sb away from sth/sb; **aleja la ropa/al niño del fuego** move the clothes/child away from the fire 2 (distanciar) **~ a algn DE algn** to distance sb FROM sb; **aquella discusión lo alejó de su padre** that quarrel distanced him from his father 3 (ahuyenta) ‹*dudas/temores*› to dispel

■ **alejarse** *v pron* to move away; (caminando) to walk away; **~se DE algo/algn**: **¡aléjate de allí!** get away from there!; **no se alejen demasiado** don't go too far; **el huracán se aleja de nuestra zona** the hurricane is moving away from our region; **nada hará que me aleje de ti** nothing will take me away from you; **~se del buen camino** to wander from the straight and narrow; **se alejó de sus padres** he drifted apart from his parents; **necesito ~me de todo** I need to get away from everything

alelado -da *adj* 1 (fascinado, absorto) spellbound, transfixed 2 (atontado) dazed 3 (fam) (sorprendido) speechless, amazed

alelar [A1] *vt* (dejar estupefacto) to overwhelm, stupefy; (dejar confuso) to bewilder

■ **alelarse** *v pron* (quedar estupefacto) to be overwhelmed, be stupefied; (quedar confuso) to be bewildered

alelí *m* wallflower

aleluya[1] *m* (Mús) hallelujah, alleluia

aleluya[2] *interj* hallelujah!

alemán[1] -mana *adj/m,f* German

alemán[2] *m* (idioma) German

Alemania *f* Germany

(Compuestos)

- **Alemania Occidental** *or* **Federal** (Hist) West Germany
- **Alemania Oriental** *or* **del Este** (Hist) East Germany

alentado -da *adj* (AmL fam) (con buena salud): **se ve de lo más ~** he looks a lot better

alentador -dora *adj* encouraging

alentar [A5] *vt* 1 (dar ánimo) to encourage; (con gritos, aplausos) to cheer … on 2 ‹*esperanza/ilusión*› to cherish

■ **alentar** *vi* (liter) (respirar) to breathe

■ **alentarse** *v pron* (AmS fam) (mejorarse) to get better

alerce *m* larch

alergia *f* allergy; **le produce ~** she's allergic to it; **~s alimentarias** food allergies; **~ A algo** allergy TO sth; **tiene ~ a la penicilina** he's allergic to penicillin

alérgico -ca *adj* 1 [SER] ‹*persona*› allergic; **~ A algo** allergic TO sth 2 ‹*afección/reacción*› allergic

alero *m* 1 (de tejado) eaves (*pl*); ***estar en el ~*** to be up in the air 2 (Dep) winger 3 (Chi) (amparo) protection

alerón *m* aileron

alerta¹ *adj or adj inv* alert; **estar ~(s)** (tener cuidado) to be alert; (estar en guardia) to be on the alert; **mantener el ojo/el oído ~** to keep watch/keep one's ears open

alerta² *adv* on the alert

alerta³ *f* alert; **dar la (voz de) ~** to raise the alarm; **poner a algn en ~** to alert sb; **en estado de ~** on alert

(Compuesto) **alerta roja** red alert

alertar [A1] *vt* **~ a algn DE algo** to alert sb TO sth; **nos alertó del peligro** he alerted us to the danger

aleta *f* 1 (de pez) fin; (de foca) flipper 2 (para natación) flipper 3 (de la nariz) wing 4 (de flecha) flight; (de hélice) blade 5 (Auto) quarter panel (AmE), wing (BrE)

aletargado -da *adj* lethargic, drowsy

aletargamiento *m* (apatía) lethargy; (somnolencia) drowsiness

aletargar [A3] *vt* ‹*persona*› to make … feel lethargic *o* drowsy

■ **aletargarse** *v pron* to feel lethargic *o* drowsy

aletazo *m* 1 (de ave) flap (of the wing); **dando ~s** flapping *o* beating its wings 2 (de pez) movement of the fin

aletear [A1] *vi* «*pájaro/gallina*» to flap its wings; «*mariposa*» to flutter its wings

aleteo *m*: **el ~ de las palomas** the flapping of the pigeons' wings; **el ~ de las mariposas** the fluttering of butterflies' wings

alevín, alevino *m*

A (Zool) fry, young fish

B (principiante) beginner; (Dep) junior

alevosía *f* (traición) treachery; (premeditacion) premeditation, malice aforethought

alevoso -sa *adj* 1 (Der) premeditated 2 (Col fam) (arrogante) cocky (colloq)

alfa *f‡* alpha

alfabéticamente *adv* alphabetically

alfabético -ca *adj* alphabetical

alfabetización *f* teaching of basic literacy; **campaña de ~** literacy campaign

alfabetizar [A4] *vt* 1 (Educ) to teach … to read and write 2 ‹*sistema/fichero*› to put … in alphabetical order, to alphabetize (frml)

alfabeto *m* alphabet; **en el ~ Morse** in Morse (code); **el ~ de los sordomudos** sign language

alfajor *m*: *type of candy or cake varying from region to region*

alfalfa *f* alfalfa, lucerne (BrE)

alfandoque *m* (Col, Per) caramel bar

alfanje *m* scimitar

alfaque *m* sandbank, sandbar

alfar *m* (taller) pottery; (arcilla) clay

alfarería *f* pottery

alfarero -ra *m,f* potter

alféizar *m* sill; **el ~ de la ventana** the windowsill

alfeñique *m* (fam) (persona) wimp (colloq)

alférez *m* second lieutenant

alfil *m* bishop

alfiler *m* (en costura) pin; (broche) brooch, pin; ***no caber ni un ~***: **no cabía ni un ~ en la sala** the hall was filled to bursting; ***prendido con ~es*** ‹*teoría*› shaky

(Compuestos)

- **alfiler de corbata** tiepin
- **alfiler de gancho** (CS, Ven) safety pin
- **alfiler de nodriza** (Col) safety pin

alfiletero *m* (estuche) needlecase; (almohadilla) pincushion

alfombra *f*

A (suelta) rug; (más grande) carpet; **~ de pie de cama** bedside rug

(Compuesto) **alfombra mágica** magic carpet

B (AmL) (de pared a pared) carpet

C ▸**alfombrilla A**

alfombrado¹ -da *adj* carpeted; **estaba totalmente alfombrada** it was fully carpeted *o* had wall-to-wall carpeting throughout

alfombrado² *m* carpeting; **con un suntuoso ~** with luxurious carpeting

alfombrar [A1] *vt* to carpet

alfombrilla *f*

A (de coche) mat; (de baño) bath mat

B (Med) *type of measles*

alforja *f* (para caballerías) saddlebag; (sobre el hombro) knapsack

alga *f‡* (en el mar) seaweed; (en agua dulce) weed, waterweed; (nombre genérico) alga

algarabía *f* (alboroto, regocijo) rejoicing, jubilation

algarada *f* brawl, commotion

algarroba *f* carob (bean)

algarrobo *m* carob (tree)

algazara *f* rejoicing, jubilation

álgebra *f‡* algebra

algebraico -ca *adj* algebraic

álgido -da *adj*

A ‹*punto/momento*› culminating (*before n*), decisive

B ‹*clima*› icy; ‹*temperatura*› freezing

algo¹ *pron* 1 something; (en frases interrogativas, condicionales, etc) anything; (esperando respuesta afirmativa) something; **quiero decirle ~** I want to tell you something; **si llegara a pasarle ~** if anything happened to her; **¿quieres ~ de beber?** do you want something *o* anything to drink?; **por ~ será** there must be some *o* a reason; **le va a dar ~** he'll have a fit; **~ así** something like that; **~ es ~** it's better than nothing; **eso ya es ~** at least that's something; **sé ~ de francés** I know some French; **¿queda ~ de pan?** is there any bread left?; **hay ~ de cierto en eso** there's some truth in that 2 (en aproximaciones): **serán las once y ~** it must be some time after eleven; **pesa tres kilos y ~** it weighs three kilos and a bit; **es enfermera o ~ así** she's a nurse or something like that; **tendrá ~ así como 30 años** she must be about 30

algo² *adv* a little, slightly; **son ~ parecidos** they're somewhat similar; **¿te duele? — algo** does it hurt? — a little *o* a bit

algo³ *m*

A 1 **un ~** (un no sé qué) something; **si no llega pronto me va a dar ~** if he doesn't turn up soon, I'll go mad; **tiene un ~ que me recuerda a su madre** she has something of her mother about her 2 (un poco): **hay un ~ de verdad en eso** there is some truth in that

B (Col) (merienda) mid-afternoon snack

algodón *m*

A (Bot) cotton; (tela) cotton

B (Farm) 1 (material) *tb* **~ hidrófilo** cotton (AmE), cotton wool (BrE) 2 (trozo) piece of cotton (AmE), piece of cotton wool (BrE); ***entre algodones***: **vivía/lo criaron entre algodones** he was pampered

(Compuestos)

- **algodón de azúcar** cotton candy (AmE), candy floss (BrE)
- **algodón en rama** raw cotton

algodonal, algodonar *m* cotton field

algodonero¹ -ra *adj* cotton (*before n*)

algodonero² -ra *m,f* 1 (agricultor) cotton planter *o* farmer; (vendedor) cotton dealer 2 **algodonero** *m* cotton plant

alguacil -cila *m,f*

A 1 (agente de autoridad) sheriff 2 (de tribunal de justicia) bailiff (AmE), constable (BrE) 3 (Taur) *person responsible for opening the bull pen at the beginning of a bullfight*

B **alguacil** *m* 1 (araña) jumping spider 2 (RPl) (libélula) dragonfly

a

alguien *pron* somebody, someone; (en frases interrogativas, condicionales, etc) anybody, anyone; (esperando respuesta afirmativa) somebody, someone; **~ con experiencia** somebody *o* someone with experience; **¿ha llamado ~?** has anybody *o* anyone called?; **si ~ preguntara** if anybody *o* anyone should ask; **¿cómo llegaste? ¿te trajo ~?** how did you get here? did somebody *o* someone bring you?

algún *adj: apocopated form of* **alguno** *used before masculine singular nouns*

alguno¹ -na *adj*
A (*delante del n*) **1** (indicando uno indeterminado) some; **algún día** some *o* one day; **en algún lugar** somewhere **2** (*en frases interrogativas, condicionales, etc*) any; **¿tocas algún instrumento?** do you play any instruments?; **si tienes algún problema** if there's any problem, if you have any problems; **¿te dio algún recado para mí?** did she give you a message for me? **3** (indicando cantidad indeterminada): **esto tiene alguna importancia** this is of some importance; **hace ~s años** some years ago *o* a few years ago; **me quedan tres tazas y algún plato** I have three cups and one or two plates; **algún** *or* **alguno que otro/alguna que otra**: **escribió algún que otro artículo** he wrote one or two articles; **algún** *or* **~ que otro lujo** the odd luxury; **he ido alguna que otra vez** I've been once or twice; **alguna que otra vez vamos al cine** we go to the cinema now and then
B (*detrás del n*) (con valor negativo): **esto no lo afectará en modo ~** this won't affect it in the slightest *o* at all

alguno² -na *pron* **1** (cosa, persona indeterminada) one: **~ de nosotros** one of us; **siempre hay ~ que no está conforme** there's always someone who doesn't agree; **en alguna de esas revistas** in one of those magazines **2** (en frases interrogativas, condicionales, etc): **buscaba una guía ¿tiene alguna?** I was looking for a guide, do you have one *o* any?; **si tuviera ~** if I had one **3** (una cantidad indeterminada — de personas) some people; (— de cosas) some; **~s creen que fue así** some (people) believe that was the case; **he visto alguna** *or* **algunas** I've seen some

alhaja *f* **1** (joya) piece of jewelry*; **iba cargada de ~s** she was laden with jewelry **2** (persona) gem, treasure

alhajar [A1] *vt* **1** ‹*persona*› to adorn (*with jewels*) **2** (CS) ‹*casa*› to decorate
■ **alhajarse** *v pron* (*refl*) to deck oneself out with jewels

alhajero *m*, **alhajera** *f* (AmL) jewel case

alharaca *f*, (Col) **alharaco** *m* fuss; **hacer ~s** to make a fuss

alharaquiento -ta *adj* melodramatic

alhelí *m* wallflower

alheña *f* privet

alhucema *f* lavender

aliado¹ -da *adj* allied

aliado² -da *m,f* (Hist, Pol) ally; **los A~s** the Allies

aliancismo *m* pro-alliance *o* pro-coalition stance

aliancista *adj* pro-alliance, pro-coalition

alianza *f*
A (pacto, unión) alliance
(Compuestos)
• **Alianza Atlántica**: **la ~ ~** the Atlantic Alliance, NATO
• **alianza matrimonial** (frml) holy matrimony (frml)
B (anillo) wedding ring

aliar [A17] *vt* to ally
■ **aliarse** *v pron* to join forces; **~se con algn** to form an alliance WITH sb, ally oneself WITH sb

alias¹ *adv* alias; **Juan Pérez, ~ 'el Rubio'** Juan Pérez alias 'el Rubio'

alias² *m* (*pl* ~) alias

alicaído -da *adj* low, down in the dumps (colloq)

alicatar [A1] *vt* (Esp) to tile

alicate *m*, **alicates** *mpl* (Tec) pliers (*pl*); (para uñas) nail clippers (*pl*); (para cutícula) cuticle clippers (*pl*)

aliciente *m* incentive; **no ven ~ en los estudios** they have no incentive to study; **volver a su pueblo no tiene ningún ~ para ella** going back to her village holds no attraction for her

alienación *f* (Der, Psic, Sociol) alienation
(Compuesto) **alienación mental** insanity

alienado¹ -da *adj* (Psic, Sociol) alienated

alienado² -da *m,f tb* **~ mental** mentally-ill person

alienador -dora, **alienante** *adj* alienating, dehumanizing

alienar [A1] *vt* (Der, Psic, Sociol) to alienate

alienígena *mf* alien

aliento *m*
A **1** (respiración, aire) breath; **sin ~** out of breath, breathless; **le faltaba el ~** he was out of breath *o* short of breath; **recuperar el ~** to get one's breath back **2** (aire espirado) breath; **mal ~** bad breath; **le huele el ~** his breath smells **3** (inspiración) inspiration; **cuentos de ~ gótico** tales with a Gothic flavor
B (ánimo, valor): **dar ~ a algn** to encourage sb; **aquello me dió ~ para seguir adelante** that gave me the strength to carry on

aligerar [A1] *vt* **1** ‹*carga*› to lighten; **lo hizo para ~ su conciencia** he did it to ease his conscience; **~ a algn DE algo** to relieve sb OF sth **2** (acelerar): **~ el paso** to quicken one's pace
■ **aligerarse** *v pron* **~se DE algo**: **se aligeró de la capa** he removed his cape; **~se de una carga** to get rid of a burden

alijo *m* (de contrabando) consignment; **un importante ~ de armas** a sizable arms cache; **un ~ de hachís** a consignment of hashish

alimaña *f* pest; **~s** vermin

alimentación *f*
A **1** (nutrición, comida) diet; **una ~ rica en proteínas** a protein-rich diet; **la ~ integral va ganando adeptos** health food *o* wholefood is growing in popularity **2** (acción): **atender a la ~ de la población** to provide food for the population; **pastos para la ~ de los animales** pastures for grazing the animals
B (de máquina, motor) fuel supply

alimentador *m* feeder

alimentar [A1] *vt*
A (nutrir) ‹*persona/animal*› to feed; **los alimentan con piensos** they are fed on pellets; **estas tierras ~on a mi familia** my family lived off this land
B ‹*ilusión/esperanza*› to nurture, cherish; ‹*ego*› to boost; **~ el odio entre dos países** to fuel the hatred between two countries
C ‹*máquina/motor*› to feed; ‹*caldera*› to stoke; **algodón para ~ la industria textil** cotton to supply the textile industry
■ **alimentar** *vi* to be nourishing
■ **alimentarse** *v pron* ‹*persona/animal*› to feed oneself; **no se alimenta bien** he doesn't eat right (AmE) *o* (BrE) properly; **~se CON** *or* **DE algo** to live ON sth

alimenticio -cia, **alimentario -ria** *adj* **1** ‹*industria*› food (*before n*); **productos ~s** foodstuffs; **hábitos ~s** eating habits **2** (nutritivo) ‹*valor*› nutritional; ‹*comida/plato*› nutritious, nourishing

alimento *m*
A (frml) (comida) food; **la leche es un ~ completo** milk is a complete food; **como ~ es pobre** it has little nutritional value
(Compuesto) **alimento chatarra** (Méx) junk food
B (valor nutritivo): **no tiene ~ ninguno** it has no nutritional value; **de mucho ~** very nutritious

alineación *f*
A (Dep) (de equipo) lineup; (de jugador) selection
B (Pol) alignment; **política de no ~** policy of non-alignment
C (Tec) alignment
D (puesta en fila) lining up

alineamiento *m* (Pol) alignment

alinear [A1] *vt*
A ‹*equipo/jugador*› to select, pick
B (poner en fila, línea) to line up
C (Tec) to align, line up
■ **alinearse** *v pron* **1** ‹‹*tropa*›› to fall in; ‹‹*niños/presos*›› to line up **2** (Pol, Rels Labs) **~se CON algo/algn** to align oneself WITH sth/sb; **países no alineados** nonaligned countries

aliñar [A1] *vt* ‹*ensalada*› to dress; ‹*carne/pescado*› to season

aliño *m* (para ensalada) dressing; (para otros alimentos) seasoning

alioli *m* (mayonesa) garlic mayonnaise; (salsa) garlic and olive oil vinaigrette

alirón *m/interj*: *soccer fans' victory chant*

alisar [A1] *vt* ‹*colcha/papel*› to smooth out; ‹*pared/superficie*› to smooth down

■ **alisarse** *v pron* (*refl*) 1 ‹*vestido/falda*› to smooth out 2 ‹*pelo*› (con la mano) to smooth down; (quitar los rizos) to straighten

alisios *mpl* trade winds

aliso *m* alder (tree)

alistamiento *m* (acción) enlistment, recruitment; (soldados alistados) call-up, draft (AmE)

alistarse [A1] *v pron* 1 (Mil) to enlist, join up; **~ en la marina/el ejército** to join the navy/the army 2 (AmL) (prepararse) to get ready

alita *f*

A (para nadar) water wing, armband

B (niña) Brownie

aliteración *f* alliteration

aliterar [A1] *vi* to alliterate

aliviadero *m* spillway, overflow channel

aliviar [A1] *vt*

A ‹*dolor*› to relieve, soothe; ‹*síntomas*› to relieve; ‹*tristeza/pena*› to alleviate; **esta medicina te ~á** this medicine will make you feel better

B (fam) (robar) **~le algo A algn** to relieve sb OF sth (hum), to lift sth FROM sb (colloq); **le ~on la cartera** someone relieved him of his wallet

■ **aliviarse** *v pron*

A 1 «*dolor*» to let up 2 «*persona*» to get better

B (Méx fam & euf) (parir): **¿cuándo te aliviaste?** when was the happy event? (colloq & euph)

alivio *m*

A (del dolor, síntoma) relief

B (de problema, preocupación) relief; **¡qué ~!** what a relief!; **sintió un gran ~** it was a great relief to him *o* he felt a great sense of relief

aljama *f* 1 (barrio — de moros) Moorish quarter; (— de judíos) Jewish quarter 2 (mezquita) mosque; (sinagoga) synagogue 3 (reunión) gathering (*of Moors or Jews*)

aljibe *m*

A (pozo) well; (depósito de agua) cistern, tank

B (Per) (cárcel) dungeon

aljófar *m* seed pearl; **~ de rocío** (liter) dewdrop

allá *adv*

A 1 (en el espacio): **ya vamos para ~** we're on our way (over); **~ en América** over in America; **esa silla está muy ~** that chair's a long way off *o* away; **lo pusiste muy ~** you've put it too far away; **¡~ voy!** here I come/go! 2 (*en locs*) **más allá** further away; **más allá de** (más lejos que) beyond; (aparte de) over and above; **más ~ del peligro que encierra** over and above the danger it entails; **~ *tú/él*** that's your/his lookout *o* problem (colloq); ***no estar muy ~*** (Esp fam): **no está muy ~** it's nothing to write home about (colloq)

B (en el tiempo): **~ por los años 40** back in the forties; **~ para enero** sometime in January

allanamiento *m* 1 (AmL) (con autorización judicial) raid; **orden de ~** search warrant 2 (Esp, Méx) (sin autorización judicial) breaking and entering

allanar [A1] *vt*

A 1 (AmL) «*autoridad/policía*» to raid 2 (Esp, Méx) «*delincuente*» to break into

B ‹*problemas*› to solve, resolve; ‹*obstáculo*› to remove, overcome; ‹*terreno*› to level out; ***~(le) el terreno a algn*** to smooth the way *o* path for sb

■ **allanarse** *v pron* **~se A algo** to agree TO sth, agree to accept sth

allegado[1] **-da** *adj* 1 (próximo) close; **fuentes allegadas a la presidencia** (period) sources close to the President; **mis amigos y parientes más ~s** my close family and friends 2 (Chi) (huésped): **está ~ en mi casa** he's staying with me

allegado[2] **-da** *m,f* 1 (amigo, pariente): **los ~s del difunto** those closest to the deceased; **un ~ de la familia** a close friend of the family 2 (Chi) (huésped): **tiene ~s en su casa** he has people staying with him; **vive de ~ en mi casa** I'm putting him up

allegar [A3] *vt* ‹*medios/recursos*› to gather together; ‹*datos*› to collect, gather

allegro /a'leɣro/ *m* allegro

allende *prep* (liter) beyond; **~ los mares** overseas

allí *adv*

A (en el espacio) there; **siéntate ~** sit there; **~ arriba/dentro** up/in there; **~ donde estés/vayas** wherever you are/go

B (en el tiempo): **~ es cuando empezaron los problemas** that's when the problems started

alma *f‡*

A (espíritu) soul; **tiene ~ de poeta** she has the soul of a poet; **tener ~ de niño** to be a child at heart; **~ mía** *or* **mi ~** (*como apelativo*) my love; ***clavársele en el ~ a algn***: **lo que me dijo se me clavó en el ~** I've never forgotten what he said; **lleva clavada en el ~ esa traición** he's never got(ten) over that betrayal; ***como (un) ~ en pena*** like a lost soul; ***con el ~ en un hilo*** worried to death; ***con toda el*** *or* ***mi/tu/su ~*** with all my/your/his/ heart; **lo odiaba con toda su ~** she hated him intensely; ***del ~***: **su amigo del ~** his bosom friend; ***de mi ~***: **¡hija de mi ~!** my darling!; ***en el ~***: **lo siento en el ~** I'm really *o* terribly sorry; **me duele** *or* **pesa en el ~** it hurts me deeply; **te lo agradezco en el ~** I can't tell you how grateful I am; ***hasta el ~*** (fam): **me dolió hasta el ~** it was excruciatingly painful; **se le vio hasta el ~** she bared her all (colloq); ***llegarle a algn al ~***: **aquellas palabras me llegaron al ~** (me conmovieron) I was deeply touched by those words; (me dolieron) I was deeply hurt by those words; ***me/le parte el ~*** it breaks my/his heart; ***no poder con su ~*** to be tired out; ***romperle el ~ a algn*** (fam) to beat the living daylights out of sb (colloq); ***romperse el ~*** (fam) to break one's neck (colloq); ***salir/ir como ~ que lleva el diablo*** to run like a bat out of hell; ***salirle a algn del ~***: **siento habérselo dicho pero me salió del ~** I'm sorry I said that, it just came out; **el suspiro le salió del ~** she sighed deeply; ***se me/le cayó*** *or* ***fue el ~ a los pies*** my/his heart sank; ***venderle el ~ al diablo*** to sell one's soul (to the Devil)

B 1 (persona) soul; **no hay un ~ por la calle** there isn't a soul on the streets; ***ni un ~ viviente*** not a living soul; ***ser ~s gemelas*** to be soul mates; ***ser un ~ bendita*** *or* ***de Dios*** to be a kind soul 2 (centro, fuerza vital): **el ~ de la fiesta** the life and soul of the party; **el ~ del movimiento nacionalista** the key figure in the nationalist movement

C (ánimo) feeling

almacén *m* 1 (depósito) warehouse 2 (CS) (de comestibles) grocery store (AmE), grocer's (shop) (BrE) 3 (AmC, Col, Ven) (de ropa, etc) store (AmE), shop (BrE) 4 (de mayorista) wholesaler's 5 **almacenes** *mpl* department store

almacenaje, almacenamiento *m* storage; **~ de datos** data storage, storage; **hicieron un buen ~ de provisiones** they built up a good stock of provisions

almacenar [A1] *vt* ‹*mercancías/datos*› to store; **tenían almacenadas enormes cantidades de armas** they had huge stockpiles of weapons

almacenero -ra *m,f* (CS) grocer

almacenista *mf* wholesaler

almácigo *m* (semillero) seedbed

almádena *f* sledgehammer

alma-máter *f‡* 1 (centro, fuerza vital) driving force; **el ~ del programa** the driving force behind the program 2 (universidad): **el ~** one's alma-mater

almanaque *m* (calendario — de escritorio) almanac, desk calendar; (— de pared) calendar

almeja *f* clam

almena *f* merlon; **~s** battlements

almendra *f*

A (fruta) almond

B (centro) kernel

almendrado -da *adj* almond-shaped; **de ojos ~s** almond-eyed

almendro *m* almond tree

almiar *m* haystack

almíbar *m* syrup

a

almibarado -da *adj* ‹*tono de voz*› sugary; ‹*palabras*› honeyed

almibarar [A1] *vt* ‹*fruta*› to preserve ... in syrup; ‹*pastel*› to soak ... in syrup

almidón *m* starch

almidonado -da *adj* (fam) ‹*persona*› (estirado) stuffy (colloq); (demasiado acicalado): **van siempre tan ∼s** they are always dressed so neat and tidy

almidonar [A1] *vt* to starch

alminar *m* minaret

almirantazgo *m* (cargo) admiralship

almirante *m* admiral

almirez *m* mortar

almizcle *m* musk

almizclera *f* muskrat

almizclero *m* musk deer

almohada *f* pillow; ***consultarlo con la*** ∼ to sleep on it

almohadilla *f*
A (para alfileres) pincushion; (para entintar) ink pad; (para sellos) damper
B (para sentarse) cushion; (en béisbol) bag

almohadón *m* (cuadrado, redondo) cushion; (cilíndrico) bolster; (en la iglesia) kneeler

almoneda *f* (subasta) auction; (liquidación) clearance sale

almorranas *fpl* (fam) piles (*pl*)

almorzar [A11] *vi* **1** (a mediodía) to have lunch **2** (en algunas regiones) (a media mañana) to have a mid-morning snack
■ **almorzar** *vt* **1** (a mediodía) to have ... for lunch **2** (en algunas regiones) (a media mañana) to have ... mid-morning

almuecín, almuédano *m* muezzin

almuerza, almuerzas, etc *see* **almorzar**

almuerzo *m* **1** (a mediodía) lunch **2** (en algunas regiones) (a media mañana) mid-morning snack

aló *interj* (Andes, Ven) (al contestar el teléfono) hello?

alocado[1] -da *adj* (irresponsable, imprudente) crazy, wild; (irreflexivo, impetuoso) rash, impetuous; (despistado) scatterbrained

alocado[2] -da *m,f* (imprudente) crazy *o* reckless fool; (irreflexivo) rash fool; (despistado) scatterbrain

alocución *f* (frml) address (frml); **la ∼ papal** the papal address

áloe, aloe *m* (planta) aloe; (sustancia) aloes

alojado -da *m,f* (Chi) guest; **pieza de ∼s** guestroom

alojamiento *m* accommodations (*pl*) (AmE), accommodation (BrE); **nos dio ∼** he put us up

alojar [A1] *vt*
A **1** (en hotel): **los hemos alojado en el hotel Plaza** we've booked them into the Plaza Hotel; **el hotel en el que estaban alojados** the hotel where they were staying **2** (en casa particular) to put ... up
B (albergar) ‹*evacuados/refugiados*› to house; **la residencia aloja a 70 estudiantes** the hostel houses 70 students
■ **alojarse** *v pron* **1** (hospedarse) to stay **2** ‹‹*proyectil/bala*›› to lodge

alón *m* wing

alondra *f* lark

alopecia *f* alopecia

alpaca *f*
A (Zool, Tex) alpaca; **lana de ∼** alpaca (wool)
B (Metal) nickel silver, German silver

alpargata *f* espadrille

alpargatería *f* shoe store (*selling espadrilles*)

Alpes *mpl*: **los ∼** the Alps

alpestre *adj* alpine

alpinismo *m* mountaineering, (mountain) climbing

alpinista *mf* mountaineer, (mountain) climber

alpino -na *adj* Alpine

alpiste *m*
A (semillas) birdseed
B (RPl fam) (bebida) booze (colloq)

alquería *f* (Esp) (granja) farm; (casa) farmhouse

alquilar [A1] *vt*
A (dar en alquiler) ‹*casa/local*› to rent (out), let; ‹*televisor*› to rent; ‹*coche/bicicleta*› to rent (out) (AmE), to hire out (BrE); **Ⓢ se alquilan esquís** skis for rent (AmE) *o* (BrE) hire
B (tomar en alquiler) ‹*casa/local/televisor*› to rent; ‹*coche/bicicleta/disfraz*› to rent (AmE), to hire (BrE)

alquiler *m* **1** (precio): **el ∼ del apartamento** the rent on the apartment; **el ∼ del televisor** the television rental **2** (acción de alquilar — una casa) renting, letting (BrE); (— un televisor) rental; (— un coche, disfraz) rental (AmE), hire (BrE); **se dedica al ∼ de coches** he's in the car-rental (AmE) *o* (BrE) car-hire business; **contrato de ∼** tenancy agreement; **tiene varios apartamentos de ∼** she has several apartments that she rents out; **coches de ∼** rental (AmE) *o* (BrE) hire cars

alquimia *f* alchemy

alquimista *mf* alchemist

alquitrán *m* tar

alquitranado *m* (acción) tarring; (superficie) tarmac

alquitranar [A1] *vt* to tar

alrededor *adv*
A (en torno) around; **a mi/tu/su ∼** around me/you/him
B **alrededor de** (*loc prep*) (en torno a) around; (aproximadamente) around, about

alrededores *mpl* **1** (de ciudad — barrios periféricos, afueras) outskirts (*pl*); (— otras localidades): **Madrid y sus ∼** Madrid and its surroundings **2** (de edificio, calle) surrounding area; **la policía está rastreando los ∼** the police are combing the surrounding area; **en los ∼ de la iglesia** in the area around the church

alsaciano -na *adj/m,f* Alsatian

alta *f‡*
A (Med) discharge; **dar el ∼ a** *or* **dar de ∼ a un enfermo** to discharge a patient
B **1** (Fisco, Servs Socs): **los dieron de ∼ en la Seguridad Social** they registered them with Social Security **2** (Esp) (ingreso) membership; **causar ∼ en el ejército** to enlist in the army; **hubo muchas ∼s en noviembre** a lot of new members joined in November

altanería *f*
A (arrogancia) arrogance; **con ∼** arrogantly
B (arc) (cetrería) falconry

altanero -ra *adj* arrogant, haughty

altar *m* altar; **la llevó al ∼** he made her his wife

(Compuesto) **altar mayor** high altar

altavoz *m* (Audio) loudspeaker; (megáfono) megaphone

alterabilidad *f* (de material) instability; (de alimento, medicina) perishability; (de colorido) tendency to discolor* *o* fade

alterable *adj* volatile

alteración *f*
A **1** (de plan, texto) change, alteration **2** (de hechos, verdad) distortion
B (del orden, de la paz) disturbance; (agitación) agitation

(Compuesto) **alteración del orden público** breach of the peace

alterado -da *adj* [ESTAR] ‹*persona*› upset; **con la voz alterada por la emoción** in a voice shaking *o* faltering with emotion

alterar [A1] *vt*
A **1** ‹*plan/texto*› to change, alter **2** ‹*hechos/verdad*› to distort; **el sentido de mis palabras fue alterado** what I said was misinterpreted *o* misrepresented **3** ‹*alimento*› to make ... go off, turn ... bad; **la exposición al sol puede ∼ el color** exposure to the sun can affect the color
B (perturbar) **1** ‹*paz*› to disturb; **∼ el orden público** to cause a breach of the peace **2** ‹*persona*› to upset; **la noticia lo alteró visiblemente** he was visibly shaken by the news
■ **alterarse** *v pron*
A ‹‹*alimentos*›› to go off, go bad
B ‹‹*pulso/respiración*›› to become irregular; **con la emoción se le alteró la voz** her voice shook with emotion
C ‹‹*persona*›› to get upset

altercado *m* argument; **tener un ∼ con algn** to have an argument with sb

álter ego *m* alter ego

alternador *m* alternator

alternancia *f* alternation; **∼ de cultivos** crop rotation

alternar [A1] *vt* **~ algo CON algo** to alternate sth WITH sth; **alternamos la gimnasia con el tenis** we alternate gymnastics with tennis; **alternan la cebada con la remolacha** they rotate crops of barley and beet

■ **alternar** *vi*

A (turnar, cambiar) to alternate; **alternaba entre la euforia y la depresión** he alternated between euphoria and depression; **~ CON algo** to alternate WITH sth; **los robles alternan con los olmos** oak trees alternate with elms

B ‹‹*persona*››: **alterna en círculos artísticos** he moves in artistic circles; **~ CON algn** to mix WITH sb

■ **alternarse** *v pron* to take turns

alternativa *f*

A (opción) alternative; **no tienes ~** you have no choice *o* alternative; **la ~ es clara** the choice is clear

B (Taur) *ceremony in which a* **novillero** *becomes a fully-fledged bullfighter*; **tomar la ~** to become a fully-fledged bullfighter

C **alternativas** *fpl*: **siguió con interés las ~s del campeonato** she followed the ups and downs of the championship with interest

alternativamente *adv* (con alternancia) alternately; (*indep*) alternatively

alternativo -va *adj* **1** ‹*medicina/prensa/música*› alternative **2** (en alternancia) in rotation; **cultivos ~s** crops in rotation

alterne *m* (Esp): **chica de ~** hostess; **bar de ~** hostess bar; **vive del ~** she makes a living as a hostess

alterno -na *adj*

A ‹*ángulos/hojas*› alternate; **sólo trabaja (en) días ~s** she only works alternate days; ▸**corriente²D**

B (Col) **1** ‹*director*› acting (*before n*) **2** ‹*sala*›: **en la sala alterna del museo** in the museum annex

alteza *f*

A (liter) (de sentimientos, pensamientos) nobility, nobleness

B **Alteza** (tratamiento) Highness; **sí, (su) A~** yes, your Highness; **su A~ real** His/Her/Your Royal Highness

altibajos *mpl* **1** (cambios bruscos) ups and downs (*pl*) **2** (del terreno) undulations (*pl*)

altillo *m* (desván) attic; (en habitación) (sleeping) loft

altilocuencia *f* grandiloquence

altilocuente *adj* grandiloquent

altímetro *m* altimeter

altiplanicie *f*, **altiplano** *m* high plateau, high plain; **el altiplano boliviano** the Bolivian altiplano

altiro *adv* (Chi fam) right away, immediately; **~ vengo** I'll be right back

altísimo *m*: **el A~** the Most High, the Almighty

altisonante *adj* highflown

altitud *f* altitude; **a 300m de ~ sobre el nivel del mar** 300m above sea level

altivez *f* (arrogancia) arrogance, haughtiness; (dignidad, orgullo) pride

altivo -va *adj* (arrogante) arrogant, haughty; (noble, orgulloso) proud

alto¹ -ta *adj*

A **1** [SER] ‹*persona/edificio/árbol*› tall; ‹*pared/montaña*› high; **zapatos de tacones ~s** *or* (AmS) **de taco ~** high-heeled shoes; **una blusa de cuello ~** a high-necked blouse **2** [ESTAR]: **¡qué ~ estás!** haven't you grown!; **está tan alta como yo** she's as tall as me now

B (indicando posición, nivel) **1** [SER] high; **los techos eran muy ~s** the rooms had very high ceilings; **un vestido de talle ~** a high-waisted dress **2** [ESTAR]: **el río está muy ~** the river is very high; **la marea está alta** it's high tide, the tide's in; **los pisos más ~s** the top floors; **salgan con los brazos en ~** come out with your hands in the air; **eso dejó en ~ su buen nombre** (CS) that really boosted his reputation; **están con la moral bastante alta** they are in pretty high spirits; **mantener ~ el espíritu** to keep one's spirits up; **en lo ~ de la montaña/de un árbol** high up on the mountainside/in a tree; **en lo ~ del árbol** high up in the tree; ***por todo lo ~*** in style; **una boda por todo lo ~** a lavish wedding

C (en cantidad, calidad) high; **tiene la tensión** *or* **presión alta** she has high blood pressure; **productos de alta calidad** high-quality products; **embarazo de ~ riesgo** high-risk pregnancy; ***tirando por lo ~*** at the most

D **1** [ESTAR] (en intensidad) ‹*volumen/televisión*› loud; **pon la radio más alta** turn the radio up **2** **en alto** *or* **en voz alta** aloud, out loud

E (*delante del n*) (en importancia, trascendencia) ‹*ejecutivo/funcionario*› high-ranking, top; **un militar de ~ rango** a high-ranking army officer; **conversaciones de ~ nivel** high-level talks

F (*delante del n*) ‹*ideales/opinión*› high; **un ~ sentido del deber** a strong sense of duty; **tiene un ~ concepto de ti** he thinks very highly of you

G (*delante del n*) **1** (Ling) high; **el ~ alemán** High German **2** (Geog) upper; **el A~ Paraná** the Upper Paraná

(Compuestos)

- **alta burguesía** *f* upper-middle classes (*pl*)
- **alta cocina** *f* haute cuisine
- **alta costura** *f* haute couture
- **alta Edad Media** *f* High Middle Ages (*pl*)
- **alta fidelidad** *f* high fidelity, hi-fi
- **alta mar** *f*: **en ~ ~** on the high seas; **flota/pesca de ~ ~** deep-sea fleet/fishing
- **altas esferas** *fpl* upper echelons (*pl*)
- **alta sociedad** *f* high society
- **altas presiones** *fpl* high pressure
- **alta tensión** *f* high tension *o* voltage
- **alto cargo** *m* (puesto) high-ranking position; (persona) high-ranking official
- **alto comisionado** *m* high commissioner
- **alto horno** *m* blast furnace
- **alto mando** *m* high-ranking officer

alto² *adv*

A ‹*volar/subir*› high

B ‹*hablar*› loud, loudly; **habla más ~** speak up a little; ***pasar por ~*** *ver* **pasar** *vt Sentido* **I F**

alto³ *interj* halt!; **¡~ (ahí)!** (Mil) halt!; (dicho por un policía) stop!, stay where you are!; **¡~ el fuego!** cease fire!

(Compuesto) **alto el fuego** *m* (Esp) (Mil) cease-fire

alto⁴ *m*

A **1** (altura) **de alto** high; **un muro de cuatro metros de ~** a four-meter high wall; **tiene tres metros de ~** it's three meters high **2** (en el terreno) high ground

B **1** (de edificio) top floor; **viven en un ~** they live in a top floor apartment *o* (BrE) flat **2** **los altos** *mpl* (CS) (en casa) upstairs; **vivo en los ~s del taller** I live above the workshop

C **1** (parada, interrupción): **hacer un ~** to stop **2** (Méx) (Auto): **pasarse el ~** (un semáforo) to run the red light (AmE), to jump the lights (BrE); (un stop) to go through the stop sign

D (Chi fam) (de cosas) pile, heap

altoparlante *m* (AmL) ▸**altavoz**

altorrelieve *m* high relief

altozano *m*

A (Geog) hillock

B (Col) (de una iglesia) parvis

altruismo *m* altruism

altruista¹ *adj* altruistic

altruista² *mf* altruist

altura *f*

A (de persona, edificio, techo) height; **el muro tiene un metro de ~** the wall is one meter high

B (indicando posición) height; **ponlos a la misma ~** put them at the same height; **tiene una cicatriz a la ~ de la sien** he has a scar on his temple; **a la ~ de los ojos** at eye level; ***a la ~ del betún*** *or* (RPl) ***felpudo*** *or* (Chi) ***del unto*** (fam): **nos dejaste a la ~ del betún** you made us look really bad; **quedó a la ~ del betún** he looked really stupid; ***estar/ponerse a la ~ de algo/algn***: **para ponernos a la ~ de la competencia** to put ourselves on a par with our competitors; **estar a la ~ de las circunstancias** to rise to the occasion; **no está a la ~ de su predecesor** he doesn't match up to his predecessor; **no estuvo a la ~ de lo que esperaban** he didn't live up to their expectations

C **1** (Aviac, Geog) (altitud) altitude; **perder ~** to lose height *o* (frml) altitude; **a 2.240 metros de ~** at an altitude of 2,240 meters; **sobrepasar los 4.000 metros de ~** to rise to (a height of) over 4,000 meters **2** **de altura** ‹*pesquero/flota*› deep-sea (*before n*); ‹*remolcador*› oceangoing (*before n*)

D (en sentido horizontal) **1** (en una calle): **¿a qué ~ de Serrano vive?** how far up Serrano do you live?; **cuando llegamos**

a

a la ~ de la plaza when we reached the square **2** (latitud): **en el Adriático, a la ~ de Florencia** on the Adriatic, on the same latitude *o* (colloq) as far up/down as Florence
E (en sentido temporal) **a estas/esas ~s**: **¡a estas ~s me vienes con eso!** you wait till now to bring this to me!; **a estas ~s del año** this late on in the year; **a esas ~s ya había perdido las esperanzas** by that stage he had already lost all hope; ***a estas ~s del partido*** (fam) by now, at this stage of the game (colloq)
F (Mús) pitch
G **alturas** *fpl* **1** (cimas) heights (*pl*) **2** (Relig): **las ~s** the highest

alturado -da *adj* (Per) calm

alubia *f* (haricot) bean

alucinación *f* hallucination

alucinado -da *adj* (fam): **los dejó a todos ~s** she left everybody stunned

alucinante *adj* **1** (Med) hallucinatory **2** (Esp, Méx fam) (increíble), amazing (colloq), mind-boggling (colloq)

alucinar [A1] *vi* «*enfermo/drogadicto*» to hallucinate

alucine *m* (Esp, Méx arg): **¡qué ~!** far-out! (colloq); **de ~** mind-boggling (colloq), amazing (colloq)

alucinógeno¹ -na *adj* hallucinogenic

alucinógeno² *m* hallucinogen

alud *m* (de nieve) avalanche; (de tierra) landslide, landslip

aludido -da *m,f*: **el ~ se volvió al oír su nombre** the person we were talking about turned around when he heard his name mentioned; **la aludida bajó la cabeza** the person in question lowered her head

aludir [I1] *vi* **1** (sin nombrar) **~ A algn/algo** to refer TO sb/sth, allude TO sb/sth; **se sintió aludido** he thought we were referring to him; **no se dio por aludido** he didn't take the hint; **no te des por aludido** don't take it personally **2** (mencionar) **~ A algn/algo** to refer TO sb/sth, mention sb/sth

alumbrado *m* lighting
(Compuestos)
- **alumbrado eléctrico** electric lighting
- **alumbrado público** street lighting

alumbramiento *m* (frml) birth

alumbrar [A1] *vt*
A (iluminar) to light, illuminate; **está muy mal alumbrado** it's very poorly lit; **un cuarto alumbrado con velas** a candlelit room; **un foco alumbra el jardín** a floodlight illuminates the garden
B (frml) (parir) to be delivered of (frml)
■ **alumbrar** *vi*
A «*sol*» to be bright; «*lámpara/bombilla*» to give off light
B (frml) (parir) to give birth

alumbre *m* alum

aluminio *m* aluminum (AmE), aluminium (BrE)

alumnado *m* (de colegio) students (*pl*) (AmE), pupils (*pl*) (BrE); (de universidad) students (*pl*)

alumno -na *m,f* (de colegio) pupil; (de universidad) student; **antiguos ~s** *or* **ex-alumnos de la universidad** ex-students *o* (AmE) alumni of the university
(Compuesto) **alumno interno, -na interna** *m,f* boarder

alunarse [A1] *v pron* (RPl fam) to sulk; **está alunado** he's sulking

alunizaje *m* moon landing

alunizar [A4] *vi* to land on the moon

alusión *f* allusion, reference; **hacer ~ a algo** to make an allusion to sth (frml); **hizo ~ a tu ausencia** he referred to your absence; **no quiero hacer alusiones personales** I don't want to point the finger at anyone

alusivo -va *adj* **~ A algo**: **unas palabras alusivas a ...** a few words regarding ...; **decorado con motivos ~s a la ocasión** decorated in keeping with the occasion

aluvial *adj* alluvial

aluvión *m*
A (Geol) alluvium
B (gran cantidad) flood; **un ~ de insultos** a barrage of insults, a torrent of abuse

alveolar *adj* alveolar

alvéolo, alveolo *m* **1** (Anat) alveolus **2** (de panal) cell

alverjilla *f* (AmL) sweet pea

alza *f‡*
A (subida) rise; **el ~ de los precios** the rise in prices; **jugar al ~** to speculate on a rising *o* bull market; **en ~**: **precios en ~** rising prices; **una escritora en ~** an up-and-coming writer; **su reputación está en ~** he has a growing reputation
B (en los zapatos) raised insole
C (Arm) rear sight

alzacristales *m* (*pl* ~) (Esp): **con ~ eléctrico** with electric windows

alzada *f* **1** (de caballo) height **2** (Col) (Arquit) elevation

alzado¹ -da *adj*
A (Andes, Ven fam) (levantisco): **la servidumbre anda medio alzada** the servants have been rather uppity lately (colloq); **un chiquillo ~** a cocky little brat (colloq)
B ‹*animal*› **1** [ESTAR] (CS fam) (en celo) in heat (AmE), on heat (BrE) **2** [SER] (Chi, Méx) (arisco, bravío) savage, vicious
C (Méx, Ven fam) (altivo) stuck-up (colloq)

alzado² *m*
A (Arquit) elevation
B **alzados** *mpl* (AmL): **los ~s en armas** the insurgents *o* rebels

alzamiento *m* uprising

alzaprima *f* **1** (palanca) lever, crowbar; (cuña) wedge **2** (Mús) bridge

alzar [A4] *vt*
A (levantar) to raise; **alzó al niño para que viera el desfile** she lifted the little boy up so he could see the parade; **todos ~on sus pancartas** they all held up their placards; **saludaron con el puño alzado** they gave the clenched fist salute; **alzó la mirada** she looked up; **el bebé quiere que lo alcen** (AmL) the baby wants to be picked up
B ‹*edificio/monumento*› to erect
C (Méx) (poner en orden) ‹*juguetes*› to pick up; ‹*cuarto/casa*› to clean (up)
■ **alzarse** *v pron*
A (sublevarse) to rise up; **~se en armas** to take up arms
B (period) (llevarse) **~se CON algo**: **se alzó con los fondos del club** he ran off with the club funds; **se alzó con el título** he carried off the title; **~se con la victoria** to triumph
C (liter) «*edificio/montaña*»: **el Aconcagua se alza majestuoso** Aconcagua rises majestically; **la torre se alza por encima de los tejados** the tower soars *o* towers high above the rooftops
D (CS fam) «*animal*» to come into *o* (BrE) on heat

Alzheimer /als'aimer/, (Esp) /alθ'eimer/ *m* Alzheimer's disease

a.m. (= **ante meridiem**) am

ama *f‡* **1** (de bebé) *tb* **~ de leche** *or* **de cría** wet nurse **2** (de niño mayor) nanny; *ver tb* **amo**
(Compuesto) **ama de casa/de llaves** housewife/housekeeper

amabilidad *f* **1** (cualidad) kindness **2** (gesto): **tuvo la ~ de invitarnos** she was kind enough to invite us; **¿tendría la ~ de cerrar la puerta?** would you be so kind as to close the door?; **tenga la ~ de esperar aquí** would you mind waiting here?

amable *adj* **1** ‹*persona/gesto*› kind; **es muy ~ de su parte** that's very kind of you; **de trato ~** kindly; **¿sería tan ~ de ...?** would you be so kind as to ...? **2** (AmS) ‹*rato/velada*› pleasant

amablemente *adv* **1** (con cordialidad): **me saludó muy ~** he greeted me in a very friendly way **2** (con generosidad) kindly; **muy ~ me cedió el asiento** he very kindly gave me his seat

amado¹ -da *adj* dear, beloved

amado² -da *m,f* love, sweetheart

amadrinar [A1] *vt* ‹*niño*› to be godmother to; ‹*boda*› to act as **madrina** at; ‹*barco*› to launch, christen

amaestrador -dora *m,f* animal trainer

amaestramiento *m* training (*of animals*)

amaestrar [A1] *vt* ‹*animales*› to train

amagar [A3] *vi* **1** (amenazar): **amagaba lluvia** it looked like rain **2** (Dep) to fake, dummy (BrE); **amagó hacia la izquierda** he faked to the left

■ **amagar** *vt* (esbozar): **amagó un saludo** he made as if he was going to wave

amago *m*: **tuvo un ~ de infarto** he had a mild heart attack; **un ~ de revuelta** a threat of revolt; **hacer un ~** (Dep) to make a feint; **~ de ataque** (Mil) diversion, diversionary attack

amainar [A1] *vi* ‹‹*lluvia*›› to ease up *o* off, abate; ‹‹*temporal/viento*›› to die down, abate; ‹‹*pasión/enfado*›› to abate

■ **amainar** *vt* ‹*velas*› to shorten

amalgama *f* amalgam

amalgamar [A1] *vt* (unir) to unite; (Quím) to amalgamate

amamantar [A1] *vt* to breastfeed

■ **amamantar** *vi* to breastfeed; **madres que amamantan** nursing mothers; **la cerda está amamantando** the sow is suckling her young

amancebado -da *adj* (ant): **están** *or* **viven ~s** they are living together

amancebarse [A1] *v pron* (ant) to start living together

amanecer[1] [E3] *v impers*: **¿a qué hora amanece?** what time does it get light?; **amanecía cuando partieron** dawn was breaking when they left

■ **amanecer** *vi* (+ *compl*) [1] ‹‹*persona*››: **amaneció con fiebre** he woke up with a temperature; **amanecieron bailando** they were still dancing at dawn [2] (aparecer por la mañana): **el día amaneció nublado** the day dawned cloudy; **todo amaneció cubierto de nieve** in the morning everything was covered in snow

■ **amanecerse** *v pron* (Chi, Méx) to stay up all night

amanecer[2] *m* [1] (salida del sol) dawn, daybreak; **al ~** at dawn *o* at daybreak [2] (liter) (comienzo) dawn

amanecido -da *adj* (Col, Ven fam): **el café se llenó de estudiantes ~s** the cafe filled up with students who had been up all night

amanerado -da *adj* (afectado) affected, mannered; (afeminado) (fam) mannered, camp (colloq)

amaneramiento *m* affectation

amanerarse [A1] *v pron* to become affected

amansar [A1] *vt* [1] ‹*caballo*› to break in; ‹*fiera*› to tame [2] (apaciguar) ‹*persona*› to calm ... down; ‹*ira*› to appease

■ **amansarse** *v pron* ‹‹*fiera*›› to become tame; ‹‹*caballo*›› to quiet (AmE) *o* (BrE) quieten down

amante[1] *adj*: **su ~ esposo** her loving husband; **es muy ~ de la buena mesa** he is very fond of good food

amante[2] *mf* lover

amanuense *mf* scribe, amanuensis (frml)

amañador -dora *adj* (Col) ‹*clima/conversación*› pleasant, agreeable; ‹*casa*› cozy*, homely

amañar [A1] *vt* (fam) ‹*elecciones*› to rig; ‹*partido/pelea*› to fix; ‹*carnet/documento*› to tamper with; ‹*informe*› to alter, doctor (pej); ‹*excusa/historia*› to dream *o* cook up, concoct

■ **amañarse** *v pron*

A *tb* **amañárselas** (ingeniarse) to manage; **se (las) amañó para llegar a fin de mes** she somehow managed to get by until the end of the month

B (Col, Ven) (acostumbrarse) to settle in

amaño *m* cunning *o* crafty trick

amapola *f* poppy

amar [A1] *vt* to love

■ **amarse** *v pron* (*recípr*) [1] (quererse) to love each other; **amaos los unos a los otros** love one another [2] (hacer el amor) to make love

amaraje *m* (Aviac) landing (*on water*); (Espac) splashdown

amaranto *m* amaranth

amarar [A1] *vi* (Aviac) to land (*on water*); (Espac) to splash down

amarga *f* (Col) beer

amargado[1] **-da** *adj* bitter, embittered

amargado[2] **-da** *m,f* bitter *o* embittered person

amargar [A3] *vt* ‹*ocasión*› to spoil; ‹*persona*› to make ... bitter; **eso me amargó la tarde** that soured *o* spoiled my evening

■ **amargarse** *v pron* to become bitter; **no te amargues la existencia** (fam) don't get all uptight about it; **te estás amargando pensando en eso** you're just upsetting yourself thinking about it

amargo[1] **-ga** *adj*

A [1] ‹*fruta/sabor*› bitter [2] (sin azúcar) unsweetened, without sugar

B ‹*experiencia/recuerdo*› bitter, painful; **me dejó un sabor ~** it left me with a bitter *o* nasty taste in my mouth

amargo[2] *m* (amargor) bitterness; (mate) maté without sugar; (licor) bitters

amargor *m* bitterness

amargura *f* bitterness; **con ~** bitterly

amariconado -da *adj* (fam) camp (colloq)

amarillento -ta *adj* yellowish

amarillismo *m* (Period) (pey) sensationalism, sensationalistic journalism

amarillista *adj* (Period) (pey): **prensa ~** sensationalist *o* yellow press

amarillo[1] **-lla** *adj*

A ‹*color/blusa*› yellow; **el semáforo estaba (en) ~** the light was yellow (AmE), the lights were (on) amber (BrE); **~ claro/fuerte** pale/bright yellow

B [1] ‹*piel*› (de raza oriental) yellow [2] ‹*piel/cara*› (por enfermedad) yellow, jaundiced

amarillo[2] *m* yellow; **el ~ combina con el azul** yellow goes with blue; **de un ~ intenso** (a) deep yellow

(Compuesto) **amarillo limón** [1] *m* lemon yellow [2] *adj inv* lemon-yellow

amarizaje *m* ▸ **amaraje**

amarizar [A4] *vi* ▸ **amarar**

amarra *f* mooring rope; **~s** moorings (*pl*); **echar (las) ~s** to moor; ***soltar (las) ~s*** (Náut) to cast off; (independizarse) to fly the nest; ***tener (buenas) ~s*** to have friends in high places

amarradero *m* [1] (poste) bollard; (argolla) mooring ring [2] (lugar) berth, slip (AmE)

amarrado -da *adj* (Col, Méx, Ven fam) stingy (colloq), tightfisted (colloq)

amarraje *m* wharfage

amarrar [A1] *vt* [1] ‹*embarcación*› to moor; ‹*animal/persona*› to tie up; **le ~on las manos** they tied his hands together; **~ algo/a algn A algo** to tie sth/sb TO sth [2] (AmL exc RPl) ‹*zapatos*› to tie; ‹*paquete*› to tie ... up

■ **amarrarse** *v pron* (AmL exc RPl) ‹*zapatos/cordones*› to tie up, do up; ‹*pelo*› to tie up; ***amarrársela*** (Col fam) to get tight (colloq)

amarre *m* (acción) mooring; (amarradero) berth, slip (AmE)

amarretas[1] *adj inv* (AmS fam) ▸ **amarrete**[1]

amarretas[2] *mf* (*pl* ~) (AmS fam) ▸ **amarrete**[2]

amarrete[1] **-ta** *adj* (AmS fam) stingy (colloq), tightfisted (colloq)

amarrete[2] **-ta** *m,f* (AmS fam) scrooge (colloq), skinflint (colloq)

amartelado -da *adj* (fam): **estaban muy ~s** they were cuddling *o* (colloq) canoodling

amartelarse [A1] *v pron* (fam) to cuddle, canoodle (colloq)

amasar [A1] *vt*

A ‹*pan*› to knead; ‹*yeso/argamasa*› to mix

B ‹*fortuna/riquezas*› to amass

amasijar [A1] *vt* (RPl arg) to beat ... to a pulp (colloq)

amasijo *m* jumble

amateur /ama'ter/ *adj/mf* (*pl* **-teurs**) amateur

amateurismo *m* amateurism

amatista *f* amethyst

amatorio -ria *adj* (liter *o* hum) ‹*poesía/carta*› love (*before n*); ‹*técnicas*› love-making (*before n*)

amazacotado -da *adj* ‹*azúcar*› lumpy; ‹*arroz*› sticky, stodgy

amazona *f* (Mit) Amazon; (Equ) horsewoman

Amazonas *m*: **el ~** the Amazon

amazónico -ca *adj* Amazonian, Amazon (*before n*)

ambages: **sin ~** (*loc adv*) ‹*hablar/decir*› without beating about the bush; **fue aceptado sin ~** it was accepted without hesitation

ámbar *m* [1] (piedra) amber [2] **(de) color ~** amber

ambición *f* ambition

ambicionar [A1] *vt* to aspire to; **sólo ambiciona llegar a la fama** her one ambition is to be famous

ambicioso -sa *adj*
A ‹*persona*› 1 (codicioso) ambitious, overambitious 2 (con empuje) enterprising, ambitious
B ‹*proyecto/plan*› ambitious

ambidextro[1] -tra *adj* ambidextrous

ambidextro[2] -tra *m,f* ambidextrous person

ambientación *f* 1 (de obra, película) atmosphere; **la ~ está muy lograda** they have captured the atmosphere very well; **la ~ musical corre a cargo de ...** incidental music is by ... 2 (de persona) adjustment

ambientador *m* air freshener

ambiental *adj* environmental

ambientalista *mf* environmentalist

ambientar [A1] *vt* 1 ‹*obra/película*› to set 2 ‹*fiesta/local*›: **para ~ el lugar** to give the place some atmosphere
■ **ambientarse** *v pron* to adjust, adapt

ambiente *m*
A 1 (entorno físico, social) environment; **la contaminación del ~** environmental pollution; **el ~ de diálogo** the atmosphere of dialogue; **se encuentra realmente en su ~** he's really in his element; **no me vendría nada mal cambiar de ~** I wouldn't mind a change of scene; **un ~ de camaradería/de fiesta** a friendly/festive atmosphere; **había una cierta tensión en el ~** there was a feeling of tension in the air; ***hacerle buen ~ a algn*** (Col) to put sb at their ease; ***hacerle mal ~ a algn*** (AmS) to make sb feel uncomfortable 2 (creado por la decoración, arquitectura) atmosphere; **un ~ acogedor** a welcoming *o* friendly atmosphere 3 (animación) life; **no había nada de ~ en la fiesta** the party was really dead, the party had no life
B (CS) (habitación) room

ambigüedad *f* ambiguity

ambiguo -gua *adj* ‹*palabras/respuesta*› ambiguous

ámbito *m* 1 (campo, círculo) sphere, field; **en el ~ de la política/la familia** within the sphere of politics/the family; **en el ~ literario** in literary circles 2 (alcance) scope, range; **el ~ (de aplicación) de la ley** the scope of the law; **fuera del ~ de su competencia** beyond the range of his competence; **una empresa de ~ nacional** a company with outlets/offices nationwide

ambivalencia *f* ambivalence

ambivalente *adj* ambivalent

ambo *m* (CS) (two-piece) suit

ambos[1] -bas *adj pl* both; **a ~ lados de la carretera** on both sides of the road

ambos[2] -bas *pron pl* both; **~ aceptaron la propuesta** they both accepted the proposal; **~ me gustan** I like both of them

ambrosía *f* (Mit, Bot, Zool) ambrosia

ambulancia *f* ambulance

ambulanciero -ra (*m*) ambulance man; (*f*) ambulance woman; **los ~s** the ambulance crew

ambulante *adj* traveling* (*before n*); **un grupo de teatro ~** a traveling *o* itinerant theater group; **biblioteca ~** bookmobile (AmE), mobile library (BrE); **es una enciclopedia ~** (hum) she's a walking encyclopedia (hum)

ambulatorio[1] -ria *adj* outpatient (*before n*)

ambulatorio[2] *m* (Esp) outpatients' department

ameba *f* amoeba

amedrentar [A1] *vt* to terrify
■ **amedrentarse** *v pron* to be *o* feel terrified; **no se amedrenta ante nada** nothing frightens her

amén *m* amen; **~ de ...** as well as ...; ***decir ~ a todo*** to agree to everything; ***en un decir ~*** in a flash *o* trice

amenaza *f* threat; **no me vengas con ~s** don't threaten me; **~ DE algo: ~ de bomba/muerte** bomb/death threat; **respondieron con ~ de huelga** they responded by threatening to strike

amenazador -dora *adj*, **amenazante** *adj* threatening, menacing

amenazar [A4] *vt* 1 «*persona*» to threaten; **lo ~on de muerte** they threatened to kill him; **nos amenazó con llamar a la policía** he threatened to call the police 2 (dar indicios de): **el edificio amenaza derrumbarse** the building is in danger of collapsing; **esas nubes amenazan lluvia** those clouds look threatening
■ **amenazar** *vi* 1 «*persona*» **~ CON algo** to threaten sth; **amenazan con una nueva huelga** they are threatening a further strike; **~ CON + INF** to threaten to + INF 2 (dar indicios de) **~ CON + INF** to threaten to + INF; **el incendio amenazaba con extenderse** the fire threatened to spread
■ **amenazar** *v impers* (Meteo): **amenaza tormenta** there's a storm brewing; **amenaza lluvia** it's threatening to rain

amenidad *f*: **sus clases carecen de ~** his classes lack sparkle *o* interest

amenizar [A4] *vt* ‹*conversación/discurso*› to make ... more enjoyable; **la fiesta fue amenizada por un payaso** a clown provided the entertainment for the party

ameno -na *adj* pleasant, enjoyable; **pasamos una tarde muy amena** we spent a very pleasant *o* nice afternoon

América *f* (continente) America; **flora que sólo se da en ~** flora found only in America *o* in the Americas

(Compuestos)
- **América Central/del Norte/del Sur** Central/North/South America
- **América Latina** Latin America

americana *f* jacket; **~ cruzada** double-breasted jacket

americanismo *m* Americanism

americanizar [A4] *vt* to Americanize
■ **americanizarse** *v pron* to become Americanized

americano -na *adj/m,f* American

amerindio -dia *adj/m,f* American Indian, Amerindian

ameritado -da *adj* (AmL) meritorious (frml)

ameritar [A1] *vt* (AmL) to deserve

amerizaje *m* ▸**amaraje**

amerizar [A4] *vi* ▸**amarar**

ametralladora *f* machine gun

ametrallamiento *m* machine-gunning

ametrallar [A1] *vt* to machine-gun; **me ametralló a preguntas** he bombarded me with questions

amianto *m* asbestos

amiba *f* amoeba

amigable *adj* ‹*persona*› friendly; ‹*trato*› friendly, amicable; **un tono poco ~** a rather unfriendly manner

amigablemente *adv* amicably

amigarse [A3] *v pron* (fam) (reconciliarse) to make up

amígdalas *fpl* tonsils (*pl*)

amigdalitis *f* tonsillitis

amigo[1] -ga *adj*: **son/se hicieron muy ~s** they are/they became good friends; **hacerse ~ de algn** to become friends with sb; **es muy ~ mío** he's a close friend of mine; **un país ~** a friendly country; **un médico ~ me lo recetó** a doctor friend (of mine) prescribed it for me; **ser ~ DE algo: es muy ~ de contradecir** he's a great one for contradicting people (colloq); **no es amiga de fiestas** she's not keen on parties; **no soy muy ~ de la comida picante** I'm not terribly fond of spicy food

amigo[2] -ga *m,f* friend; **un ~ mío** a friend of mine; **somos íntimos ~s** we're very close friends; **su ~ del alma** her best friend, her bosom friend; **no son más que ~s** they're just good friends; **¡un momento, ~!** now, just a minute, pal *o* buddy (AmE) *o* (BrE) mate! (colloq); **los ~s de lo ajeno** (hum) thieves

amigote *m* (fam) crony (colloq & pej), buddy (AmE colloq), mate (BrE colloq)

amiguismo *m*: **todo funciona a base de ~ y enchufes** it all works through contacts and string-pulling; **en esta empresa hay mucho ~** there's a lot of 'jobs for the boys' in this company

amilanar [A1] *vt* to daunt
■ **amilanarse** *v pron* to be daunted; **no se ~on ante el peligro** they were undaunted by the danger

aminoácido *m* amino acid

aminorar [A1] *vt* to reduce

amistad *f* 1 (entre personas, países) friendship; **entabló** *or* **trabó** *or* **hizo ~ con ella** he struck up a friendship with her; **nos une una gran ~** there's a great bond of friendship between us; **rompimos la(s) ~(es)** we're not friends any more 2 **amistades** *fpl* (amigos) friends (*pl*)

amistarse [A1] *v pron* (Col, Ven fam) (reconciliarse) to make up

amistosamente *adv* amicably

amistoso -sa *adj* ‹*consejo/palmadita/charla*› friendly; ‹*partido*› friendly (*before n*)

amnesia *f* amnesia

amnésico -ca *adj/m,f* amnesiac

amnistía *f* amnesty

amnistiado[1] -da *adj*: **los guerrilleros ~s** the guerrillas pardoned under the amnesty

amnistiado[2] -da *m,f*: *person pardoned under an amnesty*

amnistiar [A17] *vt* ‹*persona*› to grant an amnesty to; ‹*delito*› to amnesty

amo, ama *m,f* (de animal, criado) (*m*) master; (*f*) mistress; **aquí el ~ soy yo** I give the orders around here; **son los ~s del pueblo** they own the whole village; ***hacerse el ~ del cotarro*** (Esp fam) to become leader of the pack; *ver tb* **ama**

amoblado *m* (CS) furniture

amoblar [A10] *vt* (CS) to furnish

amodorrar [A1] *vt* to make … feel drowsy *o* sleepy

■ **amodorrarse** *v pron* to feel sleepy *o* drowsy

amohinarse [A19] *v pron* to get in a sulk

amoldable *adj* adaptable

amoldar [A1] *vt* to adjust

■ **amoldarse** *v pron* to adapt; **~se a un trabajo/una situación** to adjust to a job/a situation; **estos zapatos todavía no se me han amoldado al pie** I haven't broken these shoes in yet

amonedado -da *adj* (AmC) rich, wealthy

amonedar [A1] *vt* to stamp

amonestación *f* (reprimenda) warning; (en fútbol) caution, booking

amonestar [A1] *vt*

A (reprender) to reprimand, admonish (frml); (en fútbol) to caution, book

B (Der, Relig) ‹*novios*› to publish the banns of

amoníaco[1] -ca *adj* ammoniac (*before n*), ammoniacal

amoníaco[2] *m* ammonia

amontillado *m* amontillado

amontonamiento *m* (fam) (de objetos) stack, pile

amontonar [A1] *vt* **1** (apilar) to pile up; **amontónalos ahí** pile them up *o* put them in a pile over there **2** (juntar) to accumulate

■ **amontonarse** *v pron* «*personas*» to gather *o* crowd together; «*objetos/trabajo*» to pile up

amor *m*

A **1** (sentimiento) love; **una historia de ~** a love story; **~ no correspondido** unrequited love; **~ a primera vista** love at first sight; **¿qué tal andas de ~es?** (fam) how's your love life? (colloq); **siente un gran ~ por ti** he loves you very much; **~ al prójimo/a la patria** love for one's neighbor/one's country; **un gran ~ a la vida/a los animales** a great love of life/animals; ***de mil ~es*** with (the greatest of) pleasure; ***por ~ al arte*** (fam) just for the fun of it; ***por (el) ~ de Dios*** (mendigando) for the love of God; (expresando irritación) for God's sake!; ***~ con ~ se paga*** one good turn deserves another **2** (el acto sexual): **el ~** lovemaking; **hacer el ~ a/con algn** to make love to/with sb **3** (persona, cosa amada) love; **el gran ~ de su vida** the great love of her life; **tu ~cito está al teléfono** (fam & hum) your beloved is on the telephone (hum); **~ mío** *or* **mi ~** my darling, my love **4** (esmero, dedicación): **hacer algo con ~** to do sth lovingly; **hay mucho ~ puesto en esto** a lot of love and care has gone into this

Compuestos

- **amor cortés/libre** courtly/free love
- **amor materno** *or* **maternal** maternal love
- **amor propio** pride, self-esteem

B (fam) (persona encantadora) darling (colloq), dear (colloq)

amoral *adj* amoral

amoralidad *f* amorality

amoratado -da *adj* (de frío) blue; (por un golpe) ‹*piernas/brazos*› bruised; **ojo ~** black eye

amordazar [A4] *vt* **1** (con mordaza) ‹*persona*› to gag; ‹*perro*› to muzzle **2** «*miedo/amenazas*» to silence

amorfo -fa *adj* **1** ‹*cuerpo/masa*› amorphous, shapeless **2** ‹*persona*› characterless, insipid

amorío *m* love affair; **fue un ~ sin importancia** it was just a brief affair *o* (colloq) fling

amoroso -sa *adj* **1** (AmL) ‹*persona/casa*› lovely **2** ‹*vida*› love (*before n*); **sus relaciones amorosas** his relationships

amortajar [A1] *vt* to shroud

amortiguación *f* **1** (de golpes) absorption, cushioning; **tiene mala ~** (Auto) the shock absorbers aren't very good **2** (de sonido) muffling; (de luz) dimming

amortiguador[1] -dora *adj* shock-absorbing (*before n*)

amortiguador[2] *m* shock absorber

amortiguar [A16] *vt* **1** ‹*golpe*› to cushion, absorb; ‹*sonido*› to muffle; ‹*luz*› to dim; ‹*color*› to tone down, soften **2** (liter) ‹*dolor*› to deaden; ‹*hambre*› to take the edge off

amortizable *adj* redeemable; **~s en tres años** redeemable in three years

amortización *f* (de inversión) recovery; (de préstamo) repayment; (de bonos, hipoteca) redemption

amortizar [A4] *vt* (Com, Fin) **1** ‹*compra*› to recoup the cost of **2** (recuperar) ‹*inversión*› to recoup, recover **3** (pagar) ‹*deuda*› to repay, amortize (frml); ‹*valores/hipoteca*› to redeem

amoscarse [A2] *v pron* (Esp fam) to get into a huff (colloq)

amotinado[1] -da *adj* ‹*soldado/ejército*› rebel (*before n*), insurgent (*before n*); ‹*pueblo/ciudadanos*› rebellious, insurgent (*before n*)

amotinado[2] -da *m,f* insurgent

amotinamiento *m* (de soldados, marineros) mutiny; (de civiles) uprising, insurrection

amotinar [A1] *vt* ‹*tropa*› to incite … to mutiny *o* rebellion; ‹*población/pueblo*› to incite … to rebellion

■ **amotinarse** *v pron* «*soldados/oficiales*» to mutiny, rebel; «*población civil*» to rise up

amparar [A1] *vt* **1** (proteger) to protect; **me ampara la constitución** I am protected by the constitution; **¡que Dios nos ampare!** may the Lord help us! **2** (ofrecer refugio) to shelter, give shelter to

■ **ampararse** *v pron* **1** **~se EN algo** ‹*en la ley*› to seek protection IN sth; **se amparó en su inmunidad diplomática** he used his diplomatic immunity to protect himself; **se negó a alistarse amparándose en la objeción de conciencia** he refused to enlist on the grounds of conscientious objection **2** (resguardarse) **~se DE** *or* **CONTRA algo** to shelter FROM sth

amparo *m* **1** (protección) protection; **están bajo mi ~** they're under my protection; **al ~ de la nueva ley** under the (protection of the) new law; **al ~ de la noche** under cover of (the) night *o* of darkness **2** (refugio) refuge; **su fe fue su ~** his faith was his refuge; **dar ~ A algn** to give sb refuge

ampe *interj* (Bol) how terrible!, how awful!

amperímetro *m* ammeter

amperio *m* amp, ampere (frml)

ampliación *f* **1** (de local, carretera) extension; (de negocio) expansion **2** (Com, Fin): **una ~ de capital/de plantilla** an increase in capital/in the number of staff **3** (de conocimientos, vocabulario) widening **4** (de plazo, período) extension **5** (Fot) enlargement

ampliadora *f* enlarger

ampliamente *adv* **1** (con holgura) easily **2** (extensamente) at (great) length

ampliar [A17] *vt* **1** ‹*local/carretera*› to extend; ‹*negocio*› to expand **2** ‹*capital/plantilla*› to increase **3** ‹*conocimientos/vocabulario*› to increase; ‹*explicación*› to expand (on); ‹*campo de acción*› to widen, broaden; **versión ampliada y corregida** expanded and corrected version; **para ~ sus estudios** to further her studies **4** ‹*plazo/período*› to extend **5** ‹*fotografía*› to enlarge, blow up

amplificación *f* amplification

amplificador *m* amplifier

amplificar [A2] *vt* to amplify

amplio -plia *adj* **1** ‹*calle/valle/margen*› wide; ‹*casa*› spacious; ‹*vestido/abrigo*› loose-fitting; **con una amplia sonrisa** with a broad smile **2** ‹*criterio/sentido*› broad; **por amplia mayoría** by a large majority; **una amplia gama**

de colores a wide range of colors; **el tema tuvo una amplia difusión** the issue received wide media coverage [3] ‹*garantías/programa*› comprehensive

amplitud *f* [1] (de calle, margen) width; (de casa) spaciousness; (de vestido) looseness [2] (de miras, criterios) range; (de facultades, garantías) extent; **la ~ de sus conocimientos** the breadth *o* depth of his knowledge [3] (Fís) amplitude

ampolla *f*

A (por quemadura, rozamiento) blister; **me salió una ~ en el pie** I have a blister on my foot

B (con medicamento) ampoule (frml), vial (AmE), phial (BrE)

ampollar [A1] *vt* to cause blisters on

■ **ampollarse** *v pron* to blister; **se me ~on los pies** I got blisters on my feet, my feet blistered

ampolleta *f* [1] (con medicamento) ▸**ampolla B** [2] (Elec) (Chi) light bulb; ***se me/le prendió la ~*** (Chi) I/he had a brainwave *o* a bright idea (colloq)

ampulosidad *f* pomposity, pompousness

ampuloso -sa *adj* pompous, bombastic

amputación *f* amputation

amputar [A1] *vt* ‹*brazo/pierna*› to amputate; ‹*texto*› to cut (out)

amueblar [A1] *vt* to furnish; **casa amueblada/sin ~** furnished/unfurnished house

amuleto *m* charm, amulet

amurallar [A1] *vt* to wall, build walls around

amurrarse [A1] *v pron* (Chi fam) ▸**alunarse**

anabólico, anabolizante *m* anabolic steroid

anacarado -da *adj* pearly, mother-of-pearl (*before n*)

anacardo *m* cashew (nut)

anaconda *f* anaconda

anacoreta *mf* anchorite

anacrónico -ca *adj* anachronistic

anacronismo *m* anachronism

ánade *mf* duck

(Compuesto) **ánade real** mallard

anafe, anafre *m* (Chi, Méx) portable stove

anagrama *m* anagram

anal *adj* anal

anales *mpl* annals (*pl*)

analfabetismo *m* illiteracy

analfabeto[1] -ta *adj* illiterate

analfabeto[2] -ta *m,f* [1] (que no sabe leer) illiterate (person) [2] (fam & pey) (ignorante) ignoramus (colloq & pej)

analgésico[1] -ca *adj* analgesic, painkilling (*before n*)

analgésico[2] *m* analgesic, painkiller

análisis *m* (*pl* ~) analysis; **hacerse un ~ de sangre** to have a blood test

analista *mf* analyst

analítico -ca *adj* analytic; **mente analítica** analytic *o* analytical mind

analizar [A4] *vt*

A (examinar) to analyze*, examine

B (Med, Quím) to analyze*

C (Ling) to parse

■ **analizarse** *v pron* to undergo *o* have analysis

analogía *f* analogy; **estableció una ~ entre ...** she drew an analogy between ...; **razonar por ~** to argue by *o* from analogy

analógico -ca *adj* analogical

análogo -ga *adj* analogous, similar

ananá *m* (*pl* **-nás**) (RPl) pineapple

anaquel *m* shelf

anaranjado -da *adj* orangish (AmE), orangey (BrE)

anarco *m* (fam) anarchist

anarquía *f* anarchy

anárquico -ca *adj* anarchic

anarquismo *m* anarchism

anarquista[1] *adj* anarchist (*before n*)

anarquista[2] *mf* anarchist

anarquizar [A4] *vt* to cause chaos *o* anarchy in

anatema *m* (Relig) anathema

anatematizar [A4], **anatemizar** [A4] *vt* (Relig) to anathematize; (condenar) to condemn

■ **anatematizar** *vi* to rail; **~ CONTRA algo** to rail AGAINST sth

anatomía *f* anatomy

anatómico -ca *adj* [1] (Anat) anatomical [2] ‹*asiento/respaldo*› anatomically designed

anca *f‡* [1] (de animal) haunch; **llevar a algn en ~s** (AmL) to take sb on the crupper [2] **ancas** *fpl* (AmL fam) (de persona) behind (colloq), backside (colloq)

(Compuesto) **ancas de rana** *fpl* frogs' legs (*pl*)

ancestral *adj* ‹*costumbre*› ancient; ‹*temor*› primitive, ancient

ancestro *m* ancestor

ancho[1] -cha *adj*

A [1] ‹*camino/río/mueble*› wide; **a todo lo ~ de la carretera** right across the road; **a lo ~** breadthways *o* (BrE) widthways [2] ‹*manos/cara/espalda*› broad; **es ~ de espaldas** he's broad-shouldered [3] ‹*ropa*› loose-fitting, loose; **me queda ~ de cintura** it's too big around the waist for me

B (fam) (ufano, orgulloso) proud; **iba todo ~ del brazo de su hija** he was bursting with pride as he walked arm-in-arm with his daughter

C (cómodo, tranquilo): **allí estaremos más ~s** (Esp) we'll have more room there; **¡qué ~ me quedé después de decírselo!** (Esp) I felt really good after I'd told him; ***estar/sentirse/ponerse a sus anchas*** to be/feel/make oneself at home; ***quedarse tan ~*** (Esp fam) *ver* **pimpante**

ancho[2] *m* width; **¿cuánto tiene** *or* **mide de ~?** how wide is it?; **tiene** *or* **mide 6 metros de ~** it's 6 meters wide

(Compuesto) **ancho de vía** gauge

anchoa *f* anchovy

anchura *f* [1] (de camino, río, mueble) width [2] (de pared) thickness

anchuroso -sa *adj* (liter) ‹*llanura/mar*› wide, vast; ‹*salón*› spacious

ancianato *m* (Col, Ven) old people's home

ancianidad *f* old age

anciano[1] -na *adj* elderly; **la mujer más anciana del mundo** the oldest woman in the world

anciano[2] -na (*m*) elderly man; (*f*) elderly woman

ancla *f‡* anchor; **echar el ~** *or* **las ~s** to drop anchor; **levar ~s** to weigh anchor

anclaje *m* (acción) anchorage; (impuesto) anchorage dues (*pl*)

anclar [A1] *vt* to anchor

■ **anclar** *vi* to anchor, drop anchor

áncora *f‡*

A (Náut) anchor

B (de reloj) escapement

andadas *fpl*: ***volver a las ~*** to go back to one's old ways

andadera *f* (Méx, Ven) [1] (con ruedas) baby walker [2] **andaderas** *fpl* (arnés) baby harness, reins (*pl*)

andado -da *adj*: **llevan mucho camino ~** they've covered a lot of ground; ***desandar lo ~*** to go back to square one

andador *m*

A [1] (con ruedas) baby walker [2] **andadores** *mpl* (arnés) baby harness, reins (*pl*)

B (para ancianos) Zimmer® frame

andadora *f* baby walker

andadura *f* [1] (viaje, recorrido) journey [2] (curso, trayectoria): **en su ~ profesional** in her professional career; **esta organización comenzó su ~ en el año 1970** this organization began its activity in 1970

Andalucía *f* Andalusia

andaluz -luza *adj/m,f* Andalusian

andamiaje *m* (Const) scaffolding

andamio *m*: *tb* **~s** scaffolding

andanada *f*

A (Arm, Mil) volley; (de insultos, palabrotas) stream, volley; **le soltó una ~ de insultos** she unleashed a stream of abuse at him

B (gradería) upper tier, bleachers (*pl*) (AmE)

andante *m* andante

andanzas *fpl* adventures (*pl*)

andar¹ [A24] *vi*

A 1 (esp Esp) (caminar) to walk; **la niña ya anda** the little girl's already walking; **¿has venido andando?** did you come on foot?, did you walk?; ***a poco ~*** (Chi) before long 2 (Col, CS, Ven) (ir) to go; **anda a comprar el periódico** go and buy the newspaper; ***andá a pasear*** (RPl fam) get lost! (colloq) 3 (AmL): **~ a caballo/en bicicleta** to ride (a horse/a bicycle)

B (marchar, funcionar) to work; **el coche anda de maravilla** the car's running *o* (BrE) going like a dream

C (+ *compl*) 1 (estar) to be; **¿cómo andas?** how are you?, how's it going? (colloq); **no anda bien de salud** he isn't well; **siempre anda con prisas** he's always in a hurry; **¿quién anda ahí?** who's there?; **anda en América** he's in America; **¿cómo andamos de tiempo?** how are we doing for time?; **~ + GER** to be -ING; **anda buscando pelea** he's out for *o* he's looking for a fight; **lo andan buscando** they are looking for him *o* (colloq) are after him; ***quien mal anda, mal acaba*** if you live like that, you're bound to come to a bad end 2 **~ CON algn** (juntarse) to mix WITH sb; (salir con) to go out WITH sb; ***dime con quién andas y te diré quién eres*** a man is known by the company he keeps

D (rondar) **~ POR algo**: **~á por los 60 (años)** he must be around *o* about 60

E **~ DETRÁS DE** *or* **TRAS algn/algo** (buscar, perseguir) to be AFTER sb/sth; **anda detrás de tu dinero** he's after your money; **andan tras la fama** they are looking for fame

F 1 **~ CON algo** (esp AmL fam) ‹*con revólver/dinero*› to carry sth; ‹*con traje/sombrero*› to wear sth; **no me gusta que andes con cuchillos** I don't like you playing with *o* messing around with knives 2 (revolver) **~ EN algo** to rummage *o* poke around IN sth

G (en exclamaciones) 1 (expresando sorpresa, incredulidad): **¡anda! ¡qué casualidad!** good heavens! what a coincidence!; **¡anda! ¡mira quién está aquí!** well, well! look who's here!; **¡anda ya! ¡eso es imposible!** go on! that's impossible! (colloq) 2 (expresando irritación, rechazo): **¡anda! ¡déjame en paz!** oh, leave me alone!; **¡anda! ¡se me ha vuelto a olvidar!** damn! I've forgotten it again! (colloq) 3 (instando a hacer algo): **préstamelo, anda** go on, lend it to me!; **ándale, no seas sacón** (Méx fam) go on, don't be chicken (colloq); **¡andando, que se hace tarde!** let's get a move on, it's getting late!

■ **andar** *vt*

A (caminar) to walk; **he andado muchos caminos** (liter) I have trodden many paths (liter)

B (AmC) (llevar): **no ando dinero** I don't have any money on me; **siempre ando shorts** I always go around in *o* wear shorts

■ **andarse** *v pron*

A **~se CON algo**: **ése no se anda con bromas** he's not one to joke; **ándate con cuidado** take care, be careful

B (*en imperativo*) (AmL) (irse): **ándate de aquí** get out of here; **ándate luego** get going *o* get a move on (colloq)

andar² *m*, **andares** *mpl* gait, walk; **de ~ pausado** with an unhurried gait; **tiene ~es de princesa** she has the bearing of a princess (frml)

andariego -ga *adj* fond of walking

andarivel *m*

A (cable) ferry cable; (pasamanos) handrail; (mecanismo) cableway

(Compuesto) **andarivel de salvamento** breeches buoy

B (AmS) (en una piscina — carril) lane; (— soga) lane divider

andas *fpl* portable platform (*used in religious processions*); ***llevar a algn en ~*** (CS) to carry sb on one's shoulders

ándele, ándale *interj*: *ver* **andar¹ G3**

andén *m*

A (en estación) platform

B (AmC, Col) (acera) sidewalk (AmE), pavement (BrE)

Andes *mpl*: **los ~** the Andes

andinismo *m* (AmL) mountaineering, mountain climbing, climbing

andinista *mf* (AmL) mountaineer, mountain climber, climber

andino -na *adj* Andean

andrajo *m* rag; **vestido de** *or* **con ~s** dressed in rags

andrajoso -sa *adj* ragged

andrógeno *m* androgen

androide *m* android

andropausia *f* male menopause

andurriales *mpl* (Esp fam) godforsaken place (colloq)

anduve, anduviste, etc *see* **andar**

anécdota *f* anecdote

anecdotario *m* collection of anecdotes

anecdótico -ca *adj* 1 ‹*relato*› anecdotal; **un personaje ~** a colorful character 2 ‹*interés/valor*› incidental

anegadizo -za *adj* prone to flooding

anegar [A3] *vt* 1 ‹*campo/local*› to flood; ‹*carburador*› to flood 2 (abrumar) to overwhelm

■ **anegarse** *v pron* «*campo/terreno*» to be flooded; **con los ojos anegados en lágrimas** (liter) with her/his eyes brimming with tears (liter)

anejo¹ -ja *adj* 1 (inherente): **lleva ~s ciertos gastos/riesgos** it entails certain expenses/risks; **el puesto lleva anejas grandes responsabilidades** the post carries with it a great deal of responsibility 2 ▸**anexo¹**

anejo² *m* ▸**anexo²**

anemia *f* anemia*

anémico¹ -ca *adj* anemic*

anémico² -ca *m,f* anemic person*; **los ~s** people who suffer from anemia

anemómetro *m* anemometer, wind gauge

anémona *f* anemone

(Compuesto) **anémona de mar** sea anemone

anestesia *f* (proceso) anesthesia*; (droga) anesthetic*; **bajo los efectos de la ~** under (the) anesthetic; **lo operaron con ~** he was operated on under (an) anesthetic; **sin ~** without an anesthetic

(Compuestos)
- **anestesia general/local** (proceso) general/local anesthesia*; (droga) general/local anesthetic*
- **anestesia peridural** epidural

anestesiar [A1] *vt* ‹*encía/dedo*› to anesthetize*; **me ~on** they gave me an anesthetic

anestésico¹ -ca *adj* anesthetic*

anestésico² *m* anesthetic*

anestesista *mf* anesthetist* (*sometimes not a fully-qualified doctor*)

anexar [A1] *vt*

A (esp AmL) ‹*territorios*› to annex

B ‹*cláusula*› to add, append (frml)

anexión *f* annexation

anexionar *vt* [A1], **anexionarse** [A1] *v pron* to annex

anexo¹ -xa *adj* 1 ‹*edificio/local*› joined, annexed 2 ‹*cláusula*› added, appended (frml); ‹*documento*› (en informe) attached; (en carta) enclosed

anexo² *m* 1 (edificio) annex* 2 (documento — en informe) appendix; (— en carta) enclosure; Ⓢ **anexos** enc., enclosures 3 (Chi) (del teléfono) extension

anfeta *f* (fam) amphetamine; **~s** speed (colloq)

anfetamina *f* amphetamine

anfibio¹ -bia *adj* amphibious; **avión ~** seaplane

anfibio² *m* amphibian

anfiteatro *m* (Arquit) amphitheater*; (Geol) natural amphitheater*; (en la universidad) lecture hall

anfitrión -triona *m,f* (*m*) host; (*f*) hostess

ánfora *f*‡ 1 (cántaro) amphora 2 (Bol, Méx, Per) (urna) ballot box 3 (Méx) (botella pequeña) *tb* **anforita** flask

angarillas *fpl* (camilla) improvised stretcher; (Const) handbarrow; (de burro) panniers (*pl*)

angas (Andes, Méx fam): **por ~ o por mangas, nunca estás trabajando** for one reason or another, you're never working; **por ~ o por mangas tengo que salir** I have to go out whether I like it or not

ángel *m* 1 (Relig) angel; **que sueñes con los angelitos** sweet dreams; **pobre angelito** poor little darling; ▸**caer** 2 (encanto) charm; **tener ~** to be charming

(Compuestos)
- **ángel caído** fallen angel
- **ángel custodio** *or* **guardián** *or* **de la guarda** guardian angel

angélica *f* angelica
angelical *adj* angelic
angelito *m* (AmL) dead child; *ver tb* **ángel**
ángelus *m* angelus
angina *f*
A (Arg, Col, Ven) (de la garganta) *inflammation of the palate, tonsils and/or pharynx*
B *tb* ~ **de pecho** angina (pectoris)
anginas *fpl* **1** (Esp, Méx) (inflamación) throat infection **2** (Méx, Ven) (amígdalas) tonsils (*pl*)
angiograma *m* angiogram
anglicano -na *adj/m,f* Episcopalian (*in US and Scotland*), Anglican (*in UK*)
anglicismo *m* Anglicism
anglo¹ -gla *adj* Anglian
anglo² -gla *m,f* Angle
anglófilo¹ -la *adj* Anglophilic
anglófilo² -la *m,f* Anglophile
anglófobo¹ -ba *adj* Anglophobic
anglófobo² -ba *m,f* Anglophobe
anglófono -na *adj* anglophone (frml)
angloparlante *adj* English-speaking
anglosajón² -jona *adj/m,f* Anglo-Saxon
Angola *f* Angola
angoleño -leña *adj/m,f* Angolan
angora *f* angora
angorina *f* imitation angora
angostar [A1] *vt* (esp AmL) **1** ‹*carretera/canal*› to narrow **2** ‹*falda/pantalones*› to take ... in
■ **angostarse** *vpr* to narrow
angosto -ta *adj* ‹*calle/cama*› narrow; ‹*falda*› tight
angostura *f* **1** (cualidad) narrowness **2** (Geog, Náut) narrows (*pl*)
anguila *f* eel
angula *f* elver
angular *adj* angular
ángulo *m* (Mat) angle; (rincón, esquina) corner; (punto de vista) angle

(Compuestos)
- **ángulo agudo/obtuso/recto** acute/obtuse/right angle
- **ángulo muerto** blind spot

anguloso -sa *adj* angular
angurria *f* (CS) greed; **con** ~ greedily
angurriento¹ -ta *adj* greedy
angurriento² -ta *m,f* (fam) greedy pig (colloq)
angustia *f* **1** (congoja) anguish, distress; **gritos/mirada de** ~ anguished cries/look **2** (desasosiego) anxiety; **vive con la ~ de que...** she's constantly worried that... **3** (Psic) anxiety

(Compuesto) **angustia existencial** *or* **vital** angst, existential anxiety

angustiado -da *adj* **1** (acongojado) distressed **2** (preocupado) worried, anxious; **vive angustiada** she lives in a constant state of anxiety
angustiante *adj* ‹*experiencia*› distressing; **una situación económica** ~ a desperate situation financially
angustiar [A1] *vt* **1** (acongojar) to distress **2** (preocupar) to worry, make ... anxious
■ **angustiarse** *v pron* (acongojarse) to get distressed, get upset; (preocuparse) to get worried, become anxious
angustioso -sa *adj* ‹*situación*› distressing; ‹*mirada/grito*› anguished
anhelante *adj* (liter): **esperaba ~ su regreso** she longed *o* (liter) she yearned for his return; **una mirada** ~ a longing look; **con voz** ~ in a voice full of longing
anhelar [A1] *vt* (liter) ‹*fama/poder*› to yearn for, to long for; ~ **+ INF** to long to + INF, yearn to + INF; **anhelaba que su hijo fuera feliz** his greatest wish was for his son to be happy
anhelo *m* (liter) wish, desire; **sus ~s de paz** their yearning for peace (liter); **mi mayor** ~ my greatest wish
anhídrido *m* anhydride

(Compuesto) **anhídrido carbónico** carbon dioxide

anidar [A1] *vi* «*aves*» to nest; **el odio anidaba en su corazón** (liter) hatred dwelled in his heart (liter)
aniego *m* (Per) flood
anilla *f* **1** (de cortina, llavero) ring; (de puro) band; (de lata) ringpull; (de ave) ring **2** **anillas** *fpl* (Dep) rings (*pl*)
anillar [A1] *vt* ‹*ave*› to ring
anillo *m*
A (sortija) ring; ***caérsele los ~s a algn*** (Esp fam & iró): **se le caerían los ~s** that sort of thing would be beneath him; **no se te van a caer los ~s por hacer las camas** making the beds isn't going to kill you; ***como ~ al dedo*** (fam): **el dinero nos vino como ~ al dedo** the money was a real godsend; **te sienta como ~ al dedo** it suits/fits you perfectly

(Compuestos)
- **anillo de boda** wedding ring
- **anillo de compromiso** *or* **pedida** engagement ring

B **1** (aro, arandela) ring; (de columna) annulet; (en árbol) ring; (de gusano) ring **2** (Astron): **el** ~ *or* **los ~s de Saturno** Saturn's rings
ánima *f*‡ (liter) (alma) soul; **las ~s del Purgatorio** the souls in Purgatory
animación *f*
A (bullicio, actividad) activity; **había gran ~ en las calles** the streets were bustling with life *o* activity; **un bar con mucha** ~ a very lively bar; **se debatió con gran** ~ it was the subject of (a) lively debate
B (de una velada) entertainment
C (Cin) animation
animadamente *adv* ‹*charlar/debatir*› animatedly; **bailaron muy** ~ they danced gaily *o* merrily
animado -da *adj*
A **1** ‹*fiesta/ambiente*› lively; ‹*conversación/discusión*› lively, animated **2** (optimista, con ánimo) cheerful, in good spirits
B (impulsado) ~ **DE** *or* **POR algo** inspired *o* motivated BY sth
animador¹ -dora *adj* encouraging
animador² -dora *m,f*
A (de programa) (*m*) presenter, host; (*f*) presenter, hostess
B **animadora** *f* (de equipo) cheerleader
animadversión *f* antagonism, hostility; ~ **HACIA** *or* **POR algo/algn** hostility TOWARD(s) sth/sb; **siento ~ hacia él** I feel hostile *o* antagonistic toward(s) him
animal¹ *adj*
A ‹*instinto*› animal (*before n*); **grasas de origen** ~ animal fats
B **1** (fam) (estúpido) stupid; **¡no seas ~!** don't be so stupid! **2** (grosero) rude, uncouth
animal² *m*
A **1** (Zool) animal; ***comer como un ~*** (fam) to eat like a horse (colloq) **2** (persona con cierta característica): **no soy un ~ político** I'm not a political animal; **un ~ de costumbres** a creature of habit

(Compuestos)
- **animal doméstico** (de granja) domestic animal; (mascota) pet
- **animal salvaje** wild animal

B **animal** *mf* (fam) (persona violenta) brute, animal; (grosero) lout
animalada *f* (fam): **me contestó con una** ~ he gave me a real mouthful (colloq); **fue una ~ decírselo así** it was outrageous telling him like that (colloq)
animar [A1] *vt*
A **1** (alentar) to encourage; (levantar el espíritu) to cheer ... up; **tu visita lo animó mucho** your visit cheered him up a lot; ~ **a algn A + INF** *or* **A QUE + SUBJ** to encourage sb to + INF **2** ‹*fiesta/reunión*› to liven up; **los niños animan mucho la casa** the children really liven the house up; **el vino empezaba a ~los** the wine was beginning to liven them up **3** (con luces, colores) to brighten up
B ‹*programa*› to present, host; ‹*club/centro*› to organize entertainment in
C (impulsar) to inspire; **no nos anima el afán de lucro** we are not driven by any desire for profit
■ **animarse** *v pron* **1** (alegrarse, cobrar vida) «*fiesta/reunión*»

to liven up, warm up; «*persona*» to liven up 2 (cobrar ánimos) to cheer up; **se animó mucho al vernos** she cheered up a lot when she saw us; **si me animo a salir te llamo** if I feel like going out, I'll call you 3 (atreverse) **~se A + INF**: **¿quién se anima a decírselo?** who's going to be brave enough to tell him?; **no me animo a saltar** I can't bring myself to jump; **al final me animé a confesárselo** I finally plucked up the courage to tell her

anímicamente *adv* emotionally

anímico -ca *adj*: **su estado ~** her state of mind; **variaciones anímicas** changes of mood

ánimo *m*

A 1 (espíritu): **no estoy con el ~ para bromas** I'm not in the mood for jokes; **tu visita le levantó el ~** your visit cheered her up; **con el ~ por el suelo** in very low spirits, feeling very down-hearted; **apaciguar** *or* **calmar los ~s** to calm everyone down; ***hacerse el ~ de hacer algo*** to bring oneself to do sth; **no me hago el ~ de estudiar** I can't bring myself to study; **tengo que ir, pero no me hago el ~** I have to go, but I don't feel up to it 2 (aliento, coraje) encouragement; **darle ~(s) a algn** (animar) to encourage sb; (con aplausos, gritos) to cheer sb on; **¡~, que ya falta poco para llegar!** come on! it's not far now!; **el equipo cobró ~** the team rallied; **no tengo ~(s) de** *or* **para nada** I don't feel up to anything; **¿te sientes con ~(s) para seguir?** do you feel up to going on?

B 1 (intención, propósito) intention; **con ~ de calmar las tensiones** with the aim *o* intention of easing tensions; **lo dije sin ~ de ofender** I meant no offense, no offense intended (colloq) 2 (mente, pensamiento) mind; **en el ~ del jurado** in the minds of the jury; **su recuerdo perdura en el ~ de todos** his memory lives on in everyone's hearts

animosidad *f* animosity, hostility; **~ CONTRA algn** animosity *o* hostility TOWARD(s) sb

animoso -sa *adj* spirited

aniñado -da *adj* 1 ‹*facciones*› childlike 2 (Chi fam) (valentón) cocky (colloq)

aniñarse [A1] *v pron* (Chi fam) to act tough

aniquilación *f* annihilation; **la ~ de algunas especies** the extinction of some species

aniquilador -dora *adj* destructive

aniquilamiento *m* annihilation

aniquilar [A1] *vt* ‹*enemigo/población*› to annihilate, wipe out; ‹*defensas/instalaciones*› to destroy

anís *m* 1 (Bot) (planta) anise; (semilla) aniseed 2 (licor) anisette; ***estar hecho un ~*** (Per fam) to be dressed (up) to the nines; ***llegar a los anises*** (Per fam) to show up *o* turn up (too) late

anisado *m* anisette

aniversario *m* anniversary; **~ de boda** wedding anniversary

ano *m* anus

anoche *adv* last night; **el periódico de ~** yesterday evening's newspaper

anochecer¹ [E3] *v impers* to get dark; **ya había anochecido** it was already dark

■ **anochecer** *vi* «*persona*»: **anochecimos camino a Puebla** when it got dark *o* when night fell we were on our way to Puebla

■ **anochecerse** *v pron* (Chi, Méx): **nos anochecimos estudiando** we stayed up studying till really late

anochecer² *m* nightfall; **al ~** at nightfall

anodino -na *adj* ‹*persona*› bland, insipid; ‹*película/comentario*› anodyne, bland

ánodo *m* anode

anomalía *f* anomaly

anómalo -la *adj* anomalous

anonadado -da *adj* dumbfounded, speechless

anonadar [A1] *vt*: **la noticia lo anonadó** he was dumbfounded by the news

anonimato *m* anonymity; **permanecer en el ~** to remain anonymous; **salir del ~** to rise from obscurity

anonimia *f* anonymity

anónimo¹ -ma *adj* anonymous

anónimo² *m* (carta) anonymous letter; (obra) anonymous work

anorak /ano'rak/ *m* parka (AmE), anorak (BrE)

anorexia *f* anorexia

(Compuesto) **anorexia nerviosa** anorexia nervosa

anoréxico -ca *adj/m,f* anorexic

anorexígeno *m* anorectic

anormal¹ *adj* abnormal

anormal² *mf* (fam) idiot

anormalidad *f* abnormality

anotación *f* 1 (nota) note 2 (AmL) (en fútbol) goal; (en fútbol americano) touchdown; (en básquetbol) point

anotador -dora *m,f* (AmL) (en fútbol) scorer, goalscorer; (en fútbol americano, básquetbol) scorer

anotar [A1] *vt*

A 1 (tomar nota de) ‹*dirección/nombre*› to make a note of 2 ‹*texto*› to annotate 3 (RPl) (en curso) to enroll*; (para excursión, actividad) to put ... down

B (AmL) ‹*gol/tanto*› to score

■ **anotar** *vi* (AmL) to score

■ **anotarse** *v pron*

A (AmL) ‹*gol/tanto*› to score

B (RPl) (inscribirse) ▸ **apuntarse A1**

anquilosado -da *adj* 1 ‹*articulación*› (atrofiado) ankylosed; (entumecido) stiff 2 ‹*ideas/economía*› stagnant

anquilosamiento *m* (atrofia) ankylosis; (entumecimiento) stiffness; (estancamiento) stagnation

anquilosarse [A1] *v pron* 1 «*miembro/articulación*» (atrofiarse) to ankylose; (entumecerse) to get stiff 2 «*ideas/economía*» to stagnate

anquilostoma *m* hookworm

ánsar *m* goose

ansia *f*‡ 1 (avidez): **comer con ~** to eat eagerly; **desear algo con ~** to want sth desperately; **~ DE algo** ‹*de paz/libertad*› longing FOR sth, yearning FOR sth; **sus ~s de poder** her thirst *o* craving for power; **sentir ~ de hacer algo** to long *o* yearn to do sth 2 (Psic) anxiety 3 **ansias** *fpl* (Col, Ven fam) (náuseas) nausea

ansiar [A17] *vt* (liter) ‹*libertad/poder*› to long for, yearn for; **el tan ansiado reencuentro** the long-awaited reunion; **~ + INF** to long to + INF; **ansiaba que regresara** he longed *o* yearned for her to return

ansiedad *f* 1 (preocupación) anxiety; **con ~** anxiously 2 (Med, Psic) anxiety

ansiolítico *m* anxiolytic, tranquilizer*

ansiosamente *adv* (con preocupación) anxiously; (con deseo, entusiasmo) eagerly; **deseaba ~ que fuera niña** she desperately wanted a girl

ansioso -sa *adj* 1 (deseoso) eager; **estar ~ DE** *or* **POR + INF** to be eager to + INF; **está ~ por saberlo** he's eager *o* (colloq) dying to know; **estoy ~ de verlos** I can't wait to see them; **estoy ansiosa de que lleguen** I can't wait for them to come, I'm really looking forward to them arriving 2 [SER] (fam) (voraz) greedy

antagónico -ca *adj* conflicting

antagonismo *m* antagonism

antagonista¹ *adj* antagonistic

antagonista² *mf* antagonist

antagonizar [A4] *vt* to antagonize

antaño *adv* (liter) in days gone by; **las costumbres de ~** the customs *o* traditions of yesteryear (liter)

antártico -ca *adj* Antarctic

Antártida *f*: **la ~** Antarctica, the Antarctic

ante¹ *prep*

A 1 (frml) (delante de) before; **comparecer ~ el juez** to appear before the judge; **desfilaron ~ el rey** they marched past the king 2 (frente a): **~ la gravedad de la situación** in view of the seriousness of the situation; **~ la proximidad de las elecciones** with the elections so close; **iguales ~ la ley** equal in the eyes of the law; **nos hallamos ~ un problema** we are faced with a problem

B **ante todo** (primero) first and foremost; (sobre todo) above all; **se considera ~ todo madre** she thinks of herself as a mother above all else

ante² *m* 1 (Zool) (especie europea) elk; (especie norteamericana) moose 2 (cuero) suede

anteanoche *adv* the night before last

anteayer *adv* the day before yesterday

antebrazo *m* forearm

antecámara *f* anteroom

antecedente *m*

A 1 (precedente) precedent; **no hay ningún ~ de la enfermedad en mi familia** there's no history of the illness in my family; **una victoria así no tenía ~s** such a win was completely unprecedented 2 (causa) cause; **un problema con profundos ~s históricos** an issue which has deeply rooted historical causes; ***estar/poner a algn en ~s*** to be/to put sb in the picture

B (Fil, Ling) antecedent

C **antecedentes** *mpl* (historial) background, record

(Compuesto) **antecedentes penales** *or* **policiales** *mpl* (police *o* criminal) record; **sin ~ ~** without a criminal record

anteceder [E1] *vt* to precede, come before; **~ A algo** to come BEFORE sth, precede sth

■ **anteceder** *vi*: **el párrafo que antecede** the preceding paragraph

antecesor -sora *m,f* (predecesor) predecessor; (antepasado) ancestor

antecocina *f*: *room adjoining kitchen where dishes, cooking utensils, etc are kept*

antecomedor *m* (Méx) breakfast room

antedatar [A1] *vt* 1 ‹*documento/carta*› to backdate 2 (ser anterior a) to predate, antedate

antedicho¹ -cha *adj* (frml) aforesaid (frml), aforementioned (frml)

antedicho² -cha *m,f* (frml): **el ~** the aforementioned *o* aforesaid person (frml)

antediluviano -na *adj* (hum) ancient

antelación *f*: **con ~** ‹*reservar/pagar*› in advance; ‹*avisar/salir*› in plenty of time; **saqué la entrada con un mes de ~** I got the ticket one month in advance; **llegó con dos días de ~** she arrived two days early; **con ~ A algo** prior TO sth; **con ~ a su boda** prior to her wedding

antemano: **de ~** (*loc adv*) in advance; **agradeciendo de ~ su colaboración** (Corresp) thanking you in advance for your cooperation

antena *f*

A (de radio, televisión, coche) antenna (AmE), aerial (BrE); **el programa lleva ya cuatro años en ~** the program has been on the air for four years

(Compuestos)

- **antena colectiva** communal antenna *o* aerial
- **antena de radar** radar dish
- **antena direccional/emisora/receptora** directional/transmitting/receiving antenna *o* aerial
- **antena repetidora** relay mast

B (Zool) antenna; (Náut) lateen yard

antenoche *adv* (AmL) the night before last

anteojeras *fpl* blinders (*pl*) (AmE), blinkers (*pl*) (BrE); ***ver las cosas con ~*** (fam) to suffer from tunnel vision

anteojo *m* 1 (telescopio) telescope 2 **anteojos** *mpl* (esp AmL) ▸ **gafas**

antepasado¹ -da *adj*: **el año ~** the year before last

antepasado² -da *m,f* ancestor, forebear (liter);

antepecho *m* (de puente, balcón) parapet; (de ventana) ledge

antepenúltimo¹ -ma *adj* (*delante del n*) third from last, antepenultimate (frml)

antepenúltimo² -ma *m,f*: **fue el ~ en la carrera** he came third from last on the race; **es el ~ en la lista** he's third from bottom on the list

anteponer [E22] *vt* **~ algo A algo** (poner delante) to put sth BEFORE *o* IN FRONT OF sth; (dar preferencia) to put sth BEFORE sth; **el artículo se antepone al sustantivo** the article goes in front of *o* before the noun; **antepone sus intereses a los de su familia** he puts his own interests before those of his family

antepresente *m* (Méx) present perfect

anteproyecto *m* draft

(Compuesto) **anteproyecto de ley** bill

anterior *adj*

A 1 (en el tiempo) previous; **el día ~** the previous day, the day before; **en épocas ~es** in earlier times; **~ A algo** prior TO sth; **sucesos ~es a la revolución** events prior to *o* preceding the revolution 2 (en un orden) previous, preceding; **~ A algo**: **el capítulo ~ a éste** the previous chapter

B (en el espacio) front (*before n*); **la parte ~** the front (part); **las patas ~es** the forelegs *o* front legs

anterioridad *f* (frml) anteriority (frml); **con ~** (antes) before *o* previously; (con antelación) beforehand *o* in advance; **con ~ a su llegada** before he arrived *o* prior to his arrival

anteriormente *adv* (frml) before, previously; **~ a que fuera abolido** prior to its being abolished

antes *adv*

A 1 (con anterioridad) before; **me lo deberías haber dicho ~** you should have told me before *o* earlier; **lo ~ posible** as soon as possible; **lo compré el día ~** I bought it the day before 2 (*en locs*) **antes de** before; **~ de las tres/del accidente** before three/before the accident; **~ de Jesucristo** before Christ, BC; **no van a llegar ~ de dos horas** they won't be here for two hours; **le daré la respuesta ~ de una semana** I will give you my reply within a week; **antes de anoche** the night before last; **antes de ayer** the day before yesterday; **~ DE + INF** before -ING; **llámame ~ de salir** call me before leaving *o* you leave; **antes (DE) QUE + SUBJ**: **~ (de) que me olvide** before I forget; **no se lo des ~ (de) que yo lo vea** don't give it to him until I've seen it; **~ (de) que tú nacieras** before you were born

B (en tiempos pasados) before, in the past; **~ salíamos más** we used to go out more before; **ya no es el mismo de ~** he's not the same person any more; **las casas de ~ eran más sólidas** in the past houses were more solidly built

C 1 (indicando orden, prioridad) first; **yo estaba ~** I was here first; **~ que** before; **el señor está ~ que yo** this gentleman is before me; **~ que nada** first of all; **mis hijos están ~ que tú** my children come before you 2 (indicando preferencia): **¡~ me muero!** I'd rather *o* sooner die!; **cualquier cosa ~ que eso** anything but that; **~ que verlos pasar hambre robaría** I'd steal rather than see them go hungry

D (en el espacio) before; **me bajo dos paradas ~** I get off two stops before

E 1 **antes bien** (liter) on the contrary 2 **antes no** (Chi, Méx fam): **~ no te apuñalaron** you were lucky you didn't get stabbed

antesala *f* 1 (Arquit) anteroom; **en la ~ de la muerte** (liter) on the threshold of death; ***hacer ~*** (frml) to wait (*to be received*) 2 (precursor) prelude; **fue ~ de un gran escándalo** it was the prelude to a great scandal

antevíspera *f* (frml): **(en) la ~** two days before *o* previously

antiabortista¹ *adj* antiabortion (*before n*)

antiabortista² *mf* antiabortionist

antiácido *m* antacid

antiadherente *adj* nonstick

antiaéreo -rea *adj* antiaircraft (*before n*)

antialérgico -ca *adj* antiallergenic

antiamericano -na *adj* anti-American

antiarrugas *adj inv* anti-wrinkle (*before n*)

antibalas *adj inv* bulletproof

antibiótico *m* antibiotic

anticaspa *adj inv* anti-dandruff, dandruff (*before n*)

antichoque *adj inv* ‹*reloj*› shockproof; ‹*parabrisas*› shatterproof

anticiclón *m* anticyclone

anticipación *f* (antelación): **con (mucha) ~** (well) in advance; **con un mes de ~** a month in advance

anticipadamente *adv*: **llegó ~** he arrived early; **agradeciéndole ~ su interés** (Corresp) thanking you in advance for your interest

anticipado -da *adj* ‹*pago*› advance (*before n*); ‹*elecciones*› early; **por ~** in advance

anticipar [A1] *vt* 1 ‹*viaje/elecciones*› to move up (AmE), to bring forward (BrE) 2 ‹*dinero/sueldo*› to advance 3 ‹*información*›: **¿nos podría ~ de qué se trata?** could you give us an idea of what it is about?; **te puedo ~ que ...** I can tell you that ... 4 (indicar): **esto anticipa un incremento de la población** because of this the population is expected to increase; **estas nubes anticipan tormenta** these clouds are a sign that a storm is coming

■ **anticiparse** *v pron* [1] ‹‹*verano/lluvias*›› to be *o* come early [2] (adelantarse) **~se A algo**: **se anticipó a su tiempo** he was ahead of his time; **no nos anticipemos a los acontecimientos** let's not jump the gun; (+ *me/te/le etc*) **se nos ~on** they anticipated us (frml)

anticipo *m*
A [1] (del sueldo, dinero) advance; **me dio un ~** he gave me an advance [2] (pago inicial) down payment; ⊖ **sin anticipo** no down payment
B (de noticia, suceso): **estas imágenes son un ~ de ...** these pictures give you an idea *o* a taste of ...; **nos ofreció un ~ de su colección de verano** he gave us a foretaste of his summer collection

anticlerical *adj* anticlerical
anticlímax *m* anticlimax
anticoagulante *adj/m* anticoagulant
anticomunista *adj/mf* anticommunist
anticoncepción *f* contraception, birth control
anticonceptivo[1] -va *adj* contraceptive (*before n*); **métodos ~s** methods of contraception
anticonceptivo[2] *m* contraceptive
(Compuestos)
• **anticonceptivo de barrera** barrier method of contraception
• **anticonceptivo oral** oral contraceptive

anticongelante *adj/m* antifreeze
anticonstitucional *adj* unconstitutional
anticorrosivo -va *adj* anticorrosive
anticristo *m*: **el ~** the Antichrist
anticuado[1] -da *adj* old-fashioned
anticuado[2] -da *m,f*: **eres un ~** you're so old-fashioned
anticuario -ria *m,f* [1] (persona) antique dealer [2] **anticuario** *m* (tienda) antique shop
anticucho *m* (Bol, Chi, Per) kebab
anticuerpo *m* antibody
antidemocrático -ca *adj* (poco democrático) undemocratic; (opuesto a la democracia) antidemocratic
antideportivo -va *adj* unsportsmanlike
antidepresivo *m* antidepressant
antideslizante *adj* ‹*superficie/suela*› nonslip; ‹*neumático/freno*› antiskid (*before n*)
antidisturbios[1] *adj inv* riot (*before n*)
antidisturbios[2] *mpl*: **los ~** the riot police *o* squad
antídoto *m* antidote
antidroga *adj inv* ‹*campaña*› antidrug; **brigada ~** drug squad
antier *adv* (AmL) the day before yesterday
antiespasmódico *m* antispasmodic
antiestático -ca *adj* antistatic
antiestético -ca *adj* unsightly
antifaz *m* mask
antifeminista *adj/mf* antifeminist
antifranquista[1] *adj* anti-Franco
antifranquista[2] *mf* opponent of Franco
antígeno *m* antigen
antigripal[1] *adj* ‹*vacuna*› flu (*before n*)
antigripal[2] *m* flu remedy
antigualla *f* (fam) piece of junk (colloq)
antiguamente *adv* in the past, in the old days
antigüedad *f* [1] (de monumento, objeto) age; **esas ruinas tienen varios siglos de ~** those ruins are several centuries old [2] (en el trabajo) seniority [3] **la Antigüedad** (Hist) antiquity [4] **antigüedades** *fpl* antiques (*pl*); **tienda de ~es** antique shop

antiguo -gua *adj*
A [1] (viejo) ‹*ciudad/libro*› old; ‹*ruinas/civilización*› ancient; ‹*mueble/lámpara*› antique, old; ‹*coche*› vintage, old; ‹*costumbre/tradición*› old [2] (veterano) old, long-standing; **uno de nuestros más ~s clientes** one of our oldest customers [3] (*en locs*) **a la antigua** in an old-fashioned way; ***chapado a la antigua*** old-fashioned; **de** *or* **desde antiguo** from time immemorial
(Compuestos)
• **antiguo régimen** *m* ancien régime
• **Antiguo Testamento** *m* Old Testament
B (*delante del n*) (de antes) old (*before n*), former (*before n*); **visité mi ~ colegio** I visited my old school; **la antigua capital del Brasil** the former capital of Brazil
C (anticuado) old-fashioned

antiguos *mpl*: **los ~** the ancients
antihéroe *m* antihero
antihigiénico -ca *adj* unhygienic
antihistamínico -ca *adj* antihistamine
antiimperialismo *m* anti-imperialism
antiincendios *adj inv* firefighting (*before n*)
antiinflacionario -ria, **antiinflacionista** *adj* anti-inflation (*before n*)
antiinflamatorio *m* anti-inflammatory
antillano -na *adj/m,f* West Indian
Antillas *fpl*: **las ~** the West Indies
(Compuesto) **Antillas Mayores/Menores** Greater/Lesser Antilles

antílope *m* antelope
antimanchas *adj inv* stain-resistant
antimateria *f* antimatter
antimilitarismo *m* antimilitarism
antimisil[1] *adj* antiballistic (*before n*)
antimisil[2] *m* antiballistic missile
antimonárquico[1] -ca *adj* antimonarchical, antimonarchist (*before n*)
antimonárquico[2] -ca *m,f* antimonarchist
antimonopolista *adj*, **antimonopolio** *adj inv* antitrust (*before n*)
antimotines *adj inv* (Col) riot (*before n*)
antinatural *adj* unnatural
antiniebla *adj inv* fog (*before n*)
antinomia *f* antinomy
antinuclear *adj* antinuclear
antioxidante *adj* (Quím) antioxidant (*before n*); ‹*pintura*› antirust (*before n*)
antiparasitario -ria *adj* antiparasitic
antiparras *fpl* (fam & hum) specs (*pl*) (colloq)
antipasto *m* (AmL) hors d'oeuvre
antipatía *f* dislike, antipathy; **tomarle ~ a algo/algn** to take a dislike to sth/sb
antipático[1] -ca *adj* [1] ‹*persona*› unpleasant; **¡qué tipo más ~!** what a horrible man!; **estuvo muy ~** he was very unfriendly [2] (fam) ‹*tarea*›: **esto de planchar es de lo más ~** ironing is such a drag (colloq)
antipático[2] -ca *m,f*: **es un ~** he's really unpleasant
antipatriótico -ca *adj* unpatriotic
antipedagógico -ca *adj* pedagogically unsound
antiperspirante *m* antiperspirant
antipirético *m* antipyretic, antifebrile
antípodas *fpl*: **las ~** the antipodes; ***estar en las ~ de algo*** to be diametrically opposed to sth
antipolilla *adj inv* antimoth (*before n*)
antiquísimo -ma *adj* ancient, very old
antirrábico -ca *adj* antirabies (*before n*)
antirracista *adj* antiracist
antirreflejos *adj inv* antiglare
antirreglamentario -ria *adj* (Dep): **una jugada antirreglamentaria** a foul; **estaba en posición antirreglamentaria** (period) he was offside
antirrevolucionario -ria *adj/m,f* antirevolutionary
antirrino *m* antirrhinum
antirrobo *m* antitheft device
antisemita[1] *adj* anti-Semitic
antisemita[2] *mf* anti-Semite
antisemítico -ca *adj* anti-Semitic
antiséptico *m* antiseptic
antisocial[1] *adj* antisocial
antisocial[2] *mf* (Andes period) delinquent
antisudoral *m* (CS) antiperspirant
antiterrorista *adj* antiterrorist (*before n*)
antítesis *f* (*pl* ~) antithesis

a

antitetánica *f* antitetanus *o* tetanus injection

antivariólica *f* antismallpox *o* smallpox vaccination

antojadizo -za *adj*: **es muy antojadiza** she wants everything she sees; **no seas tan ~** you can't have everything you see/want

antojarse [A1] *v pron (en 3ª pers)*
A (apetecer) (+ *me/te/le etc*): **se me antojó una cerveza** I felt like (having) a beer; **de embarazada se me antojaban las uvas** when I was pregnant, I had a craving for grapes; **hace lo que se le antoja** he does as he pleases; **porque no se me antoja** because I don't feel like it
B (liter) (parecer) (+ *me/te/le etc*): **el camino se me antojaba eterno** the road seemed never-ending to me

antojitos *mpl* (Méx) *typical Mexican snacks, usually bought at street stands*

antojo *m* **1** (capricho) whim; **tiene que hacerlo todo a su ~** she has to do everything her own way; **maneja al marido a su ~** she has her husband twisted around her little finger **2** (de embarazada) craving **3** (en la piel) birthmark

antología *f* anthology; **de ~** (muy bueno) excellent, fantastic (colloq); (muy malo) terrible

antológico -ca *adj* ‹*recopilación*› anthological; ‹*partido/discurso*› memorable, brilliant

antónimo *m* antonym

antonomasia *f* antonomasia; **por ~** par excellence

antorcha *f* torch

antracita *f* anthracite

ántrax *m* anthrax

antro *m* (local sórdido) dive (colloq); **~ de perdición** den of iniquity

antropofagia *f* cannibalism

antropófago[1] -ga *adj* cannibalistic

antropófago[2] -ga *m,f* cannibal

antropología *f* anthropology

antropológico -ca *adj* anthropological

antropólogo -ga *m,f* anthropologist

antropomórfico -ca *adj* anthropomorphic

anual *adj* **1** ‹*cuota/asamblea*› annual, yearly; ‹*interés/dividendo*› annual; **cinco mil pesos ~es** five thousand pesos a year **2** ‹*planta*› annual

anualidad *f* (inversión) annuity; (cuota anual) annual payment (*o* subscription *etc*)

anuario *m* yearbook

anudar [A1] *vt* ‹*cordón/corbata*› to tie
■ **anudarse** *v pron* (*refl*) ‹*corbata/pañuelo*› to tie; **con la camisa anudada a la cintura** with her shirt knotted at the waist

anuencia *f* (frml) consent, knowledge

anulación *f* (de contrato, viaje) cancellation; (de matrimonio) annulment; (de sentencia) quashing, overturning; **protestó la ~ del gol** he protested when the goal was disallowed

anular[1] *adj* ‹*forma*› ring-shaped

anular[2] [A1] *vt*
A **1** ‹*contrato/viaje*› to cancel; ‹*matrimonio*› to annul; ‹*fallo/sentencia*› to quash, overturn; ‹*resultado*› to declare … null and void; ‹*tanto/gol*› to disallow **2** ‹*cheque*› (destruir) to cancel; (dar orden de no pagar) to stop
B ‹*persona*› to destroy
■ **anularse** *v pron* (*recípr*): **las dos fuerzas se anulan** the two forces cancel each other out

anular[3] *m* ring finger

Anunciación *f*: **la ~** the Annunciation

anunciador -dora *m,f*, **anunciante** *mf* advertiser

anunciar [A1] *vt*
A **1** ‹*noticia/decisión*› to announce, make … public; ‹*lluvias/tormentas*› to forecast **2** (frml) ‹*persona*› to announce; **¿a quién tengo el gusto de ~?** whom do I have the pleasure of announcing? (frml)
B «*señal/indicio*» to herald (frml), to announce; **esas nubes anuncian tormenta** those clouds presage a storm (liter)
C ‹*producto*› to advertise, promote
■ **anunciarse** *v pron* **1** (prometer ser) (+ *compl*): **el debate se anuncia interesante** the debate promises to be interesting; **el fin de semana se anuncia lluvioso** the weekend looks like being wet **2** (*refl*) (frml) «*persona*»: **sírvase ~se en recepción** (frml) kindly report to reception (frml); **se anunció dando un bocinazo** he announced his arrival by tooting the horn

anuncio *m*
A (de noticia) announcement; (presagio) sign, omen
B (Com, Marketing) (en periódico) advertisement, ad (colloq); (en televisión) commercial; **insertar un ~ en el periódico** to place *o* put an advertisement in the newspaper; ⊗ **prohibido fijar anuncios** bill stickers *o* posters will be prosecuted
(Compuesto) **anuncios clasificados** *or* **por palabras** *mpl* classified advertisements (*pl*), classified section

anverso *m* obverse

anzuelo *m* hook; **un ~ para atraer clientes** a gimmick to attract customers; ***morder*** *or* ***tragarse el ~*** to swallow *o* take the bait

añadidura: **por ~** (*loc adv*) in addition; **y el resto se os dará por ~** (Bib) and all these things shall be added unto you

añadir [I1] *vt* to add

añares *mpl* (RPl) ages (*pl*), years (*pl*); **hace ~ que no lo veo** I haven't seen him for ages

añejar [A1] *vt* to age, mature

añejo -ja *adj* ‹*vino/queso*› mature; ‹*costumbre*› old, ancient

añicos *mpl*: **tiró el florero y lo hizo ~** he knocked the vase over and smashed it to smithereens; **el parabrisas se hizo ~** the windshield shattered; **estoy hecho ~** I'm shattered (colloq)

añil *m* (Bot) indigo; (para lavar) blue, bluing

año *m*
A (período) year; **en el ~ 1492** in (the year) 1492; **los ~s 50** the 50s; **el ~ pasado/próximo** last/next year; **una vez al ~** once a year; **por ti no pasan los ~s** you don't seem to get any older; **los ~s no pasan en vano** the years take their toll; **hace ~s que no lo veo** I haven't seen him for *o* in years; ***el ~ del catapún*** *or* ***de la pera*** *or* ***de Maricastaña*** *or* ***de la nana*** (fam): **ese peinado es del ~ de la pera** that hairstyle went out with the ark (colloq), that hairstyle is really old-fashioned; **un disco del ~ de la pera** a record that's really ancient *o* that's years old; ***el ~ verde*** (RPl fam) that'll be the day (colloq); ***dentro de cien ~s todos calvos*** eat, drink and be merry (for tomorrow we die)
B (indicando edad): **soltero, de 30 ~s de edad** single, 30 years old *o* (frml) 30 years of age; **¿cuántos ~s tienes?** how old are you?; **tengo 14 ~s** I'm 14 (years old); **¿cuándo cumples (los) ~s?** when's your birthday?; **hoy cumple 29 ~s** she's 29 today; **ya debe de tener sus añitos** he must be getting on (a bit); **un hombre entrado en ~s** an elderly man; **en sus ~s mozos** in his youth; **a sus ~s y todavía sale a bailar** he still goes out dancing at his age; ***quitarse ~s***: **se quita ~s** she's older than she admits *o* says
C (curso) year; **¿qué ~ haces?** *or* **¿en qué ~ estás?** what year are you in?
(Compuestos)
- **año académico/escolar** academic/school year
- **año bisiesto/civil/sabático** leap/calendar/sabbatical year
- **año de gracia** year of grace
- **año fiscal** fiscal year (AmE), tax year (BrE)
- **año luz** light year
- **Año Nuevo** New Year; **¡Feliz A~ N~!** Happy New Year!; **A~ N~, vida nueva** make (*o* I'm making *etc*) a fresh start for the new year
- **año santo** Holy Year

añoranza *f* yearning; **~ DE** *or* **POR algo** yearning FOR sth; **siente ~ por su país** he yearns for his country

añorar [A1] *vt* ‹*patria/tranquilidad*› to yearn for; ‹*persona*› to miss

aorta *f* aorta

aovar [A1] *vi* to lay eggs

apa *interj* (Méx fam) wow!; **¡~ cochecito!** wow! what a car!

apabullante *adj* ‹*victoria/éxito*› resounding, overwhelming; ‹*rapidez/habilidad*› incredible, extraordinary; ‹*personalidad*› overpowering

apabullar [A1] *vt* (vencer) to overwhelm, crush; (dejar confuso) to overwhelm; **su generosidad me dejó apabullada** his generosity overwhelmed me

apacentar [A5] *vt* to graze, pasture

apache[1] *adj* Apache (*before n*)

apache[2] *mf* Apache

apacheta *f* shrine (*marked by a pile of stones*)

apachurrar [A1] *vt* (AmL fam) to squash

apacible *adj* ‹*carácter/persona*› calm, placid; ‹*vida*› quiet, peaceful; ‹*clima*› mild; ‹*mar*› calm; ‹*viento*› gentle

apaciguador -dora *adj* pacifying (*before n*)

apaciguar [A16] *vt* ‹*persona/ánimos*› to pacify; **a ver si tú puedes ~lo** see if you can pacify him *o* calm him down

■ **apaciguarse** *v pron* «*persona*» to calm down; «*mar*» to become calm; «*temporal/viento*» to abate, die down

apadrinamiento *m* (de artista) sponsorship; (de político, idea) backing, support; (de barco) launch, christening

apadrinar [A1] *vt* [1] ‹*niño*› to be godfather/godparent to; ‹*boda*› to act as **padrino** at; ‹*artista/novillero*› to sponsor, be patron to; ‹*político/idea/candidatura*› to support, back; ‹*barco*› to launch, christen [2] (en duelo) to act as second to

apagado -da *adj*

A ‹*persona*› [SER] spiritless, lifeless; [ESTAR] subdued

B [1] ‹*sonido*› muffled; **con voz apagada** in a subdued voice [2] ‹*color*› muted, dull

C [1] (no encendido): **la luz está apagada** the light is off; **el horno está apagado** the oven is switched off; **con el motor ~** with the engine off [2] ‹*volcán*› extinct

apagar [A3] *vt*

A ‹*luz/televisión/motor*› to turn off, switch off; ‹*cigarrillo/fuego*› to put out, extinguish (frml); ‹*vela/cerilla*› to put out; (soplando) to blow out

B (liter) ‹*sed*› to quench; ‹*ira*› to appease (liter)

■ **apagarse** *v pron*

A «*luz/fuego/vela*» to go out; **se ha apagado el brillo de sus ojos** (liter) the sparkle has gone out of her eyes

B (liter) «*ira*» to abate; «*pasión*» to fade; «*entusiasmo/fervor*» to wane

apagón *m* power cut, blackout

apaisado -da *adj* ‹*libro/tarjeta*› landscape (*before n*)

apalabrar [A1] *vt*: **lo había apalabrado pero no llegué a firmar nada** it was all arranged *o* fixed but I never actually signed anything; **ya tengo apalabrado a un albañil** (fam) I've already fixed up with a builder

■ **apalabrarse** *v pron*: **se ~on para construirlo juntos** they came to an arrangement to build it together; **ya me he apalabrado** *or* **ya estoy apalabrado** I've already said I'll do it

Apalaches *mpl*: **los (montes) ~** the Appalachians

apalancamiento *m* leverage

apalancar [A2] *vt* [1] (para levantar) to jack up (AmE), to lever up (BrE) [2] (para abrir) to force open

apalear [A1] *vt* [1] ‹*persona, alfombra*› to beat; ‹*árbol*› to beat the branches of; **niños apaleados** battered children [2] ‹*arena/carbón*› to shovel

apanado *m* (Per fam) beating; **hacer ~ a algn** to give sb a beating, to beat sb up (colloq)

apanar [A1] *vt* (Andes) ▸ **empanar**

apando *m* (Esp fam) punishment cell

apantallar [A1] *vt*

A (Méx) (impresionar) to impress

B (RPl) (abanicar) to fan

apañado -da *adj* [1] (Esp fam) ‹*persona*› resourceful; **¿te lo hiciste tú? ¡qué apañada!** did you make it yourself? aren't you smart *o* clever!; ***estar*** *or* ***ir ~*** (fam & iró): **estás ~ si crees que puedes ganarle** if you think you can beat him, you've got another think coming! (colloq); **si tengo que esperar a que él acabe estoy ~** if I have to wait till he's finished I'm done for [2] (Esp fam) (arreglado) nice, neat

apañar [A1] *vt*

A (fam) ‹*elecciones*› to fix (colloq), to rig

B (AmS fam) (encubrir) to cover up for

■ **apañarse** *v pron* (Esp fam) *tb* **apañárselas** to manage; **ya me (las) ~é** I'll manage, I'll be OK; **él se metió en el lío, ahora que se las apañe** he got himself into this mess, now he can get himself out of it

apaño *m* [1] (fam) (chanchullo) scam (colloq); **tiene que tener algún ~** he must be on the make (colloq) [2] (Esp fam) (arreglo): **le he hecho un ~** I've managed to patch it up (colloq)

apapachar [A1] *vt* (Méx fam) (abrazar) to cuddle; (acariciar) to stroke, caress

apapacho *m* (Méx fam) [1] (abrazo) cuddle; (caricia) caress [2] **apapachos** *mpl* (alabanzas) praise

aparador *m* [1] (mueble) sideboard [2] (AmL exc CS) (vitrina) store window (AmE), shop window (BrE)

aparato *m*

A [1] (máquina): **uno de esos ~s para hacer pasta** one of those pasta machines; **~s eléctricos** electrical appliances; **eso requiere ~s especiales** that requires special equipment [2] (de televisión) set; (de radio) receiver

B (para gimnasia) piece of apparatus; **los ~s** the apparatus, the equipment

C [1] (audífono) *tb* **~ auditivo** hearing aid [2] (Odont) *tb* **~s** braces (*pl*)

D (teléfono) telephone; **ponerse al ~** to come to the phone; **¡al ~!** speaking!

E (frml) (avión) aircraft

F (estructura, sistema) machine; **el ~ del partido** the party machine; **el ~ represivo** the machinery of repression

G (ceremonia) pomp

H (fam & euf) (pene) weenie (AmE colloq), willy (BrE colloq); (genitales masculinos) equipment (euph)

Compuestos

- **aparato circulatorio/digestivo/respiratorio** circulatory/digestive/respiratory system
- **aparato ortopédico** surgical appliance

aparatosamente *adv* ‹*caer/volcarse*› spectacularly; ‹*reírse*› in an exaggerated manner; **se vino ~ al suelo** she fell dramatically to the ground; **fueron detenidos ~ por la policía** the police arrested them in a great show of force

aparatoso -sa *adj* ‹*gesto*› flamboyant; ‹*sombrero*› showy, flamboyant; ‹*caída/accidente*› spectacular, dramatic

aparcamiento *m* (Esp) [1] (acción) parking [2] (lugar — en ciudad) parking lot (AmE), car park (BrE); (— en carretera) rest area *o* stop (AmE), lay-by (BrE)

Compuesto **aparcamiento disuasorio** (Esp) (para más vehículos) overflow parking lot (AmE) *o* car park (BrE); (que enlaza con transporte público) park-and-ride

aparcar [A2] *vt* (Esp) [1] ‹*vehículo*› to park [2] ‹*proyecto/idea*› to shelve, put ... on ice

■ **aparcar** *vi* (Esp) to park; **Ⓢ prohibido aparcar** no parking

aparcería *f* sharecropping

aparcero -ra *m,f* sharecropper

apareamiento *m* (Zool) mating; (de cosas) matching

aparear [A1] *vt* ‹*animales*› to mate; ‹*objetos*› to match, pair up

■ **aparearse** *v pron* to mate

aparecer [E3] *vi*

A [1] «*síntoma/mancha*» to appear [2] «*objeto perdido*» to turn up; **hizo ~ un ramo de flores** he produced a bouquet of flowers [3] (en documento) to appear; **mi nombre no aparece en la lista** my name doesn't appear on the list [4] «*revista*» to come out; «*libro*» to come out, be published

B «*persona*» [1] (fam) (llegar) to appear, turn up [2] (fam) (dejarse ver) to appear, show up (colloq); **no ha vuelto a ~ por aquí** he hasn't shown his face round here again [3] (en película, televisión) to appear

C (liter) (parecer) to seem

■ **aparecerse** *v pron* [1] «*fantasma/aparición*» **~se A algn** to appear TO sb [2] (AmL fam) «*persona*» to turn up; **¡no te vuelvas a ~ por aquí!** don't you dare show your face round here again!

aparecido *m* (espectro) ghost

aparejado -da *adj*: **esto trae ~ cierto riesgo** this entails a certain amount of risk; **la pena lleva aparejada ...** the punishment also includes *o* entails ...

aparejador -dora *m,f* quantity surveyor

aparejar [A1] *vt* [1] ‹*embarcación*› to rig [2] ‹*caballos*› (para montar) to saddle; (a carro) to harness

a

aparejo *m*
A (de embarcación) rig; (de caballo) tack; (de pesca) tackle; (polea) block and tackle
B (Const) bond

aparentar [A1] *vt* **1** (fingir) ‹*indiferencia/interés*› to feign; **quiere ~ que no le importa** he's trying to make out he's not bothered about it **2** (parecer): **no aparentas la edad que tienes** you don't look your age; **aparenta ser el líder** he seems *o* appears to be the leader
■ **aparentar** *vi* **1** «*persona*» to show off; **sólo por ~** just for show **2** «*regalo/joya*» to look impressive; **aparenta más de lo que vale** it looks more expensive than it really is

aparente *adj*
A (que parece real) ‹*timidez/interés*› apparent (*before n*); **su amabilidad era sólo ~** his kindness was all show; **la ~ victoria se tornó en derrota** what had seemed like victory turned into defeat
B (obvio, palpable) apparent, obvious

aparición *f*
A (acción) appearance; **dos libros de reciente ~** two recently published books
B (fantasma) apparition

apariencia *f* appearance; **un hombre de ~ fuerte** a strong-looking man; **en ~ estaba sano** he appeared to be in good health; **a juzgar por las ~s** judging by appearances; **guardar** *or* **cubrir las ~s** to keep up appearances; **las ~s engañan** appearances can be deceptive

apartado[1] -da *adj* **1** ‹*zona/lugar*› isolated **2** ‹*persona*› **~ DE algo/algn**: **se mantuvo ~ de la vida pública** he stayed out of public life; **vive ~ de la familia** he has little to do with his family

apartado[2] *m*
A (Corresp) *tb* **~ de correos** *or* **~ postal** post office box, P.O. Box
B (de artículo, capítulo) section

apartamentero -ra *m,f* (Col) burglar

apartamento *m* **1** (AmL) (departamento) apartment **2** (Esp) (piso — pequeño) small apartment; (— frente al mar) apartment

apartamiento *m* (retiro) withdrawal

apartar [A1] *vt*
A **1** (alejar) to move away; **aparta la ropa del fuego** move the clothes away from the fire; **aparta eso de mi vista** get that out of my sight; **sus amigos lo ~on del buen camino** his friends led him astray; **apartó los ojos** *or* **la mirada** he averted his eyes **2** ‹*obstáculo*› to move, move ... out of the way; **aparte ese coche** move that car (out of the way) **3** (frml) (de un cargo) to remove; **fue apartado del servicio activo** he was removed from active service **4** (separar) to separate; **si no los apartamos se van a matar** if we don't separate them they'll kill each other
B (guardar, reservar) to set aside; **aparté lo que me iba a llevar** I set aside what I was going to take; **aparta un poco de comida para él** put a bit of food aside for him
■ **apartarse** *v pron* (*refl*) **1** (despejar el camino) to stand aside; **¡apártense!** stand aside! **2** (alejarse, separarse) **~se DE algo/algn**: **el satélite se apartó de su trayectoria** the satellite strayed from its orbit; **apártate de ahí** get/come away from there; **no se aparta de su lado** he never leaves her side; **¡apártate de mi vista!** get out of my sight!; **se apartó bastante de su familia** she drifted away from her family; **nos estamos apartando del tema** we're going off the subject

aparte[1] *adv*
A (a un lado, por separado): **pon las verduras ~** put the vegetables to *o* on one side; **¿me lo podría envolver ~?** could you wrap it separately?; **lo llamó ~ y lo reprendió** she called him aside and reprimanded him; **dejando ~ la cuestión del dinero** leaving aside the question of money; **bromas ~** joking aside; **~ de** apart from; **~ de que no tiene experiencia ...** apart from the fact that she has no experience ...
B (además): **y ~ tiene una casa en el campo** and she has a house in the country as well; **y ~ yo no soy su criada** and anyway *o* besides I'm not his maid

aparte[2] *adj inv*: **esto merece un capítulo ~** this deserves a separate chapter; **es un caso ~** he's a special case

aparte[3] *m* aside

apartheid /a'partej/ *m* apartheid

apartotel *m* apartment hotel (AmE), serviced flats (*pl*) (BrE)

apasionado[1] -da *adj* ‹*amor/persona*› passionate; ‹*discurso*› impassioned

apasionado[2] -da *m,f* enthusiast; **los ~s de la ópera** opera lovers

apasionamiento *m* passion; **con ~** passionately; **sin ningún ~** dispassionately

apasionante *adj* ‹*obra*› exciting, enthralling; ‹*tema*› fascinating

apasionar [A1] *vi*: **la música le apasiona** she has a passion for music; **no es un tema que me apasione** the subject doesn't exactly fascinate me
■ **apasionarse** *v pron* **~se POR algo**: **se apasiona por los toros** he's a tremendous bullfighting enthusiast; **se apasionó por la música** she developed a passionate interest in music

apatía *f* apathy

apático -ca *adj* apathetic

apátrida[1] *adj* **1** (sin patria) stateless **2** (RPl) (que no ama a su país) unpatriotic

apátrida[2] *mf* **1** (sin patria) stateless person **2** (RPl) (que no ama a su país) unpatriotic person

apdo. (= **apartado de Correos**) PO Box

apeadero *m* halt, unstaffed station

apearse [A1] *v pron* (frml) (bajarse) to get off, alight (frml); **~ DE algo** ‹*de un tren*› to alight FROM sth, get OFF sth; **se apeó del caballo** he got off the horse

apechugar [A3] *vi* (fam) to grin and bear it (colloq), to put up with it (colloq); **~ CON algo**: **~ con las consecuencias** to put up with *o* suffer the consequences; **tengo que ~ con todo el trabajo yo sola** I have to cope with all the work myself

apedrear [A1] *vt* **1** (tirar piedras a) to throw stones at **2** (matar a pedradas) to stone (to death)

apegado -da *adj* **ser/estar ~ A algo/algn** to be attached TO sth/sb

apegarse [A3] *v pron* **~ A algo** to grow *o* become attached TO sth; **~ A algn** to become attached TO sb

apego *m* **~ A algo/algn** attachment TO sth/sb; **el ~ a la familia** attachment to one's family; **me tiene mucho ~** she's very attached to me; **le tiene muy poco ~ al trabajo** she is not very committed to her work; **les tiene poco ~ a las cosas materiales** he attaches little importance *o* value to material things

apelable *adj* subject to appeal, appealable

apelación *f* appeal; **presentar** *or* **interponer una ~** to appeal, lodge an appeal

apelante *mf* appellant

apelar [A1] *vi* **1** (Der) to appeal; **~ ante el Tribunal Supremo** to appeal to the Supreme Court; **~ DE** *or* **CONTRA algo** to appeal AGAINST sth **2** (invocar, recurrir a) **~ A algo/algn** to appeal TO sth/sb; **apelé a su generosidad** I appealed to her generosity **3** (apodar) to call; **Pedro I, apelado el Cruel** Peter I, known as Peter the Cruel

apelativo *m* **1** (sobrenombre) name; **se le conoce por el ~ de ...** he is known as ... **2** (Ling) form of address; **un ~ cariñoso** a term of endearment

apellidarse [A1] *v pron*: **se apellida López** his surname is López

apellido *m* surname, last name (AmE); **~ de soltera/de casada** maiden/married name

apelmazado -da *adj* **1** ‹*arroz/pasta*› stodgy; **el arroz quedó ~** the rice all stuck together **2** ‹*bizcocho/pan*› heavy **3** ‹*pelo/lana*› matted; ‹*cojín*› lumpy

apelmazarse [A4] *v pron* **1** «*arroz/pasta*» to stick together **2** «*colchón/cojín*» to go lumpy; «*lana*» to get *o* become matted

apelotonar [A1] *vt* to roll ... into a ball
■ **apelotonarse** *v pron* **1** «*gente*» to mass, crowd together; **íbamos todos apelotonados en el autobús** we were all packed together in the bus **2** «*almohada*» to go lumpy

apenar [A1] *vt* to sadden; **me apenó que se quedara solo** it saddened me that he was left on his own
■ **apenarse** *v pron*
A (entristecerse): **se sintió apenado por su muerte** he was

saddened by her death; **se apenó mucho cuando lo supo** he was very upset *o* sad when he learned of it
B (AmL exc CS) (sentir vergüenza) to be embarrassed

apenas¹ *adv* **1** (a duras penas) hardly; **~ podíamos oírlo** we could hardly *o* barely hear him; **hace ~ dos horas** only two hours ago; **sin ~ trámites** with a minimum of formalities **2** (no bien): **apenas había llegado cuando ...** no sooner had he arrived than ... **3** (Méx, Ven fam) (recién): **~ el lunes la podré ir a ver** I won't be able to go and see her until Monday

apenas² *conj* (esp AmL) (en cuanto) as soon as; **~ termines, me avisas** let me know as soon as you've finished

apendectomía *f* appendectomy

apendejarse [A1] *v pron* **1** (AmL exc CS fam) (volverse estúpido) to go soft in the head (colloq) **2** (Col fam) (ensimismarse): **se apendejaron mirando el cuadro** they became completely absorbed by the painting; **están como apendejados con la nieta** they are besotted with their granddaughter

apéndice *m*
A (del intestino) appendix; (de otro miembro) appendage; **lo operaron del ~** his appendix was removed
B (de texto, documento) appendix

apendicitis *f* appendicitis

apercibimiento *m* **1** (advertencia) warning **2** (sanción) disciplinary measure *o* sanction

apercibir [I1] *vt* **1** (advertir) **~ a algn DE algo** to warn sb OF sth **2** (Der) to order
■ **apercibirse** *v pron* **~se DE algo** to notice sth

apercollado -da *adj* (Col fam): **parejas apercolladas** couples necking *o* (AmE) making out (colloq)

apergaminado -da *adj* ‹*papel*› parchment-like; ‹*piel*› leathery; ‹*cara*› wizened

apergaminarse [A1] *v pron* «*piel*» to dry up, go leathery

aperitivo *m* **1** (bebida) aperitif; **nos invitaron a tomar el ~** they invited us for drinks before lunch (*o* dinner *etc*) **2** (comida) snack, appetizer

apero *m* **1** (utensilio) implement; **~s de labranza** farming implements (*o* tools *etc*); **~s de pesca** fishing tackle; **~s de caza** hunting gear **2** (AmL) (Equ) harness

apersonarse [A1] *v pron* **1** (comparecer) to appear **2** (Col) **~ DE algo** to take charge OF sth, take sth in hand **3** (RPl, Ven fam) (presentarse) to appear in person

apertura *f*
A **1** (de caja, sobre) opening; **S caja fuerte con apertura retardada** strongbox with time-delay mechanism **2** (de cuenta bancaria) opening; (de testamento) reading **3** (comienzo, inauguración) opening; **la sesión de ~** the opening session; **la ~ del plazo de matrícula** the opening date for registration; **la ~ del diálogo con la guerrilla** the commencement of talks with the guerrillas **4** (Fot) aperture **5** (en ajedrez) opening
B (actitud abierta) openness; (proceso) opening-up; **~ a nuevas ideas** this opening-up to new ideas

aperturismo *m* (policy of) openness

aperturista *adj* open, progressive

apesadumbrar [A1] *vt*: **no quería ~lo con sus problemas** she did not want to burden him with her problems; **la noticia lo ha apesadumbrado** the news has saddened *o* distressed him greatly

apestado -da *adj* **1** (con la peste): **gente apestada** plague victims **2** ‹*lugar*› **~ DE algo**: **~ de turistas** crawling *o* infested with tourists; **el barrio está ~ de propaganda política** the whole area is plastered with political posters **3** (AmS fam) (enfermo): **está apestada con la gripe** she has come down with the flu (AmE) *o* (BrE) with flu; **me pasé todo el invierno ~** I had the flu (*o* a cold *etc*) all winter; **esta planta está apestada** this plant has blight **4** (Méx fam) (con mala suerte): **estar ~** to be jinxed

apestar [A1] *vi* (fam) to stink (colloq); **~ A algo** to stink *o* reek OF sth (colloq)
■ **apestar** *vt* (fam) to stink out (colloq)
■ **apestarse** *v pron* (AmS fam) «*persona*» to catch (the) flu (*o* a cold *etc*); «*planta*» to become blighted

apestoso -sa *adj* (maloliente) stinking

apetecer [E3] *vi* (esp Esp): **me apetece un helado/pasear** I feel like an ice-cream/going for a walk; **¿qué te apetece cenar?** what do you feel like for dinner?; **haz lo que te apetezca** do whatever you like
■ **apetecer** *vt* to feel like; **nunca apeteció la fama** (liter) she never sought fame

apetecible *adj* ‹*manjar*› appetizing, mouthwatering; ‹*puesto*› desirable

apetencia *f* **~ DE algo**: **no tiene ~ de nada** nothing appeals to him, he doesn't feel like anything

apetito *m* **1** (ganas de comer) appetite; **no tengo ~** I don't feel *o* I'm not hungry; **tiene muy buen ~** he has a good appetite; **esta caminata me ha abierto el ~** this walk has given me an appetite; **se me ha ido** *or* **quitado el ~** I've lost my appetite **2** **apetitos** *mpl* (liter) (instintos) instincts (*pl*); **los ~s de la carne** the desires of the flesh (liter)

(Compuesto) **apetito sexual** sexual appetite

apetitoso -sa *adj* ‹*plato/manjar*› appetizing, mouthwatering

ápex *m* apex

apiadar [A1] *vt* to move ... to pity
■ **apiadarse** *v pron* **~se DE algn** to take pity ON sb

apiario *m* (AmL) apiary

ápice *m* **1** **(ni) un ~**: **no cedieron ni un ~** they didn't give an inch; **sin un ~ de malicia** without a hint of malice; **no mostró (ni) un ~ de interés** he didn't show the slightest bit of interest; **no tiene un ~ de tonta** she's certainly no fool **2** (de la lengua) tip, apex (tech); (de una pirámide) apex **3** (punto culminante) peak

apicultura *f* beekeeping, apiculture (tech)

apilar [A1] *vt* to pile up, put ... into a pile
■ **apilarse** *v pron* to pile up

apiñar [A1] *vt* to cram, pack
■ **apiñarse** *v pron* «*gente*» to crowd together; **un pueblo apiñado en torno a una iglesia** a village clustered *o* huddled around a church

apio *m* celery

apiolarse [A1] *v pron* (RPl fam) to wise up (colloq); **¿y recién te apiolás?** you mean to say you've only just caught on? (colloq)

apisonadora *f* road roller, steamroller

apisonar [A1] *vt* (con apisonadora) to roll, steamroll; (con pisón) to tamp

aplacar [A2] *vt* **1** ‹*ira*› to soothe; **para ~ a los dioses** to placate the gods; **ella supo ~ los ánimos** she was able to calm people down **2** ‹*sed*› to quench; ‹*hambre*› to satisfy; ‹*dolor*› to soothe
■ **aplacarse** *v pron* «*persona*» to calm down; «*furia*» to subside; «*tempestad*» to abate, die down

aplanacalles *mf* (*pl* ~) (AmL fam) layabout, bum (AmE colloq)

aplanadora *f* (AmL) road roller, steamroller

aplanar [A1] *vt* (con niveladora) to level; (con apisonadora) to roll

aplanchado -da *adj* (Col fam) fed up (colloq), down (colloq)

aplastamiento *m*
A (de rebelión) crushing
B (CS fam) (del ánimo) lethargy

aplastante *adj* ‹*mayoría*› overwhelming; ‹*victoria/derrota*› overwhelming, crushing; ‹*lógica*› devastating

aplastar [A1] *vt*
A ‹*sombrero/caja*› to squash, crush; **~ los plátanos con un tenedor** mash the bananas with a fork
B **1** ‹*rebelión*› to crush, quash **2** ‹*rival*› to crush, overwhelm; (moralmente) to devastate
■ **aplastarse** *v pron* (Col, Méx, Per fam) (arrellanarse) to sprawl

aplaudir [I1] *vt* to applaud
■ **aplaudir** *vi* to applaud, clap

aplauso *m* **1** (ovación) applause; **los ~s duraron varios minutos** the applause went on for several minutes **2** (elogio) praise; **recibió el ~ de la crítica** it received critical acclaim; **su tenacidad es digna de ~** his tenacity is commendable *o* praiseworthy

aplazamiento *m* 1 (de reunión — antes de iniciarse) postponement; (— una vez iniciada) adjournment 2 (de pago) deferment

aplazar [A4] *vt*

A 1 ‹*viaje*› to postpone, put off 2 ‹*juicio/reunión*› (antes de iniciarse) to postpone; (una vez iniciado) to adjourn 3 ‹*pago*› to defer

B (RPl, Ven) ‹*estudiante*› to fail

aplazo *m* (RPl) fail

aplicable *adj* applicable

aplicación *f*

A 1 (frml) (de crema) application (frml); (de pintura, barniz) coat, application (frml) 2 (frml) (de sanción) imposition; (de técnica, método) application; (de plan, medida) implementation; **en este caso será de ~ el artículo 12** (frml) in this case article 12 shall apply (frml)

B (uso práctico) application, use

C (esfuerzo, dedicación) application; **~ A algo** application TO sth

D (Andes) (solicitud) application

aplicado -da *adj* ‹*ciencias/tecnología*› applied (*before n*); ‹*estudiante*› diligent, hard-working

aplicador *m* applicator

aplicar [A2] *vt*

A (frml) ‹*pomada/maquillaje/barniz*› to apply (frml)

B ‹*sanción*› to impose; ‹*descuento*› to allow; **se ~á todo el rigor de la ley** the full weight of the law will be brought to bear; **se le ~á la tarifa 4A** you will be charged at rate 4A; **el acuerdo se aplica a los afiliados al sindicato** the agreement applies to union members

C (frml) ‹*método/sistema*› to put into practice

■ **aplicar** *vi* (Col, Ven) to apply; **~ a un puesto/una beca** to apply for a job/a scholarship

■ **aplicarse** *v pron* to apply oneself

aplique, apliqué *m* 1 (lámpara) wall light 2 (adorno — en mueble) overlay; (— en prenda) appliqué

aplomado -da *adj* ‹*persona*› self-assured, composed

aplomarse [A1] *v pron* (cobrar aplomo) to gain confidence

aplomo *m* composure; **nunca pierde el ~** he never loses his composure

apocado -da *adj* 1 [SER] (de poco carácter) timid 2 [ESTAR] (deprimido) depressed, down (colloq)

apocalipsis *m* apocalypse; **el Libro del A~** Revelations

apocalíptico -ca *adj* apocalyptic

apocamiento *m* 1 (falta de carácter) timidity, lack of self-confidence 2 (depresión) depression

apocarse [A2] *v pron*: **se apocó** she lost all her self-confidence; **no se apoca ante** *or* **por nada** nothing intimidates *o* daunts him

apocopar [A1] *vt* to apocopate

apócope *f or m* (fenómeno) apocope; (vocablo) apocopated form

apócrifo -fa *adj* apocryphal

apodar [A1] *vt* to nickname, call; **lo apodan El Puma** they call him The Puma

apoderado -da *m,f* 1 (Der) proxy, representative; **nombré ~ a mi hermano** I gave my brother power of attorney 2 (de deportista) agent, manager

apoderar [A1] *vt* ‹*persona*› to authorize, grant power of attorney to

■ **apoderarse** *v pron* 1 «*persona*» **~ DE algo** ‹*de ciudad/fortaleza*› to seize sth, take sth; **se ~on de la planta baja** they seized *o* took over the ground floor; **se apoderó del control de la empresa** he took control of the company 2 (liter) «*miedo*» **~se DE algn** to seize sb; **la ira se apoderó de ella** she was seized with anger

apodo *m* nickname

apogeo *m* 1 (auge) height; (de civilización) height, zenith; **en el ~ de su carrera** at the peak *o* height of her career 2 (Astron) apogee

apolillado -da *adj* ‹*ropa*› moth-eaten; ‹*madera*› worm-eaten; ‹*ideas*› antiquated, fusty

apolilladura *f* moth hole

apolillar [A1] *vi* (RPl fam) to snooze (colloq)

■ **apolillarse** *v pron* «*ropa*» to get moth-eaten; «*madera*» to get infested with woodworm

apolíneo -nea *adj* 1 (Mit) Apollonian 2 (bello) handsome, Apollo-like

apolítico -ca *adj* apolitical

apologética *f* apologetics

apología *f* apologia (frml); **hizo ~ del terrorismo** he made a statement (*o* speech *etc*) justifying terrorism; **una ~ del difunto escritor** a eulogy for the dead writer

apologista *mf* apologist

apoltronarse [A1] *v pron* (en asiento) to settle oneself; **consiguió ese puesto y se apoltronó** he got that job and settled into an easy life

apoplejía *f* apoplexy; **ataque de ~** stroke

apoplético -ca *adj* apoplectic

aporrear [A1] *vt* ‹*puerta/mesa*› to bang *o* hammer on; (fam) ‹*persona*› to beat

■ **aporrearse** *v pron* (Andes fam) to take a tumble (colloq)

aportación *f* 1 (contribución) contribution; **su ~ al mundo de la música** her contribution to the world of music 2 (de socio) investment

aportar [A1] *vt* 1 (contribuir) ‹*dinero/tiempo/idea*› to contribute; **aporta calcio y vitaminas** it provides calcium and vitamins 2 «*socio*» to invest

■ **aportar** *vi* (RPl) (a la seguridad social) to pay contributions

aporte *m* 1 (esp AmL) ▸**aportación** 2 (RPl) (a la seguridad social) social security contribution, ≈ National Insurance contribution (*in UK*)

aposentarse [A1] *v pron* 1 (arc) (alojarse) to lodge 2 (hum) (instalarse) to settle

aposento *m* (arc *o* hum) (habitación) chamber (dated); **me retiro a mis ~s** (hum) I'm going to retire (hum)

aposición *f* apposition; **en ~** in apposition

apósito *m* dressing

apostadero *m* station

apostar[1] [A10] *vt* to bet; **~ algo POR algo/algn** to bet sth ON sth/sb; **te apuesto una cerveza** I bet you a beer; **~ía cualquier cosa (a) que se ha olvidado** I bet you anything she's forgotten

■ **apostar** *vi*

A to bet; **~ a** *or* **en las carreras** to bet on the horses; **te apuesto (a) que gana** I bet (you) he wins

B (period) (por una opción) **~ POR algo**: **los delegados ~on por la renovación del partido** the delegates pledged their commitment to the modernization of the party; **diseñadores que apuestan por una línea romántica** designers who are going for the romantic look

■ **apostarse** *v pron* 1 (recípr): **se ~on una comida** they bet a meal on it 2 (enf) to bet; **¿qué te apuestas (a) que llega tarde?** I'll bet (you) he arrives late

apostar[2] [A1] *vt* ‹*soldados/centinela*› to station

■ **apostarse** *v pron* «*policía/soldado*» to position oneself, take up position; **dos policías apostados a la salida** two policemen positioned at the exit

apóstata *mf* apostate

apostatar [A1] *vi* to apostatize

a posteriori *loc adv* with hindsight; **un argumento ~ ~** (*loc adj*) an a posteriori argument

apostilla *f* comment, note

apostillar [A1] *vt* 1 ‹*texto*› to annotate 2 (agregar) to add

apóstol *m* 1 (Relig) apostle 2 **apóstol** *mf* (de idea) advocate, apostle (frml)

apostolado *m* (Relig) ministry, preaching; **la docencia es un verdadero ~** teaching is a true vocation

apostólico -ca *adj* apostolic

apóstrofo *m* apostrophe

apostura *f* (liter) (elegancia) elegance, gracefulness; (porte) bearing; **perdió toda su ~** he lost his fine looks

apoteósico -ca *adj* tremendous

apoteosis *f* 1 (exaltación) apotheosis; **cuando salió en escena aquello fue la ~** (fam) the audience went wild when she came on stage (colloq) 2 (Teatr) finale

apoyabrazos *m* (*pl* ~) armrest

apoyacabezas *m* (*pl* ~) headrest

apoyador -dora *m,f* linebacker

apoyalibros *m* (*pl* ~) bookend

apoyapiés *m* (*pl* ~) footrest

apoyar [A1] *vt*
A (hacer descansar) to rest; **apóyalo contra la pared** lean *o* rest it against the wall
B [1] (respaldar) ‹*propuesta/persona*› to back, support; **nadie la apoyó en su iniciativa** no one backed *o* supported her initiative [2] ‹*teoría*› to support, bear out
■ **apoyarse** *v pron*
A (para sostenerse, descansar) **~se EN algo** to lean ON sth; **camina apoyándose en un bastón** she walks using a cane for support; **se apoya mucho en su familia** he leans heavily on his family
B (basarse, fundarse) **~se EN algo** to be based ON sth; **¿en qué se apoya para hacer tal acusación?** what are you basing your accusation on?

apoyo *m* support; **contar con el ~ popular** to have the support of the people; **~ A algo** support FOR sth; **una campaña de ~ al desarme nuclear** a campaign in support of nuclear disarmament

apozarse [A4] *v pron* (Andes, CS) to collect, form a pool

apreciable *adj* ‹*cambio/mejoría*› appreciable, substantial; ‹*suma/cantidad*› considerable, substantial

apreciación *f*
A [1] (percepción, enfoque) interpretation; **es cuestión de ~** it is a matter of interpretation [2] (juicio) appraisal, assessment
B (aprecio, valoración) appreciation; **~ musical** musical appreciation
C (frml) (de moneda) appreciation (frml)

apreciado -da *adj* ‹*amigo*› valued; **su piel es muy apreciada** its fur is highly prized

apreciar [A1] *vt*
A ‹*persona*› to be fond of; **un amigo al que aprecio mucho** a very dear friend
B ‹*interés/ayuda/arte*› to appreciate; **sabe ~ la buena comida** she appreciates good food
C (percibir, observar) to see; **en la foto se aprecian unas manchas oscuras** some dark areas are visible in the picture; **para ~ la magnitud de los daños** in order to appreciate the extent of the damage
■ **apreciarse** *v pron* (frml) «*moneda*» to appreciate (frml)

apreciativo -va *adj* ‹*gesto/público*› appreciative; ‹*cálculo*›: **hacer un cálculo ~ de los daños** to appraise *o* estimate the damage; **cálculos ~s** estimates

aprecio *m* [1] (estima) esteem; **siente gran ~ por él** she holds him in great esteem; **goza del ~ de sus compañeros** she is highly regarded by her colleagues [2] (valoración) **~ DE algo** appreciation OF sth

aprehender [E1] *vt* (frml) ‹*delincuente*› to apprehend (frml); ‹*contrabando*› to seize; ‹*idea/concepto*› to grasp

aprehensión *f* (frml) (de delincuente) apprehension (frml); (de contrabando) seizure

apremiante *adj* ‹*necesidad*› pressing, urgent

apremiar [A1] *vt* (presionar): **me están apremiando para que lo termine** they are putting pressure on me to get it finished; **estamos apremiados de tiempo** we are pushed for *o* short of time; **lo ~on con preguntas** they badgered *o* harassed him with questions
■ **apremiar** *vi*: **el tiempo apremia** time is getting on *o* is pressing; **apremia una solución** a solution is urgently needed

apremio *m* [1] (urgencia) pressure [2] (mandamiento gubernativo) final demand; (procedimiento judicial) legal proceedings (*pl*); (mandamiento judicial) court order, liability order

aprender [E1] *vi* to learn
■ **aprender** *vt* ‹*lección/oficio*› to learn; **tienes que ~lo de memoria** you have to learn it (off) by heart; **~ algo DE algn/algo** to learn sth FROM sb/sth; **~ A + INF** to learn to + INF; **aprendió a leer** he learned to read
■ **aprenderse** *v pron* (*enf*): **se aprendió el papel en una tarde** she learned the part in an afternoon; **tienen que ~se la lección para mañana** you have to learn the lesson (by heart) for tomorrow

aprendiz -diza *m,f* apprentice, trainee; **es ~ de mecánico** he's an apprentice mechanic; ***ser ~ de todo y oficial de nada*** to be a jack of all trades and master of none

aprendizaje *m* [1] (proceso) learning; **el ~ de una lengua** learning a language [2] (período como aprendiz) apprenticeship, training period; **hacer el ~** to serve one's apprenticeship *o* one's training period

aprensión *f* [1] (preocupación, miedo) apprehension; **se lo dije con cierta ~** I told him somewhat apprehensively [2] (asco) squeamishness; **me da ~ ver sangre** I get squeamish at the sight of blood; **me da ~ beber de un vaso sucio** I don't like the idea of drinking out of a dirty glass

aprensivo -va *adj*: **es muy ~** he's such a worrier

apresador -dora *m,f* captor

apresar [A1] *vt* [1] ‹*nave*› to seize, arrest; ‹*delincuente*› to capture, catch [2] «*animal*» ‹*presa*› to capture, catch

aprestar [A1] *vt* [1] (preparar) to prepare [2] ‹*tela*› to size
■ **aprestarse** *v pron* (*refl*) (frml) **~se PARA algo** to prepare FOR sth; **~se A + INF** to prepare to + INF

apresto *m* size

apresuradamente *adv* [1] (con prisa) hurriedly; **salió ~** she rushed off *o* left in a hurry; **trabajan ~ para terminarlo** they are hurrying *o* rushing to get it finished [2] (precipitadamente) hastily

apresurado -da *adj* [1] ‹*despedida*› quick, hurried; ‹*visita*› rushed, hurried; **caminaba con paso ~** she walked quickly *o* at a brisk pace [2] ‹*decisión*› rushed, hasty; ‹*respuesta/comentario*› hasty

apresuramiento *m* hurry, haste

apresurar [A1] *vt* [1] (meter prisa a) to hurry [2] (acelerar) to speed up; **apresuré el paso** I quickened my pace [3] (precipitar) to hasten
■ **apresurarse** *v pron*: **apresúrate, que llegamos tarde** hurry up or we'll be late; **no nos apresuremos demasiado** let's not be hasty; **se ~on a desmentir la noticia** they were quick to deny the news; **se apresuró a defenderla** he hastened *o* rushed to her defense

apretado -da *adj*
A [1] (ajustado) tight; **esta falda me queda muy apretada** this skirt is too tight for me [2] (sin dinero): **andamos** *or* **estamos algo ~s** we're a little short of money (colloq) [3] (apretujado) cramped; **íbamos muy ~s** it was *o* we were very cramped
B ‹*calendario/programa*› tight; ‹*victoria*› narrow
C (fam) (tacaño) tight (colloq), tightfisted (colloq)
D (Ven fam) (estricto) strict

apretar [A5] *vt*
A [1] ‹*botón*› to press, push; ‹*acelerador*› to put one's foot on, press; ‹*gatillo*› to pull, squeeze [2] ‹*nudo/venda/tornillo*› to tighten; **apretó bien la tapa** he screwed the lid on tightly; **aprieta el puño** clench your fist; **apreté los dientes** I gritted my teeth [3] **~ el paso** *or* **la marcha** to quicken one's pace *o* step
B [1] (apretujar): **apretó al niño contra su pecho** he clasped *o* clutched the child to his breast; **me apretó el brazo con fuerza** he squeezed *o* gripped my arm firmly [2] (presionar) to put pressure on
■ **apretar** *vi*
A «*ropa/zapatos*» (+ *me/te/le etc*) to be too tight; **el vestido le aprieta** the dress is too tight for her
B (hacer presión) to press down (*o* in *etc*)
C (ser fuerte): **¡cómo aprieta el calor!** it's incredibly hot!; **cuando el hambre aprieta ...** when people are in the grip of hunger ...
D [1] (esforzarse) to make an effort [2] «*profesor/jefe*» to be demanding; ***~ a correr*** (fam) to break into a run
■ **apretarse** *v pron* to squeeze *o* squash together

apretón *m* [1] (abrazo) hug [2] (de gente) crush
(Compuesto) **apretón de manos** handshake; **se dieron un ~ de ~** they shook hands

apretujado -da *adj*: **tuvimos que comer todos ~s** we had to eat all squashed together round the table; **~ entre dos gordos** sandwiched *o* squashed between two fat men; **viven muy ~s en ese apartamento** they're very cramped in that apartment

apretujar [A1] *vt* (fam): **no me apretujes, que me haces daño** don't squeeze me so hard, you're hurting me; **me ~on mucho en el tren** I got squashed on the train
■ **apretujarse** *v pron* to squash *o* squeeze together

apretujón *m* [1] (agolpamiento) crush [2] (abrazo) hug

aprieta, aprietas, etc *see* **apretar**

aprieto *m* predicament; **estar/verse en un ~** to be/to find oneself in a predicament; **esto lo pone en un ~** this puts him in an awkward situation; **la saqué del ~** I got her out of it

a

a priori *loc adv* a priori (frml); **un argumento ~ ~** (*loc adj*) an a priori argument

apriorístico -ca *adj* a priori (*before n*)

aprisa *adv* ▸**deprisa**

aprisco *m* fold, pen

aprisionar [A1] *vt* to trap; **se siente aprisionado** he feels trapped

aprobación *f* (de proyecto de ley, moción) passing; (de préstamo, acuerdo, plan) approval, endorsement; (de actuación, conducta de algn) approval; **cuentas con mi ~** you have my approval

aprobado *m* (Educ) pass

aprobar [A10] *vt*

A ‹*proyecto de ley/moción*› to pass; ‹*préstamo/acuerdo/plan*› to approve, sanction; ‹*actuación/conducta*› to approve of

B «*estudiante*» ‹*examen*› to pass; «*profesor*» ‹*estudiante*› to pass

■ **aprobar** *vi* «*estudiante*» to pass

aprobatorio -ria *adj* ‹*mirada*› approving (*before n*); **un gesto ~** a gesture of approval

aproblemar [A1] *vt* (Chi) to worry

■ **aproblemarse** *v pron* (Chi) to worry, get worried

aprontarse [A1] *v pron* (CS) (*refl*) to get ready; **se lo contaré a tu mamá y aprόntate** (fam) I'll tell your mother and then you'll be for it (colloq)

apropiación *f* appropriation

(Compuesto) **apropiación indebida** misappropriation, embezzlement

apropiado -da *adj* suitable; **el discurso fue muy ~ a la ocasión** the speech was very fitting for the occasion; **este libro no es ~ para tu edad** this book is unsuitable for someone of your age; **¡podrías haber elegido un momento más ~!** you could have chosen a better *o* (frml) more appropriate time

apropiarse [A1] *v pron* **~ (DE) algo** to appropriate sth (frml); **es para todos, así que no te apropies de él** (fam) it's for everyone so don't keep it all to yourself; **te lo presto, pero no te lo apropies** (fam) I'll lend it to you, but don't get too attached to it

aprovechable *adj* usable

aprovechado[1] -da *adj*

A (oportunista) opportunistic; **no seas ~** don't take advantage (of the situation)

B ‹*estudiante*› hardworking

aprovechado[2] -da *m,f* opportunist; **es un ~ con sus padres** he takes advantage of his parents; **es un ~, viene aquí sólo a comer** he's a real scrounger, he just comes here for the food (colloq)

aprovechamiento *m* (utilización): **el ~ de los recursos naturales** the exploitation of natural resources; **para un mejor ~ del espacio** to make better use of the space

aprovechar [A1] *vt* **1** ‹*tiempo/espacio/talento*› to make the most of; **aprovecha tu juventud** make the most of your youth; **no aprovechan los recursos que tienen** they don't fully exploit the resources at their disposal; **dinero/tiempo bien aprovechado** money/time well spent; **es espacio mal aprovechado** it's a waste of space **2** ‹*oportunidad*› to take advantage of; **voy a ~ que hace buen tiempo para ...** I'm going to take advantage of the good weather to ...; **aprovecho la ocasión para decirles que ...** I would like to take this opportunity to tell you that ... **3** (usar) to use; **aproveché los restos para ...** I used the leftovers to ...; **éstas todavía se pueden ~** these can still be put to good use; **no tira nada, todo lo aprovecha** she doesn't throw anything away, she makes use of everything

■ **aprovechar** *vi*: **aproveché para venir a verte** I thought I'd take the opportunity to come and see you; **¡que aproveche!** enjoy your meal, bon appétit; **aprovechen ahora, que no tienen niños** make the most of it now, while you don't have children

■ **aprovecharse** *v pron* **1** (abusar) **~se DE algo/algn** to take advantage OF sth/sb, to exploit sth/sb **2** (abusar sexualmente) **~se DE algn** ‹*de una mujer*› to take advantage OF sb; ‹*de un niño*› to abuse sb

aprovisionador -dora *m,f* supplier

aprovisionamiento *m* (acción) provisioning; (provisiones) supplies (*pl*), provisions (*pl*)

aprovisionar [A1] *vt* ‹*buque/tropas*› to provision, to supply ... with provisions

■ **aprovisionarse** *v pron* **~se DE algo** to stock up WITH sth

aprox. (= **aproximadamente**) approx.

aproximación *f* **1** (Mat) approximation; **con una ~ del 99%** with 99% accuracy **2** (acercamiento): **la ~ de los dos países** the rapprochement between the two countries; **un intento de ~** an attempt to improve relations

aproximadamente *adv* around, about, approximately

aproximado -da *adj* ‹*cálculo/traducción/idea*› rough (*before n*); **hora aproximada de llegada** estimated time of arrival

aproximar [A1] *vt* **1** (acercar): **aproximó la mesa a la ventana** she moved (*o* brought *etc*) the table over to the window; **aproxima la silla** bring your chair closer **2** ‹*países*› to bring ... closer together

■ **aproximarse** *v pron* **1** (acercarse) «*fecha/persona/vehículo*» to approach; **se aproxima un frente frío** a cold front is approaching; **a medida que nos aproximábamos a la ciudad** as we approached *o* neared the town; **se aproximó a mí** she came up to me; **se aproximan malos tiempos** there are hard times ahead **2** **~se A algo** ‹*a la realidad/una cifra*› to come close TO sth; **el total se aproxima a los dos millones** the total comes close to two million

aproximativo -va *adj* approximate, rough

aprueba, apruebas, etc *see* **aprobar**

aptitud *f* flair; **tener ~ para los negocios/idiomas** to have a flair for business/languages; **carece de ~es para el ballet** she shows no talent for ballet

(Compuesto) **aptitud legal** legal competence

apto -ta *adj* **1** [SER] ‹*libro/película*› **~ PARA algn** suitable FOR sb; **no ~ para el consumo** not fit for consumption **2** ‹*persona*› **~ PARA algo** fit FOR sth; **~ para el servicio militar** fit for military service; **no es ~ para el cargo** he's not suitable *o* right for the job

apuesta[1] *f* bet; **le hice una ~** I had a bet with him

apuesta[2], apuestas, etc *see* **apostar**

apuesto -ta *adj* (liter) ‹*hombre/figura*› handsome

apunamiento *m* (AmS) altitude *o* mountain sickness

apunarse [A1] *v pron* (AmS) to get altitude *o* mountain sickness

apuntado -da *adj* pointed

apuntador -dora *m,f* prompter, prompt

apuntalamiento *m* (de edificio) shoring-up, bracing; (de cimientos) underpinning

apuntalar [A1] *vt* ‹*edificio/túnel*› to shore up, brace; ‹*cimientos*› to underpin; **los banqueros que ~on el régimen** the bankers who propped up the regime

apuntamiento *m* summary

apuntar [A1] *vt*

A **1** (tomar nota de) to make a note of, note down; **tengo que ~ tu dirección** I must make a note of your address; **apúntelo en mi cuenta** put it on my account **2** (para excursión, actividad) to put ... down; **apúntame para el sábado** put me down for Saturday

B (Teatr) to prompt; (Educ): **mi amiga me apuntaba las respuestas** (fam) my friend whispered the answers to me

C (señalar, indicar) to point at; **no la apuntes con el dedo** don't point (your finger) at her; **apuntó con el dedo dónde estaba el error** he pointed (his finger) to where the mistake was

D (afirmar) to point out; **apuntó la necesidad de un cambio** he pointed out the need for a change

■ **apuntar** *vi*

A **1** (con arma) to aim; **preparen ... apunten ... ¡fuego!** ready ... take aim ... fire!; **~ A algn/algo** to aim AT sb/sth; **le apuntó con una pistola** she pointed/aimed a gun at him **2** (indicar, señalar) to point; **la aguja apunta al** *or* **hacia el norte** the needle points north

B (anotar): **apunta: comprar limones, leche ...** make a note, you need to buy lemons, milk ...; **¿tienes lápiz? pues apunta** have you got a pencil? well, take *o* jot this down

C (Teatr) to prompt

D (liter) ‹‹*día*›› to break; ‹‹*barba*›› to appear, begin to show; ‹‹*flor/planta*›› to sprout; **al ~ el alba** at the break of day (liter)

■ **apuntarse** *v pron*

A 1▸ (inscribirse) **~se A or EN algo** ‹*a curso*› to enroll* ON sth; ‹*a clase*› to sign up FOR sth; **me apunté para ir a la excursión** I put my name down for the outing; **vamos a la discoteca ¿te apuntas?** we're going to the disco, do you want to come (along)?; **me voy a tomar un café ¿quién se apunta?** I'm going out for a coffee, anyone want to join me? (colloq) 2▸ (obtener) ‹*tanto*› to score; ‹*victoria*› to chalk up, achieve; **se apuntó el gol de la victoria** he scored the winning goal

B (manifestarse) ‹‹*tendencia*›› to become evident

apunte *m*

A 1▸ (nota) note 2▸ **apuntes** *mpl* (Educ) notes (*pl*); (texto preparado) handout; **tomar** *or* (CS) **sacar ~s** to take notes; ***no llevar a algn el*** *or* **de ~** (CS fam): **reclamé pero no me llevaron el** *or* **de ~** I complained but they didn't take a blind bit of notice (colloq)

B 1▸ (Art) sketch; (Lit) outline 2▸ (AmL) (Teatr, TV) sketch

C (Com) entry

apuñalar [A1] *vt* to stab; **~ a algn con la mirada** to look daggers at sb (colloq)

apuradamente *adv*

A (con dificultad) with difficulty

B (AmL) (con prisa) hurriedly; **trabajan ~ para terminarlo** they're rushing *o* hurrying to finish it

apurado -da *adj*

A (avergonzado) embarrassed

B (AmL) (con prisa) in a hurry; **andaba ~** he was in a hurry; **se casaron ~s** they got married because she got pregnant (colloq); ***a las apuradas*** (RPl): **lo hizo a las apuradas** she did it in a rush; **andar a las apuradas** to be in a rush

C 1▸ (en apuros): **se vio muy ~ para contestar las preguntas** he was hard put to answer the questions; **si te encuentras ~, dímelo** if you run into any difficulties, let me know 2▸ ‹*situación*› difficult

D 1▸ (de trabajo) overwhelmed with work 2▸ (de dinero): **anda ~ de dinero** he's short of money

E 1▸ ‹*victoria*› narrow 2▸ (Esp period) ‹*afeitado*› close, smooth

apurar [A1] *vt*

A ‹*copa/botella*›: **apura esa botella que todavía queda aceite** there's still some oil left in that bottle, use it up; **apuró la cerveza y se fue** he finished (off) his beer and left

B (apremiar): **nos están apurando para que lo terminemos** they're pushing us to finish it; **no me apures** (AmL) don't hurry *o* rush me; **fue buena, si me apuran, excelente** it was good, if pressed, I'd say it was excellent

■ **apurar** *vi* (Chi) (+ *me/te/le etc*) (urgir): **no me apura** I'm not in a hurry for it; **le apura mucho la entrega** he needs it delivered very urgently

■ **apurarse** *v pron*

A (preocuparse) to worry

B (AmL) (darse prisa) to hurry; **¡apúrate!** hurry up!, get a move on! (colloq)

apuro *m*

A (vergüenza): **¡qué ~!** how embarrassing!; **me daba ~ pedirle dinero** I was too embarrassed to ask him for money

B (aprieto, dificultad): **se vio en ~s** he found himself in a predicament *o* a tight spot; **me sacó del ~** he got me out of it *o* off the hook; **me puso en un ~** she put me in a real predicament; **pasaron muchos ~s** they had an uphill struggle *o* they went through a lot

C (AmL) (prisa) rush; **esto tiene ~** this is urgent; ***casarse de ~*** (RPl): **se casó de ~** she had to get married (*because she was pregnant*); **se casaron de ~** they had a shotgun wedding

apurruñar [A1] *vt* (Ven fam) ‹*persona*› to squeeze

aquejado -da *adj* (frml) **~ DE algo** suffering FROM sth

aquejar [A1] *vt* (frml): **lo aqueja un fuerte dolor de espalda** he is suffering from severe back pain; **los problemas que nos aquejan** the problems which afflict us

aquel, **aquella** *adj dem* (*pl* **aquellos, aquellas**) that; (*pl*) those; **en aquellos tiempos** in those days

aquél, **aquélla** *pron dem* (*pl* **aquéllos, aquéllas**) [*According to the Real Academia Española the written accent may be omitted when there is no risk of confusion with the adjective*] 1▸ (refiriéndose a cosa) that one; (*pl*) those; **ése no, ~** not that one, the *o* that other one 2▸ (refiriéndose a persona): **... y de los dos sería ~ quien lo lograría** (liter) ...and of the two it was the former who was to be successful; **todo ~ que lo necesite** (frml) anyone *o* (frml) any person needing it; **el cuento de ~ que ...** the story about the man who ...

aquelarre *m* witches' sabbath

aquello *pron dem* (*neutro*) **¿qué es ~ que se ve allá?** what's that over there?; **~ que te dije el otro día** what I told you the other day

aquellos, **aquellas** *adj dem*: *ver* **aquel**

aquéllos, **aquéllas** *pron dem*: *ver* **aquél**

aquerenciarse [A1] *v pron* **~ A algo/algn** to become attached TO sth/sb

aquí *adv*

A (en el espacio) here; **está ~ dentro/arriba** it's in/up here; **la tienda de ~, de la esquina** the shop just here, on the corner; **~ Pepe, mi primo** this is my cousin Pepe; **¡tú por ~!** what are you doing here?; **no soy de ~** I'm not from these parts *o* from around here; **pase por ~** come this way; **viven por ~** they live around here; **dando vueltas de ~ para allá** going to and fro *o* from one place to another; **~ y ahora** right here and now; **he ~ el motivo del descontento** (liter) herein lies/lay the cause of their discontent (liter)

B (en el tiempo): **de ~ a 2015** from now until 2015; **de ~ en adelante** from now on; **de ~ a que termine van a pasar horas** it'll take me hours to finish

aquiescencia *f* (frml) acquiescence (frml)

aquietar [A1] *vt* (liter) ‹*temores*› to allay, ease; ‹*conciencia*› to ease; **~los ánimos de los manifestantes** to calm the demonstrators down

■ **aquietarse** *v pron* (liter) ‹‹*aguas*›› to calm (liter), to become calm; **los ánimos se ~on** people calmed down

aquilatar [A1] *vt* ‹*oro/piedra preciosa*› to assay; **para ~ sus méritos** in order to assess her merits; **un hombre de aquilatada honradez** a man of proven honesty

ara[1] *f*‡ (altar) altar; (piedra consagrada) altar stone; **en ~s de** (frml): **en ~s de un mejor entendimiento entre...** in the interests of achieving better understanding between...; **en ~s de un futuro mejor** in order to secure a better future; **en ~s del progreso** in the name of progress

ara[2] *m* (Zool) macaw

árabe[1] *adj* 1▸ ‹*país/plato*› Arab; ‹*escritura/manuscritos*› Arabic; **una palabra de origen ~** a word of Arabic origin 2▸ (Hist) (de Arabia) Arabian; (de los moros) Moorish

árabe[2] *mf*

A 1▸ (de país árabe) Arab 2▸ (Hist) (de Arabia) Arabian; (moro) Moor

B **árabe** *m* (idioma) Arabic

arabesco[1] **-ca** *adj* arabesque

arabesco[2] *m* arabesque

Arabia Saudí, Arabia Saudita *f* Saudi Arabia

arabismo *m* Arabic expression

arabista *mf* Arabist

arácnido *m* arachnid

arada *f* (acción) plowing* (AmE), ploughing (BrE); (tierra) plowed land (AmE), ploughed land (BrE)

arado *m* plow* (AmE), plough (BrE); ***más bruto que un ~*** as dumb as an ox (AmE colloq), as thick as two short planks (BrE colloq)

aragonés -nesa *adj* Aragonese

arancel *m* (tarifa) tariff; (impuesto) duty; **~es de aduanas** customs duties

arancelario -ria *adj* ‹*derecho/tarifa/barrera*› customs (*before n*); **recibe protección arancelaria** it is protected by import duties *o* tariffs

arándano *m* bilberry, blueberry

arandela *f* washer

araña *f*

A (Zool) spider; ***ser picado de la ~*** (Chi fam) to be a flirt

B (lámpara) chandelier

arañar [A1] *vt* 1▸ ‹*persona/cara*› to scratch; ‹*suelo/superficie*› to scratch 2▸ (Esp fam) ‹*nota/resultado*› to manage to

a

get; **~on un aumento del 3%** they managed to squeeze a 3% increase out of them
■ **arañar** *vi* [1] «*gato*» to scratch [2] **arañando** *ger* (Ur fam) (con dificultad): **salvó el examen arañando** she just scraped through the exam

arañazo *m* scratch

arar [A1] *vt/vi* to plow (AmE), to plough (BrE)

araucano -na *adj/m,f* Araucanian

araucano
▸ mapuche

arbitraje *m* [1] (en fútbol, boxeo) refereeing; (en tenis, béisbol) umpiring [2] (Der, Rels Labs) (acción) arbitration; (resolución) decision, judgment

arbitral *adj*: **el juicio ~** the arbitration; **el papel ~ que desempeñó** the mediating role that he played

arbitrar [A1] *vt*
A [1] (en fútbol, boxeo) to referee; (en tenis, béisbol) to umpire [2] ‹*conflicto/disputa*› to arbitrate (in)
B (frml) ‹*recursos*› to furnish (frml), to provide; ‹*medidas*› to introduce; ‹*solución*› to find
■ **arbitrar** *vi* (en fútbol, boxeo) to referee; (en tenis, béisbol) to umpire; (en conflicto) to arbitrate, act as arbitrator

arbitrariedad *f* [1] (cualidad) arbitrariness, arbitrary nature [2] (acción): **la ejecución del preso fue una ~** the execution of the prisoner was an arbitrary, unjust act

arbitrario -ria *adj* arbitrary

arbitrio *m* (frml): **se someterá al ~ del director** the decision will be taken by the director; **eso lo dejo a tu ~** I leave that to your discretion
(Compuesto) **arbitrio judicial** adjudication

árbitro -tra *m,f* [1] (en fútbol, boxeo) referee; (en tenis, béisbol) umpire; **los ~s de la moda** the arbiters of fashion [2] (en conflicto) arbitrator

árbol *m*
A (Bot) tree; **el ~ de la ciencia/vida** the tree of knowledge/life; ***quien a buen ~ se arrima buena sombra le cobija*** it's always useful to have friends in high places; ***los ~es no dejan ver el bosque*** you can't see the forest (AmE) *o* (BrE) wood for the trees
(Compuesto) **árbol de Navidad** *or* (Andes) **de Pascua** Christmas tree
B (Auto, Mec) shaft
(Compuesto) **árbol de levas** camshaft
C (diagrama) *tb* **diagrama de ~** tree (diagram)
(Compuesto) **árbol genealógico** family tree

arbolado¹ -da *adj*
A ‹*terreno*› wooded; **una calle arbolada** a tree-lined street
B ‹*mar*› rough, heavy

arbolado² *m* trees (*pl*)

arboladura *f* spars (*pl*)

arboleda *f* grove

arbóreo -rea *adj* [1] ‹*vegetación*›: **una zona de vegetación arbórea** a wooded area, an area of woodland [2] ‹*forma*› arboreal (frml), treelike

arborescente *adj* arborescent (liter)

arborícola *adj* arboreal, tree-dwelling (*before n*)

arboricultura *f* forestry, arboriculture (frml)

arbotante *m* flying buttress

arbusto *m* shrub, bush

arca *f‡*
A (cofre) chest
(Compuestos)
• **Arca de la Alianza** Ark of the Covenant
• **Arca de Noé**: **el A~ de N~** Noah's Ark
B **arcas** *fpl* (de institución) coffers (*pl*)

arcabuz *m* harquebus

arcada *f*
A (Med): **tener ~s** to retch; **aquel olor me provocó ~s** that smell made me retch
B (Arquit) arcade; (de puente) arch

arcaico -ca *adj* archaic

arcaísmo *m* archaism

arcaizante *adj* archaic

arcángel *m* archangel

arcano¹ -na *adj* (liter) arcane (liter)

arcano² *m* (liter) mystery

arce *m* maple

arcediano *m* archdeacon

arcén *m* shoulder (AmE), hard shoulder (BrE)

archiconocido -da *adj* very well-known; **el ~ conjunto musical** the legendary group

archidiácono *m* archdeacon

archidiócesis *f* (*pl* ~) archdiocese

archiduque -quesa (*m*) archduke; (*f*) archduchess

archipiélago *m* archipelago

archisabido -da *adj* very well-known

archivador -dora *m,f*
A (persona) filing clerk
B **archivador** *m* (mueble) filing cabinet; (carpeta) ring binder, file

archivar [A1] *vt* ‹*documentos*› to file; ‹*investigación/asunto*› (por un tiempo) to shelve; (para siempre) to close the file on

archivero -ra *m,f*
A (persona) archivist
B **archivero** *m* (Méx) filing cabinet

archivo *m*
A (local) archive; (conjunto de documentos) *tb* **~s** archives (*pl*), archive; **los ~s de la policía** the police files *o* records
B (Inf) file

arcilla *f* clay; **~ de alfarería** potter's clay

arcilloso -sa *adj* clayey

arcipreste *m* archpriest

arco *m*
A (Arquit) arch
(Compuestos)
• **arco de herradura/de medio punto/ojival** horseshoe/semicircular/lancet arch
• **arco de triunfo** triumphal arch
• **arco iris** rainbow
B (AmL) (en fútbol) goal
C [1] (Anat) arch [2] (Mat) arc
D [1] (Arm, Dep) bow [2] (de violín) bow
E (Elec) arc

arcón *m* large chest

arder [E1] *vi*
A (quemarse) to burn; **ardía en deseos de verla** (liter) he burned with desire to see her (liter)
B (estar muy caliente) to be boiling (hot); **~ *en fiestas*: Zaragoza arde en fiestas** the festivities in Zaragoza are in full swing; ***estar que arde*** «*persona*» to be fuming; **la cosa está que arde** things have reached boiling point
C (escocer) ‹*herida/ojos*› to sting, smart; **le ardían los hombros** her shoulders were burning; **me arde el estómago** I've got heartburn

ardid *m* trick, ruse

ardiente *adj* ‹*defensor*› ardent; ‹*deseo*› ardent, burning; ‹*amante*› passionate; **una ~ defensa de los derechos humanos** an impassioned defense of human rights

ardilla *f* squirrel
(Compuesto) **ardilla rayada** *or* **listada** chipmunk

ardor *m* [1] (fervor) ardor* (liter); **defendía su causa con ~** she defended her cause ardently; **trabaja con ~** he works with great zeal [2] (dolor) burning; (escozor) smarting; **~ de estómago** heartburn

ardoroso -sa *adj* ardent

arduo -dua *adj* arduous

área *f‡* area
(Compuestos)
• **área chica** *or* **pequeña** goal area
• **área de castigo** penalty area
• **área de reposo** rest area, lay-by (BrE)
• **área de servicio** service area, services (*pl*)
• **área metropolitana** metropolitan area

arena *f*
A (Const, Geol) sand
(Compuesto) **arena movediza** quicksand
B [1] (palestra) arena; **en la ~ política** in the political arena [2] (Taur) ring

arenal *m* sandy area

arenga *f* harangue

arengar [A3] *vt* to harangue

arenilla *f* 1 (arena menuda) fine sand 2 (Med) *tb* **~s** gravel stones (*pl*)

arenisca *f* sandstorm

arenoso -sa *adj* ‹*playa/terreno*› sandy

arenque *m* herring; **~ ahumado** kipper

areola, aréola *f* areola

arepa *f*: *cornmeal roll*; **hay que garantizar la ~ al país** (Ven) the nation must be guaranteed its daily bread; ***ganarse la ~*** (Ven fam) to earn one's living

arequipe *m* (Col) ▸**dulce de leche**

arete *m* (AmL) earring

argamasa *f* mortar

Argel *m* Algiers

Argelia *f* Algeria

argelino -na *adj/m,f* Algerian

argentado -da, **argénteo -tea** *adj* (liter) silvery (liter)

Argentina *f*: *tb* **la ~** Argentina

argentino[1] **-na** *adj* ‹*gobierno/presidente*› Argentine (*before n*); ‹*escritor/música*› Argentinian

argentino[2] **-na** *m,f* Argentinian

argolla *f* 1 (aro) ring 2 (AmL) (anillo) ring; ***tener ~*** (AmC fam) to have contacts (colloq)

Compuesto **argolla de compromiso/de matrimonio** (AmL) engagement/wedding ring

argot *m* (*pl* **-gots**) slang

argucia *f* cunning argument

argüende *m* (Méx fam) 1 (habladuría) gossip 2 (fiesta) party

argüendero -ra *m,f* (Méx fam) gossip

argüir [I19] *vt* 1 ▸**argumentar** 2 «*hechos/pruebas*» to point to

■ **argüir** *vi* «*hechos/pruebas*»: **los hechos arguyen a mi favor** the facts support me; **no hay pruebas que arguyan en su contra** there is no evidence against him

argumentable *adj* arguable

argumentación *f* line of argument (frml)

argumentar [A1] *vt* to argue; **se podría ~ que ...** it could be argued that ...

argumento *m* 1 (razón) argument; **me dejó sin ~s** she demolished all my arguments 2 (Cin, Lit) plot, story line

aria *f*‡ aria

aridez *f* aridity, dryness

árido -da *adj* arid, dry

áridos *mpl* (Com) dry goods (*pl*); (Agr) grain

Aries[1] *m* (signo, constelación) Aries; **es (de) ~** she's an Aries *o* an Arian

Aries[2], **aries** *mf* (*pl* **~**) (persona) Aries, person born under (the sign of) Aries

ariete *m*

A (Arm, Hist) battering ram

B (period) (Dep) striker

ario -a *adj/m,f* Aryan

arisco -ca *adj* 1 [SER] (huraño) ‹*persona*› unfriendly, unsociable; ‹*animal*› unfriendly 2 [ESTAR] (Méx fam) (enojado) upset, angry

arista *f*

A (Mat) edge; (de viga) arris; (de bóveda) groin; (en montañismo) arête, ridge

B (Bot) beard

C **aristas** *fpl*: **las ~s propias de las tensiones socio-culturales** the thorny problems associated with sociocultural unrest; **los años han limado las ~s de su carácter** time has knocked the rough edges off him

aristocracia *f* aristocracy

aristócrata *mf* aristocrat

aristocrático -ca *adj* (noble) aristocratic; (fino) (pey) posh (pej)

aristotélico -ca *adj* Aristotelian

aritmética *f* arithmetic

aritmético -ca *adj* arithmetic

arlequín *m* harlequin

arma *f*‡

A 1 (Arm, Mil) weapon; **~ nuclear/convencional/biológica** nuclear/conventional/biological weapon; **tenencia ilícita de ~s** illegal possession of arms; **¡a las ~s!** to arms!; **rendir las ~s** to lay down one's arms; **tomar (las) ~s** to take up arms; ***de ~s tomar*** formidable, redoubtable (frml); ***ser un ~ de doble filo*** *or* ***de dos filos*** to be a double-edged sword 2 (instrumento, medio) weapon

Compuestos

- **arma blanca** *any sharp instrument used as a weapon*
- **arma de destrucción masiva** weapon of mass destruction
- **arma de fuego** firearm
- **arma reglamentaria** regulation firearm

B (cuerpo militar) arm; **el ~ de artillería/infantería** the artillery/infantry arm

armada *f* navy; **la A~ Invencible** the (Spanish) Armada

armadijo *m* trap, snare

armadillo *m* armadillo

armado -da *adj* ‹*lucha/persona*› armed; **~ DE** *or* **CON algo** armed WITH sth

armador -dora *m,f* shipowner

armadura *f*

A (Hist, Mil) armor*

B (Const) framework

armaduría *f* (Chi) assembly plant

armamentista *adj* arms (*before n*)

armamento *m* armaments (*pl*)

armar [A1] *vt*

A 1 (Mil) ‹*ciudadanos/país*› to arm, supply ... with arms 2 (equipar) ‹*embarcación*› to fit out, equip

B 1 ‹*estantería/reloj*› to assemble; ‹*tienda/carpa*› to pitch, put up 2 (AmL) ‹*rompecabezas*› to do, piece together 3 (Col, RPl) ‹*cigarro*› to roll 4 (dar cuerpo a) ‹*chaqueta/solapa*› to stiffen

C (fam) ‹*alboroto/ruido/lío*› to make; **~ jaleo** to kick up *o* make a racket (colloq); **~on un escándalo porque...** they caused a real scene *o* commotion because...; **~*la*** (fam): **no tengo ganas de ~la otra vez** I don't want to stir things up again (colloq); **¡buena la has armado!** you've really done it now! (colloq); **la que me armó porque llegué tarde** you should have seen the way he went on because I was late

■ **armarse** *v pron*

A 1 (Mil) to arm oneself 2 (proveerse) **~se DE algo** ‹*de utensilios/herramientas*› to arm oneself WITH sth; **tendrás que ~te de paciencia** you will have to be patient *o* (liter) arm yourself with patience; **tuvo que ~se de valor** he had to pluck up courage

B 1 (fam) «*lío/jaleo*»: **¡qué lío/jaleo se armó!** there was a real commotion, it was pandemonium; **se armó una discusión terrible** a terrible argument broke out 2 (fam) «*persona*» ‹*lío*›: **me armé un lío** I got into a mess (colloq)

armario *m* 1 (para ropa — mueble) wardrobe; (— empotrado) closet (AmE), wardrobe (BrE) 2 (de cocina) cupboard; (de cuarto de baño) cabinet

Compuestos

- **armario de luna** *closet/wardrobe with mirrors on either sides of the doors*
- **armario empotrado** (para ropa) built-in closet (AmE), fitted wardrobe (BrE); (de cocina etc) fitted cupboard

armatoste *m* (fam) huge great thing (colloq)

armazón *m or f*

A (Const) skeleton; (de avión) airframe; (de barco, mueble) frame; (de gafas) frames (*pl*)

B (de obra literaria) framework, outline

armella *f* eyebolt

Armenia *f* Armenia

armenio[1] **-nia** *adj/m,f* Armenian

armenio[2] *m* (idioma) Armenian

armería *f* gunsmith's (shop)

armisticio *m* armistice

armonía *f* harmony; **en ~ con la naturaleza** in harmony with nature

armónica *f* harmonica, mouth organ

armónico[1] **-ca** *adj* 1 (Mús) harmonic 2 (armonioso) harmonious

armónico[2] *m* harmonic

a

armonio *m* harmonium

armonioso -sa *adj* harmonious

armonización *f* 1 (Mús) harmonization 2 (de estilos, colores) blending together; (de tendencias, opiniones) harmonization

armonizar [A4] *vt* 1 (Mús) to harmonize 2 ‹*tendencias/opiniones*› to reconcile, harmonize; ‹*diferencias*› to reconcile; **~ algo con algo** to harmonize sth WITH sth, bring sth into line WITH sth

■ **armonizar** *vi* «*estilos/colores*» to blend in, harmonize; **~ con algo** «*color/estilo*» to blend (in) WITH sth

ARN *m* (= **ácido ribonucleico**) RNA

arnés *m*

A (para niño) baby reins (*pl*); (Dep) harness; (arreos) harness

B (Hist, Mil) armor*

aro *m* 1 (Jueg) hoop; ***pasar*** *or* ***entrar por el ~*** (en el circo) to jump through the hoop; (someterse) to toe the line 2 (pendiente) (Arg, Chi) earring; (en forma de aro) (Esp) hooped earring 3 (Ven) (anillo) wedding ring 4 (de servilleta) napkin ring

(Compuesto) **aro de émbolo** piston ring

aroma *m* (de flores) scent, perfume; (del café, de hierbas) aroma; (del vino) bouquet

aromaterapia *f* aromatherapy

aromático -ca *adj* aromatic

aromatizador *m* air freshener

aromatizar [A4] *vt* (Coc) to aromatize; ‹*ambiente/aire*› to scent, perfume

arpa *f*‡ harp

arpegio *m* arpeggio

arpía *f* (mujer perversa) dragon, harpy (liter); (Mit) harpy

arpillera *f* sacking, hessian, burlap (AmE)

arpista *mf* harpist

arpón *m* harpoon

(Compuesto) **arpón submarino** speargun

arponear [A1], **arponar** [A1] *vt* to harpoon

arponero -ra *m,f* harpooner

arqueado -da *adj* ‹*espalda*› curved; **tiene las piernas arqueadas** he's bowlegged

arquear [A1] *vt* ‹*espalda*› to arch; ‹*cejas*› to raise, arch; ‹*estante*› to bow, bend

■ **arquear** *vi* to retch

■ **arquearse** *v pron* «*estante*» to sag, bend; «*persona*» to arch one's back

arqueolítico -ca *adj* Stone Age (*before n*)

arqueología *f* archaeology

arqueológico -ca *adj* archaeological

arqueólogo -ga *m,f* archaeologist

arquería *f*

A (Arquit) series of arches

B (RPl) (Dep) archery

arquero *m*

A (Hist, Mil) archer

B (AmL) (en fútbol) goalkeeper

arquetípico -ca *adj* archetypal

arquetipo *m* archetype

arquitecto -ta *m,f* architect

(Compuesto) **arquitecto técnico -ta técnica** architect (*who has completed a 3 year course*)

arquitectónico -ca *adj* architectural

arquitectura *f* architecture

arrabal *m* poor quarter *o* area

arrabalero[1] **-ra** *adj* 1 (del arrabal) *from or relating to the poor areas of a city*; **quiere ocultar su origen ~** he doesn't want people to know about his humble origins; **el lenguaje ~** the language of the common people 2 (Esp) (ordinario) vulgar, common (pej)

arracada *f* pendant earring

arracimarse [A1] *v pron* to bunch together

arraigado -da *adj* ‹*costumbre*› deeply rooted, deep-rooted; ‹*vicio*› deeply entrenched; **no se siente ~ aquí** he doesn't feel that he really belongs here

arraigar [A3] *vi* «*costumbre*» to become rooted, take root; «*vicio*» to become entrenched; «*planta*» to take root

■ **arraigarse** *v pron* «*costumbres/ideas*» to take root; «*persona*» to settle

arraigo *m*: **de fuerte ~ popular** with strong popular support; **una entidad de ~** a prestigious firm; **una tradición de mucho ~** a deep-rooted tradition

arramblar [A1] *vi* **~ con algo** to make off WITH sth

arrancar [A2] *vt*

A ‹*hoja de papel*› to tear out; ‹*etiqueta*› to tear *o* rip off; ‹*botón*› to tear *o* pull off; ‹*planta*› to pull up; ‹*flor*› to pick; ‹*diente/pelo*› to pull out; ‹*esparadrapo*› to pull off; **hubo un forcejeo y le arrancó la pistola** there was a struggle and he wrenched the pistol away from her; **le arrancó el bolso** he snatched her bag

B ‹*confesión/declaración*› to extract; **no hay quien le arranque una palabra** no one can get a word out of him; **consiguió ~le una sonrisa** she managed to get a smile out of him

C ‹*motor/coche*› to start; (Inf) to boot up

■ **arrancar** *vi*

A 1 «*motor/vehículo*» to start; **el tren está a punto de ~** the train is about to leave; **¡no arranques en segunda!** don't try and move off in second gear! 2 (moverse, decidirse) (fam) to get going; **no hay quien lo haga ~** it's impossible to get him going 3 (empezar) **~ a + inf** to start to + INF, to start -ING

B (provenir, proceder) 1 «*costumbre*» to originate; **esta tradición arranca del siglo XIV** this tradition dates from the 14th century; **de allí arrancan todas sus desgracias** that's where all his misfortunes stem from 2 «*carretera*» to start

C (Chi fam) (huir) to run off *o* away; **~ de algo/algn** to get away FROM sth/sb

■ **arrancarse** *v pron*

A (*refl*) ‹*pelo/diente*› to pull out; ‹*piel/botón*› to pull off

B (Taur) to charge

C (Chi fam) (huir) to run away; **~se de algo/algn** to run away FROM sth/sb

arranque *m*

A (Auto, Mec) starting mechanism; **el coche tiene problemas de ~** I have problems starting it; ***ni para el ~*** (Méx fam): **con un kilo no tenemos ni para el ~** one kilo won't get us far (colloq)

B (de arco) base

C 1 (arrebato) fit; **un ~ de celos/ira** a fit of jealousy/rage; **un ~ de actividad/energía** a burst of activity/energy 2 (brío, energía) drive

arras *fpl* (Der) deposit, security

arrasar [A1] *vi*: **nuestro equipo volvió a ~** our team swept to victory again; **~ con algo**: **la inundación arrasó con las cosechas** the flood devastated the crops; **el PP arrasó en las urnas** the PP won a crushing victory in the elections; **~on con toda la comida** they polished off all the food (colloq)

■ **arrasar** *vt* ‹*zona*› to devastate; ‹*edificio*› to destroy; **el sistema que fue arrasado por la revolución** the system that was swept away by the revolution

■ **arrasarse** *v pron*: **los ojos se le ~on en** *or* **de lágrimas** tears welled up in her eyes

arrastrado -da *adj* 1 ‹*vida*› wretched, miserable 2 ‹*persona*› (desgraciado) wretched

arrastrar [A1] *vt*

A 1 (por el suelo) to drag; **caminaba arrastrando los pies** she dragged her feet as she walked 2 ‹*remolque/caravana*› to tow 3 (llevar consigo): **el río arrastraba ramas** branches were being swept along by the river; **la corriente lo arrastraba mar adentro** the current was carrying him out to sea

B 1 ‹*problema/enfermedad*›: **arrastra esa tos desde el invierno** that cough of hers has been dragging on since the winter; **~on esa deuda muchos años** they had that debt hanging over them for many years 2 (atraer) to draw; **está arrastrando mucho público** it is drawing big crowds; **se dejan ~ por la moda** they are slaves to fashion

C (en naipes) to draw

■ **arrastrar** *vi*

A «*mantel/cortina*» to trail along the ground

B (en naipes) to draw trumps (*o* spades *etc*)

■ **arrastrarse** *v pron*

A (por el suelo) «*persona*» to crawl; «*culebra*» to slither; **se**

arrastró hasta el teléfono she dragged herself *o* crawled to the telephone
B (humillarse) to grovel, crawl

arrastre *m* 1 (acción) dragging; ***estar para el*** ~ (fam) to be done in (colloq) 2 (Náut) trawling; **la flota de** ~ the trawlers 3 (CS fam) (atractivo) appeal; **ese chico tiene mucho** ~ that guy's a real hit with the girls (colloq)

arrayán *m* myrtle

arre *interj* (a un caballo) gee up!, giddy up!

arreada *f* (RPl) round-up

arrear [A1] *vt*
A (fam) (pegar): **te voy a** ~ **un tortazo/puntapié** I'm going to smack you/kick you
B 1 ‹*ganado*› to drive, herd; ‹*caballerías*› to spur, urge on 2 (AmL fam) ‹*gente*› to chivy* (colloq), to hurry … along 3 (AmL fam) (llevar) ~ CON **algo/algn** to cart sth/sb off (colloq)
■ **arrear** *vi*
A (fam) (pegar): ~**le a algn** to smack sb
B **arreando** *ger* (rápido): **¡vamos arreando!** let's get moving! (colloq)

arrebatado -da *adj*
A 1 ‹*discurso*› impassioned; ‹*orador*› passionate; ‹*imaginación*› wild 2 (impetuoso) impulsive
B ‹*rostro/mejillas*› flushed; **un rojo** ~ blood red

arrebatador -dora *adj* ‹*belleza*› breathtaking; ‹*sonrisa*› dazzling; ‹*mirada*› captivating

arrebatar [A1] *vt*
A (quitar) to snatch; **esa experiencia le arrebató la fe** this experience shattered her faith
B (embelesar) to enrapture, captivate
■ **arrebatarse** *v pron* ‹‹*persona*›› to get annoyed, get worked up (colloq)

arrebato *m* 1 (arranque) fit; **un** ~ **de ira/pasión** a fit of anger/passion; **le dio un** ~ he flew into a rage 2 (éxtasis) ecstasy, rapture

arrebol *m* 1 (liter) (en el cielo) crimson glow; (en las mejillas) rosy blush (liter) 2 **arreboles** *mpl* red *o* reddish clouds (*pl*)

arrebolar [A1] *vt* (liter) to turn … red *o* crimson
■ **arrebolarse** *v pron* (liter) to turn red *o* crimson

arrebujar [A1] *vt* (liter) ‹*ropa*› to crumple; ‹*niño*› to swathe (liter), to wrap up
■ **arrebujarse** *v pron* (liter) to wrap oneself up; (en la cama) to snuggle up

arrechar [A1] *vt*
A (AmL vulg) (excitar sexualmente) to turn … on (colloq)
B (AmL fam) (enojar) to bug (colloq); **me arrecha** it really bugs me, it really gets up my nose (colloq)
■ **arrecharse** *v pron*
A (AmL vulg) (sexualmente) ‹‹*persona*›› to get horny (sl); ‹‹*animal*›› to come in (AmE) *o* (BrE) on heat
B (AmL fam) (enfurecerse) to get furious

arrechera *f*
A (AmL vulg) (excitación sexual): **tenía una** ~ **impresionante** he was really horny (sl)
B (AmL fam) (enojo) bad temper; **le dio/cogió una** ~ **…** he had a fit! (colloq)

arrecho -cha *adj*
A 1 (AmL vulg) (sexualmente excitado) ‹*persona*› horny (sl), turned-on (colloq); ‹*animal*› in heat (AmE), on heat (BrE) 2 (Col, Ven fam) (valiente) gutsy (colloq)
B (AmL fam) (enojado) furious, mad (AmE colloq)
C 1 (Ven arg) (sensacional) great, fantastic 2 (Ven fam) (grande, intenso): **¡qué hambre/sed tan arrecha tengo!** I'm absolutely starving/parched (colloq); **tenía unas ganas arrechísimas de hacerlo** I had the most incredible urge to do it (colloq) 3 (AmC, Ven fam) (difícil) tough

arrechucho *m* 1 (fam) (indisposición): **me dio un** ~ I had a funny turn (colloq) 2 (fam) (arranque) fit (colloq)

arreciar [A1] *vi* 1 ‹‹*tormenta*›› to grow worse; ‹‹*viento*›› to get stronger 2 ‹‹*críticas*›› to become more intense *o* severe

arrecife *m* reef; ~ **de coral** coral reef

arredrar [A1] *vt* 1 (intimidar) to intimidate 2 (hacer retroceder) to drive back
■ **arredrarse** *v pron* to be daunted; **sin** ~**se, dio un paso adelante** undaunted, she took a step forward

arreglado -da *adj*
A 1 (limpio, ordenado) tidy 2 (ataviado) smartly turned out, smart; **¿dónde vas tan arreglada?** where are you going all dressed up like that?; ***estar*** ~ (fam): **está** ~ **si se cree que …** if he thinks that … he's got another think coming (colloq); **estamos** ~**s si perdemos el tren** if we miss the train we're in trouble
B (AmL fam) ‹*partido/elecciones*› fixed (colloq)

arreglar [A1] *vt*
A 1 ‹*aparato/reloj*› to mend, fix; ‹*ropa/zapatos*› to mend, repair; **tengo que** ~ **esta falda** I must get this skirt altered; **compró la casa muy barata, pero tiene que** ~**la** she bought the house very cheaply, but it needs a lot of work; **están arreglando la calle** they're repairing the road; **el dentista me está arreglando la boca** (fam) the dentist is fixing my teeth (colloq); **esto te** ~**á el estómago** (fam) this'll sort your stomach out (colloq) 2 (Chi fam) ‹*documento*› to doctor
B 1 ‹*casa/habitación*› to tidy (up), clean up 2 ‹*niño/pelo*›: **ve arreglando a los niños ¿quieres?** can you start getting the children ready?; **voy a ir que me arreglen el pelo** I'm going to have my hair done 3 (preparar, organizar): **tengo todo arreglado para el viaje** I've got everything ready for the trip; **un amigo me está arreglando todos los papeles** a friend is sorting out all the papers for me 4 (disponer) ‹*flores/muebles*› to arrange
C (solucionar) ‹*situación*› to sort out; ‹*asunto*› to settle, sort out; **ya está todo arreglado** it's all sorted out *o* settled now; **a ver si lo puedes** ~ **para que venga hoy** see if you can arrange for her to come today; **lo quiso** ~ **diciendo que …** she tried to put things right by saying that …
D (fam) (como amenaza): **ya te** ~**é yo a ti** I'll show you! (colloq)
■ **arreglarse** *v pron*
A (*refl*) (ataviarse): **tarda horas en** ~**se** she takes hours to get ready; **no te arregles tanto** you don't need to get so dressed up; **sabe** ~**se** she knows how to make herself look good
B ‹*pelo/manos*› 1 (*refl*) to do; **me tengo que** ~ **las manos** I have to do my nails (colloq) 2 (*caus*): **tengo que ir a** ~**me el pelo** I must go and have my hair done; **me estoy arreglando la boca** I'm getting my teeth fixed
C 1 (solucionarse) ‹‹*situación/asunto*›› to get sorted out; **ya verás como todo se arregla** you'll see, everything will turn out all right 2 ‹‹*pareja*›› (tras una riña) to make (it) up
D (fam) (amañarse): **ya me** ~**é para volver a casa** I'll make my own way home; **la casa es pequeña pero nos arreglamos** it's a small house, but we manage; ~**se** CON **algo**: **nos tendremos que** ~ **con tu sueldo** we'll have to get by *o* manage on your wages; **se tendrán que** ~ **con lo que hay** they'll have to make do with what there is; ***arreglárselas*** (fam) to manage; **no sé cómo se las arreglan** I don't know how they manage; **arréglatelas como puedas** sort *o* work it out as best you can; **sabe arreglárselas solo** he can look after himself; **ya me las** ~**é para llegar** I'll find a way of getting there
E ‹‹*día/tiempo*›› to get better, clear up

arreglista *mf* arranger

arreglo *m*
A 1 (reparación) repair; **con unos pequeños** ~**s quedará como nuevo** with a few minor repairs it'll be as good as new; **la casa necesita algunos** ~**s** the house needs some work done on it; ***tener*** ~: **este reloj no tiene** ~ this watch is beyond repair; **esta chica no tiene** ~ this girl's a hopeless case; **todo tiene** ~ there's a solution to everything; **eso tiene fácil** ~ that's easy enough to sort out 2 (de ropa) alteration 3 (Mús) *tb* ~ **musical** musical arrangement

Compuestos
- **arreglo floral** flower arrangement
- **arreglo personal** personal appearance

B (acuerdo) arrangement, agreement; **los** ~**s que tenía con uno de los policías** the little arrangement he had with one of the policemen (colloq); **con** ~ **a** (frml) in accordance with
C (fam) (lío amoroso) affair

arrejuntarse [A1] *v pron* (fam) to shack up together (colloq)

a

arrellanarse [A1] *v pron* (en asiento, cargo) to settle; **estaba arrellanada en el sofá** she was sprawled on the sofa

arremangar [A3] *vt* ▸**remangar**

arremeter [E1] *vi* (embestir) to charge; (atacar) to attack; **~ CONTRA algo/algn** (acometer) to charge AT sth/sb; (atacar, criticar) to attack sth/sb

arremetida *f* (embestida) charge; (ataque) attack, onslaught; **la ~ de las olas** the crashing *o* pounding of the waves

arremolinarse [A1] *v pron* «*agua/hojas*» to swirl; «*personas/animales*» to mill around

arrendador -dora (*m*) landlord, lessor (frml); (*f*) landlady, lessor (frml)

arrendajo *m* (europeo) jay; (americano) blue jay

arrendamiento *m* 1 (de casa) renting, letting; (de tierras, local) renting, leasing; **tomé el local en ~** I leased *o* rented the premises; **contrato de ~** lease 2 (de otra cosa — por el propietario) renting (out); (— por el que la recibe) renting 3 (precio — de casa, local) rent; (— de otra cosa) rental

(Compuesto) **arrendamiento financiero** *or* **con opción a compra** leasing

arrendar [A5] *vt*

A (Der) 1 (dar en arriendo) ‹*casa*› to rent, let; ‹*local/tierras*› to rent, lease 2 (tomar en arriendo) ‹*casa*› to rent; ‹*local/tierras*› to rent, lease 3 (contratar) ‹*servicios*› to hire

B (Andes) ‹*coche/máquinas*› (dar en arriendo) to rent; (tomar en arriendo) to hire, rent; Ⓢ **se arriendan coches** cars for rent (AmE), car hire (BrE)

arrendatario -ria *m,f* (de propiedad) lessee, tenant; (de contrata) contractor

arreo *m*

A (AmL) (Agr) (acción) driving; (recorrido) drive; (manada) herd, drove

B **arreos** *mpl* (Equ) tack

arrepentido¹ -da *adj* ‹*pecador*› repentant; **un terrorista ~** a reformed terrorist; **~ de lo que había hecho** sorry for *o* feeling remorse for what he had done; **estoy ~ de haberlo dicho** I regret having said it

arrepentido² -da *m,f* reformed terrorist

arrepentimiento *m* remorse, repentance; **su ~ era sincero** he was truly sorry

arrepentirse [I11] *v pron* 1 (lamentar) to be sorry; **~ DE algo** to regret sth; **no me arrepiento de nada** I have no regrets; **~ DE + INF** to regret -ING; **no te arrepentirás de comprarlo** you won't regret buying it 2 (cambiar de idea) to change one's mind

arrepienta, arrepintió, etc *see* **arrepentirse**

arrestar [A1] *vt* to arrest; **queda arrestado** you're under arrest

arresto *m*

A (Der, Mil) 1 (detención) arrest; **bajo ~** under arrest 2 (prisión) detention

(Compuestos)
- **arresto domiciliario** house arrest
- **arresto preventivo** preventive detention

B **arrestos** *mpl* (audacia) boldness, daring; **no tiene ~s para...** she's not daring *o* bold enough to...

arriar [A17] *vt* 1 ‹*bandera/vela*› to lower 2 ‹*cabo/cable*› (aflojar) to slacken off; (soltar) to let go, release

arriba *adv*

A 1 (lugar, parte): **está aquí ~** it's up there; **en el estante de ~** (el siguiente) on the shelf above; (el último) on the top shelf; **la sábana de ~** the top sheet; **ponlo un poco más ~** put it a little higher up; **como se dijo más ~** as stated above; **la parte de ~** the top (part); ***de ~*** (RPl fam) free; **vive de ~** he doesn't work for a living; ***de ~ abajo***: **me miró de ~ abajo** he looked me up and down; **limpiar la casa de ~ abajo** to clean the house from top to bottom; **me empapé de ~ abajo** I got soaked from head to toe; ***para tirar para ~*** (AmL fam): **tienen dinero para tirar para ~** they have money to burn (colloq); **hay hoteles para tirar para ~** there are hotels galore 2 (en edificio) upstairs; **los vecinos de ~** the people upstairs 3 (en escala, jerarquía) above; **órdenes de ~** orders from above; **los de ~ opinan que ...** the people at the top believe that ...; **las puntuaciones de 80 para ~** scores of 80 or over; **los Lakers 13 puntos ~** Lakers 13 points up *o* ahead

B (expresando dirección, movimiento): **corrió escaleras ~** he ran upstairs; **calle ~** up the street; **río ~** upstream; **miró hacia ~** he looked up; ***para ~ y para abajo*** (fam) to and fro, back and forth

C **arriba de**: **tiene ~ de 60 años** she's over 60; **con ~ de 50 alumnos** with more than 50 pupils; **~ del ropero** (AmL) on top of the wardrobe; **~ de la cocina está el baño** (AmL) the bathroom is above the kitchen

D (en interjecciones) 1 (expresando aprobación): **¡~ la democracia!** long live democracy! 2 (expresando estímulo) come on!; (llamando a levantarse) get up!

arribada *f* arrival (in port)

arribar [A1] *vi* **~ A algo** to arrive AT, come TO sth

arribismo *m* (ambición social) social ambition; (progreso, movimiento) social climbing

arribista¹ *adj* socially ambitious

arribista² *mf* arriviste, social climber

arribo *m* (liter) arrival

arriendo *m* (esp Andes) ▸**arrendamiento**

arriero *m* mule driver *o* skinner

arriesgado -da *adj* ‹*acción/empresa*› risky, hazardous; ‹*persona*› brave, daring

arriesgar [A3] *vt* 1 ‹*vida/dinero*› to risk; ***quien nada arriesga nada gana*** nothing ventured, nothing gained 2 ‹*opinión*› to venture

■ **arriesgarse** *v pron*: **¿nos arriesgamos?** shall we risk it *o* take a chance?; **se arriesgan al fracaso** they run the risk of failing *o* of failure; **~se A + INF** to risk -ING; **te arriesgas a que te multen** you risk getting a fine

arrimar [A1] *vt*

A (acercar): **arrima la silla, estás muy lejos** bring your chair closer, you're too far away; **arrima una silla** pull up a chair; **arrimó la cama a** *or* **contra la pared** he pushed *o* moved the bed up against the wall

B (Méx fam) (pegar): **le arrimó una santa tranquiza** he gave him a real beating *o* thrashing (colloq); **me arrimó un codazo** he elbowed me

■ **arrimarse** *v pron*

A (*refl*) (acercarse): **arrímate al fuego** come (up) closer to the fire; **se arrimó a** *or* **contra la pared** he moved up against the wall; **bailaban muy arrimados** they were dancing very close; **~se A algn** to move closer TO sb; (buscando calor, abrigo) to snuggle up TO sb

B 1 (Méx, Ven fam) «*pareja*»: **están arrimados** they're living together 2 (Méx, Ven fam) (en casa de algn): **se ~on en mi casa** they came to live *o* stay with me, they dumped themselves on me (pey)

arrimo *m* protection; **al ~ de** thanks to, with the help of

arrinconado -da *adj* 1 (bloqueado) blocked in, boxed in 2 (acorralado, acosado) cornered 3 (arrumbado) lying around; **es demasiado valioso para tenerlo ~** it's too valuable to be left lying around

arrinconar [A1] *vt* 1 (poner en rincón) to put ... in a corner 2 (acosar, acorralar) to corner; **lo ~on contra una pared** they got him up against a wall 3 (marginar) to exclude 4 (arrumbar) to leave, dump (colloq)

■ **arrinconarse** *v pron* (fam) to cut oneself off

arriscado -da *adj*

A ‹*paisaje/terreno*› rugged, craggy

B (audaz) bold

arriscar *vi* (Col): **~ CON algo** to be up to sth; **ese caballo no arrisca con tanta carga** that horse isn't up to carrying a load like that

arritmia *f* arrhythmia

arroba *f*

A 1 (medida de peso) *unit of weight of between 11 and 16 kg (24-36 lbs) according to region* 2 (medida de capacidad) *unit of liquid measure of between 12 and 16 liters (US 25-34 pts, Brit. 21-28 pts) according to region*

B (en dirección electrónica) at, @

arrobar [A1] *vt* (liter) to entrance

■ **arrobarse** *v pron* to become entranced

arrobo *m* (liter) (éxtasis) bliss (liter), rapture (liter); (trance) trance

arrocero¹ -ra *adj* ‹*cultivo/producción*› rice (*before n*); ‹*región*› rice-growing (*before n*)

arrocero² **-ra** *m,f* rice grower
arrodillarse [A1] *v pron* to kneel (down); **estaba arrodillado** he was kneeling *o* on his knees
arrogancia *f* (soberbia) arrogance; **con ∼** arrogantly
arrogante *adj* (soberbio) arrogant, haughty
arrogarse [A3] *v pron* (frml) to assume, arrogate (frml)
arrojadizo **-za** *adj*: **armas arrojadizas** throwing weapons
arrojado **-da** *adj* brave, daring
arrojar [A1] *vt*
A **1** (tirar) to throw; **arrojaban piedras contra la policía** the demonstrators hurled *o* threw stones at the police; **⊗ prohibido arrojar objetos a la vía** do not throw objects onto the track **2** ‹*lava*› to spew (out); ‹*humo*› to belch out; ‹*luz*› to shed **3** (liter) (expulsar) ‹*persona*› to cast out (liter)
B (frml) ‹*resultado/pruebas*› to produce; **la catástrofe arrojó 18 muertos** the disaster left 18 people dead; **el sondeo arroja un balance favorable a los Liberales** the poll gives the Liberals a favorable lead
C (vomitar) to vomit
■ **arrojar** *vi* to vomit
■ **arrojarse** *v pron* (*refl*) to throw oneself; **se ∼on al agua** they threw themselves *o* jumped into the water; **∼se SOBRE algo/algn** to throw oneself ONTO sth/sb; **el perro se arrojó sobre el intruso** the dog pounced on the intruder
arrojo *m* bravery, daring; **con ∼** bravely
arrollado *m* (RPl) **1** (dulce) jelly roll (AmE), Swiss roll (BrE) **2** (de verduras) roulade
(Compuesto) **arrollado de chancho** (Chi) rolled pork
arrollador **-dora** *adj* **1** ‹*éxito*› overwhelming; ‹*victoria*› crushing, overwhelming; **una mayoría ∼a** an overwhelming majority **2** ‹*fuerza/ataque*› devastating **3** ‹*personalidad/elocuencia*› overpowering
arrollar [A1] *vt*
A **1** «*vehículo*» to run over; «*muchedumbre/agua/viento*» to sweep *o* carry away **2** (derrotar, vencer) to crush, overwhelm
B ‹*papel/cable*› ▸**enrollar A**
arropar [A1] *vt* **1** ‹*niño/enfermo*› (abrigar) to wrap … up; (en la cama) to tuck … in **2** (proteger) to protect
■ **arroparse** *v pron* (abrigarse) to wrap up warm; (en la cama) to pull the covers up
arrope *m* (de mosto) grape syrup; (de miel) honey syrup
arrorró *m* lullaby; **∼ mi niño** hushaby baby
arrostrar [A1] *vt* ‹*peligros/penalidades*› to face up to, confront; ‹*consecuencias*› to face
arroyo *m* **1** (riachuelo) stream **2** (cuneta) gutter; ***poner*** *or* ***plantar a algn en el ∼*** (fam) to kick sb out (colloq); ***sacar a algn del ∼*** to drag sb up from the gutter **3** (AmC) (torrentera) gully **4** (Méx) (Auto) slow lane
arroyuelo *m* brook, small stream
arroz *m* rice
(Compuestos)
- **arroz a la cubana** *rice with fried egg, plantain and tomato sauce*
- **arroz blanco** (tipo de arroz) white rice; (arroz hervido) (plain) boiled rice
- **arroz con leche** rice pudding
- **arroz integral** brown rice

arrozal *m* ricefield, paddy
arruga *f* (en piel) wrinkle, line; (en tela, papel) crease
arrugado **-da** *adj* ‹*persona/manos/piel*› wrinkled; ‹*ropa*› wrinkled (AmE), creased (BrE); ‹*papel*› crumpled
arrugamiento *m* crumpling
arrugar [A3] *vt* ‹*piel*› to wrinkle; ‹*tela*› to wrinkle (AmE), to crease (BrE); «*papel*» to crumple; ‹*ceño*› to knit; ‹*nariz*› to wrinkle; ‹*cara*› to screw up; **arrugó el entrecejo** he frowned, he knitted his brow
■ **arrugarse** *v pron*
A **1** «*persona/piel*» to become wrinkled **2** (por acción del agua) «*piel/manos*» to shrivel up, go wrinkled **3** «*tela*» to wrinkle *o* get wrinkled (AmE), to crease *o* get creased (BrE); «*papel*» to crumple
B **1** (fam) (achicarse) to be daunted *o* frightened **2** (Chi fam) (inmutarse): **ni se arruga para mentir** he thinks nothing of lying; **le gritan y ni se arruga** they shout at him and he doesn't bat an eyelid (colloq)
arruinar [A1] *vt*
A (empobrecer) to ruin
B (estropear) ‹*vida/salud/reputación*› to ruin, wreck; ‹*proyecto/cosecha*› to ruin; ‹*velada/sorpresa*› to spoil, ruin
■ **arruinarse** *v pron*
A (empobrecerse): **se arruinó** he lost everything *o* he was ruined; **por invitarme a una copa no te vas a ∼** (hum) buying me one drink isn't going to break you (hum)
B «*proyecto/cosecha*» to be ruined
arrullador **-dora** *adj* soothing, lulling
arrullar [A1] *vt* (cortejar) to whisper sweet nothings to; (adormecer) to lull … to sleep; **arrullado por el sonido del agua** lulled by the sound of the water
■ **arrullar** *vi* «*paloma*» to coo
arrullo *m* (de palomas) cooing; (para adormecer) lullaby
arrumaco *m* (fam) **1** (de enamorados) petting; **se hacían ∼s** they were kissing and petting **2** (zalamería): **déjate de ∼s** stop trying to sweet-talk me
arrumar *vt* (Náut) to stow
■ **arrumarse** *v pron* to cloud over
arrumbar [A1] *vt* ▸**arrinconar 3, 4**
■ **arrumbar** *vi* to fix a course
arrume *m* (Col) pile, heap
arruncharse [A1] *v pron* (Col, Ven) to curl up; **estaban arrunchados, temblando de frío** they were huddled together, shivering with cold
arrurrú *m* (Andes) ▸**arrorró**
arrurruz *m* arrowroot
arsenal *m* **1** (Mil) arsenal **2** (colección) armory*; **un ∼ de datos** a mine of information **3** (Esp) (Náut) navy yard (AmE), naval dockyard (BrE)
arsenalero **-ra** *m,f* (Chi) nurse (AmE), theatre nurse (BrE)
arsénico *m* arsenic
arte (*gen m en el singular y f en el plural*)
A (Art) art; **el ∼ medieval** medieval art; **las ∼s** the arts; **el ∼ por el ∼** art for art's sake; **no trabajo por amor al ∼** (hum) I'm not working for the good of my health (hum); ***(como) por ∼ de magia*** as if by magic; ***no tener ∼ ni parte***: **no tuve ∼ ni parte en el asunto** I had nothing whatsoever to do with it
(Compuestos)
- **arte dramático** dramatic arts (*pl*)
- **arte poética** poetics (*pl*)
- **artes gráficas/plásticas** *fpl* graphic/plastic arts (*pl*)
- **artes marciales** *fpl* martial arts (*pl*)
- **artes menores** *fpl* crafts (*pl*)
- **artes y oficios** *fpl* arts and crafts (*pl*)

B **1** (habilidad, destreza): **el ∼ de mentir** the art of lying; **tiene ∼ para arreglar flores** she has a flair *o* gift for flower arranging **2** **artes** *fpl* (astucias, artimañas) trick; **empleé todas mis ∼s para …** I used every trick I could think of to …; **usó todas sus ∼s para seducirlo** she used (all) her feminine wiles to seduce him
artefacto *m* (instrumento) artefact; (dispositivo) device
(Compuestos)
- **artefactos de baño** *or* **sanitarios** *mpl* (CS) bathroom fixtures (*pl*), sanitary ware (frml)
- **artefactos eléctricos** *mpl* (CS) small electrical appliances (*pl*)

arteria *f* artery; **una importante ∼ fluvial** a major artery for river transport
artería *f* artfulness
arterial *adj* arterial
arterioesclerosis, arteriosclerosis *f* arteriosclerosis (tech)
artero **-ra** *adj* artful, cunning
artesa *f* trough
artesanado *m* artisans (*pl*)
artesanal *adj*: **muebles de fabricación ∼** handcrafted furniture; **quesos de fabricación ∼** farmhouse cheeses; **productos ∼es** handicrafts, craftwork; **una feria ∼** a craft fair
artesanía *f* **1** (actividad): **fomentar la ∼ tradicional** to encourage traditional crafts; **objetos de ∼ popular** traditional craftwork *o* handicrafts **2** **artesanías** *fpl* (AmL)

(productos artesanos) handicrafts (*pl*), craftwork; **~s en barro/cuero** traditional earthenware/leather goods; **mercado de ~s** craft market

artesano¹ -na *adj* ▸**artesanal**

artesano² -na (*m*) craftsman, artisan; (*f*) craftswoman, artisan

artesiano *adj* artesian

artesón *m* 1 (panel) coffer, caisson 2 (moldura) molding* 3 (techo) coffered ceiling

artesonado *m* (conjunto de artesones) coffering; (techo) coffered ceiling

ártico -ca *adj* Arctic

Ártico *m*: **el ~** (región) the Arctic; (océano) the Arctic Ocean

articulación *f*

A 1 (Anat, Mec) joint, articulation (tech) 2 (organización) organization, coordination

B (Ling) articulation

articulado -da *adj* articulated

articular¹ *adj* of/in the joint, articular (tech)

articular² [A1] *vt* 1 (Tec, Ling) to articulate 2 ‹*reglamento*› to formulate, draw up; ‹*ley*› to draft 3 (organizar, coordinar) to organize, coordinate

articulista *mf* feature writer, columnist

artículo *m*

A (Com): **~s del hogar** household goods; **S artículos para regalo** gifts; **rebajas en todos nuestros ~s** reductions on all items; **~s de punto** knitwear

(Compuestos)

- **artículo de primera necesidad** essential item, essential
- **artículos de consumo** *mpl* consumer goods (*pl*)
- **artículos de escritorio** *mpl* stationery
- **artículos de tocador** *mpl* toiletries (*pl*)

B 1 (escrito — en periódico, revista) article; (— en diccionario) entry, article 2 (de ley) article

(Compuestos)

- **artículo de fe** article of faith
- **artículo de fondo** editorial

C (Ling) article

(Compuestos)

- **artículo determinado** *or* **definido** definite article
- **artículo indeterminado** *or* **indefinido** indefinite article

artífice *mf* 1 (responsable, autor): **fue el ~ del secuestro** he planned the kidnapping; **el ~ de esta victoria** the architect of this victory 2 (artista) (*m*) craftsman, artisan; (*f*) craftswoman, artisan

artificial *adj* ‹*flor/satélite/sonrisa*› artificial; ‹*fibra*› man-made, artificial

artificiero -ra *m,f* (experto en explosivos) explosives expert; (experto en desactivarlos) bomb disposal expert

artificio *m* 1 (artimaña) trick, artful device; **una belleza sin ~s** a natural beauty 2 (afectación) affectation 3 (artilugio) device

artificioso -sa *adj* affected, contrived

artillería *f* artillery

(Compuesto) **artillería antiaérea/ligera/pesada** anti-aircraft/light/heavy artillery

artillero¹ -ra *adj* artillery (*before n*)

artillero² *m* (Mil) artilleryman; (Náut) gunner; (Dep) striker

artilugio *m* 1 (aparato) device, contraption 2 **artilugios** *mpl* (de oficio) equipment

artimaña *f* trick

artista *mf*

A (Arte) artist; **es una ~ cocinando** she's a real artist in the kitchen (colloq)

B (actor) actor; (actriz) actress; (cantante, músico) artist; **una ~ de cine** a movie star (AmE) *o* (BrE) film star

artístico -ca *adj* artistic

artrítico¹ -ca *adj* ‹*dolor*› arthritic; ‹*enfermo*› arthritis (*before n*)

artrítico² -ca *m,f* arthritis sufferer

artritis *f* arthritis

(Compuesto) **artritis reumatoide** rheumatoid arthritis

artrópodo *m* arthropod

artrosis *f* degenerative osteoarthritis

aruñar [A1] *vt/vi* (AmC, Col, Ven) ▸**arañar**

arveja *f* 1 (AmL) (guisante) pea 2 (algarroba) vetch

arvejilla, arverjilla *f* (RPl) sweet pea

arzobispado *m* archbishopric

arzobispal *adj* ‹*sede/comisión*› archiepiscopal (frml); **el palacio ~** the archbishop's palace

arzobispo *m* archbishop

as *m* 1 (Jueg) ace; ***tener/guardar un ~ en la manga*** to have/keep an ace *o* a trick up one's sleeve 2 (fam) (campeón) ace (colloq); **un ~ del volante** an ace *o* a crack driver (colloq)

(Compuesto) **as de guía** bowline

asa *f*‡ (asidero) handle

asadera *f* (RPl) roasting pan *o* dish *o* tin

asadero *m* (Coc) griddle

asado¹ -da *adj*

A (en horno) roast (*before n*); (con espetón) spit-roast (*before n*); (a la parrilla) barbecued, grilled; **castañas asadas** roast chestnuts; **papas asadas** roast/baked potatoes

B (fam) (acalorado) roasting (colloq)

asado² *m* 1 (al horno) roast; **~ de cordero** roast lamb 2 (AmL) (a la parrilla) barbecued meat 3 (AmL) (reunión) barbecue

asador¹ *m* (espetón) spit; (aparato — de espetones) rotisserie; (— de parrilla) barbecue; (restaurante) grillroom, steakhouse

asador² -dora *m,f* (RPl) cook (*person who cooks the meat at a barbecue*)

asadura, asadurilla *f*: *tb* **~s** offal

asaetear [A1] *vt* 1 (disparar a) to shoot arrows at; (herir) to wound (*with an arrow*) 2 (acosar): **lo ~on a** *or* **con preguntas** they bombarded him with questions; **sus admiradoras lo asaeteaban** he was besieged by fans

asalariado¹ -da *adj* wage-earning (*before n*)

asalariado² -da *m,f* wage *o* salary earner

asaltante¹ *adj* attacking (*before n*)

asaltante² *mf* 1 (ladrón) robber; **los ~s del banco** the bank robbers 2 (atacante) attacker; **los ~s de la embajada** those who stormed the embassy

asaltar [A1] *vt* 1 (robar) ‹*banco/tienda*› to rob, hold up; ‹*persona*› to rob, mug 2 (tomar por asalto) ‹*ciudad/embajada*› to storm 3 (atacar) to attack, assault 4 (acosar) to accost, assail (frml); **lo ~on a preguntas** they bombarded him with questions 5 «*idea*» to strike; **me asaltó una duda** I was struck *o* seized by a sudden doubt

asalto *m*

A 1 (robo) holdup, robbery; **un ~ a mano armada** an armed robbery *o* raid 2 (ataque) attack, assault; **el ~ a** *or* **de la embajada** the storming of the embassy; **lo tomaron por ~** they took it by storm

B 1 (en boxeo) round 2 (en esgrima) bout

C 1 (RPl) (fiesta) potluck party *o* dinner 2 (AmC) (fiesta sorpresa) surprise party

asamblea *f* 1 (reunión) meeting; **celebrar una ~** to hold a meeting 2 (cuerpo) assembly; **constituirse en ~ permanente** to meet in permanent session

(Compuesto) **Asamblea Nacional** *or* (en Ur) **General**: **la ~ ~** Parliament, the National Assembly

asambleísta *mf* assembly member

asar [A1] *vt* (en horno) to roast; (a la parrilla) to grill; (con espetón) to spit-roast

■ **asarse** *v pron* 1 (Coc) ▸**asar** *vt* 2 (fam) (de calor) to roast (colloq)

asaz *adv* (liter) (muy) very; (bastante) rather

asbesto *m* asbestos

ascendencia *f* 1 (origen, linaje) ancestry; **es de ~ francesa** he is of French descent; **de ~ noble** of noble ancestry; **su ~ humilde** her humble origins 2 (AmL) ▸**ascendiente B**

ascendente¹ *adj* ‹*movimiento/tendencia*› upward; ‹*astro*› rising; **la marea ~** the flood *o* rising tide

ascendente² *m* ascendant; **es Capricornio con ~ Libra** she's Capricorn with Libra in the ascendant

ascender [E8] *vi*

A (frml) (subir, elevarse) «*temperatura/precios*» to rise; «*globo*» to rise, ascend (frml); **ascendieron por la ladera oeste** they made their ascent by the west face

B (frml) (cifrarse) «*gastos/pérdidas*» **~ A algo** to amount TO sth; **el número de muertos asciende a 48** the number of dead has reached 48

C «*empleado/oficial*» to be promoted; **ascendió rápidamente en su carrera** he advanced rapidly in his career; **ascendió a capitán** he was promoted to the rank of captain; **~ a primera división** to go up to *o* be promoted to the first division; **~ al trono** to ascend the throne

■ **ascender** *vt* ‹*empleado/oficial*› to promote

ascendiente *mf*

A (antepasado) ancestor

B **ascendiente** *m* (frml) (influencia) **~ SOBRE algn** influence OVER sb

ascensión *f* ascent

Ascensión *f*: **la ~** the Ascension; **la fiesta de la ~** Ascension Day

ascenso *m* **1** (subida — de temperatura, precios) rise; (— a montaña) ascent; **una industria en ~** a growing industry **2** (de empleado, equipo) promotion; (Mil) promotion

ascensor *m* elevator (AmE), lift (BrE)

ascensorista *mf* elevator operator (AmE), lift attendant (BrE)

asceta *mf* ascetic

ascética *f* asceticism

ascético -ca *adj* ascetic

ascetismo *m* asceticism

ASCII /'aski/ *m* ASCII

asco *m* **1** (repugnancia): **¡qué ~!** how revolting!, how disgusting!; **me dio ~** it made me feel sick; **poner cara de ~** to make *o* (BrE) pull a face; **tanta corrupción da ~** all this corruption is sickening; **le tengo ~** I really loathe him; ***hacerle ~s a algo*** (fam) to turn one's nose up at something; ***poner a algn del ~*** (Méx fam) to rip sb to shreds *o* pieces **2** (fam) (cosa repugnante, molesta): **la película es un ~** the movie is disgusting; **tienen la casa que es un ~** their house is like a pigsty; **el parque está hecho un ~** the park is in a real state (colloq); **¡qué ~ de tiempo!** what foul *o* lousy weather!; **¡qué ~ de vida!** what a (rotten) life!

ascua *f*‡ ember; ***arrimar el ~ a su sardina*** (fam) to work things to one's own advantage; ***estar en*** *or* ***sobre ~s*** (fam) to be on tenterhooks; ***tener a algn en ~s*** (fam) to keep sb on tenterhooks

aseado -da *adj* (limpio) clean; (arreglado) neat, tidy

asear [A1] *vt* (limpiar) to clean; (arreglar) to clean ... up, to straighten (AmE), to tidy ... up (BrE)

■ **asearse** *v pron* (*refl*) (lavarse) to wash; (arreglarse) to clean (AmE) *o* (BrE) tidy oneself up

asechanza *f* trap

asediar [A1] *vt* **1** (Mil) ‹*ciudad*› to lay siege to, besiege; ‹*ejército*› to surround, besiege **2** (acosar) ‹*persona*› to besiege; **la ~on con preguntas** they besieged her with questions

asedio *m* **1** (Mil) siege, blockade **2** (acoso): **escapó del ~ de sus admiradoras** he escaped from the mob of fans that surrounded him; **el ~ de sus acreedores** the harassment from his creditors

asegurable *adj* insurable

asegurado[1] -da *adj* insured; **tengo el coche ~ a** *or* **contra todo riesgo** I have fully comprehensive insurance for the car; **está ~ a todo riesgo** it is fully insured

asegurado[2] -da *m,f* (persona que contrata el seguro) policyholder; (persona asegurada): **el ~/la asegurada** the insured

asegurador[1] -dora *adj* ‹*compañía*› insurance (*before n*)

asegurador[2] -dora *m,f* **1** (persona) insurer **2** **aseguradora** *f* (compañía) insurance company

asegurar [A1] *vt*

A **1** (afirmar, prometer) to assure; **le aseguro que ...** I assure you that ...; **asegura no haberlo visto** she maintains that she did not see **2** (garantizar) ‹*funcionamiento/servicio*› to guarantee; **tendremos buen tiempo asegurado** we'll be guaranteed good weather

B (Com, Fin) ‹*persona/casa*› to insure; **aseguró el coche a** *or* **contra todo riesgo** she took out fully comprehensive insurance for *o* on the car

C **1** (sujetar, fijar) ‹*puerta/estante*› to secure; **lo ~on con una cuerda** they secured it with a rope; **aseguró bien el pie en la roca** she got a firm foothold in the rock **2** ‹*edificio/entrada*› to secure, make ... secure

■ **asegurarse** *v pron*

A **1** (cerciorarse) to make sure; **asegúrate de que no falta nada** make sure there's nothing missing **2** (garantizarse, procurarse): **con ese gol se ~on el triunfo** by scoring that goal they guaranteed themselves victory

B (Com, Fin) to insure oneself

asemejar [A1] *vt* **1** (hacer parecido) to make ... (look) like; **ese peinado la asemeja a su madre** that hairstyle makes her look like her mother **2** (comparar) to compare, liken

■ **asemejarse** *v pron* «*personas*» to be *o* look alike; «*objetos*» to be similar; **~se A algo/algn** to resemble sth/sb, look like sth/sb

asenso *m* (frml) approval, assent (frml)

asentaderas *fpl* (euf & fam) behind (euph)

asentado[1] -da *adj* **1** [ESTAR] (situado): **el pueblo está ~ a orillas de un río** the village lies on the banks of a river; **la oficina central está asentada en Nueva York** the headquarters is located in New York **2** [ESTAR] (establecido) ‹*creencia/tradición*› deep-rooted, deeply rooted; ‹*persona*› settled (in) **3** [SER] (esp AmL) (maduro, juicioso) mature

asentado[2] -da *m,f* (Chi) peasant farmer (*who works his/her own land*)

asentamiento *m* settlement

asentar [A5] *vt*

A ‹*campamento*› to set up; ‹*damnificados/refugiados*› to place

B **1** ‹*objeto*› to place carefully (*o* firmly *etc*); **asienta bien la escalera** make sure the ladder's steady **2** ‹*tierra*› to firm down **3** ‹*válvula*› to seat **4** ‹*costura/dobladillo*› to press **5** ‹*conocimientos/postura*› to consolidate

C (Com, Fin) to enter

D (frml) **1** ‹*pauta/principio/criterio*› to establish, lay down **2** (Esp, Méx) (afirmar) to affirm, state

■ **asentarse** *v pron*

A «*café/polvo/terreno*» to settle

B (estar situado) «*ciudad/edificio*» to be situated, be built

C **1** (establecerse) to settle **2** (esp AmL) (adquirir madurez) to settle down

asentimiento *m* approval, consent

asentir [I11] *vi* to agree, consent; **asintió con la cabeza** she nodded; **~ A algo** to agree *o* consent TO sth

asentista *m* contractor, supplier

aseñorada *adj* (fam): **se viste de forma ~** she wears clothes that are too grown-up for her; **¡es tan ~!** she looks so ladylike!

aseo *m* **1** (limpieza) cleanliness; **~ personal** personal cleanliness *o* hygiene **2** (Esp) (retrete) toilet; Ⓢ **aseos** rest room (AmE), toilets (BrE)

aséptico -ca *adj* aseptic

asequible *adj* ‹*precio*› affordable, reasonable; ‹*meta*› attainable, achievable; ‹*proyecto*› feasible; ‹*persona*› approachable; ‹*obra/estilo*› accessible; **la educación debe ser ~ a todos** education should be accessible to all

aserción *f* assertion

aserradero *m* sawmill

aserrador -dora *m,f* sawyer

aserrar [A5] *vt* to saw

aserrín *m* (esp AmL) sawdust

aserrío *m* (Col, Ec) sawmill

aserruchar [A1] *vt* (Chi) to saw

aserto *m* assertion

asesinar [A1] *vt* to murder; (por razones políticas) to assassinate

asesinato *m* murder; (por razones políticas) assassination

asesino[1] -na *adj* ‹*instinto/odio*› murderous, homicidal; ‹*animal*› killer (*before n*); **el arma asesina** the murder weapon; **me lanzó una mirada asesina** (fam) he gave me a murderous look

a

asesino² **-na** *m,f* murderer; (por razones políticas) assassin

Compuestos
- **asesino -na a sueldo** *m,f* hired killer
- **asesino -na en serie** *m,f* serial killer

asesor¹ **-sora** *adj* ‹consejo› advisory; **ingeniero ~** consultant engineer

asesor² **-sora** *m,f* advisor*, consultant

Compuestos
- **asesora del hogar** *f* (Chi frml) maid
- **asesor -sora de imagen** *m,f* public relations consultant *o* advisor
- **asesor -sora fiscal** *m,f* tax consultant
- **asesor -sora militar** *m,f* military advisor*
- **asesor técnico -sora técnica** *m,f* technical consultant

asesoramiento *m* advice

asesorar [A1] *vt* to advise; **se hizo ~ por un abogado** she took legal advice

■ **asesorarse** *v pron* **~se CON** *or* **DE algn** to consult sb; **me asesoré con un abogado** I consulted a lawyer

asesoría *f* consultancy

Compuestos
- **asesoría financiera** financial advice
- **asesoría fiscal/jurídica** tax/legal consultancy

asestar [A1] *vt*: **me asestó una puñalada/un puñetazo** he stabbed/punched me; **le asestó un duro golpe a su orgullo** it dealt a harsh blow to his pride

aseveración *f* assertion, statement

aseverar [A1] *vt* (frml) to assert, state

asexuado -da *adj* asexual

asexual *adj* asexual

asfaltado¹ **-da** *adj* asphalt (*before n*), asphalted

asfaltado² *m* (acción) asphalting; (pavimento) asphalt

asfaltar [A1] *vt* to asphalt

asfalto *m* asphalt

asfixia *f* 1 (Med) asphyxia; **muerte por ~** death by asphyxia *o* suffocation 2 (fam) (agobio) suffocation; **las ciudades me producen una sensación de ~** I find towns suffocating *o* stifling

asfixiante *adj* 1 ‹*gas/humo*› asphyxiating (*before n*) 2 (fam) ‹*calor*› suffocating, stifling 3 (fam) ‹*ambiente/relación*› oppressive, stifling

asfixiar [A1] *vt* 1 (ahogar) to asphyxiate, suffocate; **murió asfixiado** he died of asphyxiation *o* suffocation 2 (agobiar) to suffocate, stifle

■ **asfixiarse** *v pron* 1 (ahogarse) to be asphyxiated, suffocate; (por obstrucción de la tráquea) to choke to death; **tosía tanto que se asfixiaba** he was coughing so much that he couldn't get his breath; **aquí se asfixia uno** (fam) it's suffocating in here; **me asfixiaba de calor** (fam) I was suffocating in the heat 2 (fam) (agobiarse) to suffocate, feel stifled; **está asfixiado de trabajo** he's snowed under with work (colloq)

así¹ *adj inv* like that; **si es ~ te pido disculpas** if that's the case, I'm sorry; **yo soy ~** that's the way I am; **~ es la vida** (fr hecha) that's life; **es un tanto ~ de hojas** it's about *that* many pages; **esperamos horas ¿no es ~?** we waited for hours, didn't we?; **tan** *or* **tanto es ~ que ...** so much so that ...

así² *adv*

A (de este/ese modo): **no le hables ~ a tu padre** don't talk to your father like that; **¡~ cualquiera!** that's cheating! (colloq & hum); **¿~ me lo agradeces?** is this how you thank me?; **no te pongas ~** don't get so worked up; **~ me podré comprar lo que quiera** that way I'll be able to buy whatever I want; **~ me llaman** that's what people call me; **~ es** that's right; **¿está bien ~ o quieres más?** is that enough, or do you want some more?; **¿fue ~ cómo ocurrió?** is that how it happened?; **y ~ sucesivamente** and so on; **¿dimitió? — ~ como lo oyes** you mean he resigned? — believe it or not, yes

B **~ de + ADJ/ADV**: **¡~ de fácil!** it's as easy as that; **debe ser ~ de grueso** it must be about *this* thick; **¿~ de egoísta me crees?** do you think I'm that selfish?

C (expresando deseo): **~ se muera** I hope she drops dead!

D (*en locs*) **así así** (fam) so-so; **así como**: **~ como el mayor trabaja mucho, el pequeño es un vago** while *o* whereas the older boy works very hard, the younger one is really lazy; **por su módico precio ~ como por su calidad** both for its low price and its high quality; **sus familiares, ~ como sus amigos** his family as well as his friends; **así como así** just like that; **¡así me gusta!** (fr hecha) that's what I like to see!; **¿le dijiste que no? ¡~ me gusta!** you said no? good for you!; **así mismo** ▸**asimismo**; **así nomás** (AmL) just like that; **hace los deberes ~ nomás** he dashes his homework off any which way (AmE) *o* (BrE) any old how; **así o asá** (fam): **puedes ponerlo ~ o asá** (fam) you can put it any way you like; **así pues** so; **así que** (por lo tanto) so; (en cuanto) as soon as; **¡~ que te casas!** so, you're getting married ...; **así sea** (Relig) amen; **así y todo** even so; **no así**: **se mostraron muy satisfechos. No ~ los Vives, que ...** they were very pleased, unlike the Vives, who ...; **o así**: **tendrá 30 años o ~** he must be about 30; **cien al mes o ~** around a hundred a month; **por así decirlo** so to speak

así³ *conj* (aunque) **~ + SUBJ**: **lo encontraré, ~ se esconda en el fin del mundo** I'll find him, no matter where he tries to hide; **no pagaré ~ me encarcelen** I won't pay even if they put me in prison

Asia *f*‡ Asia

Compuesto **Asia Menor** Asia Minor

asiático -ca *adj/m,f* Asian, Asiatic

asidero *m* 1 (asa) handle 2 (punto de sujeción) hand (hold) 3 (apoyo): **la religión se convirtió en su ~** religion became her support; **sin ~s en la realidad** with no grip on reality

asiduidad *f* (persistencia) assiduity; (regularidad) regularity

asiduo¹ **-dua** *adj* 1 (persistente) ‹*estudiante/lector*› assiduous; ‹*admirador*› devoted 2 (frecuente) ‹*cliente*› regular

asiduo² **-dua** *m,f* regular, habitué (frml); **~s de la ópera** regular operagoers

asiento *m*

A 1 (para sentarse) seat; **me cedió su ~** he gave up his seat to me; **~ delantero/trasero** front/back seat; **por favor, tome ~** (frml) please take a seat (frml); ***calentar el ~*** (fam): **no tuvo tiempo ni de calentar el ~** he was only here two minutes; **venía a clase sólo para calentar el ~** he only came to school to pass the time 2 (de bicicleta) saddle 3 (de silla) seat 4 (emplazamiento): **una organización con ~ en Roma** an organization based in Rome; **fue ~ de muchas culturas** it was the home *o* seat of many cultures 5 (base, estabilidad) base

Compuestos
- **asiento abatible** recliner (AmE), reclining seat (BrE)
- **asiento anatómico** (fully) adjustable seat
- **asiento expulsor** *or* **proyectable** *or* **de eyección** ejection (AmE) *o* (BrE) ejector seat

B (en contabilidad) entry

C (poso) sediment

D (de válvula) seat

E (Const) settling

asignación *f*

A 1 (de tarea, función) assignment; **la ~ del puesto a su sobrino** the appointment of his nephew to the post 2 (de fondos, renta) allocation, assignment

B (sueldo) wages (*pl*); (paga) allowance

Compuesto **asignación familiar** (CS) benefit (*payable for children and other dependants*)

C (AmC) (Educ) homework

asignar [A1] *vt* 1 (dar, adjudicar) ‹*renta/función/tarea*› to assign; ‹*valor*› to ascribe; ‹*fondos/parcela*› to allocate; **le ~on el papel de mediador** he was assigned the role of mediator; **me ~on la vacante** I was appointed to the post; **le ~on una beca** he was awarded a grant; **un hecho al que se asigna especial importancia** a fact to which special importance is attached 2 (destinar) ‹*persona*› to assign; **~ a algn A algo** to assign sb TO sth

asignatario -ria *m,f* (de herencia) heir; (de legado) legatee; (de bien) assignee

asignatura *f* subject

Compuesto **asignatura pendiente** (Educ) subject which one has to retake; (asunto sin resolver) unresolved matter

asilado -da *m,f* inmate

Compuesto **asilado político -da política** political refugee (*who has been granted asylum*)

asilar [A1] *vt* 1 (acoger) ‹*anciano/huérfano*› to take … into care; ‹*refugiado*› to grant … asylum 2 (internar) to put … in a home

■ **asilarse** *v pron* «*anciano/huérfano*» to take refuge; «*refugiado*» to seek asylum

asilo *m*

A (Servs Socs) home, institution; **un ~ para vagabundos** a shelter for down-and-outs

(Compuesto) **asilo de ancianos** *or* **de la tercera edad** old people's home

B (protección) refuge

(Compuesto) **asilo político** political asylum

asimetría *f* asymmetry

asimétrico -ca *adj* asymmetric

asimilable *adj* ‹*alimentos*› assimilable; **presentar la información de manera fácilmente ~** to present the information in a way that makes it easy to take in *o* to assimilate

asimilación *f* assimilation

asimilado -da *adj* (AmL) ‹*médico/sacerdote*› military (*before n*)

asimilar [A1] *vt*

A ‹*alimentos/ideas/cultura*› to assimilate

B (equiparar) **~ algo/a algn CON** *or* **A algo/algn** to put sth/sb on an equal footing WITH sth/sb

C (en boxeo) ‹*golpes*› to take, soak up (colloq)

asimismo *adv* 1 (también) also; **es ~ necesario crear empleo** it is also necessary to create jobs 2 (igualmente) likewise; **esto facilitará, ~, un aumento de la productividad** likewise, this will increase productivity

asintomático -ca *adj* asymptomatic

asir [I10] *vt* (liter) to seize, grasp; **~ a algn DE** *or* **POR algo**: **la asió de un brazo** he seized *o* grasped her arm

■ **asirse** *v pron* (liter) **~se DE** *or* **A algo**: **se asió a la cuerda** she grabbed (hold of) *o* seized the rope; **caminaban asidos de la mano** they walked hand in hand

asísmico -ca *adj* earthquake-resistant

asistencia *f*

A (presencia) attendance; **~ A algo** attendance AT sth

B (frml) (ayuda) assistance; **prestarle ~ a algn** to give sb assistance

(Compuestos)

- **asistencia en carretera** breakdown service
- **asistencia médica** (servicio) medical care; (atención médica) medical attention
- **asistencia pública** (en CS) municipal health service (*esp for emergencies*)
- **asistencia sanitaria** medical care
- **asistencia social** *university course/degree in social work*
- **asistencia técnica** after-sales service

C (Dep) assist

asistencial *adj* welfare (*before n*)

asistenta *f* (Esp) cleaning lady *o* woman

asistente[1] *adj*: **entre el público ~** among those present; **los delegados ~s a la asamblea** the delegates present at *o* attending the conference

asistente[2] *mf*

A 1 (ayudante) assistant 2 (Mil) batman

(Compuesto) **asistente social** social worker

B (frml) **los/las ~s** (a una reunión) those present; (a un espectáculo) the audience

asistido -da *adj* assisted

asistir [I1] *vi*

A 1 (a reunión, acto) **~ A algo** to attend sth, be present AT sth; **asistió a una sola clase** he only came/went to one class; **~ a misa** to go to *o* attend Mass 2 (frml) (presenciar) **~ A algo** to witness sth, be witness TO sth (frml)

B (Esp) (limpiar) to work as a cleaning lady *o* woman

■ **asistir** *vt* 1 (frml) (ayudar): **en el consulado lo ~án** you will receive assistance at the consulate (frml); **~ a los pobres** to care for the poor 2 (frml) (en un parto) to deliver

asma *f‡* asthma

asmático -ca *adj/m,f* asthmatic

asno[1] **-na** *adj* (fam) dumb (colloq)

asno[2] *m* (Zool) donkey; (tonto) (fam) dimwit (colloq); *para modismos ver* **burro**[2]

asociación *f* association; **en ~ con** in association *o* collaboration with; **derecho de ~** freedom of association *o* assembly; **~ de ideas** association of ideas; **~ cultural/deportiva** cultural/sports association; **una ~ sin ánimo** *or* **afán de lucro** a non-profit association (AmE), a non-profit-making association (BrE)

(Compuestos)

- **asociación de padres de alumnos** parents association
- **asociación de vecinos** residents association
- **asociación sindical** labor (AmE) *o* (BrE) trade union

asociado[1] **-da** *adj* associate (*before n*)

asociado[2] **-da** *m,f* (Com) associate; (de club, asociación) member

asocial *adj* asocial

asociar [A1] *vt* ‹*ideas/palabras*› to associate; **~ algo/a algn CON algo/algn**: **no logro ~la con nada** I can't place her; **asociaba aquel lugar con su niñez** he associated that place with his childhood

■ **asociarse** *v pron* 1 «*empresas/comerciantes*» to collaborate; **~se CON algn** to go into partnership WITH sb 2 «*hechos/factores*» to combine 3 (a grupo, club) **~se A algo** to become a member OF sth 4 (a idea, sentimiento) **~se A algo**: **nos asociamos al duelo nacional** we share in the nation's grief; **me asocio a lo expresado por mi colega** I agree with *o* (frml) concur with the views expressed by my colleague

asocio *m* (Col) association

asolador -dora *adj* devastating

asolar [A1 *or* A10] *vt* «*guerra/huracán/sequía*» to devastate; **un país asolado por el hambre** a country ravaged *o* devastated by hunger

asoleada *f* (Andes) (de una persona): **pegarse una ~** (fam) to sunbathe

asoleado -da *adj* sunny

asolear [A1] *vt* 1 (exponer al sol) ‹*ropa*› to hang … out in the sun; ‹*uvas*› to dry … in the sun 2 (Col fam) (derrotar) to thrash (colloq)

■ **asolearse** *v pron* (AmL) to sunbathe

asomado -da *adj* (Ven) nosy

asomar [A1] *vi* to show; **empiezan a ~ los primeros brotes** the first shoots begin to show *o* appear; **asomaba por entre las páginas** it was sticking out from between the pages; (+ *me/te/le etc*) **la combinación le asomaba por debajo de la falda** her slip was showing below her skirt; **ya le ha asomado el primer diente** he's just cut his first tooth; **le asomaba la cabeza por entre las sábanas** her head was sticking out from under the sheets; **una sonrisa le asomó a los labios** (liter) a smile flickered across her lips

■ **asomar** *vt* ‹*cabeza*›: ⊘ **no asomar la cabeza por la ventanilla** do not lean out of the window; **abrió la puerta y asomó la cabeza** she opened the door and stuck her head out/in

■ **asomarse** *v pron*: ⊘ **es peligroso asomarse** do not lean out of the window; **~se POR algo** to lean out OF sth; **~se A algo**: **asómate a la ventana a ver si vienen** have a look out (of the window) and see if they are coming; **cuando se asomó a la ventana le dispararon** when he appeared at the window they fired at him; **estaba asomada a la ventana** she was looking out of the window; **se habían asomado al balcón para ver el desfile** they had come out onto the balcony to watch the procession

asombrar [A1] *vt* to amaze, astonish; **me dejó asombrada** I was stunned *o* amazed; **me asombró su reacción** I was astonished *o* taken aback by his reaction

■ **asombrarse** *v pron* to be astonished *o* amazed; **~se DE/POR/CON algo**: **se asombró con los resultados** she was amazed *o* astonished at the results; **yo ya no me asombro por nada** nothing surprises me any more; **se asombró de que …** he was very surprised that …

asombro *m* astonishment; **miraba con ~ cómo caía la nieve** she watched the falling snow in wonderment; **no salía de su ~** he couldn't get over his surprise

asombroso -sa *adj* amazing, astonishing

asomo *m* (*gen en frases negativas*): **sin el menor ~ de duda** without a shadow of a doubt; **no tiene el más mínimo ~ de pudor/decencia** he doesn't have an ounce of

a

shame/a shred of decency in him; **al primer ~ de violencia** at the first sign of violence; ***ni por ~***: **no es el mejor ¡ni por ~!** it isn't the best, not by a long shot (colloq); **no se parecen ni por ~** there isn't the slightest resemblance between them; **eso no se me ocurriría ni por ~** I wouldn't dream of it

asonada *f* 1 (intentona) attempted coup 2 (motín) violent protest

asonante *adj* assonant

asorocharse [A1] *v pron* 1 (Chi, Per) (por la altura) to get mountain *o* altitude sickness 2 (Chi) (por calor, vergüenza) to flush

aspa *f‡* 1 (de molino) sail; (de ventilador) blade; (cruz) cross 2 (Arg) (asta) horn

aspaventero -ra *adj* excitable

aspaviento *m*: **deja de hacer ~s** stop getting in such a flap

aspecto *m*

A 1 (de persona, lugar) appearance; **un hombre de ~ distinguido** a distinguished-looking man; **le da ~ de intelectual** it makes him look rather intellectual *o* gives him an intellectual look; **¿qué ~ tiene?** what does he look like?; **esa herida tiene muy mal ~** that wound looks nasty 2 (de problema, asunto): **no me gusta el ~ que van tomando las cosas** I don't like the way things are going *o* looking

B (rasgo, faceta): **quisiera aclarar algunos ~s del asunto** there are a few aspects of the matter I'd like to get cleared up; **en ese ~ tienes razón** in that respect you're right

ásperamente *adv* harshly

aspereza *f*

A 1 (al tacto) roughness; (de terreno) roughness, unevenness 2 (de sabor) sharpness; (de voz, clima) harshness

B (parte áspera): **usar papel de lija para quitar las ~s** use sandpaper to remove any roughness; **un terreno lleno de ~s** a very uneven *o* rough piece of ground; ***limar ~s***: **el tiempo limó las ~s de su personalidad** time knocked the rough edges off her; **en un intento de limar ~s** in an attempt to iron out their differences

C (brusquedad) abruptness, surliness

asperjar [A1] *vt* (Agr) to spray; (Relig) to sprinkle ... with holy water

áspero -ra *adj*

A 1 ‹*superficie/piel*› rough; **una tela áspera** a coarse material 2 ‹*terreno*› uneven, rough

B 1 ‹*sabor*› sharp 2 ‹*voz/sonido/clima*› harsh

C 1 (en el trato) abrupt, surly 2 ‹*discusión*› acrimonious

aspersión *f* 1 (Agr) spraying; **riego por ~** irrigation by sprinkler 2 (Relig) sprinkling of holy water

aspersor *m* sprinkler

áspid *m* asp

aspillera *f* loophole

aspiración *f*

A (deseo, ambición) aspiration

B (Fisiol) inhalation; (Ling) aspiration; (Mús) breath; (Tec) draft (AmE), draught (BrE)

aspiradora *f*, **aspirador** *m* 1 (electrodoméstico) vacuum cleaner; **pasé la ~ por la habitación** I vacuumed *o* (BrE) hoovered the bedroom 2 **aspirador** *m* (Med) aspirator

aspirante¹ *adj* 1 ‹*persona*› **~ A algo**: **los alumnos ~s a becas** students who wish to be awarded scholarships 2 ‹*bomba*› suction (*before n*)

aspirante² *mf* **~ A algo**: **las ~s al título** the contenders for the title; **ocho ~s al puesto de redactor** eight candidates *o* applicants for the post of editor

aspirar [A1] *vi*

A (desear, pretender) **~ A algo/+ INF** to aspire to sth/+ INF; **aspira a (ser) alcalde** he aspires to become mayor; **~ a la mano de una chica** to seek a girl's hand in marriage (frml)

B 1 «*aparato*» to suck; «*aspiradora*» to pick up 2 (Fisiol) to breathe in 3 (AmL) (pasar la aspiradora) to vacuum, hoover (BrE)

■ **aspirar** *vt* 1 «*aparato*» to suck up *o* in; «*aspiradora*» to pick up 2 (Fisiol) to inhale 3 (Ling) to aspirate

aspirina *f* aspirin

asqueante *adj* sickening, nauseating

asquear [A1] *vt* (dar asco a) to sicken; (aburrir, hartar): **está asqueado de todo** he's fed up with everything (colloq); **me asquea tanta corrupción** I find all this corruption sickening

asquerosamente *adv*: **nos trató ~** the way he treated us was disgusting; **~ atractivo/rico** (fam & hum) sickeningly attractive/disgustingly rich (colloq & hum)

asquerosidad *f*: **tiene la casa hecha una ~** his house is in an absolutely filthy state; **¡que ~ de comida!** what disgusting food!

asqueroso¹ -sa *adj*

A 1 ‹*libro/película*› disgusting, filthy 2 ‹*olor/comida/costumbre*› disgusting, revolting; **estaba ~ de sucio** it was absolutely filthy

B 1 (fam) (malo, egoísta) mean (colloq), horrible (BrE colloq) 2 (lascivo): **¡viejo ~!** you dirty old man!

asqueroso² -sa *m,f*

A (sucio): **eres un ~** you're disgusting

B (fam) (malo, egoísta) meany (colloq); **es un ~** he's such a meany

asquiento -ta *adj*

A (AmL) ▸**asqueroso¹**

B (Chi fam) (delicado, aprensivo) squeamish

asta *f‡* 1 (de bandera) flagpole; **con la bandera a media ~** with the flag at half-mast 2 (cuerno) horn; ***dejar a algn en las ~s del toro*** to leave sb in the lurch 3 (de lanza, flecha) shaft

astabandera *f* (Méx) flagpole

astado -da *adj* horned

áster *m* aster

asterisco *m* asterisk

asteroide *m* asteroid

astigmático -ca *adj* astigmatic

astigmatismo *m* astigmatism

astil *m* (de herramienta) handle; (de flecha, pluma) shaft; (de balanza) beam

astilla *f* 1 (fragmento) chip; **se me ha metido una ~ en el dedo** I have a splinter in my finger 2 **astillas** *fpl* (para el fuego) kindling

astillar [A1] *vt* to splinter

■ **astillarse** *v pron* «*madera/hueso*» to splinter; «*piedra*» to chip

astillero *m* shipyard

astracán *m* astrakhan

astral *adj* astral

astringente¹ *adj* ‹*loción*› astringent; ‹*alimento/medicamento*› binding (*before n*)

astringente² *m* astringent

astringir [I7] *vi* to bind

astro *m* (Astrol, Astron) heavenly body; (Espec) star

astrofísica *f* astrophysics

astrología *f* astrology

astrológico -ca *adj* astrological

astrólogo -ga *m,f* astrologist

astronauta *mf* astronaut

astronave *f* spaceship

astronomía *f* astronomy

astronómico -ca *adj* astronomical

astrónomo -ma *m,f* astronomer

astroso -sa *adj* shabby, down at heel

astucia *f* 1 (cualidad — de sagaz) astuteness, shrewdness; (— de taimado) (pey) craftiness, cunning; **la ~ del zorro** the slyness of a fox 2 (ardid) trick, ploy

asturiano -na *adj/mf* Asturian

> **asturiano**
> ▸bable

astutamente *adv* (con sagacia) cleverly, astutely; (con malicia) (pey) craftily, cunningly

astuto -ta *adj* (sagaz) shrewd, astute; (pey) (taimado) crafty, cunning

asueto *m* time off; **tomarse un día de ~** to take a day off

asumir [I1] *vt*
A 1 ‹*cargo/tarea/responsabilidad*› to take on, assume (frml); **asumió el mando del regimiento** he assumed command of the regiment; **no estoy dispuesto a ~ ese riesgo** I am not prepared to take that risk 2 (adquirir) ‹*importancia/dimensiones*› to assume (frml); **la situación asumió una gravedad inusitada** the situation became unusually serious; **el incendio asumió grandes proporciones** it turned into a major fire 3 (adoptar) ‹*actitud*› to assume (liter); **asumió un aire de indiferencia** he assumed an air of indifference 4 (aceptar) to come to terms with; **ya tengo asumido el problema** I've come to terms with the problem now; **debe ~ las consecuencias de sus errores** he must accept the consequences of his mistakes
B (AmL) (suponer) to assume

asunceno¹ -na, asunceño -ña *adj* of/from Asunción

asunceno² -na, asunceño -ña *m,f* person from Asunción

asunción *f*
A 1 (de responsabilidad) taking on, assumption (frml); **desde su ~ del cargo** since he took on *o* (frml) assumed the post 2 (aceptación) acceptance; **esta ~ de valores occidentales** this adoption *o* acceptance of western values
B (Relig) **la Asunción** the Assumption

Asunción *f* (Geog) Asunción

asunto *m* 1 (cuestión, problema) matter; **un ~ muy delicado** a very delicate matter *o* issue; **se pelearon por el ~ de la herencia** they fell out over the inheritance; **está implicado en un ~ de drogas** he's mixed up in something to do with drugs; **~s de negocios** business matters; **no es ~ tuyo** it's none of your business; ***y ~ concluido***: **te he dicho que no y ~ concluido** I've said no and that's that; **te quedarás en casa y ~ concluido** you're staying at home and that's all there is to it 2 (pey) (relación amorosa) affair; **tuvo un asuntillo con la secretaria** he had a brief fling with his secretary 3 (CS fam) (razón, sentido): **¿a ~ de qué se lo dijiste?** what did you go and tell him for? (colloq), why on earth did you tell him? (colloq); **¿a ~ de qué voy a ir?** what on earth's the point of my going? (colloq)

asustadizo -za *adj* ‹*persona*› nervous, jumpy; ‹*animal*› skittish, easily frightened

asustado -da *adj* (atemorizado) frightened; (preocupado) worried; **los niños estaban muy ~s** the children were very frightened; **tiene algo del pulmón y está ~** he has something wrong with his lung and he's really worried

asustar [A1] *vt* to frighten; **me asustó cuando se puso tan serio** he gave me a fright when he went all serious; **nada lo asusta** he's not frightened *o* scared by anything
■ **asustarse** *v pron* to get frightened; **me asusté cuando vi que no estaba allí** I got a fright *o* I got worried when I saw he wasn't there; **no se asuste, no es nada grave** there's no need to worry *o* to be alarmed, it's nothing serious

atabal *m* kettledrum

atacador *m* tamper

atacante¹ *adj* (Chi, Ur fam) infuriating; **su machismo me resulta ~** his male chauvinism really gets on my nerves (colloq)

atacante² *mf* attacker, assailant (frml)

atacar [A2] *vt*
A ‹*país/enemigo/ideas*› to attack; **la atacó por la espalda** he attacked her from behind
B «*ácido/virus/enfermedad*» to attack; **ataca el sistema nervioso** it attacks the nervous system
C 1 (combatir) ‹*problema/enfermedad*› to attack 2 (acometer) ‹*tarea*› to tackle; ‹*pieza musical*› to launch into 3 (Ven fam) (cortejar) to go after
■ **atacar** *vi* to attack

ataché *m* (RPl) briefcase, attaché case

atacón -cona *m,f* (Ven fam) (persona) (*m*) woman-chaser; (*f*) man-chaser

atadijo *m* loose bundle

atado *m* 1 (de ropa) bundle 2 (CS) (de espinacas, zanahorias) bunch; ***ser un ~ de nervios*** (CS) to be a bundle of nerves 3 (RPl) (de cigarrillos) pack (AmE), packet (BrE)

ataduras *fpl* ties (*pl*); **romper las ~ familiares** to break the family ties

atafagar [A3] *vt* (Col fam) to hassle (colloq)

atafago, atafague *m* (Col fam): **hubo un ~ horrible en la oficina** things were really hectic in the office; **el ~ de manejar en Bogotá** the hassle of driving in Bogota

atajada *f* (CS) save

atajador -dora (Méx) (*m*) ballboy; (*f*) ballgirl

atajar [A1] *vt*
A 1 (AmL) (agarrar) ‹*pelota*› to catch 2 (Esp) (interceptar) ‹*pase/pelota*› to intercept
B 1 ‹*golpe/puñetazo*› to parry, block 2 ‹*persona*› (agarrar) to stop, catch; (interrumpir, detener) to stop; **¡atájalo!** catch *o* stop him!
C ‹*enfermedad*› to keep ... in check; ‹*incendio*› to contain, check the spread of; ‹*rumor*› to quell; **la manera de ~ este problema** the way to keep this problem under control *o* in check
■ **atajar** *vi*
A (por calle, camino): **~on por una callejuela** they took a short cut down an alley; **podemos ~ por el parque** we can cut across the park
B (Méx) (en tenis) to pick up the balls

atajo *m* short cut; **vamos por el ~** let's take the short cut; **~ de teclado** shortcut key; ***echar*** *or* ***salir por el ~*** to take the easy way out; ***ponerle ~ a algo*** (Chi) to put a stop to sth

atalaya *f*
A (torre) watchtower; (lugar) vantage point
B **atalaya** *mf* (persona) sentinel, lookout

atañer [E7] *vi* (*en 3ª pers*) to concern; **por lo que a mi atañe** as far as I'm concerned

atapuzarse [A4] *v pron* (Ven fam) to guzzle (down) (colloq); **~se DE algo** to stuff oneself WITH sth (colloq)

ataque *m*
A 1 (Dep, Mil) attack; **~ aéreo** air raid; **~ por sorpresa** surprise attack 2 (verbal) attack; **lanzó un duro ~ contra el gobierno** he launched a sharp *o* fierce attack on the government
B (acceso) fit; **un ~ de celos/ira** a fit of jealousy/rage; **si la ves te va a dar un ~ de risa** you'll die laughing if you see her (colloq)

Compuestos
- **ataque cardíaco** *or* **al corazón** heart attack
- **ataque de nervios**: **me dio un ~ de nervios** I got into a panic

atar [A1] *vt*
A 1 ‹*caja/planta*› to tie; **le até el pelo con una cinta** I tied her hair back with a ribbon; **con un pañuelo atado al cuello** with a scarf (tied) round his neck 2 ‹*persona/caballo*› to tie ... up; ‹*cabra*› to tether; **lo ~on de pies y manos** they bound him hand and foot; *ver tb* **pie¹ A2**; **ató al perro a una farola** she tied the dog to a lamppost
B «*trabajo/hijos*» to tie ... down; **no hay nada que me ate a esta ciudad** there's nothing to keep me in this town; ***~ corto a algn*** to keep sb on a tight rein
■ **atar** *vi* «*trabajo/hijos*»: **es un trabajo que ata mucho** it's a job that really ties you down; ***ni ata ni desata*** (es inútil) he's useless; (no tiene autoridad) he has no say *o* authority
■ **atarse** *v pron* (*refl*) ‹*zapatos/cordones*› to tie up, do up; ‹*pelo*› to tie up

atarantado -da *adj* 1 (Col, Méx, Per fam) (tonto) dopey (colloq) 2 (Col, Méx, Per fam) (por golpe) dazed, stunned 3 (Méx, Per fam) (confundido) in a spin, dazed 4 (Chi fam) (precipitado) harum-scarum (colloq)

atarantar [A1] *vt* (Col, Méx, Per fam): **con tantas preguntas me ~on** they made my head spin with all their questions; **el golpe lo atarantó** the blow left him dazed
■ **atarantarse** *v pron* 1 (Col, Méx, Per fam) (aturdirse, confundirse) to get flustered, get in a dither 2 (Chi fam) (precipitarse): **no te atarantes** don't rush into it (colloq)

atarazana *f* shipyard

atardecer¹ [E3] *v impers* to get dark

atardecer² *m* dusk; **al ~** at dusk; **un ~ de otoño** one autumn evening at dusk

atareado -da *adj* busy

atarraya *f* (Col) fishnet

a

atarugarse [A3] *v pron* (Méx fam) to get flustered (colloq)

atascadero *m*
A (de tráfico) bottleneck
B ▸**atolladero 2, 3**

atascar [A2] *vt*
A ‹*cañería*› to block
B (Méx) ‹*motor*› to stall
■ **atascarse** *v pron*
A 1 «*cañería/fregadero*» to block, get blocked 2 «*tráfico*» to get snarled up; **nos atascamos a la entrada de la ciudad** we got stuck in a traffic jam coming into the city 3 (fam) «*persona*» (al hablar) to dry up; (en examen) to get stuck; **estamos atascados con esto** we're bogged down *o* stuck on this point
B 1 «*mecanismo*» to jam, seize up; **la cerradura está atascada** the lock's jammed 2 (Méx) «*motor*» to stall

atasco *m* 1 (de tráfico) traffic jam; (en proceso) holdup, delay 2 (en tubería) blockage

ataúd *m* coffin

ataviar [A17] *vt* (liter) ~ **a algn con algo** to attire sb IN sth (liter)
■ **ataviarse** *v pron* (liter) ~**se con algo** to attire oneself IN sth (liter)

atávico -ca *adj* atavistic

atavío *m* (liter) attire (liter); **en ~s muy poco adecuados** very unsuitably attired (frml)

ateísmo *m* atheism

atembado -da *adj* (Col fam) dozy (colloq), dopey (colloq); (por un golpe) dazed

atemorizar [A4] *vt* (liter) ‹*persona*› to frighten, intimidate; ‹*barrio/población*› to terrorize
■ **atemorizarse** *v pron* (liter) to take fright (liter)

atemperar [A1] *vt* to temper

Atenas *f* Athens

atenazar [A4] *vt* (liter) to grip (liter); **el miedo los atenazaba** they were gripped by fear (liter)

atención[1] *f*
A 1 (concentración) attention; **quisiera dedicarle más ~ a esto** I'd like to give this more attention; **con ~** attentively; **pon ~ en lo que haces** concentrate on *o* pay attention to what you're doing; **presta ~ a esto** pay attention *o* listen carefully to this; **atraer la ~ del camarero** to attract *o* get the waiter's attention; **ser el centro de (la) ~** to be the center of attention 2 **llamar la ~: se viste así para llamar la ~** he dresses like that to attract attention (to himself); **una chica que llama la ~** a very striking girl; **lo dulce no me llama la ~** I'm not very fond of sweet things; **me llamó la ~ que estuviera sola** I was surprised she was alone; **llamarle la ~ a algn** (reprenderlo) to reprimand sb (frml), to give sb a talking to; (hacerle notar algo): **les llamé la ~ sobre ...** I drew their attention to ... 3 (*en locs*) **a la atención de** (Corresp) for the attention of; **en atención a algo** (frml) in view of sth
B 1 (servicio): **la ~ que recibimos en el consulado** the way we were treated *o* the treatment we received in the consulate; Ⓢ **horario de atención al público** (en banco) hours of business; (en oficina pública) opening hours; Ⓢ **departamento de atención al cliente** customer service department (AmE), customer services department (BrE) 2 (cortesía): **nos colmaron de atenciones** we were showered with attention *o* (BrE) attentions; **no tuvo ninguna ~ con ella a pesar de su hospitalidad** he didn't show the slightest appreciation despite her hospitality; **¡cúantas atenciones! estoy abrumado** how kind! I'm overwhelmed

atención[2] *interj* 1 (Mil) attention! 2 (para que se atienda): **¡~! están dando los resultados** listen! they're reading out the results; **¡~, por favor!** (your) attention, please! 3 (para avisar de peligro) look out!, watch out!; Ⓢ **¡atención!** danger!, warning!

atender [E8] *vi*
A 1 (prestar atención) to pay attention; **~ A algo/algn** to pay attention TO sth/sb; **atiéndeme cuando te hablo** listen to me *o* pay attention when I'm talking to you 2 (cumplir con) **~ A algo** ‹*a compromisos/gastos/obligaciones*› to meet sth; **no pudo ~ a sus deberes** he was unable to carry out his duties 3 (tener en cuenta, considerar) **~ A algo: atendiendo a su estado de salud ...** given his state of health *o* bearing in mind his state of health ...; **atendiendo a sus instrucciones** in accordance with your instructions 4 (prestar un servicio): **el doctor no atiende los martes** the doctor does not see anyone on Tuesdays; **en esa tienda atienden muy mal** the service is very bad in that store
B **atender por** (frml) (responder): **atiende por (el nombre de) Sinda** she answers to the name of Sinda
■ **atender** *vt*
A 1 ‹*enfermo*›: **¿qué médico la atiende?** which doctor usually sees you?; **el médico que me atendió durante mi enfermedad** the doctor who treated me while I was sick; **los atendieron enseguida en el hospital** they were seen immediately at the hospital; **no tiene quien lo atienda** he has no one to look after him 2 ‹*cliente*› to attend to, see to; (en tienda) to serve; **¿la están atendiendo?** are you being served?; **el Sr Gil no lo puede ~ en este momento** I'm afraid Mr Gil can't see you *o* is unavailable at the moment 3 ‹*asunto*› to deal with; ‹*llamada*› to answer; ‹*demanda*› to meet
B ‹*consejo/advertencia*› to listen to, heed (frml)
■ **atenderse** *v pron* (AmL) **~se con algn: ¿con qué médico se atiende?** which doctor usually sees you?

atenerse [E27] *v pron* 1 (ajustarse, someterse) **~ A algo: ~ a las reglas** to abide by *o* comply with the rules; **me atengo a las órdenes recibidas** I am obeying orders; **no sé a qué atenerme** I don't know what I should be doing; **~ a las consecuencias** to live with *o* abide by the consequences 2 (limitarse) **~ A algo: si nos atenemos a lo que dijeron ellos ...** if we go by what they said ...; **aténgase a los hechos** confine yourself to the facts

atenido -da *m,f* (Col fam) impractical person

atentado *m* 1 (ataque): **un ~ terrorista** a terrorist attack; **un ~ contra el presidente** an assassination attempt on the president 2 (afrenta) **~ A** *or* **CONTRA algo:** ‹*a honor/dignidad/moral*› affront TO sth

atentamente *adv* 1 ‹*escuchar/mirar*› attentively, carefully 2 (amablemente) thoughtfully, kindly; **lo saluda ~** (Corresp) sincerely (AmE), yours faithfully/sincerely (BrE)

atentar [A1] *vi* **~ CONTRA algo: ~on contra su vida** they made an attempt on her life; **estás atentando contra tu salud** you're putting your health at risk; **~ contra la seguridad del Estado** to threaten national security

atento -ta *adj*
A 1 (que presta atención) ‹*alumno/público*› attentive; **estáte ~** pay attention; **estar ~ A algo** to pay attention TO sth 2 (alerta): **estáte ~ y avísame si viene alguien** stay alert and let me know if anyone comes; **estar ~ A algo** to be on the alert FOR sth; **¡~! ¡que te quemás!** (*como interj*) (RPl) watch out, you'll burn yourself!
B 1 (amable) ‹*esposo/anfitrión/camarero*› attentive; **ser ~ CON algn** to be kind TO sb; **en respuesta a su atenta carta** (Corresp) (frml) in reply to your kind letter 2 (cortés) courteous

atenuación *f* (moderación) toning down; (de responsabilidad) reduction

atenuante[1] *adj* extenuating

atenuante[2] *m* or *f* mitigating factor, extenuating circumstance

atenuar [A18] *vt* 1 (disminuir, moderar) ‹*luz*› to dim; ‹*color*› to tone down; **deberías ~ el tono de tus críticas** you should tone down your criticism 2 (Der) ‹*responsabilidad*› to reduce, lessen
■ **atenuarse** *v pron* «*dolor*» to ease; **su optimismo se ha visto últimamente atenuado** his optimism has been tempered of late

ateo[1], **atea** *adj* atheistic

ateo[2], **atea** *m,f* atheist

aterciopelado -da *adj* velvety

aterido -da *adj* frozen; **~ de frío** numb with cold, frozen stiff

aterrador -dora *adj* terrifying

aterrar [A1] *vt* ‹*persona*› to terrify; **le aterra la idea** she's terrified at the thought

aterrizaje *m* landing; **hacer un ~ forzoso** to make a forced *o* an emergency landing

aterrizar [A4] *vi* to land, touch down

aterrorizado -da *adj* terrified

aterrorizador -dora *adj* terrifying

aterrorizar [A4] *vt* to terrorize

atesoramiento *m* hoarding
atesorar [A1] *vt* ‹*dinero*› to amass
atestado[1] **-da** *adj* packed, crammed; **~ DE algo** packed *o* crammed full OF sth; **seis cajas atestadas de libros** six boxes crammed *o* packed full of books; **el salón estaba ~ (de gente)** the hall was packed *o* crammed (with people)
atestado[2] *m* statement, attestation (frml); **hacer un ~** to make a statement
atestar *vt*
A [A5 *or* A1] (llenar) ‹*local/plaza*› to pack; ‹*caja/cajón*› **~ algo DE algo** to pack WITH *o* full OF sth
B [A1] (Der) ‹*firma*› to witness
■ **atestar** *vi* [A1] (Der) to testify
■ **atestarse** *v pron* [A5 *or* A1] **~se DE algo** to stuff oneself WITH sth
atestiguar [A16] *vt* **1** (Der) to testify **2** (probar) to bear witness to; **los resultados atestiguan el esfuerzo realizado** the results bear witness to the amount of effort involved
■ **atestiguar** *vi* to testify
atezado -da *adj* (liter) bronzed
atiborrar [A1] *vt* **~ algo/a algn DE algo** to stuff sth/sb WITH sth; **la habitación estaba atiborrada de libros** the room was stuffed *o* crammed full of books; **atiborrado de gente** packed *o* jam-packed with people
■ **atiborrarse** *v pron* **~se DE algo** to stuff oneself WITH sth, to stuff oneself full OF sth
ático *m* **1** (apartamento) top-floor apartment *o* (BrE) flat; (de lujo) penthouse; (de techo bajo) garret (AmE), attic flat (BrE) **2** (desván) attic, loft (BrE)
atienda, atiendas, etc *see* **atender**
atigrado -da *adj* ‹*gato*› tabby; ‹*pelaje*› striped
atildado -da *adj* (liter): **una mujer muy atildada** a woman of immaculate appearance (liter)
atinado -da *adj* ‹*respuesta/comentario*› pertinent, spot-on (colloq); ‹*decisión/medida*› sensible, wise; ‹*solución*› sensible; **no estuviste muy ~ al decirle eso** it wasn't very clever of you to tell her that
atinar [A1] *vi*: **~ en el blanco** to hit the target; **¡atinaste!** you're dead right!; **~ A + INF**: **no atino a enhebrar la aguja** I can't (seem to) get the needle threaded; **no atiné a decir nada** I couldn't say a word; **por suerte atinó a agarrarla de un brazo** luckily he managed to grab hold of her arm; **~ CON algo** ‹*con solución/respuesta*› to hit ON *o* UPON sth, come up WITH sth; **atiné con la talla** I got the size right; **atinaste con el regalo** the gift you got him/her was perfect; **no atinaba con la calle** I couldn't find the street; **los médicos no atinan con el diagnóstico** the doctors can't work out what's wrong with her
atingencia *f*
A (AmL) (relación): **no tiene ~ con el tema** it has no bearing on *o* relevance to the subject
B (Per) (acotación) comment, observation (frml)
atípico -ca *adj* atypical
atiplado -da *adj* high-pitched
atirantar [A1] *vt* to tighten
atisbar [A1] *vt* **1** (vislumbrar): **~on a lo lejos unas casas** (liter) they sighted *o* (liter) discerned a few houses in the distance; **se atisban indicios de mejoría** (period) we are beginning to detect signs of improvement **2** (espiar) to spy on, watch; (mirar furtivamente) to peep at
■ **atisbar** *vi* (liter) to look out
atisbo *m*: **hay ~s de mejoría** there are signs of improvement; **una poesía con pequeños ~s de inspiración** poetry with occasional glimpses of inspiration
atiza *interj* golly! (dated), wow! (colloq)
atizador *m* poker
atizar [A4] *vt*
A ‹*fuego*› to poke; ‹*pasiones/discordia*› to stir up
B (fam) (pegar): **le atizó un bofetón/un puñetazo** she slapped/punched him
■ **atizar** *vi* (Méx arg) (fumar marihuana) to smoke pot *o* dope (colloq)
■ **atizarse** *v pron*
A (fam) ‹‹*comida*›› to put away (colloq); ‹‹*cerveza/whisky*›› to knock back (colloq)
B (Méx arg) (drogarse) to get stoned *o* wasted (sl)

Atlántico *m*: **el (océano) ~** the Atlantic (Ocean)
Atlántida *f*: **la ~** Atlantis
atlas *m* (*pl* **~**) atlas
atleta *mf* athlete
atlético -ca *adj* **1** ‹*club/competición*› athletics (*before n*) **2** ‹*figura*› athletic
atletismo *m* athletics
atmósfera *f* atmosphere; **~ cargada** stuffy atmosphere; **se respira una ~ de tensión** one feels an atmosphere of tension
atmosférico -ca *adj* atmospheric
atochamiento *m* (Chi) (de vehículos) traffic jam, tailback; (de mercaderías) backlog, build-up
atole *m* (Méx) hot corn *o* maize drink; ***darle ~ con el dedo a algn*** (Méx fam) to string sb along (colloq)
atolladero *m* **1** (lugar cenagoso) mire **2** (aglomeración): **la estación era un ~** the station was horribly congested; **la plaza era un ~ de coches** the square was jam-packed with cars **3** (aprieto, apuro) predicament, awkward situation
atollarse [A1] *v pron* to get bogged down *o* stuck
atolondrado[1] **-da** *adj* **1** [SER] (impetuoso) rash, impetuous; (despistado) scatterbrained **2** [ESTAR] (por golpe) dazed, stunned
atolondrado[2] **-da** *m,f* scatterbrain
atolondrar [A1] *vt* **1** (confundir) to fluster **2** ‹‹*golpe*›› to daze, stun
■ **atolondrarse** *v pron* **1** (confundirse) to get flustered **2** (precipitarse): **no te atolondres** don't rush
atómico -ca *adj* atomic
atomizador *m* spray, atomizer
atomizar [A4] *vt* **1** (fragmentar) ‹*organización*› to fragment **2** (con atomizador) to spray
átomo *m* atom; ***ni un ~ de*** (fam): **no tiene ni un ~ de sensatez** he hasn't an ounce *o* an iota of sense
atonal *adj* atonal
atonía *f* lethargy, atony (tech)
atónito -ta *adj* astonished, amazed; **me quedé ~** I was astonished *o* (colloq) flabbergasted; **se quedó mirándola ~** he stared at her in amazement
átono -na *adj* atonic, unstressed
atontado -da *adj* (por golpe, asombro) stunned, dazed; (distraído): **contesta, que estás medio ~** answer me, you're in a daze; **está como ~** he's in a world of his own
atontamiento *m* daze
atontar [A1] *vt* ‹‹*golpe*›› to stun, daze; **las pastillas me ~on** the pills made me feel groggy; **la televisión los atonta** television turns them into vegetables *o* zombies
atorar [A1] *vt*
A (esp AmL) ‹*cañería*› to block (up)
B (Méx) (sujetar): **atoramos la puerta con una silla** we jammed the door shut/open with a chair; **atóralo con este alambre** secure it with this bit of wire
C (Ven fam) (acosar) to go on at
■ **atorarse** *v pron* (esp AmL) **1** (atragantarse) to choke **2** ‹‹*cañería*›› to get blocked; ‹‹*puerta/cajón*›› to jam; (+ *me/te/le etc*): **se me atoró el cierre** my zipper got stuck; **se le atoró el chicle en la garganta** the chewing gum got stuck in her throat
atormentar [A1] *vt* **1** ‹‹*persona*›› (físicamente) to torture; (mentalmente) to torment **2** ‹‹*dolor/celos*››: **este dolor me está atormentando** this pain is driving me crazy; **atormentado por los celos/el remordimiento** tormented by jealousy/guilt
■ **atormentarse** *v pron* (*refl*) to torment oneself
atornillar [A1] *vt* to screw on (*o* down *etc*); **~ algo A algo** to screw sth TO sth
atorrante[1] *adj*
A (Andes, CS fam) (holgazán) lazy; (desaseado) scruffy
B (Bol, RPl fam) (sinvergüenza) crooked
C (Col, Per fam) (pesado, cargante): **no seas ~** don't be such a pain in the neck (colloq)
atorrante[2] *mf*
A (Andes, CS fam) **1** (vagabundo) tramp **2** (holgazán) good-for-nothing, layabout; (desaseado) slob (colloq)
B (Bol, RPl fam) (sinvergüenza): **es un ~** he's a bit of a crook (colloq); **a ver, ~, que te lavo esa cara** come on you little

terror, let's wash that face (colloq)
C (Col, Per fam) (pesado, cargante) pain in the neck (colloq)

atortolado -da *adj*
A (fam) ‹*enamorados*› lovey-dovey (colloq)
B (Col fam) (sorprendido) flabbergasted (colloq), amazed; (nervioso) in a state (colloq)

atortolar [A1] *vt* (Col fam) to amaze
■ **atortolarse** *v pron* (Col fam) to lose one's cool (colloq), to get in a state (colloq)

atosigar [A3] *vt* (importunar) to pester, hassle (colloq); (presionar) to pressure (AmE), to pressurize (BrE)

atrabancado -da *adj* (Méx fam) (precipitado) rash, reckless

atracada *f* (Per fam) ▸**atracón**

atracadera *f* (Per fam) traffic jam

atracadero *m* mooring

atracador -dora *m,f* (de banco) bank robber, raider (journ); (de persona) mugger

atracar [A2] *vi* «*barco*» to dock, berth
■ **atracar** *vt*
A (asaltar) ‹*banco*› to hold up; ‹*persona*› to mug
B (Chi fam) (acercar, aproximar): **atrácalos más** shove them closer together (colloq); **atracó la silla a la pared** she put the chair against the wall
■ **atracarse** *v pron*
A (fam) **~se DE algo** ‹*de comida*› to stuff oneself WITH sth, gorge oneself ON sth
B (Per, Ven) (al hablar) to dry up
C (*refl*) (Chi fam) (aproximarse): **atrácate a mí** stick close to me; **se atracó al fuego** he drew near to the fire

atracción *f* attraction; **siente una gran ~ por ella** he feels strongly attracted to her; **París ejerce una ~ irresistible sobre él** Paris holds an irresistible attraction for him; **la ~ más concurrida** the most popular attraction; **las atracciones están en la playa** the funfair is on the beach

atraco *m* (a banco) robbery, raid (journ); (a persona) mugging; **¡qué precios, esto es un ~!** (fam) these prices are ridiculous, it's daylight robbery! (colloq)
(Compuesto) **atraco a mano armada** armed robbery

atracón *m* (fam): **se dio un ~ de paella** he stuffed himself with paella (colloq)

atractivo¹ -va *adj* attractive

atractivo² *m* charm, attractiveness; **tiene mucho ~** she's very charming; **el mayor ~ de la ciudad** the city's main attraction *o* appeal; **la oferta no tiene ningún ~ para mí** I don't find the offer at all attractive

atraer [E23] *vt* **1** (Fís) to attract **2** (traer, hacer venir) to attract; **un truco para ~ al público** a gimmick to attract the public; **la atrajo hacia sí** he drew her toward(s) him **3** (cautivar, gustar): **se siente atraído por ella** he feels attracted to her; **no me atrae la idea** the idea doesn't attract me *o* appeal to me; **no me atraen mucho las fiestas** I'm not very fond of parties **4** ‹*atención/miradas*› to attract
■ **atraerse** *v pron* **1** (ganarse) ‹*amistad*› to gain; ‹*interés*› to attract **2** (*recípr*) to attract (each other); **los polos opuestos se atraen** opposite poles attract

atragantarse [A1] *v pron* **1** (al tragar) to choke; **se le atragantó una espina** he choked on a fish bone **2** (fam) (caer antipático): **tengo esta asignatura atragantada** I can't stand this subject (colloq); **la mujer esa se me ha atragantado** I can't stomach that woman

atraiga, atrajo, etc *see* **atraer**

atrancar [A2] *vt* ‹*cañería*› to block (up); ‹*puerta/ventana*› to bar
■ **atrancarse** *v pron* **1** «*cañería*» to get blocked **2** (fam) «*persona*» (en tarea) to get stuck

atrapada *f* catch

atrapar [A1] *vt* ‹*conejo/ladrón*› to catch; **quedé atrapada en el ascensor** I was trapped in the elevator

atraque *m*
A (Náut) **1** (maniobra) docking **2** (muelle) berth, mooring
B (Chi fam) (besuqueo) necking (colloq), snogging (BrE colloq); **pegarse un ~** to have a necking session, to have a snog (BrE colloq)

atrás *adv*
A (en el espacio) **1** (expresando dirección) back; **muévelo para** *or* **hacia ~** move it back; **da un paso ~** take one step back **2** **¡~!** (*como interj*) get back! **3** (lugar, parte): **está allí ~** it's back there; **la parte de ~** the back; **me estaba quedando ~** I was getting left behind; **dejamos ~ la ciudad** we left the city behind us; **tiene los bolsillos ~** (esp AmL) the pockets are at the back; ***estar hasta ~*** (Méx fam) to be as high as a kite (colloq); ***saberse algo de ~ para adelante*** (CS fam) to know sth backwards
B (en el tiempo): **sucedió tres años ~** it happened three years ago; **había sucedido tres años ~** it had happened three years earlier *o* before
C **atrás de** (*loc prep*) (AmL) behind; **~ de mí/ti** behind me/you

atrasado -da *adj*
A **1** [ESTAR] ‹*reloj*› slow **2** (con respecto a lo esperado) **estar ~** to be behind; **está muy ~ en los estudios** he's really behind in his studies; **el proyecto está ~** the project is behind schedule; **está muy ~ para su edad** he's very backward for his age; **el tren llegó/salió ~** (AmL) the train arrived/left late; **apúrate que voy ~** (AmL) hurry up, I'm late
B (acumulado, pasado): **tengo mucho sueño ~** I have a lot of sleep to catch up on; **todas las cuotas atrasadas** all outstanding payments; **números ~s de la publicación** back numbers of the publication
C **1** (anticuado, desfasado) ‹*ideas/persona*› old-fashioned **2** ‹*país/pueblo*› backward

atrasar [A1] *vt* **1** ‹*reloj*› to put back; **~ los relojes una hora** to put the clocks back one hour **2** ‹*reunión/viaje*› to postpone, put back; **han atrasado la salida** the departure has been delayed
■ **atrasar** *vi* «*reloj*» to lose time; **atrasa un minuto cada hora** it loses a minute every hour
■ **atrasarse** *v pron*
A «*reloj*» to lose time; **se me ha atrasado 15 minutos** it's 15 minutes slow
B (en estudios, trabajo, pagos) to fall behind, get behind; **se ~on en el pago del alquiler** they fell behind *o* got into arrears with the rent
C «*país/industria*» to fall behind; **nos estamos atrasando respecto a nuestros competidores** we are falling behind our competitors
D (esp AmL) (llegar tarde) «*avión/tren*» to be late, be delayed; «*persona*» to be late; **me atrasé porque había mucho tráfico** I was delayed *o* held up by the traffic
E «*menstruación*» to be late

atraso *m*
A **1** (en desarrollo) backward state; (en ideas) backwardness **2** (esp AmL) (retraso) delay; **salió con unos minutos de ~** it left a few minutes late; **tenemos un ~ terrible con el trabajo** we have an awful backlog of work; **~ en el pago de las facturas** delay in payment of invoices
B **atrasos** *mpl* (deudas) arrears (*pl*)

atravesado -da *adj*
A (cruzado): **el piano estaba ~ en el pasillo** the piano was stuck (*o* placed *etc*) across the corridor; **un camión ~ en la carretera** a truck blocking the road; ***tener algo/a algn ~*** (fam): **lo tengo ~** I can't stand him (colloq); **tengo atravesada la física** I can't stand physics (colloq)
B **1** (AmL fam) (obstinado) bloody-minded; (malintencionado): **es muy ~** he's a real troublemaker **2** (Col, Ven fam) (agresivo) vicious, mean (colloq)

atravesar [A5] *vt*
A **1** ‹*río/frontera*› to cross; **la carretera atraviesa el pueblo** the road goes through the town; **atravesó el río a nado** she swam across the river **2** «*bala/espada*» to go through **3** ‹*crisis/período*› to go through
B (colocar) to put … across
■ **atravesarse** *v pron*: **se nos atravesó un camión** a truck crossed right in front of us; **¡no te vuelvas a ~ en mi camino!** don't (you) get in my way again!; **se me atravesó una espina en la garganta** I got a fish bone stuck in my throat

atraviesa, atraviesas, etc *see* **atravesar**

atrayente *adj* appealing

atreverse [E1] *v pron* to dare; **¡anda, atrévete!** go on then, I dare you (to); **~ CON algn**: **¿a que conmigo no te atreves?** I bet you wouldn't dare take me on; **~ CON algo**: **¿te atreves con esta tarea?** can you handle this task?; **¿te atreves con este filete?** can you manage this steak?; **~ A + INF**: **a que no te atreves a robar uno** I bet you wouldn't dare (to) steal one; **¿cómo te atreves a pegarle?** how dare you hit him?

atrevido¹ -da *adj* 1 (insolente) sassy (AmE colloq), cheeky (BrE colloq) 2 (osado) ‹*escote/persona*› daring; ‹*chiste*› risqué; **el ~ diseño del edificio** the bold *o* adventurous design of the building 3 (valiente) brave

atrevido² -da *m,f* 1 (insolente): **es un ~ y un maleducado** he is sassy (AmE) *o* (BrE) cheeky and bad-mannered 2 (valiente): **el mundo es de los ~s** fortune favors the brave

atrevimiento *m* nerve; **¡qué ~!** what nerve! (AmE), what a nerve! (BrE)

atribución *f* 1 (de hecho, delito) attribution 2 (de poderes): **la ~ de estas competencias a la comisión** the conferring of these powers on *o* the vesting of these powers in the committee 3 **atribuciones** *fpl* (poderes, funciones) powers (*pl*); **no está dentro de mis atribuciones** it is not within my powers

atribuible *adj* **~ A algo** attributable *o* ascribable TO sth

atribuir [I20] *vt* 1 **~ algo A algn/algo** to attribute *o* ascribe sth TO sb/sth; **le atribuyen algo que no dijo** they attribute words to him which he did not say, they put words in his mouth; **todo lo atribuye a su mala suerte** he blames everything on bad luck 2 ‹*funciones/poder*› to confer 3 ‹*cualidades/propiedades*› **~ algo A algn/algo**: **le atribuyen propiedades curativas** it is held *o* believed to have healing powers

■ **atribuirse** *v pron* (*refl*) 1 ‹*éxito/autoría*› to claim; **se atribuyeron la autoría del atentado** they claimed responsibility for the attack 2 ‹*poderes/responsabilidad*› to assume

atribulado -da *adj* (frml) ‹*persona*› afflicted (frml); ‹*expresión/mirada*› anguished (frml)

atribular [A1] *vt* to trouble

atributivo -va *adj* ‹*adjetivo*› (usado — con cópula) predicative; (— sin cópula) attributive; **verbo ~** copula, linking verb (AmE)

atributo *m*

A (cualidad) attribute, quality; (símbolo) insignia

B (Ling) predicate

atrición *f* attrition

atril *m* (para partituras) music stand; (para libros) lectern

atrinca *adj*(Ven fam) (difícil) difficult

atrincar [A2] *vt* (Chi fam) to push

atrincheramiento *m* entrenchment

atrincherar [A1] *vt* to entrench

■ **atrincherarse** *v pron* (Mil) to entrench oneself; (escudarse) **~se EN algo** to hide BEHIND sth

atrio *m* (patio interior) atrium; (de templo, palacio) portico, vestibule

atrocidad *f*

A (cualidad) barbarity; (acto) atrocity

B (uso hiperbólico): **¡qué ~!** how atrocious! *o* how awful!

atrofia *f* (de órgano, músculo) atrophy; (de facultad) degeneration

atrofiar [A1] *vt* to atrophy

■ **atrofiarse** *v pron* «*órgano/músculo*» to atrophy; «*facultad*» to degenerate

atronador -dora *adj* thunderous, deafening

atronar [A10] *vi* «*avión/cañones*» to thunder

atropelladamente *adv*: **hablaba ~** he was gabbling, his words came out in a jumble; **corrieron ~ hacia la salida** they bolted *o* rushed towards the exit

atropellado -da *adj*: **¡qué ~ eres!** you always do things in such a rush!

atropellar [A1] *vt* 1 «*coche/camión*» to knock … down; (pasando por encima) to run … over 2 ‹*libertades/derechos*› to violate, ride roughshod over; **no duda en ~ a quien sea para …** she has no qualms about riding roughshod over people to …

■ **atropellarse** *v pron* 1 (al hablar, actuar) to rush 2 (*recípr*) (empujarse): **salieron corriendo, atropellándose unos a otros** they came running out, pushing and shoving as they went

atropello *m* 1 (abuso) outrage; **esto es un ~** this is an outrage; **~ DE** *or* **A algo** violation OF sth 2 **atropellos** *mpl* (empujones) pushing and shoving; (prisas): **hazlo despacio y sin ~s** do it slowly, don't try to rush things

atroz *adj* (brutal, cruel) appalling; (uso hiperbólico) atrocious, awful; **un dolor de cabeza ~** an atrocious headache

atrozmente *adv* (con brutalidad) appallingly; (uso hiperbólico) atrociously, awfully

atte. (Corresp) (= **atentamente**): **lo saluda ~** sincerely yours (AmE), yours sincerely/faithfully (BrE)

attrezzista, atrezzista /atre'sista/ (*m*) propman; (*f*) propwoman

attrezzo, atrezzo /a'treso/ *m* props (*pl*)

atuendo *m* (frml) outfit

atufado -da *adj* (Méx, RPl fam) grouchy (colloq), grumpy

atufar [A1] *vt* (fam) to make … stink (colloq)

atún *m* tuna (fish)

atunero¹ -ra *adj* tuna (*before n*)

atunero² *m* tuna (fishing) boat

aturdimiento *m* (perplejidad) bewilderment; (por golpe, noticia) daze

aturdir [I1] *vt* 1 «*música/ruido*»: **la música te aturdía** the music was deafening; **este ruido me aturde** I can't think straight with this noise 2 (dejar perplejo) to bewilder, confuse 3 «*golpe/noticia/suceso*» to stun, daze

■ **aturdirse** *v pron* (atolondrarse) to get confused *o* flustered; (por golpe, noticia) to be stunned *o* dazed

aturrullar [A1], **aturullar** [A1] *vt* (fam): **tanto trabajo me aturrulla** I'm getting in a state *o* all confused with all this work (colloq)

■ **aturrullarse, aturullarse** *v pron* (fam) to get in a state (colloq), to get confused

atusarse [A1] *v pron* ‹*pelo*› to smooth; ‹*vestido/falda*› to smooth down

audacia *f* (valor) courage, daring; (osadía) boldness, audacity

audaz *adj* (valiente) brave, courageous; (osado) daring, bold

audazmente *adv* (valientemente) bravely, courageously; (con osadía) boldly, daringly

audible *adj* audible

audición *f*

A (facultad de oír) hearing

B (prueba) audition; **le hicieron una ~** he was auditioned, he had an audition

C (RPl) (Rad) program*

audiencia *f*

A (cita) audience; **pedir/conceder ~** to seek/grant an audience

B (Der) 1 (tribunal) court 2 (sesión) hearing

Compuestos

- **audiencia nacional** (Esp) ≈ supreme court (*in US*), ≈ high court (*in UK*)
- **audiencia pública** public hearing
- **audiencia territorial** (Esp) ≈ police court (*in US*), ≈ magistrate's court (*in UK*)

C (espectadores, oyentes) audience; **un programa de mucha ~** a program with a large audience

audífono *m* 1 (para sordos) hearing aid, deaf-aid (BrE) 2 (de radio) earphone 3 **audífonos** *mpl* (AmL) headphones (*pl*)

audio *m* 1 (campo, área) audio 2 (CS) (Cin, TV) sound

audiometría *f* audiometry (frml)

audiovisual¹ *adj* audiovisual

audiovisual² *m* audiovisual presentation

auditar [A1] *vt* to audit

auditivo -va *adj* 1 ‹*nervio/conducto*› auditory 2 ‹*problemas*› hearing (*before n*), auditory (tech)

auditor -tora *m,f* 1 (persona) auditor 2 **auditora** *f* (empresa) auditors (*pl*), firm of auditors

auditoría *f* audit

auditorio *m* (público) audience; (sala) auditorium

auditorium *m* auditorium

auge *m* 1 (punto culminante) peak; **en el ~ de su carrera** at the peak *o* height of his career 2 (aumento): **la comida vegetariana está en ~** vegetarian food is on the increase; **el español está tomando un gran ~** Spanish is rapidly gaining in importance; **un período de ~ económico** a period of economic growth

augur *m* augur

a

augurar [A1] *vt* «*futuro*» to predict, foretell; **este silencio no augura nada bueno** this silence does not bode *o* (frml) augur well; **esos nubarrones auguran tormenta** those clouds herald *o* (liter) presage a storm

augurio *m* 1 (presagio): **sus ~s no se cumplieron** his predictions did not come true; **es un ~ de mala suerte** it's (a sign of) bad luck *o* a bad omen 2 (deseo): **con nuestros mejores ~s** with best wishes

augusto -ta *adj* (liter) august (liter)

aula *f‡* 1 (en escuela) classroom; **el regreso a las ~s** the return to school 2 (en universidad) lecture (*o* seminar *etc*) room

(Compuesto) **aula magna** main lecture theater* *o* hall

aulaga *f* gorse

aullar [A23] *vi* «*lobo/viento*» to howl

aullido *m* howl; **los ~s del perro** the howling of the dog; **el ~ del viento** the howling of the wind

aumentar [A1] *vt* 1 ‹*precio/sueldo*› to increase, raise; ‹*cantidad/velocidad/tamaño*› to increase; ‹*producción/dosis*› to increase, step up; «*dolor/miedo/tensión*» to increase; **el microscopio aumenta la imagen** the microscope enlarges *o* magnifies the image 2 ‹*puntos*› (en tejido) to increase

■ **aumentar** *vi* «*temperatura/presión*» to rise; «*velocidad*» to increase; «*precio/producción/valor*» to increase, rise; **el niño aumentó 500 gramos** the child put on *o* gained 500 grams; **su popularidad ha aumentado** his popularity has grown; **~á el frío** it will become colder; **~ DE algo** ‹*de volumen/tamaño*› to increase IN sth; **aumentó de peso** he put on *o* gained weight

aumentativo[1] -va *adj* augmentative

aumentativo[2] *m* augmentative

aumento *m* 1 (incremento) rise, increase; **pedir un ~** to ask for a raise (AmE) *o* (BrE) rise; **las tarifas sufrirán un ligero ~** there will be a small increase *o* rise in fares; **~ DE algo**: **~ de peso** increase in weight; **~ de temperatura** rise in temperature; **~ de precio** price rise *o* increase; **~ de sueldo** salary increase, pay raise (AmE), pay rise (BrE) 2 (Ópt) magnification; **lentes con** *or* **de mucho ~** glasses with very strong lenses

aun *adv* even; **ni ~ trabajando 12 horas al día** (not) even if we worked 12 hours a day; **~ así, creo que...** even so, I think...; **y ~ así nos costó una fortuna** and even then it cost us a fortune

aún *adv*

A (todavía) 1 (en frases afirmativas o interrogativas) still; **¿~ estás aquí?** are you still here?; **eso ~ está por verse** that remains to be seen 2 (en frases negativas) yet; **~ no ha llamado** she hasn't called yet; **son las once y ~ no llega** it's eleven o'clock and she still hasn't arrived

B (en comparaciones) even

C (fam) (encima) still; **¿y ~ tuvo la frescura de...?** you mean she still had the nerve to...?

aunar [A23] *vt* ‹*ideas/esfuerzos*› to combine

■ **aunarse** *v pron* to unite, come together

aunque *conj*

A (refiriéndose a hechos) 1 (+ *indicativo*) although; **~ llegué tarde conseguí entradas** although *o* even though I got there late I managed to get tickets; **es simpático, ~ algo tímido** he's very likable, if somewhat shy 2 (respondiendo a una objeción) (+ *subjuntivo*): **es millonario, ~ no lo parezca** he's a millionaire though he may not look it; **~ no lo creas ...** believe it or not ...

B (refiriéndose a posibilidades, hipótesis) (+ *subjuntivo*) even if; **cómetelo, ~ no te guste** eat it, even if you don't like it; **dale ~ más no sea unos pesos** (RPl) at least give him a few pesos

aúpa *interj* (fam) (al levantar a un niño) up (you go/come)!; (para animar) come on!; ***de*** **~** (Esp fam) tremendous (colloq)

au pair /o'per/ *mf* (*pl* **-pairs**) au pair

aupar [A23] *vt* 1 (fam) ‹*niño*› to lift up 2 ‹*político*› to raise *o* bring ... to power

■ **auparse** *v pron*: **se aupó a una silla** she got up on a chair

aura *f‡*

A (halo) aura; **envuelto en un ~ de misterio** surrounded by an aura of mystery

B (liter) (brisa) gentle breeze

C (Zool) turkey buzzard

áureo -rea *adj* (liter) (de oro) gold; (dorado) golden

aureola *f* 1 (Relig) halo, aureole (liter) 2 (de gloria, fama) aura 3 (Astron) aureole, corona 4 (CS) (de mancha) ring

aurícula *f* auricle

auricular *m* 1 (del teléfono) receiver 2 **auriculares** *mpl* (Audio) headphones (*pl*), earphones (*pl*)

aurífero -ra *adj* gold-bearing, auriferous (frml)

auriga *m* charioteer

aurora *f* dawn; **la ~ de una nueva era** the dawning of a new age

(Compuesto) **aurora austral/boreal** aurora australis/borealis

auscultación *f* auscultation

auscultar [A1] *vt* to auscultate (tech); **el médico me auscultó** the doctor listened to my chest (with a stethoscope)

ausencia *f* 1 (de persona) absence; **durante mi ~** in *o* during my absence; **lo condenaron en su ~** he was sentenced in absentia *o* in his absence; ***brillar por su*** **~** to be conspicuous by one's absence; **el orden brilla por su ~** there's a distinct lack of order 2 (no existencia) lack, absence 3 (frml) (inasistencia) absence; **tiene tres ~s** he has been absent three times

ausentarse [A1] *v pron* (frml) to go away; **se ausentó un mes de su domicilio** he was away from home for a month; **pidió permiso para ~ un momento** he asked to leave the room (*o* class *etc*)

ausente[1] *adj* [ESTAR] 1 (no presente) absent; **todos los alumnos ~s** all those pupils who are absent; **García — ausente** García — he's absent *o* away; **estaba ~ de su domicilio** (period) she was not at home; **~ con aviso** apology for absence 2 (distraído) ‹*persona*› distracted; ‹*mirada/expresión*› absent (*before n*); **estaba como ~** he looked rather distracted 3 (euf) (difunto): **nuestros hermanos ~s** our brothers who are no longer with us (euph)

ausente[2] *mf* 1 (persona que falta): **no está bien criticar a los ~s** it's not right to criticize people in their absence; **uno de los grandes ~s fue ...** one notable absentee was ... 2 (Der) missing person

ausentismo *m* absenteeism

(Compuestos)

- **ausentismo escolar** absenteeism, truancy
- **ausentismo laboral** absenteeism

ausentista *adj* absentee (*before n*)

auspiciador -dora *m,f* sponsor, backer

auspiciar [A1] *vt* 1 (patrocinar) ‹*exposición/función*› to back, sponsor 2 (propiciar, facilitar) to foster, promote

auspicio *m*

A (patrocinio, apoyo) sponsorship; **bajo el ~** *or* **los ~s de ...** under the auspices of ...

B **auspicios** *mpl* (indicios): **el viaje empezó con buenos ~s** the journey began auspiciously

auspicioso -sa *adj* auspicious, promising; **el futuro se presenta ~** the future looks bright *o* promising

austeridad *f* austerity

austero -ra *adj* ‹*vida/costumbres/estilo*› austere; **es ~ en el comer** he is frugal in his eating habits

austral *adj* southern

Australia *f* Australia

australiano -na *adj/m,f* Australian

Austria *f‡* Austria

austriaco -ca, **austríaco -ca** *adj/m,f* Austrian

austro-húngaro *adj* Austro-Hungarian

autarquía *f* autarky

autárquico -ca *adj* autarkic

autenticación *f* authentication

autenticar [A2] *vt* 1 ‹*firma/documento*› to authenticate 2 (RPl) ‹*fotocopia*› to attest

autenticidad *f* authenticity

auténtico -ca *adj* 1 ‹*cuadro*› genuine, authentic; ‹*perla/piel*› real; ‹*documento*› authentic 2 ‹*interés/cariño/persona*› genuine 3 ‹*pesadilla/catástrofe*› (delante del n) real (*before n*)

autentificación *f* authentication

autentificar [A2] *vt* to authenticate

autillo *m* tawny owl
autismo *m* autism
autista *adj* autistic
auto *m*
A (esp CS) (Auto) car, automobile (AmE)
(Compuestos)
- **autos de choque** *or* (CS) **autitos chocadores** *mpl* bumper cars, dodgems (*pl*) (BrE)
- **auto de carrera** (CS) racing car
- **auto sport** (CS) sports car

B (Der) (resolución) decision; (orden) order, writ
(Compuestos)
- **auto de comparecencia** subpoena, summons
- **auto de embargo** attachment order
- **auto de fe** auto-da-fé
- **auto de prisión** committal
- **auto de procesamiento** committal for trial

C **autos** *mpl* (documentación) proceedings (*pl*); **constar en ~s** to be stated on file; **el día/la fecha de ~s** the day/date of the offense
D (Lit, Teatr) play
(Compuestos)
- **auto de la pasión** passion play
- **auto sacramental** *17th century allegorical religious play*

autoabastecerse [E3] *v pron* to be self-sufficient; **~ DE** *or* **EN algo** to be self-sufficient IN sth
autoabastecimiento *m* self-sufficiency; **~ de petróleo** self-sufficiency in oil
autoadhesivo -va *adj* self-adhesive
autoalarma *f* car alarm
autoayuda *f* self-help
autobiografía *f* autobiography
autobiográfico -ca *adj* autobiographical
autobomba *m* (RPl) water tender, fire engine
autobús *m* bus; **~ de dos pisos** double-decker bus
(Compuestos)
- **autobús de línea** (inter-city) bus
- **autobús foráneo** (Méx) intercity bus

autocalificarse [A2] *v pron* to describe oneself
autocar *m* (Esp) bus, coach (BrE)
autocine *m* drive-in
autoclave *f or m* autoclave
autocontrol *m* self-control
autocracia *f* autocracy
autócrata *mf* autocrat
autocrático -ca *adj* autocratic
autocrítica *f* self-criticism
autocross *m* autocross
autóctono -na *adj* ‹*flora/fauna*› indigenous, native; **el elefante es ~ de la India** the elephant is indigenous *o* native to India
autodefensa *f* self-defence
autodefinirse [I1] *v pron* to define oneself
autodegradación *f* self-abasement
autodenominarse [A1] *v pron* to call oneself
autodestruirse [I20] *v pron* to self-destruct
autodeterminación *f* self-determination
autodidacta[1] *adj* ‹*método*› autodidactic; ‹*persona*› self-taught
autodidacta[2] *mf* self-taught person, autodidact (frml)
autodisciplina *f* self-discipline
autodisciplinarse [A1] *v pron* to discipline oneself
autodisparador *m* self-timer
autódromo *m* racetrack, circuit
autoedición *f* desktop publishing
autoempleo *m* self-employment
autoencendido *m* self-ignition
autoengaño *m* self-deception
auto-escuela, autoescuela *f* driving school
autoestima *f* self-esteem
autoestop *m* ▸ **autostop**
autoestopista *mf* hitchhiker
autoevaluación *f* self-assessment
autofinanciarse [A1] *v pron* to finance oneself
autógeno -na *adj* autogenous
autogestión *f* self-management
autogobierno *m* self-government
autogol *m* own goal
autogolpe *m*: *coup organized by the government itself to allow it to take extra powers*
autografiar [A17] *vt* to autograph
autógrafo *m* autograph
autohipnosis *f* self-hypnosis
autoinculpación *f* self-incrimination
autolavado *m* car wash
automarginación *f* dropping-out
autómata *m* automaton
automaticidad *f* automatic nature
automático[1] **-ca** *adj* automatic; **es ~, se sienta a ver la tele y se queda dormido** (fam) it happens every time, he sits down in front of the TV and falls asleep
automático[2] *m* **1** (Fot) self-timer; (Elec) circuit breaker, trip switch **2** (cierre) snap fastener (AmE), press-stud (BrE)
automatismo *m* automatism
automatizado -da *adj* automated
automatizar [A4] *vt* to automate
automedicarse [A2] *v pron*: **se automedica con antibióticos** he takes antibiotics without a prescription
automercado *m* (AmC) supermarket
automoción *f* self-propulsion
automotor[1] **-triz** *or* **-tora** *adj* (frml) ‹*vehículo/industria*› motor (*before n*)
automotor[2] *m* (Ferr) railcar (*diesel or electric motor unit*)
automóvil[1] *adj* motor (*before n*)
automóvil[2] *m* car, automobile (AmE); **la industria del ~** the car *o* motor industry
(Compuesto) **automóvil club** automobile club
automovilismo *m* motoring
(Compuesto) **automovilismo deportivo** motor racing
automovilista *mf* motorist
automovilístico -ca *adj* ‹*carrera*› motor (*before n*); ‹*accidente*› car (*before n*)
autonomía *f*
A **1** (independencia) autonomy; **obran con ~** they act autonomously **2** (en Esp, comunidad autónoma) autonomous region; *see also* **Comunidad Autónoma**
B (Aviac, Náut) range
C (de portátil, móvil, etc) battery life

> **autonomía**
> ▸ Comunidad Autónoma

autonómico -ca *adj* **1** (independiente) autonomous **2** ‹*presidente/elecciones*› (en Esp) regional
autonomista *adj/mf* autonomist
autónomo[1] **-ma** *adj* **1** ‹*departamento/entidad*› autonomous **2** (Pol) (en Esp) ‹*región*› autonomous **3** ‹*trabajador*› self-employed; ‹*fotógrafo/periodista*› freelance
autónomo[2] **-ma** *m,f* (trabajador) self-employed worker *o* person; (fotógrafo, periodista) freelancer
autopista *f* expressway (AmE), motorway (BrE); **~ de peaje** *or* (Méx) **de cuota** turnpike, toll motorway
(Compuesto) **autopista de la información** (Inf): **la ~ de la ~** the information superhighway
autopsia *f* autopsy, post mortem; **hacerle la ~ a algn** to perform an autopsy *o* a post mortem on sb
autopullman *m*: *luxury, long-distance bus*
autor -tora *m,f* **1** (de libro, poema) author, writer; (de canción) writer; (de obra teatral) playwright **2** (de delito) perpetrator (frml); **el ~ del gol** the goalscorer; **el ~ intelectual del robo** (AmL) the brains *o* mastermind behind the robbery
autoría *f* **1** (de delito) responsibility; **se atribuyeron la ~ del atentado** (period) they claimed responsibility for the attack **2** (de libro, canción) authorship
autoridad *f*
A **1** (poder) authority; **no tengo ~ para hacerlo** I do not

a

have the authority to do it 2 (persona, institución): **la máxima ~ en el ministerio** the top official in the ministry; **se entregó a las ~es** she gave herself up to the authorities; **la ~ competente** the proper authority *o* authorities

(Compuesto) **autoridad moral** moral authority

B 1 (experto) authority; **una ~ en la materia** an authority on the subject 2 (competencia) authority; **habla con mucha ~** she speaks with great authority

C (Der): **el tratado tiene ~ de ley** the agreement is legally binding *o* has the power of law

autoritario -ria *adj* authoritarian

autoritarismo *m* authoritarianism

autorización *f* authorization (frml); **necesitan la ~ paterna** they need their parents' consent; **el tutor debe firmar la ~** the guardian must sign the consent form

autorizado -da *adj* ‹*fuente/portavoz*› official; ‹*distribuidor*› authorized, official; ‹*opinión*› expert (*before n*), authoritative

autorizar [A4] *vt* 1 ‹*manifestación/documento/firma*› to authorize; ‹*aumento/pago/obra*› to authorize, approve; **la película está autorizada para todos los públicos/para mayores de 18 años** the film has been authorized for general release/has been rated 18 and over 2 ‹*persona*› **~ a algn A** *or* **PARA + INF** to authorize sb to + INF; **eso no te autoriza a** *or* **para hablarme de ese modo** that doesn't give you the right to talk to me like that; **fue autorizado para negociar con ellos** he was given authority to negotiate with them

autorretrato *m* self-portrait

autoservicio *m* (tienda) supermarket; (restaurante) self-service restaurant, cafeteria

autostop, auto-stop /auto'(e)stop/ *m* hitchhiking; **hacer ~** to hitchhike; **me cogió en ~** (esp Esp) he gave me a lift *o* ride

autosuficiencia *f* 1 (Econ) self-sufficiency 2 (presunción) smugness

autosuficiente *adj* 1 (Econ) self-sufficient 2 (presumido) smug, self-satisfied

autosugestión *f* autosuggestion

autovagón *m* (Per) railcar

autovía *f* divided highway (AmE), dual carriageway (BrE)

auxiliar[1] *adj* 1 ‹*profesor*› assistant (*before n*); ‹*personal/elementos*› auxiliary (*before n*) 2 ‹*servicios*› auxiliary; **la tripulación ~ del avión** the cabin crew on the aircraft 3 (Tec) auxiliary 4 (Inf) peripheral

auxiliar[2] *mf*

A (persona) assistant

(Compuestos)

- **auxiliar administrativo/de laboratorio** administrative/laboratory assistant
- **auxiliar de vuelo** flight attendant

B **auxiliar** *f* (RPl) (Auto) spare tire*

auxiliar[3] [A1] *vt* 1 (socorrer) to help 2 ‹*moribundo/herido*› to attend

auxilio *m* 1 (ayuda) help; **nos prestó ~** he helped us; **¡~!** help!; **acudieron en ~ de las víctimas** they went to the aid of the victims 2 (RPl) (grúa) recovery *o* breakdown truck

(Compuesto) **auxilio en carretera** breakdown *o* recovery service

a/v. = a vista

Av. *f* (**= Avenida**) Ave.

aval *m* (Com, Fin) guarantee; (respaldo) backing, support; (recomendación) reference

(Compuesto) **aval bancario** bank guarantee

avalancha *f* avalanche

avalar [A1] *vt* 1 (Com, Fin) ‹*documento*› to guarantee; ‹*persona/préstamo*› to guarantee, act as guarantor for 2 (respaldar): **avalado por la experiencia** backed up *o* borne out by experience; **estas críticas están avaladas por la mayoría** these criticisms are endorsed by the majority

avalista *mf* guarantor

avaluar [A18] *vt* (AmL) to value

avalúo *m* (AmL) valuation

avance *m*

A 1 (adelanto) advance; **un ~ en este campo** a step forward in this field; **hubo ~s significativos en las negociaciones** significant progress was made in the negotiations 2 (movimiento) advance; (Mil) advance; (Dep) move forward

B 1 (Esp) (Cin, TV) trailer; **un ~ de la programación del domingo** a preview of Sunday's programs 2 **avances** *mpl* (Méx) (Cin, TV) trailer

(Compuesto) **avance informativo** news summary

avante *adv* ahead; **~ a toda máquina** full speed *o* steam ahead

avanzada *f*

A (Mil) advance party

B **de avanzada** advanced

avanzadilla *f* (Esp) advance party

avanzado -da *adj* advanced; **de avanzada edad** of advanced years, advanced in years; **a horas tan avanzadas** at such a late hour

avanzar [A4] *vi* 1 «*persona/tráfico*» to advance, move forward; **~ hacia la democracia** to move *o* advance toward(s) democracy; **las tropas avanzan hacia la capital** the troops are advancing on the capital 2 «*ciencia/medicina*» to advance 3 «*cinta/rollo*» to wind on 4 «*persona*» (en los estudios, el trabajo) to make progress; «*negociaciones/proyecto*» to progress 5 «*tiempo*» to draw on

■ **avanzar** *vt* 1 (adelantarse) to move forward, advance; **~on unos pasos** they moved forward a few steps 2 (mover) to move … forward, advance; **avanzó un peón** he moved *o* pushed a pawn forward 3 ‹*propuesta*› to put forward

avaricia *f* avarice; ***la ~ rompe el saco*** if you're too greedy you end up with nothing

avaricioso[1] -sa, avariento -ta *adj* greedy, avaricious

avaricioso[2] -sa, avariento -ta *m,f* greedy *o* avaricious person

avaro[1] -ra *adj* miserly

avaro[2] -ra *m,f* miser

avasallador -dora, avasallante *adj* 1 ‹*persona/actitud*› domineering, overbearing; **la fuerza ~a de las olas** the overwhelming force of the waves 2 ‹*triunfo*› resounding

avasallamiento *m* subjugation

avasallar [A1] *vt* 1 ‹*pueblo*› to subjugate 2 (fam) (apabullar): **no te dejes ~ por ellos** don't let them push you around (colloq)

■ **avasallar** *vi* (Esp) to be pushy

avatar *m* 1 (Relig) avatar 2 **avatares** *mpl* (altibajos) ups and downs (*pl*), vicissitudes (*pl*)

Avda. *f* (**= Avenida**) Ave.

ave *f‡* bird

(Compuestos)

- **ave de corral** fowl; **las ~s de corral** poultry
- **ave del paraíso** bird of paradise
- **ave de mal agüero** bird of ill omen
- **ave de paso** bird of passage
- **ave migratoria** migratory bird
- **ave negra** (Ur fam) trickster (colloq)
- **ave nocturna** (Zool) nocturnal bird; (persona) night owl *o* bird
- **ave rapaz** *or* **de rapiña** (Zool) bird of prey; (persona) shark
- **ave zancuda** wading bird, wader

AVE *m* (**= Alta Velocidad Española**) high-speed train

AVE – Alta Velocidad Española

This is a high-speed train service linking major Spanish cities. The first service was between Madrid and Seville in 1992. The Madrid-Barcelona service opened in 2008 and links to Albacete, Cuenca and Valencia are due in 2010. In the long run 6,250 miles of high-speed track are scheduled to be in service by 2020

avechucho *m* (Col fam) (insecto) bug (colloq), creepy-crawly (colloq); (ave) bird; (otro animal) creature, critter (AmE colloq)

avecinarse [A1] *v pron* to approach

avecindarse [A1] *v pron* to settle
avefría *f* lapwing
avejentado -da *adj*: **la encontré muy avejentada** she looked much older; **un rostro ~** an old face
avejentar [A1] *vt* to age, make ... look older
avellana *f* hazelnut
avellanedo *m* hazel wood
avellano *m* hazel
ave María *interj* (expresando sorpresa, disgusto) (fam) dear me! (colloq); **¡~ ~ Purísima!** (saludo) (ant) God bless this house; (en confesión) hail Mary, full of grace
Avemaría *f‡* (Relig) Hail Mary; (Mús) Ave Maria
avena *f* oats (*pl*)
avenencia *f* (acuerdo) agreement; (Com) deal
avenida *f* 1 (calle) avenue, boulevard 2 (de río) freshet, flood
avenido -da *adj*: **bien ~** well-matched; **una pareja mal avenida** they don't get on well as a couple
avenir [I31] *vt* (frml) to reconcile
■ **avenirse** *v pron* 1 (ponerse de acuerdo) **~se EN algo** to agree ON sth 2 (aceptar, acceder) **~se A algo**: **no se aviene a razones** he won't listen to reason; **se avinieron a negociar** they agreed to negotiate 3 (llevarse bien) **~se CON algn** to get on WITH sb
aventajado -da *adj* outstanding, excellent
aventajar [A1] *vt* (estar por delante de) to be ahead of; (adelantarse) to overtake, get ahead of
aventar [A5] *vt*
A 1 (Col, Méx, Per) ‹*pelota/piedra*› to throw; **le aventé un sopapo** (fam) I smacked *o* (BrE) thumped him (colloq) 2 (Méx) (empujar) to push
B ‹*fuego/lumbre*› to fan; ‹*grano*› to winnow
■ **aventarse** *v pron* 1 (Méx fam) (atreverse) to dare; **~se A + INF** to dare to + INF 2 (Méx fam) (lograr): **se ~on un partidazo** they produced *o* played a tremendous game 3 (*refl*) (Col, Méx) (arrojarse, tirarse) to throw oneself; **se aventó al agua** he dived into the water
aventón *m* (Méx) (fam) lift; **darle un ~ a algn** to give sb a lift *o* ride; **pedir ~** to hitch *o* thumb a lift *o* ride; **ir de ~** to go hitching
aventura *f* 1 (suceso extraordinario) adventure; **en busca de ~s** in search of adventure 2 (riesgo) venture; **se embarcaron en esta ~** they embarked on this venture 3 (relación amorosa — pasajera) fling; (— ilícita) affair
aventurado -da *adj* risky, hazardous
aventurar [A1] *vt* 1 ‹*opinión*› to venture, put forward; ‹*conjetura*› to hazard; **no podemos ~ cifras** we cannot speculate on the figures 2 ‹*dinero*› to risk, stake
■ **aventurarse** *v pron* to venture; **se aventuró por el desierto** she ventured into the desert; **~se A + INF**: **no me aventuré a hablarle** I didn't dare (to) speak to her; **me ~ía a decir que ...** I would go so far as to say that ...
aventurero¹ -ra *adj* adventurous
aventurero² -ra *m,f* adventurer
avergonzado -da *adj* 1 (por algo reprensible) ashamed; **~ POR** *or* **DE algo** ashamed OF sth 2 (en situación embarazosa) embarrassed
avergonzar [A13] *vt* 1 (por algo reprensible): **¿no te avergüenza salir así a la calle?** aren't you ashamed to go out looking like that? 2 (en situación embarazosa) to embarrass
■ **avergonzarse** *v pron* to be ashamed (of oneself); **~se DE algo** to be ashamed OF sth; **se avergonzó de haberle mentido** she was ashamed of herself for having lied to him
avergüenza, avergüenzas, etc *see* **avergonzar**
avería *f* (Auto, Mec) breakdown; **el coche sufrió una ~** the car broke down
averiado -da *adj* [ESTAR] ‹*coche/máquina*› broken down; **el ascensor/teléfono estaba ~** the elevator/telephone was out of order
averiarse [A17] *v pron* to break down
averiguación *f* inquiry; **hacer averiguaciones** to make inquiries
averiguar [A16] *vt* to find out; **averigua a qué hora sale el tren** find out *o* check what time the train leaves
■ **averiguar** *vi* (Méx) to quarrel, argue; ***averiguárselas*** (Méx): **me las ~é para conseguir el dinero** I'll manage to get the money somehow; ***averiguárselas con algn*** (Méx) to deal with sb
aversión *f* aversion; **siento ~ por ella** I loathe her, I have a real aversion to her
avestruz *m* ostrich
avezado -da *adj* ‹*combatiente/político*› seasoned; **un ~ delincuente** a hardened criminal
aviación *f* (civil) aviation; (Mil) air force
aviado -da *adj* (ant) (listo) ready
aviador -dora *m,f*
A (Aviac, Mil) pilot, aviator (dated)
B (Chi) (Agr, Min) backer
C (Méx) (empleado) *person who is paid a salary without actually doing any work*
aviar [A17] *vt*
A (ant) ‹*equipaje/caballo*› to prepare
B (AmL) (Agr, Min) to stake
■ **aviarse** *v pron* (*refl*) (ant) 1 (prepararse) to prepare oneself 2 (arreglárselas) to get by, manage
aviario¹ -ria *adj* bird (*before n*), avian (tech)
aviario² *m* collection of birds
avícola *adj* poultry (*before n*)
avicultor -tora *m,f* poultry farmer
avicultura *f* poultry farming
ávidamente *adv* avidly, eagerly
avidez *f* eagerness, avidity; **lee con ~** he reads avidly
ávido -da *adj* **~ DE algo** ‹*de noticias/aventuras*› eager FOR sth; ‹*de poder*› hungry FOR sth; **~ de sabiduría** thirsty for knowledge
aviejarse [A1] *v pron* to age
avieso -sa *adj* (frml *o* liter) ‹*persona*› malicious, wicked; ‹*intenciones*› wicked, evil
avinagrado -da *adj* ‹*vino*› vinegary; ‹*persona/carácter*› sour, bitter
avinagrar [A1] *vt* ‹*vino*› to make ... taste vinegary; ‹*carácter*› to make ... sour *o* bitter
■ **avinagrarse** *v pron* «*vino*» to turn *o* go vinegary; «*persona*» to become bitter *o* sour
avío *m*
A (utilidad): **me ha hecho mucho ~** it has been very useful, it has come in very handy (colloq)
B (fam) **los avíos** *mpl* (lo necesario) the gear (colloq)
(Compuesto) **avíos de pesca** *mpl* fishing tackle
C (AmL) (Agr, Min) loan, stake
avión *m*
A (Aviac) plane, aircraft (frml), airplane (AmE), aeroplane (BrE); **viajar en ~** to fly; **un ~ de reconocimiento** a spotter plane; ❸ **por avión** (Corresp) air mail
B (Méx) (Jueg) hopscotch
(Compuestos)
- **avión a chorro** *or* **a reacción** jet (plane)
- **avión cisterna** *o* **nodriza** tanker
- **avión de carga** freight plane, cargo plane
- **avión de combate/de pasajeros/militar** fighter/passenger/military plane

avionazo *m* (Méx) plane crash
avioncito *m* paper dart, paper airplane
avioneta *f* light aircraft
aviónica *f* avionics
avisado -da *adj* 1 [SER] (sagaz) informed; **el lector ~** the informed reader 2 [ESTAR] (advertido): **quedas** *or* **estás ~** you've been warned
avisar [A1] *vt* 1 (notificar): **¿por qué no me avisaste que venías?** why didn't you let me know you were coming?; **nos han avisado que...** they've notified us that... 2 (Esp, Méx) (llamar) to call; **~ al médico/a la policía** to call the doctor/the police 3 (advertir) to warn; **le ~on que venía la policía** they warned him that the police were coming
■ **avisar** *vi*: **llegó sin ~** she showed up without any prior warning *o* unexpectedly; **avísame cuando acabes** let me know when you've finished; **~ a algn DE algo** to let sb know ABOUT sth, inform sb OF sth
aviso *m*
A 1 (notificación) notice; ❸ **aviso al público** notice to the

public; **dio ~ a la policía** he notified *o* informed the police; **sin previo ~** without prior warning; **hasta nuevo ~** until further notice; **último ~ para los pasajeros ...** last call for passengers ... 2 (advertencia) warning; ***sobre* ~**: **estás sobre ~** you've been warned; **me puso sobre ~ de lo que ocurriría** he warned me what would happen 3 (Cin, Teatr) bell 4 (Taur) warning
B (AmL) (anuncio, cartel) advertisement, ad
(Compuestos)
- **aviso clasificado** *or* (Méx) **de ocasión** *or* **oportuno** classified advertisement
- **aviso fúnebre** death notice

avispa *f* wasp
avispado -da *adj* (fam) sharp, bright
avispar [A1] *vt* to make ... wise up (colloq)
■ **avisparse** *v pron* (espabilarse) to wise up (colloq)
avispero *m* 1 (nido) wasps' nest; **esa oficina es un ~** (RPl) that office is a madhouse (colloq); ***alborotar*** *or* ***revolver el*** **~** to stir up a hornet's nest 2 (lío) mess 3 (Med) carbuncle
avispón *m* hornet
avistar [A1] *vt* to sight
avitaminosis *f* vitamin deficiency
avituallamiento *m* provisioning
avituallar [A1] *vt* to provision, supply ... with food
avivado -da *m,f* (CS fam) wise guy (colloq)
avivar [A1] *vt* ‹*fuego*› to get ... going; ‹*color*› to make ... brighter; ‹*pasión/deseo*› to arouse; ‹*dolor*› to intensify
■ **avivarse** *v pron* 1 «*fuego*» to revive, flare up; «*debate*» to come alive, liven up 2 (AmL fam) (despabilarse) to wise up (colloq)
avivato -ta *m,f* (AmS fam) wise guy (colloq)
avocastro *m* (Chi fam) ugly mug (colloq)
axial *adj* axial
axila *f* 1 (Anat) armpit, axilla (tech) 2 (Bot) axillary bud
axilar *adj* underarm (*before n*), axillary (tech)
axioma *m* axiom
axiomático -ca *adj* axiomatic
ay *interj* 1 (expresando — dolor) ow!, ouch!; (— susto, sobresalto) oh! 2 (expresando aflicción) oh dear!; **¡~ de mí!** (liter) woe is me! (liter) 3 (expresando amenaza): **¡~ del que se atreva!** woe betide anyone who tries it!
aya *f*‡ (ant) governess
ayatolah *m* ayatollah
ayer[1] *adv*
A (refiriéndose al día anterior) yesterday; **~ hizo un mes** a month ago yesterday; **~ por** *or* (esp AmL) **en** *or* (RPl) **a la mañana** yesterday morning; **~ tarde** (period) yesterday afternoon; **antes de ~** the day before yesterday; **de ~ acá** *or* **a hoy** overnight, since yesterday; **el periódico de ~** yesterday's paper; ***no nací* ~** I wasn't born yesterday
B (liter) (refiriéndose al pasado): **~ era un joven idealista** he was once a young idealist; **las modas de ~** the fashions of yesteryear *o* of years gone by
ayer[2] *m* past; **en un ~ muy lejano** (liter) a long, long time ago (liter)
ayte. (= **ayudante**) asst.
ayuda *f*
A (asistencia) help; **nadie fue** *or* **acudió en su ~** nobody went to his aid; **pedir ~** to ask for help; **~s para la inversión** incentives for investment; **organizaciones de ~ internacional** international aid agencies; **ha sido de gran ~** it has been a great help; **poca ~ no es estorbo** every little helps
(Compuesto) **ayuda de cámara** *m* valet
B (fam & euf) (enema) enema
ayudante *mf* assistant
(Compuestos)
- **ayudante de campo** aide-de-camp
- **ayudante de cátedra** assistant professor (AmE), (junior) lecturer (BrE)
- **ayudante de cocina** kitchen assistant
- **ayudante de dirección/producción** director's/production assistant
- **Ayudante Técnico Sanitario** (en Esp) Registered Nurse

ayudar [A1] *vt* to help; **~ al prójimo** to help one's neighbor; **¿te ayudo?** do you need any help?; **vino a ~me** she came to help me out; **~ a algn con algo** to help sb WITH sth; **~ a algn a + inf** to help sb (to) + INF; **ayúdame a poner la mesa** help me (to) set the table
■ **ayudar** *vi* to help; **¿puedo ~ en algo?** can *o* shall I give you a hand?, can I do anything to help?; **~ a** *or* **en misa** to serve at mass
■ **ayudarse** *v pron* to help oneself; **~se de** *or* **con algo**: **camina ayudándose de** *or* **con un bastón** he walks with the aid *o* help of a stick
ayunar [A1] *vi* to fast
ayunas: **en ~** (*loc adv*): **estoy en ~** I haven't eaten anything; **debe tomarse en ~** it should be taken on an empty stomach; ***estar/quedarse en*** **~** (no entender) to be/to be left completely in the dark
ayuno *m* fast, fasting; **hacer ~** to fast
ayuntamiento *m* (corporación) town/city council; (edificio) town/city hall
(Compuesto) **ayuntamiento carnal** (ant) carnal knowledge (arch)
ayuntar [A1] *vt* (Col) (Agr) to yoke ... together
azabache *m* (Min) jet; **negro como el ~** jet black
azada *f* hoe
azadón *m* mattock
azafata *f*
A (en avión) flight attendant, air hostess; (en programa, concurso) hostess
(Compuestos)
- **azafata de congresos** conference hostess
- **azafata de tierra** ground stewardess

B (Per) (bandeja) tray
azafate *m* (AmS) tray
azafrán *m* saffron
azahar *m* (del naranjo) orange blossom; (del limonero) lemon blossom
azalea *f* azalea
azar *m* 1 (casualidad) chance; **dejar algo al ~** to trust sth to chance; **no es por ~ que ...** it's no chance *o* coincidence that ...; **quiso el ~ que coincidieran** fate decreed that they should meet; **al ~** at random 2 **azares** *mpl* (vicisitudes) ups and downs (*pl*), vicissitudes (*pl*)
azaroso -sa *adj* ‹*viaje*› hazardous; ‹*proyecto*› risky; ‹*vida*› eventful
Azerbaiyán, Azerbaiján *m* Azerbaijan, Azerbaidzhan
azerbaiyaní[1] *adj/mf* Azerbaijani, Azeri
azerbaiyaní[2] *m* (idioma) Azerbaijani
azogar [A3] *vt* to silver
azogue *m* mercury, quicksilver
azor *m* goshawk
azorado -da *adj* 1 (turbado) embarrassed 2 (Col, Méx, RPl) (asombrado) amazed, astonished
azorar [A1] *vt* 1 (turbar) to embarrass 2 (Col) (distraer) to distract
■ **azorarse** *v pron* to get embarrassed, be covered in confusion (liter)
azotador *m* (Méx) caterpillar
azotaina *f* (fam) spanking
azotar [A1] *vt*
A (con látigo) to whip, flog
B «*viento/mar*» to lash; **un temporal azota la ciudad** a storm is battering the town; **el hambre azotaba la zona** the region was in the grips of famine
C (Méx) ‹*puerta*› to slam; Ⓢ **favor de no azotar la puerta** please do not slam the door
azote *m*
A 1 (látigo) whip, lash; (latigazo) lash 2 (fam) (a un niño): **te voy a dar unos ~s** I'm going to spank you
B (del viento, mar): **los ~s de las olas** the lashing of the waves; **la ciudad sufre los ~s de los temporales** the city is lashed by storms
C (calamidad) scourge
azotea *f* terrace roof, flat roof; ***estar mal de la*** **~** (fam) to be off one's rocker (colloq)
azteca *adj/mf* Aztec

Aztecas

A Náhuatl-speaking people of Central America who in the fourteenth century established a brilliant but tyrannical civilization in central and southern Mexico. The capital was Tenochtitlán, built on reclaimed marshland which became Mexico City. Renowned for their jewelry, the Aztecs were also skilled architects and used a writing system based on pictographs and hieroglyphs. The Aztec calendar followed a 52-year astronomical cycle. They worshipped the plumed serpent Quetzalcóatl and the war-god Huitzilopochtli, whom their priests appeased by human sacrifice. The Aztec empire collapsed in 1521 after defeat by the Spanish under Hernán Cortés and Pedro de Alvarado

azúcar *m or f* sugar; **~ de remolacha/caña** beet/cane sugar; **el nivel de ~ en la sangre** the blood-sugar level; **chicle sin ~** sugar-free gum

(Compuestos)
- **azúcar blanca** *or* **blanquilla** white sugar
- **azúcar en cubos** *or* **terrones** *or* (RPl) **pancitos** sugar lumps *o* cubes (*pl*)
- **azúcar glasé** *or* (Méx) **glas** *or* (Chi) **flor** *or* (Col) **en polvo** *or* (Bol, RPl) **impalpable** confectioners' sugar (AmE), icing sugar (BrE)
- **azúcar granulada** granulated sugar
- **azúcar lustre** castor* sugar
- **azúcar morena** brown sugar

azucarado -da *adj* ‹*zumo*› sweetened; ‹*miel*› crystallized; ‹*voz/sonrisa*› (pey) sugary (pej)

azucarar [A1] *vt* ‹*café/leche*› to add sugar to; ‹*fruta*› to sprinkle … with sugar

■ **azucararse** *v pron* to crystallize

azucarera *f* [1] (AmL) (recipiente) sugar bowl [2] (fábrica) sugar refinery

azucarero[1] -ra *adj* ‹*industria*› sugar (*before n*); ‹*zona*› sugar-producing (*before n*)

azucarero[2] *m* sugar bowl

azucena *f* Madonna lily, Annunciation lily

azuela *f* adz, adze (BrE)

azufre *m* sulfur*

azul[1] *adj* blue; **ojos ~ verdoso** greenish-blue eyes; **unas camisas ~ claro/oscuro** light/dark blue shirts

azul[2] *m* blue; **el ~ le sienta muy bien** blue looks good on you; **de un ~ intenso** deep blue

(Compuestos)
- **azul añil** (color) indigo blue; (para la ropa) bluing, blue
- **azul cielo** *or* **celeste** [1] *m* sky blue [2] *adj inv* sky-blue (*before n*)
- **azul cobalto** [1] *m* cobalt blue [2] *adj inv* cobalt-blue (*before n*)
- **azul eléctrico** [1] *m* electric blue [2] *adj inv* electric-blue (*before n*)
- **azul marino** [1] *m* navy blue [2] *adj inv* navy-blue (*before n*)

azulado -da *adj* bluish

azulejo *m* (glazed ceramic) tile

azulete *m* blue, bluing

azuloso -sa *adj* (AmL) bluish

azur *adj/m* azure

azurita *f* azurite

azuzar [A4] *vt* [1] ‹*perros*› to sic; **~le los perros a algn** to set the dogs on sb [2] ‹*persona*› to egg … on

Bb

B, b *f* (*read as* /be ('larγa)/) *the letter* **B, b**

baba *f*

A 1 (de niño) dribble, drool (AmE) 2 (de adulto) saliva; ***caérsele a algn la ~ por*** *or* ***con algn*** to drool over sb 3 (de perro, caballo) slobber

B (de caracol) slime; (de cactus) sap

babear [A1] *vi*

A 1 «*persona*» to dribble, drool (AmE) 2 «*animal*» to slaver, slobber

B (Chi, Méx fam) (mirar con embeleso) **~ POR algn** to drool OVER sb

■ **babearse** *v pron* (RPl) ▶ **babear B**

babel *m* complete bedlam (colloq)

babero *m* bib

Babia *f*: **estar en ~** to have one's head in the clouds

bable *m*: *Asturian dialect*

> **bable**
>
> Or *asturiano*, *bable* is a variety of Castilian spoken in Asturias. It went into decline when the kingdom of Castile achieved political dominance and imposed Castilian on what became Spain. By the twentieth century it was confined to rural areas.
>
> With the revival of Spanish regional languages *bable* has seen a resurgence in use

babor *m* port; **virar a ~** to turn to port; **¡tierra a ~!** land to port!

babosa *f* slug; *ver tb* **baboso²**

babosada *f* (AmC, Col, Méx) drivel; **no digas ~s** don't talk drivel *o* nonsense; **se pelearon por una ~** they fought over some stupid little thing

babosear [A1] *vt* «*niño*» to dribble down *o* over; «*animal*» to slobber over

■ **babosear** *vi*

A (Col) (decir tonterías) to talk drivel

B (Méx fam) (distraerse) to daydream

baboseo *m* 1 (de niño) dribbling, drooling (AmE) 2 (de animal) slobbering, slavering

babosería *f* (Per fam): **era una ~** it was a load of drivel; **sólo dice ~s** he talks nothing but drivel

baboso¹ -sa *adj*

A (con babas) slimy

B (AmL fam) (estúpido) 1 ‹*persona*› dim (colloq) 2 ‹*libro/espectáculo*› ridiculous

C (CS fam & pey) (pegajoso) ‹*persona*› lovey-dovey (colloq & pej); **estar ~ CON** *or* **POR algn** to be besotted WITH sb

baboso² -sa *m,f* (AmL fam) (tonto) dimwit (colloq)

babucha *f* (zapatilla) slipper; ***llevar a algn a ~(s)*** (RPl fam) to give sb a shoulder ride

baca *f* roof-rack, luggage-rack

bacaladero¹ -ra *adj* cod (*before n*)

bacaladero² *m* cod trawler

bacalao *m* cod, codfish (AmE); **~ seco** salt cod

bacán¹ -cana *adj* 1 (RPl fam) (cómodo) cushy (colloq) 2 (Per fam) (estupendo) fantastic (colloq), great (colloq)

bacán² -cana *m,f* 1 (RPl fam) (ricachón) moneybags (colloq) 2 (Per fam & pey) (vanidoso) bighead (colloq)

bacanal *f* (juerga) wild party, orgy (colloq)

bacenilla *f* (Col, Ven) chamber pot

bache *m* 1 (Auto) pothole 2 (Aviac) air pocket 3 (mal momento) bad time *o* (BrE) patch

bachicha *mf* (CS fam) wop (colloq & pej)

bachiller *mf* 1 (de escuela secundaria) ≈ high school graduate (*in US*), ≈ school leaver with A levels (*in UK*) 2 (Per) (licenciado) university graduate

bachillerato *m* 1 (educación secundaria) *secondary education and the qualification obtained*, ≈ high school diploma (*in US*) 2 (Per) (licenciatura) bachelor's degree

bacilo *m* bacillus

bacinica *f* (AmL exc RPl) (fam) chamber pot, potty (colloq)

bacteria *f* bacterium; **~s** bacteria (*pl*)

bactericida *m* bactericide

bacteriología *f* bacteriology

báculo *m* 1 (bastón) walking stick 2 (liter) (apoyo) support

(Compuesto) **báculo pastoral** crosier

badajo *m* clapper

badana *f* 1 (piel) poor-quality leather (*usually used for lining*) 2 (Chi, Per) (franela) flannel

baden *m* (Chi) speed bump

badén *m* 1 (vado) ford 2 (depresión) dip

bádminton /'baðminton/ *m* badminton

badulaque *mf* (fam) (tonto) moron (colloq & pej)

baffle /'bafle/, **bafle** *m* (altavoz) speaker, loudspeaker

bagaje *m*: **~ cultural** (de persona) cultural knowledge; (de un pueblo) cultural heritage; **un ~ de conocimientos/experiencias** a wealth of knowledge/experience

bagatela *f* 1 (alhaja) trinket; (adorno) knickknack 2 (asunto sin importancia) triviality

bagre *m*

A (Coc, Zool) catfish

B (AmS fam & pey) (mujer fea) ugly hag (colloq & pej)

bagual -guala *m,f* (RPl)

A 1 (caballo) unbroken horse 2 **bagual** *m* (toro) wild bull

B **baguala** *f* (canción) *Argentinian folk song*

bah *interj* (expresando — desprecio) huh!, bah!; (— conformidad) oh well!

bahareque *m* (AmC, Col, Ven) adobe

bahía *f* bay

bailable *adj*: **música ~** music you can dance to

bailaor -laora *m,f* flamenco dancer

bailar [A1] *vi*

A (Mús) to dance; **salir a ~** to go out dancing; **la sacó a ~** he asked her to dance; ***¡que me quiten lo bailado!*** (fam) I'm going to enjoy myself while I can

B «*trompo/peonza*» to spin

C (fam) (estar flojo) (+ *me/te/le etc*): **tus zapatos me bailan** your shoes are miles too big for me (colloq)

D (Méx fam) **andar/quedar/estar bailando** «*dinero*» to be unaccounted for; «*asunto*» to be up in the air

■ **bailar** *vt*

A (Mús) to dance; **~ un tango** to (dance a) tango

B (Méx fam) (quitar, robar) to swipe (colloq), to pinch (BrE colloq)

■ **bailarse** *v pron* (Méx fam): **se los ~on en tres sets** they were thrashed in three sets

bailarín¹ -rina *adj* 1 ‹*persona*› fond of dancing 2 ‹*mono/perro*› dancing (*before n*)

bailarín² **-rina** *m,f* dancer

Compuestos

- **bailarín de ballet** *m* ballet dancer
- **bailarina de ballet** *f* ballerina, ballet dancer

baile *m*

A 1 (acción) dancing; **abrir el ~** to start the dancing 2 (arte, composición, fiesta) dance

Compuestos

- **baile de disfraces/máscaras** fancy-dress/masked ball
- **baile de San Vito** (Med): **el ~ de ~ ~** St Vitus's dance; **parece que tienes el ~ de ~ ~** (fam) you look like you've got ants in your pants

B (CS, Ven fam) (asunto): **yo no me meto en este ~** I'm not getting involved in this business; **ya que estamos en el ~ ...** while we're about it ...

bailongo *m* (AmL fam) dance

bailotear [A1] *vi* (fam & hum) to dance, bop (colloq)

bailoteo *m* 1 (fam & hum) (acción) dancing, bopping (colloq) 2 (Chi fam) (fiesta) party (*with dancing*), hop (dated)

baja *f*

A (descenso) fall, drop; **su popularidad está en ~** his popularity is waning *o* declining; **la ~ de las tasas de interés** the cut in interest rates; **a la ~**: **tendencia a la ~** downward trend; **los que juegan a la ~** those who are selling for a fall, the bears

B 1 (Esp) (Rels Labs) (permiso) sick leave; (certificado) medical certificate; **está (dado) de ~** he's off sick *o* on sick leave 2 (Dep): **el equipo tiene varias ~s** the team is missing several regulars 3 (Mil) (muerte) loss, casualty; **los rebeldes tuvieron trece ~s** the rebels lost thirteen men

Compuesto **baja por maternidad** (Esp) maternity leave

C 1 (en entidad): **ha habido varias ~s** (en clase) several students have dropped out *o* left; (en asociación) several members have left; **darse de ~** (en club) to cancel one's membership; (en partido) to resign; (de sitio web) to unsubscribe; **lo dieron de ~ en el club por no pagar la cuota** they canceled his membership to the club for not paying his fees; **causó ~ en nuestra empresa** (Esp) he left our employment 2 (Mil) (cese) discharge; **dar de ~** to discharge; **pidió la ~ en el ejército** he applied to be discharged from the army 3 (en puesto): **el equipo lo dio de ~** the club cut him (AmE), the club released him (BrE); **lo dieron de ~ por invalidez** he was dismissed because of illness *o* on health grounds

Compuestos

- **baja incentivada** (Esp) voluntary redundancy (*with incentive payment*)
- **baja voluntaria** (Esp) voluntary redundancy

bajada *f*

A (acción) descent; **al atardecer emprendimos la ~** as evening fell we began the descent; **en la ~ me fallaron los frenos** my brakes failed on the way down; **la ~ de los tipos de interés** the cut in interest rates; **tuvo una ~ de tensión** his blood pressure dropped

Compuesto **bajada de bandera** minimum fare

B (camino): **la ~ a la playa es muy empinada** the path (*o* road *etc*) down to the beach is very steep

bajamar *f* low tide

bajar [A1] *vi*

A 1 ‹‹*ascensor/persona*›› (alejándose) to go down; (acercándose) to come down; **yo bajo por la escalera** I'll take the stairs; **espérame, ya bajo** wait for me, I'll be right down; **¿bajas a la playa con nosotros?** are you coming (down) to the beach with us?; **~ A + INF** to go/come down to + INF; **bajé a despedirlos** I went down to see them out; **bajó a saludarnos** he came down to say hello 2 (apearse) **~ DE algo** ‹*de tren/avión*› to get off sth; ‹*de coche*› to get out OF sth; ‹*de caballo/bicicleta*› to get off sth 3 (Dep) ‹‹*equipo*›› to go down

B 1 ‹‹*marea*›› to go out 2 ‹‹*fiebre/tensión*›› to go down, drop; ‹‹*hinchazón*›› to go down; ‹‹*temperatura*›› to fall, drop; **le ha bajado la fiebre** her fever *o* temperature has gone down 3 ‹‹*precio/valor*›› to fall, drop; ‹‹*cotización*›› to fall; ‹‹*calidad*›› to deteriorate; ‹‹*popularidad*›› to diminish; **~ de precio** to go down in price; **seguro que no baja de los dos millones** I bet it won't be *o* cost less than two million 4 ‹‹*menstruación*›› to start

■ **bajar** *vt*

A ‹*escalera/cuesta*› to go down

B ‹*brazo/mano*› to put down, lower; **bajó la cabeza avergonzado** he bowed his head in shame

C (Inf) to download

D 1 **~ algo (DE algo)** ‹*de armario/estante*› to get sth down (FROM sth); ‹*del piso de arriba*› to bring/take down sth; **¿me bajas las llaves?** can you bring down my keys?; **hay que ~ estas botellas al sótano** we have to take these bottles down to the basement 2 **~ a algn DE algo** ‹*de mesa/caballo*› to get sb off sth

E 1 ‹*persiana/telón*› to lower; ‹*ventanilla*› to open 2 ‹*cremallera*› to undo

F ‹*precio*› to lower; ‹*fiebre*› to bring down; ‹*volumen*› to turn down; **baja la voz** lower your voice

■ **bajarse** *v pron*

A (apearse) **~se DE algo** ‹*de tren/autobús*› to get off sth; ‹*de coche*› to get out of sth; ‹*de caballo/bicicleta*› to get off sth; **¡bájate del muro!** get down off the wall!

B ‹*pantalones*› to take down; ‹*falda*› to pull down

bajativo *m* (CS) liqueur, digestif

bajel *m* (liter) ship

bajero **-ra** *adj* ‹*sábana*› bottom; **falda bajera** underskirt

bajetón **-tona** *adj* (Per fam) short

bajeza *f* 1 (acción) despicable act 2 (cualidad) baseness; **nunca creí que fuera capaz de tanta ~** I never thought her capable of being so vile

bajial *m* (Per) floodplain

bajío *m* 1 (zona poco profunda) shallows (*pl*); (banco de arena) sandbank 2 (AmL) (terreno bajo) low-lying area

bajista *mf* bass player, bassist

bajo¹ **-ja** *adj*

A [SER] ‹*persona*› short

B (indicando posición, nivel) 1 [SER] ‹*techo*› low; ‹*tierras*› low-lying 2 [ESTAR] ‹*lámpara/cuadro/nivel*› low; **la parte baja de la estantería** the lower shelves of the bookcase; **la marea está baja** the tide is out 3 (bajado): **tener las persianas bajas** to have the blinds down; **caminar con la mirada baja** to walk (along) with one's eyes on the ground

C 1 ‹*calificación/precio/número*› low; ‹*temperatura*› low; **una bebida baja en calorías** a low-calorie drink; **tiene la tensión** *or* **presión baja** he has low blood pressure; **artículos de baja calidad** poor-quality goods 2 ‹*volumen/luz*› low; **en voz baja** quietly, in a low voice; **pon la radio bajita** put the radio on quietly

D **estar ~ DE algo** (falto de): **están ~s de moral** their morale is low; **está ~ de defensas** his defenses are low

E (grave) ‹*tono/voz*› deep, low

F (vil) ‹*acción/instinto*› low, base; ***caer* ~**: **¡qué ~ has caído!** how could you stoop so low!

Compuestos

- **baja cuna** *f* humble origins (*pl*)
- **baja forma** *f*: **estoy en ~ ~** I'm in bad shape
- **baja frecuencia** *f* low frequency
- **bajas presiones** *fpl* low pressure
- **bajos fondos** *mpl* underworld
- **bajo vientre** *m*: **el ~ ~** the lower abdomen

bajo² *adv* 1 ‹*volar/pasar*› low 2 ‹*hablar/cantar*› softly, quietly; **¡habla más ~!** keep your voice down!

bajo³ *m*

A 1 (planta baja) first (AmE) *o* (BrE) ground floor 2 **los bajos** (CS) the first (AmE) *o* (BrE) ground floor

B 1 (de falda, vestido) hem 2 **bajos** *mpl* (Auto) underside

C (contrabajo) (double) bass

bajo⁴ *prep* 1 (debajo de) under; **~ techo** under cover, indoors; **tres grados ~ cero** three degrees below zero; **~ el cielo estrellado** (liter) beneath the starry sky (liter) 2 (expresando sujeción, dependencia) under; **~ juramento** under oath; **~ los efectos del alcohol** under the influence of alcohol; **~ el título ...** under the title ...

bajón *m* (fam) 1 (descenso fuerte) sharp drop *o* fall; **la Bolsa ha dado un ~** the Stock Exchange index has dropped *o* fallen sharply; **ha dado un ~ este semestre** he has gone downhill this semester 2 (de ánimo) depression; **en los últimos meses ha dado un ~** he's gone downhill in the last few months 3 (de salud): **dio un ~ tremendo la semana pasada** she took a turn for the worse last week

bajorrelieve *m* bas-relief

b

bajura *f* ▸ **flota, pesca**

bakalao *m* (Esp fam) rave *o* club music; **la ruta del ~** clubbers' weekend trail of discos

bala *f*

A (Arm) (de pistola, rifle) bullet; (de cañón) cannon ball; **a prueba de ~s** bulletproof; **una ~ perdida** a stray bullet; ***como (una) ~*** ‹*salir/entrar*› like a shot (colloq); **pasar como (una) ~** to shoot past; ***echar ~*** (Méx) (disparar) to fire shots; (estar furioso): **no la nombres, se pone que echa ~** don't say her name or he'll go through the roof (colloq); ***llevar ~*** (Méx fam) to be in a hurry; ***no me/le entran ~s*** (Chi fam) I'm/he's as tough as old boots; ***ser como*** *or* ***una ~ para algo*** (Chi, Méx fam): **es como ~ para las matemáticas** she's a whizz at math (AmE) *o* maths (BrE); **es una ~ para el dominó** he's a tremendous domino player; ***ser un(a) ~ perdida*** to be a good-for-nothing

Compuestos

- **bala de fogueo** blank (round *o* cartridge)
- **bala de goma/plástico** rubber/plastic bullet

B (AmL) (Dep) shot; **lanzamiento de ~** shot put

balaca *f* (Col) 1 (Indum) hairband 2 (Dep) sweatband, headband

balacera *f* (AmL) shooting; **se armó una ~ entre policías y asaltantes** there was a shootout between the police and the bank raiders

balada *f* ballad

baladí *adj* petty, trivial

baladronada *f*: **dijo/soltó una ~ que no impresionó a nadie** his boasting *o* bragging didn't impress anybody

balalaica *f* balalaika

balance *m*

A 1 (resumen, valoración) assessment, evaluation; **hacer ~ DE algo** to take stock OF sth, to evaluate sth 2 (resultado) result, outcome; **un ~ positivo/negativo** a positive/negative result *o* outcome

B (Com, Fin) 1 (inventario) stocktaking 2 (cálculo, cómputo) balance 3 (documento) balance sheet; **cuadrar un ~** to balance (off) the accounts 4 (de cuenta) balance

balancear [A1] *vt*

A ‹*paquetes/carga*› to balance

B ‹*pierna/brazo*› to swing; ‹*barco*› to rock

■ **balancearse** *v pron* 1 «*árbol/ramas*» to sway; «*objeto colgante*» to swing 2 «*barco*» to rock; **¡deja de ~te en la silla!** stop rocking your chair!

balanceo *m* (de hamaca) swinging; (de árboles) swaying; (de barco) rocking

balancín *m*

A (mecedora) rocking chair; (de jardín) couch hammock; (de niños) seesaw, teeter-totter (AmE)

B (de acróbata) balancing pole

balandrismo *m* yachting, sailing

balandrista (*m*) yachtsman; (*f*) yachtswoman

balandro *m*, **balandra** *f* yacht, sloop

balanza *f* scales (*pl*); (de dos platillos) scales (*pl*), balance; ***inclinar la ~ a favor de algn*** to tip the balance in favor of sb; ***poner en la ~*** to weigh (AmE), to weigh up (BrE)

Compuestos

- **balanza comercial/de pagos** balance of trade/of payments
- **balanza de baño/de cocina** bathroom/kitchen scale (AmE) *o* (BrE) scales (*pl*)
- **balanza de precisión** precision balance, precision scales (*pl*)

balar [A1] *vi* to bleat, baa

balata *f* (Chi, Méx) brake lining

balaustrada *f* balustrade

balay *m* (Bol) (canasta) flat wicker basket

balazo *m* (Arm) (tiro) shot; (herida) bullet wound; **recibió un ~** he was shot; ***coser a algn a ~s*** to riddle sb with bullets

balboa *m* balboa (*Panamanian unit of currency*)

balbucear [A1] *vt*: **balbuceó unas palabras de agradecimiento** he stammered out a few words of thanks; **—yo no lo sabía —balbuceó** I didn't know, he stammered

■ **balbucear** *vi* «*adulto*» to mutter, mumble; «*bebé*» to babble

balbuceo *m* (de adulto) mumbling, muttering; (de bebé) babble; **los primeros ~s del niño** the child's first faltering words

balbuciente *adj* stammering (*before n*), stuttering (*before n*)

balbucir [I1] *vt* ▸ **balbucear**

balcón *m* 1 (Arquit) balcony 2 (mirador) observation point 3 (Chi, Ven) (Teatr) circle

baldado[1] **-da** *adj* 1 (tullido) crippled 2 (Esp fam) (molido) shattered (colloq)

baldado[2] *m* (Col) bucketful; ***caer como un ~ de agua fría*** to come as a complete shock

baldaquín, baldaquino *m* baldachin, baldaquin

balde *m*

A (cubo) bucket, pail; ***caer como un ~ de agua fría*** to come as a complete shock

B (*en locs*) **de balde** ‹*trabajar*› for nothing, for free; ‹*viajar*› for nothing, (for) free; **en balde** in vain; **nos quejamos pero fue en ~** we complained but to no avail *o* in vain; **no en balde** no wonder

baldío[1] **-día** *adj* 1 (sin cultivar): **terreno ~** waste land 2 ‹*esfuerzo*› vain, useless

baldío[2] *m* 1 (terreno sin cultivar) area of waste land 2 (Bol, Méx, RPl) (solar) piece *o* plot of land, vacant lot (AmE)

baldosa *f* floor tile; **suelo de ~s** tiled floor

baldosín *m* tile

baleado -da *m,f* (AmL): **hay varios ~s** several people have been shot *o* have received gunshot wounds

balear [A1] *vt* (AmL) to shoot; **murió baleado** he was shot dead

baleo *m* ▸ **balacera**

balero *m*

A (Méx, RPl) (juguete) *cup-and-ball toy*

B (Méx) (rodamiento) bearing

balido *m* bleat, baa

balín *m*

A (perdigón) pellet; (bala pequeña) shot

B (Méx) (rodamiento) bearing

balística *f* ballistics

balístico -ca *adj*

A (Arm, Mil) ballistic

B (Chi) (Dep) ‹*torneo*› shooting (*before n*)

baliza *f* (Náut) (boya) buoy; (señal fija) marker; (Aviac) beacon

ballena *f* (Zool) whale

Compuesto **ballena azul** blue whale

ballenato *m* whale calf

ballenero[1] **-ra** *adj* whaling (*before n*)

ballenero[2] **-ra** *m,f* 1 (persona) whaler 2 **ballenero** *m* (barco) whaleboat, whaler

ballesta *f* (Arm) crossbow

ballestero *m* crossbowman

ballet /ba'le/ *m* (*pl* **-llets**) (arte, representación) ballet; (agrupación) (corps de) ballet

balneario *m*

A (de baños medicinales) spa

B (en costa) 1 (establecimiento) private beach/club 2 (AmL) (pueblo, urbanización) seaside resort, (holiday) resort

balompié *m* soccer, football (BrE)

balón *m* 1 (Dep) ball; ***echar*** *or* ***tirar balones fuera*** to dodge the issue 2 (recipiente) cylinder

Compuesto **balón de oxígeno** oxygen cylinder; (fuerza que reanima) fillip, boost

balonazo *m*: **recibió un fuerte ~** he was hit hard by the ball

baloncesto *m* basketball

balonmano *m* handball

balonvolea *m* volleyball

balota *f* (Per) (para votar) ballot

balotar [A1] *vi* (Per) to vote

balsa *f*

A (embarcación) raft; **~ inflable/neumática** inflatable/rubber raft

Compuesto **balsa salvavidas** life raft

B (charca) pool (*where water is stored for irrigation purposes*); ***como una ~ de aceite*** as calm *o* smooth as a millpond

balsámico -ca *adj* soothing

bálsamo *m* 1 (Farm, Med) balsam, balm; **actuó como un ∼ para su espíritu** it had a soothing effect on his spirit 2 (Chi) (para el pelo) conditioner

balsero -ra *m,f*
A (conductor de balsa) (*m*) boatman; (*f*) boatwoman
B (refugiado) boatperson; **los ∼s** the boatpeople

> **balsero**
> A name for Cubans who try to enter the US by sailing to Florida in small boats and rafts

baluarte *m* (Arquit, Mil) bastion; **un ∼ de los valores tradicionales** a bastion of traditional values; **el último ∼ español en América** the last Spanish stronghold in America; **un ∼ inexpugnable** an impregnable fortress

balurdo -da *adj* (AmC, Ven arg) ‹*ropa/fiesta*› uncool (sl), naff (BrE sl); ‹*película*› crummy (colloq), schlocky (AmE colloq), naff (BrE sl); ‹*persona*› uncool (sl)

bambalina *f* (Teatr) drop (curtain); ***entre ∼s*** behind the scenes

bambolearse *v pron* «*persona/árbol/torre*» to sway; «*objeto colgante*» to swing; «*barco/tren*» to rock; «*avión/ascensor*» to lurch

bamboleo *m* (de árbol, torre) swaying; (de objeto colgante) swinging; (de barco, tren) rocking; (de avión, ascensor) lurching

bambú *m* (*pl* **-búes** *or* **-bús**) bamboo

banal *adj* banal

banana *f* (Per, RPl) banana

bananal, bananar *m* (AmL) banana plantation

bananero[1] **-ra** *adj* (AmL) banana (*before n*)

bananero[2] *m* (AmL) banana tree

banano *m* (árbol) banana tree; (fruta) (AmC, Col) banana

banca *f*
A **la ∼** 1 (sector) banking; **trabaja en la ∼** he's in banking 2 (bancos) the banks; **la nacionalización de la ∼** the nationalization of the banks
B (Jueg) bank; **hacer saltar la ∼** to break the bank; **tienes la ∼** you're banker
C 1 (Col, Ven, Méx) (asiento) bench; (pupitre) desk 2 (AmL) (Dep) (asiento) bench; (jugadores) substitutes (*pl*)
D (RPl) (en parlamento) seat; ***tener ∼*** (RPl fam) to have clout

(Compuestos)
- **banca en línea** online banking
- **banca telefónica** telephone banking

bancada *f*
A (superficie) worksurface; (Mec) bedplate
B (AmL) (Pol) 1 (nacional) delegation 2 (de partido): **la ∼ socialista/conservadora** the socialists/conservatives

bancal *m* (terraza) terrace; (huerto) plot

bancar [A2] *vt* (RPl fam)
A ‹*problema/persona*› to put up with
B (costear) to pay for
■ **bancarse** *v pron* (*enf*) (RPl fam): **ese viaje no me lo banco más** I can't bear *o* stand that journey any more

bancario[1] **-ria** *adj* ‹*interés/préstamo*› bank (*before n*); ‹*sector*› banking (*before n*)

bancario[2] **-ria** *m,f* (CS) bank employee

bancarrota *f* bankruptcy; **en ∼** bankrupt; **ir a la ∼** to go bankrupt

banco *m*
A 1 (de parque) bench; (de iglesia) pew; (de barca) thwart; (pupitre) (Chi) desk 2 (de taller) workbench

(Compuesto) **banco de carpintero** workbench

B (Com, Fin) bank; (de órganos) bank; (de información) bank

(Compuestos)
- **banco central/de inversiones** central/investment bank
- **banco de datos** data base *o* bank
- **banco de esperma/sangre/órganos** sperm/blood/organs bank

C (de peces) shoal; (bajío) bar, bank

(Compuestos)
- **banco de arena** sandbank
- **banco de coral** coral reef
- **banco de niebla** fog bank
- **banco de nieve** snowdrift

banda *f*
A (en la cintura, cruzando el pecho) sash; (franja, lista) band; (para pelo) (Méx) hairband; (en brazo) armband

(Compuestos)
- **banda ancha** broadband
- **banda de frecuencias** frequency band
- **banda del ventilador** (Méx) fan belt
- **banda magnética** magnetic strip
- **banda salarial** salary band
- **banda sonora** (Cin) sound track
- **banda transportadora** (Méx) conveyor belt

B (de barco) side; (en billar) cushion; (en fútbol, rugby) touchline; **saque de ∼** (en fútbol) throw-in; (en rugby) put-in; **lanzó el balón fuera de ∼** he kicked the ball into touch *o* (AmE) out of bounds; ***cerrarse en ∼*** to refuse to listen; ***irse en ∼*** (CS fam): **el equipo se fue en ∼** the team did terribly
C 1 (de delincuentes) gang; **∼ armada** armed gang; **∼ terrorista** terrorist group 2 (Mús) band

bandada *f* (de pájaros) flock; (de peces) shoal

bandazo *m*: ***dar ∼s*** «*equipaje*» to move about; «*coche*» to swerve about

bandear [A1] *vt* (CS) ‹*río/lago*› to cross; ‹*cerco*› to get over

bandeja *f* 1 (para servir) tray; **∼ de plata** silver salver; ***servirle*** *or* ***ponerle algo a algn en ∼*** to hand sb sth on a platter (AmE) *o* (BrE) plate; **le sirvió el gol en ∼** he set him up with an open goal 2 (de nevera, horno) tray 3 (en coche) rear shelf

(Compuesto) **bandeja de entrada/salida** in-tray/out-tray

bandejón *m* (Chi) (Auto) *tb* **∼ central** median strip (AmE), central reservation (BrE)

bandera *f*
A 1 (de nación, club) flag; (de regimiento) colors* (*pl*); **izar la ∼** to run up *o* raise the flag; **arriar la ∼** to lower *o* strike the flag; **con la ∼ a media asta** with the flag at half mast; **jurar (la) ∼** to swear allegiance to the flag; ***lleno hasta la ∼*** packed to the rafters 2 (para señales) flag, pennant; **el código** *or* **lenguaje de ∼s** the flag code 3 (de taxi): **llevaba la ∼ bajada** he didn't have the For Hire light on; **bajar la ∼** to start the meter

(Compuestos)
- **bandera ajedrezada** *or* **a cuadros** checkered* flag
- **bandera blanca/roja** white/red flag
- **bandera negra** Jolly Roger

B (Inf) flag

banderazo *m* (Dep) (de salida) starting signal; (de llegada) checkered* flag

banderilla *f* (Taur) banderilla (*barbed dart stuck into the bull's neck*)

banderillear [A1] *vt*: *to stick the banderillas into the bull's neck*

banderillero *m* banderillero (*person who sticks the banderillas into the bull's neck*)

banderín *m* (de adorno) pennant; (del juez de línea) flag; (colgando en hilera) bunting

banderita *f* flag (*sold for charity*); **día de la ∼** flag day

banderola *f* 1 (enseña) banderole 2 (RPl) (encima de puerta) transom; (en el techo) skylight

bandido -da *m,f* (delincuente) bandit; (granuja) crook; (pícaro) rascal

bando *m*
A (edicto) edict
B (facción) side, camp; **están en ∼s contrarios** they're on opposing sides; ***ser del otro ∼*** (fam) to be one of them (colloq & pej)

bandolera *f* (cinturón) Sam Browne (belt); (para cartuchos) bandolier; **en ∼** slung across one's shoulder

bandolerismo *m* banditry

bandolero -ra *m,f* bandit

bandoneón *m*: *type of accordion*

bandurria *f*: *type of mandolin*

banjo /ˈbandʒo/ *m* banjo

banquero -ra *m,f* banker

banqueta *f* 1 (taburete) stool; (para los pies) footstool 2 (Méx) (acera) sidewalk (AmE), pavement (BrE)

b

banquete *m* banquet; **nos dio un verdadero ~** she laid on a real feast for us

(Compuesto) **banquete de bodas/de gala** wedding/gala reception

banquillo *m* 1 (Der): **el ~ (de los acusados)** the dock 2 (Dep) bench

banquina *f* (RPl) 1 (lado) verge; (en autopista) shoulder (AmE), hard shoulder (BrE) 2 (cuneta) ditch

bañadera *f* (Arg fam) (bañera) bath, bathtub

bañado *m* (Bol, RPl) area of marshland

bañador *m* (Esp) (de mujer) bathing suit (esp AmE), swimming costume (BrE); (de hombre) swimming trunks

bañar [A1] *vt*

A ‹*niño/enfermo*› to bath, give … a bath

B 1 ‹*pulsera/cubierto*› to plate; **~ algo EN algo** to plate sth WITH sth 2 **bañado EN algo** (en salsa/sangre) covered WITH sth; ‹*en sudor*› bathed *o* covered IN sth; ‹*en lágrimas*› bathed IN sth

C 1 (liter) «*mar/río*» to bathe (liter), wash (liter) 2 (liter) «*luz/sol*» to bathe (liter)

■ **bañarse** *v pron* (*refl*) 1 (en bañera) to have *o* take a bath, to bathe (AmE) 2 (en mar, río) to swim, bathe; ⊘ **prohibido bañarse** no bathing; ***mandar a algn a ~se*** (CS fam) to tell sb to get lost (colloq)

bañera *f* bath, bathtub

bañero -ra *m,f* (RPl) lifeguard

bañista *mf* bather

baño *m*

A (en bañera) bath; (en mar, río) swim; **¿nos damos un ~ en la piscina?** shall we go for a swim in the pool?

(Compuestos)

- **baño (de) María**: **calentar al ~ (de) ~** heat in a double boiler *o* (BrE) in a double saucepan
- **baño de sangre** bloodbath
- **baños públicos** *mpl* public baths (*pl*)
- **baño turco** Turkish bath

B 1 (cuarto de baño) bathroom 2 (bañera) bath 3 (esp AmL) (wáter) (en casa privada) bathroom (AmE), lavatory *o* toilet (BrE), loo (BrE colloq); (en edificio público) restroom (AmE), toilet (BrE); (— de señoras) ladies; (— de caballeros) men's room (AmE), gents (BrE)

(Compuesto) **baño público** (AmL) public toilet, public convenience (BrE frml)

C 1 (de metal) plating; **tiene un ~ de oro** it's gold-plated 2 (Coc) coating

baptista[1] *adj* Baptist (*before n*)

baptista[2] *mf* Baptist

baptisterio *m* baptistry

baquelita *f* Bakelite®

baqueta *f* 1 (Arm) ramrod 2 (Méx) (Mús) drumstick

baqueteado -da *adj*

A: **una mujer baqueteada por la vida** a woman who has taken a few knocks in her life; **estos zapatos están muy ~s** I've nearly worn these shoes out

B (en trabajo, negocio) experienced

baquiano[1] **-na** *adj* (RPl): **un jinete muy ~** a very skillful rider, an expert rider

baquiano[2] **-na** *m,f* (AmL) guide

báquiro *m* (Col, Ven) peccary

bar *m*

A (local) bar; (mueble) liquor cabinet (AmE), drinks cabinet (BrE)

B (Fís) bar

barahúnda *f* pandemonium; **se armó la ~** pandemonium *o* chaos broke out

baraja *f* deck *o* (BrE) pack (of cards); ***jugar con dos ~s*** to play a double game; ***o jugamos todos o se rompe la ~*** either we all do it or nobody does

barajar [A1] *vt*

A ‹*cartas*› to shuffle

B ‹*nombres/posibilidades*› to consider, look at; ‹*cifras*› to talk about, mention

C 1 (Col, Méx, Ven fam) (explicar) to explain; **barájamela más despacio** explain it *o* (colloq) give it to me more slowly 2 (Col fam) (enredar): **el nuevo jefe le barajó la vida** his new boss made life very complicated for him

baranda *f*

A (de balcón) rail; (de escalera) handrail, banister

B (en billar) cushion

barandilla *f* (Esp) (de balcón) rail; (de escalera) handrail

barata *f*

A (Chi) (cucaracha) cockroach

B (Méx) (liquidación) sale

baratija *f* (alhaja) trinket; (adorno) knickknack

barato[1] **-ta** *adj* 1 ‹*vestido/restaurante/viaje*› cheap, low-priced; ***lo ~ sale caro*** cheap things cost you more in the long run 2 ‹*periodismo*› cheap; ‹*música*› commercial 3 (como adv) ‹*costar/comprar*› **el coche nos costó muy ~** we got the car really cheap; **las compré baratísimas en una liquidación** I got them really cheap in a sale

barato[2] *adv* ‹*comer/vivir*› cheaply; **en esa tienda venden muy ~** prices are really low in that shop; **se compra más ~ en el mercado** you can get things cheaper in the market

baraúnda *f* ▸**barahúnda**

barba *f*

A 1 (de quien se la afeita) stubble; **~ de dos días** two days' growth of stubble 2 (de quien se la deja) beard; **dejarse (la) ~** to grow a beard; **el de la ~** the one with the beard; ***con toda la ~***: **es un líder con toda la ~** he's a true *o* real leader; ***en sus (mismísimas) ~s*** (fam) right under his nose (colloq); ***hacerle la ~ a algn*** (Méx fam) to suck up to sb (colloq); ***por ~*** (fam) each; ***subírsele a algn a las ~s*** (fam) to get fresh (AmE) *o* (BrE) cheeky with sb (colloq); ***cuando las ~s de tu vecino veas pelar pon las tuyas a remojar*** you should learn from other people's mistakes 3 (mentón, barbilla) chin

B *tb* **barbas** *fpl* 1 (de raíz) beard 2 (de cabra) beard; (de pez) barbels (*pl*); (de ave) wattle

barbacoa *f* 1 (parrilla) barbecue; (carne) barbecued meat; **a la ~** barbecued 2 (Méx) *meat roasted in an oven dug in the earth*

barbado -da *adj* (liter): **un hombre ~** a bearded man, a man with a beard

barbaján -jana *m,f* (Méx) boor

barbaridad *f*

A (acto atroz) atrocity

B (disparate): **pagar tanto es una ~** it's madness to pay that much; **lo que hiciste es una ~** what you've done is outrageous; **es capaz de cualquier ~** he's quite capable of doing something really terrible *o* stupid; **¡qué ~!** good heavens!; **¡cómo puedes decir semejante ~!** how can you say such an outrageous (*o* stupid *etc*) thing!; **su examen estaba lleno de ~es** his exam paper was full of terrible mistakes; ***una ~*** (fam) ‹*comer*› like a horse; ‹*fumar*› like a chimney; **nos costó una ~** it cost us a fortune; **pesa una ~** it weighs a ton; **una ~ de algo** loads of sth

barbarie *f* (de tribu, pueblo) barbarism, savagery; (brutalidad) barbarity

barbarismo *m* (extranjerismo) loan word, borrowing; (solecismo) barbarism

bárbaro[1] **-ra** *adj*

A (Hist) barbarian

B 1 (imprudente): **no seas ~, no te tires de ahí** don't be an idiot *o* don't be so stupid, don't try jumping off there 2 (bruto): **el muy ~ la hizo llorar** the brute made her cry; **no seas ~, no se lo digas** don't be crass *o* cruel, don't tell him

C (fam) (como intensificador) ‹*casa/coche*› fantastic; **tengo un hambre bárbara** I'm starving

bárbaro[2] *adv* (fam): **lo pasamos ~** we had a fantastic time (colloq)

bárbaro[3] **-ra** *m,f*

A (Hist) Barbarian

B (fam) (bruto) lout, thug; **esos ~s me la destrozaron** those louts ruined it; **esos ~s me rompieron los vidrios del coche** those vandals *o* thugs smashed my car windows; ***comer como un ~*** (fam) to eat like a horse

barbecho *m* 1 (estado): **dejar la tierra en ~** to leave the land fallow; ***estar en ~*** (CS) to be in preparation; **el proyecto está en ~** the project is in gestation *o* is taking shape 2 (campo) *field that is left fallow*

barbería *f* barber's (shop)

barbero[1] *m* barber

barbero² **-ra** *m,f* (Méx fam) toady

barbijo *m* (RPl) (cinta) chin strap; (mascarilla) surgical mask

barbilampiño *adj*: **un hombre ~** a man with a light beard; **es muy ~** he has a very light beard

barbilla *f* chin

barbitúrico¹ **-ca** *adj* barbituric

barbitúrico² *m* barbiturate

barbo *m* barbel

barbudo¹ **-da** *adj*: **un hombre ~** a bearded man, a man with a beard

barbudo² *m* bearded man, man with a beard

barca *f* boat

(Compuesto) **barca de remos** rowboat (AmE), rowing boat (BrE)

barcaza *f* (en canales, ríos) barge; (entre barco y tierra) lighter

(Compuesto) **barcaza de desembarco** landing craft

Barcelona *f* Barcelona

barchilón **-lona** *m,f* (Bol, Per fam) auxiliary nurse

barco¹ *adj inv* (Méx fam): **es una profesora muy ~** that teacher is a real soft touch

barco² *m* (Náut) boat; (grande) ship, vessel (frml); **un viaje en ~** a journey by sea (*o* river *etc*); **ir/viajar en ~** to go/travel by boat/ship; **abandonar el ~** to abandon ship; ***como ~ sin timón*** like a ship without a rudder, aimlessly

(Compuestos)
- **barco de carga/pasajeros** cargo/passenger ship/boat
- **barco de guerra** warship
- **barco de pesca** fishing boat
- **barco de vapor** steamboat, steamer
- **barco de vela** sailing boat, sailboat (AmE)
- **barco mercante** merchant ship

barda *f* (Méx) (de cemento) wall; (de madera) fence

bardo *m* bard

baremo *m* scale

bargueño *m* (escritorio) bureau; (aparador) sideboard

bario *m* barium

barítono **-na** *adj/m* baritone

barlovento *m* windward

barman /'barman/ *m* (*pl* **-mans**) barman, bartender (AmE)

barniz *m* [1] (para madera) varnish [2] (de cultura, educación) veneer

(Compuesto) **barniz de** *or* **para las uñas** nail varnish (esp BrE), nail polish (AmE)

barnizado *m* varnishing

barnizar [A4] *vt* to varnish

baro *m* (Méx fam) peso

barómetro *m* barometer

barón *m* (título nobiliario) baron; (de organización) influential member

baronesa *f* baroness

baronía *f* barony

barquero **-ra** (*m*) boatman; (*f*) boatwoman

barquilla *f* (de globo) basket, carriage; (Náut) log

barquillo *m* (galleta) wafer; (cono) ice-cream cone *o* (BrE) cornet

barra *f*

A [1] (de armario) rail; (para cortinas) rod, pole; (de bicicleta) crossbar [2] (de oro) bar; (de turrón, helado) block; (de jabón) bar; (de desodorante) stick; (de chocolate) bar; (de pan) (Esp, Méx) stick, French loaf

(Compuestos)
- **barra de cambios** (Col) gear shift (AmE), gear lever *o* stick (BrE)
- **barra de labios** lipstick
- **barra espaciadora** space bar

B [1] (banda, franja) bar; **las ~s y estrellas** the Stars and Stripes [2] (Mús) bar (line) [3] (signo de puntuación) oblique, slash

C (para ballet, gimnasia) bar; **ejercicios en la ~** bar exercises

(Compuestos)
- **barra de equilibrio** beam
- **barra fija** horizontal bar
- **barras asimétricas/paralelas** *fpl* asymmetric/parallel bars (*pl*)

D (de bar, cafetería) bar; **nos sentamos en la ~** we sat (down) at the bar

(Compuesto) **barra americana/libre** hostess/free bar

E (AmL fam) [1] (de hinchas, seguidores) supporters (*pl*); **¿qué gritan la(s) ~(s)?** what are the supporters shouting?; ***hacerle ~ a algn*** (Andes fam) to cheer sb on [2] (de amigos) gang (colloq)

(Compuesto) **barra de abogados** (Méx) bar

F (Geog) [1] (banco de arena) sandbank, bar [2] (CS) (desembocadura) mouth

barrabasada *f* (fam) prank; **hacer ~s** to play pranks

barraca *f*

A (puesto) stall; (caseta) booth

B (Mil) barrack hut

C (casa) adobe house (*typical of Valencia and Murcia*)

D (CS) (de materiales de construcción) builders merchant *o* yard

barracón *m* (Mil) barrack hut; (construcción rústica) hut, cabin

barranca *f* [1] (RPl) (pendiente, cuesta) hill, slope; **~ *abajo*** downhill [2] (barranco) gully; (más profundo) ravine

barranco *m* gully; (más profundo) ravine

barranquismo *m* canyoning

barredor **-dora** *m,f* (Per) road sweeper, street cleaner

barreminas *m* (*pl* ~) minesweeper

barrena *f* (punzón) gimlet; (taladro, perforadora) drill

barrenar [A1] *vt* (perforar) to drill; (volar) ‹*roca*› to blast

barrendero **-ra** *m,f* road sweeper, street cleaner

barreno *m* (barrena) drill; (para explosivo) shot hole

barreño *m* (Esp) washbowl (AmE), washing-up bowl (BrE)

barrer [E1] *vt*

A ‹*suelo/cocina*› to sweep

B [1] (arrastrar) to sweep away; **una ola lo barrió de la cubierta** a wave swept him off the deck [2] ‹*rival*› to thrash, trounce

C (Méx) (mirar) to look … up and down

■ **barrer** *vi*

A (con escoba) to sweep; **~ *para dentro*** (fam) to look after number one (colloq)

B (arrasar) to sweep the board; **barrieron en las últimas elecciones** they swept the board in the last election; **barrió en la primera etapa** he swept to victory on the first stage; **la tormenta barrió con todo** the storm swept everything away; **barrió con todos los premios** she walked off with all the prizes

■ **barrerse** *v pron* (Méx) [1] «*vehículo*» to skid [2] (en fútbol, béisbol) to slide

barrera *f* [1] barrier; **~ psicológica** psychological barrier; **ha superado la ~ del 10%** it has gone above the 10% mark [2] (Ferr) barrier, crossing gate [3] (Taur) (valla) barrier; (localidad) front row

(Compuestos)
- **barrera aduanera** *or* **arancelaria** customs barrier
- **barrera del sonido** sound barrier; **superar** *or* **romper la ~ del ~** to break the sound barrier
- **barrera de peaje** toll barrier
- **barrera generacional** generation gap
- **barrera idiomática** *or* **del idioma** language barrier

barriada *f* [1] (barrio) area, district (*often poor or working-class*) [2] (AmL) (barrio marginal) slum area, shantytown

barrial *m* (AmL) quagmire

barrica *f* barrel, cask

barricada *f* barricade

barrida *f*, **barrido** *m*

A [1] (con escoba) sweep; ***servir lo mismo para un barrido que para un fregado*** to be a jack of all trades [2] (Cin) wipe

B (en béisbol) slide

C (AmL) (redada) police raid

barriga *f*

A (fam) (vientre) belly (colloq), tummy (colloq); **dolor de ~** bellyache (colloq), tummy ache (colloq); **tiene mucha ~** she has quite a belly *o* tummy (colloq); **echar ~** to develop a paunch *o* (colloq) gut; ***rascarse*** *or* ***tocarse la ~*** (fam) to sit on one's backside *o* (AmE) butt (colloq)

B (de vasija) belly, rounded part

barrigón[1] **-gona** *adj* (fam): **se está volviendo barrigona** she's getting a bit of a belly *o* tummy (colloq); **un viejo ~** an old man with a paunch

barrigón[2] **-gona** *m,f* (fam): **es un ~** he's got a bit of a paunch *o* (colloq) gut; **es una barrigona** she's got a bit of a belly (colloq)

b

barrigudo -da *adj/m,f* (fam) ▸**barrigón**[1,2]

barril *m* 1 (de metal) barrel, keg; (de madera) barrel, cask; ***ser un ~ sin fondo*** (AmC, Chi, Méx fam) to be a bottomless pit (colloq) 2 (de pólvora) powder keg; (de petróleo) barrel

barrilete *m*
A (de revólver) chamber
B (de carpintero) clamp, dog

barrio *m* (zona) neighborhood*; **la gente del ~** people in the neighborhood, local people; **el mercado del ~** the local market; **vive en un ~ de las afueras** she lives out in the suburbs

(Compuestos)
- **barrio alto** (Chi) smart neighborhood
- **barrio chino** (de chinos) Chinatown; (zona de prostitución) (Esp) red-light district
- **barrio de invasión** (Col) shanty town
- **barrio de tolerancia** (Andes) red-light district
- **barrio espontáneo** (AmC) shanty town
- **barrio obrero/residencial** working-class/residential neighborhood *o* area
- **barrio periférico** suburb
- **barrios bajos** *mpl* poor neighborhoods (*pl*)

barriobajero -ra *adj* (pey) common (pej)

barrista *mf* (AmL) (Dep) fan, supporter

barrizal *m* quagmire, muddy area

barro *m* 1 (lodo) mud; **traes los zapatos llenos de ~** your shoes are covered in mud; **arrastraron su buen nombre por el ~** they dragged his reputation through the mud 2 (Art) clay, earthenware (*before n*)

(Compuesto) **barro cocido/refractario** fired/refractory clay

barroco[1] **-ca** *adj* ‹*estilo*› baroque; (recargado) overelaborate

barroco[2] *m* 1 (estilo) baroque (style) 2 (período) Baroque period

barroquismo *m* (Arquit, Art, Lit, Mús) baroque style; (rebuscamiento) overelaborate language (*o* style *etc*)

barrote *m* (de celda, ventana) bar; (en carpintería) crosspiece

barruntar [A1] *vt* to suspect
■ **barruntarse** *v pron* (*enf*) to suspect

barrunto *m* (sospecha) suspicion

bartola *f*: ***echarse*** *or* ***tumbarse a la ~*** (fam) (acostarse) to hit the sack *o* hay (colloq); (estar sin trabajar) to laze about; ***hacer algo a la ~*** (CS fam) to do sth any old how (colloq)

bártulos *mpl* (fam) gear (colloq), stuff (colloq); ***liar los ~*** (fam) to pack one's bags *o* things

barullo *m*
A (alboroto) racket (colloq), ruckus (AmE)
B (desorden) muddle, mess; (confusión): **me armé un ~** I got all muddled up *o* (AmE) messed up (colloq)

basa *f* base

basalto *m* basalt

basamento *m* plinth

basar [A1] *vt* ‹*teoría/idea*› **~ algo EN algo** to base sth ON sth
■ **basarse** *v pron* 1 «*persona*» **~se EN algo**: **¿en qué te basas para decir eso?** and what basis *o* grounds do you have for saying that?; **se basó en esos datos** he based his argument (*o* theory *etc*) on that information 2 «*teoría/creencia/idea/opinión*» **~se EN algo** to be based ON sth

basca *f* (Esp arg) 1 (gente) people (*pl*) 2 (pandilla) gang

báscula *f* scales (*pl*); **~ de baño** bathroom scales

bascular [A1] *vi* 1 (oscilar) to swing 2 (levantarse) to tilt

base[1] *f*
A 1 (parte inferior) base 2 *tb* **~ de maquillaje** foundation
B 1 (fundamento): **tengo suficiente ~ para asegurar eso** I have sufficient grounds to claim that; **la ~ de una buena salud es una alimentación sana** the basis of good health is a balanced diet; **sentar las ~s de algo** to lay the foundations of sth; **un movimiento sin ~ popular** a movement without a popular power base; **tomar algo como ~** to take sth as a starting point; **sobre la ~ de estos datos** on the basis of this information 2 (componente principal): **la ~ de su alimentación es el arroz** their diet is based on rice; **la ~ de este perfume es el jazmín** this perfume has a jasmine base 3 (conocimientos básicos): **tiene una sólida ~ científica** he has a sound grounding in science; **llegó al curso sin ninguna ~** he didn't have the basics when he began the course

(Compuestos)
- **base de datos** database
- **base imponible** tax base (AmE), taxable income (BrE)

C (*en locs*) **a base de**: **a ~ de descansar se fue recuperando** by resting she gradually recovered; **un régimen a ~ de verdura** a vegetable-based diet; **vive a ~ de pastillas** he lives on pills; **de base** ‹*planteamiento/error*› fundamental, basic; ‹*militante*› rank-and-file (*before n*), ordinary (*before n*); ‹*movimiento*› grass-roots (*before n*); **en base a** (crit) on the basis of; ***a ~ de bien*** (Esp fam): **comimos a ~ de bien** we ate really well
D (centro de operaciones) base; **~ aérea/naval/militar** air/naval/military base

(Compuesto) **base de lanzamiento** launch site

E **las ~s** (Pol) the rank and file (*pl*)
F (Mat, Quím) base
G **bases** *fpl* (de concurso) rules (*pl*)
H 1 (en béisbol) base 2 **base** *mf* (en baloncesto) guard

base[2] *adj inv* 1 (básico, elemental) basic; ‹*documento/texto*› draft (*before n*) 2 ‹*campamento*› base (*before n*)

básica *f* (Esp) primary *o* elementary education

básicamente *adv* basically

básico -ca *adj*
A 1 (fundamental, esencial) basic; **alimento ~** staple food 2 ‹*conocimientos/vocabulario*› basic; ‹*requisito*› essential, fundamental
B (Quím) basic

basílica *f* basilica

basilisco *m* (Mit) basilisk; ***estar hecho un ~*** (fam) to be seething (colloq); ***ponerse como un ~*** (fam) to hit the roof (colloq)

basket, básquet *m* basketball

básquetbol, basquetbol *m* (AmL) basketball

basquetbolista *mf* (AmL) basketball player

bastante[1] *adj*
A (suficiente) enough; **~s vasos/~ vino** enough glasses/wine
B (cantidad o número considerable) plenty of, quite a lot of; **había ~ gente** there were plenty of people

bastante[2] *pron*
A (suficiente) enough; **ya tenemos ~s** we already have enough; **ya he visto ~** I've seen enough
B (demasiado): **deja ~ que desear** it leaves a lot to be desired

bastante[3] *adv*
A (suficientemente) enough; **no te has esforzado ~** you haven't tried hard enough
B (considerablemente) (*con verbos*) quite a lot; (*con adjetivos, adverbios*) quite; **le gusta bastante** she likes him quite a lot; **me pareció ~ aburrido/agradable** I thought he was rather boring/quite pleasant; **llegó ~ cansado** he was quite tired when he arrived; **es ~ fácil de curar** it's quite *o* fairly easy to cure

bastar [A1] *vi* to be enough; **¿basta con esto?** will this be enough?; **basta con marcar el 101** just dial 101; **baste con decir que ...** suffice it to say that ...; **¡basta ya!** that's enough!; **¡basta de tonterías!** that's enough nonsense!; (+ *me/te/le etc*): **me basta con tu palabra** your word is good enough for me; ***~ que ... para que ...***: **basta que digas sí para que él diga no** whatever you say he's bound to say the opposite; ***~ y sobrar*** to be more than enough; ***hasta decir basta*** (fam): **comimos hasta decir basta** we ate so much we were ready *o* fit to burst (colloq); **llovió hasta decir basta** it poured *o* bucketed down (colloq)
■ **bastarse** *v pron*: **ella sola se basta** she can manage on her own

bastardilla *f* italic type, italics (*pl*)

bastardo[1] **-da** *adj*
A (ilegítimo) illegitimate
B (innoble) base

bastardo² **-da** *m,f* bastard

bastidor *m*

A (Teatr) wing; ***entre ~es*** (Teatr) offstage, in the wings; (sin transcender al público) behind the scenes

B 1 (de ventana) frame 2 (de lienzo) stretcher 3 (para bordar) frame 4 (Esp) (Auto) chassis

bastión *m* bastion

basto¹ **-ta** *adj* coarse

basto² *m* 1 **bastos** *mpl* (palo) *one of the suits in a Spanish pack of cards* 2 (carta) *any card of the* **bastos** *suit*

bastón *m* (para caminar) walking stick, cane; (en desfiles) baton; (de esquí) ski stick *o* pole

(Compuesto) **bastón de mando** (ceremonial) staff

bastoncillo *m*

A (de algodón) cotton swab (AmE), cotton bud (BrE)

B (Anat) (retinal) rod

basura *f*

A 1 (recipiente) garbage *o* trash can (AmE), dustbin (BrE); **echar** *or* **tirar algo a la ~** to throw sth in the garbage *o* trash (can) *o* dustbin 2 (desechos) garbage (AmE), trash (AmE), rubbish (BrE); (en sitios públicos) litter; **sacar la ~** to take out the garbage *o* trash *o* rubbish; **la recogida de la ~** the garbage *o* rubbish *o* (frml) refuse collection; **Ⓢ prohibido arrojar basura(s)** no dumping

B (fam) (porquería) trash (AmE colloq), rubbish (BrE colloq); **la comida era una ~** the food was lousy (colloq)

basural *m* (AmL) ▸ **basurero B1**

basurear [A1] *vt* (CS, Per fam) 1 (tratar mal): **~ a algn** to treat sb like dirt; **me basureaban por ser pobre** they used to give me a hard time because I was poor (colloq) 2 (Dep) (vencer) to thrash, trounce

basurero **-ra** *m,f*

A (persona) garbage collector (AmE), dustman (BrE)

B **basurero** *m* 1 (vertedero) garbage dump (AmE), rubbish dump *o* tip (BrE) 2 (Chi, Méx) (recipiente) trash can (AmE), dustbin (BrE)

basuriento **-ta** *adj* (CS fam) dirty, mucky (colloq)

bata *f* (para estar en casa) dressing gown, robe; (de médico) white coat; (de farmacéutico) lab coat; (de colegio) work coat (AmE), overall (BrE)

batacazo *m*

A (fam) (golpe) thump; **se pegó un ~** he fell over and banged his arm (*o* head *etc*)

B (RPl fam) (triunfo inesperado) shock *o* surprise win

bataclana *f* (CS) showgirl

batahola *f* (esp AmL fam) racket, din, ruckus (AmE)

batalla *f* 1 (lucha) battle; **librar ~** to do battle; **libraron una larga ~ contra el analfabetismo** they waged a long battle against illiteracy; **de ~** (fam) ‹*zapatos/abrigo*› everyday (*before n*); ***dar ~*** (Méx, Ven fam): **estos niños dan ~ todo el día** these kids don't let up for one minute (colloq); **un problema que le ha dado mucha ~** a problem which has caused her a lot of hassle (colloq); ***dar la ~*** to put up a fight 2 (interior) struggle, battle

(Compuestos)

- **batalla campal** pitched battle
- **batalla naval** (Náut) naval battle

batallar [A1] *vi* 1 (luchar) to battle; **~ CON algn** to battle WITH sb; **~ CON algo** to wrestle *o* struggle WITH sth; **todavía está batallando con el mismo problema** she's still wrestling with the same problem 2 (Mil) to fight

batallón *m* (Mil) battalion; (grupo numeroso) (fam) gang (colloq)

> **batasuna**
>
> The banned political wing of Eta

batasuno **-na** *m,f* (en Esp) (Pol) member *or* supporter of Batasuna

batata *f* sweet potato, yam

batatazo *m* 1 (Andes fam) (golpe de suerte) stroke of luck 2 (Chi) (triunfo inesperado) shock *o* surprise win 3 (Col) (idea genial) stroke of genius, brainstorm (AmE), brainwave (BrE)

batea *f*

A 1 (bandeja) tray; (para mariscos) bed 2 (barco) flat-bottomed boat

B (AmL) 1 (recipiente) shallow pan *o* tray (*for washing*) 2 (comedero) trough

bateador **-dora** *m,f* (en béisbol, softbol) batter; (en cricket) batsman

(Compuesto) **bateador designado** **-dora designada** *m,f* designated hitter

batear [A1] *vi* to bat

■ **batear** *vt* to hit

batería *f*

A (Auto) battery; **se me descargó la ~** my battery went dead (AmE) *o* (BrE) flat; ***aparcar*** *or* ***estacionar en ~*** to park front/rear to the curb (AmE), to park nose/tail to the kerb (BrE); ***(re)cargar las ~s*** (fam) to recharge one's batteries

B (Mús) drums (*pl*), drum kit

C (de artillería) battery

(Compuesto) **batería de cocina** *set of saucepans and kitchen utensils*

D **batería** *mf* drummer

baterista *mf* (AmL) drummer

batiburrillo *m* (fam) (de objetos) jumble; (de ideas) mishmash

batida *f*: **los cazadores dieron una ~** the hunters beat the area; **los detenidos durante la ~** those detained during the raid; **el ejército está haciendo una ~ en la zona** the army is combing *o* searching the area

batido¹ **-da** *adj* ‹*camino*› well-trodden, well-worn

batido² *m* (de leche) (milk) shake; (para panqueques) (AmL) batter

batidor **-dora** *m,f*

A (Mil) scout

B (en la caza) beater

C **batidor** *m* 1 (manual) whisk, beater; (eléctrico) mixer, blender 2 (peine) wide-toothed comb

D **batidora** *f* (máquina eléctrica) mixer, blender

batiente *m*

A (marco) jamb; (hoja) leaf, panel

B (en la costa) exposed place

batifondo *m* (RPl fam) uproar

batín *m* dressing gown

batir [I1] *vt*

A ‹*huevos*› to beat, whisk; ‹*crema/nata*› to whip; ‹*mantequilla*› to churn; **~ las claras a punto de nieve** beat *o* whisk the egg whites until stiff

B ‹*marca/récord*› to break; ‹*enemigo/rival*› to beat

C 1 ‹*ala*› to beat, flap 2 **~ palmas** to clap 3 ‹*metal*› to beat 4 (liter) «*viento/lluvia*» to beat against; «*olas/mar*» to beat *o* crash against 5 (Mil) ‹*muralla/posición*› to pound, batter

D ‹*lugar*› «*ejército/policía*» to comb, search; «*cazador*» to beat

■ **batir** *vi* «*viento/lluvia/mar*» **~ SOBRE/CONTRA algo** to beat ON/AGAINST sth

■ **batirse** *v pron*

A 1 (enfrentarse): **~se a** *or* **en duelo** to fight a duel 2 (Chi) ***batírselas*** to manage

B (Méx) (ensuciarse) to get dirty; **llegó batido de lodo** he was covered in mud when he arrived

batiscafo *m* bathyscaphe

batracio *m* batrachian

batuque *m* (RPl) racket, din; **meter ~** to make a racket *o* din

batuta *f* baton; ***llevar la ~*** (fam) to be the boss (colloq); ***tomar la ~*** (fam) to take charge

baúl *m* 1 (arca) chest 2 (de viaje) trunk 3 (Col, Ven, RPl) (del coche, carro) trunk (AmE), boot (BrE)

bausa *f* (Per fam): **estar de ~** to be off school (*o* work)

bautismal *adj* baptismal

bautismo *m* (de bebé) baptism, christening; (de adulto) baptism

(Compuesto) **bautismo de fuego** baptism of fire

bautizar [A4] *vt* 1 (Relig) ‹*bebé*› to baptize, christen; ‹*adulto*› to baptize; **la ~ron con el nombre de Ana** she was christened Ana 2 ‹*barco*› to name 3 (fam) (poner mote) to nickname

bautizo *m* 1 (Relig) (de bebé) christening, baptism; (de adulto) baptism; (fiesta) christening party 2 (de barco) naming, launching

bauxita *f* bauxite
baya *f* (Bot) berry
bayeta *f* 1 (para limpiar) cloth 2 (Bol, Col) (tela) baize
bayo -ya *adj* cream (*before n*), cream-colored*
bayoneta *f* 1 (Arm) bayonet; **calar las ~s** to fix bayonets 2 (Mec) bayonet
baza *f*
A (en naipes) trick; **hacer** *or* **ganar una ~** to win a trick; ***meter ~*** (fam) to butt in (colloq); **Pedro nunca deja meter ~ a nadie** Pedro never lets anybody get a word in edgewise (AmE) *o* (BrE) edgeways
B (recurso, arma): **parece la mejor ~ del equipo** he could prove to be the team's trump card; **jugaron su última ~** they played their last card
bazar *m*
A (mercado oriental) bazaar
B 1 (tienda) hardware store (*often selling a wide range of electrical goods and toys*) 2 (Col, Ven) (de caridad) fête, bazaar
bazo *m* spleen
bazofia *f* (fam) garbage (AmE colloq), rubbish (BrE colloq)
bazooka /ba'suka, ba'θuka/, **bazuca** *f* bazooka
be *f*: *name of the letter* **b**, *often called* **be larga** *or* **grande** *to distinguish it from* **v**
beatería *f* (pey) affected piety
beatificación *f* beatification
beatificar [A2] *vt* to beatify
beatífico -ca *adj* beatific
beatitud *f* beatitude
beato¹ -ta *adj* (Relig) blessed; (piadoso) pious; (santurrón) (pey) excessively devout
beato² -ta *m,f* 1 (Relig): **~ Roque González** the blessed Roque González 2 (piadoso) pious person; (pey) excessively devout person
bebe -ba *m,f* (RPl, Per) baby
bebé *m* baby
(Compuesto) **bebé probeta** test-tube baby
bebedera *f* (AmC, Méx fam) drinking spree
bebedero *m* (paraje) watering hole; (recipiente) trough; (para personas) (CS, Méx) drinking fountain
bebedizo *m* (bebida — mágica) magic potion, philter*; (— envenenada) poisoned drink; (— medicinal) potion
bebedor -dora *m,f* drinker; **un ~ empedernido** a hardened drinker; **es buen/mal ~** he can/can't hold his drink
beber¹ [E1] *vt* to drink; **¿quieres ~ algo?** do you want something to drink?; **bébelo a sorbos** sip it
■ **beber** *vi* to drink; **si bebes no conduzcas** don't drink and drive; **~ a la salud de algn** to drink sb's *o* (BrE) to sb's health; **~ POR algn** to drink TO sb, toast sb; **~ POR algo** to drink TO sth; **~ DE algo** to drink FROM sth
■ **beberse** *v pron* (*enf*) to drink up; **nos bebimos la botella entera** we drank the whole bottle
beber² *m* 1: **el buen ~ y el buen comer** good food and drink 2 (acción) drinking
bebida *f* (líquido) drink, beverage (frml); (vicio) drink
bebido -da *adj* [ESTAR] (borracho) drunk; **llegó a casa ~** he came home drunk
beca *f* (ayuda económica) grant; (que se otorga por méritos) scholarship
becado -da *m,f* (AmL) ▸ **becario**
becar [A2] *vt* (dar ayuda ecónomica) to give *o* (frml) award a grant to; (dar beca por méritos) to give *o* (frml) award a scholarship to
becario -ria *m,f* recipient of a grant; (por méritos) scholarship holder, scholar
becerrada *f* bullfight (*using young bulls*)
becerro -rra *m,f* (Agr, Taur) calf, young bull; (piel) calfskin
(Compuesto) **becerro de oro** golden calf
bechamel *f* white sauce
bedel *mf* ≈ porter
beduino -na *adj/m,f* bedouin
beee *interj* baa
begonia *f* begonia
beige, (Esp) **beis** /beʒ, beis/ *adj inv/m* beige; (más oscuro) fawn
béisbol, (Méx) **beisbol** *m* baseball
beldad *f* (liter) (mujer bella) beauty; (cualidad) beauty
belén *m*
A (nacimiento) nativity scene, crib, crèche (AmE)
B (lugar desordenado) mess; ***meterse en belenes*** (fam) to get into a jam *o* fix (colloq)
Belén *m* Bethlehem
belga *adj/mf* Belgian
Bélgica *f* Belgium
Belgrado *m* Belgrade
Belice *m* Belize
belicismo *m* warmongering
belicista *adj* militaristic
bélico -ca *adj* military; **preparativos ~s** preparations for war
belicosidad *f* aggressiveness
belicoso -sa *adj* 1 ‹*pueblo*› warlike, bellicose (liter) 2 ‹*persona/carácter*› bellicose, belligerent
beligerancia *f* belligerency
beligerante *adj* belligerent; **los países ~s** the belligerent *o* warring nations
bellaco -ca *m,f* (fam & hum) rogue (colloq & hum)
belladona /beja'ðona, bela'ðona/ *f* (planta) deadly nightshade, belladonna; (extracto) belladonna
belleza *f*
A (cualidad) beauty
B 1 (cosa bella): **este paisaje es una ~** this is beautiful countryside 2 (mujer bella) beauty
bellísimo -ma *adj* wonderful; *ver tb* **bello**
bello -lla *adj* ‹*mujer/paisaje/poema*› (liter) beautiful; **la Bella Durmiente (del Bosque)** (Lit) Sleeping Beauty; ***ser una bella persona*** to be a good person
(Compuestos)
- **bellas artes** *fpl* fine art, beaux-arts (*pl*)
- **bello sexo**: **el ~ ~** the fair sex

bellota *f* acorn
bemba *f* (AmL fam) thick lips (*pl*)
bembo *m* (AmL) thick lower lip
bembón -bona, **bembudo -da** *adj* (AmL fam) (de labios gruesos) thick-lipped
bemol¹ *adj* flat; **si ~** B flat
bemol² *m* (signo) flat (sign); (nota) flat; ***tener ~es*** (fam): **parece fácil pero tiene (sus) ~es** it looks easy but in fact it's quite tricky *o* quite difficult; **¡tiene ~s!** (Esp) this is too much!
benceno *m* benzene
bencina *f* 1 (Quím) benzine, petroleum ether 2 (Andes) (gasolina) gasoline (AmE), petrol (BrE)
bencinera *f* (Andes) filling station, gas station (AmE), petrol station (BrE)
bencinero¹ -ra *adj* (Andes) ‹*motor*› gasoline (AmE) (*before n*), petrol (BrE) (*before n*)
bencinero² -ra *m,f* (Andes) filling station attendant
bendecir [I25] *vt* to bless; **¡que Dios te bendiga!** God bless you!; **~ la mesa** to say grace; **bendigo la hora en que lo conocí** I bless the day that I met him
bendice, etc *see* **bendecir**
bendición *f* 1 (Relig) blessing, benediction; **nos dio** *or* (fam) **echó la ~** he gave us the blessing, he blessed us 2 (aprobación) blessing 3 (regalo divino) godsend
bendiga, bendijo, etc *see* **bendecir**
bendito¹ -ta *adj* 1 (Relig) blessed; **¡~ sea Dios!** (expresando contrariedad) good God *o* grief!; (expresando alivio) thank God! 2 ‹*agua/pan*› holy; (afortunado) lucky 3 (*delante del n*) (iró) (maldito) blessed (*before n*) (euph)
bendito² -ta *m,f* simple soul; ***dormir como un ~*** to sleep like a baby
benedictino -na *adj/m,f* Benedictine
benefactor -tora *m,f* benefactor
beneficencia *f* (caridad) charity; **asociación/obra de ~** charitable organization/work; **concierto de ~** charity *o* benefit concert
beneficiar [A1] *vt*
A (favorecer) to benefit, to be of benefit to; **esto beneficia a**

ambas partes this benefits both sides, this is of benefit to both sides; **salir beneficiados con algo** to be better off with sth; **verse beneficiado con algo** to benefit from sth **B** ‹*efectos/créditos*› to sell ... below par (AmE), to sell ... off (BrE) **C** ‹*res/cerdo*› (AmL) to dress; ‹*mineral*› (Chi) to extract
■ **beneficiarse** *v pron* (sacar provecho) to benefit; **~se CON/DE algo** to benefit FROM sth

beneficiario -ria *m,f* beneficiary; (de cheque) payee

beneficio *m*
A **1** (Com, Fin) profit; **producir** *or* **reportar ~s** to yeild *o* bring returns *o* profits; **margen de ~(s)** profit margin **2** (ventaja, bien) benefit; **no va a sacar gran ~ del asunto** he's not going to benefit much from this affair; **a ~ de** in aid of; **en ~ de todos** in the interests of everyone; **todo lo hace en ~ propio** everything he does is for his own gain *o* advantage
Compuestos
• **beneficio bruto** gross profit
• **beneficio líquido** *or* **neto** net profit
B **1** (AmL) (de animal) dressing **2** (AmC) (Agr) coffee processing plant **3** (Chi) (de mineral) extraction

beneficioso -sa *adj* beneficial

benéfico -ca *adj* ‹*influencia*› benign, beneficial; ‹*espectáculo*› charity (*before n*), benefit (*before n*)

benemérito -ta *adj* (frml) ‹*profesor/obra*› distinguished; ‹*institución*› estimable (frml)

beneplácito *m* approval; **con el ~ de su familia** with her/his parents' blessing *o* approval

benevolencia *f* (indulgencia) leniency, indulgence; (bondad) kindness, benevolence (frml)

benevolente, benévolo -la *adj* (indulgente) lenient, indulgent; (bondadoso) kind, benevolent (frml)

bengala *f* flare

benignidad *f* (del clima) mildness; (de tumor) benignancy

benigno -na *adj* ‹*clima/invierno*› mild; ‹*tumor*› benign

benjamín -mina *m,f* (*m*) youngest son, (*f*) youngest daughter

beodo[1] -da *adj* (frml *o* hum) inebriated (frml *or* hum)

beodo[2] -da *m,f* (frml *o* hum) drunkard, toper (liter *o* hum)

berberecho *m* cockle

berberisco -ca *adj/m,f* Berber

berbiquí *m* brace

berebere, bereber *adj/mf* Berber

berenjena *f* (Bot, Coc) eggplant (AmE), aubergine (BrE)

berenjenal *m* eggplant field (AmE), aubergine field (BrE); ***meterse en un ~*** (fam) to get oneself into a real mess *o* jam (colloq)

bergante *m* (fam) scoundrel (colloq), rogue (colloq)

bergantín *m* brigantine

berilo *m* beryl

Berlín *m* Berlin

berlina *f* berlin (carriage)

berlinés[1] -nesa *adj* of/from Berlin

berlinés[2] -nesa *m,f* Berliner

berma *f* (Andes) (de asfalto) shoulder (AmE), hard shoulder (BrE); (de tierra) verge

bermejo -ja *adj* (liter) red

bermellón *m* vermillion

bermudas *fpl or mpl* Bermuda shorts (*pl*)

Bermudas *fpl*: **las ~** Bermuda; **el triángulo de las ~** the Bermuda Triangle

Berna *f* Berne

berrear [A1] *vi* «*becerro/ciervo*» to bellow; «*niño*» (fam) to bawl

berrido *m* (de becerro, ciervo) bellow; (de niño) (fam): **deja de dar esos ~s** stop that bawling

berrinche *m* (fam) (rabieta) tantrum; **le dio un** *or* (Méx) **hizo un ~** he threw *o* had a tantrum; ***coger*** *or* ***llevarse un ~*** (Esp fam) to have a fit (colloq)

berro *m* watercress

berza *f* cabbage

berzal *m* cabbage patch

besamanos *m* (*pl* ~) (recepción) royal audience; (saludo) hand-kissing

besamel, besamela *f* (Esp) white sauce, béchamel sauce (frml)

besar [A1] *vt* to kiss; **la besé en la mejilla** I kissed her on the cheek; **le besó la mano** he kissed her hand
■ **besarse** *v pron* (*recípr*) to kiss (each other)

beso *m* kiss; **le dio un ~ en la frente** she kissed him *o* gave him a kiss on the forehead; ***comerse a algn a ~s*** (fam): **cuando llegué casi me comieron a ~s** when I arrived they smothered me with kisses; ***el ~ de Judas*** the kiss of Judas

bestia[1] *adj*
A (fam) **1** (ignorante, estúpido): **es tan ~ que no distingue un Picasso de un Velázquez** he's so ignorant he can't tell a Picasso from a Velázquez; **¡no seas ~ que vas a chocar!** watch out, you're going to crash! **2** (grosero) rude; **no seas ~ ¿cómo le vas a decir eso?** don't be so crass, you can't say that to him! **3** (violento, brusco): **¡qué hombre más ~! ha vuelto a pegarle** what a brute *o* an animal! he's hit her again; ***a lo ~*** (fam): **comen a lo ~** they eat an incredible *o* a massive amount!; **conducen a lo ~** they drive like madmen (colloq)
B (fam) (expresando admiración, asombro) amazing (colloq); **¡qué ~! mira cuánto ha comido** this guy's incredible! look how much he's eaten

bestia[2] *f* beast; **~ salvaje** *or* **feroz** wild animal; **~ de carga** beast of burden; ***ser una mala ~*** (fam) to be a nasty piece of work (colloq)
Compuesto **bestia negra** bête noire

bestia[3] *mf* **1** (fam) (ignorante): **es un ~ que no sabe ni usar el cuchillo** he's so uncouth, he can't even hold his knife properly **2** (persona violenta) animal, brute

bestial *adj* (fam) (muy grande): **tengo un hambre ~** I'm starving; **tiene una capacidad ~ para el trabajo** she gets through an incredible amount of work

bestialidad *f* **1** (barbaridad): **es una ~ tratar así a un niño** it's disgusting *o* barbaric to treat a child like that; **comimos una ~** we ate a massive *o* an incredible amount **2** (cualidad) brutality

bestialismo *m* bestiality

bestiario *m* bestiary

best-seller /bes'seler/ *m* (*pl* **-llers**) best-seller

besucón[1] -cona *adj* (fam): **este niño es muy ~** this child's always kissing everybody

besucón[2] -cona *m,f* (fam): **su novio es un ~** her boyfriend is always kissing her

besugo *m* (Coc, Zool) red bream

besuquear [A1] *vt* (fam) to smother ... with kisses
■ **besuquearse** *v pron* (*recípr*) (fam) to neck (colloq)

beta *f* (letra griega) beta

betabel *m* (Méx) beet, beetroot (BrE)

betún *m*
A (para calzado) shoe polish; **dales ~ a esos zapatos** give those shoes a polish
B (Tec) bitumen
Compuesto **betún de judea** asphalt
C (Chi, Méx) (Coc) icing, topping

biaba *f* (RPl fam) (paliza) beating; (derrota) hammering (colloq)

bianual *adj* biannual

biberón *m* baby's bottle, feeding bottle; **hay que darle el ~** I have to give the baby his bottle *o* feed

biblia *f* bible; **la B~** the Bible; ***la ~ en verso*** (fam): **se sabe la ~ en verso** he knows everything under the sun

bíblico -ca *adj* biblical

bibliófilo -la *m,f* bibliophile

bibliografía *f* (en libro, informe) bibliography; (para curso) booklist

bibliográfico -ca *adj* bibliographic

bibliorato *m* (RPl) lever arch file

biblioteca *f* **1** (institución, lugar) library; **~ pública/de consulta** public/reference library **2** (colección) book collection **3** (mueble) bookshelves (*pl*), bookcase

bibliotecario -ria *m,f* librarian

bicameral *adj* bicameral (frml); **sistema ~** two-chamber *o* (frml) bicameral system

b

bicampeón -peona *m,f* twice champion

bicarbonato *m* bicarbonate

(Compuesto) **bicarbonato de soda** *or* **de sodio** (Coc) bicarbonate of soda; (Quím) sodium bicarbonate

bicéfalo -la *adj* two-headed, bicephalous (tech)

bicentenario *m* bicentenary

bíceps *m* (*pl* ~) biceps

bicho *m*

A (fam) 1 (insecto) insect, bug (colloq), creepy-crawly (colloq) 2 (animal) animal, creature, critter (AmE colloq); **me picó** *or* (Esp) **ha picado un ~** I've been bitten by something; **todo ~ viviente** everyone

B (fam) (persona maligna) nasty piece of work (colloq), mean son of a bitch (AmE sl); **me miró como si fuera un ~ raro** he looked at me as if I was some kind of weirdo (colloq)

bici *f* (fam) bike (colloq)

bicicleta *f* bicycle; **va en ~ al trabajo** she cycles to work; **¿no sabes montar** *or* (AmL) **andar en ~?** can't you ride a bicycle?; **salimos a pasear en ~** we went for a bicycle ride *o* (colloq) a bike ride *o* (AmE) a bike hike

(Compuestos)

- **bicicleta de carreras/montaña** racing/mountain bike
- **bicicleta fija** *or* **de ejercicio** exercise cycle *o* bike

bicimoto *m* (Méx) moped

bicoca *f*

A (fam) 1 (ganga): **era una ~** it was a real bargain *o* (AmE) steal (colloq) 2 (cosa fácil): **este trabajo es una ~** this is a cushy job

B (Chi) (de cura) skullcap

bicolor *adj* two-colored*

BID /bið/ *m* (= **Banco Interamericano de Desarrollo**) IDB

bidé, bidet /bi'ðe/ *m* bidet

bidimensional *adj* two-dimensional

bidireccional *adj* bidirectional

bidón *m* 1 (para gasolina, agua) can; (más grande) jerry can 2 (barril) barrel

biela *f* connecting rod

bien[1] *adj inv*

A [ESTAR] (sano) well; **no me siento** *or* **encuentro ~** I don't feel well; **¡tú no estás ~ de la cabeza!** you're not right in the head!

B [ESTAR] (fam) (refiriéndose al atractivo sexual) good-looking, attractive

C [ESTAR] (cómodo, agradable): **¿vas ~ ahí atrás?** are you all right in the back?; **se está ~ a la sombra** it's nice in the shade

D (agradable) ‹*oler/saber*›: **¡qué ~ huele!** it smells really good!; **este café sabe muy ~** this coffee tastes very good *o* nice

E [ESTAR]: **¿está ~ así, señorita?** is that all right, miss?; **saliste muy ~ en esta foto** you look really good in this photo; **ese cuadro no queda ~ ahí** that painting doesn't look right there; **podríamos ir mañana, si te parece ~** we could go tomorrow, if you like; **la casa está muy ~** the house is very nice; **¿lo has leído? está muy ~** have you read it? it's very good; **¡está ~! si no quieres hacerlo no lo hagas** all right *o* okay, then! don't do it if you don't want to; **¡qué ~ mañana es fiesta!** great! tomorrow's a holiday!; **no funciona — ¡pues qué ~!** (iró) it's not working — oh, great! (iro)

F [ESTAR] (correcto, adecuado) right; **está ~ que se premie la iniciativa** it's right and proper that initiative should be rewarded

G 1 (suficiente) **estar** *or* **andar ~ DE algo** to be all right FOR sth; **¿estamos ~ de aceite?** are we all right for oil?; **no ando ~ de tiempo** I'm a bit short of time 2 **ya está ~** that's enough; **ya está ~ de jugar, ahora a dormir** you've been playing long enough, now go to bed

H 1 (fam) (de buena posición social) ‹*familia/gente*› well-to-do; **un barrio ~** a well-to-do *o* (BrE) posh area 2 (RPl fam) ‹*gente/persona*› (honrado) respectable, decent

bien[2] *adv*

A (de manera satisfactoria) ‹*dormir/funcionar/cantar*› well; **no le fue ~ en Alemania** things didn't work out for her in Germany; ***quien ~ te quiere te hará llorar*** you have to be cruel to be kind

B (ventajosamente) well; **vendió el coche muy ~** she got a good price for the car

C (favorablemente): **pensar ~ de la gente** to think well of people; **hablar ~ de algn** to speak highly of sb

D 1 (a fondo, completamente) well, properly; **~ cocido** well *o* properly cooked; **¿cerraste ~?** did you lock the door properly?; **~ sabes que ...** you know perfectly well that ...; **~ se ve que está enamorado** it's obvious that he's in love 2 (con cuidado, atención) ‹*escuchar/mirar*› carefully

E (correctamente) well; **¡~ hecho/dicho!** well done/said!; **pórtate ~** behave yourself; **hiciste ~ en decírselo** you were right to tell him; **siéntate ~** sit properly

F (como intensificador) 1 (muy) very; **canta ~ mal** he sings really badly; **llegó ~ entrada la noche** she arrived very late at night; **¿estás ~ seguro?** are you positive?; **ser ~ de adentro** (Per fam) to be a good sort 2 (fácilmente) easily; **~ pudo suceder** it could well *o* easily have happened 3 (en recriminaciones, protestas): **~ podías haberlo ayudado** you *could o might* have helped him! 4 **bien que ...**: **~ que llama cuando necesita dinero** he soon calls when he needs money

G (*en locs*) **más bien**: **es más ~ delgada** she's quite slim; **no bien** as soon as; **si bien** although; ***estar a ~ con algn*** to be on good terms with sb; ***tener a ~ hacer algo*** (frml): **le rogamos tenga a ~ abonar esta suma** we would ask you to pay this sum (frml)

bien[3] *interj* 1 (como enlace): **~, sigamos adelante** right then *o* fine, let's continue; **~, ... ¿dónde estábamos?** right, ... where were we?; **pues ~, como te iba diciendo ...** so, as I was telling you ... 2 **¡bien!** (expresando aprobación) well done!; **no habrá clases hoy — ¡bieeeen!** there won't be any lessons today — yippee *o* hurrah!

bien[4] *conj*: **puede abonarse o ~ al contado o ~ en 12 cuotas mensuales** (frml) payment may be made either in cash or in twelve monthly installments

bien[5] *m*

A (Fil) good; **el ~ y el mal** good and evil; **hacer el ~** to do good deeds; ***haz ~ y no mires a quién*** do good to all alike; **un hombre de ~** a good man

B 1 (beneficio, bienestar) good; **es por tu ~** it's for your own good; **por el ~ de todos** for the good of all 2 **hacer bien** (+ *me/te/le etc*): **esto te hará ~** this will do you good; **sus palabras me hicieron mucho ~** what he said did me a lot of good

C (en calificaciones escolares) *grade of between 6 and 6.9 on a scale of 1-10*

D 1 (posesión): **le dejó todos sus ~es** she left him everything she owned; **mi ~ más preciado** my most precious possession 2 **bienes** *mpl* (Fin) assets (*pl*); **la orden afecta a todos sus ~es** the order applies to all his assets

(Compuestos)

- **bien de consumo** consumer article *o* item; **~es de ~** consumer goods
- **bien de equipo** capital item *o* asset; **~es de ~** capital goods *o* assets
- **bien ganancial** joint asset (*acquired during marriage*); **~es ~es** joint property, community property (AmE)
- **bien inmueble** immovable item *o* asset
- **bien mueble** movable item; **~es ~s** personal property, goods and chattels
- **bien raíz** immovable item *o* asset; **~es raíces** real estate, realty (AmE)

bienal *adj* biennial

bienaventurado -da *adj* blessed

bienaventuranzas *fpl* Beatitudes (*pl*)

bienestar *m* well-being, welfare; **estado de ~** social welfare state

(Compuestos)

- **Bienestar Familiar** (en Col) Welfare Service
- **bienestar social** social welfare

bienhablado -da *adj* well-spoken

bienhechor -chora *m,f* benefactor

bienintencionado -da *adj* well-meaning, well-intentioned

bienio *m* 1 (período) two-year period 2 (incremento) two-yearly increment

bien parecido -da *adj* (ant) well-favored* (dated), fine-looking

bienvenida *f* welcome; **darle la ~ a algn** to welcome sb; **un discurso de ~** a welcoming speech
bienvenido -da *adj* welcome; **ser ~** to be welcome
bifásico -ca *adj* two-phase
bife *m*
A (Bol, RPl) (Coc) steak
B (RPl fam) (bofetada) slap
bífido -da *adj* forked
bifocal *adj* bifocal
bifocales *mpl or fpl* bifocals (*pl*)
bifurcación *f* (en carretera) fork; (en la vía férrea) junction
bifurcarse [A2] *v pron* «*camino*» to fork, diverge (frml); «*vía férrea*» to diverge
bigamia *f* bigamy
bígamo[1] -ma *adj* bigamous
bígamo[2] -ma *m,f* bigamist
bigote *m*
A (de persona) *tb* **~s** mustache*
B (de gato, ratón) whisker
bigotón -tona *adj* (Méx) ▸**bigotudo**
bigotudo -da *adj* (fam): **un hombre ~** a man with a big mustache*
bigudí *m* (*pl* **-díes -dís**) curler, roller
bikini *m*, (AmL) *m or f* bikini
bilabial *adj/f* bilabial
bilateral *adj* bilateral
biliar *adj* biliary
bilingüe *adj* bilingual
bilingüismo *m* bilingualism
bilioso -sa *adj* bilious
bilis *f* 1 (Fisiol) bile; ***hacer* ~** (Méx fam) (enojarse) to get mad (colloq); (disgustarse): **hizo tal ~ que ...** he took it so badly that ... 2 (fam) (mal humor) bad mood, spleen; **no descargues tu ~ en mí** don't take it out on me (colloq)
billar *m* (con tres bolas) billiards; (con 16 bolas) pool; (con 22 bolas) snooker
billarista *mf* billiard player
billete *m*
A 1 (Fin) bill (esp AmE), note (BrE) 2 (Andes fam) (dinero) money, dough (colloq); **trabaja aquí por el puro ~** (Andes) she only works here for the money *o* dough; ***estar/andar cargado al* ~** (Chi fam) to be flush (colloq)
B 1 (de lotería, rifa) ticket 2 (Esp) (transporte) ticket; **reservar/sacar/pagar un ~** to book/get/pay for a ticket

Compuestos

- **billete de ida y vuelta** (Esp) round-trip ticket (AmE), return (ticket) (BrE)
- **billete sencillo** *or* **de ida** (Esp) one-way ticket, single (ticket) (BrE)

billetera *f*, **billetero** *m* wallet, billfold (AmE); (con monedero) change purse (AmE), purse (BrE)
billetero -ra *m,f* (Méx, Ven) lottery ticket vendor
billón *m* trillion (AmE), billion (BrE)
billonario -ria *m,f* billionaire
bimensual *adj* (dos veces al mes) twice-monthly, fortnightly (BrE)
bimestral *adj* 1 (cada dos meses) bimonthly 2 (que dura dos meses) two-month (*before n*)
bimestre *m* (period of) two months; (pago) bimonthly payment
bimotor *m* twin-engined aircraft
binario -ria *adj* binary
bingo *m* (juego) bingo; (sala) bingo hall
binocular *adj* binocular
binoculares *mpl* binoculars (*pl*)
binóculos *mpl* (Col, Ven) binoculars (*pl*)
binomio *m* (Mat) binomial; (period) (dúo) couple
biocarburante *m* biofuel
biocombustible *m* biofuel
biodegradable *adj* biodegradable
biofísica *f* biophysics
biogenética *f* genetic engineering
biografía *f* biography
biográfico -ca *adj* biographical
biógrafo -fa *m,f* biographer
biología *f* biology
biológico -ca *adj* (Biol) biological; ‹*verduras*› organic
biólogo -ga *m,f* biologist
biombo *m* folding screen
biomédico -ca *adj* biomedical
biopsia *f* biopsy
bioquímica *f* biochemistry
bioquímico[1] -ca *adj* biochemical
bioquímico[2] -ca *m,f* biochemist
biorritmo *m* biorhythm
biosfera, biósfera *f* biosphere
biosíntesis *f* biosynthesis
bioterrorismo *m* bioterrorism
biotopo *m* biotope
bióxido *m* dioxide
bip *m* pip, beep
bipartidismo *m* two-party system
bipartidista *adj* two-party (*before n*)
bipartito -ta *adj* bipartite
bípedo *m* biped
biplano *m* biplane
biplaza *m* two-seater
biquini *m* bikini
BIRD *m* /birð/ (= **Banco Internacional para la Reconstrucción y el Desarrollo**) IBRD
birlar [A1] *vt* (fam) to swipe (colloq), to pinch (BrE colloq); **me ~on el paraguas** I had my umbrella swiped *o* pinched
Birmania *f* Burma
birmano[1] -na *adj/m,f* Burmese; **los ~s** the Burmese
birmano[2] *m* (idioma) Burmese
birome *f* (RPl) ballpoint pen, Biro®
birreactor *m* twin-jet plane
birrete *m* 1 cap (*worn by lawyers, professors, etc*) 2 (birreta) biretta
birria *f*
A (fam) (cosa fea, inútil): **¡qué ~ de vestido!** what a horrible dress!; **sus poemas son una ~** his poems are garbage (AmE) *o* (BrE) rubbish (colloq)
B (Méx) (Coc) *goat's meat in chili sauce*
bis[1] *adj* (en direcciones): **vivo en el 18 ~ y no en el 18** ≈ I live at number 18A, not at number 18
bis[2] *m* encore
bisabuelo -la (*m*) great-grandfather; (*f*) great-grandmother; **mis ~s** my great-grandparents
bisagra *f* hinge
bisel *m* bevel, beveled* edge
biselar [A1] *vt* to bevel
bisexual *adj/mf* bisexual
bisexualidad *f* bisexuality
bisiesto *adj*: **1992 fue (año) ~** 1992 was a leap year
bisílabo -ba, **bisilábico -ca** *adj* bisyllabic
bismuto *m* bismuth
bisne *m* (AmC fam) hustling (colloq), black marketeering
bisnieto -ta (*m*) great-grandson; (*f*) great-granddaughter; **mis ~s** my great-grandchildren
bisonte *m* bison
bisoñé *m* toupee, hairpiece
bisoño -ña *adj* inexperienced; **soldados ~s** raw recruits
bistec /bi'stek/ *m* (*pl* **-tecs**) steak, beefsteak
bisturí *m* scalpel
bisutería *f* costume *o* imitation jewelry*
bit *m* (Inf) bit
bitácora *f*
A (Náut) binnacle
B (en Internet) blog
bivalvo -va *adj* bivalve
bividí, B.V.D.® /biβi'ði/ *m* (Per) undershirt (AmE), vest (BrE)
bizantino -na *adj* 1 (Hist) Byzantine 2 (insoluble): **una discusión bizantina** a convoluted argument

b

bizarría *f* (liter) dash
bizarro -rra *adj* (liter) dashing
bizco[1] **-ca** *adj* cross-eyed
bizco[2] **-ca** *m,f* cross-eyed person
bizcochería *f* (Col) patisserie, cake shop
bizcocho *m* (pastel) sponge (cake); (galleta) sponge finger; (bollo) (Ur) bun
bizcochuelo *m* (CS) sponge (cake)
bizquear [A1] *vi* to be cross-eyed
bizquera *f* squint; **tiene una marcada ~** he has a pronounced squint; **no le noté la ~** I didn't notice that he was cross-eyed
blanca *f*
A (Mús) half note (AmE), minim (BrE)
B (en dominó) blank; (en ajedrez) white piece
(Compuesto) **blanca doble** double blank
C (Esp fam): **estar sin ~** to be broke (colloq)
Blancanieves Snow White
blanco[1] **-ca** *adj*
A 1 ‹*color/vestido/pelo*› white; **en ~: entregó el examen en ~** she handed in a blank exam (paper); **rellenar los espacios en ~** fill in the blanks; **voté en ~** I returned a blank ballot (AmE), I left my voting paper blank (BrE); ***quedarse en ~*** or ***quedársele a algn la mente en ~***: **me quedé en ~** or **se me quedó la mente en blanco** my mind went blank 2 (pálido) [SER] fair-skinned, pale-skinned; [ESTAR] white; **estoy muy ~** I'm very white *o* pale
B ‹*persona/raza*› white
blanco[2] **-ca** *m,f* white person
blanco[3] *m*
A (color) white; **en ~ y negro** black and white
(Compuesto) **blanco del ojo** white of the eye
B (Dep, Jueg) (objeto) target; (centro) bullseye; **tirar al ~** to shoot at the target; **fue el ~ de todas las miradas** everyone was looking at her; ***dar en el ~*** (literal) to hit the target; (acertar): **diste en el ~ con ese regalo** you were right on (AmE) *o* (BrE) spot-on with that present (colloq)
C (vino) white (wine)
blancura *f* whiteness
blancuzco -ca *adj* 1 ‹*camisa/pintura*› off-white, whitish 2 ‹*persona*› pale
blandengue[1] *adj* (fam) 1 ‹*mezcla*› soft, runny 2 ‹*persona*› soft
blandengue[2] *mf* (fam) (persona débil) softy (colloq)
blandir [I1] *vt* to brandish, wave
blando -da *adj*
A 1 ‹*carne*› tender; ‹*queso/mantequilla*› soft; **ponerse ~** to go soft 2 ‹*cama/almohada*› soft; **de carnes blandas** flabby 3 ‹*madera/metal*› soft; **un cepillo de cerdas blandas** a soft brush 4 ‹*agua*› soft
B ‹*carácter*› (débil) weak; (poco severo) soft
blandura *f*
A (de la carne) tenderness; (de cama, almohada) softness; (del agua) softness
B (falta de severidad) leniency; **trata a sus alumnos con demasiada ~** she's too lenient with/soft on her pupils
blanqueada *f*
A (de pared) (CS) whitewashing; (de dinero) laundering
B (Méx) (Dep) blank, shutout (AmE)
blanqueado *m* ▸**blanqueo A**
blanqueador *m* (para visillos) whitener; (lejía) (Col, Méx) bleach
blanquear [A1] *vt*
A 1 ‹*ropa*› to bleach; ‹*pared*› to whitewash 2 ‹*dinero*› to launder; ‹*objetos robados*› to fence
B (Dep) to blank, shut out (AmE)
blanquecino -na *adj* off-white, whitish
blanqueo *m*
A 1 (con lejía) bleaching; (de paredes) whitewashing 2 (de dinero, de capitales) laundering
B (Ven) (Dep) blank, shutout
blanquiazul *adj* 1 ‹*agua*› white and blue 2 (Dep) (period) ‹*equipo/jugador*› whose colors are white and blue
blanquillo *m*
A (Chi, Per) (Bot) white peach
B (Méx fam) (huevo) egg (*with a white shell*)
blasfemar [A1] *vi* to blaspheme
blasfemia *f* blasphemy
blasfemo -ma *m,f* blasphemer
blasón *m* (escudo) coat of arms; (divisa) blazon
bledo *m* ▸**importar**
blindado -da *adj* ‹*coche*› armor-plated*, armored*; ‹*puerta*› reinforced
blindaje *m* armor* plating
blindar [A1] *vt* ‹*barco/coche*› to armor-plate*; ‹*puerta*› to reinforce
bloc *m* (*pl* **blocs**) (de papel) pad; **~ de notas** note pad
blocar [A2] *vt* (Esp) (Dep) ‹*balón*› to stop; ‹*adversario*› to tackle; ‹*golpe*› to block
blof *m* (Col, Méx) bluff; ***ser puro ~*** (fam) to be all talk (colloq)
blofear [A1] *vi* (Col, Méx) 1 (en el juego) to bluff 2 (fam) (alardear) to show off
blogger /'bloger/ *mf* (*pl* **-s**) blogger
blonda *f*
A (encaje) (blond) lace
B (CS) (onda) scallop; (conjunto de ondas) scalloping
bloque *m*
A (de piedra, hormigón) block
B (edificio) block; (manzana de edificios) (esp Esp) block; **un ~ de departamentos** (AmL) *or* (Esp) **pisos** an apartment block, a block of flats (BrE)
C 1 (period) (de noticias) section 2 (Inf) block
D (fuerza política) bloc; **el ~ del Este** (Hist) the Eastern bloc; **en ~** (*loc adv*) en bloc, en masse
E (Auto) cylinder block
bloquear [A1] *vt*
A 1 ‹*camino/acceso*› to block; ‹*entrada/salida*› to block, obstruct; **estamos bloqueados por un camión** there's a truck blocking our way; **nos quedamos ~s a causa del temporal** we were cut off by the storm 2 (Mil) to blockade 3 ‹*proceso/iniciativa*› to block; **su negativa bloqueó las negociaciones** her refusal blocked negotiations 4 (Dep) to block
B 1 ‹*mecanismo*› to jam 2 (Auto) ‹*dirección*› to lock
C ‹*cuenta/fondos*› to freeze, block
■ **bloquearse** *v pron*
A «*mecanismo*» to jam; «*frenos*» to jam, lock on; «*ruedas*» to lock
B «*negociaciones*» to reach deadlock
bloqueo *m*
A (de ciudad) blockade, siege; (de puerto) blockade; (Dep) block
(Compuestos)
• **bloqueo mental** (fam) mental block (colloq); **tuve un ~ ~ en el examen** my mind went blank in the exam
• **bloqueo naval** naval blockade
B (de gestiones) deadlock
C (de mecanismo) jamming; (de las ruedas) locking
D (Com, Fin) freezing, blocking
blufear [A1] *vi* (CS) ▸**blofear**
bluff /bluf/ *m* (*pl* **bluffs**) 1 (Jueg) bluff 2 (fam) (fanfarronería): ***ser puro ~*** to be all talk (colloq)
blusa *f* blouse
blusón *m* loose shirt *o* blouse
blvar. *m* (= **bulevar**) Blvd (*in US*)
BM *m* = **Banco Mundial**
B° = **Banco**
boa[1] *f* (Zool) boa; ***comer como una ~*** (Per) to eat like a horse
boa[2] *m or f* (Indum) feather boa
boato *m* show, ostentation
bobada *f*: **deja de hacer ~s** stop being so stupid *o* silly; **deja de decir ~s** that's enough nonsense; **¡qué ~!** what a silly thing to say!
bobalicón -cona *m,f* (fam) fool, twit (colloq)
bobina *f* 1 (de hilo) reel 2 (de magnetofón) reel, spool 3 (Auto, Elec) coil; **~ del encendido** ignition coil
bobinado *m* winding
bobinar [A1] *vt* to wind
bobo[1] **-ba** *adj* (fam) silly

bobo² -ba *m,f* (fam) fool; **deja de hacer el ~** stop playing the fool, stop being so silly

boca *f*

A **1** (Anat, Zool) mouth; **tener la ~ seca/pastosa** to have a dry/furry mouth; **la ~ te huele a ajo** your breath smells of garlic; **tengo que ir a arreglarme la ~** I have to go and get my teeth seen to *o* fixed; **como no te calles te voy a partir la ~** if you don't shut up I'll smash your face in (colloq) **2** (*en locs*) **boca abajo/arriba** ‹*dormir/echarse*› on one's stomach/back; **puso los naipes ~ arriba** she laid the cards face up; **de boca de** from; **lo supimos de ~ de ella** we heard it (directly) from her; **uno no espera oír palabras así de ~ de un cura** you don't expect to hear such words from (the mouth of) a priest; **en boca de**: **la pregunta que anda en ~ de todos los niños** the question which is on every child's lips; **el escándalo andaba en ~ de todos** the scandal was common knowledge; **por boca de**: **la organización ha dejado claro por ~ de su secretario general ...** the organization has made it clear through its general secretary ...; **lo supe por ~ de su hermana** I heard it from his sister; ***abrir la ~*** to open one's mouth; **mejor es que no abra la ~** it's best if he keeps his mouth shut; ***andar/correr de ~ en ~***: **la noticia ya corría de ~ en ~** the news was spreading like wildfire; ***a pedir de ~*** just fine; **todo salió a pedir de ~** everything turned out just fine; ***callar(se) la ~*** to shut up; **en situaciones así más vale callarse la ~** in situations like that it's best to keep your mouth shut; ***cerrarle*** *or* ***taparle la ~ a algn*** to keep sb quiet, shut sb up (colloq); ***hablar por ~ de ganso*** to repeat other people's opinions (*o* ideas *etc*) parrot fashion; ***hacer*** *or* ***abrir ~*** (fam) to whet the *o* one's appetite; ***hacerle el ~ a ~ a algn*** to give sb the kiss of life; ***hacérsele la ~ agua a algn*** (Esp): **se le hacía la ~ agua mirando los pasteles** looking at the cakes made her mouth water; ***llenársele la ~ a algn con algo*** (fam): **se le llena la ~ con su apellido** she's always boasting about her surname; ***meterse en la ~ del lobo*** to take one's life in one's hands; ***no decir esta ~ es mía***: **no dijo esta ~ es mía** he didn't say a word; ***no tener qué llevarse a la ~***: **no tienen qué llevarse a la ~** they haven't got a penny to their name, they don't have a red cent to their name (AmE); ***(oscuro) como ~ de lobo*** pitch-black, pitch-dark; ***quedarse con la ~ abierta*** to be dumbfounded *o* (colloq) flabbergasted; ***quitarle algo a algn de la ~*** to take the words (right) out of sb's mouth; ***ser pura ~*** (Chi fam) to be all talk; ***tener una boquita de piñón*** (fam) to have a little mouth; ***en ~ cerrada no entran moscas*** if you keep your mouth shut, you won't put your foot in it (colloq); ***por la ~ muere el pez*** talking too much can be dangerous; ***quien*** *or* ***el que tiene ~ se equivoca*** (fam) to err is human **3** (persona): **tiene muchas ~s que alimentar** she has a lot of mouths to feed **4** (Vin) flavor•

B (de buzón) slot; (de túnel) mouth, entrance; (de puerto) entrance; (de vasija, botella) rim

Compuestos

- **boca de dragón** *or* (Ur) **sapo** snapdragon
- **boca de incendios** fire hydrant, fireplug (AmE)
- **boca del estómago** (fam) pit of the stomach
- **boca de metro** *or* (RPl) **subte** subway entrance (AmE), underground *o* tube station entrance (BrE)
- **boca de riego** hydrant

> **La Boca**
>
> A neighborhood on the Riachuelo River in Buenos Aires, near the mouth of the River Plate. It was the city's first port, where Genoese immigrants settled in the early twentieth century. Its brightly painted wooden houses with corrugated iron roofs make it a major tourist destination

bocacalle *f*: *entrance to a street*; **la primera ~ a la derecha** the first turning on the right

bocadillo *m*

A (Esp) (emparedado) roll

B (Col, Ven) (dulce) guava jelly

C (en comics) bubble, balloon

bocado *m*

A **1** (de comida) bite; **de un ~** in one bite; **estuve 24 horas sin probar ~** I went for 24 hours without a bite to eat **2** (comida ligera) snack

B (mordisco) (Esp): **le pegó un ~ en el brazo a su hermano** he sank his teeth into his brother's arm

C (Equ) bit

bocajarro: **a ~** (*loc adv*) **1** ‹*disparar*› at point-blank range **2** ‹*decir/preguntar*› point-blank

bocamanga *f* cuff

bocanada *f* (de humo, aliento) puff, mouthful; (ráfaga) gust, blast

bocatería *f* (Esp fam) sandwich bar, snack bar

bocatoma *f* (Andes) water inlet

bocazas *mf* (*pl* ~) (fam) big mouth (colloq)

boceto *m* (dibujo) sketch; (de proyecto) outline

bocha *f*

A (RPl fam) (cabeza) head, nut (colloq)

B **bochas** *fpl* (RPl) (Jueg) bowls

bochar [A1] *vt* **1** (RPl fam) ‹*sugerencia/propuesta*› to squash (colloq) **2** (RPl arg) (en examen) ‹*estudiante*› to fail, to flunk (AmE colloq); **me ~on en historia** I failed history, I flunked history (AmE colloq)

boche *m* (Andes) ▸**bochinche**

bochinche *m* (esp AmL fam) **1** (riña, pelea) fight, brawl **2** (barullo, alboroto) racket (colloq), ruckus (AmE colloq), row (BrE colloq); **los vecinos meten mucho ~** our neighbors are always making such a row *o* racket (colloq); **tanto ~ para nada** all that fuss about nothing (colloq) **3** (confusión, lío) muddle, mess (colloq)

bochinchear [A1] *vi* (AmL fam) to fight

bochinchero¹ -ra *adj* (AmL fam) rowdy

bochinchero² -ra *m,f* (AmL fam) brawler, troublemaker

bocho *m* (RPl fam) brainbox (colloq), brain (colloq)

bochorno *m*

A (calor) sultry *o* muggy weather

B (vergüenza) embarrassment; **¡qué ~!** how embarrassing!

bochornoso -sa *adj*

A ‹*tiempo*› sultry, muggy; ‹*calor*› sticky; **hacía un día ~** it was a close *o* muggy day

B ‹*espectáculo/situación*› embarrassing

bocina *f*

A (de coche) horn; (de fábrica) hooter, siren; (de faro) foghorn

B (AmL) (auricular) receiver

C (Méx) (Audio) loudspeaker

bocinazo *m* toot (on the horn); (más fuerte) blast *o* honk on the horn

bocio *m* goiter•

bocón¹ -cona *adj* **1** (Andes, Méx fam) (hablador) bigmouthed (colloq) **2** (Méx fam) (mentiroso) lying (*before n*)

bocón² -cona *m,f* **1** (Andes, Méx fam) (hablador) bigmouth (colloq); (chivato) squealer (colloq), grass (BrE colloq) **2** (Méx fam) (mentiroso) liar, fibber (colloq)

boda *f* wedding; **~s de oro/plata** (de matrimonio) golden/silver wedding anniversary; (de organización) golden/silver jubilee

bodega *f*

A **1** (Vin) (fábrica) winery; (almacén) wine cellar; (tienda) wine merchant's, wine shop **2** (taberna) bar **3** (en casa) cellar

B **1** (AmC, Per, Ven) (tienda de comestibles) grocery store (AmE), grocer's (BrE) **2** (Andes, Méx, Ven) (almacén) store, warehouse

C (Aviac, Náut) hold

bodegón *m* (Art) still life

bodeguero -ra *m,f*

A (Vin) (productor) wine-producer

B **1** (AmC, Per, Ven) (tendero) shopkeeper **2** (Andes, Méx, Ven) (de almacén) warehouseman

bodoque *mf*

A (fam) (tonto) dimwit (colloq)

B (Méx fam) (niño) kid (colloq)

bodrio *m* (fam): **es un ~** it is garbage (AmE) *o* (BrE) rubbish (colloq)

bóer *mf* (*pl* **bóers**) Boer

bofetada *f* **1** (en la cara) slap; **le di** *or* **pegué una ~** I slapped him (in the face) **2** (desaire) slap in the face

bofetón *m* slap

bofo -fa *adj* (Méx fam) flabby

boga *f*: **estar en ~** to be in fashion *o* in vogue, be in (colloq)

b

bogar [A3] *vi* (liter) to row

bogavante *m* (Esp) lobster

Bogotá *m* Bogotá

bogotano -na *adj* of/from Bogotá

bohemio¹ -mia *adj* 1 ‹*vida/artista*› bohemian 2 (de Bohemia) Bohemian

bohemio² -mia *m,f* bohemian

bohío *m* (AmC, Col, Ven) hut

boicot /boj'kot/ *m* (*pl* **-cots**) boycott; **organizar un ~ contra algo** to organize a boycott of sth

boicotear [A1] *vt* 1 ‹*producto/empresa*› to boycott; ‹*reunión/clases*› (no asistir a) to boycott 2 (impedir, dificultar) ‹*reunión/clases*› to disrupt

boina *f* beret

boite /bwat/ *f* night club

bol *m* bowl

bola *f*

A 1 (cuerpo redondo) ball; (de helado) scoop; **se hacen ~s con la masa** form the dough into balls; **máquina de escribir de ~** golf ball typewriter 2 (Dep) ball; (de petanca) boule; (canica) (Col, Per) marble; ***parar*** *or* ***poner ~s*** (Col fam) to pay attention, listen up (AmE colloq); ***tener la cabeza como una ~ de billar*** to be as bald as a cue ball (AmE) *o* (BrE) as bald as a coot (colloq) 3 **bolas** *fpl* (fam: en algunas regiones vulg) (testículos) balls (*pl*) (colloq *or* vulg); ***estar en ~s*** (fam *o* vulg) to be stark naked (colloq); ***estar hasta las ~s*** (vulg) to be pissed off (sl); ***hacerse ~s con algo*** (Méx) to get in a mess over sth; ***pillar a algn en ~s*** (fam *o* vulg) to catch sb with their pants (AmE) *o* (BrE) trousers down (colloq) 4 (fam) (músculo — del brazo) biceps; (— de la pantorrilla) calf muscle; **sacar ~** (Esp) to flex one's muscles

(Compuestos)

- **bola de cristal** crystal ball
- **bola de nieve** snowball
- **bola de partido/de set** match/set point
- **bolas criollas** *fpl* (Ven) *game similar to petanque*

B (fam) (mentira) lie, fib (colloq); **me metió una ~** he told me a fib; **contar/decir ~s** to fib (colloq), to tell fibs (colloq); **¡se tragó la ~!** she swallowed it! (colloq)

C (Andes, RPl fam) (atención): **no me dio ~** he didn't take the slightest bit of notice (colloq); **no me da ~** he's not interested in me

D (Méx fam) (montón): **una ~ de** loads of (colloq)

E (Méx) revolution, uprising (*esp the Mexican Revolution*); ***armarse la ~*** (Méx): **se armó la ~** all hell broke loose (colloq)

bolada *f* (RPl fam): **aprovechar la ~** to take advantage of the situation

bolchevique *adj/mf* Bolshevik

boleador -dora *m,f*

A (Méx) (lustrabotas) bootblack

B (en las pampas) *person who uses bolas to catch cattle*

boleadoras *fpl* bolas

bolear [A1] *vi* (Col) to knock up, knock a ball about ■ **bolear** *vt* (Méx) to polish, shine

bolera *f* bowling alley

bolero¹ *m*

A (Mús) bolero

B (Indum) bolero jacket/top

bolero² -ra *m,f* (Méx) bootblack

boleta *f* 1 (AmL) (en rifa) ticket 2 (CS) (de multa) ticket 3 (CS) (recibo) receipt 4 (Col) (entrada) ticket

(Compuestos)

- **boleta de calificaciones** (Méx) school report, report card (AmE)
- **boleta de depósito** (RPl) deposit slip (AmE), paying-in slip (BrE)
- **boleta electoral** (Méx, RPl) ballot paper

boletaje *m* (Méx, Per) tickets (*pl*)

boletería *f* (AmL) (de teatro, cine) box office; (de estación, estadio) ticket office

boletero -ra *m,f* 1 (Chi) (vendedor) ticket-seller 2 (Arg fam) (mentiroso) fibber (colloq)

boletín *m* bulletin, report; **~ informativo** *or* **de noticias** news bulletin

(Compuesto) **boletín de calificaciones** *or* **notas** school report, report card (AmE)

boleto *m*

A (de lotería, rifa) ticket; (de quinielas) coupon; (de tren, autobús) (AmL) ticket; (de cine, teatro, fútbol) (Chi, Méx) ticket; ***agarrar*** *or* ***sacar ~*** (Méx fam) to get into trouble; ***de ~*** (Méx fam): **vete de ~ por la leche** dash out and get some milk (colloq)

(Compuestos)

- **boleto de ida** (AmL) one-way ticket, single (ticket) (BrE)
- **boleto de ida y vuelta** (AmL) round trip (ticket) (AmE), return (ticket) (BrE)
- **boleto de viaje redondo** (Méx) round trip (ticket) (AmE), return (ticket) (BrE)

B (Méx fam) (asunto, problema): **no es ~ nuestro** it's not our concern; **eso es otro ~** that's another matter *o* that's different

boliche *m*

A 1 (en petanca) jack 2 (juguete) *cup-and-ball toy*

B 1 (Méx) (juego) bowling, ten pin bowling (BrE); (lugar) bowling alley 2 (Col) (bolo) tenpin

C (Bol, RPl) (taberna) bar

D (CS) (tienda pequeña) (fam) small store (AmE), small shop (BrE)

bólido *m* (Auto) racing car; ***salió/pasó como (un) ~*** he went out/shot by like greased lightning (colloq)

bolígrafo *m* ballpoint pen, Biro®

bolilla *f* 1 (Bol, RPl) (Educ) topic, subject 2 (RPl) (atención) ▸ bola C

bolillo *m* 1 (en pasamanería) bobbin; **encaje de ~s** bobbin lace 2 (Col) (porra) truncheon 3 (Col) (Coc) rolling pin 4 (Méx) (pan) bread roll

bolita *f* 1 (en tejido) bobble; **se me hicieron ~s en el pullover** my sweater got all balled up (AmE) *o* (BrE) went all bobbly 2 (AmS) (Jueg) marble; **jugar a las ~s** to play marbles; ***echarse la ~*** (Méx) to pass the buck

bolívar *m* bolivar (*Venezuelan unit of currency*)

Bolivia *f* Bolivia

boliviano -na *adj/m,f* Bolivian

bollería *f* (tienda) bakery; (bollos) pastries (*pl*)

bollo *m* (Coc) (bread) roll, bun; ***ser un ~*** (RPl fam) to be a piece of cake (colloq)

bolo¹ -la *adj* (AmC fam) 1 (borracho) sloshed (colloq) 2 (roto): **el motor está ~** the engine's had it (colloq)

bolo² -la *m,f* (AmC fam) old soak (colloq)

bolo³ *m*

A 1 (palo) skittle, tenpin 2 **bolos** *mpl* (juego) bowling, tenpin bowling (BrE); **jugar a los ~s** to play skittles, to go bowling

B (Méx) 1 (monedas) coins (*thrown by godfather to children at christening*) 2 (recuerdo) *token given to people at christening*

bolsa *f*

A 1 (para llevar, guardar algo) bag; **~ de plástico/papel** plastic/paper bag; **~ de la compra** shopping bag; **~ de (la) basura** garbage bag (AmE), trash bag (AmE), rubbish bag (BrE), bin liner (BrE); **una ~ del supermercado** a grocery bag (AmE) *o* (BrE) carrier bag; **~ de deportes** sports bag; ***hacerse ~*** (CS) ‹‹*zapatos*›› to get ruined; ‹‹*coche*›› to get badly damaged 2 (envase) bag; **una ~ de patatas fritas** (Esp) a bag of chips (AmE), a packet *o* bag of crisps (BrE); ***a la ~*** (Chi) at someone else's expense 3 (Méx) (bolso) handbag, purse (AmE) 4 (dinero): **¡la ~ o la vida!** your money or your life!

(Compuestos)

- **bolsa de agua caliente** hot-water bottle
- **bolsa de dormir** (RPl) sleeping bag
- **bolsa del correo** (AmL) mailbag (AmE), postbag (BrE)

B 1 (de marsupial) pouch 2 (de los testículos) scrotum 3 (en la cara): **tiene ~s debajo de los ojos** she has bags under her eyes 4 (Méx) (bolsillo) pocket

C 1 (de aire, gas, agua) pocket 2 (zona, agrupación aislada) pocket; **~s de extranjeros ilegales** pockets *o* communities of illegal immigrants

D (Econ, Fin) *tb* **B~** stock exchange, stock market; **jugar a la ~** to play the market; **se cotizará en ~** it will be listed on the stock exchange; **sacar a ~** to float

(Compuestos)

- **bolsa de empleo** (Col) employment agency
- **bolsa de trabajo** *job vacancies*
- **bolsa de valores** stock exchange, stock market
- **bolsa negra** (Chi) black market

E (beca) grant; **~ de estudios/de viajes/para libros** study/travel/book grant

bolsear [A1] *vt* 1 (Méx fam) (robar): **me ~on en el camión** I had my pocket picked on the bus 2 (Chi fam) (gorronear) to scrounge (colloq); **~le algo a algn** to scrounge sth off *o* from sb

bolsillo *m* 1 (de pantalón, chaqueta) pocket; **el ~ interior de la chaqueta** the inside jacket pocket; **de ~** pocket (*before n*); **una calculadora/un diccionario de ~** a pocket calculator/dictionary; ***meterse a algn en el ~*** to get sb eating out of one's hand; **se metió a su jefe en el ~ en dos semanas** she had her boss eating out of her hand within two weeks; ***tener algo en el ~*** to have sth sewn up; ***tener a algn en el ~*** to have sb in one's pocket 2 (dinero, presupuesto) pocket; **de mi/su/tu ~** out of my/his/her/your own pocket; ***rascarse el ~*** (fam) to dip into one's pocket (colloq)

bolsiquear [A1] *vt* (Per fam): **lo ~on** he had his pocket picked

bolso *m* (de mujer) (Esp) handbag, purse (AmE)

Compuestos

- **bolso de mano** (de viaje) (overnight) bag; (de mujer) (Esp) handbag, purse (AmE)
- **bolso de viaje** (overnight) bag

bolsón *m*

A (de viaje) (RPl) (overnight) bag; (de deporte) (RPl) sports bag; (de colegial) (Chi) school bag, satchel

B (Andes) (Geol, Min) pocket

Compuesto **bolsón de aire** (Andes) air pocket

boludo[1] -da *adj* (Col, RPl, Ven arg *o* vulg) (imbécil): **es tan ~ que ni la sacó a bailar** he's such a jerk (colloq) *o* (vulg) prick he didn't even ask her to dance

boludo[2] -da *m,f* (Col, RPl, Ven vulg) asshole (vulg), dickhead (BrE vulg)

bomba *f*

A 1 (Arm, Mil) bomb; **lanzar/arrojar ~s** to drop bombs; **pusieron una ~ en el hotel** they planted a bomb in the hotel; ***caer como una ~***: **la noticia cayó como una ~** the news came as a bombshell; ***pasarlo ~*** (Esp fam) to have a great time *o* a ball (colloq); ***ser una ~*** (RPl fam) to be gorgeous (colloq) 2 (notición) big news 3 (en fútbol americano) bomb

Compuestos

- **bomba atómica/de cobalto/de neutrones** atom *o* atomic/cobalt/neutron bomb
- **bomba de tiempo** time bomb; **este asunto es una ~ de ~** this issue is a time bomb
- **bomba fétida** stink bomb
- **bomba H** *or* **de hidrógeno** hydrogen bomb, H-bomb
- **bomba incendiaria** incendiary bomb
- **bomba lacrimógena** tear gas canister
- **bomba lapa** car bomb

B (Tec) pump; (para insecticidas, pesticidas) spray

Compuestos

- **bomba de aire** pump
- **bomba de combustible/agua** fuel/water pump

C (de chicle) bubble; **hacer ~s** to blow bubbles

D (Andes, Ven) (gasolinera) gas station (AmE), petrol station (BrE)

E (Chi) (vehículo) fire engine, fire truck (AmE); (estación) fire station; (cuerpo) fire department (AmE), fire brigade (BrE)

F (Col) (en baloncesto) area

G (Per fam) (borrachera): **se pegó una ~** he got plastered (colloq)

bombacha *f* 1 (CS) (de gaucho) baggy trousers (*pl*) 2 (RPl) (de mujer) panties (*pl*), knickers (*pl*) (BrE)

bombachos *mpl* baggy trousers (*pl*) (*which come in at the ankle*)

bombardear [A1] *vt* 1 ‹*territorio/ciudad*› (desde avión) to bomb; (con artillería) to bombard, shell; **me ~on a preguntas** they bombarded me with questions 2 ‹*átomo*› to bombard; ‹*nubes*› to seed

bombardeo *m*

A 1 (desde aviones) bombing; (con artillería) bombardment, shelling; **sufrimos un intenso ~ publicitario** we were bombarded with *o* subjected to a barrage of advertising 2 (Fís) bombardment

B (Meteo) seeding

bombardero *m* bomber

bombazo *m*

A (Méx) (explosión) bomb explosion

B (fam) (noticia) bombshell

bombear [A1] *vt* to pump

bombero *mf*, **bombero -ra** *m,f*

A (de incendios) (*m*) firefighter, fireman; (*f*) firefighter; **llamar a los ~s** to call the fire department (AmE) *o* (BrE) brigade; **cuerpo de ~s** fire department (AmE) *o* (BrE) brigade

Compuesto **bombero torero** comic bullfighter

B (Ven) (de surtidor de gasolina) filling station attendant

bombilla *f*

A (Esp) (Elec) light bulb

B (para el mate) *tube through which mate tea is drunk*

bombillo *m* (AmC, Col, Ven) light bulb; ***se me/le encendió el ~*** (Ven fam) I/he had a flash of inspiration

bombín *m*

A (Indum) derby (AmE), bowler hat (BrE)

B (para inflar) pump; **~ de pie** *or* **a pedal** foot *o* pedal pump

bombita *f* (RPl) (Elec) light bulb

bombo *m*

A (Mús) (instrumento) bass drum; (músico) bass drummer; **tengo la cabeza como un ~** my head's about to explode; ***con ~s y platillos*** *or* (Esp) ***a ~ y platillo*** with a great fanfare; ***darle ~ a algo***: **se le ha dado mucho ~ a la película** the movie's been given a lot of hype (colloq)

B (de sorteo) drum

bombón *m* 1 (confite) chocolate 2 (fam) (persona) stunner (colloq) 3 (Méx) (malvavisco) marshmallow

bombona *f* gas cylinder *o* canister

bombonera *f* candy box (AmE), sweet box (BrE)

bombonería *f* candy store (AmE), sweet shop (BrE)

bonachón[1] -chona *adj* (fam) (amable) good-natured, kind

bonachón[2] -chona *m,f* (fam) (persona amable) good-natured *o* kind person

bonaerense *adj*: *of/from the province of Buenos Aires*

bonanza *f* 1 (en el mar) fair weather 2 (prosperidad) prosperity

bonche *m*

A (AmC, Col fam) (riña) fight; (contienda) contest

B (Ven) (fiesta) party, rave-up (BrE sl); **ir de ~** to party (esp AmE fam)

bonchear [A1] *vi* (AmC, Col fam) to have a fight

bonchón -ona *m,f* (Ven fam) party animal (AmE), raver (BrE)

bondad *f* 1 (Fil) goodness; (afabilidad, generosidad) goodness, kindness; **¿tendría la ~ de cerrar la puerta?** (frml) would you mind closing the door?; **tengan la ~ de no fumar** (frml) kindly *o* please refrain from smoking (frml) 2 (del clima) mildness

bondadoso -sa *adj* kind, kindhearted, kindly

bonete *m* (Hist) hat, cap; (de graduado) mortarboard; (de eclesiástico) biretta

bongó, bongo *m* bongo

bonhomía *f* (frml) kindheartedness, good nature

boniato *m* sweet potato

bonificación *f* 1 (aumento, beneficio) bonus 2 (descuento) discount; **los pagos al contado llevan una ~ del 10%** there is a 10% discount for cash payments

bonificar [A2] *vt* (dar un descuento de) ‹*cantidad/porcentaje*› to give a discount of; **en las compras al por mayor, bonificamos el 6%** we give a 6% discount on wholesale purchases

bonito[1] -ta *adj*

A (hermoso) ‹*vestido/flor*› pretty, nice; ‹*mujer/niño*› pretty; ‹*canción/apartamento*› nice, lovely; **le quedaba muy ~** it really suited her; **¡la has hecho llorar! ¿te parece ~?** you've made her cry, I suppose you think that's clever!

B (*delante del n*) ‹*suma/cantidad*› nice, tidy (*before n*)

bonito[2] *adv* (CS) ‹*bailar/cantar*› nicely, well; **borda muy ~** she does lovely embroidery

bonito[3] *m* tuna, bonito

bono *m*

A (vale) voucher; (Econ, Fin) bond

Compuestos

- **bono de carbono** carbon credit
- **bono del Estado/Tesoro** Government/Treasury bond

- **bono de tesorería** debenture bond

B **bonos** *mpl* (Chi) (de político) prestige; (de actor) popularity

bonoloto *m* (en Esp) state-run lottery

> **bonoloto**
>
> A Spanish state lottery established in 1988. The others are the **Lotería Nacional** and the **Lotería Primitiva**. As with the *Lotería Primitiva* six numbers are marked on a ticket showing forty-nine numbers and win the main prize if all the numbers come up in the draw

bonsai *m* bonsai

boñiga *f* (cow) dung

boñigo *m* cowpat

boom /bum/ *m* boom; **el ~ de las computadoras** the computer boom

boomerang /bume'ran/ *m* (*pl* **-rangs**) boomerang; **la oferta se ha vuelto como un ~ contra ellos** the offer has boomeranged on them

boqueada *f* gasp; **dar la última ~** to breathe one's last

boquear [A1] *vi* (abrir la boca) to open one's mouth; (estar moribundo) to be at death's door

boquera *f* cold sore

boquerón *m* anchovy

boquete *m* hole; **abrieron** *or* **hicieron un ~ en la pared** they made a hole in the wall; **abrieron un ~ en el muro** (Mil) they made an opening in the wall

boquiabierto -ta *adj*: **su desfachatez me dejó ~** I was astonished at *o* by his nerve; **se quedó ~ al ver el paisaje** he gazed open-mouthed at the view

boquilla *f* (de instrumento musical) mouthpiece; (de pipa) stem; (para cigarrillos) cigarette holder; (para tomar mate) ▸**bombilla B**; ***de* ~**: **nos apoya, pero sólo de ~** he supports us but in name only

bórax *m* borax

borbollón *m* [1] ▸**borbotón** [2] (AmS fam) (tumulto) commotion, confusion

Borbón *mf* Bourbon

borbónico -ca *adj* Bourbon (*before n*)

borbotar [A1], **borbotear** [A1] *vi* to bubble

borboteo *m* bubbling

borbotón: **a borbotones** ‹*hervir*› fiercely; ‹*salir*› «*sangre/agua*» to gush out; **hablaba a borbotones** the words came tumbling out

borda *f* gunwale, rail; ***echar*** *or* ***tirar algo por la ~*** to throw sth overboard; **no puedes tirar por la ~ tantos esfuerzos** you can't just waste all the effort you've put into it; ***irse por la ~*** to go out of the window

bordado¹ -da *adj* ‹*mantel/sábana*› embroidered; **~ a máquina** machine-embroidered; ***salir ~*** (Esp fam): **la traducción le salió bordada** he did an excellent translation

bordado² *m* embroidery

bordar [A1] *vt* [1] ‹*sábana/blusa*› to embroider; **lo bordó a mano** she embroidered it by hand [2] ‹*papel*› to play ... brilliantly

borde¹ *adj* (Esp fam) rude, stroppy (BrE fam)

borde² *m* (de mesa, cama) edge; (de moneda, pieza, plato) edge, rim; (de taza, vaso) rim; (de andén, piscina) edge; **había un sauce al ~ del río** there was a willow tree on the river bank; **llenó el vaso hasta el ~** she filled the glass to the brim; **al ~ de algo** ‹*de la guerra/locura*› on the brink of sth; ‹*del caos/ruina*› on the verge of sth; **al ~ de la muerte** on the point of death; **al ~ de las lágrimas** on the verge of tears

bordear [A1] *vt* [1] (seguir el borde de) ‹*costa/isla*› to skirt, go around; **la carretera que bordea el lago** the road that goes along the edge of the lake; **navegar bordeando la costa** to hug the coast [2] (rodear, lindar con): **las barriadas pobres que bordean la ciudad** the poor districts on the outskirts of the city; **un camino bordeado de álamos** a road lined with poplars [3] ‹*peligro/fracaso*› to come close to [4] (acercarse a): **bordea los cincuenta** he's approaching *o* around fifty

bordillo *m* curb (AmE), kerb (BrE)

bordo *m*: **a ~** on board; **estar a ~** to be on board; **subir a ~** to go aboard *o* on board; **¡todos a ~!** all aboard!

boreal *adj* northern, boreal

Borgoña¹ *f* (Geog) Burgundy

Borgoña², **borgoña** *m* (Vin) Burgundy, burgundy

borla *f* (de gorro) pompom; (de cortina, birrete) tassel; (de polvera) powder puff

borlote *m* (Méx fam) row (colloq), ruckus (AmE colloq); **armar un ~** to kick up a row *o* create a ruckus

boro *m* boron

borra *f*

A (para relleno) flock; (de polvo) fluff; (Bot) down

B (sedimento — del café) dregs; (— del vino) lees (*pl*), sediment

borrachera *f*: **pegarse** *or* (Esp) **cogerse** *or* (esp AmL) **agarrarse una ~** to get drunk; **aquélla fue su última ~** that was the last time he got drunk

borrachín -china *m,f* (fam) (aficionado a la bebida): **es un ~** he likes his drink

borracho¹ -cha *adj* [1] [ESTAR] drunk; **~ de gloria/poder** drunk with glory/power [2] [SER]: **es muy ~** he is a drunkard *o* a heavy drinker

borracho² -cha *m,f* drunk; (habitual) drunkard, drunk

borrado *m* erasure

borrador *m*

A [1] (de redacción, carta) rough draft; (de contrato, proyecto) draft; (de dibujo) sketch; **lo hice en ~** I did a rough draft [2] (cuaderno) scratch pad (AmE), rough book (BrE)

B (para la pizarra) eraser (AmE), board rubber (BrE); (goma de borrar) (Col, Méx, Ven) eraser

borraja *f* borage

borrar [A1] *vt* [1] ‹*palabra/dibujo*› (con goma) to rub out, erase; (con líquido corrector) to white out, tippex out (BrE); (con esponja) to rub ... off; ‹*pizarra*› to clean; ‹*huellas digitales*› to wipe off [2] ‹*cassette/disquete*› to erase, wipe; ‹*canción*› to erase; ‹*información/ficha*› to delete, erase [3] ‹*recuerdos/imagen*› to blot out [4] ‹*persona*› (de lista, club): **la ~on de la lista** they took her (name) off the list; **lo borramos del club porque nunca iba** we cancelled his club membership because he never went

■ **borrarse** *v pron*

A [1] «*inscripción/letrero*» to fade; **se borró con la lluvia** the rain washed it away *o* off [2] «*temores/dudas*» to disappear; «*imagen/recuerdo*» to fade; **se le borró la sonrisa** her smile vanished [3] «*persona*» (de club) to cancel one's membership, resign; (de clase) to drop out; (de lista) to cross one's name off a list

B (Méx, RPl arg) (irse) to split (colloq); **yo me borro** I'm taking off (AmE), I'm off (BrE colloq)

borrasca *f* [1] (área de bajas presiones) area of low pressure; **una fuerte ~** an area of very low pressure [2] (tormenta) squall

borrascoso -sa *adj* ‹*viento*› squally; ‹*tiempo*› stormy, squally

borrego -ga *m,f*

A (cordero) lamb; (oveja) sheep

B **borrego** *m* (Méx) (noticia falsa) false rumor*; **soltaron** *or* **lanzaron el ~ de que ...** it was rumored that ...

borreguil *adj* (pey) sheeplike (pej)

borrico -ca *m,f* [1] (animal) donkey [2] (fam) (persona tonta) dummy (colloq)

borrón *m* (mancha) inkblot; (mancha borroneada) smudge; ***~ y cuenta nueva*** let's make a fresh start

borronear [A1] *vt* to smudge

borroso -sa *adj* [1] ‹*foto/imagen*› blurred; ‹*inscripción*› worn; ‹*contorno*› indistinct, blurred [2] ‹*idea/recuerdo*› vague, hazy

boscaje *m* thicket

boscoso -sa *adj* wooded

bosque *m* wood; (más grande) forest, woods (*pl*); (terreno) woodland

(Compuesto) **bosque ecuatorial** *or* **pluvial** (equatorial) rainforest

bosquecillo *m* copse, coppice; (plantado) grove

bosquejar [A1] *vt* (Art) to sketch, make a sketch of; ‹*idea/proyecto*› to outline, sketch out

bosquejo *m* (Art) sketch; (de novela) outline; **presentó** *or* **hizo un ~ de sus planes** he outlined his plans, he gave a brief outline of his plans

bostezar [A4] *vi* to yawn

bostezo *m* yawn

bota *f*
A (calzado) boot; **~s de caña alta/de media caña** knee-high/calf-length boots; ***colgar las ~s*** to hang up one's boots; ***morir con las ~s puestas*** to die with one's boots on; ***ponerse las ~s*** (Esp fam): **como pagaba la compañía se pusieron las ~s** the company was paying so they really made pigs of themselves
Compuestos
- **botas camperas** *or* **tejanas** cowboy boots
- **botas de agua** *fpl* rubber boots (*pl*), wellingtons (*pl*) (BrE)
- **botas de esquiar** *or* **de esquí** *fpl* ski boots (*pl*)
- **botas de montar** *fpl* riding boots (*pl*)

B (para vino) *small wineskin*

botadero *m* (Andes) *tb* **~ de basura** garbage dump (AmE), rubbish dump *o* tip (BrE)

botado -da *adj*
A [ESTAR] (Andes, Ven fam) (barato) dirt cheap (colloq)
B (Andes, Ven fam) (fácil) dead easy (colloq); **el examen estaba ~** the exam was a cinch *o* a piece of cake

botadura *f* launching

botafumeiro *m* censer

botagorra *adj* (AmC fam) short-tempered, quick-tempered

botamanga *f* (CS) **1** (del pantalón) cuff (AmE), turn-up (BrE) **2** (de la manga) cuff

botana *f* (Méx) snack, appetizer; **de ~ te sirven caracoles** they give you snails as an appetizer *o* with your drink; ***agarrar a algn de ~*** (Méx fam) to make fun of sb

> **botana**
> In Central America and Mexico, a small portion of food, olives, peanuts etc, usually served with a drink at parties, bars, or social occasions

botánica *f* botany

botánico -ca *adj* botanical

botar [A1] *vt*
A ‹*barco*› to launch
B ‹*pelota*› to bounce
C **1** (AmL exc RPl fam) (echar — de lugar) to throw … out (colloq); (— de trabajo) to fire (colloq), to sack (BrE colloq); **la ~on del trabajo** she was fired *o* sacked, she got the sack (BrE colloq) **2** (AmL exc RPl) (desechar) to throw … out; **no lo botes al suelo** don't throw it on the ground; **bótalo a la basura** chuck *o* throw it out (colloq); ⓢ **se prohíbe botar basura** no dumping *o* (BrE) tipping; **~ el dinero** to throw your money away **3** (Per fam) (vomitar) to bring up; **~ *el gato*** (Per arg) to throw up (colloq)
D (AmL exc RPl fam) (abandonar) ‹*novio/novia*› to chuck (colloq), to ditch (colloq); ‹*marido/esposa*› to leave; ***dejar botado a algn*** (fam) (en carrera) to leave sb miles behind; **el tren nos dejó botados** we missed the train
E (AmL exc RPl fam) (derribar) ‹*puerta/árbol*› to knock down; ‹*botella/taza*› to knock over; **no empujes que me botas** stop pushing, you're going to knock me over
F **1** (AmL exc RPl) (perder) ‹*aceite/gasolina*› to leak **2** (Col, Ven fam) (extraviar) ‹*llaves/lápiz*› to lose
■ **botar** *vi* (Esp) **1** ‹‹*pelota*›› to bounce **2** ‹‹*persona*›› to jump; **botaba de alegría** she was jumping for joy
■ **botarse** *v pron*
A (AmL exc CS fam) **1** (apresurarse) to rush; **no te botes, piénsatelo un poco** don't be too hasty *o* don't rush into anything, think it over **2** (arrojarse) to jump; **se botó de cabeza a la piscina** she dived into the pool; ***~se a algo*** (Chi fam): **se bota a duro** he likes to think of himself as a tough guy (colloq)
B (Col, Ven fam) ‹‹*leche*›› to boil over

botaratas *mf* (*pl* ~) (Col, Ven fam) spendthrift

botarate *mf* **1** (fam) (irresponsable) irresponsible fool **2** (AmL exc RPl) (derrochador) spendthrift

bote *m*
A (Náut) boat
Compuestos
- **bote de** *or* **a remos** rowboat (AmE), rowing boat (BrE)
- **bote salvavidas** lifeboat

B **1** (envase — de lata) (Esp) can, tin (BrE); (— de vidrio) jar; **un ~ de mermelada** a jar of jelly (AmE) *o* (BrE) jam; ***chupar del ~*** (Esp fam) to feather one's nest, line one's pocket; ***de ~ en ~*** packed **2** (recipiente — de lata) tin; (— de vidrio, plástico) storage jar; **el ~ de la basura** (Méx) the trash can (AmE), the rubbish bin (BrE) **3** (para gastos comunes, en juegos) kitty; (en bar, restaurante) box (*for tips*)
C (Méx arg) jail, slammer (sl)
D **1** (salto) jump; **dio** *or* **pegó un ~ de alegría** he jumped for joy; **se levantó de un ~** she leapt to her feet; ***a ~ pronto*** (Esp) off the top of one's head (colloq) **2** (de pelota) bounce; **dio dos ~s** it bounced twice **3** (Col) (vuelta, giro): **dar el ~** ‹‹*canoa*›› to capsize; ‹‹*persona*›› to (do a) somersault

botella *f* **1** (para vino, agua) bottle; **una ~ de litro** a liter* bottle; **una ~ de vino** (recipiente) a wine bottle; (con contenido) a bottle of wine; ***darle a la ~*** (fam) to hit the bottle **2** (de oxígeno, aire comprimido) cylinder

botellazo *m* blow with a bottle; **me pegó un ~** he hit me with a bottle

botellero *m*
A (para guardar botellas) bottle rack
B (CS) (trapero) ragman (AmE), rag-and-bone man (BrE)

botellín *m* small bottle of beer (*usually one-fifth of a liter*)

botica *f* (en algunas regiones ant) (farmacia) pharmacy

boticario -ria *m,f* (en algunas regiones ant) pharmacist, druggist (AmE), apothecary (arch)

botijo *m*: *drinking jug with spout*

botillería *f* (Chi) liquor store (AmE), off licence (BrE)

botín *m*
A (bota corta) ankle boot; (de bebé) bootee; (de futbolista) (CS) boot
B (de guerra) plunder, booty; (de ladrones) haul, loot

botiquín *m* **1** (armario — para medicinas) medicine chest *o* cabinet; (para colonias, jabón, etc) bathroom cabinet **2** (maletín) *tb* **~ de primeros auxilios** first-aid kit

botón *m*
A (Indum) button; **coser un ~** to sew on a button; ***como ~ de muestra*** (just) to give you an idea
Compuesto **botón de presión** (AmL) snap fastener (AmE), press stud (BrE)
B (de mecanismo) button; **dale al** *or* **aprieta el ~** press the button; **el ~ del volumen** the volume control
C (AmL) (insignia) badge, button (AmE)
D (de flor) bud

botones *mf* (*pl* ~) (de hotel) bellboy; (de oficina) (*m*) office boy; (*f*) office girl

botulismo *m* botulism

bouquet /bu'ke/ *m* (*pl* **-quets**) **1** (del vino) bouquet **2** (ramillete) bouquet

boutique /bu'tik/ *f* boutique

bóveda *f*
A (Arquit) vault
Compuestos
- **bóveda celeste** (frml & liter): **la ~ ~** the vault *o* canopy of heaven (liter), the firmament
- **bóveda de arista/de cañón/de crucería** groin/barrel/ribbed vault
- **bóveda de seguridad** (AmL) bank vault

B (RPl) (sepulcro) tomb

bóvido *m* bovid; **los ~s** the bovidae

bovino -na *adj* bovine

bowling /'boulin/ *m* **1** (deporte) tenpins (AmE), tenpin bowling (BrE) **2** (lugar) bowling alley

box /boks/ *m* (*pl* **boxes**)
A **1** (en carreras de coches) pit; **entrar en ~es** to go/come into the pits **2** (Equ) stall; **los ~es de salida** the starting gate (AmE) *o* gates (BrE)
B (CS, Méx) (boxeo) boxing

boxeador -dora *m,f* boxer

boxear [A1] *vi* to box

boxeo *m* boxing

boya *f* (Náut) buoy; (en pesca) float

boyante *adj* **1** ‹*situación/economía*› buoyant **2** (Náut) high in the water

bozal *m* (de perro) muzzle; (de caballo) halter

bozo *m* down (*on upper lip*)

bracear [A1] *vi* **1** (agitar los brazos) to wave one's arms about **2** (al nadar): **intenta ~ más largo** try to make your strokes longer

b

bracero -ra *m,f* temporary farm worker
bragas *fpl* (Esp) (de mujer) panties (*pl*), knickers (*pl*) (BrE)
braguero *m* truss
bragueta *f* fly, flies (*pl*)
brahmán *m* Brahman, Brahmin
braille[1] /'brajle/ *adj* braille (*before n*)
braille[2] /'brajle/ *m* braille
bramante *m* twine, string
bramar [A1] *vi* 1 «*toro*» to bellow, roar; «*ciervo*» to bell, bellow; «*elefante*» to trumpet 2 (liter) «*viento*» to howl, roar; «*mar*» to roar
bramido *m* 1 (del toro) bellowing, roaring; (del ciervo) bellowing, bell; (del elefante) trumpeting; **dio un ~** it bellowed/trumpeted 2 (liter) (del viento, mar) roaring
branquia *f* gill
braquicéfalo -la *adj* brachycephalic
brasa *f* ember; **carne/pescado a la(s) ~(s)** charcoal-grilled meat/fish
brasero *m* (de carbón — para interiores) small brazier; (— para la intemperie) brazier; (eléctrico) electric heater
brasier *m* (Col, Méx, Ven) bra
Brasil *m*: *tb* **el ~** Brazil
brasileño -ña, (AmL) **brasilero -ra** *adj/m,f* Brazilian
bravata *f* (amenaza) threat; (fanfarronada) boast; **es otra más de sus ~s** it's just more of his big talk
bravío -vía *adj* ‹*toro*› fierce, wild; ‹*potro*› wild, unmanageable
bravo[1] -va *adj*
A 1 [SER] ‹*toro*› fierce; ‹*perro*› fierce; **toros ~s** fighting bulls; **sus toros son muy ~s** his bulls put up a good fight 2 [ESTAR] ‹*mar*› rough 3 [ESTAR] (AmL fam) (enojado) angry
B (liter) ‹*guerrero*› brave, valiant
C (RPl fam) ‹*situación*› tricky; ‹*examen*› tough, hard; **hoy los chicos están bravísimos** the children are being really difficult today
bravo[2] *interj* (expresando aprobación) well done!, good job! (AmE); (tras actuación) bravo!
bravucón[1] -cona *adj* (fam) bragging (*before n*); **son todos muy bravucones** they're all full of bluster
bravucón[2] -cona *m,f* (fam & pey) braggart
bravuconada *f* piece of bravado; **no son más que ~s** it's all just bravado
bravura *f* 1 (de toro) fighting spirit; (de perro) fierceness 2 (de persona) bravery; **con ~** bravely 3 (del mar) roughness
braza *f* (Esp)
A (en natación) breaststroke; **nadar a ~** to swim (the) breaststroke
B (medida) fathom
brazada *f* 1 (al nadar) stroke; **en dos ~s llegó a la orilla** with two strokes she reached the shore 2 (cantidad) armful
brazal *m* 1 (Dep, Indum) armband 2 (Geog) (brazo de río) channel; (en época de lluvias) (Col) flood stream
brazalete *m* 1 (pulsera — de una pieza) bangle, bracelet; (— de eslabones) bracelet 2 (de tela) armband; **~ negro/de gala** black/ceremonial armband
brazo *m*
A 1 (Anat) arm; (parte superior) upper arm; **llevaba una cesta al** *or* **colgada del ~** she had a basket on one arm; **caminaban del ~** they walked arm in arm; **llevaba al niño en ~s** he was carrying the child in his arms; ***con los ~s abiertos*** with open arms; ***cruzado de ~s*** *or* ***con los ~s cruzados*** (literal) with one's arms crossed; (sin hacer nada): **no te quedes ahí cruzado de ~s** don't just stand/sit there (doing nothing); ***dar el ~ a torcer***: **no dio el** *or* **su ~ a torcer** he didn't let them/her twist his arm; ***luchar a ~ partido*** to fight tooth and nail; ***ser el ~ derecho de algn*** to be sb's right-hand man/woman 2 (de caballo) foreleg
B (de sillón) arm; (de tocadiscos) arm; (de grúa) jib; (de río) branch, channel
(Compuestos)
• **brazo armado** military arm
• **brazo de gitano** jelly roll (AmE), swiss roll (BrE)
• **brazo de mar** inlet, sound
C **brazos** *mpl* (trabajadores) hands (*pl*)
brea *f* pitch, tar
brebaje *m* potion; **un ~ mágico** a magic potion
brecha *f* (en muro) breach, opening; (en la frente, cabeza) gash; **se hizo una ~ en la cabeza** he split his head open; **se ha abierto una profunda ~ entre el gobierno y el ejército** there is now a serious rift between the army and the government; ***abrir ~*** to break through, blaze a trail; ***estar en la ~*** to be in the thick of things; ***seguir en la ~*** to stand one's ground
(Compuesto) **brecha generacional** generation gap
brécol *m* broccoli
brega *f* 1 (lucha) struggle; ***andar a la ~*** to be hard at work 2 (trabajo) work
bregar [A3] *vi* (luchar) to struggle; (trabajar) to work hard
breke, breque *m* (AmC) brake
brete *m* 1 (fam) (situación difícil) jam (colloq), tight spot (colloq); **nos puso en un ~** he put us on the spot 2 (RPl) (para el ganado) chute
bretel *m* (CS) strap
bretón[1] -tona *adj/m,f* Breton
bretón[2] *m* (idioma) Breton
breva *f* (Bot) early fig, black fig
breve *adj*
A 1 (frml) (corto) ‹*discurso/vacaciones*› brief, short; ‹*distancia*› short; **tras un ~ almuerzo continuó la reunión** after a short break for lunch, the meeting continued; **dentro de ~s momentos** in a few moments; **sea usted ~, por favor** please be brief; **en ~** shortly, soon 2 ‹*sonido/vocal*› short
B (liter) ‹*cintura*› dainty, slender
brevedad *f* 1 (de discurso, texto) brevity 2 (frml) (prontitud): **con la mayor ~** *or* **a la ~ posible** as soon as possible *o* (frml) at your earliest convenience
brevemente *adv* briefly, concisely
brevete *m* (Per) driver's license (AmE), driving licence (BrE)
breviario *m* breviary
brezal *m* moor, heathland
brezo *m* heather, heath (AmE)
bribón -bona *m,f* (fam) rascal (colloq), scamp (colloq)
bricolaje, bricolage *m* do-it-yourself, DIY
brida *f* bridle
briega *f* (Col) hard work, struggle
brigada[1] *m* warrant officer
brigada[2] *f* (Mil) brigade; (de policía) squad
(Compuestos)
• **brigada de estupefacientes/de explosivos** drug/bomb squad
• **Brigada de Investigación Criminal** ≈ Federal Bureau of Investigation *o* FBI (*in US*), ≈ Criminal Investigation Department *o* CID (*in UK*)
• **brigada de salvamento** rescue team
brigadier *m* 1 (ant) (en el ejército) brigadier general (AmE), brigadier (BrE); (en la marina) rear admiral 2 (Arg) (en la fuerza aérea) brigadier general (AmE), air commodore (BrE)
brillante[1] *adj* 1 ‹*luz/estrella/color*› bright; ‹*zapatos/metal/pelo*› shiny; ‹*pintura*› gloss (*before n*); ‹*papel*› shiny, glossy; **el fregadero está ~ de limpio** the sink is sparkling clean; **una tela ~** material with a sheen 2 ‹*escritor/porvenir*› brilliant; **su abogado tuvo una actuación ~** his lawyer performed brilliantly
brillante[2] *m* 1 (diamante) diamond; **un anillo de ~s** a diamond ring 2 **brillantes** *mpl* (Arg) (polvo brillante) glitter
brillantez *f* brilliance
brillantina *f* (para el pelo) brilliantine; (polvo brillante) (Ven, Ur) glitter
brillar [A1] *vi* 1 «*sol/luz*» to shine; «*estrella*» to shine, sparkle; «*zapatos/suelo/metal*» to shine, gleam; «*diamante*» to sparkle; **le ~on los ojos de alegría** her eyes lit up with joy 2 (destacarse) «*persona*» to shine; **brilla por su astucia/inteligencia** she's particularly shrewd/intelligent
■ **brillar** *vt* (Col) to polish

brillo *m* [1] (de estrella) brightness, brilliance; (de zapatos, suelo, metal) shine; (de diamante) sparkle; (del pelo) shine; (de seda, satén) sheen; **darle ~ al suelo** to polish the floor; **¿quiere las fotos con ~?** do you want a gloss finish on the photos?; **dale un poco de ~** (TV) turn the brightness up a bit; **el ~ de sus ojos** the sparkle in his eyes [2] (esplendor, lucimiento) splendor*; **un discurso/una interpretación sin ~** a dull *o* an unexceptional speech/performance [3] (para labios) lip gloss; (para uñas) clear nail polish

brilloso -sa *adj* (AmL) shiny

brincar [A2] *vi* «*niño*» to jump up and down; «*cordero*» to gambol, skip around; «*liebre*» to hop
▪ **brincar** *vt* (Méx) ‹*valla/obstáculo*› to jump

brinco *m* jump, leap, bound; **pegó** *or* **dio un ~ del susto** (fam) he jumped with fright

brindar [A1] *vi* to drink a toast; **~ POR algn/algo** to drink a toast TO sb/sth, to toast sb/sth
▪ **brindar** *vt*
A (frml) (proporcionar) (+ *me/te/le etc*) to give, to afford (frml); **me brindó su apoyo** she gave *o* (frml) lent me her support; **me brindó una oportunidad única** it gave *o* afforded me a unique opportunity; **la confianza que me brindan** the trust they are placing in me
B ‹*toro*› to dedicate
▪ **brindarse** *v pron* (frml) to volunteer; **~se A + INF** to offer to + INF, volunteer to + INF; **se brindó a acompañarme** he offered *o* volunteered to accompany me

brindis *m* (*pl* ~) toast; **hacer un ~ por algn** to drink a toast to sb

brinzar [A1] *v impers* (Ven) to drizzle

brío *m* [1] (ánimo, energía) spirit; **tocaron el primer movimiento con gran ~** they played the first movement with great gusto *o* verve; **luchó con ~** he fought with great spirit *o* determination [2] (de caballo) spirit

briosamente *adv* with spirit

brioso -sa *adj*
A (enérgico) ‹*persona*› energetic; ‹*caballo*› spirited
B ‹*andar/movimiento*› jaunty

brisa *f* breeze; **una ~ suave** a gentle breeze; **~ marina** sea breeze

británico¹ -ca *adj* British

británico² -ca *m,f* British person, Briton; **los ~s** the British, British people

brizna *f* (hebra) strand; (de hierba) blade; (llovizna) (Ven) drizzle

briznar [A1] *v impers* (Ven) to drizzle

broca *f* (drill) bit

brocado *m* brocade

brocal *m* curb, parapet

brocha *f* (de pintor) paintbrush, brush; (de afeitar) shaving brush; (en cosmética) blusher brush

broche *m* [1] (joya) brooch [2] (de collar, monedero) clasp; (para tender la ropa) (Arg) clothespin (AmE), clothes peg (BrE); (para el pelo) (Méx, Ur) barrette (AmE), hair slide (BrE) [3] (Arg) (grapa) staple

(Compuestos)
- **broche de oro** *or* **final** perfect end
- **broche de presión** (AmL) snap fastener (AmE), press stud (BrE)

brocheta *f* (aguja) brochette, skewer; (plato) kebab

brócoli *m* broccoli

broma *f* [1] (chiste) joke; **hacerle** *or* **gastarle una ~ a algn** to play a (practical) joke on sb; **déjate de ~s** stop kidding around (colloq); **no estoy para ~s** I'm not in the mood for jokes; **fuera de ~(s)** *or* **~s aparte** joking apart; **lo dije de** *or* **en ~** I was joking, I said it as a joke; **¿que yo se lo diga? ¿estás de ~?** me tell him? are you kidding? (colloq); ***ni en ~*** no way (colloq) [2] (fam & iró) (asunto) business (colloq); **la bromita nos costó un dineral** that little business *o* episode cost us a fortune

bromear [A1] *vi* to joke; **no es momento para ~** this is no time for jokes

bromista¹ *adj*: **es muy ~** he's always joking; **¡qué ~ eres!** you're such a joker

bromista² *mf* joker

bromuro *m* bromide

bronca *f* (fam)
A [1] (disputa, lío) row; **armar** *or* **montar una ~** to kick up a fuss (colloq), to create a ruckus (AmE colloq); **buscar ~** to look for trouble *o* a fight [2] (alboroto, bullicio) racket (colloq)
B (esp Esp) (regañina) scolding, telling off (colloq); **echarle la ~ a algn** to tell sb off
C (AmL fam) (rabia): **está con una ~** he's in a foul mood; **me da mucha ~** it really gets to *o* bugs me (colloq); **tenerle ~ a algn** to have it in for sb (colloq)

bronce *m* [1] (para estatuas, cañones) bronze; **una medalla de ~** a bronze medal [2] (para llamadores, placas) (AmL) brass

bronceado¹ -da *adj* tanned, suntanned

bronceado² *m* (de la piel) tan, suntan; (Metal) bronzing

bronceador¹ -dora *adj* suntan (*before n*)

bronceador² *m* suntan lotion

broncear [A1] *vt*
A «*piel*» to tan
B ‹*estatua/metal*› to bronze
▪ **broncearse** *v pron* to get a tan *o* a suntan

bronco -ca *adj* [1] ‹*sonido*› harsh; ‹*voz*› gruff, rough, gravelly; ‹*tos*› rasping, harsh [2] ‹*terreno*› rugged, rough [3] ‹*caballo*› wild

bronconeumonía *f* bronchopneumonia

bronquio *m* bronchial tube

bronquítico -ca *adj* bronchitic

bronquitis *f* bronchitis

brotar [A1] *vi* [1] «*planta*» to sprout, come up; «*hoja*» to appear, sprout; «*flor*» to come out [2] «*manantial/río*» to rise; **le brotaba sangre de la herida** blood oozed from the wound; **las lágrimas que brotaban de sus ojos** the tears that began to flow from her eyes [3] «*duda/sentimiento*» to arise; «*rebelión/violencia*» to break out [4] «*sarampión/grano*» to appear
▪ **brotarse** *v pron* (AmL) to come out in spots, break *o* come out in a rash (BrE)

brote *m* [1] (Bot) shoot; **echar ~s** to sprout, put out shoots [2] (de violencia, enfermedad) outbreak [3] (Col) (sarpullido) rash

broza *f* (maleza) undergrowth, scrub; (hojarasca) dead leaves

bruces: **de ~** (*loc adv*) face down; **se cayó de ~** he fell flat on his face

bruja *f*
A (mujer antipática) (fam) witch (colloq), old hag (colloq); *ver tb* **brujo²**
B (AmC, Col) (Zool) moth

brujería *f* witchcraft

brujo¹ -ja *adj* [1] ‹*ojos*› bewitching, beguiling; ‹*amor*› bewitching [2] (AmC, Méx fam) (sin dinero) broke (colloq)

brujo² -ja (*m*) warlock; (*f*) witch; *ver tb* **bruja**

brújula *f* compass

bruma *f* (marina) (sea) mist; (del alba) mist

brumoso -sa *adj* misty

bruñido -da *adj* burnished, polished

bruñir [I9] *vt* ‹*piedra*› to polish; ‹*metal*› to polish, burnish

brusco -ca *adj* [1] ‹*movimiento/cambio*› abrupt, sudden; ‹*subida/descenso*› sharp, sudden, abrupt; **el ~ giro de los acontecimientos** the sudden turn of events [2] ‹*carácter/modales*› rough; ‹*tono/gesto*› brusque, abrupt; ‹*respuesta*› curt, brusque; **no seas tan ~ que lo vas a romper** don't be so rough or you'll break it

Bruselas *f* Brussels

brusquedad *f* [1] (en el trato) roughness; **con ~** ‹*hablar/actuar*› abruptly [2] (de movimiento) abruptness, suddenness; **frenó con ~** he braked sharply

brutal *adj* ‹*crimen*› brutal; ‹*atentado*› savage

brutalidad *f* [1] (violencia) brutality, savageness [2] (acto, dicho): **¡qué ~, pegarle así a la pobre criatura!** what a brute, hitting the poor child like that!; **¡qué ~, preguntarle eso!** how insensitive can you get, asking him a question like that!

bruto¹ -ta *adj*
A ‹*persona*› [1] (ignorante) ignorant [2] (grosero) uncouth [3] (violento, brusco): **¡qué hombre más ~! ha vuelto a**

b

b

pegarle what a brute! *o* what an animal! he's hit her again
B ‹*peso/sueldo*› gross; **en ~** ‹*diamante*› uncut; ‹*mineral*› crude

bruto[2] **-ta** *m,f* **1** (ignorante) ignorant person; **¿cómo aprobaron a un ~ como él?** how could they pass someone as ignorant *o* as stupid as him? **2** (grosero): **es un ~** he's very rude **3** (persona violenta) brute, animal

Bs. As. = Buenos Aires

bubónico -ca *adj* bubonic

bucal *adj* ‹*lesión*› mouth (*before n*), buccal (tech); ‹*antiséptico/higiene*› oral (*before n*)

bucanero *m* buccaneer

buceador -dora *m,f* diver

bucear [A1] *vi* to swim underwater, to dive

buceo *m* underwater swimming, diving

buchaca *f* (Col) pocket

buche *m*
A **1** (de aves) crop **2** (de otros animales) maw **3** (fam) (de persona) belly (colloq); ***guardar*** *or* ***tener algo en el ~*** to keep sth under one's hat; ***sacarse algo del ~*** (Chi fam) to come out with sth
B (Med, Odont): **hacer ~s con algo** to rinse one's mouth out with sth
C (Méx fam) (boca) mouth; **cierre el ~** shut your mouth (colloq) *o* (sl) trap

bucle *m* **1** (en el pelo) ringlet; (en un cable, una cuerda) loop **2** (Inf) loop

bucólico -ca *adj* bucolic, pastoral

buda *m* **1** buddha **2** **Buda** (the) Buddha

budín *m* **1** (dulce) pudding; **~ de pan/manzana** bread/apple pudding **2** (salado) pie; **~ de pescado/carne** fish/meat pie

(Compuesto) **budín inglés** (RPl) fruitcake (AmE), fruit cake (BrE)

budismo *m* Buddhism

budista *adj/mf* Buddhist

buen *adj ver* **bueno**

buenamente *adv* **1** (sin demasiado esfuerzo): **trae lo que ~ puedas** bring whatever you can (manage); **ven si ~ puedes** come if you can (manage it) **2** (indicando buena voluntad): **yo hago lo que ~ puedo** I do what I can, I do the best I can; **cada uno da lo que ~ puede** everybody gives what they can *o* as much as they can

buenaventura *f* **1** (buena suerte) good fortune **2** (futuro): **me dijo/leyó la ~** she told my fortune

buenazo -za *m,f* (persona) kindhearted person; **el ~ de Pedro me llevó a casa** good old Pedro drove me home; **este perro es un ~** this dog's just a big softie (colloq)

buen mozo -na moza *adj* ‹*hombre*› good-looking, handsome; ‹*mujer*› attractive, good-looking

buenmozura *f* (AmL) looks (*pl*), good looks (*pl*)

bueno[1] **-na** *adj* [**buen** *is used before masculine singular nouns*]

(Sentido I)
A **1** [SER] (de calidad) ‹*hotel/producto*› good; **tiene buena memoria** she has a good memory; **ropa buena** good-quality clothes; **hizo un buen trabajo** she did a good job; ***lo ~ si breve dos veces ~*** brevity is the soul of wit **2** (valioso) good; **¡qué buena idea!** what a good idea!; **~s consejos** good *o* useful advice **3** (válido, correcto) ‹*razón/excusa*› good; ***~ está lo ~ (pero no lo demasiado)*** (fam) you can have too much of a good thing
B **1** [SER] (competente) ‹*médico/alumno*› good; **ser ~ EN algo** to be good AT sth; **es muy buena en francés** she's very good at French; **ser ~ PARA algo: es muy buena para los negocios** she's got a very good head for business **2** ‹*padre/marido/amigo*› good **3** (eficaz, efectivo) ‹*remedio/método*› good; **es ~ para la gripe/los dolores de cabeza** it's good for the flu/headaches
C (favorable) ‹*oferta/suerte*› good; **buenas noticias** good news; **la novela tuvo muy buena(s) crítica(s)** the novel got very good reviews; **están en buena posición económica** they're comfortably off; ***en las buenas*** (CS) in the good times; ***estar de buenas*** (de buen humor) (fam) to be in a good mood; (afortunado) (Col fam) to be lucky; ***por las buenas*** willingly
D [SER] (conveniente) good; **no es buena hora para llamar** it's not a good time to phone; **sería ~ que hablaras con él** it would be a good idea if you spoke to him; **no es ~ comer tanto** it isn't good to eat so much
E (ingenioso, divertido) ‹*chiste/idea*› good, great (colloq); **lo ~ fue que ...** the funny thing was ...
F **1** (agradable) nice; **hace muy buen tiempo** the weather's lovely **2** (agradable al paladar — en general) **ser ~** to be good, be nice; (— de algo en particular) **estar ~** to be good, be nice; **el guacamole es buenísimo** guacamole is really good; **¡qué buena está la carne!** the meat is delicious **3** **¡qué ~!** (AmL) great!; **¡qué ~ que lo trajiste!** it's a good thing you brought it
G [ESTAR] (en buen estado): **esta leche no está buena** this milk is off *o* sour; **¿este pescado estará ~?** do you think this fish is all right?
H [ESTAR] (fam) (sexualmente atractivo): **está muy buena** she's gorgeous (colloq); **está buenísimo** he's really gorgeous *o* hunky (colloq)
I (saludable, sano) ‹*costumbre/alimentación*› good; **tiene muy buen semblante** she looks very well; ***~ y sano*** (Chi) (sin novedad) safe and sound; (sobrio) sober
A (en fórmulas, saludos) good; **¡~s días!** *or* (RPl) **¡buen día!** good morning; **¡buenas tardes!** (temprano) good afternoon; (más tarde) good evening; **¡buenas noches!** (al llegar) good evening; (al despedirse) good night; **dale las buenas noches a la abuela** say good night to Grandma; **¡buen viaje!** have a good trip!; **¡buen provecho!** enjoy your meal, bon appetit; ***de buenas a primeras*** (de repente) suddenly

(Sentido II) **1** [SER] (en sentido ético) good; **fueron muy ~s conmigo** they were very good to me **2** [SER] ‹*niño*› good; **sé ~** behave (yourself)

(Sentido III)
A (iró & fam): **¡estaría ~ que ahora dijera que no!** it'd be just great if he said no now! (iro & colloq); **¡en buena nos hemos metido!** this is a fine mess we've got(ten) ourselves into; ***de los ~s/de las buenas*** (fam): **nos echó un sermón de los ~s** she gave us a real dressing down (colloq)
B (*delante del n*) (uso enfático): **se llevó un buen susto** she got a terrible fright; **se metió en un buen lío** he got himself into a fine mess; **todavía nos falta un buen trecho** we still have a fair way to go; **una buena cantidad** a fair amount
C **un buen día** one day; **un buen día se va a cansar y ...** one day *o* one of these days she's going to get fed up and ...; **un buen día llegó y dijo ...** one (fine) day she came home and said ...

(Compuestos)
- **buena forma** *f* physical fitness; **está en muy ~ ~** she's very fit
- **buena mesa** *f*: **la ~ ~** good cooking
- **buena pieza** *f* (iró & fam): **¡~ ~ resultó ser Ernesto!** a fine one Ernesto turned out to be! (iro & colloq)

bueno[2] **-na** *m,f* **1** (hum *o* leng infantil) (en películas, cuentos) goody (colloq); **los ~s y los malos** the good guys and the bad guys (colloq) **2** (bonachón, buenazo): **el ~ de Juan/la buena de Pilar** good old Juan/Pilar

bueno[3] *interj*
A **1** (expresando conformidad, asentimiento) OK (colloq), all right; **¿un café? — bueno** coffee? — OK *o* all right **2** (expresando duda, indecisión, escepticismo) well; **~ ... ¿qué quieres que te diga?** well ... what can I say? **3** (expresando resignación): **~, otra vez será** never mind, maybe next time
B **1** (expresando irritación): **~, se acabó ¡a la cama!** right, that's it, bed!; **pero, ~ ¿lo quiere o no?** well, do you want it or not?; **¡y ~! ¿qué querías que hiciera?** (RPl) well, what did you expect me to do? **2** (expresando sorpresa, desagrado) (well) really!; **¡~! esto era lo único que faltaba** (iró) oh, great! that's all we needed (iro)
C **1** (introduciendo o reanudando un tema) now then, right then; **~, ¿dónde estábamos?** now (then) *o* right (then), where were we? **2** (calificando lo expresado) well; **no es un lugar turístico, ~, no lo era** it isn't a tourist resort, well *o* at least, it didn't use to be
D (Méx) (al contestar el teléfono) **¡~!** hello

Buenos Aires *m* Buenos Aires

buey[1] *adj* (Méx fam) dumb (colloq)

buey[2] *m*
A (Agr, Zool) ox; ***hablar de ~es perdidos*** (RPl) to chat; ***entre***

~es no hay cornadas (RPl) birds of a feather stick together
B (Méx fam) (idiota) idiot, imbecile (colloq)
búfalo¹ -la *adj* (AmC fam) great (colloq), fantastic (colloq)
búfalo² *m* buffalo
bufanda *f* scarf
bufar [A1] *vi* 1 «*toro/caballo*» to snort 2 (fam) «*persona*» to snort; **papá está que bufa** dad's hopping mad *o* fuming (colloq)
bufet /bu'fe/, **bufé** *m*
A 1 (Coc) buffet; **~ frío** cold buffet 2 (restaurante) cafeteria
(Compuesto) **bufet libre** set price buffet
B (Andes) (aparador) sideboard
bufete *m* (Der) (despacho) lawyer's office; (negocio) legal practice, law firm
bufido *m* snort
bufo -fa *adj* ‹*espectáculo*› comedy (*before n*); ‹*actor*› comedy (*before n*), comic
bufón *m* (Hist) jester; (gracioso) (fam) clown (colloq)
bufonada *f* stupid joke; **se puso a hacer ~s** he started clowning around
buhardilla *f* 1 (desván) attic 2 (apartamento) attic apartment (AmE) *o* (BrE) room 3 (ventana) dormer window
búho *m* owl
buhonero *m* (ant) peddler*
buitre *m* (Zool) vulture; (persona avariciosa) vulture
bujía *f* 1 (Auto) spark plug 2 (AmC) (Elec) light bulb 3 (ant) (vela) candle
bula *f* (Relig) bull; **~ papal** papal bull
bulbo *m* bulb
buldozer, bulldozer /bul'ðoser/ *m* (*pl* **-zers**) bulldozer
bulevar *m* boulevard
Bulgaria *f* Bulgaria
búlgaro¹ -ra *adj/m,f* Bulgarian
búlgaro² *m* (idioma) Bulgarian
bulín *m*
A (RPl fam) 1 (de soltero) bachelor pad 2 (vivienda): **se compraron un bulincito** they bought a little place of their own (colloq) 3 (habitación) sanctum (colloq), den (colloq)
B (Per) (burdel) brothel
bulla *f* (ruido) racket (colloq), ruckus (AmE colloq); (actividad) bustle; **armar** *or* **hacer** *or* **meter ~** to make a racket, to create a ruckus; ***quitado de ~*** (Chi fam) mild-mannered
bullado -da *adj* (Chi) much talked-about
bullanguero -ra *adj* (fam) ‹*persona*› fun-loving; ‹*música/ambiente*› lively
bullaranga *f* (Col) racket
bullicio *m* 1 (ruido) racket, noise 2 (jaleo, actividad): **el ~ de la gran ciudad** the hustle and bustle of the city
bullicioso -sa *adj* ‹*calle/barrio*› busy, noisy; ‹*niño*› boisterous
bullir [I9] *vi*: **me bulle la sangre cuando oigo esas cosas** it makes my blood boil when I hear things like that; **las ideas bullían en su mente** his mind was bubbling (over) with ideas; **la calle bullía de gente** the street was teeming *o* swarming with people; **el lugar bullía de actividad** the place was a hive of activity
bullying /'bu:liin/ *m* bullying
bulto *m*
A 1 (cuerpo, forma): **a lo lejos vi un ~ que se movía** I saw a shape moving in the distance; **se le notaba el ~ de la pistola debajo de la chaqueta** you could see the bulge *o* form of the gun under his jacket; ***escurrir el ~*** (fam) (en el trabajo) to duck out; (en entrevista) to dodge the issue 2 (volumen) bulk; **cosas ligeras y de poco ~** light things that aren't too bulky; **errores de ~** glaring errors; ***a ~*** (fam): **así, a ~, yo diría unas 500 personas** at a guess, I'd say about 500 people; ***hacer ~*** to swell the numbers
B (Med) lump
C 1 (paquete, bolsa) piece of luggage; **~ de mano** piece *o* item of hand baggage *o* luggage; **cargada de ~s** laden with packages (*o* bags *etc*) 2 (Col) (saco) sack; ***llevar del ~*** (Col fam): **nos tocó llevar del ~** we got a raw deal; **¿cómo andas? — llevado del ~** how are you? — I'm having a bit of a rough time of it (colloq)

bumerán *m* boomerang
bungalow /bunɣa'lo/ *m* (*pl* **-lows**) cabin, chalet
búnker /'buŋker/ *m* (*pl* **-kers**)
A (fortificación) bunker; (refugio) shelter, bunker
B (en golf) bunker
buñuelo *m* fritter
buque *m* ship, vessel
(Compuestos)
- **buque cisterna** tanker
- **buque de guerra/insignia** warship/flagship
- **buque de pasaje** passenger liner
- **buque factoría** factory ship
- **buque mercante/nodriza** merchant/mother ship *o* vessel
- **buque portacontenedores** container ship

burbuja *f* (de gas, aire) bubble; **una bebida sin ~s** a still drink; **este vino tiene ~s** this wine is fizzy *o* bubbly
burbujeante *adj* bubbly, bubbling
burbujear [A1] *vi* 1 «*champán/agua mineral*» to fizz 2 (al hervir) to bubble
burdel *m* brothel
burdeos *adj inv* burgundy
Burdeos *m* (Geog, Vin) Bordeaux
burdo -da *adj* 1 ‹*persona/modales*› coarse 2 ‹*mentira*› blatant; ‹*imitación*› crude; **una burda calumnia** a base calumny (frml); **una burda excusa** a flimsy excuse, a cock-and-bull story 3 ‹*paño/tela*› rough, coarse
burgués¹ -guesa *adj* (Hist) bourgeois; (de clase media) middle-class; (pey) bourgeois (pej)
burgués² -guesa *m,f* 1 (Hist) member of the bourgeoisie, bourgeois; **los burgueses** the bourgeoisie 2 (persona de clase media) member of the middle class; (pey) bourgeois
burguesía *f* (Hist) bourgeoisie; (clase media) middle class, middle classes (*pl*); (pey) bourgeoisie
buril *m* burin, engraver's chisel
burla *f* 1 (mofa): **era objeto de las ~s de todos** he was the butt of everyone's jokes; **todos le hacen la ~** everyone makes fun of her *o* mocks her 2 (atropello): **esto es una ~ del reglamento** this makes a mockery of the regulations; **esta ley es una ~ a la opinión pública** this law flies in the face of public opinion
burladero *m*: *barrier behind which the bullfighter takes refuge*
burlar [A1] *vt* 1 ‹*medidas de seguridad*› to evade, get around; **~on la vigilancia de la policía** they slipped past the police 2 ‹*enemigo*› to outwit
■ **burlarse** *v pron* **~se DE algo/algn** to make fun OF sth/sb; **¡de mí no se burla nadie!** no-one makes fun of *me!*
burlesco -ca *adj* 1 ‹*género*› burlesque; ‹*espectáculo*› comic 2 ‹*tono*› mocking
burlete *m* draft* excluder
burlón -lona *adj* 1 (de mofa) ‹*actitud*› mocking; ‹*risa*› sardonic, derisive 2 (de broma) ‹*actitud*› joking, teasing
buró *m* 1 (escritorio) writing desk, bureau (BrE) 2 (Méx) (mesa de noche) bedside table
(Compuesto) **buró ejecutivo** *or* **político** executive, politburo
burocracia *f* administration, bureaucracy; (pey) bureaucracy (pej), red tape (pej)
burócrata *mf* 1 (pey) bureaucrat (pej) 2 (Méx) (funcionario) civil servant, official
burocrático -ca *adj* 1 (pey) ‹*trámite/proceso*› bureaucratic 2 (Méx) ‹*empleado/jerarquía*› government (*before n*), state (*before n*)
burra *f* (Chi fam) jalopy (AmE), old banger (BrE); *ver tb* **burro²**
burrada *f* (fam) (necedad, barbaridad): **deja de decir ~s** stop talking such nonsense *o* drivel; **me dieron ganas de contestarle una ~** I felt like saying something rude; **¿cómo pudiste hacer semejante ~?** how could you do such a stupid thing?
burrero -ra *m,f*
A (persona) (CS fam) horse racing fan
B (Chi arg) (que lleva droga) mule (arg)
burro¹ -rra *adj*
A 1 (fam) (ignorante) stupid, dumb (AmE colloq), thick (BrE

b

colloq) 2 (fam) (bruto, tosco) rough; **¡no seas ~, me has hecho daño!** careful, that hurt! 3 (fam) (obstinado, cabezón) pigheaded (colloq)

B (Col arg) (marihuanero): **son muy ~s** they are real dope fiends (colloq)

burro[2] **-rra** *m,f*

A (Zool) 1 (asno) (*m*) donkey; (*f*) female donkey, jenny; **me tienen de ~ de carga** I get landed with all the donkey work; ***apearse*** *or* ***bajarse del ~*** to back down; ***no ver tres en un ~*** (fam) to be as blind as a bat (colloq); ***trabajar como un ~*** to slog one's guts out; ***ver ~s negros*** (Chi fam) to be in agony, see stars (colloq); ***quien nace para ~ muere rebuznando*** a leopard never changes its spots 2 (CS fam) (caballo de carrera) racehorse

B (fam) 1 (ignorante) idiot 2 (bruto, tosco) oaf; **es un ~ trabajando** he can take any amount of work 3 (cabezón, obstinado) stubborn mule, obstinate pig (colloq); *ver tb* **burra**

burro[3] *m* 1 (en carpintería) sawhorse; (en herrería) workbench 2 (Méx) (para planchar) ironing board 3 (Méx) (caballete) trestle

bursátil *adj* stock market *o* exchange (*before n*); **mercado ~** stock market *o* exchange

bus *m* (Auto, Transp) bus; (Inf) bus

(Compuesto) **bus de control/datos/direcciones** control/data/address bus

busca[1] *f* (búsqueda) search; **en ~ de algo** in search of sth; **salieron en su ~** they set out to look for him; **anda en ~ de marido** she's looking for a husband; **andar a la ~ de algo/algn** (Chi fam) to be after sth/sb (colloq)

busca[2] *m* (Esp fam) pager, beeper (AmE), bleeper (BrE)

buscabullas (*pl* ~) *mf* (Chi, Méx fam) troublemaker

buscador -dora *m,f*: **~ de oro** gold prospector; **~ de tesoros** treasure hunter

buscapleitos *mf* (*pl* ~) (fam) troublemaker

buscar [A2] *vt*

A (intentar encontrar) 1 ‹*persona/objeto*› to look for; ‹*fama/fortuna*› to seek; ‹*trabajo/apartamento/solución*› to look for, try to find; **no trates de ~ excusas** don't try to make excuses; **la policía lo está buscando** the police are looking for him, he's wanted by the police; **S se busca** wanted; **te buscan en la portería** someone is asking for you at reception; **busca una manera más fácil de hacerlo** try and find an easier way of doing it 2 (en libro, lista) to look up; **busca el número en la guía** look up the number in the directory

B 1 (recoger) to collect, pick up; **vengo a ~ mis cosas** I've come to collect *o* pick up my things 2 (conseguir y traer) to get; **fue a ~ un médico/un taxi** he went to get a doctor/a taxi

C 1 (intentar conseguir): **una ley que busca la igualdad de los sexos** a law which aims to achieve sexual equality; **¿qué buscas con eso?** what are you trying to achieve by that?; **~ + INF** to try to + INF, set out to + INF; **el libro busca destruir ese mito** the book sets out *o* tries *o* attempts to explode that myth 2 (provocar) ‹*bronca/camorra*› to look for

■ **buscar** *vi* to look; **busca en el cajón** look *o* have a look in the drawer; **¿has buscado bien?** have you looked properly?; ***el que busca encuentra*** *or* ***busca y encontrarás*** seek and ye shall find

■ **buscarse** *v pron*

A (intentar encontrar) to look for; **debería ~se (a) alguien que le cuidara los niños** she should look for *o* find somebody to look after the children

B ‹*problemas*›: **no quiero ~me complicaciones/problemas** I don't want any trouble; **tú te lo has buscado** you've brought it on yourself, it serves you right; **se está buscando problemas** she's asking for trouble; ***buscársela(s)*** (fam): **te la estás buscando** you're asking for trouble, you're asking for it (colloq)

buscavidas *mf* (*pl* ~) (CS) go-getter (colloq)

buscón -cona *m,f*

A (ant) (rufián) rogue (dated), scoundrel (dated)

B **buscona** *f* (pey) (prostituta) whore (pej)

busero -ra *m,f* bus driver

buseta *f* (Col, Ven) small bus

búsqueda *f* search; **~ DE algo/algn** search FOR sth/sb

busquillas *mf* (*pl* ~) (Chi, Per) go-getter (colloq)

busto *m* 1 (de mujer) bust; **¿cuánto mide de ~?** what size (bust) are you?, what's your bust size? 2 (Art) bust

butaca *f* 1 (con respaldo) (esp Esp) armchair; (sin respaldo) (esp AmL) stool 2 (en teatro, cine) seat; **~ de patio** (Esp) orchestra (AmE) *o* (BrE) stall seat

butano *m* butane (gas)

butifarra *f* 1 (embutido) *type of sausage* 2 (Per) (bocadillo) ham, lettuce and onion sandwich

buzo[1] *adj* (Méx fam) (astuto): **es bien ~** he's really on the ball (colloq); **ponte ~** keep on your toes

buzo[2] *m*

A (Náut) diver

B (Indum) 1 (Chi, Per) (para hacer ejercicio) track suit 2 (Col) (suéter de cuello alto) turtleneck sweater (AmE), polo-neck jumper (BrE) 3 (Arg, Col) (camiseta) sweatshirt 4 (Ur) (jersey) sweater, jumper (BrE)

buzo[3] *interj* (Méx fam) 1 (para avisar) look out!, watch out! 2 (expresando enojo) watch it!

buzón *m* (en la calle) postbox, mailbox (AmE), letter-box (BrE); (en una casa) mailbox (AmE), letter-box (BrE); **echar una carta al** *or* **en el ~** to mail (AmE) *o* (BrE) post a letter; ***venderle un ~ a algn*** (RPl fam) to take sb for a ride (colloq)

Cc

C, c *f* (*read as* /se/ *or* (Esp) /θe/) *the letter* **C, c**

c/ (= **calle**) St, Rd

C *m* (= **centígrado** *or* **Celsius**) C, Centigrade, Celsius

cabal *adj* 1 ‹*noción/comprensión*›: **una noción ~ del problema** an exact idea of the problem; **5.000 pesos ~es** exactly 5,000 pesos 2 ‹*persona*› fine, upright

cábala *f* (Esp) 1 (Rel) cabala; (intriga) intrigue 2 **cábalas** *fpl*: **hacer ~s** to speculate

cabales *mpl*: **no está en sus ~** he's not in his right mind

cabalgadura *f* (liter) mount (liter)

cabalgar [A3] *vi* (liter) «*jinete*» to ride

cabalgata *f* (desfile) parade, cavalcade; **la ~ de los Reyes Magos** the Epiphany parade *o* procession

cabalístico -ca *adj* cabalistic

caballa *f* mackerel

caballada *f* (CS) ▸ **animalada**

caballeresco -ca *adj* gentlemanly, gallant

caballería *f* 1 (Mil) cavalry 2 (caballo) horse; (montura) mount (liter)

Compuestos
- **caballería andante** (actividad) knight-errantry; (gente) knights errant (*pl*)
- **caballería ligera** light cavalry

caballeriza *f* 1 (edificio) stable 2 (caballos) stable, stables (*pl*)

caballerizo -za *m,f* groom

caballero *m*

A (frml) (hombre, señor) gentleman; **sección de ~s** men's department; **¿en qué puedo servirle, ~?** how can I help you, sir?; **damas y ~s** ladies and gentlemen; Ⓢ **caballeros** Men *o* Gentlemen *o* Gents

B (hombre cortés, recto) gentleman; **es todo un ~** he's a perfect gentleman

C (Hist) knight; **fue armado ~** he was knighted

Compuesto **caballero andante** knight errant

caballerosidad *f* chivalry

caballeroso -sa *adj* gentlemanly, gallant

caballete *m* 1 (de la nariz) bridge 2 (para mesa) trestle; (para lienzo, pizarra) easel; (de moto) kickstand; (del tejado) ridge

caballito *m* 1 (juguete — que se mece) rocking horse; (— con palo) hobbyhorse; ***hacerle ~ a algn*** to bounce sb up and down on one's knee; *ver tb* **caballo** 2 **caballitos** *mpl* (carrusel) carousel, merry-go-round

Compuestos
- **caballito del diablo** dragonfly
- **caballito de mar** sea horse

caballo¹ -lla *adj* (AmC fam) (estúpido) stupid

caballo² *m*

A (Equ, Zool) horse; **¿sabes montar** *or* (AmL) **andar a ~?** can you ride (a horse)?; **fueron a ~ hasta el pueblo** they rode to the village (on horseback); **dieron un paseo a ~** they went for a ride (on horseback); ***a ~ entre ...*** halfway between ...; ***como ~ desbocado***: **salieron de clase como ~s desbocados** they charged *o* tore out of the classroom; ***estar de a ~ en algo*** (Chi fam) to be an expert on sth; ***llevar a algn a ~*** to give sb a piggyback; ***a ~ regalado no se le miran los dientes*** don't look a gift horse in the mouth

Compuestos
- **caballo de batalla** (de persona): **el inglés es su ~ de batalla** English is his real bugbear *o* is a constant battle for him; (en discusión) controversial issue
- **caballo de carga** packhorse
- **caballo de carreras** *or* (CS) **carrera** racehorse
- **caballo de tiro** carthorse
- **caballo de Troya** Trojan horse

B (en ajedrez) knight; (en naipes) ≈ queen (*in a Spanish pack of cards*)

C (Auto, Fís, Mec) *tb* **~ de vapor** (metric) horsepower

Compuesto **caballo de fuerza** (British) horsepower

D (arg) (heroína) horse (sl)

E (Méx) (en gimnasia) horse

F (AmC fam) 1 (estúpido) idiot 2 (pantalón vaquero) jeans (*pl*)

caballuno -na *adj* ‹*facciones*› horsey

cabaña *f*

A (choza) cabin, shack

B (Agr) (RPl) (estancia) cattle-breeding ranch

C (Méx) (Dep) goal

cabaré, cabaret /kaβa're/ *m* (*pl* **-rets**) cabaret

cabaretera *f* cabaret dancer

cabás *m* (Esp) lunch box

cabe *prep* (arc) beside, next to

cabeceada *f* 1 (AmL) (al dormitar): **dar ~s** to nod off; **echarse una ~** to take *o* have a nap 2 (CS) (Dep) header

cabecear [A1] *vi* 1 «*persona*» to nod off 2 «*caballo*» to toss its head; «*barco*» to pitch

■ **cabecear** *vt* ‹*balón*› to head

cabecera *f*

A 1 (de la cama) headboard; **a la ~ del enfermo** at the patient's bedside; **había un crucifijo en la ~** there was a crucifix over the bed 2 (de una mesa) head, top 3 (de un río) headwaters (*pl*) 4 (de una manifestación) head, front

B (Adm, Pol) *tb* **~ de comarca** administrative center*

C (Esp) (de periódico) masthead, flag; (de página) head, top

cabecero *m* headboard

cabecilla *mf* ringleader

cabellera *f* 1 (melena) hair 2 (de un cometa) tail

cabello *m* hair; *para modismos ver* **pelo**

Compuestos
- **cabello de ángel** *m* (dulce) *sweet pumpkin filling*
- **cabellos de ángel** *mpl* (fideos) vermicelli

cabelludo -da *adj* hairy, furry

caber [E15] *vi*

A 1 (en un lugar) to fit; **esto aquí no cabe** this won't fit *o* go (in) here; **no cabemos los cuatro** there isn't room for all four of us; **~ EN algo**: **no cabe en la caja** it won't fit in the box; **en esta botella caben diez litros** this bottle holds ten liters; **¿cabe otro en el coche?** is there room for one more in the car?; ***no ~ en sí***: **no cabía en sí de alegría** she was beside herself with joy 2 (pasar) to fit, go; **~ POR algo** to go THROUGH sth; **no cabe por la puerta** it won't go through the door 3 «*falda/zapatos*» (+ *me/te/le etc*) to fit; **estos pantalones ya no me caben** these trousers don't fit me any more

B (*en 3ª pers*) (frml) (ser posible): **cabe la posibilidad de que haya perdido el tren** he may have missed the train; **no cabe duda de que ...** there is no doubt that ...; **este es mejor, no cabe duda** this one is better, without a doubt;

sólo me cabe una solución: renunciar I have no option but to resign; **es, si cabe, aún mejor** it is even better, if such a thing is possible; ~ + INF: **cabe suponer que ha habido un error** it is possible that there has been a mistake; **cabría decir que ...** it could be said that ...; **una de las épocas más sangrientas que cabe imaginar** one of the bloodiest eras imaginable; **cabe esperar que ...** it is to be hoped that ...; **cabría cuestionarse si ...** we should ask ourselves whether ...; **cabe mencionar que ...** it is worth mentioning that ...; ***dentro de lo que cabe*** all things considered

C C (frml) (corresponder) (+ *me/te/le etc*): **le cupo la satisfacción de ...** he had the satisfaction of ...; **el papel que le cupo en las negociaciones** the role she played in the negotiations

D (Mat): **2 entre 3 no cabe** 3 into 2 won't *o* doesn't go; **17 entre 5 cabe a 3 y sobran 2** 5 into 17 goes 3 times and 2 over

cabestrillo *m* sling; **llevaba el brazo en ~** he had his arm in a sling

cabestro *m* (buey) bullock (*used for leading fighting bulls into or out of the ring*)

cabeza *f*

A 1 (Anat) head; **me duele la ~** I've got a headache; **marcó de ~** he scored with a header; **un día vas a perder la ~** (fam & hum) you'd lose your head if it wasn't screwed on (colloq & hum); **de la ~ a los pies** from head to toe *o* foot; **pararse en la** *or* **de ~** (AmL) to do a headstand 2 (medida) head; **ganó por una ~** he won by a head; **le lleva** *or* **saca una ~ a su hermana** he's a head taller than his sister 3 (pelo) hair; **me lavé la ~** I washed my hair 4 (inteligencia): **tiene ~** he's bright, he has a good head on his shoulders; **usa la ~** use your head; **¡qué poca ~!** have you/has he no sense? 5 (mente): **¡que ~ la mía! se me había olvidado** what a memory! I had forgotten; **tenía la ~ en otra cosa** my mind was on other things; **tú estás mal de la ~** you're out of your mind; **se me ha ido de la ~** it's gone right out of my head; **se le ha metido en la ~ que ...** she's got it into her head that ...; **lo primero que me vino a la ~** the first thing that came into my head; **no se me pasó por la ~** it didn't cross my mind; ***andar*** *or* ***ir de ~*** (fam): **ando de ~ con tanto trabajo** I'm up to my eyeballs *o* eyes in work; **anda de ~ por ella** he's crazy about her; ***calentarle a algn la ~ con algo*** (fam) to fill sb's head with sth; ***calentarse la ~*** (fam) to get worked up (colloq); ***cortar ~s***: **en cuanto asumió el cargo entró a cortar ~s** as soon as she took up her post, heads started to roll; ***darse (con) la ~ contra la pared*** ver **cabezazo**; ***ir con la ~ (bien) alta*** to hold one's head high; ***írsele a algn la ~***: **se me va la ~** I feel dizzy; ***jugarse la ~*** (RPl fam): **va a llegar tarde, me juego la ~** you can bet your bottom dollar she'll be late (colloq); ***levantar ~*** (fam) (superar problemas) to get back on one's feet; ***levantar la ~***: **ha estado estudiando sin levantar la ~** she's had her head buried in her work; **¡si tu padre levantara la ~!** if your father was alive today ...!; ***meterse de ~ en algo*** (fam) to throw oneself into sth; ***no caberle a algn en la ~*** (fam): **no me cabe en la ~ que te guste** I just can't understand how you can like it; **¡en qué ~ cabe!** how could anyone be so stupid!; ***perder la ~***: **no perdamos la ~** let's not panic *o* lose our heads; **perdió la ~ por esa mujer** he lost his head over that woman; ***quebrarse la ~*** (Andes fam) to rack one's brains; ***quitarle a algn algo de la ~*** to get sth out of sb's head; ***quitarse algo de la ~*** ‹*idea*› to get sth out of one's head; ***romperse la ~*** (fam) ***(***preocuparse***)*** to rack one's brains; (lastimarse) to break one's neck (colloq); ***sentar (la) ~*** (fam) to settle down; ***subírsele a algn a la ~*** «*vino/éxito*» to go to one's head; ***tener la ~ sobre los hombros*** (fam) to have one's head screwed on tight (AmE colloq) *o* (BrE colloq) screwed on; ***tener la ~ llena de pájaros*** (fam) to have one's head in the clouds; ***tengo/tiene la ~ como un bombo*** (fam) (me/le duele) my/his/her head feels ready to burst (colloq); (estoy/está confundido) my/his/her head's spinning; ***traer*** *or* ***llevar a algn de ~*** (fam) to drive sb crazy (colloq); ***nadie escarmienta en ~ ajena*** people only learn from their own mistakes

(Compuestos)

- **cabeza de chorlito** *mf* (fam) scatterbrain (colloq)
- **cabeza de jabalí** headcheese (AmE), brawn (BrE)
- **cabeza de turco** *mf* scapegoat
- **cabeza dura** 1 *mf* (fam): **es un ~ ~** he's so stubborn *o* (colloq) pigheaded 2 *adj* pigheaded (colloq), stubborn
- **cabeza hueca** *mf* (fam) scatterbrain (colloq); airhead (colloq)
- **cabeza rapada** *mf* skinhead

B 1 (individuo): **por ~** each, a head 2 (de ganado) head; **50 ~s de ganado** 50 head of cattle

C (primer lugar, delantera): **a la** *or* **en ~**: **estamos a la ~ del sector** we are the leading company in this sector; **se colocaron a la ~ de los otros partidos** they took the lead over the other parties; **iban a la ~ de la manifestación** they were at the front *o* head of the demonstration; **el equipo va en ~ de la clasificación** the team is at the top of the division

(Compuestos)

- **cabeza de familia** *mf* head of the family
- **cabeza de la Iglesia** *m* head of the Church
- **cabeza de lista** *mf*: *candidate heading an electoral list*
- **cabeza de partido** *f*: *administrative center of a* **partido² E**
- **cabeza de puente** *f* bridgehead
- **cabeza de serie** *mf* seed; **derrotó a Guillén, ~ de ~ número cuatro** he beat Guillén, seeded number four

D 1 (de alfiler, clavo, fósforo) head 2 (de misil) warhead

(Compuestos)

- **cabeza atómica** atomic warhead
- **cabeza nuclear** nuclear warhead

E (Audio, Video) head

F (de plátanos) hand, bunch

(Compuesto) **cabeza de ajo** bulb of garlic

cabezada *f* 1 (movimiento) nod; **iba dormido, dando ~s** his head kept nodding in his sleep; ***dar*** *or* ***echar una ~*** (fam) to have a nap (colloq) 2 (Equ) headstall 3 (Náut) pitch; **dar ~s** to pitch up and down

cabezal *m*

A (de un torno) headstock

B 1 (almohada) bolster 2 (de sillón) headrest

C (AmL) (de cama) headboard/footboard

D (AmL) (terminal) terminal

E (Audio, Video) head

cabezazo *m*

A 1 (golpe): **se dio un ~ en el estante** he hit *o* banged his head on the shelf; **le di un ~** I headbutted him; ***darse (de) ~s contra la pared***: **podría darme ~s contra la pared** I feel like kicking myself (colloq) 2 (Dep) header; **marcó de un ~** he scored with a header

B (Col fam) (buena idea) brainwave

cabezón¹ -zona, cabezota *adj* 1 (fam) (terco) pigheaded (colloq) 2 (fam) (de cabeza grande): **¡qué ~ es!** what a big head he has! 3 ‹*vino*› heady

cabezón² -zona *m,f*, **cabezota** *mf* (fam): **¡eres un ~!** you're so pigheaded! (colloq)

cabezudo¹ -da *adj* (de cabeza grande): **es ~** he has a very large head

cabezudo² *m*: *carnival figure with a large head*

cabida *f*

A (capacidad de recipiente, estadio, teatro) capacity; **sólo hay ~ para diez pasajeros** there's only room *o* space for ten passengers; **el estadio puede dar ~ a casi 100.000 personas** the stadium can hold almost 100,000 people; **una publicación que da ~ a diversas tendencias** a publication that accommodates a range of opinions; **ese tipo de conducta no tiene ~ en la sociedad** there is no place for that kind of behavior in society

B (de un terreno) area

cabildo *m* 1 (Relig) chapter 2 (Hist) town council 3 (en Canarias) inter-island council

cabina *f*

A 1 (vestuario) cubicle, stall (AmE) 2 (de laboratorio de idiomas, estudio de radio) booth

(Compuestos)

- **cabina de prensa** press box
- **cabina de proyección** projection room
- **cabina telefónica** *or* **de teléfonos** telephone booth *o* (BrE) box

B 1 (de camión, grúa) cab 2 (Aviac) (para pilotos) ▸ **cabina de mando**; (para pasajeros) cabin

(Compuesto) **cabina de mando** (de avión grande) flight deck; (de avión pequeño) cockpit

cabinero -ra *m,f* (Col) flight attendant

cabizbajo -ja *adj*: **caminaba ∼** he walked along, head bowed; **se lo veía ∼** he looked downcast

cable *m*

A 1 (Elec, Telec) cable; ***cruzársele*** *or* (Méx) ***cuatrapeársele los ∼s a algn*** (fam) to get mixed up 2 (para levantar, tirar) cable; ***echarle un ∼ a algn*** (fam) to help sb out, give sb a hand

B (ant) (telegrama) cable, wire

cablegrama *m* (ant) cablegram (dated), cable

cablevisión *f* cable television

cabo *m*

A (Geog) cape

B 1 (Mil) corporal 2 (en remo) stroke

(Compuestos)

- **cabo de segunda** seaman (AmE), leading seaman (BrE)
- **cabo de primera** petty officer
- **cabo primero** corporal

C (extremo) end; (trozo pequeño) bit, piece; **han quedado muchos ∼s sueltos** there are a lot of loose ends; **atar los ∼s sueltos** to tie up the loose ends; **al ∼ de** after; ***atar*** *or* ***unir ∼s*** (fam) to put two and two together; ***de ∼ a rabo*** (fam) from beginning to end; ***estar al ∼ de algo*** to know all about sth; ***estar al ∼ de la calle*** (Esp fam) to know the score (colloq); ***llevar a ∼*** ‹*tarea/misión*› to carry out; **llevó a ∼ un duro entrenamiento** he trained very hard; **lleva a ∼ una excelente labor** he does an excellent job

cabotaje *m* (Náut) cabotage

cabra *f* goat; ***estar como*** *or* ***más loco que una ∼*** (fam) to be completely nuts (colloq); *ver tb* **cabro²**

(Compuesto) **cabra montés** Spanish Ibex

cabrá, cabré, etc *see* **caber**

cabrahigar [A22] *vt* to hang strings of wild figs on

cabreado -da *adj* (fam) furious (colloq), mad (colloq); **anda** *or* **está ∼** (enojado) he's furious; (harto) (Chi) he's fed up

cabreante *adj* (fam) really annoying

cabrear [A1] *vt* 1 (fam) (enfadar) to make … mad (colloq), to piss … off (sl) 2 (Chi fam) (hartar) **∼ + INF**: **me cabreó comer tanta palta** I got fed up with *o* sick of eating avocado all the time

■ **cabrearse** *v pron* 1 (fam) (enojarse) to get mad (colloq) 2 (Chi fam) (hartarse) **∼se DE** *or* **CON algo/algn** to get fed up WITH sth/sb, get sick OF sth/sb

cabreo *m* (fam) 1 (enojo, irritación): **¡qué ∼ tiene** *or* **lleva encima!** he's in a foul *o* a terrible mood! (colloq); **agarrarse un ∼** to get mad (colloq), to hit the roof (colloq) 2 (Chi) (aburrimiento) boredom

cabrerizo -za *m,f* goatherd

cabrero¹ -ra *adj* (RPl fam) furious, mad (colloq)

cabrero² -ra *m,f* goatherd

cabría, etc *see* **caber**

cabrillas *fpl* (esp Esp) (olas) white horses *o* caps (*pl*); **hacer ∼** to skim stones, to play ducks and drakes (BrE)

cabriola *f*: **hacer ∼s** «*niño*» to caper *o* jump around; «*caballo*» to buck, prance around

cabriolé, cabriolet /kaβrjo'le/ *m* (*pl* **-lets**) (Auto) convertible, cabriolet

cabritas *fpl* (Chi) popcorn

cabritilla *f* kid, kidskin

cabrito *m*

A (Zool) kid

B (Esp fam & euf) (cabrón) swine (colloq); *ver tb* **cabro²**

cabro¹ -bra *adj* (Chi fam): **es muy ∼ para eso** he's too young for that

cabro² -bra *m,f* (Chi fam) (niño) kid (colloq)

cabrón¹ -brona *adj* (Esp, Méx vulg): **el muy ∼/la muy cabrona** the bastard *o* (AmE) son of a bitch (vulg)/the bitch (vulg)

cabrón² -brona *m,f*

A (Esp, Méx vulg) (*m*) bastard (vulg), son of a bitch (AmE vulg); (*f*) bitch (vulg)

B **cabrón** *m* 1 (vulg) (cornudo) cuckold 2 (Andes fam *o* vulg) (proxeneta) pimp, ponce (BrE)

cabronada *f* (fam) mean trick

cábula *m* (Méx fam) crook (colloq)

cabús *m* (Méx) caboose (AmE), guard's van (BrE)

cabuya *f* 1 (Bot) pita 2 pita fiber* 3 (cuerda) (Col, Ven) rope (*esp made from pita fiber*)

caca *f* 1 (fam *o* leng infantil) (excremento): **hacer ∼** to go to the bathroom (AmE) *o* (BrE) toilet (euph), to do a poop (AmE) *o* (BrE) pooh (used to or by children); **hacerse ∼** to mess oneself; **el niño se hizo ∼** the baby dirtied his diaper (AmE) *o* (BrE) nappy (colloq); **∼ de perro** dog mess; **¡no toques eso! ¡∼!** don't touch that, it's dirty! 2 (fam) (porquería): **su último libro es una ∼** his last book is trash *o* rubbish

cacahual *m* cocoa plantation

cacahuete, cacahuate *m* peanut, monkey nut; ***me, te, etc importa un (reverendo) ∼*** (Méx fam) I, you, etc couldn't give a damn (colloq)

cacao *m*

A 1 (Coc) (polvo, bebida) cocoa 2 (Bot) (planta) cacao; (semillas) cocoa beans (*pl*) 3 (Esp) (para los labios) lipsalve

B (fam) (jaleo) ruckus (AmE), to-do (BrE); **¡qué ∼ se armó!** all hell broke loose (colloq); ***tener un ∼ mental*** (fam) to be all mixed up

cacaotal *m* cocoa plantation

cacarear [A1] *vi* 1 «*gallo*» to crow; «*gallina*» to cluck 2 (fam) (presumir) to brag

■ **cacarear** *vt* (fam) ‹*triunfo*› to crow about; **una victoria muy cacareada** a much-trumpeted victory

cacareo *m* 1 (de gallo) crowing; (de gallina) clucking 2 (fam) (fanfarroneo) bragging

cacarizo -za *adj* (Méx) pockmarked

cacatúa *f* (Zool) cockatoo; (vieja) (fam & pey) old bag (pej)

cacayaca *f* (Méx fam) insult

cacería *f* (de zorro, jabalí) hunt; (de conejo, perdiz) shoot; **salir** *or* **ir de ∼** to go hunting (*o* shooting *etc*)

cacerola *f* saucepan, pan

cacerolazo *m*, **caceroleada** *f* demonstration (*where saucepans are banged as a sign of protest*)

cacha *f* (Esp arg) (muslo) thigh

cachacascán *f* (Chi) catch-as-catch-can

cachaco -ca *m,f* (Col, Ven fam) (bogotano) person from Bogotá

cachada *f*

A (AmL) (Taur) goring

B (RPl) (broma) joke; **hacerle una ∼ a algn** to play a joke on sb

cachador -dora *m,f* (RPl) joker

cachalote *m* sperm whale

cachapa *f* (Ven) *corn-based pancake*

cachapera *f* (Ven vulg) dyke (colloq & pej)

cachar [A1] *vt* 1 (AmL fam) ‹*pelota*› to catch; ‹*persona*›: **la caché del brazo** I caught *o* grabbed her by the arm 2 (AmL fam) (sorprender, pillar) to catch 3 (RPl fam) (gastar una broma) to kid (colloq); **me estás cachando** you're kidding me 4 (Andes fam) (enterarse) to get (colloq); **no cachas ¿cierto?** you don't get it, do you? 5 (Chi fam) (mirar) to look at; **¡cacha las piernas de esa mina!** look at those legs! (colloq)

cacharpas *fpl* (RPl fam & hum) junk (colloq)

cacharrazo *m* ▸ **cachiporrazo**

cacharrería *f* (Col) hardware store, ironmonger's (BrE)

cacharriento -ta *adj* (Chi fam) ‹*vehículo*› old and slow

cacharro *m*

A (de cocina) pot

B (fam) (cachivache) thing; (coche viejo) jalopy (AmE), old banger (BrE colloq); (aparato) gadget

cachas¹ *adj inv* (Esp fam) strong, muscly (colloq)

cachas² *m* (Esp fam) he-man (colloq), hunk (colloq)

cachaza *f*

A (lentitud): **todo lo hace con esa ∼** he does everything so slowly and deliberately; **¡vaya ∼ que tienes!** you really take your time!

B (bebida) *type of rum*

C (Ven fam) (descaro) nerve (colloq)

caché /ka'tʃe, ka'ʃe/ *m* 1 (sello distintivo) prestige, cachet; **ropa de mucho ∼** clothes with real cachet 2 (de un artista) fee

C

C

cachear [A1] *vt*
A (fam) (registrar) to frisk, search
B (AmL) (Taur) to gore

cachemir *m*, **cachemira** *f* cashmere

cacheo *m* (fam) frisking, search

cachet *m* ▸**caché**

cachetada *f* (AmL) (en la cara) slap; **me/le cayó como una ~** (AmL fam) I/he was very put out *o* upset

cachete *m*
A (mejilla) (esp AmL) cheek; (nalga) (CS fam) cheek
B (esp Esp) ▸**cachetada**

cachetear [A1] *vt* (AmL) to slap

cachetón -tona *adj* (Andes, Méx fam) (carrilludo) chubby-cheeked

cachetudo -da *adj* (RPl fam) chubby-cheeked

cachifo -fa *m,f* (jovenzuelo) (Col fam) kid (colloq); (criado) (Ven fam & pey) servant

cachimba *f* (pipa) pipe; **fumar en ~** to smoke a pipe

cachimbo *m* 1 (AmC fam) (montón): **un ~ de reales** tons of money 2 (AmL) (pipa) pipe

cachiporra[1] *adj* (Chi fam & pey) bigheaded (colloq)

cachiporra[2] *mf*
A (Chi fam) (engreído) bighead (colloq)
B **cachiporra** *f* (palo) billy club (AmE), truncheon (BrE)

cachiporrazo *m* (fam) (choque) crash; (golpe con la cachiporra) blow (*dealt with a billy club* (AmE) *o* (BrE) *truncheon*); **me di un ~** I banged my arm (*o* head *etc*)

cachirulo *m*
A (cosa) ▸**cachivache**
B (Chi fam) (rizo) curl; (para rizar) curler, roller
C (Méx fam) (trampa): **me hizo ~** he cheated me; **metieron dos jugadores de ~** they fielded two players who weren't eligible

cachito *m*
A (Méx) (de una lotería) *one twentieth of a lottery ticket; ver tb* **cacho**
B (Ven) (Coc) croissant

cachivache *m* (fam) 1 (trasto inútil) piece of junk; **ese ~ no sirve para nada** that's just a useless piece of junk (colloq); **tiró todos los ~s que tenía** she threw out all her old junk (colloq) 2 (objeto insignificante): **con cuatro ~s puso una habitación preciosa** with just a few bits and pieces he made the room look really nice

cacho *m*
A 1 (fam) (pedazo) bit; **un cachito de queso** a little bit of cheese 2 (Esp fam) (*como adj inv*): **¡qué ~ chuleta!** that's some *o* one hell of a chop! (colloq); **¡~ bruto!** you great oaf! (colloq)
B 1 (AmS) (cuerno) horn; ***poner*** (Per) *or* (Ven) ***montar ~s a algn*** (fam) to be unfaithful to sb, cheat on sb (colloq); ***tener algo de un ~*** (Col fam): **ya lo tengo de un ~** I've nearly finished it 2 (Andes) (juego) poker dice; (cubilete) shaker 3 (Chi) (para beber) drinking horn
C (Ec) (escarabajo) beetle
D (Col, Ven arg) (cigarrillo de marihuana) joint (colloq)
E (Chi fam) (cosa inútil, molesta) nuisance
F (RPl) (de bananas) hand

cachondearse [A1] *v pron* (Esp fam) **~ DE algn/algo** to make fun OF sb/sth

cachondeo *m* (Esp fam): **tú estás de ~** you're joking; **se lo toma a ~** he treats it as a joke; **venga, menos ~** come on, less of this fooling around; **¿qué ~ es éste?** is this some kind of a joke? (colloq)

cachondo[1] **-da** *adj* (Esp)
A (fam) (divertido, gracioso): **es un tío muy ~** he's a real scream
B (fam) (caliente) horny (colloq)

cachondo[2] **-da** *m,f* (Esp fam): **es un ~ mental** he's a real scream

cachorro[1] **-rra** *adj* (Col arg) hopping mad (colloq); **ponerse ~** to go berserk

cachorro[2] **-rra** *m,f* (de perro) puppy, pup; (de león) cub

cachucha *f* (Col, Méx, Ven) (Indum) cap
(Compuesto) **cachucha militar** (fam) dictatorship

cachudo -da *adj*
A (Andes) ‹*toro*› long-horned
B (Chi fam) (desconfiado) suspicious

cachumbo *m* (Col) ringlet

cachurear [A1] *vi* (Chi fam) to rummage

cachureo *m* (Chi fam) 1 (acción) rummaging, rooting around 2 (cosas inservibles) junk (colloq); **está lleno de ~** it's full of junk

cacillo *m* (cacerola) small saucepan; (cucharón) ladle

cacique *m* (Hist) chief, cacique; (Pol) local political boss; (hombre poderoso) tyrant

caciquismo *m* 1 (Hist) chieftainship 2 (Pol) position as local political boss 3 (despotismo) tyranny (*by local political bosses*)

> **caciquismo**
>
> Pejorative term for rule by local bosses (*caciques*) in Latin America and Spain. The word *cacique*, of Caribbean origin, was used by the Spanish conquistadors to describe tribal chiefs or district governors in their colonies

cacle *m* (Méx fam) (zapato) shoe; (sandalia) sandal

caco *m* (fam) thief

cacofonía *f* cacophony

cacofónico -ca *adj* cacophonous

cactus (*pl* ~), **cacto** *m* cactus

cacumen *m* (fam) brains (*pl*), nous (colloq); **usa el ~** use your brain

cada *adj inv*
A 1 (con énfasis en el individuo o cosa particular) each; (con énfasis en la totalidad del conjunto) every; **los ganadores de ~ grupo pasan a la final** the winners from each group go on to the final; **hay un bar en ~ esquina** there's a bar on every corner; **~ día** every day, each day; **~ dos días** every other day, every two days; **¿~ cuánto viene?** how often does she come?; **~ uno** each; **hay cinco para ~ uno** there are five each; **volvimos a casa ~ uno por su lado** we each made our own way home; **cuestan $25 ~ uno** they cost $25 each; **~ uno** *or* **~ cual sabe qué es lo que más le conviene** everyone *o* each individual knows what's best for him or her 2 (delante de numeral) every; **~ cuatro kilómetros** every four kilometers; **siete de ~ diez** seven out of (every) ten
B 1 (indicando progresión): **~ vez más rápido** faster and faster; **la gente va ~ vez menos** people are going less and less; **lo hace ~ vez mejor** she's getting better all the time; **hace ~ día más calor** it's getting hotter every day *o* by the day 2 (fam) (con valor ponderativo): **¡ tienes ~ idea ...!** the things you come out with!

cadalso *m* (patíbulo) scaffold; (horca) gallows (*pl*)

cadáver *m* (de persona) corpse; (de animal) carcass; **ingresó ~** he was dead on arrival; **¡tendrás que pasar por encima de mi ~!** over my dead body!

cadavérico -ca *adj* cadaverous, ghastly

caddie, caddy /'kaði/ *mf* (*pl* **-dies**) caddy

cadena *f*
A 1 (de eslabones) chain; **una ~ de oro** a gold chain; **iban atados con ~s** they were chained up; **es necesario el uso de ~s** (Auto) (snow) chains should be used 2 (del wáter) chain; **tirar de la ~** to flush the toilet

(Compuestos)
- **cadena antirrobo** bicycle lock
- **cadena de seguridad** safety chain
- **cadena perpetua** life imprisonment; **fue condenado a ~ ~** he was sentenced to life imprisonment, he was given a life sentence

B 1 (de hechos, fenómenos) chain; **una larga ~ de atentados** a long series of attacks 2 (Geog) *tb* **~ montañosa** *or* **de montañas** mountain range, chain of mountains 3 (Inf) string

(Compuestos)
- **cadena alimentaria** *or* **alimenticia** food chain
- **cadena de fabricación** *or* **producción** production line
- **cadena de montaje** *or* (Chi, Méx) **de ensamblaje** assembly line

C (Com) chain; **una ~ de supermercados** a chain of supermarkets; **~ de radiodifusión** radio network

(Compuesto) **cadena de distribución** distribution chain
D (TV) channel
E (Audio) *tb* ~ **de sonido** stack system
cadencia *f* (ritmo) cadence, rhythm; (terminación de una frase musical) cadence
cadencioso -sa *adj* ‹*música*› rhythmic, rhythmical; ‹*voz/ritmo*› lilting
cadeneta *f* (labor) chain stitch; (de papel) paper chain
cadera *f* hip
cadete *m* (Mil, Náut) cadet
cadmio *m* cadmium
caducar [A2] *vi* **1** «*carné/pasaporte*» to expire; **el plazo caduca el 17 de noviembre** the closing date (for enrollment, etc) is November 17; **este vale está caducado** this voucher is no longer valid *o* is out of date **2** «*medicamento*» to expire (frml); **S caduca a los tres meses** use within three months; **este yogur está caducado** this yogurt is past its sell-by date/use-by date
caducidad *f*
A (Farm, Med) expiration (AmE), expiry (BrE)
B (de testamento, ley) expiry
caduco -ca *adj*
A ‹*hoja*› deciduous
B ‹*teoría/costumbres/valores*› outdated; ‹*belleza*› (liter) faded
caer [E16] *vi*
A (de una altura) to fall; (de posición vertical) to fall over; **caí mal** I fell badly *o* awkwardly; **cayó cuan largo era** he fell flat on his face; **el coche cayó por un precipicio** the car went over a cliff; **cayó muerto allí mismo** he dropped down dead on the spot; **se dejó ~ en el sillón/en sus brazos** she flopped into the armchair/fell into his arms; **se dejó ~ desde el borde del precipicio** he jumped off from the edge of the cliff; **el avión cayó en picada** *or* (Esp) **en picado** the plane nosedived; **cayó en el mar** it came down in the sea; ~ ***parado*** (AmL) (literal) to land on one's feet; (tener suerte) to fall *o* land on one's feet; ***dejar ~ algo*** ‹*objeto*› to drop; ‹*noticia*› to let drop *o* fall; ‹*indirecta*› to drop
B «*chaparrón/nevada*»: **cayó un chaparrón** it poured down; **cayó una fuerte nevada** it snowed heavily; **cayó una helada** there was a frost; **cayeron unas pocas gotas** there were a few drops of rain; **el rayo cayó cerca** the lightning struck nearby
C **1** «*cortinas/falda*» to hang; **el pelo le caía suelto hasta la cintura** her hair hung down to her waist **2** «*terreno*» to drop; ~ **en pendiente** to slope down
D **1** (incurrir) ~ **EN algo**: **no caigas en ese error** don't make that mistake; **cayó en la tentación de mirar** she succumbed to the temptation to look; **la obra por momentos cae en lo ridículo** at times the play lapses into the ridiculous; ~ ***muy bajo*** to stoop very low; **qué bajo has caído** you've really sunk low this time **2** (en engaño, timo): **todos caímos (en la trampa)** we all fell for it; ~ ***como angelitos*** (fam): **cayeron como chinos** *or* **angelitos** they swallowed it hook, line and sinker
E (fam) (entender, darse cuenta): **¡ah, ya caigo!** (ya entiendo) oh, now I get it! (colloq); (ya recuerdo) oh, now I remember; **no caigo** I can't think *o* I'm not sure what (*o* who *etc*) you mean; **no caí en que tú no tenías llave** I didn't realize *o* (fam) I didn't click that you didn't have keys
F (en un estado): ~ **en desuso** «*palabra*» to fall into disuse; «*costumbre*» to die out; ~ **en el olvido** to sink into oblivion; **caer enfermo** to fall ill; **cayó en cama** he took to his bed
G **1** «*gobierno/ciudad*» to fall; ~ **en poder de algn** to fall to sb **2** (perder el cargo) to lose one's job; **se hará una investigación, caiga quien caiga** an inquiry will be held, however many heads have to roll **3** «*soldado*» (morir) to fall, die; (ser apresado) to be caught
H **1** «*desgracia/maldición*» ~ **SOBRE algn** to befall sb (frml *or* liter); ***la que me (te, etc) ha caído encima*** (fam): **no sabes la que te ha caído encima** you don't know what's in store for you **2** **al caer la tarde/la noche** at sunset *o* dusk/nightfall; **antes de que caiga la noche** before it gets dark *o* before nightfall
I (fam) (tocar en suerte): **le cayó una pregunta muy difícil** he got a really difficult question; **le cayeron tres años (de cárcel)** he got three years (in jail); **el gordo cayó en Bilbao** the jackpot was won by someone in Bilbao
J (+ *compl*) **1** (sentar): **el pescado me cayó mal** the fish didn't agree with me; **le cayó muy mal que no la invitaran** she was very upset about not being invited **2** (en cuestiones de gusto): **tu primo me cae muy bien** I really like your cousin; **me cae de gordo** *or* **de mal ...** (fam) I can't stand him (colloq)
K **1** (fam) (presentarse) to show up, turn up (BrE); **de vez en cuando cae** *or* **se deja ~ por aquí** she drops by *o* in now and then; ***estar al ~***: **los invitados están al ~** the guests will be here any minute *o* moment (now) **2** (abalanzarse) ~ **SOBRE algn** to fall upon *o* on sb; ***~le encima a algn*** (fam) to pounce *o* leap on sb
L **1** (estar comprendido) ~ **DENTRO DE algo** to fall WITHIN sth; **cae dentro de nuestra jurisdicción** it comes under *o* falls within our jurisdiction; **cae dentro de sus obligaciones** that's one of her duties **2** «*cumpleaños/festividad*» to fall on; **el 20 cae en (un) domingo** the 20th falls on a Sunday *o* is a Sunday; **¿el 27 (en) qué día cae** *or* **en qué cae?** what day's the 27th? **3** (Esp fam) (estar situado) to be; **¿por dónde cae?** whereabouts is that?
M «*precios/temperatura*» to fall, drop
N (Ven) (aportar dinero) (fam) to chip in (colloq)
O (Ven fam) «*llamada*»: **la llamada no me cayó** I couldn't get through
■ **caerse** *v pron*
A **1** (de una altura) to fall; (de la posición vertical) to fall, to fall over; **te vas a ~** you'll fall; **me caí por las escaleras** I fell down the stairs; **~se del caballo/de la cama** to fall off one's horse/out of bed; **se cayó redondo** (fam) he collapsed in a heap; **está que se cae de cansancio** (fam) she's dead on her feet (colloq) **2** (+ *me/te/le etc*) **oiga, se le cayó un guante** excuse me, you dropped your glove; **se me cayó de las manos** it slipped out of my hands; **cuidado, no se te vaya a ~** be careful, don't drop it; **por poco se me cae el armario encima** the wardrobe nearly fell on top of me; **se me están cayendo las medias** my stockings are falling down; ***~se con algn*** (Col fam) to go down in sb's estimation; ***no tiene/tienen dónde ~se muerto/muertos*** (fam) he hasn't/they haven't got a penny to his/their name; ***se cae por su propio peso*** *or* ***de maduro*** it goes without saying
B (desprenderse) «*diente*» to fall out; «*hojas*» to fall off; «*botón*» to come off, fall off; **se le ha empezado a ~ el pelo** he's started to lose his hair; **la ropa se le caía a pedazos** her clothes were falling to pieces
café[1] *adj* (*gen inv*) **1** (marrón claro) ‹*color*› coffee (*before n*); ‹*vestido/zapato*› coffee-colored* **2** (AmC, Chi, Méx) (marrón) brown; **ojos ~(s)** brown eyes
café[2] *m*
A (cultivo, bebida) coffee; **me sirvió un ~** he gave me some *o* a cup of coffee, he gave me a coffee (BrE)
(Compuestos)
- **café americano** large black coffee
- **café cerrero** (Col) large strong black coffee
- **café con leche** regular coffee (AmE), white coffee (BrE)
- **café cortado** *coffee with a dash of milk*
- **café descafeinado** decaffeinated coffee
- **café en grano** coffee beans (*pl*)
- **café expreso** *or* (Esp) **solo** espresso
- **café instantáneo** *o* **soluble** instant coffee
- **café molido** ground coffee
- **café natural/torrefacto** light roast/high roast coffee
- **café negro** (AmL) *or* (Chi) **puro** *or* (Col) **tinto** black coffee

B (cafetería) café
(Compuestos)
- **café bar** café
- **café concert** *or* **concierto** café (*with live music*)
- **café teatro** ≈ dinner theatre (*in US*), ≈ pub theatre (*in UK*)

C **1** **(de) color ~** coffee-colored* **2** (AmC, Chi, Méx) (marrón) brown
D (RPl fam) (regañina) telling-off
cafeína *f* caffeine
cafetal *m* coffee plantation
cafetalero[1] -ra, cafetalista *adj* coffee (*before n*)
cafetalero[2] -ra *m,f*, **cafetalista** *mf* coffee grower
cafetera *f* **1** (para hacer café) coffee maker; (para servir café) coffeepot; ***estar como una ~*** (fam) to be off one's rocker *o*

head (colloq) 2 (fam) (coche viejo) old heap (colloq)

cafetería *f* (café) café; (en museo, fábrica) cafeteria

cafetería

In Spain, a place to have a coffee, other drinks, and pastries and cakes. *Cafeterías* are frequently combined with *bares* and are very similar. However, *cafeterías* are usually smarter, and serve a wider variety of dishes

C

cafetero[1] **-ra** *adj* ‹*industria/finca*› coffee (*before n*); ‹*país*› coffee-producing (*before n*), coffee-growing (*before n*); **ser muy ~** to be a real coffee addict

cafetero[2] **-ra** *m,f* coffee planter *o* grower

cafeto *m* coffee tree

cafiche, caficho *m* (AmL arg) pimp, ponce (BrE colloq)

caficultor -tora *m,f* (Col) coffee grower

cafre[1] *adj*

A (de África) Kaffir (*before n*)

B (ignorante) moronic (colloq & pej); (vándalo) **los muy ~s** the vandals *o* (AmE) hoodlums

cafre[2] *mf*

A (de África) Kaffir

B (ignorante) idiot, moron (colloq & pej); (vándalo) lout, punk (AmE)

caftán *m* caftan*

cagada *f*

A (vulg) (excremento) shit (sl); **~s de pájaro** bird shit (sl); ***quedar la ~*** (Chi vulg): **quedó la ~** the shit hit the fan (vulg)

B (vulg) 1 (porquería): **el disco es una ~** the record is crap (sl) 2 (desacierto) screwup (AmE sl), balls-up (BrE sl)

cagadera *f* (AmL vulg): **andaba con** *or* **tenía (una) ~** I had the trots (colloq) *o* (sl) the shits

cagado -da *adj*

A (vulg) ‹*calzoncillos/sábana*› dirty, shitty (colloq & hum)

B (vulg) 1 [SER] (miedoso, cobarde) gutless (colloq) 2 [ESTAR] (asustado) scared stiff (colloq), shit-scared (vulg)

C (CS vulg) (jodido): **estamos ~s** we're in deep trouble *o* (vulg) in deep shit

D (*delante del n*) (Col vulg) (uso enfático) goddamn (AmE sl), bloody (BrE sl)

cagalera *f* (Esp vulg) ▸ **cagadera**

cagar [A3] *vi*

A (vulg) (defecar) to have a shit (vulg)

B (CS vulg) 1 (embromarse): **¡cagamos!** we've had it! (colloq) 2 (fracasar) ‹‹*plan/huelga*›› to be a flop (colloq)

■ **cagar** *vt*

A (vulg) (arruinar) ***~la***: **ahora sí que la hemos cagado** now we've really screwed up (sl); (más grave) now we're really in the shit *o* up shit creek (sl)

B (vulg) ‹*persona*› 1 (RPl) (defraudar, engañar) to cheat, rip … off 2 (CS) (vencer) to floor

■ **cagarse** *v pron* (vulg) (defecar) to shit oneself (vulg); **se estarán cagando de miedo** they'll be scared shitless (sl), they'll be shitting themselves (vulg); ***~ en algn/algo*** (vulg): **¡me cago en las autoridades!** screw the authorities! (sl); ***¡me cago en diez*** *or* ***en la mar!*** (fam *o* vulg) shit! (vulg), damn! (colloq); ***que te cagas*** (vulg): **hace un frío que te cagas** it's goddamn freezing (AmE sl), it's bloody freezing (BrE) (sl)

cagarruta *f* pellet; **~s de pájaro** bird droppings

cagón[1] **-gona** *adj* (fam *o* vulg) 1 (miedoso) wimpish (colloq), wet (colloq) 2 (Méx) (afortunado) lucky

cagón[2] **-gona** *m,f* (fam *o* vulg) 1 (bebé) *baby that keeps dirtying his/her diapers* 2 (miedoso) wimp (colloq) 3 (Méx) (afortunado) lucky devil (colloq)

caguama *m* (Méx) *measure of beer roughly equivalent to a liter*

caída *f*

A (accidente) fall; **sufrir una ~** ‹‹*persona*›› to have a fall; **fue una mala ~** it was a nasty fall

(Compuesto) **caída libre** free fall

B (del cabello): **la ~ del cabello** hair loss

C (de tela, falda): **necesitas una tela con más ~** you need a heavier material; **tiene buena ~** it hangs well

D (de gobierno, de ciudad) fall; **la ~ del Imperio Romano** the fall *o* collapse of the Roman Empire

E (descenso) fall, drop; **la ~ del dólar** the fall in the dollar

(Compuesto) **caída de agua** waterfall

F **a la caída del sol** *or* **de la tarde** at sunset, at dusk

G (de terreno, de superficie) slope; (más pronunciada) drop

caído[1] **-da** *adj*

A 1 (en el suelo) fallen; **recogieron las manzanas caídas** they picked up the windfalls 2 ‹*pechos*› drooping, sagging; **tener los** *or* **ser de hombros ~s** to be round-shouldered; **tiene el útero ~** she has a prolapsed womb

B (en la guerra): **soldados ~s en combate** soldiers who fell in combat

C (Col) ‹*vivienda*› dilapidated, run-down

caído[2] *m*: **los ~s** the fallen

caiga, caigas, etc *see* **caer**

caimán *m*

A (Zool) caiman, cayman, alligator

B (Chi, Méx) (Tec) alligator wrench

Caín *m* Cain; ***pasar las de ~*** (fam) to go through hell (colloq)

caipiriña, caipirinha /kaipi'riɲa/ *f*: *drink made with rum, sugar, lemon and ice*

Cairo *m*: **El ~** Cairo

caja *f*

A 1 (recipiente) box; **una ~ de fósforos** (con fósforos) a box of matches; (vacía) a matchbox; **una ~ de vino** a crate of wine 2 (de reloj) case, casing 3 (Mús) (de violín, guitarra) soundbox; (tambor) drum; ***echar*** *or* ***despedir a algn con ~s destempladas*** to send sb packing (colloq) 4 (fam) (ataúd) coffin

(Compuestos)

- **caja china** Chinese box
- **caja de cambios** *or* **velocidades** gearbox
- **caja de caudales** *or* (Chi) **de fondos** safe, strongbox
- **caja de embalaje** packing case
- **caja de empalmes** junction box
- **caja de fusibles** fuse box
- **caja de herramientas** toolbox
- **caja de la escalera** stairwell
- **caja de música** music box
- **caja de resonancia** (Mús) soundbox
- **caja de ritmos** drum machine
- **caja de seguridad** safe-deposit box, safety deposit box
- **caja de sorpresas** (juguete) jack-in-the-box; **eres una ~ de ~** you're full of surprises
- **caja fuerte** safe, strongbox
- **caja negra** black box, flight recorder
- **caja tonta** (fam) goggle box (colloq)
- **caja torácica** thoracic cavity

B (Com) 1 (lugar — en banco) window; (— en supermercado) checkout; (— en tienda, restaurante) cash desk, till; **sírvase pagar en** *or* **pasar por ~** pay at the cash desk *o* till 2 (máquina) till, cash register; **¿cuánto dinero ha ingresado en ~ hoy?** how much money have we/you taken today? 3 (dinero) cash; **hicimos una ~ de medio millón** we took half a million pesos (*o* euros *etc*); ***hacer (la) ~*** to cash up

(Compuestos)

- **caja de ahorros** savings bank
- **caja de pensiones** *or* **jubilaciones** (state) pension fund
- **caja registradora** cash register

C (Mil): **entrar en ~** to be drafted *o* called up

D (Impr) case

E (Arm) stock

cajero -ra *m,f* (en tienda) cashier; (en banco) teller, cashier; (en supermercado) check out operator

(Compuesto) **cajero automático** *or* **permanente** *m* cash dispenser, automated *or* automated teller machine (AmE)

cajeta *f* (Méx) caramel topping/filling

cajetilla *f* pack (AmE), packet (BrE)

cajetín *m*

A (sello) stamp (*with spaces for writing date, invoice number, etc*)

B (Elec) junction box

cajón *m*

A 1 (en un mueble) drawer; **el ~ de arriba/abajo** the top/bottom drawer; ***~ de sastre***: **este capítulo es un ~ de sastre** this chapter is a bit of a hodgepodge (AmE) *o* (BrE) a hotchpotch (colloq); **esa sección es el ~ de sastre del**

periódico that's the miscellaneous *o* oddments section of the newspaper; **de ~** (fam) ‹*respuesta/pregunta*› obvious; **eso es de ~** that's obvious [2] (caja grande) *tb* **~ de embalaje** crate; (para mudanzas) packing case; **~ de fruta** fruit box [3] (AmL) (ataúd) coffin, casket (AmE)

(Compuesto) **cajón de arena** sandpit, sandbox

B [1] (Méx) (en un estacionamiento) parking space [2] (Chi) (Geog) gulley, ravine

cajuela *f* (Méx) trunk (AmE), boot (BrE)

cajuelita *f* (Méx) glove compartment

cal *f* lime; **ahogar** *or* **apagar la ~** to slake lime; **pintado a la ~** (RPl) whitewashed; ***cerrar algo a ~ y canto*** to close sth firmly *o* tight; ***una de ~ y otra de arena*** (Esp) something nice followed by something less pleasant

(Compuestos)

- **cal apaguda** *or* **muerta** slaked lime
- **cal viva** quicklime, caustic lime

cala *f*

A (ensenada) cove

B (Náut) hold

calabacín *m*, (Méx) **calabacita** *f* zucchini (AmE), courgette (BrE)

calabaza *f* (Bot, Coc) (fruto — redondo) pumpkin; (— alargado) squash (AmE), marrow (BrE); ***dar ~s*** (fam) (a un pretendiente) to give … the brush-off (colloq); (a un estudiante) to fail, flunk (AmE colloq)

calabobos *m* (fam) drizzle

calabozo *m* (en una comisaría, cárcel) cell; (en un cuartel) guardroom; (Hist) dungeon

calada *f* (Esp fam) (de cigarro) drag (sl), puff (colloq)

caladero *m* fishing ground

calado[1] **-da** *adj*

A (empapado) soaked

B ‹*jersey/tela*› openwork (*before n*)

calado[2] *m*

A (en costura) openwork

B [1] (de barco) draft; **un barco de gran/poco ~** a ship with a deep/shallow draft [2] (altura del agua) depth

calamar *m* squid; **~es a la romana** squid fried in batter

calambrazo *m* (fam) (espasmo) attack of cramp; (sacudida eléctrica) electric shock

calambre *m* [1] (espasmo) cramp; **me ha dado un ~ en el pie** I have a cramp (AmE) *o* (BrE) I've got cramp in my foot [2] (sacudida eléctrica) electric shock; **me dio un ~** I got *o* it gave me an electric shock

calamidad *f* [1] (desastre, desgracia) disaster, calamity; **¡las ~es que ha pasado!** the terrible things he's gone through! [2] (persona inútil) disaster (colloq)

calamina *f*

A [1] (Min) smithsonite [2] (Med) calamine

B (aleación) zinc alloy; (para techos) (Chi, Per) corrugated iron

calamita *f* lodestone

calamitoso -sa *adj* disastrous, calamitous

calandria *f* (Zool) calandra lark

calaña *f*: **los de tu ~ …** your sort *o* kind … (colloq); **un tipo de mala ~** a bad sort *o* lot (colloq)

calar [A1] *vt*

A «*líquido*» (empapar) to soak; (atravesar) to soak through

B [1] ‹*sandía*› to cut a piece out of (*in order to taste it*) [2] (fam) ‹*persona/intenciones*› to rumble (colloq), to suss … out (BrE colloq); **te tenemos muy calado** we've got you sussed

C «*barco*» to draw

D ‹*bayoneta*› to fix

E (Esp) ‹*coche/motor*› to stall

■ **calar** *vi*

A «*moda*» (penetrar) to catch on; **estos cambios calan lentamente en la sociedad** these changes permeate society slowly; **los países donde ha calado esta religión** the countries where this religion has taken root; **aquellas palabras ~on hondo en él** those words made a deep impression on him

B «*zapatos/tienda de campaña*» to leak, let water in

■ **calarse** *v pron*

A (empaparse) to get soaked, get drenched; **me calé hasta los huesos** I got soaked to the skin

B (liter) ‹*sombrero/gorra*› to pull … down

C (Esp) «*coche/motor*» to stall

calavera[1] *f*

A (Anat) skull

B (Méx) (Auto) taillight

calavera[2] *m* (fam) rake

calcado -da *adj* [1] [SER] (fam) **~ A algo/algn: es ~ a su madre** he's the spitting image of his mother (colloq); **esta canción es calcada a la que ganó el festival** this song's exactly the same as the one that won the festival [2] [ESTAR] (fam): **están ~s** one is a carbon copy of the other; **~ DE algo: está ~ del de Serra** it's a straight copy of Serra's

calcar [A2] *vt* [1] ‹*dibujo/mapa*› to trace [2] (plagiar) to copy

calcáreo -rea *adj* calcareous

calce *m* wedge; **poner un ~ a la mesa** to wedge something under the leg of the table, to wedge the table

calceta *f* (labor) knitting; **hacer ~** to knit

calcetín *m* sock

(Compuestos)

- **calcetines altos** *mpl* knee-length *o* long socks (*pl*)
- **calcetines cortos** *mpl* ankle *o* short socks (*pl*)

cálcico -ca *adj* calcic

calcificar [A2] *vi* to calcify

■ **calcificarse** *v pron* to calcify

calcinación *f* calcination

calcinar [A1] *vt* [1] (abrasar) «*fuego*» to burn; «*sol*» (liter) to scorch; **murieron calcinados** they burned *o* were burned to death; **cadáveres calcinados** charred bodies [2] (Quím) to calcine

calcio *m* calcium

calco *m* [1] (copia) exact replica; **es un ~ de su padre** he's the spitting image of his father [2] (Ling) calque, loan translation

calcomanía *f* transfer, decal (AmE)

calculador -dora *adj* calculating

calculadora *f* calculator

calcular [A1] *vt*

A [1] (Mat) ‹*precio/cantidad*› to calculate, work out; **calculando por lo bajo** at a conservative estimate; **calculé mal** I miscalculated [2] (considerar, conjeturar) to reckon; **yo le calculo unos sesenta años** I reckon *o* guess he's about sixty; **se calcula que asistieron más de cien personas** over a hundred people are estimated to have attended [3] (fam) (imaginar) to imagine; **calcula mi sorpresa** imagine how surprised I was; **debes estar contento — ¡calcula!** you must be pleased — you bet!

B (planear) to work out; **lo tenía todo calculado** he had it all worked out; **un gesto calculado** a calculated gesture

cálculo *m*

A (Mat) [1] (operación) calculation; **según mis ~s** according to my calculations; **hizo un ~ aproximado** she made a rough estimate [2] (disciplina) calculus

(Compuesto) **cálculo mental** mental arithmetic

B (plan, conjetura): **eso no entraba en mis ~s** I hadn't allowed for that in my plans *o* calculations; **le fallaron los ~s** things didn't work out as he had planned; **superó los ~s más optimistas** it exceeded even the most optimistic estimates; **fue un error de ~** I/he/they misjudged *o* miscalculated

C (Med) stone, calculus (tech)

(Compuestos)

- **cálculo biliar** gallstone, bilestone
- **cálculo renal** kidney stone

caldeado -da *adj* heated; **los ánimos están ~s** feelings are running high

caldear [A1] *vt* [1] ‹*habitación/local*› to heat, heat … up [2] (enardecer): **el discurso caldeó los ánimos de los obreros** the speech inflamed the feelings of the workers; **esas palabras caldearon el ambiente** these words added fuel to the flames

■ **caldearse** *v pron* [1] «*habitación/local*» to warm up, heat up [2] (enardecerse): **se estaban empezando a ~ los ánimos** things were beginning to get heated; **se caldeó el ambiente** feelings started to run high

caldera *f*

A (industrial, de calefacción) boiler

B (caldero) caldron*, copper (BrE)
C (Geol) crater
calderero -ra *m,f* (Náut, Tec) boilermaker
caldereta *f* (de pescado) fish stew; (de cordero) lamb stew
calderilla *f* change, small *o* loose change
caldero *m* caldron*, copper (BrE)
calderón *m* (Mús) pause
caldo *m*
A (Coc) (para beber) clear soup; (con arroz, etc) soup; (para cocinar) stock; (salsa de asado, etc) juices (*pl*); **~ de pollo/verduras** chicken/vegetable stock; ***poner a algn a ~*** (Esp fam) to tell sb what you think of him/her (colloq)
(Compuesto) **caldo de cultivo** (Biol) culture medium; (ambiente propicio) breeding ground
B (Vin) wine
caldoso -sa *adj* ‹*arroz*› soggy; ‹*salsa*› runny, watery
calé¹ *adj* gypsy (*before n*)
calé² *mf* gypsy
calefacción *f* heating; **~ eléctrica** electric heating; **~ de** *or* **a gas** gas heating
(Compuesto) **calefacción central** central heating
calefactor *m* heater
calefón *m* (*pl* **-fones** *or* **-fóns**) (RPl) water heater, boiler
caleidoscopio *m* kaleidoscope
calendario *m* 1 (de pared, mesa) calendar; **~ de taco** tear-off calendar 2 (programa de actividades) schedule; **el ~ para el proyecto** the schedule *o* timetable for the project; **tiene un ~ de lo más apretado** she has a very tight schedule; **el ~ para las negociaciones** the agenda for the negotiations 3 (con días festivos de una actividad) calendar; **~ escolar/laboral** school/work calendar
calendas *fpl* calends (*pl*)
caléndula *f* pot marigold
calentadita *f* (Méx fam): **darle una ~ a algn** to rough sb up (colloq)
calentador *m* 1 (para agua) (water) heater; (estufa) heater 2 **calentadores** *mpl* (Dep, Indum) legwarmers (*pl*)
(Compuesto) **calentador de aire/de inmersión** fan/immersion heater
calentamiento *m* 1 (Dep) warm-up; **ejercicios de ~** warm-up exercises 2 (Fís) warming
(Compuesto) **calentamiento global** *or* **del planeta** global warming
calentar [A5] *vt*
A 1 ‹*agua/comida*› to heat, heat up; ‹*habitación*› to heat; **~ algo al rojo** to make sth red-hot 2 (Dep): **~ los músculos** to warm up 3 ‹*motor/coche*› to warm up
B (fam) (zurrar) to give … a good hiding (colloq)
C (vulg) (excitar sexualmente) to turn … on (colloq)
D (AmL fam) (enojar) to make … mad (colloq); **lo que me calienta es ...** what really makes me mad is … (colloq)
■ **calentar** *vi*: **¡cómo calienta hoy el sol!** the sun's really hot today!; **la estufa casi no calienta** the heater is hardly giving off any heat
■ **calentarse** *v pron*
A 1 «*horno/plancha*» to heat up; «*habitación*» to warm up, get warm 2 «*motor/coche*» (al arrancar) to warm up; (en exceso) to overheat
B (vulg) (excitarse sexualmente) to get turned on (colloq)
C «*debate*» to become heated; **los ánimos se ~on** tempers flared
D (AmL fam) (enfadarse) to get mad (colloq)
calentera *f* (Ven fam) ▸**calentura 3**
calentón -tona *m,f* (vulg) (en sentido sexual) horny devil (sl), randy devil (BrE colloq)
calentura *f* 1 (fiebre) temperature 2 (en la boca) cold sore 3 (RPl fam) (rabia): **se agarró una ~ bárbara** she had a fit *o* she was livid (colloq)
calenturiento -ta, calenturoso -sa *adj* feverish
calesa *f* calash
calesita *f* (Per, RPl) merry-go-round, carousel
caleta *f*
A (ensenada) cove, small bay
B (Col, Ven) (escondite) cache
caletear [A1] *vt* (Ven) to transport, move
caletearse *v pron* (Per fam) to strip, strip off (BrE)
caleto -ta *v pron* (Per fam) naked, nude; **nos bañamos ~s** we swam in the nude
caletrearse [A1] *v pron* (Ven arg) to learn … parrot fashion
calibrador *m* 1 (para medir) gauge, gage (AmE); **~ de mordazas** caliper* gauge 2 (de tubo, cilindro) borer
calibrar [A1] *vt* 1 ‹*arma/tubo*› to calibrate 2 ‹*consecuencias/situación*› to weigh up
calibre *m*
A 1 (de arma, proyectil) caliber*; **de grueso/pequeño ~** large-bore/small-bore; **de ~ 22** 22 caliber 2 (de tubo, conducto) caliber*; (de alambre) gauge
B (importancia) caliber*; **un artista de ese ~** an artist of that caliber; **de grueso ~** (AmL) ‹*error*› serious; **vocabulario de grueso ~** strong language
caliche *m* (Chi) caliche
calichera *f* (Chi) caliche deposit
calidad *f*
A (de producto, servicio) quality; **un artículo de primera ~** a top-quality product; **productos de mala** *or* **baja ~** poor-quality products; **es una obra de ~** it is a work of high quality
(Compuesto) **calidad de vida** quality of life
B (condición) status; **en ~ de** (frml) as; **asistió en ~ de observador** he attended as an observer; **en su ~ de presidente** in his capacity as president
calidez *f* (AmL) warmth
cálido -da *adj* 1 (Meteo) hot 2 ‹*acogida/bienvenida*› warm 3 ‹*color/tono*› warm
calidoscopio *m* kaleidoscope
calienta, etc *see* **calentar**
calientabiberones *m* (*pl* ~) bottle-warmer
calientabraguetas *f* (*pl* ~) (Méx, RPl vulg) pricktease (vulg)
calientahuevos *f* (*pl* ~) (Col, Ven vulg) pricktease (vulg)
calientapiernas *mpl* legwarmers (*pl*)
calientaplatos *m* (*pl* ~) plate warmer
calientapollas *f* (*pl* ~) (Esp vulg) pricktease (vulg)
caliente *adj*
A ‹*agua/comida/horno*› hot; **aquí estaremos más calentitas** we'll be warmer here; **comer ~** to have a hot meal; **~, ~** (Jueg) you're hot, getting hotter; **tomó la decisión en ~** she made the decision in the heat of the moment; ***agarrarle a algn en ~*** (Méx fam) to catch sb red-handed; ***pagar en ~ y de repente*** (Méx fam) to pay cash on the nail
B (fam) (excitado sexualmente) hot (colloq), horny (sl)
caliento *see* **calentar**
califa *m* caliph
califato *m* caliphate
calificación *f*
A (Educ) grade (AmE), mark (BrE)
B 1 (descripción) description 2 (de película) rating
calificado -da *adj* (esp AmL) ‹*mano de obra*› skilled; ‹*profesional*› qualified; **los más ~s** the most highly qualified; **~ PARA + INF** qualified to + INF
calificar [A2] *vt*
A (describir) **~ algo/a algn DE algo** to describe sth/sb AS sth
B (Educ) 1 ‹*examen*› to grade (AmE), to mark (BrE); ‹*alumno*› to give a grade (AmE) *o* (BrE) mark to 2 «*título/diploma*» **~ a algn PARA + INF** to qualify sb TO + INF
C (Ling) to qualify
calificativo *m*: **no encuentro ~s para describirlo** I can find no words to describe it; **se le aplicó el ~ de reaccionario** he was described as a reactionary; **sólo merece el ~ de ...** the only way to describe it/him/her is …
California *f* California
californiano -na *adj/m,f* Californian
caligrafía *f* (arte) calligraphy; (de persona) writing, handwriting; **ejercicios de ~** handwriting exercises
calilla *f* (Chi fam) debt
calima, calina *f* (nube) cloud of dust (*from the Sahara*); (neblina) mist
calipso *m* (Mús) calypso
calistenia *f* calisthenics*

cáliz *m*
A (Relig) chalice; ***apurar el ~ de la amargura*** (liter) to drain the cup of sorrow (liter)
B (Bot) calyx

caliza *f* limestone

calizo -za *adj* ‹*tierra*› limy; **piedra caliza** limestone

callada *f*: **dio la ~ por respuesta** he didn't reply

calladamente *adv* (en secreto) secretly; (silenciosamente) silently; **se reía ~** she was laughing quietly

callado -da *adj* [ESTAR] quiet; **estuvo ~ durante toda la reunión** he didn't say a thing *o* he kept quiet throughout the whole meeting; **lo escucharon ~s** they listened to him in silence; ***para ~*** (Chi fam) ‹*contar*› in secret; ***tener algo ~*** *or* ***calladito*** **to keep sth quiet**

callampa *f* (Chi) 1 (hongo) mushroom; ***brotar*** *or* ***surgir como ~s*** (fam) to spring up everywhere 2 (vivienda) shanty (dwelling) 3 **callampas** *fpl* (poblaciones marginales) shantytown

callandito *adv* (fam) quietly; **~ ~, que duermen** shh *o* quiet, they're sleeping

callar [A1] *vi* to be quiet, shut up (colloq); **no pude hacerlo ~** I couldn't get him to be quiet; **hacer ~ a la oposición/prensa** to silence the opposition/the press; **ya tiene tres niños — ¡calla!** (fam) she has three children now — never! *o* she hasn't't! (colloq); ***quien calla otorga*** silence implies *o* gives consent
■ **callar** *vt* 1 ‹*secreto/información*› to keep … quiet 2 (AmL) ‹*persona*› to get … to be quiet, to shut … up (colloq)
■ **callarse** *v pron* 1 (guardar silencio) to be quiet; **¡cállate la boca!** (fam) shut your mouth! (sl); **cuando entró todos se ~on** when he walked in everyone went quiet *o* stopped talking; **la próxima vez no me ~é** next time I'll say something 2 (no decir) ‹*noticia*› to keep … quiet, keep … to oneself

calle *f*
A 1 (camino, vía) street; **esa ~ no tiene salida** that's a no through road, that street *o* road is a dead end 2 (en sentido más amplio): **hoy no he salido a la ~** I haven't been out today; **el libro saldrá a la ~ mañana** the book comes out tomorrow; **me encontré con él en la ~** I bumped into him in the street; **el hombre de la ~** the man in the street; **el lenguaje de la ~** colloquial language; **se crió en la ~** she grew up on the streets; **de ~: traje/vestido de ~** everyday suit/dress; ***aplanar ~s*** (AmL fam) to loaf around; ***echar a algn a la ~*** to throw sb out (on the street); ***echarse*** *or* ***salir a la ~*** to take to the streets; ***echar*** *or* ***tirar por la ~ de en medio*** to take the middle course; ***en la ~*** ‹*estar/quedar*› (en la ruina) penniless; (sin vivienda) homeless; (sin trabajo) out of work; ***hacer la ~*** (fam) to work the streets (colloq); ***llevarse a algn de ~*** (fam): **se las lleva a todas de ~** he has all the girls chasing after him (colloq); ***llevar*** *or* ***traer a algn por la ~ de la amargura*** (fam) to make sb's life a misery (colloq)
(Compuestos)
- **calle de dirección única** *or* **sentido único** one-way street
- **calle de una vía** (Col) one-way street
- **calle peatonal** pedestrian street
- **calle sin salida** *or* (Andes, Ven) **calle ciega** *or* (RPl) **cortada**

B (Esp) (en atletismo, natación) lane; (en golf) fairway

callejear [A1] *vi* to hang around the streets (colloq)

callejero¹ -ra *adj* 1 ‹*riña/venta/músico*› street (*before n*); ‹*perro*› stray (*before n*) 2 ‹*persona*›: **es muy ~** he goes out a lot

callejero² *m* (Esp) street map *o* plan

callejón *m* alley, narrow street
(Compuesto) **callejón sin salida** 1 (calle) dead end, blind alley 2 (situación desesperada): **el gobierno se encuentra en un ~ sin salida** the government can't see its way out of its present situation

callejuela *f* alley, narrow street

callicida *m* corn remover

callista *mf* chiropodist

callo *m*
A (en los dedos del pie) corn; (en la planta del pie, en las manos) callus; (en una fractura) callus; ***dar el ~*** (Esp fam) to slave away (colloq)
B (Esp pey) (persona fea): **es un ~** he's got a face like the back end of a bus
C **callos** *mpl* (Esp) (Coc) tripe

callosidad *f* callus

calma *f* calm; **con ~** calmly; **procura mantener la ~** try to keep calm; **tómatelo con ~** take it easy; **no hay que perder la ~** the thing is not to lose your cool; **la ~ ha vuelto a la ciudad** the city is calm again; **el mar está en ~** the sea is calm; **¡~, por favor!** (en situación peligrosa) please, keep calm! *o* don't panic!; (en discusión acalorada) calm down, please!; ***la ~ que precede a la tormenta*** the lull *o* calm before the storm
(Compuesto) **calma chicha** dead calm

calmante *m* (para dolores) painkiller; (para los nervios) tranquilizer

calmar [A1] *vt* 1 (tranquilizar) ‹*persona*› to calm … down; ‹*nervios*› to calm; **esto calmó los ánimos** this eased the tension 2 (aliviar) ‹*dolor*› to relieve, ease
■ **calmarse** *v pron* 1 «*persona*» to calm down; **ahora que los ánimos están más calmados** now that people have calmed down 2 «*mar*» to become calm

calmo -ma *adj* (esp AmL) calm

calmoso -sa *adj* (tranquilo) calm; (lento) slow

caló *m* gypsy slang

calor *m* [*Use of the feminine gender, although common in some areas, is generally considered to be archaic or non-standard*]
A (Fís) heat
B 1 (Meteo) heat; **con este ~ no puedo trabajar** I can't work in this heat; **hoy hace ~** it's hot today; **hacía un ~ agobiante** the heat was stifling *o* suffocating; **hace un ~cillo agradable** it's pleasantly warm 2 (sensación): **tener ~** to be hot; **pasamos un ~ horrible** it was terribly *o* unbearably hot; **entrar en ~** to get warm; **esta chaqueta me da mucho ~** I feel very hot in this jacket; **al ~ del fuego/de la lumbre** by the fireside
C (afecto) warmth; **un hogar falto de ~** a home lacking in warmth and affection
D **calores** *mpl* (de la menopausia) hot flashes (*pl*) (AmE), hot flushes (*pl*) (BrE)

caloría *f* calorie

calórico -ca *adj* caloric; **con bajo contenido ~** with a low calorie content

calorífero -ra *adj* heat-producing

calorífico -ca *adj* calorific

calostro *m* colostrum

calumnia *f* (oral) defamation, slander, calumny (frml); (escrita) libel; **levantaron ~s contra la institución** they spread slanderous rumors about the institution

calumniador -dora *adj* slanderous, defamatory

calumniar [A1] *vt* (por escrito) to libel; (oralmente) to slander

calumnioso -sa *adj* ‹*discurso/rumor*› defamatory, slanderous; ‹*escrito/libro*› defamatory, libelous

caluroso -sa *adj* 1 ‹*día/clima*› hot 2 ‹*acogida/aplauso*› warm; **recibe un ~ saludo** (Corresp) best wishes

calva *f* (cabeza sin pelo) bald head; (parte sin pelo) bald patch

calvario *m*
A 1 (Relig) Stations of the Cross (*pl*) 2 (fam) (sufrimiento, martirio): **es un ~** it is torture *o* hell
B **el Calvario** (Bib) Calvary

calvicie *f* baldness

calvinismo *m* Calvinism

calvinista *adj/mf* Calvinist

calvo¹ -va *adj* ‹*persona*› bald; **quedarse ~** to go bald

calvo² -va *m,f* bald person

calypso *m* ▸**calipso**

calza *f*
A (cuña) chock
B (Col) (en una muela) filling
C **calzas** *fpl* (calzones) hose (*pl*), breeches (*pl*)

calzada *f* 1 (camino) road; **~s romanas** Roman roads 2 (de una calle) road; (de una autopista) side, carriageway

calzado¹ -da *adj*: **ir bien ~** to wear good shoes; **iba ~ con botas** he wore boots

C

calzado[2] *m* (frml) footwear (frml); **la industria del ~** the shoe industry

calzador *m* shoehorn

calzar [A4] *vt*

A **1** ‹*persona*› (proveerla de calzado) to provide ... with shoes; (ponerle los zapatos): **calza a los niños** put the children's shoes on **2** (llevar): **calzo (un) 39** I take (a) size 39, I'm a 39; **calzaba zapatillas de deporte** he was wearing training shoes

B ‹*rueda*› to chock, wedge a block under

C (Col) ‹*muela*› to fill

■ **calzarse** *v pron* (*refl*) **1** (ponerse los zapatos) to put one's shoes on **2** ‹*zapato*› to put on

C

calzo *m* chock

calzón *m*, **calzones** *mpl*

A **1** (antiguo) long underwear, long johns (*pl*) (colloq) **2** (AmS) (moderno) panties (*pl*), pants (*pl*) (BrE)

B **calzón** *m* (Esp) (para deporte) shorts (*pl*)

calzonazos *m* (*pl* ~) (fam) (marido dominado) henpecked husband (colloq); (cobarde) wimp (colloq)

calzoncillos *mpl*, **calzoncillo** *m* underpants, shorts (*pl*) (AmE), pants (*pl*) (BrE)

(Compuesto) **calzoncillos largos** *mpl* long underwear, long johns (*pl*) (colloq)

calzoncitos *mpl* (Col) panties (*pl*), pants (*pl*) (BrE)

calzonudo[1] *adj* (AmL fam) (dominado por la mujer) henpecked; (débil) wimpish (colloq)

calzonudo[2] *m* (AmL) ▸ **calzonazos**

cama *f* (para dormir) bed; **hacer** *or* (AmL) **tender la ~** to make the bed; **estirar la ~** to straighten the covers; **¡métete en la ~!** get into bed!; **guardar ~** to stay in bed; **está en ~** she's in bed; ***caer en ~*** to fall ill; ***estar de ~*** (RPl fam) to be dead (colloq), to be knackered (BrE sl); ***irse a la ~ con algn*** (fam) to go to bed with sb (colloq); ***llevarse a algn a la ~*** (fam) to get sb into bed (colloq)

(Compuestos)

- **cama camarote** (AmL) bunk bed
- **cama de agua** water bed
- **cama doble** *or* **de matrimonio** *or* (AmL) **de dos plazas** double bed
- **cama individual** *or* (AmL) **de una plaza** single bed
- **cama elástica** trampoline
- **cama nido** trundle bed, truckle bed
- **cama redonda** group sex
- **camas gemelas** *fpl* twin beds (*pl*)
- **cama solar** sunbed
- **cama turca** (sin respaldo) divan (bed)

camada *f* (Zool) litter; (de ladrones, sinvergüenzas) (pey) gang

camafeo *m* cameo

camaleón *m* chameleon

camama *f* (fam) (mentira) lie; (burla) joke

camanchaca *f* (en el Atacama) thick fog

cámara *f*

A (arc) (aposento) chamber (frml)

(Compuestos)

- **cámara acorazada** *or* **blindada** strongroom, vault
- **cámara de combustión/compresión/descompresión** combustion/compression/decompression chamber
- **cámara de gas** gas chamber
- **cámara de oxígeno** oxygen tent
- **cámara frigorífica** cold store
- **cámara mortuoria** funeral chamber

B (Gob, Pol) house

(Compuestos)

- **cámara alta/baja** upper/lower house
- **Cámara de los Comunes/de los Lores** House of Commons/of Lords
- **Cámara de los Diputados** Chamber of Deputies
- **Cámara de Representantes** House of Representatives
- **Cámara de Senadores** Senate

C (Com, Fin) association

(Compuestos)

- **cámara agraria** *or* **agrícola** farmers' union
- **cámara de comercio** chamber of commerce

D (aparato) camera; **en** *or* (Esp) **a ~ lenta** in slow motion

(Compuestos)

- **cámara de cine** film camera
- **cámara de televisión** television
- **cámara de video** *or* (Esp) **vídeo** video camera
- **cámara de viglancia** *or* **videovigilancia** security *or* CCTV camera
- **cámara fotográfica** camera

E **cámara** *mf* (Esp) (camarógrafo) (*m*) cameraman; (*f*) camerawoman

F **1** (Fís, Mec) chamber **2** (de un arma) chamber

G (de un neumático) inner tube

camarada *mf* **1** (de un partido político) comrade; **el ~ Nieves** Comrade Nieves **2** (de colegio) school friend; (de trabajo) colleague

camaradería *f* camaraderie, comradeship; **una comida de ~** (CS) a reunion dinner, an alumni dinner (AmE)

camarero -ra *m,f*

A (esp Esp) (en bar, restaurante) (*m*) waiter; (*f*) waitress; (detrás de mostrador) (*m*) barman; (*f*) barmaid

B **1** (en un hotel) (*m*) bellboy; (*f*) maid **2** (Transp) (*m*) steward; (*f*) stewardess

camarilla *f* group; (pey) clique (pej); (de jefe, presidente) cronies (*pl*) (colloq & pej)

camarín *m* (CS) **1** (Teatr) dressing room **2** (en vestuarios) changing cubicle **3** **camarines** *mpl* (Chi) (Dep) changing rooms (*pl*), locker rooms (*pl*)

camarógrafo -fa (*m*) cameraman; (*f*) camerawoman

camarón *m* (crustáceo pequeño) shrimp; (— más grande) shrimp (AmE), prawn (BrE)

camarote *m* cabin

cambalache *m* **1** (fam) (trueque) swap (colloq); **hacer ~s** to swap (colloq) **2** (RPl fam & pey) (tienda) thrift store (AmE), junk shop (BrE)

cambiable *adv* **1** (variable) changeable **2** ‹*bono/vale*› exchangeable

cambiante[1] *adj* ‹*tiempo*› changeable, unsettled; ‹*persona/carácter*› moody, temperamental

cambiante[2] *mf* moneychanger

cambiar [A1] *vt*

A **1** (alterar, modificar) ‹*horario/imagen/persona*› to change; **eso no cambia nada** that doesn't change anything **2** (de lugar, posición) **~ algo/a algn DE algo**: **~ los muebles de lugar** to move the furniture around; **nos van a ~ de oficina** they're going to move us to another office; **cambié las flores de florero** I put the flowers in a different vase **3** (reemplazar) ‹*pieza/fecha/sábanas*› to change; **le cambió la pila al reloj** she changed the battery in the clock; **~le el nombre a algo** to change the name of sth **4** ‹*niño/bebé*› to change

B (canjear) ‹*sellos/estampas*› to swap, to trade (esp AmE); ‹*compra*› to exchange, change; **si no le queda bien lo puede ~** if it doesn't fit, you can exchange *o* change it; **~ algo POR algo** ‹*sellos/estampas*› to swap *o* (esp AmE) trade sth FOR sth; ‹*compra*› to exchange *o* change sth FOR sth; **te cambio este libro por tu pluma** I'll swap you *o* trade this book for your pen; **~le algo A algn**: **¿quieres que te cambie el lugar?** do you want to change places?

C (Fin) to change; **¿me puedes ~ este billete?** can you change this bill (AmE) *o* (BrE) note for me?; **~ algo A** *or* (Esp) **EN algo** to change sth INTO sth; **cambié 100 libras a** *or* (Esp) **en dólares** I changed 100 pounds into dollars

■ **cambiar** *vi*

A **1** «*ciudad/persona*» (alterarse) to change; **~ para peor/mejor** to change for the worse/better; **está/lo noto muy cambiado** he's changed/he seems to have changed a lot; **así la cosa cambia** oh well, that's different; **le está cambiando la voz** his voice is breaking **2** (Auto) to change gear **3** (hacer transbordo) to change **4** (en transmisiones): **cambio** over; **cambio y corto** *or* **fuera** over and out

B **cambiar de** to change; **~ de color** to change color; **~ de idea** *or* **opinión** to change one's mind; **~ de marcha** to change gear; **cambió de canal** he changed channel(s)

■ **cambiarse** *v pron* **1** (*refl*) (de ropa) to change, to get changed **2** (*refl*) ‹*camisa/nombre/peinado*› to change; **¿te cambiaste los calcetines?** did you change your socks? **3** **~se POR algn** to change places WITH sb **4** (*recípr*) ‹*sellos/estampas*› to swap, to trade (esp AmE) **5** **cambiarse de** to change; **me cambié de sitio** I changed places;

~se de casa to move house; **cámbiate de camisa** change your shirt 6 (CS) (mudarse de casa) to move

cambiazo *m* (fam) change; **¡ qué ~ has dado!** how you've changed!; ***darle*** *or* ***hacerle el ~ a algn*** (Esp fam): **le habían dado el ~** they had switched it for a fake one

cambio *m*

A 1 (alteración, modificación) change; **~ DE algo** ‹*de planes/domicilio*› change OF sth; **un brusco ~ de temperatura** a sudden change in temperature; **un ~ de aires** *or* **ambiente** a change of scene; **una operación de ~ de sexo** a sex-change operation; ***a la primera de ~*** (fam) at the first opportunity 2 (Auto) gearshift (AmE), gear change (BrE); **meta el ~** (AmL) put it in gear; **un coche con cinco ~s** (AmL) a car with a five-speed gearbox

Compuestos

- **cambio de escena** scene change
- **cambio de guardia** change of guard
- **cambio de marchas** *o* **velocidades** (dispositivo) transmission (AmE), gearbox (BrE); (acción) gearshift (AmE), gear change (BrE)
- **cambio de marchas automático** automatic gearshift (AmE) *o* (BrE) gearbox
- **cambio de rasante** brow of a hill
- **cambio de vía** switch (AmE), points (*pl*) (BrE)

B 1 (canje) exchange; **saliste perdiendo con el ~** you lost out in the deal; Ⓢ **no se admiten cambios** goods cannot be exchanged 2 (*en locs*) **a cambio (de)** in exchange (for), in return (for); **en cambio**: **a él le gusta a mí en ~ no** he likes it but I don't; **el autobús es agotador, en ~ el tren es muy agradable** the bus is exhausting; the train however *o* on the other hand is very pleasant

C 1 (Fin) (de moneda extranjera) exchange; **~ de divisas** foreign exchange; **¿a cómo está el ~?** what's the exchange rate?; Ⓢ **cambio** bureau de change, change; **al ~ del día** at the current exchange rate; ▸**libre**[1] **A** 2 (diferencia) change; **me ha dado mal el ~** he's given me the wrong change 3 (dinero suelto) change; **¿tienes ~ de mil?** can you change a thousand pesos?; **necesito ~** I need some change

cambista *mf* moneychanger

cambur *m* (Ven) (fruta) banana

camelar [A1] *vt* (Esp fam) to sweet-talk (colloq); **~ a algn** PARA QUE + SUBJ to sweet-talk sb INTO + ING

camelia *f* camellia

camellear [A1] *vi* (arg) to push drugs

camello *m*

A (Zool) camel

B (Col fam) (trabajo) work; (empleo) job; (esfuerzo) hard work

C **camello** *mf* (arg) (traficante) pusher (sl), dealer (colloq)

camellón *m* (Méx) (en la calle) traffic island

camelo *m* (fam) (timo) con (colloq); (mentira) lie; **es puro ~** it's a pack of lies *o* (colloq) a load of bull; **esa noticia me huele a ~** that news sounds *o* smells fishy to me (colloq)

camembert *m* Camembert

camerino *m* 1 (Teatr) dressing room 2 **camerinos** *mpl* (Col) (Dep) changing rooms (*pl*)

camilla *f*

A (de lona) stretcher; (con ruedas) trolley, gurney (AmE); (en un consultorio) couch

B (Esp) (mesa) round table (*with a space for a heater beneath*)

camillero -ra *m,f* stretcher-bearer; **ahora vienen los ~s** now they are bringing the stretchers

caminador *m* (Col) babywalker

caminante *mf* (liter) traveler*

caminar [A1] *vi*

A 1 (andar) to walk; **le gusta ~ por el campo** he likes going for walks *o* (going) walking in the country; **salieron a ~** they went out for a walk; **podemos ir caminando** we can walk, we can go on foot; **el nene ya camina** the baby's walking now; **¡camina derecho!** stand up straight when you walk, don't slouch; **a ti te hace falta alguien que te haga ~ derecho** what you need is someone to keep you in line (colloq) 2 (hacia una meta, fin): **caminamos hacia una nueva era social** our society is moving into a new age; **~ hacia un futuro mejor** to head toward a better future

B (AmL) «*reloj/motor*» to work; «*asunto*» (fam): **el asunto va caminando** the matter is progressing, things are moving (colloq)

■ **caminar** *vt*

A ‹*distancia*› to walk; **caminamos dos kilómetros todos los días** we walk two kilometers every day

B (Col fam) ‹*persona*› to chase (colloq)

caminata *f* long walk; (en el campo) long walk, ramble, hike; **después de darme** *or* **pegarme semejante ~** after walking *o* (colloq) trekking all that way; **hay una buena ~ hasta allá** it's a fair walk *o* quite a trek (colloq)

camino *m*

A (de tierra) track; (sendero) path; (en general) road; **sigan por ese ~** continue along that path (*o* road *etc*); **están todos los ~s cortados** all the roads are blocked; ***abrir nuevos ~s*** to break new *o* fresh ground; ***allanar*** *or* ***preparar*** *or* ***abrir el ~*** to pave the way, prepare the ground; ***el ~ trillado*** the well-worn *o* well-trodden path; ***la vida no es un ~ de rosas*** life is no bed of roses; ***tener el ~ trillado***: **tenía el ~ trillado** he'd had the ground prepared for him; ***todos los ~s llevan*** *or* ***conducen a Roma*** all roads lead to Rome

Compuestos

- **Caminos, Canales y Puertos** civil engineering
- **camino vecinal** minor road (*built and maintained by local council*)

B 1 (ruta, dirección) way; **el ~ más corto** the shortest route *o* way; **saberse el ~** to know the way; **me salieron al ~** «*asaltantes*» they blocked my path *o* way; «*amigos/niños*» they came out to meet me; **éste es el mejor ~ a seguir** this is the best course to follow; **el ~ a la fama** the road *o* path to fame; **por ese ~ no vas a ninguna parte** you won't get anywhere that way *o* like that; **siguen ~s muy diferentes** they're taking very different paths; **se me fue por mal ~** *or* **por el otro ~** it went down the wrong way; ***abrir ~ a algo*** to clear the way for sth; ***abrirse ~*** to make one's way; **se abrió ~ entre la espesura** she made her way through the dense thickets; **abrirse ~ en la vida** to get on in life; ***buen/mal ~***: **este niño va por mal ~** *or* **lleva mal ~** this boy's heading for trouble; **ibas por** *or* **llevabas buen ~ pero te equivocaste** you were on the right track but you made a mistake; **las negociaciones van por** *or* **llevan muy buen ~** the negotiations are going extremely well; **llevar a algn por mal ~** to lead sb astray; ***cruzarse en el ~ de algn***: **superó todos los obstáculos que se le cruzaron en el ~** he overcame all the problems that arose; ***errar el ~*** to be in the wrong job *o* the wrong line of work; ***tirar por el ~ de en medio*** to take the middle path 2 (trayecto, viaje): **el ~ de regreso** the return journey; **se me hizo muy largo el ~** the journey seemed to take for ever; **lo debí perder en el ~ al trabajo** I must have lost it on my *o* on the way to work; **se pusieron en ~** they set off; **llevamos 300 kms/una hora de ~** we've done 300 kms/been traveling for an hour; **todavía estamos a** *o* **nos quedan dos horas de ~** we still have two hours to go; **paramos a mitad de ~** *or* **a medio ~** we stopped halfway; **cortar** *o* **acortar ~** to take a shortcut; **hizo todo el ~ a pie** he walked the whole way; **queda aún mucho ~ por recorrer** there's still a long way to go; ***a mitad de*** *or* ***a medio ~*** halfway through 3 (*en locs*) **camino de/a**: **me encontré con él ~ del** *or* **al mercado** I ran into him on the *o* on my way to the market; **ya vamos ~ del invierno** winter's on the way *o* on its way; ***llevar*** *or* ***ir ~ de algo***: **una tradición que va ~ de desaparecer** a tradition which looks set to disappear; **de camino** on the way to; **pilla de ~** it's on the way; **me queda de ~** I pass it on my way; **de camino a** on the way; **está de ~ a la estación** it is on the way to the station; **en el ~** *or* **de ~ al trabajo** on my/his/her way *o* the way to work; **en camino** on the way; **tiene un niño y otro en ~** she has one child and another on the way; **deben estar ya en ~** they must be on their way already; **por el camino** on the way

Compuesto **Camino de Santiago**: **el ~ de ~** (Hist, Relig) the road to Santiago; (Astron) the Milky Way

Camino de Santiago

A pilgrimage route since the Middle Ages across northwestern Spain to Santiago de Compostela in Galicia. The city was founded at a place where a shepherd is said to have discovered the tomb of St James the Apostle, and its cathedral reputedly houses the saint's relics

C

camión *m*
A (de carga) truck, lorry (BrE); (contenido) truckload; ***estar como un ~*** (Esp fam) to be hot stuff (colloq)
(Compuestos)
• **camión articulado** semi (AmE), semitrailer (AmE), articulated lorry (BrE)
• **camión blindado** armored truck
• **camión celular** (Esp) patrol wagon (AmE), police van (BrE)
• **camión cisterna** tanker
• **camión de la basura** garbage truck (AmE), dustcart (BrE)
• **camión de mudanzas** moving van (AmE), removal van (BrE)
• **camión frigorífico** refrigerated truck
B (AmC, Méx) (autobús) bus

camionero -ra *m,f*
A truck driver, lorry driver (BrE)
B (AmC, Méx) (conductor de autobús) bus driver

camioneta *f*
A (furgoneta) van; (camión pequeño) light truck, pickup truck
B (AmL) (coche familiar) station wagon (AmE), estate car (BrE)

camión-grúa *m* (de un taller) wrecker (AmE), breakdown lorry (BrE); (de la policía) tow truck

camisa *f*
A (Indum) shirt; **en mangas de ~** in shirtsleeves; ***cambiar de ~*** to change sides; ***me jugué/se jugó hasta la ~*** I/he put my/his shirt on it; ***meterse en ~ de once varas*** (fam) to get oneself into a mess *o* jam (colloq); ***no me/le llegaba la ~ al cuerpo*** I/he/she was scared stiff; ***perder hasta la ~*** to lose one's shirt
(Compuesto) **camisa de fuerza** *f* straitjacket
B [1] (de un libro) jacket [2] (de un cilindro) sleeve; (de un horno) lining [3] (de una lámpara) mantle

camisería *f* shirtmaker's

camisero -ra *m,f* [1] (persona) shirtmaker [2] **camisero** *m* (vestido) shirtwaist (AmE), shirtwaister (BrE)

camiseta *f* [1] (prenda interior) undershirt (AmE), vest (BrE) [2] (prenda exterior) T-shirt; (de fútbol) shirt, jersey (AmE); (de atletismo — de manga corta) shirt, jersey (AmE); (— sin mangas) jersey (AmE), vest (BrE)

camisola *f* loose-fitting shirt

camisón *m* nightdress

camomila *f* camomile, chamomile

camorra *f* [1] (fam) (bronca, riña) fight; **armar ~** to start a fight; **buscar ~** to look for a fight (colloq) [2] **la Camorra** the Camorra, the Sicilian mafia

camorrero -ra *adj/mf* (Col, CS) ▸**camorrista**[1,2] **1**

camorrista[1] *adj* [1] (fam) (pendenciero): **no seas ~** stop being a troublemaker [2] (mafioso) *of the Camorra*

camorrista[2] *mf* [1] (fam) (pendenciero) troublemaker (colloq) [2] (mafioso) *member of the Camorra*

camote *m*
A (Bot) [1] (Andes, Méx) (batata) sweet potato; ***hacerse ~*** (Méx fam) to get mixed up, get in a muddle (colloq); ***poner a algn como ~*** (Méx fam); (reprenderlo) to give sb a telling off; ***ser un ~*** (Chi, Méx fam) to be a pain in the neck (colloq) [2] (Méx) (cualquier tubérculo o bulbo) tuber
B (Andes, Méx) (lío) mess (colloq), fix (colloq)
C (Andes, RPl fam) (con una persona) crush (colloq); **tener un ~ con algn** to have a crush on sb

camotiza *f* (Méx fam): ***ponerle*** *or* ***darle una ~ a algn*** to give sb a good telling-off (colloq)

campamento *m* camp; **nos fuimos a Bariloche de ~** we went camping in Bariloche; ***levantar ~*** (CS fam) to make tracks (colloq)
(Compuesto) **campamento de instrucción/de verano** training/summer camp

campana *f*
A [1] (de iglesia) bell, church bell; ***echar las ~s al*** *or* ***a vuelo*** (literal) to set the bells ringing; (anunciar jubilosamente): **aún es pronto para echar las ~s al vuelo** it's too soon to start shouting about it; **tampoco es como para echar las ~s al vuelo** it's not worth getting that excited about; ***me/te/lo salvó la ~*** saved by the bell; ***oír ~s y no saber dónde***: **ese tipo ha oído ~s y no sabe dónde** that guy is talking through his hat (colloq) [2] (en el colegio) bell; **tocar la ~** to ring the bell; **¿ya ha sonado la ~?** has the bell gone yet?
B [1] (de chimenea) hood; (de cocina) extractor hood [2] (para proteger alimentos) cover
(Compuesto) **campana de buzo** *or* **de inmersión** diving bell

campanada *f* [1] (de campana) chime, stroke; (de reloj) stroke; **el reloj dio las 12 ~s** the clock struck 12 [2] (fam) (sorpresa): **la noticia fue una ~** the news came like a bolt from the blue (colloq); ***dar la ~*** to cause a stir

campanario *m* bell tower, belfry

campanazo *m* (AmL) ▸**campanada**

campanero -ra *m,f* bell ringer

campanilla *f*
A (campana pequeña) small bell, hand bell; ***de ~s*** high-class, classy (colloq)
B (Anat) uvula
C (Bot) campanula, bellflower

campante *adj*: **se quedó tan ~** he didn't bat an eyelid; **nosotros muertos de miedo y él tan ~** we were scared stiff but he was as cool as a cucumber

campaña *f*
A (en una guerra) campaign
B (Col) (maniobras) maneuvers* (*pl*)
C (Marketing, Pol) campaign; **hacer una ~** to run *o* conduct a campaign
(Compuestos)
• **campaña de imagen** campaign to improve one's image
• **campaña denigratoria** *or* **de desprestigio** smear campaign
• **campaña electoral** electoral *o* election campaign
• **campaña publicitaria** advertising campaign

campar [A1] *vi* (Esp) (andar): **los niños campan a sus anchas por el jardín** children can be seen playing freely in the garden; ***~ por sus respetos*** to do exactly as one pleases

campear [A1] *vi*: **en los edificios ~on las banderas** flags could be seen flying from the buildings

campechano -na *adj* (sin complicaciones) straightforward; (bondadoso) good-natured

campeón[1] **-peona** *adj* champion (*before n*)

campeón[2] **-peona** *m,f* champion

campeonato *m* championship; **ganar/perder un ~** to win/lose a championship; ***de ~*** (Esp fam): **tengo una resaca de ~** I have a terrible hangover

cámper *f* (Chi, Méx) camper, camper van

campera *f* [1] (RPl) (chaqueta) jacket [2] **camperas** *fpl* (Esp) (botas) cowboy boots

campero[1] **-ra** *adj* ‹*costumbres*› rural; ‹*estilo*› country (*before n*)

campero[2] **-ra** *m,f*
A (AmL) (persona) farm worker
B **campero** *m* (Col) (Auto) jeep

campesinado *m* peasantry, peasants (*pl*)

campesino[1] **-na** *adj* ‹*vida/costumbre*› rural, country (*before n*); ‹*modales/aspecto*› peasant-like

campesino[2] **-na** *m,f* (persona del campo) country person; (con connotaciones de pobreza) peasant; **una campesina vestida de negro** a peasant woman dressed in black; **son ~s** they are country people *o* folk; **los obreros y los ~s** the manual workers and the agricultural workers

campestre *adj* ‹*escena/vida*› rural, country (*before n*); ‹*casa/club*› country (*before n*)

camping /'kampin/ *m* (*pl* **-pings**) [1] (actividad) camping; **irse de ~** to go camping [2] (lugar) campsite, campground (AmE)

campiña *f* countryside, landscape

campirano -na *mf* ▸**campesino**

campista *mf* camper

campo *m*
A (zona no urbana) country; (paisaje) countryside; **viven en el ~** they live in the country; **la gente del ~** the country people; **el ~ se ve precioso** the countryside looks beautiful; **~ a través** *or* **a ~ traviesa** ‹*cruzar/ir*› cross-country
B [1] (zona agraria) land; (terreno) field; **trabajar el ~ de**

forma eficaz to work the land efficiently; **las faenas del ~** farm work; **los ~s de cebada** the field of barley 2▸ **de campo** field (*before n*); **investigaciones** *or* **observaciones de ~** a field study ▸**trabajo**

Compuestos
- **campo de aterrizaje** landing field
- **campo de batalla** battlefield
- **campo de vuelo** airfield
- **campo minado** *or* **de minas** minefield
- **campo petrolífero** oilfield

C (Dep) (de fútbol) field, pitch; (de golf) course; **perdieron en su ~** *or* **en ~ propio** they lost at home

Compuestos
- **campo a través** cross-country running
- **campo de juego** (en fútbol) field, pitch
- **campo de tiro** firing range

D (ámbito, área de acción) field; **esto no está dentro de mi ~ de acción** this does not fall within my area *o* field of responsibility; ***dejarle el ~ libre a algn*** to leave the field clear for sb

Compuestos
- **campo de fuego** field of fire
- **campo de pruebas** testing ground
- **campo magnético/de gravedad** magnetic/gravitational field
- **campo semántico** semantic field
- **campo visual** field of vision

E (campamento) camp; ***levantar el ~*** to make tracks (colloq)

Compuestos
- **campo de concentración/de refugiados** concentration/refugee camp
- **campo de trabajo** work camp, working vacation (AmE) *o* (BrE) holiday
- **campo de trabajos forzados** labor camp

F (Andes) (espacio, lugar): **hagan** *or* **abran ~** make room; **siempre le guardo ~** I always save her a place

G (Inf) field

camposanto *m* (liter) graveyard, cemetery

campus *m* (*pl* ~) campus

camuflado -da *adj* camouflaged

camuflaje *m* camouflage

camuflajear [A1] *vt* (AmL) ▸**camuflar**

camuflar [A1] *vt* ‹*tanques/contrabando*› to camouflage; ‹*intenciones*› to disguise

■ **camuflarse** *v pron* «*soldado*» to camouflage oneself; «*animal*» to be camouflaged

can *m* (perro) (liter *o* hum) hound (liter *or* hum), dog

cana *f*

A (pelo) gray* hair, white hair; **ya tiene ~s** she already has gray hairs *o* gray hair; ***echar una ~ al aire*** to let one's hair down; (colloq); ***respetar las ~s*** to respect one's elders; ***sacarle ~s verdes a algn*** to drive sb to an early grave

B (AmS arg) (cárcel) slammer (sl), nick (BrE colloq)

C 1▸ (RPl arg) (cuerpo de policía): **la ~** the cops (*pl*) (colloq) 2▸ (RPl arg) **cana** *mf* (agente) cop (colloq)

canaca *mf* (Chi, Per fam & pey) (chino) chink (sl & pej)

Canadá *m*: *tb* **el ~** Canada

canadiense *adj/mf* Canadian

canal[1] *m*

A (Náut) (cauce artificial) canal; (Agr, Ing) channel; **~ de desagüe** drain

Compuestos
- **Canal de la Mancha** English Channel
- **Canal de Panamá** Panama Canal
- **Canal de San Lorenzo** St Lawrence Seaway
- **Canal de Suez** Suez Canal

B 1▸ (Rad, Telec, TV) channel; **cambia de ~** change *o* switch channels 2▸ (medio) channel; **~es de distribución** distribution channels

canal[2] *f or m* (canalón) gutter; (ranura) groove

canalé *m* rib; **en ~** in rib

canalización *f* 1▸ (de un río) canalization 2▸ (de ideas, esfuerzos, fondos) channeling*

canalizar [A4] *vt* to channel

canalla *mf* 1▸ (fam) (bribón, granuja) swine (colloq) 2▸ **canalla** *f* (pey) (chusma): **la ~** the rabble *o* riffraff

canallada *f* (fam): **¡qué ~!** what a rotten *o* mean thing to do (colloq)

canalón *m* (Esp) gutter

canana *f* cartridge belt

canapé *m*

A (Coc) canapé

B (sofá) couch

canar [A1] *vi* (Col) ▸**encanecer**

Canarias *fpl*: *tb* **las (Islas) ~** the Canaries, the Canary Islands

canario[1] **-ria** *adj* of/from the Canary Islands

canario[2] **-ria** *m,f*

A 1▸ (de las Canarias) person from the Canary Islands 2▸ (Ur fam & pey) (pueblerino) country bumpkin (colloq), hick (AmE)

B **canario** *m* (Zool) canary

canasta *f*

A 1▸ (para la compra) basket 2▸ (AmL) (en rifa) hamper

Compuesto **canasta familiar** (AmL) family shopping basket (*used to calculate the retail price index*)

B (en baloncesto) basket; **meter** *or* **hacer** *or* **anotar una ~** to make *o* score a basket

C (Jueg) canasta

canastilla *f* layette

canasto *m* basket (*gen large and with a lid*)

canastos *interj* (fam) good heavens!

cancán *m* (baile) cancan; (Indum) frilly petticoat

cancel *m* (contrapuerta) inner door; (tabique) (Col, Méx) partition; (biombo) (Méx) folding screen

cancela *f* gate (*of wrought iron*)

cancelación *f*

A (suspensión) cancellation

B (liquidación) payment; **lograron la ~ de su deuda** they managed to pay off *o* settle their debt

cancelar [A1] *vt*

A ‹*reunión/viaje/pedido*› to cancel

B ‹*deuda*› to settle, pay off; ‹*cuenta*› to pay

cáncer *m* (Med) cancer; **tiene (un) ~ de pulmón/mama** she has lung/breast cancer

Cáncer[1] *m* (signo) Cancer; **es (de) ~** he's a Cancer *o* Cancerian

Cáncer[2], **cáncer** *mf* (persona) Cancerian, Cancer

cancerígeno[1] **-na** *adj* carcinogenic

cancerígeno[2] *m* carcinogen

canceroso -sa *adj* cancerous

cancha *f*

A 1▸ (Dep) (de baloncesto, frontón, squash, tenis) court; (de fútbol, rugby) (AmL) field, pitch; (de golf) (CS) course; (de polo) (AmL) field 2▸ (CS) (de esquí) slope 3▸ (Chi) (Aviac) *tb* **~ de aterrizaje** landing strip, runway

B (AmL fam) (desenvoltura): **un político con mucha ~** a politician with a great deal of experience, a seasoned politician

C (CS) (espacio) space, room; **¡abran ~!** make way!; ***darle ~ a algn*** (Col fam) to give sb an advantage; ***dejarle la ~ libre a algn*** (CS fam) to leave sb room to maneuver; (hacerse a un lado) to leave the way clear for sb; ***sentirse en su ~*** (CS fam) to be in one's element

canchero -ra *adj* (AmL fam) (experto) ‹*jugador*› skillful; **es muy ~ con las mujeres** he has a way with women (colloq)

canchita *f* (Per) popcorn

canciller *m* 1▸ (jefe de estado) chancellor 2▸ (AmS) (ministro) ≈ Secretary of State (*in US*), ≈ Foreign Secretary (*in UK*)

cancillería *f* 1▸ (de embajada) chancery, chancellery 2▸ (AmS) (ministerio) ≈ State Department (*in US*), ≈ Foreign Office (*in UK*)

canción *f* song; **ya estamos otra vez con la misma ~** here we go again! (colloq)

Compuestos
- **canción de cuna** lullaby
- **canción nacional** (Chi) national anthem

cancionero *m* (Mús) song book; (Lit) anthology (*of 15th/16th century verse*)

cancro *m* 1▸ (Med) cancer 2▸ (Bot) canker

candado *m* (cerradura) padlock; **está cerrada con ~** it is padlocked

C

candeal *m* (CS) (bebida) eggnog

candela *f* 1 (fuego) fire; **¿tienes ~?** (fam) have you got a light?; **no te acerques a la ~** don't go too near the fire; ***dar ~*** (AmL fam) to be annoying, be a nuisance; ***echar ~*** (Ven fam): **estaba que echaba ~** she was absolutely livid (colloq); ***jugar con ~*** (Col) to play with fire 2 (vela) candle

candelabro *m* candelabra

candelero *m* candlestick; ***estar en el ~*** to be in the limelight

candente *adj* 1 ‹*hierro*› red-hot 2 ‹*tema*› burning; ▸**actualidad**

candidato -ta *m,f* (aspirante) candidate; **~ a la presidencia** presidential candidate

candidatura *f* 1 (propuesta) candidacy, candidature; **presentó su ~ para el puesto** she put herself forward as a candidate for the post 2 (Esp) (lista) list of candidates

candidez *f* naivety

cándido -da *adj* naive

candil *m* oil lamp

candilejas *fpl* footlights (*pl*)

candombe *m*: *African-influenced dance*

candonga *f* (Col) dangly earring

candor *m* innocence, naivety

candorosamente *adv* innocently, naively

candoroso -sa *adj* innocent, naive

caneca *f* (Col) (papelera) wastebasket, waste-paper basket (BrE); (cubo de la basura) garbage *o* trash can (AmE), dustbin (BrE)

canela *f* 1 (Bot, Coc) cinnamon; ***ser ~ fina*** «*futbolista*» to be brilliant; «*vino/queso*» to be absolutely delicious; «*mujer*» to be outstandingly beautiful 2 (color) cinnamon; **(de) color ~** cinnamon-colored•

(Compuesto) **canela en polvo/en rama** ground/stick cinnamon

canelo, canelero *m* cinnamon tree

canelón *m*
A (Const) gutter
B **canelones** *mpl* canneloni

canesú *m* yoke

canevá *m* (RPl) canvas

cangilón *m* bucket

cangrejo *m* (de mar) crab; (de río) crayfish; ***ir para atrás como el ~*** to go from bad to worse; ***rojo como un ~*** (por el sol) as red as a lobster; (de vergüenza) as red as a beet (AmE), as red as a beetroot (BrE)

canguro *m*
A (Zool) kangaroo
B 1 (anorak) cagoule 2 (para llevar a un niño) sling
C (Esp) **canguro** *mf* (persona) babysitter; **hacer de ~** to babysit

caníbal[1] *adj* 1 (antropófago) cannibal (*before n*), man-eating 2 (Col fam) (bruto): **no sea ~** don't be so rough

caníbal[2] *mf* 1 (antropófago) cannibal 2 (Col fam) (bruto) savage, monster

canica *f* marble

caniche *mf* /ka'nitʃe, ka'niʃ/ poodle

canicie *f* grayness• (*of hair*)

canijo -ja *adj*
A (fam) (pequeño) tiny, puny (hum *or* pej)
B (Méx fam) (terco) stubborn, pig-headed (colloq)
C (Méx fam) (intenso) incredible (colloq); **el hambre era canija** I (*o* he *etc*) was ravenous (colloq)

canilla *f*
A (espinilla) shinbone
B (RPl) (grifo) faucet (AmE), tap (BrE); **agua de la ~** tap water; **cerrar la ~** to turn off the faucet *o* tap
C (bobina) bobbin

canillera *f* (AmL) shin pad, shinguard

canillita *mf* (Bol, CS) newspaper vendor *o* seller

canino[1] **-na** *adj* (Zool) canine, dog (*before n*); **tengo un hambre canina** (fam) I'm ravenous (colloq)

canino[2] *m* 1 (Odont) canine, canine tooth 2 (Zool) canine; **los ~s** the canines

canje *m* exchange

canjeable *adj* exchangeable; **este cupón es ~ por un regalo** this coupon can be exchanged for a gift

canjear [A1] *vt* 1 ‹*prisioneros/rehenes*› to exchange 2 (Fin) to exchange, trade

cannabis *m* (planta) hemp; (droga) cannabis

cano -na *adj* white; **un hombre de pelo ~** a man with gray/white hair

canoa *f* canoe

canódromo *m* greyhound stadium, dog track (colloq)

canon *m*
A (norma) rule, canon (frml)
B (Mús) canon
C (Econ, Fisco) levy, tax

canónico -ca *adj* canonical, canonic

canónigo *m* (Relig) canon

canonización *f* canonization

canonizar [A4] *vt* to canonize

canoso -sa *adj* ‹*persona*› gray-haired•, white-haired; ‹*pelo/barba*› gray•, white

canotier /kano'tje(r)/, **canotié** *m* boater, straw hat

cansadamente *adv* (con cansancio) wearily; (con pesadez) tiresomely

cansado -da *adj*
A 1 [ESTAR] (fatigado) tired; **tienes cara de ~** you look tired; **en un tono ~** in a weary tone of voice; **tengo los pies ~s** my feet are tired 2 [ESTAR] (aburrido, harto) **~ DE algo/+ INF** tired OF sth/-ING; **estoy ~ de decírtelo** I'm tired of telling you; ***a las cansadas*** (RPl) at long last
B [SER] ‹*viaje/trabajo*› tiring

cansador -dora *adj* (AmS) tiring

cansancio *m* tiredness; **me caigo** *or* **me muero de ~** I'm absolutely worn out *o* exhausted; ***hasta el ~***: **lo repitió hasta el ~** she repeated it over and over again

cansar [A1] *vt* 1 (fatigar) to tire, tire … out, make … tired; **le cansa la vista** it makes her eyes tired, it strains her eyes 2 (aburrir, hartar): **¿no te cansa oír siempre la misma música?** don't you get tired of listening to the same music all the time?

■ **cansar** *vi* 1 (fatigar) to be tiring; **un trabajo que cansa mentalmente** a job which is mentally tiring 2 (aburrir, hartar) to get tiresome

■ **cansarse** *v pron* 1 (fatigarse) to tire oneself out; **se le cansa la vista** her eyes get tired 2 (aburrirse, hartarse) to get bored; **~se DE algo/algn** to get tired OF sth/sb, get bored WITH sth/sb, **~se DE + INF** to get tired OF -ING

cansera *f* (RPl fam): **¡qué ~ tengo!** I'm dead beat

cansino -na *adj* weary

cantábrico -ca *adj* Cantabrian

Cantábrico *m*: **el (mar) ~** the Bay of Biscay

cantaleta *f* ▸**cantinela**

cantamañanas *mf* (*pl* ~) (Esp fam & pey): **es un ~** he's all talk and no action (colloq)

cantante[1] *adj* singing (*before n*)

cantante[2] *mf* singer

cantaor -ora *m,f* flamenco singer

cantar[1] [A1] *vt*
A 1 ‹*canción*› to sing; ***cantárselas claras a algn*** (fam): **se las canté claras** I gave it to her *o* told her straight (colloq) 2 (en béisbol) to call
B (liter) (ensalzar) to sing the praises of, extol the virtues of; **el tan cantado mar** the oft-praised sea (liter)
C (RPl fam) (pedirse): **canto la cama de arriba** bags I *o* bags the top bunk (colloq)

■ **cantar** *vi*
A 1 (Mús) to sing; **habla cantando** she has a singsong voice 2 «*pájaro*» to sing; «*gallo*» to crow; «*cigarra/grillo*» to chirp, chirrup
B 1 (fam) (confesar) to talk (colloq) 2 (Jueg) to declare 3 (anunciar, pregonar): **las cifras cantan** the figures speak for themselves
C (Esp fam) (apestar) to stink (colloq)

cantar[2] *m* poem (*gen set to music*); ***¡eso es otro ~!*** that's another matter, that's a different kettle of fish

(Compuesto) **cantar de gesta** chanson de geste

cántara *f* churn

cantarín -rina (CS) **cantarino -na** *adj* ‹*voz/tono/risa*› singsong; ‹*fuente/aguas*› (liter) babbling; ‹*persona*›: **es muy**

cantarina she's always singing

cántaro *m* pitcher, jug; ***llover a ~s*** to pour with rain

cantata *f* cantata

cantautor -tora *m,f* singer-songwriter

cante *m*

A (Mús) Andalusian folk song; **~ flamenco** flamenco (singing); ***quedarse con el ~*** (fam) to see what is/was going on

(Compuesto) **cante jondo** *traditional style of flamenco singing*

B (Esp fam) (extravagancia): **dar el ~** (fam) to make an exhibition of oneself

cantegril *m* (Ur) shantytown

cantera *f*

A (de piedra) quarry

B (Esp) (de deportistas, profesionales) pool; **la ~ del club** the club's youth team

cantero *m* (RPl) flowerbed

cántico *m* canticle

cantidad¹ *adv* (esp Esp fam) ‹*comer*› a lot; **sabe ~** she/he knows a lot about everything; **me gustó el libro ~** I really liked the book

cantidad² *f* 1 (volumen) quantity 2 (suma de dinero) sum, amount 3 (número, volumen impresionante): **~ de** lots of; **una ~ de mosquitos impresionante** an incredible number of mosquitoes; **no te puedes imaginar la ~ de gente/de comida que había** you wouldn't believe how many people there were/how much food there was; **tiene amigos en ~** she has lots *o* loads of friends (colloq); **tenemos ~** *or* **~es** (fam) we have lots *o* tons (colloq); ***cualquier ~ de*** (AmS) lots of, loads of (colloq)

cantilena *f* ▸ **cantinela**

cantimplora *f* water bottle, canteen

cantina *f*

A 1 (cafetería — en estación) buffet, cafeteria; (— en universidad) refectory; (— en fábrica) canteen; (— en cuartel) mess 2 (AmL exc RPl) (bar) bar 3 (RPl) (restaurante italiano) trattoria

B (Col) (para la leche) churn

cantinela *f*: **siempre la misma ~** always the same old story (*o* thing *etc*)

cantinflada *f* (fam) babble, gibberish

cantinflear [A1] *vi* (fam) to babble, talk gibberish

cantito *m* (AmL) lilt

canto *m*

A (Mús) (acción, arte) singing; (canción) chant

B (de pájaro) song; (del gallo) crowing; **se levantó con el ~ del gallo** she got up at first light *o* (liter) at cockcrow

(Compuesto) **canto de** *or* **del cisne** swan song

C (Lit) (canción) hymn; (división) canto

D (borde, filo) edge; **colocó el ladrillo de ~** he lay the brick on its side; ***faltar el ~ de un duro*** (Esp): **faltó el ~ de un duro para que se le cayera** she came very close to dropping it

E (Geol) *tb* **~ rodado** (roca) boulder; (guijarro) pebble; ***darse con un ~ en los dientes*** (fam) to think *o* count oneself lucky

cantón *m* (de Suiza) canton

cantonal *adj* cantonal

cantonés -nesa *adj* Cantonese

cantor¹ -tora *adj* singing (*before n*); **pájaro ~** songbird

cantor² -tora *m,f* (cantante) singer

cantoral *m* choir book

canturrear [A1] *vi* to sing softly to oneself

■ **canturrear** *vt* to sing … softly to oneself

canturreo *m*: **oía su ~** I could hear him singing to himself

canuto¹ -ta *adj* (Chi fam & pey) protestant; ***pasarlas canutas*** (Esp fam) to have a terrible time

canuto² *m*

A (tubo) document tube

B (Esp arg) (de hachís) joint (colloq)

caña *f*

A 1 (planta) reed 2 (tallo — del bambú) cane; (— del trigo) stalk; **muebles de ~** cane furniture; ***darle*** *or* ***meterle ~ a algo*** (fam): **hay que darle ~ a este trabajo** we'll have to get a move on with this job; **¡dale ~!** get a move on!; (conduciendo) step on it!; ***darle ~ a algn*** (criticarlo) to have a go at sb (colloq); (meter prisa) to hurry sb up *o* along (colloq); ***echar*** *or* ***hablar ~*** (Col fam) (mentir) to tell lies; (charlar) to chat

(Compuesto) **caña dulce** *or* **de azúcar** sugar cane

B (de pescar) rod

C (de la bota) leg; **botas de media ~** calf-length boots

D 1 (vaso): **una ~ (de cerveza)** (Esp) a small (glass of) beer; **una ~ de vino blanco** (Chi, Esp) a tall glass of white wine; ***ir de ~s*** (Esp fam) to go for a few beers 2 (CS) (aguardiente) eau-de-vie (*made from sugar cane*)

E (de un hueso) shaft

cañabrava *f* (AmL) reed (*used in construction of houses*)

cañada *f* 1 (Geog) gully; (más profunda) ravine 2 (camino) cattle (*o* sheep *etc*) track 3 (AmL) (arroyo) stream

cañamazo *m* embroidery canvas

cáñamo *m* (planta) cannabis plant, hemp; (tela) canvas

cañaveral *m* (de juncos) reedbed; (de caña de azúcar) (Col) sugar-cane plantation

cañería *f* (tubo) pipe; (conjunto de tubos) piping, pipes (*pl*)

cañero¹ -ra *adj* (AmL) (Agr) sugarcane (*before n*)

cañero² -ra *m,f* (Agr) (propietario) sugar plantation owner; (trabajador) sugar plantation worker, cane cutter

cañizal *m* reedbed

caño *m* (conducto) pipe; (de una fuente) spout; (grifo) (Per) faucet (AmE), tap (BrE); **agua del ~** tap water

cañón *m*

A (Arm) (arma) cannon; (de una escopeta, pistola) barrel; ***ni a ~ rayado*** *or* ***ni a cañones*** (CS fam) no way (colloq); ***pasárselo ~*** (Esp fam) to have a great time *o* a ball (colloq)

(Compuestos)

- **cañón de agua** water cannon
- **cañón antiaéreo** anti-aircraft gun
- **cañón de proyección** data projector

B (valle) canyon; **el Gran C~ del Colorado** the Grand Canyon

C (de pluma) quill; (de la barba): **se le notan los cañoncitos de la barba** you can see the stubble on his chin

cañonazo *m*

A (Arm, Mil) cannonshot; **una salva de 21 ~s** a 21-gun salute

B (fam) (en fútbol) drive; (en béisbol) blast

cañonear [A1] *vt* 1 ‹*fortín/plaza*› to shell, bombard 2 (Méx) (encañonar) to point a gun at

cañoneo *m* shelling, bombardment

cañonera *f* gunboat

cañonero -ra *m,f* (AmL) (Dep) (fam) striker

caoba *f* 1 (árbol) mahogany tree; (madera) mahogany 2 **(de) color ~** mahogany

caobo *m* (AmL) mahogany tree

caolín *m* kaolin, china clay

caos *m* chaos; **será un verdadero ~** there'll be absolute chaos

caótico -ca *adj* chaotic; **la casa estaba en un estado ~** the house was in chaos

cap. *m* (= **capítulo**) ch., chapter

capa *f*

A 1 (revestimiento) layer; **una ~ de nieve** a layer *o* carpet *o* blanket of snow; **recubierto de una ~ de chocolate** covered in chocolate 2 (veta, estrato) layer; **dos ~s de verduras y una de pasta** two layers of vegetables and one of pasta; **papel higiénico de tres ~s** 3-ply toilet paper; **la ~ de ozono** the ozone layer; **lleva el pelo cortado en** *or* (Esp) **a ~s** she has layered hair 3 (de la población) sector; **las ~s altas/bajas de la sociedad** the upper/lower strata of society 4 (Geol) stratum

B 1 (Indum) cloak, cape; (para la lluvia) cape, rain cape; ***de ~ caída*** downcast, down (colloq); ***defender algo a ~ y espada*** to fight tooth and nail to defend sth; ***hacer de su ~ un sayo*** to do as one pleases 2 (Taur) cape

(Compuesto) **capa de agua** raincape

capacha *f* (Chi fam) slammer (sl), nick (BrE colloq)

capacho *m* (cesta) basket; ***llevar a algn a ~*** (Per) to carry sb on one's back

capacidad *f*

A 1 (competencia) ability; **una persona de gran ~** a person of great ability 2 (potencial) capacity; **~ DE algo** capacity

FOR sth: **su gran ~ de trabajo** her great capacity for work; **~ DE** *or* **PARA + INF** ability *o* capacity to + INF; **su ~ de entender** her ability to understand; **están en ~ de despachar más pasajeros** (Col) they have the capacity to handle more passengers **3** (Der) capacity

Compuestos
- **capacidad adquisitiva** purchasing power
- **capacidad de pago** creditworthiness
- **capacidad física** physical capacity

B (cupo) capacity; **la ~ del depósito es de unos 40 litros** the tank has a capacity of *o* holds about 40 liters; **el teatro tiene ~ para 8000 personas** the theatre has a capacity of *o* holds 8000 people

capacitación *f* training

capacitado -da *adj* **~ PARA algo/+ INF** qualified FOR sth/ to + INF

capacitador -dora *adj* (Chi) preparatory

capacitar [A1] *vt* **1** (formar) to prepare; **esa experiencia me capacitó para enfrentarme con el mundo** that experience prepared me to go out into the world **2** (profesionalmente) **~ a algn PARA algo** to qualify sb FOR sth; **~ a algn PARA + INF** to qualify *o* entitle sb to + INF

■ **capacitarse** *v pron* (formarse) to train; (obtener un título) to qualify, become qualified

capar [A1] *vt*

A (castrar) to castrate

B (Col fam) **~ clase** to play hooky (esp AmE colloq), to skive off (school) (BrE colloq)

caparazón *m or f* shell

capataz *mf*, **capataz -taza** *m,f* (*m*) foreman; (*f*) forewoman

capaz *adj*

A **1** (competente) capable, able **2** (Der) **~ PARA + INF** with the capacity to + INF

B (de una hazaña) capable; **lo creo muy ~** I think he's quite capable of it, I wouldn't put it past him; **~ DE algo** capable OF sth; **es ~ de grandes logros** he's capable of great things; **~ DE + INF**: **¿te sientes ~ de enfrentarte con ella?** do you feel able to face her *o* feel up to facing her?; **¿a qué no eres ~ de saltar esto?** I bet you can't jump over this; **es (muy) ~ de irse sin pagar** he's quite capable of leaving without paying

C (AmS fam) **~ que** (puede que, a lo mejor): **~ que llueve** it may rain; **~ que se olvidó** maybe *o* perhaps he forgot

capazo *m* (cesta) basket; (para un niño) portacrib® (AmE), carrycot (BrE)

capcioso -sa *adj* artful, cunning; **preguntas capciosas** trick questions

capea *f*: *amateur bullfight using young bulls*

capear [A1] *vt*

A (Taur) to make passes at (*with the cape*); **~ una crisis** to ride out *o* weather a crisis

B (Chi fam) ‹*trabajo*› to skip, to skive off (BrE colloq); **~ clase** to play hooky (esp AmE colloq), to skive off (school) (BrE colloq)

capellán *m* chaplain

Caperucita Roja Little Red Riding Hood

caperuza *f*

A (Indum) pointed hood

B (de un bolígrafo) top, cap

C (en cetrería) hood

capicúa¹ *adj* ‹*número*› palindromic (frml); **era un número ~** the number read the same both ways

capicúa² *m* palindromic number

capilar¹ *adj* **1** ‹*loción*› hair (*before n*) **2** ‹*vaso/tubo*› capillary (*before n*)

capilar² *m* capillary

capilla *f*

A (Relig) chapel; ***estar en ~*** to be on tenterhooks

Compuesto **capilla ardiente** funeral chapel

B (Impr) proof sheet, galley proof, galley

capirote *m* **1** (Indum) pointed hood; ***ser tonto de ~*** to be really dumb **2** (en cetrería) hood

capital¹ *adj* ‹*importancia*› cardinal, prime; ‹*influencia*› seminal (frml); ‹*obra*› key, seminal (frml); ‹*letra*› capital

capital² *m*

A (Com, Fin) capital

Compuesto; **capital fijo/social** fixed/share capital

B (recursos, riqueza) resources (*pl*)

capital³ *f* **1** (de país) capital; (de provincia) provincial capital, ≈ county seat (*in US*), ≈ county town (*in UK*); **Valencia ~** the city of Valencia **2** (centro) capital; **la ~ del vino** the wine capital

capitalino¹ -na *adj* (AmL): **es ~** he's from the capital; **las calles capitalinas** the streets of the capital

capitalino² -na *m,f* (AmL): inhabitant of the capital

capitalismo *m* capitalism

capitalista¹ *adj* capitalist (*before n*)

capitalista² *m,f* capitalist

capitalizar [A4] *vt*

A (Fin) **1** (incorporar al capital) ‹*ganancias*› to capitalize; ‹*intereses*› to reinvest **2** ‹*empresa*› to capitalize

B ‹*hecho/circunstancia*› to capitalize on

capitán¹ *m* **1** (del ejército) captain; (de la Fuerza Aérea) captain (AmE), flight lieutenant (BrE) **2** (Náut) (de transatlántico, carguero) captain, master; (de buque de pesca) skipper **3** (Aviac) captain

Compuestos
- **capitán de corbeta** lieutenant commander
- **capitán de fragata** lieutenant commander
- **capitán de navío** captain
- **capitán general** (del ejército) general of the Army (AmE), field marshal (BrE); (de la fuerza aérea) general of the Air Force (AmE), Marshal of the Royal Air Force (BrE)

capitán² -tana *m,f*

A (de equipo) captain

B **capitana** *f* (buque) flagship

capitana *f* flagship

capitanear [A1] *vt* ‹*soldados*› to command; ‹*transatlántico*› to captain; ‹*buque de pesca*› to skipper; ‹*expedición*› to lead; ‹*equipo*› to captain; ‹*banda*› to lead

capitanía *f* (cargo) captaincy; (edificio) headquarters

capitel *m* capital

capitolio *m* (acrópolis) acropolis; (edificio grande) large, majestic building; **el C~** the Capitol

capitonado -da *adj* (Col) padded

capitoste *m* (Esp fam & pey) (de una fábrica) big boss (colloq & hum); (de un partido) bigwig (colloq & pej)

capitulación *f* **1** (Mil) surrender, capitulation **2** **capitulaciones** *fpl* (Der) marriage contract

capitular [A1] *vi* to surrender, capitulate

capítulo *m* **1** (de libro) chapter; (de serie) episode; **eso es ~ aparte** that's another matter altogether **2** (Econ, Pol) (sector) area; **los fondos destinados al ~ de vivienda** funds earmarked for housing **3** (Relig) chapter; ***llamar a algn a ~*** to bring *o* call sb to account

capo -pa *m,f* (mandamás) boss, chief

capó *m* hood (AmE), bonnet (BrE)

capón¹ *adj* castrated

capón² *m*

A (gallo) capon

B (fam) (golpe) rap on the head

caporal *m* (Méx) foreman, charge hand (BrE)

capot /ka'po/ *m* hood (AmE), bonnet (BrE)

capota *f* (de automóvil) convertible top; (de cochecito de bebé) canopy, hood

capote *m*

A (capa) cloak; (de militar, torero) cape; ***echarle un ~ a algn*** (Esp fam) to give sb a hand (colloq)

B (Méx) (Auto) hood (AmE), bonnet (BrE)

capricho *m*

A (antojo) whim, caprice (liter); **le consienten todos los ~s** they indulge his every whim; **un ~ de la naturaleza** a quirk of nature; **los ~s de la moda** the caprices *o* whims of fashion; **se lo compró por puro ~** he bought it on a whim; **hace siempre su santo ~** (fam) she always does exactly what she wants; **a ~: los libros están colocados a ~** the books are arranged any which way (AmE) *o* (BrE) any old how; **entran y salen a ~** they come in and go out at will *o* as they please

B (Mús) capriccio

caprichoso¹ -sa *adj* **1** (inconstante) ‹*carácter/persona*› capricious; ‹*tiempo/moda*› changeable; **formas caprichosas** fanciful shapes **2** (difícil, exigente) fussy

caprichoso² **-sa** *m,f*: **es un ~** (es inconstante) he's always changing his mind; (es difícil, exigente) he's so fussy

Capricornio¹ *m* (signo, constelación) Capricorn; **es (de) ~** she's a Capricorn *o* Capricornean

Capricornio², **capricornio** *mf* (persona) Capricornean, Capricorn

cápsula *f*
A (Farm) capsule
B (Audio) cartridge
C (Espac) capsule

captación *f*
A (de recursos) raising; (de clientes) winning, gaining; (de miembros) recruitment
B (de aguas) collecting
C (Rad) picking up, reception

captar [A1] *vt*
A ‹*atención/interés*› to capture; ‹*clientes*› to win, gain; ‹*partidarios/empleados*› to attract, recruit
B ‹*sentido/matiz*› to grasp; ‹*significado/indirecta*› to get
C ‹*emisora/señal*› to pick up, receive
D ‹*aguas*› to collect, take in

captura *f* (de delincuente, enemigo, animal) capture; (de un alijo) seizure; (en pesca) catch

capturar [A1] *vt* ‹*delincuente, enemigo, animal*› to capture; ‹*alijo*› to seize, confiscate; ‹*peces*› to catch

capucha *f* hood

capuchino **-na** *m,f*
A (Relig) capuchin
B **capuchino** *m* (café) cappuccino

capuchón *m* (de pluma, bolígrafo) top, cap; (Indum) hood

capullo *m*
A (Bot) bud
B (Zool) cocoon

caput *adj* kaput

caqui *adj inv/m* khaki

cara *f*
A 1 (Anat) face; **las mismas ~s conocidas** the same old faces; **dímelo a la ~** say it to my face; **se le rió en la ~** she laughed in his face; **mírame a la ~** look at me; **no lo pienso mirar más a la ~** I don't ever want to set eyes on him again 2 (*en locs*) **cara a cara** face to face; **de cara**: **llevaban el viento de ~** they were running (*o* riding *etc*) into the wind; **el sol me da de ~** the sun is in my eyes; **de cara a**: **se puso de ~ a la pared** she turned to face the wall, she turned her face to the wall; **la campaña de ~ a las próximas elecciones** the campaign for the forthcoming elections; **las medidas a tomar (de) ~ a esta situación** the measures to take in view of *o* in the light of this situation; ***a ~ descubierta*** openly; ***cruzarle la ~ a algn*** to slap sb's face; ***dar*** *or* (Col) ***poner la ~***: **nunca da la ~** he never does his own dirty work; ***dar*** *or* ***sacar la ~ por algn*** to stand up for sb; ***echarle algo en ~ a algn*** to throw sth back in sb's face; ***echarle ~ a algo*** (Esp fam) to be bold; ***echarse algo a la cara*** (Esp fam): **es lo más antipático que te puedes echar/que me he echado a la ~** he's the most unpleasant person you could ever wish to meet/I've ever met (colloq); ***hacer ~ a algo*** to face (up to) sth; ***hacerle caritas a algn*** (Méx) to give sb the eye; ***me/le/nos volteó*** (AmL) *or* (Esp) ***volvió*** *or* (CS) ***dio vuelta la ~*** she turned her head away; ***partirle*** *or* ***romperle la ~ a algn*** (fam) to smash sb's face in (colloq); ***plantarle ~ a algn*** (resistir) to stand up to sb; ***por tu ~ bonita*** *or* (CS) ***tu linda ~***: **si crees que por tu ~ bonita vas a conseguirlo todo ...** if you think everything is just going to fall into your lap ...; ***se te/le debería caer la ~ de vergüenza*** you/he should be ashamed of yourself/himself; ***verse las ~s***: **ya nos veremos las ~s tú y yo** you haven't seen the last of me
B 1 (expresión): **no pongas esa ~ que no es para tanto** don't look like that, it's not that bad; **alegra esa ~** cheer up; **no pongas ~ de bueno** don't play *o* act the innocent; **puse ~ de circunstancias** I tried to look serious; **anda con ~ de pocos amigos** *or* (fam) **de vinagre** he has a sour look on his face; **poner ~ de perro** *or* **de sargento** (fam) to look fierce; **andaba con/puso ~ larga** (fam) he had/he pulled a long face; **puso mala ~** he pulled a face; **tiene ~ de cansado/de no haber dormido** he looks tired/as if he hasn't slept; **tienes mala ~** you don't look well 2 (aspecto) look; **¡qué buena ~ tiene la comida!** the food looks delicious!
C 1 (Mat) face 2 (de disco, papel) side; **salió ~** it came up heads; **~ o cruz** *or* (Arg) **ceca** *or* (Andes, Ven) **sello** heads or tails; **lo echaron a ~ o cruz** they tossed for it; ***la otra ~ de la moneda*** the other side of the coin 3 (de situación) face, side
D 1 (fam) (frescura, descaro) nerve (colloq), cheek (BrE colloq); **¡qué ~ (más dura) tienes!** you have some nerve!; **lo dijo con toda la ~ del mundo** he said it as cool as you like; **tiene más ~ que espalda** he has such a nerve! (colloq) 2 **cara** *mf*: *tb* **~ dura** (fam) (persona) sassy devil (AmE colloq), cheeky swine (BrE colloq)

carabela *f* caravel

carabina *f* 1 (Arm) carbine 2 (Esp fam) (acompañante): **ir/hacer de ~** to play gooseberry (colloq)

carabinero **-ra** *m,f*
A 1 (agente de policía) (*m*) police officer, policeman; (*f*) police officer, policewoman 2 (agente fronterizo) border guard 3 **carabineros** *mpl* (institución) police (force); (policía fronteriza) border police
B **carabinero** *m* (Coc, Zool) *large red prawn*

Caracas *m* Caracas

caracho *interj* (Col euf) shoot! (AmE euph), sugar! (BrE euph); **¡qué ~s!** what the heck! (colloq)

caracol *m*
A 1 (Zool) (de mar) winkle; (de tierra) snail 2 (AmL) (concha) conch
B (rizo) ringlet

caracola *f* conch

caracolada *f* snails (*pl*) (*cooked in sauce*)

caracolear [A1] *vi* (Equ) to caracole; «*camino/río*» (AmL) to twist, snake

caracoles *interj* (euf) gosh! (colloq & euph)

carácter *m* (*pl* **-racteres**)
A 1 (modo de ser, genio) character; **el ~ latino** the Latin character *o* temperament; **una persona de buen ~** a good-natured person; **un ~ abierto** an open nature; **tener mal ~** to have a (bad) temper 2 (firmeza) character; **tiene mucho/poco ~** she has a lot of/doesn't have much personality 3 (originalidad, estilo) character
B 1 (índole, naturaleza) nature; **una visita de ~ oficial/privado** a visit of an official/a private nature; **con ~ gratuito** free of charge; **con ~ retroactivo** retroactively; **heridas de ~ leve** (period) minor wounds; **le daba un ~ especial al cuadro** it lent the painting a special quality 2 (Biol) characteristic

(Compuesto) **carácter dominante/recessivo** dominant/recessive characteristic

C (Col, Méx) (personaje) character
D (Impr, Inf) character; **en caracteres de imprenta** in block letters; **escrito en caracteres cirílicos/góticos** written in the Cyrillic alphabet/Gothic script

(Compuesto) **carácter comodín** wildcard character

característica *f*
A (rasgo) feature, characteristic
B (Mat) characteristic
C (RPl) (Telec) exchange code

característico **-ca** *adj* characteristic

caracterización *f* 1 (descripción) description; **hizo una excelente ~ del acusado** she gave an excellent character sketch of the defendant 2 (Teatr) (por el actor) portrayal; (por el autor) characterization

caracterizar [A4] *vt*
A (distinguir, ser típico de) to characterize; **con la franqueza que lo caracteriza** with his characteristic frankness
B (describir) to portray, depict
C (Teatr) (encarnar) to play, portray
■ **caracterizarse** *v pron*: **~se POR algo** «*enfermedad/región/raza*» to be characterized BY sth; «*persona*» to be noted FOR sth; **el discurso se caracterizó por un tono del firmeza** the speech was notable for its frank tone

caradura¹ *adj* (fam) sassy (AmE colloq), cheeky (BrE colloq)

caradura² *mf*
A (fam) ▸ **cara D2**
B **caradura** *f* (fam) ▸ **cara D1**

carajal *m* (Méx): **un ~ de** (vulg) a hell of a lot of (colloq)

carajillo *m* (café) *coffee with brandy or similar*

carajito¹ **-ta** *adj* (Ven fam) young

carajito² **-ta** *m,f* (Ven fam) (niño) kid (colloq)

C

carajo[1] *m* 1 (uso expletivo) (vulg *o* fam): **no entiendo ni un ~** I don't understand a damn thing (colloq); **hace un frío del ~** it's goddamn (AmE) *o* (BrE) bloody freezing (sl) ; **¿que le pida yo disculpas? ¡un ~!** me apologize to him? like hell I will! (colloq); ***al ~***: **mis planes se han ido al ~** my plans have gone to pot (colloq); **la empresa se fue al ~** the company went bust (colloq); **¡vete al ~!** piss off! (vulg), fuck off! (vulg); **mandó todo al ~** he chucked it all in 2 (expresando sorpresa) (fam *o* vulg) jeez (AmE colloq), bloody hell (BrE sl) 3 (expresando enojo, mal humor) (fam *o* vulg): **¡vámonos ya, ~!** for heaven's sake, come on! (colloq); **ya te dije que no voy ¡qué ~!** I've already told you I'm not going, damn it! (colloq); **~ con el niño** that goddam (AmE) *or* (BrE) bloody kid! (sl); **¿qué/quién/dónde ~...?** what/who/where the hell...? (colloq); **¡que exámen ni que ~! tú te vienes conmigo** to hell with the exam (colloq) *o* (sl) screw the exam, you're coming with me!

carajo[2] **-ja** *m,f* (Ven arg) (muchacho) (*m*) guy (colloq); (*f*) girl (colloq)

caramanchel *m* (AmC fam) stall

caramba *interj* (expresando — sorpresa) good heavens!; (— disgusto) dammit! (colloq)

carámbano *m* icicle

carambola *f* 1 (en billar) carom (AmE), cannon (BrE) 2 (fam) (casualidad): **fue de ~** it was pure chance 3 (Méx) (choque múltiple) pileup

carameleo *m* (Col fam): **ya basta de ~** stop beating about the bush

caramelizar [A4] *vt* to coat ... in caramel

caramelo *m* 1 (golosina) candy (AmE), sweet (BrE); **un ~ de menta** a mint 2 (azúcar fundida) caramel 3 **(de) color ~** caramel-colored*, caramel

carantoña *f* caress; **deja de hacerme ~s** stop trying to butter me up (colloq)

caraota *f* (Ven) bean

carapacho *m* shell, carapace

carapálida *mf* (AmL) paleface

carapintada *adj/mf* (AmL) ▸**golpista** [1,2]

caraqueño -ña *adj* of/from Caracas

carátula *f*

A 1 (página) title page 2 (de disco) jacket (AmE), sleeve (BrE); (de video) case

B (Méx) (de reloj) face, dial

C (máscara) mask

caravana *f*

A 1 (de tráfico — retención) backup (AmE) tailback (BrE); (— hilera) convoy; **había una gran ~ a la entrada de la ciudad** there was a huge backup (AmE) *o* (BrE) tailback on the approach to the city; **ir en ~** to drive in (a) convoy 2 (remolque) trailer (AmE), caravan (BrE)

B (Méx) (reverencia) bow; ***hacer ~ con sombrero ajeno*** (fam) to claim credit for sb else's achievements

caravaning /kara'βanɪn/ *m* (Esp) trailering (AmE), caravanning (BrE)

caray *interj* good heavens!

carbón *m*

A (Min) *tb* **~ mineral** *or* **de piedra** coal; ***negro como el ~*** as black as coal

B 1 *tb* **~ vegetal** *or* **de leña** charcoal 2 (Art) charcoal; **un retrato al ~** a portrait drawn in charcoal

carbonato *m* carbonate

carboncillo *m* charcoal; **dibujo al ~** charcoal drawing

carbonera *f* (habitación) coal cellar; (depósito) coal bunker; (mina) (Col) coalmine

carbonería *f* coalyard

carbonero[1] **-ra** *adj* coal (*before n*)

carbonero[2] *m* (vendedor) coal merchant; (barco) collier

carbónico -ca *adj* (Quím) carbonic

carbonífero -ra *adj* ‹*estrato*› carboniferous; ‹*producción/yacimiento*› coal (*before n*)

carbonilla *f* 1 (polvo de carbón) cinders (*pl*) 2 (RPl) (Art) charcoal

carbonizar [A4] *vt* to carbonize

■ **carbonizarse** *v pron* 1 «*edificio/muebles*» to be reduced to ashes; **los cuerpos carbonizados de las víctimas** the victims' charred remains; **el asado se me carbonizó** (fam) the roast got burned to a cinder 2 (Quím) to carbonize

carbono *m* carbon

carbonoso -sa *adj* carbonaceous

carbunclo, carbunco *m* anthrax

carburador *m* carburetor*

carburante *m* fuel

carburar [A1] *vi*

A «*motor*» to carburet

B (fam) (funcionar) «*electrodoméstico/coche*» to work; «*persona*» (Esp): **hoy no carburas ¿eh?** you're not with it today, are you?

■ **carburar** *vt* (Andes) ‹*motor*› to tune

carburo *m* carbide

carca[1] *adj* (fam) old-fashioned, fuddy-duddy (colloq)

carca[2] *mf* (fam) old fogey (colloq)

carcacha *f* (Andes, Méx fam) (auto viejo) wreck (colloq), old heap (colloq); (otro aparato) contraption (colloq)

carcaj *m* quiver

carcajada *f* guffaw; **soltar una ~** to burst out laughing; **reírse a ~s** to roar with laughter

carcajeante *adj* ‹*risa*› loud, guffawing (*before n*)

carcajearse [A1] *v pron* (fam) to roar with laughter

carcamal[1], (Méx, RPl) **carcamán -mana** *adj* (fam & pey) decrepit

carcamal[2], (Méx, RPl) **carcamán** *m* (fam & pey) (hombre) old crock (colloq & pej); (mujer) old hag (colloq & pej)

carcasa *f* 1 (armazón, estructura) frame; (de aparato) casing; **la ~ de un barco abandonado** the hulk of an abandoned ship 2 (esqueleto de animal) skeleton

cárcel *f* (prisión) prison, jail; **fue condenado a cinco años de ~** he was sentenced to five years imprisonment; **la metieron en la ~** she was put in prison

carcelario -ria *adj* prison (*before n*)

carcelero -ra *m,f* jailer

carcinoma *m* carcinoma

carcoma *f* 1 (Zool) woodworm 2 (preocupación, ansiedad) anxiety

carcomer [E1] *vt* 1 «*carcoma*» to eat away (at); **el marco está totalmente carcomido** the frame is completely worm-eaten 2 ‹*salud*› to undermine; **los celos/la envidia le carcomían** he was eaten up *o* consumed with jealousy/envy; **es una duda que me carcome** it is something that constantly preys on my mind; **un vicio que carcome las bases de nuestra sociedad** a vice which eats away at the fabric of our society

cardamomo *m* cardamom

cardar [A1] *vt* 1 ‹*lana*› to card; *ver tb* **lana** 2 ‹*pelo*› to backcomb, tease

■ **cardarse** *v pron* (*refl*) to backcomb

cardenal *m*

A (Relig) cardinal

B (fam) (moretón) bruise

cardenalicio -cia *adj* of/or relating to a cardinal

cardíaco[1], **cardiaco -ca** *adj* heart (*before n*), cardiac (tech)

cardíaco[2], **cardiaco -ca** *m,f* heart patient; **los ~s** heart patients, people with a heart condition; **es una película no apta para ~s** (hum) it's not a movie for the fainthearted

cárdigan *m* (*pl* **-gans**) cardigan

cardinal *adj* cardinal

cardiograma *m* cardiogram

cardiología *f* cardiology

cardiológico -ca *adj* cardiological

cardiólogo -ga *m,f* cardiologist

cardiovascular *adj* cardiovascular

cardo *m* (Bot) thistle

(Compuesto) **cardo borriquero** (Esp fam) cotton thistle; ***ser un ~ borriquero*** (ser antipático) to be a prickly character (colloq); (ser feo) to be as ugly as sin

carear [A1] *vt* to bring ... face to face

carecer [E3] *vi* (frml) **~ DE algo** to lack sth; **carece de interés** it is lacking in interest, it lacks interest; **carece de valor** it has no value, it is worthless; **sus palabras carecen de todo sentido** her words make no sense

carencia *f* 1 (escasez) lack, shortage; **~ de recursos financieros** lack of financial resources 2 (Med) deficiency; **~ de vitamina A** vitamin A deficiency

carente *adj* (frml): **una respuesta ~ de todo sentido** a completely nonsensical reply; **son lugares ~s de interés** they are places which are of no interest

careo *m* confrontation (*in court*)

carero[1] **-ra** *adj* (fam) ‹*comerciante*› pricey (colloq); **en esa tienda son muy ~s** that shop's very pricey

carero[2] **-ra** *m,f* rip-off artist (AmE colloq), rip-off merchant (BrE colloq)

carestía *f* 1 (costo elevado) high cost; **la ~ de la vida** the high cost of living 2 (escasez) dearth, scarcity; **un periodo de ~** a period of shortage

careta *f* mask; ***quitarle la ~ a algn*** to unmask sb

carey *m* (Zool) hawksbill turtle; (material) tortoiseshell

carga *f*

A 1 (Transp) (de barco) cargo; (de camión) load; (de tren) freight; **Ⓢ zona de carga y descarga** loading and unloading only 2 (peso) load; **Ⓢ carga máxima: ocho personas, 550 kilos** maximum load: eight people, 550 kilos; **no lleves tanta ~** don't carry such a heavy load

(Compuesto) **carga útil** payload

B 1 (de escopeta, cañón) charge; **una ~ explosiva** an explosive charge 2 (de bolígrafo, pluma) refill; **al encendedor se le está acabando la ~** the lighter is running out of fuel 3 (de lavadora) load 4 (de reactor) charge

(Compuesto) **carga de profundidad** depth charge

C (Elec) (de cuerpo) charge; (de circuito) load; **un discurso con una enorme ~ emocional** a highly emotional speech

D (responsabilidad) burden; **es una ~ para la familia** he is a burden to his family; **lleva una gran ~ sobre los hombros** he carries a great deal of responsibility on his shoulders

(Compuesto) **carga familiar** dependent relatives (*pl*)

E (Der, Fin) charge; **libre de ~s** not subject to any charges

(Compuesto) **carga impositiva** *or* **fiscal** *or* **tributaria** tax burden

F 1 (de tropas, policía) charge; **¡a la ~!** charge!; ***volver a la ~*** to return to the attack 2 (Dep) *tb* **~ defensiva** blitz

cargada *f*

A (RPl fam) practical joke

B (Pol) (en Méx) 1 (apoyo) *unconditional support for a political candidate* 2 (grupo): ***ir*** *or* ***irse a la ~*** (Méx) *to voice support for a candidate*

cargaderas *fpl* (Col) suspenders (*pl*) (AmE), braces (*pl*) (BrE)

cargadero *m* loading bay

cargado -da *adj*

A 1 (que lleva peso): **iba muy cargada** she was loaded down *o* laden (with parcels/shopping); **~ DE algo**: **vino ~ de regalos** he arrived loaded down with presents; **mujeres cargadas de hijos** women weighed down by children; **~ de deudas** heavily in debt; **un ciruelo ~ de fruta** a plum tree laden with fruit 2 ‹*ambiente/atmósfera*› (pesado, bochornoso) heavy, close; (con humo, olores desagradables) stuffy; (tenso) strained, tense; **una atmósfera cargada de humo/tensión** a very smoky/tense atmosphere 3 ‹*dados*› loaded 4 ‹*café*› strong; ‹*combinado*› strong, with plenty of rum (*or* gin, *etc*)

B **~ de hombros** *or* **de espaldas** with bowed shoulders

cargador -dora *m,f*

A 1 (de camiones) loader 2 (de barcos) (*m*) longshoreman (AmE), docker (BrE); (*f*) longshorewoman (AmE), docker (BrE) 3 (de aviones) baggage handler

B **cargador** *m* 1 (Arm) clip, magazine 2 (de pilas, baterías) battery charger

C **cargadores** *mpl* (Col) ▸**cargaderas**

cargamento *m* 1 (de camión) load; (de barco, avión) cargo; **llegó el segundo ~** the second shipment arrived 2 (cantidad enorme) load; **compró un ~ de comida** he bought loads of food

cargante *adj* 1 (CS fam) (antipático) unpleasant, horrible (colloq) 2 (Esp fam) ▸**cargoso**

cargar [A3] *vt*

A 1 ‹*barco/avión/camión*› to load 2 ‹*pistola/escopeta*› to load; ‹*pluma/encendedor*› to fill; ‹*cámara*› to load, put a film in; **cargué la estufa de leña** I filled the stove with wood; **no cargues tanto ese baúl** don't put so much into that trunk 3 (Elec) to charge

B 1 ‹*mercancías*› to load 2 ‹*combustible*› to fuel; **el avión hizo escala para ~ combustible** the plane stopped to refuel; **tengo que ~ nafta** (RPl) I have to fill up with gasoline (AmE) *o* (BrE) petrol 3 (Inf) ‹*programa/aplicación*› to load; (subir) to upload

C 1 (de obligaciones) **~ a algn DE algo** to burden sb WITH sth 2 ‹*culpa*› (+ *me/te/le etc*): **me ~on la culpa** they put *o* laid the blame on me

D (llevar) 1 ‹*paquetes/bolsas*› to carry; ‹*niño*› (AmL) to carry 2 (AmL exc RPl) ‹*armas*› to carry 3 (Ven fam) (llevar puesto) to wear; (tener consigo): **cargo las llaves** I have the keys

E (a una cuenta) to charge; **me lo ~on en cuenta** *or* **lo ~on a mi cuenta** they charged it to my account

F 1 (Esp fam) «*profesor*» to fail, flunk (AmE colloq) 2 (Méx fam) (matar) to kill

■ **cargar** *vi*

A 1 (con un bulto) **~ CON algo** to carry sth 2 (con responsabilidad) **~ CON algo**: **tiene que ~ con todo el peso de la casa** she has to shoulder all the responsibility for the household; **acabó cargando con la culpa** he ended up taking the blame

B «*tropas/policía*» to charge; **~ CONTRA algn** to charge AT sb

C «*batería*» to charge

D (fam) (+ *me/te/le etc*) (fastidiar): **me cargan los fanfarrones** I can't stand show-offs

cargarse *v pron*

A 1 «*pilas/flash*» to charge; «*partícula*» to become charged 2 (de peso, obligaciones) **~se DE algo**: **no te cargues de equipaje** don't take too much luggage; **~se de responsabilidades** to take on a lot of responsibilities; **se cargó de deudas** he saddled himself with debts; **ya se ha cargado de hijos** she's had too many children

B 1 (fam) (matar) to kill 2 (Esp fam) (romper, estropear) ‹*motor*› to wreck, ‹*jarrón*› to smash; ***cargársela(s)*** (fam): **te la vas a ~** you'll be in trouble (colloq) 3 (*enf*) (Esp fam) (suspender) «*profesor*» to fail, flunk (AmE colloq)

cargazón *f* (fam) heaviness

cargo *m*

A (puesto) post, position (frml); **un ~ de mucha responsabilidad** a very responsible job *o* post

(Compuesto) **cargo público**: **tener un ~ ~** to hold public office; **los que ostentan ~s ~s** those who hold public office

B (responsabilidad, cuidado) 1 **a cargo de algn**: **los niños están a mi ~** the children are in my care *o* (frml) charge; **el negocio quedó a su ~** he was left in charge of the business; **dejé/puse las ventas a ~ de Luque** I left/put Luque in charge of sales; **tiene cuatro hijos a su ~** *or* (Col) **a ~** he has four children to support; **tiene a su ~ la división comercial** she is responsible for *o* in charge of the sales department 2 **al cargo de algo** in charge of sth 3 **correr a ~ de algn**: **los gastos corren a ~ de la empresa** expenses will be paid *o* met by the company; **la organización del concierto corre a mi ~** I'm responsible for organizing the concert 4 **hacerse ~ de algo** (hacerse responsable) ‹*de puesto/tarea*› to take charge of sth; ‹*de gastos*› to take care of sth; (comprender) (Esp) to undertand sth, to appreciate sth

(Compuesto) **cargo de conciencia**: **no tengo ningún ~ de ~** my conscience is clear; **me da/quedó un ~ de ~ horrible** I feel/felt terribly guilty

C (Com, Fin) charge; **sin ~ adicional** at no additional cost; **sin ~** free of charge; **con ~ a mi cuenta** to be debited against *o* charged to my account

D (Der) charge

E (Chi, Per) *date-and-time stamp for documents*

cargosear [A1] *vt* (CS, Per fam) to pester (colloq)

cargoso -sa *adj* (CS, Per fam) annoying

cargue *m* (Col, Ven) loading; **Ⓢ zona de cargue y descargue** loading and unloading only

carguero[1] **-ra** *adj* cargo (*before n*)

carguero[2] *m* freighter, cargo ship *o* vessel

cariacontecido -da *adj* (fam) down in the mouth (colloq)

cariátide *f* caryatid

Caribe *m* 1 **el (mar)** ~ the Caribbean (Sea) 2 (región): **el ~** the Caribbean
caribeño¹ -ña *adj* Caribbean
caribeño² -ña *m,f: person from the Caribbean region*
caribú *m* caribou
caricatura *f* (dibujo) caricature
caricaturesco -ca *adj*: **sus personajes son ~s** his characters are like caricatures; **tiene rasgos ~s** he has very exaggerated features
caricaturista *mf* caricaturist
caricaturización *f* caricature; **hacer una ~ de algo** to caricature sth
caricaturizar [A4] *vt* to caricature
caricia *f* caress; **le hizo una ~ al perro** she stroked the dog
caridad *f* charity; **vivía de la ~** she lived on charity; **¡qué falta de ~!** how uncharitable!; **por ~** for pity's sake
caries *f* (*pl* ~) 1 (proceso) tooth decay, caries (*pl*) (tech); **la ~ dental** tooth decay 2 (cavidad) cavity; **tengo tres ~** I have three cavities
carilla *f* side
carillón *m* (de campanas) carillon; (instrumento) glockenspiel
cariño *m* 1 (afecto) affection; **niños sedientos de ~** children starved of affection; **fue la única persona que me dio ~** she was the only person who showed me any affection; **le tengo mucho ~ a este anillo** I'm very fond of this ring; **siento muchísimo ~ por ella** I have a great affection *o* fondness for her, I am very fond of her; **te ha tomado mucho ~** he's become very fond of you; **trátame el coche con ~** take good care of my car; **~s por tu casa/a tu mujer** (AmL) (send my) love to your family/your wife; **~s, Beatriz** (en cartas) (AmL) love, Beatriz; ***como sea su ~*** (Chi fam) whatever you can spare 2 (caricia): **le hice un cariñito al niño** I gave the little boy a cuddle (*o* kiss *etc*); **la pareja se hacía ~** (AmL) the couple were having a little cuddle (*o* a hug and a kiss *etc*) 3 (como apelativo) dear, honey, love (BrE); **no llores ~** don't cry, dear
cariñoso -sa *adj* ‹*persona*› affectionate; ‹*bienvenida*› warm; **un ~ saludo de mi parte** regards
carioca *adj* of/from Rio de Janeiro
carisma *m* charisma
carismático -ca *adj* charismatic
caritativo -va *adj* charitable; **es muy ~** he's very generous; **una organización con fines ~s** a charitable organization
cariz *m*: **no me gusta el ~ que están tomando las cosas** I don't like the way things are going *o* developing; **la situación está tomando mal ~** the situation is beginning to look bad
carlinga *f* (Aviac) cockpit
carmelita *adj/mf* Carmelite
carmelito *m* (Col) brown
carmesí *adj inv* crimson
carmín¹ *adj inv* carmine
carmín² *m* (para labios) lipstick; (color) carmine
carminativo -va *adj* carminative
carnada *f* bait
carnal¹ *adj* ‹*amor/deseo*› carnal
carnal² *m* (Méx arg) buddy (AmE colloq), mate (BrE colloq)
carnaval *m* (Relig) Shrovetide; (fiesta) carnival; **deberías ir en C~** you should go at carnival time

> **Carnaval**
>
> The three days of festivities preceding Lent, characterized by costumes, masks, drinking, music, and dancing. Spain's most colorful carnival is in Santa Cruz, Tenerife, and Cadiz's carnival is also famous. In Spanish-speaking Latin America, the carnivals of Uruguay, Bolivia, and Venezuela are very well known

carnavalesco -ca *adj* carnival (*before n*)
carnaza *f* 1 (Coc) *low grade meat* 2 (carnada) bait
carne *f*
A 1 (de mamífero, ave) meat; (de pescado) flesh; ***echar*** *or* ***poner toda la ~ en el asador*** to put all one's eggs in one basket; ***no ser ni ~ ni pescado*** to be neither fish nor fowl 2 (de fruta) flesh

Compuestos
- **carne blanca** white meat
- **carne de cerdo** *or* (Chi, Per) **chancho** *or* (Ven) **cochino** pork
- **carne de cordero** lamb
- **carne de ternera** veal
- **carne de vaca** *or* (AmC, Col, Méx, Ven) **res** beef
- **carne de venado** venison
- **carne mechada** (con tocino) larded meat; (en hilachas) (Ven) shredded meat
- **carne molida** *or* (Esp, RPl) **picada** ground beef (AmE), mince (BrE)

B 1 (de una persona) flesh; **es ~ de mi ~** he's my flesh and blood; ***de ~ y hueso***: **¿crees que no sufro? yo también soy de ~ y hueso** do you think I don't suffer? I have feelings too; ***en ~ propia***: **lo he vivido/sufrido en ~ propia** I've been through it/suffered it myself; ***en ~ viva***: **tenía la herida en ~ viva** her wound was raw; ***en ~ y hueso*** in the flesh 2 **carnes** *fpl* (gordura): **de ~s abundantes** of ample proportions (euph); **de pocas ~s** skinny; ***echar ~s*** to put on *or* gain weight; ***entrado*** *or* ***metido en ~s*** fat 3 **(de) color ~** flesh-colored* 4 (Relig) (cuerpo) flesh; **la ~ es débil** the flesh is weak

Compuestos
- **carne de cañón** cannon fodder
- **carne de gallina** gooseflesh, goose pimples (*pl*); **sólo pensarlo me pone la ~ de ~** it gives me goose pimples just to think about it (colloq)

carné *m* identity card; **sacar/renovar el ~** to have one's identity (*o* membership *etc*) card issued/renewed

Compuestos
- **carné de conducir** driver's license (AmE), driving licence (BrE)
- **carné de estudiante** student card
- **carné de identidad** identity card
- **carné de socio** (de club, mutual) membership card; (de biblioteca) library card
- **carné escolar** (Chi) bus/train pass

> **carné de identidad**
>
> Identity card that all residents over a certain age in Spain and Latin America must carry at all times. Holders must quote their identity card number on most official forms. In Latin America the card is also known as the *cédula de identidad*, and in Spain as the *DNI* (*Documento Nacional de Identidad*)

carnear [A1] *vt* (CS) to slaughter
■ **carnear** *vi* (CS) to slaughter a cow (*o* lamb *etc*)
carnecería *f* butcher's shop (*o* stall *etc*)
cárneo -nea *adj* (CS) meat (*before n*)
carnero *m* ram
carnet /kar'ne/ *m* (*pl* **-nets**) ▸**carné**
carnicería *f* 1 (tienda) butcher's shop (*o* stall *etc*) 2 (fam) (matanza, destrozo) slaughter
carnicero¹ -ra *adj* carnivorous
carnicero² -ra *m,f* 1 (vendedor) butcher 2 (fam & pey) (cirujano) butcher (colloq & pej)
cárnico -ca *adj* meat (*before n*)
carnitas *fpl* (Méx) pieces of barbecued pork (*pl*)
carnívoro¹ -ra *adj* carnivorous, meat-eating
carnívoro² *m* carnivore
carnoso -sa *adj* ‹*fruta*› fleshy; ‹*pollo*› meaty
caro¹ -ra *adj*
A 1 ‹*coche/entrada/ciudad*› expensive; **nos salió carísimo** it cost us a small fortune; **la vida está muy cara** everything costs so much *o* things are so expensive nowadays 2 (*como adv*): **pagarás ~ tu error** you'll pay dearly for your mistake; **esa actitud le costó caro** his attitude cost him dear; **venden sus tapices carísimos** they sell their tapestries at very high prices; **me costó muy ~** I had to pay a lot of money for it
B (liter) (querido) dear
caro² *adv* ‹*comprar/vender*›: **en esa tienda venden muy ~** they charge a lot in that store; *ver tb* **caro¹ A2**
carón -rona *adj* (AmL fam): **es muy carona** she has a very big face
carota *adj/mf* (Esp fam) ▸**caradura¹,²**
carótida *f* (carotid) artery

carpa *f*
A 1 (de circo) big top; (para actuaciones) marquee 2 (AmL) (para acampar) tent
B (Zool) carp

carpeta *f* (para documentos, dibujos) folder; ***cerrar la ~*** to close the file; ***tener algo en ~*** to have sth under consideration
Compuesto **carpeta de anillos** *or* (Esp) **anillas** *or* (RPl) **ganchos** ring binder

carpetazo *m*: **dieron ~ al incidente** they closed the file on the incident; **han dado ~ al plan** they've shelved the project

carpintería *f* 1 (taller) carpenter's workshop, joiner's workshop; (actividad) carpentry, joinery 2 (de construcción, casa) woodwork
Compuesto **carpintería metálica** metalwork

carpintero -ra *m,f* carpenter, joiner

carraca *f*
A (matraca) rattle
B (fam) (trasto, cacharro) wreck (colloq))

carraspear [A1] *vi* to clear one's throat

carraspera *f*: **tener ~** to have a rough throat

carrasposo -sa *adj* 1 ‹*garganta*› rough 2 (Col) ‹*superficie*› rough

carrera *f*
A (Dep) (competición) race; **~ de caballos** horse race; **las ~s** the races; **la ~ de los 100 metros vallas** the 100 meters hurdles; **te echo** *or* (RPl) **te juego una ~** I'll race you
Compuestos
- **carrera armamentista** *or* **-tiśtica** arms race
- **carrera contra reloj** (Dep) time trial; **una ~ ~ ~ para salvar el monumento** a race against time to save the monument
- **carrera de armamentos** arms race
- **carrera de fondo** long-distance race
- **carrera de obstáculos** steeplechase; (para niños) obstacle race
- **carrera de postas** *or* **de relevos** relay race
- **carrera de sacos** *or* (Col) **de costales** *or* (RPl) **de embolsados** *or* (Chi) **de ensacados** sack race
- **carrera espacial** space race

B 1 (fam) (corrida): **tendremos que echar una ~ si queremos alcanzar el tren** we'll have to run if we want to catch the train (colloq); **darse** *or* **pegarse una ~** to run as fast as one can; **me fui de una ~ a su casa** I tore *o* raced *o* rushed round to her house (colloq); ***a la(s) ~(s)*: siempre anda a la(s) ~(s)** she's always in a hurry *o* rush; **hice la última parte a la(s) ~(s)** I really rushed through the last part 2 (Esp fam): **hacer la ~** to turn tricks (AmE sl), to be on the game (BrE sl)
C 1 (Educ) degree course; **seguir** *or* **hacer una ~ universitaria** to do a degree course, to study for a degree; **está haciendo la ~ de Derecho** he's doing a degree in law; **tiene la ~ de Física(s)** she has a degree in physics; **dejó la ~ a medias** he dropped out halfway through college (AmE) *o* (BrE) university; **les dieron (una) ~ a sus hijos** they put their children through college (AmE) *o* (BrE) university 2 (profesión, trayectoria) career; **es una mujer de ~** she's a career woman; **un diplomático/militar de ~** a career diplomat/officer; **hizo su ~ en el cuerpo diplomático** he pursued a career in the diplomatic corps; ***hacer ~*** to carve out a career; ***no poder hacer ~ de*** *or* ***con algn***: **no puedo hacer ~ de este hijo mío** I can't do a thing with this son of mine
Compuesto **carrera media/superior** *three-year/five-year university course*
D (recorrido) 1 (de taxi) ride, journey 2 (AmL) (en baloncesto): **hacer ~** to travel
Compuesto **carrera ascendente/descendente** upstroke/downstroke
E (en la media) run, ladder (BrE); (en el pelo) (Col, Ven) part (AmE), parting (BrE)
F (en nombres de calles) street

carrerear [A1] *vt* (Méx fam) to push (colloq)

carrerilla *f*: **se lo saben de ~** they know it (off) by heart; **me lo dijo de ~** he reeled it off parrot-fashion; ***coger ~*** (Esp) to take a run-up

carreta *f*
A (con toldo) wagon; (sin toldo) cart
B (CS fam) (persona lenta) slowpoke (AmE), slowcoach (BrE); (vehículo lento): **ese tren es una ~** that train is very slow
C (Col fam) 1 (cháchara): **¿cuál es la ~?** what are you talking about? 2 (mentira): **es pura ~** it's all lies

carretada *f* wagonload, cartload

carrete *m* (de hilo, cinta) spool, reel (BrE); (de película) roll of film, film; (de caña de pescar) reel; ***darle ~ a algn*** (fam) to engage sb in conversation

carretear [A1] *vi* (AmL) (Aviac) to taxi
■ **carretear** *vt* (Chi) (llevar en auto) to take (*by car*); **¿me podrías ~ hasta el centro?** can you give me a lift *o* take me to the centre?

carretela *f* (Chi) cart

carretera *f* road; **~ de acceso** access road; **la ~ de Burgos** the Burgos road; **fuimos por ~** we went by road
Compuestos
- **carretera comarcal** secondary road, ≈ B-road (*in UK*)
- **carretera de circunvalación** *or* (Col) **carretera circunvalar** bypass, beltway (AmE), ring road (BrE)
- **carretera de doble calzada** divided highway (AmE), dual carriageway (BrE)
- **carretera general** main road
- **carretera nacional** ≈ highway (*in US*), ≈ A-road (*in UK*)

carretero -ra *m,f* cart driver; ***fumar como un ~*** (fam) to smoke like a chimney

carretilla *f*
A (de mano) wheelbarrow; ***de ~*** (Esp) *ver* **carrerilla**; ***hacer la ~*** to do a wheelbarrow
B (CS) (quijada) jaw, jawbone

carricito -ta *m,f* (Ven fam) kiddie (colloq)

carricoche *m* covered wagon

carriel *m* (Col) *rawhide shoulder bag*

carril *m* 1 (Auto) (de tránsito) lane; **conducir por el ~ de la derecha** to drive on the right *o* the right-hand side of the road 2 (Ferr) rail 3 (AmL) (Dep) lane
Compuestos
- **carril bus** bus lane
- **carril de adelantamiento** overtaking lane, fast lane
- **carril de bicicletas** cycleway, cycle path

carril-bici *m* (Esp) cycle lane

carrilera *f* (Col) track

carrillo *m* cheek; ***comer a dos*** *or* ***cuatro ~s*** (fam) to stuff oneself (colloq)

carriola *f* (Méx) baby carriage (AmE), baby buggy (BrE)

carrito *m* 1 (para el equipaje) trolley; (en supermercado) shopping cart (AmE), trolley (BrE); (de la compra) shopping trolley *o* (AmE) cart 2 (mesita de servir) trolley 3 (fam) (para la venta ambulante) van
Compuesto **carrito chocón** (Méx) bumper car

carrizo *m*
A (Bot) giant reed
B (Ven fam) (nada): **no sabe un ~** he hasn't a clue (colloq); **¿qué hiciste ayer? — un ~** what did you do yesterday? — not a lot; ***del ~*** (Ven fam): **esta muchacha del ~** this darned girl; ***más ... que el ~*** (Ven fam): **es más sucia que el ~** she's so filthy! (colloq)

carro *m*
A 1 (carreta) cart; **un ~ de tierra** a cartload of earth; ***aguantar ~s y carretas*** to put up with anything; ***¡para el ~!*** (fam) cool it! (colloq), hold your horses! (colloq); ***subirse al ~*** to jump on the bandwagon 2 (AmL exc CS) (Auto) car, automobile (AmE) 3 (Chi, Méx) (vagón) coach, carriage (BrE) 4 (Hist) (romano) chariot
Compuestos
- **carro alegórico** (CS, Méx) float
- **carro bomba** (Col) car bomb
- **carro comedor/dormitorio** (Méx) dining/sleeping car
- **carro de bomberos** (Andes, Méx) fire engine, fire truck
- **carro de combate** tank
- **carro lanza-agua** (Chi) water cannon
- **carro libre** (Ven) cab, taxi
- **carro loco** (Chi, Col, Méx) bumper car
- **carro sport** (AmL exc CS) sports car

B (de máquina de escribir) carriage

carrocería *f* (de automóvil) bodywork

carromato *m* (carro cubierto) covered wagon

C

C

carroña *f* 1 (de animal muerto) carrion 2 (gente despreciable) riffraff (+ *sing or pl vb*)

carroñero -ra *m,f* scavenger

carroza *f*

A 1 (coche de caballos) carriage 2 (de carnaval) float 3 (Chi, Ur) (coche fúnebre) hearse

B **carroza** *mf* (Esp fam) (persona anticuada) old fogey (colloq)

carruaje *m* carriage; **prohibido estacionar: paso de carruajes** no parking, access road

carrusel *m* 1 (para diapositivas) carousel, slide tray 2 **~ deportivo/de noticias** back-to-back sports/news program 3 (AmL) (para niños) merry-go-round, carousel (AmE)

carta *f*

A (Corresp) letter; **¿hay ~ para mí?** are there any letters for me?, is there any mail for me?; **echar una ~ al correo** to mail (esp AmE) *o* (esp BrE) post a letter; **~ de despido/renuncia** letter of dismissal/resignation; **~ de solicitud** letter of application

(Compuestos)
- **carta abierta** open letter
- **carta blanca** carte blanche
- **carta bomba** letter bomb
- **carta certificada** registered letter
- **carta de agradecimiento** thank-you letter
- **carta de amor** love letter
- **carta de ciudadanía** naturalization papers (*pl*)
- **carta de nacionalización** *or* **de naturaleza** naturalization papers (*pl*)
- **carta de pago** receipt, official receipt
- **carta de presentación** letter of introduction
- **carta de recomendación** reference, letter of recommendation
- **carta urgente** special-delivery letter
- **carta verde** green card

B (naipe) card; **jugar a las ~s** to play cards; **dar las ~s** to deal the cards; ***a ~ cabal***: **es honrado a ~ cabal** he's completely honest; ***echarle las ~s a algn*** to tell sb's fortune; ***jugar bien las ~s*** to play one's cards right; ***jugárselo todo a una ~*** to risk everything on one throw; ***no saber a qué ~ quedarse***: **no sé a qué ~ quedarme** I don't know what to think; ***poner las ~s boca arriba*** *or* ***sobre la mesa*** to put *o* lay one's cards on the table; ***tomar ~s en el asunto*** to intervene

(Compuesto) **cartas del Tarot** *fpl* Tarot cards (*pl*)

C (de organización) charter; (de país) constitution

(Compuestos)
- **Carta Magna** (Hist) Magna Carta; (constitución) (frml) constitution
- **Carta Social** (de la UE) Social Chapter

D (en restaurante) menu; **comer a la ~** to eat à la carte

(Compuesto) **carta de vinos** wine list

E (ant) (mapa) map

(Compuestos)
- **carta astral** astral chart
- **carta de ajuste** test card
- **carta de navegación** chart
- **carta de vuelo** flight plan

cartabón *m* (de dibujo) set square, triangle

cartapacio *m* folder

cartearse [A1] *v pron* to write to each other; **~ con algn** to correspond WITH sb

cartel[1] *m* 1 (de publicidad, propaganda) poster; (letrero) sign; **lleva dos meses en ~** «*obra/película*» it has been on for two months 2 (fama): **de ~** ‹*cantante/actor*› famous; ‹*torero*› star (*before n*); **una corrida de mucho ~** a bullfight with some big names

(Compuesto) **cartel luminoso** neon sign

cartel[2], **cártel** *m* cartel

cartelera *f*

A 1 (Cin, Teatr) publicity board; **la película sigue en ~** the movie is still on *o* still showing,; **la obra estuvo en ~ durante cuatro años** the play ran for four years 2 (en el periódico) listings (*pl*); **~ de espectáculos** entertainment guide

B (AmL) (tablón de anuncios) bulletin board (AmE), notice board (BrE)

carteo *m* (esp AmL) correspondence

cárter *m* (del cigüeñal) crankcase, sump; (del embrague) housing

cartera *f*

A 1 (billetera) wallet, billfold (AmE) 2 (para documentos) document case, briefcase; (de colegial) satchel; (de cobrador) money bag; (de cartero) sack, bag 3 (AmS) (bolso de mujer) purse (AmE), handbag (BrE)

B (Com, Fin) portfolio; ***tener algo en ~*** to have sth in the pipeline

(Compuestos)
- **cartera de acciones** stock *o* share portfolio
- **cartera de pedidos** order book
- **cartera de valores** securities portfolio

C (period) (Pol) (cargo) portfolio (journ); (departamento) department

carterear [A1] *vt* (Chi): **me ~on en la micro** my handbag was picked on the bus

carterista *mf* pickpocket

cartero (*m*) mailman (AmE), postman (BrE); (*f*) mailwoman (AmE), postwoman (BrE)

cartesiano -na *adj/m,f* Cartesian

cartílago *m* cartilage

cartilla *f* (para aprender a leer) reader, primer; ***cantarle*** *or* ***leerle la ~ a algn*** to take sb to task

(Compuestos)
- **cartilla de ahorros** passbook, savings book
- **cartilla de racionamiento** ration book

cartografía *f* cartography

cartógrafo -fa *m,f* cartographer

cartomancia, cartomancía *f* fortune-telling, cartomancy

cartón *m*

A (material) cardboard

(Compuestos)
- **cartón ondulado** *or* **corrugado** corrugated cardboard
- **cartón piedra** (Esp) papier-mâché

B (de cigarrillos, leche) carton; (de huevos) tray

C (en bingo) card

cartoné *m*: **en ~** hardback

cartuchera *f*

A 1 (estuche — para cartuchos) cartridge clip; (— para pistola) holster 2 (cinturón — para cartuchos) cartridge belt; (— para pistola) gun belt

B 1 (RPl) (de escolar) pencil case 2 (Chi) (para los anteojos) glasses *o* spectacle case

cartucho *m*

A (Arm) cartridge; ***quemar el último ~*** to play one's last card

(Compuesto) **cartucho en blanco** blank cartridge

B (de estilográfica) cartridge

C (para monedas) roll

cartuja *f* charterhouse, monastery

cartulina *f* card

casa *f*

A 1 (vivienda) house; **está buscando ~** she's looking for somewhere to live; **casita del perro** kennel 2 (hogar) home; **a los 18 años se fue de ~** *or* (AmL) **de la ~** she left home at 18; **no está nunca en ~** *or* (AmL) **en la ~** he's never (at) home; **¿estarás en casa esta tarde?** will you be at home *o* in this afternoon?; **están en casa de Ana** they're (over) at Ana's (house); **¿por qué no pasas por ~** *or* (AmL) **por la ~?** why don't you drop in *o* by?; **está en su ~** make yourself at home; **lo invito a cenar a su ~ de usted** (Méx) please come over to dinner; **vivo en Lomas 38, su ~ de usted** (Méx) I live at number 38 Lomas, where you will always be most welcome; **no soy de la ~** I don't live here; **decidió poner ~ en Toledo** she decided to go and live in Toledo; **le ha puesto ~ a su querida** he's set his mistress up in a house (*o* an apartment *etc*); **los padres les ayudaron a poner la ~** their parents helped them to set up house; ***de*** *or* ***para andar por ~*** ‹*vestido*› for wearing around the house; ‹*definición/terminología*› crude, rough; ***se me/se le vino la ~ encima*** the bottom fell out of my/her world; ***como Pedro por su ~*** as if you/he/she owned the place (colloq); ***como una ~*** (fam): **una mentira como una ~** a whopping great lie (colloq), a whopper (colloq); ***echar** or **tirar la ~ por la ventana*** to push the boat out; ***empezar la ~ por el tejado*** to put the cart before the horse; ***en la ~ de la Guayaba*** (Méx fam) miles away (colloq); ***ser muy de su ~*** (hogareño) to be very homeloving; (hacendoso) to be very houseproud; ***en ~ del herrero, cuchillo de palo*** the shoemaker's son always goes barefoot; ***cada uno en su ~ y Dios en la de todos*** each to his own and God watching over everyone

B (Com) 1 (empresa) company, firm (BrE) 2 (bar, restaurante): **especialidad de la ~** house specialty (AmE), speciality of the house (BrE); **invita la ~** it's on the house; **es un obsequio de la ~** with the compliments of the management

C (dinastía) house; **la ~ de los Borbones** the House of Bourbon

D 1 (Dep): **perdieron en ~** they lost at home; **los de ~** the home team 2 (Jueg) home

Compuestos

- **casa adosada** semi-detached *o* terraced house
- **Casa Amarilla** (en CR, Ven) Presidential Palace
- **Casa Blanca** White House
- **casa central** head office, headquarters (*sing o pl*)
- **casa consistorial** town hall
- **casa cuartel** police station (*including living quarters*)
- **casa de cambio** bureau de change
- **casa de campo** country house
- **casa de citas** *hotel where rooms are rented by the hour*
- **casa de comidas** (Esp) restaurant (*serving economically priced meals*)
- **casa de discos** *or* **discográfica** record company
- **casa de estudios** (CS) (universidad) university, college; (facultad) faculty
- **Casa de Gobierno** (en algunos países) Presidential Palace
- **casa de huéspedes** boardinghouse
- **Casa de la Moneda** 1 (Fin) mint 2 (en Chi) Presidential Palace
- **casa de locos** (fam) madhouse (colloq)
- **casa de modas** fashion house
- **casa de muñecas** dollhouse (AmE), doll's house (BrE)
- **casa de orates** lunatic asylum
- **casa de putas** (vulg) whorehouse (vulg)
- **casa de reposo** *or* **salud** (CS) nursing home
- **casa de socorro** first-aid post
- **casa de tolerancia** (AmL) brothel
- **casa de vecinos** *or* (Méx) **de vecindad** tenement house
- **casa editorial** publishing house
- **casa habitación** (Chi) dwelling
- **casa piloto** *or* (Méx) **modelo** model home (AmE), show house (BrE)
- **Casa Real** Royal Household
- **casa refugio** refuge *o* hostel for battered women
- **casa rodante** (CS) trailer (AmE), caravan (BrE)
- **casa rural** (Esp) holiday cottage
- **casa solariega** ancestral home

Casa Amarilla

The headquarters of the Venezuelan State Department in Caracas. Originally a colonial prison, it was made the presidential palace in the nineteenth century and was painted yellow, the color of the Liberal Party, hence the name.

Casa Amarilla is also the name of the presidential palace in San José, Costa Rica

Casa Rosada

The Argentinian president's official residence in the Plaza de Mayo in Buenos Aires. Its façade was painted pink as a sign of national unity by President Sarmiento in the nineteenth century, to symbolize the coming together of two opposing political factions, one of whose banners was red, the other white

casabe *m* (Col, Ven) cassava bread

casaca *f* (chaqueta) jacket; (Equ) riding jacket

casación *f* annulment, cassation (tech)

casadero -ra *adj* marriageable; **está en edad casadera** she is of marriageable age

casado[1] -da *adj* married; **está ~ con una japonesa** he's married to a Japanese woman

casado[2] -da (*m*) married man; (*f*) married woman; **los recién ~s** the newlyweds

casamentero[1] -ra *adj* (fam) matchmaking (*before n*)

casamentero[2] -ra *m,f* (fam) matchmaker

casamiento *m* (unión) marriage; (boda) wedding

casar [A1] *vt*

A 1 «*cura/juez*» to marry 2 «*padres*» to marry (off)

B (Der) ‹*sentencia*› to quash

■ **casar** *vi* 1 (encajar) «*dibujos*» to match up; «*piezas*» to fit together; «*cuentas*» to match, tally 2 (armonizar) «*colores/estilos*» to go together; **~ con algo** to go well WITH sth

■ **casarse** *v pron* to get married; **se casó con un abogado** she married a lawyer; **~se en segundas nupcias** to marry again, to remarry; ***no ~se con nadie*** to refuse to align oneself to any power (*o* ideology *etc*)

cascabel[1] *m* 1 (campanita) bell; ***poner el ~ al gato*** to stick one's neck out; ***ser alegre como un ~*** to be as happy as a clam (AmE) *o* (BrE) a sandboy 2 (Chi) (sonajero) rattle

cascabel[2] *f* (Zool) rattlesnake

cascabeleo *m* (sonido — de cascabeles) jingle, jingling; (— de motor, piezas) (AmL) rattle

cascada *f* (Geog) waterfall, cascade

cascado -da *adj* 1 ‹*voz*› hoarse 2 (Esp fam) ‹*persona*› worn-out; ‹*coche/radio*› broken-down

cascajo *m* (fam)

A (trasto viejo) wreck (colloq); **ando hecho un ~** I feel a complete wreck (colloq)

B (Col) (Const) piece of gravel

cascanueces *m* (*pl* ~) (a pair of) nutcrackers

cascar [A2] *vt*

A ‹*nuez/huevo*› to crack; ‹*taza*› to chip

B (fam) to knock … about; **su marido le casca** her husband knocks her about; **obedece o te casco** do as I tell you or I'll give you a clout

C (Esp fam) ‹*multa/pena*›: **me ~on una multa de 1.000 euros** I got a 1,000 euro fine; **le ~on 10 años de cárcel** he got 10 years; ***~la*** (fam) to peg out (colloq), to kick the bucket (colloq)

■ **cascar** *vi*

A (Esp fam) (charlar) to chat

B (Chi fam) (huir) to run away

■ **cascarse** *v pron* 1 «*huevo*» to crack; «*taza*» to chip 2 (pegarse) (*recípr*): **se ~on de lo lindo** they knocked the living daylights out of each other 3 (Esp fam) (estropearse) to break

cáscara *f* (de huevo, nuez) shell; (del queso) rind; (de naranja, limón) peel, rind; (de plátano, papa) skin; (de manzana) peel

cáscaras *interj* (fam) wow! (colloq)

cascarazo *m* (Col, RPl fam) thump (colloq)

cascarilla *f* (de cacao) roasted cacao husks (*pl*) (*used in infusions*); (de cereal, frutos secos) husk

cascarón *m* (de huevo, nuez) shell; **recién salido del ~** (fam) still wet behind the ears (colloq)

Compuesto **cascarón de nuez** cockleshell, flimsy vessel

cascarrabias[1] *adj inv* (fam) cantankerous, grumpy

cascarrabias[2] *mf* (*pl* ~) (fam) cantankerous *o* grumpy person; **es un viejo ~** he's a cantankerous old devil *o* sod (colloq)

cascarudo *m* (RPl) beetle

casco *m*

A (para la cabeza) helmet; ***calentarse los ~s*** (fam) to agonize, worry

Compuestos

- **casco azul** *mf* blue helmet (*member of the U.N. peacekeeping force*)
- **casco protector** (de obrero) safety helmet; (de motorista) crash helmet

B **cascos** *mpl* (Audio) headphones (*pl*)

C (Equ, Zool) hoof; ***ligera de ~s*** (coqueta) flight

D (Náut) hull

E (de ciudad) heart, central area; (de estancia) (RPl) farmhouse and surrounding buildings

Compuestos

- **casco antiguo** *or* **viejo** old quarter
- **casco urbano** urban area, built-up area

C

F 1 (trozo — de metralla) piece of shrapnel; (— de vasija) fragment, shard 2 (Col) (gajo) segment
G (Esp, Méx) (envase) bottle;

cascote *m* piece of rubble; **~s** rubble

caserío *m* (poblado) hamlet; (finca) farmhouse (Esp)

casero[1] **-ra** *adj* 1 ‹*vino/flan*› homemade; ‹*reparación*› amateur; **remedio ~** home *o* household remedy 2 ‹*trabajo*› domestic 3 ‹*persona*› home-loving; **¡es tan ~!** he such a homelover *o* (AmE) homebody

casero[2] **-ra** *m,f*
A 1 (propietario) (*m*) landlord; (*f*) landlady 2 (cuidador) caretaker
B (Chi) (cliente) customer; (vendedor) storekeeper (AmE), stallholder

caserón *m* big, rambling house

caseta *f* 1 (en la playa, de guardia etc) hut 2 (en exposición) stand; (en fiestas populares) *building or marquee gen with music* 3 (para perro) kennel 4 (Ferr) gateman's box (AmE), crossing keeper's box (BrE) 5 (en fútbol) dugout

casete *m or f* 1 (cinta) cassette 2 **casete** *m* (Esp) (grabador) cassette recorder/player

casetero *m* cassette box

cash-flow /'kas'flou/ *m* cash flow

casi *adv*
A 1 (cerca de) almost, nearly; **es ~ imposible** it's virtually *o* almost impossible; **~ me caigo** I nearly fell over 2 (*delante del n*) (frml): **la ~ totalidad de la población** almost the entire population
B (en frases negativas): **~ no se le oía** you could hardly hear him; **~ nunca** hardly ever; **no nos queda ~ nada de pan** there's hardly any bread left; **¿pudiste dormir? — ~ nada** did you manage to sleep? — hardly at all; **¿200? ¡~ nada!** (iró) $200? is that all? (iro); **no había ~ nadie** there was hardly anyone; **~ no vengo** I almost didn't come
C (expresando una opinión tentativa): **yo ~ te diría que lo vendas** I'd be inclined to say, sell it; **~ sería mejor esperar** maybe it would be better to wait

casilla *f*
A (para cartas, llaves) pigeonhole
(Compuesto) **casilla postal** *or* **de correo** (CS, Per) post office box, P.O. Box
B (en ajedrez, crucigrama) square; (en formulario) box
C 1 (de guardia, sereno) hut 2 (de perro) kennel 3 (Méx) (de votación) polling booth; ***sacar a algn de sus ~s*** to drive sb crazy; ***salirse de sus ~s*** to fly off the handle (colloq)

casillero *m* 1 (mueble) set of pigeonholes; (compartimento) pigeonhole 2 (CS) (en formulario) box 3 (Ven) (buzón) mailbox (AmE), letterbox (BrE)

casino *m*
A (de juego) casino
B (club social) club

casis *m* blackcurrant

casitas *fpl* (Chi fam & euf) (cuarto de baño) bathroom (euph)

caso *m*
A (situación, coyuntura) case; **en esos ~s** in cases like that; **en último ~** if it comes to it, if the worst comes to the worst; **es un ~ límite** it is a borderline case; **en el mejor de los ~s** at (the very) best; **en el peor de los ~s te pondrán una multa** the worst they can do is fine you; **a veces se da el ~ de ...** from time to time it happens that ...; **si se diera el ~ de que tuvieras que quedarte ...** if you did have to stay ...; **para el ~ es igual** what difference does it make?; **ponte en mi ~** put yourself in my place; **lo que dijo no venía al ~** what she said had nothing to do with what we were talking about; **pongamos por ~ que ...** let's assume that ...
B (*en locs*) **el caso es que**: **el ~ es que están todos bien** the important *o* main thing is that everybody is all right; **el ~ es que no sé si ...** the thing is that I don't know whether ...; **en caso de**: Ⓢ **en caso de incendio rómpase el cristal** in case of fire break glass; **en ~ de que no pueda asistir ...** if you are unable to attend ...; **en caso contrario** otherwise; **en cualquier caso** in any case; **en tal caso** in such a (frml) *o* in that case; **en todo caso**: **no estará para mañana, en todo ~ para el jueves** it won't be done for tomorrow, maybe Thursday; **quizá venga, en todo ~ dijo que llamaría** she might come, in any case she said she'd ring; **llegado el caso** if it comes to it; **según el caso** as appropriate; ***no hay/hubo caso*** (AmL fam) it is no good *o* no use/it was no good *o* no use; ***no tiene ~*** it is absolutely pointless
C (Der, Med) case; **el ~ Solasa** Solasa affair *o* case; **el suyo es un ~ especial** his is a special case; ***ser un ~*** (fam): **es un ~** he's/she's something else (colloq); ***ser un ~ perdido*** (fam) to be a hopeless case (colloq)
(Compuesto) **caso fortuito** (en lo civil) act of God; **muerte por ~** death by misadventure
D (atención): **hacerle ~ a algn** to pay attention to sb, take notice of sb; **maldito el ~ que me hace** she doesn't take the slightest notice of what I say; **hacer ~ DE algo** to pay attention TO sth; to take notice OF sth, **no hizo ~ de las señales de peligro** she took no notice of *o* paid no attention to the warning signs; **hacer ~ omiso de algo** to take no notice of sth, ignore sth
E (Ling) case

casona *f* big house

casorio *m* (fam & hum): **están de ~** they're at a wedding

caspa *f* dandruff

cáspita *interj* ▸**caramba**

casposo -sa *adj* covered with dandruff

casquería *f* butcher's shop (*specializing in offal*)

casquete *m* skullcap
(Compuestos)
- **casquete glaciar** *or* **de hielo** icecap
- **casquete polar** polar icecap

casquillo *m* 1 (de bala, cartucho) case 2 (portalámparas) lampholder, bulbholder; (de bombilla): **~ de rosca/bayoneta** screw-in/bayonet fitting

casquivano -na *adj* flighty, loose (pej)

cassette *m or f* ▸**casete**

casta *f* caste; **le viene de ~** it's in his blood; **de ~** ‹*toro*› thoroughbred; ‹*torero*› top-class

castaña *f*
A (fruto) chestnut; ***sacarle las ~s del fuego a algn*** to get sb out of trouble; ***¡toma ~!*** (Esp fam) (expresando — regodeo) so there! (colloq); (— sorpresa) wow! (colloq)
(Compuestos)
- **castaña de Indias** horse chestnut
- **castaña de Pará** (RPl) Brazil nut
- **castaña pilonga** dried chestnut

B (Esp fam) 1 (borrachera): **cogió una ~** he got plastered (colloq) 2 (golpe, choque) bump

castañazo *m* (fam) (puñetazo, tortazo) thump; (golpe, choque) bump

castañero -ra *m,f* chestnut seller

castañeta *f* (castañuela) castanet; (con los dedos) click

castañetear [A1] *vi* (+ *me/te/le etc*): **me castañetean los dientes** my teeth are chattering

castaño[1] **-ña** *adj* ‹*pelo*› chestnut; ‹*ojos*› brown

castaño[2] *m*
A (Bot) chestnut tree
(Compuesto) **castaño de Indias** horse chestnut
B (color) chestnut; ***pasarse de ~ oscuro*** (fam) «*comentario*» to be out of line (colloq); «*situación*» to be beyond a joke

castañuela *f* castanet; ***como unas ~s*** as happy as a clam (AmE) *o* (BrE) a sandboy

castellanizar [A4] *vt* to hispanicize

castellano[1] **-na** *adj* (de Castilla) Castilian; (español) Spanish

castellano[2] **-na** *m,f*
A (persona) Castilian
B **castellano** *m* (idioma — de Castilla) Castilian; (— español) Spanish

> **castellano**
>
> In Spain the term *castellano*, rather than *español*, refers to the Spanish language as opposed to Catalan, Basque etc. The choice of word has political overtones: *castellano* has separatist connotations and *español* is considered neutral. In Latin America *castellano* is another term for Spanish

casticismo *m*: *quality of being* **castizo**

castidad *f* chastity

castigar [A3] *vt*
A 1 ‹*criminal*› to punish; **crímenes castigados con la**

pena de muerte crimes punishable by death; **fueron castigados con la pena máxima** they received the maximum sentence 2 ‹niño› (a quedarse en el colegio) to keep … in detention; (a quedarse en casa) to keep … in as a punishment, to ground (esp AmE colloq); **se quedó castigado por contestarle al profesor** he was kept in detention for answering the teacher back; **mi padre me ha castigado** my father's keeping me in, my father's grounded me; **lo ~on sin postre** as a punishment he was made to go without dessert
B «*crisis/enfermedad*» to affect; **la zona más castigada por la sequía** the area worst affected by the drought

castigo *m*
A (de un delincuente, estudiante, niño) punishment; **se les impondrán ~s severos** they will be severely punished; **levantar un ~** to lift a punishment
(Compuesto) **castigo corporal** corporal punishment
B (daño, perjuicio): **el ~ que recibió en el último asalto** the punishment he took in the last round; **el ~ que la crisis ha infligido a esta zona** the severe *o* terrible effects the crisis has had on this area

Castilla *f* Castile

castillo *m* castle; ***hacer*** *or* ***construir ~s en el aire*** to build castles in the air
(Compuestos)
- **castillo de arena** sandcastle
- **castillo de cartas** house of cards
- **castillo de fuego** *or* **de fuegos artificiales** firework display
- **castillo de popa/proa** aftercastle/forecastle

castizo -za *adj* 1 (puro, tradicional) ‹*estilo/costumbre*› traditional 2 (típicamente castellano): **un apellido muy ~** a very Spanish/Castilian surname; **un lenguaje muy ~** very pure Castilian/Spanish

casto -ta *adj* chaste

castor *m* beaver

castración *f* castration

castrado *m* castrato

castrar [A1] *vt* ‹*caballo*› to geld; ‹*toro/hombre*› to castrate; ‹*gato*› to neuter

castrense *adj* military, army (*before n*)

castro *m* fort

casual[1] *adj* chance (*before n*)

casual[2] *m*: **por un ~** (fam) by any chance

casualidad *f* chance; **de** *or* **por (pura) ~** by (sheer) chance; **pasé por ahí de ~** I happened to pass by there, I passed there by chance; **si por ~ la ves** if you happen to see her; **¡qué ~!** what a coincidence!; **da la ~ de que …** as it happens *o* actually …; **ni por ~**: **no se baña ni por ~** he wouldn't dream of having a bath; **no le doy a la bola ni por ~** I just can't hit the ball

casualmente *adv* as it happens

casuca *f* (pey) hovel (pej)

casucha *f* 1 (pey) (choza) hovel (pej) 2 (Chi) (de perro) kennel

casuística *f* casuistry

casulla *f* chasuble

cata *f* (Coc, Vin) tasting
(Compuesto) **cata ciega** blind tasting

cataclismo *m* natural disaster, cataclysm (frml)

catacumbas *fpl* catacombs (*pl*)

catador -dora *m,f* taster

catadura *f* 1 (Coc, Vin) tasting 2 (pey) (aspecto) look; **un tipo de muy mala ~** (fam) a very shady-looking guy (colloq)

catafalco *m* catafalque

catalán[1] **-lana** *adj/m,f* Catalan

catalán[2] *m* (idioma) Catalan

> **catalán**
>
> The language of Catalonia. Like Castilian, Catalan is a Romance language. Variants of it include **mallorquín** of the Balearic Islands and **valenciano** spoken in the autonomous region of Valencia.
>
> Banned under Franco, Catalan has enjoyed a ▸▸▸
>
> ▸▸▸ revival since Spain's return to democracy and now has around 11 million speakers. It is the medium of instruction in schools and universities and its use is widespread in business, the arts, and the media. Many books are published in Catalan. *See also* **lenguas cooficiales**

catalanismo *m* Catalan word/expression

catalejo *m* (ant) telescope, spyglass

catalepsia *f* catalepsy

cataléptico -ca *adj/m,f* cataleptic

catálisis *f* (*pl* ~) catalysis

catalítico -ca *adj* catalytic

catalizador[1] **-dora** *adj* catalytic; **fue un factor ~ de sus sentimientos** it was a catalyst for his feelings

catalizador[2] *m*
A (Quím) catalyst
B (Auto) catalytic converter

catalizar [A4] *vt* to catalyze

catalogable *adj* classifiable

catalogar [A3] *vt* 1 (en un catálogo) to catalog (AmE), to catalogue (BrE); (en una lista) to record, list 2 (considerar) to class; **el edificio está catalogado como de interés histórico** the building is classed as being of historical interest; **lo ~on de grotesco** they described it as grotesque

catálogo *m* (Art, Com) catalog (AmE), catalogue (BrE); **compra por ~** mail-order shopping

Cataluña *f* Catalonia

catamarán *m* catamaran

cataplasma *f* poultice, cataplasm (tech)

catapulta *f* catapult
(Compuesto) **catapulta de lanzamiento** catapult

catapultar [A1] *vt* to catapult

catar [A1] *vt* 1 ‹*vino*› to taste 2 (mirar) to look at

catarata *f*
A (Geog) waterfall; **las ~s del Iguazú** Iguaçú Falls
B (Med) cataract

catarriento -ta *adj* (Chi, Méx): **está ~** he has a cold

catarro *m* 1 (resfriado) cold; **pescarse** *or* (esp Esp) **coger un ~** to catch a cold 2 (inflamación) catarrh

catarsis *f* catharsis

catártico -ca *adj* cathartic

catastral *adj* cadastral

catastro *m* (censo) land registry; (impuesto) property tax

catástrofe *f* catastrophe, disaster

catastrófico -ca *adj* catastrophic, disastrous

catastrofista *mf* doomwatcher, prophet of doom

catatónico -ca *adj* catatonic

catavinos *mf* (*pl* ~) (persona) wine taster

cate *m* (Esp) (suspenso) (arg) fail; (golpe) (fam) bang, knock

cateador -dora *m,f* (AmS) prospector

catear [A1] *vt*
A (Esp arg) (suspender) to fail
B 1 (Chi fam) (observar) to peep at; (mirar) to look at 2 (Chi) (Min) to prospect 3 (Méx) (registrar) ‹*persona*› to frisk; ‹*vivienda*› to search

catecismo *m* catechism

catecúmeno -na *m,f* catechumen

cátedra *f* (en universidad) professorship, chair; (en colegio) post of head of department; **dictar** *or* (AmL) **dar ~** to lecture; ***sentar ~*** to pontificate, sound off (colloq)

catedral *f* cathedral; ***como una ~*** (fam) huge, massive; **una mentira como una ~** a real whopper (colloq)

catedrático -ca *m,f* (de universidad) professor; (en colegio) head of department

categoría *f* 1 (clase, rango) category; **hotel de primera ~** first-class hotel; **~ profesional** professional standing; **tiene ~ de embajador** he has ambassadorial status; **un huracán de ~ cuatro** a category four hurricane 2 (calidad): **un actor de mucha ~** a distinguished actor; **una revista de mucha/poca ~** a first/second-rate magazine; **el hotel de más ~** the finest *o* best hotel; ***de ~***: **artistas de ~** fine *o* first-rate artists; **un producto de ~** a quality *o* prestige product; **gente de cierta ~** people of some standing 3 (Fil) category

Compuestos
- **categoría fiscal** tax bracket
- **categoría gramatical** part of speech

categórico -ca *adj* ‹*respuesta*› categorical: **afirmó en términos ~s que ...** he stated categorically that ...
categorización *f* categorization
categorizar [A4] *vt* to categorize
cateo *m* 1 (AmS) (Min) prospecting 2 (Chi fam) (acción de mirar): **su primera labor es de ~** her first job is to take a look round 3 (Chi, Méx) (cacheo) body search
catequesis *f*: *teaching of the catechism*
catequista *mf* catechist
catequización *f* catechization
catequizar [A4] *vt* to catechize
caterva *f*: **una ~ de imbéciles** a bunch of idiots (colloq)
catéter *m* catheter
cateto *m* (Mat) leg
catire[1] **-ra** *adj* (Ven) (de piel blanca) fair-skinned; (de pelo rubio) fair, fair-haired
catire[2] **-ra** *m,f* (Ven) (de piel blanca) fair-skinned person; (de pelo rubio) fair-haired person; **una catira a juro** a peroxide blonde (pej)
catita *f* (CS) budgerigar
catiusca *f* (Esp) wellington, rubber boot (AmE)
cátodo *m* cathode
catolicismo *m* Catholicism
católico[1] **-ca** *adj* 1 (Relig) Catholic; **es ~** he's a Catholic 2 (ortodoxo) orthodox; **este método no es muy ~ pero ...** this method is rather unorthodox but ...; ***no estar muy ~*** (fam) ‹‹*persona*›› to feel out of sorts
católico[2] **-ca** *m,f* Catholic
catorce[1] *adj inv/pron* fourteen; *para ejemplos ver* **cinco**
catorce[2] *m* (number) fourteen
catre *m* 1 (cama — plegable) folding bed; (— de campaña) camp bed 2 (CS) (armazón) bedstead; ***caído del ~*** (CS fam) dumb (colloq)
catsup *m* ketchup, catsup (AmE)
caucásico -ca *adj* Caucasian
cauce *m* 1 (Geog) bed; **el río se salió de su ~** the river burst its banks; **desviaron el ~ del arroyo** they changed the course of the stream; **las aguas volvieron a su ~** the river returned to a safe level 2 (rumbo, vía): **desvió la conversación hacia otros ~s** he steered the conversation onto another tack; **abrir un ~ para el diálogo** to open the way for talks; **seguir los ~s establecidos** to go through the normal channels
cauchal *m* rubber plantation
cauchera *f* (Col) 1 (tirachinas) (fam) slingshot (AmE), catapult (BrE) 2 (Ven) (Auto) tire* fitter's
cauchero[1] **-ra** *adj* rubber (*before n*)
cauchero[2] **-ra** *m,f* rubber tapper *o* worker
caucho *m*
A (sustancia) rubber; (árbol) (Col) rubber tree
B (neumatico) (Ven) tire*; (gomita) (Col) rubber band
cauda *f* (Col, Méx) trail
caudal[1] *adj* caudal
caudal[2] *m* 1 (de un fluido) volume of flow; **el río tiene muy poco ~** the water level *o* the river is very low 2 (riqueza) fortune 3 (abundancia) wealth; **un inmenso ~ de conocimientos** an immense wealth of knowledge
caudaloso -sa *adj* ‹*río*› large
caudillaje *m* leadership
caudillo *m* (líder) leader; **el C~** (Hist) *General Franco*
causa *f*
A (motivo) cause; **la ~ de todas mis desgracias** the cause of *o* the reason for all my misfortunes; **aún no se conocen las ~s del accidente** the cause of the accident is still unknown; **sería ~ suficiente de divorcio** it would be adequate grounds for divorce; **se enfadó sin ~ alguna** she got annoyed for no good reason *o* for no reason at all; **una relación de causa-efecto** a cause and effect relationship; **a** *or* **por ~ de** because of
Compuesto **causa final/primera** final/first cause
B (ideal, fin) cause; **una ~ perdida** a lost cause; ***hacer ~ común con algn*** to make common cause with sb
C (Der) (pleito) lawsuit; (proceso) trial; **seguir una ~ contra algn** to try sb

Compuestos
- **causa civil** lawsuit
- **causa criminal** criminal proceedings (*pl*), trial

causal *adj* causal
causalidad *f* causality
causante[1] *adj*: **el virus ~ de la enfermedad** the virus responsible for *o* which causes the disease; **los factores ~s de la crisis** the factors which caused the crisis
causante[2] *mf*
A (causa) cause
B (Der) originator; (de una sucesión) decedent (AmE), deceased (BrE)
causar [A1] *vt* ‹*daños/problema/sufrimiento*› to cause; ‹*indignación*› to cause, arouse; ‹*alarma*› to cause, provoke; ‹*placer*› to give; **el incidente causó gran inquietud** the incident caused great unease; **me causó muy buena impresión** I was very impressed with her
cáustico -ca *adj/m* caustic
cautela *f* caution
cautelar *adj* ‹*acción*› preventative; ‹*medidas*› preventive
cauteloso -sa *adj* [SER] ‹*persona*› cautious
cauterizar [A4] *vt* to cauterize
cautivador -dora *adj* captivating
cautivar [A1] *vt* (atraer) to captivate
cautiverio *m*, **cautividad** *f* captivity
cautivo -va *adj m,f* captive
cauto -ta *adj* careful, cautious
cava[1] *f* cellar
cava[2] *m* cava (*sparkling wine*)
cavador -dora *m,f* digger
cavar [A1] *vt* 1 ‹*fosa/zanja*› to dig; ‹*pozo*› to sink 2 ‹*tierra/huerto*› to hoe; ***~ su propia fosa*** *or* ***tumba*** to dig one's own grave
caverna *f* cave, cavern
cavernícola[1] *adj* 1 (Hist) cave-dwelling; **hombre ~** caveman 2 (pey) (retrógrado) reactionary
cavernícola[2] *mf* 1 (Hist) cave dweller 2 (pey) (retrógrado) reactionary
cavernoso *adj* ‹*sonido/voz*› deep, booming
caviar *m* caviar
cavidad *f* cavity
cavilación *f*: **tras profundas cavilaciones** after much deliberation *o* consideration
cavilar [A1] *vi* to ponder, deliberate, think deeply; **después de mucho ~** after much thought *o* deliberation
cayado *m* (de pastor) crook; (de obispo) crosier
cayena *f* cayenne (pepper)
cayera, cayese, etc *see* **caer**
cayo *m* cay
cayuco *m* open boat; (as used by illegal immigrants to the Canary Islands)
caza[1] *f* 1 (para subsistir) hunting; (como deporte — caza mayor) hunting; (— caza menor) shooting; **ir de ~** to go hunting/shooting; ***a la ~ de algo/algn***: **andaba a la ~ de trabajo** I was job-hunting; **anda a la ~ de marido** she's out to find herself a husband (colloq); **salieron a la ~ del ladrón** they set off in pursuit of the thief; ***dar ~ a algn*** (perseguir) to pursue sb; (alcanzar) to catch sb 2 (animales) game

Compuestos
- **caza de brujas** witch-hunt
- **caza del tesoro** treasure hunt
- **caza furtiva** poaching
- **caza mayor** (acción) (game) hunting; (animales) big game
- **caza menor** (acción) shooting; (animales) small game
- **caza submarina** underwater fishing
- **caza y captura**: **una operación para la ~ y ~ de los delincuentes** an operation to track down and capture the criminals

caza[2] *m* fighter
cazabombardero *m* fighter-bomber
cazador -dora *m,f*
A hunter

Compuestos
- **cazador -dora de cabezas** *m,f* headhunter
- **cazador de dotes** *m* dowry hunter

• **cazador -dora de fortunas** *m,f* fortune hunter
• **cazador -dora de pieles** *m,f* trapper
• **cazador furtivo -dora furtiva** *m,f* poacher
B **cazadora** *f* (Esp) (Indum) jacket

cazafortunas *f* (*pl* ~) (fam) gold digger (colloq)

cazamariposas *m* (*pl* ~) butterfly net

cazamoscas *m* (*pl* ~) flycatcher

cazar [A4] *vt*
A 1 (para subsistir) to hunt; (como deporte) (—caza mayor) to hunt; (— caza menor) to shoot 2 ‹*mariposas*› to catch
B (fam) 1 (conseguir, atrapar): **ha cazado un millonario/buen empleo** she's landed herself a millionaire/good job 2 (entender, oír) ‹*palabra/frase*› to catch; ‹*indirecta*› to take 3 (atrapar) to catch
■ **cazar** *vi* to hunt; (con fusil) to shoot; **salimos a ~** we went out hunting/shooting

cazarrecompensas *mf* (*pl* ~) bounty hunter

cazatalentos *mf* (*pl* ~) talent scout

cazatendencias *mf* (*pl* ~) trendspotter

cazo *m* (cacerola) small saucepan; (cucharón) ladle

cazoleta *f* 1 (cazuela pequeña) small saucepan 2 (de pipa) bowl

cazuela *f* casserole

(Compuesto) **cazuela de ave/vacuno** (Chi) *soup made with chicken/meat and vegetables*

cazurro¹ -rra *adj* (fam) (huraño) sullen, surly; (obstinado) stubborn, pig-headed (colloq)

cazurro² -rra *m,f* (fam) (huraño) sullen *o* surly person; (obstinado) stubborn

c.c. (= **centímetros cúbicos**) cc

c/c = **cuenta corriente**

CC¹ *f* (= **corriente continua**) DC

CC² *m*
A = **Cuerpo Consular**
B (Esp) (Auto) = **Código de la Circulación**
C (en Esp) (Pol) = **Comité Central**

CD *m*
A (= **cuerpo diplomático**) CD
B (= **compact disc**) CD

C.D. *m* = **Club Deportivo**

CDM *f* = **Confederación Deportiva Mexicana**

ce *f*: *name of the letter* **c**

CE *m* (= **Consejo de Europa**) Council of Europe

cebada *f* barley

cebado -da *adj* [ESTAR] (fam) gross, very fat

cebar [A1] *vt*
A ‹*animal*› to fatten … up
B ‹*anzuelo/cepo*› to bait
C (CS) ‹*mate*› to prepare (*and serve*)
■ **cebarse** *v pron* 1 (ensañarse) **~se CON algn** to vent one's anger ON sb 2 (alimentarse) to feed; **el miedo se ceba en la ignorancia** fear feeds on ignorance

cebo *m* 1 (en pesca, caza) bait 2 (Arm) primer

cebolla *f* onion

cebolleta *f*, **cebollino** *m* 1 (con tallo verde) scallion (AmE), spring onion (BrE) 2 (hierba) chive

cebón¹ -bona *adj* fattened (*before n*)

cebón² *m* (pavo) fattened turkey; (cerdo) fattened pig

cebra *f* zebra

cebú *m* (*pl* **-bús** *or* **-búes**) zebu

ceca *f*: **de la ~ a la meca** from one place to another

cecear [A1] *vi* 1 (Ling) *to pronounce the Spanish* /s/ *as* [θ] 2 (como defecto) to lisp

ceceo *m* (Ling) *pronunciation of the Spanish* /s/ *as* [θ]; (como defecto) lisp

cecina *f* (carne seca) cured meat; (embutido de cerdo) (Chi) pork sausage

cedazo *m* sieve; **pasar por el ~** ‹*harina*› to sift; ‹*salsa*› to sieve

ceder [E1] *vt*
A 1 ‹*derecho*› to transfer, assign; ‹*territorio*› to cede; ‹*puesto/título*› (voluntariamente) to hand over; (obligatoriamente) to give up; **me cedió el asiento** he let me have his seat; ▸ **palabra C2, paso A2** 2 ‹*balón/pelota*› to pass
B (prestar) ‹*jugador*› to loan; **me cedieron una casa en el pueblo** they gave me the use of a house in the village
■ **ceder** *vi*
A (cejar) to give way; **cedieron ante sus amenazas** they gave in to his threats; **no cedió ni un ápice** she didn't give *o* yield an inch; **~ EN algo** to give sth up; **~ A algo** to give in TO sth
B «*fiebre*» to go down; «*dolor*» to ease; «*tormenta*» to ease up; «*viento*» to drop
C 1 «*muro/puente/cuerda*» to give way 2 «*zapatos/muelles*» to give

cedilla *f* cedilla

cedro *m* cedar

cédula *f* (Fin) bond, warrant

(Compuesto) **cédula de identidad** identity card

cefalea *f* migraine, severe headache, cephalalgia (tech)

céfiro *m* (liter) zephyr (liter)

cegador -dora *adj* blinding

cegar [A7] *vt*
A 1 (deslumbrar) to blind 2 (ofuscar) to blind; **cegado por los celos** blinded by jealousy
B ‹*conducto/cañería*› to block

cegato -ta, **cegatón -tona** *adj* (fam) blind (colloq)

ceguera *f* blindness

CEI *f* (= **Comunidad de Estados Independientes**) CIS

ceja *f*
A (Anat) eyebrow; **arquear las ~s** to raise one's eyebrows; ***metérsele a algn entre ~ y ~*** (fam): **cuando se le mete algo entre ~ y ~ …** when he gets an idea into his head …; ***quemarse las ~s*** (fam) to burn the midnight oil; ***tener a algn entre ~ y ~*** (fam): **me tiene entre ~ y ~** she can't stand *o* bear me
B (Mús) capo

cejar [A1] *vi* to give up, cease (frml); **lucharon sin ~** they fought relentlessly; **~ EN algo** to cease IN *o* let up IN sth

cejijunto -ta *adj*: **es ~** his eyebrows meet in the middle

cejilla *f* capo

celada *f* 1 (trampa) trap 2 (de la armadura) helmet

celador -dora *m,f* 1 (en un museo, una biblioteca) security guard 2 (en la cárcel) (AmL) prison guard (AmE), prison warder (BrE) 3 (RPl) (Educ) monitor 4 (en un hospital) orderly, porter

celaje *m* (liter) cloudscape; ***como un ~*** (Chi) like lightning

celda *f* cell

(Compuesto) **celda de castigo** punishment cell

celdilla *f* cell

celebérrimo -ma *adj* (frml) extremely famous

celebración *f*
A (de éxito, festividad) celebration
B **celebraciones** *fpl* (festejos) celebrations (*pl*)
C 1 (frml) (de reunión, acto): **el mal tiempo impidió la ~ del concurso** bad weather prevented the contest from being held *o* taking place; **la ~ anual de este acto** the annual celebration of this ceremony (frml) 2 (Relig) celebration

celebrado -da *adj* celebrated, famous

celebrante¹ *adj* officiating (*before n*)

celebrante² *m* officiating priest, celebrant

celebrar [A1] *vt*
A 1 (festejar) ‹*éxito/cumpleaños/festividad*› to celebrate; **¡esto hay que ~lo!** this calls for a celebration! 2 (liter) ‹*belleza/valor/hazaña*› to celebrate (liter) 3 ‹*chiste/ocurrencia*› to laugh at
B (frml) (alegrarse) to be delighted at, be very pleased at; **lo celebro mucho** I'm absolutely delighted *o* really pleased; **celebro su éxito** I'm delighted to hear about your success
C 1 (frml) ‹*reunión/elecciones/juicio*› to hold; ‹*partido*› to play; **la reunión se celebró en Caracas** the meeting was held in Caracas 2 ‹*misa*› to say, celebrate; ‹*boda*› to perform, solemnize (frml) 3 (frml) ‹*acuerdo/pacto/contrato*› to sign
■ **celebrar** *vi* «*sacerdote*» to say *o* celebrate mass

célebre *adj* 1 (famoso) famous, celebrated 2 (Col) ‹*mujer*› elegant

celebridad *f* (fama) fame; (persona) celebrity

celeridad *f* swiftness, speed

C

celeste[1] *adj*
A (del cielo) heavenly, celestial
B ‹*ojos*› blue; ‹*pintura/vestido*› (claro) light *o* pale blue; (intenso) sky-blue
celeste[2] *m* (claro) light *o* pale blue; (intenso) sky-blue
celestial *adj* 1 (Relig) celestial 2 ‹*placer*› heavenly; **lo que me decía sonaba a música ~** his words were sweet music to my ears
celestina *f* (fam & hum) go-between
celibato *m* celibacy
célibe *adj/mf* celibate
celo *m*
A (esmero, fervor) zeal; **~ patriótico** patriotic zeal
B (Zool) 1 (de los machos) rut 2 (de las hembras) heat; **estar en ~** to be in season, to be in heat (AmE) *o* (BrE) on heat
C **celos** *mpl* jealousy; **sentir** *or* **tener ~s DE algn** to be jealous OF sb; **darle ~s a algn** to make sb jealous
D (Esp) (cinta adhesiva) Scotch® tape (AmE), Sellotape® (BrE)
celofán *m* cellophane
celosía *f* lattice, latticework
celoso -sa *adj*
A ‹*marido/novia*› jealous; **estar ~ DE algn** to be jealous OF sb
B (diligente, esmerado) conscientious, zealous
C (protector): **es muy celosa de sus crías** she's very protective of her young
celta[1] *adj* Celtic
celta[2] *mf*
A (persona) Celt
B **celta** *m* (Ling) Celtic
célula *f*
A (Biol) cell; (Elec) cell
(Compuestos)
- **célula fotoeléctrica** photoelectric cell
- **célula madre** *or* **primordial** *or* **troncal** stem cell

B (de una organización) cell; **una ~ terrorista** a terrorist cell
celular[1] *adj* cellular
celular[2] *m* 1 (AmL) (teléfono) cell phone 2 (Esp) (furgoneta para presos), patrol wagon (AmE), police van (BrE)
celulitis *f* (gordura) cellulite; (inflamación) cellulitis
celuloide *m* (Cin) celluloid; **una estrella del ~** a star of the silver screen
celulosa *f* cellulose
cementar [A1] *vt* 1 (Metal) to case-harden 2 (AmL) ‹*patio/suelo*› to cement
cementerio *m* cemetery; (al lado de una iglesia) graveyard
(Compuesto) **cementerio de coches** salvage *o* wrecker's yard (AmE), scrapyard (BrE)
cemento *m*
A (Const) cement
(Compuesto) **cemento armado** reinforced concrete
B 1 (AmL) (pegamento) glue, adhesive 2 (Odont) cement
cena *f* dinner, supper; (en algunas regiones del Reino Unido) tea; (formal, fuera de casa) dinner; **¿qué hay de ~?** what's for dinner *o* supper?
(Compuestos)
- **cena de gala** banquet
- **cena de negocios/trabajo** business/working dinner

cenáculo *m* (Relig) cenacle; (círculo, reunión) circle
cenagal *m* (barrizal) bog, mire
cenagoso -sa *adj* boggy
cenar [A1] *vi* to have dinner *o* supper; (en algunas regiones del Reino Unido) to have tea; **nos han invitado a ~** they've invited us for *o* to dinner; **salimos a ~** we went out for dinner; **nos dieron muy bien de ~** they gave us a great meal, they fed us very well (colloq)
■ **cenar** *vt*: **sólo cenó una tortilla** he only had an omelet for dinner *o* supper
cencerro *m* cowbell; ***estar loco como un ~*** (fam) to be nuts *o* crackers (colloq)
cenefa *f* 1 (en ropa, sábanas) border 2 (en techos, muros) frieze
cenicero *m* ashtray
cenicienta *f* drudge; **la C~** Cinderella
ceniciento -ta *adj* ash-gray*, ashen
cenit *m* zenith
ceniza *f* 1 (residuo) ash; ***reducir algo a ~s*** to reduce sth to ashes 2 **cenizas** *fpl* (restos mortales) ashes (*pl*)
cenizo *m* ***ser un ~*** (fam) to be a wet blanket (colloq)
cenotafio *m* cenotaph
cenote *m* deep pool (in limestone rock formations)
censar [A1] *vt* to take a census of
■ **censarse** *pron* (Esp) to register to vote
censo *m*
A 1 (de población) census; **hacer un ~** to conduct a census 2 (Esp) *tb* **~ electoral** electoral roll *o* register
B (Der, Fin) charge; (sobre una finca) ground rent
censor -sora *m,f*
A 1 (Cin, Period) censor 2 (crítico) critic
B (Der, Fin) *tb* **~ de cuentas** auditor
(Compuesto) **censor jurado de cuentas** certified public accountant (AmE), chartered accountant (BrE)
censura *f* 1 (reprobación) censure (frml), condemnation 2 (de libros, películas) censorship
censurable *adj* reprehensible
censurador -dora *m,f* censor
censurar [A1] *vt* 1 (reprobar) to censure (frml), to condemn 2 ‹*libro/película*› to censor, ‹*escena/párrafo*› to cut
centauro *m* centaur
centavo *m* 1 (en AmL) *hundredth part of many currencies*; ***estar sin un ~*** to be penniless 2 (del dólar) cent
centella *f* (rayo) flash of lightning; (chispa) spark; ***como una ~*** like greased lightning
centelleante *adj* ‹*estrella*› twinkling; ‹*luz/joya*› sparkling; ‹*ojos*› blazing
centellear [A1] *vi* «*luz/joya*» to sparkle, «*estrella*» to twinkle
centelleo *m* (de estrellas) twinkling; (de luz) sparkling, twinkling; (de joya) sparkling, glittering
centena *f*: **una ~** a hundred; **unidades, decenas y ~s** units, tens and hundreds
centenar *m*: **un ~ de personas** a hundred people; **~es de cartas** hundreds of letters
centenario[1] **-ria** *adj* centenarian; **un árbol ~** a hundred-year-old tree
centenario[2] **-ria** *m,f* 1 (persona) centenarian 2 **centenario** *m* (aniversario) centenary, centennial (AmE)
centeno *m* rye
centésima *f* hundredth
centesimal *adj* centesimal
centésimo[1] **-ma** *adj/pron* 1 (ordinal) hundredth; *para ejemplos ver* **vigésimo** 2 (partitivo): **la centésima parte** a hundredth
centésimo[2] *m* 1 (Fin, Mat) (partitivo) hundredth 2 (moneda) *hundredth part of the Uruguayan peso and the Panamanian balboa*
centígrado -da *adj* centigrade, Celsius; **30 grados ~s** 30 degrees centigrade *o* Celsius
centigramo *m* centigram
centilitro *m* centiliter*
centímetro *m* centimeter*
céntimo *m*: *hundredth part of many currencies*; ***no tener un ~*** to be broke; ***no vale ni un ~*** it's worthless
centinela *mf* (Mil) guard, sentry; (no militar) lookout; **estar de ~** (Mil) to be on sentry duty
centolla *f*, **centollo** *m* spider crab
centrado -da *adj* (equilibrado) stable, well-balanced; (en un trabajo, lugar) settled
central[1] *adj* central
central[2] *f* head office
(Compuestos)
- **central azucarera** (Per) sugar mill
- **central de correos** main post office
- **central telefónica** *or* **de teléfonos** telephone exchange
- **central hidroeléctrica/nuclear** hydroelectric/nuclear power station
- **central sindical** labor union (AmE), trade union (BrE)
- **central térmica** power station (*fueled by coal, oil or gas*)

centralismo *m* centralism
centralista *adj/mf* centralist
centralita *f* switchboard
centralización *f* centralization
centralizador -dora *adj* centralizing (*before n*)
centralizar [A4] *vt* to centralize
centrar [A1] *vt* 1 ‹*imagen*› to center* 2 (Dep) to center* 3 ‹*atención/investigación*› ~ **algo EN algo** to focus sth ON sth: **~on las conversaciones en el tema de ...** in their talks they focused on the issue of ...
■ **centrar** *vi* (Dep) to center*, cross
■ **centrarse** *v pron* **~se EN algo** «*investigación/atención*» to focus *o* center* ON sth; **hay que ~se más en este tema** we must focus in greater detail on this subject
céntrico -ca *adj* central; **un bar ~** a downtown bar (AmE), a bar in the centre of town (BrE)
centrifugado *m* spin
centrifugar [A3] *vt* ‹*ropa*› to spin; (Tec) to centrifuge
centrífugo -ga *adj* centrifugal
centrípeto -ta *adj* centripetal
centrista *adj/mf* centrist
centro¹ *m*
A 1 (Mat) center* 2 (área central) center*; **los países del ~ de Europa** the countries of Central Europe; **ir al ~ de la ciudad** to go downtown (AmE), to go into town *o* into the town centre (BrE); Ⓢ **centro ciudad/urbano** downtown (AmE), city/town centre (BrE)
(Compuestos)
- **centro de gravedad** center* of gravity
- **centro del campo** midfield
- **centro de mesa** centerpiece*

B (foco) 1 (de atención) center*; **es el ~ de todos los comentarios** it is the main talking point; **fue el ~ de todas las miradas** all eyes were on him; **se convirtió en el ~ de interés** it became the focus of attention; **fue el ~ de atracción** she was the center of attention 2 (de actividades, servicios) center*; **un gran ~ cultural/industrial** a major cultural/industrial center; **un ~ turístico** an tourist resort *o* center
(Compuestos)
- **centro de interés turístico** center* of interest to tourists
- **centro de población/urbano** urban center*, population center*
- **centro nervioso** nerve center*
- **centro recreacional** (AmL) leisure center*

C (establecimiento, institución) center*; **el ~ anglo-peruano** the Anglo-Peruvian center;
(Compuestos)
- **centro cívico** civic center*
- **centro comercial** shopping mall (AmE), shopping centre (BrE)
- **centro de acogida para mujeres maltratadas** refuge for battered women
- **centro de estudios** private school
- **centro de internamiento** detention center*
- **centro de planificación familiar** family planning clinic
- **centro de trabajo** (frml) workplace (frml)
- **centro docente** (frml) educational establishment *o* de enseñanza (frml)
- **centro espacial** space center*
- **centro hospitalario** *or* **sanitario** (frml) hospital
- **centro penitenciario** (frml) prison, penitentiary (AmE)

D (Pol) center*
E (en fútbol) cross, center*
(Compuesto) **centro delantero*** center* forward
centro² *mf* (Dep) center*
Centroamérica *f* Central America
centroamericano -na *adj/m,f* Central American
centrocampista *mf* midfield player
centroeuropeo -pea *adj/m,f* Central European
céntuplo *m* centuple, centuplicate
centuria *f* century
centurión *m* centurion
ceñido -da *adj* tight; **me queda muy ~** it's very tight on me

ceñir [I15] *vt* 1 «*falda/vestido*»: **esa falda te ciñe demasiado** that skirt is too tight for you; **el vestido le ceñía el talle** the dress clung to *o* hugged her waist 2 (liter) ‹*corona*› to take, put on
■ **ceñirse** *v pron*
A (limitarse, atenerse) **~se A algo**: **~se al reglamento** to adhere to *o* (colloq) stick to the rules; **cíñase al tema** keep to the subject
B (liter) ‹*espada*› to gird on (liter); ‹*corona*› to take, put on
ceño *m*: **frunció** *or* **arrugó el ~** he frowned; **me miró con el ~ fruncido** she frowned at me
ceñudo -da *adj* frowning (*before n*)
cepa *f* (Bot) stump; (Vin) stock (*of a vine*); **es un español de pura ~** he's Spanish through and through
CEPAL /'sepal, 'θepal/ *f* = **Comisión Económica para América Latina**
cepillado *m* 1 (de ropa, de pelo, de dientes) brush, brushing 2 (de madera) planing
cepillar [A1] *vt*
A 1 ‹*ropa/dientes/pelo*› to brush 2 ‹*madera*› to plane
B (Col fam) (adular) to butter ... up (colloq)
■ **cepillarse** *v pron*
A (*refl*) ‹*ropa*› to brush; ‹*dientes*› to brush, clean
B (*enf*) (Esp) 1 (arg) (matar) to bump ... off (colloq) 2 (terminar) ‹*comida*› to polish off (colloq)
cepillo *m*
A (para ropa, zapatos, pelo) brush; (para suelo) scrubbing brush; **lleva el pelo cortado al ~** he has a crew cut; ***echarle ~ a algn*** (Col fam) to butter sb up (colloq)
(Compuesto) **cepillo de dientes/uñas** toothbrush/nailbrush
B (de carpintería) plane
C (en la iglesia) collection box (*o* plate *etc*)
cepo *m* (para animales) trap; (Auto) wheel clamp; (Hist) stocks (*pl*)
ceporro *m* 1 ***dormir como un ~*** (fam) to sleep like a log; ***estar como un ~*** to be very fat 2 (fam) (persona torpe) dimwit
cera *f* (para velas) wax; (para pisos, muebles) wax polish; (de abejas) beeswax; (de los oídos) wax; **le di ~ al suelo** I polished the floor
(Compuestos)
- **cera depilatoria** depilatory wax
- **cera virgen** pure wax

cerámica *f* (arte) ceramics, pottery; (pieza) piece of pottery
ceramista *mf* ceramicist, ceramist
cerbatana *f* (arma) blowpipe; (juguete) peashooter
cerca¹ *adv*
A 1 (en el espacio) near, close; **¿hay algún banco ~?** is there a bank nearby *o* close by?; **queda aquí cerquita** it's very near (here); **está por aquí ~** it's near here (somewhere); **~ DE algo/algn** near sth/sb; **viven ~ de Tampico/de casa** they live near Tampico/near us 2 **de cerca** close up, close to; **ver algo de ~** to see sth close up *o* close to; **no veo bien de ~** I'm longsighted; ***seguir algo de ~*** to follow sth closely
B (en el tiempo) close; **los exámenes ya están ~** the exams aren't far away now; **~ DE algo/+ INF** close TO sth/-ING; **serán ~ de las dos** it must be nearly 2 o'clock *o* getting on for 2
C (indicando aproximación) **~ de** almost, nearly; **~ de 1.000** almost *o* nearly 1,000
cerca² *f* (de alambre, madera) fence; (de piedra) wall
cercado *m*
A 1 (de alambre, madera) fence; (de piedra) wall 2 (terreno) enclosure
B (Per) (distrito) district
cercanía *f*
A (en el espacio) closeness, proximity; (en el tiempo) proximity, imminence
B **cercanías** *fpl*: **Madrid y sus ~s** Madrid and its environs, Madrid and the surrounding area; **tren de ~s** local *o* suburban train; **en las ~s del aeropuerto** in the vicinity of the airport, near the airport
cercano -na *adj*
A 1 (en el espacio) nearby, neighboring*; **~ A algo** near sth, close TO sth; **los pueblos ~s a Durango** the villages in

the vicinity of *o* close to *o* near Durango; **una suma cercana al millón** an amount close to *o* close on a million 2 (en el tiempo) close, near; **en fecha cercana** soon; **~ a algo** close TO sth; **se sentía ~ a su fin** he felt the end was near

(Compuesto) **Cercano Oriente** *m* Near East

B ‹*pariente/amigo*› close

cercar [A2] *vt* 1 ‹*campo/terreno*› to enclose, surround; (con valla) to fence in 2 ‹*persona*› to surround 3 (Mil) ‹*ciudad*› to besiege; ‹*enemigo*› to surround

cercenar [A1] *vt* (frml) (cortar — un miembro) to sever; (— el borde de) cut off; **un artículo cercenado por la censura** an article which had been cut by the censor

cerciorarse *v pron* **~ se DE algo** to make certain OF sth

cerco *m*

A (asedio) siege; **poner ~ a una plaza** to lay siege to a town; **levantar el ~** to raise the siege; **un ~ policial** a police cordon; **la rodeaba un ~ de admiradores** she was besieged by a group of admirers; **estrecharon el ~ en torno al grupo** they tightened the net around the group

B (de una mancha) ring

C 1 (borde, aro) rim 2 (Esp) (marco) frame

D (AmL) (valla) fence; (seto) hedge

cerda *f*

A 1 (animal) sow 2 (fam) (mujer — sucia) slob (colloq); (— despreciable) bitch (sl)

B (pelo) bristle

cerdada *f* (fam) dirty trick (colloq)

cerdo *m*

A (animal) pig, hog (AmE); ***comer como un ~*** (comer mucho) to stuff oneself (colloq)

B (carne) pork

C (fam) (hombre — sucio) slob (colloq); (— despreciable) bastard (sl), swine (colloq)

cereal *m* (planta, grano) cereal; (para desayunar) (AmL) cereal

cereales *mpl* (Esp) (para desayunar) cereal

cerebelo *m* cerebellum

cerebral *adj* ‹*actividad/tumor/derrame*› brain (*before n*); ‹*persona*› cerebral

cerebro *m* 1 (Anat) brain; ***estrujarse el ~*** (fam) to rack one's brains (colloq); ***lavarle el ~ a algn*** to brainwash sb 2 (persona) brains; **el ~ de la operación** the brains behind the operation; ***ser un ~*** *or* ***cerebrito*** (fam) to be brainy *o* a brain box (colloq)

ceremonia *f* ceremony; **no andemos con ~s** let's not stand on ceremony; **lo hizo todo sin ~** she did it all without any fuss (colloq); **se lo solté sin ~** I told him in plain language

ceremonial *adj/m* ceremonial

ceremonioso -sa *adj* ceremonious

cereza *f* (fruta) cherry; (del café) (AmC, Col, Ven) coffee bean

cerezo *m* cherry tree

cerilla *f*

A (esp Esp) (fósforo) match

B (de los oídos) wax

cerillo *m* (esp AmC, Méx) match

cerner [E8] *vt* (harina) to sift, sieve; (arena) to sieve

■ **cernerse** *v pron* **~se SOBRE algn/algo** «*ave*» to hover OVER sb/sth; «*peligro/amenaza*» to hang *o* hover OVER sb/sth

cernícalo *m*

A (Zool) kestrel

B (fam) (bruto) boor; (tonto) dimwit (colloq)

cernir [I12] *vt* ▸**cerner**

cero *m* 1 (Fís, Mat) zero; (en números de teléfono) zero (AmE), oh (BrE); **tres grados bajo ~** three degrees below zero, minus three degrees; **a las ~ horas de hoy** at midnight last night; **~ coma cinco** zero point five; **empezar/partir de ~** to start from scratch; ***ser un ~ a la izquierda*** to be useless; (ser un don nadie) (Esp) to be a nobody 2 (en fútbol, rugby) zero (AmE), nil (BrE); (en tenis) love; **ganan por tres a ~** they're winning three-zero (AmE) *o* (BrE) three-nil; **ganaba 40 a ~** she was winning 40-love 3 (Educ) zero, nought (BrE); **me puso un ~ en física** he gave me zero *o* nought out of ten in physics

ceroso -sa *adj* ‹*sustancia*› waxy; ‹*cara/tez*› waxen (liter)

cerote *m* (AmC fam) (de excremento) turd (vulg)

cerquillo *m* (AmL) (flequillo) bangs (*pl*) (AmE), fringe (BrE)

cerrado -da *adj*

A 1 ‹*puerta/ventana/ojos/boca*› closed, shut; ‹*mejillones/almejas*› closed; ‹*sobre/carta*› sealed; ‹*puño*› clenched; ‹*cortinas*› drawn, closed; **estaba cerrado con llave** it was locked 2 ‹*válvula*› closed, shut off; ‹*grifo*› turned off

B ‹*tienda/restaurante/museo*› closed, shut; Ⓢ **cerrado** closed; Ⓢ **cerrado por defunción/reformas** closed owing to bereavement/for alterations

C 1 ‹*espacio/recinto*› enclosed 2 (cargado) ‹*ambiente*› stuffy 3 ‹*grupo*› closed 4 (Mat) ‹*serie/conjunto*› closed

D (Ling) ‹*vocal*› close, closed; ‹*acento/dialecto*› broad

E ‹*curva*› sharp

F (nublado) overcast; (refiriéndose a la noche): **ya era noche cerrada** it was already completely dark

G ‹*barba*› thick

H (enérgico): **una cerrada ovación** an ecstatic reception; **una cerrada descarga** a burst of gunfire

I 1 (poco receptivo, intransigente) set in one's ways; **estar ~ A algo**: **está ~ a todo cambio** his mind is closed to change; **el país ha estado ~ a influencias externas** the country has been shut off from outside influence 2 (poco comunicativo) uncommunicative 3 (fam) (torpe) dense (colloq), thick (colloq); **es muy ~ de mollera** he's very dense (colloq)

A (Esp) (Fin): Ⓢ **apartamentos de lujo, precio cerrado** apartments, price guaranteed

cerradura *f* lock; **el ojo de la ~** the keyhole

cerrajería *f* locksmith's shop

cerrajero -ra *m,f* locksmith

cerrar [A5] *vt*

A 1 ‹*puerta/ventana*› to close, shut; ‹*ojos/boca*› to shut, close; **cierra la puerta con llave** lock the door 2 ‹*botella*› to put the top on/cork in; ‹*frasco*› to put the lid on; **un frasco herméticamente cerrado** an airtight container 3 ‹*paraguas/abanico/mano*› to close; ‹*libro*› to close, shut; ‹*puño*› to clench 4 ‹*cortinas*› to close, draw; ‹*persianas*› to lower, pull down; ‹*abrigo*› to fasten, button up; ‹*cremallera*› to do up

B ‹*grifo/agua/gas*› to turn off; ‹*válvula*› to close, shut off

C 1 ‹*fábrica/comercio/oficina*› (en el quehacer diario, por obras, vacaciones) to close; (definitivamente) to close (down) 2 ‹*aeropuerto/carretera/frontera*› to close; **cerrado al tráfico** closed to traffic

D ‹*cuenta bancaria*› to close; ‹*caso/juicio*› to close; ‹*acuerdo/negociación*› to finalize; **han cerrado el plazo de inscripción** enrollment has closed *o* finished

E 1 ‹*acto/debate*› to bring … to an end; ‹*jornada*› to end; **los acontecimientos que han cerrado el año** the events with which the year has ended 2 ‹*desfile/cortejo*› to bring up the rear of 3 ‹*circuito*› to close 4 ‹*paréntesis/comillas*› to close

■ **cerrar** *vi*

A (hablando de puerta, ventana): **cierra, que hace frío** close *o* shut the door (*o* window *etc*), it's cold; **¿cerraste con llave?** did you lock up?

B «*puerta/ventana/cajón*» to close, shut; «*grifo/llave de paso*» to turn off; «*abrigo/vestido*» to fasten, do up (BrE); **la ventana no cierra bien** the window doesn't close *o* shut properly

C «*comercio/oficina*» (en el quehacer diario, por obras, vacaciones) to close, shut; (definitivamente) to close (down); Ⓢ **cerramos los lunes** we are closed on Mondays

D (Fin) «*dolar/peso*» to close

E (en dominó) to block; (en naipes) to go out

■ **cerrarse** *v pron*

A 1 «*puerta/ventana*» (+ *compl*) to shut, close; **la puerta se cerró sola/de golpe** the door closed by itself/slammed shut 2 «*ojos*» (+ *me/te/le etc*) to close; **se me cierran los ojos de cansancio** I'm so tired I can't keep my eyes open 3 «*flor/almeja*» to close up 4 «*herida*» to heal (up)

B (*refl*) ‹*abrigo*› to fasten, button up

C (terminar) «*acto/debate/libro*» to end, conclude; «*jornada/año*» to end

D (mostrarse reacio, intransigente): **se cerró y no quiso saber nada más** she closed her mind and refused to listen to any more about it; **se cerró en su actitud** he dug his heels in; **~se A algo**: **sería ~se a la evidencia** it would be turning our back on the evidence; **se cierran a todo**

cambio they're not open to change
cerrazón *m* (terquedad) stubbornness; (mentalidad poco flexible) blinkered attitude
cerril *adj* ‹*ganado*› wild; ‹*caballo*› wild, unbroken; ‹*persona*› uncouth, rough
cerro *m* (Geog) hill; ***irse por los ~s de Úbeda*** to go off at a tangent
cerrojazo *m*: **dar (el) ~ a algo** to put an end to sth
cerrojo *m* 1 (de puerta) bolt; **echar** *or* **correr el ~** to bolt the door 2 (de fusil) bolt 3 (Dep) defensive tactics (*pl*); **jugar al ~** to play defensively
certamen *m* competition, contest
certero -ra *adj* 1 ‹*tiro*› accurate; ‹*golpe*› well-aimed; **es un tirador ~** he's a crack shot 2 ‹*juicio*› sound; ‹*respuesta*› good
certeza, certidumbre *f* certainty; **tengo la ~ de que ...** I'm quite sure *o* certain that ...; **no lo sé con ~** I'm not sure, I don't know for sure
certificación *f* certification
certificado[1] **-da** *adj* ‹*paquete/carta*› registered; **mandé la carta certificada** I sent the letter by registered mail
certificado[2] *m* certificate
(Compuestos)
- **certificado de defunción/nacimiento** death/birth certificate
- **certificado de estudios** school-leaving certificate
- **certificado médico** medical certificate

certificar [A2] *vt* to certify
cerumen *m* cerumen (tech), earwax
cerval *adj*: **sentía un miedo ~** (liter) she was terrified
cervantino -na, cervantesco -ca *adj* of/relating to Cervantes, Cervantine
cervantista *mf* Cervantes scholar
cervatillo *m* fawn
cervecera *f* brewery
cervecería *f* bar (*gen selling a wide variety of beers*)
cervecero -ra *adj* ‹*industria*› brewing (*before n*), beer (*before n*)
cerveza *f* beer
(Compuestos)
- **cerveza tirada** *o* **de barril** draft beer (AmE), draught beer (BrE)
- **cerveza rubia/negra** lager/dark beer

cervical *adj* 1 ‹*músculo/vértebra*› neck (*before n*), cervical (tech) 2 (del útero) cervical
cérvido *m* cervid
cerviz *f* nape of the neck; ***bajar la ~*** to give in
cesación *f* ▸ **cese A**
cesante[1] *adj* 1 (frml *o* period) (en un cargo): **quedó ~** he lost his job; (por racionalización, reducción de personal) he was laid off, he was made redundant (esp BrE) 2 (Chi) (sin empleo) unemployed
cesante[2] *mf* 1 (frml *o* period) (en cargo) *person who has lost his or her job* 2 (Chi) (sin empleo) unemployed person
cesantía *f* (desempleo) (Chi) unemployment; (despido) (RPl frml) dismissal; (pago) (Col) severance pay
cesar [A1] *vi*
A (parar) to stop; **~ DE + INF** to stop -ING; **no cesó de interrumpirme** he continually interrupted me; **sin ~** incessantly; **trabajaron sin ~ durante 36 horas** they worked for 36 hours nonstop; **le contestó sin ~ de trabajar** she kept on working while she answered
B (frml *o* period) (dimitir): **cesó en su cargo** she left her post, she resigned
■ **cesar** *vt* (frml *o* period) (despedir) to dismiss
cesárea *f* cesarean* (section); **le tuvieron que hacer una ~** she had to have a cesarean
cese *m*
A (frml *o* period) (fin, interrupción) cessation (frml); **el ~ de las hostilidades** the cessation of hostilities; **el ~ de pagos** the suspension of payments; **~ de la actividad laboral** a stoppage of work
(Compuesto) **cese del fuego** (AmL) ceasefire
B (frml *o* period) 1 (despido) dismissal; **darle el ~ a algn** to dismiss sb 2 (renuncia) resignation

cesio *m* cesium*
cesión *f* (de derecho) assignment, cession (frml); (de territorio) transfer
(Compuestos)
- **cesión arrendamiento** leaseback
- **cesión de bienes** surrender *o* (frml) cession of goods

césped *m* 1 (planta) grass; (extensión) lawn, grass; Ⓢ **prohibido pisar el césped** keep off the grass 2 (Dep) field, pitch (BrE); (en tenis) (AmL) grass
cesta *f*
A (recipiente) basket
(Compuestos)
- **cesta de la compra** (Esp) (canasta) shopping basket; (Econ) *average cost of a week's shopping*
- **cesta de Navidad** Christmas hamper
- **cesta punta** (deporte) pelota; (canasta) basket (*for playing pelota*)

B (esp AmL) (en baloncesto) basket
cestería *f* 1 (tienda) basketwork shop (*o* factory *etc*) 2 (artesanía) basketwork
cesto *m*
A (esp Esp) (recipiente) basket; **el ~ de la ropa sucia** the laundry basket
B (esp AmL) (en baloncesto) basket
cetáceo *m* cetacean
cetorrino *m* basking shark
cetrería *f* falconry
cetrino -na *adj* ‹*rostro/piel*› (de aspecto sano) olive; (de aspecto enfermizo) sallow
cetro *m* (del rey, emperador) scepter*; ***empuñar el ~*** to ascend the throne
cf. (= **confróntese**) cf
cg. (= **centigramo**) cg
Ch, ch *f* (*read as* /tʃe/ *or* /se 'atʃe/ *or* (Esp) /θe 'atʃe/) *combination traditionally considered as a separate letter in the Spanish alphabet*
chabacanada *f*, **chabacanería** *f* (cualidad) tackiness (colloq), vulgarity; (acto, dicho) **decir ~s** to be crude; **hacer eso fue una ~** what you did was in very bad taste
chabacano[1] **-na** *adj* ‹*ropa/decoración*› gaudy, tasteless; ‹*espectáculo/persona*› vulgar; ‹*chiste/cuento*› coarse, tasteless
chabacano[2] *m* (Méx) (árbol) apricot tree; (fruta) apricot
chabola *f* (Esp) (en los suburbios) shack, shanty dwelling; **~s** shanty town
chabolismo *m* (Esp): **el problema del ~** the shanty town problem
chacal *m* jackal
chácara *f* (Col) (monedero) change purse (AmE), purse (BrE)
chacarera *f*: *South American folk dance*
chacarero -ra *m,f* (CS, Per) farmer (*who works a* chacra)
chacha *f* (Esp fam) maid, housemaid
chachachá *m* cha-cha, cha-cha-cha
chachalaca *f* chachalaca (*type of guan*)
cháchara *f*
A (fam) (conversación) chatter; **se pasa la mañana de ~** she spends the whole morning chattering
B (Méx) (objeto de poca importancia) piece of junk: **un cajón lleno de ~s** a drawer's full of junk; Ⓢ **compro cháchara(s) en general** general bric-a-brac bought
chacharear [A1] *vi* (fam) to chatter, to gab (AmE colloq), to natter (BrE colloq)
chacharero -ra *m,f*
A (fam) (parlanchín) chatterbox (colloq)
B (Méx) (de baratijas) junk dealer
chacho -cha *m,f* (Col fam) (persona importante) big shot (colloq); (en deporte, juego) champ (colloq), ace
Chaco *m*: *tb* **Gran ~** *region of scrub and swamp plains covering parts of Paraguay, Bolivia and Argentina*
chacolí *m*: *light, sharp wine*
chacota *f* (fam): **estar de ~** to be in a joking mood; ***tomar(se) algo a (la) ~*** to treat sth as a joke
chacotearse [A1] *v pron* (fam) **~ DE algo/algn** to make fun of sth/sb

C

C

chacotero -ra *adj* (fam): **es muy ~** he's very fond of a joke
chacra *f* (CS, Per) (granja) small farm; (casa) farmhouse
chacuaco *m* (Méx) 1 (chimenea) factory chimney; ***fumar como (un) ~*** to smoke like a chimney 2 (horno) furnace
chafa *adj* (Méx fam) shoddy (colloq)
chafar [A1] *vt*
A (fam) 1 ‹*peinado*› to flatten; ‹*plátano/pulpa*› to mash; ‹*huevos*› to break; ‹*ajo*› to crush 2 ‹*vestido/falda*› to wrinkle (AmE), to crumple (BrE)
B (Esp fam) 1 (en conversación) to squash (colloq), to crush 2 (desilusionar) to disappoint 3 (estropear) ‹*plan/vacaciones*› to spoil, ruin
■ **chafarse** *v pron* to get squashed
chafear [A1] *vi* (Méx fam): **el restaurante ya chafeó** the restaurant has gone downhill (colloq); **mi coche anda chafeando** my car's giving out (colloq); **el sindicato ya chafeó** the union's gone to the dogs (colloq)
chafirete *m* (Méx fam): **ya manejas como todo un ~** you drive like a madman (colloq)
chaflán *m* (Tec) chamfer, beveled* edge; (esquina) corner; **el banco que hace ~** the bank on the corner
chagualo *m*, **chaguala** *f* (Col fam & hum) shoe
chaise longue /ʃes'loŋ/ *f or m* chaise longue
chal *m* shawl, wrap
chala *f* 1 (RPl) (Bot) corn husk 2 (Chi) (Indum) sandal
chalado¹ -da *adj* (fam) [ESTAR] crazy (colloq), nuts (colloq)
chalado² -da *m,f* nutter (colloq)
chalán *m* (Col) (jinete) skilled horseman
chalanear [A1] *vi* to bargain, haggle
chalaneo *m*
A (en negocios) shady deals (*pl*)
B (Col, Per) (Equ) (doma) horsebreaking; (adiestramiento) training; (exhibición) display of horsemanship
chale *interj* (Méx fam) you're kidding! (colloq)
chalé *m* ▸**chalet**
chaleca *f* (Chi) cardigan
chaleco *m* (de traje) vest (AmE), waistcoat (BrE); (jersey sin mangas) sleeveless sweater; (acolchado) body warmer; (chaqueta de punto) (CS) cardigan; ***a ~*** (Méx) no matter what
(Compuestos)
• **chaleco antibalas** bulletproof vest
• **chaleco de fuerza** straitjacket
• **chaleco salvavidas** lifejacket,
chalequear [A1] *vt* (Ven fam) ‹*negocio*› to muscle in on (colloq); ‹*idea*› to pinch; **me chalequeó el puesto** he did me out of my job (colloq)
chalet /tʃa'le/ *m* (*pl* **-lets**) (en urbanización) house; (en el campo) cottage; (en la montaña) chalet; (en la playa) villa
(Compuesto) **chalet adosado/independiente** (Esp) semi-detached/detached house
chalona *f* (Per) jerked mutton
chalote *m*, **chalota** *f* shallot, scallion (AmE)
chalupa *f*
A (barca) skiff; (canoa) (AmL) small canoe
B (Méx) (Coc) stuffed tortilla
chamaco -ca *m,f* (Méx fam) (niño, muchacho) kid (colloq), youngster (colloq); (novio) (*m*) boyfriend; (*f*) girlfriend
chamagoso -sa *adj* (Méx fam) dirty, filthy
chamal *m* woolen* tunic (*worn by Araucanian women*)
chamanto *m*: *short multicolored blanket worn by Chilean peasants*
chamarra *f* (chaqueta) jacket
chamba *f*
A (Méx, Per, Ven fam) (trabajo) work; (lugar) work; **una buena ~** a good job; **tengo mucha ~** I have a lot of work to do; **en la ~** at work
B (Col) 1 (zanja) ditch 2 (herida) wound, gash; **se abrió una ~ en la cabeza** he gashed his head
chambear [A1] *vi* (Méx, Per fam) to work; **entro a ~ a las 9** I start work at 9
chambelán *m* chamberlain
chambero -ra *m,f* (Andes) scavenger
chambón¹ -bona *adj* (AmL fam) clumsy, klutzy (AmE colloq)
chambón² -bona *m,f* (AmL fam) clumsy clot (colloq), klutz (AmE colloq)
chambonada *f* (AmL fam) botch (colloq), botched job (colloq)
chambonear [A1] *vi* (Andes fam) to do a botched job (colloq)
chamboneo *m* (Col fam) botched job (colloq)
chambra *f* (Méx) matinée coat, matinée jacket
chamín *m* (Ven fam) buddy (AmE colloq), mate (BrE colloq)
chamizo *m*
A 1 (leña quemada) charred log 2 (Col) (ramas secas) *tb* **~s** brushwood
B (choza) thatched hut
chamo¹ -ma *adj* (Ven fam) young
chamo² -ma *m,f*
A (Ven fam) (niño, muchacho) kid (colloq)
B (Ven arg) (amigo) buddy (AmE colloq), mate (BrE colloq); **muéstramelas, chama** come on, let's see them
champa *f*
A (Andes) (de hierba) piece of turf; (de pelo) (fam) tuft
B (AmC) (choza) hut
champán *m*, **champaña** *m or f* champagne
champanera *f* champagne bucket
champiñón, champignon *m* mushroom
champión® *m* (RPl) sneaker (AmE), plimsoll (BrE)
champú *m* (*pl* **-pús** *or* **-púes**) shampoo
champurrado *m*
A (Méx) (Coc) *thick hot drink made with ground corn and chocolate*
B (Méx fam) (revoltijo) jumble
champurrear [A1] *vt* (CS) ▸**chapurrear**
chamuchina *f* (AmS) 1 (fam) (chusma) rabble (colloq) 2 (fam) (alboroto) rumpus (colloq), ruckus (AmE colloq)
chamullar [A1] *vi* (Chi fam) 1 (contar patrañas) to tell stories 2 (hablar) to talk; (de manera confusa) to burble on
chamullo *m* (Chi fam) (mentira) cock and bull story (colloq); (acción ilícita) scam (colloq)
chamuscar [A2] *vt* to scorch, singe; **madera chamuscada** charred wood
■ **chamuscarse** *v pron*: **~se el pelo** to singe one's hair
chamusquina *f* singeing, scorching; **aquello me olía a ~** it sounded fishy to me
chamuyar [A1] *vi* (RPl fam) to chatter
■ **chamuyar** *vt* (RPl fam) to mutter
chan *m* (AmC) mountain guide
chancaca *f* 1 (Andes) (melaza) brown sugarloaf; ***ser ~*** (Chi fam) to be a piece of cake (colloq) 2 (Per) (dulce de maíz) maize cake
chancacazo *m* (a una persona) (Andes fam) wallop (colloq); (contra algo) (Chi fam) bang
chancadora *f* (Chi) crusher, grinder
chancar [A2] *vt*
A (Andes) (triturar) to crush, grind
B (Chi fam) (pegar) to beat … up (colloq)
C (Per arg) (estudiar) to cram, to swot up on (BrE colloq)
chance *f or m* (AmL) (oportunidad) chance; **no hay ningún ~ de que se libre** he has no chance of escaping; **dar ~ a algn** to give sb the chance; **tiene pocas ~s de ganar** he doesn't have *o* stand much chance of winning
chancear [A1] *vi* (Col fam) to joke, kid around (colloq)
■ **chancearse** *v pron* **~se DE algn** to make fun OF sb
chancero -ra *adj* (Chi fam): **es muy ~** he's always joking
chanchada *f* (AmL fam) 1 (porquería, suciedad) mess; **deja de hacer ~s** stop making such a mess 2 (acción indigna) dirty trick (colloq); **hacerle una ~ a algn** to play a dirty trick on sb
chanchería *f* (AmL) pork butcher's shop
chanchero -ra *m,f* (AmL) (criador) pig farmer; (vendedor) pork butcher
chanchito¹ -ta *adj* (Chi fam): **lo pillaron ~** they caught him red-handed; **cayó ~ a la cama** he collapsed onto the bed
chanchito² *m* (fam)
A (Andes, CS) (Zool) woodlouse
B (CS) (alcancía) piggy bank

chancho¹ -cha *adj* (AmL fam) (sucio) filthy, gross (colloq); (miserable, ruin) mean

chancho² -cha *m,f*
A (AmL) (Zool) pig; ***gordo como un ~*** (CS fam) as fat as a pig (colloq); ***hacerse el ~ rengo*** (RPl fam) to act dumb (colloq); ***querer la chancha y los cinco reales*** *or* ***los veinte*** (RPl fam) to want to have one's cake and eat it (colloq); ***a cada ~ le llega su sábado*** (AmC) everyone gets their just deserts sooner or later; ***~ limpio nunca engorda*** (Bol, CS fam) a few germs never hurt anyone (colloq)
B (AmL fam) (persona sucia) dirty *o* filthy pig (colloq)

chancho³ *m*
A (Chi, Per) (Coc) *tb* **carne de ~** pork
B (Chi, Per vulg) (trasero) butt (AmE colloq), bum (BrE colloq)

chanchullero¹ -ra *adj* (fam) shady (colloq), crooked

chanchullero² -ra *m,f* (fam) crook (colloq)

chanchullo *m* (fam) racket (colloq), fiddle (BrE colloq)

chancla *f* (sandalia) flip-flop; (pantufla) (Col) slipper

chancleta *f*
A (sandalia) thong (AmE), flip-flop (BrE); (zapato viejo) (Chi fam) worn-out old shoe
B (Andes, CS fam) (niña) baby girl
C (Ven fam) (acelerador) accelerator

chancletear [A1] *vi* (CS fam) to slop around

chancletudo -da *adj* (CS, Ven fam & pey) common (pej)

chanclo *m* (de madera) clog; (de goma) galosh, overshoe

chancludo -da *adj* (Méx fam) scruffy, sloppy

chancón -cona *adj* (Per arg) hardworking

chancro *m* chancre

chancuco *m* (Col fam) swindle; **me hicieron ~** they swindled me

chándal *m* (*pl* **-dals**) (Esp) tracksuit

chanfaina *f* (fam) (Per) (lío) shambles (colloq)

chanfle *m* (AmL) spin; **darle ~ a la pelota** to put spin on the ball

chanfleado -da *adj* (AmL) ‹*tiro*› curving

changa *f* (RPl fam) odd job

changador *m* (RPl) porter

changarro *m* (Méx) small store

chango -ga *m,f* (Méx) monkey

changuito® *m* (Arg) (para las compras) shopping cart (AmE), shopping trolley (BrE); (para el bebé) stroller (AmE), pushchair (BrE)

chanquetes *mpl* whitebait (*pl*)

chanta¹ *adj* (RPl arg) (informal) unreliable; (mentiroso) deceitful

chanta² *mf* (RPl arg) (informal) unreliable person; (mentiroso) liar

chantaje *m* blackmail; **le hacen ~** he is being blackmailed

chantajear [A1] *vt* to blackmail

chantajista *mf* blackmailer

chantar [A1] *vt*
A 1 (Andes, CS fam) ‹*beso*› to plant; **le chantó un coscorrón** she whacked him on the head *o* gave him a whack on the head (colloq); **me chantó un pellizco** she pinched me; **le chantó el sombrero hasta las orejas** he jammed her hat firmly on her head 2 (Col, CS fam) ‹*trabajo/tarea*›: **siempre me chantan estos trabajos** I always get landed with these jobs (colloq)
B (Chi fam) ‹*persona*› to walk out on (colloq); ***dejar chantado a algn*** (Chi fam) to stand sb up (colloq)
■ **chantarse** *v pron*
A (Chi, Per fam) ‹*vestido*› to put on
B (Chi fam) 1 (quedarse) to instal* oneself 2 (detenerse) to stop dead 3 (dejar un vicio): **hace tiempo que se chantó** she quit *o* gave up some time ago; **no tomo más, me chanto por hoy** I'm not drinking any more, I've had enough for today

chantillí, chantilly /ʃanti'ʝi, tʃanti'ʝi/ *m*: *tb* **crema ~** (*f*) whipped cream, chantilly

chantre *m* precentor

chanza *f* derisive comment

chao *interj* (fam) bye (colloq), bye-bye (colloq)

chapa *f*
A 1 (plancha — de metal) sheet; (— de madera) panel; **techo de ~** corrugated iron roof 2 (lámina de madera) veneer 3 (carrocería) bodywork
B 1 (distintivo) badge; (de policía) shield (AmE), badge (BrE); (con el nombre) nameplate; (de perro) identification disc *o* tag 2 (RPl) (de matrícula) license plate (AmE), numberplate (BrE)
C (de botella) cap, top
D (AmL) (cerradura) lock
E **chapas** *fpl* (AmL fam) (en las mejillas): **le salieron ~s** (por vergüenza) her cheeks flushed (red); (por el aire fresco) her cheeks were red *o* rosy
F (AmC fam) (joya) earring; (dentadura postiza) false teeth (*pl*)

chapado -da *adj* ‹*metal*› plated; **un reloj ~ en oro** a gold-plated watch

chapapote *m* (Esp) oil (*on beach, coast*)

chapar [A1] *vt*
A ‹*mueble*› to veneer; ‹*reloj/pulsera*› to plate
B (Per fam) (agarrar, sorprender) to catch
■ **chapar** *vi* (Esp arg) (estudiar) to cram

chaparral *m* chaparral, thicket

chaparrastroso -sa *adj* (Méx fam) scruffy

chaparreras *fpl* (Méx) chaps (*pl*)

chaparro¹ -rra *adj* (AmL fam) short, squat; **quedarse ~** to stop growing

chaparro² -rra *m,f*
A (AmL fam) shorty (colloq), titch (colloq)
B **chaparro** *m* (arbusto) dwarf evergreen oak

chaparrón *m* (Meteo) downpour, cloudburst

chape *m* (Chi) (trenza) braid (AmE), plait (BrE); (pelo atado) bunch

chapeado -da *adj* (Col, Méx) flushed

chapeau /ʃa'po, tʃa'po/ *m* (fam *o* period): **la organización merece un ~** we should take our hats off to the organizers (journ); **¡~** bravo!, well done!

chapela *f* (Esp) beret

chapero *m* (Esp arg) ass peddler (AmE sl), rent boy (BrE colloq)

chaperón -rona *m,f* chaperon

chapetes *mpl* (Méx) ▸**chapa E**

chapiollo -lla *adj* (AmC fam) humble

chapista *mf* panel beater

chapitel *m* (de torre) spire; (de columna) capital

chapó *m* ▸**chapeau**

chapopote *m* (Méx) (alquitrán) tar; (asfalto) asphalt

chapotear [A1] *vi* (en agua) splash (around); (en barro) squelch (around)

chapoteo *m* (en agua) splashing; (en barro) squelching

chapucería *f* ▸**chapuza 1**

chapucero¹ -ra *adj* ‹*persona*› sloppy, slapdash; ‹*trabajo/reparación*› botched

chapucero² -ra *m,f*: **es un ~** his work is very slapdash

chapulín *m* (AmC, Méx) (Zool) locust

chapurrear [A1], **chapurrar** [A1] *vt* (fam): **~ el inglés** to speak broken *o* poor English

chapuza *f* 1 (fam) (trabajo mal hecho) botched job (colloq), botch (colloq); **me hizo una ~** he made a botch of the job (colloq) 2 (Esp fam) (trabajo ocasional) odd job 3 (Méx) (trampa) trick

chapuzas *mf* (*pl* ~) (Esp) ▸**chapucero²**

chapuzón *m* dip; **darse un ~** to have a dip

chaquet (*pl* **-quets**), **chaqué** *m* morning coat

chaqueta *f*
A (Indum) jacket; ***cambiar de ~*** *or* (Chi) ***darse vuelta la ~*** (fam) to change sides

Compuestos
- **chaqueta americana** (Esp) blazer
- **chaqueta de punto** cardigan

B (Col) (Odont) crown

chaquete *m* (Esp) backgammon

chaquetero -ra *m,f*
A (Esp fam) (en política) turncoat, opportunist
B (Chi fam) (envidioso) envious person

chaquetilla *f* bolero

chaquetón *m* three-quarter length coat

charada *f* charade

C

charal *m* (Méx) *small lake fish*; ***como** or **hecho un** ~* as thin as a rake (colloq)

charamusca *f*
A (Méx) (Coc) candy twist
B (Méx fam) (mujer fea) ugly hag (colloq)

charanga *f* brass band; (militar) military band; **la España de ~ y pandereta** the Spain of bullfighters and flamenco dancers

charango *m* small five-stringed guitar

charape *m* (Méx): *fermented drink made from cactus juice and brown sugar*

charca *f* pond, pool

charco *m* 1 puddle, pool 2 **el ~** (fam) (océano Atlántico) the Atlantic, the Pond (colloq & hum)

charcutería *f* delicatessen, charcuterie (AmE)

charcutero -ra *m,f* pork butcher

charla *f* 1 (conversación) chat; **estábamos de ~** we were having a chat; **su ~ me aburre** his chatter bores me 2 (conferencia) talk

charlar [A1] *vi* to chat, talk

charlatán¹ -tana *adj* (fam) talkative

charlatán² -tana *m,f* (fam) 1 (parlanchín) chatterbox (colloq) 2 (vendedor deshonesto) dishonest hawker; (curandero deshonesto) charlatan

charlatanear [A1] *vi* to chatter away

charlatanería *f* 1 (locuacidad) talkativeness 2 (arte de vender) clever *o* cunning salesmanship; (palabras) patter

charlestón *m* charleston

charlotada *f* (Taur) comic bullfight

charlotear [A1] *vi* (fam) to chat

charloteo *m* (fam) chatting, chatter; **están de ~** they are chatting

charme /ʃarm/ *m* charm

charnel *m* (AmC) piece of shrapnel

charol *m*
A 1 (barniz) lacquer 2 (cuero) patent leather
B (Col, Per) (bandeja) tray

charola *f* (Bol, Méx, Per) tray

charquear [A1] *vt*
A (Bol, Chi) ‹*carne*› to jerk
B (Chi fam) ‹*persona*› to beat … up

charqui *m* (AmS) charqui, jerked beef

charrasquear [A1] *vt*
A (AmL) ‹*guitarra*› to strum
B ‹*persona*› to stab

charrería *f* (Méx) *the culture of horsemanship and rodeo riding*

charretera *f* epaulette

charro¹ -rra *adj*
A (fam) (de mal gusto) gaudy, garish
B (en Méx) ‹*tradiciones/música*› of/relating to the **charro²**

charro² -rra *m,f* (en Méx) (jinete) (*m*) horseman, cowboy; (*f*) horsewoman, cowgirl

> **charro, charra**
>
> A Mexican cowboy or cowgirl skilled in horsemanship. The traditional *charro* costume is very elaborate and trimmed with silver. A man's outfit consists of a high-crowned, wide-brimmed hat, tight trousers, a white shirt, waistcoat and short jacket. A woman's outfit is a similar but with a long, wide skirt. *Charros* originated *charrerías*, the culture associated with horse-riding and rodeo skills. They also take part in festivals known as *charreadas*

charrúa *adj/mf* (CS period) Uruguayan

chárter¹ *adj inv* charter (*before n*)

chárter² *m* charter (flight)

chascar [A2] *vt* ▸**chasquear**

chascarrillo *m* (fam) joke, funny story

chas chas *m*
A (RPl leng infantil): **mamá te va a hacer ~ ~** Mommy's going to smack your bottom
B (Méx fam) (efectivo): **pagar al ~ ~** to pay cash

chasco *m*
A (decepción) disappointment, let-down (colloq); **me llevé un ~** I felt let down *o* disappointed
B (broma) joke

chascón -cona *adj* (Chi fam): **¡qué ~ estás!** your hair's a mess! (colloq)

chasis, chasís *m* (*pl* ~) (Auto) chassis; (Fot) plateholder

chasquear [A1] *vt* 1 ‹*lengua*› to click; ‹*dedos*› to click, snap 2 ‹*látigo*› to crack

chasqui *m* (Andes, RPl) courier, messenger

chasquido *m* 1 (de la lengua) click; (de los dedos) click, snap 2 (de látigo) crack; (de rama seca) crack, snap

chasquilla *f* (Chi) bangs (*pl*) (AmE), fringe (BrE)

chat *m* (Inf) chat room

chatarra¹ *adj inv* (Méx): **comida ~** junk food; **productos ~** cheap goods; **empresas ~** second-rate companies

chatarra² *f*
A (Metal) scrap (metal); **el coche es pura ~** the car is just a heap of scrap
B (fam) (calderilla) change, small *o* loose change

chatarrería *f* scrapyard

chatarrero -ra *m,f* scrap merchant

chatel -tela *m,f* (AmC fam) (*m*) little boy; (*f*) little girl

chateo *m* (Esp fam): **ir de ~** to go out for a few glasses of wine

chato¹ -ta *adj*
A 1 ‹*nariz*› snub (*before n*) 2 ‹*embarcación*› flat-bottomed 3 (Per fam) (bajo) short
B (AmS) ‹*nivel*› low; ‹*obra*› pedestrian; **un ambiente ~** an atmosphere lacking intellectual/artistic interest

chato² *m* (Esp) *tb* **~ de vino** glass of wine

chatura *f* (AmS) low intellectual/artistic level

chaucha *f*
A (RPl) (Bot, Coc) French bean
B (Chi fam): **estar sin una** *or* **sin ni ~** to be broke (colloq); ***caerle la ~ a algn*** (fam): **al final le cayó la ~** the penny finally dropped

chauchera *f* (Bol, Chi fam) change purse (AmE), purse (BrE)

chauvinismo /tʃoβi'nismo/ *m* chauvinism

chauvinista¹ /tʃoβi'nista/ *adj* chauvinistic

chauvinista² /tʃoβi'nista/ *mf* chauvinist

chaval -vala *m,f* 1 (esp Esp fam) (niño) kid (colloq), youngster; ***estar hecho un ~*** (fam) to be as young as can be 2 (Esp fam) (como apelativo) kid (colloq)

chavalo -la *m,f* (AmC, Méx) ▸**chaval**

chaveta *f* 1 (clavija) pin, cotter pin; ***estar mal de la ~*** (fam) to have a screw loose (colloq); ***perder la ~*** (fam) to go off one's rocker (colloq) 2 (Per fam) (navaja) switchblade (AmE), flick-knife (BrE)

chavo¹ -va *adj* (Méx fam) young

chavo² -va *m,f*
A 1 Méx (fam) (muchacho) guy (colloq); (muchacha) girl 2 (como apelativo) kid (colloq)
(Compuesto) **chavos banda** *mpl* (Méx) street gang
B **chavo** *m* (fam) (dinero): **estoy sin un ~** I'm broke (colloq)

chayote *m* (planta, fruto) chayote, mirliton; ***parir ~s*** (Méx fam) to have a terrible time of it

che¹ *interj* (RPl fam): **no te hagas el bobo, ~** come on, don't act the innocent; **¡qué frío hace, ~!** brrr, it's so cold!; **~, ¿qué hacemos?** look, what are we going to do?; **~, Marta, ¿qué tal?** hey Marta, how are you?; **¡pero ~! ¡cómo le dijiste eso!** for Heaven's sake! whatever made you tell him that?

che² *mf* (Chi fam) Argentinian

checada *f* 1 (Méx, Per) (comprobación) check; **hacer una ~ de algo** to check sth 2 (Méx) (Med) checkup

checar [A2] *vt* (Méx) 1 (revisar, mirar) to check; **me chequé la presión** (Med) I had my blood pressure checked; **¿por qué no vas a que te chequen?** why don't you go for a checkup?; **¡checa eso! ¡qué sombrero!** (fam) check that out! what a hat! (colloq) 2 (verificar) to check 3 (vigilar) to check up on 4 (marcar): **voy a ~ el boleto del estacionamiento** I'm going to get the parking ticket stamped; **tengo que ~ tarjeta a las 9** I have to clock in at nine o'clock

chécheres *mpl* (Col fam): **recoge tus ~** get your stuff together (colloq); **el cuarto de los ~** the junk room

checo¹ -ca *adj/m,f* Czech

checo² *m* (idioma) Czech
checoslovaco -ca *adj/m,f* (Hist) Czechoslovakian, Czechoslovak
Checoslovaquia *f* (Hist) Czechoslovakia
chef /ʃef, tʃef/ *m* chef
chele¹ -la *adj* (AmC) (de piel) light-skinned; (de pelo) blond-haired
chele² -la *m,f* (AmC) (de piel blanca) light-skinned person; (de pelo rubio) blond-haired person
cheli¹ *adj* slang (*before n*)
cheli² *m* (Ling) slang (*used in certain areas of Madrid*)
chelín *m* (moneda británica) (Hist) shilling; (moneda austríaca) schilling
chelista *mf* cellist
chelo *m* cello
chepa *f*
A (fam) (joroba) hump
B (Per fam) (tregua): **pedir ~** to beg ... to lay off
chepibe *m* (RPl fam & hum) errand boy
chépica *m* (Chi) turf
cheque *m* check (AmE), cheque (BrE); **me extendió un ~** she made out a check; **pagar con ~** to pay by check; **un ~ a nombre de ...** a check made out to ... *o* made payable to ...
Compuestos
• **cheque a fecha** (Chi) postdated check•
• **cheque al portador** bearer check•
• **cheque bancario** *or* **de gerencia** banker's draft
• **cheque cruzado/en blanco** crossed/blank check•
• **cheque de viaje** *or* **de viajero** traveler's check (AmE), traveller's cheque (BrE)
• **cheque nominativo** order check•; **un ~ ~ a favor de Don Juan Sánchez** a check made out to *o* made payable to Mr Juan Sánchez
• **cheque sin fondos** bad *o* (frml) dishonored• check•
chequeada *f* (Chi, Per fam) check
chequear [A1] *vt*
A 1 (revisar) to check; **~on los frenos** they checked the brakes 2 (verificar) to check; **~ la hora de salida** to check the departure time 3 (cotejar) **~ algo CON algo** to check sth AGAINST sth
B (AmL) ‹*equipaje*› to check in
■ **chequearse** *v pron* 1 (Col, Ven) (Aviac) to check in 2 (Ven) (Med) to have a checkup
chequeo *m* 1 (Med) checkup; (para entrar en el ejército, a trabajar) medical; **someterse a un ~ médico** to have a medical/a checkup; **les harán un ~** they will be given a medical/a check-up 2 (control, inspección) check; **rigurosos ~s de precios** rigorous price-checks; **mostradores de ~ de tiquetes** (Col) check-in desks
chequera *f* checkbook (AmE), chequebook (BrE)
cheve *f* (Méx fam) beer
chévere *adj* (AmL exc CS fam) great (colloq), fantastic (colloq); **¡qué ~!** that's great!
chibolo -la *m,f* (Per fam) kid (colloq)
chic¹ /ʃik, tʃik/ *adj inv* chic, fashionable
chic² /ʃik, tʃik/ *m* chic; **tiene ~** she's very chic
chica *f* (fam) maid; *ver tb* **chico**
Compuestos
• **chica de alterne** (Esp) hostess
• **chica de servicio** maid
chicanear [A1] *vi* (Andes, Méx): **deja de ~** cut out the tricks (colloq) (colloq)
chicanero -ra *adj* (Andes, Méx) tricky, crafty
chicano -na *adj/m,f* Chicano

> **Chicano**
> *Chicanos* are Mexican Americans, the descendants of Mexican immigrants living in the United States. For long looked down on by Americans of European descent, Chicano society has found a new pride in its origins and culture. There are numerous Chicano radio stations and cultural organizations in the United States and many universities and colleges now offer courses in Chicano Studies

chicha *f*
A (bebida alcohólica) *alcoholic drink made from fermented maize, also called* **chicha bruja**; ***ni ~ ni limonada*** (fam) neither one thing nor the other; ***sacarle la ~ a algn*** (Ven fam) to make sb work for his (*o* her *etc*) money; ***volver ~ a algn*** (fam) to beat sb to pulp
Compuestos
• **chicha andina** *alcoholic drink made with corn flour and pineapple juice*
• **chicha de manzana/uva** *alcoholic drink made from apple/grape juice*
B (bebida sin alcohol) *cold drink made with maize or fruit*
C (AmC vulg) (teta) tit (sl)

> **chicha**
> A Latin American drink, typically alcoholic, made of fermented maize. In some South American countries, *chicha* is drunk out of a bull's horn during fiestas patrias.
> In Peru, the term *lo chicha* is used to denote anything relating to ordinary life and the common people. It also refers to a mixture of *cumbia*, a fast music of Colombian origin, and *huayno*, Andean music

chícharo *m* (esp Méx) pea
chicharra *f* 1 (Zool) cicada 2 (timbre) buzzer 3 (monedero) wallet, billfold (AmE)
chicharrón *m*
A (Coc): **chicharrones** cracklings (*pl*) (AmE), pork scratchings (*pl*) (BrE); ***darle ~ a algo/algn*** (Méx fam) (eliminar) to get rid of sth/sb; ***tronar los chicharrones*** (Méx) to crack the whip
B (Ven fam) (rizo) curl
chiche¹ *adj* (AmC fam) dead easy (colloq); **me salió ~** it was dead easy *o* a pushover (colloq)
chiche² *m*
A (juguete) (CS fam) toy; (adorno) (Chi) trinket
B (AmC fam) (pecho) tit (sl)
chichero -ra *m,f* chicha seller
chichi *f* (Méx fam) (de mujer) tit (sl); (de animal) teat
chichicuilote *m* (Méx) sandpiper; ***piernas de ~*** long, thin legs
chichifear [A1] *vi* (Méx arg) to work as a prostitute, peddle ass (AmE vulg)
chichifo *m* (Méx arg) ass peddler (AmE sl), rent boy (BrE colloq)
chichigua *f* (Col fam) pittance (colloq)
chichiguatero -ra *m,f* (Col fam) skinflint (colloq), tightwad (AmE colloq)
chicho -cha *adj* (Méx fam) 1 (bonito) nice, neat (AmE colloq) 2 ‹*persona*›: **es muy chicha para los deportes** she's brilliant at sport (colloq)
chichón *m* swelling *o* bump on the head
chichona *adj* (AmC, Méx fam & hum) well-endowed, busty (colloq & hum)
chicle, chiclé *m* chewing gum
chiclero -ra *m,f*
A (Méx) (vendedor) street vendor (*selling chewing gum, candy, etc*)
B (AmC) (Agr) rubber tapper
chico¹ -ca *adj* (esp AmL) 1 (joven) ‹*persona*› young; **es muy ~ para salir solo** he's too young to go out on his own; **íbamos de ~s** *or* **cuando éramos ~s** we used to go there as children *o* (colloq) when we were small *o* little 2 (bajo) ‹*persona*› small; ***dejar ~ a algn*** (fam) to put sb to shame 3 (pequeño) small; **los pantalones le quedan ~s** the trousers are too small for him; **un pedacito chiquito** a tiny piece
chico² -ca *m,f*
A 1 (niño) (*m*) boy; (*f*) girl; **unos ~s** (varones) some boys; (varones y hombras) some children 2 (hijo) (*m*) son, boy; (*f*) daughter, girl; **mis ~s van a ese colegio** my children go to that school 3 (joven) (*m*) guy (colloq), boy (colloq), bloke (BrE colloq); (*f*) girl; **vino con su ~** she came with her boyfriend 4 (empleado joven) (*m*) boy; (*f*) girl 5 (como apelativo): **¡~! ¿tú por aquí?** well, well! what brings *you* here?; **~, no seas tonto** come on, don't be so silly
Compuesto **chico de los recados** messenger boy
B **chico** *m* (AmL) (en billar) frame; (en bolos) game
chicoco -ca *m,f* (Chi fam) 1 (niño) kid (colloq) 2 (persona baja) shorty (colloq), titch (BrE colloq)

C

chicoria *f* chicory
chicotazo *m* (AmL) whipping; **les impuso la obediencia a ~s** he whipped them into obedience
chicote *m* (fam)
A (AmL) (látigo) whip; **darle ~ a algn** to give sb a whipping, to whip sb
B (Náut) (de un cabo) end
C (Col) (fam) (cigarrillo) cigarette, fag (BrE colloq); (colilla) butt
chicotear [A1] *vt* (AmL) to whip
chicuelo -la *m,f* little kid
chido -da *adj* (Méx fam) fantastic (colloq)
chifa *m* (Per fam) (restaurante) Chinese restaurant; (comida) Chinese (food)
chiffon /tʃi'fon/ *m* chiffon
chifla *f* whistling, catcalls (*pl*)
chiflado[1] -da *adj* (fam) crazy (colloq), mad (BrE colloq); **ese viejo está ~** that old guy's crazy, that old guy's a nutter (colloq); **estar ~ POR algo/algn** to be crazy *o* nuts *o* mad ABOUT sth/sb (colloq)
chiflado[2] -da *m,f* (fam) nutcase (colloq), nutter (colloq)
chifladura *f* (fam): **¡qué ~ la de este tipo!** this guy's completely nuts (colloq); **le ha dado esa ~** he's got that crazy idea into his head (colloq)
chiflamicas *m* (*pl* ~) (Col fam) bad musician
chiflar [A1] *vt* ‹*actor/cantante*› to whistle at (*as sign of disapproval*) ≈ to boo
■ **chiflar** *vi*
A (silbar) to whistle
B (fam) (gustar mucho): **le chiflan los coches** he's crazy *o* nuts *o* mad about cars (colloq)
■ **chiflarse** *v pron* (fam) **~se POR algo** to be crazy ABOUT sth (colloq); **se chifló por esa chica** he flipped his lid over that girl (colloq)
chiflón, (RPl) **chiflete** *m* draft (AmE), draught (BrE)
chigüín -güina *m,f* (AmC fam) kid (colloq)
chihuahua *mf* chihuahua
chiíta, chiita *adj/mf* Shiite; **los ~s** the Shia
chilaba *f* djellaba
chilacayote *m* chilacayote (*type of gourd*)
chilango -ga *adj* (Méx) of/from Mexico City
chilaquiles *mpl* (Méx) *corn tortilla in tomato and chili sauce*
chilcano *m* (Per) pisco/cherry brandy with cola
chile *m*
A (AmC, Méx) (Bot, Coc) chili, hot pepper; ***andar a medios ~s*** (Méx fam) to be tipsy
(Compuesto) **chile con carne** chili con carne
B (AmC fam) (chiste) joke
Chile *m* Chile
chilear [A1] *vi* (AmC fam) to tell jokes
chilena *f* (AmL) (Dep) scissors kick
chileno -na *adj/m,f* Chilean
chilicote *m* (AmS) cricket
chilindrina *f* (Méx) sugar-coated bun
chilindrón *m* tomato and pepper sauce
chilla *f*
A (tabla) thin board; ***andar en la quinta ~*** (Méx fam) to be broke (colloq)
B (Chi) (Zool) fox
chillar [A1] *vi*
A «*pájaro*» to screech; «*cerdo*» to squeal; «*ratón*» to squeak
B 1 «*persona*» to shout, yell (colloq); (de dolor, miedo) to scream; **~le A algn** to yell *o* shout AT sb 2 «*bebé/niño*» (llorar) to scream
C (Col) «*colores*» to clash
chillido *m*
A (de ave) screech; (de cerdo) squeal; (de ratón) squeak
B (grito) shout, yell; (de dolor, miedo) scream, shriek; **dar** *o* **pegar ~s** *o* **un ~** (fam) to shout, to yell
chillón -llona *adj* (fam) 1 ‹*niño*›: **es muy ~** he never stops screaming (colloq) 2 ‹*voz*› shrill, piercing 3 ‹*color*› loud
chilote *m* (AmC) baby sweetcorn
chilpayate *m* (Méx fam) kid (colloq)
chiltoma *f* (AmC) sweet pepper
chimbear [A1] *vt* (Col fam) to con
chimbo -ba *adj* 1 (Col fam) (falsificado) ‹*perfume*› fake (*before n*); ‹*whisky/grabación*› bootleg (*before n*); **un cheque ~** a dud check (colloq) 2 (Ven arg) (malo) lousy (colloq)
chimbomba *f* (AmC) balloon
chimenea *f*
A 1 (de casa) chimney; (de barco) smokestack (AmE), funnel (BrE); (de locomotora, fábrica) smokestack (AmE), chimney (BrE); ***fumar como (una) ~*** (fam) to smoke like a chimney (colloq) 2 (de volcán) vent
B (hogar) fireplace, hearth
(Compuestos)
- **chimenea de aire/de ventilación** air/ventilation shaft
- **chimenea refrigeradora** cooling tower

chimento *m* (RPl fam) story
chimiscolear [A1] *vi* (Méx fam) to gossip
chimpancé *mf* chimpanzee
chimpún *m* (Per) football boot
chimuelo *adj* (Méx fam) toothless
china *f*
A 1 (piedra) pebble, small stone; ***me/te/le tocó la ~*** I/you/he got *o* drew the short straw 2 (Esp arg) (de hachís) lump
B (AmL) (en el folklore de algunos países) *wife or girlfriend of a* **gaucho** *or of a* **charro** *or of a* **huaso**
C (Esp) (porcelana) porcelain
D (Col) (abanico) fan
China *f*: *tb* **la ~** China; ***acá y en la ~*** (fam): **eso es así acá y en la ~** that's the way things work, not just here but all over the world; ***ni aquí*** *or* ***acá ni en la ~*** (fam) neither here nor anywhere
chinamo *m* (AmC fam) (en una feria) stall; (bar) small bar
chinampa *f* (Méx) (terreno) man-made island; (embarcación) riverboat
chinchar [A1] *vt* (fam) to pester (colloq)
■ **chincharse** *v pron* (fam): **para que te chinches: yo aprobé y tú no** I passed and you didn't, so there! (colloq)
chinche[1] *adj* 1 (fam) (pesado) irritating; (quisquilloso): **es muy ~** he's a real nit-picker 2 (Chi fam) (hediondo) smelly (colloq)
chinche[2] *f or m*
A (insecto) bedbug; ***caer*** *or* ***morir como ~s*** (fam) to drop like flies (colloq)
B (RPl fam) (mal humor) bad mood
chinche[3] *mf* 1 (fam) (pesado) nuisance, pain in the neck (colloq) 2 (fam) (quisquilloso) nit-picker (colloq)
chinche[4] *f* (AmC, Méx, RPl) (clavito) thumbtack (AmE), drawing pin (BrE)
chinche[5] *m* (Andes) ▸**chinche[4]**
chincheta *f* (Esp) thumbtack (AmE), drawing pin (BrE)
chinchilla *f* chinchilla
chin-chin[1] *interj* (fam) cheers!
chin-chin[2] *adv* (Ven fam) in cash
chinchona *f* quinine
chinchorro *m* 1 (bote — de remos) rowboat (AmE), rowing boat (BrE); (— de motor) motorboat 2 (red) fishnet (AmE), fishing net (BrE) 3 (Col, Ven) (hamaca) hammock
chinchudo -da *adj* (Arg fam) grumpy
chinchulines *mpl* (Bol, RPl) chitterlings (*pl*)
chincol *m* (Chi) (pájaro) crown sparrow
chinear [A1] *vt* (AmC) ‹*niño*› to cradle … in one's arms
chinela *f* (pantufla) slipper; (chancla) (AmC) thong (AmE), flip-flop (BrE)
chinesco -ca *adj* Chinese; ▸**sombra A**
chinga *f* (Méx fam): **es una ~ mudarse de casa** moving house is a real pain (colloq); **la vida es una ~** life's a bitch (sl)
chingada *f* (Méx vulg): **está pa' la ~** he's/she's had it (colloq); **¡vete a la ~!** screw you! (vulg); **la casa estaba en la ~** the house was in the middle of nowhere (colloq); **¡hijo de la ~!** you son-of-a-bitch! (sl); **¡es una hija de la ~!** she's a low-down bitch! (sl); ***estar de la ~*** (Méx vulg) to be crap (sl)
chingadazo *m* (Méx fam): **¡qué ~ me di!** I gave myself a real bang on the head (colloq); **te voy a dar un ~** I'm going to thump you (colloq)

chingadera *f* (Méx vulg) trash (colloq), crap (sl); **son puras ~s** it's trash *o* crap; **ya no digas tanta ~** stop talking crap

chingado -da *adj* (Méx vulg): **¿de dónde ~s quieres que lo saque?** where the hell (colloq) *o* (vulg) the fuck do you expect me to get that from?; **¡chingada madre! te dije que no se lo dijeras!** fucking hell! I told you not to tell him! (vulg)

chingana *f* (Andes) dive (colloq)

chingar [A3] *vi*
A (esp Méx vulg) (copular) to screw (vulg), to fuck (vulg)
B (Méx vulg) (molestar): **te lo dijo para ~ nada más** he only said it to annoy you; **¡deja de ~!** stop being such a pain in the ass! (vulg); **¡no chingues!** you're kidding! (colloq)

■ **chingar** *vt*
A (AmL vulg) (en sentido sexual) to fuck (vulg), to screw (vulg); ▸**madre**[2] **A2**
B (Méx vulg) (jorobar) to screw (vulg); **si no lo haces te van a ~** if you don't do it, they'll screw you (vulg); ***~la*: ¡no la chingues! ya cerraron el banco** (Méx vulg) shit! the bank's already closed! (vulg); **¡la chingué!** (RPl fam) I really put my foot in it (colloq)

■ **chingarse** *v pron*
A (*enf*) (AmL vulg) (en sentido sexual) to fuck (vulg), to screw (vulg)
B (esp Méx vulg) (jorobarse): **creyó que ganaría pero se chingó** he thought he'd win but he got a shock; **se chingó el motor** the engine's had it (colloq); **estamos chingados** we're in deep shit *o* up shit creek
C (Méx vulg) (aguantarse): **si no te gusta, te chingas** if you don't like it, tough (colloq)
D (Méx vulg) **1** (castigar) to give … a hard time **2** (robar) to rip … off (colloq)

chingaste *m* (AmC) coffee grounds (*pl*)

chingo[1] **-ga** *adj* (AmC fam) (desnudo) stark naked (colloq)

chingo[2] *m* (Méx fam *o* vulg): **un ~ de** loads of (colloq); **me costó un ~** it cost me a bundle *o* packet (BrE) (colloq); **me gustó un ~** I loved it (colloq)

chingo[3] **-ga** *m,f* (Ven fam) flat-nosed *o* snub-nosed person (*o* guy *etc*)

chingón[1] **-gona** *adj* (Méx vulg) ‹*partido/película*› fantastic (colloq); ‹*persona*› cool (sl)

chingón[2] **-gona** *m,f* (Méx vulg): **ser un ~ para algo** to be fucking good at sth (sl); **es una chingona bailando** she's a fucking good dancer (sl)

chingue *m*
A (Chi) **1** (Zool) skunk **2** (fam) (persona hedionda) smelly person
B (Col) (traje de baño — de hombre) swimming trunks (*pl*); (— de mujer) swimsuit

chinguear [A1] *vi/vt* (AmC) ▸**chingar**

chinguirito *m* (Méx): *alcoholic drink made from sugar cane*

chinita *f* (Chi) ladybug (AmE), ladybird (BrE)

chino[1] **-na** *adj*
A (de la China) Chinese; ***estar ~ de risa*** (Per fam) to be in stitches (colloq)
B (Méx) ‹*pelo*› curly

chino[2] **-na** *m,f*
A (de la China) (*m*) Chinese man; (*f*) Chinese woman; **los ~s** the Chinese, Chinese people; ***engañar a algn como a un ~*** to take sb for a ride; ▸**trabajar** *vi* **B**
B **1** (Arg, Per) (mestizo) mestizo, person of mixed Amerindian and European parentage **2** (Col fam) (joven) kid (colloq) **3** (Méx) (de pelo rizado) curly-haired person

chino[3] *m*
A (idioma) Chinese; **es ~ *para mí*** it's all Greek to me
B (fam) (de hachís) lump, piece
C (Méx) (pelo rizado) curly hair; (para rizar el pelo) curler, roller
D (Per fam) (tienda) convenience store, corner shop (BrE)

chip *m* (*pl* **chips**) **1** (Inf) chip; ***te/le falta un ~*** (Esp fam) you have/he has a screw loose (colloq); ***cambiar de ~*** (Esp fam) to change one's mindset **2** (papa frita) potato chip (AmE), crisp (BrE) **3** (Arg) (pancito) bridge roll

chipe *m* (Chi fam): **~ *libre*** carte blanche

chipichipi *m* (Méx fam) (llovizna) drizzle

chipirón *m* small cuttlefish

chipocludo *adj* (Méx) fantastic (colloq), great (colloq)

chipote *m* (Méx fam) bump, lump

Chipre *f* Cyprus

chipriota *adj/mf* Cypriot

chiqueado[1] *adj* (Méx fam) spoilt

chiqueado[2] *m* (Méx fam) spoilt brat (colloq)

chiqueador -dora *m,f* (Méx fam) (persona) indulgent person

chiquear [A1] *vt* (Méx fam) to spoil
■ **chiquearse** *v pron* (Méx fam) to play hard to get (colloq)

chiquero *m* **1** (Taur) pen **2** (AmL) (pocilga) pigpen (AmE), pigsty (BrE)

chiquilicuatro *m* (fam) nobody (colloq)

chiquilín[1] **-lina** *adj* (AmL fam) (infantil) childish; **ser ~** to be childish, to act like a kid (colloq)

chiquilín[2] **-lina** *m,f* (fam) (persona infantil) (AmL) big kid (colloq); (niño) (Ur) kid (colloq)

chiquilinada *f* (RPl): **estoy harto de sus ~s** I'm tired of her childishness

chiquillada *f*: **se pelearon por una ~** they fought over something really silly; **déjate de ~s** stop being so childish

chiquillería *f* (fam) kids (*pl*) (colloq)

chiquillo[1] **-lla** *adj*: **no seas ~** don't be childish

chiquillo[2] **-lla** *m,f* kid (colloq)

chiquito[1] **-ta**, **chiquitito -ta** *adj* (esp AmL fam) small

chiquito[2] **-ta** *m,f* (esp AmL fam) (niño) (*m*) little boy; (*f*) little girl; ***no andarse con chiquitas*** (fam): **no se anduvo con chiquitas y se lo dijo** she certainly didn't beat about the bush and she told him (colloq)

chiquito[3] *m* **1** (Esp) (de vino) small glass **2** (RPl fam) (pedacito) little bit (colloq)

chircal *m* (Col) brickworks

chiribita *f* **1** (chispa) spark; ***echar ~s*** (fam) to be livid (colloq) **2** **chiribitas** *fpl* (en la vista) spots in front of the eyes; **los ojos le hacían ~s** his eyes glowed

chiribitil *m* tiny room

chirigota *f* (fam) (broma) joke; **todo se lo toma a ~** he takes everything as a joke; **están siempre de ~** they're always kidding around (colloq)

chirimbolo *m* (fam) thingamajig (colloq)

chirimiri *m* fine drizzle

chirimoya *f* custard apple

chirimoyo *m* (Bot) custard apple tree

chiringuito *m* (Esp) stall, kiosk (*selling drinks and snacks*)

chiripa *f*
A (fam) (casualidad) fluke; **de** *or* **por ~** (fam) by sheer luck, by a fluke
B (Ven) **1** (insecto) cockroach **2** (palmera) palm

chiripá *m garment worn by gauchos over trousers*

chiripazo *m* (AmL fam) ▸**chiripa A**

chirla *f* (Coc, Zool) baby clam

chirle *adj* (RPl) watery, thin

chiro -ra *adj* (Méx fam) cool (sl)

chirona *f* (Esp fam) jail; **lo metieron en ~** they put him in the can (AmE colloq) *o* in the nick (BrE colloq)

chiros *mpl* (Col) rags (*pl*)

chiroso -sa *adj* (Col) ragged

chirriado -da *adj* (Col) decent (colloq), nice

chirriar [A17] *vi* «*puerta/gozne*» to squeak, creak; «*frenos/neumáticos*» to screech

chirrido *m* (de puerta) squeaking, creaking; (de frenos, neumáticos) screech, screeching

chirrión *m* (Méx) whip; ***¡ay*** *or* ***ah ~!*** (Méx) you're kidding! (colloq), you must be joking!

chirusa *f* (RPl fam) vulgar *o* common woman

chis, chist *interj* shush!, ssh!, hush!

chiscón *m* boxroom

chisme *m* **1** (chismorreo) piece of gossip; **~s** gossip, tittle-tattle (colloq); **no me vengas con ~s** don't come gossiping to me **2** (Esp, Méx fam) (trasto, cacharro) thing, thingamajig (colloq); **tiene su cuarto lleno de ~s** his room's full of junk *o* stuff (colloq)

chismear, chismorrear [A1] *vi* (fam) to gossip; **se juntan a ~** they get together for a gossip (colloq)

chismorreo *m* (fam) gossip, tittle-tattle (colloq)

chismoso¹ -sa *adj* gossipy (colloq); **es terriblemente ~** he's a terrible gossip

chismoso² -sa *m,f* gossip, scandalmonger (colloq)

chispa¹ *adj inv* (Esp fam) tipsy (colloq)

chispa² *f*

A 1 (del fuego) spark; ***está/están que echa/echan ~s*** (fam) he's/they're hopping mad (colloq) 2 (Auto, Elec) spark; **lo enchufé y empezaron a saltar ~s** I plugged it in and it started sparking *o* giving off sparks

B (fam) (pizca): **¿más vino? — una chispita** more wine? — just a drop; **no tiene ni ~ de inteligencia** he doesn't have an ounce of intelligence

C (gracia, ingenio) wit; **sus chistes tienen mucha ~** his jokes are very funny *o* witty

chisparse [A1] *v pron* (Méx) to come loose

chispazo *m* (Elec, Tec) spark

chispeante *adj* 1 ‹*leña/fuego*› crackling 2 (gracioso) ‹*lenguaje/personalidad*› witty; ‹*ingenio*› lively, sparkling 3 ‹*ojos*› (de alegría) sparkling; (de ira) flashing

chispear [A1] *vi* 1 «*leña*» to spark 2 (Elec) to spark, give off sparks

■ **chispear** *v impers* (fam) (lloviznar) to spit, spot

chispero *m* (AmC) (encendedor) (fam) lighter; (Auto) spark plug

chisporrotear [A1] *vi* «*leña/fuego*» to spark, crackle; «*aceite*» to spit, splutter; «*carne/pescado*» to sizzle

chisporroteo *m* (de leña, fuego) sparking, crackling; (de aceite) spitting, spluttering; (de la carne) sizzling

chistar [A1] *vi*: **¡y sin ~!** and not another word!; **no chistó** he didn't say a word; **soportó el dolor sin ~** he bore the pain without a word of complaint

chiste *m*

A (cuento gracioso) joke; **contar** *or* (Col) **echar un ~** to tell a joke; **¡suena a ~!** it's unbelievable!; **¡es de ~!** it's a joke! (colloq)

(Compuestos)

- **chiste colorado** (Bol, Méx) dirty joke
- **chiste picante** *or* **verde** dirty joke

B (Bol, CS, Méx) (broma) joke; **hacerle un ~ a algn** to play a joke *o* trick on sb; **me lo dijo en ~** he was joking; **el ~cito nos costó un dineral** the little business cost us a fortune; ***ni de ~*** (Méx fam) no way (colloq)

C (Col, Méx fam) (gracia): **el ~ está en** *or* **es hacerlo rápido** the idea *o* point is to do it quickly; **no le encuentro el ~ sin chile** (Méx) there's not much point without the chili; ***tener su ~*** (Méx) to be tricky

D **chistes** *mpl* (RPl) (historietas) comic strips (*pl*), funnies (*pl*) (AmE colloq)

chistera *f* top hat

chistoso¹ -sa *adj* funny, amusing

chistoso² -sa *m,f* comic, joker; ***hacerse el ~*** (hacerse el gracioso) (Andes) to act up, play the fool; (hacerse el loco) (Méx) to act dumb (colloq)

chita¹ *f*: ***a la ~ callando*** (Esp fam) (sin llamar la atención) on the quiet; (sin hacer ruido) quietly

chita² *interj* (Chi fam) (expresando — sorpresa, admiración) wow! (colloq); (— disgusto, preocupación) hell! (colloq); ***¡por la ~ (diego)!*** (Chi fam) damn it! (colloq)

chitón *interj* shush!, ssh!, hush!

chiva *f*

A (AmL) (barba) goatee

B (Col) (bus) rural *o* country bus

C (Col period) (primicia) scoop, exclusive

D (Chi fam) (mentira) cock-and-bull story (colloq) *ver tb* **chivo**

E **chivas** *fpl* (Méx fam) (cachivaches) junk (colloq)

chivarse [A1] *v pron* (Esp fam) (a la policía) to squeal (sl); **me voy a chivar a mamá** I'm going to tell Mom

chivatazo *m* (Esp fam) tip-off (colloq); **les dieron el ~** they were tipped off

chivatear [A1] *vi*

A (Col fam) (molestar) to be a pest (colloq)

B (Per fam) (corretear) to run around

chivato¹ -ta *m,f*

A (Esp, Ven fam) 1 (informador) informer, stool pigeon (colloq) 2 (acusica) tattletale (AmE colloq), telltale (BrE colloq)

B (Col fam) (niño travieso) rascal (colloq)

chivato² *m* (Esp fam) (dispositivo sonoro) bleeper; (luz piloto) pilot light

chiveado -da *adj* (Col fam): **un reloj ~** a dud watch (colloq); **un pasaporte ~** a false passport

chivear [A1] *vi* (RPl fam) to run around

■ **chivear** *vt* (Méx fam) to scare, give … a fright

■ **chivearse** *v pron* (Méx) (fam) (turbarse) to get embarrassed

chivera *f*

A (Col) (barba) goatee

B (Ven) (Auto) wrecker's yard (AmE), scrapyard (BrE)

chivo -va *m,f*

A 1 (cría de la cabra) kid 2 (Ven) (cabra) goat; ***estar como una chiva*** (fam) to be crazy (colloq); *ver tb* **chiva** 3 **chivo** *m* (AmL) (macho cabrío) billy goat

(Compuesto) **chivo expiatorio** *or* **emisario** scapegoat

B **chivo** *m* (Per fam & pey) (maricón) faggot (colloq & pej)

chivudo *adj* (Ven fam) bearded; **estar ~** to have a beard

choapino *m* (Chi) woolen* rug

chocado -da *adj* (AmL fam) smashed up (colloq); (superficialmente) dented

chocante *adj* 1 (que causa impresión): **su reacción me pareció ~** I was shocked *o* taken aback by his reaction, his reaction shocked me 2 (en cuestiones morales) shocking 3 (Col, Méx, Ven fam) (desagradable) unpleasant

chocar [A2] *vi*

A 1 (colisionar) to crash; (entre sí) to collide; **~ de frente** to collide *o* crash head-on; **nunca he chocado** (CS) I've never had an accident; **~ CON** *or* **CONTRA algo** «*vehículo*» to crash *o* run INTO sth; (con otro en marcha) to collide WITH sth; **~on con** *or* **contra un árbol** they crashed *o* ran into a tree; **el balón chocó contra el poste** the ball hit the goalpost; **las olas chocaban contra el espigón** the waves crashed against the breakwater; **~ CON algn** «*persona*» to run INTO sb, collide WITH sb 2 (entrar en conflicto) **~ CON algn** to clash WITH sb; **esta idea choca con su conservadurismo** this idea conflicts with *o* is at odds with his conservatism 3 **~ CON algo** ‹*con problema/obstáculo*› to come up AGAINST sth

B 1 (causar impresión, afectar) (+ *me/te/le etc*): **me chocó que no me invitara** I was taken aback that he didn't invite me; **le chocó que lo recibieran de esa manera** he was taken aback by the reception he was given 2 (extrañar): **me chocó que no me lo dijera** I was surprised that he hadn't told me 3 (escandalizar) to shock; **me chocó su lenguaje** I was shocked by her language

C (Col, Méx, Ven fam) (irritar, molestar) (+ *me/te/le etc*) to annoy, bug (colloq); **me choca ese actor** I can't stand that actor

■ **chocar** *vt* 1 ‹*copas*› to clink; ***~la***: **estaban enojados pero ya la ~on** (Méx fam) they had fallen out but they've made it up again now (colloq); **¡chócala!** (fam) put it there! (colloq), give me five! (colloq) 2 (AmL) ‹*vehículo*›(que se conduce) to crash; (de otra persona) to run into; **choqué el coche del vecino** I ran into my neighbor's car

■ **chocarse** *v pron*

A (Col) (en vehículo) to have a crash *o* an accident

B (Col fam) (molestarse) to get annoyed

chocarrero -ra *adj* coarse, crude

chochada *f* (AmC fam) silly little thing (colloq)

chochear [A1] *vi* (fam) 1 «*anciano*» to be gaga (colloq) 2 (sentir adoración) **~ POR algn** to dote ON sb

chochera *f* 1 (fam) (de anciano): **¡tiene una ~ …!** he's completely gaga (colloq) 2 (fam) (adoración): **tener ~ por algn** to dote on sb (colloq)

chochez *f* (fam) (de anciano) senile prattle; (tontería) nonsense

chochín *m* wren

chocho -cha *adj*

A 1 (fam) ‹*viejo*› gaga (colloq) 2 (fam) (encantado, entusiasmado): **está ~ por** *or* **con su hijita** he dotes on his daughter; **se quedó ~ con el regalo** he was delighted with his present

B (*como interj*) (AmC fam): **¡~! ¡qué montón de trabajo tenemos!** gosh, have we got a lot of work! (colloq)

choclo *m*

A (CS, Per) (mazorca) corn cob; (granos) sweet corn; (cultivo) corn (AmE), maize (BrE)

B (Méx fam)(Indum) brogue

choclón *m* (Chi fam) (grupo) crowd; (reunión política) rally

choco¹ -ca *adj* (Chi fam) (de rabo corto) short-tailed; (manco) one-armed

choco² *m* cuttlefish

chocolate *m*
A 1 (para comer) chocolate; **sirvieron unos ~s con el café** (AmL) they gave us chocolates with our coffee; ***¡~ por la noticia!*** (RPl fam) you don't say! (iro) 2 (bebida) hot chocolate; ***darle a algn agua*** *or* ***una sopa de su propio ~*** (Méx fam) to give sb a taste of his/her own medicine 3 **(de) color ~** chocolate-colored•
Compuestos
- **chocolate blanco/con leche** white/milk chocolate
- **chocolate de algarroba** carob
- **chocolate negro** plain chocolate, dark chocolate

B (Esp arg) (hachís) dope (sl), pot (colloq)
chocolatera *f: a vessel for making and/or serving hot chocolate*
chocolatería *f* (cafetería) *café serving hot chocolate as a speciality*
chocolatina *f*, (RPl) **chocolatín** *m* chocolate bar
chocoyo *m* (AmC) parakeet
chofer, (Esp) **chófer** *mf* 1 (asalariado — de coche particular) chauffeur; (— de transporte colectivo) driver; **coches con ~** chauffeur-driven cars; **coches sin ~** drive-yourself (AmE) *o* (BrE) self-drive cars 2 (persona que maneja) driver
chole *interj* (Méx fam): **¡ya ~!** that's it, I've had enough!
cholga *f* (Chi) mussel
cholla *f* (Méx fam) head
chollo *m* (Esp fam) (trabajo fácil) cushy job *o* number (colloq); (ganga) steal (colloq), bargain
cholo¹ -la *adj*
A (Andes) of/relating to a **cholo²**
B (Chi fam) (tímido, vergonzoso) shy, timid
cholo² -la *m,f* (Andes) 1 (persona) *term used throughout Andean region to refer to person of mixed race, sometimes used pejoratively* 2 (fam) (apelativo) dear, honey (AmE colloq)
chomba *f* (sin botones) (Chi) sweater; (con botones) (Arg) polo shirt
chompa *f* (chaqueta) (Col, Ec) jacket; (suéter) (Bol, Per) sweater
chompipe *m* (AmC, Méx) turkey
choncho -cha *adj* (Méx fam) 1 ‹*problema/situación*› serious 2 ‹*persona*› hefty (colloq), big
chonchón *m* (Chi) (farol) oil lamp; (juguete) paper kite
chongo *m*
A (Méx) (moño) bun; ***agarrarse del ~*** (fam) to scratch each other's eyes out (colloq)
B (Méx) (Coc) *dessert made of fried bread, topped with cheese or cinnamon*
chonta *f* (Andes) palm tree
chopera *f* poplar grove
chopo *m*
A (Bot) black poplar
B (Esp arg) (fusil) piece (AmE sl), shooter (BrE sl)
choque *m*
A 1 (de vehículos) crash, collision 2 (conflicto) clash; **se produjeron algunos ~s violentos** there were some violent clashes; **fuerzas de ~** shock troops
Compuestos
- **choque conjunto** *or* **múltiple** pile-up
- **choque frontal** (Auto) head-on collision; (enfrentamiento) head-on confrontation

B 1 (sorpresa, golpe) shock; **ha sido un ~ muy fuerte para él** it has come as a terrible shock to him 2 (Med, Psic) shock; **en estado de ~** in a state of shock
chorcha *f* (Méx fam): **andar en la ~** to party (colloq)
chorear [A1] *vt* (fam)
A (CS, Per) (robar) to swipe (colloq)
B (Chi) 1 (aburrir): **esto ya me choreó** I'm already fed up with this (colloq) 2 (molestar, enojar) (+ *me/te/le etc*) to annoy
■ **chorearse** *v pron* (fam)
A (CS) (robarse) to swipe (colloq)
B (Chi) 1 (fam) (aburrirse) to get bored, get fed up 2 (molestarse, enojarse) to get annoyed
choreo *m* (fam)
A (CS, Per) (robo) stealing
B (Chi) (aburrimiento): **tengo un ~ ...** I'm so fed up ...
choreto -ta *adj* (Ven fam) crooked
choricear [A1] *vt* (Esp fam) to swipe (colloq)
chorito *m* (Chi) baby mussel
chorizar [A4] *vt* ▸ **choricear**
chorizo *m*
A 1 (embutido curado) chorizo (*highly-seasoned pork sausage*); (salchicha) (RPl) sausage 2 (Méx, RPl) (corte de carne) *cut of beef*
B (vulg) (de excremento) turd (vulg)
C (Esp) (fam) (ratero) petty thief
chorlito *m* plover; ▸ **cabeza**
choro¹ -ra *adj* (Chi fam) (resuelto, audaz) gutsy (colloq); (digno de admiración) great (colloq), cool (sl)
choro² *m* (Chi, Per)
A (Coc, Zool) mussel
B (fam) (delincuente) crook (colloq)
chorra¹ *adj* (Esp fam) silly
chorra² *mf* (Esp fam)
A (tonto) fool, idiot; ***hacer el ~*** to play the fool
B **chorra** *f* (suerte) luck; **tener ~** to be lucky
chorrada *f* (Esp fam) 1 (estupidez): **decir ~s** to talk drivel *o* twaddle (colloq) 2 (cosa insignificante) little thing; **se enfadó por una ~** he got angry over a silly little thing; **le compraré cualquier ~** I'll buy him any old thing
chorrear [A1] *vi* to drip; **las sábanas todavía están chorreando** the sheets are still dripping wet; **llegó chorreando de sudor** she arrived dripping with sweat; **la sangre le chorreaba de la nariz** blood was pouring from his nose
■ **chorrear** *vt*
A (AmL fam) (manchar): **el mantel está todo chorreado de café** the tablecloth is covered in coffee stains
B (Col, RPl arg) (robar) to swipe (colloq)
■ **chorrearse** *v pron*
A (*refl*) (CS, Per fam) (mancharse): **cuidado con ~te** mind you don't get it all over yourself
B (Col, RPl arg) (robar) to swipe (colloq)
chorrera *f*
A (de una camisa) frill
B (AmS fam) (montón): **una ~ de** loads of (colloq); **una ~ de mentiras** a pack of lies; **las cosas malas siempre vienen en ~** it never rains but it pours (colloq)
chorrillo *m* (Méx fam) diarrhea•; **tener ~** to have diarrhea *o* (colloq) the runs
chorro¹ *m*
A (de agua) stream, jet; (de vapor, gas) jet; **un chorrito de agua** a trickle of water; **agregar un chorrito de vino** add a splash of wine; **cayó un ~ de monedas** coins poured out; **a ~** ‹*motor/avión*› jet (*before n*); **con propulsión a ~** jet-propelled; **a ~s: la sangre salía a ~s** blood poured *o* gushed out; **sudaba a ~s** he was sweating buckets (colloq); ***como los ~s del oro*** (Esp fam) as clean *o* bright as a new pin
B (AmC, Ven) (del agua) faucet (AmE), tap (BrE); **agua del ~** tap water
C (Méx fam) (cantidad): **¡qué ~ de gente!** what a lot of people!; **tiene ~s de dinero** he's got loads of money (colloq); **me gusta un ~ salir** I really love going out
chorro² -rra *m,f* (CS arg) thief
chotearse [A1] *v pron* (fam) 1 (Esp) (burlarse) **~se DE algn** to make fun OF sb 2 (Méx fam) (quemarse) to lose one's mystique
choteo *m* (Esp fam): **se montó un ~ enorme** there was complete havoc; **esto es un ~, aquí nadie hace nada** this is a joke, nobody here does anything
chotis *m* schottische
choto -ta *m,f*
A (Esp) (cabrito) kid; (ternero) calf
B **choto** *m* (RPl) (vulg) (pene) cock (vulg), dick (vulg)
chovinismo *m* chauvinism
chovinista¹ *adj* chauvinist, chauvinistic
chovinista² *mf* chauvinist
choza *f* hut, shack
christmas /'krismas/ *m* (*pl* ~) (Esp) Christmas card
chubasco *m* heavy shower; ***aguantar el ~*** (Chi) to weather the storm
chubasquero *m* slicker (AmE), cagoule (BrE)
chúcaro -ra *adj* (AmS) ‹*caballo*› untamed, wild; ‹*persona*› unsociable, unfriendly

C

chuchería *f* 1 (alhaja) trinket; (adorno) knickknack 2 (dulce) tidbit (AmE), titbit (BrE)

chucho -cha *m,f*
A (Esp fam) (perro) mutt (colloq), mongrel
B **chucho** *m* (RPl fam) (escalofrío) shiver; **tengo ~s de frío** I have the shivers (colloq)

chuchumeca *f* (Per fam) hooker (colloq)

chucrut *m* sauerkraut

chucuto -ta *adj* (Ven fam) 1 (incompleto) half-finished 2 (deficiente) inadequate

chueca *f* (Chi) (juego) *game similar to hockey, and the stick with which it's played*

chueco¹ -ca *adj*
A (AmL) (torcido) crooked, askew
B (Chi, Méx fam) (deshonesto) ‹*persona*› crooked (colloq); ‹*escritura/documento*› false; ‹*elecciones*› rigged; ***comprar/vender de ~*** (Méx fam) to buy/sell stolen goods; **tiene un stereo comprado de ~** he bought a stolen stereo
C 1 (Méx, Ven fam) (cojo) lame 2 (RPl) (patizambo) knock-kneed 3 (Per) (patituerto) bow-legged

chueco² -ca *m,f*
A (Chi, Méx fam) (deshonesto): **los ~s son los políticos** it's the politicians who are crooked (colloq)
B (Méx fam) (cojo) cripple (pej)

chueco³ *adv* (AmL fam) 1 (torcido): **camina/escribe ~** he can't walk/write straight 2 ‹*jugar/pelear*› dirty (colloq); **seguro que la consiguió ~** I'm sure she came by it dishonestly (colloq)

chufa *f* tiger nut, earth almond

chufla *f* (Esp) joke; **estar de ~** to be cracking jokes (colloq)

chuico *m* (Chi) demijohn; ***caerse al ~*** (Chi fam) to hit the bottle (colloq)

chulada *f* (fam) 1 (Esp, Méx) (cosa bonita): **ese vestido es una ~** that dress is gorgeous *o* really nice 2 (Méx) (persona bonita): **¡qué ~ de chamaca!** what a cute girl!

chulear [A1] *vt*
A (Arg fam) (provocar) to needle (colloq)
B (Méx fam) (piropear) to compliment; ‹*vestido/peinado*› to make nice comments about
C (Col) (con un signo) to check (AmE), to tick (BrE)

chulería *f* (Esp fam) (bravata) threat; **no me vengas con ~s** don't you threaten me (colloq)

chuleta *f*
A (Coc) chop; **~ de cordero** lamb chop
B (Esp arg) (para copiar) crib (colloq)
C (Chi fam) (patilla) sideburn

chuletón *m* T-bone steak

chulillo *m* (Per) delivery boy

chulla *mf* (Ec) (quiteño) *person from Quito*

chullo *m* (Andes) *woolen* cap (with earflaps)*

chulo¹ -la *adj*
A (fam) (bonito) 1 (Esp, Méx) ‹*vestido/casa*› neat (AmE colloq), lovely (BrE); **¡qué chulas flores te regalaron!** (Méx) what nice flowers they gave you! 2 (Méx) ‹*hombre*› good-looking, cute (esp AmE); ‹*mujer*› pretty, cute (esp AmE); **¿por qué llora, chula?** why are you crying, sweetheart *o* love?
B (Esp fam) (bravucón) nervy (AmE colloq), cocky (BrE colloq); **no te me pongas ~** don't get nervy *o* cocky with me (colloq)
C (Esp) (satisfecho, garboso): **¡qué chula va!** doesn't she look pretty!
D (Chi fam) (de mal gusto) tacky (colloq)

chulo² -la *m,f* (Esp fam) (bravucón) flashy type

chulo³ *m* (Esp fam)
A (proxeneta) *tb* **~ de putas** pimp
B (Col) (Zool) black vulture
C (Col) (signo) check mark (AmE), tick (BrE)

chumbar [A1] *vi* (RPl) «*perro*»: **¡chúmbale!** get 'em!, attack!

chumbe *m* (Col) woven sash

chumbera *f* prickly pear

chumero -ra *m,f* (AmC) apprentice

chuminada *f* (Esp arg) ▸**chorrada**

chumpipe *m* (AmC) turkey

chunche *m* (AmC) (fam) (cosa) thing, thingamajig (colloq)

chuncho¹ -cha *adj* (Per fam) unsociable, unfriendly

chuncho² -cha *m,f*
A (indio) chuncho (*member of a tribe indigenous to Peru*)
B **chuncho** *m* (Chi) (Zool) pygmy owl; (persona) (fam) jinx

chunga *f* (fam): **se lo toma todo a ~** he treats everything as a joke; **te lo dijo en ~** he was only joking; **estar de ~** to be in high spirits

chungo -ga *adj* (Esp arg) 1 [SER] ‹*persona*› (de mal corazón) nasty (colloq); (no de fiar) slippery, dodgy (BrE colloq) 2 [ESTAR] ‹*persona*› in a bad way (colloq) 3 ‹*situación/asunto*› dicey (colloq), dodgy (BrE colloq)

chuño *m* (CS) (fécula de papa) potato flour

chupa *f*
A (Esp fam) jacket
B (Col) (desatascador) plunger

chupa-chupa *m* (RPl) lollipop

chupachups® *m* (*pl* ~) (Esp) lollipop

chupada *f* (fam) (de helado) lick; (de cigarrillo) puff; **le dio unas ~s a la pipa** he puffed on his pipe a few times; ***creerse la última ~ del mate*** (Chi fam) to think one is the bee's knees (colloq)

chupado¹ -da *adj*
A [ESTAR] (fam) (flaco) skinny; **tiene la cara chupada** he's looking gaunt
B [ESTAR] (Esp fam) (fácil) dead easy (colloq)
C [ESTAR] (AmL fam) (borracho) plastered (colloq)
D 1 [ESTAR] (Chi, Per) (inhibido) withdrawn 2 [SER] (Chi, Per fam) (tímido) shy

chupado² -da *m,f* (Per fam) mouse (colloq)

chupalla *f* (Chi) straw hat

chupamedias *mf* (*pl* ~) (CS, Ven fam) bootlicker (colloq)

chupar [A1] *vt*
A 1 (extraer) ‹*sangre/savia*› to suck 2 ‹*biberón/chupete*› to suck (on); ‹*naranja/caramelo*› to suck; ‹*pipa/cigarrillo*› to puff on 3 (AmL fam) (beber) to drink
B (fam) ‹*dinero*› (+ *me/te/le etc*): **le están chupando todo el dinero** they're milking him dry (colloq)
■ **chupar** *vi* 1 «*bebé/cría*» to suckle 2 (AmL fam) (beber) to booze (colloq)
■ **chuparse** *v pron*
A ‹*dedo*› to suck; ***¡chúpate ésa!*** (fam) so there! (colloq)
B (Esp fam) (soportar): **me chupé tres conferencias/una caravana enorme** I had to sit through three lectures/sit in a huge traffic jam for ages
C (Andes fam) (inhibirse) to chicken out (colloq)

chupatintas *mf* (*pl* ~) (fam & pey) pen-pusher (colloq & pej)

chupeta *f* (Col) (golosina) lollipop

chupete *m*
A 1 (de bebé) pacifier (AmE), dummy (BrE) 2 (CS) (del biberón) nipple (AmE), teat (BrE)
B (Chi, Per) (golosina) lollipop
C (Chi) (Auto) choke
D (Méx fam) (en la piel) hickey (AmE colloq), lovebite (BrE)

chupetear [A1] *vt* (fam) ‹*helado*› to lick

chupetín *m* (RPl) lollipop

chupetón *m* (Esp fam) hickey (AmE colloq), lovebite (BrE)

chupo *m*
A (Per fam) (Med) boil
B (Col fam) pacifier (AmE), dummy (BrE)

chupón¹ -pona *m,f* (Esp fam) (aprovechado) scrounger (colloq)

chupón² *m*
A (Bot) sucker
B 1 (AmL) ▸**chupete A1** 2 (Méx) (del biberón) teat
C 1 (CS fam) (en la piel) hickey (AmE colloq), lovebite (BrE) 2 (Col) (chupada) lick

churrasco *m* (filete a la parrilla) barbecued steak; (filete) (CS) steak

churrasquería *f* (AmS) steak house

churrería *f*: *shop or stall selling* **churros**

churrias *fpl* (Col fam) diarrhea*

churriento -ta *adj* (Andes fam): **estaba ~** I had the runs

churrigueresco -ca *adj* (Arte) churrigueresque; (recargado) fussy, over-elaborate

churro¹ *adj* (AmS fam) gorgeous (colloq)

churro² *m*
A (Coc) *strip of fried dough*; ***venderse como ~s*** to sell like hot cakes

B (Esp fam) (chapuza) botched job (colloq)
C (AmS fam) (mujer) stunner (colloq); hombre) hunk (colloq)
D (AmC fam) (de marihuana) joint (colloq)

churro

A typical Spanish food, consisting of a long thin cylinder of dough, deep-fried in olive oil and often dusted with sugar. *Churros* are usually eaten with thick hot drinking chocolate, especially for breakfast

churruscarse [A2] *v pron* to get crisp
churrusco[1] *adj* (Col fam) frizzy (colloq)
churrusco[2] *m* (Col) (Zool) caterpillar; (cepillo) bottle brush
churumbel *m* (Esp fam) kid (colloq)
churumbela *f*
A (Mús) flageolet
B (AmL) (para el mate) cup
chus: **no dijo ~ ni mus** (fam) he didn't say a word
chusca *f* (Chi fam) tramp (AmE colloq), slag (BrE colloq)
chusco[1] **-ca** *adj*
A (gracioso) ‹*persona/humor*› earthy
B (Chi, Per fam & pey) 1 (ordinario) ‹*persona*› common (pej); ‹*perro*› mongrel; ‹*barrio/lugar*› plebeian (pej) 2 ‹*mujer*› loose (colloq)
C (Col fam) (agradable, bonito) lovely (colloq)
chusco[2] *m* crust
chusma *f* (gentuza) rabble (*pl*), plebs (*pl*) (colloq)
chuspa *f* (Col) (para lápices) pencil case; (para gafas) glasses case
chut *m* shot
chutar [A1] *vi* (Dep) to shoot
■ **chutarse** *v pron* (*refl*) (Esp arg) (inyectarse) to shoot up (sl)
chute *m*
A (Dep) shot
B (Esp arg) (de droga) fix (sl)
chuteador *m* (CS) (Dep) striker; (Indum) football boot
chutear [A1] *vt/vi* (CS) to shoot
■ **chutearse** *v pron* (Col arg) to shoot up (sl)
chuza *f*
A (Méx) (Dep) (jugada) strike; (marca) mark
B **chuzas** *fpl* (RPl fam) (greñas) rats' tails (*pl*) (colloq)
chuzo[1] *adj* (CS fam) ‹*pelo*› dead straight (colloq); ‹*persona*› hopeless (colloq)
chuzo[2] *m*
A: ***llover a ~s*** *or* ***caer ~s (de punta)*** (fam) to pour, chuck it down (BrE colloq)
B (Col) (del escorpión) sting
CI *m* (= **coeficiente intelectual** *or* **de inteligencia**) IQ
Cía. *f* (= **Compañía**) Co
cian *m* cyan
cianuro *m* cyanide
ciática *f* sciatica
cibercafé *m* Internet café, cybercafé
ciberespacio *m* (Inf) cyberspace
cibernauta *mf* cybernaut, Internet user
cibernética *f* cybernetics
cibernético -ca *adj* cybernetic
ciberpirata *mf* hacker
cicatería *f* (fam) stinginess (colloq), meanness
cicatero[1] **-ra** *adj* (fam) tightfisted (colloq)
cicatero[2] **-ra** *m,f* (fam) skinflint (colloq)
cicatriz *f* scar; **la herida le dejó ~** the wound left her with a scar
cicatrización *f* formation of scar tissue, cicatrization (tech)
cicatrizar [A4] *vi*, **cicatrizarse** [A4] *v pron* to heal (up), cicatrize (tech)
cicerone *mf* (liter) guide, cicerone (liter)
cicla *f* (Col fam) bike (colloq), bicycle
cíclico -ca *adj* cyclical
ciclismo *m* cycling, biking (colloq)
ciclista[1], (Andes) **ciclístico -ca** *adj* cycle (*before n*)
ciclista[2] *mf* cyclist
ciclo *m* 1 (de fenómenos, sucesos) cycle 2 (de películas) season; (de conferencias) series 3 (Lit) cycle 4 (Educ): **el primer ~** primary school 5 (Elec) cycle
(Compuesto) **ciclo menstrual** menstrual cycle
ciclocross *m* cyclo-cross; **bicicleta de ~** mountain bike
ciclomotor *m* moped
ciclón *m* cyclone; ***como un ~*** (fam): **entró/salió como un ~** he stormed in/out; **pasó como un ~** she rushed *o* flew past
cíclope *m* Cyclops
ciclostil, ciclostilo *m* (Esp) 1 (aparato) cyclostyle 2 (cliché) stencil
cicloturismo *m* bicycle touring
ciclovía *f* (Col) cycle path
cicuta *f* hemlock
ciego[1] **-ga** *adj*
A 1 (invidente) blind; **es ~ de nacimiento** he was born blind; **se quedó ~** he went blind; ***a ciegas***: **anduvimos a ciegas por el pasillo** we groped our way along the corridor; **lo decidió a ciegas** he decided without thinking it through; **comprar a ciegas** to buy sth without seeing it first; ***más ~ que un topo*** as blind as a bat; ***ponerse ~ a*** *or* ***de algo*** (Esp fam) to stuff oneself with sth (colloq) 2 (ante una realidad) **estar ~ A algo** to be blind to sth
B (ofuscado) blind; **~ de ira** blind with fury
C ‹*fe/obediencia*› blind
D ‹*conducto/cañería*› blocked; ‹*arco*› blank; ‹*muro*› blind
E (Esp fam) (por alcohol) blind drunk (colloq); (por la droga) stoned (sl)
ciego[2] **-ga** *m,f*
A (invidente) (*m*) blind man; (*f*) blind woman; ***en el país*** *or* ***el reino de los ~s el tuerto es (el) rey*** in the land of the blind the one-eyed man is king
B **ciego** *m* (Anat) cecum*
C **ciego** *m* (Esp arg). **¡qué ~ llevaba/se cogió!** (por droga) he was/got stoned out of his mind (sl); (por alcohol) he was/got totally plastered (colloq)
cielo *m*
A (firmamento) sky; **~ cubierto** overcast sky; **a ~ abierto** (Min) opencast (*before n*); ***a ~ descubierto*** in the open; ***cambiar del ~ a la tierra*** (Chi) to change out of all recognition; ***como caído*** *or* ***llovido del ~*** (oportunamente): **este dinero me viene como caído del ~** this money must be heaven-sent; ***remover ~ y tierra*** to move heaven and earth; ***tocar el ~ con las manos*** (AmS): **sería tocar el ~ con las manos** it would be a dream come true; **sentí que tocaba el ~ con las manos** I was over the moon (colloq)
B (Relig) 1 **el ~** (Paraíso) heaven; **ir al ~** to go to heaven; **¡que el ~ no lo permita!** heaven *o* God forbid!; ***clama al ~***: **una injusticia que clama al ~** a gross injustice, an outrage; **clama al ~ que ...** it's outrageous that ...; ***estar/sentirse en el séptimo ~*** to be in seventh heaven; ***ganarse el ~*** to earn oneself a place in heaven; ***ver el ~ abierto*** to see one's chance 2 (*como interj*): **¡~s!** (good) heavens!; **¡~ santo!** *or* **¡santo ~!** heavens above!
C (techo) ceiling
(Compuesto) **cielo raso** ceiling
D 1 (aplicado a personas) angel 2 (como apelativo) sweetheart, darling; **¡mi ~!** my darling
ciempiés *m* (*pl* **~**) centipede
cien[1] *adj inv/pron* a/one hundred; **~ mil** a/one hundred thousand; **es ~ por ~ algodón** (esp Esp) it's a hundred percent cotton; **sólo tengo ~** I only have a hundred; **se venden de a ~** they are sold by the hundred
cien[2] *m*: **el ~** (number) one hundred
ciénaga *f* swamp
ciencia *f* 1 (rama del saber) science; (saber, conocimiento) knowledge, learning; ***a ~ cierta*** for sure, for certain; ***no tiene ninguna ~*** there's nothing complicated about it 2 **ciencias** *fpl* (Educ) science
(Compuestos)
- **ciencia ficción** science fiction
- **Ciencias Empresariales/de la Información** *fpl* Business/Media Studies
- **ciencias ocultas** *fpl* occultism
- **Ciencias Políticas/de la Educación** *fpl* Politics/Education

Cienciología *f* Scientology

cienciólogo -ga *m,f* Scientologist

cieno *m* silt, mud

científico¹ -ca *adj* scientific

científico² -ca *m,f* scientist

cientista social *mf* (CS) social scientist

ciento¹ *adj/pron (delante de otro número)* a/one hundred; **~ dos/cincuenta** a/one hundred and two/and fifty; *para ejemplos ver* **quinientos**

ciento² *m* 1 (número): **~s de libros/miles** hundreds of books/of thousands; **a ~s: vinieron a ~s** they came in the (AmE) *o* (BrE) in their hundreds 2 **por ciento** percent; **cien por ~** a hundred percent; **un descuento del 20%** a 20% discount

ciernes: **en ~** *(loc adv)* in the making

cierra, cierras, etc *see* **cerrar**

cierre *m*

A (acción) 1 (de fábrica, empresa, hospital) closure 2 (de establecimiento) closing; **la hora de ~** closing time 3 (de frontera) closing 4 (de emisión) end, close; **al ~ de esta edición** at the time of going to press; **hora de ~** close, closedown 5 (de negociación) end 6 (Fin) close

Compuesto **cierre patronal** lockout

B 1 (de bolso, pulsera) clasp, fastener; (de puerta, ventana) lock; **frasco con ~ hermético** airtight container 2 (cremallera) zipper (AmE), zip (BrE)

Compuestos

- **cierre centralizado** central locking
- **cierre de dirección** steering lock
- **cierre metálico** (en tienda) metal shutter *o* grille
- **cierre relámpago** (CS, Per) zipper (AmE), zip (BrE)

cierro¹ *m* (Chi) fence

cierro² *see* **cerrar**

cierto -ta *adj*

A (verdadero) true; **no hay nada de ~ en ello** there is no truth in it; **una cosa es cierta** one thing's certain; **¡ah!, es ~** oh yes, of course; **mañana es su cumpleaños — ¡cierto!** it's her birthday tomorrow — so it is!; **parece más joven, ¿no es ~?** he looks younger, doesn't he *o* don't you think?; **estabas en lo ~** you were right; **lo ~ es que ...** the fact is that ...; **es ~ que ...** it is true that ...; **si bien es ~ que ...** while *o* although it's true to say that ...; **por ~** (a propósito) by the way, incidentally; (por supuesto) of course; **dinero que, por ~, nunca me devolvió** money which, of course, he never paid back

B *(delante del n)* (que no se especifica, define) certain; **cierta clase de gente** a certain kind of people; **de cierta edad** of a certain age; **en cierta ocasión ...** on one occasion ...; **en ~ modo** in some ways; **hasta ~ punto** up to a point; **se sentía un ~ malestar en el ambiente** there was a sense of unease in the atmosphere; **durante un ~ tiempo** for a while *o* a time; **camina con cierta dificultad** she has some difficulty walking

ciervo -va *m,f* (especie) deer; (macho) stag; (hembra) hind

Compuesto **ciervo volante** *or* **volador** *m* stag beetle

cifra *f*

A 1 (signo) figure; **un número de cinco ~s** a five-figure number 2 (número, cantidad) number; **la ~ de muertos** the number of dead, the death toll (period) 3 (de dinero) figure, sum; **pagaron una ~ astronómica** they paid an astronomical amount *o* sum of money

B (clave) code, cipher; **en ~** in code

cifrar [A1] *vt*

A ‹*mensaje/carta*› to write ... in code, encode (frml)

B ‹*esperanza*› to place, pin

■ **cifrarse** *v pron*

A «*esperanza*» **~se EN algo** to be pinned ON sth

B «*sueldo/beneficios*» **~se EN algo**: **se cifra en un 12%** it stands at 12%

cigala *f* crawfish, crayfish

cigarra *f* cicada

cigarrera *f* (de mesa — para puros) cigar box; (— para cigarrillos) cigarette box; (de bolsillo para cigarrillos) cigarette case

cigarrería *f* (Andes) tobacco shop (AmE), tobacconist's (BrE)

cigarrillo *m* cigarette; **~ con filtro** filter tipped cigarette

cigarro *m* (puro) cigar; (cigarrillo) cigarette

cigoto *m* zygote

cigüeña *f* stork

cigüeñal *m* crankshaft

cilantro *m* coriander; ***es bueno el ~, pero no tanto*** (Chi, Ven) there's no need to overdo it

cilicio *m* (vestimenta) hair shirt; (cinturón) cilice

cilindrada *f*, **cilindraje** *m* cubic capacity; **un motor de pequeña/gran ~** a small/powerful engine

cilíndrico -ca *adj* cylindrical

cilindro *m* cylinder; **un motor de cuatro ~s** a four-cylinder engine

cima *f* (de montaña) top, summit; (de árbol) top; (de profesión) top; (de carrera) peak, height; ***dar ~ a algo*** to round sth off

cimarra *f* (Chi): **hacer la ~** to play hooky (esp AmE colloq); to skive off (school) (BrE colloq)

cimarrón¹ -rrona *adj*

A ‹*ganado/planta*› wild

B (AmL) (Hist) ‹*esclavo*› runaway *(before n)*

cimarrón² -rrona *m,f*

A (animal) wild animal

B (AmL) (Hist) (esclavo) runaway, fugitive

C **cimarrón** *m* (CS) (mate) *unsweetened maté*

címbalo *m* cymbal

cimborio, cimborrio *m* dome

cimbrear [A1], **cimbrar** [A1] *vt* 1 ‹*vara*› to shake 2 ‹*caderas*› to sway

■ **cimbrearse, cimbrarse** *v pron* to sway

cimbrón *m* (AmL) ▸**cimbronazo**

cimbronazo *m*, **cimbrón** *m* (AmL) (sacudida) jolt; (de temblor de tierra) tremor, shake (colloq); **el ~ de la explosión** the shock of the explosion

cimentación *f* (acción) foundation laying; (cimientos) foundations *(pl)*

cimentar [A1] *or* [A5] *vt* 1 ‹*edificio*› to lay the foundations of 2 (consolidar) to consolidate, strengthen 3 (basar) **~ algo EN algo** to base sth ON sth

■ **cimentarse** *v pron* 1 (consolidarse) «*paz*» to be consolidated; **la democracia se ha cimentado** democracy has established itself 2 (basarse) **~se EN algo** to be based ON sth

cimientos *mpl* foundations *(pl)*; **abrir** *or* **excavar los ~** to dig the foundations; **poner** *or* **echar los ~ de algo** to lay the foundations of sth

cimitarra *f* scimitar

cinc *m* ▸**zinc**

cincel *m* (de escultor, albañil) chisel; (de orfebre) graver

cincelado *m* (de piedra) chiseling*; (de metal) engraving

cincelar [A1] *vt* ‹*piedra*› to chisel, carve; ‹*metal*› to engrave

cincha *f* (Equ) girth, cinch (AmE); (cinturón) (Chi) belt

cinchar [A1] *vt* to girth, cinch (AmE)

■ **cinchar** *vi* (RPl fam) 1 (tirar) to tug 2 (trabajar duro) to work hard 3 (Dep) **~ POR algn** to support sb

cinco¹ *adj inv/pron* five; [*nótese que algunas frases requieren el uso del número ordinal 'fifth' en inglés*] 1 (en cifras, cantidades, direcciones): **noventa y ~** ninety-five; **quinientos ~** five hundred and five; **la fila ~** row five, the fifth row; **vinieron/vinimos los ~** the five of them/of us came; **somos ~** there are five of us; **entraron de ~ en ~** they went in five at a time; **me costó ~ libras y pico** I paid five pounds something for it; **es el número ~ en la lista** he's fifth *o* number five on the list; **vive en el número ~** he lives at number five; ***ni ~*** (fam): **no tengo ni ~** I'm broke (colloq); **no sabe/entendió ni ~** (AmL) he doesn't know/he didn't understand a thing; ***venga/choca esos ~*** (fam) shake my hand; put it there! (colloq) 2 (en la hora, en fechas): **son las ~ de la mañana/tarde** it's five (o'clock) in the morning/afternoon; **~ para las dos** five to two; *ver* ▸**menos⁴**2; **las ocho y ~** five after (AmE) *o* (BrE) past eight; **serían las ~ y pico** it must have been just after five (o'clock); **son las ~ pasadas** it's just after five; **hoy estamos a** *or* **hoy es ~** today is the fifth; **el día ~ es su cumpleaños** her birthday is on the fifth, the fifth is her birthday; **en el siglo ~** in the fifth century

cinco² *m*

A (número) five; **me tocó el ~** I got number five; **aprieta el**

~ press (number) five; **hace los ~s al revés** he writes his fives backward(s); **el ~ de corazones** the five of hearts
B (Per) (momento) moment

cincuenta¹ *adj inv/pron* fifty; **los (años) ~** *or* **la década de los ~** the fifties; **tiene unos ~ años** she's about 50 years old; **~ y tantos/pico** fifty-odd, fifty something; **~ y cinco** fifty-five; **el número/la página ~** number/page fifty; **el ~ aniversario** the fiftieth anniversary

cincuenta² *m* (number) fifty

cincuentena *f*: **habrá una ~ de personas** there must be about fifty people there

cincuentenario *m* fiftieth anniversary

cincuentón¹ -tona *adj* (fam): **es ~** he's in his fifties

cincuentón² -tona *m,f* (fam): **una cincuentona** a woman in her fifties

cine *m* [1] (arte, actividad) cinema; **el mundo del ~** the movie *o* film world; **hacer ~** to make movies *o* films; **actor de ~** movie *o* film actor [2] (local) movie house *o* theater (AmE), cinema (BrE); **¿vamos al** *or* (Col) **a ~?** shall we go to the movies (AmE) *o* (BrE) cinema?

(Compuestos)
- **cine de barrio** local movie theater (AmE), local cinema (BrE)
- **cine de estreno** *movie theater where new releases are shown*
- **cine de verano** open-air movie theater (AmE), open-air cinema (BrE)
- **cine hablado** *or* **sonoro** talkies (*pl*)
- **cine mudo** silent movies *o* films (*pl*)
- **cine negro** film noir

cineasta *mf* filmmaker, moviemaker (AmE)

cineclub, cine-club *m* film club

cinéfilo¹ -la *adj* movie-going (*before n*), cinema-going (BrE) (*before n*)

cinéfilo² -la *m,f* movie buff, cinema buff (BrE)

cinegético -ca *adj* (frml) hunting (*before n*)

cinemascope® *m* Cinemascope®

cinemática *f* (Fís) kinematics

cinematografía *f* cinematography; **la ~ actual** current movie *o* film making

cinematografiar [A17] *vt* to make a movie *o* film (version) of; **la versión cinematografiada del libro** the movie *o* film version of the book

cinematográfico -ca *adj* movie (*before n*), film (BrE) (*before n*)

cinematógrafo *m* (ant) [1] (proyector) projector [2] (arte) cinema

cinética *f* kinetics

cinético -ca *adj* kinetic

cínico¹ -ca *adj* cynical

cínico² -ca *m,f* cynic

cinismo *m* cynicism; **¡qué ~ el suyo!** he's so cynical!

cinta *f*
A [1] (para adornar, envolver) ribbon [2] (en gimnasia rítmica) ribbon; (en carreras) tape; **tocar la ~** to breast the tape

(Compuestos)
- **cinta adhesiva** (en papelería) adhesive tape; (Med) sticking plaster
- **cinta aislante** *or* (Chi) **aisladora** insulating tape
- **cinta durex®** (AmL excl CS) *or* (AmL) **scotch** *or* (Col) **pegante** Scotch tape® (AmE), Sellotape® (BrE)
- **cinta magnética** magnetic tape
- **cinta métrica** tape measure
- **cinta negra** *mf* (Méx) (Dep) black belt
- **cinta transportadora** conveyor belt

B [1] (Audio, Video) tape [2] (period *o* ant) (Cin) *tb* **~ cinematográfica** movie (AmE), film (BrE)

(Compuestos)
- **cinta limpiadora** head-cleaning tape
- **cinta magnetofónica** magnetic tape
- **cinta virgen** blank tape

cinto *m* belt

cintura *f* [1] (de la persona) waist; **adelgazar la ~** to reduce the waistline; **me tomó** *or* (esp Esp) **cogió de la ~** he grabbed me round the waist; **¿cuánto tienes de ~?** what do you measure round the waist? [2] (de prenda) waist; **me queda grande de ~** it's too big for me round the waist; ***meter a algn en ~*** (Esp fam) to take sb in hand

(Compuesto) **cintura de avispa** wasp waist

cinturilla *f* waistband

cinturón *m*
A (Indum) belt; ***apretarse el ~*** to tighten one's belt

(Compuestos)
- **cinturón de castidad** chastity belt
- **cinturón de seguridad** seat belt, safety belt
- **cinturón negro/verde/azul** (Dep) black/green/blue belt

B (de ciudad) belt; **el ~ industrial** the industrial belt

(Compuesto) **cinturón verde** green belt

cipote¹ *adj*
A (fam) (estúpido) stupid
B (*delante del n*) (Col fam) (como intensificador) fabulous, fantastic; **¡~ estupidez con la que viene a salir!** what a stupid thing to say!

cipote² *m* (Esp vulg) (pene) prick (vulg)

ciprés *m* cypress

circense *adj* circus (*before n*)

circo *m*
A [1] (Espec) circus [2] (Hist) circus
B (Geol) cirque

circuito *m*
A (pista) track, circuit; (de circo, exposición) circuit

(Compuesto) **circuito urbano** urban cycle

B (Elec, Electrón) circuit

(Compuestos)
- **circuito cerrado** closed circuit
- **circuito en serie** series *o* serial circuit

circulación *f*
A (movimiento) movement; (Auto) traffic

(Compuesto) **circulación rodada** vehicular traffic

B (Biol, Med) circulation; **la ~ sanguínea** the circulation of the blood
C (Fin) circulation

(Compuesto) **circulación fiduciaria** fiduciary money, fiat money (AmE)

circulante¹ *adj*
A ‹*líquido/corriente*› flowing
B ‹*tráfico*› moving
C ‹*rumor/noticia*›: **los rumores/las noticias ~s en la política** the rumors*/news going around in political circles
D (Econ) **pasivo ~** current liabilities (*pl*); **dinero ~** money in circulation

circulante² *m* (Econ) money supply

circular¹ *adj* circular; **de forma ~** circular

circular² [A1] *vi*
A «*sangre/savia*» to circulate, flow; «*agua/corriente*» to flow
B [1] «*transeúnte/peatón*» to walk; «*conductor*»: **circulan por la izquierda** they drive on the left; **¡circulen, por favor!** move along please! [2] «*autobús/tren*» (estar de servicio) to run, operate
C «*dinero/billete/sello*» to be in circulation
D «*noticia/rumor/memo*» to circulate, go around
■ **circular** *vt* to circulate

circular³ *f* circular

circulatorio -ria *adj* circulation (*before n*)

círculo *m*
A [1] (Mat) circle [2] (circunferencia) circle; **coloca las mesas en ~** arrange the tables in a circle

(Compuestos)
- **círculo de giro** turning circle
- **Círculo Polar Antártico/Ártico** Antarctic/Arctic Circle
- **círculo vicioso** vicious circle

B [1] (grupo) circle [2] (ambiente, esfera) circle; **en (los) ~s teatrales** in theatrical circles [3] (asociación): **~ de Bellas Artes** Fine Arts Association *o* Society

circuncidar [A1] *vt* to circumcise

circuncisión *f* circumcision

circundante *adj* surrounding (*before n*)

C

circundar [A1] *vt* to surround, encircle
circunferencia *f* circumference
circunlocución *f* circumlocution (frml)
circunloquio *m*: **contestar con ~s** to answer in a roundabout way
circunnavegación *f* circumnavigation
circunnavegar [A3] *vt* to circumnavigate
circunscribir [I34] *vt* to circumscribe
■ **circunscribirse** *v pron* (frml) [1] (ceñirse) **~se A algo** to limit *o* confine oneself TO sth [2] «*problema/competencia*» **~se A algo** to be limited TO sth; **el problema se circunscribe a esta zona** the problem is restricted *o* limited to this area
circunscripción *f* (distrito) district
(Compuesto) **circunscripción electoral** electoral district, constituency (BrE)
circunscrito -ta, **circunscripto -ta** *adj* [1] [ESTAR] (frml) (limitado): **~ A algo** limited TO sth [2] (Mat) circumscribed
circunspección *f* circumspection, caution
circunspecto -ta *adj* ‹*persona/actitud*› circumspect, cautious; ‹*comentario*› guarded
circunstancia *f*
[A] (factor, particularidad): **si por alguna ~ no puede ir** if for any reason you cannot go; **no es una ~ relevante en este caso** it is not a relevant factor in this case; **se da la ~ de que ...** as it happens ...
[B] **circunstancias** *fpl* (situación) circumstances (*pl*); **bajo** *or* **en ninguna ~** under no circumstances; **en ~s en** *or* **de que** (CS) as; **dadas las ~s** under *o* given the circumstances; **debido a sus ~s familiares** due to her family situation
(Compuesto) **circunstancia agravante/atenuante/eximente** aggravating/extenuating/exonerating circumstance
circunstancial *adj*
[A] ‹*factor/hecho*› circumstantial, incidental; **fue testigo ~ de los hechos** she was a chance witness to the events
[B] (Ling) **complemento A**
cirílico -ca *adj* Cyrillic
cirio *m* candle; ***armar*** *or* ***montar un*** **~** (Esp fam) to kick up *o* raise *o* create a stink (colloq)
cirquero -ra *m,f* (Chi, Méx) circus performer
cirro *m* (nube) cirrus
cirrosis *f* cirrhosis
ciruela *f*
[A] (Bot, Coc) plum
(Compuesto) **ciruela pasa** *or* (CS) **seca** prune
[B] **(de) color ~** plum-colored*
ciruelo *m* plum tree
cirugía *f* surgery; **se hizo la ~ en la nariz** (CS fam) she had her nose done (colloq)
(Compuesto) **cirugía estética/plástica** cosmetic/plastic surgery
ciruja *mf* (RPl) [1] (trapero) junkman (AmE), rag-and-bone man (BrE) [2] (fam) (pillo) little devil (colloq)
cirujano -na *m,f* surgeon
(Compuesto) **cirujano -na dentista** *m,f* dental surgeon
cisco *m* (Min) slack; ***armar un*** **~** (Esp) to kick up *o* raise *o* create a stink (colloq); ***hacerse*** *or* (Col) ***volverse*** **~** (fam) «*jarrón*» to smash to pieces; ***hecho*** **~** (Esp fam): **estoy hecha ~** I feel completely shattered (colloq); **tengo el estómago hecho ~** I've got a bad stomach
Cisjordania *f* the West Bank
cisjordano -na *adj* West Bank (*before n*)
cisma *m* (Rel) schism; (en partido) split
cisne *m*
[A] (Zool) swan
[B] (RPl) (para polvos) powder puff
cisterciense *adj/mf* Cistercian
cisterna *f* (depósito) tank; (subterránea) cistern; (del retrete) cistern
cistitis *f* cystitis
cita *f*
[A] [1] (con profesional) appointment; **pedir ~** to make an appointment; **concertar una ~** to arrange an appointment [2] (con novio, amigo): **tengo una ~ con mi novio/con un amigo** I have a date with my boyfriend/I'm going out with a friend; **no llegues tarde a la ~** don't be late; **faltó** *or* **no acudió a la ~** he didn't show up [3] (period) (reunión) meeting; **tuvo una ~ con el presidente** he had a meeting with the president; ***darse*** **~**: **se dieron ~ en la estación** they arranged to meet at the station; **cientos de famosos se dieron ~ en el estreno** (period) hundreds of celebrities were gathered at the premiere
[B] (en texto, discurso) quote; **una ~ del diario** a quote from the newspaper; **una ~ de Cervantes** a quotation *o* quote from Cervantes
citación *f* subpoena, summons
citadino[1] **-na** *adj* (AmL) urban, city (*before n*)
citadino[2] **-na** *m,f* [1] (AmL) (ciudadano) city dweller [2] (Méx) (defeño) *inhabitant of Mexico City*
citado -da *adj*: **el caso anteriormente ~** the aforementioned case (frml); **los hechos acaecidos en la citada ciudad** the events which took place in that town
citar [A1] *vt*
[A] [1] (dar una cita) «*doctor/jefe de personal*» to give ... an appointment; **estar citado con algn** to have an appointment with sb [2] (convocar): **nos citó a todos a una reunión** she called us all to a meeting [3] (Der) to summon; **~ a algn como testigo** to call sb as a witness
[B] [1] (mencionar) to mention; **no quiero ~ nombres** I don't want to mention any names [2] (repetir textualmente) to quote
■ **citarse** *v pron* [1] **~se CON algn** to arrange to meet sb [2] (*recípr*): **se ~on en la plaza** they arranged to meet in the square; **se ~on para verse** they arranged to see each other
cítara *f* zither
citófono *m* (Andes) internal phone system
citología *f* (ciencia) cytology; (análisis) smear test; **hacerse una ~** to have a smear test
citoplasma *m* cytoplasm
cítrico[1] **-ca** *adj* citrus (*before n*)
cítrico[2] *m* citrus
ciudad *f* town; (de mayor tamaño) city; **la gran ~** the (big) city; Ⓢ **centro ciudad** town *o* city center
(Compuestos)
- **ciudad balneario** (AmL) coastal resort
- **Ciudad del Vaticano/de México** Vatican/Mexico City
- **ciudad dormitorio** bedroom community (AmE), dormitory town (BrE)
- **ciudad perdida** (Méx) shanty town
- **ciudad residencial** *town or development in the commuter belt*
- **ciudad sanitaria** hospital complex
- **Ciudad Santa**: **la ~ ~** the Holy City
- **ciudad satélite** satellite town
- **ciudad universitaria** university campus

ciudadanía *f* [1] (nacionalidad) citizenship [2] (conjunto de ciudadanos) citizens (*pl*); (civismo) civic responsibility
ciudadano[1] **-na** *adj* ‹*vida*› city (*before n*); **la inseguridad ciudadana** the lack of safety in towns *o* cities; **es un deber ~** it's the duty of every citizen; **con la colaboración ciudadana** with the cooperation of the people
ciudadano[2] **-na** *m,f*
[A] (habitante) citizen
(Compuesto) **ciudadano de a pie**: **el ~ de a ~** the man in the street
[B] (Ven frml) (al dirigirse — a un hombre) sir; (— a una mujer) madam; **todos los ~s deben acudir a la taquilla** everyone should go to the ticket office
ciudadela *f*
[A] (fortificación) citadel, fortress
[B] (Col) (de viviendas) residential complex
cívico -ca *adj* [1] ‹*deberes/derechos*› civic [2] ‹*acto*› public-spirited, civic-minded
civil[1] *adj* [1] ‹*derechos/responsabilidades*› civil [2] (no religioso) civil; **se casaron por lo ~** *or* (Per, RPl, Ven) **sólo por ~** *or* (Chi, Méx) **por el ~** they were married in a civil ceremony (AmE), they had a registry office wedding (BrE) [3] (no militar) civilian (*before n*); **iba (vestido) de ~** he was in civilian clothes

civil² *mf*
A 1 (persona no militar) civilian 2 (Esp) (guardia civil) Civil Guard
B **civil** *m* (RPl) (matrimonio civil) *civil marriage ceremony*
civilismo *m* (CS) antimilitarism
civilista *mf* lawyer (*specializing in civil law*)
civilización *f* civilization
civilizado -da *adj* civilized
civilizador -dora *adj* civilizing (*before n*)
civilizar [A4] *vt* ‹*país/pueblo*› to civilize; ‹*persona*› to teach ... to behave properly
▪ **civilizarse** *v pron* «*pueblo*» to become civilized; «*persona*» to learn to behave properly
civismo *m* public-spiritedness
cizaña *f* darnel; ***meter*** *or* ***sembrar*** ~ to cause trouble
cl. (= **centilitro**) cl.
clac *m* crack
clamar [A1] *vi* ~ **CONTRA algo** to protest AGAINST sth; ~ **POR algo** to clamor* FOR sth, cry out FOR sth
▪ **clamar** *vt*: ~ **venganza** to cry out for vengeance
clamor *m* clamor*
clamorosamente *adv* ‹*demandar/pedir*› noisily; **ha triunfado** ~ she has been resoundingly successful; **fueron** ~ **recibidos** they got a rousing reception; **ha vuelto** ~ **a las pantallas** she has returned to the screen in triumph
clamoroso -sa *adj* ‹*acogida*› rousing; ‹*ovación*› rapturous, thunderous; **un éxito** ~ a resounding success
clan *m* clan
clandestinidad *f* secrecy, secret nature; **trabajar en la** ~ to work underground; **pasar a la** ~ to go underground
clandestino¹ -na *adj* ‹*reunión/relación*› clandestine, secret; ‹*periódico*› underground
clandestino² -na *m,f* (fam) illegal immigrant
claque *f* 1 (en el teatro) claque 2 (camarilla) clique
claqué *m* tap dancing, tap
claqueta *f* clapperboard
clara *f*
A *tb* ~ **de huevo** (egg) white
B (Esp) (bebida) shandy
claraboya *f* skylight
clarear [A1] *v impers* 1 (amanecer): **estaba clareando** it was getting light *o* day was breaking 2 (Meteo): **comenzó a** ~ the sky/the clouds began to clear
▪ **clarear** *vi* «*pelo*» to go gray*/white
clarete *m* (rosado) rosé; (tinto) claret
claridad *f*
A 1 (luz) light; **en la** ~ **del crepúsculo** in the twilight 2 (luminosidad) brightness
B (de explicación, imagen, sonido) clarity; **con** ~ clearly
clarificación *f* (de situación) explanation, clarification
clarificador -dora *adj* illuminating, enlightening
clarificante *adj* ‹*información/explicación*› clarifying (*before n*)
clarificar [A2] *vt* to clarify
▪ **clarificarse** *v pron* to become clearer
clarín *m* bugle
clarinete *m* clarinet
clarinetista *mf* clarinetist
clarisa *f* nun of the Order of Saint Clare
clarividencia *f* (percepción paranormal) clairvoyance; (perspicacia) discernment
clarividente¹ *adj* (que adivina el futuro) clairvoyant; (perspicaz) discerning, clear-sighted
clarividente² *mf* clairvoyant
claro¹ -ra *adj*
A (luminoso) ‹*cielo/habitación*› bright
B (pálido) ‹*color/verde/azul*› light, pale; ‹*piel*› fair; **tiene los ojos** ~**s** she has blue/green/gray eyes
C ‹*salsa/sopa*› thin
D ‹*agua/sonido*› clear; ‹*ideas/explicación/instrucciones*› clear; ‹*situación/postura*› clear; **tener algo** ~ to be clear about sth; **que quede bien** ~ **que ...** I want it to be quite clear that ...; **¿está** ~**?** is that clear?; **quiero dejar (en)** ~ **que** ... I want to make it very *o* quite clear that ...; ***a las claras*: díselo a las claras** tell her straight; ***llevarlo*** ~ (Esp fam) to be in for a shock; ***sacar algo en*** ~ ***de algo*** to make sense of sth
E (evidente) clear, obvious; **hay pruebas claras** there is clear evidence; **está** ~ **que ...** it is clear *o* obvious that ...; **a no ser,** ~ **está, que esté mintiendo** unless, of course, he's lying
claro² *adv*
A ‹*ver*› clearly; **voy a hablarte** ~ I'm not going to beat around *o* about the bush; **me lo dijo muy** ~ he made it very *o* quite clear (to me)
B (*indep*) 1 (en exclamaciones de asentimiento) of course; **¡~ que lo sabe!** of course she knows!; **¡~ que no!** no, of course not!; **¡~ que sí!** of course, absolutely! 2 (como enlace) mind you; **nadie le creyó,** ~ **no es de extrañar** nobody believed him. Mind you, it's not surprising; ~**, así cualquiera puede** well, of course anyone can do it like that; **díselo —** ~**, para que me regañe ¿no?** (iró) tell him — oh sure, and have him tell me off, right? (iro)
claro³ *m*
A (en bosque) clearing; (en el pelo, la barba) bald patch
B (Meteo) sunny spell *o* period *o* interval
claroscuro *m* chiaroscuro
clase *f*
A 1 (tipo) kind, sort, type 2 (categoría): **productos de primera** ~ top-quality products
B (Transp) class; **viajar en primera/segunda** ~ to travel (in) first/second class

Compuestos
- **clase económica** *or* **turista** economy *o* tourist class
- **clase ejecutiva** *or* **preferente** business class

C (Sociol) class; **la** ~ **política** politicians

Compuestos
- **clase alta/baja/media** upper/lower/middle class
- **clase dirigente** *or* **dominante** ruling class
- **clase obrera** *or* **trabajadora** working class
- **clases pasivas** *fpl*: **las** ~ ~ *people receiving state pensions*

D (distinción, elegancia) class; **tiene** ~ she has class
E (Educ) 1 (lección) class; **ha faltado a** ~ **diez veces** he's missed ten classes; ~**s de conducir** *or* **manejar** driving lessons; **dictar** ~ **(DE algo)** (AmL fml) to lecture (IN sth); **dar** ~ *or* (Chi) **hacer** ~**s (DE algo)** «*profesor*» (en colegio) to teach (sth); (en universidad) to lecture in (sth), teach (sth); **¿quién te da** ~ **de latín?** who takes you for Latin?; **da** ~**s de latín/piano con un profesor privado** (Esp) she has latin classes/piano lessons with a private tutor 2 (grupo de alumnos) class; **es el primero de la** ~ he's top of the class; **un compañero de** ~ a classmate, a school friend 3 (aula — en escuela) classroom; (— en universidad) lecture hall *o* room

Compuestos
- **clase magistral** master class
- **clase particular** private class *o* lesson

F (Bot, Zool) class
clásicas *fpl* (esp Esp) classics
clasicismo *m* classicism
clasicista¹ *adj* classicistic
clasicista² *mf* classicist
clásico¹ -ca *adj* 1 ‹*decoración/estilo/ropa*› classical 2 ‹*música*› classical; ‹*método*› standard, traditional; ‹*error/malentendido/caso*› classic 3 ‹*lengua/mundo*› classical
clásico² *m* 1 (obra) classic 2 (autor): **los** ~**s de la música pop** the giants of pop music 3 (AmL) (Dep) traditional big game
clasificación *f*
A (de documentos, libros) classification; (de cartas) sorting
B (de película —acción) classification; (— certificado): **¿qué** ~ **(moral) tiene?** what certificate has it got?
C (de elemento, animal, planta) classification
D (Dep) 1 (para una etapa posterior) qualification; **esta victoria le supone la** ~ **para la fase final** this victory means that he will go through to *o* has qualified for the finals 2 (tabla) placings (*pl*); (puesto) position, place; **quinto en la** ~ **final del rally** fifth in the final placings for the rally; **obtuvo una buena** ~ he finished among the leaders

C

clasificador *m* (carpeta) ring binder; (máquina) sorter; (mueble) filing cabinet

clasificadora *f* sorter

clasificar [A2] *vt* 1 ‹*documentos/datos*› to sort, put in order; ‹*cartas*› to sort 2 ‹*planta/animal/elemento*› to classify 3 ‹*hotel*› to class, rank; ‹*fruta*› to class; ‹*persona*› to class, rank

■ **clasificarse** *v pron* (Dep) 1 (para etapa posterior) to qualify; **~ para la final** to qualify for the final 2 (en tabla, carrera): **se clasificó en sexto lugar** he finished in sixth place; **con esta victoria se clasifica en quinto lugar** with this victory she moves into fifth place

clasificatorio -ria *adj* qualifying (*before n*)

clasismo *m* classism

clasista *adj* ‹*actitud/sociedad*› classist; **es un hombre muy ~** he's very class-conscious

claudicación *f* 1 (de principios) renunciation, abandonment 2 (rendición) capitulation

claudicar [A2] *vi* (ceder, transigir) to give in; **~ DE algo** to abandon sth

claustro *m*
A (Arquit, Relig) cloister
B (Educ) (de universidad) senate; (de colegio) staff; (reunión) senate/staff meeting

(Compuesto) **claustro materno** (liter) womb

claustrofobia *f* claustrophobia; **siento ~ allí dentro** I get claustrophobia in there

claustrofóbico -ca *adj* claustrophobic

cláusula *f* (Der, Ling) clause

clausura *f*
A 1 (de congreso, festival) closing ceremony; **de ~** ‹*ceremonia/discurso*› closing (*before n*) 2 (de local) closure
B (Relig) cloister

clausurar [A1] *vt* 1 ‹*congreso/sesión*› «*acto/discurso*» to bring … to a close; «*persona*» to close 2 ‹*local/estadio*› to close … down

clava *f* club

clavada *f* (Méx) (en natación) dive

clavadista *mf* (Méx) diver

clavado¹ -da *adj*
A 1 **~ EN algo** ‹*puñal/tachuela/espina*› stuck IN sth; ‹*estaca*› driven INTO sth 2 (fijo) **~ EN algo**: **con la vista clavada en un punto** staring at a point, with his gaze fixed on a point; **tenía los ojos ~s en el cuadro** she couldn't take her eyes from the painting; **se quedó ~ en el lugar** he was rooted to the spot
B 1 (fam) (idéntico) **ser ~ A algn** «*persona*» to be the spitting image of sb (colloq); **ser ~ A algo** «*objeto*» to be identical TO sth; **esos zapatos son ~s a los míos** those shoes are identical to mine 2 (fam) (en punto): **llegó a las cinco clavadas** he arrived on the dot of five (colloq)

clavado² *m* (AmL) dive

clavar [A1] *vt*
A 1 **~ algo EN algo** ‹*clavo*› to hammer sth INTO sth; ‹*puñal/cuchillo*› to stick sth IN sth; ‹*estaca*› to drive sth INTO sth; **me clavó los dientes/las uñas** he sank his teeth/dug his nails into me 2 ‹*cartel/estante*› to put up (*with nails, etc*) 3 ‹*ojos/vista*› to fix … on
B (fam) 1 (cobrar caro) to rip … off (colloq); **nos ~on $10,000** they stung us for $10,000 2 (CS fam) (engañar) to cheat 3 (Méx fam) (robar) to swipe (colloq), to filch (colloq)
C (RPl fam) (dejar plantado) to stand … up (colloq)
D (Ven fam) ‹*estudiante*› to fail, to flunk (AmE colloq); **lo ~on en física** he was flunked in physics (colloq)

■ **clavarse** *v pron*
A 1 ‹*aguja/espina*›: **me clavé la aguja** I stuck the needle into my finger (*o* thumb *etc*); **se clavó una espina en el dedo** she got a thorn in her finger 2 (*refl*) ‹*cuchillo/puñal*›: **se clavó el puñal en el pecho** he plunged the dagger into his chest
B (CS fam) **~se CON algo** (por no poder venderlo) to get stuck WITH sth (colloq); (por ser mala compra): **se clavó con el auto que compró** the car turned out to be a bad buy
C (Per fam) (colarse): **se clavó en la cola** he jumped the line (AmE) *o* (BrE) the queue; **siempre se clava en las fiestas** he's always gatecrashing parties (colloq)
D (Col arg): **~se estudiando** *or* **a estudiar** to study like crazy (colloq)
E (Méx) (Dep) to dive

clave¹ *adj* (*pl* **~** *or* **-ves**) key (*before n*)

clave² *f*
A 1 (código) code; **en ~** in code 2 (de problema, misterio) key

(Compuesto) **clave de usuario** (AmL) user's password

B (Mús) clef; **~ de fa/sol** bass/treble clef
C (Arquit) keystone

clave³ *m* harpsichord

clavecín *m* spinet, harpsichord

clavel *m* carnation

clavelina *m*, **clavellina** *f* pink

clavetear [A1] *vt* to decorate *o* adorn … with studs

clavicémbalo *m* harpsichord

clavicordio *m* clavichord

clavícula *f* collarbone, clavicle (tech)

clavija *f* 1 (Mec) pin 2 (Elec) (enchufe) plug; (de enchufe) pin 3 (de guitarra) tuning peg; ***apretarle las ~s a algn*** (fam) to tighten up on sb

clavo *m*
A 1 (Tec) nail; ***agarrarse a un ~ ardiendo***: **se agarraría a un ~ ardiendo** he'd take (*o* do *etc*) anything; **se agarró a ella como a un ~ ardiendo** he clung to her as if she were his last hope; ***como un ~***: on the dot; ***dar en el ~*** to hit the nail on the head; **diste en el ~ con tu regalo** your present was just what I/he/they wanted; **siempre da en el ~ con sus predicciones** his forecasts are always right on the mark; ***no dar*** *or* ***pegar ni ~*** (fam) not to do a stroke of work 2 (Med) pin 3 (en montañismo) piton
B (Bot, Coc) *tb* **~ de olor** clove
C (CS fam) (expresando fastidio): **tener animales es un ~** having animals is a drag (colloq); **el auto que me vendió es un ~** the car he sold me is a dead loss

claxon /'klakson/ *m* (*pl* **-xons**) horn; **tocar el ~** to sound *o* blow one's horn, to honk

clemencia *f* mercy, clemency (frml)

clemente *adj* (liter) clement (liter)

clementina *f* clementine

cleptomanía *f* kleptomania

cleptómano -na *m,f* kleptomaniac

clerical *adj* clerical

clericalismo *m* clericalism

clérigo -ga *m,f*
A (en el clero protestante) (*m*) clergyman, cleric; (*f*) clergywoman, cleric
B **clérigo** *m* (en el clero católico) clergyman, priest

clero *m* clergy

clic *m* (*pl* **clics**)
A (al cerrarse algo) click; (al romperse algo) snap
B (Inf) click; **hacer ~ (en** *or* **sobre algo)** to click (on sth); **hacer doble ~ (en** *or* **sobre algo)** to double-click (on sth)

cliché *m*
A (expresión, idea) cliché
B (de multicopista) stencil; (Impr) plate; (Fot) negative

cliente -ta *m,f* (de tienda, de restaurante) customer; (de empresa, de abogado) client, customer; (de hotel) guest; (en taxi) fare, customer; **~ asiduo** *or* **habitual** regular customer (*o* client *etc*)

clientela *f* (de restaurante, tienda) clientele, customers (*pl*); (de hotel) guests (*pl*); (de abogado) clients (*pl*)

clientelismo *m* (AmL) *practice of obtaining votes with promises of government posts etc*

clima *m*
A (Meteo) climate; **un ~ malsano** an unhealthy climate

(Compuesto) **clima polar/tropical** polar/tropical climate

B (ambiente) atmosphere; **en un ~ festivo** in a festive atmosphere; **el ~ económico** the economic climate; ***al ~*** (Col) at room temperature

climático -ca *adj* climatic

climatizado -da *adj* ‹*local/casa*› air-conditioned; ‹*piscina*› heated

climatizador *m* climate control, air-conditioning unit

climatizar [A4] *vt* ‹*local*› to air-condition; ‹*piscina*› to heat

climatología *f* climatology
climatológico -ca *adj* climatological
clímax *m* (*pl* ~) climax
clínica *f*
A (establecimiento) private hospital *o* clinic
Compuestos
- **clínica dental** dental office (AmE), dental surgery (BrE)
- **clínica de reposo** convalescent *o* rest home

B (especialidad) clinical medicine
clínico¹ -ca *adj* ‹*ensayo*› clinical (*before n*); ▸**hospital**
clínico² -ca *m,f* (RPl) general practitioner
clip *m* (*pl* **clips**)
A 1 (sujetapapeles) paperclip 2 (para el pelo) bobby pin (AmE), hairgrip (BrE) 3 (cierre) clip; **aretes** *or* **pendientes de ~** clip-on earrings
B (Video) (pop) video
clíper *m* clipper
cliquear [A1] *vi* (fam) to click; **~ EN** *or* **SOBRE algo** to click ON sth; **~ con el botón derecho (del ratón) en algo** to right-click sth
■ **cliquear** *vt* ‹*ícono*› to click; **~ aquí** click here
clítoris *m* (*pl* ~) clitoris
cloaca *f*
A (alcantarilla) sewer
B (de ave, reptil) cloaca
cloche *m* (Ven) clutch
clon *m* clone
clonar [A1] *vt* (Biol) to clone; ‹*tarjeta de crédito*› to skim
clonación *f*, **clonaje** *m* cloning
clónico -ca *adj* clonal, clone (*before n*)
cloración *f* chlorination
clorhídrico -ca *adj* hydrochloric
cloro *m* (Quím) chlorine; (lejía) (AmC, Chi) bleach
clorofila *f* chlorophyll
clorofílico -ca *adj* chlorophyllous
cloroformo *m* chloroform
cloruro *m* chloride
clóset *m* (*pl* **-sets**) (AmL exc RPl) (en dormitorio) built-in closet (AmE), fitted *o* built-in wardrobe (BrE)
clotch /'klotʃ/ *m* (AmC) clutch
clown /'klaun/ *m* (*pl* **clowns**) clown
club *m* (*pl* **clubs** *or* **-es**) club; **~ náutico** yacht club
Compuesto **club nocturno** nightclub
clueca *adj* broody
cm. (= **centímetro**) cm.
coa *m* (en Chi) underworld slang
coacción *f* coercion; **bajo ~** under duress
coaccionar [A1] *vt* to coerce; **lo ~on para que interviniera** he was coerced into intervening
coactivo -va *adj* coercive
coadjutor¹ -tora *adj* coadjutant
coadjutor² *m* coadjutor
coadyuvar [A1] *vt* (frml) to contribute
coagulación *f* coagulation, clotting
coagulante¹ *adj* clotting (*before n*)
coagulante² *m* coagulant
coagular [A1] *vt* to clot, coagulate
■ **coagularse** *v pron* (Med) to clot, coagulate; (Quím) to coagulate
coágulo *m* 1 (Fisiol, Med) clot, coagulum (tech) 2 (grumo) clot
coalición *f* coalition; **gobierno de ~** coalition government
coalicionarse [A1] *v pron* to form a coalition
coartada *f* alibi
coartar [A1] *vt* ‹*persona*› to inhibit; ‹*libertad/voluntad*› to restrict
coautor -tora *m,f* coauthor
coba *f* (Ven arg) (mentira, engaño) lie; ***darle ~ a algn*** (adular) (Esp, Méx, Ven fam) to suck up to sb (colloq)
cobalto *m* cobalt
cobarde¹ *adj* cowardly
cobarde² *mf* coward
cobardía *f* cowardice
cobaya *f*, **cobayo** *m* guinea pig
cobear [A1] *vi* (Ven arg) to lie, bullshit (sl)
cobertizo *m* shed
cobertor *m* (colcha) bedspread; (manta) blanket
cobertura *f*
A (Fin) (protección) hedge; (de seguro) cover
B (Period, Rad, TV) coverage; **~ informativa** news coverage; **programación de ~ regional** regional programing
C (Telec) range; **estar fuera de ~** to be out of range
cobija *f* (AmL) 1 (manta) blanket 2 **cobijas** *fpl* (ropa de cama) bedclothes (*pl*)
cobijar [A1] *vt*
A ‹*persona*› (proteger) to shelter; (hospedar) to give … shelter, take … in
B (liter) ‹*sentimientos/esperanzas*› to harbor*
■ **cobijarse** *v pron* to shelter, take shelter
cobijo *m* shelter; **darle ~ a algn** to shelter sb
cobista *mf* (Esp fam) (zalamero) bootlicker (colloq)
cobra *f* cobra
cobrable *adj* recoverable
cobrador -dora *m,f* (a domicilio) collector; (de autobús) bus conductor
cobrar [A1] *vt*
A 1 ‹*precio/suma*› to charge; **nos cobran 30.000 pesos de alquiler** they charge us *o* we pay 30,000 pesos in rent; **~ algo POR algo/+ INF** to charge sth FOR sth/-ING 2 ‹*sueldo*› to earn; **cobra 4.000 euros al mes** he earns 4,000 euros a month; **todavía no hemos cobrado junio** we still haven't been paid for June; **~ la pensión** to collect *o* draw one's pension; **cobra subsidio de desempleo** he receives unemployment benefit
B ‹*alquiler*› to charge; **nos cobra un alquiler altísimo** he charges us a very high rent; **vino a ~ el alquiler** she came to collect the rent; **le ~on intereses** he was charged interest; **¿me cobra estas cervezas?** can I pay for these beers, please?; **me cobró el vino dos veces** he charged me twice for the wine; **está cobrando las entradas** he's taking the money for the tickets
C 1 ‹*deuda*› to recover; **nunca llegó a ~ esas facturas** he was never paid for those bills 2 ‹*cheque*› to cash
D 1 (Chi) (pedir): **le cobré los libros que le presté** I asked him to give back the books I'd lent him 2 (Chi) ‹*gol/falta*› to give
E 1 (adquirir): **~ fama de algo** to get a reputation for being sth; **las negociaciones ~on un nuevo impulso** the negotiations were given fresh impetus; **el tema ha cobrado actualidad** the issue has taken on a new topicality; **~ fuerzas** to gather strength 2 (tomar): **~le cariño a algn** to grow fond of sb
F (en caza) (matar) to shoot, bag
G 1 (period) ‹*vidas/víctimas*› to claim 2 ‹*botín*› to carry off 3 (Náut) to haul in
■ **cobrar** *vi* 1 **~ POR algo/+ INF** to charge FOR sth/-ING; **el lechero vino a ~** the milkman came to be paid; **¿me cobra, por favor?** can you take for this, please?, can I pay, please?; **llámame por ~** (Chi, Méx) call collect (AmE), reverse the charges (BrE) 2 (recibir el sueldo) to be paid 3 (fam) (recibir una paliza): **¡vas a ~!** you're going to get it! (colloq)
■ **cobrarse** *v pron*
A (recibir dinero): **tenga, cóbrese** here you are; **cóbrese las cervezas** can you take for the beers, please?
B ‹*víctimas*› to claim
cobre *m* 1 (Metal, Quím) copper; ***mostrar*** *or* ***pelar el ~*** (Col, Méx) to show one's true colors 2 **(de) color ~** copper (*before n*), copper-colored* 3 (AmL fam) penny; **estoy sin un ~** I'm broke (colloq)
cobrizo -za *adj* coppery, copper-colored*
cobro *m* 1 (de cheque) cashing; (de sueldo, pensión): **para el ~ de la pensión** in order to collect your pension 2 (Telec): **llamó a ~ revertido** she called collect (AmE), she reversed the charges (BrE)
coca *f* (Bot) coca; (cocaína) (arg) coke (sl)

C

coca

Andean peasants in Peru, Bolivia, and Ecuador chew coca leaves mixed with bicarbonate of soda to combat cold and tiredness while working. They also make *mate de coca*, an infusion effective against altitude sickness. Much of the coca grown in the region goes to Colombia and reaches Europe and the US as cocaine. Governments in the region are now under heavy international pressure to stop its cultivation, but coca farmers defend their right to grow it, both for their own use and because it is so profitable

cocaína *f* cocaine

cocainómano -na *m,f* cocaine addict

cocal *m* coca plantation

cocaví *m* (Chi) things (*pl*) to eat

cocción *f* 1 (Coc) cooking; **necesita 20 minutos de ~** it needs 20 minutes cooking time 2 (de ladrillos, cerámica) firing

cóccix *m* (*pl* ~) coccyx

cocear [A1] *vi* to kick

cocer [E10] *vt*
A (Coc) (cocinar) to cook; (hervir) to boil; **~ algo a fuego lento** to cook sth over a low heat
B ‹*ladrillos/cerámica*› to fire
C (Chi) ‹*bebé*› to give … a rash
■ **cocerse** *v pron*
A 1 «*verduras/arroz*» (hacerse) to cook; (hervir) to boil; **tardan unos 15 minutos en ~se** they take about 15 minutes to cook 2 (fam) «*persona*» to be roasting (colloq)
B (fam) (tramarse) to brew (colloq); **algo se está cociendo** something's brewing (colloq)
C (Chi fam) (emborracharse) to get plastered (colloq)

cochambre *f or m* (fam) filth, muck (colloq); **¡que ~ de cocina!** this kitchen is filthy!

cochambroso -sa *adj* (fam) filthy

cochayuyo *m* (AmS) edible seaweed

coche *m*
A (Auto) car, auto (AmE), automobile (AmE); **nos llevó en ~ a la estación** he drove us to the station; **~s usados** *or* **de segunda mano** *or* **de ocasión** used *o* (BrE) secondhand cars; ***en el ~ de San Fernando*** on shanks's mare (AmE) *o* (BrE) pony
(Compuestos)
- **coche bomba** car bomb
- **coche celular** patrol wagon (AmE), police van (BrE)
- **coche de bomberos** fire truck (AmE), fire engine (BrE)
- **coche de carreras** racing car
- **coche de choque** bumper car
- **coche de línea** long-distance bus (AmE), coach (BrE)
- **coche fúnebre** hearse
- **coche patrulla** patrol car, police car

B 1 (Ferr) car (AmE), carriage (BrE) 2 (de bebé) baby carriage (AmE), pram (BrE); (en forma de sillita) stroller (AmE), push-chair (BrE) 3 (carruaje) coach, carriage
(Compuestos)
- **coche cama** *or* (CS) **dormitorio** sleeper, sleeping car
- **coche de caballos** carriage
- **coche restaurante** dining car

cochecho -cha *adj* (Chi fam) sloshed (colloq)

cochecito *m* ▸**coche B2**

cochera *f* 1 (para autobuses) depot, garage; (para trenes) shed; **las ~s** the depot 2 (garaje) (Esp, Méx) garage

cochero *m* coachman

cochinada *f* (fam) (palabra, acción): **¡no digas esas ~s!** don't use such filthy language!; **eso es una ~** that's a disgusting *o* filthy thing to do

cochinería *f* (fam) 1 (cualidad) filthiness 2 ▸**cochinada**

cochinilla *f* 1 (crustáceo) woodlouse 2 (Coc, Tex) (colorante) cochineal

cochinillo *m* suckling pig, sucking pig

cochino[1] **-na** *adj*
A 1 (fam) (sucio) ‹*persona/manos*› filthy 2 (fam) (indecoroso) ‹*persona*› disgusting; ‹*revista/película*› dirty (colloq) 3 (Chi) (Dep, Jueg) (violento) dirty (colloq); (tramposo): **es muy ~** he's a terrible cheat
B (fam) (malo, asqueroso) lousy (colloq); **¡estoy harto de esta cochina vida!** I'm tired of this lousy life! (colloq)

cochino[2] **-na** *m,f*
A (Zool) pig, hog (AmE)
B (fam) (persona — sucia) filthy pig (colloq), slob (colloq); (— grosera) dirty beast (colloq)

cochiquera *f* (Esp) pigsty

cocido[1] **-da** *adj*
A (Coc) 1 (hervido) ‹*huevos/verduras*› boiled 2 (CS) (no crudo) cooked; **muy/poco ~** well done/rare; **esas salchichas ya vienen cocidas** those sausages are ready-cooked
B ‹*arcilla*› fired
C (fam) (borracho) plastered (colloq)

cocido[2] *m* (Cul) 1 (Esp) stew (*made with meat and chickpeas*) 2 (Col, Ven) stew (*made with meat, plantains and cassava*)

cociente *m* quotient
(Compuesto) **cociente intelectual** *or* **de inteligencia** IQ, intelligence quotient

cocina *f*
A (habitación) kitchen; **armario de ~** kitchen cupboard
B (aparato) range (AmE), stove (AmE), cooker (BrE)
(Compuestos)
- **cocina de** *or* **a gas** gas range *o* cooker
- **cocina eléctrica** electric range *o* cooker

C (arte) cookery; **la ~ vasca** Basque cuisine; **la ~ casera** home cooking; **libro de ~** cookbook, cookery book (BrE)

cocinar [A1] *vt* to cook
■ **cocinar** *vi* to cook; **¿quién cocina en tu casa?** who does the cooking in your house?
■ **cocinarse** *v pron* 1 (Coc) «*carne/arroz*» to cook 2 (fam) «*persona*» to bake (colloq)

cocinero -ra *m,f* cook

cocineta *f*
A (Méx) (cocina) kitchenette
B (Col) ▸**cocinilla**

cocinilla *f* camp stove (AmE), camping stove (BrE)
(Compuesto) **cocinilla de alcohol** alcohol (AmE) *o* (BrE) spirit stove

cocktail /'koktel/ *m* (*pl* **-tails**) ▸**cóctel**

coco[1] **-ca** *adj* (AmC) bald

coco[2] *m*
A (Bot, Coc) coconut; ***caerse de un ~*** (Ven fam) to be disappointed
B (fam) (cabeza) head; **anda** *or* **está mal del ~** he's off his head (colloq); ***comerle el ~ a algn*** (Esp fam): **no me comas el ~** stop trying to talk me into it; **los políticos sólo quieren comerte el ~** politicians just try to brainwash you; ***comerse el ~ con algo*** (Esp fam) to worry about sth
C (fam) (fantasma, espantajo) boogeyman (AmE), bogeyman (BrE); (persona fea) ugly person; **es un ~** he's so ugly
D (bacteria) coccus

cocoa *f* (AmL) cocoa

cocodrilo *m* crocodile

cocol *m* (Méx) (bizcocho) cookie (*covered in sesame seeds*); ***del ~*** (fam) (muy mal) terrible

cocolazos *mpl* (Méx fam): **le pusieron sus ~** he got beaten up (colloq); **se van a armar los ~** there's going to be a fight

cocoliche *m* (RPl pey) pidgin Spanish (*spoken by Italian immigrants*)

cocorota *f* (Esp fam) head

cocotal *m* coconut plantation

cocotero *m* coconut palm

cóctel *m* (*pl* **-teles** *or* **-tels**)
A (bebida) cocktail
(Compuestos)
- **cóctel de frutas** (AmC, Col) fruit salad, fruit cocktail
- **cóctel de gambas** (Esp) shrimp (AmE) *o* (BrE) prawn cocktail
- **cóctel Molotov** Molotov cocktail

B (fiesta) cocktail party

coctelera *f* cocktail shaker

cocuyo *m* 1 (AmL) (insecto) firefly, glowfly (AmE) 2 (Col, Ven) (Auto) parking light (AmE), sidelight (BrE)

coda *f* coda

codaste *m* sternpost

codazo *m*: **darle un ~ a algn** (leve) to nudge sb; (fuerte) to elbow sb; **se abrió camino a ~s** he elbowed his way through

codearse [A1] *v pron* **~ CON algn** to rub shoulders WITH sb

codeína *f* codeine

codera *f* (Indum) elbow patch

códice *m* codex

codicia *f* (avaricia) greed, avarice

codiciado -da *adj* coveted

codiciar [A1] *vt* to covet

codicioso[1] -sa *adj* ‹*persona/mirada*› covetous, greedy

codicioso[2] -sa *m,f* covetous *o* greedy person

codificación *f*
A (de leyes) codification
B (Inf) (de información) coding; (Ling) (de un mensaje) encoding

codificador *m*, **codificadora** *f* encoder

codificar [A2] *vt*
A ‹*leyes/normas*› to codify
B 1 (Inf) ‹*información*› to code 2 (Ling) ‹*mensaje*› to encode

código *m*
A (de signos) code; **descifrar un ~** to decipher a code
(Compuestos)
- **código barrado** *or* **de barras** bar code
- **código genético** genetic code
- **código morse** morse code
- **código postal** zipcode (AmE), postcode (BrE)
- **código territorial** area code, dialling code

B (de leyes, normas) code
(Compuestos)
- **código civil/militar/penal** civil/military/penal law
- **código de conducta** code of practice
- **código de la circulación** Highway Code

codillo *m* 1 (Zool) elbow 2 (Coc) knuckle

codirector -tora *m,f* codirector

codirigir [I7] *vt* to codirect

codo[1] -da *adj* (Méx fam) tightfisted (colloq)

codo[2] *m* (Anat) elbow; (de prenda) elbow; ***a fuerza*** *or* ***a base de ~s*** (fam) through sheer hard slog *o* graft (colloq); ***~ con*** *or* ***a ~*** side by side; ***empinar el ~*** (fam) to prop up the bar; ***hablar (hasta) por los ~s*** (fam) to talk nineteen to the dozen (colloq); ***hincar*** *or* ***romperse los ~s*** (fam) to knuckle down (colloq); **tuvo que hincar los ~s para el examen** she had to cram (colloq); ***ser del ~*** *or* ***duro de ~*** (Arg fam) to be tightfisted *o* stingy (colloq)
(Compuesto) **codo de tenista** tennis elbow

codorniz *f* quail

coedición *f* joint publication, co-publication

coeditar [A1] *vt* to copublish

coeficiente *m* (Mat) coefficient
(Compuestos)
- **coeficiente de amortización** amortization rate
- **coeficiente de incremento** rate of increase
- **coeficiente intelectual** *or* **de inteligencia** IQ

coercer [E2] *vt* (frml) to constrain (frml)

coerción *f* constraint

coercitivo -va *adj* coercive

coetáneo -nea *adj/m,f* contemporary

coexistencia *f* coexistence

coexistir [I1] *vi* to coexist

cofia *f* cap

cofinanciación *f* joint financing

cofinanciar [A1] *vt* to finance … jointly

cofrade *mf* member (*of a* **cofradía**)

cofradía *f* 1 (Relig) brotherhood 2 (Hist) (gremio) guild

cofre *m*
A 1 (joyero) jewel case, jewelry* box 2 (baúl — para ropa) trunk; (— para dinero, joyas) chest
B (Méx) (capó) hood (AmE), bonnet (BrE)

cofundador -dora *m,f* co-founder

cogeculo *m* (Ven vulg): **tenemos un ~ horrible** it's total chaos *o* havoc

cogedor *m* (esp Esp) dustpan

cogeolla *f* (Col) potholder, ovencloth (BrE)

coger [E6] *vt*
(Sentido I)
A (esp Esp) 1 (tomar) to take; **lo cogió del brazo** she took him by the arm; **coge un folleto** pick up *o* take a leaflet; **esto no hay** *or* **no tiene por donde ~lo** (fam) I just don't know where to start with this 2 (quitar) (+ *me/te/le etc*) to take; **siempre me está cogiendo los lápices** she's always taking my pencils 3 ‹*flores/fruta*› to pick; (levantar) to pick up; **coge esa revista del suelo** pick that magazine up off the floor; **cogió al niño en brazos** she picked the child up in her arms; **~ a algn en autostop** (Esp) to pick up a hitchhiker; **no cogen el teléfono** (Esp) they're not answering the phone
B (esp Esp) (alcanzar, atrapar) 1 ‹*ladrón/terrorista*› to catch 2 ‹*pelota*› to catch 3 ‹*pescado/liebre*› to catch 4 «*toro*» to gore
C (esp Esp) 1 (descubrir) to catch; **lo cogieron in fraganti/robando** he was caught red-handed/stealing 2 (encontrar) to catch; **me cogió de buenas** she caught me in a good mood; **la noticia nos cogió en París** we were in Paris when we got the news
D 1 ‹*tren/autobús/taxi*› to catch, take 2 ‹*calle/camino*› to take; **coge la primera a la derecha** take the first right
E (Esp fam) 1 (sacar, obtener) ‹*billete/entrada*› to get; **~ hora para el médico** to make an appointment to see the doctor 2 (traer): **vete a ~ el coche** go and get *o* bring the car 3 (ocupar): **~ sitio** to save a place; **coge la vez en la cola** take your turn in the line (AmE) *o* (BrE) queue; **cogió la delantera** he took the lead
(Sentido II)
A (Esp) 1 (aceptar) ‹*dinero/trabajo/casa*› to take; **no puedo ~ más clases** I can't take on any more classes 2 (admitir) to take; **ya no cogen más niños en ese colegio** they're not taking any more children at that school now 3 (atender): **no pudieron ~me en la peluquería** they couldn't fit me in at the hairdresser's
B (esp Esp) (adquirir) 1 ‹*enfermedad*› to catch; ‹*insolación*› to get; **vas a ~ frío** you'll catch cold; **cogí una borrachera** I got plastered (colloq); **cogió un berrinche** she had a temper tantrum 2 ‹*polvo/suciedad*› to collect, gather; **~ algo de color** (broncearse) to get a bit of color 3 ‹*acento*› to pick up; ‹*costumbre/vicio*› to pick up; ‹*ritmo*› to get into; **le cogí cariño** I got quite fond of him; **~le manía a algn** to take a dislike to sb; ***~la con algn*** to take it out on sb; ***~la por hacer algo*** (Ven fam) to take to doing sth
C (esp Esp) (captar) 1 ‹*sentido/significado*› to get 2 ‹*emisora*› to pick up, get
D (Méx, RPl, Ven vulg) to screw (vulg), to fuck (vulg)

■ **coger** *vi*
A (esp Esp) «*planta*» to take; «*tinte/permanente*» to take
B 1 (esp Esp) **cojo/cogió y …** (fam): **si empiezas con eso cojo y me voy** if you're going to start talking about that, I'm off *o* (AmE) I'm taking off (colloq); **de repente cogió y se fue** suddenly he upped and went (colloq); **cogió y se puso a llorar** she (suddenly) burst into tears 2 (esp Esp) (por un camino): **coge por esta calle y …** take this street and … 3 (Esp fam) (caber) to fit
C (Méx, RPl, Ven vulg) to screw (vulg), to fuck (vulg)

■ **cogerse** *v pron* (esp Esp) 1 (agarrarse, sujetarse) to hold on; **cógete de la barandilla** hold on to the railing 2 (*recípr*): **ir cogidos de la mano** to walk hand in hand

cogestión *f* joint management

cogida *f* (Taur) goring; **sufrió una ~** he was gored

cognac *m* brandy

cognitivo -va *adj* cognitive

cognoscible *adj* cognizable

cogollo *m*
A (Bot) 1 (de lechuga, col) heart; (de hinojo) bulb 2 (brote) bud
B (fam) (meollo) heart; **el ~ de la cuestión** the heart of the matter
C (Ven fam) (de organización) bigwigs (*pl*) (colloq)

cogote *m* (fam) (nuca) scruff of the neck; (cuello) (AmL) neck

cogotear [A1] *vt* (Chi fam) to mug

cohabitación *f* (frml) cohabitation (frml)

C

cohabitar [A1] *vi* (frml) to cohabit (frml)

cohechar [A1] *vt* to bribe

cohecho *m* bribery

coheredero -ra (*m*) coheir; (*f*) coheiress

coherencia *f*
A 1 (congruencia) coherence, logic; **con ~** coherently *o* logically 2 (consecuencia) consistency; **actuar con ~** to be consistent; **¡qué falta de ~!** he's/it's so inconsistent
B (Fís) coherence

C

coherente *adj*
A 1 (congruente) ‹*discurso/razonamiento/ideas*› coherent, logical 2 (consecuente) ‹*actitud*› consistent; **una mujer ~** a woman who acts according to her beliefs
B (Fís) coherent

coherentemente *adv* 1 ‹*discutir/hablar*› coherently 2 ‹ *comportarse/actuar*› consistently

cohesión *f*
A 1 (de ideas, pensamientos) coherence 2 (en grupo) cohesion
B (Fís) cohesion

cohesionar [A1] *vt* (frml) to unite

cohete *m*
A (Espac, Mil) rocket
Compuestos
- **cohete anticarro** *or* **antitanque** anti-tank rocket
- **cohete espacial** space rocket
- **cohete sonda** space probe

B **cohetes** *mpl* fireworks (*pl*); *ver tb* **cuete² B**

cohibido -da *adj* (tímido) shy; (inhibido) inhibited; (incómodo) awkward

cohibir [I22] *vt* 1 (inhibir) to inhibit; **la presencia de su padre lo cohíbe** he feels inhibited in front of his father 2 (hacer sentir incómodo): **hablar en público lo cohíbe** he feels embarrassed about speaking in public
■ **cohibirse** *v pron*: **se cohibió al verme** he went all shy when he saw me (colloq)

cohorte *f* cohort

C.O.I *m* (= **Comité Olímpico Internacional**) IOC

coima *f* (CS, Per fam) (soborno) bribe; (acción) bribery

coime *m* (Col fam & pey) waiter

coimear [A1] *vt* (CS, Per fam) (sobornar) to bribe; (aceptar sobornos de) to get *o* take bribes from
■ **coimear** *vi* (fam): **coimeando se hizo rico** he got rich taking bribes

coimero¹ -ra *adj* (CS, Per fam) bent (colloq)

coimero² -ra *m,f* (CS, Per fam): **son todos unos ~s** they all take bribes

coincidencia *f* 1 (casualidad) coincidence; **se dio la ~ de que él también estaba allá** by coincidence *o* chance he was there too, he happened to be there too; **¡que ~!** what a coincidence! 2 (de opiniones) agreement

coincidencial *adj* (Col) coincidental

coincidente *adj* ‹*líneas*› coincident; **en esto tenemos opiniones ~s** we are of the same opinion in this matter (frml)

coincidir [I1] *vi*
A «*fechas/sucesos*» to coincide; «*versiones/resultados*» to coincide, match up, tally; **~ CON algo** to coincide (*o* match up *etc*) WITH sth
B «*personas*» 1 (en opiniones, gustos) **~ EN algo**: **coinciden en sus gustos** they share the same tastes; **todos coincidieron en que ...** everyone agreed that ...; **~ CON algn** to agree WITH sb 2 (en un lugar): **a veces coincidimos en el supermercado** we sometimes see each other in the supermarket; **muchos famosos coincidieron allí** there were a lot of famous people there
C «*líneas*» to coincide; «*dibujos*» to match up

cointérprete *mf* 1 (Cin, Teatr) (m) co-actor, (f) co-actress; **fueron ~s en esa obra** they were on the same bill in that play 2 (Mús) co-singer

coinversión *f* joint investment

coipo *m* coypu, nutria

coito *m* intercourse, coitus (frml)

coitus interruptus *m* coitus interruptus

cojear [A1] *vi*
A 1 «*persona/animal*» (por herida, dolor) to limp; (permanentemente) to be lame; **entró cojeando** he limped *o* hobbled in 2 «*silla/mesa*» to wobble, rock
B (fam) «*explicación/definición*» to fall short

cojera *f* limp

cojín *m* cushion

cojinete *m*
A (Mec) bearing
Compuesto **cojinete de bolas/rodillos** ball/roller bearing
B (Ferr) chair, rail clip

cojo¹ -ja *adj*
A 1 ‹*persona/animal*› lame; **está ~ del pie derecho** he's lame in his right leg; ***andar a la pata coja*** (fam) to hop; ***brincar de cojito*** (Méx fam) to hop 2 ‹*mesa/silla*› wobbly
B (fam) ‹*razonamiento*› shaky, weak; **anda un poco ~ en inglés** he's rather weak at English

cojo² -ja *m,f* lame person

cojones *mpl*
A (vulg) (testículos) balls (*pl*) (sl *or* vulg); ***decir/hacer algn lo que le sale de los ~*** (Esp) to say/do what one damn well likes (colloq); ***estar hasta los ~*** (vulg) to be pissed off (sl); ***hincharle los ~ a algn*** (vulg) to piss sb off (sl); ***tener ~*** (vulg) to have guts (colloq), to have balls (sl); ***tocarse los ~*** (vulg): **yo trabajo y él se toca los ~** I do all the work and he just sits around on his butt (AmE) *o* (BrE) backside (colloq)
B (vulg) (uso expletivo): **hoy le toca a él, ¡qué ~!** it's *his* damned turn today! (colloq); **tiene que pasar por aquí por ~** he has to come this way; **el coche de los ~** the damned car (colloq); **hace un frío de ~** it's goddam (AmE sl) *o* (BrE sl) bloody freezing cold

cojonudo -da *adj*
A (arg) (estupendo) ‹*tipo/película/fiesta*› great (colloq), amazing (colloq)
B 1 (Col, RPl fam) (valiente) gutsy (colloq) 2 (RPl fam) (tonto) dense, dumb

cojudo -da *adj* (Andes vulg) (bobo) stupid

col *f* (Esp, Méx) cabbage
Compuestos
- **col de Bruselas** Brussels sprout
- **col rizada** curly kale, collard

cola¹ *f*
A 1 (de un animal, pez) tail; ***traer*** *or* ***tener ~*** to have repercussions 2 (de vestido) train; (de frac) tails (*pl*) 3 (de avión) tail; (de cometa) tail 4 (RPl fam) (nalgas) bottom (colloq) 5 (Esp fam) (pene) weenie (AmE colloq), willy (BrE colloq)
Compuesto **cola de caballo** ponytail
B 1 (fila, línea) line (AmE), queue (BrE); **no hay mucha ~** there isn't much of a line *o* queue; **hacer ~** to line up (AmE), to queue (up) (BrE); **¡a la ~!** get in line! *o* in the queue!; **pónganse a la ~ por favor** please join the (end of the) line *o* queue; **brincarse** *or* **saltarse la ~** (Méx) to cut the line, to jump the queue (BrE) 2 (de una clasificación, carrera): **en lo que se refiere a la investigación estamos a la ~** as far as research is concerned, we are at the bottom of the pile *o* the league (colloq); **a la ~ del pelotón** at the tail end of the group
C (pegamento) glue; ***no pegar ni con ~***: **esos colores no pegan ni con ~** those colors just don't go together; **aquí no pega ni con ~** it just doesn't look right here (colloq)
Compuestos
- **cola de carpintero** wood glue *o* adhesive
- **cola de contacto/impacto** contact/impact adhesive
- **cola de pescado** fish glue, isinglass (tech)

D (bebida) Coke®, cola
E (Ven) (Auto): **pedir ~** to hitchhike; **darle la ~ a algn** to give sb a lift *o* a ride

cola² *m* (Chi fam & pey) fag (AmE colloq & pej), poof (BrE colloq & pej)

colaboración *f* collaboration; **en ~ con algn/algo** in collaboration with sb/sth

colaboracionismo *m* collaboration

colaboracionista *mf* collaborator

colaborador -dora *m,f* (en revista) contributor; (en tarea) collaborator

colaborar [A1] *vi* 1 to collaborate; **~ CON algn/algo** to collaborate WITH sb/sth; Ⓢ **colabore con nosotros, mantenga limpia la ciudad** help us keep the city clean; **~ EN algo** ‹*en proyecto*› to collaborate ON sth; **colabore**

en la lucha contra el hambre help fight hunger; **colabora en una revista** he contributes to a magazine 2 (contribuir) ~ A **algo** to contribute TO sth

colación *f*

A a ~: **sacar** *or* **traer algo a** ~ to bring sth up; **salir a** ~ «*tema/asunto*» to come up

B 1 (frml) (comida ligera) light meal (*o* lunch *etc*) 2 (Col) (galleta) cookie (AmE), biscuit (BrE)

colada *f* (Esp) (lavado) laundry, washing; **tender la** ~ to hang out the washing

coladera *f* 1 (Méx) (sumidero) drain 2 (Col) ▸**colador**

coladero *m* (arg): **ese examen es un** ~ that exam's a cinch (colloq); **esta ley se convertirá en un** ~ this law will be used as a loophole

colado -da *adj*: **estar** ~ **por algn** (Esp fam) to be crazy about sb (colloq)

colador *m* (para té) tea strainer; (para pastas, verduras) colander; ***dejar algo como un*** ~: **las polillas dejaron el suéter como un** ~ (fam) the moths left the sweater full of holes; ***dejar a algn como un*** ~ (fam) to riddle sb with bullets

colágeno *m* collagen

colapís, colapiz *mf* (Chi) ▸**cola de pescado**

colapsar [A1] *vt* (paralizar) ‹*tráfico*› to bring ... to a standstill

colapso *m* 1 (Med) collapse; **sufrió/le dio un** ~ he collapsed 2 (paralización) standstill; **provocó un** ~ **en todo el país** it brought the country to a standstill

colar [A10] *vt* 1 ‹*verdura/pasta*› to strain, drain; ‹*caldo/té*› to strain 2 ‹*billete falso*› to pass; **les coló el cuento de que ...** he spun them a yarn about ... (colloq)

■ **colar** *vi* (fam) «*cuento/historia*»: **no va a** ~ it won't wash (colloq)

■ **colarse** *v pron*

A (fam) 1 (en cola) to jump the line (AmE) *o* (BrE) queue 2 (en fiesta) to gatecrash; (en cine, en autobús) to sneak in without paying (colloq); **los ladrones se ~on por una ventana** the burglars slipped *o* sneaked in through a window

B 1 (fam) (entrar, penetrar): **se cuela una corriente de aire por debajo de la puerta** there's a draft coming in under the door 2 (Esp fam) (equivocarse) to get it wrong (colloq)

colateral *adj* 1 ‹*calle/pasillo*› side (*before n*) 2 ‹*pariente/línea*› collateral 3 ‹*efecto*› collateral (frml), secondary; **los efectos ~es del medicamento** the side effects of the drug

colcha *f* bedspread

colchón *m* (de cama) mattress; ~ **de espuma/muelles/plumas** foam/sprung/feather mattress

(Compuesto) **colchón de aire** (Tec) air cushion

colchonería *f: store selling mattresses*

colchoneta *f* (de playa) air bed, Lilo® (BrE); (de gimnasia) mat; (de cama) (Méx) comforter (AmE), duvet (BrE)

cole *m* (Esp fam) school

colear [A1] *vi* 1 (fam) (no estar resuelto): **todavía colea el asunto** the matter hasn't yet been settled 2 (Col, CS) «*coche*» to fishtail

colección *f* 1 (de sellos, monedas, cuadros) collection 2 (fam) (gran cantidad): **tiene una** ~ **de pulseras** she has lots of bracelets 3 (Lit) collection 4 (de modas) collection

coleccionable[1] *adj* collectable

coleccionable[2] *m* pull-out section

coleccionar [A1] *vt* to collect

coleccionista *mf* collector

colecta *f* (de donativos) collection; **hicimos una** ~ we had a collection

colectar [A1] *vt* to collect

colectivero -ra *m,f* (de autobús) (Arg) bus driver; (de taxi) (Andes) driver of a collective taxi

colectividad *f* group, community; **en** ~ collectively

colectivización *f* collectivization

colectivizar [A4] *vt* to collectivize

colectivo[1] **-va** *adj* collective

colectivo[2] *m*

A (period) (agrupación) group

B (Ling) collective noun

C 1 (Andes) (taxi) collective taxi (*with a fixed route and fare*) 2 (Arg) (autobús) bus

D (Per, Ur) (para regalo) collection

colector *m*

A (cañería) sewer

(Compuesto) **colector de drenaje** drainpipe

B (Elec) collector

C (Auto, Tec) manifold

colega *mf* 1 (compañero de profesión) colleague 2 (homólogo) counterpart 3 (fam) (amigo) buddy (AmE), mate (BrE colloq)

colegiado[1] **-da** *adj* collegial

colegiado[2] **-da** *m,f* 1 (profesional) member (*of a professional association*) 2 (period) (en fútbol) referee

colegial -giala *m,f* (de colegio) (*m*) schoolboy; (*f*) schoolgirl; **los ~es** (the) schoolchildren

colegiarse [A1] *v pron* to become a member (*of a professional association*)

colegiata *f* collegiate church

colegiatura *f* (Méx) school fees (*pl*)

colegio *m*

A (Educ) school; ~ **de monjas** convent school; **un** ~ **de curas** a Catholic boys' school

(Compuestos)

- **colegio mayor** (Esp) residence hall (AmE), hall of residence (BrE)
- **colegio privado** *or* **de pago** fee-paying *o* private school
- **colegio público** *or* **estatal** *or* **del estado** public school (AmE), state school (BrE)
- **Colegio Universitario** University College

B (de profesionales): **C~ de Abogados** ≈ Bar Association; **C~ Oficial de Médicos** ≈ Medical Association

(Compuesto) **colegio electoral** electoral college

colegir [I8] *vt* to deduce

cólera[1] *m* cholera

cólera[2] *f* rage, anger; **descargó su** ~ **en mí** she vented her anger *o* rage on me; **montar en** ~ to fly into a rage

colérico -ca *adj* 1 [ESTAR] (furioso) furious 2 [SER] (malhumorado) quick-tempered

colesterol *m* cholesterol

coleta *f* 1 (de pelo — atrás) ponytail; (— a los lados) bunch 2 (de torero) braid (AmE), pigtail (BrE); ***cortarse la*** ~ (Taur) to retire from bullfighting; (abandonar una tarea) (fam) to pack it in (colloq)

coletazo *m* 1 (con la cola) thrash of the tail; **dar ~s** to thrash about 2 (Auto): **el coche dio un** ~ the rear of the car skidded 3 (de movimiento, régimen): **dar los últimos ~s** to be in its death throes

coletilla *f* tag, filler (tech); *tb* ~ **interrogativa** question tag, tag question

coleto *m*

A (Indum) jerkin; ***echarse algo al*** ~ (fam) ‹*comida*› to put away; ‹*bebida*› to knock back (colloq)

B (Ven) 1 (tela) canvas 2 (fam) (trapo) floorcloth; **pasar el** ~ to clean

colgado -da *adj* (*ver tb* **colgar**)

A (plantado): **lo dejó** ~ she didn't show up; **me dejó** ~ **y tuve que hacerlo todo yo** she left me in the lurch and I had to do it all myself

B 1 (Esp arg) ‹*asignatura*›: **tiene una asignatura colgada para septiembre** he has to do retakes in September 2 (Esp arg) (por drogas) spaced out (colloq) 3 (Chi, Esp fam *or* arg) (que no entiende, no sabe): **estar** ~ to be completely lost (colloq) 4 (Col fam) (atrasado) behind 5 (Col, Esp fam *or* arg) (de dinero) short of money

colgajo *m* (fam): **una cortina con ~s** a curtain with dangly bits hanging from it (colloq)

colgante[1] *adj* hanging; ▸**puente**

colgante[2] *m* pendant

colgar [A8] *vt*

A ‹*cuadro*› to hang, put up; ‹*lámpara*› to put up; **está colgando la ropa** she's hanging the washing out; ~ **algo DE algo** to hang sth ON sth

B (ahorcar) to hang; **lo ~on en 1807** he was hanged in 1807

C ‹*teléfono/auricular*› to put down; **tienen el teléfono mal**

colgado their phone is off the hook
D (Internet) ‹*fotos/archivos de sonido*› to post
■ **colgar** *vi*
A (pender) to hang; **el vestido me cuelga de un lado** my dress is hanging down on one side
B (Telec) to hang up; **no cuelgue, por favor** hold the line please, please hold; **me colgó** he hung up on me
■ **colgarse** *v pron* (*refl*)
A (ahorcarse) to hang oneself
B (agarrarse, suspenderse) **~se DE algo**: **no te cuelgues de ahí** don't hang off there; **se le colgó del cuello y le dio un beso** he put his arms around her neck and gave her a kiss; **se pasó la tarde colgada del teléfono** (fam) she spent all afternoon on the phone
C (Inf) to crash
D 1 (Chi) (Telec): **se ~on al satélite** they linked up with the satellite 2 (Chi, Méx) (Elec): **~se del suministro eléctrico** to tap into the electricity supply

colibrí *m* hummingbird

cólico *m* colic
(Compuestos)
- **cólico hepático** hepatic *o* biliary colic
- **cólico nefrítico** *or* **renal** renal colic

coliflor *f*, (RPl) *m* cauliflower

coligar [A3] *vt* (frml) to unite
■ **coligarse** *v pron* (frml) to form an alliance

colilla *f* (de cigarrillo) cigarette end *o* butt

colimba¹ *f* (Arg fam) military service

colimba² *m* (Arg fam) conscript

colín *m* (Coc) bread stick

colina *f* hill

colindante *adj* adjoining

colindar [A1] *vi* ‹‹*terrenos*›› to adjoin; **~ CON algo** to adjoin sth

colirio *m* eye drops (*pl*)

colisión *f* 1 (de trenes, aviones) collision, crash; **se produjo una ~ entre dos trenes** two trains collided *o* crashed 2 (conflicto) conflict, clash
(Compuesto) **colisión en cadena** pileup

colisionar [A1] *vi* (frml) to collide

colitis *f* colitis

colla *mf*: *Indian from the Andean region of Bolivia, Peru and the NW of Argentina*

collado *m* (colina) hill; (entre montañas) pass

collage /ko'laʒ/ *m* (*pl* **-llages**) collage

collar *m*
A 1 (alhaja) necklace; (condecoración) chain; **~ de perlas** string of pearls 2 (para animales) collar 3 (plumaje) collar, ruff
(Compuestos)
- **collar antipulgas** flea collar
- **collar ortopédico** surgical collar, cervical collar
B (Tec) collar, hose clip

collarín *m* surgical collar, cervical collar

collera *f*
A (Per fam) (pandilla) gang (colloq)
B **colleras** *fpl* (Chi) (gemelos) cuff links (*pl*)

colmado¹ -da *adj* ‹*cucharada*› heaped; *ver tb* **colmar**

colmado² *m* (Esp ant) grocery store (AmE), grocer's shop (BrE)

colmar [A1] *vt* 1 ‹*vaso/cesta*› to fill ... to the brim 2 ‹*deseos/aspiraciones*› to fulfill* 3 ‹*paciencia*› to stretch ... to the limit; **~ a algn de algo** ‹*de atenciones*› to lavish sth on sb; **me ~on de regalos** they gave me lots of presents; **una vida colmada de éxitos** a life filled with *o* full of success

colmena *f* beehive

colmenero -ra *m,f* beekeeper

colmillo *m* (de persona) eyetooth, canine (tech); (de elefante, jabalí, morsa) tusk; (de perro, lobo) fang, canine; ***enseñar los ~s***; ▸**diente 1**

colmo *m*: **el ~ de la vagancia** the height of laziness; **para ~ de desgracias** *or* **males** to top *o* cap it all; **sólo falta que para ~ (de males) nos corten el gas** all we need now is for them to cut the gas off; **sería el ~ que ...** it would be too much if ...; **¡esto es el ~!** this is the last straw!; **¡esto ya es el ~ de los ~s!** this really is the limit!

colocación *f*
A (empleo) job; **buscar ~** to look for a job
B 1 (acción) positioning, placing; (de losas, baldosas) laying 2 (Fin) investment, deposit

colocado -da *adj*
A (en un trabajo): **está muy bien ~** he has a very good job
B (Esp arg) (con drogas) stoned (colloq)

colocar [A2] *vt*
A 1 (en lugar) to place, put; ‹*losas/alfombra*› to lay; ‹*cuadro*› to hang 2 (Com, Fin) ‹*acciones*› to place; ‹*dinero*› to place, invest; ‹*producto*› to put
B ‹*persona*› 1 (en lugar) to put 2 (en trabajo) to get ... a job; **el padre lo colocó como jefe de departamento** his father placed him in charge of the department
■ **colocarse** *v pron*
A (situarse, ponerse): **se colocó a mi lado** she stood/sat beside me; **si gana se ~á en tercer lugar** if he wins he'll move into third place
B (en trabajo) to get a job
C (Esp arg) (con drogas) to get stoned (colloq)
D (*refl*) 1 (arreglarse) ‹*sombrero*› to adjust; ‹*falda*› to straighten 2 (Chi) (ponerse) ‹*reloj/abrigo*› to put on

colocho -cha *m,f*
A (AmC) (persona) curly-haired person
B **colocho** *m* (AmC) (rizo) curl

colofón *m* 1 (culminación, término): **el ~ de una brillante carrera** the culmination of a brilliant career; **el congreso tuvo como ~ una cena de gala** the convention was rounded off with a gala dinner; **como ~ a estos acontecimientos** as a coda to these events 2 (Impr) colophon

Colombia *f* Colombia

colombianismo *m* Colombianism, Colombian word/expression

colombiano -na *adj/m,f* Colombian

colombino -na *adj* of/relating to Columbus

colombófilo -la *m,f* pigeon breeder (AmE), pigeon fancier (BrE)

colon *m* colon

colón *m* colon (*Costa Rican and Salvadoran unit of currency*)

Colón 1 (Hist) Columbus; **Cristóbal ~** Christopher Columbus 2 (*como interj*) (Per fam) **¡~!** obviously!

colonia *f*
A (Hist, Pol) colony
B (de animales, células) colony
C 1 (de viviendas) residential development; **~ militar** housing estate (*for service families*) 2 (Méx) (barrio) quarter, district 3 (campamento) camp; **~ de vacaciones** holiday camp
(Compuesto) **colonia penal** (Per) penal colony
D (perfume) cologne, eau de cologne

coloniaje *m* (AmL) (período) colonial period; (sistema de gobierno) colonial government

colonial *adj* colonial

colonialismo *m* colonialism

colonialista *adj/mf* colonialist

colonización *f* colonization

colonizador¹ -dora *adj* colonizing

colonizador² -dora *m,f* colonizer

colonizar [A4] *vt* to colonize

colono *m*
A (inmigrante) colonist
B (Agr) (en tierras baldías) settler; (en tierras arrendadas) tenant farmer

coloquial *adj* colloquial

coloquio *m*
A 1 (debate) discussion, talk; (simposio) (AmL) colloquium, symposium 2 (*como adj inv*): **conferencia ~** talk (*followed by discussion*)
B (Lit) dialogue

color *m*
A 1 color*; **ha cambiado de ~** it has changed color; **¿de qué ~ es?** what color is it?; **un sombrero de un ~ oscuro/claro** a dark/light hat; **las banderitas de ~ amarillo/verde** the yellow/green flags; **una blusa (de) ~ carne** a flesh-colored blouse; **ilustraciones a todo ~** full color illustrations; **papeles de ~es** pieces of colored paper; **cintas de ~es** colored ribbons; **globos de todos**

los ~es *or* (CS, Méx) **de todos ~es** balloons of all different colors; **televisión en ~es** *or* (Esp) **en ~** *or* (Andes, Méx) **a ~** color television; **fotos en ~es** *or* (Esp) **en ~** color photos; **dar ~ a algo** to add color* to sth; ***~ de hormiga*** (AmL): **la cosa se puso ~ de hormiga** things started looking pretty grim *o* black; ***no hay ~*** (Esp) there's no comparison; ***ponerse de mil ~es*** *or* ***de todos los ~es*** to blush to the roots of one's hair; ***subido de ~*** (chiste) risqué; ***subírsele el ~*** *or* ***los ~es a algn*** (por esfuerzo) to flush, become flushed; (por vergüenza) to blush, turn red, go red (BrE) 2 **tomar** *or* (esp AmL) **agarrar** *or* (esp Esp) **coger ~** ‹‹*pollo*›› to brown; ‹‹*cebolla frita/pastel*›› to turn golden-brown; ‹‹*fruta*›› to ripen; ‹‹*piel*›› to become tanned 3 (tintura) color*, dye 4 **colores** *mpl* (lápices) colored* pencils (*pl*), crayons (*pl*) 5 **colores** *mpl* (señal distintiva) colors* (*pl*); **los ~es nacionales** the national colors; ***correr con ~es propios*** (Chi, Ven) to act on one's own initiative

(Compuesto) **color complementario/primario** complementary/primary color*

B (raza) color*; **sin distinción de credo ni ~** regardless of creed or color; **una chica de ~** (euf) a colored girl (dated)

C (colorido de relato, de fiesta) color*; **una celebración de gran ~** a celebration full of color

D (cúrcuma) turmeric

coloración *f* (color) coloration; **adquirió una ~ rojiza** it took on a reddish color

colorado¹ -da *adj* 1 red; ***ponerse ~*** to blush, turn red, go red (BrE); ▸**tomate A** 2 (Méx fam) ‹*chiste*› risqué

colorado² *m* red

colorante¹ *adj* coloring*

colorante² *m* coloring*; ⊖ **no contiene colorantes** no artificial colors

coloreado -da *adj* colored*

colorear [A1] *vt* (Art) to color*; **~ algo DE algo** to color* sth IN sth

colorete *m* blusher, rouge

colorido *m* colors* (*pl*); **el ~ de las fiestas locales** the colorful atmosphere of the local festivities

colorín¹ -rina *m,f* (Chi) red-haired person

colorín² *m*

A (fam) (color llamativo) bright color*; **y ~ colorado, este cuento se ha acabado** (fr hecha) and that is the end of the story

B (Zool) goldfinch

colorinche¹ *adj* (RPl fam) colorful*; (pey) garish (pej)

colorinche² *m* (AmL): **una manta llena de ~s** a really colorful blanket; (pey) a really garish blanket (pej)

colosal *adj* ‹*estatua/obra/fortuna*› colossal; ‹*ambiente/idea*› (fam) great (colloq)

coloso *m* (estatua) colossus; (gigante) giant

columbrar [A1] *vt* (liter) to begin to see

columna *f*

A (Arquit) column, pillar

B (Anat) spine, backbone

(Compuesto) **columna vertebral** (Anat) spine, spinal *o* vertebral column; (de sistema) backbone

C (Impr, Period) column; **un artículo a dos ~s** a two-column article

D (Mil) column; **marchar en ~ de a cuatro** to march four abreast

columnista *mf* columnist

columpiar [A1] *vt* to push (*on a swing*)

■ **columpiarse** *v pron* (*refl*) to swing

columpio *m* 1 (Jueg, Ocio) swing; **jugar a los ~s** (fam) to play on the swings 2 (sofá de jardín) couch hammock

colusión *f* collusion

colza *f* rape, colza; **aceite de ~** rapeseed oil

coma¹ *m* (Med) coma; **entrar en (estado de) ~** to go into a coma; **~ profundo** deep coma

coma² *f*

A 1 (Ling) comma; **nos lo contó sin dejarse ni una ~** he told us all about it in great detail; ▸**punto** 2 (Mat) point; **cuatro ~ cinco** four point five

B (Mús) comma

comadre *f*

A (madrina) *godmother of one's child or mother of one's godchild*

B (esp AmL fam) (amiga, vecina): **las ~s del pueblo** the village women; **¿cómo está, ~?** how are you, dear *o* (BrE) love?

comadreja *f* (mustélido) weasel

comadreo *m* (fam) chatting, nattering (BrE colloq)

comadrona *f* midwife

comal *m* (Méx) *ceramic dish or metal hotplate for cooking* **tortillas**

comandancia *f*

A (edificio) command headquarters (*sing o pl*); (territorio) command

B (RPl) (mando) command; **ejercía la ~ del ejército** he was in command of the army

comandante *mf*

A 1 (en el ejército) major; (en las fuerzas aéreas) major (AmE), squadron leader (BrE) 2 (oficial al mando) commanding officer

(Compuesto) **comandante en jefe** commander in chief

B (Aviac) captain

comandar [A1] *vt* to command

comandita *f* ▸**sociedad**

comando *m*

A 1 (grupo de combate) commando group; **~ de reconocimiento** reconnaissance commando; **~ terrorista** terrorist cell *o* squad 2 (AmL) (mando militar) command

(Compuesto) **comando de acción/información** active-service/intelligence unit

B (Inf) command

comarca *f* region

> **comarca**
>
> In Spain, a geographical, social, and culturally homogeneous region, with a clear natural or administrative demarcation. *Comarcas* are normally smaller than regiones. They are often famous for some reason, for example Ampurdán (Catalonia) for its wines, or La Mancha (Castile) for its cheeses

comarcal *adj* regional; ▸**carretera**

comatoso -sa *adj* comatose

comba *f*

A (de viga, cable) sag; (de pared) bulge

B (Esp) (Jueg) jump rope (AmE), skipping rope (BrE); **saltar la ~** to jump rope (AmE), to skip (BrE)

combado -da *adj* ‹*viga/cable*› sagging; ‹*pared*› bulging

combarse [A1] *v pron* ‹‹*viga/cable*›› to sag; ‹‹*disco*›› to warp; ‹‹*espalda/piernas*›› to bend

combate *m* 1 (Mil) combat; **zona de ~** combat zone 2 (en boxeo) fight; ***dejar a algn fuera de ~*** (en boxeo) to knock sb out; (en debate, competición) to crush sb

combatiente¹ *adj* fighting (*before n*) combatant (*before n*) (frml)

combatiente² *mf* combatant (frml); **antiguo** *or* **ex ~** veteran

combatir [I1] *vi* ‹‹*soldado/ejército*›› to fight

■ **combatir** *vt* ‹*enemigo/enfermedad/fuego*› to fight, to combat (frml); ‹*proyecto/propuesta*› to fight; ‹*frío*› to fight off

combatividad *f* fighting spirit

combativo -va *adj* 1 (luchador) spirited, combative; **espíritu ~** fighting spirit 2 (agresivo) combative

combi® *f* (Méx, Per, RPl) *VW® van*

combinación *f*

A 1 (de colores, sabores) combination 2 (Mat) permutation 3 (de caja fuerte) combination

B (Indum) slip

C (Transp) connection

combinada *f* (Col) combine harvester

combinado *m* 1 (bebida) cocktail 2 (Andes period) (Dep) team, line-up (journ)

combinar [A1] *vt* 1 ‹*ingredientes*› to combine, mix together 2 ‹*colores*› to put together; **no sabe ~ la ropa** he isn't very good at coordinating clothes; **~ algo CON algo**: **~ el rojo con el violeta** to put red and purple together; **no puedes ~ esa falda con ese jersey** you can't wear that skirt with that sweater 3 (Quím) to combine 4 (reunir) to combine

■ **combinar** *vi* ‹‹*colores/ropa*›› to go together; **~ CON algo** to go WITH sth

C

■ **combinarse** *v pron* 1 ‹‹*personas*›› (ponerse de acuerdo): **se ~on para sorprenderlo** they got together to give him a surprise; **nos combinamos para estar allí a las seis** we all arranged to be there at six 2 (Quím) to combine

combinatorio -ria *adj* combinatorial

combo¹ -ba *adj* ▸**combado**

combo² *m*

A (Chi, Per) (mazo) sledgehammer

B (Chi, Per fam) (puñetazo) punch

C (Col) 1 (Mús) band 2 (fam) (pandilla) gang (colloq)

combustible¹ *adj* combustible

combustible² *m* (Fís, Quím) combustible; (Transp) (carburante) fuel

combustión *f* combustion

comecocos *m* (*pl* ~) ▸**comedura de coco**

comedero *m* 1 (Agr) (para el ganado) feeding trough 2 (Col) (taberna, restaurante) roadside cafe, diner (AmE)

comedia *f* 1 (Teatr) (obra) play; (cómica) comedy; **no hagas tanta ~** stop being so dramatic 2 (serie cómica) comedy series 3 (AmL) (telenovela) soap opera, soap; (radionovela) radio serial

Compuestos

• **comedia de costumbres/de enredo** comedy of manners/of intrigue

• **comedia musical** musical

comediante -ta *m,f* 1 (Teatr) (*m*) actor; (*f*) actress 2 (farsante) fraud; **es un ~** he's such a fraud

comedido -da *adj* 1 (moderado) moderate, restrained 2 (AmL) (atento) obliging, well-meaning

comediógrafo -fa *m,f* playwright

comedirse [I14] *v pron* 1 (moderarse) to show *o* exercise restraint 2 (CS) (ofrecerse) to offer

comedor¹ -dora *adj* (fam): **son todos muy ~es** they're all big eaters

comedor² *m* (sala — en casa, hotel) dining room; (— en colegio, universidad) dining hall, refectory; (— en fábrica, empresa) canteen, cafeteria

comedura de coco *f* (Esp fam) 1 (lavado de cerebro): **la tele es una ~ de ~** TV just tries to brainwash you 2 (preocupación): **tener una ~ de ~** to worry nonstop

comején *m* (Col) termite

comelón¹ -lona *adj* (AmL fam) ‹*persona*› with a big appetite

comelón² -lona *m,f* (AmL fam): **es un ~** he's a big eater

comendador *m* commander

comensal *mf* (frml) guest

comentador -dora *m,f* (Per) commentator

comentar [A1] *vt* 1 ‹*suceso/noticia/película*› to talk about, discuss; ‹*obra/poema*› to comment on 2 (mencionar) to mention; (hacer una observación) to remark on; **comentó que ...** he remarked that ...; **¡qué joven es! — comentó** he's so young! — he remarked 3 (CS) (Rad, TV) ‹*partido*› to commentate on

■ **comentar** *vi* (fam): **ya sabes que la gente comenta** you know how people talk

comentario *m*

A 1 (observación) comment; **hacer un ~** to make a comment; **¿quiere hacer algún ~?** do you have any comments?; **fue un ~ de mal gusto** it was a tasteless remark; **sin ~(s)** no comment; **sobran** *or* **huelgan los ~s** it's best not to say anything 2 (mención): **no hagas ningún ~ sobre esto** don't mention this 3 (análisis) commentary; **~ de texto** textual analysis

B (Rad, TV) commentary

comentarista *mf* commentator

comenzar [A6] *vt* to begin, commence (frml)

■ **comenzar** *vi* to begin; **al ~ el día** at the beginning of the day; **~ + GER** to begin BY -ING; **~ A + INF** to start -ING *o* to + INF; **~on a disparar** they started firing *o* to fire; **~ POR algo** to begin WITH sth; **~ POR + INF** to begin BY -ING

comer¹ [E1] *vi*

A 1 (tomar alimentos) to eat; **no tengo ganas de ~** I'm not hungry; **este niño no me come nada** (fam) this child won't eat anything (colloq); **~ *como un sabañón*** *or* (Esp) ***una lima*** *or* (Méx) ***un pelón de hospicio*** (fam) to eat like a horse 2 **dar de ~** to feed; **dar(le) de ~ a algn (en la boca)** to spoonfeed sb; **darle de ~ al gato/al niño** to feed the cat/the kid; ***¡come y calla!*** shut up and do as you're told

B 1 (tomar una comida) to eat; **todavía no hemos comido** we haven't eaten yet; **salir a ~ (fuera)** to go out for a meal, to eat out; **¡a ~!** lunch (*o* dinner *etc*) is ready!; **¿qué hay de ~?** (a mediodía) what's for lunch?; (por la noche) what's for dinner *o* supper?; **aquí se come muy bien** the food here is very good 2 (esp Esp, Méx) (almorzar) to have lunch, have dinner (BrE colloq); **nos invitaron a ~** they asked us to lunch 3 (esp AmL) (cenar) to have dinner; **comemos a las nueve** we have *o* eat dinner at nine

■ **comer** *vt*

A ‹*fruta/verdura/carne*› to eat; **no puedo ~ chocolate** I can't have *o* eat chocolate; **come un poco de queso** have a little cheese; **¿puedo ~ otro?** can I have another one?; **no tienen qué ~** they don't have anything to eat; **mira el suéter, me lo comió la polilla** look at my sweater, the moths have been at it; **como un cáncer que le come las entrañas** (liter) like a cancer gnawing away at his insides; ***sin ~lo ni beberlo*** (Esp): **me llevé el castigo sin ~lo ni beberlo** I got punished even though I didn't have anything to do with it; ***¿(y) eso con qué se come?*** (Esp fam) what on earth's that? (colloq)

B (fam) (hacer desaparecer) ▸**comerse C**

C (en ajedrez, damas) to take

■ **comerse** *v pron*

A (al escribir) ‹*acento/palabra*› to leave off; ‹*línea/párrafo*› to miss out; (al hablar) ‹*letra*› to leave off; ‹*palabra*› to swallow

B 1 (*enf*) ‹*comida*› to eat; **cómetelo todo** eat it all up; **~se algo de un bocado** to gulp sth down in one go; **está para comérsela** (fam) she's really tasty (colloq); **~se las uñas** to bite one's nails; **se lo come la envidia** he's eaten up *o* consumed with envy; ***~se a algn vivo*** (fam) to skin sb alive (colloq) 2 (fam) (ser muy superior) to surpass, overshadow

C (*enf*) (fam) (hacer desaparecer) 1 ‹‹*acido/óxido*›› to eat away (at); ‹‹*polilla/ratón*›› to eat away (at) 2 ‹‹*inflación/alquiler*›› ‹*sueldo/ahorros*› to eat away at; **el colegio de los niños se come casi todo el sueldo** almost all my salary goes on the children's school fees

D (Col fam) (poseer sexualmente) to have (colloq)

comer² *m* eating; **una persona de buen ~** someone who enjoys his/her food

comercial¹ *adj* 1 ‹*zona/operación/carta*› business (*before n*); **una firma ~** a company; **el desequilibrio ~ entre los dos países** the trade imbalance between the two countries; **el déficit ~** the trade deficit; **nuestra división ~** our sales *o* marketing department; ▸**galería, centro** 2 ‹*película/arte*› commercial

comercial² *m*

A (AmL) commercial, advert (BrE)

B (CS) (Educ) business school

comercial³ *f or m* (tienda): Ⓢ **Comercial Hernández** Hernandez's Stores

comercializable *adj* marketable

comercialización *f* (de producto) marketing; (de lugar, deporte) commercialization

comercializar [A4] *vt* ‹*producto*› to market; ‹*lugar/deporte*› to commercialize

■ **comercializarse** *v pron* to become commercialized

comerciante *mf* 1 (Com) (dueño de tienda) storekeeper (AmE), shopkeeper (BrE); (negociante) dealer, trader 2 (mercenario) money-grubber (colloq)

comerciar [A1] *vi* to trade, do business; **~ EN algo** to trade *o* deal IN sth

comercio *m* 1 (actividad) trade; **el mundo del ~** the world of commerce; **el ~ de armas/pieles** the arms/fur trade 2 (tiendas): **hoy cierra el ~** the stores (AmE) *o* (BrE) shops are closed today 3 (tienda) store (AmE), shop (BrE)

Compuestos

• **comercio carnal** sexual intercourse

• **comercio exterior/interior** foreign/domestic trade

• **comercio justo** fair trade

comestible *adj* edible

comestibles *mpl* food; **este tipo de ~** this sort of food; **tienda de ~** grocery store (AmE), grocer's (shop) (BrE)

cometa¹ *m* comet

cometa[2] *f* kite; **hacer volar una ~** *or* (RPl) **remontar una ~** to fly a kite

cometer [E1] *vt* ‹*crimen/delito/pecado*› to commit; ‹*error/falta*› to make; **cometí la estupidez de decírselo** I made the stupid mistake of telling him

cometido *m* [1] (tarea, deber) task, mission [2] (Chi) (actuación) performance

comezón *f* [1] (Med) itching, itch; **tenía ~ en la espalda** his back was itching [2] (desasosiego) itch; **ya le estaba empezando la ~ de** *or* **por irse** he was already itching to leave

comible *adj* (fam) eatable

comic /ˈkomik/, **cómic** *m* (*pl* **-mics**) (esp Esp) (tira ilustrada) comic strip; (revista) comic

comicidad *f* humor*

comicios *mpl* elections (*pl*)

cómico[1] **-ca** *adj* ‹*actor/género/obra*› comedy (*before n*); ‹*situación/mueca*› comical, funny; **lo ~ de la historia es ...** the funny thing about the story is ...

cómico[2] **-ca** *m,f* (actor) comedy actor, comic actor; (humorista) comedian, comic

comida *f*

A (alimentos) food; **~ para perros** dog food

B [1] (ocasión en que se come) meal; **hago tres ~s al día** I have *o* eat three meals a day; **la ~ fuerte del día** the main meal of the day [2] (AmL) (menú, platos) food; **hacer** *or* **preparar la ~** to get the food ready *o* cook the food

Compuestos

- **comida basura/rápida** junk/fast food
- **comida de negocios/de trabajo** business/working lunch

C [1] (esp Esp, Méx) (almuerzo) lunch, dinner (BrE) [2] (esp AmL) (cena) dinner, supper; (en algunas regiones del Reino Unido) tea

comidilla *f*: **ser la ~ del pueblo** to be the talk of the town

comido -da *adj*: **volvió/llegó ~** when he returned/arrived he had (already) eaten

comience, comienza, etc *see* **comenzar**

comienzo *m* beginning; **al ~** at first, in the beginning; **el proceso fue muy lento en sus ~s** initially, the process was very slow; **los ~s son siempre difíciles** the first months (*o* steps *etc*) are always difficult; **dar ~** to begin; **dar ~ a algo** «*persona*» to begin sth; «*ceremonia/acto*» to mark the beginning of sth

comillas *fpl* quotation marks (*pl*), inverted commas (BrE) (*pl*); **poner algo entre ~** to put sth in quotation marks *o* in inverted commas; **son amigos entre ~** (son más que amigos) they are friends in quotation marks *o* inverted commas; (no son verdaderos amigos) they are friends, or so they say

comilón -lona *adj/m,f* (CS, Esp fam) ▸**comelón**[1,2]

comilona *f* (fam) feast (colloq); **nos dimos/pegamos una ~** we had a blowout

comino *m* (Bot, Coc) cumin; ***no valer (ni) un ~*** (fam) to be worthless; ▸**importar 1**

comiquita *f* (Ven fam) (historieta) comic strip (dibujos animados) cartoon

comisaría *f*

A (edificio) *tb* **~ de policía** (police) station

B (Gob) (en Col) province

comisariado *m* commission

comisario *m*

A (de policía) captain (AmE), superintendent (BrE)

B (delegado) commissioner

comisión *f*

A (delegación, organismo) committee

Compuestos

- **Comisión Europea** *or* **de las Comunidades Europeas** European Commission
- **Comisiones Obreras** (en Esp) *communist labor union*
- **comisión mixta/permanente** joint/standing committee

B (Com) commission; **trabajar a ~** to work on a commission basis; **cobra un 20% de ~** she gets 20% commission

C (misión) assignment; **en ~** on assignment

comisionado -da *m,f* commissioner; ▸**alto**[1]

comisionar [A1] *vt* to commission

comisionista *mf* commission agent

comiso *m* (Col) packed lunch

comisura *f* corner; **la ~ de los labios** the corner of the mouth

comité *m*

A (junta) committee

Compuestos

- **comité de empresa** (Esp) works committee
- **comité de redacción** editorial board *o* committee

B (RPl) (sede) local headquarters (*sing o pl*)

comitiva *f* [1] (séquito) procession [2] (grupo) delegation

Compuesto **comitiva fúnebre** funeral procession, cortège

Commonwealth /ˈkomonwelθ/ *m or* (Esp) *f*: **el** *or* **la ~** the Commonwealth

como[1] *prep*

A [1] (en calidad de) as; **quiero hablarte ~ amigo** I want to speak to you as a friend; **el director tendrá ~ funciones ...** the director's duties will be ...; **está considerado ~ lo mejor** he's considered (to be) the best [2] (con el nombre de) as; **se la conoce ~ 'flor de luz'** it's known as 'flor de luz' [3] (por ejemplo) like; **en algunos lugares ~ Londres** in some places such as *o* like London

B (en comparaciones, contrastes) like; **uno ~ el tuyo** one like yours; **pienso ~ tú** I agree with you; **fue ella, ~ que me llamo Beatriz** it was her, as sure as my name's Beatriz; **bailó ~ nunca** she danced as *o* like she'd never danced before; **me trata ~ a un imbécil** he treats me like an idiot; **¡no hay nada ~ un buen coñac!** there's nothing like a good brandy!; **~ PARA + INF: es ~ para echarse a llorar** it's enough to make you want to cry; **fue ~ para pegarle** I could have hit him

C (*en locs*) **así como** (frml) as well as; **como él solo/ella sola**: **es egoísta ~ él solo** he's so *o* he's incredibly selfish!; **como mucho/poco** at (the) most/at least; **como nadie: cocina ~ nadie** nobody cooks like her; **como que ...**: **conduce muy bien — ~ que es piloto de carreras** he drives very well — well, he *is* a racing driver, after all; **y no me lo dijiste — ¡~ que no lo sabía!** and you didn't tell me about it — that's because I didn't know about it!; **como ser** (CS) such as, for example; **como si** (+ *subj*) as if, as though; **ella está grave y él ~ si nada** *or* **~ si tal cosa** she's seriously ill and he doesn't seem at all *o* in the least worried

como[2] *conj*

A (de la manera que) as; **tal ~ había prometido** just as he had promised; **~ era de esperar** as was to be expected; **~ dice el refrán** as the saying goes; **no me gustó ~ lo dijo** I didn't like the way she said it; **(tal y) ~ están las cosas** as things stand; (+ *subj*) **hazlo ~ quieras/~ puedas** do it any way you like/as best as you can; **no voy — ~ quieras** I'm not going — please yourself *o* as you like; **~ quiera que sea** no matter what; **la buganvilla, o ~ quiera que se llame** bougainvillea or whatever it's called

B (puesto que) as, since; **~ era temprano, nos fuimos a dar una vuelta** since *o* as it was early, we went for a walk

C (si) (+ *subj*) if; **~ te pille ...** if I catch you ...

D (en oraciones concesivas): **cansado ~ estaba, me ayudó** tired though *o* tired as he was, he helped me

E (que): **vimos ~ se los llevaban** we saw them being taken away; **vas a ver ~ llega tarde** he'll be late, you'll see

como[3] *adv*

A (expresando aproximación) about; **está ~ a cincuenta kilómetros** it's about fifty kilometers away; **un sabor ~ a almendras** a kind of almondy taste

B (uso expletivo) kind of (colloq); **me da ~ vergüenza ...** I find it kind of embarrassing ...

cómo[1] *adv*

A (de qué manera) how; **¿~ estás?** how are you?; **¿~ es tu novia?** what's your girlfriend like?; **¿~ es de grande?** how big is it?; **¿~ te llamas?** what's your name?; **ya sabes ~ es** you know what he's like

B (por qué) why, how come (colloq); **¿~ no me lo dijiste antes?** why didn't you tell me before?

C (al solicitar que se repita algo) sorry?, pardon?; **¿~ dijo?** sorry, what did you say?

D [1] (en exclamaciones): **¡~ llueve!** it's really raining!; **¡~ comes!** the amount you eat!; **está nevando — ¡y ~!** it's snowing — and how! (colloq) [2] (*como interj*) what!; **¡~!**

¿no te lo han dicho? what! haven't they told you?
E (*en locs*) **¿a cómo ...?**: **¿a ~ están los tomates?** (fam) how much are the tomatoes?; **¿a ~ estamos hoy?** (AmL) what's the date today?; **¿cómo así?** how come? (colloq); **¡cómo no!** (esp AmL) of course!; **¿cómo que ...?** *or* **¡cómo que ...!**: **¿~ que no fuiste tú?** what do you mean it wasn't you?; **aquí no está — ¡~ que no!** it isn't here — what do you mean it isn't there?

cómo[2] *m*: **el ~ (y el cuando)** the how (and when)

cómoda *f* chest of drawers

cómodamente *adv* **1** (cómodamente) comfortably **2** (convenientemente) conveniently

comodidad *f*
A **1** (confort) comfort; **la ~ del hogar** the comfort of home **2** (conveniencia) convenience; **la ~ de vivir en una zona céntrica** the convenience of living centrally; **por ~** for the sake of convenience
B (holgazanería): **no lo hace por ~** he doesn't do it because he's lazy
C **comodidades** *fpl* (aparatos, servicios) comforts (*pl*); **las ~es de la vida moderna** the comforts of modern life; **un apartamento con todas las ~es** a well-appointed apartment

comodín *m* **1** (Jueg) (mono) joker; (otra carta) wild card; **esa excusa se está convirtiendo en un ~** that excuse seems to be getting used rather a lot recently; **esta palabra se usa como** *or* **de ~** this word is used to refer to anything and everything **2** (Inf) wildcard

cómodo -da *adj*
A **1** (confortable) comfortable, comfy (colloq); **ponte ~** make yourself comfortable; **no me siento ~** I feel uncomfortable **2** (conveniente, fácil) ‹*horario/sistema*› convenient; **ésa es una actitud muy cómoda** that's a very easy attitude to take; **eligió el camino más ~** she took the easy option
B (holgazán) lazy, idle

comodón -dona *adj* (fam) lazy, idle

comodoro *m* (Náut) commodore; (Aviac) brigadier general (AmE), air commodore (BrE)

comoquiera, como quiera *ver* **querer**[2] *Sentido* **II B**

Comp. (= **compárese**) cf

compa *mf* (fam) friend, buddy (AmE colloq), mate (BrE colloq)

compact /'kompak(t)/ *m* (*pl* **-pacts**) ▸ **compact disc**

compactar [A1] *vt* to crush, flatten

compact disc /kompac'ðis(k)/ *m* (*pl* **-discs**) (disco) compact disc, CD; (aparato) compact disc player, CD player

compacto[1] **-ta** *adj* **1** ‹*tejido*› close; ‹*estructura/coche*› compact **2** ‹*muchedumbre*› dense

compacto[2] *m* stack system

compadecer [E3] *vt* to feel sorry for; **pobre, la compadezco** poor thing, I feel sorry for her; **te compadezco** I feel for you
■ **compadecerse** *v pron* (apiadarse) **~se DE algn** to take pity ON sb; **~se de sí mismo** to feel sorry for oneself

compadre *m*
A (padrino) *godfather of one's child or father of one's godchild*
B (esp AmL fam) (amigo) buddy (AmE colloq), mate (BrE colloq); ***a lo ~*** (fam): **entró a lo ~ a la oficina** he got a job in the office by knowing the right people

compadrear [A1] *vi* (RPl) to show off

compadreo *m* (RPl) (fanfarroneo) showing off

compadrismo *m* ▸ **amiguismo**

compaginable *adj* compatible

compaginación *f*
A (concordancia) combining, combination
B (Impr) makeup, page makeup

compaginar [A1] *vt*
A (armonizar) ‹*actividades/soluciones*› to combine; **compagina el trabajo con los estudios** she combines work with studying
B (Impr) to make up
■ **compaginar** *vi* **1** (combinar) to go together; **esta idea compagina muy bien con su propuesta** this idea fits in very well with her proposal **2** (llevarse bien) to get on; **~ CON algn** to get on well WITH sb
■ **compaginarse** *v pron* (armonizar) «*estilos/colores*» to go together; **dos estilos que no se compaginan** two styles which do not go together; **sus horarios se compaginan bastante bien** their work schedules fit in with each other quite well

compañerismo *m* comradeship

compañero -ra *m,f* **1** (en actividad): **un ~ de equipo** a fellow team member; **fuimos ~s de universidad** we were at college together; **~ de cuarto** *or* **habitación** roommate; **~ de juegos/de clase/de trabajo** playmate/classmate/workmate **2** (pareja sentimental, en juegos) partner **3** (fam) (de guante, calcetín) pair; **¿dónde está el ~ de este guante?** where's the other glove? **4** (Pol) comrade

Compuestos
• **compañero de armas** comrade-in-arms
• **compañero de viaje** (en un viaje) traveling* companion; (Pol) fellow traveler*

compañía *f*
A **1** (acompañamiento) company; **llegó en ~ de sus abogados** he arrived accompanied by his lawyers; **hacerle ~ a algn** to keep sb company **2** **compañías** *fpl* (amistades): **andar en malas ~s** to keep bad company; **trata de evitar las malas ~s** be careful of the company you keep
B (empresa) company, firm; Ⓢ **Muñoz y Compañía** Muñoz and Co.
C (Mil) company

Compuestos
• **Compañía de Jesús** Society of Jesus
• **compañía de seguros** insurance company
• **compañía de teatro** theater* company

comparable *adj* comparable; **~ A** *or* **CON** comparable TO *o* WITH

comparación *f*
A (acción, efecto) comparison; **hacer** *or* **establecer una ~** to make *o* draw a comparison; **en ~ con el año pasado** compared to *o* with last year; **no tienen ni punto de ~** you cannot even begin to compare them; **adverbio de ~** comparative adverb
B (Lit) simile

comparado -da *adj* ‹*gramática/estudio*› comparative; *ver tb* **comparar**

comparar [A1] *vt* **1** (contrastar) to compare; **~ algo/a algn CON algo/algn** to compare sth/sb WITH sth/sb **2** (asemejar) to compare; **~ algo/a algn A algo/algn** to compare sth/sb TO sth/sb; **no puede ni ~se al otro** it doesn't even compare at all to *o* with the other one
■ **comparar** *vi* to make a comparison, to compare

comparativo[1] **-va** *adj* comparative

comparativo[2] *m* comparative

comparecencia *f* appearance in court; **orden de ~** subpoena, summons

comparecer [E3] *vi* to appear (in court)

comparecimiento *m* appearance (*in court*)

comparsa *mf* **1** (Teatr) extra; **fui a la reunión de ~** (fam) I just sat in on the meeting **2** **comparsa** *f* (conjunto musical) group; (en carnaval) krewe (AmE) (*group of people participating in a carnival parade*)

compartimentar [A1] *vt* to compartmentalize

compartimento, compartimiento *m* **1** (Ferr) compartment **2** (de cartera, cajón) section, compartment

Compuesto **compartimento estanco** (Náut) watertight compartment

compartir [I1] *vt* **1** ‹*oficina/comida/ganancias*› to share; **comparten los gastos de teléfono entre todos** they split the phone bill between them; **~ algo CON algn** to share sth WITH sb; Ⓢ **se comparte casa** room to let in shared house **2** ‹*opinión/responsabilidad*› to share

compás *m*
A (Mús) **1** (ritmo) time, meter (esp AmE); **marcar/llevar el ~** to beat/keep time; **perder el ~** to get out of time; **se movía al ~ de la música** she moved in time to the music **2** (división) measure (AmE), bar (BrE); **~ de dos por cuatro** two-four time; **los primeros compases de un tango** the opening bars of a tango

Compuestos
• **compás de espera** (Mús) bar rest; **abrir un ~ de ~** to call a temporary halt; **encontrarse en un ~ de ~** «*negociaciones*» to be on hold; «*persona*» to be waiting

• **compás mayor/menor** four-four/two-four time
B (Mat) (instrumento) compass, pair of compasses
C (Náut) compass

compasión *f* pity, compassion; **¡tenga ~ de mí!** have pity on me! (liter); **lo hace por ~** he does it out of compassion; **no siente ~ por nadie** she feels no compassion for anybody

compasivo -va *adj* compassionate

compatibilidad *f* compatibility

compatibilizar [A4] *vt* **~ algo CON algo** to combine sth with sth

■ **compatibilizar** *vi* (Chi) to get along *o* on, be compatible

compatible *adj* compatible

compatriota (*m*) fellow countryman, compatriot; (*f*) fellow countrywoman, compatriot

compeler [E1] *vt* (frml) to compel, oblige

compendiar [A1] *vt* to summarize

compendio *m* (libro) textbook, coursebook; (resumen) summary, compendium (BrE)

compenetración *f* (con persona) rapport, understanding

compenetrarse [A1] *v pron* «*persona*» 1 **~ CON algo** ‹*con ideas/objectivos*› to identify WITH sth; **el actor no ha logrado ~ con el personaje** the actor hasn't managed to get into the part successfully 2 **~ CON algn** to have a good relationship WITH sb; (en trabajo) to work well WITH sb; **se han compenetrado a la perfección** they understand each other perfectly

compensación *f*
A (contapartida) compensation; **en ~** by way of compensation; **en ~ por algo** in compensation for sth; **¿qué puedo ofrecerles como ~?** how can I make it up to you?
B (Fin) clearance, clearing

compensar [A1] *vi*: **no compensa hacer un viaje tan largo** it's not worth making such a long journey; (+ *me/te/le etc*) **no me compensa hacerlo por tan poco dinero** it's not worth my while doing it for so little money

■ **compensar** *vt*
A 1 (contrarrestar) ‹*pérdida/deficiencia*› to compensate for, make up for; ‹*efecto*› to offset; **su entusiasmo compensa su falta de experiencia** his enthusiasm makes up for his lack of experience 2 ‹*persona*› **~ a algn POR algo** to compensate sb FOR sth; **la compañía nos compensará por el retraso** the company will compensate us for the delay; **lo ~on con $2.000 por los daños** he was awarded $2,000 compensation in damages; **quisiera ~te de alguna manera por la molestia** I would like to repay you in some way for all your trouble
B ‹*cheque*› to clear

■ **compensarse** *v pron* 1 «*fuerzas*» (*recípr*) to compensate each other, cancel each other out 2 «*pérdida/efecto*» **~se CON algo** to be offset BY sth; **se compensa con una rebaja en los impuestos** it is offset by *o* compensated for by tax cuts

compensatorio -ria *adj* 1 ‹*financiación*› compensatory; **indemnización compensatoria** compensatory damages (*pl*); **pago ~** deficiency payment 2 ‹*enseñanza/educación*› remedial

competencia *f*
A 1 (pugna) competition, rivalry; **siempre ha habido ~ entre ellos** there's always been rivalry *o* a lot of competition between them; **hacerse la ~** to be rivals *o* in competition; **hacerle la ~ a algn** to compete with sb; **la ~ es feroz** competition is fierce 2 (persona, entidad) competition; **la ~ se nos adelantó** our competitors *o* the competition got in first

(Compuesto) **competencia desleal** unfair competition

B (de juez, tribunal) competence; **es ~ del consejo** this is a matter for the council; **este asunto no es de mi ~** I have no authority *o* say in this matter; **tienen ~s plenas en materia educativa** they have complete authority on educational issues
C 1 (habilidad, aptitud) competence, ability 2 (Ling) competence
D (AmL) (Dep) (certamen) competition

(Compuesto) **competencia de atletismo** track and field meet (AmE), athletics meeting (BrE)

competente *adj* competent

competer [E1] *vi* (*en 3ª pers*) **~ A algn** «*responsabilidad*» to be incumbent on sb (frml); «*decisión*» to be the responsibility of sb; **eso no me compete** that's not my responsibility

competición *f* (Esp) 1 (acción): **espíritu/juegos de ~** competitive spirit/games 2 (Dep) (certamen) competition

competidor¹ -dora *adj* rival (*before n*)

competidor² -dora *m,f* competitor, rival

competir [I14] *vi* 1 (pugnar, luchar) to compete; **~ CON** *or* **CONTRA algn (POR algo)** to compete WITH *o* AGAINST sb (FOR sth) 2 (estar al mismo nivel) **~ EN algo**: **los dos modelos compiten en calidad** the two models rival each other in quality

competitividad *f* competitiveness

competitivo -va *adj* competitive

compilación *f*
A 1 (acción) compilation, compiling 2 (de leyes) compilation; (de cuentos) collection, anthology
B (Inf) compiling

compilador -dora *m,f*
A (de datos, hechos) compiler
B **compilador** *m* (Inf) compiler

compilar [A1] *vt* to compile

compinche *mf* (compañero) (fam) buddy (AmE colloq), mate (BrE colloq); (cómplice en crimen) partner in crime

complacencia *f* (agrado) satisfaction, pleasure; (excesiva tolerancia) indulgence

complacer [E3] *vt* to please; **me complace presentarles a ...** (frml) it gives me great pleasure to welcome ... (frml)

■ **complacerse** *v pron* **~se EN algo** to take pleasure IN sth; **nos complacemos en anunciar la boda de ...** (frml) we have great pleasure in announcing the marriage of ... (frml)

complacido -da *adj* pleased; **sonrió ~** he smiled with pleasure; **se fué ~** he went away happy *o* pleased

complaciente *adj* indulgent

complejidad *f* complexity

complejo¹ -ja *adj*
A (complicado) complex
B ‹*número/oración*› complex (*before n*)

complejo² *m*
A (de edificios) complex

(Compuestos)
• **complejo deportivo/hotelero/industrial** sports/hotel/industrial complex
• **complejo de viviendas** housing *o* residential development
• **complejo turístico** tourist development/resort

B (Quím) complex

(Compuesto) **complejo vitamínico** vitamin complex

C (Psic) complex; **tiene ~ porque es bajito** he's got a complex about being short

(Compuestos)
• **complejo de culpa** *or* **culpabilidad** guilt complex
• **complejo de inferioridad/superioridad** inferiority/superiority complex
• **complejo edípico** *or* **de Edipo** Oedipus complex

complementar [A1] *vt* to complement; **~ la dieta** to supplement one's diet

■ **complementarse** *v pron* (*recípr*) to complement each other

complementario -ria *adj*
A ‹*trabajos/personalidades*› complementary; ‹*ángulos/colores*› complementary
B (adicional) additional; **información complementaria** additional information

complemento *m*
A (Ling) complement

(Compuestos)
• **complemento circunstancial de tiempo/lugar** adverbial of time/place
• **complemento directo/indirecto** direct/indirect object

C

B (Mat) complement
C (del sueldo) supplementary payment
D 1 (acompañamiento) accompaniment; **el ~ de una buena comida** the essential accompaniment to a good meal 2 (parte que completa): **sería el ~ perfecto de su dicha** it would complete her happiness 3 **complementos** *mpl* (Auto, Indum) accessories (*pl*)

completamente *adv* completely

completar [A1] *vt*
A (terminar) to finish, complete; **los fuegos artificiales ~on las fiestas** the fireworks rounded off the festivities
B (AmL) ‹*cuestionario/impreso*› to complete, fill out *o* in

completo[1] **-ta** *adj*
A 1 (entero) complete; **la baraja no está completa** this deck isn't complete; **las obras completas de Neruda** the complete works of Neruda; **la serie completa** the whole series 2 (total, absoluto) complete, total; **por ~** completely 3 (exhaustivo) ‹*explicación*› detailed; ‹*obra/diccionario*› comprehensive; ‹*tesis/ensayo*› thorough 4 ‹*deportista/actor*› complete, very versatile
B (lleno) full; **el tren iba ~** the train was full; Ⓢ **completo** (en hostal) no vacancies; (en taquilla) sold out

completo[2] *m* (Chi) hot dog (with all the trimmings)

complexión *f* constitution; **es de ~ débil** he has a weak constitution

complicación *f*
A 1 (contratiempo, dificultad) complication; **surgieron ~s** complications arose; **sin complicaciones** uncomplicated 2 (Med) complication 3 (cualidad) complexity
B (esp AmL) (implicación) involvement

complicado -da *adj* 1 ‹*problema/sistema/situación*› complicated, complex 2 ‹*carácter*› complex; ‹*persona*› complicated 3 (rebuscado): **¡no seas tan ~!** don't make life *o* things difficult for yourself! 4 ‹*diseño/adorno*› elaborate

complicar [A2] *vt*
A ‹*situación/problema/asunto*› to complicate, make ... complicated; ▸**vida A1**
B (implicar) ‹*persona*› to involve, get ... involved
■ **complicarse** *v pron*
A «*situación/problema/asunto*» to get complicated; «*enfermedad*»: **se le complicó con un problema respiratorio** he developed respiratory complications; ▸**vida A1**
B (implicarse) **~se EN algo** to get involved IN sth

cómplice[1] *adj* conspiratorial

cómplice[2] *mf* accomplice; **~ EN algo** accomplice TO sth

complicidad *f* complicity

compló, complot *m* (*pl* **-plots**) plot, conspiracy

complotar [A1] *vi* to plot
■ **complotarse** *v pron* to plot

compondré, compondría, etc *see* **componer**

componedor -dora *m,f* (Andes) *person who sets broken bones, etc*

componenda *f* shady deal; **~s políticas** political chicanery *o* wheeler dealing

componente[1] *m* 1 (de sustancia) constituent (part), component (part); (de equipo, comisión) member 2 (Tec) component

componente[2] *f* (Fís) component

componer [E22] *vt*
A (constituir) ‹*jurado/equipo/plantilla*› to make up; **componen el conjunto una falda y una chaqueta** the outfit consists of a skirt and a jacket; **el tren estaba compuesto por ocho vagones** the train was made up of eight cars
B 1 ‹*sinfonía/canción*› to compose; ‹*verso*› to compose, write 2 (Impr) ‹*texto*› to compose
C 1 (esp AmL) (arreglar) ‹*reloj/radio/zapatos*› to repair 2 (AmL) ‹*hueso*› to set
■ **componer** *vi* to compose
■ **componerse** *v pron*
A (estar formado) **~se DE algo** to be made up OF sth
B 1 «*tiempo*» (arreglarse) to improve, get better 2 (esp AmL fam) «*persona*» to get better; ***componérselas*** (fam): **que se las componga como pueda** that's *his* problem, he'll have to sort that out himself; **se las compone para trabajar y estudiar a la vez** she manages to combine work and study

comportamiento *m* 1 (conducta) behavior*; **mal/buen ~** bad/good behavior 2 (Mec) performance 3 (Fin) (de valores) performance

comportar [A1] *vt* (frml) ‹*obligaciones/riesgo*› to entail; ‹*beneficios*› to bring
■ **comportarse** *v pron* to behave; **~se en público** to behave *o* (frml) conduct oneself in public; **~se mal** to behave badly, misbehave

composición *f*
A 1 (de grupo, equipo) composition, makeup 2 (de sustancia) composition
B (Art, Fot, Mús) composition; (Educ) (redacción) composition; ***hacerse una ~ de lugar*:** **para que te hagas una ~ de ~, la cocina es alargada** just to give you an idea, the kitchen is long and narrow; **se hizo una ~ de ~ y decidió irse** he took stock of the situation and decided to leave

(Compuesto) **composición de textos** typesetting

compositor -tora *m,f* composer

compostura *f* 1 (circunspección) composure; **guardar la ~** to maintain *o* keep one's composure; **perder la ~** to lose one's composure 2 (RPl) (arreglo) repair; **taller de ~s** repair shop

compota *f* compote

compra *f* 1 (acción): **están muy ocupados con la ~ de la casa** they're very busy with buying the house *o* (frml) with the house purchase; **ir de ~s** to go shopping; **hicimos algunas ~s** we did some shopping; **hacer las ~s** *or* (Esp) **la ~** to do the shopping *o* (colloq) shop; **jefe de ~s** chief buyer; **un obsequio con la ~ de dos artículos** purchase two items and get a free gift 2 (cosa comprada) buy, purchase (frml); **fue una buena/mala ~** it was a good/bad buy

comprador -dora *m,f* buyer, purchaser (frml)

comprar [A1] *vt*
A ‹*casa/regalo/comida*› to buy, purchase (frml); **~le algo A algn** (a quien lo vende) to buy sth FROM sb; (a quien lo recibe) to buy sth FOR sb; **se lo voy a ~ para su cumpleaños** I'm going to buy it for his birthday; **~ algo al por mayor/al por menor** *or* **al detalle** to buy *o* purchase sth wholesale/retail
B (fam) (sobornar) to buy (colloq); **un árbitro comprado** a crooked *o* (esp BrE) bent referee

compraventa *f* buying and selling; **se dedica a la ~ de coches** he's a car dealer; **contrato de ~** contract of sale

comprender [E1] *vt*
A 1 (entender) to understand, comprehend (frml); **nadie me comprende** nobody understands me; **¿comprendido?** do you understand? (colloq); **como usted ~á ...** as I'm sure you will appreciate ... 2 (darse cuenta) to realize, understand; **comprendió que lo habían engañado** he realized that he had been tricked
B (abarcar, contener): «*libro*» to cover; «*factura/precio*» to include; **personas de edades comprendidas entre los 19 y los 23 años** people between the ages of 19 and 23
■ **comprender** *vi* (entender) to understand; **hacerse ~** to make oneself understood

comprensible *adj* understandable

comprensión *f* understanding; **un texto de difícil/fácil ~** a text which is difficult/easy to understand; **capacidad de ~** comprehension

(Compuesto) **comprensión auditiva** listening comprehension

comprensivo -va *adj* understanding

compresa *f* 1 (Med) compress 2 (Esp) *tb* **~ higiénica** *or* **femenina** sanitary napkin (AmE), sanitary towel (BrE)

compresión *f* compression

compresor[1] **-sora** *adj*: **cámara ~a** compression chamber; **un aparato ~** a compressor

compresor[2] *m*, **compresora** *f* compressor

comprimido[1] **-da** *adj* compressed

comprimido[2] *m*
A (Farm) pill, tablet
B (Col, Per fam) (para examen) crib (colloq)

comprimir [I1] *vt* ‹*gas*› to compress; ‹*vena*› to apply pressure to, compress (tech); ‹*información*› to compress
■ **comprimirse** *v pron* (hum) to squash together *o* up

comprobable *adj* demonstrable, verifiable

comprobación *f* 1 (acción) verification, checking 2 (Col) (examen) test

comprobante *m* proof; **~ de pago/compra** proof of payment/purchase, receipt

comprobar [A10] *vt* 1 (verificar) ‹*operación/resultado*› to check; **comprueba si funciona** see *o* check if it works 2 (demostrar) to prove; **¿tiene algún documento que compruebe su identidad?** do you have any proof of identity? 3 (darse cuenta) to realize; **comprobó que le faltaba un pedazo** he realized that a piece was missing; **comprobé con tristeza que era cierto** I was sad to discover that it was true 4 «*prueba*» (confirmar) to confirm

comprometedor -dora *adj* compromising

comprometer [E1] *vt*

A 1 (poner en un apuro) to compromise 2 ‹*vida/libertad*› to jeopardize, threaten

B (obligar) **~ a algn A algo** to commit sb TO sth; **esto no te compromete a aceptarlo** this does not commit you to accept

■ **comprometerse** *v pron* 1 (dar su palabra) **~se A + INF** to promise to + INF; **se comprometió a ayudarlo** she promised to help him; **me he comprometido para salir esta noche** I've arranged to go out tonight 2 «*autor/artista*» to commit oneself politically 3 «*novios*» to get engaged; **~se CON algn** to get engaged TO sb

comprometido -da *adj*

A [SER] ‹*asunto/situación*› awkward, delicate

B [SER] ‹*cine/escritor*› politically committed

C [ESTAR] (para casarse) engaged; **~ CON algn** engaged TO sb

compromisario -ria *m,f* elector, delegate

compromiso *m*

A 1 (obligación): **el ~ que ha adquirido con el electorado** the commitment *o* pledge he has made to the electorate; **sin ~ alguno** without obligation; **los invitó por ~** she felt obliged to invite them; **no voy a ir, yo con ellos no tengo ningún ~** I'm not going to go, I'm under no obligation to them; **no le regales nada, lo pones en un ~** don't buy him anything or you'll make him feel he has to buy *you* something 2 (de artista, escritor) political commitment

B (cita) engagement; **~s sociales** social engagements *o* commitments; **no pudo ir porque tenía otro ~** he couldn't go because he had arranged to do something else; **tiene que atender otros ~s** he has other matters *o* business to attend to

C (de matrimonio) engagement, betrothal (frml); **romper el ~** to break off the engagement

D (acuerdo) agreement; (con concesiones recíprocas) compromise; **llegaron a un ~** they came to *o* reached an agreement/a compromise; **una solución de ~** a compromise (solution)

E (apuro) awkward situation; **me puso en un ~** he put me in an awkward position

compuerta *f* 1 (de presa) sluicegate; **~ de esclusa** lockgate 2 (de submarino) hatch

compuesto¹ -ta *adj*

A ‹*oración/número/flor*› compound (*before n*)

B (acicalado) dressed up, spruced up (colloq)

C (sereno) composed; *ver tb* **componer**

compuesto² *m* compound

compulsa *f* (acción) certification; (copia) certified *o* (frml) attested copy

compulsar [A1] *vt* to certify, attest (frml); **una fotocopia compulsada** a certified *o* an attested photocopy

compulsión *f* compulsion

compulsivo -va *adj* 1 ‹*necesidad/impulso*› pressing, urgent 2 (Der) (obligatorio) compulsory

compungido -da *adj* (arrepentido) remorseful, contrite; (triste) sad

compungirse [I7] *v pron* (arrepentirse) to feel remorseful *o* sorry; (entristecerse) to feel sad

compuse, compuso, etc *see* **componer**

computación *f* 1 (Inf) computing 2 (cálculo) ▸**cómputo 1**

computadora *f*, **computador** *m* (esp AmL) computer

(Compuestos)

- **computadora personal/de mesa** personal/desktop computer
- **computadora portátil** portable computer; (más pequeña) laptop (computer)

computar [A1] *vt* (frml) to take into consideration

computerización *f* computerization

computerizado *adj* computerized

computerizar [A4] *vt* to computerize

computista *mf* (Ven) computer programer*

cómputo *m* 1 (frml) (cálculo) calculation; (recuento) count; **realizaron el ~ de los votos** they calculated/counted the number of votes; **el ~ final** the final count 2 (Col) (de calificaciones) overall average mark

comulgar [A3] *vi*

A (Relig) to receive *o* take communion

B (coincidir) **~ CON algn EN algo**: **no comulgo con ella en nada** I have nothing in common with her; **comulgaban en los mismos principios** they shared the same principles

común *adj*

A 1 ‹*intereses/características*› common (*before n*); ‹*amigo*› mutual; **el bien ~** the common good; **un sentimiento ~ a todos los hombres** a sentiment shared by all mankind 2 (*en locs*) **de común acuerdo** by common consent; **de ~ acuerdo con algn** in agreement with sb; **en común**: **no tenemos nada en ~** we have nothing in common; **una cuenta bancaria en ~** a joint bank account; **le hicimos un regalo en ~** we gave her a joint present; **hicieron el trabajo en ~** they did the work together; **no está acostumbrada a la vida en ~ con otras personas** she is not used to living with other people

B (corriente, frecuente) common; **es un nombre muy ~** it's a very common name; **un modelo fuera de lo ~** a very unusual model; **este fenómeno no es ~** this phenomenon is unusual; **tiene una inteligencia poco ~** she is unusually intelligent; **por lo ~** as a rule; **~ *y corriente*** (normal, nada especial) ordinary; ‹*expresión*› common; **es una casa ~ y corriente** it's just an ordinary house, the house is nothing special

comuna *f*

A (de convivencia) commune

B (CS, Per) (municipio) town, municipality (frml)

comunal *adj*

A (de todos) communal

B (CS, Per) (del municipio) town (*before n*), municipal

comunicación *f*

A 1 (enlace) link; **las comunicaciones por carretera** road communications *o* links; **el barrio tiene muy buena ~ con el centro** the city center is easily accessible by road or by public transport; **una ~ entre dos océanos** a passage between two oceans 2 (contacto) contact; **estar/ponerse en ~ con algn** to be/get in contact *o* in touch with sb 3 (por teléfono): **se ha cortado la ~** I've/we've been cut off 4 **comunicaciones** *fpl* (por carretera, teléfono, etc) communications (*pl*); **todas las comunicaciones quedaron cortadas** all means of communication were cut off

B (entendimiento, relación) communication; **tiene problemas de ~** she has problems communicating

C (frml) (escrito, mensaje) communication (frml); **mandar** *or* **cursar una ~** to send a communication

comunicacional *adj* communication (*before n*)

comunicado *m* communiqué

(Compuesto) **comunicado de prensa** press release

comunicante¹ *adj* ▸**vaso**

comunicante² *mf* (period) informant; **un ~ anónimo** an anonymous *o* unnamed source

comunicar [A2] *vt*

A (frml) 1 (informar) to inform; **~le algo A algn** to inform sb OF sth; **siento tener que ~le que ...** I regret to inform you that ...; **se comunica a los señores socios que ...** shareholders should note that ... 2 (AmL) (por teléfono) ‹*persona*› to put ... through

B (transmitir) 1 ‹*entusiasmo/miedo*› to convey, communicate 2 ‹*conocimientos*› to impart, pass on; ‹*información*› to convey, communicate; ‹*idea*› to put across 3 ‹*fuerza/calor*› to transmit

C

C

C ‹*habitaciones/ciudades*› to connect, link; **un barrio bien comunicado** an area easily accessible by road/well served by public transport; **~ algo CON algo** to connect sth WITH sth

■ **comunicar** *vi*

A «*habitaciones*» to be connected

B (Esp) **1** (ponerse en contacto) **~ CON algn** to get in touch *o* contact WITH sb **2** «*teléfono*» to be busy (AmE) *o* (BrE) engaged

■ **comunicarse** *v pron*

A **1** (*recípr*) (relacionarse) to communicate; **~ por señas** to communicate using sign language; **~se CON algn** to communicate WITH sb **2** (ponerse en contacto) **~se CON algn** to get in touch *o* in contact WITH sb

B «*habitaciones/ciudades/lagos*» (*recípr*) to be connected; **~se CON algo** to be connected TO sth

comunicativo -va *adj* communicative

comunidad *f*

A **1** (sociedad) community; **para el bien de la ~** for the good of the community **2** (grupo delimitado) community; **la ~ polaca** the Polish community; **vivir en ~** to live with other people **3** (Relig) community **4** (asociación) association

Compuestos

- **Comunidad Británica de Naciones** (British) Commonwealth
- **Comunidad Económica Europea** European Economic Community
- **Comunidad Europea** European Community

B (coincidencia) community; **~ de ideales/objetivos** community of ideals/objectives

comunidad autónoma

In 1978 power in Spain was decentralized and the country was divided into *comunidades autónomas* or *autonomías* (autonomous regions). The new communities have far greater autonomy from central government than the old *regiones* and were a response to nationalist aspirations, which had built up under Franco.

Some regions have more autonomy than others. The Basque Country, Catalonia, and Galicia, for example, had political structures, a desire for independence and their own languages which underpinned their claims to distinctive identities. Andalusia gained almost complete autonomy without having had a nationalist tradition. Other regions, such as Madrid, are to some extent artificial, having been created largely to complete the process.

The *comunidades autónomas* are: Andalusia, Aragon, Asturias, Balearic Islands, the Basque Country (Euskadi), Canary Islands, Cantabria, Castilla y León, Castilla-La Mancha, Catalonia, Extremadura, Galicia, Madrid, Murcia, Navarre, La Rioja, Valencia and the North African enclaves of Ceuta and Melilla

comunión *f*

A (Relig) communion; **recibir la ~** to receive *o* take communion; **dar la ~** to administer *o* take communion; **hacer la primera ~** to make one's first Holy Communion

B (de ideas, principios) communion, community

comunismo *m* communism

comunista *adj/mf* communist

comunitariamente *adv* ‹*vivir/trabajar*› communally; ‹*luchar*› as a community

comunitario -ria *adj* **1** ‹*bienes*› communal; ‹*espíritu*› community (*before n*); **trabajos ~s** community work **2** (de la CE) EC (*before n*), Community (*before n*)

con *prep*

A **1** (expresando relaciones de compañía, comunicación, reciprocidad) with; **vive ~ su novio** she lives with her boyfriend; **hablar ~ algn** to talk to sb; **está casada ~ mi primo** she's married to my cousin **2** (indicando el objeto de comportamiento, actitud): **te portaste muy mal ~ ellos** you behaved very badly toward(s) them; **he tenido mucha paciencia ~tigo** I have been very patient with you **3** (indicando el acompañamiento de algo) with; **se sirve ~ arroz** serve with rice; **pan ~ mantequilla** bread and butter

B **1** (indicando una relación de simultaneidad): **una cápsula ~ cada comida** one capsule with each meal; **se levanta ~ el alba** he gets up at the crack of dawn **2** (indicando una relación de causa): **¿cómo vamos a ir ~ esta lluvia?** how can we go in this rain?; **~ tanta prisa se me olvidó** I was in such a hurry that I forgot; **ella se lo ofreció, ~ lo que** *or* **~ lo cual me puso a mí en un aprieto** she offered it to him, which put me in an awkward position; **¿no lo vas a llevar, ~ lo que le gusta el circo?** aren't you going to take him? you know how much he likes the circus; **¡~ las veces que te lo pedí!** the (number of) times I asked you!; **~ lo tarde que es, ya se debe haber ido** it's really late, he should have gone by now; **¡~ todo lo que tengo que hacer!** on top of everything else I have to do!; ▸**todo**[3] **B**

C **1** (indicando instrumento, medio, material) with; **córtalo ~ la tijera** cut it with the scissors, use the scissors to cut it; **lo estás malcriando ~ tanto mimo** you're spoiling him with all this pampering; **¡caray ~ la niña (***or* **el vecino, etc)!** well would you believe it!; **~ + INF: ~ llorar no se arregla nada** crying won't solve anything; **~ llamarlo por teléfono ya cumples** if *o* as long as you call him, that should do; **¡~ decirte que ...** I mean, to give you an example ...; **me contento ~ que apruebes** as long as you pass I'll be happy; ▸**tal**[3] **B** **2** (indicando modo) with; **andaba ~ dificultad** she was walking with difficulty; **¡~ mucho gusto!** with pleasure! **3** (al describir características, un estado): **amaneció ~ fiebre** he woke up with a temperature; **ya estaba ~ dolores de parto** she was already having labor pains; **andaba ~ ganas de bronca** he was looking for a fight; **~ las manos en los bolsillos** with his hands in his pockets; **¿vas a ir ~ ese vestido?** are you going in that dress?; **una mujer ~ aspecto de extranjera** a foreign-looking woman

D (AmL) (indicando el agente, destinatario): **me peino ~ Gerardo** Gerardo does my hair; **se estuvo quejando ~migo** she was complaining to me

conato *m*: **un ~ de rebelión** an attempted uprising; **varios ~s de violencia** several small *o* minor outbreaks of violence; **hubo un ~ de incendio** there was a small fire which came to nothing

concatenación *f* (acción) linking, concatenation (frml); (serie) chain, concatenation (frml)

concatenar [A1] *vt* to link together, to concatenate (frml)

concavidad *f* (cualidad) concavity; (hueco) hollow

cóncavo -va *adj* concave

concebible *adj* conceivable

concebir [I14] *vt*

A (Biol) to conceive

B ‹*plan/idea*› to conceive; **me hizo ~ falsas esperanzas** she gave me false hope

C (entender, imaginar): **no concibe la vida sin él** she can't conceive of life without him; **no concibo que le hayas dicho eso** I can't believe you said that (to him); **yo concibo la amistad de modo distinto** I have a different conception of friendship

■ **concebir** *vi* to conceive

conceder [E1] *vt*

A **1** ‹*premio/beca*› to give, award; ‹*descuento/préstamo*› to give, grant (frml); ‹*privilegio/favor/permiso*› to grant; **concedieron el triunfo al irlandés** they awarded victory to the Irishman; **sin ~ un solo tanto** without conceding a single point; **el honor que me concedieron** the honor they conferred *o* bestowed on me; **nos concedió una entrevista** she agreed to give us an interview; **¿me podría ~ unos minutos?** could you spare me a few minutes? **2** ‹*importancia/valor*› to give

B (admitir, reconocer) to admit, acknowledge, concede

concejal -jala *m,f* town/city councilor*

concejalía *f* (cargo) post of town/city councilor*, councilorship*; (departamento) department

concejero -ra *m,f* (AmL) ▸**concejal**

concejo *m* council; **~ municipal** town/city council

concentración *f*

A (Psic) concentration; **tiene un gran poder de ~** she has great powers of concentration

B **1** (Quím) concentration **2** (acumulación) concentration; **grandes concentraciones urbanas** large urban areas

C (Pol) rally, mass meeting

D (Dep) pre-game *o* pre-match preparation

concentrado[1] **-da** *adj* concentrated (*before n*)

concentrado² *m* concentrate; **~ de tomate** tomato concentrate; **~ de carne** meat extract

concentrar [A1] *vt*
A 1 ‹*solución/caldo*› to make … more concentrated 2 ‹*esfuerzos*› to concentrate; ‹*atención*› to focus
B 1 (reunir) to hold; **el poder está concentrado en pocas manos** all the power is held by a few people *o* is concentrated in the hands of a few 2 (congregar) ‹*multitud/tropas*› to assemble, bring … together 3 (Dep) to bring … together (*to prepare for a game*)
■ **concentrarse** *v pron*
A (Psic) to concentrate; **~se EN algo** to concentrate ON sth
B 1 (Pol) (reunirse) to assemble, gather together 2 (estar reunido) to be concentrated 3 (Dep) «*equipo/jugadores*» to gather together (*to prepare for a game*)

concéntrico -ca *adj* concentric

concepción *f* (Biol) conception

conceptismo *m*: *17th-century conceit-based literary style*

conceptista *mf*: *exponent of* **conceptismo**

concepto *m*
A (idea): **el ~ de la libertad/justicia** the concept of freedom/justice; **tener un ~ equivocado de algo/algn** to have a mistaken idea of sth/sb; **tengo (un) mal ~ de su trabajo** I have a very low opinion of her work; **me merece el mejor de los ~s** I have a high opinion of him; ***bajo*** *or* ***por ningún*** **~** on no account
B (Com, Fin): **el dinero se le adeuda por diversos ~s** the money is owed to him in respect of various items/services; **recibieron $50.000 en** *or* **por ~ de indemnización** they received $50,000 in *o* as compensation
C (Lit) conceit

conceptual *adj* conceptual

conceptualización *f* conceptualization

conceptualizar [A4] *vt* to conceptualize

conceptuar [A18] *vt* to regard

conceptuoso -sa *adj* (CS) (amable, elogioso): **una conceptuosa felicitación** warm congratulations; **le enviaron una conceptuosa nota** they sent him a note praising his work (*o* his performance *etc*)

concerniente *adj* **~ A algo** concerning sth; **en lo ~ a este problema** as far as this problem is concerned

concernir [I12] *vi* (*en 3ª pers*) to concern; **~ A algn** to concern sb; **por** *or* **en lo que a mí concierne** as far as I'm concerned; **en lo que concierne a su pedido** with regard to your order

concertación *f* (acto) coordination, harmonization; (pacto) agreement

concertada *f* (Esp) state-aided private education sector

concertar [A5] *vt*
A ‹*cita/entrevista*› to arrange, set up; ‹*casamiento*› to arrange; ‹*precio*› to fix; **~ un plan de acción** to make agree upon a plan of action; **~ + INF** to agree to + INF
B (Mús) ‹*instrumentos*› to tune (up); ‹*voces*› to harmonize
■ **concertar** *vi* 1 (Ling) to agree 2 (Mús) to be in tune
■ **concertarse** *v pron* **~se (CON algn) PARA + INF** to get together (WITH sb) TO + INF

concertina *f* concertina

concertino *m* first violin

concertista *mf* soloist; **~ de piano** concert pianist

concerto grosso /kon'tʃerto 'groso/ *m* concerto grosso

concesión *f*
A (de premios) awarding; (de préstamo) granting
B (en una postura) concession
C (Com) dealership, concession, franchise

concesionario¹ -ria *adj* concessionary

concesionario² *m* dealer, concessionaire

concha *f*
A (de moluscos) shell; ***hacer*** **~** (Méx) to become hardened *o* toughened; ***meterse en su*** **~** to retreat into one's shell
(Compuesto) **concha nácar** (Méx) *or* (Chi) **de perla** mother-of-pearl
B (carey) tortoise shell; **gafas de ~** tortoiseshell glasses
C (Teatr) prompt box
D (Ven) (cáscara — de verduras, fruta) skin; (— del queso) rind; (— del pan) crust; (— de maníes) shell; **~ *de mango*** (Ven fam) trick question
E (Méx) (Dep) protection box, box
F (AmS vulg) (de mujer) cunt (vulg); ***¡la ~ de su madre!*** (AmS vulg) shit! (vulg), fucking hell! (vulg)
G (AmL exc CS fam: en algunas regiones vulg) (descaro) nerve (colloq), cheek (BrE colloq); **¡qué (tal) ~ la de Jorge!** Jorge's got a lot of nerve!

conchabar [A1] *vt* (CS fam) ‹*peón*› to hire
■ **conchabarse** *v pron*
A (fam) (confabularse) to plot, conspire; **~se CONTRA algn** to plot *o* conspire AGAINST sb; **estar conchabado CON algn** to be in league WITH sb
B (CS fam) (encontrar empleo) to get (oneself) a job
C (Méx fam) (ganarse, conquistarse) ‹*persona*› to get on the right side of (colloq)

cónchale *interj* (Ven fam) good heavens!

concho¹ *m*
A (Chi) (del vino) lees (*pl*); (del café) dregs (*pl*)
B (Andes fam) (hijo menor) youngest (child)
C (Chi) 1 (parte final) end, last bit; **se tomó hasta el último ~** he drank it down to the last drop 2 **conchos** *mpl* (restos) leftovers (*pl*)

concho² *interj* (euf) shoot! (AmE euph), sugar! (BrE euph)

conchudo¹ -da *adj* (AmL exc CS fam *o* vulg) (aprovechado, caradura): **¡qué tipo tan ~!** what a nerve of a guy! (AmE), he's got a bloody nerve! (BrE sl)

conchudo² -da *m,f* (AmL exc CS fam *o* vulg): **es un ~** he's got a lot of nerve

conciencia *f*
A (en moral) conscience; **tener la ~ limpia** *or* **tranquila** to have a clear *o* clean conscience; **tener mala ~** *or* **la ~ sucia** to have a bad *o* guilty conscience; **en ~ no puedo quedarme callada** in all conscience I can't remain silent; **me remuerde la ~** my conscience is pricking me; **no siente ningún cargo** *or* **remordimiento de ~** she feels no remorse; ***hacer algo a*** **~** to do something conscientiously
B (conocimiento) awareness; **lo hizo con plena ~ de que la iba a herir** he did it in the full knowledge that it would hurt her; **tener ~ de algo** to be aware of sth; **tengo plena ~ de eso** I'm well aware of that; **quieren crear ~ del peligro entre la población** they aim to make the population aware of the danger; **tomar** *or* **adquirir ~ de algo** to become aware of sth
(Compuesto) **conciencia de clase** class consciousness

concienciación *f* (Esp) ▸**concientización**

concienciador -dora *adj* (Esp) ▸**concientizador**

concienciar [A1] *vt* (Esp) ▸**concientizar**

concientización *f* (esp AmL): **una campaña de ~** a campaign to increase *o* raise public awareness, a campaign to make people more aware

concientizado -da *adj* (esp AmL) aware; **niños muy ~s acerca del daño** children who are very aware of the danger

concientizador -dora *adj* (esp AmL) consciousness-raising (*before n*)

concientizar [A4] *vt* (esp AmL) ‹*población/sociedad*› to make … aware; **~ a algn DE algo** to raise sb's consciousness ABOUT *o* awareness OF sth
■ **concientizarse** *v pron* (esp AmL) **~se DE algo** to become aware OF sth

concienzudamente *adv* ‹*trabajar/estudiar*› conscientiously; ‹*repasar*› thoroughly

concienzudo -da *adj* ‹*trabajador/estudiante*› conscientious; ‹*estudio/repaso/análisis*› thorough, painstaking

concierto *m*
A (Mús) 1 (obra) concerto; **~ para oboe** oboe concerto 2 (función) concert, recital
B (acuerdo) agreement, accord (frml)
C (frml) (conjunto armónico) concord (frml)

conciliábulo *m* secret meeting/discussion

conciliación *f* conciliation

conciliador -dora *adj* conciliatory

conciliar¹ *adj* council (*before n*)

conciliar² [A1] *vt*
A 1 ‹*personas*› to conciliate 2 ‹*ideas*› to reconcile; ‹*actividades*› to combine; **son ideas imposibles de ~** these ideas are irreconcilable
B ‹*sueño*›: **~ el sueño** to get to sleep

conciliatorio -ria *adj* conciliatory

C

C

concilio *m* council; **~ ecuménico** ecumenical council; **el C~ Vaticano II** the Second Vatican Council

concisión *f* concision, conciseness

conciso -sa *adj* concise

concitar [A1] *vt* to arouse

conciudadano -na *m,f* (de una misma ciudad) fellow citizen; (de un mismo país) (*m*) fellow countryman; (*f*) fellow countrywoman

cónclave *m* 1 (Relig) conclave 2 (reunión) meeting, conference

concluir [I20] *vt*

A (frml) (terminar) ‹*obras*› to complete, finish; ‹*trámite*› to complete; ‹*acuerdo/tratado*› to conclude

B (frml) (deducir) to conclude, come to the conclusion; **~ algo DE algo** to conclude sth FROM sth

■ **concluir** *vi* (frml) 1 «*congreso/negociaciones*» to end, conclude; **el plazo concluyó el día 17** the time limit expired on the 17th; **~ EN/CON algo** to end IN/WITH sth; **las conversaciones concluyeron en un acuerdo** the talks ended in agreement; **concluyó con una concentración** it ended with a rally 2 «*persona*» **~ DE + INF** to finish -ING; **~ CON algo** to finish sth

conclusión *f*

A 1 (terminación) completion 2 **conclusiones** *fpl* (Der) summing-up

B (deducción) conclusion; **llegar a una ~** to reach a conclusion; **saqué la ~ de que ...** I came to the conclusion that ...; **tú saca tus propias conclusiones** you can draw your own conclusions; **en ~** (en suma) in short; (en consecuencia) so; **o acepta o la echan, (en) ~: no sabe qué hacer** she either accepts or they fire her, so she just doesn't know what to do

conclusivo -va *adj* conclusive

concluyente *adj* ‹*razón/respuesta/prueba*› conclusive; **sus palabras fueron ~s** he was quite categorical; **fue ~ al responder** he answered categorically

concomitante *adj* concomitant (frml)

concordancia *f*

A (Ling) agreement, concord (tech)

B (conformidad) consistency, concordance (frml); **no hubo ~ entre las declaraciones** there was no consistency between the statements; **actúa en ~ con sus principios** he acts in accordance with his principles

C (listado) concordance

D (Mús) harmony

concordante *adj* concordant (frml), concurrent

concordar [A10] *vi* 1 (Ling) to agree; **~ CON algo** to agree WITH sth 2 «*cifras*» to tally; «*versiones*» to agree, coincide; **~ CON algo** ‹*con documento/versión*› to coincide WITH sth; **su comportamiento no concuerda con sus principios** his behavior is not in keeping with his principles

■ **concordar** *vt* to make ... agree, reconcile

concordato *m* concordat

concorde *adj* in agreement

concordia *f* harmony, concord (frml)

concreción *f*

A 1 (precisión): **expresarse con ~** to be precise 2 (AmL) (de proyectos, sueños) realization

B (Min) concretion

concretamente *adv* specifically; **vive en Wisconsin, ~ en Madison** he lives in Wisconsin, in Madison to be precise; **no sé ~ a qué ha venido** I don't know exactly why he has come

concretar [A1] *vt*

A 1 (concertar) ‹*fecha/precio*› to fix, set; **~ los términos del contrato** to agree on the terms of the contract 2 (precisar, definir) to be specific about; **no fue capaz de ~ lo que quiere hacer** he was unable to be specific about what he wants to do; **no concretamos nada** we didn't settle on anything definite 3 (materializar) ‹*oferta/esperanzas*› to realize, fulfill*; ‹*sueños*› to realize, make ... come true

B (Chi) (Const) to concrete

■ **concretar** *vi*: **a ver si concretas** try and be more specific; **bueno, concretemos** right, let's get things clear; **llámame para ~** give me a call to arrange the details

■ **concretarse** *v pron* «*cambios/amenazas*» to become a reality; «*sueños*» to be realized, come true; **la reunión nunca llegó a ~se** the meeting never took place

concretizar [A4] *vt* (Chi) ▸ **concretar**

concreto[1] **-ta** *adj* 1 (específico) ‹*política/acusación*› concrete, specific; ‹*motivo/ejemplo/pregunta*› specific; ‹*fecha/hora*› definite; ‹*lugar*› specific, particular; **en tu caso ~** in your particular case; **en ~** specifically; **quiero saber, en ~, cuánto cuesta** what I want to know specifically is how much it costs; **una conferencia sobre historia, en ~, el siglo XV** a lecture on history, the XV century to be precise; **en una zona en ~** in a particular *o* specific area; **no sé nada en ~** I don't know anything definite 2 (no abstracto) concrete

concreto[2] *m* (AmL) concrete

(Compuesto) **concreto armado** reinforced concrete

concubina *f* concubine

concubinato *m* concubinage; **vivir en ~** to cohabit

conculcar [A2] *vt* (frml) ‹*derecho/ley/norma*› to violate

concuñado -da *m,f*: **mi ~** my wife's brother-in-law; **mi concuñada** my husband's sister-in-law

concupiscencia *f* lustfulness, concupiscence (liter)

concupiscente *adj* lustful, concupiscent (liter)

concurrencia *f*

A (frml) 1 (público, asistentes) audience; **una numerosa** *or* **nutrida ~** a large audience 2 (asistencia) attendance

B (frml) (de opiniones, circunstancias) concurrence (frml)

concurrente[1] *adj* (frml) ‹*factores/circunstancias*› concurrent (frml)

concurrente[2] *mf* (frml): **los/las ~s** (a un acto) the audience; (a un concurso) the contestants; **entre los ~s al acto** among those present at the event

concurrido -da *adj* 1 [ESTAR] (con mucha gente) ‹*discoteca/local*› busy, crowded; ‹*concierto/exposición*› well-attended 2 (frecuentado) popular; **es un bar muy ~** it's a very popular bar

concurrir [I1] *vi* (frml)

A 1 (asistir, acudir) **~ A algo** ‹*a acto/concierto*› to attend sth 2 (tomar parte) **~ A algo** ‹*a concurso/examen*› to take part in sth; ‹*a elecciones*› «*partido*» to take part in sth; **concurre como candidato independiente** he is running (AmE) *o* (BrE) standing as an independent candidate; **50 novelas concurren al premio** 50 novels are in the running for the prize

B (confluir) 1 «*factores/circunstancias*» to come together, combine; **si concurren circunstancias agravantes** in the event of aggravating circumstances; **~ EN algo: diversos factores han concurrido en el fracaso de las negociaciones** various factors have combined *o* have come together to bring about the breakdown in negotiations; **~ A algo** to contribute TO sth 2 «*calles/avenidas*» to meet, converge

C (coincidir) to agree; **~ CON algn** to be in agreement WITH sb (frml)

concursante *mf* (en concurso) competitor, contestant; (para empleo) candidate

concursar [A1] *vi* (en concurso) to take part; (para puesto) to compete (*through interviews and competitive examinations*)

concurso *m*

A 1 (certamen) competition; **presentarse a un ~** to take part in a competition 2 (para puestos, vacantes) *selection process involving interviews and competitive examinations*

(Compuestos)

- **concurso de acreedores** creditors' meeting
- **concurso de belleza** beauty contest
- **concurso de méritos** *selection process not involving competitive examination*
- **concurso (de** *or* **por) oposición** (Esp, Ven) *selection process involving competitive examinations and interviews*
- **concurso hípico** show jumping competition

B (licitación) tender; **sacar algo a ~** to put sth out to tender

(Compuesto) **concurso subasta** competitive tendering (*with pre-determined maximum price*)

C (frml) (de circunstancias, factores) combination, concurrence (frml)

concusión *f* concussion

condado *m* 1 (división territorial) county 2 (dignidad — en Gran Bretaña) earldom; (— en otros países) countship

conde -desa (en Gran Bretaña) (*m*) earl; (*f*) countess; (en otros países) (*m*) count; (*f*) countess; **el señor ~** the Count

condecoración *f* decoration
condecorar [A1] *vt* to decorate
condena *f*
A (Der) sentence; **está cumpliendo su ~** he is serving his sentence
B (reprobación) **~ DE** *or* **A algo** condemnation OF sth
condenación *f* 1 (Relig) damnation; **~ eterna** eternal damnation 2 (reprobación) ▸**condena B**
condenado[1] **-da** *adj*
A 1 (destinado) **~ A algo** doomed TO sth 2 (obligado) **~ A + INF** condemned *o* forced to + INF
B (fam) (expresando irritación) wretched (colloq), damn (colloq)
condenado[2] **-da** *m,f*
A 1 (Der) convicted person; **el ~ a muerte** the condemned man 2 (Relig): **los ~s** the damned; ***como (un)* ~** (fam) ‹*correr*› like hell (colloq); **trabajaron como ~s** they worked like maniacs
B (fam) (maldito) wretch; **el ~ de tu hermano** that wretched brother of yours (colloq)
condenar [A1] *vt*
A 1 (Der) to sentence, condemn; **~ a algn A algo** to sentence sb TO sth; **lo ~on a tres años de cárcel** he was sentenced to three years imprisonment; **~ a algn a muerte** to condemn *o* sentence sb to death; **lo condenaron al pago de $100.000** they ordered him to pay $100,000; **lo ~on por robo** he was found guilty of robbery 2 (obligar) **~ a algn A algo** to condemn sb TO sth 3 (reprobar, censurar) to condemn
B 1 ‹*puerta/ventana*› (con ladrillos) to brick up; (con tablas) to board up 2 (inhabilitar) ‹*habitación/sala*› to close up
■ **condenarse** *v pron* to be damned
condenatorio -ria *adj* 1 ‹*mirada/gesto*› condemnatory 2 (Der): **una sentencia condenatoria** a conviction
condensación *f* condensation
condensado -da *adj* condensed
condensador *m* condenser
condensar [A1] *vt* to condense
■ **condensarse** *v pron* to condense
condesa *f* ▸**conde**
condescendencia *f* 1 (con aires de superioridad) condescension; **hablar con ~** to speak condescendingly 2 (con amabilidad, comprensión) understanding
condescender [E8] *vi* 1 (con aires de superioridad) **~ A + INF** to condescend *o* deign to + INF 2 (ceder) to acquiesce, agree, consent
condescendiente *adj* 1 ‹*actitud/respuesta*› (con aires de superioridad) condescending 2 (comprensivo) understanding
condición *f*
A (requisito) condition; **sin condiciones** unconditionally; **a ~** *or* **con la ~ de que** on condition (that); **acepto con una ~** I accept on one condition; **te lo presto a ~ de que me lo devuelvas mañana** I'll lend it to you as long as *o* provided (that) you give it back tomorrow; **las condiciones de un contrato** the terms *o* conditions of a contract
(Compuestos)
• **condiciones de venta** *fpl* conditions of sale (*pl*)
• **condición sine qua non** sine qua non (frml)
B 1 (calidad, situación): **en su ~ de sacerdote** as a priest; **en su ~ de jefe de la delegación** in his capacity as head of the delegation; **su ~ de extranjero le impide participar** as *o* being a foreigner he is not allowed to take part 2 (naturaleza) condition; **la ~ femenina** the feminine condition 3 (clase social) condition (dated), class; **de ~ humilde** of humble condition *o* origins; **alguien de su ~** someone of your social position 4 (Med) condition
(Compuesto) **condición humana**: **la ~ ~** the human condition
C **condiciones** *fpl* (estado, circunstancias) conditions (*pl*); **condiciones meteorológicas** weather conditions; **Ⓢ refrigerar para conservar en óptimas condiciones** refrigerate to keep (product) at its best; **estar en perfectas condiciones** ‹‹*coche/mueble*›› to be in perfect condition; ‹‹*persona*›› to be in good shape; **la carne estaba en malas condiciones** the meat was unfit for consumption; **deja tu cuarto en condiciones** leave your room neat and tidy; **todo tiene que estar en condiciones para el comienzo del curso** everything must be ready for the beginning of the school year; **estar en condiciones de jugar/trabajar** to be fit to play/work; **no estoy en condiciones de hacer un viaje tan caro** I am not in a position to go on such an expensive trip
(Compuesto) **condiciones de trabajo/de vida** *fpl* working/living conditions (*pl*)
D **condiciones** *fpl* (aptitudes) talent; **tiene condiciones para la música** she has a talent for music; **no tiene condiciones para ese trabajo** he is not suited to that job
condicional *adj* conditional
condicionamiento *m* (Psic) conditioning
condicionante[1] *adj* determining
condicionante[2] *m* determinant (frml)
condicionar [A1] *vt* 1 (determinar) to condition, determine 2 (supeditar) **~ algo A algo** to make sth conditional ON sth
condimentar [A1] *vt* to season
condimento *m*: **el comino es un ~** cumin is a condiment; **le falta ~** it needs some seasoning; **los ~s usados en la cocina india** the herbs and spices used in Indian cooking
condiscípulo -la *m,f* (de escuela) classmate; (de universidad) fellow student
condolencia *f* (frml) condolence (frml)
condolerse [E9] *v pron* (frml) to offer one's condolences (frml), to sympathize
condominio *m* 1 (propiedad) joint ownership, joint control 2 (Pol) (territorio) condominium 3 (AmL) (edificio) condominium (esp AmE), block of flats (BrE)
condón *m* condom
condonar [A1] *vt* (frml) ‹*deuda*› to cancel, write off; **le ~on la pena** he was pardoned
cóndor *m* condor
conducción *f*
A 1 (Elec, Fís) conduction 2 (esp Esp) (Auto) driving
B 1 (AmL) (dirección): **si se me confía la ~ de los destinos de la nación ...** if I am entrusted with managing the nation's destiny ...; **está a cargo de la ~ del programa** he's in charge of presenting the program 2 (Arg) (cúpula) leadership
conducente *adj* **~ A algo** leading TO sth
conducir [I6] *vi*
A (llevar) **~ A algo** ‹‹*camino/sendero*›› to lead TO sth; **~ a error** to lead to mistakes; **esa actitud no conduce a nada** *or* **ninguna parte** that attitude won't achieve anything *o* (colloq) won't get us anywhere
B (esp Esp) (Auto) to drive; **¿sabes ~?** can *o* do you drive?; **~ por la izquierda** to drive on the left
■ **conducir** *vt*
A 1 (guiar, dirigir) to lead; **~ a algn A algo** to lead sb TO sth; **~ a algn ANTE algn** to take sb BEFORE sb; **fue elegido para ~ los destinos de la nación** he was chosen to steer the nation's destiny 2 (AmL) ‹*programa*› to host, present; ‹*debate*› to chair
B (esp Esp) ‹*vehículo*› to drive
C ‹*electricidad/calor*› to conduct
■ **conducirse** *v pron* to behave, conduct oneself (frml)
conducta *f* behavior*, conduct; **mala ~** bad behavior, misconduct (frml)
conductibilidad, conductividad *f* conductivity
conductismo *m* behaviorism*
conductista *adj/mf* behaviorist*
conducto *m*
A 1 (Anat) duct, tube; (Odont) root canal 2 (Tec) (canal, tubo) pipe, tube
(Compuestos)
• **conducto auditivo** ear canal
• **conducto de desagüe** drain
B (frml) (medio, vía) channels (*pl*); **por ~ oficial/regular** through official/the proper channels; **por ~ de nuestro representante** through our representative
conductor[1] **-tora** *adj* conductive; **materiales ~es de la electricidad/del calor** materials which conduct electricity/heat
conductor[2] **-tora** *m,f*
A 1 (de vehículo) driver 2 (AmL) (de programa) host
B **conductor** *m* (Elec, Fís) conductor

conduje, condujiste, etc *see* **conducir**
conduzca, conduzcas, etc *see* **conducir**
conectar [A1] *vt*
A ‹*cables/aparatos*› to connect (up); ‹*luz/gas/teléfono*› to connect; ~ **algo a la red** to connect sth to the mains supply *o* plug sth in
B (relacionar) ‹*hechos/sucesos*› to connect, link
C (AmL) (poner en contacto) ~ **a algn CON algn** to put sb in touch *o* in contact WITH sb
■ **conectar** *vi*
A 1 (Rad, TV) ~ **CON algn/algo** to go over TO sb/sth 2 (empalmar) to connect, link up 3 (llevarse bien, entenderse) to get along *o* on well; **un político que conecta bien con la juventud** a politician young people can relate to 4 (AmL) (con vuelo, tren): **en Río conectamos con el vuelo a Asunción** in Rio we took a connecting flight to Asunción; **este vuelo/tren conecta con el de Dublín** this flight/train connects with the Dublin one
B (Méx arg) (conseguir droga) to score (sl)
conecte *mf* 1 (Méx arg) (traficante) dealer (sl) 2 (AmC fam) (contacto) friend on the inside (colloq)
conector *m* connector
coneja *f* (fam): **es una** ~ she's a real babymachine (colloq & hum)
conejera *f* (madriguera individual) burrow; (red de túneles) warren; (para crianza) rabbit hutch, hutch
conejillo de Indias *m* guinea pig
conejo -ja *m,f* (Zool) rabbit; **los cazaron como ~s** they were caught like rats in a trap; ***hacer*** ~ (Col fam) to run off without paying, do a runner (BrE colloq)
conexión *f* 1 (Elec) connection; ~ **a tierra** ground (AmE), earth (BrE); ~ **a la red** connection to the mains; **devolvemos la ~ a nuestros estudios** and now, back to the studios 2 (relación) connection; **no existe ~ entre los dos hechos** there is no connection between the two events; **pierde su ~ con el entorno** he loses touch with the world around him 3 (Transp) connection; **perdí la ~ con Roma** I missed my connection to Rome 4 **conexiones** *fpl* (AmL) (amistades, relaciones) connections (*pl*), contacts (*pl*)
confabulación *f* conspiracy, plot
confabularse [A1] *v pron* to plot, conspire; ~ **CONTRA algn** to plot *o* conspire AGAINST sb
confección *f* 1 (de trajes) tailoring; (de vestidos) dressmaking; **industria de la** ~ clothing industry; **de** ~ ready-to-wear, off-the-peg; ⓢ **confecciones** fashions 2 (de artefactos) making 3 (de folleto, periódico) production; (de lista) drawing-up 4 (de medicina) preparation
confeccionar [A1] *vt* ‹*falda/vestido*› to make, make up; ‹*artefactos*› to make; ‹*folleto/periódico*› to produce; ‹*lista*› to draw up; ‹*medicina*› to prepare
confederación *f* confederation
confederado¹ -da *adj* confederate
confederado² *m* confederate
confederarse [A1] *v pron* to confederate
conferencia *f*
A 1 (discurso — formal) lecture; (— más informal) talk; **dar una ~ SOBRE algo** to give a lecture/talk ON sth 2 (reunión) conference; **celebrar una** ~ to hold a conference; ~ **de desarme** arms talks
(Compuestos)
• **conferencia de prensa** press conference
• **conferencia episcopal** synod
B (Esp) (Telec) long distance call; **poner una ~ interurbana/internacional** to make *o* (AmE) place a long-distance call
(Compuesto) **conferencia a cobro revertido** collect call (AmE), reverse charge call (BrE)
conferenciante *mf* lecturer
conferenciar [A1] *vi* (period) to hold talks
conferencista *mf* (AmL) lecturer
conferir [I11] *vt* (frml *o* liter) 1 ‹*honor/dignidad/responsabilidad*› to confer 2 ‹*prestigio*› to confer; ‹*encanto*› to lend; **la barba le confería un aire distinguido** the beard lent him an air of distinction
confesar [A5] *vt* 1 (Relig) ‹*pecado*› to confess; **el cura que la confiesa** the priest who hears her confession 2 ‹*sentimiento/ignorancia/delito*› to confess; ‹*error*› to admit
■ **confesar** *vi* 1 (Relig) to hear confession 2 (admitir culpabilidad) to confess, make a confession
■ **confesarse** *v pron* 1 (Relig) to go to confession; **~se DE algo** to confess sth; **~se CON algn** (Relig) to go to sb FOR confession; (hacer confidencias) to open up one's heart TO sb 2 (declararse) (+ *compl*) to confess to being, admit to being
confesión *f*
A 1 (sacramento) confession; **me oyó en** ~ he heard my confession 2 (Der) confession 3 (admisión) confession; **le voy a hacer una ~: a mí no me gusta** I must confess *o* admit (that) I don't like it
B (credo) faith, creed, denomination
confesional *adj* confessional, denominational
confesionario *m* confessional
confeso¹ -sa *adj* 1 (Der) confessed; **un marxista** ~ a self-confessed Marxist 2 (Hist) ‹*judío*› converted
confeso² -sa *m,f* (Hist) converted Jew
confesor *m* confessor
confeti *m* confetti
confiable *adj* (esp AmL) 1 ‹*estadísticas*› reliable 2 ‹*persona*› (cumplidor) reliable, dependable; (honesto) trustworthy
confiado -da *adj* 1 [SER] (crédulo) trusting 2 [ESTAR] (seguro) ~ **EN algo: está muy ~ en que lo van a llevar** he's convinced they're going to take him; **no estés tan** ~ don't get over-confident
confianza *f*
A (fe) confidence; **él/ella me inspira** ~ I feel I can trust him/her; **no despierta** ~ it does not inspire confidence; **lo considero digno de toda** ~ he has my complete trust; ~ **EN algn/algo** confidence IN sb/sth; **tiene mucha ~ en sí misma** she is very self-confident; **tengo plena ~ en que ...** I'm quite confident that ... *o* I have every confidence that ...; **había puesto toda mi ~ en él** I had put all my trust *o* faith in him; **de** ~ ‹*persona*› trustworthy, reliable; ‹*producto*› reliable; **se rodea de personas de su** ~ he surrounds himself with people he trusts; **ocupa un puesto de** ~ he has a position of trust; **nombró a alguien de su** ~ he appointed someone he trusted
B (amistad, intimidad): **tenemos mucha** ~ we are close friends, we know each other very well; **no les des tanta ~ a los alumnos** don't let your pupils be so familiar with you; **estamos en** ~ we're among friends; **te lo digo en** ~ I'm telling you in confidence; **hablando en** ~ between you and me; **tratar a algn con** ~ to be friendly with sb
C **confianzas** *fpl* (libertades): **no le des tantas ~s** don't let him be so familiar with you; **¿qué ~s son ésas?** (fam) you've got some nerve! (colloq)
confianzudo -da *adj* (esp AmL fam) forward
confiar [A17] *vi* 1 (tener fe) ~ **EN algn/algo** to trust sb/sth; ~ **en Dios** to trust (in) God; **confiamos en su discreción** we rely *o* depend on your discretion 2 (estar seguro) ~ **EN algo** to be confident OF sth; ~ **EN + INF/EN QUE + SUBJ: confiamos en poder llevarlo a cabo** we are confident that we can do it; **confiemos en que venga** let's hope she comes
■ **confiar** *vt* 1 ‹*secreto*› to confide; **siempre me confía sus preocupaciones** she always tells me *o* confides in me about her worries; ~ **algo A algn** to confide sth TO sb 2 (encomendar) ‹*trabajo/responsabilidad*› to entrust; **le ~on una misión difícil** they entrusted him with a difficult mission
■ **confiarse** *v pron* 1 (hacerse ilusiones) to be overconfident; **no te confíes demasiado** don't get overconfident *o* too confident 2 (desahogarse, abrirse) **~se A algn** to confide IN sb
confidencia *f* secret, confidence (frml); **hacer una ~ a algn** to tell sb a secret
(Compuesto) **confidencias de alcoba** *fpl* intimate secrets (*pl*)
confidencial *adj* confidential
confidencialidad *f* confidentiality; **la ~ del asunto** the confidential nature of the matter
confidente *mf* 1 (amigo) (*m*) confidant; (*f*) confidante 2 (de la policía) informer
configuración *f*
A 1 (proceso) shaping 2 (forma, estructura) shape, configur-

ation (frml *or* tech); **la ~ del nuevo gabinete** the composition of the new cabinet; **la ~ del terreno** the lie of the land
B (Inf) configuration

configurar [A1] *vt* 1 (dar forma) to shape, form 2 (constituir, conformar) to make up, form
■ **configurarse** *v pron* to take shape

confín *m* (liter) 1 (lugar lejano): **en los confines del mundo** *or* **de la tierra** at the ends of the earth; **en los confines del horizonte** on the horizon 2 (límite): **los confines de una disciplina** the confines *o* bounds of a discipline 3 (frontera) border; **los confines de España y Portugal** the border between Spain and Portugal

confinamiento *m* confinement

confinar [A1] *vt* **~ a algn A algo** ‹*a hospital/a calabozo*› to put sb INTO sth; ‹*a casa*› to confine sb TO sth; ‹*a isla*› to banish sb TO sth; **la parálisis lo confinó a una silla de ruedas** he was confined to a wheelchair because of paralysis
■ **confinar** *vi*: **~ CON algo** to border WITH sth
■ **confinarse** *v pron* to shut oneself away

confirmación *f*
A (de noticia, de boleto) confirmation
B (Relig) confirmation; **hacer la ~** to be confirmed

confirmar [A1] *vt*
A ‹*noticia/vuelo*› to confirm; **esto me confirma en mis temores** this confirms my fears; **es la excepción que confirma la regla** it's the exception that proves the rule
B (Relig) to confirm

confiscación *f* confiscation

confiscar [A2] *vt* ‹*contrabando/armas*› to confiscate, seize; (para uso del estado) to requisition

confitar [A1] *vt* to crystallize

confite *m* dragée; ***estar a partir un ~*** (fam) to be as thick as thieves

confitería *f* 1 (tienda) pâtisserie, cake shop (*also selling sweets*) 2 (Bol, RPl) (salón de té) tearoom

confitero -ra *m,f* confectioner

confitura *f* preserve, jam

conflagración *f* (frml) (guerra) war

conflictividad *f* 1 (problemas) disputes (*pl*), conflicts (*pl*); **~ laboral** labor disputes (AmE), industrial disputes (BrE) 2 (cualidad de controvertido) controversial nature

conflictivo -va *adj* 1 (problemático) ‹*situación*› difficult; ‹*época*› troubled; **una zona conflictiva** a trouble spot 2 (polémico) ‹*tema/persona*› controversial 3 (AmL) (atormentado) ‹*persona*› troubled

conflicto *m* 1 (enfrentamiento) conflict; **~ de intereses** conflict of interests; **~ de ideas** clash of ideas; **estar en ~** to be in conflict; **las partes en ~** the disputing factions; **entrar en ~ con algn/algo** to come into conflict with sb/sth 2 (Psic) conflict 3 (apuro) difficult situation

Compuestos
- **conflicto armado** *or* **bélico** armed conflict
- **conflicto laboral** industrial dispute

confluencia *f* (de dos calles) junction; (de ríos) confluence; (de ideologías, corrientes) convergence

confluente *adj* ‹*ríos*› confluent; ‹*calles*› converging; ‹*ideologías*› convergent

confluir [I20] *vi* 1 ‹‹*calles/ríos*›› to converge, meet; ‹‹*corrientes/ideologías*›› to come together, merge; **todos los partidos confluyen en este punto** all the parties agree *o* concur on this point 2 ‹‹*grupos/personas*›› to congregate, come together

conformar [A1] *vt*
A (frml) 1 (constituir) to form, make up 2 ‹*carácter*› to shape
B (contentar) ‹*persona*› to satisfy
C ‹*cheque*› to authorize payment of
■ **conformarse** *v pron* 1 (contentarse) **~se CON algo** to be satisfied WITH sth; **no se conforma con nada** he's never satisfied; **no se conformó con insultarlo, sino que también le pegó** not content with insulting him, he hit him as well; **tuvo que ~se con lo que tenía** he had to make do with what he had 2 (esp AmL) (resignarse): **no tienes más remedio que ~te** you'll just have to accept it *o* to resign yourself to it; **no se puede ~** she can't get over it

conforme[1] *adj*
A [ESTAR] 1 (satisfecho) satisfied, happy; **~ CON algo/algn** satisfied *o* happy WITH sth/sb 2 (de acuerdo); **¡~!** agreed!, fine!; **entonces, ¿estamos ~s?** are we agreed, then?; **estoy ~ EN QUE se haga así** I agree that it should be done like that; **~ CON algo**: **eso no está ~ con mis ideas** that doesn't fit in with my ideas; **esto está ~ con la línea del partido** this is in keeping with the party line 3 (en regla) in order; **confirmé el vuelo, está todo ~** I confirmed the flight, everything is in order
B **conforme a** (frml) according to, in accordance with (frml); **~ a lo previsto** as predicted

conforme[2] *m* written authorization; **dar** *or* **poner el ~ a algo** to authorize sth (*by signing it*)

conforme[3] *conj* as; **~ se entra, está a mano izquierda** it's on the left as you go in

conformidad *f*
A (aprobación) consent, approval; **dio su ~** he gave his consent; **de** *or* **en ~ con** (frml) in accordance with (frml), according to
B (esp AmL) (resignación) resignation

conformismo *m* conformism

conformista *adj/mf* conformist

confort /kom'for/ *m* comfort; **apartamento todo ~** well-appointed *o* fully equipped apartment; **todo el ~ de la vida moderna** all the comforts of modern living

confortable *adj* comfortable

confortar [A1] *vt* to reassure, comfort

confraternidad *f* (sentimiento) (spirit of) fraternity; (relación) brotherhood, fraternity

confraternización *f* fraternization

confraternizar [A4] *vi* to fraternize

confrontación *f* 1 (enfrentamiento) confrontation 2 (de textos) comparison 3 (period) (Dep) game, match

confrontar [A1] *vt* 1 ‹*textos/versiones*› to compare 2 ‹*testigos/equipos*› to bring … face to face ‹*ejércitos*› to bring … into conflict; **~on sus fuerzas** they came face to face; **~ a algn CON algn** to bring sb face to face WITH sb 3 ‹*dificultad/peligro*› to confront, face; **~ la realidad** to face up to reality
■ **confrontarse** *v pron* **~se CON algo** to face up to sth

confundible *adj*: **dos conceptos fácilmente ~s** two concepts which are easily confused

confundir [I1] *vt* 1 (por error) ‹*fechas/datos*› to confuse, get … mixed *o* muddled up; ‹*personas*› to confuse, mix up; **~ algo/algn CON algo/a algn** to mistake sth/sb FOR sth/sb; **me confundió con mi hermana** he mistook me for my sister; **creo que me confunde con otra persona** I think you are confusing me with somebody else 2 (desconcertar) to confuse; **tantas cifras confunden a cualquiera** all these numbers are enough to confuse anyone 3 (turbar) to embarrass
■ **confundirse** *v pron* 1 (equivocarse): **siempre se confunde en las cuentas** he always makes mistakes in the accounts; **~se DE algo**: **me confundí de calle/casa** I got the wrong street/house 2 (mezclarse, fundirse): **se confundió entre la multitud** he disappeared into the crowd; **varios colores se confunden en el cuadro** various colors are blended together in the painting

confusión *f* 1 (desorden, caos) confusion; **para mayor ~** to add to the confusion 2 (perplejidad) confusion; **mis palabras aumentaron su ~** what I said made him more confused 3 (turbación) embarrassment 4 (equivocación) confusion; **hubo una ~ con la factura** there was a confusion over the invoice; **se presta a ~** it is open to misinterpretation; **para que no haya más confusiones** to avoid any further confusion

confusionismo *m* (confusión) confusion

confuso -sa *adj* 1 ‹*idea/texto/explicación*› confused; ‹*recuerdo*› confused, hazy; ‹*imagen*› blurred, hazy; ‹*información*› confused 2 (turbado) embarrassed, confused

conga *f*
A (Mús) conga
B (Méx) (bebida) *drink of mixed fruit juices*

congelación *f* 1 (de alimentos, agua) freezing 2 (Med) exposure; (de extremidades) frostbite; **muerte por ~** death

C

from exposure 3 (de precios, salarios, créditos) freezing; (de proyecto, negociación) suspension

congelado -da *adj* ‹*alimentos*› frozen; *ver tb* **congelar**

congelador *m* (en el refrigerador) freezer compartment; (independiente) freezer, deepfreeze

congelamiento *m* (esp AmL) ▸**congelación**

congelar [A1] *vt* 1 ‹*alimentos/agua*› to freeze 2 ‹*precios/salarios/créditos*› to freeze; ‹*proyecto*› to put ... on ice, freeze 3 (Cin, TV) ‹*imagen*› to freeze

■ **congelarse** *v pron* 1 «*agua*» to freeze; **se le congeló la sangre en las venas** the blood froze in his veins 2 «*extremidades*»: **se le congeló el pie** he got frostbite in his foot; **enciende la calefacción que me estoy congelando** put the heating on, I'm freezing!

congénere *mf*: **mis/tus/sus ~s** my/your/his kind; **el hombre y sus ~s** man and his fellow human beings

congeniar [A1] *vi* to get along (esp AmE), to get on (esp BrE); **~ CON algn** to get along *o* on WITH sb

congénito -ta *adj* congenital

congestión *f* congestion

congestionado -da *adj* 1 (Med) congested, blocked 2 ‹*cara*› flushed 3 ‹*tráfico*› congested

congestionamiento *m* congestion

congestionar [A1] *vt* 1 ‹*cara*› to make ... flushed 2 (Med) to congest

■ **congestionarse** *v pron* 1 «*cara*» to become flushed 2 (Med) to become congested *o* blocked 3 «*calle/centro*» to become congested; «*tráfico*» to come to a standstill

conglomerado *m*

A (acumulación) conglomeration

B 1 (Geol) conglomerate 2 (de madera) conglomerate 3 (de empresas) conglomerate

conglomerar [A1] *vt* to bring together

■ **conglomerarse** *v pron* to conglomerate

Congo *m*: **el ~** (país) the Congo; (río) the Congo (River) (AmE), the (River) Congo (BrE)

congoja *f* (liter) (angustia) anguish, distress; (pena) sorrow, grief

congoleño -na *adj* Congolese

congraciarse [A1] *v pron* to ingratiate oneself; **~ CON algn** to ingratiate oneself WITH sb

congratulaciones *fpl* (frml) congratulations (*pl*)

congratular [A1] *vt* (frml) to congratulate; **~ a algn POR algo** to congratulate sb ON sth

■ **congratularse** *v pron* **~se DE** *or* **POR algo** (alegrarse) to be pleased ABOUT sth, congratulate oneself ON sth (frml)

congregación *f*

A (junta) assembly, meeting

B (orden religiosa) order; (en el Vaticano) congregation

congregar [A3] *vt* to bring together; **su recital congregó a mucha gente** his recital was very well attended

■ **congregarse** *v pron* to assemble, gather

congresista (AmS) **congresal** *mf* 1 (delegado a asamblea) congress *o* conference delegate; (en congreso) conference *o* congress member 2 (Gob, Pol) (*m*) congressman, congressperson; (*f*) congresswoman, congressperson

congreso *m*

A (de profesionales, de partido político) conference, congress

B **Congreso** (Gob, Pol) 1 (asamblea) Parliament; (in US) Congress 2 (edificio) Parliament (*o* Congress *etc*) building

(Compuesto) **Congreso de los Diputados** (Esp) Chamber of Deputies (*lower chamber of Spanish Parliament*)

congrio *m* (Coc, Zool) conger eel

congruencia *f* 1 (coherencia, concordancia) coherence; **lo que dices no tiene ~** what you're saying isn't logical *o* lacks coherence; **la falta de ~ entre lo que dice y lo que hace** the lack of consistency between what he says and what he does 2 (Der, Mat) congruence

congruente *adj* 1 (coherente) coherent; **ser ~ con algo** to be consistent with sth 2 (Mat) congruent

cónico -ca *adj* ‹*pieza/forma*› conical, conic (tech); ‹*sección*› conic

conífera *f* conifer

conjetura *f* conjecture, speculation; **hacer ~s** to surmise *o* conjecture (frml); **son simples ~s** that's pure conjecture *o* speculation

conjeturar [A1] *vi* to speculate, conjecture (frml)

■ **conjeturar** *vt* to speculate on *o* about

conjugación *f* (Ling) conjugation

conjugar [A3] *vt*

A (Ling) to conjugate

B (combinar) ‹*esfuerzos*› to combine

■ **conjugarse** *v pron* to combine

conjunción *f*

A (Ling) conjunction

B (unión) combination; **en ~ con** in conjunction with

C (Astron) conjunction

conjuntar [A1] *vt*

A ‹*prendas*› to coordinate (frml)

B (reunir) ‹*esfuerzos*› to join, combine

conjuntiva *f* conjunctiva

conjuntivitis *f* conjunctivitis

conjuntivo -va *adj*

A (Anat) ‹*tejido*› connective

B (Ling) ‹*locución*› conjunctive, connecting

conjunto¹ -ta *adj* joint

conjunto² *m*

A (de objetos, obras) collection; (de personas) group; **el ~ de los magistrados ha decidido que ...** magistrates as a body *o* group have decided that ...; **en ~** as a whole; **en su ~** (referido a — obra, exposición) as a whole; (— comité, partido) as a group

(Compuestos)

- **conjunto monumental** historical monuments (*pl*)
- **conjunto residencial** residential complex *o* development

B (Mús) *tb* **~ musical** (de música clásica) ensemble; (de música popular) pop group

C (Indum) (de un pulóver y una chaqueta) twinset; (de prendas en general) outfit; **un ~ de playa** a beach outfit; **llevaba un ~ de chaqueta y pantalón** he was wearing matching jacket and trousers; **hacer ~ con algo** to go well with sth

D (Mat) set

E (totalidad): **visto en ~** *or* **en su ~** overall *o* as a whole; **debemos hacernos una visión de ~ del problema** we must get an overview of the problem

conjura, conjuración *f* conspiracy, plot

conjurado -da *m,f* conspirator

conjurar [A1] *vt* 1 ‹*peligro/amenaza*› to avert 2 ‹*demonio*› to exorcise

■ **conjurar** *vi* to conspire, plot

■ **conjurarse** *v pron* to conspire; **los elementos se habían conjurado contra nosotros** the elements had conspired against us

conjuro *m* (fórmula mágica) spell; (poder sugestivo) (liter *o* hum) magic (hum)

conllevar [A1] *vt*

A (*en 3ª pers*) (comportar, implicar) to entail; **las responsabilidades que conlleva la paternidad** the responsibilities involved with *o* that go with being a parent; **una tarea que conlleva serias dificultades** a task which is fraught with serious difficulties

B ‹*desgracia/enfermedad*› to bear

■ **conllevar** *vi* (Ven) **~ A algo** to lead TO sth

conmemoración *f* 1 (recuerdo) commemoration; **en ~ de** in remembrance of, in commemoration of 2 (ceremonia): **asistió a la ~ del centenario** he was present at the centenary celebrations

conmemorar [A1] *vt* to commemorate

conmemorativo -va *adj* commemorative; **una ceremonia conmemorativa de ...** a ceremony in commemoration of ...

conmensurable *adj* commensurable

conmigo *pron pers* with me; **no tengo las llaves ~** I don't have the keys with *o* on me; **estoy furiosa ~ misma** I'm furious with myself; **ha sido muy bueno ~** he's been very good to me

conminar [A1] *vt* **~ a algn A + INF** *or* **A QUE + SUBJ** to order sb to + INF

conminatorio -ria *adj* warning

conmiseración *f* commiseration, sympathy; **mostrar/sentir ~ por algn** to commiserate with sb

conmoción *f* [1] (Med) concussion [2] (trastorno, agitación): **el siniestro produjo una ~ en el país** the disaster left the country in a state of shock; **la noticia produjo una ~ familiar** the news shocked the whole family [3] (Geol) shock

(Compuesto) **conmoción cerebral** concussion

conmocionar [A1] *vt* to shake; **su muerte conmocionó al país** the country was shaken *o* shocked by his death

conmovedor -dora *adj* moving, touching

conmover [E9] *vt* [1] (emocionar) to move; **su discurso nos conmovió a todos** we were all moved by his speech [2] (inducir a piedad) to move … to pity; **conmovido por sus lágrimas …** moved by her tears … [3] (estremecer, sacudir) ‹*tierra/cimientos*› to shake, rock

■ **conmoverse** *v pron* [1] (enternecerse, emocionarse) to be moved [2] (estremecerse): **el país se conmovió con la noticia** the news shocked the country

conmutación *f*
A [1] (Der) commutation [2] (trueque) substitution
B (Ling) commutation

conmutador *m* (Elec) switch; (de teléfonos) (AmL) switchboard

conmutar [A1] *vt* [1] (Der) ‹*pena*› to commute; **le ~on la pena por la de cadena perpetua** his sentence was commuted to life imprisonment [2] (trocar) **~ algo POR *or* CON algo**: **es posible ~ el servicio militar por trabajos en la comunidad** it is possible to do community work instead of military service [3] (Mat) ‹*números/términos*› to commute

conmutativo -va *adj* commutative

connatural *adj* innate, inherent; **~ al hombre** inherent in man

connivencia *f* (frml) collusion, connivance; **actuar en ~ con algn** to act in collusion *o* connivance with sb

connotación *f* connotation

connotado -da *adj*
A (AmS) (destacado) ‹*político*› distinguished, eminent; ‹*músico/escritor*› famous; ‹*ciudadano*› prominent
B (Ven) ‹*bandido*› notorious

connotar [A1] *vt* to imply, connote (frml)

connubio *m* (AmL) (complicidad): **en ~ con** in league with, in cahoots with (colloq)

cono *m* [1] (figura) cone [2] (Auto) *tb* **~ de encauzamiento** *or* **de balizamiento** traffic cone

(Compuesto) **Cono Sur** Southern Cone (*Argentina, Chile, Paraguay and Uruguay*)

conocedor -dora *m,f* connoisseur, expert

conocer [E3] *vt*
A ‹*persona*› to know; (por primera vez) to meet; ‹*ciudad/país*› to know; **¿conoces a Juan?** do you know *o* have you met Juan?; **no lo conozco de nada** I don't know him at all; **te conocía de oídas** he'd heard of you; **lo conozco de nombre** I know the name; **~ a algn de vista** to know sb by sight; **es de todos conocido** he's well known; **nunca llegué a ~lo bien** I never really got to know him; **conozco muy bien a ese tipo de persona** I know that sort of person only too well; **fui a ~ a sus padres** I went to meet his parents; **conoce bien la zona** she knows the area well; **quiero que conozcas a mi novio** I want you to meet my boyfriend; (aprender cómo es) ‹*persona/ciudad*› to get to know; **¿conoces Irlanda?** do you know *o* have you been to Ireland?; **quiere ~ mundo** she wants to see the world; **me encantaría ~ tu país** I'd love to visit your country; ***más vale malo conocido que bueno por ~*** better the devil you know than the devil you don't
B (estar familiarizado con, dominar) ‹*tema/autor/obra*› to know, be familiar with; ‹*lengua*› to speak, know; **conoce muy bien su oficio** she's knows the job inside out
C [1] (saber de la existencia de) to know, know of; **no se conoce ningún remedio** there is no known cure; **ese vestido no te lo conocía** I've never seen you in that dress before; **no le conozco ningún vicio** he doesn't have any vices as far as I know; **conocían sus actividades** they knew of *o* about his activities [2] **dar a ~** (frml) ‹*noticia/resultado*› to announce; ‹*identidad/intenciones*› to reveal; **el libro que lo dio a ~ como poeta** the book which established his reputation as a poet; **darse a ~** «*persona*» to make oneself known; **intentó no darse a ~** he tried to keep his identity a secret
D (reconocer) to recognize*; **te conocí por la voz** I knew it was you by your voice
E (experimentar) ‹*crisis*› to experience; ‹*desarrollo/cambio*› to undergo; ‹*revolución*› to see
F (*impers*) (notar): **se conoce que no están en casa** they don't seem to be in; **se conoce que ya llevaba algún tiempo enfermo** apparently he'd been ill for some time
G (Der) ‹*causa/caso*› to try
H (arc) (tener trato carnal con) to know (arch)

■ **conocer** *vi*
A (saber) **~ DE algo** ‹*de tema/materia*› to know ABOUT sth
B (Der): **~ de una causa** to try a case

■ **conocerse** *v pron*
A (*recípr*) (tener cierta relación con) to know each other; (por primera vez) to meet; (aprender cómo se es) to get to know each other
B (*refl*) [1] (aprender cómo se es) to get to know oneself [2] (saber cómo se es) to know oneself
C (*enf*) (fam) (estar familiarizado con) to know; **se conoce todos los trucos** he knows all the tricks

conocido¹ -da *adj*
A (famoso) ‹*actor/cantante*› famous, well-known
B [1] ‹*cara/voz*› familiar; **su cara me resulta conocida** her face is familiar [2] ‹*hecho/nombre*› well-known; **más ~ como …** better known as …

conocido² -da *m,f* acquaintance

conocimiento *m*
A [1] (saber) knowledge [2] **conocimientos** *mpl* (nociones) knowledge; **tiene algunos ~s de inglés** he has some knowledge of English
B (frml) (información): **dar ~ de algo a algn** to inform *o* (frml) apprise sb of sth; **poner algo en ~ de algn** to inform sb of sth; **pongo en su ~ que …** (Corresp) I am writing to inform you that …; **al tener ~ del suceso** upon learning of the incident (frml); **tener ~ de algo** to be aware of sth; **llegar a ~ de algn** to come to sb's attention *o* notice (frml); ***con ~ de causa***: **obró con ~ de causa** (frml) he took this step, fully aware of what the consequences would be; **hablo con ~ de causa** I know what I'm talking about

(Compuesto) **conocimiento de embarque** bill of landing, waybill (AmE)

C (sentido) consciousness; **perder/recobrar el ~** to lose/regain consciousness; **estar sin ~** to be unconscious
D (entendimiento): **aún es pequeño, no tiene todavía ~** he's not old enough to understand

conozca, conozco, etc *see* **conocer**

conque *conj* so; **~ ya lo sabes** so now you know

conquista *f*
A (acción) [1] (de territorio, pueblo) conquest; **la ~ del espacio** the conquest of space; **ir *or* salir a la ~ de algo** to set out to conquer sth; **lanzarse a la ~ del mercado** to set out to capture the market [2] (de victoria, fama): **se lanzó a la ~ del éxito/de la medalla** she set out to achieve success/to win the medal [3] **la Conquista** (Hist) the Spanish conquest (*of America*); **la C~ de México** the conquest of Mexico
B (logro) achievement
C (fam) (amorosa) conquest; **salir de ~** to go out on the make (AmE) *o* (BrE) pickup (colloq)
D (AmS period) (Dep) goal

conquistador¹ -dora *adj* [1] ‹*ejército*› conquering [2] (fam) ‹*persona*›: **una mujer ~a** a femme fatale; **se creía de lo más ~** he fancied himself (as) a real ladykiller

conquistador² -dora *m,f* [1] (Hist) conqueror; (en la conquista de América) conquistador [2] (fam) (en el amor) (*m*) ladykiller; (*f*) femme fatale

> **Conquistadores**
>
> The collective term for the succession of explorers, soldiers and adventurers who, from the sixteenth century onward led the settlement and exploitation of Spain's Latin American colonies. Among the best known are Hernán Cortés (Mexico), Hernando de Soto (Florida, Nicaragua), the Pizarro brothers (Panama, Peru, Ecuador), Diego de Almagro (Peru, Chile) and Pedro de Valdivia (Chile)

conquistar [A1] *vt* [1] ‹*territorio/pueblo/montaña*› to conquer; ‹*mercado*› to capture [2] ‹*victoria/título*› to win;

C

C

‹éxito/fama› to achieve 3 (AmS period) ‹gol› to score 4 ‹simpatía/respeto› to win; ‹persona/público› to captivate; ‹corazón› to capture; **acabó conquistándola** he won her heart in the end

consabido -da *adj* (*delante del n*) usual; **las consabidas anécdotas** the same *o* usual old stories

consagración *f*
A (Relig) consecration
B (de monumento, tiempo, esfuerzo) dedication
C 1 (de artista, profesional): **aquel éxito contribuyó a su ~ como dramaturgo** that success helped establish him as a playwright 2 (de costumbre) establishment

consagrado -da *adj*
A (Relig) consecrated
B 1 ‹artista› acclaimed 2 ‹costumbre/procedimiento› established

consagrar [A1] *vt*
A (Relig) to consecrate
B 1 ‹monumento/edificio› **~ algo A algo/algn** to dedicate sth TO sth/sb 2 ‹vida/tiempo/esfuerzo› **~ algo A algo/algn** to dedicate *o* devote sth TO sth/sb 3 ‹programa/publicación› **~ algo A algo/algn** to devote sth TO sth/sb
C (establecer) 1 ‹artista/profesional› to establish; **la película que la consagró como actriz** the movie that established her as an actress 2 ‹costumbre› to establish
■ **consagrarse** *v pron* 1 (*refl*) (dedicarse) **~se A algo/algn** to devote oneself TO sth/sb 2 (acreditarse): **con ese triunfo se consagró (como) campeón** that triumph established her as the champion

consanguíneo[1] **-nea** *adj* blood (*before n*)

consanguíneo[2] **-nea** *m,f* blood relation

consanguinidad *f* consanguinity (frml); **parentesco por ~** kinship, blood relationship

consciencia *f* ▸**conciencia B**

consciente *adj* 1 [ESTAR] (Med) conscious 2 (de problema, hecho) **ser** *or* (Chi, Méx) **estar ~ DE algo** to be aware *o* conscious OF sth; **una persona plenamente ~ de sus actos** a person who is fully responsible for his/her actions 3 [SER] (sensato) sensible; (responsable) responsible

conscripción *f* draft, conscription

conscripto *m* (AmL) conscript

consecución *f* (frml) (de objetivo, fin): **la ~ de este contrato** the securing of this contract; **una meta de difícil ~** a difficult goal to attain *o* achieve

consecuencia *f* 1 (resultado, efecto) consequence; **tendrás que atenerte a las ~s** you'll have to accept the consequences; **esto trajo como ~ su renuncia** this resulted in his resignation; ***llevar algo hasta sus últimas ~s***: **está decidido a llevar el asunto hasta sus últimas ~s** he's prepared to see the business through to the bitter end 2 (*en locs*) **a consecuencia de** as a result of; **en consecuencia** (frml) (por consiguiente) consequently, as a result; ‹actuar/obrar› accordingly

consecuente *adj* consistent; **hay que ser ~** you have to be consistent; **trato de ser un socialista ~** I try to live according to my socialist principles; **una mujer ~ con sus ideas** a woman who acts according to her beliefs

consecuentemente *adv* 1 (por consiguiente) consequently 2 ‹obrar› according to one's beliefs/principles

consecutivo -va *adj* 1 (seguido) consecutive; **cuatro días ~s** four consecutive days 2 (Ling) consecutive

conseguido -da *adj* (esp Esp): **una película muy conseguida** a very well-made movie; **los efectos especiales están muy ~s** the special effects are very well done

conseguir [I30] *vt* 1 ‹objetivo/fin/resultado› to achieve, obtain; ‹entrada/permiso/empleo› to get; **no ~ás nada de él** you won't get anything out of him; **si lo intentas, al final lo ~ás** if you try, you'll succeed in the end; **la película consiguió un gran éxito** the film was a great success; **consiguió el primer premio** she won first prize; **consiguió la victoria** she won 2 **~ + INF** to manage to + INF; **no consigo entenderlo** I can't work it out 3 **~ QUE + SUBJ**: **vas a ~ que me enfade** you're going to get me annoyed; **al final conseguí que me dejaran pasar** I finally got them to let me through; **conseguí que me lo prestara** I got him to lend it to me
■ **conseguir** *vi* (RPl) **~ CON algn/algo** to get through TO sb/sth

consejería *f*
A (Gob, Pol) (en Esp) ministry (*in certain autonomous governments*)
B (de una embajada) department, office
C (Chi) (de empresa) directorship

consejero -ra *m,f*
A (asesor) adviser; **mi hermano es buen ~** my brother gives very sound advice
(Compuesto) **consejero matrimonial** marriage guidance counselor
B (Adm, Com) director
(Compuesto) **consejero delegado** chief executive
C (Gob, Pol) (en Esp) minister (*in certain autonomous governments*)
D (en embajada) counselor*

consejo *m*
A (recomendación) piece of advice; **te voy a dar un ~** let me give you some advice *o* a piece of advice; **me pidió ~** he asked me for advice *o* asked (for) my advice; **sus ~s son siempre acertados** she always gives good advice; **~s prácticos de limpieza** practical cleaning tips
B (organismo) council, board
(Compuestos)
- **consejo de administración** board of directors
- **consejo de estado** council of state
- **Consejo de Europa** Council of Europe
- **consejo de guerra** court-martial; **le formaron ~ de ~** he was court-martialed
- **consejo de ministros** (grupo) cabinet; (reunión) cabinet meeting; **el ~ de ~ de la CE** the Council of Ministers of the EC
- **Consejo de Seguridad** Security Council
- **consejo escolar** school board (AmE), board of governors (BrE)

consenso *m* consensus; **llegar a un ~** to reach agreement *o* a consensus; **por ~** by general consent *o* assent; **una fórmula de ~** a formula acceptable to all involved; **someter algo a ~** to put sth to the vote

consensual *adj* consensual, joint

consensuar [A1] *vt* to reach a consensus on

consentido[1] **-da** *adj* spoiled

consentido[2] **-da** *m,f*: **es un ~** he's spoiled

consentimiento *m* 1 (autorización) consent 2 **consentimientos** *mpl* (Col) (mimos) fussing

consentir [I11] *vt* 1 (permitir, tolerar) to allow; **¡no te consiento que me hables así!** I won't have you speak to me like that; **se lo consienten todo** he's allowed to do whatever he likes 2 (mimar) ‹niño› to spoil
■ **consentir** *vi*: **~ EN algo** to consent *o* agree TO sth

conserje *mf* 1 (de establecimiento público) superintendent (AmE), caretaker (BrE) 2 (de colegio) custodian (AmE), caretaker (BrE) 3 (de hotel) receptionist

conserjería *f* reception

conserva *f*: **latas de ~** cans *o* (BrE) tins of food; **fábrica de ~s** canning factory; **piña en ~** canned *o* (BrE) tinned pineapple; **~s** canned *o* tinned food

conservación *f* 1 (de alimentos) preserving 2 (Ecol) conservation 3 (de monumentos, obras de arte) preservation; **el cuadro se halla en mal estado de ~** the painting is in a bad state of repair; ▸**instinto**

conservacionismo *m* conservation

conservacionista[1] *adj* conservation (*before n*)

conservacionista[2] *mf* conservationist

conservador[1] **-dora** *adj* conservative

conservador[2] **-dora** *m,f* 1 (Pol) conservative 2 (de museo) curator

conservadurismo *m* conservatism

conservante *m* preservative

conservar [A1] *vt* 1 (mantener, preservar) ‹alimentos› to preserve; ‹sabor/calor› to retain; ‹tradiciones/costumbres› to preserve; ‹amigo/cargo› to keep; **~ la naturaleza** to conserve nature; **conservo buenos recuerdos suyos** I have good memories of him; **~ la calma/el buen humor** to keep calm/one's spirits up; **~ la línea** to keep one's figure; **conserva intactas sus facultades mentales** he is still in full possession of his mental faculties; **conserva los ideales de su juventud** she still has her youthful ideals **2** (guardar) ‹*cartas/fotografías*› to keep; **S consérvese en lugar fresco** keep *o* store in a cool place

■ **conservarse** *v pron* **1** «*alimentos*» to keep; **se conserva durante meses** it keeps for months **2** (perdurar) «*restos/tradiciones*» to survive **3** «*persona*» (+ *compl*) to keep; **se conserva ágil** she keeps herself in trim; **está muy bien conservada** she's very well preserved

conservatismo *m* (AmL) ▸**conservadurismo**

conservatorio *m* conservatory, conservatoire

conservero -ra *adj* canning (*before n*)

considerable *adj* considerable

consideración *f* **1** (atención) consideration; **sometió el tema a su ~** he put the matter to her for her consideration; **en ~ a sus méritos** in recognition of her merits; **tomar algo en ~** to take sth into consideration *o* account **2** (miramiento) consideration; **tuvo muchas consideraciones conmigo** she treated me very considerately; **la trataron sin ninguna ~** *or* **no tuvieron ninguna ~ con ella** they treated her most inconsiderately; **¡qué falta de ~!** how thoughtless!; **por ~ a su familia** out of consideration for his family **3** (importancia): **de ~** serious **4** (AmL frml) (Corresp) **De mi mayor ~** Dear Sir/Madam **5** **consideraciones** *fpl* (razonamiento) considerations (*pl*)

considerado -da *adj* [SER] considerate; **ser ~ CON algn** to be considerate TOWARD(S) sb

considerar [A1] *vt*

A **1** ‹*asunto/posibilidad/oferta*› to consider; ‹*ventajas/consecuencias*› to weigh up, consider; **considera los pros y los contras** weigh up the pros and cons; **tenemos que ~ que ...** we must take into account that ...; **considerando que ha estado enfermo** considering (that) he's been ill **2** (frml) (tratar con respeto) to show consideration for, to consider

B (frml) (juzgar, creer) (+ *compl*) to consider; **fue considerado como una provocación** it was considered (to be) provocative; **eso se considera de mala educación** that's considered bad manners; **se le considera responsable del secuestro** he is believed to be responsible for the kidnapping; **está muy bien considerado** he is very highly regarded

■ **considerarse** *v pron* «*persona*» (juzgarse) (+ *compl*) to consider oneself; **se considera afortunado** he considers himself (to be) lucky

consiga, consigas, etc *see* **conseguir**

consigna *f*

A (eslogan) slogan

B (orden) order, instruction; **cumplir/violar una ~** to carry out/disobey an order; **tenían la ~ de ...** they had orders to ...

C (para equipaje) baggage room (AmE), left-luggage (office) (BrE)

(Compuesto) **consigna automática** (coin-operated *o* automatic) luggage locker (AmE) *o* (BrE) left-luggage locker

consignación *f*

A (depósito) **1** (de mercancías) consignment **2** (Col) (de dinero) deposit **3** (Der) payment into court

B (frml) (envío) shipment, consignment (frml)

C (frml) (Fin) (asignación) allocation

consignador *m* consignor

consignar [A1] *vt*

A (depositar) **1** ‹*mercancías*› to consign **2** ‹*equipaje*› to check (AmE), to place *o* deposit ... in left luggage (BrE) **3** (Der) to pay ... into court **4** (Col) ‹*dinero/cheques*› to deposit

B (frml) ‹*hecho/dato*› to record

C (frml) (enviar) ‹*paquete/carga*› to dispatch

D (frml) (asignar) to allocate

E (Méx) (Der) ‹*presunto delincuente*› to bring ... before the authorities

consignatario -ria *m,f* **1** (Com) consignee **2** (Der) trustee **3** (destinatario) addressee

(Compuesto) **consignatario de buques** shipping agent

consigo[1] *pron pers* **1** (con él) with him; (con ella) with her; (con uno) with you *o* one; **no llevaba las llaves ~** he didn't have the keys with *o* on him; **hablaba ~ misma** she was talking to herself; **si uno no está satisfecho ~ mismo** if one is not happy with oneself **2** (con usted, ustedes) with you; **traiga/traigan ~ todo lo necesario** bring everything you'll need with you

consigo[2] *see* **conseguir**

consiguiente *adj* resulting (*before n*), consequent (*before n*) (frml); **por ~** consequently

consistencia *f* **1** (de mezcla, masa) consistency; **tomar ~** to thicken **2** (de teoría, argumento) soundness; **un argumento sin ~** a flimsy argument

consistente *adj*

A **1** ‹*salsa/líquido*› thick; ‹*masa*› solid **2** ‹*argumentación/tesis*› sound

B (Andes, Méx) ‹*conducta*› consistent; ‹*persona*› *ver* **consecuente**

C **~ EN algo** (constituido por) consisting OF sth

consistir [I1] *vi*

A (expresando composición) **~ EN algo** to consist OF sth; **en eso consistía todo su vocabulario/su capital** that was the full extent of his vocabulary/his capital

B **1** (expresando naturaleza) **~ EN algo**: **¿en qué consiste el juego?** what does the game involve?; **~ EN + INF** to involve *o* entail -ING **2** (radicar) **~ EN algo** to lie IN sth; **en eso consiste su gracia** that is what gives it its charm

consistorial *adj* **1** (Relig) consistorial **2** (del ayuntamiento) council (*before n*) ▸**casa**

consola *f*

A (mueble) console table

B **1** (panel de controles) console **2** (de órgano) console

consolación *f* ▸**premio**

consolador[1] -dora *adj* consoling, comforting

consolador[2] *m* dildo

consolar [A10] *vt* to console, comfort; **si en algo te consuela** if it's any consolation to you

■ **consolarse** *v pron* (*refl*): **no se consuela de su pérdida** he hasn't got(ten) over his loss yet; **me consuelo pensando que ...** I take comfort *o* I find some consolation in the thought that ...; **para ~me me fui de compras** I went shopping to cheer myself up

consolidación *f* **1** (de situación, acuerdo, victoria) consolidation; (de amistad, relación) strengthening **2** (Fin) consolidation

consolidar [A1] *vt*

A ‹*situación/posición/acuerdo*› to consolidate; ‹*amistad*› to strengthen

B ‹*deuda/préstamo*› to consolidate

■ **consolidarse** *v pron* «*situación/acuerdo*» to be consolidated; «*amistad/relación*» to grow stronger

consomé *m* consommé

consonancia *f* **1** (Ling, Lit) consonance **2** (Mús) harmony **3** **en consonancia con** in keeping with

consonante[1] *adj* consonant (*before n*)

consonante[2] *f* consonant

consorcio *m* consortium; **en ~ con algo/algn** in conjunction with sth/sb

consorte *mf* (frml) spouse (frml)

conspicuo -cua *adj* eminent, distinguished

conspiración *f* conspiracy, plot

conspirador -dora *m,f* conspirator

conspirar [A1] *vi* to conspire, plot

constancia *f*

A (perseverancia) perseverance

B **1** (prueba) proof; **dejar ~ DE algo** (en registro, acta) to record sth (in writing); (verbalmente) to state sth; (atestiguar) to prove sth; **este gesto deja ~ de su generosidad** this gesture is proof of his generosity; **quiero dejar ~ de mi agradecimiento** I want to express my gratitude; **no hay ~ de ello** there is no proof of it; **que quede ~ que ...** I would like the record to show that ... **2** (AmL) (documento) documentary *o* written evidence

constante[1] *adj*

A (continuo) constant

B (perseverante) ‹*persona*› persevering

constante[2] *f* **1** (Mat) constant **2** (característica) constant feature; **una ~ en su obra** a constant theme in his work; **el malhumor es una ~ en él** he's always in a bad mood **3** **constantes** *fpl* (Med) *tb* **~s vitales** vital signs (*pl*)

constar [A1] *vi*

A **1** (figurar) **~ EN algo** ‹*en acta/documento*› to be stated *o* recorded IN sth; ‹*en archivo/catálogo*› to be listed IN sth; ‹*en libro/texto*› to appear IN sth; **en el certificado no consta su edad** the certificate doesn't state her age; **y para que así conste ...** and for the record ... 2 (quedar claro): **(que) conste que yo no fui** it certainly wasn't me; **(que) conste que yo se lo advertí** I did warn her, you know; **yo nunca dije eso, que conste** just to set the record straight, I never actually said that; (+ *me/te/le etc*) **me consta que ...** I am sure that ...; **a mí no me consta** I wouldn't vouch for that (colloq) 3 **hacer ~ algo** (manifestar) to state sth; (por escrito) to register sth, to put sth on record; **hizo que ~a en acta su oposición** he asked for his opposition to be recorded in the minutes

B (estar compuesto de) **~ DE algo** to consist OF sth; **consta de tres volúmenes** it's in three volumes

constatable *adj* verifiable

constatación *f* verification

constatar [A1] *vt* 1 (notar) to verify (frml); (establecer): **pudo ~ que la muerte se había producido por asfixia** he was able to establish that death had been caused by suffocation 2 (afirmar) to state

constelación *f* constellation

consternación *f* consternation, dismay; **lo que dijo me produjo una profunda ~** I was profoundly dismayed at *o* by what he said

consternar [A1] *vt* to fill ... with dismay; **la noticia nos dejó consternados** the news filled us with dismay

■ **consternarse** *v pron* to be dismayed; **quedó consternado al oírlo** he was dismayed to hear it

constipación *f*: *tb* **~ intestinal** *or* **de vientre** constipation

constipado[1] **-da** *adj* 1 (resfriado) **está muy ~** he has a bad cold 2 (AmL) (estreñido) constipated

constipado[2] *m* cold

constiparse [A1] *v pron* to catch a cold

constitución *f*

A (establecimiento) setting-up

B (Pol) (de país) constitution

C 1 (complexión) constitution; **un hombre de ~ fuerte/débil** a man with a strong/weak constitution 2 (composición) makeup

constitucional *adj* constitutional

constitucionalidad *f* constitutionality

constitucionalizar [A4] *vt* to enshrine ... in the constitution, write ... into the constitution

constituir [I20] *vt* (frml) 1 (componer, formar) to make up, constitute (frml) 2 (ser, representar) to represent, constitute (frml); **esta acción no constituye delito** this action does not constitute a crime; **recibir este premio constituye un honor para mí** I am very honored to receive this award; **esto constituye una excepción** this is an exception 3 (crear) ‹*comisión/compañía*› to set up, establish 4 (nombrar) to name

■ **constituirse** *v pron* (frml) 1 (erigirse) **~se EN algo** to become sth 2 (reunirse) **~se EN algo** ‹*en asamblea/consejo*› to form sth, form oneself INTO sth

constitutivo -va *adj* ‹*elemento/parte*› constituent (*before n*); **hechos ~s de delito** acts which constitute a crime

constituyente[1] *adj* 1 ▸ **constitutivo** 2 ‹*asamblea/congreso*› constituent (*before n*)

constituyente[2] *m* (Der, Pol) constituent member

constreñir [I15] *vt*

A (frml) (forzar) to constrain (frml), compel; **actuó constreñido por las circunstancias** circumstances compelled him to act as he did

B (limitar) to restrict, limit; **vivo constreñido a un mísero presupuesto** I live on a very limited budget; **el espacio nos constriñe** we're limited by space

C (Med) to constrict

■ **constreñirse** *v pron* to restrict oneself; **~se en los gastos** to cut back on spending; **~se A algo** to restrict oneself TO sth

constricción *f* constriction

construcción *f*

A (acción) construction, building; **en ~** under construction; **de mala ~** poorly built; **materiales de ~** building *o* construction materials

B 1 (sector) building, construction; **la ~ naval** shipbuilding 2 (edificio, estructura) construction

C (Ling) construction

constructivismo *m* (Art, Arquit) constructivism

constructivista *adj/mf* (Art, Arquit) constructivist

constructivo -va *adj* constructive

constructor[1] **-tora** *adj* building (*before n*), construction (*before n*)

constructor[2] **-tora** *m,f* 1 (Const) builder, building contractor 2 **constructora** *f* construction company, building firm

construir [I20] *vt* 1 ‹*edificio/barco/sociedad*› to build 2 ‹*figura/frases/oraciones*› to construct

construya, etc *see* **construir**

consubstancial *adj* (frml) **~ A algn** innate IN sb (frml); **ser ~ a algo** to be an inherent characteristic of sth

consuegro -gra (*m*) *father-in-law of one's son or daughter*; (*f*) *mother-in-law of one's son or daughter*

consuelo *m* consolation, comfort; **encontrar ~ en algo/algn** to find comfort *o* consolation in sth/sb; **lloraba sin ~** she was crying inconsolably

cónsul *mf* consul

(Compuesto) **cónsul general** consul general

consulado *m* (oficina) consulate; (cargo) consulship

consular *adj* consular

consulta *f*

A (pregunta, averiguación): **¿te puedo hacer una ~?** can I ask you something?; **este problema queda pendiente de ~** this matter is awaiting consultation; **de ~** ‹*biblioteca/libro*› reference (*before n*)

(Compuesto) **consulta popular** referendum, plebiscite

B (Med) 1 (entrevista) consultation; **¿a qué horas tiene ~s el Dr. Sosa?** what are Dr Sosa's office hours (AmE) *o* (BrE) surgery times?; **Ⓢ horas de consulta** surgery hours; **~ a domicilio** home *o* house visit 2 (reunión) conference 3 (consultorio) office (AmE), practice (AmE), surgery (BrE)

consultar [A1] *vt* ‹*persona/obra*› to consult; ‹*dato/duda*› to look up; **~ algo CON algn** to consult sb ABOUT sth

■ **consultar** *vi*: **~ CON algn** to consult sb

consultivo[1] **-va** *adj* consultative

consultivo[2] *m* (Chi) meeting

consultor -tora *m,f* consultant

consultoría *f* (servicio, oficina) consultancy; (empresa) consultancy firm

(Compuesto) **consultoría de administración** *or* **gestión** management consultancy

consultorio *m* 1 (de médico, dentista) office (AmE), practice (AmE), surgery (BrE); (de abogado) office 2 (consultoría) consultancy

(Compuesto) **consultorio sentimental** (de una revista) problem page; (en la radio) phone-in (*about personal problems*)

consumación *f* (frml) 1 (de matrimonio) consummation 2 (de crimen) perpetration (frml); **impidieron la ~ del atentado/crimen** they prevented the attack from being carried out/the crime from being committed *o* perpetrated

consumado -da *adj* ‹*deportista/artista*› accomplished, consummate (frml); ‹*mentiroso*› consummate

consumar [A1] *vt* (frml) 1 ‹*matrimonio*› to consummate 2 ‹*crimen*› to commit, perpetrate (frml); ‹*robo/atentado*› to carry out

■ **consumarse** *v pron* (frml): **con este gol se consumó la victoria** this goal sealed their win; **el golpe de estado se consumó en el 78** the coup took place in 1978

consumición *f* (esp Esp) 1 (acción de consumir) consumption 2 (bebida) drink; **la ~ es de 500 pesos** drinks cost 500 pesos

(Compuesto) **consumición mínima** minimum charge

consumido -da *adj* [ESTAR] emaciated; **lo encontré ~** he looked thin and drawn; *ver tb* **consumir**

consumidor[1] **-dora** *adj* **~ DE algo**: **los países ~es de este cereal** the countries which consume this cereal

consumidor[2] **-dora** *m,f* consumer

consumir [I1] *vt*

A 1 (frml) ‹*comida/bebida*› to eat/drink, consume (frml); **no**

vamos a ~ nada we're not going to have anything to eat/drink; **consúmase en el día** eat *o* consume within one day; **consumen cantidades industriales de mermelada** (hum) they get through vast quantities of jam (colloq & hum) **2** ‹*gasolina/energía/producto*› to consume, use; ‹*tiempo*› to take up; **este coche consume ocho litros cada 100 kilómetros** this car does 100km on 8 liters of gasoline **3** ‹*salud*› to ruin

B (destruir, acabar con) **1** «*fuego/llamas*» to consume **2** «*enfermedad*»: **el cáncer lo iba consumiendo** he was wasting away with cancer **3** «*envidia/celos*»: **la envidia/los celos la consumían** he was consumed by *o* with envy/jealousy; **la ambición la consume** she is burning with ambition

C (exasperar) to exasperate

■ **consumirse** *v pron* **1** «*enfermo/anciano*» to waste away; **~se DE algo**: **se consumía de pena** she was being consumed by grief **2** «*vela/cigarrillo*» to burn down **3** «*líquido*» to reduce

consumismo *m* consumerism

consumista *adj* ‹*persona/juventud*› materialistic; **una sociedad ~** a consumer society

consumo *m* consumption; **motores de bajo ~** engines with low gas (AmE) *o* (BrE) petrol consumption; **un alto ~ de grasas animales** a high intake of animal fats

(Compuesto) **consumo mínimo** (AmL) minimum charge

consunción *f* (enfermedad) consumption; (adelgazamiento) wasting away

contabilidad *f* **1** (ciencia) accounting **2** (profesión) accountancy **3** (cuentas) accounts (*pl*), books (*pl*); **lleva la ~** she does the accounts *o* the books

contabilizar [A4] *vt* (en contabilidad) to enter; (contar) to count

contable¹ *adj* countable

contable² *mf* (Esp) accountant

contactar [A1] *vi* **~ CON algn** to contact sb, get in touch WITH sb

■ **contactar** *vt* to contact

contacto *m*

A **1** (entre dos cuerpos) contact; **estar/entrar en ~** to be in/come into contact; **hacer ~** to make contact **2** (comunicación) contact; **mantenerse en ~** to keep in touch *o* contact; **poner a algn/algo en ~ con algn/algo** to put sb/sth in touch with sb/sth; **ponerse en ~ con algn/algo** to get in touch with sb/sth **3** (entrevista, reunión) encounter

B (persona, conocido) contact

C (Auto) ignition

D (Méx) (Elec) socket, power point

contado¹ -da *adj* few; **en contadas ocasiones** on (a) very few occasions; **salimos con los minutos ~s** we left with only a few minutes to spare; **tiene los días ~s** his days are numbered

contado² *m*

A **al contado** *or* (Col) **de contado** **1** (*loc adj*) ‹*pago/precio*› cash (*before n*) **2** (*loc adv*) ‹*pagar*› (in) cash; **lo compré/pagué al ~** I paid cash for it, I paid for it in cash; **me pagó al ~** he paid me (in) cash

B (Col) (cuota, plazo) installment*

contador¹ *m* **1** (de luz, de gas) meter; (taxímetro) meter, taximeter; **leer el ~** to read the meter **2** (AmL) (ábaco) abacus

contador² -dora *m,f* (AmL) accountant

(Compuesto) **contador público, -dora pública** (AmL) certified public (AmE) *o* (BrE) chartered accountant

contaduría *f* (oficina) accounts department *o* office; (profesión) (AmL) acccountancy

contagiar [A1] *vt* **1** ‹*enfermedad*› (+ *me/te/le etc*) to pass on, transmit (tech); **me contagió su miedo** he got me scared as well **2** ‹*persona*›: **note acerques que te voy a ~** don't come near or I'll give it to you; **~on al resto de la población** they spread the disease to the rest of the population

■ **contagiarse** *v pron* **1** «*persona/animal*» to become infected; **se ha contagiado de mí** she has caught it from me; **~se DE algo**: **se contagió de la enfermedad** she caught the disease; **se ~on de su alegría** they were infected by his cheerfulness **2** «*enfermedad*» to be transmitted; «*manía/miedo*» to spread; **se contagia con facilidad** it is very contagious

contagio *m* (por contacto directo) contagion; (por contacto indirecto) infection

contagioso -sa *adj* **1** (por contacto — directo) contagious; (— indirecto) infectious **2** ‹*risa/alegría*› infectious

container /kon'tejner/ *m* (*pl* **-ners**) container

contaminación *f* **1** (del mar, aire) pollution; (de agua potable, comida) contamination; (por radiactividad) contamination **2** (de lengua, cultura) corruption

(Compuesto) **contaminación acústica** noise pollution

contaminante *m* pollutant, contaminant

contaminar [A1] *vt* **1** ‹*mar/atmósfera*› to pollute; ‹*agua potable/comida*› to contaminate; (por radiactividad) to contaminate **2** ‹*lengua/cultura*› to corrupt

contante *adj*: **dinero ~ y sonante** hard cash

contar [A10] *vt*

(Sentido I)

A ‹*dinero/votos/dís*› to count; **a ~ desde hoy** starting from today; **sus seguidores se cuentan por millares** she has thousands of followers

B **1** (incluir) to count; **y eso sin ~ las horas extras** and that's without including overtime; **lo cuento entre mis amigos** I consider him (to be) one of my friends **2** (tener): **contaba ya veinte años** (frml *o* liter) she was then twenty years old

(Sentido II) ‹*cuento/chiste/secreto*› to tell; **no se lo cuentes a nadie** don't tell anyone; **cuéntame qué es de tu vida** tell me what you've been up to (colloq); **¡a mí me lo vas a ~!** (fam) you're telling me!; **¿y a a mí qué me cuentas?** what's that to do with me?; **es muy largo de ~** it's a long story; **un minuto más y no lo cuento** one more minute and I wouldn't be here to tell the tale; **¿qué cuentas (de nuevo)?** (fam) how're things? (colloq); **cuenta la leyenda que...** the story goes that...

■ **contar** *vi*

(Sentido I)

A (Mat) to count; **cuenta de diez en diez** count in tens; **hay cuatro tiendas ... y para de ~** there are four stores and that's it; **~ con los dedos** to count on one's fingers

B (importar, valer) to count; **¿este trabajo cuenta para la nota final?** does this piece of work count toward(s) the final grade?; **este ejercicio cuenta por dos** this exercise counts as two; **lo que cuenta es el gesto** it's the thought that counts; **ella no cuenta para nada** what she says (*o* thinks *etc*) doesn't count for anything

(Sentido II) **contar con**

A ‹*persona/ayuda/discreción*› to count on, rely on; **cuento contigo para la fiesta** I'm counting *o* relying on you being at the party; **no cuentes conmigo para mañana** don't expect me there tomorrow; **yo me opongo, así es que no cuentes conmigo** I'm against it, so you can count me out; **cuenta con que iré** rest assured that I'll be going; **eso contando con que...** assuming that...; **sin ~ con que...** without taking into account that...

B (prever) to expect; **no contaba con que hiciera tan mal tiempo** I wasn't expecting the weather to be so bad

C (frml) (tener) to have; **el hotel cuenta con gimnasio y sauna** the hotel has a gym and a sauna; **cuenta con 10 años de experiencia** she has 10 years of experience

■ **contarse** *v pron* **1** (frml) (estar incluido) **~se ENTRE algo**: **se cuenta entre los pocos que tienen acceso** she is numbered among the few who have access (frml); **me cuento entre sus partidarios** I count myself as one of their supporters; **su nombre se cuenta entre los finalistas** her name figures *o* appears among the finalists; **su novela se cuenta entre las mejores** his novel is among the best **2** **¿qué te cuentas?** how's it going? (colloq)

contemplación *f*

A (observación) contemplation

B **contemplaciones** *fpl* (miramientos): **no te andes con contemplaciones** don't bother with the niceties; **tienes demasiadas contemplaciones con él** you're too soft on him; **lo echaron sin contemplaciones** they threw him out without ceremony

contemplar [A1] *vt*

A **1** ‹*paisaje/cuadro*› to gaze at, contemplate; **a la izquierda pueden ~ el Palacio Real** on the left you can see the Royal Palace **2** ‹*obra/artista*› to examine, study **3** ‹*posibilidad/idea*› to consider; **la nueva propuesta contempla**

un aumento del 5% the new proposal envisages the possibility of a 5% rise; **la legislación no contempla este caso** there is no provision for a situation of this kind in the legislation; **no tengo contemplado ir** I'm not thinking of going
B (Esp) (mimar) to spoil

contemplativo -va *adj* contemplative

contemporáneo[1] **-nea** *adj* 1 (coetáneo) contemporary; **ser ~ DE algn** to be a contemporary OF sb, be contemporary WITH sb 2 ‹*historia/arte*› contemporary

contemporáneo[2] **-nea** *m,f* contemporary

contemporizador -dora *adj* accommodating; **~ CON algo/algn** accommodating TOWARD(s) sth/sb

contemporizar [A4] *vi* to be accommodating; **~ CON algn** to be accommodating TOWARD(s) sb

contención *f* (de gastos, precios): **la ~ del desempleo/del gasto público es nuestro objetivo** our aim is to contain unemployment/to limit public spending

contencioso[1] **-sa** *adj* 1 ‹*persona*› contentious 2 (Der) litigious

contencioso[2] *m* dispute

contender [E8] *vi* to compete, fight; **~ en unas elecciones** to fight an election

contendiente *mf* (para título, premio) contender; (en duelo, combate) adversary

contenedor *m* container; (para basuras) bin, container; (para escombros) Dumpster® (AmE), skip (BrE); **~ de recogida de vidrio** bottle bank

contener [E27] *vt*
A «*recipiente/producto/libro*» to contain
B (parar, controlar) ‹*infección/epidemia*› to contain; ‹*tendencia*› to curb; ‹*movimiento político*› to keep...in check; ‹*respiración*› to hold; ‹*risa/lágrimas*› to contain (frml), to hold back; ‹*invasión/revuelta*› to contain; **dejó estallar toda su furia contenida** he let out all his pent up *o* bottled up anger
■ **contenerse** *v pron* (*refl*) to contain oneself; **no me pude ~ y me eché a llorar** I couldn't contain myself and I burst into tears; **tuve que ~me para no insultarlo** I had to control myself to stop myself insulting him

contenido[1] **-da** *adj* self-controlled; *ver tb* **contener**

contenido[2] *m* (de recipiente, producto, mezcla) contents; (de libro, carta) content; **S contenido: 20 grageas** contents: 20 tablets; **~ vitamínico** vitamin content

contentar [A1] *vt*: **¡qué difícil de ~ eres!** you're so hard to please!; **pretenden ~nos con promesas** they're trying to keep us happy with promises
■ **contentarse** *v pron* **~se CON algo**: **se contenta con muy poco** he's easy to please; **no se contenta con nada** she's never satisfied with anything; **vas a tener que ~te con jugo de naranja** you'll have to make do with orange juice; **no se contentó con gritarle, además tuvo que insultarlo** not content with shouting at him, she then had to insult him; **me ~ía con que me llamase** I'd be happy if she just called me

contento[1] **-ta** *adj* 1 [ESTAR] (feliz, alegre) happy; **se puso muy ~ al oír que venías** he was very happy *o* pleased to hear you were coming; **~ CON algo/algn** happy WITH sth/sb 2 (satisfecho) happy, content; **~ CON algo** happy WITH sth; **no ~ con que le prestara el coche ...** not content *o* satisfied with me lending him the car ...; ***darse por ~*** to consider *o* count oneself lucky; ***quedarse tan ~*** (fam); **lo dijo mal y se quedó tan ~** he said it wrong but he wasn't in the least bit bothered (colloq)

contento[2] *m* (liter) happiness, joy; **dar muestras de ~** to show delight; **no cabía en sí de ~** he was beside himself with joy

conteo *m* (Andes, Ven) count

contertulio -lia *m,f*: *member of the same* **tertulia**

contestación *f*
A (respuesta) answer, reply; **dar una ~** to give an answer; **quedo a la espera de su ~** (Corresp) I look forward to (receiving) your reply
B (oposición) opposition; **~ A algo** opposition TO sth
C (Der) plea

contestado -da *adj* disputed, controversial

contestador[1] **-dora** *adj* (CS fam) fresh (AmE colloq), cheeky (BrE colloq); **es muy ~** he's always answering back

contestador[2] **-dora** *m,f*
A (CS fam) nervy *o* mouthy brat (AmE colloq), cheeky brat (BrE colloq)
B 1 **contestador** *m* (Tel) *tb* **~ automático** answering machine, answerphone 2 **contestadora** *f* (AmL) (Tel) *tb* **~a automática** *or* **de teléfonos** answering machine, answerphone

contestar [A1] *vt* ‹*pregunta/teléfono*› to answer; ‹*carta*› to answer, reply to; **me contestó que no** he said no
■ **contestar** *vi* 1 (a pregunta, al teléfono) to answer; (a carta, a invitación) to answer, reply; **no contesta nadie** (Telec) there's no answer; **contéstale antes del lunes** let him have an answer by Monday 2 (insolentarse) to answer back

contestatario[1] **-ria** *adj* anti-establishment

contestatario[2] **-ria** *m,f* person with anti-establishment ideas

contestón -tona *adj* (fam): **es muy ~** he's always answering back

contexto *m* context; **fuera de ~** out of context

contextura *f* (frml) (estructura) make-up

contienda *f* (entre países, facciones) conflict; (entre compañías, equipos) competition; (entre partidos políticos) contest

contigo *pron pers* with you; **¿puedo ir ~?** can I go with you?; **¿estás en paz ~ misma?** are you at peace with yourself?; **ha sido muy amable ~** she's been very kind to you

contigüidad *f* nearness, closeness

contiguo -gua *adj* adjoining

continencia *f* continence

continental *adj* continental

continente *m*
A (Geog) continent
B (envase, envoltura) container

contingencia *f* contingency, eventuality

contingente *m*
A (grupo, cuadrilla) contingent
B (cuota, cupo) quota

continuación *f*
A 1 (acción) continuation; **la lluvia impidió la ~ del espectáculo** rain made it impossible for the show to continue 2 (de calle) continuation 3 (de novela) sequel; (de serie) next part *o* episode
B **a continuación** (frml): **por los motivos que se exponen a ~** for the reasons stated below; **a ~ pasamos a la actualidad internacional** and now the foreign news; **a ~ hizo uso de la palabra el presidente** the president then addressed the meeting; **a ~ de** after, following

continuado *m* (CS) movie theater (AmE) *o* (BrE) cinema (*with continuous performances*)

continuador -dora *m,f*: **los ~es de su obra** those who will carry on/who continued his work

continuamente *adv* (con frecuencia, repetidamente) continually, constantly; (sin interrupción) continuously

continuar [A18] *vt* to continue; **continuemos la marcha** let's go on *o* carry on
■ **continuar** *vi* 1 «*guerra/espectáculo/vida*» to continue; **si las cosas continúan así** if things go on *o* continue like this; **S continuará** to be continued; **la película continúa en cartelera** the movie is still showing; **~ CON algo** to continue WITH sth; **~ + GER: su estado continúa siendo delicado** he is still in a weak condition; **continúa negándose a declarar** she is still refusing to make a statement; **continuó diciendo que ...** she went on to say that ... 2 «*carretera*» to continue
■ **continuarse** *v pron* (frml) to continue; **el camino se continúa en un sendero** the road continues as a path; **su obra se continuó en sus discípulos** his work was continued by his disciples

continuidad *f* continuity

continuo[1] **-nua** *adj* 1 (sin interrupción) ‹*dolor*› constant; ‹*movimiento/sonido*› continuous, constant; ‹*lucha*› continual 2 (frecuente) ‹*llamadas/viajes*› continual, constant 3 **de continuo** ▸ **continuamente**

continuo[2], **continuum** *m* (frml) continuum

contonearse [A1] *v pron* to swing one's hips

contoneo *m* swinging of the hips

contorno *m* 1 (forma) outline 2 (de árbol, columna) girth; **medir el ~ de cintura** to take the waist measurement 3 (de ciudad) surrounding area

contorsión *f* contortion; **hacer contorsiones** to contort one's body

contorsionista *mf* contortionist

contra[1] *prep*

A 1 (indicando posición, dirección) against; **lo puso ~ la pared/la ventana** he put it against the wall/by the window; **nos estrellamos ~ un árbol** we crashed into a tree 2 (con sentido de oposición) against; **dos ~ uno** two against one; **la lucha ~ la tiranía** the struggle against tyranny; **una vacuna ~ la gripe** a flu *o* an anti-flu vaccine; **una política ~ el paro** a policy to combat unemployment 3 (*en locs*) **en contra** against; **yo estoy en ~** I'm against it; **40 votos en ~** 40 votes against; **un gol en ~** (RPl) an own goal; **en contra de** (opuesto a) against; (contrariamente a) contrary to; **está en ~ de mis principios** it's against my principles; **en ~ de la opinión general** contrary to what everybody thinks

B 1 (Fin): **un cheque girado ~ el Banco de Pando** a check drawn on the Banco de Pando 2 (Com) (a cambio de): **envíos ~ reembolso** parcels sent cash on delivery

contra[2] *f*

A (esp AmL fam) (dificultad) snag; **llevar la ~** ▸**contrario**[1] **C**

B (Col) (antídoto) antidote

C (Pol, Hist) 1 (grupo): **la ~** the Contras (*pl*) 2 **contra** *mf* (individuo) Contra rebel

contra[3] *m* ▸**pro**[1]

contraalmirante *m* rear admiral

contraatacar [A2] *vi* to counterattack

contraataque *m* counterattack

contrabajo[1] *m* (instrumento) double bass; (cantante) basso profundo

contrabajo[2] *mf* double-bass player

contrabandista *mf* smuggler

contrabando *m* 1 (actividad) smuggling; **~ de armas** gunrunning; **pasaba relojes de ~** he smuggled watches 2 (mercancías) smuggled goods (*pl*), contraband

contracción *f* contraction

contracepción *f* contraception

contraceptivo *m* contraceptive

contrachapado *m* plywood

contracorriente *f* crosscurrent; ***ir a ~*** ⟨⟨*barco*⟩⟩ to go against the current; ⟨⟨*nadador*⟩⟩ to swim against the current; ⟨⟨*diseñador/escritor*⟩⟩ to go *o* swim against the tide

contráctil *adj* contractile

contractual *adj* contractual

contracubierta *f* back cover

contracultural *adj* alternative

contradecir [I24] *vt* ⟨*persona/argumento*⟩ to contradict; **no le gusta que lo contradigan** he doesn't like being *o* to be contradicted

■ **contradecirse** *v pron* 1 ⟨⟨*persona*⟩⟩ to contradict oneself 2 (*recípr*) ⟨⟨*afirmaciones/órdenes*⟩⟩ to contradict each other, be contradictory; **~se CON algo** to conflict WITH sth, contradict sth

contradicción *f* contradiction; **eso está en ~ con lo que predica** that is a contradiction of what he advocates

contradictorio -ria *adj* contradictory

contraer [E23] *vt*

A (frml) 1 ⟨*enfermedad*⟩ to contract (frml), to catch 2 ⟨*obligación/deudas*⟩ to contract (frml); ⟨*compromiso*⟩ to make 3 ⟨*matrimonio*⟩: **contrajo matrimonio con doña Eva Sáenz** he married *o* (frml) contracted (a) marriage with Eva Sáenz

B 1 ⟨*músculo*⟩ to contract, tighten; ⟨*facciones/cara*⟩ to contort 2 ⟨*metal/material*⟩ to cause … to contract

■ **contraerse** *v pron* to contract

contraespionaje *m* counterespionage

contrafuerte *m* (Arquit) buttress

contragolpe *m* counterattack

contragolpear [A1] *vi* to counterattack

contrahecho -cha *adj* (deforme) twisted, deformed

contraincendios *adj inv* fire-prevention (*before n*)

contraindicación *f* contraindication

contraindicado -da *adj* ⟨*remedio/preparado*⟩ contraindicated (tech); **está ~ en pacientes diabéticos** it should not be taken by diabetics

contralmirante *m* rear admiral

contralor -lora *m,f* (AmL) comptroller

contraloría *f* (AmL) finance office

contralto (*f*) (en coro) alto; (solista) contralto; (*m*) countertenor

contraluz *m or f* back light; **a ~** against the light

contramaestre *m* boatswain

contramano: **el coche venía a ~** (en calle de dirección única) the car was coming the wrong way down the street; (por el lado contrario) the car was on the wrong side of the road

contraofensiva *f* counteroffensive

contraoferta *f* counteroffer

contraorden *f* countermand (frml); **si no hay ~** unless we receive orders to the contrary

contraparte *f* (Andes) opposing party

contrapartida *f* 1 (compensación) compensation; (contraste) contrast; **como ~** in contrast 2 (Com) balancing entry

contrapelo: **cepillar a ~** ⟨*tela*⟩ to brush … against the nap; ⟨*pelo*⟩ to brush … the wrong way; **ir a ~** ⟨⟨*persona*⟩⟩ to be different

contrapeso *m* (del ascensor) counterweight; (de equilibrista) balancing pole; **siéntate al otro lado para hacer ~** sit on the other side to balance it

contraponer [E22] *vt* (contrastar) to contrast; (como contrapartida) **~ algo A algo** to counter sth WITH sth

contraportada *f* (de libro, revista) back cover; (de periódico) back page

contraposición *f* comparison; **en ~ a** *or* **con algo** in comparison to *o* with sth

contraproducente *adj* counterproductive

contrapuerta *f* inner door

contrapuesto -ta *adj*: *see* **contraponer**

contrapunto *m* counterpoint

contrariado -da *adj* (disgustado) upset; (enojado) annoyed

contrariamente *adv* **~ A algo** contrary TO sth

contrariar [A17] *vt* (disgustar) to upset; (enojar) to annoy

contrariedad *f* 1 (dificultad, problema) setback, hitch; **una serie de ~es** a succession of hitches *o* setbacks; **nos surgió una ~** something came up; **¡qué ~!** how annoying! 2 (disgusto) annoyance, vexation (frml)

contrario[1] **-ria** *adj*

A (opuesto) ⟨*opiniones/intereses*⟩ conflicting; ⟨*dirección*⟩ opposite; **vientos ~s** headwinds; **mientras no se demuestre lo ~** until proven otherwise; **~ A algo**: **mi opinión es contraria a la suya** I feel very differently to you; **soy ~ al uso de la violencia** I am against the use of violence; **se manifestó ~ a la idea** she expressed her opposition to the idea; **sería ~ a mis intereses** it would be against *o* (frml) contrary to my interests; **~ a lo que se esperaba ...** contrary to expectations, …; **en sentido ~ al de las agujas del reloj** counterclockwise (AmE), anticlockwise (BrE); **el coche venía en sentido ~** (por el otro carril) the car was coming in the opposite direction; (por el mismo carril) the car was coming straight at us

B (adversario) ⟨*equipo*⟩ opposing; ⟨*bando*⟩ opposite; **pasarse al bando ~** to change sides; **la parte contraria** (Der) the opposing party

C (*en locs*) **al contrario** on the contrary; **al contrario de**: **al ~ de su hermano ...** unlike his brother, …; **al ~ de lo que esperábamos, ...** contrary to (our) expectations, …; **todo salió al ~ de como lo planearon** it turned out just the opposite to what they had planned; **de lo contrario** or else, otherwise; **por el contrario**: **en el sur, por el ~, el clima es seco** the south, on the other hand, has a dry climate; **pensé que era rico — por el ~, no tiene un peso** I thought he was rich — on the contrary *o* far from it, he doesn't have a penny; **todo lo contrario** quite the opposite; ***llevar la contraria***: **él siempre tiene que llevar la contraria** he always has to take the opposite view; **llevarle la contraria a algn** to contradict sb

contrario[2] **-ria** *m,f* opponent

C

contrarreloj *adj* ‹*carrera/etapa*› timed; **a ~** (*loc adv*) against the clock

contrarrestar [A1] *vt* to counteract

contrarrevolución *f* counterrevolution

contrarrevolucionario -ria *adj* counterrevolutionary

contrasentido *m* contradiction in terms

contraseña *f* (Mil) watchword, password; (Teatr, Cin) stub

contrastar [A1] *vi* **~ CON algo** to contrast WITH sth

■ **contrastar** *vt*

A (colocar en contraste) to contrast; **~ algo CON algo** to contrast sth WITH sth

B ‹*oro/plata*› to hallmark; ‹*pesas/medidas*› to check

contraste *m*

A (relación, aspecto) contrast; **dale más ~ a la imagen** (TV) turn the contrast up; **hacer ~ con algo** to contrast with sth; **en ~ con algo** in contrast to sth

B 1 (marca) *tb* **sello del ~** hallmark 2 (acción) hallmarking 3 (de pesas) verification

contrata *f* contract

contratación *f* 1 (de personal, servicio) contracting, hiring 2 (en la bolsa) transactions (*pl*), trading

contratante *adj* contracting (*before n*)

contratar [A1] *vt* 1 ‹*empleado/obrero*› to hire, take on; ‹*artista/deportista*› to sign up; ‹*servicios*› to contract; **me ~on para terminarlo** I was taken on *o* hired to finish it 2 (Const) ‹*ejecución de una obra*› to put ... out to contract

contratenor *m* countertenor

contratiempo *m* (problema) setback, hitch; (accidente) mishap; **sufrir** *or* **tener un ~** to have a setback/a mishap

contratista *mf* contractor; **~ de obras** building contractor

contrato *m* contract

(Compuestos)

- **contrato de alquiler** rental agreement
- **contrato de compraventa** contract of sale and purchase
- **contrato de trabajo** contract of employment

contravalor *m* exchange value

contravención *f* contravention; **en ~ de algo** in contravention *o* violation of sth; **estacionar en ~** (RPl) to park illegally

contravenir [I31] *vt* to contravene

contraventana *f* shutter

contravía (Col): **ir en ~** to drive the wrong way down the road; **se estrellaron con un carro que venía en ~** they crashed into an oncoming car

contrayente (frml) (*m*) bridegroom; (*f*) bride

contribución *f* (colaboración, donación) contribution; (Fisco) tax

(Compuesto) **contribución (territorial) urbana** local property tax, ≈ council tax (*in UK*)

contribuir [I20] *vi* 1 (aportar) to contribute; **~ CON algo** to contribute sth 2 (cooperar) to contribute; **~ A algo** to contribute TO sth; **esto sólo contribuye a empeorar la situación** this only makes the situation worse 3 (Fisco) to pay taxes

contribuyente *mf* taxpayer

contrición *f* contrition

contrincante *mf* opponent

contrito -ta *adj* contrite

control *m*

A (dominio) control; **bajo ~** under control; **sin ~** out of control; **perdí el ~ y le di una bofetada** I lost control (of myself) and slapped him; **tener ~ sobre uno mismo** to have self-control; **hacerse con el ~ de algo** to gain control of sth

(Compuestos)

- **control de armamentos** arms control
- **control de (la) natalidad** birth control
- **control demográfico** population control

B (vigilancia): **lleva el ~ de los gastos** she keeps a check on the money that is spent; **no hay ningún ~ en esta oficina** there's no one in charge in this office

(Compuestos)

- **control de calidad** quality control *o* check
- **control de existencias** stock control
- **control de pasaportes** passport control
- **control de precios** price control(s)

C (en carretera, rally) checkpoint

D 1 (de aparato) control; **el ~ del volumen** the volume control 2 **controles** *mpl* (Rad): **con Martín en los ~es** with studio production by Martín

(Compuesto) **control remoto** remote control; **a** *or* **por ~ ~** by remote control

E 1 (Educ) test 2 (Med) check-up

(Compuesto) **control antidoping** dope test, drug test

controlador -dora *m,f* controller

(Compuesto) **controlador aéreo** *or* **de vuelo, -dora aérea** *or* **de vuelo** air traffic controller

controlar [A1] *vt*

A (dominar) ‹*nervios/impulsos/persona*› to control; **controlamos la situación** we are in control of the situation; **el incendio fue rápidamente controlado** the fire was quickly brought under control; **pasaron a ~ la empresa** they took control of the company

B (vigilar) ‹*inflación/proceso*› to monitor; **~ el peso/la línea** to watch one's weight/one's waistline; **deja de ~ todos mis gastos** stop checking up on how much I spend; **me tienen muy controlada** they keep a close watch on me; **~ las entradas y salidas** to keep a check on everyone who comes in or out; **controlé el tiempo que me llevó** I timed how long it took me

C (regular) ‹*presión/inflación*› to control

■ **controlarse** *v pron*

A (dominarse) to control oneself; **si no se controla acabará alcoholizado** if he doesn't get a grip on himself he's going to become an alcoholic

B (vigilar) ‹*peso/colesterol*› to check, monitor

controversia *f* controversy

controversial *adj* (Ven) ▸**controvertido**

controvertido -da *adj* [SER] ‹*persona/tema*› controversial; ‹*negociaciones*› full of controversy

controvertir [I11] *vt* to debate, argue about

■ **controvertir** *vi*: **~ SOBRE algo** to discuss sth, argue ABOUT sth

contubernio *m* (frml) conspiracy

contumacia *f* (frml) (obstinación) obstinacy, contumacy

contumaz *adj* (frml) 1 (obstinado) obstinate 2 (Der) in contempt (of court)

contundencia *f* 1 (de argumento) force, forcefulness 2 (de golpe) severity, force

contundente *adj* 1 ‹*objeto/instrumento*› blunt; ‹*golpe*› severe, heavy 2 ‹*argumento/respuesta*› forceful; ‹*prueba*› convincing; ‹*victoria*› resounding; ‹*fracaso*› crushing; **ganó de forma ~** he won convincingly; **un ademán ~** an emphatic gesture; **fue ~ en sus declaraciones** he was categorical in his statements

conturbar [A1] *vt* to perturb

■ **conturbarse** *v pron* to be perturbed

contusión *f* (frml) contusion (frml), bruise

contusionar [A1] *vt* to bruise

contuso -sa *adj* (frml) bruised

conuco *m* (Ven) smallholding

conurbano *m* (Arg): **el ~** the suburbs (*pl*)

convalecencia *f* convalescence

convalecer [E3] *vi* to convalesce; **~ de una intervención quirúrgica** to convalesce after an operation

convaleciente *adj* convalescent

convalidable *adv* which can be validated

convalidación *f* validation; **obtener la ~ de un título** to have one's degree validated

convalidar [A1] *vt* ‹*estudios/título*› to validate, recognize; **le ~on muchas asignaturas** they accepted *o* recognized many of the subjects he had already passed

convección *f* convection

convector *m* convector

convencer [E2] *vt*

A 1 (de hecho, idea) to convince; **no se dejó ~** she wouldn't be convinced *o* persuaded; **~ a algn DE algo** to convince

sb OF sth; **no logré ~lo de lo contrario** I couldn't persuade him otherwise; **el artículo me convenció de que era verdad** the article convinced me that it was true **2** (para hacer algo) to persuade; **yo no quería ir pero mi hermana me convenció** I didn't want to go but my sister persuaded me to; **~ a algn PARA** *or* **DE QUE + SUBJ** to persuade sb to + INF; **no pude ~lo de que me prestara dinero** I couldn't persuade him to lend me any money
B (*en frases negativas*) (satisfacer): **no me convence del todo la idea** I'm not absolutely sure about the idea; **su explicación no convenció a nadie** his explanation wasn't at all convincing; **ninguno de los diseños me convence demasiado** I'm not really sure about any of the designs; **no me convence como actriz** I don't think she's a very good actress
■ **convencerse** *v pron*: **se lo han dicho pero no se convence** he's been told but he won't be convinced; **¡convéncete, estás equivocado!** believe me, you're wrong!; **~se DE algo** to accept sth; **¿te convences de que tenía razón?** do you believe *o* accept I was right?

convencimiento *m* **~ DE algo**: **tengo el ~ de que ...** I'm convinced (that) ...; **llegué al ~ de que...** I became convinced that...

convención *f* convention; **la C~ de Ginebra** the Geneva Convention; **las convenciones sociales** social conventions

convencional *adj* conventional; **viste de manera ~** he dresses conventionally

convencionalismo *m* conventionality

convenenciero -ra *m,f* (Méx fam) user (colloq)

convenible *adj* ‹*solución*› suitable; ‹*precio*› reasonable

conveniencia *f*
A (interés, provecho): **sólo piensa en su ~ personal** he only thinks of his own interests; **lo hizo por ~** she only did it because it was in her own interest; **se casó por ~** he made *o* it was a marriage of convenience
B (de proyecto, acción) advisability

conveniente *adj* **1** (cómodo) convenient; **lo que le resulte más ~** whatever is more convenient for you **2** (aconsejable, provechoso) advisable; **sería ~ que guardaras cama** it would be advisable for you to stay in bed

convenientemente *adv*
A **1** (ventajosamente) conveniently; **está ~ situado** it's conveniently situated **2** (para la propia conveniencia) conveniently; **había sido ~ olvidado** it had been conveniently forgotten
B (debidamente) duly; **el documento debe ir ~ firmado** the document must be duly signed

convenio *m* agreement
(Compuesto) **convenio colectivo** *or* **laboral** collective agreement (*on wages and working conditions*)

convenir [I31] *vi*
A **1** (ser aconsejable): **no conviene beber alcohol durante el tratamiento** it is not advisable to drink alcohol during the treatment; **no conviene que nos vean juntos** we'd better not be seen together; **convendría que descansaras** it would be a good idea if you rest; (+ *me/te/le etc*) **te conviene hacer lo que te dicen** you'd better do as you're told; **por ese precio no te conviene venderlo** it's not worth your while selling it at that price; **no le conviene que eso se sepa** it's not in his interest for anybody to know that; **ese hombre no te conviene** that man isn't right for you **2** (venir bien) (+ *me/te/le etc*): **el jueves no me conviene** Thursday's no good for me; **te convendría tomarte unas vacaciones** it would do you good to take a vacation
B **1** (acordar) **~ EN algo** ‹*en fecha, precio*› to agree (ON) sth; **convinieron en que esperarían** *or* **en esperar un mes** they agreed to wait a month **2** (asentir, admitir) (frml) **~ EN algo** to concede sth, to admit sth
■ **convenir** *vt* ‹*precio/fecha*› to agree, agree on; **a la hora convenida** at the agreed *o* (frml) appointed time; **le pagó lo convenido** she paid him the agreed amount; **sueldo a ~** salary negotiable

conventillero -ra *m,f* (CS fam) gossip, gossipmonger

conventillo *m* (CS) tenement; **esta oficina es un ~** (fam) this office is a hotbed of gossip

convento *m* convent

conventual *adj* conventual

convergencia *f* **1** (Fís, Mat) convergence **2** (de ideas, posturas): **hay indicios de ~ entre ambas partes** there are signs that the two sides are moving closer together **3** (Econ) convergence

convergente *adj* convergent

converger [E6], **convergir** [I7] *vi* (frml) **1** «*líneas/caminos*» to converge; **todas las miradas convergen sobre nuestro país** all eyes are on our country **2** «*opiniones*» **~ EN algo** to coincide ON sth; «*personas*» **~ EN algo** to concur ON sth (frml)

conversa *f* (Andes fam) chat (colloq)

conversación *f* **1** (charla) conversation; **dar ~ a algn** to talk to sb; **trabar ~ con algn** to strike up a conversation with sb; **me las encontré de gran ~** (AmL) I found them chatting away **2** (arte) conversation; **es una persona de ~ amena** he's always very nice to talk to; **no tiene ~** she has no conversation **3** **conversaciones** *fpl* (negociaciones) talks (*pl*)

conversador¹ -dora *adj* **1** (de conversación amena) chatty; **hoy no estoy muy ~** I'm not feeling very talkative *o* chatty today **2** (AmL pey) (charlatán) talkative

conversador² -dora *m,f* **1** conversationalist **2** (AmL pey) (charlatán) chatterbox (colloq)

conversar [A1] *vi* **1** (hablar) to talk **2** (esp AmL) (charlar) to chat, gab (AmE colloq); **conversé largo rato con ella** I had a long chat *o* talk *o* conversation with her; **la echaron de la clase por ~** (CS) they sent her out of the class for talking

conversión *f*
A (cambio) conversion
B (Relig) conversion
C (en rugby) conversion
D (Mil) wheel; **hacer ~** to wheel

converso¹ -sa *adj* (frml) converted

converso² -sa *m,f* convert (*esp Jew who converts to Catholicism*)

conversor *m* converter

convertible¹ *adj* convertible

convertible² *m* (AmL) convertible

convertir [I11] *vt*
A **1** (transformar) **~ algo/a algn EN algo** to turn sth/sb INTO sth **2** (a una religión) to convert; **~ a algn A algo** to convert sb TO sth **3** ‹*medida/peso*› **~ algo A algo** *or* (Esp) **EN algo** to convert sth INTO sth
B (period) (Dep) to score
■ **convertir** *vi* (AmL period) (Dep) to score
■ **convertirse** *v pron* **1** (transformarse) **~se EN algo** to turn INTO sth; **su sueño se convirtió en realidad** her dream came true **2** (a una religión) to convert, be converted; **~se A algo** to convert TO sth

convexo -xa *adj* convex

convicción *f* **1** (convencimiento) conviction; **tengo la ~ de que lo sabe** I'm certain *o* convinced he knows it **2** (persuasión) persuasion; **poder de ~** powers of persuasion **3** **convicciones** *fpl* (ideas, creencias) convictions (*pl*)

convicto¹ -ta *adj* (frml) convicted

convicto² -ta *m,f* prisoner, convict

convidado -da *m,f*: **los ~s a la boda** the wedding guests

convidar [A1] *vt* **1** (invitar) to invite; **~ a algn A algo** ‹*a una boda/una fiesta*› to invite sb TO sth; **nos ~on a unas copas** they invited us for a few drinks; **~ a algn A + INF** to invite sb to + INF **2** (AmL) (ofrecer) to offer; **¿no me convidas?** aren't you going to offer me any?; **~ a algn CON algo** *or* (Chi, Méx) **~ algo A algn** to offer sth TO sb, offer sb sth

convincente *adj* convincing

convite *m* (fam *o* hum) do (colloq)

convivencia *f*
A (vida en común — de etnias, sectas) coexistence; (— de individuos): **la ~ pone el amor a prueba** living together puts love to the test
B **convivencias** *fpl* (encuentro — religioso) retreat; (— de jóvenes) residential weekend (*o* week *etc*)

C

convivir [I1] *vi* ⟨⟨*personas*⟩⟩ to live together; ⟨⟨*ideologías/etnias*⟩⟩ to coexist; **aprender a ~** to learn to live (in harmony) with others; **~ CON algn** to live WITH sb; **~ CON algo** to coexist WITH sth

convocar [A2] *vt* ⟨*huelga/elecciones*⟩ to call; ⟨*manifestación*⟩ to organize; ⟨*concurso/certamen*⟩ to announce; ⟨*reunión/asamblea*⟩ to call, convene (frml); **~ a algn A algo** to summon sb TO sth; **~ al pueblo a las urnas** to call an election

convocatoria *f* 1 (llamamiento): **la ~ a (la) huelga fracasó** the strike call failed; **hubo una ~ para una asamblea** a meeting was called 2 (anuncio — para una reunión) notification; (— de exámenes, concursos) official announcement 3 (Esp) (Educ) (período de exámenes): **la ~ de junio** the June exams

convoy *m* (de barcos, camiones) convoy; (Ferr) (period) train

convulsión *f*
A (Med) convulsion
B (trastorno, perturbación): **las convulsiones sociales de los años 60** the social upheaval of the sixties; **las convulsiones obreras** the violent unrest among the workers
C (de la tierra) tremor

convulsionar [A1] *vt* to throw … into confusion
■ **convulsionarse** *v pron* to be thrown into confusion

convulsivo -va *adj* convulsive

convulso -sa *adj* **~ (DE algo)** convulsed (WITH sth)

conyugal *adj* (frml) marital, conjugal

cónyuge *mf* (frml) spouse (frml); **los ~s** the married couple; **la firma de uno de los ~s** either the husband's or the wife's signature

coña *f* (Esp) 1 (fam *o* vulg) (broma): **decir algo de ~** to be joking *o* (colloq) kidding; **va de ~** it's a joke; **a** *or* **en ~** as a joke; **¡ni de ~!** no way! (colloq) 2 (fam *o* vulg) (fastidio): ***darle la ~ a algn*** (fam) to pester sb

coñac, coñá *m* brandy, cognac

coñazo *m*
A (Esp fam *o* vulg) (persona o cosa pesada): **¡qué ~ (de tía)!** she's such a pain in the neck! (colloq); ***darle el ~ a algn*** (fam): **no me des el ~ con tus desgracias** stop going on about your problems (colloq)
B (Col, Ven fam) (golpe) blow; **se agarraron a ~s** they had a fight *o* (BrE colloq) punch-up; **me di un ~ en la cabeza** I banged my head (colloq)
C (Ven fam) (gran cantidad): **un ~** loads

coñete -ta *adj* (Chi, Per fam) stingy (colloq)

coño[1] *m* (vulg) (de la mujer) cunt (vulg), beaver (AmE sl), fanny (BrE sl); ***en el quinto ~*** (Esp vulg) (en un lugar — aislado) in the back of beyond (colloq); (— lejano) miles away; ***más que el ~*** (Ven vulg): **estoy más jodido que el ~** I'm shattered (colloq), I'm knackered (BrE sl); *para frases que expresan sorpresa, fastidio, etc ver* **carajo**

coño[2] **-ña** *m,f*
A (Chi fam & pey) (español) *derogatory term for a Spaniard*
B (Ven vulg) (tipo) jerk (sl)

(Compuesto) **coño de madre** *m,f* (Ven vulg) (canalla) (*m*) bastard (vulg), son of a bitch (sl); (*f*) bitch (vulg)

cooficial *adj* official

cooperación *f* cooperation

cooperador -dora *adj* cooperative, helpful

cooperante *m,f*
A (Esp) (trabajador) (overseas) aid worker
B (Col (que informa) informant

cooperar [A1] *vi* 1 (en tarea) to cooperate; **~ (CON algn) EN algo**: **cooperamos con ellos en la introducción del sistema** we worked with *o* cooperated with them on the introduction of the system; **~on en las tareas de reconstrucción** they collaborated on the rebuilding work; **~ en la lucha contra el cáncer** to work together in the fight against cancer 2 (contribuir) **~ A algo** to contribute TO sth 3 (en colecta) **~ CON algo** to contribute sth; **~ con un donativo** to make a contribution

cooperativa *f* (asociación) cooperative; (tienda) company store

cooperativismo *m* cooperativism

cooperativista[1] *adj* cooperative

cooperativista[2] *mf* (miembro) member of a cooperative; (partidario) supporter of cooperativism

cooperativo -va *adj* cooperative

coordenada *f* coordinate

coordinación *f* coordination

(Compuesto) **coordinación motriz** motor coordination

coordinado[1] **-da** *adj* coordinate

coordinado[2] *m* 1 (conjunto) outfit 2 **coordinados** *mpl* (prendas) coordinates (*pl*)

coordinador[1] **-dora** *adj* coordinating

coordinador[2] **-dora** *m,f* 1 (organizador) coordinator 2 **coordinadora** *f* coordinating committee

coordinar [A1] *vt* 1 ⟨*movimientos/actividades/esfuerzos*⟩ to coordinate; **no lograba ~ las ideas** he couldn't speak/think coherently 2 ⟨*ropa/colores*⟩ to coordinate; **~ algo CON algo**: **el azul coordinado con el rojo** blue combined with red
■ **coordinar** *vi* 1 ⟨⟨*colores*⟩⟩ to match, go together 2 (fam) (razonar): **antes del desayuno no coordino** you can't get any sense out of me before breakfast; **tú no coordinas** you just don't think, do you!

copa *f*
A 1 (para vino) glass (*with a stem*); (para postres) parfait dish; **me llenó la ~ de vino** he filled my glass with wine 2 (contenido) drink; **me invitó a una ~** he bought me a drink; **vamos a tomar una(s) ~(s)** let's go for a drink; **lleva** *or* **tiene unas ~s de más** he's had one *o* a few too many (colloq); ***eso me/le llenó la ~*** (Col) that was the last straw; ***irse de ~s*** (fam) to go out for a drink

(Compuestos)
- **copa de champán/coñac/jerez** champagne/brandy/sherry glass
- **copa de helado** ice cream sundae
- **copa de vino** wineglass

B (Dep) cup
C 1 (de árbol) top, crown 2 (de un sostén) cup 3 (de sombrero) crown
D **copas** *fpl* (en naipes) *one of the suits in a Spanish pack of cards*

copar [A1] *vt*
A 1 (acaparar) to take; **todo los puestos están ya copados** all the jobs are already taken 2 (llenar, colmar) to fill; **la capacidad del aeropuerto se verá pronto copada** the airport will soon reach full capacity; **tiene todo su tiempo copado** she has all her time taken up
B (Jueg): **~ la banca** to go banco

copartícipe *mf* (frml): **somos ~s en los beneficios** we share the profits; **fueron ~s en el delito** they committed the crime jointly

Copenhague *m* Copenhagen

copeo *m* (Esp fam): **ir/estar de ~** to go/be out drinking

copera *f* (AmS) hostess

coperacha *f* (Méx fam) (recaudación) kitty (colloq), collection; (contribución) contribution; **hacer una ~** to get up a collection (AmE colloq), to have a whip round (BrE colloq)

copete *m* 1 (de un ave) crest; ***de alto*** *or* ***mucho ~*** ⟨*familia*⟩ aristocratic, grand; ⟨*boda*⟩ society (*before n*) 2 (de pelo) tuft, quiff

copetín *m* (RPl) aperitif

> **copetín**
>
> In the River Plate region of Latin America this can mean an aperitif or light snack, or a social occasion at which these are consumed, generally before the evening meal

copetón *m* (Col) sparrow

copetudo -da *adj*
A ⟨*ave*⟩ crested
B (fam) ⟨*persona*⟩ snooty (colloq), stuckup (colloq)

copia *f*
A (de documento, fotografía) copy; **hice** *or* **saqué dos ~s** I made two copies

(Compuestos)
- **copia autentificada** *or* **legalizada** legally validated copy
- **copia certificada** certified copy
- **copia de respaldo** *or* **de seguridad** back-up copy

B (imitación) copy, imitation

copiadora *f* photocopier, copier

copiar [A1] *vt*
A 1 ⟨*cuadro/dibujo/texto*⟩ to copy; **copió el artículo a máquina** he typed out a copy of the article 2 (escribir al dictado) to take down

B 1 (imitar) to copy; **le copia todo al hermano** he copies his brother in everything 2 ‹*respuesta/examen*› to copy; **~le algo A algn** to copy sth FROM sb
■ **copiar** *vi* to copy

copihue *m* Chile-bells (*national flower of Chile*)

copiloto *mf* (Aviac) copilot; (Auto) co-driver

copión -piona *adj* (fam): **¡qué copiona!** what a copycat! (colloq)

copioso -sa *adj* ‹*cosecha/comida*› abundant, plentiful; ‹*nevada/lluvia*› heavy; ‹*información/ejemplos*› copious; ‹*llamadas*› numerous

copista *mf* copyist

copla *f*
A 1 (Lit) stanza 2 (Mús) popular folk song
B (Chi) (Tec) joint

copo *m* (de nieve) flake, snowflake; (de algodón) ball
Compuestos
• **copos de avena** *mpl* rolled oats (*pl*)
• **copos de maíz** *mpl* cornflakes (*pl*)

copón *m* 1 (Relig) ciborium; ***del ~*** (Esp vulg *o* fam): **un tonto del ~** a complete idiot; **una bronca del ~** a hell of a row (colloq) 2 (en naipes) ace of **copas** (*in Spanish playing cards*)

coproducción *f* coproduction, joint production

coproducir *vt* to co-produce

copropietario -ria *m,f* joint owner

coprotagonista *mf* costar

coprotagonizar [A4] *vi* to costar

copucha *f* (Chi fam) (rumor, chisme) rumor*; (curiosidad) nosiness (colloq); (exageración): **lo de él es pura ~** he's just putting it on

copuchar [A1] *vi* (Chi fam) (conversar) to chat (colloq); (curiosear) to nose around (colloq)

cópula *f*
A (Biol, Zool) copulation
B (Ling) copula

copular [A1] *vi* to copulate

copulativo -va *adj* copulative

copyright /kopi'rraj(t)/ *m* (*pl* **-rights**) copyright

coque *m* coke

coquear [A1] *vi* (Bol) to chew coca leaves

coquero -ra *m,f*: *person involved in the cocaine trade*

coqueta *f*
A (chica que flirtea) flirt, coquette (liter); (presumida) vain girl/woman; **eres una ~** you are so vain
B (mueble) dressing table

coquetear [A1] *vi* to flirt; **~ CON algn** to flirt WITH sb

coqueteo *m* 1 (de mujer) flirting; **se hartó de sus ~s** he became fed up with her flirting 2 (con ideología) flirtation

coqueto -ta *adj* 1 (en el arreglo personal): **es muy coqueta y coqueta** she's very concerned about her appearance 2 ‹*casa/dormitorio*› cute, sweet 3 ‹*sonrisa/mirada/mujer*› flirtatious, coquettish (liter)

coraje *m* 1 (valor) courage 2 (fam) (desfachatez) nerve; **¡qué ~!** what a lot of nerve! (AmE), what a nerve! (BrE) 3 (Esp, Méx fam) (rabia): **me da un ~** it makes me so mad!

corajudo -da *adj* brave

coral¹ *adj* choral

coral² *m*
A (Zool) coral; **una pulsera de ~(es)** a coral bracelet; **color ~** coral (*before n*), coral-colored*
B (Mús) (composición) chorale

coral³ *f*
A (Mús) (coro) choir
B (Zool) coral snake

coralino -na *adj* (liter) coralline, coral (*before n*)

Corán *m*: **el ~** the Koran

coránico -ca *adj* Koranic

coraza *f* 1 (armadura) cuirasse; **su agresividad es sólo una ~** she uses her aggressiveness as a shield 2 (Náut) armor-plating* 3 (de tortuga) shell

corazón *m*
A 1 (Anat) heart; **lo operaron a ~ abierto** he underwent open heart surgery; **sufre del ~** she has heart trouble; ***abrirle el ~ a algn*** to open one's heart to sb; ***con el ~ en la boca*** *or* ***un puño***: **estuvimos con el ~ en la boca hasta que ...** our hearts were in our mouths until ...; ***con el ~ en la mano*** with one's hand on one's heart; ***el ~ me/le dio un vuelco*** my/his heart missed a beat; ***se me/le encogió el ~*** (de tristeza) it made my/his heart bleed; ***ser duro de ~*** to be hard-hearted; ***tener un ~ de oro/de piedra*** to have a heart of gold/of stone 2 (sentimientos) heart; **es un hombre de buen/gran~** he's very kind-hearted/big-hearted; **no tener ~** to be heartless (colloq); **tener buen ~** to be kind-hearted; **tiene su corazoncito** his heart's in the right place; **con todo mi ~** with all my heart; **de (todo) ~** sincerely; **le destrozó** *or* **partió el ~** it broke her heart; ***no caberle a algn el ~ en el pecho*** I/he was bursting with pride (*o* joy *etc*) 3 (apelativo cariñoso) (fam) sweetheart (colloq)
B 1 (de manzana, pera) core; (de alcachofa) heart 2 (de ciudad, área) heart
C (en naipes) 1 (carta) heart 2 **corazones** *mpl* (palo) hearts (*pl*)

corazonada *f*: **fue una ~** it was just a hunch; **tuve la ~ de que ibas a venir** I had a hunch *o* feeling you'd come; **tuve la ~ de que debía regresar** I had a strong feeling that I should go back

corbata *f*
A (Indum) tie, necktie (AmE); **hay que ir de** *or* **con ~** you have to wear a tie
Compuesto **corbata de lazo** *or* (AmL) **de moño** *or* (Chi) **de humita** bow tie
B (Col fam) (puesto) cushy job (colloq)

corbatero *m* tie rack

corbatín *m* bow tie

corbeta *f* corvette

corcel *m* (liter) steed (liter)

corchea *f* quaver, eighth note (AmE)

corchete *m*
A (Impr) square bracket
B 1 (en costura) hook and eye 2 (Chi) (para sujetar papeles) staple

corchetear [A1] *vt* (Chi) to staple

corchetera *f*, **corchetero** *m* (Chi) stapler

corcho *m* (corteza) cork; (de una botella) cork; (para pescar, para nadar) float

corcholata *f* (Méx) bottle top

corcova *f*
A (joroba) hunchback, hump
B (Per fam) (fiesta) party (*lasting for two or more days*)

corcovado¹ -da *adj* hunchbacked, humpbacked

corcovado² -da *m,f* hunchback

corcovear [A1] *vi* to buck

corcoveo *m* (Col, CS) bucking

corcovo *m* buck; **dar ~s** to buck

cordada *f* (roped) team

cordaje *m* 1 (Náut) cordage, rigging 2 (Mús) strings (*pl*)

cordel *m* (fino) cord, string; (cuerda) (Chi) rope; *ver tb* ▸**cuerda A2, 3**

cordelería *f* (Náut) rigging

cordero *m*
A 1 (cría) lamb; ***contar corderitos*** to count sheep 2 (carne — de cordero) lamb; (— de oveja) mutton 3 (piel) lambskin; **forrado de corderito** fleece-lined
Compuesto **cordero lechal** suckling lamb
B 1 (Relig) lamb 2 (fam) (persona dócil) *tb* **corderito**: **ser un corderito** to be as good as gold

corderoy *m* (AmS) corduroy

cordial¹ *adj* (frml) (amistoso) cordial, friendly; **recibe un ~ saludo** (Corresp) (kindest) regards; **un ambiente ~** a congenial atmosphere; **se mostró muy ~** he was very friendly

cordial² *m* cordial, tonic

cordialidad *f* (frml) cordiality

cordialmente *adv* (frml) cordially; **le saluda ~** (Corresp) sincerely yours (AmE), yours sincerely (BrE)

cordillera *f* (mountain) range; **la ~ de los Andes** the Andes

cordillerano -na *adj* (AmL) Andean, mountain (*before n*)
córdoba *m* cordoba (*Nicaraguan unit of currency*)
cordón *m*
A 1 (cuerda) cord 2 (de zapatos) shoelace, lace 3 (Elec) cord 4 (Náut) strand 5 (de personas) cordon
(Compuestos)
- **cordón policial** police cordon
- **cordón sanitario** cordon sanitaire
- **cordón umbilical** umbilical cord

B 1 (CS) (de cerros) chain 2 (RPl) (de la vereda) curb (AmE), kerb (BrE)
cordoncillo *m* (bordado) piping
cordura *f* (Psic) sanity; (sensatez) good sense; **obrar con ~** to act sensibly
Corea *f* Korea
(Compuesto) **Corea del Norte/Sur** North/South Korea
coreano -na *adj/m,f* Korean
corear [A1] *vt* ‹*consignas/insultos*› to chant, chorus; ‹*marcha/estrofa*› to sing … in unison
corebac *m* (Méx) (Dep) quarterback
coreografía *f* choreography
coreográfico -ca *adj* choreographic
coreógrafo -fa *m,f* choreographer
corintio -tia *adj/m,f* Corinthian
corista *f* (en revista musical) chorus girl
cormorán *m* cormorant
cornada *f* (golpe) thrust (*with the horns*); (herida) wound (*caused by a bull's horn*); **murió de una ~** he died after being gored; **dar una ~ a algn** to gore
cornamenta *f* (de toro) horns (*pl*); (de ciervo) antlers (*pl*)
cornamusa *f* (gaita) bagpipes (*pl*)
córnea *f* cornea
cornear [A1] *vt* «*toro*» (golpear) to butt (*with the horn(s)*); (herir) to gore
corneja *f* (cuervo) crow
córneo -nea *adj* corneous, hornlike
córner *m* (*pl* **-ners**) corner (kick); **lanzar un ~** to take a corner
corneta¹ *f*
A 1 (Mús) (sin llaves) bugle; (con llaves) cornet 2 (Ven) (Auto) horn
B (de gramófono) horn
corneta² *m* bugler
cornetín *m* ▸**corneta¹ A1**
cornetista *mf* (de corneta sin llaves) bugler; (de corneta con llaves) cornet player
cornisa *f*
A (Arquit) cornice
B (Geog): **la ~ atlántica** the Atlantic coast
corno *m*
A (Mús) horn
(Compuesto) **corno inglés** English horn (AmE), cor anglais (BrE)
B (RPl fam) (uso expletivo): **no entendí un ~** I didn't understand a word; **sobre eso no sabe un ~** he doesn't have a clue about that (colloq); **no vale un ~** it's completely worthless; **¡qué viaje ni qué ~s!** trip, what trip?; **¿qué/quién/dónde ~ ...?** what/who/where the hell …? (colloq)
cornucopia *f* cornucopia, horn of plenty
cornudo¹ -da *adj* 1 ‹*animal*› horned 2 (fam) ‹*marido*› cuckolded (liter), deceived (*before n*); ‹*mujer*› deceived (*before n*)
cornudo² -da (fam) (*m*) cuckold (liter), deceived husband; (*f*) deceived wife
coro *m*
A 1 (Mús) (conjunto — vocal) choir; (— en revista musical) chorus line; **un ~ de protestas** a chorus of protest; **a ~** ‹*repetir*› together *o* in unison, ‹*cantar*› in chorus *o* together; ***hacerle ~ a algn*** to back sb up 2 (composición) chorus 3 (Arquit) choir
B (Hist, Lit) (en la tragedia) chorus
C (de ángeles) choir
corola *f* corolla
corolario *m* corollary
corona *f*
A 1 (de soberano) crown; **el heredero de la ~** the crown prince 2 (institución): **la ~** the Crown 3 (Dep) crown
B (de flores) crown, wreath; (para funerales) wreath; **la ~ de espinas** the crown of thorns
(Compuesto) **corona de caridad** (Chi) donation to charity (*instead of sending a wreath*)
C (Astron) corona
(Compuesto) **corona solar** corona, aureole
D (moneda) crown
E (Odont) crown
coronación *f* 1 (de soberano) coronation 2 (culminación) culmination
coronar [A1] *vt*
A ‹*soberano*› to crown
B ‹*montaña/cima*› to reach the top of
C 1 (rematar) to crown; **una cúpula corona el edificio** the building is crowned by a dome 2 (en damas) to crown
■ **coronarse** *v pron*
A (Per fam) (meter la pata) to put one's foot in it
B (Ven fam) (tenerlo todo) to be set up (colloq); **ya estás coronado** you're all set up now
coronario -ria *adj* coronary
coronel -nela *m,f* 1 (en el ejército) colonel; (en las fuerzas aéreas) ≈ Colonel (*in US*), ≈ Group Captain (*in UK*) 2 **coronela** *f* (ant *o* hum) colonel's wife
coronilla *f* crown, crown of the head; ***estar hasta la ~ (de algo/algn)*** (fam) to be fed up to the back teeth (with sth/sb) (colloq)
coronta *f* (Chi, Per) *tb* **~ de choclo** *stripped corn cob*
coroto *m*
A (Col, Ven fam) (trasto) piece of junk (colloq); **recoge tus ~s** get your things *o* stuff together
B (Ven) (poder político) (political) power; ***alzarse con el ~*** (Ven fam) to take power; ***entregar el ~*** (Ven fam) to hand over power
corpacho, corpachón *m* (fam): **ha echado/tiene un buen ~** he's got(ten)/he's really solid *o* hefty (colloq)
corpiño *m* (chaleco) bodice; (del vestido) bodice; (prenda interior) (RPl) brassière
corporación *f* 1 (Hist) guild 2 (Der) association 3 (Com, Fin) corporation
(Compuesto) **corporación municipal** municipal council
corporal¹ *adj* ‹*trabajo*› physical
corporal² *m* corporal, corporale
corporativismo *m* corporatism
corporativo -va *adj* corporate
corpóreo -rea *adj* physical, corporeal (frml)
corpulencia *f* heftiness
corpulento -ta *adj* ‹*persona/animal*› hefty, burly; ‹*árbol*› solid, sturdy
corpus *m* (*pl* ~) (de datos) corpus; (de obras) body, corpus
Corpus, Corpus Christi Corpus Christi
corpúsculo *m* corpuscle
corral *m* 1 (en granja) yard, farmyard 2 (para ganado) corral 3 *tb* **corralito** (para niños) playpen 4 (Hist, Teatr) open-air theater*
corralón *m* 1 (Méx) (de la policía) car pound 2 (Per) (terreno baldío) piece of waste land (*sometimes with shanty dwellings*) 3 (Arg) (Const) lumberyard
correa *f* 1 (tira) strap; (cinturón) belt; (de perro) leash; **~ de reloj** watchband (AmE), watchstrap (BrE) 2 (para afilar) strop 3 (Mec) belt; ***tener mucha/poca ~*** (fam) to be long-suffering/to have a very short fuse
(Compuestos)
- **correa de** *or* **del ventilador** fan belt
- **correa de transmisión** (Mec) drive belt; (Pol) mouthpiece

correaje *m* belts (*pl*)
correazo *m* blow with a belt
correcaminos *m* (*pl* ~) roadrunner
corrección *f*
A 1 (buenos modales): **es un hombre de una gran ~** he is

very well-mannered *o* correct; **vestir con ~** to dress correctly *o* properly 2 (honestidad) correctness 3 (propiedad): **habla los dos idiomas con ~** he speaks both languages well *o* correctly
B 1 (de exámenes) correction 2 (enmienda, rectificación) correction
(Compuesto) **corrección de pruebas** proofreading

correccional *f or* (Esp) *m*: *tb* **~ de menores** reformatory (AmE), detention centre (BrE)

correctamente *adv* 1 (sin errores) correctly 2 (con cortesía) politely 3 (honestamente) honorably

correctivo[1] **-va** *adj* corrective

correctivo[2] *m*: **como ~** as a punishment; **esto le servirá de ~** this will teach him a lesson

correcto -ta *adj*
A 1 (educado) correct, polite 2 (honesto) correct
B 1 ‹*respuesta/solución*› correct, right; **lo dijo en un ~ alemán** he said in correct German; **¡~!** (AmC, Méx) (that's) right 2 ‹*funcionamiento/procedimiento*› correct

corrector -tora *m,f*
A (de exámenes) marker
(Compuesto) **corrector -tora de pruebas** proofreader
B **corrector** *m* 1 (Odont) braces (*pl*) (AmE), brace (BrE) 2 (líquido) correction fluid

corredera[1] *adj* ▸**puerta**

corredera[2] *f* (RPl fam): **tengo una** *or* **estoy con una ~** I've got the runs (colloq)

corredizo -za *adj* ▸**nudo, puerta**

corredor -dora *m,f*
A (atleta) runner; (en ciclismo) rider
(Compuestos)
- **corredor -dora de coches** racing driver
- **corredor -dora de fondo** long-distance runner
- **corredor -dora de vallas** hurdler

B 1 (agente) agent 2 (RPl) (viajante) sales representative
(Compuestos)
- **corredor -dora de Bolsa** stockbroker
- **corredor -dora de bienes raíces** *or* (Esp) **de fincas** real estate broker (AmE), estate agent (BrE)

C **corredor** *m* (Arquit, Geog, Pol) corridor

correduría *f* ▸**corretaje A1, B**

corregible *adj* correctable

corregidor *m* (Hist) (magistrado) judge; (alcalde) mayor (*appointed by the king*)

corregir [I8] *vt* 1 ‹*error/falta*› to correct; ‹*modales*› to improve, mend 2 ‹*examen/dictado*› to correct, grade (AmE), to mark (BrE) 3 ‹*galeradas/pruebas*› to correct 4 ‹*defecto físico/postura*› to correct 5 ‹*trayectoria*› to correct
■ **corregirse** *v pron*
A 1 (en el comportamiento) to change *o* mend one's ways 2 (*refl*) (al hablar) to correct oneself; **~se DE algo**: **se corrigió del error** she corrected her mistake
B «*defecto físico*»: **un defecto que se corrige solo** a defect which corrects itself

correlación *f* correlation

correlacionar [A1] *vt* (frml) to correlate (frml)

correlativo -va *adj* (frml) correlative (frml)

correligionario -ria *m,f*: **Maggiulli y sus ~s** Maggiulli and his fellow Socialists (*o* fellow Democrats *etc*)

correntada *f* (CS) current

correntoso -sa *adj* (CS) fast-flowing

correo *m*
A 1 mail, post (BrE); **envíamelo por ~** mail (AmE) *o* (BrE) post it to me; **a vuelta de ~** by return of post; **echar una carta al ~** to mail (AmE) *o* (BrE) post a letter 2 (tren) mail train; (autobús) postbus (*bus which also transports mail*); (barco) mail boat
(Compuestos)
- **correo aéreo** air mail
- **correo certificado** *o* (Col, Ur) **recomendado** registered mail
- **correo electrónico** electronic mail
- **correo urgente** special delivery

B (oficina) *tb* **C~s** (Esp) post office; **voy al ~** *or* (Esp) **a C~s** I'm going to the post office
C (persona) 1 (mensajero) messenger 2 (de drogas) courier

> **Correos**
>
> The name of Spain's state-run post office. Stamps can be bought in estancos, although certified or express mail must be sent from a post office (*estafeta* or *oficina de correos*). Postboxes in Spain are silver with red and yellow hoops. There are also red boxes for urgent mail. In Latin America *correo*, in the singular, means both a post office and the mail system

correoso -sa *adj* tough, leathery

correr [E1] *vi*
A 1 to run; **bajó/subió las escaleras corriendo** she ran down/up the stairs; **salieron corriendo del banco** they ran out of the bank; **echó a ~** he started to run, he broke into a run; **corrió a su encuentro** she ran to meet him; ***a todo* ~** at top speed; **salió a todo ~** he went/came shooting out 2 (Dep) «*atleta*» to run; «*caballo*» to run; **sale a ~ todas las mañanas** she goes for a run every morning 3 (Auto, Dep) «*piloto/conductor*» to race
B 1 (apresurarse): **llevo todo el día corriendo de un lado para otro** I've been rushing around all day long; **¡corre, ponte los zapatos!** hurry *o* quick, put your shoes on!; **rellénalo corriendo y entrégalo** fill it in quickly and hand it in; **no corras tanto que te equivocarás** don't rush it *o* don't do it so quickly, you'll only make mistakes ; **corrí a llamarte/a escribirte** I rushed to call you/write to you; **me tengo que ir corriendo** I have to rush off; **se fueron corriendo al hospital** they rushed to the hospital 2 (fam) (ir, moverse) (+ *compl*) «*vehículo/conductor*»: **corre mucho** he drives too/very fast; **esa moto corre mucho** that motorcycle is *o* goes really fast
C 1 (+ *compl*) «*cordillera/carretera*» to run; «*río*» to run, flow 2 «*agua*» to flow, run; «*sangre*» to flow; **corría una brisa suave** there was a gentle breeze; **corre mucho viento hoy** it's very windy today; ***dejar* ~ *algo*** to let sth go 3 «*rumor*»: **corre el rumor de que ...** there is a rumor going around that ..., rumor has it that ...; **corrió la voz de que ...** there was a rumor that ... 4 «*polea*» to run; «*puerta*» to slide; **la cremallera no corre** the zipper (AmE) *o* (BrE) zip is stuck; **el pestillo no corre** I can't bolt/unbolt the door
D «*tiempo*» 1 (pasar, transcurrir): **corren tiempos difíciles** these are difficult times; **corría el año 1939 cuando ...** it was in 1939 that ...; **con el ~ de los años** as time went/goes by; **el mes que corre** in the current month (frml) 2 (pasar de prisa) to fly
E «*sueldo/alquiler*» to be payable
F (hacerse cargo) **~ CON algo** ‹*con gastos*› to pay sth; ‹*con organización*› to be responsible FOR sth
■ **correr** *vt*
A 1 (Dep) ‹*maratón*› to run; **corrió los 1.500 metros** he ran the 1,500 meters 2 (Auto, Dep) ‹*prueba/gran premio*› to race in
B 1 (fam) (echar, expulsar) to kick ... out (colloq), to chuck ... out (colloq) 2 (fam) (perseguir) to run after
C 1 (exponerse a): **no quiero ~ riesgos** I don't want to take any risks; **corres el riesgo de perderlo** you run the risk of losing it; **aquí no corres peligro** you're safe here 2 (experimentar): **ambos corrieron parecida suerte** they both suffered a similar fate; **juntos corrimos grandes aventuras** we had some great adventures together
D (mover) 1 ‹*botón/ficha/silla*› to move 2 ‹*cortina*› (cerrar) to draw *o* close; (abrir) to open *o* pull back; **corre el cerrojo** bolt the door 3 (Inf) ‹*texto*› to scroll
■ **correrse** *v pron*
A (moverse) 1 «*silla/cama*» to move; «*pieza/carga*» to shift 2 (fam) «*persona*» to move up *o* over
B 1 «*tinta*» to run; «*rímel/maquillaje*» (+ *me/te/le etc*) to run, smudge; **se me corrió el rímel** my mascara ran 2 (AmL) «*media*» to ladder
C (Esp arg) (llegar al orgasmo) to come (colloq)

correría *f* 1 (ant) (Mil) raid, incursion 2 (viaje, excursión): **sus ~s por el mundo** her travels all over the world

correspondencia *f*
A 1 (relación por correo) correspondence; **mantener ~ con algn** to correspond with sb 2 (cartas) mail, post (BrE); **~ comercial** business correspondence
B (equivalencia) correspondence
C (en el metro) interchange; **esta estación tiene ~ con la línea tres** you can change to line three at this station

C

corresponder [E1] *vi*

A 1 (en un reparto) (+ *me/te/le etc*): **le correspondió la mitad de la herencia** half the inheritance went to him; **ésta es la parte que te corresponde** this is your part 2 (incumbir): **te corresponde a ti preparar el informe** it's your job to prepare the report; **el lugar que le corresponde** his rightful place; **a quien corresponda** (Corresp) to whom it may concern; **con los honores que corresponden a su rango** with the honors befitting his rank 3 (*en 3ª pers*) (ser adecuado): **te disculpas, como corresponde** apologize, you know you should *o* (frml) as is right and proper; **serán juzgados como corresponde** they will be tried according to the law; **según corresponda** as appropriate

B (encajar, cuadrar): **esto aquí no corresponde** this doesn't belong *o* go here; **~ A algo**: **su aspecto correspondía a la descripción** his appearance fitted *o* matched the description; **la leyenda no corresponde a la fotografía** the caption doesn't belong with *o* match this photograph

C (a favor, atención) **~ A algo**: **quisiera ~ a su generosidad** I'd like to repay them for their generosity; (+ *me/te/le etc*) **lo quiere, pero él no le corresponde** she loves him, but he doesn't feel the same way about her; **y tú le correspondes con esta grosería** and you repay him with this kind of rudeness

■ **corresponder** *vt* ‹*favor*› to return; ‹*atención*› to return, repay; **un amor no correspondido** an unrequited love

■ **corresponderse** *v pron* **~se CON algo** ‹*con los hechos/con la declaración*› to square *o* tally with sth; **eso no se corresponde con su manera de ser** that's out of keeping with her character

correspondiente *adj*: **la etiqueta ~** the corresponding label; **viene con su ~ caja** it comes with its own box; **rellene el impreso ~** complete the relevant form; **~ A algo**: **los números ~s a cada página** the numbers corresponding to each page; **los resultados ~s al año pasado** last year's results; **las cifras ~s al mes de abril** the figures for the month of April

corresponsal *mf* (de periódico, radio) correspondent

(Compuesto) **corresponsal en el extranjero/de guerra** foreign/war correspondent

corresponsalía *f* (cargo) post of correspondent; (oficina) (CS) correspondent's office

corretaje *m*

A 1 (de acciones, valores) brokerage 2 (Esp) (de pisos) property dealing 3 (RPl) (de productos) wholesaling

B (comisión) commission

corretear [A1] *vi* (correr) to run around

■ **corretear** *vt*

A 1 (esp AmL) (perseguir) to chase, pursue 2 (Chi fam) ‹*ladrones*› to keep ... away, deter

B (RPl) (Com) to wholesale

corrida *f*

A 1 (fam) (carrera): **dar** *or* **echar una ~** to run, move (it) (colloq); **a las ~s** (RPl) in a rush 2 (Fin): **una ~ bancaria** a run on the banks 3 (Dep) carry

B (Taur) bullfight

C (Chi) 1 (serie) series 2 (fila) row 3 (de bebidas) round 4 (Min) outcrop

D (Méx) (en póquer) straight

> **corrida**
>
> A bullfight. Bullfighting remains popular in many parts of Spain and some Latin American countries, and is regularly broadcast on television. During the *corrida* three bullfighters (*matadores*) fight a total of six bulls, two each

corrido¹ -da *adj* 1 (fam) ‹*persona*› worldly-wise (colloq) 2 ‹*balcón/galería*› continuous; **de ~** (fam) ▸**carrerilla** 3 (Esp fam) (avergonzado) embarrassed

corrido² *m*: *Mexican folk song*

> **corrido**
>
> In Mexico, a ballad sung to guitar and trumpet accompaniment on subjects such as battles, heroic deeds, love affairs, the fight for equality, and the lives of historical and fictional characters. *Corridos* developed from the Spanish ballad tradition. The lyrics are straightforward songs of the common people

corriente¹ *adj*

A (que ocurre con frecuencia) common; (normal, no extraño) usual, normal; **es un error muy ~** it's a very common mistake; **un método poco ~** a method not much used; **lo ~ es pagar al contado** the normal thing is to pay cash; **un coche/tipo normal y ~** an ordinary car/guy; **una persona poco ~** he's rather out of the ordinary; **es de una belleza poco ~** she's unusually beautiful

B 1 (en curso) ‹*mes/año*› current; **el día tres del ~** the third of this month; **su atenta carta del 7 del ~** (frml) your letter of the 7th of this month 2 **al corriente**: **estoy al ~ en todos los pagos** I'm up to date with all the payments; **empezó con retraso pero se ha puesto al ~** she started late but she has caught up; **tener** *or* **mantener a algn al ~ de algo** to keep sb informed *o* (colloq) posted about sth

corriente² *f*

A (de agua) current; **~s marinas** ocean currents; ***dejarse arrastrar*** *or* ***llevar por la ~*** to go along with the crowd; ***ir*** *or* ***nadar*** *or* ***navegar contra (la) ~*** to swim against the tide; ***seguirle la ~ a algn*** to humor sb

B (de aire) draft (AmE), draught (BrE); **aquí hay** *or* **hace mucha ~** there's a terrible draft in here

C (tendencia) trend; **las ~s de la moda** the trends in fashion; **una ~ de pensamiento** a school of thought; **una ~ de opinión** a current of opinion

D (Elec) current; **me dio (la) ~** I got a shock *o* an electric shock; **se cortó la ~** there was a power cut; **no hay ~** there's no electricity

(Compuesto) **corriente alterna/continua** alternating/direct current, AC/DC

corrientemente *adv* (normalmente) usually, normally; (con frecuencia) commonly, often; **vestía ~** he was dressed in ordinary clothes

corrillo *m* small group of people

corro *m* 1 (círculo) circle, ring; **hacer** *o* **formar un ~** to stand/sit in a circle; **se formó un ~ a su alrededor** a circle of people formed around her 2 (Jueg): **jugar al ~** *to play a singing game standing in a ring*

corroboración *f* corroboration

corroborar [A1] *vt* to corroborate

corroer [E13] *vt* ‹*metal*› to corrode; ‹*mármol*› to erode; **la envidia la corroe** she is eaten up with envy

■ **corroerse** *v pron* to corrode

corromper [E1] *vt* 1 ‹*persona/lengua/sociedad*› to corrupt 2 ‹*materia orgánica*› to rot

■ **corromperse** *v pron* 1 «*costumbres/persona/lengua*» to become corrupted 2 «*materia orgánica*» to rot 3 «*agua*» to become stagnant

corrompido -da *adj* 1 ‹*persona/sociedad*› corrupt 2 ‹*materia orgánica*› rotten

corrosca *f* (Col) straw hat

corrosión *f* corrosion

corrosivo -va *adj* 1 ‹*sustancia/acción*› corrosive 2 ‹*humor/ironía*› caustic; ‹*crítica*› acerbic

corrugado -da *adj* corrugated

corrupción *f* 1 (de materia) decay 2 (de moral, persona, lengua) corruption

(Compuesto) **corrupción de menores** corruption of minors

corruptela *f* corruption

corrupto -ta *adj* corrupt

corruptor -tora *m,f*: **~ de menores** (hum) cradle snatcher (colloq)

corsario *m* corsair, privateer

corsé, corset /kor'se/ *m* (*pl* **-sets**) corset

(Compuesto) **corsé ortopédico** (orthopedic*) corset

corso *m* (RPl) carnival parade

corta *f* (Chi fam) (cigarette) butt, fag end (BrE)

cortaalambres *m* (*pl* ~) wirecutters (*pl*)

cortacésped *m* lawnmower

cortacircuitos *m* (*pl* ~) circuit breaker

cortacorriente *m* circuit breaker

cortada *f* 1 (Col, Méx) (herida) cut; **hacerse una ~** to cut oneself 2 (RPl) (calle sin salida) no through road

cortado¹ -da *adj*

A ‹*persona*› 1 [ESTAR] (Chi, Esp) (turbado, avergonzado) embar-

rassed **2** [ESTAR] (Esp, CS) (aturdido) stunned; **me quedé ~ con su respuesta** I was stunned by her reply **3** [SER] (Esp) (tímido) shy
B [ESTAR] ‹*calle/carretera*› closed, closed off; **S carretera cortada por obras** road closed (for repairs)
C **1** [ESTAR] ‹*mayonesa/salsa*› separated; **la leche está cortada** the milk is curdled *o* off **2** ‹*café*› with a dash of milk
D ‹*película*› cut

cortado[2] *m* expresso with a dash of milk

> **cortado**
> Popular in Spain and known also as *café cortado*. Black coffee is "cut" by adding a little milk to it

cortador -dora *m,f*
A (persona) *tb* **~ de sastre** cutter
B **cortadora** *f* **1** (máquina) cutter **2** (cuchilla) cutter
(Compuesto) **cortadora de césped** *f* lawnmower

cortadura *f*
A **1** (corte) cut **2** **cortaduras** *fpl* cuttings (*pl*), clippings (*pl*)
B (Geog) gorge

cortafrío *m* cold chisel

cortafuego *m* (en bosque) firebreak, fireguard, fire line; (en edificio) fire wall

cortante *adj* **1** ‹*instrumento/objeto*› sharp **2** ‹*viento*› biting **3** ‹*respuesta/tono*› sharp

cortapapeles *m* (*pl* ~) (abrecartas) paperknife, letter opener; (guillotina) guillotine

cortapicos *m* (*pl* ~) earwig

cortapisa *f*: **el proyecto se llevó a cabo sin ~s** they finished the project without any setbacks; **habló sin ~s** she spoke freely; **poner ~s a algo/algn** to put obstacles in the way of sth/in sb's way

cortaplumas *m or f* (*pl* ~) penknife

cortapuros *m* (*pl* ~) cigar cutter

cortar [A1] *vt*
A (dividir) ‹*cuerda/pastel*› to cut, chop; ‹*asado*› to carve; ‹*leña/madera*› to chop; ‹*baraja*› to cut; ‹*aire/agua*› (liter) to slice *o* cut through; **~ por la línea de puntos** cut along the dotted line; **~ algo por la mitad** to cut sth in half *o* in two; **~ algo en rodajas/en cuadritos** to slice/dice sth; **~ algo en trozos** to cut sth into pieces; **¿en cuántas partes lo corto?** how many slices (*o* pieces *etc*) shall I cut it into?; **este queso se corta muy bien** this cheese cuts very easily
B (quitar, separar) ‹*rama/punta/pierna*› to cut off; ‹*árbol*› to cut down, chop down; ‹*flores*› (CS) to pick; **me cortó un trozo de melón** she cut me a piece of melon; **la máquina le cortó un dedo** the machine took off his finger; **~le la cabeza a algn** to chop off *o* cut off sb's head
C (hacer más corto) ‹*pelo/uñas*› to cut; ‹*césped/pasto*› to mow; ‹*seto*› to cut; ‹*rosal*› to cut back; ‹*texto*› to cut down; **le cortó el pelo** he cut her hair
D **1** (en costura) ‹*falda/vestido*› to cut out **2** (recortar) ‹*anuncio/receta/muñeca de papel*› to cut out
E (interrumpir) **1** ‹*agua/gas/luz/comunicación*› to cut off; ‹*película/programa*› to interrupt; **le ~on el teléfono** his phone was cut off; **~la** (Chi fam): **córtala con eso** OK, cut it out, now (colloq) **2** ‹*retirada*› to cut off **3** ‹*calle*› «*policía/obreros*» to close, block off; «*manifestantes*» to block; **han cortado el tráfico en la zona** they've closed the area to traffic; **me cortó el paso** he stood in my way **4** ‹*relaciones diplomáticas*› to break off; ‹*subvenciones/ayuda*› to cut off
F ‹*fiebre*› to bring down; ‹*hemorragia*› to stop, stem
G ‹*persona*› (en conversación) to interrupt; **me cortó en seco** he cut me short
H (censurar, editar) ‹*película*› to cut; ‹*escena/diálogo*› to cut, to cut out
I ‹*recta/plano*› to cross
J **1** ‹*heroína/cocaína*› to adulterate, cut (colloq) **2** ‹*leche*› to curdle
K «*frío*»: **el frío me cortó los labios** my lips were chapped *o* cracked from the cold weather
L (RPl) ‹*dientes*› to cut

■ **cortar** *vi*
A «*cuchillo/tijeras*» to cut
B **1** (por radio): **corto y cambio** over; **corto y fuera** *or* **corto y cierro** over and out **2** (Cin): **¡corten!** cut! **3** (CS) (por teléfono) to hang up; **no me cortes** don't hang up on me
C (terminar) **1** «*novios*» to break up, split up; **~ con algn** to break up WITH sb **2** **~ con algo** ‹*con pasado/raíces*› to break WITH sth
D (en naipes) to cut
E (en costura) to cut out
F (acortar camino) **~ por algo**: **cortemos por el bosque/la plaza** let's cut through the woods/across the square; **~on por el atajo** they took the shortcut
G (Chi fam) (ir, dirigirse): **~on para la ciudad** they headed for the city; ***no sabía para dónde*** **~** (Chi fam) I/he didn't know which way to turn (colloq)

■ **cortarse** *v pron*
A (interrumpirse) «*proyección/película*» to stop; «*llamada/gas*» to get cut off; **se ha cortado la luz** there's been a power cut; **se te va a ~ la digestión** you'll get stomach cramp; **se me cortó la respiración** I could hardly breathe
B (*refl*) **1** (hacerse un corte) to cut oneself; ‹*dedo/brazo/cara*› to cut; **me corté un dedo** I cut my finger; **se cortó afeitándose** he cut himself shaving **2** «*piel/labios*» (+ *me/te/le etc*) to crack, become chapped
C **1** (*refl*) ‹*uñas/pelo*› to cut; **se corta el pelo ella misma** she cuts her own hair; **se cortó las venas** he slashed his wrists **2** (*caus*) ‹*pelo*› to have … cut
D (*recípr*) «*líneas/calles*» to cross
E «*leche/mayonesa*» to curdle
F (Chi, Esp) «*persona*» (turbarse, aturdirse) to get embarrassed; **se corta en seguida** she gets easily embarrassed
G (Chi fam) «*animal*» to collapse from exhaustion

cortaúñas *m* (*pl* ~) nail clippers (*pl*)

cortaviento *m* windbreak

corte[1] *m*
A **1** (tajo) cut; **se hizo un ~ en la cabeza** he cut his head **2** (de carne) cut, cut of meat **3** *tb* **~ de pelo** haircut, cut
(Compuestos)
- **corte a (la) navaja** razor cut
- **corte longitudinal/transversal** lengthwise/cross section

B (interrupción): **un ~ en el suministro eléctrico** (frml) a power cut; **hemos tenido varios ~s de agua** the water has been cut off several times; **se produjeron varios ~s de carretera** several roads were blocked
(Compuestos)
- **corte de digestión** stomach cramp
- **corte de luz** power cut
- **corte publicitario** (RPl) commercial break

C (Ven) (separación) (fam) break-up, bust-up (colloq); **darle un ~ a algn** to break *o* split up with sb
D (AmL) (en el presupuesto) cut
E (Cin) (por la censura) cut
F **1** (de tela) length, length of material **2** (en costura) cut; **un traje de buen ~** a well-made *o* well-cut suit
(Compuestos)
- **corte de mangas**: **les hizo un ~ de ~** ≈ he gave them the finger
- **corte y confección** dressmaking

G (tendencia, estilo): **canciones de ~ romántico** songs of a romantic nature; **un país de ~ democrático** a country of democratic persuasion
H (Esp fam) **1** (vergüenza) embarrassment; **me da ~ ir sola** I'm embarrassed to go by myself; **es un ~** it's embarrassing **2** (respuesta tajante): **¡menudo ~!** what a put-down! (colloq)
I (fam) (Audio) track
J (RPl fam) (atención): **darle ~ a algn** to take notice of sb; ***darse*** **~** (RPl fam) to show off

corte[2] *f*
A (del rey) court; **una ~ de aduladores** a circle of admirers; ***hacerle la ~ a algn*** (cortejar) (ant) to woo sb (dated *or* liter)
B (esp AmL) (Der) Court of Appeal
(Compuestos)
- **Corte Marcial** Military Appeal Court
- **Corte Suprema (de Justicia)** (AmL) Supreme Court

C **las Cortes** *fpl* (Pol) (en Esp) Parliament, the legislative assembly

cortedad *f* shortness; **~ de miras** shortsightedness

cortejar [A1] *vt* (arc) ‹*mujer*› to woo (dated *or* liter)

C

cortejo *m*
A (comitiva — de rey) retinue, entourage; (— de ministro) entourage
Compuesto **cortejo fúnebre** funeral procession *o* (frml) cortege
B (acción) courtship, wooing
cortés *adj* polite, courteous; ***lo ~ no quita lo valiente*** politeness doesn't have to be a sign of weakness
cortesana *f* (arc) courtesan
cortesano[1] -na *adj* court (*before n*)
cortesano[2] -na *m,f* courtier
cortesía *f* 1 (urbanidad, amabilidad) courtesy, politeness; **son reglas elementales de ~** it's common courtesy; **la trató con ~** he was polite to her 2 **de cortesía** ‹*entrada*› complimentary; ‹*visita*› courtesy (*before n*) 3 (atención): **le agradezco la ~** (frml) I would like to thank you for your kind invitation (*o* offer *etc*); **es una ~ de la casa** it comes with the compliments of the house; **tuvo la ~ de invitarnos** she was kind enough to invite us
córtex *m* cortex
corteza *f* 1 (de árbol) bark; (del pan) crust; (del queso) rind; (de naranja, limón) peel, rind 2 (de átomo) shell 3 **cortezas** *fpl* (Coc) (Esp) pork rinds *o* scratchings (*pl*)
Compuestos
- **corteza cerebral** cerebral cortex
- **corteza terrestre**: **la ~ ~** the earth's crust

corticoide *m* corticosteroid, corticoid
cortijo *m* (en Esp) (finca) country estate; (casa) country house
cortina *f* curtain, drape (AmE)
Compuestos
- **cortina de ducha** shower curtain
- **cortina de hierro** (AmL) (Hist): **la ~ de ~** the Iron Curtain
- **cortina de humo** smokescreen
- **cortina metálica** (metal) shutter
- **cortina musical** (CS) theme song (AmE), signature tune (BrE)

cortinaje *m* curtains (*pl*), drapes (*pl*) (AmE)
cortisona *f* cortisone
corto[1] -ta *adj*
A 1 (en longitud) ‹*calle/río*› short; **el camino más ~** the shortest route; **de manga corta** short-sleeved; **el vestido le quedóha ~** the dress is too short for her now; **iba vestida de ~** she was wearing a short dress/skirt; **en ~** ‹*pase*› (Dep) short 2 (en duración) ‹*película/curso/viaje*› short; ‹*visita/conversación*› short, brief; **la semana se me hizo corta** I found that the week went very quickly; ***a la corta o a la larga*** sooner or later
B (escaso, insuficiente): **un niño de corta edad** a very young child; **~ DE algo**: **ando ~ de dinero** I'm a bit short of money; **~ de vista** near-sighted, shortsighted (BrE); **ando muy ~ de tiempo** I'm really pressed for time; **un café con leche ~ de café** a milky coffee; ***quedarse ~***: **costará más de un millón y seguro que me quedo ~** it must cost at least a million, in fact it could well be more; **lo llamé de todo y aun así me quedé ~** I called him all the names under the sun and I could have said more; **nos quedamos ~s con el pan** we didn't buy enough bread
C ‹*persona*› 1 (fam) (tímido) shy; ***ni ~ ni perezoso*** as bold as you like; **ni ~ ni perezoso fue y se lo dijo** he told him outright 2 (fam) (poco inteligente) stupid; **~ de entendederas** *or* **alcances** dim, dense (colloq)
corto[2] *m*
A (Cin) 1 (cortometraje) short (movie *o* film) 2 **cortos** *mpl* (Col, Méx, Ven) (de película) trailer
B (de cerveza, vino) (Esp) small glass; (de whisky etc) (Chi) shot
cortocircuito *m* short circuit; **la plancha hizo ~** the iron short-circuited
cortometraje *m* short (movie *o* film)
cortoplacismo *m* short-termism
corva *f* back of the knee
corvadura *f* curve, curvature
corvejón *m* (del caballo) hock; (del gallo) spur
corvo -va *adj* ▸ **curvo**
corzo -za *m,f* 1 (especie) roe deer 2 (*m*) roebuck; (*f*) roe deer
cosa *f*
A 1 (objeto) thing; **cualquier ~** anything; **¿alguna otra ~?** *or* **¿alguna ~ más?** anything else?; **pon cada ~ en su lugar** put everything in its place; **queda poca ~** there's hardly anything left; **preguntó por no sé qué ~** he asked for something or other 2 (acto, acción) thing; **no sé hacer otra ~** it's the only thing I know how to do; **no puedo hacer otra ~** there's nothing else I can do *o* it's the only thing I can do; **me gusta hacer las ~s bien** I like to do things properly; **dejar las ~s a medias** to do things by halves; **entre una(s) ~(s) y otra(s) ...** what with one thing and another ...; **es la ~ más natural del mundo** it's perfectly normal 3 (al hablar): **¡qué ~s dices!** really, what a thing to say!; **dime una ~ ...** tell me something ...; **oye, una ~ ...** (por cierto) by the way ...; **tengo que contarte una ~** there's something I have to tell you 4 (detalle, punto): **quiero aclarar una ~** I want to make something clear 5 (asunto, tema) thing; **tenía ~s más importantes en que pensar** I had more important things to think about; **no creo que la ~ funcione** I don't think it's going to work; **fue ~ fácil** it was easy; **se enfada por cualquier ~** he gets angry over the slightest thing; **si por cualquier ~ no puedes venir, avísame** if you can't come for any reason, let me know; **por una ~ o por otra** for one reason or another; **esto no es otra ~ que nervios** it's just nerves; **esto no es ~ de broma/risa** this is no joke/no laughing matter; **la ~ es que ...** the thing is that ...
B **cosas** *fpl* (pertenencias) things (*pl*); **todas sus ~s** all her things; **mis ~s de deporte** my sports things
C (situación, suceso): **así están las ~s** that's how things are *o* stand; **la ~ se pone negra/fea** things are starting to get unpleasant; **¿cómo te van las ~s?** how are things?; **¿cómo está la ~?** (cómo está la situación) how are things?; (cómo estás) (Ven) how are you doing?; **las ~s no andan muy bien** things aren't too good; **son ~s de la vida** that's life!; **¡lo que son las ~s!** well, well! *o* fancy that! (colloq); **son ~s que pasan** these things happen; **en mi vida he visto/oído ~ igual** I've never seen/heard anything like it; **~ rara en él, se equivocó** he made a mistake, which is unusual for him; **¡qué ~ más extraña!** how strange *o* funny!; **esto es ~ de magia** *or* **de brujería** this is witchcraft!; **una ~ es ser bueno y otra ser el mejor** being good is one thing, but being the best is quite another
D 1 (fam) (ocurrencia): **¡tienes cada ~!** the things you come up (AmE) *o* (BrE) out with!; **esto es ~ de tu padre** this is your father's doing *o* idea 2 (comportamiento típico): **son ~s de niños** children are like that; **son ~s de Ana** that's one of Ana's little ways
E (incumbencia): **no es ~ tuya** it's none of your business; **no te preocupes, eso es ~ mía** don't worry, I'll handle it; **eso es ~ de mujeres** that's women's work
F (en locs) **cosa de** (AmS fam) so as to; **cosa de terminarlo** so as to finish it; **cosa que** (AmS fam) so that; **cosa que no me olvide** so that I don't forget; **no sea** *or* **no vaya a ser cosa que**: **llévate el paraguas, no sea ~ que llueva** take your umbrella just in case; **átalo, no sea ~ que se escape** tie it up so that it doesn't get away; **o cosa así** or so; ***cada ~ a su tiempo*** one thing at a time; ***como quien no quiere la ~*** casually; ***como si tal ~***: **no puedes irte como si tal ~** you can't go just like that *o* as if nothing had happened; **le dije que era peligroso y siguió como si tal ~** I told him it was dangerous but he just carried on *o* he carried on regardless; ***~ de ...*** (fam): **es ~ de unos minutos** it'll (only) take a couple of minutes; **es ~ de intentarlo** you just have to give it a go; **está a ~ de dos kilómetros** it's about two kilometers; ***darle ~ a algn*** (fam): **me da ~ comer caracoles/ver sangre** eating snails/the sight of blood makes me feel funny; **me da ~ pedirle tanto dinero** I feel awkward asking him for so much money; ***decirle a algn un par de*** *or* ***cuatro ~s*** (fam) to tell sb a thing or two; ***no ser gran ~*** (fam) to be nothing special (colloq); ***poca ~***: **es muy poca ~** (en apariencia) he's not much to look at; (en personalidad) he's not up to much (colloq); **queda algo pero poca ~** there's some left but not much; **un trabajo así es muy poca ~ para ella** a job like that isn't good enough for her; ***poner las ~s en su lugar*** *or* ***sitio*** to put *o* set the record straight; ***ser ~ hecha*** (CS) to be a foregone conclusion; ***ser/parecer otra ~***: **¡esto es otra ~!, ahora sí se oye** this is more like it! you can hear it now; **con ese peinado parece otra ~** she looks a new woman with that hairstyle; **¿invitas tú? ¡eso es otra ~!** are you paying? oh well, that's

different, then!; ***las ~s claras*** I like to know where I stand

cosaco -ca *m,f* Cossack; ***beber como un ~*** (fam) to drink like a fish (colloq)

coscorrón *m* (fam): **darse un ~** to bump *o* bang one's head; **le dio un ~** she smacked *o* cuffed him around the head (colloq)

cosecha *f*

A 1 (acción, época) harvest; **un vino de la ~ del 70** a 1970 vintage wine 2 (producto) crop; **la sequía echó a perder la ~** the drought caused the crop to fail; ***de mi/tu/su (propia) ~***: **estas zanahorias son de mi propia ~** I grew these carrots myself; **unos poemas de su propia ~** some of his own poems

B (de premios, éxitos): **después de su ~ de éxitos** following his many successes

cosechador -dora *m,f* 1 (persona) harvester 2 **cosechadora** *f* (máquina) combine (harvester)

cosechar [A1] *vt*

A (Agr) 1 (recoger) ‹*cereales*› to harvest; ‹*legumbres*› to pick 2 (Esp) (cultivar) ‹*cereales/patatas*› to grow

B ‹*aplausos/premios/honores*› to win; ‹*éxitos*› to achieve, reap (journ); ‹*admiración/respeto*› to win, earn; **trabajó mucho y no cosechó más que disgustos** he worked hard and it brought him nothing but trouble; ***se cosecha lo que se siembra*** as you sow, so you reap

■ **cosechar** *vi* to harvest

cosechero -ra *m,f* harvester

cosedor -dora *m,f* machinist

coser [E1] *vt* 1 (Indum, Tex) ‹*dobladillo*› to sew; ‹*botón*› to sew on; ‹*agujero*› to sew (up); **cóselo a máquina** sew *o* do it on the machine; ***ser ~ y cantar*** to be as easy as pie 2 ‹*herida*› to stitch

■ **coser** *vi* to sew

cosido *m* sewing

cosignatario -ria *m,f* cosignatory

cosmética *f* cosmetics (*pl*)

cosmético¹ -ca *adj* cosmetic (*before n*)

cosmético² *m* cosmetic

cósmico -ca *adj* cosmic

cosmogonía *f* cosmogony

cosmografía *f* cosmography

cosmógrafo -fa *m,f* cosmographer

cosmología *f* cosmology

cosmonauta *mf* cosmonaut

cosmopolita *adj/mf* cosmopolitan

cosmos *m* cosmos

cosmovisión *f* (frml) view of the world

coso¹ -sa *m,f* (Bol, Col, RPl) 1 (fam & pey) (tipo) jerk (colloq & pej) 2 (fam) (sustituyendo a nombre): **le dije a ~/cosa ...** I said to what's-his-name/what's-her-name ... (colloq)

coso² *m*

A (lugar cercado) enclosure, arena

(Compuesto) **coso taurino** bullring

B (carcoma) deathwatch beetle

C (fam) (cosa) thingy (colloq)

cospel *m* (Arg) token

cosquillas *fpl*: **no le hagas ~** don't tickle him; **¿tienes ~?** are you ticklish?; ***buscarle las ~ a algn*** to rile *o* annoy sb

cosquilleo *m* tickly feeling; **tenía un ~ en la garganta** he had a tickly throat; **tengo un ~ en la pierna** I have pins and needles in my leg; **sintió un ~ en la espalda** she felt something tickle her back

costa *f*

A (Geog) 1 (del mar — área) coast; (— perfil) coastline; **una ~ muy accidentada** a very rugged coastline; **la ~ atlántica** the Atlantic coast; **veranean en la ~** they spend their summers on the coast; **la C~ Azul** the Côte d'Azur 2 (RPl) (de río) bank; (de lago) shore

B (*en locs*) **a costa de**: **lo terminó a ~ de muchos sacrificios** he had to make a lot of sacrifices to finish it; **a ~ mía/de los demás** at my/other people's expense; **a toda costa** *or* **a costa de lo que sea** at all costs

C **costas** *fpl* (Der) costs (*pl*); **condenar a algn en ~s** to order sb to pay costs

costado *m* side; **pasar de ~** to go through sideways; **duerme de ~** she sleeps on her side; **escríbelo al ~** (RPl) write it in the margin; ***por los cuatro ~s***: **mexicano por los cuatro ~s** Mexican through and through

costal *m* sack, bag

costalada *f*, **costalazo** *m* (fam): **darse una ~** to fall heavily

costanera *f* (CS) (al lado — de río) riverside path (*o* road *etc*); (— del mar) promenade; (— de lago) lakeside path (*o* road *etc*)

costanero -ra *adj* coastal

costar [A10] *vt*

A (en dinero) to cost; **¿cuánto me ~á arreglarlo?** how much will it be *o* cost to fix it?

B (en perjuicios) (+ *me/te/le etc*): **el atentado que le costó la vida** the attack in which he lost his life; **le costó el puesto** it cost him his job; **el robo le costó 10 años de cárcel** he got 10 years for the robbery

C (en esfuerzo): **me ha costado mucho trabajo llegar hasta aquí** it has taken me a lot of hard work to get this far; ; **¿qué te cuesta hacerlo?** go on, why don't you do it?; **me cuesta trabajo creerlo** I find it hard *o* difficult to believe; **lo logró, pero le costó lo suyo** he managed it in the end, but not without a struggle; ***cueste lo que cueste*** at all costs

■ **costar** *vi*

A (en dinero) to cost; **el reloj me costó caro/barato** the watch cost a lot/didn't cost much

B (resultar perjudicial): **esto te va a ~ caro** you're going to pay dearly for this

C (resultar difícil): **me cuesta creerlo** I find it hard *o* difficult to believe; **nos costó convencerla/dormirnos** we had trouble persuading her/getting to sleep; **cuesta un poco/mucho acostumbrarse** it's not easy/it's very hard to get used to; **no te cuesta nada intentarlo** it won't do you any harm to give it a try; **¿te costó mucho encontrarlo?** did you have much trouble finding it?; **la física le cuesta** he finds physics difficult

Costa Rica *f* Costa Rica

costarricense *adj/mf* Costa Rican

costarriqueño -ña *adj/m,f* Costa Rican

coste *m* (Esp) ▸**costo A**

costear [A1] *vt*

A (financiar) to finance; **le costeó los estudios** she financed his studies

B (Náut) to coast, sail along the coast of

■ **costear** *vi* to sail along the coast

■ **costearse** *v pron* (*refl*) (pagarse): **se costeó él mismo los estudios** he paid his own way through college; **yo me costeé el viaje** I paid for the trip myself

coste-eficacia *m* (Esp) ▸**costo-eficacia**

costeño¹ -ña *adj* coastal

costeño² -ña *m,f*: **los ~s** people from coastal regions

costero -ra *adj* ‹*camino/pueblo*› coastal

costilla *f*

A (Anat) rib

B (AmS) (chuleta — de vaca) T-bone steak; (— de cerdo, cordero) chop

C (Náut) rib

D 1 (fam & hum) (cónyuge) better half (colloq & hum) 2 (Per fam) (novia) girlfriend

costillar *m* 1 (Anat) ribcage 2 (Náut) frame

costino -na *adj/m,f* (Chi) ▸**costeño¹,²**

costipado -da *adj/m* ▸**constipado**

costo *m*

A (Com, Econ, Fin) cost; **de bajo ~** low-cost, budget; **precio de ~** cost price; **al ~** at cost price

(Compuestos)

- **costo de (la) vida** cost of living
- **costos de fabricación/de funcionamiento** *mpl* manufacturing/operating costs (*pl*)

B (Esp arg) (hachís) hash (sl)

costo-eficacia *m* cost-efficiency, cost-effectiveness

costoso -sa *adj*

A 1 ‹*casa/coche/joya*› expensive 2 ‹*error*› costly

B ‹*trabajo/tarea*› difficult

costra *f* 1 (de herida) scab 2 (de suciedad) layer, coating

costumbre *f*
A (de individuo) habit; **tenía (la) ~ de madrugar** he was in the habit of getting up early; **agarró la ~ de ...** she got into the habit of ...; **tiene por ~ llamarme a esta hora** he usually calls me at this time; **para no perder la ~** as always *o* usual; **se van perdiendo las buenas ~s** good manners are becoming a thing of the past; **de ~** usual; **el sitio/a la hora de ~** the usual place/time; **como de ~** as usual; **se quejó más/menos que de ~** he complained more/less than he usually does
B (de país, pueblo) custom; **eso no es ~ en nuestro país** that is not customary in our country

costumbrismo *m: literary genre dealing with local customs*

costumbrista *adj: of or relating to* **costumbrismo**

costura *f* **1** (acción) sewing; ▸**alto**[1] **2** (puntadas) seam; **sin ~** seamless

costurera *f* seamstress

costurero *m* **1** (caja, estuche) workbox; (canasta) sewing basket; **~ de viaje** sewing kit **2** (Col) (de caridad) sewing bee

cota *f*
A (altura) height above sea level; **misil de baja ~** low-level missile
B (grado, cifra): **la delincuencia ha alcanzado ~s alarmantes** crime has reached alarming levels; **quiere alcanzar ~s más altas en su carrera** she wants to scale greater heights in her career
C (Indum) doublet
(Compuesto) **cota de mallas** coat of mail

cotarro *m* (Esp fam): **se armó un ~** there was a real to-do (colloq); **dirigir el ~** to be the boss *o* leader

cotejar [A1] *vt* ‹*documentos*› to compare; ‹*información/respuesta*› to collate; **~ algo CON algo** to check sth AGAINST sth

cotejo *m*
A (comparación) comparison, collating (frml)
B (AmL period) (Dep) game, match

cotelé *m* (Chi) corduroy

coterráneo -nea *m,f* compatriot

cotidiano -na *adj* ‹*vida*› everyday, daily

cotilla *mf* (Esp fam) gossip (colloq)

cotillear [A1] *vi* (Esp fam) to gossip

cotillón *m* (fiesta) ball; (baile) cotillion

cotización *f*
A (de moneda) value; (de acciones, valores, producto) price; **su ~ llegó a 500 pesos** it reached 500 pesos; **las acciones alcanzaron una ~ de 275 pesos** the shares were quoted at 275 pesos
B (cuota, prestación) contribution
C (Andes) (evaluación) valuation; (presupuesto) estimate

cotizado -da *adj* sought-after

cotizar [A4] *vt*
A **1** (Fin) ‹*acciones*› to quote; **acciones que se cotizan a 525 pesos** shares which have been quoted at 525 pesos; **acciones que se cotizan bien últimamente** shares which have been performing well recently; **la libra se cotizaba a 1,58 euros** the pound stood at 1.58 euros; **estos apartamentos se cotizan en $500.000** these apartments are valued at $500,000 **2** (apreciar, valorar) to value
B (Andes) ‹*cuadro/joyas*› to value; ‹*obra/reparación*› to give an estimate for
C (Chi fam) (prestar atención) to notice
■ **cotizar** *vi* **1** (aportar) to pay contributions **2** (Fin): **~ en Bolsa** to be listed *o* quoted on the Stock Exchange; **al cierre ~on a 2,78 euros** they closed at 2.78 euros
■ **cotizarse** *v pron* (Col) to increase in value

coto *m*
A (Dep, Ecol) reserve; ***poner ~ a algo*** to put a stop *o* an end to sth
(Compuesto) **coto de caza/pesca** game/fishing preserve
B (Andes, Ven) (bocio) goiter*

cotón *m* (Chi) (Tex) cotton fabric

cotona *f* (Chi) thick cotton shirt

cotorra *f*
A **1** (Zool) (loro) parrot; ***hablar como una ~*** to talk a mile a minute (AmE colloq), to talk nineteen to the dozen (BrE colloq) **2** (fam) (persona) chatterbox (colloq)
B (Ven fam) (conversación) chat (colloq); (cuento, mentira) tale

cotorrear [A1] *vi* (fam) to chatter
■ **cotorrear** *vt* (Méx, Ven fam) to smoothtalk (colloq)

cotorreo *m* (fam) chatter (colloq)

cototo *m* (Chi fam) bump (*on the head*)

cottolengo /koto'leŋgo/ *m* (RPl) (para ancianos) old people's home; (para niños) children's home; (para drogadictos, desamparados, etc) shelter, refuge

cotudo -da *m,f* **1** (Andes, Ven fam) (enfermo) *person with goiter* **2** (Col fam) (tonto) cretin (colloq & pej)

cotufas *fpl* (Ven) (maíz tostado) popcorn

COU /kou/ *m* (en Esp) = **Curso de Orientación Universitaria**

courier /ku'rje(r)/ *mf* courier

covacha *f* (fam) **1** (casucha) hovel **2** (Méx) (trastero) storage room

covadera *f* (Chi, Per) guano deposit

cowboy /kau'βoj, ko'βoj/ *m* (*pl* **-boys**) cowboy

coxis *m* (*pl* ~) ▸**cóccix**

coya *mf* ▸**colla**

coyón *mf* (Méx fam) chicken (colloq), coward

coyote *m*
A (Zool) coyote
B (Méx) (intermediario) fixer (colloq); (para cruzar la frontera) *person who helps illegal immigrants enter the USA*

coyuntura *f*
A (Anat) joint
B (frml *o* period) (situación) situation; **aprovechó la ~ para irse** he took advantage of the situation to leave; **a la espera de una ~ más favorable** awaiting more favorable circumstances

coyuntural *adj* (frml *o* period) **1** (presente) current **2** (temporal): **un plan ~** an interim plan; **problemas/factores ~es** temporary problems/factors

coz *f* **1** (de un caballo) kick; **dar** *or* **pegar coces** to kick **2** (de un fusil) recoil, kick

C.P. *m* = **código postal**

cps (= **caracteres por segundo**) cps

crac *m* (*pl* **cracs**) **1** (sonido) crack, snap **2** (Fin) crash

crack *m* (*pl* **cracks**)
A (droga) crack
B (AmL) (Dep) (persona) star; (caballo) champion

cranear [A1] *vt* (Andes fam) ‹*chiste/excusa*› to think up; ‹*atraco*› to plan, plot
■ **cranearse** *v pron* (Andes fam) (planear) to figure out

cráneo *m* skull, cranium (tech)

crápula *mf* **1** (libertino): **es un ~** he leads a dissolute life **2** (AmL) (canalla) swine

craso -sa *adj*
A (*delante del n*): **¡~ error!** that was a big mistake!; **dando muestras de crasa ignorancia** demonstrating his crass ignorance
B (Bot) succulent

cráter *m* crater

crawl /krol/ *m*: *tb* **estilo ~** crawl, front crawl

crayón *m* (Méx, RPl) wax crayon

creación *f*
A **1** (acción) creation; **un siglo de ~ literaria** a century of literary activity **2** (cosa creada) creation
B (Relig) **la Creación** the Creation

creador[1] **-dora** *adj* creative

creador[2] **-dora** *m,f*
A creator; **~es de moda** fashion designers
B (Relig) **el Creador** the Creator

crear [A1] *vt*
A **1** ‹*obra/modelo/tendencia*› to create, ‹*producto*› to develop **2** ‹*sistema*› to create, establish, set up; ‹*institución*› to set up, create; ‹*comisión/fondo*› to set up; ‹*empleo*› to create; ‹*ciudad*› to build
B ‹*dificultades/problemas*› to cause, create; ‹*ambiente/clima*› to create; ‹*fama/prestigio*› to bring; ‹*reputación*› to earn; **su arrogancia le creó muchas enemistades** his arrogance made him many enemies; **no quiero ~ falsas expectativas** I don't want to raise false hopes

■ **crearse** *v pron* ‹*problema*› to create … for oneself

creatividad *f* creativity

creativo¹ -va *adj* creative

creativo² -va *m,f* creative, copywriter

crecer [E3] *vi*

A [1] (aumentar de tamaño)«*ser vivo/pelo/uñas*» to grow; **ha crecido mucho** he's grown a lot [2] (criarse) to grow up; **crecieron en un pueblo** they grew up in a village

B «*río*» to rise; «*ciudad*» to grow; «*luna*» to wax

C [1] «*sentimiento/interés*» to grow; «*rumor*» to spread; **creció en la estima de todos** he grew in everyone's estimation [2] (en número, monto): **los sueldos no han crecido al ritmo de la inflación** wages have not kept pace with inflation; **el número de desempleados ha crecido** the number of unemployed has risen; **la economía ha crecido un 4%** the economy has grown by 4% [3] (en importancia, sabiduría) ~ EN **algo** to grow IN sth

■ **crecerse** *v pron*: **el equipo se crece en los partidos coperos** the team rises to the challenge in cup games; **~se** ANTE **algo/algn**: **se crece ante el peligro** he rises to the occasion when faced with danger

creces: **le devolví con ~ su dinero** I paid him back all his money and more; **pagar con ~ un error** to pay dearly for a mistake; **superar algo con ~** ‹*nivel/previsiones*› to far exceed sth; **superó con ~ la prueba de acceso** she passed the entrance exam with flying colors

crecida *f* [1] (subida de nivel): **el río experimentó una fuerte ~** the river level rose sharply [2] (desbordamiento): **las ~s del Paraná** the flooding of the Paraná

crecido -da *adj*

A ‹*persona*›: **está muy ~ para su edad** he's very big for his age

B ‹*pelo/barba*› long; **¡qué ~ tienes el pelo!** your hair is so long!

C ‹*río*› high

D ‹*número/proporción*› large

creciente *adj* [1] ‹*interés/necesidad*› increasing [2] (Astron): **luna ~** waxing moon

crecimiento *m*

A (Biol, Fisiol) growth; **está en período de ~** he's at that age when children grow quickly; **sufre un retraso en el ~** he suffers from stunted growth

B (aumento) growth; **un bajo ~** a low growth rate; **una industria en ~** a growth industry; **el ~ del PNB** the growth in the GNP

(Compuestos)

- **crecimiento cero** zero growth
- **crecimiento vegetativo** natural increase

credencial¹ *adj* ▸**carta A**

credencial² *f* document; **la ~ de su nuevo nombramiento** the document confirming your new appointment; **la ~ de socio** (Méx) membership card

(Compuesto) **credencial cívica** (Ur) voter registration card (AmE), voting card (BrE)

credibilidad *f* credibility

crédito *m*

A [1] (en negocio) credit; **tengo ~ en esa tienda** they let me have credit in that shop; **a ~** on credit [2] (cuenta) account [3] (préstamo) loan; **conceder un ~** to give *o* grant a loan

(Compuestos)

- **crédito a la exportación** export credit
- **crédito a largo/corto plazo** long-/short-term loan
- **crédito hipotecario** *or* **de vivienda** mortgage loan

B [1] (credibilidad): **fuentes dignas de ~** reliable sources; **no di ~ a sus palabras** I doubted his words (frml); ***no dar ~ a sus ojos/oídos***: **no di ~ a mis ojos/oídos** I couldn't believe my eyes/ears [2] (prestigio, fama) reputation; **un médico que goza de mucho ~** a doctor of good reputation

C (Cin, TV) credit

D (Educ) credit

credo *m* [1] (oración) creed [2] (creencias) creed, beliefs (*pl*)

credulidad *f* credulity, gullibility

crédulo -la *adj* credulous, gullible

creencia *f* belief; **en la ~ de que …** in the belief that …

creer [E13] *vi*

A [1] (Relig) to believe [2] (tener fe, confianza) ~ EN **algo/algn** to believe IN sth/sb [3] (+ *me/te/le etc*) to believe; **¡no te puedo ~!** I don't *o* can't believe it!

B (pensar, juzgar) to think; **¿estará en casa ahora? — no creo** will she be at home now? — I don't think so; **él la quiere — ¿tú crees?** he loves her — do you think so?; **ocurrió en 1965, según creo** I believe *o* understand it took place in 1965; **no creas, es bastante difícil** believe me, it's quite hard; **esto ya pasaba antes, no crea usted** this used to happen before as well, you know

■ **creer** *vt*

A (dar por cierto) to believe; **¡quién lo hubiera creído!** who would have believed it?; **hay que verlo para ~lo** it has to be seen to be believed; **lo creas o no lo creas** *or* **aunque no lo creas** believe it or not; **si no lo veo no lo creo** if I hadn't seen it with my own eyes I wouldn't have believed it; **¡ya lo creo!** of course!; **no (le) creas nada de lo que dice** don't believe a thing *o* a word he says; **¡no lo puedo ~!** I don't believe it!

B (pensar, juzgar) to think; **creo que sí/creo que no** I think so/I don't think so; **creo que va a llover** I think it's going to rain; **creo que es mi deber ayudarlo** I believe it's my duty to help him; **quiero ~ que se lo agradeciste** I hope you thanked them; **se cree que el incendio fue provocado** the fire is thought to have been started deliberately; **les hizo ~ que estaba enfermo** he made them think he was ill; **creo que no va a poder resolverlo** I don't believe *o* think she'll be able to sort it out; **no creí necesario avisarte** I didn't think it necessary to let you know; **no la creo capaz** I do not think she is capable; **¿me crees tan estúpida?** do you really think I'm that stupid?; **no ~** QUE + SUBJ: **no creo que pueda resolverlo** I doubt if *o* I don't think I'll be able to solve it; **no creo/no puedo ~ que lo haya hecho** I don't/can't believe that he did it; **no vaya a creer que es para él** he might get the impression it's for him; **~** + INF: **creí oír un ruido** I thought I heard a noise; **creo recordar que …** I seem to remember that …; **creo haberlo visto antes** I think I've seen it before

■ **creerse** *v pron*

A (dar por cierto, figurarse) [1] (*enf*) (con ingenuidad) to believe; **se cree todo lo que le dicen** she believes everything she's told; **eso nadie se lo cree** no one believes that; **que no se crea que es fácil** he shouldn't think it's easy [2] (con arrogancia) to think; **¿quién se ~á que es?** who does he think he is?; **¿qué se habrán creído?** what do they take me (*o* us etc) for?; **¿qué te crees, que soy tu criada?** what do you think I am, your maid or something?; **se lo tiene muy creído** (Esp fam) he's very full of himself (colloq); **¡que te crees tú eso!** *or* **¡que te lo has creído!** (Esp fam) you must be kidding! (colloq)

B (*refl*) [1] (considerarse): **no me creo capaz de hacerlo** I don't think I'm capable of doing it; **se cree muy listo** he thinks he's really clever [2] (CS fam) (estimarse superior) to think one is special (*o* great *etc*)

C (Méx) (fiarse) **~se** DE **algn** to trust sb

creíble *adj* credible, believable

creído -da *adj* [1] [SER] (engreído) conceited [2] [SER] (Arg) (crédulo) gullible

crema¹ *adj inv* cream; **(de) color ~** cream, cream-colored

crema² *f*

A (Coc) [1] (plato dulce) *type of custard* [2] (esp AmL) (de la leche) cream; **~ batida** whipped cream [3] (sopa) cream

(Compuestos)

- **crema agria** *or* **ácida** (AmL) sour *o* soured cream
- **crema chantilly** *or* **chantillí** (AmL) whipped cream (*with sugar, vanilla and egg white*)
- **crema de cacao** crème de cacao
- **crema doble/líquida** (AmL) double/single cream
- **crema pastelera** crème pâtissière, confectioner's custard

B **la crema** (lo mejor) the cream

C (en cosmética) cream

(Compuestos)

- **crema bronceadora** suntan lotion *o* cream
- **crema de afeitar** shaving cream
- **crema de calzado** (Esp) shoe cream
- **crema depilatoria** hair-removing cream
- **crema hidratante** moisturizer, moisturizing cream

cremación *f* cremation

C

cremallera *f* 1 (Indum) zipper (AmE), zip (BrE) 2 (Mec, Tec) rack
cremar [A1] *vt* to cremate
crematístico -ca *adj* (frml) financial, chrematistic (frml)
crematorio[1] -ria *adj* ▸**horno**
crematorio[2] *m* crematorium
cremosidad *f* creaminess
cremoso -sa *adj* ‹*salsa*› creamy; ‹*queso*› soft, creamy
crenchas *fpl* (CS fam & pey) hair
crep *m* (*pl* **creps**) ▸**crepe A**
crepa *f* (Méx) ▸**crepe A**
crepe /krep/ *m or f*
A (Coc) crepe
B **crepe** *m* ▸**crepé**
crepé *m*
A (Tex) crepe; ▸**papel**
(Compuesto) **crepé de china** crepe de Chine
B (caucho) crepe
crepería *f* creperie
crepitación *f* crackling
crepitar [A1] *vi* to crackle
crepuscular *adj* (liter) twilight (*before n*); **luz ~** twilight
crepúsculo *m* (del anochecer) twilight; (del amanecer) dawn light
crescendo *m* crescendo; **ir in ~** «*música/aplausos*» to rise in a crescendo; «*desempleo, inflación*» to rise
crespo[1] -pa *adj* (rizado) (AmL) curly; (muy rizado) frizzy
crespo[2] *m* (AmL) curl; ***con los ~s hechos*** (Andes fam): **me dejaron con los ~s hechos** they let me down; **quedarse con los ~s hechos** to be let down
crespón *m* (tela) crepe; (lazo) band
cresta *f*
A 1 (Zool) crest; (de gallo) comb 2 (de ola, monte) crest; ***estar en la ~ de la ola*** to be on *o* be riding on the crest of the wave
B (Chi vulg) (uso expletivo) ▸**mierda B4**
creta *f* chalk
cretáceo[1] -cea *adj* cretaceous
cretáceo[2] *m*: **el ~** the Cretaceous
cretinismo *m* cretinism
cretino[1] -na *adj* cretinous
cretino[2] -na *m,f* cretin
cretona *f* cretonne
creyente[1] *adj*: **es muy ~** she has a strong faith
creyente[2] *mf* believer; **los no ~s** the nonbelievers; **soy ~ pero no practicante** I believe in God but I don't go to church
creyera, creyese, etc *ver* **creer**
cría *f*
A (Agr) rearing, raising; (para la reproducción) breeding
B (Zool) 1 (camada) litter; (nidada) brood 2 (animal): **una ~ de ciervo** a baby deer; **el macho cuida las ~s** the male looks after the young
criadero *m* farm; **~ de pollos/de truchas** poultry/trout farm; **~ de perros** kennels; **~ de ostras/mejillones** oyster/mussel bed; **se ha convertido en un ~ de ratas** it's become a breeding ground for rats
criadilla *f* testicle
criado -da (*m*) servant; (*f*) servant, maid
criador -dora *m,f* breeder
crianza *f*
A (Agr) raising, rearing; (para la reproducción) breeding
B (de niños) upbringing
C (Vin) aging*

> **crianza**
> A term which refers both to the process of ageing wines, and to a category of wines, *vinos de crianza*, which have been aged for a minimum of two years, first in barrels or the more modern stainless steel tanks, and then in the bottle

criar [A17] *vt*
A ‹*niño*› 1 (cuidar, educar) to bring up, raise; **la ~on los abuelos** she was brought up *o* raised by her grandparents; **ya tiene a sus hijos criados** her children are grown up now 2 (amamantar) to breast-feed; **criado con biberón** bottle-fed
B ‹*ganado*› to raise, rear; (para la reproducción) to breed; ‹*pollos/pavos*› to breed
C (producir): **el pan ha criado moho** the bread has gone moldy; **este perro cría pulgas** this dog is always covered in fleas
■ **criar** *vi* «*mujer*» to breast-feed; «*animal*» to suckle
■ **criarse** *v pron* to grow up; **nos criamos juntos** we grew up together; **me crié con mi abuela** I was brought up by my grandmother; ***a la que te criaste*** (CS fam) any old how
criatura *f*
A (niño pequeño) child; **pero ~ ...** you silly thing …
B (cosa creada) creature
criba *f* 1 (instrumento) sieve 2 (proceso de selección): **la primera ~** the first stage of the selection process; **hicimos una ~ de las solicitudes** we went through the applications
cribar [A1] *vt* to sieve, sift
cricket /'krike(t)/ *m* cricket
crimen *m* 1 (delito grave) serious crime; (asesinato) murder 2 (fam) (pena, lástima) crime (colloq); **es un ~ tirar esta comida** it's a crime to throw away this food; **¡qué ~!** it's wicked *o* criminal
(Compuestos)
• **crimen de guerra** war crime
• **crimen de sangre** violent crime
• **crimen organizado**: **el ~ ~** organized crime
• **crimen pasional** crime of passion
criminal *adj/mf* criminal
criminalidad *f* 1 (cualidad) criminality 2 (número de crímenes) crime; **ha aumentado la ~** there has been an increase in crime
criminalista[1] *adj* criminal (*before n*)
criminalista[2] *mf* criminal lawyer
criminólogo -ga *m,f* criminologist
crin *f*
A 1 (del caballo) *tb* **~es** mane 2 (material) horsehair
B (esparto) esparto grass
crineja *f* (Ven) braid (AmE), plait (BrE)
crío, cría (esp Esp fam) *m,f* kid (colloq); **¡no seas ~!** don't be such a baby!
criogenia *f* cryogenetics
criollo[1] -lla *adj* 1 (Hist) Creole 2 (AmL) (por oposición a extranjero) Venezuelan (*o* Peruvian *etc*); ‹*plato/artesanía/cocina*› national; ***a la criolla*** (RPl fam) informal, casual 3 ‹*lengua*› creole; ▸**viveza B**
criollo[2] -lla *m,f* 1 (Hist) Creole (*of European descent born in a Spanish American colony*) 2 (AmL) (nativo) Venezuelan (*o* Peruvian *etc*) 3 **criollo** *m* (Ling) creole; ***decir algo/hablar en ~*** (AmL fam) to say sth in plain Spanish
criónica *f* cryonics
cripta *f* crypt
críptico -ca *adj* (en clave) cryptic; (oscuro, hermético) ‹*lenguaje*› obscure
criptografía *f* cryptography
criptográfico -ca *adj* cryptographic
criptograma *m* cryptogram
criquet *m* (Dep) cricket
crisálida *f* chrysalis, chrysalid
crisantemo *m* chrysanthemum
crisis *f* (*pl* ~) 1 (situación grave) crisis; **una grave ~ energética** a serious energy crisis; **estar en ~** to be in crisis; **~ de fe** crisis of faith; **pasar por una etapa de ~** to go through a crisis 2 (Med) crisis; **hacer ~** «*enfermedad*» to become critical 3 (period) (remodelación ministerial) *tb* **~ de Gobierno** cabinet reshuffle
(Compuestos)
• **crisis cardíaca** heart failure, cardiac arrest
• **crisis de identidad** identity crisis
• **crisis de los cuarenta** midlife crisis
• **crisis ministerial** cabinet crisis (*resulting in dismissals or resignations*)
• **crisis nerviosa** nervous breakdown
crisma[1] *m* chrism

crisma[2] *f*: **romperse la ~** (fam) to crack one's head open (colloq); **romperle la ~ a algn** (fam) to smash sb's face in (colloq)

crismas *m* (*pl* ~) (Esp) Christmas card

crisol *m* [1] (Tec) crucible [2] (punto de confluencia) melting pot

crispación *f* tension

crispado -da *adj* tense

crispar [A1] *vt* [1] (contraer): **con la expresión crispada por el dolor** his face tensed/contorted with pain [2] (exasperar) to infuriate; **me crispa los nervios** it really irritates me *o* gets on my nerves

■ **crisparse** *v pron* «*rostro/expresión*» to tense up; «*persona*» to get irritated; **su rostro se crispó de dolor** her face contorted with pain

cristal *m*

A (vidrio fino) crystal; (vidrio) (Esp) glass; **puerta de ~** glass door

Compuestos

- **cristal de Bohemia/Murano** Bohemian crystal/Venetian glass
- **cristal de roca** rock crystal
- **cristal tallado** *or* (AmL) **cortado** cut glass

B [1] (lente) lens [2] (Esp) (trozo) piece of glass; **~es rotos** pieces of broken glass [3] (Esp) (de ventana) pane; **limpiar los ~s** to clean the windows; **~es antibalas/ahumados** bulletproof/smoked glass

Compuestos

- **cristal delantero** (Esp) windshield (AmE), windscreen (BrE)
- **cristal trasero** (Esp) rear windshield (AmE), rear windscreen (BrE)

C (Min, Quím) crystal

cristalera *f* (Esp) [1] (mueble) display cabinet, dresser [2] (escaparate — de tienda) shop window; (— de bar, cafetería) display window [3] (puertas) French windows (*pl*), French doors (*pl*) (AmE); (ventanas) windows (*pl*)

cristalería *f*

A (Esp) (taller) glazier's; (fábrica) glassworks

B (objetos) glassware; (juego) set of glasses

cristalero -ra *m,f* (Esp) (persona que instala) glazier; (limpiacristales) window cleaner

cristalino[1] **-na** *adj* crystalline

cristalino[2] *m* crystalline lens

cristalización *f* crystallization

cristalizar [A4] *vi* [1] (Fís, Min) to crystallize [2] «*proyecto/idea*» to crystallize; **~ EN algo** to materialize IN sth

■ **cristalizar** *vt* to crystallize

■ **cristalizarse** *v pron* to crystallize

cristalografía *f* crystallography

cristianamente *adv*: **vivir ~** to live as good Christians; **murió ~** he died in a state of grace

cristiandad *f* Christendom

cristianismo *m* Christianity

cristianizar [A4] *vt* to Christianize

cristiano[1] **-na** *adj* Christian; **¿eres ~?** are you a Christian?

cristiano[2] **-na** *m,f* [1] (Relig) Christian [2] (fam) (persona): **¡no hay ~ que la entienda!** no one can understand her!; ***en ~*** (fam) (en español) in Spanish; (sin tecnicismos) in plain Spanish (*o* English *etc*)

Compuestos

- **cristiano renacido** born-again Christian
- **cristiano viejo** *Christian with neither Jewish nor Moorish ancestry*

cristo *m* crucifix

Cristo Christ; **antes/después de ~** before Christ *o* BC/AD; ***con el ~ en la boca*** with one's heart in one's mouth; ***~ y la madre*** (fam) everyone and his brother (AmE colloq), the world and his wife (BrE colloq); ***donde ~ dio las tres voces*** *or* ***perdió la alpargata*** (en un lugar — lejano) miles away; (— remoto) in the middle of nowhere; ***ir*** *or* ***estar hecho un ~*** (Esp fam) to be absolutely filthy; ***ni ~***: **ni ~ entiende** *or* **no hay ~ que entienda su letra** absolutely nobody can understand her handwriting

criterio *m* [1] (norma, principio) criterion; **tenemos que unificar ~s** we have to agree on our criteria [2] (capacidad para juzgar, discernir) discernment (frml), judgment*; **una persona de buen ~** a person of sound judgment; **no tiene ~** he has no common sense; **usa tu propio ~** use your own judgment; **lo dejo a tu ~** I leave that to your discretion *o* judgment [3] (opinión, juicio) opinion; **su ~ es que ...** he is of the view *o* opinion that ...

crítica *f*

A (ataque, censura) criticism; **ha sido objeto de numerosas ~s** she has come in for *o* been the object of a lot of criticism; **dirigió duras ~s contra el obispo** he launched a fierce attack on the bishop

B (Art, Espec, Lit) [1] (reseña) review; (ensayo) critique; **la película ha recibido muy buenas ~s** the movie has had very good reviews [2] **la ~** (los críticos) the critics (*pl*); **recibió los elogios de la ~ internacional** it was well received by critics worldwide [3] (actividad) criticism

Compuesto **crítica literaria** literary criticism

criticable *adj* reprehensible (frml)

criticar [A2] *vt* [1] (atacar, censurar) to criticize; **fue muy criticado** it was fiercely criticized; **lo criticó duramente** he strongly criticized him [2] (Art, Espec, Lit) ‹*libro/película*› to review

■ **criticar** *vi* to gossip, backbite

crítico[1] **-ca** *adj*

A ‹*análisis/estudio*› critical; **el sentido ~ del alumno** the student's critical awareness

B (decisivo, crucial) critical; **se encuentra en estado ~** she is in a critical condition; **está en la edad crítica** (en la adolescencia) she's at that difficult age; (en la menopausia) (fam & euf) she's going through the change (colloq & euph)

crítico[2] **-ca** *m,f* critic; **~ de cine** movie critic

criticón[1] **-cona** *adj* (fam & pey) critical, hypercritical

criticón[2] **-cona** *m,f* (fam & pey) faultfinder

Croacia *f* Croatia

croar [A1] *vi* to croak

croata[1] *adj* Croatian, Croat

croata[2] *mf* Croat; **los ~s** the Croats, Croatian people

crocante[1] *adj* (esp RPl) crunchy

crocante[2] *m* (turrón) *candy made with toasted almonds and caramel*; (helado) *ice cream coated in nutty chocolate*

croché, crochet /kro'ʃe, kro'tʃe/ *m* crochet; **hacer ~** to crochet

croissant /krwa'san/ *m* (*pl* **-ssants**) croissant

crol *m* (Dep) crawl

cromado *m* chroming

cromar [A1] *vt* to chromium-plate

cromático -ca *adj* chromatic; **toda la gama cromática del verde** a complete range of greens

cromo *m* [1] (metal) chromium, chrome [2] (Esp) (estampa) picture card, sticker

cromosoma *m* chromosome

crónica *f* [1] (Period) report, article; (Rad, TV) report; **~ deportiva/de sociedad** sport(s)/society page (*o* section *etc*); **~ de sucesos** accident and crime reports [2] (Hist) chronicle

crónico -ca *adj* ‹*enfermedad/problema*› chronic; **¡lo suyo es ~!** (fam) she's a hopeless case! (colloq)

cronista *mf* [1] (esp AmL) (periodista) journalist, reporter; **~ de radio** radio broadcaster [2] (Hist) chronicler

cronología *f* chronology

cronológico -ca *adj* chronological

cronometraje *m* timekeeping; **~ manual** manual timekeeping

cronometrar [A1] *vt* to time

cronómetro *m* (Tec) chronometer; (Dep) stopwatch

croqueta *f* croquette; **~s de carne** meat croquettes

croquis *m* (*pl* ~) sketch

cross /kros/ *m* [1] (deporte — en atletismo) cross-country running; (— en motociclismo) motocross [2] (carrera — a pie) cross country, cross-country race; (— en moto) motocross race

cross-country /kros'kʌntri/ *m* (*pl* ~) (en atletismo) cross-country running; (en hípica) cross-country

crótalo *m* [1] (Zool) rattlesnake [2] **crótalos** *mpl* (liter) (castañuelas) castanets (*pl*)

croto -ta *m,f* (RPl fam): **es un ~** he's useless

C

croupier /kru'pje(r)/ *mf* (*pl* **-piers**) croupier

cruce *m*

A (acción) crossing

B (de calles) crossroads; Ⓢ **cruce peligroso** dangerous junction

(Compuesto) **cruce peatonal** *or* **de peatones** pedestrian crossing

C (Telec): **hay un ~ en las líneas** there's a crossed line; ***tener un ~ de cables*** (fam) to be in a muddle (colloq)

D (Agr, Biol) cross

cruceiro *m*

A (cruz) stone cross

B (unidad monetaria) cruzeiro (*former Brazilian unit of currency*)

crucero *m*

A (viaje) cruise; **hizo un ~ por el Caribe** he went on a Caribbean cruise

B (barco de guerra) cruiser

C (Méx) (de carreteras) crossroads; (Ferr) grade crossing (AmE), level crossing (BrE)

cruceta *f* (Náut) crosstree; (Auto, Mec) crosshead

crucial *adj* crucial

crucificar [A2] *vt* to crucify

crucifijo *m* crucifix

crucifixión *f* crucifixion

crucigrama *m* crossword, crossword puzzle

cruda *f* (AmC, Méx fam) hangover

crudeza *f* [1] (del clima) severity, harshness [2] (del lenguaje) harshness, rawness; (de imágenes) harshness; **la cámara revela con ~ la miseria del país** the camera reveals the reality of poverty in that country

crudo¹ -da *adj*

A [ESTAR] ‹*carne/verduras/pescado*› (sin cocinar) raw; (poco hecho) underdone

B [SER] [1] ‹*invierno/clima*› severe, harsh [2] ‹*lenguaje/imágenes/realidad*› harsh

C **(de) color ~** natural; ‹*lana/encaje*› ecru

D [ESTAR] (AmC, Méx fam) (con resaca): **¡estoy ~!** I have a hangover

crudo² *m* crude oil, crude

cruel *adj* cruel; **ser ~ con algn** to be cruel to sb; **la venganza será ~** (hum) just you wait! (I'll get you!) (colloq)

crueldad *f* cruelty; **los trataban con ~** they treated them cruelly; **eso es una ~** that's cruel

(Compuesto) **crueldad mental** mental cruelty

cruento -ta *adj* (liter) bloody

crujido *m* [1] (de tablas, muelles, ramas) creaking [2] (de papel, hojas secas) rustling; (de seda) rustle [3] (de los nudillos, las rodillas) cracking [4] (de la grava, nieve) crunching [5] (de los dientes) grinding

crujiente *adj* ‹*galletas/tostadas*› crunchy; **el pan está ~** the bread is nice and crusty

crujir [I1] *vi* [1] «*tabla/muelles/ramas*» to creak; «*hojas secas*» to rustle [2] «*nudillos/rodillas*» to crack [3] «*grava/nieve*» to crunch [4] «*galletas/tostadas*» to be crunchy [5] «*dientes*»: **le crujen los dientes cuando duerme** he grinds his teeth in his sleep

crupier *mf* (*pl* **-piers**) croupier

crustáceo *m* crustacean

cruz *f*

A [1] (figura) cross; **marcar con una ~** mark with a cross; **ponerse con los brazos en ~** stand with your arms stretched out to the sides; ***~ y raya*** (Esp fam): **¡con José, ~ y raya!** I'm through with José (colloq); ***hacerle la ~ a algo/algn*** (CS fam) to refuse to have anything to do with sth/sb; ***hacerse cruces*** (fam): **me hago cruces de pensarlo** it makes my blood run cold just to think about it [2] (ornamento, condecoración) cross; **la ~ de la Legión de Honor** the cross of the Legion of Honor [3] **la Cruz** (Relig) the Cross

(Compuestos)

- **cruz gamada** swastika
- **cruz griega/latina** Greek/Latin cross
- **Cruz Roja** Red Cross

B (carga) cross; **cada uno lleva su ~ a cuestas** we all have our cross to bear; **¡qué ~!** (fam) what a pain! (colloq)

C (de moneda) reverse; **cara o ~** heads or tails

cruza *f* (AmL) (de animales) cross

cruzada *f* crusade; **la ~ contra la droga** the crusade against drugs

cruzado¹ -da *adj*

A (atravesado): **había un árbol ~ en la carretera** there was a tree lying across the road

B ‹*abrigo/chaqueta*› double-breasted

C ‹*cheque*› crossed

cruzado² *m*

A (Hist) crusader

B (en boxeo) cross

cruzar [A4] *vt*

A (atravesar) ‹*calle/mar/puente*› to cross; **cruzó el río a nado** she swam across the river

B ‹*piernas*› to cross; **con los brazos cruzados** with my/your/his arms crossed *o* folded; **crucemos los dedos** let's keep our fingers crossed

C ‹*cheque*› to cross

D (tachar) to cross out

E ‹*palabras/saludos*› to exchange

F (llevar al otro lado) to take (*o* carry *etc*) ... across

G ‹*animales/plantas*› to cross

■ **cruzar** *vi* (atravesar) to cross; **~on por el puente** they went across the bridge

■ **cruzarse** *v pron*

A (*recípr*) [1] «*caminos/líneas*» to intersect, meet [2] (en un viaje, un camino): **los trenes se ~on a mitad de camino** the trains passed each other half way; **nuestras cartas se han debido de ~** our letters must have crossed in the post; **seguro que nos ~emos por el camino** (nos veremos) we're sure to meet *o* pass each other on the way; (no nos veremos) we're sure to miss each other along the way; **~se con algn** to see *o* pass sb

B (interponerse): **se le cruzó una moto** a motorcycle pulled out in front of him; **se nos cruzó otro corredor** another runner cut in front of us

CSCE *f* (= **Conferencia de Seguridad y Cooperación en Europa**) CSCE

CSF, c.s.f. *m* (= **coste, seguro y flete**) CIF, c.i.f.

cta. (= **cuenta**) a/c

cte. = **corriente**

cu *f: name of the letter* **q**

c/u = **cada uno/una**

CU *f* (en Méx) = **Ciudad Universitaria**

cua, cuac *m* quack

cuaco *m* (Méx fam & pey) nag (colloq & pej)

cuaderno *m* (de ejercicios) exercise book; (de notas) notebook

(Compuestos)

- **cuaderno de bitácora** log, logbook, ship's log
- **cuaderno (de) borrador** rough notebook
- **cuaderno de espiral** *o* (Chi) **de anillos** spiral-bound notebook
- **cuaderno TIR** TIR carnet

cuadra *f*

A (Equ) stable, stables (*pl*); **la ~ Giménez** the Giménez stable *o* stables

B (AmL) [1] (distancia entre dos esquinas) block [2] (Agr) *measurement of agricultural land*

cuadrado¹ -da *adj*

A [1] (de forma) square [2] (Mat) ‹*metro/centímetro*› square (*before n*); **22 metros ~s** 22 square meters

B [ESTAR] (fam) (fornido) well-built, big, hefty (colloq)

C [SER] (AmL) (cerrado de mente) (fam) inflexible

cuadrado² *m* square; **25 elevado al ~** 25 squared

cuadrafonía *f* quadraphonics, quadriphony

cuadrafónico -ca *adj* quadraphonic

cuadragésimo -ma *adj/pron* [1] (ordinal) fortieth; *para ejemplos ver* **vigésimo** [2] (partitivo): **la cuadragésima parte** a fortieth

cuadrangular¹ *adj* ‹*base/forma*› quadrangular; (Dep) (AmL) quadrangular

cuadrangular² *m* (Méx) home run

cuadrante *m* [1] (Astrol, Mat) quadrant [2] (instrumento) quadrant [3] (esfera — de instrumento) dial; (— de reloj) face [4] (Auto) dial

(Compuesto) **cuadrante solar** sundial

cuadrar [A1] *vi*

A [1] «*cuentas*» to tally, balance [2] «*declaraciones/testimo-*

nias» to tally; ~ **CON algo** to fit in WITH sth, tally WITH sth; **el apelativo le cuadra** the name suits him [3] «*colores/ropa*» to go together; ~ **CON algo** to go WITH sth

B [1] (convenir): **si cuadra iré a verlo** if I can fit it in, I'll go and see him; (+ *me/te/le etc*) **lo hará cuando le cuadre** he will do it when it suits him [2] (Ven) (para una cita) ~ **CON algn** to arrange to meet sb; ~ **PARA + INF** to arrange to + INF

■ **cuadrar** *vt* [1] (Com): ~ **la caja** to cash up [2] ‹*figura geométrica*› to square [3] (Col, Ven) ‹*carro*› to park

■ **cuadrarse** *v pron*

A [1] «*soldado*» to stand to attention [2] «*caballo/toro*» to stand stock-still [3] (fam) (plantarse) to stand firm

B (Col fam) (ennoviarse) to get engaged; ~**se CON algn** to get engaged TO sb

C (Chi fam) [1] (solidarizarse) ~**se CON algn** to side WITH sb [2] (colaborar) ~**se CON algo** to help out WITH sth

D [1] (Col, Ven fam) (estacionarse) to park [2] (Per fam) (enfrentarse): **cuadrársele a algn** to stand up to sb

cuadratura *f* quadrature; ***la ~ del círculo*** squaring the circle

cuadrícula *f* grid, squares (*pl*)

cuadriculado -da *adj* ‹*papel*› squared; **mapa ~** grid map

cuadricular [A1] *vt* to draw a grid on

cuadrienio *m* quadrennium

cuadrilátero[1] **-ra** *adj* quadrilateral

cuadrilátero[2] *m* [1] (Mat) quadrilateral [2] (period) (de boxeo) ring

cuadrilla *f* [1] (Taur) cuadrilla (*team of matador's assistants*) [2] (de obreros) team, gang; (de soldados) squad; (de maleantes) gang; **¡vaya ~ de vagos!** what a bunch of layabouts!

cuadro *m*

A [1] (Art) (pintura) painting; (grabado) picture [2] (Teatr) scene [3] (gráfico) table, chart

B [1] (Lit) (descripción) picture, description; **me pintó un ~ muy negro** he painted me a very bleak picture [2] (panorama) scene, sight; **el campo de batalla ofrecía un ~ desolador** the battlefield presented a scene of devastation; **se complica el ~ político** the political picture is becoming complicated

(Compuesto) **cuadro de costumbres** *description of local customs*

C [1] (cuadrado) square, check; **tela a** *or* **de ~s** checked material; **zanahorias cortadas en cuadritos** diced carrots [2] (en béisbol) diamond

D (Med) symptoms (*pl*); **uno de los ~s más frecuentes** one of the most common combinations of manifestations *o* symptoms

(Compuesto) **cuadro clínico** clinical manifestation, symptoms (*pl*)

E (tablero) board, panel

(Compuestos)

- **cuadro de distribución** control panel
- **cuadro de mandos** *or* **instrumentos** (Auto) dashboard; (Aviac) instrument panel

F (de bicicleta) frame

G (en organización): **los ~s directivos del partido** the top party officials; **~ de profesionales** team of professionals; **los ~s superiores/inferiores** (de empresa) senior/junior management; (del ejército) senior/junior officers

(Compuesto) **cuadros de mando** *mpl* (de ejército) commanders (*pl*); (de organización) leaders (*pl*)

H (RPl) (Dep) team; ***ser del otro ~*** (Ur fam) to be gay

I **cuadros** *mpl* (Chi frml) (Indum) panties (*pl*) (AmE), briefs (*pl*) (BrE frml)

cuadrúpedo -da *adj/m* quadruped (*before n*)

cuádruple[1] *adj* quadruple

cuádruple[2] *m*: **esta cifra es el ~ de la que esperábamos** this figure is four times what we expected; **su fortuna ha aumentado el ~** his wealth has increased four-fold *o* has quadrupled

cuadruplicado *adj*: **por ~** in quadruplicate

cuadruplicar [A2] *vt* to quadruple

■ **cuadruplicarse** *v pron* to quadruple

cuádruplo[1] **-pla** *adj* ▸ **cuádruple**[1]

cuádruplo[2] *m* ▸ **cuádruple**[2]

cuajada *f* junket, curd

cuajado -da *adj*

A (liter) (lleno) ~ **DE algo**: **un cielo ~ de estrellas** a sky studded with stars; **una vida cuajada de éxitos** a life crammed with achievements; **tenía la frente cuajada de gotitas de sudor** his forehead was beaded with sweat

B (Col) (musculoso) well-built, hefty (colloq)

cuajar [A1] *vi*

A [1] «*leche*» to curdle; «*flan/yogur*» to set [2] «*nieve*» to settle

B [1] «*ideología*» to be accepted; «*reforma*» to come about; «*argumento/historia*» to come together; «*plan/proyecto*» to come off; «*moda*» to catch on, take off [2] «*persona*» to fit in

■ **cuajar** *vt* [1] ‹*leche*› to curdle [2] (llenar) ~ **algo DE algo** to fill sth WITH sth

■ **cuajarse** *v pron* to curdle

cuajo *m*

A (sustancia) rennet

B (raíz): **arrancar algo de ~** ‹*planta*› to pull sth out by the roots; ‹*vicio/corrupción*› to root out (completely)

cual[1] *pron*

A [1] **el ~/la ~/los ~es/las ~es** (hablando de personas) (*sujeto*) who; (*complemento*) who, whom (frml); (hablando de cosas) which; **el motivo por el ~ lo hizo** the reason why he did it; **según lo ~ ...** by which ...; **dos/la mayoría de los ~es** (hablando de cosas) two/most of which; (hablando de personas) two/most of whom [2] **lo ~** which; **por lo ~** as a result *o* therefore; **con lo ~**: **me dijo que yo allí sobraba, con lo ~ me fui** he told me that I wasn't wanted there, whereupon *o* at which point I left; **olvidó el dinero, con lo ~ no pude comprar nada** he forgot the money, which meant that I couldn't buy anything

B (*en locs*) **cada cual** everyone, everybody; **~ cual debe hacerse cargo de lo suyo** everyone must be responsible for their own things; **cada ~ se fue por su lado** each went his separate way, everyone went their separate ways; **sea cual sea** *or* **fuera** *or* **fuere** whatever; **sea ~ sea su decisión** whatever their decision is *o* may be

cual[2] *prep* (liter) like; **~ fiera enfurecida ...** like a raging beast ... (liter)

cuál[1] *pron*

A (uno en particular) which; (uno en general) what; **¿~ quieres?** which (one) do you want?; **¿y ~ es el problema?** so, what's the problem?; **¿~ es su opinión?** what is your opinion?; **¡~ no sería su sorpresa!** you can imagine his surprise

B (*en locs*) **a cuál más**: **son a ~ más insoportable** they are all equally unbearable; **cuál más, cuál menos** to a greater or lesser degree

cuál[2] *adj* (esp AmL): **¿a ~ colegio vas?** what *o* which school do you go to?

cualesquiera[1] *adj*: *ver* **cualquiera**[1]

cualesquiera[2] *pron*: *ver* **cualquiera**[2]

cualidad *f* [1] (virtud, aptitud) quality; **tiene muchas ~es** she has many qualities; **entre sus ~es no se cuenta la paciencia** patience is not one of his virtues [2] (característica) quality

cualificado -da *adj* (Esp) ▸ **calificado**

cualificar [A2] *vt* (Esp) ▸ **calificar B2**

cualitativo -va *adj* qualitative

cualquier *adj*: *apocopated form of* **cualquiera** *used before nouns*

cualquiera[1] *adj* (*pl* **cualesquiera** *or* (crit) **cualquiera**) [*see also note under* **cualquier**] any; **en cualquier momento** (at) any time; **cualquier cosa/persona** anything/anyone; **en cualquier lado** anywhere; **de cualquier forma que se haga** whichever way you do it; **de cualquier forma** *or* **manera te llamaré** I'll call you in any case; **lo voy a hacer de ~ forma** I'm going to do it anyway; **como cualquier día** *or* **como un día ~** just like (on) any other day; **uno ~** any of them; **es un mercenario ~** he's nothing but a mercenary

cualquiera[2] *pron* (*pl* **cualesquiera** *or* (crit) **cualquiera**) [1] (refiriéndose — a dos personas o cosas) either (of them); (— a más de dos cosas) any one; (— a más de dos personas) anybody, anyone; **¿cuál de los dos? — cualquiera** which one? — either (of them); **pregúntaselo a ~** ask anybody *o* anyone (you like); **¿puedo elegir ~?** can I choose any one (I like)?; **~ que elijas estará bien** whichever (one) you choose *o* any one you choose will be fine; **cualesquiera que hayan sido sus motivos** whatever his motives may have been 2 (iró) (nadie): **¡a ti ~ te entiende!** I just don't understand you!; **¡~ sabe!** who knows!; **¡~ se atreve!** who would dare!

cualquiera³ *f* (pey): **una ~** a hussy, a floozy *o* (BrE) tart (colloq & pej)

cualquiera⁴ *m*: **un ~** a nobody

C

cuán *adv* (liter) how; **le hice ver ~ equivocada estaba** I made her see how wrong she was

cuan *adv: apocopated form of* **cuanto** *used before adjectives*: **cayó al suelo ~ largo era** he fell full-length on the floor; **quedó demostrado ~ incapaz es** his incompetence was made plain for all to see

cuando¹

A *conj* 1 (con valor temporal) when; **ahora es ~ me viene mejor** now is the best time for me; **~ estoy solo** when I'm alone; **~ éramos pequeños** when we were young; (+ *subj*) **ven ~ quieras** come when *o* whenever you like 2 (referido al futuro) (+ *subj*) when; **~ se mejore** when she gets better; **~ sea viejo** when I'm old

B 1 (si) if; **será verdad ~ él lo dice** it must be true if he says so 2 (con valor adversativo) when; **dijo 2 cuando en realidad son 3** he said 2 when what he meant was 3

C (*en locs*) **cada cuando** (esp AmL) every so often; **de vez en cuando** from time to time, every so often; **cuando más** *or* **mucho** at (the) most, at the outside; **cuando menos** at least; **cuando quiera** whenever

cuando² *prep* (fam): **yo estaba allí ~ la explosión** I was there when the explosion happened; **una ermita de ~ los moros** a hermitage from the time of the Moors

cuándo¹ *adv* when; **¿de ~ es esa foto?** when was that photo taken?; **¿para ~ estará terminado?** when will it be ready (by)?; **¿desde ~ lo sabes?** how long have you known?; **¿desde ~?** since when?; **¡~ no!** (AmL) as usual!

cuándo² *m*: **el ~** the when

cuantía *f* 1 (importe): **la rebaja de las ~s de las pensiones** the reduction in the level of pensions; **la ~ de los daños** the extent of the damage; **una ~ mínima de 20.000 euros** a minimum (amount) of 20,000 euros; **la ~ de la deuda asciende a un millón** the total of the debt amounts to one million; **un aumento de la ~ de las becas** an increase in the size of grants 2 (importancia) significance, importance; **de mayor ~** of major significance *o* importance; **de menor ~** unimportant, insignificant; **un funcionario de escasa ~** an insignificant civil servant 3 (Der) claim, sum claimed

cuántico -ca *adj* quantum (*before n*)

cuantificar [A2] *vt* 1 ‹*valor/daños/pérdidas*› to quantify, assess 2 (Fís) to quantize 3 (Fil) to quantify

cuantioso -sa *adj* substantial

cuantitativo -va *adj* quantitative

cuanto¹ *adv*

A (tanto como) as much as; **grita ~ quieras** shout as much as you like

B (*como conj*): **~s más/menos seamos, mejor** the more/the fewer of us there are the better; **~ antes empecemos, más pronto terminaremos** the sooner we begin, the sooner we'll finish

C (*en locs*) **cuanto antes** as soon as possible; **cuanto más** let alone; **es duro para una persona sana, ~ más para un enfermo** it's hard enough for a healthy person, let alone somebody who's ill; **en cuanto** (tan pronto como) as soon as; (como, en calidad de) as; **en ~ pueda** as soon as I can; **en cuanto a** (en lo que concierne) as for, as regards; **en ~ a rentabilidad** as for *o* as regards profitability; **en ~ a conocimientos del tema ...** as far as knowledge of the subject is concerned ...; **por cuanto** (liter *o* frml) insofar as (frml)

cuanto² -ta *adj*

A 1 (todo, todos): **llévate ~s discos quieras** take as many records as you want *o* like 2 (*sing*) (con valor plural): **tiene ~ libro hay sobre el tema** she has every book there is on the subject

B **unos cuantos** a few; **unos ~s amigos** a few friends; **había unas cuantas personas** there were several *o* quite a few people there

cuanto³ -ta *pron*: **le di todo ~ tenía** I gave her everything I had; **fuimos sólo unos ~s** only a few of us went; **unos ~s que yo conozco** a few people I can think of

cuanto⁴ *m* quantum

cuánto¹ *adv*

A (en preguntas) how much

B (uso indirecto): **si supieras ~ la quiero/lo siento** if you knew how much I love her/how sorry I am

C (en exclamaciones): **¡~ nos reímos!** how we laughed!; **¡~ ha sufrido!** she's suffered so much!

cuánto² -ta *adj*

A (en preguntas) (*sing*) how much; (*pl*) how many; **¿~ café queda?** how much coffee is there left?; **¿~s alumnos tienes?** how many students do you have?; **¿~s años tienes?** how old are you?; **¿~ tiempo tardarás?** how long will you take?

B 1 (uso indirecto) (*sing*) how much; (*pl*) how many; **no sé ~ dinero/~s libros tengo** I don't know how much money/how many books I have 2 (en exclamaciones): **¡~ vino/cuánta comida!** what a lot of wine/food!; **¡~ tiempo sin verte!** I haven't seen you for ages! (colloq); **¡~ dolor me has causado!** you've caused me so much suffering 3 (*sing*) (con valor plural): **¡~ imbécil hay por ahí!** there are a lot of stupid people around!

cuánto³ -ta *pron*

A (en preguntas) 1 (*sing*) how much; (*pl*) how many; **¿~ pesas?** how much do you weigh?; **¿~ mides?** how tall are you?; **¿~s quieres?** how many do you want?; **¿a ~ estamos hoy?** what's the date today? 2 (referido a tiempo) how long; **¿~ falta para llegar?** how long before we get there? 3 (referido a precios, dinero) how much; **¿~ cuesta?** how much is it?; **¿~ es?** how much is that (altogether)?; **¿a ~ están las naranjas?** how much are the oranges?

B (uso indirecto): **pregúntale ~ va a demorar** ask her how long she'll be; **no sé ~ puede costar/~s tiene** I don't know how much it might cost/how many she has; ***no sé ~s*** (fam) something-or-other; **Javier no sé ~s** Javier something-or-other

C (en exclamaciones) **¡~s murieron!** so many people were killed!; **¡~ has tardado!** it's taken you a long time!

cuáquero¹ -ra *adj* Quaker (*before n*)

cuáquero² -ra *m,f* Quaker

cuarenta¹ *adj inv/pron* forty; *para ejemplos ver* **cincuenta**; ***cantarle las ~ a algn*** to give sb a piece of one's mind

(Compuesto) **cuarenta principales** *mpl* (Esp) Top 40, charts (*pl*)

cuarenta² *m* (number) forty

cuarentena *f*

A 1 (aislamiento) quarantine 2 (después de un parto) *40-day period after giving birth*

B (número) (about) forty

cuarentón¹ -tona *adj* (fam): **un hombre ~** a man in his forties

cuarentón² -tona *m,f* (fam) person in his/her forties

Cuaresma *f* Lent; **en ~** in *o* during Lent

cuarta *f* (Auto) fourth (gear); **mete la ~** put it in fourth; *ver tb* **cuarto**

cuartear [A1] *vt* (descuartizar) to cut up

■ **cuartearse** *v pron* 1 (agrietarse) «*pared/cerámica/cuero*» to crack 2 (Taur) to dodge to one side

cuartel *m* 1 (Mil) (campamento — permanente) barracks (*sing o pl*); (— provisional) encampment 2 (tregua): **no dieron ~ a los rebeldes** they showed no mercy to the rebels; **una lucha sin ~** a merciless fight

(Compuestos)

- **cuartel de bomberos** (RPl) fire station, fire house (AmE)
- **cuarteles de invierno** *mpl* (de un ejército) winter quarters (*pl*)
- **cuartel general** headquarters (*sing o pl*)

cuartelada *f*, **cuartelazo** *m* military uprising, putsch

cuartelillo *m* (de policía) station

cuarterón -rona *m,f*

A (mestizo) quadroon (*person of mixed race*)

B **cuarterón** *m* (medida) quarter (pound), four ounces

cuarteto *m* (Mús) quartet; (Lit) quatrain (*with lines of eleven syllables*)

cuartil *m* quartile

cuartilla *f* 1 (hoja) sheet of paper 2 **cuartillas** *fpl* (manuscrito) manuscript

cuarto[1] **-ta** *adj/pron* 1 (ordinal) fourth; *para ejemplos ver* **quinto** 2 (partitivo): **la cuarta parte** a quarter

(Compuesto) **cuarta dimensión** *f* fourth dimension

cuarto[2] *m*

A (habitación) room; (dormitorio) room, bedroom

(Compuestos)

- **cuarto de aseo** ≈ downstairs lavatory *o* (BrE) cloakroom, bathroom (AmE)
- **cuarto de baño** bathroom
- **cuarto de estar** living room, parlor (AmE), sitting room (BrE)
- **cuarto de (los) huéspedes** guest room, spare room
- **cuarto de servicio** maid's room
- **cuarto intermedio** (RPl) recess; **pasar a ~ ~** to adjourn, go into recess
- **cuarto oscuro** (Fot) darkroom; (Pol) (RPl) ≈ polling booth
- **cuarto trastero** lumber room, junk room

B 1 (cuarta parte) quarter; **un ~ de kilo** a quarter (of a) kilo; **un ~ de pollo** a quarter chicken; ***de tres al ~*** (fam) third-rate; ***¡qué ... ni qué ocho ~s!*** (fam): **¡qué miedo ni qué ocho ~s!** scared, my foot!; **¡qué vacaciones ni qué ocho ~s!** it was hardly what I'd call a vacation!; ***tres ~s de lo mismo*** (fam): **tu hermana es una vaga ... y tú, tres ~s de lo mismo** your sister's bone-idle ... and you're not much better (colloq) 2 (en expresiones de tiempo) quarter; **un ~ de hora** a quarter of an hour; **tres ~s de hora** three quarters of an hour; **la una y ~** (a) quarter after (AmE) *o* (BrE) past one, one fifteen; **es un ~ para las dos** *or* (Esp, RPl) **son las dos menos ~** it is a quarter to two; ***tener su ~ de hora*** (AmS) to have had one's day

C (Impr) quarto

(Compuestos)

- **cuarto creciente/menguante** first/last quarter
- **cuarto delantero** forequarter
- **cuartos de final** *mpl* quarterfinals (*pl*)
- **cuarto trasero** hindquarter

D (Esp fam) (dinero): **estoy sin un ~** I'm absolutely broke (colloq); **tiene muchos ~s** he's loaded (colloq); **le pagan cuatro ~s** he gets paid peanuts (colloq)

cuarto[3] **-ta** *adj* (Col fam) ‹*persona*› generous and easy-going

cuartucho *m* small, dark (*o* dirty *etc*) room

cuarzo *m* quartz

(Compuesto) **cuarzo rosa** *or* **rosado** rose quartz

cuatacho *m* ▸**cuate 2**

cuate *mf* (Méx) 1 (mellizo) twin 2 (fam) (amigo) pal (colloq) 3 (fam) (tipo, tipa) (*m*) guy (colloq); (*f*) woman

cuaternario[1] **-ria** *adj* quaternary

cuaternario[2] *m*: **el ~** the Quaternary (period)

cuatrapear [A1] *vt* (Méx) to ruin

■ **cuatrapearse** *v pron* (Méx) «*aparato*» to break; «*planes*» to fall through

cuatrero -ra *m,f* rustler

cuatrienal *adj* four-year (*before n*)

cuatrienio *m* four-year period, four years (*pl*)

cuatrillizo -za *m,f* quadruplet, quad

cuatrimestral *adj* 1 (en frecuencia) ‹*exámenes/reuniones*› four-monthly; **las reuniones son ~es** the meetings are held every four months 2 (en duración) ‹*curso*› four-month (long) (*before n*)

cuatrimestre *m* four-month period

cuatrimotor[1] **-tora** *adj* four-engined

cuatrimotor[2] *m* four-engined plane

cuatro[1] *adj inv/pron* four; **¿llueve? — no, sólo son ~ gotas** is it raining? no, it's just a drop or two; **le escribí ~ líneas** I wrote him a couple of lines; *para más ejemplos ver tb* **cinco**

(Compuesto) **cuatro ojos** *mf* (fam) four-eyes (colloq)

cuatro[2] *m*

A (número) (number) four; *para ejemplos ver* **cinco**

B (Ven) (guitarra) four-stringed guitar

cuatrocientos -tas *adj/pron* four hundred; *para ejemplos ver* **quinientos**

cuba *f*

A 1 (barril) barrel, cask; ***estar como una ~*** (fam) to be plastered (colloq) 2 (tina) tub, vat

B (Col fam) (hijo menor) youngest child

Cuba *f* Cuba; ***más se perdió en ~*** (Esp hum) it's not the end of the world (colloq)

cubalibre *m* (de ron) rum and coke; (de ginebra) gin and coke

cubanismo *m* Cuban word/expression

cubano -na *adj/m,f* Cuban

cubata *m* (fam) ▸**cubalibre**

cubero -ra *m,f* cooper

cubertería *f* cutlery; **una ~ de plata** a set of silver cutlery

cubeta *f* 1 (Fot, Quím) tray; (de paredes más altas) tank 2 (para hielo) ice tray 3 (barril) keg, small cask 4 (Méx) (balde) bucket

cubetera *f* ice tray

cubicar [A2] *vt* ‹*número*› to cube; ‹*recipiente*› to measure the volume *o* capacity of

cúbico -ca *adj* cubic; **2m³** *(read as: dos metros cúbicos)* 2m³; *(léase: two cubic meters)*

cubículo *m* cubicle

cubierta *f*

A (funda) cover; (de libro) cover, sleeve

B (Auto) tire*

(Compuesto) **cubierta sin cámara** tubeless tire*

C (Náut) (en barco) deck; **salir a ~** to go up on deck

(Compuestos)

- **cubierta de aterrizaje** *or* **de vuelo** flight deck
- **cubierta de popa** poop deck
- **cubierta inferior/superior** lower/upper deck

cubierto[1] **-ta** *adj* ‹*cielo*› overcast, cloudy; *ver tb* **cubrir**

cubierto[2] *m*

A 1 (pieza) piece of cutlery; **se le cayó un ~** he dropped his knife/fork/spoon; **los ~s de plata** the silver cutlery 2 (servicio de mesa) place setting; **pon otro ~** can you set another place? 3 (en restaurante) cover charge; (en boda, banquete): **¿cuánto cuesta el ~?** how much is it per head?

B (*en locs*) **a cubierto**: **ponerse a ~ de la lluvia** to take cover *o* to shelter from the rain; **bajo cubierto** under cover

cubil *m* lair, den

cubilete *m* 1 (vaso) beaker; (para dados) shaker, cup 2 (Col) (sombrero) top hat

cubismo *m* cubism

cubista *adj/mf* cubist

cubitera *f* (bandeja) ice tray; (cubo) ice bucket

cubo *m*

A (Esp) bucket

(Compuesto) **cubo de (la) basura** (de la cocina) garbage can (AmE), (kitchen) bin (BrE); (de edificio) garbage can (AmE), rubbish bin (BrE), dustbin (BrE)

B (cuerpo geométrico) cube; **cortar en cubitos** to dice

(Compuestos)

- **cubito de hielo** ice cube
- **cubo** *or* **cubito de caldo** stock cube
- **cubo** *or* **cubito de carne/de pescado/de pollo** beef/fish/chicken stock cube

C (Mat) cube; **elevar un número al ~** to cube a number

D 1 (de rueda) hub 2 (Tec) drum

cubrecama *m* bedspread, counterpane

cubrir [I33] *vt*

A (tapar) to cover; **la niebla cubría el valle** the valley was covered in mist; **~ algo DE algo** to cover sth WITH sth; **lo cubrió de besos** she smothered him with kisses

B 1 ‹*gastos/daños/riesgos*› to cover 2 ‹*demanda/necesidad*› to meet; ‹*carencia*› to cover 3 ‹*plaza/vacante*› to fill

C 1 (Period, Rad, TV) to cover 2 (recorrer) ‹*etapa/trayecto*› to cover

D ‹*retirada/flanco*› to cover; **cúbreme** cover me

E (Zool) to cover

■ **cubrirse** *v pron*

A 1 (*refl*) (taparse) to cover oneself; **se cubrió la cara** he covered his face 2 (ponerse el sombrero) to put one's hat on

C

3 (protegerse) to take cover 4 (contra riesgo) to cover oneself
B (llenarse) **~se DE algo**: **las calles se habían cubierto de nieve** the streets were covered with snow

cucaña *f* (palo) greasy pole

cucaracha *f* (Zool) cockroach

cucha *f* (RPl fam) bed; (de perro) box (*o* basket *etc*)

cuchara *f*
A spoon; ***meter (la)*** **~** (fam) (en una conversación) to put one's oar in (colloq); (en un asunto) to get in on the act (colloq); ***meterle algo a algn con*** **~** (fam) to spoon-feed sb with sth; ***recoger a algn con*** **~**: **estoy para que me recojan con ~** I'm ready to drop (colloq)
Compuestos
- **cuchara de postre** dessertspoon
- **cuchara de servir** tablespoon
- **cuchara sopera** *or* **de sopa** soup spoon

B 1 (de excavadora) bucket 2 (para pescar) spinner, spoon 3 (RPl) (de albañil) trowel

cucharada *f* spoonful
Compuesto **cucharada sopera** ≈ tablespoonful

cucharadita *f* teaspoon, teaspoonful

cucharilla, cucharita *f* (Coc) *tb* **~ de té** teaspoon
Compuesto **cucharilla** *or* **cucharita de café** coffee spoon

cucharón *m* ladle

cucheta *f* (RPl) trundle bed, truckle bed

cuchi[1] *adj* (Per leng infantil): **¡gorda ~!** fatty! (colloq)

cuchi[2] *m* (Per leng infantil) piggy (colloq)

cuchichear [A1] *vi* (fam) to whisper

cuchicheo *m* (fam) whispering

cuchilla *f*
A 1 (de segadora, batidora, cuchillo) blade; (de arado) coulter, share 2 *tb* **~ de afeitar** (hoja) razor blade; (maquinilla) razor
B (AmL) (de montañas, colinas) range
C (Col fam) 1 (jefe, profesor) tyrant (colloq) 2 (mujer dominante) harpy (colloq)

cuchillada *f*, **cuchillazo** *m* 1 (golpe) stab; **le dio** *or* **asestó una ~** she stabbed him; **lo mataron a ~s** they stabbed him to death 2 (herida) stab wound

cuchillo *m*
A (utensilio) knife; ***pasar a algn a*** **~** to put sb to the sword
Compuestos
- **cuchillo de caza** *or* **de monte** hunting knife
- **cuchillo de cocina/de trinchar** kitchen/carving knife

B (Arquit, Const) *tb* **~ de armadura** truss

cuchipanda *f* (fam) (comilona) slap-up meal (colloq); **ir de ~** to go out on the town

cuchitril *m* hole (colloq), hovel

cucho[1] -cha *adj* (Méx fam) (torcido) crooked (colloq)

cucho[2] -cha *m,f*
A (Col fam) 1 (padre) dad (colloq); (madre) mom (AmE colloq), mum (BrE colloq) 2 (profesor) teacher 3 (viejecito) (*m*) old guy (colloq); (*f*) old girl (colloq)
B (Chi fam) (gato) puss (colloq)

cuchufleta *f* (fam) joke

cuclillas *fpl*: **en ~** squatting, crouching

cuclillo *m* cuckoo

cuco[1] -ca *adj*
A (fam) (bonito) cute (colloq)
B (Esp fam) (astuto) crafty (colloq)

cuco[2] *m*
A (Zool) cuckoo
B (de bebé) Moses basket
C (CS, Per leng infantil) bogeyman

cucú *m* cuckoo

cucufato -ta *adj* 1 (Chi fam) (chiflado) nuts (colloq) 2 (Per) (beato) sanctimonious

cucurucho *m*
A 1 (de papel, cartón) cone; (de barquillo) cone 2 (helado) cone, cornet (BrE)
B (capirote) hood, pointed hat

cuece, cuecen, etc *see* **cocer**

cuelgue *m* (Esp) 1 (arg) (por la droga) high (colloq); **cogerse un ~** to get high (colloq) 2 (arg) (chasco) bummer (sl)

cuello *m*
A 1 (Anat) neck; **alargar el ~** to crane one's neck; **le cortaron el ~** they slit *o* cut his throat; ***estar metido hasta el*** **~** ***en algo*** (fam) to be in sth (right) up to one's neck (colloq); ***jugarse*** *or* ***apostarse el*** **~** (fam): **me juego el ~ a que no lo hace** I bet you anything you like he doesn't do it (colloq) 2 (de botella) neck
Compuestos
- **cuello de botella** (Auto) bottleneck
- **cuello uterino** *or* **del útero** neck of the womb

B (Indum) 1 (pieza) collar; **sin ~** collarless 2 (escote) neck
Compuestos
- **cuello a la caja** square neckline
- **cuello alto** *or* **cisne** *or* **vuelto** *or* (AmL) **tortuga** turtleneck (AmE), polo neck (BrE)
- **cuello chino** *or* **mao** mandarin collar
- **cuello de pico** V neck
- **cuello ortopédico** surgical *o* cervical collar
- **cuello redondo** round neck

cuenca *f*
A (Geog, Geol) basin
B (Min): **una ~ minera** a coal-mining area
C (del ojo) socket

cuenco *m* 1 (recipiente) bowl 2 (concavidad) hollow; **recogió agua con el ~ de la mano** he scooped water up in his cupped hands

cuenta[1] *f*
A 1 (operación, cálculo) calculation, sum; **hacer una ~** to do a calculation *o* sum; **saca la ~** add it up, work it out; **hacer** *or* **sacar ~s** to do some calculations; ***a fin de*** **~s** after all 2 **cuentas** *fpl* (contabilidad) accounts: **lleva las ~s del negocio** he does the company's accounts, he handles the money side of the business (colloq); **ella se ocupa de las ~s de la casa** she pays the bills and looks after the money 3 (cómputo) count; **llevar/perder la ~** to keep/lose count; **~ atrás** countdown; ***más de la*** **~** too much
B 1 (factura) bill; **¿nos trae la ~, por favor?** could we have the check (AmE) *o* (BrE) bill, please?; **la ~ del gas** the gas bill; **a cuenta** on account; **entregó $2.000 a ~** she gave me/him/them $2,000 on account; **este dinero es a ~ de lo que te debo** this money is to go toward(s) what I owe you 2 (Com, Fin) (en banco, comercio) account; **depositar** *or* (Esp) **ingresar un cheque en una ~** to pay a check into an account; **abrir/cerrar/liquidar una ~** to open/close/to settle an account
Compuestos
- **cuenta corriente** checking account (AmE), current account (BrE)
- **cuenta de ahorros** savings account

C **cuentas** *fpl* (explicaciones): **no tengo por qué darte ~s** I don't have to explain *o* justify myself to you; **rendir ~s de algo** to account for sth; ***en resumidas*** **~s** in short
D (cargo, responsabilidad): **los gastos corren por ~ de la empresa** the expenses are covered *o* paid by the company; **se instaló por su ~** she set up (in business) on her own; **trabaja por ~ propia** she's self-employed
E **darse ~ (de algo)** (comprender) to realize (sth); (notar) to notice (sth); **se da ~ de todo** she's aware of everything that's going on (around her); **date ~ de que es imposible** you must realize (that) it's impossible; **tener algo en ~** to bear sth in mind; **ten en ~ que es joven** bear in mind that he's young; **sin tener en ~ los gastos** without taking the expenses into account; **tomar algo en ~** to take sth into consideration
F (de collar, rosario) bead

cuenta[2], cuentas, etc *see* **contar**

cuentagotas *m* (*pl* ~) dropper; ***dar algo con*** **~** (fam): **los permisos los dan con ~** they're very mean when it comes to giving out permits

cuentakilómetros *m* (*pl* ~) (de distancia recorrida) odometer (AmE), mileometer (BrE); (de velocidad) speedometer

cuentapasos *m* (*pl* ~) pedometer

cuentarrevoluciones *m* (*pl* ~) tachometer, rev counter (BrE)

cuentero[1] -ra *adj* (Méx, RPl fam) 1 (mentiroso): **ser ~** to be a fibber (colloq) 2 (chismoso) gossipy

cuentero[2] -ra *m,f* (Méx, RPl fam) 1 (mentiroso) fibber 2 (chismoso) gossip

cuentista[1] *adj* 1 (fam) (exagerado): **no seas ~, que no duele tanto** don't exaggerate, it doesn't hurt that much 2 (fantasioso): **ser ~** to be a fibber (colloq)

cuentista[2] *mf* 1 (Lit) short-story writer 2 (fam) (exagerado): **no te fíes de ese ~, es puro teatro** don't fall for his playacting, he's just putting it on 3 (fantasioso) fibber (colloq)

cuento[1] *m*

A 1 (narración corta) short story; (para niños) story, tale; **el ~ de Cenicienta** the tale *o* story of Cinderella; **cuéntame un ~** tell me a story; ***aplícate el ~*** (fam) take note; ***~ de nunca acabar*: esto es el ~ de nunca acabar** it just never ends, it just goes on and on; ***traer algo a ~*** to bring sth up; ***venir a ~*: eso no viene a ~** that doesn't come into it; **sin venir a ~** for no reason at all 2 (chiste) joke, story; **el ~ del elefante** the joke about the elephant

Compuestos

- **cuento corto** short story
- **cuento de hadas** fairy story, fairy tale

B 1 (fam) (chisme): **le fue con el ~ al profesor** she went and told the teacher (colloq); **siempre anda con ~s** she's always gossiping; ***comer ~s*** (Ven fam) to fall for anything 2 (fam) (mentira, excusa) story (colloq); **no me vengas con ~s** I'm not interested in your excuses *o* stories; ***hacerle al ~*** (Méx fam) to pretend 3 (fam) (exageración): **todo ese llanto es puro ~** all that crying is just put on; **¡tú lo que tienes es mucho ~!** you're just putting it on!

Compuestos

- **cuento chino** (fam): **eso es un ~ ~** what a load of baloney; **no me vengas con ~s ~s** don't give me any of your cock-and-bull stories (colloq)
- **cuento del tío** (CS fam): **el ~ del ~** a con trick
- **cuento de viejas** (fam) old wives' tale

C (número): **sin ~** countless, innumerable

cuento[2] *see* **contar**

cuerazo *m*

A (Chi, Méx fam) (mujer) stunner (colloq); (hombre) hunk (colloq)

B 1 (Col, Ven fam) (latigazo) lash 2 (Col fam) (golpe): **me di un ~ terrible** I hit my arm (*o* head *etc*) really hard

cuerda *f*

A 1 (gruesa) rope; (delgada) string; **escalera de ~** rope ladder 2 (Jueg) jump rope (AmE), skipping rope (BrE); **saltar a la ~** to jump rope (AmE), to skip (BrE) 3 (para tender ropa) washing line, clothes line 4 (de arco) bowstring; ***aflojar la ~*** to ease up; ***bajo ~*** ‹*pago*› under-the-counter; (*before n*) ***contra las ~s*** (fam) on the ropes; ***llevarle*** or ***seguirle la ~ a algn*** (AmL fam) to humor* sb, play along with sb (colloq); ***una ~ de*** (Ven fam) loads of (colloq)

Compuesto **cuerda floja** (Espec) tightrope

B (Mús) 1 (de guitarra, violín) string 2 **cuerdas** *fpl* (instrumentos) strings (*pl*)

Compuesto **cuerdas vocales** *fpl* vocal chords (*pl*)

C 1 (de reloj, juguete): **la ~ de la caja de música** the spring *o* the clockwork mechanism in the music box; **le dio ~ al despertador** she wound up the alarm clock; **un juguete de ~** a clockwork toy; ***son de la misma ~*** they are very alike 2 (impulso, energía): **no le des ~, que luego no hay quien lo haga callar** don't encourage him or you'll never get him to shut up (colloq); **el abuelo todavía tiene ~ para rato** grandpa has a good few years in him yet 3 (de tornillo) thread

cuerdo -da *adj* 1 [ESTAR] (en su sano juicio) sane; **no está ~** he is insane 2 [SER] (sensato) sensible

cuerear [A1] *vt* ‹*animal*› to skin; (azotar) (AmL) to whip

cuerna *f* 1 (Zool) horns (*pl*); (de ciervo) antlers (*pl*) 2 (Mús) hunting horn 3 (para beber) drinking horn

cuerno *m*

A 1 (de toro) horn; (de caracol) feeler; (de ciervo) antler; ***irse al ~*** (fam) «*plan*» to fall through; «*fiesta*» to be ruined *o* spoiled; ***mandar algo/a algn al ~*** (fam): **lo mandó todo al ~** he chucked it all in (colloq); **¡vete al ~!** get lost! (colloq); ***me/le supo*** or ***sentó a ~ quemado*** (fam) it was a real slap in the face for me/him (colloq); ***oler a ~ quemado*** «*comida/habitación*» to stink; «*asunto*» (fam) to smell (*o* sound *etc*) fishy (colloq); ***ponerle*** or (RPl) ***meterle los ~s a algn*** (fam) to be unfaithful to sb; ***¡y un ~!*** (fam) you must be joking! (colloq) 2 (de la luna) cusp

Compuesto **cuerno de la abundancia** horn of plenty

B (RPl fam) (uso expletivo) ▸ **cuerno B**

C (Mús) horn

Compuesto **cuerno de caza** hunting horn

cuero[1] *adj* (Méx fam) gorgeous (colloq)

cuero[2] *m*

A (piel) leather; (sin curtir) skin, hide; **artículos de ~** leather goods; **chaqueta de ~** leather jacket; ***dejar a algn como un ~*** (Col fam) to humiliate sb; ***en ~s (vivos)*** (fam) (desnudo) stark naked (colloq); ***no darle a algn el ~*** (CS fam): **no me da el ~ para comprarlo** I can't run *o* stretch to that much; ***sacarle el ~ a algn*** (CS fam) to tear sb to pieces (colloq); ***ser un ~*** (Chi, Méx fam) «*mujer*» she's a real stunner (colloq); «*hombre*» he's a real hunk (colloq)

Compuestos

- **cuero cabelludo** scalp
- **cuero de chancho** (AmL) pigskin
- **cuero de cocodrilo** (CS) crocodile skin
- **cuero de vaca** cowhide

B (odre) wineskin

C (period) (en fútbol) ball

cuerpo *m*

A 1 (Anat) body; **es de ~ menudo** she's slightly built; **tenía el miedo metido en el ~** (fam) he was scared stiff (colloq); **de ~ entero** full-length; ***a ~ de rey*** (fam): **vive a ~ de rey** he lives like a king; **nos atendieron a ~ de rey** they treated us like royalty; ***a ~ gentil*** (fam) without a coat (*o* sweater *etc*); ***~ a ~*** hand-to-hand; ***echarse algo al ~*** (fam) ‹*comida*› to have sth to eat; ‹*bebida*› to have sth to drink; ***entregarse a algo en ~ y alma*** to put one's heart and soul into sth (fam); ***pedirle el ~ algo a algn*** (fam): **cuando me lo pide el ~** when I feel like it; **el ~ le pedía un descanso** he felt he had to have a rest; ***sacar(le) el ~ a algn*** (AmL fam) to steer clear of sb; ***sacar(le) el ~ a algo*** (AmL fam) (a trabajo) to get out of sth; (a responsabilidad) to evade *o* shirk sth 2 (cadáver) body, corpse; **encontraron su ~ sin vida junto al río** (period) his lifeless body was found by the river (frml) 3 (tronco) body

Compuesto **cuerpo del delito** corpus delicti

B (Equ) length; **ganó por tres ~s de ventaja** he won by three lengths

C 1 (parte principal) main body 2 (de mueble) part; (de edificio) section; **un armario de dos ~s** a double wardrobe

D (conjunto de personas, de ideas, normas) body

Compuestos

- **cuerpo de baile** corps de ballet
- **cuerpo de bomberos** fire department (AmE), fire brigade (BrE)
- **cuerpo de doctrina/de leyes** body of teaching/of laws
- **cuerpo de policía** police force
- **cuerpo diplomático** diplomatic corps
- **cuerpo legislativo** legislative body
- **cuerpo médico** medical corps

E (Fís) (objeto) body, object; (sustancia) substance

Compuestos

- **cuerpo celeste** heavenly body
- **cuerpo geométrico** geometric shape *o* figure

F (consistencia, densidad) body; **una tela de mucho ~** a heavy cloth; **un vino de mucho ~** a full-bodied wine; ***dar/tomar ~*** «*idea/escultura*» to take shape

cuervo *m* raven; (como nombre genérico) crow

cuesco *m*

A (Bot) stone

B (Esp fam) (pedo) fart (sl)

cuesta[1] *f*

A (pendiente): **ir ~ arriba** to go uphill; **iba corriendo ~ abajo** I was running downhill; **estacionar en ~** to park on a hill; **una ~ muy pronunciada** a very steep slope; ***hacérsele muy ~ arriba a algn*: se me hace muy ~ arriba venderlo** I'm finding it very difficult to sell it; ***ir ~ abajo*** to go downhill; ***la ~ de enero*** January (*when people are traditionally short of money*)

B **a cuestas** (encima): **llevar algo a ~s** to carry sth on one's shoulders/back; **echarse algo a cuestas** ‹*carga/bulto*› to put sth on one's back; ‹*problema*› to burden oneself with sth

cuesta[2], **cuestan, etc** *see* **costar**

cuestación *f* collection

C

cuestión *f*
A 1 (tema, problema) question, matter; **otra ~ sería que** *or* **si estuviera enfermo** if he were ill, that would be another matter *o* a different matter altogether; **llegar al fondo de la ~** to get to the heart of the matter 2 (*en locs*) **en cuestión** in question; **en cuestión de** in a matter of; **la cuestión es ...** the thing is ...; **la ~ es divertirnos** the main thing is to enjoy ourselves; **la ~ es molestar** he/she only does it to annoy; **ser cuestión de** to be a matter of; **es ~ de diez minutos** it'll only take/I'll only be ten minutes; **si fuera ~ de dinero, no habría problema** if it were a question of money, there'd be no problem; **todo es ~ de ...** it's just a question of ...; **será ~ de planteárselo** we'll just have to put it to him; **tampoco es ~ de enloquecernos** there's no need to get in a flap (colloq); **tampoco es ~ de que lo hagas todo tú** there's no reason why you should do it all yourself
B (duda): **poner algo en ~** to call sth into question
C (fam) (problema) disagreement, problem; (cosa, objeto) thing, thingamajig* (colloq)

cuestionable *adj* questionable

cuestionar [A1] *vt* to question
■ **cuestionarse** *v pron* to ask oneself

cuestionario *m* (encuesta) questionnaire; (Educ) question paper, questions (*pl*)

cuete[1] *adj* (Méx fam) plastered (colloq)

cuete[2] *m*
A 1 (RPl fam & euf) (pedo) fart (sl) 2 (Méx, RPl fam) (borrachera): **agarrar un ~** to get plastered (colloq)
B (AmL fam) (petardo) firecracker; ***como ~*** (AmL fam) like a shot
C (Per fam) (pistola) shooter (colloq), rod (sl)
D (Méx) (Coc) braising steak; ***ser un ~*** (Méx fam) to be a real hassle (colloq)

cueva *f* cave
Compuesto **cueva de ladrones** rip-off joint (sl)

cueza, cuezan, etc *see* **cocer**

cuezo *m* (fam) (cuello) neck; ***meter el ~*** (fam) to put one's foot in it (colloq)

cui /kwi/, **cuí** /ku'i/ *m* (*pl* **cuises**) (AmS) guinea pig

cuico -ca *m,f* (Chi fam & pey) *pejorative term for a Bolivian*

cuidado[1] **-da** *adj* ‹*presentación*› meticulous, careful; ‹*aspecto*› impeccable; ‹*dicción*› precise

cuidado[2] *m*
A 1 (precaución): **tuvo ~ de no hacer ruido** she was careful not to make any noise; **ten ~ al cruzar la calle** be careful *o* take care when you cross the street; **lo envolvió con mucho ~** she wrapped it very carefully; **¡ándate con ~!** watch your step!; **~ CON algo/algn**: **¡~ con el escalón!** mind the step!; **~ con lo que haces** be careful what you do; **ten ~ con él, no es de fiar** watch him, he isn't to be trusted; Ⓢ **¡cuidado con el perro!** beware of the dog!; **¡cuidadito con alzarme la voz!** don't you raise your voice to me!; **cuidadito con decirle nada** make sure you don't say anything to him; ***de ~*** (fam) ‹*problema/herida*› serious; **un bromista de ~** a real joker; **ese tipo es de ~** you have to watch that guy (colloq) 2 (atención) care; **pone mucho ~ en su trabajo** he takes a great deal of care over his work
B (de objetos, niños, enfermos) **~ DE algo/algn**: **consejos para el ~ de sus plantas** hints on how to care for your plants; **no tiene experiencia en el ~ de los niños** he has no experience of looking after children; **estar al ~ de algn/algo** (cuidar) to look after sb/sth; (ser cuidado por) to be in sb's care; **ha tomado el jardín a su ~** she's taken over the care of the garden; **déjalo a mi ~** I'll take care of it
C **cuidados** *mpl* (Med) attention, care, treatment; **necesita los ~s de una enfermera** she needs to be looked after *o* taken care of by a nurse; **mejoró, gracias a los ~s de su hija** thanks to his daughter's care, he got better
Compuesto **cuidados intensivos** *mpl* intensive care
D (preocupación): **pierde ~** (AmL) don't worry; **me tiene** *or* **trae sin ~** it doesn't matter to me in the slightest

cuidado[3] *interj* be careful!, watch out!

cuidador -dora *m,f* (de niños) baby sitter (AmE), childminder (BrE); (Esp) (de discapacitados) carer; (de animales) zookeeper; (de coches) attendant

cuidadoso -sa *adj* 1 ‹*persona*› careful; **eres poco ~** you don't look after things; **~ CON algo** careful WITH sth 2 ‹*búsqueda/investigación*› careful, thorough

cuidar [A1] *vt* 1 ‹*juguetes/plantas/casa*› to look after; ‹*niño*› to look after, take care of; ‹*enfermo*› to care for, look after; **cuídame la leche un momentito** would you keep an eye on the milk for a moment?; **tienes que ~ ese catarro/la salud** you should look after that cold/your health 2 ‹*estilo/apariencia*› to take care over; **debes ~ la ortografía** you must take care over your spelling; **cuida mucho todos los detalles** she pays great attention to detail
■ **cuidar** *vi*: **~ DE algo/algn** to take care OF sth/sb; **~ DE QUE + SUBJ**: **~ré de que no les falte nada** I'll make sure they have everything they need
■ **cuidarse** *v pron* 1 (*refl*) to take care of oneself, look after oneself; **¡cuídate!** take care!; **dejó de ~se** she let herself go 2 (procurar no) **~se DE + INF**: **se cuidó mucho** *or* **muy bien de (no) volver por ahí** he took good care not to *o* he made very sure he didn't go back there; **cuídate mucho de desobedecerme** you'd better do as I tell you 3 (asegurarse) **~ se DE + INF**: **se cuidó bien de cerrar las ventanas** she made sure she shut the windows

cuije *mf* (Méx) office junior

cuita *f* (liter *o* frml) trouble, problem

culantro *m* coriander; ***bueno es ~ pero no tanto*** (Col, Per, Ven fam) there's no need to overdo it

culata *f*
A (de escopeta, revólver) butt; (de cañón) breech
B (de motor) cylinder head

culatazo *m* (al disparar) kick, recoil; (golpe): **le dieron/pegaron un ~** they hit him with the butt of a rifle

culear [A1] *vi* (Andes vulg) to screw (vulg)

culebra *f*
A (Zool) snake; ***matar la ~*** (Ven) to knock a problem on the head (colloq); ***a la ~ se le mata por la cabeza*** (Ven) you have to/you should take the bull by the horns
B (Col fam) (deuda) debt
C (Ven arg) (asunto turbio): **el tipo tiene una ~ entre sí** he's up to no good
D (Ven pey) (Rad, TV) soap opera, soap (colloq)

culebrear [A1] *vi* «*culebra*» to wriggle along; «*camino/río*» to wind

culebrón *m* soap opera, soap (colloq)

culeca *adj* (Col) ▸ **clueca**

culero -ra *m,f* (Méx vulg) (cobarde) chicken (colloq)

culillo *m* (Col, Ven fam): **darle ~ a algn** to give sb the creeps (colloq); **le tengo ~ al avión** flying makes me jittery (colloq)

culín *m* (Esp fam) (de bebida) drop

culinario -ria *adj* culinary (frml)

culmen *m* (period) (de carrera, obra) highpoint, peak; (de perversidad, egoísmo) height

culminación *f*
A 1 (clímax — de carrera, negociaciones) culmination; (— de fiesta) climax 2 (realización) fulfillment*
B (Astron) zenith

culminante *adj*: **momento** *or* **punto ~** (de carrera) peak, high point; (de historia, película) climax; (de negociaciones) crucial stage; **en el momento** *or* **punto ~ de su carrera** at the peak *o* the high point of his career

culminar [A1] *vi*
A 1 (llegar al clímax): **la novela culmina cuando ...** the novel reaches its climax when ...; **~ EN** *or* **CON algo**: **las negociaciones ~on en** *or* **con la firma del tratado** the talks culminated in the signing of the treaty 2 (acabar): **con su muerte culmina una etapa de nuestra historia** his death marks the end of a chapter in our history; **~ EN** *or* **CON algo** to end IN *o* WITH sth, to culminate IN sth
B (Astron) to reach the zenith
■ **culminar** *vt* (period) to bring ... to a climax

cúlmine *adj* (Andes) ▸ **culminante**

culo *m* (fam: en algunas regiones vulg) 1 (nalgas) backside (colloq), butt (AmE colloq), bum (BrE colloq), ass (AmE vulg), arse (BrE vulg); **te voy a dar unos azotes** *or* **pegar en el ~** I'm going to spank *o* smack you; ***caerse*** *or* (AmL) ***irse de ~*** (fam) (literal) to fall on one's backside *o* ass; (asombrarse) to be flabbergasted *o* amazed (colloq); **tiene una casa que te caes de ~** he has the most amazing house; ***darle por (el) ~ a algn*** (vulg) to screw sb (sl); **¡que te den por ~!** (vulg) screw you! (vulg); ***en el ~ del mundo*** (fam) in the back of beyond; ***ir de ~*** (fam): **el negocio va de ~** the business is going really badly; ***lamerle el ~ a algn*** (vulg) to lick sb's ass (vulg); ***mandar a algn a tomar por ~*** (Esp vulg) to tell someone to piss off (vulg); ***mandar algo a tomar por ~*** (Esp vulg) to pack *o* chuck sth in (colloq); ***meterse algo en*** *or* ***por el ~*** (vulg): **métetelo en el ~** stick it up your ass (vulg); ***pasarse algo por el ~*** (vulg): **las reglas me las paso por el ~** I don't give a shit about the rules (vulg); ***perder el ~ por algo/algn*** (fam): **pierde el ~ por él/porque la inviten** she's just crazy about him/ she's just dying to be asked (colloq); ***quedar como el*** *or* ***un ~*** (AmS fam *o* vulg) to look awful *o* terrible; **ni la llamó y quedó como el** *or* **un ~** he didn't even call her, it was so rude of him! (colloq); ***ser un ~ de mal asiento*** (fam): **es un ~ de mal asiento** *or* **sin asiento** (no se está quieto) he can't sit still for a minute; (en cuestiones de trabajo, vivienda) he never stays in one place for long 2 (de vaso, botella) bottom; **gafas de ~ de vaso** *or* **botella** pebble (lens) glasses (colloq) 3 (RPl fam) (suerte) luck

culón -lona *adj* (fam): **ser ~** to have a big bottom (colloq)

culpa *f* 1 (responsabilidad) fault; **nadie tiene la ~** it's nobody's fault; **no fue ~ tuya** it wasn't your fault; **echarle la ~ a algn (de algo)** to blame sb *o* put the blame on sb (for sth); **llegó tarde por ~ del tráfico** he arrived late because of the traffic; **no importa de quién es la ~** it doesn't matter whose fault it is; **¿y qué ~ tengo yo?** and what fault is that of mine? 2 (falta, pecado) sin; **pagar por las ~s ajenas** to pay for the sins of others *o* for other people's faults

culpabilidad *f* (Der,Psic) guilt

culpabilizar [A4] *vt* ▸ **culpar**

culpable[1] *adj* [SER] 1 ‹*persona*› guilty; **~ DE algo**: **sentirse ~ de algo** to feel guilty about sth; **ser ~ de algo** to be to blame for sth; (Der) to be guilty of sth; **confesarse ~ de algo** to plead guilty to sth 2 (Der) ‹*acto*› culpable

culpable[2] *mf* 1 (de delito) culprit 2 (de problema, situación): **tú eres el ~ de todo esto** this is all your fault, you're to blame for all of this

culpar [A1] *vt* to blame; **~ a algn DE algo** to blame sb FOR sth, blame sth ON sb

culteranismo *m*: *elaborate 16th & 17th century literary style*

cultismo *m* learned word/expression

cultivable *adj* cultivable

cultivado -da *adj*

A ‹*persona*› cultivated, cultured; ‹*pueblo*› cultured

B ‹*terreno/campo*› cultivated

cultivador -dora *m,f*

A (persona) grower

B **cultivadora** *f*, **cultivador** *m* (máquina) cultivator

cultivar [A1] *vt*

A (Agr) ‹*campo/tierras*› to cultivate, farm; ‹*plantas*› to grow, cultivate; **un huerto bien cultivado** a well-tended vegetable garden

B ‹*bacterias/perlas*› to culture

C ‹*amistad*› to cultivate; ‹*inteligencia/memoria*› to develop; ‹*artes/interés*› to encourage

D (practicar) to practice*

cultivo *m*

A (Agr) 1 (de tierra) farming, cultivation; (de plantas) growing, cultivation; **~ intensivo/extensivo** intensive/extensive farming; **~ de frutas** fruit growing 2 (cosa cultivada) crop; **~s de secano/de regadío** dry-farmed/irrigated crops

B (Biol, Med) (acción) culturing; (producto) culture

C (de las artes) promotion, encouragement

culto[1] **-ta** *adj* 1 ‹*persona/pueblo*› educated, cultured 2 (Ling) ‹*palabra*› learned; ‹*literatura/música*› highbrow

culto[2] *m* 1 (veneración) worship; **rendir ~ a algo/algn** to worship sth/sb; **~ a la personalidad** personality cult; **el ~ del dinero** the cult of money 2 (liturgia) worship; **libertad de ~(s)** freedom of worship

cultura *f*

A (civilización) culture; **~ del ocio** leisure culture

B 1 (conocimientos, ilustración): **es una persona de gran ~** she's a very well-educated *o* cultured person; **~ general/musical** general/musical knowledge; **la ~ popular** popular culture 2 (en periódico, artes) arts (*pl*), culture

cultural *adj* cultural; **un acto ~** a cultural event; **bajo nivel ~** low standard of general education

culturismo *m* bodybuilding

culturista *mf* bodybuilder

culturizar [A4] *vt* (period) to enlighten, educate

■ **culturizarse** *v pron* (*refl*) (fam & hum) to get oneself some culture (colloq & hum)

cuma *f* (AmL) curved machete

cumbia *f*: *music and dance typical of the Caribbean coast of Colombia*

cumbo *m* (AmC) cup/bowl (*made from a large gourd*)

cumbre *f*

A 1 (de montaña) top 2 (apogeo) height; **en la ~ del éxito** at the height of his success

B (Pol) summit (meeting)

C (*como adj inv*): **su novela ~** his most outstanding novel; **el momento ~** (de carrera) the peak; (de película, novela) the high point

cumiche *mf* (AmC fam) baby of the family (colloq)

cum laude *loc adj/adv* cum laude; **sobresaliente ~ ~** summa cum laude

cumpa *m* (AmL fam) buddy (AmE colloq), mate (BrE colloq)

cumpleaños *m* (*pl* ~) 1 (aniversario) birthday; **¡feliz ~!** happy birthday!; **¿qué vas a hacer el día de tu ~?** what are you going to do on your birthday? 2 (fiesta) birthday party

cumplido[1] **-da** *adj*

A [SER] 1 (atento, cortés) polite; **¡con lo ~ que es!** he's always so polite *o* correct 2 (considerado) thoughtful 3 (Col) (puntual) punctual

B [ESTAR] (frml) (amplio) ‹*información/respuesta*› full

C (acabado) ‹*misión*› accomplished; **a los dos meses ~s** after two months

cumplido[2] *m*: **hacerle un ~ a algn** to pay sb a compliment; **una visita de ~** a duty *o* courtesy call; **la invitó por ~** he invited her because he felt he ought to; **vamos, sin ~s** *or* **no te andes con ~s** don't stand on ceremony; **es precioso, de verdad, no es un ~** it's beautiful, really, I'm not just being polite

cumplidor -dora *adj* reliable

cumplimentar [A1] *vt*

A (frml) ‹*diligencia/trámite*› to perform, carry out; ‹*impreso*› to complete, fill out *o* in

B (frml) ‹*autoridad*› to pay one's respects to

cumplimiento *m*

A 1 (de ley, norma) performance; **falleció en el ~ del deber** he died in the line of duty; **en ~ con lo dispuesto por la legislación vigente** in compliance with current legislation; **la ley es de obligado ~ para todas las empresas** the law is binding on all companies (frml) 2 (logro): **esto favorecerá el ~ de nuestros objetivos** this will help to achieve our objectives

B (elogio, piropo) ▸ **cumplido**[2]

cumplir [I1] *vt*

A 1 (ejecutar) ‹*orden*› to carry out; ‹*ley*› to obey; **hacer ~ la ley** to ensure that the law is upheld; **la satisfacción del deber cumplido** the satisfaction of having done one's duty; **no se cumplió el calendario previsto** they failed to adhere to the proposed schedule 2 ‹*promesa/palabra*› to keep; ‹*compromiso*› to honor*, fulfill*; ‹*obligación/contrato*› to fulfill* 3 (alcanzar) ‹*objetivo/ambición*› to achieve; **la solicitud debe ~ los siguientes requisitos** the application must fulfill the following conditions; **el edificio no cumple las condiciones mínimas de seguridad** the building does not comply with minimum safety standards 4 (desempeñar) ‹*papel*› to perform, fulfill*

B ‹*condena/sentencia*› to serve; ‹*servicio militar*› to do

C ‹*años/meses*›: **mañana cumple 20 años** she'll be *o* she's 20 tomorrow; **¿cuándo cumples años?** when's your birthday?; **¡que cumplas muchos más!** many happy returns!; **¡que los cumplas muy feliz!** have a very happy birthday!; **mañana cumplimos 20 años de casados** (AmL) tomorrow we'll have been married 20 years; **la huelga cumple hoy su tercer día** this is the third day of the strike

■ **cumplir** *vi*

A 1 **~ CON algo** ‹*con obligación*› to fulfill* sth, satisfy sth; ‹*con tarea*› to carry out sth; ‹*con trámite*› to comply WITH sth; ‹*con requisito/condición*› to fulfill* sth; **cumple con su trabajo/deber** he does his job/duty; **~ con la iglesia** to go to church 2 (con una obligación social): **lo invité a comer, creo que cumplí** I took him out for lunch, so I think I've done my duty *o* (colloq) my bit; **nos invitó sólo por ~** she only invited us because she felt she ought to; **con los Lara ya hemos cumplido** we've done our bit as far as the Laras are concerned (colloq)

B (*en 3ª pers*) (frml) (corresponder): **me/nos cumple informarle que ...** (Corresp) I am/we are writing to inform you that ... (frml)

■ **cumplirse** *v pron*

A «*deseo/predicción*» to come true; «*ambición*» to be realized, be fulfilled

B «*plazo*»: **mañana se cumple el plazo para pagar el impuesto** tomorrow is the last day for paying the tax; **hoy se cumple el primer aniversario de su muerte** today marks the first anniversary of her death

C

cumulativo -va *adj* cumulative

cúmulo *m*

A 1 (Meteo) cumulus 2 (Astron) cluster

B (montón, reunión): **un ~ de problemas** a series *o* host of problems; **un ~ de medidas** a whole set of measures

cuna *f* 1 (tradicional) cradle; (cama con barandas) crib (AmE), cot (BrE); (portabebé) portacrib (AmE), carrycot (BrE) 2 (liter) (estirpe, linaje): **ser de ilustre/humilde ~** to be of noble/ humble birth (liter) 3 (lugar de nacimiento) birthplace 4 (origen de filosofía, movimiento) birthplace; **la ~ de la civilización** the cradle of civilization

cuncho *m* (Col) 1 (poso — del café) grounds (*pl*); (— del vino) lees (*pl*) 2 (fam) (sobras): **queda un ~ de arroz** there's a little rice left over

cuncuna *f* (Chi) (Zool) caterpillar

cundido -da *adj* (Méx) **~ DE algo**: **estaba cundida de cáncer** she was riddled with cancer; **la casa estaba cundida de insectos** the house was full of *o* swarming with insects

cundir [I1] *vi*

A «*rumor*» to spread; «*miedo*» to grow; **¡que no cunda el pánico!** don't panic!; **cundió la alarma** there was widespread alarm; **cunde el temor a una reacción violenta** there are growing fears of a violent reaction; **empieza a ~ el escepticismo** skepticism is becoming rife

B (rendir): **hoy no me ha cundido el trabajo** I haven't got much work done today; **hoy la mañana me cundió** I got a lot done this morning; **este detergente cunde más/ mucho** this detergent goes further/a long way

cuneiforme *adj* cuneiform

cuneta *f* 1 (en carretera) ditch 2 (Chi) (de calle) curb (AmE), kerb (BrE)

cunetearse *v pron* (CS) to hit the curb*

cunnilinguo, cunnilingus *m* cunnilingus

cuña *f*

A 1 (pieza triangular) wedge; **en ~** in a V-formation *o* wedge formation 2 (Col) (muesca) groove

(Compuesto) **cuña anticiclónica** *or* **de alta presión** ridge of high pressure

B (Rad) slot

C (bacinica) bedpan

D (CS fam) ▸**palanca B**

cuñado -da *m,f*

A (pariente político) (*m*) brother-in-law; (*f*) sister-in-law; **mis ~s** (sólo varones) my brothers-in-law; (varones y mujeres) my brothers and sisters-in-law

B (Per fam) (compañero) buddy (AmE colloq), mate (BrE colloq)

cuño *m* (troquel) die; (sello) stamp; ***de nuevo* ~** ‹*palabra*› newly-coined (*before n*); ‹*empresa*› new-style (*before n*)

cuota *f*

A 1 (de club, asociación) membership fees (*pl*); (de sindicato) dues (*pl*); (de seguro) premium; **pagan una ~ módica por el hospedaje** they pay a modest amount for lodging; **la ~ de enganche** the connection charge 2 (AmL) (plazo) installment*, payment 3 (Méx) (Auto) toll

(Compuestos)

- **cuota alimentaria** (Arg) maintenance
- **cuota inicial** deposit, down payment

B (parte proporcional) quota; **~s de producción** production quotas

(Compuestos)

- **cuota de mercado** market share
- **cuota patronal** employer's contribution (*to social security*)

cupe *see* **caber**

cupé *m* coupé

Cupido Cupid

cupiera, cupiese, etc *see* **caber**

cupimos, cupiste, etc *see* **caber**

cuplé *m* variety song

cupletista *mf: singer or composer of* **cuplés**

cupo¹ *m* 1 (cantidad establecida) quota; **~s de importación** import quotas 2 (AmL) (capacidad) room; **una sala con ~ para 300 personas** a hall which holds 300 people 3 (AmC, Col, Méx) (plaza) place

cupo² *see* **caber**

cupón *m*

A (vale) coupon, voucher

(Compuestos)

- **cupón de franqueo internacional** international reply coupon
- **cupón federal** ≈ food stamp (*in US*)
- **cupón obsequio** gift certificate (AmE), gift voucher *o* token (BrE)

B (Esp) (de lotería) ticket

cuponazo *m* (Esp) the big one (*weekly lottery prize*)

cuponazo

▸**Once**

cuprero -ra *adj* (Chi) copper (*before n*)

cúprico -ca *adj* cupric, copper (*before n*)

cúpula *f*

A (Arquit) dome, cupola; (Mil, Náut) (torreta) turret

B (de organización): **la ~ del partido** the party leadership; **la ~ militar** the leaders of the armed forces; **la ~ de la empresa** the upper echelons of the company

cuquillo *m* cuckoo

cura¹ *m* (sacerdote) priest; **se metió de** *or* **a ~** he became a priest

(Compuesto) **cura párroco** parish priest

cura² *f* 1 (curación, tratamiento) cure; **una enfermadad que no tiene ~** an incurable disease 2 (vendaje) dressing; (curita) (Col) Band-Aid® (AmE), (sticking) plaster (BrE)

(Compuestos)

- **cura de aguas** hydrotherapy
- **cura de reposo** rest cure
- **cura de sueño** sleep therapy
- **cura de urgencias** first aid

curable *adj* curable

curaca *m* (Per) cacique, chief

curación *f*

A (tratamiento) treatment

B (recuperación—de enfermo) recovery; (— de herida) healing

curado¹ -da *adj*

A ‹*jamón/carne*› cured; ‹*cuero/piel*› tanned; ▸**espanto A2**

B (fam) (borracho) plastered (colloq)

curado² *m* (de jamón) curing; (de cuero, piel) tanning

curador -dora *m,f* (Der) guardian; (de un museo) (RPl) curator

curandero -ra *m,f* (en medicina popular) folk healer; (hechicero) witch doctor; (charlatán) (pey) quack doctor (pej)

curar [A1] *vt*

A 1 (poner bien) ‹*enfermo/enfermedad*› to cure; ‹*herida*› to heal 2 (tratar) ‹*enfermo/enfermedad*› to treat; **no le han curado la herida** his wound hasn't been cleaned/ dressed

B ‹*jamón/pescado*› to cure; ‹*cuero/piel*› to tan

■ **curar** *vi* «*enfermo*» to recover, get better; «*herida*» to heal, heal up; **una vez curado de la enfermedad ...** once he has/had recovered from his illness ...; **tiene una gripe mal curada** he hasn't got(ten) rid of his flu yet

■ **curarse** *v pron* «*persona*» to recover, get better; **~se DE algo** to get over sth

curativo -va *adj* curative

cúrcuma *f* turmeric

curcuncho -cha *m,f* (Chi, Per fam & pey) hunchback

curda¹ *adj inv* (Esp fam) sloshed (colloq)

curda² *mf*

A (RPl fam) (borracho) soak (colloq)

B **curda** *f* (fam) 1 (borrachera): **tiene una ~ que no ve** he's blind drunk (colloq) 2 (Ven) (bebida alcohólica) booze (colloq)

curdo[1] **-da** *adj*
A (Geog) Kurdish
B (Ven fam) (borracho) ▸ **curda**[1]

curdo[2] **-da** *m,f*
A (Geog) Kurd
B (Ven fam) (borracho) ▸ **curda**[2] **A**

curí *m* (Col) guinea pig

curia *f*
A (Relig) Curia, curia; (Hist) curia
B (Der) bar

curiosamente *adv* curiously, strangely; **~, no vino** (*indep*) curiously enough *o* strangely enough, he didn't come

curiosear [A1] *vi* 1 (fisgonear) to pry; **~ en la vida ajena** to pry into other people's affairs; **estaba curioseando entre mis papeles/en mis cajones** he was going *o* looking through my papers/drawers 2 (por las tiendas, en una biblioteca) to browse; **me puse a ~ en la biblioteca/entre los archivos** I started browsing around the library/through the files

curiosidad *f*
A (cualidad) curiosity; **siente/tiene mucha ~** he is very curious; **están muertos de ~** *or* **se mueren de ~** they are dying to see him (*o* to know *etc*); **me ha picado la ~** my curiosity has been aroused
B (cosa rara) curiosity; **tienda de ~es** curio shop

curioso[1] **-sa** *adj*
A (interesante, extraño) curious, strange, odd; **es ~ que ...** it's odd *o* strange that ...; **lo ~ del caso es que ...** the strange *o* funny thing is that ...
B 1 [SER] (inquisitivo) inquisitive; (entrometido) (pey) nosy* (colloq) 2 [ESTAR] (interesado) curious
C (Esp) (pulcro) neat

curioso[2] **-sa** *m,f* 1 (espectador) onlooker; Ⓢ **abstenerse curiosos** (Esp) no timewasters 2 (fam) (fisgón) busybody (colloq)

curita *f* (AmL) Band-Aid® (AmE), (sticking) plaster (BrE)

currante *mf* (Esp fam) worker

currar [A1] *vi* (Esp fam) 1 (trabajar) to work 2 (pegar) to thump (colloq)
■ **currar** *vt* (RPl fam) to rip ... off (colloq)

curricular *adj* (AmL) curricular

currículo *m* (Educ) curriculum

curriculum, currículum *m* (*pl* **-lums**) 1 (antecedentes) *tb* **~ vitae** curriculum vitae, CV 2 (Educ) curriculum

curro *m*
A (Esp fam) (trabajo) job
B (RPl fam) (timo) rip-off (colloq)

curruña *mf* (Ven fam) buddy (AmE colloq), mate (BrE colloq)

currusco *m* crust

currutaco[1] **-ca** *adj* (Col, Ven fam) pint-sized (colloq)

currutaco[2] **-ca** *m,f* (Col, Ven fam) shortie (colloq)

curry /ˈkurri/ *m* (*pl* **-rries**) (polvo) curry powder; (plato) curry; **pollo al ~** curried chicken

cursar [A1] *vt*
A (estudiar): **~ estudios universitarios** to do *o* take a university/college course; **cursa segundo de Derecho** she is in her second year at law school
B (frml) ‹*orden*› to issue; ‹*solicitud*› to deal with

cursi[1] *adj* (fam) ‹*objeto*› corny, twee (BrE); ‹*idea*› sentimental, twee (BrE); ‹*decoración*› chichi; **la encuentro ~** she just seems affected to me

cursi[2] *mf* (fam): **es un ~** he's so affected *o* twee

cursilería, cursilada *f*: **raya en la ~** it verges on the sentimental *o* the schmaltzy; **el vestido le pareció una ~** she thought the dress was rather corny *o* (BrE) twee

cursillo *m* 1 (curso corto) short course; **~ de natación** swimming lessons 2 (ciclo de conferencias) series of lectures

cursiva *f* italics (*pl*)

curso *m*
A (Educ) 1 (año académico) year; **está en (el) tercer ~** he's in the third year; **el ~ escolar/universitario** the academic year 2 (clases) course; **un ~ de contabilidad** an accountancy course 3 (grupo de alumnos) year; **una chica de mi ~** a girl in my year

(Compuestos)
- **curso acelerado** *or* **intensivo** crash *o* intensive course
- **Curso de Orientación Universitaria** (en Esp) pre-university course
- **curso por correspondencia** correspondence course

B 1 (transcurso, desarrollo) course; **en el ~ de la reunión** in the course of the meeting; **dejar que algo siga su ~** to let sth take its course; **seguir el ~ de los acontecimientos** to follow the development of events; **el año/el mes en ~** (frml) the current year/month (frml); ***dar ~ a algo*** (a una instancia/solicitud) to start to process sth; (a la imaginación) to give free rein to sth 2 (de río) course
C (circulación): **monedas/billetes de ~ legal** legal tender, legal currency

cursor *m* cursor

curtido[1] **-da** *adj* ‹*rostro/piel*› weather-beaten; ‹*manos*› hardened

curtido[2] *m* 1 (proceso) tanning 2 (cuero, piel) tanned hide; **fábrica de ~s** tannery

curtidor -dora *m,f* tanner

curtir [I1] *vt*
A ‹*cuero/pieles*› to tan
B 1 ‹*rostro/piel*› «*sol*» to tan and harden 2 ‹*persona*› «*vida/sufrimientos*» to harden
■ **curtirse** *v pron* (por el sol) to become tanned (and hardened); (por el viento, el tiempo) to become weather-beaten

curul *f* (Col, Méx, Per) (Pol) seat

curva *f*
A 1 (línea) curve; **~ de temperatura(s)** temperature curve; **la ~ de la felicidad** (fam & hum) middle-age spread (colloq & hum) (*said to be caused by marital bliss*) 2 (en camino, carretera) curve; (más pronunciada) bend; Ⓢ **curva peligrosa** sharp bend; **una ~ cerrada/en herradura** a sharp/hairpin bend; ***agarrar a algn en ~*** (Méx fam) to take sb by surprise 3 (Dep) curveball
B **curvas** *fpl* (de una mujer) curves (*pl*); **con ~** curvaceous

curvar [A1] *vt* ‹*alambre*› to bend; ‹*estante*› to bow
■ **curvarse** *v pron* «*alambre*» to bend; «*estante*» to bow

curvatura *f* curvature

curvilíneo -nea *adj* 1 (Mat) curvilinear 2 ‹*mujer/cuerpo*› curvaceous

curvo -va *adj* curved

cuscurro *m* (Coc) crust

cuscús, cus-cus *m* (Coc) couscous

cúspide *f* 1 (de montaña) top, summit; (de pirámide) top, apex 2 (de fama, poder) height, pinnacle 3 (de organización) leadership

custodia *f*
A 1 (tutela) custody; **ejerce la ~ del niño** she has custody of the child 2 (encarcelación, vigilancia) custody; **lo tienen bajo ~** he is being held in custody
B 1 (Arg) (escolta) escort 2 **custodia** *mf* (persona) guard
C (Relig) monstrance

custodiar [A1] *vt* to guard

custodio -da *m,f* guardian

(Compuesto) **custodio del orden** (Per) police officer

cusuco *m* (AmC) armadillo

cususa *f* (AmC) *homemade corn liquor*

cutacha *f* ▸ **cuma**

cutáneo -nea *adj* skin (*before n*), cutaneous (tech)

cúter *m* (Náut) cutter

cutícula *f* cuticle

cutis *m* (*pl* **~**) skin; **~ suave** smooth complexion *o* skin

cutre *adj* (Esp fam) ‹*hotel*› seedy, shabby; ‹*persona*› shabby

cuy *m* (AmS) guinea pig

cuye *m* (Chi) guinea pig

cuyo -ya *adj*
A (indicando pertenencia) whose; **vocablos ~ uso es extendido** words which are in widespread use; **en un lugar de ~ nombre no quiero acordarme** in a place, the name of which I prefer not to recall
B (sin sentido posesivo): **en ~ caso ...** in which case, ...

CV *m* = **caballo de vapor**

C.V. *m* (= **curriculum vitae**) CV

Dd

d

D, d *f* (*read as* /de/) *the letter* **D, d**
D. = **Don**
dactilar *adj* finger (*before n*); ▸**huella**
dáctilo *m* dactyl
dactilografía *f* typing, typewriting
dactilógrafo -fa *m,f* typist
dadaísmo *m* Dadaism
dádiva *f* gift
dadivoso -sa *adj* generous
dado¹ -da *adj*
A (determinado) given; **en un momento/punto ~** at a given moment/point
B (*como conj*) given; **dadas las circunstancias** given *o* in view of the circumstances; **dado que** (frml) in view of the fact that (frml), given that
C [SER] (proclive) **~ A algo/+ INF** given TO sth/-ING
D (RPl) (abierto, extrovertido) outgoing
dado² *m*
A [1] (Jueg) dice, die (frml); **echar** *or* **tirar los ~s** to throw the dice; **jugar a los ~s** to play dice [2] (cubo): **cortar el queso en ~s** cut the cheese into cubes; **zanahoria cortada en daditos** diced carrot
B (Arquit) dado
DAFO *f* (= **Debilidades, Amenazas, Fortalezas y Oportunidades**) SWOT; **análisis ~** SWOT analysis
daga *f* dagger
daguerrotipo *m* (proceso) daguerreotype process; (fotografía) daguerreotype
dalia *f* dahlia
daltónico¹ -ca *adj* color-blind*
daltónico² -ca *m,f*: **los ~s** people suffering from color-blindness*
daltonismo *m* color-blindness*
dama *f*
A (frml) (señora) lady; **~s y caballeros** ladies and gentlemen; **la final de ~s** the ladies' final
(Compuesto) **dama de honor** (de novia) bridesmaid; (de reina) lady-in-waiting
B (figura) [1] (en damas) king; **hacer ~** to make a crown *o* king [2] (en ajedrez) queen; **hacer ~** to queen, make a queen [3] (en naipes) queen
C **damas** *fpl* (juego) checkers (AmE), draughts (BrE); **jugar a las ~s** to play checkers *o* draughts
damajuana *f* demijohn
damasco *m*
A (Tex) damask
B (AmS) (fruta) apricot; (árbol) apricot tree
Damasco *m* Damascus
damasquinado *m* damascene (work)
damasquinar [A1] *vt* to damascene, damask
damasquino -na *adj* [1] (de Damasco) Damascene [2] ‹*espada*› damascene, damask
damisela *f* (arc) damsel (arch)
damnificado -da *m,f* (frml) victim; **los ~s por la sequía** the victims of the drought
danés¹ -nesa *adj* Danish
danés² -nesa *m,f*
A (persona) (*m*) Dane, Danish man; (*f*) Dane, Danish woman
B **danés** *m* (idioma) Danish
danta *f* (AmL) (tapir) tapir
dantesco -ca *adj* (de Dante) Dantesque; (terrible) horrific
danto *m* (AmC) tapir
danza *f* [1] (arte) dance; **~ moderna** modern dance; **la ~ lo es todo para ella** dancing is everything for her [2] (pieza) dance [3] (fam) (actividad, ajetreo) rush; **es una ~ continua** it's one long rush; ***estar*** *or* ***andar en ~*** (fam) to be on the go (colloq)
danzar [A4] *vi* (frml) (bailar) to dance; ***tener a algn danzando*** to keep sb on the go
danzarín -rina *adj*: **es muy ~** he loves dancing
dañado -da *adj* damaged
dañar [A1] *vt* (hacer daño a) [1] ‹*honra/reputación*› to damage, harm [2] ‹*fruta/mercancías/instalaciones*› to damage; ‹*cosecha*› to damage, spoil [3] ‹*salud/organismo*› to be bad for, damage; **esa luz me daña la vista** that light hurts my eyes
■ **dañarse** *v pron*
A [1] «*cosecha*» to be/get damaged *o* spoiled; «*comestibles/mercancías/muebles*» to be/get damaged [2] «*persona*» ‹*salud*› to damage
B (Col, Ven) [1] «*carne/comida*» to rot, go bad [2] «*auto*» to break down; «*aparato*» to break
dañino -na *adj* [SER] ‹*planta/sustancia*› harmful; **~ PARA algo** harmful TO sth; **~ para la salud** harmful to *o* bad for one's health
daño *m*
A [1] (dolor físico): **hacerse ~** to hurt oneself; **me he hecho ~ en la espalda** I've hurt my back; **hacerle ~ a algn** «*persona*» to hurt sb; **el picante me hace ~** hot, spicy food doesn't agree with me [2] (destrozo) damage; **muchas viviendas sufrieron ~s** many houses were damaged *o* suffered damage
(Compuesto) **daños y perjuicios** *mpl* damages (*pl*)
B (CS, Méx fam) (en brujería) curse; **le hicieron un ~** they put a curse on him
dar [A25] *vt*
(*Sentido* **I**)
A (entregar) to give; **dale las llaves a Pedro** give the keys to Pedro; **se las di a Jaime** I gave them to Jaime; **déme un kilo de peras** can I have a kilo of pears?; **500 dólares ¿quién da más?** any advance on 500 dollars?; ▸**conocer** *vt* **C2**, **entender** *vt* **B2**
B (regalar, donar) to give; **¿me lo prestas? — te lo doy, no lo necesito** can I borrow it? — you can keep it, I don't need it; **¡qué no ~ía por que así fuera!** I'd give anything for that to be the case; ***donde las dan las toman*** two can play at that game; ***tener para ~ y vender*** to have plenty to spare
C ‹*cartas/mano*› to deal
D [1] (proporcionar) ‹*fuerzas/valor/esperanza*› to give; **eso me dio la idea** that's where I got the idea from; **si le dan la ocasión** if he's given the chance; **pide que te den más información** ask them to give you more information [2] (Mús) to give; **¿me das el la?** can you give me an A?
E (conferir, aportar) ‹*sabor/color/forma*› to give; **las luces le daban un ambiente festivo** the lights gave a festive atmosphere
F [1] (aplicar) to give; **dale otra capa de barniz** give it another coat of varnish; **hay que ~le cera al piso** the floor needs waxing; **dale una puntada para sujetarlo** put a stitch in to hold it [2] ‹*sedante/masaje*› to give

G 1 (conceder) ‹*prórroga/permiso*› to give; **el dentista me dio hora para el miércoles** I have an appointment with the dentist on Wednesday; **dan facilidades de pago** they offer easy repayment facilities *o* terms; **nos dieron un premio** we won *o* got a prize; **me dieron un diploma** I got a diploma; **no le doy ni un mes a esa relación** I don't think they'll last more than a month together 2 (RPl) (calcular): **¿qué edad le das?** how old do you think he is?

H 1 (expresar, decir): **¿le diste las gracias?** did you thank him?, did you say thank you?; **no me dio ni los buenos días** she didn't even say hello; **dales saludos** give/send them my regards; **~le la bienvenida a algn** to welcome sb; **me dio su parecer** *or* **opinión** she gave me her opinion; **tuve que ~le la noticia** I was the one who had to break the news to him 2 (señalar, indicar): **me da ocupado** *or* (Esp) **comunicando** the line's busy *o* (BrE) engaged; **el reloj dio las cinco** the clock struck five

Sentido **II**

A (producir) ‹*fruto/flor*› to bear; **estos campos dan mucho grano** these fields have a high grain yield; **este negocio da mucho dinero** there's a lot of money in this business; **esos bonos dan un 7%** those bonds yield 7%

B 1 (rendir): **ha dado todo lo que esperaba de él** he has lived up to my/his expectations; **ese jugador lo da todo** that player puts everything into the game 2 (AmL) (alcanzar hasta): **¿cuánto da ese coche?** how fast can that car go?; **da 150 kilómetros por hora** it can do *o* go 150 kilometers an hour; **venía a todo lo que daba** it was traveling at full speed; **ponen la radio a todo lo que da** they turn the radio on full blast

C (causar, provocar): **la comida muy salada da sed** salty food makes you thirsty; **¡estos niños dan tanto trabajo!** these kids are such hard work!; (+ *me/te/le etc*) **¿no te da calor esa camisa?** aren't you too warm in that shirt?; **el vino le había dado sueño** the wine had made him sleepy; **me da mucha pena verla tan triste** it hurts me to see her so sad; **¡qué susto me has dado!** you gave me such a fright!; **este coche no me ha dado problemas** this car hasn't given me any trouble; *ver tb* **asco, hambre, miedo, etc**; **~ QUE + INF**: **el jardín da muchísimo que hacer** there's always such a lot to do in the garden; **lo que dijo me dio que pensar** what he said gave me plenty to think about; *ver tb* **dar** *vi Sentido* **III A**

Sentido **III**

A (presentar) ‹*concierto*› to give; **¿qué dan esta noche en la tele?** what's on TV tonight? (colloq); **ayer daban una obra de Calderón** there was a Calderón play on yesterday; **¿dónde están dando esa película?** where's that film showing?

B 1 ‹*fiesta*› to give; ‹*baile/banquete*› to hold 2 ‹*conferencia*› to give; ‹*discurso*› (AmL) to make 3 (CS) ‹*examen*› to take *o* (BrE) sit; *ver tb* **clase E**

Sentido **IV** (realizar la acción que se indica): **~ lectura a un comunicado** to read out a communiqué; **~ un grito/un suspiro** to give a shout/heave a sigh; **~ un paso atrás/adelante** to take a step back/forward; **dame un beso/abrazo** give me a kiss/hug; *ver tb* **golpe, paseo, vuelta, etc**

Sentido **V** (considerar) **~ algo/a algn POR algo**: **lo dieron por muerto** they gave him up for dead; **doy por terminada la sesión** I declare the session closed; **ese tema lo doy por sabido** I'm assuming you've already covered that topic; **puedes ~ por perdido el dinero** you can say goodbye to that money; **¡dalo por hecho!** consider it done!; **si apruebo ~é el tiempo por bien empleado** if I pass it will have been time well spent

■ **dar** *vi*

Sentido **I**

A 1 (entregar): **no puedes con todo, dame que te ayudo** you'll never manage all that on your own, here, let me help you; **¿me das para un helado?** can I have some money for an ice cream? 2 (en naipes) to deal; **te toca ~ a ti** it's your deal

B (ser suficiente, alcanzar) **~ PARA algo/algn**: **este pollo da para dos comidas** this chicken will do for two meals; **con una botella no da para todos** one bottle's not enough to go round; (+ *me/te/le etc*) **eso no te da ni para un chicle** you can't even buy a piece of chewing gum with that; **no me dio (el) tiempo** I didn't have time; ***~ de sí*** to stretch; **¡qué poco dan de sí mil pesos!** a thousand pesos doesn't go very far!; ***no ~ para más***: **su inteligencia no da para más** that's as much as his brain can cope with; **lo que gano no da para más** what I earn doesn't go any further; **la fiesta no daba para más** the party was beginning to wind down

C **dar a** 1 «*puerta*» to give onto, open onto; «*ventana*» to look onto, give onto 2 «*fachada/frente*» (estar orientado hacia) to face; **la terraza da al mar** the balcony overlooks *o* faces the sea 3 (llegar hasta) «*río*» to flow into, go into; «*calle*» to lead to

D (arrojar un resultado): **el análisis le dio positivo/negativo** her test was positive/negative; **¿cuánto da la cuenta?** what does it come to?; **a mí me dio 247** I made it (to be) 247

E (importar): **da lo mismo, ya iremos otro día** it doesn't matter, we'll go another day; **¡qué más da!** what does it matter!; **¿qué más da un color que otro?** what difference does it make what color it is?; (+ *me/te/le etc*) **¿el jueves o el viernes? — me da igual** Thursday or Friday? — I don't mind *o* it doesn't make any difference to me; **¿y a ti qué más te da si él viene?** what's it to you if he comes? (colloq)

Sentido **II**

A 1 (pegar, golpear): **~le A algn** to hit sb; (como castigo) to smack sb; **le dio en la cabeza/con un palo** he hit him on the head/with a stick; **dale al balón con fuerza** kick the ball hard; **te voy a ~ (de palos)** I'm going to give you a good beating; **el balón dio en el poste** the ball hit the post 2 (fam) (a tarea, asignatura) **~le A algo**: **me pasé todo el verano dándole al inglés** I spent the whole summer working on my English; **¡cómo le da al vino!** he really knocks back *o* (AmE) down the wine (colloq); **¡cómo le han dado al queso! ¡ya casi no queda!** they've certainly been at the cheese, there's hardly any left! (colloq) 3 (acertar) to hit; **~ en el blanco/el centro** to hit the target/the bull's-eye

B (accionar, mover) **~le A algo** ‹*a botón/tecla*› to press sth; ‹*a interruptor*› to flick sth; ‹*a manivela*› to turn sth; (+ *compl*) **dale al volante hacia la derecha** turn the wheel to the right; **dale a esa palanca hacia arriba** push that lever up; **dale para atrás** back up

C 1 (fam) (indicando insistencia): **¡y dale! ya te he dicho que no voy** there you go again! I've told you I'm not going (colloq); **¡y dale con lo de su edad!** stop going on about her age!; ***¡dale que dale*** *or* (Esp) ***dale que te pego!*** (fam): **he estado todo el día dale que dale** I've been hard at it all day; **¡dale que dale con lo mismo!** stop going on about it! 2 (RPl fam) (instando a hacer algo) come on; **dale, prestámelo** come on *o* go on, lend it to me

D **dar con** (encontrar) ‹*persona*› to find; ‹*solución*› to hit upon, find; ‹*palabra*› to come up with

Sentido **III**

A (acometer, sobrevenir) (+ *me/te/le etc*): **le dio un mareo** she felt dizzy; **le dio un infarto** he had a heart attack; **me va a ~ algo** (fam) I'm going to have a fit (colloq); *ver tb* **dar** *vt Sentido* **II C, escalofrío, frío, gana, etc**

B (hablando de manías, ocurrencias) **~le a algn POR + INF** to take to -ING; **le ha dado por pintar** he's taken to painting; **le ha dado por decir que ...** he's started saying that ...; **le ha dado por el yoga** she's got into yoga; **le ha dado con que me conoce** she's got it into her head that she knows me

C «*sol/viento/luz*»: **aquí da el sol toda la mañana** you get the sun all morning here; **en esa playa da mucho el viento** it's very windy on that beach; **la luz le daba de lleno en los ojos** the light was shining right in his eyes

■ **darse** *v pron*

Sentido **I**

A (producirse) to grow; **en esta zona se da bien el trigo** wheat grows well in this area

B (presentarse) «*oportunidad/ocasión*» to arise; **se dio el caso que iba pasando por ahí** it so happened that I was passing by

C (resultar) (+ *me/te/le etc*): **se le dan los idiomas** she's good at languages; **¿cómo se te da a ti la costura?** are you any good at sewing?

Sentido **II** 1 (dedicarse, entregarse) **~se A algo**: **se dio a la bebida** she took to drink; **se ha dado por entero a su familia/a la causa** she has devoted herself entirely to her family/to the cause 2 (CS, Ven) (ser sociable) **~se CON**

algn to get on with sb; **no se da con los suegros** she doesn't have much to do with her in-laws

(Sentido III) 1 (*refl*) (realizar la acción que se indica): **me di una ducha** I took *o* had a shower; **~se un banquete** to have a feast; ***dárselas de algo***: **se las da de que sabe mucho** he likes to make out he knows a lot; **dárselas de listo** to act smart; **¿y de qué se las da ése?** who does he think he is? 2 (golpearse, pegarse): **se dio con el martillo en el dedo** he hit his finger with the hammer; **no te vayas a ~ con la cabeza contra el techo** don't hit *o* bang your head on the ceiling; **se dieron contra un árbol** they crashed into a tree; **se dio ~ un golpe en la rodilla** he hit his knee 3 (*recípr*): **se estaban dando (de) patadas/puñetazos** they were kicking/punching each other

(Sentido IV) (considerarse) **~se** POR **algo**: **con eso me ~ía por satisfecha** I'd be quite happy with that; **darse por vencido** to give up; *ver tb* **aludir 1, enterado A**

dardo *m* 1 (Jueg) dart; **jugar a los ~s** to play darts 2 (arma) small spear

dársena *f* dock

datación *f* dating; **~ por carbono 14** radiocarbon dating

datar [A1] *vi*: **data del siglo XII** it dates from the 12th century; **una amistad que data de hace muchos años** a friendship which goes back many years

■ **datar** *vt* to date

dátil *m* (Bot) date

datilera *f* date palm

dativo *m* (Ling) dative

dato *m* 1 (elemento de información) piece of information; **no dispongo de todos los ~s** I don't have all the information; **alguien le pasó el ~ a la policía** (CS) somebody informed *o* (colloq) tipped off the police; **darle un ~ a algn** (CS) to give sb a tip 2 **datos** *mpl* (Inf) data (*pl*), information

(Compuesto) **datos personales** *mpl* particulars (*pl*), personal details (*pl*)

davo *m* (AmC fam) problem

dB. (= **decibelio**) db, decibel

Dcha., dcha. = **derecha**

d. de C. (= **después de Jesucristo**) AD

DDF *m* (en Méx) = **Departamento del Distrito Federal**

de[1] *prep*

(Sentido I)

A (en relaciones de pertenencia, posesión): **la casa ~ ~ mis padres/~ la actriz** my parents'/the actress's house; **el rey ~ Francia** the king of France; **el cumpleaños ~ Luis** Luis's birthday; **no es ~ él/~ ella/~ ellos** it isn't his/hers/theirs; **su padre ~ usted** (frml) your father; **es un amigo ~ mi hijo/~ la familia** he's a friend of my son's/the family; **un estudiante ~ quinto año** a fifth-year student; **la correa ~l perro** the dog's leash; **un avión ~ Mexair** a Mexair plane; **la tapa ~ la cacerola** the saucepan lid; **las calles ~ la capital** the streets of the capital; **la subida ~ los precios** the rise in prices; **al término ~ la reunión** at the end of the meeting

B 1 (introduciendo un nombre en aposición) of; **la ciudad ~ Lima** the city of Lima; **el aeropuerto ~ Barajas** Barajas airport; **el mes ~ enero** the month of January 2 (con apellidos): **Sra. Mónica Ortiz ~ Arocena** ≈ Mrs Mónica Arocena; **los señores ~ Díaz** (frml) Mr and Mrs Díaz; **las señoritas ~ Paz** (frml) the Misses Paz (frml) [**de** *is also part of certain surnames like* **de León** *and* **de la Peña**] 3 (en exclamaciones): **¡pobre ~ él!** poor him!; **¡ay ~ mí!** (liter) woe is me! (liter)

(Sentido II)

A (expresando procedencia, origen, tiempo) from; **volvía ~l banco** I was on my way back from the bank; **es ~ Bogotá** she's/she comes from Bogotá; **una carta ~ Julia** a letter from Julia; **lo saqué ~ la biblioteca** I got it out of the library; **lo recogió ~l suelo** she picked it up off the floor; **un hijo ~ su primera mujer** a son by his first wife; **al salir ~ la tienda** as he left the store; **un amigo ~ la infancia** a childhood friend; **la literatura ~ ese período** the literature of *o* from that period; **~ un día para otro** from one day to the next; DE ... A ... FROM ... TO ...; **~ aquí a tu casa** from here to your house; **~ nueve a cinco** it's open from nine to five

B (al especificar material, contenido, composición): **son ~ plástico** they're (made of) plastic; **una mesa ~ caoba** a mahogany table; **una inyección ~ morfina** an injection of morphine, a morphine injection; **un curso ~ secretariado** a secretarial course; **un vaso ~ agua** a glass of water; **una colección ~ sellos** a stamp collection; **un millón ~ dólares** a million dollars

C (expresando causa, modo): **murió ~ viejo** he died of old age; **verde ~ envidia** green with envy; **estaba ronco ~ tanto gritar** he was hoarse from shouting so much; **temblando ~ miedo** trembling with fear; **~ memoria** by heart; **lo tumbó ~ un golpe** he knocked him down with one blow; **~ dos en dos** *or* (CS) **de a dos** two at a time; **~ a poco/~ a uno** (CS) little by little/one by one

(Sentido III)

A 1 (introduciendo cualidades, características): **es ~ una paciencia increíble** he is incredibly patient; **objetos ~ mucho valor** objects of great value; **¿~ qué color lo quiere?** what color do you want it?; **tiene cara ~ aburrido** he looks bored; **tienes cosas ~ niño** sometimes you act like a child; **una botella ~ un litro** a liter bottle; **un niño ~ tres meses** a three-month-old child; **la chica ~ azul/~l abrigo rojo** the girl in blue/in the red coat; **un hombre ~ pelo largo** a man with long hair 2 (refiriéndose a una etapa en la vida) as; **~ niño** as a *o* when he was a child

B (indicando uso, destino, finalidad): **el cepillo ~ la ropa** the clothes brush; **copas ~ vino** wine glasses; **ropa ~ cama** bed clothes; **dales algo ~ comer** give them something to eat; **¿qué hay ~ postre?** what's for dessert?

C 1 (al definir, especificar): **el botón ~ abajo** the bottom button; **el vecino ~ al lado** the next-door neighbor; **es muy bonita ~ cara** she has a pretty face; **¿qué tal vamos ~ tiempo?** how are we doing for time?; **tiene dos metros ~ ancho** it's two meters wide; **es fácil/difícil de pronunciar** it's easy/difficult to pronounce 2 (sentido partitivo) of; **¿quién ~ ustedes fue?** which (one) of you was it?; **se llevó uno ~ los míos** she took one of mine; **el mayor ~ los Soto** the eldest of the Soto children

D (con sentido ponderativo): **¡lo encontré ~ viejo ...!** he seemed so old!; **¡qué ~ coches!** (fam) what a lot of cars!

E 1 (con cifras): **el número ~ estudiantes es ~ 480** there are 480 students; **pagan un interés ~l 15%** they pay 15% interest *o* interest at 15% 2 (en comparaciones de cantidad) than; **cuesta más ~ £100** it costs more than *o* over £100; **pesa menos ~ un kilo** it weighs less than *o* under a kilo; **un número mayor/menor ~ 29** a number over/under 29 3 (con un superlativo): **es el más caro ~ todos** it's the most expensive one; **la ciudad más grande ~l mundo** the biggest city in the world

F (refiriéndose a una parte del día): **duerme ~ día y trabaja ~ noche** she sleeps during the day and works at night; **salieron ~ madrugada** they left very early in the morning

G (en calidad de) as; **trabaja ~ secretaria** she works as a secretary; **hace ~ rey en la obra** he plays (the part of) a king in the play

H (en expresiones de estado, actividad): **~ mal humor** in a bad mood; **estamos ~ limpieza general/fiesta** we're spring-cleaning/having a party

I (en oraciones pasivas) by; **una novela ~ Goytisolo** a novel by Goytisolo; **una casa rodeada ~ árboles** a house surrounded by trees

(Sentido IV) (con sentido condicional) 1 DE + INF: **~ haberlo sabido, habría venido antes** if I had known *o* had I known, I would have come earlier; **~ no ser así no será considerada** otherwise it will not be considered 2 SER DE + INF (expresando necesidad, inevitabilidad): **es ~ esperar que ...** it is to be hoped that ...; **es ~ destacar su actuación** her performance is worthy of note

de[2] *f: name of the letter* **d**

dé *see* **dar**

deambular [A1] *vi* to wander around *o* about

deambulatorio *m* ambulatory

deán *m* dean

debacle *f* 1 (fiasco) debacle, fiasco; **aquello fue la ~** it was absolute chaos 2 (derrumbamiento) collapse, downfall

debajo *adv*

A [*Latin American Spanish also uses* **abajo** *in many of these exam-*

ples] underneath; **no llevo nada ~** I'm not wearing anything underneath; **el que está ~** the one below, the next one down

B debajo de (*loc prep*) under; **~ del coche** under *o* underneath the car; **~ del agua** underwater; **por ~ de la puerte** under the door; **temperaturas por ~ de lo normal** temperatures below average; **la enagua se le asomaba por ~ de la falda** her slip was showing below her skirt; **por ~ de mí/ti/él** below me/you/him

debate *m* debate; (más informal) discussion

debatir [I1] *vt* to debate; (más informal) to discuss

■ **debatirse** *v pron*: **se debatía entre el deber y su amor por ella** he was torn between the sense of duty and his love for her; **se debate entre la vida y la muerte** he's fighting for his life; **se debatía entre el miedo y la esperanza** his feelings alternated between fear and hope

debe *m* debit; **el ~ y el haber** the debit side and the credit side

deber¹ [E1] *vt* **1** ‹*dinero*› to owe; **exigen el pago de lo que se les debe** they're demanding to be paid what is owing to them; **¿cuánto se debe?** how much do I/we owe you?; **te debo las entradas de ayer** I owe you for the tickets from yesterday **2** ‹*favor/visita/explicación*› to owe; **España le debe mucho al Islam** Spain owes a great debt to Islam; **esta victoria se la debo a mi entrenador** I have to thank my coach for this victory

■ **deber** *v aux*

A (expresando obligación) **~ + INF**: **debes decírselo** you have to *o* you must tell her; **~ías** *or* **debías habérselo dicho** you ought to have *o* you should have told her; **la trató respetuosamente, como debe ser** he treated her with respect, as he should; **no debes usarlo** you are not to *o* you must not use it; **no se debe mentir** you mustn't tell lies; **no ~ías haberlo dejado solo** you shouldn't have left him alone

B (expresando suposición, probabilidad) **1 ~ (DE) + INF**: **deben (de) ser más de las cinco** it must be after five o'clock; **deben (de) haber salido** they must have gone out; **debe (de) estar ganando mucho** she/he must be earning a lot **2** (en frases negativas): **no deben (de) saber la dirección** they probably don't know the address; **no les debe (de) haber interesado** they can't have been interested

■ **deberse** *v pron*

A (tener su causa en) **~se A algo**: **se debió a un fallo humano** it was caused by *o* was due to human error; **todo se debe a que no estudia** it's all due *o* down to the fact that she doesn't study; **¿a qué se debe este escándalo?** what's all this racket about?

B «*persona*» (tener obligaciones hacia) **~se A algn** to have a duty TO sb; **el artista se debe a su público** an artist has a duty to his/her public

deber² *m*

A (obligación) duty; **cumplió con su ~** he carried out *o* did his duty; **faltó a su ~** he failed in his duty; **siento que es un ~ de conciencia ayudarlos** I feel morally bound to help them

B deberes *mpl* (tarea escolar) homework, assignment (AmE); **¿has hecho los ~es?** have you done your homework?

debidamente *adv* correctly, properly; **la vacante no fue ~ anunciada en la prensa** the vacancy was not advertised in the press as it should have been

debido -da *adj*

A (apropiado): **a su ~ tiempo** *or* **en su ~ momento** in due course; **con el ~ respeto, creo que se equivoca** with all due respect, I think you are mistaken; **tratar a algn con el ~ respeto** to show due respect to sb; **tomó las debidas precauciones** she took the necessary precautions; **no trabaja con el ~ cuidado** he doesn't take enough care over his work; **portarse/sentarse como es ~** to behave/sit properly; **una comida como es ~** a proper meal; **más de lo ~** too much

B (*en locs*) **debido a** owing to, on account of; **debido a que** owing to the fact that

débil *adj* **1** ‹*persona*› (físicamente) weak; (falto de — firmeza) soft; (— voluntad) weak; ‹*economía/ejército/gobierno*› weak; **es de complexión ~** she has a weak constitution; **es ~ de carácter** he has a weak character **2** ‹*sonido/voz*› faint; ‹*moneda*› weak; ‹*argumento*› weak; ‹*excusa*› feeble, lame; ‹*luz*› dim, faint **3** ‹*sílaba/vocal*› unstressed, weak

debilidad *f* **1** (física): **su ~ nos impide operarla** her weak state means that we are unable to operate; **siento una gran ~** I feel terribly debilitated *o* weak **2** (de carácter): **todos se aprovechan de su ~** everyone takes advantage of his feeble nature *o* his weak character **3** (inclinación excesiva) weakness; **tener ~ por algn** to have a soft spot for sb; **tener ~ por algo** to have a weakness for sth

debilitamiento *m*, **debilitación** *f* weakening

debilitar [A1] *vt* **1** ‹*persona*› to weaken, debilitate; ‹*salud/voluntad*› to weaken **2** ‹*economía/defensa*› to weaken, debilitate

■ **debilitarse** *v pron* **1** «*persona*» to become weak; «*salud*» to deteriorate; «*voluntad*» to weaken; **se debilitó mucho con la enfermedad** the illness made him very weak **2** «*sonido*» to get *o* become faint/fainter **3** «*economía*» to grow *o* become weak/weaker

débito *m* debit

(Compuesto) **débito bancario** (AmL) direct debit, direct billing (AmE)

debutante¹ *adj*: **es una actriz ~** she is making her stage debut; **un tenista ~** a tennis player taking part in his first tournament

debutante² *mf* **1** (Dep, Espec) *player or artist making his/her public debut* **2** **debutante** *f* (en sociedad) debutante

debutar [A1] *vi* to make one's debut; **debutó como actor en 1965** he made his acting debut in 1965

década *f* decade; **la ~ de los ochenta** the eighties

decadencia *f* **1** (proceso) decline; **caer en ~** to fall into decline **2** (estado) decadence

decadente *adj* **1** ‹*moral/costumbres*› decadent **2** ‹*salud*› declining

decaer [E16] *vi* **1** «*ánimo/fuerzas*» to flag; «*interés/popularidad*» to wane **2** «*barrio/restaurante*» to go downhill; «*calidad/prestigio*» to decline **3** «*imperio/civilización*» to decay, decline **4** «*enfermo*» to deteriorate

decaído -da *adj* [ESTAR] low, down (colloq); **te encuentro muy ~** you seem very low

decaimiento *m* (abatimiento) despondency; **tengo un gran ~** I feel very despondent *o* low

decálogo *m* decalogue

decanato *m* **1** (Educ) (cargo) deanship; (despacho) deanery, dean's office **2** (Astrol) decan

decano -na *m,f* **1** (de una facultad) dean **2** (de una profesión, un grupo) senior member; **el ~/la decana de nuestros críticos de cine** the doyen/doyenne of our movie critics

decantar [A1] *vt* to decant

■ **decantarse** *v pron* **1** (mostrar preferencia) **~se POR algo** to choose sth, opt FOR sth; **~se por + INF** to choose *o* opt to + INF; **se decantan por esa hipótesis** they favor that hypothesis **2** (evolucionar): **la discusión se decantaba a su favor** the discussion was going in their favor; **se decanta como un magnífico jugador** he's developing *o* turning into a great player

decapado *m* (de pintura) stripping; (de metales) rust removal

decapitación *f* decapitation, beheading

decapitar [A1] *vt* to behead, decapitate

decatlón *m* decathlon

deceleración *f* deceleration

decelerar [A1] *vi* to decelerate

decena *f*: **unidades, ~s y centenas** (Mat) units, tens and hundreds; **los venden por ~** they're sold in tens; **una ~ de personas** about ten people; **~s de personas lo presenciaron** dozens *o* scores of people witnessed it

decencia *f* decency; **si tuviera un poco de ~** if he had any decency at all

decenio *m* decade

decente *adj* **1** (honrado, decoroso) decent, respectable **2** (aceptable) ‹*sueldo/vivienda*› decent, reasonable **3** (de apariencia aceptable) respectable; **a ver si la casa está ~ cuando vuelva** I want the house looking respectable when I get back; **no estoy ~** (fam) (no estoy arreglada) I'm not presentable; (estoy medio desnuda) I'm not decent

decepción *f* disappointment, letdown (colloq); **me llevé una gran ~** I was very disappointed

decepcionado -da *adj* disappointed; **estar ~ con algo/de algn** to be disappointed with sth/sb

decepcionante *adj* disappointing

decepcionar [A1] *vt* to disappoint; **la película me decepcionó** I was disappointed with the movie; **nos has decepcionado** you've let us down

deceso *m* (AmL frml) decease (frml), death; **el ~ se produjo a las tres** death occurred at three o'clock; **no hubo ~s que lamentar** there was no loss of life

d

dechado *m*: **un ~ de perfecciones** *or* **virtudes** a paragon of virtue

decibelio, decibel *m* decibel

decididamente *adv* 1 ‹*actuar/hablar*› decisively, resolutely 2 (*indep*) (claramente) clearly, obviously

decidido -da *adj* 1 [SER] ‹*persona/tono*› (resuelto, enérgico) decisive, determined; **pueden contar con mi ~ apoyo** you can count on my wholehearted support 2 [ESTAR] **~ A + INF** determined *o* resolved to + INF

decidir [I1] *vt*

A 1 (tomar una determinación) to decide; **iba a aceptar pero después decidí que no** I was going to accept but then I decided not to; **~ + INF** to decide to + INF; **decidieron comprarlo** they decided to buy it 2 ‹*persona*› to make ... decide; **eso fue lo que me decidió** that was what decided me *o* made me decide

B ‹*asunto*› to settle; ‹*resultado*› to decide; **lo que ~ía el futuro de la empresa** what would decide the future of the company

■ **decidir** *vi* to decide; **no sé, decide tú** I don't know, you decide; **alguien había decidido por él** someone had made the decision for him; **tiene que ~ entre dos opciones igualmente interesantes** she has to choose *o* decide between two equally attractive options; **~ SOBRE algo** to decide ON sth

■ **decidirse** *v pron* to decide, to make up one's mind; **aún no me he decidido del todo** I still haven't quite decided *o* made up my mind; **~se A + INF** to decide to + INF; **~se POR algo** to decide ON sth; **se decidió por el verde** she decided on the green one

decidor -dora *adj* (Chi) significant, telling

décima *f* (de segundo, grado) tenth; **tiene 39 y tres ~s** his temperature is 39.3 (degrees); **no tiene más que unas ~s** he only has a slight fever *o* (BrE) temperature

decimal *m* (número) decimal (number)

décimo¹ -ma *adj/pron* 1 (ordinal) tenth; *para ejemplos ver* **quinto** 2 (partitivo): **la décima parte** a tenth

décimo² *m* 1 (partitivo) tenth 2 (de lotería) *tenth share in a lottery ticket*

decimoctavo -va *adj/pron* 1 (ordinal) eighteenth; *para ejemplos ver* **quinto** 2 (partitivo): **la decimoctava parte** an eighteenth

decimocuarto -ta *adj/pron* 1 (ordinal) fourteenth; *para ejemplos ver* **quinto** 2 (partitivo): **la decimocuarta parte** a fourteenth

decimonónico -ca *adj* 1 ‹*literatura/arquitectura*› nineteenth-century 2 (anticuado) ‹*educación/costumbres/ideas*› old-fashioned

decimonoveno -na, decimonono -na *adj/pron* 1 (ordinal) nineteenth; *para ejemplos ver* **quinto** 2 (partitivo): **la decimonovena parte** a nineteenth

décimoprimero -ra *adj/pron* (crit) ▸**undécimo**

decimoquinto -ta *adj/pron* 1 (ordinal) fifteenth; *para ejemplos ver* **quinto** 2 (partitivo): **la decimoquinta parte** a fifteenth

décimosegundo -da *adj/pron* (crit) ▸**duodécimo**

decimoséptimo -ma *adj/pron* 1 (ordinal) seventeenth; *para ejemplos ver* **quinto** 2 (partitivo): **la decimoséptima parte** a seventeenth

decimosexto -ta *adj/pron* 1 (ordinal) sixteenth; *para ejemplos ver* **quinto** 2 (partitivo): **la decimosexta parte** a sixteenth

decimotercero -ra *adj/pron* 1 (ordinal) thirteenth; *para ejemplos ver* **quinto** 2 (partitivo): **la decimotercera parte** a thirteenth

decir¹ *m*: **¿cientos de personas? — bueno, es un ~** hundreds of people? — well, figuratively speaking

decir² [I24] *vt*

A ‹*palabra/frase/poema*› to say; ‹*mentira/verdad*› to tell; [*para ejemplos con complemento indirecto ver división 2*] **ya dice 'mamá'** he says 'mama' now; **no digas esas cosas, por favor** please don't say things like that; **no digas estupideces** don't talk nonsense!; **¿cómo pudiste ~ eso?** how could you say that?; **¿eso lo dices por mí?** are you referring to me?; **¡no lo dirás en serio!** you can't be serious!; **dijo que sí con la cabeza** he nodded; **dicen** *or* **se dice que es el hombre más rico del país** he is said to be the richest man in the country; **no se dice 'andé', se dice 'anduve'** it isn't 'andé', it's 'anduve'; **¡eso no se dice!** you mustn't say that!; **¿cómo se dice 'amor' en ruso?** how do you say 'love' in Russian?; **bonita, lo que se dice bonita, no es** she's not what you would call pretty; **es el sábado; ni que ~ tiene que estás invitado** it's on Saturday; you're invited, but that goes without saying; **haberlo dicho antes** why didn't you say so before?; **¿tendrá tiempo de hacerlo? — dice que sí** will he have time to do it? — he says he will; **¿no lo encontró? — dice que no** didn't he find it? — no, he says he didn't; **digan lo que digan** whatever people say; **¿qué tal? ¿qué decís?** (RPl fam) hi, how are things? (colloq)

B **~le algo A algn** to tell sb sth; **eso no es lo que me dijo a mí** that's not what he told *me*; **¿sabes qué me dijo?** do you know what he told me?; (expresando sorpresa, indignación, etc) do you know what he said to me?; **se lo voy a ~ a papá** I'm going to tell Dad; **hoy nos dicen el resultado** they're going to give us the result today; **Andrés me dijo lo de tu hermano** Andrés told me about your brother; **¡a mí me lo vas a ~!** you're telling me!; **¡ya te lo decía yo!** I told you so!; **fue algo espantoso, todo lo que te diga es poco** it was terrible, I can't begin to tell you how terrible; **¡no me digas que no es precioso!** isn't it beautiful?; ***dime con quién andas y te diré quién eres*** you can judge a man by the company he keeps

C 1 (expresando o transmitiendo órdenes, deseos, advertencias): **¡porque lo digo yo!** because I say so!; **harás lo que yo diga** you'll do as I say; **papá dice que vayas** Dad wants you; **dice que llames cuando llegues** she says (you are) to phone when you get there; **dijo que tuviéramos cuidado** she said to be careful; **~le a algn QUE + SUBJ** to tell sb to + INF; **diles que empiecen** tell them to start; **le dije que no lo hiciera** I told him not to do it 2 **decir adiós** to say goodbye; **~le adiós a algn** to say goodbye to sb; **di adiós a tu vida de estudiante** you'd better say goodbye to your student days

D (por escrito) to say; **¿qué dice aquí?** what does it say here?; **el diario no dice nada sobre el asunto** there's nothing in the paper about it

E (llamar) to call; **se llama Rosario pero le dicen Charo** her name is Rosario but people call her Charo

F (sugerir, comunicar): **la forma de vestir dice mucho de una persona** the way someone dresses says a lot/tells you a lot about them; **el tiempo lo dirá** time will tell; **algo me decía que no iba a ser fácil** something told me it wasn't going to be easy; **¿te dice algo ese nombre?** does that name mean anything to you?

G **decir misa** to say mass

H **querer decir** to mean; **¿qué quiere ~ esta palabra?** what does this word mean?; **¿qué quieres ~ con eso?** what do you mean by that?; **¿quieres ~ que ya no te interesa?** do you mean (to say) that you're no longer interested?

I (opinar, pensar) to think; **¿y los padres qué dicen?** what do her parents think of it?, how do her parents feel about it?; **¡quién lo hubiera dicho!** who would have thought *o* believed it?; **habría que regalarle algo, no sé, digo yo** we ought to buy her a present, well, I think so anyway; **es muy fácil — si tú lo dices ...** it's very easy — if you say so ...

A (*en locs*) **a decir verdad** to tell you the truth, to be honest; **como quien dice** so to speak; **con decirte que**: **no me lo perdonó nunca, con ~te que ni me saluda ...** he's never forgiven me, he won't even say hello to me; **decir por decir**: **lo dijo por ~** he didn't really mean it; **es decir** that is; **mi cuñada, es ~ la mujer de Rafael** my sister-in-law, Rafael's wife that is; **es mucho decir**: **es la mejor película del año — eso ya es mucho ~** it's the best movie of the year — I wouldn't go that far; **¡he dicho!** that's that *o* final!; **¡no me digas!** no!, you're kidding *o* joking! (colloq); **por así decirlo** so to speak; **que digamos**:

no es muy inteligente que digamos he's not exactly *o* he's hardly what you'd call intelligent; **¡que no se diga!** shame on you!; **¡que no se diga que no somos capaces!** I don't want people saying that we can't do it; **y (ya) no digamos** *or* (AmL) **y no se diga**: **le cuestan mucho las matemáticas y no digamos la física** he finds mathematics very difficult, and as for physics ...; ***el qué dirán*** (fam): **siempre le ha importado el qué dirán** she's always been worried what other people (might) think; *ver tb* **dicho**[1]

■ **decir** *vi* 1 (invitando a hablar): **papá — dime, hijo** dad — yes, son?; **quería pedirle un favor — usted dirá** I wanted to ask you a favor — certainly, go ahead; **tome asiento, usted dirá** (frml) take a seat, and now, what can I do for you? 2 (Esp) (al contestar el teléfono): **¿diga?** *or* **¿dígame?** hello?

■ **decirse** *v pron* 1 (*refl*) to say ... to oneself 2 (*recípr*) to say .... to each other; **se decían secretos al oído** they were whispering secrets to each other; **se dijeron de todo** they called each other every name under the sun 3 (*enf*): **yo sé lo que me digo** I know what I'm talking about; **tú te lo dices todo** you seem to have all the answers

decisión *f* 1 (acción) decision; **tomar una ~** to make a decision; **llegar a una ~** to decide, to reach a decision; **~ DE + INF**: **su ~ de marcharse** her decision to leave 2 (cualidad) decisiveness, decision; **una mujer con ~** a decisive woman, a woman of decision 3 (AmL) (en boxeo): **ganó por ~** he won on points *o* by a decision

decisivo -va *adj* ‹*fecha/momento*› crucial, decisive, critical; ‹*prueba*› conclusive; ‹*voto/resultado*› crucial, decisive; **jugar un papel ~** to play a decisive role

declamación *f* (Teatr) declamation

declamar [A1] *vi* to declaim

■ **declamar** *vt* to recite

declaración *f*

A 1 (afirmación) declaration; **una ~ de amor** a declaration of love 2 (a la prensa, en público) statement; **hacer una ~** to issue a statement; **hacer declaraciones a la prensa** to talk to the press 3 (proclamación) declaration; **la ~ universal de los derechos del hombre** the universal declaration of human rights

(Compuestos)

- **declaración de derechos** bill of rights
- **declaración de guerra/de la independencia** declaration of war/independence

B (Der) statement, testimony; **el policía me tomó ~** the policeman took my statement; **tuvo que prestar ~ como testigo** he was called to give evidence *o* to testify

(Compuestos)

- **declaración del impuesto sobre la renta** income tax return
- **declaración jurada** affidavit, sworn statement

declaradamente *adv* openly

declarado -da *adj* declared, professed

declarar [A1] *vt*

A 1 (manifestar) ‹*apoyo/oposición/intención*› to declare, state; **declaró que no renunciaría** he announced *o* stated that he would not resign; **le declaró su amor** he declared his love to her 2 (proclamar) to declare; **~ la guerra/el cese de las hostilidades** to declare war/a ceasefire; **el presidente declaró abierta la sesión** the chairman pronounced *o* declared the session open; **os declaro marido y mujer** I pronounce you man and wife; **el jurado lo declaró culpable/inocente** the jury found him guilty/not guilty

B 1 (en la aduana) to declare; **¿algo que ~?** anything to declare? 2 (Fisco) ‹*bienes/ingresos*› to declare

■ **declarar** *vi* to give evidence, testify; **fue llamado a ~ como testigo** he was called to give evidence *o* to testify

■ **declararse** *v pron*

A 1 (manifestarse) to declare oneself; **se declaró partidaria del divorcio** she declared herself (to be) in favor of divorce; **~se culpable/inocente** to plead guilty/not guilty; **~se en quiebra** *or* **bancarrota** to declare oneself bankrupt; **~se en huelga** to go on strike 2 (confesar amor) (+ *me/te/le etc*): **se le declaró** he declared himself *o* his love to her

B «*incendio/epidemia*» to break out

declinación *f* 1 (Ling) declension 2 (Astron, Fís) declination

declinar [A1] *vt* 1 ‹*invitación/oferta/honor*› to turn down, decline (frml); **declinó hacer declaraciones** she declined to make a statement; **Ⓢ la compañía declina toda responsabilidad ...** the company accepts no responsibility ... 2 (Ling) to decline

■ **declinar** *vi* (liter) «*día/tarde*» to draw to a close (liter); **al ~ el día** as the day draws to a close (liter)

declive *m* 1 (de una superficie) slope, incline (frml); **terreno en ~** sloping ground 2 (decadencia) decline; **una economía en ~** a declining economy, an economy in decline

decolaje *m* (AmL) take-off

decolar [A1] *vi* (AmL) to take off

decolorante *m* bleaching agent

decolorar [A1] *vt* to bleach

■ **decolorarse** *v pron* 1 (*refl*) ‹*pelo*› to bleach 2 «*pelo*» (+ *me/te/le etc*) to get bleached

decomisar [A1] *vt* to confiscate, seize

decoración *f* 1 (de pasteles, platos) decoration; (de habitación) decor; (de árbol de Navidad) (AmL) decoration; **~ de vitrinas** *or* **escaparates** window dressing 2 (interiorismo) *tb* **~ de interiores** interior decoration

decorado *m* set

decorador -dora *m,f*: *tb* **~ de interiores** interior decorator

decorar [A1] *vt* ‹*pastel*› to decorate; ‹*vitrina/escaparate*› to dress; ‹*casa/habitación*› to decorate; ‹*árbol de Navidad*› (AmL) to decorate

decorativo -va *adj* decorative

decoro *m* (pudor, respeto) decorum; **guardar el debido ~** to maintain a sense of decorum *o* propriety

decoroso -sa *adj* decent, respectable

decrecer [E3] *vi* 1 «*afición/interés*» to wane, decrease; «*importancia*» to decline 2 «*número/cantidad*» to decline, fall 3 «*aguas*» to drop, fall

decreciente *adj* decreasing (*before n*)

decremento *m* decrease

decrépito -ta *adj* decrepit

decrepitud *f* decrepitude

decretar [A1] *vt* to order, decree (frml); **decretó un día de luto** he declared *o* decreed a day of mourning; **~que ...** to decree *o* order that ...

decreto *m* decree

(Compuesto) **decreto con fuerza de ley** (Chi) law-ranking decree

decreto-ley *m* decree-law, ≈ order in council (*in UK*)

dedal *m* thimble

dedalera *f* foxglove

dédalo *m* (liter) labyrinth

dedazo *m* (Méx fam): **para estos nombramientos no habrá ~** there will be no selection of personal friends/family members for these posts

dedicación *f* (entrega) dedication; **trabaja con ~** she works with dedication; **~ A algo/algn** dedication TO sth/sb

(Compuesto) **dedicación exclusiva** full-time commitment; **trabaja en régimen de ~ ~** she works full-time

dedicar [A2] *vt* 1 **~ algo A algo/+ INF** ‹*tiempo/esfuerzos*› to devote sth TO sth/-ING; **dedicó su vida a la ciencia/ayudar a los pobres** she devoted her life to science/to helping the poor; **vamos a ~ este cuarto a archivo** we're going to set this room aside for *o* give this room over to the files 2 (ofrendar, ofrecer) ‹*obra/canción*› to dedicate; **un ejemplar dedicado** a signed copy 3 (Relig) to dedicate

■ **dedicarse** *v pron* 1 (consagrarse) **~se A algo/+ INF** to devote oneself TO sth/-ING 2 (tener cierta ocupación, profesión): **¿a qué se dedica tu padre?** what does your father do?; **se dedica a la investigación/a enseñar** he does research/he teaches; **se dedica a pintar en sus ratos libres** she spends her free time painting

dedicatoria *f* dedication

dedillo *m*: **conocer algo al ~** to know sth like the back of one's hand; **sabía la lección al ~** I knew the lesson (off) by heart

d

dedo *m*
A (de mano, guante) finger; (del pie) toe; **se podían contar con los ~s** they could be counted on the fingers of one hand; **con el ~: es de mala educación señalar con el ~** it's rude to point; ***a ~*** (fam): **ir a ~** to hitchhike, hitch (colloq); **recorrió Europa a ~** she hitchhiked around Europe; **lo colocaron a ~** they got him the job; ***chuparse el ~*** (fam) to suck one's thumb; **¿tú qué crees? ¿que me chupo el ~?** do you think I was born yesterday?; ***estar para chuparse los ~s*** (fam) to be delicious; ***hacer*** *or* (Col) ***echar ~*** (fam) to hitchhike, hitch (colloq); ***mover*** *or* ***levantar un ~*** (fam): **es incapaz de mover un ~ para ayudarme** he never lifts a finger to help me; ***no quitar el ~ del renglón*** (Méx fam) to insist; ***pillarse los ~s*** (Esp fam) (en una puerta, etc) to get one's fingers caught; (en un negocio) to get one's fingers burned (colloq); ***poner el ~ en el renglón*** (Méx) to put one's finger on the spot; ***poner el ~ en la llaga*** to hit *o* touch a raw nerve; ***ponerle el ~ a algn*** (Méx arg) to point the finger at sb; ***señalar a algn con el ~*** (literal) to point at sb; (culpar) to point the finger at sb
(Compuestos)
- **dedo anular/(del) corazón** ring/middle finger
- **dedo gordo** (fam) (del pie) big toe; (de la mano) thumb
- **dedo índice** forefinger, index finger
- **dedo meñique** little finger
- **dedo pulgar** thumb

B (como medida): **hay que subirle dos ~s al dobladillo** the hem needs taking up about an inch; **para mí sólo un ~ de whisky** just a drop of whiskey for me; ***no tiene dos ~s de frente*** (fam) he hasn't an ounce of common sense

deducción *f*
A (razonamiento) deduction; (conclusión) conclusion
B (descuento) deduction

deducible *adj*
A (que se puede inferir) deducible; **esto no es ~ de la información que tenemos** this cannot be deduced from the information we have
B (Com, Fin) deductible

deducir [I6] *vt*
A (inferir) to deduce; **como no contestaban, deduje que no había nadie** as there was no reply, I assumed there was nobody there; **~ algo DE algo** to deduce sth FROM sth
B (descontar) to deduct; **deducidos los impuestos** less tax

deduje, deduzca, etc *see* **deducir**

defecación *f* defecation

defecar [A2] *vi* to defecate

defección *f* defection

defecto *m*
A 1 (en un sistema) fault, flaw, defect; **esta tela tiene un pequeño ~** there's a slight flaw *o* defect in this material; **a todo le encuentra ~s** she finds fault with everything 2 (de una persona) fault, shortcoming; **a pesar de mis ~s** in spite of my faults; **tiene el ~ de nunca escuchar lo que se le dice** she has the bad habit of never listening to what people say to her
(Compuestos)
- **defecto de fábrica** manufacturing fault *o* defect; **tenía un ~ de ~** it was faulty *o* defective
- **defecto físico** physical handicap

B (frml) **en su defecto: presentar el carnet de identidad o, en su ~, el pasaporte** present your identity card or if this is not possible, your passport; **usar un desinfectante o, en su ~, agua limpia** use a disinfectant, or, failing that, clean water

defectuoso -sa *adj* faulty, defective

defender [E8] *vt* 1 (proteger) ‹*guarnición/nación*› to defend, protect; ‹*persona*› to defend; **siempre defiende a su hermana** he always defends *o* stands up for his sister; **~ a algn DE algo/algn** to defend sb AGAINST sth/sb 2 ‹*intereses*› to protect, defend; ‹*derechos/título*› to defend 3 (Der) to defend 4 ‹*idea/teoría/opinión*› to defend, uphold; ‹*causa/ideal*› to champion, defend; **~ la tesis** ≈ to defend one's dissertation (*in US*), ≈ to have a viva on one's thesis (*in UK*)
■ **defenderse** *v pron* 1 (*refl*) (contra una agresión) to defend *o* protect oneself; (Der) to defend oneself; **~se DE algo/algn** to defend oneself AGAINST sth/sb 2 (fam) (arreglárselas) to get by (colloq); **me defiendo bastante bien en francés** I can get by quite well in French

defendible *adj* 1 ‹*ciudad*› defensible 2 ‹*conducta*› justifiable, defensible; ‹*posición/tesis*› defensible

defendido -da *m,f* defendant

defenestración *f* (frml) downfall, defenestration (journ)

defenestrar [A1] *vt* to defenestrate (journ)

defensa *f*
A 1 (protección) defense*; **salir en ~ de algn** to come to sb's defense; **actuó en ~ propia** *or* **en legítima ~** he acted in self-defense; **~ DE algo/algn** defense* OF sth/sb 2 **Defensa** *f* the Defense Department (AmE), the Ministry of Defence (BrE)
(Compuesto) **defensa personal** self-defense*
B (Der) defense*; **los testigos de la ~** the witnesses for the defense, the defense witnesses
C **defensas** *fpl* (Biol, Med) defenses* (*pl*)
D (Náut) fender
E (Dep) 1 (conjunto) defense* 2 **defensa** *mf* (jugador) defender

defensivo -va *adj* ‹*arma*› defensive; ‹*actitud/táctica*› defensive; **estar/ponerse a la defensiva** to be/get on the defensive; **jugar a la defensiva** to play defensively

defensor¹ -sora *adj* 1 ‹*ejército*› defending (*before n*) 2 (Der) ‹*abogado*› defense* (*before n*)

defensor² -sora *m,f* 1 (Mil) defender 2 (de una causa) champion 3 (Der) defense counsel (AmE), defence lawyer (BrE)

Defensor del pueblo

An ombudsman nominated by the Spanish Parliament to defend the rights of citizens against government maladministration. If he upholds a complaint he advises the administration on appropriate compensation. This post, under the same name, also exists in some Latin American countries

defeño -ña *m,f* (Méx) person from the **Distrito Federal**

deferencia *f* (frml) deference; **tuvo la ~ de cederme su lugar** he very kindly gave up his place to me; **por ~ a algn/algo** out of *o* in deference to sb/sth

defibrilar [A1] *vt* to defibrillate

deficiencia *f* 1 (defecto) fault; **~s técnicas** technical faults *o* defects 2 (insuficiencia) deficiency; **~s en nuestra alimentación** deficiencies in our diet; **~ inmunológica** immune deficiency; **una ~ en el sistema de seguridad** a flaw in the security system
(Compuesto) **deficiencia mental** mental handicap

deficiente¹ *adj* 1 (insuficiente) poor, inadequate; **~ EN algo** deficient IN sth; **una alimentación ~ en vitaminas** a diet deficient *o* lacking in vitamins 2 (insatisfactorio) ‹*trabajo*› poor, inadequate; ‹*salud*› poor; ‹*inteligencia*› low

deficiente² *mf* (persona) *tb* **~ mental** mentally handicapped person

déficit *m* (*pl* **~** *or* **-cits**) 1 (Com, Fin) deficit; **~ presupuestario** budget deficit 2 (en la producción) shortfall; (de lluvias) shortage

deficitario -ria *adj*
A (Com, Fin) ‹*división/sector*› loss-making (*before n*); **un balance ~** a deficit, a negative balance; **la producción nacional de trigo sigue siendo deficitaria** there is still a shortfall in the country's wheat production
B (Chi frml) (Psic): **un niño ~** a child with learning difficulties

defienda, defiendas, etc *see* **defender**

definición *f* (de palabra, postura) definition

definido -da *adj* ‹*carácter/ideas*› clearly-defined, well-defined; ‹*opinión*› clearly-defined; **líneas muy definidas** sharp lines

definir [I1] *vt* 1 ‹*palabra/concepto*› to define 2 ‹*postura/actitud*› to define 3 ‹*contorno/línea*› to define, make ... sharp
■ **definirse** *v pron*: **aún no se ha definido con respecto a este problema** he has yet to define his position on this issue; **el pueblo se definió por la alternativa pacífica** the people came out in favor of a peaceful solution

definitivamente *adv* 1 ‹*resolver/rechazar*› once and for all 2 ‹*quedarse/instalarse*› permanently, for good; **dejó de bailar ~** he gave up dancing permanently *o* for good

definitivo -va *adj* ‹*texto/solución/respuesta*› definitive; ‹*cierre*› permanent, definitive; **su adiós ~ al público** her final farewell to all her fans; **ya es ~ que no viene** he's definitely not coming; **ésta es, en definitiva, la mejor opción** all things considered *o* all in all, this is the best option

deflación *f* deflation

deflacionario -ria *adj* deflationary

deflector *m* [1] (Tec) baffle [2] (Fís) deflector [3] (Esp) (Auto) air vent

defoliación *f* defoliation

deforestación *f* deforestation

deforestar [A1] *vt* to deforest

deformación *f* [1] (de imagen) distortion; (de marco, riel) distortion; **para evitar la ~ de la prenda** to stop the garment losing its shape [2] (de la verdad, los hechos) distortion [3] (Anat, Med) deformity; **sufre de una ~ de la columna** he has a twisted spine

deformar [A1] *vt* [1] ‹*imagen*› to distort; ‹*chapa/riel*› to distort [2] ‹*verdad/realidad*› to distort [3] (Anat, Med) to deform; **la artritis le ha deformado los dedos** her fingers have become twisted with arthritis

■ **deformarse** *v pron* [1] «*imagen*» to become distorted [2] «*puerta/riel*» to distort, become distorted [3] (Anat, Med) to become deformed

deforme *adj* deformed

deformidad *f* deformity

defraudación *f* fraud

(Compuesto) **defraudación fiscal** *or* **de impuestos** tax evasion

defraudador -dora *m,f* defrauder

(Compuesto) **defraudador fiscal** *or* **de impuestos** tax evader

defraudar [A1] *vt* [1] (decepcionar) to disappoint; **la película me defraudó** the movie didn't live up to my expectations; **me has defraudado** you've let me down [2] (estafar) to defraud; **defraudó al fisco** he evaded his taxes

defunción *f* (frml) death; Ⓢ **cerrado por defunción** closed owing to bereavement

degeneración *f* [1] (deterioro) degeneration [2] (cualidad) degeneracy

degenerado -da *adj/m,f* degenerate

degenerar [A1] *vi* to degenerate; **~ EN algo** to degenerate INTO sth; **la discusión degeneró en una riña** the discussion developed *o* degenerated into an argument

■ **degenerarse** *v pron* «*persona*» to become degenerate; «*costumbres*» to degenerate

deglutir [I1] *vt/vi* (frml) to swallow

degollar [A12] *vt* ‹*persona/animal*›: **lo ~on** they slit his/its throat

degradación *f* [1] (Mil) demotion [2] (envilecimiento) degradation

degradante *adj* ‹*comportamiento*› degrading; ‹*tortura*› humiliating, degrading

degradar [A1] *vt*

[A] [1] (Mil) to demote [2] (envilecer) to degrade; **estas prácticas degradan al ser humano** these practices are degrading to human beings [3] (empeorar) ‹*calidad/valor*› to diminish

[B] (Art) to gradate

■ **degradarse** *v pron* [1] «*persona*» (humillarse) to demean oneself, degrade oneself [2] (Quím) «*compuesto*» to decompose, degrade

degüello *m* slaughter, massacre

degustación *f* tasting; **~ de vino** wine-tasting

degustar [A1] *vt* to taste

dehesa *f* [1] (terreno) meadow, pasture [2] (hacienda) farm

deíctico -ca *adj* deictic

deidad *f* deity

deísmo *m* deism

deísta[1] *adj* deistical, deistic

deísta[2] *mf* deist

dejación *f* (AmC, Chi) ▸**dejadez**

dejadez *f* [1] (en el aseo personal) slovenliness [2] (en tarea, trabajo) laziness, slackness

dejado -da *adj* [1] (en aseo personal) slovenly; **un joven con un aspecto muy ~** a young man of unkempt *o* slovenly appearance [2] (en tarea, trabajo) slack, lazy; **era tan ~ que acabaron por despedirlo** he was so slack in his work that they ended up firing him

dejar [A1] *vt*

(Sentido I)

[A] [1] (en lugar determinado) to leave; **lo dejé en recepción/en la mesa** I left it in reception/on the table; **dejó a los niños en el colegio** she dropped the children (off) at school; **~ un recado** to leave a message; **~ un depósito** to put down a deposit; **¿cuánto se deja de propina?** how much do you leave as a tip?; **deja ese cuchillo** put that knife down; **déjala, ella no tuvo la culpa** leave her alone, it wasn't her fault; **~ *mucho que desear*** to leave a great deal to be desired [2] (olvidar) to leave; **dejé el paraguas en el tren** I left my umbrella on the train; **¡déjalo!** forget it! [3] (como herencia) to leave

[B] [1] ‹*marca/mancha/huella*› to leave; **deja un gusto amargo en la boca** it leaves a bitter taste in the mouth [2] ‹*ganancia*› to produce; **el negocio dejó pérdidas** the business made a loss

[C] (abandonar) ‹*novia/marido*› to leave; ‹*familia*› to leave, abandon; ‹*trabajo*› to give up, leave; ‹*lugar*› to leave; **quiere ~ el ballet** he wants to give up ballet dancing

[D] (+ *compl*) [1] (en cierto estado) to leave; **dejé la ventana abierta** I left the window open; **~ las luces apagadas** to leave the lights off; **su muerte los dejó en la miseria** his death left them in absolute poverty; **su respuesta me dejó boquiabierta** I was astonished by her reply; **el golpe lo dejó inconsciente** the blow knocked him unconscious; **me dejó esperando afuera** she left me waiting outside; **el avión/bus nos dejó** (Col, Ven) we missed the plane/bus; **¡déjame en paz!** leave me alone!; **me lo dejó en 1.000 pesos** he let me have it for 1,000 pesos; **quiero ~ esto bien claro** I want to make this quite clear; **dejó atrás a los otros corredores** she left the other runners behind; **~ *algo/a algn estar*** to let sth/sb be (colloq), to leave sth/sb alone; ▸**lado** E [2] (CS) **~ algo dicho** to leave a message

[E] [1] (posponer) leave; **no lo dejes para después, hazlo ahora** don't put it off *o* leave it until later, do it now [2] (reservar, guardar) ‹*espacio/margen*› to leave; **deja un poco para los demás** leave some for other people; **deja tus chistes para otro momento** save your jokes for some other time

(Sentido II)

[A] (permitir) **~ algo/a algn + INF** to let sth/sb + INF; **déjalo entrar/salir** let it/him in/out; **deja correr el agua** let the water run; **¿me dejas ir?** will you let me go?; **~ que algo/algn + SUBJ** to let sb/sth + INF; **dejó que lo eligiera ella** he let her choose; **déjame que te ayude** let me help you; **no dejes que se queme la carne** don't let the meat burn; **~ que espese la salsa** allow the sauce to thicken; **deja que se tranquilice un poco** let him calm down a bit

[B] [1] **dejar paso** to make way; **hay que ~ paso a las nuevas ideas** we have to make way for new ideas [2] **dejar caer** ‹*objeto*› to drop; ‹*comentario*› to let … drop; **dejó caer la noticia de que se casaba** she let it drop that she was getting married

■ **dejar de** [1] (cesar) **~ DE + INF** to stop -ING; **deja de llorar/importunarme** stop crying/bothering me; **~ de fumar** to give up smoking [2] (omitir, no hacer) **~ DE + INF**: **no dejes de escribirme en cuanto llegues** make sure you write as soon as you get there; **no dejes de recordarles que ...** be sure to remind them that …; **es algo que no deja de sorprenderme** it's something I still find surprising

■ **dejarse** *v pron*

[A] [1] (abandonarse) to let oneself go [2] **~se + INF**: **se deja dominar por la envidia** he lets his feelings of envy get the better of him; **se deja convencer fácilmente** he's easily persuaded; **~se llevar por la música** to let oneself be carried along by the music; **no te dejes, tú también pégale** (AmL exc RPl) don't just take it, hit him back (colloq); **nunca te dejas ver** we never seem to see you; **~*se estar*** (AmL): **no te dejes estar** you'd better do something; **si nos dejamos estar vamos a perder el contrato** if we

d

don't get our act together we'll lose the contract
B ‹*barba/bigote*› to grow; **quiero ~me el pelo largo** I want to grow my hair long
C (esp Esp fam) (olvidar) to leave; **me dejé el dinero en casa** I left my/the money at home
D **dejarse de** (fam): **a ver si se dejan de hablar** why don't you stop talking?; **déjate de lamentaciones/de rodeos** stop complaining/beating about the bush

deje *m* ▸**dejo 1**

dejo *m* **1** (acento) (slight) accent, lilt **2** (de una bebida, comida) aftertaste; **~ A algo** slight taste OF sth **3** (tono) touch, hint; **con un ~ de arrogancia** with a touch *o* hint of arrogance **4** (impresión, sensación): **me quedó un ~ triste tras hablar con él** I was left with a feeling of sadness after talking to him

del: *contraction of* **de** *and* **el**,

delación *f* denunciation

delantal *m* (para cocinar) apron; (de escolar) pinafore

delante *adv*
A (lugar, parte) [*Latin American Spanish also uses* **adelante** *in many of these examples*]: **yo voy ~** I'll go ahead *o* in front; **no te pongas ~** don't stand in front of me; **lo tengo aquí ~** I have it right here; **el asiento de ~** the front seat; **la parte de ~** the front; **tienes toda la vida por ~** you have your whole life ahead of you; **cualquier obstáculo que se le pusiera por ~** any obstacle that got in her way; ***llevarse algo/a algn por ~***: **el coche se lo llevó por ~** the car went *o* ran straight into it/him; **se lleva a todo el mundo por delante** he rides roughshod over everybody
B **delante de** (*loc prep*) **1** (en lugar anterior a) in front of; **~ de la ventana** in front of the window; **~ de mí/ti/él** in front of me/you/him **2** (en presencia de) in front of; **~ de todos** in front of everybody

delantera *f*
A **1** (Dep) (de equipo) forwards (*pl*), forward line **2** (Espec) front row seat/seats **3** (de prenda) front **4** (fam) (pecho) boobs (*pl*) (colloq)
B **1** (Dep) (primer puesto) lead; ***llevar la ~*** to be in the lead; ***tomar la ~*** to take the lead **2** (ventaja) lead; ***llevarle ~ a algn*** to have a lead over sb; ***tomarle la ~ a algn*** (en carrera) to overtake sb; **iba a pagar pero él me tomó la ~** (fam) I was going to pay but he beat me to it

delantero[1] **-ra** *adj* **1** ‹*asiento/rueda*› front (*before n*); **la pata delantera** the front leg **2** (Dep) ‹*línea/posición*› forward (*before n*), offensive (*before n*) (AmE)

delantero[2] **-ra** *m,f* (Dep) forward
(Compuesto) **delantero -ra centro** *m,f* center* forward

delatar [A1] *vt* **1** «*persona*» (acusar) to denounce, inform on **2** «*mirada/nerviosismo/acento*» (descubrir) to give ... away, betray
■ **delatarse** *v pron* (*refl*) to give oneself away

delator[1] **-tora** *adj* **1** ‹*prueba/arma*› incriminating **2** ‹*mirada/sonrisa*› revealing

delator[2] **-tora** *m,f* informer

delegación *f*
A (grupo) delegation; (de poderes) delegation
B (Méx) (barrio) district
C (Méx) (comisaría) police station
D (Esp) (oficina local) regional *o* local office

delegado -da *m,f*
A (representante) delegate
(Compuesto) **delegado -da de curso** *m,f* student representative
B (Esp) (director de zona) regional *o* area director

delegar [A3] *vt* **1** ‹*autoridad/poderes*› to delegate; **~ algo EN algn** to delegate sth TO sb **2** ‹*persona*› to delegate; ‹*comisión*› to appoint; **~ a algn PARA QUE + SUBJ** to delegate sb to + INF
■ **delegar** *vi* to delegate

deleitar [A1] *vt* to delight
■ **deleitarse** *v pron* **~se + GER** to delight IN -ING, enjoy -ING

deleite *m* delight; **para ~ de los niños** to the children's delight

deletrear [A1] *vt* to spell

deleznable *adj* **1** ‹*persona/actitud*› despicable **2** (insignificante) ‹*error/diferencia*› insignificant, negligible

delfín *m* (Zool) dolphin

delgadez *f* (flacura) thinness; (esbeltez) slimness

delgado -da *adj* **1** ‹*persona/piernas*› (esbelto) slim; (flaco) thin; **una mujer alta y delgada** a tall, slim *o* slender woman **2** ‹*tela*› thin, fine; ‹*hilo*› fine; ‹*lámina/pared*› thin

deliberación *f* deliberation; **todavía están en deliberaciones** they are still deliberating

deliberadamente *adv* deliberately, on purpose

deliberado -da *adj* deliberate

deliberante *adj* deliberative (frml)

deliberar [A1] *vi* **1** «*comisión/comité*» (debatir) **~ SOBRE algo** to deliberate ON sth (frml); **el jurado se retiró a ~** the jury retired to consider its verdict **2** (reflexionar) to deliberate

delicadeza *f*
A **1** (cuidado, suavidad) gentleness; **con mucha ~** very gently **2** (finura, gracia): **la ~ de sus manos** the daintiness of her hands; **la ~ del bordado** the delicacy of the embroidery
B **1** (tacto, discreción) tact; **fue una falta de ~ imperdonable** it was unforgivably tactless **2** (gesto amable): **fue una ~ de su parte traerme** it was very kind of him to bring me; **ni siquiera tuvo la ~ de llamarme** he didn't even have the decency to call me

delicado -da *adj*
A (fino) ‹*rasgos/manos*› delicate; ‹*sabor*› delicate, subtle; ‹*lenguaje/modales*› refined
B **1** (que requiere cuidados) ‹*cerámica/cristal*› fragile; ‹*tela*› delicate; ‹*piel*› sensitive; **prendas delicadas** delicates, delicate garments; **la delicada piel del bebé** the baby's delicate skin **2** (refiriéndose a la salud) delicate; **está ~ del estómago** his stomach's a little delicate; **tiene el corazón ~** he has a weak *o* bad heart
C ‹*asunto/cuestión/tema*› delicate, sensitive; ‹*situación*› delicate, tricky
D **1** (melindroso) delicate, fussy **2** (susceptible) touchy

delicia *f* delight; **estos bombones son una ~** these chocolates are delicious; **corría una brisa que era una ~** there was a pleasant breeze; ***hacer las ~s de algn*** to delight sb

delicioso -sa *adj* **1** ‹*comida/bebida/sabor*› delicious **2** ‹*tiempo*› delightful; **¿no te bañas? el agua está deliciosa** aren't you going to have a swim? the water's lovely

delictivo -va *adj* criminal (*before n*)

delimitación *f* **1** (de terreno, espacio) demarcation **2** (de atribuciones, responsabilidades) defining, specifying

delimitar [A1] *vt* **1** ‹*terreno/espacio*› to demarcate (frml), to delimit (frml) **2** ‹*poderes/responsabilidades*› to define, specify

delincuencia *f* crime, delinquency (frml)
(Compuesto) **delincuencia juvenil** juvenile delinquency

delincuente *mf* criminal
(Compuestos)
• **delincuente común/habitual** common criminal/habitual offender
• **delincuente juvenil** juvenile delinquent

delineante (*m*) draftsman (AmE), draughtsman (BrE); (*f*) draftswoman (AmE), draughtswoman (BrE)

delinear [A1] *vt* **1** ‹*dibujo/plano*› to outline, draft; ‹*contorno*› to delineate **2** ‹*programa/proyecto*› to formulate, draw up

delinquir [I3] *vi* (Der) to commit a criminal offense*, offend (frml); **es la primera vez que delinque** it is his first offense; **se ven obligados a ~** they are forced to turn to crime

delirante *adj* **1** (Med) delirious **2** ‹*imaginación*› fevered, feverish

delirar [A1] *vi* (Med) to be delirious; **la fiebre lo hacía ~** the fever made him delirious

delirio *m* **1** (Med) delirium **2** (fam) (pasión): **tiene ~ por las fresas** he's crazy *o* (BrE) mad about strawberries (colloq); **con ~** madly **3** (frenesí): **apareció en escena y aquello fue el ~** he appeared on stage and everyone went wild

(Compuesto) **delirios de grandeza** *mpl* delusions of grandeur (*pl*)

delírium tremens *m* delirium tremens, the DTs (*pl*)

delito *m* crime, offense*; **cometer un ~** to commit a crime *o* an offense; **evadir impuestos constituye ~** tax evasion is a criminal offense

(Compuestos)
- **delito común/político** common/political crime
- **delito de sangre** violent crime
- **delito fiscal/monetario** tax/currency offense*

delta¹ *m* (Geog) delta

delta² *f* (letra griega) delta

demacrado -da *adj* haggard, drawn

demacrarse [A1] *v pron* to become haggard *o* drawn

demagogia *f* demagogy, demagoguery

demagógico -ca *adj* demagogic

demagogo -ga *m,f* demagogue, demagog (AmE)

demanda *f*
A (Com) demand; **la ley de la oferta y la ~** the law of supply and demand; **tiene mucha ~** it's in great demand
B **1** (Der) lawsuit; **presentar una ~ contra algn** to bring a lawsuit against sb; **interponer una ~** to bring a lawsuit, to file suit (AmE) **2** (petición) request; **accedí a su ~** I agreed to his request; **se volvió hacia ella en ~ de ayuda** he turned to her for help; **se manifestaron en ~ de mejores condiciones de trabajo** they demonstrated for better working conditions

demandado -da *m,f* defendant

demandante *mf* plaintiff

demandar [A1] *vt*
A (Der) to sue; **lo demandé por daños y perjuicios** I sued him for damages
B (AmL) (requerir) to require; **un trabajo que demanda mucha dedicación** a job which requires great dedication

demarcación *f* **1** (acción) demarcation **2** (distrito) (Adm) district; (Educ) catchment area; **dentro de nuestra ~** within our district *o* boundaries

demarrar [A1] *vi* (Esp) (Dep) to put on a spurt *o* burst of speed

demás¹ *adj inv* (*delante del n*): **agregar los ~ ingredientes** add the remaining ingredients; **su viuda, hijos y ~ familia** (frml) his widow, children and other members of the family

demás² *pron*
A **1** **lo ~** the rest; **todo lo ~** everything else **2** (*en locs*) **por lo demás** apart from that, otherwise; **por demás** extremely; **le hablé en forma por ~ ofensiva** he spoke to her in an extremely offensive manner; **no estaría por ~ intentarlo** there's no harm in trying
B **1** **los/las ~** (referido a cosas) the rest; (referido a personas) the rest, everybody else; **las cosas de los ~** other people's things; **me dio uno y se quedó con los ~** he gave me one and kept the rest **2** **y demás** and the like; **los crustáceos: langostas, cangrejos y ~** the crustaceans: lobsters, crabs, and the like

demasía: **en ~** ‹*beber*› too much, excessively; **todo alimento, tomado en ~, es perjudicial** any food, when eaten in excess, can be harmful

demasiado¹ -da *adj* (*delante del n*): **le dio ~ dinero** he gave her too much money; **había demasiada gente/~s coches** there were too many people/cars; **hace ~ calor** it's too hot; **con demasiada frecuencia** too often

demasiado² *adv*
A ‹*pequeño/caliente/caro*› too; **fue un esfuerzo ~ grande para él** it was too much of an effort for him; **es ~ largo (como) para que lo termine hoy** it's too long for me to finish today
B ‹*comer/hablar/preocuparse*› too much; **trabajas ~** you work too hard

demasiado³ -da *pron*: **piden ~ por la casa** they're asking too much for the house; **somos ~s** there are too many of us; **hizo ~s** she made too many

demencia *f* dementia

demencial *adj* (fam) crazy (colloq); **tuvimos un tráfico ~** the traffic was chaotic

demente¹ *adj* insane

demente² *mf* insane person; **sólo a un ~ se le ocurre ...** (fam) only a madman *o* lunatic would ...

demeritar [A1] *vt* (AmL frml) **1** ‹*persona*› to discredit **2** ‹*esfuerzos/trabajo*› to detract from

demérito *m* (frml) demerit (frml); **sin ~ para sus compañeros** with all due respect to his colleagues; **esto va en ~ del instituto** this brings the institute into disrepute

democracia *f* democracy

(Compuestos)
- **democracia directa/representativa** direct/representative democracy
- **democracia popular** popular *o* people's democracy

demócrata *mf* democrat

democratacristiano -na *adj/m,f* Christian Democrat

democrático -ca *adj* democratic

democratización *f* democratization

democratizar [A4] *vt* to democratize

demografía *f* demography

demográfico -ca *adj* demographic, population (*before n*)

demógrafo -fa *m,f* demographer

demoledor -dora *adj* **1** ‹*máquina*› demolition (*before n*) **2** ‹*ataque/crítica*› devastating

demoler [E9] *vt* **1** ‹*edificio*› to demolish, pull down **2** ‹*mito/teoría*› (fam) to debunk, demolish

demolición *f* demolition

demoníaco -ca, **demoniaco -ca** *adj* demonic, demoniac

demonio *m*
A (diablo) devil; **este hijo mío es un ~** this child of mine is a little devil *o* demon; ***como (el) ~*** (fam) ‹*picar/doler*› like hell (colloq); **esto pesa como el ~** this weighs a ton (colloq); ***de (los) mil ~s*** (fam) terrible; **un carácter de los mil ~s** a terrible temper; **hace un frío de los mil ~s** it's terribly cold; ***mandar a algn al ~*** (fam) to tell sb to go to hell (colloq); ***oler/saber a ~s*** (fam) to smell/taste awful *o* foul; ***ponerse como*** *or* ***hecho un ~*** (fam) to go berserk (colloq)
B (fam) (uso expletivo): **¡cómo ~s lo hizo!** how on earth did he do it?; **¿qué/dónde ~s ... ?** what/where the hell ... ? (colloq); **¡~(s)!** (expresando enfado) damn! (colloq); (expresando sorpresa) goodness!, heavens!

demora *f*
A (esp AmL) (retraso) delay; **perdón por la ~** I'm sorry I'm late; **~ EN + INF** delay IN -ING; **sin ~** without delay
B (Náut) bearing

demorar [A1] *vt* **1** (AmL) (tardar): **demoró tres horas en llegar** he took *o* it took him three hours to arrive **2** (AmL) (retrasar) ‹*viaje/decisión*› to delay

■ **demorar** *vi* (AmL): **¡no demores!** don't be long!

■ **demorarse** *v pron* (AmL) **1** (tardar cierto tiempo): **¡qué poco te demoraste!** that didn't take you very long; **¿cuánto te demoras en llegar hasta allá?** how long does it take you to get there?; **me demoro 3 horas** it takes me 3 hours **2** (tardar demasiado) to be *o* take too long; **~se EN + INF** to take a long time TO + INF; **se demoró en decidirse** she took too long to make her mind up

demorón -rona *adj* (Andes, RPl fam) slow

demoroso -sa *adj* (Bol, Chi) ‹*persona*› slow; ‹*trabajo*› time-consuming; ‹*vehículo*› slow

demoscopia *f* public opinion research; **una ~** an opinion poll

demostrable *adv* demonstrable

demostración *f* **1** (de teorema) proof **2** (de poder, aptitudes) demonstration; **grandes demostraciones de cariño** a great show *o* display of affection **3** (de producto, método) demonstration

demostrar [A10] *vt*
A (probar) ‹*verdad*› to prove, demonstrate; ‹*teorema*› to prove; **eso demuestra su ignorancia** that shows *o* proves his ignorance; **te voy a ~ que tengo razón** I'm going to prove to you that I'm right; **ha demostrado ser** *or* **que es muy capaz** he's shown himself to be very able
B **1** ‹*interés/sentimiento*› to show **2** ‹*funcionamiento/método*› to demonstrate

demostrativo -va *adj* [1] ‹*ejemplo*› illustrative [2] ‹*adjetivo/pronombre*› demonstrative [3] (AmL) ‹*persona/carácter*› demonstrative

demudar [A1] *vt* ‹*expresión*› to alter, change; **tenía el rostro demudado por el dolor** her face was distorted by *o* contorted with pain

■ **demudarse** *v pron*: **se le demudó la expresión/el rostro al verla entrar** his expression changed when he saw her come in

denantes *adv* (Chi fam) a moment ago, just now

denegación *f* refusal

denegar [A7] *vt* (frml) ‹*permiso/autorización*› to refuse; ‹*petición*› to turn down; ‹*recurso*› (Der) to refuse

dengue *m* [1] (fam) (remilgo, melindre): **hace ~s a todo** she turns her nose up at everything (colloq) [2] (Med) dengue fever [3] (Méx fam) (berrinche) tantrum

denigrante *adj* degrading, humiliating

denigrar [A1] *vt* [1] (hablar mal de) to denigrate [2] (degradar) to degrade

denodado -da *adj* (frml) ‹*esfuerzo*› indefatigable (frml), tireless; ‹*luchador/defensor*› staunch, steadfast

denominación *f* [1] (frml) (nombre) name [2] (acción) naming

(Compuesto) **denominación de origen** *guarantee of origin and quality of a wine*

denominador *m* denominator

(Compuesto) **denominador común** (Mat) common denominator; (elemento en común) common factor

denominar [A1] *vt* (frml) [1] (dar nombre a): **un área a la que denominamos ...** an area which we call ...; **el denominado efecto invernadero** the so-called greenhouse effect [2] (con carácter oficial) to designate

■ **denominarse** *v pron* (frml) to be called

denostar [A10] *vt* (frml) to revile

denotar [A1] *vt* [1] (frml) (demostrar, indicar) to show, denote (frml); **sus modales denotan una esmerada educación** her manners are the sign of an impeccable upbringing [2] (Ling) to denote

densidad *f*

A [1] (de vegetación, niebla) thickness, denseness [2] (Fís) (de líquido, material) density

(Compuesto) **densidad de población** population density

B (Inf) density

denso -sa *adj*

A [1] ‹*vegetación/niebla*› dense, thick [2] (Fís) ‹*líquido/material*› dense

B ‹*discurso/película*› dense, weighty

dentado -da *adj* ‹*filo*› serrated; **una rueda dentada** a gearwheel, a cogwheel

dentadura *f* teeth (*pl*); **tener buena/mala ~** to have good/bad teeth

(Compuesto) **dentadura postiza** false teeth (*pl*), dentures (*pl*)

dental *adj* [1] ‹*higiene*› dental; **la caries ~** dental *o* tooth decay [2] (Ling) dental

dentellada *f* [1] (mordisco) bite; **lo destrozó a ~s** it chewed it to pieces [2] (marca) tooth mark

dentera *f* (sensación): **darle ~ a algn** to set sb's teeth on edge

dentición *f* [1] (crecimiento) teething, dentition (tech); **durante la ~** during teething [2] (conjunto de dientes) dentition (tech)

dentífrico *m* toothpaste

dentista *mf* dentist

dentística *f* (Chi) dentistry, dental surgery

dentro *adv*

A (lugar, parte) [*Latin American Spanish also uses* **adentro** *in this sense*] inside; **aquí/ahí ~** in here/there; **el perro duerme ~** the dog sleeps indoors; **es azul por ~** it's blue on the inside; **la parte de ~** the inside

B **dentro de** [1] (en el espacio) in, inside; **~ del edificio** inside *o* in the building [2] (en el tiempo) in; **se casan ~ de dos semanas** they're getting married in two weeks' time; **~ del plazo previsto** within *o* in the time stipulated [3] (de límites, posibilidades) within; **no está/está ~ de nuestras posibilidades** it is beyond/well within our means; **está ~ de lo posible** it's not impossible

denuedo *m* (liter) valor* (liter); **luchar con ~** to fight valiantly

denuesto *m* (liter) insult

denuncia *f*

A (de robo, asesinato) report; **hizo la ~ del robo del coche** he reported the theft of his car; **presentar** *or* **hacer una ~** to make a formal complaint; **presentó una ~ contra ella por malversación de fondos** he went to the police and accused her of embezzlement

B (crítica pública) denunciation

denunciante *mf*: *person who reports a crime*

denunciar [A1] *vt*

A ‹*robo/asesinato/persona*› to report

B (condenar públicamente) to denounce, condemn

denuncio *m* (Chi, Col) ▸ **denuncia A**

Dep., Dept. (= **Departamento**) Dept

D.E.P. (= **descanse en paz**) RIP

deparar [A1] *vt*: **no sabían lo que les ~ía el nuevo año** they did not know what the new year would bring; **¿qué nos ~á el destino?** what does fate have in store for us?; **el viaje me ~ía tal oportunidad** the trip would provide me with that opportunity

departamento *m*

A [1] (de empresa, institución) department; **~ de ventas/publicidad** sales/advertising department; **D~ de Inglés** Department of English, English Department [2] (provincia, distrito) department

(Compuesto) **Departamento de Estado** State Department

B (AmL) (apartamento) apartment (esp AmE), flat (BrE)

departir [I1] *vi* (frml) to converse (colloq)

depauperación *f* (frml) [1] (empobrecimiento) impoverishment [2] (debilitamiento) debilitation (frml)

depauperar [A1] *vt* (frml) to impoverish

■ **depauperarse** *v pron* (frml) [1] (empobrecerse) to become impoverished [2] (debilitarse) to become weak *o* (frml) debilitated

dependencia *f*

A (estado, condición) dependence; **~ económica** economic dependence; **~ psicológica** psychological dependence *o* dependency; **~ DE algo** dependence ON sth

B [1] (sección) department; (oficina) office [2] **dependencias** *fpl* (edificios) buildings (*pl*); (salas) rooms (*pl*); **las ~s del servicio** the servants' quarters

depender [E1] *vi*

A [1] «*resultado/solución*» to depend; **¿vendrás? — depende** will you come? — it depends; **~ DE algo/algn** to depend ON sth/sb; **si de mí dependiera** if it were up to me; **todo depende de que llegue a tiempo** it all depends on him arriving on time [2] «*persona*» **~ DE algn/algo**: **depende económicamente de sus padres** he is financially dependent on his parents; **dependía totalmente de su mujer** he depended *o* relied totally on his wife; **depende totalmente de las drogas** he's totally dependent on drugs

B (en jerarquía) **~ DE algn** to report TO sb; **la comisión ~á del Senado** the commission will report *o* be accountable to the Senate

dependiente[1] *adj*: **familiares ~s** dependents*; **~ DE algo**: **un organismo ~ del Ministerio de Cultura** an organization under the authority of the Ministry of Culture

dependiente[2] **-ta** *m,f* salesclerk (AmE), shop assistant (BrE)

depilación *f* (con cera) waxing; (con crema) hair-removal, depilation (frml); (de cejas) plucking

depilar [A1] *vt* ‹*piernas/axilas*› to wax (*o* shave *etc*); ‹*cejas*› to pluck

■ **depilarse** *v pron*: **~se las cejas** (*refl*) to pluck one's eyebrows; **~se las piernas** (*refl*) to shave (*o* wax *etc*) one's legs; (*caus*) to have one's legs waxed

deplorable *adj* deplorable; **en un estado ~** in a dreadful *o* an appalling state

deplorar [A1] *vt* [1] (condenar) to deplore [2] (lamentar) to regret

deponer [E22] *vt*
A (abandonar) ‹*armas*› to lay down; **depuso su actitud** he abandoned his stance
B ‹*rey*› to depose; ‹*gobierno/presidente*› to overthrow, topple
■ **deponer** *vi*
A (Fisiol) 1▸ (defecar) to defecate 2▸ (AmC, Méx fam) (vomitar) to throw up (colloq)
B (Der) to make a statement *o* (frml) deposition; «*testigo*» to testify

deportación *f* deportation

deportar [A1] *vt* to deport

deporte *m* sport; **no practican ningún ~** they don't play *o* do any sport(s); **hace ~ para estar en forma** she does sports (AmE) *o* (BrE) some sport to keep fit; **por ~** for the fun of it
Compuestos
• **deporte acuático** water sport
• **deporte de invierno** winter sport

deportista¹ *adj* sporty; **fue muy ~ en su juventud** he was a keen sportsman in his youth

deportista² (*m*) sportsman; (*f*) sportswoman

deportividad *f* sportsmanship

deportivo¹ -va *adj* 1▸ ‹*club/centro*› sports (*before n*); **instalaciones deportivas** sports facilities 2▸ ‹*ropa*› (para deporte) sports (*before n*); (informal) sporty, casual

deportivo² *m* sports car

deposición *f*
A (de rey) deposition; (de presidente, gobierno) overthrow
B (Fisiol) (frml) 1▸ (acto) bowel movement 2▸ **deposiciones** *fpl* (heces) stools (*pl*)
C (Der) statement, deposition (frml); (de testigo) testimony

depositar [A1] *vt*
A (frml) 1▸ (colocar) to place, put, deposit (frml); Ⓢ **deposite las monedas en la ranura** place *o* deposit coins in slot 2▸ (dejar) to leave, deposit (frml); Ⓢ **se ruega depositen las bolsas en la entrada** please leave all bags at the door 3▸ (volcar): **~ algo EN algo/algn** ‹*esperanzas*› to pin sth ON sth/sb; **deposité en él toda mi confianza** I placed *o* put all my trust in him
B (Fin) ‹*dinero*› to deposit; (en cuenta corriente) (AmL) to deposit, pay in (BrE); **~ una fianza en favor de algn** to stand bail for sb
■ **depositarse** *v pron* «*sustancia*» to form a deposit, be deposited

depositario -ria *m,f* 1▸ (de dinero) deposit taker 2▸ (Der) receiver

depósito *m*
A 1▸ (almacén) warehouse; **~ de armas** arms depot; **~ de municiones** ammunition dump; **en ~** in storage *o* (BrE) in store 2▸ (tanque) tank
Compuestos
• **depósito de cadáveres** morgue, mortuary (BrE)
• **depósito de equipajes** (Col) checkroom (AmE), left-luggage office (BrE)
• **depósito de gasolina** gas tank (AmE), petrol tank (BrE)
B (sedimento) deposit, sediment; (yacimiento) deposit
C (Fin) 1▸ (AmL) (en una cuenta) deposit; **hacer un ~** to deposit *o* (BrE) pay in some money 2▸ (garantía) deposit; **dejé un ~ de 5.000 euros** *or* **dejé 5.000 euros en ~** I left a 5,000 euro deposit
Compuesto **depósito a plazo** *or* (Col) **término fijo** time deposit (AmE), fixed-term deposit (BrE)

depravación *f* 1▸ (acto) act of depravity, depraved act 2▸ (cualidad) depravity

depravado -da *m,f* degenerate; **un ~ sexual** a (sexual) pervert

depre *f* (fam): **estar con la ~** to be under the weather; **tengo una ~ ...** I feel really low *o* down (colloq)

depreciación *f* depreciation

depreciarse [A1] *v pron* to depreciate, fall in value

depredación *f* (frml) 1▸ (Zool) predation (frml) 2▸ (daño) depredation (frml)

depredador¹ -dora *adj* (Zool) ‹*animal/ave*› predatory

depredador² *m* predator

depredar [A1] *vt* (Zool) to prey on

depresión *f*
A (Psic) depression
Compuesto **depresión posparto** postnatal depression
B (Meteo) depression
Compuesto **depresión atmosférica** *or* **barométrica** atmospheric *o* barometric depression

depresivo -va *adj* depressive (frml); **es muy ~** he tends to get depressed

deprimente *adj* depressing

deprimido -da *adj* 1▸ ‹*persona*› depressed 2▸ ‹*mercado/economía/barrio*› depressed

deprimir [I1] *vt* 1▸ (Psic) to depress, make ... depressed 2▸ ‹*mercado*› to depress
■ **deprimirse** *v pron* to get/become depressed

deprisa *adv* fast; **trabajar más ~** to work faster; **¡~! escóndelo** quick! hide it; **~ *y corriendo*** in a rush

depuesto -ta *pp*: *see* **deponer**

depuración *f*
A 1▸ (del agua) treatment, purification; (de aguas residuales) treatment 2▸ (de la sangre) cleansing 3▸ (de lenguaje, estilo) refinement
B (Pol) purge

depurado -da *adj* ‹*lenguaje/estilo*› polished, refined; ‹*gusto*› refined

depuradora *f* 1▸ (de aguas residuales) sewage treatment plant 2▸ (en piscina) filter system

depurar [A1] *vt*
A 1▸ ‹*agua*› to purify, treat; ‹*aguas residuales*› to treat 2▸ ‹*sangre*› to cleanse
B 1▸ ‹*organización/partido*› to purge 2▸ ‹*lenguaje/estilo*› to polish, refine 3▸ (Inf) to debug

derecha *f*
A 1▸ (lado derecho) right; **la primera calle a la ~** the first street on the right; **dobla a la ~** turn right; **el de la ~** the one on the right; **por la ~** ‹*conducir/caminar*› on the right; **mantenga su ~** keep to the right; ***no hago/hace nada a ~s*** (Esp fam) I/he can't do anything right 2▸ (mano derecha) right hand
B (Pol): **la ~** the Right; **un político de ~** *or* (Esp) **~s** a right-wing politician

derechamente *adv*
A 1▸ (en línea recta) straight 2▸ (directamente) straight; **se fueron ~ a su casa** they went straight home 3▸ (abiertamente) straight, openly; **díselo ~ y sin tapujos** tell him straight and without beating about the bush
B (honestamente) ‹*actuar/comportarse*› honestly

derechazo *m* (en boxeo) right; (Taur) *pass made with the cape in the right hand*; (en tenis) forehand

derechista *mf* right-winger

derechización *f* drift (*o* swing *etc*) to the right

derecho¹ -cha *adj*
A ‹*mano/ojo/zapato*› right; ‹*lado*› right, right-hand; **el ángulo superior ~** the top right-hand corner; **queda a mano derecha** it's on the right-hand side *o* on the right
B 1▸ (recto) straight; **ese cuadro no está ~** that picture isn't straight; **¡pon la espalda derecha!** straighten your back!; **siéntate ~** sit up straight 2▸ (fam) (justo, honesto) honest, straight

derecho² *adv* 1▸ (en línea recta) straight; **siga todo ~** go *o* keep straight on 2▸ (fam) (directamente) straight; **fue ~ al tema** he got straight *o* right to the point

derecho³ *m*
A 1▸ (facultad, privilegio) right; **haz valer tus ~s** stand up for your rights; **~s fundamentales** basic rights; **estás en tu ~** you're within your rights; Ⓢ **reservado el derecho de admisión** the management reserves the right to refuse admission; **miembro de pleno ~** full member; **~ A algo** right TO sth; **el ~ a la vida/al voto** the right to life/to vote; **~ A + INF: tengo ~ a saber** I have a *o* the right to know; **da ~ a participar en el sorteo** it entitles you to participate in the draw; **tiene perfecto ~ a protestar** she's perfectly within her rights to protest; **tengo ~ a que se me escuche** I have the right to be heard; ***¡no hay ~!*** (fam) it's not fair!; **no hay ~ a que la traten así a una** they've no right to treat a person like that 2▸ (Com, Fin) tax

Compuestos
- **derecho de asilo** right of asylum
- **derecho de matrícula** registration fee
- **derecho de paso** *or* **servidumbre** right of way
- **derecho de reunión** right of assembly
- **derechos arancelarios** *or* **de aduana** *mpl* customs duties (*pl*)
- **derechos cinematográficos** *mpl* film rights (*pl*)
- **derechos de autor** *mpl* royalties (*pl*)
- **derechos humanos** *mpl* human rights (*pl*)

B (Der) law; **estudio ~** I'm studying law; **no se ajusta a ~** it is legally flawed

Compuestos
- **derecho administrativo/canónico/civil** administrative/canon/civil law
- **derecho empresarial/fiscal/mercantil** business/tax/commercial law
- **derecho laboral/penal** labor*/criminal law
- **derecho privado/público** private/public law

C (de prenda) right side, outside; (de tela) right side, face; **póntelo al ~** put it on properly *o* right side out

deriva *f* drift; **a la ~** ‹barco› adrift; **navegar a la ~** to drift; **la empresa va a la ~** the company has lost its sense of direction

derivación *f* **1** (Ling, Mat) derivation **2** (de problema) consequence

derivada *f* derivative

derivado *m* (Ling, Tec) derivative; **los ~s lácteos** dairy products

derivar [A1] *vi*

A **1** (proceder) **~ DE algo** (Ling) to derive FROM sth, come FROM sth; (Quím) to derive FROM sth; «*problema/situación*» to arise FROM sth; **palabras derivadas del latín** words derived from Latin **2** (traer como consecuencia) **~ EN algo** to result IN sth, lead TO sth

B (cambiar de dirección): **la conversación derivó hacia otro temas** the conversation moved on to other topics; **la discusión derivó en pelea** the argument degenerated into a fight

■ **derivar** *vt* (Med) (AmL) **~ a algn a un especialista** to refer sb to a specialist

■ **derivarse** *v pron* (proceder) **~se DE algo** «*palabra*» to be derived FROM sth, come FROM sth; «*problema/situación*» to arise FROM sth

dermatología *f* dermatology

dermatológico -ca *adj* dermatological

dermatólogo -ga *m,f* dermatologist

dermis *f* (*pl* ~) dermis

derogación *f* abolition, repeal

derogar [A3] *vt* to abolish, repeal

derramamiento *m* (de líquido) spilling, spillage; **~ de sangre** bloodshed

derramar [A1] *vt* **1** ‹*agua/leche/azúcar*› to spill; ‹*cuentas/sangre*› to shed **2** ‹*lentejas/botones*› to spill, scatter

■ **derramarse** *v pron* **1** «*tinta/leche*» to spill; «*corriente*» to pour out **2** «*cuentas/botones*» to scatter, spread

derrame *m*

A **1** (Med): **tengo un ~ en el ojo** I have a burst blood vessel in my eye **2** (de líquido) spillage

Compuestos
- **derrame cerebral** brain hemorrhage*
- **derrame sinovial** synovitis

B (Arquit) embrasure

derrapar [A1] *vi*

A «*vehículo*» to skid; «*embrague*» to slip; «*llantas*» to spin

B (Méx fam) (estar chiflado) **~ POR algn** to be nuts *o* crazy ABOUT sb (colloq)

derrape *m* (Auto) skid

derredor: **al/en ~** (*loc adv*) around

derrengado -da *adj* exhausted

derrengarse [A3] *v pron* to collapse from exhaustion

derretir [I14] *vt* ‹*mantequilla/helado*› to melt; ‹*metales*› to melt (down); ‹*hielo/nieve*› to melt, thaw

■ **derretirse** *v pron* **1** «*mantequilla/helado*» to melt; «*nieve/hielo*» to thaw, melt **2** (fam) «*persona*» **~se POR algn** to be crazy ABOUT sb

derribar [A1] *vt* **1** ‹*edificio/muro*› to demolish, knock down; ‹*puerta*› to break down **2** ‹*avión*› to shoot down, bring down **3** ‹*persona*› to floor, knock ... down; ‹*novillo*› to knock ... over **4** «*viento*» to bring down **5** ‹*gobierno*› to overthrow, topple

derribo *m* **1** (de edificio) demolition **2** (de avión) shooting down, bringing down **3** (de gobierno) overthrow

derrocamiento *m* overthrow

derrocar [A2] *vt* to overthrow, topple

derrochador¹ -dora *adj*: **es muy ~** he's a real spendthrift

derrochador² -dora *m,f* squanderer, spendthrift

derrochar [A1] *vt*

A (malgastar) ‹*dinero*› to squander, waste; ‹*electricidad/agua*› to waste

B (tener en abundancia) ‹*buen humor/simpatía*› to radiate, exude

■ **derrochar** *vi* to throw money away, to squander money

derroche *m* **1** (de dinero, bienes) waste **2** (abundancia): **un ~ de entusiasmo** a tremendous display of enthusiasm

derrota *f*

A (Dep, Mil) defeat; **sufrir una ~** to suffer a defeat; **infligir una ~ a algn** to inflict a defeat on sb

B (Náut) course

derrotado -da *adj* **1** (vencido) ‹*ejército*› defeated; ‹*equipo*› defeated, beaten **2** (desesperanzado) despondent

derrotar [A1] *vt* ‹*ejército/partido*› to defeat; ‹*equipo*› to defeat, beat

derrotero *m* **1** course; **si sigues por esos ~s vas a terminar mal** if you carry on like that, you'll come to a bad end **2** (Náut) (rumbo) course; (libro) log

derrotismo *m* defeatism

derrotista *adj/mf* defeatist

derruido -da *adj* ‹*casa*› ruined; **una casa medio derruida** a house virtually in ruins

derruir [I20] *vt* to demolish, pull down

derrumbamiento *m* **1** (de edificio) collapse **2** (de dictadura, imperio) collapse

derrumbar [A1] *vt* **1** ‹*casa/edificio*› to demolish, pull down **2** ‹*dictadura*› to overthrow, topple

■ **derrumbarse** *v pron* **1** «*edificio*» to collapse **2** «*persona*» to go to pieces; «*esperanzas/ilusiones*» to be shattered, collapse

desabastecido -da *adj*: **~s de provisiones** out of provisions *o* supplies; **dejó al país ~ de combustible** it left the country without fuel

desabastecimiento (Méx), **desabasto** *m* shortage of supplies (*o* food *etc*)

desabotonar [A1] *vt* to unbutton, undo

■ **desabotonarse** *v pron* **1** «*prenda*» to come undone **2** (*refl*) «*persona*» ‹*camisa/abrigo*› to unbutton, undo

desabrido -da *adj*

A (comida) tasteless, bland

B ‹*persona*› (soso) (AmL) boring, dull; (desagradable) (Esp) surly, disagreeable

desabrigado -da *adj* ‹*lugar*› exposed; **estás muy ~** you're not wearing warm enough clothes

desabrigarse [A3] *v pron* (en la calle) to take one's coat (*o* sweater *etc*) off; (en la cama) to throw off the covers

desabrochar [A1] *vt* ‹*prenda/zapatos/pulsera*› to undo; **¿me desabrochas?** can you undo me? (colloq)

■ **desabrocharse** *v pron* **1** «*prenda*» to come undone **2** (*refl*) «*persona*» ‹*camisa/abrigo*› to undo

desacatar [A1] *vt* ‹*órdenes*› to disobey; ‹*autoridad*› to defy; ‹*leyes*› to defy, break

desacato *m* **~ A algo** ‹*a las órdenes/la autoridad*› defiance OF sth; **~ (al tribunal)** contempt (of court)

desaceleración *f* **1** (de vehículo, objeto) deceleration, slowing down **2** (de proceso) slowing down

desacertado -da *adj* ‹*elección/comentario*› unfortunate, unwise; ‹*estrategia*› misguided; **estuvo muy ~ al decir eso** (indiscreto) it was very tactless *o* indiscreet of him to say that; (equivocado) he made a big mistake saying that

desacierto *m* mistake; **fue un ~ invitarlo** it was a mistake to invite him; **el eslogan ha sido un ~** the slogan has proved to be a bad choice *o* a mistake

desacomodar [A1] *vt* (AmS) to untidy, mess … up
■ **desacomodarse** *v pron* (AmS) to get mixed *o* jumbled up

desacompasado -da *adj* [ESTAR] ‹*bailarín*› out of step; ‹*músico*› out of time

desaconsejar [A1] *vt* to advise against; **me lo desaconsejó el médico** the doctor advised me against it

desacoplar [A1] *vt* ‹*vagón*› to uncouple; ‹*rueda/pieza*› to remove

desacorde *adj* ‹*opiniones/versiones*› conflicting; ‹*sonidos*› discordant; ‹*instrumentos*› out of tune

desacostumbrado -da *adj* 1 (insólito): **con un entusiasmo ~ en él** with unaccustomed enthusiasm; **una práctica desacostumbrada entre los europeos** a practice which is not customary among Europeans 2 ‹*persona*› **~ A algo**: **está ~ al calor** he can't take the heat anymore

desacostumbrarse [A1] *v pron* to get out of the habit; **~ A + INF** to get out of the habit OF -ING; **se desacostumbró al tráfico de la ciudad** she forgot what city traffic was like

desacreditar [A1] *vt* 1 ‹*persona*› to discredit; ‹*buen nombre/institución*› to discredit, bring … into disrepute 2 ‹*teoría*› to discredit
■ **desacreditarse** *v pron* (*refl*) to discredit oneself, damage one's reputation

desactivar [A1] *vt* ‹*bomba/explosivo*› to defuse, deactivate; ‹*situación*› to defuse

desacuerdo *m* disagreement; **~ CON algo** opposition TO sth, disagreement WITH sth; **están en total ~ con su política** they strongly oppose *o* they are in total disagreement with his policy; **~ CON algn** disagreement WITH sb; **están en ~ con la ejecutiva** they are at odds *o* at variance with the executive

desadaptación *f* (Andes) adjustment problems (*pl*)

desadaptado -da *adj*: **un niño ~** a child who has problems settling in *o* adjusting; **sentirse ~** to feel unsettled

desadaptarse [A1] *v pron* to become disoriented *o* unsettled

desafecto¹ -ta *adj* **~ A algo** opposed *o* hostile TO sth

desafecto² *m* indifference

desafiante *adj* ‹*gesto/palabras*› defiant; **se me acercó ~** he came towards me defiantly

desafiar [A17] *vt* 1 ‹*persona*› to challenge; **~ a algn A algo** to challenge sb TO sth; **~ a algn A + INF/+ SUBJ** to dare *o* challenge sb to + INF 2 ‹*peligro/muerte*› to defy

desafilado -da *adj* blunt

desafinado -da *adj* out of tune

desafinar [A1] *vi* «*instrumento*» to be out of tune; «*músico/cantante*» to be off key *o* out of tune
■ **desafinarse** *v pron* to go out of tune

desafío *m* (a una persona) challenge; (al peligro, a la muerte) defiance

desaforadamente *adv* ‹*gritar*› at the top of one's voice; ‹*correr*› hell for leather

desaforado¹ -da *adj* ‹*ambición*› unbridled, boundless; ‹*grito*› terrible

desaforado² -da *m,f*: **como un ~** ‹*correr*› hell for leather; ‹*gritar*› at the top of one's voice

desafortunado -da *adj* 1 (desdichado) ‹*persona*› unlucky; ‹*suceso*› unfortunate 2 (desacertado) ‹*medidas/actuación*› unfortunate; **el diestro estuvo ~ con la espada** the matador performed poorly with the sword

desafuero *m* 1 (atropello) outrage 2 (desmesura) excess 3 (de parlamentario, ministro) withdrawal of parliamentary/ministerial privileges

desagradable *adj* ‹*respuesta/comentario*› unkind; ‹*ruido/sensación*› unpleasant, disagreeable; ‹*escena/sorpresa*› unpleasant; ‹*tiempo/clima*› unpleasant, horrible; **estuvo realmente ~** he was really unpleasant; **¡no seas tan ~!** don't be so mean *o* unkind!

desagradar [A1] *vt*: **me desagrada su presencia/su voz** I find his presence/his voice unpleasant *o* disagreeable; **me desagrada tener que decírselo** I don't like having to tell her

desagradecido -da *adj* ‹*persona*› ungrateful; ‹*trabajo/tarea*› thankless

desagradecimiento *m* ingratitude

desagrado *m* displeasure; **lo hizo con ~** she did it reluctantly *o* unwillingly; **puso cara de ~** she didn't look (at all) happy

desagraviar [A1] *vt* (frml): **con eso no me siento desagraviado** I don't feel that is enough to make up for it; **para ~lo, se excusó públicamente** to make amends, she apologized publicly
■ **desagraviarse** *v pron* to make amends

desagravio *m*: **exigió un ~** he demanded redress; **le envió unas flores como** *or* **en ~** he sent her some flowers to make amends

desaguadero *m* 1 (de río, lago) drain 2 ▸ **desagüe (1)**

desagüe *m* 1 (de lavabo, lavadora) wastepipe; (de patio, azotea) drain 2 (acción) drainage; **el sistema de ~** the drainage system

desaguisado *m* (fam) mess; **la peluquera me hizo un verdadero ~** the hairdresser made a mess of my hair

desahogadamente *adv* comfortably; **viven ~** they are comfortably off

desahogado -da *adj* 1 ‹*posición económica/vida*› comfortable; **viven bastante ~s** they're comfortably off 2 ‹*casa/habitación*› uncluttered, spacious; **la oficina quedó más desahogada** there's more room in the office now 3 (de tiempo): **cuando terminemos éste estaremos más ~s** once we've finished this one we can relax

desahogar [A3] *vt* ‹*penas*› to give vent to; ‹*rabia/ira*› to vent, give vent to
■ **desahogarse** *v pron*: **salí a correr para ~me** I went for a run to let off steam; **se desahogó dándole patadas a la rueda** he vented his anger (*o* frustration *etc*) by kicking the wheel; **~se CON algn** to pour one's heart out to sb

desahogo *m* 1 (alivio) relief; **llorar le servirá de ~** crying will make him feel better 2 **con ~** comfortably; **vivir con ~** to be comfortably off; **aquí podrás trabajar con más ~** you'll have more space to work in here

desahuciar [A1] *vt*
A ‹*enfermo*› to declare … terminally ill
B 1 ‹*inquilino*› to evict 2 (Chi) ‹*empleado*› (despedir) to dismiss; (notificar el despido) to give … notice

desahucio *m* 1 (de inquilino) eviction 2 (Chi) (Rels Labs) (aviso) dismissal notice; (suma de dinero) severance pay

desairar [A1] *vt* to snub

desaire *m* snub, slight; **hacerle un ~ a algn** to snub *o* slight sb

desajustar [A1] *vt* to loosen
■ **desajustarse** *v pron* 1 «*pieza*» to come *o* work loose 2 «*mecanismo*»: **el tacómetro se había desajustado** the tachometer wasn't working properly

desajuste *m*
A 1 (Econ, Fin) imbalance 2 (Psic, Sociol): **~ con el entorno** failure to adjust to one's environment
B 1 (trastorno) disruption 2 (defecto) fault

desaladora *f* desalination plant

desalar [A1] *vt* to desalt

desalentador -dora *adj* disheartening, discouraging

desalentar [A5] *vt* to discourage, dishearten
■ **desalentarse** *v pron* to become disheartened *o* discouraged

desaliento *m* dejection, despondency; **el ~ se apoderó de ellos** they became disheartened *o* discouraged

desalinización *f* desalination

desalinizadora *f* desalination plant

desalinizar [A4] *vt* to desalinate

desaliñado -da *adj* slovenly

desalmado -da *m,f*: **es un ~** he's completely heartless

desalojar [A1] *vt* 1 ‹*edificio/recinto*› «*manifestantes/ocupantes*» to vacate; «*policía/juez*» to clear 2 ‹*manifestantes*› to remove, move … away; ‹*residentes*› to evacuate; ‹*inquilino*› (esp AmL) to evict

desalojo *m* (AmL) eviction

desamarrar [A1] *vt* (AmL exc RPl) ‹*embarcación*› to cast off; ‹*zapatos/paquete*› to undo, untie; ‹*animal/persona*› to untie
■ **desamarrarse** *v pron* (AmL exc RPl)
A «*paquete/zapatos*» to come undone; «*bultos/barco*» to come untied

d

B (*refl*) ⟪*persona*⟫ to get free; ⟪*animal*⟫ to get loose *o* free

desamor *m* lack of affection, coolness

desamortización *f* freeing of encumbrance; (Hist) confiscation, seizure

desamortizar [A4] *vt* to free … from encumbrance; (Hist) to confiscate, seize

desamparado -da *adj* ‹*niño/anciano*› defenseless*; ‹*lugar*› bleak, unprotected

desamparar [A1] *vt* to abandon, desert

desamparo *m* neglect; **el ~ en el que viven** the state of neglect in which they live

desandar [A24] *vt*: **tuvo que ~ el camino recorrido** he had to retrace his steps; **~ *lo andado*** to go back to square one

desangelado -da *adj* ‹*cuarto/calle*› devoid of charm, soulless; ‹*persona*› lacking in charm, charmless

desangrar [A1] *vt* to bleed

■ **desangrarse** *v pron* to bleed to death

desanimado -da *adj* discouraged, dispirited

desanimar [A1] *vt* to discourage

■ **desanimarse** *v pron* to become disheartened *o* discouraged

desánimo *m* dejection, despondency; **sentía un gran ~** she felt very downhearted *o* discouraged

desanudar [A1] *vt* to unknot, untie

desapacible *adj* ‹*tiempo/día*› unpleasant; ‹*persona/carácter*› irritable, bad-tempered

desaparecer [E3] *vi* **1** (de lugar) to disappear; **hizo ~ el sombrero** he made the hat disappear *o* vanish **2** ⟪*dolor/síntoma/cicatriz*⟫ to disappear, go; ⟪*costumbre*⟫ to disappear, die out; ⟪*mancha*⟫ to come out; **tenía que hacer ~ las pruebas** he had to get rid of the evidence **3** (de la vista) to disappear; **desapareció entre la muchedumbre** he disappeared *o* vanished into the crowd; **desaparece de mi vista** (fam) get out of my sight

■ **desaparecerse** *v pron* (Andes) to disappear; **se desaparecieron mis anteojos** my glasses have disappeared

desaparecido[1] -da *adj* **1** (que no se encuentra) missing **2** (period) (muerto) late (*before n*), deceased (frml)

desaparecido[2] -da *m,f* **1** (en un accidente) missing person; **los ~s en el siniestro** those missing after the accident **2** (Pol): **los ~s** the disappeared *o* those who have disappeared

desaparejar [A1] *vt* ‹*caballo*› to unharness; ‹*barco*› to unrig

desaparición *f* **1** disappearance; **una especie en vías de ~** an endangered species **2** (euf & frml) (muerte) passing (euph & frml)

desapasionado -da *adj* ‹*persona*› impartial, dispassionate; ‹*crítica/decisión*› unbiased, dispassionate

desapego *m* **1** (desinterés) indifference **2** (desamor) coolness, lack of affection

desapercibido -da *adj*: **pasar ~** to go unnoticed

desaprensivo -va *adj* (sin escrúpulos) unscrupulous, cynical; (insensible) callous, uncaring

desaprobación *f* disapproval

desaprobar [A10] *vt* (frml) to disapprove of

desaprovechar [A1] *vt* ‹*oportunidad*› to waste; ‹*tiempo/comida*› to waste; **el espacio está muy desaprovechada** the space is not being put to good use

desarbolar [A1] *vt* to dismast

desarmable *adj* ‹*mueble/mecanismo*› which can be dismantled *o* taken apart

desarmado -da *adj* ‹*policía/criminal*› unarmed; **iban desarmados** they weren't armed

desarmador *m* (Méx) screwdriver

desarmar [A1] *vt*

A ‹*mueble/mecanismo*› to dismantle, take apart; ‹*carpa*› (AmL) to take down; ‹*rifle/motor*› to strip (down); ‹*rompecabezas*› to take … to pieces, break up; ‹*juguete/maqueta*› to take … apart, take … to pieces

B **1** (quitar armas, dejar sin argumentos) to disarm

desarme *m* disarmament; **~ nuclear** nuclear disarmament

desarraigado -da *adj* rootless; **se siente totalmente desarraigada** she feels she has lost her roots

desarraigarse [A3] *v pron* to uproot oneself

desarraigo *m*: **el ~ que sufre el emigrado** the feeling of having been uprooted experienced by emigrants; **una manifestación del ~ cultural** a manifestation of being uprooted from one's cultural environment

desarrapado -da *adj* ▸**desharrapado**

desarreglado -da *adj* ‹*persona/aspecto/lugar*› untidy; ‹*vida*› disorganized, chaotic

desarreglar [A1] *vt* ‹*horario/funcionamiento*› to disrupt

■ **desarreglarse** *v pron* **1** ⟪*peinado*⟫ to get messed up **2** ⟪*horarios/funcionamiento*⟫ to be disrupted, be upset; ⟪*menstruación*⟫ to become irregular

desarreglo *m*

A (desorden): **con tantos ~s de horarios está muy cansado** he's very tired because his routine has been upset so much

B (CS) **1** (exceso): **hacer ~s** to overindulge **2** (en presupuesto): **este mes no podemos hacer ningún ~** this month we mustn't allow ourselves any extravagances

desarrollado -da *adj* **1** ‹*país/economía*› developed **2** ‹*niña/niño*› well-developed; ‹*sentido*› developed

desarrollar [A1] *vt*

A **1** ‹*facultad/inteligencia*› to develop; ‹*músculos*› to develop, build up **2** ‹*industria/comercio*› to develop **3** ‹*teoría/plan*› to develop

B **1** (exponer) ‹*teoría/tema*› to explain **2** (llevar a cabo) ‹*actividad/labor*› to carry out; ‹*plan*› to put into practice

C (Chi) (Fot) to develop

■ **desarrollarse** *v pron*

A ⟪*cuerpo/planta*⟫ to develop, grow; ⟪*pueblo/economía*⟫ to develop; ⟪*teoría/idea*⟫ to develop, evolve

B ⟪*acto/entrevista/escena*⟫ to take place; **veremos cómo se desarrollan los acontecimientos** we shall see how things develop

desarrollo *m*

A **1** (Econ) development; **países en vías de ~** developing countries **2** (de facultad, capacidad) development **3** (de niño, de planta) growth, development **4** (de adolescente) development

B (de teoría, tema, estrategia) development

C (de acto, acontecimiento): **durante el ~ del acto** during *o* in the course of proceedings; **intentaron impedir el normal ~ del acto** they tried to disrupt the proceedings; **según el ~ de los acontecimientos** according to how things develop

(Compuesto) **desarrollo sostenible** sustainable development

desarroparse [A1] *v pron* (*refl*) to throw the bedclothes *o* covers off

desarrugarse [A3] *v pron*: **cuelga la ropa para que se desarrugue** hang your clothes up so that the creases fall out

desarticulación *f* (de una organización) dismantling, breaking up

desarticular [A1] *vt*

A ‹*organización*› to dismantle, break up; ‹*conspiración*› to foil, thwart

B ‹*artefacto/mecanismo*› to take … to pieces, dismantle

desaseado -da *adj* ‹*niño*› grubby; ‹*habitación*› messy

desaseo *m* uncleanliness

desasirse [I10] *v pron* **~ DE algo** to free oneself FROM sth, get free FROM sth

desasistido -da *adj* neglected

desasosegado -da *adj* restless, uneasy

desasosiego *m* (feeling *o* sense of) unease; **su presencia le producía un gran ~** his presence filled her with a terrible sense of unease

desastrado -da *adj* ‹*persona*› scruffy, untidy; ‹*habitación/trabajo*› untidy

desastre *m* **1** (catástrofe) disaster **2** (fam) (uso hiperbólico) disaster; **cocinando soy un ~** I'm a disaster when it comes to cooking (colloq); **como cantante es un ~** he's a hopeless singer; **tienes la habitación hecha un ~** your room is a shambles; **vas hecha un ~** you look a real mess (colloq)

desastroso -sa *adj* disastrous

desatado -da *adj* 1 (sin amarrar): **el perro estaba ~** the dog was off its leash *o* was loose; **llevas los cordones ~s** your shoelaces are undone 2 ‹*nervios*›: **estar con** *or* **tener los nervios ~s** to be a bundle of nerves

desatar [A1] *vt*
A 1 ‹*nudo/lazo*› to untie, undo 2 ‹*persona*› to untie; ‹*perro*› to let … loose, let … off the leash
B (desencadenar) 1 (liter) ‹*cólera/pasiones*› to unleash 2 ‹*crisis/revuelta*› to spark off; ‹*polémica*› to provoke, give rise to
■ **desatarse** *v pron*
A 1 «*nudo/cordones*» to come undone *o* untied; «*perro/caballo*» to get loose 2 (*refl*) «*persona*» to untie oneself; ‹*cordones/zapatos*› to untie, undo
B (desencadenarse) 1 (liter) «*pasiones/ira/furia*» to be unleashed 2 «*polémica/crisis*» to erupt, flare up; «*revuelta*» to break out 3 «*tormenta/temporal*» to break

desatascador *m* (instrumento) plunger; (producto) nitric acid (*o* caustic soda *etc*) (*used to clear blocked drains*)

desatascar [A2] *vt* ‹*cañería/fregadero*› to unblock, clear
■ **desatascarse** *v pron* «*cañería/fregadero*» to unblock; «*carretera*» to clear

desatender [E8] *vt* 1 ‹*trabajo/familia*› to neglect 2 ‹*tienda/mostrador*› to leave … unattended 3 (frml) ‹*consejo*› to disregard, ignore

desatento -ta *adj* 1 [SER] (desconsiderado) thoughtless, inconsiderate; **fuiste ~, deberías habérselo agradecido** it was thoughtless of you not to thank her; **no seas ~, ayúdala a bajar las maletas** be a little more helpful, help her to get her suitcases down 2 [ESTAR] (distraído) inattentive

desatinado -da *adj* 1 ‹*medida*› unwise, foolish; **su explicación no es tan desatinada** his explanation is not that far-fetched 2 ‹*persona*› (sin tacto) tactless; (sin juicio) foolish

desatino *m* mistake

desatornillador *m* (AmC, Chi) screwdriver

desatornillar [A1] *vt* to unscrew

desatracar [A2] *vi* to cast off
■ **desatracar** *vt* to cast off

desatrancar [A2] *vt* to force open; **lograron ~ la puerta dándole una patada** they managed to kick the door open

desautorización *f* (frml) disavowal

desautorizar [A4] *vt* 1 (restar autoridad a) ‹*persona*› to undermine the authority of; ‹*declaraciones*› to disavow (frml), to disaffirm (frml); **quedó totalmente desautorizado con el escándalo** he was totally discredited as a result of the scandal 2 (retirar la autorización para) to ban; **han desautorizado la manifestación** the demonstration has been banned

desavenencia *f* disagreement, difference of opinion

desavenido -da *adj*: **está ~ con sus suegros** he's on bad terms with his inlaws; **son muy ~s** they don't get on at all well

desayunar [A1] *vt* to have … for breakfast; **sólo desayuna café con tostadas** she only has coffee and toast for breakfast
■ **desayunar** *vi* to have breakfast
■ **desayunarse** *v pron*
A (AmL) (tomar el desayuno) to have breakfast; **se desayunó muy bien** he had *o* ate a good breakfast; **~se CON algo** to have sth FOR breakfast
B 1 (AmL fam) (enterarse) to find out; **recién me desayuno** I've just found out; **~se DE algo** to hear ABOUT sth 2 (Chi fam) (sorprenderse) to be amazed (colloq); **me desayuno con lo que me cuentas** I'm amazed at *o* by what you're telling me

desayuno *m* breakfast; **tomar el ~** *or* (Chi) **tomar ~** to have breakfast; **durante el ~** at *o* over breakfast

desazón *f* 1 (desasosiego) (feeling *o* sense of) unease; **sentir ~** to feel uneasy 2 (falta de sabor) insipidness

desazonado -da *adj* 1 [ESTAR] (inquieto) uneasy 2 [SER] (sin sabor) insipid

desbancar [A2] *vt*
A (de una posición) to oust; **lo ~on de la presidencia** he was ousted him from his post as president; **se sintió desbancado cuando nació su hermano** he felt displaced when his brother was born; **la madera ha sido desbancada por los plásticos** wood has been superseded by plastic
B (Jueg): **al final me desbancó** in the end he broke the bank *o* (colloq) left me completely broke

desbandada *f*: **se produjo una ~ de gente/pájaros** people ran off/birds flew off in all directions; **salir en ~** to scatter, run off in all directions

desbandarse [A1] *v pron* «*personas/animales*» to scatter, run off in all directions; «*tropas*» to scatter

desbarajustar [A1] *vt* (fam) to mess up (colloq)

desbarajuste *m* (fam) mess; **un ~ económico** an economic mess *o* chaos

desbaratar [A1] *vt* 1 ‹*planes*› to spoil, ruin; ‹*sistema*› to disrupt; **el defensa desbarató la jugada** the defender broke up the move 2 (Méx) ‹*papeles*› to jumble (up), muddle (up); ‹*mecanismo*› to ruin, destroy
■ **desbaratarse** *v pron* 1 «*plan*» to be ruined, be spoiled; «*sistema*» to be disrupted, break down; **se desbarató todo con la lluvia** the rain spoiled everything 2 (Méx) «*papeles*» to get jumbled up, get muddled (up); «*mecanismo*» to break, get broken

desbarrancarse [A2] *v pron* ‹*carro/camión*› to go over a sheer drop

desbastar [A1] *vt*
A (dar forma aproximada a) ‹*metal*› to rough down; ‹*madera/piedra*› to rough-hew
B (cepillar) to plane (down), smooth down

desbloquear [A1] *vt* 1 ‹*carretera/entrada*› to clear; ‹*mecanismo*› to release, free 2 ‹*negociaciones/diálogo*› to break the deadlock in 3 (Com, Fin) ‹*cuenta*› to unfreeze

desbloqueo *m*: **el ~ de las negociaciones** the breaking of the deadlock in the negotiations; **el ~ de una cuenta** the unfreezing of an account

desbocado -da *adj* 1 ‹*caballo*› runaway (*before n*) 2 ‹*cuello/escote*› loose, wide

desbocarse [A2] *v pron* «*caballo*» to bolt

desbordamiento *m* (de río, canal) overflowing; **las lluvias provocaron el ~ del río** the rains caused the river to burst its banks

desbordante *adj* ‹*entusiasmo/júbilo*› boundless; **está ~ de entusiasmo** he's bursting with enthusiasm; **estaba ~ de júbilo** she was brimming over with happiness

desbordar [A1] *vt* 1 (salirse de): **el río desbordó su cauce** the river burst its banks 2 ‹*límites*› to exceed, go beyond; **desborda mi capacidad de comprensión** it's quite beyond me 3 (Mil, Pol) to break through; **~ las líneas enemigas** to break through the enemy lines 4 ‹*persona*› to overwhelm; **se vio desbordado por los acontecimientos** it was all too much for him; **estoy desbordada de trabajo** I'm swamped with work; **esta casa me desborda** this house is too much for me to manage 5 ‹*alegría/entusiasmo*›: **su cara desbordaba alegría** her face shone with joy; **desbordaba entusiasmo** she was brimming with enthusiasm
■ **desbordarse** *v pron* 1 «*río/canal*» to burst its banks 2 «*vaso/cubo*» to overflow 3 «*multitud*» to get out of hand, get out of control

desborde *m* (CS) ▸ **desbordamiento**

desbrozar [A4] *vt* ‹*terreno*› to clear (the vegetation from)

descabalgar [A3] *vi* to dismount

descabellado -da *adj* crazy, ridiculous

descabellar [A1] *vt* (Taur) to deliver the coup de grace (*by severing the spinal cord with a dagger*)

descabezar [A4] *vt* to leave … without a leader

descafeinado[1] -da *adj* ‹*café*› decaffeinated

descafeinado[2] *m* decaffeinated coffee

descafeinar [A1] *vt* ‹*café*› to decaffeinate

descalabrar [A1] *vt*: **~ a algn** to split sb's head open
■ **descalabrarse** *v pron* to split one's head open

descalabro *m* 1 (desastre) disaster 2 (Mil) defeat

descalcificación *f* (proceso) decalcification; (estado) calcium deficiency

descalificación *f*
A (Dep) disqualification
B (frml) (descrédito) defamatory *o* damaging remark

descalificar [A2] *vt*
A (inhabilitar, desautorizar) ‹*deportista/equipo*› to disqualify
B (frml) (desacreditar) to discredit
descalzarse [A4] *v pron* to take off one's shoes
descalzo -za *adj* ‹*pie*› bear; ‹*persona*› barefoot; **corrió ~** he ran barefoot
descamar [A1] *vt* ‹*pescado*› to scale
■ **descamarse** *v pron* «*piel*» to flake; **se le descama la piel** his skin is flaking
descaminado -da *adj*: **ir** *or* **andar ~** to be on the wrong track
descamisado -da *adj* (sin camisa) shirtless, without a shirt; (con la camisa desabrochada) with one's shirt undone; (paupérrimo) ragged, shabby
descampado *m* **1** (terreno) area *o* piece of open ground *o* land **2** **al descampado** (AmS) ‹*dormir*› in the open (air)
descansado -da *adj* **1** [ESTAR] ‹*persona*› rested, refreshed **2** [SER] ‹*actividad/trabajo*› easy, undemanding; ‹*vida*› quiet, peaceful
descansar [A1] *vi*
A **1** (de actividad, trabajo) to rest, have a rest; **sin ~** without a break; **se pararon a ~** they stopped for a rest; **¡descansen!** (Mil) (stand) at ease!; **~ DE algo** to have a rest *o* break FROM sth **2** (en la cama) to rest, have a rest; **buenas noches, que descanses** goodnight, sleep well **3** (yacer) to lie; **aquí descansan los restos del poeta** here lie the remains of the poet; **que en paz descanse** God rest his soul; **descansan juntos en su pueblo natal** they lie buried together in their birthplace
B «*tierra*» to lie fallow
C (apoyarse) **~ EN** *or* **SOBRE algo** «*techo/bóveda*» to rest ON *o* UPON sth; «*teoría*» to rest *o* hinge ON sth
■ **descansar** *vt* **1** **~ la vista** to rest one's eyes, to give one's eyes a rest; **~ la mente** to give one's mind a break *o* rest **2** (Mil) **¡descansen armas!** order arms!
descansillo *m* (Esp) landing
descanso *m*
A **1** (reposo) rest; **debemos respetar su ~** we must let him rest; **se ha tomado cuatro días de ~** she has taken four days off; Ⓢ **lunes, descanso** (Espec, Teatr) no performance on Mondays **2** (en trabajo, colegio) break **3** (Mil): **estar en posición de ~** to be standing at ease **4** (de un muerto) rest
B (intervalo) (Dep) half time; (Teatr) interval
C (alivio, tranquilidad) relief
D (AmL) (rellano) landing
descapotable *adj/m* convertible
descaradamente *adv*: **me mintió ~** he told me a bare-faced lie; **y me lo dijo así, ~** and she had the nerve to tell me just like that
descarado[1] -da *adj* ‹*persona/actitud*› brazen, shameless; **las elecciones fueron un fraude ~** the elections were a blatant fraud
descarado[2] -da *m,f*: **no contestes así a tu madre ¡~!** don't talk back to your mother like that, you rude little boy; **es un ~** he has a lot of nerve
descarga *f*
A (de mercancías) unloading; Ⓢ **carga y descarga** loading and unloading
B (Elec) discharge; **una ~ eléctrica** an electric shock
C (de arma) shot, discharge (frml); (de conjunto de armas) volley; **recibió la ~ en plena cara** he received the impact of the shot full in the face
D (Ven fam) (de insultos) volley of abuse
descargador -dora *m,f* (de camiones, aviones) loader; (de barcos) docker, longshoreman (AmE)
descargar [A3] *vt*
A ‹*vehículo/mercancías*› to unload
B **1** ‹*pistola*› (extraer las balas) to unload; (disparar) to fire, discharge (frml); **la pistola está descargada** the pistol is not loaded **2** ‹*tiro*› to fire; ‹*golpe*› to deal, land; **le descargó seis tiros** he shot her six times
C **1** ‹*ira/agresividad*› to vent; ‹*preocupaciones/tensiones*› to relieve **2** (Ven fam) ‹*persona*›: **me lo voy a ~** I'm going to give him a piece of my mind; **no eres quien para que me descargues** who do you think you are, sounding off to me like that? (colloq)
D **~ a algn DE algo** ‹*de responsabilidad*› to clear sb OF sth; ‹*de obligación*› to relieve sb OF sth; **lo ~on de toda culpa** he was cleared of all blame
■ **descargar** *v impers* «*aguacero*» to pour down; «*temporal*» to break
■ **descargarse** *v pron*
A (Elec) «*pila*» to run down; «*batería*» to go dead *o* flat
B «*tormenta*» to break; «*lluvias*» to come down, fall
C «*persona*» **1** (desahogarse) **~se CON algn** to take it out ON sb **2** (de obligación) **~se DE algo** to get out of sth
descargo *m* defense*; **¿qué puede formular en su ~?** what can you say in your defense?
descargue *m* (Col, Ven) unloading
descarnado -da *adj* **1** ‹*rostro/persona*› emaciated, gaunt; ‹*hueso*› bare **2** ‹*realismo/relato*› stark; ‹*verdad*› naked, plain
descaro *m*: **¡qué ~!** what a nerve!; **tergiversan los hechos con un ~ ...** they misrepresent the facts so blatantly
descarozado *m* (CS) dried and pitted apricot/peach
descarriado -da *adj*: **hoy día la juventud anda descarriada** the youth of today has lost its way; ▸**oveja**
descarrilamiento *m* derailment
descarrilar [A1] *vi* to derail, be derailed; **hicieron ~ el tren** they derailed the train
■ **descarrilarse** *v pron* (AmL) to derail, be derailed
descartar [A1] *vt* ‹*plan/posibilidad*› to rule out, dismiss; ‹*candidato*› to reject, rule out
■ **descartarse** *v pron* (en cartas) to discard
descarte *m* (Jueg) (acción) discarding
descascararse [A1], (Esp) **descascarillarse** [A1] *v pron* «*pared*» to peel; «*pintura/esmalte*» to chip, peel; «*taza/plato*» to chip
descendencia *f* descendants (pl); **murió sin (dejar) ~** he died without issue (frml)
descendente *adj* ‹*curva/línea*› downward; ‹*escala*› descending
descender [E8] *vi*
A **1** «*temperatura/nivel*» to fall, drop **2** (frml) (desde una altura) «*avión*» to descend; «*persona*» to descend (frml), to come/go down; **descendieron por la ladera oeste** they went/came down the western face; **el sendero que desciende hasta el río** the path which goes down to the river; **los pasajeros descendieron a tierra** the passengers disembarked **3** (liter) «*oscuridad*» to fall, descend (liter); «*niebla*» to descend (liter)
B **1** (en jerarquía): **el hotel ha descendido de categoría** the hotel has been downgraded; **su disco ha descendido en la lista de éxitos** his record has gone down the charts **2** (Dep) (en fútbol) to go down, be relegated (BrE)
C (proceder) **~ DE algn** to be descended FROM sb; **descienden directamente de los incas** they are direct descendants of the Incas; **desciende de una familia noble** he is of noble descent
descendiente *mf* descendant; **murió sin ~s** she died without issue (frml)
descenso *m*
A **1** (de temperatura, nivel) fall, drop; (de precios) fall; **el ~ en el número de accidentes** the fall *o* decrease in the number of accidents **2** (desde una altura) descent; **la carrera** *or* **prueba de ~** the downhill
B (Dep) relegation
descentrado -da *adj* **1** ‹*eje/rueda*› off-center* **2** ‹*persona*› disoriented, disorientated (BrE)
descentralización *f* decentralization
descentralizar [A4] *vt* to decentralize
descerebrarse [A1] *v pron* (Andes) to suffer brain damage
descerrajar [A1] *vt*
A (period) ‹*tiro*› to fire, let off
B ‹*cerradura*› to force, break; ‹*puerta*› to force the lock on
deschavetado -da *adj* (AmL exc RPl fam) crazy (colloq)
descifrar [A1] *vt* **1** ‹*mensaje*› to decode, decipher; ‹*escritura/jeroglífico/código*› to decipher; **no logro ~ qué dice aquí** I can't make out what it says here **2** ‹*misterio/enigma*› to work out, figure out
descocado -da *adj* (fam) brazen, shameless
descodificador *m* decoder

descojonarse [A1] *v pron* (Esp arg) *tb* ~ **de risa** to piss oneself (laughing) (vulg)

descojone *m* (Esp arg): **su novio/la película es un** ~ her boy-friend/the film is a real scream

descolgar [A8] *vt* 1 ‹*cuadro/cortina*› to take down 2 ‹*teléfono*› to pick up; **dejar el teléfono descolgado** to leave the phone off the hook
■ **descolgar** *vi*: **lo dejó sonar dos veces antes de** ~ he let it ring twice before he picked it up *o* answered it
■ **descolgarse** *v pron*
A (por una cuerda) to lower oneself
B (en carrera) to pull away, break away

descollar [A10] *vi* to be outstanding; **esa mujer descuella por su inteligencia** she is a woman of outstanding intelligence

descolonización *f* decolonization

descolonizar [A4] *vt* to decolonize

descolorido -da *adj* ‹*tela/papel*› faded

descombro *m* clearing-up

descomedido -da *adj* 1 (desmesurado) immoderate, unrestrained 2 (AmL) (poco cortés) ▸ **desatento 1**

descomponer [E22] *vt*
A ‹*alimento/cadáver*› to rot, cause ... to decompose *o* rot
B (esp AmL) ‹*máquina/aparato*› to break; ‹*peinado*› to mess up
C ‹*persona*› 1 (producir malestar) «*olor*» to make ... queasy; **la noticia la descompuso** she felt quite ill when she heard the news 2 (producir diarrea) to give ... diarrhea•
■ **descomponerse** *v pron*
A «*luz*» to split; «*sustancia*» to break down, separate
B «*cadáver/alimento*» to rot, decompose (frml)
C «*cara*» (+ *me/te/le etc*): **se le descompuso la cara cuando se lo dije** he looked really upset when I told him
D (esp AmL) «*máquina/aparato*» to break down
E «*persona*» 1 (sentir malestar): **hacía tanto calor que se descompuso** it was so hot that he felt sick; **se descompuso cuando supo la noticia** he felt quite ill when he heard the news 2 (del estómago) to have an attack of diarrhea•
F (CS) «*tiempo*» to become unsettled; «*día*» to cloud over

descomposición *f*
A (de número) factorization; (de la luz) splitting; (de sustancia) breaking down, separating
B (putrefacción) decomposition

descompostura *f* (esp AmL) (malestar, náuseas) sickness, queasiness; (diarrea) stomach upset, diarrhea•

descompresor *m* decompression valve

descompuesto -ta *adj*
A ‹*alimento*› rotten, decomposed (frml); ‹*cadáver*› decomposed
B ‹*expresión*› changed, altered; **tenía el rostro** ~ he looked very upset
C (esp AmL) [ESTAR] ‹*máquina/aparato*› broken; ‹*teléfono*› out of order
D 1 (indispuesto): **se pasó toda la semana descompuesta** she felt sick all week 2 (del estómago): **está** ~ he has diarrhea•/an upset stomach

descompuse, descompuso, etc *see* **descomponer**

descomunal *adj* ‹*estatura/fuerza/suma*› enormous, colossal; ‹*apetito*› huge, colossal

desconcentrarse [A1] *v pron* to lose concentration

desconcertado -da *adj* disconcerted; **se quedó un momento** ~ he was momentarily taken aback

desconcertante *adj* disconcerting

desconcertar [A5] *vt* to disconcert; **sus reacciones me desconciertan** I find his reactions disconcerting; **su respuesta me desconcertó** I was disconcerted by her reply

desconchabar [A1] *vt* (Méx fam) (estropear) to break, bust (colloq)
■ **desconchabarse** *v pron* (Méx fam) «*coche*» to break down; **se desconchabó la televisión** the television's broken *o* (colloq) bust

desconchado *m* (en taza, plato) chip; (en pared) *place where plaster or paint has come off*

desconchar [A1] *vt* ‹*porcelana/taza*› to chip; ~**on la pared** they knocked some of the plaster off the wall
■ **desconcharse** *v pron* «*taza/plato*» to get chipped

desconchinflar [A1] *vt* (Méx fam) ▸ **desconchabar**

desconcierto *m*: **su llamada los llenó de** ~ they were disconcerted by his call; **el** ~ **reinante** the prevailing atmosphere of uncertainty

desconectar [A1] *vt* ‹*alarma/teléfono*› to disconnect; ‹*calefacción*› to switch off, turn off; ~ **algo DE algo** to disconnect sth FROM sth
■ **desconectar** *vi* (fam) to switch off
■ **desconectarse** *v pron* 1 «*aparato*» to switch *o* turn off; **se desconecta automáticamente** it switches *o* turns (itself) off automatically 2 «*persona*» ~**se DE algo/algn** to lose touch WITH sth/sb; (voluntariamente) to sever all ties WITH sth/sb

desconfiado -da *adj* (receloso) distrustful; (suspicaz) suspicious

desconfianza *f* distrust, suspicion; **me tiene mucha** ~ he's very wary *o* suspicious of me

desconfiar [A17] *vi* 1 (no fiarse) ~ **DE algn** to mistrust sb, to distrust sb; **yo desconfío de sus intenciones** I don't trust her intentions; **desconfía de lo que te diga** don't believe a word he says 2 (dudar) ~ **DE algo**: **desconfían de poder recuperar el dinero** they doubt whether they will be able to recover the money; **desconfío de que logremos convencerlos** I doubt we'll be able to convince them

descongelante *m* deicer

descongelar [A1] *vt*
A 1 ‹*refrigerador*› to defrost 2 ‹*alimentos*› to defrost, thaw
B ‹*créditos/salarios/cuenta*› to unfreeze
■ **descongelarse** *v pron*
A «*refrigerador*» to defrost; «*alimentos*» to defrost, thaw
B «*relaciones*» to thaw

descongestión *f* 1 (de nariz, bronquios) clearing, decongestion (tech) 2 (de tráfico) easing of congestion

descongestionante *adj/m* decongestant

descongestionar [A1] *vt* ‹*nariz*› to clear; ‹*tráfico*› to clear

desconocer [E3] *vt* 1 (no conocer): **por razones que desconocemos** for reasons unknown to us; **se desconoce su identidad/su paradero** her identity is/her whereabouts are not known; **desconocía la existencia de esta cuenta** she was unaware of the existence of this account; **su obra se desconoce fuera de Cuba** his work is unknown outside Cuba 2 (no reconocer): **te desconocí** I didn't recognize you

desconocido¹ -da *adj* 1 ‹*hecho/método/sensación*› unknown; **por razones desconocidas** for some unknown reason; **su rostro no me era** ~ his face wasn't unfamiliar to me; **técnicas hasta ahora desconocidas** hitherto unknown techniques; **de origen** ~ of unknown origin; **lo** ~ the unknown 2 ‹*artista/atleta*› unknown 3 ‹*persona*› (extraño): **una persona desconocida** a stranger 4 (fam) (irreconocible): **con ese peinado nuevo está desconocida** she looks completely different with her new hairstyle; **ahora hasta plancha, está** ~ he's like a different man, he even does the ironing

desconocido² -da *m,f* 1 (no conocido) stranger 2 (no identificado): **fue atacado por unos** ~**s** he was attacked by unknown assailants; **un** ~ **le asestó una puñalada** he was stabbed by someone whose identity has not been established

desconocimiento *m* ignorance

desconsideración *f* lack of consideration, thoughtlessness

desconsiderado -da *adj* thoughtless, inconsiderate

desconsolado -da *adj* **estar** ~ **POR algo** to be heartbroken OVER sth; **lloraba** ~ he cried inconsolably

desconstructivista *adj/mf* deconstructionist

desconsuelo *m* grief, despair

descontado *adj*: **eso dalo** *or* **puedes darlo por** ~ you can be sure of that; **doy por** ~ **que vendrás a cenar** I'm assuming that you're coming to dinner

descontaminación *f* decontamination; **la** ~ **atmosférica** the reduction of pollution in the atmosphere

descontaminar [A1] *vt* ‹*alimentos/cultivos*› to decontaminate; ‹*atmósfera*› to clean up

descontar [A10] *vt*

A 1 (rebajar): **me descontó el 15%** he gave me a 15% discount 2 (restar) to deduct; **me lo ~on del sueldo** it was deducted from my balance; **te descuentan el 20% de impuestos** you get 20% deducted for taxes; **descuenta los gastos de viaje** take off traveling costs; **el árbitro descontó un minuto** the referee only allowed a minute for stoppages; **tienes que ~ las dos horas de la comida** you have to deduct two hours for lunch

B (exceptuar): **descontando a Pedro** apart from Pedro, not counting Pedro; **si descontamos los domingos ...** if we don't count Sundays ...

C ‹*letra/pagaré*› to discount

d

descontento¹ -ta *adj* [ESTAR] dissatisfied; **~ con algo/algn** unhappy *o* dissatisfied WITH sth/sb; **quedó ~ con lo que le di** he wasn't satisfied *o* happy with what I gave him

descontento² *m* discontent

descontrol *m* 1 (fam) (desorden, caos) chaos; **en la oficina hay un ~ total** things at the office are in complete chaos 2 (falta de mesura) recklessness

descontrolado -da *adj* to be out of control; **una multitud descontrolada invadió el campo** a crowd, out of control, invaded the pitch

descontrolarse [A1] *v pron* to get out of control

desconvocar [A2] *vt* to call off

desconvocatoria *f* (de huelga, manifestación) calling off; (de reunión, asamblea) cancellation

descorazonador -dora *adj* disheartening, discouraging

descorazonar [A1] *vt* to dishearten, discourage

descorchador *m* (Col) corkscrew

descorchar [A1] *vt* to uncork, open

descorrer [E1] *vt* ‹*cortinas*› to draw (back); **descorrió el cerrojo/pestillo** he drew back the bolt

descortés *adj* ‹*persona*› impolite, ill-mannered; ‹*comportamiento*› rude, impolite; **fue bastante ~ de tu parte** it was rather rude *o* ill-mannered of you

descortesía *f* 1 (acto descortés) discourtesy 2 (cualidad) rudeness, impoliteness; **nos trataron con ~** they were rude to us

descoser [E1] *vt* to unpick

■ **descoserse** *v pron* «*prenda/costura*» to come unstitched; **llevas la falda descosido** your skirt is coming apart at the seams

descosido¹ -da *adj* ‹*dobladillo/costura*› unstitched

descosido² *m* split seam; **tienes un ~ en la manga** your sleeve is coming apart at the seam

descosido³ -da *m,f*: ***como un ~*** (fam) ‹*comer*› like a horse; **gritar/reírse como un ~** to shout/laugh one's head off (colloq)

descoyuntarse [A1] *v pron* «*articulación*» to become dislocated; **ayer hice aerobic(s) y estoy descoyuntada** (fam) I went to aerobics yesterday and I can't move today

descrédito *m* discredit; **ir en ~ de algo/algn** to bring discredit on sth/sb

descremado -da *adj* skimmed

descremar [A1] *vt* to skim

describir [I34] *vt*

A ‹*paisaje/persona*› to describe

B (frml) ‹*línea/órbita*› to trace, describe (frml)

descripción *f* description

descriptivo -va *adj* descriptive

descrito -ta *pp*: *see* **describir**

descuajeringado -da *adj* 1 (fam) ‹*objeto*›: **me lo devolvió todo ~** when she gave it back to me it was falling to bits *o* pieces 2 (AmL fam) ‹*persona*› shattered (colloq)

descuajeringar [A3] *vt* (fam) ‹*cama/silla*› to pull ... to pieces *o* apart; ‹*libro*› to tear ... apart *o* to pieces

■ **descuajeringarse** *v pron* 1 (fam) «*cama/silla*» to fall apart, collapse 2 (fam) «*persona*» *tb* **~ de risa** to split one's sides laughing

descuartizar [A4] *vt* 1 ‹*res/reo*› to quarter 2 «*asesino*»: **descuartizaba a sus víctimas** he chopped his victims' bodies (up) into pieces

descubierto¹ -ta *adj*

A 1 ‹*piscina/terraza*› open-air, outdoor (*before n*); ‹*carroza*› open-top 2 ‹*cartas*›: **las cartas se dan descubiertas** the cards are dealt face up

B ‹*cielos*› clear

C **al descubierto**: **quedar al ~** «*planes/escándalo*» to come to light; **han puesto al ~ sus chanchullos** his shady dealings have been exposed; **girar al** *or* **en ~** (Com, Fin) to overdraw; *ver tb* **girar** *vt* **B1**

descubierto² *m* overdraft

descubridor -dora *m,f* discoverer; **el ~ de la penicilina** the man who discovered penicillin, the discoverer of penicillin

descubrimiento *m*

A (hallazgo, comprobación) discovery

B (persona) discovery

descubrir [I33] *vt*

A 1 ‹*tierras/sustancia/fenómeno*› to discover; ‹*oro/ruinas/cadáver*› to discover, find; ‹*virus*› to identify 2 ‹*artista/atleta*› to discover

B 1 (enterarse de, averiguar) ‹*razón/solución*› to discover, find out; ‹*complot/engaño*› to uncover; ‹*fraude*› to detect; **aún no se han descubierto las causas del accidente** the causes of the accident have not yet been established 2 ‹*persona escondida*› to find, track down 3 ‹*culpable*› find ... out; **no dijo nada** he said nothing; **por miedo a que lo descubrieran** for fear of being found out 4 (delatar) to give ... away

C 1 ‹*estatua/placa*› to unveil 2 (liter) (dejar ver) ‹*cuerpo/forma*› to reveal 3 (revelar) ‹*planes/intenciones*› to reveal

■ **descubrirse** *v pron*

A (refl) (quitarse el sombrero) to take one's hat off; ‹*rostro*› to uncover; ***¡me descubro!*** I take my hat off to you/him/them

B (delatarse) to give oneself away

descuento *m*

A 1 (rebaja) discount; ⊗ **no se hacen descuentos** no discounts given; **un ~ del 15%** a 15% discount; **compre Cremol, ahora con ~** buy Cremol, now on special offer 2 (del sueldo) deduction

B (Dep) injury time

C (de letra, pagaré) discount

descuidado -da *adj* 1 [SER] (negligente) careless; **es muy ~ al escribir** he writes very carelessly *o* sloppily; **es muy descuidada en el vestir** she's very sloppy about the way she dresses 2 [ESTAR] (desatendido) neglected; **tiene la casa muy descuidada** his house is a mess (colloq); **al hijo lo tienen muy ~** they neglect their son terribly

descuidar [A1] *vt* ‹*negocio/jardín*› to neglect; **no descuides esa herida** be careful with that cut

■ **descuidar** *vi*: **descuide, yo me ocuparé de eso** don't worry, I'll see to that

■ **descuidarse** *v pron* 1 (no prestar atención, distraerse): **la defensa se descuidó** (Dep) the defense let their concentration go *o* slip; **se descuidó un momento y el perro se le escapó** his attention strayed for a moment and the dog ran off; **si te descuidas, te roban** if you don't watch out, they'll rob you; **como te descuides, te van a quitar el puesto** if you don't look out, they'll take your job from you 2 (en el aspecto físico) to neglect one's appearance

descuido *m* 1 (distracción): **en un ~ el niño se le escapó** she took her eyes off the child for a moment and he ran off; **basta el más pequeño ~** the smallest lapse of concentration is enough; ***en un ~*** (Méx) you never know; **en un ~ hasta podemos ganar el concurso** you never know, we might even win the competition 2 (error) slip; (omisión) oversight 3 (falta de cuidado) carelessness; **todo lo hace con ~** he's very slapdash

desde *prep*

A (en el tiempo) since; **~ entonces/~ que se casó** since then/since he got married; **¿~ cuándo te gustan los mejillones? — ¡~ siempre!** since when have you liked mussels? — I've always liked them!; **¿~ cuándo trabajas aquí?** how long have you been working here?; **~ niño** since he/I was a child; **~ que tengo memoria** for as long as I remember; **~ el primer momento** *or* **un principio** right from the start; **no los veo ~ hace meses** I haven't seen them for months; **estaba enfermo ~ hacía un año** he had been ill for a year; **~ el 15 hasta el 30** from the 15th to *o* until the 30th

B (en el espacio) from; **~ aquí/allá** from here/there; **¿~ dónde tengo que leer?** where do I have to read from?; **~ mi punto de vista** from my point of view; **~ la página 12 hasta la 20** from page 12 (up) to page 20; **~ la cabeza hasta los pies** from head to foot

C (en escalas, jerarquías) from; **blusas ~ 9 euros** blouses from 9 euros; **~ el director hasta el último empleado** from the director (down) to the lowest employee

desdecir [I24] *vi* **~ DE algo**: **este cuadro desdice del resto de su obra** this picture doesn't come up to the standard of the rest of her work; **ese calzado desdice de un vestido tan elegante** those shoes don't do justice to such a smart dress

■ **desdecirse** *v pron* to go back on one's word; **no te desdigas ahora de lo que afirmaste ayer** you can't take back now what you said yesterday

desdén *m* disdain, scorn; **sentir ~ por algn** to be scornful *o* disdainful of sb; **odio el ~ con que nos trata** I hate the disdainful way he treats us

desdentado -da *adj* **1** ‹*persona*› toothless **2** (Zool) edentate

desdeñable *adj* insignificant; **una suma de dinero nada ~** it's a sum not to be despised

desdeñar [A1] *vt* **1** (menospreciar) to scorn **2** ‹*pretendiente*› to spurn

desdeñoso -sa *adj* ‹*persona*› disdainful; ‹*gesto/actitud*› disdainful, scornful

desdibujado -da *adj* ‹*contorno/imagen*› blurred, vague; ‹*recuerdo*› vague, hazy; ‹*personaje*› sketchy, nebulous

desdibujarse [A1] *v pron* «*contorno*» to become blurred; **el recuerdo se le iba desdibujando** the memory was gradually fading (liter)

desdicha *f* (desgracia) misfortune; (infelicidad) unhappiness; **sumido en la mayor de las ~s** plunged into the deepest despair

desdichado[1] -da *adj* **1** (infeliz) unhappy; **es ~ en su matrimonio** he is unhappy in his marriage **2** (desafortunado): **aquel ~ día** that ill-fated day; **ser ~ en amores** to be unlucky in love

desdichado[2] -da *m,f*: **es un pobre ~** he's a poor unfortunate wretch

desdoblamiento *m* **1** (Ópt) splitting **2** (de funciones) splitting, dividing; **sufre ~ de la personalidad** he suffers from a split personality

desdoblar [A1] *vt*

A ‹*servilleta/pañuelo*› to unfold

B **1** ‹*imagen*› to split **2** ‹*función/cargo*› to split, divide

■ **desdoblarse** *v pron* to divide into two, split into two

deseable *adj* desirable

desear [A1] *vt*

A ‹*suerte/éxito*› to wish; **te deseo un feliz viaje** I hope you have a good trip; **les deseamos mucha felicidad** we wish them every happiness; **no se lo deseo a nadie** I wouldn't wish that on anybody

B (querer): **un embarazo no deseado** an unwanted pregnancy; **las tan deseadas vacaciones** the long-awaited holidays; **lo que más deseo es ...** my greatest wish is ...; **¿qué desea?** (frml) can I help you?; **¿desea el señor algo más?** (frml) would you like anything else, sir?; **si así lo desea** if you (so) wish (frml); **~ía una respuesta ahora** I would like a reply now; **~ + INF**: **el director desea verlo** (frml) the director wishes to see you (frml); **está deseando verte** he's really looking forward to seeing you; **~ QUE + SUBJ**: **¿desea que se lo envuelva?** (frml) would you like me to wrap it for you?; **estoy deseando que llegue el verano** I can't wait for summer; **estaba deseando que le dijeran que no** I was really hoping they'd say no to him; **sería de ~ que nos avisaran pronto** ideally we would like to know as soon as possible; ▸**dejar** *vt* *Sentido* **I A1**

C ‹*persona*› to desire, want

desecar [A2] *vt* ‹*terreno*› to drain; ‹*alimentos/flores*› to dry

desechable *adj* ‹*envases/pañales*› disposable; **la idea no es totalmente ~** the idea shouldn't be rejected *o* dismissed out of hand

desechar [A1] *vt* **1** ‹*ayuda/idea/propuesta*› to reject; **~ los malos pensamientos** to banish wicked thoughts from one's mind; **desechó la idea de ir** he abandoned *o* gave up the idea of going **2** ‹*restos/residuos*› to throw away *o* out; ‹*ropa*› to throw out

desecho *m* (despojo) waste; **materiales de ~** waste materials

Compuestos

- **desechos industriales** *mpl* industrial waste
- **desechos militares** *mpl* (CS) army surplus
- **desechos nucleares/radiactivos** *mpl* nuclear/radioactive waste

desembalar [A1] *vt* ‹*vajilla/libros*› to unpack; ‹*paquete*› to unwrap

desembarazarse [A4] *v pron* **~ DE algo/algn** to get rid OF sth/sb

desembarcar [A2] *vi* (de barco, avión) «*pasajeros*» to disembark; «*tropas*» to land, disembark

■ **desembarcar** *vt* ‹*mercancías*› to unload; ‹*pasajeros*› to disembark; (en emergencia) to evacuate

desembarco *m* (de pasajeros) disembarkation; (de tropas) landing

desembarque *m* **1** (de pasajeros) disembarkation; (en emergencia) evacuation **2** (de carga) disembarkation, landing

desembocadura *f* mouth, estuary

desembocar [A2] *vi* **1** **~ EN algo** ‹*en mar/río*› to flow INTO sth; ‹*en calle*› to come out ONTO sth; ‹*en plaza*› to come out INTO sth **2** «*situación/crisis*» **~ EN algo** to culminate IN sth

desembolsar [A1] *vt* to spend, pay out

desembolso *m* expenditure; (gasto inicial) outlay; **no estoy en condiciones de hacer ese ~** I can't afford to pay out that sort of money

desembragar [A3] *vi* to let out *o* release the clutch

desembuchar [A1] *vt* **1** «*ave*» to regurgitate **2** (fam) (revelar) to come clean about (colloq)

■ **desembuchar** *vi* (fam) to come clean (colloq); **¡vamos, desembucha! ¿dónde lo escondiste?** come on, out with it! where did you hide it?

desempacar [A2] *vt/vi* (esp AmL) to unpack

desempañar [A1] *vt* (con aire) to defog (AmE), to demist (BrE); (manualmente) to wipe

desempaquetar [A1] *vt* to unwrap

desempatar [A1] *vi* **1** (Dep) to break the tie (AmE), to break the deadlock (BrE); **lanzarán penaltys para ~** the game will be decided on penalties **2** (en una votación) to break the deadlock

desempate *m* **1** (Dep): **el ~ se produjo en el minuto 36** the breakthrough came in the 36th minute; **un partido de ~** a decider; **~ a penaltys** penalty shoot-out **2** (en concurso) tiebreak, tiebreaker; (en una votación) run-off

desempeñar [A1] *vt*

A **1** (Teatr) ‹*papel*› to play **2** ‹*funciones*› to carry out, perform; ‹*cargo*› to hold; **desempeña las funciones de asesor** he acts as a consultant; **la función que desempeñan los pulmones** the function of the lungs; **el papel que desempeñó en las negociaciones** the role he played *o* performed in the negotiations

B ‹*joyas/reloj*› to redeem

■ **desempeñarse** *v pron* (AmL): **se desempeña bien en su trabajo** she does her job well; **veamos cómo se desempeña** let's see how he makes out; **se desempeñó muy bien** she did *o* managed very well

desempeño *m* **1** (de función): **es muy diligente en el ~ de sus funciones** he carries out *o* performs his duties very diligently; **durante el ~ de su cargo** during his/her time at his/her job **2** (AmL) (actuación) performance; **su ~ como presidente** his performance as president

desempleado -da *m,f*: **un ~** someone who is out of work *o* unemployed; **el número de ~s** the number of people unemployed *o* out of work; **descuentos para ~s** reductions for the unemployed

desempleo *m* 1 (situación) unemployment; **nivel de ~** level of unemployment 2 (subsidio) unemployment benefit; **cobrar el (subsidio de) ~** to receive unemployment benefit

desempolvar [A1] *vt* ‹*libros*› to dig out, dust off; ‹*ideas/proyectos*› to revive, resurrect

desencadenamiento *m* triggering

desencadenar [A1] *vt* 1 ‹*crisis/protesta/reacción*› to trigger 2 ‹*perro*› to unleash, let … off the leash; ‹*preso*› to unchain, unshackle

■ **desencadenarse** *v pron* «*explosión/reacción*» to be triggered off; «*guerra*» to break out; «*tempestad*» to break; **se desencadenó una ola de protestas** a storm of protests erupted

desencajado -da *adj* 1 ‹*pieza*› out of position; **el cajón está ~** the drawer is off its runners 2 ‹*mandíbula/rótula*› dislocated 3 (alterado) shaken; **me dio la noticia con el rostro ~** he looked shaken when he told me the news

desencajar [A1] *vt* 1 (Mec) to knock out of position 2 ‹*mandíbula/rótula*› to dislocate

■ **desencajarse** *v pron* 1 (Mec) to be knocked/come out of position 2 «*mandíbula/rótula*» to become/get dislocated

desencaminado -da *adj* (AmL) ▸ **descaminado**

desencantar [A1] *vt* (decepcionar) to disillusion

■ **desencantarse** *v pron* to become disillusioned *o* disenchanted

desencanto *m* disillusionment, disenchantment

desenchufar [A1] *vt* to unplug, disconnect

desencontrarse [A10] *v pron* (CS) to miss each other

desencuentro *m* (falta de coordinación) mix-up; (desavenencia) misunderstanding, disagreement

desenfadado -da *adj* 1 (seguro de sí mismo) self-assured, confident; (sin inhibiciones) uninhibited 2 ‹*estilo/moda/actitud*› free-and-easy, carefree

desenfado *m* 1 (seguridad en sí mismo) self-assurance, confidence; (falta de inhibiciones) lack of inhibition 2 (de estilo, moda): **visten con gran ~** they are very free and easy in the way they dress

desenfocado -da *adj* out of focus

desenfrenado -da *adj* ‹*pasión*› unbridled; ‹*baile/ritmo*› frenzied; **a un ritmo ~** at a hectic *o* frenetic pace; **sus ansias desenfrenadas de éxito** his intense *o* burning desire to succeed

desenfreno *m*: **bailaban con ~** they danced with wild abandon; **una vida de ~** a wild life

desenfundar [A1] *vt* to draw

desenganchar [A1] *vt*

A ‹*caballos/remolque*› to unhitch; ‹*vagones*› to uncouple

B (Chi) ‹*auto*› to take … out of gear, put … in neutral

■ **desengancharse** *v pron* (arg) to come off drugs, kick the habit (sl); **~se DE algo** to come off sth

desengañar [A1] *vt* (decepcionar) to disillusion; (sacar del engaño, error): **hay que ~lo, no lo van a llamar** we must get him to face facts, they aren't going to call him

■ **desengañarse** *v pron* 1 (decepcionarse) **~se DE algo** to become disillusioned WITH *o* ABOUT sth 2 (salir del engaño, error): **desengáñate, no vas a conseguir ese puesto** stop kidding yourself, you're not going to get that job (colloq)

desengaño *m* disappointment; **me llevé un ~ cuando me enteré de la verdad** it was a big disappointment when I found out the truth; **sufrió un ~ amoroso** she had an unhappy love affair

desengarzar [A4] *vt* (Col, Ven) to unhook

desengranar [A1] *vt* (AmL) to take … out of gear, put … in neutral

desengrasar [A1] *vt* to remove the grease from

desenlace *m* (de película, libro) ending; (Lit) denouement; **el trágico ~ de su aventura** the tragic outcome of their adventure

desenmarañar [A1] *vt* ‹*pelo/madeja*› to untangle, disentangle; ‹*asunto/embrollo*› to straighten out, sort out

desenmascarar [A1] *vt* ‹*bandido/encapuchado*› to unmask; ‹*estafador/culpable*› to expose, unmask

desenredar [A1] *vt* ‹*pelo/lana*› to untangle, disentangle; ‹*lío*› to straighten out, sort out

■ **desenredarse** *v pron* (*refl*): **~se el pelo** to get the knots out of one's hair

desenrollar [A1] *vt* ‹*alfombra/póster*› to unroll; ‹*persiana*› to let down; ‹*ovillo/cuerda*› to unwind

■ **desenrollarse** *v pron* «*alfombra/póster*» to unroll, come unrolled; «*ovillo/cuerda*» to unwind, come unwound

desenroscar [A2] *vt* to unscrew

desensillar [A1] *vt* to unsaddle

desentenderse [E8] *v pron* **~ DE algo** ‹*de un asunto*› to wash one's hands OF sth; **tú siempre te desentiendes de estos problemas** you never want to have anything to do with these problems; **se desentiende de los hijos** he doesn't take an interest in the children

desentendido -da *m,f*: **se hizo el ~** (pretendió — no concernirle) he acted as if it had nothing to do with him; (— ignorar) he pretended not to notice

desenterrar [A5] *vt* 1 ‹*cadáver*› to exhume, dig up; ‹*hueso/tesoro*› to unearth, dig up 2 ‹*recuerdo/rencor*› to rake up, dig up

desentonar [A1] *vi* 1 (Mús) to go out of tune *o* off key 2 «*color*» to clash; **~ CON algo** to clash WITH sth 3 «*atuendo/comentario*» to be out of place

desentrañar [A1] *vt* ‹*misterio*› to unravel, get to the bottom of; ‹*significado/sentido*› to decipher, work out

desentrenado -da *adj* out of condition *o* training

desentumecer [E3] *vt* ‹*músculos*› to loosen up; ‹*piernas*› to stretch

desenvainar [A1] *vt* to unsheathe, draw

desenvoltura *f*: **se maneja con ~** she conducts herself in a relaxed and natural manner; **respondió con mucha ~ a las preguntas** he replied to the questions with great self-assurance

desenvolver [E11] *vt* to unwrap, open

■ **desenvolverse** *v pron* 1 «*persona*»: **se desenvuelve muy bien en el trabajo** she copes very well with her work; **se desenvuelve con soltura en inglés y español** she speaks English and Spanish fluently; **se desenvolvió bien en la entrevista** he performed well in the interview; **no sabrán ~se en la vida** they won't know how to get by in life 2 «*hechos/sucesos*» to develop; **la conferencia se desenvolvió sin incidentes** the conference took place without incident

desenvolvimiento *m*

A (de persona) ease, self-assurance

B (de un acto, acontecimiento) development

desenvuelto -ta *adj* ‹*persona*› self-assured, confident; **es muy desenvuelta y puede viajar sola** she's quite capable of traveling on her own

deseo *m* 1 (anhelo) wish; **formular un ~** to make a wish; **que se cumplan todos tus ~s** may all your wishes come true; **tus ~s son órdenes para mí** (fr hecha) your wish is my command (set phrase); **~s DE algo**: **con mis mejores ~s de felicidad/éxito** wishing you every happiness/success; **ardía en ~s de verla** (liter) he had a burning desire to see her 2 (apetito sexual) desire

deseoso -sa *adj* **~ DE algo**: **un niño ~ de afecto** a child who is longing for affection; **~ DE + INF** eager TO + INF; **estaba ~ de salir a la calle** he was longing to get out; **~ DE QUE + SUBJ**: **estaba ~ de que volvieses** I couldn't wait for you to get back

desequilibrado -da *adj* ‹*rueda/mecanismo*› out of balance; ‹*persona*› unbalanced

desequilibrar [A1] *vt* 1 ‹*embarcación/vehículo*› to unbalance, make … unbalanced; ‹*persona*› (físicamente) to throw … off balance; (mentalmente) to unbalance 2 ‹*fuerzas/poder*› to upset the balance of

■ **desequilibrarse** *v pron* «*ruedas/mecanismo*» to get out of balance

desequilibrio *m* 1 (desigualdad) imbalance; **el ~ de la balanza de pagos** the balance of payments deficit/surplus 2 (Psic) unbalanced state of mind

deserción *f* (Mil) desertion; (de partido) defection

(Compuesto) **deserción escolar** (CS) *leaving school before the legal age*

desertar [A1] *vi* (Mil) to desert; (de partido) to defect

desértico -ca *adj* 1 (Geog) ‹*zona/clima*› desert (*before n*) 2 (vacío, despoblado) deserted

desertización *f* desertification

desertizar [A4] *vt* to turn into desert

desertor -tora *m,f* (Mil) deserter; (de un partido) defector

desesperación *f* 1 (angustia) desperation; **me vino una ~ terrible** I got desperate; **CON ~** ▸**desesperadamente**; **llorar DE ~** to cry OUT OF desperation 2 (desesperanza) despair 3 (exasperación): **¡qué ~ estos trenes!** these trains drive you mad!

desesperadamente *adv* ‹*luchar/gritar*› desperately; ‹*mirar/suplicar*› despairingly; ‹*llorar*› bitterly

desesperado[1] **-da** *adj* desperate; **en un intento ~ por salvarse** in a desperate attempt to save himself; **miraba ~ cómo se hundía** he looked on in desperation as it sank; **estaba ~ de dolor** he was in excruciating pain; ***a la desesperada*** in desperation

desesperado[2] **-da** *m,f*: **corrió como un ~** he ran like crazy (colloq)

desesperante *adj* 1 (exasperante) exasperating 2 (angustioso) distressing

desesperanzador -dora *adj* bleak

desesperar [A1] *vt* to drive ... to distraction *o* despair; **me desespera que nunca me haga caso** it's exasperating the way she never takes any notice of me

■ **desesperar** *vi* to despair, give up hope; **~ DE algo** to despair *o* give up hope OF sth

■ **desesperarse** *v pron* to become exasperated; **se desespera (de) ver que va tan lento** it exasperates him to see it going so slowly

desespero *m* (AmS) ▸**desesperación**

desestabilización *f* destabilization

desestabilizador -dora *adj* destabilizing

desestabilizar [A4] *vt* to destabilize

desestimar [A1] *vt* (frml) ‹*propuesta/recurso*› to reject; ‹*pruebas*› to disallow

desexilio *m* (CS) 1 (vuelta) return from exile 2 (readaptación) readaptation (*to one's native country after exile*)

desfachatez *f* audacity, nerve (colloq)

desfalcar [A2] *vt* to embezzle

desfalco *m* embezzlement

desfallecer [E3] *vi* 1 (flaquear) «*persona*» to become weak; «*fuerzas*» to fade, fail; **sintió ~ su ánimo** she felt her spirits falling *o* flagging; **lucharon sin ~** they fought tirelessly 2 (desmayarse) to faint, pass out; **desfallecía de agotamiento/hambre** he was faint with exhaustion/hunger

desfallecimiento *m* 1 (debilitación): **en un estado de ~** in a very weak state 2 (pérdida del conocimiento) faint; **sufrió un ~** he fainted, he passed out

desfasado -da *adj* 1 (Fís) out of phase; ‹*mecanismo/ritmo*› out of sync; ‹*planes/etapas*› out of step 2 ‹*ideas/persona*› old-fashioned

desfase *m* (Fís) phase lag; (falta de correspondencia): **existe un gran ~ ideológico entre ellos** ideologically they are totally out of phase *o* step

desfavorable *adj* ‹*circunstancia/crítica/opinión*› unfavorable*; **el tiempo nos ha sido ~** we had unfavorable weather conditions

desfavorecer [E3] *vt* 1 (perjudicar) to work against 2 (afear): **ese peinado la desfavorece** that hairstyle isn't at all flattering

desfavorecido -da *adj* 1 ‹*grupos/clases*› underprivileged, disadvantaged 2 (afeado): **salió muy ~ en esa foto** that's a very bad photograph of him

desfibrilador *m* defibrillator

desfigurado -da *adj* disfigured; **un rostro ~ por el terror** a face contorted with terror

desfigurar [A1] *vt*

A ‹*persona*› to disfigure; **las quemaduras le ~on el rostro** the burns disfigured his face; **la sombra le desfiguraba las facciones** the shadow distorted her features

B ‹*hechos*› to distort, twist; ‹*realidad*› to distort

desfiguro *m* (Méx fam) silly stunt (colloq)

desfiladero *m* (barranco) ravine, narrow gorge; (puerto) narrow pass

desfilar [A1] *vi* 1 «*soldados*» to parade 2 «*manifestantes*» to march; **la manifestación desfiló por la Gran Vía** the demonstration passed along the Gran Via; **miles de turistas desfilan cada año por el museo** thousands of tourists pass through the museum every year 3 «*modelo*» to parade up and down the catwalk 4 (por la mente) to pass through

desfile *m* (de carrozas) parade, procession; (Mil) parade, march past

(Compuesto) **desfile de modelos** *or* **modas** fashion show

desfinanciar [A1] *vt* (CS) to leave ... short of funds

■ **desfinanciarse** *v pron* to run short of funds

desflorar [A1] *vt* (liter) ‹*muchacha*› to deflower (liter)

desfogar [A3] *vt* 1 ‹*ira/pasiones/frustraciones*› to vent; **~ algo CON** *or* **EN algn** to vent sth ON sb 2 (Col) ‹*cañería*› to bleed

■ **desfogarse** *v pron* to vent one's anger (*o* frustration *etc*)

desfogue *m* (Col) (de un motor) exhaust; (de una cañería) outlet

desfondarse [A1] *v pron* «*cajón/bolsa/silla*» to give way; «*jugador/corredor*» to flag

desgajar [A1] *vt* **~ algo DE algo** ‹*rama*› to break *o* snap sth OFF sth; ‹*páginas*› to tear *o* rip sth OUT OF sth

■ **desgajarse** *v pron* 1 «*rama*» to break off, snap off; **~se DE algo: se ~on del grupo** they broke away from the group 2 (fam) (Col) «*aguacero*» to pour *o* (colloq) bucket down

desgana *f* 1 (inapetencia) lack of appetite; **comer con** *or* **a ~** to eat without much appetite 2 (falta de entusiasmo): **trabajar con** *or* **a ~** to work half-heartedly *o* without much interest; **obedecer con** *or* **a ~** to obey reluctantly

desganado -da *adj* 1 (inapetente): **estoy** *or* **me siento ~** I'm not hungry 2 (apático) lethargic

desgano *m* (AmL) ▸**desgana**

desgañitarse [A1] *v pron* (fam) to shout oneself hoarse

desgarbado -da *adj* ‹*persona/aspecto*› gangling, gawky; ‹*movimientos/andar*› ungainly

desgarrador -dora *adj* heartbreaking, heartrending

desgarrar [A1] *vt* 1 ‹*vestido/papel*› to tear, rip; **el clavo le desgarró el vestido** she tore *o* ripped her dress on the nail 2 (destrozar anímicamente) ‹*corazón*› to break

■ **desgarrarse** *v pron* 1 «*vestido/camisa*» to tear, rip 2 (Med) to tear; **se desgarró un músculo** he tore a muscle

desgarriate *m* (Méx fam) 1 (desorden, desbarajuste) mess 2 (alboroto, escándalo) ruckus (AmE colloq), kerfuffle (BrE colloq); **armar un ~** to go wild *o* crazy (colloq)

desgarro *m*

A (Med) (de ligamento, músculo): **sufrió un ~** she tore a muscle; (en parto) tear; (de flema, sangre) (Chi): **tiene constantes ~s** he is constantly coughing up phlegm/blood

B (en tela) tear

desgastar [A1] *vt* 1 (gastar) ‹*suelas/ropa*› to wear out; ‹*roca*› to wear away, erode 2 (debilitar) to wear ... down

■ **desgastarse** *v pron* 1 (gastarse) «*ropa*» to wear out; «*roca*» to wear away; «*tacón*» to wear down 2 «*persona*» to wear oneself out; «*relación*» to grow stale

desgaste *m* 1 (de ropa, suelas) wear; (de rocas) erosion, wearing away 2 (debilitamiento): **~ físico** debilitation; **indicios del ~ de la dictadura** signs that the dictatorship is weakening

desglosar [A1] *vt* 1 ‹*gastos/suma*› to do a breakdown of, itemize; ‹*tema*› to break down 2 (Der) ‹*documento/hoja*› to detach, extract

desglose *m* (de cifra, suma) breakdown, itemization; (de tema) breakdown

desgracia *f*

A 1 (desdicha, infortunio) misfortune; **ha tenido muchas ~s** she's had her share of misfortunes; **tener la ~ de + INF** to have the misfortune to + INF; **bastante ~ tiene con su enfermedad** he has enough to bear with his illness; ***caer en ~*** to fall from favor *o* grace 2 **por desgracia** (*indep*) unfortunately

B (suceso adverso): **han tenido una ~ tras otra** they've had one piece of bad luck after another; **y para colmo de ~s ...** and to crown *o* cap it all ...; ***las ~s nunca vienen solas*** when it rains, it pours (AmE), it never rains but it pours (BrE)

(Compuesto) **desgracias personales** *fpl* (period) casualties (*pl*)

desgraciadamente *adv* (*indep*) unfortunately

desgraciado[1] **-da** *adj* 1 [SER] (infeliz) unhappy; **lleva una vida muy desgraciada** she leads a miserable life 2 [SER] (desafortunado) ‹*viaje*› ill-fated; **ser ~ en amores** to be unlucky in love 3 (desacertado) ‹*elección/coincidencia*› unfortunate, unwise

desgraciado[2] **-da** *m,f*
A (desdichado) wretch
B (persona vil) swine (colloq)

desgraciar [A1] *vt* (fam) (estropear) to ruin, spoil
■ **desgraciarse** *v pron* 1 (fam) (hacerse daño) to do oneself an injury (colloq) 2 (*refl*) (fam) ‹*pelo*› to ruin

desgranar [A1] *vt* ‹*habas*› to shell, pod; ‹*maíz*› to separate the kernels from

desgravable *adj* tax-deductible

desgravación *f* tax exemption (AmE), tax relief (BrE); **desgravaciones por gastos de viaje** tax deductions for traveling expenses

desgravar [A1] *vt* 1 ‹*gastos/suma*› to claim tax exemption on (AmE), to claim tax relief on (BrE); **estos bonos desgravan un 15%** these bonds qualify for 15% tax exemption (AmE) *o* (BrE) relief 2 ‹*producto/importación*› to eliminate the tax *o* duty on
■ **desgravar** *vi* to be tax-deductible

desguace *m* (de barco) scrapping, breaking up; (de avión, coche) scrapping

desguanzado -da *adj* (Méx fam) ‹*persona*› washed out (colloq); ‹*fiesta*› flat, dull

desguarnecer [E3] *vt* to withdraw the garrison *o* troops from; **la ciudad quedó desguarnecida** the city was left undefended

desguazar [A4] *vt*
A ‹*barco*› to break up, scrap; ‹*avión/coche*› to scrap
B (Ven fam) ‹*casa/pueblo*› to destroy

deshabitado -da *adj* ‹*región*› uninhabited; ‹*edificio*› empty, unoccupied

deshabituarse [A18] *v pron* to get out of the habit; **~ A + INF** to get out of the habit OF -ING; **estoy deshabituada a este horario** I'm not used to this schedule any more

deshacer [E18] *vt*
A 1 ‹*costura/bordado*› to unpick 2 ‹*nudo/lazo*› to undo, untie; ‹*ovillo*› to unwind; ‹*trenza*› to undo; **el viento me deshizo el peinado** the wind ruined *o* messed up my hair
B 1 (desarmar, desmontar) ‹*maqueta/mecanismo*› to take ... apart; ‹*paquete*› to undo, unwrap 2 ‹*cama*› (para cambiarla) to strip; (desordenar) to mess up; ‹*maleta*› to unpack
C 1 (derretir) ‹*nieve/helado*› to melt 2 (desmenuzar) to break up
D 1 (destrozar, estropear): **la lejía te deshace las manos** bleach ruins your hands; **tengo los nervios deshechos** my nerves are in shreds; **la muerte de su hijo le deshizo la vida** her life was shattered by the death of her son; **la guerra deshizo el país** the war tore the country apart 2 ‹*ejército*› to rout, crush; ‹*contrincante*› to thrash (colloq); **aquella derrota lo deshizo moralmente** he was shattered by that defeat 3 (fam) (cansar, agotar) to wear ... out
E ‹*acuerdo/trato*› to break; ‹*noviazgo*› to break off; ‹*sociedad*› to dissolve; ‹*planes/compromiso*› to cancel
■ **deshacerse** *v pron*
A «*dobladillo/costura*» to come undone *o* unstitched; «*nudo*» to come undone *o* untied; «*trenza/moño*» to come undone; «*peinado*» to get messed up, be ruined
B 1 (desintegrarse) to disintegrate; **cocina las verduras hasta que se deshacen** she cooks the vegetables until they are *o* go mushy; **dejar ~se en la boca** allow it to dissolve in your mouth 2 (destruirse): **el vaso se cayó y se deshizo** the glass fell and smashed 3 «*nieve/helado*» to melt 4 «*sociedad*» to dissolve
C (desvivirse) **~se POR algn/algo**: **me deshago por complacerla** I go out of my way to please her
D **~se EN algo**: **~se en llanto** *or* **lágrimas** to dissolve into tears; **me deshice en cumplidos** I went out of my way to be complimentary
E **deshacerse de** 1 (librarse de) to get rid of; **logró ~se de sus perseguidores** he managed to shake off *o* lose his pursuers 2 (desprenderse de) to part with

deshaga, deshagas, etc *see* **deshacer**

desharrapado -da *adj* ragged; **andar ~** to be shabbily dressed *o* dressed in rags

deshecho -cha *adj* [ESTAR] 1 (cansado, agotado) exhausted; **llega ~ del trabajo** he's exhausted when he gets back from work 2 (destrozado moralmente) shattered, devastated; **quedó ~ con la noticia** he was shattered *o* devastated by the news 3 (estropeado) ruined

deshelar [A5] *vt* ‹*cañería*› to thaw out, unfreeze; ‹*nevera/congelador*› to defrost; ‹*parabrisas*› to deice
■ **deshelarse** *v pron* «*hielo*» to melt; «*nieves*» to thaw, melt; «*río/lago*» to thaw; «*relaciones*» to thaw

desheredado -da *m,f*: **los ~s** the dispossessed

desheredar [A1] *vt* to disinherit

deshice, deshiciera, etc *see* **deshacer**

deshidratación *f* 1 (Med) dehydration 2 (de alimentos) drying, dehydration

deshidratar [A1] *vt* ‹*persona*› to dehydrate; ‹*piel*› to dry up, dehydrate; ‹*alimentos*› to dehydrate, dry
■ **deshidratarse** *v pron* to become dehydrated

deshielo *m* 1 (de ríos, nieves) thaw; **agua de ~** meltwater 2 (de relaciones) thaw, thawing-out

deshilacharse [A1] *v pron* to fray

deshilvanado -da *adj* ‹*discurso/narración*› disjointed

deshilvanar [A1] *vt* to take out *o* remove the basting (AmE) *o* (BrE) the tacking from

deshinchar [A1] *vt* (Esp) ▸ **desinflar**
■ **deshincharse** *v pron* 1 «*pies/tobillos*»: **se le ~on los tobillos** the swelling in her ankles has gone down 2 (Esp) ▸ **desinflarse**

deshizo *see* **deshacer**

deshojar [A1] *vt* ‹*flor*› to pull the petals off; ‹*cuaderno*› to tear *o* rip the pages out of

deshollinador -dora *m,f* 1 (persona) chimney sweep 2 **deshollinador** *m* (escoba) chimney brush

deshollinar [A1] *vt* to sweep

deshonestidad *f* (falta de honestidad) dishonesty

deshonesto -ta *adj* 1 (tramposo, mentiroso) dishonest 2 (indecente) ‹*proposiciones*› improper, indecent; ▸ **abuso**

deshonor *m* ▸ **deshonra 1**

deshonra *f* 1 (vergüenza) dishonor* (frml); **ese chico es una ~ para su familia** that boy is a disgrace to his family 2 (pérdida de la honra) dishonor*

deshonrar [A1] *vt* ‹*familia/patria*› to dishonor*, disgrace; ‹*mujer*› to dishonor*

deshonroso -sa *adj* dishonorable*, disgraceful

deshora: **a ~(s)** off hours (AmE), out of hours (BrE)

deshuesadero *m* (Méx) scrapyard

deshuesar [A1] *vt*
A 1 ‹*aceitunas*› to pit 2 ‹*pollo*› to bone
B (Méx) ▸ **desguazar A**

deshumanizar [A4] *vt* to dehumanize

desidia *f* 1 (apatía) slackness, indolence (frml); **no soporto su ~** I can't stand his lax *o* slack attitude; **la ~ que lo invadió** the feeling of total apathy which took hold of him 2 (desaseo) slovenliness

desidioso -sa *adj* ‹*empleado/actitud*› slack, lax; ‹*aspecto*› slovenly

desierto[1] **-ta** *adj*
A ‹*lugar*› deserted; **en verano Madrid se queda ~** Madrid is deserted in summer
B (frml) ‹*premio/vacante*›: **el premio fue declarado ~** the prize was not awarded; **la vacante quedó desierta** the vacancy remained unfilled

desierto[2] *m* desert; ***predicar*** *or* ***clamar en el ~*** to preach in the wilderness

designación *f* (frml) 1 (de persona) appointment, designation (frml); **fueron nombrados mediante libre ~** they were appointed without having to sit competitive exams 2 (de fecha, lugar): **la ~ de la fecha/lugar para la reunión** the fixing of a date/place for the meeting

designar [A1] *vt*
A (frml) (elegir) 1 ‹*persona*› to appoint, designate (frml) 2 ‹*lugar/fecha*› to fix, set; (con carácter oficial) to designate; **fue designada como sede de los próximos Juegos Olímpicos** it was designated as the venue for the next Olympics
B (frml) (denominar): **designamos estos productos con nom-**

bres ingleses we give these products English names; **el punto que ~emos B** the point which we will call *o* (frml) designate B; **el proyecto fue designado con el nombre de 'Galaxia'** the project was named *o* (frml) designated 'Galaxy'

designio *m* plan; **los ~s del Señor son inescrutables** God moves in mysterious ways

desigual *adj*
A **1** (diferente): **las mangas quedaron ~es** one sleeve turned out longer (*o* wider *etc*) than the other; **reciben un trato muy ~** they are treated very differently **2** (desequilibrado) ‹*lucha*› unequal; ‹*fuerzas*› unevenly-matched
B (irregular) ‹*terreno/superficie*› uneven; ‹*letra*› uneven, irregular; ‹*calidad*› variable, varying (*before n*); ‹*rendimiento*› inconsistent, erratic

desigualar [A1] *vt* (Dep) ‹*partido*› to alter *o* change the balance of; **~on el marcador con un penalty** their penalty broke the scoreboard stalemate
■ **desigualar** *vi* to pull ahead

desigualdad *f*
A **1** (diferencia) inequality; **no debería existir ~ ante la ley** everyone should be equal before the law **2** (desequilibrio) inequality, disparity
B (de superficie) unevenness
C (Mat) inequality

desilusión *f* (decepción) disappointment; **¡qué ~!** what a disappointment!, how disappointing!; **se llevó una ~** she was disappointed

desilusionado -da *adj* (decepcionado) disappointed; **~ CON algo/algn** disappointed WITH sth/sb

desilusionar [A1] *vt* to disappoint; **el libro me desilusionó** I found the book disappointing
■ **desilusionarse** *v pron* (decepcionarse) to be disappointed; (perder las ilusiones) to become disillusioned

desincentivo *m* (para el comercio, la empresa) disincentive; (para la corrupción, un delincuente) deterrent

desinencia *f* ending, desinence (tech)

desinfección *f* disinfection

desinfectante *m* disinfectant

desinfectar [A1] *vt* to disinfect

desinflar [A1] *vt* ‹*globo/balón/neumático*› to let the air out of, to deflate, let down (esp BrE)
■ **desinflarse** *v pron* «*globo/balón/neumático*» to deflate, go down

desinformación *f* (falta de información) disinformation; (información erronea) misinformation

desinformado -da *adj* [ESTAR] (sin información) lacking in information; (mal informado) misinformed

desinhibición *f* lack of inhibition; **habló con ~** she spoke with a total lack of inhibition

desinhibido -da *adj* uninhibited

desintegración *f* **1** (de grupo, partido) disintegration, breakup; (de familia) breakup **2** (de estructura) disintegration; **la ~ del átomo** the splitting of the atom

desintegrarse [A1] *v pron* **1** «*grupo/partido*» to break up, disintegrate; «*familia*» to break up **2** «*cuerpo/materia*» to break up, disintegrate; «*átomo*» to split, disintegrate

desinterés *m* (falta de interés) lack of interest; (altruismo) unselfishness

desinteresadamente *adj* unselfishly, selflessly (frml)

desinteresado -da *adj* ‹*consejo/ayuda*› disinterested; ‹*persona*› selfless

desinteresarse [A1] *v pron* (perder interés) to lose interest; **~ DE algo** to lose interest IN sth

desintoxicación *f* detoxification

desintoxicar [A2] *vt* to detoxify
■ **desintoxicarse** *v pron* to undergo detoxification; **necesito irme al campo para ~me** I need to go out into the countryside to clean out my system

desistir [I1] *vi* to give up; **no ~ía en su empeño** he would not give up the pursuit of his objective; **~ DE algo** ‹*de propósito*› to give up sth, desist FROM sth (frml); ‹*de demanda/derecho*› to relinquish sth; **~ DE + INF** to give up -ING, desist FROM -ING (frml)

deslavazado -da *adj* ‹*tela/vestido*› limp; ‹*discurso/argumento*› disjointed, rambling (*before n*); ‹*persona*› dull, colorless*

desleal *adj* [SER] disloyal, untrue (liter); **~ CON** *or* **A algn/algo** disloyal TO sb/sth

deslealtad *f* disloyalty

desleído -da *adj* ‹*discurso*› weak

desleír [I18] *vt* ‹*sólido*› to dissolve; ‹*líquido*› to dilute

deslenguado -da *adj* foulmouthed

desligado -da *adj* (distanciado): **está ~ de su familia** he isn't very close to his family; **estar ~ de algo** to be cut off from sth

desligar [A3] *vt* **1** (separar) to separate; **hay que ~ el punto de vista económico del social** economic considerations should not be confused with social ones **2** (alejar, apartar) **~ a algn DE algn/algo** to cut sb off FROM sb/sth **3** (librar) **~ a algn DE algo** to free sb FROM sth
■ **desligarse** *v pron* **1** (librarse) **~se DE algo** ‹*de obligaciones*› to free oneself OF sth; **compromisos sociales de los que no puede ~se** social commitments which she cannot get out of **2** (apartarse) **~se DE algo/algn** to cut oneself off FROM sth/sb

deslindar [A1] *vt* **1** ‹*terrenos*› to demarcate, mark the boundaries of **2** (separar) ‹*ideas/conceptos*› to separate; **~ algo DE algo**: **no se puede ~ este problema de la situación económica** this problem cannot be viewed in isolation from the economic situation **3** (definir) ‹*campo de acción*› to define the bounds of; **la dificultad de ~ responsabilidades en este asunto** the difficulty of determining responsibility in this matter

desliz *m* **1** (error, falta) slip **2** (al hablar) gaffe, faux pas **3** (ant *o* hum) (aventurilla) indiscretion (dated *or* hum)

deslizador *m* (Méx) (ala delta) hang glider

deslizamiento *m* glide, gliding; **engrase sus esquís para un mejor ~** wax your skis so that they slide more easily *o* run more smoothly
(Compuesto) **deslizamiento de tierras** landslide

deslizar [A4] *vt* (hacer resbalar) to slip, slide; **lo deslizó por debajo de la puerta** he slipped *o* slid it under the door; **le deslizó una nota en la mano** she slipped a note into his hand
■ **deslizarse** *v pron*
A **1** «*patinador/bailarines*» to glide; «*esquiador*» to ski, slide; «*serpiente*» to slither, glide; **~se POR algo** to slide down sth; **una lágrima se deslizó por su mejilla** a tear slid down his cheek **2** «*barco/cisne*» to glide; **~se SOBRE algo** to glide OVER sth **3** «*cajón/argollas de cortina*» to slide **4** «*agua/arroyo*» to flow gently **5** (escurrirse, escaparse) to slip away; **se deslizó por la puerta trasera** he slipped out (by) the back door
B (liter) (transcurrir) to slip by

deslocalización *f* relocation (to a low-pay labor* market)

deslocalizar [A4] *vt* to relocate … to a low-pay labor* market

deslomar [A1] *vt* (fam) to wear … out, do … in (colloq); **~ a algn a patadas** to kick sb's head in (colloq)
■ **deslomarse** *v pron* (agotarse) to break one's back (colloq)

deslucido -da *adj* ‹*actuación/desfile*› dull, lackluster*; ‹*colores/paredes*› faded, drab; ‹*plata*› tarnished

deslucir [I5] *vt* ‹*actuación/desfile*› to spoil; ‹*colores/cortinas*› to fade, cause … to fade; **el polvo deslucía los muebles** the dust made the furniture look dull

deslumbrante, deslumbrador -dora *adj* ‹*luz*› blinding; ‹*belleza*› dazzling, stunning

deslumbrar [A1] *vt* to dazzle

deslustrado -da *adj* ‹*vidrio*› ground, frosted; ‹*metal*› tarnished; ‹*zapatos*› unpolished

desmadejado -da *adj* (fam) worn out (colloq), exhausted

desmadrarse [A1] *v pron* (fam) «*persona*» to go wild (colloq), to get out of hand

desmadre *m* (fam) chaos; **fue el ~ total** it was complete chaos; **la fiesta fue un ~** the party was really wild

desmalezar [A4] *vt* (AmL) to weed

desmán *m*
A (exceso, abuso) outrage, excess; **los desmanes cometidos durante la guerra** the excesses *o* outrages committed during the war; **los desmanes de los hinchas** the disorderly (*o* violent *etc*) behavior of the fans
B (Zool) desman

desmanchar [A1] *vt* (AmL) to get the stains out of

d

desmandarse [A1] *v pron* «*niños/tropas*» to get out of control *o* hand; **no se le desmanda ningún alumno** none of his pupils dares disobey him; **el caballo se le desmandó** he lost control of the horse

desmano: **a ~** (*loc adv*) ‹*estar/quedar*› out of the way; **me pilla a ~** it's out of my way

desmantelamiento *m* dismantling

desmantelar [A1] *vt* 1 ‹*fortificación*› to dismantle; ‹*stand/escenario*› to take down, dismantle; **le ~on la casa/el coche** they stripped his house/car 2 ‹*organización*› to dismantle 3 ‹*barco*› (desarbolar) to dismast; (desaparejar) to unrig

desmañado -da *adj* clumsy, awkward

desmaquillador, desmaquillante *m* makeup remover

desmaquillarse [A1] *v pron* to remove one's makeup; **~ los ojos** to remove one's eye makeup

desmarcado -da *adj* unmarked

desmarcarse [A2] *v pron* 1 (Dep) to slip the coverage (AmE), to slip one's marker (BrE) 2 (apartarse) **~se DE algo/algn** to dissociate oneself FROM sth/sb

desmayado -da *adj* ‹*persona*› unconscious (*from having fainted*); **estaba ~ de hambre** (fam) he was faint with hunger

desmayar [A1] *vi* to lose heart, become demoralized

▪ **desmayarse** *v pron* to faint

desmayo *m* 1 (Med) faint; **sufrir un ~** to faint 2 **sin ~** ‹*luchar/trabajar*› resolutely, tirelessly

desmedido -da *adj* excessive; **le han dado una importancia desmedida** they have attributed too much importance to it

desmedirse [I14] *v pron* to go too far; **~ EN algo** to go too far WITH sth; **se desmidió en la bebida** she drank too much, she had too much to drink

desmejorado -da *adj* 1 (de salud): **lo encontré muy ~** he didn't look at all well to me; **me apenó verla tan desmejorada** it was sad to see her looking so unwell 2 (de atractivo): **está desmejorada** she's lost her looks

desmejoramiento *m* (de la salud) decline; (de la economía) decline, deterioration; (en las relaciones) worsening, deterioration

desmejorar [A1] *vi* 1 (de salud) to get worse, to deteriorate; **sigue desmejorando** she's getting worse 2 (de atractivo) to lose one's looks

▪ **desmejorar** *vt* 1 ‹*salud/enfermo*› (debilitar) to weaken; (empeorar) to make … worse 2 (de atractivo) to make … look less attractive

desmelenado -da *adj* disheveled*

desmembración *f* (de partido) breakup; (de país) dismemberment; (de imperio) dismemberment, dismantling

desmembrar [A5] *vt* ‹*partido*› to break up; ‹*país*› to tear … apart; ‹*imperio*› to dismember, dismantle

desmemoriado -da *adj* forgetful, absent-minded

desmentido *m* denial; **publicar un ~** to issue a denial

desmentir [I11] *vt* ‹*noticia/rumor*› to deny; ‹*acusación*› to deny, refute

desmenuzar [A4] *vt* ‹*pescado*› to flake; ‹*pollo*› to shred; ‹*pan*› to crumble

desmerecer [E3] *vi*: **el cuadro desmerece con ese marco** that frame doesn't do the painting justice; **no ~ DE algo** to compare favorably WITH sth; **su voz no desmerece de la de los mejores tenores** his voice compares favorably with the best tenors

desmesura *f* (liter) lack of moderation

desmesuradamente *adv*: **~ grande** enormously big; **me miró con los ojos ~ abiertos** he looked at me, eyes wide open

desmesurado -da *adj* (enorme) vast, enormous; (excesivo, exagerado) excessive; **una ambición desmesurada** an excessive ambition

desmigajarse [A1] *v pron* to crumble

desmilitarización *f* demilitarization

desmilitarizar [A4] *vt* to demilitarize

desmirriado -da *adj* (fam) puny, weedy (colloq)

desmitificación *f* demystification (frml)

desmitificar [A2] *vt* to demystify, destroy the myths surrounding

desmontable *adj* 1 (desarmable) ‹*mecanismo/mueble*› which can be dismantled *o* taken apart 2 (separable) ‹*forro/pieza*› detachable, removable 3 ‹*remolque*› demountable

desmontar [A1] *vt* 1 (desarmar) ‹*mueble/mecanismo*› to dismantle, take apart; ‹*motor/rifle*› to strip (down); ‹*tienda de campaña*› to take down 2 (separar) ‹*forro/pieza*› to detach, remove

▪ **desmontar** *vi* «*jinete*» to dismount

desmoralización *f* demoralization

desmoralizador -dora *adj* demoralizing, disheartening

desmoralizar [A4] *vt* to demoralize, dishearten

▪ **desmoralizarse** *v pron* to get demoralized *o* disheartened, to lose heart

desmoronamiento *m* (derrumbamiento) collapse; (de fe, moral) breakdown

desmoronarse [A1] *v pron* 1 «*muro/edificio*» to collapse; «*imperio/sociedad*» to crumble, collapse 2 «*fe/moral*» to crumble; **se desmoronó física y psicológicamente** she went to pieces completely

desmotivado -da *adj* demotivated

desmovilización *f* demobilization

desmovilizar [A4] *vt* to demobilize

desnacionalización *f* privatization, denationalization

desnacionalizar [A4] *vt* to privatize, denationalize

desnatado -da *adj* (Esp) skimmed

desnaturalizado -da *adj* 1 ‹*aceite/vino*› denatured 2 ‹*madre*› unnatural

desnivel *m*

A (en superficie) 1 (irregularidad) unevenness, irregularity; **es un terreno lleno de ~es** it is a very uneven piece of land; **un ~ entre la cocina y el comedor** a difference in floor level between the kitchen and the dining room 2 (inclinación, pendiente) slope, incline (frml); **la mesa está en ~** the table is not level 3 (depresión) drop (*in the level of the ground*)

B (diferencia) difference, disparity

desnivelado -da *adj* 1 (irregular) ‹*terreno*› uneven 2 (fuera de nivel): **la mesa/la repisa está desnivelada** the table/shelf isn't level

desnivelar [A1] *vt*

A ‹*balanza*› to tip

B ‹*presupuesto/situación*› to upset

desnucarse [A2] *v pron* to break one's neck

desnuclearización *f* denuclearization

desnuclearizar [A4] *vt* to denuclearize; **zona desnuclearizada** nuclear-free zone

desnudar [A1] *vt* (desvestir) to undress

▪ **desnudarse** *v pron* (*refl*) (desvestirse) to undress, take one's clothes off; **se desnudó delante de todos** he stripped (off) *o* undressed in front of everyone; **~se de (la) cintura para arriba** to strip to the waist

desnudez *f*

A (de persona) nakedness, nudity; **consideran la ~ como algo natural** they consider nudity as something natural

B (de habitación, árbol, paisaje) bareness

desnudo[1] -da *adj*

A 1 (sin ropa) ‹*persona*› naked; **le gusta nadar ~** he likes swimming in the nude; **totalmente ~** stark naked; **~ de la cintura para arriba** naked to the waist 2 (descubierto) ‹*hombros/brazos/torso*› bare; **con los pies ~s** barefoot 3 (liter) ‹*espada*› naked (liter)

B 1 (sin adornos, aditamentos) ‹*pared/cuarto*› bare; **la verdad desnuda** the naked *o* plain truth; **no perceptible al ojo ~** not visible to the naked eye 2 ‹*árbol/paisaje*› bare

C **al desnudo**: **la verdad al ~** the truth plain and simple; **el cable quedó al ~** the wire was left bare *o* exposed

desnudo[2] *m* (Art) nude; **un ~ de mujer** a female nude

desnutrición *f* malnutrition, undernourishment

desnutrido -da *adj* malnourished, undernourished

desobedecer [E3] *vt/vi* to disobey

desobediencia *f* disobedience

(Compuesto) **desobediencia civil** civil disobedience

desobediente *adj* disobedient

desocupación *f*
A (desempleo) unemployment
B (desalojo) clearing

desocupado -da *adj*
A (vacío, libre) ‹*casa/habitación*› unoccupied, vacant; **¿está ~ este asiento?** is this seat free?
B (ocioso): **pasa mucho tiempo ~** he spends a lot of time doing nothing
C (desempleado) unemployed

desocupar [A1] *vt*
A **1** ‹*armario*› to empty, clear out **2** ‹*casa/habitación*› to vacate, leave
B **1** (desalojar) ‹*recinto/sala*› to clear **2** (despejar) ‹*camino/paso*› to clear
C (Chi) ‹*libro/tijeras*› to finish using, finish with
■ **desocuparse** *v pron* «*casa*» to become available *o* vacant; **ya se desocupó el baño** the bathroom's free now

desodorante *m* deodorant; **~ en barra/spray** stick/spray deodorant
(Compuesto) **desodorante ambiental** (CS) air freshener

desoír [I28] *vt* to ignore, disregard; **desoyó la voz de su conciencia** he did not heed the voice of his conscience (liter)

desolación *f*
A (devastación) devastation, destruction
B (aflicción) grief

desolado -da *adj*
A ‹*paisaje/campos*› desolate; ‹*ciudad*› devastated
B (afligido) desolated, devastated

desolador -dora *adj*
A (devastador) ‹*tormenta/epidemia*› devastating
B (triste, penoso) ‹*noticia*› devastating; ‹*espectáculo*› distressing; **un panorama ~** a bleak prospect

desolar [A10] *vt* ‹*país/campos*› to lay waste (to) (liter)

desollar [A10] *vt* ‹*animal*› to skin, flay; **~ vivo a algn** to pull sb to pieces

desorbitado -da *adj* **1** ‹*precios*› exorbitant, astronomical **2** **con los ojos ~s** with her eyes popping out of her head (colloq)

desorbitante *adj* exorbitant

desorden *m*
A **1** (de persona, cuarto, cajón) untidiness; **no soporto el ~** I can't stand untidiness; **perdona el ~** sorry about the mess; **en ~** ‹*salir/entrar*› in a disorderly fashion; **todo estaba en ~** everything was in disorder *o* in a mess; **dejó los naipes en ~** she left the cards out of order; **no dejes el cuarto en ~** don't leave the room in a mess **2** (confusión) disorder
B **desórdenes** *mpl* **1** (disturbios) disturbances (*pl*), disorder **2** (Med) disorders (*pl*)

desordenadamente *adv* ‹*entrar/salir*› in a disorderly fashion; **guardar algo ~** to put sth away untidily

desordenado -da *adj*
A **1** ‹*persona/habitación*› untidy, messy (colloq); **tengo la casa toda desordenada** my house is in a mess *o* is very untidy **2** [ESTAR] ‹*naipes/hojas*› out of order
B ‹*vida*› disorganized
C (Chi) (en el colegio) ‹*niño*› naughty, badly-behaved

desordenar [A1] *vt* ‹*mesa/habitación*› to make … untidy, mess up (colloq); ‹*naipes/hojas*› to get … out of order

desorganización *f* lack of organization

desorganizado -da *adj* disorganized

desorganizar [A4] *vt* to disrupt

desorientación *f* disorientation, confusion

desorientado -da *adj* disoriented, disorientated (BrE)

desorientar [A1] *vt* to confuse; **pistas falsas para ~ a la policía** false clues to throw the police off the trail
■ **desorientarse** *v pron* to become disoriented

desosar [A14] *vt* ▸ **deshuesar**

desovar [A1] *vi* «*insectos*» to lay eggs; «*peces/anfibios*» to spawn

desove *m* (de insectos) egg-laying; (de peces, anfibios) spawning

desoxidar [A1] *vt* **1** (Quím) to deoxidize **2** (Metal) to remove the rust from

desoxigenar [A1] *vt* to deoxidize

despabilado -da *adj* ▸ **espabilado**[1]

despabilar [A1] *vt* ▸ **espabilar**

despachante *m* (RPl) *tb* **~ de aduanas** customs officer

despachar [A1] *vt*
A **1** ‹*asunto/tarea/*› to take care of, deal with; ‹*correspondencia*› to deal with, attend to; **este asunto se debe ~ con el jefe** this matter has to be sorted out *o* cleared with the boss **2** ‹*carta/paquete*› to send; ‹*mercancías*› (por barco) to ship; (por avión, tren) to send, dispatch
B (Com) (en tienda) to serve, deal with; **~ un pedido** to deal with an order
C **1** (fam) (echar, despedir) to fire, to let … go (euph) **2** (fam) (matar) to get rid of (euph); (rematar) to dispatch (euph), to finish … off
■ **despachar** *vi* (Com) **1** «*dependiente*» to serve **2** «*comercio*» to be open (for business *o* to the public)
■ **despacharse** *v pron* (fam) ‹*paella/vino*› to polish off (colloq); ‹*libro*› to get through

despacho *m*
A **1** (oficina) office; (estudio) study **2** (mobiliario) office furniture
B (envío) dispatch, despatch; **se encarga del ~ de las cartas** he is responsible for dispatching the mail
C (Com) **1** (atención): **permite el rápido ~ de pasajeros** it allows passengers to be dealt with more quickly **2** (venta) sale **3** (tienda) shop; **~ de pan** baker's shop (*selling bread made off the premises*); **~ de lotería** lottery agency/kiosk; **el ~ de localidades** the box office
D (comunicado) communiqué; (Mil) dispatch; (Period) report

despachurrar [A1] *vt* ▸ **espachurrar**

despacio *adv*
A (lentamente) slowly
B **1** (CS) (en voz baja) quietly, softly; (sin hacer ruido) quietly; **habla ~** keep your voice down; **entró ~ para no despertarlos** he crept in so as not to wake them **2** (Chi) (con poca fuerza) gently

despacioso -sa *adj* (AmL) slow

despampanante *adj* (fam) ‹*mujer/vestido*› stunning (colloq)

despancar [A2] *vt* (Per) to husk

despanzurrado -da *adj* (fam): **un sillón viejo y ~** an old armchair with all the stuffing coming out

desparejado -da *adj* odd, unpaired

desparpajo *m* (desenvoltura) self-confidence; (desfachatez) impudence, nerve (colloq); **tuvo el ~ de negarlo todo** he had the nerve to deny everything; **me lo dijo con todo ~** he said it to me impudently

desparramado -da *adj* **1** (esparcido) scattered **2** (extendido) ‹*ciudad/barrio*› sprawling (*before n*); **estaba ~ en un sillón** he was sprawled (out) in an armchair

desparramar [A1] *vt* **1** ‹*líquido/azúcar*› to spill; ‹*botones/monedas*› to spill, scatter; ‹*papeles*› to scatter **2** (fam) ‹*noticia*› to spread … around
■ **desparramarse** *v pron* (esparcirse) «*líquido/azúcar*» to spill; «*botones/monedas*» to scatter, spill

desparramo *m* (CS) (desorden, desbarajuste) mess; (de líquidos) spillage

despatarrado -da *adj*: **estaba ~ en un sillón** he was sprawled (out) in an armchair; **siempre se sienta toda despatarrada** she always sits with her legs splayed *o* spread out

despatarrarse [A1] *v pron* (fam) «*persona/mula*» to splay one's legs; **se despatarró en el sofá** he sprawled on the sofa with his legs spread out

despavorido -da *adj* terrified, petrified

despecho *m* spite; **por ~** out of spite; **hacer algo a ~ de algn** to do sth in defiance of sb; **a ~ de las críticas** despite *o* in spite of all the criticism

despechugado -da *adj* (fam) **1** (de torso desnudo) ‹*hombre*› bare-chested; ‹*mujer*› topless **2** (con la camisa, etc desabrochada) with one's shirt (*o* blouse *etc*) unbuttoned

despechugarse [A3] *v pron* (fam) «*hombre*» to bare one's chest; «*mujer*» to bare one's breasts; (en la playa) to go topless

despectivamente *adv* ‹*tratar*› contemptuously; **nos habla a todos muy ~** she really talks down to us

despectivo -va *adj* ‹*trato/gesto/actitud*› contemptuous; ‹*tono*› disparaging, contemptuous; ‹*término*› pejorative, derogatory

despedazar [A4] *vt* ‹*res*› to joint, cut … into pieces; ‹*presa*› to tear … to pieces *o* shreds; ‹*juguete*› to pull … apart

despedida *f* 1 (acción) goodbye, farewell (liter); **no me gustan las ~s** I don't like goodbyes 2 (celebración) farewell party; **cena/regalo de ~** a farewell dinner/gift

(Compuesto) **despedida de soltera/soltero** hen/stag night *o* party

despedir [I14] *vt*

A (decir adiós): **vinieron a ~me al aeropuerto** they came to see me off at the airport; **~ los restos de algn** to pay one's last respects to sb

B (del trabajo) to dismiss, fire (colloq); (por reducción de personal) to lay off; **despidieron a 300 trabajadores** they laid off 300 workers

C ‹*olor*› to give off; ‹*humo/vapor*› to emit, give off; **salir despedido** «*corcho/pelota*» to shoot out; **el conductor salió despedido de su asiento** the driver was thrown out of his seat

■ **despedirse** *v pron*

A (decir adiós) to say goodbye; **se despide atentamente** (Corresp) sincerely yours (AmE), yours sincerely (BrE); **~se DE algn** to say goodbye TO sb

B (dar por perdido) **~se DE algo: si se lo prestate ya te puedes ~ de él** if you lent it to him, you can kiss it goodbye; **despídete de la idea** you can forget the whole idea

despegado -da *adj* [SER] unaffectionate, distant

despegar [A3] *vt* 1 ‹*etiqueta/esparadrapo*› to remove, peel off; ‹*piezas/ensambladura*› to get … unstuck *o* apart; **no despegó los labios** she didn't say a word 2 ‹*manga/cuello*› to unpick; ‹*botones*› to remove

■ **despegar** *vi* «*avión*» to take off; «*cohete*» to lift off, be launched

■ **despegarse** *v pron*

A «*sello/etiqueta*» to come unstuck, peel off; «*esparadrapo*» to come unstuck; **no se me despega ni un minuto** he won't leave my side for a minute

B (distanciarse, separarse) «*persona*» **~se DE algn** to distance oneself FROM sb

despegue *m* (de avión) takeoff; (de cohete) launch, lift-off

despeinado -da *adj* ‹*pelo/melena*› unkempt, dishevele d*; **estar/andar ~** to have one's hair in a mess

despeinar [A1] *vt*: **~ a algn** to mess up sb's hair

■ **despeinarse** *v pron* to mess one's hair up

despejado -da *adj*

A (Meteo) ‹*día/cielo*› clear; **cielos totalmente ~s** cloudless skies

B (libre, vacío) ‹*carretera/camino*› clear; **quedó mucho más ~ sin el piano** it felt much more spacious without the piano

C 1 (despierto): **todavía no estoy ~** I'm not properly awake yet; **se sentía con la mente despejada** he felt clearheaded 2 [ESTAR] (sobrio) sober

despejar [A1] *vt*

A 1 (desocupar, desalojar) to clear; **despejen la sala** clear the room 2 ‹*nariz*› to unblock, clear

B 1 (espabilar) to wake … up 2 (desembotar): **el paseo me despejó** the walk cleared my head 3 ‹*borracho*› to sober … up

C ‹*incógnita*› (Mat) to find the value of

D ‹*balón*› (en fútbol) to clear; (en fútbol americano) to punt

■ **despejar** *vi* (en fútbol) to clear; (en fútbol americano) to punt

■ **despejar** *v impers* (Meteo) to clear up; **ya despejó** it has cleared up now

■ **despejarse** *v pron* (espabilarse) to wake (oneself) up; (desembotarse) to clear one's head; «*borracho*» to sober up

despeje *m*

A (de camino, espacio) clearing

B (Dep) clearance; (en fútbol americano) punt

despellejar [A1] *vt* 1 ‹*animal*› to skin 2 (fam) (criticar) to tear … to shreds *o* pieces (colloq) 3 (Col) ‹*papas*› to peel

■ **despellejarse** *v pron* to peel; **se me despellejó la nariz** my nose peeled

despelotado -da *adj* (AmL fam) messy (colloq), chaotic

despelote *m* (AmL fam) (caos, lío) shambles (colloq), mess (colloq); **¡qué ~ tengo en la cabeza!** I'm in such a muddle; **su casa es un verdadero ~** her house is a complete shambles *o* a real mess

despelucar [A2] *vt*

A (Col, Ven fam) ▸ **despeinar**

B (Chi fam) (en el juego) to fleece (colloq)

■ **despelucarse** *v pron* (Col, Ven fam) ▸ **despeinarse**

despenalización *f* legalization, decriminalization

despenalizar [A4] *vt* to legalize, decriminalize

despensa *f* larder, pantry; **tengo la ~ vacía** I haven't a thing to eat in the house

despeñadero *m* cliff, precipice

despeñarse [A1] *v pron* «*persona/mula*» to go *o* fall over a cliff (*o* precipice *etc*); «*coche*» to go over a cliff (*o* precipice *etc*)

desperdiciar [A1] *vt* ‹*comida/papel/tela*› to waste; ‹*oportunidad*› to miss, waste

desperdicio *m* 1 (de comida, papel) waste; ***no tener ~***: **este carne no tiene ~** there's no waste on this meat; **el elepé no tiene ~** the LP doesn't have a single bad track on it; **nada tiene ~** nothing goes to waste *o* is wasted 2 **desperdicios** *mpl* (residuos) scraps (*pl*)

desperdigado -da *adj* scattered; **viñas desperdigadas por la colina** (liter) vines dotted around the hillside

desperdigarse [A3] *v pron* (esparcirse) to be scattered, to scatter

desperezarse [A4] *v pron* to stretch

desperfecto *m* 1 (daño): **sufrir un ~ mecánico** to have a mechanical breakdown; **esto podría causar ~s en el aparato** this could damage the appliance 2 (defecto) flaw; **artículos con pequeños ~s** slightly flawed articles

despersonalizado *adj* depersonalized; **un sistema despersonalizado** an impersonal system

despertador *m* alarm clock; **poner el ~** to set the alarm

despertar [A5] *vt* 1 ‹*persona*› to wake, wake … up; **despiértame a las ocho** wake me (up) at eight o'clock 2 ‹*sentimientos/pasiones*› to arouse; ‹*apetito*› to whet; ‹*recuerdos*› to evoke; ‹*interés*› to awaken, stir up; **un discurso que despertó fuertes polémicas** a speech which sparked off fierce controversy

■ **despertar** *vi* 1 (del sueño) to wake (up); (de la anestesia) to come round 2 (liter) (a la realidad, al amor) to wake up to

■ **despertarse** *v pron* 1 (del sueño) to wake (up) 2 (espabilarse) to wake (oneself) up

despiadadamente *adv* mercilessly, relentlessly

despiadado -da *adj* ‹*persona*› ruthless, heartless; ‹*ataque/crítica*› savage, merciless

despida, despidas, etc *see* **despedir**

despido *m* dismissal; (por falta de trabajo) redundancy, layoff (AmE)

(Compuesto) **despido colectivo** mass dismissal (AmE) *o* (BrE) redundancy

despierta, despiertas, etc *see* **despertar**

despierto -ta *adj* 1 [ESTAR] (del sueño) awake 2 [SER] ‹*persona/mente*› bright, alert

despiezar [A4] *vt* to quarter

despilfarrador -dora *m,f* spendthrift

despilfarrar [A1] *vi* to waste *o* squander money

■ **despilfarrar** *vt* to squander, waste

despilfarro *m* waste; **me parece un ~ ir en taxi** it seems a waste of money to take a taxi

despintar [A1] *vt* 1 (quitar la pintura) to take the paint off 2 (Chi fam) (quitar): **nada le ~á los diez años en la cárcel** nothing will save him from ten years in jail

■ **despintarse** *v pron*

A (Méx) (desteñirse) to run; **¿esta camisa se ~á al lavarla?** will this shirt run in the wash?

B (Chi fam) (quitar): **no se me despinta del lado** she never leaves my side; **no se despinta la chaqueta** he never takes his jacket off

despiojar [A1] *vt* to delouse

despistado[1] -da *adj*

A 1 [SER] vague, absentminded; **soy muy ~ para los nombres** I never remember names 2 [ESTAR]: **estaba** *or* **iba**

~ I was miles away (colloq) *o* daydreaming
B [ESTAR] (desorientado, confuso) bewildered, lost; **todavía anda un poco ~** he hasn't quite found his feet yet
despistado[2] **-da** *m,f* scatterbrain (colloq); **no te hagas el ~** don't act as if you don't know what I'm talking about
despistar [A1] *vt* **1** (desorientar, confundir) to confuse **2** ‹*perseguidor*› to shake off; ‹*sabueso*› to throw … off the scent
■ **despistarse** *v pron* (confundirse) to get confused *o* muddled; (distraerse) to lose concentration, start daydreaming
despiste *m* **1** (distracción) absentmindedness; **fue un ~** it was a lapse of concentration; **en un momento de ~ le robaron la maleta** he took his eye off his suitcase for a moment and someone stole it; **¡qué ~ tengo hoy!** I can't seem to concentrate today! **2** (equivocación) slip, mistake
desplantar [A1] *vt* to uproot
desplante *m*
A (insolencia) rudeness; **¡tiene unos ~s … !** she's so rude!
B (Chi) ▸**desenvoltura**
desplazado[1] **-da** *adj* **1** (de un lugar) displaced; (fuera de su ambiente): **sentirse ~** to feel out of place **2** (desbancado) displaced; *ver tb* **desplazar**
desplazado[2] **-da** *m,f* displaced person
desplazamiento *m*
A (movimiento) movement, displacement (frml)
B (frml) (traslado, viaje) trip; **gastos de ~** traveling expenses; **sus frecuentes ~s al extranjero** her frequent trips abroad
C (del voto) swing, shift
desplazar [A4] *vt*
A **1** (frml) (mover, correr) to move; **el choque desplazó el vehículo unos 20 metros** the impact moved *o* shunted the vehicle a distance of some 20 meters **2** (Fís) to displace **3** (Náut) to displace
B (suplantar, relegar) ‹*persona*› to displace, **la nueva secretaria la ha venido a ~** the new secretary has come to displace her; **~ A algo**: **las computadoras han desplazado a las máquinas de escribir** typewriters have been superseded by word processors
■ **desplazarse** *v pron*
A (frml) (trasladarse, moverse) «*animal*» to move around; «*avión/barco*» to travel, go; «*persona*» to get around
B «*voto*» to swing, shift
desplegar [A7] *vt*
A **1** ‹*alas*› to spread; ‹*mapa*› to open out, spread out, unfold; ‹*velas*› to unfurl; *ver tb* **vela** **2** (demostrar) ‹*talento/ingenio*› to display
B (Mil) ‹*tropas/misiles*› to deploy
C (llevar a cabo) ‹*campaña*› to mount; ‹*esfuerzo*› to make
D **1** (emplear) ‹*encantos/poder*› to use **2** (dar muestras de) to show, display
■ **desplegarse** *v pron* (Mil) to deploy
despliegue *m*
A (de tropas, recursos) deployment
B (de riqueza, sabiduría) display; **haciendo ~ de gran elocuencia** with great eloquence
desplomarse [A1] *v pron*
A «*persona/edificio*» to collapse; **cayó desplomado al suelo** he collapsed onto the floor
B «*precio/cotización*» to crash; «*ilusiones*» to be shattered; «*esperanzas*» to be dashed; «*sistema/régimen*» to collapse
desplome *m*
A (de edificio) collapse
B (de precio) fall, drop; **el ~ de los salarios** the drop in salaries
desplumar [A1] *vt* **1** ‹*ave*› to pluck **2** (fam) ‹*persona*› to fleece (colloq)
despoblación *f* depopulation; **la ~ rural** rural depopulation
despoblado -da *adj*
A (sin habitantes) deserted, uninhabited; (subpoblado) underpopulated, sparsely populated
B ‹*cejas*› thin, sparse
despoblar [A10] *vt* to depopulate; **~on el campo de árboles** they cleared the land of trees
■ **despoblarse** *v pron* to become depopulated *o* deserted
despojar [A1] *vt* (frml) **~ A algn DE algo** ‹*de privilegios/poderes*› to divest sb OF sth (frml); ‹*de título/posesiones*› to dispossess (frml) *o* strip sb OF sth
■ **despojarse** *v pron* (frml *o* liter) **~se DE algo** ‹*de ropa*› to remove sth; ‹*de bienes*› to relinquish sth
despojo *m*
A (frml) (desposeimiento) dispossession (frml)
B **despojos** *mpl* **1** (restos) remains (*pl*) **2** (presa, botín) spoils (*pl*), loot **3** (de aves) *head, wings, feet and giblets*; (de reses) *head, feet and offal*
desportillado -da *adj* chipped
desportillarse [A1] *v pron* «*bañera/taza*» to chip, get chipped
desposado -da *m,f* (frml): **los ~s** the newlyweds, the bride and groom
desposar [A1] *vt* (frml) «*sacerdote*» to marry; «*novio*» to marry
■ **desposarse** *v pron* (frml) to be wed (frml), to be married
desposeer [E13] *vt* (frml) **~ A algn DE algo** to dispossess sb OF sth (frml)
■ **desposeerse** *v pron* (frml) **~se DE algo** to relinquish sth
desposeído -da *m,f*: **los ~s** the destitute, the dispossessed
desposorios *mpl* (liter) nuptials (*pl*) (liter)
déspota *mf* (Pol) tyrant, despot
despótico -ca *adj* despotic, tyrannical
despotismo *m* despotism
(Compuesto) **despotismo ilustrado** enlightened despotism
despotricar [A2] *vi* (fam) to rant and rave; **~ CONTRA algo/algn** to sound off *o* rant and rave ABOUT sth/sb
despreciable *adj* **1** ‹*persona/conducta*› despicable, contemptible **2** **no/nada despreciable** ‹*suma/número*› not inconsiderable, significant
despreciar [A1] *vt* **1** (menospreciar) ‹*persona*› to look down on; **lo desprecio profundamente** I despise him **2** (rechazar) ‹*oferta/ayuda*› to spurn (liter), to reject; **es un trabajo que todos desprecian** it's a job which everyone feels is beneath them **3** (no tener en cuenta) ‹*posibilidad/consejo*› to disregard, discount
despreciativo -va *adj* ‹*persona*› disdainful; ‹*tono/gesto*› disdainful, scornful; **una mirada despreciativa** a look of disdain *o* scorn
desprecio *m* **1** (menosprecio) disdain; **un gesto de ~** a disdainful gesture; **me miró con ~** she gave me a disdainful *o* scornful look; **sentía un ~ infinito por él** she felt profound contempt for him **2** (indiferencia) disregard; **sienten un profundo ~ por la autoridad** they have a deep-seated contempt for authority **3** (desaire) snub, slight; **hacerle un ~ a algn** to snub *o* slight sb
desprender [E1] *vt*
A (soltar, separar) ‹*teja*› to dislodge; ‹*etiqueta*› to detach; **los golpes desprendieron parte del revoque** part of the plaster came away *o* off with all the banging; **el botón estaba medio desprendido** the button was hanging off
B ‹*gases/chispas/olor*› to give off
■ **desprenderse** *v pron*
A «*teja*» to come loose; «*botón*» to come off; «*retina*» to become detached; **se desprendió del soporte** it came away from *o* (frml) detached itself from the support
B **1** (renunciar, entregar) **~se DE algo** to part WITH sth; **no piensa ~se del bebé** she has no intention of giving up the baby **2** (apartarse, separarse) **~se DE algo** to let go OF sth; **no se desprende de su osito** he won't let go of his teddy bear; **no se le desprende del lado** she won't leave his side for a minute
C (deshacerse) **~se DE algo/algn** to get rid OF sth/sb; **~se de los prejuicios** to shake off one's prejudices
D (inferirse) **~se DE algo** to emerge FROM sth; **de lo que se desprende que …** what can be gathered from it is that …
desprendido -da *adj* [SER] generous, open-handed; *ver tb* **desprender**
desprendimiento *m*
A (de una pieza) detachment

d

Compuestos
- **desprendimiento de retina** detachment of the retina
- **desprendimiento de tierras** landslide

B (generosidad) generosity, open-handedness

despreocupación *f* lack of concern

despreocupado -da *adj* 1 (sin preocupaciones) ‹*vida*› carefree 2 (descuidado) negligent 3 (indiferente) unworried

despreocuparse [A1] *v pron* 1 (desentenderse): **se despreocupó de la educación de sus hijos** he didn't bother about his children's education; **se despreocupó de todo y se fue de vacaciones** she washed her hands of everything and went off on vacation 2 (dejar de preocuparse): **despreocúpate del qué dirán** don't worry about what other people say

despresar [A1] *vt* (Andes) to cut up, joint; **pollos despresados** chicken pieces

desprestigiar [A1] *vt* to discredit; **desprestigian la profesión** they bring the profession into disrepute

■ **desprestigiarse** *v pron* «*persona/producto/empresa*» to lose prestige; **se ha desprestigiado como abogado** his reputation *o* prestige as a lawyer has been damaged

desprestigio *m* 1 (pérdida de prestigio) loss of prestige; **ir en ~ de algo/algn** to bring discredit on *o* upon sth/sb; **sería un ~ para el partido** it would bring the party into disrepute 2 (falta de prestigio): **el ~ de los políticos era tal que ...** the politicians had such a bad name *o* reputation that ...

desprevenido -da *adj*: **estar ~** to be unprepared *o* unready; **pillar a algn ~** «*pregunta*» to catch sb unawares *o* off guard; «*lluvia*» to catch sb by surprise

desprolijo -ja *adj* (CS) 1 [ESTAR] ‹*trabajo*› careless, untidy, messy 2 [SER] ‹*persona*› careless

desproporción *f* disparity, disproportion

desproporcionado -da *adj* out of proportion; **una indemnización desproporcionada al daño sufrido** compensation disproportionate to the damage incurred

despropósito *m*

A (desatino) silly thing to say/do; **no dice más que ~s** he talks nothing but nonsense

B (Col frml) (desaire) snub, slight

desprotección *f* lack of protection; **menores en situación de ~** minors in a vulnerable situation; **la ~ legal** the lack of legal protection

desprotegido -da *adj* unprotected, vulnerable

desprovisto -ta *adj* **~ DE algo** lacking IN sth; **la escuela se halla desprovista de material** the school lacks equipment; **~ de recursos** without means; **niños ~s de cariño** children deprived of affection

después *adv*

A 1 (más tarde) later 2 (en una serie de sucesos) then, afterwards; **y ~ me vino a ver a mí** and then he came to see me; **~ no lo he vuelto a ver** I haven't seen him since then 3 (*en locs*) **después de** after; **~ de Cristo** AD; **~ DE + INF** after -ING; **~ de hablar contigo** after talking to you; **~ de pelar el limón** once you have peeled the lemon; **después de todo** after all; **después (de) que** when, after; **~ (DE) QUE + SUBJ** (refiriéndose al futuro) once, when; **~ (de) que todos se hayan ido** once *o* when everybody has left; **~ (de) que te bañes** once *o* when you've had a bath; **después que** after; **usted llegó ~ que yo** you arrived after me

B (en el espacio): **bájate dos paradas ~** get off two stops after that; **hay una casa y ~ está el colegio** there is a house and then you come to the school; **está justo ~ del puente** it's just past the bridge

C 1 (indicando orden, prioridad) then; **~ de ti** *or* **~ que tú, voy yo** I'm after you 2 (además) then; **~ tenemos éstos, que son más baratos** then we have these, which are cheaper

despuntado -da *adj* blunt

despuntar [A1] *vt* to blunt

■ **despuntar** *vi* 1 «*día*» to break, dawn; **al ~ el día/alba** at daybreak/dawn 2 «*flores*» to bud; «*plantas*» to sprout 3 «*persona*» **~ EN algo** to excel AT *o* IN sth; **despunta por su belleza** she's outstandingly beautiful

desquiciado -da *adj*: **vivimos en un mundo ~** we live in a mad *o* crazy world; **tengo los nervios ~s** my nerves are in tatters; **está ~ con tanto trabajo** he's going crazy with all the work he has (colloq)

desquiciante *adj* maddening, infuriating

desquiciar [A1] *vt*

A (trastornar, perturbar) ‹*persona*› to drive ... crazy *o* mad (colloq); **vas a conseguir ~me los nervios** you are going to drive me crazy *o* mad

B ‹*puerta/ventana*› to take ... off its hinges, unhinge

■ **desquiciarse** *v pron*

A 1 (trastornarse, perturbarse) «*persona*» to lose one's mind 2 «*situación*» to get out of control

B «*puerta/ventana*» to come off its hinges

desquicio *m* (RPl fam) chaos

desquitarse [A1] *v pron* to get even; **~ DE algn**: **lo hizo para ~ de él** she did it to get even with him; **~ CON algn** to take it out ON sb

desratizar [A4] *vt* to clear ... of rats *o* rodents

desregulación *f* deregulation

desregular [A1] *vt* to deregulate, remove controls from

desrielar [A1] *vt* (Chi) to derail

destacado -da *adj*

A ‹*profesional/artista*› prominent, distinguished; ‹*actuación*› outstanding; **la nota más destacada del día** the highlight of the day; **destacadas personalidades** prominent *o* distinguished figures

B [ESTAR] ‹*tropas*› stationed; **nuestro equipo ~ en el lugar** our team on the spot; **el cuerpo diplomático ~ en ...** the diplomatic staff in ...

destacamento *m* (tropas) detachment, detail; (instalación) outpost

Compuesto **destacamento policial** (Arg) rural police station

destacar [A2] *vt*

A (recalcar, subrayar) to emphasize, stress

B (realzar) ‹*belleza/figura*› to enhance; ‹*color/plano*› to bring out

C 1 (Mil) ‹*tropas*› to post; **~ a algn PARA + INF** to detail sb to + INF 2 ‹*periodista/fotógrafo*› to send

■ **destacar** *vi* to stand out; **~ EN algo** to excel AT *o* IN sth; **destaca por su inteligencia** her intelligence sets her apart from the rest; **el marco hace ~ aún más la belleza del cuadro** the frame further enhances the beauty of the picture; **destacó como autor teatral** he was an outstanding playwright; **nunca destacó como estudiante** he never excelled as a student

destajo *m* (Com, Rels Labs) piecework; **trabajar a ~** to do piecework; **cobran a ~** they are paid per item; ***a* ~** ‹*comer/dormir*› (Chi) to one's heart's content

destapado -da *adj* 1 (sin tapa): **cocinarlo ~** cook uncovered *o* without the lid; **¿quién ha dejado el vino ~?** who left the top off the wine? 2 (en la cama): **siempre duerme ~** he always sleeps with the covers thrown back

destapador *m* (AmL) bottle opener

destapar [A1] *vt*

A 1 ‹*botella/caja*› to open, take the top/lid off; ‹*olla*› to uncover, take the lid off 2 (descubrir) ‹*mueble*› to uncover; ‹*escándalo*› to uncover 3 (en la cama) to pull the covers off

B (AmL) ‹*cañería/inodoro*› to unblock

■ **destaparse** *v pron* (*refl*)

A (en la cama) to throw the covers *o* bedclothes off

B «*nariz/oídos*» to unblock

C (abrirse, confesarse) **~se CON algn** to open up TO sb

destape *m* 1 (desnudo) nudity; **el ~ en el cine** nudity in the movies 2 (en las ideas, costumbres) liberalization

destaponar [A1] *vt* ‹*botella*› to uncork, open; ‹*cañería*› to unblock

destartalado -da *adj* (fam) ‹*coche*› beat-up (AmE colloq), clapped-out (BrE colloq); ‹*mueble*› shabby; ‹*casa*› ramshackle, rundown

destazar [A4] *vt* (Col) (descuartizar) to quarter

destejer [E1] *vt* to unravel, undo

destellar [A1] *vi* «*brillante/joya*» to sparkle, glitter; «*estrella*» to twinkle, sparkle; «*ojos*» to sparkle; **los ojos le destellaban de alegría/rabia** her eyes sparkled with happiness/flashed with anger

destello *m* **1** (de estrella) twinkle, sparkle; (de brillante, joya) sparkle, glitter; **en un ~ de lucidez** in a flash of lucidity; **hay un ~ de maldad en sus ojos** he has an evil gleam in his eyes **2** (fam) (indicio, atisbo) atom (colloq); **no hay un ~ de sensatez en eso** there isn't an ounce *o* an atom of sense in it (colloq)

destemplado -da *adj*
A ‹*persona*›: **estoy** *or* **ando ~** (con fiebre) I have a slight fever; (indispuesto) I'm feeling off-color*
B **1** ‹*instrumento*› discordant, out-of-tune **2** ‹*voz/tono*› harsh, discordant **3** ‹*nervios*› frayed; **los ánimos están ~s** tempers are frayed

destemplanza *f* **1** (fiebre) slight fever; (malestar) indisposition **2** (del tiempo) unpleasantness

destemplar [A1] *or* (Col, Per, Ven) [A5] *vt*
A ‹*guitarra/violín*› to make … go out of tune
B ‹*ánimos/nervios*› to fray; **solo logró ~ los ánimos** all he did was to make things even more fraught
C (AmL) ‹*dientes*› to set … on edge
■ **destemplarse** *v pron*
A ‹‹*tiempo*›› to change for the worse
B (Mús) ‹‹*instrumento*›› to go out of tune
C (Andes, Méx) ‹‹*dientes*›› (+ *me/te/le etc*): **con ese ruido se me destemplan los dientes** that noise sets my teeth on edge

desteñir [I15] *vi* ‹‹*prenda/color*›› to run; (decolorarse) to fade
■ **desteñir** *vt* to fade
■ **desteñirse** *v pron* to run; (decolorarse) to fade

desternillarse [A1] *v pron* (fam): **~ de risa** to split one's sides (laughing) (colloq)

desterrado -da *m,f* exile

desterrar [A5] *vt* **1** (expulsar) to exile, banish (liter) **2** (liter) ‹*temor/duda*› to banish; ‹*costumbre/creencia*› to stamp out, eradicate

destetar [A1] *vt* to wean
■ **destetarse** *v pron* ‹‹*niño/cría*›› to be weaned

destete *m* weaning

destiempo: **a ~** ‹*marchar*› out of step; ‹*tocar*› out of time; **habló a ~** she picked the wrong moment to say it

destierro *m* exile, banishment; **lo condenaron al ~** he was sent into exile; **murió en el ~** he died in exile

destilación *f* distillation

destiladora *f* (Col) distillery

destilar [A1] *vt* **1** ‹*alcohol/petróleo*› to distill*; ‹*hulla/madera*› to char **2** (rezumar) to ooze; **sus palabras destilan veneno** his words ooze *o* exude venom

destilería *f* distillery

destinado -da *adj*
A **1** (predestinado) **~ A algo** destined FOR sth; **estar ~ a la vida religiosa** to be destined for religious life; **~ al fracaso** destined to fail **2** (dirigido, asignado): **~ a algn** ‹*carta/paquete*› addressed to sb; **~ A algo**: **las cajas destinadas a Montevideo** the boxes for *o* bound for Montevideo; **los aviones ~s a este fin** the planes used for this purpose; **una política destinada a estrechar estos lazos** a policy aimed at strengthening these links
B **1** ‹*militar*›: **~ en Ceuta** stationed in Ceuta **2** ‹*funcionario/diplomático*›: **ahora está ~ en Lima** now he's been posted to Lima

destinar [A1] *vt*
A ‹*funcionario/militar*› to post, send, assign; **está esperando que lo destinen** he's waiting for his posting *o* assignment to come through; **lo han destinado a Cartagena** he's been posted *o* sent to Cartagena
B (asignar un fin) **~ algo A algo**: **destina una parte de su sueldo a ayudar a su familia** part of her salary goes to helping her family; **~on parte de los fondos a mejorar las instalaciones** they earmarked part of the funds for improving the facilities; **~ algo PARA algo** to set sth aside FOR sth; **esta habitación la tenía destinada para …** I had planned to use this room for …

destinatario -ria *m,f* (de carta, paquete) addressee; (de giro, transferencia) payee

destino *m*
A (sino) fate; **su ~ era acabar en la cárcel** he was destined to end up in prison; **una jugada del ~** a twist of fate
B **1** (de avión, autobús) destination; **el vuelo 421 con ~ a Roma** flight 421 to Rome; **los pasajeros con ~ a Santiago** passengers traveling to Santiago; **los trenes con ~ a San Juan** trains to San Juan; **salieron con ~ a Lima** they set off for Lima **2** (puesto) posting, assignment; **solicitó un ~ en el extranjero** she asked for a foreign posting
C (uso, fin): **no se sabe qué ~ se les dará a esos fondos** it is not known what those funds will be allocated to; **debería dársele un mejor ~ a esto** this should be put to better use

destitución *f* removal from office, dismissal

destituir [I20] *vt* (frml) (despedir) to dismiss; **fue destituido de su cargo** he was removed *o* dismissed from office

destornillador *m* screwdriver

destornillar [A1] *vt* to unscrew
■ **destornillarse** *v pron* ‹‹*tuerca/tornillo*›› to come loose; **~se de risa** ▸ **desternillarse**

destreza *f* skill; **demostró mucha ~ con el florete** he showed great dexterity *o* skill in his handling of the foil; **con gran ~** very skillfully

destripar [A1] *vt* **1** ‹*res/ave/caza*› to gut, disembowel **2** (fam) (matar): **el toro destripó al caballo** the bull ripped the horse's guts out

destronamiento *m* dethronement, overthrow

destronar [A1] *vt* ‹*rey*› to dethrone, depose; ‹*líder/campeón*› to depose, topple

destrozado -da *adj* **1** (roto, deteriorado) ‹*zapatos*› ruined; **el coche quedó ~** the car was a total wreck; **éstos sillones están ~s** these armchairs are falling apart; **tenía los nervios ~s** her nerves were in tatters; **tengo los pies ~s** (fam) my feet are killing me; **el conductor tenía la cara destrozada** the driver's face was a real mess **2** ‹*persona*› (físicamente) exhausted; (moralmente) devastated, shattered **3** ‹*corazón*› broken

destrozar [A4] *vt* **1** (romper, deteriorar) to break; **la bomba destrozó varios edificios** the bomb destroyed *o* wrecked several buildings; **vas a ~ los zapatos** you'll ruin your shoes **2** ‹*felicidad/armonía*› to destroy, shatter; ‹*corazón*› to break; ‹*matrimonio*› to ruin, destroy; **me está destrozando los nervios** she's making me a nervous wreck; **su muerte la destrozó** she was devastated *o* shattered by his death
■ **destrozarse** *v pron* (*refl*) **1** (romperse): **se cayó al suelo y se destrozó** it fell to the ground and it smashed; **se me ~on los zapatos** my shoes are ruined **2** ‹*estómago/hígado*› to ruin; **te vas a ~ los pies con esos zapatos** you're going to ruin your feet wearing those shoes

destrozo *m*: **las inundaciones han causado grandes ~s** the floods have caused widespread damage; **los ~s causados por el temporal** the storm damage; **los ~s causados por la guerra** the ravages of war

destrucción *f* destruction

destructividad *f* destructiveness

destructivo -va *adj* destructive

destructor *m* destroyer

destruir [I20] *vt* **1** ‹*documentos/pruebas*› to destroy; ‹*ciudad*› to destroy; ‹*medio ambiente*› to damage **2** (echar por tierra) ‹*reputación*› to ruin; ‹*plan*› to wreck; ‹*esperanzas*› to dash, shatter; **los problemas económicos destruyeron su matrimonio** financial problems wrecked their marriage; **le destruyó la vida** it/he wrecked *o* destroyed his/her life

desubicación *f* (AmS) (desplazamiento) displacement; (desorientación) confusion, disorientation

desubicado -da *adj* (AmS) **1** [ESTAR] (desplazado) out of position **2** [ESTAR] (desorientado) confused, disoriented; **adolescentes ~s** teenagers who lack a purpose in life **3** [SER] (en cuestiones sociales): **es tan ~** he just doesn't have a clue (colloq)

desubicar [A2] *vt* (AmS) to disorient, disorientate (BrE); **estas calles son tan parecidas que te desubican** these streets are so similar that you get disoriented; **el tiro desubicó al arquero** the shot wrongfooted the goalkeeper
■ **desubicarse** *v pron* (AmS) **1** (desplazarse) to get (*o* move *etc*) out of position **2** (desorientarse) to get confused, to get disoriented

desuello *m* skinning, flaying

desunión *f* lack of unity, disunity

desunir [I1] *vt* ‹*organización*› to divide, split; **el problema desunió a la familia** the problem caused a rift within the family

desusado -da *adj*
A (anticuado): **costumbres desusadas entre nosotros** customs which have fallen into disuse in our society
B (insólito) unusual

desuso *m* disuse; ***caer en*** **~** to fall into disuse

desvaído -da *adj* ‹*color*› faded, washed-out; ‹*persona*› colorless*, insipid

desvalido -da *m,f* helpless person; **los ~s** the destitute, the helpless

desvalijar [A1] *vt* **1** ‹*casa/tienda*› to ransack **2** ‹*persona*› (robar) to rob; (en juego) (fam) to clean … out (colloq); **dejamos la puerta abierta y nos ~on** (fam) we left the door open and they cleaned us out (colloq)

desvalorización *f* (de moneda) devaluation; (de propiedad) depreciation, drop in value

desvalorizarse [A4] *v pron* to decrease in value

desván *m* attic, loft

desvanecer [E3] *vt* **1** ‹*dudas/temores/sospechas*› to dispel **2** ‹*figura/contorno*› to blur

■ **desvanecerse** *v pron*
A **1** «*humo/nubes/niebla*» to clear, disperse; «*dudas/temores/sospechas*» to vanish, be dispelled; «*fantasma/visión*» to disappear, vanish **2** «*color*» to fade
B (Med) to faint

desvanecimiento *m* (desmayo) faint; **sufrir un ~** to faint

desvariar [A17] *vi* (Med) to be delirious; (decir tonterías) to talk nonsense, rave

desvarío *m* **1** (Med) delirium **2** **desvaríos** *mpl* (disparates) ravings (*pl*); **~s de una mente trastornada** ravings of a disturbed mind; **ahí no hay nada, sólo son ~s tuyos** there's nothing there, you're just imagining things

desvelado -da *adj*: **pasé la noche ~** I had a sleepless night; **estoy ~** I can't sleep

desvelar [A1] *vt*
A ‹*persona*› to keep … awake, stop … from sleeping; **el café me desvela** coffee keeps me awake
B (esp Esp) (revelar) to reveal, disclose; (descubrir) to discover, uncover

■ **desvelarse** *v pron*
A (perder el sueño): **me desvelé anoche** I couldn't sleep last night
B (desvivirse) **~se POR algo/algn**: **se desvela por que no les falte nada a sus hijos** she does her utmost *o* very best to make sure her children do not lack for anything; **yo me desvelo por él** I go out of my way for him

desvelo *m*
A (insomnio) sleeplessness; **noches de ~** sleepless nights
B **desvelos** *mpl* (esfuerzos): **¡así me pagas todos mis ~s!** this is the thanks I get for my pains *o* for all I've done for you; **el fruto de sus ~s** the fruit of his efforts

desvencijado -da *adj* ‹*silla/cama*› rickety; ‹*coche*› dilapidated, beat-up (AmE colloq), clapped-out (BrE colloq)

desvencijarse [A1] *v pron* to fall apart

desventaja *f* disadvantage; **estar en ~** to be at a disadvantage; **poner a algn en ~** to put sb at a disadvantage; **con una ~ de dos goles** two goals down

desventura *f* misfortune

desventurado -da *adj* ‹*día*› unfortunate; ‹*viaje*› ill-fated; ‹*matrimonio*› unhappy

desvergonzado -da *m,f* **1** (impúdico): **es una desvergonzada** she has no shame **2** (descarado): **eres un ~** you're very impertinent

desvestir [I14] *vt* to undress

■ **desvestirse** *v pron* to undress, get undressed; **~se por completo** to take all one's clothes off, to strip off; **~se de la cintura para arriba** to strip to the waist

desviación *f*
A **1** (de río) diversion **2** (de fondos) diversion **3** (Med) curvature; **una ~ de columna** curvature of the spine **4** (Auto) (desvío) detour (AmE), diversion (BrE) **5** (alejamiento) **~ DE algo** deviation FROM sth; **no tolera ninguna ~ de la línea del partido** he doesn't tolerate any departure from the party line
B (frml) (aberración) deviation

desviado -da *adj* ‹*conducta*› deviant; ‹*ojo*›: **tiene un ojo ~** he has a squint

desviar [A17] *vt*
A ‹*tráfico/vuelo*› to divert; ‹*río*› to alter the course of; ‹*golpe/pelota*› to deflect, parry; ‹*fondos*› to divert; **~ la conversación** to change the subject; **desvió la mirada** he looked away, he averted his gaze
B (apartar) **~ a algn DE algo**: **~ a algn del buen camino** to lead sb astray; **aquello me desvió de mi propósito** that deflected me from my goal

■ **desviarse** *v pron*
A «*carretera*» to branch off; «*vehículo*» to turn off; **el coche se desvió hacia el centro de la ciudad/hacia la derecha** the car turned off toward(s) the city center/turned off to the right; **la conversación se desvió hacia otros temas** the conversation turned to other things
B «*persona*» **~se DE algo** to stray OFF sth; **nos estamos desviando del tema** we're getting off the point

desvincular [A1] *vt* **~ algo/A algn DE algo** to dissociate sth/sb FROM sth

■ **desvincularse** *v pron* **~se DE algn/algo** to dissociate oneself FROM sth/sb; **está desvinculado de toda actividad política** he is no longer active in politics

desvío *m* **1** (por obras) diversion, detour (AmE); **S desvío provisional** temporary diversion; **tomar un ~** to make a detour **2** (Esp) (salida, carretera) turning; **toma el ~ de Algete** take the turning for Algete

desvirgar [A3] *vt* to deflower (liter)

desvirtuar [A18] *vt* ‹*verdad/hechos*› to distort

desvivirse [I1] *v pron* **~ por algn** to be completely devoted TO sb; **~ POR + INF** to go out of one's way to + INF

detalladamente *adv* in detail

detallado -da *adj* ‹*factura/cuenta*› itemized, detailed; ‹*estudio/descripción*› detailed

detallar [A1] *vt* to detail

detalle *m*
A **1** (pormenor) detail; **entrar en ~s** to go into details; **describir algo con todo ~** to describe sth in great detail; **no perdimos ~ de lo que pasó** we didn't miss a thing; **no me dio ~s** he didn't go into detail **2** (elemento decorativo) detail
B **1** (pequeño regalo) little gift; **me trajo un ~** he brought me a little gift *o* something **2** (Esp, Méx) (atención, gesto) nice (*o* thoughtful *etc*) gesture; **¡qué ~!** how thoughtful of her (*or* you *etc*)!; **tener un ~ con algn** to do sth nice FOR sb; **en todo el tiempo que vivió en mi casa no tuvo ni un ~ conmigo** he made no gesture of appreciation in all the time he stayed with me
C (Com) **al detalle** retail; **vender al ~** to sell retail

detallismo *m* attention to detail; **un hombre de un ~ increíble** a man who pays incredible attention to detail

detallista[1] *adj*
A (minucioso) precise, meticulous
B (Com) retail (*before n*)

detallista[2] *mf* (Com) retailer

detalloso -sa *adj* (Per fam) vain

detección *f* detection

detectar [A1] *vt* to detect

detective *mf* detective; **~ privado** private detective

detector *m* detector

(Compuesto) **detector de mentiras/metales/minas** lie/metal/mine detector

detención *f*
A (arresto) arrest; (encarcelamiento) detention

(Compuestos)
- **detención preventiva** police custody
- **detención domiciliaria** house arrest

B **1** (parada): **provocó la ~ del tren** it brought the train to a halt **2** ▸ **detenimiento**

detener [E27] *vt*
A (parar) ‹*vehículo/máquina*› to stop; ‹*trámite/proceso*› to halt; ‹*hemorragia*› to stop, staunch; ‹*lanzamiento/gol*› to stop; **~ el avance de la enfermedad** to check the development of the disease; **vete, nadie te detiene** go then, nobody's stopping you
B (arrestar) to arrest; (encarcelar) to detain; **¡queda usted**

detenido! you're under arrest!
■ **detenerse** *v pron* 1 (pararse) ‹‹*vehículo/persona*›› to stop; **no te detengas por el camino** don't stop off on the way; **~se A + INF** to stop to + INF 2 (tomar mucho tiempo) **~se EN algo: no nos detengamos demasiado en los detalles** let's not spend too much time discussing the details

detenidamente *adv* at length; **la miró larga y ~** he looked at her long and hard

detenido¹ -da *adj* 1 ‹*vehículo/tráfico*› held up 2 ‹*investigación/estudio*› detailed, thorough 3 (Der): **las personas detenidas** those under arrest

detenido² -da *m,f* arrested person, person under arrest; (durante un período más largo) detainee, person held in custody; **los ~s esperaban fuera** the people who had been arrested waited outside

detenimiento *m*: **con ~** carefully *o* in detail

detentar [A1] *vt* (period) ‹*poder/título/récord*› to hold

detentor -ora *m,f* (Dep) (period) holder **; el ~ del récord mundial** the world record holder

detergente *m* 1 (para ropa) laundry detergent (AmE), washing powder (BrE) 2 (Bol, CS) (para vajilla) dishwashing liquid (AmE), washing-up liquid (BrE)

deteriorado -da *adj* ‹*mercancías*› damaged; ‹*edificio*› dilapidated, run down; **el cuadro está muy ~** the picture is in very bad condition

deteriorar [A1] *vt* ‹*relaciones/salud/situación*› to cause ... to deteriorate
■ **deteriorarse** *v pron* ‹‹*relaciones/salud/situación*›› to deteriorate, worsen; **las mercancías se ~on en el viaje** the goods were damaged in transit

deterioro *m* 1 (de edificio, muebles) deterioration, wear 2 (empeoramiento) deterioration, worsening; **su salud ha sufrido un ~** his health has deteriorated; **el ~ de la calidad de la enseñanza** the decline in the quality of education

determinación *f* (cualidad) determination, resolve; (decisión) decision; **tomar una ~** to make a decision

determinado -da *adj* (definido, preciso) ‹*fecha/lugar*› certain; **en determinadas circunstancias** in certain circumstances; **una determinada dosis** a particular dosage

determinante¹ *adj*: **la causa ~ del accidente** the main cause of the accident; **el factor ~ de nuestra decisión** the deciding factor in our decision

determinante² *m* (Mat) determinant; (Ling) determiner

determinar [A1] *vt*
A (establecer, precisar) 1 ‹‹*ley/contrato*›› to state; ‹‹*persona*›› to determine 2 (por deducción) to establish, determine; **~ las causas del accidente** to determine *o* establish what caused the accident; **se ha determinado que ...** it has been established that ...
B (motivar) to cause, bring about
C 1 (decidir) ‹‹*persona*›› **~ + INF** to decide *o* (frml) determine to + INF 2 (hacer decidir) **~ a algn A + INF** to make sb decide to + INF, to decide *o* determine sb to + INF (frml)

determinativo -va *adj* determinative

determinismo *m* determinism

determinista¹ *adj* deterministic

determinista² *mf* determinist

detestable *adj* ‹*persona/carácter*› hateful, detestable; ‹*proceder*› abominable

detestar [A1] *vt* to hate, detest

detiene, detienes, etc *see* **detener**

detonación *f* 1 (ruido) explosion; (acción) detonation 2 (Auto) (de motor) backfire

detonador *m* detonator

detonante *m* (explosivo) explosive; (causa): **el ~ de la protesta** what sparked off *o* triggered the protest

detonar [A1] *vi* to detonate, explode; **hicieron ~ la bomba** they detonated the bomb

detractor -tora *m,f* detractor, critic

detrás *adv*
A (lugar, parte) [*Latin American Spanish also uses* **atrás** *in this sense*]: **iba corriendo ~** he ran along behind; **las cajas de ~** the boxes at the back; **se abrocha por ~** it does up at the back; **me atacó por ~** he attacked me from behind
B **detrás de** (*loc prep*) behind; **~ de la casa** at the back of the house; **~ de mí/ti/él** behind me/you/him; **fumaba un cigarrillo ~ de otro** he smoked one cigarette after another; **las razones que había ~ de su decisión** the reasons that lay behind his decision; ***andar* ~ *de algo/algn*** to be after sth/sb

detrimento *m* detriment; **en ~ de algo/algn** to the detriment of sth/sb

detritus (*pl* ~), **detrito** *m* 1 (Geol) detritus 2 **detritus** *mpl* (desechos, residuos) debris, detritus (frml)

detuve, detuvo, etc *see* **detener**

deuda *f* 1 (Com, Fin) debt; **pagar** *or* **saldar una ~** to pay (off) a debt; **contraer una ~** to run up *o* (frml) contract a debt; **cargarse DE ~s** to get oneself heavily INTO debt 2 (compromiso moral) **~ CON algn: estoy en ~ con usted** I am indebted to you 3 (Relig): **perdónanos nuestras ~s** forgive us our trespasses

(Compuestos)
• **deuda del Estado** (títulos emitidos) government stock; (suma adeudada) public sector borrowing
• **deuda externa/pública** foreign/national debt
• **deudas incobrables/morosas** *fpl* bad/doubtful debts (*pl*)
• **deuda soberana** sovereign debt

deudor¹ -dora *adj* debtor (*before n*); **la empresa ~a** the debtor company; **la parte ~a** the debtor/debtors

deudor² -dora *m,f* debtor

(Compuesto) **deudor moroso** defaulter, slow payer

deudos *mpl* (frml) relatives

devaluación *f* devaluation

devaluar [A18] *vt* to devalue
■ **devaluarse** *v pron* ‹‹*moneda*›› to fall; ‹‹*terrenos/propiedad*›› to depreciate, fall in value

devanar [A1] *vt* ‹*hilo/lana/alambre*› to wind; **~ una madeja** to wind wool into a ball

devaneo *m* 1 (amorío) affair; (pasajero) fling 2 (pasatiempo frívolo) idle pursuit; **déjate de ~s** stop wasting your time

devastación *f* devastation

devastador -dora *adj* devastating

devastar [A1] *vt* to devastate

develar [A1] *vt* (AmL) ‹*secreto*› to reveal, disclose; ‹*misterio*› to uncover; ‹*monumento/placa*› to unveil

devengar [A3] *vt* ‹*beneficios*› to yield; ‹*interés*› to bear; **los intereses devengados** the interests accrued

devenir¹ [I31] *vi* (liter) to become

devenir² *m* (Fil) becoming; (liter) (desarrollo) evolution

devis (Méx fam): **de a ~** (*loc adv*) really, honestly

devoción *f* 1 (Relig) devotion; **rezar con ~** to pray devoutly 2 (amor, fervor) devotion; **lo quiere con ~** she's devoted to him; **siente ~ por sus hijos** she's devoted to her children

devocionario *m* prayer book

devolución *f* 1 (de artículo) return; (de dinero) refund; ❺ **no se admiten devoluciones** goods may not be exchanged, no refunds given 2 (Espec) return, returned ticket

devolver [E11] *vt*
A 1 (restituir) ‹*objeto prestado*› to return, give back; ‹*dinero*› to give back, pay back; ‹*envase*› to return, take back; ‹*objeto comprado*› to bring/take ... back; **tengo que ~ los libros a la biblioteca** I have to take the books back to the library; **~ al remitente** return to sender; **devuélvelo a su lugar** put it back in its place; (+ *me/te/le etc*) **me devolvieron los documentos, pero no el dinero** I got my papers back, but not the money; **le di diez pesos, me tiene que ~ dos** I gave you ten pesos, you need to give me two back; **el teléfono me devolvía las monedas** the telephone kept rejecting my coins; **la operación le devolvió la vista** the operation restored his sight; **aquel triunfo le devolvió la confianza en sí mismo** that triumph gave him back his self-confidence 2 ‹*preso*› to return; ‹*refugiado*› to return, send back 3 (Fin) ‹*letra*› to return
B (corresponder) ‹*visita/favor*› to return
C (vomitar) to bring up, throw up
■ **devolver** *vi* to be sick; **tengo ganas de ~** I feel sick
■ **devolverse** *v pron* (AmL exc RPl) (regresar) to go/come/turn back

devorador -dora *adj* ‹*pasión*› all-consuming; **tengo un hambre ~a** I'm ravenous

devorar [A1] *vt* 1 (comer) «*animal*» to devour; «*persona*» to devour, wolf down (colloq); **~ a algn con los ojos** *or* **la mirada** to devour sb with one's eyes (colloq); **devoró el libro** he devoured the book; **me ~on los mosquitos** I was eaten alive by the mosquitoes (colloq) 2 (consumir) «*celos/pasión*» to consume; **lo devora la pasión** he is consumed with passion; **fue devorado por las llamas** it was consumed by the flames

d

devoto[1] -ta *adj* ‹*persona*› devout; ‹*lugar/obra*› devotional; **es muy ~ de la Virgen** he's a devout follower of the Virgin

devoto[2] -ta *m,f* 1 (Relig) **~ DE algn** devotee OF sb 2 (aficionado) **~ DE algo** devotee OF sth; **~ DE algn** admirer OF sb

devuelto *m* (fam) vomit, puke (colloq)

devuelva, devuelvas, etc *see* **devolver**

DF *m* (en Méx) = **Distrito Federal**

di *see* **dar, decir**

día *m*

A 1 (veinticuatro horas) day; **todos los ~s** every day; **el ~ anterior** the day before, the previous day; **el ~ siguiente** the next *o* the following day; **el ~ de ayer/hoy** (frml) yesterday/today; **una vez/dos veces al ~** once/twice a day; **trabaja doce horas por ~** she works a twelve-hour day; **un ~ sí y otro no** every other day, on alternate days; **~ (de) por medio** (AmL) every other day, on alternate days; **dentro de quince ~s** in two weeks *o* (BrE) a fortnight; **cada ~** every day; **el pan nuestro de cada ~** our daily bread; **la lucha de cada ~** the daily struggle; **buenos ~s** *or* (RPl) **buen ~** good morning; **~ a ~ lo veía envejecer** day by day she saw him getting older; **~ tras ~** day after day; ***al ~***: **estoy al ~ en los pagos** I'm up to date with the payments; **ponerse al ~ CON algo** ‹*noticias/trabajo*› to get up to date ON/WITH sth; **ponga al ~ su correspondencia** bring your correspondence up to date; ***de un ~ para otro*** overnight, from one day to the next; ***~ y noche*** day and night, continually; ***hoy en ~*** nowadays, these days; ***mantenerse al ~*** to keep abreast of things, keep up to date; ***todo el santo ~*** all day long; **se pasa todo el santo ~ en el teléfono** he's on the phone all day long; ***vivir al ~*** to live from hand to mouth 2 (jornada) day; **trabajan cuatro ~s a la semana** they work four days a week, they work a four-day week; **un ~ laborable de 8 horas** an eight-hour working day 3 (fecha): **¿qué ~ es hoy?** what day is it today?; **empieza el ~ dos** it starts on the second; **hasta el ~ 5 de junio** until June fifth, until the fifth of June

(Compuestos)

- **día de Año Nuevo**: **el ~ de ~ ~** New Year's Day
- **día de entresemana** weekday
- **día de la madre** Mother's Day
- **día del juicio final**: **el ~ del ~ ~** Judgment Day, the Day of Judgment
- **día de los enamorados** (St) Valentine's Day
- **día festivo** *or* (AmL) **feriado** public holiday
- **día hábil/laborable** working day
- **día lectivo** school (*o* college *etc*) day
- **día libre** (sin trabajo) day off; (sin compromisos) free day

B (horas de luz) day; **duerme durante el ~** it sleeps during the day *o* daytime; **ya era de ~** it was already light *o* day; **al caer el ~** at dusk, at twilight; **nunca ve la luz del ~** he never sees the daylight; **en pleno ~** in broad daylight; **de ~ claro** (Chi) in broad daylight

C (tiempo indeterminado) day; **pásate por casa un ~** why don't you drop in sometime *o* one day?; **ya me lo agradecerás algún ~** you'll thank me for it one day; **el ~ que tengas hijos** when you have children of your own; **si el plan se realiza algún ~** if the plan is ever put into effect; **lo haremos otro ~** we'll do it some other time; **cualquier ~ de estos** any day now; **un ~ de estos** one of these days; **¡hasta otro ~!** so long!, see you!; ***el ~ menos pensado*** when you least expect it; ***en su ~***: **se lo contaré en su ~** I'll tell him in due course; **dio lugar a un gran escándalo en su ~** it caused a huge scandal in its day *o* time; ***un buen ~*** one fine day

D días *mpl* (vida, tiempo) days (*pl*); **tiene los ~s contados** his days are numbered, he won't last long; **desde el siglo XVII hasta nuestros ~s** from the 17th Century to the present day; ***estar en sus ~s*** (Méx fam) to have one's period

E (tiempo atmosférico) day; **hace un ~ nublado/caluroso** it's cloudy/hot

Día de la Hispanidad

▸ Día de la Raza

Día de la Raza

In Latin America, the anniversary of Columbus's discovery of America, October 12. In Spain it is known as *día de la Hispanidad*. It symbolizes the cultural ties shared by Spanish-speaking countries

Día de los (Santos) Inocentes

On December 28 people in the Spanish-speaking world celebrate the Feast of the Holy Innocents, a religious festival commemorating the New Testament story of the massacre of the "Innocents", by playing practical jokes, or *inocentadas*, on one another. The classic *inocentada* is to hang paper dolls on someone's back without their knowing. Spoof news stories also appear in newspapers and the media

Día del Trabajo

In Latin America and Spain, Labor Day is celebrated on May Day. In many Latin American countries, where workers still suffer greatly from low wages and bad working conditions, May Day celebrations often have strong overtones of protest

Día de todos los Santos *or (in Spain)* **de los Difuntos** *or (in Latin America)* **de los Muertos**

Celebrated on November 1, is a day on when people place flowers on the graves of loved ones. In Mexico it is common to hold a party by the grave. A feast is prepared, in which the dead person is symbolically included

diabetes *f* diabetes

diabético -ca *adj/m,f* diabetic

diabla *f* (Chi fam) whore

diablesa *f* she-devil

diablillo *m* (fam) scamp (colloq), imp (colloq)

diablo[1] -bla *adj* (Chi fam) 1 (avispado) smart (colloq) 2 ‹*mujer*› loose

diablo[2] *m*

A (demonio) devil; **este niño es el mismo ~** this child is a real devil; ***como (el*** *or* ***un) ~*** like crazy *o* mad (colloq); ***del ~*** *or* ***de todos los ~s*** *or* ***de mil ~s*** (fam) devilish (colloq); **está de un humor de mil ~s** she's in a devil of a mood (colloq); ***donde el ~ perdió el poncho*** (AmS fam) (en un lugar — aislado) in the back of beyond; (— lejano) miles away (colloq); ***irse al ~*** (fam): **¡vete al ~!** go to hell! (colloq); ***mandar a algn al ~*** (fam) to tell sb to go to hell (colloq); ***mandar algo al ~*** (fam) to pack sth in (colloq); ***tener el ~ en el cuerpo*** to be a devil; ***el ~ las carga*** don't play with guns; ***más sabe el ~ por viejo que por ~*** there's no substitute for experience; ***más vale ~ conocido que ciento*** (Chi) *or* (Arg) ***santo por conocer*** better the devil you know than the devil you don't

(Compuesto) **diablos azules** *mpl* (Andes fam) pink elephants (*pl*) (hum)

B (fam) (uso expletivo): **¿qué/quién/donde ~s ... ?** what/who/where the hell ... ? (colloq); **¿cómo ~s se habrá enterado?** how the hell can he have found out? (colloq)

diablura *f* (fam) prank

diabólico -ca *adj* (del diablo) diabolic, satanic; ‹*persona*› evil; ‹*plan/intenciones*› devilish, fiendish

diábolo *m* diabolo

diácono *m* deacon

diacrónico -ca *adj* diachronic

diadema *f* (para el pelo) hairband; (corona) crown, diadem; (media corona) tiara

diáfano -na *adj* 1 (liter) ‹*agua*› limpid (liter) 2 ‹*luz*› bright; ‹*cielo*› clear 3 (traslúcido) ‹*porcelana*› translucent; ‹*tela*› diaphanous 4 ‹*conducta/proceder*› impeccable; ‹*explicación*› crystal clear

diafragma *m* (Anat, Fot, Med) diaphragm

diagnosis *f* diagnostics

diagnosticar [A2] *vt* to diagnose; **le ~on un cáncer** he was diagnosed as having cancer

diagnóstico *m* diagnosis

diagonal *f* 1 (Mat) diagonal; **trazar una ~** to draw a diagonal (line) 2 (en fútbol americano) endzone

diagrama *m* diagram; **hacer un ~ de algo** to draw a diagram of sth

diagramador -dora *m,f*

A (persona) designer, layout artist

B **diagramador** *m* (Inf) designer

(Compuesto) **diagramador de datos** data diagrammer

dial *m* (Rad, Tec) dial; (del teléfono) dial

dialectal *adj* dialectal

dialéctica *f* dialectics

dialéctico -ca *adj* dialectical

dialecto *m* dialect

diálisis *f* dialysis

dialogar [A3] *vi* to talk; **no pueden ~ como dos personas civilizadas** they are unable to hold a civilized conversation; **~ CON algn** to talk TO sb; **el sindicato está dialogando con la patronal** the union is holding talks with the management

diálogo *m* 1 (conversación) conversation; (Lit) dialogue, dialog (AmE) 2 (Pol, Rels Labs) talks (*pl*), negotiations (*pl*); **el ~ Norte-Sur** the North-South dialogue

(Compuesto) **diálogo de sordos** dialogue of the deaf; **esto parece un ~ de ~** nobody is listening to anyone else

diamante *m* 1 (Min) diamond; **un anillo de ~s** a diamond ring 2 (en béisbol) diamond 3 **diamantes** *mpl* (en naipes) diamonds (*pl*)

(Compuesto) **diamante en bruto** (Min) uncut diamond; (persona) rough diamond

diametral *adj* diametric, diametrical

diametralmente *adv* diametrically

diámetro *m* diameter; **mide dos centímetros de ~** it measures *o* it is two centimeters in diameter

diana *f*

A (Mil) reveille; **tocan (a) ~ a las seis** they sound reveille at six

B (Dep, Jueg) (objeto) target; (para dardos) dartboard; (centro) bull's-eye; ***dar en la ~*** «*proyectil*» to hit the/its target; «*respuesta/comentario*» to hit home

diantre *interj* (euf) 1 (expresando desagrado) damn it! (colloq), hang it! (colloq *or* dated) 2 (uso expletivo) ▸ **diablo² B**

diapasón *m* (para afinar) tuning fork; (de instrumento de cuerda) fingerboard

diapositiva *f* slide, transparency

diariamente *adv* daily, every day

diariero -ra *m,f* (CS) (vendedor) newspaper vendor; (repartidor) (*m*) newspaper delivery man/boy; (*f*) newspaper delivery woman/girl

diario¹ -ria *adj* 1 (de todos los días) ‹*tarea/clases*› daily; ‹*gastos*› everyday, day-to-day; **las clases son diarias** classes are held daily/every day 2 (por día): **trabaja cuatro horas diarias** she works four hours a day 3 **a diario** (*loc adv*) every day; **visita a sus padres a ~** her parents daily she visits *o* every day

diario² *m*

A (periódico) newspaper

(Compuestos)

- **diario de la mañana/vespertino** morning/evening paper
- **diario hablado** news program*
- **diario mural** (Chi) bulletin board (AmE), notice board (BrE)

B (libro personal) diary, journal (AmE)

(Compuestos)

- **diario de a bordo** *or* **de navegación** log, logbook
- **diario de sesiones**: record of parliamentary proceedings, ≈ Congressional Record (*in US*), ≈ Hansard (*in UK*)

C 1 (Méx, Col, Ven) (gastos cotidianos): **el ~** day-to-day expenses 2 (uso cotidiano): **para ~** for everyday (use); **de ~** ‹*ropa/vajilla*› everyday (*before n*)

diario³ *adv* (Méx, Per fam) every day

diarrea *f* diarrhea*

diáspora *f* Diaspora

diatriba *f* diatribe; **~ CONTRA algn/algo** diatribe AGAINST sb/sth

dibujante *mf* 1 (Art) (*m*) draftsman*; (*f*) draftswoman*; (de cómics) comic book artist, strip cartoonist 2 (AmL) (Arquit, Ing) (*m*) draftsman*; (*f*) draftswoman*

(Compuesto) **dibujante publicitario** commercial artist

dibujar [A1] *vt* 1 (Art) to draw, sketch; ‹*plano*› to draw; **~ a mano alzada** to draw freehand 2 (describir): **nos dibujó un cuadro pesimista del futuro** he painted a gloomy picture of the future; **los personajes están muy bien dibujados** the characters are very well drawn *o* portrayed

■ **dibujar** *vi* to draw

■ **dibujarse** *v pron* 1 (liter) (perfilarse) «*forma/contorno*» to be outlined 2 (liter) (mostrarse) «*sonrisa*» to appear; **con la tristeza dibujada en el rostro** with a look of sadness on her (*or* his *etc*) face

dibujo *m* 1 (arte) drawing; **clase de ~** drawing class 2 (representación) drawing; **un ~ a lápiz/al carboncillo** a pencil/charcoal drawing 3 (estampado) pattern; **un ~ de flores** a floral pattern

(Compuestos)

- **dibujo lineal/técnico** line/technical drawing
- **dibujo publicitario** commercial drawing
- **dibujos animados** *mpl* cartoons (*pl*); **una película de ~ ~** a cartoon, an animated film

dic. (= **diciembre**) Dec

dicción *f* (pronunciación) diction; (empleo de la lengua) language

diccionario *m* dictionary

(Compuestos)

- **diccionario bilingüe** bilingual dictionary
- **diccionario ideológico** *or* **de ideas afines** ≈ thesaurus
- **diccionario de autoridades** *dictionary containing attributed quotations*
- **diccionario de sinónimos** dictionary of synonyms, ≈ thesaurus

dice, dices, etc *see* **decir**

dicha *f* 1 (felicidad) happiness; **¡qué ~ verlos a todos reunidos!** what a joy to see you all together!; **¡qué ~! dejó de llover** (AmL fam) fantastic *o* wonderful! it's stopped raining! 2 (suerte) good luck, good fortune; ***nunca es tarde si la ~ es buena*** better late than never

dicharachero -ra *adj* (que habla mucho) chatty (colloq), talkative; (gracioso) witty

dicho¹ -cha *pp* [*ver tb* **decir²**]: **~ esto, se fue** having said this, he left; **con eso queda todo ~** that says it all; **me remito a lo ~ antes** I refer to what was said before; **bueno, lo ~, nos vemos el domingo**oright, that's settled then, I'll see you on Sunday; **eso no se hace, te lo tengo ~** I've told you before, you mustn't do that; **¿le quiere dejar algo ~?** (CS) do you want to leave a message for her?; **~ así parece fácil** if you put it like that it sounds easy; **~ de otro modo** to put it another way, in other words; **~ sea de paso** incidentally, by the way; **dijo que ella lo prepararía y ¡~ y hecho! en diez minutos estaba listo** she said she would get it ready and, sure enough, ten minutes later there it was; **me quedan tres días, mejor ~, dos y medio** I have three, or rather, two and a half days left; **propiamente ~** strictly speaking; **la pintura cubista propiamente dicha** Cubist painting in the strict sense of the term

dicho² -cha *adj dem* (frml): **en dichas cuidades ...** in these cities ...; **~s documentos deben presentarse inmediatamente** the above *o* (frml) said documents must be submitted immediately; **no existía dicha dirección** there was no such address

dicho³ *m* saying; **como dice el ~** as the saying goes; ***del ~ al hecho va*** *or* ***hay mucho trecho*** it's one thing to say something and another to actually do it

dichoso -sa *adj*

A (feliz) happy; (afortunado) fortunate, lucky

B (*delante del n*) (fam) (maldito) blessed (colloq), damn (sl); **este ~ teléfono no para de sonar** this blessed *o* damn phone never stops ringing

diciembre *m* December; *para ejemplos ver* **enero**
diciendo *see* **decir**
diciente *adj* (Col) significant, telling
dicotomía *f* dichotomy
dictación *f* (Chi) pronouncement
dictado *m* 1 (ejercicio) dictation; **nos hizo un ~** she gave us a dictation; **escribir al ~** to take dictation 2 **dictados** *mpl* (preceptos) dictates (*pl*)
dictador -dora *m,f* dictator
dictadura *f* dictatorship

(Compuestos)
- **dictadura del proletariado** dictatorship of the proletariat
- **dictadura militar** military dictatorship

dictáfono® *m* Dictaphone®, dictating machine
dictamen *m* report
(Compuesto) **dictamen facultativo** *or* **médico** medical report
dictaminar [A1] *vt* «*juez/tribunal*» to rule; **el tribunal dictaminó su ingreso en prisión** the court ruled that he be sent to prison; **el forense dictaminó que murió asfixiado** according to the forensic report, he was asphyxiated
■ **dictaminar** *vi* to pass judgment
dictar [A1] *vt* 1 ‹*carta/texto*› to dictate 2 ‹*leyes/medidas*› to announce; ‹*sentencia*› to pronounce, pass 3 ‹*acción/tendencia/moda*› to dictate; **el sentido común nos dicta cautela** common sense advises caution 4 (AmL) ‹*clase/curso*› to give; ‹*conferencia*› to deliver, give
■ **dictar** *vi* to dictate
dictatorial *adj* ‹*gobierno/carácter*› dictatorial
didáctica *f* didactics (frml), art of teaching
didáctico -ca *adj* ‹*juguete/programa*› educational; ‹*poema/exposición*› didactic
diecinueve¹ *adj inv/pron* nineteen; *para ejemplos ver* **cinco**
diecinueve² *m* (number) nineteen
dieciochavo¹ -va *adj/pron* 1 (partitivo): **la dieciochava parte** an eighteenth 2 (crit) (ordinal) eighteenth; *para ejemplos ver* **veinteavo**
dieciochavo² *m* eighteenth
dieciochesco -ca *adj* eighteenth-century
dieciocho¹ *adj inv/pron* eighteen; *para ejemplos ver* **cinco**
dieciocho² *m* (number) eighteen
dieciséis¹ *adj inv/pron* sixteen; *para ejemplos ver* **cinco**
dieciséis² *m* (number) sixteen
diecisiete¹ *adj inv/pron* seventeen; *para ejemplos ver* **cinco**
diecisiete² *m* (number) seventeen
diente *m* 1 (Anat, Zool) tooth; **le están saliendo los ~s** he's cutting his teeth, he's teething; **ya le salió el primer ~** his first tooth has come through; **lavarse** *or* **cepillarse los ~s** to clean *o* brush one's teeth; ***armado hasta los ~s*** armed to the teeth; ***daba ~ con ~*** my/his teeth were chattering; ***de (los) ~s para afuera*** (Andes, Méx fam): **siempre habla de (los) ~s para afuera** he never means what he says; ***enseñar*** *or* ***mostrar los ~s***: **el perro les enseñó los ~s** the dog bared its teeth at them; ***entretener el ~*** (CS fam): **comí una manzana para entretener el ~** I had an apple to keep me going *o* as a snack; ***hablar*** *or* ***murmurar entre ~s*** to mutter (under one's breath); ***hincarle el ~ a algo*** ‹*comida*› to sink one's teeth into sth; ‹*fortuna*› to get one's hands on sth; ‹*asunto*› to come *o* (BrE) get to grips with sth; ***pelar el ~*** (Méx, Ven fam) to smile; ***pelar los ~s*** (Andes, Ven fam) (sonreír) to smile; «*perro*» to bare its teeth; ***ponerle los ~s largos a algn*** (fam) to make sb green with envy (colloq); ***tener buen ~*** (fam) to have a healthy appetite 2 (de engranaje, sierra) tooth; (de tenedor) prong, tine

(Compuestos)
- **diente canino/incisivo/molar** canine tooth/incisor/molar
- **diente de ajo** clove of garlic
- **diente de leche** milk tooth
- **diente de león** dandelion

dientudo -da *adj* (AmL fam) toothy, bucktoothed
diera, dieras, etc *see* **dar**
diéresis *f* (*pl* ~) diaeresis
diese, dieses, etc *see* **dar**
diesel /'disel/ *m* (*pl* ~) 1 (motor) diesel engine 2 (automóvil) diesel, diesel-engined car 3 (combustible) diesel (oil)
diestra *f* (liter *o* period) right hand; **se sentó a la ~ del presidente** she sat on the president's right, she sat to the right of the president; ***a ~ y siniestra*** *or* (Esp) ***a diestro y siniestro*** left and right (AmE), left, right and centre (BrE)
diestro¹ -tra *adj* 1 (frml) ‹*mano*› right; ‹*persona*› right-handed 2 (hábil) ‹*persona*› skillful*, adroit; ‹*jugada*› skillful*
diestro² *m* matador, bullfighter; ***a ~ y siniestro*** *ver* **diestra**
dieta *f*
A (alimentación, régimen) diet; **estar/ponerse a ~** to be/go on a diet
B 1 (para viajes) allowance; **cobra unas ~s muy elevadas** he gets generous traveling expenses *o* a generous subsistence allowance 2 (de parlamentario) salary
dietética *f* dietetics
diez¹ *adj inv/pron* ten; *para ejemplos ver* **cinco**; ***estar en las ~ de última(s)*** (RPl fam) to be on one's last legs
diez² *m* ten
diezmar [A1] *vt* to decimate
diezmo *m* tithe
difamación *f* (por escrito) libel, defamation (frml); (oral) slander, defamation (frml)
difamar [A1] *vt* (Der) (por escrito) to libel, defame (frml); (oralmente) to slander, defame (frml)
difamatorio -ria *adj* ‹*palabras/discurso*› slanderous, defamatory; ‹*artículo/carta*› libelous*, defamatory
difariar [A1] *vi* (Chi) ▸**desvariar**
diferencia *f*
A (disparidad) difference; **salieron con una ~ de pocos minutos** they left a few minutes apart: **a ~ del marido, ella es encantadora** unlike her husband, she's really charming; **la ~ de precio** the difference in price; ***con ~***: **es, con ~, la mejor** she's easily *o* by far the best
B (desacuerdo) difference; **trataron de resolver sus ~s** they tried to resolve their differences
C (resto) difference; **yo pagaré la ~** I'll pay the difference *o* the rest
diferenciación *f* differentiation
diferencial¹ *adj* ‹*cálculo/ecuación*› differential; ‹*tarifa/servicio*› premium (*before n*)
diferencial² *f* (Mat) differential
diferencial³ *m* (Auto, Fin) differential
diferenciar [A1] *vt* ‹*colores/sonidos*› to tell the difference between, differentiate between; **~ algo DE algo**: **no diferencia lo que está bien de lo que está mal** he can't distinguish between right and wrong
■ **diferenciarse** *v pron*: **¿en qué se diferencia esta especie?** what makes this species different?; **~se DE algo/algn** to differ FROM sth/sb; **sólo se diferencia del otro en** *or* **por el precio** the only difference between this one and the other one is the price
diferendo *m* (AmL frml) dispute
diferente *adj* 1 (distinto) different; **ser ~ A** *or* **DE algn/algo** to be different FROM sb/sth; **mi familia es ~ a** *or* **de la tuya** my family is different from *o* to yours; **es un lugar ~ de todos los que he visitado hasta ahora** it is unlike any other place I have visited so far 2 (*en pl, delante del n*) ‹*motivos/soluciones/maneras*› various; **~s personas fueron testigos** various (different) people witnessed it; **nos vimos en ~s ocasiones** we've met on several occasions; **por ~s razones** for a variety of reasons
diferido: **una transmisión en ~** a prerecorded broadcast; **el debate será transmitido en ~** the debate will be recorded and shown later on
diferir [I11] *vt* ‹*reunión/acto*› to postpone; ‹*pago*› to defer; **un cheque diferido** (RPl) a postdated check
■ **diferir** *vi* 1 (frml) (diferenciarse) to differ; **~ DE algo** to differ *o* be different FROM sth 2 (frml) (disentir) to disagree; **~ DE algn** to disagree WITH sb, be at odds WITH sb

difícil *adj*

A 1 [SER] ‹*problema/situación*› difficult; ‹*examen*› hard, difficult; **corren tiempos ~es** these are difficult times; **con tu actitud me lo estás poniendo más ~** you're making it harder for me by being like that; **lo tiene ~ para convencerlo** she'll have a hard job convincing him; **me fue muy ~ decírselo** it was very hard *o* difficult for me to tell him; **resulta ~ evaluar las pérdidas** it is difficult *o* hard to put a figure on the losses; **esto se hace cada vez más ~** this is becoming more and more difficult; **~ DE + INF** difficult *o* hard to + INF; **es ~ de entender** it's difficult to understand 2 [ESTAR] (fam): **está la cosa ~** things are pretty difficult *o* tricky (colloq)

B [SER] (poco probable) unlikely; **es posible pero lo veo ~** it's possible, but I don't think it's very likely; **va a ser muy ~ que acepte** it's very unlikely that he'll accept; **veo ~ que gane** I doubt if she'll win

C [SER] ‹*persona/carácter*› difficult

difícilmente *adv*: **si no estudias, ~ podrás aprobar** if you don't do some work, you'll have trouble passing; **~ te puedes negar** you can hardly say no

dificultad *f* 1 (cualidad de difícil) difficulty; **un ejercicio de escasa ~** a fairly easy exercise; **respira con ~** he has difficulty breathing 2 (problema): **superar** *or* **vencer ~es** to overcome difficulties; **tiene ~s en hacerse entender** she has difficulty in making herself understood; **me pusieron muchas ~es para entrar** they made it very hard for me to get in

dificultar [A1] *vt* to make … difficult; **la niebla dificultó la conducción** the fog made driving difficult; **las obras dificultaban la circulación** the roadworks held up the traffic; **dificultaba los intentos de rescate** it hindered the rescue attempts; **estos obstáculos dificultan el progreso** these obstacles stand in the way of progress

dificultoso -sa *adj* difficult, problematic

difteria *f* diphtheria

difuminar [A1] *vt* (Art) to shade (off); ‹*luz*› to diffuse
■ **difuminarse** *v pron* to fade

difundir [I1] *vt* ‹*noticia/rumor*› to spread; ‹*ideas/doctrina*› to spread, disseminate; ‹*comunicado*› to issue; **la noticia fue difundida por la radio** the news was broadcast on the radio; **~ la cultura** to disseminate culture; **son creencias muy difundidas** such beliefs are very widespread

difunto¹ -ta *adj* (frml) late (*before n*), deceased (frml); **su ~ marido** her late husband

difunto² -ta *m,f* (frml) deceased (frml); **los ~s** the deceased

difusión *f* (de noticia, rumor) spreading; (de ideas, doctrina) spreading, diffusion (frml); **los medios de ~** the media; **se ha dado amplia ~ al conflicto** the conflict has been given widespread coverage

difuso -sa *adj* ‹*luz*› dim, diffused; ‹*idea/conocimientos*› vague

difusor -sora *adj*: **un organismo ~ de nuestra cultura** an organization that disseminates our culture; **los medios ~es** the media

diga, digas, etc *see* **decir**

digerible *adj* digestible

digerir [I11] *vt* ‹*alimentos/comida*› to digest; ‹*información/noticia*› to digest, absorb

digestión *f* digestion; **no te bañes, aún no has hecho la ~** don't go in the water, you haven't let your food go down

digestivo¹ -va *adj* ‹*aparato*› digestive

digestivo² *m* (bebida) digestif, liqueur; (Med) digestive

digital *adj* 1 (dactilar) finger (*before n*), digital (frml) 2 ‹*aparato/sonido*› digital

digitalizar [A4] *vt* to digitize, digitalize; **cuadro de mandos digitalizado** digital instrument panel

digitar [A1] *vt* (RPl) ‹*concurso*› to rig, fix (colloq); ‹*conspiración*› to orchestrate

dígito *m* digit

dignamente *adv* (mereciendo respeto) honorably*, with dignity; (decentemente) decently; (como uno se merece) fittingly, worthily

dignarse [A1] *v pron* **~ (A) + INF: no se dignaron (a) contestar** they didn't even condescend *o* deign to reply

dignatario -ria *m,f* dignitary

dignidad *f*

A (cualidad) dignity; **no lo aceptará, su ~ se lo impide** he won't accept it, he's too proud; **¡qué poca ~ la suya!** has he no dignity *o* self-respect?

B (título) rank; (cargo) position

dignificar [A2] *vt* 1 (ennoblecer): **el trabajo dignifica al hombre** work gives man self-respect; **acciones que dignifican a una persona** acts that ennoble a person 2 (dar categoría a) to dignify

digno -na *adj*

A 1 (merecedor de respeto) ‹*persona/actitud*› honorable* 2 (decoroso, decente) ‹*sueldo*› decent, living (*before n*); ‹*vivienda*› decent

B 1 (merecedor) **~ DE algo/algn: una persona digna de admiración** a person worthy of admiration; **una medida digna de elogio** a praiseworthy measure; **ejemplos ~s de resaltar** noteworthy examples; **un espectáculo ~ de verse** a show worth seeing; **no es ~ de ti/de tu cariño** he's not worthy of you/of your affection; **una cena digna de un rey** (hum) a feast fit for a king (hum) 2 (adecuado): **~ DE algo: una recompensa digna de su esfuerzo** a fitting reward for his efforts; **un trabajo ~ de su capacidad** a job worthy of his abilities

digresión *f* digression; **hace muchas digresiones** he goes off the point *o* digresses a lot

dije¹ *adj* (Chi fam) 1 (agradable) lovely 2 (bondadoso) kind

dije² *m* charm

dije³, dijera, etc *see* **decir**

dilación *f* (frml) delay; **sin más ~** without further delay

dilapidar [A1] *vt* (frml) ‹*fortuna/bienes*› to squander; ‹*energía*› to waste, squander

dilatación *f* (Fís) expansion; (Fisiol, Med) dilation

dilatado -da *adj*

A ‹*pupila/conducto*› dilated

B (extenso): **una dilatada trayectoria política** a long political career; **una dilatada experiencia profesional** extensive experience in the field

dilatar [A1] *vt*

A (Fís, Fisiol) ‹*metal/sólido*› to cause … to expand; ‹*pupilas*› to dilate

B (prolongar) to prolong

C (diferir) to postpone, put off; **no puedo ~ más mi regreso** I cannot put off *o* postpone my return any longer
■ **dilatarse** *v pron*

A (Fís, Fisiol, Med) «*cuerpo/metal*» to expand; «*corazón*» to expand, dilate; «*pupila*» to dilate; «*embarazada*» to dilate

B (prolongarse) to be prolonged

C (diferirse) to be postponed, be put off

D (Méx, Ven) (demorarse): **no me dilato** I won't be long

dilatorio -ria *adj* ‹*maniobra/acción*› delaying (*before n*), dilatory (frml)

dilema *m*

A (disyuntiva) dilemma

B **dilema**® *m* (Chi) (Jueg) Scrabble®

diletante *mf* 1 (amante de las artes) dilettante 2 (pey) (no profesional) dilettante (pej), amateur (pej)

diligencia *f*

A 1 (aplicación) diligence, conscientiousness; **realiza su trabajo con ~** she is diligent *o* conscientious in her work 2 (liter) (rapidez) speed

B 1 (gestión): **activas ~s del gobierno** active steps by the government 2 (Der) procedure; **~s judiciales** judicial procedures *o* formalities; **instruir ~s** to institute proceedings 3 (Adm) (en documento oficial) acknowledgment, stamp

C (Hist, Transp) stagecoach, diligence

diligente *adj* 1 (trabajador) diligent, conscientious 2 (liter) (rápido) fast, swift (liter)

dilucidar [A1] *vt* ‹*asunto/cuestión*› to clarify, elucidate (frml); ‹*enigma/misterio*› to solve, clear up

diluir [I20] *vt* ‹*líquido*› to dilute; ‹*pintura*› to thin (down); ‹*sólido*› to dissolve

diluviar [A1] *vi* to pour (with rain)

diluvio *m* 1 (lluvia) heavy rain, deluge; (inundación) flood; **el D~ Universal** the Flood 2 (fam) (de cartas, quejas) flood

dimensión *f*

A 1 (Fís, Mat) dimension; **una figura en tres dimensiones**

a three-dimensional figure; **la cuarta ~** the fourth dimension **2▸ dimensiones** *fpl* (tamaño) dimensions (*pl*); **las dimensiones de la habitación** the measurements *o* (frml) dimensions of the room
B (alcance, magnitud — de problema) magnitude, scale; (— de tragedia) scale
C (aspecto) dimension, aspect
dimes y diretes *mpl* (fam) tittle-tattle (colloq), gossip
diminutivo *m* diminutive
diminuto -ta *adj* tiny, minute
dimisión *f* resignation; **presentó su ~** he handed in *o* (frml) tendered his resignation
dimisionario -ria *adj* (frml) resigning (*before n*), outgoing (*before n*)
dimitir [I1] *vi* to resign; **~ DE algo** to resign FROM sth
dimos *see* **dar**
dina *f* (Fís) dyne
Dinamarca *f* Denmark
dinámica *f* **1▸** (Fís) dynamics **2▸** (funcionamiento): **la ~ de la organización** the way the organization works; **la ~ de los acontecimientos lo obligó a dimitir** events *o* circumstances forced him to resign
(Compuesto) **dinámica de grupo** group dynamics
dinámico -ca *adj* dynamic
dinamismo *m* dynamism, energy
dinamita *f* dynamite
dinamitar [A1] *vt* to dynamite, blow ... up (*with dynamite*)
dínamo, dinamo *m or* (Esp) *f* dynamo
dinar *m* dinar
dinastía *f* dynasty
dinástico -ca *adj* dynastic
dineral *m* fortune, huge amount of money
dinero *m* money; **anda escaso de ~** he's short of money; **gente de ~** well-off *o* wealthy people; **~ *contante y sonante*** (fam) hard cash; ***hacer* ~** to make money; ***tirar el* ~** (fam) to throw money away
(Compuestos)
- **dinero de bolsillo** pocket money
- **dinero efectivo** *or* **en efectivo** cash
- **dinero electrónico** electronic cash
- **dinero negro** *or* (Méx) **sucio** undeclared income (*o* profits *etc*)
- **dinero suelto** change

dinosaurio *m* dinosaur
dintel *m* lintel
diñar [A1] *vt* (Esp fam): **~*la*** to snuff it (colloq)
dio *see* **dar**
diocesano -na *adj* diocesan
diócesis *f* diocese
diodo *m* diode
dionisiaco -ca, dionisíaco -ca *adj* Dionysian
dioptría *f* diopter*; **¿cuántas ~s tiene?** what's your correction *o* gradation?
dios, diosa *m,f*
A (Mit) (*m*) god; (*f*) goddess
B **Dios** *m* (Relig) God; **el D~ de los cristianos/musulmanes** the Christian/Muslim God; **D~ Todopoderoso** Almighty God, God Almighty; **D~ Padre** God the Father; **gracias a D~** *or* **a D~ gracias** thank God *o* heaven; **si D~ quiere** God willing; **D~ mediante** God willing; **sólo D~ sabe lo que me costó** you've no idea how difficult it was; **D~ dirá** we'll just have to wait and see; **D~ te oiga!** I hope so! *o* I pray to God you're right!; **te lo juro por D~** I swear to God; **¡por (el) amor de D~!** for God's sake *o* for heaven's sake!; **que D~ se lo pague** God bless you; **ve con D~** God be with you; **que D~ te bendiga** God bless you; **que D~ lo tenga en su gloria** God *o* the Lord rest his soul; **¡D~ me libre!** God *o* heaven forbid!; **¡sabe D~!** God knows!; **¡alabado** *or* **bendito sea D~!** (Relig) praise God *o* the Lord!; **¡bendito sea D~, mira cómo te has puesto!** (fam) good God *o* good heavens! look at the state you're in! (colloq); **¡vaya por D~!** oh dear!; **¡válgame D~!** oh my God!, good God!; **¡por D~!** for God's *o* heaven's sake!; **¡D~ mío!** *or* **¡D~ santo!** (expresando angustia) my God!, oh God!; (expresando sorpresa) (good) God!; ***armar la de D~ es Cristo*** (fam) to cause an almighty row (colloq); ***como D~ manda***: **cómprate un coche como D~ manda** buy yourself a real *o* a proper car; **pórtate como D~ manda** behave properly; ***como D~ me/lo trajo al mundo*** in my/his birthday suit; ***como que hay (un) D~*** (CS) you can bet your bottom dollar (colloq); ***costar D~ y (su) ayuda*** (fam) to take a lot of work; ***hacer algo a la buena de D~*** to do sth any which way (AmE) *o* (BrE) any old how; ***menos pregunta D~ y perdona*** (AmL) don't ask so many questions; ***ni D~*** (fam) nobody; **esto no lo entiende ni D~** *or* **no hay D~ que lo entienda** this is completely incomprehensible; ***todo D~*** (fam) absolutely everybody; ***D~ aprieta pero no ahoga*** *or* (RPl) ***ahorca*** these things are sent to try us; ***D~ los cría y ellos se juntan*** birds of a feather flock together; ***a D~ rogando y con el mazo dando*** God helps those who help themselves; ***D~ da pan a quien no tiene dientes*** it's an unfair world; ***al que madruga, D~ lo ayuda*** the early bird catches the worm; ***tener a D~ agarrado por las chivas*** (Ven fam) to have the upper hand
dióxido *m* dioxide
diploma *m* diploma, certificate
diplomacia *f*
A (Pol) (carrera) diplomacy; (cuerpo) diplomatic corps
B (tacto) diplomacy, tact; **díselo con ~** be tactful *o* diplomatic
diplomado[1] -da *adj* qualified
diplomado[2] -da *m,f*: **~ en peluquería** qualified hairdresser
diplomarse [A1] *v pron* **1▸** (AmL) (obtener un título universitario) to graduate; **~ DE/EN algo** to graduate AS/IN sth; **me diplomé de arquitecto** *or* **en arquitectura** I graduated as an architect *o* in architecture **2▸** (obtener otro título) to obtain a diploma (*o* certificate *etc*); **se diplomó de traductor** he qualified as a translator
diplomático[1] -ca *adj*
A (Pol) ‹*carrera/pasaporte*› diplomatic
B (en el trato) diplomatic, tactful
diplomático[2] -ca *m,f* diplomat; **un ~ de carrera** a career diplomat
díptero *m* dipteran
díptico *m* (Art) diptych
diptongo *m* diphthong
diputación *f* **1▸** (delegación) deputation, delegation **2▸** (Gob) (en Esp) council
(Compuesto) **diputación general/provincial** regional/provincial council
diputado -da *m,f* deputy, ≈ representative (*in US*), ≈ member of parliament (*in UK*); **~ por** *or* **de León** representative *o* member of parliament for León
dique *m* dike*
(Compuestos)
- **dique de contención** dam, dike*
- **dique seco** dry dock

Dir.[1] *mf* = **director/directora**
Dir.[2] *f* = **dirección**
diré, dirá, etc *see* **decir**
dirección *f*
A (señas) address; **nombre y ~** name and address
(Compuestos)
- **dirección electrónica** e-mail address
- **dirección particular** private address
- **dirección postal** postal address

B (sentido, rumbo) direction; **ellos venían en ~ contraria** they were coming the other way *o* from the opposite direction; **¿en qué ~ iba?** *or* **¿qué ~ llevaba?** which way was he heading *o* going?; **cambiar de ~** to change direction; **señal de ~ prohibida** no-entry sign; **~ obligatoria** one way only
C (Auto) (mecanismo) steering
(Compuesto) **dirección asistida** power steering
D (Adm) **1▸** (cargo — en escuela) principalship (AmE), headship (BrE); (— en empresa) post *o* position of manager **2▸** (cuerpo directivo — de empresa) management; (— de periódico) editorial board; (— de prisión) authorities (*pl*); (— de partido) leadership **3▸** (oficina — en escuela) principal's office (AmE), headmaster's/headmistress's office (BrE); (— en empresa) manager's/director's office; (— en periódico) editorial office

E 1▸ (de obra, película) direction; **la ∼ es de Saura** it is directed by Saura 2▸ (de orquesta): **bajo la ∼ de Campomar** conducted by Campomar 3▸ (de empresa, proyecto) management; **bajo la ∼ de su profesor** under the guidance of her teacher

direccional *f* (Col, Méx) turn signal (AmE), indicator (BrE); **poner las ∼es** to indicate *o* signal

directa *f* high (AmE), top gear (BrE)

directamente *adv* (derecho) straight; (sin intermediarios) directly

directiva *f*
A (de empresa) board (of directors); (de partido) executive committee, leadership
B (directriz) guideline

directivo *m* (gerente) manager; (ejecutivo) executive, director

directo¹ -ta *adj*
A ‹*vuelo*› direct, nonstop; ‹*ruta/acceso*› direct; **un tren ∼** a direct *o* through train; **descendiente por línea directa** direct descendant; **es mi jefe ∼** he is my immediate superior
B (Rad, TV): **en ∼** live; **transmitido en ∼** broadcast live
C ‹*lenguaje/pregunta*› direct; ‹*respuesta*› straight; ‹*persona*› direct, straightforward

directo² *m* (en boxeo) straight punch

director -tora *m,f* 1▸ (de escuela) (*m*) head teacher, principal (AmE), headmaster (BrE); (*f*) head teacher, principal (AmE), headmistress (BrE); (de periódico, revista) editor (in chief); (de hospital) administrator; (de prisión) warden (AmE), governor (BrE) 2▸ (Com) (gerente) manager; (miembro de junta directiva) director, executive 3▸ (Cin, Teatr) director

(Compuestos)
- **director adjunto -tora adjunta** *m,f* deputy director
- **director -tora de escena** *m,f* stage manager
- **director -tora de orquesta** *m,f* conductor
- **director ejecutivo -tora ejecutiva** *m,f* executive director
- **director -tora general** *m,f* (de empresa) general manager; (de organismo oficial) director-general
- **director -tora gerente** *m,f* managing director

directorio *m* (AmL exc CS) (guía telefónica) telephone directory, directory

directriz *f* (Mat) directrix; (guía) guideline, principle; (instrucción) directive

dirigencia *f* (AmL frml) (acción) leadership; (dirigentes) leaders (*pl*)

dirigente¹ *adj*: **las clases ∼s** the ruling classes; **cargos ∼s** management/leadership posts

dirigente² *mf* (de partido, país) leader

dirigible *m* airship, dirigible

dirigir [I7] *vt*
A 1▸ ‹*empresa*› to manage, run; ‹*periódico/revista*› to run, edit; ‹*investigación/tesis*› to supervise; ‹*debate*› to lead, chair; **∼ el tráfico** to direct *o* control the traffic 2▸ ‹*obra/película*› to direct 3▸ ‹*orquesta*› to conduct
B 1▸ **∼ algo A algn** ‹*mensaje/carta*› to address sth TO sb; ‹*críticas*› to direct sth TO sb; **el presidente ∼á un mensaje a la nación** the president will address the nation; **el folleto va dirigido a los padres** the booklet is aimed at parents; **la pregunta iba dirigida a usted** the question was meant for you; **no me dirigió la palabra** he didn't say a word to me 2▸ **∼ algo HACIA** *or* **A algo/algn** ‹*telescopio*› to point sth TOWARD(S) sth/sb; ‹*pistola*› to point sth TOWARD(S) sth/sb; **∼ la mirada hacia** *or* **a algo/algn** to look at sth/sb; **le dirigió una mirada de reproche** she gave him a reproachful look; **dirigió sus pasos hacia la esquina** he walked toward(s) the corner
C (encaminar) **∼ algo A + INF** ‹*esfuerzos*› to channel sth INTO -ING; ‹*energía/atención*› to direct sth TOWARD(S) -ING; **acciones dirigidas a aliviar el problema** measures aimed at alleviating the problem

■ **dirigirse** *v pron*
A (encaminarse): **∼se HACIA algo** to head FOR sth
B **∼se A algn** (oralmente) to speak *o* talk TO sb; (por escrito) to write TO sb; **me dirijo a Vd. para solicitarle ...** (Corresp) I am writing to request ...

dirimir [I1] *vt*
A (frml) ‹*disputa/pleito*› to resolve (frml), to settle
B (Der) ‹*contrato*› to cancel, declare ... void; ‹*matrimonio*› to dissolve, annul

discado *m* (AmL) dialing*

(Compuesto) **discado automático** *or* **directo** (AmL) direct dialing*

discapacidad *f* handicap, disability

discapacitado -da *m,f* disabled person, handicapped person; **los ∼s** the disabled, handicapped people; **∼ físico/psíquico** physically/mentally handicapped person

discar [A2] *vt/vi* (AmL) to dial

discernimiento *m* discernment; **obró con ∼** he was very discerning, he acted wisely

discernir [I12] *vi* to distinguish, discern; **∼ entre el bien y el mal** to distinguish *o* discern between good and evil *o* between right and wrong
■ **discernir** *vt* 1▸ (percibir) ‹*forma*› to discern (frml), to perceive 2▸ (distinguir) **∼ algo DE algo** to distinguish sth FROM sth

disciplina *f*
A (reglas) discipline; **mantener la ∼** to keep *o* maintain discipline

(Compuesto) **disciplina de partido** *or* **voto** (Pol) party discipline; **romper la ∼ de ∼** to defy the whip, to go against the party line

B 1▸ (ciencia) discipline 2▸ (Dep) discipline

disciplinado -da *adj* ‹*alumno*› disciplined

disciplinar [A1] *vt* to discipline

disciplinario -ria *adj* ‹*comisión/medida*› disciplinary (*before n*)

discípulo -la *m,f* disciple

disco¹ *m*
A 1▸ (Audio) record, disc (colloq); **grabar un ∼** to make a record *o* disc; **poner un ∼** to put on a record; ***parecer un ∼ rayado*** (fam) to be like a worn-out gramophone record (colloq) 2▸ (Inf) disk

(Compuestos)
- **disco compacto** CD, compact disc
- **disco de larga duración** album, LP
- **disco duro** hard disk
- **disco flexible** *or* **floppy** floppy disk
- **disco óptico** video disk
- **disco sencillo** single
- **disco volador** (CS) flying saucer

B 1▸ (Dep) discus; **lanzamiento de ∼** (throwing) the discus 2▸ (Med) disk* 3▸ (Auto, Mec): **frenos de ∼** disk* brakes 4▸ (del teléfono) dial
C 1▸ (señal de tráfico) (road) sign 2▸ (semáforo) (Ferr) signal; (Auto) traffic light

disco² *f* (fam) (discoteca) disco

discografía *f* 1▸ (frml) (catálogo) discography (frml) 2▸ (period) (de cantante) records (*pl*)

discográfico -ca *adj* ‹*casa/sello*› record (*before n*); ‹*contrato*› recording (*before n*)

díscolo -la *adj* unruly, disobedient

disconforme *adj* 1▸ (no satisfecho) dissatisfied; **∼ CON algo/algn** dissatisfied WITH sth/sb 2▸ (en desacuerdo) **estar ∼ CON algo** to disagree WITH sth (frml)

disconformidad *f* 1▸ (insatisfacción) dissatisfaction; **∼ CON algo/algn** dissatisfaction WITH sth/sb 2▸ (desacuerdo) disagreement; **∼ CON algo** disagreement WITH sth; **la medida está en ∼ con lo establecido en la ley** the measure is against the law

discontinuidad *f* (Mat, Tec) discontinuity

discontinuo -nua *adj* ‹*línea*› broken; ‹*sonido*› intermittent

discordancia *f* conflict; **hubo ∼ de opiniones** there was a difference of opinion; **está en ∼ con lo que manifestó antes** it is at variance with what he stated before

discordante *adj* (Mús) discordant; ‹*opiniones/versiones*› conflicting (*before n*)

discordar [A10] *vi* 1▸ (Mús) to be out of tune 2▸ «*personas*» to differ 3▸ «*opiniones*» to conflict

discorde *adj*
A (Mús) discordant
B (frml) (en desacuerdo) in disagreement; **se mostró ∼ con la**

nueva disposición he indicated that he disagreed with the new arrangement

discordia *f* discord

discoteca *f* [1] (local) discotheque [2] (colección de discos) record collection [3] (AmC) (tienda) record store *o* shop

discreción *f*

A [1] (tacto, mesura) tact, discretion [2] (reserva) discretion; **obrar** *or* **actuar con ~** to be discreet

B **a discreción**: **esto queda a ~ del juez** this is left to the discretion of the judge; **¡fuego a ~!** fire at will!

discrecional *adj* ‹*facultades/poderes*› discretionary, discretional

discrepancia *f* [1] (diferencia) discrepancy, difference; **mantienen ~s sobre este tema** there are differences between them on this subject [2] (desacuerdo) disagreement

discrepante *adj* dissenting (*before n*)

discrepar [A1] *vi* [1] (disentir) to disagree; **~ CON** *or* **DE algn/algo** to disagree with sb/sth [2] (diferenciarse) to differ

discretamente *adv* discreetly; **hace su labor ~** she quietly gets on with her work

discreto -ta *adj* [1] ‹*persona/carácter/comportamiento*› discreet; **se mostró discreta en sus acusaciones** she was restrained in her accusations [2] ‹*color/vestido*› discreet [3] ‹*cantidad/sueldo*› modest

discriminación *f* discrimination; **ser objeto de discriminaciones** to be the object of discrimination

discriminar [A1] *vt* [1] ‹*persona/colectividad*› to discriminate against [2] (distinguir) to differentiate, distinguish

discriminativo -va *adj* (Ven) discriminatory

discriminatorio -ria *adj* discriminatory

disculpa *f* apology; **me debe una ~** she owes me an apology; **un error que no tiene** *or* **no admite ~** an inexcusable error; **pedir(le) ~s (a algn) POR algo** to apologize (to sb) FOR sth

disculpar [A1] *vt* to excuse; **disculpa mi tardanza** I am sorry I'm late; **no se puede ~ algo así** there can be no excuse for doing something like that; **su madre siempre lo está disculpando** his mother's always making excuses for him

■ **disculpar** *vi*: **disculpe, no lo volveré a hacer** I'm sorry *o* (frml) I apologize, I won't do it again

■ **disculparse** *v pron* to apologize; **se disculpó con ella** he apologized to her, he said sorry to her

discurrir [I1] *vi* [1] (frml *o* liter) «*tiempo/vida*» to pass, go by; «*reunión*» to pass off; «*conversación*» to flow [2] (frml *o* liter) (pasar) to pass; **una senda que discurre entre los naranjos** a path which runs between the orange trees [3] (reflexionar) to reflect, ponder

discursivo -va *adj* discursive

discurso *m* [1] (alocución) speech; **pronunciar un ~** to give *o* make a speech; **~ de apertura** opening speech; **me soltó un ~** (fam) he gave me a real lecture [2] (retórica) discourse [3] (Ling) speech, discourse (tech); **análisis del ~** discourse analysis [4] (liter) (del tiempo) passing, passage (frml *or* liter)

(Compuesto) **discurso directo/indirecto** direct/indirect speech

discusión *f* [1] (de asunto, tema) discussion; **eso no admite ~** that leaves no room for discussion [2] (altercado, disputa) argument

discutible *adj*: **eso es ~** that's debatable *o* that's a matter of opinion

discutido -da *adj* controversial

discutir [I1] *vt* [1] (debatir) ‹*problema/asunto*› to discuss; ‹*proyecto de ley*› to debate, discuss; **esto habría que ~lo con el director** this would have to be discussed with the manager [2] (cuestionar) ‹*derecho*› to challenge, dispute; **todo lo que digo me lo discute** he questions *o* challenges everything I say

■ **discutir** *vi* to argue, quarrel; **discutieron y no se han vuelto a hablar** they had an argument *o* a quarrel and haven't spoken to each other since; **discutió de política con su padre** he argued with his father about politics; **~ POR algo** to argue ABOUT sth; **~le A algn** to argue WITH sb; **¡no me discutas!** don't argue with me!

disecación *f* [1] (de animal — para estudiarlo) dissection; (— para conservarlo) stuffing [2] (de planta) preservation (*by pressing, drying etc*)

disecar [A2] *vt* [1] ‹*animal muerto*› (para estudiarlo) to dissect; (para conservarlo) to stuff [2] ‹*planta*› to preserve

disección *f* dissection; **hacer la ~ de una rana** to dissect a frog

diseccionar [A1] *vt* [1] ‹*animal*› to dissect [2] ‹*obra/personaje*› to dissect

diseminación *f* [1] (de semillas — por el viento) dispersal, spreading (frml); (Agr) scattering [2] (de ideas, una cultura) spreading, dissemination (frml)

diseminado -da *adj*: **los pueblos ~s por la región** the villages scattered throughout the region; **los hoteles están muy ~s** the hotels are very spread out

diseminar [A1] *vt* [1] ‹*semillas*› «*viento*» to disperse, scatter; (Agr) to scatter [2] ‹*ideas/doctrina/cultura*› to spread, disseminate (frml)

■ **diseminarse** *v pron* «*personas*» to scatter, disperse; «*ideas/cultura*» to spread

disensión *f* disagreement; **las primeras disensiones dentro de la comisión** the first signs of dissension *o* disagreement within the committee

disentería *f* dysentery

disentir [I11] *vi* to dissent, disagree; **~ DE algo** to disagree WITH sth; **~ CON algn** to disagree WITH sb; **~ EN algo** to disagree ABOUT sth

diseñador -dora *m,f* designer; **~ de moda(s)** fashion designer

diseñar [A1] *vt* ‹*moda/mueble/máquina*› to design; ‹*parque/edificio*› to design, plan; **una ciudad muy bien diseñada** a very well-planned city

diseño *m* design; **~ gráfico** graphic design; **~ de interiores** interior design; **~ de moda** fashion design; **el ~ de esta tela es muy llamativo** this fabric has a very striking design; **blusas de ~ francés** French-designed blouses; **muebles/ropa de ~** designer furniture/clothes

disertación *f* lecture

disertar [A1] *vi* to speak, discourse (frml); **~ ACERCA DE/SOBRE algo** to speak ABOUT sth, discourse ON sth (frml)

disforzarse [A11] *v pron* (Per fam) to clown around

disfraz *m* [1] (Indum) (para jugar, fiestas) costume, fancy dress outfit (BrE); (para engañar) disguise; **cruzó la frontera con un ~ de mujer** he crossed the border disguised as a woman; **un baile/fiesta de disfraces** a costume *o* (BrE) fancy dress ball/party [2] (simulación) front; **es un ~ para ocultar su inseguridad** it's just a pretense *o* a front to hide his insecurity

disfrazar [A4] *vt* [1] **~ a algn DE algo** (para fiesta) to dress sb up AS sth; (par engañar) to disguise sb AS sth [2] (disimular, ocultar) ‹*sentimiento/verdad*› to conceal, hide; ‹*voz/escritura/intención*› to disguise

■ **disfrazarse** *v pron* [1] (por diversión) to dress up; **todo el mundo se disfrazó para la fiesta** everyone went to the party in costume *o* (BrE) fancy dress; **~se DE algo/algn** to dress up AS sth/sb; **¿de qué te disfrazaste en carnaval?** what did you go to the carnival as? [2] (para engañar) to disguise oneself; **~se DE algo/algn** to disguise oneself AS sth/sb, dress up AS sth/sb

disfrutar [A1] *vi* [1] (divertirse) to enjoy oneself, have fun; **~ CON algo** to enjoy sth; **~ + GER** to enjoy -ING; **disfruto viéndolos comer** I enjoy watching them eat; **~ DE algo** to enjoy sth; **espero que hayan disfrutado de la travesía** I hope you have had a pleasant crossing [2] **~ DE algo** ‹*de privilegio/derecho*› to enjoy, have; **~on de buen tiempo** they had good weather; **disfruta de buena salud** he enjoys good health; **con este vale ~á de un descuento del 5%** with this voucher you will receive a 5% discount

■ **disfrutar** *vt* ‹*viaje/espectáculo*› to enjoy; ‹*beneficio/derecho*› to have, enjoy

disfrute *m* enjoyment

disfuerzos *mpl* (Per fam) clowning around, antics (*pl*)

disfunción *f* dysfunction

disfuncional *adj* dysfunctional

disgregación *f* (de grupo) breaking up; (Tec) disintegration

disgregar [A3] *vt* ‹*grupo/familia*› to break up, split up; (Tec) to disintegrate
■ **disgregarse** *v pron* [1] «*grupo/familia*» to break up, split up; «*multitud/manifestantes*» to break up, disperse [2] (Tec) to disintegrate

disgustado -da *adj* [ESTAR] upset

disgustar [A1] *vt*: **me disgustó mucho que me mintiera** I was very upset that he lied to me; **me disgusta tener que decírselo** I don't like having to tell her
■ **disgustarse** *v pron* to get upset

disgusto *m*
A (sufrimiento, pesar): **tiene un ~ tremendo** he's very upset; **me vas a matar a ~s** you'll be the death of me; **lo hizo a ~** she did it reluctantly; **si te vas a quedar a ~ es mejor que te vayas** if you really don't want to be here, you might as well go
B [1] (discusión) argument, quarrel [2] (incidente desagradable): **si sigues conduciendo así vas a tener un ~** if you keep on driving like that you're going to have an accident

disidencia *f* (desacuerdo) dissent; **las ~s en el seno del partido** the disagreements within the party

disidente[1] *adj* [1] ‹*persona*› (que discrepa) dissident (*before n*) [2] ‹*grupo/sector*› (que discrepa) dissident (*before n*); (escindido) breakaway (*before n*)

disidente[2] *mf* (que discrepa) dissident; (escindido) member of a splinter *o* breakaway group

disimuladamente *adv* surreptitiously; **se fue ~ de la fiesta** she sneaked *o* slipped away from the party

disimulado[1] -da *adj* [1] (disfrazado, oculto) disguised; **una cicatriz muy bien disimulada** a cleverly disguised scar; **un mal ~ descontento** ill-concealed displeasure [2] (discreto) discreet

disimulado[2] -da *m,f*: **me vio pero se hizo la disimulada** she saw me but she pretended she hadn't

disimular [A1] *vt* [1] ‹*alegría/rabia/dolor*› to hide, conceal; **será muy tímida, pero lo disimula muy bien** if she is shy, she certainly hides it well [2] ‹*defecto/imperfección*› to hide, disguise
■ **disimular** *vi*: **no sabe ~** she's no good at hiding things *o* pretending; **disimula, que nos están mirando** act normal, we're being watched

disimulo *m*: **salió con ~** he slipped away (without anyone noticing); **la miraba sin ningún ~** he was staring at her quite openly; **con mucho ~ se lo metió en el bolsillo** she surreptitiously slipped it into her pocket

disipación *f*
A (libertinaje) dissipation; **una vida de ~** a dissipated life
B [1] (de temores, dudas) dispelling [2] (de fortuna) squandering

disipado -da *adj* ‹*vida/comportamiento*› dissolute, dissipated

disipar [A1] *vt* [1] ‹*temores/dudas*› to dispel [2] ‹*fortuna/dinero*› to squander
■ **disiparse** *v pron* «*nubes/niebla*» to clear; «*temores/sospechas*» to be dispelled; «*ilusiones*» to vanish, disappear

dislate *m*: **esto es un ~** this is insane

dislexia *f* dyslexia

disléxico -ca *adj/m,f* dyslexic

dislocación *f* dislocation

dislocado -da *adj* ‹*articulation*› dislocated

dislocar [A2] *vt* ‹*articulation*› to dislocate
■ **dislocarse** *v pron* ‹*articulation*› to dislocate

disminución *f* [1] (de gastos, salarios, precios) decrease, drop, fall; (de población) decrease, fall; **una ~ de las temperaturas** a drop in temperature; **la ~ de las tarifas** the reduction in charges [2] (de entusiasmo, interés) waning, dwindling [3] (al tejer) decreasing

disminuido -da *m,f*: **~ psíquico** mentally handicapped person; **~ físico** physically handicapped person

disminuir [I20] *vi*
A (menguar) «*número/cantidad*» to decrease, drop, fall; «*entusiasmo/interés*» to wane, diminish; «*precios/temperaturas*» to drop, fall; «*poder/fama*» to diminish; «*dolor*» to diminish, lessen; **los impuestos no disminuyeron** there was no cut in taxes; **disminuyó la intensidad del viento** the wind died down *o* dropped; **la agilidad disminuye con los años** one becomes less agile with age
B (al tejer) to decrease
■ **disminuir** *vt*
A (reducir) ‹*gastos/costos/impuestos*› to reduce, cut; ‹*velocidad*› to reduce; ‹*número/cantidad*› to reduce, diminish; **el alcohol disminuye la rapidez de los reflejos** alcohol slows down your reactions
B (al tejer) ‹*puntos*› to decrease

disociación *f* dissociation

disociar [A1] *vt* (Quím) to dissociate (separar) **~ algo DE algo** to separate *o* dissociate sth FROM sth
■ **disociarse** *v pron* **~se DE algo/algn** to dissociate *o* disassociate oneself FROM sth/sb

disoluble *adj* [1] ‹*matrimonio/asamblea*› dissoluble [2] (Quím) soluble

disolución *f* [1] (de contrato, matrimonio) annulment; (de organización) dissolution; (del parlamento) dissolution [2] (de manifestación) breaking up [3] (Quím) (solución) solution; (acción) dissolving

disoluto -ta *adj* dissolute

disolvente *m* solvent; **~ de grasas** grease solvent; **~ de pintura** paint thinner

disolver [E11] *vt* [1] ‹*matrimonio/contrato*› to annul; ‹*parlamento*› to dissolve [2] ‹*manifestación/reunión*› to break up [3] (en líquido) to dissolve; Ⓢ **disuélvase en la boca** (*impers*) allow to dissolve in the mouth [4] (Med) to dissolve, break up
■ **disolverse** *v pron* «*manifestación/reunión*» to break up; «*azúcar/aspirina*» to dissolve

disonancia *f* dissonance

disonante *adj* (Mús) dissonant; ‹*voz*› discordant; ‹*colores*› clashing

disonar [A10] *vi* (Col) to look out of place

dispar *adj* [1] (irregular) uneven; **el trato que reciben es muy ~** the treatment they receive varies a great deal [2] (diferente) different, disparate (frml)

disparada *f* (RPl): **a la(s) ~(s)** at top speed, at breakneck speed; **salir a la(s) ~(s)** to shoot off (colloq); **todo lo hace a la(s) ~(s)** she rushes things

disparado -da *adj* (fam): ***salir disparado*** (irse de prisa) to shoot off (colloq); **con el choque salió ~ del asiento** the impact catapulted him from his seat; ***pasó* ~** he shot by like greased lightning

disparador *m* (de arma) trigger; (Fot) shutter release; (de reloj) escapement

(Compuesto) **disparador automático** delayed action release

disparar [A1] *vi*
A [1] (con arma) to shoot, fire; **~ al aire** to fire *o* shoot into the air; **~ a matar** to shoot to kill; **le disparó por la espalda** he shot him in the back; **~ a quemarropa** *or* **a bocajarro** to fire at point-blank range; **¡no disparen!** don't shoot!; **¡alto o disparo!** stop or I'll shoot!; **~ CONTRA algn** to shoot *o* fire AT sb [2] (Dep) to shoot
B (Méx fam) (pagar) to pay
■ **disparar** *vt*
A [1] ‹*arma/flecha*› to shoot, fire; ‹*tiro/proyectil*› to fire; **le ~on un tiro en la nuca** they shot him in the back of the head [2] (Dep): **disparó el balón a portería** he shot at goal [4] (fam) ‹*pregunta*› to fire (colloq)
B (Méx fam) (pagar) to buy; **nos disparó un café** he treated us to a cup of coffee
■ **dispararse** *v pron*
A [1] «*arma*» to go off [2] (*refl*): **se disparó un tiro en la sien** he shot himself in the head
B (fam) «*precio*» to shoot up, rocket

disparatado -da *adj* ‹*acto/proyecto/idea*› crazy, ludicrous; ‹*gasto/precio*› outrageous, ridiculous, excessive

disparate *m* [1] (acción insensata, cosa absurda): **hacer ~s** to do stupid things; **decir ~s** to make foolish remarks; **cometió el ~ de conducir bebido** he was stupid enough to drink and drive; **es un ~ casarse tan joven** it's crazy to get married so young; **temo que haga algún ~** I'm afraid he might do something crazy [2] (fam) (cantidad exagerada) ridiculous (*o* crazy *etc*) amount

disparidad *f* **~ DE algo**: **dada la ~ de criterios** given the difference *o* disparity in people's opinions; **hay ~ de opiniones al respecto** there are many different opinions on this subject

disparo *m* [1] (de arma) shot; **~s de advertencia** *or* **aviso** warning shots [2] (Dep) shot

dispendio *m* waste, extravagance
dispendioso -sa *adj* (Col) ‹*trabajo*› laborious
dispensa *f* dispensation; **~ papal** papal dispensation
dispensar [A1] *vt*
A ‹*honor*› to give, accord (frml); ‹*acogida*› to give, extend (frml); ‹*ayuda/protección*› to give, afford (frml); ‹*asistencia médica*› to give; ‹*medicamentos*› to dispense; **le ~on un caluroso recibimiento** he was given *o* (frml) extended a warm reception
B 1 (eximir) **~ a algn DE algo** to exempt sb FROM sth; **la ~on de asistir a misa** she was excused from attending mass 2 (perdonar) to forgive
■ **dispensar** *vi* to forgive; **dispense, por favor** excuse me
dispensario *m* 1 (Med) clinic (*gen for the poor*) 2 (Col) (de caridad) *establishment providing food and clothing for the poor*
dispersar [A1] *vt* 1 ‹*manifestantes*› to disperse; ‹*manifestación/multitud*› to disperse, break up; ‹*enemigo*› to disperse, rout 2 ‹*rayos*› to scatter, diffuse; ‹*niebla/humo*› to clear, disperse
■ **dispersarse** *v pron* 1 «*manifestantes/manifestación/multitud*» to disperse 2 «*rayos*» to diffuse, scatter; «*niebla/humo*» to disperse, clear
dispersión *f* 1 (de manifestación) dispersion, breaking up 2 (Fís) diffusion
disperso -sa *adj* (diseminado) dispersed (frml); **mi familia está dispersa por el mundo** my family is scattered all over the world
displicencia *f* (indiferencia) indifference; (frialdad) disdain, offhand manner; **nos atendió con ~** his service was rather offhand
displicente *adj* (indiferente) indifferent, blasé; (frío) disdainful, offhand
disponer [E22] *vt*
A (frml) (establecer, ordenar) «*ley*» to provide (frml), to stipulate (frml); «*rey*» to decree; «*general/juez*» to order; **en cumplimiento con lo dispuesto en el artículo primero** in accordance with the provisions of article one; **la junta ha dispuesto subir la cuota de los socios** the committee has decided to increase membership fees; **~ QUE + SUBJ**: **dispuso que todos sus bienes pasaran a la Iglesia** he stipulated that his entire estate should go to the Church; **el juez dispuso que fuera puesta en libertad** the judge ordered her release
B (frml) (colocar, arreglar) to arrange, set out, lay out
■ **disponer** *vi*: **~ DE algn/algo** to have sb/sth at one's disposal; **puede ~ de mí para lo que guste** (frml) I am at your disposal (frml); **¿dispones de un minuto?** do you have a minute?, have you got a minute?; **con los recursos de que dispongo** with the means available to me *o* at my disposal
■ **disponerse** *v pron* (frml) **~se A + INF**: **mientras se disponían a tomar le tren** as they were about to catch the train; **la tropa se dispuso a atacar** the troops prepared to attack
disponibilidad *f* 1 (de productos, plazas) availability 2 **disponibilidades** *fpl* (Com, Fin) liquid assets (*pl*)
disponible *adj* 1 ‹*fondos/apartamento/espacio*› available; ‹*habitación*› available, free; ‹*tiempo*› free (*before n*), available; **no tenemos ningún puesto ~** we have no vacancies; **cuando estés ~ me llamas** call me when you're free 2 ‹*funcionario/militar*› available (for duty)
disposición *f*
A (norma) regulation; **las disposiciones legales** the regulations, the legal requirements; **~ testamentaria** provision of a will
B 1 (actitud) disposition 2 (talento) aptitude 3 (inclinación, voluntad) willingness; **~ A + INF** readiness *o* willingness to + INF
(Compuesto) **disposición de ánimo** attitude of mind
C 1 (de un bien) disposal 2 **a ~ de algn** at sb's disposal; **quedo a su entera ~** (frml) I am at your disposal (frml); **estoy a tu ~ para lo que sea** I'm here to help if you need anything; **será puesto a ~ del juez** he will appear before the judge; **puso su casa a mi ~** he offered me his house; **pondremos un despacho a su ~** we will place an office at your disposal (frml); **tengo un coche a mi ~** I have the use of a car
D (colocación): **no me gusta la ~ de los muebles** I don't like the way the furniture is arranged; **la ~ de los cuartos** the layout of the rooms
dispositivo *m*
A (mecanismo) mechanism; (aparato) device; **el ~ de arranque** the starting mechanism
(Compuestos)
• **dispositivo intrauterino** intrauterine device, IUD
• **dispositivo de seguridad** (Tec) safety device *o* mechanism; (medidas de seguridad) security measures (*pl*)
B (frml) (destacamento): **han reforzado el ~ militar en la zona** they have reinforced their military presence in the area; **un fuerte ~ policial** a large police presence; **aumentará el ~ de vigilancia en las carreteras** the number of highway patrols will be increased
dispuesto -ta *adj* 1 (preparado) ready 2 (con voluntad) willing; **es un tipo muy ~** he's a very willing lad; **~ A + INF** prepared to + INF
dispuse, dispuso, etc *see* **disponer**
disputa *f* 1 (discusión, pelea) quarrel, argument 2 (controversia) dispute; **es, sin ~, la mejor** she is, without question, the best
disputar [A1] *vt* 1 ‹*derecho/título*› **~le algo A algn**: **le disputó el título** he challenged him for the title; **le disputaban su derecho al trono/a la herencia** they contested his right to the throne/the inheritance 2 ‹*partido*› to play; ‹*combate*› to fight
■ **disputar** *vi* to dispute; **~ CON algn POR algo** to dispute sth WITH sb
■ **disputarse** *v pron*: **se disputan el primer puesto** they are competing for first place; **se disputaban al mismo hombre** they were fighting over the same man
disquería *f* (CS) record store, record shop (BrE)
disquete, disquette /dis'kete/ *m* diskette, floppy disk
disquetera *f* disk drive
disquisición *f* 1 (estudio, exposición) treatise 2 (comentario marginal) digression; **déjate de disquisiciones filosóficas** (iró) never mind the lengthy explanations
distancia *f*
A (en el espacio) distance; **la ~ que separa dos puntos** the distance between two points; **¿qué ~ hay de Tijuana a Tucson?** how far is it from Tijuana to Tucson?; **¿a qué ~ está Londres?** how far is it to London?, **se situó a una ~ de un metro** she stood a meter away; **una llamada de** *or* **a larga ~** a long-distance call
B (*en locs*) **a distancia**: **se situó a ~ para verlo en conjunto** she stood back to see it as a whole; **se veía a ~** one could see it from a distance; **mantenerse a ~** to keep at a distance; **en la distancia** in the distance; ***guardar*** *or* ***mantener las ~s*** to keep one's distance; ***salvando las ~s***: **es como París, salvando las ~s** it's like Paris, up to a point (colloq)
(Compuestos)
• **distancia de frenado** braking distance
• **distancia de seguridad** (safe) stopping distance
C (en el tiempo): **la ~ que nos separa de la Reconquista** the distance (in time) between the Reconquest and the present day; **con la ~ el incidente le pareció una tontería** looking back the incident seemed insignificant
D (afectiva) distance; **una gran ~ los separa** a rift has opened up between them
distanciado -da *adj* (afectivamente): **estamos algo distanciadas** we're not as close as we were
distanciamiento *m* (acción) distancing; (efecto): **se nota un cierto ~ entre ellos** they seem to have grown *o* drifted apart
distanciar [A1] *vt* 1 (espaciar) to space ... out 2 ‹*amigos/familiares*›: **la discusión lo distanció de su familia** the quarrel distanced him from his family
■ **distanciarse** *v pron* 1 **~se DE algo**: **no nos distanciemos del grupo** let's not get too far from the rest of the group; **se estaban distanciando de la casa** they began to get further and further away from the house; **debes ~te de los problemas** you have to step back from problems 2 (*recípr*) «*amigos/familiares*» to grow *o* drift apart
distante *adj* ‹*lugar*› distant, remote; ‹*recuerdos/imágenes*› distant; ‹*persona*› distant, aloof; ‹*actitud*› distant

distar [A1] *vi* (*en 3ª pers*) ~ **DE algo**: **el colegio dista unos dos kilómetros de su casa** the school is about two kilometers from her house; **esta historia dista mucho de ser cierta** this story is far from (being) true

diste, etc *see* **dar**

distender [E8] *vt* ‹*cuerda/arco*› to slacken; ‹*relaciones/ambiente*› to ease

■ **distenderse** *v pron*

A «*relaciones/ambiente*» to ease

B «*vientre*» to become distended

distendido -da *adj*

A (relajado) ‹*ambiente/clima*› relaxed; ‹*rostro/cuerpo*› relaxed

B (Med) ‹*vientre*› distended

distensión *f*: **el diálogo a favor de la ~** the talks aimed at bringing about détente; **un clima de ~** a relaxed atmosphere

disticoso -sa *adj* (Per fam) fussy, picky (colloq)

distinción *f* 1 (diferencia) distinction; **hacer una ~ entre ...** to draw *o* make a distinction between ...; **sin ~ de raza o credo** regardless of race or creed; **no hago distinciones con nadie** I don't give anyone preferential treatment 2 (elegancia) distinction, elegance 3 (honor, condecoración) award; **le otorgaron una ~ por su valor** she was given an award for her bravery

distingo *m* (CS): **no hace ~s con nadie** he doesn't give anyone preferential treatment; **sin ~s de religión** regardless of religion; **esta ley no hace ~s entre argentinos y extranjeros** this law makes no distinction between Argentinian citizens and foreigners

distinguido -da *adj* 1 ‹*escritor/actor*› distinguished; **un alumno ~** an outstanding pupil; **hoy contamos con la distinguida presencia de ...** today we are honored to have with us ...; **~ público ...** ladies and gentlemen ... 2 ‹*modales*› refined; ‹*aspecto*› distinguished; **con un aire ~** with a distinguished air

distinguir [I2] *vt*

A 1 (diferenciar) to distinguish; **~ una cosa de otra** to tell *o* distinguish one thing from another; **es muy difícil ~los** it's very difficult to tell them apart *o* to tell one from the other 2 (caracterizar) to characterize

B (percibir) to make out; **a lo lejos se distingue la catedral** the cathedral can be seen in the distance; **se distinguía claramente el ruido de las olas** we/he/they could clearly make out the sound of the waves

C (con medalla, honor) to honor*

■ **distinguirse** *v pron* (destacarse): **~se POR algo**: **se distinguió por su valentía** he distinguished himself by his bravery; **nuestros productos se distinguen por su calidad** our products are distinguished by their quality; **~se EN algo** to distinguish oneself IN sth

distintivo¹ -va *adj* ‹*rasgo/característica*› distinctive

distintivo² *m* (insignia) emblem; (símbolo) sign; **es un ~ de calidad** it is a sign of quality

distinto -ta *adj*

A (diferente) different; **ser ~ A** *or* **DE algo/algn** to be different from *o* (AmE) than sth/sb; **estas/te encuentro ~** you look different

B (*en pl, delante del n*) (varios) several, various

distorsión *f* (de la verdad, los hechos) distortion, twisting; (de las facciones) distortion; (Tec) distortion

distorsionar [A1] *vt* to distort

distracción *f* 1 (entretenimiento) entertainment; **te servirá de ~** it'll give you something to do; **una buena ~ para los niños** a good way of entertaining children 2 (descuido): **en un momento de ~se la robaron** she took her eye off it for a moment and someone stole it; **la más mínima ~ puede ser fatal** the slightest lapse of concentration could be fatal 3 (de fondos) embezzlement

distraer [E23] *vt* 1 ‹*persona/atención*› to distract; ❸ **no distraer al conductor** do not distract the driver's attention; **~ a algn DE algo** to distract sb FROM sth; **la música me distrajo de la lectura** I was distracted from my reading by the music; **traté de ~lo de sus preocupaciones** I tried to take his mind off his worries 2 (entretener) ‹*persona*› to keep ... amused; **la lectura lo distrae en sus ratos de ocio** he enjoys reading in his free time 3 ‹*fondos/dinero*› to embezzle

■ **distraerse** *v pron* 1 (despistarse, descuidarse) to get distracted; **no te distraigas y terminarás antes** keep your mind on what you're doing you'll finish sooner 2 (entretenerse): **necesitas ~te un poco** you need to find something to do ; **se distraen viendo la televisión** they pass the time watching television; **se distrae con cualquier cosa** she doesn't need much to keep amused

distraído -da *adj* 1 [**SER**] ‹*persona*› absentminded, vague; **una mirada distraída** an absent look 2 [**ESTAR**]: **perdona, estaba ~** sorry, I wasn't paying attention; **iba ~ y no me vio** he was miles away and didn't see me (colloq)

distribución *f* 1 (reparto) distribution; **la ~ de la riqueza** the distribution of wealth; **la ~ de las tareas domésticas** the allocation of the household chores 2 (de producto, película) distribution 3 (disposición, división) layout, arrangement 4 (Auto) valve-operating gear

distribuidor¹ -dora *m,f* (Com) distributor

distribuidor² *m*

A (Auto, Mec) distributor

B (Ven) (en una carretera) interchange, cloverleaf

distribuidora *f* (empresa) distributor, distribution company

distribuir [I20] *vt* 1 ‹*dinero/víveres/panfletos*› to hand out, distribute; ‹*ganancias*› to distribute; ‹*tareas*› to allocate, assign; ‹*carga/peso*› to distribute, spread; **la riqueza está mal distribuida** wealth is unevenly distributed 2 ‹*producto/película*› to distribute 3 «*canal/conducto*» ‹*agua*› to distribute 4 (disponer, dividir): **las habitaciones están muy bien distribuidas** the rooms are very well laid out; **los distribuyeron en tres grupos** they divided them into three groups

■ **distribuirse** *v pron* (*refl*) to divide up

distributivo -va *adj* distributive

distrital *adj* (Ven) local

distrito *m* district

(Compuestos)

- **distrito electoral** electoral district, constituency
- **distrito postal** postal district

> **Distrito Federal**
>
> A district of central Mexico, the seat of the federal government. It includes most of Mexico City and its suburbs, and comes under the direct supervision of the Mexican president

distrofia *f* dystrophy

(Compuesto) **distrofia muscular** muscular dystrophy

disturbio *m* 1 (perturbación del orden) disturbance 2 **disturbios** *mpl* (motín) riot, disturbances (journ)

disuadir [I1] *vt* to deter, discourage; **~ A algn DE algo** to dissuade sb FROM sth; **intentó ~lo de su propósito** she tried to talk him out of it *o* to dissuade him; **~ A algn DE QUE + SUBJ** to dissuade sb FROM -ING

disuasión *f* 1 (Mil, Pol) deterrence; **como ~** as a deterrent 2 (acción de convencer) dissuasion

disuasorio -ria, **disuasivo -va** *adj* ‹*tono/palabras*› dissuasive, discouraging; **medidas disuasorias** measures designed to act as a deterrent

disuelto -ta *pp*: *see* **disolver**

disyuntiva *f* dilemma

disyuntivo -va *adj* disjunctive

diuca *f* (Zool) diuca finch

diurético¹ -ca *adj* diuretic

diurético² *m* diuretic

diurno -na *adj* day (*before n*); **clases diurnas** daytime classes

diva *f* diva, prima donna; *ver tb* **divo**

divagación *f* digression; **déjate de divagaciones** stop rambling

divagar [A3] *vi* 1 (desviarse del tema) to digress 2 (hablar sin sentido) to ramble; **bebió mucho y empezó a ~** he drank a lot and he started to ramble

diván *m* couch

divergencia *f* difference; **han surgido ~s** differences *o* disagreements have arisen

divergente *adj* 1 ‹*opiniones*› differing (*before n*) 2 ‹*líneas/rayos*› divergent; ‹*caminos*› diverging (*before n*)

d

divergir [I7] *vi* «*opiniones/gustos*» to differ; «*líneas/rayos*» to diverge

diversidad *f* diversity; **existe una ~ de opciones** there is a variety *o* diversity of options

diversificación *f* diversification

diversificar [A2] *vt* to diversify
■ **diversificarse** *v pron* to diversify

diversión *f* 1 (esparcimiento) fun; **por ~** for fun; **te hace falta un poco de ~** you need a bit of enjoyment *o* fun 2 (espectáculo, juego): **aquí hay pocas diversiones** there isn't much to do here

diverso -sa *adj*
A (variado, diferente): **su obra es muy diversa** his work is very diverse; **seres de diversa naturaleza** various types of creatures; **ha desempeñado las más diversas actividades** she has engaged in a very wide range of activities
B (*pl*) (varios) various, several

divertido -da *adj* 1 (que interesa, divierte) ‹*espectáculo/fiesta*› fun, enjoyable; ‹*momento/situación*› entertaining; **es un tipo muy ~** he's a really fun guy, he's really fun to be with 2 (gracioso) funny

divertimento *m* (Mús) divertimento

divertir [I11] *vt* to amuse; **me divirtió muchísimo su reacción** I was greatly amused by his reaction
■ **divertirse** *v pron* (entretenerse) to amuse oneself; (pasarlo bien) to have fun; **¡que te diviertas!** have fun!, enjoy yourself!; **nos divertimos mucho en la fiesta** we had a really good time at the party; **sabe ~se solo** he knows how to keep himself amused

dividendo *m* 1 (Fin) dividend; ***dar ~s*** to pay off, pay dividends 2 (Mat) dividend 3 (Chi) (cuota) payment

dividir [I1] *vt* 1 (partir) to divide; **lo dividió en partes iguales/por la mitad** he divided it (up) into equal portions/in half; **seis dividido por** *or* **entre dos es igual a tres** (Mat) six divided by two equals *o* is three 2 (repartir) to divide, share (out); **dividieron la herencia entre los hermanos** the inheritance was shared (out) among the brothers 3 (separar): **el río divide el pueblo en dos** the river cuts the village in two 4 (enemistar) ‹*partido/familia*› to divide; ***divide y vencerás*** divide and conquer
■ **dividir** *vi* (Mat) to divide
■ **dividirse** *v pron* 1 «*célula*» to split; «*grupo/partido*» to split up; «*camino/río*» to divide; **nos dividimos en dos grupos** we split up into two groups 2 «*obra/período*»: **su obra se divide en cuatro períodos** his work can be divided into four periods; **el cuerpo humano se divide en ...** the human body is made up of ... 3 (repartirse) to divide up, share out

divierta, divirtió, etc *see* **divertir**

divinamente *adv* divinely, wonderfully

divinidad *f* 1 (deidad) deity, god 2 (cualidad) divinity 3 (fam) (preciosidad) delight

divinizar [A4] *vt* to deify

divino -na *adj* 1 (Relig) divine (*before n*) 2 (fam) ‹*chica/vestido*› delightful, divine

divisa *f*
A (Com, Fin) currency; **~s fuertes** strong currencies; **la fuga de ~s** the flight of capital; **el turismo es una fuente de ~s** tourism is a source of foreign currency
B 1 (emblema) emblem, insignia 2 (Taur) colored ribbons (*which indicate the bull's breeder*) 3 (lema) motto

divisar [A1] *vt* ‹*tierra/barco*› to sight, make out; **a lo lejos se divisaba un poblado** they (*or* he *etc*) could make out a village in the distance

divisible *adj* **~ POR algo** divisible BY sth

división *f* 1 (Mat) division; **hacer una ~** to do a division 2 (desunión) division 3 (del átomo) splitting; (de célula) division, splitting; (de herencia) division, sharing (out) 4 (Adm, Dep, Mil) division

divisor *m* divisor; **el máximo común ~** the highest common denominator

divisorio -ria *adj* dividing (*before n*); **pared/línea divisoria** dividing wall/line; **la línea divisoria de las aguas** the watershed

divo -va *m,f* (estrella) celebrity, star; (con actitud soberbia) prima donna; *ver tb* **diva**

divorciado¹ -da *adj* 1 ‹*persona*› divorced; **¿es usted ~?** are you divorced? 2 [ESTAR] ‹*ideas/actitudes*› incompatible

divorciado² -da (*m*) divorcé (esp AmE), divorcee (esp BrE); (*f*) divorcée (esp AmE), divorcee (esp BrE)

divorciar [A1] *vt* to divorce
■ **divorciarse** *v pron* to get divorced; **~se DE algn** to divorce sb, get divorced FROM sb

divorcio *m* 1 (Der) divorce; **demanda/sentencia de ~** divorce petition/ruling; **conceder el ~** to grant a divorce 2 (ruptura — entre dos planteamientos, ideas) discrepancy, difference; (— entre dos personas) split

divulgación *f* spreading

divulgar [A3] *vt* ‹*noticia/información*› to spread, circulate; ‹*secreto/plan*› to divulge
■ **divulgarse** *v pron* to spread

divulgativo -va *adj*: **programas de carácter ~** news programs (*o* documentaries *etc*)

dizque, diz que *adv* (AmL) 1 (según parece) apparently; **~ van a cerrarlo** apparently they're planning to close it down 2 (expresando escepticismo): **esta ~ democracia** this so-called democracy; **estaban allí, ~ trabajando** they were there, supposedly working

DJ /'di(d)ʒej/ *mf* (Méx) DJ

dl. (= **decilitro**) dl, deciliter*

dm. (= **decímetro**) dm, decimeter*

Dn. = **Don**

DNA *m* DNA

DNI *m* (Esp) = **Documento Nacional de Identidad**

> **DNI – Documento Nacional de Identidad**
> ▸ **carné de identidad**

Dña. = **Doña**

do¹ *m* (nota) C; (en solfeo) do, doh (BrE); **~ bemol/sostenido** C flat/sharp; **en ~ mayor/menor** in C major/minor
(Compuesto) **do de pecho**: **el ~ de ~** high C, top C; ***dar el ~ de ~*** to give one's best

do. (= **domingo**) Sun

D.O. *f* = **Denominación de Origen**

doberman *mf* /'doβerman/ (*pl* **-mans**) Doberman (pinscher)

dobladillo *m* hem; **subirle/bajarle el ~ a un vestido** to take up/let down the hem of a dress

doblaje *m* dubbing

doblar [A1] *vt*
A ‹*camisa/papel*› to fold; ‹*brazo/vara*› to bend
B ‹*esquina*› to turn, go around; ‹*cabo*› to round
C (aumentar al doble) ‹*oferta/apuesta/capital*› to double; (tener el doble que): **le dobla la edad** *or* **la dobla en edad** he's twice her age
D 1 ‹*película*› to dub; **una película doblada al castellano** a film dubbed into Spanish 2 ‹*actor*› (en banda sonora) to dub; (en escena) to double for
■ **doblar** *vi*
A (torcer, girar) «*persona*» to turn; «*camino*» to bend, turn; **dobla a la izquierda** turn left
B «*campanas*» to toll; **~ a muerto** to knell (liter), to sound a death knell
■ **doblarse** *v pron*
A «*rama/alambre*» to bend; **~se de dolor/risa** to double up with pain/laughter
B «*precios/población*» to double

doble¹ *adj*
A ‹*whisky/flor/puerta*› double; ‹*café*› large; ‹*costura/hilo/consonante*› double; **lo veo todo ~** I'm seeing double; **cerrar con ~ llave** to double-lock; **apostar ~ contra sencillo** to bet two to one; **tiene ~ sentido** it has a double meaning; **calle de ~ sentido** *or* **dirección** two-way street
(Compuestos)
- **doble crema** *f* (Méx) double cream
- **doble fondo** *m* false bottom
- **doble imposición** *f* double taxation
- **doble juego** *m* double-dealing
- **doble moral** *f* double standard
- **doble nacionalidad** *f* dual nationality
- **doble personalidad** *f* split personality
- **doble tracción** *f* four-wheel drive

- **doble ve** *or* **doble u** *f: name of the letter* **W**
- **doble ventana** *f* double glazing

B (Andes, Ven fam) ‹*persona*› two-faced

doble² *m*

A (Mat): **los precios aumentaron el ~** prices doubled; **tardó el ~** she took twice as long; **el ~ de tres es seis** two threes are six; **lo hizo el ~ de rápido** she did it twice as quickly; **lleva el ~ de tela** it uses double the amount of fabric; **es el ~ de largo que de ancho** it's twice as long as it is wide; **~ o nada** double or quits; **el ~ QUE algn/algo** twice as much AS sb/sth; **tengo el ~ que tú** I have twice as much as you have

B dobles *mpl* (en tenis) doubles

(Compuestos)

- **dobles caballeros/damas** *mpl* men's/ladies' doubles
- **dobles mixtos** *mpl* mixed doubles

C (en béisbol) double

D (de campanas) toll, knell (liter)

doble³ *mf* [1] (actor, actriz) stand-in, double; (en escenas peligrosas) (*m*) stuntman; (*f*) stuntwoman [2] (persona parecida) (fam) double

doblegar [A3] *vt* (liter) ‹*voluntad*› to break; ‹*espíritu*› to crush; ‹*persona*› to humble; **no pudieron ~los** they were unable to crush their spirit

■ **doblegarse** *v pron* (liter) to yield (liter); **no se doblega ante nadie/por nada** she won't give in to anyone/anything

doblez *m*

A (en tela, papel) fold

B doblez *m or f* (falsedad) deceitfulness

doblón *m* doubloon

doce¹ *adj inv/pron* twelve; *para ejemplos ver* **cinco**; **son las ~ de la noche** it's twelve o'clock, it's midnight

doce² *m* (number) twelve

docena *f* dozen; **una ~ de huevos** a dozen eggs; **media ~** half a dozen

docencia *f* teaching

docente *adj* ‹*personal*› teaching (*before n*)

dócil *adj* ‹*niño/comportamiento*› meek, docile; ‹*perro/caballo*› docile, well-trained; ‹*pelo*› manageable

docilidad *f* meekness, docility

docto -ta *adj* learned, erudite; **~ EN algo** well versed IN sth

doctor -tora *m,f* doctor; **~ en derecho/filosofía** Doctor of Law/Philosophy

(Compuesto) **doctor honoris causa** honorary doctor

doctorado *m* doctorate, PhD

doctoral *adj* [1] (Educ) doctoral [2] (pey) ‹*tono/lenguaje*› pompous, pedantic

doctorarse [A1] *v pron* to earn *o* get one's doctorate, do one's PhD

doctrina *f* (ideología) doctrine; (enseñanza) teaching

doctrinal *adj* doctrinal

doctrinario -ria *adj* doctrinaire

documentación *f*

A (de persona) papers (*pl*); (de vehículo, envío) documents (*pl*), documentation (frml)

B (información) information, data (*pl*)

documentado -da *adj*

A ‹*informe/hecho*› documented; **están muy bien ~s sobre el tema** they're very well informed about the subject

B (frml) (con documentación): **la carga no iba documentada** the load did not have the necessary documentation *o* papers

documental¹ *adj* [1] (Cin, TV) ‹*programa/serie*› documentary (*before n*) [2] (Der) ‹*prueba*› documentary

documental² *m* documentary

documentar [A1] *vt*

A ‹*trabajo/hipótesis/solicitud*› to document

B (Méx) ‹*equipaje*› to check in

■ **documentarse** *v pron*

A (informarse) to do research; **se documentó bien** he did a lot of research

B (Méx) «*pasajero*» to check in

documento *m* [1] (Adm, Der) document; **no hay ningún ~ que lo pruebe** there is no documentary evidence to support it; **¿lleva algún ~ que pruebe su identidad?** do you have any (means of) identification? [2] (testimonio): **estas imágenes constituyen un ~ de la situación** these images bear witness to *o* are testimony to the situation

(Compuesto) **Documento Nacional de Identidad** (en Esp) National Identity Card

dodecafónico -ca *adj* twelve-tone, dodecaphonic (tech)

dodecasílabo *m* dodecasyllable

dogma *m* dogma

dogmático -ca *adj* dogmatic

dogmatismo *m* dogmatism

dogo *mf* mastiff

(Compuesto) **dogo alemán** Great Dane

dólar *m* dollar

dolencia *f* ailment, complaint

doler [E9] *vi* [1] «*inyección/herida/brazo*» to hurt; (+ *me/te/le etc*) **le duele una muela/la cabeza** she has (a) toothache/a headache; **me dolía el estómago** I had (a) stomachache; **me duele la garganta** I have a sore throat; **me duelen los pies** my feet ache; **¿dónde le duele?** where does it hurt?; **me duele todo (el cuerpo)** I ache all over [2] (apenar) (+ *me/te/le etc*): **me duele tener que decirte esto** I'm sorry to have to tell you this; **me duele tu deslealtad** I find your disloyalty very hurtful; **me dolió muchísimo lo que me dijo** I was deeply hurt by what he said; ***ahí te/le duele*** (fam) that's what's wrong with you/him [3] (importar): **no me duele el dinero que me he gastado** I don't regret spending that much money

■ **dolerse** *v pron* **~se DE algo** (sentirse herido) to be hurt BY sth; (arrepentirse) to regret sth; **se dolía de tantos años desperdiciados** he deeply regretted all those wasted years

dolido -da *adj* hurt; **estar ~ POR algo** to be hurt AT sth

dolmen *m* dolmen

dolor *m* [1] (físico) pain; **sentía mucho ~** he was in a lot of pain; **un ~ sordo** a dull ache; **~es reumáticos/de parto** rheumatic/labor* pains; **tener ~ de muelas/cabeza/garganta** to have a toothache/a headache/a sore throat; **fuertes ~es de estómago** sharp *o* severe stomach pains; **no me has dado más que ~es de cabeza** you have been a constant worry to me [2] (pena, tristeza) pain, grief; **el ~ de perder a un ser querido** the pain *o* grief of losing a loved one; **con todo el ~ de mi corazón tuve que decirle que no** it broke my heart, but I had to turn him down; **no sabes el ~ que me causa su indiferencia** you have no idea how much his indifferent attitude hurts *o* upsets me

dolorido -da *adj* [1] (físicamente): **estoy toda dolorida** I'm aching all over; **tengo el brazo muy ~** I've got a very sore arm [2] (afligido) hurt

doloroso -sa *adj* [1] ‹*tratamiento/enfermedad*› painful [2] ‹*decisión/momento/recuerdo*› painful; ‹*separación/espectáculo*› distressing, upsetting

doma *f* (de fieras) taming; (de caballos) breaking-in

domador -dora *m,f* (de fieras) tamer; (de caballos) horsebreaker, broncobuster (AmE)

domar [A1] *vt* [1] ‹*fieras*› to tame; ‹*caballo*› to break in [2] (fam) ‹*niño*› to bring *o* get … under control [3] (fam) ‹*zapatos*› to break in

domeñar [A1] *vt* (liter) ‹*pasiones/instintos*› to check, restrain; ‹*persona*› to subdue

domesticado -da *adj* tame, domesticated

domesticar [A2] *vt* ‹*animal*› to domesticate

domesticidad *f* domesticity

doméstico -ca *adj*

A ‹*vida/problemas/servicio*› domestic; ‹*gastos*› household; **tareas domésticas** housework; **para uso ~** for household use

B ‹*vuelo*› domestic

domiciliación *f* (Esp): **~ de la nómina** payment of one's salary direct into one's bank account; **~ de los pagos** payment by direct debit *o* (AmE) direct billing; Ⓢ **domiciliación bancaria** bank details

domiciliar [A1] *vt* (Esp) ‹*pago/letras*› to pay … by direct debit *o* (AmE) direct billing; ‹*sueldo*› to have … paid direct into one's bank account

■ **domiciliarse** *v pron* (frml) (residir) to reside (frml), to be domiciled (frml); **Juan Gallo, domiciliado en la calle Cita 29** Juan Gallo of 29 Cita Street; **están domiciliados en Inglaterra** they are domiciled in England (frml)

domiciliario -ria *adj* ‹*visita/cuidados*› home (*before n*)

domicilio *m* (frml) address; **en su ~ particular** at his home address; **sin ~ fijo** of no fixed abode (frml); **Pat Lee, con ~ en Londres/en el número 23 de Watson Rd** Pat Lee currently living in London/at 23 Watson Rd; **Ⓢ reparto a domicilio** home delivery service

(Compuestos)
- **domicilio fiscal** domicile for tax purposes
- **domicilio social** registered office

dominación *f* [1] (Pol) domination [2] **dominaciones** *fpl* (Relig) dominions (*pl*)

dominante *adj*
A [1] ‹*color/tendencia*› predominant, dominant; ‹*opinión*› prevailing (*before n*); ‹*cultura*› dominant; **el rasgo ~ de su carácter** the dominant feature of his personality; **la nota ~ de la jornada fue la tranquilidad** calm prevailed throughout the day [2] (Biol, Mús, Astrol) dominant
B ‹*persona*› domineering

dominar [A1] *vt* [1] (controlar) ‹*nación/territorio/persona*› to dominate; ‹*pasión/cólera*› to control; ‹*vehículo/caballo*› to control; **dominado por la ambición/los celos** ruled by ambition/consumed by jealousy; **la policía dominó la situación en todo momento** the police had the situation under control at all times [2] ‹*idioma*› to have a good command of; ‹*tema/asignatura*› to know ... very well; **no domino el tema** I'm no expert on the subject; **quería llegar a ~ el inglés** she wanted to master English; **domina un amplio vocabulario** she has a wide vocabulary [3] (abarcar con la vista): **desde allí se domina toda la bahía** there's a view over the whole bay from there [4] «*montaña/torre*» to dominate

■ **dominar** *vi* «*color/tendencia*» to predominate; «*opinión*» to prevail; «*equipo*» to dominate; **el tema que dominó en las negociones** the subject which dominated the talks

■ **dominarse** *v pron* «*persona*» to control oneself

domingo *m* (día) Sunday; (Relig) Sabbath; *para ejemplos ver* **lunes**; **ropa/traje de ~** Sunday best; **vestido de ~** dressed in one's Sunday best; ***salir con un ~ siete*** (AmL fam): **ahora me sale con este ~ siete** now he springs this on me (colloq)

(Compuestos)
- **Domingo de Pascua** *or* **de Resurrección** Easter Sunday
- **Domingo de Pasión/Ramos** Passion/Palm Sunday

dominguero -ra *m,f* (fam) (conductor) Sunday driver; (excursionista) Sunday tripper

dominical *adj* Sunday (*before n*)

dominicano -na *adj/m,f* (Geog) Dominican

dominio *m*
A [1] (control) control; **perdió el ~ de sí mismo** he lost his self-control; **en pleno ~ de sus facultades** in full command of her faculties [2] (de idioma, tema) command; **se requiere perfecto ~ del inglés** fluent English *o* perfect command of English required; ***ser del ~ público*** to be public knowledge [3] (ámbito de ciencia, arte) sphere; **el ~ de la fantasía** the realms of fantasy
B [1] (Hist, Pol) dominion [2] **dominios** *mpl* (colonias) dominions (*pl*)

dominó *m* (*pl* **-nós**) [1] (juego) dominoes; **jugar** *or* (Esp, RPl) **al ~** to play dominoes [2] (ficha) domino

don¹ *m* [1] (liter) (dádiva) gift [2] (talento) talent, gift; **el ~ de la palabra** the gift of speech

(Compuestos)
- **don de gentes** ability to get on well with people; **tiene ~ de ~** he has a way with people
- **don de mando** leadership qualities (*pl*)

don² *m*
A [1] (con el nombre de pila, tratamiento de cortesía) ≈ Mr [2] (fam) (en motes) Mr

(Compuesto) **don nadie** *m* nobody

B (AmL) (uso popular): **¿qué le vendo, ~?** what can I do for you, buddy (AmE) *o* (BrE) guv? (colloq)

> **don/doña**
>
> The words *don*, for men, and *doña*, for women, are courtesy titles used before someone's name, when they are being spoken or written to. They are used for someone who is senior professionally, in age or socially. *Doña* is usually used only for married or widowed women, except in official documents, when it refers to any woman.*Don* and *doña* always precede a person's first name. "*¿Se va ya, don Juan?*" When talking about a third person you can use *don* and *doña* before their first name, which is followed by their surname: "*Don Juan Montesinos*". In correspondence, *don* and *doña* can be abbreviated to *D.* and *Dn.*, or *Dña.* and *Dª*, respectively, and can be preceded by the appropriate title *señor* or *señora*: "*Sr. Dn. Juan Montesinos*"; "*Sra. Dña. Ana Castellón*"

dona *f* (Méx) (Coc) doughnut, donut (AmE)

donación *f* donation; **~ de órganos/sangre** organ/blood donation; **hacer ~ de algo** to donate *o* give sth

donador -dora *m,f* donor

donaire *m* [1] (liter) (en los movimientos) grace, gracefulness; **moverse con ~** to move gracefully [2] (liter) (en la expresión): **está escrito con ~ y soltura** it is written with great charm and fluency

donante *mf* donor

donar [A1] *vt* ‹*bienes/dinero*› to donate, give; ‹*sangre*› to give, donate; ‹*órganos*› to donate

donativo *m* donation

doncella *f* [1] (arc) (virgen) maiden (liter) [2] (ant) (criada) maid

donde¹ *conj*
A [1] where; **la ciudad ~ se conocieron** the city where they met; (+ *subj*) **siéntate ~ quieras** sit wherever *o* where you like; **déjalo ~ sea** leave it anywhere [2] (con prep) where; **el café (en) ~ nos reuníamos** the café where we used to meet; **buscamos un lugar desde ~ ver el desfile** we looked for a place to watch the procession; **el país de ~ procede** the country it comes from; **de ~ se deduce que ...** from which it can be deduced that ...; **la ventana por ~ había entrado** the window through which he had got in; **sigue ~ mismo** (Chi fam) he's still in the same place
B (esp AmL fam) (+ *subj*) (si) if; **~ lo vuelvas a hacer ...** if you do it again ...
C (Chi fam) (porque) because

donde² *prep* (esp AmL, en algunas regiones crit): **ve ~ tu hermana y dile que ...** (a su casa) go over to your sister's and tell her ...; (al lugar donde está ella) go and tell your sister ...; **es allí ~ el semáforo** it's there by *o* at the traffic lights

dónde *adv*
A where; **¿~ está?** where is it?; **¿de ~ es?** where is he from?; **¿por ~ quieres ir?** which way do you want to go?; **no sé por ~ queda** I don't know where it is; **no sé ~ lo guardé** I don't know where I put it
B (Chi, Méx, Per) (cómo) how; **¡~ íbamos a imaginar que ...!** how were we to imagine that ...!

dondequiera *adv*: **~ QUE** wherever; **la encontraré, ~ que esté** I'll find her wherever she is *o* wherever she may be

donjuán *m* (tenorio) womanizer, Don Juan

donoso -sa *adj* (en los movimientos) graceful; (en el habla) amusing, witty

doña *f* ▸ **Don**
A (tratamiento de cortesía, con el nombre de pila) ≈ Mrs/Ms; **~ Cristina Fuentes** Mrs/Ms Cristina Fuentes; **~ Cristina** Mrs Fuentes; **Sra D~ Cristina Fuentes Girón** (Corresp) Mrs/Ms C Fuentes Girón
B (fam) (en motes) Miss
C (AmL) (uso popular): **no me toque la fruta, ~** don't handle the fruit, dear *o* (AmE) lady

dopado -da *adj* [ESTAR] drugged; **el corredor estaba ~** the runner had taken drugs

dopar [A1] *vt* ‹*enfermo*› to drug, dope (colloq); ‹*caballo*› to dope

■ **doparse** *v pron* (*refl*) to take drugs

doping *m* (Equ) doping; (Dep) drug-taking

doppler *m* /'dopler/ [1] (ecografía) (ultrasound) scan; **le hicieron un ~** they gave him a scan [2] (instrumento) scanner

doquier *adv* (liter): **por ~** everywhere, all around

doquiera *adv* (liter) wherever; **~ que tú vayas** wherever you (may) go

dorada *f* gilthead (bream)

dorado[1] -da *adj* 1 ‹*botón/galones*› gold; ‹*pintura*› gold, gold-colored*; ‹*cabello*› (liter) golden 2 ‹*época*› golden

dorado[2] *m* (acción) gilding; (capa) gilt

dorar [A1] *vt* ‹*marco/porcelana*› to gild; (Coc) ‹*cebolla/papas*› to brown

■ **dorarse** *v pron* (Coc) to brown; **rehogar la cebolla hasta que se dore** sauté the onion until golden brown

dórico -ca *adj* Dorian, Doric

dormida *f* (AmL) sleep; **paramos para echar una ~** we stopped for a sleep *o* to have a sleep

dormido -da *adj* 1 (durmiendo) asleep; **estar/quedarse ~** to be/to fall asleep 2 (fam) (distraído) half asleep 3 (sin sensibilidad): **tengo la pierna dormida** my leg's gone to sleep (colloq)

dormilón[1] -lona *adj* (fam): **es muy ~** he's a real sleepyhead (colloq)

dormilón[2] -lona *m,f* 1 (fam) (persona) sleepyhead (colloq) 2 **dormilona** *f* (Ven) (camisón) nightdress

dormir [I16] *vi* to sleep; **¡niños, a ~!** it's time for bed, children!; **no dormí nada** I didn't sleep a wink; **necesito ~ ocho horas** I need eight hours' sleep; **no me deja ~ (en** *or* (Esp) **por la noche)** it keeps me awake at night; **dormimos en un hotel** we spent the night in a hotel; **durmió de un tirón** she slept right through (the night); **se fue a ~ temprano** he went off to bed early, he had an early night; ***~ a pierna suelta*** (fam) to sleep the sleep of the dead; ***~ como un lirón*** *or* ***un tronco*** *or* ***un bendito*** to sleep like a log (colloq)

■ **dormir** *vt* 1 (hacer dormir): **durmió al niño** she got the baby off to sleep; **sus clases me duermen** his classes send *o* put me to sleep; ***~ la mona*** *or* ***~la*** (fam) to sleep it off (colloq) 2 (anestesiar) to give … a general anesthetic, to put … out (colloq); **todavía tengo este lado dormido** this side is still numb 3 **~ la siesta** to have a siesta *o* nap

■ **dormirse** *v pron* 1 (conciliar el sueño) to fall asleep; (lograr conciliar el sueño) to get to sleep; **casi me duermo en la clase** I almost fell asleep *o* (colloq) dropped off in class; **no podía ~me** I couldn't get (off) to sleep 2 (no despertarse) to oversleep, sleep in (AmE) 3 ‹‹*pierna/brazo*›› (+ *me/te/le etc*) to go to sleep (colloq); **se me durmió el pie** my foot went to sleep 4 (fam) (distraerse, descuidarse): **no te duermas** don't waste any time

dormitar [A1] *vi* to doze, snooze (colloq)

dormitorio *m* (en casa) bedroom; (en colegio, cuartel) dormitory

dorsal[1] *adj* dorsal

dorsal[2] *m* (Esp) number; **Prieto, con el ~ 2** Prieto, wearing the number 2 shirt

dorso *m* 1 (de un papel) back; **instrucciones al ~** instructions overleaf; **escriba su dirección al ~** write your address on the back; Ⓢ **sigue al dorso** please turn over, P.T.O. 2 (de la mano, animal) back; **nadar de ~** (Méx) to swim (the) backstroke

dos[1] *adj inv/pron* two; **lo hicimos entre los ~** we did it between the two of us; **ellos ~ que se queden** the two of them should stay; **sujétalo con las ~ manos** hold it with both hands; **se rompió las ~ piernas** he broke both (his) legs; **cantaron los ~** they both sang; **llamó ~ veces** he called twice; **caminaban de ~ en ~** they walked in pairs; **entraron de ~ en ~** *or* (CS) **de a ~** they came in two at a time *o* two by two; (*para más ejemplos ver tb* **cinco**) ***cada ~ por tres***: **me llama cada ~ por tres** he phones me up every five minutes; **se me avería cada ~ por tres** it's always breaking down on me; ***como (que) ~ y ~ son cuatro*** as sure as the day is long (AmE), as sure as night follows day (BrE); ***no hay ~ sin tres*** misfortunes/these things always come in threes; ***ya somos ~*** that makes two of us

(Compuestos)

- **dos piezas** *m* suit, two-piece suit
- **dos puntos** *mpl* colon

dos[2] *m* (number) two; *para ejemplos ver* **cinco**; ***en un ~ por tres*** in a flash; ***hacer del ~*** (Méx, Per fam) to do a pooh (used to or by children)

doscientos[1] -tas *adj/pron* two hundred; *para ejemplos ver* **quinientos**

doscientos[2] *m* (number) two hundred

dosel *m* (de cama) canopy; (de trono, púlpito) baldachin

dosificar [A2] *vt* 1 ‹*medicamento*› to dose 2 ‹*esfuerzo/cariño*› to be sparing with; **van a tener que ~ sus viajes al extranjero** (fam) they're going to have to cut down on *o* ration their trips abroad

dosis *f* (*pl* ~) 1 (Med) dose; **la ~ máxima/recomendada** the maximum/recommended dose *o* dosage 2 (cantidad): **con una buena ~ de paciencia/humor** with a good deal of patience/humor; **lo aguanto pero en pequeñas ~** I can put up with him but only in small doses

dossier *m* /do'sje(r)/ (expediente) dossier, file; (Period) report

dotación *f* 1 (frml) (de dinero, equipamiento): **una ~ de ayuda de $500 millones** an aid package of $500 million; **piden mejores dotaciones** they are asking for increased funding 2 (de personal): **la ~ de profesores del colegio es insuficiente** the school is understaffed; **una ~ de 50 bomberos** a team of 50 firefighters 3 (Náut) crew

dotado -da *adj* ‹*persona*› gifted; **es una chica muy bien dotada** (hum) she's very well-endowed (hum); **estar ~ DE algo** ‹‹*persona*›› to be blessed WITH sth; ‹‹*cocina/oficina*›› to be equipped WITH sth

dotar [A1] *vt* 1 (frml) ‹*institución/organismo*› **~ (A) algo DE** *or* **CON algo** to equip/provide sth WITH sth; **ha sido dotada de plenos poderes** it has been invested with *o* given full powers; **~ algo de fondos** to fund sth; **~ a algn de fondos** to provide sb with funds; **~on el premio con cinco millones de pesos** (frml) they set the prize money at five million pesos 2 ‹‹*naturaleza/Dios*›› **~ a algn DE** *or* **CON algo** to endow *o* bless sb WITH sth 3 ‹*mujer*› **~ a algn CON algo** to give sb a dowry of sth

dote *f*

A (de novia) dowry

B **dotes** *fpl*: **~s para el canto** a talent for singing; **~s de mando** leadership qualities; **es un alumno con excelentes ~s** he's a very gifted pupil

doy *see* **dar**

Dpto. *m* (= **Departamento**) Dept

Dr. *m* (= **Doctor**) Dr

Dra. *f* (= **Doctora**) Dr

dracma *m* drachma

draga *f* (máquina) dredge, dredger; (barco) dredger

dragado *m* dredging

dragaminas *m* (*pl* ~) minesweeper

dragar [A3] *vt* ‹*río*› to dredge; ‹*minas*› to sweep for

dragón *m*

A (Mit) dragon; (Hist, Mil) dragoon

B (Bot) snapdragon

drama *m*

A (Lit, Teatr) (género teatral) drama, theater*; (obra) play, drama

B (catástrofe, desgracia) drama; **hacer un ~ de algo** (fam) to make a big deal out of sth

dramático -ca *adj* dramatic; **un autor ~** a playwright *o* dramatist

dramatismo *m* dramatic quality *o* character

dramatización *f* dramatization

dramatizar [A4] *vt* to dramatize

dramaturgo -ga *m,f* dramatist, playwright

drástico -ca *adj* ‹*remedio/medida*› drastic; **de manera drástica** drastically

drenaje *m* drainage

drenar [A1] *vt* (Agr, Med) to drain

driblar [A1], **driblear** [A1] *vt* to dribble past *o* around

drible *m* dribble

dril *m* drill

droga *f*

A drug; **el problema de la ~** the drug problem; **~s duras/blandas** hard/soft drugs

B (Méx fam) (deuda) debt

drogadicción *f* (drug) addiction

drogadicto[1] -ta *adj* addicted to drugs; **tiene un hijo ~** her son is a drug addict

drogadicto[2] -ta *m,f* drug addict

d

d

drogar [A3] *vt* to drug
■ **drogarse** *v pron* (*refl*) to take drugs
drogata *mf* (fam) junkie (colloq)
drogodependencia *f* (frml) drug dependency *o* dependence
drogodependiente[1] *adj* (frml) drug-dependent
drogodependiente[2] *mf* (frml) drug addict
drogómano -na *adj/m,f* (Ven) ▸**drogadicto**[1,2]
droguería *f* 1 (Esp) (tienda) *store selling cleaning materials and other household goods* 2 (Col) (farmacia) drugstore (AmE), chemist's (BrE) 3 (RPl) (de productos químicos) pharmaceutical wholesaler's
dromedario *m* dromedary
druida *m* druid
dto. *m* = **descuento**
dual *adj/nm* dual
dualidad *f* duality
dubitativo -va *adj* doubtful
Dublín *m* Dublin
dublinés -nesa *m,f* Dubliner
ducado *m* 1 (título) dukedom; (territorio) duchy, dukedom 2 (moneda) ducat
ducha *f* shower; **darse** *or* (fam) **pegarse una ~** to take *o* (BrE) have a shower; **fue como una ~ de agua fría** it came like a bolt from the blue.
(Compuesto) **ducha de teléfono** hand-held shower
duchar [A1] *vt*: **~ a algn** to give sb a shower
■ **ducharse** *v pron* (*refl*) to take *o* (BrE) have a shower
ducho -cha *adj* **~ EN algo** (bien informado) knowledgeable ABOUT sth, well versed IN sth; (experimentado) experienced IN sth
dúctil *adj* 1 ‹*metal*› ductile; ‹*material/arcilla*› malleable, ductile 2 ‹*persona/carácter*› malleable, easily influenced
ductilidad *f* 1 (de metal) ductility; (de otro material) malleability, ductility 2 (de persona) malleability
ducto *m* 1 (Méx) (de gas, petróleo) pipeline 2 (Ur) (para la basura) garbage chute (AmE), rubbish chute (BrE) 3 (Col, Ven) (de ventilación) duct, shaft
duda *f*
A (interrogante, sospecha) doubt; **expuso sus ~s sobre ...** he expressed his reservations about ...; **tengo unas ~s para consultar** I have a few points I'd like to check; **me ha surgido una ~** there's something I'm not sure about; **¿tienen alguna ~?** are there any queries *o* questions?; **lo asaltó una ~** he was seized by doubt; **no hay ni sombra de ~ sobre su culpabilidad** there can be no doubt about his guilt; **nunca tuve la menor ~ de que tenía razón** I never doubted that he was right; **su honestidad está fuera de (toda) ~** his honesty is beyond (all) doubt; **de eso no cabe la menor ~** there's absolutely no doubt about that; **no cabe ninguna ~** *or* **la menor ~** there cannot be the slightest doubt; **no te quepa la menor ~** make no mistake!; **lo pongo en ~** I doubt it; **sin ~** *or* **sin lugar a ~s** undoubtedly; **sin ~ ya te lo habrás preguntado** no doubt you'll have already asked yourself that question; **para salir de ~s** just to be doubly sure; **su manera de actuar no dejaba lugar a ~s** his behaviour left little room for doubt; ***ante*** *or* ***en la ~, abstente*** if in doubt, don't
B (estado de incertidumbre, indecisión): **ahora me has hecho entrar en (la) ~** now you've made me wonder; **no sé que hacer, estoy en (la) ~** I don't know what to do; I'm of (AmE) *o* (BrE) in two minds about it; **a ver si puedes sacarme de la ~** do you think you can clear something up for me?; **si estás en (la) ~ no lo compres** if you're not sure don't buy it
dudar [A1] *vt* to doubt; **nunca lo dudé** I never doubted it; **dudo que te haya dicho la verdad** I doubt if *o* whether he's told you the truth; **es el mejor, no lo dudes** it's the best one, take it from me; **yo hice todo lo que pude — no lo dudo, pero ...** I did everything I could — I'm sure you did, but ...
■ **dudar** *vi*: **cómpralo, no sigas dudando** go ahead and buy it, stop dithering; **está dudando entre comprar y alquilar** she can't make up her mind whether to buy or rent; **~ EN + INF** to hesitate to + INF; **no dudes en llamarme** don't hesitate to call me; **~ DE algo/algn** to doubt sth/sb
dudoso -sa *adj* 1 (incierto) doubtful; **lo veo ~** it's doubtful, I doubt it; **su participación aún está dudosa** it is still uncertain whether they will take part 2 ‹*costumbres/moral*› dubious, questionable; ‹*victoria*› dubious; ‹*decisión*› dubious; **de ~ gusto** in dubious taste 3 (indeciso) hesitant, undecided
duela *f* (Méx) (del suelo) floorboard
duele, duelen, etc *see* **doler**
duelo *m*
A 1 (dolor) sorrow, grief; (luto) mourning; **estar de ~** to be in mourning; ⓢ **cerrado por duelo** (AmL) closed owing to bereavement; **~ nacional** national mourning 2 (Esp frml): **el ~** (el cortejo) the cortege; (los deudos) the mourners (*pl*)
B (desafío) duel; **retar a ~** to challenge ... to a duel; **batirse en ~** to fight a duel
(Compuesto) **duelo a muerte** duel to the death
duende *m* 1 (en cuentos) goblin, imp 2 (espíritu) spirit (*which inhabits a house or room*) 3 (encanto, magia): **un pueblo con ~** an enchanting village; **un cantante que tiene ~** a singer with a certain magic about him
dueño[1] **-ña** *adj*
A [SER] (libre) **~ DE + INF** free to + INF, at liberty to +INF (frml); **eres muy ~ de hacer lo que te parezca** you're free *o* you are perfectly at liberty to do what you like
B [SER] (indicando control): **fueron ~s de la situación en todo momento** they were in control of the situation at all times; **la policía se hizo dueña de la situación** the police brought the situation under control *o* gained control of the situation; **no era ~ de sí mismo** he was not in control of himself
dueño[2] **-ña** *m,f* 1 (de casa, pensión) (*m*) owner, landlord; (*f*) owner, landlady; (de negocio) (*m*) owner, proprietor; (*f*) owner, proprietress; **¿tiene ~ esto?** does this belong to anyone? 2 (de perro) owner
(Compuestos)
• **dueña de casa** *f* (Chi) (ama de casa) housewife
• **dueño de casa, -ña de casa** *m,f* (AmL) (propietario) householder; (en fiesta) (*m*) host; (*f*) hostess; **los ~s de ~** (Dep) the home team
duerma, duermas, etc *see* **dormir**
duermevela *m* light sleep
dueto *m* duet
dulce[1] *adj* 1 ‹*fruta/vino*› sweet; **está muy ~** it's very/too sweet; **prefiero lo ~ a lo salado** I prefer sweet things to savory ones 2 ‹*agua*› fresh; **pez de agua ~** freshwater fish 3 ‹*persona*› gentle, kind; ‹*sonrisa/voz*› sweet; ‹*música*› soft, sweet; **tiene un carácter muy ~** she has a very sweet nature
(Compuesto) **dulce espera** *f* (esp AmL): **durante la ~ ~** while I/she was expecting
dulce[2] *m* 1 (AmL exc RPl) (golosina) candy (AmE), sweet (BrE) 2 (RPl) (mermelada) jam; **~ de frutilla/durazno** strawberry/peach jam 3 (AmC) (azúcar) *type of sugarloaf* 4 **dulces** *mpl* (cosas dulces) sweet things (*pl*)
(Compuestos)
• **dulce de leche** (RPl) caramel spread (*made by boiling down milk and sugar*)
• **dulce de membrillo** quince jelly
dulcificar [A2] *vt* ‹*persona*› to mellow; ‹*vejez*› to make ... more pleasant
■ **dulcificarse** *v pron* «*carácter/persona*» to mellow, soften
dulzaina *f*: *instrument similar to a clarinet*
dulzón -zona *adj* ‹*pastel/licor*› sickly sweet; ‹*música/palabras*› slushy (colloq), schmalzy (colloq)
dulzor *m* sweetness, sweet taste
dulzura *f* sweetness; **la ~ de su mirada** the sweetness of his eyes; **habló con ~** she spoke kindly *o* gently; **los trata con mucha ~** she's very sweet *o* gentle with them
duna *f* dune
dundo -da *adj* (AmC fam) dumb (colloq)
dúo *m* 1 (composición) duet, duo 2 (de músicos, instrumentos) duo; **a ~**: **lo cantaron a ~** they sang it as a duet; **contestaron a ~** they answered in unison

duodécimo -ma *adj/pron* [1] (ordinal) twelfth [2] (partitivo): **la duodécima parte** a twelfth; *para ejemplos ver* **quinto**

duodeno *m* duodenum

dupleta *f* (Per, Ven) double

dúplex *m* (*pl* ~) [1] (apartamento) duplex apartment, maisonette (BrE) [2] (Méx) (casa) semi-detached house

duplicado[1] -da *adj* duplicated; **por ~** in duplicate

duplicado[2] *m* copy, duplicate

duplicar [A2] *vt* ‹*documento/llave*› to copy, duplicate

■ **duplicarse** *v pron* «*número*» to double

duplicidad *f* duplicity, deceitfulness

duplo *m*: **el ~ de dos es cuatro** two times two is four

duque *m* duke

duquesa *f* duchess

duración *f* [1] (de película, acto, curso) length, duration [2] (de pila, bombilla) life; **pila de larga ~** long-life battery; ▸**disco[1] A**

duradero -ra *adj* ‹*amistad/recuerdo*› lasting (*before n*); ‹*ropa/zapatos*› hardwearing, longwearing (AmE)

duramente *adv* ‹*castigar/tratar*› harshly; ‹*trabajar*› hard

durante *prep* (en el transcurso de) during; (cuando se especifica la duración) for; **~ 1980** during *o* in 1980; **gobernó el país ~ casi dos décadas** she governed the country for almost two decades; **~ la semana** during the week; **trabajé en casa ~ toda esa semana** I worked at home all that week; **los precios aumentaron un 0,3% ~ el mes de diciembre** prices rose by 0.3% in December; **su condición ha empeorado ~ los últimos días** his condition has worsened over the last few days

durar [A1] *vi* [1] «*reunión/guerra/relación*» to last; **¿cuánto dura la película?** how long is the film?; **no le duró nada el entusiasmo** his enthusiasm didn't last long [2] «*coche/zapatos*» to last; **~ más** to last longer; **las secretarias no le duran nada** her secretaries don't stay long [3] (Col, Ven) (tardar) to take; **duró una semana a llegar** it took a week to arrive

■ **durarse** *v pron* (Ven): **no te dures tanto en el baño** don't take so long in the bathroom; **me duré muchísimo haciendo el mercado** it took me ages to do the shopping

durazno *m* (esp AmL) (fruto) peach; (árbol) peach tree

durex® *m* (AmL) Scotch tape® (AmE), Sellotape® (BrE), sticky tape (BrE)

dureza *f*

A (de mineral, del agua) hardness; (de material) hardness, toughness; (de la carne) toughness

B [1] (severidad, inflexibilidad) harshness; **nos trataban con ~** they treated us harshly; **fue castigado con ~** he was severely punished; **me miró con ~** he gave me a stern look [2] (en el deporte) roughness

durmiera, durmió, etc *see* **dormir**

duro[1] -ra *adj*

A ‹*mineral*› hard; ‹*material*› hard, tough; ‹*asiento/colchón*› hard; ‹*carne*› tough; ‹*músculo*› hard; ‹*pan*› stale; **las peras todavía están duras** the pears aren't ripe yet

B ‹*luz/voz*› harsh; ‹*facciones*› hard, harsh; ‹*agua*› hard

C [1] (severo, riguroso) ‹*persona*› harsh, hard; ‹*castigo/palabras*› harsh, severe; ‹*crítica/ataque*› harsh; ‹*clima*› harsh; ‹*juego*› rough, hard; **estuviste** *or* **fuiste demasiado ~ con él** you were too hard on him; **una postura más dura** a tougher line; **los defensores de la línea dura** the hardliners [2] (difícil, penoso) ‹*trabajo/vida*› hard, tough; **fue un golpe muy ~ para ella** it was a very hard blow for her; ***a las duras y a las maduras*** through thick and thin (colloq); ***estar ~*** (Méx fam) (poco probable) to be unlikely; (muy difícil) to be tough; **está ~ que nos aumenten el sueldo** it's unlikely that we'll get a pay rise; ***estar ~ de pelar*** (fam) ‹*problema*› to be tough *o* hard (colloq); ***ser ~ de pelar*** (fam) ‹*persona*› to be a hard *o* tough nut to crack

D (Per) (tacaño) (fam) tight (colloq), stingy (colloq)

duro[2] *adv* (esp AmL) ‹*trabajar/estudiar/llover*› hard; **¡pégale ~!** hit him hard!; **le estamos dando ~** we're working hard on it; **hable más ~** (Col, Ven) speak up!; **reírse ~** (Col, Ven) to laugh loudly; **agárrense ~** (Col, Ven) hold on tight; ***~ y parejo*** (AmL fam) flat out; **darle ~ y parejo al trabajo** to work flat out

duro[3] *m*

A (en España) (Hist) five-peseta coin; ***estar sin un ~*** (Esp fam) to be broke (colloq)

B [1] (fam) (en películas) tough guy [2] (Pol) hardliner

D/V., d.v. (Com, Corresp) = **días vista**

Ee

e

E, e *f* (*pl* **es**) (*read as* /e/) *the letter* **E, e**

e *conj* [*used instead of* **y** *before* **i-** *or* **hi-**] and; **España e Italia** Spain and Italy

E. (= **Este**) E, East

ea *interj* (expresando resolución) so there!; (para animar) come on!

EAU *mpl* (= **Emiratos Árabes Unidos**) UAE

ebanista *mf* cabinetmaker

ebanistería *f* (oficio, arte) cabinetmaking; (taller) cabinetmaker's workshop

ébano *m* ebony

ébola, ebola *m* Ebola fever

ebonita *f* ebonite, vulcanite

ebriedad *f* (frml) inebriation (frml), drunkenness

ebrio, ebria *adj* (frml) inebriated (frml), drunk; **~ de ira** (liter) blind with rage

ebullición *f* [1] (Coc, Fís): **cuando entre en ~** when it comes to the boil; **punto de ~** boiling point [2] (agitación) turmoil

eccema *m* eczema

echada *f* (Méx fam) [1] (mentira) lie [2] (fanfarronada) boast

echado -da *adj* [ESTAR] (acostado): **está ~ en el sofá** he's lying down on the sofa; ***ser ~ para atrás*** (fam) to be full of oneself (colloq); ***ser muy ~ p'alante*** (fam) (ser audaz, luchador) to be assertive; (ser descarado) to be pushy (colloq)

echador[1] **-dora** *adj* (Méx fam) boastful

echador[2] **-dora** *m,f* (Méx fam) boaster (colloq)

(Compuesto) **echador -dora de cartas** *m,f* fortune-teller (*who reads cards*)

echar [A1] *vt*

(*Sentido* **I**)

A [1] (lanzar, tirar) to throw; **lo eché a la basura** I threw it out *o* away; **echó la moneda al aire** he tossed the coin; **~on el ancla/la red** they cast anchor/their net; **echó la cabeza hacia atrás** she threw her head back; **le echó los brazos al cuello** she threw her arms around his neck; ***~ a algn a perder*** to spoil sb; ***~ algo a perder*** to ruin sth; ***~ de menos algo/a algn*** to miss sth/sb [2] (soltar): **les ~on los perros** they set the dogs on them [3] (Jueg) ‹*carta*› to play, put down; **~le las cartas a algn** to read sb's cards

B (expulsar) ‹*persona*› (de trabajo) to fire (colloq), to sack (BrE colloq); (de bar, teatro) to throw … out; (de colegio) to expel; **me echó de casa** he threw me out (of the house)

C ‹*carta*› to mail (AmE), to post (BrE)

D [1] (pasar, correr) ‹*cortinas*› to pull, draw; **échale (la) llave** lock it; **la persiana estaba echada** the blinds were down; **¿echaste el cerrojo?** did you bolt the door? [2] (mover): **lo echó para atrás** she pushed (*o* moved *etc*) it backward(s)

E (expeler, despedir) ‹*olor, humo, chispas*› to give off; **echaba espuma por la boca** he was foaming at the mouth

F (producir) [1] ‹*hojas*› to sprout; **ya está echando flores** it's flowering already [2] ‹*dientes*› to cut; **estás echando barriga** (fam) you're getting a bit of a tummy (colloq)

(*Sentido* **II**)

A [1] (poner) ‹*leña/carbón*› to put; ‹*gasolina*› to put in; **¿le echas azúcar al café?** do you take sugar in your coffee?; **échale valor y díselo** (fam) just pluck up your courage and tell him [2] (servir, dar) to give; **¿te echo más salsa?** do you want some more sauce?; **~ de comer a los cerdos** to feed the pigs

B [1] (decir, dirigir) ‹*sermón/discurso*› (+ *me/te/le etc*): **me echó un sermón** (fam) he gave me a real talking-to (colloq); **le echó una maldición** she put a curse on him [2] (fam) (imponer) ‹*condena/multa*› (+ *me/te/le etc*) to give; **le ~on una multa** he got a fine, they gave him a fine; **me ~on dos años** I got two years (colloq)

C (fam) (calcular) (+ *me/te/le etc*): **¿cuántos años me echas?** how old do you think I am?; **de aquí a tu casa échale una hora** it's *o* it takes about an hour from here to your house

D (Esp fam) (dar, exhibir) ‹*programa/película*› to show; **¿qué echan en la tele?** what's on TV?

(*Sentido* **III**) ‹*cigarillo/trago*› to have; **~ una firma** to sign; **~ el freno** to put the brake on; **me echó una mirada furibunda** she gave me a furious look; **~le la culpa a algn** to put *o* lay the blame on sb

(*Sentido* **IV**) **echar abajo** ‹*edificio*› to pull down; ‹*gobierno*› to bring down; ‹*proyecto*› to destroy; ‹*esperanzas*› to dash; ‹*moral*› to undermine; **~on la puerta abajo** they broke the door down

■ **echar** *vi*

A (empezar) **~ A + INF** to start *o* begin to + INF, start *o* begin -ING; **echó a correr** he started to run *o* started running; **las palomas ~on a volar** the doves flew off

B (dirigirse): **echó calle abajo** she went off down the street; **echa por aquí** go down here

C **~ para adelante** *or* (fam) **p'alante**: **echa para adelante un poco** go forward a little; **echa p'alante, que ya llegamos** keep going, we're nearly there

■ **echarse** *v pron*

(*Sentido* **I**)

A [1] (tirarse, arrojarse) to throw oneself; **me eché al suelo** I threw myself to the ground; **~se de cabeza al agua** to dive into the water; **échate hacia atrás** lean back; **la noche se nos echó encima** night fell suddenly; ***~se a perder*** «*comida*» to go bad, go off (BrE); «*cosecha/proyecto/plan*» to be ruined [2] (tumbarse, acostarse) to lie down [3] (apartarse, moverse) (+ *compl*): **se echó a un lado** she moved to one side; **échate un poco para allá** move over that way a bit; ***~se atrás*** to back out; ***echárselas*** (Chi fam): **se las echó** he upped and left (colloq); ***echárselas de algo*** (fam): **se las echa de culto** he likes to think he's cultured [4] «*aves*» to brood

B [1] (ponerse) to put on; **~se crema** to put cream on; **se echó el abrigo por los hombros** she put the coat around her shoulders [2] (Esp fam) ‹*novio/novia*›: **se ha echado novia** he's found *o* got himself a girlfriend [3] (Méx fam) (beberse) to drink

C (expulsar): **~se un pedo** to fart (colloq)

D (Méx fam) (romper) to break; ***~se a algn*** (Méx fam) to bump sb off (colloq)

E (Col fam) (tardar) ‹*horas/días*› to take

(*Sentido* **II**) (empezar) ▶**echar** *vi* **A**

echarpe *m* shawl, stole

echazón *m* (Náut) jetsam

echón[1], **echona** *adj* (Ven fam) bigheaded (colloq)

echón[2], **echona** *m,f* (Ven fam) bighead (colloq)

ECJ *f* (= **enfermedad de Creutzfeld Jakob**) CJD

eclecticismo *m* eclecticism

ecléctico -ca *adj/m,f* eclectic
eclesial *adj* (Méx) eclesiastical, church (*before n*)
eclesiástico[1] -ca *adj* ecclesiastical, church (*before n*)
eclesiástico[2] *m* (clérigo) ecclesiastic
eclipsar [A1] *vt* 1 (Astron) to eclipse 2 ‹*persona*› to outshine, eclipse
■ **eclipsarse** *v pron* to disappear
eclipse *m* eclipse; **~ lunar** *or* **de luna** eclipse of the moon, lunar eclipse; **~ solar** *or* **de sol** eclipse of the sun, solar eclipse
eclosión *f* 1 (frml) (de larva) hatching, eclosion (tech) 2 (aparición, comienzo): **la ~ de la primavera** (liter) the dawn of spring (liter); **la crisis hizo ~ en julio** (period) the crisis broke *o* emerged in July
eco *m* (Fís) echo; **la cueva tiene ~** there's an echo in the cave; **hacer ~** to echo; **tuvo escaso ~ comercial** it made little commercial impact; ***hacerse ~ de algo*** to echo sth
(Compuesto) **ecos de sociedad** *mpl* society news
ecografía *f* ultrasound scan
école *interj* (fam) exactly!
ecología *f* ecology
ecológicamente *adv* ecologically, environmentally; **~ sería desastroso** it would be environmentally disastrous; **cultivar algo ~** to grow sth organically
ecológico -ca *adj* ‹*problema/estudio*› ecological; **deterioro ~** damage to the environment
ecologista[1] *adj* ecology (*before n*), environmentalist (*before n*)
ecologista[2] *mf* ecologist, environmentalist
ecólogo -ga *m,f* ecologist
economato *m* 1 (de empresa) company store 2 (Mil) PX (AmE), NAAFI shop (BrE)
economía *f*
A (ciencia) economics
(Compuestos)
• **economía doméstica** home economics, domestic science
• **economía política** political economy
B (de país) economy
(Compuesto) **economía de (libre) mercado** (free) market economy
C (ahorro): **hacer ~s** to economize; **con ~ de palabras** succinctly *o* concisely
(Compuesto) **economías de escala** *fpl* economies of scale
D (de persona, familia) finances (*pl*)
económicamente *adv* financially; **~, están muy bien** they are very well off financially
económico -ca *adj*
A ‹*crisis/situación*› economic (*before n*); ‹*problema/independencia*› financial
B 1 ‹*piso/comida*› cheap; ‹*restaurante/hotel*› cheap, inexpensive 2 (que gasta poco) ‹*motor*› economical; ‹*persona*› thrifty
economista *mf* economist
economizar [A4] *vt* ‹*tiempo*› to save; ‹*combustible/recursos*› to economize on, save; **~ palabras** to be very sparing with words
■ **economizar** *vi* to economize, save money
ecosistema *m* ecosystem
ecoturismo *m* ecotourism
ECU, ecu /'eku/ *m* ECU, ecu
ecuación *f* equation; **~ de primer/segundo grado** simple/quadratic equation
ecuador *m*
A (línea) equator
B **Ecuador** (país) Ecuador
ecualizador *m* equalizer
ecuánime *adj* (sereno) equable, even-tempered; (imparcial) impartial, unbiased
ecuanimidad *f* (serenidad) equanimity; (imparcialidad) impartiality
ecuatorial *adj* equatorial
ecuatoriano -na *adj/m,f* Ecuadorean
ecuestre *adj* equestrian
ecuménico -ca *adj* ecumenical
ecumenismo *m* ecumenicalism
eczema *m* eczema
Ed. 1 = **editorial** 2 (= **edición**) ed.
edad *f*
A (de persona, árbol) age; **un joven de unos quince años de ~** a boy of about fifteen; **¿qué ~ tiene?** how old is he?; **tienen la misma ~** they are the same age; **me dobla la ~** she is twice my age; **se saca** *or* **quita la ~** (AmL) he makes out (that) he's younger than he actually is; **aún no tiene la ~ suficiente** he's still not old enough ...; **de ~ madura** *or* **de mediana ~** middle-aged; **una persona de ~** an elderly person; **una niña de corta ~** a young girl; **desde temprana ~** from an early age; **niños en ~ escolar** children of school age; **la ~ adulta** adulthood; ***estar en ~ de merecer*** (ant *o* hum) to be of courting age (dated)
(Compuestos)
• **edad del pavo** (fam): **están en la ~ del ~** they're at that awkward age
• **edad mental** mental age
• **edad penal** age of criminal *o* legal responsibility
B (Hist) (época) age, period
(Compuestos)
• **edad antigua**: **la ~ ~** ancient times (*pl*)
• **edad contemporánea**: **la ~ ~** *the period from the French Revolution to the present day*
• **edad de bronce/de hierro/de piedra** Bronze/Iron/Stone Age
• **edad de oro** golden age
• **edad media**: **la ~ ~** the Middle Ages (*pl*)
• **edad moderna**: **la ~ ~** *the period from the last decade of the 15th Century up until the French Revolution*
edecán *m*
A (Mil) aide-de-camp
B **edecán** *mf* (Méx) (acompañante) escort
edema *m* edema*
Edén *m*: **el ~** (the Garden of) Eden
edición *f*
A (Impr, Period) (tirada) edition; (acción) publication; **una nueva ~** a new edition; **Ediciones Rivera** Rivera Publications; **al cerrar la ~ nos llegó la noticia** the news came in just as we were going to press
(Compuesto) **edición limitada/de bolsillo** limited/pocket edition
B (Rad, TV) program*, edition
C (frml) (de certamen, curso): **la cuarta ~ del Trofeo Carranza** the fourth Carranza Trophy; **la tercera ~ de estos cursos** the third series *o* round of these courses
edicto *m* edict
edificable *adj* ‹*terreno/superficie*› that can be built on
edificación *f* (edificio) building; (acción) construction, building
edificado -da *adj* built-up
edificante *adj* edifying
edificar [A2] *vt*
A ‹*edificio/pueblo*› to construct (frml), to build
B ‹*persona*› to edify (frml)
■ **edificar** *vi* to build
edificio *m* building
edil, edila *m,f* (Pol) councilor*
Edimburgo *m* Edinburgh
edípico -ca *adj* ‹*relación*› oedipal
editaje *m* editing
editar [A1] *vt*
A (publicar) ‹*libro/revista*› to publish
B (modificar) ‹*película/grabación/texto*› to edit; (Inf) to edit
editor[1] -tora *adj* publishing (*before n*)
editor[2] -tora *m,f*
A (que publica) publisher; (que revisa, modifica) editor
B **editor** *m* (Inf) editor
C **editora** *f* (empresa) publishing company *o* house
editorial[1] *adj* ‹*casa/actividad*› publishing (*before n*); ‹*puesto/decisión*› editorial
editorial[2] *f* (empresa) publishing company *o* house
editorial[3] *m* (en periódico) editorial, leading article

editorialista *mf* editorialist

edredón *m* eiderdown, comforter (AmE); (que se usa sin mantas) duvet, continental quilt (BrE)

educación *f*

A (enseñanza) education; (para la convivencia) upbringing

(Compuestos)

- **educación a distancia** correspondence courses (*pl*), distance learning
- **educación especial** special education, education for children with special needs
- **educación estatal/privada** state/private education
- **educación física/sexual** physical/sex education
- **educación preescolar** preschool education, nursery education (BrE)
- **educación primaria/secundaria/superior** primary/secondary/higher education
- **educación universitaria** university education, college education (AmE)
- **educación vocacional** (AmS) careers guidance

B (modales) manners (*pl*); **no tiene ~** he has no manners; **es una falta de ~** it's rude, it's bad manners

educacional *adj* educational, education (*before n*)

educado -da *adj* polite, well-mannered

educador¹ -dora *adj* educational (*before n*)

educador² -dora *m,f* (frml) teacher, educator (frml)

educando -da *m,f* (frml) pupil, student

educar [A2] *vt*

A 1 (Educ) to educate, teach; **los quieren ~ en un colegio bilingüe** they want them to be educated at a bilingual school 2 (para la convivencia) ‹*hijos*› to bring up; ‹*ciudadanos*› to educate

B ‹*paladar*› to educate; ‹*oído/voz*› to train

■ **educarse** *v pron* (hacer los estudios) to be educated; **me eduqué viajando por el mundo** I learned about life traveling around the world

educativo -va *adj* ‹*programa/juego*› educational; ‹*establecimiento*› educational, teaching (*before n*); ‹*sistema*› education (*before n*)

edulcorante *m* sweetener

edulcorar [A1] *vt* to sweeten

EEB *f* (= **encefalopatía espongiforme bovina**) BSE

EEUU *or* **EE.UU.** (= **Estados Unidos**) USA

efe *f*: *name of the letter* **f**

efectista *adj* theatrical, dramatic; **es un recurso puramente ~** it's purely for dramatic effect

efectivamente *adv* 1 (realmente) really; **si ~ es así ...** if that is really the case ... 2 (*indep*) **sí, ~, así fue** yes, that's right, that's how it was; **dijo que estaría allí y, ~, allí estaba** he said he'd be there and, sure enough, there he was

efectividad *f* (eficacia) effectiveness; (validez, vigencia): **una disposición con ~ desde el 5 de julio** a regulation which becomes effective *o* takes effect from July 5th

efectivo¹ -va *adj*

A ‹*remedio/medio/castigo*› effective; **hacer ~** ‹*cheque*› to cash; ‹*pago*› to make; ‹*amenaza/plan*› to carry out; **su dimisión se hará efectiva mañana** her resignation will take effect *o* become effective tomorrow

B (real) real, genuine, true

efectivo² *m*

A (Fin) cash; **~ en caja** cash in hand; **premios en ~** cash prizes; **pagar en ~** to pay cash; **dinero en ~** cash

B **efectivos** *mpl* (fuerzas) (frml): **numerosos ~s de la policía** a large police contingent; **~s militares** troops (*pl*)

efecto *m*

A (resultado, consecuencia) effect; **el castigo surtió ~** the punishment had the desired effect; **un calmante de ~ inmediato** a fast-acting painkiller; **hacer ~** to take effect; **bajo los ~s del alcohol** under the influence of alcohol; **llevar a ~ una operación** to carry out an operation; **de ~ retardado** ‹*mecanismo*› delayed-action (*before n*)

(Compuestos)

- **efecto bumerán**: **puede tener un ~ ~** it may boomerang *o* backfire
- **efecto invernadero/secundario** greenhouse/side effect
- **efecto óptico** optical illusion
- **efecto retroactivo**: **tener ~ ~** to be retroactive *o* retrospective; **el aumento se aplicará con ~ ~** the increase will be backdated
- **efectos especiales/sonoros** *mpl* special/sound effects (*pl*)

B (impresión): **su conducta causó muy mal ~** his behavior made a very bad impression *o* (colloq) didn't go down at all well; **no sé qué ~ le causaron mis palabras** I don't know what effect my words had *o* what impression my words made on him

C (Der) (vigencia) **la nueva ley tendrá ~ a partir de...** the new law will take effect *o* come into effect from...; **con ~ a partir de...** with effect from...

D (frml) (fin): **construido expresamente al** *or* **a tal** *or* **a este ~** specially designed for this purpose; **a ~s legales** legally (speaking) *o* in the eyes of the law; **a todos los ~s es un adulto** to all intents and purposes he is an adult

E (Dep) 1 (movimiento rotatorio) spin; **le dio a la bola con ~** she put some spin on the ball 2 (desvío) swerve; **tiró la pelota con ~** he made the ball swerve

F 1 (Fin) (valores) bill of exchange, draft; **~s negociables** commercial paper 2 **efectos** *mpl* (frml) (de comercio) stock; (de local) contents (*pl*)

(Compuestos)

- **efectos bancarios** *mpl* bank bills (*pl*), bank paper
- **efectos personales** *mpl* personal effects (*pl*)

efectuar [A18] *vt* (frml) ‹*maniobra/redada*› to carry out, execute (frml); ‹*pago*› to make; ‹*viaje/cambio*› to make; ‹*disparo*› to fire; **el tren ~á su salida a las 10.50** the train will depart at 10:50; **~ un recorrido de 10 kilómetros** to cover a distance of 10 kilometers

efeméride, efemérides *f* (Period): **las ~s del día** anniversaries of events which took place on this day in history; **conmemorar la ~s patria** (AmL frml) to commemorate the declaration of independence

efervescencia *f* 1 (de líquido) effervescence 2 (agitación): **la ~ política de la región** the political volatility of the area 3 (vivacidad) vivacity; (excitación) high spirits (*pl*)

efervescente *adj* 1 ‹*pastilla*› effervescent; ‹*bebida*› sparkling, fizzy (colloq) 2 ‹*situación*› volatile 3 (vivaz) bubbly, vivacious; (excitado) high-spirited

eficacia *f* 1 (de acción, remedio) effectiveness, efficacy (frml) 2 (eficiencia) efficiency

eficaz *adj* 1 ‹*fórmula/remedio*› effective, efficacious (frml) 2 (eficiente) efficient

eficiencia *f* efficiency

eficiente *adj* efficient

efigie *f* (cuadro) image, picture; (estatua) statue, effigy; **sellos con la ~ del Rey** stamps bearing a portrait of the King

efímera *f* mayfly

efímero -ra *adj* ephemeral

efluvio *m* (emanación) emanation; **los ~s de la prima-vera** (liter) the sweet breath of spring

efusión *f* (entusiasmo) effusiveness, warmth

efusivo -va *adj* ‹*temperamento/recibimiento*› effusive; ‹*persona*› demonstrative; **un ~ apretón de manos** a warm handshake

égida *f*: **bajo la ~ de** (frml) under the aegis of (frml)

egipcio -cia *adj/m,f* Egyptian

Egipto *m* Egypt

egiptólogo -ga *m,f* Egyptologist

eglefino *m* haddock

ego *m* ego

egocéntrico -ca *adj* egocentric, self-centered*

egoísmo *m* selfishness, egotism

egoísta¹ *adj* selfish, egotistic; **no seas egoistón** (fam) don't be mean (colloq)

egoísta² *mf* (Psic) egotist; **es una ~** she is very selfish

ególatra *adj* egomaniacal

egotismo *m* egotism

egregio -gia *adj* (frml) illustrious, eminent

egresado¹ -da *adj* (AmL): **los alumnos ~s** (de universidad) the graduates; (de colegio) the high school graduates (AmE), the school leavers (BrE)

egresado² -da *m,f* (AmL) (de universidad) graduate; (de colegio) high school graduate (AmE), school leaver (BrE)

egresar [A1] *vi* (AmL) (de universidad) to graduate; (de colegio) to graduate from high school (AmE), to leave school (*o* college *etc*) (BrE)
■ **egresar** *vt* (Andes) (Fin) to withdraw, take out

egreso *m*
A (AmL) (de universidad) graduation; (de colegio) graduation (AmE)
B (Andes) (Fin) debit; **ingresos y ~s** income and expenditure

eh *interj* **1** (para llamar la atención) hey! **2** (expresando amenaza, advertencia) eh?, huh?, OK? **3** (contestando una pregunta) eh?, what?

eider *m* eider (duck)

Ej., ej. (*read as* **por ejemplo**) eg

eje *m*
A **1** (Astron, Fís, Mat) axis; ***partir a algn por el ~*** (fam) (con cambio) to ruin *o* mess up sb's plans; (con pregunta) to stump *o* floor sb (colloq) **2** (Auto, Mec) (barra) axle

Compuestos
- **eje de simetría** axis of symmetry
- **eje de transmisión** drive shaft, propeller shaft
- **eje vial** (Méx) main artery, arterial road

B (de asunto, política) core, central theme

ejecución *f*
A (de persona) execution
B **1** (de plan) implementation, execution (frml); (de orden) carrying out **2** (Mús) performance, execution (frml)

ejecutable *adj* practicable, feasible

ejecutante *mf* performer

ejecutar [A1] *vt*
A ‹*condenado/reo*› to execute
B ‹*plan*› to implement, carry out; ‹*orden/trabajo*› to carry out; ‹*sentencia*› to execute, enforce; ‹*ejercicio/salto*› to perform; ‹*sinfonía/himno nacional*› to play, perform

ejecutiva *f* (junta) executive; *ver tb* **ejecutivo² A**

ejecutivo¹ -va *adj* ‹*función/comisión*› executive

ejecutivo² -va *m,f*
A (Adm, Com) executive
B **ejecutivo** *m* (Gob) executive

ejecutor -tora *m,f* executor

ejecutoria *f*
A (frml) (logros) accomplishments (*pl*)
B (Der) final judgment

ejecutorio -ria *adj* executory

ejem *interj* ahem!

ejemplar¹ *adj* ‹*conducta/vida*› exemplary; ‹*trabajador/padre*› model (*before n*); ‹*castigo*› exemplary

ejemplar² *m*
A (de libro, documento) copy; **~ de promoción** advance copy
B (Bot, Zool) specimen; **su novio es un ~ de mucho cuidado** her boyfriend's a really nasty character *o* a nasty piece of work

ejemplaridad *f* exemplary nature

ejemplarizador -dora *adj* (Chi, Per) exemplary

ejemplificar [A2] *vt* to give examples of, illustrate ... with examples

ejemplo *m* example; **debería servirnos de** *or* **como ~** it should serve as *o* should be an example to us; **dar (el) ~** to set an example; **pongamos por ~ el caso de Elena** let's take Elena's case as an example; **por ejemplo** for example; ***predicar con el ~*** to set a good example, practice* what one preaches

ejercer [E2] *vt*
A **1** ‹*profesión*› to practice* exercise (frml) **~ la medicina/abogacía** to practice medicine/law; **~ la docencia** to be in the teaching profession **2** ‹*derecho*› to exercise
B ‹*influencia/poder/presión*› to exert
■ **ejercer** *vi* «*abogado/médico*» to practice*; **es maestra pero no ejerce** she's a teacher but she doesn't practice her profession; **ejerce de abogado** he practices law

ejercicio *m*
A (actividad física) exercise; **hacer ~** to exercise
B **1** (de profesión) practice; **abogado en ~** practicing lawyer **2** (de función) **decisiones tomadas en el ~ de su cargo** decisions taken in the course of his duties **3** (de derecho, poder) exercise (frml)
C (Educ) **1** (trabajo de práctica) exercise **2** (prueba, examen) test, exam

Compuestos
- **ejercicio de tiro** shooting/rifle practice
- **ejercicios espirituales** *mpl*: **ir de ~ ~** to go on a retreat

D (Mil) exercise, maneuver*
E (Econ, Fin) fiscal year (AmE), financial year (BrE)

ejercitación *f*
A (de un músculo): **para la ~ de los dedos** for exercising the fingers
B (de derecho) exercising
C (Educ) (práctica) practice

ejercitar [A1] *vt*
A ‹*músculo/dedos*› to exercise; ‹*memoria/inteligencia*› to exercise
B ‹*derechos/prerrogativas*› to exercise
C ‹*caballos*› to train; ‹*tropa*› to drill, train; ‹*alumnos*› to train
■ **ejercitarse** *v pron* **~se EN algo** to practice* sth

ejército *m* army

Compuestos
- **ejército del aire** air force
- **Ejército de Salvación** Salvation Army
- **ejército de tierra** army
- **ejército regular** regular army

ejidal *adj* (en Méx) cooperative (*before n*)

ejidatario -ria *m,f* (en Méx) member of a cooperative

ejido *m*
A (Hist) common
B (en Méx) (sistema) *system of communal or cooperative farming*; (sociedad) cooperative; (terreno) *land belonging to a cooperative*

ejote *m* (Méx) green bean

el (*pl* **los**), **la** (*pl* **las**) *art* [*the masculine article* **el** *is also used before feminine nouns which begin with accented* **a** *or* **ha**, *e.g.* **el agua pura, el hada madrina**]
A **1** (con un referente único) the; **el sol** the sun; **la Tierra** the Earth **2** (con sustantivos en sentido genérico): **odio el pescado** I hate fish; **así es la vida** that's life; **(nosotros) los mexicanos** we Mexicans; **¿ya vas a la escuela?** do you go to school yet?; **en el mar** at sea **3** (con un referente conocido o que se define): **en la calle Solis** in Solis street; **el mío/las tuyas** mine/yours; **el rojo/último** the red/last one; **el estúpido del marido** that stupid husband of hers; **los nacidos entre...** those born between...
B **1** **el + DE...**: **la del sombrero** the one with the hat; **el de Valencia** the one from Valencia; **el de las nueve** the nine o'clock one; **el de Juan/de mi hijo** Juan's/my son's **2** **el + QUE...**: **el que acaba de entrar** the one who's just come in; **las que yo ví** the ones I saw; **los que estén cansados**; those who are tired, anyone who's tired; **la que te guste** whichever you like; **el que lo haya hecho** whoever has done it
C (en expresiones de tiempo): **ocurrió el domingo** it happened last Sunday; **mi cumpleaños es el 28 de mayo** my birthday's on May 28; **el mes pasado/que viene** last/next month; **no trabajo los sábados** I don't work (on) Saturdays; **toda la mañana** all morning; **a las ocho** at eight o'clock
D (cada): **$80 el metro/kilo** $80 a meter/a kilo
E (con fracciones, porcentajes, números): **la mitad/la cuarta parte del dinero** half the money/a quarter of the money; **el 20% de ...** 20% of ...; **el cuarto piso** the fifth floor (AmE) *o* (BrE) fourth floor
F (refiriéndose a partes del cuerpo, prendas de vestir, artículos personales, etc): **tenía las manos en los bolsillos** she had her hands in her pockets; **¡te cortaste el pelo!** you've had your hair cut!; **tienes la falda sucia** your skirt is dirty; **tiene los ojos azules** he has blue eyes
G (con nombres propios) **1** (con apellidos acompañados de título, adjetivos, etc): **el señor Ortiz/la doctora Vidal** Mr Ortiz/Doctor Vidal **2** (en plural): **los Ortega** the Ortegas **3** (con algunos nombres geográficos): **en la India** in India; **en (el) Perú** in Peru; *ver* **Africa, Argentina, etc** **4** (al calificar): **la España de Franco** Franco's Spain; **el Buñuel que todos conocemos** the Buñuel we all know **5** (con algunos equipos deportivos): **juegan contra el Juventus** they're playing against Juventus
H **el** (con infinitivo): **odiaba el tener que pedírselo** he hated

having to ask her; **es cuidadoso en el hablar** he's careful in the way he speaks; **el frenético girar de los bailarines** the frenzied spinning of the dancers

él *pron pers* 1 (como sujeto) he; **~ me lo dijo** he told me; **¿quién se lo va a decir? — él** who's going to tell her? — he is; **lo hizo ~ mismo** he did it himself; **fue ~** it was him, it was he (frml) 2 (en comparaciones, con preposiciones) him; (refiriéndose a cosas) it; **llegué antes que ~** I arrived before him *o* before he did; **eres tan alto como ~** you are as tall as him *o* as he is; **con/contra/para ~** with/against/for him; **son de ~** they're his

elaboración *f*
A 1 (de producto, vino) production, making; (de pan) baking, making; **de ~ casera** homemade 2 (de metal, madera) working
B 1 (de plan): **los responsables de la ~ del plan** those responsible for drawing up *o* devising the plan 2 (de informe, estudio) preparation
C (Biol) production

elaborado -da *adj* elaborate; **un diseño muy ~** a very elaborate *o* intricate design

elaborar [A1] *vt*
A 1 ‹*producto/vino*› to produce, make; ‹*pan*› to bake, make 2 ‹*metal/madera*› to work
B ‹*plan/teoría*› to devise, draw up; ‹*informe/estudio*› to prepare, write
C ‹*hormona/savia*› to produce

elasticidad *f* (de material) elasticity; (de horario) flexibility

elástico¹ -ca *adj* ‹*membrana/cinta*› elastic; ‹*medias/venda*› elastic, stretch (*before n*); ‹*horario*› flexible

elástico² *m* (material) elastic; (cordón) piece of elastic; (en géneros de punto) rib, ribbing; (goma) (Chi) rubber band

elastizado -da *adj* (RPl) elasticized (AmE), elasticated (BrE)

ele *f*: *name of the letter* **l**

ELE *m* (= **español como lengua extranjera**) Spanish as a foreign language

elección *f*
A 1 (acción de escoger) choice; **dejo la fecha a su ~** I will leave it up to you to choose the date; **llévate tres, a tu ~** take *o* choose any three 2 (Pol) (de candidato) election
B **elecciones** *fpl* (Pol) election; **convocaron elecciones** they called an election; **elecciones legislativas/municipales** legislative/local elections

eleccionario -ria *adj* (CS) ▸ **electoral**

electivo -va *adj* elective

electo -ta *adj*: **el presidente ~** the president elect

elector -tora *m,f* (Pol) voter, elector

electorado *m* electorate

electoral *adj* ‹*campaña/discurso*› election (*before n*)

electoralista *adj* electioneering (*before n*), vote-catching (*before n*)

electoralmente *adv* electorally

eléctrica *f* electricity company

electricidad *f* electricity

electricista *mf* electrician

eléctrico -ca *adj* ‹*tren/motor/luz*› electric; ‹*instalación/aparato*› electrical; ‹*carga*› electrical, electric

electrificar [A2] *vt* to electrify

electrizante *adj* electrifying

electrizar [A4] *vt* to electrify

electrocardiograma *m* electrocardiogram

electrocución *f* electrocution

electrocutar [A1] *vt* to electrocute
■ **electrocutarse** *v pron* to be electrocuted

electrodo *m* electrode

electrodoméstico *m* electrical appliance

electroencefalograma *m* electroencephalogram

electroimán *m* electromagnet

electrólisis, electrolisis *f* electrolysis

electromagnético -ca *adj* electromagnetic

electromotor -triz *adj* electromotive

electrón *m* electron

electrónica *f* electronics

electrónico -ca *adj* electronic

electroshock *m* electroshock

electrotren *m* electric express train

elefante -ta *m,f* elephant
(Compuesto) **elefante marino** *m,f* elephant seal, sea elephant

elegancia *f*
A (buen gusto en el vestir) smartness; (garbo, gracilidad) elegance, stylishness; (de barrio, restaurante) smartness, fashionableness
B (de estilo) elegance; (de solución) elegance, neatness

elegante *adj*
A 1 ‹*moda/vestido*› elegant, smart; **iba muy ~** (bien vestido) he was very well *o* very smartly dressed; (garboso) he looked very elegant 2 ‹*barrio/restaurante/fiesta*› smart, fashionable
B ‹*estilo/frase*› elegant, polished; ‹*solución*› elegant, neat

elegantemente *adv* ‹*vestir*› smartly; ‹*hablar/moverse*› elegantly; **~ amueblado** elegantly furnished

elegantoso -sa *adj* (fam) stylish, natty (colloq)

elegía *f* elegy

elegíaco -ca *adj* elegiac

elegible *adj* eligible

elegido -da *m,f* (Relig) chosen one

elegir [I8] *vt* 1 (escoger) to choose; **me dieron a ~** I was given a *o* the choice 2 (por votación) to elect

elemental *adj* 1 (esencial) ‹*norma/principio*› fundamental 2 (básico) ‹*curso/nivel/texto*› elementary; ‹*conocimientos/nociones*› rudimentary, basic

elemento¹ *m*
A (Elec, Fís, Quím) element; (fuerza natural): **los ~s** the elements
B 1 (componente) element; **el ~ sorpresa** the element of surprise 2 (medio): **los ~s básicos para llevarlo a cabo** the basic resources with which to carry it out
(Compuesto) **elementos de juicio** *mpl* facts (*pl*)
C (ambiente): **está/se siente en su ~** he's in his element
D **elementos** *mpl* elements (*pl*); **~s de física** elements of physics, basic physics
E (de secador, calentador) element
F 1 (persona): **es un ~ pernicioso** he's a bad influence; **~s subversivos** subversive elements; 2 (RPl) (tipo de gente) crowd; **el ~ que va a ese club** the crowd that goes *o* the people who go to that club

elemento² -ta *m,f* (Esp fam & pey): **es una elementa de cuidado** she's a nasty piece of work (colloq); **su hijo está hecho un ~** her son is a little monster *o* brat (colloq)

elenco *m* (de actores) cast; (de deportistas) side, team

elepé *m* album, LP

elevación *f*
A (frml) 1 (acción de levantar) raising 2 **la Elevación** (Relig) the Elevation
B (frml) (aumento) rise, increase
C (a dignidad) elevation
D (frml) (de protesta, recurso) presentation, submission
E (Geog) (colina, altura) elevation
F (frml) (de pensamiento, sentimiento) nobility; (de estilo) loftiness, elevation (frml)

elevado -da *adj*
A ‹*terreno/montaña*› high; ‹*edificio*› tall, high
B ‹*cantidad*› large; ‹*precio/impuestos/índice*› high; ‹*pérdidas*› heavy, substantial
C ‹*categoría/calidad*› high; ‹*puesto/posición*› high
D ‹*ideas/pensamientos*› noble, elevated; ‹*estilo*› lofty, elevated

elevador *m* (montacargas) hoist; (ascensor) (Méx) elevator (AmE), lift (BrE)

elevadorista *mf* (Méx) elevator operator (AmE), lift attendant (BrE)

elevalunas *m* (*pl* ~): **dotado de ~ eléctrico** with electric *o* automatic windows

elevar [A1] *vt*
A (frml) 1 (levantar) ‹*objeto*› to raise, lift; **elevó los brazos al cielo** (liter) he raised (up) his arms to heaven (liter) 2 ‹*espíritu/mente*› to uplift; **música que eleva el espíritu** (spiritually) uplifting music 3 ‹*muro/nivel*› to raise, make … higher
B (frml) 1 (aumentar) ‹*precios/impuestos*› to raise, increase; ‹*nivel de vida*› to raise 2 ‹*voz/tono*› to raise

C (frml) (en jerarquía) to elevate (frml)
D (Mat): **~ un número a la sexta potencia** to raise a number to the power of six; **~ al cuadrado** to square; **~ al cubo** to cube
E (frml) (presentar, dirigir) **~ algo A algn** ‹*informe/protesta*› to present *o* submit sth TO sb; **~on el recurso al Tribunal Supremo** they appealed to the Supreme Court
■ **elevarse** *v pron*
A (tomar altura) «*avión/cometa*» to climb, gain height; «*globo*» to rise, gain height
B (frml) (aumentar) «*temperatura*» to rise; «*precios/impuestos*» to rise, increase; «*tono/voz*» to rise
C (frml) (ascender) **~se A algo**: **la cifra se elevaba ya al 13%** the figure had already reached 13%
D (liter) «*montaña/edificio*» to stand, rise (liter)

elidir [I1] *vt* to elide

elige, elija, etc *see* **elegir**

eliminación *f* elimination; **solucionaron el problema por ~** they solved the problem by (a) process of elimination; **la ~ de los residuos** the disposal of the waste products

eliminar [A1] *vt*
A 1 ‹*obstáculo*› to remove; ‹*párrafo*› to delete, remove 2 ‹*candidato*› to eliminate; (Dep) to eliminate, knock out 3 (euf) (matar) to eliminate (euph), to get rid of (euph) 4 ‹*residuos*› to dispose of
B ‹*toxinas/grasas*› to eliminate
C (Mat) ‹*incógnita*› to eliminate

eliminatoria *f* (en torneo) qualifying round; (para carrera) heat; (certamen) qualifying competition

eliminatorio -ria *adj* ‹*examen*› qualifying (*before n*); ‹*fase*› qualifying (*before n*), preliminary (*before n*); **las pruebas eliminatorias de la carrera** the heats for the race

elipse *f* ellipse

elipsis *f* ellipsis

elíptico -ca *adj* elliptical

elisión *f* elision

elite /e'lit/, **élite** /'elite e'lit/ *f* elite, élite

elitista *adj* ‹*sociedad/actitud*› elitist; ‹*colegio/club*› exclusive

elixir *m*
A (Mit) elixir
B (Esp) (Farm) mouthwash

ella *pron pers* 1 (como sujeto) she; **~ me lo dijo** she told me; **¿quién lo va a hacer? — ella** who's going to do it? — she is; **lo hizo ~ misma** she did it herself; **fue ~** it was her, it was she (frml) 2 (en comparaciones, con preposiciones) her; (referido a cosas) it; **salí después que ~** I left after her *o* after she did; **es tan listo como ~** he's as clever as her *o* as she is; **con/contra/para ~** with/against/for her; **son de ~** they're hers; **con/contra/para ella** with/against/for her

ellas *pron pers pl: ver* **ellos**

elle *f: name of the letter* **ll**

ello[1] *pron pers*: **ya que estamos en ~** while we're at it; **todo ~ exquisitamente presentado** all beautifully presented; **para ~ hay que obtener un permiso** (frml) you need a permit for this; **debido a ~ que ...** for which reason ..., owing to which ...; **¡a por ~!** go for it!

ello[2] *m* (Psic): **el ~** the id

ellos, ellas *pron pers pl* 1 (como sujeto) they; **~ me lo dijeron** they told me; **lo hicieron ~ mismos** they did it themselves; **fueron ellas** it was them, it was they (frml) 2 (en comparaciones, con preposiciones) them; **llegué antes que ~** I arrived before them *o* before they did; **es tan alto como ~** he's as tall as them *o* as they are; **con/contra/para ~/ellas** with/against/for them; **son de ellas/de ~** they're theirs, they belong to them

elocución *f* elocution

elocuencia *f* eloquence; **con ~** eloquently; **las cifras lo expresan con ~** the figures speak for themselves

elocuente *adj* ‹*persona/discurso*› eloquent, articulate; ‹*mirada/gesto/silencio*› eloquent

elogiable *adj* praiseworthy

elogiar [A1] *vt* to praise

elogio *m* praise; **hacer ~(s) de algo** to sing the praises of sth, to extol sth; **se deshizo en ~s para con ella** he showered her with praise; **digno de ~** praiseworthy

elogioso -sa *adj* ‹*palabras*› complimentary, laudatory (liter); ‹*acción/comportamiento*› praiseworthy

elote *m* (mazorca) (AmC, Méx) corncob, ear of corn (AmE); (granos) (Méx) corn (AmE), sweetcorn (BrE)

El Salvador *m* El Salvador

elucidar [A1] *vt* to elucidate, clarify

elucubración *f* lucubration (frml); **no pierdas tiempo en elucubraciones filosóficas** don't waste time philosophizing

elucubrar [A1] *vi* to muse
■ **elucubrar** *vt* to muse on, ponder over

eludir [I1] *vt* 1 ‹*problema/compromiso/pago*› to evade, avoid; **me eludió la mirada** she avoided my gaze 2 ‹*persona*› to avoid

elusivo -va *adj* evasive

e.m. (Com, Corresp) = **en mano**

email /'imeil/ *m* e-mail; **mandarle un ~ a algn** to e-mail sb; **mandarle algo a algn en un ~** to e-mail sth to sb, e-mail sb sth

(Compuesto) **email basura** spam

emanación *f* emanation (frml); **emanaciones tóxicas** toxic emissions

emanar [A1] *vi* (frml) **~ DE algo** «*radiación/olor/gas*» to emanate FROM sth (frml), to come FROM sth; «*poder/decisión*» to emanate *o* derive FROM sth (frml)
■ **emanar** *vt* to exude

emancipación *f* (Der) emancipation; (de nación) liberation, emancipation; (de esclavo) emancipation, freeing; **la ~ de la mujer** the emancipation of women *o* women's liberation

emancipado -da *adj* ‹*esclavo*› freed, emancipated; ‹*menor/mujer*› emancipated

emancipar [A1] *vt* ‹*esclavo*› to emancipate, free; ‹*pueblo*› to free, liberate
■ **emanciparse** *v pron* «*mujer/hijo*» (Der) to become emancipated; «*colonia*» to gain independence; **las mujeres se han emancipado mucho** women have become a great deal more liberated

emascular [A1] *vt* (frml) to emasculate (frml)

embadurnar [A1] *vt* **~ algo DE algo** to smear sth WITH sth; **dedos embadurnados de chocolate** fingers covered in chocolate
■ **embadurnarse** *v pron* (*refl*) **~se DE algo** to plaster *o* smear oneself WITH sth

embajada *f* (sede, delegación) embassy; (cargo) ambassadorship

embajador -dora *m,f* 1 (Adm, Pol) ambassador 2 **embajadora** *f* (esposa) ambassador's wife

embalado -da *adj*
A (fam) (con velocidad): **el coche venía ~** the car was hurtling *o* racing along; **salieron ~s** they shot off *o* ran for it (colloq)
B (RPl fam) (con idea) excited, keen (BrE); **está de lo más ~ con ella** he really likes her

embalador -dora *m,f* packer

embalaje *m*
A (acción) packing; (costo) packing charge; (envoltura) packaging, wrapping
B (Col) (Dep) sprint; **~ final** sprint finish

embalar [A1] *vt* to pack
■ **embalar** *vi* (Per, Ur fam) to get a move on (colloq)
■ **embalarse** *v pron* (fam) 1 (cobrar velocidad): **no te embales** don't go too fast; **el coche se embaló cuesta abajo** the car sped *o* (colloq) zoomed off down the hill 2 (entusiasmarse): **no es muy hablador pero cuando se embala ...** he's not very talkative, but when he gets going ...

embaldosado *m* (acción) tiling; (suelo) tiled floor

embaldosar [A1] *vt* to tile

embalsamar [A1] *vt* to embalm

embalsar [A1] *vt* ‹*río*› to dam, dam up; **embalsan el agua en una presa** they collect the water in a reservoir

embalse *m* (depósito) reservoir

embancarse [A2] *v pron* 1 «*barco*» to run aground 2 (Andes) «*río/canal*» to silt up

embarazada[1] *adj* pregnant; **quedó** *or* (Esp) **se quedó ~** she got *o* became pregnant; **está ~ de dos meses** she's two months pregnant; ~ **de su segundo hijo** pregnant with her second child; **la dejó** ~ he got her pregnant

embarazada² *f* pregnant woman

embarazar [A4] *vt*

A ‹*mujer*› to get … pregnant

B (ant) (cohibir) to embarrass; (impedir) to hamper, restrict

embarazo *m*

A (Med) pregnancy

(Compuesto) **embarazo ectópico** *or* **extrauterino** ectopic pregnancy

B (frml) (apuro) embarrassment; (estorbo) obstacle, hindrance

embarazoso -sa *adj* embarrassing, awkward

embarcación *f* (frml) vessel (frml), craft (frml)

embarcadero *m* (atracadero) jetty; (para mercancías) wharf

embarcar [A2] *vi* (Aviac) to board; (Náut) to embark, board

■ **embarcar** *vt*

A 1 ‹*mercancías/equipaje*› to load 2 (en asunto, negocio) ~ **a algn EN algo** to get sb involved IN sth

B (Ven) to let … down

■ **embarcarse** *v pron* 1 «*pasajero*» (en barco) to board, embark; (en tren, avión) to board, get on; **se ~on para América** they set sail for America 2 (en asunto, negocio) **~se EN algo** to embark ON sth, embark UPON sth (frml)

embarco *m* embarkation

embargar [A3] *vt*

A ‹*bienes*› to seize, to sequestrate (frml); ‹*vehículo*› to impound

B 1 (sobrecoger): **lo embargó la emoción** he was overcome by emotion; **la pena que nos embarga** the overwhelming grief we feel 2 (absorber) ‹*tiempo*› to take up

embargo *m*

A 1 (Der) (incautación, decomiso) seizure, sequestration (frml); **levantar un** ~ to lift a seizure order 2 (Mil, Pol) embargo

B **sin embargo**: **sin ~, tiene algunas desventajas** however *o* nevertheless, it has some disadvantages; **sin ~, ayer no decías eso** you weren't saying that yesterday, though; **es difícil, sin ~ disfruto haciéndolo** it's difficult but I enjoy doing it all the same *o* anyway

embarque *m* (de mercancías) loading; (de pasajeros) embarkation, boarding; (carga) shipment

embarrada *f*

A (AmS fam) (metedura de pata) blunder, boo-boo (colloq)

B (Méx) (de un molde) greasing

(Compuesto) **embarrada de mano** (Méx fam) backhander (colloq)

embarrado -da *adj*

A ‹*calle/zapatos*› muddy

B (Méx fam) (ceñido) tight, tight-fitting

embarrancar [A2] *vi*, **embarrancarse** [A2] *v pron* (Náut) to run aground; «*vehículo*» to get bogged down

embarrar [A1] *vt* to cover … in mud; **~la** (AmS fam) to mess up (AmE colloq), to mess things up (BrE colloq)

■ **embarrarse** *v pron* «*persona*» to get covered in mud; ‹*prenda/ropa*› to get…muddy

embarullar [A1] *vt* (fam) ‹*persona*› to muddle, confuse; ‹*asunto/problema*› to complicate, confuse

■ **embarullarse** *v pron* (fam) to get mixed up, get in *o* into a muddle

embate *m* (del mar, viento) battering; (acometida): **proteja su piel de los ~s del tiempo** protect your skin from the ravages of time; **la industria supo neutralizar el ~ japonés** the industry managed to counter the Japanese onslaught

embaucador¹ -dora *adj* deceitful

embaucador² -dora *m,f* trickster

embaucamiento *m* (acción) swindling; (efecto) swindle

embaucar [A2] *vt* to trick, con (colloq)

embeber [E1] *vt* 1 (en líquido) ‹*bizcocho/esponja*› to soak 2 «*secante/toalla*» ‹*líquido*› to soak up 3 ‹*tela*› to gather in

■ **embeber** *vi* to shrink

■ **embeberse** *v pron* 1 (enfrascarse) **~se EN algo** to become wrapped up *o* absorbed IN sth 2 (imbuirse) **~se DE algo** to become imbued WITH sth (frml)

embeleco *m*, **embelequería** *f*

A (fam) (engaño) con (colloq), rip-off (colloq)

B (AmC, Col fam) (cosa exagerada) frippery

C (Chi fam) (cosa de poco valor) knick-knack (colloq), trinket; (golosina): **se gasta la plata en ~s** she spends all her money on candy (AmE) *o* (BrE) on sweets/on junk food

embelesado -da *adj* spellbound

embelesar [A1] *vt* to captivate

embeleso *m*: **la escuchaba con** ~ he listened to her captivated *o* spellbound

embellecedor¹ -dora *adj* beauty (*before n*)

embellecedor² *m* (tapacubos) hubcap; (adorno) trim

embellecer [E3] *vt* ‹*persona*› to make … beautiful; ‹*campiña/ciudad*› to beautify, improve the appearance of

■ **embellecer** *vi* (liter) to become *o* grow more beautiful

■ **embellecerse** *v pron* (*refl*) to make oneself beautiful, beautify oneself

embellecimiento *m* beautification

embestida *f* (del toro) rush, charge; (de personas) charge, onslaught

embestir [I14] *vi* to charge; ~ **CONTRA algo/algn** to charge AT sth/sb; **las olas embestían contra el malecón** the waves were crashing *o* pounding against the pier

■ **embestir** *vt* «*toro*» to charge (at); **el coche fue embestido por un camión** a truck ran into the car

embetunar [A1] *vt*

A ‹*zapatos*› to polish, put polish on

B (CS) (ensuciar) to get … dirty

emblema *m* emblem

emblemático -ca *adj* emblematic

embobado -da *adj* spellbound; **miraban ~s a los trapecistas** they sat open-mouthed watching the trapeze artists; **está ~ con ella** he's besotted with her

embobar [A1] *vt* to fascinate, hold … spellbound

■ **embobarse** *v pron* to be captivated *o* fascinated

embobinar [A1] *vt* to wind

embocadura *f*

A (de río) mouth; (de calle) entrance

B (de vino) flavor*, taste

C (Mús) (boquilla) mouthpiece

embocar [A2] *vt*

A ‹*pelota*› (en baloncesto) to get *o* put … in the basket; (en golf) to hole

B (Andes, RPl fam) (acertar) ‹*pregunta*› to get … right

■ **embocar** *vi*: **embocamos por una callejuela** we went down/turned into a narrow street

embojotar *vt* [A1] (Ven fam) to wrap … up

■ **embojotarse** *v pron* (Ven fam) to wrap oneself up; (en la cama) to snuggle up

embolado *m* (fam) mess (colloq); **meterse en un** ~ to get into a mess *o* a tight spot (colloq)

embolador -dora *m,f* (Col) bootblack

embolar [A1] *vt*

A ‹*toro*› to put protective balls on the horns of

B (RPl arg) (fastidiar) to bug (colloq), to piss … off (sl)

C (Col) ‹*zapatos*› to shine, polish

■ **embolarse** *v pron* (AmC fam) to get plastered (colloq)

embolatar [A1] *vt* (Col fam) ‹*libros*› to mess up (colloq); ‹*cuentas*› to get … in a mess

embolia *f* embolism

émbolo *m* piston

embolsarse [A1] *v pron* ‹*dinero ajeno*› to pocket; ‹*premio*› to collect, receive; ‹*ganancia*› to make

embonar [A1] *vi* (Méx) ‹*tubos/ventana/piezas*› to fit; ~ **CON algo** to fit in WITH sth

emboque *m* (Chi) *cup and ball game*

emboquillado -da *adj* filter-tipped, tipped

emborrachar [A1] *vt* «*bebida*» to make … drunk; «*persona*» to get … drunk

■ **emborracharse** *v pron* to get drunk

emborronar [A1] *vt* (manchar) to smudge; (con tinta) to make blots on, to blot

■ **emborronarse** *v pron* to smudge, get smudged

emboscada *f* ambush; **caer en una** ~ to walk into an ambush

emboscar [A2] *vt* to ambush

■ **emboscarse** *v pron* to position oneself for an ambush

embotado -da *adj* ‹*punta/filo*› dull, blunt; **estoy totalmente** ~ my brain's seized up *o* I can't take in any more;

tienes la mente embotada con tanta televisión all that television has dulled your mind

embotar [A1] *vt* ‹*mente/sentidos*› to dull

■ **embotarse** *v pron*: **se embotó de tanto estudiar** his brain seized up from so much studying

embotellado¹ -da *adj* 1 ‹*agua/vino*› bottled 2 ‹*calle/tráfico*› jammed solid

embotellado² *m* bottling

embotelladora *f* bottling plant

embotellamiento *m* (del tráfico) traffic jam

embotellar [A1] *vt* to bottle

embozarse [A4] *v pron* (con pañuelo) to cover one's nose and mouth; (en manta) to wrap oneself (up)

embozo *m* (de sábana) turndown; (de abrigo) collar

embragar [A3] *vi* to engage the clutch

embrague *m* clutch

embravecerse [E3] *v pron* (liter) 1 «*mar*» to become stormy *o* (liter) wild 2 (enfurecerse) to become enraged

embrear [A1] *vt* to pitch, tar

embriagado -da *adj* 1 (frml) (borracho) inebriated (frml) 2 (liter) (extasiado): **~ de placer** intoxicated with pleasure; **~ de felicidad** drunk with happiness

embriagador -dora *adj* ‹*vino*› heady; ‹*sensación*› (liter) intoxicating (liter)

embriagar [A3] *vt* (liter) «*perfume/sensación*» to intoxicate

■ **embriagarse** *v pron* (frml) (con alcohol) to become intoxicated (frml)

embriaguez *f* 1 (frml) (borrachera) inebriation (frml), intoxication (frml) 2 (liter) (éxtasis) rapture (liter), euphoria

embridar [A1] *vt* to bridle

embriología *f* embryology

embrión *m* (Biol) embryo; **en ~** in its embryonic stage

embrionario -ria *adj* embryonic

embrollar [A1] *vt* 1 ‹*hilo/madeja*› to tangle (up) 2 (confundir) ‹*situación*› to complicate; ‹*persona*› to muddle, confuse 3 (implicar) **~ a algn EN algo** to embroil sb IN sth, get sb involved IN sth

■ **embrollarse** *v pron* «*hilo/madeja*» to get tangled; «*situación*» to get confused *o* muddled; «*persona*» to get muddled, to get mixed up (colloq)

embrollo *m* (de hilos, cables) tangle; (de callejuelas, pasillos) maze; (de ideas, situaciones): **el argumento es un ~** the plot is extremely involved *o* complicated; **se metió en un ~** he got himself into a mess

embrollón -llona *adj* trouble-making (*before n*)

embromado -da *adj*

A [ESTAR] (AmS fam) 1 (enfermo, delicado): **está embromada con esa gripe** she's feeling pretty rough with that flu (colloq); **anda muy ~** he's in a bad way; **está ~ del corazón** he has heart trouble; **tiene un pie ~** she has a bad foot 2 (perjudicado): **el que siempre resulta ~ soy yo** I always seem to be the one who comes off worst (colloq)

B 1 (AmS fam) ‹*situación*› tricky; ‹*problema*› thorny 2 (Chi fam) (fastidioso) ‹*persona*› tiresome, irritating

embromar [A1] *vt* 1 (AmS fam) (molestar) to pester 2 (AmS fam) (estropear) ‹*aparato*› to ruin (colloq); ‹*plan*› to ruin, spoil 3 (AmS fam) (perjudicar): **la guerra nos embromó a todos** we all suffered because of the war; **¡me embromaste!** now you've really landed me in it! (colloq) 4 (CS fam) (tomar el pelo) to fool, trick; (timar, estafar) to rip… off; **¡no me embromes!** you're kidding *o* joking! (colloq)

■ **embromar** *vi* (CS fam): **¡no embromes!** (no molestes) stop being a pest *o* a pain! (colloq); (no digas) you're kidding!

■ **embromarse** *v pron* 1 (AmS fam) (jorobarse): **que se embrome por estúpido** it serves him right for being so stupid; **si no te gusta, te embromas** if you don't like it, tough! 2 (AmS fam) (hacerse daño) to hurt oneself; ‹*rodilla/hígado*› to damage, to do … in (BrE colloq) 3 (AmS fam) «*aparato/frenos*» to go wrong 4 (AmS fam) (enfermarse) to get ill (colloq)

embrujado -da *adj* [ESTAR] ‹*persona*› bewitched; ‹*casa/lugar*› haunted

embrujar [A1] *vt* 1 (hechizar) to bewitch, put … under a spell 2 (fascinar, enamorar) to bewitch

embrujo *m* 1 (hechizo) spell; (maleficio) curse 2 (encanto, atractivo) magic, enchantment

embrutecedor -dora *adj* soul-destroying

embrutecer [E3] *vt* «*trabajo*» to stultify; «*televisión*» to make … mindless

embuchar [A1] *vt* 1 (Coc) to stuff 2 (fam) ‹*comida*› to rush

■ **embucharse** *v pron*

A (CS) (guardarse para sí) to bottle … up (colloq)

B (Chi fam) ‹*dinero/fondos*› to pocket

C (Col, Ven) (con bebida) to get bloated

embudo *m* funnel

embuste *m* tall story, story (colloq)

embustero¹ -ra *adj*: **¡qué niño más ~!** what a little fibber (colloq)

embustero² -ra *m,f* fibber (colloq), liar

embutido *m*

A (Coc) 1 (salchicha) sausage; (fiambre) cold meat 2 (acción) stuffing

B 1 (de madera, metal) inlaying 2 (de una chapa) pressing

embutir [I1] *vt*

A **~ algo DE algo** to stuff sth WITH sth; **~ algo EN algo** to stuff *o* cram sth IN *o* INTO sth

B 1 ‹*madera/metal*› to inlay 2 ‹*chapa*› to press

■ **embutirse** *v pron* (AmL fam) to polish off (colloq); **~se DE algo** to stuff oneself WITH sth

eme *f*: *name of the letter* **m**

emergencia *f* emergency

emergente *adj* ‹*clase/nación*› emergent, emerging (*before n*); ‹*daño*› consequent, resulting (*before n*)

emerger [E6] *vi* 1 «*submarino*» to surface 2 «*persona*» to emerge 3 (sobresalir) to emerge

emérito -ta *adj* emeritus

emigración *f* (de personas) emigration; (de animales) migration

emigrado -da *m,f* emigré

emigrante *adj/mf* emigrant

emigrar [A1] *vi* «*persona*» to emigrate; «*animal*» to migrate

eminencia *f* 1 (personalidad) expert 2 (frml) (Relig) Eminence (frml); **su/vuestra E~** His/Your Eminence

eminente *adj* eminent

emir *m* emir

emirato *m* emirate

Emiratos Árabes Unidos *mpl* United Arab Emirates

emisario -ria *m,f* emissary

emisión *f*

A (Tec) emission; **compraventa de emisiones de carbono** trading in carbon emissions

B (Fin) issue

C (Rad, TV) (acción) broadcasting; (programa) (frml) program*, broadcast

emisor¹ -sora *adj*

A ‹*banco/entidad*› issuing (*before n*)

B ‹*centro/estación*› broadcasting (*before n*), transmission (*before n*)

emisor² -sora *m,f*

A (Fin) issuer

B **emisor** *m* (aparato) transmitter; (de gases) emitter

C **emisora** *f* (Rad) radio station

emitir [I1] *vt* ‹*sonido/luz/señal*› to emit, give out; ‹*acciones/sellos*› to issue; ‹*programa*› to broadcast; ‹*película*› to show; ‹*comunicado*› to issue; ‹*veredicto*› to deliver; ‹*voto*› to cast

emoción *f* (sentimiento) emotion; (expectación, excitación) excitement; **¡qué ~!** how exciting!

emocionado -da *adj* (conmovido) moved; (entusiasmado) excited

emocional *adj* emotional

emocionante *adj* (conmovedor) moving; (excitante, apasionante) exciting

emocionar [A1] *vt* to move, affect

■ **emocionarse** *v pron* (conmoverse) to be moved; (entusiasmarse) to get excited

emolumento *m* (frml) emolument (frml)

emoticono *m* emoticon

emotividad *f*: **escenas de gran ~** very emotional scenes, scenes of great emotion

emotivo -va *adj* ‹*desarrollo/mundo*› emotional; ‹*acto/discurso*› moving, emotional; ‹*persona*› emotional

empacador -dora *m,f* 1 (persona) packer 2 **empacadora** *f* (máquina) baler, baling machine

empacar [A2] *vt* 1 (empaquetar) to pack 2 ‹*algodón/heno*› to bale 3 (AmL) ‹*maleta*› to pack

■ **empacar** *vi* to pack

■ **empacarse** *v pron*

A (empecinarse) to dig one's heels in, refuse to budge

B (Col, Méx fam) ‹*comida*› to wolf down (colloq); ‹*libros*› to polish … off (colloq), to devour (colloq)

empachar [A1] *vt* (fam) 1 (indigestar) to give … an upset stomach 2 (hartar): **¿no te empacha tanta televisión?** don't you get sick of watching so much television? (colloq)

■ **empacharse** *v pron* (fam) 1 (indigestarse) **~se DE** *or* **CON algo** to get an upset stomach FROM sth 2 (hartarse) **~se DE** *or* **CON algo** to overdose ON sth (colloq)

empacho *m* 1 (fam) (indigestión): **agarrarse un ~** to get *o* have an upset stomach 2 (fam) (hartazgo): **¡tengo un ~ de niños!** I've had a bellyful of kids (colloq) 3 (*en frases negativas*) (reparo): **no tuvo ~ en reconocerlo** he wasn't ashamed to admit it

empadronamiento *m* registration

empadronar [A1] *vt* to register

■ **empadronarse** *v pron* to register

empajar [A1] *vt* (Chi) 1 (techar con paja) to thatch 2 ‹*barro*› to mix … with straw

empalagar [A3] *vt*: **los bombones me empalagan** chocolates are too sweet *o* sickly for my taste; **tantas atenciones me empalagan** I find so much kindness cloying

■ **empalagar** *vi* «*estilo/obra*» to be cloying; «*licor/dulce*» to be too sweet *o* sickly; **su sentimentalismo empalaga** its sentimentality palls *o* is rather cloying

■ **empalagarse** *v pron* «*persona*»: **me empalagué con tanto dulce** I ate so many sweet things, I couldn't face any more

empalagoso -sa *adj* ‹*tarta/licor*› sickly; ‹*persona/sonrisa*› sickly sweet, cloying

empalar [A1] *vt* to impale

■ **empalarse** *v pron* (Chi) to get frozen stiff

empalizada *f* palisade

empalmar [A1] *vt* ‹*cuerdas/películas/cintas*› to splice; ‹*cables*› to connect; ‹*temas/ideas*› to dovetail; ‹*trabajos/vacaciones*› to combine

■ **empalmar** *vi* «*líneas/carreteras*» to converge, meet

empalme *m* (de cables) connection; (de cuerdas) splice; (de carreteras, líneas) junction

empanada *f* 1 (AmL) (individual) pasty, pie 2 (Esp) (grande) pie; **tener una ~ mental** (fam) to be confused

(Compuesto) **empanada gallega** sardine/tuna pie

empanadilla *f* (Esp) tuna/meat pasty

empanar [A1], (Méx) **empanizar** [A4] *vt* to coat … in breadcrumbs

empantanado -da *adj* 1 ‹*camino/campo*› swampy 2 (con problema, trabajo) ‹*persona*› bogged down; **las obras de reconstrucción están empantanadas** there's a hold up in the reconstruction work

empantanar [A1] *vt* ‹*camino/campo*› to swamp

■ **empantanarse** *v pron* «*camino/campo*» to become swamped; «*coche*» to get bogged down

empañar [A1] *vt* ‹*cristal/espejo*› to steam *o* mist up; ‹*reputación/imagen*› to sully, tarnish

■ **empañarse** *v pron* «*vidrio/espejo*» to steam *o* mist up

empañetar [A1] *vt* (AmC, Col) to plaster

empapar [A1] *vt* 1 (embeber) ‹*esponja/toalla/galleta*› to soak; **~ algo EN algo** to soak sth IN sth 2 (mojar mucho) ‹*persona*› to soak, drench

■ **empaparse** *v pron* 1 (mojarse mucho) «*persona/zapatos/ropa*» to get soaking wet, get wet through 2 (imbuirse) **~se DE** *or* **EN algo** to be/become imbued WITH sth (frml); **empapado de la filosofía de la secta** imbued with *o* steeped in the philosophy of the sect 3 (instruirse) **~se DE** *or* **EN algo**: **se había empapado del tema** he had learned a lot about the subject

empapelado *m* (acción) wallpapering, papering; (resultado) wallpaper

empapelar [A1] *vt* ‹*habitación/pared*› to wallpaper, paper; **calles empapeladas de propaganda** streets plastered with progaganda

empaque *m*

A (distinción) (imposing) presence; (pomposidad) pomposity

B (Col) (acción de empaquetar) packing; (de regalo) wrapping

C (Col, Méx, Ven) (Tec) seal; (de llave de agua) washer

D (Col fam) (aspecto) look

empaquetado *m* packing

empaquetador -dora *m,f* 1 (persona) packer 2 **empaquetadora** *f* (máquina) packer

empaquetar [A1] *vt* (embalar) to pack

emparamar [A1] *vt* (Col, Ven fam) to soak; **emparamé todo el piso** I got *o* made the floor all wet

■ **emparamarse** *v pron* (Col, Ven fam) to get drenched, get soaked (to the skin) (colloq)

emparar [A1] *vt* (Per fam) to catch

emparedado *m* sandwich

emparedar [A1] *vt* to wall … up

emparejar [A1] *vt*

A ‹*personas*› to pair … off; ‹*calcetines/zapatos*› to pair up

B (nivelar) ‹*pelo*› to make … even; ‹*dobladillo*› to even up; ‹*pared/suelo*› to level, make … level; ‹*montones/pilas*› to make … the same height, make … level

■ **emparejar** *vi*: **~ CON algn** to catch up WITH sb

■ **emparejarse** *v pron* 1 (formar parejas) to pair off 2 (nivelarse) to level off, even up

emparentado -da *adj* [ESTAR] related; **~ CON algn** related TO sb

emparentar [A1] *vi* **~ CON algn** to become related TO sb (*through marriage*)

emparrandarse [A1] *v pron* (Col, Ven fam) (irse de juerga) to go out on the town (colloq); (soltarse el moño) to let one's hair down

empastador -dora *m,f* bookbinder

empastar [A1] *vt* ‹*diente/muela*› to fill; ‹*lienzo*› to prime, size; ‹*libro*› to bind

empaste *m* (Odont) filling; (Chi) (pasta) filler

empatar [A1] *vi*

A 1 (durante un partido) to draw level, equalize; (como resultado) to tie, draw (BrE); **~on a dos** they tied two-two (AmE), it was a two-all draw (BrE); **estamos** *or* **vamos empatados** we're equal *o* level at the moment; **~ CON algn** to tie WITH sb 2 (en una votación) to tie

B (Col, Ven) «*listones/piezas*» to fit together

■ **empatar** *vt* 1 (Ven) (amarrar) to tie *o* join … together 2 (Col, Per, Ven) ‹*cables*› to connect; ‹*tubos*› to join, connect

■ **empatarse** *v pron*

A (Ven) (unirse) «*calles/líneas*» to join, meet (up); «*huesos*» to knit together

B (Ven fam) «*personas*» to get together (colloq), to start going out together; **está empatado con mi hermana** he's going out with *o* he's dating my sister; ***empatársele a algn*** (Ven fam) to follow sb closely, tail sb (colloq)

empate *m*

A 1 (en partido, certamen) tie (AmE), draw (BrE); **terminó con ~ a cero** it finished in a scoreless tie (AmE) *o* (BrE) goalless draw; **el gol del ~** the equalizer *o* (AmE) the tying goal 2 (en una votación) tie

B (Col, Per, Ven) (empalme, unión — en carpintería) joint; (— de tubos) join, connection; (— de cables) connection

C (Ven fam) (novio) boyfriend; (novia) girlfriend

empatía *f* empathy

empavar [A1] *vt* (Ven fam) to bring … bad luck, bring bad luck to

■ **empavarse** *v pron* (Ven fam) to have bad luck

empavonar [A1] *vt* ‹*metal*› to blue

empecinado -da *adj* (esp AmL) (terco) stubborn; (determinado) determined

empecinamiento *m* (terquedad) stubbornness; (determinación) determination

empecinarse [A1] *v pron* (obstinarse) to get an idea into one's head; (empeñarse) to persist; **cuando se empecina …** once he gets an idea into his head …; **~ EN algo**: **se empecinó en que tenía que ser rojo** he got it into his head that it had to be red

empedar [A1] *vt* (Méx, RPl arg) to get … smashed (sl)
■ **empedarse** *v pron* (Méx, RPl arg) to get smashed (sl)

empedernido -da *adj* ‹*bebedor/fumador*› hardened, inveterate; ‹*jugador*› compulsive; ‹*solterón*› confirmed

empedrado[1] **-da** *adj* paved

empedrado[2] *m* (de adoquines) paving; (de piedras irregulares) cobbled paving

empedrar [A5] *vt* to pave

empegostar [A1] *vt* (Ven fam) ‹*pared*› to paste, put paste on; **no vayas a ~me el vestido con esas manos** don't get your sticky fingers all over my dress (colloq)
■ **empegostarse** *v pron* (*refl*) (Ven fam) ‹*manos/dedos*› to make *o* get … sticky; **¡no te vayas a ~ con ese helado!** don't get that ice cream all over yourself!

empeine *m* instep

empellón *m* shove; **se abrió paso a empellones** she shoved her way through

empelotado -da *adj*
A (CS fam) (desnudo) stark naked (colloq)
B (Per fam) (pesado, insistente) pesky (*before n*) (colloq); **¡qué ~es!** he's a real pest!
C (Méx fam) (enamorado): **estar ~ POR algn** to be mad ON *o* ABOUT sb

empelotar [A1] *vt*
A (Col, CS, Ven fam) (desnudar) to undress
B (Per fam) (hacer caso) to take notice of
■ **empelotarse** *v pron*
A (*refl*) (Col, CS, Ven fam) (desnudarse) to strip, strip off (BrE colloq)
B (Per fam) (buscar atención) to be an attention seeker; **lo hace para ~se** he does it to attract attention (to himself)

empeñado -da *adj*
A 1 (esforzado) **~ EN algo** committed TO sth; **~ en la búsqueda de una solución** committed to finding a solution 2 (resuelto) determined; **~ EN + INF** determined to + INF; **está ~ en hacerlo** he's determined to do it 3 (obstinado): **está ~ en que nos quedemos** he's insistent that we should stay
B (endeudado) in debt; **estamos demasiado ~s** we're too heavily *o* deep in debt

empeñar [A1] *vt* 1 ‹*joyas/pertenencias*› to pawn, hock (colloq); **~ *hasta la camisa*** *or* ***camiseta*** (fam) to get *o* go heavily *o* deep in(to) debt 2 ‹*palabra*› to give
■ **empeñarse** *v pron*
A (endeudarse) to get *o* go into debt
B 1 (esforzarse) **~se EN + INF** to strive to + INF (frml), to make an effort to + INF; **~se en hacer las cosas bien** to strive to do things well 2 (proponerse) **~se EN + INF** to be determined to + INF; **se ha empeñado en lograrlo** he's determined to achieve it 3 (obstinarse) to insist; **~se EN + INF** to insist ON -ING; **se empeñó en que estudiara medicina** she insisted that he studied medicine

empeño *m*
A 1 (afán) determination; (esfuerzo) effort; **trabajar/estudiar con ~** to work/study hard; **pondré todo mi ~ en conseguirlo** I will do my best to achieve it; **poner ~ en una tarea** to put every effort into a task, to apply oneself to a task 2 (obstinación) **~ EN algo** insistence ON sth 3 (intento, empresa) undertaking, endeavor*; **nunca ceja en su ~** (frml) he never wavers in his endeavor (frml)
B (de valores) pawning, hocking (colloq); **sacar algo del ~** (fam) to get sth out of hock (colloq)

empeñosamente *adv* (AmL) determinedly, with great determination

empeñoso -sa *adj* (AmL) hard-working

empeoramiento *m* (de la salud) deterioration, worsening; (del tiempo, de una situación) worsening

empeorar [A1] *vi* «*salud*» to deteriorate, get worse; «*tiempo/situación*» to get worse, worsen
■ **empeorar** *vt* to make … worse

empequeñecer [E3] *vi* to become smaller; **él empequeñeció ante mis ojos** he went down *o* fell in my estimation
■ **empequeñecerse** *v pron* 1 (hacerse pequeño) to become smaller 2 (acobardarse) to be/feel daunted 3 (sentirse insignificante) to feel small *o* insignificant; **se te empequeñece la visión del mundo** your vision of the world becomes narrower

emperador *m*
A (soberano) emperor
B (Coc) swordfish

emperatriz *f* empress

emperejilarse [A1] *v pron* (ant) to spruce oneself up

emperifollarse [A1] *v pron* (hum) to titivate oneself (hum), to preen oneself (hum)

empero *adv* (liter) nevertheless, nonetheless

emperolarse [A1] *v pron* (Ven fam) to dress up

emperrarse [A1] *v pron* (fam): **se emperró con ese coche** she got it into her head that she wanted that car; **se emperró en hacerlo** he was determined to do it; **se emperró en que fuera** he insisted that I should go

empezar [A6] *vi*
A «*película/conferencia/invierno*» to begin, start; **al ~ el siglo** at the turn of the century; **ya han empezado los fríos** the cold weather has arrived *o* started; **~ A + INF** to start to + INF, start -ING; **empezó a nevar** it started to snow *o* snowing; **me empezó a entrar hambre** I began *o* started to feel hungry
B «*persona*» to start; **~ de nuevo** *or* **volver a ~** to start again; **todo es (cuestión de) ~** it'll be fine once we/you get started; **¡ya empezamos otra vez!** here we go again!; **no sé por dónde ~** I don't know where to begin; **vamos a ~ por ti** let's start with you; **~ A + INF** to start -ING, start to + INF; **empezó a llorar** he began *o* started to cry; **~ + GER** to start BY -ING; **empezó diciendo que …** she started *o* began by saying that …; **empezó trabajando de mecánico** he started out as a mechanic; **~ POR + INF** to start *o* begin BY -ING; **empecemos por estudiar el contexto histórico** let's begin *o* start by looking at the historical context
C **para empezar** first of all, to start with
■ **empezar** *vt*
A ‹*tarea/actividad*› to start
B ‹*frasco/mermelada*› to start, open

empicharse [A1] *v pron* (Ven fam) «*alimento/bebida*» to go bad *o* (BrE) off; «*planta*» to rot

empiece, empieza *etc see* **empezar**

empinado -da *adj* ‹*calle/pendiente*› steep; ‹*rascacielos/torre*› towering (*before n*); ‹*cumbre/montaña*› soaring (*before n*)

empinar [A1] *vt* ‹*bota/botella/vaso*› to raise
■ **empinarse** *v pron*
A 1 (de puntillas) to stand on tiptoe 2 «*camino/cuesta*» to get steep, to rise; «*edificio/torre*» to tower, soar; «*montaña*» to rise
B (Chi, Méx fam) (beberse) to knock back (colloq)

empírico[1] **-ca** *adj* empirical

empírico[2] **-ca** *m,f* empiricist

empirismo *m* empiricism

emplaste *m* (Méx) (de colores, objetos) mess, hodge-podge (AmE), hotch-potch (BrE)

emplasto *m* 1 (Farm, Med) dressing 2 (fam) (cosa blanda, pegajosa) sticky mess (colloq)

emplazamiento *m* (frml)
A (acción) 1 (de edificio, monumento) siting 2 (Mil) (de batería) positioning; (de misiles) siting
B (sitio) 1 (de edificio, circo) location, site 2 (Mil) (de batería) emplacement, position; (de misiles) site
C (Der) (citación) summons, subpoena

emplazar [A4] *vt* (frml)
A 1 ‹*edificio/circo*› to site, locate 2 (Mil) ‹*batería*› to position; ‹*misiles*› to site
B 1 (Der) (citar) to summon, subpoena 2 (frml) (conminar) **~ a algn A + INF** *or* **A QUE + SUBJ** to call upon sb to + INF

empleada *f* maid; *ver tb* **empleado**

Compuestos
• **empleada de planta** (Méx) live-in maid
• **empleada doméstica** *or* **de servicio** (frml) maid, domestic servant (frml)

empleado -da *m,f* 1 (trabajador) employee; **una nómina de 300 ~s** a staff of 300; **se ruega notificar a todos los ~s** please notify all members of staff 2 (en oficina) office *o* clerical worker; (en banco) bank clerk, teller; (en tienda) (AmL) clerk (AmE), shop assistant (BrE)

(Compuestos)
- **empleado -da de hogar** *m,f* (Esp frml) domestic servant
- **empleado público -da pública** *m,f* civil servant

empleador -dora *m,f* employer

emplear [A1] *vt*
A 1 «*empresa/organización*» to employ 2 (colocar) ‹*hijo/sobrino*› to fix … up with a job; **su padre lo empleó en una tienda** his father fixed him up with *o* got him a job in a shop
B (usar) ‹*energía/imaginación/material*› to use; **no sabe cómo ~ su tiempo** he doesn't know how to occupy his time; **~on tres años en la construcción** it took them three years to build it; ***dar algo por bien empleado***: **me llevó toda una tarde, pero la doy por bien empleada** it took me a whole evening, but (I consider) it was time well spent; ***estarle bien empleado a algn*** (Esp) to serve sb right (colloq)
■ **emplearse** *v pron* (esp AmL) to get a job

empleo *m*
A 1 (trabajo) employment; **la creación de ~** job creation 2 (puesto) job; **tiene un buen ~** she has a good job; **está sin ~** she's out of work
(Compuesto) **empleo comunitario** community work
B (uso) use; **S modo de empleo** instructions for use

emplomadura *f* (RPl) filling

emplomar [A1] *vt* (RPl) to fill

emplumar [A1] *vi* to grow feathers, fledge
■ **emplumar** *vt* 1 (Esp fam) ‹*delincuente*› to pick up (colloq) 2 ***emplumárselas*** (Chi fam) to split (sl)

empobrecer [E3] *vt* ‹*población/tierra/lenguaje*› to impoverish
■ **empobrecer** *vi* to become impoverished, become poor
■ **empobrecerse** *v pron* «*país/lenguaje/vocabulario*» to become impoverished

empobrecimiento *m* impoverishment

empoderar [A1] *vt* empower

empollar [A1] *vi*
A «*gallina*» to brood
B (Esp fam) «*estudiante*» to cram (colloq), to swot (BrE colloq)
■ **empollar** *vt*
A ‹*huevos*› to hatch, sit on
B (Esp fam) «*estudiante*» to cram (colloq), to swot up (on) (BrE colloq)

empollón -llona *m,f* (Esp fam & pey) grind (AmE colloq), swot (BrE colloq & pej)

empolvado -da *adj* 1 ‹*libro*› dusty, dust-covered 2 (con maquillaje) powdered

empolvarse [A1] *v pron* 1 «*libros*» to gather dust 2 (*refl*) ‹*nariz/cara*› to powder

emponchado -da *adj* (CS): **un hombre ~** a man in a poncho *o* wearing a poncho

emponzoñar [A1] *vt* to poison

emporio *m* 1 (Hist) trading center* 2 (artístico, cultural) center* 3 (de riqueza) empire; **un ~ financiero** a financial empire

emporrado -da *adj* [**ESTAR**] (Esp fam) high (colloq)

empotarse [A1] *v pron* (Chi fam) **~ CON algn** to become infatuated WITH sb

empotrado -da *adj* built-in, fitted (*before n*)

empotrar [A1] *vt* ‹*mueble/caja fuerte*› **~ algo EN algo** to build sth INTO sth
■ **empotrarse** *v pron*: **el coche se empotró en el muro** the car crashed into the wall

empozarse *v pron* (Col, Per, Ven) «*agua*» to form pools/a pool

emprendedor -dora *adj* enterprising

emprender [E1] *vt* ‹*viaje*› to embark on; ‹*proyecto/aventura*› to undertake; ‹*ataque/ofensiva*› to launch; **~ la retirada** (Mil) to beat a retreat; **~ la marcha** to set out; **el pájaro emprendió el vuelo** the bird took flight; **~ el regreso** to begin one's return journey; **~*la con algn***: **estaba de mal humor y la emprendió conmigo** she was in a bad mood and she took it out on me; **la emprendió a puñetazos con él** he started punching him

empresa *f*
A 1 (compañía) company, firm (BrE); **~ filial** subsidiary company 2 (dirección) management; **la ~ no se hace responsable** the management cannot accept liability
(Compuestos)
- **empresa de servicios públicos** public utility company, public utility
- **empresa privada/pública** private/public sector company

B (tarea, labor) venture, undertaking

empresariado *m* management, managers (*pl*)

empresarial *adj* business (*before n*); **la parte ~** the management; **organizaciones ~es** employers' organizations

empresariales *fpl* (Esp) business studies

empresario -ria *m,f* 1 (Com, Fin) (*m*) businessman; (*f*) businesswoman; **una asociación de ~s** an employers' organization; **el ~ decidió vender el negocio** the owner decided to sell the business; **~ de pompas fúnebres** undertaker 2 (Teatr) impresario 3 (en boxeo) promoter

empréstito *m* (frml) loan

empujar [A1] *vt* 1 ‹*coche/columpio*› to push; **¡empújame!** give me a push! 2 (incitar, presionar) to spur … on; (obligar) to force; **no tenía ganas, pero yo la empujé un poco** she didn't feel like it, but I gave her a bit of a push (colloq) 3 (Tec) to drive
■ **empujar** *vi* 1 (hacer presión) to push; **un actor que viene empujando fuerte** (period) an up-and-coming actor 2 (dar empellones) to push, shove; **¡sin ~!** stop pushing!

empuje *m* 1 (iniciativa): **le falta ~** she lacks drive *o* initiative 2 (fuerza moral) spirit; **tiene mucho ~** she has a lot of spirit 3 (entusiasmo) enthusiasm 4 (Arquit, Aviac, Fís) thrust

empujón *m* 1 (empellón) shove, push; **abrió la puerta de un ~** he pushed the door open; **abrirse paso a (los) empujones** to shove one's way through 2 (fam) (para animar, incitar) prod (colloq); **si le damos un empujoncito seguro que viene** if we give her a gentle prod *o* a bit of encouragement I'm sure she'll come; **voy a darle un ~ al asunto** I'm going to push things along a bit (colloq)

empuñadura *f* (de espada) hilt; (de daga, navaja) handle; (de bastón, paraguas) handle

empuñar [A1] *vt* 1 ‹*arma/espada*› to take up; ‹*bastón/palo*› to brandish 2 (Chi): **empuñó la mano** he clenched his fist

emú *m* emu

emulación *f* emulation

emulador *m* emulator

emular [A1] *vt* to emulate

émulo -la *m,f* (frml) emulator

emulsión *f* emulsion

emulsionante *m* emulsifier

emulsionar [A1] *vt* to emulsify

en *prep*
A (en expresiones de lugar) 1 (refiriéndose a ciudad, edificio): **viven ~ París/~ una granja/~ el número diez/~ un hotel** they live in Paris/on a farm/at number ten/in a hotel; **~ el último piso** on the top floor; **viven ~ la calle Goya** they live on *o* (BrE) in Goya Street; **nos quedamos ~ casa** we stayed home (AmE), we stayed at home (BrE); **de puerta ~ puerta** from door to door 2 (dentro de) in; **~ una caja** in a box; **métete ~ la cama** get into bed 3 (sobre) on; **~ la mesa** on the table; **~ una silla** on a chair; **se le nota ~ la cara** you can see it in his face
B (expresando circunstancias, ambiente, medio) in; **~ armonía con la naturaleza** in harmony with nature; **~ peligro** in danger
C 1 (indicando tema, especialidad, cualidad): **un experto ~ la materia** an expert on the subject; **es muy bueno ~ historia** he's very good at history; **doctor ~ derecho** Doctor of Law; **la supera ~ inteligencia** he surpasses her in intelligence 2 (indicando proporción, precio): **~ un diez por ciento** by ten per cent; **lo vendió ~ $30** he sold it for $30; **~ dólares** in dollars; **las pérdidas se calcularon ~ $50.000** the losses were calculated at $50,000
D 1 (indicando estado, manera) in; **~ buenas/malas condiciones** in good/bad condition; **~ llamas** in flames, on fire; **estaba ~ camisón** she was in her nightdress; **con los músculos ~ tensión** with (his) muscles tensed; **~ tono sarcástico** sarcastically 2 (en forma de): **termina ~ punta** it's pointed; **colóquense ~ círculo** get into *o* in a circle 3 (en el papel de) as; **Luis Girón en el Alcalde** Luis Girón as the Mayor 4 (con medios de transporte) by; **ir**

~ **taxi/barco** to go by taxi/by boat; **fueron ~ bicicleta** they cycled, they went on their bikes; **dimos una vuelta ~ coche** we went for a ride in the car

E [1] (expresando el material): ~ **seda natural** in natural silk; **una escultura ~ bronce** a bronze (sculpture) [2] (indicando el modo de presentación o expresión) in; **¿lo tienen ~ azul?** do you have it in blue?; ~ **ruso** in Russian

F (con expresiones de tiempo): ~ **verano** in (the) summer; ~ **varias ocasiones** on several occasions; **justo ~ ese momento** just at that moment; ~ **la mañana/tarde/noche** (esp AmL) in the morning/afternoon/at night

G [1] (con construcciones verbales) in; **no hay nada de malo ~ lo que hacen** there's nothing wrong in what they're doing; **tardó media hora ~ resolverlo** it took her half an hour to work it out; **fui el último ~ salir** I was the last to leave [2] (con complementos de persona) in; ~ **él ha encontrado un amigo** she's found a friend in him; **no sé qué ve ~ ella** I don't know what he sees in her

en. (= **enero**) Jan

enaceitar [A1] *vt* to oil

enagua *f*, **enaguas** *fpl* [1] (prenda interior) petticoat, underskirt [2] (AmC) (falda) skirt

enajenable *adj* (frml) alienable (frml)

enajenación *f*

A (Der) alienation (frml)

B (alienación) alienation

C (Psic) *tb* ~ **mental** derangement

enajenado -da *adj* [ESTAR] out of one's mind, deranged; **enajenada de furia** beside herself with rage

enajenamiento *m* ▸ **enajenación**

enajenante *adj* ‹*trabajo*› alienating, dehumanizing

enajenar [A1] *vt*

A (Der, Fil) to alienate

B (alienar) to alienate, dehumanize

■ **enajenarse** *v pron*

A (volverse loco) to go out of one's mind, become unhinged

B ‹*simpatías/amistad*› to alienate

enaltecer [E3] *vt* [1] (frml) (honrar) to ennoble (frml) [2] (alabar) to praise, extol (frml)

enamoradizo -za *adj*: **es muy ~** he falls in love very easily

enamorado[1] -da *adj* [1] [ESTAR] in love; ~ **DE algn** in love WITH sb; **están muy ~s** they are very much in love [2] [SER] (CS fam) ▸ **enamoradizo**

enamorado[2] -da *m,f* [1] (amante, novio) lover; **actúan como una pareja de ~s** they're acting like a pair of lovebirds; **una pareja de ~s** two lovers; **vino con su ~** (Bol, Per) she came with her boyfriend [2] (aficionado) ~ **DE algo**: **es un ~ de su profesión** he loves his work

enamoramiento *m* infatuation

enamorar [A1] *vt* to make … fall in love, get … to fall in love

■ **enamorarse** *v pron* to fall in love; **~se DE algo/algn** to fall in love WITH sth/sb

enamoricarse [A2], **enamoriscarse** [A2] *v pron* (fam) ~ **DE algn** to get a crush ON sb (colloq), to become infatuated WITH sb

enanismo *m* dwarfism

enano[1] -na *adj* ‹*especie/planta*› dwarf (*before n*); ‹*ración*› (fam) minute, tiny

enano[2] -na *m,f* [1] (de proporciones normales) midget; (de cabeza más grande) dwarf; (en los cuentos) dwarf; **los siete enanitos** the Seven Dwarfs *o* Dwarves; ***disfrutar*** *or* ***divertirse como un ~*** to have a whale of a time (colloq); ***ser un trabajo de ~s*** (CS, Esp fam) to be very hard work; ***trabajar como un ~*** (fam) to work like a dog (colloq) [2] (fam) (niño) little one (colloq), nipper (colloq)

enarbolar [A1] *vt* [1] ‹*bandera*› (levantar) to hoist, raise; (llevar) to fly [2] ‹*palo/bastón*› to brandish

enarcar [A2] *vt* ‹*cejas*› to raise, arch; ‹*espalda*› to arch

enardecer [E3] *vt*: **la discusión enardeció los ánimos** the discussion aroused a great deal of passion; **una multitud enardecida** an angry crowd

■ **enardecerse** *v pron*: **los ánimos se enardecieron** passions became aroused *o* (liter) inflamed; **~se de pasión** (liter) to become inflamed with passion (liter)

encabalgamiento *m* enjambment*

encabestrar [A1] *vt* [1] (Equ) to halter, put a halter on [2] (Taur) to lead

encabezado *m* (Chi, Méx) headline

encabezamiento *m* [1] (en carta — saludo) opening; (— dirección, fecha) heading [2] (en ficha, documento) heading

encabezar [A4] *vt*

A ‹*artículo/escrito*› to head

B [1] ‹*liga/clasificación/lista*› to head, be at the top of; ‹*carrera/movimento/revolución*› to lead; **una pancarta encabezaba la manifestación** the demonstration was headed by a banner [2] ‹*delegación/comité*› to head, lead

encabritarse [A1] *v pron* [1] «*caballo*» to rear up [2] (fam) «*persona*» to get mad (colloq), to blow one's top (colloq) [3] (fam) «*mar*» to get *o* become choppy

encabronar [A1] *vt* (Esp, Méx vulg) to piss … off (sl)

■ **encabronarse** *v pron* (vulg) to get pissed off (sl)

encachado -da *adj* (Chi fam) [1] (simpático) nice [2] (bonito) ‹*ropa/lugar*› lovely, nice; ‹*persona*› attractive [3] (arreglado) well-dressed [4] (entretenido) ‹*historia*› entertaining

encachar [A1] *vt* (Chi fam) to make … look nice

■ **encacharse** *v pron* (Chi fam)

A (resistirse): **encachársele a algn** to stand up to sb

B (Chi fam) (acicalarse) to spruce oneself up

encachimbado -da *adj* (AmC fam) mad (AmE colloq), cross (BrE colloq); **está muy ~ conmigo** he's mad at *o* cross with me; **me tiene muy ~ este carro** I'm fed up with this car (colloq)

encachorrarse [A1] *v pron* (Col fam) to throw a tantrum

encadenado -da *adj* linked

encadenar [A1] *vt*

A [1] ‹*prisionero/bicicleta*› to chain (up) [2] «*obligación/trabajo*» to tie (down) [3] ‹*ideas/pensamientos*› to link

B (Cin) ‹*escenas/secuencias*› to fade … together

■ **encadenarse** *v pron* (*refl*) **~se A algo** to chain oneself TO sth

encajar [A1] *vt*

A (meter, colocar) to fit

B (esp AmL fam) (endilgar): **me ~on a mí el trabajito** I got saddled *o* landed with the job (colloq); **siempre le encaja los hijos a la suegra** she always dumps the kids on her mother-in-law (colloq); **me encajó tremenda patada** he gave me a hell of a kick (colloq); **les ~on tres goles** they put three goals past them

C [1] ‹*broma/críticas*› to take; ‹*desgracia/situación*› to accept [2] (Dep) ‹*gol*› to let … in; ‹*derechazo/golpe*› to take

■ **encajar** *vi* [1] «*pieza/cajón*» to fit; ~ **EN algo** to fit IN sth; **no encaja bien** it doesn't fit properly; **las piezas ~on** the pieces fitted together [2] (cuadrar) to fit; **esto no encaja dentro de ninguna categoría** this doesn't fit into any category [3] (armonizar, casar): **su versión no encaja con la de otros testigos** his version does not square with *o* correspond to that of other witnesses; **no encaja con la decoración** it doesn't fit in with the decor

■ **encajarse** *v pron*

A (*refl*) (fam) ‹*prenda*› to put on

B (Méx) (aprovecharse) to take advantage; **~se CON algn** to take advantage OF sb

encaje *m*

A (Indum) lace; **pañuelo de ~** lace handkerchief; **con ~s en el cuello** with a lacy collar

B (Fin) *tb* ~ **bancario** reserve

C (Mec) socket

encajonar [A1] *vt* [1] ‹*mercancías*› to box, put into boxes (*o* crates *etc*) [2] ‹*toro*› to pen [3] (en lugar estrecho) ~ **algo/algn EN algo** to cram *o* pack sth/sb INTO sth; **me ~on el coche** my car *o* I got boxed in [4] (Tec) to encase, box in

■ **encajonarse** *v pron* «*río*» to narrow

encalado *m* whitewashing

encalar [A1] *vt* to whitewash

encaletar [A1] *vt* (Col, Ven) ‹*droga/armas*› to stash (colloq); ‹*cerveza/comida*› to hide … away

encalillarse [A1] *v pron* (Chi fam) to get into debt

encalladero *m* (zona de poca profundidad) shallows (*pl*); (banco de arena) sandbank; (rocas) rocks (*pl*)

encallar [A1] *vi* to run aground

encallecerse [E3] *v pron* to become callused

encallecido -da *adj* ‹*manos*› callused

encalmarse [A1] *v pron* ‹‹*mar*›› to become calm; ‹‹*viento*›› to drop

encamar [A1] *vt* (Méx) to confine … to bed
■ **encamarse** *v pron* (CS, Per fam) to go to bed together; **~se CON algn** to go to bed WITH sb

encamburarse [A1] *v pron* (Ven fam) to get oneself a job in the civil service

encaminado -da *adj*: **el proyecto va bien ~** the project is shaping up well *o* is going well; **iba bien ~** he was on the right track; **~ A + INF** designed to + INF, aimed AT -ING; **medidas encaminadas a reducir ...** measures designed to reduce *o* aimed at reducing …

encaminador *m* (Telec) router

encaminar [A1] *vt* [1] ‹*intereses/esfuerzos*› to direct, channel; **~on sus esfuerzos a ...** they channeled their efforts into … [2] ‹*estudiante/niño*› to point … in the right direction
■ **encaminarse** *v pron* (liter) **~se HACIA algo** [1] ‹‹*persona*›› (dirigirse a) to head FOR/TOWARD(S) sth; (emprender el camino) to set off FOR/TOWARD(S) sth [2] ‹‹*esfuerzos*›› to be aimed AT sth, be directed TOWARD(S) sth

encamotarse [A1] *v pron* (AmL fam) **~ CON algn** to fall for sb (colloq)

encanar [A1] *vt* (AmS arg) to lock … up (colloq)

encandilar [A1] *vt* [1] ‹‹*luz*›› to dazzle [2] (asombrar, pasmar) to dazzle [3] (avivar, exacerbar) to stir up, arouse

encanecer [E3] *vi* to (go) gray•

encantado -da *adj*
A [1] (muy contento) delighted; **estoy ~ de haber venido** I am delighted *o* very glad that I came [2] (en fórmulas de cortesía): **te lo presto encantada** I'd be only too happy to lend it to you; **podemos vernos mañana — yo ~** we can meet tomorrow — that's fine by me; **~ de conocerla** pleased to meet you; **~ de poder ayudarte** I'm glad to be/to have been of help
B ‹*bosque/castillo*› enchanted

encantador¹ -dora *adj* ‹*persona/lugar*› charming

encantador² -dora *m,f* magician; **~ de serpientes** snake charmer

encantamiento *m* spell, enchantment

encantar [A1] *vi* (+ *me/te/le etc*): **me encantó la obra** I loved *o* I thoroughly enjoyed the play; **me ~ía que me acompañaras** I'd love you to come with me
■ **encantar** *vt* to cast *o* put a spell on, bewitch

encanto *m*
A [1] (atractivo) charm; **utilizó todos sus ~s para conquistarlo** she used all her charms to win him over; **su sencillez es su mayor ~** its most appealing feature is its simplicity [2] (fam) (maravilla, primor): **eres un ~** you're a darling (colloq); **¡qué ~ de hombre!** what a lovely *o* charming man!; **tienen un jardín que es un ~** they have a lovely garden
B [1] (hechizo) spell; **como por ~** as if by magic [2] (Ven fam) (fantasma) ghost

encañada *f* gully; (más profundo) ravine

encañizada *f* weir (*for fishing*)

encañonar [A1] *vt*: **lo encañonó con el revólver** she pointed the gun at him
■ **encañonarse** *v pron* ‹‹*río*›› to narrow

encapotado -da *adj* overcast, cloudy

encapotarse [A1] *v pron* to cloud over, become overcast

encapricharse [A1] *v pron* **~ CON** *or* (Esp) **DE algo**: **se ha encaprichado con ese juguete** (es su preferido) he's really taken a liking to that toy; (porque quiere tenerlo) he's got his heart set on that toy; **~ CON** *or* (Esp) **DE algn** to fall for sb (colloq)

encapuchado -da *m,f* (*m*) hooded man; (*f*) hooded woman

encapuchar [A1] *vt*: **~on al reo** they placed a hood over the prisoner's head
■ **encapucharse** *v pron* (*refl*) to put a hood on

encarado -da *adj* (Méx): **mal ~** (enojado) bad-tempered; (de mal aspecto) nasty-looking

encaramarse [A1] *v pron* **~ A** *or* **EN algo** ‹*a árbol/valla*› to climb up; ‹*a taburete*› to climb on to

encarar [A1] *vt*
A (enfocar) ‹*tarea*› to approach; (afrontar) ‹*desgracia/problema*› to face up to; ‹*futuro*› to face
B ‹*piezas*› to marry, fit … together
C (AmL) ‹*persona*› to stand up to
■ **encararse** *v pron* **~se CON algn** to face up to *o* stand up to sb

encarcelamiento *m*, **encarcelación** *f* imprisonment

encarcelar [A1] *vt* to imprison, jail

encarecer [E3] *vt*
A (hacer más caro): **el envase encarece el producto** the container makes the product more expensive; **~á los alquileres** it will push rents up
B (frml) (pedir, recomendar): **se lo encarecí repetidamente** I beseeched him many times (frml); **le encareció que cuidara de ellos** she begged him to take care of them; **nos encareció que fuéramos puntuales** he urged us to be punctual (frml)
■ **encarecerse** *v pron* ‹‹*precios*›› to increase, rise; ‹‹*productos/vida*›› to become more expensive

encarecidamente *adv* (frml): **le pido ~ que ...** I urge *o* (frml) beg you to …

encarecimiento *m*
A (frml) (de precios) increase, rise
B (frml) (insistencia) insistence; **con ~** insistently

encargado¹ -da *adj* **~ DE algo/+ INF** responsible FOR sth/-ING, in charge OF sth/-ING

encargado² -da *m,f* [1] (de negocio) manager; **quiero hablar con el ~** I'd like to speak to the person in charge *o* the manager [2] (de tarea): **tú serás el ~ de avisarles** it will be your responsibility to tell them

(Compuesto) **encargado -da de negocios** *m,f* chargé d'affaires

encargar [A3] *vt*
A [1] **~le algo A algn** ‹*tarea*› to entrust sb WITH sth; **le encargaste un asunto delicado** you entrusted him with a delicate matter; **me encargó una botella de whisky escocés** she asked me to buy *o* get her a bottle of Scotch [2] **~ a algn QUE + SUBJ** to ask sb to + INF; **me encargó que se lo recordara** he asked me to remind him
B [1] (pedir) ‹*mueble/paella/libro*› to order; ‹*informe/cuadro*› to commission [2] (fam & euf) ‹*hijo*›: **quieren ~ un hijo pronto** they're planning to start a family soon; **han encargado un niño** they have a baby on the way
■ **encargarse** *v pron* **~se DE algo/algn** to take care OF sth/sb; **yo me encargo de las bebidas** I'll take care of *o* see to the drinks; **me tuve que ~ del asunto** I had to take charge of the matter; **¡ya me ~é de él!** (fam) I'll take care of him! (colloq), I'll soon sort him out! (colloq); **se va a ~ de hacer la reserva** he's going to take care of the booking; **yo me encargo de que lo sepan** I'll see to it that they know, I'll make sure they know

encargatoria *f* (Chi) *tb* **~ de reo** indictment, committal for trial

encargo *m* [1] (recado, pedido): **¿te puedo hacer unos ~s?** could you buy *o* get a few things for me?; **mi hijo está haciendo un ~** my son is out on *o* is running an errand [2] (Com) order; **los hacemos por ~** we make them to order; ❸ **sólo por encargo** (en restaurante) must be ordered in advance; **muebles de ~** made-to-order *o* custom-made furniture; ***hecho de* ~** (Esp): **el sofá le va al salón que ni hecho de ~** the sofa is absolutely tailor-made *o* perfect for the living room; **eres más tonto que hecho de ~** (fam) you couldn't be more stupid if you tried (colloq) [3] (cargo, misión) job, assignment [4] (AmL fam & euf) (embarazo): **el novio la dejó con ~** her boyfriend got her into trouble (euph)

encariñarse [A1] *v pron* **~ CON algo/algn** to grow fond OF sth/sb, get very attached TO sth/sb

encarnación *f* incarnation

encarnado -da *adj*
A ‹*color/vestido*› red
B ‹*uña*› ingrowing

encarnadura *f*: **tener buena/mala ~** to heal quickly/slowly

encarnar [A1] *vt* [1] ‹‹*actor*›› ‹*personaje*› to play [2] ‹*cualidad/sentimiento*› to embody; **encarna la ambición desmedida** he is the embodiment of boundless ambition
■ **encarnarse** *v pron* [1] (Relig) to become incarnate [2] ‹‹*uña*›› to become ingrown

encarnizado -da *adj* bitter, fierce

encarnizamiento *m* 1 (en caza) blooding 2 (crueldad) viciousness, savagery

encarnizar [A4] *vt* 1 ‹*jauría*› to blood 2 ‹*atacante/enemigo*› to enrage

■ **encarnizarse** *v pron* **~se CON algn/algo** to attack sb/sth viciously

encarpetar [A1] *vt* 1 (guardar) to file 2 (dejar detenido) ‹*expediente*› to close; ‹*asunto*› to close the file on

encarrerado -da *adv* (Méx fam) at top speed

encarrilar [A1] *vt* 1 ‹*vagón/tren*› to put … onto the rails 2 ‹*trabajo/asunto*› to direct; ‹*persona*› to guide, give guidance to; **las negociaciones van bien encarriladas** the negotiations are progressing well

■ **encarrilarse** *v pron* to get back on the rails

encartado -da *adj/m,f* (Esp) accused

encartar [A1] *vt*

A (Esp) (Der) to indict, commit … for trial

B (Col fam) (encajar) **~ a algn CON algo** to saddle *o* land sb WITH sth (colloq)

■ **encartarse** *v pron*

A (en naipes) to pick up (cards)

B (Col fam) (clavarse) **~se CON algo/algn** to get stuck *o* saddled WITH sth/sb (colloq); **ahora tengo que ~me con estos librotes a la biblioteca** now I have to hump these great big books over to the library (colloq)

encarte *m* (Col fam) (molestia) nuisance

encasillar [A1] *vt* to class, categorize, pigeonhole

■ **encasillarse** *v pron*: **no quiso ~se dentro de ninguna tendencia** he didn't want to be identified with any particular group *o* faction

encasquetar [A1] *vt* ‹*sombrero*› to pull down; **~le algo/algn A algn** (fam): to dump sth/sb ON sb (colloq); **le encasquetan los trabajos más pesados** he gets landed *o* saddled with the most boring jobs (colloq)

■ **encasquetarse** *v pron* ‹*sombrero/gorra*› to pull down

encasquillarse [A1] *v pron* «*fusil/pistola*» to jam; «*bala*» to get jammed

encatrado *m* (Chi fam) platform

encatrinarse [A1] *v pron* (*refl*) (Méx fam) to get dressed up

encausado -da *m,f* defendant

encausar [A1] *vt* to charge

encauzar [A4] *vt* to channel; **~ algo HACIA algo** to channel sth INTO sth

■ **encauzarse** *v pron* «*tendencia/actividad*» to be channeled*; «*persona*» **~se EN algo** to channel one's energies INTO sth

encefálico -ca *adj* brain (*before n*), encephalic (tech)

encéfalo *m* brain

encefalograma *m* encephalogram

enceguecedor -dora *adj* (AmL) blinding

enceguecer [E3] *vt* (AmL) to blind

■ **enceguecerse** *v pron* (AmL) (por la luz) to be blinded; (de ira) to become furious

encelar [A1] *vt* to make … jealous

■ **encelarse** *v pron* to get jealous

encenagar [A3] *vt* to cover with *o* in mud; **encenagados en el vicio** sunk in depravity

encendedor *m* lighter

encender [E8] *vt* 1 ‹*cigarrillo/hoguera/vela*› to light; ‹*fósforo*› to strike, light 2 ‹*luz/calefacción*› to switch on, turn on; ‹*motor*› to start; **no dejes el televisor encendido** don't leave the television on 3 ‹*deseos/pasiones*› to awaken, arouse (liter); **~ el fanatismo** to stir up fanaticism

■ **encender** *vi* «*fósforo*» to light; «*leña*» to catch light; «*luz/radio*» to come on

■ **encenderse** *v pron*

A «*aparato/luz*» to come on; «*fósforo/piloto*» to light; «*leña*» to catch light; **se encendió la llama de su pasión** (liter) his passions were aroused *o* (liter) inflamed

B «*persona*» to blow one's top (colloq), to get mad (colloq); «*rostro*» to go red

encendido¹ -da *adj* 1 ‹*rostro/mejillas*› flushed; **de un rojo ~** bright red 2 ‹*discurso*› fiery, passionate; ‹*polémica*› heated

encendido² *m* ignition

encerado *m* 1 (de suelos) polishing, waxing 2 (pizarra) blackboard

enceradora *f* polisher, polishing machine

encerar [A1] *vt* to polish, wax

encerrado -da *adj*: **está ~ en su habitación** he's shut away *o* shut up in his room; **se quedó ~ en el cuarto de baño** he got locked in the bathroom; **siguen ~s en la universidad** they are still occupying the university; **oler a ~** (AmL) to be stuffy

encerrar [A5] *vt*

A ‹*ganado*› to shut up, pen; ‹*persona*› (con llave) to lock up, to shut; **me encerró en mi habitación** he shut me *o* locked me in my room; **encierra al perro** shut the dog in; **me dejaron encerrada en la oficina** I got locked in the office; **está para que lo encierren** (fam) he's crazy *o* a nut (colloq)

B 1 (contener) to contain 2 (conllevar) to involve, entail; **el peligro que ello encierra** the danger which it involves *o* entails

■ **encerrarse** *v pron* (*refl*) (en una habitación) to shut oneself in; (en una fábrica, universidad) «*obreros/estudiantes*» to lock oneself in

encerrona *f* 1 (trampa) trap; **le habían preparado** *or* **tendido una ~** they had set *o* laid a trap for her 2 (protesta) sit-in

encespedar [A1] *vt* (con tepes) to grass over, turf; (con semillas) to plant … with grass, grass over

encestar [A1] *vi* to score (a basket)

enchapado *m* 1 (de metal) plating 2 (de madera — acción) veneering; (— chapa) veneer

enchapar [A1] *vt* (de metal) to plate; (de madera) to veneer

encharcar [A2] *vt* to waterlog, flood

■ **encharcarse** *v pron* «*terreno/zona*» to become waterlogged *o* flooded; «*agua*» to form a pool/pools

enchastrar [A1] *vt* (RPl fam) ‹*ropa/cocina*› to make a mess of; **enchastró la mesa de pintura** he got paint all over the table (colloq)

■ **enchastrarse** *v pron* (RPl fam) to get dirty; **se enchastró todo de helado** he got ice cream all over himself

enchastre *m* (RPl fam) mess

enchilada *f* enchilada (*tortilla with a meat or cheese filling, served with a tomato and chili sauce*)

enchilado¹ -da *adj* (Méx) 1 (Coc) seasoned with chili 2 ‹*persona*›: **acabé enchilada** the food was too hot for me

enchilado² *m* stew (*with chili*)

enchilar [A1] *vt* (Méx) 1 (Coc) to add chili to 2 (fam) (enojar) to annoy

■ **enchilarse** *v pron* (Méx) 1 (comiendo): **ya me enchilé** my mouth's burning; **con este plato me enchilo** this dish is too hot for me 2 (fam) (enojarse) to get angry, to get shirty (BrE colloq)

enchiloso -sa *adj* (Méx fam) hot

enchinar [A1] *vt* (Méx) to perm

■ **enchinarse** *v pron* (Méx): **se me enchina la piel** I come out in goose bumps *o* goose pimples

enchinchar [A1] *vt* (Méx fam) to pester, bug (colloq)

■ **enchincharse** *v pron* (RPl fam) (enfadarse) to get in a mood *o* huff (colloq)

enchinchorrarse [A1] *v pron* (Ven fam) (acostarse) to lie in a hammock

enchuecar [A2] *vt* (AmL fam) ‹*metal*› to bend; ‹*madera/lámina*› to warp; ‹*cara/boca*› to twist; ‹*cuadro*› to tilt

■ **enchuecarse** *v pron* (Chi fam) «*metal*» to bend, get bent; «*madera/lámina*» to warp; «*cara/boca*» to become twisted

enchufado¹ -da *adj* (fam): **está ~** he knows all the right people; **estar ~ con …** to be well in with … (colloq)

enchufado² -da *m,f* (fam): **los ~s** those who have jobs because they have friends in the right places

enchufar [A1] *vt*

A 1 (conectar mediante enchufe) to plug in 2 (fam) (encender) ‹*radio/televisión*› to switch *o* turn on

B (fam) ‹*persona*›: **me enchufó en la empresa** he set me up with a job in the company (colloq)

■ **enchufarse** *v pron* 1 (AmL fam) (adaptarse) **~se EN algo** to settle INTO sth 2 (Esp fam) (en puesto): **se ha enchufado**

en el Ministerio he's got a job in the Ministry thanks to his connections

enchufe *m*

A (Elec) (macho) plug; (hembra) socket, power point (BrE); (del teléfono) socket, point (BrE)

(Compuesto) **enchufe múltiple** two-way adaptor

B (Esp fam) (influencia): **necesitas algún ~** you need to have connections; **por ~** through connections, by pulling some strings

enchumbar [A1] *vt* (Ven fam) to drench, soak

encía *f* gum

encíclica *f* encyclical

enciclopedia *f* encyclopedia*; **una ~ ambulante** (hum) a walking encyclopedia (hum)

enciclopédico -ca *adj* encyclopedic*

encienda, enciendas, etc *see* **encender**

encierra, encierras, etc *see* **encerrar**

encierro *m* 1 (en fábrica, universidad) sit-in 2 (reclusión): **tienes que salir de tu ~** you must get out and about a bit (colloq); **salió de su ~ después de ocho meses** she emerged after being holed up for eight months 3 (Taur) (conducción) *running of bulls through the streets*; (toros) *bulls to be used in a bullfight* 4 (para el ganado) enclosure, pen

encima *adv*

A (en el espacio): **le puso una piedra ~** he put a stone on it; **no llevo dinero ~** I don't have any money on me; **se tiró el café ~** she spilled the coffee over herself; **lo vi cuando ya lo tenía ~** I didn't see it until it was on top of me; **el autobús se nos venía ~** the bus was coming straight at us; **se me vino el armario ~** the cupboard came down on top of me

B (en el tiempo): **los exámenes ya estaban ~** the exams were already upon us; **se nos echaba ~ la noche** night was falling (around us)

C (además): **¡y ~ se queja!** and then she goes and complains!; **y ~ no me lo devolvió** and on top of that, he didn't give it back

D (*en locs*) **encima de**: **~ de la mesa** on the table; **~ del armario** on top of the cupboard; **llevaba un chal ~ de la chaqueta** she wore a shawl over her jacket; **viven ~ de la tienda** they live over *o* above the shop; **~ de caro es feo** not only is it expensive, it's also ugly; ***echarse algo ~*** ‹*deuda*› to saddle *o* land oneself with sth; ‹*problema*› to take … upon oneself; ***echarse ~ a algn*** (AmL): **se echó ~ a todos los profesores** he turned all the teachers against him; ***estar ~ de algn*** *or* ***estarle ~ a algn*** (fam) to be on at sb (colloq); ***hacerse ~*** (fam & euf) (orinarse) to wet oneself; (hacerse caca): **todavía se hace ~** he still messes his pants; ***por ~***: **esparcir las almendras por ~** sprinkle the almonds over it *o* on top; **volaban por ~ del pueblo** they flew over the town; **está por ~ del jefe de sección** she's higher up than *o* she's above the head of department; **temperaturas por ~ de lo normal** above-average temperatures; **lo leí por ~** I just skimmed through it; **le eché un vistazo muy por ~** I just looked over it very quickly; **una limpieza por ~** a quick clean; ***por ~ de todo***: **por ~ de todo, que no se entere él** above all *o* most important, he mustn't find out; **pone su carrera por ~ de todo** she puts her career before anything else; ***quitarse*** *or* ***sacarse algo de ~*** ‹*problema/tarea*› to get sth out of the way; ***quitarse*** *or* ***sacarse a algn de ~*** to get rid of sb

encimar [A1] *vt*

A (Col) (regalar): **me encimó dos más** she gave me two extra

B (Méx, RPl) ‹*cajas/libros*› to put *o* pile … one on top of the other, to stack up

■ **encimarse** *v pron* (Méx): **se me encima esa clase con otra** that class clashes *o* coincides with another

encimera *f* (Esp) 1 (sábana) top sheet 2 (cocina) stove top (AmE), hob (BrE) 3 (mostrador) (kitchen) counter (AmE), worktop (BrE)

encina *f* holm oak, ilex

encinar *m* oak wood/grove

encinta *adj* expecting; **~ de tres meses** three months pregnant

encizañar [A1] *vt* to stir up *o* cause trouble between/among

■ **encizañar** *vi* to cause *o* make trouble

enclaustrarse [A1] *v pron* to shut oneself away

enclavado -da *adj*: **~ en el corazón del bosque** buried deep in the heart of the forest

enclave *m* enclave

enclavijar [A1] *vt* to peg

enclenque *adj* 1 ‹*persona*› (enfermizo) sickly; (delgado) weak, weedy (colloq) 2 ‹*estructura*› rickety

enclítico -ca *adj* enclitic

encochinarse [A1] *v pron* (Chi fam) to get mucky (colloq)

encofrado *m* (en mina) timbers (*pl*); (Const) formwork, shuttering (BrE)

encofrar [A1] *vt* to put formwork *o* (BrE) shuttering around

encoger [E6] *vi* to shrink

■ **encoger** *vt* 1 ‹*ropa*› to shrink 2 ‹*cuerpo*›: **~ las piernas** to tuck one's legs in; **encogió el cuerpo de miedo** he shrank back in fear

■ **encogerse** *v pron*

A «*ropa/tela*» to shrink

B «*persona*» 1 (físicamente): **~se de hombros** to shrug one's shoulders; **caminar encogido** to walk with one's shoulders hunched 2 (por la edad) to shrink, get shorter 3 (acobardarse) to be intimidated

encogido -da *adj* shy; *ver tb* **encoger**

encolar [A1] *vt* (para pegar) to glue, paste; (para pintar) to seal, size

encolerizar [A4] *vt* to enrage, make … furious

■ **encolerizarse** *v pron* to get furious

encomendar [A5] *vt* 1 (frml) (encargar) **~le algo A algn** to entrust sb WITH sth; **le ~on la dirección de la empresa** she was entrusted with managing the company 2 (Relig) to commend

■ **encomendarse** *v pron* to commend oneself

encomendería *f* (Per) grocery store (AmE), grocer's shop (BrE)

encomendero *m*

A (Hist) *colonist granted control of land and Indians to work for him*

B (Per) (tendero) grocer

encomiable *adj* commendable, laudable (frml)

encomiar [A1] *vt* to praise

encomienda *f*

A (Hist) *control over land and Indians granted to an* **encomendero A**

B (AmL) (Corresp) package (AmE), parcel (BrE)

encomio *m* praise, eulogy; **digno de ~** praiseworthy, laudable (frml)

encomioso -sa *adj* (AmL) eulogistic, laudatory (frml)

enconado -da *adj* ‹*lucha/disputa*› fierce; ‹*discusión*› heated, passionate

enconar [A1] *vt* ‹*lucha*› to intensify; ‹*discusión/ánimos*› to inflame

■ **enconarse** *v pron* «*lucha*» to become fierce, intensify; «*discusión*» to become heated; «*ánimos*» to become inflamed

enconchar [A1] *vt* (Ven fam) to hide

■ **enconcharse** *v pron* 1 (Col, Méx fam) (ensimismarse) to withdraw into one's shell 2 (Ven fam) (esconderse) to go into hiding

encono *m* 1 (fiereza): **lucharon con ~** they fought fiercely 2 (enojo) anger, fury; (rencor) spite

encontradizo -za *m,f*: **se hizo el ~** (fam) he acted as though it was a chance meeting

encontrado -da *adj gen* **~s** conflicting, opposing

encontrar [A10] *vt*

(Sentido I)

A 1 (buscando) ‹*casa/trabajo/persona*› to find; **no encontré entradas para el teatro** I couldn't get tickets for the theater; **no le encuentro lógica** I can't see the logic in it 2 (casualmente) ‹*cartera/billete*› to find, come across

B (descubrir) ‹*falta/error*› to find, spot; ‹*cáncer/quiste*› to find, discover

C ‹*obstáculo/dificultad*› to meet (with), encounter; **allí encontró la muerte** (period) he met his death there

(*Sentido* **II**) (+ *compl*): **te encuentro muy cambiado** you look very different; **¡qué bien te encuentro!** you look so well!; **lo encuentro ridículo** I find it ridiculous; **¿cómo encontraste el país?** how did the country seem to you?; **encontré la puerta cerrada** I found the door shut

■ **encontrarse** *v pron*

(*Sentido* **I**)

A 1 (por casualidad) **~se con algn** to meet sb, bump INTO sb (colloq) 2 (*refl*) (Psic) *tb* **~se a sí mismo** to find oneself

B (*recípr*) 1 (reunirse) to meet; (por casualidad) to meet, bump into each other (colloq); **quedamos en ~nos en la estación** we arranged to meet at the station 2 «*carreteras/líneas*» to meet

C (*enf*) (inesperadamente) ‹*persona*› to meet, bump into (colloq); ‹*billete/cartera*› to find, come across; **se encontró la casa patas arriba** he found the house in a terrible state; **me encontré con que todos se habían ido** I found they had all gone

(*Sentido* **II**) (frml) (estar) to be; **me encuentro mejor** I am feeling better; **se encuentra indispuesto** he's unwell; **se encuentra detenido en la comisaría** he's being detained in the police station; **el hotel se encuentra cerca de la estación** the hotel is (located) near the station; **la crisis en que nos encontramos** the crisis in which we find ourselves (frml)

encontronazo *m* (fam) 1 (entre coches) smash (colloq), crash 2 (discusión) set-to (colloq), row (colloq)

encopetado -da *adj* (fam & pey) grand, posh (BrE colloq)

encopetarse [A1] *v pron* (Col) to get merry

encorajinar [A1] *vt* (Méx fam) to make … angry *o* (esp AmE colloq) mad

■ **encorajinarse** *v pron* (Méx fam) to get mad (colloq)

encordado *m* (CS) strings (*pl*)

encordar [A10] *vt* to string

■ **encordarse** *v pron* (en alpinismo) to rope up

encorsetar [A1] *vt* to restrict

encorvado -da *adj*: **anda ~** he walks with a stoop; **tiene la espalda encorvada** he has a stoop

encorvadura *f*, **encorvamiento** *m* curvature

encorvar [A1] *vt* to hunch

■ **encorvarse** *v pron* to develop a stoop

encrespar [A1] *vt* 1 ‹*pelo*› to make … go curly; ‹*mar*› to make … rough *o* choppy 2 ‹*pasiones*› to arouse, inflame (liter); **los ánimos estaban muy encrespados** tempers were frayed 3 ‹*persona*› to irritate, annoy

■ **encresparse** *v pron* «*pelo*» to curl, go curly; «*mar*» to get rough *o* choppy; «*pasiones*» to be aroused, be inflamed (liter); «*persona*» to become irritated

encrucijada *f* crossroads; **en la ~ del camino** at the crossroads; **estoy en una ~** I'm in a dilemma *o* a quandary

encuadernación *f* 1 (cubierta) binding; **~ en cuero/rústica** leather/paperback binding 2 (acción) book binding

encuadernador -dora *m,f* bookbinder

encuadernar [A1] *vt* to bind

encuadrar [A1] *vt*

A (clasificar) to class, classify, categorize

B 1 (Cin, Fot, TV) to frame, center* 2 ‹*lámina/pintura*› to frame

C (Mil) to post

encuadre *m* framing

encubierto -ta *pp*: *see* ▸**encubrir**

encubridor -dora *m,f* (de delicuente) accesory after the fact; (de objeto robado) receiver; **fue condenado como ~ del asesinato** he was sentenced as an accessory to murder

encubrir [I33] *vt* 1 ‹*delincuente*› to harbor*; **ella lo encubre** she covers up for him 2 ‹*delito*› to cover up 3 ‹*temor/verdad/problema*› to mask

encuclillarse [A1] *v pron* to squat (down)

encuentra, encuentras, etc *see* **encontrar**

encuentro *m* 1 (acción) meeting, encounter; **salir al ~ de algn**: **una secretaria le salió al ~** he was met by a secretary; **salió a su ~ con los brazos abiertos** she went to greet him with open arms 2 (period) (reunión) meeting; (congreso) conference 3 (Dep) (period) game

encuerado -da *adj* 1 (AmL fam) (desnudo) nude, stark naked (colloq) 2 (period) (con ropa de cuero) leather-clad (*before n*)

encuerar [A1] *vt* (Chi, Méx fam) (desnudar) to undress

■ **encuerarse** *v pron* (*refl*) (AmL fam) (desnudarse) to strip off (colloq), get undressed; (en el escenario) to strip

encuesta *f* 1 (sondeo) survey; **~ de opinión** opinion poll; **~ a pie de urna** exit poll 2 (investigación) inquiry

encuestado -da *m,f*: **el 50% de los ~s** 50% of those polled

encuestador -dora *m,f* pollster, survey taker

encularse [A1] *v pron* (Arg fam) (ponerse de mal humor) to get in a mood (colloq), to get pissed off (sl)

encumbrado -da *adj* (alto) high, lofty; (eminente) eminent, distinguished

encumbrar [A1] *vt* (Chi) 1 ‹*volantín*› to fly 2 (fam) (reprender) to tell … off (colloq)

encunetarse [A1] *v pron* (Col, Ven) to go into a ditch

encurtidos *mpl* pickles (*pl*)

encurtir [I1] *vt* to pickle

ende: **por ~** (*loc adv*) (frml) therefore, consequently (frml)

endeble *adj* ‹*persona*› weak, feeble; ‹*salud*› delicate, poor; ‹*personalidad*› weak; ‹*argumento/fundamento*› weak, feeble

endémico -ca *adj* endemic

endemoniado -da *adj*

A (inaguantable) ‹*niño/asunto*› wretched (*before n*); ‹*genio/humor*› foul, wicked; **estos ~s zapatos** these wretched *o* darned shoes (colloq)

B (poseído del demonio) possessed (by the devil)

endenantes *adv* (AmL crit) a moment ago, just now

enderezar [A4] *vt*

A 1 (destorcer) ‹*clavo*› to straighten 2 (poner vertical) ‹*poste/espalda*› to straighten, ‹*planta*› to stake; ‹*barco*› to right

B ‹*situación/asunto*› to sort out, straighten out; **para ~ su matrimonio** in order to sort out *o* straighten out their marriage

C ‹*persona*› to straighten … out

■ **enderezarse** *v pron*

A «*persona*» (ponerse derecho) to stand up straight; (corregirse) to sort oneself out, straighten oneself out

B (arreglarse): **las cosas se ~on** things sorted themselves out

endeudado -da *adj* in debt; **~ con algn** indebted TO sb; **quedo ~ contigo** I am indebted to you

endeudamiento *m* (estado) indebtedness, debts (*pl*)

endeudar [A1] *vt* to get … into debt

■ **endeudarse** *v pron* to get (oneself) into debt; **~se con algn** to get into debt WITH sb

endiabladamente *adv* extremely

endiablado -da *adj* 1 (malo) ‹*carácter/genio*› terrible; **¡este ~ niño/ruido!** this wretched child/noise! 2 (difícil) ‹*problema*› thorny, difficult; ‹*asunto*› complicated, tricky 3 (peligroso) ‹*velocidad*› reckless, dangerous

endibia *f* endive, chicory (BrE)

endilgar [A3] *vt* (fam): **nos endilgó un sermón de media hora** he lectured us for half an hour; **me ~on el trabajito** I got saddled *o* landed with the job (colloq); **me endilgó a los niños** she dumped the kids on me (colloq)

endiñar [A1] *vt* (Esp fam) 1 ‹*golpe/patada*›to give; **me endiñó una bofetada** she slapped me 2 ▸**endilgar**

endiosar [A1] *vt* to deify

■ **endiosarse** *v pron* to become conceited

endivia *f* endive, chicory (BrE)

endocrino -na *adj* endocrine

endomingarse [A3] *v pron* to put on one's Sunday best; **iba todo endomingado** he was in his Sunday best

endosante *mf* endorser

endosar [A1] *vt* 1 ‹*cheque/letra*› to endorse 2 (fam) ▸**endilgar**

endosatario -ria *m,f* endorsee

endoscopia *f* endoscopy

endoso *m* endorsement

endrina *f* sloe

endrino *m* blackthorn, sloe

endrogar [A3] *vt* (Méx) to get … into debt
■ **endrogarse** *v pron* (Méx) to get into debt

endulzante *m* sweetener

endulzar [A4] *vt* ‹*café*› to sweeten; ‹*tono/respuesta*› to soften; ‹*vida/vejez*› to brighten up; ‹*carácter*› to mellow

endurecer [E3] *vt*
A ‹*arcilla/cemento*› to harden; ‹*músculos/uñas*› to strengthen; ‹*arterias*› to harden
B 1 ‹*persona/carácter*› (volver insensible) to harden; (fortalecer) to toughen … up; **ese corte te endurece las facciones** that haircut makes you look harsher 2 ‹*actitud/castigo*› to toughen
■ **endurecerse** *v pron* 1 «*arcilla*» to harden; «*cemento*» to set, harden; «*pan*» to go stale 2 «*persona/carácter*» (volverse insensible) to harden; (fortalecerse) to toughen up 3 «*facciones*» to become harder *o* harsher

endurecimiento *m* 1 (de arcilla) hardening; (de cemento) setting, hardening; (de músculos, uñas) strengthening; (de arterias) hardening 2 (del carácter — insensibilización) hardening; (— fortalecimiento) toughening up 3 (de postura, castigo) toughening

ene *f: name of the letter* **n**

enea *f* reed mace, cattail (AmE), cat's-tail (BrE)

eneas *adj inv* (Ven fam) (de mal carácter): **tu jefe es ~** your boss is a real tyrant (colloq); ***ser ~ con burrundanga*** (hum) to be a little terror (colloq), to be nothing but trouble (colloq)

enebro *m* juniper

eneldo *m* dill

enema *m* enema

enemigo¹ -ga *adj* 1 ‹*tropas/soldados/país*› enemy (*before n*) 2 **ser ~ DE algo** to be against sth; **era enemiga de pegarles a los niños** she was against hitting children; ***lo mejor es ~ de lo bueno*** let well alone

enemigo² -ga *m,f* enemy; **pasarse al ~** to go over to the enemy; **~ DE algo** enemy OF sth; ***~ público número uno*** public enemy number one

enemistad *f* enmity

enemistado -da *adj* [ESTAR]: **hace años que están ~s** they've been at odds (with each other) for years; **quedó ~ con ellos** she fell out with them

enemistar [A1] *vt* ‹*dos facciones*› to make enemies of; **este incidente enemistó a los dos países** this incident made enemies of the two countries; **~ un país con otro** to turn one country against the other; **ella los enemistó** she turned them against each other; **eso me enemistó con mi hermano** I fell out with my brother over it
■ **enemistarse** *v pron* to fall out; **~se CON algn (POR algo)** to fall out WITH sb (OVER sth)

energético -ca *adj* ‹*crisis/política/recursos*› energy (*before n*); ‹*alimento*› energy-giving, fuel (*before n*) (AmE)

energía *f*
A (Fís) energy; **consumo de ~** energy consumption
Compuestos
- **energía atómica/eólica/hidráulica/nuclear/solar** atomic/wind/water/nuclear/solar power
- **energía cinética** kinetic energy
- **energía eléctrica** electricity, electric power

B 1 (vigor, empuje) energy; **estoy cansada y sin ~(s)** I'm tired and listless; **protestar con ~** to protest vigorously 2 (firmeza) firmness; **tienes que tratarlo con más ~** you must be firmer *o* stricter with him

enérgico -ca *adj* 1 (físicamente) ‹*ejercicio/movimiento*› energetic, strenuous; ‹*persona*› energetic, vigorous 2 (firme, resuelto) ‹*carácter*› forceful; ‹*protesta/ataque*› vigorous; ‹*medidas*› firm, strong; ‹*desmentido/rechazo*› flat, firm

energúmeno *m* (fam) lunatic; **como un ~** ‹*comer*› like crazy; ‹*trabajar*› like a slave; ‹*gritar*› like a maniac

enero *m* January; **a principios/finales de ~** at the beginning/end of January; **a mediados de ~** in the middle of January, in mid-January; **el tres de ~** the third of January, January the third, January third (AmE); **en (el mes de) ~** in (the month of) January; **durante el mes de ~** in *o* during the month of January; **Lima, 8 de ~ de 1987** (Corresp) Lima, January 8 *o* January 8th, 1987; **llegaron el 8 de ~** they arrived on the 8th of January *o* January the 8th *o* (AmE) January 8th

enervante *adj* 1 (fam) (irritante): **ese ruido es ~** that noise is driving me crazy; **una vocecita chillona y ~** a grating, high-pitched voice 2 (que quita fuerzas) enervating

enervar [A1] *vt* 1 (irritar) to irritate 2 (debilitar) to enervate

enésimo -ma *adj* nth; **por enésima vez** for the nth *o* umpteenth time (colloq)

enfadado -da *adj* (esp Esp) angry; (en menor grado) annoyed; **están ~s** they've fallen out; **está ~ contigo** he's angry/annoyed with you

enfadar [A1] *vt* (esp Esp) (enojar, disgustar) to anger, make … angry; (en menor grado) to annoy
■ **enfadarse** *v pron* (esp Esp) 1 (enojarse) to get angry, get mad (esp AmE colloq); (en menor grado) to get annoyed, get cross (BrE colloq); **no te enfades, pero te queda mal** don't be offended but it doesn't suit you; **~se CON algn** to get angry/annoyed WITH sb 2 «*novios*» to fall out

enfado *m* (esp Esp) anger; (menos serio) annoyance; **¿a qué se debe tu ~?** what are you so angry/annoyed about?; **con ~** angrily

enfangar [A3] *vt* ▸ **enlodar**

enfardar [A1] *vt* to bale

énfasis *m* emphasis; **puso ~ en este problema** she stressed *o* emphasized this problem

enfático -ca *adj* emphatic

enfatizar [A4] *vt* to emphasize, stress

enfermante *adj* (CS) exasperating

enfermar [A1] *vi* to fall ill, get sick (AmE); **si sigue así va a ~** if he carries on like that he's going to make himself ill *o* to get ill
■ **enfermar** *vt* (fam) to drive … mad (colloq)
■ **enfermarse** *v pron* 1 (AmL) (ponerse enfermo) to fall ill, get sick (AmE); **~se del estómago** to develop stomach trouble 2 (CS euf) (menstruar) to get one's period

enfermedad *f* illness; **contraer una ~** to contract an illness/a disease (frml); **está con permiso por ~** he's off sick; **los que están ausentes del trabajo por ~** those who are off work owing to sickness; **~es de la piel** skin diseases; **~ contagiosa** contagious disease
Compuestos
- **enfermedad de Parkinson** Parkinson's Disease
- **enfermedad de transmisión sexual** sexually transmitted disease
- **enfermedad infantil/profesional/venérea** childhood/occupational/venereal disease
- **enfermedad mental** mental illness
- **enfermedad nerviosa** nervous disorder

enfermería *f*
A (sala) infirmary, sickbay
B (carrera) nursing

enfermero -ra *m,f* nurse
Compuestos
- **enfermero domiciliario -ra domiciliaria** *m,f* ≈ visiting nurse (AmE), ≈ district nurse (BrE)
- **enfermero -ra jefe** *m,f* ≈ head nurse (AmE), ≈ charge nurse (BrE)

enfermizo -za *adj* unhealthy, sickly; **de aspecto ~** unhealthy-looking, sickly-looking

enfermo¹ -ma *adj* 1 (Med) ill, sick; **gravemente ~** *or* **~ de gravedad** seriously ill; **está enferma de los nervios** she suffers with *o* has trouble with her nerves; **cayó** *or* **se puso ~** he fell *o* got ill, he got sick (AmE); ***poner ~ a algn*** (fam) to get on sb's nerves (colloq), to get sb (colloq) 2 (CS euf) (con la menstruación): **estoy enferma** I've got my period, it's the time of the month (euph)

enfermo² -ma *m,f*: **quiere cuidar ~s** she wants to care for sick people *o* the sick; **~s del corazón** people with heart trouble; **~s de cáncer** cancer sufferers; **un ~ del Dr Moliner** one of Dr Moliner's patients

enfermucho -cha *adj* (fam) sickly

enfervorizado -da *adj* ecstatic, frenzied

enfervorizar [A4] *vt*: **su discurso enfervorizó a las masas** her speech fired the enthusiasm of the crowd *o* aroused the fervor of the crowd

enfiestado -da *adj* (Andes, Méx, Ven): **se pasa ~** his life's just one big party (colloq); **todavía están ~s** they're still living it up *o* partying (colloq)

enfilar [A1] *vi*: **~on hacia la plaza** they set off toward(s) the square; **enfiló por la calle principal** he made his way along the main street
■ **enfilar** *vt* 1 ‹*calle/autopista*› to take 2 ‹*cuentas/perlas*› to string, thread 3 ‹*mira/cañón*› to aim; **~ algo** HACIA **algo** to aim sth AT sth

enflaquecer [E3] *vi* to lose weight, get thin

enflusarse [A1] *v pron* (Ven fam) to wear a suit

enfocar [A2] *vt*
A (con cámara, telescopio) to focus on; **los ~on con la linterna** they shone the torch on them
B 1 (Fot, Ópt) ‹*telescopio/cámara*› to focus 2 ‹*tema/asunto*› to approach, look at

enfoque *m* 1 (Fot, Ópt) (acción) focusing*; (efecto) focus 2 (de asunto) approach; **todo depende del ~ que se le dé** everything depends on the way you look at it; **~** DE **algo** approach TO sth; **un ~ nuevo del tema** a new approach to the subject

enfrascarse [A2] *v pron* **~** EN **algo** ‹*en el trabajo/los estudios*› to bury oneself IN sth; ‹*en discusión*› to become immersed IN sth

enfrentado -da *adj* conflicting

enfrentamiento *m* clash
(Compuesto) **enfrentamiento bélico** military confrontation

enfrentar [A1] *vt*
A ‹*problema/peligro/realidad*› to confront, face up to; ‹*futuro*› to face
B 1 ‹*contrincantes/opositores*› to bring ... face to face; **~ a algn** CON **algn** to bring sb face to face WITH sb 2 (enemistar) to bring ... into conflict
■ **enfrentarse** *v pron* 1 (hacer frente a) **~se** A/CON **algn**: **se ~on con la policía** they clashed with the police; **se enfrentó con el enemigo** he confronted the enemy; **el equipo se enfrenta hoy a Paraguay** today the team comes up against *o* meets Paraguay; **~se** A **algo** ‹*a dificultades/peligros*› to face sth; **no quiere ~se a la realidad** he doesn't want to face up to reality 2 (*recípr*) «*equipos/atletas*» to meet; «*tropas/oponentes*» to clash

enfrente *adv*
A (al otro lado de una calle, etc) opposite; **vive justo ~** he lives just opposite, he lives just across the street; **~** DE **algo/algn**: **~ del parque** opposite the park; **~ de mí** facing *o* opposite me
B (delante) in front; **~** DE **algo** in front of sth

enfriamiento *m* 1 (catarro) chill 2 (de amor, entusiasmo, relaciones) cooling (off)

enfriar [A17] *vt*
A 1 ‹*alimento*› to cool; (en el refrigerador) to chill, cool 2 ‹*entusiasmo/relación*› to cool, cause ... to cool
B (Per fam) (matar) to bump off (colloq), to ice (AmE sl)
■ **enfriar** *vi*: **no dejes ~ el café** don't let your coffee go *o* get cold; **deja ~ el motor** let the engine cool down; **ponlo a ~** put it in the refrigerator to chill
■ **enfriarse** *v pron*
A 1 «*comida/bebida*» (ponerse — demasiado frío) to get cold, go cold; (— lo suficientemente frío) to cool down; **espera que se enfríe** wait till it cools down 2 «*manos*» to get cold 3 «*entusiasmo/relaciones*» to cool (off)
B (tomar frío) to catch *o* get cold; (resfriarse) to catch a cold, catch a chill
C (Per fam) (morirse) to croak (colloq), to drop dead (colloq)

enfundar [A1] *vt* ‹*espada/puñal*› to sheathe; **enfundó la pistola** he put the pistol into his holster
■ **enfundarse** *v pron* **~se** EN **algo** to put sth on; **enfundada en un ceñido traje** in *o* wearing a tight suit

enfurecer [E3] *vt* to infuriate, make ... furious
■ **enfurecerse** *v pron* to fly into a rage, get furious

enfurecido -da *adj* [ESTAR] ‹*persona*› furious; ‹*mar/aguas*› (liter) raging (liter)

enfurruñarse [A1] *v pron* (fam) to go into a sulk (colloq), to get into a huff (colloq)

engalanar [A1] *vt* to decorate, deck; **~ algo/a algn** CON **algo** to deck sth/sb (out) WITH sth
■ **engalanarse** *v pron* (*refl*) to get all dressed up, dress up in one's Sunday best

engalletarse [A1] *v pron* (Ven fam) 1 (enredarse) to get muddled (colloq) 2 «*tráfico*» to become congested

enganchado¹ -da *adj* 1 (prendido): **la falda se me quedó enganchada en el rosal** my skirt got caught *o* hooked on the rosebush 2 (fam) (adicto) hooked (colloq); **~** A **algo** to be hooked ON sth

enganchado² -da *m,f* drug addict

enganchar [A1] *vt* 1 ‹*cable/cadena*› to hook 2 ‹*remolque*› to hitch up, attach; ‹*caballos*› to harness; ‹*vagón*› to couple, attach 3 ‹*pez*› to hook 4 (fam) (atraer): **se dejó ~ por una francesa** some Frenchwoman got him in her clutches (colloq); **lo ~on para que les ayudara** they got him to help them 5 (Taur) to gore
■ **engancharse** *v pron* 1 (quedar prendido) to get caught; **se me enganchó la media en el clavo** my tights got caught on the nail 2 (fam) (Mil) to join up 3 (fam) (hacerse adicto): **~se** (A **algo**) to get hooked (ON sth)

enganche *m*
A 1 (acción de enganchar — caballos) harnessing; (— un remolque) hitching up; (— vagones) coupling 2 (pieza, mecanismo) (Auto) towing hook; (Ferr) coupling
B (Esp) (de la luz, del teléfono) connection
C (Méx) (Fin) down payment

engañabobos *m* (*pl* ~) (fam) con (colloq), swindle (colloq)

engañapichanga *f* (RPl fam) ▸**engañabobos**

engañar [A1] *vt* 1 (hacer errar en el juicio) to deceive, mislead; **me engañó la vista** my eyes deceived me; **no te dejes ~** don't be deceived *o* mislead; **tú a mí no me engañas** you can't fool me; **lo engañó haciéndole creer que ...** she deceived him into thinking that ...; **~ a algn** PARA QUE + SUBJ to trick sb INTO -ING; **~ *el hambre*** *or* ***el estómago*** to stave off hunger, to keep the wolf from the door (colloq) 2 (estafar, timar) to cheat, con (colloq) 3 (ser infiel a) to be unfaithful to, cheat on
■ **engañarse** *v pron* 1 (*refl*) (mentirse) to deceive oneself, kid oneself (colloq) 2 (equivocarse) to be mistaken; **duró, si no me engaño, hasta junio** it lasted until June, if I'm not mistaken

engañifa *f* (fam) con (colloq), swindle (colloq)

engañito *m* (Chi fam) little present

engaño *m*
A 1 (mentira) deception; **fue víctima de un cruel ~** she was the victim of a cruel deception *o* swindle; **vivía en el ~ pensando que la amaba** she was under the delusion that he loved her; ***llamarse a* ~** to claim one has been cheated *o* deceived 2 (timo, estafa) swindle, con (colloq) 3 (ardid) ploy, trick; **se vale de todo tipo de ~s** he uses all kinds of tricks
B (Taur) cape

engañoso -sa *adj* ‹*palabras*› deceitful; ‹*apariencias*› deceptive

engarce *m* setting

engarrotar [A1] *v pron* ▸**agarrotar**

engarzar [A4] *vt*
A ‹*piedra/brillante*› to set
B (Col, Ven) (enganchar) to hook; **engarzó la carnada al anzuelo** he put the bait on the hook
■ **engarzarse** *v pron* 1 (Col) (engancharse) to get caught 2 (Chi) (*recípr*) (trabarse) **~** EN **algo** to get involved IN sth

engaste *m* setting, mount

engatusar [A1] *vt* to sweet-talk; **~ a algn** PARA QUE + SUBJ to sweet-talk sb INTO -ING; **no me vas a ~ con zalamerías** flattery will get you nowhere

engavetar [A1] *vt* (Ven fam) to shelve, put ... on ice

engendrar [A1] *vt* ‹*hijos*› to father; ‹*odio/sospecha*› to breed, engender (frml); **ese episodio engendró la duda en él** that incident sowed the seeds of doubt in his mind

engendro *m* 1 (feto) fetus* 2 (criatura malformada) malformed creature 3 (creación monstruosa) freak, monster

engentado -da *adj* (Méx) dazed, confused

englobar [A1] *vt* to embrace, include

engolado -da *adj* pompous

engomado -da *adj* 1 ‹*etiqueta*› gummed, self-adhesive; ‹*sobre*› gummed, self-sealing 2 (Chi fam) (estirado) stuck-up (colloq)

engomar [A1] *vt* ‹*papel*› to gum, glue

engominado -da *adj* slicked down

engorda *f* (Chi, Méx) fattening

engordar [A1] *vt*
A 1 (aumentar) to put on, gain; ~ **cinco kilos** to put on *o* gain five kilos 2 ‹‹*pan/azúcar*›› to make … fat
B 1 (cebar) to fatten (up) 2 ‹*cifras/estadísticas*› to swell
■ **engordar** *vi* 1 ‹‹*persona*›› to put on *o* gain weight; ‹‹*animales*›› to fatten 2 ‹‹*alimentos*›› to be fattening
engorde *m* fattening
engorro *m* (fam) nuisance, hassle (colloq)
engorroso -sa *adj* ‹*problema*› complicated, thorny; ‹*situación*› awkward, difficult; ‹*asunto*› trying, tiresome
engranaje *m*
A (Mec) gear assembly (*o* mechanism *etc*), gears (*pl*); **el ~ del reloj** the cogs of the watch
B (sistema, estructura): **los ~s de la actividad política** the wheels of the political machine; **afectó a todo el ~ del partido** it affected the whole machinery of the party
engranar [A1] *vt* ‹*piezas/dientes*› to mesh, engage; ‹*marcha*› to engage
■ **engranar** *vi* ‹‹*piezas*›› to engage, mesh; ‹‹*marcha*›› to engage (frml)
engrandecer [E3] *vt* (ennoblecer) to ennoble (frml); **aquel gesto lo engrandeció ante todos** with that gesture he grew in stature in everyone's eyes
engrandecimiento *m*: **ello contribuye al ~ de nuestro ejército** that contributes to the greater glory of our army; **el ~ del espíritu a través del sacrificio** the uplifting of the spirit through sacrifice
engrane *m* (Méx) cog, cogwheel
engrapadora *f* (AmL) stapler
engrapar [A1] *vt* (AmL) to staple
engrasado *m* lubrication, greasing
engrasador *m* grease gun
(Compuesto) **engrasador a pistola** *or* **presión** grease gun
engrasar [A1] *vt* 1 (Auto, Mec) (con grasa) to grease, lubricate; (con aceite) to oil, lubricate 2 (Coc) ‹*molde*› to grease
■ **engrasarse** *v pron* to get stained with grease
engrase *m* (con grasa) greasing; (con aceite) lubrication
engreído¹ -da *adj* 1 (vanidoso) conceited, bigheaded (colloq) 2 (Per) (mimado) spoiled•
engreído² -da *m,f* 1 (vanidoso) bighead (colloq) 2 (Per) (mimado) spoiled• brat
engreimiento *m* 1 (arrogancia) conceit, bigheadedness (colloq) 2 (Per) (mimos) spoiling
engreír [I18] *vt* 1 (hacer vanidoso) to make … conceited, make … bigheaded (colloq) 2 (Per) (mimar) to spoil
■ **engreírse** *v pron* to become conceited, become bigheaded (colloq)
engrifarse [A1] *v pron* (Chi, Méx fam) (encolerizarse) to fly off the handle (colloq), to blow one's top (colloq)
engripado -da *adj* (CS fam): **estar ~** to have (the) flu
engriparse [A1] *v pron* (CS fam) to get *o* catch (the) flu, go down with (the) flu
engrosar [A10] *vt* to swell; **pasaron a ~ las filas del partido** they swelled *o* joined the ranks of the party
engrudo *m* (flour and water) paste
engrupido -da *m,f* (Arg fam) show-off (colloq)
engrupir [I1] *vt* (CS fam) to fool (colloq); **la tiene engrupida** he's leading her up the garden path (colloq)
enguantado -da *adj* ‹*mano*› gloved
enguatarse *v pron* (Chi fam) to fill oneself up (colloq)
enguayabado -da *adj* (Col, Ven fam) 1 (por la tierra natal) homesick; **estaba ~ por ella** he was missing her 2 (con resaca) hungover
engullir [I9] *vt* to bolt (down)
■ **engullirse** *v pron* (*enf*) ‹*comida*› to bolt (down), wolf (down)
enharinar [A1] *vt* ‹*pescado/carne*› to coat … with flour; ‹*mesa/molde*› to flour
enhebrar [A1] *vt* ‹*aguja*› to thread; ‹*perlas*› to string
enhiesto -ta *adj* (liter) ‹*persona/figura*› erect, upright; ‹*torre*› soaring (liter), lofty (liter); ‹*árbol*› towering (*before n*), lofty (liter)
enhorabuena¹ *f* congratulations (*pl*); **darle a algn la ~** to congratulate sb; **reciba mi más cordial ~** (frml) please accept my warmest congratulations (frml)
enhorabuena² *interj* congratulations!
enigma *m* enigma, mystery
enigmático -ca *adj* enigmatic, mysterious
enjabonar [A1] *vt* to soap
■ **enjabonarse** *v pron* (*refl*) to soap oneself; **~se las manos** to soap one's hands
enjaezar [A4] *vt* to harness
enjalbegar [A3] *vt* to whitewash
enjambrar [A1] *vi* to swarm
enjambre *m* 1 (Zool) swarm; **un ~ de periodistas** a swarm of reporters 2 (Astron) cluster
enjaretar [A1] *vt* ▸**endilgar**
enjaular [A1] *vt* 1 ‹*pájaro/fiera*› to cage, put … in a cage; **una fiera enjaulada** a caged animal 2 (fam) (meter en la cárcel) to lock … up, throw *o* put … in prison
enjoyado -da *adj* bejeweled• (liter); **iba muy enjoyada** she was wearing lots of jewelry
enjuagado *m* rinsing
enjuagar [A3] *vt* ‹*boca/ropa/vajilla*› to rinse; ‹*palangana/cubo*› to swill out
■ **enjuagarse** *v pron* (*refl*) to wash off the soap; **~se el pelo** to rinse one's hair
enjuague *m*
A 1 (acción de enjuagar) rinse 2 (AmL) (para el pelo) conditioner
(Compuesto) **enjuague bucal** mouthwash
B **enjuagues** *mpl* (fam) (tejemanejes) funny business (colloq)
enjugar [A3] *vt* 1 (liter) ‹*lágrimas/sudor*› to wipe away 2 (absorber) ‹*deuda/gastos*› to recoup, cover
■ **enjugarse** *v pron* (*refl*) (liter): **se enjugó las lágrimas** she wiped away her tears; **~se la frente** to mop *o* wipe one's brow
enjuiciado -da *m,f*: **el ~** the accused, the defendant
enjuiciamiento *m* (acusación) indictment; (juicio, proceso) trial
enjuiciar [A1] *vt*
A (Der) (acusar) to indict, commit for trial; (juzgar) to try
B (en cuestiones morales) to judge
enjundia *f* substance; **un tema con mucha ~** a very weighty *o* substantial subject
enjuto -ta *adj* lean, gaunt
enlace *m*
A 1 (conexión, unión) link; **~ telefónico/por satélite** telephone/satellite link 2 (de vías, carreteras) intersection, junction
(Compuesto) **enlace en trébol** cloverleaf
B (frml) (casamiento) *tb* **~ matrimonial** marriage
C (persona) liaison; **actúa de ~ entre …** he acts as liaison *o* as a link between …
(Compuesto) **enlace sindical** *mf* (Esp) shop steward, union rep
D (Quím) linkage, bond
enladrillar [A1] *vt* to pave … with bricks
enlatado¹ -da *adj* 1 ‹*alimentos*› canned, tinned (BrE) 2 ‹*música/programa*› canned 3 (Inf) ‹*programa*› stored
enlatado² *m*
A 1 (proceso) canning 2 **enlatados** *mpl* (productos) canned *o* (BrE) tinned goods (*pl*)
B (AmL pey) (TV) poor-quality program
enlatar [A1] *vt*
A ‹*alimentos/bebidas*› to can
B ‹*programa*› to prerecord
enlazar [A4] *vt*
A 1 ‹*ciudades*› to link, link up; ‹*ideas/temas*› to link, connect; **caminaban con las manos enlazadas** (liter) they walked along hand in hand; **~ algo CON algo** to link sth WITH *o* TO sth 2 ‹*cintas*› to tie … together
B (Col, RPl) ‹*res/caballo*› to lasso, rope (AmE)
C (Méx frml) (casar) to marry
■ **enlazar** *vi*: **~ CON algo** ‹‹*tren/vuelo*›› to connect WITH sth; ‹‹*carretera*›› to link up WITH sth
enlentecer [E3] *vt* to slow down
■ **enlentecerse** *v pron* ‹‹*proceso/marcha*›› to slow down; ‹‹*reflejos*›› to get slower
enlistado *m* (Méx) list

enlistar [A1] *vt* (Méx) to draw up *o* make a list of
▪ **enlistarse** *v pron* (AmC, Col, Ven) to enlist, join up

enlodar [A1], **enlodazar** [A4] *vt* ‹*ropa/suelo*› to get ... muddy; ‹*reputación*› to tarnish, sully
▪ **enlodarse, enlodazarse** *v pron* to get muddy

enloquecedor -dora *adj* ‹*dolor*› excruciating; **el ruido era ~** the noise was enough to drive you crazy

enloquecer [E3] *vt* to drive ... crazy *o* mad; **el dolor la tiene enloquecida** the pain is driving her crazy
▪ **enloquecer** *vi*
A (perder el juicio) to go crazy *o* mad; **enloqueció de celos** he was driven crazy *o* insane with jealousy
B (fam) (gustar mucho): **me enloquece el jazz** I'm crazy about jazz (colloq)
▪ **enloquecerse** *v pron* **1** (entusiasmarse) to go crazy, go mad; **~se POR algo** to be crazy *o* mad ABOUT sth (colloq) **2** (perder el juicio) to go crazy *o* mad

enlosado *m* (de losas) paving; (de baldosas) floor tiling

enlosar [A1] *vt* (con losas) to pave; (con baldosas) to tile

enlozado -da *adj* (AmL) ‹*cacerola*› enameled*; ‹*fuente*› glazed

enlucido *m* plaster

enlucir [I5] *vt*
A (enyesar) to plaster
B (limpiar) to polish

enlutado -da *adj* ‹*persona*› dressed in mourning; ‹*bandera*› black-fringed; **el país está ~** the country is in mourning

enlutar [A1] *vt*: ‹*país*› to plunge...into mourning; ‹*fiesta/niñez*› to cast a pall over
▪ **enlutarse** *v pron* to go into mourning

enmaderar [A1] *vt* ‹*pared*› to panel, cover with wood paneling*; ‹*suelo*› to lay wooden flooring on

enmarañado -da *adj* **1** ‹*pelo/lana*› tangled **2** (complicado, confuso) complicated, involved

enmarañar [A1] *vt* ‹*pelo/lana*› to tangle; ‹*asunto*› to complicate; ‹*persona*› to confuse
▪ **enmarañarse** *v pron* «*pelo/lana*» to get tangled; «*persona*» **~se EN algo** to get embroiled *o* entangled IN sth

enmarcar [A2] *vt*
A ‹*lámina/foto*› to frame
B **1** (dentro de un contexto): **esto quedará enmarcado en la nueva ley** this will be enshrined in the new law **2** (servir de contexto para): **la ciudad que enmarca el festival** the city which forms the backdrop to the festival; **el ambiente de cordialidad que enmarca la firma del acuerdo** the cordial atmosphere in which the agreement was signed
▪ **enmarcarse** *v pron*: **esta iniciativa se enmarca en el contexto de ...** this initiative is in line with *o* in keeping with ...; **su obra se enmarca dentro del expresionismo** his work can be classified as expressionist

enmascarado¹ -da *adj* masked

enmascarado² -da (*m*) masked man; (*f*) masked woman

enmascarar [A1] *vt* to hide, disguise
▪ **enmascararse** *v pron* (*refl*) to put on a mask, cover one's face with a mask

enmasillar [A1] *vt* to putty

enmendar [A5] *vt* ‹*conducta*› to improve, amend (frml); ‹*actitud*› to change; ‹*error*› to amend, rectify; ‹*texto/proyecto de ley*› to amend
▪ **enmendarse** *v pron* (*refl*) to mend one's ways

enmienda *f* **1** (modificación, corrección) amendment, correction; **valen las ~s** the amendments stand **2** (Der, Pol) amendment

enmohecer [E3] *vt* ‹*ropa*› to make ... moldy*, make ... go moldy*; ‹*metal*› to rust
▪ **enmohecerse** *v pron* «*ropa/pan/queso*» to become *o* (BrE) go moldy*; «*metal*» to rust, become *o* (BrE) go rusty

enmontarse [A1] *v pron* (Col) **1** «*terreno*» to become overgrown **2** «*animal*» to run away, run off into the wild **3** «*revolucionario*» to join the guerrillas (*in the bush*)

enmoquetar [A1] *vt* (Esp) to carpet

enmudecer [E3] *vi* to fall silent
▪ **enmudecer** *vt* to silence

enmugrar [A1] *vt* (AmL fam) to get ... dirty; **no me enmugres la alfombra** don't go getting dirt all over the carpet
▪ **enmugrarse** *v pron* (fam) to get dirty; **se enmugró las manos** he got his hands dirty *o* (colloq) mucky

ennegrecer [E3] *vt* (poner negro) to blacken; (oscurecer) to darken; **la noticia ennegreció la jornada** the news cast a shadow over the day
▪ **ennegrecerse** *v pron* **1** (ponerse negro) to go black **2** (ponerse oscuro) «*cielo/nubes*» to darken, go dark; «*plata*» to tarnish

ennoblecer [E3] *vt* ‹*persona*› to ennoble (frml); **ese gesto lo ennoblece** such a gesture does him credit; **este estilo ennoblece la fachada** the style lends an air of distinction to the façade

ennotado -da *adj* (Ven arg) [**ESTAR**] out of it (sl), spaced out (sl)

enojadizo -za *adj* (esp AmL) irritable, touchy

enojado -da *adj* (esp AmL) angry, mad (esp AmE colloq); (en menor grado) annoyed, cross (BrE colloq); **contestó ~** he replied angrily; **esta ~ contigo** he's angry/annoyed with you; **están ~s y no se hablan** they've fallen out and they aren't speaking to each other

enojar [A1] *vt* (esp AmL) to make ... angry; (en menor grado) to annoy
▪ **enojarse** *v pron* (esp AmL) to get angry, get mad (esp AmE colloq); (en menor grado) to get annoyed, get cross (BrE colloq); **no te enojes pero te queda mal** don't be offended but it doesn't suit you; **~se CON algo** to get angry/annoyed WITH sb; **no te enojes conmigo** don't get angry with *o* mad at me

enojo *m* (esp AmL) anger; (menos serio) annoyance; **¿ya se te pasó el ~?** are you still angry/annoyed?

enojón -jona *adj* (Chi, Méx fam) irritable, touchy

enojoso -sa *adj* (esp AmL) (violento) awkward; (aburrido) tedious, tiresome

enorgullecer [E3] *vt*: **mi hijo me enorgullece** I am proud of my son; **nos enorgullece pensar que ...** we are proud *o* it fills us with pride to think that ...
▪ **enorgullecerse** *v pron* to be proud; **no es para ~se** it's nothing to be proud of; **~se DE algo** to take pride IN sth; **no me enorgullezco de lo que hice** I am not proud of what I did

enorme *adj* ‹*edificio/animal/suma*› huge, enormous; ‹*zona*› vast, huge; **sentí una pena ~** I felt tremendously sad

enormemente *adv* ‹*crecer/isfrutar/beneficiarsec*› enormously; **había cambiado ~** he had changed greatly *o* tremendously; **me preocupa ~** it worries me a lot *o* a great deal; **me disgustó ~ que ...** I was extremely upset that ...

enormidad *f* **1** (de crimen) enormity **2** (gran cantidad) huge *o* vast amount; **una ~ de dinero** a huge *o* vast amount of money; **me gustó una ~** I liked it enormously

enquistarse [A1] *v pron* (Med) to develop into a cyst

enraizado -da *adj* ‹*prejuicio*› deep-seated, deep-rooted; ‹*tradición*› deeply rooted

enraizar [A21] *vi* «*plantas/árboles*» to take root

enramada *f* (pérgola) arbor*; (follaje) canopy

enrarecer [E3] *vt* to rarefy
▪ **enrarecerse** *v pron* **1** «*atmósfera/aire*» to become rarefied **2** «*ambiente/relaciones*» to become strained

enrarecido -da *adj* **1** ‹*atmósfera/aire*› rarefied **2** ‹*ambiente/relaciones*› strained, tense

enratonado -da *adj* (Ven fam) hungover

enrazar [A4] *vt* (Col) to cross

enredadera *f* (como nombre genérico) creeper, climbing plant; (planta convolvulácea) bindweed

enredado -da *adj*
A ‹*lana/cuerda*› tangled; ‹*pelo*› tangled, knotted; ‹*asunto/idea*› complicated
B **1** (involucrado) involved; **~ EN algo** mixed up *o* caught up IN sth; **se vio ~ en el escándalo** he found himself mixed *o* caught up in the scandal **2** (fam) (en lío amoroso) **~ CON algn** involved WITH sb

enredador¹ -dora *adj* (fam): **es muy ~a** she's a real troublemaker *o* (colloq) stirrer

enredador² -dora *m,f* (fam) troublemaker, stirrer (colloq)

e

e

enredar [A1] *vt* 1 ‹*cuerdas/cables*› to get … tangled up, tangle up 2 (embarullar) ‹*persona*› to muddle … up, confuse; ‹*asunto/situación*› to complicate; **no enredes más las cosas** don't complicate things any further 3 (fam) (involucrar) ~ **a algn EN algo** to get sb mixed up *o* caught up IN sth
■ **enredar** *vi* (fam) 1 (intrigar) to make trouble, stir up trouble 2 (Esp) (molestar) to fidget; ~ **CON algo** to fiddle around WITH sth, fiddle WITH sth
■ **enredarse** *v pron*
A «*lana/cuerda*» to get tangled, become entangled; «*pelo*» to get tangled *o* knotted; «*planta*» to twist itself around
B 1 (fam) (en lío amoroso) ~**se CON algn** to get involved WITH sb 2 (fam) (involucrarse) ~**se EN algo** to get mixed up *o* involved IN sth; **se enredó en un negocio sucio** he got mixed up in some funny business 3 (fam) (enfrascarse) ~**se EN algo** to get INTO sth (colloq); **se** ~**on en una acalorada discusión** they got into a heated discussion 4 (fam) (embarullarse) to get mixed up get muddled up

enredo *m* 1 (de hilos) tangle; (en el pelo) tangle, knot 2 (embrollo): **tengo un** ~ **en las cuentas ...** my accounts are in a terrible mess; **está metido en un** ~ **de dólares** he's involved in some shady currency deals 3 (fam) (lío amoroso) affair

enrejado *m* (de verja, balcón) railing, railings (*pl*); (rejilla) grating, grille; (para plantas) trellis

enrevesado -da *adj* ‹*problema*› complex, complicated; ‹*explicación/instrucciones*› complicated, involved; ‹*carácter/persona*› awkward, difficult

enrielar [A1] *vt* ▸**encarrilar**

enriquecedor -dora *adj* enriching

enriquecer [E3] *vt*
A ‹*país/población*› to make … rich
B ‹*espíritu/lengua/alimento*› to enrich
■ **enriquecerse** *v pron*
A (hacerse rico) to get rich; **se enriqueció con la venta de armas** he got rich through arms dealing
B «*cultura/relación/lengua*» to be enriched

enriquecido -da *adj* enriched

enriquecimiento *m* enrichment

enristrar [A1] *vt*
A ‹*ajos*› to string, string … together
B ‹*lanza*› to couch

enrojecer [E3] *vt* ‹*rostro/mejillas*› to redden, make … go red; ‹*pelo*› to turn … red, make … go red
■ **enrojecer** *vi* (liter) (ruborizarse) to redden, blush; (de ira, rabia) to go red in the face
■ **enrojecerse** *v pron* «*rostro/mejillas*» (+ *me/te/le etc*) to redden, blush; «*pelo*» to go red; «*cielo*» to turn red

enrojecido -da *adj* red, reddened

enrolar [A1] *vt* to enlist, recruit
■ **enrolarse** *v pron* 1 to enlist; ~**se en la marina** to enlist in *o* join the navy 2 (en organización): ~**se en un partido** to join a party

enrollado -da *adj*
A 1 ‹*papel*› rolled up 2 ‹*cable*› coiled, coiled up
B (Esp) 1 (fam) [ESTAR] (con una chica, un chico): **están** ~**s** they've got sth going between them (colloq); **estar** ~ **CON algn** to have a thing (going) WITH sb (colloq) 2 (fam) [ESTAR] (en actividad): **estaban** ~**s haciendo una maqueta** they were busy making a model; **estaba** ~ **hablando de política** he was deep in a conversation about politics; ~ **CON algo** ‹*con exámenes/preparativos*› wrapped up IN sth 3 (arg) (en la onda) ‹*persona/música*› cool (sl), hip (sl); ‹*película/coche*› cool (sl)
C (Ven fam) (preocupado) uptight (colloq), freaked out (sl)

enrollar [A1] *vt*
A ‹*papel/persiana*› to roll up; ‹*cable/manguera*› to coil; ~ **el hilo en el carrete** wind the thread onto the spool
B (Esp arg) (confundir) to confuse, get … confused; (en asunto) to involve, get … involved; **no me enrolles en esto** leave me out of this
■ **enrollarse** *v pron*
A «*papel*» to roll up; «*cuerda/cable*» to coil up; **la cadena se enrolló en la rueda** the chain wound itself around the wheel
B (Esp) 1 (fam) (hablar mucho): **no te enrolles** stop jabbering on (colloq) 2 (fam) (tener relaciones amorosas): **se** ~**on en la discoteca** they made out (AmE colloq) *o* (BrE colloq) they got off together in a disco; ~**se CON algn** to make out WITH sb (AmE colloq), to get off WITH sb (BrE colloq) 3 (arg) (con una actividad) ~**se CON algo** to get into sth (colloq); **se** ~**on hablando** they got deep into conversation 4 (arg) (animarse) to get into the swing (colloq); ~**se *bien*** (Esp arg): **se enrolla muy bien con la gente** he gets on very well with people; **se enrolla muy bien** he's really cool (colloq)

enronquecer [E3] *vi* to go hoarse

enroque *m* (en ajedrez) castling; **hacer un** ~ **largo/corto** to castle (on the) queen's/king's side

enroscar [A2] *vt* ‹*tornillo*› to screw in; ‹*cable/cuerda*› to coil; ~ **algo EN algo** to wind sth AROUND *o* ONTO sth
■ **enroscarse** *v pron* 1 «*víbora*» to coil up; **se enroscó alrededor de su presa** it coiled *o* twisted itself round its prey 2 «*gato/persona*» to curl up 3 (RPl fam) (en conversación) ~**se con algn** to start talking to sb; ~**se con algo** to start talking about sth

enrostrar [A1] *vt* (AmL) ~**le algo A algn** to reproach sb FOR sth

enrular [A1] *vt* (Col, CS) to curl
■ **enrularse** *v pron* (Col, CS) to go curly

enrumbar [A1] *vi* (Andes): ~**on para la montaña** they headed for *o* toward(s) the mountain

enrutador *m* (Telec) router

ensalada *f* 1 (Coc) salad; ~ **de fruta(s)** fruit salad 2 (fam) (lío): **tiene una** ~ **mental** he's really mixed up; **me hice una** ~ (RPl) I got terribly mixed up (colloq)
(Compuesto) **ensalada** *or* (Esp) **ensaladilla rusa** Russian salad

ensaladera *f* salad bowl

ensalmo *m* incantation, spell; ***como por*** ~ as if by magic

ensalzar [A4] *vt* ‹*virtudes*› to extol; ‹*persona*› to praise, sing the praises of

ensamblador[1] **-dora** *adj* assembly (*before n*)

ensamblador[2] **-dora** *m,f* 1 (persona) assembler, assembly worker 2 **ensamblador** *m* (Inf) assembler

ensambladura *f*, **ensamblaje** *m* (acción) assembly; (tipo de unión) joint

ensamblar [A1] *vt* to assemble

ensanchar [A1] *vt* 1 ‹*calle*› to widen; ‹*vestido*› to let out 2 (ampliar): **ello ensancha nuestras posibilidades de exportación** it extends *o* expands our export openings
■ **ensancharse** *v pron* «*calle/acera*» to widen, get wider; «*jersey*» to stretch

ensanche *m* 1 (de calle) widening 2 (esp Esp) de ciudad urban expansion area, (new) suburb

ensangrentado -da *adj* bloodstained

ensangrentar [A5] *vt* to stain … with blood
■ **ensangrentarse** *v pron* to get stained with blood

ensañamiento *m* cruelty, malice; **un crimen con** ~ (Der) a very vicious attack (*o* crime *etc*) (frml)

ensañarse [A1] *v pron* ~ **CON algn**: **se ensañaron con los prisioneros** they showed the prisoners no mercy *o* pity; **no te ensañes con él** don't take it out on him (colloq)

ensartar [A1] *vt*
A 1 ‹*perlas/cuentas*› to string 2 (con pincho) to skewer 3 (enhebrar) to thread 4 (clavar) ~ **algo EN algo** to stick sth IN(TO) sth
B ‹*disparates*› to reel off, trot out; ‹*insultos*› to come out with a string *o* stream of
■ **ensartarse** *v pron* 1 (AmL fam) (en discusión, asunto) to get involved 2 (CS fam) (engañarse) ~**se CON algn** to be wrong ABOUT sb; **me ensarté con el auto que compré** the car turned out to be a bad buy

ensayar [A1] *vt* 1 ‹*obra/baile*› to rehearse 2 ‹*método*› to test, try out 3 ‹*metales*› to assay
■ **ensayar** *vi* to rehearse

ensayista *mf* essayist

ensayo *m*
A 1 (Espec) rehearsal 2 (prueba) trial, test; (intento) attempt 3 (de metales) assay
(Compuesto) **ensayo general** (de obra teatral) dress rehearsal; (de concierto) final rehearsal
B (Lit) essay
C (en rugby) try

enseguida *adv* at once, immediately, right away; **¡~ voy!** I'll be right with you; **le regalas un juguete y ~ lo rompe** you give him a toy and he breaks it right away; **casi ~** almost immediately; **~ DE + INF** (esp AmL): **~ de almorzar** right *o* straight after lunch

ensenada *f* inlet, cove

enseña *f* (insignia) emblem, insignia; (bandera) flag; (estandarte) standard, banner

enseñado -da *adj*: **bien/mal ~** ‹*niño*› well/badly brought up; ‹*animal*› well/badly trained

enseñanza *f*

A **1** (docencia) teaching; **métodos de ~** teaching methods **2** (educación) education

(Compuestos)

- **enseñanza a distancia** distance learning
- **enseñanza media** *or* **secundaria** high school (AmE) *o* (BrE) secondary education
- **enseñanza primaria** elementary (AmE) *o* (BrE) primary education
- **enseñanza superior** higher education
- **enseñanza universitaria** college (AmE) *o* (BrE) university education

B **enseñanzas** *fpl* (doctrina) teachings (*pl*)

enseñar [A1] *vt*

A **1** ‹*asignatura*› to teach; **~le a algn A + INF** to teach sb to + INF; **les enseñan a buscar drogas** they train them to search for drugs **2** (dar escarmiento) to teach; **eso te ~á a callar** that'll teach you to be quiet

B (mostrar) to show; **me enseñó el camino** she showed me the way; **vas enseñando la combinación** your slip's showing

■ **enseñarse** *v pron* (Méx fam) **~se A + INF** (aprender) to learn to + INF; (acostumbrarse) to get used TO -ING

enseres *mpl* (de la casa) *tb* **~ domésticos** household equipment, furniture and fittings; (de oficina) equipment; (de artesano) tools and equipment; **~ de valor** valuables; **~ de limpieza** cleaning materials/equipment

ensillar [A1] *vt* to saddle, saddle up

ensimismado -da *adj* [ESTAR] lost in thought; **~ EN algo** engrossed IN sth, absorbed IN sth

ensimismarse [A1] *v pron* to become lost in thought; **~ EN algo** to become engrossed *o* absorbed IN sth

ensoberbecer [E3] *vt* (liter) to make … arrogant *o* haughty

■ **ensoberbecerse** *v pron* to become arrogant *o* proud *o* haughty

ensombrecer [E3] *vt* **1** ‹*felicidad/juventud*› to cloud, cast a shadow over **2** ‹*cielo*› to darken

■ **ensombrecerse** *v pron* (liter) **1** «*vida/día*» to be saddened **2** «*cielo/paisaje*» to darken, grow dark

ensoñación *f* fantasy

ensoñador -dora *adj* dreamy

ensoñar [A10] *vi* to dream; **~ CON algo** to dream OF sth

ensopar [A1] *vt* (Col, CS, Ven fam) to drench, soak

■ **ensoparse** *v pron* (Col, CS, Ven fam) to get drenched *o* soaked

ensordecedor -dora *adj* deafening

ensordecer [E3] *vt* ‹*persona*› to deafen; ‹*ruido/música*› to muffle

■ **ensordecer** *vi* to go deaf

ensortijado -da *adj* (liter) ‹*pelo*› curly

ensuciar [A1] *vt* **1** ‹*ropa/mantel*› to get … dirty, dirty, soil (frml); **lo vas a ~ todo de barro** you'll get mud everywhere **2** (liter) ‹*honor/nombre*› to sully, tarnish

■ **ensuciarse** *v pron*

A **1** «*falda/suelo*» to get dirty; (+ *me/te/le etc*) **que no se te ensucie** don't get it dirty; **se me ensució el vestido de grasa** I got grease on my dress **2** (*refl*) «*persona*» to get dirty; **no te ensucies los dedos** don't get your fingers dirty

B (*refl*) (euf) (hacerse caca) to soil oneself (frml); **el bebé se ensució** the baby has a dirty diaper (AmE) *o* (BrE) nappy

C (en asunto turbio) to get one's hands dirty

ensueño *m* daydream, fantasy; ***de*** **~: un mundo/una casa de ~** a dream world/house

entablar [A1] *vt* **1** (iniciar) ‹*conversación*› to strike up, start; ‹*amistad*› to strike up; ‹*negociaciones*› to enter into, start; **~on relaciones comerciales** «*países*» they opened up trade links «*empresas*» they started doing business together **2** ‹*partida*› to set up

entablillar [A1] *vt* to splint, put … in a splint

entallado -da *adj* ‹*chaqueta/vestido*› waisted; ‹*camisa*› tailored, fitted

entallar [A1] *vt* to tailor

■ **entallar** *vi* to fit; **este vestido entalla bien** this dress is a good fit *o* fits well

entarimado *m* **1** (suelo — de tablas) floorboards (*pl*); (— de parqué) parquet flooring; **2** (plataforma) stage, platform

entarimar [A1] *vt* (con tablas) to lay floorboards on; (con parqué) to lay parquet flooring on

ente *m*

A (ser) being, entity

B (organismo, institución) body; **~ estatal/público** state/public body; **~s con personalidad jurídica** legal entities

enteco -ca *adj* (delgado) gaunt; (enfermizo) frail

entelerido -da *adj* (Méx) sickly, weak

entendederas *fpl* (fam): **ser corto** *or* **duro de ~** to be dumb (AmE) *o* (BrE) dim (colloq)

entendedor *m*: ***a buen ~ pocas palabras (bastan)*** a word to the wise is enough

entender[1] [E8] *vt*

A **1** ‹*explicación/idioma/actitud*› to understand; **no te entiendo la letra** I can't read your writing; **no se le entiende nada** you can't understand anything she says; **lo entendió todo al revés** he got it all completely wrong; **todavía no he entendido el chiste** I still haven't got(ten) the joke; **¿entiendes lo que quiero decir?** do you know what I mean?; **se entiende que no quiera ir** it is understandable that he doesn't want to go **2** ‹*persona*› to understand; **tú ya me entiendes** you know what I mean; **me has entendido mal** you've misunderstood me; **se hace ~** *or* (AmL) **se da a ~** he makes himself understood; **¡no hay quien te entienda!** you're impossible!; **te entiendo perfectamente** I know exactly what you mean

B (frml) **1** (concebir, opinar): **no es así como yo entiendo la amistad** this is not how I see *o* understand friendship **yo entiendo que deberíamos esperar** in my view *o* as I see it, we should wait **2** (interpretar, deducir): **¿debo ~ que te vas?** am I to understand that you're leaving?; **me dio a ~ que …** she gave me to understand that …; **lo dio a ~** she implied it

■ **entender** *vi*

A (comprender) to understand; **(ya) entiendo** I understand, I see

B (saber) **~ DE algo** to know ABOUT sth; **¿tú entiendes de estas cosas?** do you know anything about these things?

C (Der): **~ en un caso** to hear a case

■ **entenderse** *v pron*

A **1** (comunicarse) **~se CON algn** to communicate WITH sb; **se entienden por señas** they communicate (with each other) through signs; **a ver si nos entendemos ¿quién te pegó?** let's get this straight, who hit you? **2** (llevarse bien); **lo que pasa es que no nos entendemos** the thing is we just don't get on very well; **~se CON algn** to get along *o* on WITH sb **3** (tratar) **~se CON algn** to deal WITH sb; **es mejor ~se directamente con el jefe** you are advised to deal directly with the boss; ***allá se las entienda*** (fam) that's his/her problem; ***entendérselas con algn*** to fix sth up with sb **4** (fam) (tener un lío amoroso) **~se CON algn** to have an affair WITH sb

B (*refl*): **déjame, yo me entiendo** leave me alone, I know what I'm doing

entender[2] *m*: **a mi/tu/su ~** in my/your/his opinion, to my/your/his mind

entendido[1] -da *adj*

A [ESTAR] (comprendido) understood; **tengo ~ que …** I understand *o* gather that …; **según tengo ~** as I understand it; **que quede bien ~** this must be clearly understood; **tenía ~ que …** I was under the impression that …; **eso se da por ~** that goes without saying; **bien ~ que …** (frml) on the understanding that …

B [SER] (experto) **~ EN algo**: **no soy muy ~ en estos temas** I'm not very well up on these subjects; **es muy ~ en política** he knows a lot about politics

entendido[2] -da *m,f* expert

e

entendimiento *m*
A (acuerdo) understanding
B (razón, inteligencia) mind; **tiene el ~ de un niño** he has the mind *o* intelligence of a child; **todavía no tiene suficiente ~** he's not old enough to understand

entente /ɔn'tɒnt/ *f or m* entente
(Compuesto) **entente cordial** entente cordiale

enterado -da *adj*
A (de hecho, suceso): **¿estás ~ de lo ocurrido?** have you heard what's happened?; **no estoy enterada de nada** I have no idea what's going on; ***darse por ~*** to get the message, take the hint
B (Esp) (que sabe mucho) knowledgeable, well-informed

enterar [A1] *vt*
A (frml) (informar) **~ a algn DE algo** to inform *o* notify sb OF sth
B (Chi, Méx) ‹*deuda*› to pay
C (Chi) (completar): **ya enteró dos meses en su nuevo empleo** he's been in his new job for two months now; **y con esto entero los cien** and that makes a hundred
■ **enterarse** *v pron*
A (de suceso, noticia): **ahora me entero** this is the first I've heard of it; **me enteré por tus padres** I found out from your parents; **le robaron el reloj y ni se enteró** they stole her watch and she didn't even notice *o* realize; **a lo mejor no se han enterado** they may not have heard; **¡que no te enteras ...!** (Esp fam) wake up! (colloq); **~se DE algo**: **me enteré de la noticia por la radio** I heard the news on the radio; **si papá se entera de esto ...** if Dad finds out about this ...; **nunca te enteras de nada** you never know what's going on; ***te vas/se va a ~ (de quién soy yo)*** you'll/he'll get what for (colloq)
B (averiguar) to find out; **~se DE algo** to find out ABOUT sth
C (esp Esp fam) (entender): **te voy a castigar ¿te enteras?** I'll punish you, have I made myself clear? *o* do you hear me?; **¡para que te enteres!** (fam) so there! (colloq); **~se DE algo** to understand sth

entereza *f* (serenidad, fortaleza) fortitude; (rectitud) integrity; (firmeza) determination, strength of mind

enteritis *f* enteritis

enterito *m* (RPl) (de bebé) rompers (*pl*); (prenda interior) teddy; (de pantalones) jumpsuit

enterizo -za *adj* one-piece (*before n*); (en costura) seamless

enternecedor -dora *adj* moving, touching

enternecer [E3] *vt* to move, touch
■ **enternecerse** *v pron* to be moved *o* touched

entero[1] -ra *adj*
A [1] (en su totalidad) whole; **una caja entera de bombones** a whole *o* an entire box of chocolates; **eso es así en el mundo ~** it's like that all over the world; **por ~** completely, entirely [2] (*delante del n*) (absoluto, total) complete, absolute; **a mi entera satisfacción** to my complete satisfaction [3] (intacto) intact; **la porcelana llegó entera** the china arrived intact *o* in one piece [4] ‹*número*› whole
B ‹*persona*› (íntegro) upright

entero[2] *m*
A (Fin) point; (Mat) whole number, integer
B (de lotería) (whole) lottery ticket

enterradero *m* (RPl) hideout, safe house

enterrador -dora *m,f* gravedigger

enterrar [A5] *vt* to bury; **lo entierran mañana** the funeral is tomorrow; **~ algo EN algo** to bury sth IN sth
■ **enterrarse** *v pron*: **~se en vida** to become a recluse

entibiar [A1] *vt* [1] ‹*líquido*› (enfriar) to cool; (calentar) to warm (up) [2] ‹*afecto*› to cool
■ **entibiarse** *v pron* [1] «*líquido*» (enfriándose) to cool down; (calentándose) to get warm; [2] «*afecto*» to cool

entidad *f*
A (frml) (organización, institución) entity, body; **una importante ~ bancaria** a major bank; **~es financieras** financial institutions; **~ jurídica** legal entity; **~ deportiva** sporting body
B (importancia) significance
C (Fil) entity, being

entienda, entiendas, etc *see* **entender**

entierro *m* (acto) burial; (ceremonia) funeral; (procesión) funeral procession; **ir a un ~** to attend a funeral

entintar [A1] *vt* [1] (Impr) ‹*tipos*› to ink; ‹*espacio*› to ink in [2] (manchar) to stain ... with ink; **con los dedos entintados** with inky *o* ink-stained fingers

entizar [A4] *vt* to chalk

entoldado *m* (marquesina) awning; (carpa) marquee

entoldar [A1] *vt* to put an awning over

entomología *f* entomology

entomólogo -ga *m,f* entomologist

entonación *f* intonation

entonado -da *adj*
A (Mús) in tune
B [ESTAR] (fam) (por el alcohol) tipsy (colloq), merry (BrE colloq)

entonar [A1] *vt*
A ‹*canción*› to intone, sing; ‹*voz*› to modulate; ‹*nota*› to sing, give
B (animar) «*café/sopa*» ‹*persona*› to perk ... up
■ **entonar** *vi*
A (Mús) to sing in tune
B «*color/estilo*» **~ CON algo** to go well WITH sth
■ **entonarse** *v pron* (fam) to get tipsy *o* (BrE) merry (colloq)

entonces *adv*
A (en aquel momento) then; **el ~ presidente** the then president; **por** *or* **en aquel ~** in those days
B [1] (introduciendo conclusiones) so; **¿~ vienes o te quedas?** so are you coming with us or staying here?; **¿él se enteró? — no — ¿~?** did he find out? — no — so *o* well then, what's the problem? [2] (uso expletivo) well, anyway; **~, como te iba diciendo ...** well *o* anyway, as I was saying ...

entornado -da *adj* ‹*puerta*› ajar, half-open; ‹*ventana*› slightly open; ‹*ojos*› half-closed

entornar [A1] *vt* ‹*puerta*› to leave ... ajar; ‹*ventana*› to leave ...slightly open; ‹*ojos*› to half close

entorno *m* [1] (situación) environment; **~ social** social milieu *o* environment; **~ familiar** home environment; **los restos hallados en su ~** the remains found around it *o* in the vicinity [2] (Lit) setting; (Mat) range; (Inf) environment

entorpecer [E3] *vt* [1] (dificultar) ‹*tráfico*› to hold up, slow down; ‹*planes/movimiento*› to hinder; **estas cajas entorpecen el paso** these boxes are (getting) in the way [2] ‹*entendimiento*› to dull; ‹*reacciones*› to dull, slow down
■ **entorpecerse** *v pron* «*entendimiento*» to become dulled; «*reacciones*» to become dulled, be slowed down

entrada *f*
A (acción) entrance; **vigilaban sus ~s y salidas** they watched his comings and goings; **Ⓢ prohibida la entrada** no entry; **la ~ es gratuita** admission *o* entrance is free; **Ⓢ entrada libre** admission free; **la ~ de divisas** the inflow of foreign currency; **~ EN** *or* (esp AmL) **A algo** entry INTO sth; **tuvieron que forzar su ~ en el** *or* **al edificio** they had to force an entry into the building; **su ~ en** *or* **a escena** her entrance, her appearance on stage; ***de ~***: **dijo que no de ~** he said no right from the start; **lo calé de ~** (fam) I sized him up right away *o* (BrE) straightaway
B (en etapa, estado) **~ EN algo**: **la ~ en vigor del nuevo impuesto** the coming into effect of the new tax
C [1] (ingreso, incorporación) entry; **~ EN** *or* (esp AmL) **A algo**: **la ~ de Prusia en la alianza** Prussia's entry into the alliance; **la fecha de su ~ en el club** the date he joined the club; **esto le facilitó la ~ a la universidad** that made it easier for him to get into university [2] (Mús) entry; **dio ~ a los violines** he brought the violins in
D [1] (lugar de acceso) entrance; **Ⓢ entrada** entrance, way in; **Ⓢ entrada de artistas** (en teatro) stage door; (en sala de conciertos) artists' entrance; **a la ~ del estadio** at the entrance to the stadium; **repartían folletos a la ~** they were handing out leaflets at the door; **las ~s a León** the roads (leading) into León [2] (vestíbulo) hall [3] (de tubería) intake, inlet; (de circuito) input
(Compuesto) **entrada de aire** air intake *o* inlet
E (Espec) [1] (ticket) ticket; **¿cuánto cuesta la ~?** how much are the tickets?; **los niños pagan media ~** it's half-price for children [2] (concurrencia) (Teatr) audience; (Dep) attendance, gate; **la plaza de toros registró media ~** the bullring was half full [3] (recaudación) (Teatr) takings (*pl*); (Dep) gate receipts (*pl*)

F (comienzo) beginning; **con la ~ del invierno** with the beginning *o* onset of winter

G (Com, Fin) [1] (Esp) (depósito) deposit; **dar una ~ para una casa** to put down a deposit on a house; **pagas $50 de ~** you pay a $50 down payment *o* deposit [2] (ingreso) income; **~s y salidas** income and expenditure, receipts and outgoings [3] (anotación) entry; (en diccionario — artículo) entry; (— cabeza de artículo) headword

H (de comida) starter

I [1] (en fútbol) tackle; **hacerle una ~ a algn** to tackle sb; [2] (en béisbol) inning

J (en el pelo): **tiene ~s muy pronunciadas** he has a badly receding hairline

entrado -da *adj*: **era entrada la noche** it was dark *o* night-time; **duró hasta bien entrada la tarde** it went on well into the evening; **está ya ~ en años** (euf) he's getting on; **una mujer entrada en carnes** (euf) a rather plump woman

entrador -dora *adj* [1] (AmL fam) (lanzado) daring, forward [2] (RPl fam) (simpático) likable*, nice

entramado *m* [1] (Arquit, Const) framework; (estructura, trabazón) framework, structure; **el ~ jurídico** the judicial framework *o* structure [2] (Tec) network

entrambos -bas *adj pl* (liter) both

entrampar [A1] *vt* (engañar) to trick, catch … out; (endeudar) to burden *o* saddle … with debts

■ **entramparse** *v pron* to get into debt

entrante[1] *adj* [1] (próximo): **el año ~** next year, the coming year [2] (nuevo) ‹*gobierno/presidente*› new, incoming (*before n*)

entrante[2] *m or f*

A (AmL) (Arquit) recess; (Geog) inlet

B **entrante** *m* (Esp) (Coc) starter

entraña *f*

A (de un asunto) heart, core

B **entrañas** *fpl* (vísceras) entrails (*pl*); **hijo de mis ~s** my dear child; **una persona sin ~s** *or* **de malas ~s** a heartless *o* callous person; **las ~s de la tierra** the bowels of the earth; ***dar (hasta) las ~s*** to give one's all

entrañable *adj* [1] ‹*amistad*› close, intimate; ‹*amigo*› very close, bosom (*before noun*); **guardo un recuerdo ~ de …** I have fond memories of … [2] ‹*persona*› pleasant, likable*

entrañar [A1] *vt* to entail, involve

entrar [A1] *vi*

A (acercándose) to come in; (alejándose) to go in; **¡entra!** come in!; **quiero ~ a comprar cigarrillos** I want to go in to buy some cigarettes; **déjame ~** let me in; **hazla ~** tell her to come in, show her in; **entró corriendo** he ran in, he came running in; **¿se puede ~ con el coche?** can you drive in?; **~ a puerto** to put into port; **había gente entrando y saliendo** there were people coming and going; **fue ~ y salir** I was in and out in no time; **¿cómo entró?** how did he get in?; **~ EN** *or* (esp AmL) **A algo**: **entró en el** *or* **al banco** she went into the bank; **nunca he entrado en** *or* **a esa tienda** I've never been into *o* in that shop; **no los dejaron ~ en** *or* **a Francia** they weren't allowed into France; **las tropas ~on en** *or* **a Varsovia** the troops entered Warsaw

B [1] (en etapa, estado) **~ EN algo** to enter sth; **~ en una nueva década** to enter a new decade; **entró en contacto con ellos** he made contact with them; **~ en calor** to get warm; **entró en coma** he went into a coma; **el reactor entró en funcionamiento** the reactor began operating *o* became operational [2] (en tema) **~ EN algo** to go into sth; **sin ~ en los aspectos técnicos** without going into the technical aspects; **~ en juicios de valor** to get involved in value judgments

C [1] (introducirse, meterse): **cierra la puerta, que entra frío** close the door, you're letting the cold in; **le entra por un oído y le sale por el otro** it goes in one ear and out the other; **me entró arena en los zapatos** I've got sand in my shoes [2] (poderse meter): **¿entrará por la puerta?** will it get through the door?; **estos clavos no entran en la pared** these nails won't go into the wall [3] (ser lo suficientemente grande) (+ *me/te/le etc*): **estos vaqueros ya no me entran** I can't get into these jeans anymore; **el zapato no le entra** he can't get his shoe on [4] (fam) «*materia/lección/idea*» (+ *me/te/le etc*): **la física no le entra** he just can't get the hang of *o* get to grips with physics (colloq); **ya se lo he explicado, pero no le entra** I've explained it to him but he just doesn't understand *o* he just can't get it into his head [5] (Auto) «*cambios/marchas*»: **no me entra la segunda** I can't get it into second (gear)

D «*hambre/miedo*» (+ *me/te/le etc*): **le entró hambre/miedo** she felt *o* got hungry/frightened; **me ha entrado la duda** I'm beginning to have my doubts; **me entró sueño/frío** I got *o* began to feel sleepy/cold

E (empezar) to start, begin; **entró de** *or* **como aprendiz** he started *o* began as an apprentice; **entró a trabajar a los 18 años** he started working when he was 18; **~ a matar** (Taur) to go in for the kill

F [1] (incorporarse) **~ EN** *or* (esp AmL) **A algo** ‹*ejército/empresa/convento*› to enter sth; **el año que entré en** *or* **a la universidad** the year I started college; **acabo de ~ en** *or* **a la asociación** I've just joined the association; **~ EN algo** ‹*guerra/campeonato/negociación*› to enter sth [2] (Mús) «*instrumento/voz*» to come in, enter

G [1] (estar incluido): **el postre no entra en el precio** dessert is not included in the price; **¿cuántas entran en un kilo?** how many do you get in a kilo?; **eso no entraba en mis planes** I hadn't allowed for that, that wasn't part of the plan; **esto ya entra en lo ridículo** this is becoming *o* getting ridiculous [2] (ser incluido): **creo que ~emos en la segunda tanda** I think we'll be in the second group; **estos números ~án en un sorteo** these numbers will be included in *o* be entered for a draw

H [1] «*toro*»: **~ al capote** to charge at the cape [2] «*futbolista*» to tackle; **recoge Márquez, le entra Gordillo** Márquez gets the ball and he is tackled by Gordillo

I (en costura): **hay que ~le de los costados** it needs taking in at the sides

■ **entrar** *vt* (traer) to bring in; (llevar) to take in; **hay que ~ la ropa** we'll have to bring the washing in; **voy a ~ el coche** I'm going to put the car in the garage; **¿cómo van a ~ el sofá?** how are they going to get the sofa in?; **lo entró de contrabando** he smuggled it in

entre[1] *prep*

A [1] (indicando posición en medio de) between; **se sienta ~ Carlos y yo** he sits between Carlos and me; **~ estas cuatro paredes** within these four walls; **~ paréntesis** in brackets; **se me escapó por ~ los dedos** it slipped through my fingers; **abierto ~ semana** open during the week; **comer ~ horas** to eat between meals [2] (en relaciones de comunicación o cooperación) between; **que quede ~ tú y yo** this is just between you and me; **~ los tres logramos levantarlo** between the three of us we managed to lift it; **¿por qué no le hacemos un regalo ~ todos?** why don't we all get together to buy him a present? [3] (con verbos recíprocos) among; **cuando hablan ~ ellos** (dos personas) when they talk to each other; (más de dos personas) when they talk among themselves; **~ ellos se entienden** they understand each other *o* one another

B [1] (en el número, la colectividad de) among; **~ los trabajadores** among the workers; **hay un traidor ~ nosotros** there's a traitor among us; **~ otras cosas** among other things [2] (mezclado con) among; **~ las monedas que me dio** among the coins he gave me; **se perdió ~ la muchedumbre** he got lost in the crowd [3] (sumando una cosa a otra) with; **hay unas cien personas ~ alumnos y profesores** with *o* including pupils and teachers there are about a hundred people; **~ una cosa y otra …** (fam) what with one thing and another … (colloq) [4] (en distribuciones) among; **repártelos ~ los niños** share them out among the children [5] (Mat): **diez ~ dos es (igual a) cinco** two into ten goes five (times)

C **entre tanto** meanwhile, in the meantime

entre[2] *adv* (esp AmL): **~ más … menos/más …** the more … the less/more …

entreabierto -ta *adj* ‹*puerta*› ajar, half-open; ‹*ventana/ojos/boca*› half-open

entreabrir [I33] *vt* to half-open

entreacto *m* interval

entrecano -na *adj* graying*

entrecasa (AmL): **zapatos de ~** shoes that I/you wear around the house

entrecejo *m* space between the eyebrows; **arrugar** *or* **fruncir el ~** to frown; **tiene el ~ muy poblado** his eyebrows meet in the middle

entrecerrado -da *adj* ‹*puerta*› ajar, half-closed; ‹*ventana/ojos*› half-closed
entrecerrar [A5] *vt* to half-close
entrechocarse [A2] *v pron* to collide
entrecomillado *m* word/phrase in inverted commas
entrecomillar [A1] *vt* ‹*cita*› to put … in quotation marks; ‹*frase/palabra*› to put … in single quotes (AmE) *o* (BrE) in inverted commas
entrecortado -da *adj* ‹*respiración*› difficult, labored*; **con la voz entrecortada** in a voice choked with emotion; **oía su llanto ~** he could hear her choking sobs
entrecot /entre'ko(t)/ *m* (*pl* **-cots**) entrecote
entrecruzar [A4] *vt* to intertwine, interweave
■ **entrecruzarse** *v pron*
A «*hilos/cintas*» to intertwine, interweave
B «*razas*» to interbreed
entredicho *m*
A (duda): **estar en ~** to be in doubt *o* question; **poner algo en ~** «*persona*» to question sth; **esto pone su integridad en ~** this calls his integrity into question
B (CS, Per) (entre dos personas) argument, difference of opinion; (entre dos países) dispute
entredós *m* (de encaje) lace insert
entrega *f*
A (acción) (de envío, paquete) delivery; (de premio) presentation; (de rehén) return; (de ciudad) surrender; (de documento, solicitud): **la ~ de estos documentos** the handing over of these documents; **el plazo para la ~ de solicitudes** the deadline for handing in *o* (frml) submitting applications; ⓢ **entrega de llaves inmediata** vacant possession, ready for immediate occupancy; **servicio de ~ a domicilio** delivery service; **le hizo ~ de la copa** (frml) she presented him with the cup
B 1 (partida) delivery, shipment 2 (plazo, cuota) installment*; **sin ~ inicial** no downpayment *o* deposit necessary 3 (de enciclopedia) installment*, fascicle; (de revista) issue
(Compuesto) **entrega contra reembolso** COD, cash on delivery
C (dedicación) dedication, devotion; (abandono) surrender
entregado -da *adj* 1 [SER] (sacrificado) selfless 2 [ESTAR] (dedicado) **~ A algo/algn** devoted *o* dedicated TO sth/sb; (abandonado) given over TO sth; **una vida entregada a la ciencia** a life dedicated to *o* devoted to science; **~ a los placeres de la carne** (liter) given over to the pleasures of the flesh (liter) 3 (RPl) (resignado): **está entregada** she's given up
entregar [A3] *vt*
A (llevar) to deliver; **entregamos los pedidos en el día** we offer same-day delivery
B 1 (dar) to give; **me/le entregó un cuestionario** she gave me/her *o* handed me/her a questionnaire; **hoy nos entregan las llaves** they're handing over the keys today; **entregó su alma a Dios** (euf) he passed away (euph); **~las** (Chi fam) to kick the bucket (colloq) 2 ‹*premio/trofeo*› to present; **~le algo A algn** to present sb WITH sth
C ‹*trabajo/deberes*› to hand in, give in; ‹*solicitud/impreso*› to hand in, submit (frml)
D 1 ‹*ciudad/armas*› to surrender; ‹*poder/control*› to hand over 2 (dedicar) to devote; **entregó su vida a los pobres** she devoted *o* dedicated her life to the poor
E 1 ‹*delincuente/prófugo*› to turn in, hand over; ‹*rehén*› to hand over; **el juez entregó al niño al padre** the judge put the child into his father's care 2 ‹*novia*› to give away
■ **entregarse** *v pron*
A (dedicarse) **~se A algo/algn** to devote oneself TO sth/sb
B 1 (rendirse) to surrender, give oneself up; (a vicio) to succumb, give in; **~se A algo** to give oneself over TO sth; **se entregó a la bebida** he gave himself over to drink; **me entregué al sueño** (liter) I succumbed to sleep (liter) 2 (sexualmente) **~se A algn** to give oneself TO sb
entreguerras: **el período de ~** the interwar period
entreguista *adj* (CS) submissive, supine
entrejuntar [A1] *vt* 1 (en carpintería) to join 2 (Chi) ‹*puerta/ventana*› to half-close
entrelazar [A4] *vt* ‹*cintas/hilos*› to interweave, intertwine; **con las manos entrelazadas** hand in hand
■ **entrelazarse** *v pron* to intertwine, interweave

entremedio *adv* 1 (en el espacio): **eran verdes, pero ~ había alguna roja** they were green, but in among them there were a few red ones; **~ de mis papeles** in among my papers 2 (en el tiempo) in between
entremés *m* (Coc) hors d'oeuvre, starter
entremezclar [A1] *vt* to intermingle
■ **entremezclarse** *v pron* «*recuerdos*» to intermingle, become intermingled; «*culturas*» to mix, intermingle
entrenador -dora *m,f* (manager) coach (AmE), manager (BrE); (preparador físico) trainer
entrenamiento *m* 1 (por el entrenador) coaching, training 2 (ejercicios) training 3 (sesión) training session
entrenar [A1] *vt* ‹*soldado/caballo*› to train; ‹*equipo/atleta*› to coach, train
■ **entrenar** *vi* to train
■ **entrenarse** *v pron* to train
entreoír [I28] *vt* to half-hear
entrepaño *m* 1 (trozo de muro) pier, stretch 2 (en puertas, ventanas) panel 3 (estante) shelf
entrepierna *f* (Anat) crotch; (medida) inside leg measurement, inseam (measurement) (AmE)
entrepiso *m* (AmL) mezzanine
entrépito -ta *adj* (Ven fam) nosy (colloq)
entreplanta *f* mezzanine
entresacar [A2] *vt* 1 (seleccionar) to extract, select 2 (en peluquería) to thin out
entresemana *adv* during the week
entresijos *mpl* (secretos) details (*pl*), ins and outs (*pl*)
entresuelo *m* (en edificio) mezzanine; (en cine) dress circle
entretanto[1] *adv* meanwhile, in the meantime; **~ (que) lo hacen** while they do it
entretanto[2] *m*: **en el ~** meanwhile, in the meantime
entretecho *m* (Chi) attic (AmE), loft (BrE)
entretejer [E1] *vt* ‹*hilos*› (en tela) to weave; (entrelazar) to interweave
entretela *f* 1 (Tex) interlining, interfacing 2 **entretelas** *fpl* (entresijos) ins and outs (*pl*)
entretelones *mpl* (CS, Per) (de un caso) ins and outs (*pl*); **los ~s de la política** what goes on behind the scenes in politics
entretención *f* (AmL) ▸**entretenimiento**
entretener [E27] *vt*
A (divertir) to entertain; **pintar me entretiene** I enjoy painting; **es una tontería pero a mí me entretiene** it's silly but it keeps me amused *o* entertained
B (distraer, apartar de una tarea) to distract; (hablando) to stall (colloq)
C (retener) to keep, detain; **no te entretengo más** I won't keep *o* detain you any longer; **un amigo me entretuvo** a friend kept me talking
D ‹*soledad/ocio*› to while away
E ‹*esperanza*› to entertain
■ **entretenerse** *v pron*
A 1 (divertirse) to amuse oneself; **se entretiene con cualquier cosa** «*adulto*» she's easily amused; «*niño*» she's happy playing with anything 2 (pasar el tiempo) to keep (oneself) busy *o* occupied
B (demorarse) to hang around, to dally about
entretenido -da *adj*
A [SER] ‹*película/conversación*› entertaining, enjoyable; ‹*persona*› entertaining
B [ESTAR] ‹*persona*› (ocupado) busy
entretenimiento *m* entertainment; **me sirve de ~** it keeps me amused *o* entertained; **lo hace por** *or* **como ~** he does it for pleasure *o* for fun; **su ~ favorito** her favorite activity *o* pastime
entretiempo *m*
A (período entre estaciones): **un abrigo de ~** a lightweight coat; **vestidos de ~** spring/autumn dresses
B (Chi) (Dep) halftime
entrever [E29] *vt* 1 (ver confusamente) to make out 2 ‹*solución/acuerdo*› to begin to see; **ha dejado ~ que …** she has hinted *o* suggested that …; **esto deja ~ una posible solución** this gives a glimpse of a possible solution; **todo deja ~ que …** everything seems to suggest that …

entreverado -da *adj* 1 (intercalado) interspersed 2 (fam) (desordenado, mezclado) muddled up, mixed up

entrevero *m* (AmS fam) jumble, mess

entrevía *f* gauge

entrevista *f*

A (para trabajo, en periódico) interview; **le hicieron una ~ por radio** he was interviewed on the radio

B (period) (reunión) meeting; **mantuvieron una ~ con él** they met (with) him

entrevistado -da *m,f* interviewee

entrevistador -dora *m,f* interviewer

entrevistar [A1] *vt* to interview

■ **entrevistarse** *v pron* (period) (reunirse) to meet; **~se CON algn** to meet (WITH) sb

entripado *m* (RPl fam) terrible problem

entristecer [E3] *vt* to sadden; **su partida la entristeció mucho** she was very sad when he left

■ **entristecerse** *v pron* to grow sad

entrometerse [E1] *v pron* to meddle; **no te entrometas** keep out of it *o* stop meddling; **~ EN algo** to meddle IN sth

entrometido¹ -da *adj* meddling (*before n*), interfering (*before n*)

entrometido² -da *m,f* meddler, busybody (colloq)

entrona *adj* (Méx fam) (coqueta): **es bien ~** she's a real flirt (colloq)

entroncar [A2] *vi*

A 1 ‹‹*familia/linaje*›› **~ CON algn** (estar emparentado) to be related TO sb; (adquirir parentesco) to become related TO sb 2 (relacionarse, enlazar) **~ CON algo** to be linked *o* connected TO sth

B (esp AmL) (empalmar) ‹‹*vías férreas*›› to connect, meet

entronización *f* (Chi, Méx frml) (establecimiento) entrenchment

entronizar [A4] *vt* (Chi, Méx frml) (establecer) to entrench

■ **entronizarse** *v pron* (Chi, Méx frml) to become entrenched

entronque *m*

A (parentesco) relationship; (enlace) connection, link

B (AmL) (Ferr) junction

entubar [A1] *vt* ‹*arroyo/acequia*› to channel, pipe; ‹*enfermo*› to put tubes into, intubate (frml)

entuerto *m*

A (fam) (perjuicio) wrong, injustice; **deshacer un ~** to right a wrong

B (Med) afterpains (*pl*)

entumecerse [E3] *v pron* (perder la sensibilidad) to go numb; (perder la flexibilidad) to get stiff

entumecido -da *adj* (insensible) numb; (sin flexibilidad) stiff; **~ de frío** numb with cold

enturbiar [A1] *vt* ‹*agua*› to cloud; ‹*relación/felicidad*› to mar, cloud

■ **enturbiarse** *v pron* ‹‹*agua*›› to become *o* go cloudy; ‹‹*relación/felicidad*›› to be marred

entusiasmado -da *adj* excited, enthusiastic; **~ con la idea** very excited about *o* enthusiastic about the idea; **aplaudió ~** he applauded enthusiastically

entusiasmante *adv* thrilling, exciting

entusiasmar [A1] *vt* 1 (apasionar): **me entusiasma el proyecto** I'm really excited about the project; **lo entusiasma el fútbol** he's crazy about football; **no me entusiasma mucho la idea** I'm not very enthusiastic about the idea 2 (infundir entusiasmo) to make … enthusiastic, get … excited

■ **entusiasmarse** *v pron* **~se CON algo** to get excited *o* enthusiastic ABOUT sth; **no te entusiasmes demasiado** don't get too excited *o* carried away

entusiasmo *m* enthusiasm; **con gran ~** enthusiastically

entusiasta¹ *adj* enthusiastic

entusiasta² *mf* enthusiast; **un ~ de la ópera** an opera enthusiast

entusiástico -ca *adj* enthusiastic

enumeración *f* enumeration

enumerar [A1] *vt* to list, enumerate (frml)

enunciación *f* statement, enunciation (frml)

enunciado *m* (Ling) statement; (Mat) formulation

enunciar [A1] *vt* ‹*idea/teoría*› to state, enunciate (frml); ‹*problema/teorema*› to formulate

enunciativo -va *adj* expository

envainar [A1] *vt* ‹*espada*› to sheathe

■ **envainarse** *v pron* (Col, Ven arg) to run *o* get into trouble

envalentonar [A1] *vt* to make … bolder, encourage

■ **envalentonarse** *v pron* (ponerse valiente) to become bolder *o* more daring; (insolentarse) to become defiant

envanecer [E3] *vt* to make … conceited

■ **envanecerse** *v pron* to become conceited

envanecimiento *m* conceit, vanity

envasado *m* (en botellas) bottling; (en latas) canning; (en paquetes, cajas) packing

envasador -dora *m,f* 1 (persona) packer 2 **envasadora** *f* (compañía) packer

envasar [A1] *vt* (en botellas) to bottle; (en latas) to can; (en paquetes, cajas) to pack; **envasado al vacío** vacuum-packed

envase *m* (botella) bottle; (lata) can, tin (BrE); (caja) box; **en ~s de cartón** in cartons; **~ de plástico** plastic container

envejecer [E3] *vi* 1 ‹‹*persona*›› (hacerse más viejo) to age, grow old; (parecer más viejo) to age 2 ‹‹*vino/queso*›› to mature, age

■ **envejecer** *vt* 1 ‹*persona*› ‹‹*tragedia/experiencia*›› to age; ‹‹*ropa/peinado*›› to make … look older 2 ‹*madera*› to make … look old; ‹*vaqueros*› to give … a worn look

■ **envejecerse** *v pron* (*refl*) to make oneself look older

envejecido -da *adj* 1 [ESTAR] ‹*persona*›: **está tan ~** he's aged so much *o* he looks so old 2 ‹*cuero/madera*› distressed

envejecimiento *m* aging*

envenenamiento *m* poisoning

envenenar [A1] *vt* to poison

■ **envenenarse** *v pron* (involuntariamente) to be poisoned; (voluntariamente) to poison oneself

envergadura *f*

A (importancia) magnitude (frml), importance; **de gran/cierta ~** of great/some importance

B (de avión, ave) wingspan

envés *m* (de tela) back, wrong side; (de hoja) underside, reverse; (de espada) back

enviado -da *m,f* (Pol) envoy; (Period) reporter, correspondent

(Compuesto) **enviado especial** (Pol) special envoy; (Period) special correspondent

enviar [A17] *vt* 1 ‹*carta/paquete*› to send; ‹*pedido/mercancías*› to send, dispatch; **te envía recuerdos** she sends you her regards; **envió el balón al fondo de las mallas** (period) he put the ball in the back of the net 2 ‹*persona*› to send; **lo ~on a Londres de agregado cultural** he was sent *o* posted to London as cultural attaché; **me envió por pan** she sent me out for bread; **~ a algn A + INF** to send sb to + INF

enviciarse [A1] *v pron* to become addicted, get hooked (colloq); **~ CON algo** to become addicted TO sth *o* (colloq) hooked ON sth

envidia *f* envy, jealousy; **le da ~ que yo saque mejores notas** he's envious *o* jealous because I get better marks; **le tienes ~** you are jealous of him; **siente ~ de su belleza** she is envious of her beauty; **me muero de ~** I'm green with envy; **¡qué ~!** I'm so jealous!

envidiable *adj* enviable

envidiar [A1] *vt* to envy; **~le algo A algn** to envy sb sth; **nuestro hospital no tiene nada que ~le a los mejores del mundo** our hospital can stand alongside the best in the world; **no tienes nada que ~le** you've no reason to be envious of him

envidioso -sa *adj* envious

envilecer [E3] *vt* to degrade, debase

■ **envilecer** *vi* to degrade, be degrading

■ **envilecerse** *v pron* to degrade *o* debase oneself

envilecimiento *m* degradation, debasement

envío *m*

A (acción): **el ~ de los fondos** the remittance *o* sending of the money; **le hace ~s periódicos de dinero** he sends him money periodically; Ⓢ **envíos a domicilio** home delivery; **fecha de ~** date of dispatch, date sent

(Compuesto) **envío contra reembolso** COD, cash on delivery

B (partida — de mercancías) consignment, shipment; (— de dinero) remittance

envión *m* 1 (empujón) push, shove (colloq) 2 (RPl) (impulso): **del** *or* **con el ~ salió despedida** the jolt sent her flying; **tomar** *or* **darse ~** take a run-up 3 (Col) (esfuerzo) spurt, effort; ***de un*** **~** (Col fam) in one go (colloq); **trabajamos 12 horas de un ~** we work 12 hours at a stretch

enviudar [A1] *vi* to be widowed

envoltijo *m* bundle

envoltorio *m* 1 (de paquete, regalo) wrapping; (de caramelo) wrapper 2 (bulto) bundle

envoltura *f* (Biol, Bot) casing, covering; (de paquete, regalo) wrapping; (de caramelo) wrapper

envolvente *adj* ‹*mirada/movimento*› sweeping; (Mil) ‹*maniobra*› enveloping, encircling

envolver [E11] *vt*

A ‹*paquete/regalo*› to wrap (up); **¿me lo puede ~ para regalo?** could you gift wrap it?; **~ algo/a algn EN algo** to wrap sth/sb (up) IN sth

B (rodear) «*membrana/capa*» to surround; «*humo/tristeza*» to envelop; **un velo de misterio envuelve el caso** the case is cloaked *o* shrouded in mystery

C (implicar) ‹*crítica/opinión*› to imply

D (involucrar) to involve; **~ a algn EN algo** to involve sb IN sth, get sb involved IN sth

■ **envolverse** *v pron* 1 (*refl*) (en manta) to wrap oneself (up) 2 (en delito, asunto) to become involved

envolvimiento *m*

A (de paquete) wrapping

B (participación) involvement

envuelto -ta *adj*

A [ESTAR] ‹*paquete/regalo*› wrapped; **~ para regalo** gift-wrapped

B 1 (rodeado) **~ EN algo**: **~ en un manto de humo** enveloped in smoke; **~ en misterio** cloaked *o* shrouded in mystery 2 (en una manta) **~ EN algo** wrapped (up) IN sth

C (involucrado) **~ EN algo** involved IN sth

enyesado *m* plastering

enyesar [A1] *vt* 1 (Const) to plaster 2 ‹*brazo/pierna*› to put … in plaster, put … in a plaster cast

enzarzarse [A4] *v pron* **~ EN algo** to get involved IN sth

enzima *f* enzyme

eñe *f*: *name of the letter* ñ

eólico -ca *adj* wind (*before n*), eolian* (tech)

epa *interj* (fam) 1 (para llamar la atención) hey! 2 (AmS) (ante accidente) whoops! 3 (Ven fam) (saludo) hi! (colloq)

épale *interj* (Chi fam) hey!

epatar [A1] *vt* (deslumbrar) to dazzle, impress; (escandalizar) to shock

EPD, e.p.d. (= **en paz descanse**) RIP

épica *f* (género) epic poetry

epicentro *m* epicenter*

épico -ca *adj* epic

epicúreo¹ -rea *adj* epicurean

epicúreo² -rea *m,f* epicure

epidemia *f* epidemic

epidémico -ca *adj* epidemic

epidérmico -ca *adj* epidermal

epidermis *f* epidermis

Epifanía *f* 1 (Bib): **la ~ (del Señor)** the Epiphany 2 (Relig) (fiesta) Epiphany

epígrafe *m* epigraph

epigrama *m* epigram

epilepsia *f* epilepsy

epiléptico -ca *adj/m,f* epileptic

epílogo *m* (Lit) epilogue; (de suceso) conclusion

episcopado *m* (dignidad) bishopric, episcopate; (conjunto de obispos) episcopate

episcopal *adj* episcopal

episódico -ca *adj* episodic

episodio *m* (Cin, Rad, TV) episode; (suceso) episode, incident

epístola *f* (frml *o* hum) epistle (frml *or* hum)

epistolar *adj* epistolary

epitafio *m* epitaph

epitelio *m* epithelium

epíteto *m* (Ling) epithet; (calificativo) name, epithet (frml)

epítome *m* summary, epitome (frml)

época *f* 1 (período de tiempo — en la historia) time, period; (— en la vida) time; **en la ~ de Franco** in Franco's time, under Franco; **muebles de ~** period furniture; **en aquella ~** in those days *o* at that time; **está pasando por una buena ~** she's doing very well; ***hacer*** **~**: **un grupo musical que hizo ~** a group which marked a new era in musical history 2 (parte del año) time of year; **la ~ de lluvias** the rainy season; **no es ~ de naranjas** oranges are not in season at the moment 3 (Geol) epoch

(Compuestos)

- **época de celo** mating season
- **época dorada** *or* **de oro** golden age

epopeya *f* 1 (Lit) (poema) epic, epic poem; (género): **la ~** epic poetry 2 (empresa difícil): **el viaje fue toda una ~** the journey turned out to be a real ordeal

equidad *f* fairness, equity (frml)

equidistante *adj* equidistant

equidistar [A1] *vi* **~ DE algo** to be equidistant FROM sth

equilátero -ra *adj* equilateral

equilibrado¹ -da *adj* ‹*persona/dieta*› well-balanced, balanced; ‹*lucha/partido*› close

equilibrado² *m* balancing

(Compuesto) **equilibrado de ruedas** wheel balancing

equilibrar [A1] *vt* 1 ‹*peso/carga/ruedas*› to balance; **para ~ las fuerzas de los partidos** in order to achieve a balance *o* an equilibrium between the parties 2 (Com, Fin): **~ las diferencias económicas** to redress economic imbalances; **~ la balanza comercial** to restore the balance of trade

■ **equilibrarse** *v pron* «*fuerzas*» to even up; «*balanza de pagos*» to be restored; «*platillos de la balanza*» to balance out

equilibrio *m*

A (de fuerzas, estabilidad) balance; **la balanza está en ~** the scales are (evenly) balanced; **el ~ entre la oferta y la demanda** the balance between supply and demand; **perdió/mantuvo el ~** he lost/kept his balance; **en estado de ~** in equilibrium; ***hacer*** **~s** to do a balancing act

B (sensatez, juicio): **una persona de gran ~** a very level-headed *o* well-balanced person; **~ mental** mental stability

equilibrismo *m*: **un espectáculo de ~** a balancing act; (sobre la cuerda floja) a tightrope act

equilibrista *mf* (Espec) tightrope walker

equino¹ -na *adj* equine

equino² *m* (erizo de mar) sea urchin, equinus (tech); (caballo) horse; **~s y ovinos** horses and sheep

equinoccio *m* equinox; **~ de primavera/de otoño** vernal/autumnal equinox

equipaje *m* baggage (esp AmE), luggage (BrE); **facturar el ~** to check in one's baggage *o* luggage; **viaja con poco ~** he travels light

(Compuesto) **equipaje de mano** hand baggage *o* luggage

equipal *m* (Méx) *chair with leather seat*

equipamiento *m* (acción de equipar — un laboratorio) equipping; (— una oficina) fitting out

equipar [A1] *vt* 1 ‹*persona*› to equip, fit … out; **están bien equipados para estas situaciones** they are well-equipped to deal with these situations; **~ a algn CON** *or* **DE algo** to equip sb WITH sth 2 ‹*casa*› to furnish; ‹*local/barco*› to fit out; (de víveres) to provision; **una cocina equipada con …** a kitchen equipped with …

■ **equiparse** *v pron* (*refl*) to equip oneself; **se ~on de armas** they equipped themselves with weapons

equiparable *adj* comparable; **~ A** *or* **CON algo** comparable TO *o* WITH sth

equiparación *f* comparison

equiparar [A1] *vt* 1 (poner al mismo nivel) ~ **algo/a algn** A *or* CON **algo/algn** to put sth/sb on a level WITH sth/sb 2 (comparar): **esta situación no se puede ~ con la existente en Nicaragua** this situation cannot be compared to *o* compared with that which exists in Nicaragua

equiparidad *f* (Chi) ▸ **igualdad**

equipo *m*

A (de trabajadores, jugadores) team; **el ~ local** *or* **de casa** the home team; **el ~ de fuera** *or* **visitante** the away *o* visiting team; **un ~ de salvamento** a rescue team; **trabajo en ~** team work; **trabajar en ~** to work as a team; **el ~ directivo** the management team; **hacer ~ con algn** (AmL) to team up with sb; ***ser del otro*** ~ (AmL fam & pey) to be one of them (colloq & pej)

(Compuesto) **equipo móvil** outside broadcasting unit

B (de materiales, utensilios) equipment; **~ de pesca** fishing tackle; **~ de fotografía** photographic equipment; **~ de gimnasia** gym kit; ***caerse con todo el*** ~ (fam) to mess things up (colloq), to screw up (AmE sl)

(Compuestos)

- **equipo de alta fidelidad** hi-fi system
- **equipo de música** *or* **de sonido** *or* (Chi) **modular** sound system
- **equipo de serie** standard fittings (*pl*)

equis *f*: *name of the letter* **x**

equitación *f* riding, horseback riding (AmE), horse riding (BrE); **practica (la) ~** he rides; **escuela de ~** riding school; **el arte de la ~** the art of horsemanship

equitativo -va *adj* ‹*persona*› fair; ‹*reparto*› equitable; **reciben un trato ~** they receive equal *o* fair treatment

equivalencia *f* equivalence; **tabla de ~s** conversion table

equivalente[1] *adj* equivalent; **~ A algo** equivalent TO sth

equivalente[2] *m* equivalent; **~ A** *or* **DE algo** equivalent OF sth

equivaler [E28] *vi* 1 (ser igual) ~ **A algo** to be equivalent TO sth; **¿a cuánto equivalen mil pesos en libras?** how much is a thousand pesos equivalent to *o* worth in pounds? 2 (suponer, significar) ~ **A algo** to be equivalent TO sth, to amount TO sth; **eso equivale a decir que ...** that's equivalent to saying that ...

equivocación *f* mistake; **por ~** by mistake, in error (frml)

equivocadamente *adv*: **actuó ~** she acted wrongly *o* mistakenly; **lo juzgué ~** I misjudged him

equivocado -da *adj* 1 ‹*dato/número/respuesta*› wrong 2 [ESTAR] ‹*persona*› mistaken, wrong

equivocar [A2] *vt* 1 ‹*persona*› to make ... make a mistake, to make ... go wrong; **no interrumpas que me equivocas** don't interrupt me, you'll make me go wrong 2 (elegir mal): **equivocó el camino dedicándose a la enseñanza** he chose the wrong career when he went in for teaching

■ **equivocarse** *v pron* (cometer un error) to make a mistake; (estar en un error) to be wrong *o* mistaken; **te equivocas, no se lo dije** you're wrong *o* mistaken, I didn't tell him; **me equivoqué con él** I was wrong about him; **no te equivoques de día** don't get the day wrong; **me equivoqué de paraguas** I picked up the wrong umbrella; **se equivocó de camino** he went the wrong way

equívoco[1] **-ca** *adj* (frml) ‹*palabra*› ambiguous, equivocal (frml)

equívoco[2] *m* (malentendido) misunderstanding; (error) mistake

era[1] *f*

A (período, época) era, age; **la ~ cristiana** the Christian era; **la ~ espacial** the space age

B (Agr) threshing floor

era[2], **éramos, etc** *see* **ser**

erario *m* treasury, public funds (*pl*)

eras *see* **ser**

erección *f*

A (Fisiol) erection

B (de edificio, monumento) erection (frml); (de tribunal) establishment, setting-up

eréctil *adj* erectile

erecto -ta *adj* erect

eremita *mf* hermit

eres *see* **ser**

ergonomía *f* ergonomics

erguido -da *adj* upright

erguir [I26] *vt* (liter) ‹*cabeza*› to raise, lift; ‹*cuello*› to straighten; ‹*orejas*› to prick up

■ **erguirse** *v pron* (liter) «*persona*» to stand up; «*edificio/torre*» to rise; **se yergue majestuosamente sobre la ciudad** it rises majestically above the city

erial *m* uncultivated land

erigir [I7] *vt* 1 (frml) ‹*edificio*› to build, erect (frml); ‹*monumento*› to erect (frml), to raise (frml) 2 (frml) (convertir, elevar) ~ **algo/a algn** EN **algo** to set sth/sb up AS sth

■ **erigirse** *v pron* (llegar a ser) **~se** EN **algo** to become sth; (atribuirse funciones de) to set oneself up AS sth

erizado -da *adj* 1 (de punta): **tenía el pelo ~** her hair was standing on end 2 (lleno) ~ **DE algo** ‹*de espinas*› bristling WITH sth; **un proyecto ~ de problemas** a project fraught with problems

erizar [A4] *vt* 1 ‹*pelo/vello*› to make ... stand on end 2 (AmL) ‹*persona*›: **ese ruido me eriza** that noise sets my teeth on edge

■ **erizarse** *v pron* 1 «*pelo*» to stand on end 2 (AmL) «*persona*» to get goose bumps (AmE) *o* (BrE) goose pimples (colloq)

erizo *m* hedgehog

(Compuesto) **erizo marino** *or* **de mar** sea urchin

ermita *f* chapel

ermitaño -ña *m,f*

A (asceta) hermit

B **ermitaño** *m* (Zool) hermit crab

erogación *f* (frml) 1 (distribución) distribution 2 (AmL) (gasto) expenditure, outlay 3 (Chi) (contribución) contribution, donation

erogar [A3] *vt* (frml) 1 (distribuir) to distribute 2 (AmL) ‹*deuda*› to settle, pay 3 (Chi) (contribuir) to contribute

erógeno -na *adj* erogenous

erosión *f* erosion

erosionar [A1] *vt* to erode

■ **erosionarse** *v pron* to be/become eroded

erosivo -va *adj* erosive

erótico -ca *adj* erotic

erotismo *m* eroticism

erotizar [A4] *vt* to eroticize

errabundo -da *adj* ▸ **errante** (A)

erradicación *f* (frml) eradication (frml)

erradicar [A2] *vt* (frml) to eradicate

errado -da *adj*

A (desacertado): **cinco tiros ~s** five misses; **un golpe ~** a mishit; **terminó con un remate ~ de Sánchez** it ended with Sánchez missing his shot

B (esp AmL) 1 [ESTAR] ‹*persona*› mistaken, wrong; **están muy ~s en estos cálculos** they're way off the mark *o* miles out with these calculations (colloq) 2 [SER] ‹*decisión*› wrong; ‹*política*› misguided

errante *adj* 1 ‹*persona*› wandering (*before n*), roaming (*before n*); ‹*pueblo*› wandering (*before n*) 2 ‹*mirada*› faraway, distant; **una vida ~** a nomadic existence

errar [A26] *vt* ‹*tiro/golpe*› to miss; **erró su vocación** she chose the wrong vocation/career

■ **errar** *vi*

A (fallar): **(le) erré otra vez** missed again! (colloq), I've missed again; **erró en su decisión** he made the wrong decision; **le erraste feo** (RPl fam) you were way out *o* off the mark (colloq); ~ ***es humano*** to err is human

B (liter) «*persona*» (vagar) to wander, roam; «*mirada/imaginación*» to wander

errata *f* (error) mistake, error; (error de imprenta) misprint, printer's error; (error de mecanografía) typing error

errático -ca *adj* erratic

erre *f*: *name of the letter* **r**

erróneo -nea *adj* (frml) ‹*decisión/afirmación*› wrong, erroneous (frml); **debido a un cálculo ~** owing to a miscalculation

error *m* mistake; **cometer un ~** to make a mistake *o* an error; **¡craso ~!** (that was a) big *o* bad mistake!; **estás en**

e

un ∼ you're wrong *o* mistaken; **¿quién lo va a sacar de su ∼?** who's going to put him right?; **∼ de ortografía** spelling mistake; **∼ de cálculo** miscalculation; **salvo ∼ u omisión** (fr hecha) errors and omissions excepted; **por ∼** by mistake, in error (frml)

(Compuesto) **error de imprenta** misprint, printer's error

Ertzaintza *f* Basque police force

> **Ertzaintza**
>
> The Basque autonomous police force. Its members, called *ertzainas*, wear a uniform of red sweaters and berets, and white jackets. Despite the *Ertzaintza*'s wide range of responsibilities, the **Guardia Civil** and *Policía Nacional* still operate in the Basque Country

e

eructar [A1] *vi* to belch, burp (colloq)

eructo *m* belch, burp (colloq)

erudición *f* erudition (frml), learning

erudito[1] **-ta** *adj* ‹*lenguaje/obra*› erudite; ‹*persona*› learned, knowledgeable; **∼ EN algo** learned IN sth, knowledgeable ABOUT sth

erudito[2] **-ta** *m,f* scholar; **los ∼s en la materia** experts in the subject

erupción *f* 1 (de volcán) eruption; **el volcán entró en** *or* **hizo ∼** the volcano erupted 2 (en la piel) rash, eruption (frml)

es *see* **ser**

esbeltez *f* slenderness

esbelto -ta *adj* slender

esbirro *m* (secuaz) henchman; (Hist) bailiff, constable

esbozar [A4] *vt* 1 ‹*figura*› to sketch 2 ‹*idea/tema*› to outline 3 ‹*sonrisa*›: **esbozó una sonrisa** she gave a hint of a smile

esbozo *m* 1 (Art) sketch 2 (de proyecto) outline, rough draft 3 (de sonrisa) hint

escabechar [A1] *vt* ‹*pescado*› to pickle, souse

escabeche *m* pickling brine (*made with oil, vinegar, peppercorns and bay leaves*)

escabechina *f* 1 (matanza) massacre 2 (Esp arg) (en examen): **el profesor hizo una ∼** the teacher failed half the class (*o* the whole class *etc*)

escabel *m* footstool

escabrosidad *f*

A (del terreno) ruggedness, roughness

B (de un asunto, tema) awkward nature, thorny nature

escabroso -sa *adj*

A ‹*terreno*› rugged, rough

B ‹*asunto/problema/tema*› thorny, tricky; ‹*escena/relato*› shocking

escabullirse [I9] *v pron* (escaparse) to escape; **logró ∼ entre la multitud** he managed to slip away *o* slip off into the crowd; **se nos escabulló** he gave us the slip (colloq); **no puedes escabullirte de tus responsabilidades** you can't get away from your responsibilities; **trató de ∼ entre la gente** she tried to slip through the crowd

escacharrarse [A1] *v pron* (Esp fam) to break down

escafandra *f* diving suit

escaguearse [A1] *v pron* (Esp fam) 1 (de lugar) to slope off (colloq); **∼se de clase** to play hooky (esp AmE colloq), to skive off (school) (BrE colloq) 2 (de obligación) **∼ DE algo** to get out OF sth

escala *f*

A (para mediciones) scale

(Compuestos)

- **escala centígrada** *or* **Celsius/Fahrenheit** centigrade *o* Celsius/Fahrenheit scale
- **escala de valores** set of values
- **escala móvil** sliding scale
- **escala salarial** salary *o* wage scale

B (Mús) scale

C (escalafón): **la ∼ social** the social scale

D 1 (de mapa, plano) scale; **hecho a ∼** done to scale; **una reproducción a ∼ natural** a life-size *o* life-sized reproduction 2 (de fenómeno, problema) scale; **a ∼ nacional** on a nationwide *o* national scale; **a** *or* **en gran ∼** on a large scale

E (Aviac, Náut) stopover; **hicimos ∼ en Roma** we stopped over in Rome

(Compuesto) **escala técnica** refueling* stop

F (escalera) ladder

escalada *f*

A (Dep) (de montaña) climb, ascent

(Compuesto) **escalada en roca/libre** rock/free climbing

B (aumento, subida): **su ∼ hacia el poder** his rise to power; **una ∼ de** *or* **en la violencia** an escalation of violence; **la ∼ de los precios** the increase *o* escalation in prices

escalador -dora *m,f* (de montañas) mountaineer, climber; (de rocas) rock-climber; (en ciclismo) climber, mountain rider

escalafón *m*: **los puestos más altos del ∼** the highest posts on the scale; **subir un puesto en el ∼** to go up one step on the promotion ladder

escalar [A1] *vt*

A ‹*montaña/pared*› to climb, scale; (en jerarquía, clasificación) to climb (up)

B (Inf) (reducir) to scale down; (aumentar) to scale up

■ **escalar** *vi*

A (Dep) to climb, go climbing

B (Náut): **∼ en un puerto** to put in at a port

escaldado -da *adj* 1 (quemado) scalded 2 (por la orina): **tiene las nalgas escaldadas** she has diaper (AmE) *o* (BrE) nappy rash 3 (escarmentado): **salió ∼ de la experiencia** he learned his lesson

escaldar [A1] *vt* 1 ‹*acelgas/tomates*› to blanch, scald 2 ‹*manos/persona*› to scald

■ **escaldarse** *v pron* 1 (con agua, vapor) to scald oneself 2 ‹‹*bebé*›› to get diaper (AmE) *o* (BrE) nappy rash

escaleno *adj* scalene

escalera *f*

A (de edificio) stairs (*pl*), staircase; **bajó las ∼s** he came downstairs *o* down the stairs; **subí las ∼s corriendo** I ran up the stairs; **el hueco de la ∼** the stairwell; **le ayudé a empapelar la ∼** I helped him to paper the stairway

(Compuestos)

- **escalera (de) caracol** *or* **espiral** spiral staircase
- **escalera de incendios** fire escape
- **escalera mecánica** escalator

B (portátil) *tb* **∼ de mano** ladder; (de tijera) stepladder

C (en naipes) run; (juego de tablero) snakes and ladders

(Compuesto) **escalera real** royal flush

escalerilla *f* (de avión) steps (*pl*); (de barco) gangway

escalfar [A1] *vt* to poach

escaliche *m* (AmC fam) pig latin (colloq)

escalinata *f* staircase, steps (*pl*)

escalofriante *adj* ‹*crimen/escena*› horrifying; ‹*cifra*› staggering, incredible

escalofrío *m* shiver; **me da** *or* **produce ∼s** it makes me shiver *o* shudder; **tiene ∼s** she's shivering

escalón *m* (peldaño) step; (travesaño) rung; (en carrera): **sigue subiendo escalones** he continues to climb higher up the ladder

escalonadamente *adv* step by step, in a series of steps

escalonado -da *adj* ‹*vacaciones*› staggered; ‹*pelo*› layered

escalonar [A1] *vt* ‹*pagos/vacaciones*› to stagger; ‹*terreno*› to terrace

escalope *m* escalope

escalpelo *m* scalpel

escama *f* 1 (Zool) scale 2 (en la piel) flake

escamar [A1] *vt*

A ‹*pescado*› to remove the scales from

B (producir desconfianza) to make … suspicious

■ **escamarse** *v pron* to become suspicious *o* wary

escamoso -sa *adj*

A 1 (Zool) scaly 2 ‹*piel*› flaky

B (Col fam) (susceptible) touchy; (enojado) angry, mad (esp AmE colloq)

escamotear [A1] *vt* 1 (ocultar) ‹*naipe*› to palm; ‹*informe*› to keep … secret; **la navaja que había escamoteado** the knife he had slipped through *o* had kept hidden 2 (no dar) (+ *me/te/le etc*): **le escamotean al espectador algo**

que ha pagado they are cheating the audience out of something they have paid for; **nos escamoteaban la información** they were keeping the information (secret) from us

escamoteo *m* [1] (destreza) sleight of hand; (de naipe) palming [2] (ocultación) concealment; (acción de quitar) removal

escampar [A1] *v impers* to stop raining, to clear up

■ **escampar** *vi* (Col) to shelter

escanciador *m* (de vino) wine waiter; (Hist) cupbearer; (de sidra) *person who pours cider*

escanciar [A1] *vt* (frml) ‹*vino*› to serve; ‹*sidra*› to pour (*from a height*)

escandalizante *adj* shocking, scandalous

escandalizar [A4] *vt* to shock; **vas a ~ a tus padres** your parents will be shocked

■ **escandalizar** *vi* [1] (causar escándalo) to shock [2] (fam) (armar jaleo) to make a row *o* racket (colloq)

■ **escandalizarse** *v pron* to be shocked

escándalo *m*

A (hecho, asunto chocante) scandal; **un ~ financiero** a financial scandal; **¡qué ~! ¡qué manera de vestir!** what a shocking *o* an outrageous way to dress!

(Compuesto) **escándalo público** public indecency

B (alboroto, jaleo): **no armen** *or* **hagan tanto ~** don't make such a racket *o* row (colloq); **cuando lo sepa va a armar un ~** when she finds out she'll kick up a fuss *o* she'll create a scene (colloq); **nada de ~s dentro del local** we don't want any trouble in here

escandalosamente *adv* [1] ‹*comportarse*› in a shocking way, outrageously; ‹*vestir*› outrageously [2] (ruidosamente) ‹*reírse*› loudly; ‹*gritar*› noisily, loudly

escandaloso -sa *adj* [1] ‹*conducta*› shocking, scandalous; ‹*ropa*› outrageous; ‹*película*› shocking; ‹*vida*› scandalous; ‹*color*› loud [2] (ruidoso) ‹*persona/griterío*› noisy; ‹*risa*› loud, uproarious

Escandinavia *f* Scandinavia

escandinavo -va *adj/m,f* Scandinavian

escáner *m* (*pl* **-ners**) scanner

escaño *m* (Esp) (Pol) (cargo, asiento) seat; (banco) bench

escapada *f*

A (huida) breakout, escape

B (en ciclismo) breakaway

C (fam) (salida rápida): **hicimos una ~ a la sierra** we escaped *o* got away to the mountains (colloq); **me voy a hacer una ~ hasta el banco** I'm just going to run out to the bank

D (de un peligro) escape

escapar [A1] *vi*

A [1] (huir) to escape; **~ DE algo** ‹*de cárcel/rutina/peligro*› to escape FROM sth; **necesito ~ de todo esto** I need to get away from all this; **una forma de ~ de la realidad** a way of escaping from reality [2] (librarse) **~ DE algo** ‹*de castigo/muerte*› to escape sth [3] **~ A algo** ‹*a influencia/castigo*› to escape sth

B **dejar escapar** ‹*carcajada/suspiro*› to let out, give; ‹*oportunidad*› to pass up; ‹*persona/animal*› to let … get away

■ **escaparse** *v pron*

A [1] (huir) «*prisionero*» to escape; «*animal/niño*» to run away; **siempre te escapas cuando hay trabajo** you always disappear *o* vanish when there's work to be done; **~se DE algo** ‹*de cárcel/jaula*› to escape FROM sth; **~se de casa** to run away from home; (+ *me/te/le etc*) **se me escapó** he got away from me; **no te me escapes** don't run away (from me); **~se DE algn** ‹*de policía/perseguidor*› to escape (FROM) sb [2] (librarse) **~se DE algo** ‹*de situación/castigo*› to escape sth; **de ésta sí que no te escapas** you're not getting out of this one (colloq)

B (+ *me/te/le etc*) [1] (involuntariamente): **se le escapó un grito** he cried out, he let out a cry; **se le escapó un eructo** he burped; **¡que no se te vaya a ~ delante de ella!** don't let it slip out in front of her! [2] (pasar inadvertido): **no se le escapa nada** he doesn't miss anything; **se me escapó ese detalle** that detail escaped my notice [3] (en tejido): **se me ~on dos puntos** I dropped two stitches

C «*gas/aire/agua*» to leak

escaparate *m*

A (esp Esp) (de tienda) shop window; **salir a ver ~s** to go window-shopping

B (Col) (vitrina) display cabinet; (aparador) sideboard

C (Ven) (armario) wardrobe

escaparatista *mf* (esp Esp) window dresser

escapatoria *f* (salida, solución) way out

escape *m*

A (fuga) escape; ***salir/ir a ~*** (Esp fam) to rush out/off

B (de gas, fluido) leak

C (Auto) exhaust

D (Chi) (en cine, teatro) emergency exit

escapero -ra *m,f* (Chi) sneak thief

escapismo *m* escapism

escapista *adj/m,f* escapist

escápula *f* scapula

escapulario *m* scapular

escaque *m* square

escarabajo *m* beetle

escaramujo *m* [1] (rosal) wild rose; (fruto) rosehip, hip [2] (Zool) goose barnacle

escaramuza *f* (Mil) skirmish; (Dep) scrimmage

escarapela *f* rosette

escarapelarse *v pron* (fam) (Per) (erizarse): **se me escarapela todo el cuerpo** it makes my hair stand on end

escarbadientes *m* (*pl* ~) toothpick

escarbar [A1] *vi* [1] (en la tierra — haciendo un hoyo) to dig; (— superficialmente) to scrabble *o* scratch around [2] (buscando algo) **~ EN algo** ‹*en cajón/armario*› to rummage (about *o* around) IN sth; **lo encontré escarbando en mi bolso** I caught him rummaging in my handbag; **perros escarbando en la basura** dogs rummaging through the garbage [3] (fisgar) **~ EN algo** ‹*en asunto*› to pry INTO sth

■ **escarbar** *vt*: **~ la tierra** (hacer un hoyo) to dig a hole; (superficialmente) to scratch around in the soil

■ **escarbarse** *v pron* (*refl*) ‹*nariz/dientes*› to pick

escarceos *mpl* [1] (del caballo) prancing [2] (actividad) dabbling; **tener ~s con el periodismo/la política** to dabble in journalism/politics

(Compuesto) **escarceos amorosos** *mpl* romantic adventures (*pl*)

escarcha *f* frost

escarchado -da *adj* [1] ‹*fruta*› crystallized [2] ‹*jardín*› frosty, frost-covered

escarchar [A1] *vt* to crystallize

escarda *f* hoe

escardar [A1] *vt* to hoe

escarlata *adj inv/m* scarlet

escarlatina *f* scarlet fever, scarlatina

escarmentado -da *adj*: **está ~** he's learned his lesson

escarmentar [A5] *vi* to learn one's lesson; **¡para que escarmientes!** that'll teach you!; **no escarmienta** she never learns; ***nadie escarmienta en cabeza ajena*** one learns from one's own mistakes

■ **escarmentar** *vt* to teach … a lesson

escarmiento *m* lesson; **esto te servirá de ~** let this be a lesson to you; **habrá que darle un buen ~** he needs to be taught a good lesson

escarnecer [E3] *vt* (liter) to mock, ridicule

escarnio *m* (liter) ridicule, derision

escarola *f* endive, escarole

escarpa *f* [1] (cuesta) escarpment, scarp [2] (Mil) scarp

escarpado -da *adj* ‹*montaña/terreno*› precipitous; ‹*pared/acantilado*› sheer, steep

escarpia *f* hook

escarpín *m* (AmL) (calcetín — de bebé) bootee; (— de adulto) bed sock

escasear [A1] *vi*: **empiezan a ~ los alimentos** food is running short; **va a ~ el café** there's going to be a coffee shortage; **escasea el agua** water is in short supply

escasez *f* shortage; **una época de ~** a time of shortages; **por ~ de medios** owing to a lack of resources; **hubo ~ de agua** there was a water shortage

escaso -sa *adj* [1] ‹*recursos económicos*› limited, scant; ‹*posibilidades*› slim, slender; ‹*visibilidad*› poor; ‹*conocimientos/experiencia*› limited; **la comida resultó escasa** there wasn't enough food; **de escasa calidad** of mediocre quality [2] (en expresiones de medida, peso): **pesa un kilo ~** it

e

weighs barely *o* scarcely a kilo; **a ~s tres días/dos meses** (AmL) barely three days/two months away ③ [ESTAR] (falto) ~ **DE algo** ‹*de dinero/tiempo*› short OF sth; **andamos ~s de personal** we're short-staffed

escatimar [A1] *vt* ‹*comida/tela*› to skimp on, be sparing with; **no ~on esfuerzos** they spared no effort

escayola *f* (Esp) (material) plaster; (Med) plaster cast; **me quitaron la ~** I had my cast *o* (BrE) my plaster taken off

escayolar [A1] *vt* (Esp) to put ... in a (plaster) cast, to put ... in plaster (BrE); **tenía la pierna escayolada** his leg was in a cast

escena *f*
A (Cin, Teatr) ① (de obra) scene; **la ~ se desarrolla en Berlín** the action takes place in Berlin ② (*sin art*) (escenario): **no había nadie en ~** there was no one on stage; **poner en ~** to stage; **entrar a** *or* **en ~** to come/go on stage ③ (actividad, profesión): **el mundo de la ~** the theater; **decidió volver a la ~** she decided to return to the stage
(Compuesto) **escena retrospectiva** flashback
B (en la vida real) scene; **conmovedoras ~s** moving scenes; **la ~ del accidente/crimen** (period) the scene of the accident/crime; **la ~ política** the political scene; **no me hagas una ~** there's no need to make a scene

escenario *m* ① (Teatr) stage; **salir al ~** to go on stage ② (period) (de suceso) scene; **llegaron al ~ de los hechos** they arrived on the scene

escénico -ca *adj* stage (*before n*)

escenificación *f* staging

escenificar [A2] *vt* ① (representar) ‹*comedia/pieza*› to stage ② (adaptar) ‹*biografía*› to dramatize, adapt ... for the stage

escenografía *f* (decorado) scenery; (arte) scenography, set design

escenógrafo -fa *m,f* scenographer, set designer

escepticismo *m* skepticism*

escéptico[1] **-ca** *adj* skeptical*

escéptico[2] **-ca** *m,f* skeptic*

escindirse [I1] *v pron* ① (dividirse) to split; ~ **EN algo** to split INTO sth ② (separarse) ~ **DE algo** to break away FROM sth; **el grupo pro-europeo se escindió del partido** the pro-European group broke away from the party

escisión *f* split

esclarecedor -dora *adj* illuminating, enlightening

esclarecer [E3] *vt* ‹*situación/hechos*› to clarify, elucidate (frml); ‹*crimen/misterio*› to clear up

esclarecimiento *m* (de situación) clarification

esclava *f* (de cadena) identity bracelet; (rígida) bangle; *ver tb* **esclavo**

esclavina *f* short cape

esclavitud *f* slavery

esclavizar [A4] *vt* ① (Hist) to enslave ② (absorber): **no te dejes ~ por tus hijos** don't let your children rule your life; **está esclavizado por el trabajo** he's a slave to his work

esclavo -va *m,f* slave; **es un ~ del trabajo** he is a slave to his work

esclerosis *f* sclerosis
(Compuesto) **esclerosis múltiple** multiple sclerosis

esclusa *f* (de canal) lock; (de presa) floodgate, sluicegate

escoba *f*
A (para barrer) broom; (de bruja) broomstick; **pasar la ~ por la habitación** to sweep the room; ***no vender una ~*** to get nowhere, to achieve nothing; ~ ***nueva barre bien*** (CS) a new broom sweeps clean
B (en naipes) *tb* ~ **de quince** *card game in which players try to combine cards to total 15 points*
C (Bot) broom

escobazo *m*: **le dio un ~** she hit him with the broom; ***echar a algn a ~s*** (fam) to kick *o* boot sb out (colloq)

escobilla *f*
A (de motor) brush; (del limpiaparabrisas) wiper-blade, blade
B ① (del inodoro) toilet brush ② (Andes) (para los dientes) toothbrush

escobillón *m* (Med, Arm) swab

escocedura *f* irritation; (de bebé) diaper rash (AmE), nappy rash (BrE)

escocer [E10] *vi* ① ‹‹*herida/ojos*›› to sting, smart ② (moralmente) to irritate, irk

escocés[1] **-cesa** *adj* ① ‹*ciudad/persona*› Scottish; ‹*dialecto*› Scots ② ‹*whisky*› Scotch; ‹*tela/manta*› tartan

escocés[2] **-cesa** (*m*) Scotsman, Scot; (*f*) Scotswoman, Scot

Escocia *f* Scotland

escocido -da *adj* ‹*cuello/axila*› sore, chafed; **tiene las nalgas escocidas** he has diaper rash (AmE) *o* (BrE) nappy rash

escofina *f* (Tec) rasp, file; (para los pies) callus file

escoger [E6] *vt* to choose; **escoge el libro que quieras** pick *o* choose whichever book you want; **tener mucho (de) donde ~** to be spoilt for choice; **no hay mucho (de) donde ~** there isn't a great deal of choice, there isn't much to choose from

escogido -da *adj* ① (selecto) ‹*mercancía*› choice; ‹*clientela*› select ② (Méx fam) (manoseado) picked over

escolar[1] *adj* school (*before n*)

escolar[2] (*m*) schoolboy, schoolchild; (*f*) schoolgirl, schoolchild

escolaridad *f* education, schooling

escolarización *f* education, schooling

escolarizar [A4] *vt* to educate, provide schooling for; **eran niños sin ~** there were children without any (formal) education *o* schooling

escolástica *f*, **escolasticismo** *m* scholasticism

escolástico -ca *adj* ① (Fil) scholastic ② ‹*lenguaje*› scholarly

escoleta *f* (Méx) ① (banda) band (*of amateur musicians*) ② (ensayo) rehearsal ③ (para aprender a bailar) dance practice *o* rehearsal

escollar [A1] *vi* to hit a reef

escollera *f* breakwater

escollo *m* (Náut) reef; (dificultad) obstacle, hurdle

escolopendra *f* centipede

escolta *mf*
A (persona) escort; (en baloncesto) guard
B **escolta** *f* (grupo) escort

escoltar [A1] *vt* (para proteger) to escort; (para vigilar) to guard, escort; (en ceremonia) to escort, accompany

escombrera *f* dump, tip (BrE)

escombros *mpl* rubble

esconder [E1] *vt* to hide, conceal (frml)
■ **esconderse** *v pron*
A (*refl*) ‹‹*persona*›› to hide; **~se DE algn** to hide FROM sb; **el sol se escondió tras las nubes** the sun disappeared behind the clouds
B (estar oculto) to hide, lie hidden

escondidas *fpl*
A (AmL) (Jueg): **jugar a las ~** to play hide-and-seek
B **a escondidas** in secret, secretly; **a ~ DE algn**: **fumaba a ~ de sus padres** she smoked behind her parents' backs; **lo hice a ~ de María para darle una sorpresa** I kept it a secret from María so that it would be a surprise for her

escondido -da *adj* ① (oculto) hidden; **el club está muy ~** the club is really out of the way ② (lejano) remote; **en un ~ rincón del planeta** in a remote corner of the planet

escondite *m* ① (para personas) hideout; (para cosas) hiding place ② (Jueg): **jugar al ~** to play hide-and-seek

escondrijo *m* hidden place, recess (liter)

escoñar [A1] *vt* (Esp arg) ‹*aparato*› to screw up (AmE sl), bugger up (BrE sl)
■ **escoñarse** *v pron* (Esp arg) ① (*refl*) (dañarse) to hurt oneself; **me escoñé un brazo** I screwed my arm up (AmE sl), I did my arm in (BrE colloq) ② ‹‹*aparato*›› to bust (colloq)

escopeta *f* shotgun
(Compuestos)
- **escopeta de aire comprimido** air gun *o* rifle
- **escopeta de dos cañones** double-barreled* shotgun
- **escopeta recortada** *or* **de cañones recortados** sawed-off shotgun (AmE), sawn-off shotgun (BrE)

escopetado -da *adj* (Esp fam): **salió ~** he shot *o* dashed off/out, he was off like a shot (colloq)

escoplo *m* chisel

escora *f* (línea) load line; (puntal) prop; (inclinación) heel

escorar [A1] *vi* 1 «*barco*» to heel (over) 2 «*político/partido*» (period) to lean 3 «*marea*» to reach its lowest point *o* ebb

■ **escorar** *vt* ‹*barco*› (apuntalar) to shore (up); (al navegar) to heel … over

escorbuto *m* scurvy

escoria *f* (de fundición) slag; **la ~ de la sociedad** the dregs of society

Escorpio[1] *m* (signo) Scorpio; **es (de) ~** he's a Scorpio

Escorpio[2], **escorpio** *mf* (*pl* ~ *or* **-pios**) (persona) Scorpio

escorpión *m* scorpion

escorrentía *f* run-off (rain water)

escorzar [A4] *vt* to foreshorten

escorzo *m* foreshortening

escotado -da *adj* 1 ‹*blusa/vestido*› low-cut, décolleté (frml); **~ por detrás** cut low at the back 2 (RPl) ‹*zapato*› strapless

escotar [A1] *vt*: **¿me lo escota un poquito más?** can you cut the neckline a little lower?

escote *m* 1 (Indum) neck, neckline; (profundo) low-cut neck *o* neckline; **con un gran ~ en la espalda** cut very low at the back *o* with a very low back; **un ~ indecente** an indecently low-cut dress (*o* gown *etc*) 2 (parte del cuerpo): **un collar adornaba su ~** a necklace adorned her neck/bosom; ***pagar a ~*** (Esp fam) to go Dutch

Compuestos

- **escote barco** *or* **bote** bateau *o* boat neck
- **escote en pico** *or* **en V** V neck
- **escote redondo** round neck; (en suéters) crew neck

escotilla *f* hatch, hatchway

escotillón *m* (Teatr) trapdoor

escozor *m* 1 (Med) stinging, burning sensation 2 (resentimiento, amargura) bitterness

escriba *m* scribe

escribanía *f*

A (mueble) escritoire, writing desk; (juego de escritorio) inkstand

B (RPl) (Der) (oficina) notary's office; (profesión): **ejerce la ~** he is a practicing notary (public)

escribano -na *m,f* 1 (Hist) (amanuense) scribe 2 (RPl) (notario) notary (public)

escribiente *mf* clerk

escribir [I34] *vt*

A 1 (anotar) to write; **escríbelo antes de que se te olvide** write it down before you forget it; **escríbelo con lápiz** write it in pencil 2 (ser autor de) ‹*libro/canción/carta*› to write

B (*pas*) (deletrear): **no sé cómo se escribe** I don't know how you spell it; **se escribe sin acento** it's written without an accent

■ **escribir** *vi* to write; **~ a máquina** to type; **nunca le escribe** she never writes him (AmE) *o* (BrE) writes to him

■ **escribirse** *v pron* (*recípr*): **nos escribimos** we write to each other; **se escribe con un peruano** she has a Peruvian penfriend *o* penpal

escrito[1] **-ta** *adj* ‹*examen*› written; **por ~** in writing; ***estar ~***: **estaba ~ que iba a acabar mal** he was destined to come to a bad end; ***tener/llevar algo ~ en la cara*** to have sth written all over one's face

escrito[2] *m* 1 (documento) document 2 **escritos** *mpl* (obras) writings (*pl*), works (*pl*)

escritor -tora *m,f* writer, author

escritorio *m* 1 (mueble) desk 2 (AmL) (oficina, despacho) office; (en casa particular) study

Compuesto **escritorio público** (en Méx) *office or stall offering letter writing, form-filling or typing services*

escritura *f*

A (sistema de signos) writing; (letra) writing, handwriting; (obra escrita) writings (*pl*), works (*pl*)

B (Der) (documento) deed; **la ~ de la casa** the deeds to *o* of the house

Compuesto **escritura privada/pública** private/public instrument *o* deed

escriturar [A1] *vt* to register

escroto *m* scrotum

escrúpulo *m* scruple; **no tuvo ningún ~ en …** he had no scruples *o* qualms whatsoever about …

escrupulosamente *adv* 1 (honestamente) honestly, scrupulously 2 (con meticulosidad) meticulously

escrupulosidad *f* meticulousness, attention to detail

escrupuloso -sa *adj* 1 (honrado) honest, scrupulous 2 (meticuloso) meticulous 3 (Esp) (aprensivo) fastidious

escrutador[1] **-dora** *adj* penetrating, piercing

escrutador[2] **-dora** *m,f* scrutineer, ≈ returning officer (*in UK*)

escrutar [A1] *vt*

A (liter) (mirar) ‹*horizonte*› to scan; ‹*persona*› to scrutinize, examine

B ‹*votos*› to count

escrutinio *m* 1 (Pol) count; **efectuar un ~ de los votos** to count the votes; **los resultados del ~** the results of the ballot 2 (inspección) scrutiny

escuadra *f*

A 1 (instrumento — triangular) set square; (— de carpintero) square; ***a*** *or* ***en ~*** square; ***fuera de ~*** out of square, out of true 2 (refuerzo) bracket

B (en el ejército) squad; (en la marina) squadron

escuadrar [A1] *vt* to square

escuadrilla *f* (Náut) squadron; (Aviac) flight

escuadrón *m* 1 (Aviac) squadron 2 (de caballería) squadron; (más pequeño) troop

Compuesto **escuadrón de la muerte** death squad

escuálido -da *adj* ‹*persona/animal*› skinny, scrawny

escualo *m* dogfish

escucha *f*

A (acción): **los servicios de ~ de la marina** the navy's monitoring services; **permanezcan a la ~** stay tuned

Compuesto **escucha telefónica** wire tap (AmE), phone tap (BrE)

B **escucha** *mf* 1 (Mil) scout 2 (AmL) (oyente) listener

escuchar [A1] *vt* 1 (prestar atención) ‹*música*› to listen to; **no te va a ~** she won't listen to you 2 (esp AmL) (oír) to hear

■ **escuchar** *vi* to listen

■ **escucharse** *v pron* (*refl*): **le encanta ~se** she loves the sound of her own voice

escudar [A1] *vt* to shield

■ **escudarse** *v pron* **~se EN algo**: **quiso ~se en su inmunidad diplomática** he tried to hide behind his diplomatic immunity; **se escuda en sus compromisos familiares** he uses his family commitments as an excuse

escudería *f* motor-racing team

escudilla *f* bowl

escudo *m*

A (Hist, Mil) shield

Compuesto **escudo antidisturbios** riot shield

B (emblema) *tb* **~ de armas** coat of arms

C (en la solapa, etc) badge

D (Fin) escudo

escudriñar [A1] *vt* 1 (liter) (mirar intensamente) ‹*horizonte*› to scan 2 (examinar) ‹*persona*› to scrutinize, examine; ‹*casa/habitación*› to search … thoroughly

escuela *f*

A 1 (institución) school; **la ~ de la vida** the school *o* university of life 2 (edificio) school 3 (facultad) faculty, school; **E~ de Medicina** Medical Faculty *o* School 4 (*como adj inv*): **granja ~** college farm; **hotel ~** hotel school, training hotel

Compuestos

- **Escuela de Bellas Artes** art school, art college
- **escuela de conductores** *or* **choferes** (AmL) driving school
- **escuela de párvulos** infant school
- **escuela primaria** *or* **de primera enseñanza** primary school
- **escuela de verano/nocturna** summer/night school
- **escuela diferencial** (RPl) school for children with special needs
- **escuela militar/naval** military/naval academy
- **escuela normal** teachers' college (AmE), teacher training college (BrE)

- **Escuela Oficial de Idiomas** *state-run language school*
- **escuela pública** public (AmE) *o* (BrE) state school
- **escuela técnica** *or* **vocacional** technical college

B (formación) coaching, training; **le falta ~** he needs more coaching

C (de pensamiento, doctrinas) school; **ha creado ~** his theories (*o* ideas *etc*) have many followers; **es de la vieja ~** she's one of the old school

escuerzo *m*
A (Zool) toad
B (persona delgada) (fam): **es un ~** she's all skin and bone(s) (colloq)

escueto -ta *adj* ‹*explicación*› succinct; ‹*lenguaje/estilo*› concise, plain; **fue muy ~** he was very succinct

escuincle -cla *m,f* (Méx fam) kid (colloq)

esculcar [A2] *vt* (AmC, Col, Méx, Ven) ‹*cajones/papeles*› to go through; ‹*persona/casa*› to search

esculpir [I1] *vt* ‹*estatua/busto*› to sculpt, sculpture; ‹*inscripción*› to engrave, carve
■ **esculpir** *vi* to sculpt, sculpture

esculque *m* (Méx) search

escultor -tora *m,f* sculptor

escultórico -ca *adj* sculptural; **grupo ~** group of sculptures; **una exposición escultórica** an exhibition of sculpture; **su obra escultórica** his sculpture(s)

escultura *f* sculpture; **~ en madera** wood carving

escultural *adj* statuesque

escupida *f* (RPl) gob (of spit) (colloq); ***como ~*** (RPl fam) like a shot (colloq); **salió como ~** he shot *o* dashed out, he came/went shooting out; ***ser la ~ de su padre/madre*** (Arg fam) to be the spitting image of one's father/mother

escupidera *f* 1 (para escupir) spittoon 2 (AmL euf) (orinal) chamber pot

escupir [I1] *vi* to spit; **⊗ prohibido escupir** no spitting; **~le a algn** to spit at sb; **le escupió en la cara** he spat in her face
■ **escupir** *vt* 1 ‹*comida*› to spit out; ‹*sangre*› to spit, cough up 2 ‹*llamas/lava*› to belch out

escupitajo *m* gob (of spit) (colloq); **hay un ~ en el suelo** someone has spat *o* (colloq) gobbed on the floor

escupo *m* (Chi, Ven) ► **escupida**

escurreplatos *m* (*pl* ~) (mueble) *cupboard with built-in plate rack*; (rejilla) plate rack

escurridera *f* ► **escurreplatos**

escurridero *m* (lugar) drainboard (AmE), draining board (BrE); (rejilla) plate rack

escurridizo -za *adj* ‹*piel/jabón*› slippery; ‹*persona/respuesta*› evasive; ‹*idea/concepto*› elusive

escurrido -da *adj* (delgado): **es muy escurrida de caderas** she has very narrow hips; **escurrida de pecho** flat-chested

escurridor *m*, **escurridora** *f* 1 ► **escurreplatos** 2 (colador) colander

escurrir [I1] *vt* ‹*ropa*› to wring out, wring; ‹*verduras/pasta*› to strain, drain; ‹*líquido/vaso*› to drain
■ **escurrir** *vi* to drain; **deja que los platos escurran** leave the plates to drain; **dejé ~ la camisa** I left the shirt to drip-dry
■ **escurrirse** *v pron*
A 1 «*líquido*»: **cuelga la camisa para que se escurra el agua** hang the shirt out to drip-dry; **déjalas en una servilleta de papel para que se escurra el aceite** leave them to drain on some kitchen paper 2 «*verduras/vajilla*» to drain
B 1 (fam) (escaparse, escabullirse) to slip away; **~se DE algo** to wriggle *o* get out OF sth 2 (resbalarse, deslizarse) to slip; **se le escurrió de (entre) las manos** it slipped through her fingers

escúter *m* scooter

escutismo *m* scouting movement, scouting

esdrújula *f* word with the stress on the antepenultimate syllable

esdrújulo -la *adj* stressed on the antepenultimate syllable

ese[1] *f*: *name of the letter* **s**; ***hacer ~s*** to zigzag (along)

ese[2], **esa** *adj dem* (*pl* **esos, esas**) that; (*pl*) those; **¿quién es el gordo ~?** (fam) who's that fat guy?; **el coche ~ que está allí** that car over there

ése, **ésa** *pron dem* (*pl* **ésos, ésas**) [*According to the Real Academia Española the written accent may be omitted when there is no risk of confusion with the adjective*] 1 that one; (*pl*) those; **~ es el tuyo** that (one) is yours; **~ es el que me gusta** that's the one I like; [*usually indicates disapproval when used to refer to a person*] **ésa no sabe lo que dice** (fam) she doesn't know what she's talking about 2 **ésa** (Corresp) (frml) *the city to which the letter is addressed*; **reside en ésa** he resides in Seville (*o* Lima *etc*) 3 **ésas** (fam) (esas cosas, esos asuntos): **¡conque ésas tenemos!** so *that's* it!; **¿todavía estás en ésas?** are you still at it?; **¡no me vengas con ésas!** don't give me that! (colloq)

esencia *f*
A (fondo, base) essence; **en ~** essentially, in essence
B (Coc, Quím, Fil) essence
(Compuesto) **esencia de café/vainilla** coffee/vanilla essence

esencial *adj*
A (fundamental) essential; **estábamos de acuerdo en lo ~** we agreed on the essentials *o* on the main points; **lo ~ es ...** the main *o* the most important thing is ...; **~ PARA algo** essential FOR *o* TO sth
B ‹*aceite*› essential

esfera *f*
A (Astron, Mat) sphere
(Compuestos)
- **esfera celeste** celestial sphere
- **esfera terrestre** globe

B (de reloj) face
C (ámbito) sphere; **en las altas ~s de la política** in the highest political circles; **~ de acción** sphere of action

esférico[1] **-ca** *adj* spherical

esférico[2] *m* (period) ball

esfero *m* (Col fam) ballpoint pen, biro® (BrE)

esferoide *m* spheroid

esfinge *f* sphinx

esfínter *m* sphincter

esforzado -da *adj* ‹*persona*› hard-working; ‹*trabajo*› hard; **gracias a la esforzada labor de los cooperantes** thanks to the hard work of the aid workers

esforzar [A11] *vt* ‹*voz/vista*› to strain
■ **esforzarse** *v pron*: **se esforzó mucho** he tried very hard, he put in a lot of effort; **tienes que ~te más** you'll have to work harder; **~se POR *o* EN + INF** to strive to + INF; **debemos ~nos por complacerlos** we must strive to please them

esfuerzo *m* effort; **hizo el ~ de ser amable** he made an effort *o* tried to be friendly; **me costó muchos ~s** it took a lot of effort

esfumar [A1] *vt* ‹*contorno*› to blur; ‹*color*› to tone down, soften
■ **esfumarse** *v pron* 1 «*ilusiones/sueños*» to evaporate; «*temores*» to melt away, be dispelled; **la sonrisa se esfumó de su rostro** the smile faded from his lips 2 (fam) «*persona/dinero*» to vanish, disappear

esgrima *f* fencing

esgrimidor -dora *m,f* fencer

esgrimir [I1] *vt* 1 ‹*arma/navaja*› to brandish, wield 2 (frml) ‹*argumento*› to put forward, use; ‹*documento/prueba*› to use

esgrimista *mf* fencer

esguince *m* sprain; **sufrió un ~ en el tobillo** he sprained his ankle

eskai® *m* imitation leather

eslabón *m*
A (de cadena, serie) link
(Compuestos)
- **eslabón giratorio** swivel
- **eslabón perdido** missing link

B (para sacar chispas) steel

eslabonar [A1] *vt* ‹*piezas*› to link (together); ‹*ideas/hechos*› to link, connect
■ **eslabonarse** *v pron* to link up

eslálom (*pl* **-loms**), **eslalon** *m* slalom

eslavo[1] **-va** *adj* Slavic, Slavonic

eslavo[2] **-va** *m,f* Slav

eslip *m* (*pl* **-lips**) underpants (*pl*), briefs (*pl*)

eslogan *m* (*pl* **-lóganes**) slogan
eslora *f* length
eslovaco¹ -ca *adj* Slovakian
eslovaco² -ca *m,f*
A (persona) Slovak
B **eslovaco** *m* (idioma) Slovak
Eslovaquia *f* Slovakia
Eslovenia *f* Slovenia
esloveno¹ -na *adj/m,f* Slovene
esloveno² *m* (idioma) Slovene
esmaltado *m* **1** (acción) enameling* **2** (capa — sobre metales) enamel; (— sobre cerámica) glaze
esmaltar [A1] *vt* ‹*metal*› to enamel; ‹*cerámica*› to glaze
esmalte *m*
A **1** (capa — sobre metales) enamel; (— sobre cerámica) glaze **2** (Odont) enamel
Compuesto **esmalte de** *or* **para uñas** nail polish *o* (BrE) varnish
B (Art) enamel
esmeradamente *adv* carefully, painstakingly; **objetos ~ restaurados** lovingly restored objects
esmerado -da *adj* ‹*persona*› conscientious, painstaking; ‹*presentación*› careful, painstaking; **presentó un trabajo ~** she submitted an excellent, beautifully presented piece of work
esmeralda *f* emerald
esmerarse [A1] *v pron* to go to a lot of trouble; **~ EN algo**: **se ha esmerado mucho en esta tarea** he has put a lot of effort into this assignment; **se esmera en hacerlo bien** she goes to great pains to do it properly
esmeril *m* emery
esmerilado -da *adj* frosted
esmerilar [A1] *vt* to grind
esmero *m* care; **puso mucho ~ en la presentación** he took enormous trouble over the presentation
esmirriado -da *adj* (fam) ‹*persona*› skinny (colloq), scrawny (colloq); ‹*animal*› scrawny
esmog *m* smog
esmoquin *m* (*pl* **-móquines**) tuxedo (AmE), dinner jacket (BrE)
esnifada *f* ▸ **esnife**
esnifar [A1] *vt* ‹*cocaína*› (arg) to snort (sl); ‹*pegamento*› to sniff (colloq)
esnife *m* (arg) (de cocaína) snort (sl); (de pegamento) sniff (colloq)
esnob¹ *adj* (*pl* **-nobs**) snobbish
esnob² *mf* (*pl* **-nobs**) snob
esnobismo *m* snobbery, snobbishness
eso *pron dem* **1** (*neutro*) that; **no digas ~** don't say that; **¡ah, no! ¡~ sí que no!** oh, no! definitely not!; **~ que te contaron** what they told you; **lo hiciste por él ¿no es ~?** you did it for him, didn't you? *o* isn't that right?; **¿qué es ~ de que no vas?** what's all this about you not going? **2** (*en locs*) **a eso de** (at) around *o* about; **en eso**: **en ~ llegó su madre** (just) at that moment her mother arrived; **en ~ estaba cuando ...** I was just in the middle of doing that when ... **¡eso es!** that's it!; **y eso que ...** even though ... **3** **¡eso!** (*interj*) exactly!
ESO *f* (en Esp) = **Educación Secundaria Obligatoria**
esófago *m* esophagus*
esos, esas *adj dem*: *ver* **ese²**
ésos, ésas *pron dem*: *ver* **ése**
esotérico -ca *adj* esoteric
espabilado¹ -da *adj* **1** (despierto) awake **2** (vivo, listo) bright, smart; **tienes que ser más ~** you have to keep more on the ball
espabilado² -da *m,f* smart ass (sl)
espabilar [A1] *vt* **1** (quitar el sueño) to wake ... up **2** (avivar) to wise ... up (colloq); **ella lo espabiló** she helped him get his act together
■ **espabilar** *vi* **1** (sacudirse el sueño) to wake up **2** (darse prisa) to get a move on (colloq) **3** (avivarse) to wise up (colloq) **4** (Ven fam) (pestañear) to blink
■ **espabilarse** *v pron* **1** (sacudirse el sueño) to wake (oneself) up **2** (darse prisa) to get a move on (colloq) **3** (avivarse) to wise up (colloq)
espachurrar [A1] *vt* (fam) to squash, crush
■ **espachurrarse** *v pron* to get squashed, get crushed
espaciado -da *adj* **1** (en el espacio): **los párrafos deben quedar más ~s** there should be more space between the paragraphs; **los árboles están muy ~s** the trees are too far apart **2** (en el tiempo): **tuvo a sus hijos muy ~s** there were quite a few years between each of her children; **sus visitas se hicieron más espaciadas** her visits became more infrequent
espaciador *m* space bar
espacial *adj*
A ‹*cohete/vuelo*› space (*before n*)
B (Fís, Mat) spatial
espaciar [A1] *vt* **1** (en el espacio) to space ... out **2** (en el tiempo): **empezó a ~ sus visitas** her visits became more and more infrequent
espacio *m*
A **1** (amplitud, capacidad) space, room; **hay mucho ~ para jugar** there is plenty of space to play; **ocupan demasiado ~** they take up too much space *o* room **2** (entre líneas, palabras) space; (entre objetos) space, gap; **un folio mecanografiado a doble ~/a un ~** a sheet of double-spaced/single-spaced typing; **rellenar los ~s en blanco** fill in the blank spaces *o* the blanks **3** (recinto, área) area; **un ~ cercado** a fenced-off area; **~s cerrados** confined spaces *o* areas
Compuestos
- **espacios abiertos/verdes** *mpl* open/green spaces (*pl*)
- **espacio vital** lebensraum, living space

B (Espac): **el ~** space
Compuestos
- **espacio aéreo** airspace
- **espacio exterior** *or* **sideral** outer space

C (de tiempo): **un corto ~ de tiempo** a short space of time; **por ~ de 24 horas** for 24 hours *o* for a period of 24 hours
D **1** (Rad, TV) (hueco) slot; (programa) program*; **~ deportivo/informativo** sports/news program; **~ publicitario** advertising slot **2** (en periódico, revista) space
espacioso -sa *adj* spacious
espada¹ *f*
A (arma) sword; **~ de esgrima** épée; ***estar entre la ~ y la pared*** to be (caught) between the devil and the deep blue sea
B **1** (carta) *any card of the* **espadas** *suit* **2** **espadas** *fpl* (palo) *one of the suits in a Spanish pack of cards*
espada² *m* matador
espadachín *m* skilled swordsman
espadaña *f*
A (campanario) belfry
B (Bot) bulrush
espagueti, espaguetti *m* piece of spaghetti; **~s** spaghetti
espalda *f*
A (Anat) back; **ancho de ~s** broad-shouldered; **perdona, te estoy dando la ~** sorry, I've got my back to you; **de ~s a nosotros** with his/her back to us; **vuélvete de ~s** turn around *o* (BrE) round; **nadar de ~(s)** to swim backstroke; **los 100 metros ~** the 100 meters backstroke; **tumbarse** *or* **tenderse de ~s** to lie on one's back; **lo atacaron por la ~** he was attacked from behind; ***caerse de ~s*** (*literal*) to fall flat on one's back; (de sorpresa): **por poco me caigo de ~s** I nearly died of shock *o* fainted (colloq); ***cubrirse las ~s*** to cover one's back; ***echarse algo a la ~*** (literal) to sling sth on one's back; ‹*responsabilidad/trabajo*› (fam) to take on; ‹*problemas/pesares*› (fam) to cast ... aside; ***hacer algo a ~s de algn*** to do sth behind sb's back; ***romperse la ~*** to break one's back; ***tener buena ~*** (Col) to bring good luck; ***tener cubiertas las ~s*** to have one's back covered; ***volverle la ~ a algn*** to turn one's back on sb
Compuesto **espalda mojada** *mf* wetback
B (de prenda) back

espalda mojada

The name in Mexico for people who try to enter the US illegally by crossing the Rio Grande that separates Mexico from the USA.

In Spain the term refers to illegal immigrants from Morocco who cross the Straits of Gibraltar to enter Spain. In both countries *espaldas mojadas* are a source of cheap unskilled labor

espaldar *m*
A (Coc) loin
B (en gimnasia) wall bars (*pl*)
C (AmL) (de asiento) back

espaldarazo *m* (reconocimiento) recognition

espaldera *f* 1 (para plantas) trellis, espalier 2 (corset) corset 3 **espalderas** *fpl* (para gimnasia) wall bars (*pl*)

espaldilla *f* shoulder blade

espantada *f*: **pegar(se) una ~** «*animal*» to bolt; «*persona*» (fam) to make a run for it (colloq)

espantadizo -za *adj* easily frightened *o* startled

espantado -da *adj* 1 (asustado) frightened, scared; **salieron ~s** they ran off in fright 2 (uso hiperbólico) horrified, appalled; **quedé ~ con su vocabulario** I was horrified *o* appalled at his language

espantajo *m* scarecrow

espantapájaros *m* (*pl* ~) scarecrow

espantar [A1] *vt*
A 1 (ahuyentar) ‹*peces/pájaros*› to frighten away 2 (asustar) ‹*caballo*› to frighten, scare 3 (apartar de sí): **se tomó un café para ~ el sueño** she had a coffee to keep herself awake; **cantando se espantan las penas** by singing you drive your troubles away; **no podía ~ el miedo que sentía** he could not shake off his feeling of fear
B (fam) (uso hiperbólico) to horrify, appall*; **le espanta la idea de vivir allí** the idea of living there appalls *o* horrifies him

■ **espantar** *vi* 1 (fam) (asustar): **es tan feo que espanta** he's absolutely hideous (colloq) 2 (Bol, Col, Ven fam) «*fantasma*»: **en esa casa espantan** that house is haunted

■ **espantarse** *v pron*
A «*pájaro/peces*» to get frightened away; «*caballo*» to take fright, be startled
B (fam) (uso hiberbólico) to be horrified *o* appalled

espanto *m*
A 1 (miedo) fright, horror 2 (uso hiperbólico): **la noticia nos llenó de ~** we were horrified *o* appalled at the news; **¡qué ~!** how awful!; **¡qué ~ de mujer!** (fam) what a dreadful *o* frightful woman! (colloq); **hace un frío de ~** (fam) it's freezing *o* terribly cold (colloq); ***estar curado de ~*** (fam): **ya está curada de ~** she's seen/heard it all before
B (Bol, Col, Ven fam) (espíritu) ghost, spook (colloq)

espantoso -sa *adj* 1 ‹*escena/crimen*› horrific, appalling 2 (fam) (uso hiperbólico) ‹*comida/letra/tiempo*› atrocious; ‹*vestido/color*› hideous; ‹*ruido/voz*› terrible, awful; **hace un calor ~** it's boiling *o* roasting hot (colloq); **pasé un frío ~** I was absolutely freezing (colloq); **tengo un hambre espantosa** I'm starving (colloq)

España *f* Spain; ***como cuando salimos de ~*** (Arg fam) we're still no further on (colloq)

español¹ -ñola *adj* Spanish

español² -ñola *m,f*
A (persona) (*m*) Spaniard, Spanish man; (*f*) Spaniard, Spanish woman; **los ~es** the Spanish, Spaniards, Spanish people
B **español** *m* (idioma) Spanish

españolada *f*: *movie, etc which presents a clichéd image of Spain*

españolizar [A4] *vt* ‹*persona/costumbres*› to make ... Spanish; ‹*palabra/término*› to spell/pronounce ... in a Spanish way

■ **españolizarse** *v pron* «*persona*» to adopt Spanish ways; «*palabra*» to come to be spelled/pronounced in a Spanish way

esparadrapo *m* surgical tape

esparcimiento *m*
A (recreo) recreation, relaxation; (diversión) leisure activity
B (diseminación) dissemination, spreading

esparcir [I4] *vt* 1 ‹*libros/juguetes*› to scatter 2 ‹*rumor*› to spread; **no lo vayas esparciendo por ahí** don't go spreading it around 3 (Chi) ‹*mantequilla*› to spread

■ **esparcirse** *v pron*
A 1 «*líquido*» to spread; «*papeles/semillas*» to be scattered 2 «*noticia/rumor*» to spread
B (recrearse) to enjoy oneself, relax

espárrago *m* asparagus; **puntas de ~** asparagus tips; ***estar hecho un ~*** (fam) to be thin as a rail (AmE) *o* (BrE) rake (colloq); ***mandar a algn a freír ~s*** (fam) to tell sb to get lost (colloq); **¡que se vayan a freír ~s!** they can get lost! (colloq)

esparring /es'parin/ *m* sparring partner

espartano -na *adj* ‹*condiciones/disciplina*› spartan

esparto *m* esparto grass, esparto

espasmo *m* spasm

espasmódico -ca *adj* spasmodic

espástico -ca *adj* spastic

espatarrarse [A1] *v pron* ▸ **despatarrarse**

espátula *f* 1 (paleta) spatula; (Art) palette knife 2 (para quitar pintura, papel) scraper

especia *f* (condimento) spice

especial¹ *adj* 1 (para uso específico) special; **en ~** especially, particularly; **nada/nadie en ~** nothing/nobody in particular 2 (excepcional) special; **un día muy ~ para mí** a very special day for me 3 (difícil) ‹*persona/carácter*› fussy; **¡qué ~ eres para comer!** you're so picky *o* fussy about your food! (colloq)

especial² *m* (TV) special (program*); **~ informativo** news special

especialidad *f*
A 1 (actividad, estudio) specialty (AmE), speciality(BrE); **tiene que hacer dos años de ~** she has to do two years' specialization; **su ~ es romper platos** (hum) he specializes in breaking plates (hum) 2 (de restaurante) specialty (AmE), speciality (BrE); **~ de la casa** specialty of the house
B (frml) (Farm) medicine

especialista¹ *adj* specialist (*before n*); **un médico ~** a specialist

especialista² *mf*
A 1 (experto) specialist, expert; **los ~s en la materia dicen que ...** experts *o* specialists on the subject say that ...; **es ~ en meter la pata** (hum) he's an expert at putting his foot in it (hum) 2 (Med) specialist; **un ~ de(l) corazón** a heart specialist
B (Cin, TV) (*m*) stuntman; (*f*) stuntwoman

especialización *f* specialization

especializado -da *adj* 1 **~ EN algo** specializing IN sth; **una librería especializada en ...** a bookshop specializing in ... 2 ‹*lenguaje*› technical, specialized 3 ‹*obrero*› skilled, specialized (*before n*)

especializarse [A4] *v pron* to specialize; **~ EN algo** to specialize IN sth

especialmente *adv* 1 (en especial) especially, particularly 2 (para un fin específico) specially; **~ diseñado para ella** specially designed for her

especie *f*
A (Biol, Bot, Zool) species
B (clase) kind, sort; **una ~ de sopa** a sort *o* a kind of soup
C **en especie** *or* **especies** in kind

especiero *m* spice rack

especificación *f* specification

especificar [A2] *vt* to specify; **especifique el modelo que desea** specify which model you require

especificativo -va *adj* (Ling) defining (*before n*)

específico¹ -ca *adj*
A (preciso) specific
B (Farm, Med) specific

específico² *m* specific

espécimen *m* (*pl* **-pecímenes**) 1 (ejemplar) specimen; (muestra) sample, specimen 2 (fam) (persona): **¡qué ~ te fuiste a elegir de novio!** (fam & hum) your boyfriend's a weird specimen (colloq)

espectacular *adj* spectacular

espectacularmente *adv* spectacularly; **se recuperó ~** he made a spectacular recovery

espectáculo *m*
A (representación) show; **un ~ de variedades** a variety show; ❸ **espectáculos** (en periódicos) entertainment guide; **el**

mundo del ~ showbusiness; ***dar un*** *or* ***el ~*** (fam) to make a spectacle of oneself

B (visión, panorama) sight; **el ~ los llenó de horror** the spectacle *o* sight filled them with horror

espectador -dora *m,f* **1** (Dep) spectator; (Espec) member of the audience; **asistieron al estreno dos mil ~es** two thousand people attended the premiere **2** (observador) observer; **fui como ~** I went along as an observer

espectral *adj* **1** ‹*aparición/luz/silencio*› ghostly **2** (Fís) spectral; **análisis ~** spectrum analysis

espectro *m*

A (Fís) spectrum; (gama) spectrum; **el ~ político** the political spectrum; **un antibiótico de amplio ~** a broad-spectrum antibiotic

B (fantasma) specter*, ghost; (amenaza) specter*; **el ~ de la muerte** the specter of death

espectroscopio *m* spectroscope

especulación *f* speculation; **la ~ del suelo** land speculation; **~ bursátil** speculation on the Stock Exchange

especulador -dora *m,f* speculator

especular [A1] *vi*

A (Com, Fin) to speculate

B (conjeturar) to speculate

especulativo -va *adj* speculative

espejear [A1] *vi* (liter) to shimmer

espejismo *m* (fenómeno óptico) mirage; (ilusión) illusion

espejo *m* **1** (para mirarse) mirror; **~ de aumento/de cuerpo entero/de mano** magnifying/full-length/hand mirror; **mirarse al** *or* **en el ~** to look (at oneself) in the mirror; ***como un ~*** spotless; **la dejó (limpia) como un ~** he left it spotlessly clean **2** (reflejo, imagen) mirror; **la obra es ~ de esa sociedad** the play is a mirror of that society, the play mirrors that society **3** (modelo) model; **se mira en él como en un ~** he looks up to him as a model

(Compuesto) **espejo lateral/retrovisor** wing/rear-view mirror

espeleología *f* spelunking, potholing (BrE)

espeleólogo -ga *m,f* spelunker, potholer (BrE)

espeluznante *adj* ‹*tragedia/estado/experiencia*› horrific, horrifying; ‹*grito*› terrifying, blood-curdling

espeluznar [A1] *vi* (fam): **un disfraz que espeluznaba** a disguise which was enough to make your hair stand on end

■ **espeluznar** *vt* to scare, frighten

espera *f*

A **1** (acción, período) wait; **la ~ se me hizo eterna** the wait seemed to go on forever **2** (*en locs*) **a la espera** waiting; **estoy a la ~ de una oferta concreta** I am waiting for a concrete offer; **en espera**: **en ~ de la decisión del comité** pending the committee's decision; **en ~ de su respuesta saluda a Vd. atte.** (frml) I look forward to hearing from you, yours faithfully

B (Der) respite

esperado -da *adj* **1** (aguardado) ‹*acontecimiento/carta*› eagerly awaited; **su tan esperada llegada** his long-awaited arrival **2** (que es de esperar): **no obtuvo los resultados ~s** he didn't get the results he expected

esperantista *mf* Esperantist

esperanto *m* Esperanto

esperanza *f* hope; **no quiero darles ~s vanas** I don't want to build your hopes up; **cifró** *or* **puso todas sus ~s en su hijo** he pinned all his hopes on his son; **~ DE algo** hope OF *o* FOR sth; **ello suscita nuevas ~s de un acuerdo** that raises new hopes for *o* of a settlement; **hay ~s de éxito** there are hopes that he/it/they will succeed; **~ DE + INF** hope OF -ING; **perdimos toda ~ de encontrarlos vivos** we gave up *o* lost hope of finding them alive; **tengo ~s de encontrar algo mejor** I hope to find *o* I have hopes of finding something better; **~ DE QUE**: **ya no abrigaba ninguna ~ de que volviera** (liter) she no longer held out any hope of him returning (liter); **fue con la ~ de que ...** he went in the hope that ...; **me dio ~s de que el niño mejoraría** he gave me hope that the child would recover; ***alimentarse*** *or* ***vivir de ~s*** to live on hopes; ***¡qué ~(s)!*** (fam) you must be joking! (colloq); ***la ~ es lo último que se pierde*** we live in hope

(Compuesto) **esperanza de vida** life expectancy

esperanzado -da *adj* hopeful

esperanzador -dora *adj* encouraging

esperanzar [A4] *vt*: **no quiso ~los** he didn't want to raise their hopes

esperar [A1] *vt*

A **1** ‹*autobús/persona/acontecimiento*› to wait for; **la esperé dos horas** I waited for her for two hours; **esperaban con impaciencia su llegada** they were really looking forward to her coming; **le encanta hacerse ~** he loves to keep people waiting; **¿qué estás esperando para decírselo?** tell him! what are you waiting for?; **no me esperes para cenar** don't wait for me to eat **2** (recibir) to meet; **la fuimos a ~ al aeropuerto** we went to meet her at the airport **3** «*sorpresa*» to await; **su reacción no se hizo ~** he was swift to react; **le espera un futuro difícil** he has a difficult future ahead of him; **¡ya verás la que te espera en casa!** (fam) you'll catch it *o* you'll be for it when you get home! (colloq)

B **1** (contar con, prever) to expect; **tal como esperábamos** just as we expected; **cuando uno menos lo espera** when you least expect it; **te espero alrededor de las nueve** I'll expect you around nine; **estoy esperando una llamada** I'm expecting a call; **~ QUE + SUBJ**: **¿esperabas que te felicitara?** did you expect me to congratulate you?; **era de ~ que el proyecto fracasara** the project was bound to fail; **no esperes que cambie de idea** don't expect me to change my mind; **~ algo DE algn/algo** to expect sth OF sb/sth; **esperaba otra cosa de ti** I expected more of you; **de ella no puedes ~ ayuda** don't expect her to help **2** ‹*niño/bebé*› to be expecting; **está esperando familia** she's expecting

C (con esperanza) to hope; **eso espero** *or* **espero que sí** I hope so; **espero que no** I hope not; **~ + INF** to hope to + INF; **espero no haberme olvidado de nada** I hope I haven't forgotten anything; **~ QUE + SUBJ**: **espero que no llueva/que te guste** I hope it doesn't rain/you like it; **espero que tengas suerte** I wish you luck; **esperemos que no sea nada grave** let's hope it's nothing serious

■ **esperar** *vi* **1** (aguardar) to wait; **no podemos ~ más** we can't wait any longer; **espera, que bajo contigo** wait a minute *o* (colloq) hold on, I'll come down with you; **~ A + INF**: **espera a estar seguro** wait until you're sure; **~ (A) QUE + SUBJ**: **~on (a) que él se fuera para entrar** they waited for him to go before they went in; **espera (a) que te llamen** wait until they call you; **~ *sentado*** (fam): **si piensa que lo voy a llamar puede ~ sentado** if he thinks I'm going to call him he's got another think coming (colloq); **¿que él cambie de idea? mejor espera sentada** him change his mind? some hope!; ***quien espera desespera*** waiting's the worst part **2** «*embarazada*»: **estar esperando** to be expecting; **¿para cuándo espera?** when's the baby due?

■ **esperarse** *v pron*

A (fam) (aguardar) to hang on (colloq), to hold on (colloq); **espérate ¿no ves que estoy ocupada?** wait a minute! can't you see I'm busy?

B (fam) (prever) to expect; **no me esperaba eso de él** I didn't expect that of *o* from him; **¡quién se lo iba a ~!** who would have thought it!

esperma *m or f*

A (Biol) sperm

(Compuesto) **esperma de ballena** spermaceti

B **esperma** *f* (Col) (vela) candle

espermatozoide, espermatozoo *m* spermatozoon, sperm

espermicida[1] *adj* spermicidal

espermicida[2] *m* spermicide

esperpéntico -ca *adj* grotesque

esperpento *m* **1** (Lit) theater* of the grotesque (*created by Valle Inclán*) **2** (fam) (mamarracho): **¿quién es ese ~?** who's that weird-looking guy? (colloq)

espesante *m* thickener

espesar [A1] *vt* to thicken

■ **espesar** *vi* to thicken, become thick

■ **espesarse** *v pron* «*salsa*» to thicken; «*vegetación*» to become thick, become dense

espeso -sa *adj* **1** ‹*salsa*› thick; ‹*vegetación/niebla*› dense, thick; ‹*nieve*› thick, deep; ‹*cabello/barba*› bushy, thick **2** ‹*libro/obra*› (fam) heavy (colloq), dense (colloq) **3** (Per fam)

e

(cargoso) annoying; **¡no seas ~!** don't be such a pain! (colloq)

espesor *m* thickness; **tiene dos centímetros de ~** it's two centimeters thick

espesura *f*: **salió de en medio de la ~** he came out from among the bushes; **se abrieron paso por entre la ~** they hacked a path through the vegetation

espetar [A1] *vt*
A (fam) 1 (soltar de repente) ‹*grosería*› to spit … out; ‹*noticia*› to blurt … out; **le ~on la noticia así** they blurted the news out to him just like that 2 (hacer escuchar) ‹*discurso/sermón*› to inflict … on
B ‹*carne/pescado*› (con asador) to put … on a spit; (con pincho) to skewer

espetón *m* 1 (asador) spit; (pincho) skewer 2 (para la lumbre) poker

espía[1] *adj inv* ‹*avión/satélite*› spy (*before n*); ‹*cámara*› hidden (*before n*), secret (*before n*)

espía[2] *mf* (persona) spy

espiantar [A1] *vt* (RPl arg) to get rid of (colloq)
■ **espiantarse** *v pron* (RPl arg) to split (sl)

espiar [A17] *vt* ‹*enemigo/movimientos*› to spy on, keep watch on
■ **espiar** *vi* to spy

espichar [A1] *vt* 1 (Col fam) (oprimir) ‹*botón/tecla*› to press, push; ‹*tubo/espinilla*› to squeeze 2 (Col, Ven fam) (aplastar) ‹*fruta/escarabajo*› to squash; **lo espichó un carro** he was run over by a car
■ **espicharse** *v pron*
A 1 (Col fam) (machacarse) to get squashed 2 (Ven fam) (desinflarse) to burst
B (Méx fam) (emaciarse) to get skinny (colloq)
C (Méx fam) (cohibirse) to get all embarrassed (colloq)

espiga *f*
A 1 (Agr, Bot) (de trigo) ear, spike; (de flores) spike 2 (diseño) ▸**espiguilla**
B (Tec) (clavo — de madera) peg; (— de metal) pin, brad

espigado -da *adj* willowy, tall and slim

espigador -dora *m,f* gleaner

espigar [A3] *vt* (Agr) (recoger) to glean; (recopilar) to gather
■ **espigar** *vi* 1 «*cereales*» to ear (up), form ears 2 «*persona*» to glean
■ **espigarse** *v pron* 1 «*persona*» to grow tall and slim 2 «*hortalizas*» to go to seed

espigón *m*
A (rompeolas) breakwater
B (Per, RPl) (en aeropuerto) terminal (building)

espiguilla *f* herringbone; **una falda de ~** *or* **de ~s** a herringbone (pattern) skirt

espina *f*
A 1 (de rosal, zarza) thorn; (de cactus) prickle 2 (de pez) bone 3 (Anat) spine
(Compuestos)
• **espina bífida** spina bifida
• **espina dorsal** spine, backbone
B 1 (de disgusto): **tiene clavada la ~ de aquel desengaño** he hasn't got over *o* (colloq) he's still smarting from that disappointment 2 (duda, resquemor) nagging doubt; **tenía que sacarme la ~** I just had to know; ***darle a algn mala ~*** to make sb feel uneasy; **esto me da mala ~** I don't like the look of this

espinaca *f* spinach

espinal *adj* spinal

espinazo *m* spine, backbone; ***romperse el ~*** (fam) to break one's neck; (trabajando) to break one's back

espinilla *f*
A (Anat) shin
B 1 (de cabeza negra) blackhead 2 (AmL) (barrito) pimple, spot

espinillera *f* shinpad

espino *m* hawthorn
(Compuesto) **espino negro** blackthorn

espinoso -sa *adj*
A 1 ‹*rosal/zarza*› thorny; ‹*cactus*› prickly 2 ‹*pescado*› bony
B ‹*problema/asunto*› thorny, knotty

espinudo -da *adj* (Chi) ▸**espinoso**

espionaje *m* spying, espionage; **novela de ~** spy novel
(Compuesto) **espionaje industrial** industrial espionage

espira *f* 1 (espiral) spiral 2 (vuelta — de bobina, espiral) turn; (— de concha) whorl

espiración *f* exhalation

espiral *f* 1 (forma, movimiento) spiral; **un cuaderno de ~(es)** a spiral-bound notebook; **una ~ de violencia** a spiral of violence; **escalera ~** *or* **en ~** *or* **de ~** spiral staircase; **la avioneta cayó en ~** the plane spun downward(s) 2 (muelle) hairspring 3 (dispositivo intrauterino) coil

espirar [A1] *vi* to breathe out, exhale

espiritismo *m* spiritualism; **sesión de ~** séance

espiritista *adj/mf* spiritualist

espiritoso -sa *adj* ▸**espirituoso**

espíritu *m*
A (alma, ser inmaterial) spirit; **un ~ maligno** an evil spirit; **el ~ del rey asesinado** the ghost of the murdered king; ***entregar el ~*** (euf) to pass away (euph)
(Compuesto) **Espíritu Santo** Holy Ghost *o* Spirit
B 1 (disposición, actitud) spirit; **con ~ de sacrificio** in a spirit of self-sacrifice 2 (naturaleza, carácter) nature; **tiene un ~ rebelde** she has a rebellious nature
(Compuestos)
• **espíritu de cuerpo** esprit de corps
• **espíritu de equipo** team spirit
C (valor, ánimo) spirit
D (esencia) spirit; **el ~ de la ley** the spirit of the law
(Compuesto) **espíritu de vino** spirits of wine (*pl*), alcohol

espiritual[1] *adj* spiritual

espiritual[2] *m*: *tb* **~ negro** (Negro) spiritual

espirituoso -sa *adj*: **bebidas espirituosas** *or* **licores ~s** spirits

espita *f* spigot (AmE), tap (BrE)

espléndidamente *adv* 1 (muy bien) ‹*portarse*› wonderfully; **nos trataron ~** they treated us marvelously; **allí se come ~** the food (there) is marvellous *o* splendid 2 (generosamente) lavishly 3 (lujosamente) magnificently

esplendidez *f* (magnificencia) splendor*, magnificence; (generosidad) generosity

espléndido -da *adj* 1 ‹*fiesta/comida*› splendid, magnificent; ‹*día/tiempo*› splendid, marvelous*; ‹*regalo/joya/abrigo*› magnificent; **estaba espléndida con aquel vestido** she looked magnificent *o* wonderful in that dress 2 (generoso) ‹*persona*› generous; ‹*regalo*› lavish, generous

esplendor *m* 1 (magnificencia) splendor*, magnificence; **el ~ de su belleza** her radiant beauty 2 (apogeo) splendor*; **cuando alcanzó su máximo ~** when it achieved its greatest splendor

esplendoroso -sa *adj* ‹*boda/fiesta*› magnificent, grand; ‹*día*› splendid, magnificent; ‹*luz/sol*› magnificent

espliego *m* lavender

espolada *f*, **espolazo** *m* dig (*with a spur*)

espolear [A1] *vt* ‹*caballo*› to spur (on); **espoleado por la ambición** spurred on by ambition

espoleta *f*
A (Arm) fuse
B (Anat) wishbone

espolón *m*
A (de ave) spur
B (de puente) cutwater; (malecón) breakwater
C (Geog) spur

espolvorear [A1] *vt* ‹*azúcar/perejil*› to sprinkle; ‹*tarta/pasta*› **~ algo CON** *or* **DE algo** to sprinkle sth WITH sth

esponja *f*
A (Zool) sponge; (para limpiar, lavarse) sponge; ***tirar la ~*** to throw in the towel, throw in the sponge (AmE)
(Compuesto) **esponja vegetal** *or* **de luffa** loofa (AmE), loofah (BrE)
B (fam & hum) (bebedor) old soak (colloq & hum); ***beber*** *or* ***chupar como una ~*** to drink like a fish (colloq)

esponjado -da *adj* spongy

esponjar [A1] *vt* to fluff up, make … fluffy
■ **esponjarse** *v pron* «*masa*» to rise; «*pelo*» to go fluffy; «*toalla*» to become fluffy

esponjoso -sa *adj* ‹*masa/bizcocho*› spongy, fluffy; ‹*tejido*› soft; ‹*lana*› fluffy

esponsales *mpl* (frml) betrothal (frml)

espónsor *mf* sponsor

espontaneidad *f* spontaneity

espontáneo[1] **-nea** *adj* ‹*persona/gesto/ayuda*› spontaneous; ‹*actuación*› impromptu; ‹*vegetación*› spontaneous

espontáneo[2] **-nea** *m,f: spectator who jumps into the ring to join in the bullfight*

espora *f* spore

esporádico -ca *adj* ‹*sucesos/visitas*› sporadic, intermittent

esposado -da *adj* handcuffed, in handcuffs

esposas *fpl* handcuffs (*pl*)

esposo -sa *m,f* (*m*) husband; (*f*) wife; **acompañado de su señora esposa** (frml) accompanied by his wife; **los nuevos ~s** the newly-weds

espray *m* (*pl* **-prays**) 1 (atomizador) spray; **¿esta colonia viene en ~?** does this perfume come in a spray?; **desodorante en ~** spray deodorant 2 (pintura) spray paint; **pinta con ~s** he paints with aerosols

esprint *m* (*pl* **-prints**) sprint; **el ~ final** the final sprint

esprintar [A1] *vi* to sprint

esprínter *mf* sprinter

espuela *f* spur; **dio** *or* **picó ~s al caballo** he spurred on his horse

espuelear [A1] *vt* (AmL) to spur (on)

espuerta *f* basket; ***a ~s*** (fam): **toma café a ~s** she drinks gallons of coffee (colloq); **compró libros a ~s** he bought tons of books (colloq); **ganar dinero a ~s** to earn pots of money (colloq)

espulgar [A3] *vt* to delouse

espuma *f*
A 1 (del mar) foam; (al romper las olas) surf; (en agua revuelta) foam, froth 2 (del jabón) lather; **este jabón no hace ~** this soap doesn't lather; **un baño de ~(s)** a foam *o* bubble bath; ***crecer como la ~*** «*rumor*» to spread like wildfire; «*número/popularidad*» to grow exponentially; ***echar ~ por la boca*** to foam *o* froth at the mouth; ***subir como la ~*** to soar, go sky-high 3 (de la cerveza) head, froth
Compuestos
- **espuma de afeitar** shaving foam
- **espuma seca** carpet shampoo
B (Coc) (capa) scum
C 1 (caucho celular) foam rubber; **un colchón de ~** a foam-rubber mattress 2 (tejido elástico) stretch nylon

espumadera *f* skimmer, slotted spoon

espumajo *m* ▸**espumarajo**

espumante *m* sparkling wine

espumar [A1] *vt* to skim

espumarajo *m* froth, foam; ***echar ~s por la boca*** to froth *o* foam at the mouth

espumillón *m* tinsel

espumoso[1] **-sa** *adj* ‹*ola*› foaming; ‹*cerveza*› frothy; ‹*vino*› sparkling

espumoso[2] *m* sparkling wine

espurio -ria, espúreo -rea *adj* (frml) spurious (frml)

esputar [A1] *vt* to expectorate

esputo *m* sputum

esqueje *m* (para plantar) cutting; (para injertar) scion

esquela *f*
A 1 (AmL) (carta) note 2 (Andes) (papel) stationery set
B (Esp) (aviso fúnebre) *tb* **~ mortuoria** death notice

esquelético -ca *adj* skeletal; **estaba verdaderamente ~** he was an absolute skeleton

esqueleto *m*
A 1 (Anat) skeleton; ***estar hecho un ~*** (fam & hum) to be all skin and bone(s) (colloq); ***menear el ~*** (fam & hum) to shake a leg (colloq & hum) 2 (de edificio, novela) framework
B (Méx) (formulario) blank form

esquema *m*
A (croquis) sketch, diagram; (sinopsis) outline
B (de ideas): **el ~ liberal** liberal philosophy *o* thinking; **no se sale de sus ~s** she doesn't change her way of thinking; ***romperle los ~s a algn*** (fam) (echar abajo — conceptos) to shatter sb's preconceptions; (— planes) to ruin sb's plans

esquemático -ca *adj* schematic; **un plano ~ del motor** a diagram of the engine; **el libro es algo ~** the book is a little oversimplified

esquematizar [A4] *vt* to schematize, describe ... in simple terms
■ **esquematizar** *vi* to schematize

esquí *m* (*pl* **-quís** *or* **-quíes**) (tabla) ski; (deporte) skiing; **hacer ~** to ski, go skiing; **pista de ~** ski run, piste
Compuestos
- **esquí acuático** *or* **náutico** waterskiing; **hacer ~ ~** to water-ski
- **esquí alpino/fuera de pista** downhill/off-piste skiing
- **esquí nórdico** *or* **de fondo** cross-country skiing, nordic skiing

esquiador -dora *m,f* skier

esquiar [A17] *vi* to ski

esquife *m* skiff

esquila *f*
A (de ovejas) shearing, clipping
B (cencerro, campanilla) bell; (de vaca) cowbell

esquilador -dora *m,f* 1 (persona) sheepshearer, clipper 2 **esquiladora** *f* (máquina) shearing *o* clipping machine

esquilar [A1] *vt* to shear, clip

esquilmar [A1] *vt*
A (Agr) to harvest
B ‹*riquezas/recursos*› to exhaust; ‹*fortuna*› to squander; ‹*persona*› to suck ... dry

esquimal *adj/mf* Eskimo

esquina *f* 1 (en calle) corner; **en la calle Vidal, ~ (a) Cádiz** on the corner of Vidal (Street) and Cadiz; **doblar la ~** to go round *o* turn the corner; **hace ~ con la plaza** it's on the corner of the square; ***a la vuelta de la ~*** (literal) around the corner; (muy cerca) just around the corner 2 (Dep): **sacar de ~** to take a corner (kick)

esquinado -da *adj* (en diagonal): **coloca el sofá ~** put the sofa across the corner

esquinazo *m*
A (Esp): **darle (el) ~ a algn** (dejar plantado) to stand sb up; (esquivar) to give sb the slip
B (Chi) (serenata) *serenade of traditional singing and dancing*

esquinero -ra *m,f*
A (Dep) corner back
B **esquinero** *m* (mueble) corner unit *o* module; (armario) corner cupboard

esquirla *f* splinter; **~s de metal** shards of metal

esquirol *mf* (pey) strikebreaker, scab (pej)

esquites *mpl* (Méx) (maíz tostado) *toasted corn/maize kernels*; (palomitas de maíz) popcorn

esquivar [A1] *vt* ‹*persona*› to avoid; ‹*golpe/pregunta*› to dodge, evade; ‹*problema/dificultad*› to avoid; ‹*responsabilidad*› to avoid, evade

esquivo -va *adj* 1 ‹*persona*› (difícil de encontrar) elusive; (huraño) aloof, unsociable; (tímido) shy; **se mostró ~ ante los periodistas** he was very evasive with the journalists 2 ‹*respuesta*› elusive, evasive

esquizofrenia *f* schizophrenia

esquizofrénico -ca *adj/m,f* schizophrenic

esquizoide *adj/mf* schizoid

estabilidad *f* stability

estabilización *f* stabilization

estabilizador[1] **-dora** *adj* stabilizing (*before n*)

estabilizador[2] *m* stabilizer

estabilizar [A4] *vt* to stabilize; **ha logrado ~ su peso** he has managed to keep his weight stable
■ **estabilizarse** *v pron* to stabilize

estable *adj* ‹*situación/persona/gobierno*› stable; ‹*trabajo*› steady; ‹*estructura/relación*› stable, steady; ‹*gas/compuesto*› stable

establecer [E3] *vt*
A 1 ‹*colonia/dictadura*› to establish; ‹*campamento*› to set up; **estableció su residencia en Mónaco** he took up residence in Monaco 2 ‹*relaciones/contacto*› to establish
B (dejar sentado) 1 ‹*criterios/bases*› to establish, lay down;

‹*precio*› to fix, set; ‹*precedente*› to establish, set; **conviene dejar establecido que ...** we should make it clear that ...; **~ un precedente** to establish *o* set a precedent **2** (frml) «*ley/reglamento*» (disponer) to state, establish **3** ‹*uso*› to establish **4** ‹*récord/marca/moda*› to set
C (determinar) to establish
■ **establecerse** *v pron* «*colono/emigrante*» to settle; «*comerciante/empresa*» to set up; **se estableció por su cuenta** he set up on his own

establecimiento *m* establishment
Compuestos
- **establecimiento comercial** (frml) establishment (frml), business
- **establecimiento penitenciario** (frml) penal institution (frml)

establo *m* stable

estaca *f*
A **1** (poste) stake, post **2** (para carpa) tent peg **3** (garrote) club, stick
B (esqueje) cutting
C (clavo) nail; (de madera) peg

estacada *f* stockade, palisade; ***dejar a algn en la ~*** to leave sb in the lurch (colloq); ***quedar(se) en la ~*** to be left in the lurch (colloq)

estacar [A2] *vt* **1** (clavar) ‹*pieles*› to stake ... out **2** (atar) ‹*toro/caballo*› to tether, stake

estación *f*
A (de tren, metro, autobús) station
Compuestos
- **estación central** main station
- **estación de bomberos** (Col, Méx, Ven) fire station
- **estación de esquí/de invierno** ski/winter resort
- **estación de policía** (Col, Ven) police station
- **estación de servicio** service station, gas (AmE) *o* (BrE) petrol station
- **estación depuradora (de aguas residuales)** sewage farm *o* plant *o* (BrE) works
- **estación espacial/meteorológica/de seguimiento** space/weather/tracking station
- **estación ferroviaria** railroad (AmE) *o* (BrE) railway station
- **estación terminal** *or* **término** terminal, terminus (BrE)

B (del año) season; **la ~ seca/de las lluvias** the dry/rainy season
C (Relig) station; **recorrer las estaciones** to visit the stations of the Cross
D (AmL) (emisora) radio station

estacional *adj* seasonal

estacionamiento *m*
A **1** (acción de estacionar) parking; Ⓢ **zona de estacionamiento vigilado/limitado** attended/restricted parking zone **2** (espacio para estacionar) parking space; (en centro comercial) (AmL) parking lot (AmE), car park (BrE)
B (en el desarrollo de algo): **se produjo un ~ en el curso de la enfermedad** the development of the disease halted; **un ~ en el crecimiento de la economía** a leveling-off in the growth of the economy

estacionar [A1] *vt* to park
■ **estacionar** *vi* to park; Ⓢ **prohibido estacionar** no parking; **~ en doble fila** to double-park
■ **estacionarse** *v pron* **1** (dejar de progresar): **el crecimiento económico se ha estacionado en un 2%** economic growth has leveled off at 2%; **el desarrollo de la enfermedad se ha estacionado** the progress of the disease has halted; **se ha estacionado en los 80 kilos** her weight has stabilized at 80 kilos **2** (Chi, Méx) «*conductor*» to park

estacionario -ria *adj* ‹*situación/temperaturas*› stable; ‹*órbita/satélite*› stationary

estadía *f* (AmL) (en un lugar) stay

estadio *m*
A (lugar) stadium; **~ de fútbol** football stadium
B (frml) (fase) stage, phase

estadista *mf* (*m*) statesman; (*f*) stateswoman

estadística *f* **1** (estudio) statistical study; **según las últimas ~s** according to the latest statistics **2** (cifra) statistic, figure **3** (disciplina) statistics

estadístico[1] -ca *adj* statistical

estadístico[2] -ca *m,f* statistician

estado *m*
A **1** (situación, condición) state; **la casa está en buen ~** the house is in good condition; **en avanzado ~ de descomposición** (frml) in an advanced state of decomposition; **en ~ de embriaguez** (frml) under the influence of alcohol; ***tomar ~ público*** (RPl frml) to become public (knowledge) **2** (Med) condition; **en avanzado ~ de gestación** (frml) in an advanced state of pregnancy (frml); **no debería fumar en su ~** she shouldn't smoke in her condition; ***estar en ~*** (euf) to be expecting (colloq); ***estar en ~ de buena esperanza*** (euf or hum) to be expecting a happy event (euph); ***quedarse en ~*** (euf) to get pregnant
Compuestos
- **estado civil** marital status
- **estado de ánimo** state of mind
- **estado de cuenta** bank statement
- **estado de emergencia** *or* **excepción/de guerra/de sitio** state of emergency/of war/of siege
- **estado de gracia** state of grace
- **estado sólido** solid state

B (nación, gobierno) state; **la seguridad del E~** national *o* state security; **un asunto de ~** a state matter; **el E~** the State
Compuestos
- **estado benefactor** *or* **de bienestar** welfare state
- **estado ciudad** city-state
- **estado de derecho** democracy
- **Estado Mayor** (Mil) general staff

Estados Unidos *m*: *tb* **los ~ ~** *mpl* the United States (+ *sing or pl vb*); **los ~ ~ de América** (frml) the United States of America (frml)

Estados Unidos Mexicanos *mpl* (frml) United States of Mexico (frml)

estadounidense[1] *adj* American, US (*before n*)

estadounidense[2] *mf* American

estafa *f* **1** (Der) fraud, criminal deception **2** (fam) (timo) rip-off (colloq), con (colloq)

estafador -dora *m,f* **1** (Der) fraudster **2** (fam) (timador) con man (colloq)

estafar [A1] *vt* **1** (Der) to swindle, defraud; **~le algo A algn** to defraud sb OF sth, swindle sb OUT OF sth **2** (fam) (timar) to rip ... off (colloq), to con (colloq); **¡qué manera de ~ a la gente!** what a con *o* rip-off! (colloq)

estafeta[1] *f*: *tb* **~ de correos** mail office (AmE), sub-post office (BrE)

estafeta[2] *m* (Col) courier, messenger

estafilococo *m* staphylococcus

estalactita *f* stalactite

estalagmita *f* stalagmite

estalinismo *m* Stalinism

estalinista *adj/mf* Stalinist

estallar [A1] *vi* **1** «*bomba*» to explode; «*neumático*» to blow out, burst; «*globo*» to burst; «*cristal*» to shatter; **hizo ~ el dispositivo** he detonated the device; **un día de estos voy a ~** one of these days I'm going to blow my top (colloq) **2** «*guerra/revuelta*» to break out; «*tormenta/escándalo/crisis*» to break **3** «*persona*» **~ EN algo** ‹*en llanto/carcajadas*› to burst INTO sth

estallido *m* **1** (de bomba) explosion; (de neumático) bursting; (de cristal) shattering; **un ~ de aplausos** a burst of applause **2** (de guerra) outbreak

estambre *m*
A (Bot) stamen
B (Tex) worsted

Estambul *m* Istanbul

estamento *m* (de sociedad) stratum, class; **~s sociales** social strata *o* classes; **el ~ castrense** the military; **diversos ~s universitarios** several university bodies

estampa *f*
A **1** (en libro) picture, illustration **2** (Relig) (tarjeta) *card bearing a religious picture* **3** (para coleccionar) picture card **4** (Lit) (escena) scene
B (aspecto) appearance; **un caballero de fina ~** a fine-looking gentleman; ***¡maldita sea tu ~!*** (fam) damn you! (colloq); ***ser la viva ~ de algn*** to be the spitting image of sb

estampado[1] **-da** *adj* patterned, printed; **~ a mano** hand printed

estampado[2] *m* 1 (motivo) pattern 2 (tela): **los ~s están de moda** patterned *o* printed fabrics are in fashion 3 (proceso — sobre tela, papel) printing; (— sobre metal) stamping; (— formando relieve) embossing

estampar [A1] *vt*

A (imprimir) ‹*tela/diseño*› to print; ‹*metal*› to stamp; (formando relieve) to emboss; **escenas que quedaron estampadas en su memoria** scenes that remained engraved *o* stamped on his memory

B (fam) (arrojar): **estampó el libro contra el suelo** she threw *o* hurled the book to the floor; **lo estampó contra la pared** he slammed it against the wall

C (fam) ‹*beso*› to plant

■ **estamparse** *v pron* (fam) **~se CONTRA algo/algn** to crash INTO sth/sb

estampida *f* stampede; **salir en** *or* **de ~** to stampede out

estampido *m* (de pistola) bang, report; (de bomba) bang

estampilla *f*

A (AmL) (sello — postal) postage (stamp); (— fiscal) tax stamp

B (sello de goma) rubber stamp

estampillado *m*

A (acción) stamping

B (Esp) (con sello de goma) rubber stamping

C (AmL) 1 (estampillas) stamps (*pl*) 2 (sello — postal) (postage) stamp; (— fiscal) tax *o* fiscal stamp

estampilladora *f* (AmL) postage meter (AmE), franking machine (BrE)

estampillar [A1] *vt* 1 (AmL) (con sello fiscal o de correos) to stamp 2 (Esp) (con sello de goma) to rubber-stamp

estampita *f* ▸**estampa A2**

estancado -da *adj* 1 ‹*agua*› stagnant 2 (detenido): **las negociaciones están estancadas** negotiations are at a standstill 3 (con un problema) stuck, bogged down

estancamiento *m* stagnation

estancar [A2] *vt* 1 ‹*río*›: **~on el río con un tronco** they dammed (up) the river with a log; **el derrumbe estancó las aguas del río** the landslide blocked the river 2 ‹*negociación/proceso*› to bring to a halt *o* standstill

■ **estancarse** *v pron* 1 «*agua*» to become stagnant, to stagnate 2 «*negociación/proceso*» to come to a halt *o* standstill 3 (con un problema) to get bogged down *o* stuck

estancia *f*

A (frml) (habitación) large room

B (Esp, Méx) (permanencia) stay; **su ~ se prolongará hasta el lunes** he will stay until Monday

C (en el CS) (Agr) farm; (de ganado) ranch

estanciero -ra *m,f* (en el CS) (Agr) farmer; (de ganado) rancher

estanco *m* (tienda) tobacconist's

> **estanco**
>
> An establishment selling tobacco, stamps, bus and subway passes and other products whose sale is restricted. Cigarettes etc are sold in bars and cafés but at higher prices. *Estancos* also sell stationery and sometimes newspapers

estándar *adj/m* standard

(Compuesto) **estándar de vida** standard of living

estandarizar [A4] *vt* to standardize

estandarte *m* standard, banner

estanque *m* pond

estanquero -ra *m,f* tobacconist

estanquillo *m* (Méx) general store (AmE), grocer's shop (BrE)

estante *m* shelf

estantería *f* shelves (*pl*); (para libros) bookcase, bookshelves (*pl*)

estañar [A1] *vt* (cubrir de estaño) to tin-plate; (soldar) to solder

estaño *m* (elemento) tin; (para soldar) solder; (peltre) pewter

estaquilla *f* peg

estar[1] [A27] *cópula*

A (seguido de adjetivos) [**Estar** *denotes a changed condition or state as opposed to identity or nature, which is normally expressed by* **ser**. **Estar** *is also used when the emphasis is on the speaker's perception of things, of their appearance, taste, etc. The examples given below should be contrasted with those to be found in* **ser**[1] *cópula* **A**] to be; **¡qué gordo está!** isn't he fat!, hasn't he got(ten) fat!; **¡pobre abuelo! está viejo** poor grandpa! he's really aged; **la sopa está deliciosa/muy caliente** the soup is delicious/very hot; **está muy simpático conmigo** he's being *o* he's been so nice to me (recently); **¡todo está tan caro!** things are *o* have become so expensive!; **está cansada/furiosa/embarazada** she is tired/furious/pregnant

B (*con* **bien, mal, mejor, peor**): **están todos bien, gracias** they're all fine, thanks; **¡qué bien estás en esta foto!** you look great in this photo!; **está mal que no se lo perdones** it's wrong of you not to forgive him; *ver tb* **bien, mal, mejor, peor**

C (hablando de estado civil) to be; **está casada con un primo mío** she's married to a cousin of mine

D (seguido de participios) **~ sentado/echado/arrodillado** to be sitting/lying/kneeling (down); **estaban abrazados** they had their arms around each other; *ver tb v aux* **B**

E (con predicado introducido por preposición) to be; *(para más ejemplos ver tb la preposición o el nombre correspondiente)*; **estoy a régimen** I'm on a diet; **¿a cómo está la uva?** how much are the grapes?; **estamos como al principio** we're back to where we started; **está con el sarampión** she has (the) measles; **siempre está con lo mismo** he's always going on about the same thing; **está de buen humor** she's in a good mood; **están de limpieza/viaje** they're spring-cleaning/on a trip; **hoy estoy de cocinera** I'm doing the cooking today; **estaba de secretaria** she worked as a secretary; **no estoy para bromas** I'm not in the mood for jokes; **estamos sin electricidad** the electricity is off at the moment; **está sin pintar** it hasn't been painted yet; ***~ con algn*** (estar de acuerdo) to agree with sb; (apoyar) to support sb, be on sb's side; **el pueblo está con nosotros** the people are with us; ***~ en algo***: **no lo hemos solucionado pero estamos en ello** *or* **eso** we haven't solved it but we're working on it

F (introducido por **que**): **el agua está que pela** the water's scalding hot; **está que no hay quien lo aguante** he's (being) unbearable

■ **estar** *vi*

(*Sentido* I) (en un lugar)

A «*edificio/pueblo*» (estar ubicado) to be; **¿dónde está Chiapas?** where's Chiapas?; **está a 20 kilómetros de aquí** it's 20 kilometers from here

B 1 «*persona/objeto*» (hallarse en cierto momento) to be; **¿sabes dónde está Pedro?** do you know where Pedro is?; **¿a qué hora tienes que ~ allí?** what time do you have to be there?; **¿dónde estábamos la clase pasada?** where did we get to in the last class? 2 (figurar) to be; **yo no estaba en la lista** I wasn't on the list, my name didn't appear on the list

C (hallarse en determinado lugar): **¿está Rodrigo?** is Rodrigo in?; **¿estamos todos?** are we all here?

D 1 (quedarse, permanecer): **sólo ~é unos días** I'll only be staying a few days; **¿cuánto tiempo ~ás en Londres?** how long are you going to be in London (for)? 2 (vivir): **ahora estamos en Soca** we're in *o* we live in Soca now; **de momento estoy con mi hermana** at the moment I'm staying with my sister

(*Sentido* II) (en el tiempo): **¿a qué (día) estamos?** what day is it today?; **¿a cuánto estamos hoy?** what's the date today?; **estamos a 28 de mayo** it's May 28th (AmE) *o* (BrE) the 28th of May; **estamos en primavera** it's spring; **¿en qué mes estamos?** what month are we in *o* is it?

(*Sentido* III)

A (existir, haber): **y después está el problema de ...** and then there's the problem of ...; **luego están los niños, hay que pensar en ellos** then there are the children to think about

B (tener como función, cometido) **~ PARA algo**: **para eso están los amigos** that's what friends are for; **estamos para ayudarlos** we're here to help them

C (radicar): **ahí está el quid del asunto** that's the crux of the matter; **~ EN algo**: **en eso está el problema** that's where the problem lies; **todo está en que él quiera** it all depends on whether he wants to or not

D (estar listo, terminado): **la carne todavía no está** the meat's not ready yet; **lo atas con un nudo y ya está** you tie a

knot in it and that's it *o* there you are; **enseguida estoy** I'll be right with you; **¡ya está! ¡ya sé la repuesta!** I've got it! I know the answer!; ***¡ahí está!*** that's it!
E (quedar entendido): **que no vuelva a suceder ¿estamos?** don't let it happen again, understand? *o* (colloq) got it?
F **ya que estamos/estás** while we're/you're at it
G (Esp) (quedar) (+ *me/te/le etc*) (+ *compl*): **te está grande/pequeña** it's too big/too small for you; **la 46 te está mejor** the 46 fits you better
■ **estar** *v aux*
A (con gerundio): **está lloviendo** it's raining; **se está afeitando** he's shaving; **estoy viendo que va a ser imposible** I'm beginning to see that it's going to be impossible
B (con participio): **la foto está tomada con flash** the photo was taken with flash; **ese asiento está ocupado** that seat is taken; **ya está hecho un hombrecito** he's a proper young man now; *ver tb* **estar** *cópula* **D**
■ **estarse** *v pron*
A (*enf*) (permanecer) to stay; **se estuvo horas ahí sentado** he remained sitting there for hours; **¿no te puedes ~ quieto?** can't you stay *o* keep still?; **estése tranquilo** don't worry
B (*enf*) (llegar) to be; **estáte allí media hora antes** be there half an hour before

estar² *m* (esp AmL) living room

estarcir [I4] *vt* to stencil

estárter *m* choke

estatal *adj* state (*before n*)

estático -ca *adj* 1 (inmóvil) static; **quedarse ~** to freeze, stand stock still 2 (Elec) static

estatificar [A2] *vt* to nationalize

estatización *f* (AmL) nationalization

estatizar [A4] *vt* (AmL) to nationalize

estatua *f* statue

estatuilla *f* statuette

estatuir [I20] *vt* (frml) to establish

estatura *f* height; **mide dos metros de ~** he's two meters (tall); **de mediana ~** of medium height; **¿qué ~ tenía?** how tall was she?

estatus *m* status

estatutario -ria *adj* statutory

estatuto *m* 1 (Der, Pol) statute; (regla) rule 2 **estatutos** *mpl* (de empresa) articles of association (*pl*)
(Compuesto) **estatuto de autonomía** (en Esp) statute of autonomy (relating to Spain's 17 autonomous regions)

este¹ *adj inv* ‹región› eastern; **en la parte ~ del país** in the eastern part *o* the east of the country; **iban en dirección ~** they were heading east *o* eastward(s); **el ala/la costa ~** the east wing/coast

este² *m* 1 (parte, sector): **el ~** the east; **en el ~ del país** in the east of the country; **al ~ de Lima** to the east of Lima 2 (punto cardinal) east, East; **vientos del E~** easterly winds; **caminaron hacia el E~** they walked east *o* eastward(s); **las ventanas dan al ~** the windows face east 3 **el Este** (Hist, Pol) the East; **los países del E~** the Eastern Bloc countries

este³, **esta** *adj dem* (*pl* **estos, estas**) 1 this; (*pl*) these; **este chico** this boy; **esta gente** these people; [*usually indicates a pejorative or emphatic tone when placed after the noun*] **la estúpida esta no me avisó** (fam) this idiot here didn't tell me 2 (como muletilla) well, er

éste, **ésta** *pron dem* (*pl* **éstos, éstas**) [*According to the Real Academia Española the written accent may be omitted when there is no risk of confusion with the adjective*] 1 this one; (*pl*) these; **~ es el mío** this (one) is mine; **un día de éstos** one of these days; **~ es el que yo quería** this is the one I wanted; **Alfonso y Andrés, ~ de pie, aquél sentado** (liter) ... Alfonso and Andrés, the former sitting down and the latter standing; [*sometimes indicates irritation, emphasis or disapproval*] **¡qué niña ésta!** (fam) honestly, this child! 2 **ésta** (frml) (en cartas, documentos) *the city in which the letter is written*; **residente en ésta** resident in Seville (*o* Lima *etc*)

estela *f* 1 (de barco) wake; (de avión, cohete) trail; **una ~ de destrucción y muerte** a trail of death and destruction 2 (Auto) slipstream

estelar *adj* 1 (Espec) star (*before n*); **con la participación ~ de ...** with the special guest appearance of ... 2 (Astron) stellar

estelarizar [A4] *vt* (Méx) to star in

esténcil *m* (AmS) stencil

estenógrafo -fa *m,f* (ant) stenographer

estenotipia *f* (máquina) Stenotype®; (actividad) shorthand typing

estenotipista *mf* shorthand typist

estentóreo -rea *adj* booming, stentorian

estepa *f* steppe

estepario -ria *adj* steppe (*before n*)

estera *f* mat

estercolero *m* dunghill, dung heap

estéreo¹ *adj inv* stereo

estéreo² *m* stereo; **grabación en ~** stereo recording

estereofonía *f* stereophony

estereofónico -ca *adj* stereophonic

estereotipado -da *adj* ‹*frase*› clichéd; ‹*idea/personaje*› stereotyped

estereotipar [A1] *vt* to stereotype

estereotipo *m* stereotype

estéril *adj* 1 ‹*animal/persona*› sterile; ‹*terreno*› infertile, barren 2 ‹*esfuerzo/discusión*› futile 3 ‹*gasa/jeringa*› sterile

esterilidad *f* 1 (de persona, animal) sterility; (de terreno) barrenness, infertility 2 (de esfuerzo, discusión) futility 3 (asepsia) sterility

esterilización *f* sterilization

esterilizar [A4] *vt* to sterilize

esterilla *f* 1 (alfombrilla) mat 2 (AmS) (mimbre) wicker

esternón *m* sternum, breastbone

estero *m* 1 (estuario) estuary 2 (AmS) (laguna, pantano) marsh 3 (Chi) (arroyo) stream

esteroide *m* steroid
(Compuesto) **esteroide anabólico** *or* **anabolizante** anabolic steroid

estertor *m* (de moribundo) death rattle; (Med) rale

esteta *mf* aesthete

estética *f*
A (Art) aesthetics
B (Med) cosmetic surgery; **se hizo la ~ en la nariz** she had a nose job (colloq)

esteticien, esteticista *mf* aesthetician, beautician

esteticismo *m* aestheticism

estético -ca *adj* aesthetic

estetoscopio *m* stethoscope

estevado -da *adj* ▸**patizambo**

estiaje *m* low water level

estibador -dora *m,f* stevedore

estibar [A1] *vt* (cargar) to load; (descargar) to unload

estiércol *m* (excremento) dung; (abono) manure

estigma *m* stigma; **~s** (Relig) stigmata (*pl*)

estilar [A1] *vi* (Chi) (gotear) to drip; (escurrir) to drain
■ **estilarse** *v pron* «*moda/peinado*» to be fashionable; **ya no se estila hacer ese tipo de fiestas** people don't have those kind of parties any more

estilete *m* (puñal) stiletto; (punzón) stylus

estilista *mf* 1 (Lit) stylist 2 (diseñador de modas) designer 3 (AmL) (peluquero) hairstylist

estilístico -ca *adj* stylistic

estilizado -da *adj* 1 (Art) stylized 2 ‹*cuerpo/figura*› slender, slim

estilizar [A4] *vt* 1 (Art) to stylize 2 ‹*figura/cuerpo*› to make ... look slender *o* slim

estilo *m*
A 1 (Art) style; **~ barroco** baroque style 2 (manera, tipo) style; **ropa de ~ deportivo** casual wear; **hecho al ~ de mi tierra** done the way they do it back home; ***por el ~***: **no es que me desagrade ni nada por el ~** it isn't that I don't like him or anything (like that); **y otras cosas por el ~** and other things of that sort *o* kind; **dijo eso o algo por el ~** he said that or words to that effect; **son todos**

por el ~ they are all the same 3 (calidad distintiva) style; **se viste con mucho ~** he dresses very stylishly

(Compuestos)

- **estilo de vida** way of life, lifestyle
- **estilo directo** (Ling) direct speech
- **estilo indirecto** (Ling) indirect *o* reported speech

B (en natación) stroke, style; **los 200 metros ~s** the 200 meter medley

(Compuestos)

- **estilo libre** freestyle
- **estilo mariposa** butterfly
- **estilo pecho** *or* (Esp) **braza** breaststroke

C (Bot) style

D (punzón) stylus

estilográfica *f*, **estilógrafo** *m* fountain pen

estiloso *adj* (AmL fam) stylish

estima *f* respect; **se ha ganado la ~ de todos** he's gained everyone's respect; **tenerle ~ a algn** to think highly of sb; **tiene en gran** *or* **mucha ~ tu amistad** he values your friendship very highly

estimable *adj* 1 (digno de estima) ‹*persona/contribución*› estimable (frml) 2 (considerable) considerable

estimación *f*

A (cálculo) estimate

B (aprecio) respect, esteem; **se ha ganado mi ~** he has earned my respect

estimado -da *adj* dear; **~ señor Díaz** (Corresp) Dear Mr Díaz

estimar [A1] *vt*

A (apreciar) 1 ‹*persona*› to respect, hold … in high *o* great esteem (frml); **lo estimo mucho, pero sólo como amigo** I'm very fond of him, but only as a friend 2 ‹*objeto*› to value; **estima mucho ese anillo** she values that ring highly; **su piel es muy estimada** its skin is highly prized

B (frml) (considerar) (+ *compl*) to consider, deem (frml); **no lo estimé necesario** I did not consider it necessary

C (calcular) ‹*valor/costo/pérdidas*› to estimate; **~ algo EN algo** to estimate sth AT sth; **pérdidas estimadas en varios millones** losses estimated at several million

estimativo -va *adj* ‹*cálculos*› rough; ‹*cifras*› approximate, rough

estimulación *f* stimulation

estimulante[1] *adj* stimulating; **bebidas ~s** stimulants

estimulante[2] *m* stimulant

estimular [A1] *vt*

A 1 «*clase/lectura*» to stimulate 2 (alentar) ‹*persona*› to encourage 3 ‹*apetito/circulación*› to stimulate 4 (sexualmente) to stimulate

B ‹*inversión/ahorro*› to encourage, stimulate

estímulo *m* 1 (incentivo) encouragement; **sirve de ~ a la inversión** it acts as an incentive to investment, it encourages investment 2 (Biol, Fisiol) stimulus

estío *m* (liter) summertime

estipendio *m* (frml) (salario) salary; (honorarios) fee

estipulación *f* stipulation

estipular [A1] *vt* to stipulate

estirada *f* (Dep) full-length save

estirado -da *adj* (fam) stuck-up (colloq), snooty (colloq)

estiramiento *m* 1 (de músculos) stretching 2 (de la piel) *tb* **~ facial** face-lift 3 (del pelo) straightening

estirar [A1] *vt*

A 1 ‹*goma/elástico/suéter*› to stretch; ‹*cable/soga*› to pull out, stretch 2 ‹*sábanas/mantel*› (con las manos) to smooth out; (con la plancha) to run the iron over

B ‹*brazos/piernas*› to stretch; **estiró el cuello para poder ver** she craned her neck to be able to see

C ‹*dinero/comida/recursos*› to make … go further

■ **estirarse** *v pron* 1 (en gimnasia, para desperezarse) to stretch; (para alcanzar algo) to stretch, reach up/out 2 «*goma/elástico/suéter*» to stretch

estirón *m*: **dar** *or* **pegar un/el ~** (fam) to shoot up (colloq)

estirpe *f* stock, lineage

estítico -ca *adj* (Chi) constipated

estitiquez *f* (Chi) constipation

estival *adj* summer (*before n*)

esto *pron dem* (*neutro*) 1 this; **~ es lo más difícil** this is the most difficult part; **el 10%, ~ es, el doble** 10%, that is to say, twice as much; **en ~ llega Daniel** just at this moment *o* just then Daniel arrives; **no tiene ni *esto* de sentido común** he hasn't an ounce of common sense 2 (Esp) (como muletilla) well, er

estocada *m* (Taur) *final thrust with the* **estoque**; (en esgrima) sword thrust; (herida) sword wound

Estocolmo *m* Stockholm

estofa *f* (pey) sort, type; **gente de baja ~** the riffraff (pej)

estofado[1] **-da** *adj* stewed; (con menos líquido) braised

estofado[2] *m* stew

estoicismo *m* stoicism

estoico[1] **-ca** *adj* stoic, stoical

estoico[2] **-ca** *m,f* stoic

estola *f* stole

estólido -da *adj* (liter) dull, slow-witted

estomacal *adj* stomach

estómago *m* (Anat) stomach; **me duele el ~** *or* **tengo dolor de ~** I have a stomachache, my stomach hurts; **beber con el ~ vacío** to drink on an empty stomach; ***revolverle el ~ a algn*** to turn sb's stomach; ***tener (buen) ~*** (fam) to have a strong stomach

estomatólogo -ga *m,f* stomatologist

estopa *f* (fibra) tow; (tela) burlap

estoperol *m*

A (Andes) (en carretera) cat's eye

B (Chi) (Dep) stud

estoque *m* sword (*used for killing bull*)

estoquear [A1] *vt* to stab (*with the* **estoque**)

estorbar [A1] *vi* to be/get in the way

■ **estorbar** *vt* to obstruct; **el vehículo estorbaba la circulación** the vehicle was blocking the traffic; **el piano estorbaba el paso** the piano was in the way

estorbo *m* hindrance, nuisance; **no soy más que un ~** I'm just a nuisance; **los niños serían un ~ en su carrera** children would be a hindrance to her career plans

estornino *m* starling

estornudar [A1] *vi* to sneeze

estornudo *m* sneeze

estos -tas *adj dem*: *ver* **este**[3]

éstos -tas *pron dem*: *ver* **éste**

estoy *see* **estar**

estrabismo *m* squint, strabismus (tech)

estrada *f* road

estrado *m* 1 (tarima) platform, dais; **subió al ~ a declarar** he took the stand to give evidence 2 **estrados** *mpl* (Der) law courts (*pl*)

estrafalario[1] **-ria** *adj* ‹*persona/ideas/conducta*› eccentric; ‹*vestimenta*› outlandish, bizarre

estrafalario[2] **-ria** *m,f* eccentric

estragón *m* tarragon

estragos *mpl*: **los ~ de la guerra** the ravages of war; **causar/hacer ~s** «*terremoto/inundación*» to wreak havoc; **la epidemia causó ~ entre la población** the epidemic devastated the population; **causa ~ entre las quinceañeras** he drives fifteen-year-old girls wild

estrambótico -ca *adj* ‹*persona/idea/conducta*› eccentric; ‹*vestimenta*› outlandish, bizarre

estrangulación *f* strangulation; **muerte por ~** death by strangulation *o* strangling

estrangulador -dora *m,f* strangler

estrangulamiento *m* ▸**estrangulación**

estrangular [A1] *vt* 1 (ahogar) to strangle, throttle 2 ‹*vena/conducto*› to strangulate

■ **estrangularse** *v pron* 1 (ahogar) to strangle oneself, be strangled 2 «*hernia*» to become strangulated

estraperlear [A1] *vi* to deal in black market goods; **~ CON algo** to sell sth on the black market

■ **estraperlear** *vt* sell ... on the black market

estraperlista *mf* black marketeer

estraperlo *m* black market; **de ~** on the black market

estratagema *f* stratagem

estratega *mf* strategist

estrategia *f* strategy
estratégico -ca *adj* strategic
estratificado -da *adj* stratified
estratificar [A2] *vt* to stratify
estrato *m* 1 (Geol, Sociol) stratum; **los ~s sociales** the social strata 2 (Meteo) stratus
estratosfera *f* stratosphere
estrechamente *adv* 1 (íntimamente) ‹*relacionado/vinculado*› closely 2 ‹*vivir*› frugally
estrechamiento *m*
A (de relaciones) strengthening
B (reducción del ancho) narrowing
estrechar [A1] *vt*
A ‹*falda/pantalones*› to take ... in; ‹*carretera*› to make ... narrower
B (apretar, abrazar) ‹*persona*›: **la estrechó entre sus brazos** he held her tightly in his arms; **me estrechó la mano** he shook my hand
C ‹*relaciones/lazos*› to strengthen
■ **estrecharse** *v pron*
A «*carretera/acera*» to narrow, get narrower
B (*recípr*) (apretarse): **se ~on en un abrazo** they embraced; **se ~on la mano** they shook hands
C «*relaciones/lazos*» to strengthen
estrechez *f*
A (de criterio) narrowness; (de política) lack of vision, shortsightedness; **~ de miras** *or* **horizontes** narrow outlook
B **estrecheces** *fpl* (dificultades económicas) financial difficulties (*pl*); **vivir sin estrecheces** to live comfortably; **pasar estrecheces** to have financial difficulties
estrecho[1] -cha *adj*
A 1 (angosto) ‹*calle/pasillo*› narrow; ‹*falda*› tight; **es estrecha de caderas** she has narrow hips 2 (apretado) tight; **íbamos muy ~s** it was very cramped
B ‹*amistad/colaboración/vigilancia*› close
C (limitado) ‹*criterio*› narrow; **es muy ~ de miras** he's very narrow-minded
estrecho[2] *m* (Geog) strait, straits (*pl*); **el E~ de Magallanes** the Strait of Magellan
estrechura *f* narrowness
estrella *f*
A 1 (Astron) star; **un cielo sin ~s** a starless sky; ***ver (las) ~s*** to see stars 2 (suerte): **no quiso mi ~ que fuera así** fate would not have it so; **tener buena/mala ~** to be born lucky/unlucky; ***unos nacen con ~ y otros nacen estrellados*** (fam & hum) some are born under a lucky star and some are born seeing stars (hum)

Compuestos
- **estrella de Belén** star of Bethlehem
- **estrella de mar** starfish
- **estrella fugaz** shooting star
- **estrella polar** Pole Star

B 1 (como símbolo) star; **un hotel de tres ~s** a three-star hotel 2 (asterisco) asterisk
C (ídolo) star; **una ~ de cine** a movie star
estrellado -da *adj* (lleno de estrellas) starry; (en forma de estrella) star-shaped
estrellar [A1] *vt*: **estrelló un plato contra la pared** he smashed a plate against the wall; **estrelló el coche contra un árbol** he smashed his car into a tree
■ **estrellarse** *v pron* 1 (chocar) to crash; **se estrelló con la moto** he had a motorcycle accident; **~se CONTRA algo** to crash INTO sth; **el balón se estrelló contra el poste** the ball slammed into the post; **se estrelló contra el cristal** he walked smack into the glass door 2 (toparse, tropezar) **~se CON algo/algn** to come up against sth/sb
estrellato *m* (period) stardom; **la película que la lanzó al ~** the movie which brought her stardom
estrellón *m* 1 (Col fam) (Auto) smash-up (colloq) 2 (Chi) (golpe): **me di un ~ con la puerta** I walked smack into the door (colloq); **nos dimos un ~** we bumped into each other
estremecedor -dora *adj* ‹*escena/noticia*› horrifying; ‹*grito/relato*› spine-chilling, hair-raising
estremecer [E3] *vt* to make ... shudder; **~ la conciencia colectiva** to shock people into awareness
■ **estremecer** *vi* to shudder; **hacer ~ a algn** to make sb shudder; **hacer ~ los cimientos de la sociedad** to shake the foundations of society
■ **estremecerse** *v pron* 1 «*persona*» **~se DE algo** ‹*de miedo/horror*› to shudder WITH sth; ‹*de frío*› to shiver *o* tremble WITH sth; **se estremeció sólo de pensarlo** he shuddered at the mere thought of it 2 «*edificio/ventana*» to shake
estremecimiento *m*: **un ~ de horror** a shudder of horror; **tenía ~s de frío** he was shivering with cold
estrenar [A1] *vt*
A (Cin, Teatr); **la película se estrenó en marzo** the movie opened *o* (journ) had its premiere in March; **acaban de ~ la obra en Madrid** the play's just started showing *o* just opened in Madrid
B (usar por primera vez): **todavía no he estrenado la blusa** I still haven't worn the blouse; **todavía no hemos estrenado el gimnasio** we still haven't tried out the gymnasium; Ⓢ **oficina de 90 metros, a estrenar** brand new office, 90 meters
■ **estrenarse** *v pron*
A (iniciarse) to make one's debut; **se estrenó como director** he made his debut as a director
B ‹*ropa/zapatos*› ▸**estrenar B**
estreno *m*
A (Cin, Espec, Teatr) premiere; **entradas para el ~ de la obra** tickets for the opening *o* first night of the play
B 1 (primer uso): **estar/ir de ~** to be wearing new clothes; **el ~ del local** the opening of the new premises 2 (primera actuación): **su ~ como chef** his debut as a chef
estreñido -da *adj* constipated
estreñimiento *m* constipation
estreñir [I15] *vi* to cause constipation
■ **estreñir** *vt* to make ... constipated, bind (colloq)
estrépito *m*: **un ~ de vasos rotos** a crash of broken glasses; **el ~ de las bocinas** the din of the car horns
estrepitosamente *adv* with a (loud) crash
estrepitoso -sa *adj* 1 ‹*aplausos*› tumultuous; ‹*risa*› loud, noisy; **carcajadas estrepitosas** roars of laughter 2 ‹*fracaso*› resounding; ‹*caída/colisión*› almighty (colloq)
estreptococo *m* streptococcus
estreptomicina *f* streptomycin
estrés *m* stress
estresado -da *adj* under stress; **está muy ~** he's been under a lot of stress
estresante *adj* stressful
estresar [A1] *vt* stress, cause stress to
estría *f* 1 (en la piel) stretch mark) 2 (Min) stria, striation 3 (de columna) groove, stria (tech); **~s** fluting 4 **estrías** *fpl* (de fusil) rifling
estriado -da *adj* 1 ‹*piel*› stretch-marked 2 ‹*mineral*› striated 3 ‹*columna*› fluted 4 ‹*cañón de fusil*› rifled
estribación *f* spur; **en las estribaciones de la cordillera** in the foothills of the range
estribar [A1] *vi*
A **~ EN algo** «*problema/encanto*» to stem FROM sth, lie IN sth
B (Arquit, Const) **~ EN algo** «*arco/edificio/columna*» to rest ON sth
estribillo *m* (Lit) refrain; (Mús) chorus
estribo *m*
A 1 (Equ) stirrup; ***con un pie en el ~*** ready to go; ***perder los ~s*** to fly off the handle, lose one's cool; ***tomarse la del ~*** to have one for the road (colloq) 2 (de vehículo) running board; (de moto) footrest
B (de arco) abutment; (de muro) buttress; (de puente) support
estribor *m* starboard; **¡tierra a ~!** land to starboard!
estricnina *f* strychnine
estricto -ta *adj* ‹*persona/disciplina*› strict; ‹*significado*› precise, strict
estridencia *f* shrillness
estridente *adj* 1 ‹*pitido/chirrido*› shrill 2 ‹*voz*› (agudo) shrill; (fuerte) strident; **su ~ protesta** her strident *o* vociferous protest 3 ‹*color*› garish, loud; **un rosa ~** a shocking pink
estrofa *f* stanza, verse
estrógeno *m* estrogen*
estroncio *m* strontium
estropajo *m* scourer
estropajoso -sa *adj* wiry, straw-like

estropeado -da *adj*: **esos zapatos están muy ~s** those shoes are falling apart; **lo encontré muy ~** I thought he looked a wreck (colloq); *ver tb* **estropear**

estropear [A1] *vt*

A 1 ‹*aparato/mecanismo*› to damage, break; ‹*coche*› to damage 2 (malograr) ‹*plan/vacaciones*› to spoil, ruin

B (deteriorar, dañar) ‹*piel*› to damage, ruin; ‹*juguete*› to break; ‹*ropa*› to ruin; **el calor estropeó la fruta** the heat made the fruit go bad; **estropeó la comida echándole mucha sal** he spoiled the food by putting too much salt in it

■ **estropearse** *v pron*

A 1 (averiarse) to break down; **la lavadora está estropeada** the washing machine is broken 2 «*plan*» to go wrong

B 1 (deteriorarse) «*fruta*» to go bad; «*leche/pescado*» to go off; **los zapatos se me ~on con la lluvia** the rain ruined my shoes 2 (Esp) «*persona*» (afearse) to lose one's looks

estropicio *m*: **dejaron todo hecho un ~** they left everything in a real mess; **los ~s causados por el huracán** the damage *o* havoc caused by the hurricane

estructura *f* 1 (de edificio, puente) structure, framework; (de mueble) frame; (de célula, mineral) structure 2 (de oración, novela) structure 3 (de empresa) structure; (de sociedad) structure, framework

estructuración *f* (acción) structuring; (resultado) structure

estructural *adj* structural

estructuralismo *m* structuralism

(Compuesto) **estructuralismo lingüístico** structural linguistics

estructurar [A1] *vt* to structure, to organize

estruendo *m* (de las olas) roar; (de cascada, tráfico) thunder, roar; (de maquinaria) din; **se derrumbó con un gran ~** it came down with a great crash

estruendoso -sa *adj* ‹*aplausos*› thunderous; ‹*fracaso*› resounding, massive; ‹*ruido*› deafening

estrujar [A1] *vt*

A 1 (apretar arrugando) ‹*papel*› to crumple up, scrunch up; ‹*tela*› to crumple (up) 2 (para escurrir) to wring (out) 3 ‹*uvas*› to press

B ‹*persona*› to squeeze, hold … tightly

estrujón *m* (fam) squeeze

estuario *m* estuary

estucado *m* plasterwork, stucco

estucar [A2] *vt* to plaster, stucco

estuche *m* (de gafas, lápices, violín) case; (de cubiertos) canteen; (de collar, reloj) box, case

estuco *m* (Art) stuccowork, stucco

estudiado -da *adj* ‹*pose/modales*› studied

estudiantado *m* students (*pl*)

estudiante *mf* (de universidad) student; (de secundaria) (high-school) student (AmE), (secondary school) pupil (BrE); **~ de Derecho/Inglés** law/English student

estudiantil *adj* student (*before n*)

estudiantina *f*: *traditional student music group*

estudiar [A1] *vt*

A 1 ‹*asignatura*› to study; **estudia música** he's studying music; (en la universidad) to study, read (frml); **estudia medicina** she's studying *o* doing *o* reading medicine; **¿qué carrera estudió?** what subject did he do at college/university? 2 ‹*instrumento*› to learn

B ‹*lección/tablas*› to learn

C (observar) ‹*rostro/comportamiento*› to study

D (considerar, analizar) ‹*mercado/situación/proyecto*› to study; ‹*propuesta*› to study, consider; **~on sus posibles causas** they looked into its possible causes

■ **estudiar** *vi* to study; **tengo que ~ para el examen** I have to do some work *o* studying for the test; **estudia en un colegio privado** he goes to a private school; **debes ~ más** you must work harder; **dejó de ~ a los 15 años** she left school at 15; **~ PARA algo** to study to be sth

■ **estudiarse** *v pron* 1 (*enf*) ‹*lección*› to study; ‹*papel*› to learn 2 (*recípr*) (observarse): **se ~on largo rato** they watched each other closely for a long time

estudio *m*

A 1 (Educ) (actividad): **primero está el ~** your studies *o* work must come first 2 (investigación, análisis) study; **el ~ de la fauna de la zona** the study of the area's fauna 3 (de asunto, caso) consideration; **le presentaron un proyecto para su ~** they put forward a plan for his consideration; **está en** *o* (RPl) **a ~ en el Parlamento** it is being considered in parliament

(Compuesto) **estudio de mercado** market research

B (lugar) 1 (de artista) studio; (de arquitecto) office, studio; (de abogado) (CS) office 2 (Cin, Rad, TV) studio 3 (en casa) study; (apartamento) studio apartment

(Compuestos)

- **estudio fotográfico/de grabación** photographic/recording studio
- **estudio jurídico** (RPl) (oficina) lawyer's office; (grupo) legal practice

C (Mús, Art) study

D **estudios** *mpl* (Educ) education; **~s primarios/superiores** primary/higher education; **quiso darle ~s a su hijo** she wanted to give her son an education; **no hace falta tener ~s superiores** you don't need a degree; **dejar los ~s** to give up one's studies; **me pagaron los ~s** they paid for my schooling

estudioso¹ -sa *adj* studious

estudioso² -sa *m,f* scholar

estufa *f* 1 (de calefacción) stove; **~ eléctrica/de gas** electric/gas heater 2 (Col, Méx) (cocina) stove; **~ de gas** gas stove, gas cooker (BrE)

estupefacción *f* astonishment, stupefaction (frml)

estupefaciente¹ *adj* narcotic

estupefaciente² *m* narcotic (drug); **tráfico de ~s** drug trafficking

estupefacto -ta *adj* astonished, amazed; **la noticia me dejó ~** the news left me speechless *o* amazed me

estupendamente *adv* ‹*cantar/desenvolverse*› marvelously*; **lo pasamos ~** we had a wonderful *o* marvelous time; **me siento ~** I feel great; **¿te viene bien el viernes? — sí, ~** is Friday all right with you? — yes, great (colloq)

estupendo¹ -da *adj* 1 (excelente) marvelous*, fantastic (colloq), great (colloq); **¡~!** great! 2 (guapo) gorgeous

estupendo² *adv*: **se viste ~** he dresses really well; **lo pasé ~** I had a great *o* wonderful time

estupidez *f* 1 (cualidad) stupidity, foolishness 2 (dicho): **no digas estupideces** don't talk nonsense 3 (acto): **hizo la ~ más grande de su vida** she made the biggest mistake of her life; **eso sería una ~** that would be stupid *o* foolish

estúpido¹ -da *adj* ‹*persona/argumento*› stupid, silly; **¡ay, qué estúpida soy!** oh, how stupid of me!

estúpido² -da *m,f* idiot, fool; **el ~ de mi hermano** my stupid brother

estupor *m* 1 (estupefacción) astonishment; **la noticia lo llenó de ~** the news left him speechless 2 (Med) stupor

esturión *m* sturgeon

estuve, estuviste, etc *see* **estar**

esvástica *f* swastika

ETA /'eta/ *f* (= **Euskadi ta Azkatasuna**) ETA

> **ETA – Euskadi ta Askatasuna**
>
> *ETA*, meaning "Basque homeland and liberty", is a terrorist organization founded in 1959 to fight for Basque independence. Its political wing, established in 1978 as *Herri Batasuna* (Popular Unity) and now called **batasuna** (Unity), has been banned since 2003. Opinion polls show a majority of Basques are opposed to the political violence and murder campaigns espoused by *ETA*

etapa *f*

A (en viaje) stage; (en ciclismo, rally) leg, stage; **por ~s** in stages

B (de proceso) stage, phase; **la ~ más feliz de mi vida** the best *o* happiest time of my life

etarra¹ *adj*: *of or relating to ETA*

etarra² *mf*: *member of ETA*

etc (= **etcétera**) etc

etcétera etcetera, and so on (and so forth); **... y un largo ~ de ensayos** (frml) … and a long list of essays

éter *m* ether; **el ~** (liter) the ether (liter)

e

etéreo -rea *adj* ethereal

eternidad *f* eternity; **me pareció una ~** it seemed like an eternity to me

eternizar [A4] *vt*

A ‹*escena/momento*› to immortalize

B ‹*control/situación*› to perpetuate, to prolongue indefinitely

eternizarse [A4] *v pron* (fam) «*reunión/espera*» to go on forever (colloq); «*persona*»: **se eterniza hablando por teléfono** he spends ages on the phone (colloq)

eterno -na *adj* eternal; **la conferencia se me hizo eterna** the conference seemed to go on forever; **se juraron amor ~** they swore everlasting love

(Compuesto) **eterno femenino** *m*: **el ~ ~** the eternal feminine *o* woman

ética *f* ethics

(Compuesto) **ética profesional** professional ethics (*pl*)

ético -ca *adj* ethical

etileno *m* ethylene

etílico -ca *adj* (Quím) ethyl (*before n*), ethylic

etilo *m* ethyl

etimología *f* etymology

etimológico -ca *adj* etymological

etiología *f* etiology

etíope, etiope *adj/mf* Ethiopian

Etiopía *f* Ethiopia

etiqueta *f*

A 1 (pegada) label 2 (atada) tag; (en prenda, con instrucciones de lavado, etc) label; **le pusieron la ~ de 'rojo'** they labeled him a 'red'

B (protocolo) etiquette; **baile/traje de ~** formal ball/dress; **vestir de ~** to wear formal dress

etiquetado, etiquetaje *m* labeling•

etiquetador -dora *m,f*

A (persona) labeler•

B **etiquetadora** *f* (máquina) labeling• machine

etiquetar [A1] *vt* ‹*producto*› to label; ‹*persona*› **~ a algn DE algo** to label sb (AS) sth

etnia *f* ethnic group

étnico -ca *adj* ethnic

etnocéntrico -ca *adj* ethnocentric

etnografía *f* ethnography

etnología *f* ethnology

etnológico -ca *adj* ethnological

eucalipto *m* eucalyptus

Eucaristía *f* Eucharist; **recibir la ~** to take communion

eucarístico -ca *adj* eucharistic

eufemismo *m* euphemism

eufemístico -ca *adj* euphemistic

eufonía *f* euphony

euforia *f* elation, euphoria

eufórico -ca *adj* ecstatic, euphoric

euforizante *adj*: **drogas ~s** drugs that produce euphoria; **el efecto ~** the euphoric effect

eugenesia *f* eugenics

eunuco *m* eunuch

Eurasia *f* Eurasia

eureka *interj* eureka!

euro *m* euro

eurobono *m* Eurobond

Eurocámara *f* European Parliament

eurócrata *mf* Eurocrat

eurodiputado -da *m,f* Euro MP, MEP, Member of the European Parliament

eurodólar *m* Eurodollar

euroescéptico -ca *m,f* Euroskeptic (AmE), Eurosceptic (BrE)

Europa *f* Europe

(Compuesto) **Europa Central/Occidental/Oriental** Central/Western/Eastern Europe

europarlamentario -ria *m,f* ▸ **eurodiputado**

europeísmo *m* Europeanism

europeísta *adj* pro-European

europeización *f* Europeanization

europeo -pea *adj/m,f* European

Eurotunnel®, eurotúnel *m* Channel Tunnel

Eurovisión *f* Eurovision; **el Festival de ~** the Eurovision Song Contest

eurozona *f* eurozone

Euskadi *f* the Basque Country

Euskadi

The most widely accepted term in the Basque language for the Basque country. The present **comunidad autónoma** includes the three Basque provinces of Vizcaya, Guipúzcoa and Álava, but not neighboring Navarra which also has substantial numbers of Basque-speakers and retains many Basque cultural traditions. For this reason the most uncompromising of Basque separatists prefer the term *Euskal Herria*, which includes Euskadi, Navarra and also the Basque *départements* of south-west France, known as Iparralde

euskera, eusquera *adj/m* Basque

euskera

The language of the Basque Country and Navarre, spoken by around 750,000 people; in Spanish *vasco* or *vascuence*. It is also spelled *euskara*. Basque is unrelated to the Indo-European languages and its origins are unclear.

Like Spain's other regional languages, Basque was banned under Franco. With the return of democracy, it became an official language alongside Spanish, in the regions where it is spoken. It is a compulsory school subject and is required for many official and administrative posts in the Basque Country. There is Basque language television and radio and a considerable number of books are published in Basque. *See also* **lenguas cooficiales**

eutanasia *f* euthanasia

evacuación *f*

A (desalojo) evacuation

B (frml) (defecación) bowel movement

evacuar [A1] *vt*

A ‹*local/zona/población*› to evacuate

B (frml) **~ el vientre** to have a bowel movement

■ **evacuar** *vi* (frml) to have a bowel movement

evadido¹ -da *adj* escaped (*before n*), fugitive (*before n*)

evadido² -da *m,f* fugitive

evadir [I1] *vt*

A ‹*dificultad/peligro/responsabilidad*› to avoid, evade; ‹*pregunta*› to avoid, sidestep; ‹*tema*› to dodge, evade; **logró ~ el cerco policial** he managed to get past the police cordon

B ‹*impuestos*› to evade

■ **evadirse** *v pron* 1 «*preso*» to escape 2 **~se DE algo** ‹*de responsabilidad/problema*› to run away FROM sth; ‹*de la realidad*› to escape FROM sth

evaluación *f* 1 (de daños, situación) assessment; (de datos, informes) evaluation, assessment 2 (Educ) (acción) assessment; (prueba, examen) test

(Compuesto) **evaluación continua** continuous assessment

evaluar [A18] *vt* ‹*pérdidas/situación*› to assess; ‹*datos*› to evaluate; ‹*alumno*› to assess

evanescente *adj* (liter) evanescent (liter)

evangélico¹ -ca *adj*

A (del evangelio) evangelical

B (protestante) protestant (*before n*)

evangélico² -ca *m,f* Protestant

evangelio *m* gospel; **los ~s sinópticos** the Synoptic Gospels

evangelista *m*

A (Bib) Evangelist; **San Juan E~** Saint John the Evangelist

B (Méx) *person who writes letters for people unable to write*

evangelizador¹ -dora *adj* ‹*misión*› evangelizing (*before n*); **la obra ~a de los jesuitas** the Jesuits' missionary work

evangelizador² **-dora** *m,f* evangelist
evangelizar [A4] *vt* to evangelize
evaporación *f* evaporation
evaporar [A1] *vt* to evaporate
■ **evaporarse** *v pron* «*líquido*» to evaporate; «*ayuda/dinero*» to evaporate; «*persona*» (fam) to vanish *o* disappear into thin air
evasión *f* escape, breakout; **literatura de ~** escapist literature
(Compuesto) **evasión fiscal** *or* **de impuestos** tax evasion
evasiva *f*: **me contestó con ~s** she avoided *o* dodged the issue
evasivo **-va** *adj* evasive, noncommital
evento *m* 1 (period) (suceso) event 2 (caso) case; **en este ~** in such a case
eventual *adj*
A (posible) ‹*problema/conflicto*› possible; ‹*gastos*› incidental; ‹*riesgos/pasivos*› contingent; **en el caso ~ de que llueva** in the event of rain
B ‹*trabajo/trabajador*› casual, temporary; ‹*cargo*› temporary
eventualidad *f* eventuality, contingency; **en la ~ de que no se resuelva el problema** (frml) in the event that the problem is not resolved, should the problem not be resolved
eventualmente *adv* (posiblemente) possibly
evidencia *f* 1 (pruebas) evidence, proof; **negar la ~** to deny the obvious *o* the facts; ***rendirse ante la ~*** to bow to the evidence 2 (cualidad) obviousness; ***dejar*** *or* ***poner a algn en ~*** to show sb up; ***poner algo en ~*** to demonstrate sth; ***ponerse*** *o* ***quedar en ~*** to show oneself up
evidenciar [A1] *vt* to show, bear witness to
■ **evidenciarse** *v pron* to become evident; **con este hecho se evidenció su falta de organización** this incident was proof of his lack of organization; **según se evidencia en ...** as can be clearly seen in ...
evidente *adj* obvious, clear
evitar [A1] *vt* 1 (eludir, huir de) to avoid; **evita entrar en discusiones con él** avoid getting into arguments with him 2 (impedir) to avoid, prevent; **haremos lo posible para ~lo** we'll do everything we can to avoid *o* prevent it; **para ~ que sufran** to avoid *o* prevent them suffering 3 (ahorrar) **~le algo A algn** ‹*molestia/preocupación*› to save *o* spare sb sth
■ **evitarse** *v pron* ‹*problemas*› to save oneself; **evítese la molestia de ir a la tienda** avoid the inconvenience of going to the store; **me ~ía tener que pintarlo** it would save me having to paint it
evocación *f*
A (recuerdo) evocation
B (de espíritu) invocation
evocador **-dora** *adj* evocative
evocar [A2] *vt*
A (liter) 1 «*persona*» (recordar) to recall 2 «*perfume/hecho*» to evoke, bring to mind
B ‹*espíritu*› to invoke, call up
evocativo **-va** *adj* evocative
evolución *f*
A 1 (Biol) evolution 2 (de ideas, sociedad) development, evolution; (de enfermedad) development; (de enfermo) progress
B (de avión, pájaro) circle; (de gimnasta, patinador) evolution (frml)
evolucionado **-da** *adj* ‹*especie*› highly developed *o* evolved; ‹*sociedad/ideas*› advanced, highly developed
evolucionar [A1] *vi*
A 1 (Biol) to evolve 2 «*ideas/sociedad/ciencia*» to develop, evolve 3 «*enfermo*» to progress; **su estado evoluciona favorablemente** (frml) his condition is improving
B «*avión/pájaro*» to circle; «*gimnasta*» to move; «*patinador*» to skate
evolucionismo *m* evolutionism
evolucionista *adj* evolutionary
evolutivo **-va** *adj* evolutionary
ex *mf* (*pl* ~) (fam) ex (colloq), ex-girlfriend (*o* ex-husband *etc*)
exabrupto *m* outburst; **me contestó con ~s** he was really sharp with me
exacción *f* levying, exaction (frml); **~ fiscal** levying of taxes
exacerbación *f* aggravation, exacerbation
exacerbado **-da** *adj*: **los ánimos estaban ~s** feelings were running high
exacerbante *adj*
A (agravante) (frml) ‹*factor*› aggravating, exacerbating
B (irritante, exasperante) ‹*ruido/situación*› exasperating, intolerable
exacerbar [A1] *vt*
A (agravar, empeorar) (frml) ‹*problema/enfermedad/dolor*› to aggravate, exacerbate
B (irritar) ‹*persona*› to exasperate
■ **exacerbarse** *v pron*
A (agravarse) (frml) «*enfermedad/dolor/problema*» to worsen
B «*persona*» to become exasperated
exactamente *adv* exactly; **se visten ~ igual** they dress identically *o* exactly the same
exactitud *f* 1 (precisión) accuracy, precision **utiliza el vocabulario con mucha ~** she uses words with great precision *o* exactness; **las órdenes se cumplieron con ~** the orders were carried out to the letter 2 (veracidad, rigor) accuracy
exacto¹ **-ta** *adj* 1 (no aproximado) ‹*medida/cantidad*› exact; **40 kilos ~s** exactly 40 kilos; **hay que ser muy ~ en los cálculos** you have to be very accurate *o* precise in your calculations; **para ser ~s** to be exact 2 (verdadero, riguroso) ‹*informe/mapa/descripción*› accurate 3 (idéntico) ‹*copia*› exact; ‹*reproducción*› accurate
exacto² *interj* exactly!, precisely!
exageración *f* exaggeration; **es una ~ lo que trabaja** he works far too hard
exagerado **-da** *adj* 1 ‹*persona*›: **¡qué ~ eres!** you do exaggerate!; **es muy exagerada con la comida** she always makes far too much food 2 ‹*historia/relato*› exaggerated 3 (excesivo) ‹*precio*› exorbitant, excessive; ‹*cariño/castigo*› excessive; ‹*moda*› extravagant, way-out (colloq)
exagerar [A1] *vt* ‹*suceso/noticia*› to exaggerate
■ **exagerar** *vi* (al hablar) to exaggerate; (al hacer algo): **tampoco hay que ~, no tienes que acabarlo todo hoy** there's no need to overdo it, you don't have to finish it all today
exaltación *f*
A (excitación): **la ~ de los ánimos hacía temer ...** feelings were running so high that there were fears of ...; **presa de ~** in an excited *o* agitated state
B (frml) (alabanza) exaltation (frml)
exaltado¹ **-da** *adj*
A (vehemente) ‹*discurso*› impassioned
B (excitado): **los ~s manifestantes** the angry demonstrators; **los ánimos estaban ~s** feelings were running high; **estaba muy ~** he was really worked up
C [SER] ‹*persona*› hotheaded
exaltado² **-da** *m,f* hothead
exaltar [A1] *vt*
A (excitar) ‹*personas*› to excite; ‹*pasiones*› to arouse; **la intervención policial exaltó a los manifestantes** the police intervention angered the demonstrators
B (frml) (alabar) to extol (frml)
■ **exaltarse** *v pron* to get worked up
exalumno **-na** *m,f* (de colegio) ex-pupil; (de universidad) ex-student
examen *m*
A (Educ) exam, examination (frml); **~ oral/escrito** oral/written exam; **hacer** *or* (CS) **dar un ~** to take an exam; **aprobar** *or* (esp AmL) **pasar un ~** to pass an exam *o* a test; **presentarse a un ~** to take *o* (BrE) sit an exam
(Compuestos)
• **examen de admisión** *or* **de ingreso** entrance examination *o* test
• **examen final** final examination
• **examen parcial** modular exam *o* test
B (análisis, reconocimiento): **efectuaron un detallado ~ del área** they carried out a detailed search of the area; **un minucioso ~ de la situación** an in-depth study of the situation; **someter algo a ~** to subject sth to examination (frml)
(Compuestos)
• **examen de conciencia**: **hacer un ~ de ~** to examine one's conscience

- **examen médico** medical examination, medical

examinador[1] **-dora** *adj* examining (*before n*)

examinador[2] **-dora** *m,f* examiner

examinando -da *m,f* (frml) examinee (frml), candidate

examinar [A1] *vt*
A ‹*alumno/candidato*› to examine
B (mirar detenidamente, estudiar) ‹*objeto*› to examine, inspect; ‹*documento/proyecto/propuesta*› to examine, study; ‹*situación/caso*› to study, consider; ‹*enfermo*› to examine
■ **examinarse** *v pron* (Esp) to take an exam; **me examiné de latín** I had *o* took my Latin exam

exangüe *adj* (liter) spent (liter), exhausted

exánime *adj* (liter) (sin vida) lifeless, inanimate; (exangüe) exhausted, spent (liter)

exasperación *f* exasperation

exasperante *adj* exasperating

exasperar [A1] *vt* to exasperate; **su torpeza me exaspera** I find his clumsiness exasperating
■ **exasperarse** *v pron* to get worked up *o* exasperated

excarcelar [A1] *vt* to release ... (from prison)

ex cátedra *loc adv* ex cathedra

excavación *f* excavation

excavadora *f* excavator

excavar [A1] *vt* 1 ‹*túnel/fosa*› to dig; **una piscina excavada en la roca** a swimming pool dug out of the rock; **las máquinas excavan la tierra** the machines dig up the earth 2 (Arqueol) to excavate
■ **excavar** *vi* to dig, excavate

excedencia *f* (Esp) extended leave of absence; **estar de ~** to be on extended leave of absence

excedentario -ria *adj* surplus

excedente[1] *adj* 1 ‹*producción*› excess (*before n*), surplus (*before n*) 2 ‹*mano de obra*› (frml) redundant 3 (con permiso) (Esp) on extended leave of absence

excedente[2] *m* surplus; **~s agrícolas/laborales** farming/manpower surpluses

exceder [E1] *vt* 1 ‹*límite/peso*› to exceed; **excede la cantidad prevista** it is higher than the figure expected 2 (superar, aventajar) **~ A algo** to be superior TO sth
■ **exceder** *vi*: **~ DE algo** to exceed sth; **excede del peso permitido** it exceeds the weight limit
■ **excederse** *v pron*: **no te excedas** don't overdo it *o* get carried away; **se excedió en sus críticas** she went too far in her criticism

excelencia *f*
A (cualidad) excellence; **alabó las ~s del vino** she praised the excellent qualities of the wine; **por ~** par excellence
B (frml) (tratamiento): **Su E~** (*m*) His Excellency; (*f*) Her Excellency; **gracias, (Vuestra) E~** thank you, (Your) Excellency

excelente *adj* excellent

excelentísimo -ma *adj* (frml) *form used when addressing holders of the title* **excelencia**; **el E~ señor Presidente de la República** the President of the Republic

excelso -sa *adj* (frml *o* liter) lofty, sublime

excentricidad *f* eccentricity

excéntrico -ca *adj/m,f* eccentric

excepción *f* 1 (caso) exception; **esta norma tiene una ~** there is an exception to this rule; **sin ~** without exception; **la ~ confirma la regla** (fr hecha) the exception proves the rule (set) 2 (acción) exception; **hacer una ~/hacer excepciones (con algn)** to make an exception/to make exceptions (for sb); **~ hecha de ...** with the exception of ..., except for ... 3 (*en locs*) **a** *or* **con excepción de** with the exception of, except for; **de excepción** ‹*medidas*› extraordinary (frml); ‹*invitado*› special

excepcional *adj* exceptional; **realizó una ~ labor en ese campo** he performed outstanding work in that field; **el proyecto despertó un interés ~** the project aroused unusual interest

excepcionalmente *adv* 1 (más de lo normal) exceptionally 2 (*indep*) as an exception

excepto *prep* except; **todos los días ~ los lunes** every day except Mondays; **las contesté todas ~ las dos últimas** I answered them all except (for) *o* apart from the last two; **todos ~ yo** everyone but me

exceptuar [A18] *vt* to except (frml); **exceptuando un pequeño incidente** except for *o* with the exception of a minor incident; **~ algo/a algn DE algo** to except sth/sb FROM sth (frml)

excesivo *adj* excessive; **el precio me parece ~** the price seems excessive to me; **llevaba un peso ~** it was overloaded *o* overweight; **no mostró ~ entusiasmo** he wasn't overly enthusiastic

exceso *m* 1 (excedente) excess; **~ de equipaje/peso** excess baggage/weight 2 (demasía): **un ~ de ejercicio** too much exercise; **me multaron por ~ de velocidad** I was fined for speeding; **mostraba un ~ de optimismo** he was overly optimistic; **con** *or* **en ~** ‹*beber/comer*› to excess, too much; ‹*fumar/trabajar*› too much; **es generoso en ~** he's excessively generous; ***pecar por ~***: **al hacer los cálculos pecaron por ~** they were overambitious in their calculations 3 **excesos** *mpl* (abusos) excesses (*pl*); **los ~s en la comida** eating to excess, overindulgence in food

excipiente *m* excipient

excitable *adj* excitable

excitación *f* 1 (agitación): **presa de una gran ~** in an excited *o* agitated state 2 (entusiasmo) excitement 3 (sexual) arousal, excitement 4 (Biol) stimulation 5 (Fís) excitation

excitante[1] *adj* ‹*espectáculo/libro*› exciting; **el café es una bebida ~** coffee is a stimulant

excitante[2] *m* stimulant

excitar [A1] *vt*
A 1 (hacer enojar): **la discusión lo excitó mucho** he got very excited *o* worked up during the argument 2 (sobreexcitar) to get ... overexcited; **el café me excita** coffee makes me jumpy 3 (en sentido sexual) to arouse, excite 4 ‹*deseo/odio/curiosidad*› to arouse
B 1 ‹*célula*› to stimulate; ‹*molécula*› to excite 2 ‹*dínamo*› to energize, excite
■ **excitarse** *v pron* 1 (enojarse) to get agitated, get worked up 2 (sobre excitarse) to get overexcited; **no se podía dormir porque estaba muy excitado** he couldn't sleep because he was so excited 3 (sexualmente) to get aroused, get excited

exclamación *f* exclamation

exclamar [A1] *vt* to exclaim

exclaustrar [A1] *vt* (secularizar) to secularize; (expulsar) to expel (*from a monastery or convent*)

excluir [I20] *vt* 1 (no incluir) to exclude; **~ algo/a algn DE algo** to exclude sth/sb FROM sth 2 ‹*posibilidad/solución*› to rule out, exclude

exclusión *f* exclusion; **~ hecha de** *or* **con ~ de** (frml) with the exclusion of, excluding

exclusiva *f* 1 (Period) (derechos) exclusive rights (*pl*); (reportaje) exclusive 2 (Esp) (Com) exclusive rights (*pl*); **tendrán la ~ de nuestros productos** they will be sole distributors of our products

exclusive *adj inv* (*detrás del n*): **del tres al quince, ambos ~** from the third to the fifteenth not inclusive

exclusividad *f* 1 (de club, colegio, diseño) exclusiveness, exclusivity 2 (AmL) (Com) exclusive rights (*pl*), sole rights (*pl*)

exclusivista *adj* exclusivist

exclusivo -va *adj* ‹*distribuidor*› sole; ‹*derechos*› exclusive, sole; ‹*club/ambiente*› exclusive; ‹*diseño/modelo*› exclusive; **este problema no es ~ de Chile** this problem is not exclusive to Chile

excluyente *adj* ‹*medidas/leyes*› exclusive; **las dos cosas no son ~s** the two things are not mutually exclusive

Excmo. Excma. (frml) (Corresp) = **excelentísimo, -ma**

excombatiente *mf* (*m*) veteran (AmE), ex-serviceman (esp BrE); (*f*) veteran (AmE), ex-servicewoman (esp BrE)

excomulgar [A3] *vt* to excommunicate

excomunión *f* excommunication

excoriar [A1] *vt* to chafe, excoriate (tech)

excreción *f* excretion

excremento *m* excrement

exculpar [A1] *vt* exonerate

excursión *f* (viaje organizado) excursion, day trip; (paseo, salida) trip, excursion; **ir de ~ al campo** to go on a trip to the countryside

excursionismo *m* hiking

excursionista *mf* (que hace una excursión) tripper; (que hace excursionismo) hiker

excusa *f* 1 (pretexto) excuse; **inventé una ~** I made up an excuse 2 **excusas** *fpl* (disculpas) apologies (*pl*); **presentó sus ~s** (frml) he made his apologies

excusable *adj* excusable

excusado[1] *adj* (frml): **~ es decir que ...** it goes without saying that ..., needless to say ...

excusado[2] *m* (ant) toilet, lavatory

excusar [A1] *vt* 1 (disculpar) to excuse; **eso no excusa tu comportamiento** that does not excuse *o* justify your behavior 2 (eximir) **~ a algn DE algo/+ INF** to excuse sb (FROM) sth/-ING; **me ~on de asistir** I was excused from attending; **fue excusado del servicio activo** he was exempted from active service 3 (Esp frml) (evitar, omitir): **excuso decirle lo mal que me sentó** I hardly need tell you how much that upset me; **excusé los detalles más desagradables** I omitted the more unpleasant details

■ **excusarse** *v pron* (frml) 1 (pedir perdón) to apologize 2 (ofrecer excusas) to excuse oneself; **se excusó y se fue** she excused herself and left

execrable *adj* execrable (frml), abominable

exégesis *f* (*pl* ~) exegesis

exención *f* exemption

exento -ta *adj* (frml) [ESTAR] exempt; **~ DE algo** exempt FROM sth; **~ de impuestos** tax-exempt, tax-free (BrE); **no está ~ de culpa** he isn't free of blame; **es una situación no exenta de riesgos** the situation is not without risk

exequias *fpl* (frml) funeral

exfoliación *f* exfoliation

exfoliador *m* (Col) notepad

exfoliar [A1] *vt* to exfoliate

exhalación *f* exhalation; ***como una ~***: **pasó como una ~** he rushed *o* shot past

exhalar [A1] *vt* (liter) 1 ‹*suspiro*› to breathe, heave; ‹*queja*› to utter; **exhaló el último suspiro** (euf) she breathed her last (euph) 2 ‹*olor*› to give off

exhaustivo -va *adj* exhaustive; **analizó el tema de forma exhaustiva** he made a comprehensive analysis of the subject

exhausto -ta *adj* exhausted

exhibición *f* 1 (demostración) display; **haciendo ~ de su fuerza** showing off *o* displaying his strength 2 (de cuadros, artefactos) exhibition, display; **estar en ~** to be on show *o* display 3 (Cin) screening, showing

exhibicionismo *m* exhibitionism

exhibicionista *mf*
A (pervertido) exhibitionist, flasher (colloq)
B (ostentoso) exhibitionist, show-off (colloq)

exhibir [I1] *vt* 1 ‹*colección/modelos*› to show, display; **no siente reparos en ~ su gordura** he's not ashamed to let people see how fat he is 2 ‹*película*› to show, screen; ‹*cuadro/obras de arte*› to exhibit; **la sala exhibe cuadros de Goya** the gallery is exhibiting paintings by Goya 3 (con orgullo) ‹*regalos/trofeos*› to show off

■ **exhibir** *vi* (period) (Art) to exhibit

■ **exhibirse** *v pron* (mostrarse en público) to show oneself; (hacerse notar) to draw attention to oneself; **le gusta ~se con su coche** she likes showing off her car

exhortación *f* exhortation (frml), appeal

exhortar [A1] *vt* to exhort (frml), urge; **~ a algn A + INF** *or* **A QUE + SUBJ** to exhort sb to + INF (frml), to urge sb to + INF

exhumación *f* exhumation, disinterment

exhumar [A1] *vt* to exhume, disinter

exigencia *f* 1 (pretensión) demand; **¡no me vengas con ~s!** don't start making demands 2 (requisito) demand, requirement

exigente *adj* ‹*persona*› demanding; ‹*prueba*› demanding, exacting; **eres demasiado ~ con él** you're too demanding with him; **para paladares ~s** for the discerning palate

exigir [I7] *vt* 1 ‹*pago/respuesta/disciplina*› to demand; **~ QUE + SUBJ**: **exigió que lo dejaran hablar** he demanded to be allowed to speak; **exigió que las tropas invasoras se retiraran** he demanded that the invading troops (should) withdraw 2 (requerir) to call for, demand; **mi trabajo exige mucha concentración** my job requires *o* demands great concentration 3 (esperar de algn) (+ *me/te/le etc*): **nos exige puntualidad** she requires us to be punctual; **le exigen demasiado en ese colegio** they ask too much of him at that school

exiguo -gua *adj* ‹*salario*› meager*, paltry; ‹*cantidad*› trifling

exiliado[1] **-da** *adj* exiled, in exile

exiliado[2] **-da** *m,f* exile; **los ~s en Suecia** those who were/are in exile in Sweden

exiliarse [A1 *or* A1] *v pron* to go into exile

exilio *m* exile; **vivir en el ~** to live in exile; **ir al ~** to go into exile

eximio -mia *adj* (liter) illustrious, eminent

eximir [I1] *vt* (frml) to exempt; **~ a algn DE algo + INF** to exempt sb FROM sth -ING; **lo eximieron de la asistencia al curso** he was exempted from attending the course; **esto me exime de toda culpa** this relieves *o* absolves me of all responsibility

■ **eximirse** *v pron* (AmL) to get an exemption

existencia *f*
A 1 (hecho de existir) existence 2 (vida) life; **amargarle la ~ a algn** to make sb's life a misery
B (Com) stock; **no lo tenemos en ~** we don't have it in stock; **S liquidación de existencias** clearance sale, stock clearance

existencial *adj* existential

existencialismo *m* existentialism

existencialista *adj/mf* existentialist

existente *adj* ‹*materiales/técnicas*› existing; **la situación ~ en la zona** (en el presente) the present *o* current situation in the area; (en el pasado) the situation in the area at the time

existir [I1] *vi* 1 (en 3ª pers) (haber): **siempre ha existido rivalidad entre ellos** there has always been rivalry between them; **no existen pruebas** there is no evidence 2 (ser) to exist; **ya no existe** it doesn't exist anymore; **pienso, luego existo** I think, therefore I am; 3 (vivir) to live; **dejó de ~** (period) he passed away (euph)

exitazo *m* smash hit, big hit

éxito *m* success; **con ~** successfully; **las negociaciones no tuvieron ~** the negotiations were not successful *o* were unsuccessful; **tuvo mucho ~ en la fiesta** he/it was a great success *o* (colloq) hit at the party; **la operación fué un ~** the operation was successful *o* a success

(Compuesto) **éxito de ventas** best-seller

exitosamente *adv* (AmL) successfully

exitoso -sa *adj* (AmL) ‹*campaña/gira*› successful

éxodo *m* 1 (viaje) exodus 2 **Éxodo** (Bib) Exodus

exonerar [A1] *vt* (frml) to exonerate (frml); **~ a algn DE algo** to exonerate sb FROM sth

exorbitante *adj* exorbitant

exorcismo *m* exorcism

exorcista *mf* exorcist

exorcizar [A4] *vt* to exorcize

exótico -ca *adj* exotic

exotismo *m* exoticism

expandible *adj* (Fís, Inf) expandable

expandir [I1] *vi* to expand

■ **expandirse** *v pron* «*cuerpo/gas*» to expand; «*empresa/sector*» to expand; «*noticia*» to spread

expansión *f*
A 1 (Fís) expansion 2 (de empresa) expansion; **S una empresa en ~** an expanding business 3 (de noticia, doctrina) spread
B (distracción) relaxation

expansionar [A1] *vt* to expand

■ **expansionarse** *v pron* (recrearse) to relax; (desahogarse) **~se CON algn** to unburden oneself TO sb

expansionista *adj* expansionist

expansivo -va *adj* expansive

expatriado -da *m,f* expatriate

expatriarse [A1] *or* [A17] *v pron* (emigrar) to leave one's country; (exiliarse) to go into exile

expectación *f* sense of expectancy *o* anticipation

expectante *adj* expectant; **esperaba ~** she waited expectantly

expectativa *f* 1 (espera): **estar a la ~ (de algo)** (a la espera) to be waiting (for sth); (pendiente): **siempre está a la ~ de lo que hagan los demás** he always waits to see what other people are going to do 2 (esperanza) expectation; **defraudó las ~s de su padre** he failed to live up to his father's expectations 3 **expectativas** *fpl* (perspectivas) prospects (*pl*); **no tengo muchas ~s** my prospects aren't very good; **tienen pocas ~s de ganar** they have little hope of winning

(Compuesto) **expectativas de vida** *fpl* life expectancy

expectorante *m* expectorant

expectorar [A1] *vi* to expectorate

■ **expectorar** *vt* to cough up

e

expedición *f*

A expedition

(Compuestos)

- **expedición de reconocimiento** reconnaissance expedition *o* mission
- **expedición de salvamento** (misión) rescue mission; (equipo) rescue party

B (de documentos, billetes) issuing, issue

C (frml) 1 (de telegrama) sending; (de mercancías) sending, shipping 2 (mercancías) shipment

expedicionario[1] **-ria** *adj* expeditionary

expedicionario[2] **-ria** *m,f* (Geog) member of an expedition

expedidor[1] **-dora** *adj*

A (que emite) issuing (*before n*)

B (frml) (que envía) sending (*before n*), dispatching (*before n*)

expedidor[2] **-dora** *m,f* (frml) sender

expedientar [A1] *vt*

A ‹*empleado/estudiante*› to take disciplinary action against

B «*policía*» to open a dossier *o* file on

expediente[1] *adj* (frml) expedient (frml)

expediente[2] *m*

A 1 (documentos) file, dossier; **~ académico** student record; **un brillante ~ profesional** a brilliant track record 2 (investigación) investigation, inquiry; **se abrirá un ~ informativo** an inquiry *o* investigation will be held 3 (medidas disciplinarias) disciplinary action; **le abrieron** *or* (frml) **incoaron ~** disciplinary action was taken against him

(Compuestos)

- **expediente de crisis** (Esp) statement of financial difficulties (*as required by law prior to laying off staff*)
- **expediente de regulación de empleo** (Esp) labor* force adjustment plan

B (medio) expedient (frml); **recurrieron a ~s drásticos** they resorted to drastic measures

expedir [I14] *vt*

A (emitir) to issue

B (frml) (enviar) ‹*telegrama*› to send; ‹*paquete/mercancías*› to dispatch, send

■ **expedirse** *v pron* (RPl frml): he did not want to express an opinion; **aún no se han expedido sobre ...** they have not yet announced their decision as to ...

expeditar [A1] *vt* to expedite (frml), to facilitate

expedito -ta *adj* 1 (frml) ‹*vía/camino*› free, clear 2 (AmL) (fácil) easy

expeler [E1] *vt* (frml) to expel (frml)

expendedor[1] **-dora** *adj* (frml): **máquina ~a de tabaco** cigarette (vending) machine

expendedor[2] **-dora** *m,f* (frml) 1 (persona): **~ de tabaco** tobacconist; **~ de lotería** lottery ticket seller 2 **expendedor** *m* (máquina) vending machine

expendeduría *f* (frml): **~ de lotería** lottery ticket agency; Ⓢ **expendeduría de tabaco** tobacconist's (shop)

expender [E1] *vt* (frml)

A (vender) to sell

B (gastar) ‹*energía*› to expend, use up

expendio *m* (AmL) (tienda) store (AmE), shop (BrE); (venta) sale; **un ~ de licores** a package store (AmE), an off-licence (BrE); **sólo se consigue en ~s autorizados** only available at authorized points of sale *o* outlets; Ⓢ **expendio bajo receta** available (only) on prescription

expensas *fpl*

A (Der) costs (*pl*), expenses (*pl*)

B **a expensas de**: **triunfó a ~ de sus ideales** she succeeded at the expense of her ideals; **vive a ~ de su familia** he lives off his family

experiencia *f*

A (conocimiento, suceso) experience; **con mucha ~** very experienced; **~ profesional/docente** professional/teaching experience; **saber algo por ~** to know sth by *o* from experience; **lo sé por ~ propia** I know from my own experience

B (experimento) experiment

(Compuesto) **experiencia piloto** pilot scheme

experimentación *f* experimentation

experimentado -da *adj* experienced

experimental *adj* experimental

experimentar [A1] *vi* **~ CON algo** to experiment ON *o* with sth

■ **experimentar** *vt*

A (probar) to try out, experiment with

B 1 ‹*sensación*› to experience, feel; ‹*tristeza/alegría*› to feel 2 (sufrir) ‹*cambio*› to undergo; **la inflación experimentó un alza** inflation rose; **la situación no experimentó variación alguna** there was no change in the situation; **ha experimentado una leve mejoría** there's been a slight improvement in his condition

experimento *m* experiment; **realizar un ~** to do *o* carry out an experiment

experto[1] **-ta** *adj*: **es ~ en casos de divorcio** he's an expert on divorce cases; **mi marido es ~ en cocina** my husband is an expert at cooking; **~ EN + INF** very good AT -ING

experto[2] **-ta** *m,f* expert; **un ~ en física nuclear** an authority *o* an expert in nuclear physics; **Juan es el ~ en política** Juan is the expert on politics

expiación *f* expiation, atonement

expiar [A17] *vt* to expiate, atone for

expiatorio -ria *adj* expiatory (frml)

expiración *f* expiry, expiration

expirar [A1] *vi* to expire

explanada *f* (plataforma) raised area, terrace; (delante de un edificio) leveled* area; (al lado del mar) esplanade

explanar [A1] *vt* to level, grade

explayarse [A1] *v pron* 1 (sobre un tema) to speak at length 2 (desahogarse) to unburden oneself; **se explayó conmigo** she opened up to me 3 (esparcirse) to relax

expletivo -va *adj* expletive

explicable *adj* ‹*fenómeno*› explicable (frml)

explicación *f* explanation; **se fue sin dar ninguna ~** he left without giving an explanation

explicar [A2] *vt* to explain; **no sé ~lo** I don't know how to explain it

■ **explicarse** *v pron* 1 (comprender, concebir) to understand; **no me lo explico** I can't understand it *o* (colloq) I just don't get it 2 (hacerse comprender) to express oneself; **se explica muy bien** he expresses himself very well; **explícate** explain what you mean; **¿me explico?** is that clear? *o* do you understand what I mean?

explicativo -va *adj* explanatory

explicatorio -ria *adj* explanatory

explicitar [A1] *vt* to specify, state explicitly

explícito -ta *adj* 1 [SER] (claro) explicit 2 [ESTAR] (expresado) explicit, clearly stated

exploración *f* 1 (de territorio) exploration; **~ submarina** underwater exploration; **la ~ de nuevos yacimientos** prospecting for new deposits 2 (Mil) reconnaissance 3 (Med) examination, exploration

explorador -dora *m,f*

A (expedicionario) explorer; (Mil) scout

B **exploradora** *f* (Col) (Auto) fog lamp

explorar [A1] *vt*

A 1 ‹*región*› to explore; ‹*yacimientos*› to prospect for 2 ‹*posibilidades*› to explore, investigate; ‹*situación*› to investigate, examine 3 (Mil) to reconnoiter*, scout

B (Med) ‹*órgano*› to examine, explore

exploratorio -ria *adj* 1 (Mil) ‹*misión*› reconnaissance (*before n*), scouting (*before n*) 2 (Med) ‹*operación*› exploratory

explosión *f* 1 (de bomba) explosion; **la bomba hizo ~** (period) the bomb exploded *o* went off 2 (de cólera, júbilo) outburst 3 (crecimiento brusco) explosion

(Compuesto) **explosión demográfica** population explosion

explosionar [A1] *vi* (Esp period) to explode, go off

explosivo¹ -va *adj* 1 ‹*artefacto/situación/tema*› explosive; **materiales ~s** explosives 2 (Ling) plosive

explosivo² *m* explosive

explotación *f*

A 1 (de tierra, mina) exploitation, working; (de negocio) running, operation; **una mina en ~** a working mine; **gastos de ~** running *o* operating costs 2 (instalaciones): **explotaciones petrolíferas** oil installations; **una ~ agrícola** a farm

(Compuesto) **explotación a cielo abierto** (actividad) strip mining (AmE), opencast mining (BrE); (mina) strip mine (AmE), opencast mine (BrE)

B (de trabajador) exploitation

explotador¹ -dora *adj* (que explota a un trabajador) exploitative

explotador² -dora *m,f* (de persona) exploiter

explotar [A1] *vt*

A 1 ‹*tierra*› to exploit, work; ‹*mina*› to operate, work; ‹*negocio*› to run, operate 2 ‹*idea/debilidad*› to exploit

B ‹*trabajador*› to exploit

■ **explotar** *vi* 1 «*bomba*» to explode, go off; «*caldera/máquina*» to explode, blow up 2 (fam) «*persona*» to explode, to blow a fuse (colloq)

expoliación *f* (frml) plundering, pillaging

expoliar [A1] *vt* (frml) to plunder

expolio *m* (frml) plundering; **los ~s de la guerra** the spoils of war

exponencial *adj* exponential

exponente *mf*;

A (persona) exponent; **el máximo ~ de su arte** the greatest exponent of his art

B **exponente** *m* 1 (Mat) exponent 2 (indicador) indicator

exponer [E22] *vt*

A ‹*cuadro/escultura/productos*› to exhibit, show; **los zapatos expuestos en la vitrina** the shoes displayed in the window

B ‹*razones/hechos*› to set out, state; ‹*ideas/teoría*› to put forward, expound (frml); ‹*tema*› to present

C 1 (poner en peligro) to put … at risk 2 (al aire, sol) **~ algo A algo** to expose sth TO sth

■ **exponer** *vi* to exhibit, exhibit *o* show one's work

■ **exponerse** *v pron* 1 (a riesgo, peligro) to expose oneself; **~se A algo** to expose oneself TO sth; **te expones a que te multen** you're risking a fine 2 (al aire, sol) **~se A algo** to expose oneself TO sth

exportable *adj* exportable

exportación *f* 1 (acción) exportation, export; **una compañía de ~** an export company; **artículos de ~** export goods 2 **exportaciones** *fpl* (mercancías) exports (*pl*)

exportador¹ -dora *adj*: **países ~es de petróleo** oil-exporting countries; **una región ~a de cítricos** a region that exports citrus fruit

exportador² -dora *m,f* exporter

exportar [A1] *vt* to export

exposición *f*

A 1 (acción) exhibition, showing 2 (muestra — de cuadros, esculturas) exhibition; (— de productos, maquinaria) show

(Compuestos)

- **exposición canina** dog show
- **exposición comercial** *or* **industrial** trade fair

B (de hechos, razones) statement, exposition (frml); (de tema, teoría) exposition (frml), presentation; **hizo una ~ detallada de lo ocurrido** she gave a detailed account of what had happened

C (al aire, sol) exposure; (Fot) exposure

exposímetro *m* light meter, exposure meter

expositor -tora *m,f*

A exhibitor

B (Col, Ven) (conferenciante) speaker

exprés¹ *adj inv* (Esp) ‹*servicio/envío*› express (*before n*)

exprés² *m*

A (Ferr) express train, fast train

B (café) espresso

expresamente *adv* 1 (explícitamente) ‹*decir/pedir/prohibir*› specifically, expressly (frml) 2 (precisamente): **~ con fines delictivos** purely for criminal purposes; **¿viniste ~ a eso?** did you come specially for that?

expresar [A1] *vt* ‹*ideas/sentimientos*› to express; **expresó su descontento** she voiced *o* expressed her dissatisfaction; **permítame ~le mi más sentido pésame** (frml) please accept my deepest sympathy (frml); **por las razones que se expresan a continuación** for the reasons shown *o* given below

■ **expresarse** *v pron* to express oneself

expresión *f* 1 (palabra) term; (frase) expression 2 (de sentimiento, idea) expression; **como ~ de mi agradecimiento** as an expression *o* a token of my gratitude 3 (de la cara, los ojos) expression 4 (Mat) expression; ***quedó reducido a la mínima ~*** it shrank to almost nothing

(Compuesto) **expresión corporal** movement, self-expression through movement

expresionismo *m* expressionism

expresionista *adj/mf* expressionist

expresividad *f* expressiveness

expresivo -va *adj* 1 ‹*persona/rostro/lenguaje*› expressive; **un silencio muy ~** an eloquent silence 2 (de expresión): **modalidades expresivas** forms of expression

expreso¹ -sa *adj*

A (explícito) express (*before n*)

B ‹*tren*› express (*before n*), fast (*before n*)

C ‹*carta/envío*› express (*before n*)

D ‹*café*› espresso

expreso² *adv* express; **envíamela ~** send it (to me) express (mail)

expreso³ *m*

A (Ferr) express train, fast train

B (café) espresso

exprimelimones *m* (*pl* ~) reamer (AmE), lemon squeezer (BrE)

exprimidor *m* (manual) reamer (AmE), lemon squeezer (BrE); (eléctrico) juicer

exprimir [I1] *vt* 1 ‹*naranja/limón*› to squeeze; ‹*ropa*› to wring 2 (explotar) ‹*trabajadores*› to exploit

ex profeso *loc adv*: **lo hizo ~ ~** he did it deliberately *o* on purpose; **fue a Roma ~ ~ para esa reunión** she went to Rome expressly for that meeting

expropiación *f* (sin indemnización) expropriation; (con indemnización) compulsory purchase

expropiar [A1] *vt* (sin indemnización) to expropriate; (con indemnización) to acquire … by compulsory purchase

expuesto -ta *adj*

A [ESTAR] (al viento, a un riesgo) exposed; **~ A algo** exposed TO sth

B [SER] (peligroso) risky, dangerous

expugnar [A1] *vt* to take … by storm

expulsar [A1] *vt*

A 1 (de institución) to expel; (de local) to throw … out, eject (frml) 2 (de territorio) ‹*individuo*› to expel; ‹*grupo/pueblo*› to expel, drive out 3 (Dep) to send off

B ‹*aire*› to expel; ‹*cálculo*› to pass, expel; ‹*placenta*› to expel, push out

expulsión *f*

A (de institución, territorio) expulsion; (Dep) sending-off

B (de aire) expulsion; (de cálculos) passing, expulsion; (de la placenta) expulsion, delivery

expurgación *f* expurgation

expurgar [A3] *vt* to expurgate

exquisitez *f*

A (cualidad) exquisiteness, deliciousness; (comida deliciosa): **el pastel es una ~** the cake is absolutely delicious *o* superb

B (refinamiento): **con ~** exquisitely; **un bordado de una ~ extraordinaria** a quite exquisite piece of embroidery

exquisito -ta *adj* ‹*comida*› delicious; ‹*tela/poema/música*› exquisite; ‹*persona*› refined

Ext. *f* (= **extensión**) ext.

extasiado -da *adj* in ecstasies, captivated

extasiarse [A17] *v pron*: **se extasiaba escuchando música** he would go into ecstasies *o* raptures listening to music; **me extasié ante aquel magnífico paisaje** I was captivated by that magnificent landscape (liter)

éxtasis *m* ecstasy

extático -ca *adj* ecstatic

extemporáneo -nea *adj* ‹*comentario*› untimely; ‹*lluvia*› unseasonable

extender [E8] *vt*

A ‹*periódico/mapa*› to open … up *o* out; **extendió la toalla en la arena** he spread the towel out on the sand

B ‹*brazos*› to stretch out; ‹*alas*› to spread; **le extendió la mano** he held out his hand to her

C ‹*pintura/mantequilla*› to spread

D (ampliar) ‹*poderes/influencia*› to broaden, extend; ‹*plazo/permiso*› to extend

E (frml) ‹*factura/cheque*› to issue (frml); ‹*receta*› to make out, write; ‹*documento/escritura*› to issue; **¿a nombre de quién extiendo el cheque?** to whom do I make the check payable?

■ **extenderse** *v pron*

A (en el espacio) 1 (propagarse, difundirse) «*fuego/epidemia/noticia*» to spread; **la humedad se extendió a la habitación de al lado** the dampness spread to the next room 2 (abarcar, ocupar) «*territorio*» stretch; **sus tierras se extienden hasta el río** her land extends as far as the river 3 «*influencia/autoridad*» to extend; **~se A algo** to extend TO sth; **mis conocimientos no se extienden a ese campo** my knowledge does not extend to that field

B (en el tiempo) 1 «*época/período*» to last; **el período que se extiende hasta la Reforma** the period up to the Reform 2 (en explicación, discurso): **se extendió demasiado en** *or* **sobre ese tema** he spent too much time on that subject; **¿quisiera ~se en** *or* **sobre ese punto?** would you like to expand on that point?

extendido -da *adj*

A ‹*costumbre/error*› widespread; **es de uso muy ~** it's widely used; **tiene el cáncer muy ~** the cancer has spread throughout his body

B ‹*brazos/alas*› outstretched

extensamente *adv* ‹*hablar*› at length; ‹*viajar*› widely

extensible *adj* extendable, extensible

extensión *f*

A 1 (superficie): **una gran ~ de terreno** a large expanse *o* stretch of land; **veíamos el parque en toda su ~** we could see the park in its entirety; **una ~ de 20 hectáreas** an area of 20 hectares 2 (longitud) length; **la ~ de la novela/carretera** the length of the novel/road; **un ensayo cuya ~ no supere las 200 palabras** an essay of no more than 200 words; **por ~** by extension

B (grado, importancia) extent; **en toda la ~ de la palabra** in every sense of the word

C (acción) extension; **pidió una ~ del plazo** she asked for an extension on the deadline

D (de cable) extension lead; (línea telefónica) extension

extensivo -va *adj*

A (aplicable) (frml): **ser ~ A algn/algo** to apply *o* be applicable TO sb/sth; **hacer ~** to extend (frml)

B (Agr) extensive

extenso -sa *adj* ‹*territorio/zona*› extensive, vast; ‹*informe/análisis*› lengthy, extensive; ‹*vocabulario/conocimientos*› extensive, wide

extensor *m* (Anat) extensor; (Dep) chest expander

extenuación *f* exhaustion

extenuado -da *adj* exhausted

extenuante *adj* exhausting

extenuar [A18] *vt* to exhaust, tire … out

■ **extenuarse** *v pron* to exhaust oneself, tire oneself out

exterior[1] *adj*

A 1 ‹*aspecto*› external (*before n*), outward (*before n*); ‹*bolsillo/temperatura*› outside (*before n*); ‹*revestimiento/capa*› outer (*before n*); **la parte ~ de la casa** the outside *o* the exterior of the house; **el mundo ~** the outside world 2 ‹*habitación/apartamento*› outward-facing

B ‹*comercio/política*› foreign (*before n*); **asuntos ~es** foreign affairs

exterior[2] *m*

A (fachada) outside, exterior; (espacio circundante) outside; **desde el ~ de la iglesia** from outside the church

B **el exterior** (países extranjeros): **la influencia del ~** foreign influence; **las relaciones con el ~** relations with other countries

C **exteriores** *mpl* (Cin) location shots (*pl*); **rodar en ~es** to film on location

exteriorizar [A4] *vt* to externalize, exteriorize

exterminación *f* extermination

exterminar [A1] *vt* to exterminate

exterminio *m* extermination

externalizar [A4] *vt* ‹*servicio*› to outsource

externar [A1] *vt* (Méx) to display, show

externo[1] **-na** *adj*

A ‹*apariencia/signos*› outward (*before n*), external; ‹*influencia*› outside, external; ‹*superficie*› external; ‹*ángulo*› exterior

B ‹*alumno*› day (*before n*)

externo[2] **-na** *m,f* day pupil

extinción *f*

A (de especie, volcán) extinction

B (de fuego) **trabajaron en la ~ del fuego** they took part in putting out *o* (frml) extinguishing the fire

C (Der) (de contrato, plazo) expiry

extinguidor *m* (AmL) fire extinguisher

extinguir [I2] *vt*

A ‹*especie*› to wipe out; ‹*violencia/injusticia*› to put an end to

B ‹*fuego*› to extinguish, put out

■ **extinguirse** *v pron*

A «*especie*» to become extinct, die out

B «*fuego*» to go out; «*volcán*» to become extinct; «*sonido*» to die away

C «*entusiasmo/amor*» to die

D (Der) to expire

extinto[1] **-ta** *adj* 1 ‹*especie/volcán*› extinct 2 (AmL frml) (difunto) late (*before n*), deceased

extinto[2] **-ta** *m,f* (AmL frml) **el ~/la extinta** the deceased

extintor *m* (Esp): *tb* **~ de incendios** fire extinguisher

extirpación *f* 1 (Med) removal, extirpation (frml) 2 (de vicio, mal) eradication

extirpar [A1] *vt* 1 (Med) to remove, extirpate (frml) 2 ‹*vicio/terrorismo*› to eradicate, extirpate (frml)

extorsión *f* extortion

extorsionar [A1] *vt* to extort money from

extra[1] *adj* 1 (Com) top quality, fancy grade (AmE) 2 (adicional) ‹*gastos/ración*› additional, extra; ‹*edición*› special

extra[2] *adv* extra

extra[3] *mf*

A (Cin) extra

B **extra** *m* (gasto) extra expense; (paga) bonus

extracción *f*

A 1 (de muela) extraction; (de bala) removal, extraction; (de sangre) extraction, taking 2 (de petróleo, resina) extraction; (de mineral) mining, extraction 3 (de humos) extraction 4 (de número de lotería) drawing

B (Mat) (de una raíz) extraction

C *tb* **~ social** background, origins (*pl*); **de ~ humilde** of humble origins

extracomunitario -ria *adj* ‹*origen/ciudadano*› from outside the EU; **países ~s** non-EU countries, countries outside the EU

extraconyugal *adj* extramarital

extracto *m*

A (resumen) summary, abstract

(Compuesto) **extracto de cuenta** (bank) statement

B (esencia) extract; **~ de rosas** rose essence

(Compuestos)

- **extracto de carne** beef extract
- **extracto de tomate** tomato paste, tomato purée

extractor[1] **-tora** *adj* extractor (*before n*)

extractor[2] *m* extractor; **~ de aire** extractor fan; **~ de humos** smoke extractor

extradición *f* extradition

extraditable *adj* extraditable (frml)

extraditar [A1] *vt* to extradite

extraer [E23] *vt*
A [1] ‹*muela*› to extract, pull out; ‹*bala*› to remove; ‹*sangre*› to take, extract [2] ‹*mineral*› to extract, mine; ‹*petróleo/resina*› to extract [3] ‹*humo/aire*› to extract [4] ‹*información/cita*› to extract [5] (en lotería) to draw
B (Mat) to extract
C ‹*conclusión*› to draw

extraescolar *adj* extramural, out-of-school (*before n*)

extrajudicial *adj* extrajudicial (frml)

extrajudicialmente *adv* out of court

extralargo -ga *adj* ‹*cigarrillo*› king-size

extralimitarse [A1] *v pron* to exceed one's authority; **ese chico se está extralimitando** (fam) that boy is overstepping the mark (colloq)

extramarital, extramatrimonial *adj* extramarital

extramuros, extra muros *adv* outside the town (*o* village *etc*)

extranjería *f* **ley de ~** (en Esp) immigration laws (*pl*)

extranjerismo *m foreign word, phrase, etc used in another language*

extranjerizante *adj*: **términos ~s** terms which make the language sound foreign; **modas ~s** imported fashions which are alien to our tradition

extranjero[1] **-ra** *adj* foreign

extranjero[2] **-ra** *m,f* [1] (persona) foreigner [2] **extranjero** *m*: **vive en el ~** she lives abroad; **viajar al ~** to travel abroad; **noticias del ~** foreign news

extranjis (Esp fam): **los vendía de ~** he was selling them on the sly (colloq); **me traje dos cartones de tabaco de ~** I smuggled in two cartons of cigarettes

extrañamente *adv* strangely, oddly

extrañar [A1] *vt* (esp AmL) ‹*amigo/país*› to miss; **te extrañé mucho** I missed you badly
■ **extrañar** *vi*
A (sorprender) (+ *me/te/le etc*) to surprise; **me extraña que no lo sepas** I'm surprised you didn't know that; **ya me extrañaba a mí que ...** I thought it was strange that ...; **no es de ~ que ...** it's hardly surprising that ...
B (RPl) (tener nostalgia) to be homesick
■ **extrañarse** *v pron* **~se DE algo** to be surprised AT sth; **no me extraño de nada** nothing surprises me; **se extrañó de que no le hubiera avisado** he was surprised that she hadn't told him

extrañeza *f* surprise; **me miró con ~** she looked at me in surprise

extraño[1] **-ña** *adj* [1] (raro) strange, odd; **es ~ que no haya llamado** it's strange *o* odd that she hasn't called; **últimamente está muy ~** he's been a bit strange lately; **eso no tiene nada de ~** there's nothing unusual about that [2] (desconocido): **no me siento bien entre gente extraña** I feel uncomfortable with people I don't know *o* strangers

extraño[2] **-ña** *m,f* (desconocido) stranger

extraoficial *adj* unofficial

extraordinaria (Esp) *f* extra month's pay (*gen at Christmas and in the summer*)

extraordinario -ria *adj* [1] ‹*suceso*› extraordinary, unusual; ‹*circunstancias/facultades*› extraordinary, special [2] ‹*asamblea*› extraordinary, special; ‹*edición*› special; ‹*contribución*› extra, additional [3] ‹*belleza/fuerza/éxito*› outstanding, extraordinary; **la película no fue nada ~** the movie was nothing special *o* nothing out of the ordinary

extraplano -na *adj* ‹*reloj/calculadora*› slimline; ‹*compresa*› extra-slim

extrapolación *f* extrapolation

extrapolar [A1] *vt* to extrapolate

extrarradio *m* outlying districts (*pl*), outskirts (*pl*)

extrasensorial *adj* extrasensory

extraterrestre *adj/mf* alien, extraterrestrial

extraterritorial *adj* extraterritorial

extravagancia *f* (acto) outrageous thing (to do); (cualidad) extravagance; **su ~ en el vestir** the outlandish *o* extravagant way he dresses

extravagante *adj* ‹*comportamiento/ideas*› outrageous, extravagant; ‹*persona/ropa*› flamboyant, outrageous

extraviado -da *adj* [1] ‹*objeto/niño*› lost, missing; **con la mirada extraviada** with a lost *o* faraway look in her eyes [2] (Med): **tiene un ojo ~** he has a cast in one eye, he has a squint

extraviar [A17] *vt* (frml) to mislay (frml), to lose
■ **extraviarse** *v pron* (frml) «*persona*» to get lost, lose one's way; «*animal*» to go missing, get lost; «*documento*» to go missing *o* astray

extravío *m* (frml) loss

extremado -da *adj* [1] (*gen delante del n*) (máximo) extreme [2] ‹*clima*› extreme

extremar [A1] *vt* (frml) ‹*precauciones*› to maximize (frml); **han extremado las medidas de seguridad** security measures have been maximized *o* stepped up

extremaunción *f* extreme unction

extremeño -ña *adj/m,f* Extremaduran

extremidad *f* [1] (extremo) end [2] **extremidades** *fpl* (Anat) extremities

extremista[1] *adj* (extremo) extreme; (Pol) extremist

extremista[2] *mf* (Pol) extremist

extremo[1] **-ma** *adj* [1] (*gen delante del n*) ‹*pobreza/cuidado*› extreme; **un caso de extrema gravedad** an extremely serious case [2] ‹*caso/medida*› extreme; **en caso ~** as a last resort

Compuestos
- **extrema derecha/izquierda** *f* (Pol) extreme right/left
- **extremo derecho/izquierdo** *mf* (Dep) right/left wing
- **Extremo Oriente** *m* Far East

extremo[2] *m*
A [1] (de palo, cable) end; **al otro ~ del pasillo** at the other end of the corridor [2] (postura extrema) extreme; **va de un ~ a otro** she goes from one extreme to the other; **son ~s opuestos** they are complete opposites; **los ~s se tocan** (fr hecha) extremes meet [3] (límite): **si se llega a ese ~ ...** if it gets that bad *o* to that point ...; **su descaro alcanzó ~s insospechados** her effrontery reached unimagined extremes; **es cuidadoso al ~** he is extremely careful; **en último ~** as a last resort [4] **en extremo** in the extreme
B (period) (punto, cuestión): **en ese ~ no estoy de acuerdo** I do not agree on that point

extremo[3] **-ma** *m,f* (en fútbol, rugby) winger

Compuesto **extremo cerrado/defensivo** tight/defensive end

extrínseco -ca *adj* extrinsic

extroversión *f* extroversion

extrovertido -da *adj/m,f* extrovert

exuberancia *f* exuberance, lushness

exuberante *adj* ‹*vegetación*› exuberant, lush; ‹*belleza*› exuberant; ‹*mujer*› voluptuous; ‹*vida/gesto*› exuberant, flamboyant

exudar [A1] *vt* to exude

exultante *adj* exultant (frml), elated

exultar [A1] *vi* to exult (frml), to rejoice

exvoto, ex voto *m* ex-voto, votive offering

eyaculación *f* ejaculation

Compuesto **eyaculación precoz** premature ejaculation

eyacular [A1] *vi* to ejaculate

eyectar [A1] *vt* to eject
■ **eyectarse** *v pron* to eject

e

f

F, **f** *f* (*read as* /'efe/) *the letter* **F, f**

f (= **femenino**) F, female

F 1 (= **Fahrenheit**) F 2 (= **febrero**): **23-F** (en Esp) 23 February (*date of attempted coup in 1981*)

fa *m* (nota) F; (en solfeo) fa, fah (BrE); **~ bemol/sostenido** F flat/sharp; **en ~ mayor/menor** in F major/minor

f.a.b. (= **franco a bordo**) f.o.b.

fabada *f* bean stew (*with pork etc*)

fábrica *f* factory; **~ de zapatos** shoe factory; **~ de textiles/papel** textile/paper mill; **~ de cerveza** brewery; **~ de conservas** cannery

fabricación *f* manufacture; **televisores de ~ japonesa** Japanese-made TV sets; **de ~ casera** home-made; **productos de ~ nacional** British-made (*o* Mexican *etc*) goods; Ⓢ **fabricación propia** all our products are made on the premises

(Compuesto) **fabricación en serie** mass production

fabricante *mf* manufacturer

fabricar [A2] *vt* to manufacture; **~ en cadena/serie** to mass-produce; Ⓢ **fabricado en Perú** made in Peru

fábula *f* (Lit) fable; (mentira) fabrication, invention

fabuloso -sa *adj* (maravilloso) (fam) fabulous (colloq), fantastic (colloq); (Lit, Mit) mythical, fabulous (liter)

facción *f*

A (Pol) faction

B **facciones** *fpl* (rasgos) features (*pl*); **es de facciones delicadas** he has delicate features

faccioso[1] -sa *adj* seditious, rebel (*before n*)

faccioso[2] -sa *m,f* (period) (agitador) agitator, troublemaker; (alzado en armas) rebel

faceta *f* facet

facha[2] *mf* (Esp fam) fascist

facha[3] *f* (fam) (aspecto) look; **tiene muy buena ~** he looks good; **¿vas a salir con esa ~?** are you going out looking like that?; **¡qué ~ tan espantosa!** what a sight! (colloq); ***estar hecho una ~*** to be *o* look a sight (colloq)

fachada *f* 1 (de edificio) facade (tech), front; **un edificio con 30 metros de ~** a building with a 30 meter frontage 2 (apariencia) facade; **su amabilidad es pura ~** her kindness is nothing but a facade *o* all for show

facho -cha *adj/m,f* (AmL fam) fascist

fachoso -sa *adj* 1 (fam) (extravagante) bizarre, weird (colloq) 2 (Chi fam) (de buen aspecto) nice-looking (colloq) 3 (Méx fam) (desaliñado) scruffy

facial *adj* ‹*vello/rasgos*› facial

fácil[1] *adj*

A 1 ‹*problema/lección*› easy; **un libro de lectura ~** a book which is easy to read; **~ DE + INF** easy to + INF; **~ de entender** easy to understand 2 ‹*vida/trabajo*› easy; **dinero ~** easy money 3 ‹*chiste/metáfora*› facile 4 (pey) (en lo sexual) easy (pej), loose (pej)

B (probable): **es ~ que no quiera** he'll probably not want to; **no es ~ que me lo den** they are unlikely to let me have it

fácil[2] *adv* (fam) easily (colloq); **deben haber pagado ~ un millón** they must have paid a million, easily

facilidad *f*

A 1 (cualidad de fácil) ease; **con ~** easily; **¿viste con qué ~ lo hizo?** did you see how easily he did it? 2 (de una tarea) simplicity

B (aptitud) **~ PARA algo** gift FOR sth; **tener ~ para los idiomas/los números** to have a gift for languages/to be good at figures

(Compuesto) **facilidad de palabra**: **tiene ~ de ~** he has a way with words

C **facilidades** *fpl* 1 (posibilidades, oportunidades): **se le dieron todas las ~es del mundo** they gave her every chance 2 (Fin) facilities (*pl*); **¿dan ~es?** do you give credit (facilities)?

(Compuesto) **facilidades de pago** *fpl* credit facilities (*pl*); **amplias ~ de ~** easy payment terms

facilitar [A1] *vt*

A (hacer más fácil) ‹*tarea*› to make … easier, facilitate (frml)

B (frml) (proporcionar) ‹*datos/información*› to provide; **le ~on los documentos** they provided him with the documents (frml); **no ha sido facilitada su identidad** his identity has not been disclosed

■ **facilitarse** *v pron* (Col): **se le facilita la física** he's good at physics

facilón -ona *adj* (fam) dead easy

facineroso -sa *adj/m,f* criminal

facsímil, facsímile *m* 1 (copia) facsimile 2 (Telec) facsimile, fax

factible *adj* possible, feasible

fáctico -ca *adj* (frml) factual

factor *m*

A (elemento, causa) factor; **intervino el ~ suerte** there was an element of luck *o* chance

(Compuestos)

- **factor humano** human factor
- **factor Rh** Rh factor, rhesus factor

B (Mat) factor

factoría *f* (fábrica) factory; (astillero) shipyard; (fundición) foundry

factorial *f or m* factorial

factótum *m* factotum

factura *f*

A (Com) invoice (frml), bill; **según ~** as per invoice; **presentarle** *or* **pasarle ~ a algn** (Fin) to invoice sb; **te hace un favor y luego te pasa la ~** he'll do you a favor and then he expects something in return

B (RPl) (Coc) *rolls, croissants, etc*

facturación *f*

A (Com) 1 (acción) invoicing 2 (volumen) turnover; **~ anual** annual turnover

B (Ferr) registration; (Aviac) check-in

facturar [A1] *vt*

A (Com) 1 ‹*mercancías/arreglo*› to invoice for, bill for 2 (refiriéndose al volumen de ventas) to turn over, have a turnover of

B (Ferr) to register; (Aviac) to check in

■ **facturar** *vi* (Ferr) to register; (Aviac) to check in

facultad *f*

A (capacidad, don) faculty; **con los años se van perdiendo ~es** as you get older you start to lose your faculties

(Compuesto) **facultades mentales** *fpl* (mental) faculties (*pl*); **tiene perturbadas sus ~ ~** he is mentally disturbed; **en pleno uso de sus ~ ~** in full possession of his faculties

B (autoridad, poder) power, authority

C (Educ) faculty; **F~ de Filosofía y Letras** Faculty of Arts

facultar [A1] *vt* (frml) **~ A algn PARA + INF** «*jefe/presidente*» to authorize sb to + INF; «*carnet/documento*» to entitle sb to + INF; «*ley*» to allow sb to + INF; **queda facultado para tomar decisiones** he is authorized to make decisions; **el carnet lo faculta para entrar gratis** the card entitles you to free admission

facultativo[1] **-va** *adj*
A (optativo) optional
B (frml) (Med) ‹*personal/dictamen*› medical; **según prescripción facultativa** as prescribed by your physician

facultativo[2] *m,f* (frml) doctor, physician

faena *f*
A (trabajo) task, job; **~s domésticas** *or* **de la casa** housework; **la dura ~ diaria** the daily grind; **~s agrícolas** farm work
B (Taur) series of passes
C (fam) [1] (mala pasada) dirty trick; **hacerle una ~ a algn** to play a dirty trick on sb (colloq) [2] (contratiempo) drag (colloq), pain (colloq)
D (Chi) (grupo de trabajadores) team, gang; (lugar de trabajo) workplace (frml)

faenar [A1] *vi*
A (pescar) to fish
B (trabajar) to labor*, work
■ **faenar** *vt* (CS) ‹*ganado*› to slaughter

fagot /fa'ɣo(t)/ *m* [1] (instrumento) bassoon [2] **fagot** *mf* (músico) bassoonist

faisán *m* pheasant

faja *f*
A [1] (prenda interior) girdle [2] (cinturón — de traje regional) wide belt; (— de sotana) sash; (— de smoking) cummerbund
(Compuesto) **faja presidencial** presidential sash
B (de puro) band; (de un periódico) newswrapper
C (franja, zona) strip

fajar [A1] *vt* (CS, Per fam) (dar una paliza) to beat up (colloq)
■ **fajarse** *v pron*
A (ponerse faja) to put on a girdle (*o* belt *etc*)
B [1] (Méx, Ven fam) (dedicarse) to knuckle down (colloq); **vas a tener que ~te como los buenos** you're really going to have to knuckle down; **se ~on a trabajar** they worked their butts off (AmE) *o* (BrE) slogged their guts out (colloq) [2] (Méx, Ven fam) (pelearse) to get into a fight
C (Méx fam) «*pareja*» to pet (colloq), make out (AmE colloq)
D (Col fam) (lucirse) to excel oneself

fajín *m* sash

fajina *f* (RPl) chore; **ropa de ~** work clothes

fajo *m* (de billetes) wad, roll (AmE); (de papeles) bundle, sheaf

fakir *m* fakir

falacia *f* fallacy

falange *f*
A (Anat) phalanx, phalange
B (Hist, Mil, Pol) phalanx; **la F~** the Spanish Falangist Movement

falangista *adj/mf* Falangist

falaz *adj* false

falda *f*
A (Indum) skirt; ***estar pegado a las ~s de su madre*** to be tied to one's mother's apron strings
(Compuestos)
- **falda de tubo** straight skirt
- **falda escocesa** (de mujer) tartan skirt, kilt; (de hombre) kilt
- **falda pantalón** split skirt, culottes (*pl*)

B **faldas** *fpl* (de cubrecama) valance; (de mesa camilla) (Esp) tablecloth
C [1] (regazo) lap [2] (Coc) flank (steak) (AmE), skirt (BrE)
D (de montaña) side
E **faldas** *fpl* (fam) (mujeres) women (*pl*); **se enemistaron por un asunto de ~s** they fell out over a woman

faldeo *m* (CS) mountainside

faldón *m*, **faldones** *mpl* [1] (de camisa) shirttails; (de frac, chaqué) coattails [2] (de bebé) christening robe

falencia *f* (CS, Per) bankruptcy

falibilidad *f* fallibility

falible *adj* fallible

fálico -ca *adj* phallic

falla *f*
A [1] (de tela, cristal) flaw; **la pieza tenía una ~** the part was defective [2] (Geol) fault
B [1] (de motor, máquina — en la composición) defect, fault; (— en el funcionamiento) failure; **hay una ~ en el motor** there's a fault in the engine; **una ~ de los frenos causó el accidente** the accident was caused by brake failure [2] (en organización — en composición) defect, fault; (— en el funcionamiento): **~s en el sistema de seguridad** security failures [3] (de persona) mistake; **una ~ la tiene cualquiera** anyone can make mistakes; **¡qué ~!** what a stupid mistake!; ***¡no hay ~!*** (AmC fam) no problem! [4] (Dep) miss
(Compuesto) **falla humana** (AmL) human error
C [1] (AmL exc CS fam) (lástima) pity, shame [2] (Col) (Educ) day's absence (*from school*)

> **Las Fallas**
>
> The most important festival in the autonomous region of Valencia. The *Fallas* take place every year between March 12 and 19.*Fallas* are groups of huge painted cardboard and wood figures which depict current events and famous people. The highlight is the burning of the *fallas* on the night of March 19.
>
> Each neighborhood makes its own *falla*. They are erected on one night, known as the *plantá*, and displayed the next day. A panel of judges "pardons" the best one and it is placed in the *falla* museum

fallado -da *adj* (CS) flawed, defective

fallar [A1] *vi*
A «*juez/jurado*» **~ a** *or* **en favor/en contra de algn** to rule in favor* of/against sb
B [1] «*frenos/memoria*» to fail; «*planes*» to go wrong; **algo falló y se estrellaron** something went wrong and they crashed; **otra vez llegas tarde ¡nunca falla!** you're late again, typical!; (+ *me/te/le etc*) **le falló el corazón** his heart failed; **si los cálculos no me fallan** if my calculations are right; **le falló la puntería** he missed; **me falló el instinto** my instinct failed me; **a ti te falla/a él le falla** (AmL) (fam) you've/he's got a screw loose (colloq) [2] «*persona*» (+ *me/te/le etc*) to let … down
■ **fallar** *vt*
A ‹*caso*› to pronounce judgment in; ‹*premio*› to award; ‹*concurso*› to decide the result of
B (errar) to miss; **fallé el disparo** I missed

fallecer [E3] *vi* (frml *o* euf) to pass away (frml *or* euph), to die; **el fallecido actor** the late *o* deceased actor (frml)

fallecido -da *m,f* (frml) deceased (frml); **los ~s durante la guerra** those who died *o* (frml) fell in the war

fallecimiento *m* (frml) death, passing (frml *or* euph)

fallero -ra *m,f*: *person who takes part in the preparation of the* **Fallas**
(Compuesto) **fallera mayor** *f* festival queen (*during the* **Fallas**)

fallido -da *adj* [1] ‹*intento/esfuerzo*› failed (*before n*); **un tiro ~** a shot that missed [2] (Com, Fin) ‹*comerciante*› bankrupt; **créditos ~s** bad debts

fallo *m*
A (en concurso, certamen) decision; (Der) ruling, judgment
B (Esp) ▸**falla 2**
C (Esp) (lástima): **¡qué ~! si llego a saber que estás aquí te lo traigo** what a shame! if I'd known you were going to be here I would have brought it
(Compuestos)
- **fallo cardíaco** heart failure
- **fallo humano** human error

falluca *f* (Méx fam) (comercio ilegal) black market (*gen in smuggled goods*); (mercancía) smuggled goods (*pl*)

falluquero -ra *m,f* (Méx) black marketeer (*gen selling smuggled goods*)

falluto -ta *adj* (RPl fam) two-faced (colloq)

falo *m* phallus

falsear [A1] *vt* ‹*hechos/datos*› to falsify; ‹*verdad/realidad*› to distort

falsedad *f* [1] (de afirmación) falseness; (de persona) insincerity, falseness [2] (mentira) lie, falsehood (frml)

falsete *m* (Mús) falsetto; **voz de ~** falsetto voice

falsificación *f* (firma, billete, cuadro) forgery; (acción —de copiar) forging, forgery; (—de alterar) falsification

f

falsificador -dora *m,f* forger

falsificar [A2] *vt* [1] ‹*firma*› to forge, fake; ‹*billete*› to forge, counterfeit (frml); ‹*cheque*› to forge [2] ‹*documento*› (copiar) to forge, counterfeit; (alterar) to falsify

falso -sa *adj*

A [1] ‹*billete*› counterfeit, forged; ‹*cuadro*› forged; ‹*documento*› false, forged; ‹*diamante/joya*› fake; ‹*cajón/techo*› false [2] (insincero) ‹*persona*› insincere, false; ‹*sonrisa/promesa*› false

B [1] (no cierto) ‹*dato/nombre/declaración*› false; **eso es ~** that is not true, that is untrue [2] **en falso**: **jurar en ~** to commit perjury; **golpear en ~** to miss the mark

Compuestos

- **falsa alarma** *f* false alarm
- **falso testimonio** *m* (Der) false testimony, perjury; **no levantar ~ ~** (Relig) thou shalt not bear false witness

f

falta *f*

A (carencia, ausencia) **~ DE algo** ‹*de interés/dinero*› lack OF sth; **por ~ de fondos** owing to a lack of funds; **~ de personal** staff shortage; **es por la ~ de costumbre** it's because I'm/you're not used to it; **no es por ~ de ganas** it's not that I don't want to; **siente mucho la ~ de su hijo** she misses her son terribly; **a ~ de un nombre mejor** for want of a better name; **a ~ de más información** in the absence of more information; ***a ~ de pan buenas son (las) tortas*** or (Méx) ***a ~ de pan, tortillas*** half a loaf is better than none; ***echar algo en ~***: **aquí se echa en ~ más formalidad** what's needed here is a more serious attitude; **echó en ~ sus alhajas** she realized her jewelry was missing

B (inasistencia) *tb* **~ de asistencia** absence; **le pusieron ~** they marked her down as absent; **tienes 30 ~s** you have been absent 30 times

C (de la menstruación) missed period; **es mi segunda ~** I've missed two periods

D **hacer falta**: **no hace ~ que se queden** there's no need for you to stay; **¡hace ~ ser tonto para creerse eso!** you have to be stupid to believe that!; **si hace ~ ...** if necessary ...; **no hizo ~ cambiarlo** I/we didn't need to change it; **lo que hace ~ es que nos escuchen** what they really need to do is listen to us; **lo que hace ~ aquí es una computadora** what's needed here is a computer; (+ *me/te/le etc*) **le hace ~ descansar** he/she needs to rest; **estudia que buena ~ te hace** (fam) it's about time you did some studying; **me haces mucha ~** I really need you; ***ni ~ que (me/te/le) hace*** (fam) so what? (colloq)

E (infracción, omisión) offense*; **una ~ grave** a serious misdemeanor*; **fue una ~ de respeto** it was very rude of you/him/her/them; **agarrar** or (esp Esp) **coger a algn en ~** to catch sb out; **lo traigo el jueves sin ~** I'll bring it on Thursday without fail

Compuestos

- **falta de educación** bad manners
- **falta de ortografía** spelling mistake
- **falta de pago** nonpayment

F (defecto): **sacarle** or **encontrarle ~s a algo** to find fault with sth

G (Dep) [1] (infracción — en fútbol, baloncesto) foul; (— en tenis) fault [2] (tiro libre — en fútbol) free kick; (— en balonmano) free throw

faltar [A1] *vi*

A [1] (no estar) to be missing; **falta dinero de la caja** there's some money missing from the till; **¿quién falta?** who's missing?; (en colegio, reunión de trabajo) who's absent?; **falta de su domicilio** she has been missing from home; (+ *me/te/le etc*) **te falta un botón** you have a button missing; **a esta taza le falta el asa** there's no handle on this cup [2] (no haber suficiente): **va a ~ vino** there won't be enough wine; **más vale que sobre comida y no que falte** it's better to have too much food than too little; (+ *me/te/le etc*) **nos faltó tiempo** we didn't have enough time; **le falta experiencia** he lacks experience; **me faltan palabras para expresarlo** I can't find the words to express it; **ganas no me faltan** I'd love to; **me falta el aire** I can't breathe [3] (*en frases negativas*): **no falta quien lo piensa** some people think that; **no ~á oportunidad** there will be plenty of opportunities [4] (hacer falta): **le falta alguien que la aconseje** she needs someone to advise her

B (quedar): **yo estoy lista ¿a ti te falta mucho?** I'm ready, will you be long?; **a la carne le faltan 15 minutos** the meat needs another 15 minutes; **sólo me falta pasarlo a máquina** all I have to do is type it out; **sólo falta decorarlo** it just needs decorating; **aún me falta pintarlo** I still have to paint it; **falta poco para Navidad** it's not long until Christmas; **falta poco para las diez** it's almost *o* nearly ten o'clock; **faltan cinco minutos para que empiece** there are five minutes to go before it starts; **¿te falta mucho para terminar?** will it take you long to finish?; **¿falta mucho para que llegue?** will it be long until she arrives?; **nos falta poco para terminar/llegar** we're almost finished/there; **me faltan tres páginas para terminar el libro** I have three pages to go to finish the book; **aún falta mucho** (tiempo) there's plenty of time yet; (distancia) there's a long way to go yet; **poco faltó para que me pegara** he nearly hit me; **¡esto es lo único que faltaba!** (iró) that's all I/we needed! (iro); ***¡no faltaba*** or ***~ía más!*** (respuesta — a un agradecimiento) don't mention it!; (— a una petición) of course, certainly; (— a un ofrecimiento) I wouldn't hear of it!; (expresando indignación) whatever next!

C [1] (no asistir): **te esperamos, no faltes** we're expecting you, make sure you come; **~ A algo** ‹*al colegio/a clase*› to be absent FROM sth; ‹*a una cita*› to miss sth; **ha faltado dos veces al trabajo** she's been off work twice [2] (no cumplir) **~ A algo**: **faltó a su promesa/palabra** he didn't keep his promise/word; **¡no me faltes al** or (CS) **el respeto!** don't be rude to me; **faltas a la verdad** you are not telling the truth

falto -ta *adj* **~ DE algo**: **un episodio ~ de interés** an episode lacking in interest; **el organismo está ~ de recursos** the organization is short of funds; **estamos ~s de personal** we're short-staffed

fama *f*

A [1] (renombre, celebridad) fame; **una marca de ~ mundial** a world-famous brand; **los vinos que han dado ~ a la región** the wines which have made the region famous [2] (reputación) reputation; **tener buena/mala ~** to have a good/bad reputation; **su ~ de don Juan** his reputation as a womanizer; **tiene ~ de bromista** he's well known as a joker; ***cría ~ y échate a dormir*** (hablando de buena fama) people think they can rest on their laurels; (hablando de mala fama) once you have a bad reputation it is very difficult to get rid of it

B (Col) (carnicería) butcher's

famélico -ca *adj* starving; **vengo ~** (fam) I'm famished

familia *f*

A [1] (parientes) family; **es de buena ~** or **de ~ bien** he's from a good family; **sus hijos y demás ~** her children and other members of the family; **somos como de la ~** we're just like family; **le viene de ~** it runs in the family; **pasa hasta en las mejores ~s** it can happen to the best of us; **pasamos las fiestas en ~** we spent the holidays with the family; **me siento como en ~** I feel at home; ***acordarse de (toda) la ~ de algn*** (fam & euf) to curse sb (colloq) [2] (hijos) children; **no tienen ~** they don't have any children

Compuestos

- **familia de acogida** foster family
- **familia numerosa** large family
- **familia política**: **mi ~ política** my wife's/husband's family, my in-laws (colloq)

B (Bot, Zool) family

familiar[1] *adj*

A [1] ‹*vida/vínculo*› family (*before n*); ‹*envase/coche*› family (*before n*) [2] ‹*trato/tono*› familiar, informal; ‹*lenguaje/expresión*› colloquial

B (conocido) familiar; **su cara me resulta ~** her face is familiar; **el idioma no me es ~** I'm not familiar with the language

familiar[2] *mf* relative, relation

familiaridad *f* familiarity

familiarizarse [A4] *v pron* **~ CON algo** to familiarize oneself WITH sth, become familiar WITH sth

famoso[1] -sa *adj* famous; **~ POR algo** famous FOR sth

famoso[2] -sa *m,f* celebrity, famous person

fan *mf* (*pl* **fans**) fan

fanal *m* [1] (de lámpara) chimney, globe; (campana de cristal) bell jar, bell glass [2] (Méx) (Auto) headlamp, headlight

fanático[1] -ca *adj* fanatical

fanático[2] -ca *m,f* (Pol, Relig) fanatic; (entusiasmado) fanatic (colloq); (de fútbol) (AmS period) fan

fanatismo *m* fanaticism

fandango *m* 1 (Mús) (baile) fandango 2 (Andes fam) (fiesta) party (*with dancing*) 3 (fam) (jaleo) fuss; **armar un ~** to kick up *o* create a fuss

fané *adj* (RPl arg): **estar ~** to be past one's prime

fanega *f* 1 (de capacidad) *unit of capacity (= 22.5 liters or, in some regions, 55.5)* 2 (de superficie) *unit of area (= 0.66 hectares)*

fanfarria *f* (música) fanfare; (aparato exagerado) pomp and ceremony

fanfarrón[1] **-rrona** *adj* (fam) 1 (al hablar) loudmouthed (colloq); **no seas ~** stop boasting 2 (al actuar): **niños fanfarrones luciendo el coche de papá** kids showing off in their fathers' cars

fanfarrón[2] **-rrona** *m,f* (fam) 1 (al hablar) loudmouth (colloq) 2 (al actuar) show-off (colloq)

fanfarronada *f* (fam) 1 (al hablar) boasting, bragging 2 (al actuar) showing-off (colloq); (acto): **una de sus ~s** one of the things he does to show off (colloq)

fanfarronear [A1] *vi* (fam) 1 (al hablar) to boast, brag 2 (al actuar) to show off (colloq)

fangal *m* quagmire, bog

fango *m* mud; **su nombre quedó cubierto de ~** his name was dragged through the mud

fangoso -sa *adj* muddy

fantasear [A1] *vi* to fantasize

fantasía *f*

A 1 (imaginación) imagination; **tiene mucha ~** she has a very lively imagination 2 (ficción) fantasy; **~s sexuales** sexual fantasies; **mundo de ~** a fantasy world

B (Mús) fantasia

C (bisutería): **joyas de ~** costume jewelry*; **una pulsera de ~** an imitation diamond (*o* ruby *etc*) bracelet

fantasioso -sa *adj* prone to fantasizing

fantasma[1] *m*

A 1 (aparición) ghost; **el ~ de la ópera** the Phantom of the Opera 2 (amenaza) specter*; **el ~ del cáncer** the specter of cancer

B (TV) ghost

C **fantasma** *mf* (Esp fam) (fanfarrón) show-off (colloq)

fantasma[2] *adj* bogus; ▸**gabinete, etc**

fantasmagórico -ca *adj* phantasmagoric

fantasmal *adj* ghostly, phantom (*before n*)

fantástico[1] **-ca** *adj* fantastic

fantástico[2] *adv* (CS fam): **nos llevamos ~** we get on fantastically well (colloq); **lo pasé ~** I had a great time

fantochada *f* (fam) (tontería): **decir ~s** to talk nonsense; **hacer ~s** to clown around (colloq)

fantoche *m* 1 (títere) puppet 2 (persona sin carácter): **no es más que un ~** he's a nonentity 3 (de aspecto ridículo): **vas hecho un ~** (fam) you look a real sight (colloq) 4 (fam) ▸**fanfarrón**[2]

faquir *m* fakir

farabute *m* (RPl fam) show-off (colloq)

farad, faradio *m* farad

faramalla *f* (Chi fam) fuss

farándula *f* (period): **la ~** (ambiente) show business; (gente) show-business people (*pl*)

farandulear [A1] *vi* (Ven fam) to show off (colloq)

faraón *m* Pharaoh

faraónico -ca *adj* 1 (Hist) Pharaonic, of the Pharaoh/Pharaohs 2 ‹*empresa/tarea*› mammoth (*before n*)

fardar [A1] *vi* (Esp fam) 1 «*persona*» ▸**fanfarronear** 2 (lucir): **un coche que farda mucho** a car that gets you noticed; **¡cómo fardan esos vaqueros!** those jeans are really trendy!

fardo *m* (de algodón, paja) bale; (de ropa) bundle

fardón[1] **-dona** *adj* (Esp fam) 1 ‹*persona*› ▸**fanfarrón**[1] 2 ‹*coche/ropa*› showy (colloq), classy (colloq)

fardón[2] **-dona** *m,f* (Esp fam) ▸**fanfarrón**[2]

farero -ra *m,f* lighthouse keeper

farfullar [A1] *vi/vt* (atropelladamente) to gabble, jabber; (con poca claridad) to mutter, mumble

faringe *f* pharynx

faringitis *f* pharyngitis

farisaico -ca *adj* (Bib) pharisaic; ‹*piedad/actitud*› (pey) hypocritical

fariseo -sea *m,f* (Bib) pharisee; (hipócrita) (pey) hypocrite

farmacéutico[1] **-ca** *adj* pharmaceutical

farmacéutico[2] **-ca** *m,f* druggist (AmE), chemist (BrE)

farmacia *f* (disciplina) pharmacy; (tienda) drugstore (AmE), chemist's (BrE); **~ de guardia** *or* **de turno** duty chemist

fármaco *m* medicine, drug

farmacodependencia *f* drug dependence

farmacología *f* pharmacology

farmacológico -ca *adj* pharmacological

farmacólogo -ga *m,f* pharmacologist

faro *m*

A (Náut) lighthouse

B (Auto) headlight, headlamp

(Compuestos)

- **faro antiniebla** fog light, fog lamp (BrE)
- **faro halógeno** halogen headlight *o* headlamp

farol *m*

A 1 (de alumbrado público) streetlight, streetlamp; (en jardín, portal) lantern, lamp 2 (Chi, Méx) (Auto) headlight

(Compuestos)

- **farol a gas** gaslamp
- **farol de papel** paper lantern

B (Esp fam) (Jueg) bluff; ***marcarse*** *or* ***tirarse* un ~** (en el póker) to bluff; (jactarse) to brag

farola *f* (luz) streetlight, streetlamp; (poste) lamppost

farolazo *m* (Méx fam) stiff drink

farolero[1] **-ra** *adj* (Esp): **es muy ~** he's always bragging

farolero[2] **-ra** *m,f* (Esp) boaster, bragger

farolillo *m* (de papel) Chinese lantern

(Compuesto) **farolillo rojo** (Esp): *team at the bottom of the division*

farra *f* (fam) partying (colloq); **irse de ~** to go out on the town, to go out partying

farragoso -sa *adj* 1 ‹*informe/texto/explicación*› involved 2 ‹*respiración*› labored*

farrear [A1] *vi* (AmL fam) to go out partying (colloq), go out on the town (colloq)

■ **farrearse** *v pron* (AmL fam) ‹*fortuna/dinero*› to blow (colloq); ‹*oportunidad*› to throw away

farrero -ra *adj/m,f* (AmL fam) ▸**farrista**[1,2]

farrista[1] *adj* (AmL fam): **estudiantes ~s** students who are always out living it up

farrista[2] *mf* (AmL fam): **es un ~** he's always out living it up

farruco -ca *adj* (Esp fam) (desafiante) aggressive; (ufano) smug

farsa *f* (Teatr) farce; (engaño) sham, farce

farsante *mf* fraud, fake

fascículo *m* (cuadernillo) part (*of a serialized publication*), fascicle (tech)

fascinación *f* fascination

fascinante *adj* fascinating

fascinar [A1] *vi* (fam) (+ *me/te/le etc*): **me fascinó ese programa** I found that program fascinating; **¿te gusta? — sí, me fascina** do you like him? — yes, I like him a lot; **me fascina viajar** I love travelling

■ **fascinar** *vt* to fascinate, captivate

fascismo *m* fascism

fascista *adj/mf* fascist

fase *f*

A (etapa) stage, phase; **la ~ previa del torneo** the qualifying stage of the competition; **está todavía en ~ de negociación** it is still being negotiated

B (Astron) phase; (de cohete) stage

fastidiado -da *adj* (esp Esp fam): **estoy un poco ~** I'm not too good *o* too well; **anda ~ de los riñones** he's having trouble with his kidneys; **tengo la garganta fastidiada** I've got a sore throat

fastidiar [A1] *vt* 1 (molestar, irritar) ‹*persona*› to bother, pester 2 (esp Esp fam) (estropear) ‹*mecanismo/plan*› to mess up; ‹*fiesta/excursión*› to spoil; ‹*estómago*› to upset; ***¡la hemos fastidiado!*** that's done it! (colloq)

■ **fastidiar** *vi*: **me fastidia tener que repetir las cosas** it annoys me to have to repeat things; **¡no fastidies! ¿de veras?** go on! you're kidding! (colloq)

■ **fastidiarse** *v pron*

A (AmL fam) (molestarse) to get annoyed

B 1 (fam) (jorobarse): **tendré que ~me** I'll have to put up with it (colloq); **¡hay que ~se!** (Esp) that's great! (colloq & iro); **¡te fastidias!** (Esp) tough! (colloq) 2 (Esp fam) (estropearse) ⟨⟨*velada/plan*⟩⟩ to be ruined

C (Esp fam) ⟨*pierna/espalda*⟩ to hurt; **te vas a ~ el hígado** you're going to damage your liver

fastidio *m* (molestia) annoyance; **¡qué ~!** what a nuisance!

fastidioso -sa *adj* 1 (molesto) ⟨*persona*⟩ tiresome, annoying; ⟨*trabajo*⟩ tiresome, irksome; **¡qué ruido más ~!** what an irritating noise! 2 (Méx, Per fam) (quisquilloso) fussy (colloq)

fastuosidad *f* (de casa, vestido) splendor*, magnificence; (de un banquete) sumptuousness

fastuoso -sa *adj* ⟨*salón*⟩ magnificent; ⟨*banquete*⟩ lavish

fatal[1] *adj*

A 1 ⟨*accidente/enfermedad/consecuencias*⟩ fatal; **se teme un desenlace ~** we fear the worst 2 (liter) (ineludible) inevitable, fatal (liter)

B (fam) (muy malo) terrible, awful; **me encuentro ~** I feel awful; **está ~, tendrán que operar** she's in a really bad way, they'll have to operate (colloq)

fatal[2] *adv*: (esp Esp fam): **viste ~** he dresses really badly; **me caen ~** I can't stand them (colloq)

fatalidad *f* (destino) fate, destiny; (desgracia) bad luck, misfortune

fatalismo *m* fatalism

fatalista[1] *adj* fatalistic

fatalista[2] *mf* fatalist

fatalmente *adv*

A (inevitablemente) unavoidably, inevitably; (desgraciadamente) unfortunately

B (fam) (muy mal) atrociously (colloq)

fatídico -ca *adj* fateful; **en aquel día ~** on that fateful day (liter)

fatiga *f*

A 1 (cansancio) tiredness, fatigue (frml) 2 (ahogo) breathlessness

(Compuestos)

- **fatiga del metal** metal fatigue
- **fatiga mental** mental fatigue

B **fatigas** *fpl* (trabajos) hardship, difficulties (*pl*)

fatigado -da *adj* tired, weary

fatigar [A3] *vt* (físicamente) to tire ... out; (mentalmente) to tire

■ **fatigarse** *v pron* 1 (cansarse) to get tired, wear oneself out (colloq) 2 (ahogarse) to get breathless

fatigoso -sa *adj* ⟨*trabajo*⟩ tiring, exhausting

fatuidad *f* (neciedad) fatuousness; (engreimiento) conceit

fatuo -tua *adj* (necio) fatuous; (engreído) conceited

fauces *fpl* (liter) jaws (*pl*), fauces (*pl*) (liter)

faul *m* (*pl* **fauls**) (AmL) foul

faulear [A1] *vt* (AmL) to foul

faulero -ra *m,f* (AmL) dirty player, persistent fouler

fauna *f* fauna

fauno *m* faun

fausto[1] **-ta** *adj* (frml) auspicious (frml)

fausto[2] *m* magnificence, splendor*; **se celebró con gran ~** it was a magnificent affair

favor *m*

A 1 (ayuda, servicio) favor*; **¿me puedes hacer un ~?** can you do me a favor?; **vengo a pedirte un ~** I've come to ask you (for) a favor; **¿me harías el ~ de copiarme esto?** would you copy this for me, please?; **hagan el ~ de esperar** would you mind waiting, please?; **gracias, no sabes el ~ que me haces** thanks ever so much, you're doing me a big favor; **si no te invitan, ~ que te hacen** if they don't invite you, they'll be doing you a favor; Ⓢ **favor de hacer la cola** (Méx) please stand in line (AmE), please queue here (BrE) 2 (*en locs*) **a favor** in favor*; **dos votos a ~** two votes in favor; **llevamos el viento a ~** we have the wind behind us; **estar a favor de algo/algn/+ INF** to be in favor* of sth/sb/-ING; **si es así, aún más a mi ~** that makes me all the more right; **cinco a dos, a ~ de Nacional** five-two, with Nacional ahead (AmE), five-two to Nacional (BrE); **en favor de** in favour of; **por favor** please; **pide las cosas por ~** say please; **¿y tú le creíste? ¡por ~, mujer!** and you believed him? honestly!

B (apoyo): **el ~ de la crítica** the approval of the critics; **~ del rey** the king's favor; **cuenta con el ~ del jefe** he's/she's in favor with the boss

C **favores** (liter) (sexuales) favor

favorable *adj* ⟨*resultado/opinión*⟩ favorable*; ⟨*pronóstico*⟩ good, favorable*; **las circunstancias no nos fueron ~s** circumstances were not in our favor; **~ A algo**: **un clima ~ a la negociación** a favorable climate for negotiation; **~ A + INF** in favor of -ING; **se muestra ~ a negociar** he is in favor of negotiating

favorecedor -dora *adj* becoming

favorecer [E3] *vt* 1 (ayudar, beneficiar) to favor*; **me ha favorecido la suerte** luck has been on my side; **una política para ~ la agricultura** a policy to help agriculture 2 ⟨⟨*peinado/color*⟩⟩ (sentar bien) to suit

■ **favorecerse** *v pron* (Col fam) to protect oneself

favorecido -da *adj* 1 (en foto): **en esta foto salió muy ~** this photograph flatters him, this is a very flattering photograph of him 2 (AmL frml) (en sorteo): **salió ~ con el primer premio** he was the lucky winner of the first prize

favoritismo *m* favoritism*

favorito -ta *adj/m,f* favorite*

fax *m* fax; **mándaselo por ~** fax it to him

faxear [A1] *vt* to fax, send ... by fax

faz *f* (liter) (rostro) countenance (liter), face; **desapareció de la ~ de la tierra** he vanished off the face of the earth

FC *m*

A = **ferrocarril**

B (= **fútbol club**) FC

Fdo = **firmado**

fe *f*

A (Relig) faith; (creencia, confianza) faith; **puse toda mi ~ en ti** I put all my trust in you; **le tiene una ~ ciega** he has absolute *o* blind faith in it

B (frml) (testimonio): **dar ~ de algo** to testify to sth; **doy ~ de que el documento es auténtico** I bear witness to the authenticity of the document

(Compuestos)

- **fe de bautismo** certificate of baptism
- **fe de erratas** errata
- **fe de vida** *document certifying that a person is still alive*

C (voluntad, intención): **buena/mala ~** good/bad faith; **actuar de buena/mala ~** to act in good/bad faith; **no dudo de su buena ~** I don't doubt his good intentions

fealdad *f* ugliness

feb. (= **febrero**) Feb

febrero *m* February; *para ejemplos ver* **enero**

febril *adj* feverish

fecal *adj* fecal*

fecha *f* date; **¿qué ~ es hoy?** what's the date today?, what date is it today?; **con** *or* **de ~ 7 de marzo** (Corresp) dated March 7 *o* (BrE) 7th March; **hasta la ~** to date; **le dieron/tiene ~ para Agosto** (para examen, entrevista, etc) she has her exam (*o* interview *etc*) in August; (para cita con el médico) she has an appointment in August; (para el parto) the baby is due in August; **el año pasado por estas ~s** this time last year; **en ~ próxima** soon

(Compuestos)

- **fecha de caducidad** (de medicamento) expiration date (AmE), expiry date (BrE); (de alimento) use-by date; Ⓢ **fecha de caducidad 25 junio 2005** (en medicamento) expires June 25th 2005; (en alimento) use by June 25th 2005
- **fecha de consumo preferente** best-before date
- **fecha de vencimiento** (de letra) due date, maturity date; (de carnet, licencia) expiration date (AmE), expiry date (BrE); (de medicamento, alimento) (AmL) ▸**fecha de caducidad**
- **fecha límite** *or* **tope** closing date

fechador *m* date stamp

fechar [A1] *vt* to date; **una noticia fechada en Bruselas** a news item from Brussels

fechoría *f* misdeed; **ya está haciendo otra de sus ~s** he's up to mischief again

fécula *f* starch

fecundación *f* fertilization

Compuesto **fecundación in vitro** in vitro fertilization

fecundar [A1] *vt* 1 ‹*óvulo*› to fertilize; ‹*animal*› to inseminate 2 (liter) (hacer fértil) to make … fertile; ‹*espíritu*› to enrich

fecundidad *f* 1 (Biol) fertility 2 (de la tierra) fruitfulness 3 (de trabajo, iniciativa) fruitfulness; (de escritor, imaginación): **un escritor de la ~ de Ramos** a writer as prolific as Ramos

fecundizar [A4] *vt* to fertilize

fecundo -da *adj* 1 (Biol) ‹*mujer*› fertile 2 ‹*región/tierra*› fertile; ‹*labor*› fruitful; ‹*autor*› prolific

FED /feð/ *m* (= **Fondo Europeo de Desarrollo**) EDF

FEDER /'feðer/ *m* (= **Fondo Europeo de Desarrollo Regional**) ERDF

federación *f* federation

federal *adj* federal

federalismo *m* federalism

federalista *adj/mf* federalist

federar [A1] *vt* to federate

■ **federarse** *v pron* «*estados*» (Pol) to federate, become federated; (Dep) to affiliate (*to the governing body of a sport*)

federativo -va *adj* federative (frml)

felicidad *f* 1 (alegría) happiness 2 **¡felicidades!** *interj* (por cumpleaños) Happy Birthday!; (en Navidad) Merry Christmas!; (por un logro) congratulations!

felicitación *f* 1 (escrito — por un logro) letter of congratulation; (— en Navidad) Christmas card (*or letter wishing sb Merry Christmas*) 2 **felicitaciones** *fpl* (deseo — por un logro) congratulations (*pl*); (— en Navidad) greetings (*pl*), wishes (*pl*); **reciba mis más sinceras felicitaciones por esta victoria** (frml) my sincerest congratulations on your victory 3 **¡felicitaciones!** *interj* (AmL) congratulations!

felicitar [A1] *vt* 1 (por un logro) to congratulate; **¡te felicito!** congratulations!; **me felicitó por el premio** he congratulated me on winning the prize 2 (para Navidad, por cumpleaños): **llamó en Nochebuena para ~nos** he called on Christmas Eve to wish us (a) Merry Christmas; **la felicité por su cumpleaños** I wished her (a) Happy Birthday

■ **felicitarse** *v pron* (frml) **~se DE algo** to be pleased WITH sth

feligrés -gresa *m,f* parishioner

felino -na *adj/m,f* feline

feliz *adj* 1 ‹*persona*› happy; **les deseo que sean muy felices** I wish you every happiness; **no me hace muy ~ que vaya** I'm not very happy about her going 2 ‹*día/vida*› happy; **un final ~** a happy ending; **¡~ cumpleaños!** happy birthday!; **¡~ Navidad!** Merry Christmas!; **¡~ Año Nuevo!** Happy New Year!; **¡~ viaje!** have a good trip!; **¡felices Pascuas!** (en Navidad) Merry Christmas!; **¡felices vacaciones!** have a good vacation (AmE) *o* (BrE) holiday! 3 ‹*idea/frase*› apt, felicitous

felizmente *adv* 1 (*indep*) (afortunadamente) luckily, fortunately 2 (con felicidad) happily

felonía *f* (liter) felony (tech), serious crime

felpa *f* (Tex) (para toallas) toweling*; (en tapicería) plush

felpudo *m* doormat

femenil *adj* (Méx) ‹*equipo/moda*› ladies' (*before n*), women's (*before n*)

femenino -na *adj* 1 ‹*equipo/moda*› ladies' (*before n*), women's (*before n*); ‹*hormona/sexo*› female; **el voto ~** women's votes 2 ‹*vestido/modales/chica*› feminine 3 (Ling) feminine

fémina *f* (hum) woman

femicidio *m* femicide, murder of a woman resulting from gender violence

feminidad *f* femininity

feminismo *m* feminism

feminista *adj/mf* feminist

fémur *m* femur, thighbone

fenecer [E3] *vi* 1 (frml) (morir) to expire (frml), to pass away (frml *or* euph) 2 (terminar) to come to an end

fénix *m* phoenix

fenomenal[1] *adj* (fam) great (colloq)

fenomenal[2] *adv* (fam): **nos lo pasamos ~** we had a great time (colloq); **me vino ~** it was exactly *o* just what I needed; **¡~!** great! (colloq)

fenomenalmente *adv* brilliantly; **jugó ~** he played brilliantly; **está ~ bien escrita** it's incredibly well written; **los niveles son ~ altos** the levels are incredibly high

fenómeno[1] **-na** *adj/adv* (AmL) ▸**fenomenal** [1,2]

fenómeno[2] *m* 1 (suceso) phenomenon 2 (persona — monstruosa) freak; (— excepcional) genius

feo[1], **fea** *adj* 1 ‹*persona/edificio*› ugly; ‹*peinado*› unflattering; **es fea de cara** she has a very plain face; **es un barrio/color ~** it's not a very nice neighborhood/color; **era una corbata feísima** it was the most awful tie; ***ser más ~ que Picio** or **que un pecado*** to be as ugly as sin (colloq) 2 ‹*asunto/situación*› unpleasant; ‹*olor/sabor*› (esp AmL) unpleasant; **¡qué ~ está el día!** what an awful day!; **la cosa se está poniendo fea** things are getting nasty *o* ugly; **es** *or* (Esp) **está muy ~ hablar así** it's not nice to talk like that; **tiene la fea costumbre de contestar** he has an unpleasant habit of answering back

feo[2] *adv* (AmL) ‹*oler/saber*› bad; **me miró ~** she gave me a dirty look; ***sentir ~*** (Méx) to feel terrible

feo[3] *m* (fam) (desaire): **hacerle un ~ a algn** to snub sb; **vamos, acéptalo, no me hagas ese ~** oh go on take it, I'll be hurt if you don't; **es de un ~ ...** (Esp) he's as ugly as they come (colloq)

feracidad *f* (liter) fertility, richness

feraz *adj* fertile, rich

féretro *m* coffin

feria *f*

A 1 (exposición comercial) fair; **la ~ del libro** the book fair; **~ de muestras** trade fair 2 (CS, Per) (mercado) (street) market

Compuesto **feria americana** (RPl) garage sale

B 1 (fiesta popular) festival; **en mi pueblo están en ~s** my village is holding its festival 2 (Taur) series of bullfights (*held during a festival*) 3 (parque de atracciones) fair

C 1 (Méx fam) (cambio, suelto) small change; **¿me cambia este billete por ~?** can you change this bill (AmE) *o* (BrE) note, please? 2 (Méx fam) (dinero) cash (colloq)

feriado *m* (AmL) (public) holiday; **mañana es ~** tomorrow's a public holiday

feriante *mf* (CS) (en exposición comercial) exhibitor; (en mercado) stallholder, trader

fermentación *f* fermentation

fermentar [A1] *vi/vt* to ferment

fermento *m* ferment

ferocidad *f* ferocity, fierceness

feroz *adj* 1 ‹*animal*› ferocious, fierce; ‹*ataque/mirada/odio*› fierce, vicious; ‹*viento/tempestad*› fierce, violent; **tengo un hambre ~** (fam) I'm ravenous *o* starved (colloq) 2 (Col, Méx, Ven fam) (feo) horrendous (colloq)

férreo -rrea *adj*

A ‹*voluntad*› iron (*before n*); ‹*determinación*› steely; ‹*disciplina/horario*› strict; ‹*oposición*› fierce, determined

B (de hierro) iron (*before n*)

ferretería *f* (tienda) hardware store, ironmonger's (BrE); (mercancías) hardware, ironmongery (BrE)

ferretero -ra *m,f* hardware dealer, ironmonger (BrE)

férrico -ca *adj* ferric, iron (*before n*)

ferrocarril *m* (sistema) railroad (AmE), railway (BrE)

Compuesto **ferrocarril de cremallera** cog railway, rack railway

ferrocarrilero -ra *adj/m,f* (Chi, Méx) ▸**ferroviario**[1,2]

ferroso -sa *adj* ferrous

ferroviario[1] **-ria** *adj* rail (*before n*)

ferroviario[2] **-ria** *m,f* railroad worker (AmE), rail worker (BrE)

ferry /'ferri/ *m* (*pl* **-rrys**) ferry

fértil *adj* fertile

fertilidad *f* fertility

fertilización *f* fertilization

Compuesto **fertilización in vitro** in vitro fertilization

fertilizante[1] *adj* ‹*agente*› fertilizing (*before n*); ‹*droga*› fertility (*before n*)
fertilizante[2] *m* fertilizer
fertilizar [A4] *vt* to fertilize, put fertilizer on
férula *f* (varilla) cane, rod; ***estar bajo la ~ de algn*** to be under sb's rule
ferviente *adj* ‹*admiración/creyente*› fervent; ‹*deseo*› burning; ‹*fe/defensor*› passionate
fervor *m* fervor*; **con ~** fervently
fervoroso -sa *adj* fervent
festejado -da *m,f* (CS) *person celebrating his/her birthday (o saint's day etc)*; **un brindis por el ~** a toast to the birthday boy (*o* guest of honor *etc*)
festejar [A1] *vt* 1 ‹*chiste/gracia*› to laugh at 2 (agasajar) to wine and dine, fête, entertain 3 (AmL) (celebrar) to celebrate; **le ~on el cumpleaños en el club** they celebrated her birthday at the club 4 (ant) (cortejar) to court (dated), to woo (dated *or* liter)
festejo *m* celebration, festivity
festín *m* feast, banquet
festinar [A1] *vt* (AmL) 1 (frml) (apresurar) to hurry through 2 (tratar con ligereza) to make light of
festival *m* festival; **~ de cine** film festival
festivalero -ra *adj* ‹*ambiente*› festive; ‹*público*› festival-going (*before n*)
festividad *f* 1 (fiesta religiosa) feast, festivity 2 **festividades** *fpl* (festejos) festivities (*pl*)
festivo -va *adj* festive; ▸**dia A**
festón *m* (punto) scallop trim
fetiche *m* fetish
fetichismo *m* fetishism
fetichista[1] *adj* fetishistic
fetichista[2] *mf* fetishist
fetidez *f* (cualidad) smelliness; (olor) stench
fétido -da *adj* fetid, foul-smelling
feto *m* 1 (Biol, Med) fetus* 2 (fam) (persona fea) ugly person; **es un ~** he's/she's as ugly as sin (colloq)
feúcho -cha *adj* (fam) ‹*mujer*› plain, homely (AmE colloq); **es ~** he's not much to look at
feudal *adj* feudal
feudalismo *m* feudalism
feudo *m* (Hist) fief; (coto, territorio) domain, territory
fez *m* fez
f.f. (= **franco fábrica**) **precio ~** ex-factory price
FF AA *fpl* = **Fuerzas Armadas**
FFCC *mpl* = **ferrocarriles**
fiabilidad *f* reliability
fiable *adj* reliable
fiaca[1] *adj inv* (RPl fam) bone idle (colloq), lazy
fiaca[2] *f* (Andes, CS fam) (pereza): **me da ~** I can't be bothered; **qué ~ que tengo** I'm feeling really lazy
fiado -da *adj* on credit; **comprar (al) ~** to buy on credit; **no vendemos (al) ~** we don't give credit
fiador -dora *m,f* (Com, Der, Fin) guarantor; **servirle de ~ a algn** to stand surety for sb
fiambre *m*
A (Coc): **sólo comen ~(s)** all they eat is cold cuts (AmE) *o* (BrE) cold meats; **el chorizo es un ~** chorizo is a kind of cold cut (AmE) *o* (BrE) cold meat
B (arg) (cadáver) stiff (sl); ***quedarse ~*** (fam) to snuff it (colloq)
fiambrera *f* (Esp) (recipiente) lunch box
fiambrería *f* (AmL) delicatessen
fianza *f* 1 (Der) bail; **salió bajo ~** she was released on bail; **está en libertad bajo ~** he is out on bail 2 (Com) deposit
fiar [A17] *vt* ‹*mercancías*› to sell … on credit; **¿me las fía?** can I owe you for them?; **le ~on las bebidas** they let him have the drinks on credit
■ **fiar** *vi* 1 (dar crédito) to give credit; Ⓢ **no se fía** no credit (given); **ya no le fian en la tienda** they won't let him have anything else on credit at the store 2 **ser de ~** «*persona*» (digno de confianza) to be trustworthy; (responsable) to be reliable; «*mecanismo/motor*» to be reliable
■ **fiarse** *v pron*: **no me fío de lo que dice** I don't believe what he says; **~se DE algn** to trust sb; **~se DE QUE + SUBJ**: **no me fío de que cumpla su promesa** I don't trust him to keep his promise
fiasco *m* fiasco
fibra *f* 1 (Tex) fiber*; **~s artificiales** *or* **sintéticas** synthetic *o* man-made fibers 2 (de amianto) fiber* 3 (de la madera) grain 4 (Coc, Med) fiber*; **una alimentación rica en ~** a high fiber diet 5 (Anat) fiber*; **ese tipo es pura ~** (fam) that guy's solid muscle (colloq) 6 **de fibra** (*loc adj*) ‹*político/ejecutivo*› gritty

Compuestos
- **fibra de vidrio** fiberglass*
- **fibra metálica** (Méx) steel wool
- **fibra óptica** optical fiber*

fibroma *m* fibroid, fibroma
fibrosis *f* fibrosis
Compuesto **fibrosis cística** *or* **pancreática** *or* **quística** cystic fibrosis
fibroso -sa *adj* fibrous
ficción *f* (Lit) fiction; (invención) fiction
ficha *f*
A (para datos) card; (de fichero) index card; **la policía le abrió ~** the police opened a file on him

Compuestos
- **ficha médica** medical records (*pl*)
- **ficha policial** police record

B 1 (de teléfono, estacionamiento) token 2 (Jueg) (de dominó) domino; (de damas) checker(AmE), draught (BrE); (de otros juegos de mesa) counter; (de ruleta, póker) chip
C (Dep) (contrato) signing-on fee; (pago) contract
D (AmL fam) (persona de cuidado) rat (colloq); **¡qué ~ resultó ser!** he turned out to be a real rat!
fichaje *m* (Dep) (acción) signing (up); (jugador) signing, trade (AmE)
fichar [A1] *vt* 1 «*policía*» to open a file on; **está fichado** the police have a file on him; **te tiene fichado** (fam) she's got you sussed (colloq) 2 «*equipo/club*» to sign (up); **lo fichó el Real Madrid** he was signed (up) by Real Madrid
■ **fichar** *vi* 1 (en fábrica, oficina — a la entrada) to clock in, punch in (AmE); (— a la salida) to clock out *o* (BrE) off, to punch out (AmE) 2 (Esp) **~ POR algn** (por un club) to sign up WITH sb, sign FOR sb
fichero *m*
A 1 (mueble — para carpetas) filing cabinet; (— para tarjetas) card index cabinet 2 (cajón — de carpetas) filing draw; (— para tarjetas) card index draw 3 (caja) index card file (AmE), card index box (BrE) 4 (conjunto de fichas) file
B (Inf) file
ficticio -cia *adj* ‹*personaje/suceso*› fictitious; ‹*valor*› fiduciary
ficus *m* rubber plant
fidedigno -na *adj* reliable
fideicomisario[1] **-ria** *adj* trust (*before n*)
fideicomisario[2] **-ria** *m,f* trustee
fideicomiso *m* trusteeship
fidelidad *f* 1 (de persona, de animal) fidelity, faithfulness; **jurar ~ al rey** to swear an oath of loyalty to the king 2 (de reproducción) faithfulness; (de instrumento) accuracy
fidelizar [A4] *vt* ‹*clientela/usuario*› to cultivate
fideo *m* 1 (pasta fina) noodle; **~s** noodles; (muy finos) vermicelli; **está flaco como un ~** (fam) he's as thin as a rake (colloq) 2 **fideos** *mpl* (RPl) (pasta en general) pasta
fiduciario -ria *adj/m,f* fiduciary
fiebre *f*
A (Med) fever; **tener ~** to be feverish, to have a fever (esp AmE), to have a temperature (esp BrE); **le bajó la ~** his fever *o* temperature came down

Compuestos
- **fiebre aftosa** foot-and-mouth disease
- **fiebre amarilla/del heno/reumática** yellow/hay/rheumatic fever
- **fiebre palúdica/tifoidea** malaria/typhoid
- **fiebre uterina** nymphomania

B (furor) obsession; **su ~ por las motos** his obsession with motorcycles; **le dio la ~ de la limpieza** he went crazy and started cleaning the whole house (colloq); **tiene la ~ de los video-juegos** he has the video-games bug

(Compuesto) **fiebre del oro** gold fever

fiel¹ *adj* [1] ‹*persona*› faithful; **no le es ~** she is unfaithful to him; **~ al rey** loyal to the king [2] ‹*traducción/copia*› faithful, accurate

fiel² *mf*

A (Relig) **los ~es** the faithful

B **fiel** *m* (de balanza) needle, pointer

fieltro *m* felt

fiera *f* [1] (animal) wild animal, beast (liter); ***ser una ~ para algo*** (fam) to be great *o* fantastic at sth (colloq) [2] (de mal carácter): **ese perro es una ~** that dog is fierce *o* vicious; **mi suegra es una ~** my mother-in-law is a real dragon (colloq); **se puso como** *or* **hecho una ~** he went wild (colloq); **se me acercó hecha una ~** he came towards me in a rage

fiereza *f* ferocity, fierceness

fiero -ra *adj* [1] (feroz) ‹*animal*› fierce, ferocious; ‹*huracán/tormenta*› fierce [2] (RPl fam) (feo) ugly

fierro *m*

A [1] (AmL fam) (trozo de metal) piece of metal; **le dio con un ~** he hit him with a metal bar [2] (AmL) (hierro) iron; ***meter(le) ~*** (CS fam) to step on it

B (AmL arg) (navaja) blade (fam)

C **fierros** *mpl* (Méx fam) (en los dientes) braces (*pl*) (AmE), brace (esp BrE)

fiesta *f*

A (celebración) party; **~ de cumpleaños** birthday party; **dieron una gran ~** they threw *o* had a big party; **estar de ~** to be having a party; ***aguar la ~*** to spoil the fun; ***hacerle ~s a algn*** to make a fuss of sb; ***no estoy para ~s*** I'm not in the mood for fun and games; ***tener la ~ en paz*** (Esp fam) to enjoy some peace and quiet; **tengamos la ~ en paz** that's enough!

B [1] (día festivo) (public) holiday; **el lunes es ~** Monday is a holiday; **aquí no hacemos ~ el 20 de agosto** the 20th of August is not a public holiday here [2] **fiestas** *fpl* (festejos) fiesta, festival; (de fin de año, etc) festive season; **son las ~s del pueblo** the town's holding its annual festival; **¡felices ~s!** Merry Christmas!; **¿dónde vas a pasar estas ~s?** where are you going to spend the vacation (AmE) *o* (BrE) holidays?

(Compuestos)
- **fiesta de guardar** day of obligation
- **fiesta fija/movible** fixed/movable feast
- **fiesta nacional** (día festivo) public holiday; (Taur) bullfighting

fiestas

A *fiesta* in Spain can be a day of neighborhood celebrations, a larger event for a town or city, or a national holiday, to commemorate a saint's day or some historical event. For example, Madrid has the *fiestas de San Isidro*, in honor of its patron saint. Other famous Spanish holidays include the **Fallas** in Valencia, the *Sanfermines* in July in Pamplona, and the *Feria de Sevilla*, two weeks after Easter.

They can last for a week or more, during which everyday life is often interrupted. Classes in schools may stop and banks, stores, and post offices alter their opening hours. There are often bullfights and dancing to live bands and people eat and drink plentifully

fiestas patrias

In Latin America, a period of one or more days on which each country celebrates its independence. There are usually military parades, firework displays, and folk activities typical of the country

FIFA /'fifa/ *f*: **la ~** FIFA

fifí *adj/m* (AmL fam) sissy (colloq)

figura *f*

A (objeto) figure; (en geometría) figure

B [1] (forma, silueta) figure, form [2] (tipo) figure; **tiene buena/mala ~** she has/doesn't have a good figure [3] (persona importante) figure; **una ~ de las letras** an important literary figure

(Compuesto) **figura paterna** father figure

C (en naipes) face card (AmE), picture *o* court card (BrE); (en ajedrez) piece (*except pawns*)

D (en patinaje, baile) figure

E (Mús) note

F (Ling) figure

(Compuesto) **figura retórica** figure of speech

figuración *f* (imaginación) imagining; **son figuraciones tuyas** it's all in your imagination

figurado -da *adj* figurative; **en sentido ~** figuratively

figurante -ta *m,f* extra

figurar [A1] *vi* [1] (en lista, documento) to appear [2] (en sociedad) to be prominent; (destacar): **lo hizo sólo para ~** *or* **por afán de ~** he just did it to show off *o* impress

■ **figurarse** *v pron* to imagine; **¿crees que vendrá? — me figuro que sí** do you think she'll come? — I imagine so *o* (AmE) I figure she will; **¡figúrate, tardamos dos horas!** just imagine! it took us two hours; **¿se enfadó mucho? — ¡figúrate!** did she get very angry? — what do you think?; **figúrate tú, se quedó viuda** can you imagine? she was left a widow; **ya me lo figuraba yo** I thought as much, so I thought; **ya te ~ás lo que hice** you can imagine *o* (AmE) figure what I did!

figurín *m* (ant) (dibujo) *illustration to accompany sewing or knitting pattern*; **va hecha un ~** (fam) she looks as if she's just stepped out of a fashion magazine

figurinista *mf* costume designer

figurita *f* (de adorno) figurine; (lámina) (RPl) picture card

fija *f* (fam) [1] (CS, Per) (Equ) (favorito) favorite*; (dato) tip [2] (*en locs*) **fija que** (RPl): **~ que llueve** it's bound *o* sure to rain; **(es) ~ que no viene** I bet she won't come; **a la fija** (Col): **a la ~ (que) viene** I'm sure he'll come

fijación *f*

A (Psic) fixation, obsession; **¡que ~ tienes con ese tema!** you're obsessed with that subject!

B **fijaciones** *fpl* (en esquí) (safety) bindings (*pl*)

fijador¹ -dora *adj* (Fot) fixing (*before n*)

fijador² *m* [1] (Art) fixative [2] (Fot) fixer [3] (gomina) brilliantine; (laca) hairspray

fijamente *adv* fixedly

fijar [A1] *vt*

A [1] (poner, clavar) to fix; **fija bien la estantería a la pared** fix the shelving securely to the wall; Ⓢ **prohibido fijar carteles** stick no bills; **fijó la mirada en el horizonte** she fixed her gaze on the horizon; **~ la atención en algo** to focus one's attention on sth [2] ‹*foto/dibujo*› to fix

B [1] ‹*residencia*›: **~on su residencia en París** they established their residence in Paris [2] ‹*fecha/cifra/precio*› to set; **la política fijada por el partido** the policy laid down by the party [3] «*reglamento/ley*» to state; **según fija el reglamento** as stated in *o* dictated by the regulations

■ **fijarse** *v pron* [1] (prestar atención): **fíjate bien en cómo lo hace** watch carefully how she does it; **si no te fijas en lo que haces, lo vas a hacer mal** if you don't watch *o* pay attention to what you're doing, you'll do it wrong; **fíjate bien en la decoración** look carefully at the decoration; **es muy observador, se fija en todo** he's very observant, he notices everything [2] (darse cuenta) to notice; **¿te has fijado en que no discuten nunca?** have you noticed that they never quarrel?; **se fijó en ella** he noticed her; **¡fíjate lo que ha crecido!** just look how she's grown!; **fíjate qué terrible** it was (*o* would be *etc*) awful; **fíjate que ayer mismo la ví** and I saw her only yesterday

fijativo *m* (Art) fixative; (Fot) fixer

fijo¹ -ja *adj*

A (no movible) fixed; **la estantería está fija** the shelving is fixed to the wall (*o* floor *etc*); **asegúrate de que la escalera está bien fija** make sure the ladder is steady; **tenía la mirada fija** he was staring into space; **con los ojos ~s en ella** with his eyes fixed on her; ***de ~***: **de ~ que vienen** I'm sure they'll turn up

B ‹*sueldo/precios*› fixed; ‹*trabajo/empleado*› permanent; ‹*cliente*› regular

C (definitivo) ‹*fecha*› definite, firm

fijo² *adv* (fam): **¿crees que vendrá? — fijo** do you think she'll come? — definitely *o* (colloq) sure; **en cuanto entre en la ducha, ~ que suena el teléfono** you can bet that as soon as I get in the shower, the phone will ring

fijo³ *m* land line (phone)

fila *f*

A [1] (hilera) line; **formen ~ aquí** form a line here; **formen ~s de (a) cinco** line up in fives; **ponerse en ~** to get into line; **en ~ india** in single file; **en doble ~** double-parked; **¡rompan ~s!** (Mil) fall out! 2 (en teatro, aula) row; ***de primera/segunda* ~** first-/second-rate; ***estar en primera* ~** (en teatro) to be in the front row; (figurar) to be in the limelight

B **filas** *fpl* 1 (Mil) ranks (*pl*); **incorporarse a ~s** to join up; **lo llamaron a ~s** he was drafted; ***cerrar*** *or* ***estrechar* ~s** to close ranks 2 (Pol) ranks (*pl*)

filamento *m* (Elec) filament; (hilo, fibra) thread

filantropía *f* philanthropy

filántropo -pa *m,f* philanthropist

filarmónico -ca *adj* philharmonic

filatelia *f* stamp collecting, philately

filatélico -ca *adj* philatelic (frml); **su colección filatélica** his stamp collection

filete *m*

A (de pescado) filet (AmE), fillet (BrE); (de carne — bistec) steak; (— corte entre las costillas y el lomo) (Chi, Méx) fillet

B (Mec, Tec) (de tornillo) thread

filfa *f* (Esp fam) (engaño): **las elecciones fueron una ~** the elections were a sham; **la invitación era pura ~** the invitation was nothing but a hoax

filiación *f*

A (afiliación) affiliation; **~ política** political affiliation; **de ~ comunista** linked to the communist party

B (Gob, Mil) (datos personales) particulars (*pl*), personal details (*pl*)

C (relación) filiation

filial¹ *adj* 1 ‹*amor*› filial 2 ‹*compañía/asociación*› affiliate (*before n*), subsidiary

filial² *f* subsidiary (company)

filibustero *m* filibuster, freebooter

filigrana *f* 1 (de oro, plata) filigree 2 (en deporte, danza) intricate movement; **¡a ver si se dejan de ~s y marcan un gol!** let's have less fancy footwork and more goals! (colloq) 3 ***hacer* ~s** to perform *o* work miracles 4 (en un papel) watermark

filípica *f* tirade, diatribe, philippic (liter)

Filipinas *fpl*: *tb* **las ~** the Philippines

filipino¹ -na *adj* Philippine, Filipino

filipino² -na *m,f* Filipino

film *m* (*pl* **films**) 1 (Cin, TV) movie, film (BrE) 2 (Coc) *tb* **~ transparente** Saran wrap® (AmE), clingfilm (BrE)

filmación *f* filming, shooting

filmadora *f* (AmL) movie camera (AmE), cinecamera (BrE)

filmar [A1] *vt* ‹*película*› to shoot; ‹*persona/suceso*› to film

filme *m* (period) movie, film (BrE)

fílmico -ca *adj* movie (*before n*), film (*before n*)

filmina *f* slide

filmografía *f* movies (*pl*), films (*pl*) (BrE), filmography (tech)

filmoteca *f* film library

filo *m*

A 1 (de cuchillo, espada) cutting edge, blade; **no tiene mucho ~** it isn't very sharp; **le voy a dar ~** I'm going to sharpen it; ***caminar por*** *or* ***pisar el* ~ *de la navaja*** to be on a knife-edge 2 (borde) edge; **el ~ de la mesa** the edge of the table; **al ~ de las siete** at seven o'clock sharp

B (AmL fam) (hambre): **tengo un ~ enorme** I'm ravenous

filología *f* philology; **una licenciatura en ~ francesa** a degree in French

filólogo -ga *m,f* philologist; **soy ~** I have a degree in languages

filón *m* 1 (Min) seam, vein 2 (fam) (negocio) gold mine (colloq)

filoso -sa *adj* 1 (AmL) ‹*cuchillo/hoja*› sharp 2 (AmC, Col arg) (hambriento) ravenous

filosofar [A1] *vi* to philosophize

filosofía *f* philosophy; **tómate las cosas con ~** (fam) you have to be philosophical about things

filosófico -ca *adj* philosophical

filósofo -fa *m,f* philosopher

filtración *f*

A (proceso) filtering, filtration (tech); (gotera) leak

B (de información) leak; **la ~ de un informe** the leaking of a report

filtrar [A1] *vt*

A 1 ‹*líquido/rayos*› to filter 2 ‹*llamadas*› to screen

B ‹*informaciones/noticias*› to leak

■ **filtrar** *vi* «*líquido/luz*» to filter

■ **filtrarse** *v pron*

A «*agua*» to leak; «*humedad*» to seep

B 1 «*noticia*» to leak 2 «*dinero*» to seep away, dwindle

filtro *m*

A (Tec) filter; **~ para el café** coffee filter

(Compuesto) **filtro solar** sunscreen

B (poción) philter*; **~ mágico** magic potion

fin *m*

A 1 (final) end; **a ~es de junio** at the end of June; **a ~ de mes** at the end of the month; **hasta el ~ de los siglos** *or* **tiempos** until the end of time; **no es el ~ del mundo** (fam) it's not the end of the world (colloq); **tuvo un triste ~** he came to a sad end; **puso ~ a la discusión** she put an end to the discussion; **el verano ya llega a su ~** summer is coming to an end; **con esta noticia ponemos ~ a la edición de hoy** and with that we end tonight's news; **un accidente aéreo puso ~ a su vida** he was killed in an aircrash; **llevó la empresa a buen ~** he brought the venture to a successful conclusion; Ⓢ **Fin** The End 2 (*en locs*) **por** *or* **al fin** at last; **¡al ~ lo conseguí!** at last I've done it!; **en fin** well; **en ~ ¡qué se le va a hacer!** ah well, what can you do?; **en ~ ¡sigamos!** anyway, let's carry on!; **repara electrodomésticos, pone enchufes … en ~ un poco de todo** he repairs electrical goods, puts in plugs … a bit of everything, really; ***a* ~ *de cuentas*** in the end, at the end of the day; ***al* ~ *y al cabo*** after all; ***tocar a su* ~** (liter) to draw to a close *o* to an end

(Compuestos)

- **fin de año** New Year's Eve
- **fin de fiesta** (grand) finale
- **fin de semana** (sábado y domingo) weekend

B (objetivo, finalidad) purpose; **el ~ de esta visita** the aim *o* purpose of this visit; **esto constituye un ~ en sí mismo** this constitutes an end in itself; **una institución sin ~es lucrativos** *or* **de lucro** a not-for-profit organization (AmE), a non-profit-making organisation (BrE); **a ~ de que** (frml) in order to; **con este ~** *or* **a este ~** *or* **a tal ~** (frml) with this aim (frml), to this end (frml); **con el ~** *or* **a ~ de** (frml) with the aim *o* purpose of; ***el* ~ *justifica los medios*** the end justifies the means

finado -da *m,f* (frml) deceased (frml)

final¹ *adj* ‹*decisión*› final; ‹*objetivo*› ultimate

final² *m* end; **a ~es de junio** at the end of June; **al ~ de la película** at the end of the movie; **no me gustó el ~** I didn't like the ending; **un ~ feliz** a happy ending; **al ~ de la lista** at the bottom of the list; **estábamos al ~ de la cola** we were last in line (AmE) *o* (BrE) at the back of the queue; **al ~ tendrá que decidirse** he'll have to make his mind up in the end *o* eventually

final³ *f* (Dep) 1 (en fútbol, tenis etc) final; **la ~ de copa** the cup final; **pasar a la ~** to go through to *o* make it to the final 2 **finales** *fpl* (en béisbol, baloncesto, fútbol americano) playoffs (*pl*)

finalidad *f* 1 (propósito, utilidad) purpose, aim; **¿con qué ~ se hizo?** what was the aim in *o* object of doing it? 2 (Fil) finality

finalista¹ *adj*: **los dos equipos ~s** the two teams that reach (*o* reached *etc*) the final

finalista² *mf* finalist

finalización *f* (de periodo, partido, guerra) end; (de proyecto, obras) completion

finalizar [A4] *vt* to finish; **~on el año con beneficios** they were making good profit at the end of the year; **dio por finalizada su estancia** her stay came to an end

■ **finalizar** *vi* to end; **así finaliza la emisión de hoy** and that brings us to the end of today's programming (AmE) *o* (BrE) programs; **una vez finalizada la reunión** once the meeting is/was over

finalmente *adv* 1 (*indep*) (por último) finally, lastly; **y ~, agregar el vino** and finally *o* lastly, add the wine 2 (al final) in the end; **~ llegaron a un acuerdo** they finally reached an agreement, in the end *o* eventually they reached an agreement

finamente *adv* in a refined *o* genteel way

financiación *f*
A (de empresa, obra, acción) financing, funding
B (facilidades) credit facilities (*pl*)
financiador -dora *m,f* financial backer
financiamiento *m* financing, funding
financiar [A1] *vt*
A ‹*empresa/proyecto*› to finance, fund
B (AmL) (vender a plazos) to give credit facilities for
financiera *f* finance company
financiero[1] -ra *adj* financial
financiero[2] -ra *m,f*, (AmL) **financista** *mf* financier
finanzas *fpl* finances (*pl*)
finca *f*
A (propiedad rural) 1 (explotación agrícola) farm; **~ cafetera** coffee plantation 2 (AmL) (de recreo) country estate
(Compuesto) **finca rústica** plot of land
B (Esp) (propiedad urbana) building
fincar [A2] *vt* (Méx) to build
fineza *f* 1 (refinamiento) refinement; **la ~ de sus modales** her refined manners 2 (cortesía) politeness, courtesy
fingido -da *adj* hypocritical, false
fingir [I7] *vt* 1 ‹*alegría/desinterés*› to feign, fake; **~ + INF** to pretend to + INF 2 ‹*voz*› to imitate
■ **fingir** *vi* to pretend
■ **fingirse** *v pron*: **se fingió apenado** he pretended to be sorry
finiquitar [A1] *vt* ‹*deuda/pleito*› to settle
finiquito *m* (pago) settlement; (documento) release document; **dar ~ a una cuenta** to settle an account; **firmó el ~** she signed the release document
finito -ta *adj* finite
finlandés[1] -desa *adj* Finnish
finlandés[2] -desa *m,f*
A (persona) Finn
B **finlandés** *m* (idioma) Finnish
Finlandia *f* Finland
fino[1] -na *adj*
A (en grosor) 1 ‹*papel/capa*› fine, thin; ‹*loncha*› thin 2 ‹*arena/cabellos/lluvia*› fine; ‹*labios*› thin; ‹*cintura/dedos/persona*› slender 3 ‹*punta*› fine; **un lápiz de punta fina** a fine pencil
B (en calidad) ‹*pastelería/bollería*› high quality; ‹*porcelana*› fine; ‹*lencería*› sheer
C (en modales) refined
D 1 ‹*oído/olfato*› acute 2 ‹*ironía/humor*› subtle
fino[2] *m* fino, dry sherry
finolis[1] *adj inv* (Esp) (hum & pey) affected
finolis[2] *mf* (*pl* ~) (Esp) (hum & pey) affected person
finta *f* feint
fintar, (AmL) **fintear** [A1] *vi* (en esgrima, boxeo) to feint; (en fútbol) to dummy, fake
finura *f*
A (refinamiento) refinement; **¡qué ~!** (iró) that's very nice! (iro)
B (de tejido, de porcelana) fineness
fiordo *m* fjord, fiord
firma *f*
A (nombre) signature; (acción) signing; **la ~ del tratado** the signing of the treaty
B (empresa) company, firm (BrE)
firmamento *m* (liter) firmament (liter)
firmante *mf* signatory; **los abajo ~s** the undersigned
firmar [A1] *vt* to sign
■ **firmar** *vi* (escribir el nombre) to sign; **~ con una cruz** to make a *o* one's mark; **firmó por el Barcelona** he was signed (up) by Barcelona
firme[1] *adj*
A 1 ‹*escalera/silla/mesa*› steady; **terreno ~** solid ground; **pisar terreno ~** to be on safe *o* firm *o* solid ground; **tener las carnes ~s** to have a firm body; **con paso/pulso ~** with a firm step/steady hand; **una oferta en ~** a firm offer; **de ~** ‹*estudiar/trabajar*› hard 2 (color) fast 3 ‹*candidato*› strong
B (Mil): **¡~s!** attention!; **en posición de ~s** standing at *o* (BrE) to attention
C 1 ‹*persona*› firm; **tienes que mostrarte más ~ con él** you have to be firmer with him; **se mantuvo ~** (ante las presiones, el enemigo) she stood her ground; **me mantuve ~ en mi postura/idea** I stuck *o* kept to my position/idea 2 (*delante del n*) ‹*creencia/convicción*› firm
firme[2] *m* road surface
firmeza *f* 1 (de convicciones) strength; **con ~** firmly 2 (del terreno) firmness
firulete *m* (AmL) (en la ropa) frill; (en firma) twirl, flourish; (en un baile) twirl
fiscal[1] *adj* fiscal, tax (*before n*); ▸**año, ministerio**
fiscal[2] -cala *m,f*, **fiscal** *mf* ≈ district attorney (*in US*), ≈ public prosecutor (*in UK*)
(Compuesto) **Fiscal General del Estado** ≈ Attorney General (*in US*), ≈ Director of Public Prosecutions (*in UK*)
fiscal[3] *m* (Ven) *tb* **~ de tránsito** (cuerpo) traffic police; (persona) traffic policeman
fiscalía *f* (despacho) ≈ district attorney's office (*in US*), ≈ public prosecutor's office (*in UK*); (cargo) *post of district attorney or public prosecutor*
fiscalidad *f* (impuestos) taxation; (sistema) tax system; **una ~ alta** a high level of taxation
fiscalizar [A4] *vt* to supervise, control
fisco *m* ≈ Treasury (*in US*), ≈ Exchequer (*in UK*); **declaró sus ingresos al ~** ≈ he declared his income to the Internal Revenue Service (*in US*), ≈ he declared his income to the Inland Revenue (*in UK*)
fisgar [A3] *vi* (fam) to snoop (colloq); **andaba fisgando por las oficinas** he was snooping around the offices
fisgón[1] -gona *adj* (fam) nosy (colloq)
fisgón[2] -gona *m,f* (fam) busybody (colloq)
fisgonear [A1] *vi* (fam) to nose around (colloq)
física *f* physics
(Compuesto) **física cuántica/nuclear** quantum/nuclear physics
físico[1] -ca *adj* physical
físico[2] -ca *m,f*
A (Fís) physicist
B **físico** *m* (cuerpo — de hombre, atleta) physique; (— de mujer) figure; (apariencia) appearance
fisiología *f* physiology
fisiológico -ca *adj* physiological
fisiólogo -ga *m,f* physiologist
fisión *f* fission; **~ nuclear** nuclear fission
fisionomía *f* ▸**fisonomía**
fisioterapeuta *mf* physiotherapist, physical therapist (AmE)
fisioterapia *f* physiotherapy, physical therapy (AmE)
fisonomía *f* 1 (de persona) features (*pl*) 2 (de objeto, lugar) appearance
fisonomista *mf*: **soy buen ~** I have a good memory for faces
fistol *m* (Méx) tiepin
fístula *f* fistula
fisura *f* 1 (grieta) fissure, crack 2 (Med) (en un hueso) fracture; (del ano) fissure
flaccidez *f* flaccidity
fláccido -da *adj* flaccid, flabby
flaco -ca *adj* 1 ‹*persona*› thin, skinny (colloq) 2 (AmL) (como apelativo cariñoso) skinny (colloq) 3 (insignificante) poor
flacucho -cha *adj* (fam) skinny (colloq)
flacura *f* thinness, skinniness (colloq)
flagelación *f* flagellation (frml); (Bib) scourging
flagelar [A1] *vt* to flagellate (frml); (Bib) to scourge
■ **flagelarse** *v pron* to flagellate oneself (frml), to whip oneself
flagelo *m*
A (calamidad) whip, scourge
B (desgracia) disaster, calamity
C (Biol) flagellum
flagrante *adj* ‹*mentira*› blatant; ‹*injusticia*› glaring, flagrant; **lo sorprendieron en ~ delito** they caught him red-handed *o* in flagrante (frml *or* hum)
flama *f* (Méx) flame

flamable *adj* (Méx) inflammable, flammable

flamante *adj* (*gen delante del n*) (nuevo) brand-new; (vistoso) smart (colloq)

flambeado -da *adj* flambé•

flambear [A1] *vt* to flambé

flamenco[1] **-ca** *adj*

A ‹*cante/baile*› flamenco (*before n*); ***ponerse*** **~** (Esp) to get sassy (AmE colloq), to get stroppy (BrE colloq)

B (de Flandes) Flemish

C (de aspecto sano) strong and healthy-looking

flamenco[2] **-ca** *m,f* (Geog) Fleming; **los F~s** the Flemish

flamenco[3] *m*

A (Mús) flamenco

B (idioma) Flemish

C (Zool) flamingo

> **flamenco**
>
> Flamenco is performed in three forms: guitar, singing, and dancing. Its origins lie with the gypsies, and many of the best *cantaores* (flamenco singers), *bailaores* (dancers), and guitarists are gypsies. There are also Arabic and North African influences.
>
> Modern flamenco blends traditional forms with rock, jazz, and salsa. Guitarists are soloists in their own right, not just accompanists. Most flamenco songs are folk songs, modified by oral tradition, on a wide range of subjects. The music and lyrics are improvised and never written down.
>
> An integral part of traditional flamenco is the *duende*, the idea that the performer becomes inspired by the emotion of the music or dance. But as flamenco becomes commercialized, rehearsed performances are more likely than spontaneous music and dancing

flan *m* (dulce) crème caramel; (salado — de arroz) mold•; (— de pescado, verduras) terrine; ***estar como un*** **~** to be shaking like a leaf

(Compuesto) **flan de arena** sandcastle

flanco *m* 1 (Mil) flank 2 (de animal) flank, side; (de persona) side

Flandes *m* Flanders

flanera *f* mold•

flanquear [A1] *vt* to flank

flap /'flap/ *m* (*pl* **flaps**) flap

flaquear [A1] *vi* «*persona/fuerzas*» to flag; **le flaqueaban las fuerzas** he was flagging; **su voluntad empezó a ~** she began to lose heart

flaqueza *f* weakness

flash /'flas/ *m* (*pl* **flashes**)

A (Fot) (aparato, destello) flash

B (Rad, TV) *tb* **~ informativo** newsflash

C (Esp arg) (impresión fuerte) shock (colloq)

flashback /'flasβak/ *m* (*pl* **-backs**) flashback

flato *m* 1 (Esp) (dolor en el costado): **tengo/me dio ~** I have/I got a stitch 2 (Chi fam) (eructo) burp (colloq)

flatulencia *f* flatulence, wind (colloq)

flatulento -ta *adj* flatulent

flauta[1] *f* (Mús) flute; ***sonar la ~ (por casualidad)*** (Esp): **¡sonó la ~!** what a fluke!; **le sonó la ~** he was lucky

(Compuestos)
- **flauta dulce** recorder
- **flauta traversa** *or* (Esp) **travesera** transverse flute

flauta[2] *mf* flute player, flutist (AmE), flautist (BrE)

flautín[1] *m* piccolo

flautín[2] *mf* piccolo (player)

flautista *mf* flute player, flutist (AmE), flautist (BrE)

flebitis *f* phlebitis

flecha[1] *adj* (Ven) one-way; ***ir*** **~** to go the wrong way up a one-way street

flecha[2] *f* 1 (de arco) arrow; (de ballesta) bolt; **salió como una ~** she dashed *o* shot out 2 (señal, símbolo) arrow

flechar [A1] *vt* (fam) (enamorar): **me flechó** he swept me off my feet (colloq); **quedó flechado** he was smitten

flechazo *m* 1 (fam) (enamoramiento): **le ha dado el ~** he's smitten; **fue un ~** it was love at first sight 2 (herida) arrow wound

fleco *m* (Méx) (en el pelo) bangs (*pl*) (AmE), fringe (BrE)

flecos *mpl* 1 (adorno) fringe; **un chal con ~** a fringed shawl 2 (borde deshilachado) frayed edge

flema *f* phlegm

flemático -ca *adj* phlegmatic

flemón *m* boil, abscess; (en la encía) gumboil

flequillo *m* bangs (*pl*) (AmE), fringe (BrE)

fletar [A1] *vt*

A (Com, Transp) ‹*barco/avión*› to charter; ‹*autobús/camión*› to hire, rent (AmE)

B (AmL) (transportar) to transport

C (fam) (expulsar) to chuck ... out

flete *m*

A (Transp) 1 (contratación — de barco, avión) charter; (— de autobús, camión) hire 2 (precio de contratación — de barco, avión) charter fee; (— de autobús, camión) hire charge, rental charge (AmE)

B (AmL) (de mercancías — transporte) transportation, carriage (frml); (— precio del transporte) freight, carriage (frml)

fletero -ra *adj* (AmL) ‹*buque*› cargo (*before n*); ‹*compañía*› freight (*before n*)

flexibilidad *f* flexibility

flexibilizar [A4] *vt* ‹*horario laboral/sistema*› to make ... more flexible; ‹*criterio/medida*› to relax

flexible *adj* flexible

flexión *f*

A (Dep) (de brazos) push-up, press-up (BrE); (de piernas) squat; **hacer flexiones** (de brazos) to do push-ups *o* press-ups; (de cintura) to touch one's toes

B (Ling) inflection

flexionar [A1] *vt* (Dep) ‹*pierna/rodillas*› to bend; **~ la cintura** to bend down

flipar [A1] *vi* (Esp fam): **el helado me flipa cantidad** I love ice cream (colloq); **flipo contigo, no hay quien te entienda** I can't believe you sometimes, you're impossible to understand

■ **fliparse** *v pron* 1 (Esp fam) (entusiasmarse): **se flipa por el cine** she's crazy about movies (colloq) 2 (Esp arg) (drogarse) to get high (colloq)

flipe *m* (Esp arg) 1 (experiencia impresionante): **el concierto fue un ~** the concert was something else 2 (por droga) buzz (colloq)

flipper /'fliper/ *m* (máquina) pinball machine

flirt /'flirt/ *m* (*pl* **flirts**) (relación) fling; (persona) (*m*) boyfriend; (*f*) girlfriend

flirtear [A1] *vi* to flirt

flirteo *m* flirting

flojear [A1] *vi* 1 (debilitarse) to grow *o* get weak 2 (fam) (holgazanear) to laze around; **últimamente ha estado flojeando en sus estudios** his work has gone down recently

flojera *f* 1 (fam) (debilidad) lethargy 2 (fam) (pereza) laziness; **me da ~** I can't be bothered; **tengo ~** I feel lazy

flojo[1] **-ja** *adj*

A 1 ‹*nudo/tornillo/vendaje*› loose; ‹*cuerda*› slack; **haces el punto muy ~** you knit very loosely; ***me la trae floja*** (Esp vulg) I don't give a shit (vulg) 2 (débil) weak 3 ‹*vientos*› light 4 ‹*café/té*› weak

B (mediocre) ‹*trabajo/examen*› poor; ‹*película/vino*› second-rate; ‹*estudiante*› poor; **está ~ en física** he's weak in (AmE) *o* (BrE) at physics

C (Com, Econ) slack; **el mercado estuvo ~** the market was slack

D ‹*persona*› (fam) (perezoso) lazy

flojo[2] **-ja** *m,f* 1 (fam) (perezoso) lazybones (colloq) 2 (Col fam) (cobarde) coward

floppy /'flopi/ *m* (*pl* **floppys**) floppy disk, diskette

flor *f* (Bot) flower; **~es naturales/secas** fresh/dried flowers; **~ecillas silvestres** wild flowers; **un vestido de ~es** a flowery dress; **en ~** in flower, in bloom; ***a ~ de piel***: **tenía los nervios a ~ de piel** his nerves were all on edge; **tiene la sensibilidad a ~ de piel** she's very easily hurt; ***a ~ de tierra/agua*** just below the ground/water; ***echarle ~es a algn*** to pay sb compliments; ***estar en la ~ de la vida*** to be in the prime of life; **~ de ...** (CS fam): **me hizo ~ de regalo** she gave me a wonderful present (colloq); **es un ~ de estúpido** he's a real idiot (colloq); ***ir de ~ en ~*** to flit from one man/woman to another; ***la ~ y***

nata the cream, the crème de la crème; ***ni ~es*** (Esp fam): **¿sabes dónde está? — ni ~es** do you know where he is? — no idea; **¿entendiste algo? — ni ~es** did you understand anything? — not a thing (colloq); ***ser la ~ de la canela*** to be wonderful

(Compuesto) **flor de azahar** (del naranjo) orange blossom; (del limonero) lemon blossom

flora *f* flora

floración *f* (acción) flowering; (período) flowering period

floral *adj* floral

floreado -da *adj* flowery

florear [A1] *vi* 1 (Chi, Méx) (Bot) to flower, blossom 2 (Méx) (halagar): **le ~on mucho su vestido** her dress got a lot of compliments

florecer [E3] *vi* 1 «*flor*» to flower, bloom; «*árbol*» to flower, blossom 2 (prosperar) to flourish, thrive

floreciente *adj* flourishing, thriving

florecimiento *m* flowering

Florencia *f* Florence

florentino -na *adj/m,f* Florentine

floreo *m* flourish

florería *f* (AmL) florist's, flower shop

florero *m* vase; ***estar de ~*** (Col, RPl, Ven fam) to be here/there purely for decoration

florescencia *f* florescence

floresta *f* (liter) verdant grove (liter)

florete *m* foil

floricultor -tora *m,f* flower grower

floricultura *f* flower growing

florido -da *adj* 1 ‹*campo*› full of flowers 2 ‹*estilo/lenguaje*› flowery 3 (selecto): **lo más ~ de la sociedad** the cream of society

florín *m* (moneda antigua) florin; (en Holanda) guilder

floripondio, (AmL) **floripón** *m* (fam): **con un ~ en la cabeza** with a great flowery thing on her head (colloq)

florista *mf* florist

floristería *f* florist's, flower shop

floritura *f* embellishment, frill

florón *m* ceiling rose, rosette

flota *f*

A (de barcos, camiones, aviones) fleet; **la ~ mercante/pesquera** the merchant/fishing fleet; **la ~ de altura/bajura** the deep-sea/inshore fleet

B (Col) (autobús) bus (AmE), coach (BrE)

flotación *f* flotation

flotador *m* 1 (para nadar — de corcho) float; (— para la cintura) rubber ring 2 (de hidroavión) float 3 (de pescar) float 4 (Tec) ballcock

flotante *adj* floating

flotar [A1] *vi* 1 (en un líquido) to float 2 (en el aire) «*partículas/polen*» to float; «*perfume*» to waft 3 (Econ, Fin) «*moneda*» to float

flote *m*: **a ~** afloat; **mantenerse a ~** to stay afloat; **logró mantener el negocio a ~** he managed to keep the business afloat; **salir a ~** «*cuerpo sumergido*» to float to the surface; **el país tendrá que salir a ~** the country will have to get back on its feet

flotilla *f* (Náut) flotilla; (Aviac) fleet

fluctuación *f* fluctuation

fluctuante *adj* ‹*temperatura/opinión*› fluctuating; ‹*mercado/divisa*› fluctuating; ‹*población*› floating

fluctuar [A18] *vi* to fluctuate

fluidez *f* 1 (de expresión) fluency; **habla griego con ~** she speaks Greek fluently 2 (de tráfico) smooth flow 3 (Fís, Quím) fluidity

fluido[1] *adj* 1 (líquido) fluid 2 (tráfico): **el tráfico es ~** the traffic is moving smoothly

fluido[2] *m* 1 (Fís, Quím) fluid 2 (period) (corriente) current; **un corte en el ~ eléctrico** a power failure *o* power cut

fluir [I20] *vi* to flow

flujo *m*

A (circulación, corriente) flow; **~ sanguíneo** blood flow; **un ~ emigratorio** a wave of immigrants; **el ~ de visitantes** the number of visitors

B (Med) (secreción) discharge

(Compuesto) **flujo menstrual** menstrual flow

C (Náut) tide; **~ y reflujo** ebb and flow

fluminense *adj* of/from Rio de Janeiro

flúor, fluor *m* (gas) fluorine; (fluoruro) fluoride

fluorescencia *f* fluorescence

fluorescente *adj* fluorescent

fluoruro *m* fluoride

fluvial *adj* river (*before n*), fluvial (tech)

flux *m*

A (en naipes) flush

B (Ven) (traje) suit

FM *f* (= **frecuencia modulada**) FM

FMI *m* (= **Fondo Monetario Internacional**) IMF

fobia *f* phobia; **tiene ~ a los aviones** he has a phobia about flying; **le tiene ~** (fam) she can't stand the sight of him (colloq)

fóbico -ca *adj* phobic

foca *f* 1 (animal) seal; (piel) sealskin 2 (fam) (persona gorda) fatty (colloq)

focal *adj* focal

foco *m*

A 1 (Fís, Fot, Mat) focus; **fuera de ~** (AmL) out of focus 2 (centro, núcleo) focus; **fue el ~ de todas las miradas** everybody's eyes were focused on him 3 (de incendio) seat

B 1 (Cin, Teatr) (reflector) spotlight 2 (AmL) (Auto) light 3 (Ec, Méx, Per) (de lámpara) light bulb; ***se me/le prendió el ~*** (Méx fam) I/she had a bright idea *o* (AmE) a brainstorm (colloq) 4 (AmC) (linterna) flashlight (AmE), torch (BrE)

foete *m* (AmL) horsewhip

fofo -fa *adj* (fam) flabby, pudgy (AmE)

fogata *f* bonfire

fogón *m* (quemador) burner; (cocina) (ant) stove; (fogata) (AmL) bonfire, campfire; (de caldera) firebox

fogonazo *m* flash, explosion

fogosidad *f* ardor•

fogoso -sa *adj* ardent

fogueado -da *adj* (AmS fam) experienced

foguearse [A1] *v pron* to undergo a baptism of fire

fogueo *m* (Mil): **un cartucho de ~** a blank (cartridge); **un partido de ~** (Col) a practice game

foja *f* (AmL) sheet; **~ de servicios** service record; ***volver a/estar en ~s cero*** (AmL) to go/be back to square one

folio *m* 1 (hoja) sheet (of paper); **papel tamaño ~** A4 paper 2 (de un trabajo) page

folk[1] /'fo(l)k/ *adj* folk (*before n*)

folk[2] /'fo(l)k/ *m* folk (music)

folklore *m* folklore

folklórico[1] **-ca** *adj* 1 ‹*danza/música/leyenda*› folk (*before n*) 2 (fam) (pintoresco) quaint

folklórico[2] **-ca** *m,f*: *performer of traditional Spanish songs and dances*

folklorista *mf* folklorist

follaje *m* foliage

follar [A1] *vt/vi* (Esp vulg) to screw (vulg), to fuck (vulg)

folletín *m* (en periódicos, revistas) newspaper serial; (revista mala) rag (colloq); (película, novela mala) melodrama

folletinesco -ca *adj* melodramatic

folleto *m* (hoja) leaflet, flier (AmE); (librito) brochure, pamphlet

follón *m* (Esp fam) 1 (trifulca) commotion, ruckus; (ruido) racket (colloq), din (AmE colloq); **armó** *or* **montó un buen ~** (montó una trifulca) he kicked up a hell of a fuss (colloq); (hizo ruido) he made such a racket *o* din (colloq) 2 (situación confusa, desorden) mess; **¡que ~ de papeles!** these papers are in such a mess!; **el ~ este de MEPIRESA** this MEPIRESA business (colloq) 3 (problema): **no te metas en follones** don't get into trouble

fomentar [A1] *vt*

A ‹*industria/turismo*› to promote; ‹*ahorro/inversión*› to encourage, boost; ‹*disturbio/odio*› to incite, foment (frml); **hay que ~les el gusto por la música** one has to foster *o* encourage an interest in music in them

B (Med) to foment

fomento *m* (impulso, promoción) promotion

fonda *f* (restaurant) (esp AmL) cheap restaurant; (pensión) (esp Esp) boarding house; (puesto) (Chi) refreshment stand

fondeadero *m* anchorage

fondear [A1] *vt* (Náut) to anchor

fondillo *m*, **fondillos** *mpl* (AmL) seat

fondista *mf* (Dep) long-distance runner

fondo *m*

A 1 (parte más baja) bottom; **el ~ del mar** the bottom of the sea; **una maleta de doble ~** a suitcase with a false bottom; **no toco ~** I can't touch the bottom; **en el ~ de su corazón** deep down (in his heart); **llegaré al ~ de esta cuestión** I'll get to the bottom of this matter; **hay un ~ de verdad en eso** there is an element of truth in that 2 (parte de atrás — de pasillo, calle) end; (— de habitación) back; **siga hasta el ~ del pasillo** go to the end of the corridor; **estaban al** *or* **en el ~ de la sala** they were at the back of the room 3 (profundidad): **tiene poco ~** it is not very deep; **un cajón con más ~** a deeper drawer 4 (de edificio) depth 5 (en cuadro, fotografía) background

B 1 (Lit) (contenido) content; **el ~ y la forma** the form and content 2 (Der): **una cuestión de ~** a question of law

C (Fin) 1 (de dinero) fund; **hacer un ~ común** to start a joint fund *o* (colloq) a kitty 2 **fondos** *mpl* (dinero) money, funds (*pl*); **recaudar ~s** to raise money; **un cheque sin ~s** a dud *o* (AmE) rubber check (colloq); **me dio un cheque sin ~s** the check he gave me bounced; **estoy mal de ~s** (fam) I'm short of cash (colloq) 3 **a fondo perdido** ‹*inversión/préstamo*› non-refundable, non-recoverable

(Compuestos)

- **fondo de amortización/inversión/pensiones/previsión** sinking/investment/pension/provident fund
- **fondo de escritorio** *or* **de pantalla** wallpaper
- **fondo de fondos** fund of funds
- **Fondo Monetario Internacional** International Monetary Fund, IMF
- **fondos públicos** *mpl* public funds (*pl*)

D (Dep) (en atletismo): **de ~** ‹*corredor/carrera/prueba*› long-distance

E (de biblioteca, museo) collection

(Compuesto) **fondo editorial** list of titles

F (Méx) (Indum) slip, underskirt

G (*en locs*) **a fondo** (*loc adj*) ‹*estudio/investigación*› in-depth; (*loc adv*) ‹*prepararse/entrenar*› thoroughly; **una limpieza a ~** a thorough clean; **una reforma a ~** a sweeping reform; **conoce el área/tema a ~** she knows the area/subject really well; **de fondo** ‹*ruido/música*› background (*before n*); ‹*error/discrepancia*› fundamental; ***en el ~***: **en el ~ no es malo** deep down he's not a bad person; **en el ~ nos llevamos bien** we get on all right, really; ***¡~ blanco!*** (AmL fam) bottoms up! (colloq); ***tener buen ~*** to be a good person at heart; ***tocar ~*** to bottom out; **su credibilidad ha tocado ~** his credibility has hit rock bottom

fonema *m* phoneme

fonética *f* phonetics

fonético -ca *adj* phonetic

fónico -ca *adj* phonic

fonógrafo *m* phonograph

fonología *f* phonology

fonoteca *f* music library

fontanería *f* (esp Esp) plumbing

fontanero -ra *m,f* (esp Esp) plumber

footing /'futin/ *m* jogging; **hacer ~** to jog

foque *m* jib

forajido -da *m,f* fugitive, outlaw

foral *adj* ‹*decreto/guardia*› autonomous (*of/relating to certain autonomous regions of Spain*)

foráneo -nea *adj* foreign, strange

forastero -ra *m,f* stranger, outsider

forcejear [A1] *vi* to struggle

forcejeo *m* struggle

fórceps *m* (*pl* ~) forceps (*pl*)

forense[1] *adj* forensic

forense[2] *mf* forensic scientist

forestal *adj* forest (*before n*)

forfait /for'fe/ *m* 1 (Com) fixed *o* set price; **viaje turístico a ~** package holiday 2 (abono) ski pass 3 (Dep) failure to appear

forja *f* (fragua, taller) forge; (acción) forging

forjar [A1] *vt* 1 ‹*utensilio/pieza*› to forge; ‹*metal*› to work 2 ‹*porvenir*› to shape, forge; ‹*plan*› to make; ‹*ilusiones/esperanzas*› to build up 3 ‹*nación/bases*› to create; ‹*amistad/alianza*› to forge

■ **forjarse** *v pron* ‹*porvenir*› to shape, forge; ‹*ilusiones*› to build up

forma *f*

A 1 (contorno, apariencia) shape; **tiene ~ circular** it's circular (in shape); **en ~ de cruz** in the shape of a cross; **tiene la ~ de un platillo** it's the shape of a saucer; **dar ~ a algo** (al barro) to shape sth; (a proyecto) to give shape to sth; **tomar ~** to take shape; **el suéter ha tomado la ~ de la percha** the sweater's been stretched out of shape by the coat hanger 2 (tipo, modalidad) form; **la discriminación no se tolerará bajo ninguna de sus ~s** discrimination will not be tolerated in any shape or form; **el medicamento se presenta en ~ de comprimidos** the medicine comes in tablet form

B (Lit) (de una novela, obra) form; (Fil) form

C (Ling) form

D (Dep, Med): **estar/mantenerse en ~** to be/keep fit; **está en baja ~** he's not on form; **en plena ~** on top form; ***en ~*** (AmL fam): **una comida en ~** a good square meal (colloq); **nos divertimos en ~** (AmL fam) we had a great time

E (manera, modo) way; **es su ~ de ser** it's just the way he is; **tiene una ~ de ser que desconcierta** he has a rather disconcerting manner; **¡qué ~ de gritar!** there's no need to shout!; **así no hay ~ de entenderse** we'll never get anywhere like this; **no veía la ~ de convencerlo** I couldn't see how to convince him; **de ~ que** (frml) in such a way that; ***de cualquier ~*** *or* ***de todas ~s*** anyway, in any case

(Compuesto) **forma de pago** form *o* method of payment

F **formas** *fpl* 1 (de mujer) figure 2 (apariencias) appearances (*pl*); **guardar las ~s** to keep up appearances

G (Méx) (formulario) form

formación *f*

A (de rocas, gobierno, palabras) formation

B (Geol) (conjunto, masa) formation

C (Mil) formation; **~ de combate** combat formation

D (educación recibida) education; (para trabajo) training; **tiene una buena ~** she has had a good education; **el período de ~** the training period

(Compuesto) **formación profesional** *or* (CS) **vocacional** professional *o* vocational training; **estudiantes de ~ ~** ≈ students at technical college

formador -dora *m,f* 1 (de algo) former, shaper; **el periodista como ~ de opinión** the journalist as opinion shaper 2 (de personas) formative influence; **fue un gran ~ de juventudes** he was a great formative influence on young people; **una institución que es la principal ~a de científicos** an institution which is the main formative influence on scientists

formal *adj*

A (cumplidor) reliable, dependable; (responsable) responsible; **¡sé ~ito!** behave yourself!

B 1 ‹*error*› formal 2 ‹*promesa/oferta*› firm; ‹*invitación/compromiso*› formal, official; ‹*acusación*› formal 3 ‹*recepción/cena*› formal

formalidad *f*

A (de persona) reliability; **no tiene ~** he's so unreliable; **tengamos ~** let's be serious

B (requisito) formality

formalismo *m* (Arte, Fil) formalism; (convencionalismo) conventionality

formalizar [A4] *vt* ‹*noviazgo/relación*› to make ... official; ‹*transacción/contrato*› to formalize; **los extranjeros deben ~ su situación** foreigners must legalize *o* regularize their position

■ **formalizarse** *v pron* «*persona*» to settle down; «*noviazgo*» to become official

formar [A1] *vt*

A 1 «*personas*» ‹*círculo/figura*› to make, form; ‹*asociación/gobierno*› to form, set up; ‹*barricada*› to set up; **formen parejas** (en clase) get into pairs *o* twos; (en baile) take your

partners [2] (Ling) to form [3] (Mil) ‹*tropas*› to have … fall in
B (componer) to make up; **~ parte de algo** to be part of sth, to belong to sth; **está formada por tres provincias** it is made up of *o* it comprises three provinces; **forman un ángulo recto** they form *o* make a right angle
C ‹*carácter/espíritu*› to form, shape
D (educar) to bring up; (para trabajo) to train
■ **formar** *vi* (Mil) to fall in; **¡a ~!** fall in!
■ **formarse** *v pron*
A [1] (hacerse, crearse) to form; **se formó una cola** a line (AmE) *o* (BrE) queue formed [2] (desarrollarse) «*niño/huesos*» to develop [3] ‹*idea/opinión*› to form; **se ha formado una impresión errónea** he has got the wrong impression
B (educarse) to be educated
formateado *m* formatting
formatear [A1] *vt* to format
formativo -va *adj* formative
formato *m*
A (tamaño, forma) format
B (Méx) (formulario, solicitud) form
fórmica® *f* Formica®
formidable *adj/interj* (fam) fantastic (colloq)
formol *m* formaldehyde
formón *m* chisel
fórmula *f*
A [1] (Mat, Quím) formula [2] (manera, sistema) way; **una nueva ~ para negociar** a new way of negotiating; **no existe una ~ mágica** there is no magic formula; **~s de pago** methods of payment [3] (frase, expresión) standard expression, formula; **~s de cortesía** polite expressions; **por pura ~** for form's sake [4] (de producto) formula; (de alimento) recipe
B (Auto) formula; **un coche de F~ 1** a Formula 1 car
C (Col) (receta médica) prescription
formulación *f* formulation
formular [A1] *vt*
A ‹*queja*› to make, lodge; ‹*teoría*› to formulate; ‹*plan*› to formulate, draw up
B (Col) «*médico*» to prescribe
formulario *m* form
fornicación *f* fornication
fornicar [A2] *vi* to fornicate
fornido -da *adj* well-built, big, hefty
foro *m* [1] (Hist) forum [2] (period) (organismo, reunión) forum [3] (Teatr) backstage area; ***desaparecer*** *or* ***irse por el ~*** (fam) to sneak off
forofo -fa *m,f* (Esp fam) (Dep) fan; (Taur) aficionado, enthusiast; **ser un ~ DE algn** to be crazy ABOUT sb
forrado -da *adj*
A ‹*chaqueta*› lined; ‹*sillón/libro*› covered; **un abrigo ~ de seda** a coat lined with silk
B [ESTAR] (fam) (de dinero) loaded (colloq)
forraje *m* fodder, forage
forrar [A1] *vt* ‹*abrigo*› to line; ‹*libro/sillón*› to cover; ‹*puerta*› to line
■ **forrarse** *v pron*
A (fam) *tb* **~se de dinero** to make a killing *o* mint
B (Méx fam) (llenarse) **~se DE algo** to stuff oneself WITH sth (colloq)
forro *m* [1] (de abrigo) lining; (de sillón) cover; (de libro) cover, jacket; ***ni por el ~*** (fam): **no lo entiendo ni por el ~** I don't understand the first thing about it; **no ha visto un libro ni por el ~** he's never opened a book in his life (colloq) [2] (Chi) (de bicicleta) tire*
fortachón -chona *adj* (fam) big and strong (colloq), strapping
fortalecer [E3] *vt* [1] ‹*organismo/músculos*› to strengthen, make … stronger; **una lectura para ~ el espíritu** reading matter that is spiritually uplifting [2] ‹*relación/amistad*› to strengthen [3] (Mil) (reforzar) to reinforce
■ **fortalecerse** *v pron* «*organismo/músculo*» to get stronger; «*espíritu*» to grow stronger
fortalecimiento *m* strengthening
fortaleza *f*
A (física) strength; (moral) fortitude, strength of spirit
B (Mil) fortress
fortificación *f* fortification
fortificar [A2] *vt*
A (Mil) ‹*lugar/plaza*› to fortify
B (dar fuerza) to strengthen, make … stronger
fortín *m* (fuerte pequeño) (small) fort; (emplazamiento) pillbox, bunker
fortísimo[1] -ma *adj*: *ver* **fuerte[1]**
fortísimo[2] *m/adv* (Mús) fortissimo
fortuitamente *adv* fortuitously, by chance
fortuito -ta *adj* ‹*encuentro/suceso*› chance (*before n*), fortuitous; **no es ~ que haya venido hoy** it's no accident that he happened to turn up today
fortuna *f* [1] (riqueza) fortune [2] (azar, suerte) fortune; **le sonrió la ~** fortune smiled on him; **tuvo la (buena) ~ de ganar** he had the good fortune to win; **por ~** fortunately; ***probar ~*** to try one's luck
forúnculo *m* boil, furuncle (tech)
forzado -da *adj* forced, unnatural
forzar [A11] *vt*
A (obligar) to force; **me vi forzado** I had to, I was forced
B [1] ‹*vista*› to strain; **estaba forzando la vista** I was straining my eyes [2] ‹*sonrisa*› to force
C ‹*puerta/cerradura*› to force
D (violar) to rape
■ **forzarse** *v pron* (obligarse) to make *o* force oneself
forzosamente *adv*: **~ alguien ha tenido que verlos** someone *must* have seen them
forzoso -sa *adj* [1] (necesario) necessary [2] (obligatorio) ‹*aterrizaje/anexión/paro*› forced; ‹*jubilación*› compulsory
forzudo[1] -da *adj* (fam) big and strong (colloq)
forzudo[2] -da *m,f* (fam): **un par de ~s** a couple of big, strong men (colloq)
fosa *f* (zanja) ditch; (hoyo) pit; (tumba) grave; (Auto) pit
(Compuestos)
• **fosa común** common *o* communal grave
• **fosa marina** trench
• **fosa séptica** septic tank
fosfato *m* phosphate
fosforera *f* (fábrica) match factory
fosforescencia *f* phosphorescence
fosforescente *adj* (Fís) phosphorescent; ‹*color/pintura*› fluorescent
fósforo *m*
A (Quím) phosphorus
B (cerilla) match
fósil[1] *adj* fossilized, fossil (*before n*)
fósil[2] *m* fossil
fosilización *f* fossilization
fosilizarse [A4] *v pron* to fossilize
foso *m*
A (zanja) ditch; (en fortificaciones) moat; (Equ) water jump
B (Teatr) pit
(Compuesto) **foso de la orquesta** orchestra pit
C (Auto) inspection pit
foto *f* picture, photo (esp BrE); **me sacó** *or* **tomó** *or* (Esp) **hizo una ~** he took a picture *o* photo of me; **una ~ en blanco y negro** a black-and-white photo
(Compuesto) **foto de carnet** *or* **pasaporte** passport photo
fotocomposición *f* photocomposition
fotocopia *f* photocopy, Xerox®; **hizo** *or* **sacó una ~ de la carta** he made *o* took a photocopy of the letter
fotocopiadora *f* photocopier, Xerox® machine
fotocopiar [A1] *vt* to photocopy, xerox
fotogénico -ca *adj* photogenic
fotograbado *m* photogravure
fotografía *f* (técnica, arte) photography; (retrato, imagen) photograph
fotografiar [A17] *vt* to photograph, take a photograph of
fotográfico -ca *adj* photographic
fotógrafo -fa *m,f* photographer
fotograma *m* still
fotomatón *m* photo booth
fotómetro *m* (Fot) exposure *o* light meter; (Fís) photometer

fotomontaje *m* photomontage
fotón *m* photon
fotonovela *f* photoromance (*romantic story in the form of photographs with captions*)
fotosíntesis *f* photosynthesis
fototeca *f* photographic library
foul /'faul/ *m* (*pl* **fouls**) (AmL) foul
foulard /fu'lar/ *m* (tejido) foulard; (pañuelo) scarf
foulear /faule'ar/ [A1] *vt* (CS) to foul
fox /'fos/ *m* (*pl* ~) foxtrot
fox-trot /'fostro(t)/ *m* (*pl* **-trots**) foxtrot
fr (= **franco**) fr
frac *m* (*pl* **fracs** *or* **fraques**) (chaqueta) tail coat, tails (*pl*); (traje) morning suit; **iba de** ~ he was in morning dress
fracasado¹ -da *adj* failed, unsuccessful
fracasado² -da *m,f* failure
fracasar [A1] *vi* to fail; ~ **EN algo** to fail IN sth
fracaso *m* failure; **un** ~ **amoroso** *or* **sentimental** a disappointment in love
fracción *f*
A fraction; **una** ~ **de segundo** a fraction of a second, a split second
B (de organización) faction
fraccionamiento *m*
A (de país, partido) division; (Quím) fractionation
B (Méx) **1** (de terreno) division (*into lots*) **2** (urbanización) development
fraccionar [A1] *vt* **1** ‹*pago*› to make … in installments* **2** (Quím) to fractionate
fraccionario -ria *adj* fractional
fractura *f*
A (Med) fracture; **sufrió** ~ **de peroné** he fractured his fibula
B (Geol) fault
fracturar [A1] *vt* to fracture
■ **fracturarse** *v pron* to fracture
fragancia *f* fragrance, perfume
fragante *adj* (liter) fragrant
fragata *f* frigate
frágil *adj* **1** ‹*cristal/fuente*› fragile; Ⓢ **frágil** fragile **2** ‹*salud/constitución*› delicate; ‹*economía*› fragile; **una viejecita muy** ~ a very frail old woman
fragilidad *f* **1** (de cristal, porcelana) fragility **2** (de una situación) delicacy; (de la economía) fragility; **la** ~ **de su salud** her frailty
fragmentar [A1] *vt* to fragment
■ **fragmentarse** *v pron* to fragment
fragmentario -ria *adj* sketchy
fragmento *m* **1** (de jarrón) shard; (de hueso) fragment **2** (de conversación) snippet, snatch **3** (de novela, carta — extracto) extract, passage; (— resto, pedazo) fragment
fragor *m* (liter) clamor* (liter)
fragua *f* forge
fraguar [A16] *vt* **1** (Metal) to forge **2** ‹*complot*› to hatch; ‹*plan*› to conceive
■ **fraguar** *vi* «*cemento*» to set
fraile *m* friar, monk
frailecillo *m* puffin
frailecito *m* (AmL) plover
frambuesa *f* raspberry
francachela *f* (Esp) (fam): **ir de** ~ (de juerga) to go out on the town; (de comilona) to have a blow-out (colloq)
francamente *adv* **1** ‹*decir/hablar*› frankly, honestly **2** (*indep*) frankly, quite honestly; ~, **me parece una estupidez** (quite) frankly, I think it's stupid **3** (realmente) ‹*bueno/malo*› really
francés¹ -cesa *adj* French; **a la francesa** the French way; ***despedirse a la francesa*** to leave without saying goodbye
francés² -cesa *m,f*
A (*m*) Frenchman; (*f*) Frenchwoman; **los franceses** the French, French people
B **francés** *m* (idioma) French
franchute¹ -ta *adj/m,f* (fam) Frog (*before n*) (colloq)
franchute² *m* (idioma) French, Frog (colloq)
Francia *f* France
franciscano -na *adj/m,f* (Relig) Franciscan
francmasón -sona *m,f* Freemason, Mason
francmasonería *f* freemasonry
franco¹ -ca *adj*
A (sincero) ‹*persona*› frank; ‹*sonrisa*› natural; **para serte** ~ **...** to be frank *o* honest …; **una mirada franca** an honest *o* open expression
B (*delante del n*) (patente) marked; **ha mostrado una franca mejoría** he has shown marked *o* clear signs of improvement; **un clima de franca cordialidad** an atmosphere of genuine warmth; **en franca rebeldía/oposición** in open rebellion/opposition
C (Com) free; ~ **de porte** carriage free; **paso** ~ free passage; ~ **a bordo** free on board; ~ **de derechos** duty-free
D [ESTAR] **1** (Mil) off duty **2** (RPl) (libre de trabajo) off; **el lunes estoy** ~ I have Monday off
E (Hist) Frankish
franco² -ca *m,f*
A (Hist) Frank
B **franco** *m* (unidad monetaria) franc
francocanadiense *adj/mf* French Canadian
francófilo -la *adj/m,f* francophile
francófobo -ba *m,f* francophobe
francófono -na *adj/m,f* francophone
franco-hispano -na *adj* Franco-Spanish
francote *adj* (fam) plainspoken
francotirador -dora *m,f* sniper
franela *f* **1** (Tex) flannel **2** (Ven) (camiseta) T-shirt **3** (Col) (camiseta de interior) undershirt (AmE), vest (BrE)
frangollo *m* (RPl fam) botched job (colloq)
franja *f* (banda) stripe, band; (cinta, adorno) border, fringe
(Compuesto) **franja de Gaza** Gaza Strip
franquear [A1] *vt*
A ‹*paso/entrada*› to clear; ‹*puerta*› to go through; ‹*umbral/río*› to cross
B ‹*carta*› (pagar) to pay the postage on; Ⓢ **a franquear en destino** postpaid
■ **franquearse** *v pron* ~**se CON algn** to confide IN sb
franqueo *m* postage
franqueza *f* frankness, openness; **voy a hablar con (toda)** ~ I'm going to be (perfectly) frank *o* honest
franquicia *f*
A (exención) exemption; (en seguros) excess
(Compuestos)
• **franquicia aduanera** (condición) duty-free status; (cantidad) duty-free allowance
• **franquicia postal** *exemption from payment of postage*
B (concesión) franchise
franquismo *m* years that Franco was in power
franquista¹ *adj* (relacionado con Franco) Franco (*before n*); (a favor de Franco) pro-Franco
franquista² *mf* supporter of Franco
frasco *m* bottle; (de mermelada) jar
frase *f* (oración) sentence; (sintagma) phrase; ~**s huecas** *or* **vacías** empty words
(Compuesto) **frase hecha** set phrase
fraseo *m* phrasing
fraternal *adj* brotherly, fraternal
fraternidad *f* fraternity, brotherhood
fraternización *f* fraternization
fraternizar [A4] *vi* to fraternize; ~ **CON algn** to fraternize WITH sb
fraterno -na *adj* brotherly, fraternal
fratricida¹ *adj* fratricidal
fratricida² *mf* fratricide
fratricidio *m* fratricide
fraude *m* fraud
(Compuestos)
• **fraude electoral** vote rigging, election fraud
• **fraude fiscal** tax evasion
fraudulencia *f* fraudulence
fraudulento -ta *adj* ‹*negocio*› fraudulent; ‹*elecciones*› rigged

fray *m* (*delante de n propio*) Brother

frazada *f* (AmL) blanket

frecuencia *f* frequency; **con ~** frequently

(Compuesto) **frecuencia modulada** frequency modulation, FM

frecuentar [A1] *vt* to frequent

frecuente *adj* ‹*llamada/visita*› frequent; **no es ~ verla** it is unusual to see her, you do not often see her

freelance /'frilans/ *mf* freelancer; **trabaja de ~** he works freelance

free-lance /'frilans/ *adj inv* freelance

freezer /'friser/ *m* 1 (AmL) (electrodoméstico) freezer, deep freeze 2 (Chi, Ven) (en el refrigerador) freezer (compartment)

fregada *f* (esp AmL fam) (restregadura) scrub

fregadera *f* (AmL exc CS fam) pain (colloq); **es una ~ tener que ir** it's a real hassle *o* pain having to go (colloq)

fregadero *m* (de la cocina) kitchen sink; (para lavar ropa) (Méx) sink

fregado[1] **-da** *adj*

A (AmL exc RPl fam) 1 (molesto) annoying; **¡no seas ~, hombre!** stop being such a pain *o* a bore (colloq); **¡qué niño más ~!** that kid's a real pest (colloq) 2 (difícil) ‹*examen/tema*› tricky (colloq), tough (colloq); ‹*persona/carácter*› difficult; **el asunto está ~** it's all very iffy 3 [ESTAR] (enfermo, delicado) in a bad way (colloq) 4 [ESTAR] (sin dinero) broke (colloq)

B (Andes, Ven fam) (exigente) strict

C (Col, Per fam) (astuto) sly, sneaky (colloq)

fregado[2] **-da** *m,f*

A (AmL exc RPl fam) (persona difícil) difficult person

B **fregado** *m* 1 (restregadura) scrub, scrubbing; **dar un ~ a algo** to give sth a scrub 2 (Esp) (fam) (lío) mess

fregar [A7] *vt*

A (lavar, limpiar) to wash; **fregué el suelo** (con trapo) I washed the floor; (con trapeador) I mopped the floor; (con cepillo) I scrubbed the floor; **~ los platos** to wash the dishes, to do the dishes (colloq)

B (AmL exc RPl fam) (molestar) to bug (colloq); **~le la paciencia a algn** to go *o* keep on at sb (colloq); **¡no me friegues!** (no me molestes) stop bugging me!; (no me digas) you're kidding! (colloq)

C (AmL exc RPl fam) ‹*planes/vacaciones*› to ruin

D (AmL exc RPl fam) (perjudicar): **me fregó con esa pregunta** her question really floored me (colloq); **fregó al país** he dragged the country down (colloq)

■ **fregar** *vi*

A (lavar los platos) to wash the dishes, to do the dishes (colloq); (limpiar) to clean; (restregar) to scrub

B (AmL exc RPl fam) (molestar): **¡déjate de ~!** stop being such a pest!; **¡no friegues!** (no digas) you're kidding! (colloq)

■ **fregarse** *v pron*

A (AmL fam) (fastidiarse): **¡te friegas!** tough! (colloq); **¡me fregué!** I've really done it now! (colloq); **los que se friegan son ustedes** you'll be the ones who lose out

B (AmL exc RPl fam) 1 (malograrse): **se ~on nuestros planes** that's ruined *o* messed up our plans (colloq) 2 ‹*tobillo/mano*› to do … in (colloq), to screw … up (AmE colloq)

fregón -gona *adj* (AmC, Col, Ec fam) ▸**fregado**[1] **A**

fregona *f*

A (pey) (sirvienta) drudge

B (Esp) (utensilio) mop

freidora *f* deep fryer

freiduría *f*: *bar or store selling fried fish*

freír [I35] *vt*

A (Coc) to fry; **no sabe ni ~ un huevo** he doesn't even know how to boil an egg

B (Esp fam) (asediar): **nos frieron a preguntas** they pestered us with questions; **me frieron los mosquitos** the mosquitos ate me alive

■ **freírse** *v pron* to fry

frenada *f* (esp AmL) ▸**frenazo**

frenado *m* braking

frenar [A1] *vt*

A (Transp) to brake

B ‹*proceso/deterioro*› to slow … down; ‹*alza/inflación*› to curb, check; ‹*progreso/desarrollo*› to hold … back; **para ~ la ola de refugiados** to stem the flow of refugees

■ **frenar** *vi* to brake, apply the brake(s) (frml)

■ **frenarse** *v pron* (*refl*) to restrain oneself

frenazo *m* (fam): **oí el ~** I heard the screeching of brakes; **dio un ~** she slammed *o* jammed on her brakes; **la huella del ~** the skid mark; **dar un ~ a las importaciones** to put the brake on imports

frenesí *m* frenzy; **con ~** madly *o* passionately

frenético -ca *adj* frenzied, frenetic; **ponerse ~** (fam) to go crazy *o* wild

frenillo *m*

A 1 (membrana) frenum 2 (defecto) *speech defect caused by an abnormal frenum*

B **frenillos** *mpl* (AmL) (para los dientes) braces (*pl*) (AmE), brace (esp BrE)

freno *m*

A (Mec, Transp) brake; **se quedó sin ~s** his brakes failed

(Compuestos)

- **freno de mano** emergency brake (AmE), handbrake (BrE)
- **frenos asistidos** *mpl* power brakes (*pl*)
- **frenos de aire/disco/tambor** *mpl* air/disc/drum brakes (*pl*)

B (Equ) bit

C (contención): **poner ~ a algo** ‹*a gastos/importaciones*› to curb sth; ‹*a abusos*› to put a stop to sth; **esto supondría un ~ al desarrollo del programa** this would slow the program down

D **frenos** *mpl* (Méx) (para los dientes) braces (*pl*) (AmE), brace (esp BrE)

frentazo *m* (Méx fam): **darse** *or* **pegarse un ~** to be devastated

frente[1] *f* forehead, brow (liter); **arrugó la ~** she frowned; **una ~ despejada** *or* **ancha** a broad forehead; ***con la ~ bien alta*** *or* ***en alto*** with one's head held high

frente[2] *m*

A 1 (de edificio) front, facade (frml); ***hacer(le) ~ a algo*** (a la realidad, una responsabilidad) to face up to sth; (a gastos, obligaciones) to meet sth; **le hizo ~ a la vida por sus propios medios** she stood on her own two feet; ***hacerle ~ a algn*** (a enemigo, atacante) to face sb 2 (*en locs*) **al frente**: **dio un paso al ~** she took a step forward; **la Orquesta Sinfónica, con López Morán al ~** the Symphony Orchestra, conducted by López Morán; **desfilaron llevando al ~ el emblema de la paz** they marched behind the symbol of peace; **vive al ~** (Chi) she lives opposite; **pasar al ~** (AmL) to come/go up to the front; **al frente de**: **están al ~ de la clasificación** they are at the top of the table; **iba al ~ de la patrulla** he was leading the patrol; **está al ~ de la empresa** she is in charge of the company; **de frente**: **chocaron de ~** they crashed head on; **una foto de ~** a full-face photo; **no entra de ~** it won't go in front on; **de frente a** (AmL) facing; **frente a** opposite; **viven ~ a mi casa** they live opposite me; **el hotel está ~ al mar** the hotel faces the sea; **estamos ~ a un grave problema** we are faced with a serious problem; **se mantiene estable ~ al dólar** it is holding up against the dollar

B 1 (Meteo) front 2 (en una guerra) front; **sin novedad en el ~** (fr hecha, hum) all quiet on that front (colloq & hum); **un ~ de acción contra la droga** a campaign to combat drugs 3 (Pol) (agrupación) front; **el ~ de liberación** the liberation front; ***hacer (un) ~ común*** to form a united front

(Compuesto) **frente de batalla** battlefront

frentón -tona *adj* (AmC): **es muy ~** he has a marked receding hairline

fresa *f*

A 1 (Bot, Coc) (planta) strawberry plant; (fruta) strawberry 2 **(de) color ~** strawberry-pink

B (Metal) milling cutter

fresadora *f* (Metal) milling machine

fresca *f*

A 1 (frescor): **la ~** the cool (of the morning/evening); **salimos con la ~** we set off while it was still cool 2 (aire) fresh air

B (fam) (insolencia): **lo regañé y me soltó una ~** I told him off and he had the nerve to answer me back (colloq); **le dije cuatro ~s** I gave him a piece of my mind (colloq)

frescachón -chona *adj* (Esp fam) healthy-looking

f

fresco[1] **-ca** *adj*
A 1 ‹*viento*› cool, fresh; ‹*agua*› cold; ‹*bebida*› cool, cold; **el tiempo está más bien ~** the weather is a bit chilly 2 ‹*ropa/tela*› cool
B 1 (no enlatado, no congelado) fresh; **pescado ~** fresh fish 2 (reciente) fresh; **trae noticias frescas** she has the latest news; **S pintura fresca** wet paint 3 ‹*cutis/belleza*› fresh, young 4 ‹*aire*› fresh
C ‹*persona*› 1 [SER] (fam) (descarado): **¡qué tipo más ~!** that guy sure has some nerve! (colloq); ***ir ~*** (Esp fam): **va ~ si espera eso** if he thinks that he's got another think coming 2 [ESTAR] (descansado) refreshed; (no cansado) fresh 3 (tranquilo): **él estaba tan ~** he was as cool as a cucumber; **me lo dijo, así, tan fresca** she was as cool as could be when she told me 4 [SER] (Col fam) (sencillo) relaxed, easygoing; **¡~ hermano!** cool it! (colloq)

fresco[2] **-ca** *m,f* (fam) (descarado): **¡eres un ~!** you have a lot of nerve! (colloq)

fresco[3] *m*
A (aire) fresh air; **tomar el ~** to get some fresh air
B (frío moderado): **hace un fresquito que da gusto** it's lovely and cool; **ponte una chaqueta que hace ~** put a jacket on, it's chilly out; ***traer a algn al ~*** (Esp fam): **eso me trae al ~** I couldn't care less about it (colloq)
C (Art) fresco; **pintura al ~** fresco painting
D (AmL) (gaseosa) soda (AmE), fizzy drink (BrE); (refresco de frutas) fruit drink

frescor *m* cool; **el ~ de la mañana** the cool of the morning

frescura *f*
A (de temperatura) coolness
B (descaro) nerve (colloq)
C (tranquilidad): **me lo dijo con toda ~** he told me quite calmly

fresno *m* ash (tree)

fresón *m* (long stem) strawberry

fresquera *f* meat safe

freudiano -na /froj'ðjano/ *adj* Freudian

frialdad *f*
A (frío) coldness
B 1 (insensibilidad): **lo hizo con absoluta ~** she did it without displaying any sign of emotion; **la ~ de su mirada** the cold look in his eyes; **es de una ~ impresionante** she's incredibly unemotional *o* cold 2 (falta de afecto, entusiasmo): **me trató con ~** he treated me coldly *o* frostily; **la ~ del público** the audience's lack of enthusiasm

fríamente *adv* 1 (con indiferencia) coldly; **me recibió ~** he gave me a cold *o* cool reception 2 (sin apasionamiento): **hablaba ~ de su enfermedad** he talked in a detached manner about his illness; **discutieron ~** they talked about it in a calm and collected way; **piénsalo ~** consider it objectively

fricativo -va *adj* fricative

fricción *f* 1 (Fís) friction 2 (desavenencia) friction 3 (friega, masaje) massage, rub

friccionar [A1] *vt* to massage, rub

friega[1] *f*
A (fricción) rub; **date una(s) ~(s) en el pecho con esto** rub this on your chest; **una(s) ~(s) de alcohol** a rubdown with alchohol
B (Chi, Méx fam) (molestia) ▸**fregadera**
C (Chi, Méx fam) (zurra) ▸**paliza AA**

friega[2], **friegas, etc** *see* **fregar**

friegaplatos *mf* (fam) 1 (persona) dishwasher 2 **friegaplatos** *m* (aparato) dishwasher

frigidez *f* frigidity

frígido -da *adj* frigid

frigorífico *m* 1 (Esp) (nevera) refrigerator, fridge 2 (en tiendas) cold store 3 (AmS) (de carne) meat processing plant
(Compuesto) **frigorífico congelador** (Esp) fridge-freezer

frijol *m* (AmL exc CS)
A (Bot, Coc) bean
(Compuesto) **frijol colorado/negro** kidney/black bean
B **frijoles** *mpl* (comida) food; ***ganarse los ~es*** to earn a living

frío[1] **fría** *adj*
A ‹*comida/agua/motor/viento*› cold; **tengo los pies ~s** my feet are cold; **~, ~** (en juegos) you're very cold; ***dejar ~ a algn***: **la noticia lo dejó ~** (indiferente) he was quite unmoved by the news; (atónito) he was staggered by the news; **ese tipo de música me deja fría** that sort of music does nothing for me; ***quedarse ~*** (quedarse indiferente) to be unmoved; (quedarse atónito) to be staggered; (enfriarse) (Esp) to get cold
B 1 (insensible) cold; **es ~ y calculador** he's cold and calculating 2 (poco afectuoso, entusiasta) cold; **estuvo ~ conmigo** he was cold towards me; **un público muy ~** a very unresponsive audience; **tuvieron un recibimiento muy ~** they got a very cool *o* frosty reception 3 (desapasionado): **una mente fría** a cool head
C (poco acogedor) ‹*decoración/color*› cold

frío[2] *m*
A (Meteo) cold; **una ola de ~** a cold spell; **no salgas con este ~** don't go out in this cold; **¡qué ~ hace!** it's so cold!; **con los primeros ~s** when the weather begins to turn cold; ***hace un ~ que pela*** (fam) it's freezing (colloq)
B (sensación): **tengo ~** I'm cold; **pasamos mucho ~** we were very cold; **tengo ~ en los pies** my feet are cold; **me está entrando ~** I'm beginning to feel cold; ***tomar*** *or* (Esp) ***coger ~*** to catch cold; ***en ~***: **su oferta me agarró** *or* (esp Esp) **cogió en ~** her offer took me aback; **no le des la noticia así, en ~** you can't break the news to her just like that; **esto hay que discutirlo en ~** this has to be discussed calmly; ***no darle a algn ni ~ ni calor*** (fam) to leave sb cold

friolento -ta *adj* (AmL): **es muy ~** he really feels the cold

friolera *f* (fam): **la ~ de 100 años/un millón de dólares** no less than one hundred years/a million dollars

friolero -ra *adj* (Esp) ▸**friolento**

frisar [A1] *vi* (frml): **frisaba en los 40 años** she was nearly 40, she was getting on for 40

friso *m* frieze

fritada *f* fried dish

fritanga *f* 1 (AmC, Andes, Méx) (alimento frito) fried snack 2 (pey) (comida frita) greasy fried food

fritanguería *f* (AmC, Andes) *stall selling fried snacks*

fritar [A1] *vt* (AmL) to fry

frito -ta *adj*
A (Coc) fried
B 1 (fam) (harto) fed up (colloq); **me tienes ~** I'm fed up with you 2 (CS, Méx fam) (en apuros) done for (colloq); **estamos ~s** we're done for *o* we've had it (colloq)
C (fam) (dormido) fast *o* sound asleep; **quedarse ~** to fall asleep, to doze off

fritos *mpl* fried food

fritura *f* (acción) frying; (comida frita) fried food; **~ de pescado** fried fish

frivolidad *f* (cualidad) frivolousness, frivolity; (cosa vana) triviality, frivolous thing

frívolo -la *adj* frivolous

fronda *f* (follaje) *tb* **~s** foliage

frondosidad *f* luxuriance, leafiness

frondoso -sa *adj* ‹*árbol*› leafy; ‹*vegetación*› lush; ‹*bosque*› thick

frontal *adj* 1 ‹*colisión*› head-on; ‹*ataque*› direct, frontal (frml); ‹*oposición*› direct 2 (delantero): **la parte ~** the front

frontenis *m* pelota (*played with tennis rackets*)

frontera *f* (Geog) border, frontier (frml); **se sitúa en las ~s de lo pornográfico** it borders on the pornographic

fronterizo -za *adj* border (*before n*); **conflictos ~s** border clashes; **los países ~s** bordering countries

frontispicio *m* (Arquit) (remate triangular) pediment; (fachada) facade

frontón *m* (Dep) (juego) pelota; (cancha) pelota court; (pared) fronton

frotar [A1] *vt/vi* to rub
■ **frotarse** *v pron* (*refl*) ‹*espalda/rodillas*› to rub; ▸**mano**[1] **H**

frote *m* rub

frotis *m* smear
(Compuesto) **frotis cervical** cervical smear, smear test

fructífero -ra *adj* ‹*conversaciones/reunión*› fruitful, productive; **un año muy ~** an extremely productive *o* profitable year

fructificar [A2] *vi* to be fruitful

fructosa *f* fructose

fructuoso -sa *adj* fruitful

frufrú *m* swish

frugal *adj* frugal

frugalidad *f* frugality

fruición *f* delight; **comer con ~** to eat with great relish

frunce *m* (en costura) gather; (defecto) ruck

fruncido -da *adj* ‹*falda*› gathered

fruncir [I4] *vt* 1 ‹*tela*› to gather 2 **~ el ceño** *or* **entrecejo** to frown; **frunció la boca** she pursed her lips

fruslería *f* knick-knack

frustración *f* frustration

frustrado -da *adj* 1 ‹*persona*› frustrated; ‹*actor/bailarina*› frustrated (*before n*); **sentirse ~** to feel frustrated 2 ‹*atentado/intento*› failed (*before n*)

frustrante *adj* frustrating

frustrar [A1] *vt* 1 ‹*persona*› to frustrate; ‹*planes*› to thwart; ‹*esperanzas*› to dash; **me frustra que no entiendan** I find it frustrating that they don't understand 2 ‹*atentado*› to foil

■ **frustrarse** *v pron* «*planes*» to be thwarted, fail; «*esperanzas*» to come to nothing

fruta *f* fruit

Compuestos

- **fruta confitada** *or* **escarchada** crystallized fruit, candied fruit
- **fruta del tiempo** *or* **de (la) estación** seasonal fruit

frutal¹ *adj* fruit (*before n*)

frutal² *m* fruit tree

frutera *f* (CS) fruit bowl

frutería *f* fruit store *o* shop, greengrocer's (BrE)

frutero¹ -ra *adj* fruit (*before n*)

frutero² -ra *m,f*

A (vendedor) fruit seller, greengrocer (BrE)

B **frutero** *m* (recipiente) fruit bowl

frutilla *f* (Bol, CS) strawberry

fruto *m*

A (Bot) fruit

Compuestos

- **fruto prohibido** forbidden fruit
- **frutos secos** *mpl* nuts and dried fruit (*pl*)

B (resultado, producto) fruit; **dar** *or* **rendir ~s** to bear fruit; **~ DE algo** ‹*de inversión*› return ON sth; **el ~ de su trabajo** the fruits of her labor; **todo fue ~ de su imaginación** it was all a figment of his imagination; **fue ~ de la casualidad** it came about *o* happened quite by chance

FSE *m* (= **Fondo Social Europeo**) ESF

fu *adj inv*: **ni ~ ni fa** (fam): **¿te gusta? — ni ~ ni fa** do you like it? — it's OK, I suppose; **¿es bonito? — ni ~ ni** is it nice? — so-so

fuchi *interj* (Méx fam) ugh! (colloq), pee-yoo! (AmE)

fucsia *f/adj inv* fuchsia

fue *see* **ir, ser**

fuego *m*

A fire; **¡~!** fire!; **sofocar el ~** to put out *o* extinguish the fire; ⊗ **está prohibido hacer fuego** the lighting of fires is prohibited (frml), no fires!; **le prendieron** *or* **pegaron ~ a la casa** they set the house on fire; ***echar ~ por los ojos***: **echaba ~ por los ojos** his eyes blazed; ***jugar con ~*** to play with fire

Compuestos

- **fuego fatuo** will-o'-the-wisp, ignis fatuus
- **fuegos artificiales** *or* **de artificio** *mpl* fireworks (*pl*)

B (para cigarrillo): **¿me da ~, por favor?/¿tienes ~?** have you got a light, please?; **me pidió ~** he asked me for a light

C (Coc): **cocinar a ~ lento** cook over a low heat; (apenas hirviendo) simmer; **poner la sartén al ~** put the frying pan on to heat; **dejé la comida en el ~** I left the food on (the stove); **cocina de tres ~s** a stove with three burners

D (Mil) fire; **preparen, apunten ¡~!** ready, aim, fire!; **~ a discreción** fire at will; **abrieron ~ sobre los manifestantes** they opened fire on the demonstrators

Compuesto **fuego cruzado** crossfire

fuel, fuel-oil *m* fuel oil

fuelle *m* bellows (*pl*); **una maleta de ~** an expandable suitcase

fuente *f*

A (manantial) spring; **la ~ del río** the source of the river

B (construcción, monumento) fountain; **~ de agua potable** drinking fountain

Compuesto **fuente de soda** (Chi, Méx) soda fountain (AmE), (*place where drinks and ice creams are bought and consumed*)

C (plato) dish

Compuesto **fuente de horno** ovenproof dish

D 1 (origen) source; **su principal ~ de ingresos** his principal source of income 2 (de información) source; **una información de buena ~** *or* **de ~s fidedignas** *or* **de toda solvencia** information from reliable sources

fuera¹ *adv*

A 1 (lugar, parte) [*Latin American Spanish also uses* **afuera** *in this sense*] outside; **aquí ~ se está muy bien** it's very nice out here; **comeremos ~** (en el jardín) we'll eat outside; (en un restaurante) we'll eat out; **pintar una casa por ~** to paint the outside of a house; **por ~ es rojo** it's red on the outside 2 (en el extranjero) abroad, out of the country; (del lugar de trabajo, de la ciudad, etc) away; **los de ~** (los extranjeros) foreigners; (los de otros pueblos, ciudades, etc) outsiders 3 (en interjecciones) **¡~ (de aquí)!** get out (of here)!; **¡~ los traidores!** traitors out!

B **fuera de** (*loc prep*) 1 (en el exterior de, más allá de) out of; **está ~ del país** he's out of the country; **ocurrió ~ del edificio** it happened outside the building; **el precio está ~ de mi alcance** it's out of my price range; **~ del alcance de los niños** out of reach of the children; **~ del alcance de los proyectiles** outside *o* beyond the range of the missiles 2 (excepto) apart from; **~ de eso, me encuentro bien** apart *o* (AmE) aside from that, I feel fine

C (*en otras locs*): **fuera de combate**: **lo dejó ~ de combate** (Dep) he knocked him out; **fuera de concurso**: **quedó ~ de concurso** he was disqualified; **su película se presentó ~ de concurso** his movie was shown outside the competition; **fuera de cuentas** (Esp) overdue; **fuera de la ley**: **vivían ~ de la ley** they lived outside the law; **fuera de lugar** ‹*mueble/persona*› out of place; ‹*comentario*› inappropriate, out of place; **fuera de peligro** out of danger; **fuera de serie** ‹*jugador/cantante*› exceptional, outstanding; **fuera de sí**: **estaba ~ de sí** he was beside himself; **fuera de temporada** *or* **estación** out of season

Compuestos

- **fuera de borda** *m* (*pl* **~ de ~**) outboard
- **fuera de juego** *or* (AmL) **de lugar** *m* offside
- **fuera de la ley** *mf* (Esp) (*pl* **~ de la ~**) outlaw
- **fuera de serie** *mf* (*pl* **~ de ~**): **es un ~ de ~** he is exceptionally good *o* is outstanding

fuera², fuéramos, etc *see* **ir, ser**

fueraborda *m* outboard

fuereño -ña *m,f* (Méx fam): **un ~** some guy from out of town (colloq)

fuero *m* 1 (jurisdicción) jurisdiction 2 (privilegio, derecho) privilege; ***en mi/su ~ interno*** in my/his heart of hearts, deep down inside

fuerte¹ *adj*

A ‹*persona*› 1 (físicamente) strong; **de complexión ~** well-built; **es un hombre fuertísimo** *or* **fortísimo** he's an exeptionally strong man 2 (moralmente) strong; ***hacerse ~*** to pull oneself together 3 (en asignatura) strong; **no estoy muy ~ en ese tema/en física** I'm not very strong on that topic/in physics (colloq)

B (resistente) ‹*tela/cuerda*› strong; **una silla bien ~** a good sturdy chair

C 1 ‹*viento*› strong; ‹*terremoto*› severe; ‹*lluvia/nevada*› heavy 2 ‹*dolor*› intense, bad; ‹*resfriado*› bad; **un ~ golpe** a heavy *o* hard blow 3 ‹*abrazo/beso*› big

D ‹*ruido*› loud; **la música está muy ~** the music's too loud

E 1 ‹*olor/sabor*› strong 2 ‹*licor/medicina*› strong 3 ‹*comida*› heavy

F ‹*acento*› strong, thick

G (violento) ‹*discusión*› violent, heated; **tiene escenas muy ∼s** it has some very shocking scenes; **me dijo que era un inútil — ¡qué ∼!** (fam) he said I was useless — that's a bit much (AmE) *o* (BrE) a bit over the top!
H 1 (poderoso) ‹*nación/empresa/equipo*› strong; **es más ∼ que yo** it's stronger than I am 2 ‹*moneda*› strong 3 (importante): **una ∼ suma de dinero** a large sum of money; **un ∼ contingente de la policía** a strong police contingent; **un ∼ incremento de precio** a sharp price increase; **una ∼ dosis de analgésicos** a heavy dose of painkillers
I (Ling) ‹*vocal*› stressed

fuerte[2] *adv*
A ‹*golpear/empujar*› hard; ‹*agarrar/apretar*› tightly; ‹*llover*› heavily; **una canción que está pegando ∼** a song that's a big hit at the moment
B ‹*hablar*› loudly; **pon la radio más ∼** turn the radio up; **hable más ∼** speak up
C (mucho): **desayunar ∼** to have a big breakfast
D ‹*jugar/apostar*› heavily

fuerte[3] *m*
A (Mil) fort
B (especialidad) strong point, forte

fuerza[1] *f*
A (vigor, energía): **tener ∼** to be strong; **tiene mucha ∼ en los brazos** she has very strong arms; **no tengo ∼s para abrirlo** I'm not strong enough to open it; **agárralo con ∼** hold on to it tightly; **empuja con ∼** push hard; **por más que hizo ∼, no logró abrirlo** try as she might, she couldn't open it; **tuvo que hacer mucha ∼ para levantarlo** it took all her strength to lift it; **le fallaron las ∼s** his strength failed him; **recuperar ∼s** to get one's strength back; **no me siento con ∼s** I don't have the strength; **gritó con todas sus ∼s** she shouted with all her might; **entró al mercado con gran ∼** it made a big impact on the market
(Compuesto) **fuerza de voluntad** willpower
B (del viento, de las olas) strength, force
C (de estructura, material) strength
D (violencia) force; **hubo que recurrir a la ∼** they had to resort to force
(Compuesto) **fuerza bruta** brute force
E (autoridad, poder) power; **la ∼ de la razón** the power of reason (liter); **la ∼ de sus argumentos** the strength of her argument; **por (la) ∼ de costumbre** out of *o* from force of habit
(Compuesto) **fuerza mayor**: **por causas de ∼ ∼** owing to circumstances beyond our control
F (Mil, Pol) force; **una ∼ de paz** a peacekeeping force; **∼s políticas** political forces
(Compuestos)
- **fuerza aérea** air force
- **fuerza pública** (period): **la ∼ ∼** the police
- **fuerzas armadas** *fpl* armed forces (*pl*)
- **fuerzas del orden** *or* **de orden público** *fpl* (period) police
- **fuerzas de seguridad** *fpl* (frml) security forces (*pl*)

G (Fís) force
(Compuestos)
- **fuerza de gravedad** (force of) gravity
- **fuerza hidráulica** hydraulic power
- **fuerza motriz** motive power

H (*en locs*) **a la fuerza**: **tiene que pasar por aquí a la ∼** she has no option but to come this way; **a la ∼ tuvo que verme** he must have seen me; **lo llevaron a la ∼** they dragged him there; **comí a la ∼** I forced myself to eat; **entraron a la ∼** they forced their way in; **lo hicieron salir a la ∼** they forced him to leave; **a fuerza de** by; **aprobó a ∼ de estudiar** he managed to pass by studying hard; **por fuerza**: **por ∼ tiene que saberlo** he *must* know about it; **por la fuerza** by force; ***a viva* ∼** by sheer force; ***medir sus* ∼s *con* or *contra algn*** to measure one's strength against sb; ***sacar* ∼s *de flaqueza*** to make a supreme effort

fuerza[2], **fuerzas, etc** *see* **forzar**
fuese, fuésemos, etc *see* **ir, ser**
fuetazo *m* (AmL) lash
fuete *m* (AmL exc CS) riding crop; (más largo) whip

fuga *f*
A (huida) escape; **una ∼ de prisioneros** a jailbreak; **se dieron a la ∼** they fled; ***poner a algn en* ∼** to put sb to flight
(Compuestos)
- **fuga de capitales** *or* **divisas** flight of capital
- **fuga de cerebros** brain drain

B (de líquido, gas) leak, escape (frml)
C (Mús) fugue

fugacidad *f* (de encuentro) brevity, fleetingness; (de belleza) transience
fugarse [A3] *v pron* 1 (huir) to flee, run away; «*preso*» to escape; **∼ DE algo** to escape from sth 2 «*enamorados*» to run away together; (para casarse) to elope; **su marido se fugó con su mejor amiga** her husband ran off with her best friend
fugaz *adj* ‹*sonrisa/visión/amor*› fleeting; ‹*visita/tregua*› brief; **la belleza es ∼** beauty is transient *o* ephemeral
fugitivo -va *adj* fugitive; **anda ∼** he is on the run
fui, fuimos, etc *see* **ir, ser**
fuiste, etc *see* **ir, ser**
ful *m* (Jueg) full house
fulana *f* (Esp fam) whore, hooker (colloq)
fulano -na *m,f* 1 (fam) (persona cualquiera) so-and-so; **don ∼ de tal** Mr so-and-so; **siempre tiene que invitar a ∼, mengano, zutano (y perengano)** she always invites every Tom, Dick, and Harry 2 **fulano** *m* (fam) (tipo) guy (colloq)
fulbac *mf* (*pl* **-bacs**) fullback
fulero[1] **-ra** *adj*
A 1 (fam) (de mala calidad) shoddy, poor 2 (fam) (falso) phoney (colloq) 3 (RPl fam) (feo) ugly
B 1 (Esp fam) (mentiroso, tramposo): **es muy ∼** (mentiroso) he's such a liar; (tramposo) he's full of tricks; (en el juego) he's such a cheat 2 (fam) (chapucero): **un trabajo ∼** a botched job (colloq)
C (Col fam) (presumido) swanky (colloq)
fulero[2] **-ra** *m,f* (en el juego) cheat
fulgente *adj* ▸ **fulgurante**
fúlgido -da *adj* (liter) shining
fulgor *m* (de luz, estrella) brightness, brilliance; (de los ojos — por felicidad) gleam; (— por rabia) blazing
fulgurante *adj* 1 ‹*luz/estrella*› bright, brilliant 2 ‹*ojos*› (de felicidad) gleaming; (de rabia) blazing
fulgurar [A1] *vi* 1 «*luz/estrella*» to shine brightly 2 «*ojos*» (de felicidad) to gleam; (de rabia) to blaze
full[1] /ful/ *adj* (AmL fam) (lleno, completo) full; **∼ *equipo*** (Ven fam): **un carro ∼ equipo** a car with a full range of features *o* accessories
full[2] /ful/ *m* (Jueg) full house
full-time /ful'tajm/ *adj inv/adv* full-time
fulminante *adj* 1 ‹*enfermedad*› sudden and devastating, fulminant (tech); **una mirada ∼** a withering look; **tuvo un efecto ∼** it had an immediate and devastating effect 2 (fuerte): **un golpe ∼** a crushing blow; **un tiro ∼** a thundering shot
fulminantes *mpl* (AmL) (Jueg) caps (*pl*); **pistola de ∼** cap gun
fulminar [A1] *vt* (matar): **murieron fulminados** they were struck by lightning and killed; **un cáncer lo fulminó** he developed cancer and died within a few days/weeks; **lo fulminó con la mirada** she gave him a withering look
fumadero *m* smoking room; **∼ de opio** opium den
fumado -da *adj* (arg) stoned (colloq)
fumador -dora *m,f* smoker; **los ∼es de puros** cigar smokers; **∼ pasivo** passive smoker; **sección de ∼es/de no ∼es** smoking/no-smoking section
fumar [A1] *vt*
A ‹*cigarrillo/puro*› to smoke
B (Méx fam) (hacer caso) to take notice of; **no los fumó** he didn't take any notice (of them)
■ **fumar** *vi* to smoke; **∼ en pipa** to smoke a pipe; **Ⓢ se prohibe fumar** *or* **prohibido fumar** no smoking
■ **fumarse** *v pron*
A (*enf*) ‹*cigarrillo/cajetilla*› to smoke
B (Esp fam) 1 (gastar) ‹*dinero/ahorros*› to blow (colloq) 2 ‹*clase*› to skip

fumarada *f* puff of smoke

fumata blanca *f* white smoke (*to indicate that a new Pope has been chosen*)

fumigación *f* (de campos, cultivos) spraying; (de local) fumigation

fumigar [A3] *vt* ‹*campo/cultivo*› to spray, dust; ‹*local*› to fumigate

funámbulo -la *m,f* tightrope walker

función *f*

A 1 (cometido, propósito) function; **la ~ del mediador** the role *o* function of the mediator; **cumple/tiene la ~ de ...** it performs the function of ...; **en ~ de** according to; **salario en ~ de la experiencia** salary according to experience; **diseñada en ~ de los usuarios** designed with the users in mind 2 **funciones** *mpl* duties (*pl*); **en el ejercicio de sus funciones** in the performance of her duties; **fue suspendido de sus funciones** he was suspended from duty; **se excedió en sus funciones** he exceeded his powers; **desempeña las funciones de asesor** he acts as a consultant; **en funciones** acting (*before n*); **el secretario en funciones** the acting secretary; **entrar en funciones** (AmL) «*empleado*» to take up one's post; «*presidente*» to assume office

B (Fisiol) function; (Mat) function; (Ling) function

(Compuesto) **función gramatical** part of speech

C (de teatro, circo) performance; (de cine) showing, performance

(Compuestos)

- **función benéfica** charity performance
- **función continua** (AmL exc CS) continuous performance
- **función de medianoche** late show
- **función de noche** late night performance

funcional *adj* functional

funcionalidad *f*: **un edificio de gran ~** a highly functional building

funcionamiento *m* 1 (de mecanismo): **para asegurar el buen ~ del aparato** to keep the equipment in working order; **me explicó su ~** he explained (to me) how it works (*o* worked *etc*) 2 (de sistema, organismo) running; **para el buen ~ de la escuela** for the smooth running of the school; **entrar/ponerse en ~** «*hospital/estación/fábrica*» to become operational; «*central nuclear*» to come into operation; «*autopista*» to open; «*mecanismo/máquina*» to start up; «*servicio/sistema*» to start; **poner en ~** ‹*central/fábrica*› to bring into operation; ‹*mecanismo/máquina*› to start ... up; **se puso en ~ una operación de búsqueda** a search was set in motion; **estar en ~** to be running

funcionar [A1] *vi* «*aparato/máquina*» to work; «*servicio*» to operate; **¿cómo funciona esto?** how does this work?; ⓢ **no funciona** out of order; **~ con pilas/gasolina** to run off batteries/on gasoline

funcionariado *m* 1 (empleados públicos) government employees (*pl*); **el ~ de correos** postal service employees (AmE), post office staff (BrE) 2 (de organización internacional) staff (+ *sing or pl vb*)

funcionario -ria *m,f* 1 (empleado público) *tb* **~ público** *or* **del Estado** government employee; **los ~s de correos** postal service employees (AmE), post office employees (BrE); **un alto ~** a senior *o* high-ranking official 2 (de organización internacional) member of staff, staff member 3 (RPl) (de empresa, banco) employee

funda *f* 1 (de libro) dustjacket; (de disco) sleeve 2 (de raqueta) cover; (de cojín, sillón) cover 3 *tb* **~ de almohada** pillowcase, pillowslip 4 (Odont) cap

fundación *f*

A (institución) foundation; **una ~ benéfica** a charity

B (de ciudad, escuela) founding; (de empresa, partido) establishment

fundadamente *adv* with good reason

fundado -da *adj* ‹*temor/sospecha*› justified, well founded; **no tenían motivos ~s** they had no justifiable reason

fundador -dora *m,f* founder

fundamental *adj* fundamental; **es ~ que entiendas** it is vital *o* essential that you understand

fundamentalismo *m* fundamentalism

fundamentalista *adj/mf* fundamentalist

fundamentalmente *adv* 1 (principalmente) ‹*afectar/interesar*› mainly, principally 2 (en esencia) ‹*alterar*› fundamentally

fundamentar [A1] *vt* 1 (apoyar) to support, back up 2 (basar) **~ algo EN algo** to base sth ON sth

fundamento *m*

A 1 (base, sustentación) foundation 2 **fundamentos** *mpl* (nociones básicas) fundamentals (*pl*), basics (*pl*)

B **fundamentos** *mpl* (Const) foundations (*pl*)

fundamentoso -sa *adj* (Ven fam) conscientious

fundar [A1] *vt* 1 ‹*ciudad/hospital/escuela*› to found; ‹*partido/empresa*› to establish 2 (basar) ‹*sospecha/argumento*› **~ algo EN algo** to base sth ON sth

■ **fundarse** *v pron* **~se EN algo** «*afirmación/sospecha*» to be based ON sth; «*persona*»: **se fundó en las pruebas** he based his ideas (*o* his theory *etc*) on the evidence; **¿en qué te fundas para decirlo?** what grounds do you have for saying that?

fundición *f* (de metales) smelting; (hierro colado) cast iron; (taller) foundry

fundido[1] -da *adj*

A ‹*metal/roca*› molten

B (AmL fam) (agotado) worn out, dead beat (colloq)

C (Per, RPl fam) (arruinado) broke (colloq)

fundido[2] *m* (Cin) fade, fade-in/fade-out; **~ en negro** fade-out

fundillo *m*, **fundillos** *mpl* 1 (AmS) (del pantalón) seat 2 (Col, Per, Ven fam) (nalgas) behind (colloq)

fundir [I1] *vt*

A ‹*metal/hierro*› to melt; ‹*mineral*› to smelt

B ‹*estatua/campana*› to cast

C 1 (Elec) to blow 2 (AmL) ‹*motor*› (de gasolina) to seize ... up; (eléctrico) to burn ... out

D (fam) ‹*dinero/herencia*› to blow (colloq)

E 1 (fusionar) to merge; **~ algo EN algo** to merge sth INTO sth 2 (Cin) ‹*imágenes/tomas*› to fade, merge

■ **fundirse** *v pron*

A «*metal*» to melt; «*nieve/hielo*» to melt, thaw

B 1 (Elec): **se ha fundido la bombilla** the bulb has gone (colloq); **se fundieron los fusibles** the fuses blew 2 (AmL) «*motor*» (de gasolina) to seize up; (eléctrico) to burn out

C (*enf*) (fam) (gastarse) to blow (colloq)

D 1 (fusionarse) to merge; **las dos empresas han decidido ~se** the two companies have decided to merge; **~se EN algo** to merge sth INTO sth; **una imagen se funde en otra** one image merges into another; **se fundieron en un abrazo** they embraced each other 2 (Cin, Mús) to fade

E (Per, RPl fam) (arruinarse) «*persona*» to lose everything; «*empresa*» to go bust

fundo *m* (Chi) country estate, large farm

fúnebre *adj* ‹*música/ambiente*› funereal; **¿a qué vienen esas caras tan ~s?** why all the long faces? (colloq); ▸ **coche, cortejo, etc**

funeral[1] *adj* funeral (*before n*)

funeral[2] *m*, **funerales** *mpl* (exequias) funeral; (oficio religioso) funeral service

funerala *f* ▸ **ojo**

funeraria *f* undertaker's, funeral parlor•

funerario -ria *adj* ‹*rito/pira/urna*› funeral (*before n*); ‹*instrumentos*› funerary

funesto -ta *adj* disastrous, terrible

fungir [I7] *vi* (Méx, Per) **~ COMO** *or* **DE algo** to act AS sth

funicular *m* (tren) funicular (railway); (teleférico) cable car

funky[1] /'fʌŋki, 'fuŋki/ *adj* funky

funky[2] /'fʌŋki, 'fuŋki/ *m* funk, funky music

fuñido -da *adj* (Ven fam) difficult

furcia *f* (Esp fam & pey) whore (pej)

furgón *m* (Auto) truck, van; (Ferr) boxcar (AmE), goods van (BrE)

(Compuesto) **furgón de cola** (Ferr) calaboose (AmE), guard's van (BrE)

furgoneta *f* (para carga) van; (para pasajeros) van, minibus

furia *f* 1 (rabia, ira) fury, rage; ***estar/ponerse hecho una ~*** (fam) to be/to get furious 2 (fuerza) fury; **la ~ del mar** the fury of the sea

furibundo -da *adj* ‹*ataque/combate*› furious; ‹*persona/mirada*› (fam) furious

f

fúrico -ca *adj* (Méx, Ven) ▸**furioso**

furioso -sa *adj* 1 (muy enojado) furious; **se puso ~** he was furious *o* he flew into a rage 2 (intenso): **una furiosa tempestad** a violent storm

furor *m* 1 (rabia) fury, rage 2 (de las olas, del viento, de una tempestad) fury 3 (entusiasmo) enormous enthusiasm; ***causar*** *or* ***hacer* ~** to be all the rage (colloq); ***sentir*** *or* ***tener* ~ *para algo*** (AmL) to have a passion for sth, be crazy about sth (colloq)

furtivamente *adv* 1 ‹*mirar/escribir*› furtively; **entró ~ en la habitación** he stole into the room 2 (ilegalmente): **cazar/pescar ~** to poach

furtivo -va *adj* 1 (ilegal): **la caza/pesca furtiva** poaching; **un cazador ~** a poacher 2 ‹*mirada/caricia*› furtive

furúnculo *m* boil, furuncle (tech)

fusa *f* demisemiquaver

fuselaje *m* fuselage

fusible *m* (Elec) fuse; **saltaron los ~s** the fuses blew

fusil *m*

A (Arm) rifle

(Compuesto) **fusil automático/de asalto** automatic/assault rifle

B (Méx fam) (plagio) plagiarism

fusilamiento *m* execution (*by firing squad*)

fusilar [A1] *vt*

A (Mil) to shoot; **fue fusilado** he was executed by firing squad

B (fam) (plagiar) to plagiarize, lift (colloq)

■ **fusilarse** *v pron* (fam) ‹*obra/novela*› to plagiarize, lift (colloq)

fusilero *m* rifleman, fusilier

fusión *f*

A (de empresas, partidos, organizaciones) merger; (de intereses) fusion

B 1 (de un metal) melting; (de metales, piezas) fusion, fusing together 2 (Fís) fusion

(Compuesto) **fusión fría/nuclear** cold/nuclear fusion

fusionar [A1] *vt* 1 ‹*piezas/metales*› to fuse, fuse together 2 ‹*empresas/partidos*› to merge 3 (Inf) to merge

■ **fusionarse** *v pron* 1 «*piezas/metales*» fuse (together) 2 «*empresas/partidos*» to merge; «*ideas*» to fuse; «*intereses*» to merge

fusta *f* riding crop; (más larga) whip

fustán *m* (Tex) fustian; (enagua) (Per, Ven) slip

fuste *m* (importancia): **un escritor de ~** a writer of some standing

fustigar [A3] *vt* 1 ‹*caballo*› to whip 2 (criticar) ‹*persona*› to lash, savage

futbito *m* (Esp) five-a-side soccer *o* football, ≈ indoor soccer (AmE)

fútbol, (AmC, Méx) **futbol** *m* soccer, football (esp BrE)

(Compuestos)

- **fútbol americano** American football
- **fútbol sala** five-a-side soccer *o* football, ≈ indoor soccer (≈ AmE)

futbolín *m* 1 (juego) table football 2 **futbolines** *mpl* (local) amusement arcade

futbolista *mf* soccer *o* football player

futbolístico -ca *adj* soccer (*before n*), football (*before n*); **la jornada futbolística** the day's soccer *o* football

fútil, futil *adj* (liter) trivial, trifling

futilidad *f* (liter) triviality

futón *m* futon

futre *mf* 1 (Chi, Per fam) (dandi) dandy, dude (AmE colloq) 2 (Chi fam) (persona de clase acomodada): **un ~ de la capital** a well-to-do guy from the capital (colloq)

futurismo *m* futurism

futurista[1] *adj* (Art) futurist; ‹*novela/diseño*› futuristic

futurista[2] *mf* futurist

futuro[1] **-ra** *adj* ‹*presidente*› future (*before n*); **las futuras generaciones** future generations; **la futura mamá** the mother-to-be; **mi futura esposa** my bride-to-be

futuro[2] *m*

A (porvenir) future; **¿qué nos deparará el ~?** what will the future bring?; **en un ~ cercano** *or* **próximo** in the near future; **en el** *or* **en lo ~** in future; **un empleo con/sin ~** a job with good prospects/with no prospects; **su relación no tiene ~** their relationship has no future

B (Ling) future (tense)

futuro[3] **-ra** *m,f* (fam & hum) intended (colloq & hum)

futurología *f* futurology

futurólogo -ga *m,f* futurologist

Gg

G, g *f* (*read as* /xe/) *the letter* **G, g**
g (= **gramo**) g, gr
gabacho -cha *m,f* **1** (Chi, Esp fam & pey) (francés) frog (colloq & pej) **2** (Méx fam & pey) (extranjero) foreigner (*of North American or European origin*)
gabán *m* (abrigo — largo) overcoat; (— corto) jacket
gabardina *f* (prenda) raincoat; (tela) gabardine
gabarra *f* barge
gabela *f* (Hist) tax; (carga) burden
gabinete *m*
A (de médico, dentista) office (AmE), surgery (BrE); (despacho) office; (en una casa) study; (laboratorio) laboratory
B (conjunto de profesionales) department; (Pol) cabinet
(Compuestos)
- **gabinete de imagen/prensa** public relations/press office
- **gabinete fantasma** *or* **en la sombra** shadow cabinet

C (Méx) (armario) kitchen cabinet *o* cupboard
(Compuesto) **gabinete del baño** (Col, Ven) bathroom cabinet
gacela *f* gazelle
gaceta *f* (periódico) gazette
gacetilla *f* (ant) (noticia) short news item; **~s de sociedad** gossip column
gacetillero -ra *m,f* **1** (ant) (reportero) reporter; (pey) hack (pej) **2** (de chismes) gossip columnist
gacho -cha *adj*
A **1** ‹*orejas*› drooping (*before n*); **un sombrero de alas gachas** a hat with a turned-down brim; **con la cabeza gacha** with his head bowed **2** **a gachas** (agachado) crouching; (a gatas) on all fours
B (Méx fam) (malo, feo) terrible, awful; (desagradable, molesto) annoying
gachupín *m* (Méx pey) Spaniard
gaélico¹ -ca *adj* Gaelic
gaélico² *m* (idioma) Gaelic
gafa *f*
A (Tec) (gancho) hook; (grapa) staple; (abrazadera) clamp
B **gafas** *fpl* **1** (anteojos) glasses (*pl*), spectacles (*pl*) (frml); **llevar** *or* **usar ~s** to wear glasses; **unas ~s nuevas** a new pair of glasses **2** (de protección) goggles (*pl*)
(Compuestos)
- **gafas bifocales** *fpl* bifocals (*pl*)
- **gafas de bucear/esquiar** *fpl* diving/skiing goggles (*pl*)
- **gafas de sol** *fpl* sunglasses (*pl*)
- **gafas graduadas** *fpl* prescription glasses *o* (frml) spectacles (*pl*)
- **gafas oscuras** *fpl* dark glasses (*pl*)
- **gafas progresivas** *fpl* varifocals (*pl*)

gafar [A1] *vt* (fam) to jinx
gafe¹ *adj* (Esp fam): **no la invito porque es ~** I'm not inviting her, she's jinxed *o* she has a jinx on her; **no seas ~** don't say that, you'll bring us bad luck
gafe² *mf* (Esp fam) **1** (persona): **el ~ de mi hermano ha vuelto a romperse el brazo** my brother's jinxed *o* so unlucky, he's broken his arm again **2** **gafe** *m*: **tener ~** to be jinxed
gafedad *f* (Ven fam) **1** (error) dumb move (colloq), stupid mistake **2** (tontería): **se ríen de cualquier ~** they laugh about the silliest little thing (colloq); **deja la ~** stop clowning *o* messing around (colloq)
gafo -fa *adj* (Ven fam) (estúpido) dumb (colloq)
gag *m* (*pl* **gags**) gag
gagá *adj inv*
A (fam) (senil) gaga (colloq)
B (Per fam) (elegante) smart (colloq)
gago -ga *m,f* (Col, Per, Ven fam) *person with a speech defect, esp one who cannot articulate consonants*
gaguear [A1] *vi* **1** ‹‹*niño*›› to say ga-ga-ga **2** (Col, Per, Ven fam) ‹‹*adulto*››: **es difícil entenderle porque gaguea** it's difficult to understand him because he can't pronounce his consonants properly
gaita *f*
A **1** *tb* **~ gallega/escocesa** (Galician/Scottish) bagpipes (*pl*); ***templar ~s*** (fam) to try and keep people happy **2** (Ven) (canción) *lively Christmas song*
B (Esp fam) (lata, cosa fastidiosa) drag (colloq)
gaitero -ra *m,f* (Mús) (bag)piper; (cantante) (Ven) *singer of* **gaitas A2**
gajes *mpl*: **son (los) ~ del oficio** it's all part of the job
gajo *m*
A (de naranja, limón) segment
B (Col) (de pelo) lock
gala *f*
A **1** (cena) gala; **cena de ~** gala (dinner); (en el teatro) *tb* **función de ~** gala (evening *o* performance); **vestido de ~** formal *o* full dress; **uniforme de ~** full-dress uniform; **vestirse de ~** to wear full *o* formal dress; ***hacer ~ de algo*** to display sth; ***tener algo a ~*** to pride oneself on sth **2** **galas** *fpl* (ropa) clothes (*pl*); **mis/tus mejores ~s** my/your best clothes; **~s nupciales** bridal attire
B (Esp) (concierto) concert
galáctico¹ -ca *adj* galactic
galáctico² -ca *m,f* superstar
galán *m* **1** (actor) hero, heartthrob **2** (hum) (novio) young man (hum), beau (dated *or* hum)
galano -na *adj*
A (elegante) elegant, smart
B (Méx) ‹*toro/vaca*› mottled
galante *adj* **1** ‹*hombre*› gallant, attentive **2** (pey) ‹*mujer/vida*› wanton
galantería *f* **1** (caballerosidad) gallantry **2** (piropo) compliment; (gesto cortés) polite gesture, attention
galápago *m*
A (Zool) (tortuga — gigante) giant turtle; (— europea) terrapin
B (en ciclismo) racing saddle
Galápagos *fpl* **las (Islas) ~** the Galapagos (Islands)
galardón *m* (period) award, prize
galardonado -da *m,f* (period) awardwinner, prizewinner
galardonar [A1] *vt* (period): **un nuevo premio para ~ la labor científica** a new prize awarded for scientific work; **su novela fue galardonada con el primer premio** her novel was awarded first prize; **el autor galardonado** the awardwinning author
galaxia *f* galaxy
galena *f* galena

galeno *m* (liter *o* hum) physician
galeón *m* galleon
galera *f*
A (Hist, Náut) galley
B (Impr) galley
C (RPl) (sombrero) top hat
galerada *f* galley proof
galería *f* 1 (interior) corridor; (exterior) gallery 2 (Teatr) gallery; **hacer algo cara a la ~** to play to the gallery
Compuestos
- **galería comercial** shopping mall (AmE), shopping arcade (BrE)
- **galería de arte** art gallery

galerna *f* strong northwest wind
galerón *m* (Méx) (sala) hall
Gales *m*: *tb* **el país de ~** Wales
galés[1] -lesa *adj* Welsh
galés[2] -lesa *m,f*
A (persona) (*m*) Welshman; (*f*) Welshwoman; **los galeses** the Welsh, Welsh people
B **galés** *m* (idioma) Welsh
galga *f* (Tec) gauge
galgo *mf* greyhound; ***correr como un ~*** to run like the wind; ***salir como un ~*** (fam) to shoot out/off (colloq)
galgódromo *m* (Méx) dog track
galicismo *m* gallicism
galifardo *m* (Per fam) layabout (colloq)
galimatías *m* (*pl* ~) (lenguaje incomprensible) gibberish; (de cosas, ideas) jumble
gallada *f* (Andes fam): **la ~** the crowd
gallardete *m* pennant
gallardía *f* (liter) 1 (apostura) striking appearance 2 (valor) gallantry, valor* (liter)
gallardo -da *adj* (liter) 1 ‹*estampa/joven*› striking, fine-looking 2 ‹*guerrero/comportamiento*› gallant (liter)
gallear [A1] *vi* to strut around
gallego[1] -ga *adj* 1 (de Galicia) Galician 2 (AmL fam) (español) Spanish
gallego[2] -ga *m,f* 1 (de Galicia) Galician 2 (AmL fam) (español) Spaniard 3 **gallego** *m* (Ling) Galician

> **gallego**
>
> The language of Galicia, spoken by around 3 million people. It is an official requirement for many official and academic positions, and a compulsory school subject.
>
> Galician, a Romance language close to Portuguese, was banned under Franco but with the return to democracy, it became an official language in Galicia beside Castilian. Nowadays there is Galician radio and television, and a considerable amount of publishing in the language.
>
> Galician has less social prestige than Catalan and Basque in their homelands. The middle classes have largely opted to use Castilian. *See also* **lenguas cooficiales**

gallera *f* (Col, Ven) cockpit
gallero -ra *m,f* (AmL fam) *person who breeds fighting cocks or who enjoys cockfighting*
galleta *f*
A (Coc) (dulce) cookie (AmE), biscuit (BrE); (salada) cracker
B (Méx fam) (fuerza): **¡échale ~!** put your back into it! (colloq)
gallina[1] *adj* (fam) chicken (colloq)
gallina[2] *f*
A (Zool) hen; (Coc) chicken; **caldo de ~** chicken broth; ***acostarse/levantarse con las ~s*** (fam) to go to bed early/to get up at the crack of dawn; ***estar/sentirse como ~ en corral ajeno*** (fam) to be/feel like a fish out of water; ***matar la ~ de los huevos de oro*** to kill the goose that lays the golden eggs
Compuestos
- **gallina clueca** (empollando) broody hen; (cuidando la pollada) mother hen
- **gallinita ciega** blind man's buff

B **gallina** *mf* (fam) (cobarde) chicken (colloq)
gallinazo *m* 1 (Zool) (de cabeza roja) turkey buzzard *o* vulture; (de cabeza negra) black vulture 2 (Col fam) (tenorio) womanizer
gallinero *m* 1 (Zool) (corral) henhouse, coop; ***alborotar*** *or* (CS fam) ***revolver el ~*** to set the cat among the pigeons 2 (fam) (sitio ruidoso) madhouse (colloq) 3 (fam) (en el cine, teatro): **el ~** the gods (colloq)
gallito[1] -ta *adj* (fam) cocky
gallito[2] *m*
A (fam) (persona) tough guy (colloq)
B (Col, Méx) (Dep) shuttlecock, birdie (AmE); *ver tb* **gallo[2]**
gallo[1] -lla *adj* (AmL fam) (bravucón) tough (colloq), macho; (valiente) tough (colloq)
gallo[2] *m*
A (Zool) (ave) cockerel; (más grande) rooster; **pelea de ~s** cockfight; ***comer ~*** (Méx fam) to get up on the wrong side of the bed (AmE colloq), to get out of the bed on the wrong side (BrE colloq); ***dormírsele el ~ a algn*** (Méx fam): **que no se te duerma el ~** you can't afford to rest on your laurels; **se me durmió el ~ y venció el plazo** I forgot about it and missed the closing date; ***en menos (de lo) que canta un ~*** in no time at all; ***entre ~s y medianoche*** (Arg) on the spur of the moment; ***~ duro de pelar*** (Méx fam): **resultaron ~s duros de pelar** they proved to be tough opposition; ***levantarse al cantar el ~*** to be up with the lark; ***mamarle ~ a algn*** (Col, Ven fam) to pull sb's leg (colloq); ***matarle el ~ a algn*** (Méx fam) to shut sb up (colloq); ***otro ~ cantaría*** *or* ***otro ~ me/te/nos cantara*** (fam) things would be very different; ***pelar ~*** (Méx fam) (huir) to leg it (colloq); (morirse) to kick the bucket (colloq); ***ser el (mejor) ~ de algn*** (Méx fam) to be sb's best bet (colloq)
Compuesto **gallo de pelea** *or* (AmS) **de riña** fighting *o* game cock
B (Méx fam) (bravucón) macho, tough guy (colloq)
C (fam) (de un cantante) false note; (de adolescente) (AmL): **soltó un ~** his voice went squeaky
D (Méx) (serenata) serenade
gallo[3] -lla (Chi fam) (*m*) guy (colloq); (*f*) woman; **hola ~** hi, buddy (AmE) *o* (BrE) mate (colloq)
gallón *m* (Méx fam) (en política) (political) bigwig (colloq); (en finanzas) big shot (colloq)
galo[1] -la *adj* 1 (Hist) Gallic 2 (period) (francés) French
galo[2] -la *m,f* 1 (Hist) Gaul 2 (period) (*m*) Frenchman; (*f*) Frenchwoman
galocha *f* (CS) galosh
galón *m*
A (Mil) stripe
B (medida) gallon
galopante *adj* ‹*inflación/tuberculosis*› galloping (*before n*); **el número de accidentes aumentó a ritmo ~** the number of accidents rose dramatically
galopar [A1] *vi* (Equ) to gallop
galope *m* gallop; **a** *or* **al ~** at a gallop; ***a ~ tendido*** (Equ) at full gallop; (rápidamente) at full speed
galpón *m* 1 (Hist) slave quarters (*pl*) 2 (AmL) (cobertizo) shed; (almacén) storehouse
galvanizar [A4] *vt* to galvanize
gama *f* 1 (de colores, productos) range; **en toda la ~ política** across the whole political spectrum; **distintos tonos dentro de la ~ del rojo** different shades of red 2 (de notas musicales) scale
gamba *f*
A (esp Esp) (Coc, Zool) shrimp (AmE), prawn (BrE)
B (arg) (pierna) leg; ***meter la ~*** (fam) to put one's foot in it (colloq)
gamberrada *f* (Esp) (grosería) loutish act; (acto violento) act of hooliganism
gamberrismo *m* (Esp) (comportamiento — escandaloso) loutishness; (— violento) hooliganism
gamberro -rra *m,f* (Esp) (grosero) lout; (vándalo) hooligan
gambeta *f* (AmS) dodge
gambetear [A1] *vi* (AmS) to dodge and weave
gambito *m* (en ajedrez) gambit
gameto *m* gamete
gamín -mina *m,f* (Col) street urchin
gamma *f* (letra) gamma
gamo -ma *m,f* fallow deer
gamonal *m* (Col, Per) cacique
gamonalismo *m* (Col, Per) exploitation (*of indigenous people by a cacique*)

gamulán® *m* (CS) (prenda) sheepskin coat/jacket

gamuza *f* [1] (Zool) chamois [2] (piel) chamois (leather); (de otros animales) suede [3] (paño) dustcloth (AmE), duster (BrE)

gana *f* [1] (deseo): **¡con qué ~s me comería un helado!** I'd love an ice cream!; **¡me iría a la cama con unas ~s!** what I wouldn't give to be able to go to bed now! (colloq); **lo hizo sin ~s** he did it very half-heartedly; **no tengo ~s de ir** I don't feel like going; **haz lo que te digo — no me da la ~** do as I tell you — I don't want to!; **haz lo que te dé la ~** *or* **lo que te venga en ~** do what you like; **siempre hace lo que le viene en ~** she always does just as she pleases; **quería ir pero me quedé con las ~s** (fam) I wanted to go, but it wasn't to be; **se quedó con las ~s de decirle lo que pensaba** she never got to tell him what she really thought; **si te crees que va a decir que sí te vas a quedar con las ~s** (fam) if you think he's going to say yes, you've got another think coming (colloq); ***con ~s***: **llover con ~s** to pour down; **es feo/tonto con ~s** he is so ugly/stupid!; ***de buena/mala ~*** willingly/reluctantly; ***tenerle ~s a algn*** (fam) (de pegarle, reñirlo) to be out to get sb (colloq); (sexualmente) (Col, CS) to have the hots for sb (colloq) [2] **~s DE + INF: jóvenes con ~s de pasarlo bien** young people out for a good time; **¡qué ~s de complicarte la vida!** you really like making life difficult for yourself!; **(no) tengo ~s de ir** I (don't) feel like going; **tengo ~s de volver a verte** I'm looking forward to seeing you again; **¡tengo unas ~s de decirle lo que pienso!** I'd really like to tell him what I think!; **(te) dan ~s de mandarlo todo al diablo** it makes you want to say to hell with it all; **le dieron** *or* **entraron ~s de reírse** she felt like bursting out laughing; **se me quitaron las ~s de ir** I don't feel like going any more; **tengo ~s de ir al servicio** I need to go to the bathroom, I want to go to the toilet (BrE); **me entraron ~s de vomitar** I felt sick [3] **~(s) DE QUE + SUBJ: tengo ~s de que llegue el verano** I'm looking forward to the summer

ganadería *f* (actividad) ranching, stockbreeding; (ganado) cattle (*pl*), livestock (+ *sing or pl vb*)

ganadero[1] **-ra** *adj* ranching, stockbreeding (*before n*)

ganadero[2] **-ra** *m,f* rancher, stockbreeder

ganado *m* cattle (*pl*), livestock (+ *sing or pl vb*)

(Compuestos)
- **ganado bovino** *or* **vacuno** cattle (*pl*)
- **ganado caballar** *or* **equino** horses (*pl*)
- **ganado cabrío** *or* **caprino** goats (*pl*)
- **ganado ovino** sheep (*pl*)
- **ganado porcino** pigs (*pl*)

ganador[1] **-dora** *adj* ‹equipo/caballo› winning (*before n*); **la película ~a del Oscar** the Oscar-winning film

ganador[2] **-dora** *m,f* winner

ganancia *f* (Com, Fin) profit

(Compuesto) **ganancia líquida** *or* **neta/total** *or* **bruta** net/gross profit

ganar [A1] *vt*

A [1] ‹*sueldo*› to earn; **¿cuánto ganas al mes?** how much do you earn a month?; **lo único que quiere es ~ dinero** all he's interested in is making money [2] (conseguir) to gain; **no ganas nada con preocuparte** there's no point worrying (about it)

B [1] ‹*partido/guerra/elecciones*› to win; **le gané la apuesta** I won my bet with him [2] ‹*premio/dinero*› to win

C (adquirir) ‹*experiencia*› to gain; **ganó fama y fortuna** she won fame and fortune

D [1] (conquistar) **~ a algn PARA algo** to win sb over TO sth; **lo ganó para su causa** she won him over to her cause [2] (reclamar) to reclaim; **las tierras ganadas al mar** the land that has been reclaimed from the sea

E (liter) ‹*meta*› to attain (frml); ‹*cumbre/orilla*› to gain (liter)

■ **ganar** *vi*

A (mediante el trabajo) to earn

B [1] (vencer) to win; **que gane el mejor** may the best man win; **van ganando 2 a 1** they're winning 2-1 [2] **~le A algn** to beat sb; **nos ~on por cuatro puntos** they beat us by four points; **a mentiroso nadie le gana** *or* **no hay quien le gane** when it comes to lying there's noone to touch him

C (aventajar) **~le a algn EN algo**: **le ganas en estatura** you're taller than him; **me gana en todo** he beats me on every count

D [1] (mejorar): **el salón ha ganado mucho con estos cambios** these changes have really improved the living room; **ha ganado mucho con el nuevo peinado** her new hairstyle has really done a lot for her [2] (obtener provecho, beneficiarse) to gain; **ganó mucho con su estancia en Berlín** he gained a lot from *o* got a lot out of his stay in Berlin; ***salir ganando***: **es el único que salió ganando con el trato/en ese asunto** he's the only one who did well out of the deal/who came out well in that business; **al final salí ganando** in the end I came out of it better off

■ **ganarse** *v pron*

A (*enf*) (mediante el trabajo) to earn

B (*enf*) ‹*premio/apuesta*› to win

C ‹*afecto/confianza*› to win; ‹*persona*› to win … over; **supo ~se el respeto de todos** she managed to win *o* earn everyone's respect

D (ser merecedor de) ‹*descanso*› to earn oneself; ***~se algo a pulso*** to earn sth; ***ganársela*** (Esp fam): **se la va a ~** she's going to get it *o* she's for it (colloq)

ganchillo *m* (aguja) crochet hook; (labor) crochet; **hacer ~** to crochet

gancho *m*

A (garfio) hook; ***hacerle ~ a algn con algn*** (CS fam) to set sb up with sb (colloq); ***ir de ~*** (Col) to walk along arm in arm

B [1] (clip) paperclip; (de patitas) paper fastener [2] (horquilla) hairpin [3] (Andes) (imperdible) safety pin [4] (AmL) (para la ropa) hanger

C [1] (fam) (para atrapar, seducir) bait [2] (fam) (atractivo): **un hombre con mucho ~** a very attractive man; **un artista que tiene ~** an artist who enjoys great popularity

D [1] (en boxeo) hook [2] (en baloncesto) hook shot

gandalla *mf* (Méx fam) (persona deshonesta) crook (colloq); (sinvergüenza) swine (colloq)

gandul -dula *m,f* (fam) lazybones (colloq)

gandulear [A1] *vi* (fam) to laze *o* (colloq) loaf around

ganga *f* (compra ventajosa) bargain; **a precio de ~** at a bargain *o* giveaway price

ganglio *m* (en los vasos linfáticos) gland; (de células nerviosas) ganglion

gangosear [A1] *vi* to talk through one's nose

gangoso -sa *adj* nasal

gangrena *f* gangrene

gangrenarse [A1] *v pron* to become gangrenous

gangrenoso -sa *adj* gangrenous

gángster *mf* (*pl* **-ters**) gangster

ganguear [A1] *vi* to talk through one's nose

gansada *f* (fam) [1] (dicho): **decir ~s** to talk through one's hat (colloq) [2] (acto): **hacer ~s** to clown around (colloq)

ganso[1] **-sa** *adj* (fam) (torpe) clumsy; (holgazán) lazy, idle; (tonto) stupid

ganso[2] **-sa** *m,f*

A (Zool) (*m*) goose, gander; (*f*) goose

B (fam) [1] (persona torpe) oaf (colloq) [2] (holgazán) slob (colloq) [3] (tonto) clown (colloq); **hacer el ~** to clown around

ganzúa *f* picklock

gañán *m* [1] (ant) (mozo de labranza) farmhand [2] (patán) boor

gañir [I9] *vi* «*perro*» to yelp; «*cuervo*» to caw

garabatear [A1] *vi*

A (escribir) to scribble, scrawl; (dibujar) to doodle

B (Chi) (decir palabrotas) to swear

■ **garabatear** *vt*

A (escribir) to scrawl, scribble; (dibujar) to doodle

B (Chi) (insultar) to swear at

garabato *m*

A [1] (dibujo) doodle [2] **garabatos** *mpl* (escritura) scrawl, scribble

B (gancho) hook

C (Chi) (palabrota) swearword

garaje /ga'raxe/ *m*, (esp AmL) **garage** /ga'raʒ/ *m* (de edificio) garage; (taller) garage

garante *mf* guarantor

garantía *f*

A (Com) guarantee, warranty; **dos años de ~** a two-year guarantee; **estar bajo** *or* **en ~** to be under guarantee

B (Der) (fianza) surety, guarantee

C (seguridad) guarantee; **no ofrece ~s para el inversor** it does not offer any security for the investor

g

(Compuesto) **garantías constitucionales** *fpl* constitutional rights (*pl*)

garantizar [A4] *vt*
A (Com) ‹*producto*› to guarantee, warrant (AmE); **se lo garantizamos por tres años** we give a three-year guarantee
B 1 (Der) «*garante*» to act as guarantor for, stand surety for 2 (asegurar) to guarantee

garañón *m* (AmL fam) (caballo) studhorse

garapiña *f* (Méx) pineapple squash

garbanzo *m* chickpea; ***ganarse los ~s*** (fam) to earn one's bread and butter (colloq); ***ser el ~ negro de la familia*** to be the black sheep of the family

garbo *m* (al andar, moverse — elegancia) poise, grace; (— gracia, desenvoltura) jauntiness

garbosamente *adv* 1 (con gracia y desenvoltura) jauntily 2 (con elegancia) with poise

garboso -sa *adj* ‹*andar/gesto*› (elegante) graceful; (con gracia) jaunty

gardenia *f* gardenia

garete: **irse al ~** (fam) «*embarcación*» to be adrift; «*planes*» to go down the drain

garfio *m* hook

gargajo *m* (fam) gob (sl)

garganta¹ *f*
A 1 (Anat) throat; **me dolía la ~** I had a sore throat; **tiene una buena ~** she has a good (singing) voice 2 (cuello) neck
B (desfiladero) gorge, ravine; (entre montañas) narrow pass

garganta² *mf* (Per fam) scrounger (colloq)

gargantilla *f* choker, necklace

gárgara *f* gargle; **hacer ~s** to gargle; ***mandar a algn a hacer ~s*** (fam) to tell sb to get lost (colloq)

gargarismo *m* (acción) gargling; (líquido) gargle

garguero, gargüero *m* (fam) throat; **mojarse el ~** (fam) to have a drink

garita *f* (de centinela) sentry box; (de portero) lodge; (caseta) hut, cabin

garito *m* gambling den

garlar [A1] *vi* (Col fam) to chat, talk

garra *f*
A 1 (de animal) claw; (de águila) talon 2 (pey) (de persona) paw (colloq & pej); **echarle la ~ a algo** to grab *o* seize sth
B (arrojo, valor) fighting spirit; (personalidad) personality
C **garras** *fpl* (poder, dominio) clutches (*pl*); **caer/estar en las ~s de algn** to fall into/be in sb's clutches
D (Chi, Méx fam) (ropa — vieja) rags (*pl*) (colloq); (— de mal gusto, fea) tasteless clothes (*pl*) (colloq); ***hacer ~s algo/a algn*** (Méx fam) to tear sth/sb to shreds (colloq)

garrafa *f* 1 (para vino) demijohn; **ginebra/vino de ~** cheap gin/wine 2 (RPl) (para gas) cylinder

garrafal *adj* terrible; **error ~** terrible *o* huge mistake

garrafón *m* demijohn

garrapata *f* tick

garrapiñada *f* (esp AmL) caramel-coated peanuts/almonds (*pl*)

garrapiñado -da *adj* caramel-coated

garrido -da *adj* (liter) ‹*mozo*› handsome; ‹*moza*› comely

garrobo *m* (AmC) iguana

garrocha *f*
A (Taur) lance, goad; (aguijada) (Méx) cattle prod
B (AmL) (Dep) pole

garrochista *mf* (AmL) pole-vaulter

garrón *m* (carne) shank; ***de ~*** (RPl fam) free; **entré de ~** I got in free

garronear [A1] *vi* (RPl fam) to scrounge (colloq)

garrotazo *m* (golpe) blow (*with a club*)

garrote *m* (palo) club, stick; (método de ejecución) garrotte

garrotero -ra *m,f* (Méx) (Ferr) brakeman (AmE), guard (BrE)

garrotillo *m* (Med) croup

gárrulo -la *adj* 1 (hablador) garrulous 2 (liter) ‹*ave*› noisy, twittering (*before n*); ‹*viento*› howling (*before n*)

garúa *f* (AmL) drizzle

garuar [A18] *v impers* (AmL) to drizzle

garufa *f* (RPl arg): **irse de ~** to go out on the town (colloq)

garza *f*
A (Zool) heron
B (Chi) (copa) long-stemmed glass

garzo -za *adj* (liter) azure (liter)

garzón -zona (Chi) (*m*) waiter; (*f*) waitress

gas *m*
A (Fís, Quím) gas; **~es tóxicos** toxic fumes; **asfixiar con ~** to gas; **cocina a** *or* **de ~** gas cooker; ***a todo ~*** (Esp fam) at full speed; ***darle ~*** (Auto) (fam) to step on the gas (colloq)

(Compuestos)
- **gas ciudad** (Esp) *or* (Chi) **de cañería** town gas
- **gas hilarante/lacrimógeno** laughing/tear gas
- **gas licuado** liquified gas
- **gas neurotóxico** *or* **nervioso** nerve gas

B **gases** *mpl* (Fisiol) wind, flatulence

gasa *f* (Med, Tex) gauze

gasear *vt* [A1] to gas

gaseoducto *m* gas pipeline

gaseosa *f* 1 (bebida efervescente) soda (AmE), fizzy drink (BrE) 2 (Arg) (cualquier refresco) soft drink

gaseoso -sa *adj* 1 ‹*cuerpo/estado*› gaseous 2 ‹*bebida*› carbonated, fizzy (BrE)

gasero *m* tanker (ship)

gásfiter *mf* (*pl* **-ters**) (Chi) plumber

gasfitería *f* (Chi, Per) plumbing

gasfitero -ra *m,f* (Per) plumber

gasificarse *v pron* to gasify

gasista *mf* gas fitter

gasoducto *m* gas pipeline

gas-oil, gasóleo *m* (para calefacción) (gas) oil; (para motores) diesel (fuel *o* oil)

gasolina *f* gasoline (AmE), gas (AmE), petrol (BrE); **tengo que echar** *or* **poner** *or* (Méx) **cargar ~** I have to get some gas *o* petrol

(Compuestos)
- **gasolina normal** regular gasoline (AmE), two-star petrol
- **gasolina sin plomo** unleaded gasoline (AmE), unleaded petrol (BrE)
- **gasolina super** premium gasoline (AmE), four-star petrol (BrE)

gasolinera *f*
A (estación) gas station (AmE), petrol station (BrE)
B (embarcación) motorboat

gasómetro *m* gasholder, gasometer

gastado -da *adj* ‹*ropa/zapatos*› worn-out; ‹*político/cantante*› washed-up (colloq)

gastador -dora *adj/m,f* spendthrift

gastar [A1] *vt*
A (consumir) 1 ‹*dinero*› to spend; **~ algo EN algo** to spend sth ON sth 2 ‹*gasolina/electricidad*› to use; **me vas a ~ las pilas** you're going to run the batteries down
B (desperdiciar, malgastar) ‹*dinero/tiempo/energía*› to waste
C (desgastar) ‹*ropa/zapatos*› to wear out; ‹*tacones*› to wear down
D 1 (fam) (llevar, usar) ‹*ropa/gafas*› to wear; **gasto el 37** I'm a size 37; **¿qué marca de cigarrillos gastas?** what brand of cigarettes do you smoke? 2 (fam) (tener) to have; **ése gasta un genio ...** he has a terrible temper!
E ‹*broma*› to play; **le ~on una broma** they played a joke *o* trick on him

■ **gastarse** *v pron*
A (*enf*) ‹*dinero*› to spend
B ‹*pilas/batería*› to run down; **se me gastó la tinta** I ran out of ink
C «*ropa/zapatos*» (desgastarse) to wear out
D (*enf*) (fam) (tener) to have; **¡qué modales se gasta!** that's a fine way to behave; **¡qué pinta de hippy se gasta!** he looks like a real hippy!

gasto *m* expense; **supondría un ~ de un millón** it would cost a million; **este mes he tenido muchos ~s** this has been an expensive month for me; **los ~s del juicio** the legal costs; **restringir ~s** to limit expenditure

(Compuestos)
- **gasto público** *m*: **el ~ ~** public expenditure
- **gastos bancarios** *mpl* bank charges (*pl*)
- **gastos de correo** *mpl* postage
- **gastos de envío** *mpl* postage and handling (AmE), postage and packing (BrE)

- **gastos fijos** *or* **estructurales** *mpl* overheads (*pl*)
- **gastos varios** *mpl* sundries (*pl*)

gástrico -ca *adj* gastric
gastritis *f* gastritis
gastronomía *f* gastronomy
gastronómico -ca *adj* gastronomic
gastrónomo -ma *m,f* gourmet, gastronome
gata *f*
A (Chi, Per) (Auto) jack; *ver tb* **gato¹**
B **a gatas** (*loc adv*) (a cuatro patas): **ir** *or* **andar a ~s** to crawl; **tuve que entrar a ~s** I had to go in on all fours
gatazo *m* (AmL fam): **cuando se arregla da el ~** when she dresses up she looks pretty good; **no es de oro pero pega el ~** it isn't gold but it could pass for gold
gatear [A1] *vi* (andar a gatas) to crawl; (trepar) to climb
gatera *f* cathole (AmE), cat flap (BrE)
gatillero *m* (Méx) gunman
gatillo *m* trigger; **apretar el ~** to pull the trigger
gatito -ta *m,f* kitten
gato¹ -ta *m,f*
A (Zool) cat; ***aquí hay ~ encerrado*** there's something fishy going on here; ***cuatro ~s*** (fam) a handful of people; ***defenderse como ~ panza arriba*** (fam) to defend oneself fiercely; ***el ~ escaldado del agua fría huye*** once bitten twice shy; ***estar para el ~*** (Chi fam) to be in a bad way (colloq); ***jugar al ~ y al ratón*** to play cat and mouse; ***lavarse como los ~s*** to make do with a lick and a promise (colloq); ***le dieron ~ por liebre*** he was conned *o* had! (colloq); ***llevarse el ~ al agua*** (fam) to pull it off (colloq)
(Compuestos)
- **gato con botas** *m*: **el ~ con ~** Puss in Boots
- **gato montés** wild cat

B (Méx fam) (criado) (*m*) servant; (*f*) maid
gato² *m*
A (Auto) jack
B (Mús) *folk dance from the River Plate area*
C (Chi, Méx) (Jueg) ticktacktoe (AmE), noughts and crosses (BrE)
D (Méx) (signo) hash sign
gatuno -na *adj* (relativo al gato) cat (*before n*), feline; (parecido al gato) catlike
gauchada *f* (Bol, CS fam) favor*, good turn
gauchaje *m* (RPl) (vaqueros): **el ~** the gauchos (*pl*)
gauchesco -ca *adj* gaucho (*before n*)
gaucho *m* gaucho

gaucho

A peasant of the pampas of Argentina, Uruguay, and Brazil. Modern gauchos work as foremen on farms and ranches and take part in rodeos.

Gauchos fought for Argentine independence from Spain, but later became involved in political disputes and suffered persecution.

A literary genre, *literatura gauchesca*, grew up in the eighteenth and nineteenth centuries. The most famous work is *Martín Fierro*, an epic poem by José Hernández about the misfortunes of an Argentine gaucho when the huge pampas are divided into ranches.

Traditionally gauchos wore baggy trousers, leather chaps, a *chiripá*, a garment that went over their trousers and came up around their waist, boots, a hat, a leather waistcoat, a belt with a large buckle. They carried a *facón* - a large knife with a curved blade, and used *boleadoras*, ropes weighted at each end and thrown like lassos, to catch cattle

gavera *f* (Ven) (para botellas) case (AmE), crate (BrE); (para hielo) ice tray
gaveta *f* drawer
gavia *f*
A (Náut) topsail
B (Zool) seagull
gavilán *m* sparrowhawk; **el ~ y la paloma** the hawk and the dove
gavilla *f* (de cereales) sheaf; (de bandidos, golfos) gang, band
gaviota *f* seagull, gull

gay¹ /gai, gei/ *adj* (*pl* ~ *or* **gays**) gay
(Compuesto) **gay saber** /gai/ *m* (liter) **el ~ ~** poetics (liter)
gay² /gai, gei/ (*pl* ~ *or* **gays**) (*m*) gay man, gay; (*f*) gay woman, lesbian
gayo -ya *adj* (liter) gay
(Compuesto) **gaya ciencia** *f* (liter) **la ~ ~** poesy (liter)
gayola *f* (RPl fam) (cárcel) slammer (colloq)
gazapera *f*
A (madriguera) warren; (de maleantes) den
B (fam) (pelea) brawl, scuffle
gazapo *m*
A (Zool) young rabbit
B 1 (errata) misprint, error 2 (fam) (equivocación) mistake
gazmoñería *f* (pudor) prudishness; (mojigatería) sanctimoniousness
gazmoño -ña *adj* (pudoroso) prudish; (mojigato) sanctimonious
gaznápiro¹ -ra *adj* (fam) dumb (colloq)
gaznápiro² -ra *m,f* (fam) fool, dummy (colloq)
gaznate *m* (garganta) (fam) throat, gullet; **refrescar el ~** (fam) to have a drink
gazpacho *m*: *tb* **~ andaluz** gazpacho (*cold soup made from tomatoes, peppers, etc*)
gazuza *f* (fam) hunger
ge *f*: *name of the letter* **g**
géiser, geiser *m* geyser
geisha /'gejʃa/ *f* geisha
gel *m* gel
gelatina *f* 1 (sustancia) gelatin* 2 (postre) Jell-O® (AmE), jelly (BrE); ***temblar como una ~*** (fam) to tremble like a leaf
gelatinoso -sa *adj* gelatinous
gélido -da *adj* (liter) icy, gelid (liter)
gema *f* gem
gemelo¹ -la *adj* twin (*before n*); **son almas gemelas** they're kindred spirits
gemelo² -la *m,f*
A (persona) twin
B 1 **gemelo** *m* (de camisa) cuff link 2 **gemelos** *mpl* (Ópt) binoculars (*pl*); **me prestó unos ~s** he lent me a pair of *o* some binoculars
gemido *m* 1 (de dolor, pena) groan, moan 2 (de animal) whine 3 (liter) (del viento) moaning
Géminis¹ *m* (signo, constelación) Gemini; **es (de) ~** she's (a) Gemini, she's a Geminian
Géminis², géminis *mf* (*pl* ~) (persona) Geminian, Gemini
gemir [I14] *vi* 1 «*persona*» to moan, groan; **gemía de dolor** he moaned with pain 2 «*animal*» to whine 3 (liter) «*viento*» to moan
gen *m* gene
gendarme *mf* gendarme
gendarmería *f* gendarmerie
genealogía *f* genealogy
genealógico -ca *adj* genealogical
generación *f*
A 1 (de una familia) generation 2 (Art, Lit) generation; **la ~ del 98** the generation of '98 3 (Inf) generation
B (acción) generation; **~ de puestos de trabajo** job creation
generacional *adj* generation (*before n*), generational; **brecha ~** generation gap
generador¹ -dora *adj*: **un plan ~ de empleo** a plan which will generate *o* create employment; **fuentes ~as de energía** sources of energy
generador² *m* generator
general¹ *adj* 1 (no específico, global) general; **hablando en líneas ~es** broadly speaking; **un panorama ~ de la situación** an overall view of the situation; **tiene nociones ~es de informática** he has a general idea about computing 2 (*en locs*) **en general** on the whole, in general; **el público en ~** the general public; **por lo general**: **por lo ~ llega a las nueve** she usually *o* generally arrives

at nine; **por lo ~ prefiero ir en auto** in general I prefer to drive

general² *mf* (Mil) general

(Compuesto) **general de brigada** (en el ejército) ≈ major general; (en las fuerzas aéreas) ≈ brigadier general (*in US*), ≈ air commodore (*in UK*)

generala *f* 1 (toque) call to arms; **tocar a ~** to sound the call to arms 2 (persona) general's wife

generalato *m* (cargo) rank of general; (conjunto) generals (*pl*)

generalidad *f* (vaguedad) general comment, generality; (mayoría) majority

generalísimo *m* generalissimo; **el G~** General Franco

Generalitat /dʒenerali'tat/ *f*: **la ~** *the autonomous government of Cataluña*

Generalitat

The name of the autonomous governments of Catalonia and Valencia. A great deal of power has now been transferred to them from central government.

The medieval term *generalitat* was revived in 1932, when Catalonia voted for its own devolved government. After the Civil War, it was abolished by Franco but was restored in 1978, with the establishment of comunidades autónomas. The Valencian *Generalitat* is keen to preserve the traditions of the region from Catalan influence

generalización *f* 1 (juicio general) generalization 2 (extensión): **la ~ del conflicto a otras zonas** the spread of the conflict into other areas; **la ~ del consumo de drogas** the increase in drug-taking

generalizado -da *adj* ‹*opinión*› widespread

generalizar [A4] *vi* to generalize, make generalizations

■ **generalizar** *vt* to spread

■ **generalizarse** *v pron* to spread

generar [A1] *vt* (Elec) to generate; (crear) to generate, create

generatriz *adj* generational

género *m*

A 1 (clase, tipo) kind, type 2 (Biol) genus 3 (Lit, Teatr) genre

(Compuestos)

- **género dramático**: **el ~ ~** drama
- **género humano**: **el ~ ~** the human race, mankind
- **género lírico**: **el ~ ~** (Teatr) *opera, zarzuela, etc*; (Lit) lyric poetry
- **género novelesco**: **el ~ ~** the novel

B (Ling) gender

C (mercancías) *tb* **~s** merchandise, goods (*pl*)

D (tela) cloth, material

generosidad *f* generosity

generoso -sa *adj* 1 ‹*persona/carácter*› generous 2 ‹*cantidad/propina*› generous 3 ‹*vino*› full-bodied

génesis *f* (origen) origin, genesis (frml)

genética *f* genetics

genético -ca *adj* genetic

genial *adj* 1 ‹*idea*› brilliant; ‹*escritor/pintor*› brilliant; **su última sinfonía es una obra ~** his last symphony is a work of genius 2 (fam) (estupendo) great (colloq), fantastic (colloq) 3 (fam) (ocurrente, gracioso) witty, funny

genialidad *f* (cualidad) genius; (ocurrencia) brilliant idea

genialmente *adv* brilliantly; **nos llevamos ~** we get along terribly well, we get on famously (BrE)

geniecillo *m* elf

genio *m* 1 (carácter) temper; **tener buen/mal ~** to be even-tempered/bad-tempered; ***estar con*** *or* ***tener el ~ atravesado*** (fam) to be in a bad mood *o* in a temper; ***~ y figura hasta la sepultura*** a leopard never changes its spots; ***tener el ~ pronto*** *or* ***vivo*** to be quick-tempered 2 (talento) genius; **un pintor con mucho ~** a painter of genius 3 (lumbrera) genius 4 (ser fantástico) genie

genital *adj* genital

genitales *mpl* genitals (*pl*), genital organs (*pl*)

genocida *mf* person guilty of acts of genocide

genocidio *m* genocide

genoma *m* genome; **el ~ humano** the human genome

genoterapia *f* gene therapy

Génova *f* Genoa

gente¹ *adj* (AmL) (de buenas maneras) respectable; (amable) kind, good

gente² *adv* (Chi, Méx): **se portó muy ~ conmigo** she was very good *o* kind to me

gente³ *f*

A 1 (personas) people (*pl*); **había muy poca/tanta ~** there were very few/so many people; **¿qué va a decir la ~?** what will people say?; **estas Navidades las pasaré con mi ~** I'm spending this Christmas with my family *o* (colloq) folks; **¿cómo está toda la ~ del pueblo?** how's everyone back home?; ***como la ~*** (CS fam) ‹*regalo/camisa*› decent (colloq); **habla como la ~** speak properly; ***ser buena ~*** to be nice (*o* kind *etc*); ***ser ~*** (AmS) to behave (properly) 2 (Méx) (persona) person

(Compuestos)

- **gente bien** (de respeto) respectable people; (adinerada) well-to-do people
- **gente de a pie**: **la ~ de a ~** the man in the street
- **gente linda** *or* (Esp) **guapa**: **la ~ ~** the beautiful people
- **gente menuda**: **la ~ ~** the children (*pl*)

B **gentes** *fpl* (liter) (habitantes) people (*pl*)

gentil¹ *adj*

A (amable) kind

B (Relig) gentile

gentil² *mf* gentile

gentileza *f* kindness; **tuvo la ~ de cederme el asiento** she was kind enough to let me have her seat; **tenga la ~ de esperar un momento** would you be so kind as to wait a moment (frml); **~ de Joaquín Arias** (Corresp) by courtesy of Joaquín Arias

gentilhombre *m* (*pl* **gentileshombres**) gentleman

gentilicio *m*: *name given to the people from a particular region or country*

gentío *m* crowd; **había tal ~ que me volví a casa** it was so crowded that I went home again

gentuza *f* (pey) riffraff (pej), rabble (pej)

genuflexión *f* genuflection

genuflexo *adj* (arrodillado) kneeling

genuino -na *adj* 1 ‹*lana/cuero*› genuine 2 ‹*dolor/tristeza*› genuine; **el ~ representante del pueblo** the true representative of the people

geofísica *f* geophysics

geofísico -ca *adj* geophysical

geografía *f* 1 (disciplina) geography; **~ política/humana** political/human geography 2 (topografía) geography

geográfico -ca *adj* geographic(al)

geógrafo -fa *m,f* geographer

geología *f* geology

geológico -ca *adj* geological

geólogo -ga *m,f* geologist

geometría *f* geometry

geométrico -ca *adj* geometric

geopolítico -ca *adj* geopolitical

geranio *m* geranium

gerencia *f* 1 (cargo) post *o* position of manager; **durante su ~** during his time as manager 2 (personas) management 3 (oficina) manager's office

gerencial *adj* (AmL) managerial

gerenciar [A1] *vt* (AmL) to manage

gerente *mf* manager

(Compuesto) **gerente comercial** business manager

geriatría *f* geriatrics

gerifalte *m*

A (Zool) gyrfalcon

B (persona importante) bigwig (colloq)

germanía *f* criminal slang

germánico -ca *adj* Germanic

germano¹ -na *adj* 1 (Hist) Germanic 2 (period) ‹*gobierno/equipo*› German 3 ‹*puntualidad/eficiencia*› Germanic, Teutonic (hum)

germano² **-na** *m,f* 1 (Hist) German (*member of a Germanic tribe*); **los ~s** the Germanic tribes *o* peoples 2 (period) (alemán) German
germanófilo **-la** *adj/m,f* Germanophile
germanófobo **-ba** *adj* Germanophobic
germanooccidental *adj* (Hist) West German
germanooriental *adj* (Hist) East German
germen *m*
A (microbio) germ
B 1 (embrión) germ; **~ de trigo** wheatgerm 2 (origen) seeds (*pl*); **el ~ de la revolución** the seeds of the revolution
germicida¹ *adj* germicidal
germicida² *m* germicide
germinación *f* germination
germinar [A1] *vi* 1 (Bot) to germinate 2 (liter) «*idea*» to germinate
gerontocracia *f* gerontocracy
gerundio *m* gerund
gesta *f* exploit, heroic deed; **cantar de ~** chanson de geste, epic poem
gestación *f* (Biol) gestation; (preparación) gestation; **en ~** in gestation
gestante *f* (frml) expectant mother (frml)
gestar [A1] *vt* to gestate
■ **gestarse** *v pron*: **se gestaba una revolución/una huelga** a revolution/a strike was brewing
gesticulación *f* gesticulation
gesticular [A1] *vi* to gesticulate
gestión *f* 1 (trámite): **hizo** *or* **efectuó gestiones para adoptar un niño** he went through the procedure for adopting a child; **su apoyo a las gestiones de paz** their support for the peace process; **las gestiones realizadas por ellos** the action taken by them 2 (Com, Fin) management 3 (Adm, Gob) administration 4 **gestiones** *fpl* (negociaciones) negotiations (*pl*)
gestionar [A1] *vt* 1 (diligenciar, tratar de obtener) ‹*compra/préstamo*› to negotiate; **le están gestionando el permiso de trabajo** they are getting his work permit sorted out *o* arranged; **estoy gestionando el traslado a Granada** I'm trying to get a transfer to Granada 2 (administrar): **el gobierno gestiona este impuesto** the government administers this tax
gesto *m*
A (movimiento) gesture; **hizo un ~ de aprobación con la cabeza** he nodded (his approval); **le hizo un ~ para que se callara** she gestured to him to be quiet; **con un ~ le indicó que se sentara** he motioned to her to sit down
B (liter) (expresión) expression; **tenía el ~ adusto** her face *o* expression was stern; **hacer ~s** to make faces; ***torcer el* ~** to make *o* (BrE) pull a face
C (actitud) gesture; (detalle, atención) gesture
gestor¹ **-tora** *adj* 1 (que tramita): **agencia ~a** agency (*which obtains official documents on clients' behalf*) 2 (que administra) ‹*órgano/comisión*› administrative, managing (*before n*)
gestor² **-tora** *m,f* (para trámites oficiales) agent (*who obtains official documents on clients' behalf*)
gestoría *f* agency (*which obtains official documents on clients' behalf*)
ghetto /'geto/ *m* ghetto
giba *f* (del camello) hump; (de persona) hump
gibado **-da**, **giboso** **-sa** *adj* hunchbacked
Gibraltar *m* Gibraltar
gibraltareño **-ña** *adj/m,f* Gibraltarian
giga *m* (fam) gigabyte; **mi disco duro es de 4.3 ~s** I have a 4.3 gigabyte hard disk
gigante¹ *adj* giant (*before n*)
gigante² **-ta** *m,f* 1 (en cuentos) (*m*) giant; (*f*) giantess; (persona alta) giant 2 (en fiestas populares) giant (*made of papier-maché*) 3 (persona, cosa que destaca) giant
gigantesco **-ca** *adj* huge, gigantic; **fue una empresa gigantesca** it was a massive *o* mammoth undertaking
gigantismo *m* giantism, gigantism
gigantón **-tona** *m,f* 1 (persona) giant 2 (en fiestas populares) giant (*made of papier-maché*)
gigoló, gigolo /ʒivo'lo/ *m* gigolo
gil *mf* (RPl fam *o* vulg) jerk (sl)
gili¹ *adj* (Esp fam) silly, dumb (colloq)
gili² *mf* (Esp fam) nerd (colloq), twit (colloq)
gilipollas¹ *adj inv* (Esp fam *o* vulg): **¡qué ~ es ese tío!** that guy's such a jerk! (sl & pej)
gilipollas² *mf* (*pl* ~) (Esp fam *o* vulg) jerk (sl & pej)
gilipollez *f* (Esp fam *o* vulg) 1 (estupidez): **decir gilipolleces** to talk garbage (AmE) *o* (BrE) rubbish; **no discutáis por esa ~** don't argue over a stupid *o* silly thing like that 2 (acción estúpida): **pagar tanto es una ~** it's stupid paying that much
gimnasia *f* gymnastics; **hago ~ todos los días** I do exercises every day; **los viernes tenemos clase de ~** we have gym *o* (BrE) PE on Fridays

Compuestos

- **gimnasia de mantenimiento** keep-fit
- **gimnasia jazz** (Arg) aerobics
- **gimnasia rítmica** eurhythmics
- **gimnasia rítmica deportiva** rhythmic gymnastics

gimnasio *m* gymnasium, gym
gimnasta *mf* gymnast
gimnástico **-ca** *adj* gymnastic
gimotear [A1] *vi* to whine, whimper
gimoteo *m* whining, whimpering
gincana *f* gymkhana
ginebra *f* gin
Ginebra *f* Geneva
ginecología *f* gynecology*
ginecólogo **-ga** *m,f* gynecologist*
gira *f* 1 (de turismo) tour 2 (Espec) tour; **estar/ir de ~** to be/go on tour 3 (de político) tour, visit
girador **-dora** *m,f* drawer
giralda *f* (veleta) weather vane
girar [A1] *vi*
A 1 «*rueda*» to turn, go around *o* round; «*disco*» to revolve, go around; «*trompo*» to spin; **la tierra gira alrededor del sol** the earth revolves around the sun; **hizo ~ la llave en la cerradura** he turned the key in the lock 2 (darse la vuelta) to turn 3 **~ EN TORNO A algo** «*conversación/debate*» to revolve *o* center* AROUND sth; «*discurso*» to center* *o* focus ON sth
B (torcer, desviarse) to turn; **en la próxima esquina gire a la derecha** take the next right; **giró hacia posiciones conservadoras** he moved to a more conservative stance
■ **girar** *vt*
A ‹*manivela/volante*› to turn; **giró la cabeza** he turned his head
B (Com, Fin) 1 ‹*cheque/letra de cambio*› to draw; **giró un cheque sin fondos** he issued a check without sufficient funds in the account 2 ‹*dinero*› to send; (a través de un banco) to transfer
C (frml) ‹*instrucciones*› to give, to issue (frml)
girasol *m* sunflower
giratorio **-ria** *adj* revolving (*before n*)
giro¹ **-ra** *adj* (AmL) speckled yellow
giro² *m*
A (Mec, Tec) turn
B 1 (Auto) turn; **hizo un ~ a la derecha** she made a right turn 2 (cambio) change of direction; **dieron un ~ hacia una postura más realista** they moved toward(s) a more realistic stance; **un ~ de 180 grados** a volte-face *o* an about-turn 3 (dirección) turn; **no me gusta el ~ que ha tomado esta conversación** I don't like the direction this conversation has taken
C (Fin): **poner** *or* **enviar un ~** (a través de un banco) to transfer money; (por correo) to send a money order

Compuestos

- **giro bancario** (cheque) bank draft, banker's draft; (transferencia) credit transfer
- **giro postal** money order, giro

D (Ling, Lit) expression, turn of phrase
gis *m* (Méx) chalk
gitanería *f* gypsies (*pl*)
gitano¹ **-na** *adj* gypsy (*before n*)
gitano² **-na** *m,f* gypsy

g

gitano
A member of Spain's gypsy community. Gypsies often live in camps and retain their nomadic habits. They have preserved many of their customs and do not usually integrate into the mainstream of Spanish society. Their language is *caló*. Gypsies have been a great influence on flamenco, and many of the best performers are gypsies

glaciación *f* glaciation
glacial *adj* 1 ‹*zona/período*› glacial 2 ‹*viento/temperatura*› icy; ‹*acogida/recibimiento*› icy, frosty
glaciar¹ *adj* ‹*erosión*› glacial; **casquete ~** ice cap
glaciar² *m* glacier
gladiador *m* gladiator
gladiolo *m* gladiolus
glamoroso -sa *adj* glamorous
glamour /'glamur/ *m* glamor*
glándula *f* gland
glandular *adj* glandular
glaseado *m* glaze
glasear [A1] *vt* to glaze
glauco -ca *adj* (liter) glaucous (liter), grayish* green
gleba *f* (terrón) clod; (Hist) glebe
glicerina *f* glycerin
global *adj* 1 (total, general) ‹*informe*› full, comprehensive; ‹*resultado*› overall; ‹*precio/cantidad*› total; ‹*visión/estudio*› global 2 (mundial) global; **repercusiones ~es** global *o* worldwide repercussions 3 (Inf) global
globalismo *m* globalism
globalizar [A4] *vt* (abarcar) to encompass; (extender) to globalize
globo *m*
A 1 (Jueg) balloon; ***estar como un ~*** (fam) to be like a barrel (colloq) 2 (de chicle) bubble 3 (en comics) speech balloon *o* bubble 4 (de lámpara) globe
(Compuesto) **globo ocular** eyeball
B (Aviac, Meteo) balloon
(Compuesto) **globo aerostático/sonda** hot-air/observation balloon
C (mundo) world, globe (journ); **~ terráqueo** *or* **terrestre** globe
D (Dep) (en béisbol) fly; (en tenis) lob; (en rugby) up-and-under
E (Esp fam) (preservativo) rubber (AmE colloq), johnny (BrE colloq)
globulina *f* globulin
glóbulo *m* (cuerpo esférico) globule; (corpúsculo) corpuscle
(Compuesto) **glóbulo blanco/rojo** white/red corpuscle
gloria *f*
A (Relig) glory; **que en ~ esté** God rest her/his soul; ***estar/sentirse en la ~***: **aquí dentro se está en la ~** it's wonderful in here; **me siento en la ~** I'm in seventh heaven
B 1 (fama, honor) glory; **cubrirse de ~** to win glory; **en ~ y majestad** triumphantly, victoriously 2 (acontecimiento) glorious moment
C (personalidad) figure; **es una de las ~s del deporte** he is one of the great sporting figures *o* heroes
gloriarse [A17] *v pron* (liter) **~ DE algo** to boast OF sth
glorieta *f* 1 (plaza) square; (Auto) traffic circle (AmE), roundabout (BrE) 2 (en el jardín) arbor*
glorificación *f* glorification
glorificar [A2] *vt* to glorify
glorioso -sa *adj* (Relig) glorious; ‹*hecho*› glorious; ‹*personaje*› great
glosa *f* gloss, note; **~ marginal** marginal note
glosar [A1] *vt* 1 (Lit) ‹*texto*› to gloss 2 ‹*resultados/informe*› to sum up
glosario *m* glossary
glotis *f* (*pl* ~) glottis
glotón¹ -tona *adj* gluttonous, greedy
glotón² -tona *m,f* glutton
glotonería *f* gluttony
glucosa *f* glucose
gluglú *m* gurgling; **hacer ~** to gurgle
gluten *m* gluten
glúteo *m* gluteus
gnomo *m* gnome
gobelino *m* Gobelin
gobernación *f* (gobierno) government; (en Col) provincial government
gobernador -dora *m,f* (Gob) governor
gobernanta *f* (en un hotel) staff manager; (institutriz) governess
gobernante¹ *adj* ‹*partido/organismo*› ruling (*before n*), governing (*before n*)
gobernante² *mf* leader, ruler; **nuestros ~s** those who govern *o* rule the country
gobernar [A5] *vt* ‹*país*› to govern, rule; ‹*barco*› to steer
■ **gobernar** *vi* (Gob, Pol) to govern; (Náut) to steer
gobierna, gobiernas *see* **gobernar**
gobiernismo *m* (Andes) pro-government stance
gobiernista *mf* (Andes) government supporter
gobierno *m* 1 (Pol) government 2 (ant) (administración) management, administration
(Compuestos)
- **gobierno de concentración** government of national unity
- **gobierno de transición** provisional government

goce *m* 1 (de un derecho, título) enjoyment; **en pleno ~ de sus facultades** in full possession of her faculties 2 (placer) pleasure
godo¹ -da *adj* 1 ‹*rey/pueblo*› Gothic 2 (Col, Ven) (realista) pro-Spanish (*in the War of Independence*) 3 (Col, Ven fam) (conservador) conservative
godo² -da *m,f* 1 (Hist) Goth 2 (fam) (en Canarias) *Spaniard from the mainland* 3 (Col, Ven) (realista) *supporter of the Spanish Crown* 4 (Col, Ven fam) (conservador) conservative
gol *m* goal; **marcar** *or* **meter** *or* **hacer un ~** to score a goal; ***meterle un ~ a algn*** to put one over on sb (colloq)
(Compuesto) **gol average** goal average
golazo *m* (fam) great *o* tremendous goal (colloq)
goleada *f* heavy defeat
goleador¹ -dora *adj* high-scoring
goleador² -dora *m,f* scorer, goal-scorer; **el máximo ~** the top scorer
golear [A1] *vt*: **el Madrid goleó al Osasuna** Madrid thrashed Osasuna; **el portero menos goleado** the goalkeeper who's let in fewest goals
golero -ra *m,f* (CS) goalkeeper
golf *m* golf
golfa *f* (fam) (prostituta) whore (colloq)
golfear [A1] *vi* (esp Esp) (holgazanear) to hang *o* laze around
golfillo -lla *m,f* street urchin
golfista *mf* golfer
golfístico -ca *adj* golf (*before n*)
golfito *m* (AmL) mini-golf, miniature golf
golfo¹ -fa *m,f* 1 (holgazán) good-for-nothing, layabout 2 (fam) (niño travieso) rascal (colloq), little devil (colloq)
golfo² *m* (Geog, Náut) gulf
(Compuestos)
- **Golfo de México** Gulf of Mexico
- **Golfo de Vizcaya** Bay of Biscay
- **Golfo Pérsico** Persian Gulf

golilla *f*
A (Indum) 1 (cuello fruncido) ruff 2 (RPl) (pañuelo) neckerchief
B (arandela) washer
gollete *m* neck (*of a bottle*); ***estar hasta el ~*** (fam) to be fed up to the back teeth (colloq); **no tiene ~** (RPl) it's the limit; **no tiene ~ que llame a estas horas** phoning at this hour is too much (colloq)
golondrina *f* (Zool) swallow; ***una ~ no hace verano*** one swallow does not make a summer
golosa *f* (Col) hopscotch
golosina *f* 1 (exquisitez) tidbit (AmE), titbit (BrE) 2 (dulce) candy (AmE), sweet (BrE)
goloso -sa *adj* (amante de lo dulce): **es muy ~** he has a really sweet tooth
golpe *m*
A (choque, impacto) knock; **se dio un ~ contra la pared** she

knocked into the wall; **me di un ~ en la cabeza** I hit my head; **te vas a dar un ~** you'll hurt yourself; **cerró el libro de un ~** she snapped *o* slammed the book shut; **me dio un ~ en la espalda** he slapped me on the back; **dio unos ~s en la mesa** he tapped on the table; (más fuerte) he knocked on the table; (aún más fuerte) he banged on the table; ***a ~ de*** (Ven) around; ***de ~*** (repentinamente) suddenly; (quizás) (Col fam) maybe, perhaps; **la puerta se abrió/cerró de ~** the door flew open/slammed shut; ***de ~ y porrazo*** (fam) (de repente) suddenly; ***de un ~*** (de una vez) all at once; (de un trago) in one go *o* gulp

B 1 (al pegarle a algn) blow; **le dio** *or* **pegó un ~ en la cabeza** she hit him on the head; **casi lo matan a ~s** they almost beat him to death; **siempre andan a ~s** they're always fighting 2 (marca) bruise, mark

C (Dep) (en golf) stroke; (en tenis) shot

D (desgracia, contratiempo) blow

E (fam) (atraco, timo) job (colloq); **dar el ~** to do the job

F (fam) (ocurrencia, salida) funny *o* witty remark; ***dar el ~ con algo*** (fam): **con esa indumentaria seguro que das el ~** you'll be a sensation *o* a knockout in that outfit

Compuestos

- **golpe bajo** (en boxeo) punch below the belt
- **golpe de efecto**: **su dimisión no causó el ~ de ~ que esperaba** his resignation did not create the dramatic effect he had hoped for
- **golpe de estado** coup (d'état)
- **golpe de gracia** coup de grâce
- **golpe de suerte** stroke of luck
- **golpe de vista** glance, look
- **golpe franco** (en fútbol) free kick; (en hockey) free hit
- **golpe maestro** masterstroke

golpear [A1] *vt*

A ‹*objeto/superficie*›: **no golpees la puerta al salir** don't slam *o* bang the door as you go out; **la lluvia golpeaba los cristales** the rain beat against the window panes; **golpeó el atril con la batuta** he tapped the music stand with his baton; **golpeó la mesa con el puño** he banged his fist on the table

B 1 (chocar) to hit; **algo me golpeó en la cara** something hit me in the face 2 (maltratar) to beat, hit; **su marido la golpea** her husband hits her 3 (sacudir): **la vida la ha golpeado duramente** life has treated her harshly *o* (liter) has dealt her some harsh blows; **una nueva tragedia golpea al país** a fresh tragedy has hit *o* struck the country

■ **golpear** *vi* 1 (dar, pegar) **~ CONTRA algo** to beat AGAINST sth 2 (AmS) (llamar a la puerta) to knock 3 (en fútbol americano) to scrimmage

■ **golpearse** *v pron* 1 (*refl*) (accidentalmente) ‹*cabeza/codo*› to bang, hit 2 (AmL) «*puerta*» to bang

golpeo *m* scrimmage

golpismo *m*: **se pronunciaron en contra del ~** they declared their opposition to any possible coup; **para mantener el ~ a raya** to keep in check any pro-coup tendencies

golpista¹ *adj*: **una minoría ~** a minority in favor of a coup; **los militares ~s** the soldiers who took part in the coup

golpista² *mf*: **los ~s serán enjuiciados** those who took part in the coup will be tried; **los ~s dentro del ejército** those within the army who are/were in favor of a coup

golpiza *f* (AmL) beating; **darle una ~ a algn** to give sb a real beating

goma *f*

A 1 (Bot) gum 2 (caucho) rubber; **suelas de ~** rubber soles 3 (pegamento) glue, gum

Compuestos

- **goma de mascar** chewing gum
- **goma de pegar** glue, gum
- **goma espuma** foam rubber

B 1 (para sujetar) rubber band 2 (de borrar) eraser 3 (RPl) (neumático) tire* 4 (fam) (condón) rubber (AmE colloq), johnny (BrE colloq)

C (en béisbol) home plate

D (AmC fam) (resaca) hangover; **ando de ~** I'm hungover

gomero *m* (CS) (Bot) rubber plant

gomina *f* hair gel

gomita *f*

A (para sujetar) rubber band

B (Chi, Méx, Ven) (dulce) gumdrop, gum (BrE)

gomoso -sa *adj* ‹*líquido*› gummy, sticky; ‹*textura*› rubbery

góndola *f* (embarcación) gondola; (Aviac) gondola

gondolero *m* gondolier

gong (*pl* **gongs**), **gongo** *m* gong

gonorrea *f* gonorrhea*

gordinflón¹ -flona *adj* (fam) chubby (colloq), roly-poly (colloq)

gordinflón² -flona *m,f* (fam) fatty (colloq), fatso (colloq)

gordo¹ -da *adj*

A ‹*persona/piernas*› fat; **siempre ha sido ~** he's always been overweight *o* fat; **estás más ~** you've put on weight; **es más bien gordita** she's quite plump; ***me/le/nos cae ~*** (fam) I/she/we can't stand him (colloq)

B (grueso) ‹*libro*› thick; ‹*lana/calcetines*› thick; ‹*suéter*› thick, chunky

C ‹*carne/tocino*› fatty

D (fam) (importante, serio) big; **algo ~ debe haber ocurrido** something big *o* serious must have happened; **fue una metedura de pata de las gordas** it was a terrible *o* a huge blunder (colloq); ***armarse la gorda*** (fam): **y entonces se armó la ~** and then the feathers began to fly

gordo² -da *m,f*

A 1 (persona) (*m*) fat man; (*f*) fat woman; **ese ~ simpático** that nice, rather fat man *o* guy; **es un gordito precioso** he's a cute, chubby little thing 2 (fam) (como apelativo ofensivo) fatso (colloq), fatty (colloq) 3 (AmL) (fam) (como apelativo cariñoso) dear, love;

B **gordo** *m* (Jueg) (premio mayor) jackpot, first prize (*in the state lottery*)

> **El Gordo**
>
> In Spain, the name given to the big prizes in the **Lotería Nacional** and **Lotería Primitiva**, in particular the prize for the Christmas draw of the *Lotería Nacional*. In Latin America it also means a big lottery prize

gordura *f* 1 (grasa) fat 2 (exceso de peso): **me preocupa su ~** I'm worried about how fat he is

gorgojo *m* weevil

gorgoritear [A1] *vi* «*pájaro*» to warble, trill; «*persona*» to trill

gorgorito *m* trill; **cantar haciendo ~s** to trill *o* warble

gorgotear [A1] *vi* (en cañería) to gurgle; (al hervir) to bubble

gorgoteo *m* (en cañería) gurgling; (al hervir) bubbling

gorila¹ *adj* (fam) fascist, dictatorial

gorila² *m*

A (Zool) gorilla

B (fam) 1 (matón) thug, bully-boy (colloq) 2 (guardaespaldas) heavy (colloq) 3 (reaccionario) fascist 4 (Esp) (en un club) bouncer

gorjear [A1] *vi* «*pájaro*» to trill, warble; «*niño*» to gurgle

gorjeo *m* (de pájaro) trill, warbling; (de niño) gurgling

gorra *f* cap; (con visera) peaked cap; (de bebé) bonnet; ***de ~*** (fam) ‹*vivir/comer*› gratis, for free; ***pasar la ~*** (fam) to pass the hat (around)

gorrear [A1] *vt*

A (fam) (pedir) to scrounge (colloq); **me gorreó $20** he scrounged $20 off me

B (Chi fam) ‹*conyuge*› to cheat on (colloq)

■ **gorrear** *vi* (fam) to scrounge (colloq)

gorrero -ra *m,f* (AmL fam) (aprovechado) scrounger (colloq)

gorrino -na *m,f* 1 (Agr, Zool) pig 2 (fam) (persona — sucia) pig (colloq); (— despreciable) swine (colloq)

gorrión *m* sparrow

gorro *m* cap; ***estar hasta el ~*** (fam) to be fed up to the back teeth (colloq); ***ponerle el ~ a algn*** (Chi fam) to cheat on sb (colloq)

Compuestos

- **gorro de baño** (para nadar) bathing cap; (para la ducha) shower cap
- **gorro de cocinero** chef's hat

gorrón -rrona *m,f* (Esp, Méx fam) scrounger (colloq)

gorronear [A1] *vt/vi* (Esp, Méx fam) to scrounge (colloq)

g

gota *f*
A (de líquido) drop; **~s de sudor** beads of sweat; **no tiene ni ~ de sentido común** she hasn't an ounce of common sense; ***la ~ que colma*** *or* ***rebasa el vaso*** the last straw; ***parecerse/ser como dos ~s de agua*** to be as like as two peas in a pod; ***sudar la ~ gorda*** (fam) (transpirar) to sweat buckets; (trabajar mucho) to sweat blood
(Compuestos)
- **gota a gota** *m* (Med) drip
- **gota de leche** (AmL) *child welfare institution*

B (enfermedad) gout
C **gotas** *fpl* (remedio) drops (*pl*)
gotear [A1] *vi* ‹‹*líquido/grifo*›› to drip; ‹‹*vela*›› to drip; ‹‹*cañería*›› to leak
■ **gotear** *v impers* (lloviznar) to spit, drizzle
goteo *m* (de líquido, grifo) dripping; (de vela) dripping
gotera *f* 1 (filtración) leak 2 (mancha) damp stain
gotero *m* 1 (Med) drip 2 (AmL) (Farm) dropper
gótico[1] **-ca** *adj* Gothic
gótico[2] *m* Gothic
gourde *m* gourde (*Haitian unit of currency*)
gourmet /gur'me/ *mf* (*pl* **-mets**) gourmet
gozada *f* (fam): **la excursión fue una ~** the trip was fantastic (colloq); **¡qué ~! ¡qué bien se está aquí!** mmm! it's bliss *o* wonderful here!
gozador -dora *adj* (AmL) fun-loving
gozar [A4] *vi*: **los niños gozan en la playa** the children love being on the beach; **parece que goza con la desgracia ajena** he seems to take pleasure in other people's misfortunes; **~ DE algo** to enjoy sth; **goza de perfecta salud** he enjoys perfect health
■ **gozar** *vt* (arc *o* liter) (en sentido sexual) to enjoy (arch *or* liter)
gozne *m* hinge
gozo *m*
A 1 (alegría) joy; ***no caber en sí de ~*** to be beside oneself with joy 2 (placer) pleasure, enjoyment
B **gozos** *mpl* (Relig) verses (*pl*)
gozoso -sa *adj* happy, content
gozque *mf* (Col) (Zool) mongrel
gr. (= **gramo**) g, gr.
grabación *f* recording; **~ en video** video recording
grabado[1] **-da** *adj* ‹*música*› recorded, taped
grabado[2] *m* engraving
(Compuestos)
- **grabado al aguafuerte** etching
- **grabado en cobre** copperplate
- **grabado en madera** woodcut
- **grabado en relieve** embossing

grabador[1] **-dora** *adj* 1 ‹*aparato*› recording (*before n*) 2 (Art) ‹*plancha*› engraving (*before n*)
grabador[2] *m* tape recorder
grabador[3] **-dora** *m,f*
A (Art) engraver
B **grabadora** *f* 1 (casa discográfica) record company 2 (magnetófono) tape recorder
(Compuesto) **grabadora DVD** DVD recorder
grabar [A1] *vt* 1 (Audio, TV) to record 2 (Art) to engrave
■ **grabar** *vi* 1 (Audio, TV) to record 2 (Art) to engrave; **~ al aguafuerte** to etch; **~ en relieve** to emboss
■ **grabarse** *v pron* to be engraved; **sus palabras se me ~on en la memoria** her words are etched on my memory; **su cara se me quedó grabada** I'll never forget her face
gracejada *f* (Méx) bad joke
gracejo *m*: **habla con ~ en cualquier ambiente** she talks with unaffected ease in any situation; **se expresa con mucho ~** he expresses himself with great fluency
gracia *f*
(*Sentido* **I**)
A (comicidad): **yo no le veo la ~** I don't think it's funny; **cuenta las cosas con mucha ~** he has a very amusing way of telling things; **¡pues sí que tiene ~ (la cosa)!** (iró & fam) well, that's great, isn't it! (iro & colloq); ***hacer ~*** (+ *me/te/le etc*): **¡me hizo una ~ ...!** it was so funny ...!; **me hace ~ que digas eso** it's funny you should say that; **no me hace ninguna ~ tener que ir** I don't relish the idea of having to go
B 1 (chiste) joke; (broma) joke, trick; ***reírle las ~s a algn*** to humor* sb 2 (de niño) party piece
C 1 (encanto, donaire): **baila con mucha ~** she's a very graceful dancer; **un vestido sin ~** a very plain dress 2 (habilidad especial): **tiene mucha ~ para arreglar flores** she has a real gift *o* flair for flower arranging
D (ant) (nombre) name
E 1 (favor, merced) grace; **por la ~ de Dios** by the grace of God; **le concedieron tres meses de ~** they gave him three months' grace 2 (disposición benévola) favor*; ***caer en ~***: **le has caído en ~** he has taken a liking *o* (colloq) a shine to you 3 (clemencia) clemency
F (Relig) grace; **estar en estado de ~** to be in a state of grace; **perder la ~** to fall from grace
G (Mit) **las tres ~s** the (three) Graces
(*Sentido* **II**) **gracias** *fpl* 1 (expresión de agradecimiento): **sólo quería darle las ~s** I just wanted to thank you; **demos ~s a Dios** let us give thanks to God 2 (*como interj*) thank you, thanks (colloq); **muchas ~s** thank you very much, thanks a lot (colloq); **un millón de ~s por tu ayuda** I can't thank you enough for your help 3 **gracias a** thanks to; **~s a Dios** thank God; **llegamos bien, pero ~s a que ...** we arrived on time, but only because ...
grácil *adj* graceful
graciosamente *adv*
A ‹*moverse/bailar*› gracefully
B ‹*expresarse*› amusingly; **una historia ~ contada** an amusingly related story
C ‹*conceder/otorgar*› graciously
gracioso[1] **-sa** *adj*
A (divertido) ‹*chiste/persona*› funny; **¡qué ~!** how funny!; **lo ~ del caso es que ...** the funny *o* amusing thing about it is that ...; **sería ~ que nos hicieran pagar si nos han invitado** (iró) that would be great, making us pay after they'd invited us (colloq & iro)
B 1 (atractivo) ‹*cara/figura*› attractive; **las pecas le dan un aspecto muy ~** those freckles make her look really cute *o* sweet 2 **su Graciosa Majestad** her gracious Majesty
gracioso[2] **-sa** *m,f*: **el ~ de tu hermano ...** that joker of a brother of yours ...; ***hacerse el ~*** to play the fool
grada *f*
A (peldaño) step
B **gradas** *fpl* (Dep) stand, grandstand
gradación *f* (Art, Mús) gradation
gradería *f*, (Esp) **graderío** *m* stands (*pl*); **la ~ cubierta** the covered stands
gradiente *f* (AmL) (pendiente) slope, gradient
grado *m*
A 1 (nivel, cantidad) degree; **el ~ de confusión reinante** the degree of confusion that prevails; **el asunto se ha complicado en** *or* (AmL) **a tal ~ ...** things have become so complicated ...; ***en ~ sumo***: **me preocupó en ~ sumo** it caused me great concern; **nos complace en ~ sumo comunicarle que ...** it gives us great pleasure to inform you that ... 2 (de parentesco) degree; **primo en segundo ~** second cousin
B (de escalafón) grade; **un oficial de ~ superior** a high-ranking officer
C (disposición): **de buen/mal ~** willingly/unwillingly
D 1 (Fís, Meteo) degree; **estamos a tres ~s bajo cero** it's three degrees below zero 2 (Geog, Mat) degree; **un ángulo de 60 ~s** an angle of 60 degrees; **25 ~s de latitud** 25 degrees latitude 3 (Vin) degree
(Compuesto) **grado centígrado** *or* **Celsius/Fahrenheit** degree centigrade *o* Celsius/Fahrenheit
E 1 (esp AmL) (Educ) (curso, año) year 2 (título): **tiene el ~ de licenciado** he has a degree
graduable *adj* adjustable
graduación *f* 1 (acción de regular) adjustment 2 (de bebida alcohólica) alcohol content 3 (Mil) rank; **un militar de alta ~** a high-ranking officer 4 (Educ) graduation
graduado[1] **-da** *adj* 1 ‹*gafas/lentes*› prescription (*before n*) 2 ‹*termómetro*› graduated
graduado[2] **-da** *m,f* (Educ) graduate
gradual *adj* gradual
graduar [A18] *vt* 1 (regular) to adjust 2 (marcar) ‹*instrumento/termómetro*› to calibrate
■ **graduarse** *v pron* 1 (Educ) to graduate 2 (Mil) to take a

commission; **acaba de ~se de capitán** he has just been commissioned as a captain

graffiti /gra'fiti/, **grafiti** *mpl* graffiti

grafía *f* spelling

gráfica *f* graph

gráfico¹ -ca *adj* 1 (Art, Impr) graphic 2 ‹*relato/narración*› graphic; ‹*gesto*› expressive

gráfico² *m* 1 (Mat) graph 2 (Inf) graphic

(Compuesto) **gráfico de barras** bar chart

grafista *mf* graphic artist, graphic designer

grafito *m* graphite

grafología *f* graphology

gragea *f* 1 (Farm) tablet 2 (Coc) small candy (AmE) *o* (BrE) sweet; **~s de chocolate** chocolate drops

Gral. *m* (= **General**) Gen.

grama *f* (AmC, Ven) (césped) lawn

gramática *f* (disciplina) grammar; (libro) grammar (book)

(Compuesto) **gramática parda** (fam): **tiene mucha ~ ~** he's pretty smart *o* worldly-wise

gramatical *adj* grammatical

gramático -ca *m,f* grammarian

gramo *m* gram

gramófono *m*, **gramola** *f* (ant) gramophone (dated)

gran *adj*: *ver* **grande¹**

grana *f*

A (Zool) (cochinilla) cochineal; (quermés) kermes

B 1 (tinte) cochineal; **ponerse rojo como la ~** to turn (as) red as a beet (AmE), to go as red as a beetroot (BrE) 2 (color) deep red

granada *f*

A (Bot) pomegranate

B (Arm, Mil) grenade

(Compuestos)

- **granada de mano** hand grenade
- **granada de mortero** mortar shell

Granada *f* (en España) Granada; (en el Caribe) Grenada

granadero *m*

A (Mil) grenadier

B (Méx) (policía antimotines) *gen* **~s** riot police

granadilla *f* (fruta — redonda, oscura) passion fruit; (— más grande, amarilla) granadilla

granado¹ -da *adj* select; **lo más ~ de la sociedad** the cream of society

granado² *m* pomegranate tree

granar [A1] *vi* to seed

granate¹ *adj inv* deep-red (*before n*)

granate² *m* (Min) garnet; (color) deep red

Gran Bretaña *f* Great Britain

grande¹ *adj* [**gran** *is used before singular nouns*]

A 1 (en dimensiones) large, big; ‹*boca/nariz*› big; **un tipo ~** a big guy 2 (en demasía) too big; **me queda** *or* **me está ~** it's too big for me; ***quedarle ~ a algn*** ‹‹*puesto/responsabilidad*›› to be too much for sb

B (alto) tall; **¡qué ~ está Andrés!** isn't Andrés tall!

C (Geog): **el Gran Santiago** Greater Santiago

D (en edad): **los más ~s pueden ir solos** the older *o* bigger ones can go on their own; **cuando sea ~** when I grow up; **ya son ~s** they are all grown up now

E (*delante del n*) 1 (notable, excelente) great; **un gran hombre/vino** a great man/wine 2 (poderoso) big; **los ~s bancos** the big banks; **los ~s señores feudales** the great feudal lords; ***a lo ~*** in style

F 1 (en intensidad, grado) great; **me causó una gran pena** it caused me great sadness; **un día de gran calor** a very hot day; **¡me llevé un susto más ~ ... !** I got such a fright!; **una gran explosión** a powerful explosion; **es un gran honor** it is a great honor; **una temporada de gran éxito** a very *o* a highly successful season; **son ~s amigos** they're great friends 2 (uso enfático): **eso es una gran verdad** that is absolutely true; **eres un grandísimo sinvergüenza** you're a real swine (colloq); **¡qué mentira más ~!** that's a complete lie!

G 1 (en número) ‹*familia*› large, big; ‹*clase*› big; **la gran parte** *or* **mayoría de los votantes** the great *o* vast majority of the voters 2 (elevado): **a gran velocidad** at high *o* great speed; **volar a gran altura** to fly at a great height; **un edificio de gran altura** a very tall building; **un gran número de personas** a large number of people; **objetos de gran valor** objects of great value; ***en ~***: **lo pasamos en ~** we had a great time (colloq)

(Compuestos)

- **grandes almacenes** *mpl* department store
- **gran danés** *m* Great Dane
- **Gran Guerra** *f*: **la ~ ~** the Great War, World War I
- **gran ópera** *f* grand opera
- **Gran Premio** *m* Grand Prix
- **gran público** *m*: **el ~ ~** the general public

grande² *m,f*

A (de la industria, el comercio) big *o* leading name

B 1 (mayor): **quiero ir con los ~s** I want to go with the big boys/girls; **la grande ya está casada** their eldest (daughter) is already married 2 (adulto): **los ~s** the grown-ups

(Compuesto) **Grande de España** (Spanish) nobleman

grandeza *f*

A (excelencia, nobleza) nobility

(Compuestos)

- **grandeza de alma** (liter) magnanimity
- **grandeza de ánimo** (liter) valor* (liter)

B 1 (dignidad de Grande) rank of grandee 2 (conjunto de Grandes): **la ~** the (Spanish) nobility *o* grandees

grandilocuencia *f* grandiloquence

grandilocuente *adj* grandiloquent

grandiosidad *f* grandeur

grandioso -sa *adj* 1 ‹*espectáculo/obra*› impressive, magnificent 2 (rimbombante) ‹*gesto/palabras*› grandiose

grandullón -llona *m,f* (fam) big kid (colloq)

grandulón -lona *m,f* (AmL fam) big kid (colloq)

granel: **a ~** (*loc adv*) 1 (Com) (suelto) **comprar/vender a ~** ‹*vino/aceite*› to buy/sell ... by the liter (*o* pint *etc*); ‹*galletas/nueces*› to buy/sell ... loose; (en grandes cantidades) to buy/sell ... in bulk 2 (en abundancia): **había comida y bebida a ~** there was loads *o* stacks of food and drink (colloq)

granero *m* granary, barn

granítico -ca *adj* 1 (Geol) ‹*formación*› granitic, granite (*before n*) 2 (frml) (indestructible) indestructible; (inquebrantable) unshakable

granito *m* (roca) granite

granizada *f* hailstorm

granizado *m* (bebida) *drink served on crushed ice*

granizar [A4] *v impers* to hail

granizo *m* (grano, bola) hailstone; (conjunto) hail

granja *f* (Agr) farm

(Compuestos)

- **granja agrícola** arable farm
- **granja avícola** poultry farm
- **granja escuela** farm school

granjear [A1] *vt* to earn, win; **esto le granjeó fama y respeto** this earned *o* won her fame and respect

■ **granjearse** *v pron* to earn, win

granjero -ra *m,f* farmer

grano *m*

A 1 (de azúcar, trigo, arroz) grain; (de café) bean; (de mostaza) seed; **~s de pimienta** peppercorns; ***ir al ~*** (fam) to get (straight) to the point; ***separar el ~ de la paja*** to separate the wheat from the chaff 2 (de arena) grain; ***aportar su (or mi etc) granito de arena*** to do one's bit (colloq)

B (Med) spot, pimple (esp AmE)

C 1 (de la piedra, la madera) grain 2 (Fot) grain

> **gran reserva**
>
> *Vinos de gran reserva* are those of the highest quality, selected from a particularly good vintage. To qualify for this designation, red wines must have been aged in cask and bottle for a minimum of five years, and white wines for four years. *See also* reserva

granuja *mf* rascal

granulación *f* granulation

granulado -da *adj* granulated

granular [A1] *vt* to granulate

gránulo *m* granule

granuloso -sa *adj* granular

g

grapa *f*
A 1 (para papeles) staple; (para cables) cable clip 2 (Arquit) cramp iron
B (CS) (aguardiente) grappa

grapadora *f* stapler

grapar [A1] *vt* to staple

grasa *f*
A 1 (Biol, Coc) fat; **la comida tenía mucha ~** the food was very greasy; **un corte de carne con mucha ~** a very fatty cut of meat 2 (suciedad) grease; **está lleno de ~** it's all greasy 3 (Mec) grease
B (Méx) (betún) shoe polish; **dale ~ a tus zapatos** polish your shoes
C **grasa** *mf* (RPl fam) (ordinario): **es un ~** he's so common

grasiento -ta *adj* 1 (Coc) greasy 2 ‹*pelo/cutis*› greasy

grasitud *f* (AmL) greasiness

graso -sa *adj* 1 ‹*pelo/cutis*› greasy 2 (Coc) greasy, oily, fatty; **queso ~** full fat cheese

grasoso -sa *adj* (AmL) ▸**grasiento**

gratén *m*: **al ~** au gratin

gratificación *f* 1 (bonificación) bonus; (recompensa) reward 2 (satisfacción) gratification

gratificador -dora *adj* (AmL) rewarding, gratifying (frml)

gratificante *adj* rewarding, gratifying (frml)

gratificar [A2] *vt* 1 ‹*persona*› to give … a bonus 2 ‹*deseo/necesidad*› to gratify, satisfy 3 (recompensar) to give … a reward; Ⓢ **se gratificará** reward offered

gratinado -da *adj* au gratin

gratinador *m* grill

gratis[1] *adj* free; **es ~** it is free (of charge)

gratis[2] *adv* free; **entramos ~** we got in free

gratitud *f* gratitude

grato -ta *adj* pleasant; **me es ~ comunicarles que …** I am pleased to inform you that …

gratuidad *f* (calidad de ser gratis): **se mantendrá la ~ del servicio** service will continue to be free

gratuitamente *adv* 1 (sin pagar) free 2 ‹*insultar*› gratuitously

gratuito -ta *adj* 1 (gratis) free 2 (infundado) ‹*afirmaciones*› unwarranted; ‹*insulto*› gratuitous

grava *f* gravel

gravamen *m* (impuesto) tax; (carga) burden; (sobre finca, casa) encumbrance
(Compuesto) **gravamen arancelario** customs duty

gravar [A1] *vt* 1 (con impuesto) ‹*ingresos/productos*› to tax 2 (con otra carga): **~ con una hipoteca** to mortgage; **las cargas que gravan la propiedad** the encumbrances *o* charges on the property

grave *adj*
A ‹*enfermo*› seriously ill; ‹*herida/enfermedad*› serious; **estar (en estado) ~** to be seriously ill
B ‹*situación/asunto/error*› serious
C 1 ‹*tono/expresión/gesto*› grave, solemn 2 ‹*voz*› deep
D (Ling) ‹*acento*› grave; ‹*palabra*› paroxytone

gravedad *f*
A (Med) seriousness; **la ~ de sus lesiones** the seriousness *o* severity of her wounds; **está herido de ~** he is seriously injured
B (de situación, problema) seriousness, gravity; **es un asunto de mucha ~** it is a very serious matter
C (de tono, expresión) gravity, seriousness
D (Fís) gravity

grávido -da *adj* 1 (frml) ‹*mujer*› pregnant 2 (liter) (lleno) **~ DE algo** full OF sth

gravilla *f* gravel

gravitación *f*
A (Fís) gravitation
B (CS) (influencia) influence

gravitar [A1] *vi*
A 1 (Fís) to gravitate 2 **~ EN TORNO A algo** «*conflicto*» to center* AROUND sth; «*polémica*» to center* ON sth
B 1 (apoyarse) «*peso/carga*» to rest; **toda la responsabilidad gravita sobre él** all the responsibility rests on his shoulders 2 (influir) **~ SOBRE** *or* **EN algo** to influence *o* affect sth 3 «*peligro/amenaza*» **~ SOBRE** *or* **EN algo** to hang OVER sth

gravoso -sa *adj* (frml) costly

graznar [A1] *vi* «*cuervo*» to caw; «*ganso*» to honk; «*pato*» to quack

graznido *m* (del cuervo) caw; (del ganso) honk; (del pato) quack

Grecia *f* Greece

greda *f* (para cerámica) clay

gregario -ria *adj* ‹*animal*› gregarious; ‹*persona*› sociable, gregarious

grei *m* (Col) grapefruit

greifrú, graifrú *mf* (*pl* **-frús**) (AmC, Ven fam) grapefruit

gremial[1] *adj* 1 (profesional) ‹*asociación*› professional 2 (AmL) (sindical) union (*before n*)

gremial[2] *f* (AmL) union

gremialista *mf* (AmL) trade unionist

gremio *m* 1 (Hist) guild 2 (de oficio, profesión): **protestas del ~ de los panaderos** protests by the bakers; **cualquiera que sea del ~ lo entenderá** anyone in the trade/profession will understand it 3 (CS, Per) (sindicato) union

greña *f* 1 (enredo) tangle; ***andar a la ~*** (Méx fam) to be at loggerheads 2 **en greña** (Méx) ‹*trigo*› unthreshed; ‹*plata/azúcar*› unrefined; ‹*tabaco*› leaf (*before n*); ***montar a la ~*** (Méx) to ride bareback 3 **greñas** *fpl* untidy hair; ***agarrarse de las ~s*** (AmL fam): **terminaron agarrándose de las ~s** they ended up at each others' throats

gres *m* (arcilla) potter's clay; (cerámica) earthenware

gresca *f* (fam) (jaleo) rumpus (colloq); (riña) fight

grey *f* 1 (liter) (rebaño) flock 2 (Relig) flock (liter) 3 (grupo de personas): **una ~ de famosos** (period) a galaxy of famous people

griego[1] **-ga** *adj/m,f* Greek

griego[2] *m* (idioma) Greek

grieta *f* crack

grifa *f* (arg) (hachís) dope (sl)

grifería *f* bathroom fittings (*pl*)

grifo[1] *m*
A (Esp) (del lavabo, de la bañera) faucet (AmE), tap (BrE); **abrir/cerrar el ~** to turn the faucet *o* tap on/off
B (Per) (gasolinera) filling station
C (Chi) (de incendios) fire hydrant, fireplug (AmE)

grifo[2] **-fa** *adj* (Méx fam) high (colloq)

grifo[3] **-fa** *m,f* (Méx fam) pothead (sl), dopehead (sl)

grill /gril/ *m* (electrodoméstico) grill

grillete *m* (Náut) shackle; (de los presos) fetter, shackle

grillo *m*
A (Zool) cricket
B **grillos** *mpl* (de los presos) fetters (*pl*), shackles (*pl*)

grima *f* (Esp): **los caracoles me dan ~** snails make my flesh crawl; **un chirrido que me da ~** a screech that sets my teeth on edge

gringada *f* (AmL fam & pey) 1 (conjunto) gringos (*pl*), foreigners (*pl*) 2 (acción): **la típica ~** the typical thing a gringo *o* foreigner does

gringo[1] **-ga** *adj* 1 (AmL fam & pey) gringo, foreign (*of or relating to a* **gringo**[2] 1) 2 (Andes fam) (rubio) fair-haired

gringo[2] **-ga** *m,f* 1 (AmL fam & pey) (extranjero) gringo, foreigner (*from a non-Spanish speaking country*); (norteamericano) Yank (colloq & pej), Yankee (colloq & pej) 2 (Andes fam) (rubio) (*m*) fair-haired boy/man; (*f*) fair-haired girl/woman

Gringolandia *f* (Andes fam & pey) Yankeeland (colloq & pej)

gripa *f* (Col, Méx) ▸**gripe**

gripal *adj* ‹*síntoma*› flu (*before n*)

gripe *f* flu; **tener ~** to have (the) flu; **está con (la) ~** she has the flu
(Compuesto) **gripe aviar** *or* **de pollo** bird flu

griposo -sa *adj* (fam): **estoy (medio) griposa** I'm coming down with (the) flu

gris[1] *adj* ‹*color/ojos/traje*› gray*; ‹*día*› gray*, overcast; **zapatos ~ oscuro** dark gray shoes

gris[2] *m* (color) gray*
(Compuesto) **gris marengo/metálico** 1 *m* charcoal/metallic gray* 2 *adj inv* charcoal/metallic gray*

grisáceo -cea *adj* grayish*

gritadera *f* (Andes, Méx fam) shrieking, yelling

gritar [A1] *vi* to shout; **no hace falta que grites** there's no need to shout *o* yell; **~ de dolor** to scream with pain; **~ de alegría** to shout for joy; **empezó a ~ pidiendo ayuda** he started shouting for help; **gritaba como un desaforado** he was screaming at the top of his voice; **~le A algn** to shout AT sb; (para llamarlo) to shout (out) TO sb

■ **gritar** *vt* to shout; **gritaban consignas en contra del gobierno** they were shouting anti-government slogans; **—¡cuidado! —gritó** watch out! — she shouted *o* cried

gritería *f*
A (bullicio) shouting, clamor*
B (AmC) (Relig) *festival to celebrate the Immaculate Conception*

griterío *m* shouting, clamor*

grito *m*
A 1 (de persona): **un ~ de dolor/terror** a cry of pain/terror; **dio un ~ de alegría/sorpresa** she let out a whoop of joy/a gasp of astonishment; **~s de protesta** shouts *o* cries of protest; **dame un ~ si ...** give me a shout if ...; **siempre habla a ~s** he always talks at the top of his voice; ***a ~ limpio*** *or* ***pelado*** (fam) at the top of one's voice; ***pedir*** *or* ***estar pidiendo algo a ~s*** (fam) to be crying out for sth (colloq); ***poner el ~ en el cielo*** (fam) to hit the roof *o* ceiling (colloq); ***ser el último ~*** to be the last word in fashion 2 (de pájaro, animal) call, cry
B (Hist) **el ~ (de Independencia)** declaration of independence (*in some Latin American countries*)

gritón -tona *adj* (fam): **es muy gritona** she always shouts (when she talks), she talks very loudly

groenlandés -desa *adj* of/from Greenland

Groenlandia *f* Greenland

groggy /ˈgrovi/, **grogui** *adj* (fam) (atontado, medio dormido) groggy; (por un golpe) dazed, stunned

grosella *f* redcurrant

grosería *f* 1 (acción): **fue una ~ de su parte** it was very rude of him 2 (comentario, dicho): **¡qué ~!** how rude!; **lo castigaron por decir ~s** he was punished for being coarse *o* crude

grosero¹ -ra *adj* 1 (descortés) ‹*persona/comportamiento*› rude, ill-mannered; ‹*lenguaje*› rude 2 (vulgar) crude

grosero² -ra *m,f*: **es un ~** (vulgar) he's so vulgar *o* crude!; (descortés) he's so rude!

grosor *m* thickness

grotesco -ca *adj* ‹*personaje/mueca*› grotesque; ‹*espectáculo*› hideous, grotesque

grúa *f* 1 (Const) crane 2 (Auto) (de taller) wrecker (AmE), breakdown van (BrE); (de la policía) tow truck; **se lo llevó la ~** it was towed (away)

grueso¹ -sa *adj* 1 ‹*persona*› (euf) stout 2 ‹*dedos/labios*› thick 3 ‹*jersey/papel*› thick; ‹*cristal/pared*› thick

grueso² *m* 1 (grosor) thickness 2 (parte principal): **el ~ de la manifestación** the main body of the demonstration; **el ~ de la población** the majority of the population

grulla *f* crane

grullo¹ -lla *adj* (Méx) gray*

grullo² -lla *m,f* (Méx) (Zool) gray* horse/mule, gray*

grumete *m* cabin boy

grumo *m* lump

grumoso -sa *adj* lumpy

gruñido *m* 1 (del cerdo) grunt; (del perro) growl 2 (fam) (de persona) grunt

gruñir [I9] *vi* 1 «*cerdo*» to grunt; «*perro*» to growl 2 (fam) «*persona*» to grumble; **siempre está gruñendo** she's always grumbling

gruñón¹ -ñona *adj* (fam) grumpy (colloq)

gruñón² -ñona *m,f* (fam) grump (colloq), grouse (colloq)

grupa *f* rump, hindquarters (*pl*)

grupo *m* 1 (de personas, empresas, países) group; (de árboles) clump; **~s sociales** social groups; **en ~** ‹*salir/trabajar*› in a group/in groups 2 (Mús) *tb* **~ musical** group, band

Compuestos
- **grupo de control** control group
- **grupo de interés** *or* **presión** pressure group
- **grupo de trabajo** working party
- **grupo sanguíneo** blood group

grupúsculo *m* (pey) faction

gruta *f* (natural) cave; (artificial) grotto

G.t. = **giro telegráfico**

guabina *f*: *Colombian folk dance*

guabinear [A1] *vi* (Ven fam) to be indecisive, sit on the fence

guaca *f* (Andes) *pre-Columbian tomb*

guacal *m* 1 (Col, Méx, Ven) (caja) wooden crate; *ver tb* ▸ **huacal** 2 (Ven) (medida) crate, crateload 3 (AmC) (calabaza) large gourd (*used for storing tortillas*)

guácala *interj* (Méx fam) yuck! (colloq), ugh! (colloq)

guacamaya *f* (Méx)
A (ave) macaw
B (fam) (persona) loudmouth (colloq)

guacamayo *m* macaw

guacamole, guacamol *m* guacamole

guachaca¹ *adj* (Chi) (fam & pey) ‹*persona*› common

guachaca² *mf* (Chi fam & pey) old soak (colloq & pej)

guachafita *f* (Col, Ven fam): **dejen la ~ y a trabajar** that's enough of this clowning around, get some work done (colloq); **armaron la ~** they caused a real rumpus

guacharaca *f* 1 (fam) (parlanchín) chatterbox (colloq) 2 (Mús) (en Col) *slotted board, played with a metal rod*

guache *m*
A (Art) gouache
B (Col, Ven fam & pey) (canalla) swine (colloq)

guachimán *m* (AmS fam) watchman

guachinango *m* (Méx) red snapper

guacho¹ -cha *adj*
A (Andes, RPl) 1 (fam) ‹*niño*› orphaned; ‹*perro*› stray 2 (fam & pey) ‹*hijo*› bastard (*before n*) (pej)
B (Chi, Per fam) 1 (sin novio, esposo) alone, on one's own 2 ‹*calcetín/guante*› odd

guacho² -cha *m,f*
A (Andes, RPl) 1 (fam) (niño abandonado) orphan, waif; (perro) stray 2 (fam & pey) (hijo ilegítimo) bastard (vulg) 3 (usado en insultos — a un hombre) bastard (pej); (— a una mujer) bitch (pej)
B guacho *m* (Per) (de la lotería) *tenth share in a lottery ticket*

guaco *m* (Andes) pot (*found in pre-Columbian tomb*)

guadaña *f* scythe

guadarnés *m* (ant) 1 (mozo) stable boy, ostler (arch) 2 (lugar) harness room

guagua *f* (fam)
A (Andes) (bebé) baby
B (Cu) (autobús) bus

guaipe *m* (Chi, Per fam) rag

guaira *f*
A (Náut) staysail
B (Andes) (horno) kiln, furnace
C (AmC) (Mús) panpipes (*pl*)

guaje -ja *m,f*
A (Méx fam) sucker (colloq); ***hacerle ~ a algn*** (serle infiel) to cheat on sb (colloq); (engañarlo) to rip sb off (colloq); ***hacerse ~*** to act dumb (colloq)
B guaje *m* (Méx) 1 (planta, fruto) bottle gourd 2 (vasija) gourd 3 (instrumento) maraca (*made from a bottle gourd*)

guajira *f*: *Cuban folk song*

guajiro -ra *m,f* 1 (en Cuba) peasant 2 (en Col, Ven) *native of the Guajira peninsula*

guajolote -ta *m,f* (Méx) turkey

gualdo -da *adj* yellow

gualdrapa *f* horse blanket

gualicho *m* (Bol, CS fam) evil spell

guama *f* (Col fam) (fastidio, molestia) nuisance

guampa *f* (CS) horn

guanábana *f* (fruto) soursop; (árbol) soursop tree

guanaco¹ *adj* (AmL fam) dumb (colloq)

guanaco² *m*
A (Zool) guanaco
B (Chi fam) (de la policía) water cannon

guanera *f* guano deposit

guanero -ra *adj* guano (*before n*)

guango -ga *adj* (Méx fam) ‹*suéter*› baggy; ‹*vestido/pantalones*› loose-fitting; ‹*cuerda/cordel*› slack, loose

guano *m* guano

g

guantada *f*, **guantazo** *m* (fam) slap

guante *m*

A glove; **~s de lana** woollen gloves; ***arrojarle*** *or* ***tirarle el ~ a algn*** to throw down the gauntlet to sb; ***colgar los ~s*** to hang up one's gloves; ***de ~ blanco*** non-violent; ***echarle el ~ a algn*** (fam) to nab sb (colloq); ***estar como un ~*** to be sweet as pie (colloq); ***recoger el ~*** to take up the gauntlet; ***quedar como un ~*** (fam) to fit like a glove; ***tratar a algn con ~ de seda*** *or* (CS) ***con ~ blanco*** to handle *o* treat sb with kid gloves

Compuestos

- **guantes de boxeo** *mpl* boxing gloves (*pl*)
- **guantes de cirujano** *mpl* surgical gloves (*pl*)

B (Dep) (persona) glove man

guantera *f* glove compartment

guapear [A1] *vi*

A (CS, Per fam) (hacerse el valentón) to act tough (colloq)

B (Chi, Ven fam) (mostrar valentía) to be brave, act bravely

g

guapetón -tona *adj* (fam) ‹*chico*› handsome; ‹*chica*› pretty

guapo[1] **-pa** *adj*

A 1 (hermoso) ‹*hombre*› handsome, good-looking; ‹*mujer*› attractive, good-looking; ‹*bebé*› beautiful 2 (elegante) smart, elegant

B 1 (fam) (bravucón): **ponerse ~** to get cocky (colloq) 2 (AmS fam) (valiente) gutsy (colloq)

guapo[2] **-pa** *m,f*

A (hermoso): **es el ~ de la familia** he's the good-looking one of the family

B (fam) 1 (bravucón): **el ~ del barrio** (AmS) the local tough guy (colloq); **hacerse el ~** to act the tough guy (colloq) 2 (valiente): **a ver quién es el ~ que se anima a decírselo** let's see who has the guts to tell him (colloq)

C (Esp) (como apelativo) (fam) 1 (expresando afecto) honey (AmE colloq), love (BrE colloq) 2 (expresando enfado): **oye ~ ¿quién te has creído?** hey pal, who do you think you are? (colloq)

guaquear [A1] *vi* (Andes) to plunder

guaquero -ra *m,f* (Andes) *plunderer of archaeological sites*

guaraca *f* 1 (Col, Per) slingshot (AmE), catapult (BrE) 2 (Chi) (látigo) whip

guarache *m* ▸**huarache**

guáramo *m* (Ven fam) strength of character

guarandinga *f* (AmS fam) 1 (asunto) business (colloq); (cosa) thingamajig (colloq) 2 (enredo, problema): **la ~ esta que tenemos por país** this mixed-up country of ours; **no sigas buscando ~s con esa gente** stop looking for trouble with those people

guarangada *f* (RPl, Ven fam) ▸**grosería 2**

guarango[1] **-ga** *adj* (CS, Ven fam) (grosero) rude, loutish

guarango[2] **-ga** *m,f* (CS, Ven fam) (grosero) lout (colloq)

guaraní[1] *adj/m,f* Guarani

guaraní[2] *m* (idioma) Guarani

> **guaraní**
>
> The name of a people who lived between the rivers Amazon and Plate, and their language.
>
> The Guarani language is an official language in Paraguay. It is also spoken in parts of Argentina, Bolivia, and Brazil. The Jesuit missionaries in Paraguay wrote Guarani dictionaries and grammars, hymns and catechisms. Guarani acquired a symbolic status in Paraguay during the Chaco War with Bolivia, 1932-35. Today many Paraguayans with hardly any indigenous blood speak Guarani better than Spanish

guarapear [A1] *vi* (Per fam) to get plastered (colloq)

guarda[1] *mf* (de museo, parque) keeper; (de edificio público) security guard

Compuestos

- **guarda forestal** *mf* forest ranger
- **guarda jurado** *mf* security guard

guarda[2] *f*

A 1 (de cerradura) ward 2 (de libro) flyleaf

B (acción) keeping; **manzanas de ~** apples which can be stored for long periods

guardabarrera *mf* grade crossing keeper (AmE), level crossing keeper (BrE)

guardabarros *m* (*pl* ~) 1 (Auto) fender (AmE), mudguard (BrE) 2 (de bicicleta) mudguard

guardabosque *mf* 1 (en parque nacional) forest ranger 2 (en finca particular) gamekeeper

guardacoches *mf* (*pl* ~) parking lot attendant (AmE), car park attendant (BrE)

guardacostas *mf* (*pl* ~) 1 (persona) coastguard 2 **guardacostas** *m* (buque) coastguard vessel

guardaespaldas *mf* (*pl* ~) bodyguard

guardafaro *mf* (CS) lighthouse keeper

guardafrenos *mf* (*pl* ~) brakeman (AmE), guard (BrE)

guardagujas *mf* (*pl* ~) (*m*) switchman (AmE), pointsman (BrE); (*f*) switchwoman (AmE), pointswoman (BrE)

guardalíneas *mf* (*pl* ~) (Chi) (*m*) linesman; (*f*) lineswoman

guardameta *mf* goalkeeper

guardapelo *m* locket

guardapolvo *m* (bata — de niño) overall; (— de profesor, tendero) workcoat (AmE), overall (BrE)

guardar [A1] *vt*

A (reservar) to save; **guárdale un trozo** save him a slice; **guarda esa botella para Navidad** keep *o* save that bottle for Christmas

B 1 (poner en un lugar) ‹*juguetes/libros*› to put … away; **ya guardé toda la ropa de invierno** I've already put away all my winter clothes 2 (conservar, mantener en un lugar) to keep; **lo guardó durante años** she kept it for years; **los tengo guardados en el desván** I've got them stored away in the attic

C (liter) (defender, proteger): **la muralla que guarda el castillo** the walls which defend *o* protect the castle; **los perros guardaban la entrada** the dogs were guarding the entrance; **Dios guarde al rey** God save the King

D ‹*secreto*› to keep; **no le guardo ningún rencor** I don't feel any resentment toward(s) him; **guardo muy buenos recuerdos de él** I have very good memories of him

E 1 (mostrar, manifestar): **hay que ~ la debida compostura en la Iglesia** you must show proper respect when in church; **~ las apariencias** to keep up appearances 2 ‹*leyes/fiestas*› to observe

■ **guardarse** *v pron*

A (quedarse con) to keep

B (reservar) to save, keep

C (poner en un lugar): **se guardó el cheque en el bolsillo** he put the check (away) in his pocket

D (cuidarse) **~se DE + INF** to be careful not TO + INF

guardarropa *m* 1 (en restaurantes, teatros) cloakroom 2 (ropa) wardrobe 3 (armario) dressing room

guardarropía *f* wardrobe

guardavallas *mf* (*pl* ~) (AmL) goalkeeper

guardería *f*: *tb* **~ infantil** nursery

guardia[2] (*m*) policeman; (*f*) policewoman

Compuestos

- **guardia jurado** *mf* security guard
- **guardia marina** *mf* midshipman
- **guardia tumbado** (Esp) speed bump

guardia[1] *f*

A 1 (vigilancia): **estar de ~** «*soldado*» to be on guard duty; «*médico*» to be on duty *o* call; «*empleado*» to be on duty; «*marino*» to be on watch; **montaban** *or* **hacían ~ frente al palacio** they were standing guard in front of the palace; ***bajar la ~*** to lower one's guard; ***con la ~ baja*** with one's guard down; ***estar en ~*** to be on one's guard; ***poner en ~ a algn*** to warn sb; ***ponerse en ~***: **se han puesto en ~ contra posibles fraudes** they are on the alert for fraud 2 (en esgrima): **en ~** on guard

B (cuerpo militar) guard; **cambio de ~** changing of the guard

Compuesto **guardia de honor** *f* guard of honor

> **Guardia Civil**
>
> A rural paramilitary police force founded in Spain in 1844. It has been used by different governments to fight against organized labor, republicanism, and regional autonomy, and came to be seen as an instrument of state repression.
>
> The Civil Guard has adapted to the new democratic Spain and is involved in anti-terrorist operations, ▸▸▸

▸▸▸ the coastguard service and environmental protection. Civil guards are armed and traditionally have had a distinctive uniform, including the *tricornio*, a black patent leather, three-cornered hat. In an effort to change its image, the *tricornio* is now worn only on ceremonial occasions or in front of official buildings

guardiamarina *mf* midshipman
guardián -diana *m,f* 1 (de edificio) (security) guard 2 (protector, defensor) guardian
guarecer [E3] *vt* to shelter, protect
■ **guarecerse** *v pron (refl)* to shelter, take shelter
guarén *m* water rat
guargüero *m* (AmL fam) (garganta) throat
guarida *f* (de animales) den, lair; (de personas) hideout
guarismo *m* (frml) figure
guarnecer [E3] *vt*
A 1 (liter) (adornar) ~ **algo DE algo** to adorn sth WITH sth (liter) 2 (Coc) to garnish
B ‹*plaza*› to garrison
guarnición *f*
A (Mil) garrison
B (Coc) (decoración) garnish; (verdura) accompaniment
C (en costura) trimming, edging; (de joya) setting; (de espada) guard
D **guarniciones** *fpl* (arreos) tack
guaro¹ -ra *adj* (Col fam) common (pej)
guaro² *m* (AmC fam) sugar-cane liquor; ***tiene mal*** ~ (fam) he gets aggressive/miserable when he's drunk (colloq)
guarrada *f* (Esp fam) 1 (porquería, suciedad) mess (colloq) 2 (mala pasada) dirty trick (colloq) 3 (indecencia, vulgaridad): **no digas ~s** don't be filthy; **esa película es una ~** that's a filthy movie
guarro¹ -rra *adj* (Esp fam) 1 (sucio) filthy 2 (que dice, hace guarradas) disgusting 3 ‹*revista/película*› dirty (colloq)
guarro² -rra *m,f* (Esp fam) 1 (persona sucia) filthy pig (colloq) 2 (indecente, vulgar): **es un ~** he's really disgusting
guarura *m* (Méx) bodyguard
guasa *f*
A (fam) (broma, burla) joke; **de ~** as a joke; **no te lo tomes a ~** it's no joke, it's no laughing matter
B (Col) (arandela) washer
guasca *f* (Chi, Per) (ramal de cuero) strap
guascazo *m* 1 (Andes fam) knock 2 (Chi fam) (latigazo) lash
guasear [A1] *vi* to joke
■ **guasearse** *v pron*: **~se DE algn/algo** to make fun OF sb/sth
guaso -sa *m,f* ▸ **huaso¹·²**
guasón¹ -sona *adj* 1 (fam) (bromista): **¡qué ~ es!** he's a real joker! 2 (fam & pey) (burlón) ‹*tono*› mocking
guasón² -sona *m,f* 1 (fam) (bromista) joker 2 (fam & pey) (burlón): **le rompieron la nariz por ~** they broke his nose for making fun of them
guata *f*
A (Esp) (algodón) wadding
B (Andes fam) (barriga) paunch; **echar ~** to get a paunch; **me duele la ~** I've got a tummy ache (colloq)
guatazo *m* (Chi fam)
A (al caer) belly flop
B (equivocación) blunder (colloq)
guatearse *v pron* (Chi fam) 1 (combarse) to warp 2 (equivocarse) to be wrong (colloq)
Guatemala *f* Guatemala
guatemalteco -ca *adj/m,f* Guatemalan
guateque *m* (Esp, Méx fam) (fiesta) bash (colloq), party
guatero *m* (Chi) hot-water bottle
guatitas *fpl* (Chi) tripe
guatón¹ -tona *adj* (Chi, Per fam): **está muy ~** he has a real paunch (colloq); **me tiene ~** I'm sick and tired of him/her (colloq)
guatón² -tona *m,f* (Chi, Per fam) fatty (colloq)
guau *interj* 1 (del perro) woof!, bow-wow! 2 (fam) (expresando agrado) wow! (colloq)
guay *adj* (Esp arg) cool (sl)
guaya *f* (Col, Ven) steel cable
guayaba *f*
A (fruta) guava
B (Méx fam & euf) (en insultos): **¡eres un hijo de la ~!** you s.o.b.! (colloq & euph)
guayabera *f: loose lightweight shirt*
guayabo *m*
A (Bot) guava tree
B 1 (Col, Ven fam) (nostalgia): ***tener*** ~ to be homesick 2 (Col fam) (resaca) hangover
Guayana *f*: *tb* **la ~ Francesa** French Guiana
(Compuesto) **Guayana Británica/Holandesa** (Hist) British/Dutch Guiana
guayo *m* (Col) sports lottery (AmE), football pools (*pl*) (BrE)
guayuco *m* (Col, Ven) loincloth
gubernamental *adj* ‹*orden/organismo*› governmental, government (*before n*); **organismos no ~es** non-governmental organizations
gubernativo -va *adj* government (*before n*)
gubernatura *f* (Méx) government
guepardo *m* cheetah
güero¹ -ra *adj* (Méx fam) (rubio) blond; (amarillo) yellow
güero² -ra (Méx fam) (*m*) blond *o* fair-haired man; (*f*) blonde *o* fair-haired woman
guerra *f*
A (Mil, Pol) war; **nos declararon la ~** they declared war on us; **estar en ~** to be at war; **hacerle la ~ a algn** to wage war on sb; **cuando estalló la ~** when war broke out
(Compuestos)
• **guerra abierta** open warfare
• **guerra a muerte** fight to the death
• **guerra bacteriológica** *or* **biológica** germ *o* biological warfare
• **guerra comercial** trade war
• **guerra de guerrillas** guerrilla war
• **Guerra de Secesión** American Civil War
• **Guerra de Sucesión** War of Spanish Succession
• **guerra de trincheras** trench warfare
• **guerra mundial** world war; **Primera/Segunda G~ M~** First/Second World War
• **guerra sin cuartel** all-out war
B (fam) (problemas) trouble, hassle (colloq); **estos niños me dan mucha ~** these kids give me a lot of hassle
guerrear [A1] *vi* (ant) to wage war, fight
guerrera *f* army jacket
guerrero¹ -ra *adj* ‹*pueblo/espíritu*› warlike; **canto ~** war cry
guerrero² -ra *m,f* warrior
guerrilla *f* 1 (grupo) guerrillas (*pl*) 2 (lucha) guerrilla warfare
guerrillero¹ -ra *adj* guerrilla (*before n*)
guerrillero² -ra *m,f* guerrilla
gueto *m* ghetto
guía *f*
A 1 (libro, folleto) guide (book); (de calles) map; **~ turística** tourist guide; **~ de hoteles** hotel guide 2 (orientación): **me sirven de ~** I use them as a guide
(Compuestos)
• **guía del ocio** entertainment guide, listings (*pl*)
• **guía telefónica** *or* **de teléfonos** telephone directory, phone book
B (de los scouts) guide
C **guía** *mf* (persona) guide; **~ de turismo** tourist guide; **~ espiritual** spirtual leader
guiar [A17] *vt* 1 (por un camino) to guide; **guiados por el afán de lucro** drawn by the desire to make money 2 (aconsejar) to guide; **no te dejes ~ por él** don't let yourself be led by him
■ **guiarse** *v pron* **~se POR algo** ‹*por mapa/consejo*› to follow sth; **~se por las apariencias** to be led by appearances; **~se por el instinto** to follow one's instincts
guija *f* (piedra) pebble
guijarral *m* stony ground
guijarro *m* pebble
guillado -da *adj* (Ven fam) ‹*dar/llevarse*› on the quiet
guillo *m* (Ven fam) care; **tener ~** to be careful
guillotina *f* guillotine

g

guinda *f* morello cherry; (confitada) glacé cherry; ***para ponerle la ~*** (fam) to cap it all (colloq)

guindar [A1] *vt*

A (Esp arg) (robar) ‹*novia/trabajo*› to steal

B 1 (Col, Méx, Ven fam) ‹*ropa*› to hang up 2 (Col fam) ‹*hamaca*› to hang

■ **guindarse** *v pron*

A (Col, Méx, Ven) (colgarse) to hang; **se ~on por teléfono toda la tarde** they were on the phone all afternoon

B (Ven fam) (lanzarse) **~se A algo**: **se guindó a llorar** she burst out crying; **cuando me guindo a trabajar** once I get down to work (colloq)

C (Ven fam) (pelearse) to get into a fight (colloq)

D (Ven fam) (atosigar) ‹*persona*› to hassle (colloq)

guindilla *f* chili

guindo *m* morello cherry tree

guindola *f* lifebuoy

guiñada *f* wink

guiñapo *m* 1 (harapo) rag; ***hecho un ~*** devastated 2 (persona) wreck (colloq)

guiñar [A1] *vt* to wink; **~le el ojo** *or* **un ojo A algn** to wink AT sb

■ **guiñar** *vi* to wink

guiño *m* wink; **hacerle un ~ A algn** to give sb a wink

guiñol *m* puppet theater•

guión *m*

A 1 (Cin, TV) script; **~ cinematográfico** screenplay 2 (esquema) outline, plan

B (Impr) (en diálogo) dash; (en palabras compuestas) hyphen; **lleva ~** it's hyphenated

guionista *mf* scriptwriter, screenwriter

guiri *mf* (Esp fam) foreigner

güirila *f* (AmC) maize pancake

guirnalda *f* garland

guisa *f* way; **a ~ de** by way of; **de tal ~ que ...** in such a way that ...

guisado *m* stew, casserole

guisante *m* (Esp) pea

guisar [A1] *vi* (Esp) to cook; **guisa muy bien** he's a very good cook

■ **guisar** *vt* (con bastante líquido) to stew; (con poco líquido) to braise; ***tú te lo guisas, tú te lo comes*** (Esp) you've made your bed, now you must lie in *o* on it

guiso *m* stew, casserole

guita *f* 1 (cuerda) string 2 (arg) cash (colloq), dough (sl)

guitarra *f*

A (instrumento) guitar

(Compuesto) **guitarra eléctrica/española/clásica** electric/Spanish/classical guitar

B **guitarra** *mf* guitarist

guitarrear [A1] *vi* (Mús) to play the guitar

guitarrista *mf* guitarist

guitarrón *m* 25-string guitar

gula *f* greed, gluttony

gurú *m* (*pl* **-rús** *or* **-rúes**) guru

gusanillo *m* (fam) itch; **le entró el ~ de los viajes** he got the itch to travel; **le quedó el ~ de saber quién fue** she was left still wanting to know who it was; **me entró el ~ de las apuestas** I got hooked on betting; ***matar el ~*** (fam): **fui a su concierto para matar el ~** I went to the concert out of curiosity; **voy a comer algo para matar el ~** I'm going to have a snack to keep me going

(Compuesto) **gusanillo de la conciencia** (fam) nagging conscience

gusano *m*

A 1 (como nombre genérico) worm; (lombriz de tierra) earthworm, worm 2 (larva — de mariposa) caterpillar; (— de mosca) maggot

(Compuestos)

- **gusano de luz** glowworm
- **gusano de seda** silkworm

B (pey) (persona despreciable) worm (pej)

gustar [A1] *vi*

A 1 (+ *me/te/le etc*): **¿te gustó el libro?** did you like *o* enjoy the book?; **me gusta su compañía** I enjoy her company; **no me/te/nos gustan los helados** I/you/we don't like ice cream; **le gusta mucho la música** he likes music very much; **¡así me gusta!** that's what I like to see (*o* hear *etc*)!; **creo que a Juan le gusta María** I think Juan likes María; **hazlo como te guste** do it however you like; **es el que más me gusta** he's/it's the one I like best 2 **~le a algn + INF**: **le gusta tocar la guitarra** she likes to play the guitar (AmE), she likes playing the guitar (BrE); **le gusta mucho viajar** she's very fond of traveling (colloq); **me gusta mucho jugar al tenis** I love playing *o* to play tennis; **nos gusta dar un paseo después de comer** we like to have a walk after lunch; **¿te ~ía visitar el castillo?** would you like to visit the castle? 3 **~le a algn QUE + SUBJ**: **no le gusta que le toquen sus papeles** he doesn't like people touching *o* to touch his papers; **me ~ía que vinieras temprano** I'd like you to come early

B 1 (en frases de cortesía) to wish (frml); **puede llamar o escribir, como guste** you may call or write, as you wish; **cuando usted guste** whenever it is convenient for you; **¿usted gusta? están muy buenas** would you like some? they're very nice 2 **~ DE algo** to like sth; **no gusta de bromas** he doesn't like jokes 3 **~ DE + INF** to like to + INF (AmE), to like -ING (BrE); **gusta de jugar a las cartas** he likes to play *o* he likes playing cards

■ **gustar** *vt* 1 (liter) (saborear) to taste; **~on las mieles del triunfo** they tasted the sweet taste of victory (liter) 2 (AmL) (querer) to like; **¿gustan tomar algo?** would you like something to drink?

gustativo -va *adj* taste (*before n*)

gustazo *m*: **me ha dado un ~ verte** it's been so good see you; ***darse el ~ de algo*** to take great pleasure in sth

gusto *m*

A 1 (sentido) taste; **resulta amargo al ~** it has a bitter taste 2 (sabor) taste; **tiene un ~ medio raro** it has a funny taste to it; **~ A algo**: **tiene ~ a fresa** it tastes of strawberry; **esto no tiene ~ a nada** this doesn't taste of anything; **deja un ~ a menta** it has a minty aftertaste

B 1 (placer, agrado) pleasure; **tendré mucho ~ en acompañarlos** (frml) it will be a pleasure for me to accompany you (frml); **¡se las comió con un ~ ...!** he tucked into them with such relish *o* delight!; **da ~ estar aquí** it's so nice (being) here; **me dio mucho ~ volverlo a ver** it was lovely to see him again; **por ~** for fun, for pleasure; ***tomarle*** *or* ***agarrarle (el) ~ a algo*** to take a liking to sth 2 (deseo, voluntad): **satisface todos los ~s de sus hijos** he indulges all his children's whims; **maneja al marido a su ~** she has her husband twisted around her little finger; **¿está a su ~ el peinado?** is the style to your liking?; **azúcar a** *or* **al ~** sugar to taste; **a ~ del consumidor** (fr hecha) however/as you like; **darle el ~ a algn**: **no le des todos los ~s** don't indulge him all the time; **hoy sí voy a darme el ~** I'm really going to treat myself today; **me di el ~ de decírselo a la cara** I took great delight *o* pleasure in telling him to his face 3 **a gusto** at ease; **un lugar en el que se está a ~** a place where you feel comfortable *o* at ease; **¿estás a ~ en tu nuevo trabajo?** are you happy in your new job? 4 (en fórmulas de cortesía): **mucho** *or* **tanto ~** pleased *o* nice to meet you; **mucho ~ (en conocerla) — el ~ es mío** pleased to meet you — the pleasure is mine (frml)

C (sentido estético) taste; **tiene muy buen ~ para vestirse** she has very good taste in clothes; **una broma de mal ~** a tasteless joke

D (inclinación, afición) taste; **ha heredado el ~ por la música** he has inherited a liking for music; **para todos los ~s** to suit all tastes; **es demasiado fuerte para mi ~** it's too strong for my taste *o* liking; ***hay ~s que merecen palos*** there's no accounting for taste; ***sobre ~s no hay nada escrito*** each to his own taste

gustosamente *adv* gladly; **acepto ~ su invitación** (frml) I am delighted to accept your kind invitation (frml)

gustoso -sa *adj* (de buen grado): **si lo tuviera, te lo prestaría gustosa** if I had it, I would willingly lend it to you; **aceptó ~ el puesto** he willingly *o* gladly accepted the job; **recibo ~ el honor que me hacen** I gladly accept the honor you bestow on me (frml)

gutapercha *f* gutta-percha

gutural *adj* ‹*consonante/sonido*› guttural; ‹*voz*› throaty

Guyana *f* Guyana

H, h *f* (*read as* /'atʃe/) *the letter* **H, h** (*ver tb* **hache**)

h. (= **hora**) hr; **a las 11h.** at 11:00 *o* 11 o'clock; **100 km/h** 100 kph, 100 km/h

ha *interj* ah!, ha!

Ha. (= **hectárea**) ha., hectare

haba *f*‡ (Bot) (broad) bean; ***en todas partes cuecen ~s*** it's the same the whole world over; ***son ~s contadas*** there are no two ways about it

Habana *f*: **La ~** Havana

habanera *f* (Mús) habanera

habanero -ra *adj/m,f* Havanan

habano *m* (cigarro) Havana cigar

haber¹ [E17] *v aux*

(*Sentido* **I**) (en tiempos compuestos) to have; **no han/habían llegado** they haven't/hadn't arrived; **como se haya olvidado lo mato** if he's forgotten, I'll kill him!; **¿se habrán perdido?** do you think they've *o* they might have got lost?; **de ~lo sabido** had I known, if I'd known; **¡deberías ~lo dicho!** you should have said so!

(*Sentido* **II**) [1] (frml) (expresando obligación, necesidad) **~ DE + INF** to have to + INF; **ha de ser firmado por ambas partes** it has to *o* must be signed by both parties [2] (expresando acción futura): **ha de llegar un día en que ...** the day will come when ... [3] (expresando probabilidad, certeza): **ha de ser tarde** it must be late; **pero ¿sabes lo que dices? — ¡no lo he de saber!** but do you know what you're saying? — of course I do!

■ **haber** *v impers*

(*Sentido* **I**) (existir, estar, darse): **hay una carta/varias cartas para ti** there's a letter/there are several letters for you; **había un cliente esperando** there was a customer waiting; **hubo dos accidentes** there were two accidents; **¿qué tomarán de postre? — ¿hay helado?** what would you like for dessert? — do you have any ice cream?; **¿cuántos kilómetros hay hasta Sevilla?** how many kilometers are there *o* is it to Seville?; **no hay como un buen descanso** there's nothing like a good rest; **no hay quien lo aguante** he's absolutely unbearable; **hay quien piensa que ...** there are those who feel that ...; **hubo varios heridos** several people were injured; **las hay rojas y verdes** there are red ones and green ones; **gracias — no hay de qué** thank you — don't mention it *o* not at all *o* you're welcome; **no hay de qué preocuparse** there's nothing to worry about; **hola ¿qué hay/hay de nuevo?** (fam) hello, how are things/what's new?; **es un poco largo — ¿qué hay?** (CS fam) it's rather long — so what?; **¿qué hubo?** (Andes, Méx, Ven fam) how are things?; **¿qué hubo de lo de Jorge y Ana?** what happened with Jorge and Ana?; ***habérselas con algn***: **tendrá que habérselas conmigo** he'll have me to deal with; ***habido y por ~***: **todos los trucos habidos y por ~** every trick in the book (colloq)

(*Sentido* **II**) (ser necesario) **~ QUE + INF**: **hay que estudiar** you/we/they must study; **hubo que romperlo** we/they had to break it; **hay que decir algo** something has to be said; **¡había que verlo!** you should have seen him!; **no hay más que apretarlo** all you have to do is press it; **no hay que darle muy fuerte** (no es necesario) you don't need *o* have to hit it too hard; (no se debe) you mustn't hit it too hard

(*Sentido* **III**) (liter) (en expresiones de tiempo): **muchos años/mucho tiempo ha** many years/a long time ago

■ **haber** *vt* **habido -da** *pp* (frml) (tenido): **los hijos habidos en el/fuera del matrimonio** children born in/out of wedlock (frml)

haber² *m* [1] (bienes) assets (*pl*) [2] (en contabilidad) credit side; ***tener algo en su ~*** (period) to have sth to one's credit [3] **haberes** *mpl* (frml) (emolumentos, paga) income, earnings (*pl*); **los ~es que se le adeudan** moneys *o* monies owed to you (frml)

habichuela *f* [1] (semilla) bean [2] (Col) (con vaina) green bean, French bean (BrE); ***ganarse las ~s*** to earn one's daily bread

hábil *adj*

A [1] (diestro) ‹*carpintero*› skilled, adept; ‹*conductor*› good, skillful*; ‹*juego/táctica*› skillful* [2] (astuto, inteligente) clever, able; **es muy ~ para los negocios** she's very good at business

B ‹*horas/días*› working (*before n*)

C (Der) competent

habilidad *f*

A [1] (para actividad manual, física) skill; **tiene gran ~ para la carpintería** he is very good *o* adept at carpentry [2] (astucia, inteligencia) skill, cleverness; **con ~** cleverly, skillfully

B (Der) competence

habilidoso -sa *adj* [SER] good with one's hands, handy

habilitación *f*

A (de lugar) fitting out

B (despacho) paymaster's office (*in government building*)

C (autorización) authorization

D (Col) (Educ): **exámenes de ~** retakes

habilitado -da *m,f* paymaster

habilitar [A1] *vt*

A ‹*lugar*› to fit out

B ‹*persona/institución*› to authorize; «*título*» to qualify, authorize; «*documento*» to authorize, empower

C (frml) (Com, Fin) **~ a algn CON algo** ‹*con fondos*› to provide sb WITH sth

D (Col) (Educ) to retake, to make up (AmE)

habiloso -sa *adj* (Chi fam) (inteligente) bright, smart (colloq)

habitable *adj* habitable

habitación *f* [1] (cuarto) room; (dormitorio) bedroom; **~ individual/doble** single/double room; **~ con baño** room with bath [2] (acción) habitation; (hábitat) habitat

habitacional *adj* (CS) housing (*before n*)

habitáculo *m* [1] (Aviac) cockpit; (Auto) interior [2] (liter) (morada) dwelling (frml)

habitante *mf* (Geog, Sociol) inhabitant; (de barrio) resident; **tiene medio millón de ~s** it has a population of half a million; **los ~s de las cavernas** the cave-dwellers

habitar [A1] *vt* ‹*vivienda*› to live in; ‹*isla/planeta*› to inhabit; **la única casa que no está habitada** the only unoccupied house

■ **habitar** *vi* (frml) to dwell (frml)

hábitat /'aβita(t)/ *m* (*pl* **-tats**) (Ecol, Zool) habitat; (Geog, Sociol) environment

hábito *m*

A (costumbre) habit; **el tabaco crea ~** smoking is addictive *o* is habit-forming; **adquirir/tener el ~ DE + INF** to get into/have the habit OF -ING

B (Relig) [1] (de religioso) habit; ***colgar los ~s*** «*sacerdote*» to give up the cloth; «*monja/monje*» to renounce one's vows; ***tomar el* ~** *or* ***los* ~*s*** «*mujer*» to take the veil; «*hombre*» to take holy orders; ***el* ~ *no hace al monje*** clothes do not make the man [2] (como ofrenda) sackcloth and ashes (*pl*)

habitual *adj* ‹*sitio/hora*› usual; ‹*cliente/lector*› regular; **con su ~ ironía** with his customary *o* usual irony

habituar [A18] *vt* **~ a algn A algo** to get sb used TO sth

■ **habituarse** *v pron* **~se A algo** to get used TO sth, get *o* become accustomed TO sth

habitué *mf* (CS) regular, habitué (frml)

habla *f‡*

A (facultad) speech; **perder/recobrar el ~** to lose/recover one's powers of speech; **al verla me quedé sin ~** when I saw her I was speechless

B [1] (idioma): **países de ~ hispana** Spanish-speaking countries [2] (manera de hablar): **el ~ de esta región** the local way of speaking; **giros propios del ~ infantil** expressions that children use; **la lengua y el ~** langue and parole

C **al habla** speaking; **¿el Sr. Ros? — al ~** Mr. Ros? — speaking; **estamos al ~ con nuestro corresponsal** we have our correspondent on the line; **estar/ponerse al ~ con algn** to be/get in contact with sb

hablado -da *adj* [1] ‹*lenguaje*› spoken [2] **bien hablado** well-spoken; **¡no seas mal ~!** don't be so rude *o* foul-mouthed!

hablador[1] -dora *adj* [1] (charlatán) talkative, chatty (colloq) [2] (chismoso) gossipy (colloq); **eres tan ~** you're such a bigmouth (colloq) [3] (Méx fam) (mentiroso): **es tan ~** he's such a fibber (colloq)

hablador[2] -dora *m,f* [1] (charlatán) chatterbox (colloq) [2] (chismoso) gossip (colloq) [3] (Méx fam) (mentiroso) storyteller, fibber (colloq)

habladurías *fpl* idle gossip *o* talk

hablante *mf* speaker

hablar [A1] *vi*

A (articular palabras) to speak; **~ en voz baja** to speak *o* talk quietly; **habla más alto** speak up; **habla más bajo** keep your voice down; **aún no sabe ~** he hasn't started to talk yet *o* isn't talking yet; **~ con la boca llena** to talk with one's mouth full

B (expresarse) to speak; **déjalo ~** let him speak, let him have his say (colloq); **~ claro** (claramente) to speak clearly; (francamente) to speak frankly; **las cifras hablan por sí solas** the figures speak for themselves; **mejor no ~** I'd better keep my mouth shut; **¡así se habla!** that's what I like to hear!; **mira quién habla** *or* **quién fue a ~** (fam) look *o* hark who's talking (colloq); **~ por señas** to use sign language; **~ en público** to speak in public; **un político que habla muy bien** a politician who is a very good speaker; ***~ por ~*** to talk for the sake of it; ***quien mucho habla mucho yerra*** the more you talk, the more mistakes you'll make

C [1] (conversar) to talk; **se pasaron toda la noche hablando** they spent the whole night talking; **tenemos que ~** we must (have a) talk; **tengo que ~te** *or* **que ~ contigo** I need to have a word with you; **hablar por teléfono/por el celular** (AmL) *or* **el móvil** (Esp) to be on the phone/cell phone (AmE) *o* mobile phone (BrE); **hablando se entiende la gente** (fr hecha) the way to work things out is by talking; **~ CON algn** to speak TO sb; ***ni* ~**: **de eso ni ~** that's totally out of the question; **¡ni ~!** no way! (colloq); **nos castigaron por ~ en clase** we were punished for talking in class [2] (murmurar) to talk; **a la gente le gusta ~** people just like to talk; ***dar que* ~** to start people talking [3] (al teléfono): **¿quién habla?** who's calling?; **¿con quién hablo?** who's speaking?

D (tratar, referirse a) **~ DE algo/algn** to talk ABOUT sth/sb; **tú y yo no tenemos nada de que ~** you and I have nothing to say to each other *o* nothing to discuss; **~ de negocios** to talk (about) *o* discuss business; **siempre habla mal de ella** he never has a good word to say about her; **lo dejamos en 10.000 y no se hable más (de ello)** let's say 10,000 and be done with it; **el viaje en tren sale caro, y no hablemos ya del avión** going by train is expensive, and as for flying ...; **háblame de tus planes** tell me about your plans; **no sé de qué me estás hablando** I don't know what you're talking about; **hablan muy bien de él** people speak very highly of him; **me ha hablado mucho de ti** she's told me a lot about you; **le hablé al director de tu caso** I spoke to the director about your case; **~ SOBRE** *or* **ACERCA DE algo** to talk ABOUT sth; **ya ~emos sobre eso luego** we'll talk about that later

E (bajo coacción) to talk

F [1] (dar discurso) to speak; **el rey habló a la nación** the king spoke to *o* addressed the nation [2] (dirigirse a) to speak; **no me hables en ese tono** don't speak to me in that tone of voice; **háblale de tú** use the 'tú' form with him

G [1] (anunciar propósito) **~ DE + INF** to talk OF -ING, talk ABOUT -ING; **mucho ~ de ahorrar y va y se compra esto** all this talk of saving and he goes and buys this! (colloq) [2] (rumorear): **se habla ya de miles de víctimas** there is already talk of thousands of casualties; **se habla de que va a renunciar** it is said *o* rumored that she's going to resign

H (Méx) (por teléfono) to call, phone

■ **hablar** *vt*

A ‹*idioma*› to speak; **Ⓢ se habla español** Spanish spoken

B (tratar): **tenemos que ~ las cosas** we must talk things over; **ya lo ~emos más adelante** we'll talk about *o* discuss that later; **háblalo con ella** speak *o* talk to her about it

C (fam) (decir): **no hables disparates** *or* **tonterías** don't talk nonsense; **no habló ni una palabra** he didn't say a word

■ **hablarse** *v pron*: **llevan meses sin ~se** they haven't spoken to each other for months; **no se habla con ella** he's not speaking *o* talking to her, he's not on speaking terms with her

habón *m* (roncha) bump; (picadura) (insect) bite

habrá, habría, etc *see* **haber**

hacedero -ra *adj* (ant) feasible, practicable

hacedor -dora *m,f* [1] (autor) creator; **~ de milagros** miracle worker [2] **el Hacedor** *m* (Relig) *tb* **el Supremo H~** the Maker, the Creator

hacendado[1] -da *adj* landowning (*before n*)

hacendado[2] -da *m,f* landowner, owner of a ranch (*o* farm *etc*)

hacendista *mf* expert in public finance

hacendoso -sa *adj* hardworking (*esp referring to housework*)

hacer [E18] *vt*

Sentido **I**

A (crear) ‹*mueble/vestido*› to make; ‹*casa/carretera*› to build; ‹*nido*› to build, make; ‹*coche*› to make, manufacture; ‹*túnel*› to make, dig; ‹*dibujo/plano*› to do, draw; ‹*lista*› to make, draw up; ‹*resumen*› to do, make; ‹*película*› to make; ‹*nudo/lazo*› to tie; ‹*pan/pastel*› to make, bake; ‹*vino/café/tortilla*› to make; ‹*cerveza*› to make, brew; **me hizo un lugar** *or* **sitio en la mesa** he made room *o* a place for me at the table; **hacen buena pareja** they make a lovely couple

B [1] (efectuar, llevar a cabo) ‹*sacrificio*› to make; ‹*milagro*› to work, perform; ‹*deberes/ejercicios/limpieza*› to do; ‹*mandado*› to run; ‹*transacción/investigación*› to carry out; ‹*experimento*› to do, perform; ‹*entrevista*› to conduct; ‹*gira/viaje*› to do; **me hicieron una visita** they paid me a visit; **me hizo un regalo** she gave me a gift; **¿me haces un favor?** will you do me a favor?; **hicimos un trato** we did *o* made a deal; **aún queda mucho por ~** there is still a lot (left) to do; **dar que ~** to make a lot of work [2] ‹*cheque/factura*› to make out, write out

C (formular, expresar) ‹*declaración/promesa/oferta*› to make; ‹*proyecto/plan*› to make, draw up; ‹*crítica/comentario*› to make, voice; ‹*pregunta*› to ask; **nadie hizo ninguna objeción** nobody raised any objections; **nos hizo un relato de sus aventuras** he related his adventures to us

D (refiriéndose a necesidades fisiológicas): **~ caca** (fam) to do a poop (AmE) *o* (BrE) a pooh (colloq); **~ pis** *or* **pipí** (fam) to have a pee (colloq); **~ sus necesidades** (euf) to go to the bathroom *o* toilet (euph)

E (adquirir) ‹*dinero/fortuna*› to make; ‹*amigo*› to make

F (preparar, arreglar) ‹*cama*› to make; ‹*maleta*› to pack; **hice el pescado al horno** I did *o* cooked the fish in the oven; **tengo que ~ la comida** I must make lunch; *ver tb* **comida B2**

G [1] (producir, causar) ‹*ruido*› to make; **este jabón no hace espuma** this soap doesn't lather; **esos chistes no me**

hacen gracia I don't find those jokes funny; **estos zapatos me hacen daño** these shoes hurt my feet 2 (refiriéndose a sonidos onomatopéyicos) to go; **las vacas hacen 'mu'** cows go 'moo'
H (recorrer) ‹*trayecto/distancia*› to do, cover
I (en cálculos, enumeraciones): **son 180 … y 320 hacen 500** that's 180 … and 320 is *o* makes 500; **el visitante que hacía el número mil** the thousandth visitor

Sentido **II**

A 1 (ocuparse en actividad) to do; **no hace más que quejarse** she does nothing but complain; **no hice más que cumplir con mi deber** I only did my duty; **le gustaría ~ teatro** she would like to work in the theater; **hacen una obra de Ibsen** they're doing *o* putting on a play by Ibsen; **deberías ~ ejercicio** you should do *o* get some exercise; **¿hace algún deporte?** do you play *o* do any sports? 2 (como profesión, ocupación) to do 3 (estudiar) to do; **hace Derecho** she's doing *o* studying *o* reading Law; **~ un curso de cocina** to do a cookery course
B 1 (realizar cierta acción, actuar de cierta manera) to do; **¡niño, eso no se hace!** you mustn't do that!; **¡qué se le va a ~!** *or* **¡qué le vamos a ~!** what can you *o* (frml) one do?; **aquí se hace lo que digo yo** around here what I say goes; ***~la*** (Méx) (fam) to make it (colloq); ***~la (buena)*** (fam): **¡ahora sí que la hice!** now I've (really) done it!; ***hacérsela buena a algn*** (Méx) to keep one's word *o* promise to sb; **soñé que te sacabas la lotería — ¡házmela buena!** I dreamed you won the lottery — if only! 2 (dar cierto uso, destino, posición) to do; **no sé qué hice con los recibos** I don't know what I did with the receipts; **y el libro ¿qué lo hice?** (CS, Méx fam) what did I do with the book? 3 (causar daño) **~le algo A algn** to do sth TO sb; **yo no le hice nada** I didn't do anything to her; **el perro no te hace nada** the dog won't hurt you
C (esp Esp) (actuar como): **~ el tonto** to act *o* play the fool
D (sustituyendo a otro verbo): **toca bien el piano — antes lo hacía mejor** she plays the piano well — she used to play better; **voy a escribirle — deja, yo lo haré** I'm going to write to him — don't bother, I'll do it
E (Méx, RPl fam) (afectar, importar): **¿qué le hace?** so what? what does it matter?; **eso no le hace nada** that doesn't matter at all

Sentido **III**

A (transformar en, volver) to make; **te hará hombre, hijo mío** it will make a man of you, my son; **la hizo su mujer** he made her his wife; **hizo pedazos la carta** she tore the letter into tiny pieces; **ella lo hizo posible** she made it possible; **~ algo DE algo** to turn sth INTO sth; **~ algo DE algn** to make sth OF sb; **quiero ~ de ti un gran actor** I want to make a great actor of you
B (dar apariencia de): **ese vestido te hace más delgada** that dress makes you look thinner
C (inducir a, ser causa de que) **~ algo/a algn + INF** to make sth/sb + INF; **me hizo llorar** it made me cry; **todo hace suponer que …** everything suggests that *o* leads one to think that …; **hizo caer al niño** he knocked the child over; **hágalo pasar** tell him to come in; **~ que algo/algn + SUBJ** to make sth/sb + INF; **¡vas a ~ que pierda la paciencia!** you're going to make me lose my temper!
D (obligar a) **~ + INF a algn** to make sb + INF; **me hizo esperar tres horas** she kept me waiting for three hours; **me hizo abrirla** he made me open it; **~ que algn + SUBJ** to make sb + INF; **hizo que todos se sentaran** he made everybody sit down
E **hacer hacer algo** to have *o* get sth done/made; **hice acortar las cortinas** I had *o* got the curtains shortened
F (suponer, imaginar): **te hacía en Buenos Aires** I thought you were in Buenos Aires; **¡yo que lo hacía casado!** I had the idea that he was married!

■ **hacer** *vi*

Sentido **I**

A 1 (obrar, actuar): **déjame ~ a mí** just let me handle this *o* take care of this; **¿cómo se hace para que te den la beca?** what do you have to do to get the scholarship?; **¿cómo hacen para vivir con ese sueldo?** how do they manage to live on that salary?; ***~le a algo*** (Chi, Méx fam): **le hace a todo** she does a bit of everything; **yo no le hago a la pintura** I don't go in for painting; ***~ y deshacer*** to do as one pleases, do what one likes 2 (+ *compl*): **hiciste bien en decírmelo** you did *o* were right to tell me; **haces mal en mentir** it's wrong of you to lie
B (refiriéndose a las necesidades fisiológicas): **¡mamá, ya hice!** (esp AmL) Mommy, I've been *o* I've finished!; **~ de cuerpo** *or* **de vientre** (frml) to have a bowel movement (frml)
C (fingir, simular): **hizo como que no me había visto** he made out *o* pretended he hadn't seen me; **hice como que no oía** I pretended not to hear; **haz como si no supieras nada** act as if *o* pretend you don't know anything about it
D (servir) **~ DE algo**: **esta sábana hará de toldo** this sheet will do for *o* as an awning; **la escuela hizo de hospital** the school served as *o* was used as a hospital
E (interpretar personaje) **~ DE algo/algn** to play (the part of) sth/sb; **hacía de 'malo'** he played the bad guy

Sentido **II**

A (+ *compl*) (sentar) (+ *me/te/le etc*): **le va a ~ bien salir un poco** it'll do her good to get out a bit; **la trucha me hizo mal** (AmL) the trout didn't agree with me
B (corresponder) **~le A algo** to fit sth; **esta tapa no le hace al frasco** this lid doesn't fit the jar
C **no le hace** (no tiene importancia) it doesn't matter; (no sirve de excusa) that's no excuse; **¿no le hace que tire la ceniza aquí?** do you mind if I drop the ash here?
D (*en 3ª pers*) (frml) (tocar, concernir): **por lo que hace a** *or* **en cuanto hace a su solicitud** as far as your application is concerned
E (Esp fam) (apetecer): **¿(te) hace una cerveza?** care for a beer?, do you fancy a beer? (BrE colloq)

■ **hacer** *v impers*

A 1 (refiriéndose al tiempo atmosférico): **hace frío/calor/sol/viento** it's cold/hot/sunny/windy; **hace tres grados** it's three degrees; **(nos) hizo un tiempo espantoso** the weather was terrible 2 (fam & hum): **hace sed ¿verdad?** it's thirsty weather/work, isn't it?; **parece que hace hambre** you/they seem to be hungry
B (expresando tiempo transcurrido): **hace dos años que murió** he's been dead for two years; **¿cuánto hace que se fue?** how long ago did she leave?; **hace poco/un año** a short time/a year ago; **hace mucho que lo conozco** I've known him for a long time; **no lo veo desde hace años** I haven't seen him for years; **hacía años que no lo veía** I hadn't seen him for *o* in years; **hasta hace poco** until recently

■ **hacerse** *v pron*

Sentido **I**

A (producirse): **hágase la luz** (Bib) let there be light; (+ *me/te/le etc*): **se me hizo un nudo en el hilo** I got a knot in the thread; **se le ha hecho una ampolla** she's got *o* she has a blister; ***hacérsele algo a algn*** (Méx): **por fin se le hizo ganar el premio** she finally got to win the award
B 1 (*refl*) (hacer para sí) ‹*café/falda*› to make oneself; **se hace toda la ropa** she makes all her (own) clothes; **se hicieron una casita** they built themselves a little house 2 (*caus*) (hacer que otro haga): **se hicieron una casita** they had a little house built; **se hizo la cirugía estética** she had plastic surgery; **voy a ~me las manos** I'm going to have a manicure
C (causarse): **me hice un tajo en el dedo** I cut my finger; **¿qué te hiciste en el brazo?** what did you do to your arm?; **¿te hiciste daño?** did you hurt yourself?
D (refiriéndose a necesidades fisiológicas): **todavía se hace pis/caca** (fam) she still wets/messes herself
E (*refl*) (adquirir) to make; **~se un nombre** to make a name for oneself; **~se enemigos** to make enemies

Sentido **II**

A 1 (volverse, convertirse en) to become; **~se famoso/monja** to become famous/a nun; **se están haciendo viejos** they are getting *o* growing old 2 (*impers*): **se hace de noche muy pronto** it gets dark very early; **se está haciendo tarde** it's getting late; (+ *me/te/le etc*) **se nos hizo de noche esperándolo** it got dark while we were waiting for him 3 (cocinarse) ‹‹*pescado/guiso*›› to cook 4 (AmL) (pasarle a): **¿qué se habrá hecho María?** what can have happened to María?
B (resultar): **esto se hace muy pesado** this gets very boring; (+ *me/te/le etc*) **se me hizo interminable** it seemed interminable; **se me hace difícil creerlo** I find it very hard to believe
C (dar impresión de) (+ *me/te/le etc*): **se me hace que está ofendida** I get the feeling *o* impression that she's upset; **se me hace que va a llover** I think *o* I have a feeling it's going to rain; ***hacérsele a algn*** (Chi fam) to back out

h

D (*caus*) **~se + INF: hazte respetar** make people respect you; **el desenlace no se hizo esperar** the end was not long in coming; **un chico que se hace querer** a likable kid; **se hizo construir una mansión** he had a mansion built; **hazte ver por un médico** (AmL) go and see a doctor
E (acostumbrarse) **~se A algo/+ INF** to get used TO sth/-ING; **no consigo ~me a la idea** I can't get used to the idea
F (fingirse): **no te hagas el inocente** don't act the innocent; **me vio pero se hizo el loco** he saw me but pretended he hadn't; **¿éste es bobo o se (lo) hace?** (fam) is this guy stupid or just a good actor? (colloq); **no te hagas el sordo** don't pretend *o* act as if you didn't hear me; **yo me hice** (Méx fam) I pretend not to notice
G (moverse) (+ *compl*) to move; **~se atrás/a un lado** to move back/to one side
H **hacerse con**: **el ejército se hizo con la ciudad** the army took the city; **tengo que ~me con esa carta** I must get hold of that letter; **logró ~se con el control de la compañía** he managed to gain control of the company
I **hacerse de** (AmL): **se hicieron de gran fama** they became very famous; **tengo que ~me de dinero** I must get *o* lay my hands on some money; **se hizo de muchos amigos** he made a lot of friends

hacha[1] *adj* (Méx fam) (diestro): **ser muy** *or* **bien ~ para algo** to be very good at sth, be an ace at sth (colloq)

hacha[2] *f‡*
A (herramienta) ax (AmE), axe (BrE); ***enterrar el ~ de guerra*** to bury the hatchet; ***estar como ~*** (Chi, Méx fam) to be well prepared; ***ni raja ni presta el ~*** (Col fam) you're/he's being a dog in the manger
B (antorcha) torch

hachazo *m* (golpe) blow of/with an ax*

hache *f*: *the name of the letter* **h**; ***llámale ~*** (fam) call it what you like *o* what you will (colloq)

hachís *m* hashish, hash (colloq)

hacia *prep* **1** (indicando dirección) toward, towards [*el inglés norteamericano prefiere la forma* **toward** *mientras que el inglés británico prefiere la forma* **towards**] **~ el sur** southward(s), toward(s) the south; **~ adentro** inward(s); **el centro queda ~ allá** the center is (over) that way; **¿~ dónde tenemos que ir?** which way do we have to go?; **empujar ~ arriba/atrás** to push upward(s)/backward(s) **2** (indicando aproximación) toward(s) [*ver nota en la sección* **1**] **llegaremos ~ las dos** we'll arrive towards *o* at around two **3** (con respecto a) toward(s); **su actitud ~ mí** his attitude toward(s) *o* to me

hacienda *f*
A **1** (esp AmL) (finca) estate; (dedicada a ganadería) ranch **2** (bienes) possessions (*pl*), property
(Compuesto) **hacienda de beneficio** (Méx) smelter
B **Hacienda** **1** (ministerio) ≈ the Treasury Department (*in US*), ≈ the Treasury (*in UK*) **2** (oficina) tax office; **el dinero que debo a H~** the money I owe the IRS (AmE) *o* (BrE) the Inland Revenue
(Compuesto) **hacienda pública**: **la ~ ~** the Treasury, public funds (*pl*)
C (RPl) (ganado) livestock

hacina *f* pile, heap

hacinamiento *m* overcrowding

hacinar [A1] *vt* ‹*mies/paja*› to stack; ‹*leña*› to pile up, stack (up)
■ **hacinarse** *v pron* to crowd together

hada *f‡* fairy; **el ~ madrina** the fairy godmother

hado *m* (liter) fate, destiny

haga, etc *see* **hacer**

hago *see* **hacer**

Haití *m* Haiti

haitiano -na *adj/m,f* Haitian

hala *interj* (Esp) **1** (para animar) come on! **2** (expresando sorpresa) wow!

halagador -dora *adj* flattering

halagar [A3] *vt* **1** ‹‹*elogios/invitación*›› to flatter; **me halaga que me lo ofrezcas a mí** I am flattered that you're offering it to me **2** (adular) ‹‹*persona*›› to flatter; **le ~on el vestido** they complimented her on her dress

halago *m* praise; **~s** praise, flattery

halagüeño -ña *adj* ‹*palabras/frases*› flattering, complimentary; ‹*situación*› promising, encouraging; ‹*noticia*› encouraging; ‹*futuro*› promising

halar [A1] *vt* **1** (Náut) ‹*cabo*› to haul in; ‹*remo*› to pull on **2** *ver tb* **jalar**

halcón *m* (Zool) falcon; (en política) (period) hawk (journ)

hálito *m* (liter) (aliento) breath; (brisa) gentle breeze

hall /'xol/ *m* (*pl* **halls**) (de casa) hall, hallway; (de teatro, cine) foyer

hallaca *f* (Ven) *cornmeal, meat and vegetables wrapped in banana leaves*

hallador -dora *m,f* finder

hallar [A1] *vt*
A **1** (frml) ‹*persona/libro/tesoro*› to find; ‹*felicidad/paz*› to find; **lo ~on en su casa** it was found at his house; **halló la muerte en un accidente** he met his death in an accident; (+ *compl*) **halló la puerta abierta** she found the door open **2** ‹*pruebas/solución*› to find; ‹*información*› to find, discover
B (esp AmL) (*en frases negativas*) (saber): **no halla cómo sentarse** she can't find a comfortable position to sit in; **no hallo cómo decírselo** I don't know how to tell her
C (esp AmL) (opinar, creer) to find
■ **hallarse** *v pron*
A (frml) (estar, encontrarse) (+ *compl*) to be; **se halla situado en las afueras de la ciudad** it is situated on the outskirts of the city
B (sentirse) (+ *compl*) to feel; **~se a gusto** to feel at ease; ***no ~se***: **no me hallo en este tipo de fiestas** I don't feel comfortable *o* at home at this type of party

hallazgo *m* find

hallulla *f*
A (Chi) (pan) *slightly leavened white bread*
B (Chi) (sombrero) straw boater

halo *m* **1** (Astron) halo **2** (aureola) halo, aureole (liter) **3** (de inocencia, santidad) aura; **envuelto en un ~ de misterio** shrouded in mystery

halógeno[1] **-na** *adj* halogen (*before n*)

halógeno[2] *m* (Quím) halogen; (faro) halogen headlight *o* headlamp

haltera *f* barbell

halterofilia *f* weightlifting

hamaca *f*
A **1** (para colgar) hammock **2** (RPl) (mecedora) rocking chair; (columpio) swing **3** (Esp) (asiento plegable) deckchair
B (archivo) suspension file

hamacar [A2] *vt* (columpiar) (RPl) to swing; (mecer) (CS) to rock
■ **hamacarse** *v pron* (columpiarse) to swing; (mecerse) to rock (oneself)

hambre *f‡*
A **1** (sensación) hunger; **tengo ~** I'm hungry; **el ejercicio da ~** exercise makes you hungry; **morirse de ~** to starve to death; **me muero de ~** (fam) I'm starving (colloq); ***matar el ~***: **comió unas galletas para matar el ~** he ate some cookies to keep him going; ***ser más listo que el ~*** (fam) to be razor sharp (colloq); ***tengo/tiene un ~ canina*** I/he could eat a horse (colloq); ***a buen ~ no hay pan duro*** beggars can't be choosers **2** (como problema) **el ~** hunger; **sueldos de ~** starvation wages
B (liter) (ansia, deseo) **~ DE algo** hunger FOR sth

hambreado -da *adj* (Andes, Méx, RPl) hungry, starving

hambrear [A1] *vt* (CS) to starve

hambriento[1] **-ta** *adj* [ESTAR] hungry, starving (colloq), famished (colloq); **los niños ~s del mundo** the world's starving children; **~ DE algo** hungry FOR sth

hambriento[2] **-ta** *m,f*: **los ~s** hungry people; **dar de comer al ~** to feed the starving *o* hungry

hambruna *f* famine

hamburguesa *f* (bistec) hamburger, beefburger (BrE); (sandwich) hamburger, burger

hamburguesería *f* hamburger bar

hampa *f‡*: **el ~** criminals (*pl*), the underworld

hampesco -ca *adj* criminal, underworld (*before n*)

hampón -pona *m,f* thug, criminal

hamponil *adj* (Ven) criminal, underworld (*before n*)

hámster /'xamster/ *m* (*pl* **-ters**) hamster

handicap /'xandikap/ *m* (*pl* **-caps**)
A (en golf) handicap; (Equ) handicap
B (desventaja) handicap, disadvantage

handling *m* baggage handling

hangar *m* hangar

haragán¹ -gana *adj* lazy, idle

haragán² -gana *m,f* shirker, layabout

haraganear [A1] *vi* to be lazy, laze *o* loaf around (colloq)

haraganería *f* laziness, idleness

harapiento -ta *adj* ragged; **un hombre ~ y sucio** a dirty-looking man, dressed in rags

harapo *m* rag

haraquiri *m* hara-kiri; **hacerse el ~** to commit hara-kiri

haras *m* (*pl* ~) (AmS) stud farm

hardware /'xar(ð)wer/ *m* hardware

haré, etc *see* **hacer**

harén *m* harem

haría, etc *see* **hacer**

harina *f* flour; ***ser ~ de otro costal*** to be a different kettle of fish
(Compuestos)
- **harina de avena/maíz** oatmeal/cornmeal
- **harina integral** wholewheat flour, wholemeal flour (BrE)

harinoso -sa *adj* floury

harnear [A1] *vt* (Andes, Méx) to sieve, sift

harnero *m* sieve

hartar [A1] *vt*
A (cansar, fastidiar): **me hartó con sus quejas** I got tired *o* (colloq) sick of his complaints
B (fam) (llenar) **~ a algn** A *or* DE **algo**: **nos hartaban a sopa** they fed us on nothing but soup; **lo ~on a palos** they gave him a real beating
■ **hartarse** *v pron*
A (cansarse, aburrirse) to get fed up; **~se DE algo** to get tired *o* sick OF sth, get fed up WITH sth; **~se DE algn** get tired OF sb, get fed up WITH sb; **~se DE + INF** to get tired *o* sick of -ING, get fed up WITH -ING; **me harté de que se burlara de mí** I got fed up with *o* I got tired of her making fun of me
B (llenarse): **comieron hasta ~se** they gorged *o* (colloq) stuffed themselves; **~se DE algo** to gorge oneself ON sth, to stuff oneself WITH sth (colloq)

hartazgo *m*: **comieron hasta el ~** they gorged themselves; **nos dimos un ~ de sardinas** (Esp fam) we stuffed ourselves with sardines (colloq)

harto¹ -ta *adj*
A 1 (cansado, aburrido) fed up; **me tienes ~ con tantas exigencias** I'm sick *o* tired of all your demands; **~ DE algo/algn** fed up WITH sth/sb, tired OF sth/sb; **~ DE + INF** tired OF -ING, fed up WITH -ING; **estaba harta de que le dijeran eso** she was tired of *o* fed up with them telling her that 2 (de comida) full
B (*delante del n*) (mucho) 1 (frml): **con harta frecuencia** very frequently; **tenían hartas ventajas** they had many advantages 2 (AmL exc RPl): **te llamé hartas veces** I phoned you lots of times; **tiene hartas ganas de verte** he really wants to see you; **había harta gente** there were a lot of people

harto² *adv*
A (modificando un adjetivo) 1 (frml) extremely, very 2 (AmL exc RPl) very; **es ~ mejor que el hermano** he's much *o* a lot better than his brother
B (modificando un verbo) (AmL exc RPl): **me gustó ~** I really liked it; **bailamos ~** we danced a lot

harto³ -ta *pron* (AmL exc RPl): **tenía ~ que hacer** I had an awful lot to do; **¿tienes amigos allí? — ¡sí, ~s!** do you have friends there? — yes, lots

hasta¹ *prep*
A (en el tiempo) 1 until; **¿~ cuándo te quedas? — ~ el viernes** how long are you staying? — until *o* till Friday; **~ hace unos años** (up) until *o* up to a few years ago; **~ ahora** *or* **~ el momento** so far, up to now; **¿siempre trabajas ~ tan tarde?** do you always work so late?; **no descansó ~ terminar** she didn't rest until she'd finished 2 **hasta que** until, till; **~ QUE + SUBJ**: **espera ~ que pare de llover** wait until *o* till it stops raining; **es inocente ~ que (no) se demuestre lo contrario** he is innocent until proven guilty 3 **hasta tanto** until such time as; **~ tanto (no) contesten** until they reply 4 (AmC, Col, Méx) (con valor negativo): **será publicado ~ mayo** it won't be published until May; **cierran ~ las nueve** they don't close until *o* till nine 5 (en saludos): **~ mañana** see you tomorrow; **~ luego** see you (colloq), bye (colloq); **~ pronto** see you soon; **~ siempre, amigos** farewell, my friends
B (en el espacio) to; **desde Puebla ~ Veracruz** from Puebla to Veracruz; **el agua me llegaba ~ los hombros** the water came up to my shoulders; **¿~ dónde va usted?** how far are you going?
C (en cantidades) up to; **~ cierto punto** up to a point

hasta² *adv* even; **~ te diría que ...** I'd even go as *o* so far as to say that ...

hastial *m* gable end

hastiante *adj* boring, sickening

hastiar [A17] *vt*: **le hastiaban aquellas fiestas** she was tired *o* weary of those parties; **hastiado de la vida** tired *o* weary of life
■ **hastiarse** *v pron* **~se DE algo** to grow tired *o* weary OF sth

hastío *m*: **el ~ de un vuelo largo** the tedium of a long flight; **su trabajo le producía ~** his job bored him intensely; **hacer algo hasta el ~** to do sth ad nauseam

hatajo *m* 1 (pey) (de gente despreciable) bunch (colloq), load (colloq); (de disparates, tonterías) load (colloq); **un ~ de mentiras** a pack of lies 2 (de ganado) herd

hatillo *m*
A (de ropa) bundle; ***ir con el ~ a cuestas*** to live out of a suitcase; ***liar el ~*** to pack one's bags
B (Agr) (de vacas) herd; (de ovejas) flock

hato *m*
A (de ropa) bundle; *para modismos ver* **hatillo**
B (de vacas) herd; (de ovejas) flock
C ▸ **hatajo 1**
D (Ven) (finca rural) cattle farm, ranch

Hawai *m* Hawaii

hawaiana /hagwai'ana/ *f* (Chi) 1 (sandalia) thong (AmE), flip-flop (BrE) 2 (camisa) Hawaiian shirt

hawaiano -na *adj/m,f* Hawaiian

hay *see* **haber**

haya¹ *f* beech

haya², hayas, etc *see* **haber**

hayaca *f* (Ven) ▸ **hallaca**

hayo *m* coca

haz¹ *m* (de leña, paja) bundle; (de trigo) sheaf; (de luz) beam

haz² *see* **hacer**

haza *f* plot (*of arable land*)

hazaña *f* (acción heróica) great *o* heroic deed, exploit; (acción que requiere gran esfuerzo) feat, achievement

hazmerreír *m* (fam) laughing stock

he¹ *see* **haber**

he² *v impers* (liter): **~ aquí las pruebas** here is *o* here I have the evidence; **~me aquí** here I am

hebilla *f* (de zapato) buckle; (de cinturón) clasp, buckle

hebra *f* 1 (Tex) thread, strand; **lana de cuatro ~s** four-ply wool 2 (fibra vegetal, animal) fiber* 3 (del gusano de seda) thread 4 (de la madera) grain

hebreo¹ -brea *adj/m,f* Hebrew

hebreo² *m* (idioma) Hebrew

hebroso -sa *adj* fibrous

hecatombe *f* (desastre) disaster, catastrophe; (mortandad) loss of life; (sacrificio) (Hist) hecatomb

heces *fpl*: *ver* **hez**

hechicería *f* (práctica) witchcraft, sorcery; (maleficio) spell

hechicero¹ -ra *adj* ‹*persona*› enchanting, captivating; ‹*ojos/sonrisa*› captivating

hechicero² -ra *m,f* 1 (brujo) (*m*) sorcerer, wizard; (*f*) sorceress, witch 2 (de tribu) witch doctor

hechizante *adj* enchanting, bewitching

hechizar [A4] *vt* 1 «*brujo*» to cast a spell on, bewitch 2 (cautivar) to captivate

hechizo¹ -za *adj* (Chi, Méx) makeshift, home-made

hechizo[2] *m* 1 (maleficio) spell 2 (atractivo, encanto) charm

hecho[1] **-cha** *pp* [*ver tb* **hacer**]

A (manufacturado) made; **~ a mano** handmade; **un traje ~ a (la) medida** a made-to-measure suit; **bien/mal ~** well/badly made

B (refiriéndose a acción): **¡bien ~!** well done!; **no le avisé — pues mal ~** I didn't let him know — well you should have (done); ***lo ~, ~ está*** what's done is done

C (convertido en): **estaba ~ una fiera** he was furious; **está hecha una vaca** she's got(ten) really fat; **tú estás ~ un vago** you've become *o* turned into a lazy devil; **se apareció ~ un mamarracho** he turned up looking a real mess

D (acostumbrado) **~ A algo** used *o* accustomed TO sth

E (*como interj*) (expresando acuerdo): **¡~!** it's a deal!, done!

hecho[2] **-cha** *adj*

A ‹*ropa*› ready-to-wear, off-the-rack (AmE), off-the-peg (esp BrE)

B (terminado) ‹*trabajo*› done; **~ *y derecho*** ‹*hombre*› (fully) grown; ‹*abogado*› fully-fledged

C (esp Esp) ‹*carne*› done; **un filete muy/poco ~** a well-done/rare steak

hecho[3] *m*

A 1 (acto, acción): **ésas son palabras y yo quiero ~s** those are just words, I want action *o* I want something done; **demuéstramelo con ~s** prove it to me by doing something about it 2 (suceso, acontecimiento) event; **el lugar de los ~s** the scene of the crime

(Compuesto) **hecho consumado** fait accompli

B (realidad, verdad) fact; **los viajes espaciales ya son un ~** space travel is already a reality; **el ~ es que ...** the fact (of the matter) is that ...

C **de hecho** in fact

hechura *f*

A 1 (de traje, vestido): **me cobró un dineral por la ~** she charged me a fortune for making it up 2 (modelo, estilo) style; **la falda tiene una ~ muy simple** the skirt is cut very simply 3 (forma) shape, form

B (de obra de arte, artesanía) craftsmanship, workmanship

C (creación): **somos ~ divina** we are God's creation; **son todos ellos ~ del profesor Ramos** they are all products of Mr Ramos' teaching

hectárea *f* hectare

hectogramo *m* hectogram

hectolitro *m* hectoliter*

heder [E8] *vi* (liter) to reek, stink

hediondez *f* stench, stink

hediondo -da *adj* (fétido) foul-smelling, stinking

hedonismo *m* hedonism

hedonista *mf* hedonist

hedor *m* (liter) stench, reek

hegemonía *f* hegemony, dominance

helada *f* frost

heladera *f* (para hacer helados) ice-cream maker; (nevera) (RPl) refrigerator, fridge; (para picnic) (Arg, Col) cool *o* cold box

heladería *f* ice-cream parlor*

heladero -ra *m,f* (esp AmL) ice-cream vendor *o* seller

helado[1] **-da** *adj*

A 1 ‹*persona/manos*› freezing (colloq), frozen (colloq); ‹*casa/habitación*› freezing (colloq); **tengo los pies ~s** my feet are frozen *o* freezing; ***dejar a algn ~***: **nos dejó ~s con la noticia** we were stunned when she told us the news; ***quedarse ~*** (de asombro) to be stunned 2 ‹*comida*› stone-cold; ‹*líquido/bebida*› (muy frío) freezing; (que se ha enfriado) stone-cold; **servir el vino bien ~** (AmL) serve the wine well chilled

B ‹*agua/estanque*› frozen

helado[2] *m* ice cream

(Compuesto) **helado de agua** (CS) water ice, sherbet (AmE); (con palo) Popsicle® (AmE), ice lolly (BrE)

helador -dora *adj* freezing, icy, bitterly cold

heladora *f* ice-cream maker

helar [A5] *vt/vi* to freeze

■ **helar** *v impers*: **anoche heló** it went below freezing last night (AmE), there was a frost last night (BrE)

■ **helarse** *v pron*

A 1 «*río/charco*» to freeze (over); «*agua*» to freeze 2 «*plantas/cosecha*» to freeze

B (fam) 1 «*persona*» to freeze; **me estoy helando** I'm freezing 2 «*comida/café*» to get *o* go cold

helecho *m* (como nombre genérico) fern; (más específico) bracken

hélice *f*

A (de barco) propeller, screw; (de avión) propeller

B (Anat, Mat) helix

helicóptero *m* helicopter

helio *m* helium

heliogábalo *m* (liter) glutton

heliograbado *m*, **heliografía** *f* photogravure

helipuerto *m* heliport

hemático -ca *adj* hematic* (tech), blood (*before n*)

hematíe *m* red blood cell

hematófago *m* bloodsucker

hematoma *m* (tumor) hematoma*; (moretón) bruise

hembra[1] *adj inv* female

hembra[2] *f*

A 1 (Zool) female; **la ~ del faisán** the hen pheasant 2 (mujer) female, woman

B (de enchufe, corchete) female (part)

hemeroteca *f* newspaper and periodicals library

hemiciclo *m* (sala del congreso) chamber; (espacio central) floor

hemisferio *m* 1 (Geog, Mat) hemisphere; **el ~ norte/sur** the northern/southern hemisphere 2 (Anat) cerebral hemisphere

hemofilia *f* hemophilia*

hemofílico -ca *adj/m,f* hemophiliac*

hemoglobina *f* hemoglobin*

hemorragia *f* hemorrhage*

hemorroides *fpl* piles, hemorrhoids (tech)

henar *m* 1 (campo) hayfield 2 (pajar) hayloft

henchir [I14], [I15] *vt* (liter) ‹*espacio*› to fill; **henchido de orgullo** swollen with pride

hender [E8] *vt* ‹*madera*› to split; ‹*olas/mar*› (liter) to cleave (liter)

hendidura *f* (en madera) crack; (en roca) fissure, crack

hendija *f* (AmS) (grieta) crack, crevice; (hueco) gap

hendir [I12] *vt* ▸**hender**

henna /'xena/ *f* henna

heno *m* hay

hepático -ca *adj* liver (*before n*), hepatic (tech)

hepatitis *f* hepatitis

heptagonal *adj* heptagonal

heptágono *m* heptagon

heráldica *f* heraldry

heráldico -ca *adj* heraldic

heraldo *m* herald

herbáceo -cea *adj* herbaceous

herbaje *m* grass

herbario *m* herbarium

herbicida *m* herbicide, weedkiller

herbívoro[1] **-ra** *adj* herbivorous

herbívoro[2] **-ra** *m,f* herbivore

herbolario[1] *m* (colección) herbarium; (tienda) herbalist's

herbolario[2] **-ria** *m,f* herbalist

herboristería *f* herbalist's

hercio *m* hertz

hercúleo -lea *adj* Herculean

heredad *f* (frml) estate

heredar [A1] *vt* ‹*bienes/título/tradiciones*› to inherit; ‹*trono*› to succeed to; **heredamos este sistema de la dictadura** this system is a legacy of the dictatorship; **heredó los ojos de su madre** he has his mother's eyes

heredero -ra (*m*) heir; (*f*) heir, heiress; **príncipe ~** crown prince; **~ DE algo** heir TO sth

(Compuesto) **heredero universal** residuary legatee

hereditario -ria *adj* hereditary

hereje *mf* heretic

herejía *f* heresy

herencia *f*
A (Der) inheritance; **le dejó en ~ la finca** he bequeathed *o* left her the farm; **nuestra ~ cultural** our cultural heritage
B (Biol) heredity

herético -ca *adj* heretical

herida *f* **1** (en el cuerpo): **sufrir ~s de carácter grave** to be seriously injured, to suffer serious injuries; **se hizo una ~ en la rodilla** he cut his knee; **~ de bala/de guerra** bullet/war wound; **curar una ~** to clean/dress a wound; ***hurgar en la ~*** to open old wounds; ***lamerse las ~s*** to lick one's wounds; ***respirar por la ~*** to reveal one's true feelings (of bitterness) **2** (pena, sufrimiento) wound

herido[1] -da *adj*
A (físicamente) injured; **está gravemente ~** (por accidente) he is seriously injured; (por agresión) he has been seriously wounded; **~ de muerte** fatally wounded
B (en sentimiento) ‹*persona*› hurt, wounded (liter); ‹*honor*› wounded (liter)

herido[2] -da *m,f*: **los ~s** the injured/wounded; **la explosión causó varios ~s** several people were injured in the explosion

herir [I11] *vt*
A **1** (físicamente) to wound; **fue herido de muerte** he was fatally wounded **2** ‹*orgullo*› to hurt; **sus palabras la hirieron profundamente** she was deeply wounded *o* hurt by his words; **esta película puede ~ la sensibilidad del espectador** this movie contains scenes/language which some viewers may find disturbing/offensive
B **1** ‹*vista*› to hurt **2** (liter) «*sol/ruido*» to pierce

hermafrodita[1] *adj* hermaphrodite (*before n*), hermaphroditic

hermafrodita[2] *mf* hermaphrodite

hermanamiento *m* twinning (BrE)

hermanar [A1] *vt* **1** (en sentimiento, propósito) to unite **2** ‹*ciudades*› to twin (BrE) **3** ‹*calcetines*› to match up, put … in pairs; ‹*fichas/naipes*› to match up

hermanastro -tra **1** (con vínculo sanguíneo) (*m*) half brother; (*f*) half sister **2** (sin vínculo sanguíneo) (*m*) stepbrother; (*f*) stepsister

hermandad *f* **1** (de hombres) brotherhood, fraternity; (de mujeres) sisterhood **2** (asociación) association

hermano[1] -na *adj* ‹*buque*› sister (*before n*); ‹*ciudades*› twin (*before n*)

hermano[2] -na *m,f*
A (pariente) (*m*) brother; (*f*) sister; **mis ~s** (sólo varones) my brothers; (varones y mujeres) my brothers and sisters; **¿tienes ~s?** do you have any brothers or sisters?; **el ~ menor** the younger/youngest brother

(Compuestos)
- **hermano -na de leche** *m,f*: *person suckled by the same woman as oneself*
- **hermano -na de sangre** (*m*) blood brother; (*f*) blood sister
- **hermano gemelo -na gemela** (*m*) twin brother; (*f*) twin sister
- **hermano político -na política** (*m*) brother-in-law; (*f*) sister-in-law

B (como apelativo) (Col, Per, Ven fam) buddy (AmE colloq), mate (BrE colloq)
C **1** (religioso) (*m*) brother; (*f*) sister **2** (prójimo) (*m*) brother; (*f*) sister
D (de guante, calcetín) pair; **¿has visto el ~ de este calcetín?** have you seen the pair for this sock?

hermético -ca *adj* **1** ‹*envase/cierre*› airtight, hermetic (tech) **2** ‹*persona/rostro*› inscrutable, secretive

hermetismo *m* inscrutability, secretiveness

hermosear [A1] *vt* to beautify, make … look beautiful
■ **hermosearse** *v pron* (hum) to make oneself (look) beautiful (hum)

hermoso -sa *adj* **1** (bello) beautiful, lovely **2** (magnífico) splendid **3** (lozano, corpulento) big and healthy, bonny (BrE) **4** (noble) noble

hermosura *f* **1** (cualidad) beauty, loveliness **2** (persona, cosa hermosa): **¡qué ~ de paisaje/niño!** what a beautiful landscape/child!

hernia *f* hernia, rupture
(Compuesto) **hernia discal** *or* **de disco** slipped disk•

herniarse [A1] *v pron* to get a hernia, rupture oneself

héroe *m* hero

heroicidad *f* heroism

heroico -ca *adj* heroic

heroína *f*
A (persona) heroine
B (droga) heroin

heroinómano -na *m,f* heroin addict

heroísmo *m* heroism

herpes *m* (*pl* ~) (en boca, genitales) herpes; (en cintura) shingles

herrador -dora *m,f* blacksmith, farrier

herradura *f* horseshoe

herraje *m tb* **~s** ironwork, iron fittings (*pl*)

herramienta *f* tool

herrar [A5] *vt* ‹*caballo*› to shoe; ‹*ganado*› to brand

herrería *f* blacksmith's, smithy

herrero -ra *m,f* blacksmith

herrete *m* aglet, tag

herrumbre *f* rust; **(de) color ~** rust, rust-colored•

herrumbroso -sa *adj* rusty

hervidero *m*: **un ~ de gente** a seething mass of people; **un ~ de moscas** a swarm of flies; **la casa era un ~** the house was buzzing; **un ~ político** a political hotbed; **un ~ de chismes** a hotbed of gossip

hervido *m* (Ven) *chicken or fish stew with vegetables, also gathering at which it is served*

hervidor *m* (de agua) kettle; (de leche) milk pan

hervir [I11] *vi* **1** «*líquido*» to boil; **romper a ~** to come to the boil; **las calles hervían de gente** the streets were seething *o* swarming with people; **hervía de rabia** she was boiling *o* seething with rage **2** **hirviendo** *adj* (muy caliente) boiling (colloq), roasting (colloq); **el niño está hirviendo** (de fiebre) the child is burning up with fever
■ **hervir** *vt* to boil

hervor *m* **1** (de líquido): **le das un ~ y lo retiras** bring to the boil and remove; **cuando rompa el ~** when it comes to the boil **2** (entusiasmo) fervor•

heterodoxia *f* heterodoxy

heterodoxo -xa *adj* heterodox

heterogéneo -nea *adj* (Quím) heterogeneous; **acudió un público muy ~** there was a wide cross section of people in the audience

heterosexual *adj/mf* heterosexual

heterosexualidad *f* heterosexuality

hexagonal *adj* hexagonal

hexágono *m* hexagon

hez *f*
A **1** (escoria) dregs (*pl*) **2** (Vin) *tb* **heces** sediment, lees (*pl*)
B **heces** *fpl* (excrementos) feces• (*pl*)

hiato *m* hiatus

hibernación *f* (Zool) hibernation; (de enfermos) artificial hibernation; (de cadáveres) deep-freezing

hibernal *adj* (liter) ‹*lluvias*› winter (*before n*); ‹*frío*› wintry

hibernar [A1] *vi* to hibernate

híbrido[1] -da *adj* ‹*animal/planta*› hybrid (*before n*); ‹*estilo*› hybrid (*before n*), composite

híbrido[2] *m* hybrid

hice, hiciera, etc *see* **hacer**

hidalgo *m* gentleman, nobleman (*from the lower ranks of the nobility*)

hidalguía *f* gentlemanliness, nobility

hidrante *m* (AmC, Col) hydrant
(Compuesto) **hidrante de incendios** fire hydrant

hidratación *f* (de verduras) hydration; (de la piel) moisturizing

hidratante *adj* moisturizing (*before n*)

hidratar [A1] *vt* ‹*verduras*› to hydrate; ‹*piel*› to moisturize

hidrato *m* hydrate; **~s de carbono** carbohydrates

hidráulico -ca *adj* hydraulic

h

hídrico -ca *adj* water (*before n*)
hidroavión *m* seaplane
hidrocarburo *m* hydrocarbon
hidroeléctrico -ca *adj* hydroelectric
hidrófilo -la *adj* 1 (Quím) hydrophilic 2 ‹*gasa*› absorbent
hidrofobia *f* hydrophobia (tech), rabies
hidrofóbico -ca *adj*, **hidrófobo -ba** *adj* hydrophobic
hidrófugo -ga *adj* damp-proof, water-resistant
hidrógeno *m* hydrogen
hidrólisis *f* hydrolysis
hidrosoluble *adj* water-soluble
hidróxido *m* hydroxide
hiedra *f* ivy
hiel *f* 1 (Fisiol) bile 2 (liter) (amargura) bile (liter), bitterness 3 **hieles** *fpl* (penas, disgustos) trials and tribulations (*pl*)
hiela, hielas, etc *see* **helar**
hielo *m* ice; **una mirada de ~** a frosty *o* an icy look; ***romper el ~*** to break the ice
(Compuesto) **hielo picado/seco** crushed/dry ice
hiena *f* hyena
hierático -ca *adj* 1 (Hist) hieratic(al) 2 ‹*rostro/expresión*› severe and inscrutable
hierba *f*
A (césped) grass; **~ *mala nunca muere*** the Devil looks after his own
(Compuesto) **hierba artificial** Astroturf®, artificial turf
B 1 (Bot, Coc, Med) herb; **malas ~s** weeds; **infusión de hierbas** herbal tea 2 (arg) (marihuana) grass (colloq)
hierbabuena *f* mint
hierbajo *m* weed
hierbero -ra *m,f* (Méx) herbalist
hierro *m* 1 (Metal) iron; **atrapados entre los ~s del tren** trapped in the wreckage of the train; ***de*** **~** iron (*before n*); ***quitar ~ a algo*** to play sth down 2 (Agr) (herramienta) branding iron; (marca) brand 3 (de lanza, flecha) head, tip; ***el que a ~ mata, a ~ muere*** he who lives by the sword, dies by the sword 4 (en golf) iron; **un ~ cuatro** a four iron
(Compuestos)
- **hierro forjado** wrought iron
- **hierro fundido** *or* **colado** cast iron

hígado *m* liver; ***echar los ~s*** (fam) to bust a gut (sl); ***ser un ~*** (Méx fam) to be a pain in the neck (colloq); ***tener mucho ~*** (Col, Ven fam) to have a lot of guts
higiene *f* hygiene
higiénico -ca *adj* hygienic
higienista *mf* hygienist
higienizar [A4] *vt* (frml) to clean, sanitize (frml)
higo *m* 1 (de la higuera) fig; ***de ~s a brevas*** (fam) once in a blue moon (colloq); ***estar hecho un ~*** (fam) to be all crumpled 2 (Col, Ven) (del nopal) prickly pear
(Compuesto) **higo chumbo** (Esp) prickly pear
higuera *f* fig tree; ***estar en la ~*** (fam) to have one's head in the clouds (colloq)
hijastro -tra (*m*) stepson; (*f*) stepdaughter; **mis ~s** my stepchildren
hijo -ja *m,f*
A (pariente) (*m*) son; (*f*) daughter; **mis ~s** (sólo varones) my sons; (varones y mujeres) my children; **espera un ~** she's expecting a baby; **¡ese ~ de su madre!** (fam & euf) that son-of-a-gun! (colloq & euph); **M. Pérez, ~** M. Pérez Junior; ***cualquier/todo ~ de vecino*** (fam): **tendrá que esperar como cualquier ~ de vecino** she'll have to wait like everybody else; **eso lo sabe todo ~ de vecino** everybody knows that; **~ *de tigre sale pintado*** (AmL fam) he's just like his father/mother
(Compuestos)
- **hijo adoptivo -ja adoptiva** (*m*) adopted son; (*f*) adopted daughter
- **hijo -ja de la guayaba** *or* **de la mañana** *or* **de su pelona** (Méx fam & euf) (*m*) bastard (vulg), swine (colloq); (*f*) bitch (colloq)
- **hijo -ja de papá** *m,f* rich kid (colloq)
- **hijo -ja de puta** *or* (Méx) **de la chingada** (vulg) (*m*) bastard (vulg), son of a bitch (AmE sl); (*f*) bitch (vulg), bastard (vulg)
- **hijo -ja natural** (*m*) illegitimate son; (*f*) illegitimate daughter
- **hijo político -ja política** (*m*) son-in-law; (*f*) daughter-in-law
- **hijo pródigo** *m* prodigal son
- **hijo único -ja única** *m,f* only child

B (de pueblo, comunidad) (*m*) son; (*f*) daughter
C (apelativo): **¡~, por Dios!** (hablándole a un niño) for heaven's sake, child!; (hablándole a un adulto) for heaven's sake, Pedro (*o* Luis *etc*)!
D (Méx fam) (interjección) jeez! (AmE colloq), gosh (colloq)
híjole *interj* (Méx) jeez! (AmE colloq), gosh (colloq)
hijuela *f* (Chi, Ec) plot
hijuelo *m* shoot
hilacha *f* loose thread; ***darle vuelo a la ~*** (Méx fam) to kick over the traces (colloq); ***mostrar*** *or* ***dejar ver la ~*** (CS fam) to show one's true colors
hilacho *m* (Méx fam) 1 (trapo) rag 2 **hilachos** *mpl* (ropa) old clothes (*pl*), rags (*pl*)
hilada *f* course
hilado *m* 1 (hilo) yarn, thread; **fábrica de ~s** spinning mill 2 (proceso) spinning
hilador -dora *adj* spinning (*before n*)
hilandería *f* spinning mill
hilandero -ra *m,f* spinner
hilar [A1] *vi* to spin; **~ *fino*** to split hairs
■ **hilar** *vt* 1 ‹*algodón/lana*› to spin; «*araña*» to spin 2 ‹*ideas/hechos*› to string together
hilarante *adj* (frml) hilarious
hilaridad *f* hilarity
hilatura *f* (proceso) spinning (*before n*); (fábrica) spinning mill
hilera *f* 1 (fila) row, line 2 (Mil) file (frml *or* liter) 3 (de ladrillos) course 4 (de semillas) row, drill
hilo *m*
A 1 (en costura) thread; ***al ~*** ‹*cortar/coser*› on the straight, with the weave; (uno tras otro) (AmL fam) in a row, on the trot (colloq); ***mover los ~s***: **es lo que mueve los ~s de su política** it is what controls their policy; **el que mueve los ~s** the one who's pulling the strings *o* calling the shots; ***pender*** *or* ***colgar de un ~*** to hang by a thread; ***por el ~ se saca el ovillo*** it's just a question of putting two and two together 2 (lino) linen 3 (de araña) thread 4 (fam) (de las judías) string
(Compuesto) **hilo dental** dental floss
B (Elec) wire
(Compuesto) **hilo musical** (Esp) piped music
C (de relato, conversación) thread; **interrumpió el ~ de sus pensamientos** it interrupted his train of thought
D (de sangre, agua) trickle; **un ~ de luz** a thread of light (liter); **con un ~ de voz** in a tiny voice
hilván *m* basting (AmE), tacking (BrE)
hilvanar [A1] *vt*
A (coser) to baste (AmE), to tack (BrE)
B ‹*frases/ideas*› to put together
himen *m* hymen
himeneo *m* (liter) nuptials (*pl*) (liter)
himno *m*
A (religioso) hymn; (de colegio) school song *o* anthem
(Compuesto) **himno nacional** national anthem
B (Lit) ode
hincada *f* (Col, Per) sharp pain
hincapié *m*: **hizo especial ~ en las ventajas económicas** she put special emphasis on the economic advantages; **hizo ~ en que ...** he stressed *o* emphasized (the fact) that ...
hincar [A2] *vt* 1 (clavar) **~ algo EN algo** ‹*estaca*› to drive *o* thrust sth INTO sth; **me hincó los dientes en la mano** it buried its teeth in *o* sunk its teeth into my hand 2 **~ la rodilla** to go down on one knee (frml *or* liter)
■ **hincarse** *v pron*: **~se de rodillas** to kneel
hincha *mf*
A (fam) (Dep) fan (colloq), supporter

B **hincha** *f* (fam) (antipatía): **tenerle ~ a algn** to have a grudge against sb
hinchada *f* (fam) supporters (*pl*), fans (*pl*) (colloq)
hinchado -da *adj* ‹*vientre/pierna*› swollen; ‹*estilo/lenguaje*› overblown
hinchador -dora *adj* (CS fam) annoying, irritating
hinchar [A1] *vt* (Esp) ‹*globo*› to inflate (frml), to blow up; ‹*rueda*› to inflate, pump up; ‹*suceso/noticia*› (fam) to blow ... up (colloq)
■ **hinchar** *vi*
A (CS fam) (fastidiar) «*persona*» to be a pain in the ass (AmE vulg) *o* (BrE vulg) arse; (+ *me/te/le etc*) **me hincha su actitud** his attitude really pisses me off (sl)
B (CS) (Dep) **~ POR algn** to cheer sb on, root for sb (colloq)
■ **hincharse** *v pron* **1** «*vientre/pierna*» (+ *me/te/le etc*) to swell up; ***~se de plata** or **dinero*** (fam) to earn *o* make a fortune (colloq) **2** (fam) (enorgullecerse) to swell with pride **3** (Esp fam) (hartarse) **~se A/DE algo**: **me hinché de ostras** I stuffed myself with oysters (colloq); **se hinchó a insultarme** she called me everything under the sun
hinchazón *f* swelling
hinchón -chona *adj* (Ven fam) annoying
hindú *adj/mf* **1** (Relig) Hindu **2** (crit) (de la India) Indian
hinojo *m*
A (Bot, Coc) fennel
B **de hinojos** (liter) on bended knee (liter)
hipar *vi* to hiccup
híper *m* (fam) large supermarket, hypermarket (BrE)
hiperactivo -va *adj* hyperactive
hipérbole *f* hyperbole
hiperbólico -ca *adj* hyperbolic
hipermercado *m* large supermarket, hypermarket (BrE)
hipermetropía *f* farsightedness (AmE), long-sightedness (BrE)
hipersensible *adj* oversensitive, hypersensitive; **~ A algo** oversensitive TO sth
hipertensión *f* high blood pressure, hypertension
hipertenso -sa *adj* hypertensive; **es ~** he has high blood pressure *o* hypertension
hipertrofia *f* (Med) hypertrophy
hípica *f* equestrian sports (*pl*); (carreras) horse racing
hípico -ca *adj* ‹*deportes*› equestrian (*before n*); **un comentarista ~** (de carreras) a horse-racing commentator; (de concursos) a showjumping commentator
hipnosis *f* hypnosis
hipnótico -ca *adj* hypnotic
hipnotismo *m* hypnotism
hipnotizador[1] **-dora** *adj* ‹*mirada*› hypnotic
hipnotizador[2] **-dora** *m,f* hypnotist
hipnotizar [A4] *vt* (Psic) to hypnotize; (fascinar) to mesmerize
hipo *m* hiccups (*pl*), hiccoughs (*pl*); **tener ~** to have hiccups; ***que quita el ~*** (fam) breathtaking
hipocampo *m* sea horse
hipocondría *f* hypochondria
hipocondríaco -ca, hipocondriaco -ca *m,f* hypochondriac
hipocorístico *m*: **Lola es un ~ de Dolores** Lola is an affectionate form of the name Dolores
hipocresía *f* hypocrisy
hipócrita[1] *adj* hypocritical
hipócrita[2] *mf* hypocrite
hipodérmico -ca *adj* hypodermic
hipódromo *m* (Equ, Ocio) racecourse, racetrack (AmE); (Hist) hippodrome
hipopótamo *m* hippopotamus
hipoteca *f* mortgage
hipotecable *adj* mortgageable
hipotecar [A2] *vt* to mortgage
hipotecario -ria *adj* mortgage (*before n*)
hipotensión *f* low blood pressure, hypotension
hipotenusa *f* hypotenuse
hipótesis *f* hypothesis
hipotético -ca *adj* hypothetical
hippy[1], **hippie** /'xipi/ *adj* (*pl* **hippies**) hippy (*before n*), hippie (*before n*)
hippy[2], **hippie** /'xipi/ *mf* (*pl* **hippies**) hippy, hippie
hiriente *adj* hurtful, wounding (*before n*)
hirsuto -ta *adj* **1** ‹*barba*› bristly; ‹*cabellera*› wiry; ‹*persona*› hairy, hirsute (liter) **2** (carácter) curt, brusque
hirviendo *see* **hervir**
hisopo *m* **1** (Bot) hyssop **2** (Med) swab; (bastoncillo) cotton swab (AmE), cotton bud (BrE)
hispánico -ca *adj* **1** (de los países de habla hispana) Hispanic **2** (relativo a España) Spanish
hispanidad *f*: **la ~** the Hispanic world
hispanismo *m* (giro propio del español de España) word/expression peculiar to Spain; (palabra derivada del español) hispanicism; (estudio) Hispanic studies
hispanista *mf* Hispanist, Hispanicist
hispanizar [A4] *vt* to hispanicize
hispano[1] **-na** *adj* **1** (español) Spanish, Hispanic (frml); **países de habla hispana** Spanish-speaking countries **2** (hispanoamericano) Spanish American, Latin American; (en EE UU) Hispanic
hispano[2] **-na** *m,f* **1** (liter) (español) Spaniard **2** (hispanoamericano) Spanish American, Latin American; (en EE UU) Hispanic
Hispanoamérica *f* Spanish America
hispanoamericano -na *adj/m,f* Spanish American
hispanófilo -la *m,f* Hispanophile
hispanohablante[1], **hispanoparlante** *adj* Spanish-speaking
hispanohablante[2], **hispanoparlante** *mf* Spanish speaker
histerectomía *f* hysterectomy
histeria *f* hysteria
(Compuesto) **histeria colectiva** mass hysteria
histérico[1] **-ca** *adj* (Med, Psic) hysterical; (exaltado): **ponerse ~** to have hysterics *o* a fit; **me pones ~** you drive me mad
histérico[2] **-ca** *m,f* (Med, Psic) hysteric; (exaltado): **es un ~** he gets quite hysterical about things
histerismo *m* hysteria
historia *f*
A (Hist) history; **la ~ se repite** history repeats itself; ***hacer ~*** to make history; ***pasar a la ~*** (por ser importante) to go down in history; (perder actualidad) (fam): **aquello ya pasó a la ~** that's ancient history now (colloq)
(Compuestos)
- **historia antigua** ancient history
- **historia clínica** (AmS) medical history
- **historia natural** natural history

B (relato) story; **la ~ de su familia/vida** his family history/the story of his life; **una ~ de amor** a love story
C (fam) **1** (cuento, excusa): **me vino con la ~ de que ...** he came up with this story *o* tale about ...; **déjate de ~s** stop making excuses **2** (asunto): **se quejó de no sé qué ~s** he complained about something or other (colloq); **una ~ de drogas** some business to do with drugs (colloq) **3** (lío amoroso) scene (colloq)
historiado -da *adj* fussy, overelaborate
historiador -dora *m,f* historian
historial *m* record
(Compuestos)
- **historial clínico** *or* **médico** medical history
- **historial personal** resumé (AmE), curriculum vitae (BrE)

historiar [A1] *vt* to tell the story of, write the history of
histórico -ca *adj* (real) historical; (importante) historic
historieta *f* comic strip, cartoon story
histriónico -ca *adj* **1** (exagerado) histrionic, theatrical, dramatic **2** ‹*talento*› dramatic
hit /'xit/ *m* (*pl* **hits**) (Mús) hit; (en béisbol) hit
hito *m* (hecho trascendental) landmark, milestone; (mojón) (ant) milestone; ***mirarle a algn de ~ en ~*** (liter) to gaze *o* stare at sb
hizo *see* **hacer**

Hnos. (= **hermanos**) Bros.

hobby /'xoβi/ *m* (*pl* **-bbies**) hobby

hocico *m* (de cerdo) snout; (de perro, lobo) snout, muzzle; ***meter el ~ en algo*** (fam) to poke one's nose into sth (colloq); *para otros modismos ver* **nariz, morro**

hocicón -cona *m,f* (CS, Méx fam & pey) bigmouth (colloq & pej), blabbermouth (colloq & pej)

hockey /'(x)oki/ *m* hockey

Compuestos

- **hockey sobre hielo** ice hockey
- **hockey sobre hierba** hockey, field hockey (AmE)

hogaño *adv* (liter) nowadays, in this day and age

hogar *m* 1 (residencia) home; **formar** *or* **fundar un ~** to set up home; **artículos para el ~** household goods; **las labores del ~** housework; **quedarse sin ~** to be left homeless; **~es deshechos** broken homes; **~, dulce ~** (fr hecha) home sweet home 2 (liter) (chimenea) hearth

Compuesto **hogar de ancianos** residential home for the elderly, old people's home (colloq)

hogareño -ña *adj* ‹*persona*› home-loving; ‹*vida/escena*› domestic (*before n*)

hoguera *f* bonfire; **murió en la ~** he was burned at the stake

hoja *f*

A (Bot) leaf; **~ de laurel** bay leaf; ***temblar como una ~*** to shake like a leaf

Compuestos

- **hoja de cálculo** spreadsheet
- **hoja de parra** (Bot) vine leaf; (Art, Bib) figleaf

B 1 (folio) sheet 2 (de libro) page, leaf; **pasar las ~s** to turn the pages 3 (formulario) form, sheet 4 (octavilla) leaflet, flier (AmE)

Compuestos

- **hoja de pedido** order form
- **hoja de ruta** (Transp) waybill; (Pol) road map
- **hoja de vida** (Col, Ven) resumé (AmE), curriculum vitae

C 1 (de puerta, mesa) leaf 2 (de madera, metal) sheet 3 (de cuchillo) blade

Compuesto **hoja de afeitar** razor blade

hojalata *f* tinplate

hojalatería *f* (Méx) body work (AmE), panel-beating (BrE)

hojalatero -ra *m,f* (que trabaja con hojalata) tinsmith; (Auto) (Méx) body shop worker (AmE), panel beater (BrE)

hojaldrado -da *adj* flaky

hojaldre *m* puff pastry, puff paste (AmE)

hojarasca *f* (hojas) fallen leaves (*pl*), dead leaves (*pl*); (palabrería) padding, waffle (BrE)

hojear [A1] *vt* to leaf *o* glance through

hojilla *f* (Ven) razor blade

hojuela *f* (Col, Méx, Per, Ven) flake

hola, ▸**Telefonear** *interj* (saludo) hello, hi! (colloq)

holá *interj* (RPl) (por teléfono) hello?

Holanda *f* Holland

holandés¹ -desa *adj* Dutch

holandés² -desa

A (*m*) Dutchman; (*f*) Dutchwoman; **los holandeses** the Dutch, Dutch people

B **holandés** *m* (idioma) Dutch

holgado -da *adj* 1 ‹*prenda*› loose-fitting, baggy 2 ‹*posición*› comfortable; **viven ~s** they're comfortably off 3 ‹*victoria*› comfortable, easy; ‹*mayoría*› comfortable 4 (de espacio): **así iremos más ~s** we'll be more comfortable like that

holganza *f* idleness; **una vida de ~** a life of leisure

holgar [A8] *vi* (*en 3ª pers*) (frml) (estar de más): **huelga decir que ...** it goes without saying that ..., needless to say ...; **huelgan los comentarios** what can one say?

holgazán¹ -zana *adj* lazy

holgazán² -zana *m,f* idler, lazybones (colloq)

holgazanear [A1] *vi* to idle, laze *o* loaf around

holgazanería *f* idleness, laziness

holgura *f* 1 (bienestar económico): **vivir con ~** to live comfortably 2 (comodidad): **ganaron con ~** they won easily *o* comfortably 3 (de prenda) fullness, looseness

hollar [A10] *vt* (liter) to tread (liter), to set foot on

hollejo *m* skin

hollín *m* soot

holocausto *m* (Hist, Relig) (sacrificio) burnt offering, sacrifice; (destrucción) holocaust; **el Holocausto** (Hist) the Holocaust

Compuesto **holocausto nuclear** nuclear holocaust

holograma *m* hologram

hombrada *f* act worthy of a man

hombre¹ *m* 1 (varón) man; **~s, mujeres y niños** men, women and children; **está hecho un ~** he's a real man, now; **hablar de ~ a ~** to talk man-to-man; **no es lo bastante ~ como para hacerlo** he's not man enough to do it; **el ejército te hará un ~** the Army will make a man (out) of you; **¡~ al agua!** man overboard!; **este ~ no sabe lo que dice** this guy doesn't know what he's talking about; ***ser un ~ de pelo en pecho*** to be a real man, be a he-man (hum); **~ *precavido vale por dos*** forewarned is forearmed 2 (especie humana): **el ~** man; **el ~ prehistórico** prehistoric man; ***el ~ propone y Dios dispone*** Man proposes and God disposes

Compuestos

- **hombre de bien** fine, upstanding man
- **hombre de confianza** right-hand man
- **hombre de estado** statesman
- **hombre del tiempo** weatherman
- **hombre de mundo** man of the world
- **hombre de negocios** businessman
- **hombre de paja** (en política) puppet; (en negocio sucio) front man, straw man (AmE)
- **hombre lobo** werewolf
- **hombre medio/de la calle** man in the street
- **hombre orquesta** (Mús) one-man band
- **hombre rana** frogman, diver

hombre² *interj*: **¡~! ¡qué sorpresa!** well! *o* hey! what a nice surprise!; **¿te gustaría venir? — ¡~!** would you like to come? — you bet! what do you think?; **~, no es lo mismo** come off it, it's not the same thing at all (colloq); **~, supongo que sí** well *o* I don't know, I suppose so

hombrecillo *m*

A (hombre pequeño) little man

B (Bot) hop

hombre-mono *m* (*pl* **hombres-mono**) apeman

hombrera *f* (almohadilla) shoulder pad; (Mil) (de uniformes) epaulet

hombretón *m* (fam) well-built guy (colloq)

hombría *f* manliness

hombrillo *m* (Ven) shoulder (AmE), hard shoulder (BrE)

hombro *m* shoulder; **tiene los ~s caídos** (hacia adelante) she has round shoulders; (hacia el costado) she has sloping shoulders; **encogerse de ~s** to shrug (one's shoulders); **lo llevaron a ~s** they carried him on their shoulders *o* shoulder high; ***arrimar el ~*** to pull one's weight, put one's shoulder to the wheel; ***echarse algo al ~*** (asumir) to shoulder sth, take sth on; **~ *con* ~** shoulder to shoulder; ***mirar a algn por encima del ~*** to look down on sb

hombrón *m* (fam) well-built guy (colloq)

hombruno -na *adj* (pey) ‹*mujer*› mannish, butch (colloq & pej); ‹*gestos/modales*› masculine, mannish

homenaje *m* 1 (tributo) tribute; **rendir(le) ~ a algn** to pay tribute *o* homage to sb; **en ~ a** in honor of 2 (acto): **le ofrecieron un ~** they held a party (*o* reception *etc*) in his honor; **el ~ que la Academia le tributó** the ceremony (*o* event *etc*) that the Academy organized as a tribute to her 3 (*como adj inv*): **una cena ~ a algn** a dinner in honor of sb; **un partido ~** a testimonial game

homenajeado -da *m,f* (frml *o* hum) guest of honor*

homenajear [A1] *vt* (frml) to honor*, pay homage *o* tribute to; **fue homenajeado con una cena** a dinner was held in his honor

homeópata *mf* homeopath

homeopatía *f* homeopathy

homeopático -ca *adj* (Med) homeopathic

homicida¹ *adj* (frml) ‹*instinto*› homicidal; **el arma ~** the murder weapon

homicida² *mf* (frml) murderer, homicide (frml)

homicidio *m* (frml) homicide

homilía *f* homily

homogeneizar [A21] *vt* to homogenize

homogéneo -nea *adj* ‹*grupo*› homogeneous; ‹*masa/mezcla*› smooth

homógrafo *m* homograph

homologable *adj* ~ **A algo** comparable WITH sth, equivalent TO sth

homologado -da *adj* approved, endorsed

homologar [A3] *vt*

A 1 ‹*producto*› (recomendar) to approve, endorse; (autorizar) to authorize, approve 2 (Dep) ‹*récord*› to ratify, recognize 3 ‹*convenio*› to recognize

B (equiparar) ~ **algo CON algo** to recognize sth as equivalent TO sth

homólogo[1] **-ga** *adj* equivalent

homólogo[2] **-ga** *m,f* (period) counterpart

homónimo[1] **-ma** *adj* ‹*palabras*› homonymous; **dos pueblos ~s** two towns with the same name

homónimo[2] *m* (Ling) homonym; (persona) namesake

homosexual *adj/mf* homosexual

homosexualidad *f* homosexuality

honda *f* (de cuero) sling; (con elástico) slingshot (AmE), catapult (BrE)

hondo[1] **-da** *adj* 1 ‹*piscina/río*› deep; **en lo ~ de su alma** in the depths of his soul; **en lo más ~ de mi corazón** deep in my heart of hearts, deep down; **en lo ~ del valle** at the bottom of the valley; ***calar ~*** to take off (colloq) 2 (*gen delante del n*) (frml) ‹*pena/pesar*› profound (frml), deep

hondo[2] *adv*: **respirar ~** to breathe deeply

hondo[3] *m*: **el ~** the depths (*pl*), the bottom

hondonada *f* hollow

hondura *f* (liter) depth; ***meterse en ~s*** to go into a lot of detail

Honduras *f* Honduras

hondureño -ña *adj/m,f* Honduran

honestamente *adv* 1 (sinceramente) honestly; **~, no sé qué puedes hacer** (*indep*) to be honest, I don't know what you can do, I don't honestly know what you can do 2 ‹*actuar/comportarse*› honestly, honorably

honestidad *f* integrity, honesty; **te lo diré con toda ~** I'm going to be completely honest *o* frank with you

honesto -ta *adj* 1 (íntegro) honest, honorable* 2 (ant *o* hum) ‹*mujer*› virtuous, honest (arch)

hongo *m* 1 (Bot) fungus 2 (AmL) (Coc) mushroom; ***aparecer*** *or* ***brotar como ~s*** to spring up all over 3 (Med) fungus; (en los pies): **tengo ~s** I have athlete's foot 4 *tb* **sombrero de ~** derby (AmE), bowler hat (BrE)

(Compuesto) **hongo atómico** *or* **nuclear** mushroom cloud

honor *m*

A 1 (dignidad moral) honor*; **un hombre/una cuestión de ~** a man/a question of honor; ***en ~ a la verdad*** to be truthful; ***hacer ~ a su fama*** *or* ***nombre*** to live up to one's reputation 2 (ant) (virginidad) honor*, virtue

B 1 (privilegio) honor*; **tengo el ~ de ...** it is my honor *o* I have the honor to ...; **una cena en ~ de ...** a dinner in honor of ...; **me hizo el ~ de recibirme** he did me the honor of receiving me 2 **honores** *mpl* (homenaje) honors* (*pl*); **le rindieron los ~es correspondientes a su rango** he was accorded the honors befitting his rank (frml); ***hacerle los ~es a algo*** to do justice to sth

honorable *adj* honorable*

honorario -ria *adj* honorary

honorarios *mpl* fees (*pl*)

honorífico -ca *adj* honorary

honoris causa *loc adj* honoris causa; **doctor ~ ~** doctor honoris causa

honra *f* 1 (dignidad moral) honor*; ***tener algo a mucha ~*** to be very proud of sth; ***¡y a mucha ~!***: **soy ecologista ¡y a mucha ~!** I'm an environmentalist and (I'm) proud of it! 2 (ant) (virginidad) honor*, virtue

(Compuesto) **honras fúnebres** *fpl* funeral rites (*pl*)

honradamente *adv* honestly, honorably*

honradez *f* (honestidad) honesty; (decencia) decency

honrado -da *adj* 1 (honesto) honest, honorable* 2 ‹*mujer*› respectable

honrar [A1] *vt*

A «*comportamiento/actitud*» to do ... credit *o* honor*; **nos honra hoy con su presencia** she is honoring us with her presence here today

B (respetar) to honor*

honroso -sa *adj* honorable*

hontanar *m* spring

hora *f*

A (período de tiempo) hour; **(una) ~ y media** an hour and a half; **media ~** half an hour, a half hour (AmE); **las ~s de mayor afluencia** the busiest time; **semana laboral de 40 ~s** 40-hour working week; **100 kilómetros por ~** 100 kilometers per/an hour; **cobrar por ~s** to be paid by the hour; **80 pesos la ~** *or* **por ~** 80 pesos an hour; Ⓢ **horas de atención al público de ocho a una** open to the public from eight to one; **se pasa ~s enteras leyendo** she reads for hours on end; **trabajar fuera de ~s** to work outside normal working hours; ***pasarse las ~s muertas*** to while away one's time

(Compuestos)

- **hora libre** free period
- **hora pico** (AmL) *or* (Esp) **punta** rush hour
- **hora puente** *or* **sandwich** (RPl) free period
- **horas de oficina/de trabajo/de visita** *fpl* office/working/visiting hours (*pl*)
- **horas de vuelo** *fpl* flying time
- **horas extra(s)** *or* **extraordinarias** *fpl* overtime
- **horas libres** *fpl* free *o* spare time

B 1 (momento puntual) time; **¿tiene ~, por favor?** have you got the time, please?; **¿me da la ~?** can you tell me the time?; **¿qué ~ es?** what's the time?, what time is it?; **pon el reloj en ~** put the clock right; **todavía no es la ~** it's not time yet; **nunca llegan a la ~** they never arrive on time; **el avión llegó antes de (su) ~** the plane arrived ahead of schedule *o* arrived early; **la decisión se conocerá a las 20 ~s** (period) they will give their verdict at 8pm; **el ataque se inició a las 20 ~s** (frml) the attack commenced at 20.00 hours (*léase: twenty hundred hours*) (frml); **desde las cero ~s** (period) from midnight; ***no dar ni la ~*** (fam): **¡ésa no da ni la ~!** I'll/you'll/he'll get nothing out of her, she's as mean as they come (colloq); **desde que es jefa, no nos da ni la ~** now that she's been made boss, she won't even give us the time of day 2 (momento sin especificar) time; **es ~ de irse a la cama** it's bedtime *o* time for bed; **a la ~ de almorzar** at lunchtime; **ya es ~ de irnos** it's time for us to go, it's time we were going; **hay trenes a toda ~** there is a frequent train service; **¡ya era ~ de que llamases!** it's about time you called; **a altas ~s de la madrugada** in the early *o* small hours of the morning; **a primera ~ de la mañana** first thing in the morning; **a última ~** at the last moment; **una noticia de última ~** a late *o* last-minute news item; ***a buena ~*** *or* ***a buenas ~s***: **¿y me lo dices ahora? ¡a buenas ~s!** *now* you tell me!, it's a bit late to tell me now!; **a buenas ~s llegas** this is a fine time to arrive!; ***a la ~ de***: **a la ~ traducirlo** when it comes to translating it; **a la ~ de la verdad** when it comes down to it; ***en buena ~***: **en buena ~ compramos esta casa** we bought this house at just the right time; ***en mala ~***: **en mala ~ se nos ocurrió invitarla** it was a really bad move inviting her; ***entre ~s*** between meals; ***hacer ~*** (Chi) to kill time; ***llegarle a algn su (última) ~***: **le llegó su (última) ~** his time had come; ***no ver la ~ de***: **no veo la ~ de que lleguen** I'm really looking forward to them coming, I can't wait for them to come

(Compuestos)

- **hora cero** *o* **H** zero hour
- **hora de cierre** (de periódico) news deadline; (de emisión) closedown
- **hora inglesa** (fam): **a las siete ~ ~** at seven o'clock on the dot (colloq)
- **hora local/oficial** local/standard time

C (cita) appointment; **me han dado ~ para mañana** they've given me an appointment for tomorrow; **pedir ~** to make an appointment

horadar [A1] *vt* ‹*roca*› to bore through; ‹*pared*› to drill a hole in

hora-hombre *f* (*pl* **horas-hombre**) man-hour

h

horario[1] **-ria** *adj* hourly
horario[2] *m*
A (de trenes, aviones) schedule (AmE), timetable (BrE); (de clases) timetable; **tiene un ~ muy flexible** his hours are very flexible; **S horario de atención al público** (en banco, comercio) business hours; (en oficina pública) hours of opening
Compuestos
- **horario continuo** *or* (AmL) **corrido** *or* (Esp) **intensivo** *continuous working day (usually from eight to three) with no break for lunch*
- **horario de visitas** visiting hours (*pl*)
- **horario estelar** (Ven) prime time
- **horario partido** *working day with a long break for lunch*

B (de reloj) hour hand
horca *f*
A (patíbulo) gallows (*pl*); (juego): **la ~** hangman
B (Agr) pitchfork, hayfork
horcajadas *fpl*: **se sentó a ~ en la pared** he sat astride the wall
horchata *f* (de chufas) horchata (*cold drink made from tiger nuts*); (en Méx) *drink made from ground melon seeds*
horcón *m* (para sostener vigas) (AmL) wooden post; (para cerca) (Ven) fence post; (para sostener ramas) (Col) forked prop
horda *f* (Hist) horde; (multitud) (fam) horde (colloq)
horizontal *adj/f* horizontal
horizonte *m* 1 (línea) horizon 2 **horizontes** *mpl* (perspectivas) horizons (*pl*); **abrirse nuevos ~s** to broaden one's horizons
horma *f* (para hacer zapatos) last; (para conservar su forma) shoetree; **zapatos de ~ ancha/estrecha** broad-fitting/narrow-fitting shoes; ***encontrar la ~ de su zapato*** to meet one's match
hormiga *f* ant; ***trabajar como ~*** to be very hardworking
Compuesto **hormiga obrera** worker ant
hormigón *m* concrete
hormigonera *f* cement mixer
hormiguear [A1] *vi* **~ DE algo** to be crawling *o* swarming WITH sth
hormigueo *m* pins and needles (*pl*), tingling; **siento un ~ en la pierna** I've got pins and needles in my leg
hormiguero *m* 1 (Zool) (nido) ant's nest; (montículo) anthill 2 (de personas): **era un ~ de gente** it was swarming with people
hormona *f* hormone
hormonal *adj* hormonal, hormone (*before n*)
hornacina *f* niche
hornada *f* (de pan, pasteles) batch; **la última ~ de diseñadores** the latest generation *o* (colloq) crop of designers
hornalla *f* (RPl) ▸**hornillo A**
horneado *m* cooking/baking time
hornear [A1] *vt* to bake
hornero *m* ovenbird
hornilla *f*
A (AmL exc CS) ▸**hornillo A**
B (Chi) ▸**hornillo B**
hornillo *m*
A (Esp) 1 (de gas) burner 2 (de una cocina eléctrica — espiral) ring; (— placa) hotplate
B (cocinilla portátil) portable electric stove
horno *m* 1 (de cocina) oven; **pollo al ~** roast chicken; **pescado al ~** baked fish; **resistente al ~** ovenproof; **esta oficina es un ~** this office is like an oven; ***no está el ~ para bollos*** (fam) it's not the right moment 2 (Metal, Tec) furnace; **~ de fundición** smelting furnace 3 (para cerámica) kiln
Compuestos
- **horno crematorio** crematorium
- **horno (de) microondas** microwave (oven)

horóscopo *m* horoscope
horqueta *f* 1 (AmL) (de río, camino, árbol) fork 2 (Chi) (de jardinero) fork; (de campesino) pitchfork
horquilla *f* 1 (para pelo) hairpin 2 (Agr) pitchfork 3 (en bicicleta) fork
horrendo -da *adj* ▸**horroroso**

horrible *adj* 1 ‹accidente/muerte› horrible, horrific 2 (feo) ‹persona› hideous, ugly; ‹camisa/adorno› horrible, hideous 3 ‹tiempo› terrible, awful 4 (inaguantable) unbearable
horripilante *adj* terrifying, horrifying
horripilar [A1] *vt* to horrify, terrify
horror *m*
A 1 (miedo, angustia) horror; **me causa ~ verlo** it horrifies me to see it; **les tengo ~ a los hospitales** I'm terrified of hospitals 2 (fam) (uso hiperbólico): **¡qué ~!** how awful *o* terrible!; **un ~ de gente** a tremendous number of people (colloq)
B **horrores** *mpl* (cosas terribles) horrors (*pl*); **dice ~es de ella** (fam) he says awful *o* terrible things about her (colloq)
horrores *adv* (fam): **te he extrañado ~** I've missed you terribly; **sabe ~ del tema** she knows an awful lot about the subject (colloq)
horrorizar [A4] *vt* to horrify, appall
■ **horrorizarse** *v pron* to be horrified, be appalled; **~se DE algo** to be horrified BY *o* AT sth
horroroso -sa *adj* ‹crimen› horrific, horrifying; ‹película/novela› terrible, awful; ‹persona/vestido› awful, ghastly, horrific (colloq); **tengo un hambre horrorosa** I'm absolutely starving (colloq)
hortaliza *f* vegetable; **~s** vegetables (*pl*), garden produce
hortelano -na *m,f* truck farmer (AmE), market gardener (BrE)
hortensia *f* hydrangea
hortera[1] *adj* (Esp fam) ‹vestido› tacky (colloq); ‹cantante› uncool (colloq)
hortera[2] *mf* (Esp fam): **es una ~** she's so uncool (colloq)
horterada *f* (Esp fam) tacky program* (*o* dress *etc*) (colloq)
horticultor -ra *m,f* horticulturalist, gardener
horticultura *f* horticulture, gardening
hosco -ca *adj* ‹persona/semblante› surly, sullen
hospedaje *m* accommodations (AmE), accommodation (BrE); **dar/encontrar ~** to provide/find accommodation(s); **da ~ a un médico** he has a doctor lodging with him
hospedar [A1] *vt* to provide … with accommodations (AmE), to provide … with accommodation (BrE)
■ **hospedarse** *v pron* to stay, put up (AmE colloq)
hospedero -ra *m,f* 1 (de hostal) hostel manager 2 **hospedero** *m* (de monasterio) guest master
hospicio *m* (para niños huérfanos) orphanage; (para peregrinos, mendigos) (Hist) hospice
hospital *m* hospital
Compuesto **hospital clínico** teaching hospital
hospitalario -ria *adj*
A ‹pueblo/persona› hospitable, welcoming
B (Med) hospital (*before n*)
hospitalidad *f* hospitality
hospitalizar [A4] *vt* to hospitalize
■ **hospitalizarse** *v pron* (AmL) to go into the hospital (AmE), to go into hospital (BrE)
hosquedad *f* sullenness, surliness
hostal *m* cheap hotel
Compuesto **hostal residencia** guesthouse, boarding house
hostelería *f* (Esp) ▸**hotelería**
hostelero -ra *m,f* owner (of a guest house)
hostería *f* small hotel
hostia *f*
A (Relig) host
B (Esp vulg *o* fam) (golpe) slap, smack in the face (*o* mouth *etc*); ***darse*** *or* ***pegarse una ~*** (Esp vulg *o* fam): **se pegó una ~ con el coche** he smashed his car up badly (colloq)
C (uso expletivo) (Esp vulg *o* fam) **¡~!** *or* **¡~s!** *or* **¡la ~!** jeez! (AmE colloq), bloody hell! (BrE sl); ***de la ~*** (Esp vulg *o* fam): **se compró un coche de la ~** she bought herself an amazing car (colloq); **hace un frío de la ~** it's goddamn (AmE) *o* (BrE) bloody freezing! (sl); ***¡qué ~s …!*** (Esp vulg *o* fam) what the hell …! (sl); ***ser la ~*** (Esp vulg *o* fam): **¡este mechero es la ~!** (expresando fastidio) this lighter is the pits! (colloq); (expresando admiración) this lighter's great! (colloq); **¡este tío**

es la ~! this guy is too much! (colloq)

hostiar [A1] *vt* (Esp vulg *o* fam) to belt, thump

hostigamiento *m* harassment

hostigar [A3] *vt*

A 1 (acosar) to bother, pester 2 (Mil) to harass 3 ‹*caballo*› to whip

B (Andes fam) «*comida/bebida*» to pall on

hostigoso -sa *adj* (Andes) ‹*comida/bebida*› sickly, sickly-sweet; ‹*persona*› annoying, irritating

hostil *adj* [SER] ‹*medio/clima*› hostile; ‹*gente/actitud*› hostile, unfriendly; **se mostró ~ a mis propuestas** he was opposed to my proposals

hostilidad *f* 1 (del clima) hostility; (de actitud) hostility, unfriendliness 2 **hostilidades** *fpl* hostilities (*pl*); **cese de ~es** cease-fire

hostilizar [A4] *vt* to harass

hotel *m* hotel

(Compuesto) **hotel residencia** guesthouse, boarding house

hotelería *f* (AmL) (negocio, industria) hotel and catering trade *o* business; (profesión) hotel management

hotelero[1] -ra *adj* hotel (*before n*)

hotelero[2] -ra *m,f* hotel manager, hotelier

hoy *adv*

A (este día) today; **~ es mi cumpleaños** it's my birthday today; **~ hace un año** a year ago today; **¿a qué** *or* **cuánto estamos ~?** what's the date today?, what's today's date?; **pan de ~** today's bread, fresh bread; **de** *or* **desde ~ en adelante** from today onward(s), as from today, starting today; **basta por ~** let's call it a day (colloq), that's enough for today

B 1 (actualmente) today, nowadays 2 (*en locs*) **hoy (en) día** nowadays, these days; **hoy por hoy** at this precise moment, at this moment in time; ***~ por ti, mañana por mí*** you can do the same for me one day

hoya *f* (AmL) river basin

hoyito *m* (AmL) dimple

hoyo *m* (agujero) hole; (depresión) hollow; (fosa) pit; (en golf) hole; (sepultura) (fam) grave

(Compuesto) **hoyo negro** (AmC, Méx) black hole

hoyuelo *m* dimple

hoz *f* sickle

huaca *f*: *pre-Colombian tomb*

huacal *m* (Col, Méx, Ven) (caja) wooden crate; ***salirse del ~*** (Méx fam) (desobedecer) to step out of line; (desviarse de un tema) to wander *o* go off the point

huachaca *adj/m,f* (Chi) ▸**guachaca[1,2]**

huachafita *f* 1 (Per fam) (mujer) jumped-up little snob (colloq) 2 (Col, Ven) ▸**guachafita**

huachafo -fa, **huachafoso -sa** *adj* (Per fam) 1 ‹*persona*› pretentious, affected 2 ‹*vestido/adorno*› tacky (colloq)

huachinango *m* (Méx) red snapper

huacho -cha *adj/m,f* ▸**guacho[1,2]**

huapango *m* 1 (Mús) *lively Mexican folk dance* 2 (fiesta veracruzana) carnival

huarache *m* (Méx) 1 (Indum) sandal 2 (Auto) patch

huasca *f* 1 (AmL) (arandela) washer 2 (Chi, Per) ▸**guasca**

huaso -sa *m,f* (Chi) 1 (campesino) peasant 2 (fam) (persona — rústica) hick (AmE colloq), country bumpkin (colloq); (—sin modales) uncouth yob (colloq)

huasteco -ca *m,f* (Chi) hick (AmE colloq), yokel (BrE colloq)

hube, hubo, etc *see* **haber**

hucha *f* (Esp) moneybox, piggybank

hueco[1] -ca *adj*

A 1 [ESTAR] ‹*árbol/bola*› hollow; ‹*nuez*› empty, hollow; **tienes la cabeza hueca** (fam & hum) you've got a head full of sawdust (colloq & hum) 2 [SER] (vacío) ‹*palabras*› empty; ‹*estilo*› superficial; ‹*persona*› shallow, superficial 3 (esponjoso) ‹*lana*› soft; ‹*colchón*› soft, spongy 4 ‹*sonido/tos*› hollow; ‹*voz*› resonant

B (orgulloso) proud

hueco[2] *m*

A 1 (cavidad): **detrás de la tabla hay un ~** there's a cavity behind the board; **suena a ~** it sounds hollow; **el ~ del ascensor** the lift shaft; **el ~ de la escalera** the stairwell; **el ~ de la puerta** the doorway 2 (espacio libre) space; **un ~ para aparcar** a parking space; **hacedme un ~ para sentarme** can you make a bit of space *o* room so I can sit down? 3 (en una organización) gap; **llenar un ~ en el mercado** to fill a gap in the market; **un ~ entre dos clases** a free period between two classes

B (concavidad) hollow

C (Andes, Ven) (agujero, hoyo) hole; (en la calle) hole, pothole

huela, huele, etc *see* **oler**

hueleguisos *mf* (*pl* ~) (Per fam) freeloader (colloq), sponger (colloq)

huelga[1] *f* strike; **declararse en ~** to come out on *o* go on strike; **hacer ~** to strike, go on strike; **estar en** *or* **de ~** to be on strike

(Compuestos)

- **huelga de celo** (Esp) work-to-rule
- **huelga de hambre** hunger strike
- **huelga general** general strike

huelga[2], huelgan, etc *see* **holgar**

huelguista *mf* striker;

(Compuesto) **huelguista de hambre** hunger striker

huelguístico -ta *adj* strike (*before n*)

huella *f* 1 (pisada — de persona) footprint, footstep; (— de rueda) track; **las ~s del animal** the animal's tracks *o* pawprints (*o* hoofmarks *etc*) 2 (vestigio) mark; **la ~ islámica en nuestra literatura** the Islamic influence on our literature; **sin dejar ~** without (a) trace 3 (de escalón) tread

(Compuestos)

- **huella ecológica** ecological footprint
- **huellas dactilares** *or* **digitales** *fpl* fingerprints (*pl*)

huelo *see* **oler**

huemul *m* deer (*native to the Southern Andes*)

huérfano[1] -na *adj* 1 ‹*persona*›: **un niño ~** an orphan; **quedó ~ a los cinco años** he was orphaned at the age of five; **es ~ de padre** he doesn't have a father 2 (carente, falto) **~ DE algo** bereft OF sth (frml)

huérfano[2] -na *m,f* orphan

huero -ra *adj* (liter) vacuous (frml)

huerta *f* 1 (huerto grande) (vegetable) garden; (con frutales) orchard 2 (explotación agrícola) truck farm (AmE), market garden (BrE); **la ~ valenciana** the fertile region of Valencia

(Compuesto) **huerta solar** solar energy farm

huertero -ra *m,f* (Chi) truck farmer (AmE), market gardener (BrE)

huerto *m* (para verduras) vegetable garden; (con frutales) orchard; ***llevarse a algn al ~*** (fam) (seducir) to have one's evil *o* wicked way with sb (hum); (engañar) to lead sb up the garden path (colloq)

hueso *m*

A 1 (Anat) bone; ***calado*** *or* ***empapado hasta los ~s*** soaked to the skin, wet through; ***dar con los*** *or* ***sus ~s en algo***: **fue a dar con sus ~s en la cárcel** he finished up *o* ended up in jail; ***en los ~s*** (fam) nothing but skin and bone(s) (colloq) 2 **(de) color ~** off-white, bone-colored 3 (Méx fam) (puesto público) safe (government) job (colloq); (sinecura) cushy job (colloq)

(Compuesto) **hueso** *or* **huesito de la suerte** wishbone

B (de fruta) pit (AmE), stone (BrE); ***ser un ~ (duro de roer)*** (ser difícil) to be a hard *o* tough nut to crack

huésped *mf*, **huésped -peda** *m,f*

A (en casa, hotel) guest

B **huésped** *m* (Biol) host

huestes *fpl* (liter) host (arch), army

huesudo -da *adj* bony

hueva *f*

A *tb* **~s** (Coc) roe; (Zool) spawn

B (Andes vulg) (testículo): **~s** balls (vulg), bollocks (BrE vulg); ***estar hasta las ~s*** (Andes vulg) to be pissed off (sl)

huevada *f*

A (Andes vulg) (estupidez) 1 (cosa, asunto): **¿dónde compraste esa ~?** where did you buy that crap (sl) *o* (vulg) that shit?; **perdí la cita ¡qué ~ más grande!** I missed the meeting, how goddamn stupid can you get! (sl) 2 (dicho): **¡no digas ~s!** don't talk crap! (sl) 3 (acto): **déjate de ~s y ponte a trabajar** stop screwing around (AmE) *o* (BrE) pissing about and get on with some work (vulg)

B (Andes vulg) (objeto determinado) thingamajig (colloq)

huevear [A1] *vi*

A (Chi, Per vulg) (perder el tiempo) to goof off (AmE colloq), to piss around (BrE sl)

B (Chi vulg) 1 (molestar): **¡hasta cuándo hueveas!** stop bugging *o* hassling me! (colloq) 2 (hacer tonterías) to screw around (AmE sl), to muck around (BrE colloq) 3 (decir tonterías) to talk crap (sl); **se sacó la lotería — ¡no estés hueveando!** he won the lottery — you're kidding! (colloq) *o* (AmE sl) no shit!

■ **huevear** *vt* (Chi vulg) ‹*persona*› (molestar) to bug (colloq), to hassle (colloq); (tomar el pelo a) to kid

hueveo *m* (Chi vulg) 1 (tomadura de pelo) pisstake(vulg); **agarrar a algn para el ~** to make fun of sb, to take the piss out of sb (BrE sl) 2 (acción de molestar): **está aburrido con los ~s del cabro** he's fed up with the kid hassling him (colloq) 3 (molestia) drag, bore

huevera *f*

A (para guardar huevos) egg box; (para servir huevos) eggcup

B (Per) (huevas) roe

huevería *f*: *store selling eggs*

huevo *m*

A (Biol, Coc, Zool) egg; ***a* ~: tuve que leer el libro a ~** (Méx vulg) I had no damn *o* (BrE) bloody choice but to read the book (sl); **comprar/vender a ~** (Andes fam) to buy/sell for peanuts (colloq); **mirar a ~** (Chi fam) to look down on; ***un huevo*: me costó un ~** (Esp vulg) it cost me an arm and a leg (colloq)

(Compuestos)

- **huevo a la copa** (Chi) boiled egg
- **huevo de Pascua** Easter egg
- **huevo duro/escalfado** hard-boiled/poached egg
- **huevo estrellado** (frito) fried egg; (revuelto) (Col) scrambled egg
- **huevo pasado por agua** *or* (Col, Méx) **tibio** soft boiled egg
- **huevo poché** (Méx, RPl) poached egg
- **huevos revueltos** *or* (Col) **pericos** *mpl* scrambled eggs
- **huevo sancochado** (Ven) hard-boiled egg

B (vulg) (testículo) ball (vulg); *para modismos ver* **cojones A**; ***¡y un ~!*** (Esp vulg) like hell! (sl)

huevón¹ -vona *adj* 1 (Andes, Ven fam *o* vulg) (tonto, estúpido) (fam) dumb (colloq) 2 (Méx vulg) (holgazán) lazy (colloq)

huevón² -vona *m,f* 1 (Andes, Ven vulg) (imbécil) jerk (sl & pej), dickhead (vulg), dumbass (AmE sl) 2 (Méx vulg) (holgazán) lazy bum (colloq)

huevonada *f* (Col, Ven vulg): **¡déjense de ~s!** stop being so goddamn (AmE) *o* (BrE) bloody stupid (sl); **no me hablen de esas ~s** I don't want to hear that boring crap (sl)

huevonear [A1] *vi* (Col, Ven vulg) ▸**huevear B2**

huida *f* 1 (fuga) flight; **emprender la ~** to take flight (frml) 2 (Equ) bolting

huidizo -za *adj* ‹*mirada*› evasive, shy; ‹*carácter/persona*› elusive; ‹*animal*› timid; **una chica tímida, de mirada huidiza** a shy girl who never looks you in the eye

huido -da *adj* 1 (prófugo): **se encuentra ~** he is on the run 2 (receloso): **anda** *or* **está ~ últimamente** he's been keeping himself to himself *o* keeping a low profile recently

huila *f* (Chi) rag; ***quedar hecho (una) ~*** (fam) to get torn to shreds

huincha *f* 1 (Andes) (cinta) ribbon; (en carrera) tape; **cruzó la meta cortando la ~ con el pecho** he breasted the (finishing) tape 2 (Andes) (para pelo) hairband 3 (Bol, Chi, Per) (para medir) tape measure

(Compuesto) **huincha aisladora** (Chi) friction tape (AmE), insulating tape (BrE)

huinche *m* (Andes) winch

huipil *m* (en AmC, Méx) huipil (*traditional embroidered dress worn by Indian women*)

> **Huipil**
>
> A traditional shirt worn by Indian and mestizo women in Mexico and Central America. *Huipiles* are generally made of richly embroidered cotton. They are very wide and low-cut, and are either waist-length or thigh-length

huir [I20] *vi* 1 (escapar) to flee (liter *or* journ), escape; **huyó de la cárcel/la policía** he escaped from prison/the police; **esperó la ocasión propicia para ~** he waited for the right moment to make his escape *o* to get away; **en cuanto los vió salió huyendo** he ran away *o* fled when he saw them; **~ del país/de las llamas** to flee the country/from the flames 2 (tratar de evitar) **~ DE algo** to avoid sth; **~le A algn** to avoid sb

■ **huirse** *v pron* (Méx) **~se CON algn** to run away *o* off WITH sb

huira *f* (Per) rope

huiro *m* (Chi, Per) seaweed

hule *m*

A (para mantel) oilcloth; (para ropa impermeable) oilskin

B (Méx) (goma) rubber; (Bot) rubber tree

hule-espuma *m* (Méx) foam rubber

hulera *f* (AmC) slingshot (AmE), catapult (BrE)

hulla *f* coal

hullero -ra *adj* coal (*before n*)

humanamente *adv* 1 ‹*posible/imposible*› humanly 2 (de manera humana) humanely

humanidad *f*

A 1 (los humanos): **la ~** the human race, humanity, mankind 2 (piedad, benevolencia) humanity

B 1 (fam & hum) (corpulencia) bulk 2 (muchedumbre): **¡qué olor a ~!** (euf) there's a tremendous smell of the great unwashed in here! (hum)

C **humanidades** *fpl* (estudios de letras) humanities (*pl*); (enseñanza secundaria) (Chi) secondary education

humanismo *m* humanism

humanista *mf* humanist

humanístico -ca *adj* humanistic

humanitario -ria *adj* humanitarian

humanizar [A4] *vt* to make … human

■ **humanizarse** *v pron* to become more human

humano¹ -na *adj*

A ‹*naturaleza*› human (*before n*)

B (benevolente) humane

humano² *m* human being; **los ~s** humans

humanoide *adj/mf* humanoid

humareda *f* cloud of smoke

humeante *adj* ‹*leño/lava*› smoking; ‹*sopa/café*› steaming (hot), piping hot

humear [A1] *vi* «*chimenea/hoguera*» to smoke; «*sopa/café*» to steam

humectador *m* humidifier

humectante¹ *adj* moisturizing

humectante² *m* moisturizer

humedad *f* 1 (Meteo) dampness; (con calor) humidity 2 (en paredes, suelo) damp

humedal *m* wetland

humedecer [E3] *vt* to moisten, dampen

■ **humedecerse** *v pron* to get damp; **se le humedecieron los ojos** his eyes filled with tears

húmedo -da *adj* 1 (Meteo) damp; (con calor) humid 2 ‹*suelo/casa/ropa*› damp 3 ‹*labios*› moist; **tenía los ojos ~s** his eyes were wet (with tears)

húmero *m* humerus

humildad *f* 1 (sumisión) humility; **con ~** humbly 2 (pobreza) humbleness, lowliness

humilde¹ *adj* ‹*carácter/tono*› meek; ‹*vivienda/ropa*› humble, lowly

humilde² *mf*: **los ~s** the meek, the humble

humildemente *adv* humbly

humillación *f* humiliation

humillante *adj* humiliating

humillar [A1] *vt* to humiliate

■ **humillarse** *v pron*: **no se humilla ante nadie** she doesn't kowtow to anyone; **está dispuesta a ~se para conseguirlo** she's prepared to swallow her pride to get it; **no me voy a ~ a pedirle que vuelva** I'm not going to demean myself by begging him to come back

humita *f*

A (CS) (Coc) *flavored corn paste wrapped in corn leaves*
B (Chi) (Indum) bow tie

humo *m*

A (de tabaco, incendio) smoke; (gases) fumes (*pl*); **echaba ~** smoke was pouring out of it; ***echar ~ por las orejas*** to be seething (colloq); ***hacerse ~*** (AmL fam) to make oneself scarce (colloq); ***llegar al ~ de las velas*** (Arg) to arrive just as everyone is leaving
B **humos** *mpl* (aires): **qué ~s que tiene!** she really gives herself airs (colloq); ***bajarle los ~s a algn*** to take sb down a peg or two; ***se te/le han subido los ~s a la cabeza*** you've/he's become very high and mighty *o* very stuck up (colloq)

humor *m*

A 1 (estado de ánimo) mood; **estar de buen/mal ~** to be in a good/bad mood; **no estoy de ~ para salir** I'm not in the mood to go out; **hay que tener ~ para ...** you have to be really enthusiastic *o* (BrE) keen to ...; ***estar de un ~ de perros*** (fam) to be in a filthy *o* foul mood (colloq) 2 (gracia) humor•
(Compuesto) **humor negro** black humor•
B (Biol, Fisiol) humor•

humorada *f* 1 (extravagancia): **hacer una ~** to do something crazy; **en una de sus ~s** in one of his crazy moments 2 (broma) little joke, witticism

humorismo *m* (cualidad) humor•; (actividad) comedy

humorista *mf* (autor) humorist, comic writer; (dibujante) cartoonist; (cómico) comic, comedian

humorístico -ca *adj* humorous

humus *m* humus

hundido -da *adj* 1 ‹*barco*› sunken 2 ‹*ojos*› deep-set; (por enfermedad) sunken 3 (deprimido) deeply depressed

hundimiento *m* 1 (de barco) sinking 2 (de negocio) collapse 3 (de edificio — bajada de nivel) subsidence; (— derrumbe) collapse

hundir [I1] *vt*

A ‹*barco*› to sink; ‹*persona*› to destroy; ‹*negocio/empresa*› to drive ... under, to drive ... to the wall
B (introducir) to bury; **hundió los pies en la arena** she buried her feet in the sand; **le hundió el cuchillo en la espalda** she plunged *o* sank the knife into his back

■ **hundirse** *v pron* 1 «*barco*» to sink 2 (en barro, nieve) to sink 3 «*empresa/negocio*» to fold, to go under 4 «*edificio*» (bajar de nivel) to sink, subside; (derrumbarse) to collapse 5 (desmoralizarse) to go to pieces

húngaro[1] -ra *adj/m,f* Hungarian

húngaro[2] *m* (idioma) Hungarian

Hungría *f* Hungary

huracán *m* hurricane

huracanado -da *adj* gale-force (*before n*), hurricane-force

huraño -ña *adj* ‹*persona*› unsociable; ‹*animal*› timid

hurgar [A3] *vi* **~ EN algo** ‹*en basura*› to rummage *o* rake THROUGH sth; **~ en una antigua herida** to open an old wound; **~ en el pasado** to delve into the past, to dig up the past

■ **hurgarse** *v pron* (*refl*) ▸ **hurguetearse**

hurguetear [A1] *vi* (CS) **~ EN algo** ‹*en papeles*› to nose THROUGH sth; ‹*en cartera*› to rummage *o* ferret around IN sth

■ **hurguetear** *vt* ‹*cajón/cartera*› to rummage around in, rummage through

■ **hurguetearse** *v pron* (*refl*) (esp AmL): **~se la nariz** to pick one's nose

hurón[1] -rona *adj* (fam) (huraño) unsociable; (fisgón) nosy (colloq)

hurón[2] -rona *m,f*

A (fam) (huraño) loner (colloq); (fisgón) busybody (colloq)
B **hurón** *m* (Zool) ferret

huronear [A1] *vi* (en caza) to ferret; (fisgar) (fam & pey) to pry, snoop around (colloq)

hurra, hurrah *interj* hurrah!, hooray!

hurtadillas *fpl*: **entrar/salir a ~** to sneak in/out

hurtar [A1] *vt* (frml) to purloin (frml), to steal

hurto *m* (frml) (robo) robbery, theft; (cosas robadas) stolen goods (*pl*), stolen property

husillo *m* screw

husmear [A1] *vt* to sniff

■ **husmear** *vi* 1 «*perro*» to sniff around 2 (fam) (fisgonear) to snoop, pry, sniff around (colloq)

huso *m* spindle

(Compuesto) **huso horario** time zone

huy *interj* (fam) (para expresar— dolor) ouch!, ow!; (— asombro) wow!; (— alivio) phew!

huya, huyas, etc *see* **huir**

h

i

I, i *f* (*pl* **íes**) (*read as* /i/) *tb* **i latina** *the letter* **i**
(Compuesto) **i griega** *the letter* **y**
ib. (= **ibídem**) ibid.
iba, íbamos, etc *see* **ir**
Iberia *f* Iberia
ibérico -ca *adj* Iberian
íbero -ra, ibero -ra *adj/m,f* Iberian
Iberoamérica *f* Latin America
iberoamericano -na *adj/m,f* Latin American
ibíd. (= **ibídem**) ibid
ibídem *adv* (frml) ibidem, ibid.
ibuprofeno *m* ibuprofen
icaco *m* (Col, Méx, Ven) coco plum
iceberg /'aɪsβer, 'iθe'βer/ *m* (*pl* **-bergs**) iceberg
ICI /'isi, 'iθi/ *m* = **Instituto de Cooperación Iberoamericana**
icono, ícono *m* icon
iconoclasta[1] *adj* iconoclastic
iconoclasta[2] *mf* iconoclast
ictericia *f* jaundice
id. (= **ídem**) id.
ida *f* 1 (viaje) outward journey; **a la ~** on the way out *o* there; **constantes ~s y venidas** constant comings and goings; **¿cuánto cuesta la ~?** how much does it cost one way?; **¿saco de ~ y vuelta?** shall I buy a round-trip ticket (AmE) *o* (BrE) return ticket? 2 (partida) departure
idea *f*
A 1 (concepto) idea; **la ~ de libertad** the idea *o* concept of freedom 2 (opinión, ideología) idea; **es de ~s conservadoras** she has conservative ideas *o* views; **es un hombre de ~s fijas** he has very set ideas about things 3 (noción) idea; **no tiene ~ de cómo funciona** he has no idea how it works; **no tengo ~** I don't have a clue; **tenía ~ de que ibas a llamar** I had a feeling you'd call; **hacerse una ~ de la situación** to get an idea of the situation; **es difícil hacerse una ~ de cómo es** it's hard to imagine what it's like; ***darse ~ para algo*** (RPl fam) to be good at sth; ***hacerse (a) la ~ de algo*** to get used to the idea of sth
B 1 (ocurrencia) idea; **se me ocurre una ~** I've got an idea; **se le metió la ~ en la cabeza** she got it into her head; **no sería buena/mala ~** it wouldn't be a good/bad idea; **~ *de bombero*** (Esp fam) crazy idea 2 (intención) intention, idea; **cambió de ~** she changed her mind 3 (sugerencia) idea
(Compuesto) **idea fija** fixed idea
ideal[1] *adj* ideal; **una sociedad ~** a perfect society; **lo ~ sería estar todos juntos** ideally, we would all be together
ideal[2] *m* 1 (prototipo) ideal 2 (aspiración) dream 3 **ideales** *mpl* (valores, principios) ideals (*pl*)
idealismo *m* idealism
idealista[1] *adj* idealistic
idealista[2] *mf* idealist
idealizar [A4] *vt* to idealize
idear [A1] *vt* ‹*proyecto/sistema*› to devise; **tenemos que ~ una manera de recaudar fondos** we have to come up with a way of raising money
ideario *m* ideology, ideas (*pl*)
ideático -ca *adj* (AmL fam): **es muy ~** he's full of strange ideas
ídem *adv* ditto, idem (frml)
idéntico -ca *adj* identical; **no has cambiado nada, estás ~** you haven't changed a bit, you're still exactly the same; **es ~ al padre** (físicamente) he looks just like his father, he's the spitting image of his father (colloq); (en el carácter) he's exactly like his father; **~ A algo** identical TO sth
identidad *f* 1 (datos personales) identity; **¿tiene algún documento que acredite su ~?** have you any identification? 2 (individualidad) identity 3 (igualdad) identity (frml); **~ de intereses** identity of interests (frml)
identificable *adj* identifiable
identificación *f* (acción) identification; (documentos) identity papers (*pl*)
identificar [A2] *vt* to identify; **un joven sin ~** an unidentified young man; **fue identificado como el autor del atraco** he was identified as the robber; **lo identifican con ese estilo** he is identified with that style
■ **identificarse** *v pron* 1 (compenetrarse, solidarizarse) **~se CON algo/algn** to identify with sth/sb 2 (demostrar la identidad) to identify oneself
ideología *f* ideology
ideológico -ca *adj* ideological
ideólogo -ga *m,f* ideologist, ideologue (pej)
idílico -ca *adj* idyllic
idilio *m* 1 (Lit) idyll 2 (romance) romance
idioma *m* language
idiomático -ca *adj* idiomatic
idiosincrasia *f* idiosyncrasy
idiota[1] *adj* 1 (fam) (tonto) stupid, idiotic; **me caí de la manera más ~** I had the most stupid fall (colloq); **¡no seas ~!** don't be such an idiot! 2 (Med) idiotic
idiota[2] *mf* (tonto) (fam) idiot, stupid fool (colloq); (Med) idiot
idiotez *f* 1 (fam) (cosa estúpida): **deja de decir idioteces** stop talking nonsense; **fue una ~ hacer eso** that was a stupid thing to do 2 (Med) idiocy
idiotizar [A4] *vt* (fam): **la televisión idiotiza a los niños** television turns children into zombies
ido, ida *adj* [ESTAR] 1 (distraído): **estás como ~** you seem miles away; **una mirada ida** a faraway look 2 (fam) (loco) crazy
idólatra[1] *adj* idolatrous
idólatra[2] *mf* idolater
idolatrar [A1] *vt* to idolize, worship
idolatría *f* idolatry
ídolo *m* idol
idoneidad *f* suitability
idóneo -nea *adj*: **la persona idónea para este cargo** the right person for this job; **un lugar ~ para filmarla** an ideal *o* a perfect location for filming it
i.e. (= **id est**) i.e.
iglesia *f* 1 (edificio) church; **no van a la ~** they don't go to church 2 (conjunto de fieles, creencias) church; **casarse por la ~** *or* (Bol, Per, RPl) **por ~** to have a church wedding 3 **la Iglesia** (institución) the Church
iglú *m* igloo
ignición *f* (combustión) combustion; (Auto) ignition

ignominia *f* (frml) 1 (vergüenza, deshonra) shame, ignominy (frml); **cubrió de ~ mi buen nombre** he brought shame on my good name 2 (cosa vergonzosa) disgrace

ignominioso -sa *adj* (frml) ‹*comportamiento*› shameful, disgraceful (frml)

ignorancia *f* 1 (falta de instrucción) ignorance; **por ~** out of *o* through ignorance 2 (desconocimiento) **~ DE algo** ignorance OF sth

ignorante[1] *adj* 1 (sin instrucción) ignorant; **soy ~ en el tema** it's not a subject I know anything about 2 (sin información) **estar ~ DE algo** to be unaware OF sth

ignorante[2] *mf* ignoramus, ignorant fool (colloq)

ignorar [A1] *vt* 1 (desconocer): **lo ignoro** I've no idea; **ignoran las causas del accidente** they have no idea what caused the accident; **ignora los peligros que le acechan** he's unaware of the dangers which await him 2 (no hacer caso de) to ignore

ignoto -ta *adj* (liter) ‹*tierra/país*› undiscovered, unknown; ‹*personaje*› unknown

igual[1] *adj*

A 1 (idéntico): **de ~ peso/~es dimensiones** of equal weight/dimensions; **son ~es** they are the same *o* alike; **estás ~ito** you're just the same (colloq); **~ A** *or* **QUE algo/algn** the same AS sth/sb; **es ~ita a** *or* **que su madre** (físicamente) she looks just like her mother; (en personalidad) she's exactly the same as *o* just like her mother; **x + y = z** (*read as: x más y igual z or es igual a z*) x + y = z (*léase: x plus y equals z*); **sigue ~ de joven** she still looks as young as ever; **de forma son ~es** they're the same shape; ***ser*** *or* ***dar* ~: me es** *or* **da ~** I don't mind; **me es** *or* **da ~ ir hoy que mañana** it makes no difference to me whether I go today or tomorrow 2 (en una jerarquía) equal; **~es ante la ley** equal in the eyes of the law 3 (semejante): **jamás había oído estupidez ~** I'd never heard anything so stupid; **¡habráse visto cosa ~!** have you ever seen anything like it!

B (constante) constant

C (en tenis): **quince ~es** fifteen all, **van ~es** they're even

igual[2] *adv*

A 1 (de la misma manera): **los trato a todos ~** I treat them all the same 2 (*en locs*) **al igual que** (frml): **el ministro, al ~ que su homólogo mexicano, acudirá a la reunión** the minister will attend the meeting, as will his Mexican counterpart (frml); **igual que**: **tiene pecas, ~ que su hermano** she has freckles, (just) like her brother; **se llama ~ que su padre** he's named after his father; **me resultó aburrido — ~ que a mí** I thought it was boring — so did I; **opino ~ que tú** I agree with you; **por igual** equally

B (de todos modos) anyway; **no le di permiso pero salió ~** I didn't give him permission but he went out anyway

C (expresando posibilidad): **~ llueve y no podemos salir** it might rain and then we won't be able to go out; **~ no viene** he may (well) not even come; **~ llamaron y no estábamos** they may have called and we weren't in

igual[3] *mf*

A (par) equal; **de ~ a ~**: **le habló de ~ a ~** he spoke to him on equal terms; **me trató de ~ a ~** she treated me as an equal; **sin ~** ‹*belleza/talento*› unequaled*, matchless (frml); **es un compositor sin ~** he's unrivaled as a composer

B **igual** *m* (signo) equals sign

igualación *f*

A (nivelación): **para conseguir la ~ de los ingresos y los pagos** to balance income and outgoings; **su objetivo es la ~ de todos los ciudadanos** its aim is to make all citizens equal

B (Mat) equating

igualada *f* (period): **el gol de la ~** the equalizing goal, the equalizer

igualado -da *adj*

A 1 (Dep): **van/están muy ~s** they're very close, they're neck and neck; **dos equipos muy ~s** two very evenly-matched teams; **quedaron ~s** they drew; **iban ~s a tres** they were level at three-three 2 ‹*superficie*› even, level

B (Méx fam) (irrespetuoso) sassy (AmE colloq), cheeky (BrE colloq)

igualar [A1] *vt*

A 1 (nivelar) ‹*superficie/terreno*› to level, level off; ‹*flequillo/dobladillo*› to even up, make ... straight 2 ‹*salarios*› to make ... equal *o* the same; **~ algo CON** *or* **A algo** to make sth the same AS sth; **ha sido igualada a Juana de Arco** she has been likened to Joan of Arc

B 1 ‹*éxito/récord*› to equal, match; Ⓢ **nadie puede igualar nuestros precios** unbeatable prices! 2 (Dep): **Pérez igualó el marcador** Pérez scored the equalizer

■ **igualarse** *v pron*: **no existe otro que se le iguale** he has no equal; **~se A** *or* **CON algo** to match *o* equal sth

igualatorio -ria *adj* equalizing

igualdad *f* equality; **~ de oportunidades** equal opportunities; **en ~ de condiciones** on equal terms

igualitario -ria *adj* egalitarian

igualmente *adv* 1 (en fórmulas de cortesía): **que lo pases muy bien — igualmente** have a great time — you too *o* and you; **saludos a tu mujer — gracias, ~** give my regards to your wife — thanks, and to yours (too) 2 ‹*bueno/malo*› equally 3 (frml) (también) likewise

iguana *f* (Zool) iguana

ijada *f*, **ijar** *m* (de animal) flank, side

ilación *f* cohesion; **historias sin ~ aparente** stories with no apparent connection

ilegal *adj* ‹*venta/comercio*› illegal, unlawful; ‹*inmigrante/huelga*› illegal; **de manera ~** illegally

ilegalidad *f* 1 (cualidad) illegality; **quedar en la ~** to remain illegal *o* outside the law 2 (acción) illegality, irregularity

ilegalización *f* banning

ilegalizar [A4] *vt* to ban, make *o* declare ... illegal

ilegible *adj* illegible, unreadable

ilegitimidad *f* illegitimacy

ilegítimo -ma *adj* ‹*hijo*› illegitimate; **sus pretensiones son ilegítimas** his claims are not legitimate

ileso -sa *adj* unhurt, unharmed; **salió ~ del accidente** he walked away from the accident unscathed

iletrado -da *adj* (analfabeto) illiterate; (inculto) uneducated

ilícito -ta *adj* illicit

ilimitado -da *adj* unlimited

Ilmo. Ilma. (frml) (Corresp) = **Ilustrísimo, -ma**

ilocalizable *adj*: **esta mañana seguía ~** he still could not be traced *o* found this morning

ilógico -ca *adj* illogical

iluminación *f* 1 (de habitación) lighting; (de monumento) illumination; (Teatr) lighting 2 **iluminaciones** *fpl* (luces) lights (*pl*), illuminations (*pl*)

iluminado -da *m,f* (lúcido, clarividente) visionary

iluminador[1] **-dora** *adj* illuminating, enlightening

iluminador[2] **-dora** *m,f*

A (Espec) lighting technician

B (de manuscritos) illuminator

iluminar [A1] *vt*

A 1 ‹*calles*› to light, illuminate; ‹*monumento*› to illuminate; ‹*escenario*› to light; **iluminado por la luz de la luna** bathed in moonlight; **iluminado por una vela** candlelit 2 (con focos muy potentes) ‹*estadio*› to floodlight 3 ‹*rostro/ojos*› (liter) to light up

B (Relig) to enlighten

C ‹*grabado*› to illuminate

■ **iluminarse** *v pron* «*cara/ojos*» to light up

ilusión *f*

A 1 (esperanza) hope; **con ~** hopefully; **no me hago muchas ilusiones** I'm not very hopeful; **no te hagas ilusiones** don't build your hopes up; **su mayor ~ es ...** her dearest *o* fondest wish is ...; **vive de ilusiones** he lives in a dream world 2 (esp Esp) (alegría, satisfacción): **me hizo mucha ~** I was thrilled; **le hace ~ el viaje** he's looking forward to the trip; **¡qué ~!** isn't it wonderful!

B (noción falsa) illusion

(Compuesto) **ilusión óptica** optical illusion

ilusionar [A1] *vt*: **me ilusiona mucho** I'm very excited about it; **no la ilusiones** don't raise her hopes

■ **ilusionarse** *v pron* 1 (hacerse ilusiones) to build one's hopes up 2 (entusiasmarse) **~se CON algo** to get excited ABOUT sth

ilusionismo *m* conjuring, magic

ilusionista *mf* conjuror, illusionist, magician

iluso[1] **-sa** *adj* naive

iluso[2] **-sa** *m,f* dreamer; **eres un ~ si crees que va a volver** you're being naive *o* (colloq) kidding yourself if you think she's going to come back

ilusorio -ria *adj* 1 (engañoso) ‹*promesa*› false; ‹*esperanza*› false, illusory 2 (imaginario) imaginary

ilustración *f*

A 1 (Art, Impr) (acción) illustration; (dibujo, imagen) illustration, picture 2 (ejemplo) illustration, example; **como ~** as an illustration

B 1 (frml) (educación, instrucción) learning, erudition (frml) 2 **la Ilustración** (Hist) the Enlightenment

ilustrado -da *adj* 1 ‹*revista/libro*› illustrated 2 (frml) ‹*persona*› erudite, learned

ilustrador -dora *m,f* illustrator

ilustrar [A1] *vt*

A 1 ‹*libro/revista*› to illustrate 2 (con ejemplos) ‹*tema/explicación*› to illustrate

B (frml *o* hum) ‹*persona*› to enlighten; **~ a algn SOBRE algo** to enlighten sb ABOUT sth

■ **ilustrarse** *v pron* (hum) to learn sth

ilustrativo -va *adj* illustrative

ilustre *adj* illustrious, distinguished

ilustrísimo -ma *adj*

A (frml) 1 (tratamiento) honorable* (frml); **el ~ señor** the honorable gentleman 2 (Corresp): **el ~ Sr Ministro de Cultura** His Excellency, the Minister of Culture

B **Su Ilustrísima** (frml) 1 (al dirigirse — a un obispo) Your Grace, Your Lordship; (— a un rector) Sir/Madam 2 (al referirse — a un obispo) His Grace; (— a un rector) ≈ the President (*in US*), ≈ the Vice Chancellor (*in UK*)

imagen *f*

A 1 (Fís, Ópt) image; (TV) picture, image 2 (foto) picture 3 (en espejo) reflection; ***a su ~ y semejanza*** in his/her own image; ***ser la viva ~ de algn*** to be the image of sb; **es la viva ~ del entusiasmo** he's enthusiasm personified 4 (en la mente) picture; **conservo una ~ muy borrosa de él** I have a very vague picture in my mind of him

B (de político, cantante, país) image

C (Art, Relig) (estatua) statue, image (arch); (estampa) picture

D (Lit) image

imaginable *adj* imaginable

imaginación *f* 1 (facultad) imagination; **¡ni (se) me pasó por la ~!** it never even crossed my mind! 2 (figuración): **es pura ~ tuya** it's all in your mind; **son imaginaciones tuyas** you're imagining things

imaginar [A1] *vt* 1 (suponer, figurarse) to imagine 2 (formar una imagen mental de) to imagine; **trata de ~lo pintado de blanco** try to imagine *o* picture it painted white 3 (idear) ‹*plan/método*› to think up, come up with

■ **imaginarse** *v pron* 1 (suponer, figurarse) to imagine; **me imagino que no querrá ir** I don't imagine *o* suppose he feels like going; **no te puedes ~ lo mal que nos trató** you've no idea how badly she treated us; **¿sabes cuánto costó? — me imagino que un dineral** do you know how much it cost? — a fortune, I should imagine; **¿quedó contento? — ¡imagínate!** was he pleased? — what do you think!; **me imagino que sí** I suppose so 2 (formar una imagen mental) to imagine; **me lo imaginaba más alto** I imagined he'd be taller

imaginario -ria *adj* imaginary

imaginativo -va *adj* imaginative

imaginería *f* (Relig) making of religious images; (Lit) imagery

imán *m*

A 1 (Fís) magnet 2 (atractivo) charisma

B (Relig) imam

imantar, imanar [A1] *vt* to magnetize

imbatible *adj* unbeatable

imbatido -da *adj* undefeated, unbeaten

imbécil[1] *adj* 1 (fam) (tonto) stupid; **¡qué ~ eres!** you're so stupid!, you're such an idiot! 2 (Med) imbecilic

imbécil[2] *mf* 1 (fam) (tonto) stupid idiot, moron (colloq & pej) 2 (Med) imbecile

imbecilidad *f* 1 (fam) (cosa estúpida): **decir/hacer ~es** to say/do stupid things 2 (Med) imbecility

imberbe[1] *adj*: **un joven ~** (sin barba) a beardless youth; (sin experiencia) a callow youth, a fresh-faced youth

imberbe[2] *m* (sin barba) beardless youth; (sin experiencia) callow youth

imbombera *f* (Ven fam) jaundice

imbombo -ba *adj* (Ven fam) 1 (Med) jaundiced 2 (tonto) stupid, thick (colloq)

imborrable *adj* lasting (*before n*), indelible

imbricado -da *adj* ‹*tejas/ladrillos*› overlapping; ‹*temas*› interwoven

imbuir [I20] *vt* **~ a algn DE algo** to imbue sb WITH sth

■ **imbuirse** *v pron* **~ DE algo** to become imbued WITH sth

imitación *f* 1 (acción) imitation 2 (parodia) impression 3 (copia) imitation; **es una burda ~** it's a very poor imitation; **bolso ~ cuero** imitation-leather bag

imitador -dora *m,f* (Teatr) impressionist, impersonator; (plagiario) imitator

imitar [A1] *vt* 1 ‹*persona*› (copiar) to copy, imitate; (para reírse) to do an impression of, mimic; **se sentó y todos lo ~on** he sat down and everyone followed suit 2 ‹*voz/gesto/estilo*› to imitate; (para reírse) to imitate, mimic; **había imitado mi firma** she had forged my signature 3 (tener el aspecto de) to simulate

imitativo -va *adj* imitative

impaciencia *f* impatience

impacientar [A1] *vt* 1 «*retraso*» to make … impatient 2 (exasperar) to exasperate

■ **impacientarse** *v pron* (por retraso) to get impatient; (exasperarse) to lose (one's) patience, get exasperated

impaciente *adj* 1 [SER] impatient 2 [ESTAR]: **estaba ~** he was (getting) impatient; **~ POR + INF** impatient to + INF; **están ~s por que llegue** they are impatient for him to arrive

impactante *adj* ‹*noticia*› shocking; ‹*libro/imagen*› powerful; ‹*espectáculo/efecto*› stunning, impressive

impactar [A1] *vt* 1 (golpear) to hit 2 (impresionar) to have a profound impact on

■ **impactar** *vi* 1 (impresionar) to shock; **se viste así para ~** she dresses like that to shock people 2 (chocar) to hit, strike

impacto *m* 1 (choque) impact; **recibió un ~ de bala** she was shot; **hacer ~** to hit 2 (huella, señal) hole, mark; **el cadáver tiene varios ~s de bala** there are several bullet wounds in the body 3 (en el ánimo, público) impact; **no tuvo mucho ~** it didn't make much of an impact

impagable *adj* (Fin) unpayable

impagado[1] -da *adj* unpaid, outstanding

impagado[2] *m* unpaid *o* outstanding item

impago[1] -ga *adj* (AmL) ‹*persona*› unpaid; ‹*deuda/impuesto*› unpaid, outstanding

impago[2] *m* non-payment

impajaritable *adj* (Andes fam & hum) inevitable

impalpable *adj* impalpable; **los velos casi ~s que la envolvían** (liter) the almost imperceptible veils enveloping her (liter)

impar[1] *adj* ‹*número*› odd

impar[2] *m* odd number

imparable *adj* unstoppable

imparcial *adj* impartial, unbiased

imparcialidad *f* impartiality

impartir [I1] *vt* (frml) 1 ‹*información*› to impart (frml), give 2 ‹*asistencia/benedición/órdenes*› to give; **imparte clases de informática** he teaches computing

impasibilidad *f* impassivity

impasible *adj* impassive

impasse /im'pas/ *m* (situación crítica) impasse

impavidez *f* composure, impassivity

impávido -da *adj* (liter) (impasible) impassive, unperturbed; (sin miedo) undaunted; **aguantó ~ mis reproches** he bore my reproaches impassively (liter)

impecable *adj* impeccable; **va siempre ~** she is always impeccably dressed

impedido[1] -da *adj* disabled

impedido[2] -da *m,f* disabled person

impedimento *m* obstacle, impediment; **si no surge ningún ~** if there are no hitches

(Compuesto) **impedimento físico** physical handicap

impedir [I14] *vt* 1 (imposibilitar) to prevent; **nadie te lo impide** nobody's stopping you; **~le a algn + INF** to prevent sb FROM -ING; **el dolor le impedía caminar** the pain prevented her from walking; **quiso ~ que nos viéramos** she tried to stop us seeing each other [2] ‹*paso*› to block; **un camión impedía la entrada** a truck was blocking the entrance [3] (dificultar) to hamper, hinder

impeler [E1] *vt* (frml) [1] «*viento/resorte*» to propel (frml), to drive [2] (obligar, empujar) to drive, impel (frml); **impelido por la necesidad** driven by necessity; **~ a algn A + INF** to impel *o* drive sb to + INF [3] (incitar) to urge

impenetrabilidad *f* (de la jungla, maleza) impenetrability; (de una persona, expresión) inscrutability

impenetrable *adj* [1] ‹*bosque*› impenetrable; ‹*fortaleza*› impregnable [2] ‹*persona/expresión*› inscrutable; ‹*misterio/secreto*› unfathomable

impenitente *adj* ‹*pecador*› unrepentant, impenitent; ‹*bebedor/jugador*› inveterate

impensable *adj* unthinkable, inconceivable

impensado -da *adj* unexpected, unforeseen

impepinable *adj* (Esp fam & hum) inevitable

imperante *adj* ‹*moda/tendencia/condiciones*› prevailing (*before n*); ‹*dinastía/régimen*› ruling (*before n*); **la normativa ~** the regulations in force

imperar [A1] *vi* «*moda/tendencia/condiciones*» to prevail; «*emperador/dinastía*» to rule

imperativo¹ -va *adj* [1] (Ling) imperative [2] ‹*voz/tono*› commanding, authoritative [3] ‹*necesidad*› pressing (*before n*), urgent

imperativo² *m* [1] (Ling) imperative [2] (exigencia) imperative

imperceptible *adj* imperceptible

imperdible *m* safety pin

imperdonable *adj* ‹*error/comportamiento*› unforgivable, inexcusable

imperecedero -ra *adj* (frml *o* liter) everlasting, undying

imperfección *f* [1] (defecto — en tela) flaw; (— en mecanismo) defect; **pequeñas imperfecciones del rostro** slight blemishes on the face [2] (cualidad) imperfection

imperfecto¹ -ta *adj*
A ‹*trabajo/tela/facciones*› flawed; **todos somos ~s** we all have our faults
B (Ling) imperfect

imperfecto² *m* imperfect (tense)

imperial *adj* ‹*dinastía/corona*› imperial

imperialismo *m* imperialism

imperialista *adj/mf* imperialist

impericia *f* lack of skill

imperio *m* [1] (territorios, período) empire; **un gran ~ hotelero** a huge hotel empire; ***gozar un ~*** (Ven fam) to have a whale of a time (colloq) [2] (preponderancia) rule; **el ~ de la ley** the rule of law

imperiosamente *adv* [1] (urgentemente) urgently [2] (con autoridad) imperiously

imperioso -sa *adj* [1] ‹*necesidad*› urgent, pressing (*before n*) [2] ‹*tono/carácter*› imperious

impermeabilidad *f* [1] (de material) impermeability [2] (insensibilidad) imperviousness

impermeabilización *f* waterproofing

impermeabilizar [A4] *vt* ‹*material/tela*› to waterproof, proof

impermeable¹ *adj* [1] ‹*material/tela*› waterproof, impermeable (tech) [2] ‹*persona*› **~ A algo** impervious TO sth; **es ~ a la crítica** she's impervious to criticism

impermeable² *m* (Indum) raincoat

impersonador -dora *m,f* (Méx) impersonator

impersonal *adj* impersonal

impersonar [A1] *vt* (Méx) to impersonate

impertérrito -ta *adj* unmoved; **escucharon ~s las acusaciones** they listened impassively to the charges

impertinencia *f* [1] (cualidad) impertinence [2] (hecho, dicho): **me dijo que me callara — ¡qué ~!** he told me to shut up — how impertinent!; **me contestó con una ~** she gave me a very cheeky reply

impertinente¹ *adj* [1] (irrespetuoso) ‹*persona/pregunta/tono*› impertinent [2] (inoportuno) ‹*momento/hora*› inopportune (frml), inappropriate; ‹*llamada*› ill-timed; ‹*comentario*› uncalled-for

impertinente² *mf*
A (persona): **eres una ~** you're extremely impertinent
B **impertinentes** *mpl* lorgnette

imperturbable *adj* [1] [SER] (sereno) imperturbable, unflappable [2] [ESTAR] (ante un peligro) unperturbed, unruffled [3] ‹*rostro/sonrisa*› impassive

impetrar [A1] *vt* (frml) [1] (rogar) to entreat, beseech [2] (obtener con ruegos) to obtain ... by entreaty

ímpetu *m* [1] (Fís, Mec) impetus, momentum [2] (energía, ardor) vigor*, energy; **con ~** energetically, vigorously [3] (violencia) force

impetuosidad *f* impetuosity, impetuousness

impetuoso -sa *adj* impetuous, impulsive

impida, impidas, etc *see* **impedir**

impiedad *f* [1] (falta de fe) ungodliness (frml), impiety (frml) [2] (falta de piedad) heartlessness, mercilessness

impío¹ -pía *adj* [1] (falto de fe) heathen (*before n*), godless [2] (irreverente) impious [3] (falto de piedad) pitiless, merciless

impío² -pía *m,f* (ant *o* hum) heathen (arch *or* hum)

implacable *adj* [1] ‹*odio/furia*› implacable; ‹*avance/lucha*› relentless; ‹*sol*› relentless; **el paso ~ del tiempo** the inexorable passage of time [2] ‹*juez/crítico*› implacable [3] ‹*enemigo/contrincante*› ruthless

implantación *f*
A (de norma, método) introduction, establishment; (de costumbres) introduction; (de régimen político) establishment
B (arraigo): **con ~ nacional** well-established nationwide
C (Med) implantation

implantado -da *adj* well-established

implantar [A1] *vt*
A ‹*método/norma*› to introduce, institute (frml); ‹*costumbre/moda*› to introduce; ‹*régimen político*› to establish; **~ el estado de excepción** to impose a state of emergency
B ‹*embrión/cabello*› to implant

implante *m* implant

implementación *f* (de medidas) implementation

implementar [A1] *vt*
A ‹*medidas/plan*› to implement
B (Ven) (instalar) to install*, set up

implemento *m* (AmL) tool, implement; **~s deportivos** sports equipment

implicación *f*
A (participación) involvement
B **implicaciones** *fpl* (consecuencias) implications (*pl*)

implicancia *f* (AmL) (consecuencia) implication

implicar [A2] *vt*
A (significar, conllevar) to entail, involve; **~ía la pérdida de puestos de trabajo** it would mean *o* entail the loss of jobs
B (envolver, enredar) to involve; **estuvo implicado en un delito** (participó) he was involved in a crime; (estuvo bajo sospecha) he was implicated in a crime
■ **implicarse** *v pron* to get involved

implícito -ta *adj* implicit

implorante *adj* imploring (*before n*), beseeching (*before n*)

implorar [A1] *vt* to beseech (liter); **~le algo A algn** to beg sth OF sb; **perdónelo, se lo imploro** forgive him, I implore you *o* I beseech you (liter); **~le a algn QUE + SUBJ** to implore *o* beg sb TO + INF

impoluto -ta *adj* [1] ‹*mar*› unpolluted [2] ‹*alma*› (liter) untainted (liter) [3] ‹*nieve*› virgin (*before n*)

imponderable¹ *adj* ‹*factores*› imponderable; ‹*consecuencias/daños*› incalculable; ‹*valor*› inestimable, incalculable

imponderable² *m* imponderable

imponencia *f* (AmL): **la ~ de las montañas** the grandeur of the mountains

imponente *adj* [1] ‹*belleza*› impressive; ‹*edificio/paisaje*› imposing, impressive; **estás ~ con ese vestido** (fam) you look terrific in that dress (colloq) [2] (como intensificador) **cayó un aguacero ~** there was an incredible *o* a terrific downpour; **hacía un frío ~** it was unbelievably cold

imponer [E22] *vt*
A [1] (frml) ‹*castigo/multa*› to impose (frml); **~ el toque de queda** to impose a curfew; **le impusieron una pena de año de cárcel** he was sentenced to one year in prison

2 (frml) ‹gravamen/impuesto› to impose, levy (frml) 3 ‹obligación› to impose, place; ‹opinión› to impose; ‹reglas/condiciones› to impose, enforce; ‹tarea› to set; **impusieron el uso obligatorio del cinturón de seguridad** safety belts were made compulsory 4 ‹respeto› to command; ‹temor› to inspire, instill* 5 ‹moda› to set
B (frml) (+ *me/te/le etc*) ‹condecoración/medalla› to confer; ‹nombre› to give
C (informar) ~ **a algn DE** or **EN algo** to inform sb OF *o* ABOUT sth
D (Esp frml) ‹dinero/fondos› to deposit
E (Chi) (a la seguridad social) to contribute
■ **imponer** *vi* (infundir respeto, admiración) to be imposing; **su mera presencia impone** he has an imposing presence
■ **imponerse** *v pron*
A 1 (*refl*) ‹horario/meta› to set oneself 2 «idea» to become established 3 (frml) «cambio/decisión» to be imperative (frml) 4 «color/estilo» to come into fashion
B (hacerse respetar) to assert oneself *o* one's authority
C (frml) (vencer) to win; **se impondrá el sentido común** common sense will prevail; **~se A algn/algo** to defeat *o* beat sb/sth
D (frml) (informarse) **~se DE algo** to acquaint oneself WITH sth
E (Méx) (acostumbrarse) **~se A algo** to become accustomed TO sth

imponible *adj* 1 [SER] (Fin, Fisco) ‹beneficios/ingresos› taxable 2 [ESTAR] (fam) ‹ropa› unwearable

impopular *adj* unpopular

impopularidad *f* unpopularity

importación *f* 1 (acción) importation; **artículos de ~** imported goods; **permiso de ~** import license 2 **importaciones** *fpl* (mercancías) imports (*pl*)

importado -da *adj* ‹producto/moda/costumbre› imported

importador¹ -dora *adj*: **la empresa ~a** the importer(s); **países ~es de petróleo** oil-importing countries

importador² -dora *m,f* importer

importancia *f* importance; **detalles sin ~** minor *o* insignificant details; **concederle** or **darle ~ a algo** to attach importance to sth; **quitarle** or **restarle ~ a algo** to play down the importance of sth; **no tiene ~** it doesn't matter; **¿y eso qué ~ tiene?** so what?; ***darse ~*** to give oneself airs

importante *adj* 1 ‹noticia/persona› important; ‹acontecimiento/cambio› important, significant; **¿qué dice la carta? — nada ~** what does the letter say? — nothing of any importance *o* nothing much; **lo ~ es ...** the important thing is ...; **es ~ que vayas** it's important that you go; ***dárselas de*** or ***hacerse el ~*** to give oneself airs 2 ‹pérdidas› serious, considerable; ‹daños› severe, considerable; ‹cantidad› considerable, significant

importar [A1] *vi* 1 (tener importancia, interés) to matter; **bueno, no importa** well, never mind *o* well, it doesn't matter; **no importa quién lo haga** it doesn't matter *o* it makes no difference who does it; **lo que importa es que te recuperes** the important thing is for you to get better; (+ *me/te/le etc*) **no me importa lo que piense** I don't care what he thinks; **¿a mí qué me importa?** what do I care?; **¿a ti qué te importa?** what business is it of yours?; **yo no le importo** I don't mean a thing to him; ***me importa un bledo*** or ***un comino*** or ***un pepino*** or ***un rábano*** (fam) I couldn't care less, I don't give a damn (colloq); ***meterse en lo que no le importa*** (fam) to poke one's nose into other people's business (colloq); **no te metas en lo que no te importa** mind your own business! 2 (molestar) (+ *me/te/le etc*): **no me ~ía venir el sábado** I wouldn't mind coming on Saturday; **si no te importa** if you don't mind; **no me importa que me llame a casa** I don't mind him calling me at home; **¿le ~ía hacerlo?** would you mind doing it?
■ **importar** *vt* (Com, Fin)
A ‹productos› to import
B (ascender a) to come to, amount to

importe *m* 1 (de factura, letra) amount; **el ~ total** the full *o* total amount; **le devolveremos el ~ de su compra** we will refund the purchase price 2 (costo) cost; **el ~ de la matrícula es ...** the registration fee is ...

importunar [A1] *vt* (frml) to inconvenience, disturb
■ **importunar** *vi*: **espero no ~** I hope it's not inconvenient, I hope I'm not disturbing you

importuno -na *adj* inopportune

imposibilidad *f* impossibility; **la ~ de llevar a cabo el proyecto** the impossibility of carrying through the plan

imposibilitado -da *adj* [ESTAR] 1 (Med) disabled; **el accidente lo dejó ~** the accident left him disabled/crippled; **quedó ~ de una pierna** he lost the use of one leg 2 (frml) (impedido) **~ PARA + INF**: **se vio ~ para asistir a la reunión** he was unable to attend the meeting; **se le declaró ~ para trabajar** he was declared unfit for work

imposibilitar [A1] *vt* 1 (hacer imposible) to make ... impossible 2 (impedir) to prevent; **la niebla imposibilitó su aterrizaje** the fog prevented its landing
■ **imposibilitarse** *v pron* (*refl*) 1 (quedar impedido) to be disabled 2 (Chi, Méx) (lastimarse) to injure *o* hurt oneself, be injured

imposible¹ *adj*
A [SER] ‹sueño/amor› impossible; **me es ~ acompañarte** I won't be able to go with you; **es ~ que lo sepan** they can't possibly know; **hicieron lo ~** they did everything they could
B (inaguantable) ‹persona› impossible; **está ~ hoy** he's (being) impossible today

imposible² *m*: **me pides un ~** you're asking the impossible of me

imposición *f*
A (frml) (de una pena) imposition; (de un impuesto) introduction
B (exigencia, obligación) imposition; **espero que no lo consideres una ~** I hope you don't think it an imposition; **no me vengas con imposiciones** don't you start telling me what to do (colloq)
C (Fin) deposit
D (Chi) (a la seguridad social) contribution

impositivo -va *adj*
A (Fin, Fisco) ‹sistema/reforma› tax (*before n*)
B ‹persona/tono› domineering, overbearing

impostor -tora *m,f* impostor

impotable *adj* ‹agua› not drinkable

impotencia *f* (falta de poder) powerlessness, helplessness, impotence; (Med) impotence

impotente¹ *adj* (incapaz, sin poder) powerless, helpless, impotent; (Med) impotent

impotente² *m* impotent man

impracticable *adj* 1 ‹operación/proyecto› impracticable, unfeasible 2 ‹camino/pista› impassable

imprecación *f* (frml) imprecation (frml), curse

imprecar [A2] *vt* (frml) to imprecate (frml), curse

imprecisión *f* 1 (cualidad) imprecision, vagueness 2 (error) inaccuracy

impreciso -sa *adj* vague, imprecise; **un número ~ de personas** an indeterminate number of people

impredecible *adj* unpredictable

impregnar [A1] *vt* 1 (empapar) ‹algodón/esponja› to soak, impregnate 2 «olor/aroma» to fill, pervade 3 (liter) «sentimiento» to pervade

impremeditado -da *adj* unpremeditated

imprenta *f* (taller) printer's; (aparato) (printing) press; (actividad) printing

imprescindible *adj* ‹requisito/herramienta/factor› essential, indispensable; **lleva lo ~** take the bare essentials; **ser ~ + INF** to be essential to + INF; **es ~ que nos acompañe** it is essential that you come with us

impresentable *adj* unpresentable; **estás ~** you're not presentable

impresión *f*
A 1 (idea, sensación) impression; **da la ~ de ser demasiado ancho** it looks (as if it might be) too wide; **nos causó** or **nos hizo muy buena ~** he made a very good impression on us; **me da/tengo la ~ de que me está mintiendo** I have a feeling he's lying to me; **cambiar impresiones** to exchange ideas 2 (sensación desagradable): **ver sangre le daba ~** she couldn't stand the sight of blood; **el accidente me produjo mucha ~** the accident really shocked me
B 1 (Impr) (acción) printing; (tirada) print run, impression (frml) 2 (Inf) (acción) printing; (producto) printout 3 (huella) imprint

Compuestos
- **impresión digital** fingerprint
- **impresión en color** color* printing

impresionable *adj* squeamish, easily affected

impresionante *adj* ‹*éxito/cantidad/paisaje*› amazing, incredible; ‹*accidente*› horrific; **la caída del dólar fue ~** the dollar suffered a dramatic fall

impresionar [A1] *vt*
A 1 (causar buena impresión): **París me impresionó** I was really taken with Paris; **me impresionó muy bien** (RPl) he made a very good impression (on me) 2 (conmover) to move; **verlo llorar me impresionó mucho** seeing him cry really moved me *o* made a deep impression on me 3 (alarmar) to shock; **me impresionó verla tan delgada** it shocked me to see her looking so thin 4 (sorprender) to strike; **lo que más me impresionó fue ...** what struck me most was ...
B (Fot) ‹*película*› to expose
■ **impresionar** *vi* to impress; **te lo dice para ~** he's only saying it to impress you
■ **impresionarse** *v pron* to be shocked (*o* moved *etc*)

impresionismo *m* impressionism

impresionista¹ *adj* ‹*movimiento/pintor*› Impressionist; ‹*estilo/descripción*› impressionistic

impresionista² *mf* Impressionist

impreso¹ -sa *pp*: *see* **imprimir**

impreso² *m* 1 (formulario) form; **~ de solicitud** application form 2 **impresos** *mpl* (Corresp) printed matter

impresor -sora *m,f*
A (persona) printer
B **impresora** *f* (Inf) printer

imprevisible *adj* ‹*hecho/factor*› unforeseeable; ‹*persona*› unpredictable

imprevisión *f* lack of foresight

imprevisto¹ -ta *adj* unforeseen, unexpected; **de modo ~** unexpectedly

imprevisto² *m* unforeseen event (*o* factor *etc*); **dinero para ~s** money for incidental expenses; **si no surge ningún ~** if nothing unexpected happens

imprimir [I36] *vt*
A 1 (Impr) to print; **impreso en Perú** printed in Peru 2 ‹*huella*›: **dejó sus huellas impresas en el barro** he left his footprints in the mud
B (comunicar, dar) (frml) to give; **le imprimió su estilo propio al personaje** he stamped his own style on the character; **experiencias que imprimen carácter** character-forming *o* character-building experiences

improbabilidad *f* improbability, unlikelihood

improbable *adj* unlikely, improbable; **es muy ~ que lo logre** it's very unlikely that he'll manage it

ímprobo -ba *adj*
A (frml) (enorme) ‹*tarea/esfuerzo*› enormous, huge
B (frml) (deshonesto) unprincipled, dishonest

improcedencia *f* (frml) inadmissibility

improcedente *adj* (frml) 1 ‹*demanda/reclamación*› inadmissible; **despido ~** unfair dismissal 2 ‹*conducta*› improper, unseemly

improductividad *f* unproductiveness, lack of productivity

improductivo -va *adj* unproductive

impronta *f* (liter) (marca, huella) stamp, mark

impronunciable *adj* unpronounceable

improperio *m* insult

impropiedad *f* (frml) 1 (cualidad) unsuitability, inappropriateness 2 (dicho, acto) impropriety (frml)

impropio -pia *adj* 1 ‹*actitud/respuesta*› inappropriate; **un libro ~ para su edad** an unsuitable book for someone his age; **un comportamiento ~ de una persona educada** behavior unbecoming to an educated person (frml) 2 (incorrecto) incorrect; **un uso ~ de la palabra** an incorrect usage of the word

improrrogable *adj*: **el plazo es ~** the deadline cannot be extended

improvisación *f* (acción) improvisation; (actuación) impromptu performance

improvisar [A1] *vt* to improvise; **~ una comida** to rustle up a meal
■ **improvisar** *vi* «*actor*» to improvise, ad-lib, extemporize (frml); «*músico*» to improvise, extemporize (frml)

improviso: **de ~** (*loc adv*) ‹*llegar/aparecer*› unexpectedly, out of the blue, without warning

imprudencia *f* 1 (acción) imprudence; **decir eso fue una ~** it was a rash *o* an imprudent thing to say; **no cometas esa ~** don't be so rash *o* reckless 2 (cualidad) imprudence; **su ~ al conducir** his reckless driving

Compuesto **imprudencia temeraria** criminal negligence

imprudente *adj* (que actúa sin cuidado) imprudent, careless; (temerario) reckless; **fuiste muy ~ al decírselo** it was very rash *o* imprudent of you to tell him

impúber *adj* (frml) prepubescent (frml)

impudicia *f* (frml) 1 (obscenidad) indecency 2 (desvergüenza) shamelessness

impúdico -ca *adj* (frml *o* hum) 1 (obsceno) indecent 2 (desvergonzado) shameless

impudor *m* (frml) shamelessness

impuesto¹ -ta *adj*
A (informado) **estar ~ EN** *or* **DE algo** to be well informed ABOUT sth
B (Méx fam) (acostumbrado) **estar ~ A algo** to be used TO sth

impuesto² *m* tax; **evasión de ~s** tax evasion; **libre de ~s** tax-free, duty-free

Compuestos
- **impuesto a** *or* **sobre la renta** income tax
- **impuesto al** *or* **sobre el valor agregado** *or* **añadido** value-added tax
- **impuesto sobre bienes inmuebles** property tax
- **impuesto de circulación/lujo** road/luxury tax

impugnable *adj* challengable, disputable

impugnación *f* challenging, contesting

impugnar [A1] *vt* ‹*decisión/fallo*› to contest, challenge

impulsar [A1] *vt* 1 ‹*motor/vehículo*› to propel, drive 2 ‹*persona*› to drive; **se sintió impulsada a decírselo** she felt impelled to tell him 3 ‹*comercio, producción*› to boost, give a boost to; **para ~ las relaciones culturales** in order to promote cultural relations

impulsivo -va *adj* impulsive

impulso *m* 1 (empuje): **un fuerte ~ para el comercio** a major boost for trade; **dar un nuevo ~ a la iniciativa** to give fresh impetus to the initiative; **tomar** *or* **darse ~** to gather momentum, to get up speed 2 (reacción, deseo) impulse; **actuó por ~** he acted on impulse; **mi primer ~ fue ...** my first instinct was ... 3 (Fís) impulse

impulsor¹ -sora *adj* driving (*before n*)

impulsor² -sora *m,f* driving force; **fue el gran ~ de esa política** he was the driving force behind that policy

impune *adj* unpunished

impunemente *adv* with impunity

impunidad *f* impunity

impuntualidad *f* unpunctuality

impureza *f* impurity

impuro -ra *adj* 1 ‹*aire/mineral*› impure 2 (Relig) ‹*pensamientos*› impure, unwholesome

impuse, impuso, etc *see* **imponer**

imputable *adj* (frml) **~ A algn/algo** attributable TO sb/sth

imputación *f* (frml) accusation, imputation (frml)

imputar [A1] *vt* (frml) **~le algo A algn** to attribute sth TO sb, impute sth TO sb (frml); **el delito que se le imputa** the crime which is attributed to her; **no se me puede ~ la responsabilidad** I cannot be held responsible

in *adj inv* ‹*discoteca*› trendy (colloq); **lo que está muy ~** the in thing (colloq), the trendy thing (colloq)

inabordable *adj* 1 ‹*persona*› unapproachable 2 ‹*tema*›: **el tema de los salarios es ~** we cannot broach *o* tackle the question of salaries

inacabable *adj* interminable, neverending

inacabado -da *adj* ‹*trabajo*› unfinished

inaccesibilidad *f* inaccessibility

inaccesible *adj* 1 ‹*montaña/persona/concepto*› inaccessible 2 (crit) ‹*precios*› prohibitive; ‹*objetivo*› unattainable

inacción *f* inaction

inaceptable *adj* unacceptable

inactivar [A1] *vt* to render … inactive

inactividad *f* inactivity

inactivo -va *adj* 1 ‹*persona/máquina*› inactive, idle 2 ‹*volcán*› inactive, dormant

inadaptable *adj* unadaptable

inadaptación *f* failure to adapt

inadaptado¹ -da *adj* maladjusted

inadaptado² -da *m,f* misfit

inadecuación *f* inadequacy

inadecuado -da *adj* ‹*color/traje*› inappropriate, unsuitable; ‹*norma/sistema*› inadequate

inadmisibilidad *f* inadmissibility

inadmisible *adj* 1 ‹*comportamiento/pretensiones*› unacceptable, inadmissible 2 (Der) inadmissible

inadvertencia *f* oversight; **por ~** inadvertently; **en un momento de ~ del profesor** while the teacher was distracted momentarily

inadvertidamente *adv* 1 (por equivocación) inadvertently, by mistake 2 (sin darse cuenta) without noticing

inadvertido -da *adj* 1 (no notado): **pasar ~** to go unnoticed 2 (distraído) distracted

inagotable *adj* ‹*fuente/reservas*› inexhaustible, endless

inaguantable *adj* unbearable

inalámbricamente *adv* wirelessly

inalámbrico -ca *adj* ‹*teléfono*› cordless; ‹*comunicaciones*› wireless

in albis *loc adv*: **me quedé ~ ~** I was totally in the dark (colloq)

inalcanzable *adj* unattainable, unachievable

inalienable *adj* inalienable

inalterable *adj* 1 ‹*expresión*› impassive; ‹*valores*› immutable (frml); **una mujer de una serenidad ~** a woman of immutable *o* unalterable serenity 2 ‹*roca*› unalterable 3 ‹*color*› fast

inanición *f* starvation

inanimado -da *adj* inanimate

inánime *adj* (frml) inanimate, lifeless

inapelable *adj* ‹*decisión*› not open to appeal

inapetencia *f* lack of appetite

inapetente *adj* lacking in appetite

inaplazable *adj*: **una reunión ~** a meeting which can't be postponed *o* put off

inapreciable *adj*
A (muy valioso) invaluable; **su ~ ayuda** her invaluable assistance; **un cuadro de un valor ~** a priceless painting
B (insignificante) negligible

inapropiado -da *adj* inappropriate

inarrugable *adj* crease-resistant

inasequible *adj* ‹*precio*› prohibitive; **una casa en esa zona es ~ para mí** a house in that area is beyond my means

inasistencia *f* absence

inastillable *adj* shatterproof

inaudible *adj* inaudible

inaudito -ta *adj* ‹*decisión/suceso*› unprecedented; **alcanza límites ~s** it is beyond belief

inauguración *f* opening, inauguration (frml); **ceremonia de ~** inauguration *o* opening ceremony; **la ~ del curso universitario** the start of the university year

inaugural *adj* opening (*before n*), inaugural (frml)

inaugurar [A1] *vt* ‹*teatro/hospital*› to open, inaugurate (frml); ‹*monumento*› to unveil; ‹*exposición/sesión*› to open; **Brasil inauguró el marcador** (period) Brazil opened the scoring

inca¹ *adj* Inca, Incaic

inca² *mf* Inca

> **Incas**
>
> Founded in the twelfth century in the region of Lake Titicaca, the Andean empire of the Quechua-speaking Incas grew until by the fifteenth century it extended from southern Colombia in the north to Argentina and central Chile in the south. Their society was rigidly divided into classes: the nobility, their servants, and the common people. The Incas worshipped the sun and the moon, and believed that Manco Capac, their first emperor or *inca*, was descended from the sun. An extensive network of roads was built to facilitate control over the empire from its capital in Cuzco. The Incas left an impressive heritage of monuments, including the palace complex of Machu Picchu. The empire collapsed in 1533 when the Spanish *conquistador* Francisco Pizarro had the emperor Atahualpa executed and occupied Cuzco

incalculable *adj* inestimable, incalculable

incalificable *adj* unspeakable; **su conducta es ~** his behavior is unspeakable *o* indescribable

incanato *m* Inca Empire

incandescencia *f* incandescence

incandescente *adj* incandescent

incansable *adj* tireless

incapacidad *f*
A 1 (física) disability, physical handicap; (mental) mental handicap 2 (Der) incapacity
Compuesto **incapacidad laboral** invalidity
B (ineptitud) incompetence; (falta de capacidad) inability; **su ~ para organizarse** his inability to organize himself
C (Col) (baja) sick leave

incapacitado -da *adj* 1 (físicamente) disabled, physically handicapped; (mentalmente) mentally handicapped 2 (Der) incapable

incapacitar [A1] *vt* «*enfermedad*» to incapacitate; **la lesión lo incapacita para su trabajo** the injury has made him unfit for work

incapaz¹ *adj*
A [SER] (de un logro, una hazaña): **no lo conseguirá nunca, es ~** he'll never do it, he simply isn't capable; **¿haría tal cosa? — no, hombre, es ~** would he do such a thing? — no way, he'd never do a thing like that (colloq); **~ DE algo** incapable OF sth; **es ~ de una cosa así** he's incapable of doing something like that; **resultó ~ de vencerla** he was unable to beat her; **es ~ de llamarme** he can't even be bothered to phone me
B (Der) incapable

incapaz² *mf* (inútil, inepto) incompetent (fool)

incautación *f* (frml) seizure, confiscation

incautarse *v pron* **~se DE algo** to seize *o* confiscate sth

incauto¹ -ta *adj* unsuspecting, unwary

incauto² -ta *m,f* unwary *o* unsuspecting person, sap (colloq)

incendiar [A1] *vt* 1 (prender fuego a) to set fire to 2 (quemar) ‹*edificio*› to burn down; ‹*coche*› to burn; ‹*pueblo/bosque*› to burn … to the ground
■ **incendiarse** *v pron* 1 (empezar a arder) to catch fire 2 (destruirse) «*edificio*» to be burned down; **la casa incendiada** the burnt-out house; **los bosques que se ~on** the forests that were destroyed by fire

incendiario¹ -ria *adj* 1 ‹*proyectil*› incendiary (*before n*) 2 ‹*discurso/palabras*› inflammatory, incendiary (frml)

incendiario² -ria *m,f* arsonist

incendio *m* fire; Ⓢ **peligro de incendio** fire hazard
Compuesto **incendio provocado** arson attack

incensario *m* censer, thurible

incentivación *f* 1 (estímulo) motivation 2 (Com) incentive scheme

incentivar [A1] *vt* (estimular) to encourage; (recompensar) to provide … with incentives, give incentives to

incentivo *m* incentive; **sueldo fijo más ~s** basic wage plus bonuses

incertidumbre *f* uncertainty

incesante *adj* incessant

incesto *m* incest

incestuoso -sa *adj* incestuous

incidencia *f*
A (frml) 1 (influencia, efecto) effect, impact; **tener ~ SOBRE** *or* **EN algo** to affect sth, have an effect *o* impact ON sth 2 (número de casos) incidence
B (episodio, suceso) incident, event

incidental *adj* incidental

incidentalmente *adv* by chance; **~ pasaba por allí** I happened to be passing by

incidente *m* incident

incidir [I1] *vi* (frml)
A (influir) **~ EN algo** to have a bearing ON sth; **eso no incidió en nuestra decisión** that did not affect our decision, that had no bearing on our decision
B (period) (insistir) **~ EN algo** to stress sth; **incidió en la necesidad de ...** he stressed the need to ...
C (frml) (incurrir) **~ EN algo** ‹*en error*› to fall INTO sth (frml)

incienso *m* incense; (Bib) frankincense

incierto -ta *adj* 1 (dudoso, inseguro) uncertain 2 (no verdadero) untrue

incineración *f* (de basura) incineration; (de cadáveres) cremation

incinerador *m*, **incineradora** *f* incinerator

incinerar [A1] *vt* ‹*basura*› to incinerate, burn; ‹*cadáver*› to cremate

incipiente *adj* (frml *o* liter) incipient (liter)

incircunciso -sa *adj* uncircumcised

incisión *f* incision

incisivo¹ -va *adj* 1 ‹*instrumento*› cutting 2 ‹*crítica/discurso*› incisive

incisivo² *m* incisor

inciso *m* 1 (paréntesis) digression 2 (Ling) interpolated clause 3 (párrafo) paragraph, subsection

incitación *f*: **~ A algo** incitement TO sth

incitador¹ -dora *adj* inflammatory, provocative

incitador² -dora *m,f* agitator

incitante *adj* provocative

incitar [A1] *vt* **~ a algn A algo** to incite sb TO sth; **los incitó a la violencia** he incited them to violence; **~ a algn CONTRA algn** to incite sb AGAINST sb

incivilizado -da *adj* uncivilized

incivismo *m* lack of public spirit

inclemencia *f* inclemency; **las ~s del tiempo** the inclemency of the weather

inclemente *adj* bad, inclement (liter)

inclinación *f*
A 1 (pendiente) slope 2 (ángulo) inclination; **la ~ de una torre** the lean *o* inclination of a tower
(Compuesto) **inclinación magnética** magnetic dip *o* inclination
B (movimiento del cuerpo) bow; **asintió con una ~ de la cabeza** he nodded (his head) in agreement
C (interés, tendencia): **tener ~ por** *or* **hacia la música** to have a musical bent *o* musical inclinations; **inclinaciones políticas/sexuales** political/sexual leanings; **inclinaciones suicidas** suicidal tendencies

inclinado -da *adj*
A ‹*tejado/terreno*› sloping; ‹*torre*› leaning (*before n*); ‹*cuadro*› crooked; **una pendiente muy inclinada** a very steep slope *o* incline; **tiene la letra inclinada** she has slanting handwriting
B (predispuesto) **sentirse ~ A + INF** to feel inclined to + INF

inclinar [A1] *vt*
A 1 ‹*botella/sombrilla/plato*› to tilt; **inclinó la cabeza a un lado** she tilted her head to one side 2 (bajar, doblar) to bow; **árboles inclinados por el viento** trees bowed by the wind; **el viento inclinaba los árboles** the wind bent the trees; **inclinó la cabeza en señal de asentimiento** he nodded (his head) in agreement
B (inducir, predisponer) ‹*persona*›: **ello me inclina a pensar que ...** this inclines me to think that ... (frml)

■ **inclinarse** *v pron*
A (tender) **~se A + INF** to be inclined to + INF; **~se POR algn/algo**: **me inclino por su candidato** I'm inclined to go for your candidate; **me ~ía por esta opción** I would tend to favor this option
B 1 (doblarse) to bend; (en señal de respeto) to bow; **~se ante algn** to bow to sb 2 (hacia adelante, hacia un lado) to lean; **se inclinó sobre la cuna** she leaned over the cradle; **~se hacia adelante/atrás** to lean forward/back

incluir [I20] *vt*
A (comprender) 1 ‹*impuestos/gastos*› to include; **sin ~ los gastos** exclusive of expenses; **$500 todo incluido** $500 all inclusive, all in 2 ‹*tema/sección*› to include, contain
B (poner, agregar) 1 (en un grupo) to include; **¿vamos a ~ a todo el personal?** are we going to include all the staff?; **¿te incluyo en la lista?** shall I put you on the list? 2 (en una carta) to enclose

inclusa *f* children's home

inclusión *f* inclusion

inclusive *adj inv* inclusive; **del 10 al 18, ambos ~** from 10 to 18 inclusive; **domingos ~** including Sundays; **hasta el sábado ~** up to and including Saturday

incluso *adv* even; **estaba muy animado, ~ hablador** he was very cheerful, in fact he was positively chatty

incoación *f* (frml) initiation (frml)

incoar [A1] *vt* (frml) to initiate (frml)

incobrable *adj* irrecoverable

incógnita *f* 1 (Mat) unknown, unknown factor *o* quantity 2 (misterio) mystery; **sus motivos siguen siendo una ~** his motives remain a mystery; ***despejar la ~*** (Mat) to find (the value of) the unknown factor *o* quantity

incógnito -ta *adj* 1 (liter) (desconocido) unknown 2 **de incógnito** ‹*viajar*› incognito

incoherencia *f* (cualidad) incoherence; **murmuraba ~s** she was mumbling incoherently

incoherente *adj* incoherent, illogical

incoloro -ra *adj* colorless*

incólume *adj* (liter) unscathed, unharmed

incombustible *adj* fireproof, incombustible (tech)

incomible *adj* inedible, uneatable

incomodar [A1] *vt* 1 (causar vergüenza) to make ... feel uncomfortable; **su pregunta me incomodó bastante** her question made me feel rather awkward *o* uncomfortable 2 (causar inconvenientes) to inconvenience, put ... out; **perdón, no quería ~la** I'm sorry, I didn't mean to put you out *o* to inconvenience you

■ **incomodarse** *v pron* 1 (sentir vergüenza) to feel uncomfortable 2 (pasar inconvenientes) to put oneself out 3 (enojarse) to get annoyed

incomodidad *f* 1 (de sillón, postura) uncomfortableness, discomfort 2 (molestia) inconvenience; **la ~ de vivir tan lejos** the inconvenience of living so far away; **no tener teléfono es una ~** it's very inconvenient not having a telephone

incómodo -da *adj* 1 ‹*silla/cama*› uncomfortable; **¿no estás ~ en esa silla?** aren't you uncomfortable in that chair? 2 (molesto, violento) uncomfortable; **se siente muy ~ en las fiestas** he feels ill at ease *o* uncomfortable at parties; ***estar ~ con algn*** (Andes) to be annoyed with sb 3 (inconveniente) inconvenient; **es muy ~ vivir tan lejos** it's very inconvenient living so far away

incomparable *adj* incomparable

incomparecencia *f* (frml) failure to appear, nonappearance

incompatibilidad *f* (cualidad) incompatibility; **~ de intereses** conflict *o* clash of interests

incompatible *adj* 1 ‹*personas/caracteres*› incompatible 2 ‹*cargo/horario*›: **los dos cargos son ~s** the two posts may not be held at the same time; **el horario de clases es ~ con el de mi trabajo** the times of the classes clash with my work hours

incompetencia *f* incompetence

incompetente *adj/mf* incompetent

incompleto -ta *adj* incomplete

incomprendido¹ -da *adj* misunderstood

incomprendido² -da *m,f*: **se consideraba un ~** he used to feel that people did not understand him

incomprensible *adj* incomprehensible

incomprensión *f* lack of understanding

incomprensivo -va *adj*: **eres muy ~** you're not being very understanding *o* sympathetic

incomunicación *f* 1 (incomprensión) lack of communication 2 (entre lugares) lack of communications 3 (de un detenido) solitary confinement

incomunicar [A2] *vt* 1 ‹*pueblo/zona*› to cut … off 2 ‹*detenido*› to put … in solitary confinement

inconcebible *adj* inconceivable; **es ~ que …** it's unbelievable *o* it seems inconceivable that …

inconciliable *adj* irreconcilable

inconcluso -sa *adj* unfinished

incondicional[1] *adj* 1 ‹*apoyo*› unconditional, wholehearted; ‹*obediencia*› absolute; ‹*aliado/admirador*› staunch; **un amigo ~** a true *o* loyal friend 2 ‹*rendición*› unconditional

incondicional[2] *mf* committed supporter, stalwart

inconexo -xa *adj* unconnected

inconfesable *adj* unmentionable

inconfeso -sa *adj* unconfessed

inconformismo *m* nonconformity

inconformista *adj/mf* nonconformist

inconfundible *adj* unmistakable

incongruencia *f* incongruity, inconsistency; **un sistema político lleno de ~s** a political system riddled with contradictions *o* incongruities; **lo que dijo fue una ~** what he said didn't make any sense

incongruente *adj*: **decía palabras ~s** his words didn't make sense; **imágenes ~s** unconnected images

inconmensurable *adj* (liter) vast, immense

inconmovible *adj*: **es ~, de nada valen las súplicas** he's implacable, no amount of pleading will make him change his mind; **~ ante mi llanto** unmoved by my tears

inconquistable *adj* ‹*fortaleza*› impregnable; ‹*tierras*› unconquerable

inconsciencia *f* 1 (Med) unconsciousness; **en estado de ~** unconscious 2 (insensatez) irresponsibility

inconsciente[1] *adj*

A [ESTAR] (Med) unconscious

B [SER] (insensato) irresponsible

C [SER] (no voluntario) ‹*movimiento/gesto*› unwitting, unconscious; **de una manera ~** unconsciously

inconsciente[2] *mf* irresponsible person; **son unos ~s** they are very irresponsible

inconsciente[3] *m* unconscious

inconscientemente *adv* unconsciously, unwittingly

inconsecuencia *f* failure to act according to one's beliefs (*o* principles *etc*)

inconsecuente *adj*: **ser ~ con uno mismo** to be inconsistent with one's principles; **no seas ~** don't betray your principles (*o* beliefs *etc*)

inconsistencia *f* 1 (de material) flimsiness, weakness 2 (de argumento — falta de solidez) weakness, flimsiness; (— falta de coherencia) inconsistency; **hay ~s en su razonamiento** there are inconsistencies *o* flaws in his reasoning

inconsistente *adj* 1 ‹*material*› flimsy, weak 2 ‹*argumento*› (falto de solidez) weak, flimsy; (falto de coherencia) inconsistent, flawed

inconsolable *adj* inconsolable

inconstancia *f* 1 (falta de perseverancia) lack of perseverance 2 (volubilidad) fickleness

inconstante *adj* 1 (falto de perseverancia) lacking in perseverance 2 (voluble) fickle

inconstitucional *adj* unconstitutional

inconstitucionalidad *f* unconstitutionality, unconstitutional nature

incontable *adj* countless, innumerable

incontaminado -da *adj* ‹*región/río*› unpolluted; **~ por el consumismo** uncontaminated by consumerism

incontenible *adj* ‹*furia/risa/llanto*› uncontrollable, uncontainable; **me entraron unos deseos ~s de pegarle** I had an uncontrollable urge to hit him

incontestable *adj* unanswerable

incontinencia *f* incontinence

incontinente *adj* incontinent

incontrolable *adj* uncontrollable

incontrolado -da *adj* 1 ‹*furia/pasión/ira*› uncontrolled, unbridled (liter) 2 ‹*llanto/risa*› uncontrollable 3 ‹*fuego*›: **el fuego sigue ~** the fire is still out of control

incontrovertido -da *adj* undisputed

inconveniencia *f* 1 (cualidad) inconvenience 2 (comentario inoportuno) tactless remark

inconveniente[1] *adj* 1 (incómodo) ‹*hora/fecha*› inconvenient 2 (inapropiado) ‹*lecturas/chistes*› unsuitable

inconveniente[2] *m* 1 (problema) problem; **si no surge ningún ~** if everything goes according to plan; if their are no problems; **¿habría algún ~ en que nos quedemos?** would it be alright if we stayed? 2 (desventaja) drawback; **el horario tiene sus ~s** the schedule has its disadvantages *o* drawbacks 3 (objeción) objection; **no tengo ~** I have no objection; **no tengo ~ en decírselo** I don't mind telling him; **no veo ningún ~ en que venga** I see no reason why he shouldn't come

incordiante *mf* (Esp fam) nuisance, pest (colloq)

incordiar [A1] *vt* (Esp fam) to annoy, to pester (colloq)

■ **incordiar** *vi* (Esp): **¡no incordies!** don't be such a nuisance!; **lo hace para ~** (fam) he does it just to be annoying

incordio *m* (Esp fam) nuisance, pain in the neck (colloq)

incorporación *f* incorporation; **buen sueldo, ~ inmediata** good salary, to start immediately

incorporado -da *adj* integral, built-in

incorporar [A1] *vt* (frml)

A 1 (agregar) to add; **~ algo A algo** to add sth TO sth, include sth IN sth; **~ las claras batidas a la mezcla** fold the whisked egg whites into the mixture 2 (integrar) to incorporate; **mi sugerencia fue incorporada al plan** my suggestion was incorporated in the plan 3 ‹*empleado*› **~ a algn A algo** to assign sb TO sth 4 ‹*recluta*› to draft, call up

B (incluir, contener) ‹*innovaciones/información*› to incorporate, include

C ‹*enfermo/niño*› to sit … up

■ **incorporarse** *v pron* (frml)

A (a equipo, puesto) to join; **~se A algo** to join sth; **~se a filas** to join up, join the army

B (levantarse) to sit up

incorpóreo -rea *adj* incorporeal

incorrección *f* 1 (error) mistake, error; **ese uso de la palabra es una ~** that use of the word is incorrect 2 (descortesía) discourtesy

incorrectamente *adv* 1 ‹*sumar/contestar*› incorrectly, wrongly 2 (con descortesía) rudely, improperly

incorrecto -ta *adj* 1 ‹*respuesta/interpretación*› incorrect, wrong 2 ‹*comportamiento*› impolite, discourteous (frml)

incorregible *adj* ‹*mentiroso/idealista*› incorrigible; ‹*defecto*› irremediable, irreparable

incorruptible *adj* incorruptible

incorrupto -ta *adj* incorrupt

incredulidad *f* skepticism*

incrédulo[1] **-la** *adj* skeptical*

incrédulo[2] **-la** *m,f* skeptic*

increíble *adj* incredible, unbelievable

incrementar [A1] *vt* (frml) to increase

■ **incrementarse** *v pron* (frml) to increase

incremento *m* (frml) increase

increpar [A1] *vt* to rebuke

incriminación *f* (frml) incrimination

incriminar [A1] *vt* (frml) 1 ‹‹*pruebas*›› to incriminate 2 (acusar, inculpar) to charge

incrustación *f* 1 (de madera, metal) inlay; **con incrustaciones de nácar** inlaid with mother-of-pearl; **la corona tiene incrustaciones de rubíes** the crown is set with rubies 2 (Col) (Odont) filling

incrustar [A1] *vt* ‹*piedra preciosa*› **~ algo EN algo** to set sth IN sth; **una tiara incrustada de** *or* **con diamantes** a tiara set *o* incrusted with diamonds

■ **incrustarse** *v pron*: **la bala se incrustó en la pared** the bullet embedded itself in the wall; **la suciedad se incrusta entre las baldosas** the dirt gets embedded between the tiles

incubación *f* incubation

incubadora *f* incubator

incubar [A1] *vt* to incubate
■ **incubarse** *v pron* «*crisis*» to brew, build up
incuestionable *adj* unquestionable
inculcar [A2] *vt* to instill*, inculcate (frml); **las ideas que les inculcan** the ideas they fill their heads with
inculpación *f* charge, accusation
inculpado -da *m,f*: **el ∼/la inculpada** the accused
inculpar [A1] *vt* (frml) to charge, accuse; **lo ∼on del robo** he was charged with *o* accused of the robbery
incultivable *adj* uncultivable
inculto[1] -ta *adj*
A (sin cultura) uncultured, uneducated; (ignorante) ignorant
B ‹*tierra*› uncultivated
inculto[2] -ta *m,f* 1 (persona sin cultura): **es un ∼** he's uneducated 2 (persona ignorante) ignorant person
incultura *f* (falta de cultura) lack of culture; (ignorancia) ignorance, lack of education
incumbencia *f* responsibility; **eso no es de tu ∼** that does not concern you
incumbir [I1] *vi* (*en 3ª pers*): **∼le a algn** to be sb's responsibility, be incumbent on *o* upon sb (frml)
incumplido -da *adj* (AmL exc CS) unreliable
incumplidor -dora *adj* (CS) unreliable
incumplimiento *m*: **el ∼ de la ley** failure to comply with the law; **∼ de contrato** breach of contract; **el ∼ de una promesa** failure to keep a promise
incumplir [I1] *vt* ‹*ley/promesa*› to break; ‹*contrato*› to breach
■ **incumplir** *vi* (AmL exc CS): **no me vayas a ∼** don't let me down; **incumplió a la cita** she didn't show *o* turn up
incurable *adj* incurable
incurrir [I1] *vi* (frml) **∼ EN algo** ‹*en error*› to fall INTO sth (frml); ‹*en gasto*› to incur sth; **los gastos en que incurrimos** the expenses we incurred; **incurrió en un delito de fraude** he committed fraud
incursión *f* (Mil) incursion, raid
incursionar [A1] *vi* (AmL) **∼ EN algo** to make incursions INTO sth
indagación *f* (frml) investigation; **hacer indagaciones** to make inquiries, to investigate
indagar [A3] (frml) *vt* to investigate
■ **indagar** *vi* to make inquiries, investigate
indagatorio -ria *adj* (frml) ‹*fase*› investigatory
indebidamente *adv* 1 (incorrectamente) improperly 2 (injustamente) wrongfully; **lo acusaron ∼** he was wrongfully accused
indebido -da *adj* 1 (impropio): **el uso ∼ de un medicamento** improper use of a medicine 2 (ilegal) wrongful; **el uso ∼ del fondo de pensiones** mhe isuse of the pension fund 3 ‹*acusación/multa*› unjust
indecencia *f* 1 (cualidad) indecency 2 (cosa, hecho): **presentarse así en público es una ∼** it's indecent to appear in public like that
indecente[1] *adj* ‹*persona/vestido*› indecent; ‹*película/lenguaje*› obscene
indecente[2] *mf* rude *o* shameless person
indecible *adj* indescribable; **ha sufrido lo ∼** he has suffered indescribable pain; **hizo lo ∼ por ayudarme** she did her utmost to help me
indecisión *f* indecision
indeciso[1] -sa *adj* ‹*persona*› 1 [SER] indecisive 2 [ESTAR] undecided; **está ∼ sobre ...** he's undecided about ...
indeciso[2] -sa *m,f* 1 (en general) indecisive person 2 (sobre un tema): **hay un gran número de ∼s** there are a lot of people who are as yet undecided
indeclinable *adj*: **es una invitación ∼** it's an invitation I can't turn down *o* decline
indecoroso -sa *adj* unseemly, indecorous (frml)
indefectible *adj* ‹*buen humor/cortesía*› unfailing; **es ∼ que llegue tarde** she invariably arrives late; **él y su ∼ bufanda de lana** him and his ever-present woolen scarf
indefectiblemente *adv* invariably, inevitably
indefendible, indefensible *adj* indefensible
indefensión *f* defenselessness*; **en un estado de total ∼** utterly defenseless
indefenso -sa *adj* ‹*niño/animal*› defenseless*; ‹*fortaleza*› undefended
indefinible *adj* indefinable
indefinidamente *adv* indefinitely
indefinido -da *adj* 1 ‹*forma*› undefined, vague; **un color ∼** a difficult color to describe 2 (ilimitado) indefinite, unlimited; **por tiempo ∼** for an indefinite *o* unlimited period
indeformable *adj*: **materiales ∼s** materials that do not lose their shape
indeleble *adj* indelible
indelicadeza *f* 1 (cualidad) indelicacy, lack of discretion 2 (acción) indiscretion; **cometió una ∼ al preguntárselo** it was indiscreet of her to ask him
indemallable *adj* (CS) runproof, ladderproof (BrE)
indemne *adj* (físicamente) unharmed, unscathed
indemnización *f* 1 (por pérdidas sufridas) compensation, indemnity (frml); (por posibles pérdidas) indemnity (frml); **cobramos una buena ∼** we received generous compensation 2 (por despido) severance pay
Compuesto **indemnización por daños y perjuicios** damages (*pl*)
indemnizar [A4] *vt* 1 (por pérdidas sufridas) to compensate, indemnify (frml); (por posibles pérdidas) to indemnify (frml); **fue indemnizado con dos millones de pesos** he was given two million pesos (in) compensation 2 (por despido) to pay severance pay to
indemostrable *adj* indemonstrable, impossible to demonstrate
independencia *f* independence; **con ∼ de ...** independently of ...
independentista[1] *adj* ‹*político/ideas*› pro-independence (*before n*)
independentista[2] *mf* supporter of the independence movement
independiente *adj/mf* independent
independientemente *adv* 1 ‹*actuar/funcionar*› independently 2 **∼ DE algo** regardless OF sth; **∼ de que tú vengas o no** (regardless of) whether you come or not
independizar [A4] *vt* to make ... independent
■ **independizarse** *v pron* to become independent, gain independence; **∼se DE algn** to become independent OF sb
indescifrable *adj* ‹*jeroglífico/mensaje*› undecipherable; ‹*misterio*› unfathomable
indescriptible *adj* indescribable
indeseable *adj/mf* undesirable
indeseado -da *adj* unwanted
indesmallable *adj* run-resistant, run-resist (AmE), ladderproof (BrE)
indestructible *adj* indestructible
indeterminación *f* indecisiveness
indeterminado -da *adj* 1 (indefinido) indefinite; **por tiempo ∼** indefinitely 2 (no establecido) undetermined 3 (vago, impreciso) ‹*contorno/forma*› indeterminate 4 (Ling) indefinite
India *f*: **la ∼** India
indiada *f*
A (Bol, CS fam) 1 (grupo de indios) Indians (*pl*), group of Indians 2 (pandilla) gang (colloq), mob (colloq)
B (Col fam) (canallada) dirty trick (colloq); **hacerle una ∼ a algn** to play a dirty trick on someone
indiano *m* (ant) *Spaniard who returned to Spain having made his fortune in Latin America*
indicación *f* 1 (instrucción) instruction; **le dio indicaciones de cómo llegar** he gave her directions as to how to get there; **tiene que descansar por ∼ médica** she is under doctor's orders to rest 2 (muestra) indication; **no dio ninguna ∼ de sus intenciones** she gave no clue as to *o* no indication of her intentions 3 (señal) signal; **me hizo una ∼ para que me acercara** he beckoned me over 4 (de instrumento) reading
indicado -da *adj* 1 (adecuado) suitable; **es el menos ∼ para hacerlo** he's the last person who should do it; **el tratamiento ∼ en estos casos** the recommended treatment in these cases; **lo más ∼ sería ...** the best thing to

do would be … 2 (señalado) ‹*hora/fecha*› specified

indicador¹ -dora *adj* warning; **señal ~a de peligro** danger *o* warning sign

indicador² *m*

A (Auto) 1 (señal de tráfico) sign 2 (dispositivo) gauge; **~ del aceite/de la gasolina** oil pressure/fuel gauge

Compuestos

- **indicador de dirección** indicator
- **indicador de velocidad** speedometer

B (Inf) flag

indicar [A2] *vt*

A (señalar) to indicate; **hay una flecha que indica el camino** there's an arrow indicating the way; **¿me podría ~ cómo llegar allí?** could you tell me how to get there?; **me indicó el lugar en el mapa** he showed me *o* pointed out the place on the map; **todo parece ~ que …** there is every indication that …

B (prescribir): **nos indicó el procedimiento a seguir** she advised us of the procedure we should follow; **las instrucciones que se indican al dorso** the instructions given on the back

C (mostrar, denotar) to indicate, show; **el asterisco indica que …** the asterisk indicates *o* shows that …; **como su nombre indica, es una flor azul** as its name suggests, it's a blue flower; **el precio no está indicado en el catálogo** the price isn't given *o* shown in the catalogue

indicativo¹ -va *adj* 1 ‹*señal/síntoma*› **~ DE algo** indicative OF sth 2 (Ling) indicative

indicativo² *m* 1 (Ling) indicative; **presente de ~** present indicative 2 (Telec) code; (Rad) call sign

Compuesto **indicativo de nacionalidad** (vehicle) nationality plate

índice *m*

A (de una publicación) index; (catálogo) catalog*

Compuestos

- **índice alfabético** alphabetical index
- **índice temático** *or* **de materias** table of contents

B (Anat) index finger, forefinger

C 1 (Mat, Inf) index 2 (tasa, coeficiente) rate

Compuestos

- **índice del costo** *or* (Esp) **coste de (la) vida** cost-of-living index
- **índice de mortalidad/natalidad** death/birth rate

D (indicio, muestra) sign, indication; **es un ~ de la crisis** it is an indication of the crisis

indicio *m*

A 1 (señal, huella) sign, indication; **al menor ~ de peligro** at the slightest sign *o* indication of danger 2 (vestigio) trace, sign; **~s de potasio** traces of potassium

B (Der) piece of circumstantial evidence

Índico *adj*: **el (Océano) ~** the Indian Ocean

indiferencia *f* indifference

indiferente *adj* 1 (poco importante, de poco interés): **es ~ que salga hoy o mañana** it doesn't matter *o* it makes no difference whether it goes today or tomorrow; **¿té o café? — me es ~** tea or coffee? — either; **todo le es ~** he's not interested in anything; **me es ~ su amistad** I'm not concerned *o* (colloq) bothered about his friendship 2 (poco interesado) indifferent; **~ A algo** indifferent TO sth; **~ al peligro** indifferent to *o* unconcerned about the danger 3 (poco afectuoso): **conmigo es fría e ~** she's cold and distant with me

indígena¹ *adj* indigenous, native (*before n*)

indígena² *mf* native

indigencia *f* (frml) poverty; **en la más completa ~** in abject poverty

indigente¹ *adj* (frml) destitute, indigent (frml)

indigente² *mf* (frml) indigent (frml); **los ~s** the destitute

indigerible *adj* indigestible, undigestible

indigestarse [A1] *v pron*

A (Med) 1 «*persona*» to get indigestion 2 «*alimentos*» (+ *me/te/le etc*): **se me indigestaron los pimientos** the peppers gave me indigestion

B (fam) «*actividad*»: **tiene la química indigestada** he can't stand chemistry

indigestión *f* indigestion

indigesto -ta *adj* ‹*alimento*› indigestible, difficult to digest; **un libro bastante ~** a book that is rather heavy going

indignación *f* indignation, anger; (más fuerte) outrage; **sentí una gran ~** I was outraged

indignado -da *adj* indignant, angry; (más fuerte) outraged, incensed

indignante *adj* outrageous

indignar [A1] *vt* to make … angry *o* indignant; (más fuerte) to outrage

■ **indignarse** *v pron* to get angry, become indignant; (más fuerte) to be outraged *o* incensed

indignidad *f* indignity

indigno -na *adj* 1 (impropio) unworthy; **~ DE algn** unworthy OF sb 2 (no merecedor) unworthy 3 (humillante) degrading, humiliating 4 (vergonzoso) shameful, disgraceful

índigo *m* indigo

indio¹ -dia *adj* 1 (de América) (American) Indian, Amerindian 2 (de la India) Indian, of/from India

indio² -dia *m,f* 1 (de América) (American) Indian, Amerindian; ***hacer el ~*** (Esp fam) to act the fool (colloq); ***~ comido, ~ ido*** (Andes) *said by or of a person who eats and then leaves immediately* 2 (de la India) Indian

indirecta *f* hint; **lanzar** *or* **soltar una ~** to drop a hint

indirectamente *adv* indirectly

indirecto -ta *adj* indirect; **una forma indirecta de decir que no** a roundabout *o* an indirect way of saying no

indisciplina *f* (de una persona) indiscipline, lack of discipline; (Mil) insubordination

indisciplinado -da *adj* ‹*alumno*› undisciplined, unruly; ‹*soldado*› insubordinate

indiscreción *f* 1 (dicho, declaración — que molesta) indiscreet *o* tactless remark; (— que revela un secreto) indiscreet *o* unguarded remark; **¿su edad, si no es ~?** how old are you, if you don't mind my asking?; **cometió la ~ de preguntárselo** he was indiscreet *o* tactless enough to ask her 2 (cualidad — al decir cosas que molestan) lack of discretion *o* tact, tactlessness; (— al revelar un secreto) lack of discretion, indiscretion

indiscreto -ta *adj* 1 (falto de tacto) indiscreet, tactless 2 (que revela un secreto) indiscreet

indiscriminado -da *adj* indiscriminate

indiscutible *adj* 1 ‹*pruebas*› indisputable, incontrovertible (frml); ‹*hecho/verdad*› indisputable, undeniable 2 ‹*líder/campeón*› undisputed

indiscutiblemente *adv* indisputably, undeniably

indiscutido -da *adj* undisputed

indisolubilidad *f* (del matrimonio, de un lazo) indissolubility; (Quím) insolubility

indisoluble *adj* ‹*matrimonio/lazo*› indissoluble; (Quím) insoluble

indispensable *adj* ‹*persona*› indispensable; ‹*objeto*› indispensable, essential; **lleva lo ~** take the bare essentials

indisponer [E22] *vt* 1 (Med) ‹*persona*› to make … unwell *o* ill 2 (enemistar) **~ a algn CON** *or* **CONTRA algn** to turn *o* set sb AGAINST sb

■ **indisponerse** *v pron* 1 (Med) (caer enfermo) to fall *o* get ill, become indisposed (frml); (empezar a menstruar) (CS euf) to start one's period 2 (enemistarse) to fall out; **~se CON algn** to fall out WITH sb

indisposición *f* 1 (Med) slight illness, indisposition (frml) 2 (falta de voluntad) unwillingness; (falta de entusiasmo) disinclination

indispuesto -ta *adj* 1 (enfermo) unwell, indisposed (frml); ‹*mujer*› (CS euf): **está indispuesta** it's the time of the month (euph) 2 (enfadado) **estar ~ CON** *or* **CONTRA algn** to be annoyed WITH sb

indisputable *adj* ‹*hecho*› indisputable, unquestionable; ‹*líder*› undisputed

indistinguible *adj* indistinguishable; **~ DE algo** indistinguishable FROM sth

indistintamente *adv* 1 (sin distinción, separación): **puede firmar uno u otro ~** either of you can sign; **todos, ~, deberán hacerlo** everyone, without distinction *o* exception, will have to do it; **los culpa a ambos ~** he blames both alike 2▸ (no claramente) ‹*percibir/recordar*› vaguely

indistinto -ta *adj* 1▸ ‹*forma/contorno*› indistinct, vague; ‹*idea/recuerdo*› hazy, vague; ‹*voz/ruido*› indistinct 2▸ (indiferente): **me es ~** it makes no difference to me

individua *f* (fam & pey) floozy (colloq & pej)

individual[1] *adj* 1▸ ‹*características/libertades*› individual 2▸ ‹*cama/habitación*› single (*before n*); **mantel ~** place mat 3▸ ‹*caso*› one-off (*before n*), isolated 4▸ (Dep) ‹*prueba/final*› singles (*before n*)

individual[2] *m* 1▸ (Dep) singles (*pl*); **~ masculino/femenino** men's/women's singles 2▸ (mantel) place *o* table mat, mat

individualidad *f* individuality

individualismo *m* individualism

individualista[1] *adj* individualistic

individualista[2] *mf* individualist

individualizar [A4] *vi*: **no voy a ~** I'm not going to mention any names *o* single anyone out

■ **individualizar** *vt* to individualize; **es preciso ~ el problema** we have to isolate the problem

individuo *m* 1▸ (persona indeterminada): **un ~ alto** a tall man 2▸ (pey) (tipo) character (colloq), individual (colloq); **dos ~s un tanto extraños** two rather strange individuals; **ese ~ que iba contigo** that guy you were with (colloq) 3▸ (Fil, Sociol): **el ~** the individual 4▸ (de una especie) individual

indivisible *adj* indivisible

indiviso -sa *adj* undivided, whole

indizar [A4] *vt* ‹*libro/revista*› to index; ‹*archivo/datos*› (Inf) to index

Indochina *f* Indo-China

indocumentado[1] **-da** *adj*: **un joven ~** a young man with no identity papers

indocumentado[2] **-da** *m,f* 1▸ *person lacking, or not carrying, identity papers* 2▸ (inmigrante) illegal immigrant

indoeuropeo[1] **-pea** *adj/m,f* Indo-European

indoeuropeo[2] *m* (idioma) Indo-European

índole *f* 1▸ (tipo, clase) kind, nature; **un problema de ~ afectiva** a problem of an emotional nature 2▸ (manera de ser) nature; **ser de buena/mala ~** to be good-natured/ill-natured

indolencia *f* laziness, slackness, indolence

indolente *adj* lazy, slack, indolent

indoloro -ra *adj* painless

indomable *adj* 1▸ ‹*animal salvaje*› untamable*; ‹*caballo*› unbreakable 2▸ ‹*pueblo/tribu*› indomitable, unconquerable; **un joven ~** an indomitable young man 3▸ (fam) ‹*pelo/remolino*› unruly, unmanageable

indomitable *adj* (AmL) indomitable

indómito -ta *adj* 1▸ ‹*animal*› untamed 2▸ ‹*persona/temperamento*› indomitable, irrepressible

Indonesia *f* Indonesia

indonesio -sia *adj/m,f* Indonesian

indubitable *adj* (frml) indubitable (frml)

inducción *f*

A (Elec, Med) induction

B (Der) inducement

inducir [I6] *vt*

A (empujar, llevar): **¿qué lo indujo a escribir este libro?** what led *o* prompted *o* induced you to write this book?; **me indujo a error** it led me into error

B (Der, Elec, Med) to induce

■ **inducir** *vi*: **esto induce a creer que ...** this leads us to believe that ...; **~ a error** to be misleading; **un factor que puede ~ a la compra de un piso** a factor that may encourage *o* induce people to buy an apartment

inductivo -va *adj*

A (Fil) inductive

B (Elec) inductive, induction (*before n*)

indudable *adj* unquestionable; **es ~ que ...** there is no doubt that ...

indudablemente *adv* undoubtedly, unquestionably

indulgencia *f*

A (tolerancia) indulgence; (para perdonar un castigo) leniency; **con ~** leniently

B (Relig) indulgence

indulgente *adj* (tolerante) indulgent; (para perdonar castigos) lenient; **~ CON algn** indulgent WITH/lenient TOWARD(S) sb

indultar [A1] *vt* (Der) to pardon; (de la pena de muerte) to reprieve

indulto *m* (Der) pardon; (de la pena de muerte) reprieve

indumentaria *f* clothing, clothes (*pl*), attire (frml)

industria *f* (Com, Econ) industry; **la ~ de la construcción** the construction industry

Compuestos

- **industria artesanal** cottage industry
- **industria automovilística/pesquera** car/fishing industry
- **industria pesada** heavy industry
- **industria siderúrgica** iron and steel industry

industrial[1] *adj* industrial

industrial[2] *mf* industrialist

industrialización *f* industrialization

industrializar [A4] *vt* to industrialize

■ **industrializarse** *v pron* to become industrialized

industrioso -sa *adj* industrious

inédito -ta *adj* 1▸ ‹*obra/autor*› unpublished 2▸ (nuevo, sin precedente) unprecedented; **una técnica inédita en nuestro país** a technique hitherto unknown in this country

inefable *adj* (liter) indescribable, ineffable (liter)

ineficacia *f* (de medida) ineffectiveness; (de método, persona) inefficiency

ineficaz *adj* 1▸ ‹*remedio/medida*› ineffectual, ineffective 2▸ ‹*método/sistema/persona*› inefficient

ineficiencia *f* inefficiency

ineficiente *adj* inefficient

inelegible *adj* ineligible

ineludible *adj* inescapable, unavoidable

inenarrable *adj* (liter) ‹*alegría*› indescribable, inexpressible; ‹*espectáculo/proeza*› indescribable

ineptitud *f* ineptitude, incompetence

inepto[1] **-ta** *adj* inept, incompetent

inepto[2] **-ta** *m,f* incompetent

inequívoco -ca *adj* unequivocal, unmistakable

inercia *f* 1▸ (Fís) inertia 2▸ **por ~** (por rutina) out of habit; (por apatía) out of inertia *o* apathy

inerme *adj* 1▸ (sin armas) unarmed 2▸ (ante críticas, calumnias) defenseless*

inerte *adj* 1▸ [SER] (Quím) inert 2▸ [ESTAR] (sin movimiento) inert (liter), motionless; (sin vida) lifeless

inescrutable *adj* inscrutable

inesperado -da *adj* unexpected; **se marchó de manera inesperada** she left unexpectedly

inestabilidad *f* 1▸ (de edificio, estructura) instability 2▸ (de país, gobierno) instability; **~ económica** economic instability 3▸ (Psic) instability, lack of stability 4▸ (Meteo) instability, changeability

inestable *adj* 1▸ ‹*edificio/estructura*› unstable 2▸ ‹*país/economía*› unstable 3▸ ‹*carácter/matrimonio*› unstable 4▸ ‹*tiempo*› changeable, unsettled 5▸ (Fís, Quím) unstable

inestimable *adj* ‹*ayuda*› invaluable

inevitabilidad *f* inevitability, unavoidability

inevitable *adj* (ineludible) inevitable; ‹*cambio/conflicto/controversia*› unavoidable; **era ~ que empeorase la situación** the situation was bound to get worse

inexactitud *f* inaccuracy

inexacto -ta *adj* 1▸ ‹*cálculo/definición*› inaccurate, inexact 2▸ (falso) untrue

inexcusable *adj* ‹*comportamiento/error*› inexcusable, unforgivable; ‹*deber*› inescapable, unavoidable

inexistencia *f*: **la ~ de pruebas en su contra** the lack of evidence against him; **la ~ de normas que lo regulen** the non-existence of regulations to control it

inexistente *adj* nonexistent

inexorable *adj* ‹*sentencia/castigo*› inexorable; ‹*juez/padre*› inflexible, unyielding; **el ~ paso del tiempo** the inexorable passing of time

inexperiencia *f* inexperience

i

inexperto -ta *adj* (falto de experiencia) inexperienced; (falto de habilidad) inexpert, unskilled
inexplicable *adj* inexplicable
inexplicado -da *adj* unexplained
inexplorado -da *adj* unexplored
inexplotado -da *adj* unexploited
inexpresable *adj* inexpressible, indescribable
inexpresivo -va *adj* expressionless, inexpressive
inexpugnable *adj* impregnable
inextinguible *adj* (liter) ‹*deseo/amor*› inextinguishable (liter), undying (liter)
inextricable *adj* ‹*problema*› inextricable; ‹*bosque/maleza*› impenetrable
infalibilidad *f* infallibility
infalible *adj* ‹*persona/método*› infallible; ‹*puntería*› unerring
infaltable *adj* (CS) inevitable
infamador -dora, **infamante** *adj* defamatory
infamar [A1] *vt* (frml) to defame (frml), to slander
infamatorio -ria *adj* defamatory
infame[1] *adj* 1 (vil, cruel) ‹*persona*› loathsome, despicable; ‹*acción/comportamiento*› unspeakable, disgraceful 2 (fam) (uso hiperbólico) horrible, terrible
infame[2] *mf* loathsome *o* despicable person
infamia *f* 1 (acción vil) disgrace 2 (fam) (uso hiperbólico) sacrilege (hum)
infancia *f* (período) childhood; **la democracia aquí está todavía en su ~** democracy is still in its infancy here
infante -ta *m,f* 1 (hijo del Rey) (*m*) prince, infante; (*f*) princess, infanta 2 (liter) (niño) infant
(Compuesto) **infante de marina** marine
infantería *f* infantry
(Compuesto) **infantería de marina** marines (*pl*), Marine Corps
infanticida *mf* child killer
infanticidio *m* infanticide
infantil *adj* 1 ‹*enfermedad*› children's (*before n*), childhood (*before n*); ‹*literatura/programa/moda*› children's (*before n*); ‹*rasgos/sonrisa*› childlike; ‹*población*› child (*before n*) 2 (pey) ‹*persona/actitud/reacción*› childish (pej), infantile (pej)
infarto *m* heart attack; **como se entere le va a dar un ~** (fam) if she finds out, she'll have a heart attack (colloq); ***de* ~** (fam): **un partido con un final de ~** a game with a heart-stopping finish (colloq); **una noticia de ~** incredible *o* staggering news
infatigable *adj* tireless, unflagging (*before n*)
infatuación *f* vanity, conceit
infatuar [A18] *vt* to make … conceited
■ **infatuarse** *v pron* to become conceited
infausto -ta *adj* (liter) ‹*suceso*› unfortunate; ‹*día*› ill-fated, ill-starred (liter)
infección *f* infection
infeccioso -sa *adj* infectious
infectar [A1] *vt* to infect
■ **infectarse** *v pron* to become infected
infectocontagioso -sa *adj* infectious
infecundidad *f* infertility
infecundo -da *adj* infertile, barren (liter)
infelicidad *f* unhappiness
infeliz[1] *adj* 1 ‹*persona/vida*› unhappy 2 ‹*intervención/tentativa*› unfortunate
infeliz[2] *mf* poor wretch, poor devil
inferencia *f* inference
inferior[1] *adj*
A (en el espacio) lower; **en los pisos ~es** on the lower floors
B (en jerarquía) ‹*especie/rango*› inferior
C (en comparaciones) lower; **~ A algo**: **temperaturas ~es a los 10°** temperatures lower than *o* below 10°; **el número de votantes fue ~ a lo previsto** the number of voters was lower than expected; **nació con un peso ~ al normal** he was below average weight when he was born; **un número ~ al 20** a number below twenty
inferior[2] *mf* inferior
inferioridad *f* inferiority
inferir [I11] *vt*
A (deducir) **~ algo DE algo** to infer *o* deduce sth FROM sth
B (frml) ‹*herida/golpe*› to inflict (frml); **le infirió una puñalada** she inflicted a stab wound on him
infernal *adj* ‹*ruido*› infernal, hideous; ‹*música*› diabolical; **hacía un calor ~** it was baking hot (colloq)
infértil *adj* infertile
infertilidad *f* infertility
infestación *f* infestation
infestado -da *adj* **~ DE algo** (de insectos, parásitos) infested WITH sth; **~ de turistas** crawling with tourists
infestar [A1] *vt* to infest
infición *f* (Méx) pollution
infidelidad *f* infidelity, unfaithfulness; **~ conyugal** marital infidelity
infidencia *f* (Andes, Ven) (secreto) intimate detail, secret
infiel[1] *adj* 1 (desleal) unfaithful; **ser ~ A algn/algo** to be unfaithful TO sb/sth 2 (Relig) unbelieving (*before n*), infidel (*before n*) (dated)
infiel[2] *mf* unbeliever, infidel (dated)
infiernillo *m* (Esp) kerosene stove, primus® stove (BrE)
infierno *m* 1 hell; **¡vete al ~!** (fam) go to hell! (sl); ***estar en el quinto* ~** (fam) (en un lugar — aislado) to be in the back of beyond (colloq); (— lejano) to be miles away 2 (suplicio, sufrimiento): **su vida es un ~** her life is hell 3 (fam) (lugar — ruidoso) madhouse (colloq), bedlam (colloq); (— horrendo) hellhole (colloq)
infílder *mf* (Col, Ven) infielder
infiltración *f* infiltration
infiltrado -da *m,f* infiltrator
infiltrar [A1] *vt* to infiltrate; **~ a algn EN algo** to infiltrate sb INTO sth
■ **infiltrarse** *v pron*
A (en partido, organización) to infiltrate; **las tropas se ~on en territorio enemigo** the troops infiltrated (into) enemy territory
B «*ideas/vocablos*»: **palabras que se han ido infiltrando en la lengua** words that have been filtering into the language
C «*luz*» to filter; **la humedad se infiltraba en la pared** the damp seeped into the wall
ínfimo -ma *adj* ‹*cantidad*› negligible; ‹*calidad*› very poor
infinidad *f* (multitud, gran cantidad): **en ~ de ocasiones** on countless occasions; **~ de veces** innumerable *o* countless times; **~ de personas** vast numbers of people
infinitamente *adv* infinitely; **te lo agradezco ~** I'm deeply *o* infinitely grateful to you; **lo siento ~** I'm terribly *o* awfully sorry
infinitesimal *adj* infinitesimal
infinitésimo -ma *adj* infinitesimal
infinitivo *m* infinitive
infinito[1] -ta *adj* 1 (Fil, Mat) infinite 2 ‹*bondad/sabiduría*› infinite; ‹*amor*› boundless; **sentí una infinita tristeza** I felt (an) immense sadness 3 (*delante del n, en pl*) (innumerables) innumerable, countless
infinito[2] *m*: **el ~** 1 (Fil) the infinite; **mirar al ~** to look into the distance 2 (Mat) infinity
infinitud *f* ▸ **infinidad**
inflable *adj* inflatable
inflación *f* inflation
inflacionario -ria, **inflacionista** *adj* inflationary
inflador *m* (Bol, Per, RPl) bicycle pump
inflamable *adj* flammable, inflammable (BrE)
inflamación *f* (Med) inflammation; (Quím) ignition
inflamar [A1] *vt* 1 (Med) to inflame 2 (Quím) to ignite, set … on fire 3 (liter) (exaltar): **la arenga inflamó los corazones de los soldados** the speech stirred the hearts of the soldiers (liter)
■ **inflamarse** *v pron* 1 (Med) to become inflamed 2 (Quím) to ignite
inflamatorio -ria *adj* inflammatory
inflar [A1] *vt*
A 1 ‹*balón/rueda*› to inflate; ‹*globo*› to blow up; **las velas**

infladas por el viento the sails filled by the wind
2 ‹*noticia/acontecimiento*› to exaggerate
B (Chi fam) (hacer caso a) to take notice of
■ **inflar** *vi*
A (RPl arg) to be a pain in the neck (colloq)
B (Méx fam) (beber) to booze (colloq), to drink
■ **inflarse** *v pron*
A «*velas*» to swell, fill; **se infla de orgullo** he swells with pride
B (Méx fam) (beberse) to drink, down (colloq)

inflexibilidad *f* inflexibility

inflexible *adj* inflexible; **tiene fama de ser ~** he has a reputation for being inflexible; **se mostró ~** he refused to give in

inflexión *f* inflection

infligir [I7] *vt* to inflict

influencia *f*
A (influjo) influence; **bajo la ~ del alcohol** under the influence of alcohol; **~ EN** *or* **SOBRE algo** influence ON *o* UPON sth; **~ SOBRE algn** influence ON sb; **ejerce una mala ~ sobre ti** she's a bad influence on you
B **influencias** *fpl* (contactos) contacts (*pl*); **tiene ~s en las altas esferas** she has friends in high places

influenciable *adj* easily influenced

influenciar [A1] *vt* to influence

influir [I20] *vi* **~ EN algo/algn** to influence sth/sb, have an influence ON sth/sb; **eso no ha influido en mi decisión** that hasn't influenced my decision
■ **influir** *vt* to influence

influjo *m* influence; **ejerce un gran ~ sobre sus nietos** he is a strong influence on his grandchildren

influyente *adj* influential

información *f*
A 1 (datos, detalles) information; **para mayor ~ ...** for further information ...; **el mostrador de ~** the information desk 2 (Telec) information (AmE), directory enquiries (BrE)
B (Period, Rad, TV) news; **y ahora pasamos a la ~ internacional** and now for the foreign news; **informaciones filtradas a la prensa** information *o* news leaked to the press; **la página de la ~ cultural** the arts page; **la ~ que llega de la zona** the news coming out of the area
C (Inf) data (*pl*)

informado -da *adj* (sobre tema, noticia) informed; **fuentes bien informadas** reliable sources; **está muy bien ~ sobre el tema** he is very knowledgeable about the subject; **me mantuvo ~** she kept me informed; **está usted muy mal informada** you have been misinformed *o* wrongly informed

informador¹ -dora *adj*: **nuestro equipo ~** our team of reporters; **la responsabilidad ~a de la prensa** the press's responsibility *o* duty to inform

informador² -dora *m,f* 1 (Period) reporter, journalist 2 ▸ **informante**

(Compuesto) **informador gráfico -dora gráfica** *m,f* press photographer

informal *adj*
A 1 ‹*persona*› unreliable 2 ‹*ropa/estilo*› informal, casual; ‹*cena/ambiente*› informal 3 (no oficial) ‹*reunión*› informal
B (AmL) ‹*economía/sector*› black (*before n*), informal (*before n*)

informalidad *f* 1 (de persona) unreliability 2 (de reunión, estilo) informality

informalmente *adv* 1 ‹*reunirse/hablar*› informally 2 ‹*vestir*› informally, casually

informante *mf* (de hecho, noticia) informant; (de la policía) informer

informar [A1] *vt* 1 ‹*persona/prensa*› to inform; **te han informado mal** you've been misinformed; **no se me había informado de esto** I had not been told about *o* informed of this; **¿podría ~me sobre los cursos de idiomas?** could you give me some information about language courses?; **me place ~le que ...** (frml) (Corresp) I am pleased to inform you that ... (frml) 2 (comunicar, hacer saber) to report; **fuentes policiales informan que ...** (period) police sources report that ...
■ **informar** *vi* (dar noticias, información) to report; **~ SOBRE algo** to report ON sth, give a report ON sth; **~ DE algo** to announce sth
■ **informarse** *v pron* to get information; **~se SOBRE algo** to find out *o* inquire ABOUT sth

informática *f* computer science, computing

informático¹ -ca *adj* computer (*before n*)

informático² *mf* computer specialist (*o* programmer *etc*)

informativo¹ -va *adj* 1 ‹*servicios/campaña*› information (*before n*); **programa ~** news program*; **desempeñamos una labor informativa** we provide information 2 (instructivo) informative; **una guía muy informativa** a very informative guidebook

informativo² *m* (news) program*

informatizar [A4] *vt* to computerize
■ **informatizarse** *v pron* to become computerized

informe *m*
A (exposición, dictamen) report; **~ policial/médico** police/medical report
B **informes** *mpl* 1 (datos) information, particulars (*pl*) 2 (de empleado) reference, references (*pl*); **pedir ~s** to ask for a reference/for references

infortunado -da *adj* ‹*persona*› unfortunate, unlucky; ‹*suceso*› unfortunate

infortunio *m* misfortune

infracción *f* offense*, infraction (frml); **una ~ contra el Fisco** a tax offense; **una ~ de la ley** an infringement *o* infraction of the law; **~ de tráfico** traffic violation (AmE), driving offence (BrE)

infraccionar [A1] *vt* (Chi, Méx frml) to fine
■ **infraccionar** *vi* (Chi, Méx frml) to offend, commit an offense*

infractor -tora *m,f* offender

infradesarrollo *m* underdevelopment

infradotado -da *adj* ‹*organismo/departamento*› underfunded, underfinanced

infraestructura *f* infrastructure

in fraganti *loc adv* red-handed; **la pescó ~ ~ con el vecino** (fam) he caught her in flagrante with their neighbor (hum)

infrahumano -na *adj* subhuman

infranqueable *adj* ‹*barrera/muro/río*› impassable; ‹*obstáculo/dificultades*› insurmountable, insuperable

infrarrojo -ja *adj* infrared

infrascrito -ta *m,f* (frml): **el ~** the undersigned

infrautilizado -da *adj* underused, underutilized

infravalorar [A1] *vt* to undervalue

infrecuente *adj* infrequent

infringir [I7] *vt* to infringe, break

infructuoso -sa *adj* fruitless

ínfulas *fpl*: **darse** *or* **tener muchas ~** to put on *o* give oneself airs; **se daba ~ de intelectual** he fancied himself as an intellectual

infundado -da *adj* unfounded, groundless

infundio *m* malicious story, lie, false rumor*

infundir [I1] *vt* ‹*confianza/respeto*› to inspire; ‹*sospechas*› to arouse; **les infundía miedo** it filled them with fear; **~ el terror entre los ciudadanos** to instill terror in the population; **para ~les ánimo** to give them encouragement

infusión *f* infusion; **~ de manzanilla** chamomile tea

Ing. = ingeniero/ingeniera

ingeniar [A1] *vt* ‹*método/sistema*› to devise, think up; ***ingeniárselas*** (fam): **se las ingenió para arreglarlo** he managed to fix it; **no sé cómo se las ingenia** I don't know how she does it

ingeniería *f* engineering

(Compuestos)
- **ingeniería civil/industrial/mecánica** civil/industrial/mechanical engineering
- **ingeniería de sistemas** systems engineering

ingeniero -ra *m,f* engineer

(Compuestos)
- **ingeniero aeronáutico -ra aeronáutica** aeronautical *o* aircraft engineer
- **ingeniero agrónomo -ra agrónoma** agriculturist
- **ingeniero -ra civil/industrial** civil/industrial engineer
- **ingeniero -ra de sistemas** systems engineer
- **ingeniero mecánico -ra mecánica** mechanical engineer

i

- **ingeniero -ra superior** engineer (*qualified after a five-year university course*)
- **ingeniero técnico -ra técnica** engineer (*qualified after a three-year university course*)

ingenio *m*
A 1 (talento) ingenuity, inventiveness; ***aguzar el ~*** to rack one's brains 2 (chispa, agudeza) wit
B (aparato) device
C (AmL) (refinería) *tb* **~ azucarero** sugar refinery

ingenioso -sa *adj* 1 (lúcido) ‹*persona/idea*› clever, ingenious 2 (con chispa, agudeza) ‹*persona/dicho/chiste*› witty 3 ‹*aparato/invención*› ingenious

ingente *adj* (frml) enormous, huge; **desarrolló una ~ labor en ese campo** she made an enormous contribution in that field

ingenuidad *f* naivety, ingenuousness

ingenuo[1] -nua *adj* naive, ingenuous; **¡qué ~ eres!** you're so naive!

ingenuo[2] -nua *m,f*: **es un ~** he's so naive

ingerencia *f* interference

ingerir [I11] *vt* (frml) ‹*alimentos/líquidos*› to consume (frml), to ingest (frml)

ingestión, ingesta *f* (frml) ingestion (frml), consumption

Inglaterra *f* England

ingle *f* groin

inglés[1] -glesa *adj* 1 (de Inglaterra) English; ***a la inglesa***: **ir a la inglesa** (Chi fam) to go Dutch; **un filete a la inglesa** (Méx) a rare steak 2 (crit) (británico) British, English (crit)

inglés[2] -glesa *m,f*
A 1 (de Inglaterra) (*m*) Englishman; (*f*) Englishwoman; **los ingleses** the English, English people 2 (crit) ▸**británico[2]**
B **inglés** *m* (idioma) English

ingobernable *adj* 1 ‹*país*› ungovernable 2 ‹*barco*› unsteerable

ingratitud *f* ingratitude

ingrato[1] -ta *adj* 1 (desagradecido) ‹*persona*› ungrateful; **~ con ella** ungrateful to her 2 (desagradable, difícil) ‹*vida*› hard; ‹*trabajo/tarea*› unrewarding

ingrato[2] -ta *m,f* ungrateful wretch (*o* swine *etc*) (colloq), ingrate (liter)

ingravidez *f* weightlessness

ingrávido -da *adj* 1 (liter) (ligero) light 2 (Fís) weightless

ingrediente *m* ingredient

ingresar [A1] *vi*
A «*persona*» 1 (en organización, club) to join; (en colegio) to enter; (en el ejército) to join; **~ en la cárcel** to be taken to jail, be placed in jail; **después de ~ en el hospital** after being admitted to (the) hospital; **ingresó cadáver** (Esp) he was dead on arrival 2 (AmL period) (entrar, introducirse): **la ventana por donde ~on los ladrones** the window through which the thieves broke in; **los jugadores ingresan al terreno de juego** the players are coming onto the field
B «*dinero*» to come in; **el dinero que ingresa en el país** the money coming into the country
■ **ingresar** *vt*
A ‹*persona*› (en hospital) to admit; **hubo que ~lo de urgencia** he had to be admitted as a matter of urgency; **fueron ingresados en esta prisión** they were taken to this prison
B (Esp) (Fin) ‹*dinero*› to pay in; **~ una cantidad en una cuenta** «*persona*» to pay a sum into an account; «*banco*» to credit an account with a sum

ingreso *m*
A 1 (en organización): **su solicitud de ~ en el club** his application to join the club; **discurso de ~** inaugural address; **el año de mi ~ a** *or* **en la universidad/el ejército/la compañía** the year I started *o* entered university/joined the army/joined the company; **examen de ~** entrance examination 2 (en hospital) admission 3 (AmL period) (entrada) entry; **fue difícil el ~ al estadio** it was difficult to get into *o* (frml) to gain access to the stadium
B (Fin) 1 (Esp) (depósito) deposit; **efectuó un ~ en el banco** he made a deposit at the bank 2 **ingresos** *mpl* (ganancias) income; **~s anuales** annual income; **los ~s del Estado** State revenue

(Compuesto) **ingresos brutos/netos** *mpl* gross/net income

íngrimo -ma *adj* (Col, Méx, Ven fam) 1 (sin compañía) all alone, all by oneself 2 ‹*lugar*› lonely, deserted

inhábil *adj*
A 1 (torpe) unskillful*, clumsy 2 (no apto) **~ PARA algo** unsuited TO sth; **es ~ para esa clase de trabajo** he's not cut out for that kind of work
B 1 ‹*día*› nonworking (*before n*) 2 (Der) (para un cargo): **fue declarado ~ para ejercer la profesión** he was disqualified from practicing the profession

inhabilidad *f*
A 1 (torpeza) lack of skill, clumsiness 2 (falta de aptitud) unsuitability
B (Der) (para un cargo) ineligibility

inhabilitación *f* disqualification, barring

inhabilitar [A1] *vt* **~ a algn PARA algo** ‹*para un cargo*› to disqualify sb FROM sth; **inhabilitado para ocupar cargos públicos** disqualified from holding public office; **el accidente lo inhabilitó para conducir** the accident left him unable to drive

inhabitable *adj* uninhabitable

inhabitado -da *adj* uninhabited

inhabitual *adj* unusual

inhalación *f* inhalation; **hacer inhalaciones** to inhale

(Compuesto) **inhalación de pegamento** *or* (Méx) **de cemento** glue sniffing

inhalador *m* inhaler

inhalar [A1] *vt* to inhale

inherente *adj* **~ A algo** inherent IN sth; **las funciones ~s al cargo** the duties attached to *o* that go with the job

inhibición *f* inhibition

inhibidor -dora *adj* inhibiting (*before n*)

inhibir [I1] *vt* to inhibit; **su actitud me inhibía** I was inhibited by her attitude
■ **inhibirse** *v pron* to become inhibited

inhóspito -ta *adj* inhospitable

inhumación *f* (frml) burial, interment (frml)

inhumanidad *f* inhumanity

inhumano -na *adj* 1 (falto de compasión) inhumane 2 (cruel) inhuman

inhumar [A1] *vt* (frml) to bury, inter (frml)

iniciación *f*
A (frml) (comienzo) beginning, start, commencement (frml)
B 1 (introducción) introduction; **curso de ~** introductory course 2 (a secta) initiation; **ceremonias de ~** initiation ceremonies

iniciado -da *m,f* initiate (frml); **para los ~s/no ~s** for the initiated/uninitiated

iniciador -dora *m,f* 1 (de técnica) pioneer; (de plan) initiator 2 (de problema): **la ~a de la disputa** the one who started *o* (frml) initiated the argument

inicial[1] *adj* ‹*plan/idea*› initial, original; ‹*temperatura/velocidad*› initial

inicial[2] *f* 1 (letra) initial 2 (en béisbol) first base 3 (Ven) (depósito) down payment

inicialar [A1] *vt* (en béisbol) to initial

inicialista *mf* (en béisbol) first base

inicializar [A4] *vt* (en béisbol) to initialize

iniciar [A1] *vt* 1 (frml) ‹*curso/viaje*› to begin, commence (frml); ‹*negociaciones/diligencias*› to initiate, commence (frml) 2 (en secta) **~ a algn EN algo** to initiate sb INTO sth 3 (en un arte) **~ a algn EN algo** to introduce sb TO sth
■ **iniciarse** *v pron*
A «*ceremonia/negociaciones*» to begin, commence (frml)
B «*persona*» 1 (en secta) **~se EN algo** to be initiated INTO sth 2 (en un arte) **~se EN algo** to take one's first steps IN sth

iniciativa *f* 1 (cualidad) initiative; **actuó por ~ propia** she acted on her own initiative 2 (propuesta) initiative 3 (ventaja, delantera): **tomó/perdió la ~** he took/lost the initiative

(Compuesto) **iniciativa privada** (Econ): **la ~ ~** the private sector, private enterprise
inicio *m* beginning, start
inicuo -cua *adj* (frml) iniquitous (frml), wicked
inidentificable *adj* unidentifiable
inigualable *adj* ‹*belleza*› matchless, incomparable; ‹*precios/oferta*› unbeatable
inigualado -da *adj* unrivaled*, unequaled*
inimitable *adj* inimitable
ininteligible *adj* unintelligible, incomprehensible
ininterrumpidamente *adv* ‹*trabajar*› without a break; ‹*llover/hablar/llorar*› nonstop
ininterrumpido -da *adj* ‹*lluvias/trabajo*› continuous, uninterrupted; ‹*sueño*› uninterrupted; ‹*línea*› continuous; **seis horas de música ininterrumpida** six hours of nonstop music
injerencia *f* interference
injerirse [I11] *v pron* **~ EN algo** to interfere IN sth
injertar [A1] *vt* to graft
injerto *m* 1 (Agr) (acción) grafting; (tallo) graft, scion 2 (Med) graft
injuria *f* 1 (frml) (insulto) insult 2 (Der) slanderous allegation; **se querelló contra ella por ~** he sued her for slander
injuriar [A1] *vt* 1 (frml) (insultar) to insult 2 (Der) to slander
injurioso -sa *adj* 1 (frml) (ofensivo) abusive, insulting 2 (Der) slanderous
injustamente *adv* unjustly, unfairly
injusticia *f* 1 (acto injusto) injustice, act of injustice; **es una ~ que te hayan dicho eso** it's unfair of them to have said that to you 2 (cualidad) unfairness, injustice
injustificable *adj* unjustifiable
injustificado -da *adj* unwarranted, unjustified; **despido ~** unfair dismissal
injusto -ta *adj* unfair; **ser ~ CON algn** to be unfair TO *o* ON sb
Inmaculada *f*: **la ~** the Blessed Virgin
inmaculado -da *adj* 1 ‹*presentación/vestido/superficie*› immaculate; **la blancura inmaculada de la nieve** (liter) the pristine whiteness of the snow (liter) 2 ‹*fama*› impeccable 3 (ant) ‹*mujer*› chaste
(Compuesto) **Inmaculada Concepción** *f* Immaculate Conception
inmadurez *f* immaturity, lack of maturity
inmaduro -ra *adj* ‹*persona/animal*› immature; ‹*fruta*› unripe
inmarchitable *adj* ‹*belleza*› unfading; ‹*ilusión/gloria*› everlasting, undying (liter)
inmaterial *adj* 1 (abstracto) ‹*problema/tema*› abstract 2 (intangible) ‹*figura/cuerpo*› ethereal, immaterial (frml)
inmediaciones *fpl* vicinity, surrounding area; **el hotel está en las ~ del aeropuerto** the hotel is in the vicinity of the airport; **en las ~ de la capital** in the area around the capital
inmediatez *f* immediacy
inmediato -ta *adj* 1 ‹*efecto/respuesta*› immediate; **de ~** immediately, right away, straightaway (BrE) 2 ‹*zona*› immediate; ‹*lugar/pueblo*› **~ A algo** close TO sth
inmejorable *adj* ‹*resultados/posición*› excellent, unbeatable; **un producto de ~ calidad** a top-quality product; **está en una situación ~** it is superbly located
inmemorial *adj* age-old (*before n*); **desde tiempo(s) ~(es)** since time immemorial
inmensidad *f* immensity
inmenso -sa *adj* ‹*fortuna/cantidad*› immense, vast, huge; ‹*casa/camión*› huge, enormous; ‹*alegría/pena*› great, immense; **sentía por ella un ~ cariño** he was extremely fond of her; **¡es ~!** it's absolutely huge!
inmensurable *adj* (liter) boundless (liter), immeasurable
inmerecido -da *adj* undeserved, unmerited
inmersión *f* 1 (de submarino, objeto) immersion 2 (en asunto, actividad) immersion, absorption
inmerso -sa *adj* 1 ‹*submarino/buzo*› submerged; ‹*objeto*› immersed 2 (en problema, actividad): **inmersa en sus tareas** absorbed in her work; **la crisis en que estamos ~s** the crisis in which we are immersed
inmesurado -da *adj* (Chi frml) immoderate, excessive
inmigración *f* immigration
inmigrado -da *m,f* immigrant
inmigrante[1] *adj* immigrant (*before n*)
inmigrante[2] *mf* immigrant
inmigrar [A1] *vi* to immigrate
inminencia *f* imminence
inminente *adj* imminent, impending
inmiscuirse [I20] *v pron* **~ EN algo** to interfere IN sth, meddle IN sth
inmobiliaria *f* 1 (agencia) real estate agency (AmE), estate agent's (BrE) 2 (empresa propietaria) real estate company (AmE), property company (BrE) 3 (empresa constructora) property developer
inmobiliario -ria *adj* real estate (*before n*) (AmE), property (*before n*) (BrE)
inmobilizador *m* immobilizer
inmoderado -da *adj* excessive, immoderate
inmodesto -ta *adj* 1 (vanidoso, presuntuoso) immodest 2 (ant) (sin recato) ‹*mujer*› unchaste (dated); ‹*escote*› immodest
inmolación *f* sacrifice
inmolar [A1] *vt* ‹*víctima*› to sacrifice
■ **inmolarse** *v pron* (frml) ‹‹*héroe*›› to sacrifice oneself
inmoral[1] *adj* immoral
inmoral[2] *mf*: **eres un ~** you have no morals
inmoralidad *f* immorality
inmortal[1] *adj* 1 ‹*alma/ser*› immortal 2 ‹*héroe/obra*› immortal; ‹*fama/amor*› eternal, undying (liter)
inmortal[2] *mf* immortal
inmortalidad *f* immortality
inmortalizar [A4] *vt* to immortalize
■ **inmortalizarse** *v pron* to achieve immortality, be immortalized
inmotivado -da *adj* ‹*ataque*› unprovoked, motiveless; ‹*preocupación*› groundless, unfounded
inmovible *adj* immovable
inmóvil *adj* still
inmovilidad *f* immobility
inmovilismo *m* resistance to change, immobilism (frml)
inmovilización *f* 1 (de persona, país, vehículo) immobilization 2 (Fin) (de capital) tying up
inmovilizar [A4] *vt*
A ‹*persona/país/vehículo*› to immobilize
B (Com, Fin) ‹*capital*› to tie up
inmueble *m* (frml) building, property (frml)
inmundicia *f* 1 (suciedad) filth 2 (dicho, cosa inmoral): **esa película es una ~** that film is absolute filth
inmundo -da *adj* 1 ‹*lugar*› filthy 2 ‹*sabor/comida*› foul, disgusting 3 (repulsivo) ‹*escena/película*› filthy, disgusting
inmune *adj* immune; **~ A algo** immune TO sth
inmunidad *f* immunity; **~ A algo** immunity TO sth
(Compuestos)
- **inmunidad diplomática** diplomatic immunity
- **inmunidad parlamentaria** parliamentary *o* congressional privilege

inmunizar [A4] *vt* to immunize; **~ a algn CONTRA algo** to immunize sb AGAINST sth
■ **inmunizarse** *v pron* 1 ‹‹*organismo*›› to become immune 2 (frml) (vacunarse) **~se CONTRA algo** to be immunized *o* inoculated AGAINST sth
inmunodeficiencia *f* immunodeficiency
inmunología *f* immunology
inmunológico -ca *adj* ‹*tolerancia*› immunological; ‹*sistema/reacción*› immune (*before n*)
inmutabilidad *f* immutability
inmutable *adj* 1 (inalterable) ‹*designios/principio*› unchanging, immutable (frml) 2 (impasible) ‹*persona*› impassive
inmutar [A1] *vt* ‹*persona*› to perturb (frml)
■ **inmutarse** *v pron* ‹‹*persona*››: **cuando se lo dije ni se inmutó** she didn't bat an eyelid when I told her (colloq); **no se inmuta por nada** he's not flustered by anything; **lo**

escuchó sin ~se she listened to him unperturbed
innato -ta *adj* innate, inborn
innavegable *adj* ‹*río*› unnavigable; ‹*embarcación*› unseaworthy
innecesario -ria *adj* unnecessary
innegable *adj* undeniable
innoble *adj* ignoble
innombrable *adj* unmentionable, unspeakable
innovación *f* innovation
innovador¹ -dora *adj* innovative
innovador² -dora *m,f* innovator
innovar [A1] *vi* to innovate
■ **innovar** *vt* to make innovations in
innumerable *adj* innumerable; **~s veces** innumerable *o* countless times
inobservancia *f* nonobservance
inocencia *f* 1 (Der) innocence 2 (ingenuidad) innocence, naivety; **lo dijo con toda la ~ del mundo** he said it in all innocence
inocentada *f* ≈ April Fools' joke (*played on 28 December*); **gastarle** *or* **hacerle ~s a algn** to play practical jokes on sb
inocente¹ *adj* [SER] 1 (sin culpa) innocent; (Der) innocent, not guilty; **lo declararon ~** he was found not guilty 2 ‹*broma*› harmless 3 (ingenuo) naive, gullible
inocente² *mf* innocent; **no te hagas el ~** don't play the innocent
inocentón -tona *adj* (fam) innocent, wet behind the ears (colloq)
inoculación *f* inoculation
inocular [A1] *vt* to inoculate
inocuo -cua *adj* ‹*sustancia/tratamiento*› harmless, innocuous
inodoro¹ -ra *adj* odorless*
inodoro² *m* 1 (wáter) toilet, lavatory 2 (taza) bowl, pan
inofensivo -va *adj* harmless, inoffensive
inolvidable *adj* unforgettable
inoperable *adj* 1 ‹*enfermo/tumor*› inoperable 2 ‹*sistema*› unworkable
inoperancia *f* 1 (inviabilidad) unworkability 2 (falta de eficacia) ineffectiveness
inoperante *adj* 1 (inviable) unworkable, inoperable 2 (ineficaz) ineffective
inopia *f* (fam): **yo, de álgebra, estoy en la ~** I don't know a thing about algebra; **me quedé en la ~** I was left in the dark; **está siempre en la ~** he's always daydreaming
inoportunidad *f* inopportuneness
inoportuno -na *adj* 1 ‹*visita/llamada*› untimely, inopportune; **llamó en un momento ~** he phoned at a bad moment 2 ‹*comentario/crítica*› ill-timed, inopportune
inorgánico -ca *adj* inorganic
inquebrantable *adj* ‹*fe*› unshakable, unyielding; ‹*lealtad*› unswerving; ‹*voluntad/salud*› iron (*before n*)
inquietante *adj* ‹*noticia/cifras*› disturbing, worrying; ‹*síntoma*› worrying
inquietar [A1] *vt* to worry, disturb
■ **inquietarse** *v pron* to worry; **~se POR algo/algn** to worry ABOUT sth/sb
inquieto -ta *adj* 1 [ESTAR] (preocupado) worried; **se sentía inquieta tan sola** she felt uneasy being all alone 2 [SER] (emprendedor) enterprising; (vivo) lively, inquiring (*before n*) 3 (que se mueve mucho) restless
inquietud *f* 1 (preocupación) worry; **~ POR algo** concern ABOUT sth 2 (interés): **es una persona sin ~es** she has no interest in anything; **su ~ filosófica** his philosophical preoccupations 3 (agitación) restlessness
inquilinaje *m* (Chi) (Agr) tenancy
inquilinato *m* 1 (arriendo) tenancy; **contrato de ~** tenancy agreement 2 (Agr) tenancy 3 (AmS) (edificio) tenement (house) 4 (Chi) (agricultores) tenant farmers (*pl*)
inquilino -na *m,f* 1 (arrendatario) tenant; **el actual ~ de la Casa Blanca** the current occupant of the White House 2 (Chi) (Agr) tenant farmer
inquina *f*: **tenerle ~ a algn** to bear ill will against sb, have a grudge against sb

inquirir [I13] *vi* (frml) **~ SOBRE algo** to make inquiries ABOUT sth, inquire INTO sth
Inquisición *f* (Hist): **la Inquisición** the Inquisition
inquisidor¹ -dora *adj* ‹*mirada/ojos*› inquiring (*before n*), searching (*before n*)
inquisidor² *m* inquisitor
inquisitivo -va *adj* inquisitive, curious
insaciable *adj* ‹*apetito*› insatiable; ‹*sed*› unquenchable; ‹*afán/deseo*› insatiable
insalubre *adj* unhealthy, insalubrious (frml)
insalubridad *f* unhealthiness, insalubrity (frml)
insalvable *adj* insurmountable, insuperable
insano -na *adj* 1 (loco) mad, insane 2 ‹*lugar/condiciones*› unhealthy
insatisfacción *f* dissatisfaction
insatisfactorio -ria *adj* unsatisfactory
insatisfecho -cha *adj* 1 (descontento) dissatisfied; **~ CON algo/algn** dissatisfied WITH sth/sb 2 ‹*hambre/deseo*› unsatisfied
inscribir [I34] *vt*
A (en registro) to register; (en curso, escuela) to register, enroll*; **inscribieron al niño/el nacimiento** they registered the child/the birth
B 1 (grabar) ‹*iniciales*› to engrave 2 (Mat) to inscribe
■ **inscribirse** *v pron*
A «*persona*» (en curso, colegio) to enroll*, register; (en concurso) to enter; (en congreso) to register
B «*acción/obra*» **~se DENTRO DE algo** to be in keeping WITH sth; **su novela se inscribe dentro del movimiento surrealista** her novel falls within the context of the surrealist movement
inscripción *f* 1 (para curso) enrollment*, registration; (para concurso) entry; (en congreso) registration; **la ~ se cierra el ...** the last day for enrollment is ... 2 (de un nacimiento) registration 3 (leyenda, lema) inscription
inscrito -ta, (RPl) **inscripto -ta** *pp*: *see* **inscribir**
insecticida *m* insecticide
insectívoro -ra *adj* insectivorous
insecto *m* insect
inseguridad *f* 1 (falta de confianza) insecurity 2 (falta de firmeza, estabilidad) unsteadiness 3 (falta de garantías) insecurity, lack of security 4 (en ciudad, barrio): **hay mucha ~ en esta ciudad** this city is very unsafe *o* dangerous; **la ~ ciudadana** the lack of safety on our streets
inseguro -ra *adj* 1 (falto de confianza) insecure 2 (falto de firmeza, estabilidad) unsteady 3 ‹*situación/futuro*› insecure 4 ‹*ciudad/barrio*› unsafe, dangerous
inseminación *f* insemination
(Compuesto) **inseminación artificial** artificial insemination
inseminar [A1] *vt* to inseminate
insensatez *f* 1 (cualidad) foolishness, senselessness 2 (dicho, hecho): **lo que has dicho/hecho es una ~** that was a stupid thing to say/do
insensato¹ -ta *adj* foolish
insensato² -ta *m,f* fool
insensibilidad *f* 1 (a emociones) insensitivity 2 (Med) (de una parte del cuerpo) numbness, lack of sensitivity
insensibilizar [A4] *vt* 1 ‹*persona*› to desensitize, harden 2 (Med) to numb, render ... insensitive
■ **insensibilizarse** *v pron* «*persona*» to become *o* grow hardened
insensible *adj* insensitive; **~ al frío** insensitive to the cold; **es ~ a mis súplicas** he is oblivious *o* insensible to my entreaties
inseparable *adj* inseparable
insepulto -ta *adj* (frml) unburied
inserción *f* insertion
insertar [A1] *vt* to insert
inservible *adj* (inútil) useless; (inutilizable) unusable; **todo tipo de trastos ~s** all kinds of useless objects
insidia *f* (malicia) malice; (engaño) deceit
insidioso -sa *adj* (malicioso) malicious; (engañoso) deceitful
insigne *adj* famous, notable

insignia *f* 1 (distintivo, emblema) insignia, emblem; (prendedor) badge, button (AmE) 2 (bandera) flag; (estandarte) standard, banner

insignificancia *f* 1 (intrascendencia) insignificance 2 (cosa insignificante): **me costó una ~** it cost me next to nothing; **es una ~, pero me dolió** it's nothing really but it hurt me; **discutir por ~s** to argue over petty things

insignificante *adj* ‹*asunto/detalle/suma*› insignificant, trivial, trifling (*before n*); ‹*objeto/regalo*› small; ‹*persona*› insignificant

insinceridad *f* insincerity, lack of sincerity

insincero -ra *adj* insincere

insinuación *f* insinuation; **por las insinuaciones que me hizo** from the hints he dropped

insinuante *adj* ‹*mirada/voz*› suggestive; ‹*escote*› provocative

insinuar [A18] *vt* to insinuate, hint at; **no lo dijo claramente pero lo insinuó** he didn't say it straight out but he hinted at it

■ **insinuarse** *v pron*

A «*barba*» to begin to show; «*problema/síntoma*» to become apparent

B **insinuársele a algn** to make advances to sb, to make a pass at sb

insípido -da *adj* insipid, bland

insistencia *f* insistence; **con ~** insistently

insistente *adj* ‹*persona*› insistent; ‹*recomendaciones/pedidos*› repeated (*before n*), persistent; ‹*timbrazos*› insistent, repeated (*before n*)

insistentemente *adv* 1 ‹*pedir*› repeatedly, persistently 2 ‹*golpear*› insistently

insistir [I1] *vi* to insist; **es inútil que insistas** there's no point going on about it; **ya que insistes, iré** if you insist, I'll go; **~ EN + INF** to insist ON -ING; **insistieron en acompañarme** they insisted on coming with me; **insiste en que lo hagamos** he insists (that) we do it; **insiste en que es suyo** she is adamant that it's hers; **~ SOBRE** *or* **EN algo** to stress sth; **insistió en su importancia** she stressed its importance

insobornable *adj* incorruptible

insociable *adj* unsociable

insolación *f* 1 (Med) sunstroke; **agarrar una ~** to get sunstroke 2 (Meteo) sunshine, insolation (frml)

insolencia *f* 1 (cualidad) insolence 2 (dicho): **no pienso tolerar sus ~s** I don't intend putting up with his insolence *o* his insolent behavior; **contestarle así fue una ~** it was very rude of you to answer him like that

insolentarse [A1] *v pron* to become insolent; **~ CON algn** to be rude *o* insolent TO sb

insolente[1] *adj* rude, insolent

insolente[2] *mf*: **es una ~** she's so rude *o* insolent

insolidaridad *f* lack of solidarity

insolidario -ria *adj* unsupportive

insólito -ta *adj* unusual; **fue ~ que viniera** it was unusual for him to come

insolubilidad *f* insolubility

insoluble *adj* insoluble

insolvencia *f* insolvency

insolvente *adj* insolvent

insomne *adj/mf* insomniac

insomnio *m* insomnia

insondable *adj* (liter) 1 ‹*abismo/mar*› bottomless 2 ‹*secreto/pensamientos*› unfathomable (liter)

insonorización *f* soundproofing

insonorizado -da *adj* soundproof

insonorizar [A4] *vt* to soundproof

insoportable *adj* unbearable, intolerable

insoslayable *adj* unavoidable, inescapable

insospechable *adj* beyond suspicion

insospechado -da *adj* ‹*reacción/consecuencias*› unforeseen; **descubrieron allí un mundo ~** there they discovered an undreamed-of world

insostenible *adj* 1 ‹*situación/gasto*› unsustainable 2 ‹*posición/tesis*› untenable

inspección *f* (verificación, examen) inspection; **una visita de ~** a tour of inspection; **~ sanitaria** health *o* sanitary inspection

inspeccionar [A1] *vt* to inspect

inspector -tora *m,f* inspector

Compuestos

- **inspector -tora de Hacienda** revenue agent (AmE), tax inspector (BrE)
- **inspector -tora de policía** (police) inspector

inspiración *f*

A (Art, Lit, Mús) inspiration; **obras de ~ clásica** works inspired by the classics

B (Fisiol) inhalation

inspirado -da *adj* inspired; **hoy no estoy muy ~** I'm not feeling very inspired today

inspirador -dora *adj* inspiring

inspirar [A1] *vt*

A ‹*confianza*› to inspire; ‹*compasión*› to arouse, inspire; **~les confianza** to inspire confidence in them *o* inspire them with confidence; **su voz les inspiraba terror** (liter) his voice filled them with fear (liter)

B «*obra/canción/persona*» to inspire

■ **inspirar** *vi* (Fisiol) to inhale

■ **inspirarse** *v pron* **~se EN algo** «*persona/obra/ley*» to be inspired BY sth

instalación *f* 1 (colocación) installation 2 (equipo, dispositivo) system; **la ~ sanitaria** the plumbing 3 **instalaciones** *fpl* (dependencias) installations (*pl*); **las instalaciones portuarias** the port installations; **instalaciones deportivas** sports facilities

instalar [A1] *vt*

A 1 (colocar y conectar) ‹*teléfono/lavaplatos*› to install; ‹*antena*› to erect, put up 2 (colocar) ‹*archivador/piano*› to put 3 ‹*oficina/consultorio*› to open, set up

B (AmL) ‹*comisión*› to set up, establish

■ **instalarse** *v pron* to settle, install oneself; **nos instalamos en la nueva oficina** we've settled into the new office

instancia *f*

A (solicitud) official request *o* application; **a ~s de** at the request of, at the instance of (frml)

B (momento) moment, happening; **en última ~** (como último recurso) as a last resort

C (period) (autoridad) authority; **las más altas ~s de la nación** the highest authorities in the land

instantánea *f* snapshot

instantáneamente *adv* instantly

instantáneo -nea *adj* 1 ‹*resultado/crédito*› instant (*before n*); ‹*reacción*› instantaneous, immediate; **le produjo la muerte instantánea** (period) it killed him instantly 2 ‹*café*› instant (*before n*)

instante *m* moment; **un ~, por favor** just a second *o* moment, please; **me llama a cada ~** he calls me all the time; **al ~** right away, straightaway (BrE)

instar [A1] *vt* (frml) **~ a algn A + INF** *or* **A QUE + SUBJ** to urge sb TO + INF

instauración *f* establishment

instaurar [A1] *vt* to establish

instigación *f* instigation; **por ~ de su hermano** at her brother's instigation

instigador -dora *m,f* instigator

instigar [A3] *vt* **~ a algn A algo/ + INF** to incite sb TO sth/ + INF; **~ al pueblo a la rebelión** to incite the people to rebellion

instintivo -va *adj* instinctive

instinto *m* instinct; **por ~** instinctively; **tiene mucho ~ para los negocios** she has a good instinct for business

Compuesto **instinto de conservación/maternal** survival/maternal instinct

institución *f* 1 (organismo) institution; **la siesta es toda una ~ aquí** (fam) the siesta is a real institution here 2 (creación, constitución) establishment 3 **instituciones** *fpl* (de una sociedad) institutions (*pl*)

institucional *adj* institutional

institucionalizar [A4] *vt* to institutionalize

instituir [I20] *vt* ‹*reforma*› to institute; ‹*norma*› to establish; ‹*premio/beca*› to set up, institute

instituto *m* institute

(Compuesto) **instituto nacional de bachillerato** (Esp) high school (AmE), secondary school (BrE)

institutriz *f* governess

instrucción *f*

A (educación) education; **una mujer sin ~** an uneducated woman; **recibieron ~ sobre estos métodos** they were trained in these methods

(Compuesto) **instrucción militar** military training

B (Der) (de una causa) hearing; **la ~ de un sumario** the preliminary investigation into a case

C **instrucciones** *fpl* 1 (de aparato, juego) instructions (*pl*); (para llegar a un lugar) directions (*pl*) 2 (órdenes) instructions

instructivo -va *adj* educational

instructor -tora *m,f* instructor

instruido -da *adj* [SER] educated

instruir [I20] *vt*

A 1 (adiestrar, educar) **~ a algn EN algo** to instruct *o* train sb IN sth; **me instruyó en su manejo** he instructed *o* trained me in its use 2 (frml) (informar) **~ a algn SOBRE algo** to apprise sb OF sth (frml)

B (Der) ‹*causa*› to try, hear; **el juez que instruye el sumario** the judge who is conducting the preliminary investigation into the case

■ **instruir** *vi*: **viajar instruye** travel broadens the mind

■ **instruirse** *v pron* (*refl*) to broaden one's mind, improve oneself

instrumentación *f* 1 (Mús) instrumentation, orchestration 2 (period) (de medidas, plan) implementation; (de una campaña) orchestration

instrumentador -dora *m,f* (RPl) nurse (AmE), theatre nurse (BrE)

instrumental[1] *adj* (Mús) instrumental

instrumental[2] *m* 1 (Med) equipment, set of instruments 2 (Mús) instruments (*pl*)

instrumentar [A1] *vt* 1 (Mús) to orchestrate, score 2 (period) ‹*medidas/resolución/plan*› to implement

instrumentista *mf* 1 (Mús) instrumentalist 2 (Med) nurse (AmE), theatre nurse (BrE)

instrumento *m*

A 1 (Mús) (musical) instrument; **~ de cuerda/de viento** string/wind instrument 2 (herramienta) instrument; (Med) instrument; **~s de medición/de precisión** measuring/precision instruments

B (medio) means

insubordinación *f* insubordination

insubordinado[1] -da *adj* 1 (desobediente) insubordinate 2 (sublevado) rebellious

insubordinado[2] -da *m,f* 1 (desobediente) insubordinate 2 (sublevado) rebel

insubordinar [A1] *vt* to rise to rebellion; **los ~on contra el dictator** they caused them to rebel against the dictator

■ **insubordinarse** *v pron* 1 (desobedecer) to be insubordinate; **~ se CONTRA algn** to be insubordinate TO sb 2 (sublevarse) to rebel; **~ se CONTRA algn** to rebel AGAINST sb

insubsistente *adj* (Col frml): **ser declarado ~** to be relieved of one's duties (frml)

insuceso *m* (Col period) unfortunate event *o* incident

insuficiencia *f* 1 (escasez): **la ~ de medios/calcio** the lack of resources/calcium; **la ~ de personal** the staff shortage 2 **insuficiencias** *fpl* (fallos, inadecuaciones) inadequacies (*pl*); **las ~s del sistema** the inadequacies of the system; **~s en la alimentación** dietary deficiencies

(Compuesto) **insuficiencia cardíaca/renal** heart/kidney failure

insuficiente[1] *adj* 1 ‹*medios/cantidad*› inadequate, insufficient 2 (Educ) ‹*trabajo*› poor, unsatisfactory

insuficiente[2] *m* fail

insufrible *adj* 1 ‹*persona*› unbearable, insufferable 2 ‹*situación*› intolerable; ‹*dolor*› unbearable

ínsula *f* (liter) isle (liter)

insular *adj* ‹*características*› insular; **la economía ~** the island's economy

insularidad *f* insularity

insulina *f* insulin

insulso -sa *adj* 1 ‹*comida*› insipid, tasteless, bland 2 ‹*persona*› insipid, dull; ‹*conversación/libro*› dull

insultante *adj* insulting

insultar [A1] *vt* 1 (proferir insultos) to insult 2 (ofender) to insult, offend; **aquello insultaba la memoria de su padre** that was an insult to the memory of her father

insulto *m* insult

insumos *mpl* (esp AmL) consumables (*pl*); **~ agrícolas como fertilizantes** agricultural inputs *o* consumables such as fertilizers; **los hospitales recibirán ayuda en ~** the hospitals will receive aid in the form of medical supplies

insuperable *adj* 1 (insalvable) ‹*problema/dificultad*› insurmountable, insuperable 2 (inmejorable) ‹*calidad/precio*› unbeatable

insurgencia *f* 1 (acto) rebellion, insurgency 2 (fuerzas) insurgent *o* rebel forces (*pl*)

insurgente[1] *adj* (frml) rebel (*before n*), insurgent (frml)

insurgente[2] *mf* (frml) rebel, insurgent (frml)

insurrección *f* (frml) uprising, insurrection (frml)

insurrecto[1] -ta *adj* (frml) rebel (*before n*), insurrectionary (frml)

insurrecto[2] -ta *m,f* (frml) rebel, insurrectionist (frml)

insustancial *adj* lightweight, insubstantial

insustituible *adj* irreplaceable

intachable *adj* impeccable, irreproachable

intacto -ta *adj* 1 (íntegro, no dañado) intact; **su reputación quedó intacta** he kept his reputation *o* his good name intact 2 (no tocado) untouched

intangible[1] *adj* intangible, impalpable

intangible[2] *m* (Com, Fin) intangible asset

integración *f* 1 (Mat, Sociol) integration; **la ~ de los immigrantes en la sociedad** the integration of immigrants into the society 2 (Fin) incorporation

integrado -da *adj* integrated

integrador -dora *adj*: **una política ~a** a policy of integration

integral[1] *adj* 1 (completo, total) comprehensive; **el desnudo ~** full-frontal nudity 2 (incorporado) built-in

integral[2] *f* (Mat) integral

integramente *adv*

A (totalmente) entirely

B ‹*actuar/comportarse*› with integrity

integrante *mf* member

integrar [A1] *vt*

A (formar) ‹*grupo/organización*› to make up; **los países que integran la organización** the countries which make up the organization

B (incorporar) ‹*idea/plan*› to incorporate

C (Mat, Sociol) to integrate; **para ~ al niño en el grupo** to integrate the child into the group

D (CS) ‹*suma/cantidad*› to pay

■ **integrarse** *v pron* 1 (asimilarse) to integrate, fit in; **~se A or EN algo** to integrate INTO sth, fit INTO sth 2 (unirse) **~se A or EN algo** to join sth; **~se a la CE** to join the EC

integridad *f*

A (totalidad, perfección): **amenaza la ~ del estado** it threatens the integrity of the state; **la ~ del producto** the (good) condition of the product

(Compuesto) **integridad física** personal safety; **un acto que atentó contra su ~ ~** an attempt against her life

B (entereza, rectitud) integrity; **~ moral** moral integrity

íntegro -gra *adj*

A 1 ‹*texto*› unabridged; **se proyectó en versión íntegra** they screened the full-length version 2 (completo, entero): **se estudió la obra íntegra en dos días** she learned the whole play in two days

B ‹*persona*› upright

intelecto *m* intellect

intelectual *adj/mf* intellectual

intelectualidad *f* (intelectuales) intelligentsia

inteligencia *f*
A (facultad, ser inteligente) intelligence
(Compuesto) **inteligencia artificial** artificial intelligence
B (comprensión) understanding
C (Mil, Pol) intelligence; **servicios de ~** intelligence services
D (intelectuales) intelligentsia

inteligente *adj* **1** (dotado de inteligencia) ‹*animal/ser*› intelligent **2** (de inteligencia superior) ‹*persona*› intelligent, clever; ‹*perro*› intelligent **3** ‹*ordenador/armas*› smart

inteligible *adj* intelligible

intemperancia *f* **1** (frml) (intransigencia) intransigence **2** (frml) (falta de moderación) intemperance **3** (Chi frml) (embriaguez) inebriation (frml)

intemperie *f*: **la ~** the elements (*pl*); **pasar la noche a la ~** to spend the night out in the open

intempestivo -va *adj* ‹*visita*› untimely, inopportune; **no lo llames a estas horas tan intempestivas** don't phone him at this ungodly *o* unearthly hour (colloq)

intemporal *adj* (frml) timeless, without time

intención *f* intention; **no fue mi ~ ofenderte** I didn't mean to offend you; **tiene buenas intenciones** she's well-intentioned, she means well; **tiene malas intenciones** he is up to no good; **lo dijo con segunda** *or* **doble ~** she had an ulterior motive for saying it; **me preguntó por ella con mala ~** he asked after her on purpose, he deliberately asked after her; **con la mejor ~** with the best of intentions; **lo que cuenta es la ~** it's the thought that counts; **vine con (la) ~ de ayudarte** I came to help you; **tiene (la) ~ de abrir un bar** she plans *o* intends to open a bar; **no tengo la menor** *or* **la más mínima ~ de devolvérselo** I have no intention whatsoever of giving it back to him

intencionadamente *adv* on purpose, deliberately

intencionado -da *adj* **1** (hecho a propósito) deliberate, intentional; **el incendio fue ~** the fire was started deliberately **2** **mal ~** malicious, hostile **3** **bien ~** ‹*plan/medida*› well-intentioned; ‹*persona*› well-meaning, well-intentioned

intencional *adj* intentional, deliberate

intencionalidad *f* intent, purpose

intendencia *f* **1** (Mil) Quartermaster Corps **2** (Andes) (división territorial) administrative division **3** (RPl) (gobierno municipal) town/city council; (edificio) town/city hall

intendente *mf* **1** (Mil) quartermaster general **2** (Andes) governor **3** (RPl) mayor

intensamente *adv* ‹*trabajar*› tirelessly; ‹*mirar/amar*› intensely; **vivió ~** he lived life to the full

intensidad *f* **1** (de terremoto) intensity, strength; (del viento) strength; (de dolor, sentimiento) intensity **2** (Elec, Fís) intensity

intensificación *f* intensification

intensificar [A2] *vt* to intensify, step up
■ **intensificarse** *v pron* «*sentimiento/dolor/sonido*» to intensify, become stronger

intensivo -va *adj* intensive; **cursos ~s** intensive *o* crash courses

intenso -sa *adj* **1** ‹*frío/luz/color*› intense; **para un bronceado más ~** for a deeper tan **2** ‹*emoción/mirada*› intense; ‹*dolor/sentimiento*› intense, acute **3** ‹*esfuerzo*› strenuous; ‹*negociaciones*› intensive; **desarrolló una intensa labor en favor de los derechos de la mujer** she campaigned tirelessly for women's rights

intentar [A1] *vt* to try; **no intentes nada** don't try anything; **¡inténtalo otra vez!** try again!; **~ un aterrizaje de emergencia** to attempt an emergency landing; **~ + INF** to try to + INF; **~é convencerlo** I'll try to persuade him; **¿has intentado que te lo arreglen?** have you tried getting *o* to get it fixed?; ***por ~lo que no quede*** (fam) there's no harm in trying

intento *m* **1** (tentativa) attempt; **un ~ de suicidio** a suicide attempt **2** (Méx) (propósito) intention, aim; ***de*** *or* ***a (puro)*** **~** (Col fam) on purpose, deliberately

intentona *f* rash attempt; **una ~ de golpe de estado** an attempted coup

interacción *f* interaction

interactivo -va *adj* interactive

interactuar [A18] *vi* to interact

interbancario -ria *adj* interbank (*before n*)

intercalar [A1] *vt* **~ algo EN algo** ‹*en texto*› to insert sth INTO sth; **intercaló algunas citas en su discurso** she interspersed her speech with some quotations; **~ algo ENTRE algo** to place sth AMONG sth; **~ algo CON algo** to alternate sth WITH sth; **intercala los ramilletes con las velas** put a bouquet between each candle

intercambiable *adj* interchangeable

intercambiar [A1] *vt* ‹*impresiones/ideas*› to exchange, swap (colloq); ‹*sellos/revistas*› to swap; **Ⓢ intercambio clases de inglés por clases de español** English lessons offered in exchange for lessons in Spanish
■ **intercambiarse** *v pron* (*recípr*) to swap (colloq), to exchange

intercambio *m* **1** (de ideas, información, bienes) exchange; **tener un ~ de palabras** to have words *o* a quarrel **2** (de sellos, revistas) swap; (de estudiantes) exchange; (de prisioneros) exchange **3** (en tenis) rally

interceder [E1] *vi* (frml) to intercede; **intercedió por ellos ante el rey** he interceded for them with the king

intercepción, interceptación *f* **1** (de correspondencia, mensaje) interception **2** (de teléfono) tapping **3** (Dep) (de balón, pase) interception **4** (de carretera, calzada) blocking

interceptar [A1] *vt* **1** ‹*correspondencia/mensaje*› to intercept **2** ‹*teléfono*› to tap **3** (Dep) ‹*balón/pase*› to intercept; ‹*golpe*› to block **4** ‹*calzada/carretera*› to block; **~ el paso** to block the way

intercesión *f* (frml) intercession (frml)

intercesor -sora *m,f* intercessor

intercomunicación *f* intercommunication, link

intercomunicar [A2] *vt* to link (up)

interconectar [A1] *vt* to link (up), interconnect

interconexión *f* interconnection, linking (up)

interconfesional *adj* interdenominational

intercontinental *adj* intercontinental

intercurricular *adj* intercurricular, cross-curricular

interdependencia *f* interdependence

interdicto *m* interdiction, ban, prohibition

interdisciplinario -ria, interdisciplinar *adj* interdisciplinary

interés *m*
A **1** (importancia, valor) interest; **de ~ turístico** of interest to tourists; **un tema de ~ humano** a human interest story; **de ~ científico** of scientific significance *o* interest **2** (actitud) interest; **despertó el ~ de todos** it aroused everyone's interest; **con gran ~** with great interest; **~ EN algo** interest IN sth; **pon más ~ en tus estudios** take more interest in your schoolwork; **tengo especial ~ en que ...** I am particularly concerned *o* keen that ...; **tienen gran ~ en verlo** they are very interested in seeing it **3** (afición, inquietud) interest
B **1** (conveniencia, beneficio) interest; **por tu propio ~** in your own interest, for your own good; **actúa sólo por ~** he acts purely in his own interest *o* out of self-interest **2** **intereses** *mpl* (objetivos) interests (*pl*); **conflicto de intereses** conflict of interests **3** **intereses** *mpl* (bienes, capital): **tiene intereses en esa empresa** he has a stake *o* an interest in that company; **administro sus intereses** I look after her investments
(Compuestos)
• **interés público** *m*: **el ~ ~** the public interest
• **intereses creados/privados** *mpl* vested/private interests (*pl*)
C (Fin) interest; **a** *or* **con un ~ del 12%** at 12% interest *o* at an interest rate of 12%; **ganar intereses** to earn interest; **tipo de ~** rate of interest
(Compuesto) **interés compuesto/simple** compound/simple interest

interesadamente *adv* selfishly

interesado[1] -da *adj* **1** [ESTAR] (que muestra interés) interested; **~ EN algo** interested IN sth; **las partes interesadas** the parties concerned, the interested parties **2** [SER] (egoísta) selfish; **su ayuda es interesada** they have ulterior motives for helping; **actuó de manera interesada** he acted selfishly **3** (parcial) biased, biassed

interesado² -da *m,f* 1 (que tiene interés) interested party (frml); **los ~s deberán ...** all those interested *o* (frml) all interested parties should ...; **nombre y dirección del ~** name and address of the applicant; **soy el principal ~ en que esto salga bien** I have the biggest interest in seeing this work out well 2 (que busca su provecho): **es un ~** he always acts in his own interest *o* out of self-interest

interesante *adj* interesting; ***hacerse el/la ~*** (fam) to try to draw attention to oneself

interesar [A1] *vi* 1 (suscitar interés): **ese tipo de programas no interesa aquí** there's no audience for that sort of program here; (+ *me/te/le etc*) **no me interesa la política** I'm not interested in politics; **¿te interesa la propuesta?** are you interested in the proposal?; **este anuncio podría ~te** this advertisement might interest you; **esto a ti no te interesa** this doesn't concern you, this is no concern of yours 2 (convenir): **~ía comprobar los datos** it would be useful/advisable to check the data; **me interesa este tipo de préstamo** this sort of loan would suit me

■ **interesar** *vt* **~ a algn EN algo** to interest sb IN sth, get sb interested IN sth

■ **interesarse** *v pron* 1 (tener interés) to take interest; **~se EN** *or* **POR algo** to take an interest IN sth; **no se interesa por nada** he isn't interested in anything, he takes no interest in anything; **~se POR algn** to care ABOUT sb; **nadie se interesa por mí** nobody cares about me 2 (preguntar) **~se POR algo/algn** to ask *o* inquire ABOUT sth/sb; **se interesó por tu salud** she asked *o* inquired about your health

interestelar *adj* interstellar

interétnico -ca *adj* interethnic

interface, interfaz *f* interface

interferencia *f* 1 (Rad, Telec) interference; (para obstaculizar la escucha) jamming 2 (Ling) interference

interferir [I11] *vt* 1 (obstaculizar) to interfere in 2 ‹*emisión*› to jam

■ **interferir** *vi* to interfere, meddle; **~ EN algo** ‹*en un asunto*› to interfere *o* meddle IN sth; **intentaron ~ en nuestra decisión** they tried to influence our decision

■ **interferirse** *v pron* **~se EN algo** to interfere *o* meddle IN sth

interfono *m* 1 (portero eléctrico) intercom (AmE), entryphone (BrE); (intercomunicador) intercom 2 (para bebés) baby alarm

interglacial *adj* interglacial

intergubernamental *adj* intergovernmental

interín, ínterin *m*: **en al ~** in the interim

interina *f* (Esp) maid (*who does not live in*)

interinamente *adv* temporarily

interinato *m* (esp AmL) (cargo) temporary post *o* position; **lo veían como un hombre de ~** he was seen as an interim *o* a stopgap president (*o* manager *etc*)

interinidad *f* temporary nature, provisional status (frml)

interino¹ -na *adj* ‹*secretario/director*› acting (*before n*); **profesor ~** substitute teacher (AmE), supply teacher (BrE); **médico ~** locum; **un gobierno ~** an interim government

interino² -na *m,f* (funcionario) temporary clerk (*o* accountant *etc*); (profesor) substitute teacher (AmE), supply teacher (BrE); (médico) locum

interior¹ *adj* 1 ‹*patio/escalera*› interior, internal, inside (*before n*); ‹*habitación/piso*› *with windows facing onto a central staircase or patio* 2 ‹*bolsillo/revestimiento*› inside (*before n*); **la parte ~ del colchón** the inside of the mattress; **en la parte ~** inside *o* on the inside 3 ‹*vida/mundo*› inner; **oyó una voz ~** she heard an inner voice 4 ‹*política/comercio*› domestic, internal

interior² *m*

A 1 (parte de dentro): **en el ~ de la habitación** inside the room; **el ~ estaba en perfectas condiciones** the interior was in perfect condition 2 (de un país) interior 3 (Méx, RPl, Ven) (provincias) provinces (*pl*) 4 (de una persona): **en su ~ estaba muy intranquilo** inside he was very worried; **allá en su ~ la amaba** deep down he really loved her

(Compuesto) **interior derecho/izquierdo** *mf* inside right/left

B **Interior** *m* (period) (Ministerio del Interior) Ministry of the Interior, ≈ Department of the Interior (*in US*), ≈ Home Office (*in UK*)

C **interiores** *mpl* (Cin) interior shots (*pl*)

D **interiores** *mpl* (Col, Ven) (Indum) underwear

interioridad *f* 1 (liter) (de una persona) inner world (liter) 2 **interioridades** *fpl* (intimidades) personal *o* private matters (*pl*)

interiorismo *m* interior decoration, interior design

interiorista *mf* interior decorator, interior designer

interiorizado -da *adj* (CS frml) well versed; **estar ~ DE** *or* **EN algo** to be well versed IN sth (frml)

interiorizar [A4] *vt*

A (Psic) to internalize

B (CS frml) (informar) **~ a algn DE** *or* **SOBRE algo** to brief sb ON sth, acquaint sb WITH sth

■ **interiorizarse** *v pron* (CS frml) **~se DE** *or* **SOBRE algo** to familiarize *o* acquaint oneself WITH sth (frml)

interiormente *adv* inwardly

interjección *f* interjection

interlocutor -tora *m,f* (frml) interlocutor (frml)

(Compuesto) **interlocutor válido** elected delegate

interludio *m* interlude

intermediario¹ -ria *adj* intermediary

intermediario² -ria *m,f* 1 (Com) middleman, intermediary 2 (mediador) intermediary, mediator, go-between

(Compuesto) **intermediario financiero -ria financiera** broker

intermedio¹ -dia *adj* 1 ‹*punto/etapa*› intermediate; **alumnos de nivel ~** students at intermediate level 2 ‹*calidad/tamaño*› medium (*before n*); **un coche de precio ~** a medium-priced car; **un color ~ entre el gris y el verde** a color halfway between gray and green

intermedio² *m* 1 (Espec) intermission, interval 2 (mediación): **por ~ de** through

intermezzo /inter'meso/ *m* intermezzo

interminable *adj* ‹*serie/discusión/espera*› interminable, never-ending; ‹*cola/fila*› endless, never-ending

intermisión *f* intermission, pause

intermitente¹ *adj* 1 ‹*lluvia*› intermittent, sporadic 2 ‹*luz*› flashing; ‹*señal*› intermittent 3 ‹*fiebre*› intermittent

intermitente² *m* turn signal (AmE), indicator (BrE)

internación *f* (CS) admission; **tras su ~ en la clínica** after his admission to the clinic; **recomendamos su ~ inmediata** we recommend immediate hospitalization

internacional¹ *adj* international; **de fama ~** internationally famous; ❸ **salidas internacionales** international departures; **las noticias ~es** the foreign *o* international news; **su política ~** their foreign policy

internacional² *mf* (Dep) international

internacionalista *adj/mf* internationalist

internacionalizar [A4] *vt* to internationalize

■ **internacionalizarse** *v pron* to become internationalized

internada *f* (Dep) run

internado¹ -da *adj* (CS): **está ~** he's been admitted to (the) hospital, he's been hospitalized

internado² *m* 1 (Educ) boarding school 2 (Med) *position or term as an intern or a houseman at a hospital*, internship (AmE)

internar [A1] *vt*: **la ~on en un manicomio** she was put in an asylum; **lo ~on en el hospital** he was admitted to (the) hospital; **tuvimos que ~lo** we had to take him to (the) hospital; **está (como) para que lo internen** (esp CS fam) he should be certified (colloq)

■ **internarse** *v pron* 1 (adentrarse) **~se EN algo** ‹*en bosque/espesura*› to penetrate INTO sth, to go deep INTO sth 2 (CS) (en hospital) to go into the hospital

Internet /inter'ne/ *m*: **el ~** the Internet

internista *mf* internist

interno¹ -na *adj*

A 1 ‹*llamada/correo/régimen*› internal 2 ‹*producción/demanda*› internal, domestic 3 ‹*dolor/hemorragia*› internal

B 1 (Educ): **está ~ en un colegio inglés** he is a boarder at an English school 2 (Med): **médico ~** ≈ intern (*in US*), ≈ houseman (*in UK*)

interno² -na *m,f*

A 1 (Educ) boarder 2 (en cárcel) inmate 3 (médico) ≈ intern (*in US*), ≈ houseman (*in UK*)

B **interno** *m* (RPl) (Telec) (extensión) extension

interpartidista *adj* ‹*comisión*› crossparty; ‹*convivencia/pugna*› between the parties

interpelación *f* (frml) question

interpelar [A1] *vt* (frml) to question; **~ a algn SOBRE algo** to question sb ABOUT *o* ON sth

interpersonal *adj* interpersonal

interplanetario -ria *adj* interplanetary

interpolación *f* (frml) interpolation (frml)

interpolar [A1] *vt* (frml) to interpolate (frml)

interponer [E22] *vt* 1 ‹*objeto/obstáculo*› to interpose (frml); **~ obstáculos en el camino de la independencia** to place obstacles in the way of independence 2 (Der) ‹*demanda*› to bring; ‹*recurso/denuncia*› to lodge, make 3 ‹*autoridad/influencia*› to exert, use 4 (frml) ‹*comentario*› to interject

■ **interponerse** *v pron*: **se interpuso y paró la pelea** he stepped in and stopped the fight; **nadie se interpone entre tú y ella** nobody is coming between you and her; **nada se interpone en su camino** nothing stands in her way; **la enfermedad se interpuso en sus planes** the illness got in the way of his plans

interpretación *f* 1 (de un texto) interpretation 2 (Cin, Mús, Teat) interpretation 3 (traducción oral) interpreting; **~ simultánea** simultaneous interpreting

interpretar [A1] *vt*

A ‹*texto/comentario/sueño*› to interpret; **interpretó mal tus palabras** she misinterpreted what you said

B 1 ‹*papel/personaje*› to play 2 ‹*pieza/sinfonía*› to play, perform; ‹*canción*› to sing

■ **interpretar** *vi* (Ling) to interpret

intérprete *mf*

A (traductor oral) interpreter

(Compuesto) **intérprete jurado -da** sworn interpreter

B 1 (Mús) performer; (cantante) singer 2 (portavoz) mouthpiece, exponent

interpuesto -ta *pp*: *see* **interponer**

interrogación *f* 1 (de un sospechoso) interrogation 2 (Chi) (Educ) test

interrogante¹ *adj* questioning (*before n*)

interrogante² *m or f* 1 (signo de interrogación) question mark 2 (incógnita) question

interrogar [A3] *vt* ‹*testigo/acusado*› to question; ‹*detenido*› to interrogate; ‹*examinando*› to examine

interrogativo -va *adj* interrogative

interrogatorio *m* (de acusado, testigo) questioning, examination; (de detenido) interrogation, questioning; **¿a qué viene este ~?** what's this grilling for? (colloq)

interrumpir [I1] *vt*

A (temporalmente) 1 ‹*persona/reunión*› to interrupt 2 ‹*suministro*› to cut off; ‹*servicio*› to suspend; ‹*tráfico*› to hold up; **las obras no ~án el paso** the work will not block the road

B 1 (acortar) ‹*viaje/vacaciones/reunión*› to cut short 2 ‹*embarazo*› to terminate

■ **interrumpir** *vi* to interrupt; **no interrumpas cuando estoy hablando** don't interrupt *o* (colloq) butt in when I'm talking

interrupción *f* interruption; **rogamos disculpen esta ~ de la emisión** we apologize for this break in transmission

(Compuesto) **interrupción (voluntaria) del embarazo** (frml) termination of pregnancy (frml)

interruptor *m* switch

intersección *f* 1 (en geometría) intersection 2 (frml) (Transp) intersection, junction

intersectarse [A1] *v pron* to intersect

intersticio *m* (frml) gap, interstice (frml)

intertanto *m*: **en el ~** (AmL) in the meantime

interurbano -na *adj* ‹*transporte/autobús/llamada*› long-distance; ‹*tren*› intercity

intervalo *m* 1 (de tiempo) interval; **un ~ de diez minutos entre clase y clase** a ten-minute recess (AmE) *o* (BrE) break between classes; **habrá ~s nubosos** it will be cloudy at times 2 (Mús) interval 3 (Teatr) (intermedio) intermission (AmE), interval (BrE) 4 (en el espacio) gap

intervención *f*

A 1 (participación) intervention; **se probó su ~ en el atraco** his involvement in the robbery was proved; **su ~ en el congreso** her speech to the conference; **su última ~ en una película** her last appearance in a film 2 (mediación) intervention, intercession (frml)

B 1 (injerencia) intervention; **una política de no ~** a policy of nonintervention 2 (de teléfono) tapping 3 (de empresa) placing in administration 4 (inspección de cuentas) auditing, official inspection 5 (de droga, armas) seizure, confiscation 6 (AmL) (de emisora, escuela) takeover

(Compuesto) **intervención quirúrgica** operation

intervencionismo *m* interventionism

intervenir [I31] *vi* 1 (en debate, operación) to take part; (en espectáculo) to appear, perform 2 (mediar) to intervene, intercede (frml); **en mi decisión intervinieron muchos factores** there were many factors involved in my decision 3 (tomar parte) to intervene; **tuvieron que ~ en la pelea** they had to intervene to stop the fight; **no quiso ~ en la pelea** he didn't want to get involved in the fight

■ **intervenir** *vt*

A 1 ‹*teléfono*› to tap 2 (tomar control de) ‹*empresa*› to place ... in administration 3 (inspeccionar) ‹*cuentas*› to audit, inspect 4 ‹*armas/droga*› to seize, confiscate 5 (AmL) ‹*universidad/emisora*› to take over the running of, take control of

B (operar) to operate on; **fue intervenido en una clínica privada** he underwent surgery in a private clinic

interventor -tora *m,f*

A (Fin) 1 (inspector) auditor 2 (administrador) administrator (*appointed by the government or by a court*)

B (en elecciones) canvasser (AmE), scrutineer (BrE)

interviú *f* interview

intestado -da *adj/m,f* intestate

intestinal *adj* intestinal

intestino¹ -na *adj* (frml) internal

intestino² *m* intestine, gut; **cáncer de ~** bowel cancer

(Compuesto) **intestino delgado/grueso** small/large intestine

inti *m* inti (*former Peruvian unit of currency*)

intimación *f* summons

intimar [A1] *vi* **~ CON algn** to get close TO sb

■ **intimar** *vt* (frml) to call on; **le intimó que moderase sus palabras** she called on him to moderate his language

intimidación *f* intimidation; **robos con ~** robberies involving threats of violence

intimidad *f*

A 1 (ambiente privado) privacy; **en la ~ del hogar** in the privacy of one's home 2 (relación estrecha) intimacy; **hay gran ~ entre ellos** they are very close

B **intimidades** *fpl* 1 (cosas íntimas) private life, personal *o* private affairs (*pl*) 2 (euf) (partes pudendas) private parts (*pl*) (euph), privates (*pl*) (colloq)

intimidante *adj* intimidating

intimidar [A1] *vt* 1 (atemorizar) to intimidate 2 (amenazar) to threaten

intimidatorio -ria *adj* threatening, intimidatory (frml)

íntimo¹ -ma *adj* 1 ‹*vida/diario/ceremonia*› private; ‹*secreto*› intimate; **un ambiente muy ~** a very intimate *o* cozy atmosphere; **aquello me tocó en lo más ~** I was deeply moved by that; **una cena íntima** a small dinner (with a few friends/members of the family); (en pareja) a candlelit *o* romantic dinner 2 ‹*amistad*› close; **amigos ~s** close *o* intimate friends

íntimo² -ma *m,f* close friend

intitular [A1] *vt* (frml) to entitle (frml)

intocable¹ *adj* 1 (sagrado) sacred, sacrosanct 2 ‹*tema*› taboo 3 ‹*casta*› untouchable

intocable² *mf* (Sociol) untouchable

intolerable *adj* intolerable; **hace un calor ~** this heat is unbearable

intolerancia *f* intolerance

intolerante *adj* intolerant

i

intoxicación *f* (Med) intoxication, poisoning
(Compuesto) **intoxicación alimenticia/etílica** food/ alcohol poisoning

intoxicar [A2] *vt* to poison
■ **intoxicarse** *v pron* to get food poisoning

intraducible *adj* untranslatable

intragable *adj* 1▸ ‹*hecho*› unpalatable, unacceptable 2▸ (fam) ‹*persona*› unbearable

intramuscular *adj* intramuscular

intranquilidad *f* 1▸ (preocupación) disquiet, (sense of) unease *o* uneasiness 2▸ (agitación) restlessness

intranquilizar [A4] *vt* to worry
■ **intranquilizarse** *v pron* to worry, get anxious

intranquilo -la *adj* 1▸ [ESTAR] (preocupado) worried, anxious 2▸ [SER] (agitado) restless

intranscendencia *f* ▸**intrascendencia**

intranscendente *adj* ▸**intrascendente**

intransferible *adj* not transferable, untransferable

intransigencia *f* intransigence

intransigente *adj* intransigent

intransitable *adj* impassable

intransitivo -va *adj* intransitive

intrascendencia *f* insignificance, unimportance; **detalles de la más absoluta ~** totally unimportant *o* insignificant details

intrascendente *adj* ‹*episodio/detalle*› insignificant, unimportant; ‹*comentario*› trivial

intratable *adj*: **hay días en que está ~** there are days when she's (just) impossible; **desde que ocurrió está ~** he's become very difficult since it happened

intrauterino -na *adj* intrauterine

intravenoso -sa *adj* intravenous

intrepidez *f* intrepidness, intrepidity

intrépido -da *adj* intrepid

intriga *f* intrigue; **~s políticas** political intrigues; **novela/película de ~** thriller

intrigante¹ *adj* 1▸ (que extraña) intriguing 2▸ (que arma intrigas) scheming

intrigante² *mf* schemer, intriguer (AmE)

intrigar [A3] *vt* to intrigue; **cuenta ya, que nos tienes intrigados** come on, tell us about it, you've got us intrigued now (colloq)
■ **intrigar** *vi* to scheme

intrincado -da *adj* 1▸ ‹*problema/asunto*› intricate, complex; ‹*laberinto/sistema*› complicated 2▸ ‹*nudo*› tangled

intríngulis *m* (fam): **tiene su ~** it's quite tricky *o* quite difficult *o* there's more to it than meets the eye

intrínseco -ca *adj* intrinsic; **~ A algo** intrinsic *o* inherent TO sth

introducción *f*
A (en libro, obra musical) introduction
B 1▸ (de cambio, medida) introduction; **la ~ de un nuevo producto en el mercado** the introduction of a new product onto the market 2▸ (inserción) insertion; **la ~ de la aguja en el músculo** the insertion of the needle into the muscle 3▸ (a tema, cultura) introduction; **~ A algo** introduction TO sth

introducir [I6] *vt*
A ‹*llave/moneda*› to insert; **introdujo la papeleta en la urna** he put his ballot paper in *o* into the ballot box
B 1▸ ‹*cambios/medidas/ley*› to introduce, bring in; **~ un nuevo producto en el mercado** to introduce a new product into *o* bring a new product onto the market 2▸ ‹*contrabando/drogas*› to bring in, smuggle in; **un solo perro podría ~ la enfermedad en el país** a single dog could bring *o* introduce the disease into the country
C 1▸ (presentar, iniciar) to introduce 2▸ ‹*persona*› (a una actividad) **~ a algn A algo** to introduce sb TO sth; **me introdujo a la lectura de los clásicos** he introduced me to the classics 3▸ (en un ambiente): **su música nos introduce en un mundo mágico** his music transports us to a magical world; **el escritor nos introduce en la Francia del siglo pasado** the writer takes us back to the France of the last century
■ **introducirse** *v pron* 1▸ (meterse): **el agua se introducía por las ranuras** the water was seeping in through the cracks; **la moneda se introdujo por una grieta** the coin fell down a crack 2▸ «*persona*» to gain access to; **se introdujeron en el banco por un túnel** they gained access to *o* got into the bank via a tunnel 3▸ (entrar en uso) «*moda*» to come in; **la costumbre se introdujo en los años 80** the practice was introduced in the eighties 4▸ (hacerse conocido) to become known; **cuando su obra se introdujo en México** when his works became known in Mexico; **ideas que se introdujeron en nuestra sociedad** ideas which found their way into our society

introductorio -ria *adj* introductory

intromisión *f* interference

introspección *f* introspection

introspectivo -va *adj* introspective

introversión *f* introversion

introvertido¹ -da *adj* introverted

introvertido² -da *m,f* introvert

intrusión *f* 1▸ (en un lugar) intrusion 2▸ (en un asunto) interference 3▸ (Geol) intrusion

intruso -sa *m,f* intruder

intuición *f* intuition; **hacer/saber algo por ~** to do/know sth intuitively; **tuve la ~ de que ...** I had a feeling that ...

intuir [I20] *vt* to sense; **intuí el peligro** I sensed the danger; **intuía que me iba a llamar** I had a feeling he was going to ring me

intuitivo -va *adj* intuitive

inundación *f* 1▸ (acción) flooding; **la ~ del mercado con coches extranjeros** the flooding of the market with foreign cars 2▸ (en área limitada, casa) flood; (en zona más amplia) floods (*pl*), flooding

inundar [A1] *vt* 1▸ «*riada/aguas*» to flood, inundate (frml); «*turistas/manifestantes*» to inundate, crowd 2▸ «*persona*» (con agua) to flood; (con productos) to flood, swamp; **me has inundado la cocina** you've flooded the kitchen; **~ algo DE** *or* **CON algo** to flood sth WITH sth
■ **inundarse** *v pron* (de agua) to be flooded; **la zona se inundó de turistas** the area was inundated with *o* swamped by tourists

inusitado -da *adj* unusual, rare, uncommon (frml)

inusual *adj* unusual

inútil¹ *adj*
A 1▸ ‹*esfuerzo/papeleo*› useless; **todo fue ~** it was all useless *o* in vain; **es ~ que insistas** there's no point (in) insisting 2▸ ‹*trasto*› useless
B 1▸ (incompetente) useless 2▸ (Mil) (no apto) unfit 3▸ (Med) disabled

inútil² *mf*: **es un ~** he's useless

inutilidad *f* 1▸ (de esfuerzo, tentativa) futility, pointlessness 2▸ (de persona) uselessness

inutilizable *adj* unusable, useless

inutilizar [A4] *vt* to make *o* render ... useless; **~on el radar** they put the radar out of action; **el brazo le quedó inutilizado** he lost the use of his arm

inútilmente *adv* uselessly

invadir [I1] *vt* 1▸ «*ejército/fuerzas*» to invade; **los manifestantes invadieron la plaza** the demonstrators poured into the square; **la televisión invade nuestros hogares** television is invading our homes 2▸ ‹*espacio aéreo/aguas*› to enter, encroach upon; **invadió nuestras aguas jurisdiccionales** it encroached upon *o* entered our territorial waters; **el autobús invadió la calzada contraria** the bus careered over onto the wrong side of the road 3▸ «*tristeza/alegría*» to overcome, overwhelm; **lo invadió un gran pesar** he was overcome *o* overwhelmed with sorrow

invalidación *f* (de documento) invalidation, nullification; (de argumento) invalidation

invalidar [A1] *vt* ‹*documento*› to invalidate, nullify; ‹*premisa/argumento*› to invalidate

invalidez *f*
A (de documento) invalidity, nullity; (de argumento) invalidity
B (Med) disability, disablement
(Compuesto) **invalidez permanente** permanent disability *o* disablement

inválido¹ -da *adj*
A ‹*documento*› invalid, null and void (frml); ‹*argumento*› invalid

B (Med) ‹*persona*› disabled, handicapped

inválido[2] **-da** *m,f* invalid, disabled person

invalorable *adj* (CS) invaluable

invariable *adj* **1** ‹*precio/estado*› constant, stable **2** (Ling) invariable

invariablemente *adv* invariably

invasión *f*

A **1** (de zona, país) invasion **2** (Der) encroachment, violation

B (Col) (chabolas) shantytown

invasivo -va *adj* invasive

invasor[1] **-sora** *adj* invading (*before n*)

invasor[2] **-sora** *m,f* invader

invencibilidad *f* invincibility

invencible *adj* **1** ‹*luchador/equipo*› unbeatable, invincible **2** ‹*miedo/timidez*› insuperable, insurmountable

invención *f* **1** (acción) invention **2** (aparato, cosa) invention **3** (mentira) fabrication

invendible *adj* unsaleable, unsellable, unmarketable

inventar [A1] *vt* **1** ‹*aparato/sistema*› to invent **2** ‹*juego/palabra*› to make up, invent; ‹*cuento/excusa/mentira*› to make up

■ **inventarse** *v pron* (*enf*) ▸**inventar** *vt*

inventario *m* (de negocio) inventory, stock list; (de casa) inventory; ❸ **cerrado por inventario** closed for stocktaking; **hizo el ~ de la casa** he made an inventory of the contents of the house; **hizo ~ de su vida** she took stock of her life

inventiva *f* inventiveness; **tiene mucha ~** she's very inventive

inventivo -va *adj* inventive

invento *m* invention; **no le creas, son puros ~s** don't believe him, it's pure fabrication *o* invention

inventor -tora *m,f* inventor

invernación *f* hibernation

invernada *f* **1** (CS) (Agr) winter pasture, wintering place; (período) wintering period **2** (Ven fam) (aguacero) downpour

invernadero *m* greenhouse

invernal *adj* ‹*lluvias*› winter (*before n*); ‹*frío*› wintry

invernar [A1 *or* A5] *vi* **1** (pasar el invierno) to winter, spend the winter **2** (hibernar) to hibernate

inverosímil *adj* implausible

inversión *f*

A (de dinero, tiempo, esfuerzos) investment

B (de posiciones, términos) reversal; (de una imagen) inversion, reversal

(Compuesto) **inversión térmica** thermal inversion

inversionista[1] *adj* investment (*before n*)

inversionista[2] *mf* investor

inverso -sa *adj* ‹*sentido/orden*› reverse; **puedes ordenarlo así o a la inversa** you can arrange it like this or the other way around; **a la inversa de lo que ocurre normalmente** contrary to what normally happens

inversor[1] **-sora** *adj* investment (*before n*), investing (*before n*)

inversor[2] **-sora** *m,f* investor

invertebrado[1] **-da** *adj* invertebrate

invertebrado[2] *m* invertebrate

invertido[1] **-da** *adj* **1** ‹*posición/orden*› reversed; ‹*imagen/figura*› inverted, reversed; **un matrimonio donde los papeles están ~s** a marriage in which the roles are reversed **2** (ant) (homosexual) homosexual

invertido[2] **-da** *m,f* (ant) invert (dated), homosexual

invertir [I11] *vt*

A ‹*dinero/capital*› to invest; ‹*tiempo*› to invest, devote

B ‹*orden/papeles/términos*› to reverse; ‹*imagen/figura*› to invert, reverse

■ **invertir** *vi* to invest; **~ EN algo** to invest IN sth

■ **invertirse** *v pron* ‹‹*papeles/funciones*›› to be reversed

investidura *f* investiture

investigación *f*

A **1** (de caso, delito) investigation; (por comisión especial) inquiry; **llevar a cabo una ~** to carry out an investigation, to hold an inquiry **2** (Educ, Med, Tec) research; **~ científica** scientific research

(Compuestos)

• **investigación de la paternidad** tests to establish paternity (*pl*)

• **investigación de mercados** market research

• **investigación y desarrollo** research and development

B **Investigaciones** *fpl* (en Chi) criminal investigation department

investigador[1] **-dora** *adj* **1** (en relación con un delito, siniestro): **una comisión ~a** a committee of inquiry; **terminaron sus tareas ~as** they finished their investigative work *o* their investigations **2** (Educ, Med, Tec) research (*before n*); **el equipo ~** the research team; **su labor ~a** their research (work)

investigador[2] **-dora** *m,f* **1** (que indaga) investigator **2** (Educ, Med, Tec) researcher

(Compuesto) **investigador privado -dora privada** private investigator

investigar [A3] *vt* **1** ‹*delito/caso*› to investigate; **se ~án las causas del accidente** there will be an investigation *o* inquiry into the causes of the accident; **tengo que ~ quién vive arriba** (fam) I have to find out who lives upstairs **2** (Educ, Med, Tec) ‹‹*persona*›› to research, do research into

■ **investigar** *vi* **1** ‹‹*policía*›› to investigate **2** (Educ, Med, Tec) **~ SOBRE algo** to do research INTO sth, to research INTO sth

investir [I14] *vt*: **fue investido presidente** he was sworn in *o* (frml) inaugurated as president; **fue investido caballero** he was knighted; **~ a algn DE** *or* **CON algo** (frml) to invest sb WITH sth (frml)

inveterado -da *adj* (frml) deeply rooted (AmE), deep-rooted (BrE)

inviable *adj* non-viable, unviable, unfeasible

invicto -ta *adj* **1** (liter) ‹*soldado/ejército*› unconquered, undefeated **2** (Dep) unbeaten, undefeated

invidente[1] *adj* blind, sightless

invidente[2] *mf* (frml) blind person

invierno *m* winter; (en la zona tropical) rainy season; **en ~** in winter, in wintertime; **en pleno ~** in the middle *o* depths of winter; **ropa de ~** winter clothes

(Compuesto) **invierno nuclear** nuclear winter

invierta, inviertas, etc *see* **invertir**

inviolabilidad *f* inviolability

(Compuesto) **inviolabilidad parlamentaria** parliamentary immunity *o* privilege

inviolable *adj* inviolable

invirtiera, invirtió, etc *see* **invertir**

invisibilidad *f* invisibility

invisible *adj* invisible

invitación *f* invitation; **hizo una ~ a la calma** he made an appeal *o* he appealed for calm

invitado -da *m,f* guest; **tenemos ~s a cenar** we have people coming to dinner; **los ~s a la boda** the wedding guests

(Compuestos)

• **invitado de piedra** *m* unwanted guest

• **invitado -da especial** *m,f* special guest

invitar [A1] *vt* to invite; **sin estar invitado** uninvited; **~ a algn A algo** to invite sb TO sth; **te invito a una copa** I'll buy *o* get you a drink; **esta vez te invito yo** this time it's my treat *o* it's on me; **~ a algn A + INF** *or* **A QUE + SUBJ** to invite sb to + INF; **me invitó a cenar** (en casa) she invited me (round) to dinner; (en restaurante) she invited me out to dinner; **la invitó a entrar** he invited her in

■ **invitar** *vi* **1** ‹‹*persona*››: **invito yo** it's on me *o* I'm buying; **invita la casa** it's on the house **2** (liter) (incitar, animar) **la tranquilidad de la tarde invitaba al reposo** the tranquility of the evening invited relaxation (liter); **el mar invitaba a bañarse** the sea looked very inviting

invite *m* (fam) invitation, invite (colloq)

in vitro *adj inv* in vitro

invocar [A2] *f*
A [1] ‹*divinidad/santos*› to invoke (frml), to call on [2] ‹*auxilio/protección*› to invoke (frml), to appeal for
B [1] ‹*amistad/circunstancias*› to cite, invoke (frml) [2] ‹*ley/derecho*› to cite, refer to

involución *f* [1] (period) (en una sociedad) involution, regression [2] (Biol, Med) involution

involucionismo *m* reactionary stance *o* attitude

involucionista *adj* (period) reactionary, involutional (frml)

involucrar [A1] *vt* [1] (en asunto, crimen) to involve; ~ **a algn EN algo** to involve sb IN sth [2] (complicar) ‹*cuestión/asunto*› to complicate [3] (AmL) (conllevar) to involve
■ **involucrarse** *v pron* «*persona*» to get involved

involuntario -ria *adj* [1] ‹*error/movimiento/gesto*› involuntary; ‹*testigo/cómplice*› unwitting [2] (Fisiol) involuntary

involutivo -va *adj* (period) regressive, reactionary

invulnerable *adj* [1] (físicamente) invulnerable [2] (a críticas, tentaciones) ~ **A algo** immune TO sth, invulnerable TO sth

inyección *f* [1] (Med) (acción) injection; (dosis) injection, shot (colloq); **le puso una ~** she gave him an injection; **~ intravenosa/intramuscular** intravenous/intramuscular injection [2] (de energía, entusiasmo, capital) injection; **una ~ financiera** an injection of funds [3] (Auto, Tec) injection; **alimentación por ~** fuel injection

inyectable *adj* injectable

inyectado -da *adj*: **ojos ~s en** *or* **de sangre** bloodshot eyes

inyectar [A1] *vt* to inject; **le ~on morfina** they gave him morphine injections/a shot of morphine; **inyectó nueva vida a la zona** it injected new life into the area
■ **inyectarse** *v pron* (*refl*) «*persona*» to give oneself an injection, inject oneself; **se inyectó heroína** he injected himself with heroin

inyector[1] **-tora** *adj* injector (*before n*)

inyector[2] *m* injector

ion *m* ion

iónico -ca *adj* ionic

ionizar [A4] *vt* to ionize

ionosfera *f* ionosphere

IPC *m* (= **Índice de Precios al Consumo** *or* **al Consumidor**) consumer prices index, ≈ RPI (*in UK*)

ipso facto *loc adv* [1] (inmediatamente) immediately, at once [2] (expresando consecuencia) ipso facto (frml)

ique *adv* (Ven fam) ▸ **dizque**

ir [I27] *vi*

(*Sentido* **I**)

A [1] (trasladarse, desplazarse) to go; ~ **en taxi** to go by taxi; **iban a caballo/a pie** they were on horseback/on foot; **~ por mar** to go by sea; **¡Fernando! — ¡voy!** Fernando! — (just) coming! *o* I'll be right there!; **lo oía ~ y venir por la habitación** I could hear him pacing up and down the room; **el ~ y venir de los invitados** the coming and going of the guests; **no hago más que ~ y venir de un lado para otro** I do nothing but run around; **voy al mercado** I'm going to the market, I'm off to the market (colloq); **vamos a casa** let's go home; **¿adónde va este tren?** where's this train going (to)?; **¿tú vas a misa?** do you go to church?; **~ de compras/de caza** to go shopping/hunting; **ya vamos para allá** we're on our way; **¿por dónde se va a ...?** how do you get to ...?; **a eso voy** I'm just coming *o* getting to that; ***¿dónde vas/va/van?*** (Esp fam) (frente a una exageración): **¿dónde vas con tanto pan?** what are you doing with all that bread?; **¿dejamos 500 de propina? — ¡dónde vas!** shall we leave 500 as a tip? — you must be joking *o* kidding!; ***~ a dar a un lugar*** *ver* **parar**; ***~ a por algn*** (Esp): **ha ido a por su madre** he's gone to get his mother, he's gone to pick his mother up; **ten cuidado, que va a por ti** watch out, he's out to get you *o* he's after you; **el perro fue a por él** the dog went for him; ***~ por*** *or* (Esp) ***a por algo***: **voy (a) por pan** I'm going to get some bread; ***no ~la con algo*** (RPl fam): **no la voy con tanta liberalidad** I don't go along with all this liberalism; ***no me/le va ni me/le viene*** (fam) (no me, le concierne) it's none of my/his/her business; (ne me, le afecta) it doesn't affect me/him/her; ***allí donde fueres haz lo que vieres*** when in Rome, do as the Romans do [2] (asistir) to go to; **voy a clases nocturnas** I go to evening classes; **ya va al colegio/a la universidad** she's already at school/university

B (expresando propósito) ~ **A + INF**: **¿has ido a verla?** have you been to see her?; **ve a ayudarla** go and help her; *ver tb* **v aux** *Sentido* **I**

C **~le a algn con algo**: **no le vayas con tus problemas** don't bother him with your problems; **le fue a la maestra con el chisme** she went and told the story to the teacher

D [1] (al arrojar algo, arrojarse): **tírame la llave — ¡allá va!** throw me the key — here you are *o* there you go!; **tírate del trampolín — ¡allá voy!** jump off the board! — here I go/come! [2] (Jueg): **ahí van otros $2.000** there's another $2,000; **¡no va más!** no more bets!; ***¡ahí va!*** (Esp fam): **¡ahí va! me he olvidado el dinero** oh no! I've forgotten the money; **ganó 20 millones en la lotería — ¡ahí va!** he won 20 million in the lottery — wow *o* (AmE) gee whiz! (colloq)

E «*comentario*»: **no iba con mala intención** it wasn't meant unkindly; **eso va por ti también** that goes for you too *o* and the same goes for you

F (estar en juego) (+ *me/te/le etc*): **le iba la vida en ello** her life depended on it *o* was at stake

G (fam) (hablando de acciones imprevistas, sorprendentes): **fue y le dio un puñetazo** she went and punched him; **y la tonta va y se lo cree** and like an idiot she believed him

(*Sentido* **II**)

A (+ *compl*) (sin énfasis en el movimiento): **iban cantando por el camino** they sang as they went along; **¿van cómodos?** are you comfortable?; **¿irán bien aquí los vasos?** will the glasses be safe here?; **íbamos sentados** we were sitting down; **vas que pareces un pordiosero** you look like some sort of beggar; **iba con miedo** she was afraid; **vas muy cargada** you have a lot to carry; **yo iba a la cabeza** I was in the lead; **hay que ~ con los ojos bien abiertos** you have to keep your eyes open; **va de chasco en chasco** he's had one disappointment after another

B (refiriéndose al atuendo) **ir DE algo**: **iban de largo** they wore long dresses; **voy a ~ de Drácula** I'm going to go as Dracula; **iba de verde** she was dressed in green

C (en calidad de) ~ **DE algo** to go (along) AS sth; **yo fui de intérprete** I went along as interpreter; **¿de qué vas, tía? ¿te crees que somos tontos o qué?** (Esp arg) hey, what are you playing at? do you think we're stupid or something?; **va de guapo/genio por la vida** (Esp arg) he really thinks he's good-looking/clever

D (Esp fam) (tratar): **¿de qué va la novela?** what's the novel about?

(*Sentido* **III**)

A «*camino/sendero*» (llevar) ~ **A algo** to lead TO sth, to go TO sth

B (extenderse, abarcar): **la autopista va desde Madrid hasta Valencia** the highway goes from Madrid to Valencia; **el período que va desde la Edad Media hasta el Renacimiento** the period from the Middle Ages to the Renaissance

(*Sentido* **IV**)

A (marchar, desarrollarse): **¿cómo va el enfermo/el nuevo trabajo?** how's the patient doing/the new job going?; **va de mal en peor** it's going from bad to worse; ; (+ *me/te/le etc*) **¿cómo te va?** how's it going?, how are things? (colloq), what's up? (AmE colloq); **¿cómo les fue en Italia?** how was Italy?, how did you get on in Italy?; **me fue mal/bien en el examen/la entrevista** I did badly/well in the exam/the interview; **¡que te vaya bien!** all the best! *o* take care!; **¡que te vaya bien (en) el examen!** good luck in the exam; **¿cómo le va con el novio?** how's she getting on with her boyfriend?

B (en juegos, competiciones): **¿cómo van? — 3-1** what's the score? — 3-1; **voy ganando yo** I'm ahead, I'm winning

C (en el desarrollo de algo) ~ **POR algo**: **¿por dónde van en historia?** where have you got (up) to in history?; **¿todavía vas por la página 20?** are you still on page 20?

D (estar en camino) ~ **PARA algo**: **¡vamos para viejos!** we're getting on *o* old!; **va para los cincuenta** she's going on fifty; **ya va para dos años que ...** it's getting on for two years since ...

E (sumar, hacer): **ya van tres veces que te lo digo** this is the third time I've told you; **con éste van seis** six, counting this one; **ya van tres pasteles que se come** that makes three cakes he's eaten now

F (haber transcurrido): **en lo que va del** *or* (Esp) **de año/mes** so far this year/month

G (haber diferencia): **de tres a ocho van cinco** eight minus three is five; **¡lo que va de un hermano a otro!** (fam) it's amazing the difference between the two brothers! (colloq)

H (CS) (depender, radicar) ~ **EN algo** to depend ON sth; **no sé en qué vá** I don't know what it depends on

(Sentido **V**)

A 1 (deber colocarse) to go; **¿dónde van las toallas?** where do the towels go?; ***¡qué va!*** (fam): **¿has terminado? — ¡qué va!** have you finished? — you must be joking!; **¿se disgustó? — ¡qué va!** did she get upset? — not at all!; **vamos a perder el avión — ¡qué va!** we're going to miss the plane — nonsense! 2 (deber escribirse): **¿va con mayúscula?** is it written with a capital letter?; **¿va con acento?** does it have an accent? 3 (RPl) (estar incluido): **todo esto va para el examen** all of this will be included in the exam

B 1 (combinar) ~ **CON algo** to go WITH sth 2 (sentar, convenir) (+ *me/te/le etc*): **el negro no te va bien** black doesn't suit you; **te ~á bien un descanso** a rest will do you good 3 ~ **en contra de algo** to go against sth

C (Esp arg) (gustar) (+ *me/te/le etc*): **esa música no me va** that music does nothing for me *o* leaves me cold

D (Méx) (tomar partido por, apoyar) **~le A algo/algn** to support sth/sb; **le va al equipo peruano** he supports the Peruvian team

(Sentido **VI**)

A **vamos** 1 (expresando incredulidad, fastidio): **¡vamos! ¿esto quién se lo va a creer?** come off it *o* come on! who do you think's going to believe that? 2 (intentando tranquilizar, animar, dar prisa): **vamos, mujer, dile algo** go on, say something to him; **¡vamos, date prisa!** come on, hurry up!; ***dar el vamos a algo*** (Chi) to inaugurate sth; ***desde el vamos*** (RPl fam) from the word go 3 (al aclarar, resumir): **eso sería un disparate, vamos, digo yo** that would be a stupid thing to do, well, that's what I think anyway; **vamos, que no es una persona de fiar** basically, he's not very trustworthy; **es mejor que el otro, vamos** it's better than the other one, anyway

B **vaya** 1 (expresando sorpresa, contrariedad): **¡vaya! ¡tú por aquí!** what a surprise! what are you doing here?; **¡vaya! ¡se ha vuelto a caer!** oh no *o* (colloq) damn! it's fallen over again! 2 (Esp) (para enfatizar): **¡vaya cochazo!** that's some car!; **¡vaya (que) si la conozco!** you bet I know her! 3 (al aclarar, resumir): **vaya, que los hay peores** well, I mean there are plenty worse

■ **ir** *v aux*

(Sentido **I**) ~ **A + INF**:

A 1 (para expresar tiempo futuro, propósito) to be going to + INF; **¡te vas a caer!** you're going to fall!; **voy a estudiar medicina** I'm going to study medicine; **va a hacer dos años que ...** it's getting on for two years since ...; **esto no te va a gustar** you're not going to like this; **te voy a pegar** I'm going to smack you 2 (en propuestas, sugerencias): **vamos a ver ¿cómo dices que te llamas?** now then, what did you say your name was?; **bueno, vamos a trabajar** all right, let's get to work

B 1 (al prevenir, hacer recomendaciones): **que no se te vaya a caer** make sure you don't drop it; **cuidado, no te vayas a caer** mind you don't fall (colloq); **lleva el paraguas, no vaya a ser que llueva** take the umbrella in case it rains 2 (expresando un deseo): **¡que te vaya bien!** all the best!

C (expresando inevitabilidad): **¡qué le iba a decir!** what else could I tell her?; **¿qué iba a pensar el pobre?** what was the poor man supposed *o* meant to think?; **¿quién iba a ser si no?** who else could it have been?

D (expresando incredulidad): **¡no ~ás a darle la razón a él!** surely you're not going to say he was right!; **¿no ~á a hacer alguna tontería?** you don't think she'll go and do something stupid, do you?

E 1 (en afirmaciones enfáticas): **¿te acuerdas? — ¡no me voy a acordar!** do you remember — of course I do *o* how could I forget? 2 (al contradecir): **¿dormiste bien? — ¡qué voy a dormir!** did you sleep well?— how could I?; **¡cómo iba a saberlo!** how was I supposed to know?; **¿por qué la voy a ayudar?** why should I help her?

(Sentido **II**) (expresando un proceso paulatino) ~ **+ GER**: **poco a poco irá aprendiendo** she'll learn little by little; **a medida que va subiendo** as it rises; **tú puedes ~ comiendo** you can start eating; **ya puedes ~ haciéndote a la idea** you'd better get used to the idea; **la situación ha ido empeorando** the situation has been getting worse and worse

■ **irse** *v pron*

A (marcharse) to leave; **¿por qué te vas tan temprano?** why are you leaving *o* going so soon?; **vámonos** let's go; **bueno, me voy** right then, I'm taking off (AmE) *o* (BrE) I'm off; **no te vayas** don't go; **vete a la cama** go to bed; **se fue de casa** she left home; **vete de aquí** get out of here; **se fue de la empresa** she left the company; **se han ido de viaje** they're away, they've gone away; **anda, vete por ahí** (fam) get lost! (colloq); (+ *me/te/le etc*) **se nos fué a vivir a Florida** he went (off) to live in Florida; **no te me vayas, quiero hablar contigo** (fam) don't run away, I want to talk to you (colloq)

B (consumirse, gastarse): **¡cómo se va el dinero!** I don't know where the money goes!; (+ *me/te/le etc*) **se me va medio sueldo en el alquiler** half my salary goes on the rent; **¡qué rápido se me ha ido la tarde!** hasn't the evening gone quickly?

C (desaparecer) «*mancha/dolor*» to go; **se ha ido la luz** the electricity's gone off; (+ *me/te/le etc*) **¿se te ha ido el dolor de cabeza?** has your headache gone?

D (salirse, escaparse) «*líquido/gas*» to escape; (+ *me/te/le etc*) **se le está yendo el aire al globo** the balloon's losing air *o* going down

E (euf) (morirse) to slip away (euph)

F (caerse, perder el equilibrio) (+ *compl*): **~se de boca/espaldas** to fall flat on one's face/back; **me iba para atrás** I was falling backwards; **frenó y nos fuimos todos para adelante** he braked and we all went flying forwards

G (andarse, actuar) (+ *compl*): **vete con cuidado/tacto** be careful/tactful

H 1 (CS) (en naipes) to go out 2 (RPl) (en una asignatura) *tb* **~se a examen** to have to take an exam

I (Andes, Ven) «*medias*» to run; **se me fueron las medias** my tights have run

ira *f* rage, anger; **ciego de ~** blinded with rage; **en un arrebato de ~** in a fit of rage *o* anger; **la ~ de los elementos** (liter) the wrath of the elements (liter)

IRA /'ira/ *m* IRA; **el ~ provisional** the Provisional IRA

iracundia *f* 1 (cólera) rage, wrath (liter), ire (liter) 2 (propensión a la ira) irascibility

iracundo -da *adj* 1 [ESTAR] (colérico) irate 2 [SER] (propenso a la ira) irascible, easily angered

Irak, Iraq *m* Iraq

Irán *m* Iran

iraní *adj/mf* Iranian

iraquí *adj/mf* Iraqi

irascible *adj* irascible

irguieron, irguió, etc *see* **erguir**

iridio *m* iridium

iridiscente *adj* iridescent

iris *m* (*pl* ~) iris

irisar [A1] *vi* to iridesce

Irlanda *f* Ireland

(Compuesto) **Irlanda del Norte** Northern Ireland

irlandés¹ -desa *adj* Irish

irlandés² -desa *m,f*

A (persona) (*m*) Irishman; (*f*) Irishwoman; **los irlandeses** the Irish, Irish people

B **irlandés** *m* (idioma) Irish (Gaelic)

ironía *f* 1 (situación irónica) irony; **las ~s del destino** the irony of fate 2 (figura retórica) irony 3 (burla) sarcasm; **con ~** ironically/sarcastically; **estoy harto de sus ~s** I'm fed up with his sarcastic remarks

irónico -ca *adj* 1 ‹*situación*› ironic 2 ‹*persona/comentario/tono*› sarcastic; **en tono ~** sarcastically

ironizar [A4] *vi* ~ **SOBRE algo** to satirize sth

■ **ironizar** *vt* to satirize, ridicule

irracional *adj* irrational

irracionalidad *f* irrationality

irradiación *f* irradiation

irradiar [A1] *vt*
A 1 ‹*calor/luz*› to radiate 2 ‹*simpatía/felicidad*› to radiate, irradiate
B (someter a radiaciones) to irradiate
irrazonable *adj* unreasonable
irreal *adj* unreal
irrealizable *adj* ‹*proyecto*› unfeasible; ‹*deseo*› unattainable, unrealizable
irrebatible *adj* irrefutable, unanswerable
irreconciliable *adj* irreconcilable
irreconocible *adj* unrecognizable; **¡cuánta amabilidad! está verdaderamente ~** he's being so friendly! it's most unlike him!
irrecuperable *adj* unrecoverable, irretrievable
irreducible *adj* 1 (Mat) ‹*fracción*› prime 2 ‹*cantidad/problema*› irreducible
irreemplazable *adj* irreplaceable
irreflexión *f* rashness
irreflexivo -va *adj* ‹*persona*› unthinking, rash; ‹*acto/impulso*› rash
irrefrenable *adj* irrepressible, uncontrollable
irrefutable *adj* irrefutable, unanswerable
irregular *adj*
A 1 ‹*trazos/facciones*› irregular; ‹*letra*› irregular, uneven; ‹*terreno/superficie*› irregular, uneven 2 ‹*rendimiento/asistencia*› irregular, erratic; ‹*pulso/ritmo*› irregular; **lleva una vida muy ~** he leads a very disorganized *o* a chaotic life
B (Der) ‹*procedimiento/acción*› irregular
C (Ling) irregular
irregularidad *f* irregularity
irrelevante *adj* irrelevant
irreligioso -sa *adj* (frml) irreligious (frml)
irremediable *adj* ‹*daños/defecto*› irreparable, irremediable; ‹*pérdida*› irreparable, irretrievable
irremediablemente *adv* inevitably; **van a perder ~** they're bound *o* certain to lose
irremisible *adj* (frml) irremissible
irreparable *adj* ‹*pérdida/daños*› irreparable; **el coche quedó ~** the car was beyond repair
irrepetible *adj* unrepeatable
irreprimible *adj* irrepressible
irreprochable *adj* irreproachable
irresistible *adj* 1 ‹*sonrisa/mujer/hombre*› irresistible; ‹*deseo/tentación*› irresistible 2 ‹*dolor*› unbearable
irresoluto -ta *adj* (frml) indecisive, irresolute (frml)
irrespetar [A1] *vt* (Col, Ven) ‹*persona*› to be disrespectful *o* rude to; ‹*lugar sagrado*› to desecrate
irrespetuoso -sa *adj* disrespectful
irrespirable *adj* unbreathable
irresponsabilidad *f* irresponsibility
irresponsable[1] *adj* irresponsible
irresponsable[2] *mf* irresponsible person
irrestricto -ta *adj* (AmL) unrestricted, unlimited
irreverencia *f* (frml) 1 (cualidad) disrespect, irreverence 2 (acto irrespetuoso) act/sign of disrespect, irreverence
irreverente *adj* (frml) disrespectful, irreverent
irreversible *adj* irreversible
irrevocable *adj* irrevocable
irrigación *f* irrigation
irrigador *m* 1 (Agr) sprinkler 2 (Med) irrigator
irrigar [A3] *vt* to irrigate
irrisión *f* (frml) derision
irrisorio -ria *adj* ‹*excusas/pretensiones*› derisory, risible (frml); **S precios irrisorios** giveaway prices
irritabilidad *f* irritability
irritable *adj* irritable
irritación *f* 1 (Med) irritation, inflammation 2 (enfado) irritation, annoyance
irritante[1] *adj* 1 ‹*situación/actitud*› irritating, annoying 2 (Med) irritant
irritante[2] *m* irritant
irritar [A1] *vt* 1 ‹*piel/garganta*› to irritate; **tiene la garganta irritada** his throat is sore *o* inflamed 2 ‹*persona*› to annoy, irritate
■ **irritarse** *v pron* 1 «*piel/ojos*» to become irritated 2 «*persona*» to get annoyed, get irritated
irrompible *adj* unbreakable
irrumpir [I1] *vi* to burst in; **la policía irrumpió en el bar** the police burst into the bar
irrupción *f*: **el tiroteo empezó con la ~ de la policía en el bar** the firing began when the police burst into the bar
isla *f* 1 (Geog) island, isle (liter) 2 (Ven) (en autopistas) median strip (AmE), central reservation (BrE)

Compuestos

- **isla desierta** desert island
- **isla peatonal** safety island (AmE), traffic island (BrE)

Isla de Pascua *f*: **la ~ de ~** Easter Island
Islam *m*: **el ~** Islam
islámico -ca *adj* Islamic
islamista *adj/m/f* Islamist
islandés[1] **-desa** *adj* Icelandic
islandés[2] **-desa** *m,f*
A (persona) Icelander
B **islandés** *m* (idioma) Icelandic
Islandia *f* Iceland
Islas Baleares *fpl* Balearic Islands (*pl*)
Islas Británicas *fpl* British Isles (*pl*)
Islas Canarias *fpl* Canary Islands (*pl*), Canaries (*pl*)
Islas Galápagos *fpl* Galapagos Islands (*pl*)
Islas Malvinas *fpl* Falkland Islands (*pl*)
isleño[1] **-ña** *adj* ‹*población/productos*› island (*before n*)
isleño[2] **-ña** *m,f* (habitante de una isla) islander
islote *m* small island, islet
isóbara, isobara *f* isobar
isósceles *adj* isosceles
isoterma *f* isotherm
isotérmico -ca *adj* 1 (Fís) isothermal 2 ‹*recipiente*› insulated; **un camión/contenedor ~** a refrigerated truck/container
isotermo -ma *adj* isothermal
isótopo *m* isotope
Israel *m* Israel
israelí *adj/mf* Israeli
istmo *m* isthmus
itacate *m* (Méx) pack, bundle; ***hacer su ~*** to pack up
Italia *f* Italy
italianada *f* ***subírsele la ~ a algn*** (RPl fam): **cuando se me sube la ~** when I get angry *o* (AmE colloq) mad
italiano[1] **-na** *adj/m,f* Italian
italiano[2] *m* (idioma) Italian
itálico -ca *adj* 1 (Hist) Italic 2 (Impr) italic
ítem *m* (*pl* **ítems**) item
itemizar [A4] *vt* (AmL) to itemize
iterar [A1] *vt* (frml) to iterate (frml), to repeat
iterativo -va *adj* 1 ‹*tema*› recurrent, repeated 2 (Inf, Ling) iterative
itinerancia *f* (Telec) roaming
itinerante *adj* ‹*exposición/muestra*› traveling* (*before n*), itinerant (frml)
itinerario *m* itinerary, route
ITS *fpl* (= **Infecciones de Transmisión Sexual**) STD
ITV *f* (en Esp) (= **inspección técnica de vehículos**) roadworthiness test, ≈ MOT (*in UK*)
IVA /'iβa/ *m* (= **Impuesto al Valor Agregado** *or* **sobre el Valor Añadido**) VAT
izar [A4] *vt* ‹*vela/bandera*› to hoist, raise, run up
izq. = izquierda
izquierda *f*
A 1 (mano izquierda): **la ~** the left hand 2 (lado) left; **la puerta de la ~** the door on the left, the left-hand door; **¡~, ar!** (Mil) by the left, quick march!; **torció a la ~** he turned left; **a la ~ de su padre** to the left of his father *o* on his father's left; **ahí enfrente a la ~** over there on the left; **conducen por la ~** they drive on the left
B (Pol) left; **de ~** *or* (Esp) **de ~s** left-wing
izquierdista[1] *adj* left-wing, leftist (*before n*)
izquierdista[2] *mf* left-winger
izquierdo -da *adj* left (*before n*)
izquierdoso -sa *adj* (pey) lefty (colloq & pej)

Jj

J, j *f (read as /'xota/) the letter* **J, j**
ja *interj* ha!
jab /dʒaβ/ *m* (AmL) jab
jaba *f* (Chi, Per) crate
jabalí *m* (*pl* **-líes**) wild boar
jabalina *f* 1▸ (Arm, Dep) javelin 2▸ (Zool) wild sow
jabato *m* (Zool) young wild boar
jábega *f* (red) dragnet; (barco) fishing smack
jabón *m*
A (producto) soap; **una barra** *or* **pastilla de ~** a bar *o* cake of soap; ***darle ~ a algn*** (Esp fam) to soft-soap sb (colloq)
(Compuestos)
• **jabón de afeitar/tocador** shaving/toilet soap
• **jabón de lavar** (en barra) household soap; (en polvo) soap powder
• **jabón de sastre** tailor's chalk
• **jabón en escamas** soapflakes (*pl*)
B (RPl fam) (susto) fright
jabonada *f*
A (con jabón): **dale una buena ~** wash it well in soapy water
B (Chi, Méx fam) (reprimenda) telling-off
jabonar [A1] *vt* ▸**enjabonar**
jabonera *f* soap dish
jabonero -ra *adj* ‹*industria*› soap (*before n*)
jabonoso -sa *adj* soapy
jaca *f* pony
jacal *m* (Méx) hut, small house (*made of adobe or reeds*)
jacalear [A1] *vi* (Méx fam) to spread gossip
jacarandá *m or f* jacaranda
jacarandoso -sa *adj* 1▸ ‹*porte/andares*› jaunty, carefree; **iba muy jacarandosa con su vestido nuevo** she looked very jaunty in her new dress 2▸ [SER] ‹*persona*› lively, vivacious
jácena *f* main beam
jacinto *m* (Bot) hyacinth
jactancia *f* (cualidad) boastfulness; (acción) boasting, bragging
jactancioso¹ -sa *adj* boastful
jactancioso² -sa *m,f* boaster, braggart
jactarse [A1] *v pron* to boast, brag; **~ DE algo** to boast *o* brag ABOUT sth
Jacuzi® /dʒa'kuzi/ *m* Jaccuzzi®
jade *m* jade
jadeante *adj*: **venía ~ por la cuesta** he came up the hill (puffing and) panting; **con voz ~** in a breathless voice
jadear [A1] *vi* to pant
jadeo *m* panting
jaez *m*
A (liter) (ralea, calaña) ilk (liter); **gente de ese ~** people of that ilk *o* kind
B **jaeces** *mpl* (Equ) trappings (*pl*)
jafbac *m* halfback
jaguar *m* jaguar
jagüey, jagüel *m* (AmL) pool
jai *f* (AmS fam) (alta sociedad) high society
jai alai *m* jai alai, pelota

jaiba *f* (AmL) crab; (de río) freshwater crab
jaibol *m* (Méx) highball (AmE), whisky and soda (BrE)
jaibón -bona *adj* (Chi fam) (encopetado) posh (colloq)
jailoso -sa *adj* (Col fam) posh (colloq)
jalada *f*
A (Méx fam) (tirón) pull, tug
B (Méx fam) (tontería, exageración): **esas son puras ~s** that's a load of garbage (AmE) *o* (BrE) rubbish (colloq)
jalado¹ -da *adj*
A (AmC, Col, Méx fam) (borracho) tight (colloq)
B (Méx fam) (descabellado) crazy (colloq)
C (Per fam) ‹*ojos*› slanting
jalado² -da *m,f* (Per fam) oriental-looking person
jalado³ *m* (Per arg) (Educ) fail
jalador¹ -dora *adj*
A (Méx fam) 1▸ (trabajador) hard-working 2▸ (animoso) willing 3▸ (que atrae) ‹*oferta*› attractive; ‹*cantante/actor*› popular
B (Per arg) ‹*profesor*› tough (colloq)
jalador² -dora *m,f*
A (Per arg) (profesor) hard taskmaster
B (Col arg) (ladrón) *tb* **~ de carros** car thief
jalapeño *m* (Méx) jalapeño pepper
jalar [A1] *vt*
A 1▸ (AmL exc CS) (tirar de) to pull; **~ la cadena** to pull the chain; **me jaló la manga** he pulled *o* tugged at my sleeve 2▸ (Méx) (agarrar y acercar) ‹*periódico/libro*› to pick up, take; ‹*silla*› to draw up 3▸ (Méx) (atraer): **lo jalan sus amigos** he's more interested in seeing his friends; **lo jalan mucho hacia sus gustos** he's drawn to their tastes
B (Per arg) ‹*alumno*› to fail, flunk (esp AmE colloq)
C (Per fam) (en automóvil, moto) to give … a lift *o* ride
■ **jalar** *vi*
A (AmL exc CS) (tirar) to pull; Ⓢ **jale** pull; **~ DE algo** to pull sth; **jaló de la cuerda para cerrarlo** he pulled (on) the cord to close it; ***~le a algo*** (Col fam) to be into sth (colloq); ***~ con algn*** (Méx fam) (llevarse bien) to get on *o* along well with sb; (unirse a): **siempre jala con nosotros los domingos** he always hangs out with us on Sundays (colloq)
B 1▸ (Méx fam) (apresurarse) to hurry up, get a move on (colloq); **¡jálale!** hurry up! 2▸ (Col, Méx fam) (irse) to go; **jálale por el pan** go and get the bread; **jala por la izquierda** keep to the left
C (Per fam) 1▸ (beber) to booze (colloq) 2▸ (inhalar cocaína) to have a snort (colloq)
D (Méx fam) ‹‹*motor/aparato*›› to work; **mi coche no jalaba en la mañana** my car wouldn't start this morning; **¿cómo van los negocios? — jalando, jalando** how's business? — oh, not so bad (colloq)
E (AmC fam) ‹‹*pareja*›› to date, go out; ‹‹*persona*›› **~ CON algn** to date sb, go out WITH sb
■ **jalarse** *v pron*
A (Méx) (*enf*) ▸**jalar** *vt* **A2**
B (Méx) (*enf*) 1▸ (irse) to go 2▸ (venir) to come; **jálate a mi casa** come round *o* over to my house
C (Col, Méx fam) (emborracharse) to get tight (colloq)
D (Col fam) (realizar) ‹*discurso*› to give, make; **se jaló un partido excelente** he played an excellent game
jalbegue *m* whitewash
jalea *f* jelly; **~ de limón** lemon jelly
(Compuesto) **jalea real** royal jelly

jalear [A1] *vt* [1] ‹*cantante/bailaor*› to encourage (*with shouts and clapping*) [2] ‹*deportista/equipo*› to cheer on

jaleo *m* (fam) [1] (alboroto, ruido) racket (colloq), row (colloq) [2] (confusión) muddle, mess; (desorden) mess; (problemas) hassle (colloq) [3] (actividad intensa): **hemos tenido mucho ~ en casa** everything's been very hectic at home; **con todo el ~ de la mudanza** with all the upheaval of the move [4] (riña) brawl

jallán *m* (AmC, Col) lout

jalón *m*

A [1] (mojón) landmark; (en topografía) ranging rod [2] (liter) (hito) milestone

B [1] (AmL exc CS fam) (tirón) pull, yank; ***de un ~*** (AmL exc CS) in one go [2] (Méx) (tramo) stretch; **aún nos queda un buen ~** we still have a fair *o* good stretch to go

C (Méx) [1] (fam) (trago) tot, shot [2] (en una media) run, ladder (BrE)

jalonar [A1] *vt* [1] (marcar) to mark; **una carrera jalonada de éxitos** a career marked by successes [2] ‹*terreno/área*› to mark *o* stake out

jalonazo *m* (AmL exc CS fam) tug, yank; **el carro iba a ~s** the car jerked *o* lurched along

jalonear [A1] *vt* (Méx, Per fam) to tug (at)

■ **jalonear** *vi* [1] (AmL exc CS fam) (dar tirones) to pull, tug [2] (AmC fam) (regatear) to haggle

jamaica *f* (Bot) hibiscus

Jamaica *f* Jamaica

jamaicano -na *adj/m,f* Jamaican

jamás *adv* never; **~ había oído cosa igual** I'd never heard anything like it; **~ volverá a suceder** *or* **no volverá a suceder ~** it will never happen again; **nunca ~** *or* (fam) **~ de los jamases** never ever; **por** *or* **para siempre ~** for ever and ever

jamba *f* jamb

jamelgo *m* nag, hack

jamón *m*

A (Coc) ham; ***¡y un ~ (con chorreras)!*** (fam): **dice que tiene 30 años — ¡y un ~ (con chorreras)!** she says she's 30 — come off it! (colloq)

(Compuestos)
- **jamón crudo** *or* **serrano** ≈ Parma ham
- **jamón de York** ≈ ham, cooked ham
- **jamón inglés** (Chi, Per) ≈ ham, cooked ham

B (fam & hum) (muslo) thigh

jamona *adj* (fam) ‹*mujer*› (grande) buxom; (muy atractiva) (Esp) stunning (colloq)

jaña *f* (AmC fam) (compañera) girlfriend; (chica) girl

Japón *m*: *tb* **el ~** Japan

japonés[1] -nesa *adj/m,f* Japanese

japonés[2] *m* (idioma) Japanese

jaque *m* check; ***tener a algn en ~*** to have sb on the rack

(Compuesto) **jaque mate** checkmate; **le dio ~ ~ a su adversario** he checkmated his opponent

jaqué, jaquet /(d)ʒa'ke(t)/ *m* (CS) morning coat

jaquear [A1] *vt* to check

jaqueca *f* migraine, severe headache

jara *f* rockrose

jarabe *m*

A [1] (Coc) syrup; **~ de frambuesa** raspberry syrup [2] (Farm, Med) syrup; **~ para la tos** cough mixture

B (Mús) *Mexican folk dance and music*

jarana *f*

A (fam) [1] (bromas): **basta de ~** that's enough fun and games *o* fooling around (colloq) [2] (juerga): **salir de ~** to go out on the town *o* out partying (colloq)

B (instrumento) *type of small guitar*

C [1] (baile) *folk dance from south-east Mexico* [2] (Per) (fiesta) party (*with folk music*)

jaranear [A1] *vi* (fam) (divertirse) to have a good time, live it up (colloq)

jaranero[1] -ra *adj* (fam): **es muy ~** he's always out on the town *o* out partying (colloq)

jaranero[2] -ra *m,f* (fam) party animal

jarcia *f* [1] (Náut) *tb* **~s** rigging [2] (AmC, Méx) (cuerda) rope

jardín *m*

A (con plantas) garden

(Compuestos)
- **jardín botánico** botanical garden
- **jardín de infancia** *or* **de niños** nursery school, kindergarten
- **jardín zoológico** zoological garden, zoo

B **los jardines** *mpl* (en béisbol) the outfield

(Compuesto) **jardín central** center* field

jardinear [A1] *vi*

A (en béisbol) to field

B (Chi) (en el jardín) to do the gardening

jardinera *f*

A (para la ventana) window box; (con pedestal) jardinière

B (Indum) (abrigo) (Col) coat; (pantalón) (Chi) overalls (*pl*) (AmE), dungarees (*pl*) (BrE)

jardinería *f* gardening

jardinero -ra *m,f*

A (persona) gardener

B (Dep) outfielder; **juega de ~ izquierdo** he plays left field

(Compuesto) **jardinero central** *or* **centro** center* fielder

C **jardinero** *m* (RPl) (pantalón) overalls (*pl*) (AmE), dungarees (*pl*) (BrE)

jareta *f* [1] (para pasar una cinta) casing; (de adorno) tuck [2] (AmC) (bragueta) fly

jaripeo *m*: *Mexican rodeo*

jarra *f*

A [1] (para servir) pitcher (AmE), jug (BrE) [2] (para beber) stein (AmE), tankard (BrE); ***en ~s***: **con los brazos en ~s** (with) arms akimbo, hands on hips; **se puso en ~s** she put her hands on her hips

B (Méx fam) bender (colloq); **irse de ~** to go on a bender; ***agarrar la ~*** (Méx fam) to get plastered (colloq)

jarrada *f* (Andes) pitcherful (AmE), jugful (BrE)

jarro *m* [1] (para servir) pitcher (AmE), jug (BrE); ***caer*** *or* ***sentar como un ~ de agua fría*** (fam) to come as a shock *o* a nasty surprise [2] (AmS) (tazón) mug; (para cerveza) beer mug

jarrón *m* vase

jarto -ta *adj* (Col fam) [1] [SER] ‹*persona/clase*› boring [2] [ESTAR] ‹*persona*› fed up (colloq)

jaspe *m* (piedra) jasper; (mármol) veined marble

jaspeado -da *adj* ‹*mármol*› veined; ‹*tela/lana*› flecked; ‹*plumaje/huevos*› speckled

Jauja *f* (fam): **piensan que la universidad es ~** they think that university is a bed of roses; **¡esto es ~!** this is the life!

jaula *f*

A (para animales) cage

B (de ascensor) cage

C (de embalaje) crate

D [1] (fam) (cárcel) jail; **está en la ~** he's doing time (colloq) [2] (Méx) (Ferr) cattletruck

E (Col, Ven fam) (furgón) Black Maria (colloq)

jauría *f* (de perros) pack (of hounds)

jayán -yana *adj* (AmC fam) foul (colloq); **no seas ~** don't be a jerk *o* creep (colloq)

jazmín *m* jasmine

(Compuesto) **jazmín de la India** *or* **del Cabo** gardenia

jazz /(d)ʒas/ *m* jazz

jazzístico -ca *adj* jazz (*before n*)

jeans /(d)ʒins/ *mpl* jeans (*pl*)

jebe *m* (Col, Per) [1] (goma) rubber; **zapatos de ~** rubber-soled shoes [2] *tb* **~cito** (para sujetar algo) rubber band

jebo -ba *m,f* (Ven) [1] (arg) (novio) (*m*) boyfriend; (*f*) girlfriend [2] **jeba** *f* (arg) (muchacha) chick (AmE colloq), bird (BrE colloq)

Jeep® /(d)ʒip/ *m* (*pl* **Jeeps**) Jeep®

jefatura *f*

A (sede) headquarters (*sing o pl*); **~ de policía** police headquarters

B (de partido) leadership; (de empresa): **ostenta la ~ de la empresa** he heads up *o* is head of the company

jefazo *m* (fam) big boss (colloq)

jefe -fa *m,f*, **jefe** *mf* [1] (superior) boss [2] (de empresa) manager; (de sección) head; (de tribu) chief [3] (Pol) leader [4] (como apelativo) buddy (AmE colloq), mate (BrE colloq) [5] **jefes** *mpl* (fam) (padres) folks (*pl*) (colloq)

(Compuestos)
- **jefe -fa de bomberos** fire chief
- **jefe -fa de cocina** chef
- **jefe -fa de estación** stationmaster
- **jefe -fa de Estado/gobierno** head of state/government
- **jefe -fa de Estado Mayor** Chief of Staff
- **jefe -fa de estudios** director of studies
- **jefe -fa de personal/ventas** personnel/sales manager
- **jefe -fa de redacción** editor-in-chief

Jehová Jehovah
jején *m: small mosquito*
jengibre *m* ginger
jeque *m* sheik, sheikh
jerarca *mf* (Relig) hierarch (frml), leader; **los ~s del partido** the party leaders
jerarquía *f* 1 (organización) hierarchy; **la ~ eclesiástica** the ecclesiastical hierarchy 2 (categoría, rango) rank
jerárquico -ca *adj* hierarchical
jerarquización *f* organization into a hierarchy
jerarquizado -da *adj* hierarchical
jerarquizar [A4] *vt* 1 ‹*organización*› to organize … into a hierarchy 2 (poner por orden) to arrange … in order of importance
jeremías *mf* (fam) moaner, whiner
jeremiquear [A1] *vi* (AmL fam) to whine, moan
jerez *m* sherry

> **jerez**
>
> Sherry is produced in an area of chalky soil known as *albariza* lying between the towns of Puerto de Santa María, Sanlúcar de Barrameda, and Jerez de la Frontera in Cádiz province. It is from Jerez that sherry takes its English name. Sherries, made from grape varieties including Palomino and Pedro Ximénez, are drunk worldwide as an aperitif, and in Spain as an accompaniment to **tapas**. The styles of *jerez* vary from the pale *fino* and *manzanilla* to the darker aromatic *oloroso* and *amontillado*. *See also* **solera**

jerga *f*
A 1 (de gremio, profesión) jargon; (de los adolescentes) slang 2 (galimatías) mumbo jumbo (colloq)
B (Méx) (trapo) floorcloth
jergón *m* straw mattress
jerigonza *f* (mezcla de idiomas) mumbo jumbo (colloq); (lenguaje en clave) secret language *o* code
jeringa *f*
A (Med) syringe
(Compuesto) **jeringa de engrase** grease gun
B (fam) (molestia) hassle (colloq)
jeringar [A3], (AmL) **jeringuear** [A1] *vt* (fam) to bug (colloq), to pester
■ **jeringar** *vi* (fam) to be a nuisance, pester
■ **jeringarse** *v pron* (fam): **si no te gusta te jeringas** if you don't like it, that's tough (colloq)
jeringuilla *f* syringe
jerma *f* (Per fam) girl
jeroglífico *m* (escritura) hieroglyphic, hieroglyph; (acertijo) rebus; **esto es un ~ para mí** this is a complete mystery to me
jersey *m* (*pl* **-seys**) 1 /'ʒersi/ (AmL) (tela) jersey 2 /xer'sei/ (Esp) (prenda) sweater
Jerusalén *m* Jerusalem
Jesucristo Jesus Christ
jesuita *adj/m* Jesuit
Jesús 1 (Relig) Jesus 2 (*como interj*) **¡~!** (expresando — dolor, fatiga) heavens!; (— susto, sorpresa) good heavens!, good grief!; (cuando alguien estornuda) (Esp) bless you!
jet /'(d)ʒet/ *m* (*pl* **jets**) (Aviac) jet
jeta *f*
A (fam) 1 (cara) face, mug (colloq); **partirle la ~ a algn** to smash sb's face in (colloq); ***tener ~*** (fam) to have a nerve (colloq) 2 (AmL fam) (boca) trap (sl); ***estirar la ~*** (Chi fam) to pull a face; **anda con la ~ estirada** he's going around with a long face (colloq)
B **jeta** *mf* (Esp fam) (caradura): **esa tía es una ~** that woman has a nerve (colloq)
jet lag /'(d)ʒetlaɣ/ *m* jet lag
jetón -tona *adj* 1 (AmL fam) (de boca grande) big-mouthed; (de labios gruesos) thick-lipped 2 (Chi fam) (estúpido) stupid
jet set /'(d)ʒetset/ *m or* (Esp) *f* jet set
jíbaro¹ -ra *adj* 1 ‹*indio/pueblo*› Jivaro 2 (AmC, Méx) (rústico) rustic
jíbaro² -ra *m,f* 1 (indio) Jivaro 2 (Col, Ven arg) (vendedor de droga) pusher (colloq)
jibia *f* cuttlefish
jícama *f* yam bean
jícara *f*
A (Méx) (Bot) calabash
B 1 (Méx) (taza) (drinking) bowl 2 (Col, Méx) (vasija — de calabaza) gourd, calabash; (— de otro material) pot
C (Méx fam) (calva) bald pate (hum)
jicote *m* (Méx) wasp
jicotera *f* 1 (Méx) (nido) wasp's nest 2 (ruido) row (colloq); ***armar una ~*** to kick up a fuss *o* row
jijez *f* (Méx fam & euf) dirty trick
jilguero *m* goldfinch
jilote *m* (Méx) green spike (*of corn/maize*)
jincharse [A1] *v pron* (Col arg) to get smashed (sl)
jincho -cha *adj* (Col) 1 (fam) (lleno) full; **estar ~ de plata** to be loaded (colloq) 2 (arg) (borracho) smashed (sl)
jineta *f* civet cat
jinete *mf* (Equ) (*m*) horseman, rider; (*f*) horsewoman, rider
jinetear [A1] *vt*
A (Equ) 1 (Chi) (montar) to ride 2 (Méx) (domar) to break
B (Méx fam) ‹*dinero*› to speculate with
■ **jinetear** *vi* (Chi) to ride
jinetera *f* (AmC fam) hooker (colloq), prostitute
jingle /(d)ʒingel/ *m* jingle
jingoísta *mf* jingoist
jiote *m* (Méx) impetigo
jipi *mf* hippy
jipijapa¹ *f* jipijapa
jipijapa² *m* panama (hat)
jipismo *m* hippy culture
jirafa *f*
A (Zool) giraffe
B (Cin, Rad, TV) boom
jirón *m*
A (de tela) shred; **hecho jirones** in tatters *o* shreds
B (Per) (avenida) avenue, street
jitomate *m* (Méx) tomato
JJ.OO. *mpl* = **Juegos Olímpicos**
jo *interj* (Esp fam) (expresando — sorpresa) wow! (colloq); (— enfado, disgusto) damn it! (colloq)
jockey /'(d)ʒoki/ *mf* (*pl* **-ckeys**) jockey
jocoque *m* (Méx) *drink or dessert made from soured milk*
jocoso -sa *adj* humorous, jocular
jocundo -da *adj* (liter) joyous (liter)
joda *f*
A 1 (AmL fam) (molestia) pain (colloq), drag (colloq) 2 (AmL fam) (broma): **en ~** as a joke
B (AmL fam) (juerga) party
C (Col) (cosa) thingamajig (colloq); **esta ~ no funciona** this thingamajig isn't working (colloq)
joder¹ [E1] *vi*
A (vulg) (copular) to screw (vulg), fuck (vulg)
B (fam: en algunas regiones vulg) (molestar): **lo hace sólo por ~** he only does it to annoy; **lo que me jode es …** what pisses me off is … (sl); ***¡no jodas!*** (fam) (no digas) you're kidding *o* joking! (colloq); (no molestes) stop being such a pest! (colloq)
■ **joder** *vt*
A (vulg) (copular con) to screw (vulg), fuck (vulg)
B (fam: en algunas regiones vulg) 1 (molestar) to bug (colloq) 2 (engañar) to rip … off (colloq)
C (fam: en algunas regiones vulg) ‹*televisor/reloj*› to bust (colloq), to fuck up (vulg); ‹*planes*› to mess up (colloq), to screw up (vulg); ***~la*** (fam) to screw up (vulg); **ahora sí que la hemos**

J

jodido now we've blown it (colloq) *o* (vulg) screwed up!
■ **joderse** *v pron* (fam: en algunas regiones vulg) 1 (fastidiarse): **y si no te gusta, te jodes** and if you don't like it, that's tough! (colloq); **¡hay que ∼se!** (Esp) can you believe it! 2 ‹*espalda*› to do … in (colloq); ‹*hígado/estómago*› to mess up (colloq) 3 ‹‹*planes*›› to get screwed up (vulg), fucked up (vulg); **se ha jodido el motor** the engine's had it (colloq)

joder² *interj* (esp Esp fam: en algunas regiones vulg) (expresando — fastidio) for heaven's sake! (colloq), for fuck's sake! (vulg); (— asombro) good grief!, holy shit! (vulg)

jodido -da *adj*
A (fam: en algunas regiones vulg) 1 [**SER**] (difícil) ‹*trabajo*› tricky, tough (colloq); ‹*persona*› difficult, pain in the neck (colloq) 2 (*delante del n*) (maldito) damn (colloq), fucking (vulg) 3 [**SER**] (AmL) (exigente) demanding, tough (colloq)
B [**ESTAR**] (fam: en algunas regiones vulg) 1 (estropeado) ‹*ascensor/radio*› bust (colloq), fucked (vulg) 2 (enfermo) in a bad way (colloq) 3 (deprimido) down (colloq) 4 (sin dinero) broke (colloq)
C [**SER**] (Col fam) (astuto) sharp

jodienda *f* (fam) pain (colloq), drag (colloq)

jodón -dona *adj* (AmL arg) (fastidioso, pesado): **¡no seas ∼!** don't be a pain in the neck! (colloq)

jofaina *f* (palangana) washbowl, washbasin; (jarra) ewer, pitcher

jogging /(d)ʒoɣin/ *m* 1 (Dep, Ocio) jogging; **hacer ∼** to jog, go jogging 2 (RPl) (Indum) jogging suit

jojoba *f* jojoba

jojoto *m* (Ven) corn (AmE), maize (BrE)

jol *m*
A (Dep) huddle
B (AmL) (vestíbulo) hall

jolgorio *m* revelry, merrymaking; **irse de ∼** (fam) to go out on the town *o* out partying (colloq)

jónico -ca *adj* ‹*columna*› Ionic; **el mar J∼** the Ionian Sea

jonrón *m* (AmL) home run

jopo *m* 1 (rabo) tail; (del zorro) brush, tail 2 (CS) (copete) quiff

Jordania *f* Jordan

jordano -na *adj/m,f* Jordanian

jornada *f*
A 1 (period) (día) day; **la ∼ de huelga convocada para hoy** the strike called for today 2 (Rels Labs) *tb* **∼ laboral** *or* **de trabajo** working day; **trabajar ∼ completa/media ∼** to work full-time/part-time; **una ∼ semanal de 40 horas** a 40-hour (working) week

(Compuestos)
- **jornada continuada** *or* **intensiva** *working day with no break for lunch so as to finish earlier*
- **jornada de puertas abiertas** open house (Ame), open day (BrE)
- **jornada partida** split shift (*working day with long break for lunch*)
- **jornada única** (Chi) ▸ **jornada continuada**

B **jornadas** *fpl* (congreso) conference, symposium; (de teatro, arte) workshop, course
C 1 (esp Col) (viaje) journey 2 (Méx) (día de viaje) day's journey; **fue una larga ∼** it was a long day's journey

jornal *m* day's wages (*pl*), day's pay; **trabajar a ∼** to be paid on a daily basis

jornalero -ra *m,f* day laborer*

joroba *f* 1 (de persona, camello) hump 2 (fam) (molestia) drag (colloq), pain in the neck (colloq)

jorobado¹ -da *adj*
A (giboso) hunchbacked
B (fam) 1 (enfermo, delicado): **todavía anda algo jorobada** she's still a bit low (colloq); **está** *or* **anda ∼ del estómago** his stomach's been playing (him) up (colloq) 2 (sin dinero) broke (colloq) 3 ‹*asunto*› tricky

jorobado² -da *m,f* hunchback

jorobar [A1] *vt* (fam) 1 (molestar) to bug (colloq) 2 (malograr) to ruin, spoil
■ **jorobar** *vi* (fam) (molestar): **lo hace sólo por ∼** he only does it to annoy; **lo que más me joroba es …** what really bugs *o* gets me is … (colloq); **¡no jorobes!** (no digas) you're kidding! (colloq); (no molestes) stop being such a pest!
■ **jorobarse** *v pron* (fam) 1 (aguantarse): **y si no te gusta, te jorobas** and if you don't like it, that's tough (colloq); **¡hay que ∼se!** (Esp) can you believe it! (colloq) 2 (dañarse) ‹*hígado/estómago*› to mess up (colloq); ‹*espalda*› to do … in (colloq) 3 ‹‹*plan*›› to be scuppered (colloq); ‹‹*fiesta*›› to be ruined

jorongo *m* (Méx) poncho

joropo *m*: *Colombian/Venezuelan folk dance*

jota *f* 1 (letra) *name of the letter* **j**; ***no entender/ver/saber ni ∼*** (fam): **no entiendo/no veo ni ∼** I don't understand/I can't see a thing; **no sabe ni ∼** he doesn't have a clue (colloq) 2 (Mús) jota (*Aragonese folk song/dance*) 3 (en naipes) jack

jote *m* (Zool) turkey buzzard

joto *m*
A (Méx fam) (homosexual) gay man
B (Col) (atado) bundle

joven¹ *adj* young

joven² *mf* (*m*) young person, young man; (*f*) young person, young woman; **de aspecto ∼** youthful looking; **los jóvenes de hoy …** young people today …

jovencito -ta (*m*) young man; (*f*) young lady; **moda para jovencitas** teenage fashions (*for girls*)

jovial *adj* jovial, cheerful

jovialidad *f* joviality, cheerfulness

joya *f*
A (alhaja) piece of jewelry*; **∼s** jewelry *o* jewels
(Compuesto) **joya de fantasía** piece *o* item of costume jewelry; **∼s de ∼** costume jewelry
B (persona) gem, treasure; (cosa): **este coche es una ∼** this is a real gem of a car; **una ∼ de la arquitectura gótica** a jewel of Gothic architecture

joyería *f* (tienda) jeweler's*; (ramo) jewelry* trade *o* business

joyero -ra *m,f* 1 (persona) jeweler* 2 **joyero** *m* (estuche) jewelry* box, jewel case

joystick /'(d)ʒojstik/ *m* joystick

jr (en Perú) (= **jirón**) street

Jr. (= **Júnior**) Jr

juana *f* (Méx fam) *tb* **juanita** grass (colloq)

juanete *m* (Med) bunion

jubilación *f* (retiro) retirement; (pensión) pension
(Compuesto) **jubilación anticipada/forzosa** early/compulsory retirement

jubilado¹ -da *adj* retired

jubilado² -da *m,f* pensioner, retired person (*o* worker etc)

jubilar [A1] *vt* 1 ‹*trabajador/empleado*› to retire, pension off 2 (fam) (desechar, tirar) ‹*silla/televisor*› to chuck out (colloq); ‹*novio*› to ditch (colloq)
■ **jubilar** *vi* (Andes) to retire
■ **jubilarse** *v pron*
A (del trabajo) to retire
B (Ven arg) (del colegio) to play hookey (esp AmE), to skive off (school) (BrE)

jubileo *m* jubilee

júbilo *m* jubilation

jubiloso -sa *adj* (liter) jubilant

jubón *m* doublet

judaico -ca *adj* Jewish, Judaic (frml)

judaísmo *m* Judaism

judas *m* Judas, traitor

judería *f* 1 (barrio) Jewish quarter, Jewry (arch) 2 (grupo) Jewry

judía *f* (Esp) bean
(Compuesto) **judía verde** green bean

judiada *f* (fam) dirty trick (colloq); **hacerle una ∼ a algn** to play a dirty trick on sb

judicatura *f* 1 (cargo) judgeship 2 (mandato) judgeship, term of office (*as a judge*) 3 (cuerpo de jueces) judiciary

judicial¹ *adj* judicial; **recurrir a la vía ∼** to have recourse to law (frml)

judicial² *m* (Méx) policeman

judío¹ -día *adj*
A (Relig, Sociol) Jewish
B (fam) (tacaño) miserly, tightfisted (colloq)

judío² **-día** *m,f* Jewish person, Jew

judo /'(d)ʒuðo/ *m* judo

juega, juegas, etc *see* **jugar**

juego *m*

A (acción) **1** (recreación) play **2** (Dep) play; **en el tercer minuto de ~** in the third minute of play *o* of the game; ***entrar en ~*** «*jugador*» to come on; «*factores/elementos*» to come into play **3** (por dinero): **el ~** gambling; **hagan ~, señores** place your bets, ladies and gentlemen; ***estar en ~*** to be at stake; ***poner algo en ~*** (arriesgar) to risk; (aportar, utilizar) to bring to bear; ***desgraciado en el ~, afortunado en amores*** unlucky at cards, lucky in love **4** (modalidad): **tienen un ~ ágil y veloz** they play a fast, free-flowing game; **~ *limpio/sucio*** fair/foul play; ***practicar un ~ limpio/sucio*** to play fair/dirty **5** (fam) (maniobras, estratagemas) game (colloq); ***hacerle/seguirle el ~ a algn*** to go *o* play along with sb; ***jugar*** *or* ***hacer un doble ~*** to play a double game **6** (en naipes) hand, cards (*pl*)

B **1** (de mesa, de niños, etc) game; ***ser un ~ de niños*** to be child's play **2** (conjunto — de cartas) pack, deck; (— de fichas) set **3** (AmL) (en la feria) fairground attraction, ride **4** **juegos** *mpl* (columpios, etc) swings, slide, etc (*in a children's playground*) **5** (en tenis) game

Compuestos

- **juego de azar** game of chance
- **juego de manos** (de prestidigitación) conjuring trick; **~ de manos, ~ de villanos** it'll only end in tears
- **juego de mesa** *or* **salón** board game
- **juego de palabras** pun, play on words
- **juegos florales** *mpl* poetry festival (*at which flowers are awarded as prizes*)
- **juegos malabares** *mpl* juggling
- **Juegos Olímpicos** *mpl* Olympic Games (*pl*), Olympics (*pl*)
- **Juegos Paralímpicos** *mpl* Paralympic Games

C **1** (de un mecanismo) play **2** (interacción): **el libre ~ de la oferta y la demanda** the free interaction of supply and demand; **~s de luces** lighting effects

D (conjunto) set; **un ~ de cuchillos** a set of knives; **un ~ de platos** a dinner service; ***hacer ~*** «*colores/cortinas*» to go together; **te hace ~ con los zapatos** it goes with your shoes

Compuestos

- **juego de café/té** coffee/tea set
- **juego de comedor/dormitorio** dining room/bedroom suite
- **juego de cubiertos** set of cutlery
- **juego de escritorio** desk set
- **juego de llaves** set of keys

juerga *f* (fam): **ir de ~** to go out on the town *o* out partying (colloq); **organizar una ~** to have *o* throw a party; ***correrse una ~*** (fam) to have a ball *o* a great time (colloq)

juerguista *mf* (fam) reveller

juev. (= **jueves**) Thurs, Thur

jueves *m* (*pl* ~) Thursday; *para ejemplos ver* **lunes**; ***nada del otro ~*** (fam) ‹*persona/casa*› nothing to write home about (colloq); ‹*examen*› not especially difficult

Compuesto **Jueves Santo** Maundy Thursday

juez *mf*, **juez -za** *m,f* **1** (Der) judge **2** (Dep) referee

Compuestos

- **juez de banda** *or* **línea** (en fútbol, tenis) (*m*) linesman; (*f*) lineswoman; (en fútbol americano, rugby) line judge
- **juez de campo** field judge
- **juez de instrucción/de primera instancia** examining magistrate
- **juez de paz** justice of the peace
- **juez de salida** starter
- **juez de silla** umpire

jugada *f* **1** (con pelota — individual) move; (entre varios) play; **las mejores ~s del partido** the highlights of the game **2** (en ajedrez, damas, etc) move; ***hacerle una (mala) ~ a algn*** to play a (dirty) trick on sb

jugado -da *adj* (Col, Méx) experienced

jugador -dora *m,f* (Dep) player; (en naipes, juegos de mesa) player; (que juega habitualmente por dinero) gambler

Compuesto **jugador de cuadro** infielder

jugar [A15] *vi*

A **1** (divertirse) to play; **~ A algo** to play sth; **~ a la pelota** to play ball; **~ al fútbol** (Esp, RPl) to play football; **¿a qué jugamos?** what shall we play?; **~ a las muñecas** to play with dolls **2** (Dep) to play; **~ *limpio/sucio*** to play fair/dirty **3** (en ajedrez, damas) to move; (en naipes) to play; (en otros juegos) to play; **me tocaba ~ a mí** it was my turn/move/go **4** (apostar fuerte) to gamble **5** (Inf) to game **6** (fam) (bromear): **se lo dije por ~** I was only joking; ***ni por ~***: **no lo hace ni por ~** she wouldn't do it (even) if you paid her **7** (Fin): **jugaban al alza/a la baja** they were betting on a bull/bear market

B **jugar con** **1** ‹*persona/sentimientos*› to play with, toy with **2** (manejar) ‹*colores/luz*› to play with; **juega con las palabras** she plays with words

C «*factores/elementos*» (actuar): **~ a favor de algn** to work in sb's favor; **~ en contra de algn** to work *o* count AGAINST sb

■ **jugar** *vt*

A **1** ‹*partido/carta*› to play; ***jugársela a algn*** to play a dirty trick on sb **2** (AmL exc RPl) ‹*fútbol/ajedrez*› to play

B **1** (apostar) **~ algo A algo** to bet sth ON sth **2** (sortear): **se juega mañana** the draw takes place tomorrow

C ‹*rol/papel*› to play

■ **jugarse** *v pron* **1** (gastarse en el juego) ‹*sueldo*› to gamble (away) **2** (arriesgar) ‹*reputación/vida*› to risk, put … at risk; **se lo jugó todo en el negocio** she staked *o* risked everything on the business; **~se el pellejo** (fam) to risk one's neck (colloq) **3** (apostarse) (*recípr*): **nos habíamos jugado una comida y gané yo** we'd bet a meal on it and I won

jugarreta *f* (fam) dirty trick (colloq); **hacerle una ~ a algn** to play a dirty trick on sb

juglar *m* minstrel, jongleur

juglaresco -ca *adj* minstrel (*before n*)

juglaría *f* minstrelsy (liter)

jugo *m*

A (líquido) juice; **~ de tomate** tomato juice; **el ~ de la carne** the meat juices

B (fam) (sustancia) substance; **este artículo tiene mucho ~** this is a very meaty article; ***sacarle (el) ~ a algo*** (fam) to make the most of sth; **les saca (el) ~ a sus obreros** he gets his money's worth from his workforce

jugoso -sa *adj* **1** ‹*fruta/carne*› juicy **2** ‹*historia/anécdota*› colorful*; ‹*chisme*› juicy **3** ‹*artículo/guión*› meaty **4** ‹*negocio*› lucrative, profitable

juguera *f* **1** (CS) (para hacer jugos) juicer **2** (Chi) (licuadora) liquidizer, blender (BrE)

juguete *m* toy; **un tren de ~** a toy train; **no es más que un ~ en sus manos** he is merely a puppet in their hands; **somos ~s del destino** (liter) we are the playthings of fate (liter)

juguetear [A1] *vi* to play

juguetería *f* (tienda) toy store; (ramo) toy trade *o* business

juguetón -tona *adj* playful

juicio *m*

A (facultad) judgment; **no está en su sano ~** he's not in his right mind; ***perder el ~*** to go out of one's mind; **me vas a hacer perder el ~** you're going to drive me crazy *o* mad

B (prudencia, sensatez) sense; **tiene muy poco ~** he's not very sensible

C (opinión) opinion; **a mi ~** in my opinion *o* to my mind; **lo dejo a tu ~** I'll leave it up to you

Compuesto **juicio de valor** value judgment

D (Der) trial; **llevar a ~ a algn** to take sb to court ; **ir a ~** to go to court

Compuestos

- **juicio civil/criminal** civil/criminal proceedings (*pl*)
- **juicio en rebeldía** judgment by default
- **Juicio Final**: **el ~ ~** the Final Judgment

juicioso -sa *adj* sensible

jul. (= **julio**) Jul

julepe *m*

A (Jueg) *card game similar to whist*

B (AmS fam) (susto) fright; **le da ~ la oscuridad** she's terrified of the dark

julepear [A1] *vt* (RPl fam) give … a fright

■ **julepearse** *v pron* (RPl fam) to get a fright

julia *f* (Méx fam) Black Maria (colloq)

j

julio *m* (mes) July; *para ejemplos ver* **enero**

jumado -da *adj* (fam) plastered (colloq)

jumar [A1] *vi* (fam) to stink (colloq)
■ **jumarse** *v pron* (AmC, Col fam) to get plastered (colloq)

jumbo /'(d)ʒumbo/ *m* jumbo jet

jumento *m* (liter) donkey, ass

jumo -ma *adj* (AmC, Col fam) plastered (colloq)

jumper /'(d)ʒumpe(r)/ *m or f* (*pl* **-pers**) (CS, Méx) jumper (AmE), pinafore dress (BrE)

jun. (= **junio**) Jun

juncal *m* reed bed

junco *m*
A (planta) rush, reed
B (Náut) *tb* ~ **chino** junk

jungla *f* jungle
(Compuesto) **jungla de asfalto** concrete jungle

junio *m* June; *para ejemplos ver* **enero**

júnior[1] /'(d)ʒunjo(r)/ *adj inv* ‹*equipo/categoría*› junior (*before n*), youth (*before n*) (BrE)

júnior[2] /'(d)ʒunjo(r)/ *mf* (*pl* ~**s**)
A 1 (Dep): **los ~s** the juniors 2 (el más joven) Junior; **Francisco Silva, J~** Francisco Silva Junior, Francisco Silva Jr
B **júnior** *m* 1 (Chi) (en oficina) office junior 2 (Méx) (hijo de papá) rich kid (colloq)

junquera *f* bulrush

junta *f*
A 1 (comité, comisión) board, committee; (de empresa) board; (reunión) meeting; **celebrar/convocar una ~ de accionistas** to hold/call a shareholders' meeting 2 (de militares) junta 3 (gobierno regional) *autonomous government in some regions of Spain*
(Compuesto) **junta directiva** board of directors
B (Mec) (acoplamiento) joint; (para cerrar herméticamente) gasket
C (CS pey) (amistad) association; **las malas ~s** bad company

juntar [A1] *vt* 1 (unir) ‹*pies/manos/camas*› to put … together 2 (reunir): **junta las fichas y ponlas en la caja** collect up the counters and put them in the box; **~ fuerzas para hacer algo** to pluck up courage to do sth; **están juntando (dinero) para el viaje** they are saving (up) for the trip; **~ monedas/sellos** (esp AmL) to collect coins/stamps 3 (cerrar) ‹*puerta*› to push … to
■ **juntarse** *v pron*
A «*personas*» 1 (acercarse) to move *o* get closer together; **júntense más, así salen todos en la foto** get (in) *o* move (in) closer together so I can get you all in the picture 2 (reunirse) to get together; **~se con algn** to join sb, meet up with sb 3 (relacionarse) **~se CON algn**: **yo no me junto con gente de su calaña** I don't mix with her sort; **se empezó a ~ con malas compañías** she fell into bad company 4 (como pareja) to live together; **se volvieron a ~** they got back together again
B 1 «*desgracias/sucesos*» to come together; **¡este mes se nos ha juntado todo!** this month it's just been one thing after another 2 «*carreteras/conductos*» to meet, join

junto -ta *adj*
A 1 (unido, reunido) together; **~s venceremos** together we shall overcome; **nunca había visto tanto dinero ~/tanta gente junta** I'd never seen so much money/so many people in one place 2 (*pl*) (cercanos, contiguos) together; **están demasiado ~s** they're too close together; **bailaban muy ~s** they were dancing very close
B (*como adv*) 1 ‹*estudiar/trabajar*› together; **éstos van ~s** these go together; **viven ~s** they live together; ***~s pero no revueltos*** (fam & hum): **viven ~s pero no revueltos** they share the same house but they lead separate lives 2 (simultáneamente) at the same time; **ahora todos ~s!** all together now!; **¡les han pasado tantas cosas juntas …!** they've just had one thing after another!
C (*en locs*) **junto a** next to; **junto con** (together) with

juntura *f* join, joint

Júpiter *m* Jupiter

jura *f* swearing in; **tuvo lugar la ~ del cargo de los nuevos ministros** the new ministers were sworn in; **la ~ de (la) bandera** *or* (AmL) **la ~ a la bandera** the ceremony at which recruits (*o* schoolchildren *etc*) swear allegiance to the flag

jurado *m*
A (cuerpo) (Der) jury; (de concurso) panel of judges, jury
B **jurado** *mf* (persona) (Der) juror, member of a jury; (de concurso) judge, member of the jury

juramentar [A1] *vt* (frml) (Der) to swear in, administer the oath to; (para un cargo) to swear in

juramento *m*
A (promesa) oath; **prestar ~** to take an oath; **tomarle ~ a algn** (Der) to swear sb in; **bajo ~** under *o* on oath
B (blasfemia) oath

jurar [A1] *vt* 1 (al prometer algo) to swear; **juró su cargo el 22 de julio** he was sworn in on July 22; **~on la Constitución/(la) bandera** *or* (AmL) **a la bandera** they swore allegiance to the Constitution/to the flag; **te juro por mi madre que es verdad** honestly, I *swear* it's true; **~ + INF** to swear to + INF; **juró vengarse** he swore to get his revenge; ***tenérsela jurada a algn*** (fam) to have it in for sb (colloq) 2 (fam) (asegurar) to swear; **habría jurado que era tu tío** I could have sworn it was your uncle; **no lo entiendo, te lo juro** I honestly don't understand
■ **jurar** *vi* 1 (maldecir) to curse, swear 2 (prometer): **~ en falso** *or* **vano** to commit perjury

jurídico -ca *adj* legal (*before n*); **sistema ~** legal system; **una laguna jurídica** a legal loophole, a loophole in the law

juriperito -ta *m,f* legal adviser

jurisdicción *f* jurisdiction

jurisdiccional *adj* ‹*ámbito*› jurisdictional; **territorio ~** jurisdiction

jurispericia *f* jurisprudence

jurisprudencia *f* (ciencia) jurisprudence; (legislación) jurisprudence, body of law; (criterio) case law

jurista *mf* jurist

juro (Ven fam): **hacer algo a ~** to be made to do sth

jurungar [A3] *vt* (Ven fam) to go *o* rummage through (colloq)

justa *f* (Hist) joust; (Dep) (period) tournament, competition
(Compuesto) **justa poética** poetry competition

justamente *adv*
A (exactamente) exactly, precisely; **~ por eso me fui** that's exactly why I left; **~ hoy que tengo invitados** today of all days, just when I have visitors
B (con justicia) fairly

justicia *f* 1 (equidad) justice; **pedir ~** to call for justice; **es de ~ que se lo hayan dado** it is only right that he should have been given it; **en ~** in all fairness, to be fair; **la ~ de su decisión** the fairness of her decision; **nunca se le ha hecho ~ como escritor** he has never received due recognition as a writer; **esta foto no le hace ~** this picture doesn't do him justice 2 (sistema, leyes): **la ~** the law; **huir de la ~** to flee from justice *o* the law; **recurrir a la ~** (frml) to have recourse to law (frml); **tomarse la ~ por su mano** to take the law into one's own hands
(Compuesto) **justicia militar** military justice system

justicialismo *m* (en Arg) *political movement founded by Juan Domingo Perón*

justiciero -ra *adj* ‹*persona*› avenging; **cayeron bajo su espada justiciera** (liter) they fell to his avenging sword

justificable *adj* justifiable

justificación *f*
A (disculpa, razón) justification; (Der) (prueba) proof
B (Impr) justification

justificante *m* receipt; **~ de pago** receipt, proof of payment; **~ de asistencia** certificate of attendance; **~ de ausencia** note explaining reasons for one's absence

justificar [A2] *vt*
A 1 «*persona*» ‹*ausencia/acción*› to justify 2 (disculpar) ‹*persona*› to find *o* make excuses for 3 «*situación/circunstancia*» to justify; **eso no justifica su actitud** that does not justify *o* that is no excuse for her attitude; **sus sospechas no estaban justificadas** his suspicions were not justified; **no hay nada que lo justifique** there's no reason for it; **trabajar por tan poco dinero no se justifica** working for such low wages just isn't worth it
B (Impr) to justify
■ **justificarse** *v pron* to justify oneself, excuse oneself

justificativo *m* (CS) note explaining reasons for one's absence

justo¹ -ta *adj*

A ‹*persona/castigo/sociedad*› just, fair; ‹*causa*› just

B 1 (exacto) ‹*medida/peso/cantidad*› exact; **me dio el dinero ~** he gave me the right money; **son 50 pesos justos** that's 50 pesos exactly; **buscaba la palabra justa** he was searching for exactly *o* just the right word 2 (apenas suficiente): **tener el dinero ~** *or* **tener lo ~ para vivir** to have just enough to live on; **andan muy ~s de dinero** they're very short of money 3 (ajustado): **estos zapatos me quedan demasiado ~s** these shoes are too tight (for me)

justo² *adv* 1 (exactamente) just; **~ a tiempo** just in time; **es ~ lo que quería** it's just *o* exactly what I wanted; **vive ~ al lado** he lives just *o* right next door; **y ~ hoy que pensaba salir** and today of all days, when I was planning to go out 2 (ajustado): **con el sueldo que gana vive muy ~** he only just manages to scrape by on what he earns; **me cupo todo, pero muy ~** I managed to get everything in, but only just

juvenil¹ *adj* ‹*moda*› young; ‹*aspecto*› youthful; ‹*categoría/competición*› junior (*before n*), youth (*before n*) (BrE)

juvenil² *mf* junior; **los ~es** the juniors

juventud *f* (edad) youth; (gente joven) youth; **¡esta ~ de hoy!** young people today!

juzgado *m* court

Compuestos

- **juzgado de instrucción/de primera instancia** court of first instance
- **juzgado municipal** county court

juzgar [A3] *vt* 1 (Der) ‹*acusado*› to try; ‹*caso*› to try, judge 2 ‹*conducta/persona*› to judge; **~ mal a algn** to misjudge sb; **juzga por ti mismo** judge for yourself 3 (considerar) to consider; **lo juzgó necesario** he considered *o* judged it (to be) necessary; **a ~ por las apariencias/los hechos** judging by appearances/the facts

Kk

K, k *f (read as /ka/) the letter* **K, k**

K 1 (= **kilobyte**) K 2 (quilate) k

ka *f: name of the letter* **k**

kaleidoscopio *m* kaleidoscope

kamikaze /kami'kase, kami'kaθe/ *m* (terrorista suicida); suicide bomber; (Hist: piloto japonés) kamikaze

kan *m* khan

kaput *adj* (fam) kaput (colloq)

karate, kárate *m* karate

karateka, karateca *mf* karate expert

kárdex *m* (archivo) file; (mueble) filing cabinet

kart *m* (*pl* **karts**) kart

karting /'kartin/ *m* karting

kartódromo *m* karting track

Kenia, Kenya *f* Kenya

keniano -na *adj/m,f* Kenyan

kepis (*pl* ~), **kepí** *m* (Esp) kepi

kermesse /ker'mes/, **kermés** *f* (CS, Méx) charity fair, fête (BrE), kermess (AmE)

ketchup /'katʃup 'katsup/ *m* ketchup, catsup (AmE)

Kg. (= **kilogramo**) kg

Khz (= **kilohertz**) kHz

kilo *m* kilogram, kilo

kilobyte /kilo'bait/ *m* (*pl* ~**s**) kilobyte

kilocaloría *f* kilocalorie

kilogramo *m* kilogram

kilometraje *m* ≈ mileage

kilométrico -ca *adj* (fam) ‹*pasillo*› endless; **había una cola kilométrica** there was a line (AmE) *o* (BrE) queue a mile long

kilómetro *m* kilometer•

kilovatio *m* kilowatt

(Compuesto) **kilovatio-hora** kilowatt-hour

kimono *m* kimono

kinder /'kinder/ *m* (*pl* ~ *or* **-ders**) (AmL fam) kindergarten

kindergarten *m* (*pl* ~ *or* **-tens**) kindergarten

kiosco, kiosko *m* 1 (Com) (de periódicos) newsstand, newspaper kiosk; (de refrescos) drinks stand; (de helados) ice-cream stand; (de caramelos, tabaco) kiosk 2 (para orquesta) bandstand

kiosquero -ra *m,f* (de periódicos) newspaper vendor; (de refrescos) drinks vendor; (de helados) ice-cream vendor; (de caramelos, tabaco) kiosk attendant

kit *m* (*pl* **kits**) kit

kitsch /kitʃ/ *adj inv/m* kitsch

kiwi /'kiwi/ *m* 1 (Bot) kiwifruit, Chinese gooseberry 2 (Zool) kiwi

Kleenex®, **kleenex** /'klineks/ *m* (*pl* ~) tissue

Km. (= **kilómetro**) km

Km/h. (= **kilómetros por hora**) kph

knock-out /'nokau(t)/ *m* (*pl* **-outs**) knockout; **dejar** *or* **poner a algn ~** to knock sb out

K.O. KO; **lo dejó ~** he knocked him out; **~ técnico** technical knock-out

koala *m* koala (bear)

kuchen /'kuxen/ *m* (Chi) (Coc) tart

Kurdistán *m* Kurdistan

kurdo[1] -da *adj* Kurdish

kurdo[2] -da *m,f* Kurd

Kuwait *m* Kuwait

Kuwaití *adj/mf* Kuwaiti

Ll

L, l *f (read as* /ˈele/) *the letter* **L, l**; **el salón hace (una) 'L'** the living room is L-shaped

l. (= **litro**) l, liter*

la¹ *art*: *ver* **el**

la² *pron pers* [1] (referido — a ella) her; (— a usted) you; (— a cosa) it; **no ~ conozco** I don't know her; **¿~ atienden?** can I help you?; **a Eva ~ veo a menudo** I see Eva often; **yo se ~ llevo** I'll take it to him [2] (*impers*) you, one (frml)

la³ *m* (nota) A; (en solfeo) la; **~ bemol/sostenido** A flat/sharp; **en ~ mayor/menor** in A major/minor

laberinto *m* (de caminos, pasillos) maze, labyrinth; (en jardín, parque) maze

labia *f* (fam) gift of the gab (colloq)

labiado -da *adj* labiate

labial *adj/f* (Ling) labial

labio *m* [1] (de la boca) lip; **~ superior** upper lip; **leer los ~s** to lip-read; **de sus ~s no salió ni una palabra** (liter) not a single word passed his lips (liter); **sin despegar los ~s** without uttering a single word [2] (de la vulva) labium

(Compuesto) **labio leporino** harelip

labiodental *adj/f* labiodental

labiolectura *f* lipreading

labor *f* [1] (trabajo) work; **una ~ de equipo** teamwork; **~es domésticas** housework; **profesión: sus ~es** (frml) occupation: housewife [2] (de coser, bordar) needlework; (de punto) knitting [3] (Agr) plowing (AmE), ploughing (BrE)

(Compuesto) **labores agrícolas** *or* **del campo** *fpl* farm work

laborable *adj* [1] ‹*día*› working (*before n*) [2] ‹*tierra*› arable

laboral *adj* ‹*problemas/conflictos*› labor* (*before n*), work (*before n*); ▸**accidente**

laboralista *adj* labor* relations (*before n*)

laborar [A1] *vi* (frml) to work

■ **laborar** *vt* (liter) ‹*tierra*› to till (liter)

laboratorio *m* laboratory

laboreo *m* farm work; **técnicas de ~** farming techniques

laborero *m* (Andes) foreman

laboriosidad *f* [1] (diligencia) diligence; **con ~** diligently [2] (dificultad) laboriousness

laborioso -sa *adj* ‹*persona*› hardworking, industrious; ‹*abejas*› industrious; ‹*tarea*› laborious

laborista¹ *adj* Labour (*before n*); **el partido ~** the Labour Party

laborista² *mf* member of the Labour Party

labrado -da *adj* ‹*madera*› carved; ‹*piedra*› cut, carved; ‹*cuero*› tooled; (Tex) patterned

labrador -dora *m,f* (Agr) (propietario) farmer; (trabajador) farmworker

labrantío -tía *adj* arable

labranza *f* farming the land, tilling the soil (liter); **herramientas de ~** farm tools; **tierras de ~** arable land

labrar [A1] *vt*

A (Agr) ‹*tierra*› to work

B ‹*madera*› to carve; ‹*piedra*› to cut; ‹*cuero*› to tool, work; ‹*metales*› to work

■ **labrarse** *v pron* (forjarse): **~se un porvenir** to carve out a future for oneself; **me labré mi propia ruina** I dug my own grave

labriego -ga *m,f* farmworker

laburar [A1] *vi* (CS fam) to work

laburo *m* (CS fam) work

laca *f* (resina) lac, shellac; (barniz) lacquer; (para el pelo) hairspray

(Compuesto) **laca de uñas** nail polish

lacar [A2] *vt* to lacquer

lacayo *m* (criado) footman; (persona servil) lackey

lacear [A1] *vt* (CS) ‹*ganado*› to lasso

lacerante *adj* (liter) ‹*dolor*› searing (liter); ‹*palabras*› cutting, wounding

lacerar [A1] *vt* (liter) ‹*piel/cuerpo*› to cut, lacerate (frml)

lacero -ra *m,f* dogcatcher

lacho -cha *m,f* (Chi fam) [1] (mujeriego) (*m*) womanizer (colloq); (*f*) man-chaser (colloq) [2] (pey) (amante) lover

lacio -cia *adj* ‹*pelo*› straight; ‹*cuerpo*› limp, weak

lacón *m* ham (*from the foreleg*)

lacónico -ca *adj* laconic

lacra *f* (Med) mark; (defecto, mancha) fault

lacrar [A1] *vt* (con cera) to seal

lacre¹ *adj* (AmL) bright-red; (Chi) red

lacre² *m* sealing wax

lacrimal *adj* tear (*before n*), lachrymal (tech)

lacrimógeno -na *adj* (fam) ‹*película*› weepy (colloq)

lacrimoso -sa *adj* ‹*persona/despedida*› tearful

lactancia *f* (secreción de leche) lactation; **durante el período de ~** while breastfeeding

lactante *adj*: **un niño ~** a child still on milk

lactar [A1] *vt* ‹*bebé*› to suckle, breastfeed; ‹*cría*› to suckle

■ **lactar** *vi* to suckle, feed

lácteo -tea *adj* dairy (*before n*), milk (*before n*)

láctico -ca *adj* lactic

lactosa *f* lactose

ladeado -da *adj* [ESTAR]: **el cuadro está ~** the picture is on a slant *o* is askew; **llevaba el sombrero ~** he wore his hat at an angle

ladear [A1] *vt* ‹*cabeza*› to tilt … to one side; ‹*objeto*› to tilt; ‹*persona*› to give … the cold shoulder

■ **ladearse** *v pron* (inclinarse) to lean to one side

ladera *f* hillside, mountainside; **la ~ norte** the northern slope *o* side

ladilla *f* [1] (Zool) crab louse [2] (persona pesada) (Ven vulg) pain in the ass (AmE vulg), pain in the arse (BrE vulg)

ladino¹ -na *adj*

A (taimado) sly, cunning

B (AmC, Méx) [1] (mestizo) mestizo, of mixed race [2] (hispanohablante) Spanish-speaking (*often used to refer to Indians who adopt Spanish ways*)

C (Méx fam) (agudo) high-pitched, piercing

ladino² -na *m,f* (AmC, Méx) [1] (mestizo) mestizo, person of mixed race [2] (hispanohablante) Spanish-speaking Indian

lado *m*

A [1] (parte lateral) side; **está en el ~ derecho** it is on the right-hand side; **a este/al otro ~ del río** on this/on the other side of the river; **¿de qué ~ de la calle?** which side of the street?; **hacerse a un ~** to move to one side; **echarse a un ~** to swerve; **ponlas a un ~** set them aside; **cambiar de ~** (Dep) to change sides (AmE) *o* (BrE) ends [2] (de papel, moneda, tela) side [3] (Mat) (de polígono) side

B (aspecto, ángulo) side; **ver el ~ positivo de las cosas** to look on the bright side of things; **todo tiene su ~ bueno y su ~ malo** there's a good side and a bad side to everything

C [1] (bando) side; **¿de qué ~ estás?** whose side are you on? [2] (rama familiar) side; **por el ~ materno** on the maternal side; **por el ~ de mi padre** on my father's side (of the family)

D (sitio, lugar): **miré en** *or* **por todos ~s** I looked everywhere; **ponlo en cualquier ~** put it anywhere; **va a todos ~s en taxi** she goes everywhere by taxi; **ir de un ~ para otro** to run around

E (*en locs*) **al lado**: **viven en la casa de al ~** they live next door; **los vecinos de al ~** the next-door neighbors; **nos queda aquí al ~** it's very near here *o* (colloq) is right on the doorstep; **al lado de algn/algo** (contiguo a) next to sb/sth, beside sb/sth; (en comparación con) compared to sb/sth; **a su ~ me siento segura** I feel safe when I'm with him; **de mi/tu/su lado**: **no te muevas de mi ~** don't leave my side, stay close to me; **de lado** ‹*meter/colocar*› sideways; ‹*tumbarse/dormir*› on one's side; **ponlo de ~** turn it sideways; **de medio lado** at an angle; **por otro lado** (en cambio) on the other hand; (además) apart from anything else; **por un ~ ..., pero por otro ~ ...** on the one hand ..., but on the other hand ...; ***dejar algo de ~*** *or* ***a un ~*** to leave sth aside *o* to one side; ***dejar a algn de ~***: **me dejan de lado en la oficina** they leave me out of things at the office; **sus amigos la dejaron a un ~** her friends gave her the cold shoulder; ***estar al*** *or* ***del otro ~*** (CS, Méx fam) to be over the worst, be laughing (colloq); ***ir cada uno por su ~***: **mejor vamos cada uno por nuestro ~ y allí nos encontramos** it's better if we all make our own way and meet each other there; **cada uno se fue por su ~** they went their separate ways; ***por cualquier ~ que se mire*** however you look at it; ***saber de qué ~ sopla el viento*** to know how the land lies

ladrar [A1] *vi* [1] «*perro*» to bark [2] (fam) «*persona*» to yell (colloq), to bark (colloq); **~ *de hambre*** (AmS fam) to be starving (colloq)

ladrido *m* bark; **~s** barking

ladrillo *m* [1] brick; **fachada de ~ a la vista** brick facade; ***ser un ~*** (fam) «*libro*» to be heavy-going [2] (Esp fam) (industria) construction industry [3] **(de) color ~** brick-red

ladrón -drona *m,f*

A (de bolsos, coches) thief; (de bancos) bank robber; (de casas) burglar; **aquí son unos ladrones** (fam) they really rip you off in here (colloq); ***el que roba a un ~ tiene cien años de perdón*** it's no crime to steal from a thief; ***piensa el ~ que todos son de su condición*** evildoers always think the worst of others

B **ladrón** *m* (Elec) adaptor

ladronzuelo -la *m,f* petty thief

lagar *m* press

lagartear [A1] *vi* (Col fam) to crawl (colloq)

■ **lagartear** *vt* (Col fam) ‹*puesto/cargo*› to finagle (colloq)

lagartija *f* wall lizard

lagarto *m*

A (Zool) lizard

(Compuesto) **lagarto de Indias** alligator

B (Col fam) (persona) crawler (colloq)

lago *m* lake

lágrima *f*

A (Fisiol) tear; **derramar ~s por algn/algo** to shed tears over sb/sth; **le caían las ~s** tears were running down her face; **se le saltaron las ~s** it brought tears to his eyes; ***llorar a ~ viva*** to cry one's eyes *o* heart out; ***llorar ~s de sangre*** to cry bitterly

(Compuesto) **lágrimas de cocodrilo** *fpl* crocodile tears (*pl*)

B (adorno) teardrop

lagrimal¹ *adj* tear (*before n*)

lagrimal² *m* [1] (extremo del ojo) corner of the eye [2] *tb* **conducto ~** tear duct

lagrimear [A1] *vi* [1] «*ojo*» to water [2] «*persona*» to sob quietly

laguna *f*

A (de agua dulce) lake, pool; (de agua salada) lagoon

B [1] (vacío, imperfección) gap; **las ~s de la legislación** the omissions in the legislation [2] (en la memoria) memory lapse

(Compuesto) **laguna jurídica** legal loophole

laicalizar [A4] *vt* (Andes) to laicize, secularize

laicizar [A4] *vt* to laicize, secularize

laico¹ -ca *adj* secular, lay (*before n*)

laico² -ca (*m*) layman, layperson; (*f*) laywoman, layperson

laísmo *m*: *use of* **la**/**las** *instead of* **le**/**les** (*as in* **la**/**las dije que no**), *common in certain regions of Spain but not acceptable to most speakers*

laja *f* (AmS) slab

lama¹ *m* lama

lama² *f* (AmL) (musgo) moss; (verdín) green slime; (moho) mold*

lambetear [A1] *vt* (Col, Méx, Ven) to lick

lambiscón -cona *m,f* (Méx fam) bootlicker (colloq)

lambisquear [A1] *vt* [1] (Col) (lamer) to lick [2] (Méx fam) (lisonjear) to suck up to (colloq)

lamé *m* lamé

lameculos *mf* (*pl* ~) (vulg) asskisser (AmE vulg), arselicker (BrE vulg)

lamentable *adj* [1] ‹*conducta/error/suceso*› deplorable, terrible [2] ‹*pérdida*› sad; ‹*estado/aspecto*› pitiful; ‹*error*› regrettable

lamentación *f* lamentation (liter); **estoy harta de oír tus lamentaciones** (fam) I'm fed up with your grumbling

lamentar [A1] *vt* to regret; **lamentamos las molestias ocasionadas** we regret any inconvenience that we may have caused you; **lo lamento mucho** I am very sorry; **no hubo que ~ daños personales** (period) there were no casualties; **lamento molestarlo** I'm sorry to disturb you; **lamentamos tener que comunicarle que ...** (frml) we regret to have to inform you that ...; **lamento que no se encuentre bien** I'm sorry to hear that you're not well; **es de ~ que ...** it is to be lamented that ... (frml)

■ **lamentarse** *v pron* to complain, to grumble (colloq); **~se DE algo** to deplore sth

lamento *m* [1] (quejido — por un dolor físico) groan; (— por tristeza) wail [2] (elegía) lament

lamer [E1] *vt* [1] «*persona/animal*» to lick [2] (liter) «*agua/olas*» to lap against

lamido -da *adj* [1] (ant) (flaco) gaunt [2] (relamido) excessively neat

lámina *f*

A (hoja, plancha) sheet; **recubierto con una ~ de oro** gold-plated

B [1] (plancha) plate; (grabado) engraving; (ilustración) plate; (estampa) picture card [2] (Educ) wall chart

laminado *m* (Metal, Tec) lamination; (plancha) sheet

laminador *m*, **laminadora** *f* rolling mill, laminator

laminar¹ *adj* laminar

laminar² [A1] *vt* [1] ‹*metal*› to laminate, roll; (recubrir con láminas) to laminate; [2] (AmC, Col, Méx) ‹*documentos/carnet*› to laminate

lampa *f* (Andes) (azada) mattock; (pala) spade

lampalagua *f* (AmS) *type of anaconda*

lámpara *f* lamp

(Compuestos)
- **lámpara de pie/mesa** standard/table lamp
- **lámpara solar** solar lamp

lamparazo *m* (Col fam) (idea brillante) brainwave (colloq)

lamparín *m* (Per) kerosene lamp

lamparita *f* (RPl) (light) bulb

lamparón *m* (fam) (mancha) stain

lampazo *m*

A (Bot) burdock

B (Náut) swab, mop; (mopa) (AmS) mop

lampiño -ña *adj* (sin barba) smooth-faced; (con poco vello) with little body hair

lamprea *f* lamprey

lana *f*

A (material) wool; (vellón, pelambre) fleece; **una bufanda de ~** a wool *o* woolen scarf; **son de ~** they're (made of) wool; ***ir (a) por ~ y volver trasquilado*** to be hoist with one's own petard; ***unos cardan la ~ y otros cobran la fama*** some do all the work and others get all the credit

(Compuesto) **lana virgen** new wool

B (AmL fam) (dinero) dough (sl); **tienen mucha ~** they're loaded (colloq)

lance *m*

A 1 (Taur) incident, move 2 (Jueg) (jugada) move; (de dados) throw; ***tirarse un ~*** (CS fam) to try one's luck

B 1 (incidente) incident; (riña) quarrel 2 (situación difícil) tight spot; **salir de un ~** to get out of a tight spot

(Compuesto) **lance de honor** duel

C (ocasión): **de ~** secondhand

lancero *m* lancer

lanceta *f* 1 (Med) lancet 2 (Andes, Méx) (aguijón) sting

lancha *f* (barca grande) launch, cutter; (bote) motorboat

(Compuestos)
- **lancha de desembarco** landing craft
- **lancha fuera borda** (outboard) launch
- **lancha motora** motor launch, motorboat
- **lancha neumática** inflatable (dinghy)
- **lancha patrullera** patrol boat
- **lancha salvavidas** *or* **de salvamento** lifeboat

lanchón *m* barge, lighter

lanero[1] **-ra** *adj* wool (*before n*)

lanero[2] **-ra** *m,f* wool merchant

langaruto -ta *m,f* (Col, Per fam) beanpole (colloq)

langosta *f* (crustáceo) lobster; (insecto) locust

langostera *f* lobster pot

langostino *m* (grande) king prawn; (pequeño) prawn

(Compuesto) **langostino de río** crayfish, crawfish (esp AmE)

langüetear [A1] *vt* (Chi) to lick

languidecer [E3] *vi* «*persona*» to languish (liter); **la conversación empezó a ~** the conversation began to flag

lánguido -da *adj* 1 (débil) listless, weak 2 ‹*mirada/aspecto*› languid

lanilla *f* (pelillo) fluff; (tela) flannel

lanolina *f* lanolin

lanudo -da *adj* long-haired, shaggy

lanza[1] *f* (arma — en las lides) lance; (— arrojadiza) spear; ***~ en ristre*** ready for action; ***ser una ~*** (AmL fam) to be on the ball (colloq)

lanza[2] *m* (Chi) (delincuente) pickpocket, thief

lanzabengalas *m* (*pl* ~) flare gun, Very pistol

lanzabombas *m* (*pl* ~) (en avión) bomb release gear; (de trinchera) trench mortar

lanzacohetes *m* (*pl* ~) rocket launcher

lanzadera *f* shuttle

(Compuesto) **lanzadera espacial** space shuttle

lanzado -da *adj*

A [SER] (fam) (precipitado) impulsive, impetuous; (decidido, atrevido) forward

B (fam) (rápido): **iban ~s** they were bombing along (colloq); **salió ~** he rushed out; **pasar ~** to shoot past

lanzador -dora *m,f* (Dep) (de disco, jabalina) thrower; (en béisbol) pitcher; **~ de bala** *or* **(Esp) de peso** shot-putter

lanzagranadas *m* (*pl* ~) grenade launcher

lanzallamas *m* (*pl* ~) flamethrower

lanzamiento *m*

A 1 (de objetos, pelota) throwing; (de misil, torpedo) launch; (de bomba) dropping 2 (de cohete, satélite) launch; (Dep) (de disco, jabalina) throw; (de bala) put; (en béisbol) pitch

(Compuestos)
- **lanzamiento de bala** *or* (Esp) **de peso** shot put
- **lanzamiento de disco/jabalina** discus/javelin throwing
- **lanzamiento de penaltys** penalty shoot-out
- **lanzamiento libre** free throw *o* shot

B (de producto, libro) launch, launching

C (CS) (Der) *tb* **orden de ~** eviction order

lanzamisiles *m* (*pl* ~) missile launcher

lanzar [A4] *vt*

A 1 ‹*pelota/objetos/jabalina*› to throw; (en béisbol) to pitch; **~ la bala** *or* (Esp) **el peso** to put the shot 2 ‹*misil/satélite*› to launch; ‹*bomba*› to drop

B ‹*producto/libro*› to launch; **el disco que lo lanzó** the record which launched him

C 1 ‹*ofensiva/ataque*› to launch 2 ‹*crítica*› to launch; **las acusaciones lanzadas contra él** the accusations made against him; **lanzó un llamamiento a la calma** he made an appeal for calm

D 1 ‹*mirada*› to shoot, give; **~ una indirecta a algn** to drop sb a hint 2 ‹*grito*› to give; **~ gritos de protesta** to shout protests; **lanzó un grito de dolor** he cried out in pain; **~ un suspiro** to sigh

■ **lanzar** *vi* (en béisbol) to pitch

■ **lanzarse** *v pron* 1 (*refl*) (arrojarse) to throw oneself; **~se al agua/al vacío** to leap into the water/the void; **~se en paracaídas** to parachute; (en una emergencia) to parachute, to bale out 2 (abalanzarse, precipitarse): **~se sobre algo/algn** to pounce on sth/sb; **se lanzó en su búsqueda** he set about looking for her; **~se a la calle** to take to the streets; **~se escaleras arriba** to charge upstairs; **~se al ataque** to attack; **se lanza a hacer las cosas sin pensar** (fam) she rushes into things without thinking 3 (emprender) **~se A algo** to undertake sth

lanzatorpedos *m* (*pl* ~) torpedo tube *o* launcher

lapa *f* 1 (molusco) limpet 2 (Ven) (mamífero) paca 3 (AmC) (ave) macaw

lapicera *f* (CS) pen

(Compuesto) **lapicera fuente** *or* **estilográfica** (CS) fountain pen

lapicero *m* 1 (portaminas) automatic pencil (AmE), propelling pencil (BrE) 2 (AmC, Per) (bolígrafo) ballpoint pen

lápida *f* (en tumba) tombstone, gravestone; (losa conmemorativa) stone plaque

lapidar [A1] *vt* to stone

lapidario[1] **-ria** *adj* 1 ‹*inscripción*› lapidary (frml) 2 (categórico) ‹*frase/afirmación*› categorical, dogmatic

lapidario[2] **-ria** *m,f* lapidary

lapislázuli *m* lapis lazuli

lápiz *m* (de madera) pencil; (portaminas) automatic pencil (AmE), propelling pencil (BrE); **con** *or* **a ~** in pencil

(Compuestos)
- **lápices de colores** *mpl* crayons (*pl*)
- **lápiz de labios** lipstick
- **lápiz de memoria** memory stick
- **lápiz de ojos** eye pencil
- **lápiz de pasta** (Chi) ballpoint pen
- **lápiz óptico** light pen

lapo *m* (fam) (Andes, Méx fam) (bofetada) wallop (colloq)

lapso *m* 1 (de tiempo) space; **un breve ~** a short space *o* period of time 2 (error, olvido) ▸ **lapsus**

lapsus *m* (*pl* ~) (error) slip, blunder; (olvido): **tuve un pequeño ~** it slipped my mind

(Compuesto) **lapsus linguae** slip of the tongue

laptop *m* laptop (computer)

laquear [A1] *vt* to lacquer

lar *m* 1 (liter) (chimenea) hearth 2 **lares** *mpl* (arc) (lugar): **¿qué haces por estos ~es?** what are you doing here?

larga *f* 1 (largo plazo): **a la ~** in the long run; ***darle ~s a algn/algo*** to put sb/sth off 2 (Auto) high beam (AmE), full *o* main beam (BrE); **dio la(s) ~(s)** he put the lights on high *o* main beam

largamente *adv* at length

largar [A3] *vt*

A 1 (Náut) ‹*amarras/cabo*› to let out, pay out 2 (RPl) (soltar, dejar caer) to let … go

B ‹*discurso/sermón*› to give; ‹*palabrota/insulto*› to let fly; **le largó que se iba** he came out with the news that he was leaving; **no me largó ni un peso** he didn't give me a penny

C (fam) (endilgar) to dump (colloq)

D (fam) (despedir) to fire, to give … the boot (colloq); **la novia lo largó** (RPl) his girlfriend ditched him

l

E (fam) (de la cárcel) to let … out
F (CS, Méx) (Dep) ‹*pelota*› to throw; ‹*carrera*› to start
■ **largar** *vi* (Andes) (Dep, Equ) to start
■ **largarse** *v pron* 1 (fam) (irse) to beat it (colloq); **lárguense antes de que venga** get out of here before he arrives; **¡yo me largo!** I'm taking off! (AmE), I'm off! (BrE) (colloq) 2 (CS fam) (empezar) to start, get going (colloq); **~se A + INF** to start to + INF, to start -ING

largavistas *m* (*pl* ~) (CS) binoculars (*pl*)

largo¹ -ga *adj*
A 1 ‹*palo/camino/pasillo*› long; ‹*pelo/piernas/ropa*› long; **una camisa de manga larga** a long-sleeved shirt; **me está largo** it's too long (for me); **se cayó cuan ~ era** he fell flat on his face 2 (*en locs*) **a lo largo** ‹*cortar/partir*› lengthways; **a lo largo de** (de camino, río) along; (de jornada, novela) throughout; **a lo ~ de su vida** in the course of her life; **a lo ~ de la semana** in the course of the week; **a lo ~ y ancho del país** throughout the country; **de largo** ‹*vestirse*› to wear a long skirt/dress; ‹*ponerse*› «*debutante*» to come out
B (extenso) long; ‹*novela/sílaba*› long; **el día se me ha hecho muy ~** it's been a long day; **es muy ~ de contar** it's a long story; **un tren de ~ recorrido** a long-distance train; ***ir para ~*** (fam): **va para ~** it's going to be a while yet; **~ *y tendido*** at great length
C (en expresiones de cantidad): **una hora larga** a good hour; **tres metros ~s** a good three meters

largo² *m*
A (longitud) length; **¿cuánto mide de ~?** how long is it?; **3 metros de ~** 3 meters long
B (en natación) lap (AmE), length (BrE)
C (Mús) largo

largo³ *interj* (fam) *tb* **¡~ de aquí!** get out of here!

largometraje *m* feature film, full-length film

larguero *m* 1 (Arquit, Const) (viga) crossbeam; (de puerta) jamb 2 (de cama) side 3 (Dep) crossbar

largueza *f* generosity; **con ~** generously

larguirucho -cha *adj* (fam) gangling (*before n*)

largura *f* (fam) length

laringe *f* larynx

laringitis *f* laryngitis

larva *f* larva, grub

larvado -da *adj* latent

larvario -ria, larval *adj* (Zool) larval

las¹ *art*: *ver* **el**

las² *pron pers*: *ver* **los²**

lasaña *f* lasagna, lasagne

lasca *f* (de una piedra) chip, chipping

lascivia *f* lasciviousness, lust

lascivo -va *adj* lascivious, lustful

láser *m* laser

lasitud *f* (liter) lassitude (liter), weariness

laso -sa *adj* (liter) weary, tired

lástima *f* 1 (pena) shame, pity; **¡qué ~!** what a shame *o* pity!; **es una ~** it's a shame *o* pity; **me da ~ tirarlo** it seems a pity *o* shame to throw it out 2 (compasión): **sentir ~ por algn** to feel sorry for sb; **da ~ verla así de triste** it's sad to see her so unhappy; **me da ~ ese hombre** I feel sorry for that man; **digno de ~** worthy of compassion

lastimadura *f* (AmL) graze

lastimar [A1] *vt* to hurt
■ **lastimarse** *v pron* (*refl*) (esp AmL) to hurt oneself; **se lastimó el pie** he hurt his foot

lastimero -ra *adj* pitiful

lastimoso -sa *adj* (triste) terrible, pitiful; (deplorable) shameful, terrible

lastrar [A1] *vt* 1 ‹*buque/globo*› to ballast 2 (entorpecer) to burden, weigh down

lastre *m* 1 (de buque, globo) ballast; **soltar** *or* **largar ~** to drop ballast 2 (carga, estorbo) burden

lat. (= **latitud**) lat.

lata *f*
A 1 (hojalata) tin 2 (envase) can, tin (BrE); **una ~ de aceite** a can of oil; **los tomates son de ~** the tomatoes are out of a can *o* tin; **sardinas en ~** canned *o* tinned sardines 3 (para galletas, etc) tin
B (fam) (pesadez) nuisance, pain (colloq); **¡qué ~!** what a nuisance!; **¡qué ~ de chico!** this boy's such a pain (in the neck)! (colloq); ***dar (la) ~*** (fam) to be a nuisance; **no hacen más que dar (la) ~** they're nothing but trouble; **¡deja ya de darme ~!** stop bugging *o* pestering me! (colloq)

latente *adj* latent

lateral¹ *adj* ‹*puerta/salida/calle*› side (*before n*); ‹*línea/sucesión*› indirect, lateral

lateral² *m*
A (Dep) (poste) goalpost
B **lateral** *m or f* (Auto) (calle perpendicular) side street; (calle paralela) service road, frontage road (AmE)
C **laterales** *mpl* (del escenario) wings (*pl*)

lateral³ *mf* (Dep) (alero) wing, winger; (defensa) left/right back

latero¹ -ra *adj* (Andes fam) boring

latero² -ra *m,f*
A (hojalatero) tinsmith
B (Andes fam) bore

látex *m* latex

latido *m* (del corazón) heartbeat; (en la sien, una herida) throbbing; (golpe) beat; (ritmo) beating

latifundio *m* large estate

latifundista *mf* owner of a large estate

latigazo *m* 1 (golpe) lash; **los hacían trabajar a ~s** they whipped them to make them work 2 (chasquido) crack of the whip 3 (reprensión) tongue-lashing

látigo *m* whip

latiguillo *m* 1 (Ling) (tópico) cliché, well-worn phrase; (muletilla) filler (*word which a person uses a lot*) 2 (frase vacía) platitude; (de político) catchphrase, slogan

latín *m* Latin; ***saber (mucho) ~*** (fam) to know what's what

latinajo, latinazgo *m* 1 (fam) (frase latina) Latin word/expression 2 (latín incorrecto) dog latin

latino¹ -na *adj* 1 ‹*literatura/gramática/pueblo*› Latin 2 (fam) (latinoamericano) Latin American

latino² -na *m,f* 1 (español, italiano, etc) Latin; **los ~s** Latin people 2 (fam) (latinoamericano) Latin American

Latinoamérica *f* Latin America

latinoamericano -na *adj/m,f* Latin American

latir [I1] *vi*
A «*corazón*» to beat; «*vena*» to pulsate; «*herida/sien*» to throb
B 1 (Chi, Méx fam) (parecer) (+ *me/te/le etc*): **me late que no vendrá** I have a feeling *o* something tells me he isn't going to come (Méx fam) 2 (parecer bien, gustar) (+ *me/te/le etc*): **¿te late ir al cine?** do you feel like going to the movies?

latitud *f* 1 (Astron, Geog) latitude 2 **latitudes** *fpl* (zona, lugar) parts (*pl*); **la flora de otras ~es** the flora of other parts of the world

lato -ta *adj* (frml) broad, wide

latón *m* 1 (Metal) brass 2 (RPl) (palangana) metal bowl

latonería *f* (Col) body shop

latonero -ra *m,f* (Col) body shop worker (AmE), panel beater (BrE)

latoso¹ -sa *adj* 1 (fam) (molesto) annoying, tiresome; **no seas ~** don't be such a pain (colloq) 2 (Andes fam) (aburrido) dull, boring

latoso² -sa *m,f* 1 (fam) (pesado) pain (in the neck) (colloq) 2 (Andes fam) (aburrido) bore

latrocinio *m* (frml) theft, larceny

laucha *f* (CS) mouse; ***aguaitar*** *or* ***catear la ~*** (Chi fam) to lie in wait

laúd *m* lute

laudable *adj* praiseworthy

láudano *m* laudanum

laudatorio -ria *adj* (frml) laudatory (frml)

laudo *m* (Der, Rels Labs) *tb* **~ arbitral** arbitration award

laureado -da *adj* (frml) prize-winning (*before n*)

laurear [A1] *vt* (frml): **~ a algn CON algo** to award sth TO sb, to honor* sb WITH sth (frml)

laurel *m*
A (árbol) laurel; (Coc) bay leaf

B **laureles** *mpl* (honores) laurels (*pl*); ***dormirse en*** *or* ***sobre los ~es*** to rest on one's laurels

lava *f* lava

lavable *adj* washable

lavabo *m* (pila) sink (AmE), washbasin (BrE); (mueble) washstand; (retrete) toilet, bathroom; **S** **lavabos** rest rooms (*in US*), toilets (*in UK*)

lavacoches *mf* (*pl* ~) **1** (persona) car washer **2** **lavacoches** *m* (lugar) car wash

lavada *f* **1** (AmL) (lavado) wash **2** (Col fam) (por la lluvia) soaking

lavadero *m* **1** (habitación) utility room, laundry room; (pila) sink; (al aire libre) washing place **2** (RPl) (lavandería) laundry **3** (Col) (tina de lavar) washtub

(Compuesto) **lavadero de oro** gold-panning site

lavado[1] **-da** *adj* **1** ‹*ropa/manos*› washed **2** (RPl fam) ‹*color*› (descolorido) washed-out; (muy claro) light; ‹*persona*› pale

lavado[2] *m*

A **1** (de ropa) wash, washing; (de coche) wash; **~ en seco** dry cleaning; **~ a mano** handwashing **2** (ropa, tanda) wash

(Compuestos)

- **lavado automático** carwash
- **lavado de cerebro** brainwashing; **hacerle un ~ de ~ a algn** to brainwash sb
- **lavado de estómago**: **le hicieron un ~ de ~** they pumped his stomach out

B (AmL) (de dinero) money laundering

lavadora *f* washing machine

lavamanos *m* sink (AmE), washbasin (BrE)

lavanda *f* lavender

lavandera *f* (mujer) washerwoman; (pájaro) wagtail

lavandería *f* laundry

(Compuesto) **lavandería automática** Laundromat® (AmE), launderette (BrE)

lavándula *f* lavender

lavaojos *m* (*pl* ~) eyecup (AmE), eyebath (BrE)

lavaplatos *mf* (*pl* ~)

A (persona) dishwasher

B **lavaplatos** *m* **1** (máquina) dishwasher **2** (Andes) (fregadero) sink

lavar [A1] *vt*

A ‹*ropa/coche*› to wash; ‹*suelo*› to mop; ‹*fruta/verdura*› to wash; **hay que ~lo en seco** it has to be dry-cleaned

B (AmL) ‹*dinero*› to launder

■ **lavar** *vi* **1** (lavar ropa) to do the laundry *o* (BrE) washing **2** (en peluquería): **~ y marcar** to shampoo and set

■ **lavarse** *v pron* **1** (*refl*) to have a wash; ‹*cara/manos*› to wash; ‹*dientes*› to clean, brush; **~se el pelo** *or* **la cabeza** to wash one's hair **2** (Col fam) (empaparse) to get soaked

lavarropas *m* (*pl* ~) (RPl) washing machine

lavativa *f* **1** (Med) enema **2** (Ven fam) (molestia) drag (colloq)

lavatorio *m*

A **1** (AmL) (mueble) washstand **2** (CS) (lavamanos) sink (AmE), washbasin (BrE)

B (Chi, Per) (palangana) washbowl (AmE), washbasin (BrE)

lavavajillas *m* (*pl* ~) (detergente) dishwashing liquid (AmE), washing-up liquid (BrE); (máquina) dishwasher

lavaza *f* (Agr) (Col, Ven) slops (*pl*)

laxante[1] *adj* laxative (*before n*)

laxante[2] *m* laxative

laxar [A1] *vi* to act as a laxative

■ **laxar** *vt*: **me laxó** it loosened my bowels

laxativo -va *adj/m* ▸ **laxante**[1,2]

laxitud *f* laxity, laxness

laxo -xa *adj* ‹*músculo*› relaxed; ‹*moral/disciplina*› lax

lazada *f* (nudo) bow

lazar [A4] *vt* (Méx) to rope, lasso

lazarillo *m* guide (*for a blind person*)

lazo *m*

A **1** (cinta) ribbon; (nudo decorativo) bow; **¿te hago un ~?** shall I tie it in a bow? **2** (Méx) (del matrimonio) *cord with which the couple are symbolically united at a wedding*

B **1** (Agr) lasso; **le echó el ~ al potro** he lassoed the colt; ***no echarle*** *or* ***tirarle un ~ a algn*** (Méx fam) not to give sb a second glance; ***poner a algn como ~ de cochino*** (Méx fam) to give sb a dressing-down **2** (cuerda) (Col, Méx) rope; (para saltar) (Col) ▸ **cuerda A2** **3** (para cazar) snare, trap

C (vínculo) bond, tie; **~s culturales** cultural ties

le *pron pers*

A **1** (como objeto indirecto) **~ dije la verdad** (a él) I told him the truth; (a ella) I told her the truth; (a usted) I told you the truth; **~ di otra mano de barniz** I gave it another coat of varnish; **el dinero ~ sería muy útil** she/he would find the money very useful; **~ robó el dinero a su padre** he/she stole the money from his father; **explícale al señor qué pasó** explain to the man what happened; **a este libro ~ faltan páginas** there are some pages missing from this book; **no te ~ pongas delante** don't stand in front of her/him **2** (*impers*): **cuando a uno ~ dicen esas cosas** when people say things like that to you

B (como objeto directo) (esp Esp) (referido — a él) him; (— a usted) you; **¿le conoces?** do you know him?; **hoy no ~ puedo recibir** I can't see you today

leal *adj* ‹*amigo/criado*› loyal, trusty; ‹*tropas*› loyal; **~ A algo/algn** loyal TO sth/sb

lealtad *f* loyalty

leasing /'lisin/ *m* (contrato) lease; (sistema) leasing

lebrel *mf* hound

lebrillo *m* bowl

lección *f* lesson; **tomarle la ~ a algn** to test sb on a lesson; **no me supe la ~** I hadn't learned the lesson; **eso te servirá de ~** let that be a lesson to you

lechada *f* (para blanquear) whitewash; (para azulejos) grout; (de papel) pulp

lechal *adj* suckling

leche *f*

A (de madre, de vaca) milk; ***más blanco que la ~*** as white as a sheet

(Compuestos)

- **leche condensada** condensed milk
- **leche descremada** *or* (Esp) **desnatada** skim milk (AmE), skimmed milk (BrE)
- **leche en polvo** powdered milk
- **leche entera** whole milk, full-cream milk

B (Bot) latex; (en cosmética) milk, lotion

(Compuestos)

- **leche humectante de pepinos** moisturising cucumber lotion
- **leche limpiadora** cleansing milk

C (vulg) (semen) cum (vulg)

D (Esp vulg) **1** (mal humor): **tiene una ~ ...** he's got a foul temper; *ver tb* **malo**[1] **2** (expresando fastidio, mal humor): **no seas pesado, ~** don't be so goddamn (AmE) *o* (BrE) bloody annoying (sl)

E (Andes fam) (suerte) luck; **estar con** *or* **de ~** to be lucky

lechecillas *fpl* sweetbreads (*pl*)

lechera *f*

A (para transportar) churn; (para servir) milk jug

B (en cuentos) milkmaid; *ver tb* **lechero**[2] **A**

lechería *f* dairy, creamery

lechero[1] **-ra** *adj*

A **1** ‹*industria/vaca*› dairy (*before n*) **2** ‹*producción*› milk (*before n*)

B (Col, Per fam) (afortunado) lucky

lechero[2] **-ra** *m,f*

A (vendedor) (*m*) milkman; (*f*) milkwoman; *ver tb* **lechera**

B (Col, Per fam) (afortunado) lucky devil (colloq)

lecho *m*

A (liter) (cama) bed; **en su ~ de muerte** on her deathbed

B (de río) bed; (capa, estrato) layer

lechón -chona *m,f* **1** (Agr) piglet **2** **lechón** *m* (Coc) (cochinillo) suckling *o* sucking pig

lechosa *f* (AmC, Col, Ven) papaya

lechoso -sa *adj* ‹*líquido*› milky; ‹*piel*› pale

lechuga *f* lettuce; ***fresco como una ~*** (fam) as fresh as a daisy; ***ser más fresco que una ~*** (fam) to have a lot of nerve (colloq)

lechuguino *m* (ant) dandy (dated), fop (dated)

lechuza *f* **1** (nombre genérico) owl **2** *tb* **~ común** barn owl

l

lectivo -va *adj* ‹*día*› school (*before n*); ‹*año*› academic (*before n*); **tiene 30 horas lectivas al mes** she has 30 hours of classes a month

lector[1] -tora *adj* reading (*before n*)

lector[2] -tora *m,f*

A (de libros, revistas) reader

(Compuestos)

- **lector de DVD** *m* DVD player
- **lector digital/óptico** *m* digital/optical scanner

B (Esp) (Educ) foreign language assistant

lectorado *m* (Esp Educ) assistantship

lectura *f* **1** (acción) reading; **dio ~ al testamento** he read the will **2** (texto) reading matter; **~s para niños** reading material for children **3** (interpretación) interpretation, reading

leer [E13] *vt* **1** ‹*libro/texto*› to read; **~ los labios** to lip-read; **~le la mano a algn** to read sb's palm; **~le el pensamiento a algn** to read sb's mind **2** (Educ) ‹*tesis doctoral*› to defend **3** (Inf) to scan

■ **leer** *vi* to read; **no sabe ~** he can't read

■ **leerse** *v pron* (*enf*) to read

legación *f* legation

legado *m*

A (Der) bequest, legacy

B (enviado) legate

legajo *m* file, dossier

legal *adj*

A (Der) **1** ‹*trámite/documentos*› legal; **por la vía ~** through legal channels **2** (lícito, permitido) lawful; **lo haré si es ~** I'll do it as long as it's within the law

B **1** (Col, Per arg) (estupendo) great (colloq) **2** (Esp arg) (de fiar) cool (sl); **es un tío ~** he's cool

legalidad *f* (de acto, medida) legality; (conjunto de leyes) law; **la ~ vigente** current legislation

legalista[1] *adj* legalistic

legalista[2] *mf* legalist

legalización *f* (Der) (de droga, aborto) legalization; (de documento) authentication

legalizar [A4] *vt* (Der) ‹*droga/aborto*› to legalize; ‹*documento*› to authenticate

légamo *m* mud, slime

legaña *f* sleep; **una ~** a bit of sleep; **tienes ~s en los ojos** you have (some) sleep in your eyes

legañoso -sa *adj*: **con los ojos ~s** with sleep in his eyes

legar [A3] *vt* (en testamento) to bequeath, leave

legatario -ria *m,f* legatee

legendario -ria *adj* legendary

legible *adj* legible

legión *f* (Hist, Mil) legion; (multitud) crowd

(Compuesto) **Legión Extranjera** Foreign Legion

legionario[1] -ria *adj* legionary

legionario[2] *m* (romano) legionary; (de otras asociaciones) legionnaire

legionella /lexjo'nela/ *f* (bacteria) legionella bacterium; (enfermedad) Legionnaire's disease

legislación *f* legislation

legislador[1] -dora *adj* legislative (*before n*)

legislador[2] -dora *m,f* legislator

legislar [A1] *vi* to legislate

legislativas *fpl* (esp Esp) parliamentary elections (*pl*)

legislativo -va *adj* legislative (*before n*)

legislatura *f* **1** (mandato) term (of office); (año parlamentario) session **2** (AmL) (cuerpo) legislature, legislative body

legista *mf* (Der) legist, jurist; (médico) forensic expert

legitimación *f* (Der) **1** (de documento, firma) authentication **2** (de hijo) legitimization

legitimar [A1] *vt* (Der) **1** ‹*documento/firma*› to authenticate **2** ‹*hijo*› legitimize

legitimidad *f* legitimacy

legítimo -ma *adj*

A ‹*hijo*› legitimate; ‹*esposa*› lawful (*before n*); ‹*heredero*› rightful (*before n*); ‹*derechos/reclamación/representante*› legitimate; **en legítima defensa** in self-defense

B ‹*cuero*› genuine, real; ‹*oro*› real

lego[1] -ga *adj*

A (seglar) lay (*before n*)

B (ignorante) **~ EN algo**: **soy ~ en la materia** I know nothing at all about the subject

lego[2] -ga *m,f*

A (Relig) **1** (fiel laico) layperson **2** (religioso) (*m*) lay brother; (*f*) lay sister

B (Col) (curandero) quack

legrado *m* (de la matriz) D and C, scrape (colloq); (de un hueso) curettage

legua *f* league; ***a la ~*** *or* (Col, Méx) ***a ~s*** (fam): **se notaba a la ~ que ...** it was patently obvious that ...

leguleyo -ya *m,f* (pey) pettifogging lawyer

legumbre *f* (garbanzo, alubia, etc) pulse, legume; (hortaliza) vegetable

(Compuesto) **legumbres secas** pulses (*pl*)

leguminosa *f* leguminous plant

lehendakari *mf First Minister of the Basque autonomous government*

leída *f* (fam) reading; **pégale una ~ rápida** give this a quick read (through)

leído -da *adj*: **ser muy ~** to be well-read

leísmo *m*: *use of* **le/les** *instead of* **lo/los/la/las** *(as in* **este libro no te le presto***), common in certain regions of Spain*

lejanía *f* remoteness; **en la ~** in the distance

lejano -na *adj* **1** ‹*época*› distant, far-off;; ‹*lugar*› remote, far-off; **en un futuro ~** in the distant future; **en un ~ país** in a distant *o* far-away country (liter) **2** ‹*pariente*› distant

(Compuesto) **Lejano Oeste/Oriente** *m* Far West/East

lejía *f* bleach

lejísimos *adv* ‹*quedar/estar*› to be very far (away); **vive ~** she lives miles away

lejos *adv*

A **1** (en el espacio): **está** *or* **queda demasiado ~ para ir a pie** it's too far to walk; **no está muy ~** it isn't very far; **~ DE algo**: **queda ~ del centro** it's a long way from the center; **estaba ~ de imaginarme la verdad** I was far from guessing the truth **2** (*en locs*) **a lo lejos** in the distance; ***muy a lo ~*** (Chi) every now and again; **de lejos** from a distance; **no veo bien de ~** I'm shortsighted; ***llevar algo/ir demasiado ~*** to take sth/to go too far; ***sin ir más ~*** for example *o* instance **3** (fam) (con mucho): **es ~** (CS) *o* (Col, Méx) **de ~** by far, easily; **es (de) ~ la mejor** she's the best by far

B (en el futuro) a long way off; (en el pasado) a long time ago; **estamos ya ~ de aquello** that all happened a long time ago; **están ~s de alcanzar una solución** they are far from finding a solution

C (señalando contraste) **~ DE + INF** far FROM -ING; **~ de molestarle, le encantó la idea** far from being upset, he thought it was a great idea

lelo -la *adj* (fam) (tonto) dim; (pasmado) speechless

lema *m* (de insignia, de persona) motto; (de partido) slogan

(Compuesto) **lema publicitario** advertising slogan

lempira *m* lempira (*Honduran unit of currency*)

lémur *m* lemur

lencería *f* lingerie

lengua *f*

A **1** (Anat) tongue; **se me traba la ~** I get tongue-tied; ***con la ~ fuera*** (fam): **llegamos con la ~ fuera** we were dead beat when we arrived (colloq); ***darle a la ~*** (fam) to chatter; ***desatársele la ~ a algn*** to start to talk; ***irse de la ~*** *or* ***írsele la ~ a algn*** (fam): **no debía haberlo dicho pero se me fue la ~** I shouldn't have said it but it just slipped out; **no te vayas a ir de la ~** make sure you don't tell anybody; ▸**malo[1]**; ***morderse la ~*** to bite one's tongue; ***soltar la ~*** to spill the beans; ***soltarle la ~ a algn*** to make sb talk; ***¿te comieron la ~ los ratones?*** (fam & hum) has the cat got your tongue? (colloq); ***tener una ~ viperina*** to have a sharp tongue; ***tirarle de*** *or* (AmL) ***tirarle*** *or* ***jalarle la ~ a algn***: **hay que tirarle (de) la ~** you have to drag everything out of him; **sé mucho sobre ti así que no me tires (de) la ~** I know a lot about you, so don't provoke me **2** (Coc) tongue **3** (de tierra) spit, tongue; (de fuego) tongue

B (Ling) language; **~ *de trapo*** baby talk

(Compuestos)
- **lengua madre** *or* **materna** mother tongue
- **lengua muerta/viva** dead/living language

lenguas cooficiales

The regional languages of Spain, **catalán**, **euskera**, and **gallego**, which now have equal status with Castilian in the regions where they are spoken. Banned under Franco, they continued to be spoken privately. They are now widely used in public life, education, and the media, cinema and literature

lenguado *m* sole

lenguaje *m* language

(Compuestos)
- **lenguaje corporal** body language
- **lenguaje gestual** *or* **de gestos** sign language

lenguaraz *adj* insolent

lengüeta *f* (de zapato) tongue; (Mús) reed

lengüetazo *m*, **lengüetada** *f* big lick

lengüetear [A1] *vt* to lick

■ **lengüetearse** *v pron* to lick oneself

lenidad *f* (frml) lenience, leniency

lenitivo -va *adj* soothing

lenocinio *m* procuring

lente *m* [*en algunas regiones f*] lens; *ver tb* **lentes**

(Compuesto) **lente de contacto** *m or f* contact lens

lenteja *f* lentil

lentejuela *f* sequin; **un vestido de ~s** a sequined dress

lentes *mpl* (esp AmL) glasses (*pl*), spectacles (*pl*)

(Compuestos)
- **lentes bifocales** bifocals (*pl*)
- **lentes de sol** sunglasses (*pl*)
- **lentes oscuros** dark glasses (*pl*)

lentilla *f* (Esp) contact lens

lentitud *f* slowness; **con ~** slowly

lento¹ -ta *adj* 1▸ ‹*proceso/trabajador/vehículo*› slow; ‹*compás/ritmo*› slow; ‹*película/argumento*› slow-moving, slow; ‹*estudiante*› slow, slow-witted; **de combustión lenta** slow-burning 2▸ (Coc): **a fuego ~** ‹*cocinar*› over a low heat; ‹*hervir*› gently

lento² *adv* slowly; **~ pero seguro** slowly but surely

leña *f* wood, firewood; ***dar/repartir ~*** (fam): **te voy a dar ~** I'm going to give you a good hiding (colloq); **en el debate le dieron ~** he took a lot of flak in the debate (colloq); **la policía repartió ~ en la manifestación** the police laid into the demonstrators (colloq); ***echar ~ al fuego*** to add fuel to the fire; ***hacer ~ del árbol caído*** to take advantage of somebody else's misfortune; ***llevar ~ al monte*** to take coals to Newcastle

leñador -dora *m,f* woodcutter

leñazo *m* (fam) 1▸ (golpe) nasty knock (colloq) 2▸ (choque) bump (colloq)

leñera *f* woodshed

leñero -ra *adj* (fam) (Dep) dirty (colloq); **lo expulsaron por ~** he was sent off for dirty play

leño *m* log

leñoso -sa *adj* woody

Leo¹ *m* (signo) Leo; **es (de) ~** he's (a) Leo

Leo², leo *mf* (*pl* ~) (persona) Leo

león -ona *m,f* 1▸ (de África) (*m*) lion; (*f*) lioness; **es un ~ para defender sus derechos** he'll fight to the death to defend his rights; ***no es tan fiero el ~ como lo pintan*** ‹*asunto*› it is not as bad as it seems; ‹*persona*› he's/she's not as bad as he's/she's made out to be; ***echar*** *or* ***arrojar a algn a los leones*** (fam) to throw sb to the lions 2▸ (AmL) (puma) puma, cougar; ***tirar a algn de a ~*** (Méx fam) to ignore sb

(Compuesto) **león marino** sea lion

leonado -da *adj* tawny

leonera *f* 1▸ (de león) lion's den 2▸ (Esp fam) (lugar desordenado) tip (colloq)

leonino -na *adj*

A ‹*condiciones/reparto*› unfair; ‹*intereses*› excessive

B (del león) leonine

leontina *f* watch chain

leopardo *m* leopard; **~ hembra** leopardess

leotardo *m tb* **~s** (woolen) tights (*pl*)

lépero -ra *adj* (Méx) coarse

lepisma *m* silverfish

lepra *f* leprosy

leprosería *f*, (CS) **leprosario** *m* leper colony

leproso¹ -sa *adj* leprous

leproso² -sa *m,f* leper

lerdo¹ -da *adj* (fam) (torpe) clumsy; (tonto) slow

lerdo² -da *m,f* (fam) (torpe) oaf (colloq); (tonto) dimwit

les *pron pers*

A (como objeto indirecto): **~ quiero mostrar algo** (a ellos, ellas) I want to show them something; (a ustedes) I want to show you something; **~ puse fundas a los muebles** I put covers on the furniture; **pregúntales a ellas** ask them; **~ han dado un ultimátum** they've been given an ultimatum

B (como objeto directo) (esp Esp) (referido — a ellos) them; (— a ustedes) you; **no ~ reconocí** I didn't recognize them/you; **¿~ atienden?** can I help you?

lesa *adj* (Der): **delito de ~ majestad** crime of lese-majesty; **delito de ~ humanidad** crime against humanity; **delito de ~ nación** *or* **patria** offense against the state

lesbiana *f* lesbian

lesbiano -na, lésbico -ca *adj* lesbian

lesear [A1] *vi* (Chi fam) (tontear) to clown *o* fool around (colloq); (bromear) to joke (colloq); (flirtear) to flirt; (perder el tiempo) to laze around

lesera *f* (Chi fam) ▸**tontería 1, 2**

lesión *f* 1▸ (Med) injury, lesion (tech); **sufrió una ~ cerebral** he suffered brain damage 2▸ (Der) injury

lesionado¹ -da *adj* injured

lesionado² -da *m,f*: **el equipo tiene varios ~s** the team has several players injured

lesionar [A1] *vt* 1▸ ‹*persona*› to injure; ‹*pierna/rodilla*›: **le ~on la pierna en el partido** his leg was hurt *o* injured in the game 2▸ ‹*derechos*› to infringe on; ‹*intereses*› to be detrimental to

■ **lesionarse** *v pron* «*persona*» to injure oneself; ‹*pierna/rodilla*› to injure

lesivo -va *adj* (frml) detrimental; ‹*sustancia*› harmful

leso -sa *adj* (Chi fam) dumb (colloq); ***hacer ~ a algn*** (fam) to make a monkey out of sb (colloq)

letal *adj* lethal, deadly

letanía *f* 1▸ (Relig) litany 2▸ (fam) (retahíla): **empezó con su ~ de siempre** he launched into his usual spiel (colloq)

letárgico -ca *adj* lethargic

letargo *m* lethargy; **cayó en un profundo ~** he became very lethargic

letra *f*

A 1▸ (Impr, Ling) letter; ***aprender las primeras ~s*** to learn how to read and write; ***la ~ con sangre entra*** spare the rod, spoil the child 2▸ (caligrafía) writing, handwriting; **no entiendo tu ~** I can't read your writing; ***despacito y buena ~*** slowly and carefully 3▸ **letras** *fpl* (carta breve): **sólo unas ~s para decirte que ...** just a few lines to let you know that ...

(Compuestos)
- **letra bastardilla** *or* **cursiva** italic script, italics (*pl*)
- **letra de molde** *or* **imprenta** print
- **letra mayúscula/minúscula** capital/lowercase letter
- **letra negrita** *or* **negrilla** boldface, bold type
- **letra pequeña** *or* (AmS) **chica** small print

B (sentido): **la ~ de la ley** the letter of the law

C (Mús) (de canción) words (*pl*), lyrics (*pl*)

D (Fin) *tb* **~ de cambio** bill of exchange, draft; **me quedan tres ~s por pagar** I still have three payments to make

E **letras** *fpl* (Educ) arts (*pl*), liberal arts (*pl*) (AmE); **licenciado en Filosofía y L~s** ≈ arts graduate

letrado¹ -da *adj* learned

letrado² -da *m,f* (frml) lawyer

letrero *m* sign, notice

(Compuesto) **letrero luminoso** neon sign

letrina *f* latrine

letrista *mf* lyricist

leucemia *f* leukemia

leucémico -ca *m,f* leukemia* sufferer
leucocito *m* leukocyte
leucoma *m* leukoma
leva *f* 1 (Mil) levy 2 (Mec) cam
levadizo -za *adj*: **una plataforma levadiza** a platform that can be raised and lowered; ▸**puente**[1]
levadura *f* yeast; **pan sin ~** unleavened bread
Compuestos
• **levadura de cerveza** brewer's yeast
• **levadura en polvo** (Esp) baking powder
• **levadura seca/de panadero** dried/fresh yeast
levantado -da *adj*: **estar ~** to be up; **está ~ desde las siete** he's been up since seven o'clock
levantador -dora *m,f* (Dep) *tb* **~ de pesas** weightlifter
levantamiento *m*
A (sublevación) uprising
B (de embargo, sanción) lifting
C (de cadáver) removal; (Geol) uplifting
Compuesto **levantamiento de pesas** weightlifting
levantar [A1] *vt*
A 1 (del suelo) ‹*bulto/peso*› to lift, pick up 2 ‹*tapadera/mantel*› to lift; ‹*cabeza/mano*› to raise; **levanta la alfombra** lift up the rug; **levanté la mano para contestar** I put up *o* raised my hand to answer 3 ‹*persiana*› to pull up, raise; **~on las copas para brindar** they raised their glasses in a toast 4 **sin ~ la vista del libro** without looking up from her book; **levantó la mirada hacia el cielo** he raised his eyes to heaven 5 ‹*voz*› to raise; ‹*polvo*› to raise 6 (Jueg) ‹*carta*› to pick up
B 1 ‹*ánimo*› to boost; ‹*moral*› to raise, boost; **¡levanta el ánimo!** cheer up! 2 ‹*industria/economía*› to help … to pick up; **conseguimos ~ este país** we got this country back on its feet
C ‹*estatua/muro/edificio*› to erect, put up
D ‹*embargo/sanción*› to lift; ‹*huelga*› to call off; **le levantó el castigo** he let him off; **se levanta la sesión** the meeting is adjourned
E ‹*rumor/protestas*› to spark (off); ‹*polémica*› to cause; **~ sospechas** to arouse suspicion
F (Der) 1 ‹*acta*› to prepare; **~ atestado de algo** to write a report on sth 2 ‹*cadáver*› to remove
G ‹*censo*› to take
H (desmontar, deshacer) ‹*campamento*› to strike; **~ la cama** to strip the bed; **~ la mesa** (AmL) to clear the table
I 1 (en brazos) ‹*niño*› to pick up 2 (de la cama) to get … out of bed 3 (poner de pie) to get … up; **ayúdame a ~lo de la silla** help me to get him up out of the chair; **el discurso levantó al público de sus asientos** the speech brought the audience to its feet
A (fam) 1 (robar) to lift (colloq); **me levantó la novia** he stole my girlfriend 2 (AmS) ‹*mujer*› to pick up (colloq)
■ **levantarse** *v pron*
A 1 (de la cama) to get up; ▸**pie A2** 2 (ponerse en pie) to stand up, to rise (frml); **¿me puedo ~ de la mesa?** may I leave the table?
B «*polvareda*» to rise; «*temporal*» to brew; **se levantó un viento muy fuerte** a strong wind began to blow
C «*torre/edificio*» (erguirse) to rise
D «*pintura*» to peel
E (sublevarse) to rise (up)
F (refl) ‹*solapas/cuello*› to turn up
G (AmS fam) ‹*mujer*› to pick up (colloq)
levante *m*
A 1 (Geog) (este) east; **viento de ~** easterly wind 2 (viento) east wind
B (AmS fam) (conquista) pick up; **salieron de ~** they went out trying to pick up (colloq)
levantisco -ca *adj* (liter) rebellious
levar [A1] *vt*: **~ anclas** to weigh anchor
leve *adj*
A 1 ‹*perfume/gasa*› delicate 2 ‹*sospecha/duda*› slight; ‹*sonrisa*› slight; ‹*brisa*› gentle, slight; ‹*golpe*› gentle, light; ‹*enfermedad*› mild
B ‹*pecado*› venial; ‹*castigo/sanción*› light; ‹*herida/lesión*› slight; ‹*infracción*› minor
levedad *f* lightness
levemente *adv* (un poco) slightly; (superficialmente) lightly
levita *f* (Indum) frock coat
levitación *f* levitation
levitar [A1] *vi* to levitate
lexema *m* lexeme
léxico[1] **-ca** *adj* lexical
léxico[2] *m* (vocabulario) vocabulary, lexis (tech); (diccionario) lexicon; (glosario) glossary, lexicon
lexicografía *f* lexicography
lexicógrafo -fa *m,f* lexicographer
ley *f*
A (disposición legal) law; **conforme a la ~** in accordance with the law; **aplicar una ~** to apply a law; **violar la ~** to break the law; **atenerse a la ~** to obey the law; ***es ~ de vida*** it is a fact of life; ***hacerle la ~ del hielo a algn*** (Chi, Méx) to give sb the cold shoulder; ***la ~ de la selva*** *or* ***de la jungla*** the law of the jungle; ***la ~ del más fuerte*** the survival of the fittest; ***la ~ del mínimo esfuerzo*** the line of least resistance; ***la ~ del talión*** an eye for an eye; ***morir en su ~*** (Andes) to die as one lived; ***quien hace la ~ hace la trampa*** every law has a loophole; ***~ pareja no es dura*** (CS) a rule isn't unfair if it applies to everyone
Compuestos
• **ley de fuga** (Col, Méx): **aplicarle a algn la ~ de ~** *the practice of allowing a prisoner to escape and then proceeding to shoot him in the back*
• **ley del embudo** unfair law/rule
• **ley seca**: **la ~ ~** Prohibition
B (justicia): **la ~** the law; **somos iguales ante la ~** we are equal in the eyes of the law; **un representante de la ~** a representative of the law; ***con todas las de la ~***: **ganó con todas las de la ~** she won very deservedly; **una comida con todas las de la ~** a proper meal; **una democracia con todas las de la ~** a fully-fledged democracy
Compuesto **ley marcial/sálica** martial/Salic law
C (Fís) law
Compuesto **ley de la oferta y la demanda** law of supply and demand
D (de oro, plata) assay value; ***de buena ~*** genuine
leyenda *f*
A (Lit) (narración) legend
Compuesto **leyenda negra** *unfavorable interpretation of Spain's colonizing role in the Americas*
B (de moneda, escudo) legend; (de ilustración) caption, legend
leyeron, leyó, etc *see* **leer**
liado -da *adj* (fam) 1 (ocupado) tied up; **~ CON algo** tied up WITH sth (colloq) 2 (relacionado) **~ CON algn** involved WITH sb
liana *f* liana
liante -ta *m,f* (Esp fam) smooth talker (colloq)
liar [A17] *vt*
A 1 ‹*cigarrillo*› to roll 2 (atar) to tie (up); (envolver) to wrap (up); (en un fardo, manojo) to bundle (up)
B (fam) 1 ‹*situación/asunto*› to complicate; ***~la*** (Esp fam) to goof (colloq) 2 (confundir) ‹*persona*› to confuse, get … in a muddle 3 (en un asunto) ‹*persona*› to involve
■ **liarse** *v pron*
A (fam) 1 «*asunto*» to get complicated 2 «*persona*» to get confused
B (Esp fam) (entretenerse): **nos liamos a hablar y …** we got talking and …; **me lié a comprobar los datos** I got held up checking the statistics; ***~se a patadas*** (Esp fam): **se ~on a patadas** they started kicking each other
libanés -nesa *adj/m,f* Lebanese
Líbano *m*: *tb* **el ~** Lebanon
libar [A1] *vt* ‹*néctar*› to suck
libelo *m* 1 (Der) (petición) petition; (demanda) lawsuit 2 (escrito difamatorio) libelous* article
libélula *f* dragonfly
liberación *f*
A (de preso, rehén) release, freeing; (de pueblo, país) liberation
Compuesto **liberación de la mujer**: **la ~ de la ~** Women's Liberation, Women's Lib
B (de precios) deregulation; (de recursos) release
C (de energía, calor) release
liberacionista *adj*
A ‹*movimiento*› women's liberation (*before n*)
B (Pol): *of the Partido de Liberación Nacional de Costa Rica*
liberado -da *adj* ‹*mujer*› liberated

liberador -dora *adj* liberating (*before n*)

liberal¹ *adj* liberal

liberal² *mf* Liberal

liberalidad *f* (liberalismo) liberalism; (generosidad) generosity, liberality (frml)

liberalismo *m* liberalism

liberalización *f* liberalization; **la ~ del comercio exterior** the relaxing of restrictions on foreign trade; **hubo una total ~ de los precios** price controls were removed

liberalizar [A4] *vt* ‹*comercio/importaciones*› to relax the restrictions on; **~ el transporte aéreo** to deregulate air fares and routes

■ **liberalizarse** *v pron* to become more liberal

liberar [A1] *vt*

A 1 ‹*preso/rehén*› to release, free; ‹*pueblo/país*› to liberate; **la policía logró ~ a los rehenes** the police managed to free the hostages 2 (de una obligación) **~ a algn DE algo** to free sb FROM sth

B ‹*precios*› to deregulate; ‹*recursos/fondos*› to release

C ‹*energía/calor*› to release

■ **liberarse** *v pron* **~se DE algo** ‹*de ataduras/deudas*› to free oneself FROM sth; **~se de los prejuicios** to get rid of one's prejudices

líbero *m* sweeper

libertad *f*

A (para decidir, elegir) freedom; **tiene plena ~ para actuar** he is at complete liberty to act; **queda usted en ~** you are free to go; **dejar/poner a algn en ~** to release sb; **exigen la ~ de los prisioneros** they are demanding the release of the prisoners

(Compuestos)

- **libertad bajo fianza** *or* **provisional** bail
- **libertad condicional** parole
- **libertad de cátedra** academic freedom
- **libertad de expresión/de prensa** freedom of speech/of the press

B **libertades** *fpl* (derechos) rights (*pl*)

C (confianza): **pídelo con toda ~** feel free to ask; **habla con toda ~** speak freely; **tomarse la ~ de hacer algo** to take the liberty of doing sth; **tomarse ~es** to take liberties

libertador¹ -dora *adj* liberating (*before n*)

libertador² -dora *m,f* liberator; **el L~** the Liberator (*title given to certain historical figures, esp Simón Bolívar*)

libertar [A1] *vt* to liberate, set … free

libertario¹ -ria *adj*

A (anarquista) libertarian

B (AmL) (libertador) liberating (*before n*); **guerra libertaria** war of liberation

libertario² -ria *m,f*

A (anarquista) libertarian

B (AmL) (libertador) liberator

libertinaje *m* licentiousness

libertino¹ -na *adj* dissolute, licentious

libertino² -na *m,f* libertine

Libia *f* Libya

libidinoso -sa *adj* lustful, libidinous (liter)

libido, líbido *f* libido

libio -bia *adj/m,f* Libyan

libra *f*

A (Fin) pound

(Compuesto) **libra esterlina** pound sterling

B (peso) pound

Libra¹ *m* (signo) Libra; **es (de) ~** she's (a) Libra, she's a Libran

Libra², libra *mf* (*pl* ~ *or* **-bras**) (persona) Libran, Libra

librado¹ -da *adj*

A (Fin): **el banco ~** the issuing bank

B 1 (dependiente) **~ A algo**: **queda ~ a tu discreción** I leave it to your discretion 2 **salir bien/mal ~ de algo** to come out of something well/badly

librado² *m* drawee

librador -dora *m,f* drawer

libramiento *m*

A (Fin) order of payment

B (Méx) (Transp) beltway (AmE), relief road (BrE)

libranza *f* (Fin) order of payment

librar [A1] *vt*

A (liberar) **~ a algn DE algo** ‹*de peligro*› to save sb FROM sth; ‹*de obligación*› to free sb FROM sth **líbranos del mal** (Relig) deliver us from evil; **¡Dios nos libre!** God forbid!; **esto me libra de toda responsabilidad** this absolves me *o* frees me from all responsibility

B ‹*batalla/combate*› to fight

C ‹*letra/cheque*› to draw, issue; ‹*sentencia*› to pass

■ **librarse** *v pron*: **se libró por poco** he had a lucky escape; **~se DE algo** ‹*de tarea/obligación*› to get out of sth; **me libré del servicio militar** I got out of doing military service (colloq); **~se de un castigo** to escape punishment; **~se DE algn** to get rid OF sb; **~se DE + INF** to get out of -ING; **se libró de tener que ayudarlo** she got out of having to help him; **se ~on de morir asfixiados** they escaped being suffocated

libre *adj*

A ‹*país/pueblo*› free; **lo dejaron ~** they set him free; **~ DE + INF** free to + INF; **eres ~ de ir donde quieras** you're free to go wherever you want

(Compuestos)

- **libre albedrío** *m* free will
- **libre cambio** *or* **comercio** *m* free trade
- **libre empresa/mercado** *m* free market

B 1 ‹*traducción/adaptación*› free; **los 200 metros ~s** the 200 meters freestyle 2 ‹*estudiante*› external; **trabajar por ~** to work freelance; ***ir por ~*** (Esp fam) to do as one pleases

C (no ocupado) ‹*persona/tiempo/asiento*› free; **¿tienes un rato ~?** do you have a (spare) moment?; **en sus ratos ~s** in her spare time; **tengo el día ~** I have the day off; **¿está ~ el cuarto de baño?** is the bathroom free?

D (exento, no sujeto) **~ DE algo**: **la empresa queda ~ de toda responsabilidad** the company does not accept any responsibility; **artículos ~s de impuestos** duty-free goods; **nadie está ~ de que le pase una cosa así** something like that could happen to any of us

librea *f* livery

librecambio *m* free trade

librecambista¹ *adj* free-trade (*before n*)

librecambista² *mf* free trader

librepensador -dora *m,f* freethinker

librería *f*

A (tienda) bookstore (AmE), bookshop (BrE)

(Compuesto) **librería de viejo** *or* **de ocasión** second-hand bookstore

B (Esp) (mueble) bookcase

librero -ra *m,f* 1 (Com) bookseller 2 **librero** *m* (Chi, Méx) (mueble) bookcase

libreta *f* notebook

(Compuestos)

- **libreta de ahorro** passbook, bankbook
- **libreta de calificaciones** (AmL) school report

libretearse [A1] *v pron* (AmC fam) to play hooky (esp AmE colloq), to skive off (school) (BrE colloq)

libretista *mf* 1 (de ópera) librettist 2 (AmL) (guionista) scriptwriter

libreto *m*

A 1 (de ópera) libretto 2 (AmL) (guión) script

B (Chi) *tb* **~ de cheques** checkbook*

libro *m*

A (Impr) book; **un ~ de arquitectura** a book on architecture; **un ~ de cocina** a cookbook; ***colgar los ~*** to quit (AmE) *o* (BrE) give up studying; ***ser (como) un ~ abierto***: **eres un ~ abierto** I can read you like a book

B **libros** *mpl* (Fin): **llevar los ~** to do the bookkeeping

C (Lit) (parte) book

(Compuestos)

- **libro animado** *or* **móvil** pop-up book
- **libro blanco** consultation document
- **libro de actas/pedidos/reclamaciones** minute/order/complaints book
- **libro de bolsillo** paperback
- **libro de caja** cashbook
- **libro de consulta** reference book
- **libro de cuentos** book of short stories
- **libro de escolaridad** school record

l

- **libro de familia** *booklet recording details of one's marriage, children's birthdates, etc*
- **libro de texto** textbook
- **libro de visitas** visitors' book

Lic. = **licenciado/licenciada**

liceal *mf* (Ur) high school student (AmE), secondary school pupil (BrE)

liceano -na *m,f* (Chi) ▸**liceal**

liceísta *mf* (Ven) ▸**liceal**

licencia *f*

A (documento) license*

(Compuestos)

- **licencia de armas** gun permit (AmE), gun licence (BrE)
- **licencia de caza** hunting permit
- **licencia de conducir** *or* (AmC, Méx, Ven) **de manejar** driver's license* (AmE), driving licence (BrE)
- **licencia de exportación/importación** export/import license*
- **licencia de obras** planning permission
- **licencia de pesca** fishing license* *o* permit
- **licencia internacional de conducir** international driver's license (AmE) *o* driving licence (BrE)

B 1 (frml) (permiso, beneplácito) permission 2 (ant) (libertad, confianza) liberty

(Compuesto) **licencia poética** poetic license*

C 1 (Mil) leave; **con ~** on leave 2 (AmL) (de un trabajo) leave; **estar de ~** to be on leave

(Compuestos)

- **licencia absoluta** absolute discharge
- **licencia por enfermedad/maternidad** (RPl) sick/maternity leave

licenciado -da *m,f* 1 (Educ) graduate; **~ en Filosofía y Letras** ≈ arts *o* (AmE) liberal arts graduate 2 (AmC, Méx) (abogado) lawyer

licenciamiento *m* discharge

licenciar [A1] *vt* to discharge

■ **licenciarse** *v pron* to graduate; **~se en Arte** to get *o* (AmE) earn a degree in Art

licenciatura *f* degree

licencioso -sa *adj* dissolute

liceo *m* (CS, Ven) high school (AmE), secondary school (BrE)

licitación *f* (esp AmL) tender; **se llamará a ~ para la construcción del puente** the construction of the bridge will be put out to tender

licitar [A1] *vt* (esp AmL) (llamar a concurso para) to invite tenders for; (presentar una propuesta para) to put in a tender for

lícito -ta *adj* 1 (dentro de la ley) ‹*acto/conducta*› legal, lawful; ‹*jugada*› legal 2 (admisible) justifiable

licor *m* (bebida dulce) liqueur; (alcohol) liquor, spirits (*pl*)

licorera *f* 1 (botella) decanter 2 (Col) (fábrica) distillery

licorería *f* (fábrica) distillery; (tienda) liquor store (AmE), off-licence (BrE)

licuado *m* (AmL) (con leche) (milk) shake; (de frutas) fruit drink

licuadora *f* blender, liquidizer (BrE)

licuar [A18] *vt* 1 (Coc) ‹*frutas/verduras*› to blend, liquidize 2 (Fís, Quím) to liquefy

licuefacción *f* liquefaction

lid *f*

A (liter) (combate) fight, combat; (discusión) wrangle, dispute; ***en buena* ~** fair and square

B **lides** *fpl* (actividades, asuntos) matters (*pl*)

líder¹ *mf*

A 1 (Dep, Pol) leader 2 (Com) leader

(Compuestos)

- **líder de la oposición** leader of the opposition
- **líder sindical** labor* leader, trade union leader (BrE)

B (*como adj*) ‹*equipo/marca/empresa*› leading (*before n*)

líder² lideresa *m,f* (Méx) (Dep, Pol) leader

liderar [A1] *vt* to lead, head

liderazgo, liderato *m* leadership; **ostentaba el ~ del partido** she was the leader of the party; **recuperó el ~ de la carrera** he regained the lead in the race

lidia *f* bullfighting; ***dar* ~** (Col): **¡qué ~ dan estos niños!** these children are a real handful!

lidiador -dora *m,f* bullfighter

lidiar [A1] *vt* to fight

■ **lidiar** *vi*: **~ CON algn/algo** to battle WITH sb/sth

liebre *f*

A (Zool) hare; ***cuando/donde menos se piensa, salta la* ~** things often happen when you least expect them to; ***levantar la* ~** to let the cat out of the bag

B (Dep) pacemaker

C (Chi) (Transp) small bus

liendre *f* nit

lienzo *m*

A 1 (Art) canvas 2 (Tex) cloth

B (Arquit) (pared) wall

lifting /'liftin/ *m* facelift

liga *f*

A (asociación, agrupación) league; (Dep) league, conference (esp AmE)

B 1 (Indum) garter 2 (AmL) (gomita) rubber *o* elastic band

C (para cazar) birdlime

ligado *adj* [ESTAR] connected, linked; **~ A algn/algo** attached TO sb/sth; **se siente muy ~ a su país** he feels a strong bond with his country; **personajes ~s al anterior gobierno** figures who have links with the previous government

ligadura *f* 1 (Med) ligature; (Mús) slur, ligature (tech); (Náut) lashing 2 **ligaduras** *fpl* (ataduras) bonds (*pl*), ties (*pl*)

(Compuesto) **ligadura de trompas**: **le hicieron una ~ de ~** she had a tubal ligation (tech), she had her tubes tied (colloq)

ligamento *m* ligament

ligar [A3] *vt*

A (unir, vincular) to bind

B (atar): **le ~on las manos** they tied his hands together; **un fajo de billetes ligados con una gomita** a bundle of bills held together with a rubber band

C ‹*metales*› to alloy; ‹*salsa*› to bind

■ **ligar** *vi* (fam) (con el sexo opuesto): **salieron a ~** they went out on the make *o* (BrE) pull (colloq); **~ CON algn** to make out WITH sb (AmE), to get off WITH sb (BrE)

■ **ligarse** *v pron*

A (fam) (conquistar) to make out with (AmE colloq), to get off with (colloq BrE)

B «*salsa*» to bind

ligazón *f* connection, link; **un texto incoherente, sin ~** an incoherent passage, without any unifying theme

ligeramente *adv* 1 (un poco) ‹*cambiar/mejorar*› slightly; **se sintió ~ mareado** he felt slightly dizzy; **sabe ~ a pescado** it has a slight taste of fish; **tostar ~ en el horno** brown lightly in the oven 2 (superficialmente) ‹*tocar*› lightly, gently; ‹*juzgar*› casually, hastily; **esto no se debe tratar ~** this shouldn't be taken lightly

ligereza *f*

A (de objeto) lightness

B 1 (de carácter) flippancy; **actuó/habló con ~** he acted/spoke flippantly 2 (acto, dicho irreflexivo): **cometió la ~ de mencionarlo** he thoughtlessly mentioned it

C (agilidad) agility, nimbleness

D (rapidez) speed

ligero¹ -ra *adj*

A (liviano) 1 ‹*paquete/gas/metal*› light; ‹*tela*› light, thin; **~ como una pluma** (as) light as a feather; **material ~** lightweight material 2 **~ DE algo**: **salió muy ligera de ropa** she went out very lightly dressed; **viajar ~ de equipaje** to travel light 3 ‹*comida/masa*› light; **comer algo ~** to have a snack

B (leve) 1 ‹*dolor/sabor/olor*› slight; ‹*inconveniente*› slight, minor; ‹*golpe*› gentle, slight; **un ~ perfume a rosas** a delicate scent of roses; **tener el sueño ~** to be a light sleeper 2 ‹*noción/sensación/sospecha*› slight

C 1 (no serio) ‹*conversación*› lighthearted; ‹*película/lectura*› lightweight; **en tono ~** lightheartedly 2 (frívolo): **una mujer ligera** (ant) a woman of easy virtue (dated *or* hum); ***a la ligera*** ‹*actuar*› without thinking, hastily; **todo se lo toma a la ligera** he doesn't take anything seriously

D (ágil) ‹*movimiento*› agile, nimble

E (rápido) ‹*persona/animal/vehículo*› fast; **es ~ como el viento** he runs like the wind

ligero² *adv* quickly, fast

light /lajt/ *adj inv* ‹*cigarrillos*› low-tar; ‹*alimentos*› low-calorie; ‹*refresco*› diet (*before n*)

ligón -gona *m,f* (Esp fam): **chica ¡qué ligona!** you always seem to have a new man in tow! (colloq); **es un ~ de cuidado** he's a real womanizer

ligue *m* (Esp, Méx fam) 1 (persona): **el nuevo ~ de Ana** Ana's new man (colloq) 2 (acción): **estar en el/ir de ~** to be on/to go out on the make *o* (BrE) pull

liguero[1] **-ra** *adj* league (*before n*)

liguero[2] *m* garter belt (AmE), suspender belt (BrE)

liguilla *f* (Esp) pool, minileague

lija *f*

A 1 (para madera, metales) *tb* **papel de ~** sandpaper 2 (Ven) ▸**lima 1B**

B (Zool) dogfish

lijadora *f* sander

lijar [A1] *vt* to sand (down)

lila[1] *f* (Bot) lilac

lila[2] *adj* (*gen inv*) ‹*color*› lilac

lila[3] *m* (color) lilac

liliácea *f* liliaceous plant

lima *f*

A 1 (herramienta) file 2 (para uñas — de metal) nail file; (—de papel) emery board

B (Bot) (fruto) lime; (árbol) lime (tree)

Lima *f* Lima

limadura *f* filing

limar [A1] *vt* 1 ‹*uñas/metal*› to file; **los prisioneros ~on los barrotes** the prisoners filed through the bars 2 ‹*obra/texto*› to polish

■ **limarse** *v pron* to file

limbo *m* 1 (Relig) limbo; ***estar en el ~*** to be in a dreamworld 2 (Bot, Astron) limb

limeño[1] **-ña** *adj* of/from Lima

limeño[2] **-ña** *m,f* person from Lima

limero *m* lime tree

limitación *f*

A (restricción) restriction, limitation; **sin limitaciones** with no restrictions; **sin limitaciones de tiempo** with no time limit; **ejerce el poder sin limitaciones** he exercises unlimited power

B (carencia) limitation; (defecto) shortcoming

limitado -da *adj*

A 1 (restringido) ‹*poder/tiempo/edición*› limited; **una visa por tiempo ~** a temporary visa; **estar ~ A/POR algo** to be restricted TO/BY sth 2 (escaso) limited; **algunos casos ~s** a few isolated cases

B ‹*persona*› slow-witted; **es un estudiante bastante ~** he's a student of limited ability

limitar [A1] *vt* ‹*funciones/derechos*› to limit, restrict; **le han limitado las salidas a dos días por mes** he's restricted to going out twice a month

■ **limitar** *vi* **~ CON algo** to border ON sth; **España limita al oeste con Portugal** Spain is bounded by Portugal to the west

■ **limitarse** *v pron* **~se A algo**: **el problema no se limita únicamente a las ciudades** the problem is not just confined *o* limited to cities; **me limité a repetir lo que tú habías dicho** I just repeated what you'd said; **limítate a hacerlo** just do it

límite *m*

A (Geog, Pol) boundary

B 1 (cifra máxima) limit; **el ~ de velocidad** the speed limit; **poner un ~ a algo** to limit *o* restrict sth 2 (tope, extremo) limit; **no tener ~** to know no limits; **bondad sin ~s** unlimited *o* boundless goodness; **la situación llegó a ~s insostenibles** the situation became untenable; **¡todo tiene un ~!** enough is enough!

C (*como adj inv*): **tiempo ~** time limit; **situación ~** extreme situation; **fecha ~** deadline

limítrofe *adj* ‹*país/provincia*› neighboring* (*before n*); ‹*conflicto*› border (*before n*)

limo *m*

A (barro) mud, slime

B (Col) (Bot) lime (tree)

limón *m* 1 (fruto amarillo) lemon 2 (AmL) (árbol) lemon tree 3 (Méx, Ven) (fruto verde) lime

limonada *f* lemonade

limonero *m* lemon tree

limosna *f* alms (*pl*) (arch): **pedir ~** to beg; **viven de ~s** they live off begging; **dar ~** to give money to beggars

limosnear [A1] *vi* (AmL) to beg

limosnera *f*, **limosnero** *m* purse

limosnero -ra *m,f* (AmL) beggar

limpia *f*: **hizo una ~ en el personal** he made sweeping staff cuts

limpiabotas *mf* (*pl* ~) bootblack; (niño) shoeshine boy

limpiacristales *m* (Esp) 1 (líquido) window cleaner 2 **limpiacristales** *mf* (persona) window cleaner

limpiada *f* clean; **dale una ~ a la mesa** give the table a wipe *o* clean

limpiador[1] **-dora** *adj* cleansing (*before n*)

limpiador[2] **-dora** *m,f*

A (persona) cleaner

B **limpiador** *m* (Méx) (Auto) ▸**limpiaparabrisas**

limpiamente *adv* honestly; **le quité el balón ~** I took the ball off him cleanly *o* fairly

limpiametales *m* (*pl* ~) metal polish

limpiamuebles *m* (*pl* ~) furniture polish

limpiaparabrisas *m* (*pl* ~) windshield wipers (*pl*) (AmE), windscreen wipers (*pl*) (BrE)

limpiar [A1] *vt*

A 1 ‹*casa/mueble/zapatos*› to clean; ‹*arroz/lentejas*› to wash; ‹*pescado*› to clean; **lo limpió con un trapo** he wiped it with a cloth; **~ algo en** *or* **a seco** to dry-clean sth; **le tuve que ~ las narices** I had to wipe his nose; **la lluvia limpió el aire** the rain cleared the air 2 ‹*nombre*› to clear; ‹*honor*› to restore

B (dejar libre) **~ algo DE algo** to clear sth OF sth

C (fam) 1 (en el juego) ‹*persona*› to clean … out (colloq) 2 «*ladrones*» ‹*casa*› to clean … out (colloq)

■ **limpiar** *vi* to clean

■ **limpiarse** *v pron* (*refl*) ‹*boca/manos/nariz*› to wipe; **se ~on los zapatos al entrar** they wiped their shoes as they came in

limpiavidrios *mf*

A (esp AmL) (persona) window cleaner

B **limpiavidrios** *m* (líquido) window cleaner

límpido -da *adj* (liter) limpid (liter)

limpieza *f*

A (estado, cualidad) cleanliness

B (acción) cleaning; **él se encarga de la ~** he does the cleaning; **la señora de la ~** the cleaning lady

(Compuestos)

- **limpieza de cutis** skin cleansing
- **limpieza en** *or* **a seco** drycleaning
- **limpieza general** spring-cleaning (AmE), spring-clean (BrE)

C (honradez, rectitud): **las elecciones se llevaron a cabo con ~** the elections were conducted fairly; **se jugó con ~** it was a clean match

D (por la policía) clean-up operation; (Pol) purge

(Compuesto) **limpieza étnica** ethnic cleansing

limpio[1] **-pia** *adj*

A 1 [ESTAR] ‹*casa/vestido/vaso*› clean 2 ‹*aire*› clean; **un cielo ~, sin nubes** a clear, cloudless sky 3 **pasar algo en** *or* (Esp) **a ~** to make a fresh copy of sth

B [SER] ‹*persona*› clean

C 1 [SER] ‹*dinero/campaña*› clean; ‹*elecciones/juego*› fair, clean; **un asunto poco ~** an underhand business 2 (libre) **~ DE algo** ‹*de impurezas/polvo*› free OF sth

D 1 ‹*perfil/imagen*› well-defined, clean; ‹*corte*› clean

E (neto): **saca unos $70 ~s por mes** she makes $70 a month after deductions; ***sacar en ~***: **no pude sacar nada en ~ de todo lo que dijo** I couldn't make sense of anything he said; **lo único que saqué en ~ es que ...** the only thing that I got clear was that …

F (fam) (uso enfático): **terminó a puñetazo ~** it degenerated into a fistfight

G (fam) (sin dinero) broke (colloq); **me dejaron ~** they cleaned me out (colloq)

limpio[2] *adv* ‹*jugar/pelear*› fairly, clean

limusina *f* limousine

linaje *m* descent, lineage (frml); **de noble ~** of noble descent

linaza *f* linseed

lince *m* (Zool) lynx; (persona): **es un ~ para los negocios** he's a very shrewd businessman

linchamiento *m* lynching

linchar [A1] *vt* to lynch

lindamente *adv*

A (iro) (tranquilamente) just like that; **le levantó ~ la novia** he swiped his girlfriend just like that *o* as cool as you please (colloq)

B (esp AmL) (muy bien) beautifully; **habitaciones ~ decoradas** beautifully decorated rooms

lindante *adj* adjoining; **~ con algo** adjoining sth

lindar [A1] *vi* 1 (limitar) **~ con algo** to adjoin sth; **el parque linda con la carretera** the park runs alongside the road 2 (asemejarse) **~ con algo** to border ON sth, verge ON sth

linde *m or f* (liter) boundary; **en los ~s del bosque** on the edges of the forest

lindero[1] **-ra** *adj* adjoining; **~ con algo** adjoining sth

lindero[2] *m* (frml) (de terreno) boundary

lindezas *fpl* (iró) (insolencias) nasty comments (*pl*)

lindo[1] **-da** *adj*

A (bonito) ‹*bebé*› cute, sweet; ‹*casa/canción*› lovely; **es muy linda de cara** she has a very pretty face; **ese vestido te queda muy ~** (AmL) you look very nice in that dress

B (esp AmL) (agradable) ‹*gesto/detalle*› nice; **la fiesta estuvo lindísima** it was a wonderful party; **fue una linda ceremonia** it was a beautiful ceremony; **¡es una persona tan linda!** she's such a lovely person; ▸**gente**[3]**A**; ***de lo ~*** (fam): **nos reímos de lo ~** we laughed till we cried; **nos divertimos de lo ~** we had a great time

lindo[2] *adv* (AmL) ‹*cantar/bailar*› beautifully; **se siente ~** (Méx) it feels wonderful

lindura *f* (AmL) delight; **me pareció una ~** I thought it was lovely

línea *f*

A 1 (raya) line; **la ~ del horizonte** the horizon; **cortar por la ~ de puntos** cut along the dotted line 2 (Art) (dibujo, trazo) line 3 (de cocaína) (fam) line (colloq)

(Compuesto) **línea de demarcación/flotación** demarcation/water line

B (Dep) 1 (en fútbol) line; **~ de gol** *or* **de fondo** goal line 2 (en béisbol) drive

(Compuestos)
- **línea de banda** sideline, touchline
- **línea de contacto** *or* **golpeo** line of scrimmage
- **línea de llegada** finishing line, wire (AmE)
- **línea de salida** starting line

C 1 (renglón) line; ***leer entre ~s*** to read between the lines 2 **líneas** *fpl* (carta breve): **escribirle unas ~s a algn** to drop sb a line

D (fila, alineación) line; ***de primera ~*** ‹*tecnología*› state-of-the-art; ‹*producto*› top-quality, high-class; ‹*actor/jugador*› first-rate; ***en primera ~***: **sigue en primera ~** she/he still ranks among the best

E 1 (Transp): **no hay ~ directa** there is no direct service; **final de la ~** end of the line; **no hay servicio en la ~ 5** (de autobuses) there are no buses operating on the number 5 bus route; (de metro) there is no service on line 5 2 (Elec, Telec) line; **~ telefónica** telephone line; **no hay ~** *or* **no me da ~** the phone *o* the line is dead; **la ~ está ocupada** the line is busy 3 (en genealogía) line; **por ~ materna** on his (*o* her *etc*) mother's side 4 (Arg) (de pescar) line

(Compuestos)
- **línea aérea** airline
- **línea de montaje** assembly line
- **línea férrea** railroad track (AmE), railway line (BrE)
- **línea regular** airline (*operating scheduled flights*)

F (sobre un tema) line; **seguir la ~ del partido** to follow the party line; **las principales ~s de su programa político** the main points of their political program; **en la ~ de ...** along the lines of ...; **en ~s generales** broadly speaking

G 1 (estilo, diseño): **un coche de ~s aerodinámicas** a streamlined car; **ésta es la ~ de moda** this is the in *o* fashionable look; **una ~ más clásica** a more classical look 2 (gama, colección) line; **nuestra nueva ~ de cosméticos** our new line *o* range of cosmetics

(Compuesto) **línea blanca** white goods (*pl*)

H (figura): **mantener/cuidar la ~** to keep/watch one's figure

lineal *adj* linear

linfático -ca *adj* lymphatic, lymph (*before n*)

lingo *m* (Per) leapfrog

lingote *m* ingot; **~ de oro** gold ingot

lingüista *mf* linguist

lingüística *f* linguistics

lingüístico -ca *adj* ‹*fenómeno/aptitud*› linguistic; ‹*barrera*› language (*before n*)

linimento *m* liniment

lino *m* (planta) flax; (tela) linen; (linaza) (AmL) linseed

linóleo *m* lino, linoleum

linotipia *f* (sistema) Linotype®; (taller) typesetter's

linotipo *m* (máquina) Linotype®; (plancha) linotype

linterna *f* (fanal) lantern; (de pilas) flashlight (AmE), torch (BrE)

linyera *mf* (CS) 1 (fam) (vagabundo) drifter 2 **linyera** *f* (atado) bundle, pack

lío *m*

A 1 (fam) (embrollo, confusión) mess; **¡qué ~!** what a mess!; **hacerse un ~ con algo** to get into a mess with sth (colloq) 2 (fam) (problema, complicación): **tiene ~s con la policía** he's in trouble with the police (colloq); **no me vengas con tus ~s** don't come to me with your problems; **¡qué ~ se va a armar!** there's going to be hell to pay! (colloq); **armó un ~** he kicked up a fuss (colloq); **meterse en un ~** to get oneself into trouble 3 (fam) (amorío) affair

B (fardo) bundle

lioso -sa *adj* (fam) confusing, muddling

lípido *m* lipid

liposucción *f* liposuction

lipotimia *f* blackout

liquen *m* lichen

liquidación *f*

A (en tienda) sale; Ⓢ **liquidación total** clearance sale; Ⓢ **liquidación de existencias** stock clearance; Ⓢ **liquidación por cierre** closeout sale (AmE), closing down sale (BrE)

B (de negocio, activo) liquidation

C 1 (de cuenta, deuda) settlement, liquidation (frml) 2 (cálculo): **preparó la ~ de mis impuestos** he worked out my tax return; **hice la ~ de lo que correspondía a cada uno** I worked out how much was due to each person 3 (Méx) (compensación por despido) severance pay

D (fam) (eliminación) liquidation

E (Quím) liquefaction

liquidar [A1] *vt*

A ‹*existencias*› to sell off

B ‹*negocio*› to wind up; ‹*activo*› to liquidate

C 1 ‹*deuda*› to settle, clear; ‹*cuenta*› to settle; ‹*sueldo/pago*› to pay; **me ~on lo que me debían** they paid me what they owed me 2 (Méx) ‹*trabajador*› to pay ... off

D (fam) 1 ‹*persona*› (matar) to do away with (colloq); (destruir) (AmL) to destroy (colloq) 2 ‹*trabajo/comida*› to polish off (colloq); ‹*dinero*› to blow (colloq); **se lo mandas y asunto liquidado** you just send it to her and ... problem solved!

■ **liquidarse** *v pron* (*enf*) (acabar con) (fam) ‹*dinero*› to blow (colloq); ‹*comida*› to polish off (colloq)

liquidez *f* liquidity; **problemas de ~** cash-flow *o* liquidity problems

líquido[1] **-da** *adj*

A ‹*sustancia*› liquid

B ‹*sueldo/renta*› net

líquido[2] *m*

A (sustancia) liquid; **una dieta a base de ~s** a liquid diet

(Compuestos)
- **líquido amniótico** amniotic fluid
- **líquido anticongelante** antifreeze
- **líquido de frenos** brake fluid

B (dinero) cash; **~ disponible/imponible** disposable/taxable income

lira *f*

A (Mús) lyre

B (Fin) lira

lírica *f* poetry

lírico -ca *adj* 1 (Lit) ‹*género/poesía*› lyric 2 (Mús) lyric, lyrical 3 (Per, RPl fam) ‹*persona*› dreamy, starry-eyed (colloq)

lirio *m* iris

(Compuestos)
- **lirio de agua** calla lily, arum lily
- **lirio de los valles** lily of the valley

lirismo *m* lyricism

lirón *m* dormouse; ▸**dormir** *vi*

lis *f* lily

lisa *f*

A (Zool) (de mar) grey mullet; (de río) loach

B (Ven arg) (cerveza) beer

Lisboa Lisbon

lisboeta, lisbonense *adj/mf* Lisboan, of/from Lisbon

lisiado¹ -da *adj* crippled

lisiado² -da *m,f* cripple; **un ~ de guerra** a disabled veteran

lisiar [A1] *vt* to damage … permanently

■ **lisiarse** *v pron* (*refl*): **se lisió la columna vertebral** he damaged his spine

liso -sa *adj*

A ‹*piel/superficie*› smooth; ‹*pelo*› straight; ‹*terreno*› flat; **los 200 metros ~s** (Esp) the 200 meter sprint

B (sin dibujos) plain; **~ y *llano*** plain and simple; ▸**llanamente**

C (fam) ‹*mujer*› flat-chested

D (Per fam) (insolente) fresh (AmE colloq), cheeky (BrE colloq)

lisonja *f* flattery

lisonjear [A1] *vt* to flatter

lisonjero -ra *adj* ‹*palabras*› flattering; ‹*persona*›: **es un hombre muy ~** he's a terrible flatterer

lista *f*

A 1 (de nombres, números) list; **lo borraron de la ~** he was crossed off the list; **la ~ de las compras** *or* (Esp) **la compra** the shopping list; **pasar ~** (Educ) to take roll call, to take the register (BrE) 2 (en restaurante) menu

(Compuestos)
- **lista de boda** wedding list
- **lista de correos** general delivery (AmE), poste restante (BrE)
- **lista de espera** waiting list
- **lista de éxitos** (Mús) charts (*pl*); (Lit) best-seller list
- **lista electoral** slate (*list of candidates put forward by a party or coalition*)
- **lista negra** blacklist

B 1 (raya) stripe; **a ~s** striped 2 (tira) strip

listado¹ -da *adj* striped

listado² *m* (Inf) printout; (lista) list

(Compuesto) **listado electoral** (RPl) electoral roll *o* register

listar [A1] *vt* to list

listeria *f* listeria

listillo -lla *m,f* (Esp fam) smart aleck (colloq)

listín *m* (Esp) list; **~ de teléfonos** telephone directory

listo¹ -ta *adj*

A [SER] ‹*persona*› clever, bright, smart (colloq); **te pasaste de ~** you've gone too far; ***estar*** *or* (Esp) ***ir* ~** (fam): **ahora sí que estamos ~s** we're in real trouble now (colloq); **está lista si cree eso** if that's what she thinks, she's got another think coming (colloq)

B 1 [ESTAR] (preparado) ready; **¡preparados** *or* (RPl) **prontos, ~s, ya!** (get) ready, set, go!; **~ PARA + INF** ready to + INF; **~ PARA algo** ready FOR sth 2 [ESTAR] (terminado) finished; **lo doblas así y ~** you fold it like this and that's it (finished) 3 (Andes fam) (manifestando acuerdo) okay (colloq)

listo² -ta *m,f* (esp Esp) 1 (inteligente) clever one; **el ~ de la clase** (pey) the class know-it-all (colloq & pej) 2 (vivo, astuto) tricky customer (colloq)

listón *m* 1 (de madera) strip; (en salto de altura) bar 2 (meta, nivel): **ponen el ~ muy alto** they have *o* set very high standards; **seguiré subiendo el ~** I will continue to set myself higher goals 3 (Méx) (cinta) ribbon

lisura *f*

A (de una superficie) smoothness

B (Per) 1 (fam) (grosería) four-letter word (colloq) 2 (gracia) gracefulness

litera *f* 1 (en dormitorio) bunk; (en barco) bunk, berth; (en tren) berth, couchette (BrE) 2 (vehículo) litter

literal *adj* literal

literalmente *adv* 1 ‹*traducir*› literally; ‹*repetir*› word for word 2 (para énfasis): **estoy ~ muerta de cansancio** I'm absolutely exhausted

literario -ria *adj* literary

literato -ta (*m*) man of letters; (*f*) woman of letters

literatura *f* literature

(Compuesto) **literatura infantil** juvenile books (AmE), children's books (BrE)

litigante *adj/mf* litigant

litigar [A3] *vi* to be at law (frml), to be in dispute

litigio *m* 1 (Der): **tener un ~ con algn** to be involved in a lawsuit with sb; **las tierras en ~** the land which is the subject of a legal dispute 2 (disputa) dispute

litografía *f* (sistema) lithography; (grabado) lithograph

litografiar [A17] *vt* to lithograph

litoral¹ *adj* coastal

litoral² *m* coast; **un largo ~** a long coastline

litosfera *f* lithosphere

litro *m* liter*

Lituania *f* Lithuania

lituano¹ -na *adj/m,f* Lithuanian

lituano² *m* (idioma) Lithuanian

liturgia *f* liturgy

litúrgico -ca *adj* liturgical

liviandad *f* lightness

liviano -na *adj* (esp AmL) 1 ‹*paquete/tela*› light; ***ser* ~ *de sangre*** (Chi fam) to be likable 2 ‹*comida*› light; **tiene un sueño muy ~** she's a very light sleeper 3 ‹*obra/película*› lightweight

lívido -da *adj* (pálido) pallid; (morado) livid; **estaba ~ de rabia** he was livid (with rage)

living /'liβin/ *m* (*pl* **-vings**) (esp AmS) living room

liza *f* (liter) (lucha) lists (*pl*), tournament field; ***entrar en* ~**: **un tercer candidato ha entrado en ~** a third candidate has entered the fray

Ll, ll *f* (*read as* /'eʎe/) Ll, ll

llaga *f* (Med) sore, ulcer; (Bib) wound

llagar [A3] *vt* to cause a sore *o* wound on

■ **llagarse** *v pron* to get a sore/sores

llama *f*

A (de fuego) flame; **el edificio en ~s** the blazing building; **la casa ardía en ~s** the house was in flames

(Compuesto) **llama piloto** pilot light

B (Zool) llama

llamada *f*

A 1 (Telec) call; **gracias por la ~** thank you for calling *o* phoning 2 (acción) call; **la ~ del deber/de la selva** the call of duty/of the wild

(Compuestos)
- **llamada al orden** call to order
- **llamada de socorro** distress call
- **llamada internacional/interurbana/urbana** international/long distance/local call

B (Impr) (en un texto) reference mark

C (Inf) call

llamado¹ -da *adj*

A (por un nombre) called; **un lugar ~ La Dehesa** a place called La Dehesa; **el 747, también ~ 'jumbo'** the 747, also known as the jumbo jet; **el ~ 'boom' de los sesenta** the so-called 'boom' of the sixties

B [ESTAR] (destinado) **~ A algo**: **está ~ a convertirse en una gran atracción** it is set to become a big attraction

llamado² *m* 1 (AmL) (al público) ▸**llamamiento** 2 (Arg) (Telec) ▸**llamada A 1**

llamador *m* door knocker

llamamiento *m* call; **las autoridades hicieron un ~ a la calma** the authorities appealed for calm

llamar [A1] *vt*

A 1 (hacer venir) ‹*bomberos/policía*› to call; ‹*médico*› to call (out); ‹*camarero/criada/ascensor*› to call; ‹*súbditos/servidores*› to summon; ‹*taxi*› (por teléfono) to call; (en la calle) to

l

hail; **lo llamó por señas** she beckoned to him; **Dios la llamó (a su lado)** (euf) God called her to him (euph); **el juez lo llamó a declarar** the judge called on him to testify; **su madre lo mandó ~** (AmL) his mother sent for him; **lo ~on para hacer el servicio militar** he was called up for military service **2** (instar): **el sindicato los llamó a la huelga** the union called them out on strike; **me sentí llamada a hacerlo** I felt driven *o* compelled to do it

B (por teléfono) to phone, to call; **la voy a ~** I'm going to give her a call; **te llamó Eva** Eva phoned (for you); **llámame al celular** (AmL) *or* **móvil** (Esp) call me on my cell phone (AmE) *o* mobile (BrE)

C **1** (dar el nombre de) to call, name; (dar el título, apodo de) to call; **la llamó de todo** he called her every name under the sun **2** (considerar) to call; **eso es lo que yo llamo un amigo** that's what I call a friend

■ **llamar** *vi*

A (con los nudillos) to knock; (tocar el timbre) to ring (the doorbell); **llaman a la puerta** there's someone at the door

B (Telec) «*persona*» to telephone, phone, call; «*teléfono*» to ring; **¿quién llama?** who's calling?

C (gustar) to appeal; **no me/le llaman las pieles** fur coats don't appeal to me/her

■ **llamarse** *v pron* to be called; **se llama Pedro** his name is Pedro; **¿cómo te llamas?** what's your name?; **... como que (yo) me llamo Ana** ... as sure as my name's Ana

llamarada *f*, (Col) **llamarón** *m* **1** (de fuego) sudden blaze, flare-up **2** (liter) (de ira, pasión) blaze

llamativo -va *adj* ‹color› bright; ‹*mujer/vestido*› striking; **ponte algo menos ~** wear something less flamboyant

llameante *adj* flaming, blazing

llamear [A1] *vi* to blaze, flame

llana *f*

A (Const) trowel

B (Geog) plain

llanamente *adv*: ***lisa*** *or* ***simple y ~*** ‹*explicar/hablar*› in straightforward terms; **lisa y ~, hay que despedirlos** they should be fired, it's as simple as that

llanero -ra *m,f* **1** (habitante del llano) (*m*) plainsman; (*f*) plainswoman **2** (vaquero) cattle herder, cowboy (*of the Colombian/Venezuelan* **llanos**)

llaneza *f* simplicity

llano¹ -na *adj*

A ‹*terreno/superficie*› (horizontal) flat; (sin desniveles) even; **los 100 metros ~s** (RPl) the 100 meters dash *o* sprint

B ‹*persona*› straightforward; ‹*trato*› natural; ‹*lenguaje*› plain

C ‹*palabra*› *with the stress on the penultimate syllable*

llano² *m* **1** (Geog) (llanura) plain **2** (extensión de terreno) area of flat ground

llanta *f* **1** (de metal) rim **2** (AmL) (neumático) tire*

(Compuesto) **llanta de repuesto** (AmL) *or* (Méx) **de refacción** spare tire*

llantera *f*, **llanterío** *m* (fam) howling, wailing

llanto *m* (de niño) crying; (de adulto) crying, weeping (liter); **déjate de ~s** stop crying

llanura *f*

A (de una superficie) evenness, smoothness

B (Geog) plain, prairie

llapa *f* ▸ **yapa**

llave *f*

A **1** (de cerradura, candado) key; **las ~s del coche** the car keys; **cierra la puerta con ~** lock the door; **bajo ~** under lock and key; **la ~ del éxito** the key to success; ***bajo siete ~s*** hidden away; ***en ~*** (Col fam): **estar en ~ con algn** «*comerciante*» to work in cooperation with sb; «*delincuente*» to be in league with sb **2** (de una propiedad): **entrega de ~s en junio** ready for occupancy (AmE) *o* (BrE) occupation in June **3** (CS) (por el alquiler) key money, premium; (por la clientela) goodwill **4** (para dar cuerda) key

(Compuestos)

- **llave de contacto** ignition key
- **llave maestra** master key, passkey

B (Mec) (herramienta) wrench (AmE), spanner (BrE)

(Compuesto) **llave inglesa** monkey wrench

C **1** (interruptor) switch; (en tubería) valve; **la ~ del gas** the gas jet (AmE) *o* (BrE) tap **2** (AmL) (de lavabo, bañera) faucet (AmE), tap (BrE) **3** (Mús) (de órgano) stop; (de trompeta) valve; (de clarinete, saxofón) key

(Compuesto) **llave de paso** (del agua) stopcock; (del gas) main valve (AmE), mains tap (BrE); **cerrar la ~ de ~** to turn the water/gas off at the main valve (AmE) *o* (BrE) at the mains

D (en un texto) brace; **entre ~s** in braces

E (en lucha, judo) hold; **lo inmovilizó con una ~ (de brazo)** she got him in an armlock; **~ de candado** (Col, Méx) hammerlock

llavero *m* key ring

llegada *f* **1** (de un viaje) arrival; **el vuelo tiene prevista su ~ para las 11 horas** the flight is due to arrive at 11 a.m. **2** (Dep) (meta) winning post

llegar [A3] *vi*

A «*persona/tren/carta*» to arrive; **tienen que estar por** *or* **al ~** they'll be arriving any minute now; **llegó (el) último** he was the last to arrive; **~on cansadísimos** they were exhausted when they arrived; **¿falta mucho para ~?** is it much further (to go)?; **siempre llega tarde** he's always late; **no me llegó el telegrama** I didn't get the telegram; **me hizo ~ un mensaje** he got a message to me; **~ A** ‹*a país/ciudad*› to arrive IN; ‹*a edificio*› to arrive AT; **los que ~on a la meta** the ones who crossed the finishing line; **~ a casa** to arrive *o* get home; **el rumor llegó a oídos del alcalde** the rumor reached the mayor; **la carta llegó a su destino** the letter reached its destination; **¿adónde quieres ~?** what do you mean?; **~ DE** to arrive FROM

B **1** «*camino/ruta*» (extenderse) **~ HASTA** to go all the way to, go as far as **2** (ir) **~ A** *or* **HASTA**: **este tren no llega hasta** *or* **a Lima** this train doesn't go as far as *o* all the way to Lima; **sólo llega al tercer piso** it only goes (up) to the third floor

C «*día/invierno*» to come, arrive; **ha llegado el momento de ...** the time has come to ...; **cuando llegue la estación de las lluvias** when the rainy season starts; **cuando llegó la noche** when night fell

D **1** (alcanzar) to reach; **~ A algo** ‹*a acuerdo*› to reach sth; **llegué a la conclusión de que...** I reached *o* came to the conclusion that ...; **los pies no le llegan al suelo** her feet don't touch the floor; **la falda le llegaba a los tobillos** her skirt came down to her ankles; **el agua le llegaba al cuello** the water came up to her neck; **su voz llegaba al fondo del teatro** her voice carried to the back of the theater **2** (Esp) «*dinero/materiales*» (ser suficiente) to be enough; **no me llega el dinero** I don't have enough money **3** (alcanzar a medir, costar, etc): **no llega a los dos metros** it is less than two meters; **no sé si ~á a tanto** I don't know if it would be as much as that; **no llegaban a 50 personas** there weren't even 50 people there **4** (expresando logro): **~á lejos** she'll go far *o* a long way; **así no vas a ~ a ningún lado** you'll never get anywhere like that; **llegó a convencerme** he managed to convince me; **quiero que llegues a ser alguien** I want you to make something of yourself; **nunca llegó a (ser) director** he never became director **5** (en el tiempo): **no ~á a las próximas elecciones** he won't survive till the next elections; **~ a viejo** to live to old age; **llegué a conocerlo mejor** I got to know him better; **¿llegó a saberlo?** did she ever find out?; **llegó a ser de gran utilidad** it proved (to be) very useful

E **~ A + INF** **1** (a un extremo): **llegó a amenazarme** she even threatened me; **llegué a pensar que ...** I even began to think that ...; **no llegó a pegarme** he didn't actually hit me; **las cosas han llegado a tal punto que ...** things have reached such a point that ...; **puede ~ a ganarle** he might beat him **2** (en oraciones condicionales): **si lo llego a saber, no vengo** if I'd known, I wouldn't have come; **si llego a enterarme de algo, te aviso** if I happen to hear anything, I'll let you know

F «*estilo/música*» (ser entendido, aceptado): **su estilo no llega a la gente** people can't relate to *o* understand his style; **un lenguaje que llega a la juventud** language that gets through to *o* means something to young people

■ **llegarse** *v pron* (fam): **se llegó hasta aquí para dármelo** she came all the way here to give it to me (colloq); **llégate a la tienda y trae algo de beber** run out to the store and get something to drink

llenador -dora *adj* (CS) ‹*comida*› filling

llenar [A1] *vt*

A **1** ‹*vaso/plato/cajón*› to fill; ‹*tanque*› to fill (up); ‹*maleta*› to fill, pack; **no me llenes el vaso** don't fill my glass right up; **siempre llena la sala** he always manages to fill the hall; ~ **algo DE/CON algo** to fill sth WITH sth [2] ‹*formulario*› to fill out, to fill in (esp BrE) [3] (cubrir) ~ **algo DE algo** to cover sth WITH sth

B (colmar) ‹*persona*› ~ **a algn DE algo**: **la noticia nos llenó de alegría** we were overjoyed by the news; **nos llenó de atenciones** he made a real fuss of us

C (hacer sentirse realizado) ‹*persona*›: **su carrera no la llena** she doesn't find her career fulfilling

■ **llenar** *vi* «*comida*» to be filling

■ **llenarse** *v pron*

A [1] «*recipiente/estadio*» to fill; **aquí el tren siempre se llena** the train always fills up here; **el teatro se llenó hasta los topes** the theater was (jam) packed; **~se DE algo** to fill WITH sth; **se le ~on los ojos de lágrimas** his eyes filled with tears [2] (cubrirse) **~se DE algo** ‹*de polvo/pelos*› to be covered IN sth; **se le llenó la cara de granos** he got very pimply (AmE colloq) *o* (BrE colloq) spotty

B ‹*bolsillo/boca*› to fill; **~se algo DE algo** to fill sth WITH sth; **no te llenes la boca de comida** don't stuff your mouth with food

C (colmarse) **~se DE algo**: **con esa hazaña se llenó de gloria** it was an achievement that covered him in glory; **se ~on de deudas** they got heavily into debt

D «*persona*» (de comida): **sólo viene a ~se la barriga** (fam) he only comes here to stuff his face (colloq); **con un plato de ensalada ya se llena** one plate of salad and she's full

lleno¹ -na *adj*

A [1] ‹*estadio/autobús/copa*› full; **no hables con la boca llena** don't speak with your mouth full; ~ **DE algo** full OF sth; **está ~ de agujeros** it's full of holes; **tiene la casa llena de gente** she has a full house at the moment; **calles llenas de gente** streets crowded with people; **una mirada llena de rencor** a resentful look [2] (cubierto) ~ **DE algo** ‹*de granos/manchas/polvo*› covered IN sth [3] (después de comer) full (up) (colloq)

B (regordete) plump

C de lleno fully; **dedicarse de ~ a algo** to dedicate oneself fully *o* entirely to sth; **el sol nos daba de ~** the sun was shining down on us

lleno² *m* sellout; **hubo un ~ total** it was completely sold out

llevadero -ra *adj* bearable

llevándola *adv* (Ven, Col fam) so-so (colloq)

llevar [A1] *vt*

Sentido I

A [1] (de un lugar a otro) to take; **le llevé unas flores** I took her some flowers; **te lo ~é cuando vaya** I'll bring it when I come; **¿qué llevas en el bolso?** what have you got in your bag?; Ⓢ **comida para llevar** take out (AmE) *o* (BrE) takeaway meals [2] (transportar) to carry; **el camión llevaba una carga de abono** the truck was carrying a load of fertilizer; **deja que te ayude a ~ las bolsas** let me help you carry your bags [3] ‹*persona*› to take; **~ a los niños al colegio** to take the children to school; **nos llevó a cenar** he took us out to dinner; **me llevó hasta la estación** she gave me a lift to the station; **lo llevaba en brazos** she was carrying him in her arms [4] (tener consigo) to have; **no llevo dinero encima** I don't have any money on me

B [1] (guiar, conducir) to take; **nos ~on por un sendero** they led *o* took us along a path; **la llevaba de la mano** I/he was holding her hand; **esto no nos ~á a ninguna parte** this won't get us anywhere; **lo ~on ante el juez** he was brought before the judge [2] (impulsar, inducir) to lead; **esto me lleva a pensar que ...** this leads me to believe that ...; **¿qué la llevó a hacerlo?** what made her do it?

C ‹*ropa/perfume/reloj*› to wear

D (tener) to have; **lleva barba** he has a beard; **llevaba el pelo corto** she had short hair; **el colegio lleva su nombre** the school bears his name; **una canción que lleva por título 'Rencor'** a song entitled 'Rencor'

Sentido II

A (tener a su cargo) ‹*negocio/tienda*› to run; ‹*caso*› to handle; **lleva la contabilidad** she does the accounts; **trabaja y lleva la casa** she works and does the housework

B [1] (conducir) ‹*vehículo*› to drive; ‹*moto*› to ride [2] ‹*pareja*› (al bailar): **no sé bailar — no importa, yo te llevo** I can't dance — it doesn't matter, I'll lead

C ‹*vida*› to lead; ~ **una vida tranquila/muy ajetreada** to lead a quiet/very hectic life; (+ *compl*) **lo llevan en secreto** they're keeping it secret; **¿cómo lleva lo del divorcio? — lo lleva muy mal** how is she coping with the divorce? — she's taking it very badly; **llevaste muy bien la entrevista** you handled the interview very well

D (seguir, mantener): ~ **el ritmo** *or* **el compás** to keep time; **¿llevas la cuenta de lo que te debo?** are you keeping track of what I owe you?; **¿qué dirección llevaban?** which direction were they going in?

Sentido III

A [1] (requerir) to take; **lleva tiempo hacerlo bien** it takes time to do it well; (+ *me/te/le etc*) **le llevó horas aprendérselo** it took her hours to learn it [2] (tener como ingrediente, componente): **¿qué lleva esta sopa?** what's in this soup?; **esta masa lleva mantequilla** this pastry is made with butter; **el tren sólo lleva dos vagones** the train has only two cars (AmE) *o* (BrE) carriages

B (aventajar, exceder en) (+ *me/te/le etc*): **me lleva un año** he's a year older than me; **nos llevan un día de ventaja** they have a one-day lead over us

C (Esp) (cobrar) to charge

■ **llevar** *v aux*: **lleva una hora esperando** she's been waiting for an hour; **lleva tres días sin comer** he hasn't eaten for three days; **el tren lleva una hora de retraso** the train's an hour late; **llevo revisada la mitad** I've already checked half of it; **llevo dos años en la empresa** I've been with the company for two years; ~ ***las de ganar/de perder*** to be likely to win/lose

■ **llevar** *vi* [1] «*camino/carretera*» to go, lead [2] (al bailar) to lead

■ **llevarse** *v pron*

A [1] (a otro lugar) to take; **la policía se llevó al sospechoso** the police took the suspect away; **¿quién se llevó mi paraguas?** who took my umbrella?; **llévate a los chicos de aquí** get the children out of here; **el agua se llevó cuanto encontró a su paso** the water swept away everything in its path [2] ‹*premio/dinero*› to win [3] (quedarse con, comprar) to take; **me llevó éste** I'll take this one; **¿cuántos se quiere ~?** how many would you like? [4] (Mat) to carry; **9 y 9 son 18, me llevo una** 9 plus 9 is 18, carry one [5] (Arg) ‹*asignatura*› to carry over

B (dirigir): **se llevó la mano al bolsillo** he put his hand to his pocket

C ‹*susto/regañina*› to get; **se llevó su merecido** he got what he deserved; **me llevé una gran decepción** I was terribly disappointed; **se llevó un buen recuerdo** he left here with pleasant memories

D ~se bien con algn to get along with sb; **se llevan a matar** they really hate each other; **se llevan como perro y gato** they fight like cat and dog

E (hablando de modas): **vuelven a ~se las faldas cortas** short skirts are back in fashion; **ya no se lleva eso de las fiestas de compromiso** people don't have engagement parties any more

llorado -da *adj* (frml) late lamented (*before n*) (frml)

llorar [A1] *vi*

A (derramar lágrimas) [1] «*persona*» to cry; **me dieron ganas de ~** I felt like crying; **lo hizo ~** she made him cry; **estaba a punto de ~** she was on the verge of tears; **se echó a ~** she started to cry; **llorábamos de (la) risa/rabia** we were crying with laughter/rage; **lloró de la emoción** he wept with emotion; ~ **POR algo/algn** to cry over sth/sb; **lloraba por la pérdida de su amigo** he wept for the loss of his friend; ***ser de*** *or* ***para ~*** to be enough to make one weep; ***el que no llora, no mama*** if you don't ask, you don't get [2] «*ojos*» (+ *me/te/le etc*) to water

B (fam) (quejarse) to grumble, whine

■ **llorar** *vt* ‹*persona/muerte*› to mourn

lloriquear [A1] *vi* (fam) to whine (colloq)

lloriqueo *m* (fam) whining (colloq); **déjate de ~s** stop whining

llorón¹ -rona *adj* (fam): **es muy ~** he cries a lot; **no seas tan ~** don't be such a crybaby (colloq)

llorón² -rona *m,f*

A [1] (fam) (que llora mucho) crybaby (colloq) [2] (Col, RPl, Ven fam) (quejón) whiner (colloq)

B la llorona *f* (Col, Méx, Ven fam) (fantasma) ghost (*of a woman said to roam the streets wailing*)

lloroso -sa *adj* ‹*tono*› tearful; **tenía los ojos ~s** her eyes were full of tears

l

llovedera *f* (Col, Ven fam) endless rain

llover [E9] *v impers* to rain; **parece que va a ~** it looks as though it's going to rain; **nos llovió todo el fin de semana** it rained all weekend; **llovió con ganas** (fam) it poured (with rain); ***ha llovido mucho desde entonces*** a lot of water has flowed *o* passed under the bridge since then; **~ *sobre mojado*: a este pobre país le llueve sobre mojado** it's just one disaster after another in this wretched country; ***llueva o truene*** come rain or shine; ***llueve/llovía a cántaros*** *or* ***mares*** it's/it was pouring (with rain); ***mandar a algn a ver si llueve*** (AmL hum) to send sb on a fool's errand

■ **llover** *vi*: **las desgracias llovieron sobre él** misfortunes rained down on him; (+ *me/te/le etc*) **le llovieron regalos** she was showered with gifts; **le han llovido las ofertas de trabajo** she's been inundated with job offers

llovida *f* (AmS fam) (rain) shower

llovizna *f* drizzle

lloviznar *v impers* [A1] to drizzle

llueva, llueve *see* **llover**

lluvia *f* 1 (Meteo) rain; **un día de ~** a rainy day; **caía una ~ menuda** *or* **fina** it was drizzling; **la estación de las ~s** the rainy season; **zonas de mucha ~** areas of heavy rainfall 2 (de balas) hail; (de críticas) hail, barrage

(Compuestos)
- **lluvia ácida** acid rain
- **lluvia radiactiva** nuclear fallout

lluvioso -sa *adj* ‹*tiempo/día/época*› rainy; ‹*región*› wet

lo¹ *art*

A : **prefiero ~ dulce** I prefer sweet things; **dejemos ~ difícil para mañana** let's leave the difficult part until tomorrow; **~ interesante del caso es que ...** the interesting thing about the case is that ...; **¿estoy en ~ cierto?** am I right?; **en ~ alto de la sierra** high up in the mountains; **ser ~ más objetivo posible** to be as objective as possible; **me dijo ~ de siempre** he came out with the same old story; **que cada cual se ocupe de ~ suyo** everyone should take care of their own things; **se ha enterado de ~ nuestro** she's found out about us; **~ de Juan fue trágico** what happened to Juan was tragic; **¿sabes ~ de Pablo?** have you heard about Pablo?; **voy a ~ de Eva** (RPl) I'm going to Eva's house

B (con oraciones de relativo): **no entiendo ~ que dices** I don't understand what you're saying; **~ que es por mí** *or* **en ~ que a mí respecta ...** (fam) as far as I'm concerned (colloq); **~ cual** *or* **que fue desmentido por el Gobierno** which was denied by the Government; **pide ~ que quieras** ask for whatever you want; **límpialo con un trapo o ~ que sea** clean it with a cloth or something *o* whatever; **¡~ que oyes!** you heard right!

C (con valor ponderativo): **¡~ que debe haber sufrido!** how she must have suffered!; **¡no te imaginas ~ que fue aquello!** you can't imagine what it was like!; **¿ves ~ mal que habla?** you see how badly he speaks?

lo² *pron pers*

A 1 (referido — a él) him; (— a usted) you; (— a cosa, etc) it; **¿~ conoces?** do you know him?; **~ encuentro muy bien, señor Lara** you're looking very well, Mr Lara; **~ compré hoy** I bought it today; **ya ~ sé** I know 2 (*impers*): **duele que a uno ~ traten así** it hurts when people treat you like that

B (*con* **ser, estar, haber**): **¿que si estoy harta? pues sí, ~ estoy** am I fed up? well, yes, I am; **si ella es capaz, yo también ~ soy** if she can, so can I

loa *f* (liter) praise

loable *adj* commendable, praiseworthy

loar [A1] *vt* (liter) to praise, laud (frml)

lobanillo *m* wen

lobato -ta *m,f* 1 (Zool) wolf cub 2 **lobato** *m* (niño) Cub (Scout)

lobby /'loβi/ *m* (*pl* **-bbies**) 1 (grupo de presión) lobby 2 (de hotel) lobby

lobezno -na *m,f* wolf cub

lobo¹ -ba *adj*

A (Col fam) ‹*vestido/color*› garish; ‹*cuadro*› tacky (colloq)

B (Chi fam) ‹*animal*› unfriendly

lobo² -ba *m,f* (Zool) wolf; ***un ~ con piel de oveja*** (fam) a wolf in sheep's clothing

(Compuestos)
- **lobo de mar** (persona) sea dog
- **lobo feroz: el ~ ~** the big bad wolf
- **lobo marino** seal

lobotomía *f* lobotomy

lóbrego -ga *adj* gloomy

lóbulo *m* lobe

LOC *m* (Inf) (= **lector óptico de caracteres**) OCR

loca *f* (*ver tb* **loco² A**) (fam) (homosexual afeminado) queen (sl)

locación *f* (Méx) (lugar): **visite el museo Rivera, ~: Calle Altavista** visit the Rivera Museum on Altavista Street; **¿en qué ~?** whereabouts?

local¹ *adj* local; **el equipo ~** the home team

local² *m* premises (*pl*); **por favor desalojen el ~** please vacate the premises

localidad *f*

A (población) town, locality (frml)

B (Espec) seat, ticket; Ⓢ **no hay localidades** sold out

localizable *adj*: **no está ~** he cannot be found *o* traced

localización *f* 1 (acción): **la tormenta dificultó la ~ del pesquero** the storm made it difficult to locate *o* to find the fishing boat 2 (lugar) location

localizador *m*

A (de personas) pager

B (de reserva) booking reference

localizar [A4] *vt* 1 ‹*persona/lugar/tumor*› to locate; **estoy intentando ~la** I am trying to get hold of her; **no logro ~lo en el mapa** I can't find it on the map 2 ‹*incendio/epidemia*› to localize

■ **localizarse** *v pron* «*dolor*» to be localized

locatario -ria *m,f* (AmL) tenant

locha *f*

A (Zool) loach

B (Col fam) (pereza) laziness

C (Ven): ***no tener una ~*** to be broke (colloq)

loción *f* lotion

(Compuestos)
- **loción capilar** hair lotion
- **loción para después del afeitado** after-shave

loco¹ -ca *adj*

A 1 (Med, Psic) mad, insane 2 (chiflado) crazy (colloq), nuts (colloq); **este tipo está medio ~** (fam) the guy's not all there (colloq); **no seas ~, te vas a matar** don't be stupid, you'll kill yourself; **eso no lo hago (pero) ni ~** there's no way I'd do that; **¿disculparme yo? ¡ni (que estuviera) ~!** what, me apologize? not in a million years!; **hacer algo a lo ~** to do sth any which way (AmE) *o* (BrE) any old how (colloq); **gasta dinero a lo ~** he spends money like water; ***estar ~ de remate*** *or* ***de atar*** (fam) to be completely nuts (colloq); ***tener*** *or* (Esp) ***traer ~ a algn*** to be driving sb crazy (colloq); ***volver ~ a algn*** to drive sb crazy (colloq); **el chocolate me vuelve loca** I adore chocolate; ***volverse ~*** to go mad 3 (contento, entusiasmado): **están ~s con el nieto** they're besotted with their grandchild; **está loca por él** she's crazy about him (colloq); **está ~ por volver** he's dying to come back (colloq) 4 (fam) (ajetreado): **anda (como) ~ con los preparativos** the preparations are driving him mad (colloq)

B 1 (indicando gran cantidad): **tengo unas ganas locas de verla** I'm dying to see her (colloq); **tuvo una suerte loca** she was incredibly lucky 2 **~ DE algo**: **estaba loca de alegría** she was blissfully happy; **está ~ de celos** he's wild with jealousy; **estaba ~ de dolor** he was racked with pain; **está loca de amor** she's madly in love

loco² -ca *m,f*

A (enfermo mental) (*m*) madman; (*f*) madwoman; **se puso como un ~** he went crazy *o* mad; **maneja** *or* (Esp) **conduce como un ~** he drives like a lunatic; **corrimos como ~s** (fam) we ran like crazy *o* mad (colloq); **gritaba como una loca** she was shouting her head off (colloq); **¡esto es de ~s!** this is sheer madness!; **el ~ de Javier se vino a pie** Javier walked here, mad fool that he is; **hay mucho ~ suelto** (fam) there are a lot of weirdos about (colloq); ***cada ~ con su tema*** (fam) to each his own; ***hacerse el ~*** to act dumb (colloq); ***la loca de la casa*** (liter) the imagination

B **loco** *m* (Zool) abalone

locomoción *f* 1▸ (acción) locomotion 2▸ (Chi) (Transp) *tb* **~ colectiva** public transport

locomotor[1] **-tora** *adj* 1▸ ‹*aparato*› locomotive (*before n*) 2▸ ‹*músculo*› locomotor (*before n*)

locomotor[2] **-triz** *adj* locomotive (*before n*)

locomotora *f* (Ferr) locomotive, engine

(Compuesto) **locomotora eléctrica/de vapor** electric/steam locomotive

locuacidad *f* talkativeness, loquacity (frml)

locuaz *adj* talkative, loquacious (frml)

locución *f* phrase

locura *f* 1▸ (Med) madness, insanity 2▸ (insensatez) crazy thing (colloq); **lo que dices es una ~** what you're saying is sheer madness; **cometió la ~ de casarse** she committed the folly of getting married 3▸ (inclinación exagerada): **siente ~ por la pequeña** she's besotted with the little one; **la quiero con ~** I'm crazy about her (colloq)

locutor -tora *m,f* announcer; **~ deportivo** sports commentator

locutorio *m* (Telec) (cabina) telephone booth; (local) shop where telephone calls can be made, often with Internet access; (Rad) studio; (en cárcel) visiting room; (en convento) parlor*

lodazal *m* quagmire

lodo *m* mud; *para modismos ver* **barro**

loft *m* (*pl* **~s**) designer apartment in an old industrial building

logaritmo *m* logarithm

logia *f* 1▸ (de los masones) lodge 2▸ (Arquit) loggia

lógica *f* 1▸ (coherencia) logic; **carece de toda ~** there is no logic to it 2▸ (Fil) logic

lógico[1] **-ca** *adj* 1▸ (normal, natural) natural, logical; **como es ~, ...** naturally *o* obviously, ...; **es ~ que así sea** it's (only) natural that it should be so; **lo ~ sería que se lo hubiera dicho** the logical thing would have been to tell him 2▸ ‹*conclusión/consecuencia*› logical 3▸ (Fil) logical

lógico[2] *adv* (*indep*) (fam) of course

lógico[3] **-ca** *m,f* logician

logística *f* logistics (*pl*)

logístico -ca *adj* logistic, logistical

logo *m* logo, logotype

logopeda *mf* speech therapist

logoterapia *f* speech therapy

logotipo *m* logo, logotype

logrado -da *adj* successful; **un retrato muy ~** a very lifelike portrait

lograr [A1] *vt* ‹*objetivo*› to attain, achieve; ‹*éxito*› to achieve; **logró el quinto puesto** she managed fifth place; **~ + INF** to manage to + INF; **no logró convencerla** he did not manage *o* he failed to persuade her; **por fin logró cobrarlo** he finally got paid for it

logro *m* (de un objetivo) achievement; (éxito) success; **los ~s de la medicina** the achievements of medicine

loísmo *m*: *use of* **lo/los** *instead of* **le/les** *(as in* **lo/los dije que no**), *common in certain regions of Spain but not acceptable to most speakers*

lolo -la *m,f* (Chi fam) teenager

loma *f* hill; (más pequeño) hillock

lomada *f* (RPl) small hill, hillock

lomaje *m* (Chi) rolling hills (*pl*)

lombarda *f* red cabbage

lombriz *f* (de tierra) worm, earthworm; (en el intestino) (fam) worm (colloq)

lomo *m*

A (de animal) back; **venía a ~s de burro** he was riding a donkey; ***jugar de ~*** (AmC fam) to be lazy *o* idle

(Compuesto) **lomo de burro** (RPl) speed bump

B (Coc) (de cerdo) loin; (de vaca) (AmL) fillet steak

C (de libro) spine; (de cuchillo) back

lona *f* (Tex) canvas; (en boxeo) canvas; (carpa del circo): **bajo la ~** under the big top, in the circus

loncha *f* slice

lonche *m* (Per) (merienda) tea

lonchera *f* (AmL) lunch box

londinense[1] *adj* ‹*público/teatro/periódico*› London (*before n*); **es ~** she's from London, she's a Londoner

londinense[2] *mf* Londoner

Londres *m* London

loneta *f* sailcloth

long. (= **longitud**) long.

longaniza *f*: *spicy pork sausage*

longevidad *f* (frml) longevity (frml)

longevo -va *adj* (frml) long-lived

longitud *f* 1▸ (largo) length; **de 30 metros de ~** 30 meters long 2▸ (Astron, Geog) longitude 3▸ (de vocal, sonido) length

(Compuesto) **longitud de onda** (Fís, Rad) wavelength

longitudinal *adj* longitudinal

lonja *f*

A 1▸ (loncha) slice 2▸ (RPl) (de cuero) strip

B 1▸ (Esp) (mercado de pescado) fish market; (mercado) marketplace 2▸ (institución mercantil) guild; **~ de propiedad raíz** (Col) association of realtors (AmE), association of estate agents (BrE)

lontananza *f*: **en ~** (liter) in the distance

loor *m* (liter) praise

loquear [A1] *vi* (AmL fam) to lark about (colloq), to horse *o* clown around (colloq)

■ **loquearse** *v pron* (Per fam) to go crazy *o* around the bend (colloq)

loquerío *m* (AmL fam) 1▸ (manicomio) madhouse (colloq), loony bin (colloq) 2▸ (situación caótica) bedlam; **aquello era un ~** it was bedlam in there

loquero -ra *m,f* (fam & hum) 1▸ (psiquiatra) shrink (colloq); (enfermero) psychiatric nurse 2▸ **loquero** *m* (manicomio) loony bin (colloq & hum); **esto es un ~** this place is a madhouse (colloq)

lor, lord *m* lord

loro[1] **-ra** *m,f* (Zool) parrot; **lo repitió como un ~** he repeated it parrot fashion; ***hablar como un ~*** (fam) to be a chatterbox (colloq)

loro[2] *m* (fam) 1▸ (charlatán) chatterbox (colloq) 2▸ (mujer fea) (Esp fam) hag

los[1], **las** *art*: *ver* **el**

los[2], **las** *pron pers*

A (referido — a ellos, ellas, cosas, etc) them; (— a ustedes) you; **las llevé al circo** I took them to the circus; **¿las atienden?** can I help you?

B (*con el verbo* **haber**): **las hay de muchos tamaños** they come in many different sizes; **también ~ hay de chocolate** we have chocolate ones too

losa *f* (de sepulcro) tombstone; (de suelo) flagstone

(Compuesto) **losa radiante** radiant heating (AmE), underfloor heating (BrE)

loseta *f* floor tile

lote *m*

A (de un producto) batch; (en subastas) lot; ***darse un ~ de algo*** (Esp fam) to stuff oneself with sth (colloq)

B (terreno) plot (of land)

(Compuesto) **lote urbanizado** serviced site

C (fam) (montón) loads (*pl*) (colloq); **un ~ de** loads of

lotear [A1] *vt* (CS) ▸**lotificar**

loteo *m* (CS) ▸**lotificación**

lotería *f* lottery; **me gané la ~** I won the lottery; **con ese trabajo le tocó** *or* (AmL) **se sacó la ~** she really struck lucky with that job; **comprarse un coche usado es una ~** buying a used car is a bit of a gamble

(Compuesto) **lotería primitiva** (en Esp) state lottery

Lotería Nacional

A Spanish state-run lottery founded in 1812. There is an "ordinary" draw on Thursdays and "special" and "extraordinary" draws, offering bigger prizes. The biggest are **El Gordo**, drawn before Christmas, and *El Niño*, drawn at Epiphany.

You can buy a complete ticket or a *participación de lotería*, worth one tenth of a ticket. It is common to buy *participaciones* collectively. Prize money is shared among the co-owners of the ticket.

Other lotteries are the **bonoloto**, **Lotería Primitiva**, and the **Once**

Lotería Primitiva *or* **Loto**

A Spanish state lottery founded in 1985. It works like the bonoloto: players mark six numbers on a ticket containing 49 numbers and win the main prize if all their numbers come up in the draw. There are "ordinary" draws on Thursdays and Saturdays, and a draw for a larger prize on the last Sunday of each month, known as El Gordo, or *El Gordo de la Primitiva*

lotero -ra *m,f* lottery ticket seller

lotificación *f* (Méx, Per) division of land into lots (AmE) *o* (BrE) plots

lotificar [A2] *vt* (Méx, Per) to divide … into lots (AmE) *o* (BrE) plots

loto *m* lotus

loza *f* 1 (material) china 2 (vajilla) crockery; (de mejor calidad) china

lozanía *f* (de persona) healthiness; (del cutis) freshness; (de las verduras) freshness

lozano -na *adj* ‹*persona*› healthy-looking; ‹*cutis*› fresh; ‹*verduras*› fresh

LSD *m or f* LSD

Ltda (= **Limitada**) Ltd, Limited

lubina *f* sea bass

lubricación *f* lubrication

lubricante[1] *adj* lubricating

lubricante[2] *m* lubricant

lubricar [A2] *vt* to lubricate

lubricidad *f* (frml) lewdness, lubricity (liter)

lucerna *f*, **lucernario** *m* skylight, fanlight

lucero *m*
A (estrella brillante) bright star
(Compuesto) **lucero del alba** morning star
B **luceros** *mpl* (liter) (ojos) eyes (*pl*)

luces *fpl* ▸ **luz**

lucha *f*
A (combate, pelea) fight; (para conseguir algo) struggle; **la ~ por la supervivencia** the struggle for survival; **las ~s internas de un partido** internal conflict within a party; **la ~ contra el cáncer** the fight against cancer
(Compuestos)
• **lucha armada** armed conflict
• **lucha de clases** class struggle
B (Dep) wrestling
(Compuesto) **lucha libre** all-in wrestling

luchador[1] **-dora** *adj*: **un hombre muy ~** a real fighter; **tienes que ser más ~** you have to fight harder

luchador[2] **-dora** *m,f*
A (persona esforzada) fighter
B (Dep) wrestler

luchar [A1] *vi*
A 1 (combatir, pelear) to fight; **~ cuerpo a cuerpo** to fight hand to hand 2 (para conseguir algo) to struggle, fight; **~ para salir adelante** struggle hard to get on in life; **~ por la paz** to fight for peace 3 (lidiar) to wrestle, struggle; **~ CON algo** to wrestle WITH sth
B (Dep) to wrestle

luche *m*
A (Bot) *type of edible seaweed*
B (Chi) (Jueg) hopscotch

lucidez *f* 1 (Psic) lucidity; **en un momento de ~** in a lucid moment 2 (inteligencia) lucidity, clarity

lucido -da *adj* 1 ‹*fiesta*› magnificent, splendid; **su actuación no fue muy lucida** her performance wasn't particularly brilliant 2 (fam) ‹*niño/bebé*› healthy

lúcido -da *adj* 1 [SER] ‹*mente/análisis*› lucid, clear; ‹*persona*› clear-thinking, clear-sighted 2 [ESTAR] ‹*enfermo*› lucid

luciérnaga *f* (insecto volador) firefly; (larva) glowworm; (insecto sin alas) glowworm

Lucifer Lucifer

lucimiento *m* 1 (acción): **permite el ~ de los gimnastas** it allows the gymnasts to show off their skills 2 (brillo) sparkle, brilliance

lucio *m* pike

lucir [I5] *vi* 1 (aparentar) to look good; **un regalo que no luce** a gift that doesn't look anything special; (+ *me/te/le etc*) **el dinero no le luce** (hum) you can't tell what he spends his money on; **gasta mucho en ropa pero no le luce** she spends a fortune on clothes but it doesn't do much for her 2 (liter) ‹‹*estrellas*›› to twinkle, shine 3 (AmL) (aparecer, mostrarse) (+ *compl*) to look; **la catedral lucía esplendorosa** the cathedral stood out in all its splendor; **te luce lindo** it looks nice on you

■ **lucir** *vt* 1 (period) ‹*vestido/modelo*› to wear, sport (journ); ‹*peinado/collar*› to sport (journ) 2 ‹*figura/piernas*› to show off, flaunt

■ **lucirse** *v pron* 1 (destacarse) to excel; **¡te luciste!** (iró) you really excelled yourself! (iro); **recetas para ~se** recipes to impress your guests 2 (presumir) to show off

lucrarse [A1] *v pron* to make a profit; **~ DE algo** to make a profit FROM sth

lucrativo -va *adj* lucrative, profitable; **una entidad sin fines ~s** a nonprofit (AmE) *o* (BrE) non-profit-making organization

lucro *m* profit, gain; **sin ánimo de ~** with no profit motive in mind

luctuoso -sa *adj* (frml) painful

lucubrar [A1] *vt* ▸ **elucubrar**

lúcuma *f* eggfruit

ludibrio *m* jeer, scoff

lúdico -ca *adj* ‹*fantasías/diversiones*› play (*before n*)

ludoteca *f* toy library

luego[1] *adv*
A (más tarde) later (on); (después de otro suceso — en el futuro) afterwards; (— en el pasado) then, next; **nos vemos ~** I'll see you later (on); **¡hasta ~!** goodbye!, see you!; **~ DE + INF** after -ING
B (Chi, Méx) (pronto) soon, quickly; **lueguito vuelvo** I'll be back in no time; **~ ~** (Méx) immediately
C 1 (en el espacio): **hay una tienda y ~ está el banco** there's a shop and then you come to the bank 2 (Méx) (cerca) nearby; **aquí ~** just here 3 (indicando orden, prioridad) then; **primero está él y ~ nosotros** he's first and then we're next
D **desde luego** of course; **desde ~ que no** of course not

luego[2] *conj* (frml) therefore

lúes *f* syphilis

lugar *m*
A (sitio) place; **no es éste el ~** this is not the place; **en cualquier otro ~** anywhere else; **cambiar los muebles de ~** to move the furniture around; **en algún ~** somewhere; Ⓢ **consérvese en lugar fresco** keep in a cool place; **el ~ del suceso** the scene of the incident
B (localidad, región): **los habitantes del ~** the local people; **~ y fecha de nacimiento** place and date of birth
C 1 (espacio libre) room; **hacer ~ para algn/algo** to make room *o* space for sb/sth 2 (asiento) seat
D 1 (situación) place; **yo en tu ~ ...** if I were you …; **ponte en mi ~** put yourself in my place 2 (en organización, jerarquía) place; **nadie puede ocupar el ~ de la madre** nobody can take a mother's place; **según el ~ que ocupan en la lista** according to their position on the list; **se clasificó en primer/quinto ~** she finished in first/fifth place
E **dar lugar a** (a una disputa, a comentarios) to provoke, give rise to; **han dado ~ a que la gente hable** their behavior has set people talking
F (Der): **no ha ~ la protesta** the objection is overruled
G (*en locs*) **en lugar de** instead of; **ella firmó en mi ~** she signed on my behalf; **en primer lugar**: **se tratarán en primer ~** they will be dealt with first; **en primer ~ porque ...** first of all *o* firstly because …; **en último lugar**: **y en último ~ ...** and finally *o* lastly …; ***a como dé/diera ~*** (AmL): **se trata de venderlo a como dé ~** the idea is to sell it any way we can; **a como diera ~ yo iba a entrar** one way or another I was going to get in; ***dejar a algn en mal ~*** to put sb in an awkward position; ***poner a algn en su ~*** to put sb in her/his place; ***sin ~ a dudas*** without doubt, undoubtedly; ***tener ~*** to take place
(Compuesto) **lugar común** cliché, commonplace

lugareño -ña *adj/mf* local

lugarteniente *mf* deputy

lúgubre *adj* ‹*habitación/ambiente/persona*› gloomy, lugubrious (liter); ‹*rostro/voz/paisaje*› gloomy

lujo *m* luxury; **no puedo permitirme el ~ de llegar tarde** I can't afford to be late; **nos dimos el ~ de viajar en primera** we treated ourselves and traveled first class; **me di el ~ de decirles que no** I had the satisfaction of saying no to them; **con ~ de detalles** with a wealth of detail

(Compuesto) **lujo asiático**: **vivir con ~ ~** to live in the lap of luxury; **eso ya es un ~ ~** that is the ultimate in luxury

lujoso -sa *adj* luxurious

lujuria *f* (liter) lust, lechery

lujuriante *adj* luxuriant, lush

lujurioso -sa *adj* lecherous, lustful

lumbago *m* lumbago

lumbar *adj* lumbar (*before n*)

lumbre *f* (de hoguera, chimenea) fire; (de la cocina): **puso el cazo en la ~** she put the saucepan on the stove; **tengo la leche en la ~** I'm heating up some milk 2▸ (ant) (para un cigarrillo): **¿tiene ~?** have you got a light?

lumbrera *f* (fam) (persona brillante) genius, whiz* (colloq); **no es ninguna ~** he's no genius

luminaria *f*

A (adorno) light; (en un altar) altar lamp

B (AmL) (persona — sabia) luminary; (— importante) prominent figure, celebrity

luminiscencia *f* luminescence

luminosidad *f* brightness, luminosity

luminoso -sa *adj* 1▸ ‹*habitación*› bright, light; ‹*fuente*› luminous; ‹*letrero*› illuminated 2▸ ‹*idea*› brilliant

luminotecnia *f* lighting

luminotécnico -ca *adj* lighting (*before n*)

lumpen¹ *adj inv* underprivileged

lumpen² *m* (*pl* ~ *or* **lúmpenes**) (grupo social) underclass

lun. (= **lunes**) Mon

luna *f*

A (Astron) moon; **a la luz de la ~** in the moonlight; **hay ~** the moon's out; ***estar en la ~*** (fam) to have one's head in the clouds; ***ladrarle a la ~*** to talk to a brick wall (colloq); ***pedir la ~*** to ask (for) the impossible

(Compuestos)

- **luna creciente/menguante** waxing/waning moon
- **luna de miel** honeymoon; **están de ~ de ~** they're on their honeymoon
- **luna llena/nueva** full/new moon

B (espejo) mirror; (de puerta, ventana) glass; (escaparate) window; (parabrisas) windshield (AmE), windscreen (BrE)

C (de la uña) half-moon, lunule (tech)

lunar¹ *adj* lunar

lunar² *m* 1▸ (en la piel) mole; **se pintó un ~ en la mejilla** she painted a beauty spot on her cheek 2▸ (en el pelo) gray* patch 3▸ (en un diseño) polka-dot; (mácula) blemish

lunático¹ -ca *adj* lunatic (*before n*)

lunático² -ca *m,f* lunatic

lunes *m* (*pl* ~) Monday; **el ~ por la mañana/noche** on Monday morning/night; **todos los ~** every Monday; **el próximo ~** next Monday; **el ~ pasado** last Monday; **el ~ es fiesta** Monday is a holiday; **nos casamos el ~ 25 de Mayo** we got married on Monday May 25th; **hasta el ~** *or* **nos vemos el ~** I'll see you on Monday; **los ~** on Mondays; **el periódico del ~** Monday's paper; ***hacer ~ de zapatero*** (Col) *or* (Chi, Méx) ***hacer san ~*** (fam & hum) to skip work *o* (BrE) skive off work on Mondays

luneta *f*

A (Auto) window; **~ trasera** rear window

B (Col, Méx) (Teatr) orchestra seats (*pl*) (AmE), front stalls (*pl*) (BrE)

lunfardo *m* Buenos Aires slang

lupa *f* magnifying glass; **lo mira todo con ~** he goes through everything with a fine tooth comb

lupanar *m* brothel

lúpulo *m* (planta) hop (plant); (fruto) hop; **el sabor del ~** the flavor of hops

luso -sa, **lusitano -na** *adj/m,f* Portuguese

lustrabotas *mf* (*pl* ~) (AmS) bootblack

lustrada *f* (AmS) polish, shine

lustrador -dora *m,f* (AmS) bootblack; (niño) shoeshine boy

lustrar [A1] *vt* (esp AmL) ‹*zapatos/muebles*› to polish

■ **lustrarse** *v pron*

A (esp AmL) ‹*zapatos*› to polish

B (AmC) (en una actividad) to excel

lustre *m* 1▸ (brillo) shine, luster*; **darle** *or* **sacarle ~ a algo** to polish sth 2▸ (distinción) glory, distinction

lustrín *m* (AmS) (cajón) bootblack's box; (puesto) shoeshine stand

lustro *m* period of five years

lustroso -sa *adj* shiny

luterano -na *adj/m,f* Lutheran

luto *m* mourning; **estar de** *or* **guardar ~** to be in mourning; **~ riguroso** deep mourning; **ir de** *or* **llevar ~** to wear mourning (clothes); **el ~ se lleva por dentro** grief is carried within; **ponerse de ~** to go into mourning

(Compuesto) **luto oficial** official mourning

luxación *f* dislocation

Luxemburgo *m* Luxembourg

luxemburgués -guesa *adj* of/from Luxembourg

luz *f*

A 1▸ (claridad) light; **la ~ del sol** the sunlight; **la habitación tiene mucha ~** the room gets a lot of light; **me da la ~ en los ojos** the light's in my eyes; **a plena ~ del día** in broad daylight; **este reflector da mucha ~** this spotlight is very bright; **no leas con tan poca ~** don't read in such poor light; **la habitación estaba a media ~** the room was in semi-darkness; **me estás tapando la ~** you're blocking the light; **luces y sombras** (Art) light and shade; (lo bueno y lo malo) the good and the bad; ***dar a ~*** to give birth; ***entre dos luces*** (liter) (al amanecer) at daybreak (liter); (al anochecer) at twilight (liter); ***sacar algo a la ~*** ‹*secreto/escándalo*› to bring sth to light; ‹*publicación*› to bring out; ***salir a la ~*** «*secreto/escándalo*» to come to light; «*publicación*» to come out; ***tener pocas luces*** (fam) to be dimwitted; ***ver la ~*** (liter) «*persona*» to come into the world (liter); «*publicación*» to be published (*for the first time*) 2▸ (que permite la comprensión): **a la ~ de los últimos acontecimientos** in the light of recent events; **arrojar ~ sobre algo** to shed light on sth; ***a todas luces***: **esto es, a todas luces, una injusticia** whichever way you look at it, this is an injustice

(Compuesto) **luz artificial/natural** artificial/natural light

B (fam) (electricidad) electricity; **les cortaron la ~** their electricity was cut off; **se fue la ~** (en una casa) the electricity went off; (en una zona) there was a power cut

C (dispositivo) light; **la ~ del cuarto de baño** the bathroom light; **encender** *or* (AmL) **prender la ~** to turn on *o* switch on the light; **apagar la ~** to turn off *o* switch off the light; **cruzar con la luz roja** to cross when the lights are red; ***comerse una*** *or* ***la ~*** (Ven fam) to go through a red light; ***dar ~ verde a algo*** to give sth the green light

(Compuestos)

- **luces de aterrizaje** *fpl* landing lights (*pl*)
- **luces de estacionamiento** *or* (Esp) **de situación** *fpl* parking lights (*pl*) (AmE), sidelights (*pl*) (BrE)
- **luces de cruce** *or* **cortas** *or* (AmL) **bajas** *fpl* dipped headlights (*pl*)
- **luces de navegación** *fpl* navigation lights (*pl*)
- **luces intermitentes** *fpl* flashing lights (*pl*)
- **luces largas** *or* **altas** *fpl*: **pon las ~ ~** put the headlights on full beam
- **luz de frenado** stoplight, brake light (BrE)
- **luz de giro** (Arg) indicator
- **luz de neón** neon light
- **luz y sonido** son et lumière

D (Arquit, Ing) span

luzca, luzcan, etc *see* **lucir**

Mm

M, m *f (read as /'eme/) the letter* **M, m**

m

A (en formularios) **1** (= **masculino**) M male **2** (= **mujer**) F female

B (= **metro**) m, meter*

maca *f* **1** (en fruta) bruise **2** (defecto) flaw, defect

macabro -bra *adj* macabre

macaco -ca *m,f*

A (Zool) macaque

B **1** (fam) (bribón) little devil (colloq), rascal (colloq) **2** (Per fam & pey) (chino) (*m*) Chinaman (colloq); (*f*) Chinese woman **3** (CS fam & pey) (persona fea) ugly person **4** (Esp arg) (chulo) pimp

macadam, macadán *m* Tarmac®

macana *f*

A (AmL) (de policía) billy club (AmE), truncheon (BrE)

B **1** (CS fam) (tontería, disparate): **decir ~s** to talk nonsense; **no hagas la ~ de renunciar** don't be so stupid as to resign (colloq) **2** (CS fam) (contrariedad): **¡qué ~ que no puedas venir!** what a shame *o* (colloq) drag you can't come!; **la ~ es que queda lejísimos** the snag *o* trouble is that it's miles away **3** (RPl fam) (mentira) lie **4** (Chi, Per fam) (porquería): **esta ~ de auto** this lousy car (colloq)

macanear [A1] *vi* (RPl fam) (mentir) to lie, tell tall stories; (decir tonterías) to talk nonsense

■ **macanear** *vt*

A (Chi fam) (molestar) to pester

B (Méx) (golpear) to beat

macanudo -da *adj* (CS, Per fam) great (colloq), fantastic (colloq)

macar [A2] *vt* to bruise

■ **macarse** *v pron* to begin to rot

macarrón *m*

A **1** (pasta) piece of macaroni; **macarrones** macaroni **2** (galleta) macaroon

B (Náut) bulwark

macarrónico -ca *adj*: **habla un inglés ~** (fam & hum) his English is absolutely terrible *o* (BrE colloq) chronic

macedonia *f* (de frutas) fruit salad, macedoine; (de verduras) mixed vegetables (*pl*), macedoine

Macedonia *f* Macedonia

macehual, macegual *m* serf (*in pre-Hispanic Mexico*)

macerar [A1] *vt* **1** (en un líquido) ‹*fruta*› to soak, macerate; ‹*carne*› to marinate, marinade **2** (machacar) ‹*ajo*› to crush

maceta *f* **1** (tiesto) flowerpot **2** (martillo) mallet **3** (Méx fam) (cabeza) nut (colloq)

maceteado -da *adj* (Chi, Per fam) burly

macetero *m* **1** (para tiestos) flowerpot holder **2** (AmS) (tiesto) large flowerpot; (jardinera) window box

macha *f*: *edible clam*

machaca *f* **1** (aparato) crusher, pounder **2** (Coc) *traditional Mexican dish made with crushed dried meat fried with egg and onion*

machacadora *f* crusher, pounder

machacar [A2] *vt*

A **1** ‹*ajo*› to crush; ‹*almendras*› to grind, crush; ‹*piedra*› to crush, pound **2** (fam) ‹*contrincante*› to thrash (colloq) **3** (fam) (pegar) to beat … to a pulp **4** ‹*precios*› to slash

B (Esp fam) **1** (repetir): **machácale bien lo que tiene que hacer** make sure you drum into her what she has to do; **~ un tema** to go on *o* harp on about a subject (colloq) **2** (estudiar) to bone up on (colloq)

■ **machacar** *vi* **1** (fam) (insistir): **~ con** *or* **sobre algo** to go on *o* harp on about sth (colloq) **2** (fam) (para un examen) to cram (colloq)

■ **machacarse** *v pron* (fam) ‹*dedo*› to crush

machacón -cona *adj* (insistente) insistent; (pesado) tiresome; **con machacona insistencia** with tiresome insistence

machada *f* (fam) stunt (colloq) **hacer una ~** to pull a stunt

machamartillo: **a ~** (*loc adj*) ‹*monárquico/feminista*› ardent, staunch; (*loc adv*) firmly; **lo creo a ~** I firmly believe it

machetazo *m* blow/slash with a machete

machete¹ *adj inv* (Ven fam) great (colloq)

machete² -ta *adj* (Ur fam) stingy (colloq)

machete³ *m*

A (cuchillo) machete

B (Arg fam) (para examen) crib (colloq)

machetear [A1] *vt*

A ‹*pasto/caña*› to cut; ‹*persona*› to slash

B (Per arg) (acariciar) to fondle

C (Ur fam) ‹*vino/comida*› to skimp on

machetero¹ -ra *adj* (Méx fam) persevering

machetero² -ra *m,f*

A (cañero) cane cutter

B (Méx) **1** (descargador) porter; (en mudanzas) removal man **2** (fam) (estudiante) plodder (colloq)

machetona *f* (Méx fam) tomboy

machi *mf* (Chi) witch doctor

machihembrado *m* (ensambladura — de caja y espiga) mortise and tenon joint; (— de cola de milano) dovetail joint; (— de ranura y lengüeta) tongue and groove joint

machín-machón *m* (Col) seesaw, teeter-totter (AmE)

machismo *m* **1** (actitud, ideología) sexism, male chauvinism **2** (cualidad) masculinity, virility

> **machismo**
>
> A concept deeply rooted in the Spanish-speaking world. It has its origin in a sense of honor, felt to depend on a man's own actions and those of his close family, particularly its female members. *Machismo* is present in the home, where even working women usually do most of the housework, and extends to the workplace. It can affect the legal status of women. In Spain legal reforms since the 1970s have contributed to undermining *machismo*

machista¹ *adj* sexist, chauvinist

machista² *mf* sexist, male chauvinist

machitún *m* (Chi) healing ceremony

macho¹ *adj*

A ‹*animal/planta*› male; **ballena/elefante ~** bull whale/elephant; **liebre ~** buck hare; **gato ~** tomcat

B (fam) (valiente, fuerte) tough, brave; (pey) macho (pej)

C ‹*pieza*› male

macho² -cha *adj* (Col fam) great (colloq)

macho³ *m*

A **1** (Biol, Zool) male **2** (fam) (hijo) boy

(Compuesto) **macho cabrío** billy goat
B (mula) mule; ***atarse los ~s*** (Esp) to pluck up courage; ***montarse en el ~*** to dig one's heels in; ***no bajarse del ~*** to stick to one's guns
C **1** (fam) (hombre fuerte) tough guy (colloq); (pey) macho man (colloq & pej); **¡aguántese como los ~s!** take it like a man! **2** (como apelativo) (Esp fam): **jo, ~ ¡qué calor hace!** boy *o* wow *o* gee *o* man, it's hot! (colloq); **oye, ~ ¡deja algo para mí!** hey you, leave some for me! (colloq)
D (Mec, Tec) pin; (Elec) male (plug); (de un corchete) hook; (en carpintería) peg, pin

machón *m* buttress

machona *f* **1** (RPl fam) (niña) tomboy **2** (Per fam & pey) (lesbiana) dyke (colloq & pej) **3** (Arg fam & pey) (mujer hombruna) butch woman (colloq & pej)

machorra *adj* **1** (estéril) sterile, barren **2** (fam & pey) (hombruna) butch (colloq & pej); (lesbiana) lesbian

machote -ta *m,f* **1** (fam) (hombre) tough guy (colloq); (pey) macho man (colloq & pej) **2** (fam & pey) (mujer) butch woman (colloq & pej)

machucadura *f* bruise

machucar [A2] *vt*
A **1** ‹*fruta*› to bruise **2** ‹*dedo*› (aplastar) to crush; (golpear) to hit, smash **3** (Méx) ‹*ajo*› to crush
B (Méx) (en béisbol) to chop
■ **machucarse** *v pron* **1** «*fruta*» to bruise, get bruised **2** (*refl*) (lastimarse) ‹*dedo*› (estrujar) to squash; (golpear) to hit, smash; ***machucárselas*** (Chi fam) to have a rough time (colloq)

machucón *m*
A (AmL fam) (moretón) bruise
B (Méx) (en béisbol) chop

Machu Picchu

An Inca fortress and sacred city in the southern Peruvian Andes. The site covers an area of around five square miles (thirteen square kilometers) at an altitude of 7,874 feet (2,400 meters). It includes a temple and citadel and is surrounded by terraces. It was rediscovered in 1911 by the American, Hiram Bingham

macicez *f* **1** (solidez) solidity **2** (robustez) sturdiness, robustness

macilento -ta *adj* **1** ‹*persona/cara*› gaunt, haggard **2** ‹*luz*› wan (liter)

macillo *m* hammer

macis *f* mace

macizo¹ -za *adj* **1** [SER] (sólido) solid **2** [ESTAR] (fam) ‹*persona*› (robusto) strapping (colloq) **3** [ESTAR] (Esp fam) (atractivo) ‹*hombre*› hunky (colloq); ‹*mujer*› gorgeous (colloq)

macizo² *m*
A **1** (de montañas) massif **2** (de flores, arbustos) clump
B (Arquit) section

maco *m* (Col) monkey

macramé *m* macramé

macro *m* (Inf) (arg) macro

macró *m* (CS) pimp

macrobiótico -ca *adj* macrobiotic; (en sentido no estricto) wholefood (*before n*)

macrocosmos, macrocosmo *m* macrocosm

macroeconómica *f* macroeconomics

macuco -ca *adj* (Chi, Per fam) cute (AmE colloq), sharp (BrE colloq)

mácula *f* **1** (liter) (mancilla) blemish (frml), taint (liter) **2** (del sol) sunspot

macuquear [A1] *vi* (Chi, Per fam) to scheme

macuto *m* back pack, rucksack (BrE)

madalena *f* ≈ cupcake (AmE), ≈ fairycake (BrE)

madama *f* madam

madame /ma'ðam/ *f* madam

madeja *f* (de lana, hilo) hank, skein; ***enredar la ~*** (fam) to complicate matters *o* things

madera *f*
A (material) wood; (para construcción, carpintería) lumber (esp AmE), timber (BrE); **es de ~** it's made of wood, it's wooden; **mesa de ~** wooden table; **~ de pino** pine (wood); ***dar ~ a algn*** (Col fam) to make mincemeat of sb (colloq); ***tener ~***: **tiene ~ de político** he has the makings of a politician, he's politician material; ***tocar ~*** to knock (on) wood (AmE), touch wood (BrE)
(Compuesto) **madera blanda/dura** softwood/hardwood
B **maderas** *fpl* (Mús) woodwind (+ *sing o pl vb*)
C (en golf) wood

maderable *adj* timber-yielding

maderamen *m* woodwork, timbering

maderero¹ -ra *adj* timber (*before n*); lumber (*before n*) (esp AmE)

maderero² -ra *m,f* timber merchant

madero *m* (piece of) timber

madona *f* Madonna

madrás *m* madras

madrastra *f* stepmother

madrazo *m* (Méx fam) blow; **darle un ~ a algn** to give sb a beating; **películas de ~** violent movies

madre¹ *adj inv* (Chi fam) great (colloq)

madre² *f*
A **1** (pariente) mother; **ser ~** to be a mother; ***ahí está la ~ del cordero*** that's the root of the problem; ***estar hasta la ~ de algo*** (Méx fam) to be fed up to the back teeth of sth; **~ de todos los vicios** mother of all vices; ***mentarle la ~ a algn*** to insult sb (*by referring to his/her mother*); ***no tener ~*** (Méx fam) to be shameless: ***ser un/una ~ para algo*** (Chi fam) to be brilliant at sth **2** (en exclamaciones): **¡~ mía!** *or* **¡mi ~!** (my) goodness!, (good) heavens!; **¡la ~ que te parió!** (fam: en algunas regiones vulg) you jerk! (colloq), you bastard! (sl); **¡tu ~!** (vulg) screw you! (vulg), up yours! (BrE sl); ***¡chinga (a) tu ~!*** (Méx vulg) screw *o* fuck you! (vulg); ***me vale ~s*** (Méx vulg) I don't give a damn (colloq) *o* (vulg) shit **3** (Relig) mother; **la ~ Soledad** Mother Soledad
(Compuestos)
- **madre alquilada** *or* **de alquiler** surrogate mother
- **madre de familia** mother
- **Madre Patria** (AmL): **la ~ ~** Spain
- **madre política** mother-in-law
- **madre soltera** single *o* unmarried mother
- **madre superiora** Mother Superior

B **1** (cauce): **el río se salió de ~** the river burst its banks; **todo se salió de ~** everything got out of hand **2** (Esp) (sedimento) lees (*pl*), sediment

madrear [A1] *vt* (Méx fam) to beat … up (colloq)

madreperla *f* mother-of-pearl

madreselva *f* honeysuckle

Madrid *m* Madrid

madrigal *m* madrigal

madriguera *f* **1** (de conejos) warren, burrow; (de zorros) earth; (de tejones) set **2** (de maleantes) den, lair

madrileño¹ -ña *adj* of/from Madrid

madrileño² -ña *m,f* person from Madrid

madrina *f*
A **1** (en bautizo) godmother; (en boda) ≈ matron of honor*; (de confirmación) sponsor **2** (de barco) *woman who launches a ship*
B (Méx fam) (coche celular) police van, paddy wagon (colloq)

madriza *f* (Méx vulg): **le dieron** *or* **pusieron una santa ~** they really beat the shit out of him (vulg)

madroño *m* **1** (Bot) tree strawberry **2** (borla) tassel

madrugada *f* **1** (amanecer, alba) dawn, daybreak, early morning; **se levantó de ~** (muy temprano) she got up very early (in the morning); (al amanecer) she got up at dawn *o* daybreak **2** (después de medianoche) early morning, morning; **la una/las tres de la ~** one/three o'clock in the morning; **llegó de ~** he arrived in the early hours of the morning *o* in the small hours

madrugador -dora *adj*: **soy muy ~** I'm an early riser

madrugar [A3] *vi* to get up early; ***a quien madruga Dios lo ayuda*** the early bird catches the worm; ***no por mucho ~ amanece más temprano*** everything at its appointed time
■ **madrugar** *vt* (AmL fam) ‹*persona*› to beat … to it (colloq)

madrugón *m* (fam): **darse** *or* **pegarse un ~** (fam) to get up very early *o* (colloq) at the crack of dawn

madruguete *m* (Méx fam): **tenderle** *or* **hacerle un ~ a algn** to get *o* have one up on sb

m

maduración *f* [1] (de fruta) ripening (process) [2] (de una persona) maturing (process) [3] (de una idea) development, maturing

madurar [A1] *vi* [1] «*fruta*» to ripen [2] «*persona*» to mature [3] «*ideas*» to mature, come to fruition

■ **madurar** *vt* [1] ‹*fruta*› to ripen [2] ‹*plan*› to develop, bring to fruition

■ **madurarse** *v pron* to ripen

madurez *f*

A (de una fruta) ripeness

B (de una persona) [1] (cualidad) maturity [2] (edad, período) maturity; **como autor tuvo una ~ prolífica** as an author he was prolific in his later years

maduro[1] **-ra** *adj*

A [1] [ESTAR] ‹*fruta*› ripe; ▸**caerse AB** [2] [ESTAR] (listo) **~ PARA algo** ripe FOR sth

B [1] [SER] (entrado en años) mature, of mature years [2] [SER] (sensato) mature; **es muy poco ~** he is very immature; **es joven pero muy ~** he's young but very mature for his age

maduro[2] *m* (Col, Ven) plantain

maese *m*

A (arc) (maestro) Master (arch)

B (Méx fam) [1] (amigo) buddy (AmE colloq), mate (BrE colloq) [2] (profesor) teacher

maestranza *f* [1] (del ejército) arsenal, armory (AmE); (de la marina) naval dockyard [2] (trabajadores) arsenal/dockyard workers (*pl*)

maestre *m* Master

maestría *f*

A (liter) (habilidad) skill, mastery

B (Educ) (postgrado) master's degree, master's

maestrillo -lla, **maestrito -ta** *m,f*: ***cada ~ tiene su librillo*** *or* ***cada maestrito con su librito*** each to his own

maestro -tra *m,f*

A [1] (Educ) teacher, schoolteacher; ***no hay mejor maestra que la necesidad*** necessity is the mother of invention [2] (en un arte, disciplina): **es un consumado ~ de la danza española** he is a master of Spanish dance; **un ~ de las letras españolas** a leading authority *o* an expert on Spanish literature [3] (en un oficio) master (*before n*); **~ carpintero** master carpenter [4] (Chi) (obrero) builder

(Compuestos)

- **maestra jardinera** *f* (Arg, Col) kindergarten teacher, nursery school teacher (BrE)
- **maestro -tra de escuela** *m,f* school teacher
- **maestro (mayor) de obras** master builder

B (Mús) maestro

C (Taur) matador

D (en ajedrez) master

E **maestro** *m* (AmL) (como apelativo) buddy (AmE colloq), mate (BrE colloq)

mafia *f* [1] (grupo de criminales) mafia; **la M~ siciliana** the Sicilian Mafia [2] (en una organización, sociedad) mafia, clique

mafioso[1] **-sa** *adj* mafia (*before n*)

mafioso[2] **-sa** *m,f* (criminal) gangster, racketeer; (de la Mafia siciliana) mafioso

magazine /maɣa'sin/ *m* [1] (TV) magazine program, magazine (AmE) [2] (Period) magazine

magdalena *f* (Esp) ▸**madalena**

Magdalena: **María ~** *or* **la ~** Mary Magdalene; ***llorar como una*** *or* ***la ~*** to cry one's eyes out

magenta *adj inv* magenta

magia *f* [1] (arte) magic; **hacer ~** to do magic (tricks) [2] (encanto, atractivo) magic; **la ~ de su voz** the magical quality *o* the magic of her voice

mágico -ca *adj* [1] ‹*poderes/número*› magic (*before n*) [2] ‹*belleza/ambiente*› magical

magín *m* (Esp fam) mind

magisterial *adj* teaching (*before n*)

magisterio *m* [1] (enseñanza) teaching; (carrera) teacher training; **estudia ~** he's training to be a teacher; **ejerció el ~ durante 20 años** she taught *o* was a teacher for 20 years [2] (conjunto de maestros) teachers (*pl*), teaching profession

magistrado -da *m,f* [1] (Der) judge, magistrate [2] (de Tribunal del Trabajo) judge

magistral *adj* ‹*actuación/libro*› masterly; ‹*tono/actitud*› magisterial (frml)

magistralmente *adv* brilliantly

magistratura *f* (cargo) judgeship/magistracy; (período) judgeship/magistracy; (conjunto de magistrados) magistracy, magistrates (*pl*), judges (*pl*)

(Compuesto) **Magistratura de Trabajo** (Esp) Industrial Tribunal

magnánimo -ma *adj* magnanimous

magnate *mf* magnate, tycoon; **los ~s de la prensa** the press barons

magnavoz *m* (Méx) bullhorn (AmE), loudhailer (BrE)

magnesia *f* magnesia

magnesio *m* magnesium

magnético -ca *adj* magnetic

magnetismo *m* magnetism

magnetizar [A4] *vt* [1] (Fís) to magnetize [2] (fascinar) to captivate, mesmerize

magnetofónico -ca *adj*: **una grabación magnetofónica** a tape recording

magnetófono, magnetofón *m* (reel-to-reel) tape recorder

magnetoscopio *m* (frml) video cassette recorder

magnicida[1] *adj* (frml): **esta acción ~** this assassination

magnicida[2] *mf* (frml) assassin

magnicidio *m* (frml) assassination

magnificar [A2] *vt*

A (liter) (alabar) to extol, laud (liter)

B (AmL) [1] ‹*imagen/objeto*› to magnify [2] ‹*problema*› to exaggerate, blow ... up (out of all proportion)

magnificencia *f* magnificence, splendor*

magnífico -ca *adj* [1] (excelente, estupendo) ‹*edificio/panorama*› magnificent, superb; ‹*espectáculo/escritor*› marvelous*, wonderful, superb; ‹*oportunidad*› wonderful, marvelous*; **¡~!** excellent! [2] (suntuoso) magnificent, splendid [3] (en títulos) honorable*

magnitud *f*

A (Astron, Fís, Mat) magnitude

B (importancia) magnitude; **consecuencias sociales de ~** far-reaching social consequences; **la ~ de la tragedia** the extent *o* magnitude of the tragedy; **una crisis de primera ~** a full-scale crisis, a crisis of the first magnitude *o* order

magno -na *adj* (*delante del n*) (frml) great

magnolia *f* magnolia

magnolio *m* magnolia (tree)

mago -ga *m,f* [1] (prestidigitador) conjurer, magician [2] (en cuentos) wizard, magician [3] (persona habilidosa) wizard [4] (Hist) (sacerdote) magus

magras *fpl* (Col) *fried eggs, ham, cheese and tomato*

magrear [A1] *vt* (Esp fam) to grope (colloq), to touch ... up (colloq)

magreo *m* (Esp fam) grope (colloq), groping (colloq)

magrez *f* leanness

magro -gra *adj*

A [1] ‹*carne*› lean [2] (liter) ‹*persona*› lean

B [1] (liter) ‹*tierra*› lean (liter), poor [2] (*delante del n*) (mezquino) meager*

magrura *f* leanness

magulladura *f* bruise

magullar [A1] *vt* to bruise

■ **magullarse** *v pron* [1] «*fruta*» to bruise [2] (*refl*) «*persona*» ‹*dedo/rodilla*› to bruise

magullón *m* (AmL) bruise

Mahoma Mohammed

mahometano[1] **-na** *adj* Islamic, Mohammedan (dated)

mahometano[2] **-na** *m,f* follower of Islam, Mohammedan (dated)

mahometismo *m* Islam, Mohammedanism (dated)

mahonesa *f* mayonnaise

maicena® *f* cornstarch (AmE), cornflour (BrE)

maicero -ra *adj* ‹*producción*› maize (*before n*), corn (*before n*) (AmE); ‹*zona*› maize-growing (*before n*), corn-growing (*before n*) (AmE)

mail /meil/ *m* (*pl* **~s**) email

mailing /'meilin/ *m* (*pl* **-lings**) mailing, mailshot (BrE); **hacer/enviar un ~** to compose/send a mailing *o* (BrE) a mailshot

(Compuestos)
- **mailing electoral** electoral mailing
- **mailing masivo** 1 (cartas) bulk mailing, mailshot (BrE) 2 (en Internet) spam

maillot /ma'ʏo(t)/ *m* 1 (traje de baño) swimsuit 2 (de ciclista) jersey

(Compuesto) **maillot amarillo** (camiseta) yellow jersey; (ciclista) yellow jersey, leader

maitines *mpl* matins (+ *sing or pl vb*)

maíz *m* (planta) maize, corn (AmE); (Coc) corn (AmE), sweet corn (esp BrE)

(Compuesto) **maíz tostado** *or* **pira** *or* **tote** (Col) popcorn

maizal *m* cornfield (AmE), maize field (BrE)

maizena® *f* cornstarch (AmE), cornflour (BrE)

maja *f* pestle; *ver tb* **majo**

majada *f* 1 (aprisco) fold 2 (estiércol — de vaca) cowpat; (— de caballo, búfalo): **una ~** some horse/buffalo dung 3 (CS) (rebaño — de ovejas) flock; (— de cabras) herd

majadería *f* 1 (fam) (cualidad) stupidity 2 (fam) (dicho, acto): **no dice más que ~s** he talks a lot of rubbish *o* nonsense (colloq); **lo que hizo fue una ~** it was a stupid thing to do

majadero[1] -ra *adj* 1 (fam) (insensato) stupid 2 (CS, Per fam) (fastidioso) whiny (colloq)

majadero[2] -ra *m,f*
A 1 (fam) (insensato) clown (colloq) 2 (CS fam) (quejoso) whiner (colloq), whinger (colloq)
B **majadoro** *m* (Tec) pestle

majar [A1] *vt* to crush

majara, majareta *adj* (Esp fam) nuts, crazy (colloq)

maje *mf*
A (AmC arg) (individuo) (*m*) guy (colloq), bloke (BrE colloq); (*f*) girl; ***hacerse el ~***: **no te hagas el ~** don't be such a pain (colloq)
B (Méx fam) (persona crédula) sucker (colloq); ***hacerle ~ a algn*** to make a sucker out of sb (colloq); ***hacerse (el/la) ~*** to play the innocent (colloq)

majestad *f*
A (aspecto grandioso) majesty
B **su Majestad** (al referirse — al rey) His Majesty; (— a la reina) Her Majesty; (al dirigirse al rey, a la reina) Your Majesty; **sus M~es los Reyes** Their Majesties the King and Queen

majestuosidad *f* majesty

majestuoso -sa *adj* majestic

majo[1] -ja *adj* (Esp fam) 1 ‹*persona*› (simpático) nice; (guapo) ‹*hombre*› handsome, good-looking; ‹*mujer*› good-looking, pretty 2 ‹*casa/vestido*› lovely, nice

majo[2] -ja *m,f* (Esp) (apelativo): **hola ~/maja!** hi, there! (colloq); **oye ~/maja, no te pases** OK, there's no need to over do it

majoleta *f* haw, hawthorn berry

majoleto *m* hawthorn

majuelo *m* 1 (Bot) hawthorn 2 (Agr) young vine

mal[1] *adj*: *ver* **malo**

mal[2] *adj inv*
A 1 (enfermo, con mal aspecto): **estar ~** to be bad *o* ill; (anímicamente) to be in a bad way (colloq); **me siento ~** I don't feel well, I feel ill; **andar ~ del estómago** to have trouble with one's stomach; **¡éste está ~ de la cabeza!** he's not right in the head; **esas cosas me ponen ~** things like that really upset me 2 (incómodo, a disgusto): **tú allí estás ~** you aren't comfortable there; **¿tan ~ estás aquí que te quieres ir?** are you so unhappy here that you want to leave?
B (fam) (*en frases negativas*) (refiriéndose al atractivo sexual): **no está nada ~** he's/she's not at all bad (colloq)
C (desagradable) ‹*oler/saber*› bad; **aquí huele ~** there's a horrible smell *o* it smells in here; **esta leche huele ~** this milk smells bad *o* off
D (insatisfactorio): **estoy** *or* **salí muy ~ en esta foto** I look awful in this photograph; **le queda ~ ese color** that color doesn't suit her; **el arroz siempre me queda ~** my rice never turns out right; **la casa no está ~, pero es cara** the house isn't bad, but it's expensive; **sacarme un millón no estaría nada ~** I wouldn't mind winning a million
E (incorrecto) wrong; **está muy ~ no decírselo** it's very wrong *o* bad not to tell her; **estuviste muy ~ en no ayudarlo** it was wrong of you not to help him
F (indicando escasez) **estar ~ DE algo** to be short OF sth; **estamos ~ de arroz** we're low on *o* almost out of rice

mal[3] *adv*
A (de manera no satisfactoria) ‹*hecho/vestido*› badly; ‹*cantar/escribir*› badly; **se expresó ~** he didn't express himself very well, he expressed himself badly; **te oigo muy ~** I can hardly hear you; **en el colegio se come muy ~** the food's terrible at school; **le fue ~ en los exámenes** his exams went badly; ***de ~ en peor*** from bad to worse
B (desventajosamente): **se casó muy ~** she made a bad marriage; **vendieron muy ~ la casa** they got a terrible price for the house; **el negocio marcha ~** the business isn't doing well
C (desfavorablemente) badly, ill; **hablar ~ de algn** to speak badly *o* ill of sb; **piensa ~ de todo el mundo** he thinks ill of everyone
D 1 (de manera errónea, incorrecta) wrong, wrongly; **lo has hecho ~** you've done it wrong; **te han informado ~** you've been badly *o* wrongly informed; **te entendí ~** I misunderstood you 2 (de manera reprensible) badly; **obró ~** he acted wrongly *o* badly; **haces ~ en no ir a verla** it's wrong of you not to go and see her; **me contestó muy ~** she answered me very rudely *o* in a very rude manner; **portarse ~** to behave badly, to misbehave
E (difícilmente): **~ puedes saber si te gusta si no lo has probado** you can hardly say whether you like it when you haven't even tried it
F (*en locs*) **hacer mal** (AmL) (a la salud): **esto hace ~ al hígado** this is bad for the liver; **comí algo que me hizo ~** I ate something which didn't agree with me; *ver tb* **mal[4] B**; **mal que bien** (fam) somehow or other; **mal que me/te/nos pese** whether I/you/we like it or not; **menos mal**: **¡menos ~!** thank goodness!; **¡menos ~ que le avisaron a tiempo!** it's just as well they told him in time!; **¡menos ~ que no se enteró!** it's a good thing she didn't find out! (colloq); ***estar a ~ con algn*** to be on bad terms with sb; ***tomarse algo a ~*** to take sth to heart

(Compuesto) **mal nacido -da** *m,f* nasty piece of work (colloq); *ver tb* **maleducado, etc**

mal[4] *m*
A (Fil) evil; **el bien y el ~** good and evil, right and wrong
B (daño, perjuicio): **el ~ que me hizo** the wrong she did me; **le estás haciendo un ~ consintiéndole todo** you're not doing her any good by giving in to her all the time; **el divorcio de sus padres le hizo mucho ~** her parents' divorce did her a lot of harm; **lo que dijo me hizo mucho ~** what he said really hurt me; *ver tb* **mal[3] F**
C (inconveniente, problema): **los ~es que aquejan a nuestra sociedad** the ills afflicting our society; **uno de los ~es de nuestro tiempo** one of the evils of our time; ***a grandes ~es grandes remedios*** desperate situations call for desperate measures; ***no hay ~ que cien años dure*** nothing goes on for ever; ***no hay ~ que por bien no venga*** every cloud has a silver lining; ***~ de muchos, consuelo de tontos***: **... pero yo no soy la única — ~ de muchos, consuelo de tontos** ... but I'm not the only one — well, if that makes you feel better about it (iro)

(Compuesto) **mal menor** (entre dos alternativas) lesser of two evils

D (Med) 1 (liter) (enfermedad) illness 2 (epilepsia): **el ~** (enfermedad) epilepsy; **cuando le da el ~** when she has a fit

(Compuestos)
- **mal de amores** (fam): **tiene ~ de ~** he's lovesick
- **mal de (las) altura(s)** altitude sickness, mountain sickness
- **mal de ojo** evil eye
- **mal de Parkinson** Parkinson's disease

E (pena) trouble

malabarismo *m* juggling; ***hacer ~s*** «*malabarista*» to juggle; (en una situación difícil) to do a juggling *o* balancing act

m

malabarista *mf* juggler
malacate *m* 1 (torno) winch 2 (Méx) (huso) spindle
malacatoso -sa *adj* (Chi fam) 1 (de mal aspecto) nasty-looking, unsavory-looking* 2 (deshonesto) crooked
malaconsejado -da *adj* [ESTAR] ill-advised
malacostumbrado -da *adj* spoiled*, pampered
malacostumbrar [A1] *vt* to spoil
■ **malacostumbrarse** *v pron* to become spoilt
malacrianza *f* (AmL) rudeness
malagradecido -da *adj* ungrateful
Malaisia *f* Malaysia
malaisio -sia *adj* Malaysian
malaleche *adj* (Esp fam) nasty (colloq), horrible (colloq)
malamente *adv* (apenas) hardly, only just; (mal) badly
malaria *f* malaria
Malasia *f* Malaysia
malasio -sia *adj/m,f* Malaysian
malavenido -da *adj* ill-matched
malaventura *f* (liter) misfortune
malaventurado -da *adj* (liter) ill-fated (liter)
malayo¹ -ya *adj/m,f* Malay
malayo² *m* (idioma) Malay
malbaratar [A1] *vt* 1 (malgastar) to squander 2 (malvender) to sell … at a loss, sell … off cheap
malcarado *adj* (con cara — de maleante) nasty looking; (— de enfado) grim-faced with anger
malcasado -da *adj* unhappily married
malcomer [E1] *vi* to eat badly
malcriado -da *adj* (mimado) spoiled*; (travieso) bad-mannered, badly brought up
malcrianza *f* (Chi, Per) rudeness
malcriar [A17] *vt* to spoil, bring … up badly
maldad *f* 1 (cualidad) evilness, wickedness 2 (acto) evil deed, wicked thing; **hacer ~es** to commit evil deeds
maldadoso -sa *adj* (fam) wicked, nasty
maldecir [I25] *vt* to curse
■ **maldecir** *vi* 1 (renegar) to curse; **~ DE algo/algn** to speak ill OF sth/sb 2 (blasfemar) to swear, curse (AmE)
maldiciente *adj* 1 (liter) (blasfemo) foulmouthed 2 (calumniador) slanderous, libelous*
maldición¹ *f* 1 (imprecación) curse; **nos echó una ~** she put a curse on us 2 (palabrota) swearword; **soltó una ~** he swore
maldición² *interj* (fam) damn (it)! (colloq)
maldiga, maldijo, etc *see* **maldecir**
maldito -ta *adj*
A (fam) (expresando irritación) damn (*before n*) (colloq), wretched (*before n*) (colloq); **maldita la gana que tengo de ir** I don't feel like going one bit; **maldita la hora en que lo acepté** I wish I'd never accepted; **¡maldita/~ sea!** damn (it)! (colloq)
B (Lit) ‹*escritor/poeta*› accursed
C (RPl fam) (egoísta) mean (colloq)
maldoso -sa *adj* (Méx) mischievous
maleabilidad *f* malleability
maleable *adj* 1 ‹*metal*› malleable 2 ‹*persona/carácter*› malleable
maleante *mf* criminal; **lo atacaron unos ~s** he was attacked by some thugs
malear [A1] *vt* to corrupt, pervert
■ **malearse** *v pron* to fall into evil ways
malecón *m* 1 (rompeolas) breakwater; (embarcadero) jetty 2 (AmL) (paseo marítimo) seafront 3 (Ferr) embankment
maledicencia *f* gossip, slander
maledicente *adj* ‹*campaña*› smear (*before n*); ‹*rumor*› slanderous; **es muy ~** he loves spreading scandal *o* malicious gossip
maleducado -da *adj* rude, bad-mannered
maleficencia *f* malice
maleficio *m* curse, spell
maléfico -ca *adj* ‹*poderes/espíritus*› evil; ‹*influencia*› harmful
malenseñado -da *adj* (CS) (maleducado) rude, bad-mannered; (mimado) spoiled
malenseñar [A1] *vt* (CS) to spoil
malentender [E8] *vt* to misunderstand; **no me malentiendas** don't misunderstand me *o* (colloq) get me wrong
malentendido *m* misunderstanding
malestar *m* 1 (Med) discomfort; **sentía un ~ general** I felt generally unwell 2 (desazón, inquietud) unease; **un profundo ~** a deep sense of unease; **el ~ que reina en el ambiente universitario** the prevailing malaise in the universities
maleta¹ *f*
A (valija) suitcase, case; **hacer la ~** to pack (one's case); ***estar de*** **~** (Chi fam) to be in a bad mood
B (Chi, Per) (Auto) trunk (AmE), boot (BrE)
maleta² *mf* (Esp fam) (persona inepta): **es un ~** he's useless *o* hopeless (colloq)
maletera *f* (Chi, Per) trunk (AmE), boot (BrE)
maletero *m* 1 (Auto) trunk (AmE), boot (BrE) 2 (mozo de estación) porter
maletilla *mf* novice bullfighter
maletín *m* (para documentos) briefcase; (maleta pequeña) overnight bag, small case; (de médico) bag
malevolencia *f* malevolence, malice
malévolo -la *adj* malevolent, malicious
maleza *f*
A 1 (espesura) undergrowth 2 (malas hierbas) weeds (*pl*)
B (AmL) (mala hierba) weed
malezal *m* (Chi) mass of weeds
malformación *f* malformation
malgastador¹ -dora *adj* wasteful, spendthrift
malgastador² -dora *m,f* squanderer, spendthrift
malgastar [A1] *vt* ‹*tiempo/esfuerzo*› to waste; ‹*dinero/herencia*› to squander
malgeniado -da *adj* (Col, Per, Ven) bad-tempered
malhablado -da *adj* foul-mouthed
malhadado -da *adj* (liter) 1 ‹*persona*› ill-fated (liter) 2 ‹*día/suceso*› ill-fated (liter), fateful
malhechor -chora *m,f* criminal, delinquent
malherir [I11] *vt* to wound … badly
malhumorado -da *adj* 1 [SER] ‹*persona/gesto*› bad-tempered 2 [ESTAR] ‹*persona*› in a bad mood
malicia *f* 1 (intención malévola) malice, malevolence 2 (picardía) mischief; **es un chico sin ninguna ~** he's completely without guile; **con ~** mischievously 3 (astucia) slyness
maliciar [A1] *vt* to suspect
■ **maliciarse** *v pron* to suspect
malicioso -sa *adj* 1 (malintencionado) malicious, spiteful 2 (pícaro) mischievous
malignidad *f* 1 (de un tumor) malignancy 2 (maldad) evil nature
maligno -na *adj* 1 ‹*tumor*› malignant 2 ‹*persona/intención*› evil; ‹*influencia*› harmful, evil
malinchista *adj* (Méx) *preferring foreign things*
malinformar [A1] *vt* (CS frml) to misinform (frml)
malintencionado -da *adj* ‹*persona/palabras*› malicious, spiteful; ‹*golpe*› malicious
malinterpretar [A1] *vt* to misinterpret
malísimo *adj* very bad, terrible
malla *f*
A 1 (Tex) (de una red) mesh; **una ~ para los insectos** a screen *o* mesh to stop insects; **una bolsa de ~** a string bag; **medias de ~ fina/gruesa** sheer/thick tights; **al fondo de las ~s** (period) (Dep) into the back of the net 2 (de armadura) (chain) mail 3 (de alambre) wire netting
B 1 (para gimnasia) leotard 2 **mallas** *fpl* (medias) tights (*pl*); (sin pie) leggings (*pl*)
(Compuesto) **malla de baño** (RPl) bathing suit, swimsuit
mallo *m* mallet
Mallorca *f* Majorca

mallorquín

The variety of catalán spoken in the Balearic Islands. Some people regard it as a separate language from Catalan, which enjoys official status, but it is not officially recognized as such

mallorquín[1] **-quina** *adj/m,f* Majorcan

mallorquín[2] *m* (idioma) Majorcan

mallugadura *f* (Méx, Ven) bruise

mallugar [A3] *vt* (Méx, Ven) to bruise

malmirado *adj*: **en ciertos círculos eso está ∼** in some circles that is not considered correct; **estaba ∼ que las mujeres fumaran** it was frowned upon for women to smoke

malnacido -da *m,f* nasty piece of work (colloq)

malnutrición *f* malnutrition

malnutrido -da *adj* malnourished

malo[1] **-la** *adj* [*The form* **mal** *is used before masculine singular nouns*]

(*Sentido* **I**)

A [SER] (en calidad) ‹*producto*› bad, poor; ‹*película/novela*› bad; **es de mala calidad** it is poor quality; **tiene mala ortografía** her spelling is bad *o* poor; ***más vale ∼ conocido que bueno por conocer*** better the devil you know (than the devil you don't)

B [SER] 1 (incompetente) ‹*alumno/actor*› bad; **soy muy mala para los números** I'm terrible *o* very bad with figures 2 ‹*padre/marido/amigo*› bad

C [SER] (desfavorable, adverso) bad; **¡qué mala suerte!** what bad luck!, how unlucky!; **lo ∼ es que ...** the thing *o* trouble is that ...; ***en las malas se conoce a los amigos*** a friend in need is a friend indeed; ***estar de malas*** (de mal humor) (fam) to be in a bad mood; (desafortunado) (esp AmL) to be unlucky; ***por las malas*** unwillingly

D [SER] (inconveniente, perjudicial) ‹*hábitos/lecturas*› bad; **las malas compañías** bad company; **llegas en mal momento** you've come at an awkward *o* a bad moment; **es ∼ tomar tanto sol** it's not good to sunbathe so much

E [SER] (sin gracia) ‹*chiste*› bad

F [SER] (desagradable) ‹*olor/aliento*› bad; **hace un día muy ∼** it's a horrible day; **hace tan ∼** (Esp) it's such horrible weather

G [ESTAR] (en mal estado) ‹*alimento*›: **el pescado/queso está ∼** the fish/cheese has gone bad, that fish/cheese is off (BrE)

H 1 (desmejorado, no saludable): **tienes mala cara/mal aspecto** you don't look well; **yo le veo muy mal color** he looks terribly pale to me 2 [SER] (serio, grave) serious; **no tiene nada ∼** it's nothing serious; **una mala caída** a bad fall 3 [ESTAR] (Esp, Méx fam) (enfermo) sick (AmE), ill (BrE); **el pobre está malito** the poor thing's not very well (colloq) 4 [ESTAR] (Esp fam & euf) ‹*mujer*›: **estoy mala** it's that time of the month (colloq & euph); **me he puesto mala** my period's started

I [SER] (difícil) **∼ DE + INF** difficult to + INF; **es muy ∼ de convencer** he's very difficult *o* hard to persuade

(*Sentido* **II**) [SER] (en sentido ético) ‹*persona*› nasty; **¡qué ∼ eres con tu hermano!** you're really horrible *o* nasty to your brother; **no seas mala, préstamelo** don't be mean *o* rotten, lend it to me (colloq); **una mala mujer** a loose woman; **una mujer mala** a wicked *o* an evil woman; ***a la mala*** (Chi fam): **se lo quitaron a la mala** they did him out of it (colloq); **pasó la cámara a la mala** she sneaked the camera through (colloq)

(*Sentido* **III**) (Esp) (uso enfático) (*delante del n*): **no nos ofrecieron ni un mal café** they didn't even offer us a cup of coffee; **no había ni una mala silla para sentarse** there wasn't a single damn chair to sit on (colloq)

(Compuestos)

- **mala hierba** *f* weed
- **mala idea** *f* (Esp): **tiene muy ∼ ∼** she's a nasty character; **lo hizo a** *or* **con ∼ ∼** he did it deliberately *o* to be nasty
- **mala leche** *f* (fam): **lo hizo con ∼ ∼** he did it deliberately *o* to be nasty; **está de ∼ ∼** (Esp) she's in a foul mood (colloq); **¡qué ∼ ∼, se ha puesto a llover!** (Esp) what a drag! it's started raining (colloq)
- **mala palabra** *f* (esp AmL) rude *o* dirty word
- **mala pata** *f* (fam) bad luck
- **mala sangre** *f*: **hacerse ∼ ∼** to get upset
- **malas artes** *fpl* guile, cunning
- **malas lenguas** *fpl* (fam): **dicen las ∼ ∼ que ...** there's a rumor going around that ..., people are saying that ...
- **malos pensamientos** *mpl* bad *o* impure thoughts
- **malos tratos** *mpl* ill-treatment

malo[2] **-la** *m,f* (leng infantil *o* hum) baddy (colloq)

malogrado -da *adj* 1 ‹*intento/proyecto*› failed 2 (period) ‹*persona*› ill-fated (journ) 3 (Per) (averiado) out of order, broken

malograr [A1] *vt*

A ‹*oportunidad*› to waste; ‹*trabajo*› to ruin, spoil

B (Ven euf) (desvirgar) to deflower

■ **malograrse** *v pron*

A «*proyecto*» to fail, miscarry; «*sueños*» to come to nothing; «*cosecha*» to fail

B 1 «*persona*» (morir joven) to die young *o* before one's time 2 «*cría*» to be stillborn 3 (Per) «*reloj*» to stop working; «*lavadora*» to break down

malogro *m* 1 (de un plan, esfuerzo) failure 2 (de una persona) untimely death 3 (de la cosecha) failure

maloliente *adj* stinking, smelly

malón *m* 1 (Hist) Indian raid 2 (CS) (grupo revoltoso) mob 3 (Chi) (fiesta) private party

malpagar [A3] *vt* to underpay; **son empleados muy malpagados** they are very badly paid employees

malparado -da *adj* 1 (maltrecho): **salió muy ∼ de esa pelea** he was in a bad way *o* in a sorry state after that fight (colloq); **él fue el que salió más ∼** he was the one who came off worst (colloq) 2 (frente a los demás): **me dejaste muy ∼** you made me look really bad (colloq); *ver tb* **parado**[1] **D**

malparido -da *m,f* (fam: en algunas regiones vulg) *m* bastard (vulg), son of a bitch (vulg), *f* bitch (vulg)

malpensado -da *adj*: **no seas ∼** don't jump to conclusions; **seré ∼, pero no puedo creer que ...** it's probably nasty of me to think this but I can't believe ...

malquerencia *f* ill will, dislike

malquerer [E24] *vt* to dislike; **los que te malquieren** those who dislike you *o* bear you ill will

malsano -na *adj* ‹*clima/lugar*› unhealthy; ‹*lectura*› unhealthy, unwholesome; ‹*influencia*› bad, unhealthy

malsonante *adj* rude

malta *f* 1 (cereal) malt 2 (bebida sin alcohol) malt drink 3 (Chi) (cerveza) stout

Malta *f* Malta

malteada *f* (AmL) milk shake

maltear [A1] *vt* to malt

maltería *f* malting, malthouse

maltraer [E23] *vi* to ill-treat, mistreat

maltratar [A1] *vt* 1 ‹*persona/animal*› to maltreat, ill-treat, mistreat; (pegar) ‹*niño/mujer*› to batter 2 ‹*juguete/coche*› to mistreat, treat ... very roughly

maltrato *m* 1 (de persona) mistreatment, poor treatment 2 (de objeto) misuse, mistreatment

maltrecho -cha *adj* [ESTAR] in a bad way (colloq); **lo dejaron muy ∼** they left him in a bad way

malucho -cha *adj* (fam) (algo enfermo): **estar ∼** be *o* feel under the weather (colloq)

malva[1] *adj inv* mauve

malva[2] *f* mallow; ***estar criando ∼s*** (Esp fam) to be pushing up daisies (colloq)

(Compuesto) **malva real** hollyhock, rose mallow (AmE)

malva[3] *m* mauve

malvado -da *adj* wicked, evil; (uso hiperbólico) wicked

malvasía *f* (uva) malvasia; (vino) malmsey

malvavisco *m* marshmallow

malvender [E1] *vt* to sell ... off cheap, sell ... at a loss

malversación *f tb* **∼ de fondos** embezzlement (of funds)

malversador -dora *m,f tb* **∼ de fondos** embezzler

malversar [A1] *vt* to embezzle, misappropriate

Malvinas *fpl*: **las ∼** the Falkland Islands, the Falklands

malvís *m* song thrush, mavis (liter)

malvivir [I1] *vi*: **lo que gana apenas le da para ∼** what he earns is barely enough to survive on; **ahora malviven en un apartamento en Bogotá** now they're struggling to make ends meet in an apartment in Bogotá; **un hombre de ∼** an unsavory character

malvón *m* (RPl, Méx) geranium

mama *f*

A (Anat) breast; (Zool) mammary gland

m

B 1 (fam) (madre) ▸**mamá** 2 (Chi, Per) (nodriza) wet-nurse

mamá *f* (*pl* **-más**) (fam) mom (AmE colloq), mum (BrE colloq); (usado por niños) mommy (AmE colloq), mummy (BrE colloq); ***creerse la ~ de los pollitos*** (Méx) to think one is the bee's knees (colloq)

mamada *f*

A (del bebé) feed

B (Méx arg) 1 (estupidez): **no me vengas con tus ~s** don't give me any of your stupid stories; **decir ~s** to talk crap (vulg) 2 (vulg) (mala pasada) dirty trick (colloq); **hacerle una ~ a algn** to play a dirty trick on sb (colloq)

C (AmS fam) (borrachera) bender (colloq), binge (colloq)

mamadera *f*

A (CS, Per) (biberón) (feeding) bottle, baby bottle

B (Andes fam) (trabajo) cushy job (colloq)

mamado -da *adj* 1 (fam: en algunas regiones vulg) (borracho) tight (colloq), sloshed (colloq) 2 (Col, Ven fam) (cansado) dead beat (colloq), shattered (colloq); (aburrido) bored

mamador -dora *adj* (Col fam) boring

mamador de gallo -dora de gallo *m,f* (Col, Ven fam) joker

mamagallista *mf* (Col fam) joker

mamagrande *f* (CS, Méx) grandmother

mamamama *f* (Per fam) grandma (colloq), granny (colloq)

mamar [A1] *vi*

A 1 «*bebé*» to feed; **a todos sus hijos les dio de ~** she breastfed all her children 2 «*gato/cordero*» to suckle

B (fam: en algunas regiones vulg) (beber alcohol) to hit the bottle (colloq), to booze (colloq)

■ **mamar** *vt*: **son cosas que uno ha mamado** they're things that one has learned/seen from childhood; **ha mamado la música** he's been surrounded by music since birth

■ **mamarse** *v pron*

A (fam: en algunas regiones vulg) (emborracharse) to get tight *o* sloshed (colloq)

B (AmS fam) ‹*discurso/programa*› to sit through

C (Col, Ven) (cansarse) to get tired

mamario -ria *adj* mammary

mamarrachada *f* (fam): **otra de sus ~s fue poner esas ventanas tan feas** another awful thing he did was put in those horrible windows; **¡qué ~ han hecho en esta pared!** what a mess *o* botch they've made of this wall! (colloq)

mamarracho *m*

A (fam) (persona) scarecrow (colloq); **estás hecho** *or* **pareces un ~** you look a sight (colloq)

B (fam) (cosa fea, ridícula): **tienen la casa que es un ~** their house looks a real mess (colloq)

mambear [A1] *vi* (Col) to chew coca

mameluco *m*

A (AmL) 1 (de niño, bebé) rompers (*pl*), romper suit (BrE) 2 (pantalón con peto) overalls (*pl*) (AmE), dungarees (*pl*) (BrE); (de trabajo) coveralls (*pl*) (AmE), overalls (*pl*) (BrE)

B (Hist) mameluke

mamerto -ta *m,f* (RPl fam) dope (colloq), twit (BrE colloq)

mamey *m* (de pulpa amarilla) mammee (apple), mamey (apple); (de pulpa roja) *tb* **~ colorado** mammee (sapote), mamey (sapote)

mamífero[1] *adj* mammalian

mamífero[2] *m* mammal

mamila *f* (Méx) 1 (biberón) (feeding) bottle 2 (tetilla) nipple (AmE), teat (BrE)

mamografía *f* (técnica) mammography; (radiografía) mammogram

mamón[1] **-mona** *adj*

A (Col fam) (aburridor) boring

B (Méx vulg) (engreído) cocky (colloq)

mamón[2] **-mona** *m,f* 1 (fam) (persona crédula) sucker (colloq), mug (BrE colloq) 2 (arg) (como insulto) ▸**cabrón**[2] **A** 3 (Méx vulg) asshole (AmE vulg), arsehole (BrE vulg)

mamotreto *m* (fam) 1 (libro) hefty volume, huge tome 2 (armatoste) huge thing, useless object

mampara *f* 1 (biombo, tabique) screen, partition 2 (Chi, Per) (puerta) inner door

mamporro *m* (Esp fam) clout (colloq); (al caer) knock, bang

mampostería *f* masonry

mampuesto *m* 1 (piedra) rough stone 2 (muro) wall

mamut *m* (*pl* **-muts**) mammoth

mana *f* (Col) spring

maná *m* manna; **~ *del cielo*** manna from Heaven

manada *f* 1 (Zool) (de elefantes) herd; (de leones) pride; (de lobos) pack 2 (fam) (de gente) herd; **los turistas llegaron a** *or* **en ~s** swarms *o* hordes of tourists arrived; ***seguir (a) la ~*** to follow the crowd *o* herd

manager /'mana(d)ʒer/ (*pl* **-gers**) *mf*, **mánager** *mf* (*pl* **-gers**) manager

Managua *f* Managua

managüense *adj* of/from Managua

manantial *m* 1 (de agua) spring 2 (origen) source

manar [A1] *vi* 1 «*sangre/sudor*» to pour 2 (liter) (abundar) **~ EN algo** to be rich IN sth

■ **manar** *vt* «*sudor/sangre*» to drip with

manare *m* (Ven) sieve

manatí *m* manatee

manaza *f*

A (fam) (mano) big mitt (colloq); **¡quítame esas ~s de encima!** take your filthy hands *o* big mitts off me! (colloq)

B **manazas** *mf* (fam) (torpe) clumsy oaf (colloq), clumsy idiot (colloq)

mancarse [A2] *v pron*

A «*caballo*» to go lame

B (RPl arg) «*persona*» to miscalculate, get it wrong

manceba *f* (arc) 1 (concubina) concubine, mistress 2 (mujer joven) maiden (arch)

mancebía *f* (arc) 1 (burdel) bawdyhouse (arch) 2 (juventud) youth

mancebo *m* (arc) youth, shaveling (arch)

mancha *f*

A 1 (de suciedad) spot, mark; (difícil de quitar) stain; **una ~ de grasa** a grease stain; **~s de humedad** damp patches; **no le pude quitar** *or* (AmL) **sacar la ~** I couldn't get the stain out 2 (borrón) blot; ***extenderse como una ~ de aceite*** «*noticia*» to spread like wildfire

Compuestos

- **mancha de petróleo** oil slick
- **mancha solar** sunspot

B 1 (en la piel) mark; **una ~ de nacimiento** a birthmark 2 (en el pelaje, las plumas) patch; **negro con ~s blancas** black with white patches; **las ~s del leopardo** the leopard's spots *o* markings

C (en pulmón) shadow

D (de vegetación) patch

E (liter) (imperfección, mácula) stain; **sin ~** ‹*alma*› pure; ‹*reputación*› spotless

F (Per fam) (pandilla) gang

G (RPl) (juego): **la ~** tag

manchado -da *adj*

A ‹*mantel/vestido*› stained; **está ~ de vino** it has wine stains/a wine stain on it; **~ de sangre** blood-stained

B ‹*pelaje/plumaje*›: **con el pelaje/plumaje ~** with different-colored markings on its coat/plumage

manchar [A1] *vt*

A (ensuciar) to mark, get … dirty; (de algo difícil de quitar) to stain

B ‹*reputación/honra*› to stain, tarnish; ‹*memoria*› to tarnish

■ **manchar** *vi* to stain

■ **mancharse** *v pron* 1 «*ropa/mantel*» to get dirty; (de algo difícil de quitar) to get stained; **~se DE** *or* **CON algo** to get stained WITH sth 2 (*refl*) «*persona*»: **me manché la blusa de aceite** I got oil stains on my blouse; **ponte un delantal para no ~te** put an apron on so you don't get dirty; **está recién pintado, no te manches** it's still wet, don't get paint on yourself

manchego -ga *adj* of/from La Mancha

mancheta *f* masthead

mancilla *f* (liter) blemish

mancillar [A1] *vt* (liter) to sully, besmirch (liter)

manco -ca *adj*: **es ~ de un brazo/una mano** he only has one arm/hand; **es ~ de los dos brazos** he has no arms; **quedó ~ del brazo derecho** he lost his right arm; ***no ser ~*** (fam) (para robar) to be light-fingered; (ser habilidoso) to be useful (colloq)

mancomún: **de ~** (*loc adv*) together

mancomunadamente *adv* (frml) together

mancomunado -da *adj* 1 ‹*países/grupos*› united 2 ‹*deudores*› joint, jointly-responsible; ‹*bienes*› common, jointly-owned

mancomunar [A1] *vt* (frml) ‹*recursos*› to join together, combine; ~ **esfuerzos** to join forces

■ **mancomunarse** *v pron* (frml) to unite, join together

mancomunidad *f* community, association

(Compuesto) **Mancomunidad Británica de Naciones** British Commonwealth

mancorna *f* (Col) cufflink

mancuerna *f*

A 1 (de bueyes) yoke 2 (Méx) (de detectives) team

B (Dep) (pesa) weight; (pequeña) dumbbell

C (Indum) cufflink

mancuernilla *f* (Méx) cufflink

manda *f* (Chi, Méx) offering, promise

mandadero -ra *m,f* (esp AmL) office boy, errand boy

mandado¹ -da *adj* (Méx fam): **es muy** ~ he's a real chancer (colloq); **no seas mandada, sólo te ofrecí uno** don't be so greedy, I only offered you one (colloq)

mandado² -da *m,f*

A (esp Esp) (subordinado) minion (hum *or* pej); **no soy más que un** ~ I'm just following orders

B **mandado** *m* 1 (esp AmL) (compra): **hacer los** ~**s** *or* (Méx) **ir al** ~ to go shopping 2 (Méx) (cosa comprada): **¿me trajiste el** ~**?** did you get the shopping *o* the things I asked you for? 3 (diligencia) errand; ***comerle el*** ~ ***a algn*** (Méx fam) to do the dirty on sb (colloq); ***comerse el*** ~ (Méx fam) to have sex (*before marriage*); ***hacerle los*** ~***s a algn*** (Méx fam): **a mí me hace los** ~**s** I don't give a damn (colloq)

mandamás *mf* (*pl* ~ *or* **-mases**) (fam) big boss (colloq), bigwig (colloq)

mandamiento *m*

A (Relig) commandment

B (orden) order; (Der) warrant, order

mandante *mf* mandator, constituent

mandar [A1] *vt*

A 1 (ordenar): **haz lo que te mandan** do as you're told; **a mí nadie me manda** nobody tells me what to do *o* orders me about; **de acuerdo a lo que manda la ley** in accordance with the law; **sí señor, lo que usted mande** as you wish, sir *o* very good, sir; ~ + INF: **la mandó callar** he told *o* ordered her to be quiet; **mandó encender una fogata** she ordered that a bonfire be lit; ~ QUE + SUBJ: **mandó que sirvieran la comida** she ordered lunch to be served; **¿quién te manda revolver en mis papeles?** who said you could go rummaging through my papers?; **¿y quién te manda ser tan tonta?** how could you be so silly! 2 (recetar) to prescribe; **el médico le mandó descansar** the doctor advised him to rest

B (enviar) to send; **la mandé por el pan** I sent her out to buy the bread

C (AmL) (tratándose de encargos): **mis padres me** ~**on llamar** my parents sent for me; **mandó decir que ...** she sent a message to say that ...; **¿por qué no mandas a arreglar esos zapatos?** why don't you get *o* have those shoes mended?

D (AmL fam) (arrojar, lanzar): **mandó la pelota fuera de la cancha** he kicked/sent/hit the ball out of play; **le mandó un puñetazo** he punched him

■ **mandar** *vi* (ordenar): **en mi casa mando yo** I'm the boss in my house; **¡mande!** yes sir/madam?, excuse me?; **¿mande?** (Méx) (I'm) sorry? *o* pardon? *o* (AmE) excuse me?; **¡María! — ¿mande?** (Méx) María! — yes?

■ **mandarse** *v pron*

A (AmS fam) ‹*hazaña*› to pull off (colloq); ‹*mentira*› to come out with (colloq); **se mandó un discurso de dos horas** she regaled us with a two hour speech; **se mandó un postre delicioso** he managed to produce a delicious dessert

B (AmS fam) (engullir) to polish off (colloq); (beberse) to knock back (colloq)

C (Méx fam) (aprovecharse) to take advantage; ~***se cambiar*** (Andes) *or* (RPl) ***mudar*** (fam): **se mandó cambiar dando un portazo** he stormed out, slamming the door; **un buen día se cansó y se mandó cambiar** one day he decided he'd had enough, and just walked out *o* upped and left (colloq); **¡mándense cambiar de aquí!** clear off! (colloq), get lost! (colloq)

mandarín *m* Mandarin (Chinese)

mandarina *f* (Bot, Coc) mandarin (orange), tangerine

mandarinero, mandarino *m* mandarin (orange tree)

mandatario -ria *m,f*

A (Pol) *tb* **primer** ~/**primera mandataria** head of state

B (Der) attorney, agent

mandato *m*

A 1 (período) term of office 2 (orden) mandate

B (Der) mandate

mandíbula *f* jaw; ***reírse a*** ~ ***batiente*** (fam) to laugh one's head off (colloq)

mandil *m* 1 (delantal) leather apron 2 (Chi) (cobertura) horse blanket

mandinga *m* (AmL fam) devil

mandioca *f* (planta) cassava; (fécula) tapioca

mando *m*

A 1 (Gob, Mil) command; **dotes de** ~ leadership qualities; **entregarle el** ~ **a algn** to hand over command to sb; **estar al** ~ to be in charge 2 **al** ~ **de algo** in charge of sth; **la expedición iba a su** ~ he was leading the expedition

B (Dep) lead; **tomar el** ~ to take the lead

C (Auto, Elec) control

(Compuesto) **mando a distancia** remote control

mandoble *m* 1 (golpe) two-handed blow 2 (espada) large sword

mandolina *f* mandolin

mandón -dona *adj* bossy

mandonear [A1] *vt* (fam) to boss ... around (colloq)

mandrágora *f* mandrake

mandril *m*

A (Zool) mandrill

B (de un torno) mandrel

manduca *f* (Esp fam) grub (colloq), nosh (colloq)

manducar [A2] *vi* (fam) to stuff oneself (colloq)

■ **manducarse** *v pron* (fam) to scoff (colloq), to guzzle (colloq)

manear [A1] *vt* (Chi) to hobble

■ **manearse** *v pron* (Chi fam) to get in a tangle (colloq), to be all fingers and thumbs (colloq)

manecilla *f* 1 (de reloj) hand; **la** ~ **grande/pequeña** the minute/hour hand 2 (de instrumento) hand, pointer

manejable *adj*

A 1 ‹*coche*› maneuverable*; ‹*máquina*› easy-to-use 2 ‹*pelo*› manageable

B ‹*persona*› easily led, easily manipulated

manejar [A1] *vt*

A (usar) ‹*herramienta/arma*› to use; ‹*máquina*› to use, operate; ‹*diccionario*› to use; ‹*explosivos*› to handle

B (dirigir, llevar) ‹*negocio/empresa*› to manage; ‹*asuntos*› to manage, handle

C (manipular) to manipulate

D (AmL) ‹*auto*› to drive

■ **manejar** *vi* (AmL) to drive

■ **manejarse** *v pron*

A (desenvolverse) to get by, manage

B (Col) (comportarse) to behave; **manéjese bien** behave yourself

manejo *m*

A (uso): **el** ~ **de la máquina es muy sencillo** the machine is easy to use *o* operate; **esto facilita el** ~ **del diccionario** this makes using the dictionary easier; **su** ~ **de la lengua** his use of the language

B (de un asunto, negocio) management; **el mal** ~ **de los fondos públicos** the mismanagement *o* mishandling of public funds

C (AmL) (Auto) driving

D **manejos** *mpl* (intrigas) scheming, schemes (*pl*)

manera *f*

A 1 (modo, forma) way; **yo lo hago a mi** ~ I do it my way, I have my own way of doing it; **¿qué** ~ **de comer es ésa?** that's no way to eat your food; **¡comimos de una** ~ **...!** you should have seen the amount we ate!; **¡qué** ~ **de malgastar el dinero!** what a waste of money!; **no saldrás a la calle vestida de esa** ~ **¿no?** you're not going out dressed like that, are you?; **se puede ir vestido de cualquier** ~ you can dress however you want; **no lo**

m

pongas así de cualquier ~, dóblalo don't just put it in any which way (AmE) *o* (BrE) any old how, fold it up; **de alguna ~ tendré que conseguirlo** I'll have to get it somehow (or other); **de una ~ u otra habrá que terminarlo** it'll have to be finished one way or another; **no hay/hubo manera** it is/it was impossible 2 (*en locs*) **a manera de** by way of; **se levantó el sombrero a ~ de saludo** he lifted his hat in greeting; ***de cualquier manera*** *or* ***de todas maneras*** anyway; **de manera que** (así que) (+ *indic*) so; (para que) (+ *subj*) so that, so; **de ninguna manera**: **¿me lo das? — de ninguna ~** will you give it to me? — certainly not; **de ninguna ~ lo voy a permitir** there's no way I'm going to allow it; **no son de ninguna ~ inferiores** they are in no way inferior; **sobre manera** ▸ **sobremanera**; ***de mala ~***: **me contestó de muy mala ~** she answered me very rudely; **la trataba de mala ~** he used to treat her badly; **los precios han subido de mala ~** (Esp) prices have shot up (colloq); **lo malcrió de mala ~** (Esp) she spoiled him terribly *o* (colloq) rotten; **querer algo de mala ~** (Esp fam) to want sth really badly

(Compuesto) **manera de ser**: **tiene una ~ de ~ que** the way she is; **su ~ de ~ le acarrea muchos problemas** the way he comes across causes him problems

B **maneras** *fpl* (modales) manners (*pl*)

manflora *f* (Méx fam) lesbian

manga *f*

A 1 (de abrigo, blusa) sleeve; **sin ~s** sleeveless; **de ~ corta/larga** short-sleeved/long-sleeved; **en ~s de camisa** in shirtsleeves; ***estar ~ por hombro*** (Esp fam) ‹*casa*› to be upside-down *o* in a mess (colloq); **un país donde todo anda ~ por hombro** a country where everything is in a state of chaos; ***sacarse algo de la ~***: **se sacó una buena respuesta de la ~** she came up with a good answer off the top of her head; ***ser más corto que las ~s de un chaleco*** (fam) (burro) to be really dumb (colloq); (tímido) to be very shy; ***tener (la) ~ ancha*** to be tolerant *o* lenient; ***tirarle la ~ a algn*** (RPl fam) to ask sb for money 2 (capa — de hule) (Méx) oilskin cape; (— de jerga) (AmC) poncho

B 1 (Coc) (filtro) strainer; (para repostería) *tb* **~ pastelera** pastry bag 2 (para pescar) net

(Compuesto) **manga de viento** 1 (indicador) windsock 2 (torbellino) whirlwind

C 1 (Dep) round; (en esquí, motocrós) run, round; (en tenis) leg, set 2 (en bridge) trick

D (manguera) hose

(Compuestos)

- **manga de incendio** fire hose
- **manga de riego** hosepipe

E (Bot) *type of mango*

F (Náut) 1 (del barco) beam 2 (red) net

G (Meteo) 1 (remolino) *tb* **~ de agua** waterspout; (chaparrón) squally shower 2 (torbellino) whirlwind

H 1 (AmL) (de langostas) swarm; (de aves) flock 2 (CS fam & pey) (grupo) bunch (colloq)

I 1 (Aviac) jetty, telescopic walkway 2 (AmL) (Agr) (para el ganado) run, chute

J (Col fam) (persona fuerte): **es chiquito pero es una ~** he's small but he's very tough

manganeso *m* manganese

mangar [A3] *vt* 1 (Esp arg) (robar) to swipe (colloq), to nick (BrE colloq) 2 (RPl fam) (gorrear) to scrounge (colloq)

manglar *m* mangrove swamp

mangle *m* mangrove

mango *m*

A (de un cuchillo, paraguas) handle

B (Bot) (árbol) mango (tree); (fruta) mango

C (CS arg) (peso) peso

D (Méx fam & hum) (persona atractiva): **es un ~** «*mujer*» she's a real stunner (colloq); «*hombre*» he's a real hunk (colloq)

mangonear [A1] *vi* (fam) 1 (mandonear) to order *o* (colloq) boss people around 2 (entrometerse) to meddle

■ **mangonear** *vt* (fam) 1 ‹*persona*› to boss ... around (colloq) 2 (robar) to swipe (colloq)

mangoneo *m* (fam) 1 (intromisión) meddling 2 (robo) thieving

mangosta *f* mongoose

manguear [A1] *vt/vi* (RPl arg) to scrounge (colloq)

manguera *f* 1 (para regar) hose, hosepipe; (de bombero) hose 2 (Náut) pump hose

manguito *m*

A 1 (del radiador) hose 2 (Tec) sleeve

B (Indum) (de mujer) muff; (de oficinista) oversleeve

maní *m* (*pl* **-níes** *or* (crit) **-nises**) (AmC, AmS) peanut

manía *f*

A (obsesión, capricho): **tiene sus ~s** he has his funny little ways; **tiene la ~ de la limpieza** she has an obsession with *o* (colloq) a thing about cleaning; **tiene la ~ de oler todo** she has this obsession with smelling everything; **ahora le ha dado la ~ de vestirse de negro** now she has this fad *o* craze of dressing in black

(Compuesto) **manía persecutoria** *or* **de persecución** persecution complex *o* mania

B (antipatía): **tenerle ~ a algn** to have it in for sb (colloq)

maniaco[1] **-ca**, **maníaco -ca** *adj* manic

maniaco[2] **-ca**, **maníaco -ca** *m,f* 1 (Psic) manic 2 (fam) (loco) maniac

(Compuesto) **maniaco sexual** sex maniac

maniacodepresión *f* manic depression

maniacodepresivo -va *adj/m,f* manic-depressive

maniatar [A1] *vt* 1 ‹*persona*›: **los ladrones lo ~on** the burglars tied his hands 2 (restringir) to hinder, shackle 3 ‹*animal*› to hobble

maniático -ca *adj* 1 (delicado, difícil) finicky, fussy; **son muy ~s con la comida** they're very picky about what they eat 2 (obsesionado) obsessive

manicero -ra *m,f* (AmC, AmS) peanut seller

manicomio *m* mental hospital, lunatic asylum; **¡esta casa es un ~!** this is a madhouse!

manicura, manicure *f* manicure; **hacerse la ~** (*refl*) to do one's nails; (*caus*) to have a manicure

manicuro -ra *m,f*, **manicurista** *mf* manicurist

manido -da *adj* ‹*frase*› hackneyed; ‹*tema*› stale

manierismo *m* mannerism

manifestación *f*

A (Pol) demonstration; **asistir a una ~** to take part in *o* go on a demonstration

B (expresión, indicio) sign; **fueron recibidos con grandes manifestaciones de júbilo** they were received with great rejoicing *o* jubilation; **las manifestaciones artísticas/culturales de la época** the artistic/cultural expression of the era

C **manifestaciones** *fpl* (period) (declaraciones) statement

manifestante *mf* demonstrator

manifestar [A5] *vt* 1 (declarar, expresar) ‹*desaprobación/agradecimiento*› to express; **lo manifestó públicamente** she declared it publicly; **~on su apoyo a esta propuesta** they expressed *o* made known their support for the proposal 2 (demostrar) ‹*emociones/actitudes*› to show; **manifestó gran entusiasmo por el proyecto** he showed *o* demonstrated a great deal of enthusiasm for the project

■ **manifestarse** *v pron*

A (hacerse evidente) to become apparent *o* evident; (ser evidente) to be apparent *o* evident; **el problema no se manifiesta hasta la pubertad** the problem does not manifest itself *o* appear until puberty

B (Pol) to demonstrate, take part in a demonstration

C (dar opinión): **se manifestó en contra/a favor de la reforma** she expressed her opposition to/support for the reform

manifiesta, manifiestas, etc *see* **manifestar**

manifiesto[1] **-ta** *adj* (frml) manifest (frml), evident (frml); **un error ~** a glaring error, an obvious mistake; **poner algo de ~** to highlight sth; **quedar de ~** to become plain *o* obvious *o* evident

manifiesto[2] *m*

A (Pol) manifesto

B (Náut) manifest

manigua *f* (AmC, Col) (marisma) swamp; (maleza) scrubland; (selva) jungle

manija *f* (esp AmL) handle; ***darle ~ a algn*** (RPl fam) to egg sb on (colloq)

Manila *f* Manila

manilargo -ga *adj*

A (fam) (ladrón) light-fingered

B (fam) (generoso) open-handed
C (fam) (pegón) fond of hitting people

manilla *f* **1** (de reloj) hand **2** (de cajón) handle **3** (Col) (guante) baseball glove

manillar *m* (esp Esp) handlebars (*pl*)

maniobra *f*
A **1** (de coche, barco, avión) maneuver* **2** **maniobras** *fpl* (Mil, Náut) maneuvers* (*pl*); **estar de ~s** to be on maneuvers
B (ardid, maquinación) ploy, maneuver*

maniobrable *adj* ‹coche› maneuverable*, easy to drive; ‹máquina› easy to handle *o* use

maniobrar [A1] *vi*
A **1** (Auto, Aviac, Náut) to maneuver* **2** «*ejército*» to carry out maneuvers*
B (intrigar) to maneuver*
■ **maniobrar** *vt* **1** ‹*vehículo*› to maneuver* **2** ‹*persona*› to manipulate

manipulación *f*
A **1** (de alimentos) handling **2** (de máquina) operation, use
B (de persona, de información, datos) manipulation

manipulador[1] -dora *adj* manipulative

manipulador[2] -dora *m,f* **1** (de mercancías) handler **2** (aprovechado) manipulator, manipulative person

manipular [A1] *vt*
A **1** ‹*mercancías*› to handle **2** ‹*aparato/máquina*› to operate, use
B ‹*persona/información/datos*› to manipulate; ‹*cifras*› to massage, manipulate; **~ los resultados** to fix *o* rig the results
■ **manipular** *vi*: **manipulaba en** *or* **con las cuentas de sus clientes** he made illicit use of his clients' accounts

maniquí *mf* **1** (persona) model **2** **maniquí** *m* (de sastre, escaparate) mannequin, dummy

manir [I1] *vt* to hang

manirroto[1] -ta *adj* **1** (fam) extravagant **2** (generoso) generous, open-handed

manirroto[2] -ta *m,f* (fam) spendthrift

manita *f*
A (Esp, Méx) *ver tb* **mano[1]**; ***estar*** *or* ***andar hasta las ~s*** (Méx fam) (estar — ebrio) to be legless (colloq); (— drogado) to be high (colloq); ***hacer ~s*** (Esp fam) to neck (colloq), to canoodle (BrE colloq); ***ser de ~ caída*** (Méx fam) to be limp-wristed (pej)
(Compuesto) **manitas de cerdo** *fpl* pig's trotters (*pl*)
B **manitas** *mf* (Esp, Méx fam) handyman (colloq)

manito[1] *m*: *ver* **mano[1]**

manito[2] -ta *m,f*: *ver* **mano[2]**

manivela *f* crank, handle

manjar *m* delicacy
(Compuesto) **manjar blanco** (Andes) ▸ **dulce de leche**

mano[1] *f*
(*Sentido* **I**)
A **1** (Anat) hand; **tengo las ~s sucias** my hands are dirty; **le dijo** *or* **hizo adiós con la ~** he waved goodbye to her; **con las dos ~s** with both hands; **entrégaselo en sus propias ~s** give it to him in person; **Ⓢ en su mano** (Corresp) by hand; **levantar la mano** to raise one's hands, put one's hand up; **lo hice yo, con mis propias ~s** I did it myself, with my own two hands; **salió con las ~s en alto** he came out with his hands in the air *o* up; **¡~s arriba!** *or* **¡arriba las ~s!** hands up!; **con la ~ en el corazón** hand on heart; **¡las ~s quietas!** keep your hands to yourself!; **su carta pasó de ~ en ~** her letter was passed around; **recibió el premio de ~s del Rey** she received the prize from the King himself; **darle la ~ a algn** (para saludar) to shake hands with sb, to shake sb's hand; (para ayudar, ser ayudado) to give sb one's hand; **dame la manito** *or* (Esp, Méx) **manita** hold my hand; **me tendió** *or* **me ofreció la ~** he held out his hand to me; **hacerse las ~s** to have a manicure; **me leyó las ~s** she read my palm; **tocaron la pieza a cuatro ~s** they played the piece as a duet **2** (Zool) (de oso, perro) paw; (de mono) hand; (Equ) forefoot, front foot
B (control, posesión) *gen* **~s** hands (*pl*); **ha cambiado de ~s varias veces** it has changed hands several times; **cayó en ~s del enemigo** it fell into the hands of the enemy; **ahora está en ~s de los socialistas** it is now held by the socialists; **el negocio está en buenas ~s** the business is in good hands; **haré todo lo que esté en mis ~s** *or* (RPl) **de mi ~** I will do everything in my power; **mi mensaje nunca llegó a sus ~s** my message never reached him; **su muerte a ~s de la policía secreta** his death at the hands of the secret police; **la situación se nos va de las ~s** the situation is getting out of hand; **la oportunidad se nos fue de las ~s** we let the opportunity slip through our fingers
C (en fútbol) handball
D (del mortero) pestle
E **1** (de papel) quire **2** (de plátanos) hand
F (de pintura, barniz) coat
G (Jueg) **1** (vuelta, juego) hand; **¿nos echamos unas ~s de dominó?** how about a game of dominoes? **2** (conjunto de cartas) hand **3** (jugador): **soy/eres ~** it's my/your lead; **tener la ~** (Andes) to lead; ***ganarle por la ~*** *or* (RPl) ***de ~ a algn*** (fam): **César me ganó por la ~** César just beat me to it (colloq)
H (*en locs*) **a mano** (no a máquina) by hand; (cerca) at hand (AmE), to hand (BrE); **hecho a ~** handmade; **escrito a ~** handwritten; **un tapiz tejido a ~** a handwoven tapestry; **las tiendas me quedan muy a ~** the shops are very close by *o* near *o* handy; **siempre tengo un diccionario a ~** I always keep a dictionary by me *o* at hand *o* to hand; **a mano** (AmL) (en paz) all square, quits; **a la mano** (AmL) close at hand; **de mano** hand (*before n*); **en mano** ‹*lápiz/copa*› in hand; **Ⓢ llave en mano** immediate possession; ***agarrar*** *or* (esp Esp) ***coger a algn con las ~s en la masa*** to catch sb red-handed; ***agarrarle*** *or* ***tomarle la ~ a algo*** (CS fam) to get the hang of sth (colloq); ***a ~ alzada*** ‹*votación*› by a show of hands; ‹*dibujo*› freehand; ‹*dibujar*› freehand; ***a ~s llenas*** ‹*dar*› generously; ‹*gastar*› lavishly; ***pedir/conceder la ~ de algn*** to ask for/give sb's hand in marriage; ***bajo ~*** on the quiet, on the sly (colloq); ***caérsele la ~ a algn*** (Méx fam & pey) to be a fairy (colloq & pej); ***cargar la ~*** (fam) to overdo; **no cargues la ~ con la sal** don't overdo the salt; ***cargarle la ~ a algn*** (en el precio) to overcharge sb; (pegar) to hit sb; ***con las ~s vacías*** empty-handed; ***con una ~ atrás y otra delante*** without a penny to one's name; ***dar la ~ derecha por algo*** to give one's right arm for sth; ***darse la ~*** (para saludar) to shake hands; (para cruzar, jugar, etc) to hold hands; (reunirse, fundirse) to come together; ***dejado de la ~ de Dios*** godforsaken; **se sentía totalmente dejado de la ~ de Dios** he felt utterly forlorn; ***de la ~***: **me tomó de la ~** she took me by the hand; **iban (tomados) de la ~** they walked hand in hand; ***de ~s a boca*** suddenly, unexpectedly; ***de primera ~*** (at) first hand; ***de segunda ~*** ‹*ropa*› secondhand; ‹*coche*› used, secondhand; ‹*información*› secondhand; ***echar*** *or* ***dar una ~*** to give *o* lend a hand; ***echarle ~ a algn*** (fam) to lay *o* get one's hands on sb (colloq); ***echar ~ a algo*** (fam) to grab sth; ***echar ~ de algo*** to resort to sth; **echamos ~ de nuestros ahorros** we dipped into our savings; ***echarse*** *or* ***llevarse las ~s a la cabeza*** (literal) to put one's hands on one's head; (horrorizarse) to throw up one's hands in horror; ***embarrarle la ~ a algn*** (Méx fam) to grease sb's palm (colloq); ***ensuciarse las ~s*** (literal) to get one's hands dirty; (en un robo, crimen) to dirty one's hands; ***estar atado de ~s*** *or* ***tener las ~s atadas*** (literal) to have one's hands tied; (no poder actuar): **la decisión es de ellos, yo tengo las ~s atadas** it's up to them, my hands are tied; ***estar/quedar a ~*** (AmL fam) to be even *o* quits (colloq); ***frotarse las ~s*** (literal) to rub one's hands together; (regodearse) to rub one's hands with glee; ***írsele la ~ a algn***: **se te fue la ~ con la sal** you overdid the salt *o* put too much salt in; **le cobré $1.000 — se te fue un poco la ~ ¿no?** I charged him $1,000 — that was a bit steep, wasn't it? (colloq); **se te fue la ~ al contestarle así** you went too far answering her back like that; ***lavarse las ~s*** to wash one's hands; ***les das la/una ~ y se toman el brazo*** give them an inch and they'll take a mile; ***levantarle la ~ a algn*** to raise one's hand to sb; ***llegar*** *or* ***irse*** *or* ***pasar a las ~s*** to come to blows; ***meter la ~ en la caja*** *or* ***lata*** to dip one's fingers in the till; ***meterle ~ a algn*** (fam) (magrear, tocar) to touch *o* feel sb up (colloq); (por un delito) to collar sb (colloq); ***meterle ~ a algo*** (fam) to get to work on sth; ***poner la(s) ~(s) en el fuego por algn*** to stick one's neck out for sb; ***ponerle la ~ encima a algn*** to lay a hand *o* finger on sb; ***ponerse ~s a la obra*** to get down to work; ***por mi/tu/su ~***: **tomó la justicia** *or* **las cosas por su ~** he took the law *o* he

m

took things into his own hands; ***quitarle algo de las ~s a algn***: **me lo quitó de las ~s** she took it right out of my hands; **tuvieron mucho éxito, nos las quitaron de las ~s** they were a great success, they sold like hotcakes (colloq); ***saber algn dónde tiene la ~ derecha*** to know what one is about; ***ser ~ ancha*** (Arg) to be generous; ***ser ~ de santo*** to work wonders; ***ser ~ larga*** (para pegar) to be free with one's hands; (para robar) to be light-fingered; ***tenderle una ~ a algn*** to offer sb a (helping) hand; ***tener algo entre ~s*** to be dealing with *o* working on sth; ***tener (la) ~ larga*** *or* ***las ~s largas*** (fam) (para pegar) to be free with one's hands; (para robar) to be light-fingered; ***tener la ~ pesada*** to be heavy-handed; ***tener ~ de seda*** to have a light touch; ***tener ~ para algo*** to be good at sth; ***traerse algo entre ~s*** to be up to sth (colloq); ***untarle la ~ a algn*** (fam) to grease somebody's palm (colloq); ***muchas ~s en un plato hacen mucho garabato*** too many cooks spoil the broth

(Compuestos)
- **mano a mano** *m* (Taur) *bullfight with two bullfighters instead of three*; **se la bebieron en un ~ a ~** (fam) between the two of them they drank it all (colloq); **el debate se convirtió en un ~ a ~ entre los dos líderes** the debate turned into a contest between the two leaders
- **mano de cerdo** pig's foot (AmE), pig's trotter (BrE)
- **mano de obra** labor*
- **mano derecha** right-hand man/woman
- **mano dura** *or* **de hierro** firm hand

(Sentido II) 1 (lado) side; **queda de esta ~** it's on this side of the street; **la segunda calle a ~ derecha** the second street on the right 2 (Auto) side of the road

(Sentido III) **manos** *mpl* (obreros) hands (*pl*)

mano² -na *m,f* (AmL exc CS fam) (apelativo) buddy (AmE colloq), mate (BrE colloq)

manojo *m* bunch; ***ser un ~ de nervios*** to be a bundle of nerves

manopla *f* 1 (guante) mitten; (para lavarse) face cloth, flannel (BrE) 2 (AmL) (puño de hierro) knuckle-duster

manoseado -da *adj* 1 ‹*libro*› well-thumbed; **fruta manoseada** fruit that has been handled by lots of people 2 ‹*tema*› hackneyed, well-worn

manosear [A1] *vt* 1 ‹*objeto*› to handle 2 (fam) ‹*persona*› to grope (colloq)

manoseo *m* 1 (de un objeto) handling, touching 2 (fam) (de una persona) groping (colloq)

manotada *f* (Col) handful

manotazo *m* swipe

manotear [A1] *vi* to wave one's hands/arms around
■ **manotear** *vt* (CS) to grab at

manotón *m* (CS) swipe, grab

mansalva : **a ~** 1 (*loc adv*) ‹*disparar*› at close range 2 (*loc adj*) (Esp fam) (en cantidad): **había gente a ~** there were loads of people (colloq)

mansarda *f* attic

mansedumbre *f* 1 (de persona) meekness, gentleness 2 (de animal) tameness, docility 3 (liter) (del tiempo) mildness

mansión *f* mansion; **~ señorial** stately home

manso -sa *adj* 1 ‹*caballo*› tame; ‹*toro*› docile; **un perro ~** a friendly dog 2 (liter) ‹*persona/carácter*› gentle, meek (liter) 3 (liter) ‹*río*› gently-flowing, peaceful; ‹*brisa*› gentle

manta¹ *f*
A (de cama) blanket; ***a ~*** (Esp): **había comida a ~** there was loads of food (colloq); ***liarse la ~ a la cabeza*** (Esp) to throw caution to the wind; ***tirar de la ~*** to reveal the truth
B (Chi) (poncho) poncho
C (Méx) (tela) *a coarse muslin-like cloth*, calico (BrE)

manta² *m* (Esp fam) layabout (colloq), bum (AmE colloq)

mantear [A1] *vt* to toss ... in a blanket

manteca *f*
A 1 (grasa) fat; (de cerdo) lard 2 (RPl) (mantequilla) butter; ***tirar ~ al techo*** (RPl) to throw a big party

(Compuestos)
- **manteca de cacao** cocoa butter
- **manteca de cerdo** lard
- **manteca de maní** (RPl) peanut butter

B (Col fam) (criada) slave (colloq), skivvy (BrE colloq)

mantecada *f* (Col, Méx) ▸ **mantecado B**

mantecado *m* 1 (Esp) (dulce) *traditional Christmas sweet made mainly from lard*; (helado) ≈ dairy ice cream 2 (RPl) (madalena) ≈ cupcake (AmE), ≈ fairy cake (BrE)

mantecoso -sa *adj* greasy

mantel *m* (de mesa) tablecloth; (del altar) altar cloth
(Compuesto) **mantel individual** place mat

mantelería *f* table linen

mantención *f* (CS) 1 (de persona) maintenance, support 2 (de vehículo, máquina) maintenance

mantener [E27] *vt*
A (económicamente) ‹*familia/persona*› to support, maintain; ‹*perro*› to keep; ‹*amante*› to keep
B 1 (conservar, preservar) to keep; **~ la calma/la compostura** to keep calm/one's composure; **para ~ su peso actual** to maintain his present weight; **~ las viejas tradiciones** to keep up the old traditions; **el euro ha mantenido su valor** the euro has held its value 2 (cierto estado, cierta situación) (+ *compl*) to keep; **~ el equilibrio** to keep one's balance; **~ algo en equilibrio** to balance sth; **S mantenga limpia su ciudad** keep Norwich (*o* York *etc*) tidy
C 1 ‹*conversaciones*› to have; ‹*contactos*› to maintain, keep up; ‹*correspondencia*› to keep up; ‹*relaciones*› to maintain; **las negociaciones mantenidas en Ginebra** the negotiations held in Geneva 2 (cumplir) ‹*promesa/palabra*› to keep
D (afirmar, sostener) to maintain
■ **mantenerse** *v pron*
A (sustentarse económicamente) to support oneself
B (en cierto estado, cierta situación) (+ *compl*) to keep; **se mantuvieron en primera división** they kept their place in the first division; **la torre aún se mantiene en pie** the tower is still standing; **~se a distancia** to keep one's distance; **~se en contacto con algn** to keep in touch with sb; **se mantuvo neutral en la disputa** he remained neutral in the dispute
C (alimentarse): **~se a base de latas** to live off tinned food; **se mantiene a base de vitaminas** he lives on vitamin pills

mantenimiento *m*
A 1 (conservación) maintenance; **ejercicios de ~** keep-fit exercises 2 (Tec) maintenance
B (de actitud, posición) maintenance; (de tradición) upholding, preservation

mantequera *f* 1 (para batir) churn 2 (RPl) (para servir) butter dish

mantequería *f* 1 (ultramarinos) grocery store (AmE), grocer's (shop) (BrE) 2 (lechería) dairy

mantequilla *f* butter; **eres de ~** (fam) you're such a crybaby (colloq)
(Compuesto) **mantequilla de cacao** (Chi, Per) cocoa butter

mantequillera *f* butter dish

mantiene, mantienes, etc *see* **mantener**

mantilla *f* 1 (de mujer) mantilla; **la España de ~ y peineta** traditional Spain; ***nacer con ~*** (Ven fam) to be born under a lucky star (colloq) 2 (de caballo) saddle cloth 3 (de bebé) terry diaper (AmE), terry nappy (BrE); ***en ~s***: **es un proyecto en ~s** the project is still in its infancy

mantisa *f* mantissa

mantis religiosa *f* praying mantis

manto *m*
A (Indum) cloak; **un ~ de nieve** (liter) a mantle of snow (liter); ***echar el ~ del olvido sobre algo*** to draw a veil over sth
B (Geol) stratum, layer
(Compuesto) **manto freático** aquifer

mantón *m* shawl

mantra *m* mantra

mantuve, mantuvo, etc *see* **mantener**

manual¹ *adj* ‹*trabajo/destreza*› manual; **tener habilidad ~** to be good with one's hands

manual² *m* manual, handbook

manualidades *fpl* handicrafts (*pl*)

manualmente *adv* manually, by hand

manubrio *m* 1 (manivela) crank, handle 2 (AmL) (de una bicicleta) handlebars (*pl*) 3 (Chi, Par) (del auto) steering wheel

manufactura *f* 1 (fabricación) manufacture 2 (artículo) product

manufacturar [A1] *vt* to manufacture; **manufacturado en México** manufactured *o* made in Mexico

manufacturero[1] -ra *adj* manufacturing (*before n*)

manufacturero[2] -ra *m,f* manufacturer

manuscrito[1] -ta *adj* hand-written, manuscript (frml)

manuscrito[2] *m* (escrito a mano) manuscript; (de un libro) manuscript, original

manutención *f* maintenance

manyar [A1] *vt/vi* (CS arg) to eat

manzana *f*

A (Bot) apple; ***la ~ de la discordia*** the apple of discord; ***una ~ podrida echa un ciento a perder*** one bad apple can spoil the whole barrel

B (de edificios) block; **dar una vuelta a la ~** to go round the block

C (AmL) (Anat) *tb* **~ de Adán** Adam's apple

manzanal *m* (huerto) apple orchard; (árbol) apple tree

manzanar *m* apple orchard

manzanilla[1] *f* (planta) camomile; (infusión) camomile tea

manzanilla[2] *m* manzanilla (*dry sherry*)

manzano *m* apple tree

maña *f*

A (habilidad) skill, knack (colloq); **tener** *or* **darse ~ para algo** to be good at sth; **no sé cómo se da ~ para mantenerlos callados** I don't know how she manages to keep them quiet; ***más vale ~ que fuerza*** brain is better than brawn

B **mañas** *fpl* (artimañas) wiles (*pl*), guile

C 1 (capricho) bad habit 2 (AmL fam) (manía): **tiene ~s de viejo** he's like an old man with all his funny little ways (colloq); **tiene la ~ de morderse las uñas** he has the annoying habit of biting his nails

mañana[1] *adv*

A (refiriéndose al día siguiente) tomorrow; **pasado ~** the day after tomorrow; **~ por la ~** tomorrow morning; **hasta ~, que duermas bien** goodnight/see you in the morning, sleep well; **adiós, hasta ~** goodbye, see you tomorrow; ***~ será otro día*** tomorrow is another day; ***no dejes para ~ lo que puedas hacer hoy*** don't put off until tomorrow what you can do today

B (refiriéndose al futuro) tomorrow; **nunca se sabe lo que pasará el día de ~** you never know what tomorrow will bring

mañana[2] *m* future; **hay que mirar el ~ con optimismo** we must look to tomorrow *o* to the future with optimism

mañana[3] *f*

A (primera parte del día) morning; **a la ~ siguiente** (the) next *o* the following morning; **a media ~ nos reunimos** we met mid-morning; **a las nueve de la ~** at nine (o'clock) in the morning; **en la(s)** *or* (esp Esp) **por la(s)** *or* (RPl) **a la ~** in the morning; **se levanta muy de ~** she gets up very early in the morning; **el tren de la ~** the morning train

B (madrugada) morning; **eran las cuatro de la ~** it was four in the morning

mañanero -ra *adj* (fam) 1 (matutino) ‹*sol*› morning (*before n*) 2 (madrugador): **soy muy ~** I'm a very early riser

mañanita *f*

A (madrugada): **de ~** very early in the morning, at the crack of dawn

B (Indum) wrap, shawl (*worn in bed*); (con mangas) bed jacket

C **mañanitas** *fpl* (en Méx) *song often sung on birthdays*

mañoco *m* (Ven) cassava *o* manioc flour

mañosear [A1] *vi* (Chi fam) 1 ‹‹*niño/viejo*›› to play *o* act up (colloq) 2 ‹‹*caballo*›› to play up (colloq)

mañoso -sa *adj*

A (habilidoso) good with one's hands

B (AmL) 1 (caprichoso) ‹*niño/anciano*› difficult; **es muy ~ para comer** he's a very fussy *o* finicky eater 2 (Chi) ‹*caballo*› difficult, stubborn

maoísta *adj/mf* Maoist

mapa *m* map; **te hago un mapita** I'll draw you a map; **estos cambios en el ~ político** these changes in the political scene *o* landscape; ***desaparecer del ~*** to disappear off the face of the earth

(Compuestos)

- **mapa de rutas** *or* **carreteras** road map
- **mapa del tiempo** weather map *o* chart
- **mapa físico/político** physical/political map

mapache *m* racoon

mapamundi *m* map of the world, world map

mapear [A1] *vt* to map

> **mapuche**
>
> The largest group of Araucanian-speaking South American Indians, living mainly in the south of Chile. The Mapuche struggled for 350 years against Spanish and Chilean domination.
>
> After Chilean independence the Mapuche were put in reservations. In the 1980s, the Chilean government transferred ownership of the land to individual Mapuche, who risk losing their land if they incur debts that they cannot repay.
>
> Originally the Mapuche were one part of the Araucanian people but nowadays the two terms are used synonymously, as most Araucanians are Mapuche.
>
> The Mapuche language, *araucano* or *mapuche*, is spoken in Chile and Argentina

mapurite *m* (AmC, Ven) skunk

maqueta *f* 1 (de edificio) model, mock-up 2 (de libro) dummy, mock-up, paste-up 3 (de disco) rough cut

maquetación *f* layout, page makeup

maquetista *mf* model maker

maquiavélico -ca *adj* Machiavellian

maquiladora *f* (Méx) (cross-border) assembly plant

maquillador -dora *m,f* makeup artist

maquillaje *m* makeup

(Compuesto) **maquillaje de fondo** foundation

maquillar [A1] *vt* ‹*persona*› to make up; (Esp) ‹*cifras/datos*› to massage, dress up

■ **maquillarse** *v pron* to put one's makeup on, to make up

maquillista *mf* (Méx) makeup artist

máquina *f*

A 1 (aparato) machine; **~ expendedora de bebidas** drinks machine; **¿se puede lavar a ~?** can it be machine-washed?; **no sé escribir a ~** I can't type; **¿me pasas esto a ~?** would you type this (up) for me? 2 (Jueg) fruit machine; (Fot) camera 3 (de café) coffee machine

(Compuestos)

- **máquina de afeitar** safety razor; (eléctrica) electric razor, shaver
- **máquina de calcular** calculator
- **máquina de coser/lavar** sewing/washing machine
- **máquina de discos** jukebox
- **máquina de escribir** typewriter
- **máquina expendedora** vending machine
- **máquina tragamonedas** *or* (Esp) **tragaperras** slot machine, fruit machine
- **máquina traganíqueles** (Col) slot machine, fruit machine

B 1 (Náut) engine; ***a toda ~*** at top speed, flat out (colloq) 2 (Ferr) engine, locomotive 3 (Ven fam) (auto) car

C (organización) machine

maquinación *f* plot, scheme; **oscuras maquinaciones** evil machinations *o* scheming

maquinador[1] -dora *adj* scheming

maquinador[2] -dora *m,f* schemer, plotter

maquinal *adj* mechanical

maquinar [A1] *vt* to plot, scheme

maquinaria *f* 1 (conjunto de máquinas) machinery 2 (mecanismo) mechanism; **la ~ del estado** the state machinery; **la ~ electoral** the electoral machine

maquinilla *f*

A *tb* **~ de afeitar** safety razor

B (Náut) winch

C (AmC) (máquina de escribir) typewriter

m

maquinista *mf*
A (operador de una máquina) machine operator
B 1 (Ferr) engine driver, engineer (AmE) 2 (Náut) engineer
C 1 (Teatr) stagehand, scene shifter 2 (Cin) cameraman's assistant, focus puller

mar *m (sometimes f in literary language and in set idiomatic expressions)*
A (Geog) sea; **la vida en el ~** life at sea; **a orillas del ~** by the sea; **surcar los ~es** (liter) to ply the seas (liter); **el fondo del ~** the seabed, the bottom of the sea; **~ abierto** open sea; **la corriente llevó la barca ~ adentro** the boat was swept out to sea by the current; **la tormenta los sorprendió ~ adentro** they were caught out at sea by the storm; **hacerse a la ~** (liter) to set sail; **por ~** by sea; ***a ~es*** (fam): **llovió a ~es** it poured with rain; **sudaba a ~es** he was streaming *o* pouring with sweat; ***arar en el ~*** to beat (AmE) *o* (BrE) flog a dead horse ; ***me cago*** (vulg) *or* (euf) ***me cachis en la*** (Esp) **~** shit! (vulg), shoot! (AmE euph), sugar! (BrE euph); ***surcar los siete ~es*** to sail the seven seas; ***quien no se arriesga no pasa la ~*** nothing ventured, nothing gained

Compuestos
- **mar Cantábrico** Bay of Biscay
- **mar de fondo** swell
- **mar de las Antillas** Caribbean Sea
- **mar del Norte** North Sea
- **mar gruesa** rough *o* heavy sea
- **mar Mediterráneo** Mediterranean Sea
- **mar patrimonial** territorial waters (*pl*) (*within a 200 mile limit*)
- **mar territorial** *or* **jurisdiccional** territorial waters (*pl*) (*within a 12 mile limit*)

B (costa): **el ~** the coast
C 1 (indicando abundancia, profusión) **un ~ de ...**: **estaba hecha un ~ de lágrimas** she was in floods of tears; **está sumido en un ~ de dudas** he's plagued by *o* beset with doubts; **tiene un ~ de problemas** he has no end of problems 2 (abismo): **hay un ~ de diferencia entre ...** there's a world of difference between ...; **los separaba un ~ de silencio** (liter) a gulf of silence lay between them (liter) 3 **la ~ de ...** (fam): **está la ~ de contento** he's over the moon (colloq); **es la ~ de simpática** she's *so* nice; **tengo la ~ de cosas que contarte** I have loads of things to tell you (colloq)

mar. (= **marzo**) Mar

mara *f* (Col) crystal ball

marabú *m* marabou stork, marabou

maraca *f* maraca; ***darle ~s a algn*** (Ven fam) (acariciar lascivamente) to grope sb (colloq); (intentar convencer) to try to get round sb; ***irse/pasarse de ~s*** (Ven fam) to go too far

maracuyá *m* passion fruit

maraña *f* 1 (de hilos, cabello) tangle; **un ovillo hecho una ~** a tangled ball of wool 2 (de arbustos, malezas) tangle of vegetation 3 (lío, confusión) tangled mess; **es una ~ de personajes y relaciones** it is a complicated *o* tangled web of characters and relationships

marasmo *m* 1 (Med) wasting, marasmus (tech) 2 (estancamiento) paralysis; **sumido en el ~ de la apatía** deep in listless apathy; **la guerra dejó al país hundido en un ~** the war left the country paralyzed *o* at a complete standstill

maratón *m or f* marathon

maratoniano -na *adj* marathon (*before n*)

maravilla *f*
A (portento, prodigio) wonder; **las siete ~s del mundo** the seven wonders of the world; **las ~s de la tecnología moderna** the wonders *o* marvels of modern technology; **la catedral/mi secretaria es una verdadera ~** the cathedral/my secretary is absolutely wonderful *o* marvelous; **borda que es una ~** she embroiders beautifully; ***a las mil ~s*** marvelously; **se llevan a las mil ~s** they get on marvelously; **nos atendieron a las mil ~s** they were extremely kind to us; **todo salió a las mil ~s** everything turned out beautifully *o* marvelously; ***de ~*** wonderfully; **ahora funciona de ~** it works beautifully now; ***hacer ~s*** to work wonders
B (asombro) amazement
C (Bot) marigold

maravillar [A1] *vt* to amaze, astonish
■ **maravillarse** *v pron* to be amazed *o* astonished; **~se DE algo/algn** to marvel AT sth/sb

maravilloso -sa *adj* marvelous*, wonderful

marbete *m* label

marca *f*
A 1 (señal, huella) mark 2 (en el ganado) brand
Compuesto **marca de agua/ley** watermark/hallmark
B (Com) (de coches, cámaras) make; (de productos alimenticios, cosméticos, etc) brand; **comprar artículos de ~** to buy brand products *o* brand names; **una ~ de prestigio** a well-known brand; **ropa de ~** designer clothes; ***de ~ mayor*** (fam) terrible (colloq)

Compuestos
- **marca de fábrica** trade name
- **marca registrada** registered trademark

C (Dep) record; **superar** *or* **batir** *or* **mejorar una ~** to break a record; **establecer una ~ mundial** to set a world record; **mi mejor ~ de la temporada** my best time (*o* height *etc*) of the season

marcación *f* 1 (Naút) bearing 2 (Chi) (Dep) ▸ **marcaje**

marcado[1] **-da** *adj* marked; **una marcada preferencia** a distinct *o* marked preference; **un ~ acento escocés** a marked *o* pronounced Scottish accent

marcado[2] *m* 1 (del pelo) set 2 (de reses) branding

marcador *m*
A (Dep) scoreboard; **¿cómo va el ~?** what's the score?; **inaugurar el ~** (period) to open the scoring
B 1 (para libros) bookmark 2 (AmL) (rotulador) felt-tip pen, fiber-tip* pen

marcaje *m* (Dep) coverage, cover, marking
Compuesto **marcaje al hombre** one-on-one coverage, man-for-man marking

marcapasos *m* (*pl* ~) pacemaker

marcar [A2] *vt*
A 1 (con señal) ‹*ropa/página/baraja*› to mark; ‹*ganado*› to brand 2 ‹‹*experiencia/suceso*›› (dejar huella) to mark 3 ‹*opción/cuadro*› to check, to tick (BrE) 4 (CS arg) ‹*persona*› to scar ... for life
B 1 (indicar, señalar) to mark; **dentro del plazo que marca la ley** within the period specified by the law; **el reloj marca las doce en punto** the time is exactly twelve o'clock; **el altímetro marcaba 1.500 metros** the altimeter showed *o* (frml) registered 1,500 meters; **hoy ha marcado un nuevo mínimo** it has reached a new low today; **seguimos la pauta marcada por nuestro fundador** we follow the guidelines established by/the standard set by our founder 2 (hacer resaltar) ‹*cintura/busto*› to accentuate 3 (Mús): **~ el compás/el ritmo** to beat time/the rhythm 4 (Fís) to mark, tag
C ‹*pelo*› to set
D (Telec) to dial
E (Dep) 1 ‹*gol/tanto*› to score 2 ‹*tiempo*› to clock 3 ‹*jugador*› to mark
■ **marcar** *vi*
A (Dep) to score
B (Telec) to dial
■ **marcarse** *v pron*
A **~se el pelo** (*refl*) to set one's hair; (*caus*) to have one's hair set
B (Náut) to take a bearing

marcha *f*
A 1 (Mil) march; (manifestación) march; (caminata) hike, walk; **ir de ~** to go walking *o* hiking; **abrir** *or* **encabezar la ~** to head the march; **cerrar la ~** to bring up the rear; **¡en ~!** (Mil) forward march!; **recojan todo y ¡en ~!** pick up your things and off you/we go!; ***ponerse en ~*** to set off 2 (en atletismo) *tb* **~ atlética** walk
B (paso, velocidad) speed; **el vehículo disminuyó la ~** the car reduced speed *o* slowed down; **llevamos una buena ~, creo que acabaremos a tiempo** we're getting through it at quite a rate, I think we'll finish on time; **acelerar la ~** to speed up; **¡qué ~ llevas!** (Esp) what a speed *o* pace you go at!; ***a ~s forzadas*** (Esp) at top speed; ***a toda ~*** at full *o* top speed, flat out; ***coger la ~*** (Esp): **en cuanto cojas la ~ te será más fácil** once you get into the rhythm of it, you'll find it easier
C (Auto) gear; **cambiar de ~** to change gear; **un coche de**

cinco ~s a car with five gears

(Compuesto) **marcha atrás** reverse, reverse gear; **meter la ~ ~** to put the car into reverse; ***dar*** *or* ***hacer*** **~ ~** (Auto) to go into reverse; (arrepentirse, retroceder) to pull out, back out

D (funcionamiento) running; ***estar en*** **~** «*motor*» to be running; «*proyecto*» to be up and running, to be under way; «*gestiones*» to be under way; **tenemos todos los operativos de seguridad en ~** all security measures are now in force *o* operation; ***poner en*** **~** ‹*coche/motor*› to start; ‹*plan/sistema*› to set … in motion; **puso en ~ un nuevo experimento** he set up a new experiment; ***ponerse en*** **~** «*tren/coche*» to move off; «*persona*»: **nos pusimos en ~ inmediatamente** we set out straightaway

E (curso, desarrollo) course; **la ~ del progreso económico** the march of economic progress; ***sobre la*** **~**: **iremos solucionando los problemas sobre la ~** we'll solve any problems as we go along

F (partida) departure

G (Mús) march; **~ militar/nupcial/fúnebre** military/wedding/funeral march

H (Esp fam) (animación, ambiente): **en esta ciudad hay mucha ~** this city is very lively *o* has a lot of night life; **¡qué ~ tiene!** he's so full of energy; ***irle a algn la*** **~** (Esp fam): **les va la ~ cantidad** they're really into having a good time *o* into the night life (colloq)

marchador -dora *m,f* walker

marchamo *m* label, tag

marchante -ta *m,f*

A (de obras de arte) art dealer

B (Méx) [1] (en un mercado — vendedor) stallholder; (— comprador) customer [2] (fam) (amante) lover

marchar [A1] *vi*

A «*coche*» to go, run; «*reloj/máquina*» to work; «*negocio/relación/empresa*» to work; **esto no marcha** this isn't working; (+ *compl*) **su matrimonio no marcha muy bien** his marriage isn't going *o* working very well

B [1] (Mil) to march [2] (caminar) to walk [3] (en un bar): **¡marchando** *or* **marchen dos hamburguesas!** two hamburgers coming up! [4] (liter) (irse) to leave

■ **marcharse** *v pron* (esp Esp) to leave; **se marcha a Roma** he's leaving for *o* going off to Rome

marchista *mf*

A (de una manfestación) marcher

B (Dep) walker

marchitar [A1] *vt* [1] ‹*flores*› to make … wither [2] (liter) (ajarse): **el tiempo había marchitado su belleza** her beauty had faded with time (liter)

■ **marchitarse** *v pron* [1] «*flores*» to wither [2] (liter) «*persona*» to fade away; «*belleza/juventud*» to fade

marchito -ta *adj* [1] ‹*flores*› withered [2] (liter) ‹*belleza/juventud*› faded

marchoso -sa *adj* (Esp fam) ‹*ambiente/ciudad*› lively; **es un tío ~** he's really into the night life (colloq), he's really into having a good time (colloq)

marcial *adj* martial

marciano -na *adj/m,f* Martian

marco *m*

A [1] (de cuadro) frame; (de puerta) doorframe [2] (Dep) goalposts (*pl*), goal [3] (Andes) (de bicicleta) frame

B (entorno, contexto): **el ~ político** the political framework; **dentro del ~ de la ley** within the framework of the law; **las conversaciones se desarrollaron en un ~ de cordialidad** the talks took place in a friendly atmosphere; **el ~ ideal para el concierto** the ideal setting for the concert

C (Fin) mark

D (*como adj inv*): **un plan ~** a draft plan

marea *f* tide; **cuando baja/sube la ~** when the tide goes out/comes in; **un río con régimen de ~** a tidal river

(Compuestos)

- **marea alta/baja/muerta/viva** high/low/neap/spring tide
- **marea creciente** rising tide, flood tide
- **marea menguante** falling tide, ebb tide
- **marea negra** oil slick

mareado -da *adj* [1] (Med): **está ~** (con náuseas) he's feeling sick *o* queasy; (con pérdida del equilibrio, etc) he's feeling dizzy *o* giddy; (a punto de desmayarse) he's feeling faint [2] (confundido): **me tienes ~ con tanta cháchara** all your chatter is making my head spin

marear [A1] *vt* [1] (Med) (con náuseas) to make … feel sick *o* queasy; (con pérdida de equilibrio, etc) to make … dizzy; **el vino lo mareó** the wine made him feel drunk *o* light-headed [2] (confundir) to confuse, get … confused *o* muddled; **me mareas con tantas preguntas** you're confusing me with all these questions

■ **marear** *vi* (arc) to navigate

■ **marearse** *v pron* [1] (Med): **siempre se marea en el coche/en barco** he always gets carsick/seasick; **miró hacia abajo y se mareó** he looked down and felt *o* went dizzy; **con dos copas se mareó** she had two drinks and started to feel drunk *o* light-headed [2] (confundirse) to get muddled *o* confused

marejada *f* heavy sea, swell; **una ~ de protestas** a wave of protests

maremágnum, mare mágnum *m*: **un ~ de fórmulas** a sea of formulae; **el ~ que siguió a la catástrofe** the chaos *o* confusion that followed the disaster; **un ~ de detalles** a welter *o* plethora of details

maremoto *m* [1] (sismo) seaquake [2] (ola) tidal wave

mareo *m* [1] (Med) (del estómago) sickness, nausea; (producido por movimiento) motion sickness; (en barcos) seasickness; (pérdida de equilibrio, etc) dizziness, giddiness; **le dan ~s en el coche** she gets carsick; **me dio un ~** I felt dizzy; **¿se te ha pasado el ~?** are you feeling less dizzy? [2] (confusión) muddle, mess

mareomotriz *adj*: **energía ~** wave *o* tidal power

marfil *m* ivory

margarina *f* margarine

margarita *f* [1] (Bot) (pequeña) daisy; (grande) marguerite; ***echar*** **~s** ***a los cerdos*** (fam) to cast pearls before swine [2] (de máquina de escribir) golf ball [3] (cóctel) margarita

margen[1] *f* (*a veces m*) (de río) bank; (de carretera) side

margen[2] *m*

A (de una página) margin

B **al margen**: **ver nota al ~** see margin note; **se mantuvo al ~ de todo** he kept out of everything; **al ~ de la ley** on the fringes of the law; **lo dejaron al ~** he was left out; **viven al ~ de la sociedad** they live on the margin *o* fringes of society; **al ~ de lo expresado** apart from what's already been said

C (franja de terreno) strip of land

D (holgura) margin; **ganó por un amplio/estrecho ~** he won by a comfortable/narrow margin; **eso nos da un ~ de tiempo** that gives us some leeway; **le han dejado un ~ de acción muy reducido** they have left him very little leeway; **un cierto ~ de autonomía** a certain degree of autonomy

(Compuestos)

- **margen de beneficio** *or* **ganancias** profit margin
- **margen de error** margin of error
- **margen de seguridad** safety margin
- **margen de tolerancia** tolerance

E **márgenes** *mpl* (límites, parámetros) limits (*pl*); **dentro de ciertos márgenes** within certain limits; **los márgenes de credibilidad de estos sondeos** the extent to which these polls can be believed

F (Com) margin, profit

marginación *f* [1] (Sociol) marginalization; **el desarraigo y la ~ social** alienation and social isolation; **a menudo viven situaciones de verdadera ~** they often find themselves marginalized *o* isolated [2] (exclusión) exclusion; **su ~ del equipo** his exclusion from the team

marginado[1] **-da** *adj* [1] (Sociol) marginalized [2] (excluido) excluded

marginado[2] **-da** *m,f*: **los ~s de nuestra sociedad** the deprived elements *o* sectors of our society; **drogadictos y todo tipo de ~s** drug addicts and all kinds of social outcasts

marginal *adj*

A [1] (Sociol): **en los barrios ~es** in the poorer areas [2] (secundario) ‹*posición*› peripheral; ‹*asunto*› marginal, peripheral

B (Fin) marginal

C (Impr): **una nota ~** a note in the margin, a marginal note

marginalidad *f* 1 (de un barrio, zona) poverty 2 (falta de integración) social exclusion, marginalization; **viven en la ~** they live in a state of social exclusion 3 (falta de importancia) marginal importance

marginalizar [A4] *vt* (AmL frml) ▸**marginar A**

marginar [A1] *vt*

A (en la sociedad) to marginalize; (en un grupo) to ostracize; **lo han marginado de la toma de decisiones** he has been left out of the decision-making

B (Impr) ‹*texto*› (anotar) to add marginal notes to; (fijar márgenes) to set margins

■ **marginarse** *v pron* **~se DE algo** to cut oneself off FROM sth

maría *f*

A (arg) (marihuana) grass (colloq)

B (Esp fam) (Educ) easy subject (*traditionally physical education, religious studies or politics*)

María: **Santa ~** *or* **la Virgen ~** the Virgin Mary

mariachi *m* mariachi musician; **sones de ~** mariachi music

mariachi

The word can mean the traditional Mexican musical ensembles, the lively mestizo music that they play, and the dance performed to it.

The instruments used by mariachis are the guitar, harp, *vihuela* (an early form of guitar), violin, and trumpet. *Mariachis* wearing costumes based on those worn by charros can be seen in the Plaza Garibaldi, in Mexico City, where they are hired for parties, or to sing *mañanitas* or serenades

marialuisa *f* (Méx) mount, passe-partout

mariano -na *adj* Marian

marica¹ *adj* 1 (fam & pey) (homosexual) faggoty (AmE colloq & pej), poofy (BrE colloq & pej) 2 (fam) (cobarde) wimpish (colloq)

marica² *m* (fam & pey) fag (AmE colloq & pej), poof (BrE colloq & pej)

maricón¹ -cona *adj* (fam & pey) 1 (homosexual) queer (colloq & pej), bent (sl & pej) 2 (como insulto): **el muy ~** the bastard *o* (AmE) the son of a bitch (vulg); **la muy maricona** the bitch (vulg) 3 (AmL) (cobarde) wimp (colloq)

maricón² *m* (fam & pey) fag (AmE colloq & pej), poof (BrE colloq & pej)

mariconada *f* (fam) dirty trick (colloq)

mariconera *f* (fam & hum) (men's) handbag

maridaje *m* (combinación) combination, marriage; (conexión) close association *o* connection

marido *m* husband

mariguana *f* marijuana

mariguanero -ra *adj/m,f* ▸**marihuanero¹,²**

marihuana, marijuana *f* marijuana

marihuanero¹ -ra, marijuanero -ra *adj* (fam): **tienen un hijo ~** one of their sons is a dope fiend (colloq)

marihuanero² -ra, marijuanero *m,f* (fam) dope fiend (colloq)

marimacho *m or f* (fam & pey) 1 (niña) tomboy (colloq) 2 (mujer hombruna) butch woman (colloq)

marimba *f* marimba (*type of xylophone*)

marimorena *f* (fam) row, ruckus (AmE colloq)

marina *f*

A 1 (organización) navy; (barcos) fleet 2 (náutica): **un término de ~** a nautical term

(Compuesto) **marina de guerra** navy

B (Art) seascape

marinar [A1] *vt* to marinate, marinade

marinera *f*

A (blusa) sailor top; (chaqueta) (Col) sailor jacket

B (baile) *Andean folk dance*

marinero¹ -ra *adj* 1 ‹*barco*› seaworthy 2 ‹*brisa*› sea (*before n*)

marinero² *m* sailor; **traje de ~** sailor suit

(Compuestos)

- **marinero de agua dulce** landlubber
- **marinero de cubierta** deckhand
- **marinero de primera/segunda** seaman (AmE), able/ordinary seaman (BrE)

marino¹ -na *adj* ‹*brisa/corriente*› sea (*before n*); ‹*fauna/biología*› marine (*before n*)

marino² *m* (marinero) sailor; (oficial) naval officer

(Compuesto) **marino mercante** merchant seaman

marioneta *f* puppet, marionette

marionetista *mf* puppeteer

mariposa *f*

A (Zool) butterfly

B *tb* **~ nocturna** 1 (Zool) moth 2 (fam & euf) (prostituta) lady of the night (euph)

C (Dep): **estilo ~** butterfly; **nadar ~** *or* (Esp) **a** *or* (Méx) **de ~** to swim butterfly

D (tuerca) wing nut

E **mariposa** *m or f* (fam) (homosexual) fairy (colloq)

mariposear [A1] *vi* 1 (fam) (alrededor de algn) to buzz around, be constantly around 2 (fam & pey) (en el trabajo) to flit from one job to another; (en el amor) to flit from one relationship to another

mariposón *m* 1 (fam) (galanteador) suitor 2 (fam & pey) ▸**marica²**

mariquita *f* 1 (Zool) ladybug (AmE), ladybird (BrE) 2 (fam & pey) ▸**marica²** 3 **mariquita** *mf* (fam & pey) (cobarde) wimp (colloq)

mariscal *m* (Hist, Mil) marshal

(Compuesto) **mariscal de campo** (Mil) field marshal; (en fútbol americano) quarterback

mariscar [A2] *vi*: *to fish for shellfish*

marisco *m* shellfish (*pl*), seafood; **el precio de los ~s** *or* (Esp) **del ~** the price of shellfish *o* seafood

marisma *f* marsh; **~s** marshes, marshland

marisquería *f* seafood restaurant/bar/shop, shellfish restaurant/bar/shop

marital *adj* ‹*relaciones*› marital (*before n*); ‹*vida*› married (*before n*)

marítimo -ma *adj* ‹*comercio*› maritime; ‹*ruta/agente*› shipping (*before n*); ‹*ciudad*› coastal, maritime; **un puerto ~** a seaport; **el transporte ~** sea transport, transport by sea

marjal *m* marsh

marketing /'marketin/ *m* marketing

(Compuesto) **marketing telefónico** telesales

marmita *f* cooking pot

mármol *m* marble

marmolado -da *adj* marbled

marmolería *f* marble mason's workshop

marmolista *mf* marble mason

marmóreo -rea *adj* (liter) marmoreal (liter)

marmota *f* 1 (Zool) marmot 2 (fam) (persona — poco espabilada) silly *o* dopey fool; (— dormilona) sleepyhead (colloq)

maroma *f*

A rope

B 1 (Andes) (acrobacia, malabarismo) trick, stunt; **las ~s del payaso** the clown's antics; ***hacer* ~s** (Andes fam) to work miracles 2 (Méx) (voltereta) somersault, tumble; **dar** *or* **echar una ~** to do a somersault

maromear [A1] *vi* (Col, Méx, Ven) to walk a tightrope

marqués -quesa *m,f*

A (persona) (*m*) marquis, marquess (BrE); (*f*) marquise, marchioness (BrE)

B **marquesa** *f* (Chi) (catre) bed

marquesina *f* (en parada, andén) shelter; (de teatro, hotel) marquee (AmE), canopy (BrE); (en estadio) roof

marquetería *f* marquetry

marrajo -ja *adj* 1 ‹*toro*› dangerous, vicious 2 ‹*persona*› sly

marranada *f* (fam) 1 (faena) dirty trick 2 (acción grosera): **hacer ~s** to do disgusting things

marrano¹ -na *adj* filthy

marrano² -na *m,f* (fam) 1 (animal) (*m*) pig, hog; (*f*) pig, sow 2 (Col) (carne) pork 3 (persona — despreciable) swine (colloq); (— grosera) dirty swine (colloq)

marraqueta *f* (Chi) bread roll

marrar [A1] *vt* to miss
■ **marrar** *vi* to go wrong, fail

marras
A : **de ~**: **el individuo de ~** the man in question; **el cuento de ~** the same old story
B (Col fam) (en expresiones de tiempo): **hace ~ que no voy al cine** I haven't been to the movies for ages; **¡~ sin verlo!** long time no see! (colloq)

marrón[1] *adj* brown; **zapatos ~ oscuro** dark brown shoes

marrón[2] *m*
A (color) brown
B (Col) (rulo) roller, curler

marroquí *adj/mf* Moroccan

marroquín *m* morocco (leather)

marroquinería *f* 1 (artículos de cuero) leather goods (*pl*) 2 (tienda) leather goods shop; (taller) leather workshop

marrueco *m* (Chi) fly, flies (*pl*)

Marruecos *m* Morocco

marrullero -ra *adj* (fam) dirty (colloq)

marsopa *f* porpoise

marsupial *adj/m* marsupial

mart. (= **martes**) Tues, Tue

marta *f* (pine) marten
(Compuesto) **marta cibelina** sable

martajar [A1] *vt* (Méx) to crush, pound

Marte *m* Mars

martes *m* (*pl* ~) Tuesday; *para ejemplos ver* **lunes**; **~ (y) trece** ≈ Friday the thirteenth
(Compuesto) **martes de carnaval** Shrove Tuesday, Mardi Gras

martillar [A1] *vt/vi* ▸ **martillear**

martillazo *m*; **le dio** *or* **pegó un ~** he hit it with a hammer; **lo clavó de un ~** he hammered it in with one blow; **lo rompió a ~s** she smashed it with a hammer

martillear [A1] *vt* 1 (con un martillo) to hammer 2 «*ruido*»: **el ruido me martilleaba la cabeza** the noise was pounding in my head
■ **martillear** *vi* to hammer

martilleo *m* hammering; **un ~ terrible en las sienes** a terrible pounding in the temples

martillero -ra *m,f* (CS, Per) auctioneer

martillo *m*
A (herramienta) hammer; (de un subastador) hammer, gavel; (Dep) hammer
(Compuesto) **martillo neumático** jackhammer, pneumatic drill
B (Anat) hammer, malleus (tech)
C (de un piano) hammer

martinete *m*
A (Zool) heron
B (del piano) hammer

martingala *f* (CS) 1 (Jueg) martingale, system 2 (maquinación) scheme

martín pescador *m* kingfisher

mártir *mf* martyr

martirio *m* 1 (muerte) martyrdom 2 (sufrimiento) torment, ordeal

martirizante *adj* ‹*dolor*› excruciating; ‹*espera*› agonizing

martirizar [A4] *vt* 1 (matar) to martyr 2 (atormentar) to torment

marullero -ra *adj* (Chi fam) 1 ‹*jugador*› cheating (*before n*) 2 (astuto) crafty (colloq), sly

marxismo *m* Marxism

marxista *adj/mf* Marxist

marzo *m* March; *para ejemplos ver* **enero**

mas *conj* (liter) but

más[1] *adv*
A 1 (comparativo): **¿tiene algo ~ barato/moderno?** do you have anything cheaper/more modern?; **duran ~** they last longer; **me gusta ~ sin azúcar** I prefer it without sugar; **ahora la vemos ~** we see more of her now; **tendrás que estudiar ~** you'll have to study harder; **cuídate ~** look after yourself better; **~ lejos/atrás** further away/back; **el que ~, el que menos, todos se beneficiaron** they all benefitted to a greater or lesser degree; **más ... QUE**: **~ que nunca/que el año pasado** more than ever/than last year; **me gusta ~ el vino seco que el dulce** I prefer dry wine to sweet, I like dry wine better than sweet; **más (...) DE**: **pesa ~ de lo que parece** it's heavier than it looks; **es ~ complicado de lo que tú crees** it's more complicated than you think; **eran ~ de las cinco** it was after five o'clock; **~ de 80 kilos** over 80 kilos; **~ de 30** over *o* more than 30 2 (especialmente) particularly, especially
B (superlativo): **es la ~ bonita/la ~ inteligente** she's the prettiest/the most intelligent; **es el que ~ sabe** he's the one who knows most; **es el que ~ me gusta** it's the one I like best; **lo ~ que puede pasar** the worst that can happen; **cuando ~ lo necesitaba** when I needed him most; **me preocupa tanto como al que ~** I'm as worried about it as anybody; **está de lo ~ entusiasmado** he's really excited; **estuvo de lo ~ divertido** it was great fun
C (*en frases negativas*) 1 (con valor limitativo): **no tiene ~ que tres meses** she's only three months old; **nadie ~ que ella** nobody but her; **no tengo ~ que esto** this is all I have; **no tienes ~ que decirlo** you have only to say so; **no fue ~ que un rasguño** it was only a scratch; **no tuve ~ remedio** I had no alternative 2 (de nuevo) any more; **no juego ~** I'm not playing any more; **nunca ~** never again; *para locs ver* **más**[3] **B**
D (con valor ponderativo): **¡cantó ~ bien...!** she sang so well!; **¡qué cosa ~ rara!** how strange!; **¡qué gente ~ amable!** what kind people!

más[2] *adj inv*
A (comparativo) more; **~ dinero** more money; **una vez/tres veces ~** once more/three times more; **ni un minuto ~** not a minute longer; **hoy hace ~ calor** it's warmer today; **tienes ~ tiempo (que yo)** you have more time (than me); **son ~ que nosotros** there are more of them than us; **sucede con ~ frecuencia de la deseable** it happens more often than one would wish
B (superlativo) most; **el equipo que ganó ~ partidos** the team that won most games; **los ~ se cansaron y se fueron** most of them got tired and left; **las ~ de las veces** more often than not
C (con valor ponderativo): **¡me da ~ rabia ...!** it makes me so mad!; **¡tiene ~ amigos/~ dinero ...!** he has so many friends/so much money!
D **¿qué/quién ~?** what/who else?; **nada/nadie ~** nothing/nobody else; **algo/alguien ~** something/somebody else; **¿quién ~ vino?** who else came?; **¿algo ~? — nada ~ gracias** anything else? — no, that's all, thank you; **no se lo digas a nadie ~** don't tell anyone else; **¿alguien ~ vino?** did anyone else come?

más[3] *pron*
A more; **¿te sirvo ~?** would you like some more?; **lo siento, no hay ~** I'm sorry, there isn't/aren't any left
B (*en locs*) **a lo más** at the most; **a más de** besides, as well as; **a más no poder**: **comieron a ~ no poder** they ate till they were fit to burst; **corrimos a ~ no poder** we ran as fast *o* hard as we could; **a más tardar** at the latest; **cuanto más** at the most; **de más**: **¿alguien tiene un lápiz de ~?** does anybody have a spare pencil?; **me dio cinco dólares de ~** he gave me five dollars too much; **de ~ está decir que ...** needless to say ...; **estoy de ~ aquí** I'm not needed here; **no está de ~ repetirlo** there's no harm in repeating it; **es más** in fact; **más bien**: **es ~ bien bajita** she's rather *o* a bit on the short side; **~ bien deberías ir tú** I would have thought it was you who should go; **más o menos** (aproximadamente) more or less; (no muy bien) so-so; **llegaremos a las cinco, poco ~ o menos** we'll arrive around five o'clock; **ni más ni menos** no less; **no más** ▸ **nomás**; **por más**: **por ~ que llores** however much you cry; **por ~ que trataba** however hard *o* no matter how hard he tried; **¿qué más da?** what does it matter?; **sin más (ni más)** just like that; ***ir a* ~** (Esp) to be on the up and up
(Compuesto) **más allá**: **el ~ ~** the other world; **voces del ~ ~** voices from beyond the grave

más[4] *prep* 1 (Mat) (en sumas) plus; **8+7 =15** (*read as: ocho más siete (es) igual (a) quince*) eight plus seven equals fifteen 2 (además de) plus; **mil pesos, ~ los gastos** a thousand pesos, plus expenses

más[5] *m* plus sign; ***tener sus ~ y sus menos***: **tienen sus ~ y sus menos** they have their good points and their bad points

masa *f*

A (Coc) **1** (para pan, pasta) dough; (para empanadas, tartas) pastry; (para bizcocho) mixture; (para crepes) batter **2** (RPl) (pastelito) pastry, cake

(Compuesto) **masa de hojaldre** puff pastry

B (volumen, conglomerado) mass; **una ~ de agua** a mass of water

(Compuesto) **masa salarial** payroll

C **en masa** **1** (*loc adj*) ‹*producción/fabricación*› mass (*before n*); ‹*despidos*› mass (*before n*), wholesale (*before n*) **2** (*loc adv*) ‹*acudir*› en masse

D (Pol, Sociol) mass; **la gran ~ de la población** the great mass of the population; **educar a las ~s** to educate the masses; **cultura/mercado de ~s** mass culture/market

E **1** (Fís) mass **2** (Elec) ground (AmE), earth (BrE)

masacrar [A1] *vt* to massacre

masacre *f* massacre

masaje *m* massage; **darle ~s** *or* **un ~ a algn** to give sb a massage

masajear [A1] *vt* to massage

masajista *mf*

A (que da masajes) (*m*) masseur; (*f*) masseuse

B (en fútbol) coach, trainer

masato *m* (Col) *drink made from fermented maize or rice*

mascada *f* **1** (Chi) (mordisco) bite **2** (Méx) (pañuelo grande) scarf

mascar [A2] *vt* to chew; ***darle todo mascado a algn*** to spoonfeed sb

máscara *f* **1** (careta) mask; **baile de ~s** masked ball **2** (apariencia) mask, appearance **3** (para bucear) face mask **4** (Chi) (de un auto) grille

(Compuestos)

- **máscara de oxígeno** oxygen mask
- **máscara facial** face pack

mascarada *f* masquerade

mascarilla *f* **1** (de cirujano, dentista) mask; (de oxígeno) mask **2** (en cosmética) face pack **3** (de un muerto) death mask

mascarón *m*: *tb* **~ de proa** figurehead

mascota *f* (talismán) mascot; (animal doméstico) pet

masculinidad *f* masculinity, manliness

masculino[1] **-na** *adj* **1** ‹*actitud/hormonas*› male; ‹*mujer/aspecto*› masculine, manly; **sexo: ~** sex: male **2** ‹*género/forma*› masculine

masculino[2] *m* masculine

mascullar [A1] *vt* to mumble, mutter

masía *f* (granja) farm; (casa) country house

masificación *f* **1** (exceso de personas) overcrowding **2** (propagación) spread, extension

masificado -da *adj* ‹*universidad*› overcrowded; **una sociedad masificada** a mass society

masificar [A2] *vt*

A **1** ‹*producción*› to apply the techniques of mass production to **2** ‹*gustos/forma de vestir*› to standardize

B ‹*información/cultura*› to give everyone access to; **~ la universidad** to open up university education to all; **~ la enseñanza de idiomas** to give everyone access to language teaching; **se debería ~ el uso de la bicicleta** everyone should be encouraged to cycle

■ **masificarse** *v pron*

A **1** «*producción*»: **cuando se masificó la producción del vehículo** when mass production of the vehicle began **2** «*gustos/forma de vestir*» to become standardized

B «*lugar*» to become *o* get overcrowded

masilla *f* (para cristales) putty; (para rellenar grietas) mastic, filler

masita *f* (CS) pastry, cake (BrE)

masitero -ra *m,f* (AmL) pastrycook

masivamente *adv* en masse

masivo -va *adj* **1** ‹*ejecución/migración*› mass (*before n*); ‹*protesta*› large-scale (*before n*), mass (*before n*); **una concurrencia masiva a las urnas** a massive turnout at the polls **2** ‹*dosis*› massive, huge

masón[1] *adj* Masonic

masón[2] *m* Freemason, Mason

masonería *f* Freemasonry

masónico -ca *adj* Masonic

masoquismo *m* masochism

masoquista[1] *adj* masochistic

masoquista[2] *mf* masochist

mastectomía *f* mastectomy

mastelero *m* topmast

master, máster /'master/ *m* (*pl* **-ters**)

A (Audio, Vídeo) master

B (Educ) master's degree

masticación *f* chewing, mastication (frml)

masticar [A2] *vt* to chew, masticate (frml); ***darle todo bien masticado a algn*** to spoonfeed sb

■ **masticar** *vi* to chew

mástil *m* **1** (Náut) mast; (para una bandera) flagpole, flagstaff **2** (de guitarra, violín) neck **3** (de carpa) centerpole*

mastín *m* mastiff

mastitis *f* (*pl* ~) mastitis

mastodonte *m* **1** (animal prehistórico) mastodon **2** (fam) (persona grande) giant

mastodóntico -ca *adj* (fam) ‹*proyecto*› mammoth; ‹*edificio*› gigantic, colossal

mastuerzo *m* **1** (planta) (garden) cress **2** (fam) (torpe) oaf

masturbación *f* masturbation

masturbar [A1] *vt* to masturbate

■ **masturbarse** *v pron* to masturbate

mata *f*

A (arbusto) bush, shrub; (planta) (AmL) plant

B **1** (ramita) sprig; (de hierba) tuft **2** (de raíces) clump **3** (bosque) thicket

C (fam) (de pelo) mane (colloq), mop (colloq)

matachín *m*

A (fam) (bravucón) bully

B (bailarín) dancer (*who performs traditional dances*)

matadero *m* slaughterhouse, abattoir

matado -da *m,f* (Méx fam & pey) grind (AmE colloq), swot (BrE colloq)

matador[1] **-dora** *adj* (fam) **1** ‹*trabajo/espera*› killing (colloq); **es una carrera ~a** it's a really tough race **2** ‹*vestido/corbata*› (horrible) (Esp) horrible, hideous; **con esa falda estás matadora** (guapísima) you look great in that skirt; (horrible) (Esp) you look terrible in that skirt

matador[2] *m* matador

matambre *m* **1** (corte de carne) flank steak (AmE), skirt (BrE) **2** (RPl) (plato) meat roulade (*filled with vegetables and hard-boiled eggs*)

matamoscas *m* (*pl* ~) **1** (paleta) flyswatter **2** (spray) fly spray, fly killer **3** (*como adj inv*) fly (*before n*); **papel ~** flypaper

matanza *f* (acción de matar) killing, slaughter; (de res, cerdo) slaughter

mataperrada *f* (Bol, Per fam) trick

mataperrear [A1] *vi* (Bol, Per fam) to hang around (colloq)

mataperro, mataperros *m* (*pl* ~) (Bol, Per fam) devil (colloq)

matapiojos *m* (*pl* ~) (Andes) dragonfly

matapolillas *m* (*pl* ~) moth killer

matar [A1] *vt*

A **1** ‹*persona*› to kill; ‹*reses*› to slaughter; **lo ~on a golpes** they beat him to death; **lo mató un coche** he was run over and killed by a car; **hubo que ~ al caballo** the horse had to be put down *o* destroyed; **entrar a ~** (Taur) to go in for the kill; **el cigarrillo acabará matándote** cigarettes will be the death of you; **entre todos la ~on (y ella sola se murió)** (fr hecha) they are all to blame; **que me maten si no es verdad lo que digo** may God strike me dead if I speak a word of a lie; ***las mata callando*** he's a wolf in sheep's clothing; **~*las*** (Chi fam) to blow it (colloq) **2** (en sentido hiperbólico): **la vas a ~ a disgustos** you'll be the death of her; **es para ~los** I could murder *o* kill them (colloq); **nos mataban de hambre** they used to starve us; **cuando se entere me mata** she'll kill me when she finds out (colloq); **me mata tener que estudiar tanto** it kills me having to study so much (colloq); **¡me mataste, no tengo ni idea!** (fam) you've really got me there, I haven't a clue! (colloq); **estos zapatos me están matando** these shoes are killing me!

B (fam) ‹*sed*› to quench; ‹*tiempo*› to kill; **compraron fruta para ~ el hambre** they bought some fruit to keep them going

C 1 ‹*pelota*› to kill 2 ‹*carta*› to cover

■ **matar** *vi* (causar muerte) to kill; **hay miradas que matan** if looks could kill; ***estar*** *or* ***llevarse a ~*** to be at daggers drawn

■ **matarse** *v pron*

A 1 (morir violentamente): **se mató en un accidente** she was killed in an accident; **casi me mato** I almost got killed 2 (*refl*) (suicidarse) to kill oneself; **se mató de un tiro** she shot herself

B (fam) 1 (esforzarse): **me maté estudiando** *or* (Esp) **a estudiar** I studied like crazy *o* mad (colloq); **se mató trabajando** he nearly killed himself working (colloq) 2 (Méx fam) (para un examen) to cram (colloq), to swot (BrE colloq)

matarife *m* 1 (en un matadero) slaughterman; (de caballos) knacker 2 (fam) (matón) thug, heavy (colloq)

matarratas *m* (*pl* ~) 1 (veneno) rat poison 2 (fam) (bebida) rotgut (colloq)

matasanos *mf* (*pl* ~) (fam) quack (colloq)

matasellar [A1] *vt* to frank, cancel

matasellos *m* (*pl* ~) 1 (marca) postmark 2 (instrumento) datestamp, stamp

matasuegras *m* (*pl* ~) party blower

matatigres *m* (*pl* ~) (Ven fam) moonlighter

matazón *f* (Col, Méx, Ven fam) massacre, slaughter

mate[1] *adj or adj inv* ‹*pintura/maquillaje*› matt; **fotos ~** photos with a matt finish

mate[2] *m*

A (en ajedrez) *tb* **jaque ~** checkmate, mate

B 1 (infusión) maté; **cebar ~** to brew maté 2 (calabaza) gourd

C (CS fam) (cabeza) head

matear [A1] *vi* (CS fam) to drink maté

■ **matearse** *v pron* (Chi fam) to cram (colloq), to swot (BrE colloq)

matemáticas *fpl*, **matemática** *f* mathematics, math (AmE), maths (BrE)

matemático[1] -ca *adj* 1 (Mat) mathematical 2 (exacto) mathematical

matemático[2] -ca *m,f* mathematician

mateo -tea *m,f* (Chi fam) (Educ) grind (AmE colloq), swot (BrE colloq)

materia *f*

A (sustancia) matter

(Compuestos)

- **materia grasa** fat
- **materia gris** gray* matter
- **materia prima** (Econ, Tec) raw material; (Fin) commodity

B 1 (tema, asunto) subject; **en ~ jurídica es un experto** he's an expert on legal matters; **en ~ de** as regards, with regard to; ***entrar en ~***: **entremos en ~** let's get straight to the matter in hand *o* straight down to business 2 (material) material 3 (esp AmL) (asignatura) subject

(Compuesto) **materia clasificada** classified information

material[1] *adj* 1 ‹*necesidades/ayuda/valor*› material; **daños ~es** damage to property, material damage 2 ‹*autor/causante*› actual 3 (uso enfático): **no tengo tiempo ~ para cosértelo** I really don't have time to sew it for you; **ante la imposibilidad ~ de ir** since it was quite impossible for her to go

material[2] *m*

A (elemento, sustancia) material; **~es para la construcción** building materials

B 1 (útiles) materials (*pl*) 2 (datos, documentos, etc) material

(Compuestos)

- **material bélico** (period) military equipment
- **material de oficina** office stationery
- **material didáctico/escolar** teaching/school materials (*pl*)
- **material fotográfico** (papel, películas) photographic materials (*pl*); (lentes, filtros) photographic equipment
- **material móvil** *or* **rodante** rolling stock

materialismo *m* materialism

materialista[1] *adj* materialistic

materialista[2] *mf*

A (persona) materialist

B (Méx) (constructor) building contractor; (camionero) truck driver, lorry driver (BrE)

materializar [A4] *vt* ‹*idea/plan*› to bring ... to fruition

■ **materializarse** *v pron* «*proyecto/plan*» to come to fruition, materialize

materialmente *adv* absolutely

maternal *adj* ‹*instinto*› maternal; ‹*amor*› motherly, maternal

maternidad *f* 1 (estado) motherhood, maternity 2 (hospital) maternity hospital; (sala) maternity ward

materno -na *adj* ‹*amor*› motherly; ‹*abuelo*› maternal; ‹*lengua*› mother; **leche materna** mother's milk

matero *m* (Ven) 1 (maceta) flower pot 2 (fam) (matas) bushes (*pl*)

mates *fpl* (Esp fam) math (AmE), maths (BrE)

matete *m* (RPl fam) 1 (lío, confusión) muddle 2 (mezcla, pegote) sticky mess

matinal[1] *adj* morning (*before n*)

matinal[2] *m* (Andes) morning performance

matinée, matiné *f* 1 (AmS) (de tarde) matinée 2 (Méx) (de mañana) morning performance

matiz *m* 1 (de color) shade, hue, nuance 2 (de palabra, frase) nuance, shade of meaning; **se diferencian en algunos matices** there are some subtle *o* slight differences between them; **tiene un cierto ~ peyorativo** it has a slightly pejorative nuance *o* has slightly pejorative connotations; **con matices políticos** with political overtones 3 (de ironía) touch, hint

matizar [A4] *vt*

A ‹*colores*› to blend

B 1 (concretar, puntualizar) to qualify, clarify 2 (dar cierto tono): **un discurso matizado de** *or* **con ironía** a speech tinged with irony 3 (variar) ‹*relato/charla*› **~ algo DE algo** to sprinkle sth WITH sth 4 (suavizar) ‹*voz/palabras*› to tone down

■ **matizar** *vi*: **aquí habría que ~ diciendo que ...** here you'd have to qualify it by saying ...

matón *m* (del barrio) thug; (en la escuela) bully; (criminal) thug, heavy (colloq)

matonería *f*, **matonismo** *m* (fam) (en barrio) thuggery; (en escuela) bullying

matorral *m* 1 (conjunto de matas) thicket, bushes (*pl*) 2 (terreno) scrubland

matraca *f*

A 1 (juguete) rattle; ***darle (la) ~*** (fam) to go on (and on) (colloq) 2 **matraca** *mf* (fam) (persona latosa) pain (colloq), nuisance

B (Méx fam) (coche) rattletrap (colloq)

matraquear [A1] *vi* (fam) to nag

matraz *m* (balloon) flask

matrero -ra *adj*

A (Col fam) (basto) shoddy

B (RPl) (fugitivo): **un gaucho ~** a gaucho on the run from the law

C (Col) (traicionero) sly, crafty

matriarca *f* matriarch

matriarcado *m* matriarchy

matriarcal *adj* matriarchal

matricida *mf* matricide

matricidio *m* matricide

matrícula *f*

A 1 (Educ) (inscripción) registration, enrollment*; **está abierta la ~** registration *o* enrollment has already begun; **derechos** *or* **tasas de ~** registration fees 2 (alumnado) roll 3 (registro) register

(Compuesto) **matrícula de honor** (Esp) ≈ distinction, ≈ magna cum laude

B 1 (Transp) (número) registration number; (placa) license* plate, number plate (BrE) 2 (Naut) registration

matriculación *f* registration

matriculado -da *m,f* registered student

m

matricular [A1] *vt* 1 ‹*persona*› to register, enroll• 2 ‹*coche/barco*› to register
■ **matricularse** *v pron* (*refl*) to register, enroll•

matrimonial *adj* marital

matrimoniar [A1] *vt* (Méx fam) to get hitched (colloq)
■ **matrimoniarse** *v pron* (Chi, Méx fam) to get hitched (colloq)

matrimonio *m* 1 (institución) marriage, matrimony (frml); **contraer ~** (frml) to marry; **nació fuera del ~** he was born out of wedlock 2 (pareja) (married) couple; **el ~ Garrido** Mr and Mrs Garrido, the Garridos 3 (AmS exc RPl) (boda) wedding

(Compuestos)
- **matrimonio civil/religioso** civil/church wedding
- **matrimonio por poder(es)** marriage by proxy

matriz *f*
A 1 (útero) womb, uterus 2 (molde) mold• 3 (de documento) original; (de disco) master 4 (de talonario) stub 5 (de un test) master copy 6 (esténcil) stencil
B (Inf, Mat) matrix
C (de empresa) headquarters (*sing or pl*)

matrona *f* 1 (mujer — distinguida) matron (liter *or* dated); (— madura) matron (pej) 2 (comadrona) midwife

matute *m* (Esp fam) (contrabando) smuggling; (artículos de contrabando) smuggled *o* contraband goods

matutino¹ **-na** *adj* morning (*before n*)

matutino² *m* morning paper

maula¹ *adj* 1 (fam) (vago) lazy, bone idle (colloq) 2 (RPl fam) (cobarde) cowardly

maula² *mf* (fam) 1 (pesado) pain in the neck (colloq) 2 (cobarde) (RPl fam) coward; (tramposo) (Chi fam) cheat

maullar [A23] *vi* to miaow

maullido *m* miaow

Mauricio *m* Mauritius

mauritano -na *adj/m,f* Mauritanian

mausoleo *m* mausoleum

máx (= **máximo**) max.

maxifalda *f* maxiskirt, maxi

maxilar¹ *adj* maxillary

maxilar² *m* jawbone, maxilla (tech)

máxima *f* maxim

máxime *adv* especially; **lo haré, ~ cuando ...** I'll do it, especially as ... *o* all the more since ...

maximizar [A4] *vt* ‹*oportunidades/beneficios*› to maximize; **~ la utilización de recursos** to make optimum use of resources

máximo¹ **-ma** *adj* ‹*temperatura/velocidad*› top (*before n*), maximum (*before n*); ‹*carga/altura*› maximum (*before n*); ‹*punto*› highest; ‹*esfuerzo*› greatest, maximum (*before n*); **el ~ galardón** the highest honor; **era su máxima ilusión/ambición** it was her great dream/greatest ambition; **el ~ dirigente francés** the French leader; **lo ~ que puede ocurrir es ...** the worst that can happen is ...

máximo² *m* maximum; **con un ~ de 20 folios** up to 20 pages long; **como ~** at the most; **100 palabras como ~** 100 words, maximum; **aprovechar algo al ~** to make the most of sth; **se esforzó al ~** she did her utmost; **rendir al ~** ‹*persona*› to give a hundred percent; ‹*máquina*› to work to its full capacity

maxisencillo, maxisingle *m* maxisingle, twelve-inch single

maya¹ *adj* Mayan

maya² *mf* Maya, Mayan; **los ~s** the Maya *o* Mayas

> **Mayas**
>
> The Mayas, possibly of North American origin, settled in the Yucatán Peninsula around 2600 BC, and established a civilization which spread through Southern Mexico, into Guatemala, Belize, parts of Honduras and El Salvador, flourishing until the arrival of the Spanish in the sixteenth century. Their society was organized on the basis of city states grouped into confederations. Though lacking metal tools, the Mayas built stepped pyramids and other stone monuments such as those at Chichén Itzá, Uxmal, Petén and Palenque

mayal *m* flail

mayestático -ca *adj* (liter) majestic; **el plural ~** the royal we

mayo *m* May; *para ejemplos ver* **enero**; **el primero de ~** May Day

mayonesa *f* mayonnaise, mayo (AmE) (colloq)

mayor¹ *adj*
A 1 (comparativo de **grande**): **vuelan a ~ altura** they fly at a greater height; **un material de ~ flexibilidad** a more flexible material; **a ~ escala** on a larger scale; **en otros países el índice es aún ~** in other countries the rate is even higher; **beneficios aún ~es** even greater benefits; **~ QUE algo** greater THAN sth; **un número ~ que 40** a number bigger *o* greater than 40 2 (superlativo de **grande**): **tienen el ~ número de accidentes** they have the greatest *o* highest number of accidents; **su ~ preocupación** her greatest *o* biggest worry; **a la ~ brevedad posible** (Corresp) as soon as possible *o* (frml) at your earliest convenience; **la ~ parte de los estudiantes** most students, the majority of students; **viven en la ~ pobreza** they live in the most terrible poverty
B (en edad) 1 (comparativo) older; **¿tienes hermanos ~es?** do you have any older *o* elder brothers or sisters?; **~ QUE algn** older THAN sb; **soy dos meses ~ que tú** I am two months older than you 2 (superlativo): **es la ~ de las dos** she is the older *o* elder of the two; **mi hijo ~** my eldest *o* oldest son; **el ~ de los residentes** the oldest of the residents 3 (anciano) elderly 4 (adulto): **hay que respetar a las personas ~es** you should treat adults *o* (colloq) grown-ups with respect; **cuando sea ~** when I grow up; **ya eres ~cito para estar haciendo esas cosas** you're a bit old to be doing things like that; **ser ~ de edad** (Der) to be of age; **soy ~ de edad y haré lo que quiera** I'm over 18 (*o* 21 *etc*) and I'll do as I please
C (*en frases negativas*) (grande): **no requiere ~es explicaciones** this doesn't need much in the way of explanation; **no tengo ~ interés en el tema** I'm not particularly interested in the subject; **no me produjo ~ inquietud** it did not worry me particularly; **sin ~es contratiempos** without any serious *o* major hitches; ***no pasar*** *or* ***llegar a ~es***: **tuvo un novio, pero el asunto no pasó a ~es** she had a boyfriend, but it didn't come to anything; **afortunadamente la cosa no llegó a ~es** fortunately it was nothing serious
D (en nombres) (principal) main; **Calle M~** Main Street (*in US*), High Street (*in UK*)
E (Mús) major
F (Com): **(al) por ~** wholesale; **hubo problemas (al) por ~** there were innumerable problems

mayor² *mf*
A (adulto) adult, grown-up (colloq); **sólo para ~es** adults only; **deben ir acompañados de un ~** they must be accompanied by an adult; **mis/tus ~es** my/your elders

(Compuesto) **mayor de edad** *mf* person who is legally of age

B **mayor** *m* (AmL) (Mil) major

mayoral *m* 1 (capataz) foreman; (de finca) farm manager, steward 2 (Hist) (cochero) coachman

mayorazgo *m* 1 (institución) primogeniture 2 (bienes) entailed estate

mayordomo *m* (criado principal) butler, majordomo; (capataz) (CS) steward, foreman; (portero) (Chi) superintendent (AmE), caretaker (BrE)

mayoreo *m* (AmL) wholesale (trade)

mayoría *f* 1 (mayor parte) majority; **la ~ de los especialistas** most of the experts, the majority of experts; **la gran ~ de ...** the great majority of ...; **ser ~** *or* **estar en ~** to be in the majority 2 (Pol) (margen) majority; **gobierno de la ~** majority rule

(Compuestos)
- **mayoría absoluta/silenciosa** absolute/silent majority
- **mayoría de edad** age of majority; **llegar a/cumplir la ~ de ~** to come of age
- **mayoría relativa** *or* **simple** simple *o* (BrE) relative majority; **consiguió una ~ ~** he achieved the highest number of votes

mayorista¹ *adj* wholesale

mayorista² *mf* wholesaler

m

mayoritariamente *adv* mainly; **la zona es ~ urbana** the area is mainly *o* chiefly urban

mayoritario -ria *adj* **1** ‹*apoyo/decisión/partido*› majority (*before n*); **los sindicatos ~s** the unions which represent most of the workers **2** (Fin) ‹*socio/accionista*› principal; **participación mayoritaria** majority holding *o* interest

mayormente *adv* **1** (principalmente) mainly, chiefly **2** (particularmente) especially, particularly; **no me preocupa ~** it doesn't worry me overmuch *o* particularly

mayúscula *f* capital (letter), uppercase letter (tech); **se escribe con ~** it is written with a capital letter; **rellenar en** *or* **con ~s** write in block capitals *o* in capital letters; ***con ~s*** ‹*amigo/profesional*› true (*before n*), real (*before n*); **se trata de dinero con D ~** we're talking serious money (colloq)

mayúsculo -la *adj* **1** ‹*letra*› capital (*before n*), uppercase (tech) **2** ‹*susto/error*› terrible; **un disparate ~** an absolutely stupid thing to do/say

maza *f* **1** (Coc) meat tenderizer **2** (Const) drop hammer **3** (en gimnasia) Indian club **4** (de bombo) drumstick **5** (arma) mace

mazacote *m*
A **1** (fam) (Coc): **un ~** a lumpy mess **2** (fam) (obra tosca) eyesore
B (Const) concrete
C (Méx) (Zool) boa

mazamorra *f* **1** (AmS) *milky pudding made with maize* **2** (Per) *pudding made with corn starch, sugar and honey* **3** (Col) *maize soup*

mazapán *m* marzipan

mazazo *m* (fam) (golpe — físico) blow, thump (colloq); (— moral) blow

mazmorra *f* dungeon

mazo *m*
A **1** (herramienta) mallet; (del mortero) pestle; (para la carne) meat tenderizer; (porra) club **2** (de una campana) clapper **3** (en croquet, polo) mallet
B (esp AmL) (manojo) bunch; (de naipes) deck (of cards) (AmE), pack (of cards) (BrE)

mazorca *f* (Bot, Coc) cob; **~ de maíz** corncob

mazurca *f* mazurka

Mc (= **megaciclo**) Mc

MCCA *m* (= **Mercado Común Centroamericano**) Central American Common Market, CACM

me *pron pers* me; **~ robaron el reloj** my watch was stolen; **¿~ lo prestas?** will you lend it to me *o* lend me it?; **~ arregló el televisor** he fixed the television for me; **~ lo quitó** he took it off me *o* away from me; **~ fue imposible** I was unable to; **~ miré en el espejo** (*refl*) I looked at myself in the mirror; **~ hice una chaqueta** (*refl*) I made myself a jacket; (*caus*) I had a jacket made; **~ equivoqué** I made a mistake; **~ alegro mucho** I'm very pleased; **se ~ murió el gato** my cat died; **no te ~ vayas** don't go away

meada *f* (vulg) piss (vulg); **echar una ~** to have a piss

meadero *m* (fam & hum) john (colloq), bog (BrE colloq)

meandro *m* meander

mear [A1] *vi* (vulg) to (have a) piss (vulg)
■ **mearse** *v pron* (fam) to wet oneself; **me estoy meando** I'm dying for a pee (colloq); ***~se de risa*** to wet *o* (colloq) pee oneself laughing

meca *f*
A (Per fam) (prostituta) prostitute, hooker (colloq), tart (BrE colloq)
B (Chi fam & euf) (caca) turd (vulg)

Meca *f*: **La ~** Mecca; **la ~** *or* **meca del cine** (fr hecha) Hollywood

mecánica *f*
A (Fís) mechanics
B (Auto, Mec) **1** (técnica) mechanics; **~ de automóbiles** car maintenance **2** (funcionamiento) mechanics (*pl*); **la ~ de la empresa** the mechanics of the firm

mecánicamente *adv* mechanically

mecanicismo *m* mechanism

mecánico¹ -ca *adj* **1** (Mec) mechanical **2** ‹*gesto/acto*› mechanical

mecánico² -ca *m,f* (de vehículos) mechanic; (de maquinaria industrial) fitter; (de fotocopiadoras, lavadoras) (*m*) engineer, repairman; (*f*) engineer, repairwoman

(Compuestos)
• **mecánico -ca dental** *or* **dentista** *m,f* dental technician
• **mecánico -ca de vuelo** *m,f* flight engineer

mecanismo *m* **1** (Mec) mechanism; **un ~ que cierra las puertas** a door-locking device *o* mechanism; **el ~ de dirección** the steering gear **2** (de proceso, sistema) mechanism; **el ~ administrativo** the administrative mechanism; **a través de los ~s de negociación** through the negotiating process

(Compuestos)
• **mecanismo de cambio europeo** *or* **de cambios** *or* **de paridades** Exchange Rate Mechanism
• **mecanismo de defensa** defense* mechanism

mecanización *f* mechanization

mecanizado -da *adj* mechanized

mecanizar [A4] *vt* to mechanize

mecanografía *f* typing

mecanografiar [A17] *vt* to type

mecanógrafo -fa *m,f* typist

mecapal *m* (Méx) headband (*used to help carry things on one's back*)

mecapalero *m* (Méx) porter

mecatazo *m* (AmC, Méx) **1** (latigazo) lash **2** (fam) (trago) swig

mecate *m* (AmC, Méx, Ven) string, cord; (más grueso) rope; ***andar como burro sin ~*** (Méx, Ven fam) to be out of control; ***jalarle ~ a algn*** (Ven fam) to suck up to sb (colloq)

mecateada *f* (AmC, Méx fam) thrashing, beating

mecatear [A1] *vt* (AmC, Méx fam) to thrash, give ... a thrashing
■ **mecatear** *vi* (Col fam) to nibble

mecato *m* (Col fam) packed lunch

mecedora *f* rocking chair

mecenas *mf* (*pl* ~) patron, sponsor

mecenazgo *m* patronage, sponsorship

mecer [E2] *vt* **1** ‹*bebé/cuna*› to rock; ‹*niño*› (en columpio) to push **2** ‹‹*olas*›› to rock; **el viento mecía las ramas** the branches swayed in the wind
■ **mecerse** *v pron* **1** (en mecedora) to rock; (en columpio) to swing **2** (bambolearse) to sway

mecha *f*
A **1** (de una vela) wick; (de armas, explosivos) fuse; ***aguantar ~*** (fam) to grin and bear it, stand the gaff (AmE colloq); ***a toda ~*** (fam) like greased lightning (colloq) **2** (RPl) (broca) bit
B **mechas** *fpl* **1** (en peluquería) highlights (*pl*) **2** (AmL fam) (pelo): **¡mira cómo tienes las ~s!** look at the state of your hair! (colloq); **la agarró de las ~s** she grabbed her by the hair; ***ser tirado de las ~s*** (CS fam) to be ridiculous

mechar [A1] *vt* to stuff, lard

mechero *m* **1** (quemador) burner **2** (Esp) (encendedor) lighter **3** (Col) (candil) oil lamp

mechón¹ *m* **1** (de pelo) lock **2** (de lana) tuft **3** **mechones** *mpl* (Col) (en peluquería) highlights (*pl*)

mechón² -chona *m,f* (Chi) (estudiante) freshman, fresher (BrE)

mechudo -da *adj* **1** (Méx fam) (con el cabello en desorden): **andas muy mechuda** your hair looks an absolute mess (colloq) **2** (Col, Ven fam) (melenudo) long-haired

medalla *f* (Dep, Mil) medal; (Relig) medallion (*with religious engraving on it*); **se adjudicó la ~ de bronce/oro** he won the bronze/gold medal

medallista *mf* medallist

medallón *m* medallion

médano *m* (duna) dune; (banco de arena) sandbank

media *f*
A (Indum) **1** (hasta el muslo) stocking; **~s con/sin costura** seamed/seamless stockings **2** **medias** *fpl* (hasta la cintura) panty hose (*pl*) (AmE), tights (*pl*) (BrE) **3** (AmL) (calcetín) sock; ***chuparle las ~s a algn*** (CS fam) to lick sb's boots (colloq)

(Compuesto) **medias bombacha(s)** (RPl) *or* (Col, Ven) **pantalón** *fpl* panty hose (*pl*) (AmE), tights (BrE) (*pl*)

B (Mat) average; **la ~ de velocidad** the average speed; **una ~ de siete horas** an average of seven hours

(Compuesto) **media aritmética** arithmetic mean

C **a medias** (*loc adv*) 1 (incompleto): **dejó el trabajo a ~s** he left the work half-finished; **me dijo la verdad a ~s** she didn't tell me the whole truth *o* story; **lo arregló a ~s** he didn't fix it properly 2 (entre dos): **pagar a ~s** to pay half each, go halves; **lo hicimos a ~s** we did it between us

mediación *f* mediation; **por ~ de** through

mediado -da *adj* 1 (a mitad de) halfway through; **mediada la tarde empezó** halfway through the afternoon 2 (medio lleno) half-full, half-empty

mediador -dora *m,f* mediator

mediados: **a ~ de mes** halfway through the month, in the middle of the month; **a ~ de los años 30** in the mid thirties; **hacia ~ de mayo** around the middle of May

mediagua *f* (Andes) hut, shack

medialuna *f* 1 (esp RPl) (Coc) croissant (*often with ham and cheese*) 2 (Chi) (corral) ring

mediana *f*

A (Mat) median

B (Auto) median strip (AmE), central reservation (BrE)

medianamente *adv* moderately, fairly; **un resultado ~ bueno** a fairly good result

medianera *f* dividing wall, party wall (BrE)

medianería *f*

A (pared divisoria) dividing wall, party wall (BrE)

B (Méx) (Agr) (contrato) sharecropping

medianero -ra *adj* ‹*muro/pared*› dividing (*before n*), party (*before n*) (BrE); ‹*cerco*› dividing (*before n*)

medianía *f*

A 1 (punto medio) half-way point 2 (mediocridad) mediocrity

B (Andes) (pared) dividing wall, party wall (BrE)

mediano -na *adj* 1 ‹*tamaño/porción*› medium; ‹*coche*› medium-sized; **de mediana estatura/inteligencia** of medium *o* average height/of average intelligence; **de mediana edad** middle-aged; **la mediana empresa** medium-sized business 2 (mediocre) average, mediocre; **un trabajo de mediana calidad** a mediocre *o* rather average essay

m

medianoche *f*

A (las doce de la noche) midnight; **a ~** at midnight

B (Coc) (Esp, Méx) *type of roll for sandwiches*

mediante *prep* (frml) through, by means of (frml); **~ un intérprete** through *o* by means of an interpreter; **los resultados obtenidos ~ este método** the results obtained by *o* using this method; **atrapa su presa ~ estas pinzas** it traps its prey with these claws

mediar [A1] *vi*

A «*persona/organización*» 1 (intervenir) to mediate; **~ EN algo** ‹*en conflicto/negociaciones*› to mediate IN sth, to act as mediator IN sth 2 (interceder) **~ POR algn** to intercede FOR sb *o* on sb's behalf; **~ ANTE algn** to intercede *o* intervene WITH sb

B 1 «*tiempo/distancia*»: **el tiempo que media entre los dos hechos** the time which separates the two incidents; **~on dos años antes de volverla a ver** two years passed *o* elapsed before he saw her again; **entre los dos pueblos median 50 kms** the two villages are separated by a distance of 50 kms; **pero de ahí a decir que es un genio media un abismo** that's a long way from saying he's a genius 2 (interponerse): **sin ~ palabra** without (saying) a word; **entre nosotros media un abismo** we are poles *o* worlds apart; **no debemos permitir que medien intereses personales** we must not allow personal interests to enter into it 3 (transcurrir): **mediaba la tarde/el mes de mayo cuando ...** it was mid-afternoon/mid-may when ...

mediasnueves *fpl* (Col) mid-morning snack, elevenses (BrE colloq)

mediático -ca *adj* media (*before n*); **el poder ~** the power of the media

mediatizar [A4] *vt* 1 (influir) to influence 2 (estorbar) to interfere with

medicación *f* (frml) (medicinas) medication; (tratamiento) treatment, medication (frml)

medicamento *m* (frml) medicine, medicament (frml)

medicamentoso -sa *adj* (frml): **alergia medicamentosa** allergy brought on by medication

medicar [A2] *vt* (frml) ‹*enfermo*› to give *o* administer medication to (frml); **está medicado** he's on medication

medicatura *f* (Ven) first aid post, clinic

medicina *f*

A (ciencia) medicine

(Compuestos)

- **medicina alternativa/homeopática** alternative/homeopathic medicine
- **medicina forense** *or* **legal** forensic medicine
- **medicina general/interna/preventiva** general/internal/preventive medicine
- **medicina naturista** naturopathy

B (medicamento) medicine

medicinal *adj* ‹*aguas/planta*› medicinal; ‹*champú/jabón*› medicated

medición *f* 1 (acción) measuring; **instrumentos de ~** measuring instruments 2 (frml) (medida) measurement

médico[1] -ca *adj* medical; **un reconocimiento ~** a medical (examination); **está en tratamiento ~** he is having *o* undergoing treatment

médico[2] -ca *m,f*, **médico** *mf* doctor

(Compuestos)

- **médico cirujano** surgeon
- **médico de cabecera** family doctor *o* (AmE) physician, general practitioner, GP
- **médico de medicina general** general practitioner, GP
- **médico forense** *or* (Chi, Per) **legista** forensic scientist
- **médico interno residente** intern (AmE), houseman (BrE)

medicucho -cha *m,f* (pey) quack (pej)

medida *f*

A (Mat) (dimensión) measurement; **tomarle las ~s a algn** to take sb's measurements; **tomar las ~s de algo** to measure something; **¿qué ~s tiene el cuarto?** what are the dimensions of the room?

B (*en locs*) **a (la) medida** ‹*traje/zapato*› custom-made (AmE), made-to-measure (BrE); **servicios diseñados a la ~** tailor-made services; **a medida que** as; **a ~ que vaya pasando el tiempo** as time goes on; **a ~ que fue creciendo** as he grew up

C (objeto) measure; (contenido) measure; **un vaso de leche por cada ~ de cacao** one glass of milk per measure of cocoa; ***colmar la ~***: **eso colmó la ~** that was the last straw

D (grado, proporción): **en gran/cierta/menos ~** to a large/certain/lesser extent; **en la ~ de lo posible** as far as possible; **irá en la ~ en que le sea posible** he'll go if it's at all possible

E (moderación): **come con ~** he eats moderately; **gastan dinero sin ~** they spend money like water

F (Lit) measure

G (disposición) measure; **tomar ~s** to take steps *o* measures; **fue una ~ demasiado drástica** it was too drastic a step; **la huelga y otras ~s de presión** the strike and other forms of pressure

medido -da *adj* (CS): **es muy ~ con la bebida** he's a very moderate drinker; **fue muy ~ en sus palabras** he was very restrained in what he said

medidor *m* (AmL) meter

mediero -ra *m,f* (Chi) sharecropper

medieval *adj* medieval

medievalista *mf* medievalist

medievo *m* Middle Ages (*pl*)

medio[1] -dia *adj*

A (*delante del n*) (la mitad de): **~ litro** half a liter, a half-liter; **~ kilo** half a kilo; **media manzana** half an apple; **pagar ~ pasaje** to pay half fare *o* half price; **un retrato de ~ cuerpo** a half-length portrait; **media hora** half an hour, a half hour (AmE); **dos horas y media** two and a half hours; **lo sabe ~ Buenos Aires** half of Buenos Aires knows; **se lo contó a ~ mundo** he told the whole world; **la falda le llega a media pierna** she's wearing a calf-length skirt; **a media mañana/tarde dio un paseo** he went for a mid-morning/mid-afternoon stroll; **está a ~ vestir** she's still getting dressed

(Compuestos)

- **media luna** *f* half-moon; **en forma de ~ ~** crescent-shaped; **la M~ L~ Roja** the Red Crescent

- **media naranja** *mf* (fam & hum): **mi/su ~ ~** (cónyuge, novio, novia, etc) my/his/her better half (colloq & hum); (hombre ideal) my/her Mr Right; (mujer ideal) my/his ideal woman
- **media pensión** *f* (en hoteles) half board; (en colegios): **los alumnos en régimen de ~ ~** pupils who have school dinners
- **media vuelta** *f* (Mil) about-face (AmE), about-turn (BrE); **(se) dio ~ ~ y se fue** she turned on her heel and left
- **medio campo** *m* midfield
- **medio del melé** *mf* scrum half
- **medio fondista** *mf* middle-distance runner
- **medio fondo** *m* middle-distance
- **medio hermano -dia hermana** (*m*) half-brother; (*f*) half-sister
- **medio luto** *m* half-mourning
- **medio pupilo -dia pupila** *m,f* (CS) day pupil; **los ~ ~s** the day pupils
- **medio tiempo** (AmL) half-time

B (mediano, promedio) average; **el ciudadano/mexicano ~** the average citizen/Mexican; **a ~ y largo plazo** in the medium and long term; **la temperatura media** the average temperature

medio² *adv* half; **está ~ loca/dormida** she's half crazy/asleep; **~ en broma ~ en serio** half joking and half serious; **todo lo deja a ~ terminar** he leaves everything half finished; **fue ~ violento encontrármelo ahí** it was rather awkward meeting him there

medio³ *m*

A (Mat) (mitad) half

B 1 (centro) middle; **en (el) ~ de la habitación** in the middle *o* center of the room; **el asiento de en** *or* **del ~** the middle seat, the seat in the middle; **el justo ~** the happy medium; **quitarse de en** *or* **del ~** to get out of the way; ***quitar a algn de en ~*** (euf) to bump sb off (colloq) 2 **los medios** *mpl* (Taur) center* (*of the ring*)

C 1 (recurso, manera) means (*pl*); **como ~ de coacción** as a means of coercion; **lo intentaron por todos los ~s** they tried everything they could; **no hay ~ de localizarlo** there's no way *o* means of locating him 2 (Art) (vehículo) *tb* **~ de expresión** medium 3 **medios** *mpl* (recursos económicos) *tb* **~s económicos** means (*pl*), resources (*pl*); **no escatimó ~s** he spared no expense; **no cuenta con los ~s necesarios para hacerlo** she does not have the means *o* resources to do it

(Compuestos)

- **medio de comunicación** *or* **difusión**: **la entrevista concedida a un ~ de ~ francés** the interview given to a French newspaper (*o* television station *etc*); **los ~s de ~** the media; **los ~s de ~ sociales** *or* **de masas** the mass media
- **medio de transporte** means of transport
- **medio informativo** ▸**medio de comunicación**
- **medios audiovisuales** *mpl* audiovisual aids (*pl*)
- **medios de producción** *mpl*: **los ~ de ~** the means of production

D (*en locs*) **de por medio**: **no puedo dejarlo, están los niños de por ~** I can't leave him, there are the children to think of; **hay intereses creados de por ~** there are vested interests involved; **había un árbol de por ~** there was a tree in the way; **en medio de**: **en ~ de tanta gente** (in) among so many people; **cómo puedes trabajar en ~ de este desorden** how can you work in all this mess; **en ~ de la confusión** in *o* amid all the confusion; **en ~ de todo** all things considered; **por medio** (CS, Per): **día/semana por ~** every other day/week; **dos o tres casas por ~** every two or three houses; **por medio de** by means of; **se comunicaban por ~ de este sistema** they communicated by means of this system; **por ~ de tu primo** from *o* through your cousin; ***de ~ a ~***: **te equivocas de ~ a ~** you're completely wrong; **le acertó de ~ a ~** she was absolutely right

E 1 (círculo, ámbito): **en ~s literarios/políticos** in literary/political circles; **no está en su ~** he's out of his element; **es desconocido en nuestro ~** he's unknown here (*o* in our area *etc*); **en ~s bien informados se comenta que ...** informed opinion has it that ... 2 (Biol) environment; **la adaptación al ~** adaptation to one's environment *o* surroundings; **animales en su ~ natural** animals in their natural habitat

(Compuesto) **medio ambiente** environment

medioambiental *adj* environmental

medioambientalista *adj/mf* environmentalist

mediocampista *mf* midfield player

mediocre *adj* mediocre

mediocridad *f* mediocrity

mediodía *m*

A 1 (las doce de la mañana) midday, noon; **a ~** *or* **al ~** at midday 2 (hora de comer) lunch time

B (Geog) south; **el ~ francés** the French Midi

medioevo *m* Middle Ages (*pl*)

mediofondista *mf* middle-distance runner

mediometraje *m* medium-length movie, medium-length film (BrE)

Medio Oriente *m* Middle East, Mid-East (AmE)

mediopensionista¹ *adj* day (*before n*)

mediopensionista² *mf* day pupil (*who has school lunch*)

medir [I14] *vt*

A to measure; **¿me mide tres metros de esta tela?** can you measure me off three meters of this material?

B (tener ciertas dimensiones) to be, measure; **mido 60 cm de cintura** I measure *o* I'm 60 cm round the waist; **la tela mide 90 cm de ancho** the cloth is 90 cm wide; **¿cuánto mide de alto/largo?** how tall/long is it?; **mide casi 1,90 m** he's almost 1.90 m (tall)

C (calcular, considerar) to consider, weigh up; **~ las consecuencias de algo** to consider the consequences of sth; **~ los pros y los contras de algo** to weigh up the pros and cons of sth

D (moderar): **mide tus palabras** you'd better choose *o* weigh your words carefully

■ **medirse** *v pron*

A (*refl*) to measure oneself; ‹*caderas/pecho*› to measure

B (Col, Méx, Ven) (probarse) to try on

meditabundo -da *adj* (liter *o* hum) pensive, thoughtful

meditación *f* meditation

(Compuesto) **meditación trascendental** transcendental meditation

meditar [A1] *vi* to meditate; **~ sobre algo** to reflect *o* meditate on sth

■ **meditar** *vt* (considerar) to think about; (durante más tiempo) to think about, ponder, meditate on; **una decisión muy meditada** a very carefully thought-out decision

meditativo -va *adj* meditative

mediterráneo -nea *adj* Mediterranean

Mediterráneo *m*: *tb* **el (mar) ~** the Mediterranean (sea)

médium *mf* (*pl* **-diums**) medium

medrar [A1] *vi* 1 «*persona/economía*» to prosper 2 (aumentar) to increase, grow

medroso -sa *adj* (liter) fearful, fainthearted (liter)

médula *f* 1 (Anat) marrow, medulla (tech); **me mojé hasta la ~** I got soaked to the skin; **británico hasta la ~** British through and through 2 (de problema) heart

(Compuestos)

- **médula espinal** spinal cord
- **médula ósea** bone marrow

medular *adj* 1 (Anat) bone-marrow (*before n*), medullary (tech) 2 (fundamental) fundamental

medusa *f* jellyfish, medusa

megabyte /'meɣaβajt/ *m* megabyte

megaciclo *m* megacycle

megafonía *f* PA system

megáfono *m* (bocina) megaphone; (altavoz) (ant) loudspeaker

megalítico -ca *adj* megalithic

megalito *m* megalith

megalomanía *f* megalomania

megalómano -na *adj/m,f* megalomaniac

megatón *m* megaton

meiga *f* witch

mejicano -na *adj/m,f* Mexican

Méjico *m* ▸**México**

mejilla *f* cheek; ***poner la otra ~*** to turn the other cheek

mejillón *m* mussel

m

mejor[1] *adj*
A 1 (comparativo de **bueno**) ‹*producto/profesor*› better; ‹*calidad*› better, higher, superior; **va a ser ~ que ...** it's better if ...; **tanto ~** *or* **~ que ~** so much the better; **cuanto más grande ~** the bigger the better; **al final todo fue para ~** it was all for *o* it all worked out for the best in the end; **es ~ que te sientes ahí** you'd be better off sitting there 2 (comparativo de **bien**) better; **sabe mucho ~ así** it tastes much better like that
B 1 (superlativo de **bueno**) (entre dos) better; (entre varios) best; **mi ~ amiga** my best friend; **productos de la ~ calidad** products of the highest quality; **lo ~ es que le digas la verdad** it's best if you tell her the truth; **le deseo lo ~** I wish you the very best *o* all the best 2 (superlativo de **bien**): **hoy es el díe en que la he encontrado ~** today is the best I've seen her

mejor[2] *adv*
A 1 (comparativo) better; **luego lo pensé ~** then I thought better of it; **pintas cada vez ~** your painting is getting better and better 2 **mejor dicho**: **me lleva dos años, ~ dicho, dos y medio** she's two years older than me, or rather, two and a half
B 1 (superlativo) best; **éste es el lugar desde donde se ve ~** this is where you can see best (from); **la versión ~ ambientada de la obra** the best-staged production of the play; **lo hice lo ~ que pude** I did it as best I could *o* (frml) to the best of my ability 2 **a lo mejor**: **a lo ~ este verano vamos a Italia** we may *o* might go to Italy this summer
C (esp AmL) (en sugerencias): **~ lo dejamos para otro día** why don't we leave it for another day?; **~ me callo** I think I'd better shut up; **~ pídeselo tú** it would be better if *you* asked him

mejor[3] *mf*: **el/la ~** (de dos) the better; (de varios) the best; **es la ~ de la clase** she's the best in the class

mejora *f*
A 1 (perfeccionamiento) improvement 2 **mejoras** *fpl* (obras) improvements (*pl*)
B (Chi) (choza): *makeshift dwelling built on another person's land*

mejorable *adj*: **la redacción es ~** the essay could be better *o* could be improved on

mejoramiento *m* improvement

mejorana *f* marjoram

mejorar [A1] *vt* 1 ‹*condiciones/situación*› to improve; **este tratamiento te ~á enseguida** this treatment will make you better right away; **intentó ~ su marca** she tried to improve on *o* beat her own record 2 ‹*oferta*› (en subastas) to increase; **los empresarios ~on la propuesta** the management improved their offer *o* made a better offer
■ **mejorar** *vi* «*tiempo*» to improve, get better; «*resultados/calidad/situación*» to improve, get better; «*persona*» (Med) to get better; **ha mejorado de aspecto** he looks a lot better; **han mejorado de posición** they've come *o* gone up in the world
■ **mejorarse** *v pron* 1 «*enfermo*» to get better; **¿ya te mejoraste de la gripe?** have you got over the flu?; **que te mejores** get well soon, I hope you get better soon 2 (Chi fam & euf) (dar a luz) to give birth

mejoría *f* improvement; **el enfermo ha experimentado una ligera ~** there has been a slight improvement in the patient's condition; **le deseamos una pronta ~** we wish him a speedy recovery

mejunje *m* (fam & pey) 1 (comida) concoction, mixture; (bebida) brew, concoction 2 (cosmético) mixture, gunk (colloq)

melado *m* (AmL) syrup

melancolía *f* 1 (tristeza) melancholy, sadness 2 (Psic) melancholia

melancólico[1] **-ca** *adj* ‹*música/versos*› melancholy, melancholic; ‹*persona*› melancholy

melancólico[2] **-ca** *m,f* melancholic

melanina *f* melanin

melanoma *m* melanoma

melaza *f* molasses

melé *f* (Dep) (libre) ruck, maul; (organizada) scrum

melena *f* 1 (pelo suelto) long hair; **con la ~ al viento** with her hair flowing in the wind 2 (estilo de corte) bob 3 (del león) mane 4 **melenas** *fpl* (fam & pey) (pelo largo) mop of hair (colloq)

melenas *m* (fam) long-haired guy

melenudo -da *adj* (fam) long-haired

melifluo -flua *adj* sickly-sweet

melindres *mpl* 1 (afectación) affectation, affected ways (*pl*) 2 (delicadeza) delicate ways (*pl*); (con la comida) finicky 3 (gazmoñería) prudishness

melindroso -sa *adj* 1 (remilgado) affected 2 (Méx) (delicado) choosy, finicky 3 (mojigato) prudish

melisa *f* lemon balm

mella *f* (en hoja de cuchillo) notch, nick; (en diente, vaso) chip; ***hacer ~ en algn/algo***: **ese fracaso no hizo ~ en él** that failure didn't affect him; **dejó ~ en su personalidad** it marked his personality; **los años no hacen ~ en ti** you haven't aged at all

mellado -da *adj* ‹*diente/taza*› chipped; ‹*cuchillo/borde*› jagged; ‹*persona*› (falto de algún diente) gap-toothed

mellar [A1] *vt* 1 ‹*cuchillo/hoja*› to notch, nick; ‹*diente/porcelana*› to chip 2 (esp AmL) ‹*honor/fama*› to damage

mellizo[1] **-za** *adj* twin (*before n*)

mellizo[2] **-za** (*m*) twin (brother); (*f*) twin (sister); **tuvo ~s** she had twins

melocotón *m* 1 (esp Esp) (fruta redonda) peach 2 (AmC) (fruta en forma de estrella) star fruit

melocotonero *m* (esp Esp) peach (tree)

melodía *f* melody, tune

melódico -ca *adj* melodic

melodioso -sa *adj* melodious, tuneful

melodrama *m* melodrama; **del menor problema hace un ~** she always makes such a drama out of everything

melodramático -ca *adj* melodramatic

melomanía *f* love of music

melómano -na *m,f* music lover

melón *m* 1 (Bot) melon 2 (fam) (cabeza) head, nut (colloq)

melopea *f* (Esp fam): **coger** *or* **agarrar una ~** to get plastered (colloq)

meloso -sa *adj* 1 (pringoso) sticky 2 ‹*persona*› sickly-sweet, sugary; ‹*música/canción*› schmaltzy, slushy; ‹*voz*› sickly-sweet

membrana *f* membrane

(Compuesto) **membrana mucosa** mucous membrane

membranoso -sa *adj* membranous

membresía *f* (AmL frml) membership (frml), members (*pl*)

membrete *m* letterhead; **papel con ~** headed paper

membrillo *m* (árbol) quince (tree); (fruta) quince; **dulce de ~** quince jelly

memez *f* (Esp fam) stupid thing to say (*o* do *etc*)

memo[1] **-ma** *adj* (Esp fam) stupid, dumb (colloq); **no seas ~** don't be so stupid *o* dumb

memo[2] **-ma** *m,f*
A (Esp fam) idiot, peabrain (colloq)
B **memo** *m* (memorándum) memo

memorable *adj* memorable

memorándum *m* (*pl* **-dums**), **memorando** *m* 1 (nota) memorandum, memo 2 (agenda) notebook

memoria *f*
A (facultad) memory; **tener mucha** *or* **buena/poca** *or* **mala ~ (para algo)** to have a good/poor *o* bad memory (for sth); **si la ~ no me falla** *or* **engaña** if my memory serves me right; **se me ha quedado grabado en la ~** it has remained etched on my memory; **desde que tengo ~** for as long as I can remember; **¡qué ~ la mía!** what a memory I have!; **aprender/saber algo de ~** to learn/know sth by heart; **estoy citando de ~** I'm quoting from memory; **se me había borrado totalmente de la ~** I'd completely forgotten about it; **la canción me trajo aquel episodio a la ~** the song brought back that whole affair; **al oír su nombre ¡cuántos recuerdos me vienen a la ~!** hearing her name brings back so many memories!; **su nombre no me viene a la ~** I can't remember his name; ***hacer ~***: **trata de hacer ~** try to remember; **seguro que te acuerdas, haz ~** of course you can remember, think hard; ***refrescarle la ~ a algn*** to refresh *o* jog sb's memory; ***tener una ~ de elefante*** to have an incredible memory
B (recuerdo) memory; **un incidente de triste ~** a lamentable

incident; **respetar/profanar la ~ de algn** to respect/blacken the memory of sb; **a la** *or* **en ~ de algn** in memory of sb; **el día más caluroso de que haya ~** the hottest day in living memory; **un monumento a la** *or* **en ~ de los caídos** a memorial to those killed

C memorias *fpl* (Lit) memoirs (*pl*)

D (Inf) memory

(Compuestos)
- **memoria RAM/ROM** RAM/ROM
- **memoria virtual** virtual memory

E 1 (Adm, Com) report; **~ anual** annual report 2 (Educ) written paper

memorial *m* memorial

memorístico -ca *adj*: **un aprendizaje netamente ~** a system based mainly on learning by heart *o* on rote learning

memorización *f* memorizing

memorizar [A4] *vt* to memorize

mena *f* ore

menaje *m*: **artículos de ~** household items; **sección de ~ del hogar** household department

mención *f* mention; **no hizo ~ de lo ocurrido** he didn't mention what had happened

(Compuesto) **mención honorífica** *or* **de honor** honorable• mention

mencionar [A1] *vt* to mention; **el tema mencionado anteriormente** the aforementioned *o* abovementioned matter (frml); **no quiero oír ~ ese nombre** I don't want to hear that name mentioned

menda *mf* (Esp fam) 1 (yo): **el/la ~** yours truly (colloq) 2 (pey) (tipo) jerk (colloq & pej); (tipa) old bag (colloq & pej)

mendacidad *f* (frml) lying, mendacity (frml)

mendaz *adj* (frml) mendacious (frml), lying (*before n*)

mendicante *adj* 1 (Relig) mendicant 2 (indigente) begging (*before n*), mendicant (frml)

mendicidad *f* begging

mendigar [A3] *vi* to beg

■ **mendigar** *vt* «*mendigo*» to beg for; **siempre tengo que andar mendigando que me ayudes** I always have to come to you hat in hand for help

mendigo -ga *m,f* beggar

mendrugo *m*: *tb* **~ de pan** piece of stale bread

menear [A1] *vt* 1 ‹*rabo*› to wag; ‹*cabeza*› to shake; ‹*caderas*› to wiggle 2 (fam) ‹*asunto/problema*› to go on about (colloq)

■ **menearse** *v pron* 1 (con inquietud) to fidget 2 (provocativamente) to wiggle one's hips 3 (fam) (apresurarse) to hurry up

meneo *m* 1 (movimiento) fidgeting; **un provocativo ~ de caderas** a provocative wiggle of the hips 2 (Esp fam) (sacudida) shake; **dar(le) un ~ a algn** to shake sb

menester *m*

A ser ~ (frml) (ser necesario) to be necessary; **es ~ que lo hagamos sin demora** we must do it without delay

B (frml) (tarea) occupation; **se ganaba la vida en los ~es más diversos** he earned his living from some very diverse activities

menesteroso -sa *m,f gen* **los ~s** the needy

menestra *f* (ingrediente) mixed vegetables (*pl*); (plato) vegetable stew

mengano -na *m,f*: *ver* **fulano**

mengua *f* (frml) decline; **una considerable ~ en el número de suscripciones** a substantial reduction *o* decline in the number of subscriptions; **sin ~ de la calidad del servicio** with no deterioration in the quality of the service

menguado¹ -da *adj* (frml) ‹*ejército*› reduced in numbers; ‹*provisiones*› diminished; **hubo una menguada asistencia** there was a low *o* poor turnout

menguado² *m* decrease

menguante *adj* ▸ **luna A, cuarto² C**

menguar [A16] *vi*

A (frml) «*temperatura/nivel*» to fall, drop; «*río*» to go down, drop in level; «*cantidad/número/reservas*» to diminish, dwindle, decrease; «*esperanzas*» to fade, dwindle; «*fuerzas*» to fade, wane, dwindle; **los embalses vieron ~ su contenido** the water level in the reservoirs dropped; **el calor no menguaba** the hot weather continued unabated

B (al tejer) to decrease

C «*luna*» to wane

■ **menguar** *vt*

A (frml) ‹*responsabilidad/influencia*› to diminish; ‹*reputación*› to damage

B ‹*puntos*› (en tejido) to decrease

menina *f*: *girl from a noble family brought up to serve at court*

meninge *f* meninx; **~s** meninges

meningitis *f* meningitis

menisco *m* cartilage, meniscus (tech)

menjurje, menjunje *m* ▸ **mejunje**

menopausia *f* menopause

menopáusico -ca *adj* menopausal

menor¹ *adj*

A 1 (comparativo de **pequeño**): **un período de ~ interés histórico** a period of less historical interest; **su poder es cada vez ~** his power is decreasing all the time; **en ~ medida/grado** to a lesser extent *o* degree; **alimentos de ~ contenido calórico** food which is lower in calories; **esta vez hay un número ~ de detenidos** this time there are fewer detainees; **un porcentaje ~** a lower *o* smaller percentage; **~ QUE algo** lower THAN sth; **un ingreso ~ que el mío** an income lower than mine; **X < Z** (Mat) (*read as: equis es menor que zeta*) X < Z; (*léase: X is less than Z*); **sucede con ~ frecuencia que antes** it happens less often *o* less frequently than before 2 (superlativo de **pequeño**): **haciendo el ~ ruido posible** making as little noise as possible; **el de ~ tamaño** the smallest one

B (en edad) 1 (comparativo): **¿tienes hermanas ~es?** do you have any younger sisters?; **~ QUE algn** younger THAN sb 2 (superlativo): **¿cuál es el ~ de los hermanos?** who's the youngest of the brothers?, **el ~ de los dos niños** the younger of the two boys

C (secundario) ‹*escritor/obra*› minor; **lesiones de ~ importancia** minor injuries

D (Mús) minor

E (Com): **(al) por ~** retail; **Ⓢ venta (al) por menor** retail sales; **los distribuidores (al) por ~** retail shops *o* outlets

menor² *mf* (Der) minor; **Ⓢ película no apta para menores** film not suitable for under-18s

(Compuesto) **menor de edad** *mf* minor

menorista¹ *adj* (Col, Méx, Ven) retail (*before n*)

menorista² *mf* (Col, Méx, Ven) retailer

menorragia *f* menorrhagia

menos¹ *adv*

A (comparativo) less; **cada vez estudia ~** she's studying less and less; **ya me duele ~** it hurts less now; **ahora lo vemos ~** we don't see him so often *o* we don't see so much of him now; **no voy a ir, y ~ aún con él** I'm not going, and certainly not with him; **menos (...) QUE**: **un hallazgo no ~ importante que éste** a find which is no less important than this one; **ella ~ que nadie puede criticarte** she of all people is in no position to criticize you; **menos (...) DE** less than; **pesa ~ de 50 kilos** it weighs less than *o* under 50 kilos; **no lo haría por ~ de cien mil** I wouldn't do it for less than a hundred thousand; **éramos ~ de diez** there were fewer than ten of us; **los niños de ~ de 7 años** children under seven; **es ~ peligroso de lo que tú crees** it's not as dangerous as you think

B (superlativo) least; **es la ~ complicada** it is the least complicated one; **éste es el ~ pesado de los dos** this is the lighter of the two; **es el que ~ viene por aquí** he's the one who comes around least (often); **es el que ~ me gusta** he's the one I like (the) least; **se esfuerza lo ~ posible** he makes as little effort as possible; **es lo ~ que podía hacer** it's the least I could do; **cuando ~ lo esperábamos** when we were least expecting it; *para locs ver* **menos³ B**

menos² *adj inv*

A (comparativo) (en cantidad) less; (en número) fewer; **alimentos con ~ fibra/calorías** food with less fiber/fewer calories; **ya hace ~ frío** it's not as *o* so cold now; **recibimos cada vez ~ pedidos** we are getting fewer and fewer orders;

m

cuesta tres veces ~ it costs a third of the price; **mide medio metro** ~ it's half a meter shorter; **menos (...) QUE**: **tengo** ~ **tiempo que tú** I haven't as *o* so much time as you; ~ **estudiantes que el año pasado** fewer students than last year; **yo no soy** ~ **que él** he's no better than me

B (superlativo) (en cantidad) least; (en número) fewest; **esos casos son los** ~ cases like that are the exception

menos[3] *pron*

A : **sírveme** ~ don't give me so much, give me less; **ya falta** ~ it won't be long now; **aprobaron** ~ **que el año pasado** fewer passed than last year

B (*en locs*) **al menos** at least; **a menos que** unless; **cuando menos** at least; **de menos**: **me ha dado 100 pesos de** ~ you've given me 100 pesos too little; **me has cobrado de** ~ you've undercharged me; **lo menos** (fam) at least; **menos mal** just as well, thank goodness; ~ **mal que no me oyó** just as well *o* it's a good thing he didn't hear me; **por lo menos** at least; ***ir a*** ~ to go downhill; ***ser lo de*** ~: **eso es lo de** ~, **a mí lo que me preocupa es ...** that's the least of it, what worries me is ...; **la fecha es lo de** ~ the date is the least of our/their problems; ***tener algo/a algn en*** ~ to think sth/sb is beneath one; **venido a** ~ ‹*barrio/hotel*› run-down; **una familia venida a** ~ a family that has come down in the world

menos[4] *prep*

A (excepto): **firmaron todos** ~ **Alonso** everybody but Alonso signed, everybody signed except *o* but Alonso; ~ **estos dos, todos están en venta** apart from *o* with the exception of these two, they are all for sale; **tres latas de pintura,** ~ **la que usé** three cans of paint, less what I used

B 1 (Mat) (en restas, números negativos) minus 2 (Esp, RPl) (en la hora): **son las cinco** ~ **diez/cuarto** it's ten to five/(a) quarter to five; **son** ~ **veinte** it's twenty to

menos[5] *m* minus sign

menoscabar [A1] *vt* ‹*autoridad/fortuna*› to diminish, reduce; ‹*derechos*› to impinge upon, infringe; ‹*honor/fama/salud*› to damage, harm

menoscabo *m*: **su salud no sufrió** ~ **alguno** his health was not impaired *o* adversely affected in any way; **sin** ~ **de nuestra amistad** without detriment to *o* without damaging our friendship; **sin** ~ **de su autoridad** without his authority being reduced *o* diminished in any way

menospreciar [A1] *vt* 1 (despreciar) ‹*persona/obra*› to despise, look down on 2 (subestimar) to underestimate; **no lo menosprecies** don't underestimate him

menosprecio *m* contempt, scorn

mensada *f* (Méx fam) stupid thing to say (*o* do *etc*)

mensaje *m* 1 (noticia, comunicación) message; **un** ~ **de paz** a message of peace; **le dejó un** ~ **sobre la mesa** she left him a note on the table 2 (de una obra, canción) message

(Compuestos)
- **mensaje de error** error message
- **Mensaje de la Corona** King's/Queen's Speech
- **mensaje de texto** text message
- **mensaje de voz** voice mail

mensajería *f* messenger company, courier company

mensajero[1] **-ra** *adj* messenger (*before n*)

mensajero[2] **-ra** *m,f* 1 (persona que lleva un mensaje) messenger 2 (Com) messenger, courier (BrE); **servicio de** ~**s** messenger service, courier service (BrE)

menso[1] **-sa** *adj* (AmL fam) stupid

menso[2] **-sa** *m,f* (AmL fam) fool

menstruación *f* menstruation; **estar con la** ~ to have one's period

menstrual *adj* menstrual

menstruar [A3] *vi* to menstruate

mensual *adj* ‹*publicación/sueldo*› monthly; **9.000 pesos** ~**es** 9,000 pesos a month

mensualidad 1 *f* (sueldo) monthly salary 2 (cuota) monthly payment *o* installment*; **debe dos** ~**es** he's two months behind with the payments

mensualmente *adv* monthly, every month

mensurable *adj* measurable

menta *f* mint; **té de** ~ mint *o* peppermint tea; **licor de** ~ crème de menthe; **helado de** ~ peppermint-flavored ice cream; **caramelos de** ~ mints, peppermints

mentada *f* (Col, Méx, Ven euf) *tb* ~ **de madre** insult (*usually about a person's mother*)

mental *adj* mental

mentalidad *f*: **una** ~ **muy abierta/cerrada** a very open/closed mind; **tiene la** ~ **de un niño de tres años** he has the mentality of a three-year-old; **tiene una** ~ **muy anticuada** she is very old-fashioned in her outlook

mentalización *f* 1 (concientización): **una campaña de** ~ a campaign to increase *o* raise public awareness 2 (preparación mental) mental preparation

mentalizado -da *adj* [ESTAR]: **están** ~**s para imponerse a cualquier dificultad** they are mentally prepared to overcome any difficulty; **está muy mentalizada de que debe esforzarse** she is well aware of the fact that she will have to exert herself

mentalizar [A4] *vt* ‹*persona*›: **lo ha mentalizado para que haga ejercicio** she has made him realize *o* see that he needs to exercise; ~ **a algn DE algo** to make sb aware OF sth

■ **mentalizarse** *v pron* 1 (prepararse mentalmente) to prepare oneself (mentally), get into the right frame of mind; **yo me había mentalizado para lo peor** I had prepared myself for the worst 2 (tomar conciencia) ~**se DE algo**: **fue muy difícil** ~**me de que se había acabado** it was very difficult to come to terms with the idea that *o* to accept that it was over

mentalmente *adv* mentally; **hizo la cuenta** ~ she added it up in her head

mentar [A5] *vt* to mention; ~ ***(a) la madre*** (euf) to insult (*referring particularly to a person's mother*)

mente *f* 1 (cerebro, intelecto) mind; **tiene la** ~ **ocupada en muchas cosas** he has a lot of things on his mind; **tenía la** ~ **en blanco** my mind was a blank; **no se le pasó por la** ~ it never entered her mind *o* occurred to her; **de repente me vino a la** ~ it suddenly came to me; **eso me trae a la** ~ **muchos recuerdos** that brings back a lot of memories; ***tener algo en*** ~ to have sth in mind; **tengo en** ~ **comprarme un apartamento** I'm thinking of buying an apartment 2 (persona) mind

mentecato[1] **-ta** *adj* silly

mentecato[2] **-ta** *m,f* fool

mentir [I11] *vi* to lie; **me mintió** he lied to me; **miente descaradamente** that's a downright lie; **no he estado nunca. ¡Miento! estuve una vez** I've never been there. No, I lie, I did go once

mentira *f*

A lie; **eso es** ~ that's a lie; **¡**~**! yo no le pegué** that's a lie, I didn't hit him!; **ya lo he agarrado** *or* **pillado en una** ~ **en varias ocasiones** I've caught him lying to me several times; **¡parece** ~**! ¡cómo pasa el tiempo!** isn't it incredible! doesn't time fly!; **aunque parezca** ~ **tiene 50 años** you may find it hard to believe but she's 50; **no quiero seguir viviendo en la** ~ I don't want to go on living a lie; **una araña de** ~ *or* (Méx) **de mentiras** (leng infantil) a toy spider; ***una*** ~ ***como una casa*** *or* ***catedral*** *or* ***un templo*** (fam) a whopping great lie (colloq), a whopper (colloq)

(Compuesto) **mentira piadosa** white lie

B (Esp fam) (en la uña) white mark

mentirijillas (Esp fam) **de** ~ (*loc adv*): **no te enfades, lo dije de** ~ don't get mad, I was only joking *o* I was only teasing

mentiroso[1] **-sa** *adj*: **es muy** ~ he's an awful *o* terrible liar; (dicho sin ánimo de ofender) he's a real fibber (colloq)

mentiroso[2] **-sa** *m,f* liar; (dicho sin ánimo de ofender) fibber (colloq)

mentís *m* (*pl* ~) (frml) denial; **dar (un)** ~ **a algo** to deny sth

mentol *m* menthol

mentolado -da *adj* menthol (*before n*)

mentón *m* chin

mentor *m* mentor

menú *m* (*pl* **-nús**)

A 1 (carta) menu 2 (comida): ~ **del día** set meal; **nos había preparado un** ~ **exquisito** he had cooked us a delicious meal

B (Inf) menu

menú del día

Common in Spain, especially at lunchtime, this consists of a selection of courses for a fixed price. A drink and coffee are often included in the price

menudear [A1] *vi*
A (abundar) to be plentiful
B (Col, Méx, Ven) (Com) to sell retail

menudencia *f*
A (cosa insignificante): **eso es una ~** that's not important
B **menudencias** *fpl* (AmL) (Coc) giblets (*pl*)

menudeo *m* (Col, Méx) retail trade; **ventas al ~** retail sales

menudillos *mpl* giblets (*pl*)

menudo[1] **-da** *adj*
A 1 ‹*persona*› slight 2 ‹*letra/pie*› small; **picar el ajo muy menudito** chop the garlic very finely
B (Esp) (en exclamaciones) (*delante del n*): **¡~ lío!** what a mess!; **¡~ cochazo!** that's some car!
C **a menudo** often

menudo[2] *m*
A **menudos** *mpl* (vísceras de aves) giblets (*pl*)
B (Col, Ven) (dinero suelto) loose change

meñique[1] *adj*: **el dedo ~** the little finger

meñique[2] *m* little finger

meollo *m* 1 (Anat) marrow 2 (de un tema) heart

meón, meona *adj* (fam): **¡que niño más ~!** that child is always wetting himself

mequetrefe *m* (fam) good-for-nothing

mercachifle *m* (buhonero) hawker; (comerciante) greedy store owner (AmE), greedy shopkeeper (BrE)

mercadear [A1] *vt* (vender) to market; (regatear) to haggle over
■ **mercadear** *vi* to deal, buy and sell

mercadeo *m* marketing

mercader *m* (ant) merchant

mercadería *f* (esp AmS) merchandise

mercadillo *m* street market

mercado *m*
A (plaza) market; **ir al ~** *or* (Col, Méx) **hacer el ~** to go to market; **día de ~** market day

Compuestos
- **mercado de abastos** *or* (RPl) **de abasto** market (*selling fresh food*)
- **mercado de las pulgas** *or* (AmL) **de pulgas** flea market
- **mercado persa** (CS) bazaar, street market

B (Com, Econ, Fin) market; **el ~ del petróleo** the oil market; **el ~ nacional/extranjero** the domestic/overseas market; **en 1985 salió al ~** it came onto the market in 1985; **un ~ alcista/bajista** a rising/falling market

Compuestos
- **mercado de divisas** foreign exchange market
- **mercado de materias primas/de valores** commodities/stock market
- **mercado emergente** emergent market
- **mercado laboral/monetario/negro** labor*/money/black market
- **mercado nicho** niche market
- **mercado paralelo** (AmL period) parallel market

mercadotecnia *f* marketing

mercancía *f*, **mercancías** *fpl* 1 (Com) goods (*pl*), merchandise; **~s perecederas** perishable goods, perishables 2 (fam) (droga) merchandise (sl), stuff (colloq)

mercante[1] *adj* merchant (*before n*)

mercante[2] *m* merchant ship

mercantil *adj* ‹*ley/operación*› commercial, mercantile

mercantilismo *m* mercantilism

mercantilista[1] *adj* mercantilist

mercantilista[2] *mf* (Econ) mercantilist; (Com, Der) *expert in mercantile law*

merced *f*
A (arc) (favor) favor*; **conceder** *or* **otorgar una ~** to grant a favor; **~ a una llamada telefónica** (frml) thanks to a telephone call; **a (la) merced de** at the mercy of
B **su/vuestra ~** Your Worship (*form of address formerly used to a person of title or rank*)

mercenario[1] **-ria** *adj* (Mil) mercenary

mercenario[2] **-ria** *m,f* 1 (Mil) mercenary 2 (pey) (persona interesada): **es un ~** he's very mercenary (pej)

mercería *f* (tienda de hilos, botones) notions store (AmE), haberdashery (BrE); (ferretería) (Chi) hardware store

mercerizar [A4] *vt* to mercerize

mercero -ra *m,f* notions dealer (AmE), haberdasher (BrE)

merco *m* (Per fam) food, grub (colloq)

Mercosur *m*: *economic community comprising Argentina, Brazil, Paraguay and Uruguay*

mercurio *m* mercury; **termómetro de ~** mercury thermometer

Mercurio *m* Mercury

merecedor -dora *adj* **~ DE algo** worthy OF sth, deserving OF sth (frml); **no es ~ de tu cariño** he is unworthy of your affection

merecer [E3] *vt* ‹*premio/castigo*› to deserve; **merece el respeto de todos** she deserves everyone's respect; **~ + INF** to deserve to + INF; **merece que le den el puesto** she deserves to get the job
■ **merecerse** *v pron* (*enf*) ‹*premio/castigo*› to deserve; **te lo tienes bien merecido** it serves you right; **~se + INF** to deserve to + INF; **se merece que la asciendan** she deserves to be promoted

merecidamente *adv* ‹*famoso/respetado*› deservedly; **fueron ~ aplaudidos** they received well-deserved applause

merecido *m*: **recibió** *or* **se llevó su ~** he got what he deserved

merecimiento *m* 1 (mérito) merit; **se impusieron con todo ~** they fully deserved to win; **acreditó el ~ del premio** he proved himself worthy of the prize; **deberá trabajar mucho y hacer ~s** she will have to work hard and be on her best behavior; **no tiene ~ suficiente para obtener el cargo** he is not good enough to get the job 2 (reconocimiento) recognition; **un ~ bien ganado** well-deserved recognition; **en ~ a su gran labor** in recognition of her great work

merendar [A5] *vi* to have a snack in the afternoon, have tea; **merendamos en el campo** we had a picnic (tea) in the country; **¡niños, a ~!** teatime, children
■ **merendar** *vt* to have … as an afternoon snack
■ **merendarse** *v pron* (fam) ‹*adversarios/contrincantes*› to thrash (colloq); ‹*trabajo*› to polish off (colloq)

merendero *m* (bar) outdoor bar; (instalaciones para picnics) picnic area

merengada *f* (Ven) milkshake

merengue *m*
A (pastel) meringue
B (baile) merengue
C (CS fam) (lío, problema) mess (colloq)
D (Chi fam & pey) (persona enclenque) weakling, weed (colloq)

meretriz *f* (frml) prostitute

meridiano[1] **-na** *adj* 1 (del mediodía) meridian; **la hora meridiana** (liter) noon 2 ‹*luz*› dazzling; **su explicación fue de una claridad meridiana** his explanation was crystal clear

meridiano[2] *m* meridian

Compuesto **meridiano cero** *or* **de Greenwich** /'grinɪtʃ/ Greenwich Meridian

meridional[1] *adj* southern

meridional[2] *mf* southerner

merienda *f*
A (por la tarde) afternoon snack, tea; (para la escuela) (RPl) snack; **ir de ~ al campo** to go for a picnic (tea) in the country; **~ *de negros*** (arreglo) (Esp fam) shady setup(colloq)

Compuestos
- **merienda campestre** picnic
- **merienda cena** *substantial early evening meal*, ≈ high tea (*in UK*)

B (Ven fam) (alboroto) pandemonium

merino[1] **-na** *adj* merino (*before n*)

merino[2] **-na** *m,f* 1 (animal) merino (sheep) 2 **merino** *m* (lana) merino wool

mérito *m* merit, worth; **una obra de ~** a commendable piece of work; **una persona de ~** a worthy person; **no le**

veo ningún ~ a eso I can't see any merit in that; **quitarle** *or* **restarle ~s a algn** to take the credit away from sb; **atribuirse el ~ de algo** to take the credit for sth; ***hacer ~s*****: va a tener que hacer ~s** (para conseguir algo) he's going to have to earn it; (para compensar algo) he's going to have to make amends

(Compuesto) **méritos de guerra** *mpl* mention in dispatches

meritocracia *f* meritocracy

meritorio¹ -ria *adj* [SER] (frml) commendable, praiseworthy (frml); **~ DE algo** worthy OF sth; **no es ~ de tales honores** he isn't worthy *o* (frml) deserving of such honors

meritorio² -ria *m,f* unpaid trainee

merluza *f* (Coc, Zool) hake

merluzo -za *m,f* (Esp fam) numskull (colloq)

merma *f* (frml) decrease, decline; **no podía volverse atrás sin ~ de su prestigio** he couldn't back down without damaging his reputation

mermar [A1] *vi* (frml) «*viento/frío*» to abate (frml); «*luz*» to fade; **el nivel del agua ha mermado** the water level has fallen

■ **mermar** *vt* (frml) ‹*suministro*› to reduce, cut down on; ‹*capital*› to reduce; **mermó las arcas de la organización** it depleted the resources of the organization

mermelada *f* (de cítricos) marmalade; (de otras frutas) jam

mero¹ -ra *adj* (*delante del n*)

A (solo, simple) mere; **el ~ hecho de ...** the mere *o* simple fact of ...; **es un ~ juego** it's only *o* just a game

B (AmC, Méx fam) (uso enfático): **¿cuántas quedaron? — una mera** how many were left? — just one; **el ~ día de su boda** the very day of her wedding; **el ~ patrón** the boss himself; **en la mera esquina** right on the corner; **¿500 pesos? — ¡eso ~!** 500 pesos? — that's right; ***el ~ ~*** (Méx fam) the boss; **se creen los ~s ~s** they think they're the tops (colloq)

mero² *adv* (Méx fam) 1 (casi) nearly, almost; **ya ~ llegamos** we're nearly there 2 (uso enfático): **así ~ me gustan los tacos** this is just how I like tacos; **ya ~** right now; **aquí merito** right here

mero³ *m* grouper

merodeador -dora *m,f* prowler

merodear [A1] *vi* to prowl

merodeo *m* prowling, snooping

merolico -ca *m,f* (Méx) (curandero) quack (colloq); (vendedor) street trader

mersa¹ *adj* (RPl fam & pey) ‹*ropa/lugar*› tacky (colloq); ‹*persona*› common (pej)

mersa² *mf* (RPl fam & pey) 1 (persona): **es un ~** he's so common (pej) 2 **la mersa** *f* the plebs (pl) (colloq & pej), the riffraff (hum *or* pej)

mersada *f* (RPl fam & pey): **ese vestido es una ~** that dress is really tacky (colloq)

mes *m* month; **el ~ pasado/que viene** last/next month; **una vez al ~** once a month; **¿cuánto pagas al ~?** how much do you pay a month?; **tiene siete ~es** he's seven months old; **está embarazada de tres ~es** she's three months pregnant; **nos deben dos ~es** they owe us two months' rent (*o* pay *etc*)

mesa *f*

A (mueble) table; **~ de comedor/de cocina** dining room/kitchen table; **poner la ~** to lay the table; **levantar** *or* **quitar** *or* **recoger la ~** to clear the table; **bendecir la ~** to say grace; **¡a la ~!** dinner (*o* lunch *etc*) is ready!; **sentarse a la ~** to sit at the table; **se levantó de la ~** he got up from *o* left the table; **reservar ~** to reserve a table; ***por debajo de la ~*** under the table; ***quedarse debajo de la ~*** (CS fam) to go hungry, miss out on the food

(Compuestos)
- **mesa auxiliar/de billar/de centro** side/billiard/coffee table
- **mesa camilla** (Esp) *small round table often with a small heater underneath*
- **mesa de dibujo** drawing board
- **mesa de noche** *or* (RPl) **de luz** bedside table
- **mesa de operaciones/partos** operating/delivery table
- **mesa nido** nest of tables
- **mesa petitoria** stand (*for charity collection, etc*)
- **mesa rodante** tea trolley

B (conjunto de personas) committee

(Compuestos)
- **mesa de examen** (RPl) examining board
- **mesa electoral** *group of people who preside over a polling station on election day*
- **mesa redonda/de negociaciones** round/negotiating table

mesada *f* (AmL) (dinero) monthly allowance; (para niños) pocket money

mesarse [A1] *v pron*: **~ la barba** to pull *o* tug one's beard

mescalina *f* mescaline

mescolanza *f* ▸**mezcolanza**

mesero -ra (AmL) (*m*) waiter; (*f*) waitress

meseta *f* (Geog) plateau; (Arquit) landing

mesiánico -ca *adj* messianic

Mesías *m* Messiah

Mesoamérica *f* Middle America (*most of Mexico and Central America*)

mesón *m*

A 1 (bar) *old-style bar/restaurant* 2 (arc) (posada) tavern (arch), inn

B (Chi) (en tienda) counter; (de bar) bar, counter; **~ de información** information desk

mesonero -ra *m,f* 1 (de bar) (*m*) landlord; (*f*) landlady 2 (arc) innkeeper 3 (Ven) (camarero) (*m*) waiter; (*f*) waitress

mestizaje *m* (conjunto de mestizos) people of mixed race (*pl*); (mezcla de razas) crossbreeding

mestizo¹ -za *adj* 1 ‹*persona*› *of mixed race, particularly of Indian and white parentage*; **de sangre mestiza** of mixed blood 2 ‹*animal*› crossbred 3 ‹*planta*› hybrid

mestizo² -za *m,f* mestizo, person of mixed race

mesura *f* moderation, restraint; **comer con ~** to eat in moderation

mesurado -da *adj* ‹*persona*› moderate, restrained; ‹*palabras*› restrained, measured

meta¹ *f*

A (Dep) 1 (en atletismo) finishing line; (en ciclismo, automovilismo) finish; (en carreras de caballos) winning post 2 (en fútbol) goal

B (objetivo) aim; **su única ~ es ganar dinero** his only aim *o* ambition is to earn money; **se ha trazado ~s inalcanzables** she has set herself impossible targets *o* goals

meta² *m* (Esp) goalkeeper

metabólico -ca *adj* metabolic

metabolismo *m* metabolism

metacarpo *m* metacarpus

metadona *f* methadone

metafísica *f* metaphysics

metafísico -ca *adj* metaphysical

metáfora *f* metaphor

metafórico -ca *adj* metaphorical

metal *m* 1 (material, elemento) metal; ***el vil ~*** filthy lucre (hum) 2 *tb* **metales** (Mús) brass (section) 3 (de la voz) timbre

(Compuestos)
- **metal noble** *or* **precioso** precious metal
- **metal pesado** heavy metal

metalenguaje *m* metalanguage

metálico¹ -ca *adj* (de metal) metallic, metal (*before n*); ‹*sonido/brillo/color*› metallic

metálico² *m*: **pagar en ~** to pay (in) cash; **un premio en ~** a cash prize

metalizar [A4] *vt* 1 (Metal) to metalize* 2 ‹*persona*› to make ... money-minded; ‹*actividad*› to commercialize

■ **metalizarse** *v pron* 1 (Metal) to become metalized* 2 «*persona*» to become money-minded; «*actividad*» to become commercialized

metalurgia *f* metallurgy

metalúrgico¹ -ca *adj* metallurgical

metalúrgico² -ca *m,f* metalworker

metamorfosearse [A1] *v pron* to metamorphose

metamorfosis, metamórfosis *f* (*pl* ~) metamorphosis

metano *m* methane

metanol *m* methanol

metástasis *f* metastasis

metate *m* (AmC, Méx) *flat stone used for grinding corn*

metazoo *m* metazoan

metedura de pata *f* (esp Esp fam) blunder, gaffe

metegol *m* (Arg) table football

metelón¹ -lona *adj*
A (Méx fam) (entrometido) nosy (colloq)
B (Col fam) (fumador de marihuana) pot-smoking (*before n*) (colloq)

metelón² -lona *m,f* (Col fam) pothead (sl)

meteórico -ca *adj* meteoric

meteorito *m* meteorite

meteoro *m* meteor

meteorología *f* meteorology

meteorológico -ca *adj* meteorological

meteorólogo -ga *m,f* meteorologist

metepatas *mf* (*pl* ~) (fam): **es una ~** she's always putting her foot in it (colloq)

meter [E1] *vt*
A 1 (introducir, poner) to put; **~ algo EN algo** to put sth IN(TO) sth; **~ la llave en la cerradura** to put the key into the lock; **quiero ~ todo esto en un folio** I want to fit all of this onto one sheet; **no le metas esas ideas en la cabeza** don't put ideas like that into her head 2 (hacer entrar) **~ a algn EN algo**: **puedo ~ cuatro personas en mi coche** I can get *o* fit four people in my car; **lo metieron en la cárcel** they put him in prison; **lo metió interno en un colegio** she sent him to (a) boarding school; **consiguió ~lo en la empresa** she managed to get him a job in the company; **~ a algn DE algo**: **lo metieron de aprendiz** they got him a job as an apprentice 3 (involucrar) **~ a algn EN algo** to involve sb IN sth, get sb involved IN sth
B 1 (invertir) to put 2 ‹*tanto/gol*› to score 3 (en costura) ‹*dobladillo*› to turn up; **métele un poco en las costuras** take it in a bit at the seams; **~le tijera/sierra a algo** to set to with the scissors/saw on sth 4 (Auto) ‹*cambio*›: **mete (la) tercera** put it into third (gear); **~ la marcha atrás** to get into reverse
C 1 (provocar, crear): **no metas ruido** keep the noise down; **~le miedo a algn** to frighten *o* scare sb; **nos están metiendo prisa** we're under a lot of pressure to do things faster; ***a todo ~*** (fam) ‹*conducir/correr/estudiar*› flat out; ***~le*** (AmL) to get a move on (colloq); **le metimos con todo** we did our utmost 2 (fam) (encajar, endilgar): **me metieron una multa** I got a ticket (colloq); **nos metió una de sus historias** she spun us one of her yarns 3 (Col arg) ‹*cocaína*› to snort (sl); ‹*marihuana*› to smoke

■ **meter** *vi* (Col arg) (consumir marihuana) to smoke (dope)

■ **meterse** *v pron*
A 1 (entrar) **~se EN algo**: **me metí en el agua** (en la playa) I went into the water; (en la piscina) I got into the water; **nos metimos en un museo** we went into a museum; **se metió en la cama** he got into bed; **no sabía dónde ~se de la vergüenza** she was so embarrassed she didn't know what to do with herself; **¿dónde se habrá metido el perro?** where can the dog have got to?; (+ *me/te/le etc*) **se me metió algo en el ojo** I got something in my eye 2 (introducirse) **~se algo EN algo**: **me metí el dedo en el ojo** I stuck my finger in my eye; **se metió el dinero en el bolsillo** he put the money in(to) his pocket; ***¡que se lo meta ahí mismo!*** *or* ***¡que se lo meta por dónde le quepa!*** (vulg) she can stuff it! (sl); ***ya sabes dónde te lo puedes ~*** (vulg) you know where you can stuff it (vulg) 3 (fam) ‹*comida/bebida*› to put away (colloq) 4 (Ven arg) ‹*cocaína*› to snort (sl); ‹*marihuana*› to smoke
B 1 (en trabajo): **se metió de secretaria** she got a job as a secretary; **~se de** *or* **a cura/monja** to become a priest/nun 2 (involucrarse) **~se EN algo** to get involved IN sth; **te has metido en un buen lío** you've got yourself into a fine mess; **se ha metido en un asunto muy turbio** she's got(ten) involved in a very shady affair; **no podemos ~nos en más gastos** we cannot take on anymore financial commitments 3 (entrometerse) to get involved; **no te metas en lo que no te importa** mind your own business; **ella empezó a ~se por medio** she started interfering; ***~se con algn*** (fam) to pick on sb: ***~se donde no lo llaman*** to poke one's nose into other people's business (colloq); **¡no te metas donde no te llaman!** mind your own business!

meterete -ta *m,f* (RPl fam) busybody (colloq)

metiche *mf* (AmL fam) busybody (colloq)

meticuloso -sa *adj* meticulous

metida de pata *f* (AmL fam) blunder, gaffe

metido¹ -da *adj*
A [ESTAR] (en ambiente, situación) **~ EN algo** involved IN sth; **está muy ~ en política** he's very involved in politics; **estoy ~ en un lío** I'm in trouble; **estuvo ~ en un asunto turbio** he was mixed up in some shady dealings
B 1 [SER] (AmS fam) (entrometido) nosy (colloq) 2 [ESTAR] (Chi fam) (intrigado) intrigued
C [ESTAR] (CS fam) (enamorado) **~ CON algn** crazy *o* mad about sb (colloq); ***dejar ~ a algn*** (Col fam) to stand sb up (colloq)

metido² -da *m,f* (AmS fam) busybody (colloq)

metilo *m* methyl

metlapil *m* (AmC, Méx) stone rolling pin

metódico -ca *adj* methodical

metodismo *m* Methodism

metodista *adj/mf* Methodist

método *m*
A (procedimiento) method; **el mejor ~ para aprobar** the best way to pass; **con ~** methodically
B (libro de texto) course book; (manual) handbook

metodología *f* methodology

metomentodo *mf* (*pl* ~) (fam) busybody (colloq)

metraje *m* length (*of film*); **película de corto/largo ~** short/feature-length movie *o* film

metralla *f* (trozos) shrapnel; (munición) grapeshot

metralleta *f* submachine gun

métrica *f* metrics

métrico -ca *adj* metric, metrical

metro *m*
A 1 (medida) meter*; **~ cuadrado/cúbico** square/cubic meter; **¿cuánto cuesta el ~?** how much is it a meter?; **vender algo por ~(s)** to sell sth by the meter; **los 100 ~s vallas** the 100-meter hurdles 2 (cinta métrica) tape measure; (regla) ruler
B (Transp) subway (AmE), tube (BrE)
C (en poesía) meter*

metrobús *m* 1 (para viajar) *combined bus and subway travel pass* 2 (vehículo) bus (*serving subway station*)

metrónomo *m* metronome

metrópolis (*pl* ~), **metrópoli** *f* 1 (ciudad grande) metropolis 2 (Hist) (capital) metropolis; (nación) mother country

metropolitano¹ -na *adj* 1 (de la ciudad) metropolitan; **área metropolitana** metropolitan area 2 ‹*iglesia*› metropolitan

metropolitano² *m* 1 (Transp) subway (AmE), underground (BrE) 2 (arzobispo) metropolitan

mexicanismo *m* Mexicanism

mexicano -na *adj/m,f* Mexican

México *m* (país) Mexico; (capital) Mexico City

mexiquense *adj* (Méx) of/from Mexico City

mezanina *f* (Ven) mezzanine

mezcal *m* mescal

mezcla *f*
A (proceso) 1 (de productos) mixing; (de vinos, tabacos, cafés) blending 2 (de razas, culturas) mixing; **estos perros son producto de una ~** these dogs are crossbreeds 3 (Audio) mixing
B (combinación) 1 mixture; (de vinos, tabacos, café) blend; (de telas) mix; **una ~ de distintos colores** a combination *o* mixture of different colors 2 (de razas, culturas) mix 3 (Audio) mix

(Compuesto) **mezcla explosiva** (Arm) explosive mixture

mezclador¹ -dora *m,f* (persona) *tb* **~ de sonido** *or* **audio** sound mixer

mezclador² *m*, **mezcladora** *f* 1 (aparato) mixing panel *o* board 2 **mezcladora** *f* (Const) mixer

mezclar [A1] *vt*
A 1 (combinar) to mix; **~ todo hasta formar una pasta** mix all the ingredients into a paste; **~ algo CON algo** to mix sth WITH sth; **~ los huevos con el azúcar** mix the eggs and the sugar together 2 ‹*café/vino/tabaco*› to blend
B ‹*documentos/ropa*› to mix up, get … mixed up; **~ algo CON algo** to get sth mixed up WITH sth
C (involucrar) **~ a algn EN algo** to get sb mixed up *o* involved IN sth
■ **mezclarse** *v pron*
A «*persona*» 1 (con un fondo, una multitud) to merge 2 (involucrarse) **~se EN algo** to get mixed up *o* involved IN sth; **~se en cuestiones políticas** to get mixed up *o* involved in politics 3 (tener trato con) **~se CON algn** to mix WITH sb
B «*razas/culturas*» to mix

mezclilla *f* 1 (tela de mezcla) cloth of mixed fibers 2 (Chi, Méx) (tela de jeans) denim

mezcolanza *f* (pey): **una ~ de francés y español** a peculiar mixture *o* (colloq) mishmash of French and Spanish; **una ~ de estilos diferentes** a hodgepodge (AmE) *o* (BrE) hotchpotch of different styles

mezquinar [A1] *vt* (esp AmL fam) to skimp on, be stingy with (colloq)

mezquindad *f* 1 (cualidad — de tacaño) meanness, stinginess (colloq); (— de ruin): **es de una ~ asombrosa** he's incredibly nasty *o* (colloq) mean 2 (acción egoísta) mean thing to do

mezquino[1] **-na** *adj* 1 (vil) mean, small-minded; (tacaño) mean, stingy (colloq) 2 (escaso) ‹*sueldo/ración*› paltry, miserable

mezquino[2] *m* (Col, Méx) wart

mezquita *f* mosque

mezzo-soprano, mezzo *f* mezzo soprano

mg. (= **miligramo**) mg

MHz (= **megaherzio**) MHz

mi[1] *adj* (*delante del n*) my; **no fue ~ intención hacerte daño** I didn't mean *o* intend to hurt you; **~ querido amigo** my dear friend (frml *or* dated); **sí, ~ vida** yes, darling; **sí, ~ capitán** yes, sir

mi[2] *m* (nota) E; (en solfeo) mi; **~ bemol/sostenido** E flat/sharp; **en ~ mayor/menor** in E major/minor

M.I. = Muy Ilustre

mí *pron pers* 1 me; **¿es para ~?** is it for me?; **por ~ no hay problema** as far as I'm concerned that's fine, that's fine by me; **¿preguntó por ~?** did she ask after me?; **¿ya ~ qué?** so what?, what do I care? 2 (uso enfático): **a ~ no me importa** I couldn't care less; **¡a ~ no me hables así!** don't speak to *me* like that! 3 (*refl*): **~ mismo/misma** myself; **todavía puedo valerme por ~ mismo** I can still look after myself

miaja *f* (fam): **no tiene ni ~ de sentido común** she doesn't have an ounce of common sense (colloq); **ponme una ~ más** give me a tiny bit more; **¡eso es una ~!** that's a tiny portion

miasma *m* miasma

miau *m* miaow; **hacer ~** to miaow

mica *f*
A 1 (Min) mica 2 (AmL) (de un reloj) crystal
B (Col) (de niño) potty (colloq)

micción *f* micturition (tech), urination

michelín *m* (fam) spare tire* (colloq), roll of fat

michicato -ta *adj* (Col fam) tight-fisted (colloq)

michino -na *m,f* (fam) puss (colloq), pussy (cat) (colloq)

micho -cha *m,f*
A (fam) (gato) puss (colloq), pussy (cat) (colloq)
B **micho** *m* (Per) (Jueg) noughts and crosses

mico -ca *m,f*
A (Zool) long-tailed monkey; (como término genérico) monkey
B **mico** *m* (fam) (persona — coqueta) vain person; (— fea) ugly devil (colloq); (— de mala pinta) (Ven) unsavory* type

micra *f* micron

micrero -ra *m,f* (Chi) bus driver

micro[1] *m*
A (fam) (microbús) small bus; (autobús) (Arg) bus, coach (BrE)
B (fam) (micrófono) mike (colloq)
C (Esp) (microordenador) microcomputer, micro

micro[2] *f* (Chi) bus

microbiano -na *adj* microbial, microbic

microbio *m* (Biol) microbe; (niño pequeño) (fam) little kid (colloq); **tú, ~, a la cama** come on, shrimp, off to bed (colloq)

microbiología *f* microbiology

microbiólogo -ga *m,f* microbiologist

microbús *m* (bus pequeño) small bus; (autobús) (Chi frml) bus

microchip /mikro'tʃip/ *m* (*pl* **-chips**) microchip

microclima *m* microclimate

microcomputadora *f* (esp AmL) microcomputer, micro

microcosmos (*pl* ~), **microcosmo** *m* microcosm

microeconomía *f* microeconomics

microelectrónica *f* microelectronics

microficha *f* microfiche, fiche

microfilm (*pl* **-films**), **microfilme** *m* microfilm

microfilmar [A1] *vt* to microfilm

micrófono *m* microphone; **hablar por el ~** to speak over the microphone

microlentilla *f* contact lens

micrómetro *m* micrometer

microonda *f* microwave

microondas *m* (*pl* ~) microwave (oven)

microordenador *m* (Esp) microcomputer, micro

microorganismo *m* microorganism

microprocesador *m* microprocessor

microscópico -ca *adj* microscopic

microscopio *m* microscope; **mirar algo al** *or* **por el ~** to look at sth under the microscope

microsurco *m* microgroove

microtecnología *f* microtechnology

mida, midas, etc *see* **medir**

miéchica *interj* (Chi, Per fam) (expresando disgusto) damn! (colloq); (uso expletivo): **¿quién/qué/dónde ~ ...?** who/what/where the hell …?

miedo *m* fear; **¡qué ~ pasamos!** we were so frightened *o* scared!; **temblaba de ~** he was trembling with fear; **casi me muero de ~** I almost died of fright; **me da ~ salir de noche** I'm afraid to go *o* of going out at night; **perder el ~** to overcome one's fear; **se cagaba de ~** (vulg) he was shit-scared (vulg); **~ A algo/algn** fear OF sth/sb; **el ~ a lo desconocido** fear of the unknown; **le tiene ~ a su padre** he's scared *o* afraid of his father; **agarrarle** *or* (esp Esp) **cogerle ~ a algo/algn** to become frightened *o* scared of sth/sb; **por ~ a** for fear of; **tener ~** to be afraid *o* frightened *o* scared; **tiene ~ de caerse** he's afraid he might fall; **tengo ~ de que se ofenda** I'm afraid he will take offense; ***de ~*** (fam) fantastic, great (colloq); **hace un frío de ~** it's freezing cold

miedoso[1] **-sa** *adj*: **¡no seas ~! no te va a hacer daño** don't be frightened *o* scared! it won't hurt you; **¡qué ~ es!** he's such a coward!

miedoso[2] **-sa** *m,f* coward, scaredy cat (colloq)

miel *f* honey; ***dejar a algn con la ~ en los labios*** to snatch sth away from under sb's nose

(Compuesto) **miel de caña/de maíz/de palma** sugarcane/corn/palm syrup

mielga *f* (Bot) alfalfa

miembro *m*
A 1 (de organización, asociación) member 2 (*como adj*) ‹*estado/países*› member (*before n*) 3 (Mat) member
B (Anat) limb; **~s anteriores/posteriores** fore/back limbs

(Compuesto) **miembro viril** (euf) male member (euph)

mienta, mientas, etc *see* **mentir**

mientes *fpl* (liter): **tener algo en ~** to have sth in mind; **me vino a las ~ que ...** it occurred to me that …; **parar** *or* **poner ~ en algo** to consider sth

mientras[1] *adv*
A (al mismo tiempo) *tb* **~ tanto** in the meantime, meanwhile
B (esp AmL) (cuanto): **~ más se le da, más pide** the more you give him, the more he wants; **~ menos coma, mejor** the less I eat the better

mientras² *conj*
A (indicando simultaneidad) while; **~ dormíamos** while we were asleep
B **1** (con idea de futuro, condición, etc) **~ + SUBJ** as long as; **mientras pueda/viva** as long as I can/live **2** **~ (que)** (siempre que) (+ *subj*) as long as; **~ (que) él no se entere ...** as long as he doesn't find out ...
C **mientras que** (con valor adversativo) whereas, while

miérc. (= **miércoles**) Wed

miércoles *m* (*pl* ~)
A Wednesday; *para ejemplos ver* **lunes**
(Compuesto) **miércoles de ceniza** Ash Wednesday
B (fam & euf) (uso expletivo): **¡~!** shoot!, sugar! (colloq & euph)

mierda *f*
A (vulg) (excremento) shit (vulg)
B (vulg) **1** (cosa despreciable): **una ~ de empleo** a crappy *o* lousy job (colloq); **la película es una ~** the movie is (a load of) crap (sl) **2** (mugre) filth, crap (sl) **3** (como interj) (Esp) (para desear suerte) break a leg! **4** (uso expletivo): **¿dónde ~ me dejaron las llaves?** where the hell have they put my keys? (colloq); ***¡a la ~ con ... !*** (vulg) to hell with ... ! (colloq); ***hacer ~ a algn*** (Méx vulg) to beat the shit out of sb (vulg); ***hecho (una) ~*** (vulg): **tiene la casa hecha una ~** his house is in a hell of a mess *o* a real state (colloq); ***irse a la ~*** (vulg) «*proyecto/empresa*» to go to the dogs, go to pot (colloq); ***mandar a algn a la ~*** (vulg) to tell sb to go to hell (colloq) *o* (vulg) to screw himself/herself; ***mandar algo a la ~*** (vulg): **decidió mandar el trabajo a la ~** she decided that work could go to hell (colloq); ***sacarle la ~ a algn*** (Chi vulg) to beat the shit out of sb (vulg); ***¡vete a la ~!*** (vulg) go to hell! (colloq), fuck off! (vulg); ***¡y una ~!*** (Esp vulg) like hell!
C (Esp vulg) (borrachera): **pillar una ~** to get rat-assed (vulg), to get shit-faced (AmE vulg)
D (arg) (hachís) shit (sl)
E **mierda** *mf* (vulg) shit (vulg)

mies *f* ripe grain; **~es** cornfields

miga *f*
A (trocito) crumb; (parte blanda) crumb; ***estar/quedar hecho ~s*** (fam) «*jarrón/vaso*» to be smashed to pieces *o* smithereens; «*persona*» to be shattered (colloq); ***hacer buenas/malas ~s (con algn)*** to get on well/badly (with sb)
B **migas** *fpl* (Coc) *breadcrumbs fried with garlic, etc*
C (contenido, sustancia) substance; (dificultad) difficulties (*pl*); **el asunto tiene su ~** it has its difficulties *o* it's quite tricky

migajas *fpl* (de pan) breadcrumbs (*pl*); (sobras) leftovers (*pl*), scraps (*pl*)

migar [A3] *vt* to crumble

migra *f* (Méx fam & pey): **la ~** the immigration police (*on the US-Mexican border*)

migración *f* migration

migrante *mf* migrant

migrar [A1] *vt/i* to migrate

migraña *f* migraine

migratorio -ria *adj* migratory

mijo¹ *m* millet

mijo² -ja *pron* (apelativo) (AmL fam): **sírvase, ~** help yourself, dear; **¿qué le pasa, mijito?** what's the matter, sweetie *o* darling? (colloq)

mil¹ *adj inv/pron* thousand; **~ quinientos pesos** fifteen hundred pesos, one thousand five hundred pesos; **20 ~ millones** 20 billion (AmE), 20 thousand million (BrE); **el año ~** the year one thousand; **una y ~ veces** a thousand and one times; **tengo ~ cosas que hacer** I have a thousand and one things to do; ***estar/ponerse a ~*** (Col, Ven fam) (nervioso) to be/get uptight (colloq); (furioso) to be/get hopping mad (colloq)

mil² *m* (number) one thousand; **el dos por ~ de la población** two people per two thousand of the population; **se lo he dicho ~es de veces** I've told him hundreds *o* thousands of times

milagrero -ra *m,f* (fam) miracle-worker

milagro *m* miracle; **tú por aquí ¡qué ~!** well, imagine *o* (BrE) fancy seeing you here!; **es un ~ que no llegaras tarde** it's a wonder you weren't late; **alcancé el tren de ~** by a miracle I caught the train; **escaparon de ~** they had a miraculous escape; ***hacer ~s*** to work wonders

milagrosamente *adv* miraculously

milagroso -sa *adj* ‹*cura/remedio*› miraculous, miracle (*before n*); (insólito, asombroso) amazing, miraculous

milanesa *f* (de ternera) Wiener schnitzel, escalope; (de otros alimentos): **~ de pollo** chicken breast fried in breadcrumbs

milano *m* kite

mildeu, mildiu *m* mildew

milenario -ria *adj* thousand-year-old (*before n*)

milenio *m* millennium

milésima *f* thousandth

milésimo -ma *adj/pron* (ordinal) thousandth; (partitivo): **la milésima parte** a thousandth

mileurista *mf* (Esp) person with higher education who has difficulty earning over €1,000 per month

milhojas *f* (*pl* ~) (Coc) millefeuille

mili *f* (Esp fam) military service

milibar *m* millibar

milicia *f* militia
(Compuesto) **milicias universitarias** *fpl* (Esp) *military service done by students in the summer vacation*

miliciano -na *m,f* militiaman

milico *m* (AmL fam & pey) soldier; **los ~s** the military

miligramo *m* milligram

mililitro *m* milliliter•

milimetrado -da *adj*: **papel ~** graph paper

milimétrico -ca *adj* (Tec) millimetric; **con precisión milimétrica** with pinpoint accuracy

milímetro *m* millimeter•

militancia *f* (filiación) political affiliation; (militantes) members (*pl*)

militante¹ *adj* politically active

militante² *mf* activist
(Compuesto) **militante de base** rank-and-file member

militar¹ *adj* military

militar² *mf* soldier, military man; **los ~es** the military
(Compuesto) **militar de carrera** career soldier

militar³ [A1] *vi* to be politically active; **~ en un partido político** to be an active member of a political party

militarismo *m* militarism

militarista *adj/mf* militarist

militarizar [A4] *vt* to militarize

milla *f* mile
(Compuesto) **milla náutica** *or* **marina** nautical mile

millaje *m* mileage

millar *m* **1** (mil unidades) thousand; **hubo un ~ de heridos** about a thousand people were injured **2** **millares** *mpl* (gran cantidad) thousands (*pl*)

millón *m* million; **15 mil millones** 15 billion (AmE), 15 thousand million (BrE); **un ~ de gracias** thank you very much; **tengo un ~ de cosas que hacer** I've got a million and one things to do

millonada *f* (fam) fortune; **les costó una ~** it cost them a fortune *o* (BrE colloq) a packet

millonario¹ -ria *adj*: **es ~** he's a millionaire; **premios ~s** prizes worth millions

millonario² -ria *m,f* millionaire

millonésima *f* millionth

millonésimo -ma *adj*: **la millonésima parte** a millionth

milonga *f*
A (Mús) *a type of dance and music from the River Plate region*
B (RPl arg) **1** (fiesta) party, bash (colloq) **2** (mujer fácil) slut (colloq & pej)

milonguero -ra *m,f* (RPl arg) reveler, raver (BrE colloq)

milpa *f* (AmC, Méx) (campo) field (*used mainly for the cultivation of maize*); (cultivo) crop

milpear [A1] *vi* (AmC, Méx) to work the land

milpero -ra *adj* (AmC, Méx) ‹*cultivo*› maize (*before n*), corn (*before n*); ‹*región/campesino*› maize-growing (*before n*), corn-growing (*before n*); ‹*agricultura*› maize-based, corn-based

milpiés *m* (*pl* ~) (cochinilla) woodlouse; (miriápodo) millipede

m

mimado[1] **-da** *adj* spoiled, pampered

mimado[2] **-da** *m,f* spoiled child; **este niño es un ~** this child is spoiled *o* (pej) is a spoiled brat; **los ~s de la prensa** the darlings of the press

mimar [A1] *vt* to spoil, pamper

mimbre *m* 1 (material) wicker/wickerwork; **silla de ~** wicker *o* basket chair 2 (varita) wicker 3 (planta) osier, willow

mimbrera *f* (arbusto) osier; (sauce) willow

mimeografiar [A17] *vt* to mimeograph

mimeógrafo *m* mimeograph

mimético -ca *adj* mimetic, imitative

mimetismo *m* mimicry, mimesis (tech)

mimetizarse [A4] *v pron*: **se mimetizó en el terreno** it merged *o* blended into the landscape

mímica *f* (Teatr) mime; (gestos, señas) sign language, mime; (imitación) imitation

mímico -ca *adj* mimic (*before n*); **lenguaje ~** sign language

mimo *m*

A 1 (caricia) cuddle; **hacerle ~s a algn** to cuddle sb 2 (trato indulgente) pampering; **lo criaron con mucho ~** he had a very pampered upbringing 3 (cuidado, celo) care; **limpiaba con ~ los adornos** she lovingly cleaned the ornaments 4 (fam) (mañas): **lo único que tiene es ~(s)** she's just a spoiled brat trying to get attention (colloq & pej)

B **mimo** *mf* mime

mimosa *f* mimosa

mimoso -sa *adj*: **es muy ~** he loves being made a fuss of *o* being pampered

min (= **minuto**) min

mina *f*

A (yacimiento, excavación) mine; **~ de carbón** coalmine; **es una ~ de información** he's a mine of information; ***ser una ~ (de oro)*** ‹‹*negocio*›› to be a real goldmine; ‹‹*persona*›› to be worth one's weight in gold

(Compuesto) **mina a cielo abierto** *or* (Andes) **a tajo abierto** strip mine (AmE), opencast mine (BrE)

B (de lápiz) lead

C (Mil, Náut) mine; **un campo sembrado de ~s** a minefield

D (Hist, Mil) (galería) underground passage

E (CS arg) (mujer) broad (AmE sl), bird (BrE sl)

minador -dora *m,f*

A (Hist) sapper

B **minador** *m* (barco) minelayer

minar [A1] *vt* 1 ‹*campo/mar*› to mine 2 (debilitar) ‹*salud*› to damage; ‹*autoridad/moral*› to undermine

minarete *m* minaret

mineral[1] *adj* mineral

mineral[2] *m* 1 (sustancia) mineral 2 (de un metal) ore 3 (Chi) (mina) mine

mineralogía *f* mineralogy

mineralogista *mf* mineralogist

minería *f* mining industry

minero[1] **-ra** *adj* mining (*before n*); **explotación minera** mining development

minero[2] **-ra** *m,f* miner

minestrón *m o f* (AmL) minestrone

minga *f* (Andes) *farm work carried out in exchange for food*

mingaco *m* (Chi) ▸ **minga**

mingitorio *m* urinal

mini[1] *m* (Esp fam) mini, minicomputer

mini[2] *f* (fam) miniskirt, mini (colloq)

miniar [A1] *vt* to illuminate

miniatura *f* (Art) miniature; (cosa diminuta) (fam) : **¡qué ~ de pie!** what a tiny little foot; **en esa ~ de oficina** in that tiny *o* poky little office (colloq)

miniaturista *mf* miniaturist

miniaturizar [A4] *vt* to miniaturize

minicomputadora *f* (esp AmL) minicomputer

minifalda *f* miniskirt

minifundio *m* (propiedad) smallholding; (sistema) *division of land into smallholdings*

minifundista *mf* small farmer, smallholder (BrE)

mini-golf *m* miniature golf

mínima *f* minimum temperature; ***a la ~*** (fam) at/for the slightest little thing

minimalista *mf* minimalist

minimizar [A4] *vt* (reducir al mínimo) to minimize; (quitar importancia) to make light of, play down

mínimo[1] **-ma** *adj* 1 ‹*temperatura/peso*› minimum (*before n*); **no le importa lo más ~** he couldn't care less; **el trabajo no le interesa en lo más ~** he is not in the least (bit) *o* slightest (bit) interested in his work; **no tengo la más mínima idea** I haven't the faintest *o* slightest idea 2 (insignificante) ‹*detalle*› minor; **los beneficios han sido ~s** profits have been minimal 3 (muy pequeño) minute, tiny

(Compuesto) **mínimo común denominador/múltiplo** lowest common denominator/multiple

mínimo[2] *m* minimum; **con un ~ de esfuerzo** with a *o* the minimum of effort; **no tiene ni un ~ de educación** she has absolutely no manners; **con un ~ de sentido común** with the least bit of (common) sense, with a modicum of sense (frml); **reducir algo al ~** to keep sth to a minimum; **como ~** at least

minimoto *f* minimoto, pocketbike

minino -na *m,f* (fam) puss (colloq), pussy (cat) (colloq)

miniserie *f* miniseries

minishorts /mini'ʃors/ *mpl* hot pants (*pl*)

ministerial *adj* ‹*reunión*› cabinet (*before n*); ‹*orden*› ministerial

ministerio *m*

A (Pol) ministry, department (AmE)

(Compuestos)

- **Ministerio de Defensa** ≈ Defense Department (*in US*), ≈ Ministry of Defence (*in UK*)
- **Ministerio de Hacienda** ≈ Treasury Department (*in US*), ≈ Treasury (*in UK*)
- **Ministerio del Interior** ≈ Department of the Interior (*in US*), ≈ Home Office (*in UK*)
- **Ministerio de Relaciones** *or* **Asuntos Exteriores** ≈ State Department (*in US*), ≈ Foreign Office (*in UK*)
- **Ministerio Fiscal** *or* **Público** Attorney General's office

B (Relig) ministry

ministro -tra *m,f* minister, government minister

(Compuestos)

- **Ministro de Defensa** ≈ Defense Secretary (*in US*), ≈ Minister of Defence (*in UK*)
- **Ministro de Hacienda** ≈ Secretary of the Treasury (*in US*), ≈ Chancellor of the Exchequer (*in UK*)
- **Ministro del Interior** ≈ Secretary of the Interior (*in US*), ≈ Home Secretary (*in UK*)
- **Ministro de Relaciones** *or* **Asuntos Exteriores** ≈ Secretary of State (*in US*), ≈ Foreign Secretary (*in UK*)
- **ministro plenipotenciario** plenipotentiary, envoy
- **ministro sin cartera** minister without portfolio

minoría *f* minority; **estar en ~** to be in a/the minority; **~s étnicas** ethnic minorities

(Compuesto) **minoría de edad** minority

minorista[1] *adj* retail (*before n*); **comerciante/vendedor ~** retailer

minorista[2] *mf* retailer

minoritario -ria *adj* minority (*before n*)

mintiera, mintió, etc *see* **mentir**

minucia *f* 1 (detalle pequeño) minor detail; **no te entretengas en ~s** don't waste time with petty details 2 (cualidad) detail; **se lo explicó con ~** she explained it to him in detail *o* thoroughly

minuciosidad *f* attention to detail; **está pintado con ~** it's painted with great attention to detail

minucioso -sa *adj* ‹*búsqueda/investigación/persona*› meticulous, thorough; ‹*informe*› detailed

minué *m* minuet

minueto *m* minuet

minúscula *f* lower case letter, minuscule (tech)

minúsculo -la *adj* 1 (diminuto) minute, tiny 2 ‹*letra*› lower case

minusvalía *f*
A (Med, Psic) (física) physical handicap *o* disability; (psíquica) mental handicap
B (Econ) drop *o* fall in value

minusválido¹ -da *adj* (físico) physically handicapped, disabled; (psíquico) mentally handicapped

minusválido² -da *m,f* (físico) disabled person, physically handicapped person; (psíquico) mentally handicapped person; **coches para ∼s** cars for the disabled

minusvalorar [A1] *vt* to undervalue, underestimate

minuta *f*
A (de abogado, notario) bill; (borrador) draft copy
B (menú) (ant) bill of fare (dated); (plato rápido) (RPl) quick meal

minutero *m* minute hand

minutisa *f* sweet william

minuto *m*
A (de tiempo) minute; **a tres ∼s (de distancia) de su casa** three minutes (away) from his house; **cuando tenga un ∼** when I have a minute *o* moment
B (de ángulos) minute

mío¹, mía *adj* (*detrás del n*) mine; **éste es ∼** this one's mine; **un primo ∼** a cousin of mine; **eso es asunto ∼** that's my business; **amor ∼** sweetheart; **Muy señor ∼** (Corresp) (frml) Dear Sir

mío², mía *pron*: **el ∼/la mía** *etc* mine; **sus hijos son amigos de los ∼s** their children and mine are friends; **los idiomas no son lo ∼** languages are not my thing; **los ∼s** my family and friends

miocardio *m* myocardium; **infarto de ∼** myocardial infarction

miope¹ *adj* 1 (Med, Ópt) myopic (tech), nearsighted (AmE), short-sighted (BrE) 2 (falto de perspicacia) short-sighted

miope² *mf* myopic person (tech), nearsighted person (AmE), short-sighted person (BrE)

miopía *f* 1 (Med, Ópt) myopia (tech), nearsightedness (AmE), short-sightedness (BrE) 2 (falta de perspicacia) short-sightedness

mira *f* 1 (Arm, Ópt) sight; 2 (intención, objetivo): **con ∼s a reducir los gastos** with a view to reducing costs; **tiene la ∼ puesta en ese cargo** he's set his sights on getting that job; **sus ∼s son egoístas** his motives are selfish; **encarar algo con amplitud de ∼s** to adopt a broad-minded approach to sth; **es muy estrecho de ∼s** he's very narrow-minded

mirada *f* 1 (modo de mirar) look; **su ∼ era triste** he had a sad look in his eyes; **tiene una ∼ penetrante** he has a penetrating gaze; ***hay ∼s que matan*** if looks could kill ... 2 (acción de mirar) look; **lo fulminó con la ∼** she looked daggers at him; **le dirigió** *or* **lanzó una ∼ reprobatoria** he looked at her disapprovingly; **sólo le eché una miradita por encima** I just had a quick glance at it; **échale una miradita al arroz** have a quick look at the rice 3 (vista): **tenía la ∼ fija en el suelo** she had her eyes fixed on the ground; **recorrió la habitación con la ∼** she cast her eyes over the room/she looked around the room; **su ∼ se posó en ella** (liter) his gaze settled on her (liter); **bajar/levantar la ∼** to look down/up 4 (mira) sights (*pl*)

miradero *m* (Col) viewpoint

mirado -da *adj*
A (visto, considerado) **bien/mal ∼**: **es muy bien ∼ en esos círculos** he's very highly regarded in those circles; **eso no está bien ∼** that's not approved of, that's looked down on; **está muy mal ∼ en el barrio** he is not at all well thought of *o* well regarded in the neighborhood; *ver tb* **mirar** *vt* **C**
B ‹*persona*› 1 (con dinero) careful with money 2 (comedido, considerado) thoughtful, considerate

mirador *m* viewpoint

miramiento *m*: **¿por qué he de tener yo ∼s con ella?** why should I show her any consideration?; **tratar a algn sin ningún ∼** to treat sb with a total lack of consideration

mirar [A1] *vt*
A 1 (observar, contemplar) to look at; **no me mires así** don't look at me like that; **se me quedó mirando** he just stared at me, he just gaped at me; **miró el reloj con disimulo** she glanced furtively at her watch; **miraba distraída por la ventana** he was gazing absent-mindedly out of the window; **∼ a algn a los ojos** to look sb in the eye; **miraba cómo lo hacía** he was watching how she did it; **he mirado el informe muy por encima** I've only had a quick look at the report; **ir a ∼ escaparates** *or* (AmL) **vidrieras** to go window shopping; ***ser de mírame y no me toques*** to be very fragile *o* delicate 2 ‹*programa/partido*› to watch; **∼ televisión** to watch television
B (fijarse) to look; **a ver si mira por dónde va** why don't you look where you're going?; **¡mira lo que has hecho!** look what you've done!; **mira bien que esté apagado** make sure *o* check it's off; **mira a ver si está listo** have a look to see if he's ready; **mira a ver si lo puedes abrir tú** see if *you* can open it
C (considerar): **míralo desde otro punto de vista** look at it from another point of view; **mira bien lo que haces** think hard about what you're doing; **bien mirado** *or* **mirándolo bien, no es una mala idea** thinking about it *o* all things considered, it's not a bad idea; **mirándolo bien creo que prefiero no ir** on second thoughts, I think I'd prefer to stay; **lo mires por donde lo mires** whatever *o* whichever way you look at it; **∼ *algo en menos*** ‹*regalo*› to turn one's nose up at sth; ‹*trabajo/idea*› to look down one's nose at sth; **∼ *a algn en menos*** to look down on sb; **∼ *mal*** *or* ***no*** **∼ *bien a algn*: lo miran mal porque lleva el pelo largo** they disapprove of him because he has long hair; **en el trabajo no lo miran bien** he's not very highly thought of at work
D (ser cuidadoso con): **mira mucho el dinero** she's very careful with her money; **mira hasta el último céntimo** he watches every penny
E 1 (expresando incredulidad, irritación, etc): **¡mira que poner un plato de plástico en el horno ...!** honestly *o* really imagine putting a plastic dish in the oven ...! (colloq); **¡mira que eres tacaño!** boy, you're mean! (colloq); **¡mira las veces que te lo habré dicho ...!** the times I've told you!; **¡mira quién habla!** look who's talking!; **¡mira si será egoísta!** talk about (being) selfish! 2 (en advertencias): **mira que mi paciencia tiene un límite** I'm warning you, I'm running out of patience; **mira que ya son las nueve** you realize *o* you (do) know it's already nine

■ **mirar** *vi*
A (observar, contemplar) to look; **no mires** don't look; **se mira y no se toca** look but don't touch; **he mirado por todas partes** I've looked everywhere; **mirar por la ventana** to look out of the window; **¿miraste bien?** did you have a good look?, did you look properly?; **∼ *atrás*** to look back
B (fijarse) to look; **mire usted, la cosa es muy sencilla** well, it's very simple; **sacó el primer premio — ¡mira tú!** he won first prize — well, well! *o* well I never!; **no, mira, yo tampoco me lo creo** no, to be honest, I don't believe it either; **mira, no me vengas con excusas** look, I don't want to listen to your excuses; ***mira por dónde*** (Esp fam): **y mira por dónde, me llevé el trofeo** and would you believe it? I won the trophy, and guess what? I won the trophy
C (estar orientado) **∼ A/HACIA algo** «*fachada/frente*» to face sth; «*terraza/habitación*» to look out over sth, overlook sth; **ponte mirando hacia la ventana** stand (*o* sit *etc*) facing the window
D **mirar por** 1 (preocuparse por) to think of 2 (Col) (cuidar) to look after

■ **mirarse** *v pron* 1 (*refl*) to look at oneself 2 (*recípr*) to look at each other

mirasol *m* sunflower

miríada *f* (frml) myriad

mirilla *f* peephole, spyhole

miriñaque *m* crinoline

miriópodo *m* myriapod

mirlo *m* blackbird

mirón¹ -rona *adj* (fam): **es muy ∼** he's always ogling people *o* eyeing people up (colloq)

mirón² -rona *m,f*: **se nos acercaron unos mirones** a few inquisitive passers-by came up to us; **¿qué haces tú ahí de ∼? ¡haz algo!** don't just stand there watching *o* looking, do something!; ***los mirones son de piedra*** if you want to watch you'd better keep quiet; ***ir de*** **∼** to go along to watch *o* as a spectator

mirra *f* myrrh

mirruña, mirrusca *f* (Col, Méx fam) tiny bit

m

mirto *m* myrtle

misa *f* mass; **están en ~** they're at mass; **ir a ~** to go to mass; **ayudar a ~** to serve at mass; **decir ~** «*sacerdote*» to say *o* celebrate mass; **como en ~** in dead silence; ***por mí como si dice*** *or* ***que diga ~*** (Esp fam) I couldn't care less what he says (colloq); ***no saber de la ~ la mitad*** *or* ***la media*** (fam): **no sabe de la ~ la mitad** he doesn't know the first thing about it; ***va a ~*** (fam): **lo que él dice va a ~** what he says goes (colloq)

Compuestos

- **misa campal** *or* **de campaña** open-air mass
- **misa de cuerpo presente** funeral mass
- **misa de** *or* **del gallo** midnight mass (*on Christmas Eve*)
- **misa de difuntos** Requiem (mass)
- **misa mayor** *or* **solemne** High Mass
- **misa rezada** Low Mass

misal *m* missal

misantropía *f* misanthropy

misantrópico -ca *adj* misanthropic

misántropo -pa *m,f* misanthrope, misanthropist

miscelánea *f* 1 (variedad) miscellany; (Lit, Period) miscellany 2 (Méx) (tienda) small general store, corner shop (BrE)

misceláneo -nea *adj* miscellaneous

miserable[1] *adj* 1 (pobre) ‹*vivienda*› miserable, wretched; ‹*sueldo*› paltry, miserable 2 (avaro) mean, stingy (colloq) 3 (malvado) malicious, nasty

miserable[2] *mf* wretch, scoundrel

miseria *f*

A (pobreza) poverty, destitution; **vivir en la más absoluta ~** to live in abject poverty

B (cantidad insignificante) miserable amount, paltry amount; **gana una ~** she earns a pittance

C (desgracia) misfortune; **las ~s de la guerra** the miseries of war; ***estar a la ~*** (RPl fam) to be in a bad way (colloq); ***quedar a la ~*** to be a write-off *o* (AmE) be totaled (colloq); ***llorar ~(s)*** (CS fam) to complain about not having any money

misericordia *f* mercy, compassion

misericordioso -sa *adj* merciful; **obras misericordiosas** charitable works

mísero -ra *adj* 1 (pobre) miserable; **en un ~ cuartucho** in a miserable *o* squalid hovel 2 (*delante del n*) (escaso) miserable, measly

misérrimo -ma *adj* (frml) 1 (muy pobre) wretched 2 (muy tacaño) miserly

misil *m* missile; **~ de corto/medio/largo alcance** short-range/medium-range/long-range missile

Compuestos

- **misil antiaéreo/balístico** antiaircraft/ballistic missile
- **misil (de) crucero** cruise missile
- **misil tierra-aire** ground-to-air missile

misilístico -ca *adj* missile (*before n*)

misión *f*

A (tarea) mission; **¡~ cumplida!** (fr hecha) mission accomplished!

Compuesto **misión de combate/de reconocimiento** combat/reconnaissance mission

B (delegación): **una ~ científica** a team of scientists; **la ~ (diplomática) española en la ONU** the Spanish diplomatic delegation to the UN

C (Relig) mission

misionero[1] -ra *adj* missionary (*before n*)

misionero[2] -ra *m,f* (Relig) missionary

Misisipí *m* (río): **el (río) ~** the Mississippi (River); (estado) Mississippi

misiva *f* (frml) missive (frml *or* liter)

mismamente *adv* (fam): **~ ayer hablábamos de ti** we were talking about you only yesterday; **¿así? — mismamente** like this? — exactly *o* that's it

mismísimo -ma *adj*: *ver* **mismo[1] B 2**

mismo[1] -ma *adj*

A 1 (*delante del n*) (expresando identidad) same; **hacer dos cosas al ~ tiempo** to do two things at once *o* at the same time; **la misma historia de siempre** the same old story; **nos gustan las mismas películas** we like the same movies 2 (*como pron*) same; **Roma ya no es la misma** Rome isn't the same any more; **¿usted es Pedro Lecue? — el ~** are you Pedro Lecue? — I am indeed *o* that's right; **es el ~ que vimos ayer** it's the same one we saw yesterday; ***en las mismas***: **no ha llegado, así que seguimos en las mismas** it hasn't arrived so we're no further on; **si vienes tú pero falta él, estamos en las mismas** if *you* come but *he* doesn't turn up, then we're no better off

B (uso enfático) 1 (refiriéndose a lugares, momentos, cosas): **en el ~ centro de Lima** right in the center of Lima; **en este ~ instante** this very minute; **eso ~ pienso yo** that's exactly *o* just what I think 2 (refiriéndose a personas): **hablé con el mismísimo presidente** I spoke to the president himself; **te perjudicas a ti ~** you're only spiting *o* hurting yourself; **él ~ lo trajo** he brought it himself; **se corta el pelo ella misma** she cuts her own hair; **él ~ se pone las inyecciones** he gives himself the injections

C **lo mismo** (la misma cosa): **siempre dice lo ~** he always says the same (thing); **lo ~ para mí** the same for me, please; **¡qué elegante te has venido! — lo ~ digo** you're looking very smart! — so are you *o* you, too; **o lo que es lo ~** in other words; **pidió lo ~ que yo** he ordered the same as me; ***dar lo ~***: **me da lo ~ si lo rompe** I don't care if he breaks it; **le da lo ~ con o sin azúcar** he doesn't mind with or without sugar; **da lo ~ quién lo haga** it doesn't matter *o* it makes no difference who does it

D **lo mismo** (*como adv*) 1 (fam) (expresando posibilidad): **te ve por la calle y lo ~ no te saluda** you can meet him in the street and sometimes he doesn't even say hello to you; **¿pregúntaselo? lo ~ dice que sí** ask him, he might (well) *o* may (well) say yes; **lo ~ puedes conseguir caramelos que una botella de whisky** you can get anything, from sweets to a bottle of whiskey 2 (RPl fam) (de todos modos) just *o* all the same, anyway

E **lo mismo que** (al igual que): **nuestra empresa, lo ~ que tantas otras** our company, like so many others; **los niños pueden ir lo ~ que los adultos** children can go as well as adults

F 1 (*como pron*) (frml): **se detuvo un coche y tres individuos bajaron del ~** a car pulled up and three individuals got out 2 (*como pron relativo*) (Méx frml): **agradecemos su donativo, ~ que fue aplicado a la compra de medicamentos** we thank you for your donation, which has been used to buy medicines

mismo[2] *adv* (uso enfático): **aquí/ahora ~** right here/now; **hoy ~ te mando el cheque** I'll send you the check today; **ayer ~ hablé con él** I spoke to him only yesterday

misoginia *f* misogyny

misógino *m* misogynist

miss /mis/ *f* beauty queen; **M~ Universo** Miss Universe; **un concurso de ~es** a beauty contest

mistela *f* (Chi) hot punch

míster *m* (Dep) coach, trainer

misterio *m*

A (enigma, secreto) mystery; **una novela de ~** a mystery novel; **¡déjate de ~s!** stop being so mysterious! (colloq)

B 1 (Relig) mystery 2 (Teatr) mystery play

misterioso -sa *adj* mysterious

mística *f* 1 (en teología) mysticism 2 (Lit): **la ~** mystic literature

misticismo *m* mysticism

místico[1] -ca *adj* ‹*experiencia*› mystic, mystical; ‹*escritor*› mystic (*before n*)

místico[2] -ca *m,f* mystic

mistificación *f* mystification

Misuri *m* (río): **el (río) ~** the Missouri (River); (estado) Missouri

mita *f* (Hist) forced labour (*by Indians for Spanish colonists*)

mitad *f*

A (parte) half; **la primera ~ del partido** the first half of the game; **¿me das la ~?** can I have half?; **a ~ de precio** half price; **lo hizo en la ~ del tiempo** she did it in half the time; **~ y ~** half and half

B (medio, centro): **cortar algo por la ~** to cut sth in half; **corta el papel por la ~** cut the paper in half *o* down the middle; **dividir algo por la ~** to halve sth; **voy por la ~ del libro** I'm halfway through the book; **dejar algo por la ~** to leave sth half finished; **a** *or* **en (la) ~ de la**

m

reunión in the middle of the meeting; **en la ~ de la película** halfway through the movie; **queda a ~ de distancia entre tu casa y la mía** it's halfway between your house and mine; ***partir a algn por la ~*** *ver* ▸ **eje**

mítico -ca *adj* mythical

mitificar [A2] *vt* to mythicize, turn ... into a legend (colloq)

mitigación *f* (frml) mitigation (frml); (del dolor) relief; (de la sed) quenching

mitigar [A3] *vt* ‹*dolor*› to relieve, ease; ‹*pena/sufrimiento*› to alleviate, mitigate (frml); ‹*sed*› to quench; **para ~ los efectos de la crisis económica** to mitigate the effects of the economic crisis

mitin, mitín *m* 1 (Pol) political meeting, rally; **llevar a cabo** *or* **celebrar un ~** to hold a meeting 2 (Esp fam) (sermón) lecture (colloq), sermon (colloq)

mito *m* 1 (leyenda) legend 2 (invención, mentira) myth

mitología *f* mythology

mitológico -ca *adj* mythological

mitón *m* mitten; (de medio dedo) fingerless glove

mitote *m* (Méx) (baile) Aztec dance; (jaleo) (fam) trouble

mitra *f* (gorro) miter*

mixto¹ -ta *adj*

A 1 ‹*escuela*› mixed, coeducational; **educación mixta** coeducation 2 ‹*partido/equido*› mixed

B 1 ‹*comisión/comité*› joint (*before n*) 2 ‹*economía/agricultura*› mixed

mixto² *m* (sandwich) toasted sandwich (*with two different fillings*); **un ~ de jamón y queso** a toasted ham and cheese sandwich

mixtura *f* (liter) blend, mixture

ml. (= **mililitro**) ml

mm. (= **milímetro**) mm

mnemotecnia, mnemotécnica *f* mnemonics

mnemotécnico -ca *adj* mnemonic

m/o. = **mi orden**

moaré *m* moiré

mobbing *m* bullying (in the workplace)

mobiliario *m* furniture, furnishings (*pl*); **renovar el ~ del comedor** to refurnish the dining room

(Compuestos)

- **mobiliario de baño** *or* **sanitario** bathroom furnishings (*pl*)
- **mobiliario de cocina** kitchen fittings *o* units (*pl*)

moblaje *m* furniture, furnishings (*pl*)

moca *m*: *tb* **café ~** mocha; **tarta de ~** coffee cake

mocasín *m* moccasin

mocedad *f* (liter) youth

mocerío *m*: **el ~** young people

mocetón -tona (*m*) strapping kid (AmE) *o* (BrE) lad; (*f*) strapping girl

mochar [A1] *vt* 1 (fam) (cercenar): **le mochó un dedo** it chopped off his finger (colloq); **le ~on el artículo** they hacked her article up (colloq) 2 (cortar mal): **me ~on en la peluquería** they sheared me at the hairdresser's (colloq)

■ **mocharse** *v pron*

A (Méx fam) (compartir): **se mochó con los cigarros** he shared out his cigarettes; **nos mochamos con la cuenta** we split the bill between us

B (Chi, Ven fam) ‹*pelo*› to chop ... off (colloq)

mochila *f* 1 (de excursionista, soldado) backpack; (de escolar) satchel 2 (Col, Ven) (que cuelga del hombro) shoulder bag

mochilear [A1] *vi* (CS) to backpack

mochilero -ra *m,f* (CS) backpacker

mocho¹ -cha *adj* (fam) ‹*buey/toro*› with its horns cut off; ‹*lápiz/cuchillo*› blunt; **dejó todos los pinos ~s** he lopped (the tops off) all the pine trees; **la máquina le dejó el dedo ~** the machine chopped the top off his finger

mocho² -cha *m,f*

A (Col, Méx, Ven): **es un ~** he only has one arm

B (Méx) (mojigato) prude

C **mocho** *m* (Col fam) (caballo) horse; (rocinante) (fam & pey) nag (colloq & pej)

mochuelo *m* little owl; ***cargar a algn (con) el ~*** (Esp) to give sb the dirty job (colloq); ***sacudirse el ~*** (Esp) to get out of doing the dirty job (colloq)

moción *f* motion; **presentar una ~** to propose *o* (BrE) table a motion; **votar una ~** to vote on a motion; **hacer una ~ de orden** to make a point of order

(Compuesto) **moción de censura** vote of no-confidence

mocionar [A1] *vi* (Méx, RPl) to propose a motion (from the floor)

mocito¹ -ta *adj* (fam): **tus niñas ya son mocitas** your daughters are very grown-up now; **tiene dos hijos ~s** he has two youngsters *o* boys (colloq)

mocito² -ta *m,f* (fam): **ya no es ningún ~** he's no longer a lad *o* a youngster; **una mocita de unos 15 años** a young girl *o* a youngster of about 15

moco *m* 1 (líquido) snot (colloq); **límpiate los ~s** wipe *o* blow your nose; **le colgaban** *or* **se le caían los ~s** he had a runny nose (colloq) *o* (sl) snotty nose; **tengo ~s** my nose is running; **suelta una especie de ~** it exudes a kind of mucus; ***llorar a ~ tendido*** (fam) to cry one's eyes out 2 (seco) booger (AmE colloq), bogey (BrE colloq)

(Compuesto) **moco de pavo** (Zool) crest; ***no es ~ de ~*** (fam) (no es nada fácil) it's no easy matter; (no es poca cosa) it's no trifle

mocoso -sa *m,f* (fam) squirt (colloq), pipsqueak (colloq); **pero si sólo eres una mocosa** but you're just a kid (colloq)

moda *f* fashion; **la ~ joven** *or* **juvenil** young fashion; **ir a la ~** to be trendy; **estar de ~** to be in fashion, be in (colloq); **estar muy de ~** to be all the rage (colloq); **ponerse/pasar de ~** to come into/go out of fashion; **estar de última ~** to be very fashionable; **revista de ~s** fashion magazine; **la ~ de los patines** the rollerskating craze; ***la ~ no incomoda*** you have to suffer in the name of fashion

modal *adj* modal

modales *mpl* manners (*pl*); **tener buenos/malos ~** to be well mannered/bad mannered; **tiene que aprender ~** she needs to learn some manners

modalidad *f*: **cualquier ~ de disidencia** any kind *o* form of dissent; **varias ~es de pago** several methods *o* modes of payment; **la medalla de oro en la ~ de esquí alpino** the gold medal for downhill skiing

modelado *m* (acción) modeling*; (resultado): **el ~ del rostro es perfecto** the face is perfectly sculpted *o* modeled

modelador -dora *m,f* modeler*

modelaje *m* (Andes, Ven) modeling*; **hacer ~** to model

modelar [A1] *vt* (Art) ‹*arcilla*› to model; ‹*estatua/figura*› to model, sculpt; ‹*carácter*› to mold*

■ **modelar** *vi*

A (Art) to model

B (Andes) (para fotos, desfiles) to model

modélico -ca *adj* (Esp) ▸ **modelo¹ 1**

modelismo *m* model-making

modelista *mf* (Art) modeler*; (de costura) pattern maker

modelo¹ *adj inv* 1 ‹*niño/estudiante*› model (*before n*); ‹*comportamiento/carácter*› exemplary 2 (de muestra): **visité la casa ~** I visited the model home (AmE) *o* (BrE) the showhouse

modelo² *m*

A 1 (ejemplo) model; **copiaron el ~ cubano** they copied the Cuban model; **su conducta es un ~ para todos** her conduct is an example to us all; **tomar/utilizar algo como ~** to take/use sth as a model; **tomó a su padre como ~** he followed his father's example 2 (muestra, prototipo) model; **~ en** *or* **a escala** scale model

B (tipo, diseño) model; **el ~ de lujo** the deluxe model

C (Indum) design; **un ~ de Franelli** a Franelli (design); **llegó con un nuevo modelito** (fam) she arrived wearing a new little number; **un sombrero último ~** the (very) latest in hats

modelo³ *mf* model; **desfile de ~s** fashion show

módem *m* (*pl* **-dems**) modem

moderación *f* moderation; **beber con ~** to drink in moderation; **obrar con ~** to act with restraint

moderadamente *adv* moderately

moderado¹ -da *adj* ‹*temperatura*› moderate; ‹*precio*› reasonable; ‹*ideología/facción*› moderate

moderado² -da *m,f* moderate

moderador¹ -dora *adj* moderating (*before n*)

moderador² **-dora** *m,f*
A (en debate) moderator, chair; (Rad, TV) presenter
B **moderador** *m* (Fís) moderator

moderar [A1] *vt*
A 1 ‹*impulsos/aspiraciones*› to curb, moderate 2 ‹*vocabulario/palabras*›: **por favor modera tu vocabulario** please mind your language; **trata de ~ tus palabras** try to tone down your language; **modera el tonito** don't use that tone of voice with me 3 ‹*gasto/consumo*› to curb; ‹*velocidad*› to reduce
B ‹*debate/coloquio*› to moderate, chair
■ **moderarse** *v pron*: **modérate, estás comiendo mucho** restrain yourself *o* (colloq) go easy, you're eating too much; **modérate, no hables así** control yourself, don't talk like that; **~se en los gastos** to cut down on spending

modernamente *adv* nowadays, in modern times

modernidad *f* 1 (calidad) modernness, modernity 2 (edad) modern age

modernismo *m* (Arquit, Art, Lit) modernism; (cualidad) modernness, modernity

modernista *adj/mf* modernist

modernización *f* modernization

modernizador **-dora**, **modernizante** *adj* ‹*efecto*› modernizing (*before n*); **un proceso ~** a process of modernization

modernizar [A4] *vt* ‹*fábrica/técnica/sociedad*› to modernize; ‹*costumbres*› to update; ‹*vestido/abrigo*› to do up
■ **modernizarse** *v pron*: **debes ~te** you have to keep up with the times

moderno¹ **-na** *adj* 1 (actual) modern; **el hombre ~** modern man; **una edición más moderna** a more up-to-date edition 2 (a la moda) ‹*vestido/peinado*› fashionable, trendy 3 ‹*edad/historia*› modern

moderno² **-na** *m,f* trendy (colloq)

modestia *f* modesty; **vivir con ~** to live modestly; **~ *aparte*** in all modesty, modesty apart

modesto **-ta** *adj* 1 (falto de pretensión) modest; **en mi modesta opinión** in my humble opinion 2 (humilde, sencillo) ‹*familia*› humble; ‹*posición social*› modest, humble 3 ‹*sueldo*› modest 4 (ant) ‹*mujer*› modest (liter)

módico **-ca** *adj* reasonable

modificable *adj* modifiable

modificación *f* (en aparato) modification; (en un plan) change; (en texto, programa) change, alteration

modificador¹ **-dora** *adj* modification (*before n*), modifying (*before n*)

modificador² *m* modifier

modificar [A2] *vt* 1 ‹*aparato*› to modify; ‹*plan*› to change; ‹*horario/ley*› to change, alter 2 (Ling) to modify
■ **modificarse** *v pron* to change, alter

modismo *m* idiom

modista *mf* (que diseña) couturier, designer; (que confecciona) dressmaker

modistería *f* (Col) (actividad) dressmaking; (establecimiento) dressmaker's shop/workshop

modisto *m* couturier, designer

modo *m*
A 1 (manera, forma) way, manner (frml); **no lo digas de ese ~** don't say it like that; **del siguiente ~** in the following manner; **a mi ~ de ver** to my way of thinking, in my opinion; Ⓢ **modo de empleo** instructions for use, directions; **me lo pidió de muy mal ~** (AmL) she asked me (for it) very rudely 2 (*en locs*) **a mi/tu/su modo** (in) my/your/his (own) way; **a modo de**: **se puso una manta a ~ de poncho** he put a blanket round his shoulders like a poncho; **a ~ de introducción** by way of introduction; **de cualquier modo** (de todas formas) (*indep*) in any case, anyway; (sin cuidado) anyhow; **del mismo** *or* **de igual modo que** just as, in the same way (that); **de modo que** (así que) so; (para que) (+ *subj*) so that; **¿de ~ que se van?** so they're going, are they?; **de ~ que se vean desde aquí** so that they can be seen from here; **de ningún modo** no way; **de ningún ~ puedo aceptar** there's no way I can accept; **de todos modos** anyway, anyhow; **en cierto modo** in a way; **ni modo** (AmL exc CS fam): **¿pudieron entrar? — no, ni ~** did they get in? — no, no way (colloq); **traté de persuadirlo pero ni ~** I tried to persuade him but it was no good; **ni ~, yo soy como soy** that's tough *o* too bad, I am the way I am (colloq); **ni ~ que te quedes aquí** there's no way you're staying here (colloq)
B **modos** *mpl* (modales) manners (*pl*); **con buenos/malos ~s** politely/rudely *o* impolitely
C (Ling) mood
D (Mús) mode

modorra *f* (fam): **qué ~ tengo hoy** I'm so sleepy today; **sacúdete la ~** wake up!

modosito **-ta** *adj* (de buen comportamiento) well-behaved, good; (educado) polite, well-mannered; (recatado) demure

modulación *f* modulation
(Compuesto) **modulación de amplitud/frecuencia** amplitude/frequency modulation

modulador *m* modulator

modular¹ *adj* modular

modular² [A1] *vt/vi* to modulate

módulo *m*
A 1 (de mueble) unit, module 2 (de prisión) unit 3 (Espac) module 4 (Educ) module
B (Fís, Mat) modulus

modus operandi/vivendi *m* modus operandi/vivendi

mofa *f* mockery; **hacer ~ DE algo/algn** to make fun of sth/sb; **en tono de ~** mockingly, in a mocking tone

mofarse [A1] *v pron* **~ DE algo/algn** to make fun of sth/sb

mofeta *f* skunk

mofle *m* (AmC, Méx) muffler (AmE), silencer (BrE)

moflete *m* (fam) chubby cheek

mofletudo **-da** *adj* (fam) chubby-cheeked

mogolla *f* (Col) bread roll

mogollón *m* (Esp arg) 1 (gran cantidad): **había (un) ~ de gente** there were loads of people there (colloq); **este ~ de papeles** this mass of papers 2 (lío) confusion

mohair /mo'er/ *m* mohair

mohín *m* face; **hacer un ~** to make *o* (BrE) pull an angry face

mohína *f* 1 (enfado) annoyance; **tener ~** to be annoyed 2 (tristeza) depression; **tener ~** to be upset *o* depressed

mohíno **-na** *adj* 1 (enfurruñado): **está ~** he's in a sulk 2 (alicaído) depressed

moho *m* 1 (en fruta, pan) mold*, mildew; ***criar ~*** «*fruta/queso*» to go moldy* 2 (en cobre) patina, verdigris; (en hierro) rust

mohoso **-sa** *adj* 1 ‹*fruta/pan/queso*› moldy* 2 ‹*cobre*› covered in patina *o* verdigris; ‹*hierro*› rusty

moisés *m* (cuna) cradle, Moses basket; (portátil) portacrib (AmE), carrycot (BrE)

mojado¹ **-da** *adj* wet; **estaba completamente ~** he was dripping *o* soaking wet

mojado² **-da** *m,f* (Méx fam) wetback (colloq & pej)

mojar [A1] *vt*
A 1 ‹*suelo/papel/pelo*› (accidentalmente) to get *o* make … wet; (a propósito) to wet; **pasó un coche y me mojó** a car went by and splashed me; **aún moja la cama** (euf) he still wets the bed; **moja la gasa con colonia** moisten the gauze with cologne 2 (sumergiendo) ‹*galleta/bizcocho*› to dip, dunk (colloq); **mojó la pluma en el tintero** she dipped the pen in the inkwell; ***no moja pero empapa*** (Ven fam) he's/she's a wolf in sheep's clothing
B (fam) (celebrar): **esto hay que ~lo** this calls for a drink (colloq)
■ **mojarse** *v pron* 1 «*persona/ropa/suelo*» to get wet; **se me ~on los zapatos** my shoes got wet; **me mojé toda** I got soaked 2 ‹*pelo/pies*› (a propósito) to wet; (accidentalmente) to get … wet 3 (orinarse): **se mojó en los pantalones** he wet his pants; **el bebé está mojado** the baby is wet

mojarra *f*: *type of sea bream*

mojicón *m*
A (Esp) (Coc) ladyfinger, sponge finger (BrE)
B (fam) (golpe) punch; (con la mano abierta) slap

mojigatería *f* prudishness; **déjate de ~s** don't be so prudish

mojigato¹ **-ta** *adj* prudish, straitlaced

mojigato² **-ta** *m,f* prude

mojón *m*
A (señal) marker, boundary stone; (hito) landmark; (Auto) *tb* **~ kilométrico** ≈ milestone
B (fam) (excremento) turd (vulg)
C (Ven fam) (mentira, cuento) story (colloq)

mojonear [A1] *vt* (Ven fam) to spin … a yarn (colloq)

mojonero -ra *m,f* (Ven fam) fibber (colloq)

molar¹ [A1] *vi* (Esp arg): **mola cantidad** it's really cool *o* amazing; **no me molan** they are seriously uncool (colloq)

molar² *m* molar, back tooth

molcajete *m* (Méx) mortar

molde *m*
A (pieza hueca) **1** (para hornear) baking pan (AmE), baking tin (BrE); (para flanes, gelatina) mold*; **~ de pan** loaf pan (AmE) *o* (BrE) tin **2** (para jugar en la arena) mold* **3** (Tec) cast; **un ~ de yeso** (Art) a plaster cast; ***de ~*** just right, perfect **4** (Impr) form; ***de ~*** just right, perfect; ***romper ~s***: **un atleta que rompe los ~s** an athlete who is in a class of his own; **los jóvenes rompen todos los ~s** young people break all the molds
B (AmL) (para coser) pattern; (para tejer) (knitting) pattern

moldeable *adj* **1** ‹*barro*› moldable*, malleable **2** ‹*persona/carácter*› malleable

moldeado *m* (Art) (en bronce) casting; (en barro) molding*, modeling*

moldear [A1] *vt* **1** (en bronce) to cast; (en barro) to mold*, model **2** ‹*persona/carácter*› to mold*, shape; ‹*pelo*› to style

moldura *f* molding*

mole¹ *f* mass; **una ~ de hormigón** a huge mass *o* block of concrete; **él es una ~** he's really huge; **se me vino encima con toda su ~** he fell with his full weight on top of me

mole² *m*
A (Méx) (salsa) chili sauce (*with chocolate and peanuts*); (plato) *turkey, chicken or pork with* **mole** *sauce*; ***darle a algn en su (mero) ~*** (Méx fam): **me dieron en mi mero ~** (con regalo, invitación) they couldn't have thought of anything better, it was a perfect choice; (en conversación) they got me onto my favorite *o* pet subject; ***ser el (mero) ~ de algn*** (Méx fam): **las matemáticas son su ~** mathematics are his forte; **ese tipo de trabajo es mi mero ~** that sort of job is right up my street (colloq)
(Compuesto) **mole de olla** (Méx fam) meat stew; ***ser ~ de ~*** to be the perfect time
B (Méx fam) (sangre) blood

molécula *f* molecule

molecular *adj* molecular

moledor¹ -dora *adj* grinding (*before n*), crushing (*before n*)

moledor² *m* grinder

moler [E9] *vt* ‹*especias/café*› to grind; ‹*trigo*› to grind, mill; ‹*aceitunas*› to crush; ‹*carne*› to grind (AmE), to mince (BrE); ‹*plátano*› (Chi, Méx) to mash; **café molido** ground coffee; ***~ a algn a golpes*** *or* ***a palos*** to beat sb to a pulp
■ **moler** *vi* (Col fam) to work

molestar [A1] *vt*
A **1** (importunar) to bother; **perdone que lo moleste** sorry to trouble *o* bother you **2** (interrumpir) to disturb
B (ofender, disgustar) to upset
■ **molestar** *vi*
A (importunar) (+*me/te/le etc*): **¿no te molesta ese ruido?** doesn't that noise bother you?; **¿le molesta si fumo?** do you mind if I smoke?; **me molesta su arrogancia** her arrogance irritates *o* annoys me; **me molesta que hables de él** it upsets me when you talk about him; **las pulseras me molestan para trabajar** bracelets get in the way when I'm working; **no me duele, pero me molesta** it doesn't hurt but it's uncomfortable
B (fastidiar) to be a nuisance; **no quiero ~** I don't want to be a nuisance *o* to cause any trouble; **vino a ayudar pero no hizo más que ~** he came to help, but he just made a nuisance of himself; **sus niños nunca molestan** her children are never any trouble
■ **molestarse** *v pron*
A (disgustarse) to get upset; **~se POR algo** to get upset about sth; **se molestó por lo que le dije** he was upset *o* offended by what I said; **~se CON algn** to get annoyed WITH sb
B (tomarse el trabajo) to bother, trouble oneself (frml); **no se moleste** it's all right *o* please, don't bother; **¿para qué vas a ~te?** why should you put yourself out?; **~se EN + INF: ni se molestó en llamarme** he didn't even bother to call me; **se molestó en venir a verme** she took the trouble to come and see me

molestia *f*
A **1** (incomodidad, trastorno) trouble; **siento causarte tantas ~s** I'm sorry to cause you so much trouble; **no es ninguna ~** it's no trouble at all; **perdona la ~, pero ...** sorry to bother you, but …; **rogamos disculpen las ~s ocasionadas** (frml) we apologize for any inconvenience caused (frml) **2** (trabajo): **¿para qué te tomaste la ~?** why did you bother to do that?; **~ DE + INF: ahórrate la ~ de ir** save yourself the trip; **se tomó la ~ de escribirnos** she took the trouble to write to us
B (malestar): **~s estomacales** stomach problems *o* upsets; **no es un dolor, sólo una ~** it's not a pain, just a feeling of discomfort; **las ~s que acompañan a estados gripales** the aches and pains symptomatic of flu

molesto -ta *adj*
A **1** [SER] (fastidioso) ‹*ruido/tos*› annoying, irritating; ‹*sensación/síntoma*› unpleasant; **resulta ~ tener que viajar con tantos bultos** it's a nuisance *o* it's very inconvenient having to travel with so much baggage **2** [ESTAR] (incómodo, dolorido): **está todavía algo ~** he's still in some pain; **está ~ por la anestesia** he's in some discomfort because of the anesthetic **3** [SER] (violento, embarazoso) awkward, embarrassing
B [ESTAR] (ofendido) upset; (irritado) annoyed; **está muy ~ por lo que hiciste** he's very upset/annoyed about what you did

molestoso -sa *adj* (AmL fam) annoying

molicie *f* **1** (comodidad): **el lujo y la ~ en que fue criado** the atmosphere of luxury and pampering in which he was brought up; **la inercia y la ~ de los que mandan** the inertia and complacency of those in charge **2** (blandura) softness

molido¹ -da *adj* **1** (fam) (agotado) bushed (AmE colloq), shattered (BrE colloq) **2** (Andes fam) (dolorido) stiff

molido² *m* (Chi fam) loose change

molienda *f* **1** (acción) grinding, milling **2** (cantidad) batch (*of corn or sugarcane*) **3** (temporada) milling season **4** (molino) (liter) mill

molinero -ra *m,f* miller

molinete *m* **1** (juguete) pinwheel (AmE), windmill (BrE) **2** (RPl) (para entrar al metro) turnstile **3** (en danza) spin (*while holding hands*)

molinillo *m* **1** (de café, especias) grinder, mill **2** (juguete) pinwheel (AmE), windmill (BrE) **3** (Col, Méx) (para batir) whisk
(Compuestos)
- **molinillo de café** coffee mill *o* grinder
- **molinillo de carne** grinder (AmE), mincer (BrE)
- **molinillo de pimienta/sal** pepper/salt mill

molino *m* **1** (máquina — para el trigo) mill; (— para la carne) grinder (AmE), mincer (BrE) **2** (fábrica) mill; **~ de papel** paper mill
(Compuestos)
- **molino de agua** waterwheel
- **molino de viento** windmill; ***luchar contra ~s de ~*** (liter) to tilt at windmills (liter)

molla *f* (del pan) crumb; (de la carne) lean, lean part; (de la fruta) flesh

molleja *f*
A (de res) sweetbread; (de ave) gizzard
B (Ven fam) (descaro) nerve (colloq)

mollera *f* (fam) head; **no le da la ~ para tanto** he hasn't got that much up top (colloq); **está mal de la ~** he's off his head *o* rocker (colloq); ***cerrado*** *or* ***duro de ~*** pigheaded (colloq)

mollete *m* muffin

molo *m* (Chi) *tb* **~ de abrigo** breakwater, mole

molón -lona *adj* (Méx fam): **¡qué mujer tan molona!** that woman's such a nuisance *o* pest!

molote *m* (Méx fam): **se hizo un ~** she put her hair up

molturar [A1] *vt* to grind, mill

molusco *m* mollusk*

m

momentáneamente *adv* momentarily, for a moment

momentáneo -nea *adj* 1 (breve) momentary 2 (pasajero) temporary

momento *m*

A 1 (instante puntual) moment; **justo en ese ~** just at that moment; **en todo ~** at all times; **a partir de ese ~** from that moment on; **en este ~ no está** she's not in right now *o* at the moment 2 (lapso breve) minute, moment; **dentro de un ~** in a minute *o* moment; **eso te lo arreglo en un ~** I'll fix that for you in no time at all; **¡un momentito!** (por teléfono) just a moment, just a minute; **no para ni un ~** she's on the go the whole time 3 (época, período) time, period; **atravesamos ~s difíciles** we're going through a difficult time *o* period; **está en su mejor ~** he is at his peak 4 (ocasión) time; **llegas en buen/mal ~** you've arrived at the right time/at a bad time; **cuando llegue el ~** when the time comes; **en ningún ~** never, at no time 5 (tiempo presente) moment; **la moda del ~** the fashion of the moment

B (*en locs*) **al momento** at once; **de momento**: **de ~ se siente bien** she feels all right at the moment; **de ~ se va a quedar en mi casa** she's going to stay with me for the time being; **dejemos este asunto de ~** let's forget this matter for the moment; **desde el momento que** (CS) since, as, seeing as (colloq); **de un momento al otro**: **están por llegar de un ~ al otro** they'll be arriving any minute now; **cambia de opinión de un ~ al otro** she changes her mind from one minute to the next; **en cualquier momento**: **puedes llamar en cualquier ~** you can call at any time; **pueden llegar en cualquier ~** they could arrive any time now *o* at any moment; **en el momento** immediately; **en el momento menos pensado** when they/you/we least expect it; **en un momento dado** at a given moment; **si en un ~ dado tu quisieras ...** if at any *o* some time you should want to ...; **por el momento** for the time being; **por momentos**: **el frío aumenta por ~s** it's getting colder by the minute; **su estado empeoraba por ~s** her condition was deteriorating from one minute to the next

C (Fís, Mec) momentum

momia *f* mummy

momificación *f* mummification

momificar [A2] *vt* to mummify

■ **momificarse** *v pron* to mummify, become mummified

momio -mia *m,f* (Chi fam & pey) right-wing reactionary

mona *f*

A (fam) (borrachera): **agarrar una ~** to get plastered (colloq); **dormir la ~** to sleep it off

B 1 (en naipes) old maid 2 (Col) (para un álbum) picture card; ***como la ~*** (CS fam) terrible 3 (Ven fam) (mujer pretenciosa) stuck-up woman

monacal *adj* monastic

monacato *m* monasticism, monastic life

monada *f* (fam) 1 (cosa bonita): **¡qué ~ de vestido!** what a lovely *o* gorgeous dress! 2 (persona bonita): **su novia es una ~** his girlfriend's gorgeous *o* a real stunner (colloq); **¡qué ~ de niño!** what a lovely *o* (colloq) cute kid 3 (RPl) (persona encantadora) angel (colloq) 4 **monadas** *fpl* (monerías): **no hagas ~s** stop monkeying *o* clowning around (colloq)

mónada *f* monad

monaguillo *m* altar boy, acolyte, server

monarca *mf* monarch

monarquía *f* monarchy

monárquico¹ -ca *adj* ‹*régimen*› monarchical; ‹*persona/ideas*› monarchist (*before n*)

monárquico² -ca *m,f* monarchist, royalist

monarquismo *m* monarchism

monasterio *m* monastery

monástico -ca *adj* monastic

monda *f*

A (Esp) 1 (de cítricos) peel; **~s de las patatas** potato peelings 2 (acción) peeling; ***ser la ~*** (Esp fam) (ser muy divertido) to be a scream (colloq); (ser el colmo) to be the limit (colloq)

B (Méx fam) (paliza) thrashing, hiding (colloq)

mondadientes *m* (*pl* ~) toothpick

mondadura *f* ▸**monda A1**

mondar [A1] *vt* (Esp) 1 ‹*fruta/patatas*› to peel; ***anda y que te monden*** (fam) get lost (colloq), go fly a kite (AmE colloq) 2 ‹*árbol*› to prune 3 (fam) (cortar el pelo) to scalp (colloq) 4 (fam) (dejar sin dinero) to fleece (colloq)

■ **mondarse** *v pron* (*refl*): **se mondaba los dientes** she was picking her teeth; ***~se de risa*** (Esp) to die laughing

mondo -da *adj* (Esp): **le dejaron la cabeza monda** they scalped him (colloq); ***~ y lirondo*** plain and simple

mondongo *m* 1 (entrañas) insides (*pl*), guts (*pl*) 2 (AmS) (callos) tripe

moneda *f*

A 1 (pieza) coin; **una ~ de cinco pesos** a five-peso coin *o* piece 2 (de país) currency; **acuñar ~** to mint money; ***pagar con la misma ~*** to pay sb back in kind

Compuestos

- **moneda blanda** *or* **débil** soft currency
- **moneda corriente** currency; ***ser ~ corriente*** to be an everyday occurrence
- **moneda de curso legal** legal tender
- **moneda fraccionaria** (Fin) fractional currency; (dinero suelto) correct *o* exact change

B **la Moneda** (en Chi) Presidential Palace

monedero *m* change purse (AmE), purse (BrE)

monerías *fpl* (fam): **hacer ~** (tontear) to mess around (colloq); (hacer payasadas) to monkey *o* clown around (colloq)

monero -ra *m,f* (Méx fam) cartoonist

monetario -ria *adj* ‹*crisis*› monetary, financial

monetarista *adj/mf* monetarist

mongol -gola *m,f* Mongol, Mongolian

mongólico¹ -ca *adj* 1 (ant *o* crit) (Med) ‹*rasgos*› mongoloid (dated *or* crit); **niños ~s** Down's syndrome children 2 (fam & pey) (tonto) moronic (colloq & pej)

mongólico² -ca *m,f* 1 (ant *o* crit) (Med) person suffering from Down's syndrome 2 (fam & pey) (tonto) moron (colloq & pej)

mongolismo *m* (ant *o* crit) Down's syndrome

monigote *m* 1 (muñeco) rag doll; (de papel) paper doll; (dibujo) doodle 2 (fam) (tonto) fool (colloq)

monitor -tora *m,f*

A 1 (CS) (Dep): **~ de esquí/natación** ski/swimming instructor; **~ de tenis** tennis coach; **es ~ en un campamento juvenil** he's a monitor at a summer camp 2 (Educ) (en la escuela) (RPl) monitor; (en la universidad) (Col) *student who acts as an assistant teacher*

B **monitor** *m* (Inf, Med, Tec) monitor

monitorear [A1], **monitorizar** [A4] *vt* to monitor

monja *f* nun; **meterse a** *or* **de ~** to become a nun

monje *m* monk

monjil *adj* 1 (Relig): **la vida ~** life in a convent 2 ‹*vestimenta*› austere; ‹*idea/actitud*› prudish

mono¹ -na *adj*

A (fam) ‹*mujer*› pretty, lovely-looking (colloq); ‹*niño*› lovely, cute (colloq); ‹*vestido/piso*› gorgeous, lovely; **es muy mona de cara** she has a lovely face

B (Col) (rubio) ‹*hombre/niño*› blond; ‹*mujer/niña*› blonde

C (Audio) mono

mono² -na *m,f*

A (Zool) monkey; **el ~ desnudo** the naked ape; ***ser el último ~*** (fam) to be the lowest of the low; ***ser un ~ de imitación*** (fam) to be a copycat (colloq); ***tener ~s en la cara*** (fam): **¿qué miras? ¿es que tengo ~s en la cara?** is there something funny about me?; ***aunque la mona se vista de seda mona se queda*** you can't make a silk purse out of a sow's ear

B **mono** *m* (monigote) doodle; **una revista de monitos** (Andes, Méx) a comic; **la página de los monitos del periódico** (Andes, Méx) the cartoon page, the funnies (AmE colloq)

Compuestos

- **mono animado** (Chi) cartoon
- **mono de nieve** (Chi) snowman

C **mono** *m* 1 (de mecánico) coveralls (*pl*) (AmE), overalls (*pl*) (BrE) 2 (de moda — de cuerpo entero) jumpsuit; (— con peto) overalls (*pl*) (AmE), dungarees (*pl*) (BrE) 3 (Méx) (malla de bailarina) leotard

D (Audio): **en ~** in mono

E (arg) (síndrome de abstinencia) cold turkey (sl); **está con el ~** he's gone cold turkey (sl)

F (en naipes) joker

monocarril *m* monorail
monocolor *adj* one-color* (*before n*)
monocorde *adj* (Mús) monotonic; (monótono) monotonous
monocromático -ca *adj* monochromatic
monocromo -ma *adj* monochrome
monóculo *m* monocle
monocultivo *m* monoculture
monodia *f* monody
monofásico -ca *adj* single-phase
monogamia *f* monogamy
monógamo[1] -ma *adj* monogamous
monógamo[2] -ma *m,f* monogamist
monografía *f* monograph
monográfico -ca *adj* monographic
monograma *m* monogram
monolingüe *adj* monolingual
monolítico -ca *adj* monolithic
monolito *m* monolith
monologar [A3] *vi* (Teatr) to soliloquize; (hablar mucho) to hold forth; (hablar consigo mismo) to talk to oneself
monólogo *m* monologue
monomanía *f* (Psic) monomania; (obsesión) (fam) obsession, mania
monomio *m* monomial
monono -na *adj* (CS fam) divine (colloq)
mononucleosis *m* mononucleosis; **mononucleosis infecciosa** glandular fever, infectious mononucleosis
monoparental *adj* (frml): **familias ~es** one-parent families
monopatín *m* (con manillar) (CS) scooter; (sin manillar) (Esp) skateboard
monoplano *m* monoplane
monoplaza *adj/m* single-seater
monopolio *m* monopoly
monopolización *f* monopolization
monopolizar [A4] *vt* to monopolize; **~ la atención de algn** to monopolize sb's attention
monorriel *m* (AmL) monorail
monosilábico -ca, **monosílabo -ba** *adj* monosyllabic
monosílabo *m* monosyllable; **respondió con ~s** she answered in monosyllables
monoteísmo *m* monotheism
monotipo *m* Monotype®
monotonía *f* (de una tarea) monotony; (de un sonido) monotone
monótono -na *adj* 1 ‹*vida/trabajo*› monotonous, humdrum; ‹*discurso/espectáculo*› monotonous, tedious 2 ‹*voz*› monotonous
monousuario -ria *adj* single-user (*before n*)
monovalente *adj* monovalent, univalent
monóxido *m* monoxide; **~ de carbono** carbon monoxide
monrero -ra *m,f* (Andes) burglar
Mons. *m* (= **monseñor**) Msgr.
monseñor *m* Monsignor
monstruo[1] *m* (Mit) monster; (persona) monster; (fenómeno) phenomenon; **un ~ de la música pop** a pop phenomenon
monstruo[2] *adj inv* (fam) fantastic (colloq)
monstruosidad *f* 1 (cosa fea, grande) monstrosity 2 (atrocidad) atrocity 3 (cualidad) monstrous nature, monstrousness
monstruoso -sa *adj* 1 ‹*crimen/comportamiento*› monstrous, atrocious 2 ‹*dimensiones*› monstrous 3 (deforme, anormal) ‹*ser/facciones*› hideous, grotesque
monta *f*
A (monto) total (value); ***de poca ~*** ‹*asunto*› of little importance *o* note; ‹*escritor*› third-rate; **los daños materiales fueron de poca ~** the damage was slight *o* minor
B (period) (caballo) mount; (jinete) rider
montacargas *m* (*pl* ~) freight *o* service elevator (AmE), service *o* goods lift (BrE)

montado -da *adj*: **iba ~ a caballo** he was riding a horse; **la policía montada** the mounted police; **estaba montada en su bicicleta** she was sitting on her bicycle; *ver tb* **montar**
montador -dora *m,f* (Mec, Tec) fitter; (Cin, TV) film editor
(Compuesto) **montador -dora de escena** *m,f* set designer
montaje *m* 1 (de máquina, mueble) assembly; **el ~ de la red** the setting up of the network 2 (de obra) staging; (de película) editing; **seguro que todo es un ~** I bet it's all a big frame-up *o* a set-up (colloq)
(Compuesto) **montaje fotográfico** photomontage
montallantas *m* (*pl* ~) (Col) (taller) *workshop where tires* are retreaded*; (mecánico) *person who retreads tires**
montante *m*
A (Fin) total (amount)
B (Const) 1 (soporte) upright, post; (de una ventana) mullion 2 (ventana) transom, fanlight
montaña *f*
A 1 (Geog) mountain; **tienen un chalet en la ~** they have a chalet in the mountains; ***hacer una ~ de un grano de arena*** to make a mountain out of a molehill; ***si la ~ no viene a Mahoma, Mahoma va a la ~*** if the mountain will not come to Mohammed, Mohammed must go to the mountain 2 (Chi) (monte) scrubland
(Compuestos)
- **montaña rusa** roller coaster
- **Montañas Rocosas** *or* **Rocallosas** *fpl*: **las ~ ~** the Rocky mountains (*pl*)

B (montón) pile
montañero -ra *m,f* mountaineer, mountain climber
montañés[1] -ñesa *adj* mountain (*before n*), highland (*before n*)
montañés[2] -ñesa *m,f* highlander
montañismo *m* mountaineering, mountain climbing
montañoso -sa *adj* ‹*cadena*› mountain (*before n*); ‹*terreno/país*› mountainous
montaplatos *m* (*pl* ~) dumbwaiter
montar [A1] *vt*
A 1 ‹*caballo*› (subirse a) to mount, get on; (ir sobre) to ride 2 (subir, colocar): **montó al niño en el poni** he lifted the boy up onto the pony
B ‹*vaca/yegua*› to mount
C 1 (poner, establecer) ‹*feria/exposición*› to set up; ‹*negocio*› to start up, set up 2 ‹*máquina/mueble*› to assemble; ‹*estantería*› to put up; **¿me ayudas a ~ la tienda de campaña?** can you help me to put up *o* pitch the tent? 3 ‹*piedra preciosa*› to set; ‹*diapositiva*› to mount 4 (organizar) ‹*obra/producción*› to stage; **~ *un número*** *or* ***lío*** *or* ***escándalo*** (Esp) to make *o* cause a scene
D 1 ‹*puntos*› to cast on 2 ‹*pistola*› to cock
E (Esp) ‹*nata*› to whip; ‹*claras*› to whisk
■ **montar** *vi*
A 1 (ir): **~ a caballo/en bicicleta** to ride a horse/bicycle 2 (Equ) to mount
B (cubrir parcialmente) **~ SOBRE algo** to overlap sth
C (sumar, importar) **~ A algo** to amount TO sth
■ **montarse** *v pron*
A (en un coche) to get in; (en un tren, autobús) to get on; (en un caballo) to mount, get on; **¿me dejas ~me en tu bicicleta?** can I have a ride on your bicycle?; **~se en las atracciones de una feria** to go on the rides in a fairground
B (arreglárselas) (Esp fam): **¡qué bien te lo montas!** you're on to a good thing (colloq); **no sé cómo se lo monta** I don't know how she manages it
montaraz *adj* ‹*animal*› wild; ‹*persona*› (tosco) coarse; (arisco) surly, unfriendly
monte *m*
A (Geog) 1 (montaña) mountain 2 (terreno — cubierto de maleza) scrubland, scrub; (— cubierto de árboles) woodland; ***batir el ~*** to beat (*for game*); ***echarse*** *or* ***tirarse al ~*** to take to the hills; ***no todo (en) el ~ es orégano*** life isn't all a bowl of cherries 3 (Ven fam) (campo): **vive en el ~** he lives out in the sticks *o* the wilds (colloq) 4 (RPl) (bosquecillo) copse, coppice

m

Compuestos
- **monte alto/bajo** forest/scrubland
- **monte de piedad** pawnshop

B (en naipes) 1 (juego) monte 2 (en el tute) last trick
C (AmC, Col, Ven fam) (marihuana) grass (colloq)

montepío *m*
A (monte de piedad) pawnshop
B 1 (mutualidad) fund (*collected by a benefit society for its members*) 2 (pensión) pension 3 (Chi) (de huérfano, viuda) dependent's pension

montera *f* (gorra) cap; (de torero) bullfighter's hat

montería *f* hunting (*of deer, wild boar, etc*)

montero -ra *m,f* 1 (cazador) hunter (*of deer, wild boar, etc*); **~ mayor** master of the hunt 2 (ojeador) beater

montés *adj* wild

montevideano -na *adj* of/from Montevideo

Montevideo *m* Montevideo

montgomery *m* (CS) duffle coat

montículo *m* mound

montilla *m*: *type of pale, dry sherry*

montón *m* 1 (pila) pile; ***(ser) del ~*** (fam): **un estudiante de los del ~** an average student; **es un escritor de los del ~** he's a rather run-of-the-mill writer; **es una chica del ~** she's (just) an ordinary girl 2 (fam) (gran cantidad): **había un ~ de gente** there were loads of people (colloq); **me duele un ~** it hurts like hell (colloq); **me gusta un ~** I'm crazy about her/it (colloq)

montonera *f*
A (fam) (montón): **una ~ de gente** masses *o* loads of people (colloq); ***tirar algo a la ~*** (Col) to throw sth into the crowd
B (Hist) peasant militia

montonero -ra *m,f* (guerrillero) guerrilla; **los M~s** *Argentinian guerrilla movement*

montura *f*
A (Equ) (silla) saddle; (animal) mount
B (de anteojos) frame; (engarce) setting, mount

monumental *adj*
A (Arquit): **la riqueza ~ de la ciudad** the wealth of monuments in the city
B (fam) (muy grande) 1 (en tamaño) huge, massive 2 (en grado) monumental
C (fam) (estupendo) fabulous (colloq)

monumento *m*
A (obra conmemorativa) monument; **~ a los caídos** war memorial

Compuestos
- **monumento funerario** commemorative stone
- **monumento histórico/nacional** historical/national monument

B (Relig) altar (*decorated for Holy Week*)
C (obra excepcional) masterpiece, classic; **un ~ de la épica española** a classic example of the Spanish epic
D (fam) (mujer atractiva) stunner (colloq)

monzón *m* monsoon

monzónico -ca *adj* monsoon (*before n*)

moña *f* (Taur) ribbon; (lazo) (RPl) bow

moñita *f* (Ur) bow tie

moño *m* 1 (peinado) bun; **se hizo un ~** she put her hair up in a bun; ***agarrarse del ~*** (fam) to go for each other's throats (colloq); **terminaron agarrándose del ~** they ended up at each other's throats (colloq); ***estar hasta el ~*** to be fed up (to the back teeth) (colloq); ***soltarse el ~*** (fam) to let one's hair down 2 (AmL) (lazo) bow

moñona *f* (Col) strike; **hacer ~** to get a strike

moquear [A1] *vi* «*nariz*» to run; «*persona*» to have a runny nose

moqueo *m* runny nose

moquera *f* (CS fam): **tener ~** to have a sniffle

moquero *m* (fam & hum) snot rag (colloq & hum), hankie (colloq)

moqueta *f* (Esp) wall-to-wall carpet, fitted carpet (BrE)

moquete *m* (fam) punch (*in the face*)

moquette /mo'ket/ *f* (RPl) wall-to-wall carpet, fitted carpet (BrE)

moquillento -ta *adj* (Andes fam) (resfriado) coldy (colloq); (con mocos) ‹*nariz*› runny, snotty (colloq); ‹*niño*› runny-nosed, snotty-nosed (colloq)

moquillo *m* distemper

mor: **por ~ de** (*loc prep*) (frml) because of, out of consideration for (frml)

mora *f*
A (fruto — de zarzamora) blackberry; (— de moral) mulberry; (— de morera) white mulberry
B (Der) (retraso) default

morada *f* (frml *o* liter) 1 (residencia, hogar) dwelling (frml), abode (frml *or* liter); **la última ~** the final resting place 2 (estancia): **hacer ~ en un lugar** to stay in a place

morado[1] **-da** *adj* ‹*color*› purple; **~ del frío** blue with cold; **ponerle a algn un ojo ~** to give sb a black eye; ***pasarlas*** *or* ***verlas moradas*** (Esp) to have a hard *o* tough time; ***ponerse ~ de algo*** (Esp fam) to stuff oneself with sth (colloq)

morado[2] *m* (Esp, Ven) bruise

morador -dora *m,f* (liter) inhabitant

moral[1] *adj* moral; **apoyo ~** moral support

moral[2] *m* mulberry (tree)

moral[3] *f*
A (Fil, Relig) 1 (doctrina) moral doctrine; **la ~ cristiana** the Christian doctrine 2 (moralidad) morality, morals (*pl*); **faltar a la ~** to commit an immoral act
B 1 (estado de ánimo) morale; **levantarle la ~ a algn** to raise sb's morale, lift sb's spirits; **tener mucha ~** to be very optimistic; **estar bajo de ~** to be feeling low; **quedaron con la ~ por los suelos** their morale hit rock bottom 2 (arrojo, determinación) will; **con una ~ de acero** with iron-willed determination

moraleja *f* moral

moralidad *f* morality, ethics (*pl*)

moralista[1] *adj* moralistic

moralista[2] *mf* moralist

moralizante *adj* moralizing (*before n*), moralistic

moralizar [A4] *vi* to moralize

morar [A1] *vi* (liter) to dwell (liter)

moratón *m* bruise

moratoria *f* moratorium

mórbido -da *adj*
A ‹*escena/historia*› gruesome; (Med) morbid
B (liter) (delicado, suave) soft, delicate

morbo *m*
A (fam) (morbosidad): **hay mucho ~ dentro del toreo** there is a lot of morbid fascination in bullfighting; **despertaba el ~ de la gente** it brought out people's ghoulish instincts; **me da ~ saber la verdad** I'm dying to know the truth
B (Med) disease

morbosidad *f* morbidity; **la ~ de la película** the morbidity *o* gruesomeness of the film; **la ~ con que contaba la historia** the relish with which she told the story

morboso[1] **-sa** *adj* 1 ‹*escena/película*› gruesome; ‹*persona/mente*› ghoulish; (truculento, retorcido) morbid 2 (Med) morbid

morboso[2] **-sa** *m,f* (fam) ghoul

morcilla *f* blood sausage (AmE), black pudding (BrE)

mordacidad *f* sharpness, causticity (liter)

mordaz *adj* ‹*estilo/lenguaje*› scathing, caustic; ‹*crítica*› sharp, scathing

mordaza *f* 1 (en la boca) gag 2 (Tec) clamp

mordedura *f* bite

morder [E9] *vt*
A 1 (con los dientes) to bite; **mordía la manzana con avidez** he was eagerly munching the apple 2 (Tec) «*lima*» to file
B (Méx fam) «*policía/funcionario*» to extract a bribe from
C (Ven fam) (captar, entender) to get
■ **morder** *vi*
A «*perro/serpiente*» to bite; ***estar que muerde*** (fam): to be hopping mad (colloq)
B (Ven fam) (entender): **no mordió** he didn't get it (colloq)
■ **morderse** *v pron* (*refl*) to bite oneself; **~se las uñas** to bite one's nails

m

mordida *f*
A (CS) (bocado) bite; (acción) bite; (huella) toothmarks (*pl*)
B (Méx fam) (soborno) bribe, backhander (BrE colloq)

mordisco *m* 1 (de animal, persona) bite; **le dio un ~ en el brazo** it bit her (on the) arm 2 (bocado) bite

mordisquear [A1] *vt* to nibble; **no mordisquees el lápiz** don't chew the pencil

morena *f*
A (Geol) moraine
B (Zool) moray (eel); *ver tb* **moreno² A**

moreno¹ -na *adj* 1 [SER] ‹*persona*› (de pelo oscuro) dark, dark-haired; (de tez oscura) dark; (de raza negra) (euf) dark-skinned (euph) 2 [ESTAR] (bronceado) brown, tanned 3 ‹*piel*› brown, dark

moreno² -na *m,f*
A 1 (persona de pelo oscuro) (*m*) dark-haired man (*o* boy *etc*); (*f*) dark-haired woman (*o* girl *etc*), brunet* 2 (persona — de tez oscura) dark person (*o* man *etc*); (— de raza negra) (euf) dark-skinned person (*o* man *etc*) (euph), coloured man (*o* woman *etc*) (BrE euph)
B moreno *m* (Esp) (bronceado) tan, suntan

morera *f* white mulberry tree

morería *f* Moorish quarter

moretón *m* bruise

morfar [A1] *vi* (RPl arg) to eat

morfema *m* morpheme

morfina *f* morphine

morfinómano -na *m,f* morphine addict

morfología *f* morphology

morganático -ca *adj* morganatic

morgue *f* (AmL) morgue, mortuary

moribundo¹ -da *adj* dying, moribund (frml)

moribundo² -da *m,f* dying man (*o* woman *etc*)

morir [I37] *vi* 1 «*persona*» to die; **~ ahogado** to drown; **murió asesinada** she was murdered; **~ DE algo** to die OF sth; **~ de vejez/de muerte natural** to die of old age/of natural causes; **murió de hambre** she starved to death; **murieron por su patria** they died for their country; **¡muera el dictador!** death to the dictator!; **¡y allí muere!** (AmC fam) and that's all there is to it!; ***hasta* ~** (Méx fam): **la fiesta va a ser hasta ~** we're going to party till we drop (colloq) 2 (liter) «*civilización/costumbre*» to die out; **cuando muere la tarde** as the day draws to a close (liter); **el río va a ~ a la mar** the river runs to the sea
■ **morirse** *v pron* to die; **se me murió la perra** my dog died; **no te vas a ~ por ayudarlo** (fam) it won't kill you to help him (colloq); **como se entere me muero** (fam) I'll die if she finds out (colloq); **¡por mí que se muera!** he can drop dead for all I care (colloq); **que me muera si miento** cross my heart and hope to die (colloq); **¡muérete! me caso el sábado** (fam) you'll never guess what! I'm getting married on Saturday! (colloq); **~se DE algo**: **se murió de un infarto** he died of a heart attack; **~ de miedo/aburrimiento** to be scared stiff/bored stiff; **me muero de frío** I'm freezing; **me estoy muriendo de hambre** I'm starving (colloq); **es para ~se de risa** it's hilariously funny; **me muero de ganas de verlos** I'm dying to see them (colloq); **~se POR algo/algn**: **me muero por una cerveza** I'm dying for a beer (colloq); **se muere por ella** he's nuts *o* crazy about her (colloq); **~se POR + INF** to be dying to + INF (colloq)

morisco¹ -ca *adj* Moorish, Morisco

morisco² -ca *m,f* Morisco (*Moorish convert to Christianity who remained in Spain after the* **Reconquista**)

morisqueta *f* (CS): **hacer ~s** to make *o* (BrE) pull faces

morlaco *m* (CS, Méx fam) (dinero): **me prestó unos ~s** she lent me some cash (colloq)

mormado -da *adj* (Méx) ‹*nariz*› blocked; **estoy ~** I'm all stuffed up *o* bunged up (colloq)

mormón -mona *adj/m,f* Mormon

moro¹ *adj*
A (Hist) Moorish
B (Esp) (de África del Norte) (fam & pey) North African; (machista) (fam) chauvinistic, sexist

moro² -ra *m,f*
A 1 (Hist) Moor; ***hay/no hay ~s en la costa*** (fam): **ya puedes salir, no hay ~s en la costa** you can come out now, the coast is clear (colloq); **cállate, hay ~s en la costa** quiet, there are people listening *o* this isn't a good moment 2 (mahometano) Muslim
B (Esp) (de África del Norte) (fam & pey) North African; (machista) (fam) sexist, male chauvinist pig

morocho¹ -cha *adj* (AmS fam) (de pelo oscuro) dark, dark-haired; (de piel oscura) dark

morocho² -cha *m,f*
A (AmS fam) (de pelo oscuro) dark-haired person (*o* man *etc*); (de piel oscura) dark person (*o* man *etc*)
B (Ven fam) (mellizo) twin

morondanga *f*: **de ~** (RPl fam) lousy (colloq)

moronga *f* (AmC, Méx) blood sausage (AmE), black pudding (BrE)

morosidad *f* (Com, Fin) (lentitud en el pago) slowness (in paying); (deudas) arrears (*pl*)

moroso¹ -sa *adj*: **cuentas morosas** delinquent accounts; ▸**deudor²**

moroso² -sa *m,f* doubtful debtor

morrada *f* ▸**morrón A**

morral *m* 1 (que cuelga — del hombro) rucksack, haversack; (— a la espalda) backpack, rucksack 2 (para el pienso) nosebag

morralla *f*
A 1 (Coc) small fish *o* fry (*pl*) 2 (cosas sin valor) junk
B (chusma) riffraff, rabble
C (Méx) (dinero suelto) loose change

morrear [A1] *vi* (Esp, Méx fam) to neck (colloq)

morrena *f* moraine

morreo *m* (Esp fam) necking (colloq)

morriña *f* (fam) homesickness; **tener ~** to feel *o* be homesick

morro *m*
A 1 (hocico) snout 2 (Esp fam) (boca) *th* **morros** mouth, chops (*pl*) (BrE colloq); **límpiate ese ~** wipe your mouth (colloq); ***beber a ~s*** (Esp fam) to drink (straight) from the bottle; ***estar de ~s (con algn)*** (Esp fam) to be in a bad mood (with sb) 3 (Esp fam) (descaro) nerve (colloq); ***echarle ~*** (Esp fam) to stick one's neck out (colloq); ***por el ~*** (Esp fam) (sin pagar) without paying; (con descaro): **llegó y me pidió dinero por el ~** he had the gall to ask me for money (colloq) 4 (Esp fam) (de coche, avión) nose
B (cerro) hill

morrocota *f* (Col, Ven) *gold coin weighing one ounce*; ***cuidar las ~s*** (fam) to be careful with one's money

morrocotudo -da *adj* (fam) ‹*paliza/susto*› terrible (colloq); (estupendo) fantastic (colloq)

morrón *m*
A (fam) (golpe): **se dio un ~** he fell flat on his face
B (CS) (pimiento) red pepper

morsa *f* walrus

morse¹ *adj inv* Morse (*before n*)

morse² *m* Morse code

mortadela *f* mortadella

mortaja *f*
A (sábana) shroud
B (Tec) mortise

mortal¹ *adj*
A 1 ‹*ser*› mortal 2 ‹*herida*› fatal, mortal; ‹*dosis*› fatal, lethal; ‹*enfermedad/veneno*› deadly; **la caída/el accidente fue ~** the fall/accident killed him *o* caused his death; **un golpe ~** a death blow
B 1 ‹*odio/enemigo*› mortal 2 ‹*aburrimiento*›: **fue un aburrimiento ~** it was lethally (AmE) *o* (BrE) deadly boring

mortal² *mf* mortal

mortalidad *f* mortality

mortalmente *adv*
A (de muerte) mortally, fatally
B (en sentido hiperbólico): **se odian ~** they hate each other bitterly; **se enemistaron ~** they became deadly *o* bitter *o* (liter) mortal enemies

mortandad *f* 1 (por causas naturales) loss of life 2 (en batalla) slaughter, carnage

mortecino¹ -na *adj* ‹*luz*› weak; ‹*color*› pale

mortecino² *m* (Col, Ven) carrion

mortero *m* mortar

mortífero -ra *adj* deadly, lethal

mortificación *f* [1] (tormento): **verlo tan feliz era una ~ para ella** it was torture *o* hell for her to see him so happy [2] (Relig) mortification

mortificar [A2] *vt* [1] (atormentar) to torment; **los celos lo mortifican** he's tortured *o* tormented by jealousy [2] (Relig) to mortify

▪ **mortificarse** *v pron* (*refl*) (atormentarse) to fret, distress oneself; (Relig) to mortify the flesh

mortuorio -ria *adj* funeral (*before n*)

mosaico[1] -ca *adj* Mosaic, Mosaical

mosaico[2] *m* [1] (Art) mosaic [2] (Méx, RPl) (baldosa) floor tile; **piso de ~** tiled floor [3] (Col) (foto) school/college photograph

mosca[1] *adj inv* [1] (Esp fam) (preocupado) uneasy, edgy (colloq); (enfadado) sore (AmE colloq), cross (BrE colloq) [2] (Ven fam) (alerta) alert

mosca[2] *f*

A [1] (Zool) fly; **no se oía ni una ~** you could have heard a pin drop (colloq); ***caer como ~s*** to drop *o* fall like flies; ***es incapaz de matar una ~*** she wouldn't harm *o* hurt a fly; ***estar con la ~ en*** *or* ***detrás de la oreja*** to be wary, be on one's guard; ***papar ~s*** (fam) to mooch around (colloq); ***por si las ~s*** (fam) just in case (colloq); ***¿qué ~ te/le ha picado?*** (fam) what's got into *o* what's up with you/him? (colloq); ***sentirse como ~ en leche*** (Andes fam) to feel like a fish out of water; ***venir*** *or* ***acudir como ~s*** to swarm round like flies; *ver tb* **mosquita** [2] (para pescar) fly

(Compuesto) **mosca tsé-tsé** *or* **tsetsé** tsetse fly

B (Esp fam) (dinero) dough (colloq); **afloja la ~** cough up (colloq)

mosca[3] *mf* (Ur fam) freeloader (colloq), sponger (BrE colloq)

moscarda *f* blowfly, bluebottle

moscardón *m* [1] (Zool) botfly [2] (fam) (charlatán) chatterbox (colloq)

moscatel[1] *adj* muscat (*before n*)

moscatel[2] *m* muscatel

moscón *m* [1] (Zool) botfly [2] (fam) (hombre) creep (colloq)

moscovita *adj/mf* Muscovite

Moscú *m* Moscow

mosqueado -da *adj* (esp Esp fam) [1] (molesto, disgustado) annoyed, sore (AmE colloq), cross (BrE colloq) [2] (desconfiado, suspicaz) suspicious, wary

mosquear [A1] *vt* (esp Esp fam) [1] (disgustar) to annoy [2] (hacer sospechar) ‹*persona*› to make … suspicious

▪ **mosquearse** *v pron* (esp Esp fam) [1] (sospechar, desconfiar) to get suspicious, smell a rat (colloq) [2] (disgustarse) to get annoyed, get sore (AmE colloq), to get cross (BrE colloq)

mosqueo *m* (esp Esp fam): **menudo ~ agarró** he was *o* got really annoyed

mosquerío *m* (fam) flies (*pl*)

mosquero *m* (Méx) ▸ **mosquerío**

mosquete *m* musket

mosquetero *m* musketeer

mosquetón *m* (Arm) musket

mosquita *f*: ***ser*** *or* ***parecer una ~ muerta*** to look as if butter wouldn't melt in one's mouth

mosquitero *m*, **mosquitera** *f* (de ventana) mosquito netting; (de tela) mosquito net

mosquito *m* mosquito

mostacho *m* (fam & hum) mustache*, 'tache (colloq & hum)

mostaza *f* [1] (Coc) mustard; ***me/le subió la ~*** (CS fam) I/he got all hot under the collar (colloq) [2] **(de) color ~** mustard, mustard-colored*

mosto *m* grape juice, must

mostrador *m* (en tienda) counter; (en bar) bar; (en aeropuerto) check-in desk

mostrar [A10] *vt* [1] (enseñar, indicar) to show; **muéstrame cómo funciona** show me how it works [2] ‹*interés/entusiasmo*› to show, display (frml)

▪ **mostrarse** *v pron* (+ *compl*): **se mostró muy atento con nosotros** he was very obliging (to us); **se mostró muy contento** he was very happy; **se ~on partidarios de la propuesta** they expressed support for the proposal; **nunca se ha mostrado agresivo con él** she's never displayed *o* shown any aggression toward(s) him

mostrenco[1] -ca *adj* (tonto) oafish

mostrenco[2] -ca *m,f* oaf

mota *f*

A (partícula) tiny bit, dot; **una ~ de polvo** a speck of dust

B (Tex) [1] (lunar) small spot; **una tela a ~s** a spotted fabric [2] (jaspeado) fleck [3] (Andes) (bolita de lana) ball, bobble [4] (Méx) (borla) pom-pom, bobble

C (AmS) (pelo) tight curls (*pl*)

D (AmC, Méx arg) (marihuana) grass (colloq), weed (sl)

E (Méx) (para empolvarse) powder puff

F (Per) (borrador de pizarrón) blackboard duster

mote *m*

A (apodo) nickname; **le pusieron como ~ 'el Oso'** they nicknamed him 'the Bear'

B (Andes) (trigo) boiled wheat; (maíz) boiled corn (AmE) *o* (BrE) maize

moteado -da *adj* ‹*tela*› (jaspeado) flecked; (a lunares) dotted, spotted; ‹*piel*› mottled; **los cerros ~s de blanco** (liter) the hills dotted with white (liter)

motear [A1] *vt* (liter) to speckle, dot

▪ **motearse** *v pron* (Col) to become covered in little balls of fluff

motejar [A1] *vt* **~ a algn DE algo** to brand sb sth

motel *m* motel

motero -ra *m,f* (fam) biker (colloq)

motín *m* (de tropas, una tripulación) mutiny; (de prisioneros) riot, rebellion

motivación *f* (incentivo) motivation; (motivo) motive

motivador -dora *adj* motivating

motivar [A1] *vt*

A (impulsar) to motivate; **¿qué te motivó a hacerlo?** what made you do it?; **motivado por la venganza** motivated by revenge

B (causar) to bring about; **el factor que motivó su derrota** the cause of *o* the reason for his defeat

motivo *m*

A [1] (razón, causa) reason, cause; **el ~ de su viaje/del accidente** the reason for her trip/the cause of the accident; **por este ~ nos hallamos aquí reunidos** that's (the reason) why we're gathered here; **yo tendré mis ~s** I have my reasons; **con ~ de algo** on the occasion of sth; **con ~ del centenario** to mark the centenary; **dar ~s para algo** to give grounds for sth; **no des ~s para que te critiquen** don't give them cause to criticize you; **hay ~s para preocuparse** there is cause for concern; **el adulterio es ~ suficiente de divorcio** adultery is sufficient grounds for divorce; **por ~s personales** for personal reasons; **sin ningún ~** for no reason at all; **sin ~ justificado** without (good) cause; ***¡que sea un ~!*** (Col fam) let's drink to that! (colloq) [2] (propósito, finalidad) reason, purpose; **¿con qué ~ se convocó la reunión?** what was the purpose of calling the meeting?; **empiezo a sospechar de sus ~s** I'm beginning to suspect his motives; **el ~ de esta carta es ...** the purpose of this letter is ...

B (Art, Lit, Mús) motif; **~s decorativos** decorative motifs

moto *f* (motocicleta) motorcycle, motorbike (BrE); (motoneta, escúter) (motor) scooter; **fue en ~** he went on his motorcycle

(Compuestos)

- **moto acuática** jet ski
- **moto de nieve** snowmobile

motobomba *f* (motorized) pump

motocarro *m* three-wheeler van

motocicleta *f* motorcycle

motociclismo *m* motorcycling

motociclista *mf* motorcyclist

motocross, moto-cross *m* motocross

motoesquí *m* (*pl* **-quís** *or* **-quíes**) motorized ski

motola *f* (Col fam) head, nut (colloq)

motonáutica *f* motorboating

motonave *f* (pequeña) motorboat; (grande) motor ship, motor vessel

motoneta *f* (AmL) (motor) scooter

motonieve *f* snowmobile

motoniveladora *f* grader

motor[1] -triz, motor -tora *adj* motor (*before n*)

motor² *m*
A (Tec) engine; **funciona con** *or* **a ~** it is motor-driven
(Compuestos)
• **motor a inyección/a reacción** fuel-injected/jet engine
• **motor de arranque** starter motor
• **motor de combustión interna** *or* **de explosión** internal combustion engine
• **motor diesel/hidráulico** diesel/hydraulic engine
• **motor fuera (de) borda** outboard motor
B (impulsor) driving force

motora *f* small motorboat, powerboat
motorismo *m* motorcycling
motorista *mf* 1 (que va en moto) motorcyclist 2 (Col) (automovilista) motorist (frml), driver
motorización *f* (acción): **la ~ de la población** the increase in car ownership
motorizado¹ -da *adj* ‹*ejército*› motorized; **hoy no ando ~** (fam) I don't have any transport today
motorizado² -da *m,f* (Ven) motorcycle messenger *o* (BrE) courier
motorizar [A4] *vt* to motorize
■ **motorizarse** *v pron* (fam) to get oneself some wheels (colloq), to get mobile (colloq)
motosegadora *f* motor mower
motosierra *f* chain saw
motoso¹ -sa *adj* (Col) ‹*suéter/bufanda*› flecked; ‹*pelo*› frizzy
motoso² *m* (Col fam) nap (colloq)
motricidad *f* motor functions (*pl*)
motriz *adj*: *ver* **motor¹**
motudo -da *adj* (CS fam) frizzy
motu proprio *loc adv*: **lo hizo (de) ~ ~** he did it on his own initiative
mousse /mus/ *f or m* mousse
mouton /mu'ton/ *m* sheepskin
movedizo -za *adj* ‹*niño*› restless, fidgety; ▸**arena A**
mover [E9] *vt*
A 1 (trasladar, desplazar) to move 2 (Jueg) ‹*ficha/pieza*› to move 3 (menear) ‹*cola*› to wag; ‹*caderas*› to wriggle; **no muevas la cámara** keep the camera still; **el viento movía las hojas de los árboles** the wind shook the leaves on the trees; **movió la cabeza** (asintiendo) he nodded (his head); (negando) she shook her head 4 (accionar) to drive; **el agua mueve la rueda del molino** the water turns the millwheel 5 (manejar) ‹*dinero*› to handle 6 (fam) ‹*droga*› to push (colloq)
B (incitar, inducir): **actuó movida por razones políticas** her actions were politically motivated; **¿qué lo movió a hacer eso?** what moved him to do that?
■ **mover** *vi*
A (Jueg) to move
B (incitar, inducir) **~ A algo**: **su situación mueve a la compasión** his predicament moves one to pity
■ **moverse** *v pron*
A 1 (desplazarse) to move; **no te muevas de ahí** stay right where you are, don't move 2 (menearse) to move; **dejá de ~te** stop fidgeting, stop moving about; **la lámpara se movía con el viento** the lamp was moving *o* swaying in the wind
B 1 (alternar) to move; **se mueve en las altas esferas** she moves in high circles 2 (hacer gestiones): **si no te mueves no encontrarás empleo** if you don't get moving you'll never find a job (colloq); **se movió como loca para sacarlo de la cárcel** she moved heaven and earth to get him out of jail 3 (apresurarse) to hurry up, get a move on (colloq)
movida *f*
A (Jueg) move
B (Esp) 1 (fam) (asunto, rollo): **no me interesa la ~ ecológica** I'm not into this ecology thing (colloq); **la ~ pacifista de los sesenta** the sixties' peace movement; **al chico le va la ~** he's really into the scene (colloq); **anda en ~s chuecas** (Méx) he's into some shady deals (colloq) 2 (actividad cultural): **la ~ madrileña** the Madrid scene; **allí es donde está la ~** that's where it's all going on
movido -da *adj* 1 (Fot) blurred 2 (agitado) ‹*mar*› rough, choppy; ‹*día/año*› hectic, busy; ‹*fiesta*› lively

móvil¹ *adj* mobile
móvil² *m*
A (frml) (impulso) motive 2 (adorno) mobile
B 1 (Fís) moving object 2 (Tel) mobile phone
movilidad *f* mobility
(Compuesto) **movilidad ascendente/social** upward/social mobility
movilización *f*
A 1 (Mil) mobilization 2 (Rels Labs): **movilizaciones obreras** protests *o* demonstrations by the workers; **han planeado un calendario de movilizaciones** they have planned a program of industrial action
B (Chi) (Transp) public transportation (AmE), public transport (BrE)
movilizar [A4] *vt*
A ‹*tropas/población*› to mobilize
B (desbloquear) to free, unblock
■ **movilizarse** *v pron*
A (Mil, Rels Labs) to mobilize
B (CS) (desplazarse) to move *o* get around
movimiento *m*
A 1 (Fís, Tec) motion, movement; **un cuerpo en ~** a body in motion; **poner algo en ~** to set sth in motion; **se puso en ~** it started moving 2 (desplazamiento) movement; **el ~ migratorio de las aves** the migratory movement of birds 3 (cambio de postura, posición) movement; **un ~ en falso** one false move; **el menor ~ de la mano** the slightest movement of the hand; **caminaba con un ligero ~ de caderas** her hips swayed slightly as she walked
(Compuestos)
• **movimiento de rotación** rotation
• **movimiento de traslación** orbital movement
• **movimiento sísmico** earth tremor
B 1 (traslado — de dinero, bienes) movement; (— de la población) shift 2 (variación, cambio) movement, change 3 (agitación, actividad) activity
C 1 (corriente, tendencia) movement; **el ~ surrealista** the surrealist movement; **~ pictórico** school of painting 2 (organización) movement
D (alzamiento) uprising, rebellion
E (Mús) (parte de obra) movement; (compás) tempo
F (Jueg) move
moviola® *f* (aparato) Moviola®; (repetición) action replay
moyo *m* (Col) flower (pot)
mozalbete *m* lad
mozárabe¹ *adj* Mozarabic
mozárabe² *mf* Mozarab
mozo¹ -za *adj*: **en mis años ~s** in my youth; **sus hijos ya son ~s** her children are quite grown-up now
mozo² -za *m,f* 1 (ant) (joven) (*m*) young boy; (*f*) young girl; **los ~s del pueblo** the young people in the village 2 (AmS) (camarero) (*m*) waiter; (*f*) waitress 3 (Col fam) (amante) (*m*) fancy man (colloq); (*f*) fancy woman (colloq) 4 (Ferr) *tb* **~ de equipajes** *or* **de estación** porter
(Compuestos)
• **mozo -za de cuadra** (*m*) stable boy, stable lad (BrE); (*f*) stable girl
• **mozo de estoques** *bullfighter's assistant*
ms. (*pl* **mss.**) (**= manuscrito**) ms
Mtro. *m*
A **= maestro**
B **= ministro**
mu *m* moo; ***no decir ni ~*** (fam): **no digas ni ~** not a word (to anyone) (colloq); **no dijo ni ~ en toda la noche** he didn't open his mouth *o* say a word all evening
muaré *m* moiré
muca *adj* (Per fam) broke (colloq)
mucamo -ma (AmL) (*m*) servant; (*f*) maid, servant
(Compuesto) **mucama de hotel** *f* (AmL) chambermaid
muchacha *f*: *tb* **~ de servicio** maid; *ver tb* **muchacho**
muchachada *f* (fam) kids (*pl*) (colloq)
muchacho -cha *m,f* (jóven) (*m*) kid (colloq), boy, guy (colloq); (*f*) girl; **es un buen ~** he's a good kid
muchedumbre *f* crowd

m

mucho[1] *adv* [1] ‹*salir/ayudar*› a lot; **me gusta muchísimo** I like it/her/him very much *o* a lot; **funciona ~ mejor** it works much *o* a lot better; **trabaja ~** he works very hard; **¿llueve ~?** is it raining hard?; **por ~ que insistas** no matter how much you insist; **después de ~ discutir** after long discussions [2] (en respuestas): **¿estás preocupado? — mucho** are you worried? — (yes, I am,) very; **¿te gusta? — sí, ~** do you like it? — yes, very much; *para locs ver* **mucho**[3] **C**

mucho[2] **-cha** *adj*

A [1] (*sing*) a lot of; (en negativas e interrogativas) much, a lot of; **¿tienes mucha hambre?** are you very hungry? [2] (*pl*) a lot of; (en negativas e interrogativas) many, a lot of; **¿recibiste ~s regalos?** did you get many *o* a lot of presents?

B (*sing*) [1] (fam) (con valor plural): **~ elogio pero no me lo van a publicar** they're full of praise but they're not going to publish it; **hay ~ sinvergüenza por ahí** there are a lot of rogues around [2] (fam) (con valor ponderativo): **era ~ jugador para un equipo así** he was much too good a player for a team like that

mucho[3] **-cha** *pron*

A (refiriéndose a cantidad, número): **~ de lo que ha dicho** much *o* a lot of what he has said; **somos ~s** there are a lot of us; **tengo ~ que hacer** I have a lot to do; **si no es ~ pedir** if it's not too much to ask; **~s creen que ...** many (people) believe that ...

B **mucho** (refiriéndose a tiempo) a long time; **hace ~ que no lo vemos** we haven't seen him for a long time; **¿falta ~ para llegar?** are we nearly there?; **¿tuviste que esperar ~?** did you have to wait long?

C (*en locs*) **como mucho** at (the) most; **con mucho** by far, easily; **ni mucho menos** in no way; **no es un buen pianista ni ~ menos** he isn't a good pianist, far from it

mucosa *f* mucus

mucosidad *f* mucus, mucosity

mucoso -sa *adj* mucous, mucose

muda *f* (de ropa) change of clothes; (de la piel) shedding, sloughing off

mudanza *f* move (AmE), removal (BrE); **camión de ~s** moving (AmE) *o* (BrE) removal van; **estoy de ~** I'm in the process of moving (house); **se perdió una caja en la ~** one box was lost in the move

mudar [A1] *vi*

A (cambiar) **~ DE algo**: **las serpientes mudan de piel** snakes slough off *o* shed their skin; **cuando mudó de voz** when his voice broke; **~ de opinión** (liter) to have a change of opinion

B (Méx) (cambiar los dientes): **ha empezado a ~** she's started to lose her milk teeth

■ **mudar** *vt*

A ‹*bebé/sábanas*› to change

B [1] (Zool) ‹*piel/plumas*› to molt, shed; **está mudando el pelo** it's shedding (its fur), it's moulting (BrE) [2] (Fisiol): **cuando haya mudado la voz** when his voice has broken

■ **mudarse** *v pron* [1] (de casa) to move (house); **se ~on a una casa más grande** they moved to a bigger house [2] (de ropa) to get changed, change (one's) clothes

mudéjar *adj/mf* Mudejar

mudo[1] **-da** *adj* [1] (Med) dumb, mute; **es ~ de nacimiento** he was born mute; **se quedó ~ de asombro** he was dumbfounded; **~ de emoción** speechless with emotion [2] ‹*letra*› silent, mute

mudo[2] **-da** *m,f* mute

mueble *m* piece of furniture; **un ~ antiguo** a piece of antique furniture; **los ~s del dormitorio** the bedroom furniture

(Compuestos)

- **mueble bar** drinks cabinet, cocktail cabinet
- **mueble cama** foldaway bed
- **mueble de cocina** piece of kitchen furniture

mueblería *f* [1] (tienda) furniture store (AmE) *o* (BrE) shop [2] (fábrica) furniture factory

mueca *f*: **le hacían ~s al profesor** they were making *o* (BrE) pulling faces at the teacher; **sus graciosísimas ~s** her funny faces; **su rostro se retorció en una ~ de dolor** she grimaced with pain; **una ~ burlona** a sneer

muecín *m* muezzin

mueco -ca *adj* (Col) gap-toothed

muégano *m* (en Méx) *caramel-covered candy*

muela *f*

A (Odont) molar, back tooth; (como término genérico) tooth; **me sacaron una ~** I had a tooth taken out; **tengo dolor de ~s** I have (a) toothache; ***tener/ser buena ~*** (Col fam): **tiene/es buena ~** he really enjoys his food

(Compuesto) **muela del juicio** wisdom tooth

B (de molino) millstone; (para afilar) whetstone

C (Geog) hill, mound

D (Col) (en calle) parking bay; (en carretera) rest stop (AmE), lay-by (BrE)

muelle[1] *adj* comfortable

muelle[2] *m*

A [1] (Náut) (saliente) pier, mole; (rústico, más pequeño) jetty; (sobre la costa) quay, wharf [2] (Ferr) freight platform; (para camiones) loading bay

B (resorte) spring

(Compuesto) **muelle real** mainspring

muera, mueras, etc *see* **morir**

muérdago *m* mistletoe

muérgano[1] **-na** *adj* (Col, Ven fam) mean (colloq), nasty (colloq)

muérgano[2] **-na** *m,f* (Col, Ven fam) mean brute

muermo *m* (Esp fam) [1] (aburrimiento) boredom; (persona aburrida) bore; (sitio aburrido) boring dump (colloq) [2] (apatía): **vaya ~ que tienes** you're so apathetic

muerte *f* [1] (de ser vivo) death; **~ natural/repentina** natural/sudden death; **el veneno le produjo la ~** the poison killed him; **condenado a ~** sentenced to death; **amenaza de ~** death threat; **a la ~ de su padre** on her father's death; **herido de ~** fatally wounded; **me dio un susto de ~** (fam) she scared the living daylights out of me (colloq), she scared me to death (colloq); **odiar a ~** to loathe, detest; ***cada ~ de obispo*** (AmL fam) once in a blue moon; ***de mala ~*** (fam) ‹*pensión*› grotty (colloq), cheesy (AmE colloq); **un pueblo de mala ~** a dump (colloq), a really grotty place; ***ser de ~ lenta*** (Ven fam) to be fantastic (colloq); ***ser la ~*** (fam) (ser atroz) to be hell *o* murder (colloq); (ser estupendo) to be great *o* fantastic (colloq) [2] (homicidio): **lo acusan de la ~ de tres personas** he is accused of killing three people; **dar ~ a algn** (frml) to kill sb [3] (fin) death

(Compuestos)

- **muerte cerebral** brain death
- **muerte clínica**: **cuando certificaron la ~ ~** when he was pronounced clinically dead
- **muerte de cuna** crib death (AmE), cot death (BrE)
- **muerte súbita** (de adulto) sudden death; (de bebé) crib death (AmE), cot death (BrE); (en fútbol, etc) sudden death; (en tenis) tiebreaker, tiebreak

muerto[1] **-ta** *adj*

A [ESTAR] [1] ‹*persona/animal/planta*› dead; **resultaron ~s 30 mineros** 30 miners died *o* were killed; **lo dieron por ~** he was given up for dead; **~ *y enterrado*** dead and buried, over and done with (colloq); ***ni ~*** *or* ***muerta*** no way (colloq), no chance (colloq) [2] (fam) (cansado) dead beat (colloq) [3] (fam) (pasando, padeciendo) **~ DE algo**: **estar ~ de hambre/frío/sueño** to be starving/freezing/dead-tired (colloq); **estaba ~ de miedo** he was scared stiff (colloq); ***~ de (la) risa*** (fam): **estaba ~ de risa** he was laughing his head off

B (*como pp*) (period): **fue ~ a tiros** he was shot dead; **las dos personas muertas por los terroristas** the two people killed by the terrorists

C [1] ‹*pueblo/zona*› dead, lifeless [2] (inerte) limp [3] ‹*carretera/camino*› disused

muerto[2] **-ta** *m,f*

A (persona muerta): **hubo dos ~s** two people died *o* were killed; **los ~s de la guerra** the war dead; **lo juro por mis ~s** (fam) I swear on my mother's grave; **hacerse el ~** to pretend to be dead; ***cargar con el ~*** (fam) (con un trabajo pesado) to do the dirty work; **se fueron sin pagar y me tocó cargar con el ~** they took off and left me to pick up the tab (colloq); ***cargarle el ~ a algn*** (fam) (responsabilizar) to pin the blame on sb; (endilgarle la tarea) to give sb the dirty work (colloq); ***hacer el ~*** to float on one's back; ***ser un ~ de hambre*** (fam) to be a nobody (colloq); ***el ~ al hoyo y el vivo al bollo*** dead men have no friends

B **muerto** *m* (en naipes) dummy

muesca *f* 1 (hendidura) nick, notch 2 (para encajar) slot, groove 3 (Agr, Taur) mark

muesli /'musli/ *m* muesli

muestra *f*
A 1 (de mercancía) sample; ***para ~ (basta) un botón*** (fam) for example, for instance 2 (de sangre, orina) specimen, sample 3 (en labores) sample of work done 4 (en estadísticas) sample; **~ de población** population sample
B (prueba, señal): **como** *or* **en ~ de mi gratitud/buena voluntad** as a token of my gratitude/goodwill; **una ~ de cansancio/falta de madurez** a sign of tiredness/immaturity
C (exposición) exhibition, exhibit (AmE); (de teatro, cine) festival

muestrario *m* collection of samples; **~ de telas** fabric sampler; **~ de colores** color chart *o* card

muestreo *m* sampling; **se hizo un ~ de la población** a sample of the population was chosen

mueva, muevas, etc *see* **mover**

mufa *f* (RPl fam) 1 (mal humor) bad mood; 2 (moho) mold*

mugido *m* moo; **los ~s de las vacas** the mooing of the cows

múgil *m* gray* mullet

mugir [I7] *vi* «*vaca*» to moo; «*toro*» to bellow

mugre *f* (suciedad) dirt, filth; (grasa) grime, grease; ***sacarle la ~ a algn*** (AmL fam) to beat sb black and blue

mugriento -ta *adj* filthy

mugrón *m* shoot

mugroso -sa *adj* (Chi, Méx fam) filthy

muguete, (RPl) **muguet** /mu'ɣe/ *m* lily of the valley

mujer *f* 1 woman; **ya es toda una ~cita** she's a young woman already; **es una ~ hecha y derecha** she's a grown woman; ***hacerse ~*** (euf) to reach puberty, become a woman (euph); ***ser una ~ de su casa*** to be a good housewife 2 (esposa) wife 3 (como apelativo): **¿se habrá ofendido? — ¡no, ~!** do you think I've offended him? — no, of course not

Compuestos
- **mujer de la limpieza** cleaning lady, cleaner
- **mujer de la vida** (euf) lady of the night (euph & dated)
- **mujer de mala vida** *or* **de mal vivir** prostitute
- **mujer de negocios** businesswoman
- **mujer de vida alegre** (euf) loose woman
- **mujer fatal** femme fatale
- **mujer policía** policewoman
- **mujer rana** diver

mujeriegas: **a ~** (*loc adv*) sidesaddle

mujeriego[1] *adj*: **es muy ~** he's a real womanizer

mujeriego[2] *m* womanizer

mujerzuela *f* (pey) slut (pej)

mújol *m* gray* mullet

mula[1] *f*
A (Zool) mule; **~ de carga** pack mule; ***bajarse de la ~*** (Ven fam) to cough up (colloq); ***mantenerse*** *or* ***sostenerse en su ~*** (Méx) to stand one's ground; ***meterle la ~ a algn*** (CS fam) (engañar) to pull a fast one on sb (colloq); ***terco/tozudo como una ~*** as stubborn as a mule (colloq); ***trabajar como una ~*** (fam) to work one's butt off (AmE colloq), to slog one's guts out (BrE colloq)
B (fam) (de droga) mule (colloq)
C (Méx) (en dominó): **tengo la ~ de seises** I have the double six; *ver tb* **mulita, mulo**

mula[2] *adj* (Méx fam) stubborn

muladar *m* garbage (AmE) *o* (BrE) rubbish dump; **su casa parece un ~** her house is like a pigsty (colloq)

mular *adj* mule (*before n*)

mulato[1] -ta *adj* of mixed race (*black and white*), mulatto (dated *or* pej)

mulato[2] -ta *m,f* person of mixed race (*of a black and a white parent*), mulatto (dated *or* pej)

mulero -ra *m,f* muleteer, mule driver

muleta *f*
A (bastón) crutch; (apoyo) crutch, prop
B (Taur) red cape (*attached to a stick*)

muletazo *m*: *movement performed with the* **muleta B**

muletilla *f* tag, filler (tech)

muletón *m* (Tex) flanelette; (para mesa) undercloth

mulita *f*
A (RPl) (armadillo) armadillo
B (Per) (de pisco) glass, shot

mullido -da *adj* ‹*colchón/sofá*› soft, springy; ‹*hierba*› springy

mulo *m* (male) mule; ***estar hecho un ~*** (Esp fam) to be as strong as an ox; *ver tb* **mula**

multa *f* fine; **le aplicaron una ~** he was fined

multar [A1] *vt* to fine

multicelular *adj* multicellular

multicentro *m* (shopping) mall

multicine *m* multiscreen movie complex (AmE), multiscreen cinema (BrE)

multicolor *adj* multicolored*

multiconferencia *f* (Telec) conference call

multicopista *f* (Esp) duplicator

multicultural *adj* multicultural

multiculturalidad *f* multiculturality

multidireccional *adj* multidirectional

multidisciplinario -ria, **multidisciplinar** *adj* multidisciplinary

multiforme *adj* multiform

multigrado *adj* multigrade

multilateral *adj* multilateral

multilingüe *adj* multilingual

multimedia *adj inv* multimedia

multimillonario[1] -ria *adj*: **es ~** he is a multimillionaire; **un contrato ~** a multi-million dollar (*o* pound etc) contract

multimillonario[2] -ria *m,f* multimillionaire

multinacional *adj/f* multinational

multipartidismo *m* multiparty system

multipartidista *adj* multiparty (*before n*)

múltiple *adj*
A ‹*aplicaciones/causas*› many, numerous
B ‹*flor/imagen/fractura*› multiple

multiplicación *f*
A (Biol, Mat) multiplication
B (incremento) increase; **la ~ de los panes y los peces** the feeding of the five thousand

multiplicar [A2] *vt* to multiply; **~ algo POR algo** to multiply sth BY sth; **12 multiplicado por 15** 12 multiplied by 15, 12 times 15
■ **multiplicar** *vi* to multiply
■ **multiplicarse** *v pron*
A «*especie*» to multiply, reproduce
B (aumentar) to increase several times over

multiplicidad *f* multiplicity, wide variety

múltiplo *m* multiple; **25 es (un) ~ de 5** 25 is a multiple of 5

multiprocesador *m* multiprocessor

multiproceso *m* multiprocessing

multiprogramación *f* multiprogramming

multipropiedad *f* time share

multirracial *adj* multiracial

multitud *f*
A (muchedumbre) crowd
B **~ DE algo** (muchos): **tengo (una) ~ de cosas que hacer** I have dozens of things to do (colloq); **una ~ de usos** an enormous variety of uses

multitudinario -ria *adj* ‹*manifestación/movilizaciones*› mass (*before n*); ‹*concierto*› with mass audiences; **una congregación multitudinaria de fieles** a multitudinous congregation of the faithful (frml)

multiuso *adj inv* multipurpose

multiusuario *adj inv* multiuser

multiviaje *adj*: **boleto** (AmL) *or* (Esp) **billete ~** multi-journey ticket; **tarjeta ~** travel pass

mundanal *adj* worldly, of the world; **lejos del ~ ruido** (liter) far from the madding crowd (liter)

mundano -na *adj* 1 ‹*problemas/placeres*› worldly 2 ‹*fiesta*› society (*before n*); **su gusto por la vida mundana** his taste for high society

mundial[1] *adj* ‹*historia/mercado*› world (*before n*); **la marca ~** the world record; **de fama ~** world-famous; **ha tenido**

m

influencia a escala ~ she has been influential worldwide; **es un problema ~** it's a global *o* worldwide problem; **la población ~** the world's population

mundial² *m*, **mundiales** *mpl* World Championship(s); **el ~ de fútbol** the World Cup

mundialista *adj* (AmL): **un atleta ~** an athlete who is competing/has competed in the World Championships

mundialización *f* globalization

mundialmente *adv* worlwide; **es ~ famoso/conocido** he is famous/known worldwide

mundo *m*

A (el universo, la Tierra): **el ~** the world; **artistas venidos de todo el ~** artists from all over the world; **el mejor del ~** the best in the world; **me parece lo más normal del ~** it seems perfectly normal to me; **así anda el ~** that's why the world is in the state it's in; ***comerse el ~***: **parece que se va a comer el ~** he looks as if he could take on the world; ***correr ~*** to get around; ***del otro ~***: **no es nada del otro ~** he's/it's nothing special *o* (colloq) he's/it's nothing to write home about; ***desde que el ~ es ~*** since time began, since time immemorial (liter); ***el ~ es un pañuelo*** it's a small world; ***hundirse*** *or* ***venirse abajo el ~***: **por eso no se va a hundir el ~** it's not the end of the world; **pensé que el ~ se me venía abajo** I thought my world was falling apart; ***partir de este ~*** (euf) to depart this life *o* world (euph); ***por nada del*** *or* ***en el ~***: **yo no me lo pierdo por nada del ~** I wouldn't miss it for the world; **no lo vendería por nada en el ~** I wouldn't sell it for anything in the world *o* (colloq) for all the tea in China; ***ponerse el ~ por montera*** to scorn the world and its ways; ***¡qué pequeño*** *or* ***chico es el ~!*** it's a small world!; ***tal y como vino al ~*** stark naked, as naked as the day he/she was born; ***traer a algn/venir al ~*** to bring sb/come into the world; ***ver ~*** to see the world

B (planeta, universo) planet, world; **él vive en otro ~** he's on another planet *o* in another world; ***por esos ~s de Dios*** here, there and everywhere

m

C 1 (porción de la realidad, de lo concebible) world; **el ~ árabe** the Arab world; **el ~ sobrenatural** the realm of the supernatural 2 (de actividad humana) world; **el ~ de los negocios/la droga** the business/drugs world; **el ~ del espectáculo** showbusiness

D (gente): **todo el ~** everybody; **el ~ entero está en peligro** the whole world is in danger; **se lo contó a medio ~** he told just about everybody

E **un ~** (mucho, muchos): **un ~ de gente** crowds *o* hordes of people; **de tu opinión a la mía hay un ~** our opinions are worlds apart; **todo se le hace un ~** he lets everything get blown up out of all proportion

F 1 (vida material): **el ~** the world; **los placeres del ~** worldly pleasures 2 (experiencia): **tienen** *or* **han visto mucho ~** they've been around; **una mujer que tiene mucho ~** a woman of the world

munición *f* 1 (carga) *tb* **municiones** ammunition, munitions (*pl*) 2 (pertrechos) supplies 3 (Chi) (perdigón) pellet

(Compuesto) **munición de boca** provisions (*pl*)

municipal¹ *adj* ‹*impuestos*› local; ‹*elecciones/piscina/mercado*› municipal

municipal² *mf* (Esp) ▸ **policía B**

municipio *m* (territorio) municipality; (entidad) town council; (edificio) town hall

munido -da *adj* (liter) **~ DE algo** armed WITH sth; **se ruega presentarse ~s del pasaporte** (RPl frml) you are requested to bring your passport (frml)

munificencia *f* munificence (frml)

munificente *adj* munificent (frml)

muñeca *f*

A 1 (Jueg) doll; **jugar a las ~s** to play with dolls; ***ser/parecer una ~*** to be a little doll 2 (fam) (como apelativo) honey, darling (colloq)

(Compuestos)
- **muñeca de trapo** rag doll
- **muñeca rusa** Russian doll

B (Anat) wrist

C (RPl fam) (influencia) pull (colloq); **tiene ~** he has a lot of pull *o* contacts (colloq); **consiguió el puesto por ~** he got the job by pulling strings (colloq)

D (Méx) (mazorca nueva) baby corn

muñeco *m*

A 1 (juguete con forma — humana) doll; (— de animal) toy animal; **~ de peluche** stuffed animal (AmE), soft toy (BrE) 2 (de ventrílocuo, sastre, etc) dummy; **un ~ que representaba al presidente** an effigy of the president 3 (dibujo) figure 4 (fam) (como apelativo) sweetie (colloq), honey (colloq)

(Compuesto) **muñeco de nieve** snowman

B **muñecos** *mpl* (Per fam): **estar con los ~s** to be very nervous

muñequear [A1] *vt* (Chi fam) to wangle (colloq)

■ **muñequearse** *v pron* 1 (RPl fam) (usando conexiones): **se muñequeó el puesto** he pulled some strings to get the job 2 (Per fam) to get jumpy (colloq), to get into a state (colloq)

muñequera *f* (Dep) wristband; (Med) wrist bandage

muñir [I15] *vt* (Esp fam) to fix (colloq)

muñón *m* (de un miembro) stump

mural¹ *adj* wall (*before n*), mural (*before n*)

mural² *m* mural

muralista *adj/mf* muralist

muralla *f* 1 (de ciudad) walls (*pl*), city wall; (de convento) wall 2 (Chi) (pared) wall

(Compuesto) **Muralla China** Great Wall of China

murciélago *m* bat

murga *f*

A (Mús) 1 (grupo) band of street musicians 2 (Col) (concurso) musical competition

B (Esp fam) (molestia) drag (colloq); ***dar la ~*** (Esp fam) to be a pain (colloq)

muriera, murió, etc *see* **morir**

murmullo *m* 1 (de voces) murmur; **hablaba casi en un ~** she spoke almost in a whisper 2 (liter) (de agua) murmur (liter); (de viento) whispering; (de hojas) rustle

murmuraciones *fpl* gossip

murmurador¹ -dora *adj* gossipy

murmurador² -dora *m,f* gossip

murmurar [A1] *vt* 1 (hablar bajo) to murmur; **murmuró que lo aceptaría** he murmured his agreement; **le murmuró algo al oído** he whispered something in her ear 2 (con enojo) to mutter; **— no pienso hacerlo — murmuró** I won't do it, she muttered 3 (en son de crítica): **andan murmurando que ...** there are rumors that ...; **cosas que se murmuran en la oficina** rumors that go around the office

■ **murmurar** *vi* 1 (criticar) to gossip (*maliciously*); **~ DE algn** to gossip ABOUT sb 2 (liter) «*agua*» to murmur (liter); «*viento*» to whisper, murmur; «*hojas*» to rustle

muro *m* wall

(Compuestos)
- **Muro de Berlín** (Hist) Berlin Wall
- **muro de carga/de contención** load-bearing/retaining wall
- **Muro de las Lamentaciones** *or* **los Lamentos** Wailing Wall

murria *f* gloom; **le entró la ~** he became depressed

mus *m*: *a Spanish card game*

musa *f* (Mit) Muse; (inspiración) muse

musaraña *f*

A (Zool) shrew; ***pensar en*** *or* ***mirar las ~s*** to daydream

B (Chi fam) (gesticulación) gesture

muscular *adj* muscular

musculatura *f* muscles (*pl*), musculature (tech)

músculo *m* muscle; **sacar ~** to flex one's muscles

musculoso -sa *adj* muscular

muselina *f* muslin

museo *m* (de pintura, escultura) museum, gallery; (arqueológico, de historia, etc) museum

(Compuestos)
- **museo de cera** wax museum, waxworks (*pl*)
- **museo de ciencias naturales** natural science museum

musgo *m* moss

música¹ *adj* (Méx fam) 1 [SER] (antipático) mean (colloq) 2 [SER] (negado) **~ PARA algo** hopeless AT sth (colloq)

música² *f*

A (Mús) music; **pon algo de ~** put some music on; **~ en**

directo *or* **en vivo** live music; **puso ~ a los versos de Machado** he set Machado's poetry to music; **la ~ amansa las fieras** (fr hecha) music has a great calming effect; ***irse con la ~ a otra parte*** (fam): **vámonos con la ~ a otra parte** let's get out of here (colloq); **vete con la ~ a otra parte** clear off! (colloq); ***sonar a/ser ~ celestial*** (fam) to be music to one's ears

(Compuestos)
- **música ambiental** background music; (en tienda, fábrica) piped *o* canned music
- **música clásica/folk/ligera** classical/folk/light music
- **música de acompañamiento/de cámara/de fondo** incidental/chamber/background music

B (Chi fam) (armónica) mouth organ, harmonica

musical *adj/m* musical

musicalidad *f* musicality

músico -ca *m,f* (compositor) composer; (instrumentista) musician

(Compuesto) **músico callejero** street musician, busker

musitar [A1] *vt* to whisper, murmur

musiú -siúa *m,f* (Ven fam) foreigner (*white and non-Spanish-speaking*)

muslera *f* thighband

muslo *m* thigh; **~s de pollo** chicken legs

mustio -tia *adj*

A ‹*flor/planta*› withered

B (fam) (triste, abatido) down (colloq), low (colloq)

C (Méx fam) (hipócrita) two-faced (colloq)

musulmán -mana *adj/m,f* Muslim, Moslem

mutabilidad *f* (frml) mutability (frml *or* tech), changeable nature; **la ~ de la lengua** the changeable nature of the language

mutable *adj* changeable, mutable (frml)

mutación *f* mutation

mutante *adj/mf* mutant

mutilación *f* mutilation

mutilado -da *m,f* disabled person; **un ~ de guerra** a disabled serviceman

mutilar [A1] *vt* **1** ‹*persona/pierna*› to mutilate; **quedó mutilado en el accidente** he was maimed as a result of the accident **2** ‹*texto/película*› to mutilate, bowdlerize; ‹*árbol/estatua*› to vandalize

mutis *m* (Teatr) exit; (silencio) silence; **tú de esto, ~** not a word to anyone about it; ***hacer ~ por el foro*** (callarse) to keep sth to oneself; (irse) to make onself scarce; **cuando se les pide soluciones, ~ por el foro** when asked what the solution is they have nothing to say

mutismo *m* silence

mutua *f* benefit society (AmE), friendly society (BrE)

(Compuesto) **mutua de seguros** mutual insurance company

mutual *f* **1** (CS) (de asistencia económica) benefit society (AmE), friendly society (BrE) **2** (RPl) (de asistencia médica) *medical care fund*

mutualidad *f* benefit society (AmE), friendly society (BrE)

mutualista[1] *adj* mutualist

mutualista[2] *mf* (miembro) *member of a* **mutualidad**

mutuamente *adv* mutually; **se insultaron/acusaron ~** they insulted/accused each other

mutuo -tua *adj* **1** (recíproco) ‹*respeto/ayuda*› mutual; **de ~ acuerdo** by mutual *o* joint agreement; **el sentimiento es ~** the feeling is mutual **2** (común) mutual; **redundará en beneficio ~** it will be to our mutual benefit

muy *adv* **1** very; **~ poca gente** very few people; **son ~ amigos** they're great friends; **~ admirado** much admired; **~ respetado** highly respected; **~ bien, sigamos adelante** OK *o* fine, let's go on; **un gesto ~ suyo** a typical gesture of his; **ella es ~ de criticar a los demás** she's very fond of criticizing others; **por ~ cansado que estés** however *o* no matter how tired you are; **el ~ sinvergüenza** the swine **2** (demasiado) too; **quedó ~ dulce** it's rather *o* too sweet

mV (= **milivoltio**) mv, mV

MV (= **megavoltio**) MV

MW (= **megawatio**) MW

Nn

N, n *f (read as /'ene/) the letter* **N, n**

n/ = nuestro

N *f* (en Esp) **= (carretera) nacional**

N. (**= norte**) North, N

nabo *m* (Bot) turnip

(Compuesto) **nabo sueco** rutabaga (AmE), swede (BrE)

naborí *mf* Indian servant

nácar *m* mother-of-pearl, nacre

nacarado -da *adj* ‹*reflejos*› pearly; ‹*esmalte de uñas*› pearlized

nacarino -na *adj* (de nácar) mother-of-pearl (*before n*); ‹*reflejos*› pearly

nacatamal *m* (AmC, Méx): (*steamed meat and vegetable pasty, cooked in banana or maize leaves*)

nacer [E3] *vi*

A [1] «*niño/animal*» to be born; **¿dónde naciste?** where were you born?; **al ~** at birth; **~ antes de tiempo** to be premature; **el niño nació muerto** the child was stillborn; **nació en el Perú, de padres españoles** she was born in Peru to *o* of Spanish parents; **~ PARA algo/+ INF** to be born to + INF; **nació para (ser) músico** he was born to be a musician; **~ *parado*** (Chi, Ven fam) to have the luck of the devil (colloq); ***no nací ayer*** I wasn't born yesterday [2] «*pollito/insecto*» to hatch [3] «*hoja/rama*» to sprout [4] «*río*» to have its source; «*carretera*» to start [5] «*pelo/plumas*» to grow

B [1] (surgir): **una gran amistad nació entre ellos** a great friendship sprung up between them; **no le nace ser amable** being nice doesn't come naturally to her: **~ DE algo** «*problema/situación*» to arise *o* spring FROM sth; **~ DE algn** «*idea/iniciativa*»: **nació de ella invitarlo** it was her idea to invite him [2] (liter) (iniciarse) **~ A algo** to be awakened TO sth (liter)

nacho *m* (Coc) nacho (*tortilla piece with topping of cheese and spices*)

nacido[1] -da *adj* born; **un niño recién ~** a newborn baby

nacido[2] -da *m,f*: **los ~s en este año** those born this year; ▸**mal[3] F**

naciente[1] *adj* [1] ‹*sol*› rising (*before n*) [2] ‹*amistad*› newly-formed; **el ~ interés por la ecología** the new interest in ecology

naciente[2] *m*: **el ~** (liter) the Orient (liter)

naciente[3] *f*, **nacientes** *fpl* (CS) source

nacimiento *m*

A [1] (de niño, animal) birth; **es argentino de ~** he's Argentinian by birth; **es sorda de ~** she was born deaf [2] (de aves) hatching

B [1] (origen) birth; **aquél fue el ~ de una amistad duradera** that was the start *o* beginning of a lasting friendship [2] (liter) (iniciación, despertar) **~ A algo** awakening TO sth [3] (cuna) birth; **de ~ noble** of noble birth *o* origins

C [1] (de río) source [2] (del pelo) hairline

D (belén) crib

nación *f* [1] (estado) nation [2] (habitantes) nation; **el presidente se dirigió a la ~** the president addressed the nation *o* the people [3] (territorio) nation, country

(Compuesto) **Naciones Unidas** *fpl* United Nations (*pl*)

nacional[1] *adj* [1] (de la nación) ‹*deuda/reservas*› national; **en todo el territorio ~** throughout the country; **un programa de difusión ~** a program broadcast nationwide [2] (no internacional) ‹*vuelo*› domestic [3] (no extranjero) ‹*industria*› national; **compre productos ~es** ≈ buy Spanish (*o* Argentinian *etc*); **la ginebra ~ es muy buena** Spanish (*o* Argentinian *etc*) gin is very good

nacional[2] *mf* (frml) (ciudadano) national

nacionalidad *f*

A (ciudadanía) nationality; **adquirió la ~ española** he took Spanish nationality *o* citizenship

B (Pol) (en Esp) people

nacionalismo *m* nationalism

nacionalista[1] *adj* nationalist (*before n*)

nacionalista[2] *mf* nationalist

nacionalización *f* (de industria) nationalization; (naturalización) naturalization

nacionalizar [A4] *vt* ‹*industria*› to nationalize; ‹*persona*› to naturalize

■ **nacionalizarse** *v pron* «*persona*» to become naturalized

nacionalsocialismo *m* National Socialism

nacionalsocialista *adj/mf* National Socialist

nacismo *m* Nazism

nacista *mf* Nazi

naco[1] -ca *adj* (Méx fam & pey) plebby (colloq & pej)

naco[2] -ca *m,f* (Méx fam & pey) pleb (colloq & pej)

nada[1] *pron*

A [1] nothing; **es mejor que ~** it's better than nothing; **de ~ sirve que le compres libros** there's no point in buying him books; **antes que** *or* **de ~** first of all; **no hay ~ como ...** there's nothing like ...; **no quiere ~** he doesn't want anything; **¡no sirves para ~!** you're useless; **no se hizo ~** he wasn't hurt; **¡perdón! — no fue ~** sorry! — that's all right; **no es por ~ pero ...** don't take this the wrong way but ...; **sin decir ~** without a word; **nadie me dio ~** nobody gave me anything; **sin ~ de azúcar** without any sugar at all; **no tiene ~ de gracia** it's not at all funny [2] (*en locs*) **de nada** you're welcome; **nada de nada** (fam) not a thing; **nada más**: **no hay ~ más** there's nothing else; **¿algo más? — ~ más** anything else? — no, that's it *o* that's all; **~ más fui yo** (Méx) I was the only one who went; **salí ~ más comer** I went out right *o* straight after lunch; **sacó (~ más ni) ~ menos que el primer puesto** she came first no less; **nada más que**: **no se lo dije ~ más que a él** he's the only one I told; **para nada**: **no me gustó para ~** I didn't like it at all; ***como si*** **~** (fam): **¡me lo dijo como si ~!** she told me as if it was nothing; **se quedó como si ~** she didn't even bat an eyelid; ***no hay ~ que hacerle*** (fam) that's all there is to it

B [1] (ninguna cosa): **antes de que digas ~** before you say anything [2] (muy poco): **con** *or* **de ~ se rompe** it breaks just like that; **en ~ de tiempo** in no time at all; **la compraron por ~** they bought it for next to nothing; **llora por ~** she cries at the slightest little thing; **dentro de ~** very soon; ***estar en*** **~**: **estuvo en ~ que perdiéramos el tren** we very nearly missed the train [3] (fam) (uso expletivo): **y ~, que al final no lo compró** anyway, in the end she didn't buy it; **pues ~, ya veremos qué pasa** well *o* anyway, we'll see what happens

C (Esp) (en tenis) love; **quince-~** fifteen-love

nada² *adv*: **no está ~ preocupado** he isn't at all *o* the least bit worried; **esto no me gusta ~** I don't like this at all *o* (colloq) one bit

nada³ *f*

A (Fil): **la ~** nothing; **se creó de la ~** it was created from nothing *o* from the void; **surgió de la ~** it came out of nowhere

B (Méx, RPl fam) (pequeña cantidad): **una ~ de sal** a tiny pinch of salt; **una ~ de agua** a tiny drop of water

nadador -dora *m,f* swimmer

nadar [A1] *vi*

A 1 «*persona/pez*» to swim; **¿sabes ~?** can you swim?; **~ (estilo) mariposa** to do (the) butterfly 2 «*ramas/hojas*» (flotar) to float

B 1 (quedar grande) (+ *me/te/le etc*): **esa falda te nada** that skirt's much *o* far too big for you 2 (en un espacio): **nadábamos en esa casa tan grande** we were lost in that great big house

C **nadar en** (tener mucho): **~ en dinero** to be rolling in money (colloq); **el pollo nadaba en grasa** the chicken was swimming in grease

■ **nadar** *vt* to swim

nadería *f* (fam) little thing, trifle; **discutir por ~s** to argue over nothing

nadie *pron* nobody, no one; **no me ayudó ~** nobody helped me; **no vi a ~** I didn't see anybody; **sin que ~ se diera cuenta** without anyone noticing; **toca el arpa como ~** he's a brilliant harpist

nado *m*

A (Méx, Ven) (natación) swimming; **tiene el récord en ~ de pecho** he holds the breaststroke record

(Compuesto) **nado sincronizado** (Méx) synchronized swimming

B **a nado**: **fueron hasta las rocas a ~** they swam out to the rocks; **cruzó el río a ~** he swam across the river

nafta *f* 1 (Quím) naphtha 2 (RPl) (gasolina) gas (AmE), petrol (BrE)

NAFTA /'nafta/ *m* NAFTA

naftalina *f* (Quím) naphthalene; (para ropa) mothballs (*pl*)

nagual *m* (Méx) sorcerer

naguas *fpl* (Méx fam) petticoat

náhuatl¹ *adj* (*pl* **nahuas**) Nahuatl

náhuatl² *mf* (*pl* **nahuas**) 1 (indígena) Nahuatl 2 **náhuatl** *m* (idioma) Nahuatl

nailon *m* nylon

naipe *m* (playing) card; **juegos de ~s** card games

naja *f* cobra

nalga *f* (Anat) buttock; **una inyección en la ~** an injection in the buttock *o* bottom; **le dio una palmada en las ~s** she smacked his bottom; **el bebé venía de ~s** it was a breech birth

nalgada *f* (Méx) smack on the bottom

nana *f*

A (canción de cuna) lullaby

B 1 (fam) (abuela) grandma (colloq), granny (colloq); ***hacerse ~*** (CS leng infantil) to hurt oneself 2 (Andes, Ven) (niñera) nanny

nao *f* (arc) vessel, ship

napa *f* (cuero — muy blando) nappa; (— más duro) leather

napia *f*, **napias** *fpl* (fam & pey) schnozzle (AmE colloq & pej), conk (BrE colloq & pej)

naranja¹ *f* (fruta) orange; ***¡~s de la China!*** (fam) (expresando incredulidad) come off it! (colloq); (expresando rechazo) no way! (colloq); ▸**medio¹ A**

(Compuesto) **naranja amarga** Seville orange

naranja² *adj* (*gen inv*) orange; **calcetines ~** orange socks; **~ chillón/intenso** lurid/bright orange

naranja³ *m* (color) orange

naranjada *f* orangeade

naranjal *m* orange grove

naranjero -ra *m,f* 1 (Agr) orange grower 2 **naranjero** *m* (naranjo) orange tree

naranjo *m* orange tree

narcisismo *m* narcissism

narcisista¹ *adj* narcissistic

narcisista² *mf* narcissist

narciso *m* 1 (Bot) daffodil; (género) narcissus 2 (persona) narcissist

narco¹ *adj* (Col, Méx fam): **dinero ~** money made from drug trafficking

narco² *mf* (fam) drug trafficker

narcodependencia *f* drug dependence

narcoguerrilla *f* drugs-linked guerrillas (*pl*), narco-guerrillas (*pl*)

narcótico¹ -ca *adj* narcotic

narcótico² *m* narcotic

narcotismo *m* narcotism

narcotizante *adj/m* narcotic

narcotizar [A4] *vt* to drug (*with narcotics*)

narcotraficante *mf* drug trafficker

narcotráfico *m* drug trafficking

nardo *m* spikenard, nard

narigón -gona, **narigudo -da** *adj* (fam): **una chica narigona** a girl with a big nose

nariguera *f* nose ring

nariz *f* 1 (Anat) nose; **sonarse la ~** to blow one's nose; **habla con** *or* **por la ~** he has a nasal voice *o* twang; **no te metas los dedos en la ~** don't pick your nose; **lo tenía delante de las narices** it was right under my nose; ***darle en*** *or* ***por las narices a algn*** (fam) to get one up on sb (colloq); ***darse de narices con algn*** (fam) to bump into sb (colloq); ***darse de narices con*** *or* ***contra algo*** (fam): **nos dimos de narices contra un árbol** we went smack into a tree (colloq); ***en mis/sus propias narices*** (fam) right under my/his nose; ***estar hasta las narices de algo/algn*** (fam) to be fed up (to the back teeth) with sth/sb (colloq); ***hincharle las narices a algn*** (Esp fam) to get on sb's nerves (colloq); ***meter las narices*** *or* ***la ~ en algo*** (fam) to poke one's nose into sth (colloq); ***no ve más allá de sus narices*** (fam) he can't see further than the end of his nose; ***por narices*** (Esp fam): **ahora te lo comes, por narices** now you're going to eat it, if it's the last thing you do (colloq); ***refregarle algo a algn por las narices*** (fam): **no tienes por qué refregármelo por las narices** there's no need to keep rubbing it in (colloq); ***romperle las narices a algn*** (fam) to smash sb's face in (colloq); ***tener narices*** (Esp fam): **¡si tendrá narices el tío!** he has some nerve! (AmE colloq), he's got a nerve *o* cheek! (BrE colloq); **¡tiene narices la cosa!** it's ridiculous! 2 (de avión) nose

(Compuesto) **nariz griega** Grecian profile

narizota *f* (fam) schnozzle (AmE colloq), conk (BrE colloq)

narración *f* (relato) story; (acción de contar) account

narrador -dora *m,f* narrator

narrar [A1] *vt* (frml) 1 «*película/libro*» ‹*hazañas/experiencias*› to tell of (frml), to relate; ‹*historia*› to tell, relate 2 «*persona*» ‹*historia*› to tell, narrate (frml)

narrativa *f* (género) fiction; (narración) narrative

narrativo -va *adj* narrative

nasal *adj/f* nasal

nata *f* 1 (sobre leche hervida) skin 2 (Esp) ▸**crema A2**

natación *f* swimming

(Compuesto) **natación sincronizada** synchronized swimming

natal *adj* 1 ‹*país*› native (*before n*); ‹*ciudad*› home (*before n*); **la casa ~ del poeta** the house where the poet was born 2 (Méx) (originario): **es ~ de Chiapas** she was born in Chiapas

natalicio *m* (frml) birth; **hoy se celebra el ~ de nuestro prócer** today we celebrate the anniversary of the birth of our national hero

natalidad *f* birthrate

natillas *fpl* custard

natividad *f* 1 **la ~** (nacimiento de Cristo) the Nativity 2 **la N~** (navidad) Christmas

nativo¹ -va *adj* 1 ‹*tierra/país/lengua*› native; Ⓢ **clases de ruso, profesor nativo** native speaker offers Russian classes 2 ‹*flora/fauna*› native; **~ DE algo** native to sth

nativo² -va *m,f* (aborigen) native; (hablante) native speaker

nato -ta *adj* 1 ‹*artista*› born (*before n*) 2 ‹*cargo*› ex officio

natural¹ *adj*

A 1 ‹*fenómeno*› natural; ‹*ingredientes*› natural; **en estado**

n

~ natural, native; **al ~** ‹*mejillones*› in brine; **es más bonita al ~** she's prettier without makeup 2 (a temperatura ambiente) ‹*cerveza/gaseosa*› unchilled; **se sirve al ~** serve at room temperature 3 (Mús) natural
B 1 (espontáneo) ‹*gesto/persona*› natural 2 (inherente) natural, innate 3 (normal) natural; **me parece lo más ~ del mundo** it seems perfectly natural to me; **es ~ que le cueste** it's quite natural that he should find it hard
C (frml) (nativo) **ser ~ DE** to be a native OF, to come FROM

natural² *m*
A (carácter) nature; **es de ~ generoso** she has a generous nature
B (nativo) native; **los ~es del lugar** people from the area
C (Art): **pintar del ~** to paint from life
D (Taur) *close pass made with the* **muleta** *held in the left hand*

naturaleza *f*
A (Ecol): **la ~** nature; **en contacto con la ~** close to nature
(Compuesto) **naturaleza muerta** still life
B (índole) nature; **la ~ humana** human nature; **es de ~ agresiva** he's aggressive by nature
C (ant) (nacionalidad) nationality

naturalidad *f*: **su ~** her natural manner; **con la mayor ~ del mundo** as if it were the most natural thing in the world
naturalismo *m* naturalism
naturalista¹ *adj* naturalistic
naturalista² *mf* naturalist
naturalización *f* naturalization
naturalizar [A4] *vt* to naturalize
■ **naturalizarse** *v pron* to become naturalized
naturismo *m* 1 (estilo de vida) natural lifestyle 2 (nudismo) nudism
naturista¹ *adj* 1 ‹*médico/tratamiento*› natural 2 ‹*playa/campamento*› nudist (*before n*)
naturista² *mf* nudist
naufragar [A3] *vi* 1 «*barco*» to be wrecked; «*persona*» to be shipwrecked 2 «*plan/negocio*» to go under
naufragio *m* 1 (Náut) shipwreck 2 (fracaso) failure
náufrago¹ -ga *adj* shipwrecked
náufrago² -ga *m,f* (Náut) shipwrecked person
nauseabundo -da *adj* nauseating
náuseas *fpl*, **náusea** *f* nausea, sickness; **~ matutinas** morning sickness; **sentir** *or* **tener ~** to feel sick *o* nauseous; **me da ~** it makes me sick
náutica *f* art of navigation
náutico -ca *adj* nautical

navaja *f*
A (de bolsillo) penknife; (para afeitar) razor
(Compuesto) **navaja automática** *or* **de resorte** switchblade (AmE), flick knife (BrE)
B (Zool) razor clam (AmE), razor-shell (BrE)

navajazo *m*, **navajada** *f* (herida) knife wound; **le pegaron un ~ en la mejilla** they slashed his cheek
navajero -ra *m,f*: *criminal armed with a knife*
naval *adj* naval
Navarra *f* Navarre
navarro -rra *adj* of/from Navarre

nave *f*
A (Náut) (arc *o* liter) ship; ***quemar las ~s*** to burn one's boats *o* bridges
(Compuestos)
• **nave capitana** *or* **insignia** flagship
• **nave espacial** spacecraft, spaceship
B (Arquit) 1 (de iglesia) nave 2 (local) premises (*pl*); (sección) section
(Compuestos)
• **nave industrial** industrial premises (*pl*)
• **nave lateral** aisle

navegabilidad *f* (de río) navigability; (de embarcación) seaworthiness
navegable *adj* ‹*río*› navigable; ‹*barco*› seaworthy
navegación *f* 1 (acción de navegar) navigation; (tráfico) shipping 2 (arc) (viaje) voyage
(Compuestos)
• **navegación aérea** aerial navigation
• **navegación a vela** sailing
• **navegación costera** (acción de navegar) coasting; (tráfico) coastal shipping
• **navegación espacial** space travel
• **navegación fluvial** river navigation

navegador -dora *m,f* 1 (marinero) mariner 2 (Aviac, Náut) **navegador automático** automatic pilot; **~ GPS** GPS system 3 **navegador** *m* (Inf) browser
navegante¹ *adj* seafaring (*before n*)
navegante² *mf* 1 (arc) (marino) mariner (arch) 2 (que determina el rumbo) navigator
navegar [A3] *vi* 1 «*nave*» to sail 2 «*persona*» (a vela) to sail 3 (determinar el rumbo) to navigate
■ **navegar** *vt* (liter) to sail
Navidad *f* Christmas; **el día de ~** Christmas Day; **¡feliz ~!** happy Christmas!; **en ~** at Christmas(-time)
navideño -ña *adj* Christmas (*before n*)
naviera *f* shipping company
naviero¹ -ra *adj* shipping (*before n*)
naviero² -ra *m,f* shipowner
navío *m* ship
(Compuesto) **navío de guerra** warship
nazareno¹ -na *adj* of/from Nazareth
nazareno² *m* (penitente) penitent (*in Holy Week processions*)
Nazaret *m* Nazareth
nazi *adj/mf* Nazi
NB (= **nota bene**) NB
N. del T. = nota del traductor
N. de R. = nota de redacción
NE (= **nordeste**) NE
neblina *f* mist
neblinero *m* (Chi) fog light
neblinoso -sa *adj* misty
nebulosa *f* nebula
nebulosidad *f* 1 (Meteo) mist 2 (de idea) haziness
nebuloso -sa *adj* 1 (Meteo) misty 2 (Astron) nebular 3 ‹*idea/imagen*› hazy, nebulous
necedad *f* 1 (cualidad) crassness 2 (dicho, acto): **decir ~es** to talk nonsense; **es una ~** it's sheer stupidity
necesariamente *adv* necessarily; **tienen que pasar por aquí ~** they *have* to come this way
necesario -ria *adj* (imprescindible) necessary; **no dispone del dinero ~** she doesn't have enough money; **me sentía ~** I felt needed; **si es ~ se lo llevaré personalmente** if necessary *o* if need be, I'll take it to him myself; **no será ~ abrir todas las cajas** it won't be necessary to open all the boxes; **no es ~ que te quedes** there's no need for you to stay
neceser *m* (estuche) toilet kit (AmE), toilet bag (BrE); (maleta pequeña) overnight bag

necesidad *f*
A 1 (urgencia, falta) need; **en caso de ~** if necessary, if need be; **una imperiosa ~** an urgent need; **no hay ~ de que se entere** there's no need for her to know; ***la ~ tiene cara de hereje*** beggars can't be choosers; ***la ~ hace maestros*** *or* ***aguza el ingenio*** necessity is the mother of invention 2 (cosa necesaria) necessity, essential
B (pobreza) poverty, need; **la ~ lo impulsó a robar** he stole out of necessity *o* need
C **necesidades** *fpl* 1 (requerimientos) needs (*pl*), requirements (*pl*) 2 (privaciones) hardship; **pasaron muchas ~es** they underwent great hardship 3 **hacer sus ~es** (euf) to relieve oneself (euph)

necesitado¹ -da *adj* 1 (falto) **~ DE algo**: **anda ~ de dinero** he's short of money; **está muy ~ de cariño** he is in great need of affection 2 (pobre) in need, needy
necesitado² -da *m,f* needy person; **los ~s** the needy
necesitar [A1] *vt* to need; Ⓢ **se necesita vendedora** saleswoman required; **~ + INF** to need to + INF; **no necesito comprarlo hoy** I don't need to *o* I needn't buy it today; **necesita que alguien le eche una mano** she needs someone to give her a hand
■ **necesitar** *vi* (frml) **~ DE algo** to need sth

necio -cia *adj*
A (tonto) stupid
B (AmC, Col, Ven fam) (travieso) naughty

necrología *f* obituary

necrológicas *fpl* deaths section/page

necrológico -ca *adj*: **artículo ~** obituary

necromancia *f* necromancy

necrópolis *f (pl ~)* **1** (Arqueol) necropolis **2** (period) (cementerio) cemetery

necropsia *f* (téc) autopsy, necropsy, postmortem (examination) (esp BrE)

néctar *m* nectar

nectarina *f* nectarine

nefando -da *adj* (liter) ‹*crimen*› heinous (liter); ‹*persona*› loathsome, odious

nefasto -ta *adj* ‹*consecuencias*› disastrous; ‹*influencia*› harmful; ‹*tiempo/fiesta*› (fam) awful (colloq)

negación *f* (acción) denial, negation; (antítesis) antithesis; (Ling) negative

negado[1] -da *adj* useless (colloq), hopeless (colloq); **es ~ para la geografía** he's useless *o* hopeless at geography

negado[2] -da *m,f* dead loss (colloq)

negar [A7] *vt*
A ‹*acusación/rumor*› to deny; **no puedo ~lo** I can't deny it; **negó que la Tierra fuera plana** he disputed the idea that the earth was flat; **~ + INF** to deny -ING; **niega habértelo dicho** she denies having told you
B (no conceder) (+ *me/te/le etc*) to refuse; **les ~on la entrada** they were refused entry; **sigue negándome el saludo** he still refuses to say hello to me
C ‹*persona*› to disown; **su madre lo negó** his mother disowned him; **lo negó tres veces** (Bib) he denied Him three times
■ **negar** *vi*: **~ con la cabeza** to shake one's head
■ **negarse** *v pron*
A (rehusar) to refuse; **~se A + INF** to refuse to + INF; **~se A QUE + SUBJ**: **se negó a que llamáramos un taxi** he refused to let us call a taxi
B (*refl*) ‹*placeres/lujos*› to deny oneself

negativa *f* **1** (ante acusación) denial; (a pregunta): **contestó con una ~** she replied in the negative, she said no **2** (a propuesta) refusal; **una ~ rotunda** a flat refusal

negativamente *adv*
A ‹*responder*› in the negative
B (con espíritu negativo) negatively

negativismo *m* negativism

negativo[1] -va *adj*
A ‹*respuesta/verbo/análisis*› negative
B (perjudicial) ‹*actitud*› negative
C (Elec, Mat) negative

negativo[2] *m* negative; **imagen en ~** negative image

neglìgé /neɣli'ʒe/ *m* negligee

negligencia *f* negligence

negligente[1] *adj* negligent

negligente[2] *mf* person guilty of negligence

negociabilidad *f* negotiability

negociable *adj* negotiable

negociación *f*
A **1** (Pol, Rels Labs) negotiation; **la ruptura de las negociaciones** the breakdown of negotiations *o* talks **2** (Fin) negotiation
B (Méx) (empresa) business

negociado *m*
A (departamento) department
B (AmS fam) (negocio sucio) shady deal (colloq)

negociador[1] -dora *adj* negotiating (*before n*)

negociador[2] -dora *m,f* negotiator

negociante[1] *adj* (pey) money-grubbing (colloq & pej)

negociante[2] *mf* **1** (Com, Fin) (*m*) businessman; (*f*) businesswoman; **un ~ en cereales** a cereals trader *o* dealer **2** (pey) (mercenario) money-grubber (colloq & pej)

negociar [A1] *vt* **1** ‹*solución/acuerdo*› to negotiate **2** (Fin) ‹*valores/títulos*› to negotiate
■ **negociar** *vi* **1** (discutir, conversar) to negotiate **2** (Com) to trade

negocio *m* **1** (empresa) business; **montar** *or* **poner un ~** to set up a business **2** (transacción) deal; **un buen ~** a good deal; ***hacer ~*** to make money **3** (CS) (tienda) store (AmE), shop (BrE) **4** **negocios** *mpl* (comercio) business; **dedicarse a los ~s** to be in business; **hablar de ~s** to talk business; **en el mundo de los ~s** in the business world **5** (fam) (asunto) business (colloq)

negra *f*
A (Mús) crotchet
B (en ajedrez): **las ~s** the black pieces
C (mala suerte): **tener la ~** (fam) to be out of luck

negrear [A1] *vi* (liter) (ponerse negro): **negreaba la noche** night was falling; **ya negrean las moras** the blackberries are already starting to ripen
■ **negrear** *vt*
A (AmC, Méx fam) (explotar) to treat … like a slave
B (Col, Ven fam) (marginar) to ostracize

negrero[1] -ra *adj*: **barco ~** slave ship, slaver

negrero[2] -ra *m,f* (Hist) slave trader; (explotador) (fam) slave driver (colloq)

negrita, negrilla *f* boldface, bold type; **en ~(s)** in boldface, in bold (type)

negro[1] -gra *adj*
A **1** ‹*pelo/ropa*› black; ‹*ojos*› dark; **~ *como el azabache*** jet-black; **~ *como el carbón*** *or* ***un tizón*** as black as coal *o* soot; ***poner ~ a algn*** (fam) to drive sb up the wall (colloq) **2** (fam) (por el sol) tanned **3** (sombrío) black, gloomy; **lo ve todo tan ~** she's always so pessimistic; ***pasarlas negras*** (fam) to have a rough time of it (colloq); ***vérselas negras*** (fam): **se las vio negras para terminarlo** he had a tough time finishing it (colloq); **me las estoy viendo negras con este trabajito** this job is a real uphill struggle (colloq)
B ‹*hombre/raza/piel*› black

negro[2] *m* (color) black

(Compuesto) **negro azabache** **1** *m* jet black **2** *adj inv* jet-black

negro[3] -gra *m,f* (de raza negra) black person; ***trabajar como un ~*** to work like a slave

negroide *adj* negroid

negrura *f* blackness

negruzco -ca *adj* blackish

nemoroso -sa *adj* (liter) (del bosque) sylvan (liter); (cubierto de bosques) wooded

nemotecnia, nemotécnica *f* mnemonics

nemotécnico -ca *adj* mnemonic

nene -na *m,f* (Esp, RPl fam) **1** (niño pequeño) (*m*) little boy; (*f*) little girl; **los ~s** the kids (colloq) **2** (apelativo cariñoso) darling, honey **3** **nena** *f* (arg) (mujer) chick (AmE colloq), bird (BrE colloq)

nené *mf* (Ven fam) (*m*) little boy; (*f*) little girl

neocelandés[1] -desa *adj* of/from New Zealand

neocelandés[2] -desa *m,f* New Zealander

neoclasicismo *m* neoclassicism

neoclásico -ca *adj* neoclassical

neofascista *adj/mf* neofascist

neófito -ta *m,f* **1** (Relig) neophyte **2** (frml) (de partido) new member; (en colegio) new student *o* pupil; (en universidad) freshman

neolítico[1] -ca *adj* neolithic

neolítico[2] *m*: **el ~** the Neolithic (period)

neologismo *m* neologism

neón *m* neon

neonazi *adj/mf* neonazi

neorrealismo *m* neorealism

neoyorquino[1] -na *adj* of/from New York

neoyorquino[2] -na *m,f* New Yorker

nepotismo *m* nepotism

Neptuno *m* Neptune

nervadura *f* (Arquit, Bot, Zool) ribs (pl)

nervio *m*
A **1** (Anat) nerve **2** (en la carne) sinew; **carne con ~s** gristly meat
B **nervios** *mpl* **1** (nerviosismo) nerves (*pl*); **tengo unos ~s …** I'm *o* I feel so nervous; **me muero de ~s** I'm a nervous wreck (colloq); **le dio un ataque de ~s** he had an attack of

nerves **2** (sistema nervioso) nerves (*pl*); **tiene los ~s destrozados** his nerves are in shreds; **está enfermo de los ~s** he suffers with his nerves; **me altera** *or* **crispa los ~s** it gets *o* grates on my nerves; ***ponerle a algn los ~s de punta*** to get on sb's nerves; ***ser puro ~*** (activo, dinámico) to be full of energy; (nervioso) to be a bag *o* bundle of nerves (colloq); ***tener los ~s de punta*** to be very tense, to be on edge; ***tener ~s de acero*** to have nerves of steel
C (impulso, vitalidad) spirit

nerviosismo *m*, **nerviosidad** *f*: **el ~ que producen los exámenes** the feeling of nervousness *o* nerves that exams produce; **noté cierto ~ entre ellos** they seemed rather agitated

nervioso -sa *adj*
A ‹*persona/animal*› **1** [SER] (excitable) nervous **2** [ESTAR] (preocupado, tenso) nervous; **estoy muy ~ por lo de los exámenes** I'm very nervous about the exams **3** [ESTAR] (agitado) agitated; **últimamente se le nota ~** he's been on edge *o* (colloq) uptight lately; **ese ruido me tiene muy nerviosa** that noise is getting on my nerves; **me pongo ~ cada vez que la veo** I get flustered every time I see her
B ‹*trastorno*› nervous

nervudo -da *adj* sinewy

neta *f* (Méx fam): **la ~** the truth; ***ser la ~*** (Méx) to be great (colloq)

netiqueta *f* (fam) netiquette

neto -ta *adj* **1** ‹*sueldo/precio*› net **2** (claro) ‹*silueta/perfil*› distinct, clear

neumático¹ -ca *adj* pneumatic

neumático² *m* tire (AmE), tyre (BrE)

neumonía *f* pneumonia

neura¹ *adj* (fam): **eso me pone ~** that drives me crazy *o* (BrE) mad (colloq); **es tan ~** he's so neurotic

neura² *mf* (fam)
A (persona): **es un ~** he's a complete neurotic (colloq)
B **neura** *f*: **está con la ~** she's in a real state (colloq)

neuralgia *f* neuralgia

neurálgico -ca *adj* **1** (Med) neuralgic **2** (clave, importante) key (*before n*)

neurastenia *f* nervous exhaustion

neurasténico -ca *adj/m,f* **1** (Med) neurasthenic **2** (fam) ► **neura¹,²**

neurocirugía *f* neurosurgery, brain surgery

neurología *f* neurology

neurólogo -ga *m,f* neurologist

neurona *f* neuron

neurosis *f* neurosis

(Compuesto) **neurosis bélica** shellshock

neurótico -ca *adj/m,f* neurotic

neutral *adj* neutral

neutralidad *f* neutrality

neutralismo *m* neutralism

neutralista *adj/mf* neutralist

neutralización *f* neutralization

neutralizador¹ -dora *adj* neutralizing (*before n*)

neutralizador² *m* neutralizer

neutralizar [A4] *vt* to neutralize

neutro¹ -tra *adj*
A (Elec, Fís, Quím) neutral
B (Biol, Ling) neuter

neutro² *m*
A (Ling) neuter
B (AmL) (Auto) neutral

neutrón *m* neutron

nevada *f* snowfall

nevado¹ -da *adj* **1** ‹*cumbres/picos*› snowcapped, snow-covered **2** (liter) (blanco) white; (plateado) silvery

nevado² *m* (AmS) snowcapped mountain

nevar [A5] *v impers* to snow

nevasca *f*, (CS) **nevazón** *f* blizzard, snowstorm

nevera *f* **1** (refrigerador) refrigerator, fridge, icebox (AmE) **2** (para picnic) cooler (AmE), cool bag/box (BrE)

(Compuesto) **nevera congelador** fridge-freezer

nevería *f* (Méx) ice-cream parlor*

nevisca *f* light snowfall

nexo *m* (enlace, vínculo) link; **actuó de ~ entre los dos equipos** she acted as a liaison between the two teams

ni *conj*
A (con otro negativo): **venía sin gabardina ~ paraguas** he wasn't wearing a raincoat or carrying an umbrella; **no se lastimó ~ nada** he didn't hurt himself or anything; **no vino él ~ su mujer** neither he nor his wife came; **yo no pienso ir — ~ yo (tampoco)** I don't intend going — neither do I; **ni ... ni**: **~ fumo ~ bebo** I don't smoke or drink, I neither smoke nor drink; **no nos avisaron ~ a Sol ~ a mí** they didn't tell Sol or me (either)
B **1** *tb* **ni siquiera** not even **2** **ni un/una**: **no vendieron ~ un libro** they didn't sell a single book; **de sus amigos no vino ~ uno** not one of his friends came
C **1** (en frases que expresan rechazo): **¡~ hablar!** out of the question!; **~ aunque me lo pida de rodillas** not even if he gets down on bended knee **2** (en frases que expresan enfado): **¡~ que fuera el jefe!** anyone would think he was the boss; **no podemos permitírnoslo ¡~ que fuéramos millonarios!** we can't afford it, we're not millionaires you know!

Niágara *m*: **las cataratas del ~** Niagara Falls

nica *adj/mf* (AmL fam) Nicaraguan

Nicaragua *f* Nicaragua

nicaragüense *adj/mf* Nicaraguan

niche *adj* (Ven pey) common (pej)

nicho *m* (Arquit) niche; (en cementerio) *deep recess in a wall used as a tomb*

nicotina *f* nicotine

nidada *f* (de huevos) clutch; (de crías) clutch, brood

nidal *m* nesting box

nido *m* **1** (de aves, insectos) nest; ***caerse del ~*** (fam): **¿tú te crees que yo me he caído del ~?** I wasn't born yesterday, you know! (colloq); ***ser un ~ de víboras*** to be a nest of vipers **2** (hogar) nest; **los hijos ya han dejado el ~** the children have already flown the nest **3** (guarida) den; **un ~ de ladrones** a den of thieves

(Compuesto) **nido de amor** love nest

niebla *f* fog; **había ~** it was foggy; **un día de ~** a foggy day

niega, niegas, etc *see* **negar**

nieto -ta (*m*) grandson, grandchild; (*f*) granddaughter, grandchild; **mis ~s** (sólo varones) my grandsons; (varones y mujeres) my grandchildren

nieva *see* **nevar**

nieve *f*
A **1** (Meteo) snow; ***blanco como la ~*** as white as snow **2** **nieves** *fpl* (nevada) snows (*pl*)
B (liter) (blancura) snowy whiteness
C **1** (Coc): **batir las claras a (punto de) ~** whisk the egg whites until stiff **2** (Méx) (helado) sorbet, water ice
D (arg) (cocaína) snow (sl)

NIF /nif/ *m* = **número de identificación fiscal**

> **NIF – Número de identificación fiscal**
>
> Tax identification code that all residents of Spain must have. People must give it when applying for a loan, opening a bank account, sending invoices, etc. It is the same as a person's identity number, with an additional letter

Nigeria *f* Nigeria

nigeriano -na *adj/m,f* Nigerian

nigromancia *f* necromancy

Nilo *m*: **el ~** the Nile River (AmE), the River Nile (BrE)

nilón *m* nylon

nimbo *m*
A (Astron, Relig) halo
B (Meteo) nimbus

nimiedad *f* **1** (cosa insignificante) triviality, trifle; **discuten por cualquier ~** they argue over the slightest little thing **2** (cualidad) triviality

nimio -mia *adj* trivial, petty

ninfa *f* (Mit) nymph; (mujer atractiva) (fam) stunner (colloq)

ninfómana *f* nymphomaniac

ningún *adj: apocopated form of* **ninguno** *used before masculine singular nouns*

ningunear [A1] *vt* (Méx fam) to treat … like dirt (colloq)

ninguno[1] -na *adj (see note under* **ningún***)* 1 *(delante del n)*: **no prestó ninguna atención** he didn't pay any attention; **en ningún momento** never; **no lo encuentro por ningún lado** *or* **ninguna parte** I can't find it anywhere; **no es tonta, pero tampoco es ninguna lumbrera** she's not stupid, but she's no genius either 2 *(detrás del n)* (uso enfático): **no hay problema** ~ there's absolutely no problem

ninguno[2] -na *pron*

A (refiriéndose — a dos personas o cosas) neither; (— a más de dos) none; ~ **de los dos vino** neither of them came; **no trajo** ~ **de los dos** she didn't bring either of them; **ninguna le pareció aceptable** he didn't find any of them acceptable; **sin que** ~ **de nosotros se diera cuenta** without any of us realizing

B (nadie) nobody, no-one; **toca mejor que** ~ he plays better than anybody *o* anyone

niña *f* pupil; ***ser la* ~ *de los ojos de algn*** to be the apple of sb's eye; *ver tb* **niño[2]**

niñada, niñería *f* (pey): **déjate de ~s** stop being so childish

niñero -ra *m,f* nanny, nursemaid (AmE)

niñez *f* childhood

niño[1] -ña *adj* 1 (joven) young; **es muy niña para casarse** she's very young to be getting married 2 (infantil, inmaduro) immature, childish

niño[2] -ña *m,f* 1 *(m)* boy, child; *(f)* girl, child; (bebé) baby; **¿te gustan los ~s?** do you like children?; **de** ~ as a child; ***estar como (un)* ~ *con zapatos nuevos*** to be like a child with a new toy 2 (con respecto a los padres) *(m)* son, child; *(f)* daughter, child; **está esperando un** ~ she's expecting a baby 3 (adulto joven) *(m)* (young) boy, (young) guy (colloq); *(f)* (young) girl 4 (AmL) (término de respeto) *(m)* young master; *(f)* young lady; **¿la niña Lupita va a cenar en casa?** will Miss Lupita be dining in this evening?

(Compuestos)

- **niña bonita** *f*: **la** ~ ~ number fifteen
- **niño -ña bien** *m,f* rich kid (colloq)
- **niño bonito -ña bonita** *m,f* (Esp) rich kid (colloq)
- **niño -ña de brazos** *m,f* babe-in-arms
- **niño -ña de pañales** *or* **de pecho** *m,f* small *o* young baby
- **Niño Jesús** *or* **Dios** *m*: **el** ~ ~ Baby Jesus
- **niño mimado -ña mimada** *m,f* favorite*, pet
- **niño -ña probeta** *m,f* test-tube baby
- **niño -ña prodigio** *m,f* child prodigy

nipón -pona *adj/m,f* Japanese

níquel *m* nickel

niquelar [A1] *vt* to nickel

niqui *m* (Esp) polo shirt

níspero *m* loquat

nitidez *f* (de imagen, del día) clarity; (de recuerdo) vividness

nítido -da *adj* ‹*foto/imagen*› clear; ‹*recuerdo*› vivid; ‹*cielo/agua*› clear

nitrato *m* nitrate

nítrico -ca *adj* nitric

nitrógeno *m* nitrogen

nitroglicerina *f* nitroglycerine

nivel *m* 1 (altura) level; **sobre el** ~ **del mar** above sea level 2 (en escala, jerarquía) level; **conversaciones de alto** ~ high-level talks; **negociaciones al más alto** ~ top-level negotiations; **un funcionario de bajo** ~ a low-ranking civil servant; **no está al** ~ **de los demás** he's not up to the same standard as the others; **estar al** ~ **de las circunstancias** to rise to the occasion

(Compuesto) **nivel de vida** standard of living

nivelación *f*, **nivelamiento** *m*

A (de superficie) leveling*

B (de presupuesto) balancing

niveladora *f*, **nivelador** *m* grader

nivelar [A1] *vt*

A (Const) ‹*suelo/terreno*› to level; ‹*estante*› to get … level

B ‹*presupuesto*› to balance

níveo -vea *adj* (liter) snow-white

nixtamal *m* (Méx) cooked maize *(used to make tortillas)*

NN (= **ningún nombre**) *initials on grave of unidentified person*

no[1] *adv*

A (como respuesta) no; (modificando adverbios, oraciones, verbos) not *[la negación de la mayoría de los verbos ingleses requiere el uso del auxiliar 'do']* **¿te gustó? — no** did you like it? — no *o* no, I didn't; **¿vienes? — no** are you coming? — no *o* no, I'm not; **pídeselo tú — ¡ah, ~! ¡eso ~!** you ask her — oh, no! no way! (colloq); **¿por qué no quieres ir? — porque** ~ why don't you want to go? — I just don't; **¿fue difícil? —** ~ **mucho** was it difficult? — not really

B (con otro negativo): ~ **veo nada** I can't see a thing *o* anything; ~ **viene nunca** she never comes; *ver tb* **ni**

C (en coletillas interrogativas): **está mejor ¿~?** she's better, isn't she?; **ha dimitido ¿~?** he has resigned, hasn't he?; **más vale tarde que nunca ¿~?** better late than never, don't you think?

D (expresando incredulidad): **se ganó la lotería — ¡~!** he won the lottery — he didn't! *o* no!

E (sustituyendo a una cláusula): **creo que** ~ I don't think so; **¿podemos ir? — he dicho que** ~ can we go? — I said no; **¿te gustó? a mí** ~ did you like it? I didn't; **yo llegaré antes — ¡a que ~!** I'll get there first — I bet you won't!

F (sin valor negativo): **nadie viajará hasta que** ~ **recibamos el dinero** no one can travel until we receive the money; **¡cuántas veces** ~ **se lo habré dicho!** how many times have I told him!; **tenía miedo** ~ **le fuese a ocurrir algo** I was afraid something might happen to him; **¿~ me lavarías esto?** do you think you could wash this for me, please?

G 1 *(delante de n)*: **los** ~ **fumadores** nonsmokers; **la** ~ **violencia** non-violence 2 *(delante de adj, pp)*: **un hijo** ~ **deseado** an unwanted child; **material** ~ **inflamable** nonflammable material

no[2] *m (pl* **noes***)* no; **contestó con un** ~ **rotundo** her answer was a categorical no

NO (= **noroeste**) NW

Nobel *m* 1 *tb* **Premio** ~ Nobel Prize 2 (ganador) Nobel prizewinner

nobiliario *m* peerage

noble[1] *adj* 1 ‹*familia/ascendencia*› noble; **un caballero de** ~ **linaje** (liter) a knight of noble lineage (liter) 2 (bondadoso) noble 3 ‹*animal*› noble 4 ‹*madera*› fine

(Compuesto) **noble bruto** *m* (liter): **el** ~ ~ the horse

noble[2] *(m)* nobleman; *(f)* noblewoman; **los** ~ the nobles, the nobility

nobleza *f*

A (clase) nobility; ~ **obliga** (fr hecha) noblesse oblige

B (de persona) nobility; (de material) quality

nocaut[1] *adj* (AmL): **lo dejó** ~ he/it knocked him out; **está** ~ he's out for the count

nocaut[2] *m (pl* **-cauts***)* (AmL) knockout

noche *f*

A (período de tiempo) night; **la** ~ **anterior** the night before, the previous evening; **a altas horas de la** ~ in the small hours; **esta** ~ tonight, this evening; **a las ocho de la** ~ at eight o'clock in the evening *o* at night

B 1 (oscuridad) night; **antes de que caiga la** ~ before it gets dark, before nightfall; **en la** ~ **de los tiempos** (liter) in the mists of time (liter) 2 (liter) (tristeza) sadness, gloom

C *(en locs)* **buenas noches** (al saludar) good evening; (al despedirse) goodnight; **de noche** ‹*trabajar/conducir*› at night; **ahora es de** ~ **en el Japón** it's night *o* nighttime now in Japan; **se hizo de** ~ it got dark, night fell; **en la** *or* (esp Esp) **en la** *or* (RPl) **a la noche**: **por la** ~ **fuimos al teatro** in the evening we went to the theater; **el lunes por la** ~ on Monday evening/night; ***de la* ~ *a la mañana*** overnight; ***hacer* ~** to spend the night; ***pasar la* ~ *en blanco*** to have a sleepless night; ***pasar la* ~ *en vela*** (vigilando, esperando a algn) to sit *o* stay up all night; (no poder dormir) to have a sleepless night; ***de* ~ *todos los gatos son pardos*** *or* (AmL) ***negros*** no one will notice (in the dark)

(Compuesto) **Noche Vieja** New Year's Eve *(in the evening)*

Nochebuena *f* Christmas Eve

Nochebuena

In Spanish-speaking countries, Christmas Eve is celebrated rather than Christmas Day. Dinner is eaten before Midnight Mass known as *misa del gallo*.

In Latin America, where many countries do not celebrate the *día de Reyes* (*see* **Reyes Magos**), Christmas gifts are given on Christmas Eve. This custom is spreading in Spain, although the *día de Reyes* is celebrated there

Nochevieja *f* New Year's Eve (*in the evening*)

Nochevieja y Año Nuevo

In Spain and other Spanish-speaking countries, it is customary to see the New Year in by eating twelve grapes for good luck, one on each chime of the clock at midnight

noción *f* 1 (idea, concepto) notion, idea; **no tiene la menor ~ del tema** he doesn't know the first thing about the subject; **ha perdido la ~ del tiempo** he has lost all sense *o* notion of time 2 **nociones** *fpl* (conocimientos): **tengo nociones de ruso** I know a little Russian; **les dio unas nociones de electrónica** she taught them the basics *o* rudiments of electronics

nocividad *f* harmfulness

nocivo -va *adj* ‹*sustancia/aditivo*› harmful; ‹*influencia*› damaging

noctambulismo *m*: **el ~ de la vida madrileña** the late-night social activity of Madrid life; **el ~ de los españoles** the Spanish custom of staying up late

noctámbulo -la *adj*: **siempre ha sido ~** he's always been a night bird *o* night owl *o* (AmE) nighthawk (colloq)

nocturno[1] **-na** *adj* 1 ‹*vuelo/tren*› night (*before n*); ‹*clases*› evening (*before n*); **sus visitas nocturnas** his nighttime visits; **vida nocturna** night life; **en el silencio ~** (liter) in the silence of the night 2 ‹*animal/planta*› nocturnal

nocturno[2] *m*

A (Mús) nocturne

B (en colegios, universidades) *courses held in the evening*

nodo *m* node

nodriza *f* (ama de cría) wet nurse; (niñera) (ant) nursemaid

nódulo *m* nodule

nogal *m* (árbol) walnut tree; (madera) walnut

nómada[1] *adj* nomadic

nómada[2] *mf* nomad

nomadismo *m* nomadism

nomás *adv*

A (AmL): **pase ~** come on in; **démelo así ~, sin envolver** don't bother wrapping it, I'll take it as it is; **no lo vas a convencer así ~** you're not going to convince him as easily as that; **vive aquí ~, a dos cuadras** she lives just two blocks away from here; **déjelo aquí ~** just leave it here; **lo dijo por molestar ~** she only said it to be difficult; **tiemblo ~ de imaginármelo** I tremble at the mere thought of it

B **nomás (que)** (Col, Méx fam) as soon as; **~ (que) tenga dinero** as soon as I have some money

nombradía *f* renown, fame

nombrado -da *adj*: **muy ~ en círculos científicos** renowned *o* very well-known in scientific circles; **una película muy nombrada** a very famous film

nombramiento *m* (designación) appointment; (documento) letter of appointment

nombrar [A1] *vt*

A (citar, mencionar) to mention; **la persona anteriormente nombrada** the aforementioned person

B (designar) to appoint

nombre *m*

A 1 (de cosa, persona, animal) name; **¿cuál es el ~ de la compañía?** what's the name of the company?; **~ completo** *o* **~ y apellidos** full name, name in full; **¿qué ~ le pusieron?** what did they call him?; **le pusieron el ~ de su padrino** they named him for (AmE) *o* (BrE) after his godfather; **responde al ~ de Bobi** he answers to the name of Bobi; **de ~** by name; **llamar a algn por el ~** to call sb by their first name; **en ~ de** (en representación de) on behalf of; (apelando a) in the name of; **a ~ de**: **un paquete a ~ de ...** a package addressed to ...; **un cheque a ~ de ...** a check made payable to *o* made out to ...; ***llamar a las cosas por su ~*** to call a spade a spade; ***no tiene ~***: **lo que ha hecho no tiene ~** what she has done is unspeakable 2 (sobrenombre): **a todos les pone ~** he gives everybody nicknames; **más conocida por el ~ de la Pasionaria** better known as la Pasionaria

(Compuestos)
- **nombre artístico** stage name
- **nombre comercial** trade name
- **nombre de guerra** *or* (AmL) **de batalla** nom de guerre
- **nombre de pila** first name, christian name
- **nombre de soltera** maiden name

B (Ling) noun

(Compuestos)
- **nombre compuesto** compound
- **nombre propio** proper noun

C (fama): **un científico de ~** a renowned scientist; **hacerse un ~ en la vida** to make a name for oneself

nomenclatura *f* nomenclature

nomeolvides *m or f* (*pl* ~) (Bot) forget-me-not

nómina *f* (lista de empleados) payroll; (hoja de pago) payslip; (suma de dinero) salary, wages (*pl*)

nominación *f* nomination

nominal *adj*

A ‹*sueldo*› nominal; **valor ~** face value

B (Ling) noun (*before n*), nominal

nominar [A1] *vt* ‹*película/candidato*› to nominate

nominativo[1] *adj* (Fin): **un cheque ~ a favor de ...** a check made out to *o* payable to ...

nominativo[2] *m* nominative

nomo *m* gnome

non[1] *adj* odd; **números ~es** odd numbers

non[2] *m* odd number; **pares y ~es** odds and evens

nonagésimo[1] **-ma** *adj/pron* 1 (ordinal) ninetieth; *para ejemplos ver* **vigésimo** 2 (partitivo): **la nonagésima parte** a ninetieth

nonagésimo[2] *m* ninetieth

nonato -ta *adj*: *born by Cesarean section especially after mother's death*

nones *adv* (fam): **le dijo que ~** she said no way (colloq)

nono -na *adj/pron* (frml) ninth

noqueada *f* knockout

noquear [A1] *vt* to knock out

noratlántico -ca *adj* north-Atlantic (*before n*)

nordeste[1], **noreste** *adj inv* ‹*región*› northeastern; **iban en dirección ~** they were heading northeast

nordeste[2], **noreste** *m* 1 (parte, sector): **el ~** the northeast, the Northeast 2 (punto cardinal) northeast, Northeast; **vientos del ~** northeasterly winds

nórdico[1] **-ca** *adj* 1 ‹*país/pueblo*› Nordic 2 (Hist) Norse

nórdico[2] **-ca** *m,f* 1 (del norte de Europa) Northern European (*esp Scandinavian*) 2 (Hist) Norseman

noria *f* 1 (para sacar agua) waterwheel 2 (Ocio) Ferris wheel (AmE), big wheel (BrE)

norma *f* 1 (regla) rule, regulation; **~s de conducta** rules of conduct; **~s de seguridad** safety regulations; **dictar ~s** to lay down rules *o* regulations; **tengo por ~ ...** I make it a rule ... 2 (manera común de hacer algo): **es ~ que** *or* **la ~ es que acudan los directivos** it is standard practice for the directors to attend

normal[1] *adj* 1 (común, usual) normal; **hoy en día es muy ~** it's very common nowadays; **no es ~ que haga tanto frío** it's unusual *o* it isn't normal for it to be so cold; **superior a lo ~** above-average; ***~ y corriente*** ordinary 2 (sin graves defectos) normal; **esa chica no es ~** (fam) there's something wrong with that girl (colloq)

normal[2] *adv* (fam) normally; **camina ~** he walks quite normally; **cocina ~** she's average cook

normal[3] *f* 1 (escuela): **la N ~** teacher training college 2 (gasolina) regular gas (AmE), two-star petrol (BrE)

normalidad *f* 1 (cualidad): **seguimos trabajando con toda ~** we carried on working normally *o* as normal; **la manifestación se desarrolló con toda ~** the demonstration passed off without incident 2 (situación) normalcy (AmE), normality (BrE); **el país ha vuelto a la ~** the country has returned to normal

normalista *mf* (Col) primary (school) teacher

normalización *f*
A (de situación) normalization
B (estandarización) standardization

normalizar [A4] *vt*
A ‹*situación/relaciones*› to normalize
B (estandarizar) to standardize
■ **normalizarse** *v pron*
A «*situación/relaciones*» to return to normal
B (estandarizarse) to become standardized

normalmente *adv* normally, usually

Normandía *f* Normandy

normando -da *adj/m,f* Norman

normar [A1] *vt* (Chi, Méx) 1 (regir): **estos principios ~án el proceso** the process will conform to these principles 2 (regular) to control, regulate

normativa *f* regulations (*pl*), rules (*pl*)

normativo -va *adj*: **sistema normativo** set of rules *o* regulations; **un régimen ~ muy estricto** very strict rules *o* regulations

noroeste[1] *adj inv* ‹*región*› northwestern; **iban en dirección ~** they were heading northwest

noroeste[2] *m* 1 (parte, sector): **el ~** the northwest, the Northwest 2 (punto cardinal) northwest, Northwest; **vientos del ~** northwesterly winds

norte[1] *adj inv* ‹*región*› northern; **en la parte ~ del país** in the northern part *o* the north of the country; **iban en dirección ~** they were heading north *o* northward(s); **la costa/el ala ~** the north coast/wind

norte[2] *m* 1 (parte, sector): **el ~** the north; **en el ~ del país** in the north of the country; **al ~ de Matagalpa** to the north of Matagalpa 2 (punto cardinal) north, North; **vientos del N~** northerly winds; **caminaron hacia el N~** they walked north *o* northward(s); **la casa da al ~** the house faces north 3 (rumbo): **perder el ~ de realidad** to lose sight of reality

Norteamérica *f* 1 (América del Norte) North America 2 (EEUU) America, the States (colloq)

norteamericano -na *adj/m,f* 1 (de América del Norte) North American 2 (estadounidense) American

norteño[1] **-ña**, (Chi, Per) **nortino -na** *adj* northern

norteño[2] **-ña**, (Chi, Per) **nortino -na** *m,f* northerner

Noruega *f* Norway

noruego[1] **-ga** *adj/m,f* Norwegian

noruego[2] *m* (idioma) Norwegian

nos *pron pers* 1 (como complemento directo, indirecto) us; **~ ayudaron mucho** they helped us a lot; **escúchanos** listen to us; **~ han robado el coche** our car's been stolen; **¿~ explicas cómo se hace?** can you tell us *o* explain to us how it's done?; **~ lo trajeron ayer** they brought it yesterday; **~ lo quitó** she took it off us *o* away from us 2 (*refl*) ourselves; **~ hicimos daño** we hurt ourselves; **sentémonos** let's sit down; **~ vamos a hacer socios del club** we're going to become members of *o* join the club 3 (*recípr*): **~ conocemos desde hace años** we have known each other for years

nosocomio *m* (frml *o* period) hospital

nosotros -tras *pron pers pl* 1 we; **¿quién lo trajo? — nosotros** who brought it? — we did; **ábrenos, somos nosotras** open the door, it's us; **~ mismos lo arreglamos** we fixed it ourselves 2 (en comparaciones, con preposiciones) us; **viven mejor que ~** they live better than we do *o* better than us; **antes/después que ~** before/after us

nostalgia *f* nostalgia; **siente ~ por** *or* **de su país** he feels homesick

nostálgico -ca *adj* nostalgic

nota *f*
A 1 (apunte) note; **tomar ~ de algo** (apuntar) to make a note of sth; (fijarse) to take note of sth; **tomar ~s** to take notes 2 (acotación) note

(Compuestos)
- **nota al margen** margin note
- **nota a pie de página** footnote

B 1 (mensaje) note 2 (noticia breve): **y ahora, la ~ deportiva ...** and now the sports roundup ...; **según una ~ que acaba de llegar** according to a report just in

(Compuestos)
- **nota de prensa** press release
- **nota necrológica** announcement of a death; **~s ~s** obituaries

C (Educ) (calificación) grade (AmE), mark (BrE); **sacar buenas ~s** to get good grades *o* marks

D 1 (rasgo): **la ~ dominante de su estilo** the dominant feature of his style; **la ~ melancólica de sus poemas** the underlying note of sadness in his poems 2 (detalle) touch; **una ~ de humor** a touch of humor; **fue la ~ de mal gusto de la reunión** it was the one thing that lowered the tone of the meeting

E (Mús) note; ***dar la ~*** (fam) to stand out; (por algo censurable) to make a spectacle of oneself; ***dar la ~ discordante*** to be difficult (*o* different *etc*); ***ser la ~ discordante*** to strike a sour note

(Compuesto) **nota musical** note

F (en restaurante) check (AmE), bill (BrE); (en tienda) (Ur) receipt

notabilidad *f* : **un músico de gran ~** a musician of great note; **su ~ ya traspasa las fronteras** his fame has spread far and wide

notable[1] *adj* notable; **una actuación ~** an outstanding performance; **posee una ~ inteligencia** she is remarkably *o* extremely intelligent

notable[2] *m* 1 (Educ) *grade between 7 and 8.5 on a scale from 1 to 10* 2 (persona importante) dignitary

notación *f* notation

notar [A1] *vt* 1 (advertir) to notice; **hacer(le) ~ algo (a algn)** to point sth out (to sb); **notó que alguien le tocaba el brazo** she became aware of somebody touching her arm; **te noto muy triste** you look very sad; **se le notaba indeciso** he seemed hesitant; ***hacerse ~*** (atraer la atención) to draw attention to oneself; (dejarse sentir) to be felt 2 (*impers*): **se nota que es novato** you can tell *o* see he's a beginner; **¿se notan las puntadas?** do the stitches show?; (+ *me/te/le etc*): **se te nota en la cara** it's written all over your face; **se le nota mucho el acento** his accent is very noticeable
■ **notarse** *v pron* (+ *compl*) to feel; **me noto muy rara con este vestido** I feel funny in this dress

notaría *f* 1 (profesión) *profession of notary*; (oficina) notary's office 2 (Col) (registro civil) registry office

notarial *adj* notarial

notario -ria *m,f* notary, notary public

noticia *f* 1 (informe): **¡es una estupenda ~!** that's wonderful news!; **la ~ de su muerte** the news of his death; **las ~s son alarmantes** the news is alarming; **buenas/malas ~s** good/bad news; **¿quién le va a dar la ~?** who's going to break the news to him?; **la última ~ del programa** the final item on the news; ***estar atrasado de ~s*** to be behind with the news; ***hacer ~*** to hit the headlines 2 **noticias** *fpl* (referencias) news; **no tenemos ~s suyas** (provenientes de él) we haven't heard from him; (provenientes de otra persona) we haven't had (any) news of him 3 (información, conocimiento): **no tenía ~ de que hubiera problemas** I didn't know (that) there were problems

(Compuesto) **noticia bomba** (fam): **lo de su divorcio fue una ~ ~** the news of their divorce was a real bombshell (colloq); **traigo una ~ ~** I have some amazing news for you

noticiario *m*, (AmL) **noticiero** *m* (Rad, TV) news; (Cin) newsreel

noticioso[1] **-sa** *adj* (Andes, RPl): **su visita fue el golpe ~ del año** his visit was the big event of the year

noticioso[2] *m* (Andes, RPl) news bulletin

notificación *f* (frml) notification (frml)

notificar [A2] *vt* (frml) ‹*resolución/sentencia*› to notify; **~ algo A algn** to notify sb OF sth (frml)

notoriedad *f*
A (frml) (conocimiento) knowledge; **es de ~ pública que...** it is common knowledge that...
B (fama) fame; (mala fama) notoriety

notorio -ria *adj* 1 (evidente) evident, obvious 2 (conocido) well-known; **la figura más notoria de la oposición** the best-known opposition figure 3 (notable) ‹*descenso/mejora*› marked

nov. (= **noviembre**) Nov

n

novatada *f* 1 (broma) practical joke (*played on a new student/recruit*); **hacerle una ~ a algn** to haze sb (AmE), to rag sb (BrE colloq) 2 (error) new boy's/girl's/guy's blunder

novato[1] **-ta** *adj* inexperienced, new

novato[2] **-ta** *m,f* novice, beginner

novecientos -tas *adj/pron* nine hundred; *para ejemplos ver* **quinientos**

novedad *f*

A 1 (cosa nueva) innovation; **este modelo trae algunas ~es** this model has some new features; **la gran ~ para esta temporada** the latest idea (*o* fashion *etc*) for this season 2 (cualidad) newness, novelty 3 **novedades** *fpl* novelties (*pl*)

B 1 (noticia): **eso no es ninguna ~** everybody knows that; **¿cómo sigue? — sin ~** how is he? — much the same 2 (percance, contratiempo): **llegamos sin ~** we arrived safely; ***sin ~ en el frente*** (hum) all quiet on the Western front (hum)

novedoso -sa *adj* ‹*idea/enfoque*› novel, original; **un ~ sistema de financiación** a completely new system of finance

novel[1] *adj* new; **para que esta ~ industria prospere** (frml) so that this fledgling industry may prosper (frml)

novel[2] *mf* novice, beginner

novela *f* 1 (Lit) novel; ***de ~*** like something (straight) out of a novel 2 (TV) soap opera

(Compuestos)

- **novela de aventuras** adventure story
- **novela policíaca** *o* **policial** detective novel *o* story
- **novela rosa** (pey) novelette (pej), romantic novel

novelar [A1] *vt* ‹*sucesos/guerra*› to write a novel about; ‹*obra*› to make *o* turn ... into a novel

novelero -ra *adj*: **es muy ~** (fantasioso) he tends to embroider his stories; (aficionado a la novela) he loves reading novels

novelesco -ca *adj* ‹*vida/historia*› like something out of a novel; ‹*viajes/andanzas*› fabulous

novelista *mf* novelist

novelística *f*: **la ~** the novel

novelístico -ca *adj* ‹*técnica*› novelistic, novel-writing (*before n*); **su obra novelística** his novels

novena *f*

A (Relig) novena

B (en béisbol) ninth

noveno[1] **-na** *adj/pron* 1 (ordinal) ninth; *para ejemplos ver* **quinto** 2 (partitivo): **la novena parte** a ninth

noveno[2] *m* ninth

noventa[1] *adj inv/pron* ninety; *ver* **cincuenta**

noventa[2] *m* (number) ninety

noviar [A1] *vi* (AmL fam) to go out together, to date (AmE); **~ CON algn** to go out WITH sb, to date sb (AmE)

noviazgo *m*: **el ~ duró un año** they went out (together) for one year; **~s a larga distancia** long-distance relationships

noviciado *m* 1 (Relig) novitiate 2 (en oficio) apprenticeship

novicio -cia *m,f* 1 (Relig) novice 2 (principiante) novice, beginner

no-vidente *adj/mf* (CS) ▸**invidente**

noviembre *m* November; *para ejemplos ver* **enero**

novillada *f*: *bullfight using young bulls*

novillero -ra *m,f* apprentice bullfighter

novillo -lla (*m*) young bull; (*f*) heifer; ***hacer ~s*** (fam) to play hooky (esp AmE colloq), to skive off (school) (BrE colloq)

novio -via *m,f* 1 (no formal) (*m*) boyfriend; (*f*) girlfriend; (después del compromiso) (*m*) fiancé; (*f*) fiancée 2 (el día de la boda) (*m*) groom; (*f*) bride; **los ~s** the bride and groom

nubarrón *m* storm cloud

nube *f*

A (Meteo) cloud; **un cielo cubierto de ~s** an overcast *o* a cloudy sky; **ninguna ~ enturbiaba su felicidad** (liter) not a single cloud marred her happiness (liter); ***como caído de las ~s*** out of the blue; ***estar*** *or* ***andar en las ~s*** (fam) to have one's head in the clouds; ***estar/ponerse por las ~s*** (fam): **las casas están por las ~s** house prices are sky-high (colloq); **la carne se está poniendo por las ~s** the price of meat is going through the roof (colloq); ***poner a algn por las ~s*** to sing sb's praises; ***vivir en las ~s*** to live in cloud-cuckoo land (colloq)

(Compuesto) **nube de verano** (Meteo) summer shower; **el enfado fue una ~ de ~** the quarrel was short-lived

B (de polvo, humo) cloud; (de insectos) cloud, swarm; **una ~ de fotógrafos** a swarm of photographers

(Compuesto) **nube atómica** mushroom cloud

núbil *adj* (liter) nubile

nubilidad *f* (liter) nubility

nublado[1] **-da** *adj* 1 ‹*cielo/día*› cloudy, overcast 2 (liter) (enturbiado) clouded

nublado[2] *m* (nube) storm cloud; (período) cloudy spell

nublar [A1] *vt* 1 ‹*vista*› to cloud 2 (liter) ‹*felicidad*› to cloud (liter)

■ **nublarse** *v pron* 1 «*cielo*» to cloud over 2 «*vista*» to cloud over 3 (liter) «*razón*» to become clouded

nubosidad *f* cloud; **la ~ irá en aumento** it will become increasingly cloudy

nuboso -sa *adj* cloudy

nuca *f* back *o* nape of the neck

nuclear[1] *adj* nuclear

nuclear[2] *f* nuclear power station

nuclearización *f* nuclearization

nuclearizado -da *adj*: **un país ~** *a country which has nuclear weapons or allows them on its territory*

núcleo *m*

A 1 (Biol, Fís, Quím) nucleus 2 (Ling) nucleus 3 (Elec) core

B 1 (de asunto) heart, core; (de conjunto) nucleus 2 (grupo) group 3 (centro) center•

(Compuestos)

- **núcleo de población** center• of population
- **núcleo familiar** family unit

nudillo *m* knuckle

nudismo *m* nudism

nudista *adj/mf* nudist

nudo *m*

A 1 (lazo, atadura) knot; **se hizo un ~ en el hilo** the thread got into a knot; **¿me haces el ~ de la corbata?** can you tie *o* do my tie for me?; **tenía un ~ en la garganta** I had a lump in my throat 2 (Náut) knot

B (en madera) knot; (en caña) node, joint; (Anat) node

C (de carreteras, vías férreas) junction

D (de trama) climax; (de problema) crux, heart

nudoso -sa *adj* ‹*manos*› knotted, gnarled; ‹*vara/tronco*› knotty

nuera *f* daughter-in-law

nuestro[1] **-tra** *adj* our; **ése es ~ coche** *or* **ése es el coche ~** that's our car; **un amigo ~** a friend of ours

nuestro[2] **-tra** *pron*: **el ~, la nuestra** *etc* ours; **los ~s son azules** ours are blue; **es de los ~s** he's one of us; **nosotros a lo ~** let's just get on with our own business; **sabe lo ~** he knows about us

nueva *f* (arc) tidings (*pl*) (arch); **las buenas ~s** the glad tidings; (Esp) ***coger a algn de ~s*** (Esp) to take sb by surprise; ***hacerse de ~s*** (Esp) to act surprised

Nueva Delhi *f* New Delhi

nuevamente *adv* again; **mañana estaremos ~ con ustedes** we'll be back (again) tomorrow

Nueva Orleáns *f* New Orleans

Nueva York *f* New York

Nueva Zelandia, Nueva Zelanda *f* New Zealand

nueve[1] *adj inv/pron* nine; *para ejemplos ver* **cinco**

nueve[2] *m* (number) nine; *para ejemplos ver* **cinco**

nueveavo[1] **-va** *adj* 1 (partitivo): **la nueveava parte** a ninth 2 (crit) (ordinal) ninth; *para ejemplos ver* **veinteavo**[1]

nueveavo[2] *m* ninth

nuevo -va *adj*

A 1 [SER] ‹*coche/casa/trabajo*› new 2 (*delante del n*) ‹*intento/cambio*› further; **ha surgido un ~ problema** another *o* a further problem has arisen 3 [SER] ‹*estilo/enfoque*› new;

¿qué hay de ~? (fam) what's new? (colloq) 4▸ [ESTAR] (no desgastado) as good as new; **todavía lo tengo nuevecito** *or* (CS) **nuevito** it's still as good as new

(Compuestos)
- **nueva ola** *f* new wave
- **nuevas tecnologías** *fpl* new technology
- **nuevo rico -va rica** *m,f* nouveau riche
- **Nuevo Testamento** *m* New Testament

B **de nuevo** again

Nuevo México *m* New Mexico

Nuevo Mundo *m* (liter): **el ~ ~** the New World (liter)

nuez *f*
A 1▸ (del nogal) walnut 2▸ (Méx) (pacana) pecan (nut)
(Compuesto) **nuez moscada** nutmeg
B (Anat) Adam's apple

nulidad *f*
A (Der) nullity
B (fam) (calamidad) dead loss (colloq); **como cocinero es una ~** he's a hopeless cook (colloq)

nulo -la *adj*
A (Der) ‹*testamento/votación/contrato*› null and void; ‹*voto*› void
B ‹*persona*› useless (colloq), hopeless (colloq)
C (inexistente): **mis conocimientos del tema son ~s** I know absolutely nothing about the subject

Núm., núm. (= **número**) no.

numen *m* 1▸ (Mit) numen 2▸ *tb* **~ poético** (liter) poetic inspiration

numerable *adj* countable

numeración *f* (acción) numbering; (números) numbers (*pl*); (sistema) numerals (*pl*)
(Compuesto) **numeración arábiga/romana** Arabic/Roman numerals (*pl*)

numeral *adj/m* numeral

numerar [A1] *vt* to number

numerario¹ -ria *adj* 1▸ ‹*empleado*› permanent 2▸ ‹*socio/miembro*› (antiguo) long-standing; (de pleno derecho) full (*before n*)

numerario² *m* (frml) cash

numérico -ca *adj* numerical

número *m*
A 1▸ (Mat) number; **vive en el ~ 15** she lives at number 15; **el ~ premiado** the winning number; **pagó una suma de seis ~s** he paid a six figure sum; **un ~ cada vez mayor de emigrantes** more and more emigrants; **problemas sin ~** innumerable *o* countless problems; ***en ~s redondos*** in round numbers; ***estar en ~s rojos*** (fam) to be in the red (colloq); ***hacer ~s*** to do one's arithmetic *o* (BrE) sums 2▸ (de zapatos) size; **¿qué ~ calzas?** what size shoe do you take? 3▸ (billete de lotería) lottery ticket

(Compuestos)
- **número arábigo/romano** Arabic/Roman numeral
- **número cardinal/ordinal** cardinal/ordinal number
- **número decimal** decimal
- **número de identificación personal** PIN number, Personal Identification Number
- **número de matrícula** license number (AmE), registration number (BrE)
- **número de serie** serial number
- **número de teléfono/fax** phone/fax number
- **número fraccionario** fraction
- **número par/impar** even/odd number
- **número uno** *mf* (de equipo) number one; (líder) leader; **es el ~ ~ de su clase** he's top of his class

B (Espec) act; ***montar un/el ~*** (Esp fam) to kick up a fuss (colloq)
C (de publicación) issue

numeroso -sa *adj* ‹*clase/grupo*› large; ‹*ocasiones/ejemplos*› numerous, many

numismática *f* numismatics, coin collecting

nunca *adv* never; **~ es tarde** it's never too late; **casi ~** hardly ever; **más que ~** more than ever (before); **como ~** like never before; **~ más** never again

nunciatura *f* nunciature

nuncio *m* 1▸ (Relig) *tb* **~ apostólico** papal nuncio 2▸ (liter) (anuncio, precursor) herald (liter), harbinger (liter)

nupcial *adj* (liter) ‹*festejos*› nuptial (liter); ‹*ceremonia*› (fam) wedding (*before n*); **el lecho ~** the marriage bed

nupcias *fpl* (liter) nuptials (*pl*) (liter)

nutria *f* otter

nutrición *f* nutrition

nutricional *adj* nutritional

nutricionista *mf* nutritionist

nutrido -da *adj*
A 1▸ (*delante del n*) (frml) (abundante): **una nutrida concurrencia** a large crowd; **~s aplausos** hearty applause 2▸ (frml) (con abundancia) **~ DE algo** full OF sth
B (alimentado): **mal ~** undernourished, malnourished; **bien ~** well-nourished

nutriente *f* nutrient

nutrir [I1] *vt*
A ‹*organismo*› to nourish; ‹*niño/planta*› to nourish, feed
B (liter) ‹*odio/celos*› to fuel, feed
■ **nutrirse** *v pron*
A «*planta/organismo*» to receive nourishment; **la organización se nutre de donativos estatales** the organization is funded by donations
B (liter) «*odio/rencor*» **~se DE algo** to be fueled BY sth

nutritivo -va *adj* ‹*alimento*› nutritious; ‹*valor*› nutritional

nylon /'najlon, ni'lon/ *m* nylon

n

Ñ, **ñ** *f (read as /'eɲe/) the letter* **Ñ, ñ**

ña *f* (AmL fam) *shortened form of* **doña** *used to refer to older women in rural communities*

ñame *m* yam

ñam ñam *interj* (fam) yum-yum (colloq)

ñandú *m* rhea

ñandubay *m* nandubay (*hardwood tree*)

ñandutí *m* nanduti (*fine Paraguayan lace*)

ñango -ga *adj* (Méx fam) wimpish (colloq)

ñaña *f* (AmC vulg) shit (vulg), crap (vulg)

ñapa *f* (AmL fam) *small amount of extra goods given free*, lagniappe (AmE); **dar algo de ~** to throw sth in (for free) (colloq); **me dio dos de ~** she threw in a couple extra

ñara *mf* (AmC arg) jerk (colloq), moron (colloq & pej)

ñata *f*, **ñatas** *fpl* (Andes, RPl fam) nose

ñatita *f* (Andes, RPl fam) snub nose

ñato[1] -ta *adj* (AmS fam) ‹*persona*› snub-nosed; ‹*animal*› pug-nosed

ñato[2] -ta *m,f* (fam) 1 (CS fam) (tipo) (*m*) guy (colloq); (*f*) woman 2 (Andes) (como apelativo cariñoso) funny face (colloq)

ñauca *f* (Chi) ▸ **ñaupa**

ñaupa *f* (RPl fam): **es del año de ~** it's really ancient (colloq); **ropa del año de ~** clothes that went out with the ark (colloq)

ñecla *f* (Chi) (volantín) small kite

ñeque *m* (Chi fam) strength, stamina; **le faltó ~** he didn't have the strength *o* the stamina; **una competencia de ~** a grueling competition; ***ponerle ~ a algo*** (Chi fam) to put a lot into sth; ***tener ~*** (Chi fam) to have guts (colloq)

ñoco -ca *adj* (Col fam): **le quedó la mano ñoca** he lost a hand; **tiene un dedo ~** he has a finger missing

ñoña *f* (Ven fam) rubbish (colloq), crap (vulg); ***como la ~*** (Chi fam) very badly; ***volver*** *or* ***hacer algo ~*** (Ven fam) to smash sth; ***volverse ~*** «*persona*» (Ven fam) to get into a mess (colloq)

ñoñería *f*: **déjate de ~s** stop whining (colloq), don't be such a crybaby *o* drip (colloq)

ñoño[1] -ña *adj* drippy (colloq)

ñoño[2] -ña *m,f* drip (colloq)

ñoquis *mpl* (Coc) gnocchi (*pl*)

ñorbo *m* (Ec, Per) passionflower

ñu *m* gnu, wildebeest

Oo

O, **o** *f (read as /o/) the letter* **O, o**

o *conj* 1 (planteando alternativa) or; **¿vienes o no?** are you coming or not? 2 (si no): **dámelo o se lo digo a la maestra** give it to me or I'll tell the teacher; **o ... o ...** either ... or ...; **o mañana o el jueves** either tomorrow or Thursday 3 (indicando aproximación) [*between two digits* **o** *is written with an accent*: **unas 100 ó 120** about 100 or 120] 4 (indicando equivalencia) or; **o sea** *ver* **ser**[1] *vi Sentido* **II D**

O. (= **oeste**) W, West

oasis *m (pl* ~) oasis

obcecación *f* blindness (to reason), obstinacy

obcecado -da *adj* 1 [ESTAR] (cegado): **está ~ con la idea** he's obsessed with the idea; **~ por los celos** blinded by jealousy 2 [SER] (porfiado) obstinate

obcecar [A2] *vt* to blind; **la ira lo obcecó** he was blinded by rage

■ **obcecarse** *v pron* to become obsessed

obedecer [E3] *vt* 1 ‹*orden/norma*› to obey, comply with 2 ‹*persona*› to obey; **obedece a tu madre** do as your mother tells you

■ **obedecer** *vi* 1 «*persona*» to obey; **para que aprendas a ~** to teach you to do as you're told 2 «*mecanismo*» to respond 3 (frml) (a motivo, causa) **~ A algo** to be due to sth

obediencia *f* obedience

obediente *adj* obedient

obelisco *m* obelisk

obertura *f* overture

obesidad *f* obesity

obeso[1] **-sa** *adj* obese

obeso[2] **-sa** *m,f* obese person

óbice *m* (frml): **no ser ~ PARA algo**: **esto no es ~ para que cumplan las normas** this does not prevent them (from) complying with the rules

obispado *m* bishopric

obispo *m* bishop

obituario *m* (en periódico) obituary; (registro) register of deaths

objeción *f* objection; **¿alguna ~?** (are there) any objections?; **nadie hizo** *or* **puso objeciones** nobody objected *o* made any objection

(Compuesto) **objeción de conciencia** conscientious objection

objetante *mf* objector

(Compuesto) **objetante de conciencia** conscientious objector

objetar [A1] *vt* to object; **¿tienes algo que ~?** do you have any objection?

■ **objetar** *vi* (Esp fam) to declare oneself a conscientious objector

objetividad *f* objectivity; **con ~** objectively

objetivo[1] **-va** *adj* objective

objetivo[2] *m*

A (finalidad) objective, aim; (Mil) objective

B (Fot, Ópt) lens

objeto *m*

A (cosa) object; **~s de valor** valuables; **~s de uso personal** items *o* articles for personal use; ⓢ **objetos perdidos** lost and found (AmE), lost property (BrE)

(Compuestos)

- **objeto de arte** objet d'art
- **objeto volador** *or* (Esp) **volante no identificado** unidentified flying object, UFO

B (finalidad) object; **tuvo por ~ facilitar el diálogo** the aim *o* objective was to make it easier to hold talks; **con el ~ de coordinar la operación** in order to coordinate *o* with the aim of coordinating the operation; **con el ~ de que se conozcan** so that they can get to know each other

C 1 (de admiración, críticas) object; **ser ~ de malos tratos** to be ill-treated; **es ahora ~ de una minuciosa investigación** it is now the subject of a detailed investigation 2 (Ling) object 3 (de ciencia) object

objetor -tora *m,f* objector

(Compuesto) **objetor -tora de conciencia** *m,f* conscientious objector

oblea *f*

A (Relig) wafer

B (Inf) chip, wafer

oblicuo -cua *adj* ‹*línea*› oblique

obligación *f*

A (deber) obligation; **tiene (la) ~ de ...** it is his duty to ..., he has an obligation to ...; **es mi ~ decírtelo** it is my duty to tell you; **lo hace por ~** she does it out of obligation; **cumplió con sus obligaciones** he fulfilled his obligations; **si sus obligaciones se lo permiten** if her commitments permit; ***antes*** *or* ***primero es la ~ que la devoción*** business before pleasure

B (Com, Fin) 1 (pasivo) obligation, liability 2 (bono) bond, debenture

obligado -da *adj*

A 1 [ESTAR] ‹*persona*› obliged; **~ A + INF** obliged to + INF; **se vio ~ a acompañarla** he was obliged to accompany her 2 (forzoso): **una disposición de ~ cumplimiento** a legally binding provision; **es de lectura obligada** it is required reading

B [SER] (normal) customary; **en estos casos es ~ llevar regalo** in such instances it is the done thing *o* it is customary to take a gift

obligar [A3] *vt* 1 «*circunstancia/persona*»: **el mal tiempo nos obligó a ...** bad weather forced *o* (frml) obliged us to ...; **nos obligan a llevar uniforme** we are required to wear uniform; **no lo obligues a comer** don't force him to eat; **lo obligué a pedirle perdón** I made him apologize to her; **~ A algn A QUE + SUBJ** to make sb + INF 2 «*ley/disposición*» to bind; **esta ley sólo obliga a los mayores de edad** only adults are legally bound by this law; **las normas obligan a los maestros a ...** the rules oblige teachers to ...

■ **obligarse** *v pron (refl)* **~se A + INF** (forzarse) to make oneself + INF, force oneself to + INF; (comprometerse) to undertake to + INF

obligatoriedad *f* obligatory nature; **la ley establece su ~** the law makes it obligatory *o* compulsory

obligatorio -ria *adj* compulsory, obligatory; **no es ~ firmarlo** it doesn't have to be signed

obliterar [A1] *vt* to obliterate

oblongo -ga *adj* ovoid, oval

obnubilar [A1] *vt* to cloud; **estaba obnubilado por el poder** power had clouded his judgment

oboe *m* 1 (instrumento) oboe 2 **oboe** *mf* (músico) oboist

óbolo *m* (moneda) obol

obra *f*
A **1** (creación artística) work; **sus primeras ~s** her earliest works; **una ~ de artesanía** a piece of craftsmanship; **la ~ cinematográfica de Buñuel** Buñuel's films; **sus ~s de teatro** *or* **su ~ dramática** her plays **2** (Mús) work, opus
Compuestos
- **obra de arte** work of art
- **obra de consulta** reference book
- **obra maestra** masterpiece

B (acción): **mi buena ~ del día** my good deed for the day; **por sus ~s los conoceréis** (Bib) by their works will you know them; **~s de misericordia** charitable deeds; **esto es ~ de Víctor** this is Víctor's doing; ***~s son amores que no buenas razones*** actions speak louder than words
Compuestos
- **obra benéfica** *or* **de beneficencia** (acto) act of charity; (organización) charity, charitable organization
- **obra social** (labor filantrópica) benevolent *o* charitable work

C (Arquit, Const) **1** (construcción) building work; **estamos de** *or* **en ~s** we're having some building work done; **⊖ peligro: obras** danger: building work in progress; **⊖ cerrado por obras** closed for repairs **2** (sitio) building *o* construction site
Compuesto **obras públicas** *fpl* public works (*pl*)
D **la Obra** (Relig) the Opus Dei

obrar [A1] *vi*
A (actuar) to act; **~ de buena fe** to act in good faith
B (frml) (Corresp, Der): **los documentos que obran en mi poder** the documents in my possession; **las pruebas obran en su poder** he is in possession of the evidence
■ **obrar** *vt* to work; **la fe obra milagros** faith works miracles

obrera *f* (hormiga) worker (ant); (abeja) worker (bee); *ver tb* **obrero²**

obrero¹ -ra *adj* ‹barrio› working-class; **el movimiento ~** the workers' movement; **la clase obrera** the working class

obrero² -ra *m,f*: **los ~s dejaron la arena en el jardín** the workmen left the sand in the garden; **~ de fábrica/de la construcción** factory/construction worker
Compuesto **obrero calificado** (AmL) *or* (Esp) **cualificado** skilled worker

O

obscenidad *f* obscenity; **una revista llena de ~es** a magazine full of obscene material

obsceno -na *adj* obscene

obscuro, etc ▸**oscuro, etc**

obsequiar [A1] *vt* (frml) **1** ‹*persona*› **~ A algn CON algo** to present sb WITH sth, give sb sth **2** (AmL) ‹*reloj/cuadro*› **~le algo a algn** to present sb WITH sth, give sb sth

obsequio *m* (frml) gift; **el libro es ~ de la casa** the book comes with the compliments of the management; **acepte esta copa, ~ de la casa** have this drink on the house

obsequioso -sa *adj* deferential; **excesivamente ~** obsequious

observación *f*
A (examen, vigilancia) observation; **tener a algn en ~** (Med) to keep sb under observation; **tener mucha/poca capacidad de ~** to be/not to be very observant
B (de leyes, preceptos) observance
C (comentario) observation, remark; (en texto) note

observador¹ -dora *adj* observant

observador² -dora *m,f* observer

observancia *f* observance

observar [A1] *vt*
A **1** (mirar, examinar) to observe; **alguien la observaba** someone was watching her **2** (notar) to observe (frml); **como pueden ~ ...** as you can see …, *o* as you will observe …; **¿has observado algún cambio?** have you observed *o* noticed any changes? **3** (comentar) to remark, observe (frml)
B ‹*leyes/preceptos*› to observe, abide by; ‹*protocolo*› to observe

observatorio *m* observatory

obsesión *f* obsession; **tenía la ~ de que ...** she was obsessed with the idea that …

obsesionar [A1] *vt* to obsess; **estaba obsesionado con** *or* **por la idea** he was obsessed with *o* by the idea
■ **obsesionarse** *v pron* to become obsessed

obsesivo -va *adj/m,f* obsessive

obseso -sa *m,f* (Psic) obsessive; **es un ~ sexual** he's obsessed with sex

obsidiana *f* obsidian

obsoleto -ta *adj* obsolete

obstaculizar [A4] *vt* ‹*progreso/trabajo*› to hinder, hamper; ‹*tráfico*› to hold up; **no obstaculice el paso** don't stand in the way

obstáculo *m* obstacle; **superar** *or* **salvar un ~** to overcome an obstacle; **no fue ~ para que ganara** it did not stop *o* prevent him (from) winning

obstante: **no obstante** (sin embargo) nevertheless, nonetheless; (a pesar de) despite, in spite of

obstar [A1] *vi* (frml) (*en 3ª pers*) **no ~ PARA QUE + SUBJ**: **eso no obsta para que sea trasladado** that should not prevent him from being transfered

obstetra *mf* (esp AmL) obstetrician

obstetricia *f* obstetrics

obstinación *f* (tozudez) obstinacy, stubbornness; (tenacidad) tenacity

obstinadamente *adv* (con tozudez) obstinately, stubbornly; (con tenacidad) tenaciously

obstinado -da *adj* **1** (tozudo) obstinate, stubborn **2** (tenaz) tenacious, dogged **3** (Ven) (harto) fed up (colloq)

obstinar [A1] *vt* (Ven fam) to drive … round the bend (colloq)
■ **obstinarse** *v pron*
A **~ EN + INF** to insist ON -ING ; **se ha obstinado en que hay que terminar hoy** he is determined that it has to be finished today
B (Ven fam) **~se CON** *or* **DE algo/algn** to get sick of sth/sb, to get fed up WITH sth/sb (colloq)

obstrucción *f* obstruction

obstruccionismo *m* obstructionism; (en debate) filibustering

obstruir [I20] *vt*
A (bloquear) ‹*conducto*› to block; ‹*salida*› to block, obstruct; **⊖ no obstruya el acceso** do not block access, keep clear
B (entorpecer) ‹*plan/proceso*› to obstruct; ‹*tráfico*› to obstruct, hold up; ‹*progreso*› to impede
C (Dep) to obstruct
■ **obstruirse** *v pron* to get blocked (up)

obtención *f* obtaining, securing

obtener [E27] *vt* ‹*premio*› to win, receive; ‹*resultado/autorización*› to obtain; ‹*calificación*› to obtain, set

obturador *m* (Fot) shutter; (Mec) plug, seal

obturar [A1] *vt* to close, seal, block

obtuso -sa *adj* obtuse

obtuve, obtuvo, etc *see* **obtener**

obús *m* (arma) mortar, howitzer; (proyectil) shell, mortar bomb

obviar [A1] *vt* to avoid, obviate (frml)

obvio -via *adj* obvious

oca *f* (Zool) goose

ocasión *f*
A **1** (vez, circunstancia) occasion; **en alguna ~** occasionally; **con ~ de** on the occasion of; **las grandes ocasiones** special occasions **2** (momento oportuno) opportunity; **no tuve ~ de hablarle** I didn't have an opportunity *o* a chance to talk to him; ***a la ~ la pintan calva*** you have to strike while the iron is hot
B (ganga) bargain; **precios de ~** bargain prices; **muebles de ~** (usados) secondhand furniture; (baratos) cut-price furniture; **coches de ~** used *o* secondhand cars

ocasionado (Ven period): **~ a** (*loc prep*) because of

ocasional *adj* ‹*encuentro*› chance (*before n*); **tengo un trabajo ~** I have some temporary work

ocasionar [A1] *vt* to cause; **espero no ~le demasiadas molestias** I do hope it doesn't cause you too much trouble

ocaso *m* (liter) (del sol) sunset; (de vida, imperio) twilight (liter)

occidental[1] *adj* ‹*zona*› western; ‹*cultura/países*› Western; **África O~** West Africa

occidental[2] *mf* westerner

occidentalizar [A4] *vt* to westernize

■ **occidentalizarse** *v pron* to become westernized

occidente *m* west; **el O~** (Hist, Pol) the West

occiso -sa *m,f* (frml) (Der) murder victim

OCDE *f* (= **Organización para la Cooperación y el Desarrollo Económico**) OECD

Oceanía *f* Oceania

oceánico -ca *adj* oceanic

océano *m* ocean

(Compuesto) **Océano Atlántico/Índico/Pacífico** Atlantic/Indian/Pacific Ocean

oceanografía *f* oceanography

oceanógrafo -fa *m,f* oceanographer

ocelote *m* ocelot

ochenta[1] *adj inv/pron* eighty; *para ejemplos ver* **cincuenta**

ochenta[2] *m* (number) eighty

ocho[1] *adj inv/pron* eight; *para ejemplos ver* **cinco**

ocho[2] *m* (number) eight; *para ejemplos ver* **cinco**

ochocientos -tas *adj/pron* eight hundred; *para ejemplos ver* **quinientos**

ocio *m* [1] (tiempo libre) spare time, leisure time; **la cultura del ~** the leisure culture [2] (inactividad, holgazanería) inactivity, idleness; ***el ~ es la madre de todos los vicios*** the devil makes work for idle hands

ociosidad *f* inactivity, idleness

ocioso -sa *adj* [1] [ESTAR] (inactivo) idle; **una vida ociosa** a life of idleness [2] [SER] (inútil, innecesario) pointless

oclusión *f* occlusion

oclusiva *f* occlusive, plosive

oclusivo -va *adj* occlusive, plosive

ocote *m* (árbol) ocote pine; (madera) ocote wood

ocre *m* [1] (Min) ocher* [2] **(de) color ~** ocher-colored*

oct. (= **octubre**) Oct

octágono *m* octagon

octanaje *m* octane number *o* rating

octano *m* octane

octava *f* octave

octavilla *f* pamphlet

octavo[1] **-va** *adj/pron* [1] (ordinal) eighth; *para ejemplos ver* **quinto** [2] (partitivo): **la octava parte** an eighth

octavo[2] *m* eighth

(Compuesto) **octavos de final** *mpl*: *round before the quarter-finals*

octeto *m* (Mús) octet; (Inf) byte

octogenario[1] **-ria** *adj* octogenarian (*before n*), eighty-year-old (*before n*)

octogenario[2] **-ria** *m,f* octogenarian

octogésimo[1] **-ma** *adj/pron* [1] (ordinal) eightieth; *para ejemplos ver* **vigésimo** [2] (partitivo): **la octogésima parte** an eightieth

octogésimo[2] *m* eightieth

octubre *m* October; *para ejemplos ver* **enero**

ocular *adj* ‹*infección/lesión*› eye (*before n*), ocular (frml)

oculista *mf* ophthalmologist

ocultar [A1] *vt* [1] ‹*noticia/verdad*› **~le algo A algn** to conceal sth FROM sb [2] ‹*sentimientos/intenciones*› to conceal, hide [3] (de la vista) to conceal, hide

■ **ocultarse** *v pron* [1] «*persona*» to hide [2] (estar oculto) to hide, lie hidden; **tras esa sonrisa se oculta una mala intención** behind that smile there lie dishonest intentions [3] «*sol*» to disappear

ocultismo *m* occult, occultism

oculto -ta *adj* [1] [ESTAR] (escondido) hidden; **permanecer ~** to stay hidden [2] [SER] (misterioso) ‹*razón/designio*› mysterious, occult

ocupación *f*

A (empleo) occupation; (actividad) activity; **el nivel de ~** the level of employment

B [1] (de vivienda) occupation [2] (de cargo): **la ~ de estos puestos** the filling of these posts [3] (de fábrica, territorio) occupation

ocupado[1] **-da** *adj* [1] (atareado) busy; **últimamente está** *or* **anda muy ocupada** she's been very busy lately; **tengo las manos ocupadas** I have *o* I've got my hands full [2] ‹*línea telefónica*› busy, engaged (BrE); **¿este asiento está ~?** is this seat taken?; Ⓢ **ocupado** engaged [3] ‹*territorio*› occupied

ocupado[2] **-da** *m,f*: **el número de ~s** the number of people at work (AmE) *o* (BrE) in work

ocupante[1] *adj* occupying (*before n*)

ocupante[2] *mf* occupant

ocupar [A1] *vt*

A ‹*espacio*› to take up

B «*persona*» [1] (situarse en): **volvió a ~ su asiento** she returned to her seat, she took her seat again; **ocupaba la cabecera de la mesa** she sat at the head of the table [2] ‹*vivienda/habitación*›: **ya han ocupado la casa** they have already moved into the house; **ocupaban la habitación del fondo** they slept in the room at the back; **¿quién ocupa la habitación 234?** who's in room 234? [3] (en clasificación): **ocupa el tercer lugar en la lista** she's third on the list; **¿qué lugar ocupan en la liga?** what position are they in the division?; **pasan a ~ el primer puesto** they move into first place [4] ‹*cargo*› to hold, occupy (frml); ‹*vacante*› to fill

C ‹*fábrica/territorio*› to occupy

D [1] ‹*trabajadores*› to provide employment for [2] (concernir) to concern

E ‹*tiempo*›: **¿en qué ocupas tu tiempo libre?** how do you spend your spare time?; **me ocupa demasiado tiempo** it takes up too much of my time

F (AmC, Chi, Méx) (usar) to use

■ **ocuparse** *v pron* **~se DE algo/algn**: **¿quién se ocupa de los niños?** who takes care of *o* looks after the children?; **este departamento se ocupa de ...** this department deals with *o* is in charge of ...; **yo me ~é de eso** I'll see to that; **yo me ocupé de hacer la reservación** I took care of the reservations; **tú ocúpate de tus cosas** you mind your own business

ocurrencia *f* (comentario gracioso) witty *o* funny remark, witticism; (idea disparatada) crazy idea

ocurrente *adj* (gracioso) witty; (ingenioso) clever

ocurrido -da *adj*: **los sucesos ~s ayer** the events that took place yesterday; **lamento lo ~** I am sorry about what happened

ocurrir [I1] *vi* (*en 3ª pers*) to happen; **lo peor que puede ~** the worst that can happen; **ocurra lo que ocurra** whatever happens; **¿ha ocurrido algo?** is anything the matter?, is anything wrong?; **lo que ocurre es que ...** the trouble is (that) ...; **¿qué te ocurre?** what's the matter?; **nunca me había ocurrido una cosa así** nothing like that had ever happened to me before

■ **ocurrirse** *v pron* (*en 3ª pers*): **se me ocurrió que ...** it occurred to me that ... (frml); **di lo primero que se te ocurra** say the first thing that comes into your head; **se me ha ocurrido una idea** I've had an idea; **no se les ocurría nada** they couldn't think of anything; **¿a quién se le ocurre dejarlo solo?** who in their right mind would leave him on his own?; **¿cómo se te ocurrió comprarlo?** whatever made you buy it?

oda *f* ode

ODECA /o'ðeka/ *f* (= **Organización de Estados Centroamericanos**) OCAS

odiar [A1] *vt* to hate; **lo odio a muerte** I really hate him; **~ + INF** to hate -ING; **odio planchar** I hate ironing

odio *m* hate, hatred; **le he tomado ~** I've come to hate him; **tenerle ~ a algn** to hate sb

odioso -sa *adj* ‹*trabajo/tema*› horrible, hateful; ‹*persona*› horrible, odious

odisea *f* odyssey; **la O~** (Lit) the Odyssey

odontología *f* dentistry, odontology

odontólogo -ga *m,f* dental surgeon, odontologist

odre *m* wineskin

OEA *f* (= **Organización de Estados Americanos**) OAS

oeste[1] *adj inv* ‹*región*› western; **en la parte ~ del país** in the western part of the country; **conducían en dirección ~** they were driving west *o* westward(s); **la costa/el ala ~** the west coast/wing

oeste[2] *m* 1 (parte, sector): **el ~** the west; **en el ~ de la provincia** in the west of the province; **al ~ de Oaxaca** to the west of Oaxaca 2 (punto cardinal) west, West; **vientos del O~** westerly winds; **caminaron hacia el O~** they walked west *o* westward(s); **el balcón da al ~** the balcony faces west 3 **el Oeste** (de los Estados Unidos) the West; **una película/novela del O~** a Western

ofender [E1] *vt* 1 (agraviar) to offend; **sus palabras me ofendieron** I was offended by what she said; **~ a Dios** to sin; **~ la memoria de algn** to insult sb's memory 2 ‹*buen gusto*› to offend against; **colores que ofenden la vista** colors which offend the eye

■ **ofenderse** *v pron* to take offense*; **no te ofendas, pero ...** don't be offended, but ...

ofensa *f* (agravio) insult

ofensiva *f* offensive; **tomar la ~** to take the offensive; **pasar a la ~** to go onto *o* over to the offensive

ofensivo -va *adj* 1 ‹*palabra/actitud*› offensive, rude 2 (Mil) ‹*táctica*› offensive (*before n*)

oferta *f*

A 1 (proposición) offer; **no recibí ninguna ~** I didn't receive any offers; Ⓢ **ofertas de trabajo** job vacancies, situations vacant 2 (Econ, Fin) supply; **la ley de la ~ y la demanda** the law of supply and demand

B (Com) offer; **están de** *or* **en ~** they are on special offer

(Compuesto) **oferta de lanzamiento** introductory offer

ofertar [A1] *vt* 1 (liquidar) to put ... on special offer 2 (esp AmL) (ofrecer) to offer

■ **ofertar** *vi* (en licitación) to tender

off *m* **en off** (*loc adj/adv*) (Teatr) offstage; (Cin) offscreen

offset /'ofset/ *m* offset

offside /of'sai/ *m* offside

oficial[1] *adj* official; Ⓢ **Concesionario Oficial** authorized dealer

oficial[2] **-ciala** *m,f*, **oficial** *mf*

A (obrero) skilled worker; **se necesita ~ tornero** time-served machinist needed

B **oficial** *mf* (de policía) police officer (*above the rank of sergeant*); (Mil) officer

(Compuesto) **oficial de guardia** officer of the day

oficialidad *f*

A (oficiales) officer corps, officers (*pl*)

B (cualidad) official nature *o* character

oficialismo *m* (AmL): **representantes del ~** representatives of the ruling *o* governing party

oficialista *adj* (AmL) ‹*periódico*› pro-government; ‹*candidato*› fielded by the party in power

oficializar [A4] *vt* to make ... official

oficiante[1] *adj* officiating (*before n*)

oficiante[2] *m* officiant, celebrant

oficiar [A1] *vt* ‹*misa*› to officiate at; ‹*servicio*› to conduct; **¿quién ofició la misa en la boda?** who officiated at your wedding?

■ **oficiar** *vi* 1 «*sacerdote*» to officiate 2 (actuar) **~ DE algo** to officiate AS sth

oficina *f*

A (despacho) office; **en horas de ~** during office hours

(Compuestos)

- **oficina de cambio** bureau de change
- **oficina de empleo/turismo** unemployment/tourist office

B (Chi) (Min) nitrate field

oficinista *mf* office worker

oficio *m*

A (trabajo) trade; **carpintero de ~** carpenter by trade; ***ser del ~*** (fam) to be a hooker (sl), to be on the game (BrE colloq); ***sin ~ ni beneficio***: **un vago sin ~ ni beneficio** a lazy bum (AmE colloq), a good-for-nothing layabout (BrE)

B 1 (comunicación oficial) official letter; **tamaño ~** (AmS) foolscap 2 (Der) **de ~** court-appointed (*before n*)

C (Relig) service, office

(Compuesto) **oficio de difuntos** mass *o* office for the dead

oficiosamente *adv* (de manera no oficial) unofficially

oficiosidad *f*

A (de noticia, declaración) unofficial nature

B 1 (frml) (diligencia) diligence 2 (solicitud) solicitousness (frml)

C (entrometimiento) officiousness

D (Der): *ability of a judge or ministry to institute proceedings*

oficioso -sa *adj* (no oficial) unofficial; (relacionado con el gobierno): **fuentes oficiosas** sources close to the government

ofimática *f* office automation

ofrecer [E3] *vt*

A 1 ‹*ayuda/cigarrillo/empleo*› to offer; **te llamo para ~te al niño** (Col, Ven) I'm ringing to let you know that the baby has been born; **~ + INF** to offer TO + INF; **ofreció prestarnos su coche** she offered to lend us her car 2 ‹*dinero*› to offer; (en una subasta) to bid 3 ‹*fiesta*› to give, throw (colloq); ‹*recepción*› to lay on, to hold 4 ‹*sacrificio/víctima*› to offer (up)

B 1 ‹*oportunidad*› to give, provide; **le ofrece la posibilidad de entablar nuevas amistades** it provides her with the chance to make new friends; ‹*dificultad*› to present 2 ‹*aspecto/vista*›: **su habitación ofrecía un aspecto lúgubre** her room had an air of gloominess about it; **el año ofrece buenas perspectivas** the coming year looks promising; **ofrecían un espectáculo desgarrador** they were a heartrending sight 3 ‹*resistencia*› «*persona*» to put up, offer; **la puerta se abrió sin ~ resistencia** the door opened easily

■ **ofrecerse** *v pron*

A «*persona*» to offer, volunteer; **~se A** *or* **PARA + INF** to offer *o* volunteer TO + INF; Ⓢ **se ofrece niñera con experiencia** experienced nanny seeks employment

B ‹*presentarse*›: **un espectáculo único se ofrecía ante nuestros ojos** a unique spectacle greeted our eyes; **en valle se nos ofrecía en todo su esplendor** the valley appeared before us in all its splendor

C (frml) (querer, necesitar) (*gen neg o interrog*) **¿se le ofrece alguna otra cosa?** can I offer *o* get you anything else?; **¿qué se le ofrece, señora?** what would you like, madam? (frml); **estoy para lo que se les ofrezca** I'm at your service; **si no se le ofrece nada más** if there's nothing else I can do for you

ofrecimiento *m* offer

ofrenda *f* offering

ofrendar [A1] *vt* (Relig) to offer (up)

oftalmología *f* ophthalmology

oftalmólogo -ga *m,f* ophthalmologist

ofuscación *f*, **ofuscamiento** *m* 1 (de razón): **en un momento de ~** in a moment of blind rage 2 (de vista) blurring

ofuscar [A2] *vt* «*celos/pasión*» to blind

■ **ofuscarse** *v pron* to get worked up

ogino, Ogino *m* rhythm method

ogro *m* ogre

ohm, ohmio *m* ohm

oídas: **de ~** (*loc adv*) **lo conozco de ~** I've heard of him, I know of him; **lo sabía de ~** I'd heard it; **lo sabemos sólo de ~** it's only hearsay

oído *m* 1 (Anat) ear; **me duelen los ~s** my ears hurt; **me lo susurró al ~** she whispered it in my ear; ***hacer*** *or* ***prestar ~s sordos a algo*** to turn a deaf ear to sth; ***llegar a ~s de algn*** to come to the attention *o* notice of sb; ***por un ~ me/te/le entra y por el otro me/te/le sale*** it goes in one ear and comes out the other; ***prestar ~s a algo*** to pay attention to sth, take notice of sth; ***regalarle el ~ a algn*** to flatter sb; ***ser todo ~s*** to be all ears; ***silbarle*** *or* ***zumbarle los ~s a algn***: **¡cómo le estarán silbando** *or* **zumbando los ~s!** his ears must be burning! 2 (sentido) hearing; (para la música, los idiomas) ear; **es duro de ~** he's hard of hearing; **aguzar el ~** to prick up one's ears; **no tiene ~** she's tone-deaf, she has no ear for music; ***tocar de ~*** (Mús) to play by ear

(Compuesto) **oído interno/medio** inner/middle ear

oiga, oigas, etc *see* **oír**

oír [I28] *vt*

A (percibir sonidos) to hear; **no oigo nada** I can't hear anything *o* a thing; **se oía el canto de un ruiseñor** you/we could hear a nightingale's song; **no se oía ni el vuelo de una mosca** you could have heard a pin drop; **ya lo has**

oído, que no se repita you've been told, don't do it again; **su último disco se oye bastante** her latest record is being played quite a lot; **he oído hablar de él** I've heard of him; **he oído decir que se va** I've heard he's leaving; **¡lo que hay que ~!** the things you hear!; ***como quien oye llover*** it's like water off a duck's back; ***me va a ~*** (fam) I'm going to give him an earful (colloq)

B (escuchar) ‹*música/radio*› to listen to

C **oír misa** to go to mass

D **oiga/oye** (para llamar la atención) excuse me; **¡oiga! se le cayó la cartera** excuse me, you've dropped your wallet; **oye, si ves a Gustavo dile que me llame** listen, if you see Gustavo tell him to call me; **oye ¿tú qué te crees?** hey, who do you think you are?

■ **oír** *vi* to hear

OIT *f* (= **Organización Internacional del Trabajo**) ILO

ojal *m* buttonhole

ojalá *interj*: **seguro que apruebas — ¡~!** I'm sure you'll pass — I hope so!; **¡~ que todo salga bien!** let's hope everything turns out all right!

ojeada *f* glance; **echar una ~ a algo** to have a quick glance *o* look at sth

ojear [A1] *vt* to (have a) look at

ojeras *fpl* rings under the eyes (*pl*)

ojeriza *f* grudge; **tenerle ~ a algn** to have a grudge against sb

ojeroso -sa *adj*: **estar ~** to have rings under one's eyes

ojete *m* (en costura) eyelet; (ano) (vulg) asshole (AmE vulg), arsehole (BrE vulg)

ojímetro (fam): **a ~** (*loc adv*) at a rough guess

ojiva *f* **1** (Arquit) ogive, pointed arch **2** (de misil) warhead

ojival *adj* ogival, pointed

ojo *m*

A **1** (Anat) eye; **un niño de ~s negros** a boy with dark eyes; **~s rasgados** slanting eyes; **de ~s saltones** bug-eyed; **se le llenaron los ~s de lágrimas** his eyes filled with tears; **le guiñó el ~** he winked at her; **mirar fijamente a los ~s** to stare straight into sb's eyes; **no me quita los ~s de encima** he won't take his eyes off me; **se le salían los ~s de las órbitas** his eyes were popping out of his head; **aceptaría con los ~s cerrados** I'd accept without a second thought; **¡dichosos los ~s (que te ven)!** it's wonderful *o* lovely to see you!; **a los ~s de la sociedad** in the eyes of society; ***cerrar los ~s a algo*** to close one's mind to sth; ***¿con qué ~s, divina tuerta?*** (Méx fam) where do you expect me to get the money from?; ***cuatro ~s ven más que dos*** two heads are better than one; *ver tb* **cuatro**[1]; ***en un abrir y cerrar de ~s*** in the twinkling of an eye; ***no pegué (el*** *or* ***un) ~ en toda la noche*** I didn't sleep a wink; ***no ver algo con buenos ~s*** not to approve of sth; ***salir por*** *or* ***costar un ~ de la cara*** (fam) to cost an arm and a leg (colloq); ***ser el ~ derecho de algn*** to be the apple of sb's eye; ***~ por ~*** an eye for an eye; ***~s que no ven, corazón que no siente*** out of sight, out of mind **2** (vista): **bajó los ~s avergonzada** she lowered her eyes in shame; **sin levantar los ~s del libro** without looking up from her book; **toda América tiene los ~s puestos en él** the eyes of all America are on him; ▸**parche 1**; ***a ~ de buen cubero*** *or* ***a ~*** *or* (AmS) ***al ~*** at a guess; **le eché el azúcar a ~** I just put the sugar in without measuring it; ***a ~s vista(s)*** visibly; **es novato, se nota a ~s vistas** he's new, you can see it a mile off (colloq); ***comer con los ~s*** to ask for/take more than one can eat; ***comerse a algn con los ~s*** to devour sb with one's eyes; ***echarle el ~ a algo*** to have one's eye on sth (colloq); ***echar un ~ a algo/algn*** (fam) to have *o* take a (quick) look at sth/sb; ***entrar por los ~s*:** **a Pepe le entra la comida por los ~s** Pepe will only eat his food if it looks nice; ***hay que estar*** *or* ***andar con cuatro ~s*** (fam) you need eyes in the back of your head; ***írsele los ~s a algn*:** **se le van los ~s detrás de las mujeres** he's always eyeing up women (colloq); ***mirar algo/a algn con otros ~s*** to look at sth/sb through different eyes; ***tener a algn entre ~s*** (fam) to have it in for sb (colloq); ***tener ~ de lince*** *or* ***de águila*** to have eyes like a hawk; ***ver algo con malos ~s*** to take a dim view of sth

(Compuestos)

- **ojo a la funerala** *or* **a la virulé** (Esp fam) ▸**ojo morado**
- **ojo avizor**: **ir/estar con ~ ~** to be alert
- **ojo de agua** (Méx) spring
- **ojo de buey** porthole
- **ojo de gallo** corn
- **ojo de gato** (CS) (Auto) cat's-eye
- **ojo del culo** (vulg) asshole (AmE), arsehole (BrE)
- **ojo de pez** fish-eye lens
- **ojo de vidrio** *or* (Esp) **cristal** glass eye
- **ojo mágico** (AmL) spyhole, peephole
- **ojo morado** *or* (Méx) **moro** *or* (CS fam) **en tinta** black eye, shiner; **le puse un ~ ~** I gave him a black eye

B (perspicacia): **¡vaya ~ que tiene!** he's pretty sharp *o* on the ball!; **una mujer con ~ para los negocios** a clever *o* sharp businesswoman; ***tener (un) ~ clínico*** to be sharp *o* clever

C (fam) (cuidado, atención): **mucho ~ con lo que haces** be careful what you do; **hay que andar** *or* **ir con mucho ~** you have to keep your eyes open; **¡~! que viene un coche** watch out! *o* be careful! there's a car coming

D (de aguja) eye

E (de tormenta, huracán) eye

F (Agr) (en tubérculo) eye

G (de arco) archway; (de puente) span

ojota *f* (CS) (para playa, piscina) thong (AmE), flip-flop (BrE); (calzado rústico) sandal

okey *interj* (esp AmL) OK!, okay!

ola *f* wave; **una ~ de violencia** a wave of violence; **una ~ de despidos** a spate of dismissals

(Compuestos)

- **ola de calor** heat wave
- **ola de frío** cold spell

olán *m* (Méx) flounce, frill

olé, ole *interj* olé!, bravo!

oleada *f* wave

oleaginoso -sa *adj* oleaginous, oily

oleaje *m* swell

óleo *m* **1** (sustancia) oil; (cuadro) oil painting; **pintura al ~** oil painting; **pintar al ~** to paint in oils **2** (Relig) holy oil

oleoducto *m* (oil) pipeline

oleoso -sa *adj* oily

oler [E12] *vi*

A (percibir olores) **~ A algo** to smell sth; **¿no hueles a humo?** can't you smell smoke?

B (despedir olores) ‹‹*comida/perfume*›› to smell; **¡qué bien/mal huele!** it smells good/awful!; (+ *me/te/le etc*) **le huelen los pies** his feet smell; **~ A algo** to smell OF sth; **huele a rosas** it smells of roses

C (fam) (expresando sospecha) (+ *me/te/le etc*): **esto me huele a cuento** I smell a rat *o* something fishy; **me huele que fue ella** I have a feeling it was her

■ **oler** *vt* ‹‹*persona*›› to smell; ‹‹*animal*›› to sniff, smell

■ **olerse** *v pron* (fam) to suspect; **ya me lo olía** I thought so; **ya me olía yo que aquí había algo raro** I had a feeling there was something funny going on

olfatear [A1] *vt* **1** (oler con insistencia) to sniff **2** ‹*rastro/presa*› to scent, follow

olfato *m* (sentido) smell; (perspicacia, intuición) nose

oligarca *mf* oligarch

oligarquía *f* oligarchy

oligofrénico -ca *adj/m,f* oligophrenic

olimpiada, olimpíada *f*: *tb* **~s** Olympic Games (*pl*), Olympics (*pl*)

olímpicamente *adv* (fam): **pasa ~ de lo que digas** he doesn't give a damn what you say (colloq); **estás perdiendo el tiempo ~** you're completely wasting your time

olímpico -ca *adj* **1** ‹*campeón/récord*› Olympic (*before n*) **2** (fam) ‹*desprecio/indiferencia*› total, utter **3** (AmL fam) ‹*pase/gol*› fantastic (colloq), sensational (colloq)

olisquear [A1] *vt* to sniff

oliva *f* olive

oliváceo -cea *adj* ‹*color*› olive-green; ‹*tez/rostro*› olive; **verde ~** olive green

olivar *m* olive grove

olivo *m* olive (tree)

olla *f* pot; **~ *de grillos*** (fam) madhouse (colloq); ***parar la ~*** (CS, Per fam): **soy yo la que para la ~** I'm the breadwinner; **no tengo con qué parar la ~** I can't make ends meet

(Compuesto) **olla a presión** pressure cooker

olmedo *m*, **olmeda** *f* elm grove

olmo *m* elm (tree)

olor *m* smell; **tiene un ~ raro** it has a funny smell; **tomarle el ~ a algo** (AmL) to smell sth; **¡qué rico ~!** what a lovely smell!; **~ A algo** smell OF sth; **tiene ~ a queso** it smells of cheese; ***en ~ de multitud(es)***: **fue recibido en ~ de multitud** he was welcomed by a huge crowd; ***en ~ de santidad***: **vivir en ~ de santidad** to lead the life of a saint; **morir en ~ de santidad** to die a saint

oloroso -sa *adj* ‹*jabón/flor*› scented, fragrant; ‹*queso/pies*› smelly

olote *m* (AmC, Méx) cob, corncob

olvidadizo -za *adj* forgetful

olvidado -da *adj* forgotten; **murió ~ de todos** (liter) he died forgotten by everyone (liter)

olvidar [A1] *vt*

A 1 (borrar de la memoria) to forget; **tienes que ~ el pasado** you must put the past behind you 2 (no acordarse) to forget; **había olvidado que ...** I had forgotten that ...; **~ + INF** to forget to + INF

B (dejar en un lugar) to forget, leave ... behind; **olvidó el pasaporte en casa** she left her passport at home

■ **olvidarse** *v pron*

A 1 (borrar de la memoria) **~se DE algo** to forget sth 2 (no acordarse) to forget; **~se DE algo** to forget sth; **me había olvidado de que ...** I had forgotten that ...; **~se DE + INF** to forget to + INF; **se olvidó de llamarlo** she forgot to call him; (+ *me/te/le etc*) **se me olvidó su cumpleaños** I forgot his birthday; **¡ah! se me olvidaba** ah! I almost forgot; **se me olvidó decírtelo** I forgot to tell you

B (dejar en un lugar) to forget, leave ... behind

olvido *m* 1 (abandono, indiferencia) obscurity; **caer en el ~** to fall *o* sink into obscurity *o* oblivion; **relegado al ~** condemned to obscurity 2 (descuido) oversight; **fue un ~** it was an oversight, I forgot

O

ombligo *m* navel, belly button (colloq); ***el ~ del mundo*** the center* of the universe

ombú *m* ombu

OMC *f* (= **Organización Mundial del Comercio**) WTO

omega *f* omega

ominoso -sa *adj* (frml) (abominable) despicable; (de mal agüero) ominous

omisión *f* omission

omitir [I1] *vt* 1 ‹*frase/nombre*› to omit, leave out 2 (frml) **~ + INF** to omit *o* fail to + INF; **omitió mencionar que ...** he omitted *o* failed to mention that ...

ómnibus *m* (*pl* ~ *or* **-buses**) (autobús — urbano) (Per, Ur) bus; (— de larga distancia) (Arg) bus, coach (BrE)

omnímodo -da *adj* (frml) absolute

omnipotencia *f* omnipotence

omnipotente *adj* omnipotent

omnipresencia *f* omnipresence

omnipresente *adj* omnipresent

omnívoro¹ -ra *adj* omnivorous

omnívoro² *m* omnivore

omoplato, omóplato *m* shoulder blade, scapula (tech)

OMS /oms/ *f* (= **Organización Mundial de la Salud**) WHO

once¹ *adj inv/pron* eleven; *para ejemplos ver* **cinco**

once² *m* (number) eleven

onces *fpl* (Andes) tea; **lo invitaron a tomar ~** they invited him to tea

> **ONCE – Organización Nacional de Ciegos Españoles**
>
> *ONCE* was founded in 1938 to create employment for the blind. The organization started fund-raising lotteries, for which blind people sold tickets throughout Spain.
>
> In 1981 *ONCE* launched a national lottery which is drawn every day except Saturday. Money raised is invested in training and social centers for blind people. The biggest of its prizes is the *cuponazo*

onda *f*

A (Fís, Rad) wave; **longitud de ~** wavelength; ***agarrar*** *or* ***captar la ~*** (fam) to understand, get it (colloq); ***agarrarle la ~ a algo*** (AmL fam) to work sth out, suss sth out (colloq); ***estar en la ~*** (fam) (a la moda) to be trendy (colloq); (al tanto) to be bang up to date (colloq); ***estar fuera de ~*** (fam) to be (way) behind the times (colloq); ***¡qué buena ~!*** (AmL fam) that's great *o* fantastic! (colloq); ***¡qué mala ~!*** (AmL fam) that's terrible *o* (AmE) too bad!; ***¿qué ~?*** (AmL fam) what's new? (colloq)

(Compuestos)
- **onda corta/larga/media** short/long/medium wave
- **onda de choque** shock wave
- **onda expansiva** blast, shock wave
- **onda sísmica** seismic wave

B (del pelo) wave; (del agua) wave; (en costura) scallop

ondear [A1] *vi* «*agua*» to ripple; «*bandera*» to fly

ondulación *f* undulation

ondulado *adj* ‹*pelo*› wavy; ‹*terreno*› undulating, rolling

ondulante *adj* ‹*movimiento*› undulatory; ‹*terreno*› undulating, rolling

ondular [A1] *vt* ‹*pelo*› to wave

■ **ondular** *vi* (liter) «*agua*» to ripple; «*terreno*» to undulate

■ **ondularse** *v pron* to go wavy

oneroso -sa *adj* (frml) onerous (frml), burdensome (frml)

ONG *f* (= **organización no gubernamental**) NGO

ónice, onix *m* onyx

onomástica *f* (Esp frml) saint's day

onomástico *m* (AmL frml) saint's day

> **onomástica, onomástico**
>
> ▸ **santo**

onomatopeya *f* onomatopoeia

onomatopéyico -ca *adj* onomatopoeic

ontología *f* ontology

ONU /'onu/ *f* (= **Organización de las Naciones Unidas**): **la ~** the UN, the United Nations

onza *f*

A (peso) ounce

B (de chocolate) square

C (Zool) ounce

Op. (= **opus**) op; **Op. cit.** op cit

opa¹ *adj* (Bol, RPl fam) (tonto, idiota) silly (colloq)

opa² *interj* (RPl fam) oops! (colloq), whoops! (colloq)

OPA *f* (= **Oferta Pública de Adquisición**) takeover bid; **lanzar una ~ sobre una empresa** to make a takeover bid for a company

opacar [A2] *vt* (AmL) 1 (hacer opaco) to make ... opaque; (oscurecer) to darken 2 (deslucir) to mar; **que nada opaque su recuerdo** let nothing darken her memory 3 (anular) to overshadow; **su personalidad me opacaba** I was overshadowed by her personality

opacidad *f* opacity

opaco -ca *adj* (no transparente) opaque; (sin brillo) dull

ópalo *m* opal

opción *f* 1 (alternativa) option; **no tenía otra ~** I had no option *o* choice 2 (derecho, posibilidad): **con ~ a compra** with option to buy; **el equipo perdió toda ~ al título** the team lost any chance of (winning) the title

opcional *adj* optional

open *m* open championship *o* tournament

OPEP /o'pep/ *f* (= **Organización de Países Exportadores de Petróleo**) OPEC

ópera *f* (obra musical) opera; (edificio) opera house

operación *f*

A 1 (Mat) operation 2 (Med) operation; **una ~ a corazón abierto** open-heart surgery

B (Fin) transaction; **una ~ bursátil** a stock market transaction *o* deal
C (misión) operation; **~ de rescate** rescue operation

(Compuestos)
- **operación limpieza** clean up (operation)
- **operación rastrillo** search operation
- **operación retorno** (Esp) *mass return by road to the cities from the seaside resorts after public holidays*
- **operación salida** (Esp) *mass exodus by road from the cities to the seaside resprts before public holidays*

operacional *adj* operational, working

operador -dora *m,f* **1** (Inf, Tec, Telec) operator **2** (Cin, TV) (de cámara) (*m*) cameraman; (*f*) camerawoman; (de proyección) projectionist **3** (Méx) (obrero) ▸ **operario**

(Compuesto) **operador turístico** *m* tour operator

operancia *f* (Chi frml) efficiency

operante *adj* operational

operar [A1] *vt*
A (Med) to operate on; **tuvieron que ~la de urgencia** she had to have an emergency operation; **me van a ~ de la vesícula** I'm having a gallbladder operation; **lo ~on de apendicitis** he had his appendix taken out
B (frml) ‹*cambio/transformación*› to produce, bring about
C (Méx) ‹*máquina*› to operate
■ **operar** *vi*
A **1** (Mat) to operate **2** (Med) to operate
B (frml) (funcionar, actuar) to operate; **este vuelo ~á todos los martes** this flight will operate every Tuesday
C (frml) (negociar) to deal, do business
■ **operarse** *v pron*
A (Med) (*caus*) to have an operation; **~se del corazón** to have a heart operation
B (frml) «*cambio/transformación*» to take place

operario -ria *m,f* (frml) operative (frml); **el ~ de la máquina** the machine operator

operatividad *f* operational capacity

operativo¹ -va *adj* operating (*before n*); **sus métodos ~s** their working *o* operating methods

operativo² *m* (AmL) operation

operatorio -ria *adj* operating (*before n*)

opereta *f* operetta

operístico -ca *adj* operatic

opinar [A1] *vi*: **todos pueden ~** everyone is allowed to express an opinion; **si puedo ~ te diré que ...** if I may venture an opinion, I think ...; **prefiero no ~** I would prefer not to comment
■ **opinar** *vt* **1** (pensar) to think; **¿qué opinas del aborto?** what are your views on *o* what do you think about abortion?; **¿qué opinas de ella?** what do you think of her?; **no opino lo mismo** I do not share that view *o* opinion **2** (expresar un juicio): **opinó que deberían aplazarlo** he expressed the view that it should be postponed; **opino que debería renunciar** in my opinion he should resign

opinión *f* opinion; **¿cuál es tu ~ sobre el programa?** what do you think of the program?; **en mi ~** in my opinion; **cambió de ~** he changed his mind

(Compuesto) **opinión pública**: **la ~ ~** public opinion; **engañar a la ~ ~** to fool people *o* the public

opio *m* (Bot, Farm) opium

opíparo -ra *adj* sumptuous

oponente *mf* opponent

oponer [E22] *vt* ‹*resistencia*› to offer, put up; ‹*objeción*› to raise; **~ algo A algo** to counter *o* answer sth WITH sth; **~ la razón a la fuerza** to counter force with reason
■ **oponerse** *v pron* **1** (ser contrario) to object; **~se A algo** to oppose sth; **nadie se opuso al plan** nobody objected to *o* opposed the plan; **nuestros caracteres se oponen** (*recípr*) we are opposites **2** (contradecir) **~se A algo** to contradict sth

oporto *m* (vino) port

oportunamente *adv*: **respondió muy ~** her reply was very much to the point *o* very appropriate; **les avisaremos ~** we will inform you at the proper time

oportunidad *f*
A **1** (momento oportuno) chance, opportunity; **aprovecha esta ~** make the most of this opportunity; **a la primera ~** at the earliest opportunity; **tiene el don de la ~** (iró) he has a knack of putting his foot in it **2** (posibilidad) chance; **tuve la ~ de conocerla** I was fortunate enough to be able to meet her; **igualdad de ~es** equal opportunities
B (AmL) (vez, circunstancia) occasion; **en aquella ~ tuvo que ceder** that time *o* on that occasion he had to give in

oportunismo *m* opportunism

oportunista¹ *adj* opportunistic

oportunista² *mf* opportunist

oportuno -na *adj* **1** ‹*visita/lluvia*› timely, opportune; **llegó en el momento ~** he arrived at just the right moment **2** (conveniente) appropriate; **se tomarán las medidas oportunas** appropriate measures will be taken; **sería ~ avisarle** we ought to inform her **3** ‹*respuesta*› appropriate; **estuvo muy ~** what he said was very much to the point; **¡tú siempre tan ~!** (iró) you can always be relied upon to put your foot in it

oposición *f*
A **1** (enfrentamiento) opposition; **~ A algo** opposition TO sth **2** (Pol) opposition
B (Esp, Ven) (concurso) (public) competitive examination; **hacer oposiciones** to take *o* (BrE) sit a competitive examination

> **oposiciones**
>
> In Spain, competitive examinations for people wanting a public-sector job, to teach in a state secondary school, or to become a judge. The large number of candidates, or *opositores* - much higher than the number of posts available - means that the exams are very difficult. Those successful obtain very secure employment. Many people have private coaching for the exams

opositor¹ -tora *adj* opposition (*before n*)

opositor² -tora *m,f*
A (de partido, régimen) opponent
B (Esp, Ven) (en concurso de oposición) candidate

opresión *f* (de un pueblo) oppression; (en el pecho) tightness

opresivo -va *adj* oppressive

opresor¹ -sora *adj* oppressive

opresor² -sora *m,f* oppressor

oprimido¹ -da *adj* ‹*pueblo*› oppressed; **tenía el corazón ~ por la pena** (liter) his heart was heavy with sadness

oprimido² -da *m,f*: **los ~s** the oppressed

oprimir [I1] *vt* **1** (frml) (apretar, presionar) to press; **la angustia le oprimía el pecho** (liter) he was wracked with anguish **2** (tiranizar) to oppress

oprobio *m* (frml) dishonor*, opprobrium (frml)

optar [A1] *vi*
A (decidirse) **~ POR algo** to choose sth, opt FOR sth; **~ POR + INF** to choose *o* opt to + INF; **optó por callarse** she chose *o* opted to keep quiet
B **~ A algo** ‹*a plaza/puesto*› to apply FOR sth

optativo -va *adj* optional

óptica *f* (Fís, Ópt) optics; (tienda) optician's; (punto de vista) viewpoint, point of view

óptico¹ -ca *adj* optical

óptico² -ca *m,f* optician

optimismo *m* optimism

optimista¹ *adj* optimistic

optimista² *mf* optimist

óptimo -ma *adj* ‹*posición*› ideal, optimum; **de óptima calidad** top-quality; **en condiciones óptimas** ‹*persona*› in peak condition; ‹*coche*› in perfect condition; ‹*alimento*› fresh

opuesto -ta *adj* ‹*versiones/opiniones*› conflicting; ‹*extremos/polos*› opposite; **tienen caracteres ~s** they have very different personalities; **venía en dirección opuesta** he was coming from the opposite direction; **el lado ~ a éste** the opposite side to this one; **es ~ a todo cambio** he is opposed to *o* he is against any change

opulencia *f* opulence, affluence; **viven en la ~** they live in the lap of luxury

opulento -ta *adj* opulent, affluent

oquedad *f* (frml) cavity, hollow

ora *conj* (liter): **cae ~ en la tierra, ~ en la roca** it falls now on the soil, now among the stones (liter)

oración *f*
A (Relig) prayer; **las campanas llaman a ~** the bells are

O

summoning the faithful to prayer
B (Ling) sentence
(Compuesto) **oración principal/subordinada** main/subordinate clause
oráculo *m* oracle
orador -dora *m,f* speaker
oral¹ *adj* **1** ‹*examen/tradición*› oral **2** (Med) oral; **administrar por vía ~** to be taken orally
oral² *m* oral (exam), orals (*pl*)
órale *interj* (Méx fam) (expresando acuerdo) right!, OK!; (para animar) come on!
orangután *m* orangutan
orar [A1] *vi* (frml) (Relig) to pray; **~ POR algo/algn** to pray FOR sth/sb
orate *mf* lunatic
oratoria *f* oratory
oratorio *m* (Relig) oratory, chapel; (Mús) oratorio
orbe *m* (esfera) sphere, orb (liter); (liter) (mundo) world
órbita *f*
A (Astron) orbit; **poner en ~** to put into orbit
B (Anat) (eye) socket, orbit (tech)
C (ámbito, esfera) field
orbital *adj* orbital
orca *f* killer whale
órdago : **de ~** (Esp fam) terrific (colloq); **una casa de ~** a lovely *o* fantastic house; **un escándalo de ~** a huge *o* terrific rumpus
orden¹ *f*
A (mandato) order; **acatar una ~** to obey an order; **deja de darme órdenes** stop ordering me about; **por ~ del Sr Alcalde** by order of His Honour (AmE) *o* (BrE) Worship the Mayor; **hasta nueva ~** until further notice; **estamos a la ~ para lo que necesite** (AmL) just let us know if there's anything we can do for you; **¡a sus órdenes!** yes, sir!; **¡a la ~!** (Mil) yes, sir!; (fórmula de cortesía) (Andes, Méx, Ven) you're welcome, not at all
(Compuestos)
- **orden de alejamiento** restraining order, protective order (AmE)
- **orden de arresto** *or* **de busca y captura** arrest warrant
- **orden de desalojo** notice to quit
- **orden del día** (Mil) order of the day
- **orden de registro** *or* (Chi, Méx) **de cateo** search warrant
- **orden judicial/ministerial** court/ministerial order

B (Fin) order; **~ bancaria** banker's order; **~ de pago** order to pay
(Compuesto) **orden permanente de pago** standing order
C (Hist, Mil, Relig) order
(Compuesto) **órdenes sagradas** *fpl* holy orders (*pl*)
D (AmL) (Com) (pedido) order
orden² *m*
A **1** (indicando colocación, jerarquía) order; **en** *or* **por ~ alfabético** in alphabetical order; **por ~ de estatura** according to height; **por ~ cronológico** in chronological order; **por ~ de antigüedad** in order of seniority; **vayamos por ~** let's begin at the beginning; **una necesidad de primer ~** a basic necessity **2** (armonía, concierto) order; **pon un poco de ~ en la habitación** straighten your room up a little (AmE), tidy your room up a bit (BrE); **poner en ~** to put in order; **tengo que poner mis ideas en ~** I have to straighten (AmE) *o* (BrE) sort my ideas out; ***llamar a algn al ~*** to call sb to order; ***sin ~ ni concierto*** without rhyme or reason **3** (disciplina) order; **mantener el ~ en la clase** to keep order in the classroom; **¡~ en la sala!** order in the court!; **la policía restableció el ~** the police reestablished order **4** (de curas/monjas order; (fraternidad) order
(Compuestos)
- **orden de batalla** battle formation
- **orden del día** agenda
- **orden natural** natural order
- **orden público** public order; **mantener el ~ ~** to keep the peace; **alterar el ~ ~** to cause a breach of the peace
- **orden sacerdotal** ordination

B **1** (frml) (carácter, índole) nature; **problemas de ~ económico** problems of an economic nature **2** (cantidad): **del ~ de** (frml) on the order of (AmE), in *o* of the order of (BrE) **3** (period) (ámbito): **en el ~ internacional** on the international front; **en este ~ de cosas** in this respect; **en otro ~ de cosas ¿qué opina de ...?** moving on to something else, what do you think about ...?
C **1** (Arquit) order **2** (Biol, Zool) order
ordenación *f*
A (de sacerdote) ordination, ordainment
B (organización) organization, regulation; (Arquit) distribution
ordenadamente *adv*: **colocó los libros ~** she arranged the books neatly *o* tidily; **salieron ~** they left in an orderly fashion
ordenado -da *adj* **1** [ESTAR] (en orden) tidy **2** [SER] ‹*persona*› (metódico) organized, orderly; (para la limpieza) tidy; **lleva una vida ordenada** she leads an ordered existence
ordenador *m* (Esp) ▸**computadora**
ordenanza¹ *f* ordinance, bylaw
ordenanza² *m* (en oficinas) porter; (Mil) orderly, batman (BrE)
ordenar [A1] *vt*
A ‹*habitación/armario*› to straighten (up) (AmE), to tidy (up) (BrE); **ordené los libros por materias** I arranged the books according to subject; **ordena estas fichas** put these cards in order
B **1** (dar una orden) to order; **le ordenó salir de la oficina** she ordered him to leave the office; **me ordenó que guardara silencio** he ordered me to keep quiet **2** (AmL) (en bar, restaurante) to order; **~ un taxi** to call a taxi
C ‹*sacerdote*› to ordain
■ **ordenarse** *v pron* to be ordained
ordeña *f* (AmL) milking
ordeñadora *f* milking machine
ordeñar [A1] *vt* to milk
ordinal *m* ordinal (number)
ordinariamente *adv*
A (por lo común) ordinarily, usually
B (groseramente) coarsely, vulgarly, rudely
ordinariez *f* **1** (falta de refinamiento) vulgarity; (grosería) rudeness, bad manners (*pl*); (en la manera de hablar) vulgarity, coarseness **2** (comentario — poco refinado) vulgar comment; (— grosero) rude comment
ordinario¹ -ria *adj*
A (poco refinado) vulgar, common (pej); (grosero) rude, bad-mannered; (en el hablar) vulgar, coarse
B (de mala calidad) poor *o* bad quality; **un vino ~** a very average wine
C (no especial) ordinary; **correo ~** regular (AmE) *o* (BrE) normal delivery
D **de ordinario** usually, normally; **hay menos gente que de ~** there are fewer people than usual *o* normal
ordinario² -ria *m,f* (persona — poco refinada) vulgar *o* (pej) common person; (— grosera) rude *o* bad-mannered person
orear [A1] *vt* ‹*habitación/ropa*› to air; ‹*carne*› to dry
■ **orearse** *v pron* (Chi fam) to sober up
orégano *m* oregano
oreja¹ *f*
A (Anat) ear; **tiene las ~s despegadas** *or* **salidas** his ears stick out; **el perro puso las ~s tiesas** the dog pricked up its ears; ***calentarle la ~ a algn*** (Ven fam) to try to talk sb into sth; ***con las ~s gachas*** with one's tail between one's legs; ***jalarle las ~s a algn*** (Méx, Per, Ven fam) to tell sb off; ***parar la ~*** (AmL fam) to pay attention; **paré la ~ para ver de qué hablaban** I pricked up my ears to hear what they were talking about (colloq); ***tirarle a algn de las ~s*** *or* (AmL) ***tirarle las ~s a algn*** (literal) to pull sb's ears; (reprender) to tell sb off; ***verle las ~s al lobo*** to realize sth is wrong
B (de sillón) wing
oreja² *mf* (Méx fam) (soplón — de la policía) stool pigeon (colloq), grass (BrE colloq); (que escucha a escondidas) eavesdropper
orejera *f* earflap
orejón *m* (Coc) *dried peach or apricot*
orejudo -da *adj* big-eared, with big ears
orfanato, (Méx) **orfanatorio** *m* orphanage
orfebre *mf* goldsmith, silversmith
orfebrería *f* (oficio) goldsmithing/silversmithing, working of precious metals; (artículos) gold/silver articles (*pl*)

orfelinato *m* orphanage

orfeón *m* [1] (coral) choral society [2] (Chi) (banda) band; **~ de carabineros/militar** military band

organdí *m* organdy (AmE), organdie (BrE)

orgánico -ca *adj* organic

organigrama *m* (Inf) flow chart *o* diagram; (de empresa) organization chart

organillo *m* hurdy-gurdy

organismo *m* (Biol) organism; (Adm, Pol) organization

organista *mf* organist

organización *f* organization; **una ~ sindical** a labor (AmE) *o* (BrE) trade union

organizado -da *adj* organized

organizador¹ -dora *adj* organizing (*before n*)

organizador² -dora *m,f* organizer

organizar [A4] *vt* to organize, arrange
■ **organizarse** *v pron* to organize oneself

órgano *m*
A (Anat) organ; (pene) (euf) organ (euph), member (euph)
B (entidad) organ; (portavoz) organ
C (Mús) organ

orgasmo *m* orgasm

orgía *f* orgy

orgullo *m* pride; **con ~** proudly

orgulloso -sa *adj* [1] [ESTAR] (satisfecho) proud; **~ DE algn/algo** proud OF sb/sth; **~ DE + INF** proud to + INF [2] [SER] (soberbio) proud

orientación *f*
A (de habitación, edificio) aspect (frml); **¿cuál es la ~ de la casa?** which way does the house face?; **la ~ de la antena** the way the antenna (AmE) *o* (BrE) aerial is pointing
B (enfoque, dirección) orientation; **le dio una ~ práctica al curso** he gave the course a practical bias; **la nueva ~ del partido** the party's new direction
C (guía) guidance, direction; (acción de guiar) orientation
(Compuesto) **orientación profesional** *or* (CS) **vocacional** (para estudiantes) vocational guidance, careers advice; (para desempleados) career guidance *o* advice
D (en un lugar) bearings (*pl*); **perder la ~** to lose one's bearings

oriental¹ *adj* (del este) Eastern; (del Lejano Oriente) Oriental; (uruguayo) (AmL) Uruguayan

oriental² *mf* (del Lejano Oriente) Oriental; (uruguayo) (AmL) Uruguayan

orientar [A1] *vt*
A [1] ‹*reflector*› to position; **oriente la antena hacia el este** position/turn the antenna (AmE) *o* (BrE) aerial to face east; **orientó el avión hacia el sur** he headed the plane south [2] ‹*edificio*›: **la casa está orientada al sur** the house faces south (frml) [3] (Náut) ‹*velas*› to trim
B (encaminar): **orienté mis esfuerzos hacia ...** I directed my efforts toward ...; **una política orientada a combatir la inflación** a policy designed to fight inflation *o* directed at fighting inflation
C ‹*personas*› «*faro/estrellas*» to guide; «*profesor/amigo*» to advise; **~ a los jóvenes en algo** to give young people guidance on sth
■ **orientarse** *v pron*
A (ubicarse) to get one's bearings, orient oneself; **~se por las estrellas** (Náut) to steer by the stars
B [1] (girar): **plantas que se orientan hacia el sol** plants that turn toward(s) the sun [2] (inclinarse): **mis hijos se ~on hacia las ciencias** my sons went in for *o* opted for science [3] (informarse) to get information

orientativo -va *adj* ‹*mapa*› outline (*before n*); ‹*diagnóstico*› initial, preliminary; ‹*test*› guiding (*before n*); **a modo ~** by way of guidance, for guidance

oriente *m*
A (punto cardinal) (liter) east; (Geog) East; (viento) east wind
(Compuesto) **Oriente Medio/Próximo** Middle/Near East
B (de las perlas) orient

orificio *m* (frml) orifice; **los ~s de la nariz** the nostrils; **un ~ de bala** a bullet hole

origen *m* [1] (principio) origin; (de palabra, tradición) origin; **en su ~** originally, in the beginning; **el tratado dio ~ a la unión** the union came into being as a result of the treaty; **aquel comentario dio ~ a ...** that remark gave rise to *o* caused ... [2] (procedencia) origin; **país de ~** country of origin; **es español de ~** he is Spanish by birth; **de ~ holandés** of Dutch origin; **de ~ humilde** of humble origin(s); **mejillones envasados en ~** mussels canned at point of origin; **embotellado en ~** bottled at source [3] (Mat) origin

original¹ *adj*
A (primero, no copiado) original
B ‹*artista/enfoque*› original; **¡tú siempre tan ~!** (iró) you always have to be different!

original² *m* original; **un ~ de Dalí** a Dalí original, an original Dalí
(Compuesto) **original de imprenta** original, manuscript

originalidad *f* (cualidad) originality; (comentario) clever remark

originar [A1] *vt* to start, give rise to
■ **originarse** *v pron* «*idea/costumbre*» to originate; «*movimiento*» to start, come into being, originate; «*incendio/disputa*» to start

originario -ria *adj* [1] (de un lugar) native; **ser ~ DE algo** «*persona*» to be a native OF sth, come FROM sth; «*especie*» to be native TO sth; come FROM sth [2] (primero, original) original

orilla *f* [1] (del mar, de lago) shore; (de río) bank; **se bañaban en la ~** they were bathing near the shore; **viven a la ~ del mar** they live by the sea *o* at the seaside; **un paseo a la ~ del mar** a walk along the seashore [2] (de mesa, plato) edge [3] (dobladillo) hem

orillar [A1] *vt*
A [1] ‹*problema/obstáculo*› to get around [2] ‹*muro/costa/zona*› to skirt (around) [3] (Col, Méx, Ven) (hacer a un lado): **orilló el coche** he pulled over
B (en costura) to hem
C (Méx) (obligar) **~ a algn a algo** to drive sb TO sth
■ **orillarse** *v pron* (Col, Méx, Ven) to move over; **se orilló para dejarlos pasar** (Auto) he pulled over to let them pass

orín *m*
A (herrumbre) rust
B (orina) urine

orina *f* urine

orinal *m* (de dormitorio) chamber pot; (para niños) pot, potty (colloq); (para enfermos) bedpan

orinar [A1] *vi* to urinate
■ **orinar** *vt*: **~ sangre** to pass blood
■ **orinarse** *v pron* to wet oneself; **se orina en la cama** he wets the bed

Orinoco *m*: **el (río) ~** the Orinoco (River)

oriundo¹ -da *adj* ▸ **originario 1**

oriundo² -da *m,f* native

orla *f* [1] (de retratos, diplomas) border; **con una ~ de armiño** trimmed *o* edged with ermine [2] (en escudo) orle

orlar [A1] *vt* ‹*tela/tapiz*› to edge, trim; ‹*página*› to decorate the borders of

ornamentación *f* ornamentation

ornamentar [A1] *vt* (frml) to adorn (frml), to ornament (frml)

ornamento *m* [1] (frml) (adorno, decoración) ornament (frml) [2] **ornamentos** *mpl* (Relig) vestments (*pl*)

ornar [A1] *vt* (frml) to adorn (frml)

ornato *m* (frml) adornment (frml)

ornitología *f* ornithology

ornitólogo -ga *m,f* ornithologist

ornitorrinco *m* duck-billed platypus

oro¹ *adj inv* gold

oro² *m*
A (metal) gold; **~ (de) 18 quilates** 18-carat gold; **lingote de ~** gold ingot; **bañado en ~** gold-plated; ***andar cargado al ~*** (Chi fam) to be loaded (colloq); ***guardar/tener algo como ~ en polvo*** (AmL) *or* (Esp) ***en paño*** to treasure sth (as if it were gold (AmE) *o* (BrE) gold dust); ***ni por todo el ~ del mundo*** not for all the tea in China (colloq); ***prometer el ~ y el moro*** to promise the earth; ***no es ~ todo lo que reluce*** all that glitters is not gold

Compuestos
- **oro batido** gold leaf
- **oro blanco/negro** white/black gold

B (en naipes) 1 (carta) *any card of the* **oros** *suit* 2 **oros** *mpl* (palo) *one of the suits in a Spanish pack of cards*

orondo -da *adj* smug, self-satisfied

oropel *m* (latón) imitation gold leaf; (ostentosidad) glitz, glitter; **sus joyas de ~** her glitzy jewels

orquesta *f* orchestra;

Compuestos
- **orquesta de cámara/sinfónica** chamber/symphony orchestra
- **orquesta de jazz** jazz band

orquestación *f* orchestration

orquestar [A1] *vt* to orchestrate

orquídea *f* orchid

ortiga *f* (stinging) nettle

ortodoncia *f* orthodontics, orthodontia

ortodoxia *f* orthodoxy

ortodoxo -xa *adj* orthodox

ortografía *f* spelling, orthography (frml); **tiene muy mala ~** her spelling is terrible

ortopedia *f* (especialidad) orthopedics*; (tienda) surgical aids shop

ortopédico -ca *adj* orthopedic*; **pierna ortopédica** artificial leg

ortopedista *mf* orthopedist*

oruga *f* (Zool) caterpillar; (Auto) caterpillar *o* crawler track

orzuela *f* (Méx): **tengo ~** I've got split ends

orzuelo *m* sty*

os *pron pers* (Esp) 1 (complemento directo, indirecto) you; **~ veo mañana** I'll see you tomorrow; **~ lo prometió** she promised it to you; **~ ha pintado la habitación** he has painted your room for you 2 (*refl*) yourselves; **no ~ engañéis** don't kid yourselves 3 (*recípr*): **creía que ~ conocíais** I thought you knew each other

osadía *f* (valor) (liter) daring, boldness; (descaro) temerity, audacity

osado -da *adj* (liter) daring, bold, audacious

osamenta *f* bones (*pl*); **la ~ de un mamut** the skeleton of a mammoth

osar [A1] *vi* (liter) **~ + INF** to dare to + INF; **no osó decirles la verdad** he dared not tell them the truth (liter)

osario *m* ossuary

oscar /'oskar/ *m* (*pl* ~ *or* **-cars**) Oscar

oscilación *f* (movimiento) oscillation; (fluctuación) fluctuation; **la ~ de los precios** the fluctuation in prices

oscilador *m* oscillator

oscilar [A1] *vi*

A «*péndulo*» to swing, oscillate (tech); «*aguja*» to oscillate; «*torre/columna*» to sway

B (fluctuar): **sus edades oscilaban entre ...** their ages ranged between ...; **la cotización osciló entre $90 y $92** the share price fluctuated between $90 and $92; **oscila entre la depresión y la euforia** he oscillates *o* fluctuates between depression and euphoria

oscilatorio -ria *adj* oscillatory

ósculo *m* (liter) kiss, osculation (frml)

oscurantismo *m* obscurantism

oscuras: **a ~** (*loc adv*) in darkness

oscurecer [E3] *v impers* to get dark

■ **oscurecer** *vt* 1 ‹*habitación/color*› to darken, make ... darker 2 ‹*significado*› to obscure

■ **oscurecerse** *v pron* «*cuero/madera*» to get darker; «*cielo*» to darken, get darker

oscuridad *f*

A (de la noche, de lugar) darkness, dark; **estaba sentada en la ~** she was sitting in the dark *o* in darkness; **le tiene miedo a la ~** he's afraid of the dark; **¡qué ~!** it's so dark in here!;

B (anonimato) obscurity; (de texto, definición) obscurity, obscureness

oscuro -ra *adj*

A 1 ‹*calle/habitación*› dark; **a las seis ya está ~** at six it's already dark; **la oscura y triste celda** the gloomy cell 2 ‹*color/ojos/pelo*› dark; **vestía de ~** she was wearing dark clothes

B 1 ‹*intenciones*› dark; ‹*asunto*› dubious; **su ~ pasado** her murky past 2 (poco claro) ‹*significado/asunto*› obscure 3 (poco conocido) ‹*escritor/orígenes*› obscure

óseo, ósea *adj* ‹*estructura/tejido*› bone (*before n*), osseous (tech); ‹*consistencia*› bony; **fragmentos ~s** fragments of bone

osezno *m* bear cub

osificación *f* ossification

osificarse [A2] *v pron* to ossify, become ossified

ósmosis, osmosis *f* osmosis

oso, osa *m,f* bear; ***hacer el ~*** (Esp fam) (hacer payasadas) to play the fool; (hacer el ridículo) to make a fool of oneself; ***peludo como un ~*** (fam) as hairy as a gorilla

Compuestos
- **Osa Mayor/Menor** *f* Great/Little Bear
- **oso de felpa** *or* **peluche** teddy bear
- **oso hormiguero** anteater, ant bear (AmE)
- **oso panda** panda
- **oso pardo** brown bear; (especie norteamericana) grizzly bear
- **oso polar** polar bear

ostensible *adj* obvious, evident

ostentación *f* ostentation; **hacen ~ de su fortuna** they flaunt *o* parade their wealth; **con ~** ostentatiously

ostentar [A1] *vt*

A (frml) (tener) ‹*cargo/título*› to hold; **la empresa ostenta el liderazgo en ...** the company is the market leader in ...

B (exhibir) ‹*alhajas/dinero*› to flaunt

■ **ostentar** *vi* to show off

ostentoso -sa *adj* ostentatious

osteópata *mf* osteopath

osteopatía *f* osteopathy

ostión *m* 1 (Esp) *type of oyster* 2 (CS) scallop 3 (Méx) oyster

ostra *f* oyster; ***aburrirse como una ~*** (fam) to get bored stiff *o* to death (colloq)

Compuesto **ostra perlífera** pearl oyster

ostracismo *m* ostracism; **condenar a algn al ~** (Hist) to ostracize sb

osuno -na *adj* bear-like

OTAN /'otan/ *f* (= **Organización del Tratado del Atlántico Norte**) NATO

otario[1] -ria *adj* (RPl arg) gullible

otario[2] -ria *m,f* (RPl arg) sap (colloq)

otate *m* (Méx) *giant grass used in basket making etc*

otear [A1] *vt* 1 ‹*horizonte/cielo*› to scan 2 (desde lo alto) to look down on *o* over

otero *m* hillock

OTI /'oti/ *f* = **Organización de las Televisiones Iberoamericanas**

otitis *f* inflammation of the ear, otitis (tech)

otoñal *adj* ‹*colores/paisaje*› autumnal, fall (*before n*) (AmE), autumn (*before n*) (BrE); ‹*belleza/amor*› (liter) autumnal

otoño *m* fall (AmE), autumn (BrE); **en ~** in the fall, in (the) autumn; **un bello día de ~** a fine fall *o* autumn day; **en el ~ de la vida** in the autumn of one's life

otorgar [A3] *vt*

A (frml) ‹*premio*› to award; ‹*favor/préstamo*› to grant; ‹*poderes*› to bestow (frml), to give

B (Der) ‹*contrato*› to sign, execute (tech); **otorgó testamento** she drew up *o* made her will

otorrinolaringólogo -ga *m,f* ear, nose and throat *o* ENT specialist, otorhinolaryngologist (tech)

otro[1], otra *adj*

A (con carácter adicional) (*sing*) another; (*pl*) other; (con numerales) another; **¿puedo comer ~ trozo?** can I have another piece?; **necesito ~s dos kilos** I need another two kilos; **prueba otra vez** try again; **una y otra vez** time and time again; *ver* **tanto[3] B**

B (diferente) (*sing*) another; (*pl*) other; **¿no sabes ninguna otra canción?** don't you know any other songs?; **no hay otra forma** there's no other way; **probar ~s métodos** to try other methods; **en ~ sitio** somewhere else; **en ~ momento** some other time

O

C (estableciendo un contraste) other; **queda del ∼ lado de la calle** it's on the other side of the street

Compuestos

- **otro mundo** *m*: **el ∼ ∼** the next world; *ver tb* **mundo A**
- **otro yo** *m* alter ego, other self

D [1] (siguiente, contiguo) next; **al ∼ día me llamó** she phoned me the following *o* (the) next day [2] **el otro día** the other day

otro², **otra** *pron*

A (con carácter adicional) (*sing*) another (one); **¿quieres ∼?** would you like another (one)?; **¡otra!** encore!

B (diferente): **parece otra** she looks like a different person; **no voy a aceptar ningún ∼** I won't accept any other; **lo dejó por ∼** she left him for another man; **∼s piensan que no es así** others feel that this is not so

C (estableciendo un contraste): **la otra es mejor** the other one is better; **los ∼s no están listos** (hablando — de personas) the others aren't ready; (— de cosas) the others *o* the other ones aren't ready; **todo lo ∼ va aquí** everything else goes in here

D (siguiente, contiguo): **un día sí y ∼ no** every other day; **de un día para (el) ∼** overnight, from one day to the next; **la semana que viene no, la otra** not next week, the week after; **uno detrás del ∼** one after the other

otrora *adv* (liter) once; **el ∼ respetado político** the once-respected politician

ovación *f* (frml) ovation

ovacionar [A1] *vt* (frml) to applaud, give ... an ovation (frml)

oval *adj*, **ovalado -da** *adj* oval

óvalo *m* oval

ovario *m* ovary

oveja *f* (nombre genérico) sheep; (hembra) ewe; **un nebaño de ∼s** a flock of sheep; ***cada ∼ con su pareja*** birds of a feather flock together

Compuestos

- **oveja descarriada** (Bib): **la ∼ descarriada** the lost sheep
- **oveja negra** black sheep

ovejuno -na *adj* sheep (*before n*), ovine (frml)

overol *m* (AmL) (pantalón con peto) overalls (*pl*) (AmE), dungarees (*pl*) (BrE); (con mangas) coveralls (*pl*) (AmE), overalls (*pl*) (BrE)

oviforme *adj* egg-shaped, oviform (frml)

ovillar [A1] *vt* to wind ... into a ball

■ **ovillarse** *v pron* to curl up (in a ball)

ovillo *m* ball (*of yarn*); ***hacerse un ∼*** to curl up (in a ball)

ovino -na *adj* sheep (*before n*), ovine

ovíparo -ra *adj* oviparous

ovni, OVNI /'oβni/ *m* (= **objeto volador** *or* **volante no identificado**) UFO

ovoide *adj/m* ovoid

ovulación *f* ovulation

ovular [A1] *vi* to ovulate

óvulo *m* (Biol) ovule; (Farm) pessary

oxidación *f* (del hierro) rusting, oxidation (tech); (de otros elementos) oxidation

oxidado -da *adj* rusty

oxidar [A1] *vt* ‹*hierro*› to rust, oxidize (tech); ‹*cobre*› to oxidize

■ **oxidarse** *v pron* «*hierro*» to rust, go rusty, oxidize (tech); «*cobre*» to oxidize, form a patina

óxido *m*; (herrumbre) rust; (Quím) oxide

oxigenación *f* oxygenation

oxigenar [A1] *vt* [1] (Quím) to oxygenate [2] ‹*pelo*› to bleach

■ **oxigenarse** *v pron* to get a breath of air, get some fresh air

oxígeno *m* oxygen

oye, etc *see* **oír**

oyente *mf* [1] (Educ) occasional student, auditor (AmE); **voy de ∼ a sus clases** I sit in on her classes [2] (Rad) listener

oyera, oyese, etc *see* **oír**

ozono *m* ozone; **la capa de ∼** the ozone layer

ozonosfera *f* ozonosphere

Pp

P, **p** *f* (*read as* /pe/) *the letter* **P, p**
p. *f* (= **página**) p, page
P. *m* (= **Padre**) Fr, Father
pa' *prep: form often used instead of* **para** *in colloquial or rustic speech*
p.a. (= **por autorización**) pp
pabellón *m*
A 1 (en hospital, cuartel) block, building; (en feria, exposición) pavilion; (de palacio) pavilion; (en jardín) summerhouse 2 (de instrumento de viento) bell
Compuestos
- **pabellón auricular** *or* **de la oreja** outer ear
- **pabellón de caza** hunting lodge
- **pabellón deportivo** *or* **de deportes** sports hall

B (frml) (bandera) flag
Compuesto **pabellón de conveniencia** flag of convenience
pabilo *m* (de vela) wick
pábulo *m* (liter) fuel; ***dar ~ a algo*** to fuel sth
PAC *f* (= **Política Agrícola Comunitaria**) CAP
paca *f*
A (Zool) paca
B (fardo) bale
pacana *f* pecan
pácatelas *interj* (Méx fam) crash!
pacatería *f* prudishness
pacato -ta *adj* prudish, prim
paceño¹ -ña *adj* of/from La Paz
paceño² -ña *m,f* person from La Paz
pacer [E3] *vi/vt* to graze
pacha *f* (AmC) baby's bottle
pachá *m* pasha; ***vivir como un ~*** to live like a lord *o* king
pachanga *f* (esp AmL fam) ▸**parranda**
pachanguero -ra *adj* (esp AmL fam) ▸**parrandero**
pacharán *m: type of sloe gin*
pacheco -ca *m,f* (Méx fam) junkie
pachocha *f* (Per fam) sluggishness, slowness
pachón -chona *adj* (Méx) ‹*suéter*› chunky; ‹*perro*› wooly*
pachorra *f* (fam) sluggishness, slowness
pachucho -cha *adj* [ESTAR] (Esp fam) ‹*persona*› poorly (colloq); ‹*fruta*› overripe
pachuco¹ -ca *adj* (Méx fam) flashily-dressed
pachuco² -ca *m,f* (Méx) *young Mexican influenced by US culture*
pachulí, pachuli *m* patchouli
paciencia *f* patience; **ten ~** be patient, have a little patience; **¡~, otra vez será!** oh well *o* never mind, maybe next time; **perder la ~** to lose patience; **se me acabó** *or* **agotó la ~** my patience ran out; ***tener más ~ que Job*** *or* ***que un santo*** to have the patience of Job *o* of a saint
paciente¹ *adj*
A (tolerante) patient
B (Ling) passive
paciente² *mf* patient
pacienzudo -da *adj* ‹*persona*› extremely patient; ‹*trabajo/labor*› painstaking
pacificación *f* pacification
pacificador¹ -dora *adj* peace (*before n*); **medidas ~as** measures designed to bring about peace
pacificador² -dora *m,f* peacemaker
pacíficamente *adv* peacefully, peaceably
pacificar [A2] *vt* (Mil) to pacify (frml); (calmar) to pacify, appease; **~ los ánimos** to calm people down
■ **pacificarse** *v pron* «*viento*» to abate; «*mar*» to become calm
pacífico -ca *adj* 1 ‹*manifestación/medios*› peaceful, pacific (frml); **por la vía pacífica** by peaceful means 2 ‹*carácter/persona*› peace-loving, peaceable; ‹*animal*› peaceful
Pacífico *m*: **el (océano) ~** the Pacific (Ocean)
pacifismo *m* pacifism
pacifista *adj/mf* pacifist
paco -ca *m,f* (Andes fam) cop (colloq)
pacota *f* (Méx) ▸**pacotilla**
pacotilla *f* trash; **de ~** ‹*escritor*› second-rate; ‹*novela*› trashy, second-rate; ‹*reloj*› cheap, shoddy; **dictadores de ~** tinpot dictators (colloq)
pacotillero -ra *m,f* (vendedor) street vendor (*gen selling shoddy goods*)
pactar [A1] *vt* ‹*paz/tregua*› to negotiate, agree terms for; ‹*plazo/indemnización*› to agree on
■ **pactar** *vi* to make a pact, negotiate an agreement
pacto *m* pact, agreement; **cumplir/romper un ~** to abide by the terms of/to break an agreement; ***hacer un ~ con el diablo*** to make a pact with the devil
Compuestos
- **Pacto Andino** Andean Pact (*agreement on economic cooperation between Andean countries*)
- **pacto de no agresión** non-aggression pact
- **Pacto de Varsovia** Warsaw Pact
- **pacto social** social contract
- **pacto de estabilidad** (en UE) stability pact

padecer [E3] *vt* ‹*enfermedad/hambre*› to suffer from; ‹*desgracias/injusticias/privaciones*› to suffer, undergo
■ **padecer** *vi* to suffer; **~ DE algo** to suffer FROM sth; **padecía de los nervios** I had trouble with my nerves; **padece del corazón** he has heart trouble
padecimiento *m* suffering
pádel *m* (RPl) paddle tennis
padrastro *m*
A (pariente) stepfather
B (Anat) hangnail
padre¹ *adj* 1 (fam) (grande) terrible (colloq); **me di** *or* **me llevé un susto ~** I got a hell of a fright (colloq); **un escándalo ~** an almighty *o* a terrible fuss 2 [ESTAR] (Méx fam) ‹*coche/persona*› great (colloq), fantastic; **¡qué ~!** great!
padre² *m*
A (pariente) father; **mis ~s** my parents; ***de ~ y (muy) señor mío*** terrible (colloq); ***no tener ~ ni madre, ni perrito que le ladre*** to be all alone in the world
Compuestos
- **padre de familia** father, family man
- **padre de la patria** (Hist) hero of the nation; **los ~s de la ~** (fundadores) the founding fathers, the founders of the nation

B (Relig) (sacerdote) father; **el ~ Miguel** Father Miguel

(Compuesto) **padre espiritual** confessor

C **Padre** (Dios): **el P~** the Father; **Dios P~** God the Father

padrenuestro *m* Lord's Prayer; ***en menos que se reza un ~*** in no time at all

padrillo *m* (AmS) stallion

padrino *m* 1 (en bautizo) godfather; (de boda) *man who gives away the bride, usually her father* 2 (en duelo) second 3 (protector) sponsor, patron; **para conseguirlo hace falta tener ~s** to achieve it you need to know the right people

padrón *m*

A (Gob, Pol) register

(Compuesto) **padrón electoral** (AmL) electoral roll *o* register

B (AmL) (Equ) stallion

C (Chi) (Auto) registration documents (*pl*)

padrote *m* (Méx fam & pey) pimp

paella *f* paella

paellada *f*: *meal of paella*; **me convidaron a una ~** they invited me round to eat paella

paellera *f* paella dish *o* pan

paf *m* splat!, wham!

pág. *f* (= **página**) p.; **760 págs.** 760 pp.

paga *f* 1 (acción de pagar) payment 2 (sueldo) pay; **¿qué tal es la ~?** what's the pay like?

(Compuestos)

- **paga de Navidad** *extra month's salary paid at Christmas*
- **paga extra** *or* **extraordinaria** *extra month's salary gen paid twice a year*

pagadero -ra *adj* payable; **~ en cuotas mensuales** to be paid in monthly installments

pagado -da *adj*: **~ de sí mismo** full of oneself, smug

pagador[1] -dora *adj*: **la entidad ~a** the payer

pagador[2] -dora *m,f* 1 payer; **es mal ~** he's a bad payer 2 (Mil) paymaster

pagaduría *f* cashier's office, accounts office

paganini *mf* (fam & hum): **el ~ siempre soy yo** I always end up footing the bill

paganismo *m* paganism

paganizar [A4] *vt* to secularize

■ **paganizarse** *v pron* to lose its religious significance, become secularized

pagano[1] -na *adj* pagan; (pey) heathen

pagano[2] -na *m,f* pagan, non-believer; (pey) heathen

pagar [A3] *vt* 1 (abonar) ‹*cuenta/alquiler*› to pay; ‹*deuda*› to pay (off), repay; ‹*comida/entradas/mercancías*› to pay for; **¿cuánto pagas de alquiler?** how much rent do you pay?; **me pagan los estudios** they are paying for my education; **no puedo ~ tanto** I can't afford (to pay) that much; ***ni que me/le paguen*** not even if you paid me/him; **~ algo POR algo** to pay sth FOR sth 2 ‹*favor/desvelos*› to repay; **¡que Dios se lo pague!** God bless you! 3 (expiar) ‹*delito/atrevimiento*› to pay for; **~ algo CON algo** to pay FOR sth WITH sth; **lo pagó con su vida** he paid for it with his life; ***el que la hace la paga*** you've made your bed and now you'll have to lie in it; ***¡me las vas a ~!*** *or* ***¡ya me las ~ás!*** you'll pay for this!

■ **pagar** *vi* 1 (Com, Fin) to pay; **pagan bien** they pay well, the pay's good 2 (corresponder) to repay; ***~le a algn con la misma moneda*** to pay sb back in their own coin *o* in kind 3 (Col fam) (rendir, compensar) to pay; **el negocio no paga** the business doesn't pay; **no paga pintar estas paredes** it's not worth painting these walls

pagaré *m* promissory note, IOU

página *f*

A (de libro) page; **los ejercicios de la ~ cinco** the exercises on page five; **en la ~ siguiente** on the next page

(Compuestos)

- **página de inicio** *or* **inicial** home page
- **páginas amarillas** yellow pages

B (episodio) chapter

paginación *f* pagination

paginar [A1] *vt* to number, paginate (tech)

pago[1] -ga *adj* [ESTAR] 1 ‹*cuenta*› paid; ‹*pedido/mercancías*› paid for 2 (RPl) ‹*empleado*› paid

pago[2] *m*

A 1 (Com, Fin) payment; **~ adelantado** *or* **anticipado** payment in advance; **~ inicial** down payment; **~ al contado/a plazos/en especie** payment in cash/by installments/in kind; **~ a cuenta** payment on account; **atrasarse en el ~ del alquiler** to get behind with the rent 2 (recompensa) reward; **en ~ a algo** as a reward for sth

(Compuesto) **pago contra entrega** cash on delivery, COD

B (fam) (lugar, región) *tb* **~s**: **¿qué haces tú por estos ~s?** what are you doing in this neck of the woods *o* in these parts (colloq); **fue a morir a su(s) ~(s)** (CS) he went back home to die

pagoda *f* pagoda

pai *m* (AmC, Méx) pie

(Compuesto) **pai de queso** (AmC, Méx) cheesecake

paila *f* 1 (sartén) large copper frying pan 2 (Chi) (plato) dish; ***irse a las ~s*** (Chi fam) to come to grief (colloq)

país *m* 1 (unidad política) country; **los ~es miembros** the member countries 2 (ciudadanos) nation 3 (en ficción) land; **en un ~ lejano** in a distant *o* faraway land; **el ~ de las maravillas** wonderland; **ciego[2]**

(Compuestos)

- **País de Gales** *m*: **el ~ ~ ~** Wales
- **país de origen** (de persona) home country, native land; (de producto) country of origin
- **Países Bajos** *mpl*: **los ~ ~** (país) the Netherlands; (región) (Geog, Hist) the Low Countries
- **país natal** native country
- **país satélite** satellite (nation)
- **País Vasco** *m* Basque Country

paisaje *m* 1 (panorama) landscape, scenery; **la belleza del ~ asturiano** the beauty of the Asturian countryside *o* landscape; **el ~ es agreste/boscoso** it is a rugged/wooded landscape 2 (Art) landscape

paisajismo *m* (Art) landscape painting; (en jardinería) landscape gardening

paisajista *mf* (Art) landscape painter; (en jardinería) landscape gardener

paisajístico -ca *adj* landscape (*before n*)

paisanada *f* (RPl fam): **la ~** the country folk (*pl*), the peasants (*pl*)

paisanaje *m* (de la misma zona, ciudad) common origin; (campesinos) peasantry

paisano[1] -na *adj* from the same country (*o* area *etc*); **somos ~s** (compatriotas) we're fellow countrymen; (de la misma zona, ciudad) we're from the same area/place

paisano[2] -na *m,f*

A 1 (compatriota) (*m*) fellow countryman, compatriot; (*f*) fellow countrywoman, compatriot 2 (de la misma zona, ciudad): **es un ~ mío** he's from the same area/place as I am

B (Indum): **ir/vestir de ~** «*soldado*» to be in/to wear civilian clothes *o* (colloq) civvies; «*policía*» to be in/to wear plain clothes; «*sacerdote*» to be in/to wear secular dress

C 1 (Chi) (árabe) Arab 2 (Per) *mountain-dweller of Indian origin* 3 (RPl) peasant

paja[1] *adj* (Per fam) great (colloq)

paja[2] *f*

A (Agr, Bot) straw; **sombrero de ~** straw hat; **techo de ~** thatched roof; ***hacerse*** *o* (Chi, Per) ***correrse una*** *or* ***la ~*** (vulg) to jerk off (vulg), to wank (BrE vulg); ***hacerse ~s mentales*** (vulg) to indulge in mental masturbation; ***tener (el) rabo*** (Col, Ven) *or* (RPl) ***(la) cola de ~*** to have a guilty conscience; ***ver la ~ en el ojo ajeno y no la viga en el propio*** to see the mote in one's neighbor's eye and not the beam in one's own

B (para beber) *tb* **pajita** (drinking) straw

C 1 (fam) (en texto, discurso) padding, waffle (BrE colloq) 2 (Col fam): **hablar** *or* **echar ~** (decir mentiras) to tell lies; (charlar) to chat, gab (colloq)

D (AmC) (grifo) faucet (AmE), tap (BrE)

pajar *m* (granero) barn; (desván) hayloft

pájara *f*

A (fam & pey) (mujer astuta) crafty woman, scheming bitch (sl & pej)

B (fam) (decaimiento brusco) collapse

pajarearse [A1] *v pron* (Per fam) to goof (colloq), to boob (BrE colloq)

P

pajarera *f* (jaula) aviary

pajarería *f* 1 (tienda) pet shop (*specializing in birds*) 2 (bandada) flock of birds

pajarero -ra *m,f* (criador) bird breeder; (vendedor) bird dealer; (cazador) bird hunter *o* trapper

pajarita *f* 1 *tb* ~ **de papel** origami bird 2 (Esp) (Indum) bow tie

pajarito *m* (cría) baby bird; (pájaro) (fam) little bird, birdie (colloq); ***comer como un*** ~ to eat like a bird; ***me lo dijo un*** ~ (fam) a little bird told me (colloq)

pájaro *m*

A (Zool) bird; ***matar dos ~s de un tiro*** to kill two birds with one stone; ***ser ~ de mal agüero*** to be a prophet of doom *o* a Jeremiah; ***tener ~s en la cabeza*** (fam) to be scatterbrained (colloq); ***más vale ~ en mano que cien*** *or* ***ciento volando*** a bird in the hand is worth two in the bush

Compuestos

- **pájaro bobo** penguin
- **pájaro carpintero** woodpecker
- **pájaro mosca** hummingbird

B (fam) (granuja) nasty piece of work (colloq); ***ser un ~ de cuenta*** (fam) to be a nasty piece of work (colloq)

C (Col) (Hist) (asesino) hired killer (*in the pay of landowners*)

pajarón -rona *adj*

A (CS fam) (tonto) silly

B (Chi fam) (distraído) scatterbrained

pajarraco *m* (fam) 1 (Zool) big, ugly bird 2 (granuja) rogue

paje *m* 1 (Hist) page; **corte de pelo a lo ~** pageboy haircut 2 (en boda) page (boy)

pajita, pajilla *f* (drinking) straw

pajizo -za *adj* straw-colored*

pajonal *m* (AmL) scrubland

pajuerano -na *m,f* (RPl fam) country bumpkin, hick (AmE colloq)

Pakistán *m* Pakistan

pakistaní *adj/mf* Pakistani

PAL *m* /pal/ PAL

pala *f*

A (para cavar) spade; (para mover arena, carbón) shovel; (para recoger la basura) dustpan

Compuesto **pala mecánica** power shovel

B (Coc) (para servir — pescado) slotted spatula (AmE), fish slice (BrE); (— tarta) cake slice

C 1 (para golpear alfombras) carpet beater 2 (de frontenis) racket; (de ping-pong) paddle, bat (BrE); (en piragüismo) paddle

D 1 (de remo, hélice) blade 2 (de zapato) upper, vamp; (de corbata) apron; **corbata de ~ ancha** wide tie

palabra *f*

A (vocablo) word; **una ~ de seis letras** a six-letter word; **en toda la extensión de la ~** in every sense of the word; **no son más que ~s** it's all talk; **en pocas ~s, es un cobarde** in a word, he's a coward; **~ por ~** word for word; **yo no sabía ni una ~ del asunto** I didn't know a thing *o* anything about it; **no entendí (ni) una ~** I didn't understand a (single) word; **sin decir (una) ~** without a word; ***comerse las ~s*** to gabble; ***con (muy) buenas ~s*** in the nicest possible way; ***decirle a algn cuatro ~s bien dichas*** to tell sb a few home truths; ***eso ya son ~s mayores*** (refiriéndose — a insulto, acusación) those are strong words; (— a propuesta excesiva) that's taking things too far; ***quitarle las ~s de la boca a algn*** to take the words right out of sb's mouth; ***tener la última ~*** to have the final say; ***tener unas ~s con algn*** to have words with sb (colloq); ***a ~s necias oídos sordos*** take no notice of the stupid things people say; ***las ~s se las lleva el viento*** actions speak louder than words

Compuestos

- **palabra clave** key word
- **palabra compuesta** compound word
- **palabra funcional** *or* **vacía** function word
- **palabras cruzadas** *fpl* (CS) crossword (puzzle)

B (promesa) word; **una mujer de ~** a woman of her word; **cumplió con su ~** she kept her word; **nunca falta a su ~** he never breaks *o* goes back on his word; **se lo devolví ¡~!** I gave it back to her, honest! (colloq); ***cobrarle la ~ a algn*** (Chi fam) to hold sb to his/her word (colloq); ***tomarle la ~ a algn***: **le tomé la ~ y le pedí un préstamo** I took him up on his offer and asked for a loan

Compuesto **palabra de honor** word of honor*

C 1 (habla) speech; **el don de la ~** the gift of speech; **un acuerdo de ~** a verbal agreement; **no me dirigió la ~** she didn't speak to me; ***dejar a algn con la ~ en la boca***: **me dejó con la ~ en la boca** (me interrumpió) he cut me off in mid-sentence; (no me dejó hablar) he didn't give me a chance to open my mouth 2 (frml) (en ceremonia, asamblea): **pedir la ~** to ask for permission to speak; **pido la ~** may I say something?, I'd like to say something; **tener/tomar la ~** to have/to take the floor (frml); **ceder(le) la ~ a algn** to give the floor to sb (frml), to call upon sb to speak

palabrear [A1] *vt* (Chi fam) 1 ‹*asunto/negocio*› to have a chat about (colloq) 2 ‹*persona*› to work on (colloq) 3 (concertar) to agree on 4 ‹*mujer*› to promise to marry

palabrería *f*, **palabrerío** *m* talk; **no dice más que ~** he's full of hot air (colloq)

palabrero -ra *m,f* (fam) gasbag (colloq), windbag (colloq)

palabrota *f* (fam) swearword; **decir ~s** to swear

palacete *m* (palacio) small palace; (casa lujosa) (fam) mansion

palaciego -ga *adj* (de palacio) palace (*before n*), court (*before n*); (magnífico) palatial

palacio *m* 1 (residencia) palace; **el personal de ~** the Royal Household; **ir a ~** to go to the (Royal) Palace 2 (edificio público) *large public building*

Compuestos

- **Palacio de Justicia** lawcourts (*pl*)
- **Palacio Episcopal** Bishop's Palace
- **Palacio Real** Royal Palace

(Palacio de) la Moncloa

The Spanish prime minister's official residence, in Madrid

(Palacio de) la Moneda

The Chilean presidential palace, in the capital, Santiago

palada *f* (con pala) spadeful, shovelful; (con remo) stroke

paladar *m* 1 (Anat) palate; (gusto) palate; **para ~es exigentes** for those with a discerning palate 2 (Vin): **tener buen ~** «*licor*» to be very smooth on the palate

paladear [A1] *vt* to savor*

paladeo *m* tasting

paladín *m* (Hist) paladin; (defensor) champion

palafrén *m* palfrey

palanca *f*

A 1 (para levantar, mover algo) lever; (para forzar, abrir algo) crowbar; **es más fácil levantarlo haciendo ~** it's easier to lift it using a lever; **abrir algo haciendo ~** ‹*baúl/ventana*› to lever sth open; ‹*tarro/lata*› to pry sth open 2 (de control) lever

Compuestos

- **palanca de cambios** gearshift (AmE), gear lever *o* stick (BrE)
- **palanca de mando** joystick

B (fam) 1 (influencia) influence; **hay que tener ~** you have to be able to pull a few strings (colloq) 2 (persona influyente) influential person, contact

palangana[1] *f* 1 (para fregar) bowl 2 (jofaina) washbowl (AmE), washbasin (BrE) 3 (Col) (fuente) serving dish

palangana[2] *mf* (fam) 1 (Andes) (fanfarrón) loudmouth (colloq), show-off 2 (RPl) (tonto) idiot

palanganear [A1] *vi* (Andes fam) to show off

palanquear [A1] *vt*

A (AmL) ▸ **apalancar**

B (AmL fam) (usando influencias): **le ~on un puesto** they pulled some strings to get him a job (colloq)

■ **palanquear** *vi* (AmL fam) to pull strings (colloq)

palanqueta *f* (palanca) jimmy (AmE), jemmy (BrE)

palapa *f* (Méx) palm shelter

palatal *adj/f* palatal

palatino -na *adj*

A (de palacio) court (*before n*), palace (*before n*); (Hist) palatine

B (del paladar) palatal

palco *m* box
(Compuestos)
- **palco de autoridades** *or* **de honor** ≈ royal box, (*box for distinguished guests*)
- **palco de platea/de proscenio** ground-floor/stage box

palear [A1] *vt*
A ‹*tierra*› to shovel; ‹*piragua*› to paddle
B (AmL) (robar) to swipe (colloq), to lift (colloq)
■ **palear** *vi* to paddle

palenque *m*
A (valla) fence, stockade
B (RPl) (poste) tethering post
C (Méx) 1 (fiesta popular) festival (*with cockfights, music, etc*) 2 (para gallos) cockpit

paleografía *f* paleography
paleolítico *adj* paleolithic
paleontología *f* paleontology
paleontólogo -ga *m,f* paleontologist
Palestina *f* Palestine
palestino -na *adj/m,f* Palestinian
palestra *f* (Hist) arena; **la ~ política** the political arena; ***salir a la*** **~** to join the fray; ***saltar a la*** **~** to come to the fore, hit the headlines

paleta *f*
A 1 (de pintor) palette 2 (de cocina) spatula 3 (de albañil) trowel 4 (Dep) (de ping-pong) paddle, bat (BrE)
B (fam) (diente) front tooth
C (Coc) shoulder; (Anat, Zool) (Andes) shoulder blade
D (Tec) (de noria) paddle, blade; (de ventilador) vane, blade
E (AmL) (Jueg) beach tennis
F 1 (Andes, Méx) (helado) Popsicle® (AmE), ice lolly (BrE) 2 (Méx) (dulce) lollipop

paletada *f* (de cemento) trowelful
paletilla *f* 1 (Anat, Zool) shoulder blade 2 (Coc) shoulder
paleto¹ -ta *adj* (Esp fam): **no seas ~** don't be such a yokel (colloq)
paleto² -ta *m,f* (Esp fam) country bumpkin, hick (AmE colloq & pej)
paletó *m* (Chi) (man's) jacket
paliacate *m* (Méx) brightly colored* scarf
paliar [A1] *or* [A17] *vt* ‹*dolor*› to ease, alleviate; ‹*efectos*› to mitigate, lessen
paliativo¹ -va *adj* palliative
paliativo² *m* 1 (Fin, Med, Pol) palliative (measure) 2 **sin ~s** (*loc adj*) inexcusable; (*loc adv*) unreservedly; **comportamiento sin ~s** inexcusable behavior; **lo condenó sin ~s** he roundly *o* unreservedly condemned it
palidecer [E3] *vi* 1 «*persona*» to turn *o* go pale 2 (liter) (eclipsarse) to pale (liter)
palidez *f* paleness
pálido -da *adj* ‹*persona/luz/color*› pale; **estás ~** you're very pale; **se puso ~** he went pale; **a la pálida luz de la luna** (liter) by the pale light of the moon (liter)
paliducho -cha *adj* (fam) pale, peaky (colloq)

palillo *m*
A 1 (mondadientes) *tb* **~ de dientes** toothpick; **tiene las piernas como ~s** her legs are like matchsticks; ***estar como un*** *or* ***hecho un*** **~** (fam) to be as thin as a rake 2 (fam) (persona flaca): **es un ~** he's as thin as a rake 3 (para comida oriental) chopstick
B 1 (de tambor) drumstick 2 **palillos** *mpl* (castañuelas) castanets (*pl*)
C (Chi) (para tejer) knitting needle

palinodia *f* palinode (liter), public recantation; ***cantar la*** **~** to make a public recantation
palio *m* 1 (dosel) canopy; ***recibir a algn bajo*** **~** to give sb a royal welcome 2 (prenda) pallium
palisandro *m* rosewood
palista *mf* canoeist

palito *m*
A (palo) small stick (*o* post *etc*)
B (RPl) (helado) Popsicle® (AmE), ice lolly (BrE)

palitroque *m* (bolo) skittle; (juego) skittles; (local) skittle alley

paliza *f*
A 1 (zurra) hiding, beating; **su padre le dio una buena ~** his father gave him a good hiding; **los matones le pegaron una ~** the thugs beat him up 2 (fam) (derrota) thrashing (colloq); **al Danubio le dieron una ~ en casa** Danubio were hammered *o* thrashed at home (colloq)
B (fam) 1 (esfuerzo): **fue una ~ de viaje** the journey was a real killer; **¡qué ~ tener que ir hasta allá!** what a trek having to go all the way over there! (colloq); ***darse la*** **~** (fam) (trabajando, estudiando) to work one's butt off (AmE colloq), to slog one's guts out (BrE colloq) 2 (aburrimiento) drag (colloq)

palizada *f* (valla) palisade; (terreno) fenced enclosure
palla *f* (Per fam) mistress
pallar *m* (Per) (Bot, Coc) butter bean
pallasa *f* (CS) straw mattress, palliasse

palma *f*
A (de la mano) palm; ***conocer algo como la*** **~** ***de la mano*** to know sth like the back of one's hand; ***untarle la*** **~** ***a algn*** to grease sb's palm
B 1 (Bot) (planta) palm; (hoja) palm leaf 2 (gloria, triunfo) distinction; ***llevarse la*** **~** (ser el mejor) to be outstanding; (ser el colmo) to take the cake (colloq)
(Compuesto) **palma de coco** (Col) coconut palm
C **palmas** *fpl*: **dar** *or* **batir ~s** (aplaudir) to clap (one's hands), applaud; **tocar las ~s** (marcando el ritmo) to clap in time

palmada *f* 1 (golpecito amistoso) pat; **le dio una ~ en la espalda** he gave him a pat on the back; **me dio unas palmaditas en la mejilla** he patted me on the cheek 2 (para llamar la atención) clap; **dio unas ~s para pedir silencio** he clapped his hands for silence 3 (AmL) (golpe, azote) smack, slap
palmado *adj* 1 (AmC fam) (sin dinero) broke (colloq) 2 (Arg fam) (cansado) worn out (colloq)
palmar¹ *m* palm grove
palmar² [A1] *vt* (Esp, Méx fam): **~la** to snuff it (colloq), to kick the bucket (colloq)
palmarés *m* (historial) record, list of achievements; (lista) list of winners/champions
palmatoria *f* candlestick
palmeado -da *adj* ‹*pata*› webbed; ‹*hoja/raíz*› palmate (*before n*)
palmear [A1] *vt* to slap … on the back
palmera *f* 1 (Bot) palm tree 2 (Coc) palmier
palmeral *m* palm grove
palmero -ra *m,f* palm farmer
palmeta *f* cane
palmípedo¹ -da *adj* webfooted
palmípedo² -da *m,f* webfoot
palmista *mf* palmist
palmito *m* (planta) European fan palm, palmetto; (tallo) palm heart
palmo *m* span, handspan; **casi un ~** several inches; ***conocer algo*** **~** ***a*** **~** to know sth like the back of one's hand; ***dejar a algn con un*** **~** ***de narices*** (fam) to take the wind out of sb's sails (colloq)
palmotear [A1] *vi* to clap (one's hands)
■ **palmotear** *vt* to slap … on the back
palmoteo *m* clapping

palo *m*
A 1 (trozo de madera) stick; (de valla, portería) post; (de herramienta) handle; (de telégrafos) pole; (de tienda, carpa) tent pole; **~ de escoba** broomstick, broomhandle; **clavar un ~ en la tierra** to drive a stake into the ground; ***(flaco) como un*** **~** (fam) as thin as a rake *o* rail; ***más tieso que un*** **~** as stiff as a board; ***de tal*** **~, *tal astilla*** a chip off the old block, like father like son (*o* like mother like daughter *etc*) 2 (AmC, Col fam) (árbol) tree 3 (Dep) (de golf) (golf) club; (de hockey) hockey stick 4 (Náut) mast; ***a*** **~** ***seco*** (fam): **se lo comió a ~ seco** she ate it on its own; **me lo dijo a ~ seco** she told me outright 5 **palos** *mpl* (Equ) rails (*pl*)
(Compuestos)
- **palo de amasar** (RPl) rolling pin
- **palo de mayo** (AmC) *style of music and dance from the Atlantic coast*
- **palo grueso** (Chi fam) fat cat (colloq)

p

- **palo mayor** mainmast

B (madera) wood; ***no está el ~ para cucharas*** (Col fam) the time isn't right

(Compuestos)
- **palo de rosa** rosewood
- **palo dulce** licorice*

C (Impr) (de la b, d) ascender; (de la p, q) descender

D **1** (fam) (golpe) blow (with a stick); **lo molieron a ~s** they beat him till he was black and blue; ***dar ~s de ciego*** (al pelear) to lash *o* strike out blindly; (al resolver un problema) to grope in the dark; ***ni a ~(s)*** (AmS) no way; ***~s porque bogas, ~s porque no bogas*** you can't win **2** (fam) (revés, daño) blow **3** (fam) (en cuestiones de dinero): **darle** *or* **pegarle un ~ a algn** to rip sb off (colloq)

E (en naipes) suit; **seguir el ~** to follow suit

F (AmL arg) (millón) million pesos (*o* soles *etc*)

G (Ven fam) (trago) drink

H (Col, Ven fam) (de agua): **cayó un ~ de agua** it poured (with rain), it poured down

paloma *f* (Zool) pigeon; (blanca) dove; (como símbolo) dove

(Compuestos)
- **paloma de la paz** dove of peace
- **paloma mensajera** carrier pigeon
- **paloma torcaz** *or* **torcaza** ringdove, wood pigeon (BrE)

palomar *m* dovecot, pigeon loft

palomear [A1] *vt* (Per fam) to shoot ... dead, blow ... away (sl)

palomero -ra *m,f* (Col fam) goalhanger (colloq)

palomilla[1] *adj* (Andes fam) ‹*niño/muchacho*› (callejero) street (*before n*); (travieso) naughty

palomilla[2] *f*

A (mariposa nocturna) moth; (crisálida) chrysalis

B (tuerca) wing nut, butterfly nut; (soporte) wall bracket

C (Méx fam) (pandilla, grupo) gang

palomilla[3] *mf* (Andes fam) (muchacho — callejero) street kid (colloq); (— travieso) little monkey (colloq), little devil (colloq)

palomino *m* **1** (Zool) young pigeon, young dove **2** (fam) (joven inexperto) upstart, pipsqueak (colloq) **3** (AmL) (caballo) palomino

palomita *f*

A **1** (bebida) anisette and water **2** (Dep) full-length dive **3** **palomitas** *fpl*: *tb* **~s de maíz** popcorn

B (Méx fam) (marca) check (AmE), tick (BrE)

palomo *m* (ave) cock pigeon

palote *m*

A (en caligrafía) line, stroke

B (RPl) (de amasar) rolling pin

palpable *adj* (claro, evidente) palpable (frml), obvious; (al tacto) palpable, tangible

palpar [A1] *vt* (Med) to palpate; (tantear) to touch, feel; **se palpa el temor del pueblo** you can feel/sense people's fear; ***~ de armas*** (RPl) to frisk (*for weapons*)

palpitación *f* palpitation

palpitante *adj* **1** ‹*corazón*› beating (*before n*); ‹*vena/sien*› throbbing (*before n*); **con el corazón ~ de alegría** her heart pounding with joy **2** ‹*tema*› burning (*before n*); **de ~ actualidad** (period) highly topical

palpitar [A1] *vi*

A **1** «*corazón*» to beat; **le palpitaba el corazón con fuerza al verlo** her heart pounded when she saw him **2** «*vena/sien*» to throb

B (RPl fam) (parecer) (+ *me/te/le etc*): **me palpita que va a llover** I have a feeling it's going to rain

■ **palpitarse** *v pron* (AmS fam): **eso ya me lo palpitaba yo** I had a hunch *o* a feeling that would happen (colloq)

pálpito *m* (AmS fam) feeling (colloq); **me dio el** *or* **tuve un ~** I had a feeling *o* a hunch

palta *f*

A (Bol, CS, Per) (Bot, Coc) avocado (pear)

B (Per fam) (equivocación) gaffe, blunder

palteado -da *adj* (Per fam) down (colloq), low (colloq)

paltearse [A1] *v pron* (Per fam) to goof (colloq), to mess up (AmE colloq)

palto *m* (Bol, CS, Per) avocado tree

paltó *m* (Chi) (man's) jacket

palúdico *adj* **1** (Med) malarial; **fiebre palúdica** malaria, marsh fever **2** (de los pantanos) marsh (*before n*)

paludismo *m* malaria

palurdo[1] **-da** *adj* (fam) boorish, uncouth

palurdo[2] **-da** *m,f* (fam) boor

palustre *m* trowel

pamela *f* picture hat

pamento *m* (RPl fam) fuss

pampa *f* pampa, pampas (*pl*); **la ~ argentina** the Argentinian Pampas; ***quedar(se) en ~ y la vía*** (RPl) to be cleaned out (colloq)

(Compuestos)
- **pampa húmeda/seca** humid/arid pampas (*pl*)
- **pampa salitrera** *region of nitrate deposits in northern Chile*

pámpana *f* vine leaf

pámpano *m* (zarcillo) tendril; (racimo) *small bunch of grapes*

pampeano -na *adj* pampas (*before n*)

pampero[1] **-ra** *adj* pampas (*before n*)

pampero[2] *m* cold South wind

pampino -na *m,f* inhabitant of the **pampa salitrera**

pamplinas *fpl* (fam) **1** (zalamerías) sweet talk (colloq); **no me vengas con ~** don't try to sweet-talk me (colloq) **2** (tonterías) nonsense

pamplinero -ra *m,f* (fam) **1** (zalamero) sweet-talker (colloq) **2** (tonto): **es un ~** he's full of nonsense

pan *m*

A (Coc) bread; (pieza) loaf; (panecillo) roll; **un ~ de medio kilo** a loaf of bread (*weighing half a kilo*); **una rebanada de ~** a slice of bread; ***con su ~ se lo coma*** (colloq) it's his/her tough luck (colloq); ***contigo ~ y cebolla*** you're all I need, all I need is you; ***dame ~ y dime tonto*** I don't care what people say as long as I get what I want; ***el ~ nuestro de cada día*** (Relig) our daily bread; **eso se ha convertido en el ~ nuestro de cada día** that's become an everyday occurrence; ***ganarse el ~*** to earn one's daily bread; ***llamar al ~, ~ y al vino, vino*** to call a spade a spade; ***quitarle el ~ de la boca a algn*** to take the food out of sb's mouth; ***ser ~ comido*** (fam) to be a piece of cake (colloq); ***ser un ~ bendito*** *or* ***más bueno que el ~*** *or* (AmS) ***más bueno que un ~ de Dios*** to be very good; **ese niño es más bueno que el ~** that child is as good as gold; ***venderse como ~ caliente*** to sell *o* go like hotcakes; ***no sólo de ~ vive el hombre*** man cannot live by bread alone; ***~ con ~, comida de tontos*** variety is the spice of life

(Compuestos)
- **pan blanco/de centeno/integral** white/rye/whole wheat bread
- **pan de azúcar** sugarloaf
- **pan de higos** block of dried figs
- **pan de molde** tin *o* pan loaf (BrE), (*bread/loaf baked gen in a rectangular tin*)
- **pan de Pascua** (Chi) panettone
- **pan dulce** (con pasas) (RPl) panettone; (bollo) (AmC, Méx) bun, pastry
- **pan francés** (tipo) French bread; (pieza) baguette
- **pan rallado** breadcrumbs (*pl*)
- **pan tostado** toast; **un ~ ~** (Chi, Méx) a piece of toast

B (de jabón) cake, bar

pana[1] *f*

A (tela) corduroy; **panatalones de ~** corduroy trousers

B (Chi) (avería) breakdown; **quedarse en ~** to break down

C (Chi) (Coc) liver

pana[2] *mf* (Ven fam) buddy (AmE colloq), mate (BrE colloq)

panacea *f* panacea

panaché *m* *tb* **~ de verduras** stewed vegetables (*pl*)

panadería *f* (tienda) bakery, baker's (shop); (fábrica) bakery

panadero -ra *m,f* baker

panadizo *m* whitlow

panal *m* honeycomb

panamá *m* panama hat

Panamá *m* **1** (país) Panama; **el Canal de ~** the Panama Canal **2** (capital) *tb* **ciudad de ~** Panama (City)

panameño -ña *adj/m,f* Panamanian

Panamericana *f*: **la ~** the Pan-American Highway

panca *f* (Per) leaf (*which covers the corn cob*)

P

pancarta *f* banner, placard
panceta *f* 1 (Esp) (sin curar) belly pork 2 (RPl) (curada) streaky bacon
pancho¹ -cha *adj* (tranquilo) calm; ***quedarse tan ~*** (fam): **se lo dije y se quedó tan ~** he didn't bat an eyelash *o* (BrE) eyelid when I told him
pancho² *m* (RPl) hot dog
pancista¹ *adj* (fam) opportunist (*before n*), opportunistic
pancista² *mf* (fam) opportunist
pancita *f* (Méx) tripe
pancito *m* (AmL) (bread) roll
páncreas *m* (*pl* ~) pancreas
pancreático -ca *adj* pancreatic
panda¹ *mf* panda
panda² *f* (Esp fam) gang
pandear [A1] *vi*, **pandearse** [A1] *v pron* «*madera*» to warp; «*pared*» to bulge, sag
pandemonio, pandemónium *m* pandemonium; **la casa era un auténtico ~** the house was in uproar
pandereta *f*
A (Mús) tambourine
B (Chi) (Arquit) brick wall
pandero *m*
A (Mús) tambourine
B (Esp fam & hum) (culo) ass (AmE colloq), bum (BrE colloq)
C (Per) (Fin) *cooperative savings scheme*
pandilla *f* (fam) gang
pandillero -ra *m,f* (esp AmL) hoodlum
A (frml) (panadería) bakery
B (máguina) bread machine
pando -da *adj*
A ‹*pared*› bulging, sagging; ‹*madera*› warped
B (Col) (poco profundo) shallow
pandorga *f* (fam) (mujer gorda) fat woman
panecillo *m* (Esp) bread roll
panecito *m* (AmL) bread roll
panegírico¹ -ca *adj* eulogistic, panegyrical
panegírico² *m* panegyric, eulogy
panegirista *mf* panegyrist, eulogist
panel *m*
A 1 (de puerta, pared) panel 2 (tablero — de anuncios) noticeboard; (— en exposición) exhibition panel; (— en estación) departures board 3 (Chi) (de auto) dashboard
(Compuestos)
- **panel de instrumentos** instrument panel *o* console
- **panel solar** solar panel

B (de personas) panel
panela *f* (Col, Ven) *brown sugarloaf*
panelista *mf* panelist
panera *f* (para servir pan) bread basket; (para guardar pan) bread box (AmE), bread bin (BrE)
pánfilo¹ -la *adj* (fam) dimwitted (colloq)
pánfilo² -la *m,f* (fam) dimwit (colloq)
panfletario -ria *adj* ‹*estilo/escrito*› cheap, demagogic
panfletista *mf* pamphleteer
panfleto *m* pamphlet
panga *f* (AmC) (bote) canoe
pánico *m* panic; **fue presa del ~** she was panic-stricken; **¡que no cunda el ~!** don't panic!; **tenerle ~ a algo** to be terrified of sth; ***sembrar el ~*** to spread panic
paniego -ga *adj* wheat-growing (*before n*)
panificadora *f*
A (frml) (panadería) bakery
B (máquina) bread machine
panizo *m*
A (Agr) millet
B (Chi) (Min) deposit; ***se me/le/nos aguó el ~*** (Chi fam) my/his/our plans were spoiled *o* ruined
panocha *f*
A (de maíz, trigo) ear
B (Méx) (melaza) *candy made from molasses*
panoja *f* ear (*of corn or millet*)
panoplia *f* (armadura) panoply
panorama *m* 1 (vista, paisaje) view, panorama 2 (perspectiva) outlook; **se presenta un ~ esperanzador** the outlook is promising *o* hopeful 3 (escenario): **el ~ político** the political scene; **el ~ económico del país** the state of the country's economy
panorámica *f* (Cin, TV) pan; (perspectiva) outlook
panorámico -ca *adj* panoramic
panque *m* (Méx) sponge cake
panqueque *m* (AmL) pancake, crepe
panquequería *f* (AmL) crêperie, pancake restaurant
pantagruélico -ca *adj* Pantagruelian (liter)
pantaletas *fpl* (AmC, Ven) panties (*pl*), knickers (*pl*) (BrE)
pantalla *f*
A (TV, Cin) screen; (Inf) monitor; **~ de radar** radar screen; **llevar una novela a la ~** to do a screen adaptation of a novel
(Compuestos)
- **pantalla chica** (AmL) small screen
- **pantalla gigante** *or* **grande** big screen
- **pantalla táctil** touch screen

B 1 (de lámpara) shade 2 (de chimenea) fireguard 3 (cobertura) front; **hacer de ~ (para algo)** to serve as a front (for sth)
(Compuesto) **pantalla acústica** baffle
C (AmL) (abanico) fan
pantallear [A1] *vi* (Col, Ven fam) to show off
pantalones *mpl*, **pantalón** *m* pants (*pl*) (AmE), trousers (*pl*) (BrE); **unos ~** a pair of pants *o* trousers; ***llevar los ~*** to wear the pants *o* trousers; ***tener*** *or* ***llevar bien puestos los ~*** to be master in one's own home
(Compuestos)
- **pantalones bombachos** baggy pants *o* trousers (*pl*)
- **pantalones cortos** shorts (*pl*)
- **pantalones de peto** overalls (*pl*) (AmE), dungarees (*pl*) (BrE)
- **pantalones tejanos** *or* **vaqueros** *or* (Chi, Méx) **de mezclilla** jeans (*pl*)
- **pantalón fuseau** stretch ski-pants (*pl*)

pantano *m*
A (natural) marsh, swamp; (artificial) reservoir
B (dificultad) mess, predicament
pantanoso -sa *adj*
A ‹*terreno*› marshy, swampy
B ‹*asunto/negocio*› difficult, tricky (colloq)
panteísmo *m* pantheism
panteísta¹ *adj* pantheistic
panteísta² *mf* pantheist
panteón *m* 1 (monumento) pantheon, mausoleum; **~ de familia** family vault 2 (AmL) (cementerio) cemetery
panteonero *m* (AmL) gravedigger
pantera *f* panther
panti *m* (*pl* **-tis**), (Méx) **pantimedia** *f* ▸ **panty**
pantomima *f* pantomime
pantomimo -ma *m,f* mime artist
pantoque *m* bilge
pantorrilla *f* calf
pants *mpl* (Méx) tracksuit, sweat suit (AmE)
pantufla *f*, **pantuflo** *m* slipper
panty *m* (*pl* **-tys**) panty hose (*pl*) (AmE), tights (*pl*) (BrE)
panza *f* 1 (fam) (barriga) belly, paunch (colloq); **tener ~** to have a belly *o* paunch; **tirarse de ~** to do a belly flop (colloq) 2 (de cántaro) belly 3 (de rumiante) rumen
panzada *f* (fam)
A (en el agua) belly flop (colloq); **se dio una ~** he did a belly flop
B 1 (comilona): **darse una ~ de algo** to pig out on sth (colloq) 2 (hartazgo): **me di una ~ de trabajar** I worked really hard, I worked my butt off (AmE colloq)
panzón -zona *adj* (fam) potbellied (colloq)
panzudo -da *adj* (fam) potbellied (colloq)
pañal *m* diaper (AmE), nappy (BrE); ***estar en ~es*** «*ciencia/industria*» to be in its infancy; «*persona*» to be a novice *o* a beginner
pañería *f* (tienda) dry goods store (AmE), draper's shop (BrE); (género) fabrics (*pl*), material
pañetar [A1] *vt* (Col) to skim … with plaster
pañito *m* doily

paño *m*
A 1 (Tex) woollen cloth; **abrigo de ~** wool coat; ***conocer(se) el ~*** to know what's what (colloq); ***en ~s menores*** (fam & hum) in my/his undies (colloq & hum); ***ser el ~ de lágrimas de algn*** to be a shoulder for sb to cry on 2 (para limpiar) cloth; ***jugar a dos ~s*** to play a double game; ***~s calientes*** half measures 3 (de adorno) antimacassar
Compuestos
- **paño de cocina** (para limpiar) dishcloth; (para secar) teatowel
- **paño higiénico** sanitary napkin (AmE), sanitary towel (BrE)
- **paño mortuorio** pall

B (de pared) stretch, length
C **paños** *mpl* (Art) drapes (*pl*), drapery
pañolenci *m* (CS) baize, felt
pañoleta *f* (de mujer) shawl; (de torero) neckerchief
pañolón *m* shawl, wrap
pañosa *f* cape
pañuelo *m* (para la nariz) handkerchief; (para la cabeza) headscarf, scarf; (para el cuello) scarf, neckerchief
papa[1] *m* pope; **el P~** the Pope
papa[2] *f*
A (esp AmL) (Bot) potato; ***ni ~*** (fam) not a thing; **no sé ni ~ de coches** I haven't a clue about cars (colloq); ***ser una ~*** (RPl fam) ‹‹*persona*›› to be a dead loss (colloq); ‹‹*tarea*›› to be a piece of cake (colloq), to be a cinch (colloq)
Compuestos
- **papa caliente** *f* hot potato
- **papa dulce** *f* (AmL) sweet potato
- **papas fritas** *fpl* (esp AmL) 1 (de paquete) potato chips (*pl*) (AmE), potato crisps (*pl*) (BrE) 2 (de cocina) French fries (*pl*) (AmE), chips (*pl*) (BrE)

B (AmL fam) (comida) food; ***ganarse la ~*** (Col) to earn a living *o* (colloq) a crust
C (Chi, Méx fam) (mentira) fib (colloq)
D (CS fam) (agujero) hole
E (Chi) (bulbo) bulb
papá *m* (*pl* **-pás**) (fam) daddy (colloq), pop (AmE colloq); **mis ~s** (AmL) my parents, my mom and dad (AmE), my mum and dad (BrE colloq)
Compuesto **Papá Noel** Santa Claus, Father Christmas
papada *f* (de persona) double chin, jowl
papado *m* papacy
papagayo *m*
A (ave) parrot; ***aprender/recitar algo como un ~*** to learn/recite sth parrot-fashion; ***hablar como un ~*** to be a chatterbox *o* windbag (colloq)
B (Per, RPl) (para enfermos) bedpan
C (Ven) (cometa) kite
papal *adj* papal
papalina *f* (cofia) cap
papalote *m* (AmC, Méx) (juguete) kite; (ala delta) hang glider
papamoscas *mf* (*pl* ~) 1 (fam) (papanatas) halfwit (colloq) 2 **papamoscas** *m* (Zool) flycatcher
papanatas *mf* (*pl* ~) (fam) halfwit (colloq)
Papanicolau *m* (AmL) smear test
paparazzi /papa'rasi, papa'raθi/ *mpl* paparazzi (*pl*)
paparrucha, paparruchada *f* (fam) nonsense; **todas esas ~s sobre Papá Noel** all that baloney about Santa Claus (AmE colloq), all that rubbish about Father Christmas (BrE colloq); **¡~s!** bullshit! (sl), rubbish! (BrE colloq)
papaya *f* papaya, pawpaw; ***de papayita*** (Col fam): **me queda de papayita** it's really handy for me (colloq); ***ser ~*** (Chi fam) to be a cinch *o* a piece of cake (colloq)
papayo *m* papaya tree, pawpaw tree
papear [A1] *vt/vi* (fam) to eat
papel *m*
A (material) paper; **un ~** a piece of paper; **toalla/pañuelo de ~** paper towel/tissue; ***sobre el ~*** on paper
Compuestos
- **papel biblia** India paper, Bible paper
- **papel carbón** carbon paper
- **papel cebolla** onionskin (paper)
- **papel celofán** cellophane®
- **papel confort** (Chi) toilet paper
- **papel continuo** continuous listing paper
- **papel cuadriculado/rayado** squared/lined paper
- **papel de aluminio** tinfoil, aluminum* foil
- **papel de arroz** rice paper
- **papel de calcar** (translúcido) tracing paper; (entintado) carbon paper
- **papel de carta** writing paper
- **papel de cera** *or* (RPl) **de manteca** *or* (Chi) **de mantequilla** waxed *o* wax paper, greaseproof paper (BrE)
- **papel de diario** *or* **de periódico** (Impr) newsprint; **lo envolvió en ~ de ~** she wrapped it in newspaper
- **papel de embalar/de envolver** wrapping paper
- **papel de estraza** gray* paper
- **papel de lija** sandpaper
- **papel de plata** silver paper
- **papel de regalo** wrapping paper
- **papel de seda** tissue paper
- **papel higiénico/de water** toilet paper
- **papel mojado**: **el contrato es ~ ~** the contract isn't worth the paper it's written on
- **papel** *or* **papelillo de fumar** cigarette paper
- **papel picado** (RPl) confetti
- **papel pintado** *o* (CS) **mural** wallpaper
- **papel secante** blotting paper
- **papel vegetal** film

B (documento) document, paper; **no tenía los ~es en regla** her papers were not in order
C (Fin) 1 (valores) commercial paper 2 (dinero) *tb* **~ moneda** paper money
Compuestos
- **papel del Estado** government bonds (*pl*), government paper
- **papel de pagos al Estado** certificate of payment (*to government agency*)

D 1 (Cin, Teatr) role, part; **hace el ~ de monja** she plays the part of the nun; **está muy bien en el ~ de Romeo** he's very good as Romeo 2 (actuación): **hizo un lamentable/triste ~ en el congreso** his performance at the conference was abysmal/terrible; **si no la invitas vas a hacer muy mal ~** it's going to look very bad if you don't invite her; **¡hizo un ~ tan ridículo!** he made such a fool of himself! 3 (función) role; **jugó un ~ decisivo en la campaña** it played a decisive role *o* part in the campaign
papeleo *m* (fam) red tape, paperwork
papelera *f* 1 (de oficina) wastepaper basket; (en la calle) litter basket (AmE), litter bin (BrE) 2 (fábrica) paper mill
papelería *f* (tienda) stationery store (AmE), stationer's (BrE); **artículos de ~** stationery
papelero[1] **-ra** *adj* paper (*before n*)
papelero[2] **-ra** *m,f*
A (fabricante) paper manufacturer; (vendedor) stationer
B **papelero** *m* (CS) ▸**papelera 1**
papeleta *f* 1 (de votación) ballot (paper); **~ en blanco** blank ballot (paper) 2 (de rifa) raffle ticket; **me tocó a mí la ~ de hacer el turno de la noche** I got stuck with doing the night shift (colloq) 3 (de calificación) grade slip 4 (de empeño) pawn ticket
papelillo *m* cigarette paper
papelina *f* sachet
papelitos *mpl* (Ur) confetti
papelón *m*
A (fam) (cosa vergonzosa): **hacer un ~** to make a fool of oneself; **¡qué ~!** how embarrassing!
B (Ven) (Coc) sugarloaf (*made from unrefined sugar*)
papeo *m* (fam) food, grub (colloq)
paperas *fpl* mumps
papero -ra *adj* (AmL) ‹*cultivo*› potato (*before n*)
papi *m* (fam) ▸**papá**
papiamento *m* creole (*spoken in Curaçao*)
papila *f* papilla
papilla *f* (para bebés) baby food, formula (AmE); (para enfermos) puree, pap; ***hacer ~*** (fam) ‹*moto/coche*› to smash up; ‹*person*› to beat … to a pulp; **estamos hechos ~** we're absolutely shattered (colloq)
papiloma *m* papilloma
papiro *m* papyrus

papirotazo *m* (fam) flick

papista¹ *adj* papist; ***ser más ~ que el Papa*** to be very extreme in one's views

papista² *mf* papist

papo *m* (fam) (de animal) dewlap; (de ave) crop; (de persona) jowl

paporreta (Per fam): **de ~** parrot-fashion (colloq)

paprika *f* paprika

paquete¹ -ta *adj* (RPl fam) smart, chic; **¡qué paqueta te has puesto!** you're looking very smart *o* chic

paquete² *m*

A **1** (bulto envuelto) package, parcel; **hacer un ~** to wrap up a parcel; ***ir de ~*** (fam) to ride on the back (*of a motorcycle*) **2** (de galletas, cigarrillos) pack (AmE), packet (BrE); **un ~ de papas fritas** (AmL) a bag of chips (AmE), a packet of crisps (BrE); ***meterle un ~ a algn*** (Esp fam) to throw the book at sb

Compuestos

- **paquete bomba** parcel bomb
- **paquete de acciones** stockholding
- **paquete postal** parcel (*sent by mail*); **envíalo como ~ ~** send it (by) parcel post

B (conjunto) package; **un ~ de software/de aplicación** (Inf) a software/an application package

C (fam) (genitales masculinos) bulge (colloq & euph)

D (Méx fam) (problema) headache (colloq); ***cargar con el ~*** (fam) to take responsibility

paquetería *f* parcels office; **servicio de ~** parcels service

paquidermo *m* pachyderm

Paquistán *m* Pakistan

paquistaní *adj/mf* Pakistani

par¹ *adj* ‹*número*› even; **jugarse algo a ~es o nones** *to decide sth by guessing whether the number of objects held is odd or even*

par² *m*

A **1** (de guantes, zapatos) pair; **un ~ de preguntas/de veces** a couple of questions/of times; ***a ~es*** two at a time **2** (comparación) equal; **sin ~** (liter) incomparable, matchless (liter); **un atleta sin ~** an athlete without equal

Compuestos

- **par de fuerzas** couple
- **par de torsión** torque

B (Arquit) rafter; ***(abierto) de ~ en ~*** wide open

C **al par** *ver* **par³**

D (en golf) par; **sobre/bajo ~** over/under par

E (Hist) (título) peer

par³ *f* par; **a la ~** (Fin) at par (value); **estar a la ~/por encima de la ~** to be at/above par; **sabroso a la ~ que sano** both tasty and healthy; **es lengua oficial a la ~ del castellano** it is an official language on a par with *o* along with Spanish; **baila a la ~ que canta** he dances and sings at the same time

para *prep*

Sentido I

A (expresando destino, finalidad, intención) for; **una carta para él** a letter for him; **¿~ qué revista escribes?** what magazine do you write for?; **lee ~ ti** read to yourself; **fue muy amable ~ con todos** he was very friendly to everyone; **¿~ qué sirve esto?** what's this (used) for?; **no sirve ~ este trabajo** he's no good at this kind of work; **¿~ qué lo quieres?** what do you want it for?; **¿~ qué se lo dijiste?** what did you tell him for?; **champú ~ bebés** baby shampoo; **jarabe ~ la tos** cough mixture; ***que ~ qué decirte/hablar*** (fam): **tenían un hambre que ~ qué decirte/hablar** they were starving

B **~ + INF** to + INF; **~ serte sincero** to tell you the truth; **esta agua no es ~ beber** this isn't drinking water; **está listo ~ pintar** it's ready to be painted *o* for painting; **~ aprobar** (in order) to pass; **entró en puntillas para no despertarla** he went in on tiptoe so as not to wake her

C **~ QUE + SUBJ**: **lo dice ~ que yo me preocupe** he (only) says it to worry me; **pídeselo — ¿~ que me diga que no?** ask him for it — so he can say no?; **cierra ~ que no nos oigan** close the door so (that) they don't hear us

D (expresando consecuencia) to; **~ su desgracia** unfortunately for him; **~ mi sorpresa** (much) to my surprise

Sentido II

A (expresando suficiencia) for; **no hay ~ todos** there isn't enough for everybody; **no es ~ tanto** it's not that bad; **~ + INF**: **soy lo bastante viejo (como) ~ recordarlo** I'm old enough to remember it; **bastante tengo yo (como) ~ estar ocupándome de ti** I've enough problems of my own without having to deal with yours as well; **¡es (como) ~ matarlo!** (fam) I'll kill him! (colloq); **~ QUE + SUBJ**: **basta con que él aparezca ~ que ella se ponga nerviosa** he only has to appear for her to get flustered

B (en comparaciones, contrastes): **hace demasiado frío ~ salir** it's too cold to go out; **son altos ~ su edad** they're tall for their age; **~ lo que come, no está gordo** considering how much he eats, he's not fat; **¡~ el caso que me hacen ...!** for all the notice they take of me ...; **~ + INF**: **~ haber sido improvisado fue un discurso excelente** for an off-the-cuff speech it was excellent; **¿quién es él ~ hablarte así?** who does he think he is, speaking to you like that ?; **~ QUE + SUBJ**: **es mucho ~ que lo haga sola** it's too much for you to do it on your own; **¡tanto esforzarme por ellos ~ que no te lo agradezcan!** after all that effort I made for them they didn't even say thankyou!

C **estar ~ algo/+ INF** (indicando estado): **no estoy ~ bromas** I'm in no mood for joking; **está ~ tirarla a la basura** it's only fit for throwing out; **no está (como) ~ salir sin abrigo** it's not warm enough to go out without a coat

D (expresando puntos de vista): **~ mí que no viene** if you ask me, he won't come; **~ su padre, es un genio** in his father's opinion *o* as far as his father's concerned, he is a genius; **lo es todo ~ él** she's everything to him; **¿qué es lo más importante ~ ti?** what's the most important thing for you?

Sentido III **1** (indicando dirección): **salieron ~ el aeropuerto** they left for the airport; **empuja ~ arriba** push up *o* upward(s); **¿vas ~ el centro?** are you going to *o* toward(s) the center?; **tráelo ~ acá** bring it over here; **córrete ~ atrás** move back **2** (en sentido figurado): **ya vamos ~ viejos** we're getting old *o* getting on; **va ~ los 50 años** she's going *o* (BrE) getting on for fifty

Sentido IV (en relaciones de tiempo)

A **1** (señalando una fecha, un plazo): **estará listo ~ el día 15** it'll be ready by *o* for the 15th; **deberes ~ el lunes** homework for Monday; **faltan cinco minutos ~ que termine** there are five minutes to go before the end; **me lo prometió ~ después de Pascua** he promised me it for after Easter; **¿cuánto te falta ~ terminar?** how much have you got left to do?; **estará listo ~ finales de agosto** it'll be ready sometime around the end of August; **~ entonces estaré en Madrid** I'll be in Madrid (by) then; **¿~ cuándo espera?** when is the baby due?; **tengo hora ~ mañana** I have an appointment (for) tomorrow **2** (AmL exc RPl) (al decir la hora) to; **son cinco ~ las diez** it's five to ten

B **1** (expresando duración): **~ siempre** forever; **tengo ~ rato** (fam) I'm going to be a while (yet); **esto va ~ largo** (fam) this is going to take some time **2** (con idea de finalidad) for; **¿qué le regalo ~ el cumpleaños?** what can I give him for his birthday?

C (en secuencias de acciones): **se fue ~ nunca volver** (liter) she went away never to return; **salió sólo ~ volver a entrar** he went out only to come in again

parabién *m* (frml) *tb* **parabienes** congratulations (*pl*); **le dio su ~** she offered him her congratulations

parábola *f* **1** (Relig) parable **2** (Mat) parabola

parabólica *f* satellite dish

parabólico -ca *adj* parabolic

parabrisas *m* (*pl* ~) windshield (AmE), windscreen (BrE)

paracaídas *m* (*pl* ~) (Aviac) parachute; **un salto en ~** a parachute jump; **les lanzaron alimentos en ~** they dropped food to them by parachute; **tirarse** *or* **lanzarse en ~** to parachute

paracaidismo *m* parachuting

paracaidista¹ *adj* parachute (*before n*)

paracaidista² *mf* **1** (Mil) paratrooper; (Dep) parachutist **2** (AmL fam) (en fiesta) gatecrasher; **llegar de ~** to come/go uninvited (*to a party*)

parachoques *m* (*pl* ~) (Auto) bumper, fender (AmE); (Ferr) buffer

parada *f*
A (Transp) **1** (acción) stop; **hicimos una ~ de media hora** we made a half-hour stop **2** (lugar) *tb* **~ de autobús** (*or* **de ómnibus** *etc*) bus stop; **me bajo en la próxima ~** I'm getting off at the next stop
(Compuestos)
• **parada de taxi** taxi stand, taxi rank (BrE)
• **parada discrecional** request stop
B (Dep) (en fútbol) save, stop
C (desfile) parade; ***ir a todas las ~s*** (Chi fam) to be game for anything (colloq)
D (Per) (mercado) street market
E (RPl fam) (presunción): **son gente de mucha ~** they are very hoity-toity (colloq)

paradero *m* **1** (frml) (de persona) whereabouts (*pl*); **se desconoce su ~** her whereabouts are not known (frml) **2** (AmL exc RPl) (de autobús) bus stop; (de tranvía) stop **3** (Chi, Cu, Per) (de tren) halt

paradigma *m* paradigm (frml)

paradigmático -ca *adj* paradigmatic

paradisíaco -ca, paradisiaco -ca *adj* heavenly

parado[1] -da *adj*
A **1** (detenido): **no te quedes ahí ~, ven a ayudarme** don't just stand there, come and help me; **un coche ~ en medio de la calle** a car sitting *o* stopped in the middle of the street; **la producción está parada** production has stopped *o* is at a standstill **2** (esp Esp) (desconcertado): **se quedó ~, sin saber qué decir** he was taken aback and didn't know what to say
B (Esp) (desempleado) unemployed
C **1** (AmL) (de pie) **estar ~** to stand, be standing; **tuve que viajar ~** I had to stand for the whole journey **2** (AmL) (erguido): **tengo el pelo todo ~** my hair's standing on end; **escuchaba con las orejas paradas** she was all ears **3** (Chi) ‹*cuesta/subida*› steep
D **bien/mal parado**: **salió bastante bien parada del accidente** she escaped from the accident pretty much unscathed; **salió muy mal ~ del accidente** he was in a bad way after the accident; **salió mal ~ de su última inversión** he lost a lot of money on his last investment; **ha dejado muy mal ~s a sus colegas** he has left his colleagues in a very difficult situation; **estar bien ~ con algn** (AmL) to be (well) in with sb (colloq)
E **1** (CS fam) (engreído) stuck up **2** (Esp fam) (soso): **no seas parada** don't be such a drip (colloq)

parado[2] -da *m,f* (Esp) unemployed person; **los ~s** the unemployed, the people out of work

paradoja *f* paradox

paradójico -ca *adj* paradoxical

parador *m*
A **1** (mesón) roadside bar/hotel **2** (en Esp) parador, state-owned hotel
B (Méx) (Dep) *tb* **~ en corto** shortstop

> **parador (nacional de turismo)**
> A national chain of hotels in Spain. *Paradores* were designed to give buildings such as former palaces, castles and monasteries a new lease of life and to bring tourism to economically disadvantaged areas. They are often luxurious but relatively inexpensive and emphasize local character and cooking

paraestatal *adj* public-sector (*before n*), public (*before n*)

parafernalia *f* (frml) paraphernalia

parafina *f* **1** (sólida) paraffin (wax) **2** (AmL) (combustible) kerosene
(Compuesto) **parafina líquida** mineral oil (AmE), liquid paraffin (BrE)

parafrasear [A1] *vt* to paraphrase

paráfrasis *f* (*pl* ~) paraphrase

paragolpes *m* (*pl* ~) (RPl) ▸ **parachoques**

paraguas *m* (*pl* ~) umbrella

Paraguay *m*: *tb* **el ~** Paraguay

paraguayo -ya *adj/m,f* Paraguayan

paragüero *m*, **paragüera** *f* umbrella stand

paraíso *m* **1** (Relig) **el ~** paradise, heaven **2** (Teatr) family circle (AmE), gods (*pl*) (BrE)
(Compuestos)
• **paraíso fiscal** tax haven
• **paraíso terrenal** Garden of Eden

paraje *m* spot, place

paralé *m* (Chi, Per fam): **darle** *or* **hacerle un ~ a algn** to put sb in their place

paralela *f*
A (línea) parallel (line)
B **paralelas** *fpl* (Dep) parallel bars (*pl*)
(Compuesto) **paralelas asimétricas** asymmetric bars (*pl*)

paralelamente *adv* ‹*correr/extenderse*› parallel; **~ A algo** ‹*crecer/subir*› in line WITH sth

paralelismo *m* parallelism, parallel

paralelo[1] -la *adj*
A **1** ‹*líneas/planos*› parallel; **~ A algo** parallel TO sth **2** (*como adv*) ‹*marchar/crecer*› parallel
B (Elec) **en ~** in parallel

paralelo[2] *m*
A (Astron, Geog) parallel
B (comparación) parallel; **sin ~** unparalleled

paralelogramo *m* parallelogram

paralímpico -ca *m,f* disabled athlete (*who takes part in Paralympics*)

parálisis *f* (Med) paralysis; (falta de actividad) paralysis
(Compuestos)
• **parálisis cerebral** cerebral palsy
• **parálisis infantil** poliomyelitis, infantile paralysis
• **parálisis progresiva** creeping paralysis

paralítico[1] -ca *adj* paralytic (*before n*); **es/se quedó ~** he is/was paralyzed

paralítico[2] -ca *m,f* paralytic

paralización *f* **1** (Med) paralyzation **2** (en una actividad): **solicitaron la ~ de las obras** they applied for the work to be stopped; **el paro provocó la ~ de la ciudad** the strike brought the city to a standstill

paralizador -dora, **paralizante** *adj* paralyzing (*before n*)

paralizar [A4] *vt* **1** (Med) to paralyze; **se quedó paralizada de un lado** she was paralyzed down one side; **el miedo me paralizó** I was paralyzed with fear **2** ‹*circulación/producción*› to bring … to a halt *o* standstill

paralogismo *m* fallacious argument, paralogism (frml)

paramento *m*
A **1** (Arquit) face **2** (colgadura) hanging
B **paramentos** *mpl* (del altar) paraments (*pl*)
(Compuesto) **paramentos sacerdotales** *mpl* ecclesiastical vestments *o* robes (*pl*)

parámetro *m* parameter

paramilitar *adj* paramilitary

paramnesia *f* paramnesia

páramo *m* high plateau, bleak upland *o* moor

paramuno[1] -na *adj* (Col) upland (*before n*)

paramuno[2] -na *m,f* (Col) *person from the high plateau*

parangón *m* comparison; **sin ~** incomparable, matchless (liter)

parangonar [A1] *vt* (frml) to compare; **~ algo/a algn CON algo/algn** to compare sth/sb WITH sth/sb

paraninfo *m* main hall *o* auditorium

paranoia *f* paranoia

paranoico -ca *adj/m,f* paranoid

paranormal *adj* paranormal

paraolimpiada ▸ **paralimpiada**

parapente *f* **1** (deporte) paragliding; **hacer** *or* **practicar ~** to go paragliding, paraglide **2** (paracaídas) paraglider

parapetarse [A1] *v pron* to take cover; **~ TRAS algo** ‹*tras muro/barricada*› to take cover BEHIND sth; **se parapetó tras la excusa de siempre** he hid behind the same old excuse

parapeto *m* (Arquit) parapet; (barricada) barricade

paraplejía, paraplejia *f* paraplegia

parapléjico -ca *adj/m,f* paraplegic

parapsicología *f* parapsychology

parapsicológico -ca *adj* parapsychological

parar [A1] *vi*
A (detenerse) to stop; **paró en seco** she stopped dead; **el autobús no nos paró** the bus didn't stop for us; ***¡dónde vas a ~!*** (Esp fam) there's no comparison!; ***ir/venir a ~*** to end up; **fue a ~ a la cárcel** he ended up in prison; **¿a dónde habrá ido a ~ aquella foto?** what can have happened to that photo?; **¡a dónde iremos a ~!** I don't know what the world's coming to
B (cesar) to stop; **para un momento** hang on a minute; **el ruido no paró en toda la noche** the noise didn't let up *o* stop all night; **ha estado lloviendo sin ~** it hasn't stopped raining; **no para quieto ni un momento** he can't keep still for a minute; **no he parado en todo el día** I've been on the go all day (colloq); **no ~ás hasta romperlo** you won't be happy until you've broken it; **no para en casa** she's never at home; **~ DE + INF** to stop -ING; **aún no ha parado de llover** it still hasn't stopped raining; **no para de comer** she does nothing but eat; **no para de criticar a los demás** he's always criticizing others; ***y para de contar*** (fam) and that's it
C (hospedarse) to stay; (en bar, club) (fam) to hang out (colloq)
D (AmL) «*obreros/empleados*» to go on strike
■ **parar** *vt*
A [1] ‹*coche/tráfico/persona*› to stop; ‹*motor/máquina*› to stop, switch off; **cuando se pone a hablar no hay quien lo pare** once he starts talking, there's no stopping him [2] ‹*hemorragia*› to stanch (AmE), to staunch (BrE) [3] ‹*balón/tiro*› to save, stop; ‹*golpe*› to block, ward off; ***~la(s)*** (Chi, Per fam) to catch on (colloq); **¿no la(s) paras?** don't you get it? (colloq)
B (AmL) [1] (poner de pie) to stand; **páralo en la silla** stand him on the chair [2] (poner vertical) ‹*vaso/libro*› to stand … up; **el perro paró las orejas** the dog pricked up its ears
■ **pararse** *v pron*
A (detenerse) [1] «*persona*» to stop; **¿te has parado alguna vez a pensar por qué?** have you ever stopped to think why? [2] «*reloj/máquina*» to stop; «*coche/motor*» to stall; **se me paró el reloj** my watch stopped
B [1] (AmL) (ponerse de pie) to stand up; **párate derecho** stand up straight; **se paró en una silla** she stood on a chair; **¿te puedes ~ de cabeza/de manos?** can you do headstands/handstands?; **se paró de un salto** she jumped to her feet [2] (AmL) «*pelo*» (hacia arriba) to stick up; (en los lados) to stick out; **se le paró el pelo del susto** he was so scared it made his hair stand on end [3] (Méx, Ven) (levantarse de la cama) to get up
C (Chi) (Rels Labs) «*obreros/empleados*» to (go on) strike

pararrayos *m* (*pl* ~), **pararrayo** *m* (en edificio) lightning rod (AmE), lightning conductor (BrE); (en circuito) lightning arrester

parasitar [A1] *vt* to parasitize
■ **parasitar** *vi*: **~ EN algo** to live as a parasite in sth

parasitario -ria *adj* parasitic

parasitismo *m* parasitism

parásito¹ -ta *adj* parasitic

parásito² *m*
A parasite
B **parásitos** *mpl* (interferencia) atmospherics (*pl*)

parasitología *f* parasitology

parasol *m* (sombrilla) parasol, sunshade

paratifoidea *f* paratyphoid

paratopes *m* (*pl* ~) (Col) buffer

parcela *f* plot (of land), lot (AmE)

parcelación *f* division (*of land into plots*)

parcelar [A1] *vt* to divide … into plots *o* (AmE) lots, to parcel up

parchado *m* (AmL) repair, patching

parchar [A1] *vt* (AmL) (arreglar) to repair; (con parche) to patch (up)

parche *m* [1] (remiendo) patch; **eso es poner ~s al problema** that's just papering over the cracks; ***¡ojo*** *or* ***oído al ~!*** (fam) watch out! (colloq) [2] (para un ojo) (eye) patch; (en herida) patch; ***colocarse el ~ antes de la herida*** (Chi fam) to take precautions [3] (en la piel) mark, blotch [4] (del tambor) drumhead
(Compuesto) **parche curita** (Chi) Band-Aid® (AmE), sticking plaster (BrE)

parchís *m* (Esp, Méx) Parcheesi® (AmE), ludo (BrE)

parcial¹ *adj*
A ‹*solución/victoria*› partial; **pago ~** part payment
B (no equitativo) biased, partial

parcial² *m* [1] (examen) assessment examination (*taken during the year and counting towards the final grade*) [2] (Dep) (tanteo) score (*during a particular period*)

parcialidad *f* [1] (cualidad) partiality, bias [2] (seguidores) supporters (*pl*)

parco -ca *adj* [1] (lacónico) laconic; **— no — fue su parca respuesta** no, he replied laconically [2] (sobrio, moderado) frugal; **ser ~ EN algo** ‹*en palabras*› to be sparing WITH sth; **fue ~ en sus alabanzas** he was sparing with his praise (liter); **son ~s en el comer** they are moderate in their eating habits [3] (escaso) ‹*sueldo*› meager*; ‹*recursos*› scant, meager*

pardiez *interj* (arc) gadzooks! (arch *or* hum)

pardillo -lla *m,f*
A (Zool) linnet
B (Esp fam) (novato) novice, beginner

pardo¹ -da *adj* ‹*color*› dun, brownish-gray*

pardo² -da *m,f* (RPl pey) *offensive term for a person of mixed race*

pardusco -ca, **parduzco -ca** *adj* brownish-gray*

pareado¹ -da *adj* [1] ‹*versos*› rhyming (*before n*) [2] ‹*casa*› semidetached

pareado² *m* rhyming couplet

parear [A1] *vt* (formar pares de) to put … into pairs

parecer¹ [E3] *vi*
A (aparentar ser): **parece mayor de lo que es** she looks older than she is; **parece fácil** it looks easy; **parecen simpáticos** they seem nice; **pareces tonto** are you stupid or something?; **no pareces tú en esta foto** this picture doesn't look like you (at all); **parecía de cuero** it looked like leather; **~ + INF** to seem to + INF; **todo parece indicar que …** everything appears *o* seems *o* (frml) would seem to indicate that …; **parece ser muy inteligente** she seems to be very clever
B (expresando opinión) (+ *me/te/le etc*): **su comentario me pareció muy acertado** I thought his remark (was) very apt; **todo le parece mal** he's never happy with anything; **¿qué te parecieron?** what did you think of them?; **deberíamos invitarlos — ¿te parece?** we ought to invite them — do you think so?; **vamos a la playa ¿te parece?** what do you think, shall we go to the beach?; **podemos reunirnos si te parece bien** we could meet up if that's alright with you; **me parece que sí** I think so; **¿a ti qué te parece?** what do you think?; **me parece importante mencionarlo** I think it's important to mention it; **¿te parece bonito contestarme así?** is that any way to speak to me?; **me/nos parece que tiene razón** I/we think she's right; **me pareció que no era necesario** I didn't think it necessary; **¿te parece que éstas son horas de llegar?** what time do you call this?; **hazlo como mejor te parezca** do it however *o* as you think best; (+ *subj*) **me parece mal que vaya sola** I don't think it's right that she should go on her own; **me parece raro que …** it seems odd *o* I find it odd that …; **me parece importante que ella esté presente** I think it's important that she (should) be here
C (haber indicios, señales) (*en 3ª pers*) **según parece** *or* **al ~ todo va bien** it looks as though everything's going well, everything seems to be going well; **así parece** *or* **parece que sí** it looks like it *o* it would seem so; **aunque no lo parezca, está limpio** it might not look like it, but it's clean; **¿le gusta? — parece que no** does he like it? — apparently not; **parece que no, pero cansa** you wouldn't think so, but it's tiring; **parece que va a llover** it looks like (it's going to) rain; **parece que fue ayer** it seems like only yesterday; **parece (ser) que tiene razón** she appears to be right, it seems she's right; **~ía que …** it would seem that …; (+ *subj*): **parece increíble que hayan sobrevivido** it seems incredible that they survived; **parece mentira que tenga 20 años** it's hard to believe *o* I can't believe that he's 20; **parece que para él no pasaran los años** he never seems to get any older; **parece que fuera mas joven** you'd think she was much younger; **no parece que le haya gustado** It doesn't look as if he liked it
■ **parecerse** *v pron* [1] (asemejarse) **~se A algn/algo** (en lo físico) to look *o* to be like sb/sth; (en el carácter) to be like

P

sb/sth; **no son ricos ni nada que se le parezca** they're not wealthy, not by any means 2 (*recípr*) to be alike; **no se parecen en nada** they're not/they don't look in the least bit alike; **se parecen mucho** they are very similar

parecer² *m* 1 (opinión) opinion; **a mi ∼** in my opinion; **son del mismo ∼** they're of the same opinion; **soy del ∼ de que ...** I believe *o* (frml) I am of the opinion that ...; **ello me hizo cambiar de ∼** it made me change my mind 2 **de buen parecer** (ant) handsome

parecido¹ -da *adj*: **no son tan ∼s** (personas) they're not so alike; (cosas) they're not that similar; **son muy parecidas de cara** they have very similar features; **tengo una muy parecida** I have one very similar; **una especie de capa o algo ∼** a cape or something like that; **∼ A algo** similar TO sth; **eres muy ∼ a tu padre** you're a lot like your father; ▸**bien parecido, mal parecido**

parecido² *m* resemblance; **tiene cierto ∼ con su hermano** he bears some *o* a certain resemblance to his brother; **no le encuentro ningún ∼ con su familia** I can't see any family resemblance; **tiene un gran ∼ con Jaime** there is a close resemblance between him and Jaime; **son de un ∼ asombroso** there's a startling resemblance *o* likeness between them

pared *f*

A 1 (Arquit, Const) wall; **viven ∼ por medio** they live next door; ***entre cuatro ∼es*** cooped up; ***es como darse contra las ∼es*** (fam) it's like banging your head against a brick wall; ***es como hablarle a la ∼*** (fam) it's like talking to a brick wall; ***hasta la ∼ de enfrente*** (Chi, Méx fam) loads (*pl*) (colloq); ***las ∼es oyen*** walls have ears; ***subirse*** *or* ***trepar por las ∼es*** (fam) (de rabia, irritación) to go through the roof (colloq); (de aburrimiento) to be climbing the walls (with boredom) (colloq) 2 (de recipiente) side 3 (Anat) wall 4 (de montaña) face

(Compuesto) **pared maestra/medianera** main/party wall

B (en fútbol) one-two; **hacer la ∼** to play a one-two, to play a wall pass (AmE)

paredón *m* 1 (de roca) rock face, wall of rock 2 (pared gruesa) thick wall 3 (de fusilamiento) wall; **¡al ∼ con ellos!** put them up against the wall and shoot them!; **mandar a algn al ∼** to put sb before a firing squad

pareja *f*

A 1 (equipo, conjunto) pair; **salieron por ∼s** they came out in pairs *o* two at a time; **formar ∼s** to get into pairs 2 (en una relación) couple; **vivir en ∼** to live together 3 (de convivencia, baile, juego) partner

(Compuesto) **pareja de hecho** (heterosexual) co-habiting couple; (homosexual co-habiting same-sex couple

B 1 (de guante, zapato): **la ∼** the other one (*of a pair*); **no encuentro la ∼ de este guante** I can't find the other glove (that goes with this one); **un calcentín sin ∼** an odd sock 2 (en naipes) pair

parejo¹ -ja *adj* 1 (esp AmL) (sin desniveles) even; **los dos ciclistas van muy ∼s** the two cyclists are neck and neck; **el nivel en la clase es muy ∼** the class are all at the same level; **los dos equipos son muy ∼s** the two teams are evenly matched 2 (afín, semejante) similar 3 (CS, Méx) (equitativo) ‹*trato*› equal; ‹*ley*› fair, impartial; 4 (AmL) (como adv) ‹*pintar/cortar*› evenly

parejo² -ja *m,f*

A (Col) (de baile) partner

B (Méx fam) **al ∼** (a la par): **trabajan al ∼** they all do the same amount of work; **al ∼ de los mejores del mundo** on a par with the world's best

parentela *f* (fam) clan (colloq), tribe (colloq)

parentesco *m* relationship; **¿qué relación de ∼ tenía contigo?** what was her relationship to you?, what relation was her to you?; **lazos de ∼** ties of kinship (frml); **no tengo ∼ directo con él** I am not directly related to him; **un cierto ∼ de estilo** a certain similarity of style

paréntesis *m* (*pl* ∼) 1 (signo) parenthesis, bracket (BrE); **cerrar el ∼** close parentheses *o* brackets; ***entre ∼*** (literal) in parentheses, in brackets; (a propósito) by the way 2 (digresión) digression, parenthesis 3 (intervalo) break, interval

parezca, parezcas, etc *see* **parecer¹**

paria *mf* pariah

parida *f* (Esp fam) stupid remark; **decir ∼s** to talk a load of garbage (AmE) *o* (BrE) rubbish (colloq)

paridad *f* (igualdad) equality, parity; (Fin) parity, exchange rate

parienta *f* (Esp fam & hum) **la ∼** the wife

pariente *mf*, **pariente -ta** *m,f* (familiar) relative, relation; **∼ lejano** distant relative *o* relation

(Compuesto) **pariente político** in-law

parietal *m* parietal bone

parihuela *f*, **parihuelas** *fpl* (para cosas) handbarrow; (para personas) stretcher

parir [I1] *vi* «*mujer*» to give birth; «*vaca*» to calve; «*yegua/burra*» to foal; «*oveja*» to lamb; ***poner a ∼ a algn*** (vulg) (insultar) to bad mouth sb (AmE colloq), to slag sb off (BrE colloq)

■ **parir** *vt* 1 «*mujer*» to give birth to, have; **lo conozco como si lo hubiera parido** (fam) I know him inside out (colloq); **¡la madre que te parió!** (vulg) you son of a bitch! (vulg) 2 «*mamíferos*» to have, bear (frml)

París *m* Paris

parisiense *adj/mf* Parisian

parisino -na *adj/m,f* Parisian

paritario -ria *adj* ‹*valor*› equal

parking /'parkin/ *m* (esp Esp) parking lot (AmE), car park (BrE)

parlamentar [A1] *vi* «*enemigos*» to talk, parley (dated); **∼ con el enemigo** to talk to the enemy

parlamentario¹ -ria *adj* parliamentary

parlamentario² -ria *m,f* member of parliament, parliamentarian

parlamento *m* (asamblea) parliament; (Lit, Teatr) speech

parlanchín¹ -china *adj* (fam) chatty (colloq)

parlanchín² -china *m,f* (fam) chatterbox (colloq)

parlante¹ *adj* talking (*before n*)

parlante² *m* (AmL) (en lugar público) loudspeaker; (de equipo de música) speaker

parlotear [A1] *vi* (fam) to prattle (colloq), to chatter (colloq)

parloteo *m* (fam) prattle (colloq), chatter (colloq)

parné *m* (Esp arg) dough (sl)

paro *m*

A (esp AmL) (huelga) strike; **hacer un ∼ de 24 horas** to go on a 24-hour strike; **están en** *or* **de ∼** (AmL) they're on strike

(Compuestos)

- **paro de brazos caídos** (AmL) sit-down strike
- **paro general** (esp AmL) general strike
- **paro patronal** (AmL) lockout

B (Esp) 1 (desempleo) unemployment; **está en ∼** he's unemployed 2 (subsidio) unemployment benefit; **cobrar el ∼** to claim unemployment benefit

(Compuestos)

- **paro forzoso** (Esp): **están en ∼ ∼** they have been laid off
- **paro registrado** (Esp) official unemployment figures (*pl*)

C (de máquina, proceso) stoppage

(Compuesto) **paro cardíaco** *or* **cardiaco** cardiac arrest

D (Col) **en ∼** (totalmente) completely, totally

parodia *f* parody, send-up (colloq)

parodiar [A1] *vt* to parody, to send up (colloq)

parón *m* sudden stop, dead stop

paroxismo *m* paroxysm

parpadear [A1] *vi* 1 «*persona*» to blink; «*ojo*» to blink, twitch; **me miró sin ∼** she stared at me without blinking 2 «*luz*» to blink, flicker; «*estrellas*» to twinkle

parpadeo *m* 1 (de los ojos) blinking, twitching 2 (de una luz) blinking, flickering; (de las estrellas) twinkling

párpado *m* eyelid

parque *m*

A (terreno) park

(Compuestos)

- **parque acuático** waterpark
- **parque de atracciones** *or* (Col, RPl) **de diversiones** *or* (Chi) **de entretenciones** amusement park, funfair
- **parque de bomberos** (Esp) fire station
- **parque nacional** national park

- **parque natural** nature reserve
- **parque zoológico** zoo

B (conjunto): **el ~ automovilístico del país/de una empresa** the number of vehicles in the country/a company's fleet of vehicles

(Compuesto) **parque móvil** fleet of official vehicles

C (para niños) playpen

D (Méx) (municiones) ammunition

parqué *m* (suelo) parquet (flooring); (en la Bolsa) floor

parqueadero *m* (Col) parking lot (AmE), car park (BrE)

parquear [A1] *vt* (Col) to park

■ **parquearse** *v pron* (Col) to park

parquedad *f* 1 (al hablar): **habló con ~** he was sparing with his words 2 (sobriedad) frugality, moderation 3 (escasez) paucity (frml), scarcity

parqueo *m* (Col) parking

parqués *m* (Col) Parcheesi® (AmE), ludo (BrE)

parquet *m* (*pl* **-quets**) ▸ **parqué**

parquímetro *m* parking meter

parra *f* vine; ***subirse a la ~*** (fam) (envanecerse) to get bigheaded (colloq)

parrafada *f* 1 (perorata) lecture (colloq), sermon (colloq); **me soltó una ~ de una hora** he lectured me for an hour (colloq) 2 (fam) (conversación) long talk; **echarse una ~ con algn** to have a long talk with sb (colloq)

párrafo *m* paragraph; **~ aparte** new paragraph; **su trabajo merece un ~ aparte** his work merits a separate mention

parral *m* (en un jardín) vine arbor*; (viñedo) vineyard

parranda *f* (fam): **estar** *or* **andar/irse de ~** to be/go out on the town *o* out partying (colloq)

parrandero -ra *adj* (fam): **es muy ~** he's always out on the town (colloq)

parricida *mf* parricide

parricidio *m* parricide

parrilla *f*

A 1 (Coc) grill, broiler (AmE); **pescado a la ~** grilled *o* (AmE) broiled fish 2 (restaurante) grillroom, grill bar 3 (de la chimenea) grate

B (AmL) (para el equipaje) luggage rack, roof rack

(Compuesto) **parrilla de salida** starting grid

parrillada *f* 1 (comida) grill, barbecue 2 (RPl) (restaurante) grillroom, grill bar

párroco *m* parish priest

parroquia *f*

A (iglesia) parish church; (área) parish; (feligreses) parishioners (*pl*)

B (clientela) customers (*pl*), clientele

parroquial *adj* (Relig) ‹*registro/boletín*› parish (*before n*); ‹*responsabilidad*› parochial; **escuela ~** parochial school (AmE), parish school (BrE)

parroquiano -na *m,f* 1 (Relig) parishioner 2 (cliente) regular customer *o* (frml) patron

parsimonia *f* 1 (calma) calm; **¡todo lo hace con una ~ ...!** she has such a relaxed approach to everything! 2 (frugalidad) parsimony

parsimonioso -sa *adj* 1 (tranquilo) phlegmatic, unhurried 2 (frugal) parsimonious

parte[1] *m*

A (informe, comunicación) report; **dar ~ de un incidente** «*particular*» to report an incident; «*autoridad*» to file a report about an incident; **dar ~ de enfermo** to call in sick

(Compuestos)

- **parte de defunción** death certificate
- **parte de guerra** dispatch
- **parte facultativo** medical report *o* bulletin
- **parte meteorológico** weather report

B (Andes) (multa) ticket (colloq), fine; **me pasaron** *or* **me pusieron un ~** I got a ticket *o* a fine

parte[2] *f*

A 1 (porción, fracción) part; **tres ~s iguales** three equal parts; **una sexta ~ de los beneficios** a sixth of the profits; **pasa la mayor** *or* **gran ~ del tiempo al teléfono** she spends most of her *o* the time on the phone; **la mayor ~ de los participantes** the majority of *o* most of the participants; **su ~ de la herencia** his share of the inheritance; **me siento ~ integrante del equipo** I feel I'm a full member of the team; **esto se debe en gran ~ a ...** this is largely due to ... 2 (de lugar) part; **la ~ antigua de la ciudad** the old part of the city; **¿de qué ~ de México eres?** what part of Mexico are you from?; **en la ~ de atrás** at the back; **atravesamos la ciudad de ~ a ~** we crossed from one side of the city to the other

(Compuesto) **parte de la oración** part of speech

B (*en locs*) **en parte** partly; **en ~ es tu culpa** it's partly your fault; **en gran ~** largely; **es, en buena ~, culpa suya** it is, to a large *o* great extent, his own fault; **de un tiempo a esta ~** for some time now; **de unos meses a esta ~ la situación ha empeorado** the situation has deteriorated over the past few months; **de parte de algn** on behalf of sb; **llamo de parte de María** I'm ringing on behalf of María; **dale recuerdos de mi ~** give him my regards; **muy amable de su ~** (that is/was) very kind of you; **de ~ del director que subas a verlo** the director wants you to go up and see him; **vengo de ~ del señor Díaz** Mr Díaz sent me; **¿de ~ de quién?** (por teléfono) who's calling?, who shall I say is calling? (frml); **¿tú de ~ de quién estás?** whose side are you on?; **se puso de su ~** he sided with her; **tienes que poner de tu ~** you have to do your share *o* part *o* (BrE colloq) bit; **formar parte de algo** «*pieza/sección*» to be part of sth; «*persona/país*» to belong to sth; **entrar a formar ~ de algo** to join sth; **por mi/tu/su parte** for my/your/his part; **yo, por mi ~ ...** I, for my part ... (frml), as far as I'm concerned ...; **por parte de**: **fue un error por parte nuestra/de la compañía** it was a mistake on our part/on the part of the company; **por ~ de** *or* **del padre** on his father's side; **por partes**: **revisémoslo por ~s** let's go over it section by section; **vayamos por ~s** let's take it step by step; **por otra parte** (además) anyway, in any case; (por otro lado) however, on the other hand; ***salva sea la ~*** (euf & hum) rear (colloq & euph)

C (participación) part; **yo no tuve ~ en eso** I played no part in that; **tomar ~** to take part

D (lugar): **vámonos a otra ~** let's go somewhere else *o* (AmE) someplace else; **esto no nos lleva a ninguna ~** this isn't getting *o* leading us anywhere; **¿adónde vas? — a ninguna ~** where are you going? — nowhere; **en cualquier ~** anywhere; **a/en todas ~s** everywhere; **en alguna ~** somewhere; **no aparece por ninguna ~** I can't find it anywhere

E (en negociación, contrato, juicio) party; **las ~s contratantes** the parties to the contract; **las ~s firmantes** the signatories; **ambas ~s quieren negociar** both sides want to negotiate; **la ~ demandante** the plaintiff/plaintiffs

F (Teatr) part, role; ***mandarse la(s) ~(s)*** (CS) (fam) to show off

G (Méx) (repuesto) part, spare (part)

H **partes** *fpl* (euf) (genitales) private parts (*pl*) (euph)

(Compuesto) **partes pudendas** (euf) private parts (*pl*) (euph), pudenda (*pl*) (frml)

parteluz *m* mullion

partenaire /parte'ner/ *mf* partner

partenogénesis *f* parthenogenesis

partición *f* (frml) (de herencia) division; (de territorio) partition

participación *f*

A (intervención) participation; **la ~ del público** audience participation; **con la ~ especial de Emilio Dávila** with a special guest appearance by Emilio Dávila; **~ EN algo**; ‹*en debate/clase/huelga*› participation IN sth; ‹*en robo/fraude*› involvement IN sth; ‹*en obra/película*› role IN sth; **tuvo una destacada ~ en las negociaciones** she played an important role in the negotiations; **el índice de ~ en las elecciones** the turnout for the elections

B 1 (en ganancias) share; **aumentaron su ~ en el mercado** they increased their market share 2 (en empresa) stockholding, interest 3 (de lotería) share (*in a lottery ticket*)

C (de casamiento, nacimiento) announcement

participante[1] *adj* ‹*empresas/artistas*› participating (*before n*); **los coros ~s en el concurso** the choirs taking part in the competition

participante[2] *mf* (en debate) participant; (en concurso) contestant; (en carrera) competitor

participar [A1] *vi*

A **~ (EN algo)** to take part (IN sth), participate (IN sth) (frml);

P

~ activamente en algo to take an active part in sth
B (en ganancias) to have a share; (en empresa) to have a stockholding
C (compartir) (frml) **~ DE algo** ‹*de una opinión/un sentimiento*› to share sth
■ **participar** *vt* (frml) (comunicar) ‹*boda/nacimiento*› to announce; **tengo que ~les que ...** I have to inform you that ...

partícipe *mf* (frml) **1** **ser ~ EN algo** (contribuir) to contribute TO sth **2** **ser ~ DE algo** (compartir) to share IN sth; **nos hizo ~s de la noticia** he informed us of the news, he shared the news with us

participio *m* participle
Compuestos
• **participio pasado** *or* **pasivo** past participle
• **participio presente** *or* **activo** present participle

partícula *f* particle

particular¹ *adj* **1** (privado) ‹*clases/profesor*› private; ‹*teléfono*› home (*before n*); **en su domicilio ~** at his home **2** (específico) ‹*caso/aspecto*› particular; **rasgos que les son ~es** characteristics (which are) peculiar *o* unique to them; **en ~** in particular, particularly **3** (especial): **tiene un estilo muy ~** she has a very individual *o* personal style; **es un tipo muy ~** (fam) he's a very peculiar guy; **no tiene nada de ~ que vaya** there's nothing unusual *o* strange in her going; **la casa no tiene nada de ~** there's nothing special about the house

particular² *m* **1** (frml) (asunto) matter, point; **sin otro ~ le saluda** sincerely yours (AmE), yours faithfully (BrE) **2** (persona) (private) individual; **de ~** (RPl) out of uniform

particularidad *f* **1** (cualidad) peculiarity **2** (rasgo) special feature *o* characteristic

particularizar [A4] *vt*
A (distinguir) to distinguish; (caracterizar) to characterize
B (especificar) to specify; (entrar en detalles) to particularize, go into detail about
■ **particularizar** *vi* **1** (personalizar): **no particularices** don't single anybody out **2** (dar detalles) to go into details *o* specifics
■ **particularizarse** *v pron* to be characterized

particularmente *adv* **1** (especialmente) particularly, especially **2** (*indep*) (personalmente) personally; **yo, ~, considero que ...** personally, I think (that) ...

partida *f*
A (Jueg) game; **una ~ de ajedrez/cartas** a game of chess/cards; **echar una ~** to have a game
B **1** (en registro, contabilidad) entry; (en presupuesto) item; **importantes ~s de dinero** large sums of money **2** (de mercancías) consignment, batch
Compuestos
• **partida bautismal/de nacimiento** certificate of baptism/birth certificate
• **partida doble** (Fin) double entry; ***por ~ ~*** twice over
C (frml) (salida) departure, leaving
D (de rastreadores, excursionistas) party, group; ***ser ~*** (Per fam) to be game (colloq)
Compuesto **partida de caza** (de caza menor) shooting party; (de caza mayor) hunting party

partidario¹ -ria *adj* **1** (a favor) **~ DE algo/+ INF** in favor* OF sth/-ING; **se mostró ~ de la medida** he expressed his support for the measure **2** ‹*militancia/ideología*› partisan

partidario² -ria *m,f* supporter; **~ DE algn/algo: los ~s de Gaztelu** Gaztelu's supporters; **los ~s de la violencia** those who favor *o* advocate the use of violence

partidismo *m* partisanship; **una política sin ~s** a nonpartisan policy

partidista *adj* partisan, party (*before n*)

partido¹ -da *adj*
A ‹*labios*› chapped; ‹*barbilla*› cleft
B (Mat): **siete ~ por diez** seven over ten; **nueve ~ por tres da ...** nine divided by three gives ...

partido² *m*
A **1** (de fútbol) game, match (BrE); (de tenis) match; **echar un ~** to have a game; **un ~ de béisbol** a baseball game **2** (AmL) (partida) game; **un ~ de ajedrez** a game of chess
Compuestos
• **partido amistoso** friendly game *o* match, friendly
• **partido de desempate** replay, deciding game
• **partido de ida/vuelta** first/second leg
B (Pol) party; **~ político** political party; **~ de la oposición** opposition party; **un ~ de izquierda/centro** a left-wing/center party; **sistema de ~ único** one-party *o* single-party system; ***tomar ~*** to take sides
C (provecho): **sacar ~ de algo** to benefit from sth; **sacarle ~ a algo** to make the most of sth
D (para casarse): **un buen ~** a good catch
E (comarca) administrative area

partir [I1] *vt* **1** (con cuchillo) ‹*tarta/melón*› to cut; **lo partió en dos/por la mitad** he cut it in two/in half; **¿me partes otro trozo?** can you cut me another piece? **2** (romper) ‹*piedra/coco*› to break, smash; ‹*nuez/avellana*› to crack; ‹*rama/palo*› to break; **el rayo partió el árbol por la mitad** the lightning split the tree in two **3** (con golpe) ‹*labio*› to split (open); ‹*cabeza*› to split open; **¡te voy a ~ la cara!** (fam) I'll smash your face in! (colloq) **4** «*frío*» ‹*labios*› to chap
■ **partir** *vi*
A **1** (frml) «*tren/avión/barco*» to leave, depart (frml); «*persona/delegación*» to leave, depart (frml); **partió ayer con destino a Londres** she left for London yesterday **2** «*auto*» (Chi) to start
B **1** **~ DE algo** ‹*de una premisa/un supuesto*› to start FROM sth; **debemos ~ de la base de que ...** we should start from the premise that ...; **partiendo de esta hipótesis** taking this hypothesis as a starting point **2** **a partir de** from; **a ~ de ahora/ese momento** from now on/that moment on; **a ~ del cambio la situación ha mejorado** since the change, the situation has improved; **a ~ de hoy** (as *o* starting) from today
■ **partirse** *v pron* **1** «*mármol/roca*» to split, smash; **se le partió un diente** she broke *o* chipped a tooth **2** (*refl*) ‹*labio*› to split; ‹*diente*› to break, chip; **te vas a ~ la cabeza** you're going to split *o* crack your head open

partisano -na *adj/m,f* partisan

partitivo¹ -va *adj* partitive

partitivo² *m* partitive

partitura *f* (de obra orquestada) score; **me olvidé de la ~** I forgot my music

parto *m* (Med) labor*; **estar de ~** to be in labor; **fue un ~ difícil** it was a difficult birth; **provocar el ~** to induce labor; **hubo que provocarle el ~** she had to be induced; **murió en el** *or* **de ~** she died in childbirth; **fue un ~ prematuro** she gave birth prematurely
Compuestos
• **parto natural** natural birth
• **parto sin dolor** pain-free labor*

parturienta *f* (durante el parto) parturient (tech), woman in labor*; (después del parto) woman who has just given birth

parva *f* (de mies) heap of grain; (de paja) haystack

parvada *f* (AmL) flock, bevy

parvulario¹ *m* kindergarten, nursery school (BrE)

parvulario² -ria *m,f* (Chi) infant teacher

párvulo *m* preschooler (AmE), infant (BrE)

pasa *f* raisin; ***estar hecho una ~*** *or* ***estar arrugado como una ~*** to be very wrinkled
Compuesto **pasa de Corinto/de Esmirna** currant/sultana

pasable *adj*
A (tolerable) passable
B ‹*río/arroyo*› (AmL) fordable

pasabordo *m* (Col) boarding pass

pasacalle *m* street band, passacaglia

pasada *f*
A **1** (con un trapo) wipe; (de barniz, cera) coat; **dale una ~ con la plancha** give it a quick run over with the iron **2** (en labores) row **3** (paso) **de ~: estuvo de ~, no se quedó mucho rato** he was just passing (by), he didn't stay long; **trató el tema de ~** he dealt with the subject in passing; ***hacerle*** *or* ***jugarle una mala ~ a algn*** to play a dirty trick on sb
B (Esp arg) (abuso) rip off (colloq)

pasadizo *m* passageway, passage

p

pasado[1] **-da** *adj*
A (en expresiones de tiempo): **el año/sábado ~** last year/Saturday; **la visita real que tuvo lugar en días ~s** the royal visit which took place a few days ago; **en tiempos ~s** in days gone by, in bygone days (liter); **lo ~, ~ está** (fr hecha) what's done is done, let bygones be bygones; **~s dos días** after two days; **son las cinco pasadas** it's after *o* past five o'clock; **pasadas las tres de la tarde** (sometime) after three o'clock in the afternoon; **~ mañana** the day after tomorrow
B **1** (anticuado) old-fashioned, passé **2** (raído) worn-out
C ‹*fruta*› overripe; ‹*arroz/pastas*› overcooked; **la leche está pasada** the milk is off; **el pescado está ~** the fish is bad; **el filete muy ~, por favor** I'd like my steak well done
D (arg) ‹*persona*› stoned (colloq)

pasado[2] *m* **1** (época pasada) past; **eso pertenece al ~** that's all in the past; **a causa de su ~ político** because of her political background **2** (Ling) past (tense)

pasador *m*
A **1** (de pelo — decorativo) barrette (AmE), hair slide (BrE); (— en forma de horquilla) (Méx) bobby pin (AmE), hair clip (BrE) **2** (de corbata) tiepin **3** (Per) (cordón) shoelace
B (de puerta, ventana) bolt; (de bisagra) pin
C (filtro) filter; (colador) strainer

pasaje *m*
A (esp AmL) **1** (Transp) ticket; **un ~ de ida/de ida y vuelta** a one-way/round-trip ticket (AmE), a single/return ticket (BrE) **2** (ant) (viaje) voyage, passage (dated)
B (callejón) passage, narrow street; (galería comercial) arcade, mall
C (Lit, Mús) passage

pasajero[1] **-ra** *adj* ‹*capricho/moda*› passing (*before n*); ‹*amor*› fleeting (*before n*); ‹*molestia/dolor*› temporary

pasajero[2] **-ra** *m,f* passenger

pasamanería *f* braids (*pl*), cords (*pl*)

pasamanos *m* (*pl* ~), **pasamano** *m* **1** (de escalera) banister **2** (CS) (en bus, tren) handrail

pasamontañas *m* (*pl* ~) balaclava

pasante *mf*
A (Esp) **1** (ayudante) assistant **2** (Der) articled clerk
B (Méx) (Educ) probationary teacher

pasantía *f* internship, work experience (BrE)

pasapalo *m* (Ven fam) nibble (colloq)

pasaporte *m* passport; **sacar el ~** to get a passport

pasapurés *m* (*pl* ~), **pasapuré** *m* (con manivela) food mill; (para aplastar) potato masher

pasar [A1] *vi*

Sentido **I**

A **1** (ir por un lugar) to come/go past; **no ha pasado ni un taxi** not one taxi has come/gone past; **¿a qué hora pasa el lechero?** what time does the milkman come?; **los otros coches no podían ~** the other cars weren't able to get past; **no dejan ~ a nadie** they're not letting anyone through; **no dejes ~ esta oportunidad** don't miss this opportunity; **~ de largo** to go right *o* straight past; **~ POR algo** to go THROUGH sth; **al ~ por la aduana** when you go through customs; **el Tajo pasa por Aranjuez** the Tagus flows through Aranjuez; **es un vuelo directo, no pasa por Miami** it's a direct flight, it doesn't go via Miami; **¿este autobús pasa por el museo?** does this bus go past the museum?; **¿el 45 pasa por aquí?** does the number 45 come this way?; **pasamos por delante de su casa** we went past her house; **pasaba por aquí y...** I was just passing by *o* I was in the area and...; **ni me pasó por la imaginación** it didn't even occur to me, it didn't even cross my mind **2** (deteniéndose en un lugar) **~ POR algo: ¿podríamos ~ por el banco?** can we stop off at the bank?; **pase usted por caja** please go over to the cashier; **pasa un día por casa** why don't you drop *o* come by the house sometime?; **~ A + INF: puede ~ a recogerlo mañana** you can come and pick it up tomorrow; **~emos a verlos** we'll call in *o* drop in and see them **3** (atravesar) to cross; **~ de un lado a otro** to go *o* cross from one side to the other; **~on de Chile a Argentina a pie** they crossed over from Chile to Argentina on foot; **la humedad pasó a la otra habitación** the damp went through to the other room **4** (caber, entrar): **no pasará por la puerta** it won't go through the door; **esta camiseta no me pasa por la cabeza** I can't get this T-shirt over my head
B **1** (transmitirse, transferirse) «*corona/título*» to pass; **una tradición que pasa de padres a hijos** a tradition that is handed *o* passed down from generation to generation; **pasó de mano en mano** it was passed around (to everyone) **2** (comunicar): **te paso con Javier** (en el mismo teléfono) I'll hand *o* pass you over to Javier; (en otro teléfono) I'll put you through to Javier
C (entrar — acercándose al hablante) to come in; (— alejándose del hablante) to go in; **pase, por favor** please, do come in; **¡que pase el siguiente!** next, please!; **haga ~ al Sr Díaz** show Mr Díaz in please; **¡no ~án!** (fr hecha) they shall not pass!; **~on al comedor** they went through into the dining room; **¿puedo ~ al baño?** may I use the bathroom please?; **¿quién quiere ~ al pizarrón?** (AmL) who's going to come up to the blackboard?
D **1** (cambiar de estado, actividad, tema) **~ (DE algo) A algo** to go (FROM sth) TO sth: **pasó del quinto al séptimo lugar** she went *o* dropped from fifth to seventh place; **ahora pasa a tercera** (Auto) now change into third; **pasando a otra cosa ...** anyway, to change the subject ...; **pasan a ocupar el primer puesto** they move into first place; **pasó a tratar el problema** he went on to deal with the problem; **pasamos a informar de otras noticias** now, the rest of the news **2** (Educ) to pass; **¿pasaste?** did you pass?; **~ de curso** to get through *o* pass one's end-of-year exams **3** (ser aceptable): **no está perfecto, pero puede ~** it's not perfect, but it'll do; **por esta vez (que) pase** I'll let it pass *o* go this time
E (exceder un límite) **~ DE algo: no pases de 100** don't go over 100; **no pasó de un desacuerdo** it was nothing more than a disagreement; **está muy grave, no creo que pase de hoy** he's very ill, I don't think he'll last another day; **no pasa de los 30** he's not more than 30; **no pasamos de nueve empleados** they're only nine of us working there/here
F **pasar por** **1** (ser tenido por): **pasa por tonto, pero no lo es** he might look stupid, but he isn't; **podrían ~ por hermanas** they could pass for sisters; **se hacía ~ por médico** he passed himself off as a doctor; **se hizo ~ por mi padre** he pretended to be my father **2** (Esp) (implicar): **la solución pasa por una reforma política** the solution lies in a political reform

Sentido **II**

A (transcurrir) «*tiempo*» to pass; **~on muchos años** many years went by *o* passed; **ya han pasado dos horas** it's been two hours now; **¡cómo pasa el tiempo!** doesn't time fly!; **por ti no pasan los años** you look as young as ever; **pasaban las horas y no llegaba** the hours went by *o* passed and still he didn't come
B (cesar) «*crisis/mal momento*» to be over; «*efecto*» to wear off; «*dolor*» to go away; **menos mal que el invierno ya ha pasado** thank goodness winter's over
C (arreglárselas) to manage, get by; **sin electricidad podemos ~** we can manage *o* get by without electricity

Sentido **III**

A (suceder) to happen; **cuéntame lo que pasó** tell me what happened; **lo que pasa es que...** the thing *o* the problem is ...; **pase lo que pase** whatever happens, come what may; **¿qué pasó con lo del reloj?** what happened about the watch?; **...y aquí no ha pasado nada** ...and let's just forget the whole thing; **en este pueblo nunca pasa nada** nothing ever happens in this town; **siempre pasa igual** *or* **lo mismo** it's always the same; **¿pasa algo?** is something the matter?; **¿qué pasa?** what's the matter?, what's up? (colloq); **¡hola, Carlos! ¿qué pasa?** (fam) hi, Carlos! how's things *o* how's it going? (colloq); **son cosas que pasan** these things happen; (+ *me/te/le etc*) **¿qué te pasa?** what's the matter with you?; **¿qué te pasó en el ojo?** what happened to your eye?; **¿qué le pasa a la tele?** what's wrong with the TV?; **eso le pasa a cualquiera** that can happen to anybody; **por suerte a él no le pasó nada** fortunately, nothing happened to him
B (experimentar) **~ POR algo** ‹*por crisis/mala racha*› to go THROUGH sth

Sentido **IV** **1** (en naipes, juegos) to pass **2** (fam) (rechazando algo): **¿vas a tomar postre? — no, yo paso** are you going to have a dessert? — no, I think I'll give it a miss; **paso de salir, estoy muy cansada** I don't feel like going out, I'm very tired (colloq) **3** (fam) (expresando indiferencia): **que se las**

P

arreglen, yo paso they can sort it out themselves, it's not my problem; **pasa ampliamente de lo que diga la gente** she couldn't care less what people say (colloq); **paso de él** (esp Esp) I don't give a damn *o* I couldn't care less what he does (colloq)

■ **pasar** *vt*

Sentido I

A 1 (hacer atravesar) ~ **algo por algo** to put sth THROUGH sth; ~ **la salsa por un tamiz** to put the sauce through a sieve; **pasa el cordón por este agujero** thread the string through this hole 2 (por la aduana —legalmente) to take through; (— ilegalmente) to smuggle 3 (hacer deslizar): **pásale un trapo al piso** give the floor a quick wipe; ~**lo primero por harina** first dip it in flour; **a esto hay que** ~**le una plancha** this needs a quick iron *o* run over with the iron

B (exhibir, mostrar) ‹*película/anuncio*› to show

C 1 (cruzar, atravesar) ‹*frontera*› to cross; ‹*pueblo/ciudad*› to go through; ~**on el río a nado** they swam across the river 2 (dejar atrás) ‹*edificio/calle*› to go past; **todavía no hemos pasado lo peor** the worst is yet to come 3 (adelantar, sobrepasar) to overtake; ~ **a algo** to overtake sth, to get past sth; **está altísimo, ya pasa a su padre** he's really tall, he's already overtaken his father

D ‹*examen/prueba*› to pass

E ‹*página/hoja*› to turn

F (fam) (tolerar): **esto no te lo paso** I'm not letting you get away with this; **no te deja** ~ **ni una** he doesn't let you get away with anything; **a ese tipo no lo paso** I can't stand *o* take that guy (colloq); **no podía** ~ **aquella sopa** I couldn't stomach *o* eat that soup; ~ ***por alto*** ‹*falta/error*› to overlook, forget about; «*tema/punto*» to leave out, omit

G (transcribir): **tendré que** ~ **la carta** I'll have to write *o* copy the letter out again; **¿me pasas esto a máquina?** could you type this for me?

Sentido II

A (entregar, hacer llegar): **pásaselo a Miguel** pass it on to Miguel; **¿me pasas el martillo?** can you pass me the hammer?; **le pasó el balón a Gómez** he passed the ball to Gómez; **el padre le pasa una mensualidad** she gets a monthly allowance from her father

B ‹*gripe/resfriado*› to give; **me lo pasó a mí** he gave it to me, he passed it on to me

Sentido III

A 1 ‹*tiempo*› to spend; **pasamos las Navidades en casa** we spent Christmas at home; **fuimos a Toledo a** ~ **el día** we went to Toledo for the day 2 (con idea de continuidad): **pasé toda la noche en vela** I was awake all night; **puede** ~ **días sin comer** he can go for days without eating

B 1 (sufrir, padecer) «*penalidades/desgracias*» to go through, to suffer; **está pasando una mala racha** he's going through bad times *o* (BrE) a bad patch; **no sabes las que pasé** you've no idea what I went through; **pasé mucho miedo/frío** I was very frightened/cold 2 **pasarlo** *or* **pasarla bien** to have a good time; **¿qué tal lo pasaste en la fiesta?** did you have a good time at the party?, did you enjoy the party?; **lo pasé mal** I didn't enjoy myself; **lo pasa muy mal con los exámenes** he gets very nervous about exams

■ **pasarse** *v pron*

Sentido I

A (cambiarse): ~**se al enemigo** to go over to the enemy; **queremos** ~**nos a la otra oficina** we want to move to the other office

B 1 (ir demasiado lejos): **nos pasamos, el banco está más arriba** we've gone too far, the bank isn't as far down as this; **nos pasamos de estación** we went past our station 2 (fam) (excederse) to go too far; **esta vez te has pasado** you've gone too far this time; **se** ~**on con los precios** the prices they charged were way over the top (colloq); **se pasó con la sal** he overdid the salt (colloq); **te pasaste con el regalo** that was a really nice present you gave me; **se pasó de listo** he tried to be too clever (colloq); **te pasas de bueno** you're too kind for your own good 3 (CS fam) (lucirse): **¡te pasaste! esto está riquísimo** you've excelled yourself! this is really delicious (colloq)

C 1 «*peras/tomates*» to go bad, get overripe; «*carne/pescado*» to go off, go bad; «*leche*» to go off, go sour 2 (recocerse): «*arroz/pasta*» to get overcooked; **no le dejes** ~**se de punto** don't let it overcook

Sentido II

A 1 (desaparecer) «*efecto*» to wear off; «*dolor*» to go away; (+ *me/te/le etc*) **ya se me pasó el dolor** the pain's gone *o* eased now; **espera a que se le pase el enojo** wait until he's calmed *o* cooled down; **hasta que se le pase la fiebre** until her temperature goes down 2 (transcurrir): **el año se ha pasado muy rápido** this year has gone very quickly; (+ *me/te/le etc*) **sus clases se me pasan volando** her classes seem to go so quickly

B (+ *me/te/le etc*) 1 (olvidarse): **se me pasó totalmente** I completely forgot; **se me pasó su cumpleaños** I forgot his birthday 2 (dejar de notar): **se le** ~**on varios errores** he overlooked several mistakes; **no se le pasó ese detalle** this detail didn't escape his attention 3 (dejar escapar): **se me pasó la oportunidad** I missed the opportunity

Sentido III

A (*enf*) (estar): **se pasa el día al teléfono** she spends all day on the phone; **me pasé toda la noche estudiando** I was up all night studying; **se pasó el domingo durmiendo** he spent the whole of Sunday evening sleeping; *ver tb* **pasar** *vt Sentido* **III A2 y B2**

B (*enf*) (fam) (ir): **pásate por casa** come round; **¿podrías** ~**te por el mercado?** could you go down to the market?

C (*refl*): **se pasó la mano por el pelo** he ran his fingers through his hair; ~**se un peine** to run a comb through one's hair

pasarela *f* 1 (en desfiles de modelos) runway (AmE), catwalk (BrE) 2 (Náut) gangway

pasatiempo *m* 1 (entretenimiento) hobby, pastime 2 **pasatiempos** *mpl* (en periódico) puzzles (*pl*)

Pascua *f* 1 (fiesta de Resurrección) Easter; ***de*** ~***s a Ramos*** (fam) once in a blue moon (colloq); ***estar más contento que unas*** ~***s*** (fam) to be over the moon (colloq); ***hacerle la*** ~ ***a algn*** (fam) to mess up sb's plans (colloq); ***y santas p***~***s*** (fam) and that's/that was that 2 (Navidad) Christmas 3 (fiesta judía) Passover

Compuesto **Pascua Florida** *or* **de Resurrección** Easter

pase *m*

A 1 (permiso) pass; ~ **de periodista** press pass 2 (para espectáculo) *tb* ~ **de favor** complimentary ticket 3 (Col) (licencia de conducción) license*

Compuestos

- **pase de abordar** (Méx) boarding pass
- **pase pernocta** overnight pass

B 1 (Dep) (en fútbol, baloncesto, rugby) pass; (en esgrima) feint; ~ **adelantado/hacia atrás** forward/back pass 2 (Taur) pass 3 (en magia) sleight of hand

Compuesto **pase de pecho** pass at chest height

C (Cin) showing, performance

paseador -dora *adj* (Col) ▸**paseandero**

paseandero -ra *adj* (CS fam): **es muy** ~ he goes out a lot

paseante *mf* stroller

pasear [A1] *vi* 1 (a pie) to go for a walk *o* stroll; **salir a** ~ to go out for a walk *o* stroll 2 (en bicicleta) to go for a (bike) ride; (en coche) to go for a drive

■ **pasear** *vt* 1 ‹*perro*› to walk; **nos paseó por todo el edificio** he showed *o* took us around the whole building 2 (lucir) ‹*sombrero/traje*› to show off

■ **pasearse** *v pron* 1 (caminar) to walk; **se paseaba de un lado a otro de la habitación** she was pacing up and down the room 2 (en coche, bicicleta etc) ▸**pasear** *vi*

paseíllo *m* (Taur) opening procession

paseo *m*

A 1 (caminata) walk; **¿salimos a dar un** ~**?** shall we go for a walk *o* (colloq) stroll?; ***mandar a algn a*** ~ (fam) to tell sb to get lost (colloq); **¡vete a** ~**!** get lost! (colloq), go to hell! (sl) 2 (en bicicleta) ride; (en coche) drive; **fuimos a dar un** ~ **en coche** we went for a drive 3 (AmL) (excursión) trip, outing; **no vivo aquí, estoy de** ~ I don't live here, I'm just visiting

B (en nombres de calles) walk, avenue

Compuesto **paseo marítimo** esplanade, seafront

pasillo *m* (corredor) corridor; (en avión) aisle

Compuesto **pasillo rodante** moving walkway

P

pasión *f* passion; **lo quiero con ~** I love him passionately; **siente** *or* **tiene verdadera ~ por ella** he's passionately in love with her; **tiene** *or* **siente ~ por el fútbol** he has a passion for football; **la Pasión** (Relig) the Passion

pasional *adj*: **un arrebato/crimen ~** a fit/crime of passion

pasito *adv* (Col, Ven) ‹*hablar*› quietly, softly; **entró pisando ~** she came in softly *o* quietly; **poner ~ la música** to turn the music down

pasiva *f* passive

pasividad *f*
A (cualidad) passivity
B (Ur frml) (pensión) pension

pasivo¹ -va *adj*
A ‹*actitud/persona*› passive
B (Econ, Servs Socs): **la población pasiva** the non-working population
C (Ling) ‹*oración*› passive
D (Esp frml) (Fisco) **~ DE algo** liable FOR sth

pasivo² *m* (en negocio) liabilities (*pl*); (en cuenta) debit side

pasmado -da *adj*
A (fam) ‹*persona*›: **¡no te quedes ahí ~!** don't stand there gaping *o* gawping (colloq); **la noticia me dejó pasmada** I was stunned by the news (colloq)
B (Chi, Méx) ‹*fruta*› stunted

pasmar [A1] *vt* (fam) to amaze, stun; **tiene unos modales que te pasman** you'd be amazed *o* stunned at his manners (colloq)
■ **pasmar** *vi*: **¡hace un frío que pasma!** (fam) it's perishing (cold)! (colloq)
■ **pasmarse** *v pron*
A (fam) ‹‹*persona*›› to be amazed, be stunned (colloq)
B (Chi, Méx) ‹‹*fruta*›› to stop growing

pasmarote *mf* (fam) dummy (colloq)

pasmo *m* (Esp fam) shock

pasmoso -sa *adj* amazing (colloq), incredible (colloq)

paso *m*
A 1 (acción): **el ~ del agua** the flow of water; **el ~ del tren** the passing of the train; **el ~ del tiempo** the passage of time; **el huracán destruyó todo a su ~** the hurricane destroyed everything in its path; **el ~ de la dictadura a la democracia** the transition from dictatorship to democracy; ***de ~***: **están de ~** they're just visiting *o* just passing through; **de ~ puedo comprar pan** I can buy some bread on the way; **fui a la oficina y de ~ hablé con él** I went to the office and while I was there I had a word with him; **me pilla de ~** it's on my way; **y dicho sea de ~ ...** and incidentally ... 2 (camino, posibilidad de pasar) way; **abran ~** make way; **me cerró el ~** she blocked my way; **dejen el ~ libre** leave the way clear; Ⓢ **ceda el paso** yield (*in US*), give way (*in UK*); Ⓢ **prohibido el paso** no entry; ***abrirse ~*** to make one's way; (a codazos) to elbow one's way; **abrirse ~ en la vida** to make one's way in life; ***salir al ~ de algn*** (abordar) to waylay sb; (detener) to stop sb; **un guardia salió a su ~** he was stopped by a security guard
B (Geog) (en montaña) pass; ***salir del ~*** to get out of a (tight) spot *o* (AmE) crack (colloq)

Compuestos
- **paso a nivel** grade (AmE) *o* (BrE) level crossing
- **paso de cebra** zebra crossing
- **paso de peatones** crosswalk (AmE), pedestrian crossing (BrE)
- **paso elevado** *or* (Méx) **a desnivel** overpass (AmE), flyover (BrE)
- **paso fronterizo** border crossing
- **paso subterráneo** (para peatones) underpass, subway (BrE); (para vehículos) underpass

C 1 (al andar, bailar) step; **dio un ~ para atrás** he took a step backward(s); **camina 50 ~s al norte** walk 50 paces to the north; **dirigió sus ~s hacia la puerta** she walked toward(s) the door; **oyó ~s** she heard footsteps; **entró con ~ firme** he came in purposefully; **no da un ~ sin consultarme** she won't do anything without asking me first; **~ a ~** step by step; ***a cada ~*** at every turn; ***andar en malos ~s*** to be mixed up in shady deals; ***a ~s agigantados*** by leaps and bounds; ***dar los primeros ~s*** (literal) to take one's first steps; (iniciarse en algo) to start out; ***dar un ~ en falso*** (literal) to stumble; (equivocarse) to make a false move; ***seguirle los ~s a algn*** to tail sb; ***seguir los ~s de algn*** to follow in sb's footsteps; ***volver sobre sus ~s*** to retrace one's steps 2 **pasos** *mpl* (en baloncesto) traveling*, steps (*pl*); **hacer ~s** to travel
D 1 (distancia corta): **vive a dos ~s de mi casa** he lives a stone's throw (away) from my house; **estuvo a un ~ de la muerte** she was at death's door; **está a un ~ de aquí** it's just around the corner/down the road from here; **de ahí al estrellato no hay más que un ~** it's only a short step from there to stardom 2 (avance) step forward; **eso ya es un ~ (adelante)** that's a step forward in itself 3 (de gestión) step; **hemos dado los ~s necesarios** we have taken the necessary steps
E (en contador) unit
F 1 (ritmo, velocidad): **apretó/aminoró el ~** he quickened his pace/he slowed down; **el tren iba a buen ~** the train was going at a fair speed; **a este ~ ...** at this rate ...; ***a ~ de hormiga*** *or* ***tortuga*** at a snail's pace; ***marcar el ~*** to mark time 2 (Equ) **al ~** at a walking pace

Compuesto **paso ligero** *or* **redoblado**: **a ~ ~** double quick, in double time

pasodoble *m* paso doble

pasón *m* (Méx arg) trip (colloq); **está en un ~** he's tripping (colloq)

pasota¹ *adj* (Esp fam): **es muy ~** he doesn't give a damn about anything (colloq); **está en plan ~** he's just loafing *o* lazing around (colloq)

pasota² *mf* (Esp fam): **ese tío es un ~** that guy couldn't give a damn about anything (colloq)

pasotismo *m* (Esp) indifference, apathy

paspadura *f* (RPl) chapped skin

pasparse [A1] *v pron* (RPl) ‹‹*cara/labios*›› to get chapped; **el bebé tiene la cola paspada** the baby has diaper (AmE) *o* (BrE) nappy rash

paspartú *m* (*pl* **-tús**) passe-partout

pasquín *m*
A (esp AmL) (periódico) rag
B (cartel) pasquinade, satirical poster

pasta *f*
A (Coc) 1 (fideos, macarrones, etc) pasta 2 (Esp) (masa de harina) pastry; (galleta) *tb* **~ de té** cookie 3 (de tomates, anchoas, etc) paste
B 1 (materia moldeable) paste; **un libro en ~** a book in boards; **libros de ~ blanda** (Méx) paperback books; ***ser de buena ~*** to be good-natured; ***tener ~ para/de algo*** to be cut out for sth; **tiene ~ de actriz** she's actress material 2 (Chi) (betún) polish

Compuestos
- **pasta dentífrica** *or* **de dientes** toothpaste
- **pasta de papel** wood pulp

C (Esp fam) (dinero) money, dough (sl)

pastar [A1] *vi* to graze

pastel¹ *adj inv* pastel; **colores ~** pastel (colors)

pastel² *m*
A 1 (dulce) cake; **~ de chocolate** chocolate cake *o* gateau 2 (cubierto de masa) pie

Compuestos
- **pastel de boda/cumpleaños** wedding/birthday cake
- **pastel de carne** (con masa) meat pie
- **pastel de papas** (CS) shepherd's pie, cottage pie

B (fam) (enredo) mess (colloq); ***descubrir el ~*** (fam) to take the lid off sth (colloq)
C (Art) pastel; **al ~** pastel (*before n*)

pastelería *f* (tienda) cake shop, patisserie (BrE); (actividad) (cake) baking

pastelero -ra *m,f*
A (fabricante) patissier, pastry cook; (vendedor) cake seller
B (Per fam) dopehead (sl)

pastelón *m* (Chi) paving stone

pasteurización, pasterización *f* pasteurization, pasteurizing

pasteurizado -da, pasterizado -da *adj* pasteurized

pasteurizar [A4], **pasterizar** [A4] *vt* to pasteurize

pastiche /pas'tiʃ, pas'titʃe/ *m* pastiche

pastilla *f*
A 1 (Farm, Med) (para tragar) pill, tablet; (para chupar) pastille, lozenge; **~s para dormir** sleeping tablets *o* pills; **~s para**

P

los nervios tranquilizers 2 (caramelo) candy (AmE), sweet (BrE); ~ **de anís** aniseed candy *o* sweet; ~ **de menta** mint; ~**s de goma** fruit pastilles/gums; ***a toda*** ~ (Esp fam) (velocidad) flat out (colloq); (volumen) on full blast (colloq)
B (de jabón) bar; (de chocolate) bar; (de caldo) cube
(Compuesto) **pastilla de freno** brake shoe *o* pad
C (Electrón) chip, microchip
(Compuesto) **pastilla de silicio** silicon chip

pastillero *m* pillbox

pastizal *m* pastureland, grazing land

pasto *m* 1 (Agr) pasture; **hay buenos** ~**s** there is good grazing *o* pasture; ***a todo*** ~ (Esp fam): **comimos a todo** ~ we ate until we were fit to burst (colloq); **fumaban a todo** ~ they smoked like chimneys (colloq); ***ser*** ~ ***de algo*** «*persona*» to be the subject of sth; **el edificio fue** ~ **de las llamas** the building was enveloped *o* engulfed in flames 2 (AmL) (hierba) grass; (extensión) lawn, grass

pastor -tora *m,f*
A (Agr) (*m*) shepherd; (*f*) shepherdess
(Compuesto) **pastor alemán** German shepherd, Alsatian
B (Relig) minister

pastoral[1] *adj* pastoral

pastoral[2] *f* 1 (Relig) pastoral (letter) 2 (fam) (escrito) screed; (discurso) sermon (colloq)

pastorear [A1] *vt* to tend
■ **pastorear** *vi* (AmL) to graze, pasture

pastoreo *m* pasture, pasturage; **tierras de** ~ pastureland, grazing land

pastoril *adj* pastoral

pastoso -sa *adj* 1 ‹*sustancia/masa*› doughy 2 ‹*boca/lengua*› furry 3 ‹*voz/tono*› rich, mellow

Pat. (= **patente**) pat.

pata[1] *f*
A (Zool) 1 (pierna — de animal, ave) leg; **las** ~**s delanteras/traseras** the front/hind legs 2 (pie — de perro, gato) paw; (— de ave) foot
B (de persona) 1 (fam & hum) (pierna) leg; ***a la*** ~ (Chi fam) word for word; ***estirar la*** ~ (fam) to kick the bucket (colloq); ***meter la*** ~ (fam) to put one's foot in it (colloq); ~***s (para) arriba*** (fam) upside down; **tengo toda la casa** ~**s arriba** the house is in a complete mess 2 (AmL fam & hum) foot; ***a*** ~ (fam & hum) on foot; ***a*** ~ ***pelada*** (Chi, Per fam) barefoot; ***hacer algo con las*** ~***s*** (Col, Méx, Ven fam) to make a botch of sth (colloq); ***hacerle la*** ~ ***a algn*** (Chi fam) to suck up to sb (colloq); ***por abajo de la*** ~ (RPl fam) at least; ***saltar a (la)*** ~ ***coja*** to hop; ***saltar en una*** ~ (CS) to jump for joy; ***ser*** ~ (RPl fam) to be game (colloq); ***ser*** ~ ***de perro*** (Chi, Méx fam) to have itchy feet (colloq); **es muy** ~ **de perro** she likes going out a lot (colloq); ***tener*** ~ (AmL fam) to have contacts; **tener** ~**s** (Chi fam) to have a lot of nerve (colloq); ▸**malo**[1]
(Compuestos)
- **pata de cabra** crowbar, prybar (AmE)
- **pata de gallo** (Esp) (tela) houndstooth check
- **pata de palo** wooden leg
- **patas de gallo** *fpl* crow's feet (*pl*)

C (de mueble) leg

pata[2] *m* (Per fam) 1 (tipo) guy (colloq), bloke (BrE colloq) 2 (amigo) buddy (AmE colloq), mate (BrE colloq); **él es mi** ~ **del alma** he's my best pal *o* (BrE) mate (colloq)

pataca *f* Jerusalem artichoke

patada *f*
A (puntapié) kick; **le dio una** ~ **al balón** he kicked the ball, he gave the ball a kick; **tiró la puerta abajo de una** ~ he kicked the door down; **dio una** ~ **en el suelo** he stamped his foot; **lo agarraron a** ~**s** (AmL) they kicked him about; **¡te voy a dar una** ~ **en el culo!** (vulg) I'm gonna kick your ass (AmE) *o* (BrE) arse (vulg); ***a las*** ~***s*** (AmL fam) terribly; **el informe está hecho a las** ~**s** the report has just been thrown together; ***a*** ~***s*** (fam): **la trata a** ~**s** he treats her like dirt (colloq); **los echaron a** ~**s** they were kicked out; **había comida a** ~**s** there was tons *o* loads of food; ***como una*** ~ (fam): **lo que dijo me sentó como una** ~ **(en el estómago** *or* **hígado)** what he said was like a kick in the teeth (colloq); **la cena me sentó como una** ~ what I had for dinner really disagreed with me; ***darle la*** ~ ***a algn*** to give sb the push *o* boot (colloq); ***darse de*** ~***s*** (fam) to clash; ***de la*** ~ (Méx fam): **me ha ido de la** ~ everything has gone wrong for me; **el estreno estuvo de la** ~ the premiere was a flop (colloq); **me cae de la** ~ I can't stand her (colloq); ***en dos*** ~***s*** (AmL fam) in a flash (colloq); ***me/le da cien*** ~***s*** (fam) I/he can't stand it; ***ni a*** ~***s*** (Chi, Méx fam) no way (colloq)
B (AmL) 1 (de arma) kick 2 (fam) (producida por la electricidad) shock (colloq); **me dio tremenda** ~ I got a real shock

Patagonia *f*: **la** ~ Patagonia; ***aquí y en la*** ~ (fam) here and anywhere else in the world

patagónico -ca *adj* Patagonian

patalear [A1] *vi* 1 (con enfado) to stamp (one's feet) 2 (en el aire, agua) to kick (one's legs in the air/water) 3 (fam) (protestar) to kick up a fuss (colloq)

pataleo *m* 1 (contra el suelo) stamping 2 (en el aire, agua) kicking 3 (fam) (protesta) protest; **el derecho al** ~ (fr hecha) the right to complain

pataleta *f*
A (fam) (de niño pequeño) tantrum; **le dio una** ~ «*niño*» he threw a tantrum; «*adulto*» he had a fit (colloq)
B (CS fam): **le dio una** ~ **al hígado** he got an upset tummy

patán[1] *adj* (fam) loutish, uncouth; **no seas** ~ don't be such a lout *o* so uncouth

patán[2] *m*
A (fam) (grosero) lout, yob (BrE colloq)
B (Chi) (holgazán) good-for-nothing

patata *f* (Esp) potato; ***ser una*** ~ (Esp fam) to be a lemon (colloq)
(Compuestos)
- **patata caliente** (Esp period) hot potato (journ)
- **patata frita** (Esp) (de sartén) French fry, chip (BrE); (de bolsita) (potato) chip (AmE), (potato) crisp (BrE)

patatín (fam): **que (si)** ~**, que (si) patatán** (*loc adv*) and so on and so forth

patatús *m* (fam) fit (colloq); **le va a dar un** ~ she'll have a fit; **me dio un** ~ **del susto** it frightened me to death

patchouli /pa'tʃuli/, **patchulí** *m* patchouli

paté, pâté *m* pâté; ~ **de hígado** liver pâté

pateador -dora *m,f* (Dep) kicker

pateadura *f* (CS, Per fam) beating; **le dio una** ~ he beat her up

patear [A1] *vt*
A 1 «*persona*» to kick, boot (colloq) 2 (AmL) «*animal*» to kick
B (Chi fam) ‹*novio/novia*› to dump (colloq)
■ **patear** *vi*
A 1 (dar patadas en el suelo) to stamp (one's feet) 2 (AmL) «*animal*» to kick 3 «*escopeta*» to kick; ~ ***para el otro lado/los dos lados*** (RPl fam) to be gay/to be bisexual
B (Dep) to putt
C 1 (CS fam) (+ *me/te/le etc*) «*comida*» to disagree with 2 (Chi) (desagradar) (+ *me/te/le etc*): **me patea ese tipo** I can't stand that guy (colloq)
■ **patearse** *v pron* (fam) (*enf*) (recorrer a pie) to traipse around

patena *f* paten; ***limpio como una*** ~ (Esp) as clean as a new pin

patentado -da *adj* ‹*invento*› patented; ▸**marca B**

patentar [A1] *vt*
A ‹*marca*› to register; ‹*invento*› to patent
B (CS) ‹*coche*› to register

patente[1] *adj* clear, evident; **era** ~ **su esfuerzo por controlarse** he was visibly trying not to lose his temper; **dejó** ~ **cuál era su objetivo** he made his aim quite clear; **es** ~ **que ...** clearly *o* obviously ...

patente[2] *f*
A (de invento) patent; **tienen la** ~ **para este diseño** they hold the patent for this design
(Compuestos)
- **patente de corso**: **le han dado** ~ **de** ~ **para actuar** he's been given carte blanche
- **patente de navegación** registration certificate

B (Auto) 1 (CS) (impuesto) road tax; (placa) license* plate, numberplate (BrE); **el número de la** ~ the (registration) number *o* (AmE) the license number 2 (Col) (carnet de conducir) driver's license*
C (Chi) (de profesional) registration fee (*paid to a professional association*)

patente[3] *adv* (CS) clearly

patentizar [A4] *vt* (period) to demonstrate

P

patera *f* 1 (de inmigrantes) (Esp) open boat (*used by illegal immigrants to reach Spain*) 2 (en la caza de patos) punt

paternal *adj* paternal

paternalismo *m* paternalism

paternalista *adj* paternalistic

paternidad *f*
A (del padre) 1 (Der) paternity (frml); **no reconoció la ~ del niño** he did not acknowledge paternity of the child 2 (circunstancia) fatherhood; **la ~ lo ha cambiado** fatherhood *o* being a father has changed him
B (de los padres) parenthood
C (autoría) authorship; **se le atribuye la ~ de este invento** this invention has been attributed to him

paterno -na *adj* 1 ‹*abuelo*› paternal (*before n*); **por línea paterna** on my (*o* your *etc*) father's side 2 ‹*autoridad/herencia*› paternal; ‹*cariño*› paternal, fatherly; **su domicilio ~** her parents' home

patero -ra *m,f* (Chi) bootlicker (colloq)

patético -ca *adj* pathetic, moving

patetismo *m* pathos (liter); **imágenes de (un) gran ~** very moving images

patíbulo *m* 1 (tablado) scaffold 2 (horca) gallows; **lo condenaron al ~** he was sent to the gallows

patidifuso -sa *adj* (fam) flabbergasted (colloq); **se quedó ~** he was flabbergasted

patilla *f*
A 1 (barba) sideburn, sideboard (BrE); **dejarse ~s** to grow sideburns 2 (de las gafas) sidepiece, arm
B (fruta) (Col, Ven) watermelon; (esqueje) (Chi) cutting

patín *m* 1 (con ruedas) (roller) skate; (para el hielo) (ice) skate; **le regalé unos patines** I gave him a pair of skates 2 (tabla) skateboard 3 (Esp) (bote) pedalo, pedal boat
(Compuesto) **patín del diablo** (Méx) scooter

pátina *f* patina

patinada *f* (AmL) ▸ **patinazo**

patinador -dora *m,f* (Dep) (sobre ruedas) (roller) skater; (sobre hielo) (ice) skater
(Compuestos)
- **patinador artístico -dora artística** *m,f* figure skater
- **patinador -dora de velocidad** *m,f* speed skater

patinaje *m* (sobre ruedas) roller skating; (sobre hielo) ice skating
(Compuesto) **patinaje artístico/de velocidad** figure/speed skating

patinar [A1] *vi*
A 1 (Dep) (con ruedas) to skate, roller-skate; (sobre hielo) to skate, ice-skate 2 (resbalar) «*persona*» to slip, slide; «*vehículo*» to skid; «*embrague*» to slip; ***a ti te patina/a éste le patina*** (CS fam) you've/he's got a screw loose (colloq)
B (fam) (equivocarse) to slip up
■ **patinarse** *v pron* (RPl fam) ‹*dinero*› to blow (colloq)

patinazo *m*
A (de vehículo) skid; **el coche dio** *or* **pegó un ~** the car skidded
B (fam) (equivocación) blunder, slip-up (colloq)

patineta *f* 1 (con manillar) scooter 2 (CS, Méx, Ven) (sin manillar) skateboard

patinete *m* scooter

patio *m*
A (en una casa) courtyard, patio; (de escuela) playground, schoolyard; ***cómo está el ~*** (Esp fam): **¡cómo está el ~!** what a state things are in!; **voy a ver cómo está el ~ allí adentro** I'm going to see what's going on inside; ***pasarse al ~*** (RPl fam) to overstep the mark
(Compuestos)
- **patio de armas** parade ground
- **patio de luces** *or* **de luz** well

B (Esp) (Cin, Teatr) orchestra (AmE), stalls (*pl*) (BrE)
(Compuesto) **patio de butacas** (Esp) orchestra (AmE), stalls (*pl*) (BrE)
C (Méx) (Ferr) shunting yard

patiperrear [A1] *vi* (Chi fam): **~ por el mundo** to go off globetrotting; **patiperreó toda la mañana** he traipsed around all morning

patita *f* leg; ***¡~s pa' qué te quiero!*** (CS fam & hum) I'm out of here! (colloq); ***poner a algn de ~s en la calle*** (fam) to kick *o* chuck sb out (colloq)

patitieso -sa *adj* (fam) 1 (paralizado): **quedarse ~ (de frío)** to freeze to death *o* (colloq) get frozen stiff 2 (patidifuso) flabbergasted (colloq)

patito -ta *m,f* duckling; ***hacer ~s*** (CS, Méx) to play ducks and drakes; **el ~ feo** the ugly duckling

patituerto *adj* (fam) bowlegged

patizambo -ba *adj* (con las piernas arqueadas — hacia adentro) knock-kneed; (— hacia afuera) bowlegged

pato[1] **-ta** *m,f* (Zool) duck; ***hacerse ~*** (Méx fam) to pretend not to know anything; ***pagar el ~*** (fam) to get the blame
(Compuesto) **pato salvaje** *or* **silvestre** wild duck

pato[2] **-ta** *adj* [ESTAR] (CS fam) broke (colloq)

pato[3] *m*
A (Esp fam) (persona) clodhopper (colloq)
B (Col fam) (en una fiesta) gatecrasher (colloq)
C (Andes, Méx) (Med) bedpan

patochada *f* (fam) piece of nonsense; **decir ~s** talk nonsense

patógeno[1] **-na** *adj* pathogenic

patógeno[2] *m* pathogen

patología *f* pathology

patológico -ca *adj* pathological

patólogo -ga *m,f* pathologist

patón -tona *adj* (AmL fam) ▸ **patudo A**

patonearse [A1] *v pron* (Col fam) to traipse around

patoso[1] **-sa** *adj* (Esp fam) clumsy

patoso[2] **-sa** *m,f* (Esp fam) clumsy idiot (colloq)

patota *f* (AmL fam) mob, gang

patotero -ra *m,f* (CS fam) hooligan

patraña *f* tall story

patria *f* homeland, motherland, fatherland; **luchar/morir por la ~** to fight/die for one's country; **¡viva la ~!** God save Colombia (*o* Spain *etc*)!; ***hacer ~*** to fly the flag (for one's country)
(Compuestos)
- **patria adoptiva** adopted country
- **patria chica** hometown
- **patria potestad** custody, guardianship

patriarca *m* patriarch

patriarcado *m* (Sociol) patriarchy; (Relig) patriarchate

patriarcal *adj* patriarchal

patricio -cia *adj/m,f* patrician

patrimonial *adj* (del patrimonio) patrimonial; (hereditario) hereditary

patrimonio *m* patrimony; **impuesto sobre el ~ de las personas físicas** capital gains tax; **~ personal** personal assets (*pl*); **el ~ social** stockholders' *o* shareholders' equity; **el ~ nacional** national wealth; **~ histórico** heritage; **~ artístico/cultural** artistic/cultural heritage; **es ~ de todos** it's a heritage we all share

patrio -tria *adj* (liter) ‹*amor*› for one's country; ‹*deber*› to one's country; ‹*suelo*› native

patriota[1] *adj* patriotic

patriota[2] *mf* patriot

patriotería *f* jingoism, chauvinism

patriotero[1] **-ra** *adj* jingoistic, chauvinistic

patriotero[2] **-ra** *m,f* jingoist, chauvinist

patriótico -ca *adj* patriotic

patriotismo *m* patriotism

patrocinado -da *m,f* (protegido) protégé; (Der) client

patrocinador[1] **-dora** *adj*: **la empresa ~a** the sponsors

patrocinador[2] **-dora** *m,f* (de acto, proyecto) sponsor; (Art) patron

patrocinar [A1] *vt*
A ‹*acto/proyecto*› to sponsor
B (Chi, Méx) «*abogado*» to represent

patrocinio *m*
A (de acto, proyecto) sponsorship; (Art) patronage
B (Chi, Méx) (de abogado) representation

P

patrón -trona *m,f*
A 1 (Rels Labs) employer (frml), boss 2 (Esp) (de casa de huéspedes) (*m*) landlord; (*f*) landlady 3 (Náut) skipper; (de buque mercante) master, skipper
B (Relig) patron saint
C (CS fam) (como apelativo) (*m*) sir; (*f*) madam
D **patrón** *m* 1 (en costura) pattern; ***cortados por el mismo ~*** cast in the same mold* 2 (para mediciones) standard
(Compuesto) **patrón oro** gold standard
E **la patrona** *f* (CS fam & hum) (esposa) the boss (colloq & hum)
patronal[1] *adj* 1 (Rels Labs) ‹*oferta*› management (*before n*); **organización ~** employers' organization 2 (Relig): **fiesta ~** patron saint's day
patronal[2] *f* (de empresa) management; (clase empresarial) employers (*pl*)
patronato *m* board, trust, council
patronímico[1] -ca *adj* patronymic
patronímico[2] *m* patronymic
patrono -na *m,f* 1 (esp AmL) (Relig) patron saint 2 (Rels Labs) employer
patrulla[1] *f* patrol; **están de ~** they are on patrol; **~ de aviones** air patrol; **la ~ costera** the coastguard (patrol)
patrulla[2] *m or f* (coche) patrol *o* squad car
patrullar [A1] *vi* to patrol; **salieron a ~** they went out on patrol
■ **patrullar** *vt* to patrol
patrullera *f* 1 (lancha) patrol boat 2 (Chi) (coche) patrol *o* squad car
patrullero[1] -ra *adj* patrol (*before n*)
patrullero[2] *m* (barco) patrol boat; (avión) patrol plane; (coche — militar) patrol car; (— policial) (CS, Per) patrol *o* squad car
patuco *m* (Esp) (para bebés) bootee
patudez *f* (Chi fam) nerve
patudo -da *adj*
A (AmL fam) (de pies grandes) with big feet;**¡qué niño tan ~!** what big feet he/she has!
B (Chi fam) (descarado) nervy (AmE colloq), cheeky (BrE colloq)
paulatinamente *adv* gradually, little by little
paulatino -na *adj* gradual; **de modo ~** gradually
paulista *adj* of/from São Paulo
pauperismo *m* (frml) pauperism (frml)
pauperización *f* (frml) impoverishment
paupérrimo -ma *adj* ‹*país*› poverty-stricken, very poor; ‹*persona*› very poor
pausa *f* 1 (interrupción) pause; (Rad, TV) break; ***con toda ~*** (Méx) unhurriedly; **hacer una ~** to pause/have a break 2 (Mús) rest
pausadamente *adv* slowly and deliberately
pausado[1] -da *adj* slow and deliberate, unhurried
pausado[2] *adv* slowly
pauta *f*
A (guía) guideline; **~s de comportamiento** rules *o* norms of behavior; **eso me dio la ~ de lo que pasaba** that gave me a clue as to what was happening
B (de un papel) lines (*pl*); (pentagrama) (Chi) stave, staff
pautar [A1] *vt* (frml) to provide guidelines *o* criteria for
pava *f*
A (para calentar agua) kettle
B (Col fam) (de cigarrillo) butt; *ver tb* **pavo[2]**
pavada *f* (RPl fam) 1 (dicho, acción) silly thing to say/do 2 (cosa insignificante) little thing
pavana *f* pavane
pavear [A1] *vi* (fam) 1 (RPl) (tontear) to clown around (colloq) 2 (Chi) (no prestar atención): **iba paveando** I was daydreaming (colloq)
pavesa *f* burning smut
pavimentación *f* (con asfalto) surfacing, asphalting; (con cemento, adoquines) paving; **obras de ~** resurfacing work
pavimentar [A1] *vt* (con asfalto) to surface, asphalt; (con cemento, adoquines) to pave
pavimento *m* (de asfalto) road surface; (de cemento, adoquines) paving
pavo[1] -va *adj* 1 (fam) (tonto, bobo) silly, dumb (AmE colloq) 2 (Chi fam) (ingenuo) naive (colloq)

pavo[2] -va *m,f*
A (Coc, Zool) turkey; ***comer ~*** (Col fam) to be a wallflower (colloq); ***de ~*** (Chi, Per fam) ‹*viajar/entrar*› without paying; ***pelar la pava*** (Esp fam) to bill and coo; ***se le sube/subió el ~*** (Esp fam) he blushes/blushed
(Compuesto) **pavo real** peacock
B (fam) (persona tonta) dummy (colloq), dope (colloq)
C **pavo** *m* 1 (Esp fam) (moneda) *five peseta coin* 2 (Chi) (volantín) large kite
pavonearse [A1] *v pron* (fam) to show off; **iba pavoneándose con una rubia** he was strutting along with a blonde on his arm (colloq); **~ DE algo** to brag *o* crow ABOUT sth (colloq)
pavoneo *m* (fam) showing-off
pavor *m* terror; **me da ~** it terrifies me; **les tiene ~ a los perros** (fam) she's terrified of dogs
pavoroso -sa *adj* terrifying, horrific
pavoso -sa *adj* (Ven fam) (desafortunado) unlucky; (que trae mala suerte) jinxed (colloq)
pay *m* (AmL) pie
paya (Chi), **payada** (RPl) *f*: *improvised musical dialogue*
payador *m* (CS) singer (*who performs* **payadas**)
payar [A1] *vi* 1 (CS) (Mús) to improvise a musical dialogue 2 (RPl) (hablando, escribiendo) waffle (colloq)
payasa *f* (Bol, Chi) straw mattress, palliasse
payasada *f*
A (bufonada): **deja de hacer ~s** stop clowning around *o* acting the clown (colloq)
B (Chi fam) 1 (tontería) stupid thing to say/do; **son puras ~s** that's utter nonsense 2 (cosa) thingamajig (colloq)
payasear [A1] *vi* (AmL fam) to clown around (colloq)
payaso -sa *m,f* 1 (Espec) clown; ***hacer*** *or* ***hacerse el ~*** to clown around (colloq) 2 (persona — cómica) clown, comedian; (— poco seria) joker (colloq & pej)
payo -ya *m,f* (Esp) *word used by gypsies to refer to a non-gypsy*
paz *f* 1 (Mil, Pol) peace; **firmar la ~** to sign a peace agreement *o* treaty; **en época de ~** in peacetime; ***estar*** *or* ***quedar en ~*** (fam) to be quits *o* even (colloq); ***hacer las paces*** to make (it) up; ***poner ~*** to make peace; ***y en ~*** (fam): **si no lo quieres me lo dices y en ~** if you don't want it, just tell me and that'll be an end to it 2 (calma) peace; **no me dejan vivir en ~** they don't give me a moment's peace; **¡deja en ~ el reloj!** leave the clock alone!; **¡déjame en ~!** leave me alone!; **vivir en ~ consigo mismo** to be at peace with oneself; **descanse en ~** (frml) rest in peace (frml); **tu abuelo, que en ~ descanse ...** your grandfather, God rest his soul ...
pazguato[1] -ta *adj* (fam) dopey (colloq)
pazguato[2] -ta *m,f* (fam) dope (colloq)
PBI *m* (en RPl) (= **Producto Bruto Interno**) GDP
PC *m or f* personal computer, PC
p/cta. = **por cuenta**
P.D. (= **post data**) PS
pe *f*: *name of the letter* **p**; ***de ~ a pa*** (fam) from beginning to end
peaje *m* (dinero) toll; (lugar) toll barrier; **carretera de ~** toll road
peana *f* (pedestal) base
pearse [A1] *v pron* (AmL fam) to fart (sl)
peatón *m* pedestrian
peatonal *adj* pedestrian (*before n*)
pebete -ta *m,f*
A (RPl fam) kid (colloq)
B **pebete** *m* (RPl) (pan) bun
pebre *m*: *sauce made with onion, chili, coriander, parsley and tomato*; ***hacer ~ a algn*** (Chi fam) to beat sb to a pulp
peca *f* freckle
pecado *m* 1 (Relig) sin; **estar en ~** to be in a state of sin; **¿y quién te contó eso? — se dice el ~, pero no el pecador** (fr hecha) and who told you that? — I'm not naming names 2 (lástima) crime, sin; **es un ~ tirar la comida** it's a crime to throw away food
(Compuestos)
• **pecado capital/original/venial** deadly/original/venial sin

- **pecado de omisión** sin of omission
- **pecado mortal** mortal sin; **está en ~ ~** he has committed a mortal sin

pecador[1] -dora *adj* sinful

pecador[2] -dora *m,f* sinner

pecaminoso -sa *adj* sinful

pecar [A2] *vi* 1 (Relig) to sin; **~ de pensamiento/palabra/obra** to sin in thought/word/deed 2 **~ DE algo**: **peca de bondadoso** he's too kind; **tú no pecas de generosidad** you're not overgenerous

pecarí, pécari *m* (AmL) peccary

pecera *f* (redonda) goldfish bowl; (rectangular) fish tank

pechar [A1] *vt* (CS fam) (pedir) to scrounge, to cadge (colloq)

■ **pechar** *vi* (fam) (esforzarse mucho) **~ (POR + INF)** to work one's butt off (AmE) *o* (BrE) to slog one's guts out (TO + INF) (colloq)

pechera *f*

A (de camisa, vestido) front

(Compuesto) **pechera postiza** dickey*

B (fam & hum) (pecho de mujer) bosom; **tiene una buena ~** she's well-endowed (hum)

pecho *m* (tórax) chest; (mama) breast; **dar (el) ~ a un niño** to breast-feed *o* suckle a child; **nadar (estilo) ~** to swim (the) breaststroke; ***a ~ descubierto*** boldly; ***echarse algo entre ~ y espalda*** (fam) ‹*comida*› to put sth away (colloq); ‹*bebida*› to knock sth back (colloq); ***sacar ~*** (literal) to stick one's chest out; (vanagloriarse) (CS fam) to brag, show off; ***tomarse algo a ~*** ‹*crítica*› to take sth to heart; ‹*responsabilidad*› to take sth seriously; ***a lo hecho, ~*** what's done is done

pechoño -ña *adj* (Chi) overpious

pechuga *f* 1 (de pollo) breast 2 (fam & hum) (tetas) boobs (*pl*) (colloq)

pechugón[1] -gona *adj*

A (fam & hum) big-breasted, busty (colloq)

B (Per fam) (aprovechador) opportunistic

pechugón[2] -gona *m,f*

A (Per fam) (aprovechador) opportunist, user (colloq & pej)

B **pechugona** *f* (fam & hum) big-breasted woman

pechugonada *f* (Per fam) piece of opportunism

pecíolo, peciolo *m* petiole

pécora *f*

A (mujer): **mala ~** bitch (colloq), Jezebel

B (Per fam) smell of cheesy feet (colloq)

pecoso -sa *adj* freckly

pectina *f* pectin

pectoral[1] *adj*

A ‹*músculos*› pectoral (*before n*)

B (Med): **jarabe ~** cough mixture *o* syrup

pectoral[2] *m* 1 (Anat) pectoral (muscle) 2 (Farm) cough mixture *o* syrup

pecuario -ria *adj* livestock (*before n*), cattle (*before n*)

peculado *m* (Chi, Méx) embezzlement

peculiar *adj*

A (característico) particular; **un rasgo ~** a particular trait; **las características ~es de este país** the characteristics peculiar to this country; **con su ~ buen humor** with his characteristic good humor

B (poco común, raro) ‹*sensación*› peculiar, unusual

peculiaridad *f* peculiarity; **esta ~ física los distingue** this physical peculiarity is a distinguishing feature; **las ~es del sistema** the particular characteristics of the system; **es una ~ suya** it is one of his little quirks

peculio *m* private wealth

pecuniario -ria *adj* (frml) financial, pecuniary (frml)

pedagogía *f* pedagogy, teaching

pedagógico -ca *adj* pedagogical, teaching (*before n*)

pedagogo -ga *m,f* (estudioso) educationalist; (educador) educator, teacher, pedagogue (frml)

pedal *m*

A (de bicicleta, coche) pedal; (de piano) pedal

(Compuestos)

- **pedal de arranque** kickstart
- **pedal de embrague/de freno** clutch/brake pedal

B (Esp fam) (borrachera): **¡menudo ~!** he's really plastered! (colloq)

pedalear [A1] *vi* to pedal

pedaleo *m* pedaling*; **ejercicio de ~** cycling exercise

pedante[1] *adj* pedantic

pedante[2] *mf* pedant

pedantería *f* pedantry

pedazo *m*

A (trozo) piece; **un ~ de pan** a piece of bread; **se hizo ~s** it smashed (to pieces); **el coche saltó** *or* **voló en ~s** the car was blown to pieces; **lo hice ~s** I smashed it; ***caerse a ~s*** to fall to pieces; ***estar hecho ~s*** (fam) ‹‹*coche/juguete*›› to be falling to pieces; ‹‹*persona*›› to be shattered (colloq); ***ser un ~ de pan*** (fam) to be a real sweetie (colloq)

B (fam) (en insultos): **¡~ de idiota/bestia!** you idiot/you great brute! (colloq)

pederasta *m* (homosexual) homosexual; (pedófilo) pederast

pedernal *m* flint

pederse [E1] *v pron* to fart (sl)

pedestal *m* pedestal; ***bajar(se) del ~*** to get off one's high horse; ***caérsele a algn del ~*** to go down in sb's estimation; ***poner a algn en un ~*** to place *o* put sb on a pedestal

pedestre *adj* ‹*estilo*› pedestrian, prosaic; ‹*lenguaje*› prosaic, ordinary

pediatra *mf* pediatrician*

pediatría *f* pediatrics*

pediátrico -ca *adj* pediatric*

pedicura *f* pedicure; **hacerse la ~** to have a pedicure

pedicuro -ra *m,f* chiropodist

pedida *f* (Esp) ▸**petición de mano**

pedido *m*

A (Com) order; **hacer un ~** to place an order

B (AmL) (solicitud) request; **a ~ de** at the request of; **a ~ del público** by popular request

pedigree /peði'vri/, **pedigrí** *m* pedigree; **un perro de** *or* **con ~** a pedigree dog; **tiene ~** it has a (good) pedigree

pedigüeño[1] -ña *adj* (fam): **¡mira si eres ~!** oh, stop asking for so many things!

pedigüeño[2] -ña *m,f* (fam): **es un ~** he's always asking for things

pedinche *mf* (Méx fam) scrounger (colloq)

pedir [I14] *vt*

A 1 ‹*dinero/ayuda*› to ask for; **pidieron un préstamo al banco** they asked the bank for a loan; **pidió permiso para salir** she asked permission to leave; **pide limosna** he begs (for money); **perdirle algo A algn** to ask sb FOR sth; **le pidió ayuda** he asked her for help; **nadie (te) ha pedido tu opinión** nobody asked (for) your opinion; **me pidió disculpas** *or* **perdón** he apologized (to me); **me pidió explicaciones** *or* **cuentas** he asked me to justify my actions; **~ hora** to make an appointment; **~ la palabra** to ask for permission to speak; **¿qué más se puede ~?** what more could you ask for?; **me pidió que le enseñara** he asked me to teach him; **pidió que lo trasladaran** he asked to be transferred; *ver* **prestado** 2 (en bar, restaurante) ‹*plato/bebida*› to order; ‹*cuenta*› to ask for

B (Com) 1 (como precio) **~ algo POR algo** to ask sth FOR sth; **¿cuánto pide por la casa?** how much is she asking for the house? 2 ‹*mercancías*› to order

C (para casarse): **~ a una mujer en matrimonio** to ask for a woman's hand in marriage (frml)

D (requerir) to need; **este pescado pide un vino blanco** this fish needs a white wine to go with it; **esta planta está pidiendo a gritos que la rieguen** this plant is crying out to be watered

■ **pedir** *vi* 1 (mendigar) to beg 2 (en bar, restaurante) to order 3 (para tener algo) (AmL) to ask; **pidió para salir temprano** he asked if he could go early; **estos niños sólo saben ~** these children do nothing but make demands

pedo[1] *adj inv* (Esp, Méx fam) plastered (colloq)

pedo[2] *m*

A (fam) (ventosidad) fart (sl); **tirarse un ~** to fart (sl), to let off (BrE colloq); ***al ~*** (RPl fam) for nothing; ***como un ~*** (AmL vulg) like a shot (colloq)

B (arg) (borrachera): **agarró un buen ~** he got really plastered (colloq); **tenía un ~ que no veía** he was blind drunk (colloq); ***estar en ~*** (RPl fam) (borracho) to be plastered (colloq); (loco) to be off one's head (colloq)

P

C (Méx fam) (problema, lío) hassle (colloq); ***hacerla de ~*** (Méx vulg) to kick up a stink (colloq); ***hacérsela de ~ a algn*** (Méx vulg) to give sb hell (colloq); ***ponerse al ~*** (Méx fam) to get tough (colloq)

pedofilia *f* pedophilia•

pedófilo *m* pedophile•

pedorreta *f* (fam) raspberry (colloq); **le hacían ~** they were blowing raspberries at him

pedorro¹ -rra *adj* (fam) annoying, irritating

pedorro² -rra *m,f* (fam) pain in the neck (colloq)

pedrada *f*

A (golpe): **me dio una ~ en la cabeza** she hit me on the head with a stone; **la ~ le dio justo en la frente** the stone caught *o* hit him right on the forehead; **lo mataron a ~s** he was stoned to death

B (Méx fam) (indirecta) hint; **¡deja de echarme ~s!** stop dropping hints!

pedregal *m* stony area, piece of stony ground

pedregoso -sa *adj* stony

pedregullo *m* (RPl) gravel

pedrera *f* stone quarry

pedrería *f* precious stones (*pl*), gems (*pl*)

pedrisco *m* hail

pedrusco *m* (piedra) rough stone; (pedazo de piedra) piece of stone

pedúnculo *m* (Bot, Zool) peduncle

pega *f*

A (Col fam) (broma) trick; **de ~** (Esp fam) ‹*araña/culebra*› joke (*before n*), trick (*before n*); ‹*revólver*› dummy (*before n*); ***estar en la ~*** (Ur fam) to be in the know (colloq)

B (Esp fam) (dificultad, inconveniente) problem, snag (colloq); **a todo le encuentra ~s** he finds something wrong with everything; **te ponen muchas ~s si intentas reclamarlo** they make it really difficult for you to claim it

C (Andes fam) 1 (trabajo) work; (empleo) work; **está sin ~** he's out of work 2 (lugar) work

D (Chi fam) (excusa tonta) feeble excuse

pegada *f* (AmL) (en boxeo) punch; **tiene buena ~** he packs a good punch

pegadizo -za *adj* catchy

pegado -da *adj* [ESTAR]

A (junto) **~ A algo**: **su casa está pegada a la mía** her house is right next to mine; **iba muy ~ al coche de delante** he was too close to the car in front; **la cama está pegada a la pared** the bed is right up against the wall

B (adherido) stuck; (con cola, goma) glued; **las piezas están pegadas** the pieces are glued together; **~ A algo**: **está ~ al suelo** it's stuck to the floor; **se pasa todo el día ~ al televisor** he spends all day glued to the television; ***quedarse ~*** (fam) (electrocutarse) to be electrocuted; (Educ) to stay *o* be kept down

pegajoso -sa *adj* 1 ‹*superficie/sustancia*› sticky; **tengo las manos pegajosas** my hands are all sticky 2 ‹*calor*› sticky 3 (fam) ‹*persona*› clinging (colloq) 4 (AmL fam) ‹*canción/música*› catchy

pegamento, (Col) **pegante** *m* glue, adhesive

pegar [A3] *vt*

A 1 ‹*bofetada/patada*› to give; **le pegó una paliza terrible** he gave him a terrible beating; **le ~on un tiro** they shot her 2 ‹*grito/chillido*› to let out; **les pegó cuatro gritos y se callaron** she shouted at them and they shut up; **~ un salto de alegría** to jump for joy; **~le un susto a algn** to give sb a fright 3 (fam) ‹*repaso*›: **pégale un repaso a este capítulo** look over this chapter again; **le pegué una miradita** I had a quick look at it

B 1 (adherir) to stick; (con cola) to glue, stick; **pegó un póster en la pared** she stuck (*o* pinned *etc*) a poster up on the wall 2 (coser) ‹*mangas/botones*› to sew on 3 (arrimar) to move … closer; **pega el coche un poco más a la raya** move the car a little closer to the line; **pegó el oído a la pared** he put his ear to the wall

C (fam) (contagiar) ‹*enfermedad*› to give; **me pegó la gripe** he gave me the flu; ***~la*** (RPl fam) to be dead on (AmE colloq), to be spot on (BrE colloq)

■ **pegar** *vi*

A 1 (golpear): **~le A algn** to hit sb; (a un niño, como castigo) to smack sb; **¡a mí no me vas a ~!** don't you dare hit me!; **si vuelves a hacer eso, te pego** if you do that again, I'll smack you; **le pega a su mujer** he beats his wife; **la pelota pegó en el poste** the ball hit the goalpost 2 (fam) (hacerse popular) «*producto/moda*» to take off; «*artista*» to be very popular; **su disco está pegando fuerte** her record is a big hit (colloq) 3 (fam) (ser fuerte) «*viento*» to be strong; **¡cómo pegaba el sol!** the sun was really beating down!; **este vino pega** this wine's strong

B 1 (adherir) to stick 2 (armonizar) to go together; **~ CON algo** to go WITH sth; **no pega con el vestido** it doesn't go (very well) with the dress; ***no ~ ni con cola*** (fam): **esos colores no pegan ni con cola** those colors don't go together at all; **este cuadro aquí no pega ni con cola** this picture looks really out of place here

■ **pegarse** *v pron*

A 1 (golpearse): **me pegué con la mesa** I knocked *o* hit myself on the table; **me pegué en la cabeza** I banged *o* knocked my head; **me pegué un golpe en la pierna** I hit my leg; **se pegó un porrazo** (fam) she gave herself a nasty knock; ***pegársela*** (Esp fam) to have a crash; ***pegársela a algn*** (Esp fam) (ser infiel) to be unfaithful to sb 2 (*recípr*) (darse golpes) to hit each other

B ‹*susto*› to get; **¡qué susto me pegué!** what a fright I got!; **~se un tiro** to shoot oneself; **~se una ducha** (fam) to take *o* have a shower; **anoche nos pegamos una comilona tremenda** we had an amazing meal (colloq); **¡me voy a ~ unas vacaciones …!** I'm going to give myself a good vacation *o* (BrE) holiday

C 1 (adherirse) to stick; **se me pegó el arroz** the rice stuck; **¡cómo se pega al teléfono!** she never stops yakking on the phone (colloq); **se pegó al** *or* **del timbre** she kept her finger on the doorbell; **~se a algn** latch on to sb 2 (contagiarse) «*enfermedad*» to be infectious; **eso se pega** you can easily catch it; (+ *me/te/le etc*): **se te va a ~ mi catarro** you'll catch my cold; **se le pegó la costumbre de …** she got into the habit of …; **se le ha pegado el acento mexicano** he's picked up a Mexican accent

pegatina *f* (Esp) sticker

pego *m* (Esp fam): **no es de oro pero da el ~** it isn't gold but it fools most people; **¿qué? ¿doy el ~?** well, do I pass inspection?

pegoste *mf* (Méx fam) hanger-on (colloq)

pegote *m* 1 (de suciedad) sticky mess; ***tirarse ~s*** (Esp fam) to brag (colloq) 2 (Esp fam) (mamarracho): **quita ese ~ del medio** take away that awful thing in the middle; **ese lazo es un ~** that bow just doesn't go

peinada *f* comb; **darse una ~** to give one's hair a quick comb

peinado¹ -da *adj*: **no estaba peinada** she hadn't combed her hair; **siempre va muy bien peinada** her hair always looks very nice

peinado² *m*

A (arreglo del pelo) hairstyle; **la lluvia me estropeará el ~** the rain will ruin my hair; **lavado y ~** shampoo and set

B (period) (por la policía) thorough search; **el ejército efectuó un ~ en la zona** the army combed the area *o* carried out a thorough search of the area

peinador -dora *m,f*

A (Méx, RPl) (persona) hairdresser, stylist

B **peinador** *m* 1 (prenda) peignoir 2 (Chi) (tocador) dressing table

C **peinadora** *f* (Ven) (tocador) dressing table

peinar [A1] *vt*

A 1 ‹*melena/flequillo*› (con peine) to comb; (con cepillo) to brush 2 «*peluquero*»: **¿quién te peina?** who does your hair?

B ‹*lana*› to card

C (period) ‹*área/zona*› to comb

■ **peinarse** *v pron* 1 (*refl*) (con peine) to comb one's hair; (con cepillo) to brush one's hair 2 (*caus*) to have one's hair done; **me peino en esta peluquería** I have my hair done at this salon

peine *m* comb; **me pasé el ~** I ran a comb through my hair; ***te vas/se va a enterar de lo que vale un ~*** (Esp fam) you'll/he'll soon find out what's what (colloq)

peineta *f* 1 (para sujetar, adornar) ornamental comb 2 (Chi) (peine) comb

peinilla *f* 1 (AmL) (peine) comb 2 (Col) (machete) machete

p. ej. (= **por ejemplo**) eg, for example

pejerrey *m* (americano) silverside; (europeo) sand smelt

P

Pekín *m* Peking, Beijing

pekinés -nesa *m,f* Pekinese

pela *f*

A (Esp fam) (peseta) peseta; **tiene muchas ~s** he's loaded (colloq)

B (Col, Méx, Ven fam) (golpe) slap, smack

pelada *f*

A 1 (fam) (corte de pelo): **¡mira la ~ que me han hecho!** look, I've been scalped! (colloq) 2 (CS fam) (calva — parcial) bald patch; (— total) bald head

B **la Pelada** (CS fam & euf) (la muerte) the Grim Reaper

peladero *m* 1 (Andes fam) (zona) wasteland 2 (Chi fam) (solar) site, lot (AmE)

peladez *f* (Méx) rude word

peladilla *f* sugared almond

pelado¹ -da *adj*

A 1 (con el pelo corto): **lo dejaron ~** *or* **con la cabeza pelada (al rape)** they cropped his hair very short 2 (CS) (calvo) bald; **se está quedando ~** he's going bald

B 1 ‹*manzana*› peeled; ‹*pollo*› plucked; ‹*hueso*› clean; **almendras peladas** blanched almonds 2 ‹*nariz/espalda*›: **tengo la nariz/espalda pelada** my nose/back is peeling

C (fam) (sin dinero) broke (colloq); **estoy ~** I'm broke *o* (BrE) skint (colloq); **salió ~ del casino** he lost his shirt at the casino

D 1 (fam) ‹*número/cantidad*› exact, round (*before n*); **cobra el sueldo ~** she earns a basic salary with no extras or bonuses 2 (Chi fam) ‹*pies/trasero*› bare; **ir a pie ~** to go barefoot

E (Méx fam) (grosero) foulmouthed

pelado² -da *m,f*

A (CS fam) (calvo): **¿quién es ese ~?** who's that bald guy? (colloq)

B **pelado** *m* 1 (Chi fam) (conscripto) conscript 2 (Esp fam) ▸ **pelada A1**

pelador -dora *m,f*

A (Chi fam) (persona) gossip

B **pelador** *m* (AmL) (utensilio) peeler

peladura *f* 1 (de fruta) peel; **~s de patata** potato peelings 2 (Andes) (en la piel) graze

pelagatos *m* (*pl* ~) (fam) nobody

pelaje *m* 1 (de animal) coat, fur 2 (fam) (aspecto) look 3 (fam) (clase) sort

pelambre *f or m*

A 1 (fam) (melena) mop (colloq) 2 (de animal) tuft of hair/fur

B **pelambre** *m* (Chi fam) (chisme) gossip

pelambrera *f* (fam) (melena) mop (colloq)

pelanas *m* (*pl* ~) (fam) nobody

pelandusca *f* (fam) whore (colloq), slut (colloq)

pelapapas (*pl* ~) *m* potato peeler

pelapatatas (*pl* ~) *m* (Esp) potato peeler

pelar [A1] *vt*

A 1 ‹*fruta/zanahoria*› to peel; ‹*habas/marisco*› to shell; ‹*caramelo*› to unwrap 2 ‹*ave*› to pluck

B (rapar): **lo ~on al cero** *or* **al rape** *or* (Méx) **a jícara** they cropped his hair very short

C (fam) (en el juego) to clean … out (colloq)

D (Chi fam) ‹*persona*› to badmouth (AmE colloq), to slag off (BrE colloq)

■ **pelar** *vi* 1 **que pela** (fam): **hace un frío que pela** it's freezing (cold) (colloq) 2 (Chi fam) (chismear) to gossip (maliciously)

■ **pelarse** *v pron* 1 (a causa del sol) «*persona*» to peel; «*cara/hombros*» (+ *me/te/le etc*) to peel; **se te están pelando los brazos** your arms are peeling 2 (*caus*) (fam) (cortarse el pelo) to get *o* have one's hair cut; ***que se las pela*** (fam) ‹*ir/correr*› like the wind (colloq)

peldaño *m* (escalón) step, stair; (travesaño) rung

pelea *f* 1 (discusión) quarrel, fight (colloq), argument; **buscar ~** to try to pick a quarrel *o* fight; **tuvimos una ~** we quarreled *o* had an argument 2 (en sentido físico) fight 3 (en boxeo) fight

(Compuesto) **pelea de gallos** (literal) cockfight

peleado -da *adj* 1 (enfadado): **están ~s** they've fallen out; **estar ~ con algn** to have quarrelled with sb, to have fallen out with sb 2 ‹*partido/carrera/elecciones*› keenly-contested

peleador -dora *adj* (fam) (que discute) argumentative; (que pelea): **es muy ~** he's always fighting

pelear [A1] *vi* 1 (discutir) to quarrel; **~on por una tontería** they quarreled *o* (colloq) had a fight over a silly little thing 2 «*novios*» (discutir) to quarrel, argue; (terminar) to break up, split up 3 (en sentido físico) to fight; **~ POR algo** to fight OVER sth; **las tropas ~on con gran valor** the troops fought bravely 4 (batallar): **tuvo que ~ mucho para lograrlo** she really had to work hard to get it; **me paso la vida peleando con los niños para que estudien** it's a constant battle trying to get the children to study 5 (en boxeo) to fight

■ **pelearse** *v pron* 1 (discutir) to quarrel; **se ~on por una chica** they quarreled over a girl 2 «*novios*» (discutir) to quarrel; (terminar) to break up, split up 3 (pegarse) to fight; **~se POR algo** to fight OVER sth

pelechar [A1] *vi* 1 (perder pelo) to molt• 2 (criar pelo) to grow hair

pelela *f* (CS fam) potty (colloq)

pelele *m* 1 (de trapo) rag doll; (de paja) straw doll 2 (persona — manipulada) puppet; (— débil) (fam) wimp (colloq)

peleón -leona *adj*

A (Esp fam) ▸ **peleador**

B (Esp) ‹*vino*› rough, cheap

peleonero -ra *adj* (Méx) ▸ **peleador**

peletería *f* (oficio) fur trade; (tienda) furrier's, fur shop; (género) furs (*pl*)

peletero¹ -ra *adj* fur (*before n*)

peletero² -ra *m,f* furrier

peliagudo -da *adj* ‹*problema*› difficult, tricky, ‹*asunto*› thorny

pelícano *m* pelican

pelicorto -ta *adj* (Col) short-haired (*before n*)

película *f*

A 1 (Cin, TV) movie, film (BrE); **hoy dan** *or* (Esp) **echan** *or* **ponen una ~ de aventuras** there's an adventure movie *o* film on today, they're showing an adventure movie *o* film today; **de ~** (fam) fantastic (colloq); **una chica de ~** a gorgeous *o* fantastic girl; **una casa de ~** a dream house (colloq); **me pasó algo de ~** something incredible happened to me 2 (Fot) film

(Compuestos)

- **película de dibujos animados** cartoon
- **película del Oeste** *or* **de vaqueros** Western
- **película de miedo** *or* **de terror** horror movie *o* film
- **película de suspenso** *or* (Esp) **suspense** thriller
- **película muda** silent movie *o* film
- **película X** X-certificate movie *o* film

B (capa fina — de aceite) film; (— de polvo) thin layer

peliculero -ra *adj* (fam) 1 (fantasioso) prone to fantasazing 2 (aficionado al cine): **es muy ~** he's a great movie fan *o* (BrE) film buff (colloq)

peliento -ta *m,f* (Chi fam) slob (colloq)

peligrar [A1] *vi* to be at risk; **hacer ~ algo** to put sth at risk

peligro *m* danger, peril (liter); **estar en** *or* **correr ~** «*persona*» to be in danger; «*vida*» to be in danger *o* at risk; **esta escalera es un ~ para los niños** this staircase is a hazard for children; **un ~ para la salud** a health risk; **poner a algn en ~** to put sb at risk, to endanger sb; **poner algo en ~** to put sth at risk, to jeopardize sth; **correr el ~ de + INF** to be in danger OF -ING; **corres el ~ de que te despidan** you run the risk of being fired; **estar fuera de ~** to be out of danger; Ⓢ **peligro de incendio** fire hazard; Ⓢ **peligro de muerte** danger

(Compuesto) **peligro público** (fam) menace, public nuisance

peligrosamente *adv* dangerously

peligrosidad *f* dangerousness; **prima de ~** danger money

peligroso -sa *adj* dangerous

pelillo *m* small hair; ***~s a la mar*** (Esp fam) let's just forget all about it (colloq)

pelín *m* (Esp fam): **un ~** a little, a bit (colloq)

pelirrojo¹ -ja *adj* red-haired, ginger-haired

pelirrojo² -ja *m,f* redhead

P

pella *f* (de masa) lump; ***hacer ~s*** (Esp arg) to play hooky (esp AmE colloq), to skive off (school) (BrE colloq)

pelleja *f* sheepskin

pellejerías *fpl* (Andes fam) hard times (*pl*)

pellejo *m* 1 (piel — de animal) skin, hide; (— de persona) (fam) skin (colloq); ***estar/ponerse en el ~ de algn*** (fam) to be/put oneself in sb's shoes; ***no ser*** *or* ***no tener más que ~*** (fam) to be all skin and bone (colloq) 2 (fam) (vida) neck (colloq); **jugarse** *or* **arriesgar el ~** to risk one's neck (colloq) 3 (odre) wineskin

pelliza *f* fur-lined coat

pellizcar [A2] *vt* 1 ‹*persona/brazo*› to pinch 2 (fam) ‹*comida*› to nibble at 3 (Ven) (en béisbol) to chop

pellizco *m* 1 (en la piel) pinch; **me dio un ~ en la pierna** she pinched my leg 2 (fam) (cantidad pequeña) little bit; **un ~ de sal** a pinch of salt; **le tocó un buen ~** she won a tidy little sum 3 (Ven) (en béisbol) chop

pelma *adj/mf* (Esp fam) ▸ **pelmazo**[1,2]

pelmazo[1] *adj* (fam) boring; **¡qué tipo más ~!** that guy's such a bore! (colloq)

pelmazo[2] *m* (fam) bore

pelo *m*

A, (de personas) hair; **~ rizado/liso** *or* **lacio** curly/straight hair; **cortarse el ~** to have one's hair cut; **tiene un ~ divino** she has lovely *o* beautiful hair; **tiene mucho ~** he has really thick hair; **llevar el ~ suelto** to wear one's hair down *o* loose; ***al ~*** (fam): **la falda le quedó al ~** the skirt looked great on her; **el dinero extra me viene al ~** the extra money is just what I need; ***andar*** *or* ***estar con los ~s de punta*** (CS fam) to be in a real state (colloq); ***caérsele el ~ a algn***: **se me cae el ~** my hair is falling out; **se le está cayendo el ~** he's losing his hair; **como te descubran se te va a caer el ~** if you get found out, you'll be for it *o* you've had it (colloq); ***con estos ~s*** (fam): **¡y yo con estos ~s!** look at the state I'm in!; ***con ~s y señales*** (fam) down to the last detail; ***de medio ~*** (fam) ‹*película/jugador*› second-rate; ***echar el ~*** (Chi fam) to live it up (colloq); ***no tiene ~s en la lengua*** (fam) he doesn't mince his words; ***no tienes/tiene (ni) un ~ de tonto*** (fam) you're/he's no fool; ***no verle el ~ a algn*** (fam) not to see hide nor hair of sb (colloq); **ya no te vemos el ~ por aquí** we never see you around here any more; ***ponerle a algn los ~s de punta*** (fam) (aterrorizar) to make sb's hair stand on end (colloq); (poner neurótico) (AmL) to drive sb crazy *o* mad; ***por los ~s*** (fam) only just; ***se me/le ponen los ~s de punta*** (fam) it sends shivers down my/his spine, it makes my/his hair stand on end; ***tirarse de los ~s*** (fam): **estaba que se tiraba de los ~s** he was at his wit's end, he was tearing his hair out (in desperation); ***tocarle un ~ a algn*** to lay a finger on sb; ***tomarle el ~ a algn*** (fam) (bromeando) to pull sb's leg (colloq); (burlándose) to mess around with sb (AmE), to mess sb around (BrE); ***traído por*** *or* ***de los ~s*** farfetched

B (fam) (poco): **se han pasado un ~** they've gone a bit too far; **no me fío (ni) un ~ de él** I don't trust him an inch; **te queda un pelito corta** it's a tiny bit short for you

C (Zool) (filamento) hair; (pelaje — de perro, gato) hair, fur; (— de conejo, oso) fur; **un perro de ~ largo** a long-haired dog; ***montar a*** *or* (CS) ***en ~*** to ride bareback

(Compuesto) **pelo de camello** camelhair

D (de alfombra) pile; **una alfombra de ~ largo** a shag-pile carpet

pelón[1] **-lona** *adj*

A 1 (fam) (sin pelo) bald 2 (Ec fam) (con mucho pelo) ‹*hombre*› hairy; **un bebé ~** a baby with a good head of hair

B (Méx fam) (difícil) tough (colloq)

pelón[2] **-lona** *m,f*

A 1 (fam) (sin pelo) bald person 2 (Ec fam) (con mucho pelo): **es un ~** he has a good head of hair

B 1 **pelón** *m* (RPl) (Bot) (durazno) nectarine 2 **la Pelona** *f* (Andes, Méx fam) (la muerte) Death, the Grim Reaper

pelota[1] *mf*

A (AmS vulg) (imbécil) jerk (sl)

B (Esp fam) (adulador) creep (colloq)

pelota[2] *f*

A (Dep, Jueg) ball; **una ~ de fútbol** (AmL) a football; **jugar a la pelota** to play ball; ***darle ~ a algn*** (CS fam) to take notice of sb; ***hacerle la ~ a algn*** (Esp fam) to suck up to sb (colloq); ***la ~ está/estaba en el tejado*** (Esp period) it's/it was all up in the air; ***le devolví/devolvió la ~*** I/she gave as good as I/she got; ***pasar la ~*** (fam) to pass the buck

B **pelotas** *fpl* (vulg) (testículos) balls (*pl*) (colloq *or* vulg); ***en ~s*** (vulg) (sin ropa) stark naked; (sin dinero) flat broke (colloq); ***estar hasta las ~s de algo/algn*** (vulg) to be really pissed off with sth/sb (sl); ***hincharle*** *or* ***tocarle las ~s a algn*** (vulg) to get up sb's nose (colloq); ***tener ~s*** (AmS arg) to have balls (vulg), to have guts (colloq)

> **pelota vasca**
>
> A ball game, also known as *jai alai*, that developed in the Basque Country. It is played in Spain, Mexico, Cuba and Florida.
>
> The game has similarities to squash and fives. It is played in a *frontón*, a court with three high walls. The players use a *cesta*, a long, concave basket attached to their hand with a strap, to throw and catch the ball against the wall. The ball reaches high speeds and spectators watch from behind a metal fence. Pelota is played by two teams of two players. It is a professional game on which spectators place bets

pelotari *mf* jai alai *o* pelota player

pelotazo *m*

A (con un pelota): **me dio un ~** he hit me hard with the ball

B (Esp fam) (de alcohol) drink, slug (fam)

C (Esp fam) (actidud): **la cultura del ~** the get-rich-quick culture

pelotear [A1] *vi* (en fútbol) to kick a ball around; (en tenis) to knock *o* hit a ball around, have a knock-up (BrE)

■ **pelotear** *vt* 1 (Per fam) ‹*persona*› to shunt … around (colloq) 2 (Chi fam) ‹*objeto*› to juggle with (colloq)

peloteo *m* 1 (en fútbol) kickabout; (en tenis) warm-up, knock-up (BrE) 2 (Per fam) (ir y venir): **ya estoy cansado de tanto ~** I'm fed up with being shunted around (colloq)

pelotera *f* (fam) 1 (lío, jaleo) ruckus (AmE colloq), rumpus (BrE colloq) 2 (riña) argument, row (colloq)

pelotero -ra *m,f* 1 (AmL) (jugador — de béisbol) baseball player; (— de fútbol) soccer *o* football player, footballer 2 (Chi) (recogepelotas) (*m*) ballboy; (*f*) ballgirl

pelotilla[1] *adj* (fam): **es muy ~** he's a real creep *o* crawler (colloq)

pelotilla[2] *f* (fam) (de moco) bogey (colloq); (de mugre) ball of dirt; ***hacerle la ~ a algn*** (fam) to suck up to sb (colloq)

pelotilleo *m* (Esp fam) fawning

pelotillero[1] **-ra** *adj* ▸ **pelotilla**[1]

pelotillero[2] **-ra** *m,f* ▸ **pelota**[1] **B**

pelotón *m* 1 (Mil) squad 2 (en ciclismo) bunch, pack; (en atletismo) pack 3 (fam) (de gente) gang (colloq)

(Compuesto) **pelotón de ejecución** *or* **fusilamiento** firing squad

pelotudo[1] **-da** *adj* (AmS vulg): **¡qué ~!** what a jerk! (sl)

pelotudo[2] **-da** *m,f* (AmS vulg) jerk (sl)

peltre *m* pewter

peluca *f* wig

peluche *m* felt, plush; **un juguete de ~** a cuddly toy; ▸ **oso**

pelucón -cona *adj* (Chi, Per fam) (con mucho pelo) hairy; (de pelo largo) long-haired

peludo[1] **-da** *adj* ‹*hombre/brazo*› hairy; ‹*barba*› bushy; ‹*animal*› hairy, furry; ‹*cola*› bushy; ‹*lana/jersey*› hairy

peludo[2] *m* (Zool) armadillo

peluquería *f* 1 (establecimiento) hairdresser's, hairdressing salon; **~ de caballeros/señoras** gentlemen's/ladies' hairdresser's 2 (oficio) hairdressing, hairstyling

peluquero -ra *m,f* hairdresser, hairstylist

peluquín *m* toupee, hairpiece; ***¡ni hablar del ~!*** (Esp fam) no way! (colloq)

pelusa[1], **pelusilla** *f*

A (en la cara) down, fuzz; (de durazno) down; (en jersey) ball of fluff *o* fuzz; (de suciedad) ball of fluff

B (Esp fam) (celos) jealousy; **tener ~** to be jealous

pelusa[2] *mf* (Chi fam) (niño — callejero) street kid (colloq); (— travieso) little rascal (colloq)

pelvis *f* (*pl* ~) pelvis

Pemex = Petróleos Mexicanos

pena *f*

A 1 (tristeza): **tenía/sentía mucha ~** he was *o* felt very sad;

P

me da ~ verlo it upsets me *o* it makes me sad to see it; **a mí la que me da ~ es su mujer** it's his wife I feel sorry for; **está que da ~** she's in a terrible state; **me da pena tener que decírselo** it hurts me to have to tell him; **lloraba con tanta ~** he was crying so bitterly [2] (lástima) pity, shame; **¡qué ~!** what a pity *o* shame!; **es una ~ que …** it's a pity (that) …; ***de ~*** (Esp) terrible; ***estar hecho una ~*** to be in a sorry *o* terrible state; ***sin ~ ni gloria*** almost unnoticed; ***vale*** *or* ***merece la ~*** it's worth it; **vale la ~ leerlo/visitarlo** it's worth reading/a visit; **no vale la ~ intentar convencerlo** there's no point *o* it's not worth trying to persuade him

B **penas** *fpl* [1] (problemas) sorrows (*pl*); **ahogar las ~s** to drown one's sorrows; **me contó sus ~s** he told me his troubles *o* (liter *or* hum) woes; ***a duras ~s*** (apenas) hardly; (con dificultad) with difficulty [2] (penalidades) hardship; **pasamos muchas ~s** we suffered great hardship

C (Der) sentence; **la ~ máxima** the maximum sentence; **bajo** *or* **so ~ de** (frml) on pain of (frml); **so ~ de repetirme** at the risk of repeating myself

(Compuesto) **pena capital** *or* **de muerte** death penalty

D (AmL exc CS) (vergüenza) embarrassment; **¡qué ~!** how embarrasing!; **me da mucha ~ pedírselo** I'm too embarrassed to ask him; ***quitado de la ~*** (Méx) blithely, gaily

E (Per) (fantasma) ghost

penacho *m* (de ave) tuft, crest; (adorno) plume

penado -da *m,f* (frml) convict

penal¹ *adj* criminal (*before n*)

penal² *m*

A (cárcel) prison, penitentiary (AmE)

B (AmL period) (Dep) penalty

C **penales** *mpl* police *o* criminal record

pénal *m* (Andes) penalty

penalidad *f*

A (Der) punishment

B **penalidades** *fpl* hardship, suffering

penalista *mf* (abogado) criminal lawyer; (estudioso) expert in criminal law

penalización *f* [1] (Der) (acción) penalization; (castigo) penalty [2] (Dep) penalty

penalizar [A4] *vt* (Der) to penalize

penalty /'penalti, pe'nalti/ *m* (*pl* **-tys**) penalty; **marcó dos goles de ~** he scored two penalties; **pitar** *or* **señalar ~** to award *o* give a penalty; ***se casó/se casaron de ~*** (Esp fam) she/they got married because she was *o* got pregnant (colloq)

penar [A1] *vt*

A (Der) ‹*delito*›: **será/está penado con dos años de cárcel/cadena perpetual** it will be/it is punishable with two years' imprisonment/by life imprisonment

B (Andes) «*difunto*» to haunt

■ **penar** *vi*

A (liter) (sufrir) to suffer

B (Andes) «*difunto*» to be in torment

penca¹ *adj inv* (Chi fam) ‹*cosa*› crappy (sl); ‹*situación*› lousy (colloq); ‹*persona*› ugly

penca² *f* [1] (de hoja) main rib [2] (del nopal) stalk [3] (Méx) (de bananas) bunch

pencar [A2] *vi* (fam) to slog away (colloq)

penco *m* nag, hack

pendejada *f* [1] (AmL exc CS fam) (estupidez) stupid thing to say/do; **¡no digas ~s!** (vulg) don't talk crap! (vulg) [2] (Per vulg) (mala jugada) dirty trick

pendejear [A1] *vi* (Méx fam) to clown around (colloq); ***~la*** (Méx) to blow it (colloq)

pendejez *f* (Méx vulg) stupidity

pendejo¹ -ja *adj* [1] (AmL exc CS fam) (estúpido) dumb (AmE colloq), thick (BrE colloq) [2] (Per fam) (listo) sly, sharp (colloq)

pendejo² -ja *m,f* [1] (AmL exc CS fam) (estúpido) dummy (colloq), nerd (colloq); ***hacerse el ~*** (fam) (hacerse el tonto) to act dumb (colloq); (no hacer nada) to loaf around (colloq) [2] (Per fam) (persona lista) sly devil [3] (CS vulg) (mocoso) snotty-nosed kid (colloq)

pendenciero¹ -ra *adj* [1] (discutidor) quarrelsome, argumentative [2] (peleador): **un chico ~** a kid who's always getting into fights

pendenciero² -ra *m,f* troublemaker

pender [E1] *vi*

A (liter) to hang; **~ DE algo** to hang FROM sth; **la amenaza que pendía sobre allos** the threat that hung over them

B (Der): **la sentencia pende ante el juez** the case awaits the judge's decision

pendiente¹ *adj*

A ‹*asunto/problema*› unresolved; **el asunto está ~ de resolución** the matter has to be resolved; **tenemos algunas cuentas ~s** (hablando — de dinero) we have some bills outstanding; (— de problemas) we have some unfinished business to settle

B (atento) **estar ~ DE algo/algn**: **está ~ del niño a todas horas** she devotes every minute of the day to the child; **estoy ~ de que me llamen** I'm waiting for them to call me; **siempre está ~ de los demás** he's always watching to see what other people are doing

pendiente² *m* (Esp) earring

pendiente³ *f* (de terreno) slope, incline; (de tejado) slope; **un camino en ~** an uphill path; **tiene mucha ~** it slopes steeply; **una ~ muy pronunciada** a very steep slope *o* incline; **la colina tiene una ~ del 20%** the hill has a one-in-five gradient

pendón *m*

A (Hist, Mil) banner, standard

B (Esp fam) [1] (juerguista) partygoer [2] (mujer de vida licenciosa) whore (colloq)

pendonear [A1] *vi* (Esp fam) (ir de juerga) to live it up (colloq); (no hacer nada) to hang out *o* around (colloq)

pendular *adj* pendular

péndulo *m* pendulum

pene *m* penis

penetración *f* [1] (acción) penetration [2] (sagacidad) insight

penetrante *adj*

A [1] ‹*mirada/voz*› penetrating, piercing; ‹*olor*› pungent, penetrating; ‹*sonido*› piercing [2] ‹*viento/frío*› bitter, biting

B ‹*inteligencia/mente*› sharp, incisive; ‹*humor/ironía*› sharp, cutting

penetrar [A1] *vi* [1] (entrar) **~ POR algo** «*agua/humedad*» to seep THROUGH sth; **la luz del sol penetraba por la ventana** the sunlight shone through the window; **la puerta por donde penetró el ladrón** the door through which the burglar entered; **el olor penetraba por todos los rincones** the smell pervaded every corner; **~ EN algo** to penetrate sth; **el frío le penetraba en los huesos** the cold was getting right into his bones; **esta crema penetra rápidamente en la piel** this cream is quickly absorbed by the skin; **es difícil ~ en su mente** it is difficult to fathom his thoughts [2] (en el acto sexual) to penetrate

■ **penetrar** *vt* [1] ‹*defensa/membrana*› to penetrate; **un ruido que penetra los oídos** a piercing noise [2] (liter) ‹*misterio/secreto*› to fathom, penetrate (liter) [3] (Com) ‹*mercado*› to penetrate [4] (en el acto sexual) to penetrate

penicilina *f* penicillin

península *f* peninsula

peninsular¹ *adj* peninsular

peninsular² *mf*: **los ~es** people from mainland Spain

penique *m* penny

penitencia *f*

A (Relig) penance; **en ~** as (a) penance

B (en juegos) (Andes) forfeit; (castigo) (RPl fam) punishment; **el maestro me puso en ~** the teacher punished me; **está en ~** she's not allowed out, she's grounded (colloq)

penitenciaría *f* penitentiary

penitenciario -ria *adj* penitentiary (*before n*), prison (*before n*)

penitente *mf* penitent

penosamente *adv* with difficulty, laboriously

penoso -sa *adj*

A (lamentable) terrible, awful

B [1] (triste) sad [2] ‹*viaje*› grueling*; ‹*trabajo*› laborious, difficult

C (AmL exc CS fam) [1] ‹*persona*› shy [2] (embarazoso) embarrassing

penquearse [A1] *v pron* (Chi fam) to drink

P

pensado -da *adj* 1 (considerado, esperado) ‹*decisión*› well-considered/well thought-out; **el día menos ~** one day when I/you least expect it; **siempre aparece en el momento menos ~** he always turns up when you least expect him to 2 (diseñado) **estar ~ PARA algo** to be designed FOR sth; *ver tb* **pensar**

pensador -dora *m,f* thinker

pensamiento *m*

A 1 (facultad) thought 2 (cosa pensada) thought; **me adivinó el ~** she read my mind *o* my thoughts 3 (doctrina) thinking 4 (máxima) thought

(Compuesto) **pensamiento lateral** lateral thinking

B (Bot) pansy

pensante *adj* thinking (*before n*)

pensar [A5] *vi* 1 (razonar) to think; **después de mucho ~ ...** after much thought ...; **déjame ~** let me think; **siempre actúa sin ~** he always does things without thinking; **¡pero piensa un poco!** just think about it a minute!; **a ver si piensas con la cabeza y no con los pies** (fam & hum) come on, use your head *o* your brains!; **pensé para mí** *or* **para mis adentros** I thought to myself; **~ EN algo/algn** to think ABOUT sth/sb; **sólo piensa en divertirse** all he thinks about is having fun; **no quiero ni ~ en lo que hubiera podido ocurrir** I don't even want to think what would have happened 2 (esperar) to expect; **cuando menos se piensa ...** just when you least expect it ... 3 (creer) to think; **~ mal/bien de algn** to think ill *o* badly/well of sb; **siempre piensa mal de los demás** he always thinks the worst of others; ***dar que*** *or* ***hacer* ~: un libro que da mucho que ~** *or* **que hace ~ mucho** a very thought-provoking book; **su amabilidad me dio que ~** his friendliness made me think *o* set me thinking; ***piensa mal y acertarás*** if you think the worst, you won't be far wrong

■ **pensar** *vt*

A 1 (creer, opinar) to think; **pienso que no** I don't think so; **es mejor ~ que todo saldrá bien** it's better to believe *o* think that things will turn out all right in the end; **¡tal como yo pensé!** just as I thought!; **no vaya a ~ que ...** I wouldn't want you thinking *o* to think that ...; **¿qué piensas del divorcio/del jefe?** what do you think about divorce/the boss? 2 (considerar) to think about; **lo ~é** I'll think about it; **¿lo has pensado bien?** have you thought it through *o* thought about it carefully?; **piénsalo bien antes de decidir** think it over before you decide; **pensándolo bien, ...** on second thought(s) *o* thinking about it, ...; **¡y ~ que ...!** (and) to think that ...!; **sólo de ~lo me pongo a temblar** just thinking about it makes me tremble; **¡ni ~lo!** *or* **¡ni lo pienses!** no way! (colloq), not on your life! (colloq); **no lo pienses dos veces** don't think twice about it 3 (Col) ‹*persona*› to think about

B (tener la intención de) **~ + INF** to think OF -ING, to plan TO + INF; **¿piensas ir?** are you thinking of going?, are you planning to go?; **no pienso esperar más** I don't intend to wait any longer

■ **pensarse** *v pron* (*enf*) (fam) ‹*decisión/respuesta*› to think about; **me lo voy a ~** I'm going to think about it; **esto hay que pensárselo dos veces** this needs to be thought through; **es como para pensárselo** I/you will need to give it some careful thought

pensativo -va *adj* pensive, thoughtful

pensión *f*

A (Servs Socs) (por haber trabajado) retirement pension; (por contribuciones de familiar) widow's/orphan's pension; **cobrar la ~** to draw one's pension

(Compuestos)

- **pensión alimenticia** maintenance
- **pensión de invalidez** disability (allowance) (AmE), invalidity benefit (BrE)
- **pensión de viudedad** *or* **viudez** widow's pension
- **pensión vitalicia** annuity

B 1 (casa — de huéspedes) guesthouse, rooming house (AmE), boarding house (BrE); (— para estudiantes) student hostel 2 (alojamiento) accommodations (*pl*) (AmE), lodging, accommodation (BrE); ▸ **medio¹**

(Compuesto) **pensión completa** full board

C (Col) (mensualidad) tuition (AmE), school fees (*pl*) (BrE)

pensionado -da *m,f*

A (Servs Socs) pensioner

B **pensionado** *m* 1 (Esp) (internado) boarding school 2 (CS) (pensión para estudiantes) student hostel 3 (Chi) (en hospital) private wing

pensionar [A1] *vt* (Per fam) (molestar) to upset, bother; (preocupar) to worry

■ **pensionarse** *v pron* (Col) to retire

pensionista *mf*

A (Servs Socs) pensioner

B (en casa de huéspedes) resident, lodger

pentágono *m* 1 (Mat) pentagon 2 **el Pentágono** the Pentagon 3 (Méx) (en béisbol) home plate

pentagrama *m* (Mús) stave, staff

pentámetro *m* pentameter

pentatleta *mf* pentathlete

pentatlón *m* pentathlon

Pentecostés *m* Pentecost

penúltima *f* (fam & hum): **la ~** one for the road (colloq)

penúltimo¹ -ma *adj* penultimate; **el ~ día** the penultimate day, the last day but one

penúltimo² -ma *m,f*: **era el ~** I was second to last, I was last but one; *ver tb* **penúltima**

penumbra *f* 1 (media luz) half-light, semidarkness 2 (Astron) penumbra

penuria *f* 1 (escasez) shortage, dearth; **una auténtica ~ de medios** a real shortage *o* dearth of resources; **pasaron verdaderas ~s** they suffered real hardship 2 (pobreza) poverty; **viven en la ~** they live in poverty

peña *f*

A (roca) crag, rock

B 1 (grupo) circle, group; **~ taurina** bullfighting club 2 (AmL) *tb* **~ folklórica** folk club 3 (Esp fam) folk club

peñascal *m* rocky area/slope

peñasco *m* crag, rocky outcrop

peñazo *m* (Esp fam): **eres un ~** you're a pain (colloq); **dar el ~** to hassle sb (colloq)

peñón *m* crag, rocky outcrop

peo *m* ▸ **pedo²**

peón *m*

A (Const) laborer*; (Agr) (esp AmL) agricultural laborer*, farm worker

(Compuestos)

- **peón albañil** (building) laborer*
- **peón caminero** road worker

B (en ajedrez) pawn; (en damas) piece, checker (AmE), draughtsman (BrE)

peonada *f* (trabajo) day's work; (equipo) (esp AmL) gang of laborers*

peonía *f* peony

peonza *f* spinning top

peor¹ *adj*

A 1 (comparativo de **malo**) ‹*producto/película/profesor*› worse; ‹*calidad*› poorer; **pues ~ para él** that's his loss; **va a ser ~ para él (como no estudie)** if he doesn't study so much the worse for him; **y si vienen los dos, tanto ~** *or* **~ que ~** and it'll be even worse if the two of them come 2 (comparativo de **mal**) worse

B 1 (superlativo de **malo**) (entre dos)worse; (entre varios) worst; **en el ~ de los casos** if the worst comes to the worst; **lo ~ de todo es que ...** the worst thing of all is that ... 2 (superlativo de **mal**): **los enfermos que estaban ~** *or* **~es** the patients who were most seriously ill; **son los que están ~** *or* **~es de dinero** they're the worst off (for money)

peor² *adv*

A (comparativo de **mal**) worse; **cuanto más lo mimas, ~ se porta** the more you spoil him, the worse he behaves; **cada vez ~** worse and worse; **~ que nunca** worse than ever

B (superlativo de **mal**) worst; **el lugar donde ~ se come** the worst place to eat in; **su novela ~ escrita** his most badly written novel

peor³ *mf*: **el/la ~** (de dos) the worse; (de varios) the worst

pepa *f*

A (AmS) (semilla — de uva, naranja) pip; (— de durazno, aguacate) stone, pit; ***ser una ~*** (Col fam) to be brainy (colloq)

B (Ven fam) (grano) zit (colloq), pimple

C (Per fam) (cara) face

Pepe: *diminutive of José*

pepé *m* (Arg leng infantil) shoe

pepenador -dora *m,f* (Méx) scavenger (*on garbage dumps*)

pepenar [A1] *vt* (Méx fam)
A 1 (recoger) to pick up; (en la basura) to scavenge 2 (agarrar) to grab hold of
B (sorprender) to catch

pepinazo *m* (fam) (choque) smash; **pegarse un ~** to have a smash

pepinillo *m* gherkin

pepino *m* cucumber; ▸**importar**

pepita *f* 1 (de uva) pip; (de tomate) seed; (de calabaza) (Méx) dried pumpkin seed 2 (de oro) nugget

pepitoria *f* (Esp): **pollo en ~** chicken in sauce with egg and almonds

pepón -pona *adj* (Per fam) (atractivo) good-looking

pepona *f* large doll

peppermint *m* créme de menthe

peque *mf* (fam) kid (colloq), little one (colloq)

pequeñajo¹ -ja *adj* (fam) tiny, small

pequeñajo² -ja *m,f* (fam) 1 (niño) kid (colloq) 2 (persona baja) midget (colloq)

pequeñez *f* 1 (de tamaño) smallness, small size; **~ de espíritu** pettiness 2 (menudencia) trifle, triviality

pequeñín¹ -ñina *adj* (fam) tiny, teeny-weeny (colloq)

pequeñín² -ñina *m,f* (fam) kid (colloq), little one (colloq)

pequeño¹ -ña *adj* 1 (de tamaño) small; **se me ha quedado ~** it's too small for me now; **en ~** in miniature 2 (de edad) young, small; **mi hermano ~** my younger *o* little brother; **de ~** *or* **cuando era ~** when I was small *o* little 3 (de poca importancia) ‹*distancia*› short; ‹*retraso*› short, slight; ‹*cantidad*› small; ‹*esfuerzo*› slight; **tienen sus pequeñas diferencias** they have their little differences; **un ~ problema** a slight *o* small problem

Compuestos
- **pequeña burguesía** *f* petite bourgeoisie
- **pequeña empresa** *f* small business
- **pequeña pantalla** *f*: **la ~ ~** the small screen (colloq), television
- **pequeño empresario -ria empresaria** (*m*) small businessperson, small businessman; (*f*) small businessperson, small businesswoman

pequeño² -ña *m,f* (tamaño) little one (colloq); (edad — de dos) younger (— de muchos) youngest; **es el ~ de la familia/de la clase** he's the baby of the family/the youngest in the class; **yo soy la pequeña** I'm the youngest

pequeñoburgués -guesa *adj/m,f* petit bourgeois

pera *f*
A (Bot) pear; ***pedirle ~s al olmo*** to ask the impossible; ***ser la ~*** (fam) to be the limit (colloq)
Compuesto **pera de agua** dessert pear
B 1 (de goma) bulb 2 (interruptor) switch 3 (Col) (para abrir, tirar, etc) ▸**perilla B**
C (en boxeo) punching ball (AmE), punchball (BrE)
D (CS fam) (mentón) chin; (barba) goatee

peral *m* pear tree

peralte *m* (en pista) banking; (en carretera) bank, cant

perborato *m* perborate

perca *f* perch

percal *m* percale; ***conocer(se) el ~*** (fam) to know the score (colloq)

percala *f* (Chi, Per) percale

percán *m* (Chi) mold*

percance *m* (contratiempo) mishap; (accidente) minor accident

per cápita *loc adj* per capita

percatarse [A1] *v pron* to notice; **~ DE algo** to notice sth; **¿te percataste de ese detalle?** did you notice *o* spot that detail?; **ni se percató de mi presencia** she didn't even notice *o* realize I was there; **no se percató de la gravedad de la situación** he failed to realize how serious the situation was

percebe *m* 1 (molusco) goose barnacle 2 (fam) (estúpido) twit (colloq)

percepción *f*
A (por los sentidos) perception
Compuesto **percepción extrasensorial** extrasensory perception, ESP
B (Fin) (cobro) receipt; (cantidad cobrada) payment

perceptible *adj*
A (por los sentidos) perceptible, noticeable
B (Fin) receivable

perceptivo -va *adj* perceptive

perceptor¹ -tora *adj* receiving (*before n*)

perceptor² -tora *m,f* recipient

percha *f*
A 1 (para el armario) (coat) hanger 2 (gancho) coat hook; (perchero) coat stand
B (figura): **tiene buena ~** she has a good figure
C (para aves) perch

perchero *m* (de pared) coat rack; (de pie) coat stand

percherón¹ -rona *adj* Percheron (*before n*)

percherón² -rona *m,f* Percheron, draft horse

percibir [I1] *vt*
A ‹*sonido/olor*› to perceive; **percibió el peligro** he sensed the danger
B (frml) ‹*sueldo/cantidad*› to receive

percudido -da *adj* (AmS) ingrained with dirt

percudirse [I1] *v pron* (AmS) to become ingrained with dirt

percusión *f* percussion

percutor, percusor *m* hammer

perdedor¹ -dora *adj* losing (*before n*)

perdedor² -dora *m,f* loser; **es un buen/mal ~** he's a good/bad loser

perder [E8] *vt*
A 1 (extraviar) ‹*llaves/documento/guante*› to lose 2 ‹*señal/imagen/contacto*› to lose
B (ser la ruina de): **lo perdió la curiosidad** his curiosity was his undoing *o* his downfall
C 1 ‹*dinero/propiedad/cosecha*› to lose; **con preguntar no se pierde nada** we've/you've nothing to lose by asking, there's no harm in asking; **más se perdió en la guerra** (fr hecha) it's not the end of the world 2 ‹*derecho/trabajo*› to lose 3 ‹*brazo/sangre/vista*› to lose; **el susto le hizo ~ el habla** the fright rendered him speechless; **~ la vida** to lose one's life, to perish; ▸**cabeza, vista² C 4** ‹*hijo/marido*› to lose
D 1 ‹*interés/entusiasmo/paciencia*› to lose; **no hay que ~ el ánimo** you mustn't lose heart; **yo no pierdo las esperanzas** I'm not giving up hope; **llegas tarde, para no ~ la costumbre** (iró) you're late, just for a change (iro); **~ la práctica/la costumbre** to get out of practice/the habit; **tienes que ~les el miedo a los aviones** you have to get over *o* to overcome your fear of flying; **~ el equilibrio** to lose one's balance; **~ el conocimiento** to lose consciousness, to pass out 2 ‹*fuerza/intensidad/calor/altura*› to lose; **~ el ritmo** (Mús) to lose the beat; (en trabajo) to get out of the rhythm 3 ‹*peso/kilos*› to lose
E 1 ‹*autobús/tren/avión*› to miss 2 ‹*ocasión/oportunidad*› to miss; **sin ~ detalle** without missing any detail 3 ‹*tiempo*› to waste; **¡no me hagas ~ (el) tiempo!** don't waste my time!; **no hay tiempo que ~** there's no time to lose; **no pierdas (el) tiempo intentándolo** don't waste your time trying; **llámalo sin ~ un minuto** call him immediately; **perdimos dos días por lo de la huelga** we lost two days because of the strike
F 1 ‹*guerra/pleito/partido*› to lose 2 ‹*curso/año*› to fail; ‹*examen*› (Ur) to fail
G ‹*agua/aceite/aire*› to lose

■ **perder** *vi*
A (ser derrotado) to lose; **no sabes ~** you're a bad loser; **perdieron 3 a 1** they lost 3-1; **llevar las de ~** to be onto a loser; **la que sale perdiendo soy yo** I'm the one who loses out *o* comes off worst
B 1 «*cafetera/tanque*» to leak 2 (RPl) «*color*» (aclararse) to fade
C **echar(se) a perder** *ver* **echar** *Sentido* **I A1, echarse** *Sentido* **I A1**

■ **perderse** *v pron*
A 1 (extraviarse) «*persona/objeto*» to get lost; (+ *me/te/le* etc) **se le perdió el dinero** he's lost the money; **que no se te pierda** don't lose it; **¿y a tí que se te ha perdido por allí?** whatever possessed you to go there; ***no hay por***

P

dónde* ~*se (Chi fam) there's no question about it 2 (desaparecer) to disappear; **se perdió entre la muchedumbre** she disappeared into the crowd 3 (en tema, conversación): **cuando se ponen a hablar rápido me pierdo** when they start talking quickly I get lost; **las cifras son tan enormes que uno se pierde** the figures are so huge that they start to lose all meaning; **empieza otra vez, ya me perdí** start again, you've lost me already 4 (en espacio): **los sillones se pierden en ese salón** the armchairs are rather lost in the sitting room
B ‹*fiesta/película/espectáculo*› to miss; **no te perdiste nada** you didn't miss anything
C «*persona*» 1 (acabar mal) to get into trouble, lose one's way (liter) 2 (Per fam) (prostituirse) to go on the streets (colloq)

perdición *f* ruin; **el alcohol será su** ~ drink will be his ruin *o* downfall *o* undoing; **el chocolate es mi** ~ I just can't resist chocolate

perdida *f* 1 (mujer inmoral) loose woman 2 (Chi, Méx) (prostituta) streetwalker

pérdida *f*
A (extravío) loss; ***no tiene*** ~ (Esp) you can't miss it
B 1 (Fin) loss; **el negocio no les deja sino ~s** the business is making a loss; **vender con** ~ to sell at a loss 2 (de memoria, vista, peso) loss; **tuvo una ~ de conocimiento** he lost consciousness, he passed out 3 (desperdicio) waste; **fue una ~ de tiempo** it was a waste of time 4 (defunción) loss; **la irreparable ~ sufrida por su familia** (frml) the irreparable loss suffered by her family

Compuestos
- **pérdidas humanas** *fpl* loss of life
- **pérdidas materiales** *fpl* damage
- **pérdidas y ganancias** *fpl* profit and loss

C (escape de gas, agua) leak
D (Chi euf) (aborto) miscarriage

perdidamente *adv*: ~ **enamorado** hopelessly in love

perdido[1] **-da** *adj*
A [ESTAR] 1 ‹*objeto/persona*› lost; ***dar algo por*** ~ to give sth up for lost; ***de*** ~ (Méx fam) at least 2 (confundido, desorientado) lost, confused; **estoy totalmente ~ en Inglés** I'm completely lost in English 3 ‹*bala/perro*› stray (*before n*)
B [ESTAR] (en un apuro): **si se enteran, estás** ~ if they find out, you've had it *o* you're done for (colloq)
C (aislado) ‹*lugar*› remote, isolated; ‹*momento*› idle, spare
D 1 ‹*idiota*› complete and utter (*before n*), total (*before n*); ‹*loco*› raving (*before n*); ‹*borracho*› out and out (*before n*) 2 (*como adv*) (totalmente) completely, totally
E (Esp fam) (sucio) filthy; **ponerse ~ DE algo** ‹*de aceite/barro*› to get covered with sth; **te has puesto ~ de aceite** you've got oil all over you

perdido[2] **-da** *m,f* degenerate

perdigón *m* (Arm) pellet; **perdigones** shot, pellets

perdigonada *f* (disparo) shot; (herida) pellet *o* shot wound

perdiguero -ra *m,f* gundog

perdiz *f* partridge; **y fueron felices y comieron perdices** (fr hecha) and they lived happily ever after

perdón[1] *m* (Der) pardon; (Relig) forgiveness; **le concedieron el** ~ he was pardoned; **me pidió ~ por su comportamiento** he apologized to me for his behavior, he said he was sorry about his behavior; ***con*** ~ if you'll pardon the expression; ***no tener ~ (de Dios)*** (acción) to be unforgivable; (persona): **no tienes ~ de Dios** what you've done is unforgivable

perdón[2] *interj* (tras encontronazo) I beg your pardon (frml), excuse me (AmE), sorry; (al iniciar conversación) excuse me, pardon me (AmE); (al pedir que se repita algo) sorry?, pardon me? (AmE); ~ **¿me puede decir la hora?** excuse me *o* (AmE) pardon me, can you tell me the time?; ~ **pero no estoy de acuerdo** I'm sorry but I don't agree

perdonar [A1] *vt* 1 (disculpar) ‹*persona/falta*› to forgive; **te perdono** I forgive you 2 (Der) to pardon 3 ‹*pecado*› to forgive 4 ‹*deuda*› to write off; ‹*castigo/obligación*›: **le perdonó el castigo/el dictado** she let him off the punishment/the dictation; **no le perdona ni una** she doesn't let him get away with anything 5 (en fórmulas de cortesía): **perdona mi curiosidad, pero ...** forgive *o* pardon my asking but ...; **perdonen las molestias que esto pueda causarles** we apologize for any inconvenience this may cause you; **perdone que lo moleste, pero ...** sorry to bother you *o* (AmE) pardon me for bothering you, but ...

■ **perdonar** *vi*: **perdone ¿me puede decir dónde está la estación?** excuse me *o* (AmE) pardon me, can you tell me where the station is?; **perdone ¿cómo ha dicho?** sorry? what did you say?, excuse *o* pardon me? what did you say? (AmE); **perdona ¿te he hecho daño?** (I'm) sorry, are you all right?, excuse me, are you all right? (AmE); **perdona, pero yo no dije eso** I'm sorry but that's not what I said

perdonavidas *mf* (*pl* ~) (fam) thug, tough (colloq)

perdurable *adj* ‹*recuerdo/relación*› lasting (*before n*); ‹*vida/amor*› everlasting

perdurar [A1] *vi* «*duda/sentimiento/recuerdo*» to remain, last; «*crisis/situación/relación*» to last; **perdura en nuestra memoria** he lives on in our memory

perecear [A1] *vi* (Col) to laze around

perecedero -ra *adj* ‹*producto/artículo*› perishable; ‹*ser*› mortal; ‹*vida*› transitory

perecer [E3] *vi* (frml) to die, perish (journ *or* liter); **pereció ahogado** he died by drowning

peregrinación *f*, **peregrinaje** *m* pilgrimage

peregrinar [A1] *vi* to make *o* go on a pilgrimage

peregrino[1] **-na** *adj*
A ‹*idea/respuesta*› outlandish, peculiar
B 1 ‹*ave*› migratory 2 ‹*monje*› wandering (*before n*)

peregrino[2] **-na** *m,f* pilgrim

perejil *m* (Bot, Coc) parsley

perenne *adj* 1 (Bot) ‹*planta*› perennial; **un árbol de hoja** ~ an evergreen (tree) 2 (constante) constant, perennial

perentorio -ria *adj* 1 ‹*tono/orden/mirada*› peremptory 2 (frml) ‹*necesidad*› urgent, compelling (frml) 3 ‹*plazo*› fixed, set

pereque *m* (Col fam) pain in the neck (colloq)

pereza *f* laziness; **me da ~ ir** I can't be bothered to go; **tengo una ~ horrible** I feel terribly lazy; **¡qué ~ tener que ir!** what a bind *o* drag having to go! (colloq)

perezosa *f* (Col, Per) deck chair

perezosamente *adv* lazily

perezoso[1] **-sa** *adj* lazy, idle, slothful (liter)

perezoso[2] **-sa** *m,f*
A (holgazán) lazybones (colloq)
B **perezoso** *m* (Zool) sloth

perfección *f* perfection; **habla francés a la** ~ she speaks perfect French

perfeccionamiento *m*: **un curso de** ~ an advanced course

perfeccionar [A1] *vt* (mejorar) to improve; (hacer perfecto) to perfect

perfeccionismo *m* perfectionism

perfeccionista *mf* perfectionist

perfectamente *adv* perfectly; **se encuentra** ~ he's absolutely fine *o* perfectly OK; **los dos sabían ~ que ...** they both knew perfectly well that ...

perfecto[1] **-ta** *adj* 1 (ideal, excelente) perfect; **en ~ estado de salud** in perfect health 2 (*delante del n*) (absoluto): **un ~ caballero** a perfect gentleman; **un ~ idiota** an absolute idiot; **es un ~ desconocido** he is completely unknown

perfecto[2] *interj* fine!

perfidia *f* (liter & hum) perfidy (liter), treachery

pérfido -da *adj* (liter & hum) perfidious (liter), treacherous

perfil *m*
A 1 (del cuerpo, la cara) profile; **una foto/un retrato de ~** a profile photograph/portrait; **visto de ~** seen from the side , if you look at it from the side; **un ~ griego** a Greek profile 2 (contorno, silueta) profile, silhouette
B (Arquit) cross section; (Tec) profile, longitudinal section
C (características) profile; **el ~ de la mujer moderna** the profile of the modern woman

perfilador *m* lip pencil

perfilar [A1] *vt* 1 ‹*plan/estrategia*› to shape 2 ‹*coche/avión*› to streamline

■ **perfilarse** *v pron* 1 «*silueta/contorno*» to be outlined; **las montañas se perfilaban a lo lejos** the mountains could be seen outlined in the distance 2 (tomar forma) «*posición/actitud*» to become clear; **se perfila como el**

P

próximo líder he is shaping up as *o* beginning to look like the next leader

perforación *f* 1 (Min) (acción) drilling, boring; (pozo) borehole 2 (en madera) drilling, boring 3 (Med) perforation 4 (en papeles, sellos) perforation

perforadora *f*
A (Min, Tec) drill
Compuesto **perforadora de percusión** hammer drill
B (de papeles) hole puncher; (de sellos) perforator

perforar [A1] *vt*
A 1 ‹*pozo*› to sink, drill, bore 2 ‹*madera*› to drill *o* bore holes/a hole in 3 «*ácido*» to perforate; «*bala*» to pierce; **la costilla le perforó el pulmón** the rib pierced *o* punctured her lung
B ‹*papel/tarjeta*› to perforate
■ **perforarse** *v pron* 1 «*úlcera/intestino*» to become perforated 2 (Tec) «*capa*» to rupture 3 (*caus*): **~se la nariz/las orejas** to have one's nose/ears pierced

performance /perfor'mans/ *f* (AmL period) performance

perfumador *m* atomizer

perfumar [A1] *vt* to perfume
■ **perfumarse** *v pron* (*refl*) to put perfume *o* scent on

perfume *m* perfume, scent

perfumería *f* (industria) perfume industry; (productos) perfumery; (tienda) perfumery, perfume store (*o* department *etc*)

perfumero *m* perfume spray

pergamino *m* (material) parchment; (documento) scroll; **un ~ egipcio** an Egyptian scroll

pergenio -nia *m,f* (CS fam) kid (colloq), squirt (colloq)

pérgola *f* pergola

pericia *f* (destreza) skill

pericial *adj* expert (*before n*)

perico *m* (Zool) parakeet; ***P~ (el) de los palotes*** anybody

pericote *m* (Chi, Per) large rat

periferia *f* 1 (de círculo) periphery, circumference 2 (de ciudad) outskirts (*pl*), periphery (frml) 3 (Inf) peripherals (*pl*)

periférico¹ -ca *adj* ‹*barrio/zona*› outlying (*before n*); **parques ~s** parks on the periphery *o* edge of the city

periférico² *m*
A (Inf) peripheral
B (AmC, Méx) (carretera) beltway (AmE), ring road (BrE)

perifollo *m* 1 (Bot) chervil 2 **perifollos** *mpl* (fam) (adornos) frills (*pl*), trimmings (*pl*)

perífrasis *f* (*pl* ~) periphrasis

perifrástico -ca *adj* periphrastic

perilla *f*
A (barba) goatee; ***venir de ~s*** (fam) to be very useful, come in very handy (colloq)
B (de puerta) doorknob; (de gaveta) knob

perímetro *m* perimeter; **dentro del ~ urbano** inside the city boundary, within the city limits

perimido -da *adj* (RPl) obsolete

periódicamente *adv* periodically

periodicidad *f* (Tec) periodicity

periódico¹ -ca *adj* periodic

periódico² *m* newspaper, paper
Compuesto **periódico dominical** *or* **del domingo** Sunday newspaper

periodiquero -ra *m,f* (Méx) news *o* newspaper vendor

periodismo *m* journalism
Compuesto **periodismo gráfico** photojournalism

periodista *mf* journalist, reporter; **los ~s** the journalists (*pl*), the press; **~ gráfico** press photographer

periodístico -ca *adj* ‹*estilo*› journalistic

período, periodo *m*
A 1 (de tiempo) period; **un ~ de tres meses** a three-month period 2 (Geol, Mat, Fís) period
B (menstruación) period

peripecia *f* 1 (incidente): **un viaje lleno de ~s** an eventful journey; **sus ~s en el extranjero** her adventures abroad 2 (problema) vicissitude

periplo *m* (period) (viaje) long journey, tour; (Náut) (long) voyage

peripuesto -ta *adj* (fam & hum) dressed up to the nines (colloq & hum)

periquete *m*: **vuelvo en un ~** (fam) I'll be back in a jiffy (colloq); **terminé en un ~** I finished it in no time

periquito *m* (americano) parakeet; (australiano) budgerigar, budgie (colloq)

periscopio *m* periscope

peritaje *m* 1 (informe) expert's report; (para el seguro) loss adjuster's report; (de casa) survey (report) 2 (inspección) inspection (*by an expert, a loss adjuster, etc*); (de casa) survey 3 (Educ) technical studies (*pl*)
Compuesto **peritaje industrial/mercantil** industrial/business studies (*pl*)

peritar [A1] *vt* to give an expert opinion on
■ **peritar** *vi* to give an expert opinion

perito¹ -ta *adj* expert; **ser ~ en algo** to be an expert on sth

perito² -ta *m,f* 1 (experto) expert 2 (en seguros) (loss) adjuster 3 (Der) expert witness
Compuestos
- **perito agrónomo -ta agrónoma** *m,f* agricultural technician
- **perito -ta industrial** *m,f* engineer
- **perito -ta mercantil** *m,f* qualified accountant

peritonitis *f* (*pl* ~) peritonitis

perjudicado¹ -da *adj*: **el que resultó ~** the one who lost out *o* who was worst hit; **los más ~s** the worst hit *o* the worst affected

perjudicado² -da *m,f*: **el ~ fui yo** I was the one who lost out

perjudicar [A2] *vt* 1 (dañar) to be detrimental to (frml); **el tabaco perjudica tu salud** smoking damages your health; **está perjudicando sus estudios** it is having an adverse effect on *o* it is proving detrimental to his schoolwork; **estas medidas perjudican a los jóvenes** these measures are prejudicial to *o* harm young people 2 (Col, Per fam & euf) (violar) to rape, have one's way with (euph)

perjudicial *adj* damaging, harmful, detrimental (frml); **el alcohol es ~ para la salud** alcohol is damaging *o* detrimental to your health; **esta sequía es ~ para el campo** this drought is bad for agriculture

perjuicio *m* 1 (daño) damage; **causó grave ~ a su reputación** it caused serious damage to his reputation; **esto le reportará a la empresa un gran ~** this will prove very damaging for the company; **no sufrió ningún ~** it did him no harm *o* damage 2 **en perjuicio de** (frml): **redunda** *o* **va en ~ de todos** it works against *o* is detrimental to everyone 3 **sin perjuicio**: **sin ~ para su salud** without detriment to his health (frml); **sin ~ de los derechos establecidos por la ley** without affecting your statutory rights

perjurar [A1] *vi* to perjure oneself, commit perjury
■ **perjurar** *vt* to swear; **juró y perjuró que no sabía nada** he swore up and down (AmE) *o* (BrE) blind that he knew nothing (colloq)

perjurio *m* perjury

perjuro¹ -ra *adj* perjured

perjuro² -ra *m,f* perjurer

perla¹ *f* (joya) pearl; ***de ~s*** (fam): **me vendría de ~s** it would suit me down to the ground; **marcha de ~s** it's going really well; **todo salió de ~s** everything went perfectly *o* (colloq) fine
Compuestos
- **perla artificial** artificial pearl
- **perla cultivada** *or* **de cultivo** cultured pearl
- **perla natural** *or* **verdadera** natural pearl

perla² *mf* 1 (fam) (persona ideal) gem (colloq) 2 (Chi fam) (fresco) sassy (AmE) *o* (BrE) cheeky devil (colloq)

perlado -da *adj* pearl (*before n*), pearled

perlero -ra, **perlífero -ra** *adj* pearl (*before n*)

permanecer [E3] *vi* (frml) 1 (en lugar) to stay, remain (frml) 2 (en actitud, estado) to remain; **permaneció en silencio** he was *o* remained silent

permanencia *f* (en lugar) stay; (en organización, cargo) continuance (frml)

P

permanente[1] *adj* permanent; **servicio ~ de información** 24-hour information service

permanente[2] *f*

A (en el pelo) perm; **hacerse la ~** to have one's hair permed, to have a perm

B (Col) (juzgado) emergency court (*for cases of violent crime*)

permanganato *m* permanganate

permeabilidad *f* permeability

permeable *adj* ‹*material*› permeable

permisible *adj* permissible

permisionario -ria *m,f* (Méx) concessionaire, official agent

permisividad *f* permissiveness

permisivo -va *adj* permissive

permiso *m*

A (autorización) permission; **me dio ~** she gave me permission; **con ~ del jefe** with the boss's permission, with permission from the boss; **(con) permiso** (al abrirse paso) excuse me; (al entrar) may I come in?; **con su ~, tengo que irme** if you'll excuse me, I have to go

B (días libres) leave; **un ~ de tres días** three days' leave; **de ~** on leave

C (documento) permit, license*

(Compuestos)

- **permiso de conducir** driver's license (AmE), driving licence (BrE)
- **permiso de obras** building permit
- **permiso de exportación/de importación** export/import permit *o* license*
- **permiso de residencia** residence permit, green card (AmE)
- **permiso de trabajo** work permit

permitir [I1] *vt* 1 (autorizar) to allow, permit (frml); **no van a ~les la entrada** they're not going to let them in; **no le permitieron ver a su esposa** he was not allowed to see his wife; Ⓢ **no se permite la entrada a personas ajenas a la empresa** staff only, no entry to unauthorized persons; **¿me permite?** (frml) may I?; **¿me permite la palabra?** may I say something?; **los indicios permiten hablar de una conspiración** the signs point to *o* indicate a conspiracy 2 (tolerar, consentir): **no te permito que me hables así** I won't have you talking to me like that; **no ~emos ninguna injerencia** we will not allow anyone to interfere; **permítame que le diga que...** with all due respect *o* if you don't mind me saying so...; **si se me permite la expresión** if you'll pardon the expression 3 (hacer posible) to make ... possible; **esto permite detectar la enfermedad** this makes it possible to detect the disease; **si el tiempo lo permite** weather permitting

■ **permitirse** *v pron* (*refl*): **puede ~se ese lujo** she can allow herself that luxury; **no puedo ~me tantos gastos** I can't afford to spend so much money; **me permito dirigirme a Vd para ...** (Corresp) I am writing to you to ...; **se permite muchas confianzas con el jefe** he's very familiar with the boss

permuta *f* exchange

permutable *adj* exchangeable

permutación *f* permutation

permutar [A1] *vt* 1 (intercambiar) ‹*bienes*› to exchange, swap; ‹*puesto*› to exchange 2 (Mat) to permute

pernera *f* (del pantalón) leg

pernicioso -sa *adj* pernicious (frml)

pernil *m* (de animal) upper leg, haunch; (de cerdo) ham

perno *m* (tornillo) bolt

pernoctar [A1] *vi* (frml) to stay overnight, stay the night

pero[1] *conj*

A but; **ella fue, ~ yo no** she went, but I didn't

B 1 (en expresiones de protesta, sorpresa): **¿~ tú estás loca?** are you crazy?; **~ bueno ... ¿vienes o no?** for goodness sake, are you coming or not?; **¡~ si me lo prometiste!** but you promised!; **¡~ si es Marta!** hey, it's Marta!; **¡~ si queda lejísimos!** but it's miles (away)! 2 (uso enfático): **no me hizo caso, ~ ningún caso** she didn't take the slightest notice (colloq), she didn't take any notice, none whatsoever; **la película está ~ que muy bien** it's a very good movie indeed

pero[2] *m* 1 (defecto) defect, bad point; (dificultad, problema) drawback; ***ponerle ~s a algo/algn*** to find fault with sth/sb 2 (excusa) objection; **no admito ~s** I won't stand for any 'ifs' or 'buts'; ***¡no hay ~ que valga!*** I don't want any excuses (*o* arguments *etc*)

perogrullada *f* (fam) platitude, truism

Perogrullo *m*: **ser de ~** to be patently obvious

perol *m* (pequeño) saucepan; (grande) pot

peroné *m* fibula

peronismo *m* Peronism

> **peronismo**
>
> A political movement, known officially as *justicialismo*, named for the populist politician Colonel Juan Domingo Perón, elected President of Argentina in 1946. An admirer of Italian fascism, Perón claimed always to be a champion of the workers and the poor, the *descamisados* (shirtless ones), to whom his first wife Eva Duarte ('Evita') became a sort of icon, especially after her death in 1952. Although he instituted some social reforms, Perón's regime proved increasingly repressive and he was ousted in an army coup in 1955. He returned from exile to become president again in 1973, but died in office a year later. His *Partido Justicialista* governed Argentina won the 2007 elections led by Cristina Fernández Kirchner

peronista *adj/mf* Peronist

perorar [A1] *vi* (fam) to hold forth

perorata *f* (fam) lecture (colloq); **nos echó una ~** she gave us a lecture

peróxido *m* peroxide

perpendicular *adj/mf* perpendicular

perpetrar [A1] *vt* to perpetrate (frml), to carry out

perpetuación *f* perpetuation

perpetuar [A18] *vt* to perpetuate

perpetuidad *f* perpetuity; **a ~** in perpetuity

perpetuo -tua *adj* perpetual

perplejidad *f* perplexity, puzzlement

perplejo -ja *adj* perplexed, puzzled; **estar ~ con algo** to be puzzled *o* perplexed by sth

perra *f*

A (Zool) dog, bitch [**bitch** *sólo se emplea cuando se quiere hacer referencia al sexo del animal*] *ver tb* **perro**[2]

B (Esp fam) (moneda) coin; **una ~** a penny (colloq); **unas ~s** a few bucks (AmE) *o* (BrE) quid (colloq); ***costar/valer cuatro ~s*** (fam) to cost/to be worth next to nothing (colloq)

(Compuesto) **perra chica/gorda** (fam) (Hist) five/ten centimo coin

C (Esp fam) 1 (rabieta) tantrum; **coger una ~** to have *o* throw a tantrum 2 (manía) obsession; **le ha dado la ~ de tener uno** he's obsessed with having one

D (Esp vulg) (prostituta) bitch

perrada *f* (AmL fam) dirty trick

perramus *m* (*pl* ~) (Bol, RPl ant) raincoat

perrera *f* 1 (lugar) dog pound, dog's home 2 (vehículo) dog catcher's van

perrería *f* 1 (fam) (acto) terrible thing (colloq); **le hacen ~s al gato** they torment the cat mercilessly 2 (insulto) terrible thing (colloq)

perrero -ra *m,f* dog catcher, dog warden (BrE)

perrito *m*

A (Zool) little dog; **nadar estilo ~** *or* (Méx) **nadar de ~** to do the dog paddle *o* the doggie-paddle (colloq)

(Compuesto) **perrito caliente** hot dog

B (AmL) (Bot) snapdragon

perro[1] **-rra** *adj* 1 (fam) ‹*vida/suerte*› rotten (colloq), lousy (colloq) 2 ‹*persona*› nasty

perro[2] **-rra** *m,f*

A (Zool) dog; Ⓢ **¡cuidado con el perro!** beware of the dog; ***a otro ~ con ese hueso*** (fam) go tell it to the marines! (AmE colloq), pull the other one! (BrE colloq); ***atar ~s con longaniza*** (fam) to have money to burn (colloq); ***como ~ en cancha de bochas*** (RPl fam & hum): **andar más perdido que ~ en cancha de bochas** to be like a fish out of water; **me tuvieron todo el día como ~ en cancha de bochas** they had me rushing around from pillar to post all day long (colloq); ***como un ~*** (fam): **terminó sus días como un ~** he ended his days in the gutter; **me dejó**

P

tirado como un ~ she abandoned me as if I were a stray dog; ***de ~s*** (fam) foul; **hace un tiempo de ~s** the weather's foul *o* horrible; **está de un humor de ~s** he's in a foul mood; ***echarle los ~s a algn*** (fam) (para ahuyentar) to set the dogs on sb; (recibir muy mal) to give sb a hostile reception (colloq); ***es el mismo ~ con diferente collar*** nothing has really changed, it's the same people (*o* regime *etc*) under a different name; ***estar meado de ~s*** (CS fam) to be plagued *o* dogged by bad luck; ***hacer ~ muerto*** (Chi fam) to do a runner (colloq); ***llevarse como (el) ~ y (el) gato*** to fight like cats and dogs (AmE) *o* (BrE) cat and dog; ***meterle a algn el ~*** (RPl fam) to con sb (colloq); ***no tener ni ~ que le ladre*** (fam) to be all alone in the world; ***~ no come ~*** (Col fam) there is honor* among thieves; ***ser como el ~ del hortelano (que ni come ni deja comer al amo)*** to be a dog in the manger; ***ser ~ viejo*** to be a wily *o* shrewd old bird (colloq); ***tratar a algn como a un ~*** to treat sb like dirt; ***a ~ flaco todo son pulgas*** it never rains but it pours; ***~ que ladra no muerde*** *or* (Esp) ***~ ladrador, poco mordedor*** his/her bark's worse than his/her bite

(Compuestos)
- **perro callejero** stray (dog)
- **perro de caza** gundog
- **perro de compañía** pet dog
- **perro de lanas** poodle
- **perro de presa** bulldog
- **perro esquimal** husky
- **perro guardián** guard dog
- **perro guía** *or* **lazarillo** guide dog
- **perro lobo** German shepherd, Alsatian (BrE)
- **perro pastor** sheepdog
- **perro pequinés** *or* **pekinés** Pekinese
- **perro** *or* **perrito caliente** (Coc) hot dog
- **perro** *or* **perrito faldero** lapdog
- **perro policía** *or* (Chi) **policial** German shepherd, Alsatian (BrE)
- **perro rastreador** (para seguir huellas) tracker dog; (para buscar drogas) sniffer dog
- **perro salchicha** dachshund, sausage dog (colloq)

B (persona) tyrant

perruno -na *adj* (fam) (del perro) dog (*before n*); (parecido al perro) doglike

persa¹ *adj/mf* Persian

persa² *m* (idioma) Persian

per saecula saeculorum *loc adv* until the end of time, for ever and ever

per se *loc adv* (frml) per se (frml)

persecución *f* [1] (en sentido físico) pursuit; **salir en ~ de algn** to set off in pursuit of sb [2] (por la ideología) persecution; **ser objeto de** *or* **sufrir persecuciones** to be subjected to persecution, to be persecuted

per sécula seculórum *loc adv* ▸ **per saecula saeculorum**

persecutorio -ria *adj* ‹*régimen*› persecutory

perseguidor -dora *m,f* (en sentido físico) pursuer; (por ideología) persecutor

perseguir [I30] *vt*

A [1] ‹*fugitivo/delincuente/presa*› to pursue, chase [2] (por la ideología) to persecute

B [1] ‹*objetivo/fin*› to pursue; **~ la fama** to be in pursuit of fame; **la finalidad que se persigue es ...** the ultimate aim is ...; **no sé qué persigues con esa actitud** I don't know what you're hoping to achieve with that attitude [2] (acosar): **me persigue para que le preste el coche** he's always pestering me to lend him the car (colloq); **la han estado persiguiendo hasta conseguir que trabaje para ellos** they've been pursuing her until they've managed to get her to work for them; **me persigue la mala suerte** I'm dogged by bad luck; **lo persiguen las enfermedades** he's be plagued by illness

perseverancia *f* perseverance, persistence

perseverante *adj* persevering, persistent

perseverar [A1] *vi* to persevere; **~ EN algo: perseveró en los entrenamientos** he persevered with his training; **si perseveras en esa actitud...** if you carry on with *o* persist with that attitude...; ***persevera y triunfarás*** if at first you don't succeed, try, try again

Persia *f* Persia

persiana *f* [1] (que se enrolla o levanta) blind; ***enrollarse como una ~*** (Esp fam) to go on and on [2] (AmL) (contraventana, postigo) shutter

(Compuesto) **persiana veneciana** *or* **de lamas** Venetian blind

persignarse [A1] *v pron* to cross oneself

persistencia *f* persistence

persistente *adj* persistent

persistir [I1] *vi*: **persiste el temporal** there is still a storm blowing; **~ EN algo** to persist IN sth

persona *f*

A [1] (ser humano) person; **una ~ muy educada** a very polite person; **había tres ~s** there were three people; **Ⓢ carga máxima: ocho personas** maximum capacity: eight persons; **¿cuántas ~s tiene a su cargo?** how many people do you have reporting to you?; **en su ~ se concentra todo el poder** all the power resides in him; **las ~s interesadas ...** all those interested ... [2] (*en locs*) **de persona a persona** person to person; **en persona** ‹*ir/presentarse*› in person; **la tarea recayó en la ~ de ...** the task was allocated to ...; **no lo conozco en ~** I don't know him personally; **es el orden en ~** he is orderliness personified; **por persona**: **20 dólares por ~** 20 dollars a head; **sólo se venden dos entradas por ~** you can only get two tickets per person

(Compuestos)
- **persona física** individual
- **persona jurídica** legal entity
- **persona no** *or* **non grata** persona non grata

B (Ling) person; **la primera ~ del singular** the first person singular

personaje *m* [1] (Cin, Lit) character [2] (persona importante) important figure, personage (frml); **un ~ de la política** an important political figure; **~s del mundo del teatro** celebrities from the world of theater; **es todo un ~** (fam) he's a real big shot (colloq)

personal¹ *adj* personal; **objetos de uso ~** personal effects

personal² *m* [1] (de fábrica, empresa) personnel (*pl*), staff (*sing or pl*); **estamos escasos de ~** we're short-staffed [2] (Esp fam & hum) (gente) people

(Compuestos)
- **personal de cabina/de tierra/de vuelo** cabin/ground/flight staff *o* crew
- **personal de maestranza** (Arg) staff (*of a building*)

personalidad *f* [1] (Psic) personality [2] (persona importante) ▸ **personaje 2**

(Compuesto) **personalidad jurídica** legal status

personalismo *m* [1] (favoritismo) favoritism*, partiality [2] (protagonismo) personal ambition [3] **personalismos** *mpl* (ofensas) personal remarks (*o* attacks *etc*) (*pl*)

personalista *adj*: **luchas ~s** personal rivalries

personalizado -da *adj* ‹*servicio*› personalized; **plan ~ de ahorro** personal savings plan

personalizar [A4] *vi*: **no quiero ~** I don't want to name names *o* mention any names

■ **personalizar** *vt* to personalize

personalmente *adv* personally; **me encargaré ~ de enviárselo** I'll send it to him personally *o* myself

personarse [A1] *v pron* [1] (frml) (en un lugar): **la policía se personó en el lugar del accidente** the police arrived at the scene of the accident; **se ruega al Sr González se persone en recepción** will Mr González please go to the front desk [2] (Esp) (Der) to appear in court

personería *f* (Col, RPl) legal capacity

(Compuestos)
- **personería gremial** (Col, RPl) legal recognition (*of a trade union*)
- **personería jurídica** (Col, RPl) legal status

personero -ra *m,f* (AmL) (representante) representative; (portavoz) (*m*) spokesman, spokesperson; (*f*) spokeswoman, spokesperson

personificación *f* [1] (encarnación) embodiment, personification; **es la ~ de la impaciencia** he is impatience personified [2] (Lit) personification

personificar [A2] *vt* to personify; **Otelo personifica los celos** Othello is the personification of jealousy; **es la**

p

bondad personificada she is kindness itself

perspectiva *f* 1 (Arquit, Art) perspective; **en ~** in perspective 2 (vista, paisaje) view, perspective (frml) 3 (punto de vista) perspective 4 (posibilidad) prospect; **las ~s son buenas** the prospects are *o* the outlook is very good; **una ~ poco halagüeña** not a very promising outlook; **ante la ~ de...** faced with the prospect of...; **no tengo ningún plan en ~** I've no plans for the immediate future

perspicacia *f* shrewdness, insight

perspicaz *adj* shrewd, perceptive

persuadir [I1] *vt* to persuade; **la persuadieron con promesas** she was won over with promises; **~ a algn DE QUE** *or* **PARA QUE + SUBJ** to persuade sb to + INF

■ **persuadirse** *v pron*: **no se persuadió** he wasn't convinced; **~se DE algo** to become convinced OF sth

persuasión *f* persuasion; **el poder de ~ de la publicidad** the persuasive power of advertising

persuasivo -va *adj* persuasive

pertenecer [E3] *vi* 1 (ser propiedad) **~ A algn** to belong TO sb 2 (formar parte) **~ A algo** to belong TO sth, be a member OF sth

perteneciente *adj*: **los países ~s al grupo** the countries belonging to *o* which are members of the group

pertenencia *f*

A 1 (a grupo, organización) membership 2 (frml) (propiedad): **los objetos de su ~** his belongings; **ese reloj es de mi ~** (hum) that watch is mine 3 **pertenencias** *fpl* belongings (*pl*), possessions (*pl*)

B (Chi) (Min) mineral rights (*pl*)

pértiga *f* 1 (vara pole 2 (Esp) (Dep) pole; **salto con ~** pole vault

pertinaz *adj* (frml) 1 (persistente) ‹*sequía*› prolonged; ‹*tos*› persistent 2 (obstinado) obstinate

pertinencia *f* 1 (lo adecuado) appropriateness 2 (relevancia) pertinence, relevance

pertinente *adj* 1 (oportuno, adecuado) ‹*medida*› appropriate; **es ~ recordar que ...** one should bear in mind that ... 2 (relevante) ‹*observación/comentario*› relevant, pertinent; **en lo ~ a** with regard to

pertrechar [A1] *vt* 1 (Mil) to equip, supply ... with military equipment; **guerrilleros pertrechados** well-equipped guerrillas 2 (proveer) to equip, supply

■ **pertrecharse** *v pron* **~se DE** *or* **CON algo** to equip oneself WITH sth

pertrechos *mpl* 1 (Mil) military equipment, military supplies (*pl*) 2 (equipo, utensilios) tackle, gear

perturbación *f* (alteración) disruption; (Psic) disturbance

(Compuestos)

- **perturbación atmosférica** atmospheric disturbance
- **perturbación del orden público** breach of the peace

perturbado¹ -da *adj* disturbed; **tiene perturbadas las facultades mentales** he is mentally disturbed

perturbado² -da *m,f*: *tb* **~ mental** mentally disturbed person

perturbador -dora *adj* 1 (inquietante) ‹*síntomas/comentarios/cifras*› disturbing, perturbing; ‹*belleza*› disquieting (liter) 2 (revoltoso) disruptive

perturbar [A1] *vt* 1 ‹*calma*› to disturb; ‹*orden*› to disrupt; **~ la marcha de algo** to disrupt the progress of sth 2 (Psic) to disturb

Perú *m*: *tb* **el ~** Peru; ***valer un ~*** «*persona*» to be worth one's weight in gold; «*cosa*» to cost a fortune

peruanismo *m* Peruvianism, Peruvian word/expression

peruano -na *adj/m,f* Peruvian

perversidad *f* (depravación) depravity; (maldad) wickedness

perversión *f* 1 (maldad) evil, wickedness 2 (corrupción) perversion; **un antro de ~** a den of iniquity; **~ sexual** sexual perversion

perverso¹ -sa *adj* evil

perverso² -sa *m,f* evil *o* wicked person

pervertido -da *m,f* pervert

pervertidor -dora *m,f* corruptor

pervertir [I11] *vt* to corrupt, pervert

■ **pervertirse** *v pron* to become corrupted

pervinca *f* periwinkle

pervivencia *f* survival

pervivir [I1] *vi* to survive, remain

pesa *f* 1 (de balanza, reloj) weight 2 (Dep) (grande) weight; (pequeña) dumbbell; **levantamiento de ~s** weight lifting; ***hacer ~s*** to do weight training 3 (balanza) scales (*pl*)

pesadamente *adv* 1 ‹*caer*› heavily; **se dejó caer ~ en el sillón** he slumped into the armchair 2 ‹*caminar/moverse*› slowly, heavily

pesadez *f*

A (fam) (aburrimiento, molestia) drag (colloq); **¡qué ~ de conversación!** what a boring conversation!

B (sensación de cansancio) heaviness; **tengo ~ en las piernas** my legs feel very heavy; **~ de estómago** bloated *o* heavy feeling in the stomach

C (Andes fam) (broma) tiresome joke; (comentario) nasty remark

pesadilla *f* 1 (sueño) nightmare, bad dream 2 (situación) nightmare

pesado¹ -da *adj*

A 1 ‹*paquete/artillería/maquinaria*› heavy 2 ‹*comida*› heavy, stodgy (colloq); ‹*estómago*› bloated; **me siento ~** I feel bloated 3 ‹*atmósfera/tiempo*› heavy, oppressive 4 ‹*ojos/cabeza*› heavy; **tengo las piernas pesadas** my legs feel very heavy 5 ‹*sueño*› deep

B (fam) (fastidioso, aburrido) 1 ‹*libro/película/trabajo*› tedious; **la conferencia me resultó un poco ~** I found the lecture rather heavy going 2 ‹*persona*›: **¡qué ~ es!** he's such a pain in the neck! (colloq); **¡qué ~, nunca no me deja en paz!** he's such a pest, he never leaves me alone (colloq); **no te pongas ~** don't be so annoying *o* (colloq) such a pest!

C (Andes fam) (antipático) unpleasant; **¡qué tipo tan ~!** what a jerk! (colloq)

pesado² -da *m,f* 1 (fam) (latoso) pain (colloq), pest (colloq) 2 (Andes fam) (antipático) jerk (colloq)

pesadumbre *f* grief, sorrow

pésame *m* condolences (*pl*); **darle el ~ a algn** to offer sb one's condolences; **mi más sentido ~** (fr hecha) my deepest sympathies

pesar¹ *m*

A 1 (pena, tristeza) sorrow; **me expresó su ~** she expressed her sorrow; **a ~ mío** *or* **muy a mi ~** much to my regret; **con ~** sorrowfully, with a heavy heart 2 (remordimiento) regret, remorse; **no siente ningún ~** he feels no remorse

B **a pesar de** despite; **a ~ de su enfermedad/de estar enfermo** despite *o* in spite of being ill; **a ~ de todo** in spite of *o* despite everything; **a ~ de los ~es** (fam) in spite of everything; **a ~ de que no sabía mucho inglés...** despite not knowing much English ...; **se lo llevó, a ~ de que yo se lo había prohibido** he took it, despite the fact that *o* even though I had forbidden him to

pesar² [A1] *vi*

A 1 «*paquete/maleta*» to be heavy; **¡cómo pesa!** it's terribly heavy!, it weighs a ton! (colloq); **estas gafas no pesan** these glasses don't weigh much; **no me pesa** it's not heavy 2 (ser una carga): **ya me pesan los años** I feel my age now; **le pesan todas esas cargas familiares** he's weighed down by all those family reponsibilities; **~ SOBRE algn/algo**: **toda la responsabilidad pesa sobre él** all the responsibility falls on his shoulders *o* on him; **la hipoteca que pesa sobre la casa** the mortgage on the house 3 (influir): **su influencia sigue pesando en la región** their influence continues to carry weight in the region; **ha pesado más su personalidad que su ideología** her personality has been more of a factor than her ideology

B (causar arrepentimiento) (+ *me/te/le etc*): **ahora me pesa mucho** now I deeply regret it; **ya te ~á no haber estudiado** you'll be sorry you didn't study, you'll regret not studying; **me pesa haberlo ofendido** I'm very sorry I offended him

C **pese a** despite, in spite of; **pese a todo, creo que su trabajo es el mejor** despite *o* in spite of everything, I still think her work is the best; **firmó pese a no estar de acuerdo** she signed even though she did not agree; **pese a que** even though; **pese a quien (le) pese** no matter who I *o* you, *etc* have to upset, no matter whose toes I *o* you, *etc* have to tread on; **mal que me/le pese** whether I like/he likes it or not

P

■ **pesar** *vt* 1 ‹*niño/maleta*› to weigh; ‹*manzanas*› to weigh (out) 2 (tener cierto peso) to weigh; **pesa 80 kilos** he weighs 80 kilos

■ **pesarse** *v pron* (*refl*) to weigh oneself

pesaroso -sa *adj* (triste) sad, sorrowful; (arrepentido) sorry

pesca *f* 1 (acción) fishing; **la ~ del atún** tuna fishing; **ir** *or* **salir de ~** to go fishing; **~ con caña** angling; **~ con red** net fishing 2 (peces) fish (*pl*); **aquí hay mucha ~** there are a lot of fish here 3 (lo pescado): **hoy hubo buena ~** the fishing was good today; ***y toda la ~*** (fam & hum): **la madre, la prima y toda la ~** her mother, her cousin, the whole lot *o* (AmE) bunch

Compuestos
- **pesca de altura/bajura** deep-sea/coastal fishing
- **pesca de arrastre** trawling
- **pesca submarina** underwater fishing

pescada *f* hake

pescadería *f* fish shop, fishmonger's (BrE)

pescadero -ra *m,f* fish dealer (AmE), fishmonger (BrE)

pescadilla *f* whiting, young hake

pescado *m* (Coc) fish; (pez) (AmL) fish

Compuesto **pescado azul/blanco** blue/white fish

pescador -dora (*m*) fisherman; (*f*) fisherwoman

pescante *m* 1 (de carruaje) driver's *o* coachman's seat 2 (Náut) davit 3 (Teatr) hoist

pescar [A2] *vt*

A ‹*trucha/corvina*› to catch; **no pescamos nada** we didn't catch anything; **fuimos a ~ trucha(s)** we went trout-fishing, we went fishing for trout

B (fam) 1 ‹*catarro/gripe*› to catch; **así ~ás una pulmonía** you'll catch your death if you go out like that (colloq) 2 ‹*novio/marido*› to get, hook (colloq & hum) 3 ‹*chiste/broma*› to get (colloq); **no pescas ni una** you're so slow on the uptake 4 (pillar) to catch; **lo ~on robando** they caught him red-handed (as he was stealing something); **la pesqué en una mentira** I caught her lying

■ **pescar** *vi* to fish; **~ a mosca** to fly-fish

■ **pescarse** *v pron* (*enf*) (fam) ‹*catarro*› to catch, get

pescozón *m* (fam) slap on the neck

pescuezo *m* (fam) neck; ***retorcerle el ~ a algn*** to wring sb's neck (colloq)

pese a *loc prep ver* **pesar² C**

pesebre *m* (en establo) manger, trough; (de Navidad) crib

pesebrera *f* (Col) stable

pesero *m* (Méx) minibus

peseta *f* peseta (*former Spanish unit of currency*)

pesetero -ra *adj* (Esp fam) money-grubbing (colloq)

pésimamente *adv* terribly, dreadfully

pesimismo *m* pessimism

pesimista¹ *adj* pessimistic

pesimista² *mf* pessimist

pésimo¹ -ma *adj* dreadful, terrible, abysmal

pésimo² *adv* ‹*jugar*› terribly; **canta ~** she has a terrible voice

pesista *mf* (Andes) weight lifter

peso *m*

A 1 (Fís, Tec) weight; **perder/ganar ~** to lose weight/gain *o* put on weight; ***tomarle el ~ a algo*** to weigh sth up; ***valer su ~ en oro*** to be worth one's weight in gold; ▸**caerse** 2 **al peso** by weight

Compuestos
- **peso bruto/neto** gross/net weight
- **peso específico** (Fís, Quím) specific gravity
- **peso muerto** deadweight

B 1 (carga) weight, burden; **lleva todo el ~ de la empresa** he carries all the burden of responsibility for the company; ***quitarle un ~ de encima a algn*** to take a load *o* a weight off sb's mind; **me he quitado un buen ~ de encima** that's a real load *o* weight off my mind 2 (influencia) weight; **las asociaciones de mayor ~** the most important associations, the associations which carry the most weight; **todo el ~ de la ley** the full weight of the law 3 **de peso** ‹*argumento*› strong, weighty; ‹*razón*› forceful

C (Dep) 1 (Esp) (en atletismo) shot; **lanzamiento de ~** shot-put, shot-putting 2 (Esp) (en halterofilia) weight; **levantamiento de ~s** weightlifting 3 (en boxeo) weight

Compuestos
- **peso gallo** bantamweight
- **peso ligero** lightweight
- **peso medio** middleweight
- **peso mosca** flyweight
- **peso pesado** (Dep) heavyweight; **un ~ ~ de la política** a political heavyweight
- **peso pluma** featherweight
- **peso welter** welterweight

D (báscula) scales (*pl*); (de balanza) (Chi) weight

E (Fin) peso (*unit of currency in many Latin American countries*); **no tiene un ~** he doesn't have a cent *o* penny

pespunte *m* backstitch

pespuntear [A1] *vt* to backstitch

pesquería *f* (CS, Per) (pesca) fishing; (compañía) fishery; (industria) fishing industry; (lugar) fishing ground, fishery

pesquero¹ -ra *adj* fishing (*before n*)

pesquero² *m* fishing boat

pesquis *m* (fam) common sense

pesquisa *f* investigation, inquiry

pestaña *f* 1 (Anat) eyelash; **~s postizas** false eyelashes; ***quemarse*** *or* ***dejarse las ~s*** (fam) to burn the midnight oil 2 (de libro) thumb index 3 (Mec) flange

pestañada, pestañeada *f* (Chi) blink; ***de una ~*** (Chi fam) in a jiffy (colloq), in a tick (BrE colloq); ***echarse*** *or* ***pegarse una ~*** (Chi fam) to have forty winks (colloq)

pestañear [A1] *vi* to blink; ***sin ~*** (literal) without blinking; (sin inmutarse) without batting an eyelash (AmE) *o* (BrE) eyelid

pestañeo *m* blinking

pestañina *f* (Col) mascara

pestazo *m* (fam) stink, stench

peste *f* 1 (Med, Vet) plague, epidemic; ***decir*** *or* ***echar*** *or* ***hablar ~s de algn*** (fam) to run sb down (colloq), to slag sb off (BrE colloq); ***huirle a algn/algo como a la ~*** (fam) to avoid sb/sth like the plague; ***ser la ~*** (fam) to be a nuisance 2 (AmL fam) (enfermedad contagiosa) bug (colloq); (resfriado) cold 3 (fam) (mal olor) stink

Compuestos
- **peste bovina** rinderpest
- **peste bubónica** bubonic plague
- **peste cristal** (Chi) chickenpox
- **peste negra** Black Death
- **peste porcina** hog cholera (AmE), swine fever (BrE)

pesticida *m* pesticide

pestilencia *f* 1 (olor) stench 2 (plaga) plague, pestilence (liter)

pestilente *adj* ‹*olor*› foul

pestillo *m* (cerrojo) bolt; (de cerradura) latch, catch; **echó** *or* **corrió el ~** she put the bolt across

pesto *m* (Coc) pesto (sauce)

petaca *f*

A 1 (cigarrera) cigarette case; (estuche de tabaco — de cuero) tobacco pouch; (— de metal) tobacco tin; ***hacerle la ~ a algn*** to short sheet sb (AmE), to make sb an apple-pie bed (BrE colloq) 2 (para bebidas alcohólicas) hipflask 3 (Méx) (maleta) suitcase 4 (Ur) (polvera) compact

B **petacas** *fpl* (Méx fam) (nalgas) butt (esp AmE colloq), bum (BrE colloq)

petacón -cona *adj* 1 (RPl fam) (gordito) dumpy (colloq), plump (colloq) 2 (Méx fam) (de nalgas grandes) broad in the beam (colloq)

pétalo *m* petal

petanca *f* petanque

petaquearse [A1] *v pron* (Col fam) to mess up (colloq)

petar [A1] *vi* (Esp fam): **no me peta** I don't feel like it

petardazo *m* (fam) bang (*of a firecracker*)

petardo *m* 1 (cohete) firecracker, banger (BrE); (Mil) petard 2 (fam) (pesado) pain in the neck (colloq)

petate *m*

A (Mil) (para dormir) bedroll; (bolsa) knapsack; ***liar el ~*** (fam) to up sticks (colloq)

B (Col, Méx) (estera) matting

C **petates** *mpl* (CS fam) (pertenencias) gear (colloq)

petatearse [A1] *v pron* (Méx fam) to kick the bucket (colloq)

petenera *f*: ***salirse por ~s*** to say sth silly

P

petición *f* 1 (acción) request; **a ~ del público** by popular request *o* demand; **a ~ fiscal** at the prosecutor's request; **consulta previa petición de hora** consultation by appointment 2 (escrito) petition

Compuestos

- **petición de divorcio** petition for divorce
- **petición de extradición** application for extradition
- **petición de mano**: *act of asking a woman's father for permission to marry her*

peticionante *adj/mf* ▸ **peticionario**

peticionar [A1] *vt* (AmL) to petition

peticionario¹ -ria *adj* petitionary

peticionario² -ria *m,f* petitioner

petimetre *m* (ant) fop (arch), dandy (arch)

petirrojo *m* robin

petiso¹ -sa *adj* (AmS fam) short, tiny

petiso² -sa *m,f*

A (AmS fam) (de baja estatura) shorty (colloq)

B petiso *m* (CS) (Equ) small horse, pony

petisú *m* cream puff

petitorio *m* (CS) list of demands

petizo -za *adj/m,f* ▸ **petiso¹,²**

peto *m* 1 (de pantalón, delantal) bib; **pantalones de ~** (Esp) overalls (*pl*) (AmE), dungarees (*pl*) (BrE) 2 (de armadura) breastplate 3 (Taur) protective covering (*for picador's horse*) 4 (en béisbol) chest protector

petrel *m* petrel

pétreo -trea *adj* stone (*before n*)

petrificación *f* petrifaction

petrificado -da *adj* ‹*madera*› petrified; ‹*animal*› fossilized; **al oírlo se quedó ~** he was thunderstruck when he heard

petrificar [A2] *vt* to petrify

■ **petrificarse** *v pron* to become petrified, turn to stone

petrodólar *m* petrodollar

petróleo *m* 1 (Min) oil, petroleum; ***sudar ~*** (Col fam) to sweat blood (colloq) 2 (combustible) kerosene, paraffin (BrE)

Compuesto **petróleo crudo** crude oil

petrolera *f* oil company

petrolero¹ -ra *adj* oil (*before n*)

petrolero² *m* oil tanker

petrolífero -ra *adj* oil (*before n*); ▸ **yacimiento**

petrolizar [A4] *vt* (Col) ‹*carretera*› to tar, tarmac; ‹*automóvil*› to underseal

petroquímica *f* petrochemistry

petroquímico -ca *adj* petrochemical (*before n*)

Petroven = **Petróleos de Venezuela**

petulancia *f* smugness

petulante¹ *adj* smug, self-satisfied

petulante² *mf* smug *o* self-satisfied fool

petunia *f* petunia

peyorativo -va *adj* pejorative

peyote *m* peyote, mescal

pez¹ *m* fish; **~ de río** freshwater fish; ***estar ~ en algo*** (Esp fam): **en cuestiones de cocina estoy ~** I don't know the first thing about cooking (colloq); ***estar*** *or* ***sentirse como ~ en el agua*** to be in one's element

Compuestos

- **pez de colores** goldfish
- **pez espada** swordfish
- **pez gordo** (fam) (persona importante) bigwig (colloq); (en delito) big shot (colloq)
- **pez martillo** hammerhead
- **pez sierra** sawfish
- **pez volador** flying fish

pez² *f* (sustancia) pitch, tar

Compuesto **pez de Castilla** (Chi) chalk

pezón *m* (Anat) nipple; (Zool) teat

pezuña *f*

A 1 (Zool) hoof 2 (de persona) (fam) paw (colloq); **¡quita tus ~s de ahí!** get your paws off!

B (Per fam) (olor) cheesy smell (*of unwashed feet*)

pH *m* pH

piadoso -sa *adj* ‹*personas*› devout, pious; ‹*obra*› kind

piafar [A1] *vi* to stamp, paw the ground

pial *m* (AmL) lasso

pianista *mf* pianist

piano¹ *adv* piano; ***piano, piano*** (CS, Méx fam) calm down, take it easy (colloq)

piano² *m* piano; ***como un ~*** (Esp fam) huge

Compuestos

- **piano de cola/de media cola** grand piano/baby grand
- **piano mecánico** Pianola®, player piano
- **piano vertical** upright piano

pianola *f* Pianola®, player piano

piar [A17] *vi* to chirp, tweet

piara *f* herd

piastra *f* piaster

PIB *m* (Esp) (= **Producto Interior Bruto**) GDP

pibe -ba *m,f* (RPl fam) kid (colloq)

pica *f*

A (Arm) pike; (Taur) lance, goad; (para cavar) pick, pickax*

B (Jueg) 1 (carta) spade 2 **picas** *fpl* (palo) spades

C (CS fam) (resentimiento) resentment; ***sacarle ~ a algn*** (Chi fam) to get on sb's nerves

picacho *m* peak

picada *f*

A (AmL) (descenso pronunciado): **caer** *or* **descender en ~** «*avión*» to nose-dive «*pájaro*» to plunge, to dive «*acciones/valores*» to plummet

B 1 (AmL) (aperitivo) nibbles (*pl*) 2 (Arg) (senda) path, trail 3 (Chi fam) (lugar) cheap restaurant (*with its own specialty*)

C (RPl) (Auto) car race

picadero *m*

A (para caballos) exercise ring; (escuela) riding school

B (Esp fam) (apartamento) bachelor pad (colloq)

picadillo *m* (Coc): **hacer un ~ con el ajo y el perejil** finely chop the garlic together with the parsley; ***hacer ~ a algn*** (fam) to beat sb to a pulp (colloq)

picado¹ -da *adj* 1 ‹*diente*› decayed, bad; ‹*manguera/llanta*› perished; **tiene una muela picada** you have a cavity in one tooth; **una cara picada de viruela** a pockmarked face 2 ‹*ajo/perejil*› chopped; ‹*carne*› (Esp, RPl) ground (AmE), minced (BrE) 3 ‹*manzana*› rotten; ‹*vino*› sour 4 (fam) (enfadado, ofendido) put out (colloq), miffed (colloq); **está ~ porque no lo llamaste** he's a bit put out that you didn't call him (colloq) 5 ‹*mar*› choppy

picado² *m* (Esp) ▸ **picada A**

picador *m* 1 (Taur) picador 2 (en mina) face worker

picadora *f* (Esp, RPl) meat grinder (AmE), mincer (BrE)

picadura *f*

A (de mosquito, serpiente) bite; (de abeja) sting; (de polilla) hole

B (tabaco) pipe tobacco

picaflor *m* (AmL) (Zool) hummingbird; (donjuán) (fam) womanizer

picahielos *m* (*pl* ~) ice pick

picana *f* (AmL) 1 (aguijada) prod 2 *tb* **~ eléctrica** cattle prod 3 (fam) (espuela) spur

picanear [A1] *vt* 1 (CS) ‹*bueyes*› to goad, prod 2 (RPl) (torturar) to torture … with a cattle prod

picante¹ *adj* 1 (Coc) ‹*comida*› hot 2 ‹*chiste/libro*› risqué; ‹*comedia*› racy

picante² *m* 1 (Coc) hot spices (*pl*); **le has puesto demasiado ~** you've made it too hot; **el médico le ha prohibido el ~** *or* **los ~s** his doctor has told him not to eat spicy food 2 (Chi, Per) (guiso) spicy meat stew

picantería *f* 1 (Per) (restaurante) restaurant (*specializing in spicy dishes*) 2 (Chi fam & pey) (puesto) stall (*drinks and food*)

picapedrero *m* (obrero de cantera) quarry worker; (artesano) stonemason

picapleitos *mf* (*pl* ~) (fam) pettifogger, shyster (AmE colloq)

picaporte *m* (manivela) door handle; (mecanismo) latch

picar [A2] *vt*

A 1 «*mosquito/víbora*» to bite; «*abeja/avispa*» to sting; **¿te ~on los mosquitos?** did you get bitten by the mosquitoes? 2 «*polilla*»: **una manta picada por las polillas** a moth-eaten blanket; **las polillas me ~on el**

poncho the moths got at my poncho **3** ⟪*ave*⟫ ⟨*comida*⟩ to peck at; ⟨*enemigo*⟩ to peck **4** ⟨*anzuelo*⟩ to bite **5** (fam) (comer) to eat; **saca algo para ~** put out some nibbles; **sólo quiero ~ algo** I just want a little snack *o* a bite to eat **6** ⟨*billete/boleto*⟩ to punch **7** (Taur) to jab

B **1** (Coc) ⟨*carne*⟩ (Esp, RPl) to grind (AmE), to mince (BrE); ⟨*cebolla/perejil*⟩ to chop (up); ⟨*pan/manzana*⟩ (Ven) to cut **2** ⟨*hielo*⟩ to crush; ⟨*pared*⟩ to chip; ⟨*piedra*⟩ (deshacer, romper) to break up, smash; (labrar, astillar) to work, chip away at

C ⟨*dientes/muelas*⟩ to rot, decay; **el azúcar pica los dientes** sugar rots your teeth *o* gives you tooth decay

D (en billar) ⟨*bola*⟩ to put spin on

E (Per fam) (obtener dinero de) to get (some) money from *o* out of

F **1** (incitar) to spur on; (enfadar) to upset, hurt **2** ⟨*amor propio*⟩ to wound, hurt; ⟨*curiosidad*⟩ to pique, arouse

G ⟨*papel*⟩ to perforate

H (Mús) to play … staccato

■ **picar** *vi*

A **1** (morder el anzuelo) to bite, take the bait; **~ *alto*** to aim high **2** (comer) to nibble

B **1** ⟪*comida*⟫ to be hot **2** (producir comezón) to itch; ⟪*lana/suéter*⟫ to itch, be itchy; **me pica la espalda** my back itches *o* is itchy; **¿te pican los ojos?** are your eyes stinging? **3** (fam) (quemar): **¡cómo pica el sol!** the sun's really burning *o* scorching!

C (AmL) ⟪*pelota*⟫ to bounce

D (RPl arg) (irse, largarse) to split (sl); **~le** (Méx fam) to get a move on (colloq)

■ **picarse** *v pron*

A **1** ⟪*muelas*⟫ to decay, rot; ⟪*manguera/llanta*⟫ to perish; ⟪*cacerola/pava*⟫ to rust; ⟪*ropa*⟫ to get moth-eaten **2** ⟪*manzana*⟫ to go rotten; ⟪*vino*⟫ to go sour

B ⟪*mar*⟫ to get choppy

C (fam) (enfadarse) to get annoyed; (ofenderse) to take offense; **anda picado** he's in a huff (colloq)

D ⟪*avión*⟫ to nose-dive; ⟪*pájaro*⟫ to dive

E (arg) (inyectarse) to shoot up (sl)

F **picárselas** (RPl arg) (irse) to split (sl)

picardía *f*

A (cualidad) craftiness, cunning; **tuvo la ~ de esconderlo** he was crafty *o* cunning enough to hide it; **un comentario hecho con ~** a mischievous comment

B (RPl fam) (lástima) shame

picardías *m* (*pl* ~) (Esp) baby-doll pajamas*

picaresca *f* **1** (Lit) **la ~** the picaresque genre **2** (cualidad de pícaro) craftiness, guile

picaresco -ca *adj* picaresque

pícaro¹ -ra *adj* **1** (ladino) crafty, cunning **2** (malicioso) ⟨*persona*⟩ naughty, wicked (colloq); ⟨*chiste/comentario*⟩ naughty, racy; ⟨*mirada/sonrisa*⟩ wicked (colloq), cheeky (BrE)

pícaro² -ra *m,f* **1** (Lit) rogue, villain **2** (astuto) cunning *o* crafty devil (colloq)

picarón *m* (Chi, Per) (buñuelo) *type of doughnut*

picatoste *m* (para sopa) crouton

picazón *f* irritation, itch; **me está dando (una) ~** it's making me itch

picha *f* (Esp vulg) cock (vulg), prick (vulg)

pichanga¹ *adj* (Bol) easy

pichanga² *f* (Chi) **1** (partido — improvisado) kickabout, friendly game; (— malo) bad game **2** (en dados, etc) dud hand (colloq)

pichear [A1] *vi/vt* to pitch

pichel *m* (AmC) pitcher, jug (BrE)

pichi *m* (Esp) jumper (AmE), pinafore (BrE)

pichí *m* (CS fam) wee-wee (used to or by children)

pichicata *f* (cocaína) (Bol, Per fam) coke (sl); (droga) (CS, Per fam) drugs (*pl*)

pichicatearse [A1] *v pron* (CS, Per fam) to take drugs

pichicatero -ra *m,f* (CS, Per fam) (adicto) drug addict; (proveedor) dealer

pichicato -ta *adj* (Col, Méx fam) stingy (colloq)

pichincha *f*

A (RPl fam) (ganga) bargain, steal (colloq)

B (Chi) **1** (pizca) tiny bit **2** (fam) (cosa fácil) cinch (colloq), piece of cake (colloq)

pichirre¹ *adj* (Ven fam) stingy (colloq)

pichirre² *mf* (Ven fam) skinflint (colloq)

picho -cha *adj* (Col) ⟨*alimento*⟩ rotten; **la leche está picha** the milk's turned (AmE) *o* (BrE) off

pichón -chona *m,f*

A (de paloma) young pigeon; (de otros pájaros) chick

B (Méx) (novato, inexperto) beginner, novice

pichulear [A1] *vi* (RPl fam) (demostrar mezquindad) to be stingy (colloq); (trabajar) to scrape a living by doing odd jobs

pichuleo *m* (RPl fam) (mezquindad) meanness, stinginess (colloq); (trabajo) odd jobs (*pl*); **vive del ~** he scrapes a living doing odd jobs

picnic *m* (*pl* **-nics**) picnic

pico *m*

A **1** (de pájaro) beak **2** (fam) (boca) mouth; **¡cierra el ~!** shut up (colloq), keep your trap shut! (colloq); **no abrió el ~** he didn't open his mouth; ***estar/irse de ~s pardos*** (fam) to be/go out on the town (colloq); ***ser puro ~ de gallo*** (Méx fam) to be all talk (colloq); ***tener un ~ de oro*** (fam) to be silver-tongued, to have the gift of the gab (colloq)

B **1** (cima, montaña) peak; **el acantilado caía a ~** the cliff fell steeply *o* sharply away **2** (en gráfico) peak **3** (en diseños, costura) point; **la chaqueta termina en un ~** the jacket tapers to a point; **cuello de ~** V neck **4** (de mesa, libro) corner **5** (de jarra, tetera) spout

C (fam) (algo): **tiene 50 y ~ de años** she's fifty odd *o* fifty something (colloq); **son las dos y ~** it's past *o* gone two; **tres metros y ~** (just) over three meters; **será unas 3.000 — y un ~ largo** it'll be about 3,000 — and the rest!; **son 3.105 pero te perdono el pico** it's 3,105 but call it 3,000 (colloq); ***salir por/costar un ~*** (fam) to cost a fortune (colloq)

D **1** (herramienta) pick **2** **picos** *mpl* (Méx) (zapatillas) spikes (*pl*)

E (Col, Ven fam) (beso) kiss, peck

F (Chi vulg) (pene) cock (vulg), prick (vulg)

picón -cona *adj* (Per fam) huffy (colloq)

picor *m* irritation, itch

picoso *adj* (Méx) hot, spicy

picota *f*

A (Hist) pillory; ***poner a algn en la ~*** to put sb on the spot

B (Bot) bigarreau cherry

C (Chi) (pico) pickax*

picotazo *m*, **picotada** *f* peck; **el pato me dio** *or* **pegó un ~** the duck pecked me

picotear [A1] *vt* to peck

■ **picotear** *vi* **1** (fam) (entre comidas) to nibble, snack **2** (Chi fam) (en actividad, tema) to dabble

pictórico -ca *adj* pictorial

picudo -da *adj*

A **1** ⟨*nariz*⟩ pointed, sharp **2** ⟨*ave*⟩ long-beaked

B (Méx fam) **1** ⟨*persona*⟩ **~ PARA algo** good AT sth **2** ⟨*zapato/coche*⟩ smart (colloq), nifty (colloq) **3** (complicado) tricky (colloq)

pida, pidas, etc *see* **pedir**

pídola *f* (Esp) leapfrog

pie¹ *m*

A **1** (Anat) foot; **un dedo del ~** a toe; **tiene (los) ~s planos** she has flat feet; **a sus ~s, señora** (frml) at your service, madam (frml) **2** (*en locs*) **a pie** on foot; **¿vamos a ~ o en coche?** shall we walk or take the car?; **hoy ando a ~** (AmL) I'm without wheels today; **al pie** (Col) very close, just round the corner; **de pie** standing; **tuve que viajar de ~ todo el camino** I had to stand all the way; **ponte de ~** stand up; **en pie**: **estoy en ~ desde las siete** I've been up since seven o'clock; **no puedo tenerme en ~** I can hardly walk/stand; **sólo la iglesia quedó en ~** only the church remained standing; **queda en ~ la cita** our date is still on; **mi oferta/promesa sigue en ~** my offer/promise still stands; **ganado en ~** (AmL) livestock, cattle on the hoof; ***andarse con ~(s) de plomo*** (fam) to tread very carefully *o* warily; ***a ~ pelado*** (Chi) barefoot, in one's bare feet; ***a ~(s) juntillas***: **seguí a ~s juntillas sus indicaciones** I followed his instructions to the letter; **creerse algo a ~s juntillas** to blindly believe sth; ***buscarle tres*** *or* ***cinco ~s al gato*** (fam) (buscar complicaciones) to complicate matters; ***cojear del mismo ~*** (fam) to be two of a kind (colloq); ***con los ~s*** (fam) badly; **lleva la**

P

empresa con los ~s he's making a hash *o* mess of running the company (colloq); ***con los ~s por*** *or* ***para delante*** (fam & euf) feet first; ***con los ~s sobre la tierra*** with one's feet on the ground; ***con mal ~*** *or* ***con el ~ izquierdo***: **empezó con mal ~** she got off to a bad start; **hoy me levanté** *or* **empecé el día con el ~ izquierdo** I got up on the wrong side of the bed today (AmE), I got out of bed on the wrong side today (BrE); **no le des ~ para que te critique** don't give him cause *o* reason to criticize you; ***dar ~ a algo*** ‹*murmuraciones/especulaciones*› to give rise to sth; **esto dio ~ a una discusión** this caused *o* was the cause of an argument; ***darle pie a algn***: ***de a ~*** common, ordinary; **el ciudadano de a ~** the man in the street, the average man/person; ***de la cabeza a los ~s*** *or* ***de ~s a cabeza*** from head to foot *o* toe, from top to toe (colloq); ***echar ~ atrás*** (Chi) to back down; ***en ~ de guerra*** on a war footing; ***en (un) ~ de igualdad*** on an equal footing; ***estar a ~*** (Chi fam) to be lost (colloq); ***estar atado de ~s y manos*** to be bound hand and foot; ***estar con un ~ en el estribo*** (fam) to be about to leave; ***estar con un ~ en la tumba*** *or* ***la sepultura*** *or* ***el hoyo*** to have one foot in the grave; ***hacer ~*** to be able to touch the bottom; ***írsele los pies a algn***: **cuando empezó la música se me iban los pies** once the music began I couldn't keep my feet still; ***leche al ~ de la vaca*** (AmL) milk fresh from the cow; ***levantarse/empezar con buen ~*** *or* ***con el ~ derecho*** to get off to a good start; ***nacer de ~*** to be born under a lucky star; ***no doy/da ~ con bola*** (fam) I/he can't get a thing right; ***no tener ni ~s ni cabeza*** to make no sense whatsoever; **un plan sin ~s ni cabeza** a crazy *o* an absurd plan; ***pararle a algn los ~s*** (Esp) to put sb in his/her place (colloq); ***perder ~*** (en el agua) to get out of one's depth; (resbalarse) to lose one's footing; ***~s de barro*** feet of clay; ***poner (los) ~s en polvorosa*** (fam) to take to one's heels (colloq); ***poner los ~s en un lugar*** to set foot in a place; ***por mi/tu/su (propio) ~*** unaided, without any help; ***saber de qué ~ cojea algn*** (Esp fam) to know sb's faults *o* weak points; ***ser más viejo que andar a ~*** (CS fam) to be as old as the hills (colloq)

(Compuesto) **pie de atleta** athlete's foot

B 1 (de calcetín, media) foot 2 (de lámpara, columna) base; (de copa — base) base; (— parte vertical) stem 3 (de página, escrito) foot, bottom; **una nota a** *or* **al ~ de página** a footnote; **al ~** *or* **a los ~s de la montaña** at the foot of the mountain; **viviendas a ~ de playa** (Esp) houses with direct access to the beach; ***al ~ de la letra*** exactly; **sigue mis instrucciones al ~ de la letra** follow my instructions to the letter *o* exactly; ***al ~ del cañón***: **Ana se quedó al ~ del cañón mientras el jefe estaba fuera** Ana stayed here to hold the fort while the boss was away 4 (de cama) *tb* **~s** foot

(Compuestos)
- **pie de firma** name and title of signatory
- **pie de fotografía** caption
- **pie de fuerza** (Col) (personal) manpower; (Mil) standing army
- **pie de imprenta** imprint

C (Bot) cutting, slip

D (medida) foot; (Lit) foot

(Compuesto) **pie quebrado**: *line of four or five syllables*

pie² /pai/ *m* (AmL) pie

piececito, (CS) **piecito** *m* tiny *o* little foot

piedad *f* 1 (compasión) mercy; **ten ~ de nosotros** have mercy on us; **no tiene ~** *or* **es un hombre sin ~** he's merciless; **¡por ~!** for pity's sake! 2 (devoción) devotion 3 (Art) pietà; **la P~** the Descent from the Cross, the Pietà

pied-de-poule /'pjeðepul/ *m* (CS) houndstooth check, dogtooth check

piedemonte *m* (Col) foothills (*pl*)

piedra *f*

A (material) stone; (trozo) stone, rock (esp AmE); **casas de ~** stone houses; **lavado a la ~** stonewashed; ***ablandar hasta las ~s*** (fam) to melt a heart of stone; ***caer como (una) ~*** (AmL fam) to go out like a light, crash out (colloq); ***darse con una ~ en el pecho*** (Chi fam) to think *o* count oneself lucky, to be thankful; ***dejar a algn de ~*** (fam) to stun sb; ***(duro) como una ~*** rock hard; **tiene el corazón duro como una ~** he has a heart of stone; ***lo saben hasta las ~s*** it's common knowledge; ***menos da una ~*** (Esp fam) it's better than nothing; ***no dejar ~ por mover*** to leave no stone unturned; ***no dejar ~ sobre ~*** ‹*ejército/enemigo*› to raze the town (*o* village *etc*) to the ground; ‹*terremoto*› to leave nothing standing; ***no soy/no es de ~*** I'm not/he's not made of stone; ***quedarse de ~*** (fam) to be flabbergasted *o* stunned (colloq); ***tirar la primera ~*** to cast the first stone; ***tirar ~s a su propio tejado*** to foul one's own nest

(Compuestos)
- **piedra angular** cornerstone
- **piedra arenisca** sandstone
- **piedra caliza** *or* **de cal** limestone
- **piedra de afilar** whetstone
- **piedra de molino** millstone
- **piedra de toque** touchstone
- **piedra filosofal** philosopher's stone
- **piedra pómez** *or* (Méx) **poma** pumice stone
- **piedra preciosa** precious stone

B 1 (de mechero) flint 2 (cálculo) stone; **tiene ~s en el riñón/la vesícula** she has kidney stones/gallstones 3 (Meteo) large hailstone

piel *f*

A (Anat, Zool) skin; **~ grasa/seca** oily *o* greasy/dry skin; **estirarse la ~** (del rostro) to have a facelift; ***dejarse la ~*** (fam) to work one's butt off (AmE colloq), to slog one's guts out (BrE colloq); ***se me/te pone la ~ de gallina*** I/you get gooseflesh *o* goose pimples; ***tener (la) ~ de gallina*** to have gooseflesh *o* goose pimples

(Compuesto) **piel roja** *mf* (fam & pey) redskin (colloq & pej), Red Indian

B (Indum) 1 (Esp, Méx) (cuero) leather; **bolso/guantes de ~** leather bag/gloves 2 (de visón, zorro, astracán) fur; **abrigo de ~(es)** fur coat 3 (sin tratar) pelt

(Compuestos)
- **piel de cocodrilo** crocodile skin
- **piel de serpiente** snakeskin
- **piel sintética** (cuero sintético) (Esp, Méx) synthetic leather; (imitación nutria, visón, etc) synthetic fur

C (Bot) (de cítricos, papa) peel; (de manzana) peel, skin; (de otras frutas) skin; **~es de patata** (Esp) potato peelings

piélago *m* (liter) **el ~** the ocean, the deep (liter)

pienso *m* (comida) fodder, feed

(Compuesto) **pienso compuesto** compound feed

piercing /'pirsin/ *m* (*pl* **~s**)

A (acción) body piercing; **hacerse un ~** to have a piercing; **hacerse un ~ en la lengua** to have one's tongue pierced

B (joya) stud; **se puso un ~ en la lengua** she had a stud put in her tongue

pierda, pierdas, etc *see* **perder**

pierde *m* (Col, Ven): **no tiene ~** you can't miss it

pierna¹ *f* 1 (Anat) leg; **con las ~s cruzadas** cross-legged; **la falda le llega a media ~** the skirt is calf length on her; ***abrirse de ~s*** (en gimnasia) to do the splits; ***dormir a ~ suelta*** to sleep the sleep of the death; ***estirar las ~s*** to stretch one's legs; ***hacer ~s*** (andar) (fam) to have a walk; ***salir por ~s*** (fam) to take to one's heels, leg it (colloq) 2 (Coc) leg; **~ de cordero** leg of lamb

pierna² *adj inv* (RPl fam): **es un tipo ~ para todo** he's the sort of guy who's game for anything (colloq); **andá, sé ~ y prestánoslo** come on, be a sport and lend it to us

pierneras *fpl* (Chi) chaps (*pl*)

pierrot *m* pierrot

pieza *f*

A 1 (elemento, parte) piece; **un bañador de dos ~s** a two-piece bathing suit; **la ~ clave de su política** the key element *o* feature of their policy; *ver tb* **dos¹** 2 (Tec) part; **las ~s de un reloj/motor** watch/engine parts *o* components; ***dejar a algn de una ~*** to leave sb speechless; ***quedarse de una ~*** to be dumbfounded; ***ser de una sola ~*** (AmL) to be as straight as a die 3 (en ajedrez) piece; (unidad, objeto) piece; ***ser una ~ de museo*** (fam) to be a museum piece (colloq)

(Compuestos)
- **pieza de convicción** piece of evidence
- **pieza dentaria** tooth
- **pieza de recambio** *or* **de repuesto** spare part

B (en caza) piece, specimen

C (de tela) roll

P

D (Mús, Teatr) piece; **¿me permite esta ~?** (ant) may I have the pleasure of this dance?
E (esp AmL) (dormitorio) bedroom; (en hotel) room

pífano *m* fife

pifia *f*
A 1 (fam) (error) boo-boo (colloq), boob (colloq) 2 (en billar) miscue 3 (Chi) (defecto) fault
B (Chi, Per) (del público) booing and hissing

pifiar [A1] *vt*
A (fam) (fallar) to fluff (colloq); **~la** (fam) to goof (colloq), to blow it (colloq)
B (Chi, Per) «*público*» to boo
■ **pifiar** *vi* (Chi, Per) «*público*» to boo and hiss

pigmentación *f* pigmentation

pigmento *m* pigment

pigmeo -mea *adj/m,f* pygmy

pignorar [A1] *vt* (Der) ‹*cosa*› to pawn; (Fin) ‹*títulos/valores*› to pledge … as security

pija *f* (RPl vulg) cock (vulg), prick (vulg)

pijada *f* (Esp fam) (cosa insignificante) little thing; (estupidez) stupid thing

pijama *m* pajamas (*pl*) (AmE), pyjamas (*pl*) (BrE)

pije *adj/mf* (Chi) ▸**pijo**

pijo¹ -ja *adj* (Esp fam & pey) ‹*persona/moda/lugar*› posh (colloq & pej)

pijo² -ja *m,f* (Esp fam & pey) rich kid (colloq & pej)

pijotero¹ -ra *adj* 1 (Esp fam) (fastidioso) annoying, irritating 2 (Arg) (tacaño) stingy (colloq), mean

pijotero² -ra *m,f* 1 (Esp fam) (incordiante) pest (colloq) 2 (Arg) (tacaño) miser, scrooge (colloq)

pijudo -da *adj* (AmC fam) gorgeous (colloq)

pila¹ *adj inv* (AmC fam): **estar ~** (muerto) to be dead; (sin dinero) to be broke (colloq)

pila² *f*
A (Elec, Fís) battery; **funciona a ~(s)** *or* **con ~s** it runs on batteries *o* is battery-operated; ***cargar las ~s*** (fam) to recharge one's batteries (colloq); ***ponerse las ~s*** (fam) to get cracking (colloq)
B (fregadero) sink; (de una fuente) basin, bowl
(Compuestos)
• **pila bautismal** baptismal font
• **pila de agua bendita** stoup
C 1 (fam) (de libros, platos) pile, stack 2 (AmS fam) (de trabajo, amigos) loads (*pl*) (colloq); **hace una ~ de años** eons ago (colloq)
D (Inf) stack

pilapuesta *adj inv* (AmC fam) on the ball (colloq)

pilar¹ *f* (Arquit) pillar, column; (de puente) pier; **los ~es de la sociedad** the pillars *o* mainstays of society

pilar² *mf* (en rugby) prop (forward)

pilastra *f* pilaster

pilchas *fpl* (CS fam) clothes (*pl*), gear (colloq)

píldora *f* 1 (pastilla) pill, tablet; ***dorar la ~*** to sweeten *o* sugar the pill 2 *tb* **~ anticonceptiva** (contraceptive) pill; **tomar la ~** to be on the pill
(Compuesto) **píldora del día siguiente** morning-after pill

pileta *f* 1 (RPl) (fregadero) kitchen sink; (del baño) washbowl (AmE), washbasin (BrE) 2 (RPl) (piscina) swimming pool 3 (Chi) (estanque) pond; (bebedero) drinking fountain

pillaje *m* pillage

pillar [A1] *vt*
A (fam) 1 (atrapar) to catch; **me pilló la policía** the police caught *o* (colloq) nabbed me; **le pilló un dedo** it caught *o* trapped her finger 2 (por sorpresa) to catch; **¡te pillé!** caught *o* got you!; **nos pilló la lluvia** we got caught in the rain 3 ‹*catarro/resfriado*› to catch
B (Esp fam) 1 «*coche*» to hit 2 «*lugar*»: **me pilla de camino** it's on my way; **me pilla lejos** it's a bit far for me
C (fam) 1 ‹*sentido/significado*› to get (colloq) 2 ‹*ganga*› to pick up (colloq)
■ **pillarse** *v pron* (fam) ‹*dedos/manga*› to catch

pillarse *m* (Chi) tag (colloq)

pillastre *m* (fam) crafty devil *o* rogue

pillería *f* (cualidad) craftiness, cunning; (acto) prank, trick

pillín -llina *m,f* (fam) crafty devil (colloq), rascal (colloq)

pillo¹ -lla *adj* (fam) (travieso) naughty, wicked (colloq); (astuto) crafty, cunning

pillo² -lla *m,f* (fam) (travieso) rascal (colloq); (astuto) crafty *o* cunning devil (colloq)

pilluelo -la *m,f* (fam) little rascal (colloq)

pilmama *f* (Méx) nanny

pilo -la *adj* (Col fam) capable, together (colloq)

pilón *m*
A 1 (de fuente) basin 2 (Arquit) pillar; (de puente) pylon
B (Coc) sugarloaf
C (Méx fam) (en la compra) *small amount of extra goods given free*; **me dio tres manzanas de ~** he threw in three extra apples (for free)

piloncillo *m* (Méx) brown sugar

piloso -sa *adj* hair (*before n*), pilose (tech)

pilotaje *m* (de avión) piloting, flying; (de barco) pilotage, steering; (de coche) driving; (de moto) riding

pilotar [A1] *vt* 1 ‹*avión*› to pilot, fly; ‹*barco*› to pilot, steer; ‹*coche*› to drive; ‹*moto*› to ride 2 ‹*empresa/país*› to guide, steer

pilote *m* pile

pilotear [A1] *vt* (AmL) ▸**pilotar**

piloto *mf*
A (Aviac, Náut) pilot; (de coche) driver; (de moto) rider
(Compuestos)
• **piloto civil** civilian pilot
• **piloto de carreras** racing driver
• **piloto de pruebas** (de avión) test pilot; (de coche) test driver; (de moto) test rider
B **piloto** *m* 1 (luz de un aparato) pilot light; (llama de un calentador) pilot light 2 (CS) (impermeable) raincoat
C (*como adj inv*) ‹*programa/producto*› pilot (*before n*)

pilsen, pilsenor *f* (Chi) beer

piltra *f* (Esp fam) bed

piltrafa *f* 1 (de comida) scrap; ***estar hecho una ~ humana*** (fam) to be a complete wreck (colloq) 2 (cosa inservible) useless thing

pilucho¹ -cha *adj* (Chi fam) naked

pilucho² *m* (Chi) (Indum) romper suit, rompers (*pl*)

pimentero *m* (Bot) pepper plant; (para la pimienta) pepper shaker (AmE), pepperpot (BrE)

pimentón *m* 1 (dulce) paprika; (picante) cayenne pepper 2 (AmS exc RPl) (fruto) capsicum, pepper

pimienta *f* pepper

pimiento *m* pepper, capsicum; **~ rojo/verde** red/green pepper; ***me importa un ~*** (fam) I couldn't care less (colloq)

pimpante *adj* (fam) cool (colloq); **lo echaron y se quedó tan ~** they fired him and he didn't turn a hair

pimpinela *f* scarlet pimpernel

pimpollo *m* 1 (Bot) (de flor) bud; (brote) shoot 2 (fam) (persona) dish (colloq), knockout (colloq); **¡está hecho un ~!** he looks great for his age

pimpón *m* Ping-Pong®, table tennis

pin *m* (broche) pin

pinacle *m* pinochle

pinacoteca *f* art gallery

pináculo *m* (Arquit) pinnacle; (apogeo) pinnacle, peak

pinar *m* pine forest

pinaza *f* pine needles (*pl*)

pincel *m* (Art) paintbrush; (para maquillarse) brush

pincelada *f* brushstroke; **le di las últimas ~s** I added the final touches

pinchadiscos *mf* (*pl* ~) (Esp fam) disc jockey, DJ (colloq)

pinchar [A1] *vt*
A 1 ‹*globo/balón*› to burst; ‹*rueda*› to puncture 2 (con alfiler, espina) to prick 3 (para recoger) to spear; ***ni ~ ni cortar*** (fam): **él en la oficina ni pincha ni corta** he doesn't have any clout in the office; **yo aquí ni pincho ni corto** my opinion doesn't count for anything around here
B 1 (fam) (poner una inyección) to give … a shot (colloq) 2 (fam) (provocar) to needle (colloq); (incitar, azuzar) to egg … on
C ‹*teléfono*› to tap, bug
D (Esp fam) ‹*discos*› to play

P

■ **pinchar** *vi*
A (herir): **esa planta pincha** that plant is prickly
B (Auto) to get a flat (tire*), get a puncture
C (period) (perder) to be/get beaten
D (Chi fam) (con el sexo opuesto) ► **ligar** *vi*
E (Esp fam) (en póker) to ante up (colloq)
■ **pincharse** *v pron*
A «*persona*» 1▸ (*refl*) (accidentalmente) to prick oneself 2▸ (*refl*) (fam) (inyectarse) to shoot up (sl), to jack up (sl)
B «*rueda*» to puncture; «*globo/balón*» to burst; **se me pinchó un neumático** I got a flat (tire) *o* a puncture

pinchazo *m* 1▸ (herida) prick; (inyección) shot (colloq) 2▸ (en una rueda) flat, puncture 3▸ (dolor agudo) sharp pain 4▸ (fam) (de droga) fix (colloq)

pinche¹ *adj* 1▸ (AmL exc CS fam) (*delante del n*) (maldito): **¡~ vida!** what a (lousy *o* rotten) life!; **por unos ~s pesos** for a few measly pesos (colloq); **¿por qué no nos vamos de este ~ sitio?** let's get out of this damn place! 2▸ (Méx fam) (de poca calidad) lousy (colloq); (despreciable) horrible 3▸ (AmC fam) (tacaño) tightfisted (colloq)

pinche² *mf* 1▸ (Coc) kitchen assistant 2▸ (Esp) (en una oficina) office junior 3▸ (fam) (de albañil) mate (colloq)

pinche³ *m*
A (Esp) (Jueg) ante, stake money
B (Chi) (para el pelo) bobby pin (AmE), hairgrip (BrE)
C (Chi fam) (persona): **tiene muchos ~s** she has a lot of admirers; **su nuevo ~** her new man

pincho *m*
A (de rosa, zarza) thorn, prickle (colloq); (de cactus) spine, prickle (colloq)
B (Esp) (de aperitivo) bar snack
(Compuestos)
• **pincho de tortilla**: *small portion of Spanish omelet**
• **pincho moruno** (Esp) pork kebab
C (Per vulg) (pene) cock (vulg), prick (vulg)

> **pincho**
> In Spain, *pinchos* are small portions of food, often on a cocktail stick, eaten in a bar or café. Often free, they are similar to **tapas**, but much smaller. There are *pinchos* of many foods, including Spanish omelet, ham, sausage, and anchovy. *See also* **ración**

pinga *f* (Andes, Méx fam) weenie (AmE colloq), willy (BrE colloq)

pingajo *m* (Esp fam) rag; **llevaba la ropa hecha un ~** her clothes were in tatters *o* rags

pinganilla *mf* (Chi fam) shady character

pingo¹ *m*
A (Esp fam) (harapo, andrajo) old rag
B (CS fam) (caballo) horse
C (Méx fam) (demonio) **el ~** the devil

pingo² -ga *m,f* (Méx fam) little scamp *o* rascal (colloq)

Ping-Pong® *m* Ping-Pong®, table tennis

pingüe *adj* ‹*beneficios*› huge, fat (colloq); ‹*negocio*› profitable, lucrative; ‹*cosecha*› bumper

pingüino *m* penguin

pininos, pinitos *mpl* (fam): **hacer los primeros ~** «*niño*» to take his first steps; «*actriz*» to make her debut

pino *m*
A (Bot) (árbol) pine (tree); (madera) pine; ***en el quinto ~*** (Esp fam) miles away
(Compuesto) **pino insigne/tea** Monterey/loblolly pine
B (Esp) (en gimnasia): **hacer el ~** to do a handstand
C (Méx) (en bolos) pin
(Compuesto) **pino central** kingpin
D (Chi) (Coc) fried ground beef and onion

pinocha *f* pine needles (*pl*)

pinol *m* (AmC): *flour made from toasted maize*

pinolillo *m* (AmC) (maíz) cornstarch (AmE), maize flour (BrE); (bebida) *drink made with cornstarch and water*

pinta¹ *f*
A 1▸ (fam) (aspecto): **¡qué buena ~ tiene el pastel!** the cake looks delicious *o* great!; **tiene ~ de extranjero** he looks foreign; **¿dónde vas con esa(s) ~(s)?** where are you going looking like that?; ***echar*** *or* ***tirar*** (Andes) *or* ***hacer*** (RPl) (fam) to impress 2▸ (Chi fam) (vestimenta) clothes (*pl*), outfit; ***ponerse la ~*** (Andes fam) to put on one's glad rags (colloq)
B 1▸ (en una tela) spot, dot 2▸ (Zool) spot
C (medida) pint
D (Méx fam) (de la escuela): **irse de ~** to play hooky* (esp AmE colloq), to skive off (school) (BrE colloq)

pinta² *m* (Esp fam) rogue (colloq)

pintada *f* piece of graffiti, graffito (frml); (Pol) slogan

pintado -da *adj*
A ‹*vaca*› spotted; ‹*caballo*› dappled, pied; ***el más ~*** (fam) anyone; ***que ni ~*** (fam): **ese vestido te queda que ni ~** you look great *o* a knockout in that dress (colloq); **el dinero me vino que ni ~** the money was a godsend
B (AmL fam) (idéntico) identical; **~ A algo** identical TO sth; **ser ~ A algn** to be identical TO sb, be the spitting image OF sb

pintalabios *m* (*pl* ~) (fam) lipstick

pintar [A1] *vt*
A 1▸ ‹*cuadro/retrato*› to paint; ‹*pared/ventana*› to paint; **pintó la puerta de rojo** she painted the door red 2▸ (fam) (dibujar) to draw 3▸ (describir) (+ *compl*) to paint; **nos pintó muy mal la situación** he painted a very black picture of the situation
B (fam) (tener relación, influencia): **¿qué pintas tú en este asunto?** and where exactly do you fit into all this? (colloq); **yo allí no pinto nada** I don't have any say in what goes on there
■ **pintar** *vi*
A 1▸ (con pintura) to paint 2▸ (fam) (dibujar) to draw
B (en naipes) to be trumps; **pintan tréboles** clubs are trumps
C (AmS fam) «*situación/negocio*» (+ *compl*) to look; **la cosa no pinta nada bien** things don't look at all good (colloq)
D (madurar) to ripen
■ **pintarse** *v pron* (*refl*) (maquillarse) to put on one's/some makeup; **yo no me pinto** I don't wear makeup; **~se los ojos** to put on eye makeup; **~se las uñas** to paint one's nails; ***pintárselas solo para hacer algo*** (Esp fam) to be an expert at doing sth (colloq)

pintarrajear [A1] *vt* to daub
■ **pintarrajearse** *v pron* (*refl*) to plaster *o* cake one's face in makeup (colloq)

pintiparado -da *adj* (Esp fam): **tu regalo me vino ~** your gift was just what I wanted; **el apodo le viene que ni ~** his nickname suits him to a T

pinto -ta *adj* pinto (*before n*)

pintor -tora *m,f* (de cuadros) painter, artist; (de paredes) (house) painter
(Compuesto) **pintor de brocha gorda** (de casas, barcos) painter; (artista) bad painter, dauber (colloq)

pintoresco -ca *adj* picturesque

pintura *f* 1▸ (arte, cuadro) painting; **~ a la acuarela/al óleo** watercolor*/oil painting; ***no poder ver algo/a algn ni en ~*** (fam): **no puedo verlo ni en ~** I can't stand the sight of him (colloq); **no puede ver el queso ni en ~** she can't stand *o* bear cheese (colloq) 2▸ (material) paint; (en cosmética) makeup 3▸ **pinturas** *fpl* (Méx) (lápices de colores) crayons (*pl*)

pinza *f*
A 1▸ (para la ropa) clothespin (AmE), clothes peg (BrE) 2▸ (para el pelo) bobby pin (AmE), hairgrip (BrE) 3▸ (de un cangrejo) pincer 4▸ (en costura) dart; **un pantalón con ~s** pleated pants (AmE) *o* (BrE) trousers
B *tb* **~s** 1▸ (para depilar) tweezers (*pl*); (de cirujano) forceps (*pl*); (para el hielo) tongs (*pl*) 2▸ (alicates) pliers (*pl*); ***tratar a algn con ~s*** (CS, Méx fam) to treat sb with kid gloves

piña *f*
A (Bot) (fruta) pineapple; (del pino) pine cone
B (fam) (puñetazo) thump (colloq); **le dio una ~** he thumped him (colloq); **agarrarse a ~s** to come to blows (colloq)

piñata *f*: *container hung up during festivities and hit with a stick to release candy inside*

piño *m* (Chi) (de vacas) herd; (de ovejas) flock

piñón *m*
A (Bot) pine kernel *o* nut; ***estar a partir (de) un ~*** (fam) to be bosom pals *o* bosom buddies (colloq)
B (Mec) pinion; (de bicicleta) sprocket wheel
(Compuesto) **piñón libre** freewheel

piñoso -sa *adj* (Per fam) unlucky

pío¹, pía *adj* devout, pious

p

pío² *m* peep, tweet; ***no decir ni*** ~ (fam) not to say a word

piocha *f*
A (para romper piedra) pickax*; (para cavar) mattock
B (Chi) (distintivo) badge
C (Méx) (barbita) goatee (beard); **por** ~ per head

piojento -ta *adj* (fam) ▸ **piojoso**

piojo *m* louse; ~**s** lice

piojoso -sa *adj* 1 (con piojos) lousy, lice-ridden; (con pulgas) flea-ridden 2 (fam) (sucio) filthy

piola¹ *adj inv* (RPl fam) 1 (divertido) fun (*before n*) (colloq); **son muy** ~ they're really good fun 2 (astuto) crafty (colloq); **¡qué** ~ **sos!** you're a crafty devil (colloq) 3 ‹*ropa*› trendy (colloq), with-it (colloq)

piola² *f* (AmL) cord

piolet /pjoˈle(t)/ *m* (*pl* **-lets**) ice ax*

pionero¹ -ra *adj* pioneering (*before n*)

pionero² -ra *m,f* pioneer

pipa *f*
A (para fumar) pipe; **fumar (en)** ~ to smoke a pipe; ***fumar la*** ~ ***de la paz*** to smoke the pipe of peace
B (tonel) cask, barrel; ***como*** ~ (Chi fam) plastered (colloq)
C (Esp) (de sandía, mandarina) pip; (de girasol, calabaza) seed; ***pasarlo*** ~ (Esp fam) to have a great time
D 1 (Col) (de gas) cylinder, bottle 2 (Col, Per fam) (barriga) belly 3 (Méx) (camión) tanker

pipeño *m*: *Chilean white wine*

pipeta *f* pipette

pipi² *f* (Bol, Col, Méx) (pene) weenie (AmE colloq). willy (BrE colloq)

pipí¹ *m* (fam) pee (colloq), wee (BrE colloq), wee-wee (used to or by children); **hacer** ~ to have a pee *o* (BrE) wee

pipián *m*
A (AmC) (verdura) *type of squash*
B (AmC) (muchacha) (fam & hum) nymphet (colloq & hum)

pipiolo -la *m,f* (fam) (novato) novice, greenhorn (colloq); (joven) kid (colloq)

pipón -pona *adj* (RPl fam) full up (colloq), stuffed (colloq)

pique *m*
A **a pique**: **el camino bajaba a** *or* (Méx) **en** ~ the road down was very steep; **una caída a** *or* (Méx) **en** ~ **hasta el mar** a vertical *o* sheer drop to the sea below; **a** ~ **de** on the point of, about to; ***irse a*** ~ «*barco*» to sink; «*negocio*» to go under, to founder; **sus ilusiones se fueron a** ~ her hopes were dashed
B (fam) 1 (enfado, resentimiento): **tener un** ~ **con algn** to be at odds with sb 2 (rivalidad) rivalry, needle
C 1 (carta) spade 2 **piques** *fpl* (palo) spades (*pl*)
D (arg) (de droga) fix (sl)
E (Auto) acceleration, pick-up (AmE); ***pegarse un*** ~ (Chi fam): **me pegué el** ~ **hasta allá y no estaba** I trailed *o* traipsed all that way and he wasn't there (colloq)
F (AmL) (rebote): **la pelota entró de** ~ the ball went in on the rebound; **la pelota dio tres** ~**s** the ball bounced three times
G (Chi) (Min) mine shaft

piqué *m* piqué

piquera *f* hole

piqueta *f* pick, pickax*

piquete *m*
A (de huelguistas) picket; (de soldados) squad, picket (arch)
Compuesto **piquete móvil** *or* **volante** flying picket
B (Méx fam) 1 (herida) prick; (inyección) shot (colloq), jab (colloq) 2 (de insecto) sting, bite 3 (de licor) drop

piquetear [A1] *vt/vi* (esp AmL) to picket

pira *f* pyre

pirado -da *adj* (Esp, Méx fam) crazy (colloq)

piragua *f* (Dep) canoe

piragüismo *m* canoeing

piragüista *mf* canoeist

piramidal *adj* pyramid (*before n*)

pirámide *f* pyramid

piraña¹ *f* (Zool) piranha

piraña² *mf* (persona) shark (colloq)

pirarse [A1] *v pron* (Esp fam) to make oneself scarce (colloq); ***pirárselas*** (Esp fam) to take to one's heels

pirata¹ *adj* 1 ‹*barco*› pirate (*before n*) 2 (clandestino) ‹*casete/copia*› pirate (*before n*), bootleg (*before n*) (colloq) 3 (Ven) (de mala calidad) poor, shoddy (colloq)

pirata² *mf* 1 (Náut) pirate 2 (de casetes, videos) pirate
Compuestos
- **pirata aéreo** hijacker, skyjacker (journ)
- **pirata informático, pirata informática** hacker

piratear [A1] *vi*
A to commit piracy
B (Ven fam) (trabajar mal) to botch things (colloq)
■ **piratear** *vt* to pirate

piratería *f*
A (Náut) piracy; (de videos, casetes) piracy
B (Ven fam) (trabajo mal hecho) botch job (colloq)

Pirineos *mpl*, **Pirineo** *m*: **los** ~ *or* **el Pirineo** the Pyrenees (*pl*)

pirinola *mf* 1 (Andes, Méx) (peonza) spinning top 2 (AmC fam) (pene) weenie (AmE colloq), willy (BrE colloq); ***andar en*** ~ (AmC fam) to go around naked *o* (colloq) without a stitch on

piripi *adj* (Esp fam) merry (colloq), tipsy (colloq)

pirita *f* pyrite

piromanía *f* pyromania

pirómano -na *m,f* pyromaniac

piropear [A1] *vt* to make flirtatious/flattering comments to

piropo *m* flirtatious/flattering comment; **le echan muchos** ~**s por la calle** she gets a lot of comments from men in the street

pirotecnia *f* fireworks (*pl*), pyrotechnics (frml)

pirrar [A1] *vi* (Esp fam) (+ *me/te/le etc*): **me pirran los helados** I love ice cream
■ **pirrarse** *v pron* (Esp fam) ~**se POR algo** to be crazy *o* wild ABOUT sth (colloq)

pirueta *f* (en danza) pirouette; (de un caballo) pesade; ***hacer*** ~***s*** to perform miracles

piruja *f* (Col, Méx fam) hooker (colloq), whore (colloq)

piruleta *f* lollipop

pirulo¹ -la *adj* (Chi fam) ‹*lugar*› ritzy (colloq), upmarket; ‹*persona*› refined

pirulo² *m* (fam) (pene), weenie (AmE colloq), willy (BrE colloq)

pis *m* (fam) pee (colloq), wee (BrE colloq); **hacer** ~ to have a pee *o* (BrE) wee

pisacorbatas *m* (Col) tiepin

pisada *f* (acción) footstep; (huella) footprint; ***no perderle*** ~ ***a algn*** to keep close tabs on sb

pisado *m* treading (*of grapes*)

pisapapeles *m* (*pl* ~) paperweight

pisar [A1] *vt*
A 1 (con el pie): **la pisó sin querer** he accidentally stepped *o* trod on her foot; ⊘ **prohibido pisar el césped** keep off the grass; **hace una semana que no piso la calle** I haven't been out (of the house) for a week; **no vuelvo a** ~ **esta casa nunca más** I'll never set foot in this house again; ~ **el escenario** to go on stage, tread the boards 2 (humillar) to trample on, walk all over
B (RPl, Ven) 1 (Coc) to mash 2 (fam) (atropellar) to run over
C (Esp fam) (adelantarsea): **me has pisado la idea** you stole *o* (BrE colloq) pinched my idea!; **otro periódico nos pisó la noticia** another newspaper beat us to the story (colloq)
D 1 «*ave macho*» to mount 2 (AmC vulg) (joder) to screw (vulg)
■ **pisar** *vi* to tread; **pisó mal y se cayó** she lost her footing and fell; **no pises ahí, está mojado** don't walk *o* tread there, it's wet; ~ ***fuerte*** to make a big impact

pisca *f* (Méx) harvest

pisciano -na *adj/m,f* Piscean, Pisces

piscicultor -tora *m,f* fish farmer

piscicultura *f* fish farming, pisciculture (frml)

pisciforme *adj* fish-shaped

piscina *f* swimming pool; ~ **cubierta/climatizada/al aire libre** covered/heated/open air swimming pool; ~ **olímpica** Olympic-sized swimming pool

Piscis¹ *m* (signo, constelación) Pisces; **es (de)** ~ he's (a) Pisces, he's a Piscean

Piscis², **piscis** *mf* (*pl* ~) (persona) Piscean, Pisces

pisco *m* (aguardiente) ≈ grappa
(Compuesto) **pisco sauer** *or* **sour** *cocktail made with* **pisco**, *lemon, egg white and sugar*

> **pisco**
> An alcoholic drink, produced by distilling grape juice, originally from Peru but now also characteristic of Chile

piscola *f* (Chi): **pisco** *with cola*
piscolabis *m* (*pl* ~) (Esp fam) snack (colloq)
piso *m*
A 1 (de edificio) floor, story*; (de autobús) deck; **una casa de seis ~s** a six-story building; **vivo en el primer ~** I live on the second (AmE) *o* (BrE) first floor; **un autobús de dos ~s** a double-decker bus 2 (— de tarta) layer
B (AmL) 1 (suelo) floor; ***serrucharle*** (RPl) *or* (Chi) ***aserrucharle el ~ a algn*** (fam) to pull the rug out from under sb's feet (colloq) 2 (de carretera) road surface
C (Esp) (apartamento) apartment (esp AmE), flat (BrE)
(Compuestos)
- **piso franco** (Esp) safe house
- **piso piloto** (Esp) show apartment *o* (BrE) flat

D (Chi) (taburete) stool; (alfombrita) rug; (felpudo) doormat
pisotear [A1] *vt* 1 (con los pies) to trample, stamp on 2 ‹*persona/derecho*› to ride roughshod over
pisotón *m* stamp; **darle un ~ a algn** (intencional) to stamp on sb's foot *o* toes; (sin querer) to tread *o* step on sb's foot *o* toes
pista *f*
A 1 (rastro) trail, track; **seguirle la ~ a algn** to be/get on sb's trail; **están sobre la ~** they're on the right track; **~ falsa** false trail 2 (indicio) clue
B 1 (carretera) road, track 2 (Chi) (carril) lane; ***se me/le puso pesada la ~*** (Chi fam) I/he found it heavy *o* tough going 3 (Audio) track
C 1 (en el circo) ring; (en el picadero) ring; (en el hipódromo) track (AmE), course (BrE) 2 (Esp) (de tenis) court; **~ de hierba/de tierra batida** grass/clay court
(Compuestos)
- **pista cubierta/de atletismo** indoor/athletics track
- **pista de aterrizaje** runway, landing strip
- **pista de baile** dance floor
- **pista de esquí** ski slope, piste
- **pista de hielo/de patinaje** ice/skating rink
- **pista de saltos** showjumping ring *o* arena

pistacho *m* pistachio (nut)
pistilo *m* pistil
pistola *f* 1 (Arm) pistol; **a punta de ~** at gunpoint; ***hacerle ~ a algn*** (Col fam) ≈ to give sb the finger (sl) 2 (para pintar) spray gun
(Compuestos)
- **pistola de engrase** grease gun
- **pistola de fogueo** starting pistol

pistolera *f* holster
pistolerismo *m* gun law
pistolero *m* gunman
pistoletazo *m* (disparo) pistol shot; (Dep) starting signal
pistón *m* 1 (émbolo) piston 2 (de arma) percussion cap 3 (de instrumento) key 4 (Chi) (de manguera) nozzle
pita *f* (Bot) pita; (hilo) pita fiber*; (cordel) (Andes) twine
pitada *f*
A 1 (pitido) beep; **las ~s de los coches** the beeping *o* hooting of the car horns 2 (en espectáculo) ≈ booing and hissing, whistling (*as sign of disapproval*)
B (AmL) (de cigarrillo) puff, drag (colloq)
pitanza *f*
A (arc) (comida) daily ration
B (Chi fam) (broma) joke
pitar [A1] *vi*
A 1 «*guardia/árbitro*» to blow one's whistle 2 «*vehículo*» to blow the horn, to hoot 3 «*público*» (como protesta) to boo and hiss
B **pitando** *ger* (Esp fam) (rápido): **salió pitando** he was off like a shot (colloq), he legged it (colloq)
C (CS fam) (fumar) to smoke
■ **pitar** *vt* ‹*falta*› to blow for, award, call (AmE)
pitazo *m*
A 1 (CS, Per) (del árbitro) whistle 2 (CS) (de tren) whistle; (de barco) boom, blast on the siren
B (Méx fam) (información) tip-off
pítcher *mf* pitcher
pitear [A1] *vi* (pitar) to blow a/one's whistle
pitido *m* (sonido agudo) whistle, whistling; (de claxon) beep, hoot, honk
pitillera *f* cigarette case
pitillo *m*
A (fam) (cigarrillo) smoke (colloq), fag (BrE colloq)
B (Col) (para beber) straw
pitiminí *m*: **de ~** trifling
pito *m*
A 1 (silbato) whistle; **tocar el ~** to blow the whistle; **tener voz de ~** (fam) to have a squeaky voice; ***entre ~s y flautas*** (fam) (what) with one thing and another (colloq); ***me importa un ~*** (fam) I don't give a damn (colloq); ***no entender/saber (ni) un ~*** (fam): **no entendí ni un ~** I didn't understand a thing (colloq); **no sabe un ~ de motores** he doesn't know the first thing about engines (colloq); ***por ~s o flautas*** (fam) somehow or other (colloq); ***tocar ~*** (AmL fam): **¿y este tipo qué ~(s) toca aquí?** what on earth's *o* what the hell's he doing here? (colloq); **nosotros ahí no tocamos un ~** that's nothing to do with us (colloq) 2 (fam) (de coche) horn, hooter; (de tren) whistle; **tocar el ~** to hoot, honk
B 1 (fam) (cigarrillo) smoke, fag (BrE colloq) 2 (Chi fam) (de marihuana) joint (colloq), spliff (sl)
C (fam) (pene) weenie (AmE colloq), willy (BrE colloq)
pitón[1] *f or m* python
pitón[2] *m* 1 (del toro) horn; (del ciervo) point, spike 2 (de un botijo) spout 3 (en alpinismo) piton
pitonisa *f* fortuneteller
pitorrearse [A1] *v pron* (Esp fam) **~ DE algn** to make fun OF sb
pitorreo *m* (Esp fam): **se lo tomó a ~** he didn't take it seriously; **siempre está de ~** he's always larking *o* clowning around (colloq)
pitorro *m* (Esp) spout
pitote *m* (Esp fam) row, din, ruckus (AmE)
pituco[1] **-ca** *adj* (CS, Per fam) 1 (elegante) posh (colloq); **¿adónde vas tan pituca?** where are you going dressed up in that posh gear? (colloq) 2 (engreído) snooty (colloq), stuck-up (colloq)
pituco[2] **-ca** *m,f* (CS, Per fam) snob
pituto *m*
A (Chi) (cilindro) short tube/cylinder
B (Chi fam) (para conseguir algo) contact
pívot *mf* (*pl* **-vots**) (Dep) center*, pivot
piyama *m or f* (AmL) pajamas (*pl*) (AmE), pyjamas (*pl*) (BrE)
pizarra *f* 1 (Min) slate 2 (en el aula) blackboard, chalkboard; (del alumno) slate 3 (Cin) clapperboard 4 (en béisbol) scoreboard
pizarral *m* slate quarry
pizarrón *m* (AmL) blackboard, chalkboard
pizca *f*
A (cantidad pequeña): **una ~ de algo** (de sal) a pinch of sth; (de vino) a drop of sth; ***ni ~***: **no tiene ni ~ de gracia** it's not the slightest bit funny; **no me gusta ni ~** I don't like it one little bit
B (Méx) (cosecha) harvest
pizcar [A2] *vt* (Méx) ‹*maíz*› to harvest; ‹*algodón*› to pick
■ **pizcar** *vi* (Méx) to take in the harvest
pizza /'pitsa, 'pisa/ *f* pizza
pizzería /pitse'ria, pise'ria/ *f* pizzeria
pizzicato /pitsi'kato/ *m* pizzicato
Pl. (= **Plaza**) Sq, Square
placa *f*
A (lámina, plancha) sheet; **una ~ de acero** a steel sheet; **tiene una ~ de metal en el cráneo** he has a metal plate in his skull; **~ de mármol** marble slab
(Compuestos)
- **placa de energía solar** solar cell
- **placa de hielo** black ice
- **placa de silicio** silicon chip
- **placa madre** motherboard

B 1 (con inscripción) plaque; **~ conmemorativa** commemorative plaque; **una ~ con el nombre** a nameplate **2** (de policía) badge

(Compuesto) **placa de matrícula** license (AmE) *o* (BrE) number plate

C (Fot, Geol) plate

D **1** *tb* **~ dental** dental plaque, tartar **2** (de infección) spot, pustule **3** (costra) scab

E (period) (Audio) record, disc

F (Chi) (dentadura) dentures (*pl*), dental plate

placaje *m* (en fútbol americano) block; (en rugby) tackle

placar [A2] *vt* (en fútbol americano) to block; (en rugby) to tackle

placard /pla'kar/ *m* (RPl) built-in closet (AmE), fitted wardrobe (BrE)

placebo *m* placebo

pláceme *m* (frml) message of congratulations, congratulatory message; **darle el ~ a algn** to congratulate sb; ***estar de ~(s)*** (Andes frml) to be delighted

placenta *f* placenta, afterbirth

placentero -ra *adj* pleasant, agreeable

placer¹ [E4] *vi* (*en 3ª pers*) (+ *me/te/le etc*): **haz lo que te plazca** do as you please; **me place informarle que ...** (frml) I am pleased *o* (frml) it is my pleasure to inform you that ...

placer² *m*

A (gusto, satisfacción) pleasure; **ha sido un ~ conocerla** (frml) it has been a pleasure to meet you; **tengo el ~ de presentarles a ...** (frml) it is my pleasure *o* I have the pleasure to introduce to you ...; ***a ~*** ‹*comer/beber*› as much as one wants

B **1** (Geol, Min) placer **2** (Náut) sandbank

placero *m* (Per) street vendor

placidez *f* placidity, placidness, calmness

plácido -da *adj* placid, calm

plaf *m* (en la mejilla) smack!; (al caerse) crash!, bang!; (al caer al agua) splash!

plafón *m* (rosetón) ceiling rose; (panel) soffit

plaga *f* **1** (de insectos, ratas) plague; **las ardillas son consideradas una ~** squirrels are considered to be a pest; **trajeron a sus hijos, que eran una ~** they brought along their horde of children **2** (calamidad, azote) plague; **la ~ del turismo** the menace *o* scourge of tourism

plagado -da *adj* **~ DE algo**: **está ~ de faltas** it is riddled with mistakes; **la playa estaba plagada de turistas** the beach was crawling *o* swarming with tourists

plagiar [A1] *vt*

A ‹*idea/libro*› to plagiarize

B (AmL) ‹*persona*› to kidnap

plagiario -ria *m,f* **1** (que copia) plagiarist **2** (AmL) (secuestrador) kidnapper

plagio *m*

A (copia) plagiarism

B (AmL) (secuestro) kidnap, kidnapping

plan *m*

A (proyecto, programa) plan; **hacer ~es** to make plans; **~ de desarrollo** development plan

(Compuestos)

- **plan de campaña** plan of action
- **plan de estudios** syllabus
- **plan maestro** master plan

B **1** (fam) (cita, compromiso): **si no tienes otros ~es podríamos ir a cenar** if you're not doing anything else we could go out for dinner; **¿tienes algún ~ para esta noche?** do you have any plans for tonight? **2** (Esp fam) (ligue): **salió en busca de ~** he went out looking for a pickup (colloq), he went out on the pull (BrE colloq); **su marido tiene un ~** her husband's having an affair

C (fam) (actitud): **no te pongas en ~ chulo** don't get cocky with me! (colloq); **lo dijo en ~ de broma** he was only kidding (colloq); **en ~ económico** cheaply, on the cheap (colloq); **salen en ~ de amigos** they're just good friends

plana *f*

A (de periódico) page; **aparece en primera ~** it has made *o* it's on the front page; **viene publicado a toda ~** it has been given a full page

B (Educ) (ejercicio) handwriting exercise

(Compuesto) **plana mayor** (Mil) staff officers (*pl*); (jefes) (fam) top brass (colloq)

plancha *f*

A **1** (electrodoméstico) iron; **pásale la ~** run the iron over it **2** (acto) ironing; (ropa para planchar) ironing

B **1** (Const, Tec) sheet; **acero en ~s** sheet steel **2** (Impr) plate **3** (Chi) (con inscripción) plaque

C (utensilio) griddle; (parte de la cocina) hotplate, griddle; **un filete a la ~** a grilled steak

D (en natación): **hacer la ~** to float

E **1** (fam) (metedura de pata) boo-boo (colloq), boob (colloq); **tirarse una ~** (Esp fam) to put one's foot in it (colloq), to goof (colloq) **2** (Chi fam) (vergüenza) embarrassment; **¡qué ~ pasé!** I was *o* felt so embarrassed!

planchada *f* (esp AmL) (planchado): **dale una planchadita al cuello** just run the iron over the collar; **con una buena ~ quedará como nuevo** it'll be as good as new once you iron it

planchado¹ -da *adj* **1** (RPl fam) (agotado) shattered (colloq), beat (AmE colloq) **2** (Chi fam) (sin dinero) broke (colloq)

planchado² *m* ironing

planchador -dora *m,f* **1** (en tintorería, fábrica) presser **2** **planchadora** *f* (máquina) press, presser

planchar [A1] *vt* ‹*sábana/mantel*› to iron; ‹*pantalones*› to press, iron; ‹*traje*› to press

■ **planchar** *vi*

A (con la plancha) to do the ironing

B **1** (Bol, CS fam) (en baile): **planchó toda la noche** nobody asked her to dance all night **2** (Chi fam) (quedar en ridículo) to look stupid

C (RPl fam) (caerse) to take a tumble (colloq), to fall over

planchazo *m* **1** (fam) (caída): **se dio un ~** she fell flat on her face **2** ▸ **plancha E1**

plancton *m* plankton

planeación *f* (Méx) planning

planeador *m* glider

planeamiento *m*

A (de proyecto, viaje) planning

B (Aviac) gliding

planear [A1] *vt* to plan

■ **planear** *vi* (Aviac) to glide; «*águila*» to soar; (Náut) to plane

planeo *m* (Aviac) gliding; (Náut) planing

planeta *m* planet

planetario¹ -ria *adj* (Astron) planetary; (global) global

planetario² *m* planetarium

planicie *f* plain

planificación *f* planning

(Compuestos)

- **planificación familiar** family planning
- **planificación urbana** urban *o* town planning

planificador¹ -dora *adj* planning (*before n*)

planificador² -dora *m,f* planner

planificar [A2] *vt* to plan, draw up a plan for

planilla *f*

A **1** (tabla) table, chart; (lista) list **2** (AmL) (nómina) payroll; **estar en ~** to be on the payroll **3** (AmL) (personal) staff

B **1** (Méx) (en elección) list of candidates **2** (Col) (censo electoral) electoral register

planisferio *m* planisphere

planning /'planin/ *m* (*pl* **~s**) agenda, schedule

plano¹ -na *adj*

A ‹*superficie/terreno/zapato*› flat; **los 100 metros ~s** (AmL) the hundred meters dash *o* sprint

B ‹*figura/ángulo*› plane

plano² *m*

A (de edificio) plan; (de ciudad) street plan, map

B (Mat) plane

C **1** (nivel) level; **se mueven en ~s sociales muy diferentes** they move in very different social circles; **en el ~ afectivo** on an emotional level; **en el ~ laboral** on the employment front **2** (Cin, Fot) shot

(Compuestos)

- **plano corto** close-up
- **plano general/largo** pan/long shot

D (de espada) flat

E **de plano** ‹*rechazar/rehusar*› flatly

P

planta *f*
A (Bot) plant
(Compuesto) **planta de interior** houseplant, indoor plant
B (Arquit) 1 (plano) plan 2 (piso) floor; **primera/tercera ~** second/fourth floor (AmE), first/third floor (BrE); **una casa de dos ~s** a two-story house; **grandes ofertas en la ~ de señoras** big savings in the ladies' fashion department
(Compuesto) **planta baja** first floor (AmE), ground floor (BrE)
C (Tec) (instalación) plant
D (del pie) sole
E (tipo, apariencia): **de buena ~** fine-looking
F (de empleados) staff

plantación *f* 1 (terreno plantado) field; (de árboles) plantation 2 (explotación agrícola) plantation 3 (acción) planting

plantado -da *adj* **~ DE algo** planted WITH sth; ***bien ~*** (ant) handsome; **un chico bien ~** a fine-looking young man; ***dejar ~ a algn*** (fam) (en una cita) to stand sb up (colloq); (el día de la boda) to jilt sb; **los invité a cenar y me dejaron ~** I invited them to dinner but they didn't turn *o* show up

plantador -dora *m,f* 1 (persona) planter 2 **plantador** *m* (utensilio) dibble, dibber

plantar [A1] *vt*
A 1 ‹*árboles/cebollas*› to plant; ‹*semillas*› to sow 2 ‹*postes*› to put in; ‹*tienda*› to pitch, put up
B (fam) 1 (abandonar) ‹*novio*› to ditch (colloq), to dump (colloq); ‹*estudios*› to give up, to quit (AmE) 2 (no acudir a una cita): **la plantó el día de la boda** he jilted her on their wedding day; **los invité a cenar y me ~on** I invited them to dinner but they didn't turn *o* show up
C (fam) 1 (poner): **lo planté en la calle** I threw *o* (colloq) chucked him out; **fue y plantó su silla delante del televisor** she went and plonked *o* stuck her chair right in front of the television (colloq) 2 ‹*beso/puñetazo*› to plant
■ **plantarse** *v pron*
A (fam) (quedarse, pararse) to plant oneself (colloq); **se plantó delante de la puerta** he planted himself in front of the door (colloq); **el caballo se plantó delante del obstáculo** the horse stopped dead in front of the fence; **se plantó en su actitud** he dug his heels in (colloq); **se plantó aquí con tres amigas** she turned *o* showed up here with three friends
B (Jueg) (en cartas, apuesta) to stick
C (Andes fam) (beberse) to down (colloq), to knock back (colloq); (comerse) to put away (colloq)

plante *m* (protesta) protest; (paro) stoppage

planteamiento *m* 1 (enfoque) approach 2 (exposición): **no les sabe dar el ~ adecuado a sus ideas** he doesn't know how to set his ideas out; **ése no es el ~ que me hicieron** that's not the way they explained the situation to me; **el ~ de su relación en la película** the depiction *o* portrayal of their relationship in the movie

plantear [A1] *vt*
A 1 (Mat) ‹*problema*› to set out 2 (exponer): **me lo planteó de la siguiente manera** he explained it to me in the following way; **planteó la necesidad de un cambio** she expressed the need for a change; **las reivindicaciones que ~on** the demands which they made; **le ~é la cuestión a mi jefe** I will bring it up with my boss; **nos ~on dos opciones** they presented us with *o* gave us two options; **le planteé la posibilidad de ir a Grecia** I suggested going to Greece
B (causar, provocar) ‹*problemas/dificultades*› to create, cause
■ **plantearse** *v pron*
A (considerar) ‹*problema/posibilidad*› to think about, consider
B (presentarse) «*problema/posibilidad*» to arise; **se nos ha planteado un nuevo problema** a new problem has arisen *o* has come up; **se me planteó una disyuntiva** I came up against *o* I was faced with a dilemma

plantel *m*
A (cuerpo) staff; **un excelente ~ de profesores** an excellent teaching staff; **el equipo se presenta con un renovado ~** the team has a new lineup
B (Agr) nursery
C (AmL frml) (escuela) educational establishment (frml)

plantificar [A2] *vt* (fam) (poner) to stick (colloq); **plantificó su silla delante del televisor** she plonked *o* stuck her chair right in front of the television (colloq); **le plantificó los niños a la abuela** she dumped the children on their grandmother (colloq); **~le un puñetazo a algn** to land a punch on sb
■ **plantificarse** *v pron* 1 (fam) (en un lugar) to plant oneself (colloq); **se plantificó delante de la puerta** he planted himself in front of the door; **me plantifiqué en su oficina hasta que me recibió** I didn't budge from her office until she saw me 2 (*refl*) (fam) «*abrigo*» to throw on; **se plantifica cada sombrero ...** the hats she wears!

plantilla *f*
A (de zapato) insole
B (Esp) (personal) staff; (nómina) payroll; **estar en ~** to be on the staff *o* payroll
C (para marcar, cortar) template; (para corregir exámenes) mask

plantío *m* field of crops

plantón *m* 1 (fam) (espera) long wait; **me di** *or* **pegué un ~ de dos horas** I had a two-hour wait (colloq); ***darle el ~ a algn*** (en cita) to stand sb up (colloq); (el día de la boda) to jilt sb 2 (Méx) (para protestar) sit-in

plañidera *f* hired mourner, weeper

plañidero -ra *adj* mournful, plaintive

plañir [I9] *vi* to moan, wail, lament

plaqué *m* plating; **de ~** plated

plaqueta *f*
A (Biol) platelet
B (de cemento) small slab

plasma *m* (Biol, Fís) plasma

plasmar [A1] *vt* (frml) to give expression to; **quiso ~ en el lienzo aquel dolor** he tried to give expression to *o* capture that pain on canvas
■ **plasmarse** *v pron* (frml) to be expressed; **esta angustia se plasmó en toda su obra** this suffering is expressed *o* manifests itself throughout his work

plasta[1] *adj* 1 (Esp fam) (pesado): **¡no seas ~, tío!** stop being such a pain in the neck! (colloq) 2 (AmL fam) (cachazudo) slow, sluggish (colloq)

plasta[2] *f*
A (fam) (masa — blanda) soft lump; (— aplastada) flat *o* shapeless lump
B 1 (AmL fam) (cachaza) laid-back attitude (colloq); **¡qué ~ tiene!** she's so laid back! (colloq) 2 (persona cachazuda) slow *o* (colloq) laid-back person; (persona inútil) useless person, waste of time (colloq) 3 (persona fea) ugly mug (colloq) 4 (persona aburrida) bore (colloq)

plástica *f* 1 (artes plásticas) plastic arts (*pl*) 2 (escultura) *sculpture and modeling*

plasticidad *f* (de material) plasticity; (de forma) elasticity, plasticity; (de movimiento) elasticity, fluency

plasticina ® *f* (CS) Plasticine®

plástico[1] **-ca** *adj*
A (de plástico) plastic; (dúctil) pliable, plastic
B 1 (Art) physical, plastic 2 (Lit) ‹*descripción*› vivid, evocative; ‹*estilo*› expressive

plástico[2] *m* 1 (material) plastic 2 (explosivo) plastic explosive, plastique 3 (Esp arg) (disco) record, disc (colloq) 4 (fam) (tarjetas de crédito) credit cards (*pl*), plastic (colloq)

plastificar [A2] *vt* ‹*tela*› to plasticize; ‹*carné/documento*› to laminate

plata *f*
A 1 (metal) silver; ***hablando en ~*** (fam) to put it bluntly 2 (vajilla) silver, silverware
(Compuesto) **plata de ley** hallmarked silver
B (AmS fam) (dinero) money; **tiene mucha ~** she has a lot of money; ***estar podrido en ~*** (fam) to be filthy rich (colloq); ***salvar la ~*** (AmL fam) «*persona*» to save the day; «*servicio/comida*» to be the saving grace

platada *f* (Chi) (de comida) plateful

plataforma *f*
A 1 (tarima) platform; **esto le sirvió de ~ para trabajar en el cine** this was his stepping stone to a career in the movies 2 (de autobús) platform 3 (de zapato) platform
(Compuestos)
- **plataforma continental** continental shelf
- **plataforma de lanzamiento** launchpad
- **plataforma de perforación** drilling platform *o* rig

B (Pol) (de un partido) platform

(Compuesto) **plataforma electoral** (conjunto de políticas) electoral platform; (documento) election manifesto

platal *m* (AmS fam) fortune (colloq)

platanal, platanar *m* banana plantation

platanera *f* 1▸ (árbol) banana tree 2▸ (empresa) banana company

platanero -ra *m,f*

A (persona) banana grower

B platanero *m* (árbol) banana tree

plátano *m*

A (árbol caducifolio) plane tree

(Compuesto) **plátano oriental** plane tree, Oriental plane

B 1▸ (fruto dulce, que se come crudo) banana; (árbol) banana tree 2▸ (fruto más grande, para cocinar) plantain; (árbol) plantain

platea *f* 1▸ (patio de butacas) orchestra (AmE), stalls (*pl*) (BrE) 2▸ (localidad) seat (*in the orchestra/stalls*)

(Compuesto) **platea alta** dress circle

plateado¹ -da *adj* 1▸ (del color de la plata) silver; **sus sienes plateadas** (liter) his silvery temples 2▸ (con baño de plata) silver-plated

plateado² *m* silver-plating

platear [A1] *vt* (Metal) to silver-plate, silver; **la luna plateaba las aguas del lago** (liter) moonlight silvered the lake (liter)

plateau /pla'to/ *m* set

plateresco -ca *adj* plateresque

platería *f* 1▸ (arte) silverwork 2▸ (objetos) silver(ware) 3▸ (taller) silversmith's workshop; (tienda) silversmith's

platero -ra *m,f* silversmith

plática *f* 1▸ (conferencia) talk 2▸ (esp AmL) (conversación) [*this noun is widely used in Mexico and Central America but is literary in other areas*] talk; **estar de ~** to talk, to chat (colloq); **reanudarán ~s con el sindicato** they will restart talks *o* negotiations with the union

platicar [A2] *vi* (esp AmL) [*this verb is widely used in Mexico and Central America but is literary in other areas*] to talk, chat (colloq)

■ **platicar** *vt* (Méx) (contar) to tell

platija *f* plaice

platillo *m*

A 1▸ (plato pequeño) saucer; (de balanza) pan; (para limosnas) collection plate *o* bowl; ***pasar el ~*** to pass the hat around 2▸ (Mús) cymbal 3▸ (Dep) clay pigeon

(Compuesto) **platillo volador** *or* (Esp) **volante** flying saucer

B (Méx) (en una comida) course

platina *f* 1▸ (de microscopio) slide 2▸ (de máquina) platen 3▸ (Impr) platen, plate 4▸ (de tocadiscos) deck

(Compuesto) **platina a cassette** tape deck

platino *m*

A (metal) platinum

B platinos *mpl* (Auto, Mec) (contact breaker) points (*pl*)

plato *m*

A 1▸ (utensilio) plate; **lavar** *or* **fregar los ~s** to wash *o* do the dishes; ***no haber roto un ~*** (fam): **tiene cara de no haber roto un ~ en su vida** she looks as if butter wouldn't melt in her mouth (colloq); ***pagar los ~s rotos*** to pay the consequences 2▸ (para taza) *tb* **platito** saucer

(Compuestos)

- **plato de postre** dessert plate
- **plato hondo** *or* **sopero** soup dish
- **plato llano** *or* (RPl) **playo** *or* (Chi) **bajo** *or* (Méx) **extendido** (dinner) plate

B (contenido) plate, plateful; **me comí dos ~s** I had two helpings *o* platefuls

C 1▸ (receta) dish; **~ típico** typical dish; ***no es ~ de gusto*** it's no fun (colloq) 2▸ (en una comida) course; **una comida de cuatro ~s** a four-course meal; **¿qué hay de segundo ~?** what's for (the) main course?

(Compuestos)

- **plato central** (Ven) main course
- **plato combinado** (Esp) *meal served on one plate*
- **plato de fondo** (AmL) main course
- **plato del día** dish of the day
- **plato fuerte** (Coc) main course; (de un espectáculo) pièce de résistance; **su conferencia fue el ~ ~ del día** his lecture was the high point of the day

D 1▸ (de balanza) (scale) pan 2▸ (de tocadiscos) turntable 3▸ (Dep) clay pigeon 4▸ (en béisbol) home plate

E (AmS fam) (situación, persona divertida) scream (colloq)

plató *m* set

platónico -ca *adj* platonic

platudo -da *adj* (AmS fam) well-heeled (colloq)

plausible *adj* 1▸ ‹*motivo/razón*› acceptable, valid 2▸ (loable) commendable, praiseworthy

playa *f* (extensión de arena) beach; (lugar de veraneo) seaside

(Compuesto) **playa de estacionamiento** (CS, Per) parking lot (AmE), car park (BrE)

play back, playback /'plejbak/ *m* playback

playboy /'plejboj/ *m* (*pl* **-boys**) playboy

playera *f* (zapatilla) canvas shoe, beach shoe; (camiseta) (Méx) T-shirt

playero -ra *adj* 1▸ ‹*vestido*› beach (*before n*) 2▸ ‹*persona*›: **es muy ~** he loves the beach

plaza *f*

A 1▸ (espacio abierto) square 2▸ (Taur) bullring; **el toro que abrió/cerró ~** the first/last bull

(Compuestos)

- **plaza de armas** (Mil) parade ground; (lugar público) (Andes) main square
- **plaza de toros** bullring
- **plaza mayor** main square

B (esp AmL) (bolsa) market

C (Esp) (mercado) market (place)

D (ciudad) 1▸ (Mil) garrison town 2▸ (frml) (Corresp): **nuestro representante en la ~** our local representative; **en dicha ~** in the abovementioned city/town

(Compuesto) **plaza fuerte** garrison town

E 1▸ (puesto — de trabajo) post, position; (— en una clase, universidad) place; **cubrir una ~** to fill a position; **hay varias ~s vacantes** there are several vacancies 2▸ (asiento) seat; **un sofá de tres ~s** a three-seater sofa

(Compuesto) **plaza de aparcamiento** *or* **de garaje** parking space

plazo *m*

A (de tiempo) period; **el ~ se cierra el próximo lunes** the deadline is next Monday; **tenemos un mes de ~ para pagar** we have one month to pay; **el ~ de admisión termina mañana** tomorrow is the closing date; **dentro del ~ estipulado** within the stipulated period; **cuenta/depósito a ~ fijo** (Fin) fixed term account/deposit; **comprar a ~ fijo** (Fin) to buy forward; **un objetivo a corto/largo/medio** *or* (CS) **mediano ~** a short-term/long-term/medium-term objective

B (mensualidad, cuota) installment*; **pagar a ~s** to pay in installments; **comprar a ~s** to buy on installments

plazoleta, plazuela *f* small square

plebe *f* 1▸ (Hist) **la ~** the masses (*pl*), the populace 2▸ (pey) (chusma) rabble (pej), plebs (*pl*) (colloq & pej)

plebeyo -ya *adj/m,f* plebeian

plebiscitar [A1] *vt* (frml) to hold a plebiscite on, decide ... by plebiscite

plebiscito *m* plebiscite

plegable *adj* folding (*before n*); **silla ~** folding *o* collapsible chair

plegadera *f* (navaja) jackknife, penknife; (abrecartas) paperknife

plegado *m* (acción) folding; (pliegues) folds (*pl*)

plegamiento *m* 1▸ (Geol) folding 2▸ (de un camión) jacknife, jackknifing

plegar [A7] *vt* ‹*papel*› to fold; ‹*silla*› to fold up

■ **plegarse** *v pron*

A (ceder) to yield, submit; **~se A algo** to yield TO sth, submit TO sth

B «*camión*» to jackknife

C (AmS) (unirse) to join in; **~se A algo** to join sth

plegaria *f* prayer

pleitear [A1] *vi*

A (Der) to go to litigation, go to court

B (AmL fam) (discutir) to argue

pleitesía *f* respect; **rendirle ~ a algn** to show respect for sb, to treat sb courteously

pleito *m*
A (Der) action, lawsuit; **entablar ~** to bring an action *o* a lawsuit; **tienen un ~ con el dueño** they're involved in a legal dispute with the landlord
B (AmL) **1** (disputa, discusión) argument, fight (colloq); ***estar de ~*** (Méx) to be arguing *o* (colloq) fighting **2** (de boxeo) fight, boxing match

plenamente *adv* fully, completely

plenario[1] -ria *adj* plenary, full

plenario[2] *m* (CS) plenary *o* full meeting/session

plenilunio *m* (frml) full moon

plenipotenciario -ria *adj/m,f* plenipotentiary

plenitud *f*: **está en la ~ de la vida** she's in the prime of life; **en la ~ de su carrera** at the height *o* peak of his career; **vivir la vida con ~** to live life to the full

pleno[1] -na *adj*
A **1** (completo, total) full; **en ~ uso de sus facultades** in full possession of his faculties; **miembro de ~ derecho** full member; **~s poderes** full powers **2** (uso enfático): **en ~ verano/invierno** in the middle of summer/winter; **le dio una bofetada en plena cara** he slapped her right across the face; **vive en ~ centro de la ciudad** she lives right in the city center; **a plena luz del día** in broad daylight; **a ~ sol** in the full sun
(Compuesto) **pleno empleo** full employment
B (liter) (lleno) **~ DE algo** full OF sth

pleno[2] *m*
A (reunión) plenary *o* full meeting/session; **asistió la corporación en ~** the entire corporation attended
B (Jueg) (en bolos) strike; (en lotería, bingo) full house; (en las quinielas) correct forecast *o* prediction

pleonasmo *m* pleonasm

plétora *f* (frml) (abundancia) plethora (frml), abundance

pletórico -ca *adj* (frml) **~ DE algo**: **~s de ilusión** full of expectation; **estaba ~ de dicha** he was bursting with *o* brimming over with happiness

plexo *m* plexus
(Compuesto) **plexo solar** solar plexus

pléyade *f* (liter) pleiad (liter); **una ~ de excelentes investigadores** an illustrious group of researchers

plica *f* (Esp) sealed tender, sealed bid

pliego *m* **1** (hoja de papel) sheet of paper **2** (Impr) section, signature **3** (documento) document
(Compuestos)
- **pliego de cargos** list of charges
- **pliego de condiciones** specifications (*pl*)
- **pliego de descargo** defense* depositions *o* submissions (*pl*)
- **pliego de peticiones** (Chi, Ven) (Rels Labs) list of demands

pliegue *m* **1** (en papel) fold, crease; (en la piel) fold; (en tela) pleat **2** (Geol) fold

plinto *m* (en gimnasia) box

plisado *m* (acción) pleating

plisar [A1] *vt* to pleat

plomada *f* **1** (Const) plumb line **2** (Náut) (línea) lead; (en red) weights (*pl*), sinkers (*pl*)

plomazo *m*
A (fam) (persona) bore (colloq); **esa tipa es un ~** that girl's a real bore; **la película es un ~** the movie's deadly boring (colloq)
B (Méx fam) (balazo) shot; **lo mataron de un ~** they shot him dead

plomería *f* (AmL) plumbing

plomero -ra *m,f* (AmL) plumber

plomífero -ra *adj* (Min) lead-bearing, plumbiferous (frml)

plomillo *m* fuse

plomizo -za *adj* ‹cielo› gray*, leaden (liter)

plomo *m*
A **1** (metal) lead; **soldado de ~** tin soldier **2** (arg) (balas) lead (sl); ***ser más pesado que el ~*** (fam) (ser latoso) to be a real pain in the neck (colloq); (ser aburrido) to be deadly boring (colloq)
B (fam) (persona, cosa pesada): **este libro/profesor es un ~** this book/teacher is deadly boring (colloq); **¡qué ~!** what a drag *o* pain! (colloq)
C **1** (plomada) plumb line; **tiene que estar a ~** it has to be plumb *o* exactly vertical; ***caer a ~*** ‹‹*tela/cortina*›› to hang straight **2** (para cortinas) weight **3** (en pesca) weight
D (Esp) (fusible) fuse
E **(de) color ~** lead-colored*, lead-gray*

pluma *f*
A (de aves) feather; (usada antiguamente para escribir) quill; (como adorno) plume, feather; **mudar la ~** to molt*; ***pesar menos que una ~*** to be as light as a feather; ***ser ligero*** *or* (esp AmL) ***liviano como una ~*** to be as light as a feather
B **1** (para escribir) pen; ***a vuela ~*** ‹*anotar*› to jot down; ***dejar correr la ~*** to let one's pen run on **2** (actividad literaria) writing; **vivir de la ~** to make a living out of writing *o* as a writer **3** (escritor) writer
(Compuestos)
- **pluma atómica** (Méx) ballpoint pen
- **pluma estilográfica** *or* (AmL) **fuente** fountain pen

C (Col, Méx) (del agua) faucet (AmE), tap (BrE)
D (Bol fam) (prostituta) tart (colloq)

plumaje *m* (de ave) plumage; (en un casco) plume, crest

plumazo *m* stroke of the pen; ***de un ~*** at a stroke

plumear [A1] *vi* to hatch

plumero *m* **1** (para limpiar) feather duster; ***se te/le ve el ~*** (Esp fam) I know what you're/he's up to (colloq) **2** (estuche) pencil case; (recipiente) pen holder

plumier *m* (estuche) pencil case; (caja) pencil box

plumilla *f*
A (para escribir) nib
B **1** (del limpiaparabrisas) blade **2** (proyectil) dart **3** (Mús) brush **4** (Dep) shuttlecock

plumín *m* nib

plumón *m*
A **1** (pluma suave) down **2** (edredón) down-filled quilt *o* (BrE) duvet
B (Chi) (rotulador) felt-tip pen

plumoso -sa *adj* feathery

plural[1] *adj* plural

plural[2] *m* plural; **tercera persona del ~** third person plural; **en ~** in the plural

pluralidad *f* plurality

pluralismo *m* pluralism

pluralista *adj* pluralist, pluralistic

pluralizar [A4] *vi* to generalize
■ **pluralizar** *vt* (Ling) to pluralize

pluriempleado -da *m,f*: **ser un ~** to have more than one job

pluriempleo *m*: *the holding of more than one job by an individual*

plurilingüe *adj* multilingual

pluripartidismo *m* multiparty system

pluripartidista *adj* multiparty

plus *m* bonus; **~ de peligrosidad** danger money; **~ por desplazamiento** relocation allowance

pluscuamperfecto *m* pluperfect, past perfect

plusmarca *f* record; **batir una ~** to break a record

plusmarquista *mf* record-holder

plusvalía *f* **1** (Fin) capital gain, added value **2** (en la teoría marxista) surplus value

plutocracia *f* plutocracy

plutócrata *mf* plutocrat

Plutón *m* Pluto

plutonio *m* plutonium

pluvial *adj* (Meteo) rain (*before n*)

pluviómetro *m* rain gauge, pluviometer (tech)

pluviosidad *f* rainfall

p.m. (= **post meridiem**) pm, PM

PM *mf* (= **policía militar**) MP

PNB *m* (= **Producto Nacional Bruto**) GNP

P° *m* = **paseo**

P.O., p.o. (Corresp) (= **por orden**) pp

poblacho *m* (fam & pey) hole (colloq & pej), one-horse town (colloq)

población *f*
A (habitantes) population; (Zool) population, colony

P

(Compuesto) **población activa/pasiva/fija/flotante** working/non-working/permanent/floating population
B (ciudad) town, city; (aldea) town, village
(Compuesto) **población callampa** (Chi) shantytown
C (acción) settlement

poblacional *adj* population (*before n*)

poblado¹ -da *adj*
A (habitado) populated; **poco/densamente ~** sparsely/densely populated
B ‹*barba/cejas*› bushy, thick; ‹*pestañas*› thick; **un bosque ~ de castaños** a wood full of *o* filled with chestnut trees

poblado² *m* village

poblador -dora *m,f* 1 settler 2 (Chi, Per) *inhabitant of a shantytown*

poblar [A10] *vt*
A ‹*territorio/región*› 1 «*colonos/inmigrantes*» (ir a ocupar) to settle, populate; «*autoridades/gobierno*» (mandar a ocupar) to populate, settle 2 (habitar) to inhabit; **las estrellas que pueblan el firmamento** (liter) the stars which populate the firmament
B ~ algo DE algo ‹*bosque*› to plant sth WITH sth; ‹*río/colmena*› to stock sth WITH sth
■ **poblarse** *v pron* 1 «*tierra/colonia*» to be settled 2 (llenarse) **~se DE algo**: **las calles se ~on de gente** the streets filled with people; **la frente se le pobló de arrugas** his forehead became very lined

pobre¹ *adj*
A 1 ‹*persona/barrio/nación*› poor; ‹*vestimenta*› poor, shabby 2 (escaso) ‹*vocabulario*› poor, limited; **~ EN algo**: **aguas ~s en minerales** water with a low mineral content 3 (mediocre) ‹*examen/trabajo/actuación*› poor; ‹*salud*› poor, bad; **un argumento bastante ~** a rather weak argument 4 ‹*tierra*› poor
B (*delante del n*) (digno de compasión) poor; **pobrecito, tiene hambre** poor little thing, he's hungry; **¡~ de mí!** poor (old) me!; **¡~ de ti si lo tocas!** if you touch it, you'll be for it
(Compuesto) **pobre diablo** (infeliz) poor devil; (necesitado) poor soul

pobre² *mf*
A (necesitado) poor person, pauper (arch); **los ~s** the poor; ***sacar de ~*** (fam) to make … rich; ***salir de ~*** (fam) to get somewhere in the world
B (expresando compasión) poor thing
(Compuesto) **pobre de espíritu** (Bib): **los ~s de ~** the poor in spirit

pobretón -tona *m,f* (fam) (*m*) poor man, pauper (arch); (*f*) poor woman, pauper (arch)

pobreza *f* 1 (económica) poverty; **extrema ~** abject poverty 2 (mediocridad) poverty, poorness; **su conversación es de una ~ deprimente** his conversation is depressingly dull; **~ cultural y espiritual** cultural and spiritual poverty 3 (de la tierra) poorness, poor quality

poceta *f* (Ven) toilet bowl *o* pan

poché /po'tʃe, po'ʃe/ *adj* poached

pochismo *m* (Méx fam) 1 (Ling): *term borrowed from American English* 2 (modo de ser): *Americanized Mexican attitude*, Pochismo (AmE)

pocho¹ -cha *adj* 1 (Esp fam) ‹*persona*› (pálido) off-color, peaked (AmE colloq); (abatido) depressed 2 ‹*fruta*› overripe; ‹*flor*› withered

pocho² -cha *m,f* (Méx fam) *person of Mexican origin who speaks Spanish heavily interspersed with English*

pochoclo *m* (Arg) popcorn

pocholada *f* (esp Esp fam): **¡qué ~ de niño!** what a gorgeous *o* adorable little boy! (colloq)

pocilga *f* pigsty

pocillo *m* 1 (bol) bowl, dish 2 (taza — pequeña) (AmL) small coffee cup; (— cualquiera) (Per) cup

pócima *f* (Farm) potion; (bebida) (fam) concoction (colloq)

poción *f* potion

poco¹ *adv*: **es muy ~ agradecido** he is very ungrateful; **un autor muy ~ conocido** a very little-known author; **me resultó ~ interesante** I didn't find it very interesting; **habla ~** he doesn't say much *o* a lot; **viene muy ~ por aquí** he hardly ever comes around; **… con lo ~ que le gusta el arroz** … and he doesn't even like rice; *para locs ver* **poco³ D**

poco² -ca *adj* (con sustantivos no numerables) little; (en plural) few; **muy ~ vino** very little wine; **muy ~s niños** very few children; **¡qué ~ sentido común tienes!** you don't have much common sense, do you?; **tengo muy poca ropa** I have very few clothes; **éramos demasiado ~s** there were too few of us

poco³ -ca *pron*
A (poca cantidad, poca cosa): **le serví sopa pero comió poca** I gave her some soup but she didn't eat much; **por ~ que gane…** no matter how little *o* however little she earns…; **se conforma con ~** he's easily satisfied; **~ faltó para que me pegara** he nearly hit me; **lo ~ que gana se lo gasta en vino** he spends the little *o* what little he earns on wine; **compra más lentejas, nos quedan muy pocas** buy some more lentils, we've hardly any left; **es un profesor como ~s** there aren't many teachers like him; **fue asombroso, todo lo que te pueda decir es ~** it was amazing, I can't (even) begin to tell you; **todo le parece ~** she is never satisfied; **~s pueden permitirse ese lujo** not many people can afford to do that
B poco (refiriéndose a tiempo): **lo vi hace ~** I saw him recently *o* not long ago; **hace muy ~ que lo conoce** she hasn't known him for very long; **tardó ~ en hacerlo** it didn't take him long to do it; **falta ~ para las navidades** it's not long till Christmas; **a ~ de venir él** soon *o* shortly after he came; **dentro de ~** soon; **~ antes de que …** a short while *o* shortly before …
C un poco 1 (refiriéndose a cantidades) a little; (refiriéndose a tiempo) a while; **espera un poquito** wait a little while; **todavía le duele un ~** it still hurts him a little *o* a bit; **es un ~ lo que está pasando en Japón** it's rather like what's happening in Japan; **un ~ porque me dio lástima** partly because I felt sorry for him 2 **un poco de**: **un ~ de pimienta/vino** a little (bit of) pepper/wine; **come un ~ de jamón** have a bit of ham 3 **un poco + ADJ/ADV**: **un ~ caro/tarde** a bit *o* a little expensive/late
D (*en locs*) **a poco** (Méx): **¿a ~ no lees los periódicos?** don't you read the newspapers?; **¡a ~ no está fabuloso Acapulco!** isn't Acapulco just fantastic!; **¡a ~ ganaron!** don't tell me they won!; **de a poco** (AmL) gradually; **agrégale la leche de a poquito** add the milk gradually *o* a little at a time; **de a poquito se lo fue comiendo** little by little she ate it all up; **en poco**: **en ~ estuvo que no viniéramos** we almost didn't come; **tienen en ~ la vida ajena** they set little value on other people's lives; **me tienes bien en ~ si crees que …** you can't think very highly *o* much of me if you think …; **poco a poco** gradually; **poco más o menos** approximately, roughly; **poco menos que** nearly; **~ menos que la mata** (fam) he almost killed her; **por poco** nearly

pocotón *m* (Per fam): **un ~ de comida** loads of food

poda *f* (acción) pruning; (temporada) pruning season

podadera *f* (cuchillo) pruner; (tijeras) pruning shears

podadora *f* (Méx) *tb* **~ de pasto** lawnmower

podar [A1] *vt* ‹*árbol*› to prune; ‹*rabo*› to dock

podcast *m* (Inf) podcast; **hacer un ~** to podcast

podenco *m* hound

poder¹ [E21] *v aux*
(Sentido I)
A (tener la capacidad o posibilidad de): **en cuanto puedas** as soon as you can; **no puedo pagar tanto** I can't pay that much; **no podía dejar de reír** I couldn't stop laughing; **no va a ~ venir** he won't be able to come; **¿cuándo podrá darme una respuesta?** when will you be able to *o* when can you give me an answer?; **no pudo asistir a la reunión** he was unable to *o* he couldn't attend the meeting; **¿pudiste hacerlo sola?** were you able to do it on your own?; **no se puede valer por sí mismo** he can't manage by himself; **con aquel ruido no se podía trabajar** it was impossible to work with that noise going on
B (expresando idea de permiso): **¿puedo servirme otro?** can *o* may I have another one?; **¿le puedo hacer una sugerencia?** may I make a suggestion?; **¿podría irme un poco más temprano hoy?** could I leave a little earlier today?; **puedes hacer lo que quieras** you can do whatever you like; **no puede comer sal** he isn't allowed to eat salt; **¿se puede? — ¡adelante!** may I? — come in; **aquí no se**

puede fumar smoking is not allowed here
C (expresando derecho moral): **no podemos hacerle eso** we can't do that to her; **bien puedes tomarte un descanso ahora** you can afford to take a rest now
D 1 (en quejas, reproches): **¿cómo pudiste hacer una cosa así?** how could you do such a thing?; **podías** *or* **podrías haberme avisado** you could *o* might have warned me! 2 (en sugerencias): **ya te puedes ir haciendo a la idea** you'd better start getting used to the idea; **podrías** *or* **podías pedírselo tú** *you* could ask him for it 3 (solicitando un favor): **¿puedes bajar un momento?** can you come down for a moment?; **¿podrías hacerme un favor?** could you do me a favor?
(Sentido **II**) (con el verbo principal sobreentendido)
A ~ CON **algo/algn**: **¿puedes con todo eso?** can you manage all that?; **no puedo con esta maleta** I can't manage this suitcase; **no pudo con el alemán y lo dejó** he couldn't get to grips with German and he gave up; **¡con este niño no hay quien pueda!** this child is just impossible!; ***podérsela con algo*** (Chi fam) to cope with sth
B (*en locs*) **a más no poder**: **comió a más no ~** he ate until he was fit to burst; **corrimos a más no ~** we ran as fast as we could; **es feo a más no ~** he's as ugly as they come; **no poder más**: **estoy que no puedo más** (cansado) I'm exhausted; (lleno) I can't eat anything else; **ya no puedo más con este niño** I'm at the end of my tether with this child; **ya no puedo más, me está desquiciando** I can't go on like this, it's driving me mad; **no poder (por) menos que**: **no pude menos que sentirme halagado** I couldn't help feeling flattered; **no pudo menos que reconocer** she had no alternative but to admit
C (fam) (+ *me, te, le etc*) 1 (ganar): **él es más alto, pero tú le puedes** he's taller than you but you can beat him 2 (Méx) (doler): **tu indiferencia le puede mucho** she's very hurt by your indifference; **nos pudo mucho la muerte de Julio** we were terribly upset by Julio's death
(Sentido **III**)
A (con idea de eventualidad, posibilidad): **puede aparecer en cualquier momento** he may turn up at any moment; **de él se puede esperar cualquier cosa** anything's possible with him; **no hagas nada que pueda resultar sospechoso** don't do anything that might look suspicious; **puede haber venido ayer** he may have come yesterday; **te podrías** *or* **podías haber matado** you could have killed yourself!; **no podía haber estado más amable** she couldn't have been kinder; **podría volver a ocurrir** it could happen again; **no pudo haber sido Pilar** it couldn't have been Pilar
B (*en 3ª pers*): **no puede ser que no lo sepa** he *must* know; **no puede ser que ya haya terminado** he *can't* have finished already; **si puede ser** *or* (Esp) **a ~ ser** if possible; **no pudo ser** it wasn't possible; **puede (ser) que tengas razón** you may *o* could be right; **puede (ser) que no nos haya visto** he may not have seen us; **— puede que sí, puede que no** maybe, maybe not

poder² *m*
A 1 (control, influencia) power; **tiene mucho ~ en el pueblo** he has a great deal of power *o* influence in the village; **estamos/nos tiene en su ~** we are/she has us in her power; **caer en ~ de algn** «*ciudad/país*» to fall to sb 2 (Pol) **el ~** power; **estar en el ~** to be in power; **tomar el ~** to take *o* seize power; **detenta el ~ desde hace 20 años** (frml) he has held power for 20 years
B (posesión): **la carta está en ~ de ...** the letter is in the hands of ...; **obra en su ~ la copia del acta** (frml) you have in your possession a copy of the minutes
C 1 (derecho, atribución): **tener amplios/plenos ~es para hacer algo** to have wide-ranging powers/full authority to do sth; **los~es de la junta son ilimitados** the junta has unlimited powers; **la entrega de ~es** the handing over of power 2 (Der) (documento) letter of authorization; (hecho ante notario) power of attorney; **casarse por ~** (AmL) *or* (Esp) **por ~es** to get married by proxy
D 1 (capacidad, facultad) power; **su ~ de convicción** her power of persuasion 2 (de motor, aparato) power
(Compuestos)
- **poder absoluto** *m* absolute power
- **poder adquisitivo** *m* purchasing power
- **poder ejecutivo** *m*: **el ~ ~** the executive
- **poderes fácticos** *mpl*: *institutions which hold effective control*
- **poderes públicos** *mpl*: **los ~ ~** the authorities
- **poder judicial** *m*: **el ~ ~** the judiciary
- **poder legislativo** *m*: **el ~ ~** the legislature

poderío *m* power
poderoso -sa *adj* ‹*nación/persona*› powerful; ‹*remedio/calmante*› powerful, effective; ‹*motivo*› powerful, strong
poderosos *mpl*: **los ~s** (los ricos) the wealthy; (los que tienen poder) the powerful
podio *m*, **pódium** *m* (*pl* **-diums**) (Dep) podium; (Mús) podium, rostrum
podología *f* chiropody, podiatry (AmE)
podólogo -ga *m,f* chiropodist, podiatrist (AmE)
podré, etc *see* **poder¹**
podredumbre *f* (mal estado) rottenness, putrefaction; (corrupción) corruption
podría, etc *see* **poder¹**
podrida *f* (RPl fam): **se armó la ~** all hell broke loose (colloq), there was a tremendous ruckus (AmE colloq)
podrido -da *adj*
A 1 (descompuesto) rotten; **huele a** *or* (AmL) **hay olor a ~** there's a smell of something rotting *o* rotten 2 (corrompido) rotten, corrupt; ***estar ~ de dinero*** *or* (AmL) ***estar ~ en plata/oro*** (fam) to be stinking *o* filthy rich (colloq)
B (RPl fam) (harto, aburrido) fed up (colloq); **me tienen podrida** I'm fed up with them; **estar ~ DE algo/algn** to be fed up WITH sth/sb (colloq)
podrir [I38] *vt* ▸**pudrir**
poema *m* poem; ***fue todo un ~*** (fam) you should have seen him/her/it!; ***ser un ~*** (AmL fam) to be lovely
poesía *f* (género) poetry; (poema) poem
poeta -tisa *m,f*, **poeta** *mf* poet
poética *f* poetics, poetic art
poético -ca *adj* poetic
póker, poker *m* ▸**póquer**
polaco¹ -ca *adj* Polish
polaco² -ca *m, f*
A (persona) Pole
B **polaco** *m* (idioma) Polish
polaina *f* (de cuero, paño) gaiter; (de lana tejida) (RPl) legwarmer
polar *adj* polar
polaridad *f* polarity
polarización *f* 1 (Fot, Ópt) polarization 2 (de atención, interés) concentration 3 (de nación, opiniones) polarization
polarizar [A4] *vt* 1 (Fot, Ópt) to polarize 2 ‹*atención*› to focus 3 ‹*nación/opiniones*› to polarize
■ **polarizarse** *v pron* (dividirse) to polarize, become polarized
polca *f* polka
pole *f* pole position; **salir de la ~** to start in pole position
polea *f* (Tec) pulley; (Náut) tackle
polémica *f* controversy, polemic (frml)
polémico -ca *adj* controversial, polemic (frml)
polemista *mf* polemicist
polemizar [A4] *vi* to argue; **se ha polemizado mucho en torno a este tema** there has been a great deal of controversy about this matter
polen *m* pollen
poleo *m* pennyroyal
polera *f* (suéter) (RPl) polo neck (camiseta); (Chi) T-shirt
poli *mf* 1 (fam) (agente) cop (colloq) 2 **la poli** *f* (fam) (cuerpo) the fuzz (*pl*) (colloq), the cops (*pl*) (colloq)
poliamida *f* (Quím) polyamide; (Tex) nylon
poliandria, poliandría *f* polyandry
polichinela *m* (títere) string puppet
policía *f*
A (cuerpo) police; **llamar a la ~** to call the police; **la ~ está investigando el caso** the police are investigating the case
(Compuestos)
- **policía antidisturbios/militar/secreta** riot/military/secret police

- **policía de tráfico** *or* (AmL) **de tránsito** traffic police, highway patrol (AmE)
- **policía municipal** local *o* city police
- **policía nacional** (state) police

B **policía** (agente) (*m*) policeman, police officer; (*f*) policewoman, police officer

(Compuestos)
- **policía de tráfico** *or* (AmL) **tránsito** (*m*) traffic officer *o* policeman; (*f*) traffic officer *o* policewoman
- **policía municipal** (*m*) city *o* local police officer, city *o* local policeman; (*f*) city *o* local police officer, city *o* local policewoman

policíaco -ca, **policiaco -ca** *adj* ‹*novela/serie*› crime (*before n*), detective (*before n*)

policial *adj* police (*before n*)

policlínica *f*, **policlínico** *m* polyclinic

policromía *f* polychromy

policromo -ma, **polícromo -ma** *adj* polychrome

polideportivo *m* sports center•

poliedro *m* polyhedron

poliéster *m* polyester

polietileno *m* polyethylene (AmE), polythene (BrE)

polifacético -ca *adj* versatile, multifaceted

polifonía *f* polyphony

polifónico -ca *adj* polyphonic

poligamia *f* polygamy

polígamo[1] **-ma** *adj* polygamous

polígamo[2] **-ma** *m,f* polygamist

políglota *mf* polyglot

polígono *m*

A (Mat) polygon

B (Esp) (zona) area, zone; (urbanización) development, housing estate

(Compuesto) **polígono industrial** (Esp) industrial zone

polígrafo *m* lie detector, polygraph (Tec)

polilla *f*

A (Zool) moth

(Compuesto) **polilla de la madera** woodworm

B (Per fam) (prostituta) hooker (colloq)

polimorfismo *m* polymorphism

polimorfo -fa *adj* polymorphous

Polinesia *f* Polynesia

polinesio[1] **-sia** *adj/m,f* Polynesian

polinesio[2] *m* (idioma) Polynesian

polinización *f* pollination; **~ cruzada** cross-pollination

polinizar [A4] *vt* to pollinate

polio *f* polio

poliomielitis *f* poliomyelitis

pólipo *m* (Med, Zool) polyp; (coral) coral

polisemia *f* polysemy

polisémico -ca *adj* polysemous

polisílabo[1] **-ba** *adj* polysyllabic

polisílabo[2] *m* polysyllable

politécnico -ca *adj* ‹*universidad*› *specializing in technical or practical subjects*; **escuela politécnica** technical college

politeísmo *m* polytheism

política *f*

A (Pol) politics; **meterse en ~** (como profesión) to go into politics; (como militante) to get involved in politics

B (postura) policy; **~ interior/exterior** domestic/foreign policy; **nuestra ~ educativa/salarial** our education/wage policy

politicastro -tra *m,f* (pey) politician, politico (pej)

político[1] **-ca** *adj*

A (Pol) political

B (diplomático) diplomatic, tactful

C (en relaciones de parentesco): **es mi sobrino ~** he's my nephew by marriage; **la familia política** the in-laws

político[2] **-ca** *m,f* politician

politiquear [A1] *vi* (fam) to indulge in politics *o* (pej) politicking

politiqueo *m*, **politiquería** *f* (fam) political maneuvering•, politicking (pej)

politizar [A4] *vt* to politicize

■ **politizarse** *v pron* to become politicized

polivalente *adj* (Quím) polyvalent; (versátil) multipurpose

póliza *f*

A (de seguros) policy; **~ de seguro de incendios/vida** fire/life insurance policy

B (esp Esp) (sello) fiscal stamp

polizón *mf* stowaway; **viajar de ~** to stow away

polla *f*

A (Esp vulg) (pene) cock (vulg), prick (vulg)

B [1] (AmL) (apuesta) bet [2] (Per) (quiniela) ≈ sports lottery (*in US*), ≈ pools (*in UK*) [3] (Chi) (lotería) lottery; *ver tb* **pollo**

> **polla**
>
> In Chile and Peru a word for an official lottery, whose proceeds go to charity. In some Latin American countries, a *polla* is a sweepstake on soccer games, horse races etc

pollera *f* [1] (CS) (Indum) skirt [2] **polleras** *fpl* (CS fam) (mujeres) women (*pl*); **un lío de ~s** woman trouble, some trouble with a woman

pollería *f* poultry store, poulterer's store

pollero -ra *m,f*

A (vendedor) poulterer; (criador) chicken farmer

B (Méx) (coyote) *person who gets illegal immigrants across the border*

pollino -na *m,f* (Zool) donkey; (persona) (fam) idiot, silly ass (colloq)

pollito -ta *m,f* chick

pollo -lla *m,f*

A (Zool) [1] (cría) chick [2] (adulto) chicken [3] (Coc) chicken; **~ asado** roast chicken; ***listo el ~*** (AmL fam) that's that!; **hago esto y listo el ~** I'll just do this and then I'm calling it a day

B (fam) (*m*) young lad; (*f*) young girl

polluelo *m* chick

polo[1] **-la** *adj* (AmC fam) country (*before n*), hick (*before n*) (AmE colloq); **no sea tan ~** don't be such a hick

polo[2] *m*

A (Geog) pole

(Compuesto) **Polo Norte/Sur** North/South Pole

B (Elec, Fís) pole; **~ positivo/negativo** positive/negative pole; ***ser el ~ opuesto de algo/algn*** (fam) to be the complete opposite of sth/sb; ***ser ~s opuestos*** (fam) to be poles apart

C (centro) center•, focus

D (Dep) polo

E (Indum) polo shirt

F (Esp) (helado) Popsicle® (AmE), ice lolly (BrE)

pololear [A1] *vi* (Chi) to have a boyfriend/girlfriend

pololo -la (Chi) (*m*) boyfriend; (*f*) girlfriend

polonesa *f* polonaise

Polonia *f* Poland

poltrona *f* armchair, easy chair

polución *f* pollution

polvareda *f* dust cloud; ***levantar una ~*** (fam) to cause an uproar *o* a commotion

polvera *f* powder compact

polvero *m* (Col, Ven) dust cloud

polvo *m*

A [1] (suciedad) dust; **limpiar** *or* **quitar el ~** to do the dusting, to dust; **la casa está llena de ~** the house is very dusty *o* full of dust; ***estar hecho ~*** (agotado) to be all in (fam); **a él no le pasó nada pero el coche está hecho ~** he was all right but the car is a wreck *o* (AmE) was totaled *o* (BrE) is a write-off (colloq); **la noticia los hizo ~** they were stunned *o* shattered by the news (colloq); ***limpio de ~ y paja*** clear; ***morder el ~*** to bite the dust (colloq) [2] (Coc, Quím) powder; **viene entera o en ~** you can buy it whole or ground *o* in powder form [3] **polvos** *mpl* (en cosmética) face powder

(Compuestos)
- **polvos (de) pica pica** *mpl* itching powder
- **polvos de talco** *mpl* talcum powder, talc (colloq)

B (vulg) (acto sexual) fuck (vulg), screw (vulg); **echar(se) un ~** to have a screw (vulg), to ball (AmE sl)

P

pólvora *f* 1 (explosivo) gunpowder; ***arder como la ~*** to go up like a torch 2 (fuegos artificiales) fireworks (*pl*)

polvoriento -ta *adj* dusty

polvorín *m* 1 (almacén de explosivos) magazine 2 (lugar, país peligroso) powder keg

pomada *f* (Farm) ointment, cream; ***hacer ~ a algn*** (Méx, RPl fam) to give sb a thrashing *o* hammering (colloq); ***hacer ~ algo*** (RPl fam) to ruin sth

(Compuesto) **pomada de zapatos** (RPl) shoe polish

pomelo *m* (fruto) grapefruit; (árbol) grapefruit tree

pomo *m* (de puerta, mueble) handle, knob; (de espada) pommel

pompa *f*

A *tb* **~ de jabón** bubble

B (esplendor) pomp, splendor*

(Compuesto) **pompas fúnebres** *fpl* (ceremonia) funeral ceremony; (funeraria) funeral parlor*, funeral director's

pompas *fpl* (Méx fam) (trasero) bottom (colloq), butt (AmE colloq)

pomposidad *f* 1 (esplendor) splendor*, pomp; (del lenguaje) pomposity 2 (ostentación) ostentation, pomposity

pomposo -sa *adj* 1 ‹*boda/fiesta*› magnificent, splendid; ‹*lenguaje/estilo*› pompous, high-sounding 2 (ostentoso) pompous, ostentatious

pómulo *m* (hueso) cheekbone; (mejilla) cheek

pon *see* **poner**

ponchada *f* (RPl fam): **me costó una ~ de plata** *or* **de pesos** it cost me a bomb *o* a fortune (colloq); **una ~ de libros** loads *o* stacks of books (colloq)

ponchadura *f* (Méx) flat, puncture

ponchar [A1] *vt*

A (Méx) ‹*llanta/balón*› to puncture; ‹*boleto*› to punch

B (en béisbol) to fan (colloq), to strike out; **¡ponchado!** out!

■ **poncharse** *v pron*

A (Méx) «*balón*» to puncture; **se nos ponchó una llanta** we had a flat *o* a puncture

B (Col, Ven) (en béisbol) to fan (colloq), to strike out

ponche *m* (bebida) punch

poncho *m* poncho

ponderable *adj* (considerable) considerable; (elogiable) praiseworthy

ponderación *f* 1 (de índice, cálculo) weighting, adjustment 2 (mesura) deliberation 3 (elogio) praise

ponderado -da *adj* ‹*índice/cálculo*› weighted, adjusted; ‹*acciones/palabras*› balanced, considered; (elogiado) praised

ponderar [A1] *vt* 1 ‹*cálculo/índice*› to weight, adjust 2 (considerar) to weigh up, consider, ponder 3 (alabar) to praise, speak highly of

pondré, pondría, etc *see* **poner**

ponedero *m* nest

ponedora *f* layer, laying hen

ponencia *f* 1 (discurso) (Pol) address; (en congreso científico) paper, presentation; **presentar una ~** to give a paper 2 (propuesta) proposal, motion 3 (comisión) committee

ponente *mf* (en congreso, asamblea) speaker

poner [E22] *vt*

(*Sentido I*)

A 1 (colocar) to put; **lo pusieron en el curso avanzado** he was put *o* placed in the advanced class; **pon agua a calentar** put some water on to boil; **no le puso la tapa** he didn't put the lid on; **ponle el collar al perro** put the dog's collar on 2 ‹*anuncio/aviso*› to place, put

B (agregar) to put; **¿cuándo se le pone el agua?** when do you put the water in?, when do you add the water?; **¿le pones azúcar al café?** do you take sugar in your coffee?

C ‹*ropa/calzado*› (+ *me/te/le etc*): **¿me pones los zapatos?** can you put my shoes on (for me)?; **le puse el vestido rojo** I dressed her in her red dress

D ‹*inyección/supositorio*› to give

E **poner la mesa** to lay *o* set the table; **pon otro cubierto para Juan** lay another place at the table for Juan

F 1 (instalar, montar) ‹*oficina/restaurante*› to open; **puso una autoescuela** he opened up a driving school; **les ayudó a ~ la casa** he helped them set up house *o* home 2 ‹*cocina/teléfono/calefacción*› to install 3 ‹*cerradura/armario*› to fit; **pusimos parqué en el salón** we laid parquet flooring in the living room

G «*ave*» ‹*huevo*› to lay

H (Esp) (servir, dar): **¿qué le pongo?** what can I get you?; **póngame un café, por favor** I'll have a coffee, please; **¿cuántos le pongo?** how many would you like?

(*Sentido II*)

A 1 (contribuir): **él pone el capital y yo el trabajo** he puts up the capital and I supply the labor; **pusimos 500 pesos cada uno** we put in 500 pesos each 2 (proporcionar) ‹*transporte*› to lay on

B ‹*atención*› to pay; ‹*cuidado/interés*› to take; **pon atención en lo que haces** pay attention to what you're doing; **pon más cuidado en la presentación** take more care over the presentation; **pone mucho entusiasmo en todo lo que hace** he puts a lot of enthusiasm into everything he does; **~ énfasis en algo** to stress sth

C 1 (imponer) ‹*deberes*› to give, set; ‹*examen/problema*› to set; **le pusieron una multa** he was fined 2 (oponer): **no puso inconveniente** he didn't have *o* raise any objections; **a todo le pone peros** *or* **pegas** she finds fault with everything 3 (adjudicar) ‹*nota*› to give; **¿qué nota te puso?** what mark did he give you?; **le pusieron un cero** he got nought out of ten

D (dar) ‹*nombre/apodo*› to give; ‹*ejemplo*› to give; **¿qué título le pusiste?** what title did you give it?; **le pusieron Eva** they called her Eva; **le pusieron el apodo de 'el cojo'** they nicknamed him 'el cojo'

E (enviar) ‹*telegrama*› to send

F (escribir) to put; **no sé que ~le** I don't know what to put *o* say

G (esp Esp) (expresar por escrito) to say; **allí pone que no se puede pasar** it says there that you can't go in

H (Esp) (exhibir, dar) ‹*obra/película*›: **¿ponen algo interesante en la tele?** is there anything interesting on TV?; **¿qué ponen en el Royal?** what's on *o* what's showing at the Royal?; **en el teatro ponen una obra de Casares** there's a play by Casares on at the theater

I (RPl) (tardar) to take; **de allí a Salta pusimos tres horas** it took us three hours from there to Salta

(*Sentido III*)

A (en estado, situación) (+ *compl*): **~ a algn nervioso** to make sb nervous; **~ a algn de mal humor** to put sb in a bad mood; **~ a algn en evidencia** to show sb up; **~ a algn en un aprieto** to put sb in an awkward position; **nos puso al corriente de lo sucedido** he brought us up to date on what had happened; **¡mira cómo has puesto la alfombra!** look at the mess you've made on the carpet!; **me lo estás poniendo muy difícil** you're making things very difficult for me

B (adoptar) «*cara/voz*»: **no pongas esa cara** there's no need to look like that; **puso voz de asustado** he sounded scared

C 1 (hacer empezar): **me pusieron a régimen** they put me on a diet; **~ a algn A + INF: puso a las hijas a trabajar** he sent his daughters out to work; **lo puse a hacer los deberes** I made him do his homework 2 **~ a algn DE algo**: **la pusieron de jefa de sección** they made her head of department; **lo pusieron de ángel** he was given the part of an angel; **siempre te pone de ejemplo** he always holds you up as an example

D (suponer): **pon que perdemos ese tren...** say we miss that train *o* if we (were to) miss that train...; **pongamos (por caso) que están equivocados** suppose *o* let's just say they're wrong; ***~le*** (esp AmL): **¿cuánto se tarda? — ponle dos horas** how long does it take? — about two hours *o* reckon on two hours

(*Sentido IV*)

A 1 (conectar, encender) ‹*televisión/calefacción*› to turn on, switch on, put on; ‹*programa/canal*› to put on; ‹*disco*› to put on; **puso el motor en marcha** she switched on *o* started the engine; **nos van a ~ la luz** we're going to have our electricity connected 2 (ajustar, graduar): **pon el despertador a las siete** set the alarm (clock) for seven; **pon la música más alta** turn the music up; **puso el reloj en hora** she put the clock right; **~ el motor a punto** to tune up the engine

B (Esp) (al teléfono): **en seguida le pongo** I'm just putting you through *o* connecting you; **~ a algn CON algo/algn** to put sb THROUGH TO sth/sb; **¿me pone con la extensión 24?** could you put me through to extension 24, please?

■ *vi* «*gallina*» to lay
■ **ponerse** *v pron*
(Sentido I)
A [1] (*refl*) (colocarse): **pongámonos a la sombra** let's sit (*o* lie *etc*) in the shade; **~se de pie** to stand (up); **~se de rodillas** to kneel (down), get down on one's knees; **ponte ahí, junto al árbol** stand over there, by the tree; ***se me/le puso que ...*** (AmS fam) I/he had a feeling that ... (colloq); **¡se le pone cada cosa ...!** he gets the strangest ideas into his head [2] (Esp) (llegar): **en una hora nos pusimos allí** we got there in one hour
B «*sol*» to set
C (*refl*) ‹*calzado/maquillaje/alhaja*› to put on; **no tengo nada que ~me** I don't have a thing to wear; **me puse el collar de perlas** I wore *o* put on my pearl necklace
(Sentido II)
A (en estado, situación) (+ *compl*): **se puso triste** she became sad; **cuando lo vio se puso muy contenta** she was so happy when she saw it; **se puso como loco** he went mad; **quiero ~me morena** I want to get a tan; **~se cómodo** to make oneself comfortable; **no te pongas así** don't get so worked up; **¡cómo te has puesto de barro!** look at you, you're covered in mud!; **la vida se está poniendo carísima** everything's getting so expensive
B [1] (empezar) **~se A + INF** to start -ING, to start + INF; **se puso a llover** it started raining *o* started to rain; **a ver si te pones a trabajar** you'd better get down to some work [2] (CS arg) (contribuir dinero): **cuando llega la cuenta hay que ~se** when the bill comes, everyone has to cough up (colloq); **yo me pongo con cien** I'll put in *o* chip in a hundred
(Sentido III) (Esp) (al teléfono): **¿Pepe? sí, ahora se pone** Pepe? OK, I'll just get him for you; **dile a tu madre que se ponga** ask your mother to come to the phone

ponga, pongas, etc *see* **poner**

poni *m* ▸**pony**

poniente *m* (occidente) west; (viento) west wind

ponqué *m* (Col, Ven) cake

pontificado *m* pontificate

pontificar [A2] *vi* to pontificate

pontífice *m* pontiff, pope

pontificio -cia *adj* papal, pontifical

pontón *m* pontoon

pony /'poni/ *m* (*pl* **-nies** *or* **-nys**) pony

ponzoña *f* poison

ponzoñoso -sa *adj* ‹*bebida*› poisonous; ‹*ataque*› venomous

pop *m*
A (Mús) pop (music)
B (Ur) (Coc) popcorn
(Compuesto) **pop salado/acaramelado** (Ur) salted/sweet popcorn

popa *f* stern

popelín *m*, **popelina** *f* (AmL) poplin

popis *adj inv* (Méx fam) posh

popó *m* (leng infantil) poop (AmE colloq), pooh (BrE colloq); **quiero hacer ~** I want (to do) a poop *o* a pooh

popoff *adj inv* (Méx fam) posh

popote *m* (Méx) straw

populachería *f* cheap populism

populacho *m* (pey) plebs (*pl*) (pej), masses (*pl*)

popular *adj*
A [1] ‹*cultura/tradiciones*› popular (*before n*); ‹*canción/baile*› traditional, folk (*before n*); ‹*costumbres*› traditional [2] (Pol) ‹*movimiento/rebelión*› popular (*before n*)
B (que gusta) ‹*actor/programa/deporte*› popular
C ‹*lenguaje*› colloquial

popularidad *f* popularity; **goza de una gran ~** she is very popular

popularizar [A4] *vt* to popularize, make ... popular
■ **popularizarse** *v pron* to become popular

populismo *m* populism

populista *adj/mf* populist

popurrí *m* (de cosas, colores) potpourri

póquer *m* (juego — de naipes) poker; (— de dados) poker dice; **un ~ de ases** four aces

poquísimo *adj*: *ver* **poco**

por *prep*
(Sentido I)
A (en relaciones causales) because of; **lo he puesto aquí ~ el gato** I've put it here because of the cat; **~ falta de dinero** because of *o* owing to lack of money; **eso te pasa ~ crédulo** that's what you get for being (so) gullible; **~ naturaleza** by nature; **~ necesidad** out of necessity; **tanto ~ su precio como ~ su calidad** both for its price and its quality; **fue ~ eso que vine** that was why I came; **si no fuera ~ mi hijo ...** if it wasn't for my son ...; **fue elogiado ~ su actuación** he was praised for his performance; **~ + INF** for -ING; **me pidió perdón ~ haberme mentido** he apologized for lying *o* for having lied to me
B (según): **~ lo que he oído** from what I've heard; **~ lo que parece ...** it seems *o* it would seem ...
C (*en locs*) **por qué** why; **¿por qué no vienes conmigo?** why don't you come with me?; **por si** in case; ▸**acaso, mosca**[2]
D (en expresiones concesivas): **~ más que me esfuerzo** however hard *o* no matter how hard I try; **~ (muy) fácil que sea** however easy *o* no matter how easy it is
E [1] (en expresiones de modo): **colócalos ~ orden de tamaño/altura** put them in order of size/height; **~ orden de altura** in order of height; **~ adelantado** in advance; **~ escrito** in writing [2] (indicando el medio): **se lo comunicaron ~ teléfono** they told him over the phone; **lo dijeron ~ la radio** they said it on the radio; **~ avión/barco/carretera** by air/sea/road; **la conocí ~ la voz** I recognized her by her voice; **me enteré ~ un amigo** I heard from *o* through a friend; **lo intenté ~ todos los medios** I tried everything possible *o* every possible way [3] (Educ) from; **es doctor honoris causa ~ Oxford** he has an honorary doctorate from Oxford
F [1] (en relaciones de proporción): **cobra $30 ~ clase** he charges $30 a *o* per class; **120 kilómetros ~ hora** 120 kilometers an *o* per hour; **lo venden ~ metro** they sell it by the meter; **tú comes ~ tres** you eat enough for three people; **había un hombre ~ cada dos mujeres** there was one man to every two women; **tiene tres metros de largo ~ uno de ancho** it's three meters long by one meter wide; **es bastante ~ hoy** it's enough for today; **uno ~ uno** one by one; ▸**ciento**[2] [2] (en multiplicaciones): **tres ~ cuatro (son) doce** three times four is twelve, three fours are twelve
G [1] (en relaciones de sustitución, intercambio, representación) for; **su secretaria firmó ~ él** his secretary signed for him *o* on his behalf; **yo puedo ir ~ ti** I can go for you *o* in your place; **podrías pasar ~ inglesa** you could pass as English *o* for an Englishwoman; **es senador ~ Sevilla** he's a senator for Seville [2] (como): **~ ejemplo** for example; **¿acepta usted ~ esposa a Carmen?** do you take Carmen to be your (lawful wedded) wife?
H (introduciendo el agente) by; **compuesto ~ Mozart** composed by Mozart; **se vieron sorprendidos ~ una tormenta** they were caught in a sudden storm
(Sentido II)
A (expresando finalidad, objetivo): **pelearse ~ algo** to fight over sth; **lo hace ~ el dinero** he does it for the money; **te lo digo ~ tu bien** I'm telling you for your own good; **no tengo ~ qué ir** there's no reason why I should go; **~ + INF**: **daría cualquier cosa ~ verla** I'd give anything to see her; **no entré ~ no molestar** I didn't go in because I didn't want to disturb him; **eso es hablar ~ hablar** that's talking for the sake of talking *o* for the sake of it; **~ QUE + SUBJ** (*here* **por que** *can also be written* **porque**): **estaba ansioso ~ que lo escucharan** he was eager for them to listen to him; **lucharon ~ que se hiciera justicia** they fought for justice to be done
B (indicando consideración, favor) for; **~ mí no lo hagas** don't do it just for me *o* for my sake
C (indicando inclinación, elección): **su amor ~ la música** her love of music; **demostró interés ~ el cuadro** he showed interest in the painting; **no siento nada ~ él** I don't feel anything for him; **opté ~ no ir** I chose not to go; **votó ~ ella** he voted for her
D (en busca de): **salió/fue ~** *or* (Esp) **a ~ pan** he went (out) for some bread, he went (out) to get some bread
E (en lo que respecta a): **~ mí no hay inconveniente** I don't mind; **~ mí que haga lo que quiera** as far as I'm concerned, he can do what he likes

P

F (indicando una situación pendiente) **~ + INF**: **tengo la casa ~ limpiar** I've got the house to clean; **estos cambios aún están ~ hacer** these changes are yet to be made; **¡eso está ~ ver!** we'll see about that!
G (esp AmL) **estar ~ + INF** (estar a punto de): **deben (de) estar ~ llegar** they should be arriving any minute; **la leche está ~ hervir** the milk's about to boil
Sentido **III**
A (indicando lugar de acceso, salida, trayectoria): **entró ~ la ventana** he came in through the window; **no va a pasar ~ la puerta** it won't go through the door; **sal ~ aquí** go out this way; **se cayó ~ la escalera** he fell down the stairs; **subieron ~ la ladera este** they went up by the east face; **¿el 121 va ~ (la) Avenida Rosas?** does the 121 go along Rosas Avenue?; **fuimos ~ el camino más largo** we took the longer route; **¿~ dónde has venido?** which way did you come?; **¿puedes pasar ~ la tintorería?** could you call in at *o* drop by the drycleaner's?
B 1 (expresando lugar indeterminado): **está ~ ahí** he's over there somewhere; **¿~ dónde está** *or* **queda el hotel?** whereabouts is the hotel?; **viven ~ mi barrio** they live around my area; **¿qué tal te fue ~ Londres?** how did you get on in London?; **~ todos lados** *or* **~ todas partes** everywhere 2 (expresando lugar determinado): **corta ~ aquí** cut here; **voy ~ la página 15** I'm up to *o* I'm on page 15; **empieza ~ el principio** start at the beginning; **agárralo ~ el mango** hold it by the handle 3 (indicando extensión): **~ todo el país** throughout the (whole) country; **viajamos ~ el norte de Francia** we travelled around *o* in the North of France; **pasa un trapo ~ el piso** give the floor a quick wipe; *ver tb* **afuera, adentro, dentro, fuera, encima, etc**
Sentido **IV**
A (expresando tiempo aproximado): **~ aquella época** *or* **~ aquel entonces** at that time; **sucedió allá ~ 1960** it happened some time back around 1960
B (Esp) (indicando una ocasión) for; **me lo regaló ~ mi cumpleaños** she gave it to me for my birthday
C (durante) for; **~ los siglos de los siglos** for ever and ever; **~ el momento** *or* **~ ahora** for the time being *o* for now; *ver tb* **mañana³, tarde², noche**

porcelana *f* 1 (material) china; (de mejor calidad) porcelain; **una taza de ~** a china/porcelain cup 2 (objeto) piece of china/porcelain

porcentaje *m* percentage; **trabaja a ~** she works on a commission-only basis

porcentual *adj* ‹*aumento/punto*› percentage (*before n*); **crecimiento ~** growth in percentage terms

porche *m* (de casa) porch; (soportal) arcade

porcino -na *adj* ‹*productos*› pork (*before n*); **ganado ~** pigs, hogs (AmE)

porción *f* (de todo) portion; (en reparto) share; (de comida) portion, helping, serving

pordiosero -ra *m,f* beggar

porfiado¹ -da *adj* stubborn, pig-headed (colloq)

porfiado² -da *m,f*
A (persona) stubborn creature (colloq)
B **porfiado** *m* (Per) (muñeco) roly-poly doll

porfiar [A17] *vi*
A (insistir): **no me porfíes, ya te dije que no** don't keep on *o* go on about it, I said no
B (perseverar): **porfió en obtenerlo** he persevered in his efforts to obtain it

pormenor *m* detail; **me contó los ~es del asunto** he explained the whole matter to me in detail

pormenorizado -da *adj* detailed

pormenorizar [A4] *vi* to go into detail
■ **pormenorizar** *vt* to describe … in detail

porno *adj inv* (fam) ‹*película/libro*› porn (*before n*) (colloq)

pornografía *f* pornography

pornográfico -ca *adj* pornographic

poro *m*
A (Anat, Biol) pore
B (Col) (mortero) mortar (*made from a gourd*)
C (Chi, Méx) (puerro) leek

pororó *m* (RPl) popcorn

porosidad *f* porosity

poroso -sa *adj* porous

porotera *f* (Chi arg) prison, can (AmE colloq), nick (BrE colloq)

poroto *m*
A (CS) bean; ***anotarse*** *or* ***apuntarse un ~*** (CS fam) to score a point; ***ganarse los ~s*** (Chi fam) to earn one's living, earn a crust (colloq)
Compuesto **poroto verde** (Chi) green bean
B (RPl fam) (insignificancia): **tu problema es un ~ al lado de esto** your problem is nothing compared to this

porque *conj* 1 (indicando causa) because; **¡porque sí!** because! (colloq); **¿por qué no vas ir? — ~ no** why don't you go? — because I don't want to 2 (indicando finalidad) *ver* **por** *Sentido* **II A**

porqué *m* reason; **quiero saber el ~ de su decisión** I want to know the reason for his decision

porquería *f*
A 1 (suciedad) dirt 2 (cochinada): **no hagas ~s** don't do disgusting *o* filthy things like that; **la casa está hecha una ~** (fam) the house is in such a state (colloq)
B 1 (cosa de mala calidad): **me regaló una ~** he gave me a really trashy gift; **el libro es un ~** the movie's a piece of junk *o* (BrE colloq) the book's a load of rubbish; **la comida es una ~** the food is dreadful *o* terrible 2 **de porquería** (AmS fam) lousy (colloq); **¡qué tiempo de ~!** what foul *o* lousy weather!; **¡cómo me duele este diente de ~!** this damn tooth is killing me (colloq) 3 (chuchería): **no te comas esa ~** don't eat that junk *o* (BrE) that rubbish

porqueriza *f* pigsty

porquerizo -za *m,f* (ant) swineherd (arch)

porra *f*
A (de guardia, policía) nightstick (AmE), truncheon (BrE)
B (fam) (expresando disgusto, enojo): **¡qué película ni qué ~s! ¡a estudiar!** watch the movie? you must be joking! get on with your schoolwork (colloq); **ya no hago más ¡qué ~s!** I'm damned if I'm doing any more! (colloq); ***mandar a algn a la ~*** (colloq) to send sb packing, tell sb to get lost (colloq); **¡vete** *or* **ándate a la ~!** go to hell! (colloq), get lost! (colloq); ***mandar algo a la ~*** (colloq) ‹*trabajo*› to chuck sth in (colloq); ***y una ~*** (Esp fam) like hell! (colloq); **lo tienes que hacer tú — ¡y una ~!** *you* have to do it — like hell I do! (colloq)
C (Jueg) draw, lottery
D (Col, Méx fam) 1 (seguidores, hinchas) fans (*pl*) 2 (canto, grito): **¡una ~ para Villalva!** three cheers for Villalva!; **la ~ de la universidad** the college chant; ***echarle ~s a algn*** (Méx fam) ‹*a equipo/corredor*› to cheer sb (on); **necesita que le echemos ~s** she needs cheering up

porrazo *m* (fam) 1 (con porra, palo etc): **le dio un ~** he whacked him with his stick (*o* truncheon *etc*) (colloq) 2 (accidente): **se pegó un buen ~** he banged his head (*o* arm *etc*); **me pegué un ~ contra un árbol** I went smack into a tree (colloq); ***de ~*** (Per fam) in one go (colloq)

porrillo *m* (Esp fam): **tener algo a ~** to have loads of sth (colloq); **hay rebajas a ~** there are sales galore (colloq)

porrista *mf* 1 (Col, Méx) (seguidor) fan 2 **porrista** *f* (Col, Méx) (animadora) cheerleader

porro¹ -rra *adj* (Chi fam) lazy

porro² -rra *m,f* (Chi fam) lazy child (*o* student *etc*); **el ~ de la clase** the laziest kid in the class (colloq)

porro³ *m*
A (Esp arg) (de hachís) joint (colloq), spliff (sl)
B (Méx fam & pey) (policía infiltrado) undercover cop (colloq), pig (sl & pej) (*who infiltrates student organizations*)

porrón *m*
A 1 (de vino) wine bottle (*with a long spout for drinking from*) 2 (Arg) (de cerveza) bottle of beer
B (CS) (pimiento) green pepper; (puerro) leek

portaaviones *m* (*pl* ~) aircraft carrier

portabebés *m* (*pl* ~) portacrib® (AmE), carrycot (BrE)

portabicicletas *m* (*pl* ~) bicycle rack

portacasetes *m* (*pl* ~), **portacassettes** *m* (*pl* ~) cassette case

portación *f* (AmL frml) carrying

portada *f*
A (de libro) title page; (de periódico) front page; (de revista) cover
B (de iglesia) front, facade

portadocumentos *m* (*pl* ~) (AmL) (grande) briefcase, attaché case; (pequeño) document wallet

portador -dora *m,f*

A 1 (Med) (de virus, germen) carrier 2 (frml) (de carta, mensaje) bearer (frml)

B (Com, Fin) bearer; **páguese al ~** pay the bearer

portaequipajes *m* (*pl* ~) 1 (Auto) (para el techo) roof-rack; (maletero) trunk (AmE), boot (BrE) 2 (en tren, autobús) luggage rack

portafolios *m* (*pl* ~), **portafolio** *m* (maletín) briefcase; (archivador) (Chi) ring binder

portahelicópteros *m* (*pl* ~) helicopter carrier

portal *m*

A 1 (de casa — entrada) doorway; (— vestíbulo) hall 2 (de iglesia, palacio) portal 3 (en muralla) gate; **el ~ de Belén** (Bib) the stable at Bethlehem

B **portales** *mpl* (soportales) arcade

portalámparas *m* (*pl* ~) bulbholder

portaligas *m* (*pl* ~) (CS) garter (AmE) *o* (BrE) suspender belt

portalón *m* 1 (Arquit) portal, monumental gate *o* entrance 2 (Náut) gangway

portamaletas *m* (*pl* ~) ▸**portaequipajes**

portaminas *m* (*pl* ~) automatic (AmE) *o* (BrE) propelling pencil

portamonedas *m* (*pl* ~) purse, change purse (AmE)

portaobjetos *m* (*pl* ~), **portaobjeto** *m* microscope slide

portapapeles *m* (*pl* ~s) 1 (fam) (de escritorio) letter rack 2 (Inf) clipboard

portaplumas *m* (*pl* ~) penholder

portar [A1] *vt* (frml) ‹*arma/bandera*› to carry, bear (frml)

■ **portarse** *v pron* 1 (comportarse): **~se bien** to behave (oneself); **~se mal** to behave badly; **~se bien/mal con algn** to treat sb well/badly 2 (cumplir): **el Zaragoza se portó en la final** Zaragoza delivered the goods in the final; **hoy te portaste** you've really excelled today

portarretratos *m* (*pl* ~) (photo) frame

portarrollos *m* (*pl* ~) (en la cocina) kitchen roll holder; (en el baño) toilet roll holder

portátil *adj* portable

portaviandas *m* (*pl* ~) lunch pail (AmE) *o* (BrE) box

portaviones *m* (*pl* ~) aircraft carrier

portavoz *mf* (*m*) spokesperson, spokesman; (*f*) spokesperson, spokeswoman

portazo *m* slam, bang; **dar un ~** to slam the door; **la puerta se cerró de un ~** the door slammed shut

porte *m*

A (aspecto, aire) bearing, demeanor*; **un joven de ~ distinguido** a distinguished-looking young man; **una mansión de ~ señorial** a very grand-looking mansion

B (tamaño) size; **es de este ~** (AmL) it's about *this* big

C 1 (costo) carriage; **la mercancía se envía a ~ pagado** the goods are sent freight paid *o* postage paid 2 (acción de portar) carrying

D **portes** *mpl* (transporte) transport; **~s pagados** freight/postage paid

porteador -dora *m,f* bearer, porter

portento *m* 1 (persona) genius; **esta niña es un ~** this girl's a prodigy 2 (prodigio) wonder; **canta que es un ~** she has a wonderful *o* marvelous voice

portentoso -sa *adj* ‹*memoria*› wonderful; ‹*representación/voz*› magnificent, superb

porteño -ña *adj* of/from the city of Buenos Aires

portería *f*

A 1 (de edificio) *desk/area from where the super/caretaker supervises the building*; **deje las llaves en ~** leave the keys at the desk 2 (vivienda) super's *o* superintendent's apartment (AmE), caretaker's flat (*o* house *etc*) (BrE)

B (Dep) goal

portero -ra *m,f*

A (que abre la puerta) doorman, porter; (que cuida el edificio) super (AmE), superintendent (AmE), caretaker (BrE)

(Compuesto) **portero eléctrico** *or* (Esp) **automático** *m* entryphone

B (Dep) goalkeeper

> **portero**
>
> A superintendent in an apartment building who looks after it, keeps it clean, delivers mail, and keeps an eye on comings and goings. *Porteros* often have an apartment in the building as part of their pay.
>
> Many buildings no longer have *porteros*. In these cases, access is regulated by a *portero automático* (intercom). The *portero*, and particularly the female *portera*, are part of popular culture. They have a reputation for being inquisitive and fond of gossip

portezuela *f* door

pórtico *m*

A (entrada) portico, porch; (galería) arcade

B (Chi period) (Dep) goal

portillo *m* (en una pared) chink, crack; (entre montañas) narrow pass

portón *m* (puerta grande) large door; (puerta principal) front door; (en cerca) gate

portorriqueño -ña *adj/m,f* Puerto Rican

portuario -ria *adj* port (*before n*), harbor* (*before n*); **trabajador ~** port worker, dockworker

Portugal *m* Portugal

portugués¹ -guesa *adj/m,f* Portuguese

portugués² *m* (idioma) Portuguese

porvenir *m* future; **de gran ~** with excellent prospects; **un joven sin ~** a young man with no future *o* no prospects

pos *m*: **en pos de** (*loc prep*) ‹*de presa/ladrón*› in pursuit of; ‹*de ilusión/fama*› in search of; **abandonó esta idea en ~ de una política más pragmática** he abandoned this idea in favor of a more pragmatic policy

posada *f* 1 (arc) (taberna) inn (arch) 2 (cobijo) hospitality

> **posada**
>
> A popular celebration in Mexico and Central America between December 16 and Christmas Day to commemorate the journey of Mary and Joseph to Bethlehem. It consists of a procession of models of religious figures that people carry on their shoulders, asking for shelter as they go by. The figures have their origin in an Aztec celebration, adapted to Christian tradition.
>
> Generally one family takes charge of organizing the models, and offers its house as the last of nine *posadas*. Other groups form, one of which goes from house to house with the figures, asking for shelter. It is turned away at each house. At the last house, the figures are taken in and put on an altar. The celebrations continue with food and drink, singing and dancing

posaderas *fpl* (fam) backside (colloq), butt (AmE colloq), bum (BrE colloq)

posadero -ra *m,f* innkeeper

posafuentes *m* (*pl* ~) (CS) (salvamanteles) table mat; (con patas) trivet

posar [A1] *vi* to pose

■ **posar** *vt* 1 (liter) ‹*mano*› to place, lay; **posó la mirada en el mar** she rested her gaze on the sea 2 ‹*bulto/carga*› to put down, set down, rest

■ **posarse** *v pron* «*pájaro/insecto*» to alight, land; «*avión/helicóptero*» to land

posavasos *m* (*pl* ~) coaster; (de cartón) beermat

posdata *f* postscript

pose *f* 1 (para foto) pose 2 (pey) (afectación) pose; **todo en él es pura ~** he's a real poseur *o* (BrE colloq) poser; **siempre adopta ~s de intelectual** he's always striking intellectual poses

poseedor -dora *m,f* (frml) (de título, récord, billete) holder; **se cree el ~ de la verdad absoluta** (iró) he believes himself to be in possession of the absolute truth (iro)

poseer [E13] *vt*

A 1 ‹*tierras/fortuna*› to own; **posee un título de propiedad** he holds title of ownership 2 ‹*conocimientos*› to have 3 ‹*récord/título*› to hold

B 1 (liter) (dominar): **lo poseían los celos** he was overcome with jealousy (liter); 2 (en sentido sexual) to possess, take

poseído¹ -da *adj* possessed; **~ por la ambición** (liter) driven by ambition (liter)

P

poseído² -da *m,f*: **gritaba como un ~** he was screaming like one possessed

posesión *f*
A 1 (con énfasis en la idea de disponer de) possession; (con énfasis en la idea de ser propietario de) ownership; **tomar posesión de algo** ‹*casa*› to take possession of sth; ‹*cargo*› to take up sth; **está en ~ de todas sus facultades** he is in full possession of his faculties; **la ~ de tanta riqueza por unos pocos** the possession of so much wealth by a few people; **se disputan la ~ de las tierras** they are in dispute over ownership of the land; **la ~ de 100 acciones le da derecho a ...** ownership of 100 shares gives you the right to ... 2 (tenencia — de drogas, armas) possession
B (objeto poseído) possession; **sus posesiones de ultramar** their overseas possessions; **tienen posesiones en Jalisco** they have estates *o* land in Jalisco
C (Psic) possession

posesionar [A1] *vt* (frml) **~ A algn DE algo** to hand over possession OF sth TO sb
■ **posesionarse** *v pron* (frml) **~se DE algo** to take possession OF sth

posesividad *f* possessiveness

posesivo -va *adj* possessive

poseso -sa *m,f* ▸ **poseído²**

posgrado *m* ▸ **postgrado**

posgraduado -da *adj/m,f* postgraduate

posguerra *f* postwar period; **los años de la ~** the postwar years, the years following the war

posibilidad *f*
A (circunstancia) possibility; **hemos previsto todas las ~es** we have anticipated every eventuality (frml); **~ DE + INF** chance OF -ING; **¿qué ~(es) tiene de ganar?** what chance does she have *o* what are her chances of winning?; **tiene muchas ~es de salir elegido** he has a good chance of being elected; **esto aumenta las ~es de que gane** this makes it more likely that he will win; **existe la ~ de que estés equivocado** you might just be wrong
B **posibilidades** *fpl* (medios económicos) means (*pl*); **vivir más allá/dentro de** *or* **por encima de las ~es de uno** to live beyond/within one's means; **la casa está por encima de mis ~es** the house is out of my price range, I can't afford the house

posibilitar [A1] *vt* to make ... possible; **su gestión posibilitó este encuentro** his work enabled us to hold this meeting *o* made this meeting possible

posible¹ *adj* possible; **¿crees que ganará? — es ~** do you think he'll win? — he might (do) *o* it's possible; **a ser ~** *or* (CS) **de ser ~** if possible; **haré lo ~ por** *or* **para ayudarte** I'll do what I can to help you; **hicieron todo lo ~** they did everything possible *o* everything they could; **prometió ayudarlo dentro de lo ~** *or* **en lo ~** *or* **en la medida de lo ~** she promised to do what she could to help (him); **¡será ~!** (fam) I don't believe this! (colloq); **¿que se ha casado? ¡no es ~!** he's got(ten) married? I don't believe it! *o* that can't be true! (colloq); **ser ~** (+ *me/te/le etc*): **en cuanto te sea ~** as soon as you can; **no creo que me sea ~** I don't think I'll be able to; **ser ~ + INF** to be possible to + INF; **no fue ~ avisarles** it was impossible to let them know; (+ *me/te/le etc*) **no me fue ~ terminarlo** I wasn't able to finish it; **¿le sería ~ recibirme hoy?** would you be able to see me today?; **ser ~ QUE + SUBJ**: **es ~ que sea cierto** it might *o* may *o* could be true; **es ~ que se haya perdido** it may have got(ten) lost; **¿será ~ que no lo sepa?** surely she must know!

posible² *adv*: **lo más pronto ~** as soon as possible; **intenta hacerlo lo mejor ~** try to do it as well as you can *o* the best you can; **ponlo lo más alto ~** put it as high as possible

posiblemente *adv* possibly; **~ no llegue hasta las 10** he may not arrive until 10

posición *f*
A 1 (lugar, puesto) position; **en (la) quinta ~ ...** he finished the race in fifth place ... 2 (Mil) position
B 1 (situación) position; **no estoy en ~ de negociar** I'm in no position to negotiate 2 (en la sociedad) social standing; **gente de buena ~** *or* **de ~ elevada** people of high social standing; **es de una familia de ~ desahogada** his family is comfortably off
C 1 (postura física) position; **en ~ vertical** in an upright position 2 (actitud) position, stance; **adoptar una ~ intransigente** to take *o* adopt a tough stance

positivismo *m* positivism

positivista *adj/mf* positivist

positivo¹ -va *adj*
A ‹*polo/número/respuesta*› positive; **saldo ~** credit balance; **el análisis dio ~** the test was *o* proved positive
B (provechoso, constructivo) positive; **el diálogo resultó muy ~** it was a very constructive *o* positive exchange of views

positivo² *m*
A (Fot) print, positive (tech)
B (Ling) positive

posmodernismo *m*, **posmodernidad** *f* (movimiento) postmodernism; (período) postmodern era

posmodernista *adj* postmodernist

posmoderno -na *adj* postmodern

poso *m* (del vino) sediment, lees (*pl*), dregs (*pl*); (del café) dregs (*pl*), grounds (*pl*)

posología *f* dosage

posoperatorio¹ -ria *adj* ‹*período*› postoperative

posoperatorio² *m* postoperative period

posparto *m* puerperium (tech)

posponer [E22] *vt*
A (aplazar) to postpone, put off; **tuvo que ~lo para el día siguiente** she had to put it off until the following day
B (Ling): **se pospone al nombre** it comes after *o* follows the noun

posta *f*
A 1 (ant) (de caballos) relay 2 (AmL) (Dep) relay (race); ***pasarle la ~ a algn*** (RPl fam) (en una carrera) to pass the baton to sb; (ante un problema) to hand over to sb
B (Arm) pellet
C (AmC) (Mil) sentry post; **estar de ~** to be on sentry duty
D (Esp) **a posta** on purpose, deliberately
E (AmC, Chi) (Coc) round
F (Chi) (centro médico) accident and emergency center*

postal¹ *adj* ‹*distrito/servicio*› postal

postal² *f* postcard

postdata *f* postscript

poste *m* 1 (de alambrado) (fence) post; (de teléfono, telégrafo) pole; ***como un ~*** (fam): **no te quedes allí como un ~** don't just stand there (like a dummy) 2 (Dep) post, upright

Compuestos
- **poste de alta tensión** electricity pylon
- **poste de (la) luz** lamp post
- **poste de llegada/salida** winning/starting post
- **poste indicador** signpost

postemilla *f* (AmL) gumboil, abscess

póster *m* (*pl* **-ters**) poster

poste restante /'poste rres'tante/ *m* (AmL) general delivery (AmE), poste restante (BrE); **me lo mandó ~ ~** he sent it to me general delivery *o* poste restante

postergación *f* (esp AmL) postponement, deferment (frml), deferral (frml)

postergar [A3] *vt*
A (esp AmL) (aplazar) ‹*juicio/reunión*› to postpone, put back; **postergó su decisión** he put off *o* (frml) deferred making a decision
B (relegar) ‹*empleado*› to pass over; **se siente postergado** he feels neglected *o* left out

posteridad *f* posterity; **pasará a la ~ como ...** posterity will remember him as *o* he will go down in history as ...; **su obra quedará para la ~** her work will be handed down to *o* will remain for posterity

posterior *adj*
A 1 (en el tiempo) later, subsequent; **ese incidente fue ~ a su llegada** that incident happened after his arrival 2 (en orden) subsequent; **ocupaba un puesto ~ al mío** she was further down than me
B 1 (trasero) ‹*patas*› back (*before n*), rear (*before n*); **la parte ~** the back *o* rear 2 (Ling) ‹*vocal*› back (*before n*)

posterioridad *f*: **con ~** subsequently, later; **con ~ a esa fecha** later than *o* subsequent to the due date

posteriormente *adv* subsequently; **reformas que se introdujeron ~** reforms which were subsequently introduced *o* were introduced at a later date

postgrado *m* postgraduate course; **hizo un ~ en turismo** she did a postgraduate course in tourism; **un curso de ~** a postgraduate course

postgraduado -da *adj/m,f* postgraduate

postguerra *f* ▸**posguerra**

postigo *m* shutter

postilla *f* scab

postín *m* (Esp): **de ~** smart; ‹*restaurante*› plush, smart; ‹*zona*› smart, posh (colloq)

postizo[1] **-za** *adj* 1 ‹*pestañas*› false; **dentadura postiza** dentures, false teeth 2 ‹*manga/cuello*› detachable

postizo[2] *m* hairpiece

postnatal[1] *adj* postnatal

postnatal[2] *m* (Chi) (permiso) maternity leave; (asignación) maternity benefit *o* allowance

postoperatorio[1] **-ria** *adj* postoperative

postoperatorio[2] *m* postoperative period

postor *m* bidder; **venderse al mejor ~** to be sold to the highest bidder

postparto *m* puerperium (tech)

postración *f* deep depression

postrar [A1] *vt* (debilitar) to weaken; **la tuberculosis lo tenía postrado** he was confined to bed with tuberculosis

▪ **postrarse** *v pron* (frml) (arrodillarse) to kneel; **se postró ante el rey** she prostrated herself before the king

postre[1] *m* dessert, pudding (BrE); **¿qué hay de ~?** (en restaurante) what desserts do you have *o* are there?; (en casa) what's for dessert *o* (BrE) pudding?; ***llegar a los ~s*** (fam) to be very late

postre[2] *f*: **a la ~** (*loc adv*) (frml) in the end; **una batalla que a la ~ decidiría la guerra** a battle which, as it turned out, was to decide the course of the war

postrer *adj*: *ver* **postrero**

postrero -ra *adj* (liter) [**postrer** *is used before masculine singular nouns*] last; **exhaló su postrer aliento** he breathed his last

postrimerías *fpl* end; **en las ~ de los sesenta** in the late sixties

postulación *f*

A (colecta) collection

B 1 (Relig) postulancy 2 (AmL) (Pol) (de candidato) proposal, nomination 3 (CS) (solicitud) application

postulado *m* postulate

postulante -ta *m,f*

A (en colecta) collector

B 1 (Relig) postulant 2 (AmL) (Pol) (candidato) candidate 3 (CS) (para puesto) applicant

postular [A1] *vt*

A (frml) 1 ‹*hipótesis*› to advance, postulate (frml) 2 (proponer) ‹*medidas/soluciones*› to propose

B (AmL) (Pol) ‹*candidato*› to nominate, propose

▪ **postular** *vi* **~ PARA algo** ‹*para puesto*› (CS) to apply FOR sth; ‹*para obra benéfica*› (Esp) to collect FOR sth

▪ **postularse** *v pron* (AmL) to stand, run

póstumo -ma *adj* posthumous

postura *f*

A (del cuerpo) position

B 1 (actitud) stance; **adoptar una ~ firme con respecto a algo** to take a tough stance on sth; **eso de no comprometerte es una ~ muy cómoda** not committing yourself like that is an easy option 2 (opinión) opinion; **~s encontradas** *or* **enfrentadas** opposing views; ***tomar* ~** to take a stand

C (AmL) (de ropa, zapatos): **se le rompieron a la primera ~** they broke the first time she wore them

(Compuesto) **postura de argollas** (Chi) (acción) exchange of rings (*to seal one's engagement*); (fiesta) engagement party

postventa, posventa *adj inv* after-sales (*before n*); **servicio ~** after-sales service

potable *adj* 1 ‹*agua*› drinkable; potable (frml; ⓢ **agua no potable** not drinking water 2 (fam) ‹*trabajo*› bearable; ‹*comida*› edible

potaje *m* (Coc) vegetable stew/soup (*gen with pulses*)

potasio *m* potassium

pote *m* (olla) pot; (de crema, maquillaje) (CS) pot, jar

potencia *f*

A 1 (fuerza, capacidad) power; **~ militar** military power; **~ sexual** sexual prowess; **este niño es un artista en ~** this child has the makings of an artist 2 (Fís, Mec) power

B (nación, organización) power; **una ~ naval/nuclear** a naval/nuclear power

C (Mat) power; **cinco elevado a la cuarta ~** five (raised) to the power of four

potenciación *f* (period): **la consiguiente ~ de las exportaciones** the resulting boost in exports; **la ~ de la música clásica** the promotion of classical music

potencial[1] *adj* (posible) potential; (Ling) conditional

potencial[2] *m*

A (capacidad, posibilidades) potential

B 1 (Fís) potential energy 2 (Elec) *tb* **~ eléctrico** potential difference

C (Ling) conditional

potencializar [A4] *vt* 1 ‹*turismo/productividad*› to boost; ‹*oferta/conocimientos*› to improve 2 ‹*medicamento*› to increase the effects of, potentiate (tech)

potenciar [A1] *vt* (period) 1 «*desarrollo/investigación/exportaciones*» to boost; «*relaciones/unidad/talento*» to foster; ‹*cultura*› to promote 2 (mejorar) ‹*seguridad*› to improve

potentado -da *m,f* tycoon; **los ~s de la industria del petróleo** the oil barons *o* magnates

potente *adj* ‹*arma/altavoz/motor*› powerful; ‹*voz*› powerful, strong; ‹*saque/golpe*› powerful; ‹*hombre*› virile

potestad *f* legal authority

potestativo -va *adj* facultative, optional

potiche *m* (Chi) earthenware pot

potingue *m* (fam) cream, lotion

potito *m* (Esp) (bote) jar of baby food

poto *m* (Andes fam) (de persona) butt (AmE colloq), bum (BrE colloq); (de botella) bottom

potosí *m*: ***valer un ~*** «*persona*» to be worth one's weight in gold; «*cosa*» to cost a fortune

potpourrí, potpurrí /popu'rri/ *m* medley

potra *f* 1 (arg) (suerte) luck; **¡qué ~ tiene!** she's so lucky! 2 (fam) (hernia) rupture, hernia; *ver tb* **potro A1**

potrero *m* 1 (AmL) (terreno cercado) field; (para pastar) pasture 2 (Chi) (terreno baldío) area of waste ground *o* land, vacant lot (AmE)

potrillo -lla *m,f* 1 (Zool) foal 2 **potrillo** *m* (Chi) (vaso) large glass

potro -tra *m,f*

A 1 (caballo joven) (*m*) colt; (*f*) filly 2 **potro** *m* (Chi) (semental) stallion

B **potro** *m* (instrumento de tortura) rack; (cepo) stocks (*pl*); (en gimnasia) vaulting horse, buck

poyo *m* stone bench/ledge

poza *f* (charco) puddle; (de río, mar) (Chi, Méx) pool

pozo *m*

A 1 (de agua) well; ***ser un ~ sin fondo*** (fam) to be (like) a bottomless pit (colloq) 2 (en mina) shaft 3 (en río) deep pool 4 (RPl) (en el camino) pothole

(Compuestos)

- **pozo artesiano** artesian well
- **pozo ciego** *or* **negro** *or* **séptico** septic tank, cesspool, cesspit
- **pozo de petróleo** oil well

B 1 (fondo común) pool; **hicieron un ~ para las propinas** they pooled all their tips 2 (en juegos, naipes) pool, kitty (colloq); (en concurso) pool; **llevarse el ~** to win the jackpot

pp. 1 (Corresp) (= **por poder, por poderes**) pp 2 (Com) (= **porte pagado**) ppd

práctica *f*

A 1 (en actividad) practice; (en trabajo) experience; **le falta ~** he needs practice; **se aprende con la ~** it comes with practice; **tiene mucha ~** he's had a lot of practice; **perder la ~** to be out of practice 2 (profesión) practicing*; **abandonó la ~ del derecho** she gave up practicing law; **es aconsejable la ~ de algún deporte** it's advisable to play *o* do some sport

P

B (aplicación) practice; **en la ~** in practice; **poner algo en ~** *or* **llevar algo a la ~** to put sth into practice
C prácticas *fpl* **1** (clase, sesión práctica): **~s de tiro** target practice; **las ~s de Anatomía** the anatomy practicals **2** (de maestro) teaching practice
D (costumbre) practice; **esta operación es hoy una ~ habitual** this operation is now common practice

practicable *adj* practicable, workable

prácticamente *adv* practically, virtually; **¿has terminado? — prácticamente** have you finished? — almost

practicante[1] *adj* (Rel) practicing* (*before n*)

practicante[2] *mf* (Med) nurse (*specializing in giving injections, dressing wounds, etc*)

practicar [A2] *vt*
A 1 ‹*idioma/pieza musical*› to practice*; **no practica ningún deporte** he doesn't play *o* do any sport(s); **hay que ~ lo que se predica** you should practice what you preach **2** ‹*profesión*› to practice*
B (frml) (llevar a cabo, realizar) ‹*corte/incisión*› to make; ‹*autopsia/operación*› to perform, do; ‹*redada/actividad*› to carry out; ‹*detenciones*› to make; **hubo que ~le una cesárea** they had to perform a Cesarean section (on her)
■ **practicar** *vi* (repetir) to practice*; (ejercer) to practice*

práctico[1] -ca *adj*
A ‹*envase/cuchillo*› useful, handy; ‹*falda/diseño*› practical; **regalémosle algo ~** let's give her something useful *o* practical; **es muy ~ tener el coche para hacer la compra** it's very handy *o* convenient having the car to do the shopping
B (no teórico) practical
C ‹*persona*› [SER] (desenvuelto) practical; **tiene gran sentido ~** she's very practical

práctico[2] *mf* (Náut) pilot

pradera *f* grassland, grasslands (*pl*); **las ~s de los Estados Unidos** the prairies of the United States

prado *m* **1** (Agr) meadow, field **2** (lugar de paseo) park (*with lawns*) **3** (Col) (jardín) garden, yard (AmE)

Praga *f* Prague

pragmático[1] -ca *adj* pragmatic

pragmático[2] -ca *m,f* pragmatist

pragmatismo *m* pragmatism

pragmatista *mf* pragmatist

praliné *m* praline

preacuerdo *m* outline *o* draft agreement

preámbulo *m* **1** (de obra) introduction; (de constitución) preamble **2** (rodeo): **sin más ~s** without further ado; **dímelo sin tanto ~** stop beating about the bush and tell me **3** (de curso, negociaciones) preliminary; **las charlas sirvieron de ~ al curso** the talks served as a preliminary to the course

preaviso *m* notice; **hay que dar 2 meses de ~** you have to give two months' notice

prebenda *f* **1** (privilegio) privilege; **una de las ~s del cargo** one of the perquisites *o* benefits of the position **2** (Relig) prebend

precalentamiento *m* **1** (Dep) warm-up; **ejercicios de ~** warm-up exercises **2** (del horno) preheating **3** (de motor) warming up

precalentar [A5] *vt* ‹*horno*› to preheat; ‹*motor*› to warm up

precandidato -ta *m,f*: *short-listed candidate*

precariedad *f* **1** (escasez): **la ~ en la que viven** the deprivation in which they live; **la ~ de recursos** the scarcity of resources
(Compuesto) **precariedad laboral** job insecurity
2 (de salud) precariousness

precario -ria *adj* ‹*vivienda*› poor; ‹*medios*› scarce, meager*; ‹*salud/situación*› precarious, unstable; ‹*gobierno/puesto*› unstable

precaución *f*
A (medida) precaution; **tomar precauciones** to take precautions
B (prudencia): **como medida de ~** as a precautionary measure; **actuar con ~** to act with caution; **lo hice por ~** I did it to be on the safe side *o* (frml) as a precautionary measure; Ⓢ **circule con precaución** drive carefully

precaver [E1] *vt* to provide against, take steps to prevent *o* avoid

precaverse [E1] *v pron* to take precautions; **~ del peligro** to guard against danger

precavido -da *adj* cautious, prudent; **fui precavida y me traje el paraguas** I came prepared, I brought my umbrella

precedencia *f* precedence, priority; **tener ~ (SOBRE algo/algn)** to take/have precedence *o* priority (OVER sth/sb)

precedente[1] *adj* previous

precedente[2] *m* precedent; **sentar ~s** *or* **(un) ~** to set a precedent; **que esto no sirva de ~** I don't want this to set a precedent; **un caso sin ~s** an unprecedented case

preceder [E1] *vt* to precede; **los días que precedieron a su muerte** the days leading up to *o* (frml) preceding his death; **su nombre precede al mío** his name comes before mine

preceptivo -va *adj* mandatory, compulsory

precepto *m* rule, precept (frml)

preceptor *m* private tutor

preces *fpl* **1** (liter) (ruegos) prayers (*pl*), supplications (*pl*) **2** (en la misa) invocations (*pl*)

preciado -da *adj* ‹*bien/objeto*› prized, valued; ‹*don*› valuable

preciarse [A1] *v pron* **1** (estimarse): **un abogado que se precie no haría eso** no self-respecting lawyer would do that **2** (jactarse) **~ DE algo** to pride oneself ON sth

precintado *m* **1** (Com) (de producto) sealing; **envasado y ~ de botellas** bottling and sealing **2** (de local — tras crimen) sealing; (— clausura) closing down

precintar [A1] *vt* **1** ‹*paquete/botella*› to seal **2** ‹*local*› (tras crimen) to seal; (clausurar) to close down (*often on health or safety grounds*)

precinto *m* seal; **~ de garantía** seal of guarantee

precio *m*
A (de producto) price; **subir los ~s** to raise prices, to put prices up; **bajar los ~s** to lower prices, to bring prices down; **¿qué ~ tiene este vestido?** how much is this dress?; **está muy bien de ~** it's very reasonable; **tiene un ~ prohibitivo** it is prohibitively expensive; **tiene un ~ irrisorio** it's ridiculously cheap; **a ~s populares** at affordable prices; **~ al contado/a plazos** cash/credit price; **a ~ de saldo** at a bargain price; ***no tener ~*** to be priceless; **su ayuda no tiene ~** her help has been invaluable; ***pagar*** *or* ***comprar algo a ~ de oro*** to pay the earth *o* a fortune for sth; ***poner ~ a la cabeza de algn*** to put a price on sb's head
(Compuestos)
• **precio al por mayor/menor** wholesale/retail price
• **precio de compra/lanzamiento/mercado** purchase/launch/market price
• **precio de costo** *or* (Esp) **coste** cost price
• **precio de salida** starting price
• **precio de venta al público** (de alimento, medicamento) recommended retail price; (de libro) published price
• **precio franco (de) fábrica** factory (gate) price
B (sacrificio, esfuerzo): **logró lo que quería ¿pero a qué ~?** she got what she wanted, but at what price *o* cost?; **a cualquier ~** whatever the cost

preciosidad *f*: **esta vista es una ~** this view is absolutely beautiful *o* wonderful; **una ~ de casa** a really lovely *o* an absolutely gorgeous house; **su hermana es una ~** his sister is gorgeous *o* really beautiful

preciosismo *m* preciosity, euphuism

precioso -sa *adj* (hermoso) beautiful, gorgeous, lovely; (de gran valor) precious, valuable

preciosura *f* (AmL) ▸ **preciosidad**

precipicio *m* (despeñadero) precipice

precipitación *f*
A (prisa) rush, hurry; **lo hizo con mucha ~** she did it in a rush *o* hurry; **no hace falta tanta ~** there's no need to rush *o* hurry
B (Meteo) precipitation (frml); **habrá precipitaciones débiles** there will be some light rain (*o* snow *etc*); **cielo nuboso, con alguna ~** overcast with occasional showers
C (Quím) precipitation

precipitadamente *adv*: **salir ~** to leave in a rush *o* hurry; **no tomes la decisión ~** don't make any hasty decisions

precipitado[1] **-da** *adj* ‹*decisión/actuación*› hasty; ‹*juicio*› snap (*before n*)

precipitado[2] *m* (Quím) precipitate

precipitar [A1] *vt*

A (acelerar) ‹‹*crisis/incidente*›› to hasten, precipitate (frml); **no precipites los acontecimientos** don't rush things

B (lanzar, arrojar): **lo precipitó al vacío** she pushed him out of the window (*o* over the cliff *etc*)

C (Quím) to precipitate

■ **precipitarse** *v pron*

A (en decisión, juicio): **no te precipites** don't rush into anything, don't be hasty; **te precipitaste juzgándolo así** you were rash to judge him like that

B (apresurarse) to rush; **~se A + INF** to rush to + INF; **~se HACIA algo** to rush TOWARD(S) sth; **el coche se precipitó contra el muro** the car hurtled into the wall

C 1▸ (caer) to plunge; **el coche se precipitó por el acantilado** the car plunged over the cliff 2▸ (*refl*) (arrojarse) to throw oneself

precisado -da *adj* (AmL frml): **verse ~ a hacer algo** to be forced *o* obliged to do sth

precisamente *adv* precisely; **llegó ~ cuando yo salía** he arrived just as I was going out; **~ estábamos hablando de eso** we were just talking about that; **~, por eso no voy** (*indep*) precisely *o* exactly, that's why I'm not going

precisar [A1] *vt*

A (determinar con exactitud) to specify; **la hora está todavía sin ~** the time has not yet been fixed *o* specified

B (necesitar) to need; **no precisa plancha** no ironing needed; **Ⓢ precisamos secretarias bilingües** bilingual secretaries required

precisión *f* 1▸ (exactitud) precision; **con la ~ de un reloj** with clockwork precision, like clockwork; **no puedo decírtelo con ~** I can't tell you exactly; **de ~** ‹*instrumento/máquina*› precision (*before n*) 2▸ (claridad, concisión) precision

preciso -sa *adj*

A 1▸ (exacto, claro) precise; **¿me puede dar datos más ~s?** can you give me more detailed information 2▸ (*delante del n*) (como intensificador) very; **en este ~ momento** right now, this very minute; **en el ~ momento en que salía** just as he was going out; **en este ~ lugar** in this very spot

B (necesario) necessary; **si es ~** if necessary, if need be; **ser ~ + INF** to be necessary to + INF; **no es ~ entregarlo hoy** it doesn't have to be handed in today; **fue ~ darle un sedante** he had to be given a sedative; **es ~ que la veas** you must see her; **no es ~ que vayamos todos** there's no need for all of us to go

preclaro -ra *adj* (frml) illustrious, eminent

precocidad *f* precociousness

precocinar [A1] *vt* to precook; **alimentos precocinados** precooked foods

precolombino -na *adj* pre-Columbian

preconcebido -da *adj* preconceived; **ideas preconcebidas** preconceptions, preconceived ideas

preconcebir [I14] *vt* to preconceive

precondición *f* precondition

preconizar [A4] *vt* (frml) (abogar por) to advocate; (elogiar) to praise, extol (frml)

precontrato *m* pre-contract

precordillera *f* (en AmS) foothills (*pl*) (*of the Andes*)

precoz *adj* ‹*niño/desarrollo*› precocious; ‹*diagnóstico*› early; ‹*fruto*› early, precocious (tech); ‹*helada*› early

precozmente *adv* 1▸ ‹*envejecer/desarrollarse*› prematurely 2▸ ‹*diagnosticar/detectar*› early 3▸ (Bot) early

precursor -sora *m,f* precursor, forerunner

predecesor -sora *m,f* predecessor

predecible *adj* predictable

predecir [I25] *vt* to predict, foretell (frml)

predestinación *f* predestination

predestinado -da *adj* predestined; **estar ~ (A algo/+ INF)** to be predestined (TO sth/+ INF)

predestinar [A1] *vt* to predestine

predeterminar [A1] *vt* to predetermine

prédica *f* (Relig) sermon

predicado *m* predicate

predicador -dora *m,f* preacher

predicamento *m*

A (prestigio) prestige; **la figura de mayor ~** the most prestigious figure

B (AmL) (situación difícil) predicament

predicar [A2] *vi* to preach; **~ con el ejemplo** to practice what one preaches

■ **predicar** *vt* (Relig) to preach; (aconsejar) to advocate

predicativo -va *adj* predicative

predicción *f* prediction, forecast; **la ~ del tiempo** the weather forecast

predicible *adj* (Andes) predictable

predilección *f* predilection; **tiene/siente ~ por su hijo** she's especially fond of her son

predilecto[1] **-ta** *adj* favorite*

predilecto[2] **-ta** *m,f* favorite*; **el ~ del profesor** the teacher's pet (colloq)

predio *m* (esp AmL frml) 1▸ (terreno) piece of land; **~s** land; **en los ~s** *or* **en el ~ de la universidad** in the university grounds, on the university campus 2▸ (local) premises (*pl*)

predisponer [E22] *vt*

A (Med) to predispose

B (influir en): **su simpatía nos predispuso en su favor** her kindness made us warm to her; **lo predispusieron en contra mía** they prejudiced him against me

predisposición *f*

A (Med) predisposition

B (inclinación): **tenía una cierta ~ contra ella** he was slightly prejudiced against her; **tienen ~ a aceptar todo lo que dice** they have a tendency to accept everything he says

predispuesto -ta *adj* 1▸ [SER] (propenso) **~ A algo** prone TO sth 2▸ [ESTAR] (prejuiciado) **~ A FAVOR/EN CONTRA DE algo/algn** biased TOWARDS/AGAINST sth/sb

predominante *adj* predominant

predominar [A1] *vi*: **el tema predominó en el congreso** the subject dominated the conference; **el tipo de cine que predomina hoy** the kind of films that dominate the market nowadays; **en el concierto predominaban los jóvenes** the audience at the concert was predominantly young; **~án los cielos despejados** the sky will be mainly clear

predominio *m* predominance; **~ SOBRE algo** predominance OVER sth

preelectoral *adj* pre-election (*before n*)

preeminencia *f* preeminence

preeminente *adj* preeminent

preescolar *adj* ‹*edad/educación*› preschool (*before n*); **centro de educación ~** kindergarten, nursery school (BrE)

preestablecer [E3] *vt* to establish … beforehand, preestablish

preestablecido -da *adj* preestablished

preestreno *m* preview

prefabricado -da *adj* prefabricated

prefacio *m* preface

prefecto *m* 1▸ (Relig) prefect 2▸ (Gob) (en Francia) prefect 3▸ (Per) (gobernador) civil governor 4▸ (Col) (Educ) *teacher responsible for discipline*

prefectura *f* 1▸ (Relig) prefecture 2▸ (Gob) (en Francia) prefecture 3▸ (RPl) (Mil, Náut) naval command

preferencia *f* 1▸ (prioridad) priority, precedence; (Auto) right of way, priority (BrE) 2▸ (predilección) preference; **tiene ~ por el más pequeño** the youngest one is her favorite; **de ~** preferably; **se dará ~ a los candidatos que hablen inglés** preference will be given to candidates who speak English 3▸ (Espec) (localidad) grandstand

preferente *adj* (especial) special; **recibí un trato ~** I received special *o* preferential treatment

preferentemente *adv* preferably

preferible *adj* [SER] preferable, better; **ser ~ A algo/+ INF** to be preferable TO sth/-ING; **es ~ a uno de plástico** it's better than *o* preferable to a plastic one; **es ~ que llegue tarde a que no llegue** I'd rather he arrived late than not at all

preferido -da *adj/m,f* favorite*; **el ~ de la maestra** the teacher's favorite *o* (colloq) pet

P

preferir [I11] *vt* to prefer; **la prefiero con el pelo largo** I like her better *o* I prefer her with her hair long; **prefiero esperar aquí** I'd rather wait here, I'd prefer to wait here; ~ **algo** A **algo** to prefer sth TO sth; **prefiero vivir sólo a compartir** I prefer living on my own to sharing; ~ **QUE + SUBJ**: **prefiero que te quedes** I'd rather you stayed, I prefer you to stay; **~ía que nevara** I'd rather it snowed, I'd prefer it if it snowed

prefiera, prefieras, etc *see* **preferir**

prefijo *m* (Ling) prefix; (de teléfono) (dialing*) code

prefiriera, prefirió, etc *see* **preferir**

pregón *m* 1 (para vender algo) cry (*of a street or market vendor*) 2 (de fiestas) opening speech 3 (Hist) (bando) proclamation

pregonar [A1] *vt* 1 ‹*noticia/secreto*› to make ... public; **no lo vayas pregonando por ahí** (fam) don't go spreading it around 2 ‹*virtudes/méritos*› to extol 3 ‹*mercancía*› to hawk, cry 4 ‹*bando/aviso*› to proclaim

pregonero -ra *m,f* 1 (Hist) (de bando) towncrier 2 (de fiestas) *person who inaugurates an event*

pregunta *f* question; **hacer/contestar una** ~ to ask/answer a question; **una** ~ **capciosa** a trick question; **si se me permite la** ~ if you don't mind my asking

(Compuesto) **pregunta temada** (Méx) essay question

preguntar [A1] *vt* to ask; **eso no se pregunta** you shouldn't ask things like that; **si no es mucho** ~ if you don't mind my asking; **la maestra me preguntó la lección** the teacher tested me on the lesson

■ **preguntar** *vi* to ask; **le preguntó sobre** *or* **acerca de lo ocurrido** he asked her (about) what had happened; ~ **POR algo/algn** to ask ABOUT sth/sb; **me preguntó por ti/por tu salud** he asked about you/how you were; **vino a** ~ **por el trabajo** he came to inquire about the job; **preguntaban por un tal Mario** they were looking for *o* asking for someone called Mario

■ **preguntarse** *v pron* (*refl*) to wonder

preguntón[1] **-tona** *adj* (fam) nosy (colloq)

preguntón[2] **-tona** *m,f* (fam) busybody (colloq), nosy parker (BrE colloq)

prehistoria *f* prehistory

prehistórico -ca *adj* prehistoric

preinstalado -da *adj* already installed

prejuiciado -da *adj* (AmL) prejudiced

prejuicio *m* prejudice; **tener ~s contra algo/algn** to be prejudiced against sth/sb; **es una persona sin ~s** he has no prejudices, he's not at all prejudiced

prejuzgar [A3] *vt/vi* to prejudge

prelación *f* precedence; **tiene** ~ **el auto que sube** (Col) the car going up the hill has right of way *o* (BrE) priority

prelado *m* prelate

prelavado *m* prewash

preliminar[1] *adj* 1 ‹*cálculo/nota/etapa*› preliminary 2 (Dep) ‹*pruebas*› qualifying (*before n*), preliminary (*before n*)

preliminar[2] *m or f* (AmL) (Dep) qualifier, qualifying *o* preliminary game (*o* competition *etc*)

preludiar [A1] *vt*: **aquella tensión no podía** ~ **nada bueno** that tense atmosphere did not bode at all well; **'Las Señoritas de Aviñón' preludia el Cubismo** 'Les Demoiselles d'Avignon' was a prelude to Cubism

preludio *m* (Mús) prelude; (comienzo, preámbulo) prelude

premamá *adj inv* (Esp fam) maternity (*before n*)

prematrimonial *adj* ‹*relaciones*› premarital; ‹*acuerdo*› prenuptial; **cursillo** ~ marriage preparation course

prematuro -ra *adj* premature; **es** ~ **hablar de ello ahora** it's too soon *o* too early to talk about it now

premeditación *f* premeditation; **el crimen fue cometido con** ~ it was a premeditated crime

premeditado -da *adj* premeditated; **con premeditada ironía** with deliberate irony

premeditar [A1] *vt* to premeditate

premiación *f* (AmL) (acción) awarding of prizes; (ceremonia) awards ceremony, prize-giving (BrE); **se hizo la** ~ **del concurso** the prizes were awarded

premiado -da *adj* ‹*número/boleto*› winning; ‹*novela/película/escritor*› prizewinning (*before n*); *ver tb* **premiar**

premiar [A1] *vt* 1 ‹*actor/escritor*› to award a/the prize to, award ... a/the prize; **~on tres películas cubanas** three Cuban films won awards; **fue premiado con el Nobel de la Paz** he was awarded the Nobel Peace Prize 2 ‹*generosidad/sacrificio*› to reward

premio *m* 1 (galardón) prize; **conceder** *or* **dar** *or* **otorgar un** ~ to award *o* give a prize; **recibir/obtener/ganar un** ~ to receive/get/win a prize; **el** ~ **a la mejor película** the award *o* prize for the best movie; **de** *or* **como** ~ as a prize; **se llevó el primer** ~ she took *o* got *o* won first prize 2 (en sorteo) prize; **¿le tocó algún ~?** did you win a prize? 3 (a esfuerzos, sacrificios) reward; **como** ~ **a su dedicación** as a reward for your dedication 4 (competición) trophy; **el P~ Inyala** the Inyala Cup/Trophy

(Compuestos)
- **premio de consolación** *or* (CS) **(de) consuelo** consolation prize
- **premio gordo** jackpot
- **Premio Nobel** (galardón) Nobel Prize; (galardonado) Nobel Prize winner

premisa *f* premise

premolar *adj/m* premolar

premonición *f* premonition

premonitorio -ria *adj* premonitory (frml)

premunirse [I1] *v pron* (Chi frml) ~ **DE algo** ‹*de armas/herramientas*› to furnish oneself WITH sth (frml); ‹*de valor/paciencia*› to arm oneself WITH sth

premura *f* haste

prenatal[1] *adj* prenatal (AmE), antenatal (BrE)

prenatal[2] *m* (Chi) 1 (permiso) maternity leave 2 (asignación) maternity benefit, maternity allowance

prenda *f*

A (de vestir) garment

(Compuesto) **prenda íntima** undergarment, item of underwear

B (señal, garantía) security, surety; **dejar algo en** ~ to leave sth as security *o* surety; **en** ~ **de mi amor** as a token *o* pledge of my love; ***no dolerle ~s a algn***: **no me duelen ~s reconocerlo** I don't mind admitting it; ***no soltar*** ~ (fam) not to say a word

C (Jueg) forfeit; **jugar a las ~s** to play forfeits

D (apelativo cariñoso) darling, pet (colloq)

prendarse [A1] *v pron* (liter) ~ **DE algn** to fall in love WITH sb; **quedé prendado de su simpatía** I was captivated by her charm

prendedor *m* brooch

prender [E1] *vt*

A ‹*persona*› to catch, seize

B (sujetar): **llevaba una flor prendida en el ojal** he was wearing a flower (pinned) in his buttonhole; **el bajo está prendido con alfileres** the hem's been pinned up

C 1 ‹*cigarrillo/cerilla*› to light; **prender fuego a** to set fire to 2 (AmL) ‹*gas*› to turn on, light; ‹*estufa/horno*› to turn on; ‹*radio/luz*› to turn on, switch on

■ **prender** *vi*

A «*rama/planta*» to take

B (arder): **la leña no prende** the wood won't catch (light)

C «*idea/moda*» to catch on

■ **prenderse** *v pron* (con fuego) to catch fire

prendería *f* (Col) pawnbroker's, pawn shop

prensa *f*

A 1 (Period) press; **leer/comprar la** ~ to read/buy the papers; **la** ~ **oral** radio and television; **la** ~ **escrita** the press; **la** ~ **deportiva** the sports press; ***buena/mala*** ~ good/bad press; **la película tuvo muy buena** ~ the film had a very good press; **los ecologistas tienen mala** ~ **por aquí** ecologists get a bad press around here 2 (imprenta) (printing) press; **estar en** ~ to be in *o* at the press 3 (periodistas) **la** ~ the press; **asociaciones de la** ~ journalists' *o* press associations

(Compuestos)
- **prensa amarilla** gutter press, yellow press
- **prensa del corazón** gossip magazines (*pl*)
- **prensa roja** (CS) sensationalist press (*specializing in crime stories*)

B (Tec) press

(Compuesto) **prensa hidráulica** hydraulic press

prensado[1] **-da** *adj* pressed

prensado² *m* pressing

prensadora *f*, **prensador** *m* press; **~ de uvas** grape press; **~ de chatarra** crusher; **~ de paja** straw baler; **~ de pantalones** pants (AmE) *o* trouser (BrE) press

prensar [A1] *vt* to press

preñado -da *adj* 1 ‹*animal*› pregnant 2 (lleno) (liter) **estar ~ DE algo** ‹*de alegría/significado/peligros*› to be pregnant WITH sth (liter)

preñar [A1] *vt* ‹*hembra*› to impregnate

preñez *f* pregnancy

preocupación *f* 1 (problema) worry; **les causa muchas preocupaciones** she causes them a lot of worry *o* problems 2 (inquietud) concern; **un motivo de ~** cause for concern

preocupado -da *adj* worried; **me tiene muy preocupada que aún no haya llegado** I'm really worried (that) he hasn't arrived yet; **~ POR algo** worried ABOUT sth

preocupante *adj* worrying

preocupar [A1] *vt* to worry; **le preocupa el futuro** she's worried *o* concerned about her future; **me preocupa que no haya llamado** it worries me that she hasn't phoned; **no me preocupa** it doesn't bother *o* worry me

■ **preocuparse** *v pron*

A (inquietarse) to worry; **no te preocupes** don't worry; **~se POR algo/algn** to worry ABOUT sth/sb; **tiene amigos que se preocupan por ella** she has friends who care *o* who are concerned about her

B (ocuparse) **~se DE algo**: **me preocupé de que no faltara nada** I made sure *o* I saw to it that we had everything; **no se preocupó más del asunto** he gave the matter no further thought

prepago de ~ *loc adj* ‹*sistema/plan*› prepayment (*before n*); **tarjeta (de) ~** (Tel) prepayment card, top-up card

prepalatal *adj* prepalatal

preparación *f*

A (de examen, discurso) preparation; **la ~ de la expedición** preparations *o* preparing for the expedition; **la ~ de este plato es muy laboriosa** there's a lot of preparation involved in this dish

B 1 (conocimientos, educación) education; (para trabajo) training 2 (de deportista) training; **su ~ física es muy buena** he's in peak condition

C (Farm, Med) preparation

preparado¹ -da *adj*

A [ESTAR] (listo, dispuesto) ready; **~ PARA algo** ready FOR sth; **no está ~ para presentarse al examen** he's not ready to take *o* not prepared for the exam; **no está ~ para recibir la noticia** he's not prepared for the news; **¡~s, listos, ya!** get ready, get set, go! (AmE), on your marks, get set, go (BrE)

B [SER] (instruido, culto) educated; **es una persona muy preparada** she's very well-educated; **un profesional muy bien ~** a highly-trained professional

preparado² *m* preparation

preparador -dora *m,f* (Dep) coach, trainer; (de caballos) trainer

preparar [A1] *vt*

A ‹*plato*› to make, prepare; ‹*comida*› to prepare, get … ready; ‹*medicamento*› to prepare, make up; ‹*habitación*› to prepare, get … ready; ‹*cuenta*› to draw up (AmE), make up (BrE); **te tengo preparada una sorpresa** I've got a surprise (waiting) for you

B ‹*examen/prueba*› to prepare

C ‹*persona*› (para examen) to tutor, coach (BrE); (para partido) to train, coach, prepare; (para tarea, reto) to prepare; **no ha sabido ~ a los hijos para la vida** he has failed to prepare his children for life

■ **prepararse** *v pron*

A «*tormenta/crisis*» to brew

B (*refl*) (disponerse): **~se PARA algo** to get ready FOR sth; **se preparó para darle la mala noticia** he got ready *o* prepared himself to give her the bad news; **prepárate que me vas a escuchar** just you listen to me!

C (*refl*) (formarse) to prepare; **~se PARA algo** ‹*para examen/competición*› to prepare FOR sth; **no se preparó bien (para) la prueba** she didn't do enough work for the test

preparativos *mpl* preparations (*pl*)

preparatorio -ria *adj* ‹*curso*› preparatory; ‹*ejercicios*› warm-up (*before n*)

preparatorios *mpl* (Ur) *former two-year pre-university course*

preponderancia *f* preponderance

preponderante *adj* predominant, preponderant (frml); **la opinión ~ en la reunión** the dominant *o* predominant view at the meeting

preponderar [A1] *vi* to predominate, preponderate (frml)

preposición *f* preposition

preposicional *adj* prepositional

prepotencia *f* arrogance

prepotente *adj* ‹*persona*› arrogant, overbearing; ‹*actitud*› high-handed

prepucio *m* foreskin, prepuce (tech)

prerrogativa *f* prerogative; **hacer uso de sus ~s** to exercise one's prerogative

presa *f*

A (en caza) prey; **~ DE algo** ‹*de terror/pánico*› seized WITH sth; ***hacer ~ en algo/algn***: **el pánico hizo ~ en los espectadores** the spectators were seized with panic; **el fuego hizo ~ en las ramas secas** the fire took hold in the dry branches

B (dique) dam; (embalse) reservoir, lake

C (AmS) (de pollo) piece

presagiar [A1] *vt* to presage (frml *or* liter), forebode

presagio *m* 1 (señal) portent (frml *or* liter), omen; **buen/mal ~** good/bad omen 2 (premonición) premonition

presbiteriano -na *adj/m,f* Presbyterian

presbiterio *m* presbytery

prescindir [I1] *vi*

A **~ DE algo/algn** (arreglárselas sin) to do WITHOUT sth/sb; **no puedo ~ de su ayuda** I can't do without *o* manage without your help; **nos vemos obligados a ~ de sus servicios** (euf) we are obliged to let you go (euph)

B **~ DE algo** ‹*de consejo/opinión*› (no tener en cuenta) to disregard sth

C **~ DE algo** ‹*de detalles/formalidades*› (omitir) to dispense with sth

prescribir [I34] *vt* to prescribe; **le prescribió reposo absoluto** he prescribed complete rest

prescripción *f* prescription; **por ~ facultativa** *or* **médica** on doctor's orders

prescrito -ta, **prescripto -ta** *pp*: *see* **prescribir**

preselección *f*: **hacer una ~ de los candidatos** to draw up a shortlist of candidates; **una vez terminada la ~** once the initial selection process is/was complete

preseleccionar [A1] *vt* «*candidatos/solicitantes*» to shortlist; **preseleccionó a 20 jugadores** he initially selected *o* named 20 players, he named a squad of 20 players

presencia *f* 1 (en lugar, acto) presence; **contaron con la ~ de 50.000 visitantes** there were 50,000 visitors; **en ~ del rey** in the presence of the king; **en ~ de tu abuela** in front of your grandmother 2 (euf) (aspecto físico) appearance; **se requiere buena ~** good *o* (BrE) smart appearance required

(Compuesto) **presencia de ánimo** (serenidad) presence of mind; (valor) courage, strength

presenciar [A1] *vt* ‹*suceso/asesinato*› to witness; ‹*acto/espectáculo*› to be present at, to attend; **yo presencié la discusión** I saw *o* witnessed the argument

presentable *adj* presentable

presentación *f*

A 1 (de personas) introduction; **hizo las presentaciones** he did *o* made the introductions 2 (de programa) presentation; **la ~ del concurso corre a cargo de …** the competition/contest is hosted by … 3 (primera exposición) presentation (frml), launch; **la ~ del libro** the book launch 4 (muestra, entrega) presentation; **hizo la ~ de credenciales** he presented his credentials; **el límite de tiempo para la ~ del trabajo** the deadline for handing in the work

B (aspecto) presentation; **la ~ de un producto** the way a product is presented

P

(Compuesto) **presentación en sociedad** coming out, debut

presentador -dora *m,f* presenter

presentar [A1] *vt*

A 1 (mostrar) to present; **un producto bien presentado** a well-presented product 2 (exponer por primera vez) ‹*libro/disco*› to launch; ‹*obra de arte*› to present; ‹*colección de moda*› to present, exhibit 3 (entregar) ‹*informe/solicitud*› to submit; **le presenté el pasaporte** I gave him my passport, I presented my passport to him 4 (enseñar) to show; **hay que ~ el carné para entrar** you have to show your membership card to get in 5 ‹*disculpas/excusas*› to make; ‹*dimisión*› to hand in, submit; ‹*queja*› to file, make; **fui a ~ mis respetos** I went to pay my respects; **~on una denuncia** they reported the matter (to the police), they made an official complaint; **~ pruebas** to present evidence; **~ cargos** to bring charges; **~ una demanda** to bring a lawsuit 6 (Mil): **~ armas** to present arms

B (TV) ‹*programa*› to present, introduce

C ‹*persona*› to introduce; **te presento a mi hermana** I'd like you to meet my sister, this is my sister

D ‹*novedad/ventaja*› to offer; ‹*síntoma*› to show

■ **presentarse** *v pron*

A 1 (en lugar) to turn up, appear; **~se (como) voluntario** to volunteer; **se presentó voluntariamente a la policía** he turned himself in to the police; **~se ante el juez** to appear before the judge 2 (a concurso, examen): **se presentó al examen** she took *o* (BrE) sat the exam; **me presenté al concurso** I entered the competition; **se presenta como candidato independiente** he's running (AmE) *o* (BrE) he's standing as an independent; **~se para un cargo** to apply for a post

B «*dificultad/problema*» to arise, come up, crop up (colloq); **si se me presenta la oportunidad** if I get the opportunity, if the opportunity arises; **el futuro se presenta prometedor** the future looks promising

C (darse a conocer) to introduce oneself; **~se en sociedad** to make one's debut (in society)

presente[1] *adj*

A (en un lugar) present; **el mineral estaba ~ en las muestras analizadas** the mineral was found in the samples analyzed; **Juan Prado — ¡~!** (al pasar lista) Juan Prado — present *o* here!; **la guerra está ~ en todas sus novelas** war is a constant feature in her novels; **S Presente** (CS) (Corresp) ≈ by hand; ***hacerle ~ a algn*** (frml) to notify sb (frml); ***mejorando lo ~***: **es muy inteligente, mejorando lo ~** he's very intelligent, as indeed are you; ***tener algo ~*** to bear sth in mind; ***tener ~ a algn*** to think of sb, remember sb

B (actual) present; **a finales del ~ año** at the end of the current *o* present year; **el día 15 del ~ mes** the 15th of this month, the 15th inst. (frml); **en su atenta carta del 3 ~** (Méx frml) (Corresp) in your letter of the 3rd of this month *o* (frml) of the 3rd inst.; **el ~ documento/contrato** (frml) (Corresp) this document/contract; *ver tb* **presente**[3]

presente[2] *m*

A 1 (en el tiempo) **el ~** the present 2 (Ling) present (tense)

B los presentes *mpl*, **las presentes** *fpl* (asistentes) those present

C (regalo) gift, present

presente[3] *f* (frml): **por la ~ me complace informarle que ...** I am pleased to inform you that ... (frml); **por la ~ pongo en su conocimiento que ...** I am writing to inform you that ... (frml)

presentimiento *m* premonition, presentiment (frml); **tengo el ~ de que ...** I have a feeling that ...

presentir [I11] *vt*: **presiento que me van a llamar** I have a feeling that they're going to call me; **presintió la muerte de su marido** she sensed beforehand *o* she had a premonition that her husband was going to die

preservación *f* preservation; **la ~ del medio ambiente** the protection of the environment

preservar [A1] *vt* 1 (proteger) to preserve; **~ algo/a algn DE algo** to protect sth/sb FROM sth 2 (AmL) (conservar, mantener) to maintain

preservativo *m*

A (condón) condom

B (Andes) (conservante) preservative

presidencia *f* 1 (Gob, Pol) (cargo) presidency; **candidato a la ~** presidential candidate; **ocupar la ~ del gobierno** to be the head of government; **la P~** the President's office 2 (de compañía, banco) presidency (esp AmE), chairmanship (BrE); (de reunión, comité) chairmanship, chair

(Compuesto) **presidencia municipal** (Méx) town hall

presidenciable *mf* (AmL) presidential hopeful

presidencial *adj* presidential; **elecciones ~es** presidential elections

presidente -ta *m,f* 1 (Gob, Pol) president; **el ~ del gobierno** the premier, the prime minister 2 (de compañía, banco) president (AmE), chairman/-woman (BrE) 3 (de reunión, comité, acto) chairperson, chair 4 (Der) (de tribunal) presiding judge/magistrate 5 (de jurado) chairman/-woman

presidiario -ria *m,f* convict, inmate, prisoner

presidio *m* (lugar) prison; (pena) prison sentence; **condenado a cinco años de ~** sentenced to five years imprisonment *o* five years in prison

presidir [I1] *vt*

A ‹*país*› to be president of; ‹*reunión*› to chair, preside at *o* over; ‹*comité*› to chair; ‹*tribunal/cortes/jurado*› to preside over; **presidió la compañía durante diez años** he was president (AmE) *o* (BrE) chairman of the company for ten years

B (reinar en) to prevail

presilla *f* (para abrochar) eye; (lazo) loop

presión *f*

A 1 (Fís) pressure; **cerveza a ~** draft beer 2 (Meteo) pressure; **altas/bajas presiones** areas of high/low pressure 3 (Med) pressure

(Compuesto) **presión arterial** *or* **sanguínea** blood pressure

B (coacción) pressure; **en su puesto está sometido a muchas presiones** he gets a lot of pressure in his job; **grupo de ~** pressure group; **confesó bajo ~** he confessed under pressure *o* under duress

presionar [A1] *vt* 1 (coaccionar) to put pressure on, to pressure (esp AmE), to pressurize (esp BrE); **lo ~on para que se retirara** he was pressured *o* pressurized into withdrawing 2 ‹*botón/timbre*› to press

■ **presionar** *vi* (Dep) to put on the pressure; **~ SOBRE algo/algn** to put pressure ON sth/sb, bring pressure to bear ON sth/sb (frml)

preso[1] **-sa** *adj*: **estuvo ~ diez años** he was in prison for ten years; **llevarse a algn ~** to take sb prisoner; **meter a algn ~** (CS, Esp) to put sb in prison

preso[2] **-sa** *m,f* prisoner

(Compuestos)
- **preso -sa común** *m,f* ordinary prisoner *o* criminal
- **preso político -sa política** *m,f* political prisoner
- **preso preventivo -sa preventiva** *m,f*: *prisoner held in preventive custody*

prestación *f*

A (de servicio) provision

B prestaciones *fpl* (Servs Socs) benefits (*pl*), assistance; **prestaciones económicas por invalidez** disability allowance; **prestaciones por desempleo** unemployment benefit *o* (AmE) compensation

C 1 (Tec) feature 2 **prestaciones** *fpl* (Auto) performance

prestado -da *adj*: **el libro está ~** the book is on loan *o* (colloq) is already out; **me pidió el coche ~** she asked if she could borrow my car; **pidió dinero ~** she asked for a loan, she asked to borrow some money; ***vivir de ~*** to live off other people

prestamista *mf* moneylender

préstamo *m*

A (Econ, Fin) (acción — de prestar) lending; (— de tomar prestado) borrowing; (cosa prestada) loan; **lo tenemos en ~** we've borrowed it, we've got it on loan

B (Ling) loanword

prestancia *f* (excelencia) excellence; (distinción en modales y movimientos) poise, elegance

prestar [A1] *vt*

A 1 ‹*dinero/coche/libro*› to lend 2 (Col) (pedir prestado) to borrow

P

B 1 ‹*ayuda*› to give; ‹*servicio*› to render; ‹*servicio militar*› to do 2 **prestar atención** to pay attention
C ‹*juramento*› to swear; **prestó declaración ante el juez** he made a statement to the judge
D (liter) ‹*alegría/colorido*› to lend
■ **prestarse** *v pron*
A **~se A algo** ‹*a críticas/malentendidos*› to be open TO sth; **el sistema se presta a abusos** the system lends itself to *o* is open to abuse
B (ser apto, idóneo) **~se PARA algo** to be suitable FOR sth; **la novela se presta para ser abreviada** the novel is ideal *o* suitable for abridgement
C (*refl*) (ofrecerse) **~se A + INF** to offer to + INF; (en frases negativas) **no me presto a negocios sucios** I won't take part in anything underhand

prestatario -ria *m,f* borrower

presteza *f* (liter) promptness, swiftness; **acudió con ~** he came swiftly *o* promptly

prestidigitación *f* conjuring

prestidigitador -dora *m,f* conjurer

prestigiado -da *adj* (Chi) prestigious

prestigio *m* prestige; **de ~** prestigious

prestigioso -sa *adj* famous, prestigious

presto[1] -ta *adj*
A (liter *o* frml) (preparado) ready
B (Mús) presto

presto[2] *adv* (liter) promptly, swiftly

presumible *adj*: **no es ~ una acción subversiva** any subversive activity seems unlikely; **era ~ su reacción** his reaction was predictable

presumido -da *adj* 1 (engreído) conceited, full of oneself; (arrogante) arrogant 2 (coqueto) vain

presumir [I1] *vi* to show off; **~ DE algo**: **presume de guapo** he thinks he's good-looking; **presume de intelectual** he likes to think he's an intellectual, he fancies himself as an intellectual (DiE), **le encanta ~ de dinero** she loves to flash her money around
■ **presumir** *vt*: **se presume una reacción violenta** there is likely to be a violent reaction; **es de ~ que ya habrán llegado** presumably they will already have arrived; **era de ~** it was quite predictable

presunción *f*
A 1 (engreimiento) presumptuousness, conceit; (arrogancia) arrogance 2 (coquetería) vanity
B (suposición) supposition; **~ de inocencia** presumption of innocence

presuntamente *adv* (frml) allegedly

presunto -ta *adj* (*delante del n*) (frml) ‹*asesino/terrorista*› alleged (*before n*)

presuntuoso -sa *adj* conceited, vain

presuponer [E22] *vt* to presuppose (frml), assume

presupuestal *adj* (AmL) ▸ **presupuestario**

presupuestar [A1] *vt*
A (Fin) to budget for; **exceder lo presupuestado** to exceed the budget
B (Chi) (planear) to plan

presupuestario -ria *adj* ‹*reforma/política*› budgetary (*before n*); ‹*déficit*› budget (*before n*)

presupuesto *m*
A 1 (Fin) budget; **~s generales del Estado** state/national budget 2 (precio estimado) estimate; **pedir/hacer un ~** to ask for/give an estimate
B (supuesto) assumption, supposition; **parten de unos ~s falsos** they are basing their theory on false assumptions *o* premises

presuroso -sa *adj* (liter): **se alejó presurosa** she rushed off, she left hastily; **andar con paso ~** to walk at a brisk *o* quick pace

pretencioso -sa *adj* 1 ‹*casa*› pretentious, showy; ‹*persona/película*› pretentious 2 (Chi) (vainidoso) vain

pretender [E1] *vt*
A 1 (intentar, aspirar): **¿qué pretendes con esa actitud?** what do you hope to gain with that attitude?; **¿qué pretendes de mí?** what do you expect of me?; **~ + INF** to try to + INF; **no ~ás hacerlo tú sola** you're not going to try to do it alone, are you?; **pretendía hacerme cambiar de opinión** she was trying to make me change my mind; **¿qué pretendes decir con eso?** what are you trying to say?, what are you getting at? 2 (esperar): **¿pretendes que te crea?** do you expect me to believe you?
B (ant) ‹*mujer*› to woo (dated)

pretendido -da *adj* (*delante del n*): **el ~ duque** the so-called duke; **con ~ interés** with false interest

pretendiente *mf*
A (al trono) pretender; (a un puesto) applicant
B **pretendiente** *m* (de una mujer) suitor

pretensión *f*
A 1 (intención) plan; (deseo) hope, wish, desire; ❸ **indíquese pretensiones salariales** indicate desired salary 2 (Der) (a trono, herencia) claim
B **pretensiones** *fpl* (ínfulas): **tener pretensiones** to be pretentious; **una película sin demasiadas pretensiones** an unpretentious film

pretérito *m* preterit*

Compuestos
- **pretérito anterior** past anterior
- **pretérito indefinido** simple past, preterit*
- **pretérito perfecto/pluscuamperfecto** present/past perfect

pretextar [A1] *vt* to claim; **pretextó desconocer el tema** he claimed he knew nothing about the subject; **pretextó otro compromiso** he claimed he had another engagement

pretexto *m* pretext; **volvió con el ~ de recoger el paraguas** he went back on the pretext of getting his umbrella; **no vino con el ~ de que ...** he excused himself from coming, saying that ...; **siempre sale con algún ~** she always comes out with some excuse; **so ~ de** (frml) on the pretext of, under pretext of

pretil *m* parapet

prevalecer [E3] *vi* to prevail; **~ SOBRE algo** to prevail OVER sth

prevalerse [E28] *v pron* **~ DE algo** to take advantage OF sth, avail oneself OF sth (frml); **~ de sus influencias/amistades** to use one's influence/friendships

prevaricación *f* corruption

prevaricar [A2] *vi* to pervert the course of justice, be guilty of corrupt practices

prevención *f*
A 1 (de un mal, problema) prevention; **la ~ de la delincuencia** crime prevention; **una campaña de ~ del alcoholismo** a campaign to fight alcoholism; **para la ~ de enfermedades infecciosas** to prevent the spread of infectious diseases 2 (medida): **tomar prevenciones** to take precautionary measures
B (prejuicio) **tener ~ CONTRA algo/algn** to be prejudiced AGAINST sth/sb

prevenido -da *adj* 1 [SER] (precavido) well-prepared, well-organized; **es muy prevenida** she likes to be prepared *o* ready for all eventualities 2 [ESTAR] (advertido) forewarned; **ahora ya estás ~** you've been warned

prevenir [I31] *vt* 1 ‹*enfermedad/accidente*› to prevent; ***más vale ~ que curar*** prevention is better than cure; ***más vale ~ que lamentar*** better safe than sorry 2 (advertir, alertar) to warn
■ **prevenirse** *v pron* **~se CONTRA algo** to take preventive *o* preventative measures AGAINST sth, take precautions AGAINST sth

preventiva *f* (Méx) yellow (AmE) *o* (BrE) amber light

preventivo -va *adj* preventive, preventative

prever [E29] *vt* 1 (anticipar) ‹*acontecimiento/consecuencias*› to foresee, anticipate; ‹*tiempo*› to forecast; **se prevé un aumento de precios** a rise in prices has been predicted; **todo hace ~ su victoria** everything points to her victory 2 (proyectar, planear): **medidas previstas por el gobierno** measures planned by the government; **la terminación del puente está prevista para enero** the bridge is due to be completed by January; **tiene prevista su llegada a las 11 horas** it is due *o* scheduled to arrive at 11 o'clock; **todo salió tal como estaba previsto** everything turned out just as planned 3 «*ley*» to envisage
■ **prever** *vi*: **como era de ~** as was to be expected

previo -via *adj*
A 1 (anterior) previous; **no se necesita experiencia previa** no previous experience required; **sin ~ aviso** without (prior) warning 2 ‹*reunión/asunto*› preliminary
B (RPl) (Educ): **me queda una materia previa** I have one

P

subject from last year to make up (AmE) *o* (BrE) retake
C (como preposición) (frml): **Ⓢ consulta previa petición de hora** consultation by appointment only; **las llaves se entregarán ~ pago de la fianza** the keys will be handed over on receipt of the deposit

previsible *adj* foreseeable

previsión *f* **1** (precaución) precaution; **en ~ de ...** as a precaution against ...; **por falta de ~** owing to a lack of foresight; **un sistema de ~ social** a welfare system **2** (predicción — de resultado) forecast, prediction; (— del tiempo) forecast

previsivo -va *adj* (Col, Méx) ▸ **previsor**

previsor -sora *adj* (con visión de futuro) farsighted; **seguro que lleva aspirinas, es muy previsora** she's bound to have some aspirins, she's always well-prepared

prieta *f* (Chi) blood sausage, black pudding (BrE)

prieto -ta *adj*
A (liter) firm
B (Méx fam) (oscuro) dark; (de piel oscura) dark-skinned

priísta *adj* of/relating to the **PRI**

prima *f* **1** (de seguro) premium **2** (pago extra) bonus; **~ de productividad/rendimiento** productivity-/performance-related bonus; **~ de** *or* **por peligrosidad** danger money

primacía *f*
A **1** (preeminencia) supremacy **2** (prioridad) priority; **~ SOBRE algo** priority OVER sth, precedence OVER sth
B (Relig) primacy

primado *m* primate

prima facie *adv* (frml) prima facie (frml)

primar [A1] *vi*: **debería ~ el interés público** the public interest should be (a) top priority *o* (frml) should be paramount; **prima la preocupación por las nuevas tecnologías** concern for new technology predominates; **~ SOBRE algo** to take precedence *o* priority OVER sth; **prima la rentabilidad sobre la calidad** profitability takes precedence *o* priority over quality
▪ **primar** *vt* (Dep) ‹*jugadores*› to give a bonus to

primaria *f*
A (Educ) elementary *o* (BrE) primary education
B (Pol) (en EEUU) primary

primario -ria *adj* **1** (básico) ‹*necesidades/objetivo*› primary, basic; ‹*deber*› fundamental, primary **2** (primitivo) ‹*instintos*› primitive **3** (Psic) primary **4** (Elec) primary

primate *m* primate

primavera *f*
A (estación) spring; **en ~** in spring, in springtime; **en la ~ de la vida** in the springtime of one's life
B (Bot) primrose

primaveral *adj* ‹*tiempo/moda*› spring (*before n*); ‹*ambiente*› spring-like

primer *ver* **primero¹**

primera *f* **1** (Auto) first (gear) **2** (Transp) (clase) first class; **viajar en ~** to travel first class; *ver tb* **primero¹**

primeramente *adv* first of all

primeriza *f* first-time mother

primerizo¹ -za *adj* **1** (fam) (poco experto) green (colloq), inexperienced; **un texto para lectores ~s** a text for the lay person *o* for the uninitiated **2** (Med): **madre primeriza** first-time mother

primerizo² -za *m,f* novice, beginner

primero¹ -ra *adj/pron* [**primer** *is used before masculine singular nouns*]
A , (en el espacio, el tiempo) first; **vivo en el primer piso** I live on the second (AmE) *o* (BrE) first floor; **en primer lugar ...** first (of all), ..., firstly, ...; **las diez primeras páginas** the first ten pages; **sus ~s poemas** her early *o* first poems; **1° de julio** (*read as: primero de julio*) 1st July, July 1st (*léase: July the first*); **Olaf I** (*read as: Olaf primero*) Olaf I (*léase: Olaf the First*); **la primera fila** the front row; **a primeras horas de la madrugada** in the early hours of the morning; **mañana a primera hora** first thing tomorrow

Compuestos
- **primera plana** *f* front page; **salir en ~ ~** to make front-page news *o* the headlines
- **primeros auxilios** *mpl* first aid
- **primer plano** *m* (Fot) close-up (shot); **en ~ ~** (Art) in the foreground
- **primer plato** *m* first course, starter

B (en calidad, jerarquía): **un artículo de primerísima calidad** a top-quality product; **de primera categoría** first-class, first-rate; **es el ~ de la clase** he is top of the class; **es el primer atleta del país** he is the country's top athlete; **la primera empresa mundial** the world's leading company; ***de primera*** first-class, first-rate

Compuesto **primer ministro -ra ministra** *m,f* Prime Minister

C (básico, fundamental): **nuestro primer objetivo** our primary objective; **artículos de primera necesidad** basic necessities; **lo ~ es ...** the most important thing is ...

primero² *adv*
A (en el tiempo) first
B (en importancia): **estar ~** to come first; **~ el deber (y después el placer)** business before pleasure

primicia *f* **1** (Bot) first fruit **2** (Period): **conseguimos la ~ del reportaje** we were the first to carry the report; **una ~ informativa** a scoop

primigenio -nia *adj* (frml) ‹*motivación*› underlying (*before n*), original (*before n*); ‹*preocupación*› basic (*before n*), original (*before n*)

primitivismo *m* primitivism

primitivo -va *adj*
A primitive; **los hombres ~s** primitive *o* early man
B (original) original
C (Art) primitive

primo¹ -ma *adj* ‹*número*› prime; ‹*materia*› raw

primo² -ma *m,f* **1** (pariente) cousin **2** (Esp fam) (bobo) sucker (colloq), patsy (AmE colloq); ***hacer el ~*** (Esp fam) to be taken for a ride (colloq), to be conned (colloq)

Compuestos
- **primo -ma carnal** *m,f* first cousin
- **primo hermano -ma hermana** *m,f* first cousin
- **primo segundo -ma segunda** *m,f* second cousin

primogénito¹ -ta *adj* firstborn (*before n*) (liter), first (*before n*)

primogénito² -ta *m,f* firstborn (liter), first *o* firstborn child

primogenitura *f* primogeniture (frml), birthright (liter)

primor *m* **1** (esmero): **está bordado con mucho ~** it is very finely *o* delicately embroidered **2** (delicadeza) delicacy **3** (maravilla, encanto): **esta porcelana/chica es un ~** this is an exquisite piece of porcelain/girl is a delight; **canta que es un ~** she sings like an angel

primordial *adj* ‹*objetivo*› fundamental, prime (*before n*); ‹*interés/importancia*› paramount; **es ~ analizar sus causas** it is essential to analyse its causes

primoroso -sa *adj* **1** (fino, esmerado) exquisite **2** (delicado) delicate **3** ‹*niño/mujer*› beautifully dressed

prímula *f* primula; (amarilla) primrose

princesa *f* princess

principado *m* (territorio) principality; (título) princedom, principality

principal¹ *adj* ‹*entrada/carretera/calle*› main; **el papel ~** the main part *o* leading role; **el personaje ~** the main character; **lo ~ es que...** the main thing is that...; **lo ~ es la salud** there's nothing more important than your health

principal² *m* **1** (Fin) principal, capital **2** (en teatro, cine) dress circle, mezzanine (AmE)

príncipe *m* prince

Compuestos
- **príncipe azul** Prince Charming (hum)
- **príncipe consorte** prince consort
- **príncipe heredero** crown prince

principesco -ca *adj* princely

principiante¹ *adj*: **es un conductor ~** he's a learner driver, he's learning to drive

principiante² *mf* beginner; **un curso para ~s** a beginners' course; **un error de ~** a basic mistakes

principiar [A1] *vt* (frml) to commence (frml), to begin

principio *m*
A (comienzo) beginning; **el ~ del verano** early summer, the beginning of summer; **a ~s de temporada** at the beginning of the season; **a ~s de siglo** at the turn of the century; **empieza por el ~** start at the beginning; **eso es un buen ~** that's a good start; **congeniamos desde el ~**

P

we got along well from the start; **al ~** at first; **en ~ la reunión es el jueves** the meeting's on Thursday unless you hear otherwise; **en ~ estoy de acuerdo** I agree in principle; **en un** *or* **al ~** at first, in the beginning

B 1 (concepto, postulado) principle; **un ~ universalmente aceptado** a universally accepted concept; **la teoría parte de un ~ erróneo** the theory is based on a false premise 2 (norma moral) principle; **es una mujer de ~s** she's a woman of principle; **por ~** on principle

pringar [A3] *vt*

A 1 (fam) (ensuciar) to get … dirty (with grease, oil etc); **dejó la cocina toda pringada** he left everything in the kitchen covered in grease; ***¡la he/hemos pringado!*** (fam) now I've/we've done it! (colloq) 2 ‹*pan*› to dip

B (fam) **~ a algn EN algo** (comprometer) to get sb mixed up in sth; **está pringado en el contrabando** he's mixed up in the smuggling racket

■ **pringarse** *v pron* (fam) 1 (ensuciarse) **~se DE algo** ‹*de grasa/mermelada*› to get covered IN sth 2 (comprometerse) **~se EN algo** ‹*en negocio*› to get mixed up IN sth

pringoso -sa *adj* greasy

pringue *m* (fam) 1 (grasa) grease; (mugre) gunk, gunge (BrE) 2 (salsa) sauce, juices (*pl*)

prior, priora (*m*) prior; (*f*) prioress

prioridad *f* 1 (precedencia) priority 2 (Auto) priority; **tener ~ (de paso)** to have right of way *o* priority

prioritariamente *adv* first and foremost

prioritario -ria *adj* priority (*before n*); **nuestra tarea prioritaria** our top priority *o* most urgent task

priorizar [A4] *vt* (dar preeminencia a) to give priority to; (decidir el orden de importancia de) to prioritize

prisa *f*

A (rapidez, urgencia) rush, hurry; **¿a qué viene tanta ~?** what's the rush *o* hurry?; **con las ~s olvidé decírselo** in the rush I forgot to tell her; **tenía ~ por llegar a casa** he was in a rush to get home; **no me metas ~** don't rush *o* hurry me; **tengo ~** (Esp, Méx) I'm in a rush *o* a hurry; **darse ~** to hurry (up)

B (*en locs*) **a** *or* **de prisa** ▸**deprisa**; **a toda prisa** as fast as possible; **huyó a toda ~** she ran away as fast as she could go; **correr prisa**: **éstos no (me) corren ~** there's no rush for these; ***sin ~ pero sin pausa*** slowly but surely; **hazlo sin ~ pero sin pausa** take your time

prisco *m* (CS) *type of peach*

prisión *f*

A (edificio) prison, jail, penitentiary (AmE)

B (pena) imprisonment; **condenado a seis años de ~** sentenced to six years' imprisonment

(Compuestos)

- **prisión mayor** long-term prison sentence (*6 to 12 years*)
- **prisión menor** medium-term prison sentence (*6 months to 6 years*)
- **prisión preventiva** *or* **provisional** preventive detention; **el juez decretó la ~ ~** the judge ordered him to be remanded in custody

prisionero -ra *m,f* prisoner; **caer ~** to be taken prisoner *o* captured; **lo hicieron ~** he was taken prisoner *o* captured

(Compuesto) **prisionero -ra de guerra** *m,f* prisoner of war

prisma *m* (Fís, Ópt) prism; (perspectiva) perspective

prismáticos *mpl* binoculars (*pl*), field-glasses (*pl*); **unos ~** a pair of binoculars

prístino -na *adj* pristine

privacidad *f* privacy

privación *f* 1 (acción) deprivation; **¿qué se consigue con la ~ de libertad?** what is to be gained by depriving someone of their freedom?; **se lo castigó con la ~ del carné** he had his license taken away 2 (falta, carencia) privation; **pasar muchas privaciones** to suffer great hardship

privada *f* (Méx) private road (*with security control*)

privado -da *adj* 1 ‹*reunión/vida*› private; **en ~** in private 2 (Col, Méx) (desmayado) unconscious 3 (Méx) ‹*teléfono/número*› unlisted (AmE), ex-directory (BrE)

privar [A1] *vt*

A **~ a algn DE algo** ‹*de derecho/libertad*› to deprive sb OF sth; **fue privado de sus bienes** all his possessions were confiscated

B (Col, Méx) (dejar inconsciente) to knock … unconscious

■ **privar** *vi*

A (destacar): **en su comportamiento privaba la honradez** her behavior was characterized by honesty; **en la casa privaba un ambiente de serenidad** a serene atmosphere prevailed in the house

B (fam) (gustar) (+ *me/te/le etc*): **me privan las manzanas** I adore *o* really love apples

■ **privarse** *v pron*

A **~se DE algo** ‹*de lujos/placeres*› to deprive oneself OF sth; **cuando tiene ocasión de comer bien, no se priva** when she gets the chance to eat well she doesn't hold back

B 1 (Col, Méx) (desmayarse) to lose consciousness, pass out 2 (Ven) (quedarse tieso): **el agua estaba tan fría que me privé** the water was so cold that I couldn't breathe properly

privativo -va *adj* [SER] (propio): **es función privativa del rey** it is the exclusive right of the king

privatización *f* privatization

privatizar [A4] *vt* to privatize

privilegiado[1] -da *adj* 1 ‹*persona/clase*› privileged 2 (excelente) ‹*posición*› privileged; ‹*clima/inteligencia/memoria*› exceptional

privilegiado[2] -da *m,f*: **unos pocos ~s** a privileged few

privilegiar [A1] *vt* 1 (favorecer) to favor*; **la ley privilegia a los ricos** the law favors the rich 2 (frml) (conceder un privilegio a) to grant a privilege to

privilegio *m* privilege; **conceder ~s** to grant privileges; **gozar de ~s** to enjoy privileges

pro[1] *m*

A (ventaja) advantage; **sopesar los ~s y los contras de algo** to weigh up the pros and cons of sth

B **de pro** (ant): **un hombre de ~** a good man and true (arch)

pro[2] *prep*: **una colecta ~ ciegos** a collection for the blind; **los sectores ~ amnistía** the sectors in favor of an amnesty

proa *f* bow, prow; **situado en la ~** situated forward *o* in the bow; **poner ~ hacia** to set course for

probabilidad *f* (Mat) probability; **con toda ~** in all probability *o* likelihood; **¿qué ~es tiene de ganar?** what are her chances of winning?; **existen pocas ~es de que sea encontrado con vida** (frml) the possibility of him being found alive is very remote (frml)

probable *adj* (posible) probable; **¿lo habrá perdido? — es ~** do you think he's lost it? — probably; **es ~ que llegue hoy** he will probably arrive today; **lo más ~ es que no se haya enterado** she most probably hasn't heard; **es muy ~ que le renueven el contrato** her contract will very probably be renewed

probablemente *adv* probably; **~ llegue** *or* **llegaré tarde** I'll probably be late

probado -da *adj* 1 (*delante del n*) (confirmado) proven; **un remedio de probada eficacia** a proven remedy; **de probada rectitud** of proven integrity 2 (Der) proven

probador *m* fitting room, changing room (BrE)

probar [A10] *vt*

A (demostrar) ‹*teoría/inocencia*› to prove

B 1 ‹*vino/sopa*› to taste; (por primera vez) to try; **no he vuelto a ~ la ginebra** I haven't touched gin since; **no probé bocado en todo el día** I didn't eat a thing *o* have a bite to eat all day 2 ‹*método*› to try; **prueba el coche antes de comprarlo** try out the car before buying it; **llevé el coche a que le ~an los frenos** I took the car to have the brakes tested 3 ‹*ropa*› to try on; **~le algo A algn** to try sth ON sb; **la modista me probó el vestido una vez** the dressmaker gave me one fitting for the dress 4 (poner a prueba) ‹*empleado/honradez*› to test

■ **probar** *vi* (intentar) to try; **~ no cuesta nada** there's no harm in trying; **¿has probado con quitamanchas?** have you tried using stain remover?; **~ A + INF** to try -ING

■ **probarse** *v pron* ‹*ropa/zapatos*› to try on; **quisiera ~me uno más grande** I'd like to try a larger size

probeta[1] *f* test tube

probeta[2] *adj inv* ‹*gemelos/hijos*› test-tube (*before n*)

P

problema *m* problem; **resolver/solucionar un ~** to solve a problem; **nos está creando muchos ~s** it is causing us a lot of problems *o* a lot of trouble; **~s económicos** financial difficulties *o* problems; **los coches viejos dan muchos ~s** old cars give a lot of trouble; **si se enteran, vas a tener ~s** if they find out, you'll be in trouble; **no te hagas ~** (AmL) don't worry about it

problemática *f* problems (*pl*); **la ~ de América Central** the problems *o* the situation in Central America; **la ~ de la pareja** the problems within a relationship

problemático -ca *adj* problematic, difficult

procacidad *f* (de chiste, comentario) indecency, lewdness; (del lenguaje) obscenity

procaz *adj* ‹*comentario/chiste*› indecent, lewd; ‹*lenguaje*› obscene

procedencia *f*
A 1 (origen) origin; **investigan la ~ de las armas** they're investigating where the weapons came from 2 (de barco) port of origin
B (Der) legitimacy

procedente *adj*
A ‹*tren/vuelo*›: **el vuelo/tren ~ de París** the flight/train from Paris, the Paris flight/train
B (Der) legitimate, fair

proceder[1] *m* (frml) behavior*, conduct (frml)

proceder[2] [E1] *vi*
A (provenir) **~ DE algo** to come FROM sth
B (actuar) to proceed (frml); **procedió con mucha corrección** he behaved very correctly; **~ contra algn** (Der) to iniciate proceedings against sb
C (frml) (iniciar) **~ A algo** to proceed TO sth; **la policía procedió a su detención** the police proceeded to arrest him; **se procedió a la votación immediatamente** they went straight into the vote
D (ser conveniente): **procede actuar rápidamente** it would be wise to act swiftly; **rellenar lo que proceda** complete as appropriate; **procede/no procede la protesta** (Der) objection sustained/overruled

procedimiento *m*
A (método) procedure; (Tec) process
B (Der) proceedings (*pl*)
C (RPl) (de la policía) operation

proceloso -sa *adj* (liter) stormy, tempestuous (liter)

prócer *m* national hero (*esp of a struggle for independence*)

procesado -da *m,f*
A (Der) accused, defendant
B **procesado** *m* (Fot, Tec) processing

procesador *m* processor
(Compuesto) **procesador de textos** word processor

procesamiento *m*
A (Der) prosecution, trial
B (Tec, Inf) processing
(Compuesto) **procesamiento de textos** word processing

procesar [A1] *vt*
A (Der) to try, prosecute
B ‹*materia prima/datos/solicitud*› to process

procesión *f* procession; ***la ~ va por dentro*** I'm (or he's, etc) going through a lot, although I don't (or he doesn't, etc) show it

proceso *m*
A 1 (serie de acciones, sucesos) process; **el ~ de paz** the peace process 2 (Med): **sufre un ~ de insuficiencia respiratoria** he has a respiratory complaint; **es una enfermedad de ~ lento** it is a long, drawn-out illness
B (Der) trial; **se le sigue ~ por robo** he is on trial for theft; **abrir un ~ contra algn** to investigate sb
C (Inf) processing
(Compuesto) **proceso de datos/textos** data/word processing
D (transcurso) course

proclama *f* (Pol) proclamation; (notificación pública) announcement

proclamación *f* proclamation, declaration

proclamar [A1] *vt* to proclaim; **fue proclamada la ley marcial** martial law was declared *o* proclaimed
■ **proclamarse** *v pron* to proclaim oneself; **se proclamó campeón por cuarta vez** he won the championship for the fourth time

proclive *adj* **~ A algo** given to sth; **políticos ~s al diálogo** politicians who are inclined toward(s) *o* who favor dialogue

proclividad *f* proclivity, inclination

procreación *f* procreation

procrear [A1] *vi* to procreate, breed

procura *f* (AmL frml): **avanzar en ~ de resolver los problemas** to make an attempt to resolve the problems; **en ~ de ayuda** to seek assistance (frml)

procurador -dora *m,f* (Der) (abogado) attorney, lawyer; (asistente) ≈ paralegal (*in US*), ≈ clerk (*in UK*)
(Compuesto) **procurador -dora general del Estado** *m,f* (AmL) attorney general

procurar [A1] *vt*
A (intentar) **~ + INF** to try to + INF, endeavor* to + INF (frml); **procura que no te vea** try not to let him see you; **~emos que llegue intacto** we'll try to make sure it gets there in one piece
B ‹*ropa/armas*› (frml) to obtain, secure, procure (frml); **el consuelo que le procuran los niños** the comfort the children bring him; **les procuró casa y comida** she found them food and lodging
■ **procurarse** *v pron* (frml) to secure

prodigalidad *f* (despilfarro)wastefulness, extravagance; (generosidad) lavishness, generosity

pródigamente *adv* (con generosidad) generously, lavishly; (con derroche) wastefully, extravagantly

prodigar [A3] *vt* (frml) **~ algo A algn** ‹*elogios/alabanzas*› to lavish sb WITH sth
■ **prodigarse** *v pron* (frml) **~se EN algo**: **no se prodiga en elogios** he is not very generous *o* lavish with his praise; **se prodigó en atenciones con ella** he lavished attention on her

prodigio *m* 1 (maravilla) wonder; **un ~ de la naturaleza** one of the wonders of nature; **un ~ de la técnica** a technological wonder; **este nuevo ~ del tenis** this new wonder boy of tennis 2 (milagro) miracle

prodigioso -sa *adj* ‹*fuerza/esfuerzo*› prodigious, incredible; ‹*memoria*› prodigious, phenomenal; ‹*éxito*› phenomenal; ‹*jugador/músico*› phenomenal, exceptional

pródigo -ga *adj* prodigal; **~ EN algo** prodigal WITH *o* (frml) OF sth; **un discurso ~ en promesas** a speech prodigal with promises

producción *f*
A 1 (Com, Econ) (proceso, acción) production; (cantidad) output, production 2 (conjunto de obras) output; **su ~ dramática es escasa** his dramatic output is small; **la ~ pictórica de Picasso** Picasso's paintings
(Compuesto) **producción en cadena** *or* **serie** mass production
B (Cin, Teatr, TV) production; **la etapa de ~** the production stage; **una ~ de la BBC** a BBC production

producir [I6] *vt*
A 1 «*región/país*» ‹*trigo/tomates/vino*› to produce; ‹*petróleo*› to produce; «*persona*» ‹*trigo/tomates*› to produce, grow; ‹*aceite/vino*› to produce, make 2 (manufacturar) to produce, make 3 ‹*electricidad/calor/energía*› to produce, generate 4 ‹*sonido*› to cause, generate
B (Com, Fin) ‹*beneficios*› to produce, generate, yield; ‹*pérdidas*› to cause, result in
C ‹*película/programa*› to produce
D (causar) ‹*conmoción/reacción/explosión*› to cause; **le produjo una gran alegría** it made her very happy; **me produjo muy buena impresión** I was very impressed with her; **la pomada le produjo un sarpullido** the ointment brought her out in a rash
■ **producirse** *v pron*
A (frml) (tener lugar) «*accidente/explosión*» to occur (frml), to take place; «*cambio*» to occur (frml), to happen; **se produjeron 85 muertes** there were 85 deaths, 85 people died *o* were killed; **se produjeron momentos de histerismo** there were moments of panic
B (*refl*) (frml) ‹*heridas*› to inflict … on oneself (frml); **se produjo heridas con un cuchillo** she deliberately cut herself with a knife; **se produjo varias fracturas al caerse** he broke several bones when he fell

P

productividad *f* (cualidad) productivity; (rendimiento) productivity, output

productivo -va *adj* ‹*tierra*› productive, fertile; ‹*empresa/negocio*› lucrative; ‹*reunión/jornada*› productive

producto *m*

A 1 (artículo producido) product; **~s nacionales** home-produced goods *o* products; **~s de granja** farm produce 2 (resultado) result, product; **su éxito es el ~ de mucho esfuerzo** her success is the result *o* product of a great deal of effort; **todo es ~ de su imaginación** it's all a product *o* a figment of his imagination

Compuestos

- **producto alimenticio** foodstuff
- **producto de belleza** beauty product, cosmetic
- **producto interior bruto** gross domestic product, GDP
- **producto lácteo** dairy product
- **producto nacional bruto** gross national product, GNP

B (Mat) product

productor[1] **-tora** *adj*

A (Agr, Com) producing (*before n*); **países ~es de café** coffee-producing countries

B (Cin, TV) production (*before n*)

productor[2] **-tora** *m,f*

A (Com) producer; (Agr) producer, grower

B (Cin, TV) 1 (persona) producer 2 **productora** *f* (empresa) production company

produje, produzca, etc *see* **producir**

proemio *m* (de libro) preface; (de canción) introduction

proeza *f* (logro) feat, exploit; (Mil) heroic deed *o* exploit

profanación *f* desecration

profanar [A1] *vt* ‹*templo/sepultura*› to desecrate, defile, profane (frml); **~ la memoria de algn** to defile *o* profane sb's memory

profano[1] **-na** *adj*

A 1 (no sagrado) ‹*escritor/música*› secular, profane (frml); ‹*fiesta*› secular 2 (antirreligioso) profane (frml), irreverent

B (no especializado): **soy ~ en la materia** I'm not an expert on the subject

profano[2] **-na** *m,f*

A (Relig) (*m*) layman; (*f*) laywoman

B (no especialista) non-specialist

profecía *f* prophecy

proferir [I11] *vt* ‹*palabras/amenazas*› to utter; ‹*insultos*› to hurl; **a ~ maldiciones** to curse and swear

profesar [A1] *vt* 1 (declarar) ‹*religión/doctrina*› to profess 2 (sentir) ‹*cariño*› to feel; ‹*respeto*› to have

■ **profesar** *vi* (Relig) to take one's vows

profesión *f*

A (ocupación) profession; **es carpintero de ~** he's a carpenter by trade; **es abogada de ~** she's a lawyer by profession; **Ⓢ profesión** (en formularios) occupation

Compuesto **profesión liberal** profession

B (Relig) profession

profesional[1] *adj* ‹*fotógrafo/deportista*› professional; **su vida ~** her work, her professional life

profesional[2] *mf* 1 (no aficionado) professional; **un ~ del crimen** a professional criminal 2 (de las profesiones liberales) professional

profesionalidad *f*, **profesionalismo** *m* professionalism

profesionalización *f* professionalization

profesionalizar [A4] *vt* to professionalize

■ **profesionalizarse** *v pron* to become a professional, turn professional

profesionista *mf* (Méx) professional

profesor -sora *m,f* (de escuela secundaria) teacher, schoolteacher; (de universidad) professor (AmE), lecturer (BrE); **~ de piano/guitarra** piano/guitar teacher; **es ~ de gimnasia** he's a physical education teacher; **tiene un ~ particular** he has a private tutor

profesorado *m* (cuerpo) faculty (AmE), teaching staff (BrE); (actividad) teaching profession

profeta *m* prophet

profético -ca *adj* prophetic

profetizar [A4] *vt* to prophesy

profiláctico -ca *adj/m* (frml) prophylactic (frml)

profilaxis *f* prophylaxis

profitar [A1] *vi* (Chi frml) **~ DE algo** to exploit *o* use sth

prófugo -ga *m,f* (Der) fugitive; (Mil) deserter

profundamente *adv* ‹*emocionado/afectado*› profoundly, deeply; **influyó ~ en el proceso** he had a profound influence on the process; **respire ~** breathe deeply; **~ dormido** sound asleep

profundidad *f*

A 1 (de pozo, río) depth; **tiene 20 metros de ~** it's 20 meters deep; **¿qué ~ tiene el armario?** how deep is the cupboard? 2 (de conocimientos, ideas) depth; **analizar un asunto en ~** to analyze a question in depth; **una reforma en ~** a radical *o* far-reaching reform

Compuesto **profundidad de campo** depth of field

B **las profundidades** *fpl* (del océano) the depths (*pl*)

profundizar [A4] *vi* **~ EN algo: no tenemos tiempo para ~ en este tema** we don't have time to go into this topic in any depth; **ha profundizado más en los personajes femeninos** he has portrayed his female characters in greater depth

■ **profundizar** *vt* to deepen

profundo -da *adj* 1 ‹*herida/pozo/raíz*› deep; **un río poco ~** a shallow river; **una tradición con profundas raíces** a deeply-rooted tradition; **lo siento en lo más ~ de mi alma** I'm deeply sorry 2 ‹*pensamiento*› profound, deep; ‹*respeto/desprecio*› profound; ‹*lazos*› strong; ‹*desengaño*› grave, terrible; **mis conocimientos de la materia no son muy ~s** I don't have an in-depth knowledge of the subject 3 ‹*misterio*› profound; ‹*silencio*› deep, profound 4 ‹*voz/suspiro*› deep 5 ‹*sueño*› deep, sound

profusamente *adv* ‹*sangrar/sudar*› profusely; **el tema fue ~ tratado** the subject was dealt with at great length

profusión *f* profusion, abundance

profuso -sa *adj* ‹*ilustraciones/explicaciones*› abundant, plentiful; **con profusas nuestras de cariño** with effusive displays of affection

progenie *f* (frml) progeny (frml)

progenitor -tora *m,f* 1 (antepasado) ancestor 2 (frml) (*m*) (padre) father; (*f*) (madre) mother

programa *m*

A 1 (Rad, TV) program*; **~ doble** (Cin) double bill, double feature 2 (folleto) program*

Compuesto **programa concurso** quiz show

B (programación, plan) program*; **un ~ de visitas muy apretado** a very tight program *o* schedule; **¡eso no estaba en el ~!** (fam) that wasn't part of the plan! (colloq)

C 1 (político) program*; **su ~ electoral** their election manifesto 2 (Educ) (de asignatura) syllabus; (de curso) curriculum, syllabus

D (Inf, Elec) program*

E (RPl fam) (conquista) pickup (colloq)

programable *adj* programmable

programación *f*

A 1 (Rad, TV) programs* (*pl*); **la ~ de hoy** today's programs 2 (de festejos, visitas — lista) program*; (— organización) organization, planning

B (Inf) programming

programador -dora *m,f* programmer

programar [A1] *vt*

A 1 (Rad, TV) to schedule 2 ‹*actividades/eventos*› to plan, draw up a program* for; ‹*horario/fecha*› to schedule, program*; ‹*viaje*› to organize; **la gira todavía no ha sido programada** the program for the tour has yet to be finalized 3 (Transp) ‹*llegadas/salidas*› to schedule, timetable (BrE)

B (Inf) to program

programático -ca *adj* ‹*discurso*› programmatic (frml); **los principales puntos ~s del partido** the main points of the party's program *o* manifesto

progre[1] *adj* (fam) (moderno) trendy (colloq); (liberal) liberal, progressive

progre[2] *mf* (fam) (persona — moderna) trendy (colloq); (— liberal) liberal; (— de izquierdas) trendy lefty (colloq)

progresar [A1] *vi* ‹‹*persona*›› to make progress, to progress; ‹‹*negociaciones/proyecto*›› to progress

P

progresión *f* (Mat, Mús) progression; **ha habido una ~ anual del 3%** there has been a 3% annual increase

(Compuesto) **progresión aritmética/geométrica** arithmetic/geometric progression

progresismo *m* progressive way of thinking, progressive ideas (*pl*), progressivism (frml)

progresista *adj/mf* progressive

progresivo -va *adj* [1] (que avanza) progressive [2] (continuo) progressive [3] (paulatino) progressive, gradual [4] (Ling) ‹*tiempo*› continuous, progressive

progreso *m* [1] (adelanto): **supuso un gran ~** it was a great step forward; **ha hecho grandes ~s** he has made great progress [2] (evolución, desarrollo) progress

prohibición *f* (acción) prohibition, banning; (orden) ban

prohibir [I22] *vt* [1] ‹*acto/venta*› to prohibit (frml); **esta ley prohíbe las huelgas** this law bans *o* prohibits strikes; **queda terminantemente prohibido** it is strictly forbidden *o* prohibited; **iba en dirección prohibida** I was going the wrong way up a one-way street; Ⓢ **prohibido el paso** *or* **prohibida la entrada** no entry; Ⓢ **prohibido fijar carteles** stick no bills, bill posters *o* bill stickers will be prosecuted; Ⓢ **prohibido fumar** no smoking [2] **~le algo A algn** to ban sb FROM sth; Ⓢ **se prohíbe la entrada a menores de 16 años** over 16s only, no admission to persons under 16 years of age; **tengo prohibido el alcohol** I've been told I mustn't drink alcohol [3] **~le A algn + INF** to forbid sb to + INF, prohibit sb FROM -ING (frml); **prohíben sindicarse a los trabajadores** workers are not allowed to form a union; **le tenemos prohibido salir** he's not allowed out [4] **~ A algn QUE + SUBJ** to forbid sb to + INF; **te prohíbo que me hables así** I forbid you to speak to me like that

prohibitivo -va *adj* prohibitive

prohijar [A19] *vt* to adopt

prohombre *m* great man, outstanding figure

prójimo *m* (semejante) fellow man; **amar al ~** to love one's neighbor; **las desgracias del ~** other people's misfortunes

prolapso *m* prolapse

prole *f* kids (*pl*) (colloq), offspring (hum)

prolegómeno *m* [1] (de texto) preface, prolegomenon (frml) [2] (de relato) introduction, preamble; (de petición) preliminaries (*pl*), introduction

proletariado *m* proletariat

proletario -ria *adj/m* proletarian

proliferación *f* proliferation, spread

proliferar [A1] *vi* to proliferate, spread

prolífico -ca *adj* prolific

prolijidad *f*
A (extensión excesiva) long-windedness; (minuciosidad) detail; **el relato es de gran ~** the story is told in great detail
B (RPl) (orden, aseo) neatness, tidiness

prolijo -ja *adj*
A (extenso) protracted, long-winded; (minucioso) detailed
B (RPl) (ordenado, aseado) ‹*persona/casa*› tidy; ‹*cuaderno*› neat

prologar [A3] *vt* to write a preface *o* a prologue to

prólogo *m* (de libro) preface, foreword; (de acto) prelude

prolongación *f*
A (de carretera, muelle) [1] (acción) extension, lengthening [2] (tramo) extension, continuation
B (de contrato) extension

prolongado -da *adj* prolonged, lengthy

prolongar [A3] *vt* [1] ‹*contrato/plazo*› to extend; ‹*vacaciones/negociaciones*› to prolong, extend [2] ‹*línea/calle*› to extend

■ **prolongarse** *v pron* [1] (en el tiempo) «*debate/fiesta*» to go on, carry on; **la espera se prolongó durante horas** we/they had to wait for hours [2] (en el espacio) «*carretera/línea*» to extend

promediar [A1] *vt* [1] (Mat) ‹*cifras*› to average out, find the average of [2] (tener un promedio de) to average; **el costo ~á cinco dólares** the average cost will be five dollars

promedio *m* [1] (Mat) average; **el ~ de ventas fue de 60.000** sales averaged 60,000; **hizo un ~ de 25 kilómetros al día** he averaged 25 kilometers a day; **el ~ de mis ingresos** my average earnings; **como ~** on average [2] (nota media) average grade *o* (BrE) mark [3] (punto medio) mid-point

promesa *f* [1] (palabra) promise; **cumplí (con) mi ~** I kept my promise *o* word; **faltaste a tu ~** you went back on your word, you didn't keep your promise; **romper una ~** to break a promise [2] (persona) hope

promesero -ra *m,f* (Andes) pilgrim

prometedor -dora *adj* promising

prometer [E1] *vt* [1] (dar su palabra) to promise; **me prometió un regalo** he promised me a present; **te lo prometo** I promise [2] (augurar) to promise; **esas nubes no prometen nada bueno** those clouds look ominous *o* don't bode well [3] (fam) (afirmar, asegurar) to tell; **estoy harta, te lo prometo** I'm fed up, I can tell you

■ **prometer** *vi* «*persona/negocio*» to show *o* have promise

■ **prometerse** *v pron* [1] (en matrimonio) to get engaged [2] (*refl*) ‹*viaje/descanso*› to promise oneself [3] (confiar en) to expect; ***prometérselas muy felices*** (Esp) to have high hopes

prometido¹ -da *adj* [1] (para casarse) engaged [2] ‹*aumento/regalo*› promised; **cumplir con lo ~** to keep one's promise *o* word

prometido² -da (*m*) fiancé; (*f*) fiancée

prominencia *f*
A (protuberancia) bump, protuberance (frml); (del terreno) rise
B (cualidad) prominence

prominente *adj* prominent; **tiene el mentón muy ~** she has a very prominent chin

promiscuidad *f* promiscuity

promiscuo -cua *adj* [1] ‹*persona/relación*› promiscuous [2] (mezclado) mixed, jumbled

promoción *f*
A [1] (de actividad, producto) promotion; **hacer la ~ de un producto** to promote a product; **~ de ventas** sales promotion [2] (ascenso) promotion
B (Educ): **somos de la misma ~** we graduated at the same time; **los médicos de la ~ de 1988** the doctors who qualified in 1988

promocional *adj* promotional

promocionar [A1] *vt* to promote

promontorio *m* (en tierra) hill, rise; (en el mar) promontory, headland

promotor¹ -tora *adj*: **la empresa ~a** (Const) the development company; (Espec) the promoters (*pl*)

promotor² -tora *m,f*
A (persona) [1] (Const) developer [2] (Espec) promoter [3] (de rebelión, huelga) instigator; **el ~ de la iniciativa** the man behind the initiative
B **promotora** *f* (compañía) *tb* **~ inmobiliaria** (property) developer, development company

promover [E9] *vt*
A [1] ‹*ahorro/turismo*› to promote, stimulate; ‹*plan*› to instigate, promote; ‹*conflicto/enfrentamientos*› to provoke; ‹*acuerdo*› to bring about, promote; **los que promovieron la manifestación** those who organized the demonstration [2] (Der) ‹*querella/pleito*› to bring
B ‹*oficial/funcionario*› to promote

promulgación *f* (de ley) enactment, promulgation (frml); (anuncio) announcement, promulgation (frml)

promulgar [A3] *vt* to enact, to promulgate (frml)

pronombre *m* pronoun

(Compuesto) **pronombre personal/posesivo/reflexivo** personal/possessive/reflexive pronoun

pronominal *adj* pronominal

pronosticar [A2] *vt* ‹*tiempo/resultado*› to forecast; **pronosticaban lluvias** rain was forecast; **pronosticó la muerte del rey** he predicted the king's death

pronóstico *m* [1] (predicción) forecast, prediction; **el ~ del tiempo** the weather forecast [2] (Med) prognosis; **sufrió lesiones de ~ grave/leve** he was seriously/slightly injured [3] (en carreras de caballos) tip

prontitud *f* promptness; **se agradece la ~ en el pago** (frml) prompt payment would be appreciated

pronto¹ -ta *adj*
A [1] (rápido) ‹*entrega/respuesta*› prompt; **le deseo una pronta mejoría** I wish you a speedy recovery, I hope you get well soon [2] (despierto, vivaz) sharp

B (RPl) (preparado) ready

pronto[2] *adv*

A (en poco tiempo) soon; **~ cumple 40 años** she'll soon be 40; **ven aquí ¡~!** come here, right now!; **¡hasta ~!** see you soon!; **lo más ~ posible** as soon as possible; **eso se dice muy ~** (fam) that's easy to say; **hizo los dos a la vez, que se dice ~** he made them both at the same time, which is not as easy as it sounds

B (Esp) (temprano) early

C (*en locs*) **de pronto** (repentinamente) suddenly; (a lo mejor) (AmS) perhaps, maybe; **por lo pronto** *or* **por de pronto** for the moment, for now; **tan pronto**: **tan ~ llueve, como hace sol** one minute it's raining and the next it's sunny; **tan pronto como** as soon as

pronto[3] *m* (fam): **le dio un ~ y me tiró el plato** he had a fit of temper and threw the plate at me; **tiene un ~ muy malo** she has a very quick temper

prontuariar [A1] *vt* (CS) to open a file on; **está prontuariada** she has a police record

prontuario *m* 1 (libro) handbook, guide 2 (CS) (Der): **abrirle ~ a algn** to open a file on sb; **tiene ~** she has a criminal record

pronunciación *f* pronunciation

pronunciado -da *adj* 1 ‹*curva*› sharp, pronounced; ‹*pendiente*› steep, pronounced 2 ‹*facciones/rasgos*› pronounced, marked 3 ‹*tendencia*› marked, noticeable

pronunciamiento *m* rebellion, military uprising

pronunciar [A1] *vt*

A 1 (Ling) to pronounce 2 ‹*discurso*› to deliver, give; **pronunció unas palabras de bienvenida** he said a few words of welcome

B (resaltar) to accentuate

■ **pronunciarse** *v pron*

A (dar una opinión) **~se A FAVOR/EN CONTRA DE algo** to declare oneself to be IN FAVOR OF/AGAINST sth; **no se ha pronunciado sobre el tema** he has not commented on the matter

B (acentuarse) to become marked, become more pronounced

C (Mil) to rebel, revolt

propagación *f* propagation; **la rápida ~ del fuego** the rapid spread of the fire

propaganda *f* 1 (Pol) (para promover o desprestigiar una causa) propaganda 2 (Com, Marketing) advertising; (en prensa): **hacer ~ de un producto/espectáculo** to advertise a product/show; **no trae más que ~** it has nothing but advertisements in it; **repartía ~ de la tienda** she was handing out advertising leaflets for the shop

propagandista *mf* propagandist

propagandístico -ca *adj* 1 (Pol) propaganda (*before n*) 2 (Com, Marketing) publicity (*before n*), advertising (*before n*)

propagar [A3] *vt* 1 ‹*doctrina/rumores*› to spread, to propagate 2 ‹*enfermedad*› to spread, propagate 3 ‹*especie*› to propagate

■ **propagarse** *v pron* 1 «*doctrina/rumores*» to spread, propagate 2 «*enfermedad*» to spread 3 «*fuego*» to spread 4 (Biol) to propagate 5 «*sonido/luz*» to propagate

propalar [A1] *vt* ‹*secreto*› to divulge, disclose; ‹*rumor*› to spread

propano *m* propane

propasarse [A1] *v pron* 1 (excederse) to go too far, overstep the mark; **no te propases bebiendo** don't overdo it with the drink 2 (en sentido sexual) **~ CON algn** to make a pass AT sb; **intentó ~ conmigo** he made a pass at me

propelente *m* propellant

propender [E1] *vi* **~ A algo** to be prone TO sth; **~ A + INF** to tend TO + INF

propensión *f* tendency, leaning, leanings (*pl*); **~ A + INF** tendency TO + INF; **tengo ~ a engordar** I have a tendency to put on weight; **tiene ~ a resfriarse** he is prone to colds

propenso -sa *adj* **~ A algo** prone TO sth; **es muy ~ a resfriarse** he catches colds very easily

propiamente *adv* exactly; **no vive en Londres ~ dicho** he doesn't live in London proper

propiciador -ra *m,f*: **los ~es del acuerdo de paz/del desarme** those in favor• of the peace agreement/of disarmament

propiciar [A1] *vt* (favorecer) to favor•; (causar) to bring about; **su muerte propició la unión de la familia** his death helped bring the family together; **las condiciones que propician una revolución** conditions that create a favorable atmosphere for revolution

■ **propiciarse** *v pron* to win, gain

propicio -cia *adj* ‹*momento*› opportune, propitious (frml); ‹*condiciones*› favorable•, propitious (frml); **no es un ambiente ~ para la meditación** the surroundings are not conducive to meditation

propiedad *f*

A 1 (pertenencia): **la casa no es de mi ~** I don't own the house; **la finca es ~ de mi hijo** the estate belongs to my son; **delito contra la ~** crime against property; **les dejó los terrenos en ~** she left them the freehold to the land; **los cuadros son ~ de la fundación** the paintings are the property of the foundation 2 (lo poseído) property

B (cualidad) property; (corrección): **hablar/expresarse con ~** to speak/express oneself correctly; **comportarse con ~** to behave with decorum

Compuestos

- **propiedad industrial** patent rights (*pl*)
- **propiedad inmobiliaria** real estate (AmE), property (BrE)
- **propiedad intelectual** copyright
- **propiedad privada/pública** private/public property

propietario -ria *m,f* 1 (de comercio) owner, proprietor; **es ~ de tres tiendas** he owns three shops 2 (de casa) owner, landlord/-lady 3 (de tierras) landowner

propina *f* 1 (a camarero, empleado) tip, gratuity (frml); **dejó 25 pesos de ~** she left a 25 peso tip; **¿cuánto se le da de ~?** what's the usual tip?, how much should I/do you usually tip him?; **dar ~ a algn** to tip sb 2 (Per) (de niño) pocket money

propinar [A1] *vt* ‹*patada/paliza*› to give; **le ~on cinco balazos** they shot him five times

propio -pia *adj*

A 1 (indicando posesión) own; **tienen piscina propia** they have their own swimming pool; **¿tu piso es ~ o alquilado?** do you own your flat or is it rented? 2 (*delante del n*) (uso enfático) own; **salió de la clínica por su ~ pie** she walked out of the clinic; **lo vi con mis ~s ojos** I saw it with my own two eyes *o* with my (very) own eyes 3 (no postizo) real 4 (de uno mismo): **lo hace todo en beneficio ~** everything he does is for selfish reasons

B (característico, típico) **~ DE algo/algn**: **esa actitud es muy ~ de él** that kind of attitude is very typical of him; **costumbres propias de los países orientales** customs characteristic of oriental countries

C **~ PARA algo** (adecuado, idóneo) suitable FOR sth; **es un vestido muy ~ para la ocasión** the dress is just right for the occasion

D (*delante del n*) (mismo): **fue el ~ presidente** it was the president himself; **debe ser el ~ interesado quien lo pida** it must be the person concerned who makes the request; **el ~ Juan se llevó una sorpresa** even Juan himself got a surprise

proponer [E22] *vt* 1 ‹*idea*› to propose, suggest; **nos propuso ir al campo** she suggested we go to the countryside; **te voy a ~ un trato** I'm going to make you a proposition; **propongo que se vote la moción** I propose that we vote on the motion 2 ‹*persona*› (para cargo) to put forward, nominate; (para premio) to nominate 3 ‹*moción*› to propose 4 ‹*teoría*› to propound

■ **proponerse** *v pron*: **cuando se propone algo, lo consigue** when he sets out to do something, he invariably achieves it; **me lo propuse como meta** I set myself that goal; **no me propongo insultar a nadie** it is not my intention to insult anybody; **se proponen alcanzar la cima** their aim *o* goal is to reach the summit; **me propuse decírselo** I made up my mind *o* I decided to tell her; **me había propuesto levantarme más temprano** I had intended to get up earlier; **te has propuesto que me enfade** you're determined to make me lose my temper

proporción *f*

A (relación) proportion; **guardar/no guardar ~ con algo** to be in/out of proportion to sth; **los sueldos no suben en**

~ a la inflación salaries are not keeping pace with inflation; **en ~ a los ingresos** in proportion to income; **en proporciones iguales** in equal proportions

B **proporciones** *fpl* (dimensiones) proportions (*pl*); **un edificio de grandes proporciones** a large building; **el horno es de proporciones gigantescas** the furnace is immense *o* massive; **un incendio de grandes proporciones** a huge *o* massive fire

proporcionado -da *adj*: **~ a la figura humana** in proportion to the human body; **mal ~** ‹*dibujo*› poorly proportioned; **es bajo pero bien ~** he's short but he's well-proportioned

proporcional *adj* proportional, proportionate; **los beneficios serán ~es a la inversión** profits will be directly related to investment

proporcionalmente *adv* proportionally, proportionately

proporcionar [A1] *vt* ‹*materiales/información/comida*› to provide; **~ algo A algn** to provide sb WITH sth; **les proporcionó un buen disgusto** it caused them great distress

proposición *f*

A 1 (sugerencia) proposal 2 (oferta) proposal, proposition; **~ de matrimonio** proposal of marriage; **le hizo proposiciones deshonestas** he made improper advances to her

B 1 (Mat, Fil) proposition 2 (Ling) clause

propósito *m* 1 (intención) intention, purpose; **tiene el firme ~ de dejar de fumar** she's determined to give up smoking; **se ha hecho el ~ de adelgazar** she's decided to lose weight; **buenos ~s** good intentions; **se fue con el firme ~ de volver** he left with the firm intention of returning; **se puso a ahorrar con el ~ de comprarse un coche** he started saving up to buy a car 2 **a propósito**: **no lo hice a ~** I didn't do it deliberately *o* on purpose; **se hizo un vestido a ~ para la ocasión** she had a dress made specially for the occasion; **a ~, Carlos te manda saludos** by the way, Carlos sends his regards; **a ~ de trenes ¿cuándo te vas?** speaking of trains *o* on the subject of trains, when are you leaving?

propuesta *f*

A (sugerencia) proposal; **formuló una ~ de diálogo** he made an offer to negotiate

B (oferta) offer; **varias ~s de trabajo** several job offers

propugnar [A1] *vt* (frml) (apoyar) to support; (proponer) to advocate, propose

propulsar [A1] *vt* ‹*desarrollo/actividad*› to promote, stimulate; ‹*avión/cohete*› to propel; ‹*vehículo*› to drive, propel

propulsión *f* propulsion; **~ a chorro** jet propulsion; **con ~ a chorro** jet-propelled

propulsor¹ -sora *adj* ‹*mecanismo*› driving (*before n*), propulsion (*before n*); ‹*cohete*› propulsion (*before n*)

propulsor² -sora *m,f* 1 (de actividad, idea) promoter; **fue el ~ de ese movimiento** he was the driving force behind that movement 2 **propulsor** *m* (Tec) propellant

propuse, propuso, etc *see* **proponer**

prorrata *f* pro rata amount; **a ~** pro rata

prórroga *f* 1 (extensión) extension; (Dep) overtime (AmE), extra time (BrE) 2 (aplazamiento) deferral, deferment

prorrogable *adj* 1 ‹*plazo/período*› extendable 2 (aplazable) deferrable; **la fecha no es ~** the date cannot be deferred *o* postponed *o* put back

prorrogar [A3] *vt* 1 (alargar) to extend; **~ el plazo de matrícula** to extend the registration period 2 (aplazar) ‹*fecha*› to postpone, put back

prorrumpir [I1] *vi* **~ EN algo**: **el público prorrumpió en aplausos** the audience burst *o* broke into applause; **prorrumpió en carcajadas** she burst out laughing; **prorrumpió en lágrimas** she burst into tears

prosa *f*

A (género literario) prose; (conjunto de obras) prose (writings) (*pl*)

B (Per fam) (pomposidad) pomposity

prosaico -ca *adj* ‹*existencia/vida*› mundane, prosaic; **le han dado un tratamiento muy ~** they have dealt with it in a very pedestrian *o* prosaic way

proscenio *m* proscenium

proscribir [I34] *vt* 1 (desterrar) to exile 2 ‹*costumbre/actividad*› to ban, outlaw, proscribe (frml); ‹*libro*› to ban; ‹*partido/organización*› to ban, proscribe (frml)

proscripción *f* 1 (destierro) exile 2 (prohibición) ban, proscription (frml)

proscrito¹ -ta *pp*: *see* **proscribir**

proscrito² -ta *m,f* (bandido) outlaw; (exiliado) political exile

prosecución *f* continuation

proseguir [I30] *vi* (frml) to continue; **prosiga, por favor** please continue, please proceed (frml); **~ CON algo** to continue WITH sth, proceed WITH sth (frml)

■ **proseguir** *vt* (frml) to continue; **prosiguió su camino** he continued on his way; **prosiguieron la discusión** they continued (with) the discussion

proselitismo *m* (Relig) proselytism (frml); (Pol) propaganda; **hacer ~** to proselytize (frml)

prosélito -ta *m,f* convert, proselyte (frml)

prosodia *f* prosody

prosódico -ca *adj* prosodic

prosopopeya *f* (Lit) prosopopeia

prospección *f* 1 (del subsuelo) prospecting; **~ petrolífera** oil prospecting, drilling for oil 2 (Com, Marketing) research; **~ de mercado** market research

prospecto *m* 1 (de fármaco) directions for use (*pl*), patient information leaflet 2 (de propaganda) pamphlet, leaflet 3 (Fin) prospectus

prosperar [A1] *vi* 1 «*negocio/país*» to prosper, thrive; «*persona*» to do well, make good 2 «*iniciativa/proyecto*» (aceptarse) to be accepted, prosper

prosperidad *f* prosperity

próspero -ra *adj* ‹*empresa/industria*› prosperous, thriving; ‹*región/comerciante/industrial*› prosperous; **¡Feliz Navidad y P~ Año Nuevo!** Merry Christmas and a Prosperous New Year!

próstata *f* prostate (gland)

prosternarse [A1] *v pron* (liter) to prostrate oneself

prostíbulo *m* brothel

prostitución *f* prostitution

prostituir [I20] *vt* to prostitute

■ **prostituirse** *v pron* to prostitute oneself

prostituto -ta *m,f* (*m*) male prostitute; (*f*) prostitute

protagonismo *m* prominence; **el ~ de los estudiantes en la revuelta** the leading *o* prominent role played by the students in the revolt; **tiene demasiado afán de ~** he always has to be center stage; **ganar ~** to become more prominent/important

protagonista *mf* 1 (Cin, Teatr): **el ~ de la nueva serie** the actor who is playing the leading role in the new series 2 (personaje) main character, protagonist 3 (de suceso): **los ~s de la revolución** those who played a leading role in the revolution; **los principales ~s de nuestra historia** the major figures of our history

protagonizar [A4] *vt* 1 (Cin, Teatr) to star in, play the lead *o* leading role in; **una película protagonizada por Marlon Brando** a film starring Marlon Brando 2 ‹*tiroteo*› to be involved in; ‹*debate*› to take part in; ‹*disturbios*› to be responsible for; **la marcha que ~on alumnos y profesores** the march staged by pupils and teachers

protección *f* protection; **brindar/dar ~ a algn** to offer/give protection to sb; **viviendas de ~ oficial** (Esp) subsidized housing

(Compuesto) **Protección Civil** civil defense• organization

proteccionismo *m* protectionism

proteccionista *adj/mf* protectionist

protector¹ -tora *adj* protective; **crema ~a** protective cream; **sociedad ~a de animales** society for the prevention of cruelty to animals

protector² -tora *m,f* 1 (defensor) protector; (benefactor) patron 2 **protector** *m* (en boxeo) gumshield, mouthpiece

(Compuesto) **protector de pantallas** screen saver

protectorado *m* protectorate

proteger [E6] *vt* 1 ‹*persona/ciudad*› to protect; ‹*derecho/propiedad*› to protect, defend; **el cerco de seguridad que los protegía** the security cordon around them; **~ algo/a algn DE *or* CONTRA algo/algn** to protect sth/sb FROM *o*

AGAINST sth/sb **2** ‹*industria/producto*› to protect **3** ‹*artes*› to champion, patronize; ‹*pintor/poeta*› to act as patron to

■ **protegerse** *v pron* (*refl*) **~se DE** *or* **CONTRA algo** to protect oneself FROM *o* AGAINST sth; **sirve para ~se contra las picaduras de mosquito** it protects against mosquito bites; **~se de la lluvia** to shelter from the rain; **se protegió la cara del golpe** he protected *o* shielded his face from the blow

protegido[1] -da *adj* **1** ‹*especie*› protected **2** ‹*vivienda*› subsidized **3** (Inf) write-protected

protegido[2] -da *m,f* (*m*) protegé; (*f*) protegée

proteína *f* protein; **rico en ~s** rich in protein

proteínico -ca *adj* proteinic (tech), protein (*before n*)

prótesis *f* prosthesis

protesta *f*

A **1** (queja) protest; **hacer una ~** to make *o* lodge a protest; **una campaña de ~** a protest campaign; **en señal de ~** in protest **2** (manifestación) demonstration, protest march (*o* rally *etc*)

B (Méx) (promesa) promise; (juramento) oath; **cumplieron con su ~** they kept their promise *o* word; **le tomaron la ~ al nuevo presidente** the new president was sworn in; **rendir ~** to take an oath; **bajo ~** under oath

protestante *adj/mf* Protestant

protestantismo *m* Protestantism

protestar [A1] *vi* **1** (mostrar desacuerdo) to protest; **~ CONTRA algo** to protest AGAINST *o* ABOUT sth; **¡protesto, su señoría!** objection, your Honor*, I object, your Honor*! **2** (quejarse) to complain; **~ POR** *or* **DE algo** to complain ABOUT sth; **nadie protestó cuando lo propuse** nobody complained *o* objected when I made the proposal

■ **protestar** *vt*

A **1** (Com, Fin) ‹*letra*› to protest; ‹*cheque*› to refer ... to drawer, dishonor* **2** ‹*actuación/decisión*› to protest about *o* at

B (frml) ‹*inocencia*› to protest

protestón -tona *m,f* (fam) grouch (colloq), moaner (BrE colloq); **no seas ~** stop moaning *o* bellyaching (colloq)

protocolario -ria, **protocolar** *adj* formal

protocolo *m*

A **1** (etiqueta) protocol; **observar el ~** to observe protocol *o* convention; **vestimenta de ~** formal dress **2** (solemnidad): **me tratan con mucho ~** they treat me very formally *o* politely

B **1** (de acuerdo) protocol **2** (Der) registry

C (Inf) protocol

protón *m* proton

prototípico -ca *adj* typical, archetypal

prototipo *m* **1** (de especie) archetype, prototype; **es el ~ del español medio** he's a typical *o* an archetypal Spaniard **2** (Tec) prototype

protuberancia *f* bulge, protuberance (frml)

provecho *m* **1** (beneficio, utilidad) benefit; **no sacó ningún ~ del curso** he derived no benefit from the course; **le sacó mucho ~ a su estancia** she got a lot out of her stay; **sólo piensa en su propio ~** he's only out for himself (colloq); **un estudiante de ~** a hardworking student; **una experiencia/visita de ~** a worthwhile experience/visit **2** (en la mesa): **¡buen ~!** (dicho por uno mismo) bon appetit!; (dicho por camarero) enjoy your meal!

provechoso -sa *adj* profitable; **no ha hecho nada ~ en su vida** he's never done a useful thing in his life

proveedor -dora *m,f* supplier, purveyor (frml); **~ de fondos** financial backer; **pídalo a su ~ habitual** ask your local dealer *o* supplier for it

proveer [E14] *vt*

A (suministrar) to provide; **~ a algn DE algo** to provide sb WITH sth; **nos proveyeron de todo lo necesario** they supplied *o* furnished us with everything we needed; **iban provistos de botes salvavidas** they were equipped with *o* they carried lifeboats

B ‹*vacante*› to fill

C (Der) to give an interim ruling on

■ **proveer** *vi* to provide

■ **proveerse** *v pron* (*refl*): **nos proveemos en la tienda del pueblo** we get our provisions at the village store; **~se DE algo** ‹*de herramientas, armas*› to equip oneself WITH sth; **tenemos que ~nos de suficiente comida** we must get *o* obtain enough food

proveniente *adj*: **estudiantes ~s de universidades extranjeras** students from foreign universities

provenir [I31] *vi* **~ DE algo/algn** to come FROM sth/sb

proverbial *adj* proverbial

proverbio *m* proverb

providencia *f*

A (Relig): **la (divina) P~** (divine) Providence

B (medida, precaución) precaution

C (Der) ruling

providencial *adj* **1** (oportuno) fortunate, lucky, providential (frml); **fue ~ que ...** it was fortunate that ... **2** (Relig) providential

provincia *f*

A **1** (Gob) province; **capital de ~** provincial capital **2** (Relig) province

B **provincias** *fpl* (por oposición a la capital) provinces (*pl*); **una ciudad de ~s** a provincial city; **la vida de ~s** provincial life

> **provincia**
>
> Each of the 55 different administrative areas into which Spain is divided. Each *provincia* includes a main city or town, sometimes more, depending on its social and economic power. The provincial capital usually has the same name as the province.
>
> Most **comunidades autónomas** comprise at least two or more *provincias*, except Madrid, Murcia and Cantabria, which consist of just one

provincial *adj* provincial

provinciano[1] -na *adj* **1** (de provincias) provincial; **se crió en un ambiente ~** she had a provincial upbringing **2** (pey) (estrecho) parochial; **su actitud es muy provinciana** she's very parochial *o* provincial in her outlook **3** (pey) (paleto): **no seas ~** don't be such a hick (AmE) *o* (BrE) country bumpkin

provinciano[2] -na *m,f* **1** (de provincias): **los ~s** people from the provinces **2** (pey) (de mentalidad estrecha) provincial **3** (paleto) hick (AmE), country bumpkin (BrE)

provisión *f*

A **1** (suministro) provision **2** (de vacante): **concurso para la ~ de la vacante** competition to fill the vacancy

B (Ur) (almacén) store, shop (BrE)

C **provisiones** *fpl* (víveres) provisions (*pl*)

provisional *adj* provisional

provisionalidad *f* provisional *o* temporary nature

provisionalmente *adv* provisionally; **vive allí ~** he's living there for the time being

provisorio -ria *adj* (AmS) temporary, provisional, makeshift

provisto -ta *pp*: *ver* **proveer**

provocación *f*

A (incitación) provocation; **las provocaciones de los manifestantes** the demonstrators' taunts *o* provocative remarks

B (de parto) induction

provocador[1] -dora *adj* provocative

provocador[2] -dora *m,f* agitator

provocar [A2] *vt*

A **1** ‹*explosión*› to cause; ‹*incendio*› to start; ‹*polémica*› to spark off, prompt **2** (Med): **~ el parto** to induce labor*; **las pastillas le ~on una reacción cutánea** the pills caused *o* brought on a skin reaction

B ‹*persona*› (al enfado) to provoke; (sexualmente) to lead ... on

■ **provocar** *vi* (Andes) (apetecer): **¿le provoca un traguito?** do you want a drink?, do you fancy a drink? (BrE colloq)

provocativo -va *adj*

A (insinuante) provocative

B (Col, Ven) (apetecible) tempting, mouthwatering

proxeneta (*m*) procurer (frml), pimp (colloq); (*f*) procuress (frml), pimp (colloq)

próximamente *adv* soon, shortly; Ⓢ **próximamente en esta sala** coming soon

proximidad *f* **1** (en el tiempo, espacio) closeness, proximity (frml); **su ~ me hace sentir incómodo** I feel uncomfortable when she's near me **2** **proximidades** *fpl*

p

(cercanías) vicinity; **en las ~es del aeropuerto** in the vicinity of the airport, around the airport

próximo -ma *adj*

A 1 (siguiente) next; **el ~ jueves** next Thursday 2 (*como pron*): **esto lo dejamos para la próxima** we'll leave this for next time; **tome la próxima a la derecha** take the next (on the) right; **me bajo en la próxima** I'm getting off at the next stop

B [ESTAR] (cercano) 1 (en el tiempo) close, near; **la fecha ya está próxima** the day is close *o* is drawing near; **en fecha próxima** in the near future; **estar ~ A + INF** to be close TO + ING, to be about TO + INF; **estaba ~ a morir** he was close *o* near to death 2 (en el espacio) near, close; **~ A algo** close *o* near TO sth

proyección *f*

A 1 (Cin) showing; **una ~ de diapositivas** a slide show; **el tiempo de ~ es de 95 minutos** the running time is 95 minutes 2 (de sombra) casting; (de luz) throwing 3 (Mat, Psic) projection

B (difusión, alcance — de ley) scope; (— de problema) implications (*pl*); **ha adquirido una ~ internacional** she has become a figure of international renown

C (de rocas, lava) discharge, throwing out

proyectar [A1] *vt*

A (planear) to plan; **~ + INF** to plan to + INF; **tiene proyectado ampliar su negocio** she is planning to expand her business

B 1 ‹*película*› to show, screen; ‹*diapositivas*› to project, show 2 ‹*sombra*› to cast; ‹*luz*› to throw, project 3 (Mat, Psic) to project

C (Arquit, Ing) to design

D (lanzar) (+ *compl*) to throw, hurl

■ **proyectarse** *v pron* «*sombra*» to be cast

proyectil *m* projectile, missile

proyecto *m* 1 (plan) plan; **tiene el ~ de formar su propia empresa** he plans to set up his own business; **¿qué ~s tienes para el próximo año?** what are your plans for next year?; **tiene varios trabajos/un viaje en ~** she has several projects in the pipeline/she's planning a trip 2 (trabajo) project; **el ~ se está retrasando** the project is falling behind schedule; **~ piloto** pilot project 3 (Arquit, Ing) plans and costing

(Compuesto) **proyecto de ley** bill

proyector *m*

A (Cin, Fot) projector; **~ de transparencias** *or* **diapositivas** slide projector

B (Teatr) spotlight; (para monumentos) floodlight; (Mil) searchlight

proyectora *f* (Chi) ▸**proyector A**

prudencia *f* (cuidado) caution; (sabiduría) wisdom, prudence; **conduce con ~** drive carefully; **gracias a su ~ en cuestiones de dinero** thanks to her prudence *o* carefulness in money matters

prudencial *adj* prudent, sensible; **un tiempo ~** a reasonable *o* sensible length of time

prudente *adj* prudent, sensible; **se marchó a una hora ~** she left at a reasonable *o* sensible hour; ; **sea ~ con la bebida** don't drink too much; **consideró ~ no decir nada** she thought it wise *o* prudent not to say anything; **una mujer ~** a sensible woman

prueba *f*

A 1 (demostración, testimonio) proof; **esto es ~ concluyente de que nos mintió** this is conclusive proof that he lied to us; **no hay ~s de que eso sea verdad** there's no proof that that's true; **tendrá que presentar ~s de ello** he'll have to prove it; **eso es ~ de que le caes bien** that proves he likes you; **dio constantes ~s de su lealtad** he proved his loyalty again and again; **no dio la menor ~ de estar sufriendo** he didn't give the slightest hint *o* indication that he was suffering; **en** *or* **como ~ de mi agradecimiento** as a token of my gratitude 2 (Der) piece of evidence; **falta de ~s** lack of evidence

(Compuestos)

- **prueba de compra** proof of purchase
- **pruebas materiales** *fpl* material evidence

B (Educ) test; (Cin) screen test, audition; (Teatr) audition

(Compuestos)

- **prueba de aptitud** aptitude test
- **prueba de fuego** acid test

C 1 (ensayo, experimento): **haz la ~ de dejarlo en remojo** try leaving it to soak; **vamos a hacer la ~** let's try 2 (circunstancia difícil): **la enfermedad de su padre fue una dura ~ para ella** her father's illness was a testing time for her 3 (*en locs*) **a prueba**: **tomar a algn a ~** to take sb on for a trial period; **tener algo a ~** to have sth on trial; **poner algo a ~** to put sth to the test; **estás poniendo a ~ mi paciencia** you're trying my patience; **a prueba de**: **un reloj a ~ de golpes** a shockproof watch; **un dispositivo a ~ de ladrones** a burglarproof mechanism; **cristal a ~ de balas** bulletproof glass 3 (en costura) fitting

(Compuestos)

- **prueba de laboratorio** laboratory trial *o* test
- **prueba del alcohol** *or* **de la alcoholemia** Breathalyzer® test, sobriety test (AmE), drunkometer test (AmE)
- **prueba del embarazo** pregnancy test
- **prueba nuclear** nuclear test

D (Fot, Impr) proof; **corregir ~s** to proofread

E (Dep): **en las ~s de clasificación** in the qualifying heats; **la ~ de los 1.500 metros** the 1,500 meters (event *o* race); **las ~s de descenso** the downhill events

prurito *m* 1 (afán): **tiene el ~ de la imparcialidad** he's got a thing about impartiality 2 (Med) itching, pruritus (tech)

psicoanálisis *m* psychoanalysis

psicoanalista *mf* psychoanalyst

psicoanalítico -ca *adj* psychoanalytic, psychoanalytical

psicoanalizar [A4] *vt* to psychoanalyze

■ **psicoanalizarse** *v pron* (*caus*) to be psychoanalyzed, have *o* undergo psychoanalysis

psicodélico -ca *adj* psychedelic

psicolingüística *f* psycholinguistics

psicología *f* psychology

psicológico -ca *adj* psychological

psicólogo -ga *m,f* 1 (Psic) psychologist 2 (fam) (persona perspicaz): **mi madre es buena psicóloga** my mother's a good judge of character

psicomotor -motora, psicomotriz *adj* psychomotor (*before n*)

psicópata *mf* psychopath

psicopatología *f* psychopathology

psicosis *f* (*pl* ~) psychosis

psicosomático -ca *adj* psychosomatic

psicoterapeuta *mf* psychotherapist

psicoterapia *f* psychotherapy

psicótico -ca *adj/m,f* psychotic

psique *f* psyche

psiquiatra *mf* psychiatrist

psiquiatría *f* psychiatry

psiquiátrico[1] -ca *adj* psychiatric (*before n*)

psiquiátrico[2] *m* psychiatric hospital, mental hospital

psíquico -ca *adj* psychic

pss *interj* 1 (expresando indiferencia, duda) mm …, well … 2 (llamando la atención) psst!

ptas, pts = pesetas

Pte., pte.

A = presente

B (**= puente**) ≈ Br.

C (**= presidente**) Pres.

pto. (**= punto**) pt

púa *f*

A 1 (de erizo) spine, quill; (de alambre) barb; (de peine) tooth 2 (Chi, Ven) (en zapatos de atletismo) spike

B (para guitarra) plectrum, pick; (de tocadiscos) (RPl) needle

puaj, puah *interj* ugh! (colloq), yuck! (colloq)

pub /puβ, pʌβ/ *m* (*pl* **pubs** *or* **pubes**) bar (*gen with music, open late at night*)

púber *adj/mf* adolescent

pubertad *f* puberty

pubis *m* (*pl* ~) pubis

publicación *f* publication

públicamente *adv* publicly

publicar [A2] *vt* 1 ‹*artículo/noticia*› to publish 2 (divulgar) to divulge, disclose; **no lo publiques mucho** don't go around telling everybody

publicidad *f* [1] (de tema, suceso) publicity; **se le dió mucha ~** it has received a lot of publicity [2] (Com, Marketing) advertising; **agencia de ~** advertising agency; **hacer ~ de algo** to advertise sth; **hay demasiada ~ en la tele** there's too much advertising on TV

(Compuesto) **publicidad estática** billboard advertising

publicista *mf* [1] (AmL) (Com) advertising executive *o* agent, publicist [2] (Period) publicist

publicitario -ria *adj* advertising (*before n*); **fue un montaje ~** it was a publicity stunt

público[1] **-ca** *adj* public; **hacer ~ algo** to announce sth; **es un peligro ~** he's a danger to the public

público[2] *m* (en teatro) audience, public; (Dep) spectators (*pl*); (de publicación) readership; **asistió poco ~ al partido** few people attended the game, there were few spectators at the game; Ⓢ **horario de atención al público** (en oficinas públicas) opening hours; (en bancos) hours of business; **la exposición está abierta al ~** the exhibit (AmE) *o* (BrE) exhibition is open to the public; **película apta para todos los ~s** *or* (CS) **para todo ~** 'G' movie (AmE), 'U' film (BrE); **el ~ en general** the general public; **un manual escrito para el gran ~** a manual written for the layperson *o* non-specialist; **hablar en ~** to speak in public; **no le gusta tocar el piano en ~** she doesn't like playing the piano in front of an audience; ***salir al ~*** (Andes) ‹‹*periódico/revista*›› to come out, appear; ‹‹*noticia/información*›› to be published

pucará *m* pre-Columbian fortress

pucha, puchacay *interj* (AmS euf & fam) (expresando — sorpresa) wow! (colloq), jeez! (AmE colloq); (— fastidio) damn! (colloq), oh, no! (colloq); **~ digo** *or* (Chi) **~ Diego, me olvidé** damn *o* oh no, I forgot!

pucherazo *m* (fam) electoral rigging; **hubo ~** the election was fixed *o* rigged

puchero *m*

A (Coc) (recipiente) pot, stewpot; (cocido) stew; ***ganarse el ~*** (fam) to earn a crust (colloq)

B (mueca) pout; **hacer ~s** to pout

pucho *m* (AmL fam) [1] (cigarrillo — de tabaco) smoke (colloq), fag (BrE colloq); (— de marihuana) joint (colloq) [2] (resto — de cigarrillo) butt, fag end (BrE colloq); (— de comida) scrap; (— de bebida) drop; ***a ~s*** (AmL fam) bit by bit (colloq), a little at a time (colloq); **se tomó la sopa a ~s** he sipped his soup; ***no valer un ~*** (Chi fam) to be completely worthless

pude *see* **poder**

pudibundo -da *adj* prudish, prim and proper

púdico -ca *adj* ‹*ropa*› modest; ‹*comportamiento/beso*› chaste

pudiente *adj* (rico) wealthy, rich; (poderoso) powerful

pudiera, pudiese, etc *see* **poder**

pudín *m* ▸**budín**

pudiste, etc *see* **poder**

pudor *m* [1] (recato sexual) modesty (arch); **no se desnudó por ~** she was too embarrassed *o* shy to take her clothes off; **es una falta de ~** it shows a lack of (a sense of) decency [2] (reserva) reserve; **nos habló sin ~ de sus problemas** he talked to us very openly about his problems

pudoroso -sa *adj* ▸**púdico**

pudrir [I38] *vt*

A (descomponer) ‹*carne/fruta*› to rot, decay; ‹*madera/tela*› to rot

B (RPl fam) [1] (fastidiar, hartar): **me tiene podrida con sus quejas** I'm fed up to the back teeth of his complaining (colloq); **me pudre que me de todos los trabajos difíciles** I'm sick and tired of being given all the difficult jobs (colloq) [2] (aburrir) to bore … to death (colloq)

■ **pudrirse** *v pron*

A (descomponerse) ‹‹*fruta/carne*›› to rot, decay; ‹‹*madera/tela*›› to rot; ‹‹*cadáver*›› to decompose, rot

B (fam) [1] (por el abandono): **~se en la cárcel** to rot in jail [2] (por el aburrimiento): **en ese pueblo te vas a ~** you'll die of boredom in that village (colloq) [3] (expresando enfado): **¡ahí te pudras!** go to hell! (colloq); **¡que se pudra!** he can go to hell! (colloq)

pueblerino -na *adj*: **¡qué ~ eres!** you're such a country bumpkin *o* (AmE colloq) hick!; **con su aire ~** with her provincial *o* small town ways

pueblo *m*

A (poblado) village; (más grande) small town; ***~ chico infierno grande*** living in a small town can be hell (colloq)

(Compuestos)

- **pueblo de mala muerte** dead-end town, one-horse town
- **pueblo joven** (Per) shantytown

B (comunidad) people; **un ~ nómada** a nomadic people; **~s primitivos** primitive peoples; **el ~ español/vasco** the Spanish/Basque people

C (clase popular): **el ~** the working class; **la voz del ~** the voice of the people; **una rebelión del ~** a popular uprising

(Compuesto) **pueblo llano**: **el ~ ~** the ordinary people

pueda, puedas, etc *see* **poder**

puente *m*

A (Ing) bridge; ***tender (un) ~*** to build bridges

(Compuestos)

- **puente aéreo** (servicio frecuente) shuttle (service); (Mil) airlift
- **puente colgante/giratorio** suspension/swing bridge
- **puente de barcas** *or* **pontones** pontoon bridge
- **puente levadizo** (en castillo) drawbridge; (en carretera) lifting bridge

B (Mús, Odont) bridge; (de anteojos) bridge

C (Elec) bridge (circuit); **le tuve que hacer el** *or* **un ~** (Auto) I had to hot-wire it

D (vacación) ≈ long weekend (*linked to a public holiday by an extra day's holiday in between*)

E (Náut) *tb* **~ de mando** bridge

> **puente**
>
> *Puentes* are very important in Spain and most of Latin America. *Hacer puente* means that when a working day falls between two public holidays, it too is taken as a holiday

puentear [A1] *vt* (Esp)

A (Elec) to install a bridge circuit in

B (fam) (obviando el orden jerárquico) to bypass

■ **puentear** *vi* (Dep) to go bungee jumping (*from a bridge*)

puenting /'puentin/ *m* (Esp) bungee jumping (*from a bridge*)

puerco[1] **-ca** *adj* (fam & pey) (sucio) dirty; (despreciable) lowdown (colloq); **el muy ~** the dirty rat (colloq)

puerco[2] **-ca** *m,f*

A [1] (animal) (*m*) pig, hog, boar; (*f*) pig, hog, sow [2] (Méx) (carne) pork

(Compuesto) **puerco espín** porcupine

B (fam) (persona — sucia) pig (colloq); (— despreciable) swine (colloq)

puericultor -tora *m,f*: *nurse or doctor who specializes in babycare/childcare*

puericultura *f* babycare, childcare

pueril *adj* [1] (infantil) childish, puerile (frml); **comportarse de manera ~** to behave childishly [2] (ingenuo) naive, naïve

puerilidad *f* childishness

puerro *m* leek

puerta *f*

A (de casa, coche, horno) door; (en jardín, valla) gate; **llamar a la ~** to ring the doorbell/knock on the door; **te espero en la ~ del teatro** I'll meet you at the entrance of the theater; **te acompaño a la ~** I'll see *o* show you out; **servicio ~ a ~** door-to-door service; **de ~ a ~ tardo media hora** it takes me half an hour, door to door; **su intransigencia cerró las ~s a un acuerdo** her intransigence put an end to *o* put paid to any hope of an agreement; **un coche de dos ~s** a two-door car; ***a ~(s) cerrada(s)*** behind closed doors; ***coger la ~ (y largarse)*** (Esp fam) to leave; ***darle con la ~ en las narices a algn*** to slam the door in sb's face; ***de ~s (para) adentro*** in private, behind closed doors; ***de ~s para fuera*** *or* (AmL) ***~s afuera*** in public; ***en ~s***: **la Navidad está en ~s** Christmas is just around the corner; ***estar a las ~s de algo***: **el ejército estaba ya a las ~s de la ciudad** the army was already at the gates of the city; **estaba a las ~s de la muerte** he was at death's door; **se quedó a las ~s del triunfo** she narrowly missed winning; ***por la ~ grande***:

P

el torero salió por la ~ grande the bullfighter made a triumphal exit; **volvió a Hollywood por la ~ grande** she returned to Hollywood in triumph

(Compuestos)
- **puerta corredera** *or* **corrediza** sliding door
- **puerta de embarque** gate
- **puerta de servicio** service entrance
- **puerta giratoria** revolving door
- **puerta principal** *or* **de la calle** (de casa) front door; (de edificio público) main door *or* entrance
- **puerta trasera** back door

B (Dep) **1** (en fútbol): **un tiro** *or* **remate a ~** a shot (at goal); **saca de ~ Zubizarreta** Zubizarreta takes the goal kick; **marcó a ~ vacía** he put the ball into the empty net **2** (en esquí) gate

puerto *m*

A (Náut) port, harbor*; **entrar a ~** to enter port *o* harbor; ***llegar*** *or* ***arribar a buen ~*** «*expedición/barco*» to arrive safely; «*negociaciones/proyecto*» to reach a satisfactory conclusion

(Compuestos)
- **puerto artificial/natural** man-made/natural harbor*
- **puerto deportivo** marina
- **puerto fluvial/marítimo** river port/seaport
- **puerto franco** *or* **libre** free port
- **puerto pesquero** fishing port
- **puerto USB** USB port

B (Geog) *tb* **~ de montaña** (mountain) pass

Puerto Príncipe *m* Port-au-Prince

Puerto Rico *m* Puerto Rico

puertorriqueño -ña *adj/m,f* Puerto Rican

pues[1] *conj*

A **1** well; **~ mira, yo si fuera tú ...** well look, if I were you ... **2** (expresando duda, vacilación) well; **~ ... no sé** well ... I don't know **3** (en exclamaciones) well; **¡~ yo no sabía nada!** well, I didn't know anything about it!; **¿a ti te interesaría? — ¡~ claro!** would you be interested? — yes, of course! *o* why, yes! **4** (indicando consecuencia) then; **no me gusta — ~ no lo comas** I don't like it — well, don't eat it then; **~ si te gusta tanto, cómpralo** if you like it that much, then buy it

B (frml) (porque) as, since

pues[2] *adv* (liter *o* frml): **ésta es, ~, mi conclusión** this, then, is my conclusion; **llegamos, ~, a nuestro destino** and so we arrived at our destination

puesta *f*

A (acción de poner): **la ~ en práctica del plan no fue fácil** putting the plan into practice wasn't easy; **hasta la ~ en servicio de los autobuses** until the buses come into service; **la ~ en libertad de los prisoneros** the freeing *o* release of the prisoners; **la fiesta de su ~ de largo** her coming-out party; **~ al día** updating

(Compuestos)
- **puesta a punto** (de vehículo) tune-up; (de máquina) adjustment
- **puesta de sol** sunset
- **puesta en escena** production;
- **puesta en marcha** (de vehículo, motor) starting (up)

B (de huevos) lay

puestero -ra *m,f* (AmL) **1** (vendedor) stallholder, market vendor **2** (en una estancia) farmer (*responsible for the running of part of a large ranch*)

puesto[1] **-ta** *adj*: **¿qué haces con el abrigo ~?** what are you doing with your coat on?; **la mesa estaba puesta** the table was laid; **iba muy ~** he was all dressed up; ***con lo ~***: **se marchó con lo ~** he left with nothing but the clothes he was wearing; ***estar ~*** (estar dispuesto) (Méx) to be ready *o* set; (estar borracho) (Chi fam) to be plastered *o* sloshed (colloq); *ver tb* **poner**

puesto[2] *m*

A **1** (lugar, sitio) place; **cada uno que ocupe su ~** (to your) places, everyone!, positions, everyone! **2** (en una clasificación) place, position; **sacó el primer ~ de su clase** she came top *o* (AmE) came out top of the class

B (empleo) position, job; **quedó vacante un ~ de mecanógrafa** there was a vacancy for a typist; **no es un ~ fijo** it isn't a permanent job *o* position

(Compuesto) **puesto de trabajo** (empleo) job; (Inf) workstation

C **1** (Com) (en mercado) stall; (quiosco) kiosk; (tienda) stand, stall **2** (de la policía, del ejército) post

(Compuestos)
- **puesto de observación** observation post
- **puesto de policía** police post
- **puesto de socorro** first-aid post/station
- **puesto fronterizo** border post

D **puesto que** (*conj*) (frml) since; **~ que así lo quieres ...** since that's the way you want it ...

puf[1] *m* (*pl* **pufs**) hassock (AmE), pouffe (BrE)

puf[2] *interj* (expresando — repugnancia) ugh! (colloq), pee-yoo! (AmE); (— cansancio, sofoco) whew!, oof!

púgil *m* (period) boxer, pugilist (frml)

pugilato *m* (period) boxing, pugilism (frml)

pugilístico -ca *adj* (period) boxing (*before n*)

pugna *f* **1** (lucha) struggle; **la ~ por el primer puesto** the battle for first place **2** (conflicto): **tendencias/intereses en ~** conflicting trends/interests; **facciones en ~ por el poder** factions vying for power; **están en ~ con la oposición** they are at odds with the opposition; **entrar en ~ con algo/algn** to clash *o* come into conflict with sth/sb

pugnar [A1] *vi* **1** (liter) (luchar) **~ POR + INF** to strive to + INF (frml) **2** (Chi frml) (contraponerse) **~ CON algo** to conflict WITH sth, run contrary TO sth

puja *f*

A (lucha) **~ POR + INF** struggle to + INF

B (Esp) (en subasta — acción) bidding; (— cantidad) bid

pujante *adj* booming (*before n*)

pujanza *f* vigor*, strength; **la industria ha cobrado gran ~** the industry is going from strength to strength

pujar [A1] *vi*

A (luchar) **~ POR + INF** to struggle to + INF

B (Esp) (en subasta) to bid

C (Méx fam) (gemir) to moan, whimper

pulcritud *f* **1** (cualidad de impecable): **la ~ de su aspecto** her immaculate appearance **2** (esmero): **trabajar con ~** to work meticulously *o* with great care

pulcro -cra *adj* ‹*persona/aspecto*› immaculate, neat and tidy; ‹*informe/trabajo*› meticulous

pulga *f* (Zool) flea; ***buscarle las ~s a algn*** (fam) to put sb on (AmE colloq), to wind sb up (BrE colloq); ***tener malas ~s*** (fam) to be bad-tempered, have a bad temper

pulgada *f* inch

pulgar *m* (de la mano) thumb; (del pie) big toe

pulgón *m* aphid, plant louse

pulgoso -sa, (CS) **pulguiento -ta** *adj* flea-ridden, flea-bitten

pulido -da *adj* **1** ‹*estilo/trabajo/lenguaje*› polished; ‹*modales*› refined **2** (Chi fam) ‹*persona*› affected

pulidor *m* (RPl) scouring powder

pulidora *f* polisher

pulimentar [A1] *vt* ▸ **pulir A**

pulir [I1] *vt*

A **1** ‹*metal/piedra/vidrio*› to polish **2** ‹*madera*› to sand **3** (lustrar) to polish

B (refinar) ‹*estilo/trabajo*› to polish up; ‹*persona*› to make ... more refined; **fue a Inglaterra a ~ su inglés** she went to England to brush up her English

■ **pulirse** *v pron* (refinarse) to improve oneself, become more refined

pulla *f* gibe, cutting comment *o* remark

pullover /pu'loβer/ *m* (*pl* **-vers**) ▸ **pulóver**

pulmón *m* lung; **gritar a pleno ~** to shout at the top of one's voice; ***tener buenos pulmones*** (fam) to have a good pair of lungs (colloq)

(Compuesto) **pulmón de acero** iron lung

pulmonar *adj* pulmonary (tech), lung (*before n*)

pulmonía *f* pneumonia; **~ doble** double pneumonia

pulóver *m* (*pl* **-vers**) (esp AmL) (suéter) pullover, sweater, jumper (BrE)

pulpa *f*

A (de fruta, vegetal) pulp; (de madera) (wood) pulp

B (Ur) (corte de carne) filet*

pulpejo *m* fleshy part

pulpería *f* (AmL) local store

pulpero -ra *m* (AmL) local storekeeper

P

púlpito *m* pulpit

pulpo *m*
A (Zool) octopus
B (Chi fam) (explotador) shark (colloq)

pulque *m* pulque (*drink made from fermented cactus sap*)

> **pulque**
> A thick, white, Mexican alcoholic drink made from fermented *maguey* juice; the sacred drink of the Aztecs. It is drunk without being aged, sometimes with added fruit or vegetable juice. *Pulquerías* are bars where it is drunk

pulquear [A1] *vi* (Méx) to drink pulque
■ **pulquearse** *v pron* (Méx) to get drunk (*on pulque*)

pulquería *f* (Méx) bar, restaurant (*serving pulque*)

pulquero -ra *m,f* (Méx) *owner of a* **pulquería**

pulquérrimo -ma *adj* (liter) impeccable, immaculate

pulsación *f*
A (latido) beat
B (en mecanografía) keystroke; **¿cuántas pulsaciones piden por minuto?** ≈ what typing speed do they want?

pulsador *m* (de timbre) (push) button; (de la luz) switch

pulsar [A1] *vt*
A 1 (Mús) ‹*cuerda*› to pluck; ‹*tecla*› to press 2 ‹*botón*› to push, press; ‹*timbre*› press, ring
B ‹*opinión/situación*› to gauge, assess

pulsear [A1] *vt* (CS) ▸**pulsar**
■ **pulsear** *vi* (echar un pulso) to arm wrestle

pulsera *f* bracelet; **~ de tobillo** ankle bracelet, anklet

pulso *m* 1 (Med) pulse; **tomarle el ~ a algn** to take sb's pulse; ***tomarle el ~ a algo*** to gauge sth; **tomarle el ~ a la opinión pública** to gauge *o* sound out public opinion 2 (firmeza en la mano): **tengo muy mal ~** I have a very unsteady hand; **me temblaba el ~** my hand was shaking; **lo levantó a ~** he lifted it with his bare hands; **una línea hecha a ~** a line drawn freehand; ***ganarse algo a ~*** to earn sth 3 (prueba): armwrestling match; **un ~ entre reformadores y tradicionalistas** a trial of strength between reformers and traditionalists

pulular [A1] *vi* 1 (bullir) «*muchedumbre*» to mill around 2 (abundar): **por aquí pululan mosquitos nucleos** there are swarms of mosquitos here; **aquí pululan los rateros** this place is teeming *o* crawling with pickpockets

pulverización *f* (de líquidos) spraying; (de sólidos) pulverization, crushing; (destrucción) crushing

pulverizador *m* (de perfume) atomizer, spray; (de pintura) spray gun; (del carburador) jet

pulverizar [A4] *vt* 1 ‹*líquido*› to atomize, spray; ‹*sólido*› to pulverize, crush 2 (destruir) to crush, pulverize (colloq)

puma *m* (animal) cougar, mountain lion, puma

puna *f* 1 (páramo) *high Andean plateau* 2 (Andes) (soroche) mountain *o* altitude sickness

punción *f* puncture

pundonor *m*: **~ profesional** sense of professional pride; **su ~ no le permite pedir ayuda económica** he is too proud to ask for money

punga *mf*
A (CS arg) 1 (ladrón) thief 2 (carterista) pickpocket
B **punga** *f* (CS arg) (robo) theft; **vivir** *or* **tirar de la ~** to lead a life of crime, live by thieving

punible *adj* (frml) punishable

punir [I1] *vt* (frml) to punish

punitivo -va *adj* (frml) punitive

punki /'puŋki, 'pʌŋki/ *adj/mf* (fam) punk

punta¹ *adj inv*: **la hora ~** the rush hour; **un sector ~ de nuestra industria** a sector which is at the forefront of our industry; **velocidad ~** top speed

punta² *f*
A 1 (de lengua, dedos) tip; (de nariz) end, tip; (de pan) end; (de pincel) tip; **en la otra ~ de la mesa** at the other end of the table; **vivo en la otra ~ de la ciudad** I live on the other side *o* at the other end of town; **con la ~ del pie** with his toes; ***a ~ (de) pala*** (Esp fam) loads (colloq); ***a ~ de pistola*** *or* (Per) ***de bala*** at gunpoint; ***ir/ponerse de ~ en blanco*** to be/get (all) dressed up; ***la ~ del iceberg*** the tip of the iceberg; ***tener algo en la ~ de la lengua*** to have sth on the tip of one's tongue 2 **puntas** *fpl* (del pelo) ends (*pl*)
B (de aguja, clavo, cuchillo, lápiz) point; (de flecha, lanza) tip; **sácale ~ al lápiz** sharpen the pencil; **de ~** point first; **en ~** pointed; **por un extremo acaba en ~** it's pointed at one end; ***mandar a algn a la ~ del cerro*** (CS fam) to send sb packing (colloq), to tell sb to get lost (colloq)
(Compuesto) **punta de lanza** spearhead
C (de pañuelo) corner
D (Dep): **juega en la ~** he's a forward *o* striker
E (Geog) point
F (CS fam) (montón): **una ~ de plata** a lot of money, a fortune (colloq); **tiene una ~ de cosas que hacer** she has loads *o* stacks of things to do (colloq); **son una ~ de asesinos** they're a bunch of murderers (colloq)
G **a punta de** (AmL fam): **a ~ de repetírselo mil veces** by telling him it a thousand times; **a ~ de palos lo hicieron obedecer** they beat him until he did as he was told; **una dieta a ~ de líquidos** a liquid-based diet

punta³ *m* (Dep) forward

puntabola *f* (Bol) ballpoint pen, Biro® (BrE)

puntada *f*
A (en costura) stitch; **le di unas ~s al dobladillo** I put a few stitches *o* a stitch in the hem; ***no da/dan ~ sin hilo*** (CS fam) he doesn't/they don't do anything for nothing; ***no dar ~*** (fam): **aún no has dado ~** you haven't done a stroke (of work) yet (colloq)
B (CS) (de dolor) stab of pain, sharp pain; **tengo una ~ en el costado** I have (a) stitch (in my side)
C (Méx fam) (comentario ingenioso) quip, witticism

puntaje *m* (AmL) score; **sacó el ~ más alto de la clase** she got the highest scores in the class

puntal *m* 1 (Const) (vertical) prop, post; (inclinado) prop, shore 2 (Náut) (soporte de cubierta) stanchion; (altura desde la quilla) height 3 (sostén, apoyo) mainstay

puntapié *m* kick; **darle** *or* **pegarle un ~ a algo/algn** to kick sth/sb, to give sth/sb a kick; *para modismos ver* **patada**

punteado -da *adj* (de puntos) dotted; (de perforaciones) perforated, dotted

puntear [A1] *vt*
A ‹*melodía*› to pluck, play ... pizzicato; **~ la guitarra** to pluck the guitar
B (AmL) (Dep) to lead

punteo *m* plucking

puntera *f* (de zapato, calcetines) toe

puntería *f*: **¡qué ~!** what a shot!; **tener buena/mala ~** to be a good/bad shot; ***afinar la ~*** (apuntar con cuidado) to take careful aim; (poner cuidado) to take care, be careful

puntero¹ -ra *adj* ‹*empresa/sector/país*› leading (*before n*); **van ~s en la división** they are the division leaders

puntero² *m*
A (para señalar) pointer; (de reloj) (Andes) hand
B (Dep) 1 (equipo) leader, leaders (*pl*) 2 (Col, CS) (en fútbol) winger

puntiagudo -da *adj* (acabado en punta) pointed; (afilado) sharp; **una nariz puntiaguda** a pointed nose

puntilla *f*
A (Taur) dagger (*used to administer the coup de grâce in a bullfight*); ***dar la ~*** (Taur) to administer the coup de grâce; **se dio la ~ a esta práctica** they put an end to this practice; **aquello la dio la ~** that was the final blow
B (punta del pie): **de ~s** *or* (AmL) **en ~s** on tiptoe; **ponerse/andar de ~s** to stand/walk on tiptoe; **entró de ~s** she tiptoed into the room
C (encaje) lace edging

puntilloso -sa *adj* particular, punctilious

punto *m*
A 1 (señal, trazo) dot; **un ~ en el horizonte** a dot *o* speck on the horizon 2 (Ling) (sobre la 'i', la 'j') dot; (signo de puntuación) period (AmE), full stop (BrE); ***a ~ fijo*** exactly, for certain; ***... y punto***: **lo harás y ~** you'll do it and that's that; ***poner los ~s sobre las íes*** (aclarar algo) to make sth crystal clear; (detallar algo) to dot the i's and cross the t's; ▸**dos¹**
(Compuestos)
- **punto decimal** decimal point
- **punto final** period (AmE), full stop (BrE); ***poner ~ ~ a algo*** to end sth
- **puntos suspensivos** *mpl* ellipsis (tech), suspension points (*pl*) (AmE), dot, dot, dot

- **punto y aparte** period, new paragraph (AmE), full stop, new paragraph (BrE)
- **punto y coma** semicolon
- **punto y seguido** period (AmE), full stop (BrE) (*no new paragraph*)

B 1 (momento, lugar) point; **en ese ~ de la conversación** at that point in the conversation; **busca un local en un ~ céntrico** he's looking for premises somewhere central; **el ~ donde ocurrió el accidente** the spot *o* place where the accident happened 2 (en geometría) point

Compuestos
- **punto álgido** crucial moment *o* point
- **punto cardinal** cardinal point;
- **punto culminante** high point
- **punto de apoyo** (de palanca) fulcrum; **no hay ningún ~ de ~ para la escalera** there is nowhere to lean the ladder
- **punto débil** weak point
- **punto de caramelo**: ***a ~ de ~*** ‹*almíbar*› caramelized; (en su mejor momento) (fam): **este queso está a ~ de ~** this cheese is just right (for eating)
- **punto de congelación/ebullición/fusión** freezing/boiling/melting point
- **punto de control** checkpoint
- **punto de mira** (de rifle) front sight; (blanco) target; (objetivo) aim, objective
- **punto de nieve**: **batir las claras a ~ de ~** beat the egg whites until they form stiff peaks
- **punto de partida** starting point
- **punto de penalty** *or* **penalti** penalty spot
- **punto de referencia** reference point
- **punto de venta** point of sale, sales outlet
- **punto de vista** (perspectiva) viewpoint, point of view; (opinión) views
- **punto fijo** (Chi) (lugar) *permanent or semi-permanent guard post*; (vigilante) guard; **estar en ~ ~** to be on guard duty
- **punto flaco/fuerte** weak/strong point
- **punto muerto** (Auto) neutral; (en negociaciones) deadlock; **llegar a un ~ ~** to reach deadlock *o* stalemate; (Fin) break-even point
- **punto neurálgico** (en ser vivo, organización) nerve center*; **uno de los ~s ~s de la ciudad** one of the busiest spots *o* points in the city

C (grado) point; **hasta cierto ~ tiene razón** she's right, up to a point; **hasta tal ~ que ...** so much so that ...

D (asunto, aspecto) point; **los ~s a tratar en la reunión** the matters *o* items on the agenda for the meeting; **analizar algo ~ por ~** to analyze sth point by point

E (*en locs*) **a punto** (a tiempo) just in time; **a ~ DE + INF**: **estábamos a ~ de cenar** we were about to have dinner; **estuvo a ~ de caerse** he almost fell over; **a ~ de llorar** on the verge of tears; **en su punto** just right; **al punto** (Esp) at once; **en punto**: **te espero a las 12 en ~** I'll expect you at 12 o'clock sharp; **son las tres en ~** it's exactly three o'clock; **llegaron en ~** they arrived exactly on time; **de todo punto** absolutely, totally

F 1 (en costura, labores) stitch; **se me ha escapado un ~** I've dropped a stitch; **artículos de ~** knitwear; **hacer ~** (Esp) to knit; ***~ en boca*** (fam): **tú ~ en boca** keep your mouth shut 2 (en cirugía) *tb* **~ de sutura** stitch

Compuestos
- **punto (de) cruz** cross-stitch
- **punto del derecho** plain stitch
- **punto del revés** purl stitch
- **punto elástico** rib, ribbing

G (Dep, Jueg) point; (Educ) point, mark; (Fin) point; **vencer por ~s** to win on points; **tiene dos ~ de ventaja sobre Clark** he is two points ahead of Clark; ***matarle el ~ a algn*** (CS fam) to go one better than sb

Compuesto **punto para partido/set** (Méx) match/set point

H (Per, RPl arg) (tonto) idiot; ***agarrar*** *or* ***tomar a algn de ~*** (Per, RPl arg): **lo agarraron de ~** (burlándose de él) they made him the butt of their jokes; (aprovechándose de él) they took him for a ride; **la profesora me ha agarrado de ~** the teacher has it in for me (colloq)

puntuable *adj*: **ser ~ para algo** to count towards sth

puntuación *f*

A (Impr, Ling) punctuation

B 1 (acción) (Educ) grading (AmE), marking (BrE); (Dep) scoring 2 (esp Esp) (puntos obtenidos) (Educ) grade (AmE), mark (BrE); (Dep) score

puntual *adj*

A 1 ‹*persona*› punctual; **es muy ~** she's very punctual, she's always on time 2 (*como adv*) punctually, on time

B (detallado) detailed; (exacto) precise

C (Ling) ‹*aspecto*› momentary, punctual

puntualidad *f* punctuality; **se ruega ~ en el pago** prompt payment is requested

puntualizar [A4] *vt* 1 (especificar) to state 2 (señalar) to point out

puntualmente *adv* (con puntualidad) punctually; (con exactitud) accurately; **siempre llega ~ al trabajo** she's always punctual *o* on time for work

puntuar [A18] *vt*

A ‹*examen/prueba*› to grade (AmE), to mark (BrE)

B ‹*texto*› to punctuate

■ **puntuar** *vi*

A 1 «*partido/prueba*» **~ PARA algo** to count TOWARD(s) sth 2 «*deportista*» score (points)

B (calificar): **puntúa muy bajo** she gives very low grades (AmE) *o* (BrE) marks

puntudo -da *adj* (Col, CS) ▸ **puntiagudo**

punzada *f* sharp pain, stab of pain; **me dio una ~ en el costado** I felt a sharp pain *o* a stab of pain in my side; **una ~ de remordimiento** a pang of remorse

punzante *adj* ‹*objeto*› sharp; ‹*dolor*› sharp, stabbing (*before n*); ‹*palabras/comentario*› biting, incisive; ‹*estilo*› caustic

punzar [A4] *vt* (agujerear) to punch a hole in; (Med) to puncture

punzón *m* (para hacer agujeros) bradawl, awl; (para hacer ojetes) hole punch; (de grabador, escultor) burin; (para monedas, medallas) stamp, die

puñado *m* handful; **había cucarachas a ~s** there were loads *o* hundreds of cockroaches

puñal[1] *adj* (Méx fam & pey) gay, faggoty (AmE colloq & pej), poofy (BrE colloq & pej)

puñal[2] *m* dagger; ***ponerle un ~ en el*** *or* ***al pecho a algn*** to hold a gun to sb's head

puñalada *f* 1 (navajazo) stab; **lo mató a ~s** she stabbed him to death; ***coser a algn a ~s*** to carve sb up (colloq) 2 (herida) stab wound

Compuesto **puñalada trapera** *or* **por la espalda** stab in the back

puñalearse [A1] *v pron* (Ven fam) to grind (AmE colloq), to swot up (BrE colloq)

puñeta *f* (Esp fam): **¿qué ~(s) hace él aquí?** what the hell's he doing here? (colloq); **¡qué resfriado ni qué ~s!** I don't give a damn if you have a cold! (colloq); ***hacerle la ~ a algn*** (Esp fam): **si no me lo trae hoy, me hace la ~** if she doesn't bring it for me today, I'll be in deep trouble; ***mandar a algn a hacer ~s*** (Esp fam) to tell sb to go to hell; **¡vete a hacer ~s!** go to hell! (colloq)

puñetazo *m* punch; **darle** *or* **pegarle un ~ a algn** to punch sb; **pegó un ~ en la mesa** he thumped the table with his fist; **terminaron la discusión a ~s** the argument degenerated into a brawl (colloq); **se dieron (de) ~s** they traded punches (colloq); **le rompió la cara de un ~** he smashed his face in (colloq)

puñetero -ra *adj* (fam) 1 (*delante del n*) (uso enfático) damn, blasted; **este ~ pueblo** this lousy *o* miserable town (colloq); **no nos hizo ni ~ caso** he didn't take a damned bit of notice of us (colloq); **vete de una puñetera vez** just get the hell out of here (colloq) 2 [SER] ‹*persona*›: **no seas ~** don't be a swine (colloq), don't be a jerk (colloq)

puño *m*

A (Anat) fist; **golpeé la mesa con el ~** I banged my fist on the table; **apretar los ~s** to clench one's fists; **cierre el ~** clench your fist; ***como ~s***: **dijo mentiras como ~s** he told some whopping great lies (colloq); ***de mi/tu/su ~ y letra*** in my/your/his own hand; ***pelear a ~ limpio*** to have a fistfight; ***tener a algn (metido) en un ~*** (fam) to have sb twisted around one's little finger

B (de camisa) cuff

C (de espada) hilt; (de bastón) handle, haft; (de moto) grip

pupa *f* 1 (fam) (en los labios) cold sore 2 (Esp leng infantil) (dolor, daño): **mamá, (tengo) ~** mummy, it hurts; **¿te has**

hecho ~? have you hurt yourself?

pupila *f* pupil; **tener ~ para los negocios** to have a good head for business

pupilo¹ -la *adj* (RPl): **está ~ en el colegio** he's a weekly boarder at the school

pupilo² -la *m,f*
A 1 (de maestro) pupil; (de tutor) ward, charge 2 (Chi frml) (Educ) (*m*) son; (*f*) daughter; (respecto del apoderado) ward 3 (RPl) (alumno interno) boarder
B (ant) (en pensión) boarder

pupitre *m* desk

puramente *adv* purely

purasangre *mf* thoroughbred

puré *m*: **~ de verduras** puréed vegetables; **~ de tomates** tomato purée *o* paste; **~ de papas** *or* (Esp) **patatas** mashed *o* creamed potatoes; (más líquido) potato purée; ***estar hecho*** **~** (fam) to be beat *o* done in (colloq)

pureza *f* purity

purga *f* (Med) purgative, laxative; (Pol) purge

purgante *adj/m* purgative, laxative

purgar [A3] *vt*
A 1 (Med) to purge 2 (Tec) ‹*tubería/depósito*› to drain; ‹*frenos*› to bleed 3 (Pol) to purge
B ‹*pecados*› to purge, expiate

purgatorio *m* purgatory; **las almas** *or* **ánimas del ~** the souls in purgatory

puridad *f* (frml): **en ~** in all honesty

purificación *f* purification

purificador *m* purifier

(Compuesto) **purificador de ambientes** (Col) air freshener

purificadora *f* (Andes) *tb* **~ de agua** water treatment plant, waterworks (*sing or pl*)

purificar [A2] *vt* to purify

purismo *m* purism

purista *adj/mf* purist

puritanismo *m* puritanism

puritano¹ -na *adj* (Relig) Puritanical, Puritan (*before n*); (mojigato) puritanical

puritano² -na *m,f* (Relig) Puritan; (mojigato) puritan

puro¹ -ra *adj*
A 1 (limpio, sin mezcla) pure; **es de pura lana** it's pure wool; **el aire ~ del campo** the fresh *o* clean country air 2 (casto, inocente) ‹*mujer*› chaste, pure; ‹*niño*› innocent; ‹*mirada/amor*› innocent, pure

(Compuesto) **pura sangre** *mf* thoroughbred

B (mero, simple) (*delante del n*) ‹*verdad*› plain, honest (colloq); ‹*casualidad/coincidencia*› pure, sheer; **es ~ músculo** he's all muscle; **lo hizo por ~ capricho** she did it purely on a whim; **de ~ cansancio** from sheer exhaustion
C (AmL fam) (sólo): **a ese bar van ~s viejos** only old men go to that bar; **son puras mentiras** it's just a pack of lies (colloq)

puro² *adv*
A (AmL fam) (muy, tan): **se murió de ~ vieja** she just died of old age; **lo tiré de ~ sucio que estaba** it was so filthy I threw it out; **lo hizo de ~ egoísta** he did it out of sheer selfishness
B (Col fam) (justo) right

puro³ *m* cigar

(Compuesto) **puro habano** Havana (cigar)

púrpura *f*: **(de) color ~** purple

purpúreo -rea *adj* purple

purpurina *f* (en pinturas) metallic powder; (para adornar) glitter

pus *m* pus

puse, pusiera, etc *see* **poner**

pusilánime¹ *adj* fainthearted, pusillanimous (frml)

pusilánime² *mf*: **este trabajo no es para los ~s** this job is not for the fainthearted

pusiste, etc *see* **poner**

puso *see* **poner**

pústula *f* pustule

puta *f* (vulg & pey) (prostituta) prostitute, whore (colloq & pej), hooker (colloq); **ir de ~s** to go whoring (colloq); **hijo (de) ~** son of a bitch (vulg), bastard (vulg)

putada *f* (vulg): **hacerle una ~ a algn** to play a dirty trick on sb (colloq); **¡qué ~! hemos perdido el tren** damn *o* shit! we've missed the train (sl)

putativo -va *adj* putative (frml), presumed

putear [A1] *vt*
A (AmL fam) (insultar) to tear into (AmE colloq), have a go at (BrE colloq)
B (Esp vulg) (maltratar, jorobar): **me putearon mucho** I had to take a lot of crap *o* shit (sl); **lo putean mucho en la oficina** they really screw him around (AmE) *o* (BrE) piss him about in the office

■ **putear** *vi*
A (vulg) 1 ‹‹*prostituta*›› to work one's beat (colloq) 2 (ir de putas) to go whoring (colloq)
B (AmL vulg) (decir palabrotas) to swear, cuss (sl)

putero *m* (Méx fam *or* vulg) whorehouse (colloq), brothel, cathouse (AmE colloq)

puto¹ -ta *adj*
A (vulg) ‹*mujer*› loose (pej); **la puta madre que te parió** you son of a bitch! (vulg); ***de puta madre*** (Esp vulg) great (colloq), fantastic; **jugó de puta madre** he was bloody brilliant (colloq)
B (*delante del n*) (vulg) (uso expletivo): **no tengo ni puta idea** I don't have a goddamn (AmE) *o* (BrE) bloody clue (sl); **no te hacen ni ~ caso** they don't take the slightest notice of you (colloq); **¡acabemos de una puta vez** let's get this damn thing finished (colloq)

puto² *m* (vulg & pey) (prostituto) male prostitute, rent boy (BrE colloq)

putrefacción *f* putrefaction

putrefacto -ta, pútrido -da *adj* putrid

puya *f* 1 (Taur) point (*of the picador's lance*) 2 (comentario irónico) gibe; **lanzar** *or* **echar una ~** to make a gibe

puyar [A1] *vt* (Col, Ven) (con alfiler, púa) to prick; (para conseguir algo) (fam) to hassle (colloq)

■ **puyarse** *v pron* (Col, Ven) (con espina) to prick oneself

puyudo -da *adj* (Ven) pointed

puzzle /'pusle/ *m* (rompecabezas) (jigsaw) puzzle; (crucigrama) (Chi) crossword (puzzle)

PVP *m* (Com) (= **precio de venta al público**) retail price

Pza. *f* (= **Plaza**) Sq

Q, q *f (read as /ku/) the letter* **Q, q**

q.e.p.d., Q.E.P.D. (= **que en paz descanse**) R.I.P.

q.m. = **quintal métrico/quintales métricos**

quásar *m* quasar

que[1] *conj*

A (introduciendo complemento, sujeto) [1] **~ + INDIC** that; **demostró ~ estuvo allí** he proved (that) he was there; **creemos ~ ésta es la solución** we believe that this is the solution; **estoy seguro de ~ vendrá** I'm sure (that) she'll come; **¿cuántos años crees ~ tiene?** how old do you think she is?; **me preguntó ~ quién era yo** he asked me who I was; **está claro ~ no te gusta** it's obvious that you don't like it; **eso de ~ estaba enfermo es mentira** (fam) this business about him being ill is a lie [2] **~ + SUBJ**: **quiero ~ vengas** I want you to come; **lamento ~ no puedas quedarte** I'm sorry (that) you can't stay; **dice ~ no vayas** she says you're not to go; **ve a ~ te ayude tu padre** go and get your father to help you; **(el) ~ sea el jefe no significa ...** just because he's the boss doesn't mean ...; **es importante ~ quede claro** it's important that it should be clear; **sería una lástima ~ no vinieras** it would be a shame if you didn't come [3] **es que**: **es ~ hoy no voy a poder** I'm afraid (that) I won't be able to today; **es ~ no tengo dinero** the trouble is I don't have any money; **¿es ~ eres sordo?** are you deaf or something?

B [1] (en expresiones de deseo): **¡~ te mejores!** I hope you feel better soon; **¡~ se diviertan!** have a good time!; **por mí ~ se muera** he can drop dead for all I care [2] (en expresiones de mandato): **¡~ te calles!** shut up! (colloq); **¡~ no!** I said no!; **¡~ pase el siguiente!** next please! [3] (en expresiones de sorpresa): **¿~ se casa?** she's getting married?; **¿cómo ~ no vas a ir?** what do you mean, you're not going? [4] (en expresiones de indignación): **¡~ tengamos que aguantar esto!** to think we have to put up with this!; **¡~ se lo haya ido a contar!** I can't believe he went and told her!

C (uso enfático) [1] (reafirmando algo): **¡~ no, ~ no voy!** no! I'm not going!; **¡~ sueltes, te digo!** I said, let go! [2] (respondiendo a una pregunta): **¿~ dónde estaba? pues aquí** where was I? right here; **¿~ cómo me llamo?** what's *my* name? [3] (indicando persistencia): **se pasa dale ~ dale con lo mismo** he goes on and on about the same old thing; **y aquí llueve ~ llueve** and over here it just rains and rains

D [1] (introduciendo una razón): **escóndete, ~ te van a ver** hide or they'll see you; **ven, ~ te peino** come here and let me comb your hair [2] (introduciendo una consecuencia) that; **se parecen tanto ~ apenas los distingo** they're so alike (that) I can hardly tell them apart; **canta ~ da gusto** she sings beautifully

E (en comparaciones): **su casa es más grande ~ la mía** his house is bigger than mine; **tengo la misma edad ~ tú** I'm the same age as you

F (fam) (en oraciones condicionales) if; **yo ~ tú** if I were you

que[2] *pron*

A (refiriéndose a personas) [1] (*sujeto*) who; **los ~ viajan, que esperen aquí** those who are traveling, wait here; **es la/el ~ manda aquí** she's/he's the one who gives the orders here [2] (*complemento*): **la mujer ~ amo** the woman (that) I love; **las chicas ~ entrevistamos** the girls (that *o* who) we interviewed; **es el único al ~ no le han pagado** he's the only one who hasn't been paid; **el paciente del ~ te hablé** the patient (that *o* who) I spoke to you about

B (refiriéndose a cosas, asuntos, etc) [1] (*sujeto*) that, which; **la pieza ~ se rompió** the part that *o* which broke; **eso es lo ~ me preocupa** that's what worries me; **me contaron lo ~ pasó** they told me what happened [2] (*complemento*): **el disco ~ le regalé** the record (which *o* that) I gave her; **la casa en ~ vivo** the house (that) I live in; **la forma/el lugar en ~ ocurrió** the way/the place (in which) it happened; **¿sabes lo difícil ~ fue?** do you know how hard it was?; *ver tb* **lo**[1] **B, C**

qué[1] *pron*

A (interrogativo) [1] what; **¿~ es eso?** what's that?; **¿y ~?** so what?; **¿y a mí ~?** what does that have to do with me?; **¿a ~ fuiste a su casa?** what did you go to her house for?; **¿a ~ viene esa pregunta?** why do you ask that?; **¿de ~ habló?** what did she talk about?; **¿sabes ~?** you know what *o* something?; **no sé ~ hacer** I don't know what to do [2] (al pedir que se nos repita algo) what; **¿qué?** what?; **¿se olvidó de traer el/la ~?** she forgot to bring the what? [3] (en saludos): **¿~ tal?** how are you?; **¿~ es de tu vida?** how's life?; ▶ **tal**[3], **tanto**[1]

B (en exclamaciones): **¡~ va a ser abogado ése!** him, a lawyer?; **¿crees que va a llover? — ¡~ va!** do you think it's going to rain? — no way! (colloq); **es difícil ¿verdad? — ¡~ va!** it's difficult, isn't it? — nonsense *o* rubbish!; **~ DE algo**: **¡~ de gente hay!** what a lot of people there are!; **¡~ de agua ha caído!** hasn't it rained heavily *o* a lot!

qué[2] *adj*

A (interrogativo) what, which; **¿~ color quieres?** what *o* which color do you want?

B (en exclamaciones) what; **¡~ noche!** what a night!; **¡~ casualidad!** what a coincidence!

qué[3] *adv*: **¡~ lindo/estupendo!** how lovely/wonderful!; **¡~ inteligente eres!** aren't you clever!; **¡~ hermosa vista!** what a beautiful view!; **¡~ bien (que) se está aquí!** it's so nice here!

quebracho *m* quebracho (*South American hardwood tree*)

quebrada *f* [1] (despeñadero) gully; (más profunda) ravine [2] (AmS) (arroyo) stream

quebradero de cabeza *m* problem, headache (colloq)

quebradizo -za *adj* [1] (frágil) fragile; ‹*uña/hueso*› brittle [2] (que se desmenuza con facilidad) crumbly

quebrado[1] **-da** *adj*

A [1] ‹*hueso*› broken; ‹*vaso/huevo*› (roto) broken; (rajado) cracked [2] ‹*voz*› faltering

B ‹*empresa/comerciante*› bankrupt

C [1] ‹*línea*› crooked, zigzag (*before n*) [2] ‹*terreno*› uneven [3] (Mat) **número ~** fraction

quebrado[2] *m* fraction

quebradora *f* (AmC fam): **la ~** dengue fever

quebradura *f* [1] (Geol) crack, fissure [2] (Med) hernia

quebrantahuesos *m* (*pl* ~) (de la montaña) lammergeier; (de la costa) white-tailed eagle

quebrantamiento *m* breaking

quebrantar [A1] *vt* (liter) ‹*salud*› to break (liter); ‹*paz/armonía*› (frml) to disturb; ‹*ley/promesa*› (frml) to break; **~le la moral a algn** to break sb's spirit

quebranto *m*

A (liter) (aflicción, dolor) suffering; **le causó penas y ~s** it caused him pain and suffering

B (liter) (debilitación, daño): **el ~ de sus esperanzas** the shattering of his hopes; **ha sufrido repetidos ~s de salud** she has suffered a series of problems with her health
C (Ven fam) (fiebre) mild *o* slight fever

quebrar [A5] *vt*
A (esp AmL) ‹*lápiz/rama*› to snap; ‹*vaso/plato*› (romper) to break; (rajar) to crack
B (AmL) ‹*cartulina*› to crease
C (Méx fam) (matar) to kill
■ **quebrar** *vi*
A (Com) «*empresa/persona*» to go bankrupt
B (cambiar de dirección) to turn
C (AmC) (romper una relación) to break up; **~ con algn** to break up WITH sb
■ **quebrarse** *v pron*
A (esp AmL) **1** «*lápiz/rama*» to snap; «*vaso/plato*» (romperse) to break; (rajarse) to crack **2** ‹*pierna/brazo*› to break; **se quebró un diente** he chipped his tooth
B (Col) (arruinarse) to go bankrupt

quebrazón *f* (AmL fam) smashing; **escuchó una ~ de vidrios** he heard the sound of glass smashing

quechear [A1] *vi* to catch

quécher *mf* catcher

quechua¹ *adj* Quechua

quechua² *mf*
A (persona) Quechuan
B **quechua** *m* (idioma) Quechua

> **quechua**
>
> The language of the Incas, Quechua is spoken today by some 13 million people in Peru, Bolivia, Chile, Colombia, Ecuador, and Argentina. Since 1975 it has been an official language in Peru. The Quechua people are one of South America's most important ethnic minorities. Words derived from Quechua include *coca*, *cóndor*, *pampa*, and *puma*

quedado -da *adj* **1** (Ven fam) **estar ~** to be out of it (colloq) **2** **ser ~** (Chi, Ven fam) to be slow

quedar [A1] *vi*

(Sentido I)
A (en un estado, una situación): **~ viudo/viuda** to be widowed; **~ huérfano** to be orphaned; **quedó paralítico** he was left paralyzed; **~ sin hogar/en la miseria** to be left homeless/destitute; **el coche quedó como nuevo** the car is as good as new (now); **ha quedado precioso pintado de blanco** it looks beautiful painted white; **todo quedó solucionado** everything was sorted out; **ha quedado acordado que ...** it has been agreed that ...; **y que esto quede bien claro** and I want to make this quite clear; **¿dónde quedamos la clase pasada?** where did we get (up) to in the last class?; **¿quién quedó en primer/último lugar?** who was *o* came first/last?; (+ *me/te/le etc*) **me quedó muy claro que ...** it was quite clear to me that ...; **el postre le quedó riquísimo** that dessert (he made) was delicious
B (en la opinión de los demás): **para no ~ mal** so as not to lose face; **si no vamos, quedamos mal** it'll look bad if we don't go; **si no voy ~é mal con ellos** it won't go down very well if I don't turn up; **lo hice para ~ bien con el jefe** I did it to get in the boss's good books; **quedé muy bien con el regalo** I made a very good impression with my present; **me hiciste ~ muy mal diciendo eso** you really showed me up saying that; **nos hizo ~ mal a todos** he embarrassed us all; **quedó en ridículo** (por culpa propia) he made a fool of himself; (por culpa ajena) he was made to look a fool; **quedé como una ignorante** I made a fool of myself
C (permanecer): **¿queda alguien adentro?** is there anyone left inside?; **le quedó la cicatriz** she was left with a scar; **quedó sin solución** it remained unsolved; **esto no puede ~ así** we can't leave things like this; **quedamos a la espera de su confirmación** (frml) we await your confirmation (frml); **quedo a sus gratas órdenes** (frml) (Corresp) Sincerely yours (AmE), Yours faithfully (BrE); **~ EN algo**: **todo quedó en suspenso** everything was left in the air; **nuestros planes ~on en nada** our plans came to nothing; **~ *atrás*** «*persona*» to fall behind; «*rencillas/problemas*» to be in the past
D (+ *me/te/le etc*) **1** «*tamaño/talla*»: **me queda grande/largo/apretado** it's too big/long/tight for me; **la talla 12 le queda bien** the size 12 fits (you/him) fine **2** (sentar): **el azul/ese peinado te queda muy bien** blue/that hairdo really suits you

(Sentido II) **1** (acordar, convenir) **~ EN algo**: **¿en qué ~on?** what did you decide?; **¿entonces en qué quedamos?** so, what's happening, then?; **quedamos en que yo iría** we agreed *o* arranged that I would go; **~ EN** *or* (AmL) **DE + INF**: **~on en no decirle nada** they agreed *o* decided not to tell him anything; **quedó en venir a las nueve** she said she would come at nine **2** (citarse): **¿a qué hora/dónde quedamos?** what time/where shall we meet?; **quedé con unos amigos para cenar** I arranged to meet some friends for dinner

(Sentido III) (estar situado) to be; **queda justo enfrente de la estación** it's right opposite the station; (+ *me/te/le etc*) **me queda muy lejos/cerca** it's very far/near from where I live (*o* work *etc*)

(Sentido IV) (*en 3ª pers*)
A **1** (haber todavía): **¿queda café?** is there any coffee left?; **no quedan entradas** there are no tickets left; **sólo quedan las ruinas** only the ruins remain; (+ *me/te/le etc*) **¿te queda algo de dinero?** do you have any money left?; **¿te queda alguna duda?** is there anything you still don't understand?; **no nos queda más remedio que ir** we have no choice but to go; **ya no me quedan fuerzas** I've no more strength left **2** (sobrar) «*comida/vino*» to be left (over)
B (faltar): **queda poco para que acabe la clase** it's not long till the end of the class; **¿cuántos kilómetros quedan?** how many kilometers are there to go?; (+ *me/te/le etc*) **todavía le quedan dos años** he still has two years to go *o* do; **me queda poco para terminar** I've almost finished; **~ POR + INF**: **queda mucho por ver/visitar** there is still a lot to see/visit; **aún quedan estudiantes por pagar** there are still some students who haven't paid; (+ *me/te/le etc*) **aún me queda todo esto por hacer** I still have all this to do; ***no me/le queda otra*** (AmL fam) I have/he has no choice; ***por ... que no quede*** (Esp fam): **venga, por intentarlo que no quede** come on, let's at least give it a try; **hazlo, por mí que no quede** go ahead, don't let me stop you

■ **quedarse** *v pron*

(Sentido I)
A **1** (en un lugar) to stay; **quedarse en casa/en la cama** to stay at home/in bed; **se ~on en París/en un hotel** they stayed in Paris/in a hotel **2** (en un estado, una situación) (+ *compl*): **te estás quedando calvo** you're going bald; **quédate tranquilo, yo me ocuparé del asunto** relax, I'll take care of it; **~se dormido** to fall asleep; **¿te quedaste con hambre?** are you still hungry?; **me quedé sin postre** I didn't get any dessert; **~se sin trabajo** to lose one's job; **~se soltera** to stay single; **no me gusta ~me sola en casa** I don't like being alone in the house; **no te quedes ahí parado** don't just stand there!; **nos quedamos charlando toda la noche** we spent the whole night chatting; **se me quedó mirando** he sat/stood there staring at me, he just stared at me; **de repente el motor se quedó** (AmL) the engine suddenly died on me
B (+ *me/te/le etc*) **1** (fam) (memorizar): **no se me quedan los nombres** I don't retain names; **no se me queda nada** I don't retain a thing **2** (Andes) (olvidarse): **se me quedó el paraguas** I left my umbrella behind **3** (Esp) (llegar a ser): **la casa se les está quedando pequeña** the house is getting (to be) too small for them

(Sentido II) **~se CON algo**: **se quedó con mi libro** she kept my book; **entre él y su mujer no sé con cuál me quedo** there's not much to choose between him and his wife; **me quedo con éste** I'll take this one; ***~se con algn*** (Esp fam) (engañarlo) to take sb for a ride (colloq)

quedito *adv* **1** ‹*entrar/hablar*› quietly; **me lo dijo bien ~** she said it to me very quietly **2** ‹*tocar/cantar*› softly; **me besó ~** he kissed me softly

quedo¹ -da *adj* ‹*voz*› soft, quiet; ‹*paso*› quiet

quedo² *adv* softly, quietly

quehacer *m* **1** (actividad, tarea) work; **el ~ diario** the daily routine; **su ~ artístico** her art *o* work **2** **quehaceres** *mpl*: *tb* **~es domésticos** *or* **de la casa** housework, household chores (*pl*)

queja *f* **1** (protesta) complaint; **presentar una ~** to make a complaint; **no tengo ~ de él** I have no complaints about him [2] (de dolor) *ver* **quejido**

quejarse [A1] *v pron* [1] (protestar) to complain; (refunfuñar) to grumble; **después no te quejes** don't go complaining afterward(s); **~ DE algo/algn** to complain ABOUT sth/sb [2] (de una afección, un dolor) **~ DE algo** to complain OF sth [3] (gemir) to moan, groan

quejica *adj/m,f* (Esp fam) ▸ **quejón[1,2]**

quejido *m* groan, moan; (más agudo) whine; **un ~ de dolor** a cry of pain; **los ~s del viento** (liter) the wailing of the wind (liter)

quejón[1] -jona *adj* (fam) whining (*before n*) (colloq)

quejón[2] -jona *m,f* (fam) crybaby (colloq)

quejoso -sa *m,f* (Méx) (persona que protesta): **de acuerdo a los ~s** according to the people who complained

quejumbroso -sa *adj* [1] ‹*tono*› plaintive, querulous; (irritante) whining [2] ‹*persona*› querulous; **hoy estás muy ~** you're complaining a lot today

quema *f*
A (acción de quemar) burning; ***huir de la ~***: **trataron de huir de la ~** they tried to get out before things got too hot
B (AmL) (Agr) burn-off
C (Arg) (basural) garbage dump (AmE), rubbish dump *o* tip (BrE)

quemada *f* [1] (Andes, Ven fam) (del sol): **pegarse una ~** to get sunburned [2] (Méx) ▸ **quemadura**

quemado -da *adj*
A [ESTAR] ‹*comida/tostada*› burnt; **esto sabe a ~** this tastes burnt; **aquí huele a ~** I can smell burning
B [ESTAR] [1] (rojo) ‹*cara/espalda*› burnt [2] (AmL) (bronceado) tanned, brown
C [ESTAR] [1] (desgastado, agotado) burned-out [2] (fam) (irritado) annoyed [3] (desprestigiado) ‹*político/cantante*› finished (colloq)
D [SER] (Chi fam) (con mala suerte) unlucky

quemador *m* burner

quemadura *f* [1] (herida causada — por fuego, ácido) burn; (— por líquido caliente) scald [2] (en prenda — de cigarrillo) cigarette burn; (— al planchar) scorch mark; (en mueble) burn mark

quemar [A1] *vt*
A [1] ‹*basura/documentos*› to burn [2] ‹*herejes/brujas*› to burn … at the stake
B ‹*leña/combustible*› to burn; ‹*calorías*› to burn up; ‹*grasa*› to burn off
C (accidentalmente) [1] ‹*comida/mesa/mantel*› to burn; (con la plancha) to scorch; **me quemó con el cigarrillo** he burned me with his cigarette [2] «*líquido/vapor*» to scald [3] «*ácido*» ‹*ropa/piel*› to burn [4] ‹*motor*› to burn… out; ‹*fusible*› to blow [5] «*sol*» ‹*plantas*› to scorch; ‹*piel*› to burn; (broncear) (AmL) to tan
D (malgastar) ‹*fortuna/herencia*› to squander

■ **quemar** *vi*
A (estar muy caliente) «*plato/fuente*» to be very hot; «*café/sopa*» to be boiling (hot) (colloq)
B «*sol*» to burn

■ **quemarse** *v pron*
A [1] (*refl*) (con fuego, calor) to burn oneself; (con líquido, vapor) to scald oneself; ‹*mano/lengua*› to burn; ‹*pelo/cejas*› to singe [2] (fam) (en juegos): **caliente, caliente … ¡te quemaste!** getting warmer, warmer … you're burning! (colloq) [3] (al sol — ponerse rojo) to get burned; (— broncearse) (AmL) to tan
B [1] (destruirse) «*papeles*» to get burned; «*edificio*» to burn down [2] (sufrir daños) «*alfombra/vestido*» to get burned; «*comida*» to burn; (+ *me/te/le etc*) **se me ~on las tostadas** I burned the toast
C «*persona*» (desgastarse) to burn oneself out; (pasar de moda): **un cantante que se quemó en un par de años** a singer who disappeared from the scene after a couple of years

quemarropa: **a ~** (*loc adv*) ‹*disparar*› at point-blank range; **se lo preguntó a ~** she asked him point-blank

quemazón *f* [1] (sensación de ardor) burning [2] (AmL) (quema): **salvé estos libros de la ~** I saved these books from being burned; **todavía quedan vestigios de la ~** traces of the fire can still be seen

quena *f* reed flute (*used in Andean music*)

quepa, etc *see* **caber**

quepis (*pl* ~), **quepi** *m* (Esp) kepi

quepo *see* **caber**

queque *m* (AmC, Andes) (pastel, torta) cake; (bizcocho) sponge cake

querella *f*
A (Der) lawsuit, action; **presentar ~ contra algn** to bring an action against sb, to take legal action against sb
B (disputa) dispute

querellado -da *m,f* defendant

querellante *mf* plaintiff

querellarse [A1] *v pron* **~ CONTRA algn** to take legal action AGAINST sb, to sue sb

querencia *f* [1] (instinto, tendencia) homing instinct [2] (liter) (hogar) home; (terruño) homeland [3] (Taur) *spot to which the bull tends to return*

querendón -dona *adj* (AmL fam) (cariñoso) affectionate; (enamoradizo) flighty

querer[1] *m* love; **las penas del ~** the pangs of love

querer[2] [E24] *vt*

Sentido **I** (amar) to love; **se hace ~** she/he endears herself/himself to people; **sus alumnos lo quieren mucho** his pupils are very fond of him; **me quiere, no me quiere** (al deshojar una margarita) she loves me, she loves me not; **¡por lo que más quieras!** for pity's sake!, for God's sake!; ***~ bien a algn*** to be fond of sb; ***~ mal a algn*** to have it in for sb (colloq); ***quien bien te quiere te hará llorar*** sometimes you have to be cruel to be kind

Sentido **II**
A [1] (expresando deseo, intención, voluntad): **quiero una casa más grande** I want a bigger house; **no sabe lo que quiere** she doesn't know what she wants; **quisiera una cerveza/habitación doble** I'd like a beer/double room; **haz lo que quieras** do as you like; **¿qué más quieres?** what more do you want?; **hazlo cuando/como quieras** do it whenever/however you like; **quiera o no quiera** whether she/he likes it or not; **iba a hacerlo pero él no quiso** I was going to do it but he didn't want me to; **será muy listo y todo lo que tú quieras, pero …** he may be very smart and all that, but …; **tráemelo mañana ¿quieres?** bring it tomorrow, will you?; **no quiero** I don't want to; **~ + INF** to want to + INF; **quiero ir** I want to go; **quisiera reservar una mesa** I'd like to book a table; **quisiera poder ayudarte** I wish I could help you; **¡ya quisiera yo estar en su lugar!** I'd change places with him any day!; **no quiso comer nada** she wouldn't eat anything; **~ QUE algn+ SUBJ** to want sb to + INF; **quiero que estudies más** I want you to study harder; **¿y qué querías que hiciera?** so what did you expect me to do *o* what was I supposed to do?; **¡qué quieres que te diga …!** quite honestly *o* frankly …; **¡qué quieres que (le) haga!** what can you do?; ***~ es poder*** where there's a will there's a way [2] (al ofrecer algo): **¿quieres un café/algo de beber?** would you like *o* (less frml) do you want a coffee/something to drink? [3] (introduciendo un ruego) **~ + INF**: **¿quieres pasarme el pan?** could you pass me the bread, please?; **¿querrías hacerme un favor?** would you mind doing me a favor?; **¿te quieres callar?** be quiet, will you?
B (*en locs*) **como quiera que** (de cualquier manera que) however; **como quiera que haya sido …** whatever happened *o* it doesn't matter what happened …; **como quiera que se mire** whichever way you look at it; **cuando quiera que** whenever; **donde quiera que** wherever; **queriendo**: **lo hizo queriendo** she/he did it on purpose *o* deliberately; **sin querer** accidentally; **perdona, fue sin ~** sorry, it was an accident *o* I didn't mean to; **querer decir** to mean; **¿qué quieres decir con eso?** what do you mean by that?; ***¡está como quiere!*** (Esp, Méx fam) (es muy guapo, guapa) he's/she's hot stuff! (colloq); (tiene mucha suerte) some people have got it made (colloq)
C (como precio) **~ algo POR algo**: **¿cuánto quieres por el coche?** how much do you want *o* are you asking for the car?
D (referido a cosas inanimadas): **el coche no quiere arrancar** the car won't start; **el destino así lo quiso** it was destined to be; **parece que quiere llover** it looks as if it's going to rain

■ **quererse** *v pron* (*recípr*): **se quieren mucho** they love each other very much; **se quieren como hermanos** they're so close, they're like brothers

querido[1] -da *adj* [1] (amado) ‹*patria*› beloved; **mis recuerdos más ~s** my fondest memories; **seres ~s** loved ones; **un profesor muy ~ por todos** a well-liked teacher [2] (Corresp) Dear [3] (Col fam) (simpático) nice

q

querido² -da *m,f* 1 (como apelativo) darling, dear, sweetheart 2 (amante) (*m*) fancy man; (*f*) fancy woman

querosén, queroseno *m* kerosene, paraffin (BrE)

querré, querría, etc *see* **querer²**

querubín *m* cherub

quesadilla *f* 1 (Méx) (tortilla): *tortilla filled with a savory mixture and topped with melted cheese* 2 (Ven) (panecillo) small roll (*flavored with cheese*)

quesera *f* (plato y campana) cheese dish; (para queso rallado) cheese bowl

quesería *f* (tienda) cheese shop; (fábrica) dairy (*specializing in cheese*)

quesero¹ -ra *adj* cheese (*before n*)

quesero² -ra *m,f* (fabricante) cheese maker; (vendedor) cheese seller

queso *m* (Coc) cheese

Compuestos

- **queso crema** (AmL) cream cheese
- **queso de bola** ≈ Edam
- **queso fresco** green cheese (*soft unripened cheese*)
- **queso fundido/rallado** processed/grated cheese
- **queso para untar** cheese spread

quetzal *m* (Fin) quetzal (*Guatemalan unit of currency*)

quevedos *mpl* (Esp) *small, round metal-rimmed glasses*

quicio *m* doorjamb; ***sacar de ~ a algn*** to drive sb crazy (colloq); ***sacar las cosas de ~*** (Esp) to blow things up out of all proportion

quid *m*: **el ~ de la cuestión es que ...** the crux *o* nub of the matter is that ...

quiebra *f* 1 (Com, Fin) (de empresa, individuo) bankruptcy; **la compañía se declaró en ~** the company went into liquidation 2 (de valores) breakdown

quiebre *m*

A 1 (AmL fam) (de relaciones) breaking off; **se produjo un ~ en las conversaciones** the talks were broken off 2 (de sistema, jerarquía) breakdown; **el ~ de valores tradicionales** the breakdown in traditional values

B (cambio de dirección) turn; **marcó un ~ en la historia del país** it marked a turning point in the country's history

C (Dep) 1 (en tenis) service break; **punto de ~** break point 2 (de marca, récord) **hubo varios ~s de marcas** several records were broken

quiebro *m* (regate) dodge; (balanceo) swaying movement

quien *pron*

A 1 (*sujeto*) who, that; (*complemento*) who, that, whom (frml); **tienes que ser tú misma ~ lo decida** *you* are the one who *o* that has to decide; **es a él a ~ debemos agradecérselo** he's the one (who) we must thank; **la chica con ~ salía** the girl (who) I was going out with 2 (frml *o* liter) (en frases explicativas) who, whom (frml); **su hermano, a ~ no había visto, ...** her brother, who *o* whom she had not seen, ...; **sus padres, para ~es esto había sido un duro golpe, ...** her parents, for whom this had been a severe blow, ...

B (la persona que): **~es hayan terminado pueden irse** those who have finished may go; **~ lo haya encontrado** the person who found it; **~ se lo haya dicho** whoever told him; **no encontré ~ me lo pudiera explicar** I didn't find anybody who could explain it to me

C **no ser quien**: **no soy ~ para opinar al respecto** I'm not the (right) person to comment on this matter; **tú no eres ~ para juzgarme** you're nobody to judge me

quién *pron* 1 who; **¿~ era/~es eran?** who was it/were they?; **¿~ de ustedes se atrevería?** which of you would dare?; **¿con ~es fuiste?** who did you go with?; **¿de ~ es esto?** whose is this?; **llegó una postal — ¿de ~?** there's a postcard — who's it from?; **~ más, ~ menos, todos somos egoístas** we're all selfish, to a greater or lesser degree; ***dime con ~ andas y te diré ~ eres*** you can tell a person by the company he keeps 2 (en exclamaciones) who; — **¡~ sabe!** — who knows!; **¡~ pudiera quedarse unos días más!** if only I could stay a few more days!

quienquiera *pron* (*pl* **quienesquiera**) whoever; **~ que se lo haya dicho** whoever told him

quiera, quieras, etc *see* **querer²**

quieto -ta *adj* still; **¡estáte** *or* **quédate ~!** keep still!; **¡todo el mundo ~!** everybody freeze!; **¡las manos quietas!** keep your hands to yourself!; **¡~!** (a un perro) down, boy!

quietud *f* (ausencia de movimiento) stillness; (tranquilidad, sosiego) calm, peace; **en la ~ de la noche** in the still of the night (liter)

quihubo *interj* (Chi, Méx fam) hi! (colloq), how's it going? (colloq)

quihúbole *interj* (Méx fam) ▸ **quihubo**

quijada *f* jaw (bone)

quijotada *f* quixotic act

quijote *m*: **es un ~** he's a hopeless idealist

Quijote *m*: **Don ~** Don Quixote

quijotería *f* (cualidad) quixotic nature; (acción) quixotic act

quijotesco -ca *adj* quixotic

quilate *m* karat (AmE), carat (BrE); **oro de 18 ~s** 18-karat gold

quilla *f* keel

quilombo *m* (Bol, RPl arg) 1 (burdel) whorehouse (colloq) 2 (lío, jaleo) mess

quiltro -tra *m,f* (Chi fam) mongrel

quimera *f*

A (ilusión) illusion, chimera (liter); **el proyecto no pasó de ser una ~** the plan was never anything but a pipe dream

B (Mit) chimera

quimérico -ca *adj* ‹*plan/idea*› fanciful, chimeric (liter)

química *f* chemistry

químico¹ -ca *adj* chemical

químico² -ca *m,f* chemist

quimioterapia *f* chemotherapy

quimono *m* kimono

quina *f* (corteza) cinchona bark

quincalla *f* 1 (ant) (Com) hardware 2 (baratijas) trash, junk

quincallería *f* (ant) hardware store

quincallero -ra *m,f* hardware dealer

quince¹ *adj inv/pron* fifteen; **dentro de ~ días** in two weeks' time, in a fortnight's time (BrE); *para ejemplos ver tb* **cinco**

quince² *m* (number) fifteen

quinceañero -ra *m,f* (de quince años) fifteen-year-old; (menos específico) teenager

quincena *f* 1 (dos semanas) two weeks (*pl*), fortnight (BrE); **la primera ~ del mes de marzo** the first two weeks in March 2 (paga) wages (*pl*) (*paid every two weeks*)

quincenal *adj* bimonthly (AmE), fortnightly (BrE)

quincha *f* (AmS) (de cañas y barro) wattle and daub; (de cañas) thatch, thatching

quincuagenario -ria *adj* 50-year-old

quincuagésimo -ma *adj/pron* 1 (ordinal) fiftieth; *para ejemplos ver* **vigésimo** 2 (partitivo): **la quincuagésima parte** a fiftieth

quiniela *f* 1 (Esp) (boleto) sports lottery ticket (AmE), pools coupon (BrE); (juego): **la ~** *or* **las ~s** the sports lottery (AmE), the football pools (BrE) 2 (RPl) *betting on the last two or three figures of the lottery*

quinientos¹ -tas *adj/pron* five hundred; **quinientas pesos** five hundred pesos; **~ cinco** five hundred and five; **~ mil** five hundred thousand; **~ y pico** five hundred odd; **el ~ aniversario** the five hundredth anniversary, the fifth centenary

quinientos² *m* (number) five hundred

quinina *f* quinine

quino *m* cinchona

quinqué *m* oil lamp

quinquenal *adj* ‹*revisión/censo*› five-yearly, quinquennial (frml); **un plan ~** a five-year plan

quinquenio *m* (frml) five-year period

quinta *f*

A 1 (casa) *house in its own grounds, usually in the country* 2 (Agr) estate, farm; ***~ del ñato*** (AmS fam) cemetery

B (Esp) (Mil) draft, call up; **lo llamaron a ~s** he was drafted *o* called up; **es de mi ~** (fam) he's my age
C (Mús) fifth
quintada *f* practical joke
quintaesencia *f* quintessence (frml); **la ~ DE algo** the quintessence OF sth
quintal *m* 100 lbs
(Compuesto) **quintal métrico** 100 kgs
quintar [A1] *vt* (Esp) to call up, draft
quintero -ra *m,f* (arrendatario) tenant farmer; (mozo) farm laborer•
quinteto *m* quintet
quintillizo -za *m,f* quintuplet
Quintín: ***se armó la de San ~*** (fam) it was chaos (colloq)
quinto¹ -ta *adj/pron* 1 (ordinal) fifth; **llegó ~** *or* **en ~ lugar** he came fifth; **Carlos V** (*read as: Carlos quinto*) Charles V (*read as: Charles the fifth*); **vive en el ~ (piso)** she lives on the sixth (AmE) *o* (BrE) fifth floor; **eres el ~ de la lista** you're fifth on the list; **está en ~ de (la) carrera** she's in the fifth year of her college/university course 2 (partitivo): **la quinta parte** a fifth
quinto² *m*
A 1 (partitivo) fifth; **tres ~s** three-fifths; **un ~ del presupuesto** a fifth *o* one fifth of the budget 2 (en Méx) (moneda) five centavo coin; ***estar sin un ~*** (Méx fam) to be broke (colloq); ***ni un ~*** (Méx fam): **no traigo ni un ~** I don't have a penny on me *o* (AmE) a dime with me (colloq)
B (Esp) (Mil) conscript
quíntuple¹ *m* quintuple
quíntuple² *mf* (Chi, Ven) quintuplet
quintuplicar [A2] *vt* to quintuplicate
■ **quintuplicarse** *v pron*: **en dos años el precio llegó a ~se** there was a fivefold price increase in two years
quíntuplo¹ -pla *adj* quintuple, fivefold
quíntuplo² *m* quintuple
quiosco *m* ▸ **kiosco**
quiosquero -ra *m,f* ▸ **kiosquero**
quiquiriquí *m* (canto) cock-a-doodle-doo
quirófano *m* operating room (AmE), operating theatre (BrE)
quiromancia *f* palmistry, chiromancy (frml)
quiromántico -ca *m,f* palmist
quiromasaje *m* chiromassage
quirúrgico -ca *adj* surgical; **fue sometido a una intervención quirúrgica** (frml) he underwent surgery (frml)
quise, quisiera, etc *see* **querer²**
quisqui, quisque *m* (Esp fam): **todo ~** everybody
quisquilla *f* shrimp
quisquilloso -sa *adj* (meticuloso, exigente) fussy, picky (colloq); (susceptible) touchy
quiste *m* cyst
quita *f* deduction
quitaesmalte *m* nail polish remover
quitamanchas *m* (*pl* ~) stain remover
quitanieves *m* (*pl* ~) snowplow (AmE), snowplough (BrE)
quitar [A1] *vt*
A 1 (apartar, retirar): **¡quítalo de aquí!** get *o* take it out of here!; **¡quita esa silla de en medio!** get that chair out of the way!; **quita tus cosas de mi escritorio** take your things off my desk; **quitó los obstáculos de mi camino** he removed the obstacles from my path; **~ la mesa** (Esp) to clear the table; (+ *me/te/le etc*) **¡quítame las manos de encima!** take your hands off me!; **le quitó la piel al pollo** he skinned the chicken; **me quitó una pelusa del hombro** she picked a bit of fluff off my shoulder; **no le puedo ~ la tapa** I can't get the top off 2 ‹*prenda/anillo*› (+ *me/te/le etc*) to take off; **quítale los zapatos** take his shoes off
B (+ *me/te/le etc*) 1 (de las manos): **le quitó la pistola al ladrón** he got *o* took the gun off the thief; **se lo quitó de un manotazo** she swiped it out of his hand; **le quité el cuchillo** I took the knife (away) from her 2 (privar de): **la policía le quitó el pasaporte** the police took his passport away 3 (robar): **me ~on la cartera del bolsillo** someone took *o* stole my wallet from my pocket; **me quitó el asiento** he took my seat
C (restar) (+ *me/te/le etc*): **me estás quitando autoridad** you're undermining my authority; **me quita mucho tiempo** it takes up a lot of my time; **no le quites méritos** give him his due; **~le años a algn** to take years off sb; **~le importancia a algo** to play sth down; **le quita valor/credibilidad** it detracts from its value/credibility
D (hacer desaparecer) ‹*mancha*› to remove, get ... out; ‹*dolor*› to relieve, get rid of; ‹*sed*› to quench; ‹*apetito*› to take away; (+ *me/te/le etc*) **eso te ~á el hambre** that will stop you feeling hungry; **hay que ~le esa idea de la cabeza** we must get that idea out of his head
E **quitando** (*ger*) (fam) except for
■ **quitar** *vi*
A (Esp fam): **¡quita (de ahí)!** get out of the way!; **¡quita ya! ¡eso no se lo cree nadie!** oh come off it, nobody believes that!
B (*en locs*) **de quita y pon** ‹*funda/etiqueta*› removable; ***eso no quita que ...***: **pero eso no quita que se pueda hacer de otra manera** but that doesn't mean that there aren't other ways of doing it; ***ni ~ ni poner*** (fam): **yo aquí ni quito ni pongo** I don't count *o* my opinion doesn't count around here; ***quien quita y ...*** (Méx fam): **quien quita y me saco la lotería** maybe I'll even win the lottery; **quien quita y lo encontramos** we might still find it
■ **quitarse** *v pron*
A (desaparecer) «*mancha*» to come out; «*dolor*» go (away); «*viento*» to die down; (+ *me/te/le etc*) **se me quitó el dolor** I got rid of the pain; **ya se me ~on las ganas** I don't feel like it any more
B (apartarse, retirarse) to get out of the way; **¡quítate de mi vista!** get out of my sight!
C (*refl*) 1 ‹*prenda/alhaja/maquillaje*› to take off 2 ‹*dolor/resfriado*› to get rid of; ‹*miedo*› to overcome, get over; **se quita años** *or* **la edad** she lies about her age; **~se algo DE algo**: **¡quítate el dedo de la nariz!** stop picking your nose!; **¡quítate las manos de los bolsillos!** take your hands out of your pockets!; **~se algo/a algn de encima/en medio** to get rid of sth/sb; **te has quitado veinte años de encima** you look twenty years younger
quitasol *m* sunshade
quitasueño *m* (fam) nagging worry
quite *m* 1 (Taur) *move to draw the bull away from a bullfighter in difficulties*; ***estar al ~*** «*torero*» to be ready to draw the bull away; «*amigo/padre*» to be on hand (to help); ***hacerle el ~ a algn*** (Andes fam) to dodge sb 2 (en esgrima) parry
quiteño -ña *adj* of/from Quito
Quito *m* Quito
quiubo *interj* (Chi, Méx fam) ▸ **quihubo**
quizá, quizás *adv* maybe, perhaps; **~ vengan mañana** maybe *o* perhaps they'll come tomorrow
quórum /'kworum/ *m* (*pl* **-rums**) quorum; **no hubo ~** they/we did not have a quorum, the meeting was inquorate (frml)

q

Rr

R, **r** *f (read as /'ere/) the letter* **R, r**

R/ = **remite**

rabadilla *f* (de ave) pope's nose (esp AmE), parson's nose (BrE); (de res) rump; (de persona) (fam) tailbone (colloq)

rábano *m* radish; ***tomar el ~ por las hojas*** to get the wrong end of the stick (colloq); ***¡y un ~!*** (fam) no way! (colloq); ▸**importar**

rabí *mf (pl* **-bíes**) rabbi

rabia *f*

A (enfermedad) rabies

B [1] (expresando fastidio): **¡me da una ~ tener que irme!** it's really annoying that I have to leave; **no sabes la ~ que me da que ...** you've no idea how much it annoys *o* irritates me that ...; **¡qué ~!** how annoying! [2] (furor, ira) anger, fury; **con ~** angrily, in a rage [3] (antipatía, manía): **tenerle ~ a algn** to have it in for sb (colloq)

rabiar [A1] *vi* [1] (de furor, envidia): **el jefe está que rabia contigo** the boss is furious with you; **no lo hagas ~** don't tease him, ***a ~*** (fam): ‹*aplaudir*› like crazy (colloq); **me gusta a ~** I'm crazy about him (colloq) [2] (de dolor): **rabiaba de dolor** she was in terrible pain [3] (desear ansiosamente) **~ POR algo** to be dying FOR sth (colloq)

rabieta *f* tantrum; **le dio una ~** he threw a tantrum

rabillo *m*

A (Zool) short tail

B (Bot) stem, stalk; (del ojo) corner; ***mirar a algn con el ~ del ojo*** to look at sb out of the corner of one's eye

rabino -na *m,f* rabbi

rabioso -sa *adj*

A (Med, Vet) rabid

B [1] (furioso) furious [2] (uso enfático): **un tema de rabiosa actualidad** a highly topical issue; **tengo unas ganas rabiosas de conocerlo** I'm dying to meet him

rabo *m*

A [1] (Zool) tail; ***irse con el ~ entre las piernas*** to go away with one's tail between one's legs [2] (de letra) tail

B (Bot) stem, stalk

rabón -bona *adj* [1] ‹*animal*› (sin rabo) tailless; (con rabo corto) short-tailed [2] (Méx) ‹*vestido/pantalones*› short

rabona *f* (prostituta) camp-follower; **hacerse (la) ~** (fam) to play hooky (esp AmE colloq), to skive off (school) (BrE colloq)

racanear [A1] *vi* (fam) to be stingy (colloq)

rácano[1] -na *adj* (fam) (tacaño) stingy (colloq)

rácano[2] -na *m,f* (fam) (tacaño) scrooge (colloq), tightwad (AmE colloq)

racha *f* [1] (secuencia): **ha pasado una ~ de mala suerte** she's had a run *o* spell of bad luck; **una ~ de enfermedades** a series *o* string of illnesses; **pasar una mala ~** to go through bad times *o* (BrE) a bad patch; **tengo una buena ~, voy a seguir jugando** I'm on a winning streak so I'm going to carry on playing; ***a*** *or* ***por ~s***: **llueve a ~s** it keeps raining on and off; **va por ~s** it goes in phases [2] (Meteo) gust of wind

racheado -da *adj* gusty

racial *adj* racial; **disturbios ~es** race riots

racimo *m* (de uvas) bunch, cluster; (de plátanos) bunch

raciocinio *m* (facultad) reason; (argumento) reasoning

ración *f* [1] (parte) share [2] (porción de comida) portion, helping [3] (en bar): **una ~ de calamares** a portion *o* plate of squid [4] (Mil) ration; **a media ~** on half rations

> **ración**
>
> In Spain, a *ración* is a serving of food eaten in a bar or café, generally with a drink. Friends or relatives meet in a bar or café, order a number of *raciones*, and share them. *Raciones* tend to be larger and more elaborate than *tapas*. They may be: Spanish omelet, squid, octopus, cheese, ham, or *chorizo*, among others. *See also* **pincho**

racional *adj* rational

racionalidad *f* rationality

racionalismo *m* rationalism

racionalista *adj/mf* rationalist

racionalización *f* rationalization

racionalizar [A4] *vt* to rationalize

racionamiento *m* rationing

racionar [A1] *vt* to ration

racismo *m* racism, racialism

racista *adj/mf* racist, racialist

radar, rádar *m* radar

(Compuesto) **radar móvil** mobile speed camera

radiación *f* radiation

radiactividad *f* radioactivity

radiactivo -va *adj* radioactive

radiado -da *adj* radiate

radiador *m* radiator

radial *adj*

A ‹*forma/neumático*› radial; ‹*carretera*› arterial

B (AmS) ‹*cadena/emisión/novela*› radio (*before n*)

radiante *adj* [1] (brillante) brilliant; **hace un sol ~** it's brilliantly *o* beautifully sunny; **un día ~** a bright, sunny day [2] [ESTAR] ‹*persona*› radiant; **~ de alegría** radiant with happiness [3] (Fís) radiant

radiar [A1] *vt*

A (period) (Rad) to broadcast (*on the radio*); **mensajes radiados** radio messages

B (Fís) to radiate; (Med) to irradiate, treat ... with radiation

radicado -da *adj*: **están ~s en París** they are based in Paris

radical[1] *adj* radical

radical[2] *mf*

A (Pol) radical

B [1] (Mat) root [2] (Ling) radical, root

radicalismo *m* radicalism

radicalizar [A4] *vt* to radicalize, toughen

■ **radicalizarse** *v pron* «*persona/partido*» to become more radical; «*situación/conflicto*» to intensify

radicar [A2] *vi* «*problema/dificultad*» to lie; **el problema radica en ...** the problem stems from *o* lies in ...

■ **radicarse** *v pron* to settle

radio[1] *m*

A [1] (Mat) radius [2] (distancia, área) range, radius; **en un ~ de diez kilómetros** within a ten kilometer radius [3] (de rueda) spoke

(Compuesto) **radio de acción** (de avión, barco) operational range; (de organización) area of operations

B (AmL exc CS) (Rad) radio; *ver tb* **radio[2]**

C (Anat) radius

D (Quím) radium

radio² *f* [1] (medio de comunicación) radio; **transmitir por (la) ~** to broadcast on the radio; **se pusieron en contacto por ~** they established radio contact; **escuchar la ~** to listen to the radio; **lo dijeron por la ~** they said it on the radio [2] (CS, Esp) (aparato) radio; **apaga la ~** turn off *o* switch off the radio [3] (emisora) radio station

(Compuesto) **radio pirata** pirate radio station

radioactividad *f* radioactivity

radioactivo -va *adj* radioactive

radioaficionado -da *m,f* radio ham

radiocassette /rraðioka'set/, **radiocasete** *m* radio cassette player

radiodespertador *m or f* radio alarm

radiodiagnóstico *m* X-ray diagnosis

radiodifusión *f* broadcasting

radiodifusor -sora *adj* (AmL) radio (*before n*)

radiodifusora *f* (AmL frml) radio station

radioemisora *f* radio station

radioescucha *mf* listener

radiofónico -ca *adj* radio (*before n*)

radiografía *f* X-ray; **hacerse** *or* **sacarse una ~** to have an X-ray taken, to be X-rayed; **le hicieron** *or* **sacaron una ~ del brazo** they took an X-ray of his arm

radiografiar [A17] *vt* to X-ray

radiográfico -ca *adj* X-ray (*before n*)

radiograma *m* radio message, radiogram

radiología *f* radiology

radiólogo -ga *m,f* radiologist

radionovela *f* radio serial

radiooperador -dora *m,f* (AmL) radio operator

radiopatrulla *m* radio patrol car

radio-taxi *m* radio taxi, radio cab

radioteléfono *m* radiotelephone

radiotelegrafista *mf* radio operator

radiotelescopio *m* radio telescope

radioterapia *f* radiotherapy

radiotransmisión *f* (acción) transmission; (mensaje) broadcast, transmission

radioyente *mf* listener

RAE *f* = **Real Academia Española**

raer [E16] *vt* ‹*superficie*› to scrape; ‹*barniz/pintura*› to scrape off

ráfaga *f* (de viento) gust; **una ~ de ametralladora** a burst of machine-gun fire

rafia *f* raffia

raid *m*

A (period) (ataque) raid

B (AmC) (en carro) ride; **pedir ~** to hitch a ride *o* lift

raído -da *adj* worn-out, threadbare

raigambre *f* [1] (tradición) roots (*pl*); **música de ~ popular** music which has its roots in the popular tradition; **una costumbre de profunda ~** a deeply-rooted custom [2] (Bot) root system, roots (*pl*)

raíz *f*

A [1] (Bot) root; ***de ~***: **arrancar una planta de ~** to uproot a plant; **arranca el vello de ~** it removes the hair at the roots; **eliminaron de ~ el problema** they eradicated the problem; ***echar raíces*** «*planta*» to take root; «*persona*» to put down roots; «*costumbre/doctrina*» to take root [2] (de diente, pelo) root

B (Ling) root

C [1] (Mat) root; **~ cuadrada/cúbica** square/cube root [2] (Inf): **el directorio ~** the root directory

D [1] (origen) root; **atacar un problema en su ~** to attack the root causes of a problem; **la tradición tiene sus raíces en Francia** the tradition originated in France [2] **a raíz de** as a result of

raja *f*

A [1] (en pared, cerámica) crack [2] (rotura — en costura) split; (— en tela) tear, rip [3] (abertura — en falda) slit; (— en chaqueta) vent

B (de melón, salami) slice

rajá *m* rajah

rajado¹ -da *adj*

A (fam) (cobarde) cowardly

B (Chi fam) [1] (tarambana) wild (colloq) [2] ‹*conductor*› reckless; ***ir*** *or* ***andar ~*** (Chi fam) to go at top speed (colloq)

rajado² -da *m,f* (fam) coward, chicken (colloq)

rajadura *f* crack

rajar [A1] *vt*

A [1] (agrietar) to crack, cause … to crack [2] (desgarrar) to tear, rip [3] (arg) ‹*persona*› to knife (colloq); **le rajó el cuello** he slit his throat (colloq)

B [1] (CS fam) (criticar) to run … down [2] (Andes) (en examen) (fam) to fail, flunk (AmE colloq)

■ **rajar** *vi* [1] (Col, Per fam) (criticar) **~ DE algn** to badmouth sb (AmE colloq), to slag sb off (BrE colloq) [2] (Bol, CS fam) (huir rápido) to run away; **rajemos de aquí** let's get out of here (colloq), let's beat it (colloq)

■ **rajarse** *v pron*

A «*pared/cerámica*» to crack; «*tela*» to split, tear, rip

B [1] (fam) (echarse atrás) to back out [2] (Col, Per fam) (en examen) to fail, flunk (AmE colloq)

rajatabla: **a ~** (*loc adv*) strictly; **siguió las instrucciones a ~** he followed the instructions to the letter; **sigue la ley a ~** she keeps strictly to the letter of the law

rajón¹ *adj* [1] (Méx fam) (cobarde) cowardly [2] (Per fam) (maldiciente): **es muy ~** he's always badmouthing people (AmE colloq), he's always slagging people off (BrE colloq)

rajón² -jona *m,f* (Méx fam) (cobarde) coward, chicken (colloq)

RAL *f* (Inf) (= **Red de Área Local**) LAN

ralea *f* (pey): **yo no me mezclo con gente de su ~** I don't mix with his sort (pej); **son todos de la misma ~** they're all as bad as each other

ralear [A1] *vi* «*hojas*» to thin (out); **le empieza a ~ el cabello** his hair is beginning to thin

ralentí *m* [1] (Auto): **dejar el motor al ~** to leave the engine idling *o* (BrE) ticking over; **hay que ajustar/subir el ~** the timing needs adjusting [2] (Cin) slow motion

ralentización *f* [1] (de imagen) slowing down [2] (período de proceso/ritmo) slowing down

ralentizar [A4] *vt* to slow down

rallado -da *adj* ‹*queso/zanahoria*› grated; **pan ~** breadcrumbs

rallador *m* grater

ralladura *f*: **~ de limón** grated lemon rind

rallar [A1] *vt* to grate

rally /'rrali/ *m* (*pl* **-llys**) rally

ralo -la *adj* ‹*bosque*› sparse; ‹*monte*› bare; ‹*pelo/barba*› thin, sparse

rama *f* branch; **una ramita de perejil** a sprig of parsley; **algodón en ~** raw cotton; **un trozo de canela en ~** a cinnamon stick; ***andarse/irse por las ~s*** to beat about the bush

ramada *f* [1] (AmS) (cobertizo) shelter (*made from branches*) [2] (Chi) (pérgola) arbor, arbour (BrE)

ramaje *m* branches (*pl*)

ramal *m* (Ferr) branch line; (Geog) branch; (cuerda) strap

ramalazo *m* [1] (acometida): **un ~ de locura/pánico** a fit of madness/panic; **me dio el ~ poético** I started to wax poetic, I came over all poetic (BrE); **un ~ de frío** a shiver; **un ~ de dolor** a stabbing pain [2] (de viento) gust, blast; (de lluvia) blast

rambla *f* [1] (cauce seco) dry riverbed, watercourse [2] (RPl) (paseo marítimo) esplanade, promenade [3] (avenida) boulevard

ramera *f* prostitute

ramificación *f*

A [1] (de árbol, planta, nervios) ramification [2] (Inf) branch

B **ramificaciones** *fpl* (derivaciones) ramifications (*pl*)

ramificarse [A2] *v pron*

A [1] «*árbol/plantas/nervios*» to branch, ramify (tech) [2] «*carretera/ciencia*» to branch

B «*problema*» to ramify (frml), to become complex

ramillete *m* [1] (de flores) posy [2] (iró) (grupo selecto) bunch (colloq)

ramo *m*

A [1] (de flores) bunch; (para novia, dignatario) bouquet [2] (rama) branch

B (en industria) industry; **el ~ de la hostelería** the hotel and catering industry

C (Chi) (Educ) subject

rampa *f* (pendiente) ramp
(Compuesto) **rampa de lanzamiento** launch pad
rampante *adj* rampant
rampla *f* (rampa) ramp
ramplón -plona *adj* (pey) coarse, basic
rana *f* (Zool) frog; ***cuando las ~s críen pelo*** (fam): **terminará cuando las ~s críen pelo** he won't finish in a month of Sundays (colloq); ***salir ~*** (Esp fam) to be a real disappointment
ranchera *f* (Mús) *Mexican folk song*
ranchería *f* 1 (Col) (poblado) settlement; (en suburbios) shanty town 2 (Méx) dairy
rancherío *m* (CS) settlement
ranchero[1] -ra *adj* (Méx) fam) shy
ranchero[2] -ra *m,f* (Méx) (hacendado) rancher; (peón) rancher, ranch hand
rancho *m*
A (comida) food (*for a group of soldiers, workers, etc*); ***hacer ~ aparte***: **no te quedes aquí haciendo ~ aparte** don't be so unsociable; **en las fiestas hacen ~ aparte** at parties they form their own little clique
B 1 (AmL) (choza) hut; (casucha) hovel; (chabola) shack, shanty 2 (Méx) (hacienda) ranch
rancio -cia *adj*
A ‹*mantequilla/tocino*› rancid
B 1 ‹*vino*› mellow 2 (*delante del n*) ‹*abolengo/tradición*› ancient, long-established
rango *m*
A 1 (Mil) rank 2 (categoría, nivel) level
B (Chi) (lujo, pompa) luxury
rangoso -sa *adj* (Chi) luxurious
ránking /'rraŋkin/ *m* (*pl* **-kings**) 1 (en boxeo) rankings (*pl*) **~ de popularidad** popularity ranking 2 (en música) charts (*pl*)
ranura *f* 1 (para monedas) slot; **la ~ del buzón** the mailbox slot *o* opening; **por la ~ de la puerta** through the chink *o* gap in the door 2 (en ensambladura) groove; (en tornillo) groove, slot
rap *m* rap; **hacer ~** to rap
rapacidad *f* rapacity
rapado -da *adj* ‹*cabeza*› shaven; ‹*persona*› shaven-headed; ‹*pelo*› closely-cropped
rapapolvo *m* (Esp) telling-off (colloq), talking-to (colloq)
rapar [A1] *vt* ‹*cabeza*› to shave; ‹*pelo*› to crop
rapaz[1] *adj* 1 (Zool) predatory; **ave ~** bird of prey 2 (ávido) greedy, rapacious 3 (que roba) thieving (*before n*)
rapaz[2] -paza *m,f* (fam) kid (colloq)
rape *m* 1 (Coc, Zool) monkfish, goosefish (AmE) 2 **al ~**: **tiene el pelo cortado al ~** he has closely-cropped hair
rapé *m* snuff
rapel, rápel *m* ▸**rappel**
rapero -ra *adj* rap (*before n*)
rápidamente *adv* quickly
rapidez *f* speed; **con ~** quickly; **¡qué ~!** that was quick!
rápido[1] -da *adv* ‹*hablar/trabajar*› quickly, fast; ‹*conducir/ir*› fast; **¡vamos, ~, que es tarde!** quick *o* hurry, we're late!; **tráemelo ¡~!** bring it to me, quick!
rápido[2] *adj* ‹*aumento*› rapid; ‹*cambio*› quick, rapid, swift; ‹*desarrollo*› rapid, swift; **a paso ~** quickly, swiftly; **comida rápida** fast food; **es muy ~ de hacer** you can make it very quickly
rápido[3] *m*
A (Ferr) express train, fast train
B **rápidos** *mpl* (Geog) rapids (*pl*)
rapiña *f* robbery, pillage
raponero -ra *m,f* (Col fam) bag-snatcher
raposa *f* vixen
rappel *m* abseil, rappel; **bajar en/hacer un ~** to abseil *o* rappel down
rapsodia *f* rhapsody
raptar [A1] *vt* (secuestrar) to kidnap, abduct (frml); (Hist, Mit) to rape (arch)
rapto *m*
A (secuestro) kidnapping, abduction (frml); (Hist, Mit) rape (arch)
B (arrebato) fit; **un ~ de ira/celos** a fit of rage/jealousy
raptor -tora *m,f* kidnapper
raqueta *f* (de tenis, squash) racket; (para nieve) snowshoe
raquítico -ca *adj* 1 ‹*niño/animal*› rickety, rachitic (tech); ‹*árbol*› stunted 2 (fam) ‹*cantidad*› paltry, measly (colloq)
raquitismo *m* rickets, rachitis (tech)
rareza *f* 1 (peculiaridad) peculiarity; **todos tenemos nuestras ~s** we all have our little quirks *o* idiosyncrasies 2 (cosa poco común) rarity 3 (cualidad) rareness
raro -ra *adj*
A 1 (extraño) strange, odd, funny (colloq); **es ~ que ...** it's strange *o* odd *o* funny that ...; **¡qué cosa más rara!** *or* **¡qué ~!** how odd *o* strange!; **es un poco rara** she's a bit odd *o* strange; **te noto muy ~ hoy** you're acting very strangely today; *ver* **bicho B** 2 (poco frecuente) rare; **salvo raras excepciones** with a few rare exceptions; **~ es el día que ...** there's rarely *o* hardly a day when ...; **aquí es ~ que nieve** it's very unusual *o* rare for it to snow here
B ‹*gas*› rare
ras *m* 1 **a ras de** (*loc prep*): **llega a ~ del suelo** it reaches down to the floor; **volar a ~ de tierra** to fly very low 2 **al ras** (*loc adj*) ‹*cucharada*› level (*before n*)
rasante[1] *adj*: **un avión en vuelo ~** a low-flying aircraft; **disparó un tiro ~** he hit a low, skimming shot
rasante[2] *f* slope, gradient
rasar [A1] *vt* to skim
rasca[1] *adj* (CS fam) 1 ‹*persona*› vulgar, common (pej); ‹*lugar*› tacky (colloq) 2 (de mala calidad) trashy (colloq)
rasca[2] *f* (Andes fam) (borrachera): **pegarse una ~** to get plastered (colloq)
rascacielos *m* (*pl* ~) skyscraper
rascar [A2] *vt*
A 1 (con las uñas) to scratch 2 (con cuchillo) ‹*superficie*› to scrape; ‹*pintura*› to scrape off 3 ‹*violín*› to scrape away at
B (Col fam) (picar) to itch; **me rasca la pierna** my leg itches
■ **rascarse** *v pron* (*refl*) to scratch (oneself)
rasero *m* measuring stick; ***medir a algn por el mismo ~*** to treat sb equally *o* the same
rasgado -da *adj*
A ‹*ojos*› almond (*before n*), almond-shaped
B (Col fam) (generoso) open-handed, generous
rasgadura *f* 1 (acción): **el tirón provocó la ~ de la tela** the tug made the cloth tear 2 (efecto) tear; **para evitar que se produzcan ~s** in order to prevent tearing
rasgar [A3] *vt* to tear, rip
■ **rasgarse** *v pron* to tear, rip
rasgo *m*
A 1 (característica) characteristic, feature 2 (gesto) gesture 3 (de la pluma) stroke; (en pintura) brushstroke; ***a grandes ~s*** in outline, broadly speaking
B **rasgos** *mpl* (facciones) features (*pl*)
rasgón *m* tear, rip
rasguear [A1] *vt* to strum
rasguñar [A1] *vt* to scratch
■ **rasguñarse** *v pron* (*refl*) (con uña, púa) to scratch oneself; (con cosa áspera) to graze oneself; **me rasguñé la rodilla** I grazed my knee
rasguño *m* scratch; **sin un ~** unscathed, without a scratch
rasmillarse [A1] *v pron* (Chi fam) to graze oneself
raso[1] -sa *adj*
A 1 ‹*taza/cucharada*› level (*before n*) 2 ‹*vuelo/tiro*› ▸**rasante[1]**
B (exterior) open country; **al ~** out in the open
raso[2] *m* satin
raspa *f* (de pescado) backbone; (de cebada) beard
raspacachos (*pl* ~) *m* (Chi fam) telling-off (colloq)
raspado *m*
A (Med) scrape, curettage
B (Col, Méx) ▸**granizado 1**
raspadura *f* (arañazo) scratch; (ralladura de madera, metal, chocolate) shavings
raspaje *m* (CS) scrape, curettage
raspar [A1] *vt*
A 1 (con espátula) ‹*superficie*› to scrape; ‹*pintura*› to scrape off 2 (limar) to file, rasp

r

B ‹*brazo/piel*› to scrape, graze

■ **raspar** *vi* 1 «*toalla/manos*» to be rough; «*barba*» to scratch, be scratchy 2 «*garganta*» (+ *me/te/le etc*) to feel rough

■ **rasparse** *v pron* ‹*rodillas/codos*› (con algo puntiagudo) to scratch; (con algo áspero) to scrape, graze

raspón *m* (AmL) (por algo puntiagudo) scratch; (por algo áspero) graze, scrape; **lleva un ~ en el codo** he has a grazed elbow; **hay un ~ en la puerta** the door is scratched

rasposo -sa *adj* 1 (áspero) rough, scratchy 2 (RPl fam) (raído) ‹*ropa*› threadbare, shabby

rastacuero *m* (CS fam) upstart

rastafario -ria *adj/m,f* Rastafarian

rastra *f*

A 1 (Agr) harrow 2 (ristra) string 3 (cinturón de gaucho) wide belt (*decorated with silver coins*)

B **a rastras** (*loc adv*): **iba con la maleta a ~s** she was dragging her suitcase along behind her; **tuve que llevarlo a ~s al médico** I had to drag him to the doctor; **siempre va con los niños a ~s** she always has the children in tow

rastreador -dora *m,f* tracker

rastrear [A1] *vt* 1 ‹*zona*› to comb 2 ‹*persona/satélite*› to track 3 ‹*río/lago*› «*pescadores*» to trawl; «*la policía*» to drag, dredge 4 ‹*causas/orígenes*› to trace

rastreo *m* 1 (de zona) thorough search 2 (de río, lago — por pescadores) trawling; (— por la policía) dragging, dredging 3 (de satélite) tracking 4 (de causas, orígenes) investigation, research

rastrero -ra *adj* 1 (despreciable) despicable, contemptible 2 ‹*tallo*› creeping (*before n*); **plantas rastreras** creepers 3 ‹*animal*› crawling (*before n*)

rastrillar [A1] *vt* 1 ‹*tierra*› (con rastrillo) to rake; (con rastra) to harrow 2 ‹*césped*› to rake; ‹*hojas*› to rake up

rastrillo *m*

A (Agr) rake

B (Méx) (para afeitarse) safety razor

rastro *m*

A (pista, huella) trail; (señal, vestigio) trace, sign; **no dejaron ni ~ de la comida** they ate every last bit of the food; **sin dejar ~** without (a) trace

B (mercado) flea market

rastrojo *m* 1 (de cereales) stubble; (de hierba) cuttings (*pl*) 2 (Col) (maleza) weeds (*pl*)

rasurador *m*, **rasuradora** *f* (AmC, Méx) electric razor *o* shaver

rasurar [A1] *vt* (AmL) to shave

■ **rasurarse** *v pron* (AmL) to shave

rata[1] *adj* (fam) (tacaño) stingy (colloq), tightfisted (colloq)

rata[2] *mf* (fam) (tacaño) miser, stingy devil (colloq), tightwad (AmE colloq)

rata[3] *f*

A (Zool) rat; ***hacerse la ~*** (RPl fam) to play hooky (esp AmE colloq), to skive off (school) (BrE colloq); ***no se salvó ni una ~*** no one escaped; ***ser más pobre que una ~*** to be as poor as a church mouse

B (Col) (Econ, Mat) (tasa) rate; (razón) ratio; (porcentaje) percentage

ratán *m* rattan

ratero -ra *m,f* (fam) (carterista) pickpocket; (ladrón) petty thief

raticida *m* rat poison

ratificación *f* ratification

ratificar [A2] *vt* ‹*tratado/contrato*› to ratify; ‹*persona*› (en un puesto) to confirm; ‹*noticia*› to confirm

■ **ratificarse** *v pron* **~se EN algo** to reaffirm sth

rato *m* 1 (tiempo breve) while; **hace un ~** a while ago; **ya hace ~ que volvieron** they've been back a while *o* some time now; **espera un ratito** wait a minute (colloq); **en mis ~s libres** *or* **de ocio** in my spare time; **pasé un mal ~** it was terrible; **iré dentro de un ~** I'll go shortly 2 (*en locs*) **a cada rato** (AmL): **me interrumpe a cada ~** he's always interrupting me; **al (poco) rato** shortly afterwards; **al poco ~ de irte tú** shortly *o* just after you left; **al ~ se me quitó el dolor** shortly afterward(s) the pain went; **sólo al ~ me di cuenta** I only realized a little while later; **a ratos** from time to time, now and again; **a ratos perdidos** now and again; ***para ~*** (fam): **tengo para ~** I'll be a while, I'll be some time; **todavía hay para ~** there's still a long way to go; ***pasar el ~*** to while away the time; ***un ~ (largo)*** (Esp fam) a lot; **saber un ~ largo de algo** to know a hell of a lot about sth (colloq)

ratón[1] -tona *m,f* (Zool) mouse

(Compuesto) **ratón de biblioteca** *m* (fam) bookworm

ratón[2] *m*

A (Inf) mouse

B (AmC) 1 (Coc) *sinewy cut of meat* 2 (fam) (bíceps) biceps; **sacar ~** to flex one's muscles

C (Ven fam) (resaca) hangover

D **ratones** *mpl* (Ur fam) (ínfulas) airs and graces (*pl*)

ratonera *f* 1 (trampa) mousetrap; (madriguera) mousehole 2 (Andes fam) (antro) dive (colloq)

raudal *m* 1 (de agua) torrent 2 **a raudales**: **la luz entraba a ~es** the light streamed in; **tiene dinero a ~es** he has pots *o* stacks of money (colloq); **tiene simpatía a ~es** he's incredibly nice

raudo -da *adj* swift; **bajaban ~s hacia el río** (liter) they rushed headlong toward(s) the river; **salgo hacia allá ~ y veloz** (hum) I'll be there in two shakes of a lamb's tail (colloq & hum)

ravioles, raviolis *mpl* ravioli

raya *f*

A 1 (línea) line; **un vestido a ~s** a striped dress; ***pasarse de la ~*** to overstep the mark, to go too far; ***tener*** *or* ***mantener a algn a ~*** to keep a tight rein on sb 2 (del pantalón) crease 3 (del pelo) part (AmE), parting (BrE); **llevar ~ al** *or* (Esp) **~ en medio** to have a center part *o* centre parting; **hacerse la ~** to part one's hair 4 (Impr) dash; (en morse) dash

B (Zool) ray, skate

rayado[1] -da *adj*

A ‹*papel*› lined, ruled (frml); ‹*tela/vestido*› striped, stripy (colloq)

B [ESTAR] (AmS fam) (loco) screwy (colloq), nutty (colloq)

rayado[2] *m* (en papel) lines (*pl*), ruling; (en tela, vestido) stripes (*pl*)

rayano -na *adj* **~ EN algo** bordering ON sth

rayar [A1] *vt* 1 ‹*pintura/mesa*› to scratch; **le ~on el coche** someone scratched her car 2 (garabatear) to scrawl

■ **rayar** *vi*

A (dejar marca) to scratch

B (aproximarse) **~ EN algo** to border ON sth, verge ON sth; **debe estar rayando (en) los cincuenta** he must be getting on for *o* pushing fifty (colloq)

C (liter) (amanecer): **al ~ el alba** at the break of day (liter)

D (Méx) «*obreros*» to get one's wages, get paid

■ **rayarse** *v pron*

A «*superficie*» to get scratched; **este suelo se raya con facilidad** this floor scratches easily

B (AmS fam) (volverse loco) to crack up (colloq)

rayo *m*

A (Fís) ray; **un ~ de luz** a ray *o* beam (of light); **un ~ de esperanza** a ray of hope; **un ~ de luna** a moonbeam

(Compuestos)

- **rayo láser** laser beam
- **rayos cósmicos** *mpl* cosmic rays (*pl*)
- **rayos gamma** *mpl* gamma rays (*pl*)
- **rayos infrarrojos/ultravioleta** *mpl* infrared/ultraviolet rays (*pl*)
- **rayos X** *mpl* X-rays (*pl*)

B (Meteo) bolt (of lightning); ***como un ~*** (fam) ‹*salir/pasar*› to go out/shoot by like greased lightning (colloq); ***echar ~s y centellas*** to fume (colloq); ***que te/lo parta un ~*** (fam) **¡que te parta un ~!** you can go to hell for all I care! (colloq)**ellos se van y a mí que me parta un ~** they go off and don't give a damn about me! (colloq)

C (fam) (persona viva, despierta): **es un ~** he's razor-sharp

D (AmL) (de rueda) spoke

rayón *m* rayon

rayuela *f* 1 (juego de adultos) *game similar to pitch-and-toss* 2 (RPl) (juego de niños) hopscotch

raza *f*

A (etnia) race; (Agr, Zool) breed; **un perro de ~** a pedigree dog

B (Per fam) (descaro) nerve (colloq)

r

razón *f*
A (motivo, causa) reason; **la ~ por la que te lo digo** the reason (that) I'm telling you; **¿por qué ~ lo hiciste?** why did you do it?; **no sé la ~ que lo movió a hacerlo** I don't know what made him do that; **se enojó y con ~** she got angry and rightly so; **con ~ o sin ella** rightly or wrongly; **se quejan sin ~/con ~** they're complaining for no good reason/they have good reason to complain; **¡con ~ no contestaban!** no wonder they didn't answer!; **por una u otra ~** for one reason or another; **~ de más para ...** all the more reason to ...; **por razones de seguridad** for security reasons; **en ~ de** because of; **en ~ de los últimos sucesos** in view of *o* owing to recent events; ***atender*** *or* ***atenerse*** *or* ***avenirse a razones*** to listen to reason
(Compuesto) **razón social** registered name
B (información): Ⓢ **razón: portería** inquiries to the doorman (AmE) *o* (BrE) porter; Ⓢ **razón: 874256** call 874256; ***dar ~ de algo/algn*** to give information about sth/sb; **nadie le dio ~** (fam) no one could help him
(Compuestos)
- **razón de ser** raison d'être (frml); **ese problema no tiene ~ de ~** there's no reason why there should be any problem
- **razones de Estado** *fpl* reasons of State (*pl*)

C (verdad, acierto): **la ~ está de su parte** he's in the right; **tener** *or* **llevar ~** to be right; **tuve que darle la ~** I had to admit she was right; **tienes toda la ~** (fam) you're absolutely right
D [1] (inteligencia) reason; **actuó guiado por la ~** he was guided by reason; **desde que tengo uso de ~** for as long as I can remember [2] (cordura) reason; **entrar en ~** to see reason *o* sense; **perder la ~** to go out of one's mind; (en sentido hiperbólico) to take leave of one's senses
E (Mat) ratio; **salimos a ~ de 500 pesos cada uno** it came out at 500 pesos each

razonable *adj* reasonable

razonado -da *adj* reasoned, well-reasoned

razonamiento *m* reasoning

razonar [A1] *vi* to reason
■ **razonar** *vt*: **¿has razonado bien tu decisión?** have you thought carefully about your decision?; **razonó que ...** she reasoned that ...

razzia *f* (CS) raid

Rbo. = **recibo**

R.D. *m* = **Real Decreto**

RDSI *f* (= **Red Digital de Servicios Integrados**) ISDN

re *m* (nota) D; (en solfeo) re, ray; **~ bemol/sostenido** D flat/sharp; **en ~ mayor/menor** in D major/minor

reabastecer [E3] *vt* (de combustible) to refuel; (de víveres) to resupply
■ **reabastecerse** *v pron* «*ejército*» to replenish supplies (frml); «*familia*» (fam) to get more supplies *o* provisions; **~se DE algo** ‹*de combustible*› to refuel; ‹*de víveres*› to get more supplies

reabrir [I33] *vt* to reopen
■ **reabrirse** *v pron* to reopen

reacción *f*
A (Fís, Quím, Med) reaction
(Compuesto) **reacción en cadena/nuclear** chain/nuclear reaction
B (ante situación, noticia) reaction
C (Pol) (AmL) right wing

reaccionar [A1] *vi*
A (Fís, Quím) to react; **~ A/CON algo** to react TO/WITH sth
B (ante situación, noticia) to react; **~ A** *or* **FRENTE A** *or* **ANTE** *or* **A algo** to react TO sth; **~ CONTRA algo** to react AGAINST sth

reaccionario -ria *adj/m,f* reactionary

reacio -cia *adj* reluctant; **se mostró ~ a aceptarlo** he was unwilling *o* reluctant to accept it

reacondicionamiento *m* (de motor) reconditioning; (de edificio) conversion; (de vehículo) adaptation; **los trabajos de ~ del puente** the renovation work on the bridge

reacondicionar [A1] *vt* ‹*motor*› to recondition; **lo ~on como museo** they converted it into a museum

reactivar [A1] *vt* to reactivate, revive

reactor *m*
A (Fís) reactor
(Compuesto) **reactor nuclear** nuclear reactor
B (Aviac) (motor) jet engine; (avión) jet (plane)

readaptación *f* (a situación) readjustment; (de obrero) retraining

readaptar [A1] *vt* ‹*obrero*› to retrain
■ **readaptarse** *v pron* [1] (a una situación) to readjust [2] «*obrero*» to retrain

readmisión *f* (de empleado) reemployment; (de alumno) readmission

readmitir [I1] *vt* ‹*trabajador*› to reemploy; ‹*alumno*› to readmit

reafirmar [A1] *vt* to reaffirm, reassert

reagrupación *f* regrouping

reagrupar [A1] *vt* to regroup
■ **reagruparse** *v pron* to regroup

reajustar [A1] *vt* (cambiar) to adjust; (cambiar de nuevo) to readjust

reajuste *m* adjustment
(Compuestos)
- **reajuste ministerial** cabinet reshuffle
- **reajuste salarial** wage settlement

real[1] *adj*
A (verdadero, no ficticio): **un hecho ~** a true story; **en la vida ~** in real life; **historias de la vida ~** true-life stories
B (de la realeza) royal; **la familia ~** the royal family
C (fam) (uso expletivo): **porque me da la ~ gana** because I damn well want to (colloq)

real[2] *m*
A [1] (Hist) real (*old Spanish coin*); ***no valer un ~*** (fam) to be worth nothing [2] (Fin) real (*Brazilian unit of currency*) [3] **reales** *mpl* (AmC fam) (dinero) cash (colloq)
B (Mil) camp; ***sentar*** *or* ***establecer sus*** *or* ***los ~es*** «*ejército*» to set up camp; «*persona*» to install oneself

realce *m*
A [1] **dar ~ A algo** ‹*a belleza/figura*› to enhance sth; **las estrellas invitadas dieron ~ al festival** the star guests added luster to the festival [2] (en costura) relief [3] (Tec) embossing
B (importancia) significance

realeza *f* [1] (cualidad) royalty [2] **la ~** (personas) the royal family

realidad *f* reality; **ésa es la dura ~** those are the harsh facts; **la ~ paraguaya** the reality of life *o* of the situation in Paraguay; **hacer frente a la ~** to face up to reality; **en ~** in reality, actually

realismo *m* realism

> **Realismo Mágico**
>
> A term applied to the work of certain twentieth-century Latin American novelists, in particular the Colombian Gabriel García Márquez, the Chilean Isabel Allende, the Argentinian Jorge Luis Borges and the Cuban Alejo Carpentier. The common characteristic, found for example in García Márquez's *Cien años de soledad* (One Hundred Years of Solitude), is the realistic treatment of unrealistic or fantasy situations

realista[1] *adj* (pragmático) realistic; (Art, Lit, Fil) realist

realista[2] *mf* realist

reality *m* (tb **~ show**) reality show

realizable *adj* feasible, practicable

realización *f*
A (de tarea) carrying out, execution (frml); (de sueños, deseos) fulfillment*, realization
B (Cin, TV) production
C (de bienes) realization, disposal; **~ de beneficios** *or* (AmL) **utilidades** profit-taking

realizado -da *adj* fulfilled*

realizador -dora *m,f* producer

realizar [A4] *vt*
A [1] ‹*tarea*› to carry out, execute (frml); ‹*viaje/visita*› to make; ‹*prueba/entrevista*› to conduct; ‹*encuesta*› to carry out; **realizan gestiones para ...** they are taking the necessary steps to ...; **realizó una magnífica labor** she did a magnificent job [2] ‹*ambiciones/ilusiones*› to fulfill*, realize

r

B (Cin, TV) to produce
C (Com, Fin) 1 ‹bienes› to realize, dispose of, sell 2 ‹compra/inversión› to make; ~ **ventas por valor de ...** to sell goods to the value of ...
■ **realizarse** *v pron* «sueños/ilusiones» to come true, be realized; «persona» to fulfill* oneself
realmente *adv* really, in fact
realzar [A4] *vt* 1 ‹belleza/figura› to enhance, set off, ‹color› to highlight, bring out 2 (Tec) to emboss
reanimación *f* (restablecimiento) revival; (tras accidente, ataque) resuscitation
reanimar [A1] *vt* to revive
■ **reanimarse** *v pron* (recobrar fuerzas) to revive; (recobrar el conocimiento) to come to *o* around
reanudación *f* (frml) resumption
reanudar [A1] *vt* (frml) ‹conversaciones/negociaciones/viaje› to resume; ‹hostilidades› to renew, resume; **~án las clases mañana** they go back to school tomorrow; **~on el viaje** they resumed their journey
■ **reanudarse** *v pron* to resume
reaparecer [E3] *vi* «publicación/persona» to reappear; «artista» to make a comeback
reaparición *f* (de publicación, persona) reappearance; (de artista) comeback
reapertura *f* reopening
rearmar [A1] *vt* to rearm
■ **rearmarse** *v pron* to rearm
rearme *m* rearmament
reasumir [I1] *vt* ‹poder/responsabilidad› to reassume, take over ... again; ‹cargo/funciones› to resume
reata *f* 1 (Méx) (cuerda) rope 2 (Méx) (Agr) lasso 3 (Col) (correa) cartridge belt
reavivar [A1] *vt* to revive
■ **reavivarse** *v pron* to be revived
rebaja *f* 1 (descuento) discount, reduction; **nos hicieron una ~ del 10%** they gave us a 10% discount *o* reduction; **Ⓢ grandes rebajas** big reductions; **¿no me haría una rebajita?** couldn't you give me a discount?, couldn't you knock a bit off the price? (colloq); **de ~** reduced 2 **rebajas** *fpl* (saldos) sale, sales (*pl*); **las ~s de verano** the summer sales; **están en** *or* **de ~s** there's a sale on, they're having a sale
rebajar [A1] *vt*
A ‹precio› to lower, bring ... down; ‹artículo› to reduce; **me rebajó $200** he took $200 off; **me lo rebajó a $3.500** he brought the price down to $3,500
B ‹pintura/solución› to dilute, thin
C 1 (achicar, acortar): **~ un poco la puerta** to cut/saw/plane a little off the door 2 ‹terreno› to lower (the level of) 3 ‹peso/kilos› to lose
D (humillar) to humiliate; (bajar): **fue rebajado de categoría** it was relegated to a lower category *o* downgraded
■ **rebajar** *vi* (humillar) to degrade, be degrading
■ **rebajarse** *v pron* **~se A + INF** to lower oneself TO -ING; **no pienso ~me a pedirle perdón** I'm not going to lower myself to asking him to forgive me; **~se ANTE algn** to humble oneself BEFORE sb
rebalsar [A1] *vi* (CS) to overflow
■ **rebalsar** *vt* (CS): **las lluvias ~on el río** the rains caused the river to burst its banks; **lo llenó hasta ~lo** she filled it to overflowing
■ **rebalsarse** *v pron* (CS) «agua/cauce/vaso» to overflow; **se rebalsó el río** the river burst its banks
rebanada *f* slice
rebanar [A1] *vt* to slice, cut
rebañar [A1] *vt* ‹salsa› to mop up (colloq); ‹plato/recipiente› to wipe ... clean
rebaño *m* (de ovejas) flock; (de cabras) herd
rebasar [A1] *vt*
A (sobrepasar): **el agua ha rebasado el límite** the water has risen above the limit; **~ un punto** to go past *o* beyond a point; **~ el límite de velocidad** to exceed *o* go over the speed limit; **había rebasado los 40 años** he was over 40 years old; **los resultados rebasan todas las previsiones** the results exceed *o* surpass all predictions; **rebasa los límites de lo verosímil** it goes beyond the bounds of credibility; **su fama rebasa nuestras fronteras** her fame extends beyond our borders
B (Méx) (Auto) to pass, overtake
■ **rebasar** *vi* (Méx) to pass, overtake (BrE)
rebatinga *f* (Méx fam) **andar** *o* **estar a la ~** to argue, quarrel
rebatir [I1] *vt* to refute
rebato *m* surprise attack; **tocar a ~** to sound the alarm
rebeca *f* (Esp) cardigan
rebelarse [A1] *v pron* to rebel; **~ CONTRA algn/algo** to rebel AGAINST sb/sth
rebelde[1] *adj* 1 ‹tropas/ejército› rebel (*before n*) 2 ‹niño/carácter› unruly, rebellious 3 ‹tos› persistent; ‹mancha› stubborn 4 (Der) defaulting (*before n*)
rebelde[2] *mf* (Mil, Pol) rebel; (Der) defaulter
rebeldía *f* 1 (cualidad) rebelliousness 2 (Der): **declarar a algn en ~** to declare sb to be in default; **juzgar a algn en ~** to try sb in his/her abscence
rebelión *f* rebellion, uprising
rebenque *m* (CS) riding crop
reblandecer [E3] *vt* to soften
■ **reblandecerse** *v pron* to become *o* go soft
reblandecimiento *m* softening
rebobinar [A1] *vt* to rewind
reborde *m* (de tela) edging, border; (de mesa) edge; (de bandeja) rim
rebosante *adj* **~ DE algo** ‹de alegría/optimismo› brimming WITH sth; ‹de vino/agua› filled to the brim WITH sth
rebosar [A1] *vi* 1 **~ DE algo** ‹de felicidad/entusiasmo› to brim *o* bubble over WITH sth; **rebosa de salud** she's bursting *o* brimming with health 2 «agua/embalse» to overflow; «lugar»: **el estadio rebosaba de gente** the stadium was full to bursting
■ **rebosar** *vt* ‹alegría/felicidad›: **rebosaba felicidad** she was radiant with happiness
rebotado -da (fam) (*m*) ex-priest (*o* ex-monk *etc*); (*f*) ex-nun
rebotar [A1] *vi* «pelota/piedra/correo electrónico» to bounce; «bala» to ricochet
rebote *m* 1 (al golpear algo): **la pelota dio un ~ en el poste** the ball bounced off the post; **de ~: esta medida nos afecta de ~** this measure has an indirect effect on us; **la pelota entró de ~** the ball went in on the rebound 2 (en baloncesto) rebound
rebozar [A4] *vt* to coat ... in batter (*o* in egg and breadcrumbs *etc*)
rebozo *m* (AmL) (Indum) shawl, wrap; **sin ~** openly, frankly
rebrotar [A1] *vi* to produce *o* sprout new shoots
rebujo *m* (de papel) ball; (de trapos, hilos) mass, tangle
rebullir [I9] *vi* «persona» to move, stir
■ **rebullir** *vt* (Col) ‹café/té› to stir
rebuscado -da *adj* (complicado) over-elaborate, roundabout; (afectado) affected, recherché
rebuscar [A2] *vi*: **rebuscó entre los papeles** he searched through the papers; **rebusqué en sus bolsillos** I went through *o* searched his pockets; **rebuscaba en la basura** he was rummaging about in the garbage
rebuznar [A1] *vi* to bray
rebuzno *m* (sonido) bray; (sucesión de sonidos) braying
recabar [A1] *vt* 1 ‹información/apoyo/votos› to obtain, gather; ‹ayuda› to obtain, get; ‹fondos› to raise; ‹firmas› to collect; **recabó el respaldo de los ciudadanos** he asked the people to support him 2 ‹derecho/libertad› to claim
recadero *m* messenger, runner
recado *m*
A 1 (mensaje) message; **le mandó ~ de que volviera** she sent word that he should return 2 (Esp) (encargo, diligencia) errand; **hacer un ~** to run an errand
B (RPl) (Equ) tack
recaer [E16] *vi*
A «enfermo» to have *o* suffer a relapse
B 1 «sospechas/responsabilidad» **~ SOBRE algn** to fall ON sb 2 «premio/nombramiento» **~ EN algn** to go TO sb
recaída *f* relapse; **tener una ~** to have a relapse
recalcar [A2] *vt* to stress, emphasize; **les recalcó que ...** she stressed *o* she emphasized that...

r

recalcitrante *adj* ‹*persona/actitud*› recalcitrant; **es enemigo ~ de la música moderna** he is a declared *o* sworn enemy of modern music

recalentamiento *m* overheating

(Compuesto) **recalentamiento global** global warming

recalentar [A5] *vt* [1] ‹*motor*› to cause … to overheat [2] ‹*comida*› to heat up, warm up; **¿puedes ~lo?** can you heat *o* warm it up?; **me dio un guiso recalentado** he gave me some reheated stew

■ **recalentarse** *v pron* to overheat, become overheated

recalificar [A2] *vt*

A ‹*clasificar de nuevo*› to reclassify

B ‹*un examen*› to regrade

C ‹*terrenos*› to redesignate

recámara *f*

A (Méx) (dormitorio) bedroom; (muebles del dormitorio): **comprar una ~** to buy some bedroom furniture

B (Arm) chamber

recamarera *f* (Méx) chambermaid

recambio *m* [1] (Auto, Mec) spare (part); **rueda de ~** spare wheel [2] (de bolígrafo) refill

recapacitar [A1] *vi* to reconsider, think again; **~ SOBRE algo** to reconsider sth

recapitulación *f* summing up, recap

recapitular [A1] *vi* to sum up, recap

■ **recapitular** *vt* to sum up

recargable *adj* ‹*batería/pila*› rechargeable; ‹*encendedor/pluma*› refillable

recargado -da *adj* ‹*decoración*› overelaborate, excessively ornate; ‹*texto*› overwritten; (de trabajo) overloaded

recargar [A3] *vt*

A [1] ‹*decoración*› to overdo; **han recargado la habitación con cuadros** they've cluttered the room up with pictures [2] ‹*texto*› to overwrite

B ‹*batería*› to recharge; ‹*mechero/estilográfica*› to refill; ‹*arma/programa*› to reload

C [1] (en un pago) (+ *me/te/le etc*): **le ~on un 10%** they charged him 10% extra [2] **~ a algn DE algo** ‹*de trabajo*› to overload sb WITH sth

■ **recargarse** *v pron* (Col, Méx, Ven) (apoyarse) **~se CONTRA algo** to lean AGAINST sth

recargo *m*: **un ~ del veinte por ciento** a twenty per cent surcharge; **entrega a domicilio sin ~** home delivery service at no extra charge

recatado -da *adj* (pudoroso) demure; (reservado) reserved

recatarse [A1] *v pron*: **lo dijo sin ~** he said it quite openly

recato *m* [1] (pudor) modesty [2] (reserva) reserve

recauchado, (Esp) **recauchutado** *m* retreading, remolding*

recauchar, (Esp) **recauchutar** [A1] *vt* to retread, remold*

recaudación *f* [1] (acción) collection [2] (ganancia — en tienda) takings (*pl*); (— en cine) box office receipts (*pl*); (— en estadio) gate

recaudador -dora *m,f*: *tb* **~ de impuestos** tax collector

recaudar [A1] *vt* to collect

recaudo: **a buen ~** in a safe place

recelar [A1] *vi* **~ DE algo/algn** to be suspicious OF sth/sb, distrust sth/sb

■ **recelar** *vt* to suspect

recelo *m* suspicion, distrust; **miran con ~ a sus líderes** they regard their leaders distrustfully

receloso -sa *adj*: **me miró ~** he looked at me distrustfully; **~ DE algo** suspicious OF sth, distrustful OF sth

recepción *f*

A [1] (de mercancías) receipt (frml) [2] (Rad, Telec) reception [3] (acogida) reception; **una calurosa ~** a warm reception

B (fiesta, ceremonia) reception

C (en hotel) reception; **pregunta en ~** ask at reception *o* at the desk

recepcionista *mf* receptionist

receptáculo *m* receptacle

receptividad *f* receptiveness, receptivity; **tener ~** to be receptive

receptivo -va *adj* receptive

receptor -tora *m,f*

A (Med, Ling) recipient

B (Dep) (en fútbol americano) receiver; (en béisbol) catcher

C **receptor** *m* (Rad) radio, receiver; (TV) television (receiver *o* set)

recesión *f* recession

recesivo -va *adj* recessive

receso *m* (AmL) recess; **estar/entrar en ~** to be/go into recess; **pidió al juez un ~** he asked the judge for an adjournment

receta *f* (Coc) recipe; (Med) prescription

recetar [A1] *vt* to prescribe

recetario *m* (Coc) recipe book, cookery book (BrE); (Farm, Med) prescription pad

rechazar [A4] *vt* [1] ‹*invitación/propuesta/individuo*› to reject; ‹*moción/enmienda*› to defeat; ‹*oferta/trabajo*› to turn down [2] ‹*ataque/enemigo*› to repel, repulse [3] (Med) ‹*órgano*› to reject

rechazo *m* (de invitación, individuo, órgano) rejection; (de moción, enmienda) defeat

rechifla *f* whistling (*as a sign of disapproval*), ≈ booing; **hubo una gran ~** there was a lot of booing from the audience

rechiflar [A1] *vt* to whistle at (*as a sign of disapproval*), ≈ to boo

rechinar [A1] *vi* «*polea/bisagra*» to creak, squeak; **le rechinan los dientes mientras duerme** he grinds his teeth in his sleep

rechinón *m* (Méx) screech

rechistar [A1] *vi* (en frases negativas): **cómetelo sin ~** eat it up and no arguments; **lo aguantó todo sin ~** he put up with it all without saying a word

rechoncho -cha *adj* (fam) dumpy (colloq), short and fat

rechupete (fam). **de ~** (*loc adj*) ‹*comida*› delicious, scrumptious (colloq)

recibí *m* receipt

recibidor *m* entrance hall

recibimiento *m* reception

recibir [I1] *vt*

A [1] ‹*carta/paquete*› to receive, get; ‹*mercancías*› to receive; **recibió muchos regalos** she got lots of gifts; **¿han recibido el libro que pedí?** has the book I ordered come in yet? [2] (Rad, TV) to receive [3] ‹*ayuda/llamada/oferta*› to receive; **¿recibiste mi recado?** did you get my message?; **ha recibido orden de …** he has been ordered *o* he has received orders to…; **recibió muchas demostraciones de afecto** people showed her a great deal of kindness; **recibe el nombre de …** it is called …; **reciba un atento saludo de …** (Corresp) sincerely yours (AmE), yours faithfully/sincerely (BrE); **recibe un fuerte abrazo…** (Corresp) best wishes; **reciba nuestra más cordial felicitación** (frml) please accept our warmest congratulations (frml)

B ‹*persona/visita*› to receive; **~ a algn con los brazos abiertos** to welcome sb with open arms; **van a ir a ~lo** they are going to meet him; **el encargado la ~á enseguida** the manager will see you right away

C (acoger) ‹*propuesta/oferta*› (+ *compl*) to receive; **recibieron la sugerencia fríamente** the suggestion met with *o* received a cold reception

D ‹*peso/carga*› to support

■ **recibir** *vi*: **recibe los jueves** she sees *o* receives visitors on Thursdays; **el doctor no recibe hoy** the doctor does not have office hours (AmE) *o* (BrE) surgery today

■ **recibirse** *v pron* (AmL) (Educ) to graduate; **~se DE algo** to qualify AS sth

recibo *m*

A (de pago) receipt; (justificante de compra) (sales) receipt; (de luz, teléfono) bill

B (acción de recibir) receipt; **al ~ de esta carta** (frml) on *o* upon receipt of this letter; ***no ser de ~*** to be unacceptable

reciclado[1] -da *adj* recycled

reciclado[2], **reciclaje** *m*

A (de papel, vidrio) recycling

B (de persona) retraining

recicladora *f* (planta) recycling plant; (empresa) recycling company *o* firm

reciclar [A1] *vt*

A ‹*papel/vidrio*› to recycle

r

B ‹*persona*› to retrain
■ **reciclarse** *v pron* «*persona*» to retrain
recién *adv*
A (con participio): **el ~ iniciado curso escolar** the school year that has just begun; **pan ~ hecho** freshly baked bread; **está ~ pintado** it's just been painted; **un huevo ~ puesto** a new-laid egg
Compuestos
• **recién casado -da** *m,f* recently married man/woman; **los ~ casados** the newlyweds
• **recién llegado -da** *m,f*: **los ~ ~s** (a población) newcomers; **lo repetiré para los ~ ~s** I'll go over it again for the benefit of the latecomers
• **recién nacido -da** *m,f* newborn baby
B (AmL) 1 (hace poco tiempo) just; **~ llegaron** they have just arrived 2 (sólo ahora) only just; **¿~ te enteras?** you mean you've only just found out? 3 (sólo) only; **¿~ vas por la página 20?** are you only on page 20?; **~ el lunes iré** the first day I'll be able to go is Monday
reciente *adj* recent; **en fecha ~** recently; **esos hechos están todavía ~s** those events are still fresh in people's minds
recinto *m*: **el público abandonó el ~** the public left the premises/building; **~ ferial** (de muestras) showground, exhibition site; (de atracciones) fairground; **el ~ diplomático** the grounds of the embassy; **el ~ donde los enterraban** the enclosure where they were buried
recio[1] -cia *adj* ‹*hombre/aspecto*› robust, sturdy; ‹*lucha*› hard, tough; **en lo más ~ del combate** at the height of the battle
recio[2] *adv* ‹*hablar*› loudly; ‹*llover*› hard
recipiente *m*
A (utensilio) container, receptacle (frml)
B **recipiente** *mf* (persona) recipient
reciprocar [A2] *vi* (AmL) to reciprocate
■ **reciprocar** *vt* (AmL) to return
recíproco -ca *adj* reciprocal; **un sentimiento ~** a mutual feeling
recital *m* (Mús) recital; (de poesía) reading, recital
recitar [A1] *vt* to recite
reclamación *f* 1 (petición, demanda) claim; **una ~ judicial** a legal claim 2 (queja) complaint; **hacer una ~** to lodge *o* make a complaint
reclamar [A1] *vt* 1 «*persona*» ‹*derecho/indemnización*› to claim; (con insistencia) to demand; **reclamó su parte** he claimed his share; **reclaman el derecho al voto** they demand the right to vote 2 «*situación/problema*» to require, demand
■ **reclamar** *vi* to complain; **reclamó ante los tribunales** she took the matter to court; **reclamé contra la multa** I appealed against the fine
réclame, reclame *m* (AmL) commercial, advertisement; **~ publicitario** advertising
reclamo *m*
A 1 (de pájaro) call 2 (para cazar — silbato) birdcall; (— señuelo) lure, decoy
B (esp AmL) (para atraer la atención, provocar interés) lure
C (AmL) (queja) complaint
reclinable *adj* reclining (*before n*)
reclinar [A1] *vt* to rest, lean
■ **reclinarse** *v pron*: **reclínate un poco** lean *o* lie back a little; **reclinado contra la pared** leaning against the wall
recluir [I20] *vt* (en prisión) to imprison; (en hospital psiquiátrico), to intern (frml)
■ **recluirse** *v pron* to shut oneself away; **desde la muerte de su mujer se ha recluido** since the death of his wife he has been a recluse/lived as a recluse; **se recluía en su cuarto para escribir** she would shut herself away in her room to write
reclusión *f* imprisonment
Compuesto **reclusión perpetua** life imprisonment
recluso[1] -sa *adj*: **la población reclusa** the prison population
recluso[2] -sa *m,f* prisoner, inmate
recluta *mf* (Mil) recruit; (en servicio militar) conscript, recruit
reclutamiento *m* recruitment, recruiting
reclutar [A1] *vt* to recruit

recobrar [A1] *vt* 1 ‹*confianza*› to regain; ‹*salud/vista*› to recover; **~ el conocimiento** *or* **el sentido** to come to *o* round, to regain consciousness; **~ las fuerzas** to recover one's strength; **la ciudad recobró la normalidad** the city returned to normal 2 ‹*dinero/botín/joyas*› to recover, retrieve 3 ‹*ciudad/plaza fuerte*› to recapture
■ **recobrarse** *v pron* **~se DE algo** ‹*de enfermedad/susto*› to recover FROM sth, get over sth; ‹*de pérdidas económicas*› to recoup sth
recocido -da *adj* overcooked, overdone
recodo *m* bend; **un ~ del camino** a bend in the road
recogedor *m* dustpan
recogepelotas *mf* (*pl* ~) (*m*) ball boy; (*f*) ball girl
recoger [E6] *vt*
A 1 (levantar) to pick up; **lo recogió del suelo** she picked it up off the floor; **recogí el agua con un trapo** I mopped the water up; **recoge estos vidrios** clear up this broken glass 2 ‹*casa/habitación*› to straighten (up) (AmE), to tidy (up) (BrE); **~ la mesa** to clear the table
B 1 ‹*dinero/firmas*› to collect 2 ‹*deberes/cuadernos*› to collect, take in; **~ la ropa del tendedero** to bring the washing in 3 ‹*trigo/maíz*› to harvest, gather in; ‹*fruta*› to pick; ‹*flores/hongos*› to pick, gather; **no llegó a ~ el fruto de su trabajo** he was unable to reap the fruits of his labor 4 ‹*tienda de campaña/vela*› to take down 5 ‹*pelo*›: **le recogió el pelo en una cola** he put her hair into a ponytail
C (recibir y retener) ‹*agua/polvo*› to collect
D (ir a buscar) ‹*persona*› to pick up, fetch, collect; ‹*paquete*› to collect, pick up; ‹*basura*› to collect; **el autobús pasará a ~nos a las ocho** the bus will come by to collect us *o* pick us up at eight; **¿puedes ~ el traje de la tintorería?** can you fetch *o* pick up the suit from the dry-cleaners?; **fui a ~ mis cosas** I went to get *o* to pick up my things
E ‹*huérfano/gatito*› to take in
F «*foto*» ‹*instantánea/momento*› to capture; «*novela*» ‹*ambiente/contexto social*› to depict; **el informe no recoge estas estadísticas** these statistics do not figure *o* appear in the report; **el espectáculo recoge tres de sus obras breves** the show brings together three of his short works
■ **recoger** *vi* (guardar) to clear up, to straighten up (AmE)
■ **recogerse** *v pron*
A (volver a casa) to go home; (ir a la cama) to go to bed, retire; (para meditar, rezar) to withdraw
B ‹*pelo*› to tie up; **~se el pelo en un moño** to put one's hair up in a bun
recogida *f* 1 (de basura, correo) collection 2 (Agr) harvest 3 (Col) (Mil) retreat
Compuesto **recogida de beneficios** profit taking
recogido -da *adj* ‹*vida*› quiet; ‹*lugar*› secluded
recogimiento *m* (meditación) withdrawal; (devoción) devotion; **una vida de ~** a secluded life
recolección *f* 1 (Agr) (acción) harvest; (temporada) harvest, harvest-time 2 (de fondos, dinero) collection
recolectar [A1] *vt* 1 ‹*trigo*› to harvest, gather in; ‹*fruta*› to pick, harvest 2 ‹*dinero*› to collect
recolector -tora *m,f* (de cereales) harvester; (de fruta) picker
recoleto -ta *adj* ‹*ambiente*› peaceful; ‹*playa*› secluded
recomendable *adj*: **es un lugar muy poco ~** it's not a place I'd recommend; **libros no ~s para niños** books not suitable for children; **es ~ reservar** it is advisable to book (in advance)
recomendación *f* 1 (consejo): **lo hizo por ~ mía** he did it on my recommendation *o* advice; **ignoró mis recomendaciones** she ignored my advice 2 (para empleo) reference, recommendation
recomendado -da *adj*
A ‹*método/producto*› recommended; **viene ~ por ...** he's been recommended by ...; ⓢ **no recomendada para menores de 15 años** not suitable for under-15s
B (Col, Ur) ‹*carta*› registered
recomendar [A5] *vt* 1 ‹*libro/restaurante*› to recommend 2 (para empleo) to recommend, put forward 3 (aconsejar) to advise; **no te lo recomiendo** I wouldn't advise it

recomienda, recomiendas, etc *see* **recomendar**

recompensa *f* reward; **le dieron 200 dólares de ~** he was given a 200-dollar reward

recompensar [A1] *vt* to reward

reconcentrar [A1] *vt* **1** ‹*solución*› to concentrate, make … more concentrated **2** ‹*ejército/tropas*› to concentrate **3** ‹*interés/cariño*› **~ algo EN algn/algo** to focus *o* concentrate sth ON sb/sth

reconciliación *f* reconciliation

reconciliar [A1] *vt* to reconcile

■ **reconciliarse** *v pron*

A **1** **~se CON algn** to make (it) up WITH sb **2** **~se CON algo** ‹*con idea/postura*› to reconcile oneself TO sth

B (*recípr*) «*amigos/novios*» to be reconciled (frml), to make (it) up

recóndito -ta *adj* ‹*lugar/rincón*› remote; **en lo más ~ de su corazón** in the very depths of her heart (liter)

reconfortante *adj* ‹*palabras/pensamientos*› comforting; ‹*baño*› relaxing

reconfortar [A1] *vt* to comfort; **esta sopa te ~á** this soup will make you feel better

reconocer [E3] *vt*

A **1** ‹*hecho/error*› to admit; **hay que ~ que...** you can't deny that …, you have to admit that …; **reconoció que existían diferencias** he acknowledged that there were differences **2** ‹*hijo/gobierno/derecho*› to recognize; **los derechos que te reconoce la ley** the rights which are yours by law

B (identificar) ‹*persona/letra/voz*› to recognize; **no te había reconocido** I didn't recognize you

C **1** ‹*paciente/enfermo*› to examine **2** ‹*terreno*› to reconnoiter*

■ **reconocerse** *v pron* (confesarse) (+ *compl*): **se reconoció culpable** he admitted that he was guilty

reconocido -da *adj* (frml) indebted (frml), obliged (frml); **le estoy** *or* **quedo muy ~** I am very much obliged to you

reconocimiento *m*

A **1** (Med) *tb* **~ médico** medical (examination) **2** (de territorio) reconnaissance

B (frml) **1** (aprobación) recognition; **en ~ por** *or* **a algo** in recognition of sth; **nunca obtuvo el ~ que merecía** he never received the recognition *o* acknowledgment he deserved; **quiero manifestar mi ~ por ...** I should like to show my appreciation for … **2** (de hecho) recognition

C (legitimación) recognition

reconquista *f* **1** (de territorio) reconquest **2** **la R~** the Reconquest

> **Reconquista**
>
> The period in Spain's history during which the Christian kingdoms slowly recovered the territories occupied by the Moslem Moors of North Africa. The Moorish invasion of the Iberian peninsula began in 711 AD and was halted at the Battle of Covadonga in Asturias, in 718. The expulsion of the last Moorish ruler of the kingdom of Granada in 1492 completed the Reconquest. The intervening 781 years saw periods of conflict and coexistence between Moors and Christians. Alliances of Moorish and Christian kingdoms against mutual enemies were not unknown

reconquistar [A1] *vt* ‹*territorio*› to reconquer, regain; ‹*cariño/afecto*› to win back

reconsiderar [A1] *vt* to reconsider

reconstituir [I20] *vt* **1** ‹*alimentos*› to reconstitute **2** ‹*escena*› to reconstruct

■ **reconstituirse** *v pron* «*tejidos*» to regenerate

reconstituyente *m* tonic, restorative

reconstrucción *f* (de edificio, ciudad) reconstruction, rebuilding; (de suceso) reconstruction

reconstruir [I20] *vt* ‹*edificio/ciudad*› to reconstruct, rebuild; ‹*suceso/hechos*› to reconstruct

reconvenir [I31] *vt* ‹*persona*› to chide, scold

reconversión *f* (reestructuración) restructuring, rationalization; (de trabajador) *tb* **~ profesional** retraining

(Compuesto) **reconversión industrial** restructuring *o* rationalization of industry

reconvertir [I11] *vt* ‹*industria*› to rationalize, restructure; ‹*profesional*› to retrain

recopilación *f* compilation, collection

recopilador -dora *m,f* compiler

recopilar [A1] *vt* to compile, gather together

récord[1], record *adj inv* record (*before n*); **en un tiempo ~** in record time

récord[2], record *m* (*pl* **-cords**) record; **batir un ~** to break a record; **posee el ~ mundial en jabalina** she holds the world javelin record

recordar [A10] *vt*

A **1** ‹*nombre/fecha*› to remember, recall; **soy muy malo para ~ fechas** I'm very bad at remembering dates; **recuerdo que lo puse ahí** I remember *o* recall putting it there **2** (rememorar) to remember; **~ viejos tiempos** to remember old times; **recuerdo esa época con cariño** I have fond memories of that time

B **1** (traer a la memoria) **~le A algn/algo QUE + SUBJ** to remind sb ABOUT sth/to + INF; **recuérdale lo de la cena/que los llame** remind him about the supper/to call them about the supper; **les recuerdo que ...** I would like to remind you that … **2** (por asociación, parecido) to remind; **su forma recuerda la de una calabaza** its shape reminds one of a pumpkin; **estos versos recuerdan a Neruda** these verses are reminiscent of Neruda; (+ *me/te/le etc*) **esto me recuerda que ...** this reminds me that …; **me recuerdas a tu hermano** you remind me of your brother

■ **recordar** *vi* (acordarse) to remember; **que yo recuerde ...** as far as I remember …; **si mal no recuerdo** if I remember right

■ **recordarse** *v pron* (Chi) (acordarse) to remember; **~se DE algo/algn** to remember sth/sb

recordatorio *m* (aviso) reminder; (de comunión, fallecimiento) card (*given as a memento of a first communion, etc*)

recorderis *m* (Col fam): **dame un ~ cuando sean las cinco** give me a shout *o* let me know when it's five o'clock

recorrer [E1] *vt* **1** ‹*país/ciudad*›: **recorrí toda España** I traveled *o* went all over Spain; **~ mundo** to travel all around the world; **recorrimos toda la costa** we went *o* traveled the whole length of the coast; **recorrimos toda la ciudad buscándolo** we scoured the whole city looking for it; **~la** (Chi fam) to live it up (colloq) **2** ‹*distancia/trayecto*› to cover, do **3** (con la mirada): **recorrió la sala con la mirada** he looked around the hall; **recorrí la carta con la vista** I ran my eyes over the letter

■ **recorrerse** *v pron* (*enf*) **1** ‹*ciudad/país*›: **se recorrió toda Europa** she went all over *o* around Europe **2** ‹*distancia/trayecto*› to cover, do

recorrido[1] -da *adj* (Andes fam): **es muy ~** he's been around (colloq); he's seen a thing or two (colloq)

recorrido[2] *m*

A **1** (viaje): **un ~ por Perú** a trip around Peru **2** (trayecto) route; **cubrir el ~** to cover the route

B (del émbolo) stroke; (de proyectil) trajectory; (de balón) path

C (en golf) round; (en esquí) run

recortable[1] *adj* cutout (*before n*)

recortable[2] *m* cutout

recortar [A1] *vt*

A **1** ‹*figura/artículo/anuncio*› to cut out; **la escopeta tenía los cañones recortados** the barrels of the shotgun had been sawed off (AmE) *o* (BrE) sawn off **2** ‹*pelo/puntas*› to trim

B ‹*gastos/plantilla*› to reduce

C (Méx fam) (criticar) to tear into (colloq), to pull … apart (colloq)

■ **recortarse** *v pron* (liter) «*perfil/figura*» **~se SOBRE algo** to be outlined *o* silhouetted AGAINST sth

recorte *m*

A (de periódico, revista) cutting, clipping

B (Fin) (acción) cutting; (efecto) cut, reduction; **~s presupuestarios** budget cuts

recostar [A10] *vt* (apoyar) to lean; **recostó la cabeza en la almohada** he laid his head back on the pillow

■ **recostarse** *v pron* **1** (acostarse) to lie down; **recuéstate en el almohadón** lie back on the pillow **2** (apoyarse) to lean; **recostados en el escritorio** leaning on the desk; **estaba recostado en un sillón** he was sitting back in an armchair

recoveco *m*: **un camino lleno de ~s** a road full of twists and turns; **en todos los ~s de la casa** in every nook and cranny of the house; **esta ley tiene muchos ~s** this law has lots of ins and outs

recrear [A1] *vt* to recreate

■ **recrearse** *v pron*: **se recreaba viéndolos jugar** she took pleasure in *o* she enjoyed watching them play

recreativo -va *adj* recreational

recreo *m* [1] (diversión): **nos servía de ~** it served as entertainment; **barco/viaje de ~** pleasure boat/trip; **en mis horas de ~** in my leisure time [2] (en el colegio) recess (AmE), break (BrE)

recriminación *f* recrimination, reproach

recriminar [A1] *vt* to reproach

recrudecerse [E3] *v pron* to intensify

recrudecimiento *m*: **se produjo un ~ de los combates** fighting intensified

recta *f* (Mat) straight line; (Dep) straight

(Compuesto) **recta final** (Dep) home stretch

rectal *adj* rectal

rectangular *adj* rectangular

rectángulo *m* rectangle

rectificación *f*

A (de información, error) correction, rectification (frml)

B (de carretera) straightening

rectificar [A2] *vt*

A ‹*persona*› to correct; ‹*información/error*› to correct, rectify (frml)

B ‹*carretera/trazado*› to straighten

■ **rectificar** *vi* (corregirse) to correct oneself

rectilíneo -nea *adj* rectilinear

rectitud *f* rectitude (frml), honesty

recto[1] -ta *adj* [1] ‹*línea/nariz/falda*› straight [2] (honrado) honest, upright

recto[2] *m*

A (Anat) rectum

B (Impr) right-hand page, recto (tech)

C (en boxeo): **un ~ de izquierda** a straight left

recto[3] *adv* straight; **todo ~** straight on

rector[1] -tora *adj* ‹*idea/principio*› guiding (*before n*); ‹*órgano*› governing (*before n*)

rector[2] -tora *m,f* (de universidad) rector (AmE), vice-chancellor (BrE)

rectorado *m* (cargo) rectorship (AmE), vice-chancellorship (BrE); (oficina) rector's (AmE) *o* (BrE) vice-chancellor's office

recua *f* (de caballerías) train; **una ~ de chiquillos** a string *o* drove of kids (colloq)

recuadro *m* box

recubrir [I33] *vt* **~ algo DE** *or* **CON algo** to cover sth WITH sth; **una pared recubierta de azulejos** a tiled wall

recuento *m* (de votos) recount; **al hacer ~ de la jornada ...** looking back at the day's events ...

recuerdo *m*

A [1] (reminiscencia) memory; **guardo un grato ~ de la infancia** I have fond childhood memories [2] (souvenir) souvenir; (regalo) memento, keepsake; **me dio una cajita de ~** she gave me a little box as a memento; **es un ~ de familia** it's a family heirloom

B **recuerdos** *mpl* regards (*pl*), best wishes (*pl*); **dale ~s** give him my regards

recular [A1] *vi*

A ‹‹*vehículo*›› to reverse, back up; ‹‹*animal*›› to move backward(s); ‹‹*persona*›› to move back

B (ante tarea, reto) to back out, withdraw

recuperación *f*

A (de enfermo, economía) recovery

B [1] (de dinero, botín) recovery, recouping [2] (de la vista) recovery

C (Esp) (Educ) *tb* **examen de ~** retake, makeup (exam) (AmE)

recuperar [A1] *vt* [1] ‹*dinero/joyas/botín*› to recover, get back; ‹*pérdidas*› to recoup [2] ‹*vista*› to recover; **~ la salud** to get better, recover; **~ fuerzas** to get one's strength back; **~ la confianza en sí mismo** to regain *o* recover one's self-confidence [3] (compensar): **~ el tiempo perdido** to make up for lost time; **tuve que ~ los días que estuve enfermo** I had to make up (for) the days I was off sick [4] ‹*examen/asignatura*› to retake, make up (AmE)

■ **recuperarse** *v pron* **~se DE algo** ‹*de enfermedad*› to recover FROM sth, recuperate FROM sth (frml); ‹*de sorpresa/desgracia*› to get over sth, recover FROM sth

recurrente *adj* [1] (Med) recurring [2] ‹*idea/tema*› recurrent

recurrir [I1] *vi*

A (frente a problema) **~ A algn** to turn TO sb; **~ A algo** to resort TO sth, have recourse TO sth (frml); **~ a la fuerza** to resort to force

B (Der) **~ CONTRA algo** to appeal AGAINST sth

■ **recurrir** *vt* to appeal against

recursivo *adj* (Col) resourceful

recurso *m*

A (medio): **agoté todos los ~s** I exhausted all the options; **como último ~** as a last resort; **un hombre de ~s** a resourceful man

B **recursos** *mpl* (medios económicos — de país) resources (*pl*); (— de persona) means (*pl*); **una familia sin ~s** a family with no means of support

(Compuestos)

- **recursos económicos** *mpl* economic *o* financial resources (*pl*)
- **recursos humanos** *mpl* human resources (*pl*)
- **recursos naturales** *mpl* natural resources (*pl*)

C (Inf) facility, resource

D (Der) appeal; **presentar** *or* **interponer un ~** to lodge an appeal

recusar [A1] *vt* [1] ‹*juez/jurado*› to challenge [2] (rechazar) to reject

red *f*

A [1] (para pescar) net; ***caer en las ~es de algn*** to fall into sb's clutches [2] (Dep) net [3] (para pelo) hairnet [4] (en tren) (luggage) rack

B (de comunicaciones, emisoras, transportes) network; (de comercios, empresas) chain, network; (de espionaje, contrabando) ring; **~ hotelera** hotel chain

C (de electricidad) power supply, mains; (de gas) mains; **antes de conectarlo a la ~** before connecting it to the house current (AmE) *o* (BrE) to the mains

D **la Red** (Inf) the Net

redacción *f*

A [1] (de carta) writing; (de borrador) drafting; (de tratado) drawing-up, drafting [2] (lenguaje, estilo) wording, phrasing

B (Educ) composition, essay

C (Period) [1] (acción) writing [2] (equipo) editorial staff *o* team [3] (oficina) editorial department *o* office

redactar [A1] *vt* ‹*informe/artículo/composición*› to write; ‹*acuerdo/tratado*› to draw up; **una carta bien/mal redactada** a well-written/badly-written letter

■ **redactar** *vi*: **redacta muy bien** she writes very well

redactor -tora *m,f* editor; **~ político/deportivo** political/sports editor; **~ jefe** editor in chief

redada *f* [1] (de policía) raid; **efectuar una ~** to carry out a raid [2] (en pesca) haul, catch

redaños *mpl* (fam) (valor) guts (*pl*) (colloq)

redecilla *f* (para pelo) hairnet

rededor (ant): **en ~** (*loc adv*) around

redención *f* redemption

redentor[1] -tora *adj* redeeming

redentor[2] -tora *m,f* redeemer; **el R~** (Relig) The Redeemer *o* Savior*; ***meterse a ~*** (fam) to poke one's nose in (colloq)

redescubrir [I33] *vt* to rediscover

redicho -cha *adj* (fam): **es muy ~** he has a very affected way of speaking

redil *m* fold, enclosure; ***volver al ~*** to return to the fold

redimir [I1] *vt*

A [1] (Relig) to redeem [2] ‹*cautivos*› to redeem (frml), to ransom; ‹*esclavos*› to redeem [3] **~ a algn DE algo** ‹*de esclavitud/ignorancia*› to redeem *o* deliver sb FROM sth (frml); **no lo redime de responsabilidad** it does not absolve him from responsibility

B ‹*hipoteca*› to repay, redeem (frml); ‹*joya*› to redeem

rédito *m* return, yield

redoblado -da *adj* ‹*esfuerzo/entusiasmo*› redoubled

redoblar [A1] *vt* (aumentar) ‹*esfuerzos/críticas*› to redouble; ‹*vigilancia*› to step up, tighten
■ **redoblar** *vi* «*tambor*» to roll

redoble *m* drumroll

redoma *f*
A (recipiente) flask
B (Ven) (Auto) traffic circle (AmE), roundabout (BrE)

redomado -da *adj* utter, out-and-out

redonda *f*
A (Impr) Roman character
B (Mús) semibreve
C **a la redonda**: **en diez metros a la ~** within a ten meter radius; **se oyó a varios kilómetros a la ~** it could be heard for miles around

redondeado -da *adj* rounded

redondear [A1] *vt*
A (dar forma curva) to round (off)
B ‹*cifra/número*› to round off; (por lo alto) to round up; (por lo bajo) to round down
■ **redondear** *vi* (hablando de números): **digamos 200, para ~** let's make it a round 200

redondel *m*
A (figura circular) ring
B (Taur) bullring

redondela *f* (Andes) ▸**redondel A**

redondez *f* [1] (de superficie, formas) roundness [2] (de persona) (euf *o* hum) rotundity (euph *or* hum)

redondo -da *adj*
A ‹*cara/espejo*› round; ***caer(se)* ~** to keel over; **cayó ~ en la cama** he collapsed *o* slumped onto the bed; ***en* ~**: **girar en ~** to turn (right) around; **negarse en ~** to flatly *o* roundly refuse
B ‹*cifra/número*› round; **en números ~** in round figures
C (perfecto): **fue un negocio ~** it was a great *o* excellent deal; **nos salió todo ~** everything turned out perfectly for us
D (Méx) ‹*boleto/pasaje*› return (*before n*), round-trip (*before n*) (AmE)

reducción *f*
A [1] (disminución) reduction; **la ~ del precio del pan** the reduction in *o* lowering of the price of bread; **~ de impuestos** tax cuts, reduction in taxes; **se solicitó la ~ de la pena** they asked for the sentence to be commuted *o* reduced [2] (Fot) reduction
B (Mat, Quím, Med) reduction
C (Chi) (de indígenas) reservation

reducido -da *adj* ‹*espacio*› limited; ‹*tamaño*› small; **a precios ~s** at reduced prices; **un número ~ de personas** a small number of people; **un presupuesto muy ~** a very limited budget; **trabaja jornada reducida** she is on short-time (working)

reducidor -dora *m,f*
A (AmS) (de objetos robados) receiver, fence (colloq)
B (de cabezas) headshrinker

reducir [I6] *vt*
A [1] ‹*gastos/costos*› to cut, reduce; ‹*velocidad/producción/consumo*› to reduce; **~ al mínimo los riesgos** to minimize *o* to reduce the risks to a minimum; **debería ~ el consumo de sal** you should cut down on salt; **le redujeron la pena** they shortened *o* reduced his sentence; **~ algo A algo** to reduce sth TO sth; **la población quedó reducida a la mitad** the population was halved; **~ algo a su mínima expresión** (Mat) to reduce sth to its simplest form; **~ algo EN algo** to reduce sth BY sth; **~ el gasto en cinco millones** to reduce costs by five million [2] ‹*fotocopia/fotografía*› to reduce
B [1] (transformar) **~ algo A algo**: **~ los gramos a milígramos** to convert the grams to milligrams; **quedaron reducidos a cenizas** they were reduced to ashes; **mis ilusiones quedaron reducidas a la nada** my dreams came to nothing [2] (Quím) to reduce [3] (AmS) ‹*objeto robado*› to receive, fence (colloq)
C (dominar) ‹*enemigo/rebeldes*› to subdue; ‹*ladrón*› to overpower; **~ a un pueblo a la esclavitud** to reduce a people to slavery
D ‹*fractura/hernia*› to set, reduce (tech)
■ **reducir** *vi*
A (Coc) to reduce, boil down
B (Auto) to shift into a lower gear
■ **reducirse** *v pron* **~se A algo**: **todo se reduce a tener tacto** it all comes down to being tactful; **todo se redujo a un paseo por el río** in the end it was just a walk by the river

reducto *m* redoubt

redundancia *f* (Ling) tautology, redundancy; **valga la ~** if you'll forgive the repetition

redundante *adj* (superfluo) superfluous, redundant; (Ling) tautologous, redundant

redundar [A1] *vi* **~ EN algo**: **esto ~á en beneficio del consumidor** this will benefit *o* will be of advantage to the consumer; **~á en sus posibilidades de trabajo** it will have a bearing on his job prospects

reduplicar [A2] *vt* [1] (repetir) to reduplicate [2] ‹*esfuerzos*› to redouble

reedición *f* reissue, reprint

reedificar [A2] *vt* to rebuild

reeditar [A1] *vt* to reprint, reissue

reelección *f* reelection

reelegir [I8] *vt* to reelect

reembolsable *adj* refundable

reembolsar [A1] *vt* ‹*gastos*› to refund, reimburse (frml); ‹*depósito*› to refund; ‹*préstamo*› to repay

reembolso *m* (de gastos) refund, reimbursement (frml); (de depósito) refund; (de préstamo) repayment; **contra ~** cash on delivery, COD

reemplazar [A4] *vt*
A ‹*persona*› (durante período limitado) to substitute for, stand in for; (durante más tiempo) to replace; **~ a algn POR *or* CON algn** to replace sb WITH *o* BY sb
B ‹*aparato/pieza*› to replace; **nada puede ~ a la seda natural** there is no substitute for real silk; **~ algo POR *or* CON algo** to replace sth WITH sth; **la miel puede ~ al azúcar** honey can be used as a subtitute for sugar

reemplazo *m*
A (acción): **el ~ del secretario es inminente** the secretary is to be replaced in the very near future; **entró en ~ del jugador lesionado** he came on as a substitute for the injured player
B (persona) replacement, substitute; (Teatr) understudy
C (Esp) (quinta) draft (*annual intake of recruits*)

reemprender [E1] *vt* (liter): **reemprendió el camino/la marcha** he took to the road again, he set out again

reencarnación *f* reincarnation

reencarnarse [A1] *v pron* to be reincarnated; **~ EN algn/algo** to be reincarnated AS sb/sth

reencauchar [A1] *vt* (AmC, Col, Ven) ▸**recauchar**

reencontrarse [A10] *v pron* to meet again

reencuentro *m* reunion

reengancharse [A1] *v pron* (Esp fam) (Mil) to reenlist

reestrenar [A1] *vt* ‹*película*› to rerelease, show again; ‹*obra teatral*› to put … on again

reestreno *m* (de película) rerelease; (de obra teatral) revival

reestructuración *f* restructuring, reorganization

reestructurar [A1] *vt* to restructure

refacción *f*
A (AmS) (para ampliar, mejorar) refurbishment; Ⓢ **cerrado por refacciones** closed for alterations *o* for refurbishment
B (Méx) (pieza de repuesto) spare part; **llanta de ~** spare tire

refaccionar [A1] *vt* (AmS) to refurbish

refaccionaria *f* (Méx) (tienda) auto spares store; (taller) garage

refajo *m*
A (ant) (Indum) underskirt
B (Col) (bebida) shandy

refectorio *m* refectory

referencia *f*
A [1] (alusión) reference; **hacer ~ a algo** to refer to *o* mention sth [2] (relación) reference; **punto de ~** point of reference; **con ~ a …** with reference to … [3] (en texto) reference; **número de ~** reference number
B (recomendación) reference

referéndum (*pl* **-dums**), **referendo** *m* referendum; **someter algo a ~** to hold a referendum on sth

referente *adj*: **las noticias ~s al golpe de estado** the news about the coup d'état; **en lo ~ a …** regarding …

réferi, referí *mf* (AmL) referee

r

referir [I11] *vt*
A (liter) (relatar) to tell; **nos refirió sus experiencias** he told us of his experiences
B (remitir) ~ **a algn A algo** to refer sb TO sth
C (situar) ~ **algo A algo** to set sth IN sth; **refiere el suceso al siglo pasado** she sets the action in the last century
■ **referirse** *v pron* 1 (aludir) ~**se A algo/algn** to refer TO sth/sb; **no me refería a ti** I wasn't referring to you; **no se refirió a la nueva ley** he made no reference to the new law 2 (estar relacionado con) ~**se A algo**: **en** *or* **por lo que se refiere a tu pregunta ...** in reference to *o* with regard to your question ..., as far as your question is concerned ...; **las denuncias se refieren al hospital** the complaints refer to *o* concern the hospital

refilón: **de** ~ (*loc adv*) 1 (oblicuamente): **el sol daba de ~ en la casa** the sun shone on the corner of the house; **la bala me tocó de ~** the bullet grazed me; **lo miré de ~** I gave him a sidelong glance 2 (de pasada): **tratamos el tema de ~** we just touched on the topic; **la vi sólo de ~** I just caught a glimpse of her

refinado -da *adj* ‹*persona/modales*› refined; ‹*crueldad*› consummate (frml), extreme; ‹*ironía*› subtle

refinamiento *m* 1 (del petróleo) refining 2 (de modales, costumbres) refinement; (de sistema) refinement

refinar [A1] *vt* 1 ‹*petróleo/azúcar*› to refine 2 ‹*modales/gustos*› to refine; ‹*estilo*› to polish; ‹*sistema*› to refine
■ **refinarse** *v pron* to become more refined

refinería *f* refinery

reflector *m*
A (pantalla reflectante) reflector
B (foco) (Teatr) spotlight; (Dep) floodlight; (Mil) searchlight; (en monumento) floodlight

reflejar [A1] 1 ‹*imagen/luz*› *vt* to reflect; **el espejo reflejaba su imagen** his image was reflected in the mirror 2 (mostrar)‹*ambiente*› to reflect; **en la película quedan reflejados los problemas de la sociedad actual** the problems of contemporary society are reflected in the movie
■ **reflejarse** *v pron* 1 «*imagen*» to be reflected 2 «*emoción/cansancio/duda*» to show

reflejo[1] **-ja** *adj* reflex (*before n*)

reflejo[2] *m*
A 1 (luz reflejada) reflected light; **los ~s del sol sobre su pelo** the reflected rays of the sun on her hair 2 (imagen) reflection; **es el ~ de su papá** (Col fam) he is the living *o* spitting image of his father 3 (de situación, sentimiento, época) reflection 4 **reflejos** *mpl* (en el pelo) highlights (*pl*)
B (Fisiol) reflex; **~s rápidos** fast reflexes; **es lento de ~s** he has slow reflexes

reflexión *f*
A 1 (acción) reflection; **entregado a la ~** deep in thought; **sin ~** without thinking 2 **reflexiones** *fpl* (consideraciones) reflections (*pl*); **después de muchas reflexiones** after much reflection *o* thought; **hizo unas reflexiones sobre ...**he made some observations on ...
B (Fís) reflection

reflexionar [A1] *vi* to reflect (frml); **reflexiona antes de tomar una decisión** reflect on it before you make a decision; **¿has reflexionado bien?** have you thought it over *o* through carefully?; **sin ~** without thinking; ~ **SOBRE algo** to think ABOUT sth, reflect ON sth (frml)

reflexivo -va *adj*
A (Ling, Mat) reflexive
B ‹*persona*› thoughtful, reflective

reflexología *f* reflexology

reflexólogo -ga *m,f* reflexologist

reflotar [A1] *vt* to refloat

reflujo *m* (de marea) ebb (tide)

refocilarse [A1] *v pron* ▸**regodearse A**

reforestación *f* reforestation

reforestar [A1] *vt* to reforest

reforma *f*
A 1 (de ley, institución) reform 2 **la Reforma** (Relig) the Reformation
(Compuesto) **reforma agraria** agrarian reform
B (en edificio, traje) alteration; ⊗ **cerrado por reformas** closed for refurbishment *o* for alterations

reformar [A1] *vt*
A ‹*ley/institución*› to reform, change
B 1 ‹*casa/edificio*› to make alterations *o* improvements to 2 ‹*abrigo/vestido*› to alter
C ‹*delincuente*› to reform
■ **reformarse** *v pron* to mend one's ways

reformatorio *m* reformatory

reformismo *m* reformism

reformista[1] *adj* ‹*espíritu/impulso*› reforming (*before n*); ‹*político/partido*› reformist

reformista[2] *mf* reformist

reforzado -da *adj* reinforced

reforzar [A11] *vt* 1 ‹*puerta/costura*› to reinforce; ‹*guardia*› to increase, strengthen; ‹*relaciones*› to reinforce; **han reforzado las medidas de seguridad** security has been stepped up *o* tightened 2 (Fot) to intensify

refracción *f* refraction

refractario -ria *adj*
A ‹*materiales*› heat-resistant, refractory (tech); ‹*fuente/molde*› ovenproof
B ‹*persona*› ~ **A algo** opposed TO sth

refrán *m* saying, proverb; **como dice** *or* **según reza el ~** as the saying goes

refranero *m* collection of sayings *o* proverbs

refregar [A7] *vt* 1 ‹*puños/cuello*› to scrub 2 (reprochar): **me refregó todo lo que había hecho por mí** she went on about how much she'd done for me (colloq)

refrenar [A1] *vt* ‹*ímpetu/deseo*› to hold back, restrain; ‹*caballo*› to rein in
■ **refrenarse** *v pron* (*refl*) to restrain oneself

refrendar [A1] *vt*
A ‹*documento*› (frml) to countersign; ‹*decisión/declaración*› to endorse
B (Col, Méx) ‹*pasaporte*› to renew

refrescante *adj* refreshing

refrescar [A2] *vt* 1 ‹*bebida*› to cool; ‹*ambiente*› to make ... fresher *o* cooler 2 ‹*conocimientos*› to brush up (on); **te voy a ~ la memoria** let me refresh your memory
■ **refrescar** *v impers* to turn cooler
■ **refrescarse** *v pron* to cool (oneself) down

refresco *m* soft drink, soda (AmE)

refriega *f* (de poca importancia) scuffle; (más grave) clash, brawl; (Mil) clash, skirmish

refrigeración *f* 1 (de alimentos) refrigeration 2 (de motor) cooling; (aire acondicionado) air-conditioning

refrigerador *m* 1 (nevera) refrigerator, fridge 2 (del aire acondicionado) cooling unit

refrigeradora *f* (Col, Per) refrigerator, fridge

refrigerar [A1] *vt* 1 ‹*alimentos/bebidas*› to refrigerate 2 ‹*motor*› to cool; ‹*cine/bar*› to air-condition; ⊗ **local refrigerado** air-conditioned premises

refrigerio *m* (frml) light refreshments (*pl*)

refrito[1] **-ta** *adj* 1 (Coc) refried 2 ‹*obra*› rehashed

refrito[2] *m* (Coc): **un ~ de tomate y cebolla** fried onions and tomato

refuerzo *m*
A 1 (para puerta, pared, costura) reinforcement 2 (de vacuna) booster 3 **refuerzos** *mpl* (Mil) reinforcements (*pl*)
B (Ur) (sandwich) French-bread sandwich

refugiado[1] **-da** *adj* refugee (*before n*)

refugiado[2] **-da** *m,f* refugee

refugiar [A1] *vt* to give ... refuge
■ **refugiarse** *v pron* to take refuge; **se refugió en el trabajo** he took refuge in his work; **siempre se refugia en las mismas excusas** she always hides behind the same excuses; **~se DE algo** ‹*de bombardeo/ataque*› to take refuge FROM sth; ‹*de lluvia/tormenta*› to take shelter from sth

refugio *m* 1 (contra la lluvia, bombardeo) shelter; (en montaña) refuge, shelter 2 (contra perseguidores) refuge; **buscar ~** to seek shelter 3 (en calzada) traffic island
(Compuestos)
• **refugio antiaéreo** air-raid shelter
• **refugio antinuclear** *or* **antiatómico** fallout shelter

refulgencia *f* (liter) refulgence (liter); radiance

refulgente *adj* (liter) ‹*luz*› refulgent (liter), resplendent

refulgir [I7] *vi* (liter) to shine brightly

refundición *f*
A (Metal) recasting
B (Lit, Teatr) (acción) reworking; (obra) adaptation

refundir [I1] *vt*
A (Metal) to recast
B (revisar) to rework; (reunir, unir) to combine
C (Andes fam) (extraviar) to lose, mislay
■ **refundirse** *v pron* (Méx fam) to hole up (colloq), hide away

refunfuñar [A1] *vi* (fam) to grumble, grouch (colloq)

refunfuñón[1] **-ñona** *adj* (fam) grouchy (colloq), grumpy (colloq)

refunfuñón[2] **-ñona** *m,f* (fam) grouch (colloq), grumbler (colloq)

refutar [A1] *vt* to refute

regada *f*
A (fam) (con agua): **le hace falta una ~ al jardín** the garden needs watering
B (Chi, Méx fam) (metida de pata) blunder

regadera *f* 1 (para jardín) watering can; ***estar como una ~*** (Esp fam) to be crazy 2 (Col, Méx, Ven) (de ducha) rose, shower head (AmE); (ducha) shower

regadío *m* (sistema) irrigation; **tierras/cultivos de ~** irrigated land/crops

regalado -da *adj* 1 (dado como regalo): **todo lo que tengo es ~** everything I have has been given to me; **no lo quiero ni ~** I wouldn't want it even if they were giving it away 2 (fam) (muy barato): **precios ~s** giveaway prices (colloq); **esos zapatos están ~s** those shoes are dirt cheap *o* are a steal (colloq) 3 (Chi, Méx, Ven fam) (muy fácil) easy

regalar [A1] *vt* 1 (obsequiar): **¿qué te ~on para tu cumpleaños?** what did you get for your birthday?; **¿por qué no me lo regalas?** why don't you give it to me?; **le ~on un reloj de oro** he was given a gold watch 2 (vender muy barato) to sell … at bargain prices
■ **regalar** *vi*
A (frml) (deleitar, agasajar) **~ a algn CON algo: nos regaló con algunas anécdotas** he regaled *o* entertained us with a few stories; **les regaló los oídos con una sonata** she delighted their ears with a sonata (frml)
B (CS) (vender muy barato) to sell things at bargain prices

regalía *f* 1 (por algún derecho) royalty 2 (de empleado) bonus, perquisite, perk 3 **regalías** *fpl* (de monarca) royal prerogative

regaliz *m* licorice (AmE), liquorice (BrE)

regalo *m* 1 (obsequio) gift, present; **compre dos y llévese otro de ~** buy two and get one free; ***un ~ del cielo*** a godsend 2 (cosa barata) steal (colloq); **es un ~** it's a steal (colloq), it's dirt cheap (colloq) 3 (deleite, festín) treat

regalón[1] **-lona** *adj* (CS fam) spoiled

regalón[2] **-lona** *m,f* (CS fam): **es la regalona de su padre** she's her daddy's pet (colloq); **es un ~** he's a spoiled brat (colloq)

regalonear [A1] *vt* (CS fam) to spoil
■ **regalonear** *vi* (CS fam): **le encanta ~ con su abuela** she loves being made a fuss of by her grandmother

regañada *f* (Col, Per, Ven fam) scolding, telling-off (colloq)

regañadientes: **a ~** (*loc adv*) reluctantly, unwillingly

regañar [A1] *vt* (esp AmL) to scold, to tell … off (colloq)
■ **regañar** *vi* (Esp) (pelearse) to quarrel; **ha regañado con el novio** (ha discutido) she's had an argument with her boyfriend; (ha roto) she's split up *o* broken up with her boyfriend

regañina, (Méx) **regañiza** *f* (fam) scolding, talking-to (colloq), telling-off (colloq)

regaño *m* (AmL fam) scolding, telling-off (colloq)

regañón[1] **-ñona** *adj* (fam) grumpy (colloq)

regañón[2] **-ñona** *m,f* (fam) grumbler (colloq)

regar [A7] *vt*
A 1 ‹*planta/jardín*› to water; ‹*tierra/campo*› to irrigate; ‹*calle*› to hose down 2 «*río*» to water
B 1 (esparcir) ‹*azúcar/café*› to spill; ‹*objetos*› to scatter; **~on los juguetes por todas partes** they scattered the toys everywhere; ***~la*** (Chi, Méx fam) to blow it (colloq) 2 (AmC, Ven) ‹*noticia/versión*› to spread

regata *f*
A (carrera) yacht race; (serie de carreras) regatta
B (arroyo) irrigation channel

regate *m* (Esp) (en fútbol) feint

regatear [A1] *vi* (Com) to bargain, haggle
■ **regatear** *vt*
A (escatimar): **no han regateado esfuerzos para…** no efforts have been spared to…; **no hay que ~ horas en este trabajo** you can't rush *o* hurry this job; **sin ~ medios** whatever it takes
B (Dep) to get past, swerve past

regateo *m*
A (Com) bargaining, haggling
B (Dep) feinting

regazo *m* (liter) lap

regencia *f* (en lugar del soberano) regency

regeneración *f* regeneration

regenerar [A1] *vt* to regenerate
■ **regenerarse** *v pron* 1 (Biol, Tec) to be regenerated 2 «*persona*» to be reformed

regenta *f*
A (esposa del regente) wife of the regent
B (Chi) (de prostíbulo) madam, brothel owner

regentar [A1] *vt* ‹*negocio/hotel*› to run; **el banco que regentaba** the bank he managed *o* ran

regente *mf* regent

regicida *mf* regicide

regicidio *m* regicide

regidor *m* (Teatr) stage manager; (Hist) alderman

régimen *m*
A (dieta) diet; **estar a** *o* **hacer ~** to be on a diet; **el médico lo puso a ~** the doctor put him on a diet; **ponerse a ~** to go on a diet
B 1 (reglamento): **presos sometidos a ~ de alta seguridad** prisoners held under a high-security regime; **cárcel en ~ abierto** open prison; **alumnos en ~ de internado** boarding pupils; **en ~ de media pensión** half board 2 (de lluvias, vientos) pattern, regime (tech)
(Compuesto) **régimen de vida** lifestyle
C (Pol) regime

regimiento *m* 1 (Mil) regiment 2 (fam) (grupo, multitud) crowd (colloq)

regio -gia *adj*
A (majestuoso) regal
B (Col, CS fam) (estupendo) great (colloq); **te queda ~** it looks fantastic on you (colloq); **¿a las ocho? —¡~!** is eight o'clock OK? — great *o* fine!; **me viene ~** it suits me fine

región *f*
A 1 (Geog) region; **una ~ montañosa** a mountainous region *o* area; **la ~ andina** the Andean region 2 (Adm) region, district
B (Anat) region, area

regional *adj* regional

regionalismo *m* regionalism

regir [I8] *vt* 1 (gobernar) to govern 2 «*ley/disposición*» to govern; **los factores que rigen la economía** the factors governing *o* which control the economy 3 (Ling) to take
■ **regir** *vi* «*ley/disposición*» to be in force, be valid; **ese horario ya no rige** that timetable is no longer valid
■ **regirse** *v pron* **~se POR algo** «*sociedad*» to be governed BY sth; «*economía/mercado*» to be controlled BY sth *o* subject TO sth

registrar [A1] *vt*
A 1 ‹*nacimiento/defunción/patente*› to register 2 ‹*sonido*› to record 3 (marcar) ‹*temperatura*› to record; ‹*temblor*› to register; **países que registran una alta tasa de inflación** countries which have *o* register a high rate of inflation
B ‹*equipaje/lugar/persona*› to search; **los ~on** they were searched; **¡a mí que me registren!** (fam) don't look at me! (colloq); **¿quién ha estado registrando mis cajones?** (fam) who's been going through my drawers?
C (Méx) ‹*carta*› to register
■ **registrarse** *v pron*
A (apreciarse): **se ~on temperaturas de hasta 40 grados** temperatures of up to 40 degrees were recorded; **se registró un descenso en las temperaturas** temperatures dropped slightly
B (haber): **no se ~on incidentes de importancia** there

r

were no serious incidents; **no se ~on víctimas mortales** there were no fatalities

C (inscribirse) to register; (en hotel) to register, check in

registro *m*

A (libro) register; (acción de anotar) registration; (cosa anotada) record, entry

(Compuestos)

- **registro civil** (libro) register of births, marriages and deaths; (oficina) registry, registry office (BrE)
- **registro de la propiedad** (libro) land register; (oficina) land registration office, land registry (BrE)
- **registro de patentes y marcas** patent office

B (por la policía) search; **orden de ~** search warrant

(Compuesto) **registro domiciliario** search (*of a house*); **efectuar un ~ ~** to carry out a search (*of a house*)

C (de reloj) regulator

D (Mús) **1▸** (de voz, instrumento) range **2▸** (pieza — de órgano) register, stop; (— de piano, clavicordio) pedal **3▸** (tono) register

E (Ling) register

F (Tec) (abertura) inspection hatch; (de agua) (Col) stopcock, shutoff valve (AmE)

regla *f*

A (utensilio) ruler

(Compuestos)

- **regla de cálculo**; slide rule
- **regla T** T square

B (norma) rule; **todo está en ~** everything is in order; **por ~ general** as a (general) rule

(Compuestos)

- **regla de oro** golden rule
- **regla de tres** (Mat) rule of three; **por esa ~ de ~ no trabajaría nadie** if we all followed that logic nobody would work
- **reglas del juego** *fpl* rules of the game (*pl*)

C (menstruación) period; **tengo la ~** I have my period

reglamentación *f* (reglas, normativa) regulations (*pl*), rules (*pl*); (acción) regulation

reglamentar [A1] *vt* to regulate

reglamentario -ria *adj* ‹*horario*› set (*before n*); ‹*uniforme/arma*› regulation (*before n*); **trabajar las horas reglamentarias** to work the set number of hours

reglamento *m* rules (*pl*), regulations (*pl*); **atenerse al ~** to abide by *o* obey the rules

(Compuesto) **reglamento de tráfico** *or* **del tránsito** traffic regulations (*pl*), highway code (BrE)

regleta *f* interlinear space, leading

reglón *m* (Chi) ▸**renglón**

regocijar [A1] *vt* to delight, fill … with joy

▪ **regocijarse** *v pron* to rejoice; **~ DE** *or* **POR algo** (por buena noticia) to rejoice AT sth; (por mal ajeno) to take delight IN sth, delight IN sth

regocijo *m* **1▸** (júbilo, alborozo) rejoicing; (alegría) delight; **sintió gran ~ al verla** he was delighted to see her **2▸** (ante el mal ajeno) pleasure; **sintió cierto ~ al verlo sufrir** she took a certain delight in seeing him suffer

regodearse [A1] *v pron*

A (complacerse) to delight in, take great delight in; **~ EN** *or* **CON algo** to delight IN sth, gloat OVER sth

B (Chi) (al elegir) to hesitate; ***haber para ~*** (Chi): **hay comida para ~** there's plenty of food

regodeo *m* (alegría) delight; (acción) gloating

regordete -ta *adj* (fam) chubby

regresar [A1] *vi* to return, come/go back; **no sé cuándo va a ~** I don't know when he'll be back

▪ **regresar** *vt* (AmL exc CS) **1▸** ‹*libro/llaves*› to return, give back; **se olvidó de ~me el cambio** she forgot to give me my change; **me ~on la carta** the letter was sent back *o* returned to me **2▸** ‹*persona*› to send …back

▪ **regresarse** *v pron* (AmL exc RPl) to return, go/come back; **ya se regresó** she's back now

regresión *f* **1▸** (retorno) return, regression **2▸** (retroceso, disminución): **una especie en ~** a species in decline; **~ económica** economic recession; **una ~ en la producción** a drop in production **3▸** (Mat) regression

regresivo -va *adj* regressive

regreso *m*

A (vuelta) return; **emprendió el ~** she set off on the return journey *o* trip; **de ~ paramos en León** on the way back we stopped in León

B **1▸** (en fútbol americano) return; **~ de patada** kickoff return **2▸** (AmL) (devolución) return

reguero *m*

A (rastro) trail; ***correr*** *or* ***difundirse como un ~ de pólvora*** to spread like wildfire

B (Agr) irrigation channel

regulable *adj* adjustable

regulación *f* (de máquina, pieza) adjustment; (de flujo, temperatura) regulation, control; (mediante normas) regulation

regulador¹ -dora *adj* **1▸** ‹*válvula/sistema*› regulating (*before n*), control (*before n*) **2▸** (Der) regulatory

regulador² *m* regulator, governor

(Compuestos)

- **regulador de corriente/tensión** current/voltage regulator;
- **regulador de luz** dimmer

regular¹ *adj*

A **1▸** ‹*ritmo/movimiento*› regular; **a intervalos ~es** at regular intervals **2▸** ‹*verbo*› regular **3▸** (Mat) regular

B **por lo regular** (*loc adv*) as a (general) rule

C **1▸** (no muy bien): **¿qué tal te va? — regular** how's it going? — so-so; **¿qué tal la película? — regular** how was the movie? — nothing special; **su trabajo está bastante ~cillo** the work he produces is pretty run-of-the-mill **2▸** (de tamaño) medium-sized, middling

regular² [A1] *vt*

A **1▸** ‹*espejo/asiento*› to adjust **2▸** ‹*caudal/temperatura/velocidad*› to regulate, control

B «*ley/norma*» to regulate

regular³ *m* (calificación) fair

regularidad *f* regularity; **con ~** regularly

regularización *f* (normalización) normalization; (legalización) regularization

regularizar [A4] *vt* (normalizar) to normalize; (legalizar) to regularize

regularmente *adv* regularly

regurgitar [A1] *vi* to regurgitate

regusto *m* aftertaste; **un ~ amargo** a bitter aftertaste

rehabilitación *f* **1▸** (de enfermo, delincuente) rehabilitation **2▸** (en cargo) reinstatement **3▸** (de vivienda) renovation, restoration **4▸** (vindicación) rehabilitation

rehabilitar [A1] *vt* **1▸** ‹*paciente/delincuente*› to rehabilitate **2▸** (en cargo) to reinstate **3▸** ‹*vivienda/local*› to renovate, restore **4▸** (vindicar) to rehabilitate

rehacer [E18] *vt*: **habrá que ~lo** it'll have to be redone; **trató de ~ su vida** she tried to rebuild her life

▪ **rehacerse** *v pron* **~se DE algo** to get over sth

rehén *m* hostage; **tomar/tener a algn como** *or* **de ~** to take/hold sb hostage

rehilete *m*

A (dardo) dart

B (Dep) **1▸** (volante) shuttlecock, birdie (AmE) **2▸** (juego) badminton

C (Méx, Per) (molinete) pinwheel (AmE), windmill (BrE)

rehogar [A3] *vt* to fry … lightly

rehuir [I21] *vt* to shy away from

rehusar [A23] *vt* to refuse; **rehusé la oferta** I refused *o* (frml) declined the offer

▪ **rehusar** *vi* to refuse

▪ **rehusarse** (esp AmL) *v pron* to refuse; **~se A + INF** to refuse to + INF

reilón -lona *adj* (Per, Ven fam) smiley (colloq)

reimplantar [A1] *vt* **1▸** ‹*sistema*› to reintroduce, reestablish; ‹*norma*› to reimpose **2▸** (Med) to reimplant

reimpresión *f* (acción) reprinting; (obra) reprint

reimprimir [I36] *vt* to reprint

reina¹ *f*

A (monarca) queen; **¿dónde está mi ~?** (fam) where's my little princess? (colloq)

(Compuestos)

- **reina de belleza** beauty queen
- **reina de las fiestas** carnival queen
- **reina madre** queen mother

B (Zool) queen; (en ajedrez) queen

r

reina[2] *adj inv* blue-ribbon (*before n*); **la prueba ~** the top *o* the blue-ribbon event

reinado *m* reign

reinante *adj* [1] ‹*casa/dinastía*› reigning [2] ‹*frío/lluvias*› prevailing; **el malestar ~ en el partido** the unease prevailing in the party

reinar [A1] *vi* [1] «*monarca/dinastía*» to reign [2] «*silencio/paz*» to reign; «*temperatura/buen tiempo*» to prevail; **reinaba la confusión** everything was in total chaos; **reinaba un ambiente de terror** an atmosphere of terror prevailed

reincidencia *f* recidivism (frml); **el juez tuvo en cuenta su ~** the judge bore in mind his previous offenses *o* his previous record

reincidente[1] *adj* recidivist (frml), reoffending (*before n*)

reincidente[2] *mf* reoffender, recidivist (frml)

reincidir [I1] *vi* (Der) to reoffend; **~ en el mismo error** to repeat the same mistake

reincorporación *f* [1] (de empleado — espués de ausenciad) return; (— después de despido) reinstatement [2] (de territorio) restoration, return

reincorporar [A1] *vt* [1] ‹*empleado*› to reinstate [2] ‹*territorio*› to restore, return

■ **reincorporarse** *v pron* to return; **~se A algo** to return TO sth; **~se a filas** to rejoin the army

reingresar [A1] *vi* **~ EN algo** to return TO sth; **reingresó en el servicio activo** he returned to active service

■ **reingresar** *vt* (Med) to readmit

reingreso *m* [1] (en un país) reentry; (Espac) reentry; **~ EN** *or* (esp AmL) **A algo** reentry INTO sth; **visa** (AmL) *or* (Esp) **visado de ~** reentry visa [2] (en hospital) readmission

reino *m* kingdom, realm (liter); **el ~ de la fantasía** the realm of fantasy; ▸**ciego**[2]

(Compuesto) **reino animal/mineral/vegetal** animal/mineral/vegetable kingdom

Reino Unido *m* United Kingdom

reinserción *f*: *tb* **~ social** social rehabilitation, reintegration into society

reinsertar [A1] *vt* to rehabilitate, reintegrate ... into society

■ **reinsertarse** *v pron* to reintegrate into society

reintegración *f* [1] (de persona — en cargo) reinstatement; (— en comunidad) reintegration [2] (frml) (de depósito) refund, return; (de gastos) reimbursement

reintegrar [A1] *vt*

A ‹*persona*› (a cargo) to reinstate; (a comunidad) to reintegrate; **~ a algn A** *or* **EN algo**: **la reintegraron a** *or* **en su puesto** she was reinstated in her post; **~ a un paciente a** *or* **en la comunidad** to reintegrate a patient into the community

B (frml) ‹*depósito*› to refund, return; ‹*gastos*› to reimburse; ‹*préstamo*› to repay; ‹*propriedad/bien*› to hand back, return

■ **reintegrarse** *v pron* to return; **~se A algo** to return TO sth; **~se en la comunidad** to reintegrate into the community

reintegro *m*

A [1] (en banco) withdrawal; (de depósito) refund; (de gastos) reimbursement; (de préstamo) repayment; **se le hará el ~ de sus gastos** your expenses will be reimbursed; **se deberá efectuar el ~ del préstamo** the loan must be repaid [2] (en lotería) refund (*of the ticket price*)

B (a cargo — después de despido) reinstatement; (— después de ausencia) return

reír [I18] *vi* to laugh; **se echaron a ~** they burst out laughing; ***el que ríe último ríe mejor*** he who laughs last laughs longest

■ **reír** *vt* ‹*gracia/chiste*› to laugh at

■ **reírse** *v pron* to laugh; **~se a carcajadas** to guffaw; **~se con ganas** to laugh heartily; **~se DE algo/algn** to laugh AT sth/sb; **se rió de él en su propia cara** she laughed in his face

reiteración *f* reiteration, repetition

reiteradamente *adv* repeatedly

reiterado -da *adj* ‹*ataques*› (*delante del n*) repeated; ‹*ocasiones*› countless, numerous; ‹*uso*› repeated

reiterar [A1] *vt* to reiterate (frml), to repeat

reiterativo -va *adj* reiterative (frml)

reivindicación *f* [1] (demanda) demand, claim; **las reivindicaciones obreras** the workers' demands; [2] (reconocimiento) recognition; **luchan por la ~ de sus derechos** they are fighting for recognition of their rights; [3] (rehabilitación): **luchó por la ~ de su buen nombre** she fought to vindicate her good name; **la ~ del general como héroe nacional** the restoration *o* rehabilitation of the general as a national hero; [4] (de atentado): **la ~ del atentado** the claiming of responsibility for the attack

reivindicar [A2] *vt* [1] ‹*derecho*› to demand; ‹*tierras*› to claim [2] (rehabilitar) to restore, rehabilitate [3] ‹*atentado*› to claim responsibility for

■ **reivindicarse** *v pron* (AmS) to vindicate oneself

reja *f*

A [1] (de ventana) grille; ***estar entre ~s*** to be behind bars [2] (para cercar) railing

B (Agr) plowshare (AmE), ploughshare (BrE)

rejego *adj* (Méx fam) ‹*persona*› mouthy (AmE), cheeky (BrE)

rejilla *f*

A (de ventilación) grille; (Auto) grille; (del confesionario) screen; (del desagüe) grating

B (para equipajes) luggage rack; (de horno) rack; (base de chimenea) grate

C (varillas entrelazadas) wickerwork

rejo *m*

A (aguijón de hierro) spike; (de abeja) sting

B (Col) (látigo) whip

rejoneador -dora *m,f* mounted bullfighter (*who uses a lance*)

rejonear [A1] *vt* to wound ... with a lance

■ **rejonear** *vi* to fight bulls from horseback

rejuntar [A1] *vt* (Méx fam) ‹*reses*› to round up; ‹*borregos*› to gather

rejuvenecedor -dora *adj* rejuvenating

rejuvenecer [E3] *vt* to rejuvenate

■ **rejuvenecer** *vi* to be rejuvenated

■ **rejuvenecerse** *v pron* to be rejuvenated

relación *f*

A [1] (conexión) connection; **con ~ a** *or* **en ~ con** (con respecto a) in connection with; (en comparación con) relative to; **en ~ con su carta ...** with regard to *o* regarding your letter ... [2] (correspondencia): **en una ~ de diez a uno** (Mat) in a ratio of ten to one; **tiene una excelente ~ calidad-precio** it is excellent value for money; **una ~ causa-efecto** a relationship of cause and effect

B [1] (trato): **tienen una buena ~** they have a good relationship; **relaciones sexuales** sexual relations; **relaciones prematrimoniales** premarital sex; **tener relaciones amorosas con algn** to have an affair with sb; **estoy en buenas relaciones con él** I'm on good terms with him; **relaciones diplomáticas/comerciales** diplomatic/trade relations; **es nulo en lo que respecta a las relaciones humanas** he's hopeless when it comes to dealing with people; **las relaciones entre padres e hijos** the relationship between parents and their children [2] **relaciones** *fpl* (influencias) contacts (*pl*), connections (*pl*)

(Compuesto) **relaciones públicas** [1] *fpl* (actividad) public relations (*pl*) [2] *mf* (persona) public relations officer; (de cantante, artista) PR

C [1] (exposición) account; **hizo una detallada ~ de los hechos** she gave a detailed account of the facts [2] (lista) list

relacionado -da *adj* [1] [ESTAR] ‹*temas/ideas*› related; **todo lo ~ con el cine** anything to do with *o* related to films [2] ‹*persona*›: **está muy bien ~** he is very well connected; **estar ~ CON algn** to be connected WITH sb; **está ~ con gente del gobierno** he has contacts in the government

relacionar [A1] *vt*

A (conectar) to relate; **~ algo A** *o* **CON algo** to relate sth TO sth; **si relacionamos los dos sucesos** if we link the two events

B (hacer una lista) to list

■ **relacionarse** *v pron* [1] **~se CON algo** ‹*con tema/asunto*› to be related TO sth [2] «*persona*» **~se CON algn** to mix WITH sb

relajación *f* (de músculos, mente) relaxation

relajado -da *adj*

A (tranquilo) relaxed

B ‹*costumbres*› dissolute, lax

relajamiento *m* (de las tensiones) easing; (de la moral) decline

relajante *adj*
A ‹*música/baño*› relaxing
B (CS fam) (empalagoso) sickly-sweet (pej)

relajar [A1] *vt*
A ‹*músculo/persona/mente*› to relax
B (RPl arg) (insultar) to lay into (colloq)
■ **relajar** *vi*
A «*ejercicio/música*» to be relaxing
B (CS fam) (empalagar): **es tan dulce que relaja** it's sickly sweet
■ **relajarse** *v pron*
A 1 (físicamente, mentalmente) to relax; (tras período de tensión) to relax, unwind 2 «*tensión*» to ease; «*ambiente*» to become more relaxed
B (degenerar) «*costumbres/moral*» to decline

relajo *m*
A (de la moral) decline
B (esp Esp fam) 1 (relax): **¡qué ~!** how relaxing! 2 (falta de seriedad) slack *o* lax attitude
C (AmL fam) (desorden, confusión): **esa clase es un ~** that class is bedlam *o* mayhem (colloq); **con tanto ~ la despertarás** you'll wake her up with that commotion; ***armar* ~** (AmL fam) (jugar) to clown around (colloq); (alborotarse) to kick up a din (colloq)
D (Méx fam) 1 (persona divertida) laugh (colloq); **eres un ~** you're such a laugh; ***de* ~** (Méx fam) for a laugh (colloq); ***echar* ~** (Méx fam) to clown around (colloq) 2 (persona problemática) troublemaker

relamerse [E1] *v pron* (por algo sabroso) to lick one's lips; (de satisfacción) to smack one's lips

relamido -da *adj* hoity-toity

relámpago *m* (Meteo) bolt *o* flash of lightning; ‹*salir/pasar*› **como un ~** like greased lightning; **pasó por mi mente como un ~** it flashed through my mind

relampaguear [A1] *v impers*: **estuvo relampagueando** there were some flashes of lightning; **relampagueó** the lightning flashed
■ **relampaguear** *vi* «*ojos*» to flash; **le relampagueaban los ojos de ira** her eyes flashed with anger

relanzamiento *m* relaunching, relaunch

relatar [A1] *vt*: **nos relató su viaje** he related *o* recounted the story of his journey (frml)

relatista *mf* (Chi) short story writer

relativamente *adv* relatively

relatividad *f* relativity

relativo¹ -va *adj*
A (no absoluto) relative; **eso es muy ~** that depends; **una dolencia de relativa gravedad** a relatively serious illness
B (concerniente) **~ A algo** relating TO sth; **todo lo ~ a la política** anything to do with *o* anything related to politics; **en lo ~ a este problema** with regard to this problem

relativo² *m* (Ling) relative

relato *m* 1 (historia, cuento) story, tale; **~s para niños** children's stories 2 (relación) account; **un ~ de lo ocurrido** an account of what had happened; **su ~ no coincide con el tuyo** his story *o* account does not tally with your version

relax *m* relaxation; **el lugar perfecto para el ~** the perfect place to relax in *o* to find relaxation; Ⓢ **relax** (Esp euf) (en anuncios de periódico) personal services (euph)

releer [E13] *vt* to reread, read again

relegación *f* relegation

relegar [A3] *vt*: **se siente relegado** he feels left out; **~ algo/a algn A algo**: **el problema quedó relegado a un segundo plano** the matter was pushed into the background; **relegado al olvido** consigned to oblivion

relente *m*: **el ~ de la noche** the cold (damp) night air; **dormir al ~** to sleep (out) in the open

relevante *adj* notable, outstanding; **ocupa un cargo ~ en la empresa** she has an important job in the company

relevar [A1] *vt*
A (sustituir) to relieve; **~ la guardia** (Mil) to change the guard; **relevó a Salinas como entrenador** he took over from *o* replaced Salinas as coach
B (destituir) to remove
C (eximir) to exempt; **~ a algn DE algo** to exempt sb FROM sth; **lo ~on de servicio** he was exempted from duty
■ **relevarse** *v pron* to take turns, take it in turn(s)

relevista *mf* relay runner

relevo *m* 1 (Mil): **el ~ de la guardia** the changing of the guard; **le hice el ~ a las dos** I relieved him at two o'clock 2 (Dep) *tb* **~s** relay (race); ***tomarle el ~ a algn*** (Dep) to take the baton from sb; (en tarea) to take over from sb

relicario *m* (para reliquias) reliquary; (para recuerdos sentimentales) locket

relieve *m*
A (Geog): **un mapa del ~ de España** a relief map of Spain; **la costa tiene un ~ muy accidentado** the coast is very rugged
B 1 (Art) relief; **en ~** in relief; **letras en ~** embossed letters 2 (parte que sobresale): **el marco tiene un centímetro de ~** the frame protrudes by a centimeter
C (importancia) prominence; **personas de ~** prominent people; **la institución de más ~ en ese campo** the leading institution in that field; **esta noticia da especial ~ a la reunión** this news makes the meeting especially important; **la presencia del Rey dio ~ a la ceremonia** the King's presence lent an added grandeur to the ceremony; ***poner de* ~** to highlight

religión *f* religion

religiosamente *adv* religiously

religiosidad *f* religiousness, religiosity

religioso¹ -sa *adj* religious

religioso² -sa *m,f* member of a religious order; **un ~ franciscano** a Franciscan friar *o* monk; **las religiosas del convento** the nuns in the convent

relinchar [A1] *vi* to neigh, whinny

reliquia *f* relic; **una ~ de familia** a family heirloom; **guardar algo como una ~** to treasure sth; **lo guardo como una ~ suya** I kept it in memory of him

rellano *m* (de escalera) landing; (de ladera, montaña) shelf

rellena *f* (Col, Méx fam) blood sausage, black pudding (BrE)

rellenar [A1] *vt*
A 1 ‹*pavo/pimientos*› to stuff; ‹*pastel*› to fill; **~ algo DE** *or* **CON algo** to stuff/fill sth WITH sth 2 ‹*cojín/muñeco*› to stuff 3 ‹*agujero/grieta*› to fill
B (volver a llenar) to refill
C ‹*impreso/formulario*› to fill out *o* in
D ‹*examen/discurso*› to pad out

relleno¹ -na *adj*
A ‹*pavo/pimientos*› stuffed; **caramelos ~s de chocolate** candies with a chocolate filling
B (regordete): **tiene la cara rellena** he has a full face; **es rellenita** she's quite plump

relleno² *m*
A (para pasteles, tortas) filling; (para pavo, pimientos) stuffing; (para cojines, muñecos) stuffing; (de ropa interior) padding; (para agujeros, grietas) filler
B (parte superflua): **dan un documental de ~** they fill up the time with a documentary; **estas estadísticas están aquí de ~** these statistics are here to pad things out

reloj *m* (de pared, mesa) clock; (de pulsera, bolsillo) watch; **mi ~ (se) adelanta/atrasa** my watch gains/loses; **funciona** *or* **marcha como un ~** it's going like clockwork; **contra ~** against the clock; ***ser un* ~** to be as regular as clockwork

(Compuestos)
- **reloj checador** (Méx) time clock
- **reloj de arena** hourglass
- **reloj de cuco** *or* (AmL) **cucú** cuckoo clock
- **reloj de pie** grandfather clock
- **reloj de pulsera** wristwatch
- **reloj de sol** sundial
- **reloj despertador/registrador** alarm/time clock

relojería *f* (tienda, taller) clockmaker's, watchmaker's; (actividad) watchmaking

relojero -ra *m,f* (de relojes — de pulsera) watchmaker; (— de pared, mesa) clockmaker

reluciente *adj* **1** (brillante): **su ~ coche nuevo** her shiny *o* gleaming new car; **una mañana ~** a bright, sunny morning; **los suelos estaban ~s** the floors gleamed **2** ‹*persona*› glowing, radiant

relucir [I5] *vi* «*sol*» to shine; «*estrellas*» to twinkle, glitter; «*plata/zapatos*» to shine, gleam; ***sacar a ~*** to bring up; ***salir a ~*** to come to the surface, come out

reluctancia *f* reluctance

relumbrante *adj* brilliant, dazzling

relumbrar [A1] *vi* to shine brightly; **cuando el sol más relumbra** when the sun is at its most dazzling

relumbrón *m*: **todo es puro ~** it's all a big show; **un cargo de ~** a job with a flashy-sounding title (colloq)

remachado *m* (de clavo) clinching; (de perno, chapa) riveting

remachador -dora *m,f*

A (jugador — en vóleibol) spiker; (— en tenis): **es un excelente ~** he's a master of the smash

B **1** (obrero) riveter **2** **remachadora** *f* (máquina) riveter, riveting machine

remachar [A1] *vt*

A ‹*clavo*› to clinch; ‹*perno/chapas*› to rivet

B (recalcar) to repeat, reiterate; (finalizar) to round off, finish off

■ **remachar** *vi* (en tenis) to smash; (en voleibol) to spike

remache *m*

A **1** (perno) rivet **2** (acción) ▸**remachado**

B (en tenis) smash; (en vóleibol) spike

remanente[1] *adj* ‹*mercancía*› surplus; ‹*líquido*› residual

remanente[2] *m*: **el ~ de la cosecha** the remainder of the crop; **liquidación de ~s** end-of-season sale

remangar [A3] *vt* ‹*pantalones*› to roll up; ‹*falda*› to hitch up

■ **remangarse** *v pron* (*refl*): **se remangó para lavar los platos** he rolled up his sleeves to wash the dishes; **se remangó los pantalones** he rolled up his trousers *o* (AmE) pants

remansarse [A1] *v pron* to form a pool

remanso *m* pool; **un ~ de paz** a haven of peace (liter)

remar [A1] *vi* (en bote) to row; (en canoa) to paddle

remarcar [A2] *vt*

A (hacer notar) to stress, emphasize

B (CS) (Com) to mark up

rematadamente *adv*: **juega ~ mal** he plays incredibly badly; **está ~ loco** he's completely *o* absolutely mad

rematado -da *adj* complete, absolute; **es un loco ~** he's a raving lunatic

rematador -dora *m,f*

A (en fútbol) goal scorer, striker

B (AmL) (subastador) auctioneer

rematante *mf* highest bidder

rematar [A1] *vt*

A **1** ‹*actuación/intervención*› to round off, finish off; ‹*negocio*› to conclude, close; ‹*torre/bastón*› to top, crown; ***y para ~la*** (fam) and to crown *o* cap it all (colloq) **2** ‹*costura*› to finish off **3** ‹*animal/persona*› to finish off

B (en tenis) to smash; (en vóleibol) to spike; (en fútbol): **remató el centro a la portería** he hit the cross straight into the goal

C (AmL) **1** (en subasta — vender) to auction; (— comprar) to buy … at an auction; **se remató en $80.000** it went for $80,000 **2** (liquidar) to sell … off cheaply

■ **rematar** *vi*

A (terminar) to end; **~ EN algo** to end IN sth

B (en tenis) to smash; (en vóleibol) to spike; (en fútbol) to shoot; **~ de cabeza** to head the ball

remate *m*

A **1** (de activades, esfuerzos) culmination; **esta cita sería un buen ~ para tu discurso** this quotation would be a nice way to round off your speech; ***y como ~*** *or* (Chi) ***y para (más) ~*** (fam) and to crown *o* cap it all (colloq) **2** (en costura) double stitch (*to finish off*)

B (en tenis) smash; (en vóleibol) spike; (en fútbol) shot; **~ de cabeza** header

C (AmL) (subasta) auction

rematista *mf* (Per) auctioneer

remb... ▸**reemb...**

remedar [A1] *vt* to mimic, ape

remediar [A1] *vt*

A ‹*situación/problema*› to remedy; ‹*daño*› to repair; **para ~ los efectos de la sequía** to repair the damage done by the drought; **sólo la muerte no se puede ~** there's a cure for everything except death; **¿qué piensas hacer para ~lo?** what are you going to do to put things right?; **con pedirle perdón no remedias nada** saying you're sorry won't solve anything

B (evitar): **no lo puedo ~** I can't help it; **perdí dinero, no pude ~lo** there was nothing else for it, I lost money

remedio *m*

A **1** (Med) (cura) remedy, cure **2** (esp AmL) (Farm) medicine; **un ~ natural/a base de hierbas** a natural/herbal remedy; ***es/fue peor el ~ que la enfermedad*** it is/was a case of the solution being worse than the problem; ***ni para (un) ~***: **no dejaron vino ni para (un) ~** they finished off every (last) drop of wine; **no encontré una habitación ni para un ~** I couldn't find a hotel room for love or money; ***santo ~*** (AmL): **hablé con él y santo ~, no me molestó más** I talked to him and that did the trick, he didn't bother me again

B (solución) solution; **no tiene ~** there's nothing we/they can do; **su matrimonio no tiene ~** her marriage is beyond hope; **poner ~ a un problema** to remedy a problem; **un caso sin ~** a hopeless case

C (alternativa, recurso) option; **no tuvo/no le quedó más ~ que …** she had no option but …; **no hay/no queda más** *or* **otro ~ que …** we have no alternative *o* choice but …; **iré si no hay otro ~** I'll go if I really have to *o* if I must; **como último ~** as a last resort

remedo *m* poor imitation, poor copy

rememorar [A1] *vt* (liter) to recall

remendar [A5] *vt* to mend

remera *f* (RPl) (camiseta) T-shirt

remero -ra (*m*) rower, oarsman; (*f*) rower, oarswoman

remesa *f* (de mercancías) consignment, shipment; (de dinero) remittance

remesar [A1] *vt* ‹*mercancías*› to consign, ship; ‹*dinero*› to remit;

remeter [E1] *vt* to tuck in

remezón *m* (Andes) (temblor) earth tremor; (sacudida brusca) shake; (suceso inesperado) shake-up

remiendo *m* (pedazo de tela, cuero) patch; **le hizo un ~** she mended *o* patched it

remilgado -da *adj* fussy

remilgo *m*: **déjate de ~s** don't be so fussy, don't be such a fusspot (colloq)

remilgón -gona, **remilgoso -sa** *adj* (delicado) (Andes, Méx) fussy; (difícil) (Méx) difficult

reminiscencia *f*: **un edificio de ~s moriscas** a building reminiscent of the Moorish style; **una carta llena de ~s literarias** letter full of literary references

remirado -da *adj* fastidious, fussy

remirar [A1] *vt*: **lo mira y remira** he keeps looking at it again and again; **miró y remiró en el bolso** she went through her bag again and again

remise /rre'mis/ *m* (RPl) chauffeur-driven car

remisión *m*

A **1** (frml) (envío): **prometió la ~ del proyecto a las Cortes** he promised to bring the bill before Parliament (frml); **la ~ del pedido se efectuó el día 19** your order was dispatched on the 19th **2** (en texto) reference; **~ A algo** reference TO sth

B (de enfermedad) remission

C (Relig, Der) remission; ***sin ~***: **van a la quiebra, sin ~** they're heading inexorably toward bankruptcy

remiso[1] **-sa** *adj* (reacio) reluctant; **~ A + INF** reluctant to + INF

remiso[2] *m* (Andes) draft dodger

remite *m* (persona) sender; (dirección) return address

remitente *mf* sender; ❺ **devuélvase al remitente** return to sender

remitido *m* (RPl) (paid) announcement (*o* article *etc*); **publicar un ~ en la prensa** to place a notice in the newspapers

remitir [I1] *vt*

A **1** (frml) (mandar) to send; **adjunto le remito los documentos** please find enclosed the documents **2** (Der)

r

(transferir) to remit, refer, transfer 3 ‹*lector/estudiante*› ~ **A algn A algo** to refer sb TO sth
B (Der) (perdonar) to remit
■ **remitir** *vi*
A «*fiebre*» to drop, go down; «*tormenta*» to abate, subside; **la ola de violencia está remitiendo** the wave of violence is subsiding
B (a obra, nota) ~ **A algo** to refer TO sth
■ **remitirse** *v pron* **~se A algo** to refer TO sth

remo *m* (con soporte) oar; (sin soporte) paddle

remoción *f* (frml) removal

remodelación *f* (Arquit) remodeling*, redesigning; (de organización) reorganization, restructuring; **una ~ del gabinete** a cabinet reshuffle

remodelar [A1] *vt* ‹*plaza/barrio*› to remodel, redesign; ‹*organización*› to reorganize, restructure

remojar [A1] *vt*
A ‹*ropa/lentejas*› to soak
B (fam) (festejar bebiendo): **¡esto hay que ~lo!** this calls for a celebration! (colloq)

remojo *m* (en agua): **poner a** *or* **en ~ algo** to put sth to soak; **dejar en ~ algo** to leave sth to soak

remojón *m*
A (fam) (en agua) soaking, drenching; **¿quién quiere darse un ~?** who's for a dip? (colloq)
B (Méx) (de algo nuevo): **nos dio el ~** (en el coche) he took us for a spin in his new car; (en la casa) he had us over for a housewarming party

remolacha *f* beet (AmE), beetroot (BrE)
(Compuesto) **remolacha azucarera** sugar beet

remolcador *m* (Náut) tug; (Auto) tow truck (AmE), breakdown van (BrE)

remolcar [A2] *vt* ‹*barco*› to tug; ‹*coche*› to tow

remoler [E9] *vi* (Chi fam) to live it up (colloq)

remolino *m*
A 1 (de viento) eddy, whirl 2 (de agua) eddy; (más violento) whirlpool
B (en el pelo) cowlick
C (CS) (juguete) pinwheel (AmE), windmill (BrE)

remolón¹ -lona *adj* (fam) idle, lazy

remolón² -lona *m,f* (fam) slacker (colloq)

remolonear [A1] *vi* to waste time

remolque *m* 1 (vehículo) trailer; **~ para transportar caballos** horsecar (AmE), horsebox (BrE) 2 (acción) towing; ***hacer algo a ~*** (fam) to do sth unwillingly; ***ir a ~*** (Auto) to be in tow 3 (Náut) (cuerda) towrope, towing line 4 (AmS) (grúa) tow truck (AmE), breakdown van (BrE)

remontadora *f* (Col) cobbler's, shoemaker's

remontar [A1] *vt*
A ‹*dificultad/problema*› to overcome, surmount (frml); **los Jets ~on un déficit de 20 puntos** the Jets came from 20 points behind
B 1 **~ el vuelo** «*avión*» to gain height; «*pájaro*» to fly *o* soar up; 2 **~ el río** to go upriver; 3 (RPl) ‹*barrilete*› to fly
C (Col) ‹*zapatos*› to mend
■ **remontarse** *v pron*
A «*avión*» to gain height; «*pájaro*» to soar up
B (en el tiempo) to go back

rémora *f*
A (Zool) remora
B (frml) (obstáculo, impedimento) hindrance

remorder [E9] *vi* (+ *me/te/le etc*): **me remuerde haberlo dicho** I feel guilty for *o* I feel bad about having said it; **¿no te remuerde la conciencia?** don't you feel guilty? don't you have a guilty conscience?

remordimiento *m* remorse; **sentir** *or* **tener ~s de conciencia** to suffer pangs of conscience

remotamente *adv* remotely; **no son ni ~ parecidos** they aren't even remotely alike; **lo recuerdo ~** I vaguely remember him

remoto -ta *adj*
A (en el tiempo): **en épocas remotas** in distant *o* far-off times
B 1 ‹*lugar/mares/tierras*› remote, far-off 2 (Inf) remote
C ‹*posibilidad*› remote, slim; ‹*esperanza*› faint; **no tengo (ni) la más remota idea** I haven't the remotest *o* faintest idea

remover [E9] *vt*
A ‹*líquido/salsa*› to stir; ‹*ensalada*› to toss; ‹*tierra/piedras*› to turn over; ‹*escombros*› to dig about in; ‹*brasas*› to poke, stir
B ‹*asunto*› to bring … up again; ‹*recuerdo/pasado*› to revive, stir up
C (frml) 1 ‹*impedimento/obstáculo*› to remove 2 (esp AmL) (destituir) **~ A algn DE algo** to remove sb FROM sth
■ **removerse** *v pron* to shift, shift around

remozar [A4] *vt* to renovate

rempl... ▸ **reempl...**

remunerable *adj* paid

remuneración *f* remuneration (frml); **~ a convenir** salary *o* remuneration to be agreed; **detallar las remuneraciones percibidas en el año** give details of income received during the year

remunerar [A1] *vt* to pay, remunerate (frml); **mal remunerado** badly paid

renacentista¹ *adj* Renaissance (*before n*)

renacentista² *mf* Renaissance artist

renacer [E3] *vi* to be reborn; **sentí ~ la esperanza** I felt renewed hope; **sintió ~ sentimientos que creía extinguidos** emotions stirred inside him which he thought were long dead

renaciente *adj* renewed, resurgent (frml)

renacimiento *m*
A (acción) revival, rebirth
B (Art, Hist) **el R~** the Renaissance

renacuajo *m* (Zool) tadpole; (niño, persona baja) (fam) shrimp (colloq)

renal *adj* renal (tech), kidney (*before n*)

rencilla *f* quarrel, row

renco -ca *adj* (Col, RPl) lame

rencor *m*: **no te guardo ~** I don't bear you any grudge; **sin ~es ¿de acuerdo?** no hard feelings, OK? (colloq); **aún siento ~ por lo que me hizo** I still feel bitter about what he did to me; **su ~ le impide perdonarlo** she still feels too bitter to forgive him

rencoroso -sa *adj* [SER] resentful

rendición *f* surrender

rendida *f* (Chi fam) stream of abuse, mouthful (colloq); **echarle una ~ a algn** to give sb a mouthful

rendido -da *adj* 1 [ESTAR] (exhausto) exhausted; **cayó ~ (de cansancio)** he collapsed from exhaustion; *ver tb* **rendir** 2 ‹*admirador*› devoted

rendidor -dora *adj* (AmL) ‹*tierra*› productive; **un detergente ~** a detergent that goes a long way

rendija *f* (grieta) crack, crevice; (hueco) gap

rendimiento *m*
A (de persona) performance; **el alto ~ de los alumnos** the pupils' excellent performance *o* high level of achievement
B (Auto) performance; (Mec, Tec) output; **funciona a pleno ~** it is working at full capacity
C (de terreno) yield
D (Fin) yield, return

rendir [I14] *vt*
A ‹*homenaje/tributo*› to pay; **~le culto a algn** to worship sb; **le rindieron honores militares** he was received with full military honors
B (Fin) to yield; (producir) to produce; **el esfuerzo rindió sus frutos** the efforts bore fruit
C ‹*persona*›: **me rindió el sueño** I was overcome by sleep; **tanto trabajo rinde a cualquiera** working that hard is enough to exhaust anyone
D 1 ‹*informe*› to present 2 (CS) (Educ) ‹*examen*› to take, sit (BrE)
E (Col, Ven) (diluir) to dilute, water down
■ **rendir** *vi*
A (cundir) (+ *me/te/le etc*): **me rindió mucho la mañana** I had a very productive morning; **trabaja mucho pero no le rinde** he works hard but he doesn't make much headway
B «*persona*» to perform well, get on well
C «*tela/arroz/jabón*» to go a long way
D (RPl) (Educ) to take *o* (BrE) sit an exam
■ **rendirse** *v pron* 1 (Mil) to surrender; **~se al enemigo** to surrender to the enemy; **vamos, no te rindas** come on,

don't give up; **~se ante la evidencia** to bow to *o* accept the evidence 2 (en adivinanzas) to give up

renegado -da *m,f* renegade; **un ~ social** a dropout

renegar [A7] *vi*

A 1 (Relig) to apostatize 2 (abjurar) **~ DE algo** ‹*de creencias/principios*› to renounce sth; **~ de Dios** to renounce God; **renegó de su familia** she disowned her family

B (maldecir) to swear, curse; (blasfemar) to blaspheme

C (quejarse, refunfuñar) to grumble; **~ DE algo** to grumble ABOUT sth

D (AmL) (enojarse) to get annoyed

■ **renegar** *vt* to deny ... vigorously

renegón -gona *adj* (fam) grumpy (colloq), grouchy (colloq)

renglón *m* (línea) line; **un cuaderno sin renglones** a plain *o* an unlined notebook; ***a ~ seguido*** immediately afterward(s); **viene señalado a ~ seguido** it is detailed immediately below

rengo[1] -ga *adj* (AmL) lame

rengo[2] -ga *m,f* (AmL) lame person, cripple (pej)

renguear [A1] *vi* (AmL) to limp

renguera *f* (AmL) limp

reno *m* reindeer

renombrado -da *adj* well-known, renowned

renombre *m* renown

renovable *adj* renewable

renovación *f*

A (de pasaporte, contrato) renewal

B (del mobiliario) complete change; (de edificio, barrio) renovation; **la ~ del personal de la empresa** the restaffing of the company; **facilita la ~ celular** it aids cell renewal

C (de organización, sistema) updating

D (reanudación) renewal

renovador -dora *adj*: **el espíritu ~ que reina en la nación** the spirit of renewal *o* change in the country; **se necesita un empuje ~** a fresh impetus is needed

renovar [A10] *vt*

A ‹*pasaporte/contrato*› to renew

B ‹*mobiliario*› to change; ‹*edificio/barrio*› to renovate

C ‹*organización/sistema*› to update, bring up to date

D ‹*ataque/esperanza/promesa*› to renew; **el volver a verlo renovó mi dolor** seeing him again brought back the pain; **con renovadas fuerzas** with renewed energy

■ **renovarse** *v pron* 1 «*sospechas/dolor/interés*» to be renewed 2 «*persona*» to be revitalized; **~se o morir** *or* (RPl) **~se es vivir** (fr hecha) adapt or die

renquear [A1] *vi* to limp

renqueo *m* limp

renta *f*

A (beneficio) income; **~s derivadas de capitales/del trabajo personal** unearned/earned income; **inversiones de ~ fija** fixed interest investments; ***vivir de las ~s***: **tiene dinero/propiedades y vive de las ~s** she has some money and lives off the interest/some properties and lives off the rents; **un escritor que lleva años viviendo de las ~s** a writer who has been living off past glories for years

(Compuestos)

- **renta gravable** taxable income
- **renta nacional** national income
- **renta per cápita** income per capita
- **renta vitalicia** life annuity

B (esp Méx) (alquiler) rent

rentabilidad *f* profitability

rentabilizar [A4] *vt* ‹*inversión*› to achieve a return on; **~ los recursos de la zona** to make the most of the area's resources

rentable *adj* ‹*inversión/negocio*› profitable: **no me es ~ viajar hasta allí** it isn't worth my while *o* it doesn't make sense financially to go all that way

rentado -da *adj* (CS) paid; **un empleo muy bien ~** a very well-paid job

rentar [A1] *vt* (Méx) 1 ‹*departamento*› «*propietario*» to let, rent out; «*usuario*» to rent 2 ‹*coche*› to rent, hire (BrE)

rentista *mf* person who lives off the income from investments (*o* real estate *etc*)

renuente *adj* reluctant, unwilling

renuncia *f*

A (dimisión) resignation; **presentar la ~** to resign, tender one's resignation (frml)

B 1 (abandono) **~ A algo** renunciation OF sth 2 (Der) relinquishment

C (abnegación) self-sacrifice

renunciar [A1] *vi*

A (dimitir) to resign; **~ A algo** ‹*a puesto*› to resign sth; **~ a la corona** to renounce the throne

B (a derecho, proyecto) **~ A algo** to give up *o* relinquish sth; **~ a la violencia** to renounce violence

reñidero *m* cockpit

reñido -da *adj*

A ‹*partido/batalla*› hard-fought, tough

B 1 [ESTAR] (peleado) **~ CON algn**: **está ~ con su novia** he has fallen out with his girlfriend (colloq) 2 (en contradicción) [ESTAR] **~ CON algo** ‹*con principios*› against sth; **un espectáculo ~ con la moral tradicional** a show (which is) at odds with conventional moral standards

reñir [I15] *vi* (esp Esp) 1 (discutir) to argue, quarrel 2 **~ CON algn** (pelearse) to quarrel *o* have a row WITH sb; (enemistarse) to fall out WITH sb

■ **reñir** *vt* (Esp) (regañar) to scold, tell ... off (colloq)

reo *mf* (en lo penal — acusado) accused, defendant; (— condenado) convicted offender; (en lo civil) (Méx) defendant

reojo: **de ~** (*loc adv*) **mirar a algn de ~** to look at sb out of the corner of one's eye

reorganización *f* reorganization

reorganizar [A4] *vt* to reorganize

reorientación *f* (de política, enfoque) reorientation; (de recursos) redeployment

reorientar [A1] *vt* ‹*política/enfoque*› to reorient (AmE), to reorientate (BrE); ‹*recursos*› to redeploy

Rep. (= **República**) Rep.

repanchigarse, repantingarse [A3] *v pron* (fam) to lounge, sprawl out

reparación *f*

A (arreglo) repair; **taller de reparaciones** repair shop; **Ⓢ reparación de calzado** shoe repairs

B (de daño, ofensa) redress, reparation; **exigió ~ de daños** she claimed damages

reparador -dora *adj* ‹*sueño/descanso*› refreshing

reparadora *f* (Chi) cobbler's, shoemaker's

reparar [A1] *vt*

A ‹*coche*› to repair, fix; ‹*gotera/avería*› to mend, fix

B ‹*fuerzas/energías*› to restore

C ‹*error*› to correct, put right; ‹*ofensa/agravio*› to make amends for, make up for; ‹*daño/perjuicio*› to make good, compensate for

■ **reparar** *vi*

A 1 (considerar, pensar) (*gen en frases negativas*) **~ EN algo**: **no repara en gastos** she spares no expense; **no ~on en sus advertencias** they took no notice of *o* paid no heed to his warnings 2 (darse cuenta) **~ EN algo** to notice sth; **les hizo ~ en la calidad del tejido** he drew their attention to the quality of the cloth

B (Méx) «*caballo/toro*» to rear, shy

reparo *m*

A 1 (inconveniente, objeción): **pone ~s a todo** she finds fault with everything; **no tengo ningún ~ en decírselo** I have no qualms about telling him 2 (duda) reservation; **accedió, pero no sin ~(s)** he agreed but not without reservation(s)

B (en esgrima) parry

C (Méx) (de caballo, toro): **el caballo dio un ~** the horse reared up *o* shied; **aguantó los ~s del caballo** he held on despite the horse's bucking/rearing

repartición *f*

A (división) distribution, share-out

B (CS) (departamento, sección) department; **las reparticiones del ejército** the army divisions

(Compuesto) **repartición pública** (CS) (institución) government department; (edificio) government building

repartidor -dora (*m*) delivery man; (*f*) delivery woman; **~ de periódicos** newspaper man (*o* boy *etc*); **~ de leche** (*m*) milkman; (*f*) milkwoman

repartimiento *m* distribution, share-out

r

repartir [I1] *vt*
A ‹*ganancias/trabajo*› to distribute, share out; **la riqueza está mal repartida** wealth is unfairly distributed
B ‹*panfletos/propaganda*› to hand out, give out; ‹*periódicos/correo*› to deliver; ‹*cartas/fichas*› to deal
C (esparcir) to spread, distribute
■ **repartir** *vi* (Jueg) to deal
■ **repartirse** *v pron* to share out

reparto *m*
A (distribución) distribution; ~ **de premios** prize-giving; **se hizo el ~ del dinero** the money was shared out *o* divided up; **le tocó poco en el ~** she didn't get very much in the share-out
(Compuesto) **reparto de utilidades** *or* (Esp) **beneficios** profit sharing
B (servicio de entrega) delivery; Ⓢ **reparto a domicilio** delivery service; ~ **de correo** mail delivery
C (Cin, Teatr) cast

repasador *m* (RPl) dish towel (AmE), tea towel (BrE)

repasar [A1] *vt*
A ‹*lección/tema*› to review (AmE), to revise (BrE); ‹*lista/cuenta*› to go over, check; **necesito ~ el discurso** I need to look *o* go over the speech; **estábamos repasando las fotos** we were looking through the photos
B ‹*ropa*› (con plancha) to iron; ‹*costura*› to reinforce; ‹*botones*› to sew … on more firmly
C (AmL) ‹*adornos/muebles*› to dust
■ **repasar** *vi* to review (AmE), to revise (BrE)

repaso *m* (revisión — para aprender algo) review (AmE), revision (BrE); (— para detectar errores) check; **hacer un ~ de un tema** to review (AmE) *o* (BrE) revise a subject; **dio un ~ a sus apuntes** she went *o* looked over her notes; **un ~ de las noticias más destacadas** a review *o* run-through of the main points of the news

repatear [A1] *vi* (Esp fam) to annoy

repatingarse [A3] *v pron* (AmL) ▸ **repanchigarse**

repatriación *f* repatriation

repatriado -da *m,f* repatriate

repatriar [A1 *or* A17] *vt* to repatriate

repecho *m* steep slope; **a ~** uphill

repelar [A1] *vi* (Méx fam) to grumble, to moan (BrE colloq)

repelente[1] *adj*
A (que ahuyenta): **una loción ~** a repellent
B ‹*persona*› repulsive, repellent; ‹*niño*› obnoxious

repelente[2] *m* insect repellent

repeler [E1] *vt*
A ‹*ataque/agresión*› to repel, repulse (frml)
B (rechazar) to resist; **una tela que repele el agua** a water-resistant fabric
C (Fís) to repel
■ **repeler** *vi* (+ *me/te/le etc*): **las serpientes me repelen** I find snakes repellent *o* repulsive; **me repele su actitud paternalista** I can't stand his paternalistic attitude

repente *m*
A (de ira, histeria) fit
B **de repente** (*loc adv*) [1] (de pronto) suddenly [2] (RPl, Per) (quizás) maybe, perhaps

repentino -na *adj* sudden

repercusión *f* [1] (de sonido) reverberation [2] (impacto): **sus diseños han tenido gran ~** her designs have made a great impact [3] (consecuencia) repercussion

repercutir [I1] *vi*
A «*sonido*» to reverberate
B (afectar) ~ **EN algo** to have an effect *o* an impact ON sth; **su fracaso repercutió en su matrimonio** his failure had repercussions on *o* affected their marriage

repertorio *m* repertoire

repesca *f* [1] (Dep) repechage [2] (Esp fam) (Educ) make up exam (AmE), resit (BrE)

repetición *f*
A (de hecho, palabra) repetition; **para evitar repeticiones** so as to avoid repetition; **la ~ de este tema en su obra** the recurrence of this theme in his work
B (de programa) repeat, rerun; (de experimento) repetition; **una ~ de las jugadas más importantes** (TV) edited highlights of the game

repetidamente *adv* repeatedly

repetido *adj*
A ‹*sello/disco*›: **éste lo tengo ~** I have two of these
B (delante del n) ‹*casos/avisos/intentos*› repeated (*before n*); **se lo había dicho en repetidas ocasiones** I'd told him again and again *o* time and again

repetidor -dora *m,f*
A (Educ) *student repeating a year*
B **repetidor** *m*, **repetidora** *f* (Rad, TV) relay station, booster station

repetir [I14] *vt*
A ‹*pregunta/explicación*› to repeat; **¿me lo puedes ~?** could you repeat it, please?; **hay que ~le las cosas diez veces** you have to tell her everything ten times; **se lo repetí hasta la saciedad** I told him until I was blue in the face (colloq); **¡que no te lo tenga que volver a ~!** don't let me have to tell you again!
B ‹*tarea*› to do … again; ‹*programa*› to repeat, rerun; ‹*experimento*› to repeat; ‹*curso/asignatura*› to repeat; **una experiencia que no quiero ~** an experience I don't want to repeat; **tuvo que ~ la pieza** he had to play the piece again
C ‹*plato*› have a second helping of, to have seconds of (colloq)
D ‹*ajo/pepino*›: **he estado repitiendo la cebolla** the onion's been repeating on me
■ **repetir** *vi*
A (volver a comer) have a second helping, to have seconds (colloq)
B «*pimientos/pepinos*» to repeat; **el ajo me repite** garlic repeats on me
C (Educ) to repeat a year/course
■ **repetirse** *v pron*
A «*fenómeno/incidente*» to recur, happen again; «*persona*» to repeat oneself; **la historia se repite** (fr hecha) history repeats itself
B (Chi) (volver a comer) to have a second helping, have seconds (colloq)

repetitivo -va *adj* repetitive

repicar [A2] *vi* to ring out, peal
■ **repicar** *vt* to ring

repipi *adj* (esp Esp fam) (cursi) affected, precious (pej); (sabihondo): **es tan ~** she's such a little know-it-all

repique *m* ringing, pealing

repiquetear [A1] *vi*
A «*campanas*» to peal, ring out; «*teléfono*» (Chi, Méx) to ring
B (golpear): **la lluvia repiqueteaba en los vidrios** the rain pattered on the window panes; **~ con los dedos en la mesa** to drum *o* tap one's fingers on the table

repiqueteo *m*
A (de campanas) ringing, pealing; (del teléfono) (Chi, Méx) ringing
B (de lluvia) pattering, pitter-patter (colloq); (con los dedos) drumming, tapping

repisa *f* (estante) shelf; (de chimenea) mantelpiece; (Arquit) corbel

repita, repitas, etc *see* **repetir**

repitente *mf* (Chi) (Educ) *student repeating the year*

replana *f* (Per) underworld slang

replantar [A1] *vt* ‹*terreno/bosque*› to replant; ‹*planta*› to transplant

replantear [A1] *vt*: **replanteó la necesidad de …** he again raised the question of the need to …; **debes ~ tu posición** you must redefine your position; **~on su sistema defensivo** they reorganized their defense
■ **replantearse** *v pron* to rethink

replegar [A7] *vt* ‹*alas*› to fold, draw in; ‹*tren de aterrizaje*› to retract, draw up
■ **replegarse** *v pron* (Dep, Mil) to withdraw, fall back

repleto -ta *adj*
A ‹*calle/vehículo/sala*› ~ **DE algo** packed WITH sth; **la ciudad está repleta de museos** the city is full of museums; **el tren iba ~** the train was packed *o* (colloq) jam-packed
B ‹*persona*› replete (frml *or* hum), full

réplica *f*
A (frml) (contestación) reply
B (copia) replica
C (Chi, Méx) (de terremoto) aftershock

r

replicar [A2] *vt* (frml) to retort, reply
■ **replicar** *vi*
A (argumentar) to argue
B (Der) to reply

repliegue *m*
A (en superficie) fold, furrow
B (Dep, Mil) withdrawal

repoblación *f* 1 (Agr) restocking; **~ forestal** reforestation 2 (con personas) repopulation, resettlement

repoblar [A10] *vt* 1 ‹*río/lago*› to restock 2 (de árboles) to reforest 3 (de personas) to repopulate, resettle

repollo *m* cabbage

reponer [E22] *vt*
A 1 (reemplazar) ‹*existencias*› to replace; ‹*dinero*› to put back, repay; **~ fuerzas** to get one's strength back 2 ‹*funcionario/trabajador*› to reinstate 3 ‹*obra*› to put … on again, revive; ‹*serie*› to repeat, rerun; ‹*película*› to show … again
B (replicar) to reply
■ **reponerse** *v pron* to recover; **~se DE algo** to recover FROM sth

reportaje *m* (en periódico, revista) article, feature; (en televisión) report, item; (entrevista) (AmL) interview; **le hicieron un ~** they interviewed him
(Compuesto) **reportaje gráfico** illustrated feature

reportar [A1] *vt*
A ‹*beneficios/pérdidas*› to produce, yield; (+ *me/te/le etc*) **le reportó grandes ganancias** it brought him large profits; **sólo me reportó disgustos** it brought *o* caused me nothing but trouble
B (AmL) (denunciar, dar cuenta de) to report
C (Méx) ▸ **reportear**
■ **reportarse** *v pron* (AmL) (presentarse) to report

reporte *m* (Méx) (informe) report; (queja) complaint

reportear [A1] *vt* (Andes) to cover, report on
■ **reportear** *vi* (Andes) to report

reportero -ra *m,f* reporter
(Compuesto) **reportero gráfico** press photographer

reposacabezas *m* (*pl* ~) headrest

reposadamente *adv* unhurriedly, calmly; **se mueve ~** her movements are unhurried

reposado -da *adj* [SER] ‹*persona/temperamento*› calm; ‹*ademanes/habla*› unhurried

reposar [A1] *vi*
A «*persona*» (descansar) to rest; **sus restos mortales reposan en Tijuana** his mortal remains lie in Tijuana; **la naturaleza reposa en invierno** (liter) in winter, nature lies dormant; **su mano reposaba sobre el libro** her hand was resting on the book
B «*líquido/solución*» to settle; **dejar ~ la masa** let the dough stand
■ **reposar** *vt*: **~ la comida** to let one's food go down *o* settle

reposición *f*
A (reemplazo) replacement
B (de serie) repeat, rerun; (de obra) revival; (de película) reshowing

reposo *m*
A 1 (descanso) rest; **me recomendó guardar ~ absoluto** he recommended complete rest 2 (Coc): **dejar en ~** leave to stand
B (Fís) rest; **moléculas en ~** molecules at rest

repostar [A1] *vt* 1 ‹*gasolina*› to fill up with; **el avión repostó combustible en Caracas** the plane refueled in Caracas 2 ‹*provisiones*› to stock up with
■ **repostar** *vi* (Auto) to fill up, to get some gas (AmE) *o* (BrE) petrol; (Aviac, Náut) to refuel

repostería *f* confectionery, baking (*of pastries, desserts*)

repostero -ra *m,f*
A (persona) confectioner, pastrycook
B **repostero** *m* (Chi) (despensa) pantry; (comedor) kitchen diner

reprender [E1] *vt* to scold, tell … off (colloq)

represa *f* 1 (en río — dique) dam; (— embalse) reservoir 2 (de molino) millpond

represalia *f* reprisal; **tomar ~s** to take reprisals; **como ~ por …** in retaliation for …

representación *f*
A (acción): **asistió en ~ del Rey** she attended as the King's representative; **en ~ de mis compañeros** on behalf of my companions; **tiene a su cargo la ~ de una editorial** he represents a publishing house
B (delegación) delegation
C (Teatr) performance, production
D 1 (símbolo) representation 2 (imagen) illustration; **hacerse una ~ mental de algo** to picture sth 3 (muestra) sample

representante *mf* representative; **es ~ de una editorial** she represents a publishing house; **ganó la ~ brasileña** the Brazilian contestant won
(Compuesto) **representante de la ley** (period) officer of the law

representar [A1] *vt*
A ‹*persona/organización/país*› to represent; **hacerse ~ por alguien** to send a representative *o* proxy
B ‹*obra*› to perform, put on; **representó el papel de Cleopatra** she played (the part of) Cleopatra
C (aparentar) to look; **no representa su edad** he doesn't look his age
D (simbolizar) to symbolize
E (reproducir) «*dibujo/fotografía/escena*» to show, depict; «*obra/novela*» to portray, depict
F (equivaler a, significar) to represent; **esto representa un aumento del 5%** this represents a 5% increase; **para él no representa ningún sacrificio** it's no sacrifice for him; **eso ~ía tres días de trabajo** that would mean *o* involve three days' work
■ **representarse** *v pron* to picture, imagine

representatividad *f*: **el gobierno carece de ~** the government does not represent the will of the people

representativo -va *adj*
A ‹*muestra*› representative; **un autor ~ del período** a representative author of the period; **este cuadro es ~ de su época cubista** this picture is a good example of his Cubist period
B (Pol) representative; **sistema ~ de gobierno** representative system of government

represión *f* repression

represivo -va *adj* repressive

represor -sora *m,f* oppressor

reprimenda *f* reprimand

reprimido¹ -da *adj* repressed

reprimido² -da *m,f*: **es un ~** he's repressed

reprimir [I1] *vt*
A ‹*rebelión*› to suppress, crush
B ‹*risa/llanto/bostezo*› to suppress, stifle; **tuvo que ~ su ira** he had to choke back his anger
C (Psic) to repress
■ **reprimirse** *v pron* (*refl*) to control oneself

reprise /rre'pris/, **repris** *m or f*
A (Auto) acceleration
B **reprise** *f* (AmL) (reposición) revival

reprobable *adj* reprehensible

reprobación *f* disapproval

reprobar [A10] *vt*
A ‹*actitud/conducta*› to condemn; **repruebo el favoritismo** I disapprove of any kind of favoritism
B (AmL) ‹*estudiante*› to fail; ‹*materia/curso*› to fail; **me ~on en física** I failed physics

réprobo -ba *adj/m,f* reprobate

reprochable *adj* reprehensible

reprochar [A1] *vt* to reproach; **no tengo nada que ~le** I have nothing to reproach him for
■ **reprocharse** *v pron* (*refl*) to reproach oneself

reproche *m*: **no merezco tus ~s** I do not deserve your reproaches; **una mirada de ~** a look of reproach, a reproachful look; **siempre me hace ~s** he's always criticizing *o* reproaching me

reproducción *f*
A (Biol, Bot) reproduction; **los órganos de la ~** the reproductive organs; **animales reservados para la ~** animals kept solely for breeding
B (de sonido) reproduction; (de modelo) reproduction, copy; (de disco) copy

r

reproducir [I6] *vt*
A (volver a producir) to repeat, reproduce
B ‹*cuadro/ambiente*› to reproduce; **van a ~ una aldea íbera** they are going to reconstruct an Iberian village
C ‹*sonido/discurso/texto*› to reproduce
■ **reproducirse** *v pron*
A (Biol, Bot) to reproduce, breed
B «*fenómeno*» to recur, occur *o* happen again

reproductor -tora *adj* **1** ‹*animal*› breeding (*before n*); **caballo ~** stud horse **2** ‹*órgano*› reproductive

reptar [A1] *vi* «*serpiente*» to slither; «*cocodrilo*» to crawl, slide; **escaparon reptando por el túnel** they escaped by crawling along the tunnel

reptil¹ *adj* reptilian, reptile (*before n*)

reptil² *m* reptile

república *f* republic
Compuestos
- **república bananera** (pey) banana republic (pej)
- **república federal** federal republic

República Checa *f* Czech Republic

República Dominicana *f* Dominican Republic

República Eslovaca *f* Slovak Republic

republicanismo *m* republicanism

republicano -na *adj/m,f* republican

República Oriental del Uruguay *f* (frml) *official name of Uruguay*

repudiar [A1] *vt*
A ‹*atentado/violencia*› to condemn
B (Der) ‹*mujer*› to disown, repudiate (frml); ‹*herencia*› to repudiate

repudio *m* repudiation

repuesto *m* (pieza) (spare) part; (reserva): **de ~** spare (*before n*)

repugnancia *f*: **me causa ~** I find him repulsive *o* repugnant; **siento ~ por** *or* **hacia las culebras** I can't stand snakes, I have an aversion to snakes; **el atentado causó ~ en todo el país** the whole country felt revulsion at the attack; **me da ~ ver cómo le miente** it's horrible *o* it makes me sick the way he's always lying to her

repugnante *adj* ‹*olor*› disgusting, revolting; ‹*crimen*› abhorrent, repugnant; ‹*persona*› (físicamente) repulsive, revolting; (moralmente) repugnant

repugnar [A1] *vi*: **me repugna beber de un vaso sucio** I find having to drink out of a dirty glass disgusting; **me repugnan sus mentiras** I find his lies repugnant; **le repugna la injusticia** she finds any form of injustice abhorrent

repujado -da *adj* embossed, repoussé

repujar [A1] *vt* to emboss, to work … in repoussé

repulsa *f* (condena) condemnation; (rechazo) rejection

repulsión *f* repulsion

repulsivo -va *adj* ‹*persona*› (físicamente) repulsive, revolting; (moralmente) repugnant; ‹*olor*› disgusting, revolting

repuntar [A1] *vi*
A **1** «*precio/cotización*» to rally, pick up **2** «*industria/economía*» to recover, pick up (colloq) **3** (AmL) «*equipo/jugador*» to recover, improve; «*estudiante/enfermo*» to improve, pick up (colloq)
B «*marea*» to turn; «*río*» (AmL) to rise

repunte *m* (Fin) (de precios, cotizaciones) recovery, rally; (de industria, economía) upturn, recovery; (de la inflación) increase

reputación *f* reputation; **tienes ~ de buen mecánico** you have a reputation as a good mechanic

reputado -da *adj* ‹*cantante/profesional*› famous, renowned; *ver tb* **reputar**

reputar [A1] *vt* to consider; **un país reputado como moderno** a country considered *o* held to be modern

requebrar [A5] *vt* (liter) to pay amorous compliments to

requemar [A1] *vt* to burn
■ **requemarse** *v pron* to burn; **el pollo se requemó** the chicken got *o* was burned

requerimiento *m*
A (Der) request; **a ~ del juez** at the judge's request
B (necesidad, requisito) requirement

requerir [I11] *vt*
A (necesitar) to require; **requiere paciencia** it requires *o* demands patience; **S se requiere buena presencia** good appearance essential
B ‹*documento*› to require; ‹*persona*› to summon; **fue requerido de pago** he was ordered to pay

requesón *m* curd (cheese)

requiebro *m* amorous compliment

réquiem /'rrekjem/ *m* (*pl* **requiems**) requiem

requintar [A1] *vt*
A (Per fam) (regañar) to tell … off
B (Méx) ‹*cuerda*› to tighten

requisa *f*
A (de vehículos, suministros) requisition; (de drogas, objetos robados) seizure
B (inspección) inspection; (registro) (AmL) search

requisar [A1] *vt*
A (expropiar) ‹*vehículo/suministros*› to requisition; (confiscar) ‹*drogas/objetos robados*› to seize
B (inspeccionar) to inspect; (cachear) (Col, Ven) to search

requisito *m* requirement; **reunir los ~s** to fulfill *o* meet the requirements; **es ~ indispensable** it is an essential requirement
Compuesto **requisito previo** prerequisite

requisitoria *f* **1** (dirigida — al acusado) summons; (— a otro juez) warrant **2** (AmL) (interrogatorio) interrogation

res *f* **1** (animal) animal; **tiene más de 100 ~es** she owns more than a hundred head of cattle; **~es bravas** fighting bulls **2** (Col, Méx, Ven) (Coc) *tb* **carne de ~** beef

resabiado -da *adj* **1** ‹*caballo/toro*› *which has acquired a particular habit* **2** ‹*persona*›: **quedé** *or* **salí ~** I learned my lesson

resabido -da *adj* **1** (fam) (bien sabido): **lo tengo sabido y ~** I know it backwards *o* inside out **2** (fam & pey) ‹*persona*›: **es muy ~** he's such a know-it-all (colloq)

resabio *m*
A (sabor desagradable) (unpleasant) aftertaste; **~s del pasado** unpleasant memories of the past
B (mala costumbre) bad habit

resaca *f*
A (de las olas) undertow
B (después de beber) hangover
C (RPl) (limo) silt; (en la orilla) jetsam; (de un grupo) (fam & pey) dregs (*pl*) (pej); **la ~ de la sociedad** the dregs of society

resaltador *m* (Col) highlighter

resaltante *adj* (AmL) outstanding

resaltar [A1] *vi*
A (sobresalir, destacarse) to stand out; **resaltaban sus grandes ojos negros** her big dark eyes were her most striking feature
B **hacer resaltar** ‹*color*› to bring out; ‹*importancia/necesidad*› to highlight, stress
■ **resaltar** *vt* ‹*cualidad/rasgo*› to highlight; ‹*importancia/necesidad*› to highlight, stress

resalte, resalto *m* projection, ledge

resarcimiento *m* (indemnización) compensation; (reembolso) reimbursement, repayment

resarcir [I4] *vt* **~ a algn DE algo** ‹*de daños/inconvenientes*› to compensate sb FOR sth; ‹*de gastos*› to reimburse sb FOR sth; **es difícil de leer pero te resarce del esfuerzo** it is difficult to read but it's worth the effort
■ **resarcirse** *v pron* **~se DE algo** (desquitarse) to get one's own back FOR sth; (compensar) to make up FOR sth

resbalada *f* (AmL) slip; **darse** *or* **pegarse una ~** to slip

resbaladilla *f* (Méx) slide, chute

resbaladizo -za *adj*
A ‹*superficie/carretera*› slippery
B ‹*asunto/tema*› delicate, tricky (colloq)

resbalar [A1] *vi*
A (caerse) to slip; **se dejó ~ por la barandilla** he slid down the banister; **las lágrimas le resbalaban por las mejillas** the tears ran *o* trickled down his cheeks
B (fam) (equivocarse) to slip up
C (fam) (ser indiferente): **todo lo que le digas le resbala** anything you say to him is just like water off a duck's back (colloq); **mis problemas/las críticas le resbalan** he couldn't care less about my problems/criticism (colloq)
■ **resbalarse** *v pron* to slip; **nos resbalamos por la pendiente** we slithered *o* slid down the slope

r

resbalín *m* (Chi) slide

resbalón *m* slip; ***dar(se)*** *or* ***pegar(se) un*** ~ (literal) to slip; (meter la pata) to put one's foot in it (colloq)

resbaloso -sa *adj* (AmL) ‹*superficie*› slippery

rescatar [A1] *vt*
A (salvar — de prisión) to rescue, free; (— de peligro) to rescue, save; **intentaba ~ sus joyas** she was trying to save her jewels
B ‹*dinero/pulsera*› to recover, get back; ‹*tierra*› to reclaim; **~on el cadáver** they recovered the body

rescate *m*
A 1 (salvamento) rescue; **equipo/operación de ~** rescue team/operation 2 (precio) ransom
B 1 (de dinero, joya) recovery 2 (de tierras) reclamation

rescindir [I1] *vt* to rescind (frml), terminate

rescoldo *m* embers (*pl*); ***avivar el ~ de algo*** to rekindle sth

resecar [A2] *vt*
A ‹*piel/ambiente*› to make … very dry; ‹*planta*› to dry up
B (Med) (extirpar) to remove, resect (tech)
■ **resecarse** *v pron* to dry up, get very dry

reseco -ca *adj* ‹*planta*› dried-up; ‹*pan*› dry; **la tierra estaba reseca** the earth was parched *o* had dried up

resentido¹ -da *adj*
A (dolorido) painful
B (disgustado) upset, hurt; (con rencor) resentful; **está ~ porque no lo ascendieron** he feels resentful that he wasn't promoted

resentido² -da *m,f*: **es un ~** he has a chip on his shoulder

resentimiento *m* resentment, bitterness

resentirse [I11] *v pron*
A 1 (sentir dolor) ~ DE **algo**: **aún se resiente de la lesión** he is still suffering the effects of the injury; **ya no me resiento de la espalda** my back doesn't give me trouble any more (colloq); **aún se resienten de la derrota** they're still smarting from the defeat 2 (sufrir las consecuencias) to suffer; **su trabajo no se resentía** his work didn't suffer; **su salud se resentía con el clima** the weather was taking its toll on his health
B (ofenderse, molestarse) to get upset

reseña *f* 1 (de congreso, reunión) summary, report; (de libro) review; **hizo la ~ del partido** he wrote the report on the game; **una ~ histórica/biográfica** a historical/biographical outline 2 (descripción) description; (sobre escritor, deportista) profile

reseñar [A1] *vt* 1 ‹*obra literaria*› to review; ‹*acto/conferencia*› to report on, write a summary of; ‹*partido*› to report on 2 ‹*persona/animal*› to describe

resero *m* (RPl) cowhand, cowboy

reserva¹ *f*
A (de habitación, pasaje) reservation; (de mesa) booking, reservation; **¿tiene ~?** do you have a reservation?, have you booked?; **hacer una ~** to make a reservation
B 1 (cantidad guardada) reserve; **~s de trigo** reserves *o* stocks of wheat; **tengo otro par de ~** I have a spare pair; **este dinero lo tengo de ~ para …** I'm keeping this money in reserve for … 2 **reservas** *fpl* (Biol) reserves (of fat) (*pl*)
C 1 (Dep) (equipo) reserves (*pl*), reserve team; (conjunto de suplentes) substitutes (*pl*) 2 (Mil): **la ~** the reserve
D (de indígenas) reservation; (de animales) reserve
(Compuesto) **reserva natural** nature reserve
E (secreto, discreción): **en la más absoluta ~** in the strictest confidence; **mantener algo en la mayor ~** to keep sth absolutely secret
F **reservas** *fpl* 1 (dudas) reservations (*pl*); **lo aceptó, pero no sin ~s** he agreed, but not without reservations 2 (reparos): **habló sin ~s** he talked openly *o* freely; **díselo sin ~s** tell her everything, don't keep anything back
G (Méx) **a ~ DE QUE + SUBJ**: **iremos a ~ de que (no) llueva** we'll go as long as *o* provided it doesn't rain

reserva² *mf* (Dep) reserve

reserva³ *m*: *wine aged for at least three years*

> **reserva**
>
> *Vinos de reserva* are those of a better than average vintage. To qualify for this designation, red wines must have been aged in cask and bottle for a minimum of three years, and white wines for two years. *See also* **gran reserva**

reservación *f* (AmL) ▸**reserva¹ A**

reservadamente *adv* in confidence

reservado¹ -da *adj* ‹*persona/actitud*› reserved; ‹*asunto/tema*› confidential; *ver tb* **reservar**

reservado² *m*
A (en restaurante, bar) private room; (en tren) reserved compartment
B (CS) (vino) vintage wine

reservar [A1] *vt*
A ‹*asiento/habitación/mesa*› to reserve, book; ‹*pasaje/billete*› to book; Ⓢ **reservado** reserved
B (guardar): **nos reservaba una sorpresa** he had a surprise in store for us; **reservó lo mejor para el final** she kept the best till last; **reservó parte del dinero** he set aside part of the money; Ⓢ **reservado el derecho de admisión** the management reserves the right to refuse admission
■ **reservarse** *v pron*
A (para sí mismo) ‹*porción/porcentaje*› to keep … for oneself; **~se la opinión** to reserve judgment
B (*refl*) (para otra tarea) to save oneself; **me reservo para el postre** I'm leaving some room for dessert

reservista *mf* reservist

reset /rri'set/ *m* reset

resfriado¹ -da *adj*: **estoy algo ~** I have a slight cold

resfriado² *m* cold; **pescar un ~** (fam) to catch a cold; **no te quiero pegar mi ~** I don't want you to catch my cold

resfriarse [A17] *v pron* to catch a cold

resfrío *m* (esp AmS) cold

resguardar [A1] *vt* 1 ~ **algo/a algn** DE **algo** ‹*de peligro/frío*› to protect sth/sb FROM sth 2 ‹*derechos/privilegios*› to safeguard
■ **resguardarse** *v pron* (de peligro) to protect oneself; (de la lluvia, el frío) to shelter, take shelter; **se ~on de la lluvia** they sheltered *o* took shelter from the rain

resguardo *m*
A (Esp) (de depósito, de dinero, bienes) deposit slip; (en tintorería, zapatería) slip, ticket
B (cobertizo, protección) shelter; **se pusieron a ~ de la lluvia** they took shelter from the rain
C (Col) (reserva) reservation, reserve
D (Méx) (control, vigilancia) control

residencia *f*
A 1 (en país, ciudad) residence; **fijar ~** to take up residence; **dos alemanes con ~ en Florida** two Germans resident in Florida 2 (derecho) right of residence 3 (documento) *tb* **permiso de ~** residence permit
B 1 (casa) residence 2 (de estudiantes) dormitory (AmE), hall of residence (BrE); (de enfermeras) hostel, home; **la ~ de oficiales** the officers' quarters 3 (hostal, fonda) boarding house, guest house (*not providing meals*)
(Compuesto) **residencia de ancianos** old people's home
C (AmL) (Med) residency (AmE), time spent as a houseman (BrE)

residencial¹ *adj* residential

residencial² *f* (CS) guesthouse, boarding house

residente¹ *adj* resident

residente² *mf*
A (en país) resident
B (médico) resident (AmE), houseman (BrE)

residir [I1] *vi* 1 «*persona*» (vivir) to live, reside (frml) 2 «*encanto/interés*» (radicar) ~ EN **algo** to lie IN sth; **la soberanía reside en el pueblo** sovereignty is vested in the people

residual *adj* ‹*sustancia/valor*› residual

residuo *m*
A (Mat) remainder; (Quím) residue
B **residuos** *mpl* (desperdicios) waste, waste materials *o* products (*pl*)

Compuestos
- **residuos nucleares/radiactivos/tóxicos** *mpl* nuclear/radioactive/toxic waste
- **residuos sólidos** *mpl* (frml) refuse, solid waste

resignación *f* resignation

resignado -da *adj* resigned; **~ A algo** resigned TO sth

resignarse [A1] *v pron* to resign oneself; **~ A + INF** to resign oneself to -ING

resina *f* resin

resinoso -sa *adj* resinous

resistencia *f*
A 1 (oposición) resistance; **sin ofrecer** *or* **oponer ~** without putting up *o* offering any resistance; **~ pasiva** passive resistance 2 **la Resistencia** (Hist, Pol) the Resistance
B 1 (aguante) **tiene una gran ~ física** she has tremendous stamina; **prueba de ~** endurance test 2 (a virus, enfermedad) resistance
C 1 (al aire, agua, a corriente eléctrica) resistance 2 (componente de circuito) resistor; (de secador, calentador) element

resistente *adj* ‹*material/metal*› resistant, tough; ‹*tela*› tough, hard-wearing; ‹*persona/animal/planta*› tough, hardy; **~ a la humedad** damp-proof; **~ al calor** heat-resistant; **~ al frío** resistant to cold

resistir [I1] *vt* 1 (aguantar) ‹*dolor/calor/presión*› to withstand, take; **¿~á otro invierno?** will it last *o* survive another winter?; **su corazón no ~ía un golpe tan fuerte** his heart couldn't take *o* stand a shock like that; **no la resisto** (Col, Per fam) I can't stand her 2 ‹*tentación/impulso*› to resist 3 ‹*ataque*› to resist, withstand; ‹*enemigo*› to resist, hold out against
■ **resistir** *vi* 1 (aguantar): **no resistió, era demasiado peso** it didn't take it *o* hold, it was too heavy; **ya no resisto más** I can't take (it) any more; **¿cuánto resistes debajo del agua?** how long can you stay underwater? 2 «*ejército*» to hold out, resist
■ **resistirse** *v pron*
A (oponer resistencia) to resist; **no hay mujer que se le resista** women find him irresistible
B (tener reticencia) **~se A + INF**: **se resiste a aceptarlo** she's unwilling *o* reluctant to agree to it; **me resisto a creerlo** I find it hard to believe; **no pude ~me a decírselo** I couldn't resist telling her
C (fam) (plantear dificultades): **la cerradura se me resistía** I couldn't get the lock open; **las cifras se me resisten** figures are beyond me (colloq)

resma *f* ream

resolana *f*, (Esp) **resol** *m* (brillo) glare of the sun; (luz) sunlight

resollar [A10] *vi* 1 (respirar fuertemente) to breathe heavily; (por agotamiento) to puff 2 (hablar): **sin ~** without (saying) a word

resolución *f*
A (de problema) solution; (de conflicto) settlement, resolution (de contrato) termination
B (decisión) decision; **tomar una ~** to make a decision; **tomaron la ~ de emigrar** they decided to emigrate
C (determinación) determination, resolve

resoluto -ta *adj* determined, resolute

resolver [E11] *vt*
A ‹*crimen/problema*› to solve; ‹*asunto/conflicto*› to resolve, settle; **¿me puedes ~ una duda?** could you clear up one point for me?; **tiene resuelto su futuro** his future is settled
B (decidir) to decide; **~ + INF** to decide *o* resolve to + INF
■ **resolver** *vi* «*juez*» to rule, decide
■ **resolverse** *v pron* to decide; **se resolvieron a aceptarlo** they decided to accept it; **no se resuelve a abandonarlo** she can't bring herself to leave him

resonancia *f* (Mús, Fís) resonance; (eco) echo; (de noticia, suceso): **tuvo gran ~** it had a huge impact

resonante *adj* ‹*sonido*› resonant; ‹*éxito*› resounding

resonar [A10] *vi* (hacer eco) to echo, resound; **sus gritos aún resuenan en mis oídos** his cries still ring in my ears

resondrar [A1] *vt* (Per fam) to tell … off (colloq), to scold

resoplar [A1] *vi* (por cansancio) to puff; (por enfado) to snort

resoplido *m* 1 (de enfado) snort 2 (de cansancio): **dando ~s** puffing and panting 3 (de caballo) snort

resorte *m*
A (muelle) spring; (medio, influencia): **los ~s del poder** the reins of power; **tocó todos los ~s** she used all her influence
B (AmC, Col, Méx) (elástico) elastic

resortera *f* (Méx) slingshot (AmE), catapult (BrE)

respaldar [A1] *vt*
A 1 ‹*persona*› (apoyar) to support, back; (en discusión) to back … up 2 ‹*propuesta/plan*› to support, back; **respaldado por la experiencia** backed by *o* with the backing of experience
B (endosar) ‹*documento*› to endorse
■ **respaldarse** *v pron*
A (en sillón) to sit back; (contra árbol, pared) to lean back
B (depender): **se respalda mucho en sus padres** he relies heavily on his parents (for support)

respaldo *m*
A (de asiento) back
B (apoyo) support, backing; (Fin) backing
C (dorso de documento) back; (lo escrito) endorsement

respectar [A1] *vi* (*en 3ª pers*): **en** *or* **por lo que a mí respecta** as far as I'm concerned; **en lo que respecta al personal** as far as the staff is concerned, with regard to the staff

respectivo -va *adj*
A (correspondiente) respective
B **en lo respectivo a** (frml) as regards, with regard to

respecto *m*: **a este ~ dijo que …** on this matter *o* (frml) in this regard he said that …; **hizo unos comentarios al ~** he made a few remarks on the matter; **no sé nada (con) ~ a este asunto** I know nothing about *o* regarding this matter; **~ de su petición** regarding *o* with regard to your request

respetabilidad *f* respectability

respetable[1] *adj* (digno de respeto) respectable; (considerable) considerable; **a una distancia ~ del centro** quite a distance *o* a fair distance from the center

respetable[2] *m* (period): **el ~** (Teatr) the audience; (Taur) the crowd, the spectators (*pl*)

respetar [A1] *vt* 1 ‹*persona*› to respect; **se hizo ~ de** *or* **por todos** he won *o* gained everyone's respect 2 ‹*opinión/tradiciones*› to respect; ‹*ley/norma*› to observe; **~ el medio ambiente** to respect the environment; **~ los límites de velocidad** to observe the speed restrictions; **lo reformaron respetando el diseño original** they renovated it conserving the original design
■ **respetarse** *v pron* (*refl*) to respect oneself, have self-respect; **un abogado que se respete no haría eso** no self-respecting lawyer would do that

respeto *m* 1 (consideración, deferencia) respect; **con ~** respectfully, with respect; **ella me merece mucho ~** I have the highest regard *o* respect for her; **por ~ a algn/algo** out of consideration *o* respect for sb/sth; **guardar el debido ~ a algn** to show due respect to sb; **faltarle al** *or* (CS) **el ~ a algn** to be rude *o* disrespectful to sb; **el ~ a los derechos humanos** respect *o* regard for human rights; **el ~ a la Constitución** respect for *o* observance of the Constitution; ***campar por sus ~s*** (Esp) to do as one pleases 2 (temor): **su presencia impone ~** her presence commands (a feeling of) respect; **les tengo mucho ~ a los perros** I have a healthy respect for dogs 3 **respetos** *mpl* respects (*pl*); **presentaron sus ~s a …** they paid their repects to … (frml)

respetuoso -sa *adj* ‹*persona/silencio*› respectful; **le envía un ~ saludo** Sincerely yours (AmE), Yours respectfully (frml), Yours faithfully (BrE)

respingado -da *adj* (AmL) ‹*nariz*› turned-up

respingar [A3] *vi*
A «*falda*» to ride up
B «*caballo*» to buck
C (Méx fam) (replicar) to answer back

respingo *m* start; **dio un ~** he gave a start

respingón -gona *adj*
A ‹*nariz*› turned-up
B (Méx fam) ‹*persona*› touchy

respiración *f*
A (Fisiol) breathing, respiration (frml); **me quedé sin ~** I was out of breath; **recobrar la ~** to get one's breath back; **contener la ~** to hold one's breath

(Compuestos)
- **respiración artificial** artificial respiration
- **respiración boca a boca** mouth-to-mouth resuscitation, kiss of life

B (ventilación) ventilation

respiradero *m* (de chimenea) flue; (de mina) ventilation shaft; (Tec) vent; (para pesca submarina) snorkel

respirar [A1] *vi*

A 1 (Fisiol) to breathe; **~ por la boca** to breathe through one's mouth; **respire hondo** take a deep breath; **respiraba con dificultad** she was having difficulty breathing; **lo escuchaban casi sin ~** they listened to him with bated breath; ***no me/le deja ni ~*** (fam) she won't give me/him a minute's peace (colloq); ***no tengo tiempo ni de ~*** (fam) I hardly have time to breathe 2 «*vino*» to breathe

B (tranquilizarse): **cuando llegó respiré** when he finally arrived I breathed a sigh of relief

■ **respirar** *vt*

A 1 ‹*aire*› to breathe; **respiran el humo de los coches** they breathe in the exhaust fumes 2 ‹*tranquilidad*›: **la paz que se respira aquí** the feeling of peace that you get here

B (rebosar) ‹*felicidad/bondad*› to radiate

respiratorio -ria *adj* respiratory

respiro *m*

A (aliento) breath

B 1 (descanso) break; **tomarse un ~** to take a break *o* (colloq) have a breather; **dame un ~** give me a break (colloq) 2 (prórroga) respite; **conceder a algn un ~** to grant sb a respite; **pidieron un ~ para cubrir la deuda** they asked for a few months' (*o* weeks' *etc*) grace to pay off the debt 3 (alivio) respite; **este dolor no le da (un) ~** she gets no respite from the pain

resplandecer [E3] *vi* 1 «*sol*» to shine; «*luna/metal/cristal*» gleam; «*hoguera*» to blaze 2 (liter) (radiar): **resplandecía de felicidad** she radiated happiness

resplandeciente *adj* 1 ‹*luna/metal/cristal*› gleaming; **un sol ~** a dazzling sun; **tiene la cocina ~** his kitchen is sparkling clean 2 (radiante): **~ de orgullo** glowing with pride; **tenía la cara ~ de felicidad** her face radiated happiness

resplandor *m* (del sol) glare, brightness; (de luna, metal, cristal) gleam; (de relámpago, explosión) flash

responder [E1] *vi*

A 1 (contestar) to reply, answer, respond (frml); **respondió con una evasiva** he gave an evasive reply; **respondió afirmativamente** she said yes, she responded in the affirmative (frml); **~ A algo** to reply TO sth, to answer sth, to respond TO sth (frml) 2 (replicar) to answer back

B (reaccionar) to respond; **~ A algo** ‹*a amenaza/estímulo*› to respond TO sth; **no respondía a los mandos** it was not responding to *o* obeying the controls; **responde al nombre de Kurt** he answers to the name of Kurt

C 1 (corresponder) **~ A algo**: **no responden a la descripción** they do not answer the description; **las cifras no responden a la realidad** the figures do not reflect the true situation; **responde a las exigencias actuales de seguridad** it meets present-day demands for safety 2 (estar motivado por algo) **~ A algo**: **responde a la demanda actual** it is a response to the current demand; **su viaje respondía al deseo de verla** his trip was motivated by the desire to see her

D (responsabilizarse): **si ocurre algo yo no respondo** if anything happens I will not be held responsible; **~ ante la justicia** to answer for one's acts in a court of law; **~ DE algo**: **yo respondo de su integridad** I will vouch for his integrity; **no respondo de lo que hizo** I am not responsible for what he did; **yo respondo de que lo haga** I will be responsible for ensuring that he does it; **~ POR algn** to vouch FOR sb

■ **responder** *vt* 1 (contestar) to reply, answer, respond (frml); **respondió que no le interesaba** he replied that he was not interested 2 ‹*pregunta*› to answer 3 ‹*llamada/carta*› to answer, reply to, respond to (frml)

respondón¹ -dona *adj* (fam) ‹*niño*› mouthy (AmE colloq), cheeky (BrE colloq)

respondón² -dona *m,f* (fam): **es un ~** he's always answering back

responsabilidad *f*

A 1 (de cargo, tarea) responsibility; **un puesto de mucha ~** a post which involves a great deal of responsibility; **tiene la ~ de mantenerlos** he is responsible for supporting them 2 (conciencia de las obligaciones) responsibility; **tener sentido de la ~** to have a sense of responsibility

B (Der) (culpa) responsibility; (obligación de indemnizar) liability; **cargó con toda la ~** she took full responsibility; **exigen ~es al alcalde por ...** the mayor is being held accountable for ...

responsabilizar [A4] *vt* **~ a algn DE algo** to hold sb responsible *o* accountable FOR sth

■ **responsabilizarse** *v pron* 1 (de tarea) to take responsibility; **~se DE algo** to take responsibility FOR sth 2 **~se DE algo** ‹*de delito*› to admit responsibility FOR sth; ‹*de accidente*› to take responsibility FOR sth; **el periódico no se responsabiliza de ...** the newspaper accepts no responsibility *o* liability for ...

responsable¹ *adj*

A [SER] 1 (concienzudo) responsible 2 (de tarea) **~ DE algo** responsible FOR sth

B (culpable) responsible; (con obligación de indemnizar) liable; **~ DE algo** responsible/liable FOR sth; **no es ~ de sus actos** he's not responsible for his actions; **eres ~ ante mí del resultado** you're answerable *o* accountable to me for the result; **nadie se ha hecho ~ del atentado** no one has claimed responsibility for the attack

responsable² *mf* 1 (de tarea): **el ~ del área de auditoría** the person responsible for audits 2 (de delito, accidente): **los ~s serán castigados** those responsible *o* the people responsible will be punished

responso *m: prayer for the dead*

respuesta *f*

A 1 (a carta, mensaje) reply, answer, response (frml) 2 (reacción) response; (Psic) response

B (solución) answer, solution

resquebrajadura *f* (en roca) crack; (en madera) split

resquebrajar [A1] *vt* ‹*loza/roca*› to crack; ‹*madera*› to split

■ **resquebrajarse** *v pron* «*loza/roca*» to crack; «*madera*» to split

resquemor *m* feeling of suspicion; **sentí un cierto ~ por habérselo ocultado** I felt a little uneasy at having hidden it from him

resquicio *m*

A (grieta) crack; (abertura) gap

B (oportunidad) opportunity, opening

C (huella, resto) trace; **quedaba un ~ de esperanza** there was still a glimmer of hope

resta *f* subtraction; **hacer una ~** to do a subtraction

restablecer [E3] *vt* ‹*relaciones/comunicaciones*› to re-establish; ‹*orden/democracia*› to restore; **se restableció la normalidad** normality was restored

■ **restablecerse** *v pron* to recover

restablecimiento *m* (de relaciones, comunicaciones) re-establishment; (de orden, paz) restoration; (de enfermo) recovery

restallar [A1] *vi* «*látigo*» to crack; «*fuego*» to crackle; «*olas*» to crash

■ **restallar** *vt* ‹*naipes*› to flick; **~ la lengua** to click one's tongue

restallido *m* (de látigo) crack; (de leña) crackle, crack

restante *adj* remaining; **lo ~** the remainder

restantes *mpl/fpl*: **los/las ~s** the rest, the remainder

restañar [A1] *vt* (liter) to stanch (AmE), to staunch (BrE); **el tiempo ~á sus heridas** time will heal his wounds

■ **restañar** *vi* (liter) to heal

restar [A1] *vt* 1 (Mat) ‹*número*› to subtract, take away; **~ algo DE algo** to take (away) *o* subtract sth FROM sth 2 ‹*gastos/cantidad*› to deduct, take away; **~ algo A algo** to take away *o* deduct sth FROM sth 3 (quitar): **~le importancia a algo** to minimize *o* play down the importance of sth; **esto resta credibilidad a la hipótesis** this detracts from the credibility of the hypothesis; **~le méritos a algn** to take the credit away from sb

■ **restar** *vi*

A (Mat) to subtract, take away

B (frml) (faltar): **restan dos etapas para el final** there are two stages left before the end; **sólo me resta darles las gracias** it only remains for me to thank you all (frml); **sólo**

r

resta formalizarlo all that remains to be done is to formalize it
C (Esp) (Dep) to return (service)
restauración *f* restoration
restaurador -dora *m,f* restorer
restaurante, restaurant *m* restaurant
restaurar [A1] *vt* to restore
restitución *f* (frml) restitution (frml)
restituir [I20] *vt* **1** ‹*bienes/dinero*› to return; ‹*derechos*› to restore **2** (en cargo) to reinstate
resto *m*
A **1** (lo demás, lo que queda) **el ~** the rest; **el ~ del dinero** the rest *o* the remainder of the money; **el ~ de sus días** the rest of his days; **¿qué importa lo que haga el ~ (de la gente)?** what does it matter what everybody else does? **2** (Mat) remainder
B **restos** *mpl* **1** (despojos) remains (*pl*); **~s arqueológicos** archaeological remains; **los ~s del avión siniestrado** the wreckage of the airplane **2** (de comida) leftovers (*pl*)
(Compuesto) **restos mortales** *mpl* (frml) mortal remains (*pl*) (frml)
C (Esp) (Dep) return (of service)
D (Col, Méx fam) (montón): **falta un ~ para llegar** we won't be there for ages (colloq); **un ~ de gente** loads of people (colloq)
restorán *m* restaurant
restregar [A7] *vt* ‹*suelo*› to scrub; ‹*ropa*› to rub, scrub
■ **restregarse** *v pron* (*refl*) to rub; **~se los ojos** to rub one's eyes
restricción *f* restriction; **restricciones de agua** restrictions on the use of water; **sin ~ de edad** with no age limit
restrictivo -va *adj* restrictive
restringido -da *adj* ‹*libertad*› restricted, limited; ‹*posibilidades/cantidad*› limited
restringir [I7] *vt* ‹*gastos*› to restrict, cut; ‹*libertad*› to restrict
■ **restringirse** *v pron* to restrict *o* limit oneself
resucitar [A1] *vt* **1** (Relig) to raise … from the dead, to bring … back to life **2** (Med) to resuscitate, revive **3** ‹*costumbres/rencores*› to revive, resurrect
■ **resucitar** *vi* «*persona*» to rise (from the dead); «*costumbre/grupo*» to take on a new lease of life
resuello *m* **1** (respiración fuerte) heavy breathing; (por agotamiento) labored* breathing **2** (aliento): **sin ~** out of breath
resueltamente *adv* resolutely, with determination
resuelto -ta *adj* **1** [SER] ‹*persona*› decisive; **en tono ~** decisively **2** [ESTAR] (decidido) determined, resolved (frml); **~ A + INF** determined *o* resolved to + INF; *ver tb* **resolver**
resultado *m*
A (de examen, análisis) result; (Mat) result
B (consecuencia, efecto) result; **los ~s de sus acciones** the outcome *o* consequences of his actions; **mi idea dio ~** my idea worked; **eran baratos, pero me han dado un ~ buenísimo** they were cheap but they've turned out to be very good; **intentó convencerlo, pero sin ~** she tried to persuade him, but without success *o* to no avail
resultante *adj* resulting (*before n*), resultant (*before n*)
resultar [A1] *vi*
A (dar resultado) to work; **su idea no resultó** his idea didn't work (out); (+ *me/te/le etc*) **no creo que te resulte** I don't think it will work
B (+ *compl*) **1** **resultar + ADJ**: **resulta más barato así** it works out cheaper this way; **resultó más cara** it proved *o* turned out to be more expensive; **~on muertas dos personas** (period) two people were killed; **resultó tal como lo planeamos** it turned out *o* worked out just as we planned; (+ *me/te/le etc*) **me resulta simpático** I think he's very nice; **la película me resultó aburrida** I found the movie boring **2** **resultar + INF** to turn out + INF; **resultó ser un malentendido** it turned out to be *o* proved to be a misunderstanding
C (*en 3ª pers*): **ahora resulta que era periodista** now it turns out that he was a journalist; **ahora resulta que tengo yo la culpa** so now it's all *my* fault
D (derivar) **~ EN algo** to result IN sth, lead TO sth; **~ DE algo** to be the result OF sth; **¿qué va a ~ de todo esto?** what will come of all this?
resultas: **a ~ de** *or* **de ~ de** (*loc prep*) as a result of
resultón -tona *adj* (Esp fam) attractive
resumen *m* summary; **hacer un ~ de un texto** to précis *o* summarize a text; **en ~** in short
resumidero *m* (AmL) drain
resumido -da *adj* summarized; **en resumidas cuentas** in short, in a word
resumir [I1] *vt* **1** (condensar) ‹*texto/libro*› to summarize **2** (recapitular) ‹*discurso/argumento*› to sum up
■ **resumir** *vi*: **resumiendo …** in short …, to sum up …
resurgimiento *m* resurgence; **el ~ de la economía** the resurgence in the economy, the economic revival
resurgir [I7] *vi* to reemerge; **este espíritu resurge en tiempos de crisis** this spirit reemerges in times of crisis; **resurge el interés por estos temas** there is a resurgence of interest in these subjects
resurrección *f* resurrection
retablo *m* (Art, Relig) altarpiece, reredos; (Teatr) tableau
retacarse [A2] *v pron* (Andes) **1** «*persona*» to back out **2** «*caballo*» to stop; (en competición) to refuse
retacear [A1] *vt* (RPl): **nos ~on los recursos** they kept a tight hold on the purse strings
retachar [A1] *vt* (Méx fam) **1** ‹*carta/trabajo*› to reject, refuse to accept **2** (no dejar entrar): **nos ~on** they turned us away
■ **retachar** *vi* (Méx) «*bala*» to ricochet
retaco *m*
A (fam) (persona): **es un ~** she's rather dumpy *o* (colloq) a real dumpling
B (escopeta) short-barrelled shotgun
retacón -cona *adj* (RPl fam) dumpy (colloq), short and fat
retador -dora *m,f* (AmL) challenger
retaguardia *f* (Mil) rearguard; **estar en la ~** (en carrera) to be at the back
retahíla *f* string; **una ~ de insultos** a stream *o* string of insults
retaliación *f* (AmL) retaliation
retama *f*, (Chi) **retamo** *m* broom
retar [A1] *vt*
A (desafiar) to challenge; **~ a algn A algo** to challenge sb TO sth; **~ a algn A + INF** to challenge sb to + INF
B (CS) (regañar) to tell … off (colloq), to scold
retardado¹ -da *adj*
A (Tec) delayed; **de apertura retardada** with time-delay lock
B ‹*persona*› mentally handicapped *o* retarded
retardado² -da *m,f* mentally handicapped *o* retarded person, retard (AmE colloq & pej)
retardar [A1] *vt* (frenar) to delay, hold up, retard (tech); (posponer) to postpone
retazo *m* (de tela) remnant; (de texto, obra) snippet
retén *m*
A (patrulla) patrol; (pelotón) squad; (puesto de policía) police post
B (Ven) (correccional) reformatory (AmE), remand home (BrE)
retención *f*
A (de información) withholding, keeping back; (de pasaporte, tarjeta) retention; (Fin, Fisco) deduction, withholding (AmE), stoppage (BrE); **las retenciones que me hacen del sueldo** the money that is deducted from my salary
B (de preso) holding, detaining
C (de calor, carga, líquidos) retention
retener [E27] *vt*
A **1** ‹*datos/información*› to keep back, withhold **2** ‹*pasaporte/tarjeta*› to retain **3** (Fin, Fisco) ‹*dinero/cuota*› to deduct, withhold
B **1** «*policía*» ‹*persona*› to detain, hold **2** (hacer permanecer): **no te retendré mucho** I won't keep you long; **el maestro nos retuvo** the teacher kept us in after class; **tres reclusos retuvieron a un funcionario** three prisoners held a prison guard hostage; **no sabe cómo ~lo** she doesn't know what to do to stop him leaving
C ‹*calor/carga/líquidos*› to retain
D ‹*atención/interés*› to keep, retain
E (recordar) to retain, keep … in one's head
■ **retenerse** *v pron* to restrain oneself

retentiva *f* memory

reticencia *f* 1 (renuencia) reluctance; **con ~** reluctantly 2 (reserva) reticence; **a pesar de su ~ inicial, ...** despite his initial reticence, ... 3 (indirecta) hint, insinuation

reticente *adj* 1 (reacio) reluctant; **~ a todo tipo de negociaciones** reluctant to get involved in any sort of negotiations; **~ A + INF** reluctant to + INF 2 (reservado) reticent 3 ‹*discurso*› full of hints *o* insinuations

retina *f* retina

retintín *m* 1 (fam) (tonillo sarcástico) sarcastic tone of voice; **lo dijo con ~** he said it sarcastically 2 (sonido) (de cascabeles) tinkling; (de pulseras) jingling, jangling

retinto -ta *adj* ‹*animal*› dark brown

retirada *f*
A 1 (separación, alejamiento) withdrawal; **esperan la ~ de las aguas** they are waiting for the waters to recede *o* retreat; 2 (Mil) retreat; **les cortamos la ~** we cut off their retreat; **batirse en ~** (Mil) to retreat, to beat a retreat; (ante situación desfavorable) to retreat 3 (de permiso, pasaporte) withdrawal
B (de propuesta) withdrawal; (de acusación) withdrawal, dropping
C (de fondos) withdrawal; (recogida) collection
D 1 (jubilación) retirement 2 (de actividad) withdrawal 3 (de competición — antes de iniciarse) withdrawal; (— una vez iniciada) retirement

retirado -da *adj*
A 1 ‹*lugar/casa*› remote, out-of-the-way; **~ DE algo**: **una casa retirada de la calle** a house set back from the road; **un barrio ~ del centro** an outlying district 2 ‹*vida*› secluded, quiet
B (jubilado) retired

retirar [A1] *vt*
A 1 (quitar) to remove, take away; (apartar) to move away; **retíralo de ahí un poco** move it a bit further away from there; **retiró la cacerola del fuego** he removed the saucepan from the heat, he took the saucepan off the heat; **el autobús fue retirado del servicio** the bus was withdrawn from service; **~ de la circulación** to withdraw from circulation 2 ‹*cabeza/mano*› to pull ... back; **retiré la mano de la bolsa** I took my hand out of the bag 3 ‹*embajador/tropas*› to withdraw, pull out 4 ‹*jugador*› to take off, pull ... out of the game; ‹*corredor/ciclista*› to withdraw, pull out 5 (+ *me/te/le etc*) ‹*apoyo*› to withdraw; ‹*pasaporte/carnet*› to withdraw, take away; **me retiró la palabra** she stopped speaking to me
B ‹*afirmaciones/propuesta*› to withdraw; **retiro lo dicho** I take back what I said
C 1 (de cuenta, fondo) ‹*dinero*› to withdraw 2 (recoger) ‹*carnet/entradas*› to collect

■ **retirarse** *v pron*
A 1 (apartarse) to move back *o* away; (irse) to leave, withdraw; **cuando las aguas se ~on** when the waters receded 2 «*ejército/tropas*» to withdraw, pull out 3 (irse a dormir) to go to bed, retire (frml)
B (jubilarse) to retire; (de actividad) to withdraw; **se retiró de la carrera** (antes de iniciarse) he pulled out of *o* withdrew from the race; (una vez iniciada) he pulled out of *o* retired from the race

retiro *m*
A (jubilación) retirement; (pensión) (retirement) pension
B (lugar tranquilo) retreat; (Relig) retreat
C (AmL) (de fuerzas, empleados) withdrawal; (de apoyo, fondos) withdrawal

reto *m*
A (desafío) challenge
B (CS) (regañina) telling-off (colloq), scolding

retobado -da *adj* (rebelde) (Méx, RPl fam) rebellious; (terco) (Méx fam) stubborn

retobar [A1] *vi* (Méx fam) to answer back
■ **retobarse** *v pron* (RPl fam) to be rude

retocar [A2] *vt* ‹*fotografía/maquillaje*› to touch up, retouch; **~ un texto** to put the finishing touches to a text

retomar [A1] *vt*: **retomó (el hilo de) la narrativa** she picked up the thread of the narrative; **el tema se retoma en el adagio** the theme is reintroduced in the adagio; **retomé mi carril** I got back in (the) lane

retoñar [A1] *vi* (Bot) to sprout, shoot; (reaparecer) to reappear

retoño *m*
A (Bot) shoot
B (fam) (hijo) little one (colloq), kid (colloq)

retoque *m*: **esta foto necesita unos ~s** this photo needs some retouching; **dar los últimos ~s a algo** to put the final *o* the finishing touches to sth

retorcer [E10] *vt*
A 1 ‹*alambre/cuerda*› to twist; ‹*alambres/hilos*› to twist ... together; ‹*ropa*› to wring 2 ‹*brazo*› (+ *me/te/le etc*) to twist; **le retorció el pescuezo** she wrung its neck
B ‹*palabras*› to twist
■ **retorcerse** *v pron*
A 1 (enrollarse) to become tangled (up) 2 «*serpiente*» to writhe 3 «*persona*»: **~se de dolor** to writhe in agony; **~se de risa** to fall about laughing
B (*refl*) ‹*manos*›: **se retorcía las manos con nerviosismo** she was wringing her hands nervously

retorcido -da *adj* ‹*persona/mente*› twisted, devious; ‹*estilo/argumento*› convoluted, involved; *ver tb* **retorcer**

retorcijón *m* (AmL) sharp pain (*in the stomach or gut*); **retorcijones de tripas** stomach cramps

retórica *f* (Lit) rhetoric; (manera de hablar) rhetoric; (palabrería) *tb* **~s** empty rhetoric

retórico -ca *adj* rhetorical

retornable *adj* returnable; **no ~** non-returnable

retornar [A1] *vi/vt* (frml *o* liter) to return

retorno *m*
A (frml *o* liter) (regreso, devolución) return; (viaje de regreso) return journey
B (Rad) return signal

retortero *m* twist; ***andar/ir al ~*** (fam) to be on the go (colloq); ***estar algo al ~*** (fam): **está toda la casa al ~** the whole house is in a mess (colloq); ***llevar a algn al ~*** (fam) to have sb wrapped around one's little finger (colloq); ***traer a algn al ~*** (fam) to keep sb on the go

retortijón *m* (Esp, Méx) ▸ **retorcijón**

retozar [A4] *vi* (liter) «*corderos*» to gambol, frolic; «*niños*» to frolic, gambol (liter)

retozón -zona *adj* ‹*cordero*› gamboling* (*before n*), frolicking (*before n*); ‹*niño*› playful

retractable *adj* retractable

retractarse [A1] *v pron*: **se retractó y admitió su equivocación** he backed down and admitted his mistake; **~ DE algo**: **se retractó de sus acusaciones/de lo dicho** he withdrew his accusations/what he said; **se retractaron de su error** they recanted

retráctil *adj* (Zool) retractile; (Tec) retractable

retraer [E23] *vt*
A (Zool) ‹*uñas*› to retract
B (traer de vuelta) to bring back
■ **retraerse** *v pron* 1 (retirarse) to withdraw; **se retrae de la gente que no conoce bien** when he's with people he doesn't know well he withdraws into his shell 2 «*demanda*» to reduce, fall

retraído -da *adj* withdrawn, retiring (*before n*)

retraimiento *m* 1 (timidez) shyness; (aislamiento) isolation, seclusion 2 (acción) withdrawal

retransmisión *f* 1 (transmisión) transmission; **~ en directo** live broadcast *o* transmission 2 (repetición) repeat

retransmisor *m* transmitter

retransmitir [I1] *vt*
A (repetir) to repeat, rebroadcast (frml)
B (Esp period) (TV) to broadcast, show; (Rad) to broadcast

retrasado¹ -da *adj* 1 [SER] (Med, Psic) mentally handicapped 2 [ESTAR] (en tarea, actividad): **va** *or* **está muy ~ con respecto a los demás** he lags a long way behind the others; **están ~s en los pagos** they are behind in their payments; **tengo trabajo ~** I have work to catch up on 3 ‹*país/sociedad*› backward 4 ‹*reloj*› slow

retrasado² -da *m,f*: *tb* **~ mental** mentally handicapped person, (mentally) retarded person, retard (AmE colloq & pej)

retrasar [A1] *vt*
A 1 ‹*persona*› to make ... late; **el tráfico nos retrasó** we got held up in the traffic 2 ‹*producción/proceso*› to delay, hold up; **la niebla retrasó la salida del avión** the departure (of the plane) was delayed by fog

B ‹*partida/fecha*› to postpone
C ‹*reloj*› to put back
■ **retrasar** *vi* «*reloj*» to run slow
■ **retrasarse** *v pron* **1** (llegar tarde) to be late; **el tren se retrasó** the train was *o* arrived late **2** «*producción/trámite*» to be delayed, be held up **3** (en trabajo, estudios, pagos) to fall behind; **se retrasó en presentarlo** she was late (in) submitting it; **me he retrasado con esta traducción** I'm behind with this translation

retraso *m* **1** (demora) delay; **viene con media hora de ~** it's (running) half an hour late; **llevamos un ~ de dos meses sobre lo previsto** we're two months behind schedule **2** (de país) backwardness **3** (Psic): **niños con ~ mental** mentally retarded *o* handicapped children

retratar [A1] *vt* **1** (pintar) to paint a portrait of; (fotografiar) to photograph; **se hizo ~ por un famoso pintor** she had her portrait painted by a famous artist **2** ‹*realidad/costumbres*› to portray, depict
■ **retratarse** *v pron* (*caus*) (en cuadro) to have one's portrait painted; (en foto) to have one's photograph taken

retratista *mf* (pintor) portrait artist *o* painter; (fotógrafo) portrait photographer

retrato *m* **1** (Art, Fot) portrait; **un ~ de cuerpo entero** a full-length portrait; ***ser el vivo ~ de algn*** to be the (spitting) image of sb (colloq) **2** (descripción) depiction, portrayal
(Compuesto) **retrato hablado** (AmS) *or* (Méx) **reconstruido** *or* (Esp) **robot** Identikit® picture, photofit® (picture) (BrE)

retreta *f*
A (Mil) **1** (toque) retreat; **tocar ~** to sound the retreat **2** (desfile) tattoo
B (AmL) (concierto) open-air concert

retrete *m* lavatory, W.C., bathroom (AmE)

retribución *f* (sueldo) salary; (recompensa) reward

retribuir [I20] *vt* **1** ‹*esfuerzos/trabajo*› to pay; **vacaciones retribuidas** paid vacation (AmE), paid holiday(s) (BrE) **2** (recompensar) to reward **3** (AmL) ‹*favor*› to return

retroactividad *f* (de ley) retroactive *o* retrospective nature

retroactivo -va *adj* retrospective, retroactive; **con efecto ~** retroactively, retrospectively; **un aumento con efecto ~ desde enero** an increase backdated to January

retroalimentación *f* feedback

retroceder [E1] *vi*
A «*persona/coche*» to go back, move back; «*ejército*» to withdraw, retreat; **al ver la pistola retrocedió** when he saw the pistol he stepped back *o* drew back; **el autor nos hace ~ tres siglos** the author takes us back three centuries
B (desistir) to give up; (volverse atrás) to back down
C (Arm) to recoil

retroceso *m* **1** (movimiento hacia atrás) backward movement; **esto supone un ~ para el equipo** this is a backward step for the team **2** (de ejército) withdrawal, retreat **3** (acción de volverse atrás) backing down **4** (Arm) recoil **5** (Ven) (Auto) reverse

retrógrado[1] -da *adj* ‹*persona/actitud*› reactionary; ‹*planteamiento/idea*› retrograde

retrógrado[2] -da *m,f* reactionary

retropropulsión *f* jet propulsion

retrospección *f* retrospection

retrospectiva *f* retrospective

retrospectivo -va *adj* ‹*análisis*› retrospective; **una escena retrospectiva** a flashback; **echó una mirada retrospectiva a su vida** she looked back over her life

retrotraer [E23] *vt* ‹*persona/sistema*› to take ... back
■ **retrotraerse** *v pron* to go back

retrovisor *m* (interior) (rear-view) mirror; (lateral) (wing) mirror

retrucar [A2] *vi* (esp CS frml) to answer back
■ **retrucar** *vt*
A (replicar) to retort
B (en billar) to kiss

retruque *m* (Per fam) witty reply

retumbante *adj* booming (*before n*)

retumbar [A1] *vi* «*voz/explosión*» to boom; «*eco*» to resound; «*paso*» to echo; «*trueno*» to roll, boom; «*habitación*» to resound; **los golpes hacían ~ las paredes** the banging was making the walls shake

reubicar [A2] *vt* (AmL)
A ‹*trabajadores*› to relocate, redeploy; ‹*empresas*› to relocate; ‹*pobladores/damnificados*› to resettle
B (cambiar de lugar) to put ... in a different place, change the position of

reuma, reúma *m or f* rheumatism

reumático -ca *adj* rheumatic

reumatismo *m* rheumatism

reunido -da *adj*: **estuvieron ~s tres horas** the meeting lasted three hours; **llevan más de una hora ~s** they've been in the meeting for over an hour; *ver tb* **reunir**

reunificar [A2] *vt* ‹*nación*› to reunify; ‹*familia*› to reunite, bring together

reunión *f*
A **1** (para discutir algo) meeting **2** (de carácter social) gathering; **~ de ex-alumnos** school reunion, old boys'/girls' reunion **3** (Dep) meeting, meet **4** (grupo de personas) meeting
(Compuesto) **reunión cumbre** summit (meeting)
B (de datos, información) gathering, collecting

reunir [I23] *vt*
A ‹*cualidades/características*› to have; ‹*requisitos*› to satisfy, meet; **reúne todas las condiciones necesarias** he fulfills all the requirements
B ‹*datos*› to gather; ‹*dinero/fondos*› to raise; ‹*información*› to gather together, collect; **reunió una colección excepcional de sellos** she built up an impressive stamp collection; **el volumen reúne sus mejores artículos** the volume is a collection of his best articles; **~ pruebas** to gather *o* assemble evidence
C ‹*personas*›: **reunió a su familia en su casa** she got her family together at her house; **reunió a los jefes de sección** he called a meeting of the heads of department; **los reunió y se lo dijo** he called them together and told them
■ **reunirse** *v pron* «*consejo/junta*» to meet; «*amigos/parientes*» to get together; **me reuní con él en Chicago** I met up with him in Chicago; **se va a ~ con los representantes** she's going to have a meeting with *o* meet the representatives

reválida *f* (RPl) (convalidación) validation; **no le dieron la ~** they didn't recognize her qualifications

revalidación *f* **1** (Chi, Méx) (convalidación) validation **2** (Col) (diploma) high-school diploma (*for mature students*) **3** (Col, Ven) (del pasaporte) renewal

revalidar [A1] *vt*
A ‹*campeonato/título*› to defend, win ... again; ‹*victoria*› to repeat
B **1** (Chi, Méx) (convalidar) to validate **2** (Col, Ven) ‹*pasaporte*› to renew

revalorización *f* (de divisa) revaluation; (de pensión) increase, adjustment; (de activo) appreciation (frml), increase in value

revalorizar [A4] *vt*
A ‹*moneda*› to revalue, revaluate (AmE); ‹*pensiones*› to increase, adjust
B ‹*sistema/situación*› to reassess, reevaluate
■ **revalorizarse** *v pron* «*acciones/propiedad*» to appreciate; **~se en un 50 %** to appreciate by 50 %; **el euro se revalorizó** the euro gained in value

revaluación *f* (esp AmL) ▸ **revalorización**

revaluar [A18] *vt* (esp AmL) ▸ **revalorizar**

revancha *f* **1** (Dep, Jueg) return game; **pido la ~** I want a rematch *o* a chance to get even **2** (desquite): **¡me tomaré la ~!** I'll get my own back! (colloq)

revelación *f*
A (de secreto, noticia) revelation, disclosure
B (éxito, figura) revelation; **la ~ literaria del año** the literary sensation of the year; **el coche fue la ~ del salón** the car was the star attraction at the show
C (*como adj inv*): **los Tigers, el equipo ~ de la temporada** the Tigers, this season's surprise success story; **el coche ~ de este año** the car of the year

revelado *m* developing

revelador[1] -dora *adj* revealing

r

revelador² *m* developer

revelar [A1] *vt*
A ‹*secreto/verdad*› to reveal
B (Cin, Fot) to develop
■ **revelarse** *v pron* to show oneself; **se reveló como una gran actriz** she proved herself to be a great actress

revendedor -dora *m,f* (que vende al por menor) retailer; (de entradas) scalper (AmE), ticket tout (BrE)

revender [E1] *vt* ‹*alimentos/artículos*› to resell; ‹*entradas*› to scalp (AmE), to tout (BrE); ‹*acciones*› to sell off

revenido -da *adj* ‹*carne/pescado*› bad, off (colloq); ‹*mantequilla*› rancid; ‹*ensalada*› limp, soggy; ‹*vino*› vinegary, sour

revenirse [I31] *v pron* «*carne/pescado*» to go bad, to go off (colloq); «*mantequilla*» to go rancid; «*ensalada*» to go limp *o* soggy; «*vino*» to turn sour, go vinegary

reventa *f* (de alimentos, articulos) resale; (de entradas) scalping (AmE), touting (BrE)

reventado -da *adj* (fam) exhausted, beat (AmE colloq), shattered (BrE colloq)

reventar [A5] *vi*
A 1 «*globo*» to burst, pop; «*neumático*» to blow out, burst; «*ampolla/tubería*» to burst; «*ola*» to break; «*capullo*» to burst open 2 (fam) «*prenda*» to split
B 1 «*persona*» (uso hiperbólico): **si sigue comiendo así va a ~** if he carries on eating like that, he'll burst!; **¡que reviente!** he can go to hell! (colloq); **reventaba de indignación** she was bursting with indignation 2 (fam) (de ganas): **cuéntamelo, que si no vas a ~** come on, I can see you're bursting to tell me (colloq) 3 (de ganas de orinar): **estoy que reviento** I'm bursting (to go) (colloq) 4 (fam) (de cansancio): **trabajan hasta ~** they work their butts off (AmE colloq), they slog their guts out (BrE colloq)
C (fam) (molestar) to rile (colloq), to make … mad (colloq); **me revienta su tonito paternal** that patronizing tone of his really gets me (colloq)
■ **reventar** *vt* 1 ‹*globo/neumático*› to burst 2 (fam) (destrozar): **reventó la puerta a patadas** he kicked the door down; **le reventó la nariz de un puñetazo** he punched him and broke *o* smashed his nose 3 (fam) (agotar) ‹*caballo*› to ride … into the ground
■ **reventarse** *v pron*
A 1 «*globo, etc*» ▸**reventar** *vi* **A1** 2 (fam) (agotarse) to work one's butt off (AmE colloq), to slog one's guts out (BrE colloq)
B (*refl*) ‹*grano*› to squeeze; ‹*ampolla*› to burst

reventón *m*
A (de neumático) blowout; (de tubería) burst
B (Méx fam) (fiesta) party

reverberación *f* (de la luz) reflection; (del sonido) reverberation

reverberar [A1] *vi* 1 (destellar): **las estrellas reverberaban** the stars twinkled; **el sol reverberaba en los vidrios** the sun glittered *o* sparkled on the windowpanes 2 «*sonido*» to reverberate, echo

reverbero *m*
A (de luz, sonido) ▸**reverberación**
B (AmL) (cocinilla) spirit stove

reverdecer [E3] *vi* 1 «*prado/planta*» to become green again 2 «*costumbre/sistema*» to revive
■ **reverdecer** *vt* to revive

reverencia *f*
A (de hombre, niño) bow; (de mujer, niña) curtsy; **hacer una ~** «*hombre*» to bow; «*mujer*» to curtsy
B (veneración) reverence; (tratamiento): **Su Reverencia** Your/His Reverence

reverenciar [A1] *vt* to revere, venerate

reverendo¹ -da *adj*
A (Relig) reverend (*before n*)
B (esp AmL fam) (como intensificador) (*delante del n*): **eso es un ~ disparate** that's utter nonsense (colloq); **su trabajo es una reverenda porquería** his work is absolutely appalling

reverendo² -da *m,f* reverend

reverente *adj* reverent

reversa *f* (Col, Méx) reverse; ***meter*** *or* ***echar*** **~** (en coche) to put the car into reverse; **iban a recortar el personal, pero metieron ~** they were going to cut staff numbers, but they reversed their decision

reversible *adj* reversible

reverso *m* 1 (de papel, cuadro) back; **ver al ~** see other side, see back, PTO 2 (de moneda, medalla) reverse; ***ser el ~ de la medalla*** *or* ***moneda*** to be the exact *o* complete opposite

revertir [I11] *vi*
A 1 «*propiedad*» **~ A algn** to revert TO sb 2 (a estado anterior) **~ A algo** to go back TO sth, revert TO sth
B (redundar) **~ EN algo: la decision ~á en beneficio/perjuicio de sus hijos** the decision will be to the benefit/detriment of their children

revés *m*
A 1 **el ~** (de prenda) the inside; (de tela) the back, the wrong side; (de papel, documento) the back 2 **al ~** (con lo de adelante atrás) back to front; (con lo de arriba abajo) upside down; (con lo de dentro fuera) inside out; (en sentido inverso) the other way around *o* (BrE) round; **te has puesto los zapatos al ~** you've put your shoes on the wrong feet; **hace la 'y' al ~** he writes his y's back to front *o* the wrong way round; **puso el cuadro al ~** he turned the picture to face the wall; **todo lo entiende al ~** she's always getting the wrong end of the stick; **todo me sale al ~** nothing goes right for me; **al ~ de lo que uno se imagina** contrary to what you might expect; **lo hizo al ~ de como le dije** she did it the opposite way to how I told her; ***saberse algo al ~ y al derecho*** to know sth (off) by heart
B 1 (bofetada) slap (*with the back of the hand*); **¡te voy a dar un ~!** you're going to feel the back of my hand! 2 (Dep) backhand
C (contratiempo) setback; **un ~ de fortuna** a reversal of fortune

revestimiento *m* (de suelo) covering, flooring; (de cable) sheathing; (de tubería) lining; **~ de madera** wooden paneling; **un ~ antiadherente** a nonstick surface; **un ~ aislante** a layer of insulating material

revestir [I14] *vt*
A (cubrir) ‹*pared/suelo*› to cover; ‹*cable*› to sheathe, cover; ‹*tubería*› to lag; **un volante revestido de cuero** a leather-covered steering wheel; **paredes revestidas de madera** wood-paneled walls; **una fachada revestida de mármol** a façade clad *o* faced with marble; **~ algo con material aislante** to line sth with insulating material
B (frml) (tener, presentar): **la ceremonia revistió gran solemnidad** the ceremony was marked by great solemnity; **su estado no revestía gravedad** her condition was not serious; **la situación reviste caracteres alarmantes** the situation has certain alarming aspects
■ **revestirse** *v pron*: **se revistieron de valor** they plucked up (their) courage; **se revistió de paciencia** she armed herself with patience

revienta, revientas, etc *see* **reventar**

revirado -da *adj* (RPl fam) (loco) loopy (colloq); (revoltoso) wild

revirarse *v pron* (RPl fam) to go loopy (colloq)

revisación *f* (RPl) (Med, Odont) examination; (periódica) checkup

revisar [A1] *vt*
A ‹*documento*› to go through, look through; ‹*traducción/cuenta*› to check, go through
B ‹*criterio/doctrina/edición*› to revise
C 1 ‹*máquina/instalación/frenos*› to check 2 (Esp) ‹*coche*› (hacer revisión periódica) to service
D (AmL) ‹*equipaje/bolsillos*› to search, go through
E (AmL) ‹*paciente*› to examine; ‹*dentadura*› to check; **se hizo ~ la dentadura** he had a dental checkup

revisión *f*
A (de trabajo, documento) checking, check; **la etapa de ~** the checking stage; **una ~ de los gastos** a check of *o* on expenses
B (de criterio, doctrina) revision; **se hace una ~ periódica de las tarifas aéreas** airfares are revised periodically
C (de instalación) inspection; (de frenos) check; **la ~ de los 5.000 kilómetros** (Esp) the 5,000 kilometer service
D (AmL) (de equipaje) inspection
E (Med, Odont) checkup
(Compuesto) **revisión médica** (Esp) (periódica) checkup; (para trabajo) medical examination
F (Der) review

revisionista *adj/mf* revisionist

revisor -sora *m,f* (Esp) ticket inspector

r

revista *f*
A (publicación ilustrada) magazine; (de profesión) journal; (crítica) review section

Compuestos
• **revista de chistes** (RPl) comic book (AmE), comic (BrE)
• **revista del corazón** real-life *o* true-romance magazine
• **revista de modas** fashion magazine

B (Espec, Teatr) revue; **teatro de ~** variety theater
C (inspección) review; **pasar ~ a las tropas** to inspect *o* review the troops; **pasó ~ a la situación** he reviewed the situation; **pasé ~ a los últimos detalles** I checked over the final details

revistero *m* magazine rack

revitalizante *adj* revitalizing

revitalizar [A4] *vt* to revitalize; **un intento de ~ las relaciones entre los dos países** an attempt to give (a) fresh impetus to relations between the two countries

revivir [I1] *vi* **1** «*persona/planta*» (físicamente) to revive; **cuando sale el sol uno revive** when the sun comes out you come alive again **2** «*sentimiento*» to revive
■ **revivir** *vt* to relive

revocar [A2] *vt*
A (Der) ‹*consentimiento/testamento*› to revoke; ‹*fallo*› to reverse, revoke
B (Const) ‹*pared interior*› to plaster; ‹*pared exterior*› to render

revolcar [A9] *vt*: **lo ~on por el suelo** they knocked him to the ground and pushed him around; **lo ~on en el debate** they wiped the floor with him in the debate (colloq)
■ **revolcarse** *v pron* to roll around; **los cerdos se revolcaban en el barro** the pigs were rolling *o* wallowing around in the mud; ***~se con algn*** (fam) to have a roll in the hay with sb (colloq); ***~se de la risa*** (fam) to roll around laughing *o* with laughter

revolcón *m*
A (caída) tumble; (vuelta) roll
B (fam) (derrota): **les dieron** *or* **pegaron un buen ~** they wiped the floor with them (colloq)
C (fam) (con amante) roll in the hay (colloq)

revolear [A1] *vt* (CS) to whirl ... round

revolotear [A1] *vi* «*mariposa*» to flutter; «*polilla*» to flit; «*pájaro*» to flutter around; «*papeles/hojas*» to fly *o* swirl around

revoloteo *m* (de mariposa, pájaro) fluttering; (de polilla) flitting

revoltijo, revoltillo *m*
A (fam) (desorden) mess, jumble
B (fam) (comida, bebida) mixture, concoction

revoltoso -sa *adj* ‹*niño*› naughty; ‹*soldados/estudiantes*› rebellious

revolución *f*
A (Hist, Pol) revolution
B (Tec) revolution; **revoluciones por minuto** revolutions *o* revs per minute

revolucionar [A1] *vt*
A ‹*costumbres/industria*› to revolutionize
B ‹*niños*› to get ... excited; ‹*estudiantes/obreros*› to stir up, create discontent among
■ **revolucionarse** *v pron* to rebel

revolucionario -ria *adj/m,f* revolutionary

revolver [E11] *vt*
A **1** ‹*salsa/guiso*› to stir; **me revuelve el estómago** it turns my stomach **2** (AmL) ‹*dados*› to shake
B ‹*cajones/papeles*› to rummage through, go through; **me revolvieron toda la casa** they turned the whole house upside down; ***~la(s)*** (Chi fam) to live it up (colloq)
■ **revolver** *vi*: **revolvió en mis cosas** he rummaged through my things
■ **revolverse** *v pron* **1** (moverse): **se revolvía inquieto sin poder dormir** he tossed and turned, unable to sleep **2** (dar la vuelta) to turn around **3** (con agresión) **~se CONTRA algn** to turn on sb

revólver *m* revolver; ***ponerle el ~ en el pecho a algn*** (CS) to hold a gun to sb's head

revoque *m* (material — para interior) plaster; (— para exterior) render, rendering

revuelo *m* (conmoción) stir; (de pájaros): **el disparo produjo un ~ de palomas** a mass *o* cloud of pigeons flew up when the shot was fired

revuelta *f* **1** (de civiles) uprising; (de tropas) uprising, revolt; **~s estudiantiles** student riots **2** (jaleo) commotion, row (colloq)

revuelto¹ -ta *adj*
A (desarreglado) in a mess; **iba con el pelo ~** her hair was all disheveled; **tener el estómago ~** to feel sick *o* nauseous
B **1** ‹*mar*› rough; ‹*tiempo*› unsettled **2** (agitado): **el ambiente está ~** there is an atmosphere of unrest; **los ánimos están ~s** people are restless *o* on edge

revuelto² *m* vegetables sautéed with egg

revulsivo *m* **1** (Med) counterirritant, revulsive (tech) **2** (sorpresa) salutary lesson

rey *m*
A **1** (monarca) king; **los R~es de Suecia** the King and Queen of Sweden; **los R~es y sus hijos** the royal couple and their children; **el ~ de la selva** the king of the jungle; **hablando del ~ de Roma ...** (fr hecha) talk of the devil!; ***a ~ muerto, ~ puesto*** no sooner has one gone than another comes along *o* comes to take their place **2** (en ajedrez, naipes) king **3** (como apelativo) pet (colloq), precious (colloq)
B **1** **Reyes** *m* Epiphany, January 6th **2** **los Reyes** *mpl*: *tb* **Los R~es Magos** the Three Wise Men, The Three Kings

> **Reyes Magos**
>
> The *cabalgata de los Reyes Magos* takes place in Spain on January 5, the day before Epiphany (*día de Reyes*). It is a parade of floats symbolizing the coming of the Three Wise Men to Bethlehem.
>
> In Spain and some Latin American countries, Epiphany is the day when gifts are exchanged

reyerta *f* brawl, fight

reyezuelo *m*
A (pey) (rey débil) kinglet (pej)
B (Zool) kinglet (AmE), goldcrest (BrE)

rezagado¹ -da *adj*: **quedar ~** to fall *o* drop behind; **iban** *or* **estaban ~s** they were lagging behind; **el trabajo está ~** the work is behind schedule; **los alumnos más ~s** the slower students

rezagado² -da *m,f* straggler

rezagarse [A3] *v pron* to fall behind, drop behind

rezago *m*
A **1** (material) unused *o* surplus material **2** **rezagos** *mpl* (mercancías) unsold *o* surplus stock; (en aduana) goods seized by customs (*resold at auction*)
B (Méx) **1** (atraso): **el ~ del campo** the backwardness of rural areas; **el ~ en los salarios** the falling behind of salaries **2** (de correos) backlog

rezar [A4] *vi*
A (Relig) to pray; **~ POR algn/algo** to pray FOR sb/sth; **reza por que todo salga bien** pray that everything turns out all right; **~le A algn** to pray TO sb
B (frml) «*texto/cláusula*» to state; **la orden reza así ...** the order reads as follows ...; **como reza el refrán** as the saying goes
C **1** (estar de acuerdo) **~ CON algo**: **eso no reza con su cargo** that is not in keeping with his post **2** (gustar) **~ CON algn**: **el soborno no reza conmigo** I don't go in for bribery (colloq)
■ **rezar** *vt* ‹*oración*› to say; **~ el rosario** to say *o* recite the rosary

rezo *m* prayer; **durante el ~ del rosario** while saying *o* reciting the rosary

rezongar [A3] *vi* to grumble
■ **rezongar** *vt* (AmC, Ur fam) (regañar) to tell ... off (colloq)

rezongo *m* (AmC, Ur fam) telling-off (colloq)

rezongón¹ -gona *adj* (fam) grumpy (colloq)

rezongón² -gona *m,f* (fam) grouch (colloq)

rezumar [A1] *vt* **1** ‹*líquido*› to ooze; **las paredes rezuman humedad** the walls are running with damp **2** (liter) ‹*nostalgia/violencia*› to ooze
■ **rezumar** *vi* to ooze; **~ DE algo** to ooze OUT OF *o* FROM sth

RFA *f* (= **República Federal de Alemania**) FRG
ría¹ *f* ria (*long, narrow, tidal inlet*)
ría², rías, etc *see* **reír**
riachuelo, riacho *m* stream, brook
riada *f* flood; (en área más extensa) flooding; **una ~ de gente** crowds of people
ribazo *m* steep bank *o* slope
ribera *f* 1 (Geog, Náut) (orilla — de río) bank; (— de lago, mar) shore 2 (vega) strand, riverside
ribereño -ña *m,f* person who lives by a river (*o* lake *etc*)
ribete *m*
A (adorno) trimming, edging; **un estilo sin ~s** a style with no embellishments
B **ribetes** *mpl* (visos, asomos): **una historia con ~s policíacos** a story with touches of crime fiction; **tiene ~s de escándalo** it has a hint of scandal
ribetear [A1] *vt* to edge, border
ricacho -cha, ricachón -chona *m,f* (fam & pey) rich guy/woman; **los ~s** the rich; **los ~s del lugar** the local fat cats (colloq)
ricamente *adv*
A (con opulencia) ‹*vestido*› splendidly; ‹*decorado*› richly
B (fam) (sin preocupación): **está durmiendo tan ~** she's sleeping like a baby; **la mandó a paseo, así, tan ~** he told her to get lost, just like that (colloq)
ricino *m* castor-oil plant
rico¹ -ca *adj*
A ‹*persona/país*› rich, wealthy
B 1 ‹*tierra*› rich; ‹*vegetación*› lush; ‹*lenguaje/historia*› rich 2 (abundante) **~ EN algo** rich IN sth
C 1 ‹*comida*› good, nice; **¡esto está riquísimo!** this is delicious! 2 (esp CS) ‹*perfume*› nice, lovely; **¡qué ~ olor tiene!** what a lovely smell!
D (fam) (mono) ‹*niño/chica*› lovely, cute; **es muy rica de cara** (CS) she has a very pretty *o* a lovely face
E (AmL exc RPl) (agradable) lovely, wonderful; **¿te vas a Acapulco? ¡ay, qué ~!** you're off to Acapulco? how lovely!
rico² -ca *m,f*
A (*m*) rich *o* wealthy man; (*f*) rich *o* wealthy woman; **los ~s** rich people, the rich
B (como apelativo) (fam & iró) sweetie (colloq & iro), honey (colloq & iro)
rictus *m* (liter) (de burla) grin; (de desprecio) sneer; **con un ~ de dolor** wincing with pain; **un ~ de amargura** a bitter smile
ricura *f* (fam): **tiene un bebé que es una ~** she has the cutest little baby (colloq); **ven, ~** come here, darling (colloq)
ridiculez *f* 1 (tontería, insignificancia): **lo que dijo fue una ~** what he said was ridiculous; **¡qué ~!** that's ridiculous!; **es una ~ pelearse por eso** it's ridiculous to fight over that; **le pagan una ~** they pay her a pittance; **pagué una ~ por esto** I paid next to nothing for this 2 (cualidad) ridiculousness
ridiculizar [A4] *vt* to ridicule; **lo ridiculizan por su acento** he is often ridiculed for his accent
ridículo¹ -la *adj* 1 ‹*persona/comentario*› ridiculous, absurd; ‹*vestimenta*› ridiculous; **lo ~ de la situación era que ...** the ridiculous thing about the situation was that ...; **es ~ decir que ...** it is an absurdity to say that ...; **no comprendía lo ~ de su situación** he didn't appreciate the absurdity of his situation 2 ‹*cantidad/precios*› ridiculous, ludicrous; ‹*sueldo*› ridiculous, laughable
ridículo² *m*: **sentido del ~** sense of the ridiculous *o* absurd; **dejar** *or* **poner a algn en ~** to make a fool of sb, to make sb look stupid *o* ridiculous; **hacer el ~** to make a fool of oneself
ríe, etc *see* **reír**
riega, riegas, etc *see* **regar**
riego *m* 1 (Agr) (de zona) irrigation; (de cultivos) irrigation, watering; **canales de ~** irrigation channels 2 (de calle) hosing, spraying
(Compuesto) **riego sanguíneo** blood flow; **falta de ~ ~** insufficient blood supply
riel *m* 1 (Ferr) rail; ***andar sobre ~es*** (fam) to go *o* run smoothly 2 (de cortina, puerta) rail
rienda *f* rein; ***aflojar*** *or* ***soltar las ~s*** to slacken the reins; ***dar ~ suelta a algo*** to give free rein to sth; **dio ~ suelta a su furia** he vented the full force of his anger; ***llevar*** *or* ***tener las ~s*** to be in charge *o* control; ***tener a algn con la ~ corta*** to keep sb on a tight rein; ***tomar*** *or* ***coger las ~s*** to take charge
riesgo *m* risk; **un ~ para la salud** a health hazard; **siempre existe el ~ de que ...** there's always a danger that ...; **aun a ~ de perder su amistad** even at the risk of losing his friendship; **heridas con ~ de muerte** injuries which could prove fatal; **fuera de ~ vital** out of danger, no longer in a life-threatening situation; **correr el ~** to run the risk; **de alto ~** high-risk; **es un ~ que hay que correr** it's a risk you have to take; **por su cuenta y ~** at your own risk; **un seguro a** *or* **contra todo ~** an all-risks *o* a comprehensive insurance policy
(Compuesto) **riesgo moral** moral hazard
riesgoso -sa *adj* (AmL) risky
rifa *f* (sorteo) raffle, draw; (papeleta) (RPl) raffle *o* draw ticket
rifar [A1] *vt* to raffle
■ **rifarse** *v pron* 1 (fam) (disputarse): **las chicas se lo rifan** all the girls are squabbling over him (colloq) 2 (Ur arg) ‹*tema/capítulo*›: **esa bolilla me la rifé** I didn't study that one
rifle *m* rifle
riflero -ra *m,f* (Mil) rifleman
rigidez *f* 1 (de material) stiffness, rigidity; (de un miembro) stiffness 2 (de ley, doctrina, horario) inflexibility; **la ~ de su educación** the strictness of his upbringing
rígido -da *adj* 1 ‹*material*› rigid, stiff 2 ‹*educación/dieta*› strict; ‹*regla/horario*› inflexible; ‹*carácter*› inflexible, unbending; ‹*actitud*› rigid, inflexible; ‹*moral/principios*› strict
rigor *m*
A (severidad) rigor*; **con todo el ~ de la ley** with the full rigor of the law; **el ~ de estas medidas** the harshness *o* severity of these measures; **el ~ del invierno** the rigors of winter
B (precisión) rigor*; **~ científico** scientific rigor; **con ~** rigorously, strictly; **los saludos de ~** the usual greetings; **en una ocasión así el frac es de ~** tails are de rigueur *o* are a must on such an occasion; **en ~** (honestamente) honestly, in all honesty; (estrictamente) strictly speaking; ***ser el ~ de las desdichas*** to be very unfortunate
rigor mortis *m* rigor mortis
rigurosamente *adv* 1 ‹*investigar*› thoroughly; **siguió ~ mis instrucciones** he followed my instructions to the letter; **es ~ cierto** it is strictly true 2 ‹*castigar*› severely; **aplicaron la ley ~** they applied the law rigorously
rigurosidad *f* (de investigación, inspección) thoroughness; (de medidas) severity, harshness; (del clima) harshness
riguroso -sa *adj* 1 ‹*método*› rigorous; ‹*dieta/control*› strict; **se vistieron de luto ~** they wore deep mourning; **rigurosas medidas de seguridad** tight security; **en ~ orden de llegada** strictly on a first come, first served basis; **en sentido ~ ...** strictly speaking ... 2 ‹*juez*› harsh; ‹*maestro*› strict; ‹*castigo*› severe, harsh 3 ‹*invierno*› hard; ‹*clima*› harsh
rima *f* 1 (de sonidos) rhyme 2 **rimas** *fpl* (composición) verse, poems (*pl*)
rimar [A1] *vi* to rhyme
rimbombante *adj* ‹*estilo*› grandiose, overblown; ‹*palabras*› high-flown; ‹*boda/fiesta*› ostentatious, showy
rímel *m* mascara
rin *m*
A (Col, Méx) (rueda) wheel; (llanta) rim
B (Per) (teléfono) public telephone; (ficha) (telephone) token
Rin *m*: **el ~** the (River) Rhine
rincón *m*
A (de habitación) corner
B (lugar): **bellos rincones de Perú** beautiful places *o* spots in Peru; **un ~ tranquilo** a peaceful spot *o* place; **registraron hasta el último ~ de la casa** they searched every nook and cranny of the house
C (en boxeo, lucha) corner
rinconera *f* (armario) corner cupboard; (sillón) corner unit *o* module
ring /rrin/ *m* (*pl* **rings**) (Dep) ring
rinoceronte *m* rhinoceros
riña *f* 1 (pelea) fight; **una ~ callejera** a street fight *o* brawl 2 (discusión) quarrel, argument, row (colloq)
(Compuesto) **riña de gallos** (AmS) cockfight

r

riñón *m* 1 (Anat) kidney; ***costar un ~*** (Esp fam) to cost an arm and a leg (colloq) 2 (Coc) kidney 3 **riñones** *mpl* (fam) (espalda baja) lower part of the back, kidneys (*pl*); **me duelen los riñones** my back hurts

riñonada *f* (carne) loin; (guiso) kidney stew

riñonera *f* money belt

río[1] *m* river; **~ abajo/arriba** downstream/upstream; **~ de lava** river *o* stream of lava; **~s de tinta/sangre** rivers of ink/blood; ***a ~ revuelto, ganancia de pescadores*** it's an ill wind that blows nobody any good; ***cuando el ~ suena agua*** *or* ***piedras trae*** there's no smoke without fire

(Compuesto) **Río de la Plata** River Plate

río[2], **rió, etc** *see* **reír**

Río de Janeiro *m* Rio de Janeiro

rioja *m* Rioja

rioplatense *adj* of/from the River Plate

R.I.P., RIP (= **Requiescat In Pace**) RIP

ripio *m*

A (escombro) rubble, debris; (grava) (CS, Per) gravel

B (en escritos, conversación) padding, waffle

riqueza *f*

A 1 (bienes) wealth; **la mala distribución de la ~** the uneven distribution of wealth; **una enorme ~ en joyas** a vast fortune in jewels; **las ~s del museo** the treasures of the museum 2 (recursos): **las ~s del suelo** the earth's riches; **las ~s naturales de un país** a country's natural resources

B (variedad, abundancia) richness

risa *f* laugh; **una risita nerviosa** a nervous giggle *o* laugh; **contener la ~** to contain one's laughter; **¡qué ~!** what a laugh!, how funny!; **entre las ~s del público** amid laughter from the audience; **soltar la ~** to burst out laughing; **¡me dio una ~ ...!** it was so funny!; **me entró la ~** I got the giggles; **da ~ oírla hablar** it's very funny hearing her talk; **no es motivo de ~** it is no laughing matter; **la situación es de ~** (iró) the whole situation is a joke (iro); ***mearse*** *or* ***cagarse de (la) ~*** (vulg) to wet oneself (laughing) (colloq); ***morirse*** *or* (CS) ***matarse de (la) ~*** (fam) to die laughing (colloq); **estábamos muertos de (la) ~** we were killing ourselves laughing (colloq); ***tomarse algo a ~*** (fam) to treat sth as a joke

risco *m* crag

risión *f* (burla) mockery, derision (frml); (objeto de burla) laughingstock

risotada *f* guffaw; **soltar una ~** to let out a guffaw

ríspido -da *adj* prickly

ristra *f* string; **me soltó una ~ de insultos** she hurled a string of insults at me

ristre *m*: **en ~** (*loc adv*) at the ready; **cámaras en ~ para captarlo** cameras at the ready to capture it on film; **apareció bastón en ~** he appeared wielding his cane

risueñamente *adv* smilingly, cheerfully

risueño -ña *adj* ‹*cara/expresión*› smiling; ‹*persona*› cheerful; ‹*porvenir/perspectivas*› bright; **le espera un futuro poco ~** his future doesn't look very bright

rítmico -ca *adj* rhythmic, rhythmical

ritmo *m*

A (cadencia, compás) rhythm; **al ~ de la música** to the rhythm of the music, in time to the music; **llevaba el ~ con los pies** he kept time with his feet; **seguir el ~** to keep in time, follow the beat; **marcar el ~** to beat time; **un ~ lento** a slow beat

B (velocidad) pace, speed; **llevan un buen ~ de trabajo** they work at a steady pace *o* speed; **a este ~ no terminaremos nunca** at this rate we'll never finish; **el ~ de crecimiento de la demanda interior** the rate of growth in the home market

rito *m* (Relig) rite; (costumbre) ritual

ritual *adj/m* ritual

rival[1] *adj* rival (*before n*)

rival[2] *mf* rival; **sin ~** unrivaled

rivalidad *f* rivalry

rivalizar [A4] *vi* **~ EN algo**: **los dos vinos rivalizan en calidad** the two wines rival each other in quality; **~ CON algo/algn** to compete WITH sth/sb

rivera *f* brook

rizado -da *adj* ‹*pelo*› curly; ‹*mar*› slightly choppy

rizador *m* (aparato eléctrico) curling tongs (*pl*); (rulo) curler

rizar [A4] *vt* ‹*pelo/melena*› to curl, perm; ‹*cinta*› to curl; ‹*lago/mar*› to ripple, ruffle the surface of

■ **rizarse** *v pron*

A 1 «*pelo*» (con la humedad) to frizz, go frizzy 2 (*refl*) ‹*pelo*› to curl

B «*lago/mar*» to ripple

rizo *m* 1 (de pelo) curl 2 (Tex) bouclé 3 (Aviac) loop; ***rizar el ~*** (Aviac) to loop the loop; (complicar) to complicate things unnecessarily 4 (Náut) reef

róbalo, robalo *m* sea bass

robar [A1] *vt*

A 1 ‹*dinero/bolso*› to steal; ‹*banco*› to rob; **~le algo A algn** to steal sth FROM sb; **les ~on todos los ahorros** all their savings were stolen; **me robó el corazón** she stole my heart; **no te quiero ~ más tiempo** I don't want to take up any more of your time 2 (raptar) ‹*niño*› to abduct, kidnap

B (estafar) to cheat, rip off (colloq); **¿$300? ¡te ~on!** $300? you were conned! (colloq)

C (Jueg) (en naipes, dominó) to draw, pick up (colloq)

■ **robar** *vi* to steal; **~on en la casa de al lado** the house next door was burglarized (AmE) *o* (BrE) was burgled; **¡me han robado!** I've been robbed!

roble *m* 1 (árbol) oak (tree); ***más fuerte que un ~*** as strong as an ox 2 (madera) oak; **una mesa de ~** an oak table

robledal, robledo *m* oak grove *o* wood

robo *m* 1 (en banco, museo) robbery; (hurto de dinero, objeto) theft 2 (en vivienda) burglary; (forzando la entrada) break-in 3 (fam) (estafa) rip-off (colloq)

(Compuesto) **robo a mano armada** armed robbery

robot *m* (*pl* **-bots**) robot

robótica *f* robotics

robotizar [A4] *vt* ‹*producción/fábrica*› to automate (*using robots*), to robotize

robustecer [E3] *vt* to strengthen

■ **robustecerse** *v pron* to become *o* grow stronger

robusto -ta *adj* ‹*árbol*› robust, strong; ‹*persona*› robust, sturdy; ‹*construcción*› sturdy

ROC *m* (= **Registro Óptico de Caracteres**) OCR

roca *f* rock; ***firme como una ~*** solid as a rock

rocalloso -sa *adj* rocky

rocambolesco -ca *adj* ‹*espectáculo/escena*› bizarre; ‹*estilo*› extravagant; ‹*imaginación*› wild; **una historia rocambolesca** a rather farfetched tale

rocanrolero -ra *adj* rock-and-roll (*before n*)

roce *m*

A (contacto) rubbing; **no soporta el ~ de la sábana** he can't bear the sheet rubbing against his skin; **el ~ de las dos piezas genera calor** friction between the two parts produces heat; **el ~ de su mejilla** the brush of her cheek; **tiene los puños gastados por el ~** his cuffs are worn

B (trato frecuente) regular contact; **de pequeños tuvimos mucho ~** when we were children we used to see a lot of each other

C (fricción, desacuerdo): **hay ~s dentro del partido** there is a lot of friction within the party; **tener un ~ con algn** to have a brush with sb

D (CS) (don de gentes) social graces (*pl*)

rociador *m* (para la ropa) spray; (para regar) sprinkler

rociar [A17] *vt*

A (humedecer): **rocía la camisa** sprinkle the shirt with water; **rocían la calle para que no se levante polvo** they spray the street with water to keep the dust down; **lo ~on de keroseno** they doused it with kerosene; **~ algo CON algo**: **~ las hojas con agua** to spray the leaves with water; **rocíelo con limón** sprinkle with lemon

B (acompañar una comida) to wash down

rocín *m* old horse, nag (colloq)

rocío *m* 1 (Meteo) dew; **una gota de ~** a dewdrop 2 (Fís) condensation, dew

rock[1] *adj inv* rock (*before n*)

rock[2] *m* rock music; **~ duro** *or* (AmL) **pesado** hard rock

rock and roll *m* rock and roll

rockero¹ -ra *adj* ‹*grupo/ambiente*› rock (*before n*); **jóvenes ~s** young rock fans

rockero² -ra *m,f* rock artist *o* musician, rocker (colloq)

rococó *adj inv/m* (Arquit) rococo

rocola *f* (AmL) jukebox

rocoso -sa *adj* rocky

rocote, rocoto *m* (AmS) hot pepper

rodaballo *m* turbot

rodachina *f* (Col) caster, roller

rodada *f*
A (de rueda) track; (más profunda) rut
B (CS fam) fall, tumble (colloq)

rodado¹ -da *adj*
A ‹*tráfico*› road (*before n*); ‹*vehículo*› wheeled (*before n*), road (*before n*); ***me/te/le vino*** ~ it couldn't have come at a better time
B (experimentado) experienced; (cosmopolita) (Col, Ven fam) cosmopolitan

rodado² *m*
A 1 (CS frml) (vehículo) vehicle 2 (Chi frml) **el** ~ (transporte) transportation (esp AmE), transport (esp BrE) 3 (CS) (para bebés) baby carriage (AmE), pram (BrE)
B (Chi) (de tierra, rocas) landslide; (de nieve) avalanche

rodaja *f* slice; **en** *or* **a ~s** sliced

rodaje *m*
A (Cin) filming, shooting
B (Auto) running-in
C (Aviac) taxiing

rodamiento *m* (Mec) bearing; (Auto) running, rolling

rodapié *m* baseboard (AmE), skirting board (BrE)

rodar [A10] *vi*
A «*moneda/pelota*» to roll; «*rueda*» to go round, turn; **rodaba por la cubierta** it was rolling around (on) the deck; **rodó escaleras abajo** she went tumbling down the stairs; **el jinete rodó por tierra** the jockey went tumbling *o* rolling along the ground; ***echar algo a*** ~ to set sth in motion; ***mandarlo todo a*** ~ (fam) to pack *o* (BrE) chuck it all in (colloq); ~ ***bien/mal*** to go well *o* smoothly/badly
B «*automóvil/moto*»: **el coche casi no ha rodado** the car has hardly been used; **los ciclistas ruedan a gran velocidad** (period) the cyclists are going at great speed
C (Cin) to film, shoot; **¡se rueda!** action!
■ **rodar** *vt*
A (Cin) to shoot, film
B ‹*coche nuevo*› to run in
■ **rodarse** *v pron* (Andes): **se rodó el tornillo** I/you/he stripped the thread on the screw

rodeado -da *adj* ~ DE **algo** surrounded BY sth; **murió ~ de su familia** he died with his family around him

rodear [A1] *vt*
A 1 (ponerse alrededor de) ‹*edificio/persona*› to surround; **todos ~on a los novios** they all crowded *o* gathered round the newlyweds 2 (poner alrededor) ~ **algo** DE **algo** to surround sth WITH sth 3 (con los brazos): **le rodeó la cintura con los brazos** he put his arms around her waist 4 (AmL) ‹*ganado*› to round up
B (estar alrededor de) to surround; **las circunstancias que ~on su muerte** the circumstances surrounding his death; **todos los que lo rodean** everyone who works with him/knows him
■ **rodearse** *v pron* **~se** DE **algo/algn** to surround oneself WITH sth/sb

rodeo *m*
A (desvío) detour; **dar un** ~ to make a detour; ***andar(se) con rodeos*** to beat about the bush
B (Agr) roundup; (Espec) rodeo

rodete *m* 1 (almohadilla) pad 2 (rueda) wheel, runner 3 (en el pelo) (RPl) bun

rodilla *f* knee; **ponerse de ~s** to kneel down, to get down on one's knees; ***hincar*** *or* ***doblar la*** ~ to go down on one's knees *o* on bended knee

rodillazo *m*: **le di un** ~ I kneed him

rodillera *f* 1 (Dep) kneepad; (Med) knee bandage 2 (parche) knee patch; (marca): **se me hicieron ~s en el pantalón** my pants (AmE) *o* (BrE) trousers went baggy at the knees

rodillo *m* (de cocina) rolling pin; (para pintar) paint roller; (de máquina de escribir) roller, platen; (de tinta) ink roller; (de lavadora) mangle, wringer

rododendro *m* rhododendron

roedor¹ -dora *adj* gnawing (*before n*)

roedor² -dora *m,f* rodent

roer [E13] *vt* 1 ‹*hueso/cable*› to gnaw (at); **los ratones han roído el queso** the mice have been nibbling the cheese; **un libro roído por los ratones** a book gnawed by mice 2 (atormentar) to gnaw at, eat away at

rogar [A8] *vt*: **te lo ruego** I beg you; ⊗ **se ruega no fumar** you are kindly requested not to smoke; **roguemos una oración por su alma** let us remember him in our prayers; **rogamos respondan a la brevedad** (frml) please reply as soon as possible; **te ruego que me perdones** please forgive me; **le rogó que tuviera misericordia** she begged him to have mercy
■ **rogar** *vi* (Relig) to pray; **roguemos al Señor** let us pray; ***hacerse (de)*** *or* (Méx) ***del*** ~: **aceptó sin hacerse (de)** ~ he accepted without any persuasion

rojizo -za *adj* reddish

rojo¹ -ja *adj*
A 1 ‹*color/vestido*› red; **ponerse** ~ «*persona*» to blush, turn red; «*semáforo*» to turn red, go red (BrE); **ponerse ~ de ira** to turn *o* (BrE) go red with anger; **un vestido ~ chillón** a bright red dress 2 ‹*piel*› (por el sol) sunburnt, red
B (pey *o* hum) (Pol) 1 (de izquierda) red (pej *or* hum), commie (pej *or* hum) 2 (en la Guerra Civil española) Republican

rojo² *m* red; **el ~ te queda muy bien** you look good in red; ***al ~ vivo*** ‹*metal*› incandescent, red-hot; **la situación está al ~ vivo** the situation is at boiling point

(Compuesto) **rojo cereza** 1 *m* cherry (red) 2 *adj inv* cherry (*before n*), cherry-red

rojo³ -ja *m,f* (pey *o* hum) 1 (izquierdista) red (pej *or* hum), commie (pej *or* hum) 2 (en la Guerra Civil española) Republican

rol *m*
A (lista) roll, list; (Náut) crew list, muster roll
B (papel) role; **~ social** social role, role in society

rolar [A1] *vi*
A 1 «*viento*» (en sentido contrario a las manecillas del reloj) to back; (en sentido de las manecillas del reloj) to veer 2 «*barco*» to roll
B (Méx fam) (dar vueltas) to wander around
■ **rolar** *vt* (Méx fam) ‹*persona*› to move; **lo ~on de turno** he was put on a different shift; ***~la de algo*** (Méx fam) to work as sth
■ **rolarse** *v pron* (*recípr*) (Méx fam) (turnarse): **nos estamos rolando para cuidarlo** we're taking it in turns to look after him; **tenemos que ~nos el libro** we have to take turns with the book *o* pass the book around

rollero *adj* (Méx fam) 1 (hablador) talkative; **¡qué ~ es!** he sure does go on! (colloq) 2 (mentiroso): **es muy** ~ he's a real fibber

rollista *adj* (Esp fam) ▸ **rollero**

rollizo -za *adj* ‹*persona/brazo*› plump, chubby; ‹*bebé*› chubby

rollo¹ *adj inv* (Esp fam) boring; **¡qué tío más ~!** that guy's such a pain *o* bore! (colloq)

rollo² *m*
A 1 (de papel, tela, película) roll 2 (de cable, cuerda) reel 3 (fam) (de gordura) roll of fat 4 (Esp) (Coc) *tb* **~ pastelero** rolling pin
B 1 (Esp fam) (cosa aburrida) bore; **las clases son un ~** the classes are dead boring (colloq); **¡qué rollazo de conferencia!** what a boring lecture! 2 (Esp, Méx fam) (lata): **¡qué ~!** what a nuisance!
C (fam) 1 (perorata) speech (colloq), lecture (colloq); **todos los días nos suelta** *or* **nos echa** *or* (Ven) **nos arma el mismo ~** he gives us the same speech *o* sermon every day (colloq); **no me sueltes el ~** you can cut the lecture (colloq); **bueno, corta el ~ ya** OK, can it, will you? (AmE colloq), OK, put a sock in it, will you? (BrE colloq) 2 (mentira) story
D (Esp arg) (ambiente) scene (colloq); **a mí este ~ no me va** this isn't my scene (colloq)
E (Esp, Méx fam) 1 (asunto) business; **el ~ ese de los impuestos nuevos** that new tax business; **no sé de qué va el ~** I don't know what it's all about

r

Roma *f* (ciudad, imperio) Rome; (el Vaticano) Rome

romance¹ *adj* Romance (*before n*)

romance² *m*

A (aventura amorosa) romance

B (Lit) ballad, romance; (Ling) Romance

romancero *m* (Lit) collection of ballads

romaní *mf* Romany

románico¹ -ca *adj* ‹*arquitectura/columna*› Romanesque; ‹*lengua*› Romance (*before n*)

románico² *m* Romanesque

romano¹ -na *adj* (Hist) Roman; (de la ciudad) of/from Rome, Roman

romano² -na *m,f* (Hist) Roman; (de la ciudad) person from Rome

romanó *m* (arg) Romany

romanticismo *m* (Art, Lit, Mús) Romanticism; (sentimentalismo) romanticism

romántico -ca *adj/m,f* (Art, Lit, Mús) Romantic; (sentimental) romantic; **es un ~ empedernido** he's an incurable romantic

romanticón -cona *adj* (pey) ‹*persona*› sentimental, soppy (BrE colloq); ‹*película*› slushy (colloq & pej)

romanza *f* romance

rombo *m*

A (Mat) rhombus

B 1 (carta) diamond 2 **rombos** *mpl* (palo) diamonds (*pl*)

romería *f* 1 (Relig) procession (*to a local shrine, gen followed by festivities*) 2 (AmL fam) (multitud) mass, crowd

romero -ra *m,f*

A (Relig) *person taking part in a* **romería**

B **romero** *m* (Bot, Coc) rosemary

romo -ma *adj*

A ‹*cuchillo/tijeras*› blunt; ‹*nariz*› snub (*before n*)

B ‹*persona*› dull

rompecabezas *m* (*pl* ~) puzzle

rompecorazones *mf* (*pl* ~) (fam) heartbreaker (colloq)

rompefilas *m* (*pl* ~) (Chi) pass

rompehielos *m* (*pl* ~) icebreaker

rompehuelgas *mf* (*pl* ~) strikebreaker, blackleg (colloq)

rompeolas *m* (*pl* ~) breakwater

romper [E30] *vt*

A 1 ‹*loza/mueble*› to break; ‹*ventana*› to break, smash; ‹*lápiz/cuerda*› to break, snap 2 ‹*puerta*› (tirándola abajo) to break down; (para que quede abierta) to break open 3 ‹*hoja/póster*› (rasgar) to tear; (en varios pedazos) to tear up 4 ‹*camisa*› to tear, split

B 1 ‹*silencio/monotonía*› to break; ‹*tranquilidad*› to disturb 2 ‹*promesa/pacto*› to break; ‹*relaciones/compromiso*› to break off

■ **romper** *vi*

A 1 «*olas*» to break 2 (liter) «*alba*» to break; «*flores*» to open, burst open; **al ~ el día** at daybreak, at the crack of dawn 3 (empezar): **~ A + INF** to begin *o* start to + INF; **rompió a llorar/reír** she burst into tears/burst out laughing; **~ en llanto** to burst into tears

B «*novios*» to break up, split up; **~ CON algn** ‹*con novio*› to split *o* break up WITH sb; **~ CON algo** ‹*con el pasado*› to break WITH sth; ‹*con tradición*› to break away FROM sth; **este verso rompe con la estructura del poema** this verse departs from the structure of the poem; ***de rompe y rasga*** ‹*decidir*› suddenly; **mujeres de rompe y rasga** strong-minded women

■ **romperse** *v pron* 1 «*vaso/plato*» to break, smash, get broken *o* smashed; «*papel*» to tear, rip, get torn *o* ripped; «*televisor/ascensor*» (RPl) to break down 2 «*pantalones/zapatos*» to wear out 3 (*refl*) ‹*brazo/pierna*› to break

rompevientos *m* (*pl* ~) (Méx, RPl) (pulóver) sweater; (anorak) windbreaker (AmE), windcheater (BrE)

rompiente *m* (escollo) shoal, rocks (*pl*) (*where waves break*); (ola) breaker

ron *m* 1 (bebida) rum 2 (Per) (combustible) methanol, methylated spirits

roncar [A2] *vi*

A (al dormir) to snore; (dormir) (fam) to sleep

B (Chi fam) (mandar) to be the boss (colloq)

roncha *f* (Med): **las ~s del sarampión** the spots you get with measles; **me picó un mosquito y me salió una ~** I was bitten by a mosquito and I came up in a bump; **le salieron unas ~s en el cuello** she came out in a rash all over her neck

ronco -ca *adj* 1 ‹*persona*› hoarse; **se quedó ~ de tanto gritar** he shouted himself hoarse 2 ‹*voz*› husky

ronda *f*

A (de soldado, guarda) patrol; (de enfermera) round; (de policía) patrol, beat

B (vuelta, etapa) round; (de bebidas) round; **pidieron otra ~** they ordered another round

C (CS, Per) (de niños): **formaron una ~ tomándose de la mano** they held hands in a circle; **danzaban en ~** they were dancing around in a circle; ***hacerle la ~ a algn*** (fam) to be *o* chase after sb (colloq)

D (Esp, Méx) (serenata) serenade

rondalla *f* group of serenaders

rondar [A1] *vt*

A «*vigilante/patrulla*» to patrol

B «*pensamiento*»: **hace días que me ronda esa idea** that idea has been going round and round in my head for days

C ‹*lugar*› to hang around; **como si lo rondase la muerte** as if death were stalking him

D (cortejar) to court (dated *or* liter)

E (acercarse a): **debe estar rondando los 60** she must be getting on for 60; **la rentabilidad ronda el 3%** the yield is hovering around the 3% mark

F (dar serenata a) to serenade

■ **rondar** *vi*

A «*vigilante/patrulla*» to be on one's round *o* beat, be on patrol

B (merodear) to hang around

C (dar serenata) to serenade

rondín *m* (Andes) watchman

ronquera *f* hoarseness

ronquido *m* snore; **¡daba unos ~s ...!** he snored so loud(ly) ...! (colloq)

ronronear [A1] *vi* to purr

ronroneo *m* purring

ronzal *m* halter

roña¹ *adj* (fam) tight-fisted (colloq), stingy (colloq)

roña² *f*

A 1 (mugre) dirt, grime; **siempre van llenos de ~** they are always grubby 2 (en metal) rust

B (del ganado) mange

C (Col fam) (pereza): **dejen la ~** stop lazing about

D (Méx) (juego) tag; **jugar a la ~** to play tag

E **roña** *mf* (fam) (tacaño) scrooge (colloq), skinflint (colloq)

roñoso¹ -sa *adj*

A [ESTAR] 1 (mugriento) dirty; **lleva el cuello de la camisa ~** his shirt collar's really grubby 2 (oxidado) rusty

B [SER] (fam) (tacaño) tight-fisted (colloq), stingy (colloq)

C [ESTAR] (Vet) mangy

roñoso² -sa *m,f* ▸ **roña E**

ropa *f* clothes (*pl*); **cambiarse de ~** to get changed, to change (one's clothes); **la ~ sucia** the dirty laundry; **~ usada** secondhand clothes; **tengo un montón de ~ para planchar** I've got a stack of ironing to do; **comprar la ~ hecha** to buy ready-to-wear clothes; **iba ligera de ~(s)** she was scantily clad; **a quema ~** *ver* **quemarropa**; ***hay ~ tendida*** (fam) walls have ears; ***la ~ sucia se lava en casa*** one shouldn't wash one's dirty linen in public; ***nadar y guardar la ~*** (fam) to hedge one's bets

Compuestos

- **ropa blanca** (sábanas, mantelería) household linen; (ropa interior) underwear, underclothes (*pl*); (para un lavado) whites (*pl*)
- **ropa de baño** ▸ **traje de baño**
- **ropa de cama** bedclothes (*pl*), bed linen
- **ropa interior** underwear, underclothes (*pl*)

ropaje *m*, **ropajes** *mpl* apparel (liter) (*pl*)

ropavejero -ra *m,f* secondhand *o* used clothes dealer

ropero *m* (armario) wardrobe; (de caridad) *church organization that distributes old clothes among the poor*

roque *adj* (Esp fam): **quedarse ~** (fam) to nod *o* doze off (colloq); **estaba ~** he was out for the count (colloq)

roquedal, (Chi) **roquerío** *m* rocky place

roquero -ra *adj/m,f* ▸**rockero**

rosa¹ *f* 1 (flor) rose 2 (rosal) rosebush; ***(fresco) como una* ~** as fresh as a daisy; ***no hay* ~ *sin espinas*** there's no rose without a thorn 3 (Chi) (nudo) bow

(Compuesto) **rosa náutica** *or* **de los vientos** compass card, rose

rosa² *adj (gen inv)* pink; **un vestido (de color) ~** a pink dress; **verlo todo de color de ~** to see things through rose-colored glasses *o* (BrE) rose-tinted spectacles; **rayas ~ claro/fuerte** pale/bright pink stripes

rosa³ *m* pink; **un ~ pálido** a pale pink

rosáceo -cea *adj* pinkish

rosado¹ -da *adj* ‹*color/vestido*› pink; ‹*mejillas*› rosy; ‹*vino*› rosé

rosado² -da *m* (color) pink; (vino) rosé

rosal *m* (árbol) rosetree; (arbusto) rosebush

(Compuesto) **rosal silvestre** wild rose

rosaleda *f* rose garden

rosario *m* 1 (Relig) (rezo) rosary; (cuentas) rosary (beads); **rezar el ~** to say the rosary; ***acabar como el* ~ *de la aurora*** (fam) to end in disaster 2 (serie, sarta) string

rosca *f*

A (de tornillo, tuerca) thread; **tapón de ~** screw top; ***pasarse de* ~: el tornillo se pasó de ~** the screw isn't biting; **te has pasado de ~** (fam) you've gone too far

B (bollo) *type of doughnut*; (pan) bread roll (*baked in a ring shape*); ***hacerse una* ~** to curl up into a ball

(Compuesto) **rosca de Reyes** ▸**roscón de Reyes**

C (Bol, Col) (círculo, grupo) clique, set; **conocer a gente en la ~** to know the right people

D (Chi fam) (riña, pelea) fight

rosco *m*

A (bollo) *type of doughnut*; (pan) bread roll (*baked in a ring shape*)

B (Esp arg) (Educ) (cero) zero, zilch (AmE colloq)

roscón *m*: *large ring-shaped bun*

(Compuesto) **roscón de Reyes** *large ring-shaped cake baked for Epiphany*

rosedal *m* (CS, Méx) rose garden

roseta *f* (Arquit) rose, rosette; (de ducha) showerhead; (de regadera) spinkler (AmE), rose (BrE)

(Compuesto) **rosetas de maíz** *fpl* popcorn

rosetón *m* (ventana) rose window, rosette; (en el techo) ceiling rose

rosquear [A1] *vi* (Chi fam) to fight

rosquete *m* (Per fam & pey) fag (AmE colloq & pej), poof (BrE colloq & pej)

rosquilla *f*: *type of doughnut*

rosticería *f* (Méx) ▸**rotisería**

rostizar [A4] *vt* (Méx) to roast; **pollo rostizado** roast chicken

rostro *m*

A (cara) face; **entró con el ~ demudado** (liter) she came in looking distraught; **una muchacha de ~ infantil** (liter) a girl with a childlike countenance (liter)

B (Esp fam) (desfachatez) nerve (colloq), cheek (BrE colloq)

rotación *f* rotation; **el movimiento de ~ de la Tierra** the rotation of the Earth, the Earth's rotation

(Compuestos)

- **rotación de cultivos** crop rotation
- **rotación de existencias** *or* **stocks** stock turnover *o* rotation

rotar [A1] *vt/vi* to rotate

■ **rotarse** *v pron*: **hay cinco personas que se rotan** there are five people working on a rota system; **se rotaban para manejar** they took it in turns to drive; **se rotan el coche** (Méx) they take it in turns to use the car

rotativa *f* rotary press

rotativo¹ -va *adj* 1 ‹*máquina/movimiento*› rotary 2 ‹*equipo/turno*› *operating on a rota system*; **equipos ~s** teams working in shifts; **exposiciones rotativas** temporary exhibitions

rotativo² *m*

A (period) (diario) newspaper

B (Chi) (Cin) movie theater (AmE), cinema (BrE) (*showing a continuous performance*)

rotatorio -ria *adj* ▸**rotativo¹**

rotería *f* (Chi) 1 (fam) (hecho): **fue una ~ no invitarlo** it was incredibly rude not to invite him; **me hizo una ~** he was rude to me 2 (fam & pey) (clase baja) plebs (*pl*) (colloq & pej), rabble (pej)

rotisería *f* (CS) *delicatessen selling spit-roast chickens*

roto¹ -ta *adj*

A 1 ‹*camisa*› torn, ripped; ‹*zapato*› worn-out 2 ‹*vaso/plato*› broken 3 ‹*papel*› torn; **me devolvió el libro ~** the book was falling apart when he gave it back to me 4 ‹*pierna/brazo*› broken

B (RPl) ‹*televisor/heladera*› broken; ‹*coche*› broken down

C (Chi fam & pey) 1 ‹*barrio/gente*› lower-class (pej), plebby (colloq & pej) 2 (mal educado) rude

roto² -ta *m,f*

A (Chi) 1 (fam) (individuo) (*m*) man, guy (colloq); (*f*) woman, girl (colloq) 2 (fam & pey) (de clase baja) pleb (colloq & pej) 3 (fam & pey) (mal educado): **es una rota, nunca saluda** she's so rude, she doesn't even say hello

B (Per fam) (chileno) Chilean

C **roto** *m* (Esp) (agujero) hole

rotonda *f* 1 (glorieta) traffic circle (AmE), roundabout (BrE) 2 (Arquit) rotunda

rotor *m* rotor

rotoso -sa *adj* 1 (CS, Per fam) ‹*persona/ropa*› scruffy 2 (Chi fam & pey) ‹*barrio/gente*› lower-class (pej)

rótula *f* 1 (Anat) kneecap, patella (tech) 2 (Mec) ball-and-socket joint

rotulación *f* (de mapas, frascos, cajas) labeling*; (confección de letreros) sign-writing, sign-painting

rotulador *m* (Esp) felt-tip pen

rotular [A1] *vt* 1 ‹*mapa/plano*› to label 2 ‹*frasco/caja*› to label, put a label on

rotulista *mf* signwriter

rótulo *m*

A 1 (etiqueta) label 2 (logotipo) logo 3 (Impr) (título) title; (encabezamiento) heading

B (letrero) sign

(Compuesto) **rótulo luminoso** neon *o* electric sign

rotundamente *adv*: **contestó ~ que no** he answered with an emphatic 'no'; **se negó ~ a hacerlo** she flatly refused to do it; **fracasó ~** he failed completely

rotundidad *f* 1 (de negativa, respuesta): **dismintió con toda ~ esos rumores** he emphatically *o* categorically denied those rumors 2 (de lenguaje) polish

rotundo -da *adj* 1 ‹*respuesta*› categorical, emphatic; ‹*negativa*› categorical; **me contestó con un 'no' ~** his answer was an emphatic 'no' 2 ‹*éxito*› resounding 3 ‹*párrafo/lenguaje*› polished

rotura *f* 1 (acción): **la explosión provocó la ~ del oleoducto** the pipeline burst as a result of the explosion; **sufrió ~ de cadera** she fractured her hip 2 (efecto): **tiene ~ de ligamentos** she has torn ligaments; **tiene una ~ en la manga** (CS) it has a rip in the sleeve

roturadora *f* Rototiller® (AmE), Rotovator® (BrE)

roturar [A1] *vt* to plough up; (con roturadora) to rototill (AmE), to rotovate (BrE)

round /rraun/ *m* (Dep) round

router /'ruter/ *m* (Telec) router

rozado -da *adj* (gastado) worn; (sucio) grubby

rozadura *f* 1 (raspadura) scratch; **le hizo una ~ al coche** he scratched the car 2 (en la piel): **los zapatos nuevos le hicieron una ~** her new shoes rubbed

rozagante *adj* (AmL) healthy

rozamiento *m* friction

rozar [A4] *vt* 1 (tocar ligeramente): **sus labios ~on mi frente** her lips brushed my forehead; **la bala le rozó el brazo** the bullet grazed his arm; **su falda rozaba el suelo** her skirt was trailing on the floor; **me roza el zapato** my shoe's rubbing; **apenas lo rocé** I hardly touched him; **el coche pasó rozando la pared** the car just scraped past the wall 2 (aproximarse a): **debe estar rozando los 60** he must be getting on for 60 (colloq); **su actitud rozaba la impertinencia** his attitude verged upon *o* bordered on rudeness

r

■ **rozar** *vi*: ~ **con algo**: **eso ya roza con la grosería** that is bordering *o* verging on rudeness
■ **rozarse** *v pron*
A (*recípr*) «*cables/piezas*» to chafe; **sus labios se ~on** their lips touched
B (*refl*) ‹*brazo/rodillas*› to graze
C «*cuello/puños*» to wear
D (Méx) «*bebé*» to get diaper rash (AmE), get nappy rash (BrE); **el bebé está rozado** the baby has diaper (AmE) *o* (BrE) nappy rash

r.p.m. (= **revoluciones por minuto**) rpm

Rte. (= **remite** *or* **remitente**) sender

RTI *f* = **Radio y Televisión Interamericana**

ruana *f* ruana (*Colombian, Venezuelan poncho*)

rubéola, rubeola *f* German measles

rubí *m* (Min) ruby; (de reloj) jewel; **(de) color ~** ruby (red)

rubia *f* (Esp fam) (peseta) peseta

rubicundo -da *adj* ‹*persona*› ruddy-complexioned, rosy-cheeked; ‹*cara*› ruddy, rosy

rubio[1] -bia *adj* ‹*pelo*› fair, blonde; ‹*hombre*› fair-haired, blond; ‹*mujer*› fair-haired, blonde

rubio[2] -bia
A (persona): (*m*) blond *o* fair-haired man; (*f*) blonde *o* fair-haired woman, blonde (colloq)
B **rubio** *m* (color): **se tiñó de ~** she dyed her hair blonde

rublo *m* ruble*

rubor *m* **1** (liter) (sonrojo) flush; **el ~ de sus mejillas la delató** her flushed cheeks betrayed her **2** (Méx, RPl) (cosmética) rouge, blusher

ruborizarse [A4] *v pron* to blush, to turn red (in the face), to flush

ruboroso -sa *adj* **1** (propenso a ruborizarse): **ser ~** to blush easily **2** (ruborizado): **estar ~** to be blushing *o* red

rúbrica *f* (de firma) flourish, paraph; (firma) signing

rubricar [A2] *vt* **1** (frml) (firmar) to sign (*gen with a decorative flourish*) **2** (period) (suscribir, apoyar) to endorse

rubro *m* (esp AmL)
A **1** (área) area; **nuestro ~ de peletería** our line in furs; **en el ~ de la computación** in computers; **se encarga del ~ de alimentación** he is in charge of the food department **2** (en contabilidad — apartado) heading; (— renglón) item
B (Impr) (título) title; (encabezamiento) heading

ruca *f* (de indio) hut (*built by Araucanian Indians*)

rucio[1] -cia *adj* **1** ‹*caballo*› gray* **2** (Chi fam) ‹*pelo*› fair, blonde; ‹*hombre*› fair-haired, blond; ‹*mujer*› fair-haired, blonde

rucio[2] -cia *m,f* (Chi fam) (*m*) blond *o* fair-haired man; (*f*) blonde *o* fair-haired woman, blonde (colloq)

ruco -ca *adj* (Méx fam) old

rudeza *f* roughness; **la ~ de sus modales** his rough *o* unpolished manners

rudimentario -ria *adj* ‹*herramienta/método*› rudimentary, primitive; ‹*conocimientos*› rudimentary, basic

rudimento *m* rudiment

rudo -da *adj* (tosco) rough, rude (arch); (duro): **fue un ~ golpe para ella** it was a cruel blow for her

rueca *f* distaff

rueda *f* **1** (de vehículo) wheel; **~ delantera/trasera** front/back wheel; **patinar sobre ~s** to roller-skate; ***ir*** *or* ***marchar sobre ~s*** to go *o* run smoothly **2** (de mecanismo) wheel; (de mueble) caster, roller **3** (corro) ring, circle; **jugar a la ~** to play ring-around-a-rosy (AmE) *o* (BrE) ring-a-ring-a-roses **4** (en gimnasia) cartwheel

Compuestos
- **rueda de auxilio** (RPl) spare wheel
- **rueda de carro** (Méx, RPl) cartwheel
- **rueda de Chicago** (Andes) *or* (Méx) **de la fortuna** *or* (Chi, Urg) **gigante** Ferris wheel (AmE), big wheel (BrE)
- **rueda de identificación** *or* **de presos** line-up (AmE), identification *o* identity parade (BrE)
- **rueda de molino** millstone
- **rueda dentada** gear wheel, cogwheel
- **rueda de prensa** press conference
- **rueda de recambio** *or* **repuesto** spare wheel

ruedo *m* **1** (Taur) bullring **2** (esp AmL) (de falda, pantalón) hem

ruego *m* request; **atendiendo a numerosos ~s** in response to popular demand; **de nada te servirán tus ~s** your pleading will get you nowhere; **apartado de ~s y preguntas** (Esp) any other business, A.O.B.

rufián *m* (granuja) rogue, scoundrel (dated); (proxeneta) pimp

rugbista *mf* (CS) rugby player

rugby /ˈrruɣbi/ *m* rugby

rugido *m* roar; **lanzó un ~** it let out a roar

rugir [I7] *vi* «*león/mar/viento*» to roar

rugosidad *f* pitted *o* bumpy texture

rugoso -sa *adj* rough, bumpy

ruibarbo *m* rhubarb

ruido *m* **1** (sonido) noise; **sin hacer ~** quietly; **no quiero oír ni un ~** I don't want to hear a sound; **no metas** *or* **hagas tanto ~** don't make so much noise; **lejos del mundanal ~** (liter *o* hum) far from the madding crowd (liter), away from it all; ***mucho ~ y pocas nueces*** all talk and no action **2** (Audio) noise

Compuestos
- **ruido de fondo** background noise
- **ruido de sables** saber-rattling*

ruidoso -sa *adj* ‹*calle/máquina/persona*› noisy; ‹*caso/proceso*› much talked-about

ruin *adj* **1** (mezquino, vil) despicable, contemptible; (avaro) miserly, mean (BrE) **2** ‹*animal*› bad-tempered

ruina *f*
A **1** (estado): **la región quedó sumida en la ~** the area was left in ruins *o* was devastated; **dejar a algn en la ~** to ruin sb; **eso lo condujo a la ~** that brought about his downfall; ***estar hecho una ~*** (fam) to be a wreck (colloq) **2** (bancarrota) ruin; **dejar a algn en la ~** to ruin sb; **la compañía está en la ~** the company has collapsed **3** (perdición) ruin; **el juego va a ser su ~** gambling will be the ruin of her
B (acción) collapse; **la casa amenaza ~** the house is on the point of collapse
C **ruinas** *fpl* (de edificio, ciudad) ruins (*pl*); **en ~** in ruins

ruinoso -sa *adj* ‹*edificio/vivienda*› dilapidated, rundown; ‹*economía/negocio*› ruinous, disastrous

ruiseñor *m* nightingale

rulemán *m* (RPl) roller bearing

rulero *m* (Per, RPl) curler

ruleta *f* roulette

Compuesto **ruleta rusa** Russian roulette

ruletear [A1] *vi* (Méx fam) to work as a cab *o* taxi driver, to hack (AmE colloq)

ruletero -ra *m,f* (Méx fam) cab *o* taxi driver, cabbie (colloq)

rulo *m*
A (para el pelo) curler, roller; (rizo) (CS, Per) curl
B (Chi) (Agr): **de ~** dry; ***ser de ~*** (fam) to be on the wagon (colloq)

rulot *f* (Esp) trailer (AmE), caravan (BrE)

ruma *f* (Chi) pile, heap

Rumania, Rumanía *f* Romania

rumano[1] -na *adj/m,f* Romanian, Rumanian

rumano[2] *m* (idioma) Romanian, Rumanian

rumba *f* rumba

rumbear [A1] *vi* **1** (Col, Ven fam) (irse de juerga) to go out on a spree **2** (RPl fam) (dirigirse) to make one's way

rumbero -ra *adj* (Col, Ven fam): **es muy ~** he really likes to party (colloq)

rumbo *m*
A (dirección) direction, course; (Náut) course; **caminar sin ~ fijo** to wander aimlessly; **partió (con) ~ a Toluca** he set off for Toluca; **navegar con ~ norte/sur** to sail a northerly/southerly course; **poner ~ a** to set a course for *o* head for; **los acontecimientos tomaron un ~ trágico** events took a tragic turn; **a partir de entonces su vida tomó un nuevo ~** that changed the whole course of his life
B (esplendidez) lavishness

rumboso -sa *adj* ‹*persona/fiesta*› lavish

rumiante *m* ruminant

rumiar [A1] *vt* **1** (liter) (cavilar) ‹*idea/problema*› to ponder (frml); ‹*venganza*› to brood over **2** (fam) (refunfuñar) to grumble about, moan about (BrE); **rumiaba entre murmullos**

que ... she muttered under her breath that ...
■ **rumiar** *vi* «*vaca*» to chew the cud, ruminate

rumor *m* 1▸ (murmuración) rumor*; **circulan ~es de que ...** rumors are circulating that ..., rumor has it that ... 2▸ (sonido) murmur; **el ~ del agua** the murmur of the water

rumorear [A1], (Col) **rumorar** [A1] *vt*: **se rumorea que ...** rumor has it that ...

rumoroso -sa *adj* (liter) ‹*aguas*› murmuring (*before n*) (liter); **un arroyo ~** a babbling brook (liter)

runrún *m* (de motor) purring, humming; (de voces) hum, murmur

rupestre *adj* ‹*pintura/dibujo*› cave (*before n*); ‹*planta*› rock (*before n*)

rupia *f* rupee

ruptura *f* 1▸ (de relaciones) breaking-off; (de contrato) breach, breaking; (de matrimonio) breakup; **eso provocó la ~ de las relaciones diplomáticas** that led to a break in diplomatic relations; **ésa fue la causa de la ~ de las negociaciones** that was what caused the negotiations to be broken off; **su ~ con Ernesto** her breakup with Ernesto; **esta ~ con el pasado** this break with the past 2▸ (Dep) (en tenis) service break

rural¹ *adj* rural

rural² *f* (RPl) station wagon (AmE), estate car (BrE)

Rusia *f* Russia

ruso¹ -sa *adj/m,f* Russian

ruso² *m* (idioma) Russian

rústica (esp Esp): **en rústica** (*loc adj*) ‹*edición*› paperback; **un libro en ~** a paperback

rústico¹ -ca *adj* (del campo) rustic; (basto) coarse

rústico² -ca *m,f* (Esp) country person

ruta *f* 1▸ (itinerario) route 2▸ (RPl) (carretera) road

ruteador *m* (Telec) router

rutilante *adj* (liter) ‹*estrella*› bright (liter), twinkling; ‹*perla*› gleaming; **de una belleza ~** of dazzling beauty

rutilar [A1] *vi* (liter) «*estrella*» to shine (brightly), twinkle; «*perla*» to gleam

rutina *f* 1▸ (hábito) routine; **por pura ~** out of habit; **inspección de ~** routine inspection 2▸ (Inf) routine

rutinario -ria *adj* 1▸ ‹*trabajo/vida*› monotonous; **¡qué ~ eres!** you're so unadventurous! 2▸ ‹*inspección/procedimiento*› routine (*before n*)

rutinizar [A4] *vt*: **debemos ~ la práctica del ejercicio** we must make taking exercise part of our routine; **la convivencia rutiniza las relaciones** living together makes relationships routine
■ **rutinizarse** *v pron* «*proceso/acto*» to become routine; «*persona*» to get into a rut

r

Ss

S, **s** *f (read as /'ese/) the letter* **S, s**
s *m* (= **segundo**) sec.
s. *m* (= **siglo**) C; **s.XX** C20
s/ = **su/sus**
S (= **sur**) S, South
S. (= **santo**) St
S.A. (= **Sociedad Anónima**) ≈ Inc (*in US*), ≈ Ltd (*in UK*), ≈ PLC (*in UK*)
sáb. (= **sábado**) Sat
sábado *m* Saturday; (Relig) Sabbath
Compuestos
- **sábado de Gloria** *or* **Santo** Easter Saturday
- **sábado inglés** (CS) *non-working Saturday*

sabana *f* (Geog) savanna*, grassland
sábana *f* sheet; **¿se te pegaron las ~s?** overslept, huh? (AmE colloq), overslept, did you? (BrE colloq)
Compuestos
- **sábana ajustable** *or* (Méx) **de cajón** fitted sheet
- **sábana bajera/encimera** bottom/top sheet

sabandija *f*
A (insecto) creepy-crawly (colloq), bug; (reptil) creepy-crawly (colloq)
B **sabandija** *mf* (AmL fam) (pícaro) rascal (colloq)
sabanear [A1] *vt* (AmC fam) **1** (aprehender) to catch **2** (adular) to flatter
sabañón *m* chilblain; ▸**comer**[1]
sabático -ca *adj* sabbatical
sabedor -dora *adj*: **~ de lo que ocurría ...** aware of *o* knowing what was happening ...
sabelotodo *mf* (fam) know-it-all (AmE colloq), know-all (BrE colloq)
saber[1] *m* knowledge; **una persona de gran ~** a person of great learning; ***el ~ no ocupa lugar*** one can never know too much
saber[2] [E25] *vt*
A **1** ‹*nombre/dirección/canción*› to know; **ya lo sé** I know; **no lo sé** I don't know; **no sé cómo se llama** I don't know his name; **así que** *or* **conque ya lo sabes** so now you know; **no sabía que tenía hijos** I didn't know he had (any) children; **para que lo sepas, yo no miento** (fam) for your information, I don't tell lies; **¡si lo sabré yo!** don't I know it!; **cállate ¿tú qué sabes?** shut up! what do you know about it?; **¡yo qué sé dónde está!** how (on earth) should I know where he/it is! (colloq); **no se sabe si ...** they don't know if ...; **no sé qué decirte** I really don't know what to say; **¿a que no sabes qué?** (fam) you'll never guess what; **tiene un no sé qué** she has a certain something; **me da no sé qué decirte esto** I feel very awkward saying this to you; **que yo sepa** as far as I know; **~ algo DE algo** to know sth ABOUT sth; **sé muy poco de ese tema** I know very little about the subject; **hacerle ~ algo a algn** (frml) to inform sb of sth; **nos hizo ~ su decisión** he informed us of his decision **2** (darse cuenta de) to know; **no sabe lo que dice** he doesn't know what he's talking about; **¡tú no sabes lo que es esto!** you can't imagine what it's like!
B (ser capaz de) **~ + INF** to know how to + INF; **¿sabes nadar/escribir a máquina?** can you swim/type?, do you know how to swim/type?; **ya sabe leer y escribir** she can already read and write; **sabe escuchar** she's a good listener; **sabe hablar varios idiomas** she can speak several languages; **no saben perder** they're bad losers; **sabe defenderse** she knows how to *o* she can look after herself
C (enterarse) to find out; **lo supe por mi hermana** I found out about it through my sister; **si es así, pronto se va a ~** if that's the case, we'll know *o* find out soon enough; **sin que lo supiéramos** without our knowing; **¡si yo lo hubiera sabido antes!** if I had only known before!; **¡cómo iba yo a ~ que ...!** how was I to know that ...!; **¿se puede ~ por qué?** may I ask why?; **¿y tú dónde estabas, si se puede ~?** and where were you, I'd like to know?
D **a saber** (frml) namely
■ **saber** *vi*
Sentido I **1** (tener conocimiento) to know; **vete tú/vaya usted a ~** but who knows; **¿quién sabe?** who knows?; **~ DE algo/algn** to know OF sth/sb; **yo sé de un sitio donde te lo pueden arreglar** I know of a place where you can get it fixed **2** (tener noticias, enterarse) **~ DE algn/algo**: **no sé nada de ella desde hace más de un mes** I haven't heard from her for over a month; **yo supe del accidente por la radio** I heard about the accident on the radio; **no quiero ~ de él** I want nothing to do with him
Sentido II **1** (tener sabor) (+ *compl*) to taste; **sabe dulce/bien/amargo** it tastes sweet/nice/bitter; **~ A algo** to taste OF sth; **sabe a ajo** it tastes of garlic; **no sabe a nada** it has no taste to it; **sabe a podrido** it tastes rotten **2** (causar cierta impresión) **~le mal/bien a algn**: **no le supo nada bien que ella bailara con otro** he wasn't at all pleased that she danced with someone else; **me sabe mal tener que decírselo** I don't like having to tell him
■ **saberse** *v pron* (*enf*) ‹*lección/poema*› to know; **se sabe todo el cuento de memoria** he knows the whole story off by heart; ***sabérselas todas*** (fam) to know every trick in the book (colloq)
sabido -da *adj* [SER] well-known; **es cosa sabida que ...** it's a well-known fact that ...; **como es ~** as everybody knows
sabiduría *f* wisdom; **la ~ popular** popular wisdom
sabiendas: **a ~** (*loc adv*) **lo hizo a ~ de que me molestaba** he did it knowing full well *o* perfectly well that it annoyed me
sabihondo -da *m,f* (fam) know-it-all (AmE colloq), know-all (BrE colloq)
sabio[1] **-bia** *adj* (con grandes concocimientos) learned, wise; (sensato) ‹*persona/medida*› wise; ‹*consejo*› sound, wise
sabio[2] **-bia** (*m*) wise man, sage (liter); (*f*) wise woman
sablazo *m* saber* slash; ***darle el*** *or* ***un ~ a algn*** (fam) (cobrar de más) to rip sb off (colloq); (pedir dinero) to scrounge money off sb (colloq)
sable *m*
A (Arm) saber*; (Náut) batten
B (en heráldica) sable
sablear [A1] *vt* (fam) ‹*persona*› to scrounge off (colloq); ‹*dinero*› to scrounge (colloq)
sablista *mf* (fam) scrounger (colloq), sponger (BrE colloq)
sabor *m* **1** (de comida, bebida, etc) taste, flavor*; **con ~ a menta** mint-flavoured; **viene en tres ~es** it comes in

S

three flavors; **no tiene ~** it doesn't taste of anything; **me dejó un ~ amargo en la boca** it left a bitter taste in my mouth; ***dejar a algn con mal ~ de boca*** to leave a bad taste in one's mouth [2] (carácter) flavor*

saborear [A1] *vt* [1] ‹*comida/bebida*› to savor* [2] ‹*éxito/triunfo*› to relish, savor*; ‹*venganza*› to savor*, enjoy

sabotaje *m* sabotage

saboteador -dora *m,f* saboteur

sabotear [A1] *vt* to sabotage

sabré, sabría, etc *see* **saber**

sabroso -sa *adj*
A ‹*comida*› tasty, delicious; ‹*chisme/historia*› spicy (colloq), juicy (colloq)
B [1] (AmL fam) (agradable) ‹*música/ritmo*› pleasant, nice; ‹*clima/agua*› beautiful [2] (Andes fam) ‹*persona*› lively, fun

sabrosón -sona *adj* [1] (AmL fam) ‹*guiso*› tasty, delicious; ‹*fruta*› delicious [2] (AmL fam) ‹*clima*› mild [3] (Andes, Ven fam) ‹*mujer*› gorgeous (colloq), tasty (sl) [4] (Col, Méx, Ven fam) ‹*música*› pleasant [5] (Per fam) (divertido) fun

sabueso *m* [1] (Zool) bloodhound [2] **sabueso** *mf* (fam) (detective) sleuth (colloq), gumshoe (AmE colloq)

saca *f* sack
(Compuesto) **saca del correo** (Esp) mailbag

sacacorchos *m* (*pl* ~) corkscrew; ***sacarle algo a algn con ~*** (fam) to drag sth out of sb (colloq)

sacacuartos *m* (*pl* ~) (Esp fam) [1] (timo) rip-off (colloq) [2] **sacacuartos** *mf* (persona) con-artist (colloq)

sacadera *f* (Col, Per, Ven fam): **es una ~ de plata** it costs a fortune (colloq)

sacalagua *adj* (Per fam) *light-skinned mulatto*

sacapuntas *m* (*pl* ~) pencil sharpener

sacar [A2] *vt*
(Sentido I)
A (extraer) [1] ‹*billetera/lápiz*› to take out, get out; ‹*pistola/espada*› to draw; **~ algo DE algo** to take sth OUT OF sth; **lo saqué del cajón** I took *o* got it out of the drawer; **~on agua del pozo** they drew water from the well [2] ‹*muela*› to pull out, take out; ‹*riñón/cálculo*› to remove; **me ~on sangre** they took some blood [3] ‹*diamantes/cobre*› to extract, mine; **~ petróleo de debajo del mar** to get oil *o* (frml) extract petroleum from under the sea [4] ‹*carta/ficha*› to draw
B (poner, llevar fuera) [1] ‹*maceta/mesa/basura*› to take out; **saca las plantas al balcón** put the plants out on the balcony; **sácalo aquí al sol** bring it out here into the sun; **tuvimos que ~lo por la ventana** we had to get it out through the window; **~ el perro a pasear** to take the dog out for a walk; **los saqué a dar una vuelta en coche** I took them out for a ride (in the car); **~ algo/a algn DE algo** to get sth/sb OUT OF sth; **~ el coche del garaje** to get the car out of the garage; **¡sáquenme de aquí!** get me out of here! [2] (invitar): **el marido no la saca nunca** her husband never takes her out; **~ a algn a bailar** to ask sb to dance [3] ‹*parte del cuerpo*› to put out; **me sacó la lengua** he stuck *o* put his tongue out at me; **no saques la cabeza por la ventanilla** don't put your head out of the window
C (retirar) to take out; **~ dinero del banco** to take out *o* withdraw money from the bank; **sólo puede ~ tres libros** you can only take out *o* borrow three books
D (de una situación difícil) **~ a algn DE algo** to get sb OUT OF sth; **me sacó de un apuro** he got me out of a tight spot; **aquel dinero los sacó de la miseria** that money released them from their life of poverty
E (Esp) ‹*dobladillo*› to let down; ‹*pantalón/falda*› (alargar) to let down; (ensanchar) to let out
(Sentido II) (obtener)
A ‹*pasaporte/permiso*› to get; ‹*entrada*› to get, buy; **ya saqué el pasaje** *or* (Esp) **he sacado el billete** I've already bought the ticket *o* got my ticket
B [1] ‹*calificación/nota*› to get; **saqué un cinco en química** I got five out of ten in chemistry [2] ‹*votos/puntos*› to get [3] (en juegos de azar) ‹*premio*› to get, win; **tiró los dados y sacó un seis** she threw the dice and got a six [4] ‹*conclusión*› to draw [5] ‹*suma/cuenta*› to do, work out
C ‹*beneficio*› to get; ‹*ganancia*› to make; **no vas a ~ nada hablándole así** you won't get anywhere talking to him like that; **¿qué sacas con eso?** what do you gain by doing that?; **saco $3.000 mensuales** I take home $3,000 a month; **le sacó diez segundos (de ventaja) a Martínez** he took a ten-second lead over Martínez; **el hijo ya le saca 10 centímetros** (fam) his son is already 10 centimeters taller than he is; **~ algo DE algo**: **~on mucho dinero de la venta** they made a lot of money from the sale; **no ha sacado ningún provecho del curso** she hasn't got anything out of the course
D **~ algo DE algo** ‹*idea/información*› to get sth FROM sth; ‹*porciones/unidades*› to get sth OUT OF sth; **~le algo A algn** ‹*dinero/información*› to get sth OUT OF sb
E ‹*brillo*› to bring out; **~le brillo a algo** to polish sth to a shine
(Sentido III)
A [1] ‹*libro*› to publish, bring out; ‹*disco*› to bring out, release; ‹*modelo/producto*› to bring out; **~on el reportaje en primera plana** the report appeared on the front page [2] ‹*tema*› to bring up [3] ‹*foto*› to take; ‹*copia*› to make, take; ‹*apuntes*› to make, take [4] (Esp) ‹*defecto/falta*› (+ *me/te/le etc*) to find; **a todo le tiene que ~ faltas** he always has to find fault with everything
B **sacar adelante** ‹*proyecto*› (poner en marcha) to get sth off the ground; (salvar de la crisis) to keep sth going; **luché tanto para ~ adelante a mis hijos** I fought so hard to give my children a good start in life
C (Dep) ‹*tiro libre/falta*› to take
(Sentido IV) (quitar)
A (esp AmL) [1] **~le algo A algn** ‹*botas/gorro*› to take sth OFF sb; ‹*juguetes/plata*› (RPl) to take sth FROM sb; **no se lo saques, que es suyo** don't take it (away) from him, it's his; **¿cuánto te sacan en impuestos?** how much do they take off in taxes? [2] **~le algo A algo** ‹*tapa/cubierta*› to take sth OFF sth [3] (retirar): **saca esto de aquí** take this away; **saquen los libros de la mesa** take the books off the table
B (esp AmL) (hacer desaparecer) ‹*mancha*› to remove, get … out; **me sacas un peso de encima** you've taken a great weight off my mind

■ **sacar** *vi* (Dep) (en tenis, vóleibol) to serve; (en fútbol) to kick off; **~ de puerta/de esquina** to take the goal kick/to take the corner; **~ de banda** to take the throw-in

■ **sacarse** *v pron* (*refl*)
A (extraer): **ten cuidado, te vas a ~ un ojo** be careful or you'll poke *o* take your eye out; **me saqué la astilla con unas pinzas** I got the splinter out with a pair of tweezers; **me tengo que ~ una muela** (*caus*) I have to have a tooth out; **~se algo DE algo** to take sth OUT OF sth; **sácate las manos de los bolsillos** take your hands out of your pockets
B (AmL) (quitarse) ‹*ropa/zapatos*› to take off; ‹*maquillaje*› to remove, take off; **sácate el pelo de la cara** get *o* take your hair out of your eyes; **no pudimos sacárnoslo de encima** we just couldn't get rid of him
C [1] (*caus*) ‹*foto*›: **tengo que ~me una foto** I have to get a photo taken [2] (AmL) ‹*calificación/nota*› to get

sacarina *f* saccharin

sacerdocio *m* priesthood

sacerdote *m* priest

sacerdotisa *f* priestess

saciar [A1] *vt* ‹*hambre*› to satisfy; ‹*sed*› to quench; ‹*deseo*› (liter) to satiate (liter); ‹*ambición*› to fulfill*, realize

■ **saciarse** *v pron*: **comer/beber hasta ~se** to eat/drink one's fill

saciedad *f*: **comer/beber hasta la ~** to eat/drink one's fill; **repetir algo hasta la ~** to repeat sth ad nauseam

saco *m*
A (continente) sack; (contenido) sack, sackful; **comprar algo por ~s** to buy sth by the sackful *o* sack; ***echar a algn al ~*** (Chi fam) to swindle sb (colloq); ***caer en ~ roto*** «*consejo*» to go unheeded; **estos errores no deben caer en ~ roto** we should learn from these mistakes; ***echar algo en ~ roto*** ‹*esfuerzo/trabajo*› to let sth go to waste; ‹*consejos*› to ignore sth; ***~ de papas*** (Chi fam) fat lump (colloq); ***ser un ~ de huesos*** (fam & hum) to be all skin and bones (colloq)
(Compuesto) **saco de dormir** sleeping bag
B (AmL) (de tela) jacket; **al que le venga el ~ que se lo ponga** (fr hecha) if the cap fits, wear it
(Compuesto) **saco sport** (AmL) sports coat (AmE), sports jacket (BrE)

sacón[1] -cona *adj* (Méx fam) chicken (colloq)

S

sacón² *m* (RPl) three-quarter-length coat

sacralizar [A4] *vt* to idolize, regard … as sacred

sacramento *m* sacrament; **administrar/recibir los ~s** to administer/receive the sacraments; **los últimos ~s** the last rites

sacrificado -da *adj* ‹*persona*› selfless, self-sacrificing; **tuvo una vida muy sacrificada** she had a really hard life

sacrificar [A2] *vt* 1 (Relig) ‹*cordero/víctimas*› to sacrifice 2 ‹*res/ganado*› to slaughter; ‹*perro/gato*› (euf) to put … to sleep (euph), to put away (AmE), to put down (BrE) 3 ‹*carrera/juventud*› to sacrifice; **ha sacrificado los mejores años de su vida** he has given up *o* sacrificed the best years of his life

■ **sacrificarse** *v pron* to make sacrifices; **se sacrificó por sus hijos** she sacrificed everything for her children

sacrificio *m* 1 (privación, renuncia) sacrifice; **lo ha conseguido a costa de muchos ~s** she's achieved it by making a lot of sacrifices 2 (inmolación) sacrifice; **ofrecer algo/a algn en ~** to offer (up) sth/sb as a sacrifice 3 (de res) slaughter

sacrilegio *m* sacrilege

sacrílego -ga *adj* sacrilegious

sacristán *m* sacristan, verger

sacristía *f* vestry, sacristy

sacro -cra *adj* sacred

sacrosanto -ta *adj* sacrosanct

sacudida *f* 1 (agitando) shake, shaking; (golpeando) beating 2 (de terremoto) tremor; (de explosión) blast; (de tren, coche) jerk, jolt; **avanzaba dando ~s** it bumped *o* jolted along 3 (fam) (descarga) electric shock; **me dio una ~** I got a shock

sacudir [I1] *vt*

A 1 (agitar) ‹*toalla/alfombra*› to shake; (golpear) ‹*alfombra/colchón*› to beat; **sacudió la arena de la toalla** he shook the sand out of the towel 2 (fam) ‹*niño*› to clobber (colloq); **~ la cabeza** (para negar) to shake one's head; (para afirmar) to nod (one's head) 3 (hacer temblar) to shake; **un escalofrío la sacudió de pies a cabeza** a shiver ran through her 4 (CS, Méx) (limpiar) to dust, do the dusting

B (conmover, afectar) to shake; **una revolución que sacudió los cimientos de la sociedad** a revolution which shook society to its foundations

■ **sacudir** *vi* (CS, Méx) to dust

■ **sacudirse** *v pron* (*refl*) 1 (apartar de sí) ‹*problema*› to shrug off; ‹*sueño/modorra*› to shake off; **no sé cómo ~me a este tipo** I don't know how to get rid of this guy (colloq) 2 (quitarse) ‹*arena/polvo*› to shake off; **sacúdete los pelos del perro** (CS) brush the dog hairs off you

sacudón *m*

A (AmL fam) 1 (sacudida violenta) shake, shaking; **me dio un ~** he shook me 2 (de terremoto) tremor; (de vehículo) lurch; **el coche avanzaba a sacudones** the car lurched forward

B (Andes fam) 1 (revuelo, conmoción) upheaval, turmoil 2 (golpe) blow

sádico¹ -ca *adj* sadistic

sádico² -ca *m,f* sadist

sadismo *m* sadism

sadomasoquismo *m* sadomasochism

sadomasoquista *mf* sadomasochist

saeta *f*

A (dardo) dart; (flecha) arrow

B (copla) *Flamenco verse sung at processions in Holy Week*

safari *m* 1 (gira, viaje) safari; **ir de ~** to go on safari 2 (zoológico) safari park

saga *f* (Lit) saga

sagacidad *f* astuteness, shrewdness

sagaz *adj* shrewd, astute

Sagitario¹ *m* (signo, constelación) Sagittarius; **es (de) ~** she's (a) Sagittarian

Sagitario², sagitario *mf* (*pl* ~ *or* **-rios**) (persona) Sagittarian, Sagittarius

sagrado -da *adj*

A (Relig) ‹*altar*› holy; ‹*lugar*› holy, sacred; **te lo juro por lo más ~** I swear to God

(Compuestos)
- **Sagrada Familia** *f* Holy Family
- **Sagradas Escrituras** *fpl or* **Sagrada Escritura** *f* Holy Scriptures (*pl*)

B (fundamental, intocable) sacred; **el derecho a la vida es ~** the right to life is sacred

sagrario *m* (tabernáculo) tabernacle; (capilla) side chapel

Sahara /sa'ara/ *m*: **el (desierto del) ~** the Sahara (Desert)

saharaui /saxa'rawi/ *adj/mf* Saharan; **los ~s** the Saharan people

sainete *m* comic *o* comedy sketch, one-act farce

sajón -jona *adj/m,f* Saxon

sal¹ *f*

A (Coc) salt; **mantequilla sin ~** unsalted butter; ***caerle (la) ~ a algn*** (Méx fam): **le cayó la ~ con la venta de la casa** she was unlucky *o* she had bad luck when she sold the house; ***echarle la ~ a algn*** (Méx fam) to put a jinx on sb; ***la ~ de la tierra*** the salt of the earth

(Compuestos)
- **sal de mesa** *or* **fina** table salt
- **sal gorda** *or* (CS) **gruesa** *or* **de cocina** cooking salt

B (Quím) salt

(Compuestos)
- **sal de fruta** liver salts (*pl*)
- **sales de baño** *fpl* bath salts (*pl*)

C (fam) (gracia, chispa): **esa ~ que tiene para contar anécdotas** her witty *o* funny way of telling stories; **la ~ de la vida** the spice of life

sal² *see* **salir**

sala *f* 1 (de casa) *tb* **~ de estar** living room, lounge (BrE) 2 (de hotel) lounge 3 (en hospital) ward 4 (para reuniones, conferencias) hall; (Teatr) theater*; (Cin) movie theater (AmE), cinema (BrE); **la película se exhibe en la ~ 1** the movie is showing on Screen 1 5 (sede de tribunal) courtroom, court

(Compuestos)
- **sala cuna** (Chi) day nursery, creche
- **sala de clases** (CS frml) classroom
- **sala de conferencias** assembly *o* conference *o* lecture hall
- **sala de embarque** departure lounge
- **sala de espera** waiting room
- **sala de exposiciones** gallery, exhibition hall
- **sala de fiestas** night club (*usually featuring dancing and cabaret*)
- **sala de juntas** boardroom
- **sala de lectura** reading room
- **sala de profesores** staff room

salado -da *adj*

A (Coc) 1 (con sal) salted; **la carne está demasiado salada** the meat is too salty; **las anchoas son muy saladas** anchovies are very salty; **le gusta la comida poco salada** he doesn't like too much salt in his food 2 [SER] (no dulce) ‹*plato/comida*› savory*; **me gusta más lo ~** I prefer savory things

B 1 (fam) ‹*persona*› (gracioso) funny, witty 2 (fam) ‹*chiste*› risqué; ‹*anécdota*› spicy

C (CS fam) (caro) pricy; **la multa le salió bastante salada** the fine was pretty steep *o* heavy

D 1 (AmL fam) (desafortunado) jinxed (colloq) 2 (Méx fam) (que trae mala suerte) jinxed (colloq)

salamandra *f* (Zool) salamander; (estufa) salamander stove

salame *m* 1 (CS) (Coc) salami 2 (RPl fam) (tonto) idiot

salar¹ [A1] *vt* 1 (para conservar) ‹*carne/pescado*› to salt (down); ‹*pieles*› to salt 2 (para condimentar) to salt, add salt to

■ **salarse** *v pron* (Méx fam) (echarse a perder) «*planes*» to fall through; «*negocio*» to go bust; **se me ~on las vacaciones** my vacation plans fell through

salar² *m* (Chi) salt pan, salt flat

salarial *adj* wage (*before n*), salary (*before n*)

salario *m* (frml) wage, salary

(Compuesto) **salario base/mínimo** basic/minimum wage

salaz *adj* (frml) salacious (frml)

salazón *f* salting

S

salchicha *f* sausage

salchichón *m: spiced sausage similar to salami*

salchichonería *f* (Méx) delicatessen

saldar [A1] *vt* [1] ‹*cuenta*› to settle; ‹*deuda*› to settle, pay (off) [2] ‹*mercancías/productos*› to sell off

■ **saldarse** *v pron* (period) **~se CON algo: el encuentro se saldó con un empate** the game ended in a tie; **el accidente se saldó con cinco víctimas mortales** five people died in the accident

saldo *m*

A [1] (de cuenta) balance; **~ a (su favor/nuestro) favor** credit/debit balance; **el ~ es de $4.000 a nuestro favor** we are $4,000 in credit [2] (period) (de incidente, confrontación): **la pelea terminó con un ~ de tres heridos** the fight resulted in three people being injured

(Compuestos)

- **saldo acreedor** *or* **positivo** credit balance
- **saldo deudor** *or* **negativo** debit balance

B [1] (artículo): **los ~s no se cambian** sale goods cannot be exchanged; **precios de ~** sale prices; Ⓢ **venta de saldos** clearance sale [2] **saldos** *mpl* (rebajas) sales (*pl*); **las tiendas estaban de ~s** the sales were on

saldré, saldría, etc *see* **salir**

salero *m*

A (recipiente) salt shaker (AmE), saltcellar (BrE)

B (fam) (gracia): **tiene mucho ~ contando chistes** he's so funny when he starts telling jokes; **¡qué ~ tienes bailando!** you're a really stylish dancer! (colloq)

C (Méx) (persona): **yo estoy de ~ en (medio de) su discusión** they're arguing and I'm stuck in the middle

saleroso -sa *adj* ▸**salado B1**

salga, salgas, etc *see* **salir**

salida *f*

(*Sentido* I) (hacia el exterior)

A (lugar) [1] (de edificio, lugar) exit; Ⓢ **salida** exit; **dimos mil vueltas buscando la ~** we went round and round looking for the way out *o* the exit; **todas las ~s de Bilbao** all the roads out of Bilbao; **Bolivia no tiene ~ al mar** Bolivia has no access to the sea; **mi habitación tenía ~ a la terraza** my bedroom opened onto the terrace; **es una calle sin ~** it's a dead end [2] (de tubería) outlet, outflow; (de circuito) outlet

(Compuesto) **salida de emergencia/incendios** emergency/fire exit

B [1] (acción): **me lo encontré a la ~** I met him on my way out; **a la ~ del concierto** after the concert; **el gobierno les ha negado la ~ del país** the government has refused to allow them to leave the country; **impedir la ~ de divisas** to prevent currency being taken out of *o* leaving the country; **la ~ del primer toro** the entry of the first bull [2] (como distracción): **es su primera ~ desde que la operaron** it's the first time she's been out since her operation; **una ~ al campo** an outing *o* a trip to the country [3] (de líquido, gas, electricidad) output [4] **la ~ del sol** sunrise

(*Sentido* II) (partida)

A (de tren, avión) departure; **el tren efectuará su ~ por la vía cinco** the train will leave from track five; Ⓢ **salidas nacionales/internacionales** domestic/international departures

B (Dep) (en una carrera) start

(*Sentido* III)

A [1] (solución): **no le veo ninguna ~ a esta situación** I can see no way out of this situation; **no nos queda otra ~** we have no other option [2] (posibilidades): **la informática tiene muchas ~s** nowadays there are many job opportunities in computing; **esta prenda no tiene mucha ~** this garment doesn't sell very well

B (Com, Fin) (gasto) payment; **entradas y ~s** income and expenditure

C (ocurrencia): **este chico tiene cada ~ ...** this child comes out with the funniest things ...; **fue una ~ que nos hizo reír mucho** his remark *o* comment had us all in stitches

(Compuesto) **salida de tono**: **fue una ~ de ~** it was a totally inappropriate thing to say/do

salido[1] **-da** *adj*

A ‹*ojos*› bulging; ‹*frente/mentón*› prominent; ‹*dientes*› projecting (*before n*), sticky-out (colloq)

B (fam) ‹*yegua/perra*› in heat (AmE), on heat (BrE); ‹*persona*› (Esp) horny (colloq), randy (BrE colloq)

salido[2] **-da** *m,f* [1] (Esp fam) (obseso sexual) sex maniac (colloq) [2] (Ven fam) (persona entrometida) busybody (colloq), nosy parker (BrE colloq)

salidor -dora *adj* (AmL fam): **estás muy ~a últimamente** you're always out on the town these days (colloq); **es muy ~a** she likes going out a lot (colloq)

saliente[1] *adj* ‹*pómulo/hueso*› prominent; ‹*cornisa/balcón*› projecting

saliente[2] *f or* (Esp) *m* (de edificio, muro) projection

salina *f* (instalación costera) saltworks (*sing or pl*), saltern; (mina) saltmine; (marisma) salt marsh

salinidad *f* salinity, saltiness

salino -na *adj* saline

salir [I29] *vi*

(*Sentido* I)

A (partir) to leave; **¿a qué hora sale tu tren/tu vuelo?** what time is your train/flight?; **el jefe había salido de viaje** the boss was away; **salió corriendo** *or* **disparada** (fam) she was off like a shot (colloq); **~ DE algo** to leave FROM sth; **¿de qué andén sale el tren?** what platform does the train leave from?; **salgo de casa a las siete** I leave home at seven; **~ PARA algo** to leave FOR sth

B (al exterior — acercándose al hablante) to come out; (— alejándose del hablante) to go out; **no salgas sin abrigo** don't go out without a coat; **no puedo ~, me he quedado encerrado** I can't get out, I'm trapped in here; **~ DE algo** to come out/get out OF sth; **¡sal de ahí!** come out of there!; **¡sal de aquí!** get out of here!; **sal ya de la cama** get out of bed; **¿tú de dónde has salido?** where have you sprung from?; **¿de dónde salió este dinero?** where did this money come from?; **nunca ha salido de España** he's never been out of Spain; **no puede ~ del país** she can't leave the country; **~ POR algo** to leave BY sth; **salió por la puerta de atrás** he went out *o* left by the back door; **tuvo que ~ por la ventana** she had to get out through the window; **~ A algo**: **salieron al balcón/al jardín** they went out onto the balcony/into the garden; **~ A + INF** to go out/come out to + INF; **¿sales a jugar?** are you coming out to play?; **salió a hacer las compras** she's gone out (to do the) shopping

C (habiendo terminado algo) to leave; **no salgo de trabajar hasta las siete** I don't finish *o* leave work until seven; **¿a qué hora sales de clase?** what time do you get out of class *o* finish your class?; **¿cuándo sale del hospital?** when is he coming out of (the) hospital?

D [1] (como entretenimiento) to go out; **estuvo castigado un mes sin ~** he wasn't allowed to go out for a month; **salieron a cenar fuera** they went out for dinner [2] (tener una relación) to go out; **salen juntos** they're going out together; **~ CON algn** to go out WITH sb; **¿estás saliendo con alguien?** are you going out with anyone?

E (a calle, carretera): **¿por aquí se sale a la carretera?** can I get on to the road this way?; **¿esta calle sale al Paseo Colón?** does this street come out onto the Paseo Colón?

F «*clavo/tapón*» to come out; «*anillo*» to come off

(*Sentido* II)

A (aparecer, manifestarse) [1] «*cana/sarpullido*» to appear; (+ *me/te/le etc*) **me empiezan a ~ canas** I'm starting to go gray; **ya le ha salido el primer diente** her first tooth has already come through; **le están saliendo los dientes** she's teething; **me ha salió una ampolla** I've got a blister; **le salió un sarpullido** he came out in a rash; **me salieron granos** I broke out *o* (BrE) come out in spots; **¿te sale sangre?** are you bleeding *o* is it bleeding?; **me sale sangre de la nariz** my nose is bleeding; **a la planta le están saliendo hojas nuevas** the plant's putting out new leaves [2] «*sol*» (por la mañana) to rise, come up; (de detrás de una nube) to come out [3] (surgir) «*tema/idea*» to come up; **yo no se lo pedí, salió de él** I didn't ask him to do it, it was his idea *o* he offered; **ya salió aquello** you (*o* he *etc*) had to bring that up; (+ *me/te/le etc*) **le salió así, espontáneamente** he just came out with it quite spontaneously; **me salió en alemán** it came *o* I said it in German; **me salió otro compromiso** something (else) came up [4] «*carta*» (en naipes) to come up; **¿ha salido ya el 15?** have they called number 15 yet?

B [1] (tocar en suerte) (+ *me/te/le etc*): **me salió un tema que no había estudiado** I got a subject I hadn't studied

S

2 (en un reparto) ~ A **algo** to get sth; **salimos a dos pastelitos cada uno** we get two cakes each; **salen a tres mil el par** it works out at three thousand a pair
C «*mancha*» (aparecer) to appear; (quitarse) to come out
D 1 «*revista/novela*» to come out; «*disco*» to come out, be released; ~ **al mercado** to come on to the market 2 (en televisión, el periódico) to appear; **salió en primera página** it appeared on the front page; **salió por** *or* **en (la) televisión** she was *o* appeared on television 3 (en una foto) to appear; (+ *compl*) **¡qué bien saliste en esta foto!** this photo of you is really good 4 (desempeñando un papel): **sale de pastor** he plays *o* he is a shepherd
E (expresando irritación, sorpresa): **¡ya salió la niña!** her again!; ~ CON **algo**: **¡mira con qué sale éste ahora!** did you hear what he just said?; **no me salgas ahora con eso** don't give me that (colloq)

Sentido III

A (expresando logro) (+ *me/te/le etc*): **¿te salió el crucigrama?** did you finish the crossword?; **no me sale esta ecuación** I can't do this equation; **no te sale bien el acento** you haven't got the accent right; **ahora mismo no me sale su nombre** (fam) I can't think of her name right now; **no le salían las palabras** he couldn't get his words out
B (resultar): **de aquí no va a ~ nada bueno** no good is going to come of this; **¿a ti te da 40? a mí me sale 42** how do you get 40? I make it 42; (+ *compl*): **las cosas salieron bien** things turned out *o* worked out well; **el plan no salió como esperábamos** the plan didn't work out as we expected; **no salió ninguna de las fotos** none of the photographs came out; **la foto salió movida** the photograph has come out blurred; **tenemos que acabarlo salga como salga** we have to finish it no matter how it turns out; **sale muy caro** it works out *o* is very expensive; **salió elegido tesorero** he was elected treasurer; **¿qué número salió premiado?** what was the winning number?; ~ **bien/mal en un examen** (Chi fam) to pass/fail an exam; (+ *me/te/le etc*) **el postre no me salió bien** the dessert didn't come out right; **las cosas no nos han salido bien** things haven't gone right for us; **no lo hagas deprisa que te va a ~ todo mal** don't try to do it too quickly, you'll do it all wrong; **¿cómo te salió el examen?** how did you get on *o* do in the exam?; **el niño les salió muy inteligente** their son turned out (to be) really bright
C (de situación, estado) ~ DE **algo**: **para ~ del apuro** in order to get out of an awkward situation; **está muy mal, no sé si saldrá de ésta** she's very ill, I don't know if she'll pull through; **no sé cómo vamos a ~ de ésta** I don't know how we're going to get out of this one; **me ayudó a ~ de la depresión** he helped me get over my depression; (+ *compl*) **salió bien de la operación** she came through the operation well; **salieron ilesos del accidente** they were not hurt in the accident; **salió airosa del trance** she came through it with flying colors; ~ ***adelante*** «*negocio*» to stay afloat, survive; «*propuesta*» to prosper; **fue una época muy dura, pero lograron ~ adelante** it was a difficult period but they managed to get through it
D (con preposición) 1 **salir a** (parecerse a) to take after 2 **salir con** (Col) (combinar con) to go with 3 **salir de** (Col, Ven) (deshacerse de) to get rid of

■ **salirse** *v pron*

A 1 (de recipiente, límite): **cierra el grifo, que se va a ~ el agua** turn off the faucet (AmE) *o* (BrE) tap, the water's going to overflow; **vigila que no se salga la leche** don't let the milk boil over; ~**se** DE **algo**: **el camión se salió de la carretera** the truck came/went off the road; **el río se salió de su cauce** the river overflowed its banks; **la pelota se salió del campo de juego** the ball went into touch *o* out of play; **procura no ~te del presupuesto** try to keep within the budget; **te estás saliendo del tema** you're getting off the point 2 (por orificio, grieta) «*agua/tinta*» to leak (out), come out; «*gas*» to escape, come out; ~**se** DE **algo**: **se está saliendo el aire del neumático** the air's coming *o* leaking out of the tire; **se me salió el hilo de la aguja** the needle's come unthreaded 3 (Chi, Méx) «*pluma/recipiente*» to leak
B (soltarse) to come off; (+ *me/te/le etc*) **estos zapatos se me salen** these shoes are too big for me; **se le salían los ojos de las órbitas** his eyes were popping out of his head
C (irse) to leave; ~**se** DE **algo** ‹*de asociación*› to leave sth; **se salió del cine a la mitad de la película** she walked out halfway through the movie; ~***se con la suya*** to get one's (own) way

salitre *m* 1 (Min, Quím) saltpeter*, niter* 2 (del agua de mar) salt residue

saliva *f* saliva, spit (colloq); ***gastar*** ~ to waste one's breath; ***tragar*** ~ to swallow hard

salivadera *f* (CS) spittoon

salivar [A1] *vi* to salivate

salmo *m* psalm

salmón¹ *adj inv* salmon-pink, salmon, salmon-colored*

salmón² *m* salmon

salmonelosis *f* salmonella (poisoning), salmonellosis

salmonete *m* red mullet, surmullet (AmE)

salmuera *f* brine

salobre *adj* briny, brackish

salón *m* 1 (en casa particular) living room, sitting room (BrE), lounge (BrE) 2 (en hotel) reception room, function room 3 (en palacio) hall 4 (de clases) classroom

Compuestos

- **salón de actos** auditorium (AmE), assembly hall (BrE)
- **salón de baile** ballroom
- **salón de belleza** beauty salon, beauty parlor
- **salón de exposiciones** exhibition hall
- **salón de fiestas** (AmL) function room, reception room
- **salón de té** tearoom, teashop
- **salón náutico/del automóvil** boat/motor show
- **salón recreativo** amusement arcade

salpicadera *f* (Méx) (de coche, bicicleta) fender (AmE), mudguard (BrE)

salpicadero *m* (Esp) dashboard

salpicado -da *adj* ~ DE **algo** dotted WITH sth; **un texto ~ de citas** a text sprinkled with quotations

salpicadura *f* splash; **había ~s de barro en el auto** the car was spattered *o* splashed with mud

salpicar [A2] *vt*

A 1 (de agua) to splash; (de barro, aceite) to splash, spatter 2 (afectar): **el escándalo salpicó a todos los ministros** all the ministers were implicated in the scandal
B ‹*discurso/conversación*› ~ **algo** DE **algo** to pepper sth WITH sth

salpicón *m* (de pescado, ave) *chopped seafood or meat with onion, tomato and peppers*

salsa *f*

A (Coc) sauce; (de jugo de carne) gravy; ***estar en su (propia)*** ~ to be in one's element

Compuestos

- **salsa bechamel** *or* **blanca** bechamel (sauce)
- **salsa de tomate** (sofrito) tomato sauce; (catsup) (Col) ketchup, catsup (AmE)
- **salsa verde** parsley sauce

B (Mús) salsa

salsamentaría *f* (Col) delicatessen

salsera *f* gravy boat, sauceboat

saltador -dora *m,f* jumper; ~ **de altura/longitud** high/long jumper; ~ **de pértiga** pole vaulter; ~ **de triple** triple jumper

saltamontes *m* (*pl* ~) grasshopper

saltante *adj* (Per) notable, salient (frml)

saltar [A1] *vi*

A 1 (brincar) to jump; (más alto, más lejos) to leap; ~ **a la cuerda** *or* (Esp) **comba** to jump rope (AmE), to skip (BrE); **saltaban de (la) alegría** they were jumping for joy; **salté por encima de las cajas** I jumped over the boxes; **miraba ~ las truchas en el río** he watched the trout leaping in the river; ~ **con** *or* **en una pierna** to hop 2 (en atletismo) to jump; **tendrá que ~ 1,85m** he will have to jump *o* clear 1.85m 3 «*pelota*» to bounce 4 (lanzarse) to jump; ~ **en paracaídas** to parachute; **saltó desde una ventana** he jumped from a window; ~ **a tierra/al suelo** to jump to the ground; ~ **al agua** to jump into the water; **¿sabes ~ del trampolín?** can you dive off the springboard?; **saltó al vacío** he leapt into space; ~ SOBRE **algo/algn** to jump ON sth/sb; **la pantera saltó sobre su presa** the panther jumped *o* leapt on its prey 5 (levantarse): ~ **de la cama/del sillón** to jump out of bed/off one's chair
B 1 (aparecer) ~ A **algo**: **ambos equipos saltan al terreno**

de juego the two teams are now coming out onto the pitch; **salta a la vista que ...** it's patently obvious that ...; **la noticia saltó a primera plana** the story hit the headlines *o* made front-page news [2] (pasar) ~ DE **algo** A **algo** to jump FROM sth TO sth; **saltaba de una idea a otra** she kept jumping from one idea to the next

C [1] ‹‹*botón*›› to come off, pop off; ‹‹*chispas*›› to fly; ‹‹*aceite*›› to spit; ‹‹*corcho*›› to pop out; ‹‹*fusibles*›› to blow; **le hizo ~ tres dientes de un puñetazo** he knocked out three of his teeth with one punch; **hacer ~ la banca** to break the bank [2] (estallar): **la bomba hizo ~ el coche por los aires** the bomb blew the car into the air; **hicieron ~ el edificio con dinamita** they blew up the building with dynamite

D (fam) ‹‹*persona*›› [1] (enojarse) to lose one's temper, get angry [2] (decir, soltar) to retort; **—eso no es verdad —saltó Julián** that's not true, retorted Julián; ~ CON **algo**: **¿y ahora saltas con eso?** and now you come out with that?

■ **saltar** *vt* [1] ‹*obstáculo/valla/zanja*› to jump (over); (apoyándose) to vault (over); **el caballo se negó a ~ la valla** the horse refused the fence [2] (omitir) ‹*pregunta/página*› to skip, miss out; **me saltó al pasar lista** he missed me out when he was taking the register

■ **saltarse** *v pron*

A [1] (omitir) ‹*línea/página/nombre*› to skip; ‹*comida*› to miss, skip [2] ‹*semáforo/stop*› to jump; ‹*leyes*› to bypass, circumvent

B ‹‹*botón*›› to come off, pop off; ‹‹*pintura*›› to chip; **se le ~on las lágrimas** her eyes filled with tears

C (Chi) ‹‹*diente/loza*›› to chip

saltarín -rina *adj* ‹*cordero*› frolicking (*before n*)

salteado -da *adj*: **¿se pueden contestar las preguntas salteadas?** can we answer the questions in any order?; **leí unos capítulos ~s** I read a few odd chapters

salteador *m* highwayman

saltear [A1] *vt*

A (Coc) to sauté

B (ant) (asaltar) to hold up

■ **saltearse** *v pron* (RPl) to skip, jump

salterio *m* [1] (libro) psalter [2] (Mús) psaltery

saltimbanqui *m* (Espec, Hist) tumbler, acrobat

salto *m*

A [1] (brinco) jump; **atravesó el arroyo de un ~** he jumped (over) the stream; **se levantó de un ~** (de la cama) he leapt *o* sprang out of bed; (del suelo) he leapt *o* jumped up from the floor; **se puso en pie de un ~** she leapt *o* sprang to her feet; **los pájaros se acercaban dando saltitos** the birds were hopping closer to me/us; **dar** *or* **pegar un ~** (dar un brinco) to jump; (de susto) to start, jump; **el corazón le daba ~s de la emoción** her heart was pounding with excitement; **daban ~s de alegría** they were jumping for joy; **dos años más tarde dio el ~ de productor a director** two years later he made the jump from producer to director; **el país ha dado un enorme ~ atrás** the country has taken a huge step backward(s); ***dar un ~ en el vacío*** to take a leap in the dark; ***hacer algo a ~ de mata*** to do sth in a haphazard way; ***vivir a ~ de mata*** to take each day as it comes [2] (Dep) (en atletismo, esquí, paracaidismo) jump; (en natación) dive

(Compuestos)

- **salto con pértiga** *or* (AmL) **garrocha** pole vault
- **salto de altura/longitud** high/long jump
- **salto de cama** (Indum) (ligero) negligée; (bata) (CS) dressing gown
- **salto (en) alto/(en) largo** (AmL) high/long jump
- **salto mortal** somersault

B (Geog) *tb* **~ de agua** waterfall

saltón -tona *adj*

A ‹*ojos*› bulging

B (Andes fam) (receloso, desconfiado) wary, jumpy

salubre *adj* healthy, salubrious (frml)

salubridad *f* healthiness, salubriousness (frml)

salucita *interj* (AmL fam) cheers!, your health!

salud *f*

A (Med) health; **estar bien de ~** to be in good health; **gozar de buena ~** to enjoy good health; ***curarse en ~*** to be on the safe side, play safe

(Compuesto) **salud pública** public health

B **¡~!** (al brindar) cheers!; (cuando alguien estornuda) (AmL) bless you!; **¡a su ~!** good health!

saludable *adj* ‹*clima/alimentación*› healthy; ‹*experiencia*› salutary

saludar [A1] *vt*

A ‹*persona*› [1] (de palabra) to greet, say hello to; **se acercó a ~lo** she went up to say hello to him *o* to greet him; **como pasaba por allí, fui a ~los** since I was passing, I dropped in on them; **saluda a tu hermano de mi parte** give my regards to your brother; **lo saluda atentamente** (Corresp) Sincerely (yours) (AmE), Yours sincerely (BrE), Yours faithfully (BrE) [2] (con un gesto): **los saludó con la mano** she waved to them; **los artistas salieron a ~ al público** the performers came out to take a bow [3] (Mil) to salute

B (aplaudir) ‹*innovación/medida*› to welcome

■ **saludar** *vi* [1] (de palabra) to say hello (*o* good morning *etc*) [2] (con un gesto) to wave [3] (Mil) to salute

■ **saludarse** *v pron* (*recípr*) to greet each other; **ya ni se saludan** they don't even say hello to each other now, they're not on speaking terms any more

saludo *m* [1] (fórmula verbal) greeting; **dirigió un cálido ~ a la concurrencia** he greeted the audience warmly; **~s a tu hermana** give my regards to your sister, say hello to your sister for *o* from me; **te mandan** *or* **envían ~s** they send (you) their regards *o* best wishes; **reciba un ~ cordial de** (Corresp) with best wishes; **~s** (Corresp) best wishes; ***retirarle*** *or* ***quitarle el ~ a algn*** to stop speaking to sb [2] (gesto) wave; **le hice un ~ con la mano** I gave him a wave *o* I waved to him [3] (Mil) salute

salva *f*: **una ~ de 21 cañonazos** a 21-gun salute *o* salvo; **una ~ de aplausos** a burst *o* round of applause

salvación *f* salvation; **ese dinero fue mi ~** that money saved my life (colloq); **no tiene ~** there is no hope for him

salvada *f*

A [1] (Chi fam) (de la muerte, un peligro) escape [2] (Per) (rescate) rescue

B (Chi fam) (Dep) save

salvado *m* bran

salvador -dora *m,f* savior•

Salvador *ver* **El Salvador**

salvadoreño -ña *adj/m,f* Salvadoran, Salvadorean

salvaguarda *f* ▸ **salvaguardia**

salvaguardar [A1] *vt* to safeguard

salvaguardia *f* safeguard, defense•

salvajada *f* [1] (acto) atrocity; **las ~s de los hinchas de fútbol** the mindless violence of the football fans [2] (fam) (grosería): **le soltó una ~** he said something nasty to her (colloq) [3] **ser una ~** (fam) (exageración, insensatez): **pagó una ~ por el coche** he paid an outrageous amount for the car; **es una ~ intentar acabarlo todo hoy** it's crazy to try to do it all today

salvaje[1] *adj*

A [1] ‹*animal*› wild [2] (primitivo) ‹*tribu*› savage [3] ‹*vegetación/terreno*› wild

B (cruel) ‹*persona/tortura*› brutal; ‹*ataque/matanza*› savage

salvaje[2] *mf* (primitivo) savage; (bruto) (pey) animal, savage

salvajismo *m* savagery

salvamanteles *m* (*pl* ~) (para platos, fuentes) tablemat; (para vasos) coaster

salvamento *m* rescue; **bote de ~** lifeboat; **equipo/operación de ~** rescue team/operation

salvapantalla *m* screen saver

salvar [A1] *vt*

A [1] (de la muerte, de un peligro) to save; **lograron ~le la vida** they managed to save her life; **~ algo/a algn** DE **algo** to save sth/sb FROM sth; **salvó al niño de perecer ahogado** she saved the child from drowning [2] (fam) (librar) to save; **~ a algn** DE **algo** to save sb FROM sth [3] (Relig) to save

B [1] ‹*dificultad/obstáculo*› to overcome [2] ‹*distancia*› to cover [3] (Per, Ur) ‹*examen*› to pass

■ **salvarse** *v pron* [1] (de la muerte, de un peligro): **sólo se ~on tres personas** only three people got out alive, only three people survived; **¡sálvese quien pueda!** every man for himself!; **~se** DE **algo** to escape FROM sth [2] (fam) (librarse): **de la familia, el único que se salva es Alejandro** the only one of the family who's all right is Alejandro; **sólo se salva él porque no lo sabía** he's the only one who

S

can be excused because he didn't know; **~se DE algo**: **se salvó de hacer el servicio militar** he got out of doing his military service 3 (Relig) to be saved

salvataje *m* (CS) ▸**salvamento**

salvavidas *mf* (*pl* ~) 1 (persona) lifeguard 2 **salvavidas** *m* (flotador) life jacket, life preserver (frml)

salvedad *f* 1 (excepción): **hechas estas ~es, ...** apart *o* aside from that, ...; **con la ~ de ...** apart from ..., except ... 2 (condición) condition, proviso (frml); **con una ~** on one condition, with one proviso 3 (aclaración): **quisiera hacer una ~** I would like to make one thing clear

salvia *f* sage

salvo[1] **-va** *adj* safe, unharmed

salvo[2]: **a ~** (*loc adv*) **poner algo a ~** to put sth in a safe place; **los niños están a ~** the children are safe *o* unharmed; **lograron ponerse a ~** they managed to get themselves to safety *o* to reach safety

salvo[3] *prep* (excepto) except, apart from; **todos estaban presentes ~ el secretario** everyone was there except *o* apart from the secretary; **sus canciones son bastante malas ~ excepciones** with a few exceptions his songs are pretty poor; **~ que** unless

salvoconducto *m* safe-conduct

samba *m or f* samba

sambenito *m* (fam) label; **me colgaron** *or* **pusieron el ~ de timador** they branded *o* labeled me a con man

SAMUR *m* (en Esp) = **Servicio de Asistencia Municipal de Urgencia y Rescate**

San *adj* (*apócope de* **santo** *usado delante de nombres de varón excepto Domingo, Tomás y Tomé*) St, Saint; **el 19 de marzo es ~ José** March 19th is St Joseph's Day

sanar [A1] *vi* ⟨⟨*enfermo*⟩⟩ to get well, recover; ⟨⟨*herida*⟩⟩ to heal; **~ DE algo** to recover from sth

■ **sanar** *vt* to cure

sanatorio *m* 1 (para convalecientes) nursing home, sanitarium (AmE), sanatorium (BrE) 2 (hospital) clinic, hospital (*usually private*) 3 (Col, Ven) (hospital psiquiátrico) mental hospital, psychiatric hospital

sanción *f*

A (castigo): **una ~ de tres partidos** a three-game ban *o* suspension; **le será aplicada la ~ correspondiente** (a obrero) appropriate disciplinary measures will be taken; (Der) the appropriate sanction *o* penalty will be applied; **impusieron sanciones económicas a Sudáfrica** economic sanctions were imposed on South Africa

(Compuestos)

- **sanción económica** (multa) fine
- **sanciones económicas** (a país) economic sanctions

B (de ley) sanction; (de costumbre) sanction (frml), authorization; **ha dado su ~ a esta práctica** he has sanctioned this practice

sancionar [A1] *vt*

A (multar) to fine; (castigar): **está sancionado por tres partidos** he has been banned *o* suspended for three games

B ⟨*ley/disposición/acuerdo/huelga*⟩ to sanction; ⟨*costumbre*⟩ to approve, sanction

sancochar [A1] *vt* (AmL) (cocer a medias) to parboil

■ **sancocharse** *v pron* (AmS fam) ⟨⟨*persona*⟩⟩ (achicharrarse) to boil (colloq), to roast (colloq)

sancocho *m* (Coc) *soup/stew made with fish or chicken, plantain and cassava*

sandalia *f* sandal

sándalo *m* sandalwood

sandez *f* (fam) silly *o* stupid thing to say; **¡no digas sandeces!** don't talk nonsense!

sandía *f* watermelon

sánduche *m* (Andes, Ven) sandwich

sandunga *f*

A (fam): **¡qué poca ~ tienes!** you've got no spark *o* oomph! (colloq); **tiene tanta ~** he's a real live wire (colloq)

B (AmL) (juerga) party, rave-up (esp BrE colloq); **sus clases eran una ~** his classes were a riot (colloq)

C (baile) *Southern Mexican folk song/dance*

sandunguear [A1] *vi* to party

sandunguero -ra *adj*: **es muy ~** he's a real party animal *o* (esp BrE) raver (colloq)

sándwich /'saŋgwitʃ/ *m*, **sándwiche** /'saŋgwitʃe/ *m* (esp AmL) (de pan de molde) sandwich; (de pancito) (filled) roll

saneamiento *m*

A 1 (de empresa) reorganization, rationalization 2 (de zona, río) cleaning up 3 (Der) compensation

B (Esp) (fontanería) plumbing

sanear [A1] *vt* 1 ⟨*empresa*⟩ to reorganize, rationalize; **~ la economía** to get the economy into shape *o* on to a sound footing 2 ⟨*edificio/barrio*⟩ to clean up 3 (Der) to compensate

sanfasón *f* (RPl fam): **todo es un poco a la ~** it's all a bit hit-and-miss; **iba peinada a la ~** her hair was all over the place

sanfermines *mpl*: *festivity in Pamplona in which bulls are run through the streets*

sangrante *adj* ⟨*herida*⟩ bleeding; ⟨*injusticia*⟩ gross, flagrant

sangrar [A1] *vi* ⟨⟨*persona/herida/nariz*⟩⟩ to bleed

■ **sangrar** *vt*

A ⟨*enfermo*⟩ to bleed; ⟨*árbol*⟩ to tap

B ⟨*renglón/texto*⟩ to indent

sangre *f*

A (Biol) blood; **una transfusión de ~** a blood transfusion; **no me salió ~** it didn't bleed; **la ~ le salía a borbotones** (the) blood was pouring *o* gushing from him; **te sale ~ de** *or* **por la nariz** your nose is bleeding; **los ojos inyectados en ~** bloodshot eyes; **no hubo derramamiento de ~** there was no bloodshed; **corrió mucha ~** there was a lot of bloodshed; **animales de ~ fría/caliente** cold-blooded/warm-blooded animals; ***a ~ y fuego*** with great violence; ***chuparle la ~ a algn*** (fam) (explotarlo) to bleed sb white *o* dry; (hacerle pasar malos ratos) (Méx) to cause sb a lot of heartache; ***dar*** *or* ***derramar ~ por algo/algn*** to give one's life for sth/sb; ***hervirle a ~ a algn***: **me hierve/hirvió la ~** it makes/made my blood boil; ***lavar algo con ~*** to avenge sth with blood; ***no llegar la ~ al río***: **se gritaron mucho, pero no llegó la ~ al río** there was a lot of shouting, but it didn't go beyond that; ***no tener ~ en las venas*** to be a cold fish (colloq); ***~, sudor y lágrimas*** blood, sweat and tears; ***se me/le fue la ~ a los pies*** (Méx) my/his blood ran cold; ***se me/le heló la ~ (en las venas)*** my/his blood ran cold; ***se me/le sube la ~ a la cabeza*** it makes me/him see red; ***sudar ~*** to sweat blood; ***tener (la) ~ en el ojo*** (CS fam) to bear a grudge; ***tener la ~ ligera*** *or* (Méx) ***ser de ~ ligera*** *or* (Chi) ***ser liviano de ~*** to be easygoing; ***tener la ~ pesada*** *or* (Méx) ***ser de ~ pesada*** *or* (Chi) ***ser pesado de ~*** to be a nasty character *o* a nasty piece of work (colloq); ***tener ~ de horchata*** *or* (Méx) ***atole***: **Juan tiene la ~ de horchata, no se emociona por nada** Juan is such a cold fish, he never shows any emotion; ▸**malo**[1], **puro**[1]

(Compuesto) **sangre fría** calmness, sangfroid; **a ~ ~** ⟨*matar*⟩ in cold blood; **ha sido una venganza a ~ ~** it was cold-blooded revenge

B (linaje) blood; **era de ~ noble** he was of noble blood *o* birth; **es de ~ mestiza** he is of mixed race; **no desprecies a los de tu misma ~** don't despise your own kind *o* your own family; **no son de la misma ~** they are not from the same family; ***la ~ tira*** blood is thicker than water; ***llevar*** *or* (Méx) ***traer algo en la ~*** to have sth in one's blood; **lo lleva en la ~** it's in his blood

(Compuesto) **sangre azul** blue blood

sangría *f*

A (bebida) sangria (*type of red wine punch*)

B 1 (Med) bleeding 2 (de capital, recursos) outflow, drain

C (Impr) indentation

D (acequia) irrigation channel; (zanja) ditch

sangriento -ta *adj* bloody

sangrón[1] **-grona** *adj* (Méx fam) annoying

sangrón[2] **-grona** *m,f* (Méx fam) nuisance

sangronada *f* (Méx fam) 1 (dicho inoportuno) silly remark 2 (hecho desagradable): **deja de hacer ~s** stop being so annoying, stop being such a pain in the neck (colloq)

sanguaraña *f*: *Peruvian folk dance*

sanguijuela *f* 1 (Zool) leech 2 (fam) (persona) leech, bloodsucker

sanguinario -ria *adj* ⟨*persona*⟩ cruel, bloodthirsty; ⟨*animal*⟩ vicious, ferocious

sanguíneo -nea *adj* 1 (Med) blood (*before n*) 2 ⟨*persona*⟩ sanguine, ruddy-complexioned

S

sanguinolento -ta *adj* 1 ‹*flujo/secreción*› bloody, containing blood; **su cara era una masa sanguinolenta** her face was covered in blood 2 ‹*ojos*› bloodshot 3 ‹*carne*› bloody, underdone

sanidad *f*
A (calidad de sano) health, healthiness
B 1 (salud pública) public health; **inspector de ~** public health inspector 2 **Sanidad** (*sin art*) (departamento) Department of Health

sanitario¹ -ria *adj* ‹*medidas*› public health (*before n*); **condiciones sanitarias** sanitary conditions; **servicios ~s** sanitation; **asistencia sanitaria** health-care

sanitario² -ria *m,f*
A (persona) health worker
B **sanitario** *m* (Col, Méx, Ven) (retrete) toilet, lavatory
C **sanitarios** *mpl* (para cuarto de baño) bathroom fittings (*pl*)

sanjacobo *m* (Esp) *breaded pork or ham slices stuffed with cheese and fried*

sano -na *adj*
A ‹*persona/planta/cabello*› healthy; ‹*clima*› healthy; ‹*alimentación*› healthy, wholesome; **lleva una vida muy sana** he leads a very healthy life; ***cortar por lo ~*** to take drastic action; ***~ y salvo*** safe and sound
B (en buen estado): **pon aquí las peras sanas** put the good pears here; **sólo quedaron dos vasos ~s** only two glasses were left intact
C (en sentido moral) ‹*lecturas/ideas*› wholesome; ‹*ambiente*› healthy; ‹*persona*› good

San Salvador *m* San Salvador

sánscrito *m* Sanskrit

sanseacabó *interj* (fam): **vas porque te lo digo yo y ~** you'll go because I say so and that's that!; **¡lo despides y ~!** fire him and have done with it *o* let that be an end to it!

Santa Sede *f*: **la ~ ~** the Vatican, the Holy See (frml)

santateresa *f* mantis, praying mantis

Santiago (de Chile) *m* Santiago

Santiago (de Compostela) *m* Santiago (de Compostela)

santiaguino -na *adj* of/from Santiago (*Chile*)

santiamén *m*: **en un ~** (fam) in no time at all

santidad *f* (de lugar) sanctity, holiness; (de persona) saintliness, godliness

santificación *f* sanctification

santificar [A2] *vt* 1 (venerar): **~ las fiestas** to observe feast days; **santificado sea tu nombre** hallowed be Thy name 2 ‹*matrimonio/unión*› to consecrate

santiguarse [A16] *v pron* (*refl*) to cross oneself, make the sign of the cross

santísimo -ma *adj*
A (Relig) most holy
B (fam) (uso enfático): **hay que hacer su santísima voluntad** we have to do everything he damn well wants

Santísimo *m*: **el ~** the Holy Sacrament

santo¹ -ta *adj*
A (Relig) 1 ‹*lugar/mujer/vida*› holy; **la santa misa** holy mass; **tu abuelo fue un ~ varón** your grandfather was a saint 2 (con nombre propio) St, Saint; **Santa Teresa** Saint Theresa; **S~ Domingo** Saint Dominic; *ver tb* **San**

Compuestos
- **santo patrón** *or* (AmL) **patrono** *m* patron saint
- **Santos Inocentes** *mpl* Holy Innocents (*pl*)

B (fam) (uso enfático): **llovió todo el ~ día** it rained the whole blessed day (colloq); **siempre tenemos que hacer su santa voluntad** we always have to do what *he* wants

santo² -ta *m,f*
A (persona) saint; **se ha portado como una santa** she's been a little angel; **no te hagas el ~** don't come over all virtuous; **se necesita una paciencia de ~** you need the patience of a saint; **¡por todos los ~s!** for Heaven's *o* goodness' sake!; ***¿a ~ de qué?*** (fam) why on earth? (colloq); ***darse de ~s*** (Méx fam) to think oneself lucky (colloq); ***desnudar a un ~ para vestir a otro*** to rob Peter to pay Paul; ***no es ~ de mi/tu/su devoción*** he/she is not my/your/his favorite person; ***quedarse para vestir ~s*** to be left on the shelf; ***se me/le fue el ~ al cielo*** it went right out of my/his head; ***ser llegar y besar el ~*** (fam) (ser rápido) to be incredibly quick; (ser fácil): **no te creas que fue llegar y besar el ~** don't think it was just handed to me/him on a plate

Compuesto **santo y seña** password

B **santo** *m* (festividad) name day, saint's day; (cumpleaños) (esp AmL) birthday

> **santo**
>
> Most first names in Spanish-speaking countries are those of saints. A person's *santo*, (also known as *onomástico* in Latin America and *onomástica* in Spain) is the saint's day of the saint that they are named for. Children were once usually named for the saint whose day they were born on, but this is less common now

Santo Domingo *m* Santo Domingo

santoral *m* (lista de santos) calendar of saints' (feast) days; (libro) hagiography

santuario *m* (Relig) sanctuary, shrine; (refugio) sanctuary

santurrón -rrona *m,f* (fam) overpious *o* excessively devout person

saña *f* viciousness, brutality; **con ~** brutally, viciously

São Paulo *m* São Paulo

sapear [A1] *vt*
A (Andes fam) (delatar) ‹*persona*› to squeal on (colloq); ‹*robo*› to squeal about (colloq)
B (Chi fam) (espiar) to spy on

sapo¹ -pa *adj*
A (Andes fam) (astuto) sharp (colloq)
B (Chi fam) (mirón) nosy (colloq)

sapo² *m* (Zool) toad; ***echar ~s y culebras por la boca*** (fam) to curse and swear

sapo³ -pa *m,f*
A (Andes fam) (astuto): **es una sapa** she's very sharp (colloq)
B (Andes fam) (delator) informer, grass (BrE colloq)

saque *m* 1 (en tenis, vóleibol) serve, service 2 (en fútbol) kickoff; ***tener buen ~*** (Esp fam) to have a good appetite

Compuestos
- **saque de banda** (en fútbol) throw-in; (en rugby) line-out
- **saque de esquina** corner (kick)
- **saque de puerta** *or* (CS) **valla** goal kick
- **saque inicial** kickoff

saquear [A1] *vt* ‹*ciudad/población*› to sack, plunder; ‹*tienda/establecimiento*› to loot

saqueo *m* (de pueblo) sacking, plundering; (de tienda) looting

S.A.R. (= **Su Alteza Real**) HRH

sarampión *m* measles

sarao *m* soirée, party

sarape *m* (Guat, Méx) ▸**zarape**

sarcasmo *m* 1 (cualidad) sarcasm; **lo dijo con ~** he said it sarcastically *o* in a sarcastic tone 2 (comentario) sarcastic remark

sarcástico -ca *adj* sarcastic

sarcófago *m* sarcophagus

sardina *f* sardine; **íbamos como ~s en lata en el tren** (fam) we were packed into the train like sardines (colloq)

sardinel *m* (Col) 1 (de la acera) curb (AmE), kerb (BrE) 2 (de ventana) windowsill

sardinero -ra *adj* ‹*barco/industria*› sardine (*before n*)

sardónico -ca *adj* sardonic, ironic

sargazo *m* gulfweed, sargasso

sargento *mf* 1 (Mil) (en el ejército) sergeant; (en las fuerzas aéreas) ≈ staff sergeant (*in US*), ≈ sergeant (*in UK*) 2 (fam & pey) (persona autoritaria) tyrant (colloq)

sari *m* sari

sarita *f* (Per) straw hat

sarmentoso -sa *adj* 1 ‹*planta*› sarmentous (tech), creeping (*before n*) 2 ‹*manos*› (liter) gnarled

sarmiento *m* vine shoot

sarna *f* (Med) scabies; (Vet) mange

sarnoso -sa *adj* ‹*persona*› suffering from scabies, scabious; ‹*perro*› mangy

sarpullido *m* rash, hives (*pl*)

sarraceno -na *adj/m,f* Saracen

sarro *m* (en los dientes) plaque, tartar; (en la lengua) fur; (en tetera eléctrica, cañería) scale, fur (BrE)

S

sarta *f* [1] (serie) string; **una ~ de insultos** a string of insults [2] (de perlas) string

sartén *f*, (AmL) *m or f* frying pan, fry pan (AmE), skillet; ***tener la ~ por el mango*** to call the shots (colloq)

sastre *mf*, **sastre -tra** *m,f* [1] (persona) tailor [2] **sastre** *m* (Col) (traje) woman's suit

sastrería *f* tailor's shop

Satanás, Satán *m* Satan

satánico -ca *adj* (del diablo) satanic; (malvado) evil, satanic

satélite *m* (Astron, Espac) satellite; (país) satellite (state)

(Compuestos)
- **satélite artificial/de comunicaciones** artificial/communications satellite
- **satélite meteorológico** meteorological *o* weather satellite

satén (AmL) **satín** *m* satin

satinado -da *adj* ‹*papel*› satin (*before n*), satin-finish (*before n*); ‹*hilo/tela*› with a satin sheen

sátira *f* satire

satírico -ca *adj* satirical

satirizar [A4] *vt* to satirize

sátiro *m* (Mit) satyr

satisfacción *f*

[A] (agrado, placer) satisfaction; **la ~ del deber cumplido** the satisfaction of a job well done; **esperamos que sea de su entera ~** we hope it will be to your complete satisfaction; **es una ~ para mí estar aquí** it is a pleasure to be here; **recibió con ~ la noticia** she was pleased when she heard the news

[B] [1] (de necesidad, deseo) satisfaction, fulfillment* [2] (por ofensa) satisfaction; **exijo una ~** I demand satisfaction [3] (de deuda) payment, settlement

satisfacer [E20] *vt* [1] ‹*persona*› to satisfy; **su respuesta no me satisface** I am not satisfied *o* happy with your reply [2] ‹*necesidad/deseo*› to satisfy, fulfill*; ‹*instintos*› to satisfy; **~ el hambre/la curiosidad** to satisfy one's hunger/one's curiosity [3] (frml) ‹*requisitos/condiciones*› to satisfy, fulfill*, meet [4] (frml) ‹*cantidad/cuota*› to pay; ‹*deuda*› to pay off, settle

■ **satisfacerse** *v pron* [1] (contentarse) to be satisfied; **no se satisface con nada** she's never satisfied [2] (de agravio) to obtain satisfaction

satisfactorio -ria *adj* satisfactory

satisfaga, satisfará, etc *see* **satisfacer**

satisfecho -cha *adj*

[A] [ESTAR] (complacido, contento) satisfied, pleased; **los resultados me han dejado muy ~** I am very pleased *o* happy with the results

[B] [ESTAR] (saciado, lleno): **no, gracias, estoy ~** no thanks, I've had plenty; **no queda nunca ~** he never seems to be full

saturación *f* saturation

saturado -da *adj* [1] (Fís, Quím) saturated [2] ‹*mercado*› saturated; ‹*líneas telefónicas*› busy, engaged (BrE) [3] (fam) ‹*persona*›: **están ~s de trabajo** they're up to their eyes in work (colloq); **acabamos ~s de cine** we had our fill of cinema

saturar [A1] *vt* [1] (Fís, Quím) to saturate [2] ‹*mercado*› to saturate, flood

Saturno *m* Saturn

sauce *m* willow

(Compuesto) **sauce llorón** weeping willow

saudí, saudita *adj/mf* (Saudi) Arabian

sauna *f or* (AmL) *m* sauna

savia *f* [1] (Bot) sap [2] (energía, vitalidad) vitality, life

sávila *f* (Méx) aloe vera

saxo *m* (fam) [1] (instrumento) sax (colloq) [2] **saxo** *mf* (persona) sax player (colloq)

saxofón, saxófono *m* saxophone

saxofonista *mf* saxophonist

sayo *m* smock; ***al que le caiga*** *or* ***venga el ~ que se lo ponga*** (CS) if the cap fits, wear it;

sazón¹ *f*

[A] [1] (condimento) seasoning; (sabor) flavor* [2] (de la fruta) ripeness; **estar en ~** to be ripe

[B] **a la sazón** (liter) at that time

sazón² *m or f* (Méx) ▸**sazón¹ A**

sazonado -da *adj* [1] ‹*guiso/plato*› seasoned; **un guiso muy bien ~** a well-seasoned stew [2] ‹*discurso/relato*› **~ DE algo** peppered WITH sth

sazonar [A1] *vt* to season

s/c. [1] = **su cargo** [2] = **su cuenta**

schop /ʃop/ *m* (Chi) (vaso) beer mug; (cerveza) keg beer

Scotch® /(e)s'kotʃ/ *m* (Andes) Scotch® tape (AmE), Sellotape® (BrE)

scout /(e)s'kau(t)/ *mf* scout

se *pron pers*

[A] [*seguido de otro pronombre: sustituyendo a* **le**]: **ya ~ lo he dicho** (a él) I've already told him; (a ella) I've already told her; (a usted, ustedes) I've already told you; (a ellos) I've already told them; **el vestido tenía cuello pero ~ lo quité** the dress had a collar but I took it off

[B] (*en verbos pronominales*): **quejarse** to complain; **~ queja de todo** «*él/ella*» he/she complains about everything; «*usted*» you complain about everything; **¿no ~ arrepienten?** «*ellos/ellas*» aren't they sorry?; «*ustedes*» aren't you sorry?; **el barco ~ hundió** the ship sank; **~ cortó** (*refl*) he cut himself; **~ cortó el dedo** (*refl*) he cut his finger; **~ hizo un vestido** (*refl*) she made herself a dress; (*caus*) she had a dress made; **no ~ hablan** (*recípr*) they're not on speaking terms, they're not speaking to each other; **~ lo comió todo** (*enf*) he ate it all

[C] [1] (*voz pasiva*): **~ oyeron unos gritos** there were shouts, I (*o* we *etc*) heard some shouts; **~ estudiarán sus propuestas** your proposals will be studied; **~ publicó el año pasado** it was published last year; Ⓢ **se habla inglés** English spoken here [2] (*impersonal*): **aquí ~ está muy bien** it's very nice here; **~ iba poco al teatro** people didn't go to the theater very much; **~ ha llegado a un punto en que ...** we've/they've now reached a point where ..., a point has now been reached where ...; **~ los acusa de subversión** they are accused of subversion; **~ castigará a los culpables** those responsible will be punished [3] (en normas, instrucciones): **¿cómo ~ escribe tu nombre?** how is your name spelled?, how do you spell your name?; **~ pica la cebolla bien menuda** chop the onion finely; Ⓢ **sírvase bien frío** serve chilled

SE (= **sureste**) SE

S.E. (= **su excelencia**) H.E.

sé *see* **saber, ser**

sea, seas, etc *see* **ser**

sebáceo -cea *adj* sebaceous

sebo *m* (grasa) grease, fat; (para jabón, velas) tallow; (Coc) suet

seboso -sa *adj* (grasiento) greasy; (mugriento) grimy

secado *m* drying

secador *m*

[A] *tb* **~ de pelo** hairdryer

[B] (Per) (paño) dishtowel (AmE), tea towel (BrE); (toalla) towel

secadora *f* (de ropa, tabaco) dryer; (para el pelo) (Méx) hairdryer

secamanos *m* (*pl* **~s**) hand dryer

secamente *adv* curtly; **me trató muy ~** he was very curt *o* short with me

secano *m*: **de ~** ‹*campo/tierra*› dry, unirrigated

secante¹ *m* blotting paper

secante² *f* (Mat) secant

secar [A2] *vt* [1] ‹*ropa/pelo/platos*› to dry; ‹*pintura/arcilla*› to dry; **le secó las lágrimas con un pañuelo** she dried his tears with a handkerchief [2] ‹*tierra/plantas/hierba*› to dry up; **el sol seca la piel** the sun makes your skin dry

■ **secar** *vi* to dry

■ **secarse** *v pron*

[A] [1] «*ropa/pintura/pelo*» to dry; **se me secó la garganta** my throat is really dry; **se me seca mucho la piel** my skin gets very dry [2] «*herida*» to heal (up) [3] «*tierra/planta/hierba*» to dry up [4] «*río/pozo/fuente*» to dry up [5] «*arroz/guiso*» to go dry

[B] (*refl*) «*persona*» ‹*manos/pelo*› to dry; ‹*lágrimas*› to dry, wipe away; **se secó el sudor de la frente** he mopped his brow; **se secó con la toalla** she dried herself (off) with the towel

S

sección *f*
A (corte) section; **~ longitudinal/transversal** longitudinal/cross section
B 1 (división, área — en general) section; (— de empresa) department, section; (— en grandes almacenes) department 2 (de periódico, orquesta) section
C (Mil) platoon

seccional *f*
A (Col, Ven) (de organización) section
B (RPl) *tb* **~ de policía** (territorio) police district, precinct (AmE); (edificio) police station, precinct house (AmE)

seccionar [A1] *vt* (cortar) to cut off; (dividir en secciones) to section

secesión *f* secession; **la Guerra de S~** the (American) Civil War

seco -ca *adj*
A 1 [ESTAR] ‹*ropa/platos/pintura*› dry; **Ⓢ manténgase en lugar seco** store in a dry place; **tengo la boca/garganta seca** my mouth/throat is dry 2 [ESTAR] ‹*planta/río/comida*› dry 3 [SER] ‹*clima/región*› dry
B (disecado) ‹*higos/flores*› dried; **bacalao ~** stockfish, dried salt cod
C [SER] (no graso) ‹*piel/pelo*› dry
D [SER] (no dulce) ‹*vino/licor/vermut*› dry
E ‹*golpe/sonido*› sharp; ‹*tos*› dry
F 1 ‹*respuesta/carácter*› dry; **estuvo muy ~ conmigo** he was very short with me 2 (fam) (delgado) thin; **está más ~ que un palo** he's as thin as a rake 3 [ESTAR] (fam) (sediento) parched (colloq)
G (*en locs*) **en seco** ‹*frenar*› sharply, suddenly; **me paró en ~** he stopped me in my tracks; **limpieza en ~** dry cleaning; ***a secas*** (fam): **llámeme Roberto a secas** just call me (plain) Roberto; **comimos pan a secas** we ate bread on its own; ***dejar a algn ~*** (matar) (fam) to kill sb stone dead (colloq); «*noticia/respuesta*»: **la noticia me dejó ~** when I heard the news I was absolutely staggered

secoya *f* sequoia

secreción *f* (de glándula) secretion; (de herida) discharge

secretar [A1] *vt* to secrete

secretaría *f*
A 1 (cargo) office of secretary; **asumió la ~ del club** she took over as secretary of the club 2 (oficina) secretary's office 3 (departamento administrativo) secretariat
(Compuesto) **secretaría general** general secretariat
B (Méx) (ministerio) department, ministry (BrE)

secretariado *m* secretarial work; **estudia ~ bilingüe** she's doing a bilingual secretarial course

secretario -ria *m,f*
A 1 (trabajador administrativo) secretary; **soy secretaria bilingüe** I'm a bilingual secretary 2 (de asociación, sociedad) secretary
(Compuestos)
- **secretario -ria de dirección** *m,f* secretary to the director
- **secretario -ria general** *m,f* secretary general

B (Méx) (Gob, Pol) secretary of state, minister
(Compuestos)
- **Secretario -ria de Economía** *or* **de Hacienda** *m,f* (en Méx) Finance Minister, ≈ Treasury Secretary (*in US*), ≈ Chancellor of the Exchequer (*in UK*)
- **Secretario -ria de Gobernación** *m,f* (en Méx) Minister of the Interior, ≈ Home Secretary (*in UK*)

secretear [A1] *vi* (AmL fam) to whisper
■ **secretearse** *v pron* (AmL fam) to whisper

secreteo *m* (AmL fam) whispering; **estaban de mucho ~** they were whispering away

secreter *m* writing desk

secretismo *m* excessive secrecy

secreto¹ -ta *adj* secret

secreto² *m* 1 (información confidencial) secret; **guardar un ~** to keep a secret; **los preparamos en ~** we prepared them secretly *o* in secret; **revelar un ~** to give away *o* reveal a secret; **te lo dije en ~** I told you in confidence; **no es ningún ~ que ...** it is no secret that ... 2 (truco) secret; **el ~ está en la manera de doblarlo** the secret is in the way you fold it; **y no tiene más ~** and that's all there is to it
(Compuestos)
- **secreto a voces** open secret
- **secreto de confesión** secret of the confessional
- **secreto de estado** state secret
- **secreto de familia** family secret
- **secreto de sumario**: **el ~ de ~ me impide dar más detalles** I am unable to give further details because the matter is sub judice

secta *f* sect

sectario -ria *adj* sectarian

sectarismo *m* sectarianism

sector *m* 1 (grupo) sector, group; **ningún ~ social se va a beneficiar** no social group will benefit 2 (Mat) sector 3 (de ciudad) area; **el ~ norte de la ciudad** the northern area *o* part of the city 4 (Com, Econ) sector; **la empresa líder en su ~** the leading company in its field; **el ~ agrario** the agricultural sector *o* industry
(Compuestos)
- **sector de servicios** service *o* tertiary sector
- **sector industrial** (Col, Ven) industrial estate
- **sector privado/público** private/public sector

sectorial *adj* sectorial

secuaz (*m*) follower, henchman; (*f*) follower

secuela *f* (de guerra, decisión) consequence; **esta enfermedad tiene sus ~s** this illness has long-term effects

secuencia *f* 1 (Mat) sequence, series 2 (Cin, TV) sequence

secuestrador -dora *m,f* (de persona) kidnapper; (de avión) hijacker

secuestrar [A1] *vt* 1 ‹*persona*› to kidnap; ‹*avión*› to hijack 2 ‹*periódico/revista*› to seize; ‹*bienes*› to sequestrate, confiscate

secuestro *m* 1 (de persona) kidnapping; (de avión) hijack(ing) 2 (de periódico) seizure; (de bienes) sequestration, confiscation

secular *adj*
A (laico) secular, lay (*before n*); **clero ~** lay clergy
B (antiguo) ‹*tradición/lucha*› centuries-old, age-old

secularizar [A4] *vt* to secularize

secundar [A1] *vt* 1 (en proyecto) ‹*persona/esfuerzos*› to support, back 2 ‹*moción/propuesta*› (al proponerla) to second; (en la votación) to support 3 ‹*huelga*› to join, support

secundaria *f* 1 (AmL) (enseñanza media) secondary education, high school (AmE) 2 (Méx) (instituto) middle school

secundario -ria *adj* ‹*factor/problema*› secondary; **una de las actrices secundarias** one of the supporting actresses

secuoya, secuoia *f* sequoia

sed *f* thirst; **el agua le quitó la ~** the water quenched his thirst; **tengo mucha ~** I'm very thirsty; **me da mucha ~** it makes me (feel) really thirsty; **su ~ de venganza/riqueza** her thirst for vengeance/riches

seda *f* silk; ***estar como la*** *or* ***una ~*** to be as meek as a lamb; ***ir/funcionar como la ~*** to go/work perfectly *o* like a dream
(Compuesto) **seda dental** dental floss

sedal *m* fishing line

sedán *m* sedan

sedante *adj/m* (Med) sedative

sedar [A1] *vt* to sedate

sede *f* 1 (del gobierno) seat 2 (Relig) see 3 (de organización internacional) headquarters (*sing or pl*); (de compañía) headquarters (*sing or pl*), head office 4 (de congreso, feria) venue; **México fue la ~ de los Juegos Olímpicos en 1968** Mexico was the venue for *o* Mexico hosted the Olympic Games in 1968
(Compuesto) **sede social** (de empresa) headquarters (*sing or pl*), head office; (de club) headquarters (*sing or pl*)

sedentario -ria *adj* sedentary

sedición *f* sedition, insurrection

sedicioso -sa *m,f* rebel, seditious element (frml)

sediento -ta *adj* thirsty; **~ de venganza/poder** thirsty for revenge/power

sedimentación *f* sedimentation

sedimento *m* sediment, deposit

S

sedoso -sa *adj* ‹*aspecto*› silky, sleek; (al tacto) silky, silky-smooth

seducción *f* seduction

seducir [I6] *vt* 1 (en sentido sexual) to seduce 2 (fascinar, cautivar) to captivate; **no te dejes ~ por sus palabras** don't be seduced by fine words 3 ‹‹*idea/proposición*›› (atraer) to attract, tempt; **no me seduce nada la idea** the idea doesn't appeal to me at all

seductor¹ -tora *adj* 1 (en sentido sexual) ‹*persona*› seductive; ‹*manera/gesto*› seductive, alluring 2 (que cautiva, fascina) enchanting, charming 3 ‹*idea/proposición*› attractive, tempting

seductor² -tora (*m*) seducer; (*f*) seducer, seductress

sefardí¹, **sefardita** *adj* Sephardic

sefardí², **sefardita** *mf* Sephardi

seg. *m* (= **segundo**/**segundos**) sec.

segador -dora *m,f* 1 (persona) reaper, harvester 2 **segadora** *f* (máquina) harvester

segar [A7] *vt* 1 ‹*mies*› to reap (liter), to cut 2 (liter *o* period) ‹*cabeza/miembro*› to sever, cut off 3 (liter *o* period) ‹*esperanzas*› to shatter, dash; **una vida segada en la plenitud** a life cut short in its prime

seglar¹ *adj* lay (*before n*)

seglar² (*m*) layman; (*f*) laywoman

segmentación *f* segmentation

segmentarse [A1] *v pron* to divide into segments

segmento *m* (Mat) segment; (Zool) segment; (Com) sector

(Compuesto) **segmento de edad** age group

segregación *f*

A (de personas, grupos) segregation

(Compuesto) **segregación racial** racial segregation

B (secreción) secretion

segregacionismo *m* policy of segregation, segregationist policy

segregacionista *adj* ‹*grupo*› segregationist; **una política ~** a policy of segregation, a segregationist policy

segregar [A3] *vt*

A ‹*personas/grupos*› to segregate

B (secretar) to secrete

seguida: **en ~** (*loc adv*) immediately; **vinieron en ~** they came at once *o* right away; **en ~ voy/vuelvo** I'll be right there/straight back

seguidamente *adv*: **~ fue interrogado** (frml) he was interrogated immediately afterward(s)

seguido¹ -da *adj* consecutive; **ha faltado a clase tres días ~s** she's missed school three days running *o* three days in a row; **lleva dos semanas seguidas con fiebre** she's had a fever for two weeks now; **van a dar las dos obras seguidas** the two plays will be performed consecutively; **pasaron tres autobuses ~s** three buses went by one after the other; **~ DE algo/algn** followed BY sth/sb

seguido² *adv*

A (recto, sin desviarse) straight on; **vaya todo ~** go straight on *o* straight ahead

B (AmL) (a menudo) often; **viene ~ a visitarnos** he often comes to visit us

seguidor -dora *m,f* (de teoría, filósofo) follower; (Dep) supporter, fan; **su música tiene muchos ~es** her music has a large following; **los ~es del método escolástico** those who follow the scholastic method

seguimiento *m* (de animal, satélite) tracking; (de proceso) monitoring

seguir [I30] *vt*

A ‹*persona/vehículo/presa*› to follow; **la hizo ~ por un detective** he had her followed by a detective; **camina muy rápido, no la puedo ~** she walks very fast, I can't keep up with her; **creo que nos están siguiendo** I think we're being followed; **seguidos cada vez más de cerca por los japoneses** with the Japanese catching up on them all the time; **la mala suerte la seguía a todas partes** she was dogged by bad luck wherever she went; ***el que la sigue la consigue*** (fam) if at first you don't succeed, try, try again

B ‹*camino/ruta*›: **siga esta carretera hasta llegar al puente** go along *o* follow this road as far as the bridge; **la saludé y seguí mi camino** I said hello to her and went on (my way); **si se sigue este camino se pasa por Capileira** if you take this route you go through Capileira; **seguimos las huellas del animal hasta el río** we tracked the animal to the river; **la enfermedad sigue su curso normal** the illness is running its normal course

C (en el tiempo) to follow; **~ A algo/algn** to follow sth/sb; **el hermano que me sigue** the brother (who comes) after me

D 1 ‹*instrucciones/consejo/flecha*› to follow; **~ el dictamen de la conciencia** to be guided by one's conscience 2 (basarse en) ‹*autor/teoría/método/tradición*› to follow; **sus esculturas siguen el modelo clásico** her sculptures are in the classical style; **sigue a Kant** she's a follower of Kant's philosophy; **sigue los pasos de su predecesor** he follows in the footsteps of his predecessors

E 1 ‹*trámite/procedimiento*› to follow; **va a tener que ~ un tratamiento especial** you will have to undergo special treatment 2 (Educ) ‹*curso*› to take; **estoy siguiendo un curso de fotografía** I'm doing *o* taking a photography course

F 1 ‹*explicaciones/profesor*› to follow; **dicta demasiado rápido, no la puedo ~** she dictates too quickly, I can't keep up; **¿me siguen?** are you with me? 2 (permanecer atento a): **no sigo ese programa** I don't watch that program, I'm not following that program; **seguimos muy de cerca su desarrollo** we are following its development very closely

■ **seguir** *vi*

A 1 (por un camino) to go on; **siga derecho** *or* **todo recto hasta el final de la calle** keep *o* go straight on to the end of the street; **sigue por esta calle hasta el semáforo** go on down this street as far as the traffic lights; **desde allí hay que ~ en mula** from there you have to go on by mule; **~ de largo** (AmL) to go straight past 2 **seguir adelante** to carry on; **sigamos adelante** let's carry on; **resolvieron ~ adelante con los planes** they decided to go ahead with their plans 3 (Col, Ven) (entrar): **siga por favor** come in, please

B (en lugar, estado): **¿tus padres siguen en Ginebra?** are your parents still in Geneva?; **espero que sigan todos bien** I hope you're all keeping well; **sigo sin entender** I still don't understand; **sigue soltera/tan bonita como siempre** she's still single/as pretty as ever; **si las cosas siguen así ...** if things carry on like this ...; **si sigue así de trabajador, llegará lejos** if he carries on working as hard as this, he'll go a long way

C 1 ‹‹*tareas/buen tiempo/lluvia*›› to continue; ‹‹*rumores*›› to persist 2 **~ + GER**: **sigo pensando que deberíamos haber ido** I still think we ought to have gone; **sigue leyendo tú** you read now; **~é haciéndolo a mi manera** I'll go on *o* carry on doing it my way, I shall continue to do it my way (frml)

D 1 (venir después, estar contiguo): **lee lo que sigue** read what comes next; **el capítulo que sigue** the next chapter; **sigue una hora de jazz** there follows an hour of jazz; **un período de calma ha seguido a estos enfrentamientos** these clashes have been followed by a period of calm 2 ‹‹*historia/poema*›› to continue; **¿cómo sigue la canción?** how does the song go on?; Ⓢ **sigue en la página 8** continued on page 8; **la lista definitiva ha quedado como sigue** the final list is as follows

■ **seguirse** *v pron* (*en 3ª pers*) **~se DE algo** to follow FROM sth; **de esto se sigue que ...** it follows from this that ...

según¹ *prep*

A (de acuerdo con) according to; **~ la ley** according to the law; **~ parece ...** it would appear *o* seem (that) ...; **así que está en la India — ~ parece** so he's in India — so it seems *o* apparently; **~ las órdenes que me dieron** in accordance with the orders I was given; **~ me dijo, piensa quedarse** from what he told me, he intends to stay

B (dependiendo de) **~ + SUBJ**: **~ te parezca** as you think best; **obtendrás distintos resultados ~ cómo lo hagas** you will get different results depending (on) how you do it; **¿me llevas a casa? — ~ dónde vivas** will you take me home? — (it) depends where you live

según² *adv* it depends; **este método puede resultar o no, ~** this method may or may not work, it depends

según³ *conj* 1 (a medida que) as; **~ van entrando** as they come in 2 (en cuanto): **~ llegamos a la ventanilla,**

S

pusieron el cartel de cerrado just as we reached the window they put up the closed sign; **~ llegues sube a verme** come up and see me as soon as you arrive

segunda *f*
A 1 (Auto) (marcha) second (gear); **mete (la) ~** put it in second (gear) 2 (Transp) (clase) second class; **viajar en ~** to travel second class
B **segundas** *fpl*: **todo lo dice con ~s** there's a hidden meaning to everything he says
C (Ven) (en béisbol) bottom; **la ~ del noveno** the bottom of the ninth (inning)

segundero *m* second hand

segundo[1] **-da** *adj/pron* 1 (ordinal) second; **~ plano**: **en un ~ plano está ...** in the background is ...; **quedar relegado a un ~ plano** to be pushed into the background; *para ejemplos ver tb* **quinto** 2 ‹*categoría/clase*› second

segundo[2] **-da** *m,f* deputy, second-in-command
(Compuesto) **segundo -da de a bordo** *m,f* (Náut) first mate, first officer; (en empresa) (fam) second-in-command

segundo[3] *m* 1 (de tiempo) second; **no tardo ni un ~** I won't be a second; **un ~, ahora te atiendo** just a second, I'll be right with you 2 (medida de ángulo) second

segundón -dona *m,f* (fam) second-rater (colloq)

seguramente *adv* (*indep*): **¿llegarán hoy? — seguramente** will they arrive today? — probably; **compramos veinte aunque, ~, gastaremos menos** we bought twenty although I'm sure they won't all be used

seguridad *f*
A (ausencia de peligro) safety; (protección contra robos, atentados) security; **cierre de ~** safety catch; **por razones de ~** for safety reasons; **medidas de ~** (contra accidentes, incendios) safety measures; (contra robos, atentados) security measures; **como medida de ~** as a safety precaution; **una prisión de alta ~** a high security prison
(Compuestos)
- **seguridad ciudadana** public safety
- **seguridad del estado**: **la ~ del ~** state *o* national security
- **seguridad vial** road safety

B (estabilidad, garantía) security
(Compuesto) **seguridad social** social security
C 1 (certeza): **no te lo puedo decir con ~** I can't tell you for certain *o* for sure 2 (confianza, aplomo) confidence, self-confidence; **tener ~ en uno mismo** to be sure of oneself, to be self-confident

seguro[1] **-ra** *adj*
A 1 [SER] (exento de riesgo) safe; **ese aeropuerto no es muy ~** it's not a very safe airport; **ese ascensor no es ~** that elevator is not safe; **ponlo en un lugar ~** put it in a safe place 2 (estable) secure; **un trabajo ~** a secure job; **una inversión segura** a safe *o* secure investment; **esa escalera no está segura** that ladder isn't safe *o* steady; ***sobre* ~**: **un político que sabe jugar sobre ~** a politician who knows how to play safe; **sabía que iba sobre ~** he knew he was onto a sure thing (colloq) 3 [SER] (fiable): **un método anticonceptivo poco ~** not a very reliable *o* safe method of birth control; **el cierre de la pulsera es muy ~** the fastener on the bracelet is very secure 4 [ESTAR] (a salvo) safe; **el dinero estará ~ aquí** the money will be safe here; **a su lado se siente ~** he feels safe when he's beside her
B 1 [ESTAR] (convencido) sure; **no estoy ~** I'm not sure; **~ DE algo** sure *o* certain OF sth; **estoy absolutamente ~ de haberlo dejado aquí** I'm absolutely sure *o* certain (that) I left it here; **no estaba ~ de haber elegido bien** he wasn't sure that he'd made the right choice 2 [SER] (que no admite duda): **su triunfo es ~** his victory is assured; **iban a una muerte segura** they were heading for certain death; **no me han dado fecha segura** they haven't given me a definite day; **todavía no es ~** it's not definite yet; **se da por ~** there seems to be little doubt about it; **no te preocupes, ~ que no es nada** don't worry, I'm sure it's nothing; **~ que se le olvida** he's sure *o* bound to forget; ***a buen* ~** (ciertamente) for certain; (a salvo) safe; **guárdalo a buen ~** keep it safe, put it away for safe keeping 3 (con confianza en sí mismo) self-assured, self-confident; **es una persona muy segura de sí misma** he's a very self-confident person

seguro[2] *m*
A 1 (mecanismo — de armas) safety catch; (— de una pulsera, un collar) clasp, fastener; **poner el ~** to do up the clasp *o* fastener; **echó el ~ antes de acostarse/arrancar** he locked the door before going to bed/starting the car 2 (Méx) (imperdible) safety pin
B 1 (contrato) insurance; **se sacó** *or* **se hizo un ~** she took out insurance *o* an insurance policy 2 (Seguridad Social): **el ~** *or* **el S~** the state health care system, ≈ Medicaid (*in US*), ≈ the National Health Service (*in UK*); **se operó por el ~** he had his operation through Medicaid/on the National Health; **me lo recetó el ~** I got the prescription on Medicaid (AmE), I got it on prescription (BrE)
(Compuestos)
- **seguro contra** *or* **a todo riesgo** comprehensive insurance, all-risks insurance
- **seguro contra** *or* **de incendios** fire insurance
- **seguro contra terceros** liability insurance (AmE), third-party insurance (BrE)
- **seguro de desempleo** unemployment benefit
- **seguro de enfermedad** medical insurance
- **seguro de vida** life assurance, life insurance

seguro[3] *adv*: **dijo que llegaría mañana ~** she said she'd definitely be arriving tomorrow; **no lo sabe ~** she doesn't know for sure *o* certain; **~ que sospecha lo nuestro** I'm sure he suspects we're up to something; **¿~ que basta? — sí, ~** (are you) sure that's enough? — yes, positive; **esta vez dice la verdad — ¡sí, ~!** (iró) this time he's/she's telling the truth — oh yeah, sure (he/she is)! (colloq & iro)

seibó *m* (Ven) sideboard

seis[1] *adj inv/pron* six; *para ejemplos ver* **cinco**

seis[2] *m* (number) six; *para ejemplos ver* **cinco**

seiscientos -tas *adj/pron* six hundred

seísmo *m* (Esp) (temblor) tremor; (terremoto) earthquake

SELA /'sela/ *m* = **Sistema Económico Latinoamericano**

selección *f* selection; **la ~ de los candidatos fue muy difícil** selecting *o* choosing the candidates was very difficult; **hizo una ~ de los mejores** she selected the best ones; **la ~ nacional** (Dep) the national team; **hoy juega la ~** Spain (*o* Colombia *etc*) are playing today
(Compuesto) **selección natural** natural selection

seleccionador -dora *m,f* (Dep) 1 (entrenador) coach (AmE), manager (BrE) 2 (miembro de una junta) selector

seleccionar [A1] *vt* to select, choose

selectividad *f* (Educ) (en Esp) *university entrance examination*

selectivo -va *adj* selective

selecto -ta *adj* ‹*fruta/vino*› select, choice; ‹*ambiente/club*› select, exclusive; **lo más ~ de la sociedad** the cream *o* the elite of society

selector *m* selector

self-service /sel(f)'serβis/ *m* self-service restaurant

sellado *m* 1 (de pasaporte) stamping 2 (del oro) hallmarking

sellar [A1] *vt*
A 1 ‹*pasaporte*› to stamp 2 ‹*plata/oro*› to hallmark
B (cerrar) to seal

sello *m*
A (de correos) (postage) stamp; (útil de oficina) rubber stamp; (marca) stamp
(Compuesto) **sello fiscal** fiscal *o* revenue stamp
B 1 (en el oro) hallmark 2 (AmL) (de una moneda) reverse; **¿cara o ~?** (Andes, Ven) heads or tails? 3 (anillo) signet ring, seal ring 4 (elemento distintivo) hallmark 5 (Mús) *tb* **~ discográfico** record label
C (precinto) seal

selva *f* (bosque) forest; (de vegetación tropical) jungle; **~ virgen** virgin forest; **la ~ amazónica** the Amazonian jungle *o* rainforest
(Compuestos)
- **Selva Negra** Black Forest
- **selva tropical** tropical rainforest, selva

selvático -ca *adj* (del bosque) forest (*before n*); **la región selvática del Amazonas** the Amazonian jungle *o* rainforest

S

semáforo *m* 1 (Auto) traffic lights (*pl*); **se pasó un ~ en rojo** she went through *o* (AmE) ran a red light; **después encuentras otro ~** after that you come to another set of (traffic) lights 2 (Ferr) stop signal 3 (Náut) semaphore

semana *f*
A (periodo) week; **la ~ próxima** *or* **que viene** *or* (Méx) **que entra** next week; **una vez a la ~** *or* **por ~** once a week; **no salgo entre ~** I don't go out during the week; **S semana del juguete en la Galería** toy week at the Galería

(Compuestos)
- **semana inglesa** five-day week
- **semana laboral** workweek (AmE), working week (BrE)
- **Semana Santa** Holy Week; **fuimos a Escocia en ~ ~** we went to Scotland at Easter

B (Col) (dinero) allowance, pocket money

Semana Santa

The most famous celebrations of Holy Week in the Spanish-speaking world are held in Seville. Lay brotherhoods, *cofradías*, process through the city in huge parades between Palm Sunday and Easter Sunday. *Costaleros* bear the *pasos*, huge floats carrying religious figures made of painted wood. Others, *nazarenos* (Nazarenes) and *penitentes* (penitents) walk alongside the *pasos*, in their distinctive costumes. During the processions they sing *saetas*, flamenco verses mourning Christ's passion. The Seville celebrations date back to the sixteenth century

semanal *adj* weekly

semanalmente *adv* every week, once a week

semanario *m* weekly magazine (*o* newspaper *etc*), weekly

semántica *f* semantics

semántico -ca *adj* semantic

semblante *m* (liter) countenance (liter)

semblantear [A1] *vt* (Méx fam): **~ a algn** to look at sb straight in the eye, to come face to face with sb

semblanza *f* biographical sketch

sembradío *m* (Andes) sown field

sembrado¹ *m* sown field

sembrado² -da *m,f* (Méx) (Dep) seed

sembrador -dora *m,f* 1 (persona) sower 2 **sembradora** *f* (máquina) seeder, sower

sembrar [A5] *vt* 1 ‹*terreno/campo*› to sow; ‹*trigo/hortalizas*› to sow, plant; **~ algo DE algo** to plant sth WITH sth; ***el que siembra recoge*** as you sow, so shall you reap 2 (liter) ‹*pánico/odio*› to sow (liter) 3 (llenar) **~ algo DE algo**: ‹*de flores/papeles*› strewn *o* covered WITH sth; **los huelguistas ~on de tachuelas la calle** the strikers scattered tacks across the road

sembrío *m* (Per) sown field

semejante¹ *adj* 1 (similar) similar; **~ A algo** similar TO sth; **sus costumbres son ~s a las nuestras** their customs are similar to ours 2 (Mat) similar 3 (*delante del n*) (para énfasis): **nunca había oído ~ estupidez** I'd never heard such nonsense *o* anything so stupid; **no pienso trabajar con ~ imbécil** I'm not going to work with an idiot like that

semejante² *m*: **tus/nuestros ~s** your/our fellow men

semejanza *f* similarity; **a ~ de sus antepasados** like his ancestors

semejar [A1] *vi* to resemble, look like

semen *m* semen

semental¹ *adj* stud (*before n*)

semental² *m* (caballo) stud horse; (toro) stud bull

sementera *f* (acción) sowing; (temporada) sowing season; (campo sembrado) sown field

semestral *adj* 1 (en frecuencia) ‹*exámenes/reuniones*› half-yearly, six-monthly; **una publicación ~** a publication which comes out every six months 2 (en duración) ‹*curso*› six-month (*before n*)

semestre *m* 1 (seis meses): **el balance del primer ~** the balance for the first half of the year; **cada curso dura un ~** each course lasts six months 2 (Educ) (en algunos países latinoamericanos) *tb* **~ lectivo** semester (AmE), term (BrE)

semiautomático -ca *adj* semiautomatic

semicircular *adj* semicircular

semicírculo *m* semicircle

(Compuesto) **semicírculo graduado** (RPl) protractor

semicircunferencia *f* semicircumference

semiconductor *m* semiconductor

semiconsonante *f* semiconsonant

semicorchea *f* sixteenth note (AmE), semiquaver (BrE)

semidescremado -da *adj* semi-skimmed

semidesnatado -da *adj* (Esp) semi-skimmed, half-cream (*before n*)

semifinal *f* semifinal

semifinalista *mf* semifinalist

semilla *f* 1 (Agr, Bot) seed; **uvas sin ~s** seedless grapes 2 (causa, origen) seed; **la ~ de la libertad/discordia** the seeds of liberty/discord

semillero *m* 1 (Agr, Bot) seedbed 2 (de discordias) source; (de delincuencia) hotbed, breeding ground

seminal *adj* seminal

seminario *m* 1 (Relig) seminary 2 (Educ) seminar

seminarista *m* seminarian

semiología *f* semiology

semiológico -ca *adj* semiotic, semiological

semiólogo -ga *m,f* semiologist

semiótica *f* semiotics

semiótico -ca *adj* semiotic

semiseco -ca *adj* demi-sec

semita¹ *adj* Semitic

semita² *mf* Semite

semítico -ca *adj* Semitic

semivocal *f* semivowel

semivolea *f* half volley

sémola *f* semolina

(Compuesto) **sémola de arroz** ground rice

sempiterno -na *adj* perennial

Sena *m*: **el ~** the Seine, the Seine River (AmE), the River Seine (BrE)

senado *m* (cámara alta) senate; (edificio) senate, senate building *o* (AmE) house

senador -dora *m,f* senator

S.en C. *f* = **Sociedad en Comandita**

sencillamente *adv* simply

sencillez *f* simplicity; **habla con ~** she uses plain language; **viste con ~** she dresses simply *o* modestly; **se comporta con gran ~** he behaves with great modesty

sencillo¹ -lla *adj*
A 1 ‹*ejercicio/problema*› simple, straightforward; **no fue ~ hacerlos entrar** it wasn't easy getting them in 2 ‹*persona*› modest, unassuming; ‹*vestido/estilo*› simple, plain; ‹*casa/comida*› simple, modest; **son gentes sencillas y trabajadoras** they are simple, hardworking people
B (Esp, Méx) ‹*billete*› one-way (AmE), single (BrE)

sencillo² *m*
A (disco) single
B (AmL) (dinero suelto) change
C (Esp, Méx) (Transp) one-way ticket (AmE), single (ticket) (BrE)

senda *f* 1 (camino) path; **siguió la ~ del bien** he followed the path of good 2 (Ur) (de carretera) lane

senderismo *m*
A (Dep) hiking, trekking
B (en Perú) *ideology of Sendero Luminoso*

senderista *mf*
A (Dep) hiker
B (en Per): *a member or follower of Sendero Luminoso*

sendero *m* path, track; **el ~ de la libertad** the path *o* way to freedom

sendos -das *adj pl* 1 (cada uno): **llevaban sendas pistolas** each of them was carrying *o* they were each carrying a gun; **con sendas fiestas en Madrid y Barcelona** with parties in both Madrid and Barcelona 2 (crit) (ambos) both

Senegal *m* Senegal

senegalés -lesa *adj/m,f* Senegalese

S

senil *adj* (liter) senile

senilidad *f* senility

sénior, senior /'senjor/ *adj inv* senior

seno *m*

A 1 (mama) breast; (pecho) bosom; **los ~s** the breasts; **le extirparon el ~ izquierdo** she had her left breast removed; **lo apretó contra su ~** she clutched him to her breast *o* bosom; **dar el ~** (Ven) to breastfeed; **que Dios lo acoja en su ~** may he be taken into the bosom of the Lord 2 (matriz) womb 3 (de organización, empresa) heart; **volvió al ~ de su familia** she returned to the bosom of her family

B (Mat) sine

sensación *f*

A (percepción, impresión) feeling; **una ~ de tristeza/impotencia** a feeling of sadness/impotence; **una vaga ~ de placer** a vague sensation of pleasure; **una ~ de pérdida/espacio** a sense of loss/space; **tengo** *or* **me da la ~ de que no vamos a ganar** I have a feeling we're not going to win

B 1 (furor) sensation; **la noticia causó ~** the news caused a sensation 2 (éxito) sensation; **ser una ~** to be a sensation

sensacional *adj* sensational; **S ¡sensacionales rebajas!** sensational *o* fantastic reductions!

sensacionalismo *m* sensationalism

sensacionalista *adj* ‹*artículo/foto*› sensationalistic; **la prensa ~** the sensationalist press, the tabloid press

sensatez *f* sense; **obró con ~** she acted sensibly; **demostraste ~** you were very sensible; **pusieron en duda la ~ del proyecto** they cast doubt on the wisdom of the project

sensato -ta *adj* sensible

sensibilidad *f*

A 1 (emotividad) sensitivity; **puede herir la ~ del espectador** it may offend viewers' sensibilities 2 (inclinación) sensitivity; **la ~ poética** a sensitivity to *o* feeling for poetry

B 1 (en brazo, pierna) feeling; **perdió la ~ en los dedos** she lost all feeling in her fingers 2 (de instrumento, aparato) sensitivity

sensibilización *f* (de la opinión pública): **una campaña de ~ ciudadana** a campaign to raise public awarenes

sensibilizado -da *adj*: **países ~s frente a la contaminación** countries that are aware of the problems of pollution; **es un hombre ~ ante el tema de los indígenas** he is a man who is aware of *o* sensitive to the problem of the Indian peoples

sensibilizar [A4] *vt*

A (concienciar) to raise … awareness; **una campaña para ~ a los ciudadanos** a campaign to raise public awareness; **~ al educador frente a las necesidades de los alumnos** to make the educator sensitive to the needs of students

B (Fot, Med) to sensitize

sensible *adj*

A (susceptible, impresionable) sensitive

B 1 ‹*piel/ojos*› (físicamente) sensitive; **~ A algo** sensitive TO sth 2 ‹*instrumento/aparato*› sensitive; (Fot) sensitive

C (*gen delante del n*) (frml) (ostensible) ‹*cambio/diferencia*› appreciable; ‹*mejoría*› noticiable; ‹*aumento/pérdida*› considerable

sensiblemente *adv* ‹*cambiar*› appreciably; ‹*mejorar/aumentar*› considerably, appreciably

sensiblería *f* (pey) sentimentality, mawkishness

sensiblero -ra *adj* (pey) ‹*persona*› overly sentimental, mawkish; ‹*novela/película*› mawkish, schmaltzy (colloq)

sensitivo -va *adj* ‹*órgano*› sensory, sense (*before n*); ‹*facultad*› sensory

sensor *m* sensor; **~es de humo** smoke detectors

sensorial *adj* sensory, sensorial

sensual *adj* ‹*boca/cuerpo*› sensual, sensuous; ‹*placeres/gesto*› sensual; ‹*descripción*› sensuous

sensualidad *f* (de boca, gesto) sensuality; (de descripción) sensuousness; **la ~ con la que bailaba** the sensual *o* sensuous way in which she danced

sentada *f* 1 (protesta) sit-in, sit-down protest 2 **de** *or* **en una sentada** ‹*leer/escribir*› in one go, at one sitting

sentaderas *fpl* (RPl fam) backside (colloq), butt (AmE colloq), bum (BrE colloq)

sentado -da *adj* sitting, seated (frml); **estaban ~s a la mesa** they were (sitting) at the table; **pueden permanecer ~s** (frml) you may remain seated (frml); **llevamos más de una hora aquí ~s** we've been sitting here for over an hour; ***dar algo por ~*** to assume sth; ***dejar algo ~***: **quiero dejar bien ~ que ...** I would like to make it quite clear that ...; ***esperar(se) ~*** (fam & iró): **si crees que voy a prestártelo, puedes esperar ~** if you think I'm going to lend it to you you've got another think coming (colloq)

sentador -dora *adj* (AmL) flattering, fetching

sentar [A5] *vi* (+ *me/te/le etc*) 1 «*ropa/color*» (+ *compl*): **ese vestido le sienta de maravilla** that dress really suits her 2 «*comida/bebida/clima*» (+ *compl*): **el café/este clima no le sienta bien** coffee/this climate doesn't agree with her; **esta sopita te ~á bien** this soup will make you feel better; **me sentó bien el descanso** the rest did me a lot of good 3 «*actitud/comentario*» (+ *compl*): **me sentó mal que no me invitaran** I was rather put out that they didn't ask me (colloq)

■ **sentar** *vt*

A ‹*niño/muñeca*› to sit; ‹*invitado*› to seat, sit

B (establecer) to establish; **~ jurisprudencia** to set *o* establish a legal precedent; **la firma del acuerdo sentó las bases para una mayor colaboración** the signing of the agreement laid the foundations for greater cooperation

■ **sentarse** *v pron* to sit; **~se a la mesa** to sit at (the) table, sit down to eat; **no había donde ~se** there was nowhere to sit; **siéntese, por favor** please sit down *o* take a seat, do sit down *o* take a seat; **siéntate bien** *or* **derechita** sit up (straight); **el bebé ya se sienta solo** the baby is sitting up on his own now

sentencia *f*

A (Der) judgement, ruling; **dictar** *or* **pronunciar ~** to pass *o* pronounce sentence; **visto para ~** ready for sentencing

B (máxima) motto, maxim

C (Inf) sentence

sentenciar [A1] *vt* to sentence; **lo ~on a dos años de prisión** (Der) he was sentenced to two years in prison, he was given a two-years sentence; **la ~on a muerte** (Der) she was sentenced to death; **la mafia lo tiene sentenciado a muerte** the mafia have got a contract out on him

■ **sentenciar** *vi*: **—más vale tarde que nunca —sentenció** better late than never, he declared sententiously

sentencioso -sa *adj* sententious

sentido[1] -da *adj*

A ‹*palabras/carta*› heartfelt; ‹*anhelo/dolor*› deep; **mi más ~ pésame** my deepest sympathy

B ‹*persona*› 1 [ESTAR] (AmL) (dolorido) hurt, offended 2 [SER] (Esp) (sensible) sensitive, touchy

sentido[2] *m*

A 1 (Fisiol) sense; ***poner los cinco ~s en algo*** to give sth one's full attention; (ante peligro) to keep one's wits about one 2 (noción, idea) **~ DE algo** sense OF sth; **su ~ del deber** her sense of duty; **tiene un gran ~ del ritmo** he has a great sense of rhythm

(Compuestos)

- **sentido común** common sense
- **sentido de (la) orientación** sense of direction
- **sentido del humor** sense of humor•
- **sentido del ridículo** sense of the ridiculous

B (conocimiento) consciousness; **el golpe lo dejó sin ~** he was knocked unconscious by the blow; **perder el ~** to lose consciousness; **recobrar el ~** to regain consciousness, to come to, to come round

C (significado): **en el buen ~ de la palabra** in the nicest sense of the word; **en el ~ más amplio del vocablo** in the broadest sense of the term; **en ~ literal/figurado** in a literal/figurative sense; **lo dijo con doble ~** he was intentionally ambiguous; **el ~ de la vida** the meaning of life; **en cierto ~ ...** in a sense ...; **no le encuentro ~ a lo que haces** I can't see any sense *o* point in what you're doing; **cobrar ~** to acquire significance; **sus palabras cobran ahora un nuevo ~** his words take on a new meaning now; **esa política ya no tiene ~** that policy doesn't make sense anymore *o* is meaningless now; **palabras sin ~** meaningless words; **no tiene ~ preocuparse por eso** it's pointless worrying about that

D (dirección) direction; **se mueve en el ~ de las agujas del**

S

reloj it moves clockwise; **gírese en ~ contrario al de las agujas del reloj** turn (round) in a counterclockwise (AmE) *o* (BrE) an anticlockwise direction; **venían en ~ contrario** *or* **opuesto al nuestro** they were coming in the opposite direction to us; **calle de ~ único** *or* (Méx) **de un solo ~** one-way street

sentimental *adj* 1 (relativo a los sentimientos) sentimental 2 ‹*persona/canción/novela*› sentimental; **ponerse ~** to get sentimental 3 ‹*aventura/vida*› love (*before n*); **tener problemas ~es** to have problems with one's love life

sentimentalismo *m* sentimentalism; **déjate de ~s** stop being so sentimental

sentimiento *m*
A 1 (emoción) feeling; **ser de buenos ~s** to be a caring person 2 (pasión): **no se deja llevar por los ~s** she doesn't let herself get carried away by her emotions; **canta con mucho ~** he sings with a lot of feeling 3 (pesar): **te/les acompaño en el ~** my commiserations
B **sentimientos** *mpl* 1 (amor): **no juegues con sus ~s** don't play with his emotions *o* feelings 2 (sensibilidad) feelings (*pl*); **herir los ~s de algn** to hurt sb's feelings

sentir[1] [I11] *vt*
A 1 ‹*dolor/pinchazo*› to feel; **~ hambre/frío/sed** to feel hungry/cold/thirsty; **sentí un dolor en la pierna** I felt a pain in my leg; **empecé a ~ los efectos de la droga** I started to feel the effects of the drug 2 ‹*emoción*› to feel; **sentimos una gran alegría** we were overjoyed; **lo hizo para que él sintiera celos** she did it to make him feel jealous; **se ve que siente lo que dice** you can tell he means what he says 3 (presentir): **sentí que nos iba a pasar algo** I had a feeling something was going to happen to us 4 (experimentar consecuencias): **los efectos de la crisis se dejarán ~ durante décadas** the effects of the crisis will be felt for decades; **el descontento se hizo ~ pronto** their discontent soon made itself felt
B 1 (oír) ‹*ruido/disparo*› to hear; **anoche te sentí llegar** I heard you come in last night 2 (esp AmL) (percibir): **siento olor a gas** I can smell gas; **le siento gusto a vainilla/ajo** I can taste vanilla/garlic
C (lamentar): **sentí mucho la muerte de tu padre** I was very sorry to hear of your father's death; **ha sentido mucho la pérdida de su madre** she has been very affected by her mother's death; **lo siento mucho** I'm really sorry; **lo siento en el alma** I'm terribly sorry, I'm so sorry; **sentí mucho no poder ayudarla** I was very sorry not to be able to help her; **el director siente no poder recibirlo** the director regrets that he is unable to see you (frml)
■ **sentirse** *v pron*
A (+ *compl*) to feel; **¿te sientes bien?** are you feeling *o* do you feel all right?; **me siento mal** I don't feel well, I'm not feeling well; **me siento enfermo/peor** I feel ill/worse; **se sintió desfallecer** she felt as if she were about to faint; **no me siento con ánimos** I don't feel up to it; **no tiene por qué ~se ofendida** she has no reason to feel hurt; **me siento vigilada** I feel as if I am being watched; **me siento identificada con él** I can identify with him
B (Chi, Méx) (ofenderse) to be offended *o* hurt; **~se CON algn** to be offended *o* upset WITH sb

sentir[2] *m* (sentimiento) feelings (*pl*), emotions (*pl*); (opinión, postura) feeling, view

seña *f*
A (gesto) sign; **hacer una ~** to make a sign, to signal; **por ~s le pedí más coñac** I gestured to him to give me more cognac; **les hice ~s de que se callaran** I gestured *o* motioned to them to keep quiet; **se comunican por ~s** they communicate by means of sign language *o* signs
B **señas** *fpl* (detalles): ***por*** *or* ***para más*** **~s** to be more specific
(Compuesto) **señas personales** physical description
C **señas** *fpl* (dirección) address
D **señas** *fpl* (indicios): **dar ~s DE algo** to show signs OF sth
E (RPl) ▸**señal E**

señal *f*
A 1 (aviso, letrero) sign; **~es de tráfico** *or* **circulación** traffic signs; **~ de peligro/stop/estacionamiento prohibido** danger/stop/no parking sign; **~es de carretera** road signs 2 (signo) signal; **dio la ~ de salida** he gave the starting signal; **nos hacía ~es para que nos acercáramos** she was signaling *o* gesturing for us to come nearer; **~es de humo** smoke signals; **~ de auxilio** *or* **socorro** distress signal 3 (Ferr) signal
(Compuesto) **Señal de la Cruz** sign of the cross
B (marca, huella): **pon una ~ en la página por dónde vas** mark the page where you've got up to; **no presentaba ~es de violencia** it showed no signs of violence
C (Rad, TV) signal; (Telec): **la ~ para marcar** the dial (AmE) *o* (BrE) dialling tone; **la ~ de ocupado** *or* (Esp) **comunicando** the busy signal (AmE), the engaged tone (BrE)
(Compuesto) **señal horaria** time signal
D (indicio) sign; **eso es mala ~** that's a bad sign; **no daba ~es de vida** he showed no signs of life; **continuó sin dar ~es de cansancio** she carried on without showing any sign of tiring; **en ~ de protesta** as a sign *o* gesture of protest; **en ~ de amor** as a token of love
E (Esp) (Com) (depósito) deposit, down payment; **dar** *or* **dejar una ~** to leave a deposit *o* down payment

señalado -da *adj*: **en una fecha tan señalada como ésta** on such a special day as this; **una victoria señalada** a signal victory; *ver tb* **señalar**

señalador *m*: *tb* **~ de libros** bookmark(er)

señalar [A1] *vt*
A (indicar): **la flecha señalaba la salida** the arrow pointed to the exit; **me estaba señalando con el dedo** he was pointing at me (with his finger); **me señaló la ruta en un mapa** he showed me the route *o* pointed out the route (to me) on a map; **me señaló con el dedo qué pasteles quería** he pointed out (to me) which cakes he wanted; **las manecillas del reloj señalaban las doce** the hands of the clock showed twelve
B (marcar con lápiz, rotulador) to mark
C (afirmar) to point out; **señaló que ...** she pointed out that ...
D (fijar) ‹*fecha*› to fix, set; **a la hora señalada** at the appointed *o* arranged time; **en el lugar señalado** in the appointed *o* agreed place
E (anunciar) to mark
■ **señalar** *vi* to point; **¡no señales!** don't point!
■ **señalarse** *v pron* to distinguish oneself

señalización *f* 1 (en carretera, calle) signposting; (en edificio, centro comercial) signs (*pl*) 2 (Ferr) signaling*

señalizar [A4] *vt* 1 ‹*carretera/calle/ciudad*› to signpost; ‹*edificio/centro comercial*› to put up directions on/in 2 (Ferr) ‹*tramo/vía*› to install signals on
■ **señalizar** *vi* to signal, indicate (BrE)

señero -ra *adj* (liter) unique

señor[1] **-ñora** *adj* (*delante del n*) (fam) (uso enfático): **es un ~ puesto** it's a really good job; **aquello era un ~ cuadro** it was a huge picture

señor[2] **-ñora** *m,f*
A 1 (persona adulta) (*m*) man, gentleman; (*f*) lady; **te busca un ~** there's a man *o* gentleman looking for you; **la ~a del último piso** the lady who lives on the top floor; **peluquería de ~as** ladies' hairdresser's; **la ~a de la limpieza** the cleaning lady; ❾ **señoras** ladies, women 2 (persona distinguida) (*m*) gentleman; (*f*) lady; **es todo un ~** he's a real gentleman; **tiene ínfulas de gran ~a** she gives herself airs and graces
(Compuesto) **señora de compañía** *f* companion
B (dueño, amo): **el ~/la ~a de la casa** the gentleman/the lady of the house (frml); **el ~ de estas tierras** (Hist) the lord of these lands
(Compuesto) **señor feudal** *m* feudal lord
C (Relig) 1 **Señor** *m* Lord; **Dios, nuestro S~** the Lord God; **Nuestro S~ Jesucristo** our Lord Jesus Christ 2 **Señora** *f*: **Nuestra S~a de Montserrat** Our Lady of Montserrat
D **señora** *f* (esposa) wife
E (tratamiento de cortesía) 1 (con apellidos) (*m*) Mr; (*f*) Mrs; **los ~es de Paz** Mr and Mrs Paz 2 (uso popular, con nombres de pila): **la ~a Cristina/el ~ Miguel** ≈ Mrs Fuentes/Mr López 3 (frml) (con otros sustantivos): **el ~ alcalde no podrá asistir** the mayor will not be able to attend; **la ~a directora está ocupada** the director is busy; **S~ Director** (Corresp) Dear Sir, Sir (frml) 4 (frml) (sin mencionar el nombre): **perdón, ~/~a ¿tiene hora?** excuse me, could you tell me the time?; **¿se lleva ésa, ~a?** will you take that one, Madam? (frml); **muy ~ mío/~es míos** (Corresp) Dear Sir/Sirs; **Teresa Chaves — ¿~a o ~ita?** Teresa Chaves —

S

Miss, Mrs or Ms?; **los ~es han salido** Mr and Mrs Paz (*o* López *etc*) are not at home 5 (uso enfático): **¿y lo pagó él?—sí ~** you mean he paid for it—he did indeed; **no ~, no fue así** no that is certainly not what happened; **no ~, no pienso ir** there's no way I'm going

Señor/Señora/Señorita

Titles used before someone's name when speaking to or about them. They are generally followed by the person's surname, or first name and surname. They can also be followed by the person's professional title, without the name: *señor arquitecto, señora doctora, señorita maestra.* They can be used on their own to attract attention. In letters they can be followed by the appropriate forms of **don/doña**: *Sr. Dn Juan Montesinos, Sra Dña. Ana Castellón.*

The full forms are written in lower case when used in the middle of a sentence; the abbreviated forms are always capitalized - for *señor, Sr.*, for *señora, Sra.*, and for *señorita, Srta.Señor* is used for men. *Señores*, can mean "sirs", "gentlemen", and "ladies and gentlemen", and when used of a married couple means "Mr and Mrs": *los señores Montesino. Señora* is used for married women and widows, and women of unknown marital status. *Señorita* is used for single women, young women of unknown marital status, and female teachers

señoría *f*: **su ~** (frml) (dirigiéndose a un juez) ≈ your Honor*; **sus ~s** (refiriéndose a diputados) ≈ the members of this house ≈ the Right Honorable* members

señorial *adj* ‹*casa*› stately; ‹*ciudad*› noble; **su porte ~** his noble bearing

señorío *m*

A 1 (Hist) (territorio) domain, manor, estate 2 (dominio) rule, dominion

B 1 (elegancia, distinción) class 2 (Esp) (gente bien): **el ~ de la capital** all the top people from the capital

señorita *f*

A 1 (mujer joven) young woman; **vino una ~ a preguntar por usted** there was a young lady *o* woman here asking for you; **residencia de ~s** hostel for young women 2 (empleada — joven) young lady; (— mayor) lady 3 (joven distinguida) young lady 4 (maestra) teacher

B (tratamiento de cortesía) 1 (con apellidos) Miss; **~ Chaves, teléfono** Miss Chaves, telephone call for you 2 (con nombres de pila): **~ Teresa ¿puede atender a la señora?** Teresa/Miss Chaves (*o* López *etc*), could you serve this lady please? 3 (maestra) Miss 4 (sin mencionar el nombre) (frml): (a una maestra) Miss; **¿qué deseaba, ~?** may I help you, miss?; **estimada ~** (Corresp) Dear Miss/Ms Chaves (*o* López *etc*)

señorito *m* 1 (ant) (tratamiento dado por subalternos) master (frml & dated); **sí, ~ Rafael** yes, Master Rafael (frml & dated) 2 (pey) rich young man, rich kid (colloq)

señorón -rona *m,f* (fam) bigwig (colloq), big shot (colloq)

señuelo *m* (persona) bait; (para aves) decoy; (en ganadería) ox (*used to lead other animals*)

sep. (= **septiembre**) Sep, Sept

sepa, sepas, etc *see* **saber**

separación *f*

A 1 (división) division; **el río sirve de ~ entre las dos fincas** the river marks the division between the two estates; **mamparas de ~** dividing *o* partition screens; **la ~ de la Iglesia y del Estado** the separation of the Church and the State 2 (espacio) space, gap

B 1 (ausencia): **se reunieron después de dos meses de ~** they met up again after being apart for two months 2 (del matrimonio) separation

(Compuesto) **separación de bienes** division *o* separation of property

C (frml) (de un cargo) dismissal

separado¹ -da *adj*

A ‹*persona*› separated

B 1 ‹*camas*› separate; **tiene los dientes muy ~s** her teeth are very widely spaced 2 **por separado** separately

separado² -da *m,f*: **es hijo de ~s** his parents are separated, he's the child of separated parents

separador *m*

A (de carpeta) divider

B (Col) (Auto) median strip (AmE), central reservation (BrE)

separar [A1] *vt*

A 1 (apartar, alejar) to separate; ‹*boxeadores*› to separate, part; **separa la cama de la pared** move the bed away from the wall; **no se aconseja ~ a la madre de su ternero** it is not advisable to take the calf away from its mother 2 (dividir un todo) to divide; **~ las palabras en sílabas** divide the words into syllables

B 1 (deslindar) to separate, divide; **una valla separa los dos campos** there is a fence separating the two fields; **los separan profundas diferencias** they are divided by deepseated differences; **~ algo DE algo** to separate sth FROM sth 2 (despegar): **no puedo ~ estas dos fotos** I can't get these two photographs apart; **separa las lonchas de jamón** separate the slices of ham

C (frml) (destituir) to dismiss (frml); **fue separado de su cargo/sus funciones** he was removed from office/relieved of his duties (frml)

■ **separarse** *v pron* 1 «*matrimonio*» to separate; **se ~on hace un mes** they separated *o* split up a month ago; **es hijo de padres separados** his parents are separated; **~se DE algn** to separate FROM sb 2 (apartarse, alejarse) to split up; **a mitad de camino nos separamos** we split up half way; **no se separen, que los pequeños se pueden perder** please stay together in case the children get lost; **~se DE algo/algn: esta niña no se separa del televisor** this child is always glued to the television; **no me he separado nunca de mis hijos** I've never been away *o* apart from my children; **no se separen de su equipaje** do not leave your luggage unattended 3 (guardar, reservar) to put *o* set aside

separata *f* offprint

separatismo *m* separatism

separatista¹ *adj* separatist (*before n*)

separatista² *mf* separatist

separo *m* (Méx) cell

sepelio *m* burial, interment (frml)

sepia¹ *f* 1 (Coc, Zool) cuttlefish, sepia (tech) 2 (en pintura) sepia

sepia² *m* (color) sepia

septentrional *adj* northern

septicemia *f* septicemia* (tech), blood poisoning

séptico -ca *adj* septic

septiembre *m* September; *para ejemplos ver* **enero**

séptimo¹ -ma *adj/pron* 1 (ordinal) seventh; *para ejemplos ver* **quinto** 2 (partitivo): **la séptima parte** a seventh

(Compuesto) **séptimo arte** *m*: **el ~ ~** the movies (*pl*) (AmE), the cinema (BrE)

séptimo² *m* seventh

septuagenario -ria *adj/m,f* septuagenarian (frml)

septuagésimo -ma *adj/pron* 1 (ordinal) seventieth; *para ejemplos ver* **vigésimo** 2 (partitivo): **la septuagésima parte** a seventieth

sepulcral *adj* 1 (liter) ‹*silencio*› deathly; **hacía un frío ~** it was deathly cold 2 ‹*inscripción*›: **la inscripción ~** the inscription on the tomb; **piedras/túmulos ~es** tombstones/burial mounds

sepulcro *m* tomb, sepulcher* (liter)

sepultar [A1] *vt* 1 (frml) ‹*muerto*› to inter (frml), to bury 2 (period) (cubrir): **el pueblo quedó sepultado bajo las aguas** the town was totally submerged; **fue sepultado por un alud de nieve** he was buried by an avalanche

sepultura *f* 1 (acción) burial; **le dieron ~ en el panteón familiar** she was buried in the family vault 2 (tumba) tomb, grave

sepulturero -ra *m,f* gravedigger

sequedad *f* 1 (de terreno, región, piel) dryness 2 (de respuesta, tono) curtness; **nos saludó con ~** he greeted us curtly

sequía *f* drought

séquito *m* (de rey) retinue, entourage

ser¹ [E26] *cópula*

A (seguido de adjetivos) to be [**ser** *expresses identity or nature as opposed to condition or state, which is normally conveyed by* **estar**. *The examples given below should be contrasted with those to be found in* **estar¹** *cópula* **A**] **es bajo** he's short; **es muy callada** she's very quiet; **mi padre es calvo** my father's bald; **es sorda de nacimiento** she was born deaf; **es**

inglés/rubio/católico he's English/fair/(a) Catholic; **era cierto/posible** it was true/possible; **sé bueno, estáte quieto** be a good boy and keep still; **que seas muy feliz** I hope you'll be very happy; (+ *me/te/le etc*) **para ~te sincero** to be honest with you, to tell you the truth; **siempre le he sido fiel** I've always been faithful to her; *ver tb vi* **A E**; **¿éste es o se hace?/¿tú eres o te haces?** (AmL fam) is he/are you stupid or something? (colloq)

B (hablando de estado civil) to be; **el mayor es casado/divorciado** the oldest is married/divorced; **es viuda** she's a widow; *ver tb* **estar**[1] *cópula* **C**

C (seguido de nombre, pronombre, sintagma nominal) to be; **soy peluquera/abogada** I'm a hairdresser/a lawyer; **es madre de dos niños** she's a mother of two; **ábreme, soy Mariano/yo** open the door, it's Mariano/it's me; **el que fuera presidente** the former president; **años más tarde sería mi asistente** years later she would become my assistant; **por ~ usted, haremos una excepción** for you *o* since it's you, we'll make an exception; **dame cualquiera que no sea ése** give me any one except *o* but that one; **ya no soy lo que era** I'm not what I used to be

D (con predicado introducido por 'de'): **esos zapatos son de plástico** those shoes are (made of) plastic; **soy de Córdoba** I'm from Cordoba; **es de los vecinos** it belongs to the neighbors, it's the neighbors'; **este libro no es de aquí** this book doesn't go *o* belong here; **ésa es de las que ...** she's one of those people who ..., she's the sort of person who ...; **~ *de lo que no hay*** (fam) to be incredible (colloq)

E (hipótesis, futuro): **será un error** it must be a mistake; **¿será cierto?** can it be true?; **¡pero será animal!** he must be a complete idiot

■ **ser** *vi*

(Sentido I)

A 1 (existir) to be 2 (liter) (en cuentos): **érase una vez ...** once upon a time there was ...

B 1 (tener lugar, ocurrir): **la fiesta va a ~ en su casa** the party is going to be (held) at her house; **¿dónde fue el accidente?** where did the accident happen?; **el asunto fue así ...** it happened like this ... 2 (en preguntas) **~ DE algo/algn**: **¿qué habrá sido de él?** I wonder what happened to *o* what became of him; **¿qué es de Marisa?** (fam) what's Marisa up to (these days)? (colloq); **¿qué va a ser de nosotros?** what will become of us?

C (sumar): **¿cuánto es (todo)?** how much is that (altogether)?; **son 3.000 pesos** that'll be *o* that's 3,000 pesos; **cuatro y cuatro son ocho** four and four are *o* make eight; **somos diez en total** there are ten of us altogether

D (causar, significar) to be; **aquello fue su ruina** that was his downfall

E (resultar): **me va a ~ imposible venir** I'm not going to be able to come; **me fue muy difícil entenderlo** I found it very difficult to understand

F (consistir en) to be; **lo importante es participar** the important *o* main thing is to take part

G (indicando finalidad, adecuación) **~ PARA algo** to be FOR sth; **este agua es para beber** this water is for drinking; **este traje no es para usarlo mucho** this suit is not for frequent wear

(Sentido II)

A (usado para enfatizar): **así es como queda mejor** like that it looks best; **fue aquí donde lo vi** this is where I saw him, it was here that I saw him; **era él el que quería** he was the one who wanted to; **fueron los bancos los que se beneficiaron** it was the banks that benefited; **fui yo quien** *or* **la que lo dije, fui yo quien** *or* **la que lo dijo** I was the one who said it, it was me that said it

B **es que ...**: **¿es que no lo saben?** do you mean to say they don't know?; **es que no sé nadar** the thing is I can't swim; **díselo, si es que te atreves** tell him, if you dare

C **lo que es ...** (fam): **lo que es yo, no pienso hablarle más** I certainly have no intention of speaking to him again; **¡lo que es saber idiomas!** it sure is something to be able to speak languages! (AmE), what it is to be able to speak languages! (BrE)

D (*en locs*) **a no ser que** (+ *subj*) unless; **como debe ser**: **¿ves como me acordé? — ¡como debe ~!** see, I did remember— I should think so too!; **los presentó uno por uno, como debe ~** she introduced them one by one, as you should; **¿cómo es eso?** why is that?, how come? (colloq); **como/cuando/donde sea**: **tengo que conseguir ese trabajo como sea** I have to get that job no matter what; **hazlo como sea, pero hazlo** do it any way *o* however you want but get it done; **puedo dormir en el sillón o donde sea** I can sleep in the armchair or wherever you like *o* anywhere you like; **como ser** (CS) such as; **de no ser así** (frml) should this not be the case (frml); **de ser así** (frml) should this be so *o* the case (frml); **de no ser por ...**: **de no ~ por él, ...** if it hadn't been *o* if it weren't for him, ...; **¡eso es!** that's it!, that's right!; **lo que sea**: **cómete una manzana, o lo que sea** have an apple or something; **tú pagas tus mil pesos o lo que sea ...** you pay your thousand pesos or whatever ...; **estoy dispuesta a hacer lo que sea** I'm prepared to do whatever it takes *o* anything; **no sea que** *or* **no vaya a ser que** (+ *subj*) in case; **cierra la ventana, no sea** *or* **no vaya a ser que llueva** close the window in case it rains; **ten cuidado, no sea** *or* **no vaya a ~ que lo eches todo a perder** be careful or you'll ruin everything; **o sea**: **los empleados de más antigüedad, o sea los que llevan aquí más de ...** longer serving employees, that is to say those who have been here more than ...; **o sea que no te interesa** in other words, you're not interested; **o sea que nunca lo descubriste** so you never found out; **(ya) sea ..., (ya) sea ...** either ..., or ...; **(ya) sea por caridad, (ya) sea por otra razón, ...** whether he did it out of charity or for some other reason, ...; **sea como sea**: **hay que impedirlo, sea como sea** it must be prevented now matter how *o* at all costs; **sea cuando sea** whenever it is; **sea quien sea le dices que no estoy** whoever it is, tell them I'm not in; **si no fuera/hubiera sido por ...** if it wasn't *o* weren't/hadn't been for ...

(Sentido III), (en el tiempo) to be; **¿qué fecha es hoy?** what's the date today?, what's today's date; **¿qué día es hoy?** what day is it today?; **es miércoles** it's Wednesday; **serían las cuatro cuando llegó** it must have been (about) four (o'clock) when she arrived; *ver tb v impers*

■ **ser** *v impers* to be; **era primavera** it was spring(time); **es demasiado tarde para llamar** it's too late to phone

■ **ser** *v aux* (en la voz pasiva) **ser + PP** to be + PP; **fue construido en 1900** it was built in 1900

ser[2] *m*

A 1 (ente) being; **~es sobrenaturales** supernatural beings 2 (individuo, persona): **un ~ querido** a loved one; **un ~ muy especial** a very special person

(Compuesto) **ser humano/vivo** human/living being

B 1 (naturaleza): **desde lo más profundo de mi ~** from the bottom of my heart 2 (carácter esencial) essence

C (Fil) being; **la mujer que te dio el ~** the woman who brought you into this world

serafín *m* seraph

Serbia *f* Serbia

serbio[1] **-bia** *adj/m,f* Serbian

serbio[2] *m* (idioma) Serbian

serbocroata[1] *adj/mf* Serbo-Croat, Serbo-Croatian

serbocroata[2] *m* (idioma) Serbo-Croat

seré, seremos, etc *see* **ser**

serenar [A1] *vt* to soothe, calm

■ **serenarse** *v pron*

A (calmarse) to calm down

B (Col) (exponerse al sereno) to go out in the damp night air

serenata *f* serenade; **dar (una)** *or* (Méx) **llevar ~** to serenade

serenidad *f* calmness, serenity; **no pierdas la ~** keep calm

sereno[1] **-na** *adj*

A 1 ‹*rostro/expresión/belleza*› serene; ‹*persona*› serene, calm 2 ‹*cielo*› cloudless, clear; ‹*tarde*› still; ‹*mar*› calm, tranquil (liter)

B (no borracho) sober

sereno[2] *m*

A (vigilante nocturno) night watchman

B (Meteo) night dew; **dormir al ~** to sleep out in the open

sería, etc *see* **ser**

serial *m*, (CS) **serial** *f* ▸ **serie B**

seriamente *adv* seriously

serie *f*

A 1 (sucesión) series; **~ numérica** (Mat) numerical sequence 2 (clase) series; **coches/motores de ~** production cars/

S

engines; **ofrece dirección hidráulica de ~** it offers power-assisted steering as standard; **producción** *or* **fabricación en ~** mass production; **producir/fabricar en ~** to mass produce; ***fuera de*** **~** (fam) out of this world (colloq) [3] (Dep) heat

B (Rad, TV) series; (historia continua) serial

seriedad *f* [1] (falta de jocosidad) seriousness [2] (sensatez, responsabilidad): **se comportó con mucha ~** she behaved very sensibly *o* responsibly; **¡un poco de ~!** come on, let's be serious now!; **es una falta de ~ que nos tengan esperando así** it's no way to treat people keeping us waiting like this [3] (gravedad, importancia) seriousness

serigrafía *f* (proceso) silk screen printing; (cuadro) silk screen (print)

serio -ria *adj*

A (poco sonriente) serious; **qué cara más seria ¿qué te ha pasado?** what a long face, what's the matter? (colloq); **se puso muy ~** his expression became very serious *o* grave; **voy a tener que ponerme ~ con este niño** I'm going to have to start getting strict with this child

B ‹*empleado*› responsible, reliable; ‹*empresa*› reputable; **no confío en él, es muy poco ~** I don't trust him, he's very unreliable

C [1] ‹*cine/tema*› serious [2] (grave) ‹*enfermedad/problema*› serious; **tengo mis serias dudas acerca de él** I have serious doubts about him [3] **en serio** ‹*hablar*› seriously, in earnest; **¿lo dices en ~?** are you (being) serious?, do you really mean it?; **tomarse algo en ~** to take sth seriously; **esto es ~, está muriéndose** this is serious, he's dying; **y esto va en ~** and I really mean it

sermón *m* sermon; **me echó un ~ por llegar tarde** (fam) he gave me a lecture for being late (colloq)

sermonear [A1] *vi* (fam) to sermonize (colloq & pej), to lecture (colloq)

seronegativo -va *adj* (en general) seronegative; (sin el VIH) HIV negative

seropositivo -va *adj* (en general) seropositive; (con el VIH) HIV positive

serpenteante *adj* ‹*río/camino*› winding

serpentear [A1] *vi* «*río*» to meander, wind; «*camino*» to wind, twist

serpentín *m* coil

serpentina *f* streamer

serpiente *f* snake, serpent

(Compuestos)

- **serpiente (de) cascabel** rattlesnake
- **serpiente pitón** python

serrado -da *adj* serrated

serrallo *m* (ant) seraglio (dated), harem

serranía *f* mountain range

serrano -na *adj* [1] ‹*aire/gente*› mountain (*before n*); **un pueblo ~** a village in the mountains, a mountain village [2] (Esp fam) ‹*cuerpo*› shapely, attractive

serrar [A5] *vt* to saw (up)

serrín *m* sawdust; ***tener la cabeza llena de*** **~** (fam) to be soft in the head (colloq)

serruchar [A1] *vt* (AmL) to saw; **~*le el piso a algn*** (AmL fam) to pull the rug out from under sb/sb's feet

serrucho *m* handsaw; ***hacer*** **~** (Col fam) to have underhand dealings

servicentro *m* (Andes) service station

servicial *adj* helpful, obliging

servicio *m*

A [1] (acción de servir) service; **estaremos a su ~ de nuevo el próximo lunes** we will reopen (for business) next Monday; **estamos a su ~ las 24 horas del día** we are at your service 24 hours a day; **prestó ~ como médico en el frente** he served as a doctor at the front; **cumplió 20 años de ~** he completed 20 years' service; **estar de ~** to be on duty; **un policía libre de ~** an off-duty policeman; Ⓢ **servicio permanente** *or* **de 24 horas** round-the-clock *o* 24-hour service [2] (favor) favor*, service; **me prestó un ~ inestimable** she did me a really good turn *o* a very great service [3] **servicios** *mpl* (asistencia) services (*pl*); **recurrieron a los ~s de un abogado** they sought the advice of a lawyer; **les agradecemos los ~s prestados** we would like to thank you for all your work *o* help

(Compuestos)

- **servicio a domicilio** (home) delivery service
- **servicio diplomático/secreto/de inteligencia** diplomatic/secret/intelligence service
- **servicio postventa** after-sales service
- **servicio público** public service
- **servicios informativos** *mpl* broadcasting services (*pl*)
- **servicios mínimos** *mpl* minimum *o* skeleton service
- **servicios sociales** *mpl* social services (*pl*)

B [1] (funcionamiento) service, use; **han puesto en ~ el nuevo andén** the new platform is now in use *o* is now open; **¿cuándo entra en ~ la nueva estación depuradora?** when is the new purifying plant coming into operation *o* service?; Ⓢ **fuera de servicio** out of service [2] (sistema) service; **~ postal** postal service; **el ~ de la línea 19 es pésimo** the number 19 is a terrible service

C [1] (en hospital) department; **~ de urgencias** accident and emergency department, casualty department; **es jefe del ~ de cirugía** he is the chief surgeon [2] **servicios** *mpl* (Econ) public services (*pl*); **el sector (de) ~s** the public service sector

D (en restaurante, hotel) [1] (atención al cliente) service [2] (propina) service (charge); Ⓢ **servicio e impuestos incluidos** tax and service included

E (servidumbre): **sólo hablan de los problemas del ~** all they talk about is the problems of having servants; **escalera de ~** service staircase; **entrada de ~** tradesman's entrance; **habitación** *or* **cuarto de ~** servant's quarters (frml), maid's room

(Compuesto) **servicio doméstico** (actividad) domestic service; (personas) servants (*pl*), domestic staff; **las habitaciones destinadas al ~ ~** the servants' quarters

F (Mil) service; **estar en ~** to be in service

(Compuesto) **servicio activo/militar** active/military service

G (retrete) restroom (AmE), bathroom (esp AmE), toilet (esp BrE)

H [1] (juego de loza): **~ de café** coffee set; **~ de té** tea service *o* set [2] (juego de cubiertos) set of cutlery; (cubierto para cada comensal): **una cubertería de doce ~s** a set of cutlery for twelve people; **este juego no tiene ~ de pescado** there are no fish knives in this set; **pon otro servicio en la mesa** set another place

I (en tenis) service, serve; **~ de Fortín** Fortín to serve; **tiene que mejorar su ~** she needs to work on her serve

A (Relig) service

A (AmL) (Auto) service

servidor -dora *m,f*

A [1] (sirviente) servant [2] (en fórmulas de cortesía): **¿quién se encarga de esto? — (su/un) ~** (frml *or* hum) who is in charge of this? — I am, Sir (*o* Madam *etc*) (frml), yours truly (hum); **su (atento y) seguro ~** (Corresp) (frml) your humble servant (frml); **Chaves — servidora** (frml) (al pasar lista) Chaves — present; **¿quién es el último? — servidor** who's last in line (AmE) *o* (BrE) in the queue? — I am

B **servidor** *m* (Inf) server

servidumbre *f*

A (esclavitud) servitude

B (conjunto de criados) (domestic) staff, servants (*pl*)

servil *adj* [1] ‹*persona/actitud*› servile, obsequious (frml) [2] ‹*trabajo*› menial

servilismo *m* servility, obsequiousness (frml)

servilleta *f* napkin, serviette (esp BrE); **~ de papel** paper napkin, paper serviette (BrE)

servilletero *m* napkin ring, serviette ring (BrE)

servir [I14] *vi*

A (ser útil): **esta caja no sirve** this box won't do *o* is no good; **tíralo, ya no me sirve** throw it away, it's (of) no use to me anymore; **~ PARA algo**: **¿para qué sirve este aparato?** what's this device for?; **no lo tires, puede ~ para algo** don't throw it away, it might come in useful for something; **este cuchillo no sirve para cortar pan** this knife is no good for cutting bread; **no sirves para nada** you're useless; **no creo que sirva para este trabajo** I don't think he's right *o* suitable for this job; **yo no sirvo para mentir** I'm a hopeless liar, I'm not good at lying; **~ DE algo**: **de nada sirve llorar** it's no use *o* good crying; **¿de qué sirve hablarle si no te escucha?** what's the point in *o* the use of talking to him if he doesn't listen to

S

you?; **esto te puede ~ de mesa** you can use this as a table

B 1 (en la mesa) to serve; **se sirve a los invitados primero** guests are served first 2 (trabajar de criado) to be in (domestic) service; **empezó a ~ a los catorce años** she went into service at the age of fourteen 3 (Mil) to serve (frml)

C (Dep) (en tenis) to serve

■ **servir** *vt*

A ‹*comida*› to serve; ‹*bebida*› to serve, pour; **~ la comida** to serve (out) *o* (colloq) dish out the food; **la cena está servida** dinner is served; **~ a temperatura ambiente** serve at room temperature

B 1 (estar al servicio de) **~ A algo/algn** to serve sth/sb; **se cree que todos la tienen que ~** she expects to be waited on hand and foot; **¿en qué puedo ~le?** (frml) how can I help you?; **para ~le** at your service; ***no se puede ~ a Dios y al diablo*** no man can serve two masters 2 (Com) ‹*pedido*› to process; ‹*cliente*› to serve; ‹*mercancías*› to send

■ **servirse** *v pron*

A (*refl*) ‹*comida*› to help oneself to; ‹*bebida*› to pour oneself, help oneself to; **sírvete otro trozo** help yourself to another piece

B (frml) (hacer uso) **~se DE algo** to make use of sth, use sth

C (frml) (hacer el favor de) **~se + INF: sírvase rellenar la solicitud** please fill in the application form; **les rogamos se sirvan enviarnos esta información** we would ask you to send us this information (frml)

servodirección *f* power(-assisted) steering

servofreno *m* power-assisted brake, servoassisted brake

(Compuesto) **servofreno de emergencia** brake assist system, BAS

sésamo *m* sesame

sesear [A1] *vi*: *to pronounce the Spanish [θ] as* [s], *eg* /ser 'βesa/ *instead of* /θer'βeθa/ *for* **cerveza**

sesenta¹ *adj inv/pron* sixty; *para ejemplos ver* **cincuenta**

sesenta² *m* (number) sixty

sesentón -tona *m,f* sexagenarian (frml); **un ~** a man in his sixties

seseo *m*: *pronunciation of the Spanish [θ] as* /s/, *eg* /ser'βesa/ *instead of* /θer'βeθa/ *for* **cerveza**

sesera *f* (fam) brains (*pl*) (colloq); **estar mal de la ~** to be soft in the head (colloq); **no tiene nada en la ~** he's got nothing up top at all (colloq)

sesgado -da *adj*

A 1 (al bies): **la falda tiene un corte ~** the skirt is cut on the bias 2 (inclinado, ladeado): **cabe si la colocamos sesgada** it should fit if we put it in crosswise *o* at an angle

B (parcial) biased, slanted

sesgar [A3] *vt* 1 ‹*tela/paño*› (cortar al bies) to cut … on the bias; (colocar al bies) to place … diagonally *o* at an angle 2 (liter) ‹*vida*› to cut short

sesgo *m*

A 1 (de falda) bias; **se corta al ~** you cut it on the bias 2 (diagonal): **al ~** crosswise, diagonally

B (tendencia, enfoque) bias, slant; (rumbo) direction

sesión *f* 1 (reunión) session; **abrir/levantar/cerrar la ~** to open/adjourn/close the session *o* meeting; **~ inaugural** *or* **de apertura** inaugural *o* opening session; **~ de clausura** closing session 2 (de tratamiento, actividad) session; (de fotografía, pintura) sitting 3 (Cin, Teatr) (de cine) showing, performance; (de teatro) show, performance; **~ de tarde/noche** evening/late evening performance

(Compuestos)
- **sesión continua** continuous performance
- **sesión de espiritismo** séance
- **sesión numerada** separate performances (*pl*)
- **sesión solemne** (Col) prizegiving

sesionar [A1] *vi* (AmL) to be in session

seso *m* 1 (Anat, Zool) brain; ***devanarse*** *or* ***estrujarse los ~s*** (fam) to rack one's brains (colloq); ***haber perdido el ~ por algn*** (fam) to be crazy about sb (colloq); ***sorberle el ~ a algn*** (fam) to bowl sb over (colloq); **esa chica le tiene sorbido el ~** he's completely bowled over by that girl; ***tener poco ~*** (fam) to be brainless (colloq) 2 **sesos** *mpl* (Coc) brains (*pl*)

sesquicentenario *m* sesquicentennial (frml), 150th anniversary

sesudo -da *adj* (fam) (sensato) sensible, wise; (inteligente) bright, brainy (colloq)

set *m* (*pl* **sets**)

A (en tenis) set

B (escenografía) set

seta *f* (comestible) mushroom; (venenosa) toadstool

setecientos -tas *adj/pron* seven hundred; *para ejemplos ver* **quinientos**

setenta¹ *adj inv/pron* seventy; *para ejemplos ver* **cincuenta**

setenta² *m* (number) seventy

setentón -tona *m,f* septuagenarian (frml); **es un ~** he is a man in his seventies

setiembre *m* September; *para ejemplos ver* **enero**

seto *m* hedge

seudónimo *m* (de artista) pseudonym; (de escritor) pen name, pseudonym

severidad *f* (de castigo, pena) severity, harshness; (de padre, educador) strictness; **la ~ del clima** the harshness of the climate

severo -ra *adj* ‹*padre/profesor*› strict; ‹*castigo*› severe, harsh; ‹*invierno*› hard, severe; **sigue un régimen muy ~** he's on a very strict diet

Sevilla *f* Seville; ***el que se fue a ~, perdió su silla*** if you go off you lose your place

sexagenario -ria *adj/m,f* sexagenarian

sexagésimo -ma *adj/m,f* sixtieth

sexismo *m* sexism

sexista *adj/mf* sexist

sexo *m* 1 (condición, género) sex; **~ masculino/femenino** male/female sex 2 (órganos genitales) sexual organs (*pl*) 3 (sexualidad) sex

(Compuestos)
- **sexo débil**: **el ~ ~** the weaker sex
- **sexo seguro** safe sex

sexología *f* sexology

sexólogo -ga *m,f* sexologist

sextante *m* sextant

sexto¹ -ta *adj/pron* 1 (ordinal) sixth; *para ejemplos ver* **quinto** 2 (partitivo): **la sexta parte** a sixth

(Compuesto) **sexto sentido** sixth sense

sexto² *m* sixth

sexual *adj* ‹*relaciones/órganos/comportamiento*› sexual; ‹*educación/vida*› sex (*before n*)

sexualidad *f* sexuality

sexy /'seksi, 'sesi/ *adj* (fam) ‹*persona/vestido*› sexy; ‹*espectáculo*› titillating

s/f = su favor

SFC *m* (= **síndrome de fatiga crónica**) CFS, ME

Sgto. *m* (= **sargento**) Sgt

sh, shh *interj* shush!, ssh!, hush!

sha, shah *m* shah

sheriff /'ʃerif/ *mf* sheriff

shock /ʃok/ *m* 1 (Med) shock; **en estado de ~** in (a state of) shock 2 (sorpresa desagradable) shock

show /ʃou, tʃou/ *m* (*pl* **shows**) show; ***montar/dar un ~*** (fam) to make a scene (colloq)

si¹ *conj*

A 1 (introduciendo una condición) if; **~ lo sé, no vengo** (fam) if I'd known, I wouldn't have come; **~ pudiera, se lo compraba** (fam) if I could, I'd buy it for him; **~ lo hubiera** *or* **hubiese sabido …** if I'd known …, had I known …; **empezó a decir que ~ esto, que ~ lo otro** he said this, that and the other 2 (*en locs*) **si bien**: **~ bien el sueldo es bueno, el horario es malísimo** the pay may be good but the hours are terrible; **si no** otherwise; **pórtate bien, ~ no, te vas a la cama** behave yourself, or else you're going straight to bed; **date prisa, que ~ no nos vamos sin ti** hurry up, otherwise we're going without you

B 1 (planteando un hecho) if; **~ no ha venido por algo será** if she hasn't come there must be some reason for it 2 (cada vez que) if; **~ hacía sol salíamos a pasear** if *o* when it was sunny we used to go out for a walk

C 1 (en frases que expresan deseo) **~ + SUBJ: ¡~ yo lo supiera!** if only I knew!; **¡~ me hubieras avisado a tiempo!** if

only you had let me know in time! [2] (en frases que expresan protesta, indignación, sorpresa): **¡~ tendrá cara!** she really has a nerve!; **¡pero ~ te avisé ...!** but I warned you ...! [3] (fam) (uso enfático): **¡~ lo sabré yo!** don't I know it!, you're telling me! [4] (planteando eventualidades, sugerencias): **y ~ no quiere hacerlo ¿qué?** and if she doesn't want to do it, what then?; **¿y ~ lo probáramos?** why don't we give it a try?
D (en interrogativas indirectas) whether; **no sé ~ marcharme o quedarme** I don't know whether to go or to stay; **me pregunto ~ lo encontrarán** I wonder if *o* whether they'll find it

si² *m* (nota) B; (en solfeo) ti, te (BrE); **~ bemol/sostenido** B flat/sharp; **en ~ mayor/menor** in B major/minor

sí¹ *adv*
A (respuesta afirmativa) yes; **¿has terminado? — sí** have you finished? — yes *o* yes, I have; **¿te sirvo un poco más? — ~, gracias** do you want a bit more? — yes, please; **decir que ~ con la cabeza** to nod; **¿por qué lo hiciste? — porque ~** why did you do it? — because I felt like it; **¿por qué lleva tanto tiempo? — porque ~** why does it take so long? — it just does
B (uso enfático): **ahora ~ que lo has hecho bien** now you've really done it! (colloq); **tú ~ que sabes vivir** you certainly know how to live!; **lo que ~ quiero es que lo pienses bien** what I *do* want you to do is to think it over carefully; **no puedo — ¡~ que puedes!** I can't — yes, you can! *o* of course, you can!; **que ~ cabe** it does fit; **no es tuyo — ~ que lo es** it isn't yours — oh yes, it is!; **¡ah, no! ¡eso ~ que no!** oh no! I'm not having that! (colloq) (colloq); **es de muy buena calidad — eso ~** it's very good quality — (yes,) that's true; **son pobres pero, eso ~, comen bien** they are poor, but they certainly eat well
C (sustituyendo a una cláusula): **creo que ~** I think so; **me temo que ~** I'm afraid so; **¿lloverá? — puede que ~** do you think it will rain? — it might; **un día ~ y otro no** every other day; **se fue sin permiso — ¿ah ~?** he left without asking permission — is that so? *o* did he now?; **¿te gusta? a mí ~** do you like it? *I* do; **no puedo ir pero María ~** I can't go but María can; **¡que no vas! — ¡que ~!** you're not going! — oh, yes I am!; **¿a que no te atreves? — ¡a que ~!** I bet you wouldn't dare — (do you) want to bet?

sí² *m* yes; **con el ~ del encargado** with the manager's approval; ***darle el ~ a algn*** to accept sb's proposal; **aún no me ha dado el ~** she still hasn't said yes; **dar el ~ quiero** to say 'I do' (*in wedding*); ***no tener (ni) un ~ ni un no*** (CS, Méx) never to exchange a cross word

sí³ *pron pers*
A (3ª *pers sing*) [1] (*refl*): **sólo piensa en ~ mismo** he only thinks of himself; **lo hizo por ~ mismo** *or* **por ~ solo** he did it by himself *o* on his own; **parece muy segura de ~ misma** she seems very sure of herself; **cerró la puerta tras de ~** (liter) she closed the door behind her [2] (*impers*): **uno tiene que ver por ~ mismo** you have to see it for yourself
B (3ª *pers pl*) [1] (*refl*): **lo hacen para convencerse a ~ mismos** they do it just to convince themselves; **saben reírse de ~ mismos** they know how to laugh at themselves [2] **entre sí** (entre dos) between themselves; (en un grupo) among themselves; **todos son muy diferentes entre ~** they are all very different (from one another); **no se respetan entre ~** they don't have respect for each other *o* respect each other
C (*refl*) [1] (usted) yourself; **guárdese los comentarios para ~** keep your comments to yourself [2] (ustedes): **léanlo para ~ (mismos)** read it (for) yourselves
D (*en locs*) **de por sí**: **es de por ~ nervioso** he is nervous by nature; **el sistema es de por ~ complicado** the system is in itself complicated; **en sí**: **el hecho en ~ (mismo) no tenía demasiada importancia** this in itself was not so important; **el sueldo en ~ no es maravilloso, pero ...** the salary itself isn't great but ...

siamés¹ -mesa *adj* Siamese

siamés² -mesa *m,f* (gemelo) Siamese twin

sibarita *mf* (amante de los lujos) lover of luxury, sybarite (frml); (en cuestiones de comida) gourmet, epicure (frml)

Siberia *f* Siberia; **ahí fuera hace más frío que en ~** it's like the North Pole out there!

sibilante *adj* sibilant

sibilino -na *adj* (liter) (profético) sibylline; (misterioso) enigmatic, sibylline (liter)

sicario -ria *m,f* hired assassin

SICAV *f* (= **Sociedad de Inversión Mobiliaria de Capital Variable**) mutual fund, unit trust (in Uk)

Sicilia *f* Sicily

siciliano -na *adj/m,f* Sicilian

sicómoro, sicomoro *m* sycamore

sida *m* (= **Síndrome de Inmunodeficiencia Adquirida**) AIDS

sidecar /siðe'kar, 'saikar/ *m* (*pl* **-cares** *or* **-cars**) sidecar

sideral *adj*, **sidéreo -rea** *adj* [1] (Astron) sidereal [2] (CS fam) ‹*suma/precio*› astronomical (colloq)

siderometalúrgico -ca *adj* iron and steel (*before n*)

siderurgia *f* iron and steel industry

siderúrgico -ca *adj* iron and steel (*before n*)

sidra *f* hard cider (AmE), cider (BrE)

siega *f* [1] (acción — de cortar a mano) reaping, cutting; (— de cortar a máquina) mowing; (— de cosechar) harvesting [2] (época) harvest time

siembra *f* (acción) sowing; (época) sowing season

siempre *adv*
A always; **~ se sale con la suya** he always gets his own way; **casi ~ acierta** he's almost always right; **como ~** as usual; **pasó lo de ~** the usual thing happened; **a la hora de ~** at the usual time; **los amigos de ~** the usual crowd; **los conozco desde ~** I've known them for as long as I can remember; **¿regresas para ~?** are you back for good?; **por ~ jamás** for ever and ever
B (en todo caso) always; **~ podemos modificarlo después** we can always modify it later
C (AmL) (todavía) still; **¿~ viven en Malvín?** do they still live in Malvín?
D (*en locs*) **siempre que** (cada vez que) whenever; (a condición de que) (+ *subj*) provided (that), providing (that); **podrá entrar ~ que llegue antes de las siete** she'll be able to get in provided *o* as long as she arrives before seven; **siempre y cuando** (+ *subj*) provided (that)
E (Méx) (uso enfático) after all

sien *f* temple

sienta, sientas, etc *see* **sentar, sentir**

sierpe *f* (liter) serpent (liter)

sierra *f*
A (Tec) saw

Compuestos
- **sierra de cadena** chain saw
- **sierra de mano** handsaw
- **sierra de marquetería** coping saw
- **sierra eléctrica/mecánica** electric/power saw

B (Geog) (cordillera) mountain range; (zona montañosa): **la ~** the mountains

Sierra Leona *f* Sierra Leone

sierraleonés -nesa *adj* of/from Sierra Leone

siervo -va *m,f* serf, slave

siesta *f* siesta, nap; **dormir la ~** *or* **echar una ~** to have a siesta *o* nap; **a la hora de la ~** during siesta-time

siete¹ *adj inv/pron* seven; *para ejemplos ver* **cinco**; ***de la gran ~*** (CS fam) ‹*resfrío/carácter*› terrible; **hace un frío de la gran ~** it's absolutely freezing

siete² *m* [1] (cardinal) (number) seven; *para ejemplos ver* **cinco** [2] (rotura) tear (*L-shaped*); **se hizo un ~ en la chaqueta** he tore his jacket

sietemesino¹ -na *adj* premature (*esp two months premature*)

sietemesino² -na *m,f* premature baby (*esp when born two months early*)

sífilis *f* syphilis

sifilítico¹ -ca *adj* syphilitic

sifilítico² -ca *m,f* person with *o* suffering from syphilis, syphilitic

sifón *m*
A [1] (botella) siphon* [2] (Esp fam) (soda) soda (water) [3] (Col) (cerveza) draft* beer
B (para trasvasar líquidos) siphon; (en fontanería) U-bend, trap

sifrino -na *adj* (Ven fam) grand, posh (BrE colloq)

S

sig. (= **siguiente/siguientes**) following; **los ~ productos** the following *o* foll. products; **pág. 48 y ~** p. 48 et seq, p. 48 ff

siga, sigas, etc *see* **seguir**

sigilo *m* stealth; **se acercó con ~** he crept up stealthily; **se negoció con mucho ~** the negotiations were carried out amid great secrecy

sigiloso -sa *adj* stealthy

sigla *f* abbreviation; (pronunciado como una palabra) acronym; **SDN son las ~s de Secretaría de la Defensa Nacional** SDN stands for Secretaría de la Defensa Nacional

siglo *m* century; **data del ~ XV** it dates from *o* is from the 15th century; **mi madre es de otro ~** my mother is really old-fashioned; **hace ~s** *or* **un ~ que no le escribo** (fam) I haven't written to her for ages (colloq); ***por los ~s de los ~s*** for ever and ever

Compuestos
- **Siglo de las Luces** Age of Enlightenment
- **Siglo de Oro** Golden Age

signatario¹ -ria *adj* (frml) signatory (*before n*) (frml)

signatario² -ria *m,f* (frml) signatory (frml)

signatura *f* (en bibliotecas) catalog* *o* call number; (Impr) signature

significación *f* (importancia) significance, importance; **los hechos de mayor ~** the most significant *o* important events

significado¹ -da *adj* (frml) ‹*político/científico*› noted (*before n*), well known, renowned

significado² *m*
A (de palabra) meaning; (de símbolo) meaning, significance
B (importancia) ▸**significación**

significante *m* signifier

significar [A2] *vt*
A 1 (querer decir) «*palabra/símbolo*» to mean; «*hecho*» to mean, signify (frml) 2 (suponer, representar) ‹*mejora/ruina*› to represent; ‹*esfuerzo/riesgo*› to involve; **para mí no significa ningún sacrificio** it's no sacrifice for me 3 (valer, importar) to mean; **no significo nada para ti** I mean nothing to you
B (frml) (expresar) ‹*condolencias*› to express; ‹*importancia*› to stress; ‹*opinión*› to state, make clear
C (frml) (distinguir, destacar) **~ A algo/algn COMO algo** to establish sth/sb AS sth
■ **significarse** *v pron* (frml) (destacarse — positivamente) to distinguish oneself; (— negativamente) to draw attention to oneself

significativo -va *adj*
A ‹*cambio/detalle*› significant
B ‹*gesto/sonrisa*› meaningful

signo *m*
A (señal, indicio) sign
B (Mat) sign

Compuestos
- **signo de admiración** exclamation point (AmE), exclamation mark (BrE)
- **signo de igual** equal sign (AmE), equals sign (BrE)
- **signo de interrogación** question mark
- **signo de la victoria** V-sign
- **signo (de) más/menos** plus/minus sign
- **signo de puntuación** punctuation mark
- **signo ortográfico** diacritic

C (Astrol) *tb* **~ del zodiaco** sign; **¿de qué ~ eres?** what sign are you?
D (frml) (carácter): **dos sucesos de ~ positivo** two positive events; **dos exposiciones de muy distinto ~** two very different exhibitions

sigo, sigue, etc *see* **seguir**

siguiente *adj*
A 1 (en el tiempo) following (*before n*); **al día ~** the next *o* the following day; **el jueves ~** the following Thursday 2 (en secuencia) next; **en el capítulo ~** in the next *o* following chapter 3 (*como n*): **¡(que pase) el ~!** next please!; **este jueves no, ¿qué tal el ~?** not this Thursday, how about next Thursday?
B (que se va a nombrar) following (*before n*); **con los ~s jugadores** with the following players

sílaba *f* syllable

silabear [A1] *vt* pronounce ... syllable by syllable

silábico -ca *adj* syllabic

silbante *adj* (que silba) whistling (*before n*); **su respiración ~** his wheezing

silbar [A1] *vt* 1 ‹*melodía*› to whistle 2 ‹*cantante/obra*› (en señal de desaprobación) to whistle at, catcall
■ **silbar** *vi* 1 (Mús) to whistle 2 «*viento*» to whistle; **la bala pasó silbando** the bullet whistled past 3 «*oídos*»: **me silban los oídos** I've got a ringing *o* whistling in my ears

silbato *m* 1 (pito) whistle; **tocar el ~** to blow the whistle 2 (Col period) (árbitro) referee

silbido *m* 1 (con la boca, un silbato) whistle; **dio un ~** he whistled 2 (del viento) whistling; (de respiración) wheezing; **el ~ de las balas** the whistling of the bullets 3 (en los oídos) ringing, whistling 4 **~s** (en señal de desaprobacion) catcalls

silenciador *m* 1 (Auto) muffler (AmE), silencer (BrE) 2 (de arma) silencer

silenciar [A1] *vt* 1 ‹*persona/opinión/prensa*› to silence 2 (period) ‹*suceso*› to keep ... secret, hush up (colloq) 3 ‹*motor*› to muffle (AmE), to silence (BrE), to fit a muffler *o* silencer to 4 ‹*pistola*› to silence, fit a silencer to

silencio *m*
A 1 (ausencia de ruido) silence; **se hizo un ~ sepulcral** there was a deathly silence; **se guardó un minuto de ~** there was a minute's silence; **deben guardar ~** you must remain silent; **¡qué ~ hay!** isn't it quiet?; Ⓢ **silencio, hospital** quiet, hospital; **en el ~ más absoluto** in dead *o* total silence; **el ~ de la noche** the silence *o* quiet of the night 2 (ausencia de declaraciones) silence
B (Mús) rest

silencioso -sa *adj*
A ‹*máquina/motor*› quiet, silent, noiseless; ‹*persona*› silent, quiet
B ‹*calle/barrio*› quiet

sílex *m* (*pl* ~) silex, flint

sílfide *f* sylph; **es una ~** (liter *o* hum) she has a sylphlike figure (liter *or* hum)

silicato *m* silicate

sílice *f* silica

silicio *m* silicon

silicona *f* silicone

silicosis *f* silicosis

silla *f* 1 (mueble) chair 2 (Equ) *tb* **~ de montar** saddle

Compuestos
- **silla abuelita** (AmC) *or* (AmL) **de hamaca** rocking chair
- **silla de ruedas** wheelchair
- **silla eléctrica** electric chair
- **silla giratoria** swivel chair
- **silla plegable** *or* **de tijera** folding chair
- **silla presidencial** (Ven): **la ~ ~** the Presidency

sillar *m*
A (Const) ashlar
B (Equ) back

sillería *f*
A 1 (de salón, comedor) chairs (*pl*) 2 (del coro) stalls (*pl*) 3 (taller) chairmaker's workshop
B (Arquit, Const) masonry

sillín *m* (de bicicleta) saddle

sillón *m* armchair, easy chair

silo *m* silo

silogismo *m* syllogism

silueta *f* 1 (cuerpo) figure; **tenía una ~ perfecta** she had a perfect figure 2 (contorno) silhouette; **en el horizonte se recortaba la ~ de un velero** a sailing boat was silhouetted against the horizon 3 (Art) silhouette

silvestre *adj* ‹*flor/fruta*› wild

silvicultura *f* forestry, silviculture (frml)

sima *f*
A (grieta) sink, sinkhole, pothole; (cueva) pothole, cave; (abismo) chasm, pit
B (roca) sima, mantle

simbiosis *f* symbiosis

simbiótico -ca *adj* symbiotic

simbólico -ca *adj* symbolic; **un paro ~** a token strike

S

simbolismo *m* (Art, Lit) symbolism; (movimiento) Symbolism

simbolista *adj/mf* symbolist

simbolizar [A4] *vt* to symbolize, represent

símbolo *m* symbol

simbología *f* symbols (*pl*), system of symbols, symbology (frml)

simetría *f* symmetry; **plano/eje de ~** plane/axis of symmetry

simétrico -ca *adj* symmetric, symmetrical

simiente *f* (en algunas regiones: liter) seed

símil *m* 1 (comparación) comparison; **establecer** *or* **hacer un ~** to draw *o* make a comparison 2 (Lit) simile

similar *adj* similar; **~ A algo** similar TO sth

similitud *f* similarity, resemblance

simio *m* ape, simian (tech)

simonía *f* simony

simpatía *f*

A 1 (de una persona) friendliness; **los conquistó a todos con su ~** she won everyone over with her warm, friendly personality 2 (sentimiento): **se ganó** *or* **granjeó la(s) ~(s) de todos** everyone came to like him; **no le tengo mucha ~** I don't really like him

B (Fís, Med) sympathy

C **simpatías** *fpl* (Pol) sympathies (*pl*); **~s POR algo**: **sus ~s por la izquierda** her left-wing sympathies

simpático -ca *adj* 1 ‹*persona*› nice; **me cae** *or* **me resulta muy ~** I really like him, I think he's really nice; **es un hombre de lo más ~** he's a very nice *o* pleasant man; **estuvo de lo más ~** he was extremely nice *o* pleasant 2 ‹*gesto/detalle*› nice, lovely 3 ‹*ambiente*› pleasant, congenial; ‹*paseo*› pleasant, delightful, nice

simpatizante *mf*: **un ~ del partido comunista** a communist party sympathizer *o* supporter; **es ~ de la extrema derecha** he has extreme right-wing sympathies

simpatizar [A4] *vi* 1 (caerse bien): **~ CON algn** to get on well WITH sb; **la persona con quien más simpatizaba** the person I got on best with; **~on desde el primer momento** they took to each other right from the start 2 (sentir simpatía) **~ CON algn** to like sb 3 (Pol) **~ CON algo** to be sympathetic TO sth, to sympathize WITH sth

simple[1] *adj*

A 1 (sencillo, fácil) ‹*sistema/procedimiento*› simple; **no puede ser más ~** it couldn't be (any) simpler *o* more straightforward; ▸**llanamente** 2 (Quím) ‹*sustancia*› simple 3 (Ling) ‹*tiempo*› simple

B (*delante del n*) (mero) simple; **es un ~ resfriado** it's just a common cold; **un ~ soldado** an ordinary soldier

C (tonto) simple, simple-minded; **no seas ~** don't be silly

simple[2] *mf* simpleton

simplemente *adv* just, simply; **~ hay que extremar las precauciones** it's simply a question of taking better precautions; **dile, ~, que no vas a poder ir** just *o* simply tell him you won't be able to go

simpleza *f* 1 (falta de inteligencia) simpleness; (ingenuidad) gullibility 2 (tontería): **deja de hacer/decir ~s** stop being silly; (insignificancia): **no voy a discutir por esa ~** I'm not going to argue over such a trifling matter

simplicidad *f* simplicity; **es de una ~ impresionante** it's amazingly simple *o* straightforward

simplificación *f* simplification

simplificar [A2] *vt* to simplify

simplismo *m* oversimplification

simplista *adj* simplistic

simplón[1] **-plona** *adj* (fam) gullible, dumb (colloq)

simplón[2] **-plona** *m,f* (fam) dope (colloq); gullible fool

simposio, simposium *m* symposium

simulación *f* simulation

simulacro *m* 1 (cosa fingida): **no era de verdad, sólo fue un ~** it wasn't for real, they (*o* he *etc*) were (*o* was *etc*) just pretending 2 (farsa) sham; **las elecciones fueron un ~** the elections were just a sham

(Compuestos)

- **simulacro de ataque/combate** mock attack/battle
- **simulacro de incendio** fire drill, fire practice

simulador *m* simulator

(Compuesto) **simulador de vuelo** flight simulator

simular [A1] *vt* ‹*sentimiento*› to feign; ‹*accidente*› to fake; ‹*efecto/sonido*› to simulate

simultánea *f*

A (en ajedrez) simultaneous match

A (Espec): **en ~** (AmL) simultaneously

simultáneamente *adv* simultaneously

simultanear [A1] *vt*: **quiere ~ sus estudios con un trabajo** he wants to get a job and go on studying at the same time; **es imposible ~ los dos cargos** it is impossible to hold *o* do both jobs at the same time

simultaneidad *f* simultaneity; **con ~** simultaneously

simultáneo -nea *adj* simultaneous

sin *prep*

A without; **lo tomo ~ azúcar** I don't take sugar; **seguimos ~ noticias** we still haven't had any news; **~ previo aviso** with no advance warning; **¡salta! ¡~ miedo!** jump! don't be scared!; **agua mineral ~ gas** still mineral water; **cerveza ~ alcohol** non-alcoholic beer, alcohol-free beer; **una pareja ~ hijos** a couple with no children, a childless couple; **me quedé ~ pan** I ran out of bread; **se quedó ~ trabajo** he lost his job

B 1 **~ + INF** (con significado activo) without -ING; **se fue sin pagar** he left without paying; **son diez ~ contar éstos** there are ten not counting these (ones); **estuvo una semana ~ hablarme** she didn't speak to me for a week; **sigo ~ entender** I still don't understand; **la pisé ~ querer** I accidentally trod on her foot; **a la cama ~ cenar** off to bed without dinner 2 **~ + INF** (con significado pasivo): **preguntas ~ contestar** unanswered questions; **esto está aún ~ terminar** it still isn't finished

C **~ QUE + SUBJ**: **no voy a ir ~ que me inviten** I'm not going if I haven't been invited; **quítaselo ~ que se dé cuenta** get it off him without his *o* without him noticing

sinagoga *f* synagogue

sinalefa *f* synaloepha, elision

sinceramente *adv* ‹*hablar*› sincerely; **~, me parece un disparate** (*indep*) to be honest, I think it's crazy

sincerarse [A1] *v pron* **~ CON algn** to open one's heart TO sb

sinceridad *f* sincerity; **te voy a contestar con toda ~** I'm going to be quite honest *o* frank with you; **con toda ~ no te lo recomendaría** in all honesty *o* sincerity I wouldn't recommend him

sincero -ra *adj* sincere

síncopa *f* (Ling) syncope; (Mús) syncopation

sincopar [A1] *vt* to syncopate

síncope *m*

A (Med) syncope; **casi me da un ~** (fam) I nearly fainted (colloq)

B (Ling) syncope

sincronía *f* synchrony

sincrónico -ca *adj* 1 ‹*sucesos*› simultaneous, synchronous 2 (Ling) synchronic

sincronismo *m* sychronism

sincronización *f* synchronization

sincronizar [A4] *vt* 1 ‹*frecuencias/relojes*› to synchronize; **~ algo CON algo** to synchronize sth WITH sth 2 (Col) ‹*carro*› to tune

sindicación *f*

A (esp Esp) (Rels Labs) unionization

B (Fin) syndication

C (AmL frml) (acusación) accusation, charge

sindicado -da *m,f* (AmL frml) defendant, accused

sindical *adj* union (*before n*), labor union (*before n*) (AmE), trade union (*before n*) (BrE)

sindicalismo *m* 1 (movimiento) labor union movement (AmE), trade union movement (BrE) 2 (sistema, ideología) unionism, trade unionism (BrE) 3 (doctrina) *tb* **~ revolucionario** syndicalism

sindicalista[1] *adj* ‹*teoría*› syndicalist

sindicalista[2] *mf* 1 (Rels Labs) member of the unions, trade unionist (BrE) 2 (Pol) syndicalist

sindicalización *f* unionization

sindicalizar [A4] *vt* to unionize

■ **sindicalizarse** *v pron* (formar un sindicato) to unionize,

S

form a union; (afiliarse a un sindicato) to join a union

sindicar [A2] *vt*

A (Rels Labs) ▸**sindicalizar**

B (AmL frml) (acusar) ~ **a algn DE algo** to accuse sb OF sth; (formalmente) to charge sb WITH sth

■ **sindicarse** *v pron*

A (Rels Labs) ▸**sindicalizarse**

B (Fin) to form a syndicate

sindicato *m*

A (Rels Labs) union, labor union (AmE), trade union (BrE)

B (Fin) syndicate

síndico *m* trustee; (de quiebras) receiver

síndrome *m* syndrome

Compuestos

- **síndrome de abstinencia** withdrawal symptoms (*pl*)
- **síndrome de inmunodeficiencia adquirida** Acquired Immune Deficiency Syndrome, AIDS
- **síndrome del shoc tóxico** toxic shock syndrome
- **síndrome de muerte infantil súbita** sudden infant death syndrome
- **síndrome premenstrual**: **el ~ ~** premenstrual syndrome *o* (BrE) tension, PMS, PMT (BrE)

sinfín *m*: **un ~ de** a great many; **hemos tenido un ~ de problemas** we've had no end of problems

sinfonía *f* symphony

sinfónica *f* symphony orchestra

sinfónico -ca *adj* ‹*música*› symphonic; ‹*orquesta*› symphony (*before n*)

Singapur *m* Singapore

singladura *f* 1 (Náut) (jornada) nautical day; (recorrido) day's run 2 (de persona, partido, país): **su ~ como coreógrafa** her career as a choreographer; **la larga ~ hacia la recuperación** the long road to recovery

single /'siŋgel/ *m*

A (Mús) single

B (en tenis) 1 (CS) (partido) singles (match) 2 **singles** *mpl* (AmL) (partido) singles (match)

singular[1] *adj*

A 1 (frml) (extraordinario, especial) singular (frml); **un cuadro de ~ colorido** a singularly colorful picture 2 (peculiar, raro) peculiar, odd 3 (frml) (excepcionalmente bueno) singularly good (frml)

B (Ling) singular

singular[2] *m* singular; **en ~** (Ling) in the singular

singularidad *f* (cualidad de especial) special nature, singularity (frml); (rareza, peculiaridad) peculiarity, singularity (frml)

singularizar [A4] *vt* (frml) to make … special

■ **singularizarse** *v pron* (frml) (por una acción) to distinguish oneself

siniestrado -da *adj* (frml): **los restos del avión ~** the wreckage of the airplane; **los vehículos ~s** the vehicles involved in the accident *o* crash

siniestro[1] **-tra** *adj*

A (liter) ‹*mano/lado*› left (*before n*)

B ‹*mirada/aspecto*› sinister; ‹*intenciones*› sinister, evil

siniestro[2] *m* (frml) (accidente) accident; (causado por una fuerza natural) disaster, catastrophe; **el coche fue declarado ~ total** the car was declared a total wreck (AmE) *o* (BrE) a write-off

sinnúmero *m* ▸**sinfín**

sino[1] *conj* 1 (corrigiendo una impresión errónea): **se comió no uno, ~ tres** he ate not one, but three; **no vino, ~ que llamó** he didn't come, he telephoned; **no nos ayudó, ~ todo lo contrario, …** he didn't help us, on the contrary *o* quite the opposite, … 2 (nada más que): **en toda la tarde no ha entrado ~ un cliente** in the whole of the afternoon we've only had one customer; **no hace ~ criticar a los demás** he does nothing but criticize everybody else 3 **no sólo … sino que** not only … but; **no sólo baila ~ que también canta** she not only sings but she also dances

sino[2] *m* (liter) fate

sínodo *m* synod

sinonimia *f* synonymity, synonymy

sinónimo[1] **-ma** *adj* synonymous; **~ DE algo** synonymous WITH sth

sinónimo[2] *m* synonym; **~ DE algo** synonym FOR sth

sinopsis *f* (*pl* ~)

A (resumen) synopsis

B (CS) (Cin) preview, trailer

sinóptico -ca *adj* synoptic

sinrazón *f* injustice, wrong

sinsabores *mpl* (problemas) troubles (*pl*); (experiencias tristes) heartaches (*pl*), upsetting experiences (*pl*)

sinsonte *m* mockingbird

sintáctico -ca *adj* syntactic

sintagma *m* syntagm, syntagma

Compuesto **sintagma nominal** noun phrase

sintaxis *f* syntax

síntesis *f* (*pl* ~)

A 1 (resumen) summary; **hacer una ~ de algo** to summarize sth; **en ~** in short 2 (deducción) synthesis

B (Fil, Quím) synthesis; (combinación) synthesis, combination

sintético -ca *adj*

A ‹*fibra*› synthetic, man-made; ‹*suelas*› man-made

B ‹*análisis/explicación*› synthetic

sintetizador *m* synthesizer

sintetizar [A4] *vt*

A 1 (resumir) to summarize 2 (combinar) to synthesize, combine

B (Fil, Quím) to synthesize

sintiera, sintió, etc *see* **sentir**

síntoma *m* (Med) symptom; (señal) sign, indication

sintomático -ca *adj* symptomatic

sintonía *f* 1 (Rad, TV): **botón de ~** tuning knob; **están ustedes en la ~ de Radio Victoria** you are listening to Radio Victoria; **para una mejor ~** for better reception; **la música de ~** the theme music *o* tune 2 (audiencia): **un programa de mucha ~** a popular program 3 (armonía): **en ~ con el pueblo** in tune with the people

sintonización *f* (Rad, TV) tuning

sintonizador *m* tuner

sintonizar [A4] *vt* ‹*emisora*› to tune (in) to

■ **sintonizar** *vi* 1 (Rad, TV) to tune in; **~ con una emisora** to tune in to a station 2 (con persona, idea): **un político que sintoniza con la sensibilidad popular** a politician who is in tune with people's feelings

sinuosidad *f* (liter) 1 (de camino) sinuosity (liter) 2 (de intenciones, conducta) deviousness

sinuoso -sa *adj* (liter) 1 ‹*camino/carretera*› winding, sinuous (liter) 2 ‹*personalidad/conducta*› devious

sinusitis *f* sinusitis

sinvergüenza[1] *adj* 1 (canalla): **¡qué tipo más ~!** what a swine! (colloq) 2 (hum) (pícaro) naughty

sinvergüenza[2] *mf* 1 (canalla) swine (colloq), scoundrel (dated); (estafador, ladrón) crook (colloq) 2 (hum) (pícaro) rascal (hum), little devil *o* rascal (hum)

sionismo *m* Zionism

sionista *adj/mf* Zionist

síper *m* (Méx) zipper (AmE), zip (BrE)

siquiera[1] *adv*

A (por lo menos) at least; **dile ~ adiós** at least say goodbye to her; **¡si (tan) ~ me hubiera avisado …!** if only you'd warned me …!; **dale (tan) ~ unos centavos** give him something, even if it's only a few cents

B (en frases negativas) even; **ni ~ nos saludó** he didn't even say hello to us

siquiera[2] *conj* **~ + SUBJ** even if; **que descanse ~ sea una hora** let him rest even if it's only for an hour

sirena *f*

A (Mit) mermaid; (en mitología clásica) siren

B (de fábrica, ambulancia, alarma) siren

C (Col) (en pirotecnia) rocket

Siria *f* Syria

sirio -ria *adj/m,f* Syrian

siroco *m* sirocco

sirope *m* syrup

sirviente -ta (*m*) servant; (*f*) maid, servant; **los ~s** the servants

sisa *f*

A (en ropa) armhole

B (Esp fam) (acción de robar) pilfering, petty thieving; (robo individual) petty theft

S

sisar [A1] *vt* (Esp fam): **me sisaba unas pesos en la compra** she used to diddle me out of a few pesos from the shopping money

sisear [A1] *vi* to hiss

siseo *m* hiss

sísmico -ca *adj* seismic

sismo *m* (terremoto) earthquake; (temblor) earth tremor

sismografía *f* seismography

sismógrafo *m* seismograph

sistema *m*
A (método) system; **trabajar con ~** to work systematically *o* methodically; **por ~** as a matter of course
B (conjunto organizado) system; **el ~ educativo/impositivo** the education/tax system

(Compuestos)
- **sistema métrico decimal** metric system
- **sistema montañoso** mountain range
- **sistema nervioso** nervous system
- **sistema operativo de disco** disk operating system
- **sistema solar** solar system

sistemático -ca *adj* ‹*persona*› systematic, methodical; ‹*método*› systematic

sistematizar [A4] *vt* to systematize

sitial *m* seat *o* place of honor*

sitiar [A1] *vt* 1 (Mil) to besiege; **estamos sitiados** we are under siege 2 (acorralar) to corner

sitio *m*
A 1 (lugar) place; **pon ese libro en su ~** put that book back in its place; **cambié la tele de ~** you moved the TV; **déjalo en cualquier ~** leave it anywhere; **tiene que estar en algún ~** it must be around somewhere; ***en el ~*** (Esp fam) dead; **lo dejaron en el ~ de un balazo** they shot him dead; **le dio un infarto y se quedó en el ~** he dropped dead of a heart attack; ***poner a algn en su ~*** (fam) to put sb in his/her place 2 (espacio) room, space; **¿hay ~ para todos?** Is there (enough) room for everyone?; ***hacer ~*** to make room 3 (plaza, asiento): **guárdame el ~** keep my seat *o* place; **le cambié el ~** I changed places with him; **déjale el ~ a esa señora** let the lady sit down; **no hay ~ para estacionarse** there's nowhere to park 4 (Méx) (parada de taxis) taxi stand *o* rank 5 (Chi) (terreno urbano) vacant lot
B (Mil) siege; **levantar el ~** to raise *o* lift the siege; **poner ~ a una ciudad** to lay siege to a city, to besiege a city

sito -ta *adj* (frml) situated (frml), located (frml)

situación *f*
A 1 (coyuntura) situation; **no está en ~ de poder ayudarnos** she is not in a position to be able to help us; ***salvar la ~*** to save the day 2 (en la sociedad) position, standing
B (emplazamiento) position, situation (frml), location (frml); **la ~ del local es excelente** the premises are ideally situated *o* located

situado -da *adj* 1 (ubicado) situated; **está ~ al oeste del río** it lies *o* is situated to the west of the river 2 ‹*persona*›: **estar bien ~** to have a good position in society

situar [A18] *vt*
A 1 (colocar, ubicar) ‹*fábrica/aeropuerto*› to site, to locate (frml); **esta novela la sitúa entre los grandes de la literatura** this novel places her among the greatest writers 2 (Lit) ‹*obra/acción*› to set 3 ‹*soldados*› to post, station
B (Fin) to invest, place
■ **situarse** *v pron*
A 1 (colocarse, ubicarse): **con esta victoria se sitúan en primer lugar** this victory puts them in first place; **ha logrado ~se entre los cinco mejores** she has succeeded in establishing a position for herself among the top five 2 (socialmente): **se ha situado muy bien** he has done very well for himself
B (frml) (cifrarse): **la tasa de desempleo se sitúa en un 22%** unemployment stands at 22%; **el precio podría llegar a ~se en 20 dólares** the price could reach 20 dollars

siútico -ca *adj/m,f* (Chi) ▸**cursi**

skai®, **skay**® /(e)s'kai/ *m* imitation leather

skin
A (de cabeza rapada) (fam) skinhead
B (Inf) skin

S.L. *f* = **Sociedad Limitada**

slalom /(e)s'lalom/ *m* (*pl* **-loms**) slalom

(Compuesto) **slalom gigante** giant slalom

slip /(e)s'lip/ (*pl* **slips**) *m*
A (prenda interior) 1 (de hombre) underpants (*pl*), briefs (*pl*) (frml), pants (*pl*) (BrE) 2 (de mujer) panties (*pl*), briefs (*pl*) (frml), knickers (*pl*) (BrE)
B (bañador) swimming trunks (*pl*)

s.m. = **siglo** C; **s. XX** C20

S.M. = **Su Majestad**

SMIS *m* (= **síndrome de muerte infantil súbita**) SIDS

smog /(e)s'moɣ/ *m* (AmL) smog

SMS *m* text message, SMS

s/n = **sin número**

s.n.m. = **sobre el nivel de mar**

snob /(e)s'noβ/ *adj/mf* (*pl* **snobs**) ▸**esnob**[1,2]

so[1] *prep*: **~ pena de ser expulsado/de muerte** on pain of expulsion/of death (frml); **~ pretexto de ...** (frml) under the pretext of ...

so[2] *interj* 1 (para detener a un caballo) whoa! 2 (*delante del n*) (intensificando un insulto): **¡~ animal!** you great *o* big brute!

s/o = **su orden**

SO (= **sudoeste**) SW

soba *f* (fam) beating (colloq), walloping (colloq)

sobaco *m* armpit

sobado -da *adj* 1 ‹*tapizado/cortinas/prenda*› worn, shabby; ‹*libro*› dog-eared, well-thumbed 2 ‹*excusa*› well-worn; ‹*cliché*› hackneyed, well-worn

sobajear [A1] *vt* (AmL fam) ▸**sobar A1, 2**

sobaquera *f*
A (Indum) (sisa) armhole; (para proteger la prenda) dress shield
B (arg) (para pistola) shoulder holster

sobar [A1] *vt*
A 1 (manosear) ‹*tela/ropa/tapizado*› to handle, finger, dirty (*through excessive handling*) 2 (fam) ‹*chica*› to feel up (colloq), to grope (esp BrE colloq) 3 (Méx, Per fam) (adular) to suck up to (colloq)
B (Col, Ven) (dar masajes) to massage
■ **sobar** *vi* (Esp fam) to sleep

soberanamente *adv*: **aburrirse ~** to be bored to death *o* tears

soberanía *f* sovereignty

soberano[1] **-na** *adj*
A ‹*estado/pueblo/poder*› sovereign
B (fam) (enorme) tremendous; **eso es una soberana estupidez** that's an absolutely ridiculous thing to say/do

soberano[2] **-na** *m,f* (Gob, Pol) sovereign

soberano[3] *m* (moneda) sovereign

soberbia *f* (orgullo) pride; (altivez) arrogance, haughtiness

soberbio -bia *adj*
A ‹*persona/carácter*› (orgulloso) proud; (altivo) arrogant, haughty
B (magnífico) superb, magnificent

sobornar [A1] *vt* to bribe, suborn (frml)

soborno *m* (acción) bribery; (dinero, regalo) bribe

sobra *f*
A **de sobra** 1 (mucho): **hay comida de ~** there's plenty of food; **tiene dinero de ~** he has plenty of money; **tengo motivos de ~ para pensarlo** I have every reason to think so 2 (de más): **tengo una entrada de ~** I have a spare *o* an extra ticket; ***estar de ~***: **tú aquí estás de ~** you're not wanted/needed here 3 (muy bien): **saber de ~ que ...** to know full well *o* perfectly well that ...
B **sobras** *fpl* (de comida) leftovers (*pl*)

sobradamente *adv*: **ayer hablamos ~ de esto** we went through all this yesterday in detail; **es ~ conocido que ...** it is common knowledge that ...; **sabes ~ que ...** you know perfectly well *o* full well that ...

sobrado[1] **-da** *adj*
A 1 ‹*experiencia*›: ample, more than enough; **un escritor con ~s méritos para el premio** a writer who is more than worthy of the prize; **tengo ~s motivos para sospechar** I have every reason to be suspicious 2 [ESTAR] ‹*persona*› **~ DE algo**: **está sobrada de dinero** she has plenty of money; **no ando muy ~ de dinero** I'm a bit short of money at the moment; **no estoy muy ~ de tiempo** I'm a bit short of time
B (Andes fam) (engreído) full of oneself (colloq)

S

sobrado² *adv* (Andes): **llegó ~ a la meta** he crossed the finishing line well ahead of the rest; **lo sé ~** I know that only too well

sobrado³ -da *m,f* (Andes fam) bighead (colloq)

sobrados *mpl* (Col, Ven fam) (sobras) leftovers (*pl*)

sobrante¹ *adj* remaining; **el material ~** the spare *o* surplus material; **con la masa de pan ~** with the leftover dough

sobrante² *m* remainder, surplus

sobrar [A1] *vi* 1 (quedar, restar): **sobró mucha comida** there was a lot of food left over; **¿te ha sobrado dinero?** do you have any money left?; **no me sobra el tiempo** I don't have all that much time 2 (estar de más): **ya veo que sobro** I can see I'm not wanted/needed here; **a mí no me sobra el dinero** I don't have money to burn (colloq); **sobra un cubierto** there's an extra place; ***salir sobrando*** (Méx) to be superfluous *o* unnecessary

sobrasada *f*: *spicy pork sausage*

sobre¹ *m*

A 1 (Corresp) envelope; **~ aéreo** *or* **(de) vía aérea** airmail envelope 2 (envase): **un ~ de sopa** a package of soup (AmE), a packet of soup (BrE)

B (AmL) (cartera) clutch bag

sobre² *prep*

A (indicando posición) 1 (con contacto): **lo dejé ~ la mesa** I left it on the table; **los puso uno ~ otro** she placed them one on top of the other; **letras en azul ~ (un) fondo blanco** blue letters on *o* upon a white background; **prestar juramento ~ la Biblia** to swear on the Bible; **se abalanzaron ~ él** they leapt on him; **estamos ~ su pista** we're on their trail 2 (sin contacto) over; **en el techo justo ~ la mesa** on the ceiling right above *o* over the table; **4.000 metros ~ el nivel del mar** 4,000 meters above sea level; ***estar ~ algn*** (vigilar) to check up on sb 3 (alrededor de) on; **gira ~ su eje** it spins on its axis

B (en relaciones de jerarquía): **su victoria ~ el equipo local** their victory over the local team; **amar a Dios ~ todas las cosas** to love God above all else

C 1 (en relaciones de efecto, derivación, etc) on; **su influencia ~ él** her influence on him; **una opereta ~ libreto de Sierra** an operetta with libretto by Sierra 2 (Com, Fin) on; **un incremento del 11% ~ los precios del año pasado** an increase of 11% on *o* over last year's prices; **la hipoteca que pesa ~ la casa** the mortgage on the house

D (acerca de) on; **legislación ~ impuestos** tax legislation, legislation on taxes; **escribió ~ el espinoso tema de …** she wrote on *o* about the thorny topic of …

E (Esp) (con cantidades, fechas, horas) around, about (BrE); **~ unos 70 kilos** around *o* about 70 kilos

F **sobre todo** above all

sobreabundancia *f* superabundance, overabundance

sobreabundante *adj* superabundant, overabundant

sobreactuar [A18] *vi/vt* to overact

sobrealimentación *f* (de persona) overfeeding; (de motor) supercharging

sobrealimentar [A1] *vt* ‹*persona*› to overfeed; ‹*motor*› to supercharge

sobrecalentar [A5] *vt* to overheat

sobrecama *f or m* (AmL exc CS) bedspread, counterpane

sobrecarga *f* 1 (en vehículo) excess load *o* weight 2 (de circuito, motor) overload; (de batería) overcharging

sobrecargado -da *adj* 1 ‹*vehículo*› overloaded 2 ‹*circuito*› overloaded 3 ‹*persona*› **~ DE algo** ‹*de trabajo*› overburdened WITH sth; ‹*de deudas*› weighed down WITH sth

sobrecargar [A3] *vt* 1 ‹*vehículo/animal*› to overload 2 ‹*circuito/motor*› to overload; ‹*batería*› to overcharge; ‹*órgano*› to overtax; **las líneas telefónicas están sobrecargadas** the lines are all jammed 3 ‹*persona*› **~ a algn DE algo** ‹*de trabajo/responsabilidad*› to overburden sb WITH sth

sobrecargo *mf* 1 (Aviac) (supervisor) purser, chief flight attendant; (auxiliar de vuelo) flight attendant 2 (Náut) purser

sobrecogedor -dora *adj* shocking, horrific

sobrecoger [E6] *vt* 1 (conmover) to move 2 (asustar) to strike fear into

■ **sobrecogerse** *v pron* 1 (conmoverse) to be moved 2 (asustarse) to be terrified

sobrecubierta *f* dust jacket, dustcover

sobredorar [A1] *vt* to gild, gold plate

sobredosis *f* (*pl* ~) overdose

sobreentender [E8] *vt*: **no lo dijeron, pero quedó sobreentendido** they didn't say so, but it was implied *o* understood; **se sobreentiende que lo tendrá que pagar** it goes without saying that he will have to pay for it

sobreestimar [A1] *vt* to overestimate

sobregirado -da *adj* (esp AmL) overdrawn; **su cuenta está sobregirada en** *or* (Méx) **por 4.000 pesos** she is 4,000 pesos overdrawn

sobregirar [A1] *vt* (esp AmL) to overdraw (on)

■ **sobregirarse** *v pron* to overdraw; **se sobregiró en** *or* (Méx) **por $1.000** he overdrew by $1,000

sobregiro *m* (esp AmL) overdraft

sobrehumano -na *adj* superhuman

sobrellevar [A1] *vt* ‹*dolor/enfermedad*› to endure, bear; ‹*tragedia*› to bear; ‹*soledad*› to endure

sobremanera *adv* (frml) exceedingly (frml); **me molesta ~** I find it really annoying

sobremesa *f* 1 (período): **se emitirá en la ~** it will be shown in the afternoon slot; **programación de ~** afternoon viewing 2 (conversación) after-lunch/after-dinner conversation; **estuvimos de ~** we sat around the table chatting

sobrenatural *adj* supernatural; **lo ~** the supernatural

sobrenombre *m* nickname, sobriquet (frml)

sobrepasar [A1] *vt* 1 ‹*nivel/cantidad*› to exceed, go above; **~ el límite de velocidad** to exceed *o* go over *o* break the speed limit; **sobrepasó el tiempo permitido en 2 segundos** she went over *o* exceeded the time allowed by 2 seconds 2 ‹*persona*› (en capacidad) to outstrip; (en altura) to overtake 3 (Aviac) ‹*pista*› to overshoot

■ **sobrepasarse** *v pron* 1 (excederse): **me sobrepasé en los gastos** I overspent; **no te vayas a ~ con el vino** go easy with the wine 2 (propasarse) to go too far

sobrepelliz *f* surplice

sobrepeso *m* 1 (AmL) (exceso — de equipaje) excess (baggage); (— de carga) excess load *o* weight 2 (Chi, Méx) (de persona): **tiene un ~ de 7 kilos** he's seven kilos overweight

sobreponer [E22] *vt* to superimpose

■ **sobreponerse** *v pron* (recuperarse) to pull oneself together; **~se A algo** to get over sth, recover FROM sth

sobreprecio *m* surcharge

sobreproducción *f* overproduction

sobrepuesto *pp*: *see* **sobreponer**

sobrepujar [A1] *vt* (en subasta) to outbid; (exceder) to outdo

sobresaliente¹ *adj* ‹*actuación*› outstanding; ‹*noticia/hecho*› most significant *o* important

sobresaliente² *m*

A (Educ) *grade between 8.5 and 10 on a scale of 10*

B **sobresaliente** *mf* (Taur) understudy, reserve bullfighter; (Teatr) understudy

sobresalir [I29] *vi* 1 «*alero/viga*» to project, overhang; **el borde sobresale unos tres centímetros** the edge protrudes about three centimeters 2 (ser más alto) to stand out 3 **~ EN algo** ‹*en deportes, idiomas*› to excel *o* shine AT sth; **sobresale por su talento musical** his talent for music sets him apart from the rest

sobresaltar [A1] *vt* to startle, make … jump

■ **sobresaltarse** *v pron* to jump, be startled

sobresalto *m* fright; **llevarse un ~** to get a fright

sobreseer [E13] *vt* to dismiss

sobreseimiento *m* dismissal

sobresueldo *m* supplementary wage

sobretasa *f* surcharge

sobretiempo *m* (Chi, Per) 1 (horas extra, pago) overtime 2 (Dep) overtime (AmE), extra time (BrE)

sobretodo *m* overcoat

sobrevenir [I31] *vi* «*desgracia/accidente*» to strike; **me sobrevino una extraña sensación** a strange feeling came over me; **le sobrevino la muerte** he was struck down

sobrevida *f* (CS) survival

sobrevivencia *f* survival
sobreviviente *adj/mf* ▸ **superviviente**
sobrevivir [I1] *vi* to survive; ~ **a algo** to survive sth
■ **sobrevivir** *vt* ‹*persona*› to outlive, survive
sobrevolar [A10] *vt* to fly over; (Mil) to fly over, overfly
sobriedad *f* (de persona) sobriety, moderation; (de estilo) sobriety, simplicity; **viste con** ~ she dresses simply
sobrino -na (*m*) nephew; (*f*) niece; **mis** ~**s** (sólo varones) my nephews; (varones y mujeres) my nephews and nieces
sobrio -bria *adj*
A [SER] [1] ‹*persona*› sober, restrained, moderate; ‹*hábitos*› frugal; **era** ~ **en la bebida** he drank in moderation [2] ‹*decoración/estilo/color*› sober
B [ESTAR] (no borracho) sober
sobros *mpl* (AmC) leftovers (*pl*)
soca *f*
A (Col, Méx) (de caña) ratoon; (de arroz) shoot; (tabaco) top leaf *o* shoot
B (AmC) (Mús) soca
socaire *m* (fam): **al** ~ **del promontorio** in the shelter of the headland; (Náut) in the lee of the headland; **al** ~ **de algn** under sb's wing, protected by sb
socarrar [A1] *vt* to burn
■ **socarrarse** *v pron* «*comida*» to burn; **se socarró las pestañas** she burned *o* singed her eyelashes
socarrón -rrona *adj* (sarcástico) sarcastic, snide; (taimado) sly, crafty
socarronería *f* sarcastic *o* snide humor*
sócate *m* (Ven) lampholder, socket
socavar [A1] *vt* to undermine
socavón *m* (hoyo) hole; (excavación) shaft, tunnel; (cueva) cave
sociabilidad *f* [1] (cualidad) sociability [2] (Ur) (vida social) socializing; **hacer** ~ to socialize
sociable *adj* sociable
social *adj*
A [1] ‹*problemas/clase/lucha*› social; **las reivindicaciones** ~**es de los trabajadores** the workers' demands for improvements in social conditions [2] ‹*reunión/compromiso*› social
B (Fin) company (*before n*)
socialdemocracia *f* social democracy
socialdemócrata[1] *adj* social democratic
socialdemócrata[2] *mf* social democrat
socialdemocrático -ca *adj* social democratic
sociales *fpl*
A (Esp fam) (Educ) social sciences (*pl*)
B (Col, Ven, RPl fam) (Period) society column/pages (*pl*)
socialismo *m* socialism
socialista *adj/mf* socialist
socializar [A4] *vt* to socialize
sociedad *f*
A (Sociol) society
(Compuestos)
• **sociedad de consumo** consumer society
• **Sociedad Protectora de Animales** Society for the Prevention of Cruelty to Animals
B (asociación, club) society; **una** ~ **secreta** a secret society; ~ **deportiva** sports club
C (Der, Fin) company
(Compuestos)
• **sociedad anónima** ≈ public corporation (*in US*), ≈ public limited company (*in UK*)
• **sociedad comanditaria** *or* **en comandita** limited partnership
• **sociedad de crédito hipotecario** ≈ savings and loan institution (*in US*), ≈ building society (*in UK*)
• **sociedad de responsabilidad limitada** ≈ limited corporation (*in US*), ≈ (private) limited company (*in UK*)
• **sociedad estatal** state corporation
• **sociedad inmobilaria** (Esp) (que construye) construction company; (que administra) real estate (AmE) *o* (BrE) property management company
• **sociedad mercantil** trading company
• **sociedad mixta** joint venture
D (clase alta) (high) society; **presentarse en** ~ to come out (*as a debutante*)

socio -cia *m,f*
A (miembro) member; **hacerse** ~ **de un club** to join a club
(Compuestos)
• **socio -cia de número** *m,f* full member
• **socio fundador -cia fundadora** *m,f* founding member, founder member
• **socio honorario -cia honoraria** *m,f* honorary member
B (Der, Fin) partner
(Compuestos)
• **socio -cia accionista** *m,f* shareholder
• **socio -cia capitalista** *m,f* silent partner (AmE), sleeping partner (BrE)
• **socio mayoritario -cia mayoritaria** *m,f* majority shareholder
C (fam) (camarada) buddy (AmE colloq), mate (BrE colloq)
sociocultural *adj* sociocultural
socioeconómico -ca *adj* socioeconomic
sociolingüística *f* sociolinguistics
sociología *f* sociology
sociológico -ca *adj* sociological
sociólogo -ga *m,f* sociologist
sociopolítico -ca *adj* sociopolitical
socorrer [E1] *vt* to help, come to the aid of
socorrido -da *adj* ‹*excusa/recurso*› handy, useful
socorrismo *m* (en el agua) lifesaving; (en la montaña) mountain rescue; (primeros auxilios) first aid
socorrista *mf* (en el agua) lifeguard, lifesaver; (en la montaña) mountain rescue worker; (de primeros auxilios) first-aider
socorro *m* help; **pedir** ~ to ask for help; **¡~!** help!; **acudir en** ~ **de algn** to come to sb's aid; **un grito de** ~ a cry for help
soda *f* [1] (bebida) soda water, soda (AmE) [2] (Quím) *tb* ~ **cáustica** caustic soda, sodium hydroxide [3] (AmC) (cafetería) coffee bar
sódico -ca *adj* sodium (*before n*); **cloruro** ~ sodium chloride
sodio *m* sodium
sodomía *f* sodomy
sodomita *mf* sodomite
soez *adj* rude, crude, coarse
sofá *m* sofa, settee, couch
sofá-cama *m* sofa bed
sófero -ra *adj* (Per fam) almighty (colloq), huge (colloq)
sofisma *m* sophism
sofisticación *f* sophistication
sofisticado -da *adj* sophisticated
soflama *f* harangue, fiery speech
soflamero -ra *adj* (Méx fam) melodramatic
sofocación *f* suffocation
sofocante *adj* ‹*calor/temperaturas*› suffocating, stifling; ‹*relación*› stifling
sofocar [A2] *vt* ‹*fuego*› to smother, put out; ‹*motín/revolución*› to stifle, put down
■ **sofocarse** *v pron* (acalorarse) to get upset *o* (colloq) worked up
sofoco *m* [1] (fam) (disgusto): **estaba con un** ~ **terrible** I was so upset [2] (por el calor) suffocation; (en la menopausia) hot flash (AmE), hot flush (BrE)
sofocón *m* (fam): **¡vaya ~!** it was terrible!; **¡se lleva cada** ~ **por nada!** he gets into a terrible state about nothing (colloq), he gets very upset about nothing
sofreír [I35] *vt* to sauté, fry lightly
sofrito *m*: *lightly fried tomatoes, onion, garlic, etc*
software /'sofwer/ *m* software
soga *f* (cuerda) rope; ***estar con la ~ al cuello*** to have one's back to the wall, be in a real fix (colloq)
sois *see* **ser**
soja *f* (Esp) soy (AmE), soya (BrE)
sojuzgar [A3] *vt* (frml) to subjugate (frml)
sol *m*
A [1] (Astron) sun; **al salir/ponerse el** ~ at sunrise/sunset [2] (Meteo) sun; **brillaba el** ~ the sun was shining; **ayer**

S

hizo *or* **hubo** ~ it was sunny yesterday; **a pleno** ~ in the sun; **un día de** ~ a sunny day; **en esa habitación no da el** ~ that room doesn't get any sunlight *o* sun; **sentémonos al** ~ let's sit in the sunshine; **ayer hubo siete horas de** ~ we had seven hours of sunshine yesterday; ***arrimarse al** ~ **que más calienta*** to keep in with the right people; ***de** ~ **a** ~* from morning to *o* till night; ***no dejar a algn ni a** ~ **ni a sombra***: **no la deja ni a** ~ **ni a sombra** he doesn't leave her alone for a minute; ***tomar el** ~* *or* (CS) ***tomar** ~* to sunbathe; ***un** ~ **de justicia*** a blazing sun **3** (Espec, Taur): **localidades de** ~ cheaper seats (*in the sun*)

(Compuesto) **sol naciente/poniente** rising/setting sun

B (fam) **1** (persona encantadora): **es un** ~ she's an angel (colloq) **2** (como apelativo cariñoso): **ven aquí,** ~ **mío** *or* **mi** ~ come here, sweetie *o* darling (colloq)

C (Mús) (nota) G; (en solfeo) so*, sol; ~ **bemol/sostenido** G flat/sharp; **en** ~ **mayor/menor** in G major/minor

D (moneda) sol (*Peruvian unit of currency*)

solamente *adv* ▸ **sólo**

solana *f* **1** (sol fuerte) strong sun; **¡qué** ~ **hace!** the sun is really strong **2** (de casa — galería) balcony; (— terraza) sun terrace; (lugar) sunny spot, suntrap

solapa *f* (de chaqueta) lapel; (de bolsillo, libro, sobre) flap

solapado -da *adj* ‹*persona*› sly, underhand (BrE); ‹*maniobra*› surreptitious, sly

solar[1] *adj* ‹*energía/año/placa*› solar; **los rayos** ~**es** the sun's rays

solar[2] *m*

A (terreno) piece of land, site

B **1** (casa solariega) ancestral home **2** (linaje) lineage

C (Per) (casa de vecindad) tenement building

D (Col, Ven) (patio) backyard

solariego -ga *adj* ancestral

solario, solárium *m* solarium

solaz *m* (liter) (consuelo) solace; (descanso) relaxation, repose

solazarse [A4] *v pron* (liter) to relax

soldadera *f* (Méx) camp follower

soldadesca *f* (pey) (soldados indisciplinados) violent/unruly soldiers (*pl*)

soldado *mf* soldier; ~ **de caballería** cavalryman; ~ **de infantería** infantryman; **alistarse como** ~ to enlist, to join up, to join the army; **el S**~ **Desconocido** the Unknown Soldier

(Compuestos)

- **soldado raso** private
- **soldado** *or* **soldadito de plomo** tin soldier

soldador -dora *m,f*

A (operario) welder

B (utensilio) **1** **soldador** *m* (para soldar con estaño) soldering iron **2** **soldadora** *f* (para soldar sin estaño) welder, welding equipment

soldadura *f* (Tec) **1** (acción — con estaño) soldering; (— sin estaño) welding **2** (efecto) (con estaño) solder; (sin estaño) weld

(Compuesto) **soldadura autógena** autogenous welding

soldar [A10] *vt* (con estaño) to solder; (sin estaño) to weld
■ **soldarse** *v pron* «*metales*» to weld

soleado -da *adj* sunny

solear [A1] *vt* to put ... out in the sun

solecismo *m* solecism

soledad *f*: **en la** ~ **de su cuarto** in the solitude of his room; **bebe para olvidar su** ~ she drinks to forget her loneliness; **no soporta la** ~ he can't stand being alone; **pasó sus últimos años en** ~ she spent her last years alone

solemne *adj*

A **1** ‹*acto*› formal, solemn; ‹*promesa*› solemn; ‹*tono*› solemn **2** (Der) ‹*contrato*› solemn

B (*delante del n*) (fam) ‹*mentira*› complete, downright; **una** ~ **estupidez** an extremely stupid remark

solemnidad *f*

A (cualidad) solemnity; ***de** ~* (fam) extremely, seriously (colloq); **son pobres de** ~ they are extremely poor

B (requisito — formal) formality, solemnity; (— legal) solemnity (tech), legal requirement

solenoide *m* solenoid

soler [E9] *vi* ~ + INF: **suele venir una vez a la semana** she usually comes once a week; **no suele retrasarse** he's not usually late; **lo que se suele olvidar es que ...** what tends to be forgotten is ...; **solía correr todos los días** he used to go for a run every day; **como suele decirse en estos casos ...** as is usually said in these cases ...; **es, como suele decirse, ...** it is, as they say, ...

solera *f*

A (tradición, calidad): **calles con mucha** ~ streets which have a lot of character; **una familia con** ~ a family with a long pedigree, a long-established family

B (CS) (Indum) sundress

C (Chi) (de la acera) curb (AmE), kerb (BrE)

D (Per) (sábana) undersheet

> **solera**
>
> A system of blending used in the production of fortified wines such as jerez. Only a quarter of a cask of mature wine is drawn off for bottling at any one time, and the cask is then topped up from a cask of younger wine of the same variety. This second cask is topped up with a third, younger wine, and so on up to the fourth cask

solfa *f* sol-fa (syllables); ***darle una** ~ **a algn*** (fam) to give someone a hiding (colloq); ***poner algo en** ~* (fam) (ridiculizar) to mock sth; (poner en duda) to call sth into question

solfear [A1] *vt* to sol-fa

solfeo *m* (asignatura) music theory, sol-fa

solicitado -da *adj* ‹*persona*› in demand; ‹*canción*› popular

solicitante *mf* applicant

(Compuesto) **solicitante de asilo** asylum seeker

solicitar [A1] *vt* ‹*empleo/plaza*› to apply for; ‹*permiso/entrevista/información*› to request, ask for; ‹*servicios/apoyo/cooperación*› to request, ask for; **la oposición solicitó su dimisión** the opposition called for his resignation; **solicite mayor información en nuestras oficinas** further information is available on request from our offices

solícito -ta *adj* (dispuesto a ayudar) attentive, solicitous (frml); (amable) thoughtful, kind; **se mostró muy** ~ he was very attentive *o* obliging

solicitud *f*

A **1** (para trabajo) application; (para licencia) application, request; (para información, ayuda) request; **presentar una** ~ to submit an application/a request; **denegar una** ~ (frml) to reject an application/a request; **recurrieron a la ONU en** ~ **de ayuda** they turned to the UN for help **2** (formulario) application form

B (preocupación) concern, solicitude (frml); (amabilidad) kindness, thoughtfulness

solidaridad *f* **1** solidarity; **en** *or* **por** ~ **con algn** in solidarity with *o* in sympathy with sb **2** (Der) joint and several liability

solidario -ria *adj* **1** (fraterno) supportive; **un gesto** ~ a gesture of solidarity; **recibió el apoyo** ~ **de sus compañeros** she received warm support from her colleagues **2** (Der) ‹*obligación*› binding on all parties; ‹*deudor*› jointly and severally liable

solidarizar [A4] *vi* ~ CON **algn** to support sb
■ **solidarizarse** *v pron* ~**se** CON **algn** to support sb; **se** ~**on con los mineros en huelga** they gave their support to the striking miners; ~**se** CON **algo** to support sth, to back sth

solidez *f* (de muro, edificio) solidity; (de argumento) soundness, solidness; (de empresa) soundness; (de relación) strength

solidificación *f* solidification

solidificarse [A2] *v pron* to solidify, harden

sólido[1] -da *adj*

A **1** ‹*estado/alimentos*› solid **2** ‹*muro/edificio*› solid; ‹*base*› solid, firm; ‹*mueble/zapatos*› solid, sturdy **3** ‹*terreno*› solid, hard **4** ‹*color*› fast

B **1** ‹*argumento/razonamiento*› solid, sound; ‹*preparación/principios*› sound **2** ‹*empresa*› sound; ‹*relación*› steady, strong

sólido[2] *m* **1** (Fís, Mat) solid **2** **sólidos** *mpl* (Med) solids (*pl*)

soliloquio *m* soliloquy

solista *mf* soloist

S

solitaria *f* tapeworm

solitario¹ -ria *adj* 1 ‹*persona/animal*› solitary; **lleva una vida muy solitaria** he leads a very solitary existence; **tuvo una niñez muy solitaria** she had a very lonely childhood; **canta en ~** he sings solo 2 ‹*calles*› empty, deserted; ‹*paraje/lugar*› lonely, solitary

solitario² -ria *m,f*
A (persona) loner, solitary (liter)
B **solitario** *m* 1 (Jueg) solitaire (AmE), patience (BrE); **hacer un ~** to play solitaire *o* patience 2 (diamante) solitaire

soliviantar [A1] *vt* ‹*tropas*› to incite ... to mutiny; ‹*masas/trabajadores*› to stir up, incite
■ **soliviantarse** *v pron* «*tropas*» to mutiny; «*masas/trabajadores*» to rebel, rise up

sollozar [A4] *vi* to sob

sollozo *m* sob; **prorrumpió en ~s** he began sobbing

solo¹ -la *adj* 1 (sin compañía): **estar/sentirse ~** to be/feel lonely; **no tiene amigos allí, está muy ~** he doesn't have any friends out there, he's all alone; **lo dejaron ~** (sin compañía) they left him on his own *o* by himself; (para no molestar) they left him alone; **el niño ya camina ~** the baby's walking on his own now; **¡qué bonito! ¿lo hiciste tú solito?** isn't that lovely! did you do it all by yourself?; **es mentirosa como ella sola** she's the biggest liar I know; **baila como ella sola** nobody dances like her; **hablar ~** to talk to oneself; **a solas** alone; ***quedarse más ~ que la una*** (fam & hum) to be left all by oneself; ***más vale (estar) ~ que mal acompañado*** it's better to be on your own than with people you don't like 2 ‹*café/té*› black; ‹*whisky*› straight, neat; ‹*pan*› dry 3 (*delante del n*) (único): **lo haré con una sola condición** I'll do it on one condition; **no puso ni una sola objeción** she didn't raise one *o* a single objection; **su sola presencia me molestaba** her very *o* mere presence upset me

solo² *m*
A (Mús) solo; **un ~ de violín** a violin solo
B (Esp) (café) black coffee

sólo *adv* [*The accented spelling remains the norm despite the Real Academica Española's recommended form* **solo**] only; **~ quería ayudarte** I only wanted to help, I was only *o* just trying to help; **~ quiero que me lo expliques** I just want you to explain it to me; **es ~ un momento** it will only take a moment; **¡pero si es ~ un niño!** but he's just *o* only a child!; **~ de pensarlo me dan escalofríos** just *o* merely thinking about it makes me shudder; **no ~ estudia sino que también trabaja** she isn't just studying, she's working as well; **~ con mencionar su nombre me dejaron pasar** I only had to mention his name and they let me through; **podríamos ir ~ que no tengo coche** we could go except that I don't have a car

solomillo *m* fillet/tenderloin/sirloin steak

solsticio *m* solstice; **~ de invierno/de verano** winter/summer solstice

soltar [A10] *vt*
A (dejar ir) to release; **~on varios toros en las fiestas** during the festivities they let several bulls loose in the streets; **soltó al perro** he let the dog off the leash; **le solté el perro** I set the dog on him
B (dejar de tener agarrado) to let go; **aguanta esto y no lo sueltes** hold this and don't let go of it; **soltó el dinero y huyó** he dropped/let go of the money and ran; **suéltame, que me haces daño** let (me) go *o* let go of me, you're hurting me; **no suelta un peso** you can't get a penny out of him; **¡suelta la pistola!** drop the gun!; **no pienso ~ este puesto** I've no intention of giving up this position
C 1 (desatar) ‹*cuerda/cable*› to undo, untie; **~ amarras** to cast off 2 (aflojar): **suelta la cuerda poco a poco** let *o* pay out the rope gradually 3 ‹*freno*› to release; ‹*embrague*› to let out 4 (desatascar) ‹*cable/cuerda*› to free; ‹*tuerca*› to ondo, get ... undone
D (desprender) ‹*calor/vapor*› to give off; ‹*pelo*› to shed; ‹*jugo*›: **cuando la carne ha soltado el jugo** when the juice has come out from the meat
E 1 ‹*carcajada*› to let out; ‹*palabrotas/disparates*› to come out with; ‹*grito*› to let out, give; **no soltó palabra** he didn't say *o* utter a word; **siempre suelta el mismo rollo** (fam) she always comes out with the same old stuff (colloq) 2 (dar) (+ *me/te/le etc*): **le solté un tortazo** I clobbered him (colloq)
F (fam) ‹*vientre*› (+ *me/te/le etc*): **te suelta el vientre** it loosens your bowels
■ **soltarse** *v pron*
A (*refl*) «*persona/animal*» (desasirse): **no te sueltes (de la mano)** don't let go of my hand; **el perro se soltó** the dog got loose; **el prisionero consiguió ~se** the prisoner managed to free himself *o* get free
B (desatarse) «*nudo*» to come undone, come loose; (aflojarse) «*nudo*» to loosen, come loose; «*tornillo*» to work loose; **~se el pelo** let one's hair down
C (adquirir desenvoltura): **necesita práctica para ~se** she needs practice to gain confidence; **se soltó más con el francés** his French became more fluent

soltería *f*: *the fact or state of being unmarried*; (en hombre) bachelorhood (frml); (en mujer) spinsterhood (frml)

soltero¹ -ra *adj* single; **soy** *or* (esp Esp) **estoy soltera** I'm single *o* I'm not married; **quedarse ~** to stay single

soltero² -ra (*m*) single man, bachelor; (*f*) single woman, spinster (dated *or* pej)

solterón -rona (pey) (*m*) old *o* confirmed bachelor; (*f*) old maid (pej)

soltura *f* (de una persona): **habla dos idiomas con ~** he speaks two languages fluently; **se desenvuelve con ~ en cualquier situación** she is at ease in any situation

solubilidad *f* solubility

soluble *adj*
A (Quím) soluble; **~ en agua** water-soluble
B ‹*problema*› soluble, solvable

solución *f* 1 (Mat, Quim) solution 2 (salida, remedio) solution; **encontrar una ~ a algo** to resolve sth, to find a solution to sth; **una ~ negociada** a negotiated settlement *o* solution; **son asuntos de difícil ~** there are no easy answers to these problems; **este chico no tiene ~** (fam) this kid is a hopeless case (colloq)

(Compuesto) **solución de continuidad** break, interruption

solucionar [A1] *vt* ‹*problema*› to solve; ‹*asunto/conflicto*› to settle, resolve
■ **solucionarse** *v pron* «*problema*» to be resolved; **a ver si se soluciona lo de la casa** let's hope we get the problem of the house resolved *o* (colloq) sorted out; **al final todo se solucionó** everything worked out in the end

solvencia *f* (Fin) solvency

solventar [A1] *vt* 1 ‹*gastos*› to pay; ‹*cuenta*› to pay, settle; ‹*deuda*› to pay (off), settle 2 ‹*dificultad/asunto*› to resolve, settle

solvente¹ *adj* (Fin) solvent

solvente² *m* solvent

somalí *adj/mf* Somali

Somalia *f* Somalia

somanta *f* (Esp fam): **le voy a dar una ~ de palos** I'm going to give him a good thrashing *o* hiding (colloq)

somático -ca *adj* somatic

sombra *f*
A 1 (lugar sin sol) shade; (proyección) shadow; **las ~s de los árboles** the shadows of the trees; **sentarse a** *or* **en la ~** to sit in the shade; **este árbol casi no da ~** this tree gives hardly any shade; **quítate que me haces** *or* **das ~** move out of the way, you're blocking (out) the sun; **parece mi ~, me sigue a todas partes** he's like my shadow, he follows me everywhere; **no es (ni) ~ de lo que era** he's a shadow of his former self; ***a la ~ de algn*** under the protection *o* the wing of sb; ***hacerle ~ a algn*** to put sb in the shade; ***tener mala ~*** to be a nasty piece of work (colloq) 2 (Espec, Taur): **localidades a la ~** more expensive seats (*in the shade*) 3 (atisbo, indicio): **sin la menor ~ de duda** without a shadow of a doubt 4 (mancha) blemish; **en su historial no hay ninguna ~** his record is spotless

(Compuestos)
- **sombra de** *or* **para ojos** eyeshadow
- **sombras chinescas** *fpl* shadow play

B (Art) shade
C (fam) (cárcel) cooler (AmE colloq), nick (BrE colloq); **se pasó ocho años a la ~** he spent eight years inside (colloq)

sombreado *m* shading

sombrear [A1] *vt* to shade in

S

sombrerera *f* (caja) hatbox; (percha) (Per) hat rack

sombrerería *f* [1] (tienda — de caballeros) hat shop; (— de señoras) hat shop, milliner's [2] (fábrica) hat factory

sombrerero -ra *m,f* (de mujer) milliner, hatter; (de hombre) hatter

sombrero *m* hat; **entró sin ~** he came in bareheaded *o* without a hat; ***hay que sacarle el ~*** (CS) I take my hat off to him/her; ***pasar el ~*** to pass the hat around; ***quitarse el ~*** (para saludar) to raise one's hat; (en señal de admiración): **me quito el ~** I take my hat off to her/him

(Compuestos)
- **sombrero de copa** top hat
- **sombrero de jipijapa** Panama (hat)
- **sombrero de tres picos** three-cornered hat, cocked hat
- **sombrero hongo** derby (AmE), bowler (hat) (BrE)
- **sombrero jarano** Mexican sombrero

sombrilla *f* [1] (de mano) parasol; (de playa) sunshade, beach umbrella [2] (Col, Ven) (paraguas) lady's umbrella

sombrío -bría *adj* (liter) ‹*lugar*› (umbrío) dark [2] (lúgubre) cheerless, dismal; ‹*persona*› gloomy

somero -ra *adj* superficial, summary (frml)

someter [E1] *vt*

A [1] (dominar): **logró ~ a todo el país** he managed to subjugate *o* conquer the whole country; **fue necesario usar la fuerza para ~lo** they had to use force to subdue him [2] (subordinar): **los sometió a su autoridad** he forced them to submit to his authority; **quieren ~ nuestros intereses a los suyos** they are trying to put their interests before ours

B [1] (a torturas, presiones) to subject [2] (a tratamiento): **fue sometido a una intervención quirúrgica** he had surgery *o* an operation [3] (a prueba) to subject; **someten los productos a pruebas de calidad** the products are subjected to *o* undergo quality control tests; **el avión fue sometido a una minuciosa revisión** the aircraft was given a thorough overhaul [4] (a votación, aprobación): **el proyecto de ley será sometido a votación** the bill will be put to the vote; **la propuesta será sometida a la aprobación de los socios** the proposal will be submitted to *o* put before the members for approval

■ **someterse** *v pron* [1] (a autoridad) to submit to, yield to; (a capricho) to give in to; (a ley) to comply with [2] (a prueba, exámen, operación) to undergo

sometimiento *m*

A (de un pueblo) subjection, subjugation

B [1] (a autoridad) submission; (a ley) compliance [2] (a prueba, proceso) subjection; **para su ~ a pruebas bacteriológicas** so that they can undergo bacteriological tests

somier /so'mje(r)/ *m* (*pl* **-miers** *or* **-mieres**) sprung bed base

somnífero *m* sleeping pill, soporific (frml)

somnolencia *f* drowsiness, sleepiness; **me entró una ~ terrible** I started to feel terribly sleepy *o* drowsy; **el vino le produce ~** wine makes him sleepy; **este fármaco puede provocar ~** this drug may cause drowsiness

somnoliento -ta *adj* sleepy, drowsy

somos *see* **ser**

son[1] *m*

A [1] (sonido) sound; **al ~ del violín** to the strains *o* to the sound of the violin; ***bailar al ~ de la música que me/te/le tocan*** to toe the line [2] **en son de**: **lo dijo en ~ de burla** she said it mockingly *o* in a mocking tone; **venimos en ~ de paz** we come in peace

B (canción latinoamericana) *song with a lively, danceable beat*

son[2] *see* **ser**

sonado -da *adj*

A ‹*boda/suceso/noticia*› much-talked-about; **fue muy ~** everybody was talking about it

B [1] ‹*boxeador*› punch-drunk [2] (fam) (torpe) stupid (colloq)

C (AmL fam) (en dificultades) [ESTAR] in a mess (colloq), in trouble (colloq); **si no hay nadie en casa, estoy ~** if there's nobody home, I've had it (colloq)

sonaja *f* (Méx) rattle

sonajero *m* rattle

sonambulismo *m* sleepwalking, somnambulism (frml)

sonámbulo[1] **-la** *adj* somnambulistic (frml); **es ~** he sleepwalks, he walks in his sleep

sonámbulo[2] **-la** *m,f* sleepwalker, somnambulist (frml)

sonar[1] [A10] *vi*

A «*teléfono/timbre*» to ring; «*disparo*» to ring out; **el despertador sonó a las cinco** the alarm went off at five o'clock; **cuando suena la sirena** when the siren goes; **~on las doce en el reloj** the clock struck twelve; **¡cómo me suenan las tripas!** (fam) my tummy's rumbling (colloq)

B (+ *compl*) [1] «*motor/instrumento*» to sound; «*persona*» to sound; **suena a hueco/a metal** it sounds hollow/metallic *o* like metal [2] «*palabra/expresión*» to sound; **se escribe como suena** it's spelled as it sounds; ***(así) como suena*** just like that, as simple as that

C [1] (resultar conocido) (+ *me/te/le etc*): **me suena tu cara** your face is *o* looks familiar; **¿de qué me suena ese nombre?** where do I know that name from?; **¿te suena este refrán?** does this proverb ring a bell (with you) *o* sound familiar to you? [2] (parecer) **~ A algo** to sound like sth; **me suena a una de sus invenciones** it sounds to me like one of his stories

D [1] (AmL fam) (fracasar): **soné en el examen** I blew the exam (colloq), I blew it in the exam (colloq); **sonamos** we've had it now, we've blown it now (colloq) [2] (CS fam) (descomponerse, estropearse) to pack up (colloq) [3] (CS fam) (morirse) to kick the bucket (colloq)

■ **sonar** *vt*

A [1] (+ *me/te/le etc*) ‹*nariz*› to wipe; **suénale la nariz** wipe her nose for her, will you? [2] ‹*trompeta*› to play

B (Méx fam) [1] (pegar) ‹*persona*› to thump (colloq), to clobber (colloq) [2] (en competición) to beat, thrash (colloq)

■ **sonarse** *v pron*: *tb* **~se la nariz** to blow one's nose

sonar[2] *m* sonar

sonata *f* sonata

sonda *f* [1] (Med) catheter; **le pusieron una ~** he was fitted with a catheter [2] (para perforar) drill [3] (Náut) sounding line, lead line [4] (Espac, Meteo) probe

(Compuesto) **sonda espacial** space probe

sondar [A1] *vt* [1] (Med) to catheterize [2] (Min, Tec) to test drill, sink a borehole in [3] (Náut) to sound [4] (Espac, Meteo) to explore, probe

sondear [A1] *vt* ‹*opinión*› to sound out; ‹*mercado*› to test; ▸**sondar 2, 3, 4**

sondeo *m*

A (encuesta) poll, survey

(Compuesto) **sondeo de opinión** opinion poll

B (perforación) test drilling; (Náut) sounding; (Espac, Meteo) exploration

soneto *m* sonnet

sónico -ca *adj* sonic

sonido *m* sound

soniquete *m* droning

sonoridad *f* [1] (de instrumento) tone; (de voz) sonority, tone [2] (Ling) voice

sonorización *f* [1] (de película) addition of a soundtrack [2] (de lugar, recinto) installation of a sound system [3] (Ling) voicing

sonorizar [A4] *vt* ‹*local/recinto*› to install a sound system in; (Ling) to voice

sonoro -ra *adj* ‹*golpe*› resounding, loud; ‹*voz/lenguaje*› sonorous, resonant; (Ling) voiced

sonreír [I18] *vi* [1] «*persona*» to smile; **~(le) A algn** to smile AT sb [2] «*vida/fortuna*» (+ *me/te/le etc*) to smile on; **el futuro le sonríe** his future is bright

■ **sonreírse** *v pron* to smile

sonriente *adj* ‹*ojos/expresión*› smiling (*before n*); **hoy estás muy ~** you're looking very happy today

sonrisa *f* smile; **siempre tiene la ~ en los labios** she's always smiling; **con una ~ de oreja a oreja** grinning from ear to ear

sonrojar [A1] *vt* to make … blush

■ **sonrojar** *vi*: **hacer ~ a algn** to make sb blush

■ **sonrojarse** *v pron* to blush

sonrosado -da *adj* rosy, pink

sonsacar [A2] *vt*: **me costó trabajo ~le la verdad** I had a hard time getting the truth out of her; **le ~on el secreto** they wormed *o* got the secret out of him

sonsera *f* (Col, RPl fam): **no digas ~s** don't talk nonsense *o* (BrE colloq) rubbish!; **¡qué ~!** that was a really stupid *o*

S

that was a (AmE) dumb thing to do (colloq)

sonso -sa *adj/m,f* ▸ **zonzo**

sonsonete *m* 1 (tono monótono) drone, droning 2 (cantaleta): **me tienes harta con ese ~** I'm fed up with your constant nagging (*o* complaining *etc*)

soñado -da *adj* (AmL fam) divine (colloq), heavenly (colloq); *ver tb* **soñar**

soñador¹ -dora *adj* ‹*mirada*› dreamy, faraway; **soy muy ~** I'm a real dreamer

soñador² -dora *m,f* dreamer

soñar [A10] *vt* 1 (durmiendo) to dream; ***ni lo sueñes*** *or* ***ni ~lo*** (fam) no way! (colloq) 2 (fantasear) to dream; **la casa soñada** her/his/their dream house

■ **soñar** *vi* 1 (durmiendo) to dream; **~ CON algo/algn** to dream ABOUT sth/sb; **anoche soñé contigo** I dreamed *o* I had a dream about you last night; **que sueñes con los angelitos** (fr hecha) sweet dreams 2 (fantasear) to dream; **~ despierto** to daydream; **~ CON algo** to dream OF sth; **sueña con volver a su país** he dreams about *o* of going back home

soñolencia *f* ▸ **somnolencia**

soñoliento -ta *adj* ▸ **somnoliento**

sopa *f* (caldo) soup; **~ de verduras** vegetable soup; **~ de sobre** packaged soup (AmE), packet soup (BrE); ***comer*** *or* ***vivir a la ~ boba*** (Esp fam) to live at sb else's expense, live off sb; ***hasta en la ~*** (fam) all over the place (colloq); ***hecho una ~*** (fam) soaked to the skin (colloq), drenched

sopapo *m* (fam) (bofetón) slap, smack (colloq); **darle un ~ a algn** to slap *o* smack sb

sope *m* (Méx) *fried tortilla topped with refried beans, onion and hot sauce*

sopear [A1] *vt* (Chi, Méx) to mop up (*with bread etc*)

sopera *f* soup tureen

sopero -ra *adj* soup (*before n*)

sopesar [A1] *vt* ‹*situación/ventajas*› to weigh up; ‹*palabras*› to weigh

soplagaitas *mf* twit (colloq), twerp (colloq)

soplamocos *m* (*pl* ~) (fam) slap, smack (colloq)

soplar [A1] *vi*

A 1 (con la boca) to blow; **sopla fuerte** blow hard 2 «*viento*» to blow; **sopla un viento muy fuerte** there's a strong wind (blowing)

B (fam) (en examen) to whisper (*answers in an exam*)

■ **soplar** *vt*

A 1 ‹*vela*› to blow out; ‹*fuego/brasas*› to blow on; **sopló el polvo que había sobre los libros** she blew the dust off the books 2 ‹*vidrio*› to blow

B 1 (fam) ‹*respuesta*› (en examen) to whisper 2 (arg) (a la policía) to give … away; **alguien debió ~les el lugar donde se escondían** someone must have squealed and told the police where they were hiding (sl)

C (fam) 1 (robar) to swipe (colloq), to pinch (BrE colloq); (cobrar) to sting (colloq); **me ~on 10.000 pesos** they stung me (for) 10,000 pesos 2 ‹*pieza/ficha*› to take

■ **soplarse** *v pron*

A (fam) ‹*bebida*› to down (colloq); ‹*plato*› to wolf down (colloq)

B (AmL fam) (vencer) to beat

C (Méx, Per fam) (aguantar) ‹*persona*› to put up with; ‹*discurso/película*› to sit through, suffer

D (Méx, RPl fam) (matar) to do … in (colloq)

soplete *m* 1 (para soldar) gas welding torch; (para quitar pintura) blowtorch 2 (CS) (para pintar) spray gun; **pintar a ~** to spray-paint

soplido *m* puff

soplo *m*

A 1 (soplido) puff; **de un ~** with one puff, in one go; ***como un ~*** (fam): **la mañana se me ha pasado como un ~** the morning has flown past *o* whizzed by (colloq) 2 (de aire) puff; (más fuerte) blast 3 (de viento) puff; (más fuerte) gust 4 (Metal) blast

B (fam) (chivatazo): **alguien dio el ~ a la policía** someone tipped off the police (colloq); **me dieron un ~ para la carrera** they gave me a hot tip for the race (colloq)

C (Med) heart murmur

soplón -plona *m,f* 1 (fam) (en colegio) tittle-tattle (AmE colloq), telltale (BrE colloq) 2 (fam) (a la policía) informer, stoolie (AmE colloq), grass (BrE colloq)

soponcio *m* (fam) 1 (desmayo): **le dio un ~** she fainted 2 (ataque de nervios) fit (colloq); **le va a dar un ~ cuando se entere** he'll have a fit when he finds out (colloq)

sopor *m* 1 (somnolencia) drowsiness, sleepiness 2 (letargo) torpor

soporífero¹ -ra *adj* ‹*efecto/discurso/clase*› soporific

soporífero² *m* sleeping pill, soporific (frml)

soportable *adj* bearable

soportal *m* 1 (de casa) porch 2 **soportales** *mpl* (de calle) arcade, colonnade

soportar [A1] *vt*

A 1 ‹*situación/frío/dolor*› to put up with, bear, endure (frml); ‹*persona*› to put up with; **no soporto este calor/la gente así** I can't stand this heat/people like that; **soportó el dolor sin quejarse** she put up with *o* bore the pain without complaint

B ‹*peso/carga*› to support, withstand; ‹*presión*› to withstand

soporte *m* 1 (de estante) bracket; (de viga) support; (de maceta, portarretratos) stand 2 (Inf) medium

(Compuesto) **soporte físico/lógico** (Inf) hardware/software

soprano *mf* soprano

soquete *m*

A (CS) (Indum) ankle sock

B (Chi) (Elec) lampholder, socket

C (Col, Méx, RPl fam) (tonto) fool, idiot

sor *f* (Relig) sister

sorber [E1] *vt* 1 (beber) to suck in *o* up; (tomar poco a poco) to sip 2 «*esponja*» to absorb, soak up

■ **sorberse** *v pron*: **~se los mocos** (fam) to sniff *o* sniffle

sorbete *m* sherbet (AmE), sorbet (esp BrE)

sorbo *m* 1 (cantidad pequeña) sip; **bébetelo a sorbitos** sip it 2 (trago grande) gulp; **de un ~** in one gulp

sordera *f* deafness

sordidez *f* (suciedad) squalor, sordidness; (de tema, negocio) sordidness

sórdido -da *adj* ‹*lugar/ambiente*› squalid; ‹*asunto/libro*› sordid

sordina *f* (de trompeta, violín) mute; (de piano) damper

sordo¹ -da *adj*

A (Med) deaf; **se quedó ~** he went deaf; **es ~ de nacimiento** he was born deaf

B ‹*ruido/golpe*› dull, muffled; ‹*dolor*› dull; (Ling) voiceless

sordo² -da *m,f* deaf person; **una escuela para ~s** a school for the deaf; ***hacerse el ~*** to pretend not to hear

sordomudo¹ -da *adj* deaf-mute (*before n*), deaf and dumb (BrE)

sordomudo² -da *m,f* deaf-mute

sorgo *m* sorghum

soriasis *f* psoriasis

sorna *f* sarcasm; **se lo dijo con ~** she said it in a sarcastic *o* sardonic way

sorocharse [A1] *v pron* (Andes) (en la montaña) to get altitude *o* mountain sickness

soroche *m* (Andes) (en la montaña) mountain sickness, altitude sickness

sorprendente *adj* surprising

sorprender [E1] *vi* to surprise; **me sorprende que no lo sepas** I'm surprised you don't know

■ **sorprender** *vt* 1 (coger desprevenido) to surprise, catch … unawares; **nos sorprendió la lluvia** we got caught in the rain 2 ‹*mensaje*› to intercept; ‹*conversación*› to overhear

■ **sorprenderse** *v pron* to be surprised; **¿de qué te sorprendes?** what are you so surprised about?

sorprendido -da *adj* surprised; **me miró ~** he looked at me in surprise; **quedarse ~** to be surprised; **yo fui el primer ~** nobody was more surprised than me; *ver tb* **sorprender**

sorpresa¹ *f* 1 (emoción) surprise; **¡qué ~!** what a surprise!; **se va a llevar una ~** she's going to be surprised, she's in for a surprise (colloq); **causar ~** to come as a surprise; **me miró con cara de ~** he looked at me in surprise; **para mi gran ~** *or* **con gran ~ por mi parte** to my great surprise; ***tomar*** *or* (esp Esp) ***coger a algn de*** *or*

S

por ~ to take sb by surprise 2 (regalo) surprise; **te he traído una ~** I've brought you a surprise
sorpresa² *adj inv* ‹*fiesta/ataque*› surprise (*before n*)
sorpresivo -va *adj* (AmL) surprise (*before n*), unexpected
sortear [A1] *vt*
A ‹*premio/puesto*› to draw lots for; **~on los puestos de salida** they drew lots to decide the starting positions; **se ~á un coche** there will be a prize draw for a car
B 1 ‹*bache/obstáculo*› to avoid, negotiate 2 ‹*problema/dificultad*› to get around; **sorteó las preguntas con habilidad** he dealt with the questions skillfully
sorteo *m* 1 (de premio) draw; **por ~** by drawing lots 2 (Mil) (de quintos) *drawing of lots to decide draft postings*
sortija *f* 1 (anillo) ring 2 (en el pelo) ringlet
sortilegio *m* (embrujo) spell, charm; (brujería) sorcery; (adivinación) fortune-telling
sos: *equivalent of 'eres' in Central America and the River Plate area*
SOS *m* SOS, distress call
sosa *f* soda; **~ cáustica** caustic soda
sosegado -da *adj* ‹*vida*› quiet, peaceful; ‹*persona*› calm; **lo encontré más ~** he seemed calmer
sosegar [A7] *vt* to calm
■ **sosegarse** *v pron* «*persona/ánimos*» to calm down; «*niños*» to quieten down; «*mar*» (liter) to become calm
sosiego *m* peace; **un día de ~** a quiet day
soslayar [A1] *vt* ‹*dificultad/obstáculo*› to avoid, get around; ‹*pregunta*› to dodge, avoid
soslayo *m*: **mirar a algn de ~** to give sb a sidelong glance
soso -sa *adj* 1 ‹*comida*› (sin sabor) bland, tasteless; **está ~** (sin sabor) it's bland *o* tasteless; (sin sal) it needs more salt 2 ‹*persona/película*› boring, dull; ‹*estilo*› flat, drab
sospecha *f* suspicion; **tengo la ~ de que ...** I suspect *o* I have a feeling that ...; **despertar las ~s de algn** to arouse sb's suspicions; **estar por encima de toda ~** to be above suspicion
sospechar [A1] *vt* to suspect; **¡ya me lo sospechaba!** just as I suspected!
■ **sospechar** *vi*: **me hizo ~** it made me suspicious; **~ DE algn** to suspect sb, have one's suspicions ABOUT sb
sospechoso¹ -sa *adj* ‹*movimiento/comportamiento*› suspicious; ‹*paquete*› suspicious, suspect; **tres hombres de aspecto ~** three suspicious-looking men; **relojes de origen ~** watches of dubious origin; **me parece muy ~** I find it very *o* highly suspicious
sospechoso² -sa *m,f* suspect
sostén *m* 1 (físico) support; (económico) means of support 2 (Indum) bra, brassiere
sostener [E27] *vt*
A (apoyar) 1 ‹*estructura/techo*› to hold up, support; ‹*carga/peso*› to bear; **tenían que ~lo los dos** it needed both of them to support him *o* hold him up *o* prop him up 2 (en un estado) to keep; **lo único que la sostiene es su fuerza de voluntad** it's sheer willpower that keeps her going 3 (sustentar) ‹*familia*› to support, maintain
B (sujetar, tener cogido) ‹*paquete*› to hold; **no tengas miedo, yo te sostengo** don't be afraid, I've got you *o* I'm holding you; **sostén la puerta** hold the door open
C ‹*conversación/relación/reunión*› to have; **la polémica que sostiene con Godoy** the dispute that he and Godoy are engaged in
D 1 (opinar) to hold; **yo siempre he sostenido que ...** I have always maintained *o* held that ... 2 ‹*argumento/afirmación*› to support, back up
E 1 ‹*lucha/ritmo/resistencia*› to keep up, sustain; **ella sostuvo mi mirada** she held my gaze 2 (Mús) ‹*nota*› to hold, sustain
■ **sostenerse** *v pron*
A 1 (no caerse): **la estructura se sostiene sola** the structure stays up without support; **apenas se sostenía en pie** he could hardly stand 2 (en un estado) to remain; **se sostuvo en el poder** she managed to stay *o* remain in power; **la economía se ha sostenido firme** the economy has held firm; **se sostuvo en su negativa** he stuck firmly to his refusal
B (mantenerse): **no puede ~se con lo que gana** he can't support himself on what he earns; **se sostiene a base de leche** she lives on *o* survives on milk
sostenibilidad *f* sustainability
sostenible *adj* sustainable
sostenido -da *adj* sharp; **re ~** D sharp
sostuve, sostuvo, etc *see* **sostener**
sota *f* jack (*in Spanish pack of cards*)
sotana *f* cassock, soutane
sótano *m* (habitable) basement; (para almacenamiento) cellar, basement
sotavento *m* leeward; **a ~** to leeward
soterrar [A5] *vt* ‹*objeto*› to bury; ‹*recuerdo/sentimiento*› to bury, hide
soto *m* (arboleda) grove, copse; (matorral) thicket
sotobosque *m* undergrowth
sotol *m* (Méx) 1 (planta) sotol 2 (bebida) *type of pulque*
soufflé /su'fle/ *m* (*pl* **-fflés**) soufflé
souvenir /suβe'nir/ *m* (*pl* **-nirs**) souvenir
soviético -ca *adj/m,f* (Hist) Soviet
soy *see* **ser**
soya *f* (AmL) soy (AmE), soya (BrE)
sport /(e)s'por/ *m*: **ropa (de) ~** leisure wear, casual clothes (*pl*); **iban vestidos de ~** they were casually dressed
spot /(e)s'pot/ *m* (*pl* **spots**) *tb* **~ publicitario** (espacio) slot; (anuncio) commercial, advertisement (BrE)
spray /(e)s'prai/ *m* (*pl* **sprays**) spray; **desodorante en ~** spray *o* spray-on deodorant
Sr. *m* (= **señor**) Mr; **~ (Don) Miguel López Ríos** (Corresp) Mr M. López Ríos, Miguel López Ríos, Esq (frml)
Sra. *f* (= **señora**) Mrs; **~ (Doña) Ana Fuentes de Luengo** (Corresp) Mrs A. Luengo
S.R.C. (= **se ruega contestación**) RSVP
S/ref. (= **su referencia**) your ref
Sres. *mpl* = **señores**
S.R.L. *f* (= **Sociedad de Responsabilidad Limitada**) Ltd
Srta. *f* (= **señorita**) Miss
ss.
A = **siguientes**
B = **siglos**
SS 1 (= **Su Santidad**) H.H. 2 (Mil) **la ~** *or* **las ~** the SS 3 (Servs Socs) (en Méx) = **Secretaría de Salud**
SS.MM. = **Sus Majestades**
S.S.S. (ant) (Corresp) = **su seguro servidor**
Sta. (= **Santa**) St
standing /(e)s'tandin/ *m* standing; **un piso de alto ~** luxury *o* top quality apartment
status /(e)s'tatus/ *m* (*pl* ~) status
status quo *m* status quo
Sto. (= **Santo**) St
stock /(e)s'tok/ *m* (*pl* **stocks**) stock
stop /(e)s'top/ *m* (disco) stop sign; **se saltó un ~** he went through *o* (AmE) ran the stop sign
su *adj* (*delante del n*) 1 (de él) his; (de ella) her; (de usted, ustedes) your; (de ellos, ellas) their; (de animal, cosa) its; **cuando uno ha perdido ~ última esperanza** when one's last hope is gone 2 (uso enfático): **pesará ~s buenos 90 kilos** he must weigh a good 90 kilos
suave *adj*
A ‹*piel/cutis*› smooth, soft; ‹*pelo*› soft; ‹*superficie/pasta*› smooth; **~ al tacto** smooth to the touch
B 1 ‹*tono*› gentle; ‹*acento/música*› soft 2 ‹*color*› soft, pale 3 ‹*sabor*› (no fuerte) delicate, mild; (sin acidez) smooth
C 1 ‹*movimiento/gesto*› gentle, slight 2 ‹*temperaturas/clima*› mild; ‹*brisa*› gentle 3 ‹*modales/carácter/reprimenda*› mild, gentle 4 ‹*cuesta/curva*› gentle, gradual 5 ‹*jabón/champú*› gentle, mild 6 ‹*laxante/sedante*› mild
D (Méx fam): ***llevársela ~ con algo*** to go easy on sth (colloq)
E (Méx fam) (fantástico): **¡qué ~!** great!, fantastic! (colloq)
suavemente *adv* gently; **se deslizaba ~ por el agua** it slid smoothly through the water; **me habló ~** she talked softly to me

S

suavidad *f* (de la piel) smoothness, softness; (de jabón, champú) gentleness, mildness; (de tono, acento) gentleness, softness; (de color) softness, paleness; (de movimiento) gentleness; (de carácter) mildness, gentleness

suavizante *m* (para el pelo) conditioner; (para la ropa) fabric softener *o* conditioner

suavizar [A4] *vt* ‹*piel*› to leave … smooth/soft; ‹*color*› to soften, tone down; ‹*sabor*› to tone down; ‹*carácter*› to mellow, make … gentler; ‹*dureza/severidad*› to soften, temper; ‹*situación*› to calm, ease; **~on el régimen penitenciario** they relaxed the prison regulations

■ **suavizarse** *v pron* «*piel*» to become smoother/softer; «*carácter*» to mellow, become gentler; «*situación*» to calm down, ease

subacuático -ca *adj* underwater (*before n*)

subalimentación *f* undernourishment

subalimentado -da *adj* undernourished, underfed

subalterno¹ -na *adj* (Adm, Mil) subordinate; (secundario) secondary

subalterno² -na *m,f* [1] (en jerarquía) subordinate [2] (Taur) *member of a matador's support team*

subarrendar [A5] *vt* to sublease, sublet

subarrendatario -ria *m,f* subtenant, sublessee (frml)

subarriendo *m* (acción) subleasing, subletting; (acuerdo) sublease, subtenancy, sublet

subasta *f* [1] (venta) auction; **sacar algo a ~** to put sth up for auction [2] (de obras) invitation to tender

subastador -dora *m,f* [1] (persona) auctioneer [2] **subastadora** *f* (empresa) auction-house

subastar [A1] *vt* ‹*cuadro*› to auction, sell … at auction; ‹*contrato/obra pública*› to put … out to tender

subcampeón -peona *m,f* (en liga) runner-up; (en torneo eliminatorio) losing finalist

subcomisión *f* subcommittee

subcomité *m* subcommittee

subconjunto *m* subset

subconsciente *adj/m* subconscious

(Compuesto) **subconsciente colectivo** collective subconscious

subcontinente *m* subcontinent

subcontratación *f* subcontracting

subcontratar [A1] *vt* to subcontract

subcontratista *mf* subcontractor

subcutáneo -nea *adj* subcutaneous

subdesarrollado -da *adj* underdeveloped

subdesarrollo *m* underdevelopment

subdirector -ra *m,f* (de organización) deputy director; (de comercio) assistant manager, deputy manager

súbdito -ta *m,f* subject

subdividir [I1] *vt* to subdivide

subdivisión *f* subdivision

subempleado -da *adj* ‹*personas*› underemployed; ‹*recursos*› underused, underemployed

subespecie *f* subspecies

subestimar [A1] *vt* to underestimate

subfusil *m* automatic rifle

subgénero *m* subgenus

subida *f* [1] (pendiente) rise, climb [2] (a montaña) ascent, climb; (al poder) rise; **la ~ fue muy dura** going up was very hard [3] (de temperatura, precios, salarios) rise, increase; **la fuerte ~ del yen** the sharp rise in the value of the yen

subido -da *adj* ‹*color*› intense, deep

subíndice *m* subscript

subinquilino -na *m,f* subtenant, sublessee (frml)

subir [I1] *vi*

A [1] «*ascensor/persona*» (alejándose) to go up; (acercándose) to come up; **hay que ~ a pie** you have to walk up; **ahora subo** I'll be right up; **los autobuses que suben al pueblo** the buses that go up to the village; **el camino sube hasta la cima** the path goes up to *o* leads to the top of the hill [2] **~ A algo** ‹*a autobús/tren/avión*› to get ON *o* ONTO sth; ‹*a coche*› to get IN *o* INTO sth; ‹*a caballo/bicicleta*› to get ON *o* ONTO sth, to mount sth (frml); **~ a bordo** to go *o* get on board [3] (de categoría) to go up; (en el escalafón) to be promoted; **han subido a primera división** they've been promoted to *o* they've gone up to the first division [4] (en tenis) **~ a la red** to go up to the net

B [1] «*marea*» to come in; «*aguas/río*» to rise [2] «*fiebre/tensión*» to go up, rise; «*temperatura*» to rise [3] «*leche materna*» to come in

C «*precio/valor/cotización/salario*» to rise, go up; **~ en un 5%** to go up by 5%

■ **subir** *vt*

A ‹*montaña*› to climb; ‹*cuesta*› to go up, climb; ‹*escaleras*› to go up, climb; **subió corriendo la escalera** she ran upstairs

B [1] ‹*objeto/niño*› (llevar arriba — acercándose) to bring up; (— alejándose) to take up; **voy a ~ la compra** I'm just going to take the shopping upstairs; **tengo que ~ unas cajas al desván** I have to put some boxes up in the attic [2] ‹*objeto/niño*› (poner más alto): **sube al niño al caballo** lift the child onto the horse; **voy a ~ un poco este cuadro** I'm going to put this picture up a bit higher; **traía el cuello del abrigo subido** he had his coat collar turned up [3] ‹*persiana/telón*› to raise; ‹*pantalones*› to pull up; **¿me subes la cremallera?** will you zip me up?, will you fasten my zipper (AmE) *o* (BrE) zip?; **subió la ventanilla** she raised the window [4] ‹*dobladillo*› to take up; ‹*falda*› to take *o* turn up

C (Inf) to upload

D [1] ‹*precios/salarios*› to raise, put up; **¿cuánto te han subido este año?** how much did your salary go up this year? [2] ‹*volumen/radio*› to turn up; **sube un poco la calefacción** turn the heating *o* heat up a little

■ **subirse** *v pron*

A [1] (a coche, autobús, etc) ▸ *vi* **A2** [2] (trepar) to climb; **se subió al árbol/al muro** she climbed up the tree/(up) onto the walls; **estaba subido a un árbol/caballo** he was up a tree/sitting on a horse [3] (a la cabeza, cara) (+ *me/te/le etc*): **el éxito se le subió a la cabeza** the success went to his head; **se me subieron los colores** I went red *o* blushed

B (*refl*) ‹*calcetines/pantalones*› to pull up

súbitamente *adv* suddenly

súbito -ta *adj* [1] (repentino) sudden; **de ~** suddenly, all of a sudden [2] (precipitado) hasty

subjetividad *f* subjectivity

subjetivo -va *adj* subjective

subjuntivo *m* subjunctive

sublevación *f* uprising, revolt, rebellion

sublevar [A1] *vt* [1] ‹*tropas/presos*› to incite … to rebellion, stir up revolt among [2] (indignar) to infuriate

■ **sublevarse** *v pron* to revolt, rise up, rebel

sublimación *f* sublimation

sublimar [A1] *vt* ‹*deseos/instintos*› to sublimate; (Quím) to sublime, sublimate

sublime *adj* ‹*acción/sacrificio*› noble; ‹*cuadro/música*› sublime

subliminal *adj* subliminal

submarinismo *m* scuba diving

submarinista *mf* (buzo) scuba diver; (tripulante de submarino) submariner

submarino¹ -na *adj* underwater (*before n*), submarine (*before n*)

submarino² *m* submarine

subnormal¹ *adj* [1] (Psic) mentally handicapped, subnormal [2] (fam & pey) (como insulto) moronic (colloq & pej)

subnormal² *mf* [1] (Psic) mentally handicapped person [2] (fam & pey) (cretino) moron, cretin (colloq & pej)

suboficial *m* noncommissioned officer, NCO

subordinado -da *adj/mf* subordinate

subordinar [A1] *vt* to subordinate; **~ algo A algo** to subordinate sth TO sth

subproducto *m* byproduct, spin-off

subrayado *m* (con línea — acción) underlining; (— texto) underlined text; (texto en cursiva) text in italics

subrayar [A1] *vt* [1] ‹*texto*› to underline, underscore [2] (poner énfasis en) to underline, emphasize, stress

subrepticio -cia *adj* surreptitious

subrogante *mf*

A (Der) (en relación jurídica) subrogating party

B (AmC, CS) (en un cargo) temporary office-holder

S

subsanar [A1] *vt* ‹*error*› to rectify, correct; ‹*carencia*› to make up for; ‹*obstáculo/dificultad*› to overcome

subsecretario -ria *m,f* undersecretary

subsidiario -ria *adj* subsidiary, secondary

subsidio *m* subsidy; **~ de enfermedad** sickness benefit; **~ de desempleo** unemployment compensation (AmE), unemployment benefit (BrE)

subsiguiente *adj* subsequent

subsistencia *f* subsistence, survival

subsistir [I1] *vi* «*persona/planta*» to survive, subsist (frml); «*creencia/tradición*» to persist, survive

subsuelo *m* (Geol) subsoil

subte *m* (RPl fam) subway (AmE), tube (BrE colloq)

subteniente *m* ≈ second lieutenant (*in US*), ≈ sub-lieutenant (*in UK*)

subterfugio *m* subterfuge

subterráneo¹ -nea *adj* underground, subterranean

subterráneo² *m* 1 (pasaje) subway, tunnel 2 (RPl) (Transp) subway (AmE), underground (BrE)

subtitular [A1] *vt* to subtitle; **versión original subtitulada** original version with subtitles

subtítulo *m* subtitle; **~s en francés** French subtitles

subtropical *adj* subtropical

suburbano -na *adj* suburban

suburbio *m* (extrarradio) suburb; (barrio pobre) depressed area (*on the outskirts of town*)

subvención *f* subsidy, subvention (frml)

subvencionar [A1] *vt* to subsidize

subversivo -va *adj* subversive

subvertir [I11] *vt* to subvert (frml)

subyacente *adj* underlying

subyacer [E5] *vi* **~ (EN algo)** to underlie (sth)

subyugación *f* subjugation

subyugar [A3] *vt* ‹*pueblo/enemigo*› to subjugate; (fascinar) to enthrall, captivate

succión *f* suction

succionar [A1] *vt* to suck (up)

sucedáneo *m* substitute; **un ~ del café** a coffee substitute

suceder [E1] *vi*

A (ocurrir) to happen; **¿qué sucede?** what's happening?, what's going on?; **¿le ha sucedido algo?** has something happened to him?; **lo peor** *or* (fam) **lo más que puede ~ es que ...** the worst that can happen is that ...; **le expliqué lo sucedido** I explained to him what had happened; **no te abandonaré, suceda lo que suceda** I'll never leave you, come what may; **suceda lo que suceda no te muevas de aquí** whatever happens *o* no matter what happens don't move from here; **por lo que pueda ~** just in case

B (en el tiempo) «*hecho/época*» **~ A algo** to follow sth

■ **suceder** *vt* (en trono, cargo) to succeed

■ **sucederse** *v pron* to follow; **los acontecimientos se sucedían de manera vertiginosa** events followed *o* succeeded each other at a dizzy pace

sucesión *f*

A 1 (al trono, en un cargo) succession; **es el segundo en la línea de ~ al trono** he is second in line to the throne 2 (herederos) heirs (*pl*), issue (frml); **murió sin ~** he died without issue 3 (Der) (herencia) estate, inheritance

B (serie) succession, series

sucesivamente *adv* successively; **y así ~** and so on (and so forth)

sucesivo -va *adj* consecutive; **tres días ~s** three consecutive days, three days running; **~s gobiernos han intentado resolverlo** successive governments have tried to resolve it; **en lo ~** from now on, in future

suceso *m* 1 (acontecimiento) event 2 (accidente, crimen): **el lugar del ~** the scene of the incident/crime/accident

sucesor -sora *m,f* (al trono, en un puesto) successor; (heredero) heir, successor (frml)

suciedad *f* 1 (mugre) dirt; **¿cómo puedes vivir aquí, con toda esta ~?** how can you live in such a filthy place? 2 (estado) dirtiness

sucinto -ta *adj* succinct, concise

S

sucio¹ -cia *adj*

A 1 [ESTAR] ‹*ropa/casa/vaso*› dirty; **tengo las manos sucias** my hands are dirty; **¿de quién es este cuaderno tan ~?** whose is this grubby exercise book?; **hacer algo en ~** to do a rough draft of sth (AmE), do sth in rough (BrE) 2 ‹*lengua*› furred, coated

B [SER] 1 (que se ensucia fácilmente): **el blanco es muy sucio** white really shows the dirt terribly 2 ‹*color*› dirty (*before n*) 3 ‹*trabajo*› dirty; ‹*dinero/negocio/juego*› dirty 4 ‹*lenguaje*› filthy; ‹*mente*› dirty; **tener la conciencia sucia** to have a guilty conscience; **una jugada sucia** a dirty trick

sucio² *m* (Ven fam) dirty mark

sucre *m* sucre (*Ecuadorean unit of currency*)

suculento -ta *adj* succulent

sucumbir [I1] *vi* 1 «*ejército/plaza*» to succumb, surrender; **~ A algo** to succumb TO sth 2 (a tentación) to succumb; **~ A algo** to succumb TO sth

sucursal *f* (de banco, comercio) branch; (de empresa) office

sudaca *mf* (Esp) *pejorative term used to refer to a Latin American*

sudadera *f* (Dep, Indum) (suéter) sweatshirt; (conjunto) (Col, Ven) tracksuit

sudado -da *adj* sweaty

Sudáfrica *f* South Africa

sudafricano -na *adj/m,f* South African

Sudamérica *f* South America

sudamericano -na *adj/m,f* South American

Sudán *m*: *tb* **el ~** (the) Sudan

sudanés -nesa *adj/m,f* Sudanese

sudar [A1] *vi* 1 (transpirar) to sweat, perspire (frml) 2 (fam) (trabajar duro) to work flat out (colloq)

■ **sudar** *vt* ‹*camiseta*› to make ... sweaty; ***me la suda*** (Esp vulg) I couldn't give a damn (colloq) *o* (sl) a toss; **~ *tinta*** *or* ***la gota gorda*** to sweat blood (colloq)

sudario *m* shroud

sudeste¹ *adj inv* ‹*región*› southeastern; **iban en dirección ~** they were heading southeast

sudeste² *m* 1 (parte, sector): **el ~** the southeast, the Southeast 2 (punto cardinal) southeast, Southeast; **vientos del ~** southeasterly winds

sudoeste¹ *adj inv* ‹*región*› southwestern; **iban en dirección ~** they were heading southwest

sudoeste² *m* 1 (parte, sector): **el ~** the southwest, the Southwest 2 (punto cardinal) southwest, Southwest; **vientos del ~** southwesterly winds

sudor *m* 1 (transpiración) sweat, perspiration (frml); **un ~ frío** a cold sweat; **se lo ganó con el ~ de su frente** she earned it by the sweat of her brow 2 **sudores** *mpl* (fam) (gran esfuerzo): **le costó ~es terminarlo** it took him blood, sweat and tears to finish it (colloq)

sudoración *f* (frml) perspiration (frml)

sudoroso -sa *adj* sweaty

Suecia *f* Sweden

sueco¹ -ca *adj* Swedish

sueco² -ca *m,f*

A (persona) Swede; ***hacerse el ~*** (fam) to pretend not to have heard (*o* seen *etc*)

B **sueco** *m* (idioma) Swedish

suegro -gra (*m*) father-in-law; (*f*) mother-in-law; **mis ~s** my in-laws, my mother-and father-in-law

suela *f* (de zapato) sole; **medias ~s** half soles; **la carne está dura como una ~** the meat is as tough as shoeleather (AmE colloq) *o* (BrE colloq) as old boots; ***no te llega ni a la ~ del zapato*** he's not even fit to tie your shoelaces

suelazo *m* (Andes fam) (al caerse) bang, thud; **se dio un ~** she crashed to the ground; **hacer ~** (Per fam) to sleep on the floor

sueldo *m* 1 (nivel de retribución — de funcionario, oficinista) salary; (— de obrero) wage; **aumento de ~** salary/wage increase, pay raise (AmE), pay rise (BrE) 2 (dinero recibido — por funcionario, oficinista) salary; (— por obrero) wages (*pl*); **cobra un buen ~** she earns good wages *o* a good wage/a good salary; **un asesino a ~** a paid *o* hired killer

Compuestos

- **sueldo base** base salary (AmE), basic salary (BrE)
- **sueldo vital** (CS) living wage

suelo *m* 1 (tierra) ground; **se echaron** *or* **tiraron al ~** they threw themselves to the ground; **se cayó al ~** she fell over; ***arrastrarse por los ~s*** (fam) to grovel; ***estar por los ~s*** *or* ***el ~*** (fam) ‹‹*precios*›› to be rock bottom (colloq); ‹‹*moral/ánimos*›› to be at rock bottom (colloq); ***poner algo/a algn por los ~s*** *or* ***el ~*** (fam) to run sth/sb down (colloq) 2 (en casa) floor 3 (en calle, carretera) road (surface) 4 (Agr) land 5 (territorio) soil; **en ~ americano** on American soil; **el ~ patrio** one's native soil *o* land

suelta, sueltas, etc *see* **soltar**

suelto¹ -ta *adj*
A 1 ‹*animal/perro*›: **el perro está ~ en el jardín** the dog's loose in the garden; **el asesino anda ~** the murderer is on the loose 2 ‹*vestido/abrigo*› loose-fitting, full; **déjate el pelo ~** leave your hair loose *o* down 3 (separado, aislado): **ejemplares ~s** individual *o* single issues; **no los vendemos ~s** ‹*yogures/sobres*› we don't sell them individually *o* separately; ‹*caramelos/tornillos*› we don't sell them loose; **Ⓢ pares sueltos** loose pairs; **encontré un arete ~** I found an odd earring
B ‹*tornillo/tabla*› loose; ‹*cordones*› loose, untied; **esta hoja está suelta** this page has come loose *o* fallen out
C 1 ‹*dinero*› (fraccionado): **¿tienes mil pesos sueltas?** do you have a thousand pesos in change? 2 ‹*lenguaje/estilo*› fluent; ‹*movimientos*› fluid 3 (euf) ‹*vientre*› loose

suelto² *m* (Esp, Méx) (monedas) (small) change; **no tengo ~** I don't have any (loose) change

suena, suenan, etc *see* **sonar**

sueño *m*
A 1 (estado) sleep; **conciliar el ~** to get to sleep; **oyó un ruido entre ~s** she heard a noise in her sleep; **tener el ~ ligero/pesado** to be a light/heavy sleeper; **el ~ eterno** (euf) eternal rest (euf); ***descabezar*** *or* ***echar un sueñecito*** (fam) to have forty winks, have a (little) nap; ***perder el ~ (por algo)*** to lose sleep (over sth); ***quitarle el ~ a algn*** to keep sb awake; ***tener (el) ~ atrasado***: **tengo ~ atrasado** I have missed out on a lot of sleep 2 (ganas de dormir): **¿tienes ~?** are you tired/sleepy?; **¡qué ~ (tengo)!** I'm so sleepy!; **me empezó a entrar ~** I started feeling sleepy; **me estoy cayendo** *or* **muriendo de ~** I'm falling asleep on my feet; **se me ha quitado el ~** I've woken up again now, I don't feel sleepy any more; **lo venció el ~** (liter) sleep overcame him, he was overcome by sleep
B 1 (representación) dream; **que tengas dulces ~s** sweet dreams!; ***ni en ~s***: **no pienso prestarle ese dinero ni en ~s** I wouldn't dream of lending him that money 2 (ilusión) dream; **la mujer de sus ~s** the woman of his dreams; **sus ~s se hicieron realidad** her dreams came true; ***ser un ~*** (fam) to be divine (colloq)

(Compuesto) **sueño dorado**: **su ~ ~ es llegar a ser actriz** her (greatest) dream is to become an actress

suero *m* 1 (Med) (para alimentar) saline solution; (para inmunizar) serum 2 (de la sangre) blood serum 3 (de la leche) whey

suerte *f*
A 1 (azar) chance; **dejar algo en manos de la ~** to leave sth to chance; **me cayó** *or* **tocó en ~** it fell to my lot (frml *o* hum); ***echar algo a ~s*** (con monedas) to toss for sth; (con pajitas) to draw straws for sth; **la ~ está echada** (fr hecha) the die is cast 2 (fortuna) luck; **buena/mala ~** good/bad luck; **ha sido una ~ que vinieras** it was lucky you came; **¡qué mala ~!** how unlucky!; **¡qué ~ tienes!** you're so lucky!; **tiene la ~ de vivir en una casa grande** she is lucky *o* fortunate enough to live in a big house; **estamos de ~** we're in luck; **número/hombre de ~** lucky number/man; **deséame (buena) ~** wish me luck; **por ~ no estaba sola** luckily *o* fortunately I wasn't alone; **¡(que tengas) buena ~!** good luck!; ***probar ~*** to try one's luck; ***traer*** *or* ***dar mala ~*** to bring bad luck 3 (destino) fate; **quiso la ~ que nos volviéramos a encontrar** as fate would have it we met again; ***tentar a la ~*** to tempt fate *o* providence
B (tipo, clase) sort, kind; **vino toda ~ de gente** all sorts *o* kinds of people came; **de (tal) ~ que** (frml) so that
C (Taur) *each of the phases into which a bullfight is divided*

suertero¹ *adj* (Méx fam) ▸ **suertudo¹**

suertero² -tera *m,f* (Per) lottery ticket seller

suertudo¹ -da *adj* (fam) lucky, jammy (BrE colloq)

suertudo² -da *m,f* (fam) lucky *o* (BrE) jammy devil (colloq)

suéter *m* sweater, pullover, jersey (BrE), jumper (BrE)

suficiencia *f* 1 (aptitud) aptitude; **prueba de ~** aptitude test 2 (presunción) self-satisfaction, smugness; **sonrió con ~** she smiled smugly *o* complacently; **aire de ~** air of self-satisfaction

suficiente¹ *adj* 1 (bastante) enough; **con esto hay más que ~** there's more than enough here; **hay pruebas ~s para condenarlo** there is enough *o* sufficient evidence to convict him 2 ‹*persona*› self-satisfied, smug

suficiente² *m* pass (*equivalent to a grade of 5 on a scale from 0-10*)

suficientemente *adv* sufficiently; **no estaba (lo) ~ caliente** it wasn't hot enough

sufijo *m* suffix

suflé *m* soufflé

sufragar [A3] *vt* (frml) ‹*gastos/costos*› to defray (frml)
■ **sufragar** *vi* (AmL) (votar) to vote; **~ POR algn** to vote FOR sb

sufragio *m* (sistema) suffrage; (voto) (frml) vote

(Compuesto) **sufragio universal** universal suffrage

sufragista *mf* 1 (*mf*) suffragist; 2 (*f*) suffragette

sufrido -da *adj* ‹*persona*› long-suffering, uncomplaining; ‹*ropa/tejido*› hard-wearing; **un color ~** a color that doesn't show the dirt

sufrimiento *m* suffering; **después de muchos ~s** after much suffering; **pasar ~s** to suffer

sufrir [I1] *vt* 1 ‹*dolores/molestias*› to suffer; **sufre lesiones de gravedad** he has serious injuries; **sufrió una grave enfermedad** she had a serious illness 2 ‹*derrota/persecución/consecuencias*› to suffer; ‹*cambio*› to undergo; ‹*accidente*› to have; **sufrió un atentado** there was an attempt on his life; **el coche sufrió una avería** the car broke down; **son los que más sufren la crisis económica** they are the ones hardest hit by the economic crisis 3 (soportar) (*en frases negativas*) to bear; **no puedo ~ que se ría de mí** I can't bear *o* stand him laughing at me
■ **sufrir** *vi* to suffer; **~ DE algo** to suffer FROM sth; **sufre del hígado** she suffers from *o* has a liver complaint

sugerencia *f* suggestion

sugerente *adj* ‹*mirada/pose*› suggestive; ‹*vestido/blusa*› sexy

sugerir [I11] *vt*
A (aconsejar, proponer) to suggest; **me sugirió que lo probara** he suggested that I (should) try it; **sugiero dejarlo para mañana** I suggest we leave it *o* I suggest leaving it until tomorrow
B (suscitar): **¿qué te sugiere este cuadro?** what does this picture make you think of?; **aquel episodio le sugirió el argumento** that incident gave him the idea for the plot

sugestión *f* (convencimiento): **es pura ~** it's all in your (*o* his/her *etc*) mind; **tiene gran poder de ~** he is very persuasive

sugestionable *adj* impressionable, suggestible

sugestionar [A1] *vt*: **no la sugestiones** don't put ideas *o* thoughts like that into her head; **se dejó ~ por el vendedor** he allowed himself to be influenced by the salesman
■ **sugestionarse** *v pron* to get ideas into one's head; **se sugestionó con (la idea de) que iba a morir** she got the idea into her head that he was going to die

sugestivo -va *adj* ‹*mirada*› suggestive; ‹*escote*› sexy; ‹*libro/idea*› stimulating

suicida¹ *adj* suicidal

suicida² *mf* suicide victim; **un ~ no haría eso** a person about to commit suicide would not do that

suicidarse [A1] *v pron* to commit suicide

suicidio *m* suicide; **un intento de ~** a suicide attempt

suite /swit/ *f*
A (Mús) suite
B (en hotel) suite; **la ~ nupcial** the bridal suite

Suiza *f* Switzerland

suizo¹ -za *adj* Swiss

suizo² -za *m,f*
A (persona) Swiss
B **suizo** *m* AmC, Ven fam) (paliza) thrashing, beating

sujeción *f*
A (fijación): **puntos de ~** fixing points; **este cinturón ofrece mejor ~** this belt holds you in your seat better

S

B [1] (dominación) subjugation, subjection [2] (a ley): **con ~ a las normas** in accordance with the regulations

sujetador *m* (Esp) bra, brassiere

sujetalibros *m* (*pl* ~) bookend

sujetapapeles *m* (*pl* ~) (clip) paper clip; (con resorte) binder clip, bulldog clip (BrE)

sujetar [A1] *vt*

A [1] (mantener sujeto) to hold; **sujétalo mientras se pega** hold it in place while it sticks; **sujétalo bien, que no se escape** hold it tight, don't let it go; **tuvimos que ~los para que no se pegaran** we had to hold them back to stop them hitting each other; **sujétalo mientras llamo a la policía** keep hold of him while I call the police [2] (sostener) to hold; **sujétame los paquetes** hold on to the packages for me [3] (fijar, trabar): **sujeta los documentos con un clip** fasten the documents together with a paper clip; **sujetó el dobladillo con alfileres** she pinned up the hem

B (dominar) to subdue, conquer

■ **sujetarse** *v pron*

A [1] (agarrarse) **~se A algo** to hold on TO sth [2] (trabar, sostener): **se sujetaba los pantalones con la mano** he held his trousers up with his hand; **se sujetó la falda con un imperdible** she fastened her skirt with a safety pin; **se sujetó el pelo en un moño** she put *o* pinned her hair up in a bun

B (someterse) **~se A algo** ‹*a ley/reglas*› to abide BY sth

sujeto¹ -ta *adj*

A (sometido) **~ A algo** subject TO sth; **el programa está ~ a modificaciones** the program is subject to change

B (fijo) secure; **asegúrate de que la cuerda está bien sujeta** check that the rope is secure

sujeto² *m*

A (individuo) character, individual

B (Fil, Ling) subject

sulfamida *f* sulfonamide (AmE), sulphonamide (BrE)

sulfatar [A1] *vt* to sulfurize (AmE), to sulphurize (BrE)

sulfato *m* sulfate (AmE), sulphate (BrE)

sulfurarse [A1] *v pron* (fam) to blow one's top (colloq)

sulfúrico -ca *adj* sulfuric (AmE), sulphuric (BrE)

sulfuro *m* sulfur (AmE), sulphur (BrE)

sulfuroso -sa *adj* sulfurous (AmE), sulphurous (BrE)

sultán *m* sultan

sultana *f* sultana, sultan's wife

suma *f*

A (cantidad) sum

B [1] (Mat) addition; **hacer ~s** to do addition, to do sums (BrE); **hagamos la ~ de los gastos** let's add up all the expenses [2] (conjunto) combination; **la ~ de estos incidentes** the combination of these events; **en ~** in short

sumamente *adv* extremely, exceedingly (frml)

sumando *m* addend

sumar [A1] *vt*

A [1] ‹*cantidades*› to add (up) [2] (totalizar) to add up to; **8 y 5 suman 13** 8 and 5 add up to *o* make 13

B (agregar) ‹*apoyo/éxito/interés*› to add

■ **sumar** *vi* to add up; **suma y sigue** (a pie de página) balance carried forward

■ **sumarse** *v pron* [1] (agregarse) **~se A algo**: **esto se suma a los problemas ya existentes** this comes on top of *o* is in addition to any already existing problems; **a su falta de experiencia se suma su poca habilidad** he lacks both experience and ability [2] (adherirse) **~se A algo** (a protesta, celebración) to join sth

sumario¹ -ria *adj* [1] ‹*exposición*› brief, concise, summary (frml) [2] (Der) summary

sumario² *m*

A (Der) [1] (en lo penal) indictment; **abrir** *or* **instruir un ~** to conduct a preliminary investigation into a case [2] (juicio administrativo) disciplinary action

B (índice) (table of) contents

sumergible *adj* ‹*reloj*› waterproof; ‹*nave*› submersible

sumergido -da *adj* [1] ‹*submarino*› submerged; ‹*ciudad*› submerged, sunken [2] (sumido) **~ EN algo**: **vive ~ en su trabajo** he's always buried in his work; **estaban ~s en la apatía** they had sunk into a state of apathy

sumergir [I7] *vt* [1] (en líquido) to immerse, submerge; **sumergí la cabeza en el agua** I put my head under the water [2] **~ a algn EN algo** ‹*en pobreza/guerra*› to plunge sb INTO sth; (en ambiente) to immerse sb IN sth

■ **sumergirse** *v pron* [1] ‹‹*submarino/buzo*›› to dive, submerge [2] ‹*en ambiente*› to immerse oneself; **~se EN algo** to immerse oneself IN sth

sumersión *f* submersion

sumidero *m* drain

sumido -da *adj*

A (sumergido) **~ EN algo**: **~ en un mar de dudas** wracked by doubt; **me dejó ~ en la tristeza** it plunged me into sadness; **estaba ~ en un profundo sueño** he was in a deep sleep; **seguía sumida en sus reflexiones** she was still deep in thought

B (Col, Méx) (abollado) dented

suministrador -dora *m,f* supplier

suministrar [A1] *vt* (frml) [1] ‹*gas/mercancías*› to supply; **~ algo A algn** to supply sth TO sb, supply sb WITH sth [2] ‹*datos/información*› to provide, supply; **~ algo A algn** to provide sb WITH sth, provide sth FOR sb, supply sb WITH sth

suministro *m* [1] (acto de proveer) supply; **el ~ de gas/agua** the gas/water supply [2] (cosa provista) supply [3] **suministros** *mpl* (Mil) supplies (*pl*)

sumir [I1] *vt*

A (sumergir) **~ algo/a algn EN algo** ‹*en tristeza, desesperación*› to plunge sth/sb INTO sth; **lo sumió en un mar de dudas** it threw him into confusion

B (Col, Méx) (abollar) to dent, make a dent in

■ **sumirse** *v pron*

A (hundirse) **~se EN algo** ‹*en sueño*› to sink INTO sth; ‹*en tristeza*› to plunge INTO sth; ‹*en pensamientos*› to become lost IN sth

B (Col, Méx) (abollarse) to get dented

sumisión *f* (acción) submission; (actitud dócil) submissiveness

sumiso -sa *adj* submissive; **con actitud sumisa** submissively

súmmum *m*: **el ~** the ultimate; **es el ~ de la estupidez** he's as stupid as they come (colloq)

sumo -ma *adj* great; **me interesa en grado ~** I find it extremely interesting; **con ~ cuidado** with great *o* extreme care; **a lo ~** at the most; **la suma autoridad** the supreme authority

(Compuesto) **Sumo Sacerdote** *m* high priest

suntuosidad *f* sumptuousness, magnificence

suntuoso -sa *adj* ‹*palacio*› magnificent, splendid; ‹*decoración*› sumptuous, lavish; ‹*vestimentas*› sumptuous, splendid

supe *see* **saber**

supeditar [A1] *vt*: **supeditó todo a su trabajo** she put her work before everything else; **está supeditado a ...** it is subject to *o* conditional on ...

■ **supeditarse** *v pron* (a reglas, decisión) to abide by; **se ha supeditado a la voluntad de los padres** she has given in to her parents' wishes; **no sabe ~se a un horario** he's not good at keeping to fixed hours

super¹, súper *adj inv* (fam) super

super², súper *adv* (fam): **lo pasamos ~ bien** we had a great *o* fantastic time (colloq); **lo hizo ~ rápido** he did it incredibly quickly

super³, súper *f* ≈ premium grade gasoline (*in US*), ≈ four-star petrol (*in UK*)

superable *adj* ‹*problema*› that can be overcome, surmountable

superabundancia *f* superabundance, overabundance

superabundante *adj* superabundant

superación *f* (de problema) surmounting, overcoming; (de récord) breaking, beating; (de teoría) superseding

superar [A1] *vt*

A [1] (ser superior a, mayor que) to exceed, go beyond; **nadie lo supera en experiencia** no one has more experience than him; **supera en estatura a su hermano** he's taller than his brother; **nos superan en número** they outnumber us; **supera en tres puntos la cifra de ayer** it is three points higher than yesterday's figure [2] (mejorar) ‹*marca*› to beat; **ese método está totalmente superado** that method has been completely superseded

B [1] (vencer, sobreponerse a) ‹*timidez/dificultad/etapa*› to overcome; ‹*trauma*› to get over; **ya hemos superado la etapa más difícil** we've already got(ten) through *o* over the most difficult stage [2] (frml) ‹*examen/prueba*› to pass

■ **superarse** *v pron* to better oneself

superávit *m* (*pl* ~ *or* **-vits**) surplus

superbloque *m* (Ven) large apartment building

supercarburante *m* high-octane petrol

superchería *f* trick, fraud

superconductor *m* superconductor

superdotado[1] **-da** *adj* highly gifted

superdotado[2] **-da** *m,f* highly-gifted person

superestructura *f* superstructure

superficial *adj*
A (frívolo) ‹*persona*› superficial, shallow; ‹*charla/comentario*› superficial
B ‹*herida*› superficial; ‹*marca/grieta*› surface (*before n*)

superficialidad *f*
A (de persona) superficiality, shallowness; (de charla, comentario) superficiality
B (de herida) superficiality, superficial nature

superficialmente *adv* superficially

superficie *f*
A (parte expuesta, aparente) surface; **la ~ terrestre** the earth's surface; **salir a la ~** to surface, come to the surface
B (Mat) (área) area; **una ~ de diez metros cuadrados** a surface area of ten square metres

superfluo -flua *adj* superfluous, unnecessary; ‹*gastos*› unnecessary; **no gastes dinero en cosas superfluas** don't waste money on things you don't need

superior[1] *adj*
A [1] ‹*parte/piso*› top (*before n*), upper (*before n*); ‹*nivel*› higher; **el ángulo ~ derecho** the top right-hand corner [2] ‹*labio/mandíbula*› upper (*before n*)
B [1] (en calidad) superior; **~ A algo/algn** superior TO sth/sb; **se siente ~ a los demás** he thinks he's better than everyone else; **una inteligencia ~ a la media** above-average intelligence [2] (en jerarquía) ‹*oficial*› superior; ‹*clase social*› higher [3] (en cantidad, número): **los atacantes eran ~es en número** the attackers were greater *o* more in number; **~ A algo** above sth; **un número ~ a 9** a number greater than *o* higher than *o* above 9; **es ~ a mis fuerzas** it's more than I can bear

superior[2] **-riora** *m,f* [1] (Relig) (*m*) Superior; (*f*) Mother Superior [2] **superior** *m* (en rango) superior

superioridad *f* superiority; **~ SOBRE algn/algo** superiority OVER sb/sth

super-jumbo *m* (Aviat) super jumbo

superlativo[1] **-va** *adj* superlative

superlativo[2] *m* superlative

supermercado *m* supermarket

supermodelo *f* supermodel

supernumerario -ria *adj/m,f* supernumerary

superpetrolero *m* supertanker

superpoblación *f* (de región) overpopulation; (de ciudad) overcrowding

superpoblado -da *adj* ‹*mundo/país*› overpopulated; ‹*barrio/ciudad*› overcrowded

superponer [E22] *vt* to superimpose, place … on top

superposición *f* superimposition

superpotencia *f* superpower

superproducción *f*
A (Econ) overproduction
B (Cin) blockbuster

supersónico -ca *adj* supersonic

superstición *f* superstition

supersticioso -sa *adj* superstitious

supervigilancia *f* (Andes) supervision

supervigilar [A1] *vt* (Andes) to oversee, supervise

supervisar [A1] *vt* to supervise

supervisión *f* supervision

supervisor -sora *m,f* supervisor

supervivencia *f* survival

superviviente[1] *adj* surviving (*before n*)

superviviente[2] *mf* survivor

supiera, supiste, etc *see* **saber**

supino -na *adj*
A ‹*posición*› supine
B ‹*ignorancia/tontería*› crass

súpito -ta *adj* [1] (Col, Méx fam) (atónito, perplejo) stunned; **quedarse ~** to be stunned *o* dumbstruck *o* taken aback [2] (Méx fam) (dormido) fast asleep

suplantación *f* (de personalidad) impersonation; (de objeto) switch

suplantar [A1] *vt*
A ‹*objeto*› to supplant (frml), to replace; ‹*persona*› to impersonate, pass oneself off as
B (CS) (suplir) to act as a replacement for

suplementario -ria *adj* [1] ‹*información/ingresos*› additional, supplementary; ‹*trabajo*› extra; **trenes ~s** extra *o* relief trains [2] ‹*ángulo*› supplementary

suplemento *m* supplement; **~ dominical** Sunday supplement

suplencia *f* [1] (sustitución): **hacer una ~** ‹‹*profesor*›› to do substitute teaching (AmE), to do supply teaching (BrE); **le está haciendo la ~ al Dr. Suárez** she's standing in for Dr Suárez [2] (trabajo) temporary job

suplente[1] *adj*: **profesor ~** substitute teacher (AmE), supply teacher (BrE); **médico ~** covering doctor (AmE), locum (BrE); **el guardameta ~** the substitute *o* reserve goalkeeper

suplente[2] *mf* [1] (de médico) covering doctor (AmE), locum (BrE) [2] (de actor) understudy [3] (Dep) substitute [4] (de profesor) substitute (teacher) (AmE), supply teacher (BrE); **el ~ del señor Beardo** Mr Beardo's stand-in *o* replacement

supletorio[1] **-ria** *adj* ‹*cama*› extra, additional; **teléfono ~** extension

supletorio[2] *m* extension

súplica *f* (ruego) entreaty, plea; (Der) petition

suplicante *adj* imploring (*before n*); **¡ayúdeme! —dijo en tono ~** help me! — he implored

suplicar [A2] *vt* (rogar) to beg; **~le a algn QUE + SUBJ** to beg *o* implore *o* (liter) beseech sb to + INF; **te suplico que no se lo digas** I beg you not to tell him

suplicio *m* [1] (tortura) torture; **es un verdadero ~** (fam) it's absolute torture *o* a real nightmare (colloq) [2] (castigo) punishment

suplir [I1] *vt*
A (compensar, remediar) to make up for; ‹*dieta*› to supplement
B (reemplazar) ‹*profesor/médico*› to stand in for, substitute for; ‹*jugador*› to replace, substitute
C (Col, Ven) (dotar, proveer) **~ algo/a algn DE *or* CON algo** to provide *o* supply sth/sb WITH sth

suponer[1] *m*: **si quebraran, es un ~, …** suppose *o* supposing they were to go bankrupt, …; **si, es un ~, perdieses tu trabajo …** just supposing for the sake of argument that you were to lose your job

suponer[2] [E22] *vt*
A [1] (tomar como hipótesis) to suppose, assume; **supongamos que lo que dice es cierto** let's suppose *o* assume what he says is true; **suponiendo que todo salga bien** assuming everything goes OK; **supongamos que los dos ángulos son iguales** let us suppose *o* assume that both angles are equal [2] (imaginar): **supongo que tienes razón** I suppose you're right; **nada hacía ~ que …** there was nothing to suggest that …; **¿va a venir hoy? — supongo que sí** is she coming today? — I should think so *o* I imagine so; **es de ~ que se lo habrán dicho** presumably *o* I should think *o* I would imagine he's been told; **se supone que empieza a las nueve** it's supposed to start at nine [3] (atribuir) (+ *me/te/le etc*) **le suponía más edad** I imagined *o* thought he was older; **se le suponía un valor aproximado de …** it was thought to be worth approximately …
B (significar, implicar) to mean; **supuso mucho trabajo** it involved a great deal of work; **eso supondría tener que empezar desde el principio** that would mean having to start from the beginning again; (+ *me/te/le etc*): **ese negocio no le supuso ningún beneficio** that deal didn't make him any profit; **no me supone ninguna molestia** it's no trouble at all

suposición *f* supposition

supositorio *m* suppository

supranacional *adj* supranational
supremacía *f* supremacy
supremo -ma *adj* supreme
supresión *f* 1 (de impuesto) abolition; (de restricción) lifting; (de servicio) withdrawal 2 (de párrafo, capítulo) deletion 3 (de noticias, detalles) suppression
suprimir [I1] *vt* 1 ‹*impuesto/ley/costumbre*› to abolish; ‹*restricción*› to lift; ‹*servicio*› to withdraw; **debemos ~ gastos superfluos** we must eliminate *o* cut out unnecessary expenses; **le suprimieron la medicación** they stopped his medication 2 (Impr) ‹*párrafo/capítulo*› to delete 3 ‹*noticia/detalles*› to suppress
supuestamente *adv* supposedly
supuesto[1] -ta *adj* 1 (falso) false; **el ~ electricista** the so-called *o* supposed electrician 2 (que se rumorea): **la radio desmintió su supuesta muerte** reports of his death were denied on the radio; **su supuesta enfermedad** her supposed illness 3 **por supuesto** of course; **¿lo sabías? — ¡por ~ que sí!** did you know? — of course I did!; ***dar algo por ~*** to take sth for granted
supuesto[2] *m* supposition; **partiendo del ~ de que no sabían nada** working on the assumption that they knew nothing; **en el ~ de que tenga un accidente** should you have an accident, in the event of an accident
supuración *f* suppuration
supurar [A1] *vi* to weep, ooze, suppurate (tech)
supuse, supuso, etc *see* **suponer**
sur[1] *adj inv* ‹*región*› southern; **en la parte ~ del país** in the southern part *o* the south of the country; **conducían en dirección ~** they were driving south *o* southward(s); **el ala/la costa ~** the south wing/coast
sur[2] *m* 1 (parte, sector): **el ~** the south; **en el ~ de la provincia** in the south of the province; **al ~ de Cartagena** to the south of Cartagena 2 (punto cardinal) south, South; **vientos del ~** southerly winds; **viajábamos hacia el ~** we were travelling south *o* southward(s); **las ventanas dan al ~** the windows face south
Suráfrica *f* South Africa
surafricano -na *adj/m,f* South African
Suramérica *f* South America
suramericano -na *adj/m,f* South American
surazo *m* (CS) strong southerly wind
surcar [A2] *vt* 1 ‹*tierra*› to plow through (AmE), to plough through (BrE) 2 (liter) ‹*agua*› to cleave (liter), to cut through; ‹*aire/espacio*› to fly through 3 ‹*superficie*› to score
surco *m*
A 1 (en la tierra) furrow 2 (en el agua) wake, track 3 (en disco) groove; (en superficie) groove, line; (marca de rueda) ruts, track
B (Col) (de flores) flowerbed
sureño[1] -ña *adj* southern
sureño[2] -ña *m,f* southerner
sureste *adj inv/m* ▸ **sudeste**
surf /'surf/, **surfing** /'surfin/ *m* surfing
surfear [A1] *vi* (AmL) 1 (Dep) to surf 2 (Inf): **~ en Internet/la web** to surf the Internet/the World Wide Web
surfista *mf* surfer
surgir [I7] *vi* 1 «*manantial*» to rise 2 (aparecer, salir) «*problema/dificultad*» to arise, come up, emerge; «*interés/sentimiento*» to develop, emerge; «*idea*» to emerge, come up; «*tema*» to come up, crop up; «*movimiento/partido*» to come into being, arise; **me ha surgido un problema y no podré ir** something has cropped up and I won't be able to go; **el amor que surgió entre ellos** the love that sprang up between them; **han surgido muchas empresas de este tipo** a lot of companies of this kind have sprung up *o* emerged; **~ DE algo**: **una silueta surgió de entre las sombras** a shape rose up from *o* loomed up out of the shadows
suroeste *adj inv/m* ▸ **sudoeste**
surrealismo *m* surrealism
surrealista[1] *adj* ‹*artista/exposición*› surrealist (*before n*); ‹*estilo/efecto*› surrealistic
surrealista[2] *mf* surrealist

surtido[1] -da *adj* 1 ‹*bombones/galletas*› assorted 2 (provisto) stocked; **una tienda bien/mal surtida** a well-stocked/poorly-stocked shop
surtido[2] *m* (de bombones, galletas) assortment; (de herramientas, ropa) range, selection, assortment; **un gran ~ de muebles** a large selection of furniture
surtidor *m* (aparato) gas pump (AmE), petrol pump (BrE); (estación de servicio) gas station (AmE), petrol station (BrE)
surtir [I1] *vt* 1 (proveer) **~ a algn DE algo** to supply sb WITH sth 2 **surtir efecto** to take effect: **el tratamiento no surtió efecto** the treatment had no effect *o* didn't work
■ **surtirse** *v pron* **~se DE algo** ‹*de provisiones*› to stock up WITH sth; **allí puede ~se de todo lo necesario** you can stock up with *o* get everything you need there
susceptibilidad *f* sensitivity, touchiness
susceptible *adj*
A ‹*persona*› sensitive, touchy; **~ A algo** sensitive TO sth
B (frml) (capaz) **~ DE algo**: **es ~ de mejora** there is room for improvement; **órganos ~s de ser transplantados** organs which can be transplanted; **es ~ de alteraciones** it's subject to alterations
suscitar [A1] *vt* (frml) ‹*curiosidad/interés*› to arouse; ‹*dudas*› to raise; ‹*escándalo/polémica*› to provoke, cause; ‹*debate*› to give rise to
suscribir [I34] *vt*
A 1 (frml) ‹*tratado/convenio*› to sign; **el que suscribe** (frml) the undersigned (frml) 2 (frml) ‹*opinión*› to endorse, subscribe to (frml)
B ‹*bonos/acciones*› to subscribe for
C (a publicación) **~ a algn A algo** to take out a subscription TO sth FOR sb
■ **suscribirse** *v pron* (*refl*) **~ A algo** to subscribe TO sth; **me he suscrito a varias revistas** I've taken out subscriptions to various magazines
suscripción *f*
A (a publicación) subscription; **abrir una ~** to take out a subscription
B (de tratado) signing
C (de bonos, acciones) subscription
suscriptor -tora *m,f* subscriber
susodicho -cha *adj* (frml) (*delante del n*) aforementioned (frml), aforesaid (frml)
suspender [E1] *vt*
A 1 (suprimir) ‹*pagos*› to suspend; ‹*garantía/derecho*› to suspend, withdraw; ‹*sesión*› to adjourn; ‹*viaje*› (para siempre) to call off; (temporalmente) to put off; ‹*tratamiento*› to stop, suspend; ‹*servicio*› to suspend, discontinue; ‹*programa*› to cancel 2 (de sus funciones) ‹*empleado/jugador*› to suspend; ‹*alumno*› (AmL) to suspend; **fueron suspendidos sin sueldo** they were suspended without pay
B (colgar) **~ algo DE algo** to hang sth FROM sth; **estaba suspendido de una rama** he was hanging from a branch
C (Esp) ‹*asignatura/examen/alumno*› to fail
■ **suspender** *vi* (Esp) to fail
suspense *m* (Esp) ▸ **suspenso A1**
suspensión *f*
A 1 (de garantías) withdrawal, suspension; (de servicio) suspension, discontinuation 2 (de empleado, jugador) suspension; (de alumno) (AmL) suspension
Compuestos
• **suspensión de empleo y sueldo** suspension without pay
• **suspensión de pagos** bankruptcy protection
B (de partículas) suspension
C (Auto) suspension
suspenso *m*
A 1 (AmL) (Cin, Lit) suspense; **película/novela de ~** thriller 2 **en suspenso** ‹*sentencia*› suspended
B (Esp) (Educ) fail, failure; **no he tenido ningún ~** I haven't failed anything
suspensor *m* 1 (Per, RPl) (Dep) ▸ **suspensorio** 2 **suspensores** *mpl* (Chi) (tirantes) suspenders (*pl*) (AmE), braces (*pl*) (BrE)
suspensorio *m* jockstrap, athletic supporter (AmE), athletic support (BrE)
suspicacia *f* suspicion
suspicaz *adj* suspicious

S

suspirar [A1] *vi* 1 (de pena, alivio) to sigh 2 (anhelar) **~ POR algo** to yearn *o* long FOR sth

suspiro *m* sigh; **un ~ de alivio** a sigh of relief; ***exhalar el último ~*** (liter) to breathe one's last (liter)

sustancia *f*
A (materia) substance
B (contenido) substance; **el libro no tiene ninguna ~** the book has no substance to it
C (de comida) substance, goodness

sustancial *adj*
A (referente a la sustancia) substantial, fundamental
B (considerable) substantial, considerable

sustancioso -sa *adj* ‹*comida/plato*› substantial; ‹*ganancias*› substantial, considerable

sustantivo[1] -va *adj* 1 (frml) (fundamental) substantive (frml), fundamental 2 (Ling) noun (*before n*), substantive (*before n*) (frml)

sustantivo[2] *m* noun, substantive (frml)

sustentación *f*
A (mantenimiento económico) maintenance, support
B 1 (Arquit) support 2 (Aviac) lift

sustentar [A1] *vt*
A 1 ‹*peso*› to support 2 ‹*persona/familia*› to support, maintain
B ‹*opinión/teoría*› to hold, maintain; ‹*moral/esperanza*› to sustain, keep up
■ **sustentarse** *v pron* 1 (mantenerse) to support oneself 2 (alimentarse) **~se DE** *or* **CON algo** to sustain oneself WITH sth, to subsist ON sth

sustento *m* 1 (apoyo) means of support; **ganarse el ~** (liter) to earn one's living, to support oneself 2 (alimento) sustenance

sustitución *f* 1 (permanente) replacement; **fue nombrado en ~ de Ana Tamayo** he was appointed to replace Ana Tamayo; **~ DE algo/algn POR algo/algn** replacement OF sth/sb BY sth/sb 2 (transitoria) substitution; **le hice la ~ porque estaba enfermo** I stood in for him because he was ill; **~ DE algo/algn POR algo/algn**: **la ~ de Merino por Juárez** the substitution of Juárez for Merino

sustituir [I20] *vt* 1 (permanentemente) to replace; **sustituyó a Morán como líder** he replaced *o* took over from Morán as leader; **~ A algo** to replace sth; **~ algo/a algn POR algo/algn** to replace sth/sb WITH sth/sb; **sustituyó a Rubio por Guerra** he replaced Rubio with Guerra, he substituted Guerra for Rubio 2 (transitoriamente) ‹*trabajador/profesor*› to stand in for; ‹*deportista*› to come on as a substitute for; **me pidió que lo sustituyera** he asked me to stand in for him

sustituto -ta *m,f* 1 (permanente) replacement 2 (transitorio) substitute; (de médico) covering doctor (AmE), locum (BrE); (de actor) understudy; **el ~ de la profesora de alemán** the substitute (AmE) *o* (BrE) stand-in for the German teacher

sustitutorio -ria, **sustitutivo -va** *adj* (frml) substitute (*before n*); **una declaración sustitutoria del certificado** a declaration in place of the certificate

susto *m* 1 (impresión momentánea) fright; **¡qué ~ me has dado** *or* (fam) **pegado!** you gave me such a fright!; **me di** *or* **llevé un ~ de padre y señor mío** (fam) I got the fright of my life (colloq); ***no ganar para ~s*** (Esp fam): **con este niño no ganamos para ~s** it's just one thing after another with this boy 2 (miedo) fear; **está con un ~ que se muere** she's frightened *o* scared to death

sustracción *f* (frml)
A (Mat) subtraction
B (robo) theft, robbery

sustraer [E23] *vt*
A (Mat) to subtract
B (frml) 1 (robar) to steal; **le fue sustraída la cartera** his wallet was stolen 2 (llevarse) to remove, take away
■ **sustraerse** *v pron* (frml) **~se A algo** to avoid sth; **intentó ~se a las miradas del público** he tried to stay *o* keep out of the public eye; **intentó ~se a sus preguntas** she tried to elude his questions

sustrato *m* (Ling, Geol) substratum

susurrante *adj* 1 ‹*voz*› whispering (*before n*) 2 (liter) ‹*riachuelo*› murmuring (*before n*); ‹*viento*› sighing (*before n*); ‹*hojas*› rustling (*before n*)

susurrar [A1] *vi* 1 «*persona*» to whisper 2 (liter) «*agua*» to murmur; «*viento*» to sigh; «*hojas*» to rustle
■ **susurrar** *vt* to whisper; **le susurró algo al oído** she whispered something in his ear

susurro *m* 1 (murmullo) whisper 2 (liter) (del agua) murmuring; (del viento) sighing; (de las hojas) rustling

sutil *adj* 1 ‹*diferencia*› subtle, fine; ‹*ironía*› subtle; ‹*mente/inteligencia*› keen, sharp 2 ‹*gasa/velo*› fine; ‹*fragancia*› subtle, delicate

sutileza *f* subtlety

sutura *f* (Med) suture

suturar [A1] *vt* to suture, stitch

suyo[1] -ya *adj* (de él) his; (de ella) hers; (de usted, ustedes) yours; (de ellos, ellas) theirs; **Marta y un amigo ~** Marta and a friend of hers; ***ser muy ~***: **eso es muy ~** that's typical of him/her; **es muy suya** she's an odd sort (colloq)

suyo[2] -ya *pron* **el ~, la suya** *etc* (de él) his; (de ella) hers; (de usted, ustedes) yours; (de ellos, ellas) theirs; **él me prestó el ~** he lent me his; ***hacer (una) de las suyas*** (fam) to get up to one's usual *o* old tricks; ***ir a lo ~*** to look after number one; ***lo ~***: **tuvo que trabajar lo ~** he had to work very hard; **pesa lo ~** it weighs a ton; ***salirse con la suya*** to get one's own way

svástica *f* swastika

switch /(e)'switʃ/ *m* 1 (Col, Ven, Méx) (interruptor) light switch 2 (Méx) (Auto) ignition switch

Tt

T, t *f (read as /te/) the letter* **T, t**

t. (= **tonelada**) t, ton

T.

A (= **tara**) tare

B (= **tonelada**) t, ton

taba *f* 1 (Anat) anklebone 2 (Jueg) jacks

tabacal *m* tobacco plantation

tabacalera *f* cigarette factory

tabacalero[1] **-ra** *adj* tobacco (*before n*)

tabacalero[2] **-ra** *m,f* tobacco grower

tabaco *m* 1 (planta, producto) tobacco 2 (Esp) (cigarrillos) cigarettes (*pl*) 3 (Col) (puro) cigar

(Compuestos)

- **tabaco de hebra/de mascar/de pipa** loose/chewing/pipe tobacco
- **tabaco negro/rubio** dark/Virginia tobacco

tabalear [A1] *vi* to drum, tap

tabanco *m* 1 (puesto) stall (*selling food*) 2 (AmC) (desván) attic

tábano *m* horsefly

tabaquera *f* 1 (para tabaco) tobacco pouch; (para cigarrillos) cigarette case; (para cigarros) cigar case 2 (de la pipa) bowl

tabaquismo *m* nicotine poisoning

(Compuesto) **tabaquismo pasivo** passive smoking

tabarra *f* (Esp fam) nuisance, pest (colloq); **deja de dar la ~** stop pestering *o* (colloq) bugging me

tabasco *m* Tabasco® (sauce)

taberna *f* bar, tavern (arch), pub (BrE)

tabernáculo *m* tabernacle

tabernero -ra *m,f* (propietario) (*m*) bar owner, landlord (BrE); (*f*) bar owner, landlady (BrE); (camarero) (*m*) bartender; (*f*) barmaid

tabicar [A2] *vt* (con ladrillos) to wall up, brick up

tabique *m* 1 (pared) partition 2 (Méx) (ladrillo) brick

tabla *f*

A (de madera) plank; **las ~s del suelo** the floorboards; ***salvarse en*** *or* ***por una tablita*** (Méx fam) to have a narrow escape (colloq)

(Compuestos)

- **tabla de lavar** washboard
- **tabla de picar/planchar** chopping/ironing board
- **tabla de salvación** salvation
- **tabla rasa** tabula rasa; ***hacer ~ ~*** to wipe the slate clean
- **tablas de la ley** *fpl* tables of the law (*pl*)

B **tablas** *fpl* 1 (Teatr) stage; ***tener ~s*** «*actor, cantante*» (fam) to be an old hand *o* an expert, to have presence 2 (Taur) barrier

C (de surfing) surfboard; (de windsurf) sailboard, windsurfer; (para natación) float

D 1 (gráfico, listado) table; **las ~s (de clasificación) de la liga** the division *o* league tables 2 (Mat) *tb* **~ de multiplicar** multiplication table; **la ~ del 6** the 6 times table

(Compuestos)

- **tabla de logaritmos** log table
- **tabla de materias** table of contents
- **tabla periódica** *or* **de los elementos** periodic table

E (de falda) pleat; **una falda de ~s** a pleated skirt

F (de terreno) plot, lot (AmE)

G *tb* **~ de gimnasia** (serie de ejercicios) circuit training; (en competición) routine

H **tablas** *fpl* (en ajedrez): **hacer ~s** to draw; **acabar** *or* **quedar en ~s** to end in a draw; ***estar ~s*** (Méx fam) to be even *o* quits (colloq)

tablado *m* (para discursos) platform; (para espectáculos) stage

tablao *m*: *tb* **~ flamenco** *bar or club where flamenco is performed*

tablear [A1] *vt*

A ‹*tela/falda*› to pleat

B (Agr) to level

tablero *m* 1 (para anuncios, fotos) bulletin board (AmE), noticeboard (BrE) 2 (Jueg) board; **un ~ de ajedrez** a chessboard; **un ~ de damas** a checkerboard (AmE), a draughtboard (BrE) 3 (pizarra) blackboard 4 (de mesa) top 5 (Taur) barrier

(Compuestos)

- **tablero chino** Chinese checkerboard
- **tablero de dibujo** drawing board
- **tablero de instrumentos** *or* **de mandos** instrument panel

tableta *f* 1 (Farm) tablet, pill 2 (de chocolate) bar

tabletear [A1] *vi* to rattle, clack

tableteo *m* rattling, clickety-clack

tablilla *f*

A (Med) splint

B (Méx) (de chocolate) bar

tablón *m* 1 (de madera) plank 2 *tb* **~ de anuncios** (Esp) bulletin board (AmE), noticeboard (BrE)

tabú[1] *adj inv* taboo; **un tema ~** a taboo subject

tabú[2] *m* (*pl* **-búes** *or* **-bús**) taboo

tabulador *m* tabulator, tab

tabular[1] *adj* tabular

tabular[2] [A1] *vt* to tabulate

taburete *m* stool

tacada *f* (en billar) shot; ***de una ~*** (Jueg), with a single shot; (de un tirón): **lo escribió de una ~** he dashed it off

tacañería *f* stinginess, meanness (colloq)

tacaño[1] **-ña** *adj* stingy, mean

tacaño[2] **-ña** *m,f* miser, tightwad (AmE colloq)

tacar [A2] *vt* (Col) ‹*pipa*› to fill; ‹*cigarrillo*› to tap; ‹*cañón*› to tamp

■ **tacar** *vi* (Col, Ven) to hit the ball

taca-taca *m* (Chi) table football

tacha *f* stain, blemish; **sin ~** ‹*reputación*› unblemished, spotless; ‹*conducta*› irreproachable; **es una persona sin ~** he is beyond reproach

tachadura *f* crossing out, correction

tachar [A1] *vt*

A (en escrito) to cross out; **tacha éstas de la lista** cross these off the list

B (tildar) **~ a algn DE algo** to brand *o* label sb AS sth

C (Der) to impeach, discredit

tacho *m* 1 (CS) (recipiente) (metal) container 2 (CS, Per) (papelero) wastebasket (AmE), wastepaper basket (BrE); **el ~ de la basura** (en la cocina) garbage can (AmE), rubbish bin (BrE); (para la calle) garbage *o* trash can (AmE), dustbin (BrE); ***irse al ~*** (CS fam) «*negocio*» to go to the wall; «*planes*» to fall through

t

tachón *m*
A (en escrito) crossing out
B (tachuela) stud, boss
C (Ven) (en costura) pleat

tachonado -da *adj* studded; **un cielo ~ de estrellas** a sky studded with stars

tachuela *f* 1 (clavo) tack; (en cinturón) stud 2 (Chi, Méx fam) (persona baja) shrimp (colloq), shorty (colloq)

tácito -ta *adj* ‹*acuerdo*› tacit, unspoken; **la idea está tácita en el libro** the idea is implicit in the book; **el verbo está ~** the verb is understood

taciturno -na *adj* 1 [SER] (callado, silencioso) taciturn, uncommunicative 2 [ESTAR] (triste) glum, gloomy

tacle *m* (AmL) tackle

taclear [A1], **tacklear** [A1] *vt* (AmL) to tackle

taco *m*
A 1 (de madera) plug; ***a todo ~*** (Col fam) (a todo lujo) in the lap of luxury; (a todo volumen) on full blast 2 (de billetes) book; (de folletos) wad
B 1 (en billar) cue 2 (Col) (de golf) tee
C 1 (Dep) (de botas) cleat (AmE), stud (BrE) 2 (CS, Per) (tacón) heel; **zapatos de ~ alto/bajo** *or* **chato** high-heeled/low-heeled *o* flat shoes
(Compuesto) **taco aguja** *or* **alfiler** (CS) spike heel
D 1 (Coc) taco; ***hacerse ~*** (Méx) to wrap (oneself) up; ***hacer ~ a algn*** (Méx) to wrap sb up 2 (Méx) (comida ligera) snack, bite to eat (colloq); ***darse ~*** (Méx fam): **se da mucho ~** he really thinks he's it (colloq); ***echarse un ~ de ojo*** (Méx fam) to ogle the men/women (colloq), to eye up the talent (BrE colloq)
E (Esp fam) (palabrota) swearword
F (Esp fam) 1 (confusión) mess (colloq) 2 (alboroto) racket (colloq)
G (Chi) (embotellamiento) traffic jam; (en conducto, canal) blockage

tacón *m* heel; **zapatos de ~ alto/bajo** high-heeled/low-heeled *o* flat shoes
(Compuesto) **tacón de aguja** *or* **alfiler** spike heel

taconazo *m* (golpe) kick (*with the heel*); (contra el suelo) stamp (*with the heel*); (en fútbol) backheel; **dar un ~** to click one's heels

taconear [A1] *vi* 1 (al andar): **iba taconeando por la calle** she walked down the street, her heels clicking as she went 2 (en baile) to stamp (one's heel)

taconeo *m* 1 (al andar): **oíamos el ~ de la vecina de arriba** we could hear the woman upstairs walking about in her heels 2 (en baile) heel stamping

táctica *f* tactic, strategy

táctico¹ -ca *adj* tactical

táctico² -ca *m,f* tactician

táctil *adj* tactile

tacto *m*
A 1 (sentido) sense of touch 2 (acción) touch; **mecanografía al ~** touch-typing 3 (cualidad) feel
B (delicadeza) tact; **¡qué falta de ~!** how tactless!; **tiene mucho ~** he's very tactful

TAE *f*
A (= **tasa anual efectiva**) APR
B (= **trastorno afectivo estacional**) SAD

tafetán *m* taffeta

tafilete *m* morocco (leather)

taguara *f* (Ven) cheap restaurant

Tahití *m* Tahiti

tahona *f* (panadería) bakery; (molino) flourmill

tahúr *mf* gambler, cardsharp (colloq)

tailandés¹ -desa *adj/m,f* Thai

tailandés² *m* (idioma) Thai

Tailandia *f* Thailand

taimadamente *adv* craftily, cunningly

taimado -da *adj*
A (astuto) crafty, cunning
B (Chi) (malhumorado) sulky, huffy

taimarse [A1] *v pron* (Chi fam) 1 «*persona*» to get into a huff (colloq) 2 «*mula*» to balk

taita *m* (fam) (papá) dad (colloq), daddy (colloq)

taiwanés -nesa *adj/m,f* Taiwanese

tajada *f*
A 1 (de melón, queso) slice; ***sacar ~ de algo*** (fam) to take/get one's cut of sth (colloq) 2 (Ven) (de plátano frito) slice of fried plantain
B (Esp arg) (borrachera): **¡vaya ~ que llevaba!** she was smashed! (arg)

tajamar *m* 1 (Náut) cutwater 2 (de puente) cutwater 3 (CS) (malecón) breakwater

tajante *adj* ‹*respuesta*› categorical, unequivocal; ‹*tono*› sharp; **un 'no' ~** an emphatic *o* a categorical 'no'

tajantemente *adv* categorically

tajar [A1] *vt* (Col, Per) to sharpen

tajear [A1] *vt* (AmL) to slash

tajo *m*
A 1 (corte) cut 2 (CS) (en falda) slit
B 1 (Geolg) gorge, ravine 2 (en mina) face
C (Hist) block
D (Esp) (obra) site

tal¹ *adj*
A (dicho) such; **no existía ~ tesoro** there was no such treasure; **nunca dije ~ cosa** I never said anything of the kind *o* such a thing
B (seguido de consecuencia): **era ~ su desesperación que ...** such was his despair that ...; **se llevó ~ disgusto que ...** she was so upset (that) ...; **había ~ cantidad de gente que ...** there were so many people that ...
C (con valor indeterminado) such-and-such; **~ día, en ~ lugar** such-and-such a day, at such-and-such a place; **llamó un ~ Méndez** a Mr Méndez phoned

tal² *pron*: **si quieres trato de adulto, compórtate como ~** if you want to be treated like an adult, behave like one; **y como ~ es responsable** as such he is responsible; **que si ~ y que si cual** and so on and so forth; ***son ~ para cual*** (fam) he's just as bad as she is, they're as bad as each other
(Compuesto) **tal por cual** *mf* (fam) so-and-so (colloq)

tal³ *adv*
A (fam) (en preguntas): **hola ¿qué ~?** hello, how are you?; **¿qué ~ es Marisa?** what's Marisa like?; **¿qué ~ lo pasaron?** how did it go?
B (*en locs*) **con tal de + INF**: **hace cualquier cosa con ~ de llamar la atención** he'll do anything to get attention; **con ~ de no tener que volver** as long as I don't have to come back; **con tal (de) que + SUBJ**: **con ~ (de) que nadie se entere** as long as no one finds out; **con ~ (de) que me lo devuelvas** as long as *o* provided you give it back (to me); **tal (y) como**: **~ (y) como están las cosas** the way things are; **hazlo ~ (y) como te indicó** do it exactly as she told you; **tal cual**: **me lo dijo así, ~ cual** those were her exact words; **lo dejé todo ~ cual** I left everything exactly as it was *o* just as it was; **tal vez** maybe; **~ vez venga** maybe he'll come; **pensé que ~ vez querrías** I thought you might want to

tala *f* felling, cutting

talabartería *f* saddlery

talabartero -ra *m,f* saddler, leather worker

talacha *f* 1 (Méx) (reparación de llantas) flat *o* puncture repair 2 (Méx fam) (trabajo manual) work; **hacer la ~** to do the donkey work (colloq)

talachero -ra (Méx fam) (*m*) handyman; (*f*) handywoman

talador -dora *m,f* woodcutter, lumberjack

taladradora *f* pneumatic drill

taladrar [A1] *vt* 1 ‹*pared/madera*› to drill (through) 2 ‹*oído*›: **un ruido que taladra los oídos** an earsplitting *o* earpiercing noise

taladro *m* 1 (mecánico) hand drill; (eléctrico) electric *o* power drill; (neumático) pneumatic drill 2 (agujero) drill hole

talaje *m*
A (AmC, Méx) (ácaro) tick
B (Chi) (pasto) grass; (lugar) pasture

tálamo *m* (liter) (lecho) bed; **el ~ nupcial** the nuptial bed (liter)

talán, talán *m* ding, dong

talante *m* 1 (humor) mood; **estar de buen/mal ~** to be in a good/bad mood 2 (voluntad, disposición) willingness; **me ayudó de buen ~** he helped me willingly

talar [A1] *vt* ‹*árbol*› to fell, cut down
■ **talar** *vi* (Chi) «*ganado*» to graze

talco *m* talc; **polvos de ~** talcum powder

talega *f*
A (saco) sack
B **talegas** *fpl* (Méx vulg) (testículos) nuts (*pl*) (sl), balls (*pl*) (vulg)

talegada *f*, **talegazo** *m*: **se dio/pegó una buena ~** she took *o* had a nasty fall

talego *m* (saco) sack; (bolsa) (Col, Ven) bag

taleguilla *f* bullfighter's breeches (*pl*)

talento *m* **1** (aptitud) talent; **un escritor de gran ~** a very talented *o* gifted writer; **es un joven de ~** he's a talented *o* able young man **2** (persona) talented person

talentoso -sa *adj* talented, gifted

TALGO /'talɣo/ *m* (= **Tren Articulado Ligero Goicoechea Oriol**) *air-conditioned express train*

> **Talgo – Tren Articulado Ligero Goicoechea Oriol**
> This was Spain's fastest train, until the AVE came into service in 1992

talismán *m* talisman, lucky charm

talla *f*
A **1** (Indum) size; **¿cuál es su ~?** what size are you?; **de** *o* **en todas las ~s** in all sizes **2** (estatura) size, height; **de ~ mediana** of medium height; ***dar la ~*** (en altura) to be tall enough; (mostrarse competente) to make the grade, measure up **3** (categoría): **un escritor de ~ internacional** a writer of international stature; **una revista de la ~ de 'Semana'** a magazine as important as 'Semana'
B (escultura) sculpture; (de madera) carving; (de piedras preciosas) cutting
C (AmL) (Jueg) **1** (repartición) deal **2** (banca) bank
D (Chi fam) **1** (dicho) joke, wisecrack (colloq) **2** (broma) practical joke

tallado *m* (de madera) carving; (de piedras preciosas) cutting

tallador -dora *m,f*
A (de madera) carver; (de piedras preciosas) cutter
B (AmL) (en naipes) dealer

tallar [A1] *vt*
A ‹*madera*› to carve; ‹*escultura/mármol*› to sculpt; ‹*piedras preciosas*› to cut
B (Esp) ‹*reclutas*› to measure (*and kit out*)
C (Méx) **1** (para limpiar) to scrub **2** (para aliviar) to rub
■ **tallar** *vi* (Col) «*zapatos*» (+ *me/te/le etc*) to be too tight
■ **tallarse** *v pron*
A (Méx) (para limpiarse) to scrub oneself; (para aliviar) to rub oneself
B (Méx fam) (batallar mucho) to work one's butt off (AmE colloq), to slog one's guts out (BrE colloq)

tallarín *m* noodle

talle *m* **1** (cintura) waist; **de ~ esbelto** slim-waisted **2** (figura) figure **3** (en costura) trunk measurement; **es corta de ~** she's short-waisted

taller *m*
A **1** (Auto) garage, repair shop (AmE) **2** (de carpintero, técnico) workshop
(Compuestos)
- **taller de reparación de calzado** shoe repairer's
- **taller mecánico** *or* **de reparaciones** garage, vehicle repair shop (AmE frml)
- **talleres gráficos** *mpl* printing works

B (Educ) workshop

tallista *mf* woodcarver

tallo *m* stem, stalk

talludito -ta *adj* (fam) ‹*adulto*›: **ya estás ~ para esas cosas** you're getting a bit old for that sort of thing; **se casó cuando ya estaba talludita** she was getting on a bit when she married (colloq)

talón *m*
A **1** (del pie) heel; (de zapato, calcetín) heel; ***no llegarle ni a los talones a algn*** (Andes, Méx) *ver* **tobillo**; ***pisarle a algn los talones*** (fam) to be hot on sb's heels (colloq) **2** (de caballo) heel
(Compuesto) **talón de Aquiles** Achilles' heel
B **1** (AmL) (matriz) stub, counterfoil **2** (Esp) (cheque) check (AmE), cheque (BrE); (vale) chit; **~ de compra** receipt
C (Méx fam) **1** (prostitución): **anda en el** *or* **le da al ~** she's a hooker (colloq), she's on the game (BrE colloq) **2** (crédito) credit (colloq)

talonador -dora *m,f* (en rugby) hooker

talonar [A1] *vt* (en rugby) to hook

talonario *m* (de cheques) checkbook (AmE), chequebook (BrE); (de recibos) receipt book; (de volantes) book of vouchers

talonazo *m* (golpe) kick (*with the heel*); (en rugby) heel; (en fútbol) backheel

talonear [A1] *vi*
A (Méx fam) (dedicarse a la prostitución), to hustle (AmE colloq), to be on the game (BrE colloq)
B (Méx fam) (Equ) to spur one's horse on; **~le** (Méx fam) to step on it (colloq)
■ **talonear** *vt* (AmL) ‹*caballo*› to spur (on)

talonera *f*
A (de bota) heelpiece
B (Méx fam) (prostituta) whore (colloq), hooker (colloq)

talquera *f* (recipiente) talcum powder dispenser; (con borla) compact

talud *m* slope, incline, bank

tamal *m* tamale

tamaño¹ -ña *adj* (*delante del n*): **nunca vi tamaña injusticia** I've never seen such injustice; **me llevé ~ susto** I got a terrible fright

tamaño² *m* size; **de todos los ~s** in all sizes
(Compuesto) **tamaño bolsillo/carné/familiar/natural** pocket-/passport-/family-/life-size

tamarindo *m* **1** (Bot) tamarind **2** (Méx fam) (agente) traffic cop (colloq)

tambache *m* (Méx fam) (bulto) bundle; (montón) pile; ***hacer ~ a algn*** (Méx fam) to do the dirty on sb (colloq)

tambaleante *adj*: **entró con andar ~** he staggered into the room; **un anciano de paso ~** a doddery old man; **un régimen ya ~** an already shaky regime

tambalearse [A1] *v pron*, **tambalear** [A1] *vi* «*silla/botella*» to wobble; «*persona*» (de adelante a atrás) to stagger, totter; (de lado a lado) to sway; **(se) tambaleó y cayó** she tottered and fell; **caminaba tambaleándose** he was staggering *o* lurching ; **el régimen empezó a ~** the regime began to teeter; **todo empezó a ~** everything began to shake

tambaleo *m* (de persona) staggering; (de lámpara) swinging; (de mueble) shaking, rocking

también *adv* too, as well **~ habla ruso** she speaks Russian too *o* as well, she also speaks Russian; **está de baja — ¿él ~?** he's off sick — him too *o* him as well?; **que te diviertas — tú ~** have fun! — you too *o* and you; **estás invitado y tu mujer ~** you're invited and so is your wife *o* and your wife, too; **Pilar fuma — yo ~** Pilar smokes — so do I; **el ~ cirujano López Saura** (period) López Saura, (who is) also a surgeon

tambo *m*
A (RPl) (establecimiento) dairy farm; (corral) milking yard
B (Méx) **1** (recipiente) can (AmE), bin (BrE); ***mover el ~*** (Méx fam & hum) to boogie (colloq) **2** (fam) (cárcel) slammer (sl), can (AmE sl)
C (Per) **1** (Hist) (posada) wayside inn **2** (tienda) wayside stall

tambor *m*
A (Mús) **1** (instrumento) drum; **un redoble de ~es** a drum roll; ***a ~ batiente***: **el equipo volvió a ~ batiente** the team returned to a heroes' welcome **2** (persona) drummer
(Compuesto) **tambor mayor** drum major
B **1** (de freno, lavadora, revólver) drum **2** (Méx) (colchón) spring mattress
C **1** (de detergente) drum **2** (AmL) (barril, bidón) drum
D (para bordar) tambour
E (Anat) eardrum

tambora *f* bass drum

tamboril *m* tabor

tamborilear [A1] *vi* to drum, tap

tamborileo *m* drumming, tapping

tamborilero -ra *m,f* drummer

Támesis *m*: **el ~** the (River) Thames

tamiz *m* sieve; **pasar algo por el ~** ‹*harina*› to sift sth; ‹*salsa*› to sieve sth

tamizar [A4] *vt* ‹*harina*› to sift; ‹*salsa*› to sieve

tampoco *adv* **1** not … either; **yo ~ entendí** I didn't understand either; **él no va, ni yo ~** he isn't going and neither am I; **no he estado en Roma ni ~ en París** I've never been to Rome or Paris; **no lo conoce — (ni) yo ~** she doesn't know him — neither do I *o* I don't either **2** (uso expletivo): **bueno, ~ es para ponerse así** come on, there's no need to get like *that* about it; **~ estaría mal recordárselo** it wouldn't be a bad idea to remind him

tampón *m* **1** (para entintar) ink pad **2** (Farm, Med) tampon

tan *adv: form of* **tanto** *used before adjectives (except some comparatives), adverbs, and adjectival or adverbial phrases*

tanatología *f* palliative care

tanatorio *m* funeral parlor*

tanda *f*

A (grupo): **llegó otra ~ de excursionistas** another group *o* party of tourists arrived; **la nueva ~ de alumnos** the new intake of pupils; **en dos ~s** in two sittings; **cada dos minutos hay una ~ de avisos** (AmL) every couple of minutes there's another lot of commercials; **los horneamos en dos ~s** we baked them in two batches; **una buena ~ de azotes** a good thrashing

B (AmC, Méx fam) **1** (terreno) cactus plot **2** (función — de teatro) performance; (— de cine) showing, performance

C (Col, Méx) (ronda) a round (of drinks)

tandear [A1] *vi* (Chi fam) to joke

tándem *m* **1** (bicicleta) tandem **2** (dos personas) duo; **un ~ de famosos** a famous duo; **trabajan en ~** they work together *o* as a team

tanga *f* tanga

tangencial *adj* tangential

tangente *f* tangent; ***irse*** *or* ***salirse por la ~*** to go off at a tangent

tangerina *f* tangerine

tangible *adj* tangible, concrete

tango *m* tango

tanguear [A1] *vi* to tango

tanguista *m,f*

A tango singer

B **tanguista** *f* nightclub hostess

tano -na *adj/m,f* (RPl fam & pey) Italian

tanque *m*

A (Arm) (carro) tank

B (de agua, gasolina) tank; (de gas, oxígeno) cylinder, bottle

tanqueta *f* armored personnel carrier

tanquista *mf* (oficial) tank officer; (soldado) soldier in a tank unit; **hizo su servicio militar de ~** he did his military service in tanks/in a tank unit

tantarantán *m* (del tambor) rat-a-tat-tat

tanteador *m* scoreboard

tantear [A1] *vt* **1** (con el tacto) to feel **2** ‹*situación*› to weigh up, size up; ‹*persona*› to sound out **3** (calcular aproximadamente) to estimate

■ **tantear** *vi* to feel one's way

tanteo *m*

A (de situación) sizing up; **a** *or* **al** *or* **por ~** by trial and error

B (Dep) score

tantito *adv* (Méx fam) a bit; **espérame ~, ya voy** just wait a bit, I'm coming; **hazte ~ para allá** move up a bit

tanto¹ *adv*

A [*see note under* **tan**] (aplicado a adjetivo o adverbio) so; (aplicado a verbo) so much; **es tan difícil de describir** it's so difficult to describe; **¡es una chica tan amable!** she's such a nice girl!; **si es así, ~ mejor** if that's the case, so much the better; **y si no te gusta, ~ peor para ti** and if you don't like it, too bad *o* (colloq) tough!; **la tan esperada boda** the long-awaited wedding; **no es tan difícil** it's not *that* difficult; **ya no salimos ~** nowadays we don't go out so often *o* so much; **tan/tanto ... QUE** so … (THAT); **~ insistió que me quedé** he was so insistent that I stayed; **no lo reconocí de tan viejo que estaba** he had aged so much I didn't recognize him; **tan/tanto ... como** as … as; **no es tan tímida como parece** she's not as shy as she looks; **sale ~ como tú** he goes out as much *o* as often as you do; **tan pronto como le sea posible** as soon as you can; **no han mejorado ~ como para poder ganar** they haven't improved enough to win; **~ Suárez como Vargas votaron en contra** both Suárez and Vargas voted against

B (AmL exc RPl) **qué tanto/qué tan**: **¿qué tan alto es?** how tall is he?; **¿qué ~ hay de cierto en eso?** how much of it is true?

C *para locs ver* **tanto³ B**

tanto² -ta *adj*

A **1** (*sing*) so much; (*pl*) so many; **había ~ espacio/~s niños** there was so much space/there were so many children; **¡tiene tanta fuerza ...!** she has such strength …!; **¡~ tiempo sin verte!** it's been so long!; **tanto/tantos ... COMO** as much/as many…as; **sufro ~ como ella** I suffer as much as she does; **no hubo ~s turistas como el año pasado** there weren't been as many *o* so many tourists as last year; **tengo tanta suerte como tú** I'm as lucky as you are **2** (fam) (expresando cantidades indeterminadas): **tenía setenta y ~s años** he was seventy something, he was seventy-odd (colloq); **cincuenta y ~s pesos** fifty and something pesos

B (*sing*) (fam) (con valor plural) so many; **había ~ mosquitos** there were so many mosquitoes

tanto³ -ta *pron*

A **1** (*sing*) so much; (*pl*) so many; **quería azúcar, pero no tanta** I wanted sugar but not that much; **es uno de ~s** he's one of many; **¡tengo ~ que hacer!** I've so much to do!; **¿de verdad gana ~?** does he really earn that much?; ***ni ~ ni tan calvo*** *or* ***tan poco*** there's no need to go *that* far; ***no ser para ~*** (fam): **no te pongas así, no es para ~** come on, there's no need to get like that about it: **duele, pero no es para ~** it hurts, but it's not *that* bad; **~ *tienes* ~ *vales*** you are what you own **2** (fam) (expresando cantidades indeterminadas): **hasta las tantas de la madrugada** until the early hours of the morning; **en mil ochocientos treinta y ~s** in eighteen thirty-something; **cincuenta y tantas** fifty-odd, fifty or so **3** **tanto** (refiriéndose a tiempo) so long; **hace ~ que no me llama** it's been so long since she called me; **aún faltan dos horas — ¿~?** there's still two hours to go — what? that long?

B (*en locs*) **en tanto** while; **en ~ + SUBJ** as long as, so long as; **en ~ tú estés aquí** as long as you're here; **entre tanto** meanwhile, in the meantime; **hasta tanto + SUBJ** (frml): **hasta ~ (no) se solucione este conflicto** until this conflict is solved; **otro tanto** as much again; **me queda otro ~ por hacer** I have as much again still to do; **cuesta $15 y las pilas, casi otro ~** it costs $15 and then the batteries cost nearly as much again; **otro ~ cabe decir de ...** the same can be said of …; **por (lo) tanto** therefore; **tan siquiera**: **no pudo ni tan siquiera gritar** he couldn't even shout; **cómprale tan siquiera unas flores** at least buy her some flowers; **¡si tan siquiera me hubieras prevenido!** if only you'd warned me!; **tan sólo** only; **tanto es así que ...** so much so that …; **tanto más cuanto que ...** especially since …

tanto⁴ *m*

A (cantidad): **un ~ por ciento** a certain percentage; **hay que dejar un ~ de depósito** you have to put down a certain amount as a deposit

B (punto — en fútbol) goal; (— en fútbol americano) point; (— en tenis, en juegos) point; ***apuntarse un ~*** to score a point

C (*en locs*) **al tanto**: **me puso al ~** she put me in the picture; **mantenerse al ~ de** to keep up to date with; **te mantendré al ~** I'll keep you informed; **estar al ~** (pendiente, alerta) to be on the ball (colloq); **ya está al ~ de lo ocurrido** he already knows what's happened; **un tanto triste** somewhat *o* rather *o* a little sad

tañer [E7] *vt* (liter) ‹*arpa*› to strum

■ **tañer** *vi* «*campana*» to peal, ring out

tañido *m* **1** (de guitarra) strumming **2** (de campanas) pealing, ringing

taoísmo *m* Taoism

tapa *f*

A **1** (de caja, pupitre) lid **2** (de bote, cacerola) lid; (de botella, frasco) top **3** (de lente) cap; **la ~ del tanque de gasolina** the gas (AmE) *o* (BrE) petrol cap; ***levantarle*** *or* ***volarle la ~ de los sesos a algn*** (fam) to blow sb's brains out; ***ser la ~*** (Per fam) to be the latest thing (colloq)

(Compuesto) **tapa de rosca** screw top

B **1** (de libro, revista) cover; (para fascículos) binder; (de disco) sleeve; **no te lo has mirado ni por las ~s** you haven't

t

even opened the book 2 (de tacón) heelpiece; **estos zapatos necesitan ~s nuevas** these shoes need reheeling 3 (de bolsillo) flap 4 (Auto) head

C (Esp) (para acompañar la bebida) tapa, bar snack

tapas

In Spain, these are small portions of food served in bars and cafés with a drink. There is a wide variety, including Spanish omelet, seafood, different kinds of cooked potatoes, salads, cheese, ham, and *chorizo*. They can be very elaborate, and people often order several to make a meal.*Tapas* are part of a lifestyle and the social aspect is very important. The practice of going out for a drink and *tapas* is known as *tapeo*

tapabarros *m* (*pl* ~) (Chi, Per) (de coche) fender (AmE), wing (BrE); (de bicicleta) splashguard (AmE), mudguard (BrE)

tapada *f* (Andes fam) save, stop

tapadera *f* 1 (de cazo) lid 2 (de fraude, engaño) cover, front 3 (Méx) (de botella) cap, top

tapadillo: **de ~** (*loc adv*) (fam) on the quiet (colloq), secretly

tapado¹ *m*

A (RPl, Ven) (abrigo) (winter) coat

B (Méx) (Pol) potential candidate (*with official support*)

tapado² -da *adj* 1 (Col, Méx, Ven) (torpe) dim (colloq), dumb (colloq), thick (BrE colloq) 2 (Col fam) (taimado) sly

tapado³ -da *m,f* (fam) 1 (Col, Ven) (persona torpe) dimwit (colloq) 2 (Col) (persona taimada) slyboots (colloq), sneaky devil (colloq)

tapadura *f* (Andes, Méx) filling

tapar [A1] *vt*

A (cubrir) ‹*caja*› to put the lid on; ‹*botella/frasco*› to put the top on; ‹*olla*› to cover, put the lid on; **tapó al niño con una manta** she covered the child with a blanket; **le tapó la boca** he put his hand over her mouth

B 1 ‹*agujero/hueco*› to fill in; ‹*puerta/ventana*› to block up 2 (Andes, Méx) ‹*muela*› to fill; **me ~on dos muelas** I had two fillings 3 ‹*defecto/error*› to cover up

C 1 ‹*vista/luz*› to block; **nos tapa todo el sol** it completely blocks out the sun 2 ‹*salida/entrada*› to block; ‹*excusado/cañería*› (AmL) to block

■ **tapar** *vi* (Per) (Dep) to keep goal, play in goal

■ **taparse** *v pron*

A (*refl*) (cubrirse) to cover oneself up; **se tapó la cara** he covered his face

B 1 «*oídos/nariz*» (+ *me/te/le etc*) to get *o* become blocked; **tengo la nariz tapada** my nose is blocked 2 (AmL) «*cañería/excusado*» to get blocked

taparrabos *m* (*pl* ~) loincloth

tapatío -tía *adj* of/from Guadalajara (*in Mexico*)

tapete *m*

A 1 (para mesa) decorative table cloth; (para sofá) antimacassar 2 (Jueg) *tb* **~ verde** card table; ***estar sobre*** *or* ***en el ~*** to be under discussion *o* at issue; ***poner algo sobre el ~*** to bring up *o* raise sth

B (Col, Méx, Ven) (alfombra) rug

tapia *f* (muro) wall; (cerca) fence; ***ser/estar más sordo que una ~*** (fam) to be as deaf as a post (colloq)

tapiar [A1] *vt* 1 ‹*espacio*› to wall in 2 ‹*puerta/ventana*› to brick up

tapicería *f* 1 (de coches, muebles) upholstery 2 (arte) tapestry making; (tapiz) tapestry

tapicero -ra *m,f* (de muebles) upholsterer; (de tapices) tapestry maker

tapilla *f* (Chi) heelpiece

tapir *m* tapir

tapisca *f* (AmC) maize harvest

tapiz *m* (para pared) tapestry; (para suelo) carpet

tapizado *m* upholstery

tapizar [A4] *vt* ‹*sillón*› to upholster; ‹*pared*› to line; **el sendero estaba tapizado de hojas** the path was carpeted with leaves

tapón *m*

A 1 (de vidrio, goma) stopper; (de corcho) cork; (del lavabo) plug; (de botella) (Esp) top 2 (para los oídos) earplug; (en cirujía) tampon; (de cerumen) plug

B (fam) (persona) shorty (colloq)

C 1 (fam) (atasco) traffic jam, tailback (BrE) 2 (en baloncesto) block

D (CS) (Elec) fuse

taponamiento *m* 1 (de cañería) blockage 2 (Med) plugging 3 (Col, RPl) (Auto) (embotellamiento) traffic jam, tailback (BrE)

taponar [A1] *vt* 1 ‹*agujero*› to block 2 ‹*herida*› to plug

■ **taponarse** *v pron* 1 «*oídos/nariz*» (+ *me/te/le etc*) to get blocked; **se me taponó la nariz** my nose got blocked 2 «*cañería*» to get blocked 3 (Col, RPl) «*ciudad/zona*» to block

taponazo *m* (AmL) shot

tapujos *mpl*: **sin ~** openly, honestly; **no te andes con ~** don't try to pull the wool over my/his eyes (colloq)

taquear [A1] *vi*

A (Méx) (comer) to eat tacos, have a snack

B (Per fam) (Jueg) to shoot pool (colloq)

taquería *f* (Méx) taco stall/restaurant

taquicardia *f* tachycardia

taquigrafía *f* shorthand, stenography (AmE)

taquígrafo -fa *m,f* shorthand clerk (*o* typist *etc*), stenographer (AmE)

taquilla *f* 1 (de cine) box office; (en estación, estadio) ticket office 2 (cantidad recaudada) takings (*pl*); ***hacer ~*** *or* ***tener buena ~*** «*película/obra*» to be a box-office hit 3 (casillero) rack, pigeonholes (*pl*)

taquillaje *m* takings (*pl*)

taquillero¹ -ra *adj* 1 (Cin, Teatr) box-office (*before n*); **un actor ~** a box-office draw 2 (Chi fam) (de moda) trendy (colloq)

taquillero² -ra *m,f* box-office clerk

taquimecanógrafo -fa *m,f* shorthand typist, stenographer (AmE)

tara *f*

A (peso) tare

B (defecto) defect

tarabilla *mf* (fam) 1 (persona habladora) chatterbox (colloq) 2 (persona inquieta): **es una ~** she gets really hyped up (colloq)

tarado¹ -da *adj* 1 (minusválido) handicapped 2 (fam & pey) (tonto) stupid

tarado² -da *m,f* 1 (minusválido) handicapped person 2 (fam & pey) (imbécil), moron (colloq & pej)

tarambana *mf* (fam) good-for-nothing (colloq)

tarantela *f* tarantella

tarántula *f* tarantula

tarar [A1] *vt* (pesar) to tare

tararear [A1] *vt* to la-la-la

tarasca *f* 1 (fam) (mujer de carácter violento) battle-ax* (colloq) 2 (Chi fam) (boca) mouth

tarascón *m* (CS) bite

tardado -da *adj* (Méx) ‹*proceso/tarea*› time-consuming; ‹*persona*› slow; **¡qué ~!** what a slowpoke! (AmE colloq), slow coach (BrE colloq)

tardanza *f* delay; **sin ~** without delay; **perdona la ~ en contestar** forgive my delay in replying; **me preocupa su ~** I'm worried that he's so late; **su ~ se debió a ...** his lateness was due to ...

tardar [A1] *vt* (emplear cierto tiempo): **tardó tres horas más de lo previsto** she took three hours longer than expected; **no tardo ni un minuto** I won't be a minute; **¿cuánto se tarda de Moscú a Berlín?** how long does it take from Moscow to Berlin?; **está tardando mucho** she's taking a long time; **~án varios días en dármelo** it'll be several days before they give it to me; **tarda una hora en hacerse** it takes about an hour to cook; ***a más ~*** at the (very) latest

■ **tardar** *vi* (retrasarse) to be late; (emplear demasiado tiempo) to take a long time; **la obra empieza a las seis, así que espero que no tarden** the play starts at six so I hope they won't be late; **sólo ha salido a comprar pero parece que tarda** he's only gone to do some shopping but he seems to be taking a long time; **¡no tardo!** I won't be long!; **~ EN + INF**: **aún ~á en llegar** it'll be a while yet before he gets here; **no ~on en detenerlo** it didn't take them long to arrest him

■ **tardarse** *v pron* (Méx, Ven) ▸ **tardar** *vt, vi*

tarde[1] *adv* late; **llegar ~** to be late; **es ~ para eso** it's too late for that; **se está haciendo ~** it's getting late; **más ~** later; **tuvo los hijos muy ~** she had her children very late in life; ***~ o temprano*** sooner or later; ***más vale ~ que nunca*** better late than never

tarde[2] *f* (temprano) afternoon; (hacia el anochecer) evening; **a las seis de la ~** at six in the evening; **¡buenas ~s!** (temprano) good afternoon!; (hacia el anochecer) good evening!; **en la** *or* (esp Esp) **por la** *or* (RPl) **a la ~** in the afternoon/evening; ***de ~ en ~*** occasionally

tardío -día *adj* ‹*fruto*› late (*before n*); ‹*decisión/acuerdo*› belated; **uno de sus poemas ~s** one of his later poems; **tuvo un amor ~** he had a romance in his later life

tardo -da *adj* (liter) slow

tardón[1] -dona *adj* (fam) slow; **¡qué ~ es!** what a slowpoke (AmE) *o* (BrE) slowcoach he is! (colloq)

tardón[2] -dona *m,f* (fam) slowpoke (AmE colloq), slowcoach (BrE colloq)

tarea *f* [1] (trabajo) task, job; **las ~s de la casa** the housework [2] (deberes escolares) homework

tarifa *f* [1] (baremo, escala) rate; **~s eléctricas** electricity charges; **¿cuál es su ~?** what rate *o* how much do you charge? [2] (Transp) fare [3] (lista de precios) price list [4] (arancel) tariff; **~s aduaneras** customs tariffs *o* duties

(Compuestos)
- **tarifa económica** economy fare
- **tarifa plana** flat rate

tarima *f* (plataforma) dais

tarjar [A1] *vt* (Andes) to cross out, delete (frml)

tarjeta *f* card; **marcar** (AmL) *or* (Méx) **checar ~** to clock in/out, punch in/out (AmE)

(Compuestos)
- **tarjeta amarilla/roja** yellow/red card; **mostrar** *or* **sacar a algn la ~ amarilla/roja** to show sb the yellow/red card
- **tarjeta de crédito** credit card
- **tarjeta de embarque** boarding pass *o* card
- **tarjeta de Navidad** Christmas card
- **tarjeta de visita** *or* (Méx) **de presentación** (personal) visiting card; (de negocios) business card
- **tarjeta inteligente** smart card
- **tarjeta postal/telefónica** postcard/phonecard
- **tarjeta prepago** top-up card

tarjetahabiente *mf* (Méx, Ven) cardholder

tarjetero *m*, (AmL) **tarjetera** *f* credit card holder *o* wallet

tarquín *m* mud, silt

tarro *m*
A (recipiente— de vidrio) jar; (— de cerámica) pot; (— de metal) (Chi) can, tin (BrE)
B (Méx, Ven) (taza) mug
C (Esp arg) (cabeza) head

tarso *m* tarsus

tarta *f* (Esp) cake

(Compuestos)
- **tarta de cumpleaños** birthday cake
- **tarta de queso** cheesecake

tartaja *mf* (fam) stammerer, stutterer

tartajear [A1] *vi* (tartamudear) to stammer, stutter; (mezclar sílabas) to make spoonerisms

tartajoso -sa *adj/m,f* ▸ **tartamudo[1,2]**

tartaleta *f* [1] (tarta individual) tartlet [2] (porción) piece of cake

tartamudear [A1] *vi* to stutter, stammer

tartamudeo *m* stuttering, stammering

tartamudez *f*: **superó su ~** he overcame his stutter *o* stammer

tartamudo[1] -da *adj* stuttering (*before n*), stammering (*before n*); **es ~** he has a stutter *o* stammer

tartamudo[2] -da *m,f* stammerer; **tengo un ~ en mi clase** one of the boys in my class has a stutter *o* stammer

tartán *m* tartan

tartana *f* covered trap

tártaro -ra *adj/m,f* Tartar

tartera *f* (para cocinar) cake tin; (fiambrera) lunch pail (AmE), lunch box (BrE)

tartufo -fa *m,f* (liter) Tartuffe (liter), hypocrite

tarugo *m* [1] (de madera) piece; (de pan duro) piece, hunk [2] (clavija) peg, dowel [3] (fam) (persona torpe) blockhead (colloq)

tarumba *adj* crazy (colloq); **me vuelve ~** he drives me crazy (colloq); **volverse ~** (fam) to go crazy (colloq)

tasa *f* [1] (valoración) valuation [2] (impuesto) tax [3] (medida) moderation [4] (índice) rate

(Compuestos)
- **tasa de desempleo** rate of unemployment
- **tasa de interés** interest rate
- **tasa de mortalidad/natalidad** mortality rate/birthrate

tasación *f* valuation

tasador -dora *m,f* valuer, assessor

tasajear [A1] *vt* (Méx, Per) to slash

tasar [A1] *vt*
A ‹*objeto/coche*› to value
B (racionar) ‹*dinero/comida*› to ration, limit

tasca *f* (taberna) bar, tavern; (bar de poca categoría) cheap bar

tasqueo *m* (Esp fam): **ir(se) de ~** to go drinking, go pubbing (BrE colloq)

tata[1] *m* (AmL fam)
A (padre) dad (colloq), pop (AmE colloq)
B (abuelo) grandpa (colloq)

tata[2] *f* (Esp fam) (niñera) nanny

tatarabuelo -la (*m*) great-great-grandfather; (*f*) great-great-grandmother; **mis ~s** my great-great-grandparents

tataranieto -ta (*m*) great-great-grandson; (*f*) great-great-granddaughter; **mis ~s** my great-great grandchildren

tate *interj* (fam) [1] (¡despacio!) slowly!, easy does it! (colloq) [2] (al darse cuenta de algo) so that's it!, now I see!

ta-te-ti *m* (RPl) tic-tac-toe (AmE), noughts and crosses (BrE)

tatuaje *m* (acción) tattooing; (dibujo) tattoo

tatuar [A18] *vt* to tattoo

taumaturgo -ga *m,f* miracle worker

taurino[1] -na *adj*
A ‹*temporada/afición*› bullfighting (*before n*), taurine (frml)
B (Astrol) Taurean

taurino[2] -na *m,f* (Astrol) Taurean, Taurus

Tauro[1] *m* (signo, constelación) Taurus; **es (de) ~** he's (a) Taurus, he's a Taurean

Tauro[2], **tauro** *mf* (*pl* **~ -ros**) (persona) Taurean, Taurus

tauromaquia *f* (the art of) bullfighting

tautología *f* tautology

tautológico -ca *adj* tautological, redundant

taxativamente *adv* (frml) specifically

taxativo -va *adj* (frml) restricted, specific

taxi *m* taxi, cab

(Compuesto) **taxi colectivo** (Col) minibus

taxímetro *m* taximeter

taxista *mf* taxi driver, cabdriver

taxonomía *f* taxonomy

taxonómico -ca *adj* taxonomical

taza *f* [1] (recipiente) cup; **~ de café/té** coffee cup/teacup [2] (contenido) cupful; **tomar una ~ de té** to have a cup of tea [3] (del retrete) (toilet) bowl [4] (de fuente) basin

tazón *m* bowl

tb. = **también**

te[1] *f*: *name of the letter* **t**

te[2] *pron pers* [1] you; **¿~ ha mandado la cuenta?** has he sent you the bill?; **no ~ lo quiero prestar** I don't want to lend it to you; **¿~ lo paso a máquina?** shall I type it for you?; **~ lo quiere quitar** he wants to take it away from you; **voy a serte sincera** I'll be frank with you; **cuídate** (*refl*) look after yourself; **¿~ has cortado el pelo?** (*refl*) have you cut your hair?; (*caus*) have you had your hair cut?; **¿~ sientes bien?** are you feeling all right?; **no ~ muevas** don't move [2] (*impers*): **cuando ~ pasa eso ...** when that happens ...

t

té *m* 1 (infusión, planta) tea; **me invitó a tomar el ~** she invited me for tea; ***a la hora del ~*** (literal) at tea-time; (a la hora de la verdad) (Col fam) when it comes to the crunch (colloq) 2 (AmL) (reunión) tea party

(Compuesto) **té canasta** (AmL) charity tea and canasta party

tea *f* torch; ***arder como una ~*** to go up like a torch

teatral *adj* 1 (Teatr) ‹*grupo/temporada*› theater* (*before n*); **una obra ~** a play; **vi la producción ~** I saw the stage version; **un autor ~** a playwright 2 ‹*persona*› theatrical; ‹*gesto/tono*› theatrical, dramatic

teatro *m*

A (Teatr) 1 (arte, actividad) theater*; **~ de vanguardia** avant-garde theater; **el ~ de Calderón** Calderon's theater *o* plays; **una obra de ~** a play; **adaptado para el ~ por ...** adapted for the stage by ...; **actor de ~** stage actor; **el mundo del ~** the theater 2 (local) theater* 3 (cine) movie theater (AmE), cinema (BrE)

(Compuestos)

- **teatro de aficionados** amateur dramatics
- **teatro de guiñol** puppet theater*
- **teatro de la ópera** opera house
- **teatro de variedades** vaudeville (AmE), music hall (BrE)

B (fam) (exageración): **es puro ~** it's all an act

C (de batalla, guerra) theater*

(Compuesto) **teatro de operaciones** theater* of operations

tebeo *m* (Esp) comic (*for children*)

techado *m* roof

techador -dora *m,f* (de tejas) roofer; (de paja) thatcher

techar [A1] *vt* (con tejas) to roof; (con paja) to thatch

techo *m*

A 1 (cielo raso) ceiling 2 (AmL) (tejado, cubierta) roof; **bajo ~** indoors *o* under cover 3 (hogar, casa) house; **bajo el mismo ~** under the same roof; **sin ~** homeless

(Compuesto) **techo corredizo** sunroof

B (nivel, cota) ceiling; **rebasó el ~ del 8%** it exceeded the 8% ceiling *o* limit; **tratan de elevar su ~ electoral** they are trying to raise their quota of seats; **los precios tocaron ~** prices reached their highest point

techumbre *f* roof

tecla *f* 1 (Mús) key; ***dar en la ~*** to hit the nail on the head (colloq) 2 (de ordenador) key 3 (fam) (para conseguir un fin): **no me queda ninguna ~ por tocar** I've tried every avenue *o* approach; **tocaré todas las ~s** I'll pull out all the stops; **alguna ~ habrá tocado** I bet she pulled some strings (colloq)

(Compuesto) **tecla de función** function key

teclado *m* keyboard; **~ numérico** numeric keypad

tecleado *m* keyboarding, keying

teclear [A1] *vt* ‹*palabra/texto*› to key in, type in

■ **teclear** *vi* (en máquina de escribir) to type; (en ordenador) to key

tecleo *m* 1 (en máquina de escribir) typing; (en ordenador) keying, keyboarding 2 (ruido) clicking, tapping

teclista *mf* 1 (Impr, Inf) keyboarder 2 (Mús) keyboard player

técnica *f*

A 1 (método) technique 2 (destreza) skill

B (tecnología) technology

C (en baloncesto) technical foul

tecnicismo *m* (cualidad) technical nature; (palabra) technical term

técnico[1] **-ca** *adj* technical

técnico[2] **-ca** *m,f*, **técnico** *mf* 1 (en fábrica) technician 2 (de lavadoras, etc) repairman (AmE), engineer (BrE) 3 (Dep) trainer, coach (AmE), manager (BrE)

tecnicolor *m* Technicolor®

tecnificar [A2] *vt* to introduce the use of modern technology in

tecnócrata *mf* technocrat

tecnofobia *f* technophobia

tecnología *f* technology

(Compuesto) **tecnología punta** up-to-the-minute technology

tecnológico -ca *adj* technological

tecnólogo -ga *m,f* technologist

tecolines *mpl* (Méx fam) cash (colloq)

tecolote *m*

A (Méx) (Zool) owl

B (Méx fam) (policía) cop (colloq)

tedeum, Te Deum *m* thanksgiving service

tedio *m* boredom, tedium; **me produce ~** I find it boring *o* tedious

tedioso -sa *adj* tedious, boring

tegua *mf* (Col) quack

teipe *m* (Ven) sticky tape

teísmo *m* theism

teísta *adj/mf* theist

teja *f* tile; **~s de pizarra** slates; ***corrérsele a algn la ~*** (Andes) to flip one's lid (colloq); ***pagar a toca ~*** (Esp) to pay cash on the nail (colloq)

tejado *m* (esp Esp) roof

tejano -na *adj/m,f* Texan

tejar [A1] *vt* (con tejas — de barro) to tile; (— de pizarra) to slate

Tejas *m* Texas

tejaván *m* (Méx) shed

tejedor -dora *m,f* 1 (con telar) weaver 2 (con agujas, máquina) knitter

tejemaneje *m* (fam) 1 (maquinación) intrigue; **~s** skulduggery, scheming 2 (Esp) (actividad): **¿qué ~s se traen?** what are they up to?

tejer [E1] *vt*

A 1 (en telar) to weave; **tejido a mano** hand-woven 2 (con agujas, a máquina) to knit; (con ganchillo) to crochet; **máquina de ~** knitting machine 3 «*araña*» to spin

B (elaborar) ‹*plan*› to devise; **tejió una gran mentira** she spun an elaborate yarn

■ **tejer** *vi* (en telar) to weave; (con agujas, a máquina) to knit; (con ganchillo) to crochet

tejido *m* 1 (tela) fabric; **~s sintéticos** synthetic fabrics *o* textiles 2 (de tela) weave 3 (AmL) (con agujas, máquina) knitting; (con ganchillo) crochet 4 (Anat) tissue

tejo *m* 1 (disco) disc 2 (juego — de niños) hopscotch; (— de adultos) *game similar to pitch-and-toss*

tejolote *m* (Méx) pestle

tejón *m* badger

Tel. (= **teléfono**) Tel.

tela *f*

A (Tex) (material) material, fabric, cloth; **~ de lana** wool (fabric); **~ de algodón** cotton (fabric); **~ sintética** man-made *o* synthetic material; **un libro encuadernado en ~** a clothbound book; ***allí hay (mucha) ~ de donde*** *or* ***para cortar*** there's plenty that could be said about that; ***poner algo en ~ de juicio*** to call sth into question; ***tener ~ (marinera)*** (Esp fam) «*asunto*» to be tricky; **tenemos ~ para rato** we have a lot of work on our hands

(Compuestos)

- **tela de araña** spiderweb (AmE), spider's web (BrE); (polvorienta) cobweb
- **tela metálica** wire mesh

B (Art) (cuadro) canvas, painting

C (membrana) skin, film

telar *m* 1 (máquina) loom 2 **telares** *mpl* (fábrica) textile mill

telaraña *f* spiderweb (AmE), spider's web (BrE); (polvorienta) cobweb; ***mirar las ~s*** to have one's head in the clouds; ***sacudirse las ~s*** to blow the cobwebs away; ***tener ~s en los ojos*** to be blind

tele *f* (fam) TV (colloq), telly (BrE colloq)

teleadicto -ta *m,f* (fam) TV addict (colloq),telly addict (BrE colloq)

telebanco *m* cash machine *o* dispenser

teleco *f* telco

telecomedia *f* sitcom

telecomunicación *f* telecommunication

teleconferencia *f* conference call, teleconference

teleculebra *f* (Ven fam) soap opera (colloq)

telediario *m* (Esp) (television) news

t

teledifusión *f* television broadcasting

teledirigido -da *adj* ‹coche› radio-controlled, remote-controlled; **misiles ~s** guided missiles

teleférico *m* cable railway

telefilm (*pl* **-films**), **telefilme** *m* TV movie

telefonazo *m* (fam) buzz (colloq), ring, call; **darle un ~ a algn** to give sb a buzz (colloq)

telefonear [A1] *vt* to telephone, phone, call; **¿puedo ~ a Londres?** can I make a (telephone) call to London?
■ **telefonear** *vi* to telephone, phone; **telefoneé para pedir un taxi** I phoned *o* telephoned for a cab

telefónico -ca *adj* telephone (*before n*)

telefonista *mf* telephone operator

teléfono *m*
A (Telec) telephone, phone; **número de ~** phone number; **¿tienes ~?** are you on the phone?; **contestar el ~** to answer *o* (colloq) get the phone; **me colgó el ~** she hung up on me; **hablé por ~ con ella** I spoke to her on the phone; **está hablando por ~** he's on the phone; **llamar a algn por ~** to call sb (up), phone sb, ring sb (up) (BrE)
(Compuestos)
- **teléfono celular** *or* (Esp) **móvil** mobile telephone
- **teléfono fijo** land line
- **teléfono inalámbrico** cordless telephone
- **teléfono interno** extension
- **teléfono satélite** satphone

B (de la ducha) shower head

telegénico -ca *adj* telegenic

telegrafía *f* telegraphy

telegrafiar [A17] *vi/vt* to telegraph

telegráfico -ca *adj* telegraphic

telegrafista *mf* telegraphist

telégrafo *m* telegraph

telegrama *m* telegram

teleimpresor *m*, **teleimpresora** *f* teletypewriter (AmE), teleprinter (BrE)

telele *m* (fam & hum): **darle un ~ a algn** (desmayarse) to faint; (enfurecerse) to have a fit (colloq)

telenovela *f* soap opera

teleobjetivo *m* telephoto lens

telépata *mf* telepathist

telepatía *f* telepathy

telepático -ca *adj* telepathic

teleplatea *f* (CS) television audience

telequinesia *f* telekinesis

telescópico -ca *adj* telescopic

telescopio *m* telescope

teleserie *f* television series

telesilla *f or m* chair lift

telespectador -dora *m,f* viewer

telesquí *m* ski lift

teleteatro *m* (Teatro, TV) play produced for TV; (culebrón) television drama series (*usually of poor quality*)

teletexto, teletex *m* teletext, videotex

teletipo *m* teletypewriter (AmE), teleprinter (BrE)

teletrabajo *m* teleworking, telecommuting

televentas *fpl* telesales

televidente *mf* viewer

televisar [A1] *vt* to televise

televisión *f* [1] (sistema) television; **lo transmitieron por ~** it was broadcast on television [2] (programación) television; **ver ~** to watch television [3] (televisor) television (set)
(Compuestos)
- **televisión a** *or* **en color(es)** color* television
- **televisión por cable/por satélite** cable/satellite television

televisivo -va *adj* television (*before n*)

televisor *m* television (set)

télex *m* (*pl* ~) telex; **enviar algo por ~** to telex sth

telilla *f* film, skin

telón *m* curtain
(Compuestos)
- **telón de acero** (Esp) Iron Curtain
- **telón de fondo** (Teatr) backdrop; **sobre el ~ de ~ de la guerra civil** against the backdrop of the civil war

telonero[1] -ra *adj* ‹artista/grupo› support (*before n*), supporting (*before n*)

telonero[2] -ra *m,f* supporting artist (*o* band *etc*); **los ~s** the support

telúrico -ca *adj* telluric, of the earth

tema *m*
A [1] (asunto, cuestión) matter; (de conferencia, composición) topic; (de examen) subject; (Art, Cin, Lit) subject; **un ~ delicado** a delicate matter *o* subject; **~ de conversación** topic of conversation; **~s de actualidad** current affairs; **el ~ de la novela** the subject matter of the novel; **cambiar de ~** to change the subject; **no se trató ese ~** that topic wasn't discussed [2] (Mús) (motivo) theme
B (Ling) stem

temario *m* [1] (para examen) syllabus, list of topics [2] (en congreso) agenda

temática *f* subject matter

temático -ca *adj* thematic

temblar [A5] *vi* [1] «*persona*» (de frío) to shiver; (por nervios, miedo) to shake, tremble; **tiemblo de pensar lo que podría haber pasado** I shudder to think what might have happened; (+ *me/te/le etc*) **me tiembla el párpado** my eyelid is twitching; **le temblaba la mano** his hand was shaking; **la voz le temblaba de emoción** her voice was trembling with emotion; **~ *como un flan*** to shake like a jelly *o* leaf [2] «*edificio/tierra*» to shake
■ **temblar** *v impers*: **¡está temblando!** (AmL) it's an earthquake!

tembleque[1] *adj* (fam) shaky (colloq)

tembleque[2] *m* shaking; **me dio** *or* **entró un ~** (fam) I got the shakes (colloq)

temblequear [A1] *vi* (fam) to shake, tremble

temblor *m*
A (de frío, fiebre) shivering; (de miedo, nervios) trembling, shaking; **habló con un ligero ~ en la voz** he spoke in a tremulous voice
B *tb* **~ de tierra** earth (tremor)

tembloroso -sa *adj* [1] ‹manos› trembling, shaking; ‹voz› trembling, tremulous; **~ de miedo** shaking with fear; **~ de frío** shivering with cold [2] ‹llama/luz› flickering, quivering

temer [E1] *vt* ‹castigo/reacción› to fear, dread; ‹persona› to be afraid of; **sus hijos le temen** her children are afraid of her; **todos temían lo peor** they all feared the worst; **~ + INF** to be frightened *o* afraid OF -ING; **~ QUE + SUBJ**: **teme que le echen la culpa a él** he's afraid that they'll blame him for it
■ **temer** *vi* to be afraid; **no temas** don't be afraid; **estos niños son de ~** (fam) these kids are terrible! (colloq); **~ POR algo/algn** to fear FOR sth/sb
■ **temerse** *v pron* [1] (sospechar) to fear; **ya me lo temía** I knew this/that would happen; **me temo que ...** I fear that ... [2] (en fórmulas de cortesía) to be afraid; **me temo que no ha llegado** I'm afraid he hasn't arrived

temerario -ria *adj* bold

temeridad *f* [1] (acción): **eso fue una ~** that was a very rash *o* bold thing to do [2] (cualidad) temerity; **conduce con ~** she drives recklessly

temeroso -sa *adj* frightened; **huyeron ~s** they fled in fear (liter); **~ DE algn/algo** fearful OF sb/sth (liter), afraid OF sb/sth; **~ de Dios** God-fearing

temible *adj* fearsome, fearful

temor *m* fear; **no le dije nada por ~ a ofenderlo** I didn't say anything for fear of offending him
(Compuesto) **temor de Dios** fear of God

témpano *m* (plancha de hielo) ice floe; **ser como un ~ (de hielo)** to have a heart of ice; ***quedarse como un*** **~** to be chilled to the marrow *o* bone

témpera *m* tempera

temperamental *adj* (irascible, cambiable) temperamental; (de mucho carácter) spirited

temperamento *m*
A [1] (manera de ser) temperament; **son de ~s muy diferen-**

t

tes they have very different temperaments; **tiene un ~ violento** she has a violent nature 2 (vigor de carácter): **un chico/torero con mucho ~** a boy/bullfighter with a lot of spirit
B (Mús) temperament

temperancia *f* temperance

temperante[1] *adj* (Méx fam) teetotal

temperante[2] *mf* (Méx fam) teetotaler*

temperar [A1] *vt* 1 (moderar) to temper 2 (Mús) to temper
■ **temperar** *vi* (Col) to have a change of air

temperatura *f* 1 (Fís, Med) temperature; **tomar la ~ a algn** to take sb's temperature; **tiene ~** (CS) she has a fever (AmE) *o* (BrE) a temperature 2 (Meteo) temperature; **un descenso de las ~s** a drop in temperatures
(Compuesto) **temperatura ambiente** room temperature

tempestad *f* storm, tempest (liter)
(Compuesto) **tempestad de arena** sandstorm

tempestuoso -sa *adj* stormy, tempestuous

templado -da *adj*
A 1 ‹clima› mild, temperate; ‹zona› temperate; ‹temperatura› warm 2 ‹agua› warm, lukewarm; ‹comida› lukewarm
B ‹ánimo› bold, courageous; **tiene los nervios bien ~s** she has nerves of steel
C (Col) (duro, difícil) tough

templanza *f* temperance

templar [A1] *vt*
A (Tec) ‹acero› to temper
B (Mús) ‹violín/cuerda› to tune
C (entibiar — enfriando) to cool down; (— calentando) to warm up
■ **templar** *vi* (hacer más calor) to get warmer *o* milder; (refrescar) to get cooler
■ **templarse** *v pron* (enfriarse) to cool down; (calentarse) to get warmer, warm up

templario *m* (Knight) Templar

temple *m*
A (Tec) (acción) tempering; (efecto) temper
B (coraje) mettle (liter), courage; ***estar de buen/mal ~*** to be in a good/bad mood
C (Art) tempera

templo *m* temple; **un ~ del saber** a seat of learning

tempo *m* tempo

temporada *f*
A (época establecida) season; **verduras de ~** seasonal vegetables; **fuera de/en ~** out of/in season; **en plena ~ turística** at the height of the tourist season
(Compuesto) **temporada alta/baja** high/low season
B (período de tiempo) spell; **una ~ de mucho trabajo** a very busy spell *o* period

temporal[1] *adj*
A (transitorio) temporary
B (relativo al tiempo) temporal
C ‹poder› temporal; ‹bienes› worldly

temporal[2] *m* (Meteo) storm; ***capear el ~*** to ride out *o* weather the storm
(Compuesto) **temporal de nieve** snowstorm, blizzard

temporalero -ra *m,f* (Méx) seasonal worker

temporalidad *f*
A (transitoriedad) transient nature, transience
B 1 (secularidad) temporality 2 **temporalidades** *fpl* (beneficios) temporalities (*pl*)
C (por oposición al espacio) temporality

temporalmente, (AmL) **temporariamente** *adv* temporarily

temporario -ria *adj* (AmL) temporary

temporero[1] **-ra** *adj* ‹trabajador› seasonal

temporero[2] **-ra** *m,f* (trabajador) seasonal worker

temporizador *m* timer

tempranero -ra *adj* early (*before n*)

temprano[1] **-na** *adj* early; **a la temprana edad de ...** at the early age of ...

temprano[2] *adv* early; **levantarse ~** to get up early; **todavía es ~ para saberlo** it's still too early to know

ten *see* **tener**

tenacidad *f* 1 (perseverancia) tenacity 2 (de material) toughness, resilience

tenacillas *fpl* hair crimper

tenaz *adj*
A 1 ‹persona› tenacious; **su ~ propósito de ganar** in his determined bid to win 2 ‹dolor› persistent; ‹mancha› stubborn
B (Col fam) 1 ‹problema/situación› tough 2 (*como interj*) oh no!, that's too bad! (AmE colloq)

tenaza *f*, **tenazas** *fpl* 1 (Mec, Tec) pliers (*pl*) 2 (de chimenea, cocina) tongs (*pl*) 3 (del cangrejo) pincer 4 (Méx) (de pelo) curling iron (AmE), hair crimper (BrE)

tenca *f* (Zool) tench

ten con ten *m* (Esp fam) (tacto) tact

tendajón *m* (Méx) shack (*serving as a store or stall*)

tendal *m* 1 (AmL) (para el café) drying area 2 (RPl fam) (reguero) trail

tendalada *f* (Chi fam): **una ~ de gente** loads of people (colloq); ***dejar/quedar la ~*** (Chi fam): **el derrumbe dejó la ~** the landslide wreaked havoc; **quedó la ~** there was absolute chaos

tendedero *m* (cuerda) clothesline;(caballete) clotheshorse

tendencia *f* tendency; **~s homosexuales** homosexual tendencies *o* leanings; **~ A algo** trend TOWARD(s) sth; **~ a la baja/al alza** downward/upward trend; **~ A + INF** tendency to + INF; **tiene ~ a exagerar** she has a tendency to exaggerate

tendencioso -sa *adj* tendentious

tender [E8] *vt*
A ‹ropa› (afuera) to hang out; (dentro de la casa) to hang (up); **tengo ropa tendida** I have some washing on the line
B 1 (extender) ‹manta› to spread out, lay out; ‹mantel› to spread 2 (AmL) ‹cama› to make; ‹mesa› to lay, set 3 ‹persona› to lay; ‹cadáver› to lay out
C 1 ‹cable› (sobre superficie) to lay; (suspendido) to hang 2 ‹vía férrea› to lay
D (extender): **le tendió la mano** he held out his hand to him; ▸**amno**[1] **H**
E ‹emboscada› to lay, set; ‹trampa› to set
■ **tender** *vi* (inclinarse) **~ A + INF** to tend TO + INF; **~ A algo**: **tiende a la introversión** she tends to be introverted
■ **tenderse** *v pron*
A (tumbarse) to lie down
B (Jueg) (en naipes) to show

tenderete *m* 1 (en mercado) stall 2 (para tender la ropa) airer, clotheshorse

tendero -ra *m,f* storekeeper (esp AmE), shopkeeper (esp BrE)

tendido *m*
A (Elec) 1 (acción de tender cable — sobre superficie) laying; (— suspendido) hanging 2 (cables) cables (*pl*), wires (*pl*)
B (de puente) building; (de vía férrea) laying
C (Taur) section
D (Col, Ven) (ropa de cama) bedclothes (*pl*)

tendiente *adj* (esp AmL): **medidas ~s a la creación de empleos** measures aimed at creating jobs; **~ A + INF** designed to + INF

tendón *m* tendon; **~ de Aquiles** Achilles' tendon

tendré, tendría, etc *see* **tener**

tenebrosidad *f* (de lugar) darkness, gloom; (de asunto) sinisterness

tenebroso -sa *adj* ‹lugar› dark, gloomy; ‹asunto/maquinaciones› sinister; ‹porvenir/situación› dismal, gloomy

tenedor -dora *m,f*
A (Com, Der) holder
(Compuesto) **tenedor -dora de libros** *m,f* bookkeeper
B **tenedor** *m* (cubierto) fork

teneduría de libros *f* bookkeeping

tenencia *f*
A 1 (de valores) holding 2 (Der) possession
(Compuesto) **tenencia ilícita de armas** illegal possession of arms
B (de cargo) tenure

C (Méx) (Auto) road tax

tener [E27] *vt* [*El uso de 'got' en frases como 'I've got a new dress' está mucho más extendido en el inglés británico que en el americano. Éste prefiere la forma 'I have a new dress'*]

Sentido **I**

A (poseer, disponer de) ‹*dinero/trabajo/tiempo*› to have; **¿tienen hijos?** do they have any children?, have they got any children?; **no tenemos pan** we don't have any bread, we haven't got any bread; **no tengo a quién recurrir** I have nobody to turn to; **tú no tienes idea de lo que fue** you've no idea what it was like; **aquí tienes al culpable** here's *o* this is the culprit; **¡ahí tienes! yo te lo dije** there you are! I told you so; ***¿conque ésas tenemos?*** so that's the way things are, is it?

B **1** (llevar encima) to have; **¿tiene hora?** have you got the time? **2** (llevar puesto) to be wearing; **¡qué traje más elegante tienes!** that's a smart suit you're wearing!

C (hablando de actividades, obligaciones) to have; **tengo invitados a cenar** I have *o* I've got some people coming to dinner; **tenemos clases mañana** we've got school tomorrow; **tener ... QUE + INF** to have ... TO + INF; **tengo cosas que hacer** I have *o* I've got things to do

D **1** (señalando características, atributos) to have; **tiene el pelo largo** she has *o* she's got long hair; **tiene mucho tacto** he's very tactful; **la casa tiene mucha luz** the house is very light *o* gets a lot of light; **tiene un metro de largo** it is one meter long; **tiene mucho de su padre** he's very much like his father; **¿y eso qué tiene de malo?** and what's so bad about that?; **no tiene nada de extraño** there's nothing strange about it; **le lleva 15 años — ¿y eso qué tiene?** (AmL fam) she's 15 years older than he is — so what does that matter? **2** (expresando edad): **¿cuántos años tienes?** how old are you?; **tengo veinte años** I'm twenty (years old) **3** (con idea de posibilidad): **no creo que tenga arreglo** I don't think it can be fixed; **el problema tiene solución** there is a solution to the problem

E (dar a luz) ‹*bebé/gemelos*› to have

Sentido **II**

A (sujetar, sostener) to hold; **tenlo derecho** hold it upright

B (tomar): **ten la llave** take *o* here's the key

Sentido **III**

A (recibir) to have; **no hemos tenido noticias de él** we haven't heard from him; **la propuesta tuvo una acogida favorable** the proposal was favorably received

B **1** (sentir): **tengo hambre/sueño/frío** I'm hungry/tired/cold; **tiene celos de su hermano** she's jealous of her brother; **no tiene interés por nada** she's not interested in anything; **le tengo mucho cariño** I'm very fond of him; **tengo el placer de ...** it gives me great pleasure to ...; **¿qué tienes?** what's wrong?, what's the matter? **2** (refiriéndose a síntomas, enfermedades) to have; **tengo dolor de cabeza** I have *o* I've got a headache; **no saben lo que tiene** they don't know what's wrong with him **3** (refiriéndose a experiencias, sucesos) to have; **que tengas buen viaje** have a good trip; **~ una discusión con algn** to have an argument with sb

C (refiriéndose a actitudes): **ten más respeto** have a little more respect; **ten paciencia/cuidado** be patient/careful

Sentido **IV**

A (indicando estado, situación) (+ *compl*): **la mesa tiene una pata rota** one of the table legs is broken; **tengo las manos sucias** my hands are dirty; **tienes el cinturón desabrochado** your belt's undone; **lo tiene dominado** she has him under her thumb; **lo tengo terminado** I've already finished it; **me tiene muy preocupada** I'm very worried about it; **nos tuvo allí esperando** he kept us waiting there; **me tienen de sirvienta** they treat me like a maid; **tengo a la niña enferma** my little girl's sick

B (considerar) **~ algo/a algn POR algo**: **se lo tiene por el mejor** he/it is considered (to be) the best; **siempre lo tuve por tímido** I always thought he was shy; **ten por seguro que lo hará** you can be sure he'll do it

■ **tener** *v aux*

Sentido **I**

A **1** (expresando obligación, necesidad) **~ QUE + INF** to have (got) to + INF; **tengo que estudiar hoy** I have to *o* I must study today; **no tienes más que apretar este botón** all you have to do is press this button; **no tengo por qué darte cuentas a ti** I don't have to explain anything to you; **tienes que comer más** you ought to eat more **2** (expresando propósito, recomendación) **~ QUE + INF**: **tenemos que ir a verla** we must go and see her; **tengo que hacer ejercicio** I must get some exercise; **tendrías que llamarlo** you should ring him

B (expresando certeza) **~ QUE + INF**: **tiene que estar en este cajón** it must be in this drawer; **tiene que haber sido él** it must have been him; **¡tú tenías que ser!** it had to be you!

Sentido **II**

A (con participio pasado): **¿tiene previsto asistir?** do you plan to attend?; **tengo entendido que sí viene** I understand he *is* coming; **te tengo dicho que eso no me gusta** I've told you before I don't like that; **teníamos pensado irnos hoy** we intended leaving today; **tiene bastante dinero ahorrado** she has quite a lot of money saved up

B (AmL) (en expresiones de tiempo): **tienen tres años de casados** they've been married for three years; **tenía un año sin verlo** she hadn't seen him for a year

■ **tenerse** *v pron*

A (sostenerse): **no podía ~se en pie** he couldn't stand; **no ~se de sueño** to be dead *o* asleep on one's feet

B (*refl*) (considerarse) **~se POR algo**: **se tiene por muy inteligente** he considers himself to be very intelligent

tenga, tengas, etc *see* **tener**

tenia *f* (Med) tapeworm, taenia (tech)

tenida *f* (Chi) outfit

teniente *mf* **1** (en ejército) lieutenant **2** (en fuerzas aéreas) ≈ first lieutenant (*in US*), ≈ flying officer (*in UK*)

Compuestos

- **teniente coronel** **1** (en ejército) lieutenant colonel **2** (en fuerzas aéreas) ≈ lieutenant colonel (*in US*), ≈ wing commander (*in UK*)
- **teniente general** (en ejército) lieutenant general; (en fuerzas aéreas) ≈ lieutenant general (*in US*), ≈ Air Marshal (*in UK*)

tenis *m* (*pl* ~)

A (deporte) tennis

Compuesto **tenis de mesa** table tennis

B (Indum) (con suela fina) sneaker (AmE), plimsoll (BrE); (con suela más gruesa) sneaker (AmE), trainer (BrE)

tenista *mf* tennis player

tenístico -ca *adj* tennis (*before n*)

tenor *m*

A (Mús) tenor

B (de discurso, texto) meaning; **~ literal** literal meaning; **el ~ de sus declaraciones** the tone of his statement; **a ~ de** according to

tenorio *m* (fam) womanizer, Don Juan

tensar [A1] *vt* ‹*músculo*› to tense; ‹*cuerda/cable*› to tighten; ‹*arco*› to draw; ‹*relaciones/lazos*› to strain

tensión *f*

A **1** (de cuerda, cable) tautness, tension; (de músculo) tension **2** *tb* **~ arterial** blood pressure; **tomarle la ~ a algn** to take sb's blood pressure

Compuestos

- **tensión nerviosa** nervous tension
- **tensión premenstrual** premenstrual syndrome *o* (BrE) tension

B (estrés) strain, stress; (en relaciones, situación) tension

C (Elec) voltage

tensionado -da *adj* ‹*músculo/persona*› tense; ‹*región/país*› troubled

tenso -sa *adj*

A ‹*cuerda/cable*› taut, tight; ‹*músculo*› tense

B ‹*persona*› tense; ‹*relación*› strained, tense; ‹*situación*› tense

tensor *m* **1** (Anat) tensor **2** (Dep) chest pull (AmE), chest expander (BrE)

tentación *f* **1** (impulso) temptation; **~ DE + INF** temptation to + INF; **no resistió la ~ de comérselo** he couldn't resist the temptation to eat it **2** (cosa, persona): **los bombones son mi ~** I can't resist chocolates (colloq)

tentáculo *m* tentacle

tentado -da *adj* tempted; **~ DE + INF** tempted to + INF; **estuve ~ de decírselo** I was tempted to tell him

tentador[1] **-dora** *adj* tempting

t

tentador² **-dora** *m,f* 1 (Taur) *person who assesses the fighting potential of young bulls* 2 **tentadora** *f* (seductora) temptress

tentar [A5] *vt*
A (atraer, seducir) «*plan/idea*» to tempt; «*persona*» to tempt; **me tienta tu propuesta** I am very tempted by your proposal; **no me tientes con esos bombones** don't tempt me with those chocolates; **~ a algn A + INF** to tempt sb to + INF; **~ *a Dios* or *al diablo*** to tempt fate *o* providence
B (probar) 1 ‹*cuerda/tabla*› to test 2 (ant) ‹*comida*› to try, taste 3 ‹*becerro*› to test
C (palpar) to feel
■ **tentarse** *v pron* (CS fam) (caer en la tentación) to give in to temptation

tentativa *f* attempt; **~ de robo** attempted robbery

tentempié *m* (bocado) snack

tenue *adj* 1 ‹*luz*› faint, weak; ‹*voz/sonido*› faint; ‹*neblina/llovizna*› light; ‹*línea*› faint, fine; **una ~ sonrisa** a faint smile 2 ‹*color*› subdued, pale 3 (liter) ‹*hilo*› fine, slender; ‹*tela*› flimsy, fine 4 ‹*razón/relación*› tenuous, insubstantial 5 ‹*estilo*› simple, plain

teñido *m* dyeing

teñir [I15] *vt* 1 ‹*ropa/zapatos/pelo*› to dye 2 (manchar) to stain; **~ algo DE algo** to stain sth WITH sth; **sus manos estaban teñidas de sangre** their hands were stained with blood 3 (matizar): **palabras teñidas de amargura** words tinged with bitterness; **un país con una historia teñida de sangre** a country with a bloodstained history
■ **teñirse** *v pron* (*refl*) to dye; **no me tiño (el pelo)** I don't dye my hair

teocracia *f* theocracy

teocrático **-ca** *adj* theocratic

teología *f* theology

teológico **-ca** *adj* theological

teólogo **-ga** *m,f* theologian

teorema *m* theorem

teoría *f* theory; **en ~** in theory
(Compuesto) **teoría de la evolución/relatividad** theory of evolution/relativity

teóricamente *adv* theoretically

teórico¹ **-ca** *adj* ‹*existencia/valor/curso*› theoretical; **no pasó el examen ~** he didn't pass the theory (exam)

teórico² **-ca** *m,f* theoretician, theorist

teorizar [A4] *vi* to theorize; **~ SOBRE algo** to theorize ON *o* ABOUT sth

Teotihuacán

A pre-Columbian city, the ruins of Teotihuacán lie northeast of Mexico City. The Nahuatl name means "city of the gods" or "where men became gods". Little is known about the city's founders or inhabitants, but it reached its peak between 300 and 600 AD. It includes the Pyramids of the Sun and Moon, the temple of Quetzalcóatl, the Great Compound, and the central complex, the *Ciudadela*. The two main groups of buildings are linked by a road known as the Way of the Dead.

By 650 AD Teotihuacán was in decline; it was in ruins when the Aztecs found it in the fifteenth century

TEPT *m* (= **trastorno por estrés postraumático**) PTSD

tequila *m* tequila

terapeuta *mf* therapist

terapéutica *f* therapeutics

terapéutico **-ca** *adj* therapeutic

terapia *f* therapy
(Compuestos)
- **terapia de pareja** marriage counseling*
- **terapia intensiva** (Méx, RPl) intensive care
- **terapia ocupacional** occupational therapy

tercer *ver* **tercero¹**

tercera *f* 1 (Auto) third (gear); **mete (la) ~** put it into third (gear) 2 (Transp) (clase) third class

tercermundismo *m* backwardness (*conditions, attitudes, etc, considered typical of a third-world country*)

tercermundista *adj* third-world (*before n*)

tercero¹ **-ra** *adj/pron* [**tercer** *is used before masculine singular nouns*] 1 (ordinal) third; **en el tercer piso** on the third floor; **sin que intervengan terceras personas** without other people getting involved; ***la tercera es la vencida*** *or* ***a la tercera va la vencida*** third time lucky 2 (partitivo) **la tercera parte** a third; *para ejemplos ver* **quinto**
(Compuestos)
- **tercera edad** *f*: **la ~ ~** (frml) retirement years, the third age (frml); **personas de la ~ ~** senior citizens
- **Tercer Mundo** *m*: **el ~ ~** the Third World

tercero² *m* third party; **seguro contra ~s** third party insurance; **se enteró por ~s** he found out from someone else

terceto *m* (Lit) tercet; (Mús) trio

terciado **-da** *adj* 1 ‹*bolso/rifle*› slung, hung; **se puso la boina terciada** he put on his beret at a tilt *o* slant 2 (Taur) medium-sized 3 (Méx) ‹*bebida*› mixed

terciana *f* tertian (fever)

terciar [A1] *vt* 1 ‹*bolso/rifle*› to sling; ‹*sombrero*› to tilt 2 (decir, opinar) to interject
■ **terciar** *vi* (intervenir) to intervene
■ **terciarse** *v pron* (Esp): **si se tercia** if the opportunity arises; **si se tercia el tema** if the subject arises

terciario **-ria** *adj* 1 ‹*era*› Tertiary 2 ‹*sector/economía*› tertiary

tercio *m*
A 1 (tercera parte) third; ***hacer mal ~*** (Méx) to be a fifth wheel (AmE colloq), to play gooseberry (BrE colloq) 2 (Taur) *each of the three main stages of a bullfight*; ***cambiar de ~*** (Taur) to enter the next stage of the bullfight; (pasar a otra cosa) to move on to something else
B (Ven arg) (hombre): **mi ~** my man *o* guy (colloq)

terciopelo *m* velvet

terco **-ca** *adj* stubborn, obstinate; ***ser ~ como una mula*** (fam) to be as stubborn as a mule

tergiversación *f* distortion, twisting

tergiversar [A1] *vt* to distort, twist

termal *adj* thermal

termalista *mf* 1 (comerciante) spa manager/owner 2 (usuario): *person taking cures at a spa*

termas *fpl* 1 (baños) hot *o* thermal baths (*pl*); (manantial) hot *o* thermal springs (*pl*) 2 (Hist) thermae (*pl*)

térmica *f* thermal

térmico **-ca** *adj* thermal

terminación *f* 1 (finalización) termination (frml); **la ~ de las obras estaba prevista para 1990** the work was due to be finished by 1990 2 (acabado) finish 3 (Ling) ending

terminado **-da** *adj* finished; *ver tb* **terminar**

terminal¹ *adj*
A (Bot) terminal
B ‹*enfermedad/caso*› terminal; **los enfermos ~es** the terminally ill

terminal² *m*
A (Elec) terminal
B (*en algunas regiones f*) (Inf) terminal
C (Chi) ▸**terminal³**

terminal³ *f* (de autobuses) terminus, bus station; (Aviac) terminal

terminante *adj* ‹*respuesta*› categorical; ‹*orden*› strict

terminantemente *adv* strictly

terminar [A1] *vt* ‹*trabajo/estudio*› to finish; ‹*casa/obras*› to finish, complete; **terminó sus días en Sicilia** he ended his days in Sicily; **dar por terminado algo** ‹*discusión/conflicto*› to put an end to sth; **dieron por terminada la sesión** they brought the session to a close; **termina esa sopa** finish up that soup
■ **terminar** *vi*
A «*persona*» 1 (de hacer algo) to finish; **~ DE + INF** to finish -ING; **déjame ~ de hablar** let me finish (speaking); **salió nada más ~ de comer** he went out as soon as he'd finished eating 2 (en estado, situación) to end up; **terminé muy cansada** I ended up feeling very tired; **va a ~ mal** he's going to come to a bad end; **~ DE algo**: **terminó de camarero** he ended up (working) as a waiter; **~ + GER** *or* **~ POR + INF** to end up -ING; **terminó marchándose** *or* **por marcharse** he ended up leaving
B 1 «*reunión/situación*» to end, come to an end; **todo ha**

terminado it's all over; **el caso terminó en los tribunales** the case ended up in court; **esto va a ~ mal** this is going to turn out *o* end badly; **y para ~ nos sirvieron ...** and to finish we had ... 2 (rematar) **~ EN algo** to end IN sth; **la palabra termina en consonante** the word ends in a consonant

C terminar con 1 (acabar, consumir) **~ CON algo** ‹*con libro/tarea*› to finish WITH sth; ‹*con problema/abuso*› to put an end to sth; **~on con todo lo que había en la nevera** they polished off everything in the fridge 2 **~ CON algn** (pelearse) to finish WITH sb; (destruir) to kill sb; **ocho años de cárcel ~on con él** eight years in prison destroyed him

D (llegar a) **~ DE + INF**: **no termina de convencerme** I'm not totally convinced; **no terminaba de gustarle** she wasn't totally happy about it

■ **terminarse** *v pron*

A «*azúcar/pan*» to run out; (+ *me/te/le etc*) **se me terminó la lana** I've run out of wool

B «*curso/reunión*» to come to an end, be over

C (*enf*) ‹*libro/comida*› to finish, polish off

término *m*

A (frml) (final) end, conclusion (frml); **llevar algo a buen ~** to bring sth to a successful conclusion; **dio ~ a sus vacaciones** he ended his vacation; **poner ~ a algo** to put an end to sth

B (plazo) period; **en el ~ de un mes** within a month; **a ~ fijo** (Col) ‹*contrato/inversión*› fixed-term (*before n*); ***en el ~ de la distancia*** (Col fam) in the time it takes me/him to get there

C (posición, instancia): **fue relegado a un segundo ~** he was relegated to second place; **en último ~** as a last resort; **en primer ~** first *o* first of all

Compuesto **término medio** happy medium; ***por*** *or* ***como ~ ~*** on average

D (Ling) term; **en ~s de costos** in terms of costs; **en ~s generales** generally speaking; **en ~s reales** in real terms

E (Fil, Mat) term; **invertir los ~s** (Mat) to invert the terms; **invirtió los ~s de manera que ...** he twisted the facts in such a way that ...

F términos *mpl* (condiciones, especificaciones) terms (*pl*); ***estar en buenos/malos ~s con algn*** to be on good/bad terms with sb

G (Col, Méx, Ven) (Coc): **¿qué ~ quiere la carne?** how would you like your meat (done)?

terminología *f* terminology

terminológico -ca *adj* terminological

termita *f* termite

termo® *m* (recipiente) Thermos®, vacuum flask

termoeléctrico -ca *adj* thermoelectric

termómetro *m* thermometer

termonuclear *adj* thermonuclear

termostato *m* thermostat

terna *f* short list (*of three candidates*)

ternario[1] -ria *adj* ternary

ternario[2] *m*: *three days of devotion*

ternera *f* veal

ternero -ra *m,f* calf

terneza *f* 1 (ternura) tenderness 2 **ternezas** *fpl* (fam) (palabras) endearments (*pl*)

terno *m* (AmS) suit (*in some countries specifically a three-piece suit*)

ternura *f* tenderness; **me trata con mucha ~** he's very kind to *o* gentle with me

terquedad *f* obstinacy, stubbornness

terracería *f* (Méx) 1 (camino) rough dirt track 2 (tierra) earth (*used for filling in holes, etc*)

terracota *f* terra-cotta

terrado *m* flat roof

terraje *m* rent

terraplén *m* embankment, bank

terráqueo -quea *adj* earth (*before n*)

terrateniente[1] *adj* landowning (*before n*)

terrateniente[2] *mf* landowner

terraza *f*

A 1 (balcón) balcony 2 (azotea) terrace 3 (de bar) *area outside a bar or café where tables are placed*; **sentémonos en la ~** let's sit outside

B (Agr) terrace

terrazo *m* terrazzo

terregal *m* (Méx) loose topsoil

terremoteado -da *adj* (Chi fam) *damaged or destroyed by an earthquake*

terremotear [A1] *v impers* (Chi fam): **en Chile terremotea mucho** in Chile there are frequent earthquakes

terremoto *m* earthquake

terrenal *adj* worldly, earthly

terreno[1] -na *adj* 1 (Relig) earthly 2 (no marino o aéreo) terrestrial (frml), land (*before n*)

terreno[2] *m*

A (lote, parcela) plot of land, lot (AmE); **heredó unos ~s en Sonora** she inherited some land in Sonora; **un ~ plantado de viñas** a field planted with vines; **el ~ cuesta tanto como la casa** the land costs as much as the house; **el ~ llega hasta el río** the land *o* plot *o* lot extends as far as the river

Compuesto **terreno de juego** field, pitch; **perdieron en su propio ~ de ~** they lost at home

B (extensión de tierra) land; **una casa con mucho ~** a house with a lot of land

C 1 (Geog) (refiriéndose al relieve) terrain; (refiriéndose a la composición) land, soil; ***allanarle el ~ a algn*** to smooth the way *o* path for sb; ***ceder/ganar/perder ~*** to give/gain/lose ground; ***estar en su (propio) ~*** to be on one's own ground; ***minarle*** *or* ***socavarle el ~ a algn*** to cut the ground from under sb's feet; ***pisar ~ firme/peligroso*** to tread on safe/dangerous ground; ***prepararle el ~ a algn/algo*** to pave the way for sb/sth; ***recuperar ~*** to recover lost ground; ***sobre el ~***: **estudiar sobre el ~ una situación** to make an on-the-spot assessment of a situation; **haremos planes sobre el ~** we'll plan things as we go along; ***tantear el ~*** to see how the land lies 2 (Geol) terrane, terrain

Compuestos

- **terreno abonado** *or* **propicio**: **es ~ ~ para la delincuencia** it is a breeding ground for crime; **es un ~ ~ para la especulación** it gives rise to a great deal of speculation
- **terreno conocido** familiar ground

D (esfera, campo de acción) sphere, field; **en el ~ laboral** at work; **en el ~ de las artes** in the arts

terrestre *adj* 1 ‹*transportes/comunicaciones*› land (*before n*), terrestrial (frml); **por vía ~** overland *o* by land; **fuerzas ~s** ground *o* land forces; **la superficie ~** the earth's surface 2 (Relig) ‹*vida*› earthly

terrible *adj* 1 ‹*tortura/experiencia*› terrible, horrific 2 (uso hiperbólico) terrible; **tengo un sueño ~** I'm terribly tired; **este niño es ~** this child is terrible

terriblemente *adv* terribly

terrícola *mf* earthling

territorial *adj* territorial

territorialidad *f* territoriality

territorio *m* (área, superficie) territory; (división administrativa) region, territory

terrón *m* (de azúcar) lump; (de tierra) clod, lump

terror *m* 1 (miedo) terror; **me da ~** *or* **le tengo ~** it terrifies me, I find it terrifying 2 (persona) terror; **es el ~ de la ciudad** he is terrorizing the city

terrorífico -ca *adj* horrific

terrorismo *m* terrorism

terrorista *adj/mf* terrorist

terroso -sa *adj* 1 ‹*color*› earthy 2 ‹*aguas*› muddy

terruño *m* 1 (tierra natal): **volver al ~** to return to one's native land *o* (liter) soil 2 (tierras propias) land, plot of land (*which is the source of one's livelihood*)

terso -sa *adj* 1 ‹*piel/cutis*› smooth 2 ‹*lenguaje/estilo*› flowing, smooth

tersura *f* 1 (de la piel) smoothness 2 (del estilo) smoothness, flow

tertulia *f* (reunión) gathering (*to discuss philosophy, politics, art, etc*)

t

(Compuesto) **tertulia literaria** (grupo) literary circle; (reunión) literary gathering

tertulia

A discussion group. Formerly, *tertulias* were groups of men who met in a café to talk about soccer, bullfighting, literature, cinema, politics, etc. Some of these became very famous, as they included important political and cultural figures. Now *tertulias* are often televized discussion programs

tertuliano -na *m,f* member of a **tertulia**

tesauro *m* thesaurus

tesina *f* dissertation (*submitted as part of a first degree*)

tesis *f* (*pl* ~) [1] (Educ, Fil) thesis [2] (opinión): **los dos sostienen la misma ~** they are both of the same opinion; **esto confirma la ~ inicial** this confirms the initial theory

(Compuesto) **tesis doctoral** doctoral thesis

tesitura *f* [1] (actitud) frame of mind [2] (Mús) tessitura

tesón *m* tenacity, determination; **se opusieron con ~ al cierre de la fábrica** they resisted the closure of the factory tenaciously *o* with determination

tesonero -ra *adj*: **es aplicado y ~** he works hard and is determined; **un llanto ~** a persistent crying

tesorería *f* [1] (oficina) treasury; (cargo) post of treasurer [2] (Fin) (activo disponible) liquid assets (*pl*)

tesorero -ra *m,f* treasurer

tesoro *m* [1] (cosa valiosa) treasure; **un ~ escondido** hidden treasure [2] (persona) treasure, gem (colloq); **eres un ~** you're a real gem; **¿qué te pasa, ~?** what's the matter, darling? [3] (libro) thesaurus [4] **el Tesoro** *tb* **el T~ público** the Treasury

test *m* (*pl* **tests**) test; **un examen tipo ~** a multiple-choice exam

testa *f* (fam) head

testado -da *adj* testate

testador -dora (*m*) testator; (*f*) testatrix

testaferro *m* figurehead, straw man (AmE)

testamentario[1] -ria *adj* testamentary

testamentario[2] -ria (*m*) executor; (*f*) executrix

testamento *m* will, testament (frml); **hacer** *or* **otorgar ~** to make one's will

testar [A1] *vi* to make one's will; **testó en favor de sus hijos** he willed everything to his children

testarada *f*, **testarazo** *m* (fam) bump on the head; **darse** *or* **pegarse una ~** to bump one's head

testarudez *f* stubbornness, pigheadedness

testarudo -da *adj* stubborn, pigheaded

testículo *m* testicle

testigo *mf*

A [1] (que presencia algo) witness; (Der) witness; **Pablo es ~ de que no lo toqué** I didn't touch it, Pablo can vouch for me; **ser ~ de algo** to witness sth; **la historia será ~ de que ...** history will bear witness to the fact that ... [2] (en boda) witness; **fui ~ en su casamiento** I was a witness at their wedding

(Compuestos)

- **testigo de cargo/descargo** witness for the prosecution/defense
- **testigo de oídas** hearsay witness
- **testigo ocular** *or* **presencial** eyewitness

B **testigo** *m* (en carreras de relevos) baton

testimonial *adj* [1] (Der) testimonial [2] (simbólico) token (*before n*), symbolic

testimoniar [A1] *vi* to testify

■ **testimoniar** *vt* to bear witness to, testify to

testimonio *m* [1] (Der) (declaración) testimony, statement [2] (prueba) proof, testimony (frml); **como ~ de su agradecimiento** as a token of his gratitude; **cifras que dan ~ de este hecho** figures which bear witness to this fact

teta *f* (fam *o* vulg) (de mujer) tit (colloq *or* vulg), boob (colloq); (de mamífero) teat

tétanos, tétano *m* tetanus

tetera *f* [1] (para servir té) teapot [2] (Andes, Méx) (para hervir agua) kettle [3] (Méx) (biberón) baby's bottle

tetero *m* (Col, Ven) baby's bottle

tetilla *f* [1] (Anat) nipple; (Zool) teat [2] (del biberón) teat

tetina *f* teat

tetona *adj* (fam) busty (colloq)

tetralogía *f* tetralogy

tétrico -ca *adj* dismal, gloomy

teutón -tona, teutónico -ca *adj* Teutonic

texano -na *adj/m,f* Texan

textil[1] *adj* textile (*before n*)

textil[2] *m* textile

texto *m*

A (escrito) text

B (libro) text, book

textual *adj* [1] ‹*traducción*› literal; ‹*palabras*› exact; ‹*cita*› direct [2] ‹*análisis*› textual

textualmente *adv* ‹*traducir*› literally; ‹*citar/repetir*› verbatim, word for word; **dice ~ 'bajo ningún concepto'** it says, and I quote, 'under no circumstances'

textura *f* texture

tez *f* complexion

tezontle *m* (Méx) red volcanic rock

ti *pron pers* [1] you; **para ~** for you; **delante de ~** in front of you; **está interesado en ~** he's interested in you; **a mí me gusta ¿y a ~?** I like it, do you? [2] (uso enfático): **¿y a ~ qué te importa?** what business is it of yours? [3] (en oposición a otro): **¿a ~ qué te tocó?** what did he get *you*? [4] (*refl*): **piensa en ~ mismo** just think of yourself [5] (*impers*) you; **si a ~ te cuentan que ...** if someone tells you that ...

tianguis *m* (Méx) street market

TIAR /ti'ar/ *m* = **Tratado Interamericano de Asistencia Recíproca**

tiara *f* tiara

Tíbet *m*: **el ~** Tibet

tibetano -na *adj* Tibetan

tibia *f* tibia

tibieza *f* (calor) warmth; (falta de calor) lukewarmness, tepidness; (de persona) halfheartedness

tibio -bia *adj* [1] ‹*agua/baño*› lukewarm, tepid [2] ‹*atmósfera/ambiente*› warm [3] ‹*relación*› lukewarm; ‹*acogida*› unenthusiastic, cool

tiburón *m* [1] (Zool) shark [2] (fam) (persona) shark [3] (Fin) raider

tic *m*

A (movimiento) *tb* **~ nervioso** nervous tic

B (marca en escrito) tick

tico -ca *adj/m,f* (AmL fam) Costa Rican

tic-tac, tictac *m* tick-tock, ticking

tiempo *m*

(Sentido I)

A (que transcurre) time; **el ~ pasa** time passes *o* goes by; **¡cómo pasa el ~!/¡el ~ vuela!** how time flies!; **te acostumbrarás con el ~** you'll get used to it in time; **el ~ dirá** time will tell; **el ~ apremia** time is short, time is of the essence (frml); **perder el ~** to waste time; **no hay ~ que perder!** there's no time to lose!; **recuperar el ~ perdido** to make up for lost time; **pérdida de ~** waste of time; **para ganar ~** (in order) to gain time

(Compuestos)

- **tiempo compartido** time-sharing
- **tiempo universal** universal time

B [1] (duración, porción de tiempo) time; **¿cuánto ~ hace que no lo ves?** how long is it since you last saw him?; **hace (mucho) ~ que no sé de él** I haven't heard from him for a long time; **ya hace ~ que se marchó** she left quite some time ago *o* quite a while ago; **¡cuánto ~ sin verte!** I haven't seen you for ages; **estudió todo el ~** she studied the whole time; **la mayor parte del ~** most of the time; **al poco ~** soon after; **dentro de muy poco ~** very soon; **¿cada cuánto ~?** how often?; **cada cierto ~** every so often; **de ~ en ~** from time to time; **me llevó mucho ~** it took me a long time; **no pude quedarme más ~** I couldn't stay any longer; **hace algún ~ que no viene** he hasn't been around for some time; **nos quedaremos (por) un ~** we'll stay for a while; **un** *or* **algún ~ atrás** some time ago *o* back; **viene de ~ atrás** this goes back a

t

long way; **poco ~ después** a short time after; **de un ~ a esta parte está insoportable** he's been quite unbearable for some time now; **de un ~ a esta parte ha estado muy triste** he's been very sad recently; **a ~ completo/parcial** full time/part time; **de ~ completo** full-time **2** (período disponible, tiempo suficiente) time; **no tenemos mucho ~** we don't have much time; **tengo todo el ~ del mundo** I've got all the time in the world; **no sé de dónde voy a sacar el ~** I don't know where I'm going to find the time; **hay ~ de sobra** there's plenty of time; **me va a faltar ~** I'm not going to have enough time **3** (Dep) (marca) time **4** (de bebé): **¿cuánto ~ tiene?** how old is he?

(Compuesto) **tiempo libre** spare time, free time

C (*en locs*) **a tiempo** in time; **no vamos a llegar a ~** we won't get there in time; **todavía estás a ~** you still have time; **al mismo tiempo** *or* **a un tiempo** at the same time; **al tiempo que** at the same time as *o* that; **con tiempo** in good time; ***con (el) ~ y una caña ...*** everything in good time; ***dar(le) ~ al ~*** to be patient; ***hacer ~*** to while away the time; (Dep) to play for time; ***matar el ~*** (fam) to kill time; ***robarle ~ al sueño*** to burn the candle at both ends; ***el ~ es oro*** time is precious *o* money; ***el ~ todo lo cura*** time is a great healer

D **1** (época): **en mi(s) ~(s)** in my day *o* my time; **eran otros ~s** things were different then; **¡qué ~s aquellos!** those were the days!; **es del ~ de mi abuela** from my grandmother's time; **en aquellos ~s** at that time, in those days; **los problemas de nuestro ~** the problems of our time *o* age; **en los ~s que corren** these days, nowadays; ***ser del ~ de Maricastaña*** (fam) to have come out of the ark (colloq) **2** (temporada) season **3** (momento propio, oportuno): **a su (debido) ~** in due course; **cada cosa a su ~** everything in (its own) good time; **nació antes de ~** he was premature

E (Dep) (en partido) half; **primer/segundo ~** first/second half

(Compuestos)
- **tiempo extra** *or* **suplementario** (Dep) overtime (AmE), extra time (BrE); (Com) period of inactivity
- **tiempo muerto** time out

F (Mús) (compás) tempo, time; (de sinfonía) movement

G (Ling) tense

(*Sentido* **II**) (Meteo) weather; **hace buen/mal ~** the weather's good/bad; **mal ~** bad weather; **el pronóstico del ~** the weather forecast; **¿qué tal el ~ por ahí?** what's the weather like over there?; **del** *or* (Méx) **al ~** at room temperature; ***a mal ~, buena cara*** I/you/we may as well look on the bright side

tienda *f*

A (Com) (en general) store (esp AmE), shop (esp BrE); (de comestibles) grocery store (AmE), grocer's (shop) (BrE); **la ~ de la esquina** the local convenience store, the corner shop (BrE); **ir de ~s** to go shopping

(Compuestos)
- **tienda de comestibles** *or* (AmC, Andes, Méx) **abarrotes** grocery store (AmE), grocer's (shop) (BrE)
- **tienda de departamentos** (Méx) department store
- **tienda de regalos** gift shop *o* (AmE) store

B (Dep, Mil, Ocio) *tb* **~ de campaña** tent; **poner** *or* **montar** *or* **armar una ~** to put up *o* pitch a tent; **quitar** *or* **desmontar** *or* **desarmar una ~** to take down a tent

tiene, tienes, etc *see* **tener**

tienta *f*

A (tacto) **a tientas**: **andar** *or* **ir a ~s** to feel one's way; **subió las escaleras a ~s** he felt his way up the stairs; **buscó el timbre a ~s** he fumbled *o* felt around for the bell

B (Taur) trial (*to test fighting spirit of young bulls*)

tiento *m*

A (tacto, cuidado) tact, care; **andarse con ~** to tread carefully

B (afinación) tuning up

C (Esp): **darle un ~ a algo** (tocar) ‹*aguacate/melón*› to feel; (probar) ‹*vino*› to take a swig of; ‹*arroz/guiso*› to taste

D (Méx) (Equ) tether; ***está/estaba con la vida en un ~*** (Méx) his life hangs/hung by a thread

tierno -na *adj*

A ‹*carne*› tender; ‹*pan*› fresh; ‹*brote/planta*› young, tender; **un niño de tierna edad** a child of tender years (liter); **en la más tierna infancia** in early childhood

B ‹*persona*› affectionate, loving; ‹*mirada/corazón*› tender

tierra *f*

A (campo, terreno) land; **~s fértiles/áridas** fertile/arid land; **~ labrantía** *or* **de cultivo** arable *o* cultivated land; **~s baldías** wasteland; ***poner ~ de por medio*** to make oneself scarce (colloq)

B (suelo, superficie) ground; (materia, arena) earth; **clavó la estaca en la ~** he drove the stake into the ground; **ésta es muy buena ~** this is very good land *o* soil; **no juegues con ~** don't play in the dirt; **un camino de ~** a dirt road *o* track; **¡cuerpo a ~!** hit the ground! (colloq); ***echar algo por ~*** ‹*edificio/monumento*› to pull *o* knock down; ‹*planes*› to wreck, ruin; ‹*argumentos*› to demolish, destroy; ‹*esperanzas*› to dash; ***echarle ~ a algo/algn*** (Col fam) to put sth/sb to shame, make sth/sb look bad; ***echarse ~ encima*** to do oneself down; ***echar ~ a*** *or* ***sobre algo*** (ocultarlo) to cover *o* hush sth up; (olvidarlo) to forget about sth; ***tragarse la ~ a algn***: **como si se lo hubiera tragado la ~** as if he'd vanished off the face of the earth; **deseé que me tragara la ~** I just wanted the earth to open and swallow me up

C (AmL) (polvo) dust

(Compuesto) **tierra batida** (Esp) clay

D (Elec) ground (AmE), earth (BrE); **estar conectado a ~** *or* (AmL) **hacer ~** to be grounded *o* earthed

E (por oposición al mar, al aire) land; **¡~ a la vista!** land ho *o* ahoy!; **viajar por ~** to travel overland *o* by land; **gentes de ~ adentro** people from inland; **el ejército de ~** the army; **~ firme** solid ground; ***quedarse en ~*** to be left behind; ***tocar ~*** to land, put into port; ***tomar ~*** to land, touch down

F **1** (país, lugar): **decidió volver a su ~** he decided to return to his homeland *o* to his native land; **costumbres de aquellas ~s** customs in those places *o* countries **2** (territorio) soil

(Compuestos)
- **tierra de nadie** no-man's-land
- **tierra natal** native land, land of one's birth
- **Tierra Prometida/Santa** Promised/Holy Land

G (planeta) **la Tierra** (the) Earth *o* earth

tierral *m* (Andes, Méx) dustbowl

tierrero *m* (Col, Ven fam) **1** (polvareda) dustbowl **2** (montón de tierra) pile of dirt *o* earth **3** (fam) (discusión, lío) fuss (colloq); **va a armar un ~** he's going to kick up a real fuss (colloq)

tieso[1] -sa *adj*

A **1** (rígido) stiff; **con las orejas tiesas** with ears pricked up **2** (Col, Ven) (duro) ‹*pan*› hard; ‹*carne*› tough

B ‹*persona*› **1** (erguido) upright, erect; (orgulloso) stiff **2** (fam) (muerto) stone dead (colloq); ***dejar a algn ~*** (fam) (matarlo) to bump sb off (sl); (pasmarlo) to leave sb speechless; ***quedarse ~*** (fam) (morirse) to kick the bucket (colloq); (helarse) to freeze to death (colloq)

tieso[2] *adv* (Andes fam) (lleno) full up (colloq)

tiesto *m* **1** (para plantas) flowerpot **2** (Chi) (palangana) basin; ***fuera de ~*** (Chi fam) out of place

tiesura *f* (rigidez) stiffness; (dureza) hardness

tifón *m* typhoon

tifus *m* **1** (transmitido por parásitos) typhus (fever) **2** (fiebre tifoidea) typhoid

tigre -gresa *m,f*

A **1** (animal asiático) (*m*) tiger; (*f*) tigress **2** (AmL) (jaguar) jaguar

B **tigre** *m* (Ven fam) (trabajo ocasional) casual job

tigresa *f* (fam) vamp (colloq)

tijeras *fpl*, **tijera** *f* (para cortar papel, tela, etc) scissors (*pl*); (para uñas) nail scissors (*pl*); (para césped) shears (*pl*); **unas ~s** a pair of scissors; ***estar cortados por la misma ~*** (AmL) to be cut from the same cloth; **de ~** ‹*silla/cama*› folding (*before n*); **escalera de ~** stepladder

(Compuesto) **tijeras de podar** *fpl* pruning shears (*pl*)

tijereta *f*

A (Zool) earwig

B (en gimnasia) scissors (*pl*); (en fútbol) scissors kick, overhead kick

tijeretada *f*, **tijeretazo** *m* snip, cut

tijeretear [A1] *vt* to hack

tila *f* (infusión) lime (blossom) tea; (flor) lime blossom

t

tildar [A1] *vt* ~ **algo a algn DE algo** to brand sth/sb (AS) sth; **me ~on de reaccionario** I was branded *o* called a reactionary; **lo ~on de tacaño** they said he was mean

tilde *f* (acento) accent; (sobre la ñ) tilde, swung dash

tiliches *mpl* (Méx fam) stuff (colloq)

tilín *m* ting-a-ling, tinkle; ***en un*** ~ (Col) in a flash; ***hacerle ~ a algn*** (fam): **me hizo** ~ I took a liking to him

tilo *m* 1 (árbol) lime (tree) 2 (Chi) ▸**tila**

timador -dora *m,f* swindler, cheat

timar [A1] *vt* to swindle, cheat

timba *f* (fam) 1 (partida) game; **están de** ~ they're gambling 2 (garito) gambling den

timbal *m*

A (Mús) kettledrum; **los ~es** the timpani, the timps (colloq)

B (Coc) timbale

timbero -ra *adj* (RPl fam): **es muy** ~ he loves to gamble

timbrado -da *adj* ‹*voz*› well-pitched

timbrar [A1] *vt* ‹*documento*› to stamp; ‹*carta*› to frank; ***dejar timbrado a algn*** (Col, Ven fam) to bowl sb over (colloq)

■ **timbrar** *vi* (Col, Méx) to ring the bell

■ **timbrarse** *v pron* (Col, Ven fam) (ponerse nervioso) to get jumpy *o* edgy (colloq)

timbrazo *m* ring; **dar un** ~ to ring the bell

timbre *m*

A (para llamar) (door)bell; **tocar el** ~ to ring the bell; ~ **de alarma** alarm bell

B (de sonido, voz) tone, timbre; ~ **agudo** high pitch

C 1 (sello) fiscal stamp 2 (renta del estado) stamp duty *o* tax 3 (Chi) (utensilio) rubber stamp 4 (Méx) (sello postal) (postage) stamp

tímidamente *adv* (de manera retraída) shyly; (titubeando, sin atreverse) timidly

timidez *f* (retraimiento) shyness; (falta de decisión, coraje) timidity

tímido -da *adj* (retraído) shy; (falto de decisión, coraje) timid

timo *m* (fam) con (colloq), scam (colloq); **¡vaya ~ de coche!** this car has been a real rip-off! (colloq)

(Compuesto) **timo de la estampita** *con trick involving forged banknotes*; ***ser el ~ de la ~*** to be an absolute rip-off (colloq)

timón *m* 1 (Aviac, Náut) rudder; **tomó el ~ de la empresa** she took over the helm of the company 2 (Col, Per) (volante) steering wheel; **ir al** ~ to be at the wheel

timonear [A1] *vt* 1 ‹*barco*› to helm 2 (dirigir) to guide, steer 3 (Col, Per) (Auto) to steer

timonel (*m*) helmsman; (*f*) helmswoman

timonera *f* wheelhouse

timorato¹ -ta *adj*

A (temeroso) spineless, gutless

B (mojigato) prudish

timorato² -ta *m,f*

A (temeroso) coward

B (mojigato) prude

tímpano *m* (Anat) eardrum

tina *f* (bañera) bathtub, tub; (palangana) washtub; (Tec) vat

tinaco *m* (Méx) water tank

tinaja *f* large earthenware jar

tinca *f* (Andes) (fam) (empeño) effort; **ponle un poco más de** ~ put a bit more effort *o* (colloq) put your back into it

tincada *f* (Andes fam) feeling, hunch (colloq)

tincado -da *adj* (Andes fam): **es muy** ~ he likes to act on hunches (colloq)

tincar [A2] *vi* (Andes fam) (+ *me/te/le etc*) 1 (parecer): **me tinca que ya no viene** I get the feeling she's not coming 2 (parecer bien, gustar): **ese pescado me tinca** I like the look of that fish; **¿te tinca ir al cine?** do you feel like going *o* how about going to the movies?

tinglado *m*

A (tablado) platform; (cobertizo) shed; (puesto) stall

B (Esp fam) 1 (montaje) set-up (colloq); **conocer el** ~ to know the set-up; **todo el** ~ the whole caboodle (colloq) 2 (embrollo, lío) mess 3 (asunto turbio) racket (colloq); **el ~ de la droga** the drugs racket

tinieblas *fpl* 1 (oscuridad) darkness 2 (ignorancia): **estar en ~ (sobre algo)** to be in the dark (about sth)

tino *m* 1 (sentido común) sound judgment, good sense; **has tenido mucho ~ al no aceptar** you showed good sense *o* judgment in not accepting; **gastar sin** ~ to spend money foolishly 2 (tacto) tact, sensitivity; **que poco ~ tiene** she is so tactless

tinta *f* 1 (Art, Impr) ink; **escribir con** ~ to write in ink; ***medias ~s*** half-measures; **él no se anda con medias ~s** (al hablar) he doesn't beat about the bush; (al actuar) he never does things by halves; **políticos de medias ~s** wishy-washy politicians; ***saber algo de buena ~*** to have sth on good authority; ***sudar ~*** to sweat blood 2 (del calamar, pulpo) ink

(Compuesto) **tinta China** India ink (AmE), Indian ink (BrE)

tintar *vt* (fam) ‹*pelo, ropa*› to dye

tinte *m*

A (acción) dyeing; (sustancia) dye; (color) color*

B (Esp) (establecimiento) dry cleaner's

C (matiz, rasgo) overtone

tinterillo *m* (Andes) (abogado) pettifogger; (sin título) unqualified lawyer

tintero *m* inkwell; ***quedarse en el ~*** ‹‹*asunto*›› to fail to get a mention; **se me quedó en el** ~ I forgot to mention it

tintín *m* (de campanilla) tinkling, jingling; (de copa) clinking

tintinear [A1] *vi* ‹‹*campanilla*›› to tinkle, jingle; ‹‹*copa*›› to clink

tinto¹ -ta *adj* ‹*vino/uva*› red; ~ **en sangre** (liter) bloodied (liter)

tinto² *m*

A (Vin) red wine

B (Col) (café) black coffee

tintorería *f* dry cleaner's

tintorero -ra *m,f* dry cleaner

tintorro *m* (fam) cheap red wine

tintura *f* dye, tincture (frml)

tiña *f*

A (Med) ringworm; ***más viejo que la ~*** as old as the hills

B (fam) (mugre) grime, filth

tiñoso -sa *adj*

A (Med) scabby, mangy

B (fam) (mugriento) filthy

tío, tía *m,f*

A 1 (pariente) (*m*) uncle; (*f*) aunt; **mis ~s** (sólo varones) my uncles; (varones y mujeres) my aunts and uncles 2 (fam) (delante de nombre propio, como apelativo cariñoso) (*m*) Uncle; (*f*) Aunt, Auntie (colloq)

(Compuestos)

- **tía abuela** *f* great-aunt, grandaunt
- **tío abuelo** *m* great-uncle, granduncle
- **tío Sam** *m*: **el ~ ~** Uncle Sam

B (Esp) (individuo) (fam) ▸**tipo¹**

tiovivo *m* (Esp) merry-go-round, carousel (AmE)

tipazo *m* (fam): **mi jefe es un** ~ my boss is a real hunk (colloq)

tipear [A1] *vt* (AmS) to type

tipejo -ja *m,f* (fam) (persona — tonta) idiot; (— despreciable) nasty piece of work (colloq)

típico -ca *adj* typical; ‹*plato/traje*› typical, traditional; **volvió a llegar tarde — ~ de él** he was late again — typical!; **los turistas buscan lo** ~ tourists are always looking for local color*

tipificación *f* 1 (clasificación) classification, categorization 2 (de productos, calidades) standardization

tipificar [A2] *vt* 1 (clasificar) to categorize 2 (ser representativo de) to typify, epitomize 3 ‹*producto/calidad*› to standardize

tipismo *m* 1 (cualidad): **un lugar que atrae por su** ~ a place famous for the local style and architecture of its buildings 2 (costumbre y caracteres típicos) local color*

tiple *mf* (persona) soprano

tipo¹ -pa *m,f* (fam) (*m*) guy (colloq), bloke (BrE colloq); (*f*) woman

tipo² *m*

A (clase) kind, type, sort; **todo ~ de plantas** all kinds of plants; **no es mi** ~ he's not my type

B 1 (figura — de mujer) figure; (— de hombre) physique; ***jugarse el ~*** (Esp fam) to risk one's neck (colloq) 2 (aspecto)

appearance; **una mujer de ~ distinguido** a distinguished-looking woman; ***dar el ~*** (Esp) to be the type
C (Fin) rate
(Compuesto) **tipo de cambio/interés** exchange/interest rate
D (Impr) type
E (*como adj inv*) typical; **una serie ~ 'Dallas'** a 'Dallas'-type series
F (*como adv*) (CS fam) around, about; **vénganse ~ cuatro** come around about four o'clock

tipografía *f* typography

tipógrafo -fa *m,f* typographer

tique, tiquet *m* 1 (de tren, bus) ticket 2 (recibo) receipt, sales slip (AmE)

tiquete *m* (Col) ▸**tique**

tiquismiquis *mf* (Esp, Méx fam) 1 (persona) fusspot (colloq); **es un ~ para comer** he's a very fussy *o* picky eater (colloq); **es un ~ para el orden** he's a stickler for order 2 **tiquismiquis** *m* (reparos) fussing

tira[1] *f* (de papel, tela) strip; (de zapato) strap; ***hacer ~s algo*** (fam) ‹*libro*› to tear sth to shreds; ‹*vaso*› to smash sth to smithereens (colloq); ***la ~*** (Esp fam): **me divertí la ~** I had a whale of a time (colloq); **¿gastaste mucho? — sí, la ~** did you spend a lot? — yes, I spent a fortune (colloq); **hace la ~ de tiempo que ...** it's ages since ... (colloq)
(Compuesto) **tira cómica** comic strip, strip cartoon

tira[2] *mf*
A 1 (Chi, Méx fam) (agente) cop (colloq) 2 (Per, RPl arg) (detective infiltrado) police plant (colloq), undercover cop (colloq) 3 **la tira** *f* (Méx fam) (cuerpo) the cops (colloq)
B *ver* **tira y afloja**

tirabuzón *m*
A (sacacorchos) corkscrew; ***sacarle algo a algn con ~*** to drag sth out of sb (colloq)
B (rizo, bucle) ringlet
C (en béisbol) screwball

tirada *f*
A (Jueg) (en juegos de mesa) throw; **tiró todos los bolos a la primera ~** she knocked all the pins down with her first ball; ***de una ~*** (fam) in one go
B (Impr) print run; **un periódico con una ~ de 300.000 ejemplares diarios** a newspaper with a daily circulation of 300,000 copies
C (fam) (distancia) distance: **de aquí a Medina hay una buena ~** it's a fair stretch from here to Medina (colloq)
D (Méx fam) (propósito) aim, plan

tiradero *m* (Méx) (basurero) garbage (AmE) *o* (BrE) rubbish dump; (casa, habitación) mess, pigsty

tirado -da *adj*
A (en desorden): **lo dejan todo ~** they leave everything lying around; **había ropa tirada en el suelo** there were clothes all over the floor; ***dejar a algn ~*** to leave sb behind
B (fam) [ESTAR] 1 (muy fácil) dead easy (colloq) 2 (muy barato) dirt cheap (colloq)

tirador[1] *m* 1 (de cajón, puerta) knob, handle 2 (tirachinas) slingshot (AmE), catapult (BrE) 3 **tiradores** *mpl* (Arg, Bol) (de pantalón) suspenders (*pl*) (AmE), braces (*pl*) (BrE)

tirador[2] **-dora** (*m*) marksman; (*f*) markswoman; **es un buen ~** he's a good shot

tiraje *m* 1 (AmL) (Impr) ▸**tirada B** 2 (CS) (de la chimenea) damper

tiralíneas *m* (*pl* ~) drawing pen

tiranía *f* tyranny

tiránico -ca *adj* tyrannical

tirano[1] **-na** *adj* tyrannical

tirano[2] **-na** *m,f* tyrant

tirantas *fpl* (Col) suspenders (*pl*) (AmE), braces (*pl*) (BrE)

tirante[1] *adj* 1 ‹*piel/costura/cuerda*› taut 2 ‹*situación*› tense; ‹*relaciones*› tense, strained

tirante[2] *m*
A (Const) strut, brace
B (Indum) 1 (de prenda) strap, shoulder strap; **falda de ~s** jumper (AmE), pinafore dress (BrE); **pantalones de ~s** overalls (*pl*) (AmE), dungarees (*pl*) (BrE) 2 **tirantes** *mpl* (Esp, Méx, Ven) (de pantalón) suspenders (*pl*) (AmE), braces (*pl*) (BrE)

tirantez *f* 1 (de cuerda, la piel) tautness, tightness 2 (en relaciones) tension, strain

tirar [A1] *vt*
A 1 (arrojar) to throw; **tiró la pelota al aire** he threw the ball up in the air; **no tires los papeles al suelo** don't throw *o* drop the wrappers on the ground; **~le algo A algn** (para que lo agarre) to throw sb sth; (con agresividad) to throw sth AT sb; **tírame las llaves** throw me the keys; **me tiró una piedra** she threw a stone at me; **le tiró los brazos** he stretched his arms out to her; **~le un beso a algn** to blow sb a kiss 2 (desechar, deshacerse de) to throw out *o* away; **estos zapatos ya están para ~(los)** these shoes are about ready to be thrown away *o* out 3 (desperdiciar) to waste; **¡qué manera de ~ el dinero!** what a waste of money!
B 1 (hacer caer) to knock over; **¡cuidado, que vas a ~ la leche!** be careful, you're going to knock the milk over!; **tiró el jarrón al suelo de un codazo** he knocked the vase off the table (*o* shelf *etc*) with his elbow 2 (derribar) to knock down; **van a ~ (abajo) esta pared** they're going to knock this wall down; **~on la puerta abajo** they broke the door down
C 1 ‹*bomba*› to drop; ‹*cohete*› to fire, launch; ‹*flecha*› to shoot; ‹*tiros*› to fire 2 ‹*foto*› to take
D (AmL) (atrayendo hacia sí) to pull; **tiró la cadena** he pulled the chain; **no le tires el pelo** don't pull her hair; **le tiró la oreja** she tweaked his ear; **le tiraba la manga** he was tugging at her sleeve
E (Impr) to print, run off
F (Mat) ‹*línea*› to draw
G (Chi) ‹*lotería*› to draw the winning number in; ‹*rifa*› to draw

■ **tirar** *vi*
A (atrayendo hacia sí) to pull; **~ DE algo** to pull sth; **~ de la cadena** to pull the chain; **no le tires del pelo** don't pull her hair; **dos caballos tiraban del carro** the cart was drawn by two horses; **le tiró de la oreja** she tweaked his ear
B (atraer): **le sigue tirando México** she misses Mexico; **la sangre tira** blood is thicker than water; **no le tira el deporte** he's not interested in sports
C 1 (disparar) to shoot; **¡no tiren!** don't shoot!; **le tiró a traición** she shot him in the back; **~ a dar** to shoot to wound (*not to kill*); **~ al blanco** to aim at the target; **~ a matar** to shoot to kill 2 (Dep) to shoot; **~ al arco** (AmL) *or* (Esp) **a puerta** to shoot at goal; ***tirando por lo bajo/alto*** at the (very) least/most 3 (Jueg) (descartarse) to throw away; (en juegos de dados) to throw; (en dardos) to throw; (en bolos) to bowl
D 1 «*chimenea/cigarro*» to draw 2 «*coche/motor*» to pull
E 1 (fam) (arreglárselas) to get by; **con $100 podemos ~** with $100 we could get by 2 **tirando** *ger* (fam): **ganamos poco pero vamos tirando** we don't earn much but we're managing; **¿qué tal andas? — tirando ...** how are things? — not too bad
F (Esp fam) (desplazarse): **vamos, tira** get a move on; **si tiras para atrás cabe otro coche** if you back up a bit we can get another car in; **tira (p'alante) no te pares** keep going don't stop now; **tira por esta calle abajo** go *o* turn down this street
G (AmL vulg) (en sentido sexual) to screw (vulg), to fuck (vulg)
H **tirar a** (tender a): **tira más bien a azul** it's more of a bluish color; **un erotismo que tira a pornográfico** an eroticism which verged on the pornographic; **es de estatura normal, tirando a bajito** he's average to short in height; **los niños tiran más a la madre** the children take after their mother more

■ **tirarse** *v pron*
A 1 (lanzarse, arrojarse) (+ *compl*) to throw oneself; **~se en paracaídas** to parachute; (en emergencia) to bale out; **~se al agua** to dive/jump into the water; **~se del trampolín** to dive off the springboard; **~se de cabeza** to dive in, to jump in headfirst; **se le tiró a los brazos** she threw herself into his arms 2 (AmL) (tumbarse) to lie down; ***tirárselas de algo*** (AmL fam): **se las tira de valiente** he makes out he's so brave
B (fam) ‹*horas/días*› to spend; **se tiró dos años escribiéndolo** he spent two years writing it
C (vulg) (en sentido sexual) **~se a algn** to screw sb (vulg), to lay sb (sl)

t

D (fam) (expulsar): **~se un pedo** to fart (sl); **~se un eructo** to burp (colloq)

E (Col fam) (echar a perder) to ruin; **el aguacero se tiró el paseo** the downpour ruined our walk; **se tiró el examen** he flunked the exam (colloq)

tira y afloja *m* hard bargaining

tirita *f* (Esp) Band-Aid® (AmE), sticking plaster (BrE)

tiritar [A1] *vi* to shiver, tremble; **~ de frío** to shiver with cold

tiritón *m* shiver

tiritona *f* (fam): **le dio** *or* **entró una ~** she started shivering; **tener una ~** to have the shivers (colloq)

tiro *m*

A (disparo) shot; **le dispararon un ~ en la pierna** they shot him in the leg; **lo mató de un ~/a ~s** she shot him dead; **disparó tres ~s al aire** he fired three shots into the air; **ejercicios de ~** shooting practice; ***al ~*** (Chi fam) right away, straightaway (BrE); ***andar echando ~s*** (Méx fam): **anda echando ~s con su traje nuevo** he's strutting around in his new suit; ***a ~*** (Mil) within *o* in range; ***a ~ de piedra*** (Esp fam): **la playa estaba a ~ de piedra** the beach was a stone's throw away; ***como un ~*** (Esp fam): **esa hamburguesa me sentó como un ~** that hamburger really disagreed with me; **lo que dijo le sentó como un ~** what he said really upset her; **ese vestido me sienta como un ~** I look awful in that dress; **salir/pasar como un ~** (Col, RPl, Ven) to shoot out/past; ***de a ~*** (Méx fam) absolutely; ***de ~s largos*** (fam): **se puso de ~s largos** she got all dressed up (colloq); ***errar el ~*** (literal) to miss; (equivocarse) to get it wrong; ***estar a ~ de hacer algo*** (Col fam) to be about to do sth; ***me/le salió el ~ por la culata*** (fam) my/his plan backfired on me/him; ***ni a ~s*** (fam): **no va a aprobar ni a ~s** there's no way he's going to pass (colloq); ***saber por dónde van los ~s*** to have an idea of sth; ***ser un ~ al aire*** (AmL fam) to be scatterbrained (colloq)

(Compuesto) **tiro de gracia** coup de grâce

B (en fútbol, baloncesto) shot; (deporte) shooting

(Compuestos)

- **tiro al arco** (deporte) archery; (en fútbol) (AmL) shot at goal
- **tiro al blanco** (deporte) target shooting; (lugar) shooting gallery
- **tiro al plato** skeet shooting (AmE), clay-pigeon shooting (BrE)
- **tiro a puerta** shot at goal
- **tiro de esquina** (AmL) corner (kick)
- **tiro libre** (en fútbol) free kick; (en baloncesto) free shot *o* throw
- **tiro pasado** (en tenis) passing shot

C (de pantalón) top block (frml)

D (de chimenea) flue; **tiene muy buen ~** it draws well

E **animal/caballo de ~** draught animal/horse

tiroides *f* thyroid (gland)

tirón *m* 1 (movimiento) tug, pull; **pégale un ~ fuerte a la cuerda** give the string a good hard pull *o* tug; **dale un ~ de orejas** tweak his ears for him (colloq); **me dio un ~ de pelo** he pulled my hair; **el autobús avanzaba a tirones** the bus jerked along; ***de un ~***: **me arrancó la cadena de un ~** he ripped the chain from my neck; **hicimos el viaje de un ~** (fam) we did the journey without stopping; **lo leyó/bebió de un ~** (fam) she read/downed it in one go; **trabajamos 12 horas de un ~** (fam) we worked 12 hours at a stretch 2 (de músculo): **sufrió un ~ en la pierna** he pulled a muscle in his leg; **sentí un ~ en la espalda** I felt something pull in my back 3 (forma de robo): **le dieron un** *or* **el ~** they snatched her bag

tironear [A1] *vi* (AmL fam) to tug, pull

■ **tironear** *vt* (AmL fam) to tug (at)

tironero -ra *m,f*, **tironista** *mf* bag-snatcher

tirotear [A1] *vt* to shoot … repeatedly; **murió tiroteado en la calle** he was gunned down in the street

tiroteo *m* (tiros) shooting (intercambio de tiros) shoot-out, exchange of shots

tirria *f* (fam) grudge; **tenerle ~ a algn** to have a grudge against sb; **tomarle ~ a algn** to take against sb (colloq)

tisana *f* tisane, herbal tea

tísico -ca *m,f* (ant) consumptive (dated)

tisis *f* (ant) tuberculosis, consumption (dated)

tisú *m* (*pl* **-sús** *or* **-súes**) (pañuelo) tissue; (tela) lamé

titán *m* titan; **una obra de titanes** a mammoth task

titánico -ca *adj* huge, colossal (*before n*)

títere *m*

A 1 (marioneta) puppet; ***no dejar ~ con cabeza*** to spare nobody; ***no quedar ~ con cabeza***: **tras el reajuste no quedó ~ con cabeza** nobody escaped the reshuffle unscathed 2 **títeres** *mpl* (función) puppet show

B (persona) puppet

titilar [A1] *vi* 1 «*estrella*» to twinkle; «*luz*» to flicker 2 «*párpado*» to twitch

titipuchal *m* (Méx fam) (gran cantidad): **un ~ de algo** loads of sth (colloq)

titiritar [A1] *vi* to shiver, tremble

titiritero -ra *m,f* (de marionetas) puppeteer; (acróbata) acrobat

titubeante *adj* ‹*voz/respuesta*› faltering, halting; ‹*actitud*› hesitant

titubear [A1] *vi* 1 (dudar, vacilar) to hesitate; **sin ~** without hesitation 2 (balbucear) to stutter

titubeo *m* (duda, vacilación) hesitancy, hesitation; **el ~ de su voz** the hesitancy in his voice

titulación *f* qualifications (*pl*); **personas con ~ universitaria** university graduates, college graduates (AmE)

titulado[1] -da *adj* qualified

titulado[2] -da *m,f* graduate

(Compuestos)

- **titulado medio** *graduate with a qualification obtained after a three-year degree course as opposed to a five-year course*
- **titulado superior** *or* **universitario** university graduate, college graduate (AmE)

titular[1] *adj* ‹*médico/profesor*› permanent; **jugadores ~es** first-team players

titular[2] *mf*

A 1 (de pasaporte, cuenta) holder; (de bien, vivienda) owner, titleholder (frml) 2 (de cargo, plaza) holder, incumbent (frml); **el ~ de la cartera de Defensa** the Defense Secretary; **el ~ de la comisaría de la localidad** the chief of the local police

B **titular** *m* 1 (en periódico) headline 2 (Rad, TV) main story; **los ~es** the main stories, the news headlines

titular[3] [A1] *vt* ‹*obra*›: **su novela titulada 'Julia'** his novel called *o* (frml) entitled 'Julia'; **¿cómo vas a ~ la canción?** what's the title of the song going to be?

■ **titularse** *v pron*

A «*obra/película*» to be called, be entitled (frml)

B (Educ) to graduate, get one's degree; **~se EN/DE algo** to graduate IN/AS sth

titularidad *f* 1 (de bien, vivienda) ownership, title (frml) 2 (de cargo, plaza): **obtener la ~** to become permanent; **intenta recuperar la ~** he's trying to regain his place on the team

título *m*

A (de libro, película) title, name; (de capítulo) heading, title; (de una ley) title; **un poema que lleva por ~ …** a poem called *o* (frml) entitled …

(Compuesto) **título de crédito** credits (*pl*)

B (Educ) degree; (diploma) certificate

(Compuestos)

- **título académico** academic qualification
- **título universitario** university degree, college degree (AmE)

C (que refleja honor, mérito, etc) title; **el ~ de campeón juvenil** the junior title

D *tb* **~ nobiliario** title

E (en locs) **a título**: **esto lo digo a ~ personal** I'm speaking personally here; **les daré algunas cifras a ~ orientativo** I'll give you a few figures to put you in the picture *o* to give you an idea; **a título de** (a manera de) by way of; (en calidad de): **asiste a ~ de observador** he's here as an observer; **lo recibió a ~ de préstamo** he received it as a loan; **¿a ~ de qué me dices eso ahora?** (fam) what are you telling me that for now?

F (Der) title, (Econ, Fin) security, bond

(Compuestos)

- **título al portador** bearer bond
- **título de crédito** credit instrument

t

• **título de propiedad** title deed

tiza *f* (material) chalk; (barra) (piece of) chalk; (en billar) chalk

tiznajo *m* (mancha) smudge; (partícula) smut

tiznar [A1] *vt* to blacken (*with soot/coal*)
■ **tiznarse** *v pron* (*refl*) to blacken oneself (*with soot/coal*)

tizne *m* (hollín) soot; (mancha) smut

tizón *m* (leño) charred stick/log; ***más negro que un ~*** as black as coal

tlapalería *f* (Méx) hardware store

TLC *m* (= **Tratado de Libre Comercio**) FTT

TLCAN *m* (= **Tratado de Libre Comercio de América del Norte**) NAFTA

Tm., tm. (= **tonelada métrica**) tonne

Tn. (= **tonelada**) t, ton

TNT *m* (= **trinitrotolueno**) TNT

toalla *f* [1]▸ (tejido) toweling* [2]▸ (para secarse) towel; ***tirar*** *or* ***arrojar la ~*** to throw in the towel
(Compuesto) **toalla higiénica** sanitary napkin (AmE), sanitary towel (BrE)

toallero *m* (barra) towel rail; (aro) towel ring

tobillera *f* [1]▸ (Med) ankle support [2]▸ (de ciclista) cycle clip

tobillo *m* ankle; ***no llegarle a algn ni al ~*** *or* ***a los ~s***: **no le llega ni al ~ a Ricardo** he is nowhere near as good as Ricardo, he can't hold a candle to Ricardo

tobogán *m* [1]▸ (en parque) slide; (en piscina) water chute [2]▸ (Aviac) escape chute [3]▸ (trineo) toboggan

toca *f* (de religiosa) wimple; (de tocado) circlet

tocadiscos *m* (*pl* ~) record player

tocado[1] -da *adj*
[A] [1]▸ (fam) (loco) touched (colloq); **está ~ (de la cabeza)** he's not all there (colloq) [2]▸ (fam) ‹*boxeador*› punch drunk
[B] (frml) (con la cabeza cubierta): **iba tocada con mantilla española** she was wearing a Spanish mantilla
[C] ‹*fruta*› bruised

tocado[2] *m* (en la cabeza) headdress

tocador *m* (mueble) dressing table; (habitación) (ant) boudoir (dated)

tocante *adj*: **en lo ~ a** (frml) with regard to, regarding

tocar [A2] *vt*
(Sentido I)
[A] [1]▸ «*persona*» to touch; (palpar) to feel; (manosear) to handle; **¡no vayas a ~ ese cable!** don't touch that cable!; **si le toca un pelo al niño ...** if he lays a hand *o* finger on that child ...; **no ha tocado los libros** he hasn't opened the books; **no puede ~ el alcohol** he mustn't touch a drop of alcohol; **mis ahorros no los quiero ~** I don't want to touch my savings; **a los hijos no se los toques** don't say a word against her children [2]▸ (entrar en contacto con) to touch; **la planta ya toca el techo** the plant is already touching the ceiling; **la pelota tocó la red** the ball clipped the net; **el avión tocó tierra** the plane touched down
[B] (Aviac) to make a stopover in; (Náut) to put in; **no toca puerto en Lisboa** it doesn't call at Lisbon
[C] (en béisbol) to bunt
[D] ‹*tema*› (tratar) to touch on, refer to; (sacar) to bring up
[E] [1]▸ (conmover, impresionar) to touch; **tu comentario tocó su amor propio** your comment hurt his pride [2]▸ (atañer, concernir) to affect; **un problema que nos toca de cerca** a problem which affects us directly; **que ese tema no me toca en lo más mínimo** that subject doesn't concern me at all [3]▸ (Esp fam) (estar emparentado con): **¿Victoria te toca algo?** is Victoria related to you?
(Sentido II) [1]▸ (hacer sonar) ‹*timbre/campana*› to ring; ‹*claxon*› to blow, sound [2]▸ (Mús) ‹*instrumento/pieza*› to play
■ **tocar** *vi*
(Sentido I)
[A] (concernir): **por** *or* **en lo que toca a la ecología** (frml) as far as ecology is concerned
[B] (rayar) **~ EN algo** to border *o* verge ON sth
(Sentido II) [1]▸ (AmL) (llamar) «*persona*» to knock at the door; **alguien está tocando (a la puerta)** there's somebody at the door [2]▸ «*campana/timbre*» to ring; **las campanas tocaban a misa** the bells were ringing for mass; **~ a rebato/a retirada** (Mil) to sound the alarm/the retreat [3]▸ (Mús) (hacer música) to play
(Sentido III)
[A] [1]▸ (corresponder en reparto, concurso, sorteo) (+ *me/te/le etc*): **a ella le toca la mitad de la herencia** she gets half of the inheritance; **le tocó el primer premio** she won the first prize; **nos tocó (en suerte)** it fell to our lot; **me tocó la maestra más antipática del colegio** I got the most horrible teacher in the school; **nos tocó hacer la práctica en el mismo colegio** we happened to do our teaching practice at the same school; **me tocó a mí comunicárselo** I was the one who had to tell him [2]▸ (ser el turno) (+ *me/te/le etc*): **te toca a ti** it's your turn; **¿a quién le toca cocinar?** whose turn is it to do the cooking?
[B] (*en 3ª pers*) (fam): **vamos, toca ponerse a estudiar** come on, it's time we/you got down to some studying; **mañana toca historia** we've got history tomorrow
■ **tocarse** *v pron* [1]▸ (*refl*) ‹*herida/grano*› to touch; **siempre se toca la barba/la nariz** he always plays with his beard/touches his nose [2]▸ (*recípr*) «*personas*» to touch each other; «*cables*» to touch

tocateja (Esp fam): **pagar a ~** to pay (in) cash

tocayo -ya *m,f* namesake; **es ~ mío** he's my namesake; **somos ~s** we have *o* share the same name

tocho *m* (fam) weighty tome (hum)

tocino *m* (para guisar) pork fat; (con vetas de carne) fatty salt pork; (para freír) bacon

tocología *f* obstetrics

tocólogo -ga *m,f* obstetrician

tocón *m* stump

toc toc *m* knock knock

tocuyo *m* (AmS) calico

todavía *adv*
[A] [1]▸ (aún) still; **¿~ estás aquí?** are you still here?; **~ la quiero** I still love her [2]▸ (en frases negativas) yet; **¿~ no has terminado?** haven't you finished yet?; **~ no** — not yet; **~ no está lista** she isn't ready yet
[B] (en comparaciones) even, still; **sus primos son ~ más ricos** her cousins are even richer *o* still richer
[C] (fam) (encima, aun así) still; **¡le pagan hasta el alquiler y ~ se queja!** they even pay his rent and he still complains!

todero -ra *m,f* (Col, Ven fam) Jack-of-all-trades (colloq)

todo[1] -da *adj*
[A] (la totalidad de) all; **nos comimos ~ el pan/~s los bombones** we ate all the bread/chocolates; **toda la mañana** all morning, the whole morning; **invitó a toda la clase** she invited the whole class; **se recorrió ~ México** she traveled all over Mexico; **por ~s lados** all over the place; **dedicó toda su vida a la investigación** he dedicated his entire life to research; **~s ustedes lo sabían** you all knew
[B] (cualquier, cada): **~ artículo importado** all imported items, any imported item; **~ aquél que quiera** anyone who wishes to; **~s los días/los años** every day/year; **~s los que estaban presentes** all those who were present
[C] (uso enfático): **a toda velocidad** at top speed; **a ~ correr** as fast as possible; **con toda inocencia** in all innocence; **le dieron ~ tipo de facilidades** they gave him all kind of facilities; **está fuera de toda duda** it's beyond all doubt; ***a ~ esto*** (mientras tanto) meanwhile, in the meantime; (a propósito) incidentally, by the way

todo[2] *m*: **el/un ~** the/a whole; ***jugarse el ~ por el ~*** to risk *o* gamble everything on one throw

todo[3] -da *pron*
[A] [1]▸ (sin excluir nada) everything; **lo perdieron ~** they lost everything; **a pesar de ~** despite everything; **~ le parece poco** he's never satisfied; **hazlo ~ lo largo que quieras** make it as long as you like; **¿eso es ~?** is that all?; **~ o nada** all or nothing [2]▸ **~s/todas** (referido a — cosas) all; (— a personas) all, everybody; **se rompieron ~s** they all broke; **los compró ~s** she bought all of them; **vinieron ~s** they all came, everybody came; **son todos muy simpáticos** they're all very friendly; **buena suerte a ~s** good luck to everybody; **es el más alto de ~s** he's the tallest of the lot *o* of them all; **¿están ~s?** is everyone *o* everybody here?; **¿estamos ~s?** are we all here?; **~s y cada uno** each and every one
[B] (*en locs*) **con todo (y eso)** (fam) (aun así) all the same, even so; **con ~, sigo pensando que ...** all the same *o* even so I

t

still think that ...; **de todo**: **come de ~** she'll eat anything; **venden de ~** they sell everything *o* all sorts of things; **hace de ~ un poco** he does a bit of everything; **del todo** totally; **no es del ~ cierto** it's not entirely *o* totally true; **y todo**: **enfermo y ~, vino a trabajar** sick as he was, he still came to work; **tuvo que venir la policía y ~** (fam) the police had to come and everything (colloq); ***de todas, todas*** (fam): **¿es verdad? — de todas, todas** is it true? — you bet it is! (colloq); **ganó de todas, todas** he won by a mile (colloq); ***me las pagará todas juntas*** one of these days I'll get even with him for all of this; ***no tener las todas consigo*** to be a little worried *o* uneasy

C (*como adv*) **1** (completamente) all; **está ~ mojado** it's all wet; **está toda entusiasmada con el viaje** she's all *o* terribly excited about the trip **2** (en frases ponderativas) quite; **fue ~ un espectáculo** it was quite a show! **3** (indicando cualidad predominante): **el pescado era ~ espinas** the fish was full of bones; **soy toda oídos** I'm all ears

todopoderoso -sa *adj* all-powerful; **Dios T~** Almighty God

Todopoderoso *m*: **el ~** the Almighty

todoterreno *m* (Auto) four-wheel-drive vehicle, 4 x 4; (*léase: four by four*)

toga *f* (Hist) toga; (de magistrados) gown

toilette[1] /twa'le(t)/ *m* washroom (AmE), bathroom (esp AmE), toilet (esp BrE)

toilette[2] /twa'le(t)/ *f* (fam): **hacerse la ~** to perform *o* do one's ablutions (hum)

Tokio *m* Tokyo

tokiota *adj* of/from Tokyo

tolda *f* (Col) (tienda) tent; (mosquitero) mosquito net

tolderío *m*, **toldería** *f* Indian camp/village

toldo *m* **1** (de terraza) canopy; (de tienda) awning; (en la playa) awning; (en camión) tarpaulin **2** (para fiestas) tent (AmE), marquee (BrE) **3** (de los indios) hut

tolerable *adj* tolerable

tolerancia *f* **1** (respeto) tolerance; (aguante, paciencia) tolerance; **~ religiosa/política** religious/political tolerance **2** (Med, Tec) tolerance

tolerante *adj* tolerant

tolerar [A1] *vt* **1** ‹*comportamiento/persona*› to tolerate; **no pienso ~ su insolencia** I don't intend to put up with *o* to tolerate his rudeness; **¡eso no se puede ~!** that's intolerable!; **no tolera el calor** she can't stand *o* take the heat **Ⓢ tolerada (para menores de 14 años)** (Esp) ≈ PG **2** ‹*medicamento*› to tolerate

toletole *m* rumpus, commotion; **se armó un ~** (AmS fam) there was a terrible rumpus *o* ruckus *o* commotion

tolva *f* **1** (recipiente) hopper **2** (Ferr) hopper wagon

tolvanera *f* dust storm

toma *f*

A **1** (Mil) capture, taking; **la ~ de la Bastilla** the storming of the Bastille **2** (de universidad, fábrica) occupation; (de tierras) seizure

B (Cin, Fot) shot; **el director quiere repetir esa ~** the director wants to do that take again

C (de medicamento) dose

D (de datos) gathering; (de muestras) taking; **la ~ de decisiones** the decision-making

E (en yudo) hold

F (AmL) (acequia) irrigation channel

Compuestos

- **toma de agua** (de máquina) intake, inlet; (grifo) faucet (AmE), tap (BrE); (para incendios) hydrant
- **toma de aire** air intake *o* inlet
- **toma de conciencia**: **esta ~ de ~ del problema** this new awareness of the problem; **crear una ~ de ~ entre la población** to make the public aware
- **toma de contacto** (contacto) contact; (contacto inicial) first *o* initial contact
- **toma de corriente** (wall) socket, power point (BrE)
- **toma de posesión** (de presidente) inauguration; (de ministros) swearing-in ceremony; **el día de mi ~ de ~** the day I took up my post
- **toma de tierra** **1** (Elec) ground (wire) (AmE), earth (wire) (BrE) **2** (Aviac) landing, touchdown

tomado -da *adj*

A ‹*voz*›: **tengo la voz tomada** I'm hoarse

B (AmL fam) ‹*persona*› drunk

tomador -dora *m,f*

A **1** (Fin) payee **2** (de seguro): **el ~** the insured

B (AmL) (bebedor) drunkard, drinker

tomadura de pelo *f* **1** (broma, chiste) joke **2** (burla): **esto es una ~ de ~** they're just messing around with us (AmE) *o* (BrE) messing us around

tomar [A1] *vt*

Sentido I

A (asir, agarrar) to take; **toma lo que te debo** here's what I owe you; **¿lo puedo ~ prestado?** can I borrow it?; **la tomé de la mano** I took her by the hand; **~ las armas** to take up arms; **~ algo DE algo** to take sth FROM sth

B **1** (Mil) ‹*pueblo/ciudad*› to take, capture; ‹*tierras*› to seize **2** ‹*universidad/fábrica*› to occupy

C (hacerse cargo de): **tomó el asunto en sus manos** she took charge of the matter; **tomó la responsabilidad del negocio** he took over the running of the business; **tomó a su cuidado a las niñas** she took the girls into her care

D **1** (beber) to drink; **tomó un sorbito** she took a sip; **el niño toma (el) pecho** the baby's being breast-fed **2** (servirse, consumir) to have; **ven a ~ una copa** come and have a drink; **¿vamos a ~ algo?** shall we go for a drink? **3** ‹*medicamento/vitaminas*› to take

E ‹*tren/taxi/ascensor*› to take; ‹*calle/atajo*› to take

F **1** (medir, registrar) to take; **~le la temperatura/la tensión a algn** to take sb's temperature/blood pressure **2** ‹*notas/apuntes*› to take; **~ algo por escrito** to write sth down; **~le declaraciones a algn** to take a statement from sb; **la maestra me tomó la lección** the teacher made me recite the lesson **3** ‹*foto*› to take

G (adoptar) ‹*medidas/actitud*› to take, adopt; ‹*precauciones*› to take; ‹*decisión*› to make, take; **tomó la determinación de no volver a verlo** she decided not to see him again

H **1** **~ a algn por esposo/esposa** (frml) to take sb as *o* to be one's husband/wife **2** (esp AmL) (contratar) to take on; **lo ~on a prueba** they took him on for a trial period **3** «*profesor*» ‹*alumnos/clases*› to take on **4** «*colegio*» ‹*niño*› to take

I (confundir) **~ algo/a algn POR algo/algn** to take sth/sb FOR sth/sb; **¿por quién me has tomado?** who *o* what do you take me for?; **te van a ~ por tonto** they'll take you for a fool, they'll think you're stupid; **me tomó por mi hermana** he mistook me for my sister

J (reaccionar frente a) ‹*noticia/comentario*› to take; **tómalo como de quien viene** take it with a grain (AmE) *o* (BrE) pinch of salt; **lo tomó a mal/a broma** he took it the wrong way/as a joke

K ‹*tiempo*› to take; **eso toma demasiado tiempo** that takes up too much time

L (en costura) to take in

Sentido II

A (adquirir) **1** ‹*forma*› to take; ‹*aspecto*› to take on; **el pollo está empezando a ~ color** the chicken's beginning to brown; **dado el cariz que están tomando las cosas ...** the way things are going ... **2** ‹*velocidad/altura*› to gain; **3** ‹*costumbre*› to get into

B (cobrar) ‹*cariño/asco*› **~le algo A algo/algn**: **le he tomado cariño a esta casa/a la niña** I've become quite attached to this house/quite fond of the girl; **les ha tomado asco a los mejillones** he's gone right off mussels (colloq); **justo ahora que le estoy tomando el gusto** just when I was getting to like it; ***~la con algn/algo*** (fam) to take against sb/sth

Sentido III

A **1** (exponerse a): **~ el aire** *or* **el fresco** to get some (fresh) air; **~ (el) sol** to sunbathe; **vas a ~ frío** (RPl) you'll get *o* catch cold **2** ‹*baño/ducha*› to take, have

B (recibir) ‹*clases*› to take; ‹*curso*› to take, do (BrE)

■ **tomar** *vi*

A (asir): **toma, léelo tú misma** here, read it yourself; **toma, aquí tienes tus tijeras** here are your scissors; **tome, yo no lo necesito** take it, I don't need it

B (esp AmL) (beber alcohol) to drink

C (AmL) (ir) to go; **~on para el norte/por allí** they went north/that way; **~ a la derecha** to turn *o* go right

D «*injerto*» to take

■ **tomarse** *v pron*

A ‹*vacaciones/tiempo*› to take; **se tomó el día libre** he took the day off; **tómate todo el tiempo que quieras** take as long as you like

B ‹*molestia/libertad*› to take; **~se la molestia/libertad de + INF** to take the trouble to + INF/the liberty of + GER; **ya me ~é la revancha** I'll get even one of these days

C (*enf*) **1** ‹*café/vino*› to drink; **se toma todo lo que gana** (AmL) he spends everything he earns on drink **2** ‹*medicamento/vitaminas*› to take **3** ‹*desayuno/merienda/sopa*› to eat, have; ‹*helado/yogur*› to have

D ‹*autobús/tren/taxi*› to take

E (Med) **1** (*refl*) to take; **se tomó la temperatura** she took her temperature **2** (*caus*): **~se la presión** *or* **la tensión** to have one's blood pressure taken

F (*caus*) (esp AmL) ‹*foto*› to have ... taken

G (*enf*) (reaccionar frente a) ‹*comentario/noticia*› to take; **no te lo tomes a mal** don't take it the wrong way

H (Chi) ‹*universidad/fábrica*› to occupy

tomatal *m* field of tomatoes

tomate *m*

A (Bot, Coc) tomato; ***estar/ponerse (colorado) como un ~*** (de vergüenza) to be/turn as red as a beet (AmE), to be/go as red as a beetroot (BrE); (por el sol) to be/turn as red as a lobster

Compuesto **tomate (de) pera** plum tomato

B (Esp fam) (agujero) hole

tomatera *f*

A (Bot) tomato plant

B (Chi fam) (juerga) bender (colloq)

tomavistas *m* (*pl* ~) movie camera

toma y daca *m* (intercambio de favores, servicios) give-and-take; (en combate, prueba) cut-and-thrust

tombo *m* (Col, Ven fam) (policía) cop (colloq)

tómbola *f* tombola

tomillo *m* thyme

tomo *m* volume; ***de ~ y lomo*** (fam) out-and-out (*before n*)

ton *m*: **hacer algo sin ~ ni son** to do sth for no reason; **una decisión tomada sin ~ ni son** a decision taken without rhyme or reason

tonada *f* **1** (melodía) tune; (canción) ballad, song **2** (AmL) (acento) accent

tonadilla *f* popular song

tonal *adj* tonal

tonalidad *f* (Art, Mús) tonality

tonel *m* barrel; ***estar como/ser un ~*** to be like a barrel

tonelada *f* ton

tonelaje *m* tonnage

tonelero -ra *m,f* cooper, barrel-maker

tongo *m*

A (fam) (en partido, pelea) fix (colloq); **hubo ~** it was fixed (colloq)

B (Andes) (sombrero) bowler hat

toni *m* (Chi) circus clown

tónica *f*

A (bebida) tonic (water)

B (tendencia, tono) trend, tendency; **ésa es la ~ general** that is the general trend; **la ~ de su discurso** the tone of his speech

tonicidad *f* tonicity

tónico¹ -ca *adj*

A (Med) tonic (*before n*)

B **1** ‹*sílaba/vocal*› tonic (*before n*), stressed **2** (Mús) tonic

tónico² *m* (Med) tonic; (en cosmética) toner

tonificante *adj* invigorating, tonic (*before n*)

tonificar [A2] *vt* to tone up

tonillo *m* tone of voice (*often sarcastic*); **lo dijo con cierto ~** there was something about the way he said it

tono *m*

A (altura de la voz) pitch, tone; (manera de expresarse) tone; **~ grave** serious tone; **en ~ cariñoso** in an affectionate tone of voice; **se lo he dicho en todos los ~s** I've tried telling him every way I can think of; **en ~ de reproche** reproachfully; **el ~ en que lo dijo** the way he said it

B (tendencia, matiz) tone; **a ~ con la ocasión** in keeping with the occasion; **para estar a ~ con los tiempos** to keep up with the times; ***fuera de ~*** ‹*reacción*› uncalled-for; ‹*comentario*› inopportune; ***no venir a ~*** to be out of place; ***ponerse a ~*** (fam) to get in the mood (colloq); ***ser de buen/mal ~*** to be in good/bad taste

C (de color) shade; ***subido de ~*** risqué

D (Mús) key

E (Audio, Rad, TV) tone; ***bajar el ~*** (reducir el volumen) to turn the volume down; (hablar con menos arrogancia): **baja el tonito conmigo** don't take that tone with me; ***subir el ~*** (elevar el volumen) to turn up the volume; (insolentarse) to raise one's voice

F (del teléfono) tone; **este teléfono no tiene ~** I can't get a dial tone (AmE) *o* (BrE) dialling tone on this phone

Compuestos

- **tono de marcar** *or* (AmL) **de discado** *or* (AmS) **de discar** dial tone (AmE), dialling tone (BrE)
- **tono de ocupado** busy signal (AmE), engaged tone (BrE)

G (de músculos) tone

tontamente *adv* stupidly, foolishly

tontear [A1] *vi* **1** (hacer el tonto) to play the fool; (decir tonterías) to talk nonsense **2** (flirtear) to fool around (colloq)

tontera *f* ▸ **tontería**

tontería *f* **1** (cosa tonta) silly *o* stupid thing; (dicho tonto) silly remark; **¡déjate de ~s!** stop fooling around; **¡~s!** nonsense! **2** (cosa insignificante) silly thing, small thing; **se enoja por cualquier ~** she gets angry over the slightest little thing; **oye, que cien mil pesos no son ninguna ~** come on, a hundred thousand pesos is no small sum **3** (cualidad) stupidity

tonto¹ -ta *adj*

A **1** [SER] ‹*persona*› (falto de inteligencia) stupid, dumb (colloq); (ingenuo) silly; **¡no seas tonta!** don't be silly!; **fui tan ~ como para decirle que sí** I was stupid *o* foolish enough to say yes **2** [ESTAR] (intratable) difficult, silly; (disgustado) upset; ***a tontas y a locas*** without thinking; **gasta el dinero a tontas y a locas** she spends money like there's no tomorrow (colloq); ***dejar ~ a algn*** (Esp fam) to leave sb speechless; ***hacer ~ a algn*** (Chi fam) to fool sb; ***ser ~ del bote*** to be a complete idiot

B ‹*excusa/error/historia*› silly

tonto² -ta *m,f* (falto de inteligencia) idiot, dummy (colloq); (ingenuo) idiot, fool; ***hacer el ~*** (hacer payasadas) to play *o* act the fool; (actuar con necedad) to make a fool of oneself; ***hacerse el ~*** to act dumb

Compuestos

- **tonto de capirote** prize idiot, utter fool
- **tonto útil** stooge

tontorrón¹ -rrona *adj* (fam) silly

tontorrón² -rrona *m,f* silly twit (colloq)

topacio *m* topaz

topar [A1] *vi*

A ▸ **toparse**

B «*toro/carnero*» to butt

■ **toparse** *v pron* **~se CON algn** (tropezarse) to bump into sb; (encontrarse) to bump *o* run into sb; **~se CON algo** (tropezarse) to bump into sth; (encontrarse) to come across sth

tope *m*

A **1** (límite) limit; **~ máximo** upper limit; ***hasta el ~*** *or* ***los ~s***: **llené la taza hasta el ~** I filled the cup to the brim; **tenía la maleta hasta el ~** her suitcase was full to bursting; **el estadio estaba hasta los ~s** the stadium was jam-packed; **estoy hasta el ~ de trabajo** I'm snowed under with work **2** **a tope** (Esp fam) ‹*trabajar*› flat out (colloq); **vivir a ~** to live life to the full; **el club estaba a ~** the club was packed out (colloq) **3** (*como adj inv*) ‹*edad/precio*› maximum (*before n*); **fecha ~** deadline

B **1** (para las puertas) doorstop; (en trenes, estaciones) buffer **2** (Méx) (Auto) speed bump

C (Andes) (cima) top

D **1** (Andes) (golpe, choque) bump **2** (Méx fam) (cabezazo): **me di un ~** I bumped my head

topetada *f* ▸ **topetazo**

topetazo *m* bump; (más fuerte) bang; **se dio un ~ contra la pared** he bumped/banged into the wall

topetear [A1], **topetar** [A1] *vt* (golpear levemente) to bump; (dar con los cuernos) to butt

■ **topetear** *vi*: **~ contra algo** to bump *o* knock against sth

topetón *m* ▸ **topetazo**

tópico[1] -ca *adj*
A ‹*comentario/afirmación*› trite
B (Farm): **S** **uso tópico** for external use only
tópico[2] *m* **1** (tema, asunto) topic, subject **2** (tema trillado) hackneyed subject; (expresión) cliché
top-less, topless /'toples/ *m*: **se bañaba en ~** she was bathing topless; **el ~ es habitual aquí** it is quite normal for people to go topless here
topo *m* **1** (Zool) mole; ***ser más ciego que un ~*** to be as blind as a bat **2** (agente infiltrado) mole **3** (Col fam) (persona torpe) klutz (AmE colloq), clumsy clod (BrE colloq) **4** (Col) (pendiente) earring
topografía *f* topography, surveying
topógrafo -fa *m,f* topographer, surveyor
toque *m*
A **1** (de timbre) ring; (de campana) stroke, chime; **al ~ de las doce** when the clock strikes twelve; ***a ~ de campana***: **aquí hay que hacerlo todo a ~ de campana** it's like being in the army here **2** (fam) (llamada) call, ring (BrE colloq)
(Compuestos)
- **toque de atención** warning; **darle un ~ de ~ a algn** to rap sb on the knuckles
- **toque de diana** reveille
- **toque de difuntos** (de trompeta) taps (*pl*) (AmE), last post (BrE); (de campanas) death knell
- **toque de queda** curfew

B **1** (golpe suave) touch; **se aplica con unos toquecitos** you dab it on **2** (Med): **hacerse** *or* **darse unos ~s** to paint one's throat (*with antiseptic*) **3** (en béisbol) bunt
C (detalle) touch; **sólo falta darle los últimos ~s** we just have to put the finishing touches to it
D **1** (Méx arg) (de marihuana) joint (colloq), spliff (arg) **2** (Méx fam) (descarga) electric shock
toquetear [A1] *vt* (fam) to touch; (sexualmente) to touch up; **estos niños todo lo toquetean** these children get their hands on everything
toquilla *f* shawl
torácico -ca *adj* ‹*región*› thoracic
tórax *m* thorax
torbellino *m* **1** (de viento) whirlwind, twister (AmE); (de polvo) dust storm **2** (de actividad) whirl; **un ~ de sentimientos** a turmoil of emotions **3** (persona inquieta) bundle of energy
torcedura *f* sprain
torcer [E10] *vt*
A ‹*cuerpo*› to twist; ‹*cabeza*› to turn; **me torció el brazo** she twisted my arm; **tuerce un ojo** he has a squint in one eye; **torció el gesto de dolor** she grimaced in *o* winced with pain
B ‹*esquina*› to turn
C ‹*ropa*› to wring (out)
D ‹*curso/rumbo*› to change
■ **torcer** *vi* (girar) «*persona/vehículo*» to turn; **el sendero tuerce a la izquierda** the path bends *o* curves round to the left
■ **torcerse** *v pron*
A ‹*tobillo/muñeca*› to twist
B «*madera/viga*» to warp
C «*planes*» to fall through
torcido -da *adj*
A **1** [ESTAR] (con respecto a otra cosa) crooked; **tiene la nariz torcida** he has a crooked nose; **llevas la falda torcida** your skirt's twisted; **el cuadro está ~** the picture isn't straight **2** (curvo) bent; **tiene la columna torcida** she has curvature of the spine; **tiene las piernas torcidas** (para adentro) he is knock-kneed; (para afuera) he is bow-legged
B ‹*intenciones*› devious, crooked
torcijón *m* stomach cramp
tordo[1] -da *adj* dappled, dapple-gray*
tordo[2] -da *m,f* **1** (caballo) dapple, dapple-gray* **2** (pájaro) thrush
toreador -dora *m,f* (ant) toreador, bullfighter
torear [A1] *vi* to fight; **torea desde los 18 años** he has been a bullfighter since he was eighteen
■ **torear** *vt*
A ‹*toro/novillo*› to fight
B (fam) **1** ‹*persona*› (para evitar algo) to dodge **2** (AmL) (provocar) to torment, needle
toreo *m* bullfighting
torera *f* bolero; ***saltarse algo a la ~*** (fam) to flout sth
torero[1] -ra *adj* bullfighting (*before n*)
torero[2] -ra *m,f* bullfighter, matador
toril *m* bull pen
tormenta *f*
A (Meteo) storm; ***hacer frente a la ~*** to weather the storm; ***una ~ en un vaso de agua*** a tempest in a teapot (AmE), a storm in a teacup (BrE)
(Compuesto) **tormenta de nieve** snowstorm; (con viento) blizzard
B (de pasiones) storm; (de celos) frenzy
(Compuesto) **tormenta de ideas** brainstorming
tormento *m* **1** (angustia, dolor) torment; **vivía con el ~ de los celos** she lived tormented by jealousy; **ir al dentista es un ~** going to the dentist is a nightmare *o* is hell (colloq) **2** (malos tratos) torture
tormentoso -sa *adj* stormy
torna *f* **1** (regreso) return **2** (en un cauce) gate; ***se han vuelto las ~s*** it's a different story now; ***volverle las ~s a algn*** to turn the tables on sb
tornadizo[1] -za *adj* fickle
tornadizo[2] -za *m,f*: **es una tornadiza** she's always changing her mind
tornado *m* tornado
tornamesa *f or m* (Col, Méx) (plato giratorio) turntable
tornar [A1] *vi* (liter) **1** (regresar) to return; **tornó a nevar** it snowed again **2** (volver, hacer) to make, render
■ **tornarse** *v pron* (liter) to become; **~se EN algo** to turn INTO sth
tornasol *m*
A (reflejo) reflected light
B (Bot) sunflower; (Quím) litmus
tornasolado -da *adj* ‹*color/destello*› iridescent; ‹*tela*› shot
torneado -da *adj* ‹*cuerpo/piernas*› shapely; ‹*brazos*› nicely-shaped
tornear [A1] *vt* (en carpintería) to turn; (en alfarería) to throw
torneo *m* (Dep) tournament, competition
tornero -ra *m,f* lathe operator
tornillo *m* (Tec) screw; ***apretarle los ~s a algn*** (fam) to put the screws on sb (colloq); ***te/le falta un ~*** you have/he has a screw loose (colloq); ***tener un ~ flojo*** *or* ***suelto*** (fam) to have a screw loose (colloq)
(Compuesto) **tornillo sin fin** worm gear
torniquete *m* **1** (Med) tourniquet **2** (de acceso) turnstile **3** (Ven) (en béisbol) screwball
torno *m*
A **1** (de carpintero) lathe; **~ de ceramista** *or* **alfarero** potter's wheel **2** (Odont) drill **3** (para alzar pesos) winch
B **en torno a** around; **la conversación giró en ~ a ...** the conversation revolved around...
toro *m*
A (animal) bull; ***agarrar al ~ por las astas*** *or* ***los cuernos*** (AmL) *or* (Esp) ***coger el ~ por los cuernos*** to take the bull by the horns; ***fuerte como un ~*** as strong as an ox; ***ver los ~s desde la barrera*** to watch from the sidelines
(Compuesto) **toro bravo** *or* **de lidia** fighting bull
B **los toros** *mpl* (el espectáculo) bullfighting; **nunca he ido a los ~s** I've never been to a bullfight

> **(la fiesta de) los toros**
>
> Bullfighting is popular in Spain, Mexico, Colombia, Peru, and Venezuela. For some Spaniards it is crucial to Spanish identity. The season runs from March to October in Spain, from November to March in Latin America.
>
> The art of bullfighting is given the name *tauromaquia*. The bullfighters in a corrida gather in *cuadrillas*. The principal bullfighter, or *matador*, is assisted by *peones*. Their outfit, the *traje de luces*, consists of a tight silk jacket and trousers, decorated with embroidery and epaulettes, and a black, two-cornered hat known as a *montera*

toronja *f* (AmL) grapefruit

torpe *adj* [1] (en las acciones) clumsy; (al andar) awkward; **un animal lerdo y ~** a slow, ungainly animal [2] (de entendimiento) slow (colloq) [3] (sin tacto) ‹*persona/comentario*› clumsy; **de manera ~** clumsily

torpedear [A1] *vt* to torpedo

torpedero *m*
A (Mil) torpedo boat
B (en béisbol) shortstop

torpedo *m*
A (Arm) torpedo
B (Chi fam) (de estudiante) crib (note) (colloq)

torpemente *adv* [1] ‹*caminar/moverse*› clumsily; ‹*expresarse/actuar*› clumsily [2] (tontamente) stupidly

torpeza *f*
A (cualidad) [1] (en las acciones) clumsiness; (al andar) awkwardness [2] (falta de inteligencia) stupidity; **perdona mi ~, pero no entiendo** I'm sorry to be so stupid *o* dim, but I don't understand [3] (falta de tacto) clumsiness
B (dicho desacertado) gaffe; (acción desacertada) blunder

torpor *m* torpor

torrar [A1] *vt* to roast

torre *f* [1] (de castillo) tower; (de iglesia) tower; (en punta) steeple, spire [2] (de cables de alta tensión) pylon; (de pozo de petróleo) derrick [3] (en ajedrez) rook, castle [4] (edificio alto) apartment block (AmE), tower block (BrE)
(Compuestos)
- **torre de control/observación** control/observation tower
- **torre de marfil** ivory tower

torrefacción *f* roasting

torreja *f*
A (AmL) (pan frito) ▸**torrija**
B (Chi) (rodaja) slice

torrencial *adj* torrential

torrencialmente *adv* torrentially

torrente *m*
A (Geog) torrent
(Compuesto) **torrente sanguíneo** bloodstream
B (de insultos) stream, torrent; (de lágrimas) flood

torrentoso -sa *adj* (AmL) fast-flowing

torreón *m* tower

torrero *m* lighthouse keeper

torreta *f* (de submarino) conning tower, bridge; (de avión, tanque) turret

tórrido -da *adj* torrid

torrija *f* piece *o* slice of French toast; **~s** French toast

torsión *f* torsion; **con una leve ~ del tronco** with a slight twist of the upper body

torso *m* (Anat) torso, trunk; (Art) bust

torta *f*
A (Coc) [1] (AmL) (de verduras) pie; (sin tapa de masa) pie, flan, tart [2] (CS, Ven) (de cumpleaños, etc) cake; (decorada, con crema, etc) gateau
B (Méx) (bocadillo) sandwich
C (esp Esp) (bizcocho basto) sponge cake; ***me/te salió la ~ un pan*** things didn't work out the way I/you had planned; ***ni ~*** (Esp fam) not a thing; **no entiendo ni ~** I don't understand a thing; ***nos/les está costando la ~ un pan*** it's costing us/them more than we're/they're saving
D (fam) (golpe): **darle una ~ a algn** to hit *o* wallop sb (colloq); **pegarse una ~** to bang one's head (*o* arm *etc*); **liarse a ~s** to come to blows

tortazo *m* (fam) ▸**torta D**

tortícolis *f* stiff neck, torticollis (tech)

tortilla *f*
A (de huevos) omelet*; ***se ha dado (la) vuelta*** *or* ***se ha vuelto la ~*** the shoe (AmE) *o* (BrE) boot is on the other foot now
(Compuesto) **tortilla de papas** *or* (Esp) **de patatas** Spanish omelet* (*made with potatoes and sometimes onion*)
B (de maíz) tortilla

tortillera *f* (fam) dyke (sl), lesbian

tortillero -ra *m,f* tortilla seller

tórtola *f* turtledove

tórtolo *m* (fam) lovebird (colloq)

tortuga *f* (Zool) (de tierra) tortoise, turtle (AmE); (de mar) turtle; ***ser*** *or* ***parecer una ~*** (fam) to be a slowpoke (AmE) *o* (BrE) slowcoach (colloq)

tortuguismo *m* (Méx) go-slow

tortuosidad *f* [1] (sinuosidad) tortuousness (liter); **la ~ del camino** the twists and turns in the road [2] (de la mente, conducta) deviousness

tortuoso -sa *adj* [1] ‹*sendero*› tortuous, winding [2] ‹*maquinaciones/conducta*› devious; ‹*mente*› devious

tortura *f* torture; **los exámenes son una ~** (fam) exams are a real nightmare (colloq)

torturado -da *m,f* torture victim

torturador -dora *m,f* torturer

torturar [A1] *vt* (con violencia física) to torture; (angustiar) to torment, torture
■ **torturarse** *v pron* (*refl*) to torture *o* torment oneself

torvo -va *adj* ‹*mirada*› baleful; ‹*intenciones*› grim

tos *f* cough; **tener ~** to have a cough
(Compuestos)
- **tos convulsa** *or* **convulsiva** whooping cough
- **tos de perro** (AmL) barking cough

tosco -ca *adj* [1] ‹*utensilio/mueble/construcción*› crude, basic; ‹*tela*› coarse, rough [2] ‹*persona/manos*› rough; ‹*lenguaje*› unrefined; ‹*modales*› coarse

toser [E1] *vi* to cough; ***a ése no hay quien le tosa*** (Esp fam) he can't take criticism

tosquedad *f* [1] (de objeto) crudeness; (de tela) coarseness, roughness [2] (de persona) roughness; (de modales) coarseness; (del lenguaje) lack of refinement

tostada *f* [1] (de pan) piece *o* slice of toast; **~s** toast [2] (Méx) (de tortilla) tostada (*fried corn/maize tortilla*) [3] (Ven) (arepa frita) fried corn cake

tostado[1] **-da** *adj* ‹*pan/almendras*› toasted; ‹*café*› roasted; ‹*piel*› tanned; **(de) color ~** ‹*guantes/bolso*› tan

tostado[2] *m* [1] (de pan, almendras) toasting; (de café) roasting [2] (de la piel) suntan, tan [3] (Coc) toasted sandwich

tostadora *f*, **tostador** *m* (para pan) toaster; (para café) roaster

tostadura *f* (de café, cacao) roasting; (de otras semillas) toasting

tostar [A10] *vt* [1] ‹*pan/almendras*› to toast; ‹*café*› to roast [2] ‹*piel/persona*› to tan
■ **tostarse** *v pron* (broncearse) to tan

tostón *m*
A [1] (Esp) (pan frito) crouton [2] (Ven) (plátano frito) fried plantain
B (Esp fam) (cosa fastidiosa) drag (colloq); ***darle el ~ a algn*** (Esp fam) to pester somebody
C (Méx fam) (moneda) fifty-cent coin; (billete) fifty-peso bill

total[1] *adj* [1] (absoluto) ‹*desastre/destrucción*› total; ‹*éxito*› resounding, total; **un cambio ~** a complete change [2] (global) ‹*costo/importe*› total

total[2] *m* total; **¿cuánto es el ~?** how much is it altogether?; **el ~ de sus ahorros** the whole of her savings; **en ~** altogether

total[3] *adv* (*indep*) (fam) [1] (al resumir una narración) so, in the end; **~, que me di por vencida** so in the end I gave up [2] (expresando indiferencia, poca importancia): **~, a mí qué** (fam) what do I care anyway; **~, mañana no tienes que trabajar** after all, you don't have to go to work tomorrow

totalidad *f*: **la ~ de la población** the whole *o* entire population; **fue destruido en su ~** it was totally destroyed; **el acuerdo fue aprobado en su ~** the agreement was approved in its entirety; **la deuda se pagó en su ~** the debt was paid in full

totalitario -ria *adj* totalitarian

totalitarismo *m* totalitarianism

totalizar [A4] *vt* «*persona*» to total, add up, totalize (frml); «*cifras*» to total

totalmente *adv* totally; **estoy ~ de acuerdo** I agree entirely; **construido ~ en madera** built entirely of wood

totogol *m* (Col) sports lottery (AmE), football pools (*pl*) (BrE)

totopo *m* (Méx) tortilla chip

totora *f* reed mace, bulrush

t

touch /tutʃ, tuʃ/ *m* touch; **el balón va a ~** the ball goes into touch

tour /tur/ *m* (*pl* **tours**) tour

tournée, tourné /tur'ne/ *f* tour

tour operador -dora *m,f*, **tour-operator** *m,f* 1 (persona) tour operator 2 **tour operador** *m* (empresa) tour operator

toxicidad *f* toxicity

tóxico¹ -ca *adj* toxic

tóxico² *m* poison, toxin

toxicodependencia *f* (frml) drug addiction

toxicomanía *f* (frml) drug addiction

toxicómano¹ -na *adj* addicted to drugs

toxicómano² -na *m,f* drug addict

tozudez *f* obstinacy, stubbornness; **¡qué ~ la tuya!** you're so obstinate *o* stubborn!

tozudo¹ -da *adj* obstinate, stubborn

tozudo² -da *m,f*: **es un ~** he's extremely stubborn *o* obstinate

traba *f*

A (en ventana) catch; (entre dos vigas) tie; (para caballo) hobble; (para preso) shackles (*pl*); (de cinturón) belt loop

B (dificultad, impedimento) obstacle; **me puso muchas ~s** he made things really difficult for me

C (Col, Ven arg) (efecto) high (colloq)

trabajado -da *adj* ‹*diseño/bordado/plan*› elaborate; **una novela muy bien trabajada** an extremely well-crafted novel

trabajador¹ -dora *adj* (que trabaja mucho) hard-working

trabajador² -dora *m,f* worker; **un ~ no calificado** (AmL) *or* (Esp) **cualificado** an unskilled worker *o* laborer

(Compuestos)

- **trabajador autónomo -dora autónoma** *m,f* self-employed worker *o* person
- **trabajador -dora de medio tiempo** (AmL) *or* (Esp) **a tiempo parcial** *m,f* part-time worker
- **trabajador -dora independiente** *or* **por cuenta propia** *m,f* self-employed worker *o* person
- **trabajador -dora social** *m,f* (Méx) social worker

trabajar [A1] *vi*

A (en empleo) to work; **~ por cuenta propia** to be self-employed; **~ jornada completa** *or* **a tiempo completo** to work full-time; **~ media jornada** *or* (AmL) **medio tiempo** *or* (Esp) **a tiempo parcial** to work part-time; **trabaja bien** she does her job well; **~ mucho** to work hard; **¿en qué trabajas?** what do you do (for a living)?; **trabaja en publicidad** she works *o* is in advertising; **~ DE** *or* **COMO algo** to work AS sth

B (en tarea, actividad) to work; **deja de perder el tiempo y ponte a ~** stop wasting time and start doing some work; **estoy trabajando en una novela** I'm working on a novel; **~ por la paz** to promote peace; **~ *como una bestia* *or* *un negro* *or* *(un) chino*** to work like a slave

C (actuar) to act, perform; **¿quién trabaja en la película?** who are the actors *o* who's in the movie?

D (operar, funcionar) to work; **la fábrica está trabajando a tope** the factory is working *o* operating at full capacity; **haga ~ su dinero** make your money work for you; **hacer ~ el cerebro** to exercise one's mind

■ **trabajar** *vt*

A 1 ‹*campo/tierra*› to work 2 ‹*madera/cuero*› to work 3 ‹*masa*› (con las manos) to knead, work; (con tenedor) to mix

B ‹*género/marca*› to sell, stock

C (perfeccionar, pulir) to work on

D (fam) (intentar convencer) ‹*persona*› to work on (colloq)

■ **trabajarse** *v pron* (fam) 1 ‹*premio/ascenso*› to work for 2 (*enf*) (fam) ‹*persona*› to work on (colloq)

trabajo *m*

A 1 (empleo) job; **conseguir ~** to get *o* find work, to get *o* find a job; **buscar ~** to look for work *o* for a job; **quedarse sin ~** to lose one's job; **no tiene ~ fijo** he doesn't have a steady job; **un ~ de media jornada** *or* (AmL) **de medio tiempo** *or* (Esp) **a tiempo parcial** a part-time job; **~ de jornada completa** *or* **de** *or* **a tiempo completo** full-time work *o* job 2 (lugar) work; **está en el ~** she's at work; **ir al ~** to go to work

B (actividad, labor) work; **requiere años de ~** it takes years of work; **~ en equipo** teamwork; **el ~ de la casa** housework; **este bordado tiene mucho ~** a lot of work has gone into this embroidery; **los niños dan mucho ~** children are hard work; **¡buen ~!** well done!; **fue premiado por su ~ en esa película** he was given an award for his performance in that movie

(Compuestos)

- **trabajo a destajo** piece work
- **trabajo a reglamento** (CS) work-to-rule
- **trabajo de campo** fieldwork
- **trabajo de chinos** fiddly *o* laborious job
- **trabajo de parto** labor*
- **trabajo de práctica** practical work
- **trabajos forzados** *mpl* hard labor*
- **trabajos manuales** *mpl* handicrafts (*pl*)
- **trabajo voluntario** voluntary *o* (AmE) volunteer work

C 1 (tarea) job; **limpiar el horno es un ~ que odio** cleaning the oven is a job *o* chore I hate 2 (obra escrita) piece of work; **hice un ~ sobre Lorca** I did a paper on Lorca

D (esfuerzo): **con mucho ~ consiguió levantarse** with great effort she managed to get up; **me cuesta ~ creerlo** I find it hard to believe; **se tomó/dio el ~ de venir** she took the trouble to come

E (Econ) labor*

trabajoadicto -ta *m,f* workaholic

trabajosamente *adv*: **subió ~ las escaleras** he struggled up the stairs; **~ logró hacerse entender** with effort she managed to make herself understood; **respiraba ~** his breathing was labored

trabajoso -sa *adj* ‹*subida*› arduous; ‹*tarea*› laborious; **su letra es muy trabajosa de leer** it's very hard work to read his writing

trabalenguas *m* (*pl* ~) tongue twister

trabar [A1] *vt*

A 1 ‹*puerta/ventana*› (para que no se abra) to hold … shut; (para que no se cierre) to hold … back *o* open 2 ‹*vigas*› to tie, connect 3 ‹*caballo*› to hobble

B 1 ‹*conversación*› to strike up, start; ‹*amistad/relación*› to strike up; **han trabado una gran amistad** they've become great friends 2 ‹*historia*› to weave together

C ‹*proceso/negociaciones*› to impede *o* hamper the progress of

■ **trabarse** *v pron*

A «*cajón/cierre*» to get jammed *o* stuck; **se le traba la lengua** he gets tongue-tied

B (enzarzarse) **~se EN algo** to get involved IN sth

C (Col, Ven arg) (con droga) to get high *o* stoned (colloq)

trabazón *f* linking together

trabilla *f* (de pantalón) stirrup; (de chaqueta, abrigo) belt loop

trabucar [A2] *vt* to mix up, confuse

■ **trabucarse** *v pron* to get one's words jumbled up *o* mixed up

trabuco *m* blunderbuss

trácala¹ *m* (Méx, Ven fam) cheat

trácala² *f* (Méx, Ven fam) trick, swindle; **se la pasa haciendo ~** he's always cheating people

tracalada *f* (Andes fam) bunch (colloq); **una ~ de amigos/mentiras** a whole bunch of friends/lies (colloq)

tracalear [A1] *vt* (Méx, Ven fam) to cheat, swindle

tracalero -ra *adj* (Méx, Ven fam) dishonest; **no seas ~** don't be a cheat, don't cheat

tracción *f* (Auto, Mec) traction, drive

(Compuestos)

- **tracción a cuatro ruedas** *f* four-wheel drive; **un vehículo con** *or* **de ~ a ~ ~** a four-wheel-drive vehicle
- **tracción animal** *f* draft (frml)
- **tracción delantera/trasera** *f* front-wheel/rear-wheel drive

tractor *m* tractor

trad. = traducido

tradición *f* (costumbre) tradition; **seguir la ~** to keep up the tradition; **romper con la ~** to break with tradition

tradicional *adj* traditional; **mañana, como es ya ~, …** tomorrow, as is customary …

tradicionalismo *m* traditionalism

tradicionalista *adj/mf* traditionalist

tradicionalmente *adv* traditionally

traducción *f* translation; ~ **del inglés al español** translation from English into Spanish

(Compuestos)

- **traducción directa** *translation into one's native language*
- **traducción inversa** *translation into a foreign language*
- **traducción simultánea** simultaneous translation

traducible *adj* translatable

traducir [I6] *vt* ‹*texto/escritor*› to translate; ~ **DE algo A algo** to translate FROM sth INTO sth

■ **traducirse** *v pron* ~**se EN algo** ‹*en un ahorro/un beneficio*› to result IN sth

traductor -tora *m,f* translator

traductorado *m* (CS) translator's exams (*pl*)

traer [E23] *vt*

A (de un lugar a otro) to bring; **me trajo un recuerdo de su viaje** she brought me back a souvenir from her trip; **tráigame la cuenta por favor** could I have *o* would you bring me the check (AmE) *o* (BrE) bill, please?; **me trajo en la moto** he brought me on his motorbike; **traía al niño sobre los hombros** he was carrying the child on his shoulders; **¿qué te trae por aquí?** what brings you here?; ***muy traído y llevado***: **el muy traído y llevado tema de su divorcio** the tired old story about his divorce

B (ocasionar, causar) ‹*problemas/dificultades*› to cause; **la guerra trajo mucha pobreza** the war brought *o* caused much poverty; **esto trajo aparejados muchos cambios** this entailed many changes; ~ **buena suerte** to bring good luck; ***tener a algn a mal*** ~ to give sb a hard time (colloq)

C (contener) to have; **trae un artículo sobre computación** it has *o* contains an article on computing; **este diccionario no lo trae** it's not in this dictionary

D 1 ‹*ropa/sombrero*› to wear 2 (tener consigo) to bring; **traje poco dinero** I didn't bring much money (with me)

■ **traerse** *v pron*

A (*enf*) (a un sitio) to bring (along); **lo invité a él y se trajo a toda la familia** I invited him and he brought the whole family along

B (fam) (tramar) to be up to (colloq); **¿qué se ~án esas dos?** what are those two up to?; ***traérselas*** ‹‹*problema/asunto/examen*›› to be tough (colloq) *o* difficult

trafagar [A3] *vi* to be on the go (colloq)

traficante *mf* dealer, trafficker; ~ **de drogas** drug dealer *o* trafficker; ~ **de esclavos** slave trader

traficar [A2] *vi* ~ **EN** *or* **CON algo** to deal IN sth

tráfico *m*

A (de vehículos) traffic; **accidente de** ~ road accident

(Compuestos)

- **tráfico aéreo** air traffic
- **tráfico marítimo** shipping

B (de mercancías) trade; ~ **de armas** arms trade *o* dealing; ~ **de drogas** drug dealing *o* trafficking; ~ **de esclavos** slave trade

(Compuesto) **tráfico de influencias** influence peddling, spoils system (AmE)

tragaderas *fpl* (fam) gullet; ***tener buenas*** ~ (fam) (comer mucho) to eat anything and everything; (tener mucho aguante) to be prepared to put up with a lot

tragaldabas *mf* (*pl* ~) (fam) glutton (colloq)

tragaluz *m* (en el techo) skylight; (en una puerta) fanlight

tragamonedas *m or f* (*pl* ~) (Jueg) slot machine; (de discos) jukebox

traganíqueles *m* (*pl* ~) (AmC) slot machine

tragantona *f* (Esp fam) binge (colloq); **darse una** ~ to go on a binge

tragaperras *m or f* (*pl* ~) (Esp fam) slot machine

tragar [A3] *vt*

A 1 ‹*comida/agua/medicina*› to swallow 2 ‹*lágrimas*› to choke back

B (fam) (soportar) to put up with; ***no (poder)*** ~ ***a algn*** (fam): **no lo trago/traga** I/she can't stand him

■ **tragar** *vi*

A 1 (Fisiol) to swallow 2 (fam) (engullir): **¡cómo traga este niño!** this kid really puts away his food! (colloq)

B (RPI fam) (estudiar) to cram

■ **tragarse** *v pron*

A (*enf*) 1 ‹*comida*› to swallow; ~**se el humo** to inhale 2 ‹*lágrimas*› to choke back; ‹*orgullo*› to swallow; ‹*angustia*› to suppress 3 ‹‹*mar*›› to swallow up 4 ‹‹*máquina*›› ‹*dinero/tarjeta*› to swallow up 5 (fam) (engullirse) to put away (colloq)

B (fam) 1 (soportar) ‹*insulto*› to put up with; ‹*obra/recital*› to sit through 2 (creerse) ‹*excusa/cuento*› to fall for (colloq)

tragasables *mf* (*pl* ~) sword swallower

tragedia *f* tragedy

trágicamente *adv* tragically

trágico[1] **-ca** *adj* 1 ‹*actriz/obra*› tragic (*before n*); **lo ~ del caso es que ...** the tragedy of it all is that ... 2 ‹*vida/final/consecuencia*› tragic; **no te pongas** ~ don't be so melodramatic

trágico[2] *m* tragedian

tragicomedia *f* tragicomedy

tragicómico -ca *adj* tragicomic

trago *m*

A 1 (de líquido) drink, swig; **dame un traguito para probar** let me try a sip *o* a drop; **de un** ~ in one gulp 2 (esp AmL fam) (bebida alcohólica) drink; **¿vamos a tomar un ~?** shall we go for a drink?

B (experiencia): **ha pasado un** ~ **amargo** he's had a rough time; **fue un mal** ~ it was an awful experience

tragón[1] **-gona** *adj* (fam) greedy

tragón[2] **-gona** *m,f* (fam) glutton

traición *f* 1 (delito) treason; **fue acusado de** ~ **a la patria** he was accused of treason *o* of betraying his country 2 (acto desleal) treachery, betrayal; **lo mataron a** ~ they killed him by treachery

traicionar [A1] *vt* 1 ‹*patria/amigo*› to betray 2 (delatar) ‹‹*mirada/nerviosismo*›› to give ... away

traicionero -ra *adj* 1 ‹*persona/acción*› treacherous 2 ‹*mar/tiempo*› treacherous, dangerous

traidor[1] **-dora** *adj* traitorous, treacherous

traidor[2] **-dora** *m,f* traitor; ~ **A algo** traitor TO sth

traiga, traigas, etc *see* **traer**

trailer /'trajler/ *m*

A 1 (AmL) (casa rodante) trailer (AmE), caravan (BrE) 2 (para caballos) horsebox

B (Méx) (camión) semitrailer (AmE), articulated lorry (BrE)

tráiler *m*

A (Esp) (Cin) trailer

B ▸**trailer A**

trailero -ra *m,f* (Méx) truck driver

trainera *f* fishing boat (*with oars*)

traje[1] *m* (de dos, tres piezas) suit; (vestido de mujer) dress; (Teatr) costume; (de país, región) dress; ~ **típico** typical dress

(Compuestos)

- **traje de baño** (de hombre) swimming trunks (*pl*); (de mujer) bathing suit, swimsuit
- **traje de calle** business suit (AmE), lounge suit (BrE)
- **traje de campaña** battledress
- **traje de etiqueta/gala** formal/evening dress
- **traje de luces** bullfighter's costume
- **traje largo** evening dress

traje[2], **etc** *see* **traer**

trajeado -da *adj* (bien vestido) smart; **¡qué ~ has venido hoy!** you're looking very smart today!

trajera, trajese, etc *see* **traer**

trajimos, trajiste, etc *see* **traer**

trajín *m*: **un día de mucho** ~ a very hectic day; **con el ~ de las Navidades/la mudanza** with all the hustle and bustle of Christmas/the commotion of the move; **con todo este ~ ...** with all this coming and going...; **el ~ de las grandes ciudades** the hustle and bustle of big cities

trajinar [A1] *vi* (fam) to rush about (colloq); **se pasa el día trajinando** she's on the go all day (colloq)

trajinera *f* (Méx) canoe

trajiste, etc *see* **traer**

tralla *f* (látigo) whip

trallazo *m* (latigazo) lash; (chasquido) crack (*of a whip*)

trama *f*

A (de tejido) weave, weft

B 1 (Lit) plot 2 (intriga) plot

t

tramador -dora *adj* (Col) ‹*película/libro*› gripping; ‹*conferencia*› absorbing

tramar [A1] *vt* ‹*engaño*› to devise; ‹*venganza*› to plot; ‹*complot*› to hatch, lay; **¿qué andan tramando?** what are you up to? (colloq)

■ **tramarse** *v pron* (*enf*) to plot, scheme

tramitación *f* processing; **los documentos necesarios para la ~ de un permiso** the documents you need to have a permit application processed; **la ~ del divorcio tardó años** the divorce proceedings took years

tramitar [A1] *vt* ‹*préstamo*› «*funcionario*» to deal with; «*interesado*» to arrange; **tengo que ~ algunos asuntos** I have a few matters to attend to *o* to deal with; **están tramitando el divorcio** «*cónyuges*» they have started divorce proceedings; **~ un permiso de trabajo** «*organismo*» to deal with a work permit application; «*interesado*» to apply for one's work permit

trámite *m* (proceso) procedure; (etapa) step, stage; **el préstamo está en ~** the loan application is being processed; **los ~s necesarios para su obtención** all the steps *o* formalities required to obtain it; **se iniciaron los ~s para su extradición** extradition proceedings were begun; **tengo que hacer unos ~s en el centro** I have some business to attend to in the centre

tramo *m* (de carretera, vía) stretch; (de escalera) flight; **el ~ final de la campaña** the final phase of the campaign

tramontana *f* north wind

tramoya *f* 1 (Teatr) piece of stage machinery 2 (fam) (enredo, trama) scam (colloq)

tramoyista *mf* 1 (Teatr) sceneshifter, stagehand 2 (fam) (enredador) schemer; (estafador) con artist

trampa *f* 1 (para animales) trap; (de lazo) snare 2 (ardid) trap; **caer en la ~** to fall into the trap; **le tendieron una ~** they laid *o* set a trap for him 3 (en el juego): **hacer ~(s)** to cheat

trampear [A1] *vi* to cheat

trampilla *f* trapdoor

trampolín *m*

A (Dep) (en natación — flexible) springboard; (— rígido) diving board; (en gimnasia) trampoline; (en esquí) ski jump

B (para obtener algo): **ese puesto fue un ~ para llegar a la directiva** that job was a springboard to a place on the board; **esa película fue su ~ a la fama** she was catapulted to fame by that movie

tramposo[1] -sa *adj*: **ser ~** to be a cheat

tramposo[2] -sa *m,f* cheat

tranca *f*

A 1 (de puerta, ventana) bar; **poner la ~ a la puerta** to bar the door 2 (palo) cudgel, club; ***a ~s y barrancas*** (fam) with great difficulty

B (esp AmL fam) (borrachera) bender (colloq); **pegarse** *or* **agarrarse una ~** to get plastered *o* smashed (colloq)

C (Ven fam) (Auto) holdup, tailback

trancar [A2] *vt* ‹*puerta/ventana*› to bar

trancazo *m* (golpe) blow

trance *m*

A (momento crítico): **pasar por un ~ difícil** to go through a difficult time; **ya han salido de ese ~** they've come through it *o* got over it now; **en ~ DE algo**: **estar en ~ de muerte** to be at death's door; **estas costumbres están en ~ de desaparición** these customs are (in the process of) disappearing *o* are dying out; ***a todo ~*** at any cost

B (Psic, Relig) trance; **estar/entrar en ~** to be in/go into a trance

tranco *m* 1 (paso largo) stride; **andaba a ~s** she was striding along; **en dos ~s** in two shakes (AmE) *o* (BrE) in two ticks (colloq) 2 (CS) (ritmo) rate, pace; ***agarrarle el ~ a algo*** to get the hang *o* knack of sth

tranque *m* (CS) reservoir

tranquera *f* (AmL) gate

tranquilamente *adv* ‹*hablar/actuar*› calmly; ‹*descansar*› peacefully; **te los pruebas ~ en casa** you can try them on at your leisure in your own home

tranquilidad *f* 1 (calma) peace; **la ~ del campo** the peace *o* tranquility of the countryside; **ni un minuto de ~** not a moment's peace; **paz y ~** peace and quiet; **léelo con ~** read it at your leisure; **respondió con ~** she replied calmly 2 (falta de preocupación): **llámame a la hora que sea, con toda ~** feel free to call me at any time; **lo hice para mi propia ~** I did it for my own peace of mind

tranquilizador -dora *adj* ‹*palabras/noticia*› reassuring; ‹*música*› soothing; **la droga tiene un efecto ~** the drug has a tranquilizing *o* calming effect

tranquilizante[1] *adj* 1 ▸**tranquilizador** 2 (Med) tranquilizing*

tranquilizante[2] *m* tranquilizer*

tranquilizar [A4] *vt* ‹*persona/animal*› to calm … down; **intenté ~lo** I tried to calm him down; **sus palabras la ~on** his words reassured her; **la noticia nos tranquilizó a todos** we were all relieved to hear the news; **eso me tranquiliza mucho** that makes me feel a lot better

■ **tranquilizarse** *v pron* «*persona*» to calm down

tranquillo *m* (Esp) knack; ***cogerle el ~ a algo*** (fam) to get the hang *o* knack of sth (colloq)

tranquilo[1] -la *adj*

A 1 [SER] ‹*persona*› (pacífico) calm 2 ‹*mar/ambiente*› calm; ‹*lugar*› quiet, peaceful, tranquil

B [ESTAR] 1 (libre de preocupacion): **ahora que trabaja estoy más ~** I feel better *o* happier now that he's found a job; **viven ~s allí en su granjita** they lead a peaceful *o* tranquil life on their little farm; **¡tranquilo!** relax!; **tú, ~, que de eso me encargo yo** there's no need for you to worry, I'll take care of that; **lo hice para quedarme ~** I did it for my own peace of mind; **déjalo ~** leave him alone; **tengo la conciencia tranquila** my conscience is clear 2 (sin inmutarse): **su hermano en el hospital y él tan ~** his brother's in hospital and he doesn't seem at all bothered; **...y se quedó tan tranquila** ...and she didn't bat an eyelash (AmE) *o* (BrE) eyelid

tranquilo[2] *adv* (Méx fam): **te cuesta ~ unas 2,000 libras** it costs 2,000 pounds easily (colloq)

tranquiza *f* (Méx fam) hiding (colloq)

transa *adj/mf* (Méx fam) ▸**tranza[1,2]**

transacción *f*

A (Com, Fin) transaction, deal

B (Der) settlement, agreement

transandino[1] -na *adj* trans-Andean

transandino[2] *m* trans-Andean railroad *o* railway

transar [A1] *vi* (AmL) 1 (hacer concesiones) ▸**transigir (a)** 2 (llegar a un acuerdo) to reach an agreement *o* a compromise; **~ EN algo** to settle FOR sth; **no ~emos por menos del 10%** we will not settle for *o* accept less than 10%; **~on en un 5%** they settled for *o* accepted 5%

■ **transar** *vt*

A (AmL) (Com, Fin) to buy and sell; **pocas acciones se ~on hoy en la bolsa** there was little activity *o* little buying and selling on the stock market today

B (Méx) (engañar) ▸**tranzar**

transatlántico[1] -ca *adj* transatlantic; **países ~s** countries on the other side of the Atlantic

transatlántico[2] *m* ocean liner

transbordador *m* ferry

(Compuesto) **transbordador espacial** space shuttle

transbordar [A1] *vt* ‹*mercancías/equipajes*› to transfer

■ **transbordar** *vi* «*pasajeros*» to change

transbordo *m* 1 (de viajeros) change; **hacer ~** to change 2 (de equipaje, mercancías) transfer

transcribir [I34] *vt* to transcribe

transcripción *f* 1 (acción) transcription; (resultado) transcript 2 (Mús) transcription

transcultural *adj* transcultural, cross-cultural

transcurrir [I1] *vi* 1 «*tiempo/años*» to pass, go by; **han transcurrido varios meses desde …** it's (been) several months now since …; **transcurría el minuto 20 cuando se anotó el primer gol** the first goal was scored in the 20th minute 2 «*acontecimiento/acto*» to take place; **la marcha transcurrió pacíficamente** the march went *o* passed off peacefully

transcurso *m* course; **en el ~ del año** during the course of the year; **con el ~ del tiempo** as time goes/went by

transeúnte *mf* (peatón) passer-by; (no residente) non-resident

transexual *adj/mf* transsexual

transexualidad *f*, **transexualismo** *m* transsexualism

transferencia *f*
A (de propiedad, derecho) transfer, handing over; (de jugador) transfer
(Compuesto) **transferencia bancaria** credit *o* bank transfer
B (Psic) transference
transferible *adj* transferable
transferir [I11] *vt* to transfer
transfiguración *f* 1▸ (cambio radical) transformation 2▸ (Relig) Transfiguration
transfigurar [A1] *vt* to transform
■ **transfigurarse** *v pron* to be transformed
transformación *f* 1▸ (cambio) transformation, change 2▸ (en rugby) conversion 3▸ (Ling) transformation
transformador *m* transformer
transformar [A1] *vt* 1▸ (convertir) to convert; **~ algo EN algo** to convert sth INTO sth 2▸ (cambiar radicalmente) ‹*persona/situación/país*› to transform, change *o* alter … radically 3▸ (en rugby) to convert; (en fútbol) (period) to score
■ **transformarse** *v pron* 1▸ (convertirse) **~se EN algo**: **los carbohidratos se transforman en azúcar** the carbohydrates are converted into sugar; **la calabaza se transformó en un carruaje** the pumpkin turned into *o* was transformed into a carriage 2▸ (cambiar radicalmente) «*persona/país*» to change completely, be transformed
transformista *mf* quick-change artist
tránsfuga *mf*
A (Pol) turncoat
B (Col, RPl fam) (sinvergüenza) rogue (colloq)
transfundir [I1] *vt* to transfuse (frml)
transfusión *f* transfusion; **~ de sangre** blood transfusion
transgénico -ca *adj* genetically modified, transgenic
transgredir [I1] *vt* (frml) to transgress (frml)
transgresión *f* (frml) transgression (frml)
transgresor -sora *m,f* transgressor
transición *f* transition; **~ DE algo A algo** transition FROM sth TO sth; **período de ~** period of transition
transido -da *adj* (liter) racked; **~ de dolor/de pena** racked with pain/grief
transigencia *f* (acto) compromise; (cualidad) accommodating attitude
transigente *adj* accommodating
transigir [I7] *vi* 1▸ (hacer concesiones) to compromise, give way; **~ EN algo** to compromise ON sth; **en cuestiones de principios no voy a ~** I'm not going to compromise on matters of principle 2▸ (tolerar) **~ CON algo** to tolerate sth, put up WITH sth 3▸ (Der) to reach a settlement
transistor *m* transistor
transitable *adj* passable
transitar [A1] *vi* (frml) «*vehículo*» to travel, go; «*peatón*» to go, walk
transitivo -va *adj* transitive
tránsito *m*
A (tráfico) traffic; **las horas de máximo ~** peak hours; **una calle de mucho ~** a very busy road; **un accidente de ~** (AmL) a road accident; **infracción de ~** (AmL) traffic violation (AmE), motoring offense (BrE)
(Compuesto) **tránsito rodado** vehicular traffic
B (paso) passage, movement; **sólo están de ~** they're just passing through; **pasajeros en ~** passengers in transit
C (liter) (muerte) passing (euph), death
transitoriedad *f* 1▸ (provisionalidad) temporary *o* provisional nature 2▸ (cualidad efímera) transience
transitorio -ria *adj* 1▸ ‹*medida*› provisional; ‹*situación*› temporary; ‹*período*› transitional 2▸ (efímero) transitory, fleeting
translación *f* ▸**traslación**
translucir [I5] *vi* ▸**traslucir**
transmigración *f* (de personas) migration; (de almas) transmigration
transmigrar [A1] *vi* «*personas*» to migrate; «*almas*» to transmigrate
transmisible *adj* transmissible
transmisión *f*
A (Rad, TV) 1▸ (señal) transmission; (programa) broadcast; **una ~ en directo/en diferido** a live/prerecorded broadcast 2▸ (de señal) transmission; (de programa) broadcasting, transmission
B 1▸ (de sonido, movimiento) transmission 2▸ (Med) transmission; **enfermedades de ~ oral** orally transmitted diseases 3▸ (de derecho) transfer
(Compuestos)
- **transmisión de datos** data transfer
- **transmisión de dominio** transfer of ownership
- **transmisión de mando** transfer of power; **ceremonia de ~ de ~** (AmL) inauguration ceremony
- **transmisión de pensamiento** thought transference

transmisor[1] **-sora** *adj* transmitting (*before n*); **aparato ~** transmitter; **estación ~a** transmitter, radio/TV station
transmisor[2] *m* transmitter
(Compuesto) **transmisor-receptor** transceiver; (portátil) walkie-talkie
transmitir [I1] *vt*
A (Rad, TV) ‹*señal*› to transmit; ‹*programa*› to broadcast
B 1▸ ‹*sonido/movimiento*› to transmit 2▸ ‹*enfermedad/tara*› to transmit, pass on 3▸ (Der) to transfer 4▸ ‹*lengua/costumbres*› to transmit, pass on; ‹*conocimientos*› to pass on 5▸ ‹*saludos/felicidades*› to pass on
■ **transmitir** *vi* (Rad, TV) to transmit
transmutar [A1] *vt* to transmute
transnacional *adj/f* transnational
transoceánico -ca *adj* transoceanic
transparencia *f* 1▸ (cualidad) transparency 2▸ (Fot) slide, transparency; (para retroprojector) transparency
transparentar [A1] *vt* ‹*sentimientos/intenciones*› to reveal
■ **transparentarse** *v pron* 1▸ ‹*tela/blusa*›: **una tela/blusa que se transparenta** a see-through material/blouse; **con ese vestido se le transparenta el viso** her petticoat shows through that dress 2▸ ‹*intenciones*› to be evident, be apparent
transparente *adj* 1▸ ‹*cristal/agua*› transparent, clear; ‹*aire*› clear 2▸ ‹*tela/papel*› transparent; ‹*blusa*› see-through 3▸ ‹*persona/carácter*› transparent; ‹*intenciones*› clear, plain; **eres tan ~** I can see right through you
transpiración *f* (Fisiol) perspiration; (Bot) transpiration
transpirar [A1] *vi* (Fisiol) to perspire, sweat; (Bot) to transpire
transpirenaico -ca *adj* trans-Pyrenean
transportable *adj* transportable; **fácilmente ~** easily transported *o* transportable
transportación *f* transportation
transportador *m*
A (Mat) protractor
B (Mec) conveyor
(Compuesto) **transportador de correa** *or* **cinta** conveyor (belt)
transportar [A1] *vt*
A 1▸ ‹*personas/mercancías*› to transport; **~ algo por aire** to ship sth by air 2▸ ‹*energía/sonido*› to transmit; **la sangre transporta el oxígeno** oxygen is carried by the blood
B (embelesar) to mesmerize
■ **transportarse** *v pron* to be transported; **se transportó con el pensamiento al pasado** his thoughts took him back *o* transported him back to the past
transporte *m*
A 1▸ (de pasajeros) transportation (esp AmE), transport (esp BrE); **sistema de ~** transport *o* (AmE) transit system; **me pagan el ~** they pay my traveling expenses 2▸ (de mercancías) transportation (esp AmE), transport (esp BrE); **~ aéreo** airfreight; **~ por carretera** haulage; **el ~ corre por cuenta nuestra** we pay the freight
(Compuesto) **transporte público** public transportation (AmE), public transport (BrE)
B (medio, vehículo) means of transport
(Compuesto) **transporte de tropas** troop carrier
transportista *mf* haulage contractor
transposición *f* transposition
transversal[1] *adj* ‹*eje/línea*› transverse; **una calle ~ al Paseo de Recoletos** a street which crosses the Paseo de Recoletos; **un corte ~** a cross section

transversal² *f* 1 (calle); **la calle Colonia y sus ~es** Colonia street and all the streets that cross it *o* (AmE) and its cross streets 2 (Mat) transversal

tranvía *m* 1 (vehículo urbano) streetcar (AmE), tram (BrE) 2 (Esp) (Ferr) local train

tranza¹ *adj* (Méx fam) crooked

tranza² *mf* 1 (Méx fam) (persona) con artist (colloq), shark (colloq) 2 **tranza** *f* (Méx fam) (engaño, fraude) scam (colloq)

tranzar [A4] *vt* (Méx fam) ‹*persona*› to con (colloq); **le ~on todos sus ahorros** they conned him out of all his savings

trapacear [A1] *vi* to fiddle (colloq)

trapacero -ra *m,f* racketeer

trapeador *m* (AmL) mop

trapear [A1] *vt* (AmL) to mop

trapecio *m* 1 (Mat) trapezoid (AmE), trapezium (BrE) 2 (Espec) trapeze

trapecista *mf* trapeze artist

trapería *f* 1 (tienda) thrift store (AmE), secondhand clothes shop (BrE) 2 (trapos) rags (*pl*)

trapero -ra *m,f*
A 1 (ropavejero) junkman (AmE), rag and bone man (BrE) 2 (CS fam) (aficionado a la ropa): **es una trapera** she's crazy about clothes (colloq)
B **trapero** *m* (AmL) (para el suelo) floorcloth

trapiche *m* (de caña de azúcar) sugar mill; (de aceitunas) olive press; (de uvas) winepress

trapichear [A1] *vi* (fam) to buy and sell stolen goods

trapicheo *m* 1 (fam) (negocio) shady deal 2 **trapicheos** *mpl* (fam) (tejemanejes) scheming, dealing

trapío *m* 1 (Taur) power 2 (garbo, brío) grace

trapisonda *f* trickery, scheming

trapo *m*
A (para limpiar) cloth; ***a todo ~*** (sin ahorrar) (AmS fam) with no expense spared; **llorar a todo ~** to cry one's eyes out; ***dejar a algn hecho un ~*** (fam) to tear sb to shreds (colloq); ***los ~s sucios se lavan en casa*** you shouldn't wash your dirty linen in public; ***sacar los ~s sucios al sol*** *or* ***a relucir*** (fam) to reveal personal secrets (*o* inside information *etc*); ***soltar el ~*** (fam) to burst into tears

Compuestos

- **trapo de cocina** dishtowel (AmE), tea towel (BrE)
- **trapo de sacudir** dust cloth (AmE), duster (BrE)

B (fam) (Taur) cape
C **trapos** *mpl* (fam) (ropa) clothes (*pl*); (ropa vieja) rags (*pl*)

tráquea *f* windpipe, trachea

traquear [A1] *vi* (Col fam) to creak

traqueteado -da *adj* (fam) hectic, busy

traquetear [A1] *vi*
A «*tren/coche*» to clatter, jolt
B (fam) «*persona*» (ir de un sitio a otro) to rush around

traqueteo *m*
A (de tren, automóvil — movimiento) jolting; (— ruido) clatter, clattering
B (fam) (de persona) rushing around

tras *prep*
A 1 (frml) (después de) after; **~ + INF** after -ING; **~ interrogarlo lo pusieron en libertad** after questioning him they released him 2 (indicando repetición) after; **día ~ día** day after day
B (detrás de) behind; **la puerta se cerró ~ él** the door closed behind him; **la policía anda/salió ~ él** the police are/went after him

trasandino -na *adj* ▸**transandino¹**

trascendencia *f* 1 (importancia) significance, importance; (repercusión, alcance) implication; **no reconocían la ~ de estos sucesos** they did not recognize the implications of these events 2 (Fil) transcendence

trascendental *adj* 1 (importante) ‹*noticia/ocasión*› momentous; (de gran alcance) ‹*decisión/cambio/efecto*› far-reaching; **una decisión ~** a decision which has far-reaching implications 2 (Fil) transcendental

trascendente *adj* 1 (importante) ‹*hecho/suceso*› significant, important 2 (Fil) transcendent

trascender [E8] *vi* 1 (period) (darse a conocer): **según ha trascendido** according to reports; **ha trascendido que ...** it has emerged that ...; **el caso ha trascendido a la opinión pública** the case has come to public notice; **desean evitar que la noticia trascienda** they want to avoid the news leaking out 2 (frml) (extenderse) **~ A algo** «*influencia/popularidad*» to extend TO sth 3 (ir más allá) **~ DE algo** to transcend sth (frml), to go beyond sth; **esto trasciende de lo puramente filosófico** this transcends *o* goes beyond the purely philosophical
■ **trascender** *vt* to go beyond, transcend (frml)

trascendido *m* (CS) leak

trasegar [A7] *vt* 1 ‹*vino/líquido*› to decant 2 ‹*papeles/documentos*› to shuffle, move ... around; ‹*libros*› to move ... around
■ **trasegar** *vi* (moverse) to go backward(s) and forward(s), to go to and fro

trasero¹ -ra *adj* ‹*puerta/habitación/asiento*› back (*before n*); ‹*rueda*› rear, back (*before n*); ‹*motor*› rear-mounted

trasero² *m* (fam) (de persona) bottom, backside (colloq); (de animal) hindquarters (*pl*)

trasfondo *m* background; **había un ~ de resentimiento en lo que dijo** there was an undertone of resentment in her words

trasgo *m* imp, goblin

trashumar [A1] *vi* to move to winter/summer pastures

trasiego *m* 1 (de líquido) decanting; (de objetos) moving *o* shuffling around 2 (fam) (ir y venir) coming and going

traslación *f* (Astron) movement, passage; (Mat) translation

trasladar [A1] *vt*
A (cambiar de sitio) ‹*objeto/oficina/tienda*› to move; ‹*preso/enfermo*› to move, transfer; ‹*información*› to transfer; **los heridos fueron trasladados al hospital** the injured were taken to hospital
B (cambiar de destino) ‹*empleado/funcionario*› to transfer
■ **trasladarse** *v pron* 1 (mudarse) to move 2 (period) (ir) to go, travel 3 (Fís) «*luz*» to travel

traslado *m*
A (cambio de sitio — de prisioneros transferal; (— de oficina) removal; **el ~ de víveres se efectuará en avión** supplies will be taken by air; **el ~ del cuadro se llevó a cabo ayer** the picture was moved yesterday; **gastos de ~** relocation expenses; **mañana tendrá lugar el ~ de sus restos mortales al Cementerio** (period) ≈ the funeral will take place tomorrow at the Cemetery
B (cambio de destino) transfer
C (Der) (de una actuación judicial) notification

traslúcido -da *adj* translucent

traslucir [I5] *vt* to reveal; **dejar ~ algo** (insinuar) to suggest sth; (dejar ver) to reveal, betray
■ **traslucirse** *v pron* 1 (notarse, percibirse): **en sus declaraciones se traslucía el miedo** his statement betrayed his fear 2 «*ropa interior*» to show through

trasluz *m*: **al ~** against the light

trasmano: **a ~** out of the way; **vivía muy a ~** she lived in a very out-of-the-way *o* remote place

trasminar [A1] *vt/vi* to seep through
■ **trasminarse** *v pron* to seep through

trasnochada *f*: **pegarse una ~** (fam) (no acostarse) to be up all night; (acostarse de madrugada) to stay up until the early hours of the morning

trasnochado -da *adj* 1 ‹*chiste/noticia*› old, stale; ‹*idea/teoría*› outdated 2 ‹*persona*›: **está/anda ~** (no se acostó) he's been up all night; (se acostó de madrugada) he stayed up until the early hours of the morning

trasnochador -dora *adj*: **es muy ~** he's often out all night/until the early hours

trasnochar [A1] *vi* (no acostarse) to be up all night; (acostarse de madrugada): **ha trasnochado varias veces este mes** she's had several late nights this month
■ **trasnocharse** *v pron* (Col, Per, Ven) ▸**trasnochar**

trasnoche *m*: **de ~** late-night (*before n*)

traspapelar [A1] *vt* (extraviar) to mislay
■ **traspapelarse** *v pron* (extraviarse) to be/get mislaid

traspasar [A1] *vt*
A 1 «*bala/espada*» to pierce, go through; «*líquido*» to go through, soak through; **lo traspasó con la espada** he ran him through (with his sword); **unos pitidos que traspasan el oído** ear-piercing whistles; **su rostro afligido le**

traspasó el corazón her grief-stricken expression pierced him to the heart (liter) 2 (sobrepasar) to go beyond
B 1 ‹*bar/farmacia*› (vender) to sell; (arrendar) to let, lease; Ⓢ **se traspasa local** to let *o* for rent 2 ‹*negocio*› to transfer
C ‹*poderes/fondos*› to transfer
D (Dep) ‹*jugador*› to transfer, trade (AmE)

traspaso *m*
A 1 (de bar, farmacia — venta) sale; (— arrendamiento) leasing, letting; **el ~ del local** the transfer of the lease on the premises 2 (suma) premium
B (de poderes, fondos) transfer
C (Dep) 1 (de jugador) transfer 2 (suma) transfer fee

traspatio *m* (AmL) backyard

traspié *m*
A (tropezón) stumble; **dio un ~ y se cayó** she stumbled and fell
B (fam) (metedura de pata) blunder, slip-up (colloq)

trasplantable *adj* (Bot, Med) transplantable

trasplantar [A1] *vt* 1 (Bot, Med) to transplant 2 ‹*instituciones/costumbres*› to transfer

trasplante *m* (Bot, Med) transplant

trasponer [E22] *vt* (liter *o* period) ‹*límite*› to surpass; ‹*obstáculo*› to surmount; ‹*umbral*› to cross

traspontín *m*
A (asiento) tip-up *o* fold-down seat
B (fam) (trasero) seat (colloq), backside (colloq)

traspuesto -ta *adj* (fam) dazed; **quedarse ~** to go into a daze

traspunte *mf* (apuntador) prompter, prompt; (que da la entrada) callboy

trasquilador -dora *m,f* shearer, clipper

trasquilar [A1] *vt* 1 ‹*ovejas*› to shear, clip 2 (fam) ‹*pelo*› to hack ... about (colloq); ‹*persona*› to scalp (colloq)

trastabillar [A1] *vi* (dar tropezones) to stumble; (tartamudear) to stutter, stammer

trastabillón *m* stumble; **dio un ~ al subir la escalera** she tripped as she went up the stairs

trastada *f* 1 (fam) (mala pasada) dirty trick; **hacerle** *or* **jugarle una ~ a algn** to play a dirty trick on sb 2 (travesura) prank

trastazo *m* (fam) bump

traste *m*
A (Mús) fret
B (fam) (trasero) backside (colloq); ***dar al ~ con algo*** to put paid to sth; ***irse al ~*** «*plan/idea*» to fall through; «*esperanzas*» to be dashed
C (AmC, Méx) (utensilio) utensil; **lavar los ~s** to do the dishes *o* (BrE) the washing-up

trastear [A1] *vt*
A (revolver) to rummage through, rifle through (colloq)
B (Col) ‹*muebles/cajas*› to move ... around; ‹*oficina/casa*› to move
■ **trastear** *vi*
A (revolver) to rummage
B (Col) (en una mudanza) to move
■ **trastearse** *v pron* (Col) to move

trastero¹ -ra *adj*: **el cuarto ~** the junk *o* lumber room

trastero² *m* junk room, lumber room (AmE)

trastienda *f* back room (*of a shop*); ***tener mucha ~*** to be crafty

trasto *m*
A (fam) (cosa inservible) piece of junk (colloq); **tienen la casa llena de ~s** their house is full of junk; **el cuarto de los ~s** the junk room; ***tirarse los ~s a la cabeza*** (fam) to have a fight
B **trastos** *mpl* (Esp fam) (pertenencias): **mis/tus ~s** my/your stuff (colloq)

trastocar [A2] *vt* ‹*papeles/objetos*› to disarrange; ‹*planes*› to upset, disrupt
■ **trastocarse** *v pron* 1 «*folios/fichas*» to get out of order; «*planes*» to be ruined 2 (enloquecerse) to go out of one's mind

trastornado -da *adj*: **su muerte lo dejó ~** she was deeply disturbed *o* traumatized by his death; **~ por las drogas** drug-crazed

trastornar [A1] *vt*
A ‹*persona*› to disturb; **la muerte de su hijo la trastornó** her son's death left her deeply disturbed; **esa chica lo ha trastornado** (fam) he's lost his head over that girl (colloq)
B (alterar la normalidad) to upset, disrupt
■ **trastornarse** *v pron*
A «*persona*» to become disturbed
B «*planes*» to be upset

trastorno *m*
A (Med, Psic) disorder
(Compuestos)
• **trastorno afectivo estacional** seasonal affective disorder
• **trastorno biopolar** manic depression
• **trastorno por estrés postraumático** post-traumatic stress disorder
B (alteración de la normalidad) disruption; **los ~s provocados por el cambio** the upheavals *o* disruption caused by the change; **me ocasionó muchos ~s** it caused me a great deal of inconvenience

trastrocar [A9] *vt* to alter, change; **~ algo EN algo** to transform *o* change sth INTO sth
■ **trastrocarse** *v pron* 1 **se han trastrocado los papeles** their roles have been reversed 2 **~se EN algo** to be transformed INTO sth

trasuntar [A1] *vt* (frml) to reflect

trasunto *m* (frml) reflection

trasvasar [A1] *vt* 1 ‹*vino/aceite*› to decant 2 ‹*río/agua de río*› to divert 3 (Inf) to download

trasvase *m* 1 (de aceite, vino) decanting 2 (de río, de agua de río) diversion 3 (de divisas, población) transfer

trasvestismo *m* ▸**travestismo**

trata *f* trade
(Compuestos)
• **trata de blancas** white slavery
• **trata de esclavos** slave trade

tratable *adj* 1 ‹*persona*›: **es bastante ~** he's fairly easy to get on with 2 ‹*enfermedad*› treatable

tratadista *mf* writer (*of a treatise*)

tratado *m*
A (Der, Pol) treaty
(Compuestos)
• **tratado de libre comercio** free trade agreement
• **tratado de paz** peace treaty
B (libro) treatise

tratamiento *m*
A 1 (Med) treatment; **estoy en** *or* **bajo ~ médico** I am undergoing medical treatment 2 (de material, sustancia) treatment 3 (de tema) treatment; (de problema) handling; **le ha dado un ~ muy superficial al tema** he has dealt very superficially with the subject
(Compuestos)
• **tratamiento de datos/de la información** data processing
• **tratamiento de textos** text processing
B (comportamiento hacia alguien) treatment
C (título de cortesía) form of address; **le dieron el ~ de señoría** they addressed him as 'your Lordship'

tratante *mf* dealer, trader
(Compuestos)
• **tratante de blancas** white slaver
• **tratante de esclavos** slave dealer *o* trader

tratar [A1] *vi*
A (intentar) to try; **~ DE + INF** to try to + INF; **traten de no llegar tarde** try not to be late; **~ DE QUE + SUBJ**: **trata de que queden a la misma altura** try to get them level; **~é de que no vuelva a suceder** I'll try to make sure it doesn't happen again
B «*obra/libro/película*» **~ DE algo** to be ABOUT sth; **¿de qué trata el libro?** what's the book about?; **~ SOBRE algo** to deal WITH sth; **la conferencia ~á sobre medicina alternativa** the lecture will deal with alternative medicine
C (tener contacto, relaciones) **~ CON algn** to deal WITH sb; **~ con él no es nada fácil** he's not at all easy to get on with
D (Com) **~ EN algo** to deal IN sth
■ **tratar** *vt*
A 1 ‹*persona/animal/instrumento*› (+ *compl*) to treat; **me**

t

tratan muy bien they treat me very well; **trata la guitarra con más cuidado** be more careful with the guitar [2] (llamar) ~ **a algn DE algo** to call sb sth; ~ **a algn de usted/tú** *to address sb using the polite* **usted** *or the more familiar* **tú** *form*

B (frecuentar): **lo trataba cuando era joven** I saw quite a lot of him when I was young; **lo traté un par de veces** I met him a couple of times; **nunca lo he tratado** I have never actually spoken to him

C ‹*tema/asunto*› to deal with; **no podemos ~lo delante de ellos** we can't discuss this in front of them

D [1] ‹*paciente/enfermedad*› to treat [2] ‹*sustancia/metal*› to treat

■ **tratarse** *v pron*

A [1] **~se CON algn**: (ser amigo de) to be friendly WITH sb; (alternar) to socialize *o* mix WITH sb [2] (*recípr*): **somos parientes pero no nos tratamos** we're related but we are not in contact with each other

B (+ *compl*) [1] (*recípr*): **se tratan de usted/tú** they address each other as 'usted'/'tu'; **se tratan sin ningún respeto** they have *o* show no respect for each other [2] (*refl*) (cuidarse): **~se bien/mal** to look after oneself well/not to look after oneself

C (Med) to have *o* undergo treatment

D **tratarse de** (*en 3ª pers*) [1] (ser acerca de) to be about; **¿de qué se trata?** what's it about? [2] (ser cuestión de): **se trata de arreglar la situación, no de discutir** we're supposed to be settling things, not arguing; **si sólo se trata de eso ...** if that's all it is ...; **sólo porque se trata de ti** just because it's you

tratativas *fpl* (CS): **estar en ~ con algn** to be in negotiation with sb; **estar en ~s** to be negotiating *o* talking

trato *m*

A [1] (acuerdo) deal; **hacer/cerrar un ~** to make/finalize a deal; **¡~ hecho!** it's a deal! [2] **tratos** *mpl* (negociaciones): **estamos en ~s con otra compañía** we are talking to *o* negotiating with another company

B [1] (relación): **no tiene ~ (social) con los empleados** she doesn't socialize with her staff; **tengo poco ~ con ella** I don't really have much contact with her *o* much to do with her [2] (cualidad) manner: **tiene un ~ muy agradable** she has a very pleasant manner; [3] (manera de tratar) treatment; **le dan un ~ preferencial** they give him preferential treatment; **el ~ que les da a los juguetes** the way he treats his toys [4] *tb* **~ carnal** carnal knowledge

trauma *m* trauma

traumado -da *adj* traumatized

traumar [A1] *vt* to traumatize

traumático -ca *adj* traumatic

traumatismo *m* traumatism

traumatizado -da *adj* traumatized

traumatizar [A4] *vt* to traumatize

■ **traumatizarse** *v pron* (fam) to be traumatized

travelling /'traβelin/, **travelín** *m* (Cin, TV) tracking shot

través [1] **a través de** (*loc prep*) (de lado a lado) across; (por medio de) through; **pusieron barricadas a ~ de la calle** they erected barricades across the street; **se enteró a ~ de un amigo** she heard about it through a friend; **el agua pasa a ~ de un filtro** the water passes through a filter [2] **al través** (*loc adv*) ‹*cortar*› crossways, diagonally; **de través** (Méx) (*loc adv*) diagonally

travesaño *m* [1] (Const) crossbeam [2] (Dep) crossbar

travesear [A1] *vi* (fam) to kid *o* mess around (colloq)

travesía *f*

A (viaje) crossing

B (Esp) (callejuela) alleyway, side street

travesti, travestí *m* transvestite

travestido *m* transvestite, cross-dresser

travestismo *m* transvestism, cross-dressing

travesura *f* prank; **hacer ~s** to play pranks

travieso -sa *adj* naughty, mischievous

trayecto *m* [1] (viaje) journey; **cubrir el ~** to do the journey; **el tren cubría el ~ Madrid-Barcelona** the train was traveling between Madrid and Barcelona; **durmió durante todo el ~** he slept all the way [2] (ruta) route; **final de ~** end of the line [3] (trayectoria) trajectory, path

trayectoria *f* [1] (de proyectil, pelota) trajectory, path; **describir una ~** to describe a trajectory (frml) [2] (de persona, institución): **una brillante ~ profesional** a brilliant career; **tienen una amplia ~ en este campo** they have many years' experience in this field; **una larga ~ democrática** a long democratic tradition

trayendo *see* **traer**

traza *f*

A (de línea, etc) ▸ **trazado**

B [1] (aspecto) appearance; **un individuo de mala ~** a rough-looking individual [2] **trazas** *fpl* (indicios) signs (*pl*); **no había ~s de vida** these were no signs of life; **esto lleva** *or* **tiene ~s de ir para largo** this looks as if it's going to drag on and on; **tiene ~s de ser obra de Jaime** this has all the signs of being Jaime's handiwork

trazado *m* [1] (de línea, dibujo) drawing, tracing [2] (de carretera) route; (de ciudad) layout; **de ~ antiguo/moderno** of ancient/modern design [3] (de edificio) plan

trazador *m* tracer

trazar [A4] *vt*

A [1] ‹*línea*› to trace, draw; ‹*plano*› to draw ‹*ruta*› to plot; **~ el contorno de algo** to outline sth [2] (Arquit) ‹*puente/edificio*› to design

B [1] ‹*plan/proyecto/estrategia*› to draw up, devise [2] (describir) to draw; **~ un paralelo entre los dos casos** to draw a parallel between the two cases; **trazó una semblanza de la vida y obra del artista** he drew *o* sketched a picture of the life and work of the artist

■ **trazarse** *v pron* (*refl*) (frml) ‹*meta*› to set oneself

trazo *m* stroke; **está descrito con ~ magistral** it's described with a masterful touch; **escribe con ~ firme y seguro** she writes with a steady and sure hand

trébol *m*

A (Bot) clover

B (Transp) cloverleaf

C (Jueg) [1] (carta) club [2] **tréboles** *mpl* (palo) clubs (*pl*)

trece¹ *adj inv/pron* thirteen; *para ejemplos ver* **cinco**; ***mantenerse/seguir en sus ~*** to stand one's ground

trece² *m* (number) thirteen

treceavo¹ -va *adj/pron* [1] (partitivo): **la treceava parte** a thirteenth [2] (crit) (ordinal) thirteenth; *para ejemplos ver* **veinteavo**

treceavo² *m* thirteenth

trecho *m* [1] (tramo) stretch; **su carrera ha tenido ~s difíciles** her career has been through difficult periods; **a ~s** here and there; ***de ~ en ~*** every so often, at intervals [2] (distancia) distance; **aún nos queda un buen ~** we still have a good distance *o* a fair way to go; **eres joven y aún te queda un ~ por recorrer** you're still young and you have a lot of years ahead of you

tregua *f* [1] (Mil) truce; **acordar una ~** to agree to a truce [2] (interrupción): **sin ~** relentlessly; ***no dar ~***: **el dolor no le daba ~** the pain didn't let up for a moment; **los niños no le dan ~** she doesn't get a moment's rest with the children

treinta¹ *adj inv/pron* thirty; *para ejemplos ver* **cinco, cincuenta**

treinta² *m* (number) thirty

treintavo¹ -va *adj/pron* [1] (partitivo): **la treintava parte** a thirtieth [2] (crit) (ordinal) thirtieth; *para ejemplos ver* **veinteavo**

treintavo² *m* thirtieth

treintena *f*: **una ~ de personas** about 30 people; **ya entró en la ~** she's already turned 30

tremebundo -da *adj* ‹*insulto/cólera*› terrible; ‹*grito*› terrifying, fearful

tremenda *f*: **tomarse algo a la ~** (fam) to take sth to heart

tremendo -da *adj*

A (terrible) terrible, dreadful; **se hallan en una situación tremenda** they're in a terrible *o* dreadful situation; **la película tiene unas escenas tremendas** the film has some horrific scenes; **tiene (un) tremendo chichón** (AmL) he has a huge *o* massive *o* terrible bump on his head; **me dio (una) tremenda patada** (AmL) he kicked me really hard

B (fam) (travieso) terrible, naughty; (desobediente) disobedient, terrible

tremolar [A1] *vi* (liter) to flutter

tremolina *f* (fam) rumpus, commotion; **se armó una ~ ...** there was a terrible rumpus *o* commotion

trémulo -la *adj* (liter) ‹*manos*› trembling; ‹*voz*› tremulous; ‹*llama/luz*› flickering; **trémula de gozo** (liter) trembling with pleasure

tren *m*

A (Ferr) train; **tomar** *or* (esp Esp) **coger el ~** to take *o* catch the train; **ir en ~** to go by train; **cambiar de ~** to change trains; ***estar como un ~*** (Esp fam) to be gorgeous (colloq), to be hot stuff (colloq); ***perder el ~*** (refiriéndose a oportunidad) to miss the boat; ***subirse al ~ de algo***: **quieren subirse al ~ de las nuevas tecnologías** they want to jump on the new technology bandwagon; **¡hay que subirse al ~ del progreso!** we must keep up with the times

(Compuestos)

- **tren correo** *or* **postal** mail train
- **tren de alta velocidad** high-speed train
- **tren de carga** *or* **de mercancías** freight train, goods train (BrE)
- **tren de cercanías** local *o* suburban train
- **tren (de) cremallera** rack *o* cog railway
- **tren directo/de largo recorrido** through/long-distance train
- **tren expreso** *or* **rápido** express train

B (fam) (ritmo) rate; **a este ~** at this rate (colloq); **~ de vida** lifestyle; ***a todo ~*** (fam): **vivir a todo ~** to have a luxurious lifestyle; **una boda a todo ~** a lavish wedding; **lo hicimos a todo ~** we did it at top speed; ***estar en ~ de hacer algo*** (CS) to be in the process of doing sth

C (conjunto) assembly

(Compuestos)

- **tren de aterrizaje** undercarriage, landing gear
- **tren de lavado** carwash
- **tren de montaje** assembly line
- **tren nocturno** night train

trenazo *m* (Méx) train crash

trenca *f* (Esp) duffle *o* duffel coat

trenza *f* (de cintas, fibras) plait; (de pelo) braid (AmE), plait (BrE)

trenzado *m* (de cuerdas, fibras) plaiting; (de pelo) braiding (AmE), plaiting (BrE)

trenzar [A4] *vt* ‹*cuerdas/fibras*› to plait; ‹*pelo*› to braid (AmE), to plait (BrE)

■ **trenzarse** *v pron*

A (*refl*) ‹*pelo*› to braid (AmE), to plait (BrE)

B 1 (AmL) (enzarzarse) **~se EN algo** to get involved IN sth 2 (RPl fam) (pelearse) «*persona*» to get into a fight

trepada *f* climb

trepador[1] -dora *adj* 1 ‹*planta*› climbing (*before n*): **rosal ~** rambling rose 2 (Col, CS, Ven): **es ambicioso y ~** he's an ambitious social climber

trepador[2] -dora *m,f*

A (Col, CS, Ven) social climber

B **trepadora** *f* 1 (Bot) climber 2 (Zool) nuthatch

trepadores *mpl* climbing irons (*pl*), crampons (*pl*)

trepar [A1] *vi* to climb; **~ a un árbol** to climb (up) a tree; **~ a la cima de una montaña** to climb to the top of a mountain; **~ por la escala social** to climb (up) the social ladder

■ **trepar** *vt* (fam): **el equipo ha trepado varios puestos** the team has gone up *o* climbed several places

■ **treparse** *v pron* **~se A algo** ‹*a árbol*› to climb sth; ‹*a silla*› to climb ONTO sth

trepidación *f* vibration

trepidante *adj* ‹*ritmo*› fast; **un partido ~ de emoción** a furiously-paced game

trepidar [A1] *vi*

A «*suelo/máquina*» to vibrate

B (Chi) (dudar, vacilar) to hesitate; **sin ~** without hesitation

tres[1] *adj inv/pron* three; *para ejemplos ver* **cinco**; ***ni a la de ~*** (Esp fam): **no lo termino ni a la de ~** there's no way I can finish this; **no me salía ni a la de ~** I just couldn't work it out

tres[2] *m* (number) three; *para ejemplos ver* **cinco**

(Compuestos)

- **tres cuartos** *m,f* (en rugby) three-quarter
- **tres en raya** *or* (Col) **en línea** tic-tac-toe (AmE), noughts and crosses (BrE)

trescientos -tas *adj/pron* three hundred; *para ejemplos ver* **quinientos**

tresillo *m*

A (Esp) (sofá) three-seater sofa; (juego de muebles) suite

B (Jueg) ombre

C (Mús) triplet

treta *f* 1 (ardid) trick, ruse; **se valió de una ~ para convencernos** she tricked us into believing her 2 (en esgrima) feint

tríada *f* triad

trial /'trial/ *m* motocross

triangular *adj* triangular

triángulo *m*

A (Mat) triangle

(Compuesto) **triángulo rectángulo** right-angled triangle

B 1 (en relaciones amorosas) (love) triangle 2 (Mús) triangle 3 (Auto) *tb* **~ reflectante** advance-warning triangle

tribal *adj* tribal

tribu *f* tribe

tribulaciones *fpl* tribulations (*pl*)

tribuna *f* 1 (para orador) platform, rostrum 2 (para autoridades) platform; (para espectadores) grandstand, stand; **la ~ de la prensa** the press box 3 (de iglesia) gallery

(Compuesto) **tribuna pública** public gallery

tribunal *m*

A (Der) 1 (lugar) court; (jueces) judges (*pl*); **comparecer ante un ~** to appear in court 2 **tribunales** *mpl* (justicia): **acudir/recurrir a los ~es** to go to court

(Compuestos)

- **tribunal constitucional** constitutional court
- **tribunal de apelación** court of appeals (AmE), court of appeal (BrE)
- **tribunal militar** court martial, military court
- **tribunal supremo** ≈ supreme court (*in US*), ≈ high court (*in UK*)
- **tribunal (tutelar) de menores** juvenile court

B (en examen) examining board; (en concurso) panel of judges

tribuno *m*: *tb* **~ de la plebe** tribune

tributación *f* (acción) payment; (impuesto) taxation; (régimen) tax system

tributar [A1] *vt*

A 1 (Fisco) to pay 2 (rendir, ofrecer) ‹*sacrificio*› to offer (up); **~ un homenaje a algn** to pay tribute to sb

B ‹*afecto/respeto*› to profess, show

■ **tributar** *vi* to pay taxes

tributario[1] -ria *adj*

A (Fisco) tax (*before n*); **el sistema ~** the tax system

B ‹*río*› tributary (*before n*)

tributario[2] *m* tributary

tributo *m* 1 (Fisco) tax 2 (Hist) tribute 3 (ofrenda, homenaje) tribute; **rendirle ~ a algn/algo** to pay tribute to sb/sth 4 (precio) price

tricampeón -peona *m,f* triple champion

tricentenario *m* tricentenary, tricentennial

triciclo *m* tricycle

tricolor[1] *adj* tricolored•, tricolor• (*before n*)

tricolor[2] *f or m* tricolor•

tricornio *m* (Indum) tricorn

tricota *f* (RPl) (abierta) cardigan; (cerrada) sweater

tricotar [A1] *vt* (Esp) to knit

tridente *m* trident

tridimensional *adj* three-dimensional

trienal *adj* triennial

trienio *m* (período) three-year period; (bonificación) three-yearly *o* three-year increment

trifásico -ca *adj* three-phase

trifulca *f* (fam) rumpus, commotion

trifurcación *f* trifurcation

trifurcarse [A2] *v pron* to branch into three

trigal *m* wheat field

trigésimo -ma *adj* thirtieth

trigo *m* wheat; ***no es/son ~ limpio*** he's/they're not totally trustworthy

trigonometría *f* trigonometry

trigueño -ña *adj* ‹*pelo*› light brown; ‹*persona*› dark; **una niña de tez trigueña** an olive-skinned girl

t

triguero -ra *adj* ‹*tierras*› wheat-producing; ‹*producción*› wheat (*before n*)
trilingüe *adj* trilingual
trilla *f* (acción) threshing; (temporada) threshing season
trillado -da *adj* hackneyed, trite
trilladora *f* threshing machine
trillar [A1] *vt* to thresh
trillizo -za *m,f* triplet
trillo *m* thresher
trillón *m* quintillion (AmE), trillion (BrE)
trilogía *f* trilogy
trimestral *adj* ‹*publicación/pago*› quarterly; **examen ~** end-of-semester examination (AmE), end-of-term examination (BrE)
trimestralmente *adv* every three months
trimestre *m* 1 quarter, three-month period; **pago por ~s** I pay quarterly *o* every three months 2 (Educ) term, ≈ semester (*in US*)
trinar [A1] *vi* «*pájaro*» to sing; ***estar que trina*** (fam) to be seething (colloq)
trinca *f* (de objetos) trio; (de personas) trio, threesome
trincar [A2] *vt* 1 (Esp fam) (agarrar) to pick up, nab (colloq); (inmovilizar) to hold 2 (Col fam) (inmovilizar) to hold 3 (Méx fam) (estafar) to swindle
trinchante *m* (Coc) (cuchillo) carving knife; (tenedor) carving fork
trinchar [A1] *vt* to carve
trinche *m* (Méx fam) fork
trinchera *f* 1 (Mil) trench; **guerra de ~s** trench warfare 2 (Indum) trench coat
trineo *m* 1 (Dep, Jueg) sled (AmE), sledge (BrE) 2 (tirado por perros, caballos) sleigh
trinidad *f* trinity; **La T~** (Relig) the Trinity
trino *m* 1 (de pájaro) trill 2 (Mús) trill
trinomio *m* trinomial
trinquete *m*
A (palanca) pawl; (mecanismo) ratchet
B (Méx fam) (trampa, engaño) swindle; **hubo ~ en la pelea** the fight was rigged; **hace ~ en las cartas** she cheats at cards
trinquetear [A1] *vt* (Méx fam) to rig
trío *m* 1 (Mús) (composición) trio; (conjunto) trio 2 (fam) (de personas) trio, threesome
trip *m* (arg) (dosis) fix; (alucinación) trip
tripa *f*
A 1 *tb* **tripas** *fpl* (intestino) intestine, gut; (vísceras) (fam) innards (*pl*) (colloq); **se me revuelven las ~s sólo de verlo** just looking at it turns my stomach; ***echar las ~s*** (fam) (esforzarse) to work one's butt off (AmE colloq), to bust a gut (BrE sl); (vomitar) to throw up (colloq); ***hacer de ~s corazón*** to pluck up courage 2 (material) gut; **cuerda de ~** catgut
B (Esp fam) (barriga) belly (colloq); **tener/echar ~** to have/get a bit of a paunch *o* (colloq) belly
tripería *f: market stall or store selling offal*
triplano *m* triplane
triple¹ *adj* triple
triple² *m*
A (Mat): **el precio aumentó al ~** the price tripled *o* trebled; **tardó el ~** it took him three times as long; **el ~ de tres es nueve** three times three equals nine; **es el ~ de grande que el nuestro** it's three times the size of ours
B (Elec) three-way adapter *o* adaptor
C (en béisbol) three-base hit; **pegó un ~** he hit a triple
triple³ *f* triple vaccine
triplicación *f* triplication, trebling
triplicado: **por ~** (*loc adv*) in triplicate
triplicar [A2] *vt* ‹*capacidad/precio/ventas*› to treble; ‹*longitud/cifra*› to triple; **nos triplicaban en número** they outnumbered us by three to one
■ **triplicarse** *v pron* to treble, triple
trípode *m* tripod
tripón¹ -pona *adj* (fam) pudgy (AmE); podgy (BrE colloq)
tripón² -pona *m,f* 1 (fam) (persona) fatty (colloq) 2 **tripón** *m* (fam) (tripa grande) potbelly, (big) belly

tríptico *m* (Art) triptych
triptongo *m* triphthong
tripulación *f* crew
tripulado -da *adj* ‹*velero/barco*› crewed; ‹*avión*› manned
tripulante *mf* crew member; **los ~s** the crew
tripular [A1] *vt* to crew, man
triquiñuela *f* (fam) trick, dodge (colloq); **saberse las ~s del oficio** to know the tricks of the trade; **conseguir algo por medio de ~s** to obtain something through trickery
triquitraque *m*
A (fam) (ruido) clatter
B (en pirotecnia) firecracker
tris *m*: ***estar en un ~ de algo*** to be within a hair's breadth of sth; **estuve en un ~ de perder el empleo** I came very close to losing my job
triscar [A2] *vi* «*cabra/cordero*» to gambol, frolic; «*persona*» to romp, frolic
trisílabo -ba *adj* trisyllabic
triste *adj*
A 1 [ESTAR] (afligido) ‹*persona*› sad; **esa música me pone ~** that music makes me sad; **se puso muy ~ cuando se lo dije** he was very sad *o* unhappy when I told him 2 ‹*expresión/mirada*› sad, sorrowful 3 [SER] (que causa tristeza) ‹*historia/película/noticia*› sad; ‹*paisaje/color*› dismal, gloomy; ‹*lugar/ambiente*› gloomy; **un día nublado y ~** a miserable, cloudy day
B (*delante del n*) (miserable, insignificante) miserable; **es la ~ realidad** it's the sad truth; **hizo un ~ papel** he performed poorly
tristemente *adv* sadly
tristeza *f* sadness, sorrow; **qué ~ que haya terminado** how sad it's all over; **sólo me ha dado ~** he's given me nothing but heartache; **hemos compartido alegrías y ~s** we've shared good times and bad
tris tras *m*
A (ruido de las tijeras) snip snip
B (momentito) flash (colloq); **en un ~ ~** in no time
trituración *f* (al moler) crushing, grinding; (al mascar) chewing
triturador¹ -dora *adj* crushing, grinding (*before n*)
triturador² *m*: **~ de basura** garbage disposal unit (AmE), waste disposal unit (BrE); **~ de ajos** garlic press
trituradora *f* crushing machine, crusher
triturar [A1] *vt* 1 ‹*almendras/ajo*› to crush; ‹*minerales*› to grind, crush; **la crítica lo trituró** the critics tore him to shreds (colloq) 2 (mascar) to chew
triunfador¹ -dora *adj* ‹*ejército*› triumphant; ‹*equipo*› winning (*before n*), triumphant
triunfador² -dora *m,f* winner
triunfal *adj* ‹*marcha/arco*› triumphal; ‹*gesto/sonrisa/entrada*› triumphant
triunfalismo *m* triumphalism
triunfalista *adj* triumphalist
triunfante *adj* triumphant; **salir ~** to emerge triumphant
triunfar [A1] *vi* 1 (derrotar, ganar) **~ SOBRE algo/algn** to triumph OVER sth/sb; **~ EN algo**: **triunfó en el concurso** she won the competition; **México triunfó en los campeonatos** Mexico triumphed in the championships 2 (tener éxito) to succeed, be successful 3 «*justicia/verdad/razón*» (prevalecer) to prevail, win out (AmE) *o* (BrE) through 4 (en naipes): **triunfan picas** spades are trumps
triunfo *m*
A 1 (victoria) victory; **el ~ del equipo irlandés** the Irish team's victory; ***costar un ~*** (fam): **me costó un ~ llegar** I had terrible trouble getting there (colloq); **costó un ~ convencerlo** it was very difficult convincing him 2 (éxito): **sus muchos ~s discográficos** his many hits *o* chart successes; **clasificarme ya es todo un ~** just qualifying is a triumph in itself
B (en naipes) trump; **palo del ~** trumps (*pl*)
triunvirato *m* triumvirate
trivalente *f* (vacuna) triple vaccine
trivial *adj* trivial

t

trivialidad *f* 1 (cualidad) triviality 2 (dicho) trivial *o* trite remark; (cosa) triviality; **hablamos de ~es** we just made small talk

trivializar [A4] *vt* ‹asunto› to trivialize; ‹éxito› to play down

trizarse [A4] *v pron* (Chi) (rajarse) «anteojos/vaso» to crack; «diente» to chip

trizas *fpl*: **hacer ~ algo/a algn** to tear sth/sb to shreds; **el jarrón se cayó y se hizo ~** the vase fell and smashed (to bits *o* smithereens); **tengo los nervios hechos ~** my nerves are in shreds *o* tatters

trocar [A9] *vt* 1 (liter) (convertir) **~ algo EN algo** to turn sth INTO sth 2 (Com) to barter, trade

■ **trocarse** *v pron* (liter): **su amor se trocó en odio** his love turned to hatred

trocha *f*

A (sendero) path; **abrieron ~** they blazed a trail, they led the way

B (AmL) (Ferr) gauge

troche (fam): **a ~ y moche**: **gastar a ~ y moche** to spend like there's no tomorrow (colloq); **repartió golpes a ~ y moche** he lashed out left and right (AmE), he lashed out left, right and centre (BrE)

trofeo *m* 1 (premio) trophy 2 (Taur) *the ears and/or tail, awarded to a successful bullfighter* 3 (Arm) panoply

troglodita *mf* 1 (cavernícola) troglodyte 2 (fam) (bruto) lout

trola *f* (Esp fam) lie, whopper (colloq)

trole *m* (varilla) trolley; (trolebús) (fam) trolleybus

trolebús *m* trolleybus

trolero¹ -ra *adj* (Esp fam) lying (*before n*)

trolero² -ra *m,f* (Esp fam) liar, fibber (colloq)

trolley *m* (AmL) trolleybus

tromba *f* (terrestre) whirlwind, tornado; (marina) waterspout; **en ~** ‹entrar/salir› en masse; **entraron en la discoteca en ~** they poured *o* flooded into the discotheque (en masse); **los Saints se lanzaron en ~** the Saints stormed forward

(Compuesto) **tromba de agua** downpour

trombón *m*

A (instrumento) trombone

B **trombón** *mf* (músico) trombonist

trombonista *mf* trombonist

trombosis *f* thrombosis

(Compuesto) **trombosis venosa profunda** deep vein thrombosis

trompa *f*

A 1 (de elefante) trunk; (de insecto) proboscis 2 (Esp fam) (nariz) nose, conk (BrE colloq)

B (Mús) 1 (instrumento) horn 2 **trompa** *mf* (persona) hornplayer

(Compuesto) **trompa de caza** hunting horn

C (Esp fam) (borrachera): **coger una ~** to get plastered

D 1 (AmL fam) (boca) lips (*pl*), mouth; **¡qué ~ tiene ese tipo!** that guy has such thick lips! 2 (AmS fam) (gesto, expresión): **andar con ~** to go around with a long face; **no pongas esa ~** stop looking so miserable *o* grumpy (colloq)

trompada *f* (AmS fam) (puñetazo) punch; **agarrarse a ~s** to come to blows; **darle** *or* **pegarle una ~ a algn** to punch sb

trompazo *m* (fam): **me di un ~ con la puerta** I walked (*o* ran *etc*) smack into the door (colloq); **darle un ~ a algn** to punch sb

trompear [A1] *vt* (AmL fam) to thump (colloq), to punch

■ **trompearse** *v pron* (*recípr*) to have a fight

trompeta *f* 1 (instrumento) trumpet 2 **trompeta** *mf* (persona) trumpet player; (Mil) trumpeter

trompetilla *f* (Med) ear trumpet

trompetista *mf* trumpet player

trompicar [A2] *vi* to stumble

trompicón *m*: **iba dando trompicones** he was staggering; **a trompicones** in fits and starts

trompo *m* 1 (Jueg) (spinning) top 2 (Auto) spin; ***bailar como un ~*** (AmL fam) to dance very well

trompudo -da *adj* (AmL fam) (de labios gruesos) thick-lipped

trona *f* (Esp) high chair

tronado -da *adj* 1 (fam) (loco) crazy (colloq) 2 ‹*vestido/zapatos*› worn-out

tronador -dora *adj* ‹cañón› thundering; ‹cohete› cracking, banging

tronar [A10] *v impers* to thunder

■ **tronar** *vi*

A «cañones» to thunder; «voz/persona» to thunder, roar; **salió tronando de la reunión** he was seething when he came out of the meeting; ***por lo que pueda ~*** (fam) just in case

B (Méx fam) 1 (en relación) to split up (colloq) 2 (fracasar) to flop (colloq); (en examen) to fail

■ **tronar** *vt*

A (AmC, Méx fam) (fusilar) to shoot

B (Méx fam) ‹examen/alumno› to fail, flunk (AmE colloq)

troncal *adj* ‹carretera/línea› main (*before n*)

tronchante *adj* (Esp fam) hilarious

tronchar [A1] *vt* 1 ‹tallo/rama› to snap 2 (truncar) ‹*vida/relación*› to cut short; ‹esperanza/ilusión› to shatter

■ **troncharse** *v pron* 1 «tallo/rama» to break *o* snap off 2 ‹muñeca/tobillo› to sprain, twist; ***~se de (la) risa*** (Esp fam) to die laughing (colloq)

tronco *m*

A 1 (Bot) trunk 2 (leño) log; ***dormir como un ~*** to sleep like a log; ***estar como un ~*** to be dead to the world (colloq) 3 (Coc): **~ de Navidad** chocolate yule log

B (en genealogía) stock

C (Ling) branch

D (Anat) trunk, torso

E (Andes, RPl fam) (persona inepta): **es un ~** he's useless; (colloq); **es un ~ para los idiomas** he's hopeless at languages

tronera *f* 1 (Mil) (en fortificación) embrasure, porthole; (en barco) gun port 2 (en billar) pocket 3 (Col, Ven) (agujero) hole

tronío *m* extravagance

trono *m* 1 (de monarca) throne; **subir al ~** to come to *o* (frml) ascend the throne 2 (Dep period) crown

tropa *f*

A (Mil) 1 (soldados rasos): **la ~** the troops (*pl*) 2 **tropas** *fpl* (ejército, soldados) troops

(Compuesto) **tropa de asalto** assault troops (*pl*)

B (fam) (muchedumbre) horde

tropel *m* 1 (de personas) mob; **entraron al estadio en ~** they poured into the stadium 2 (de cosas) jumble; **un ~ de ideas revueltas** a mass of confused ideas

tropezar [A6] *vi* 1 (al caminar, correr) to stumble, trip; **~ CON algo** ‹con piedra/escalón› to trip OVER sth; ‹*con árbol/muro*› to walk (*o* run *etc*) INTO sth 2 (encontrarse) **~ CON algo** ‹con dificultad/problema› to come up AGAINST sth; **~ CON algn** to run *o* bump INTO sb (colloq)

■ **tropezarse** *v pron* (encontrarse) **~se CON algn** to run *o* bump INTO sb (colloq)

tropezón *m* 1 (acción de tropezar) stumble; **dio un ~ y cayó** he stumbled and fell; **a tropezones** (fam) in fits and starts 2 (equivocación) mistake, slip

tropical *adj* tropical

trópico *m* tropic

(Compuesto) **trópico de Cáncer/de Capricornio** tropic of Cancer/of Capricorn

tropiece, tropieces, etc *see* **tropezar**

tropieza, tropiezas, etc *see* **tropezar**

tropiezo *m* (contratiempo) setback, hitch; (equivocación) mistake, slip

tropo *m* trope

trotacalles *mf* (*pl* ~) (fam & pey) bum (AmE colloq & pej), layabout (BrE pej)

trotamundos *mf* (*pl* ~) globetrotter

trotar [A1] *vi* 1 «caballo/jinete» to trot 2 (fam) (ir de un lado a otro) to rush around 3 (CS, Méx) (como ejercicio) to jog

trote *m*

A (Equ) trot; **al ~** (Equ) at a trot; **terminó el trabajo al ~** (fam) he finished the job in double-quick time (colloq); **se marchó al ~** (fam) she rushed off

B 1 (fam) (ajetreo): **¡que ~ he tenido hoy!** I've been rushing around like crazy *o* mad today (colloq); **esta semana me**

t

espera un ~ bárbaro this week is going to be really hectic; ***no estar para esos/estos ~s***: **ya no estoy para esos ~s** I'm not up to that sort of thing any more 2 (fam) (uso): **este vestido tiene bastante ~** this dress has seen a lot of service; **zapatos de** *or* **para mucho ~** shoes which will stand up to a lot of wear and tear

troupe /trup/ *f* (Espec) troupe; (pandilla) (fam) gang (colloq)

trova *f* 1 (verso, poesía) poem (*composed by medieval poet or minstrel*) 2 (canción) ballad (*composed and sung by medieval minstrel*)

trovador *m* troubadour, minstrel

Troya *f* Troy; **el caballo/la guerra de ~** the Trojan Horse/War; ***allí fue ~*** there was a hell of a fuss!; ***arda ~*** to hell with the consequences!

trozar [A4] *vt* (AmL) to cut … into pieces, cut up

trozo *m* 1 (de pan, pastel) piece, bit, slice; (de madera, papel, tela) piece, bit; (de vidrio, cerámica) piece, fragment; **cortar la zanahoria en trocitos** dice the carrot 2 (Lit, Mús) passage

trucaje *m* 1 (en un juego) fixing, rigging 2 (Fot) trick photography

trucar [A2] *vt* 1 ‹*dados/juego/elecciones*› to fix, rig 2 ‹*fotografía*› to touch up

trucha¹ *f* (Coc, Zool) trout

Compuesto **trucha arco iris** rainbow trout

trucha² *adj* (Méx fam) smart (colloq); **ponte ~** watch out, keep on your toes

truco *m* trick; **debe de haber algún ~** there must be a catch; **el ~ está en...** the trick *o* secret is…; **pillarle el ~ a algo** to get the hang of sth

truculencia *f* gruesomeness, horror

truculento -ta *adj* horrifying, gruesome

trueno *m* 1 (Meteo) thunderclap, clap of thunder; **~s** thunder 2 (de cañones) thunder

trueque *m* (cambio) barter; **el ~ de maíz por frijoles** the bartering *o* exchange of corn for beans

trufa *f* truffle

trufar [A1] *vt* to stuff … with truffles

truhán¹ -hana *adj* (arc) knavish (arch)

truhán² *m* (arc) knave (arch)

trullo *m*

A (Zool) teal

B (Vin) winepress

truncado -da *adj* truncated

truncar [A2] *vt* 1 ‹*frase/discurso/texto*› to cut short 2 ‹*vida*› to cut short; ‹*planes*› to frustrate, thwart; ‹*ilusiones*› to shatter

trunco -ca *adj* truncated, incomplete

trusa *f* 1 (RPl) (faja) girdle 2 (Per) (calzoncillos) underpants (*pl*)

TSE *f* (= **Tarjeta Sanitaria Europea**) EHIC

tu *adj* (*delante del n*) your; **~s amigos** your friends

tú *pron pers* [*familiar form of address*]

A 1 (como sujeto) you; **¿quién lo va a hacer? — tú** who's going to do it? — you are; **tratar de ~ a algn** *to address sb using the familiar* **tú** *form* 2 (en comparaciones, con ciertas preposiciones) you; **llegó después que ~** he arrived after you (did); **es tan capaz como ~** he's as capable as you (are); **entre ~ y yo** between you and me; **según ~** according to you

B (uno) you; **te dan varias opciones y ~ eliges una** you're given several options and you choose one

tuba *f* tuba

tubazo *m* (Ven Dep) scoop

tubei *m* (Ven Dep) double

tuberculina *f* tuberculin

tubérculo *m* (Bot) tuber; (Anat, Med) tubercule

tuberculosis *f* tuberculosis

tuberculoso¹ -sa *adj* tubercular

tuberculoso² -sa *m,f* tuberculosis sufferer (patient *etc*)

tubería *f* (cañería) pipe; (conjunto de tubos) piping, pipes (*pl*)

tubo *m*

A 1 (cilindro hueco) tube; ***como por un ~*** (AmL fam): **pasó la prueba como por un ~** he sailed *o* waltzed through the test (colloq); **fue como por un ~** it was dead easy *o* a cinch (colloq); ***por un ~*** (Esp fam): **sabe inglés por un ~** he speaks really good English; **había gente por un ~** there were loads of people 2 (del órgano) pipe

Compuestos

- **tubo capilar** capillary
- **tubo de escape** exhaust (pipe)
- **tubo digestivo** alimentary canal

B (Elec, Fís) tube

Compuestos

- **tubo de imagen** picture tube
- **tubo fluorescente** fluorescent tube

C (RPl) (del teléfono) receiver

D (Chi, Méx) (para el pelo) roller, curler

tubular *adj* tubular

tuco *m* (Per, RPl) (Coc) tomato sauce

tudesco -ca *adj/m,f* (fam) German

tuerca *f* nut; ***apretarle a algn las ~s*** (fam) to clamp down on sb (colloq)

Compuesto **tuerca mariposa** wingnut

tuerce, tuerces, etc *see* **torcer**

tuerto¹ -ta *adj* one-eyed; **es ~** (sin un ojo) he only has one eye; (ciego de un ojo) he's blind in one eye

tuerto² -ta *m,f*: *person blind in one eye or with only one eye*

tuerza, tuerzas, etc *see* **torcer**

tueste *m* (de pan) toasting; (de café) roasting

tuétano *m* marrow; ***estar mojado hasta el ~*** *or* ***los ~s*** to be soaked to the skin; ***hasta el ~*** *or* ***los ~s***: through and through; **estaba enamorado hasta el ~ de ella** he was head over heels in love with her

tufarada *f* (fam) nasty smell, whiff (colloq); **una ~ nauseabunda** a nauseating stench

tufo *m* 1 (fam) (olor — a sucio, podrido) stink (colloq); (— a cerrado): **aquí dentro hay un ~ horrible** it smells really stuffy in here; **llegó con un ~ a vino tremendo** he arrived reeking of wine (colloq) 2 (fam) (gas, humo) fumes (*pl*)

tugurio *m* 1 (vivienda) hovel; (bar) dive 2 **tugurios** *mpl* (barrio pobre) slums (*pl*)

tul *m* tulle

tulipa *f* lampshade

tulipán *m* tulip

tullido¹ -da *adj* crippled

tullido² -da *m,f* cripple

tumba *f* (excavada) grave; (construida) tomb; **estos niños me van a llevar a la ~** (fam & hum) these kids will be the death of me (colloq & hum); ***ser (como) una ~*** (fam) to be the soul of discretion

tumbaburros *m* (*pl* ~) (Méx fam) dictionary

tumbar [A1] *vt*

A 1 (derribar) to knock down; **lo tumbó al suelo de un golpe** he punched him to the floor; **un olor que te tumbaba** a smell that was enough to knock you out 2 (AmL) ‹*árbol*› to fell, cut down; ‹*muro/casa*› to knock down

B (Esp arg) (en un examen) to fail, flunk (AmE colloq)

C (Col fam) 1 (matar) to bump off (colloq) 2 (timar) to rip … off (colloq); **me tumbó las vueltas** he shortchanged me

■ **tumbarse** *v pron* to lie down

tumbo *m*

A (vaivén): **salió del bar dando ~s** he staggered out of the bar; **el coche no paraba de dar ~** the car was constantly jolting *o* bumping around; ***a (los) ~s*** with great difficulty

B (Bol) (fruta) passion fruit

tumbona *f* (Esp) sun lounger, deck chair

tumefacción *f* tumefaction, swelling

tumefacto -ta *adj* tumescent, swollen

tumido, túmido *adj* tumid, swollen

tumor *m* tumor*

tumoral *adj* tumoral, tumorous

túmulo *m* (sepultura elevada) burial mound; (catafalco) catafalque

tumulto *m* (multitud) crowd; (alboroto) commotion; **la policía sofocó los ~s** the police quelled the disturbances

tumultuoso -sa *adj* tumultuous

tuna *f*

A (Bot, Coc) (planta, fruto) prickly pear

B (Mús) tuna (*musical group made up of university students*)

tuna

A *tuna*, also called an *estudiantina*, is a group of strolling student players. They play in bars and restaurants, or at parties and weddings. *Tunas* are one of the most deeply rooted traditions at Spanish universities dating from the seventeenth or eighteenth centuries. *Tunas* wear black velvet costumes, with doublets and capes. The instruments played are the lute, the guitar, the violin, and the tambourine. *Tunos* wear ribbons on their capes, showing the faculties that they belong to

tunda *f* (fam) thrashing (colloq)

tundir [I1] *vt* 1 ‹*pieles*› to shear, clip 2 (golpear): **~ a algn** to give sb a thrashing (colloq)

tundra *f* tundra

tunecino -na *adj/m,f* Tunisian

túnel *m* tunnel; ***hacerle el ~ a algn*** (Dep) to thread the ball through sb's legs

Compuestos

- **túnel de lavado** car wash
- **túnel del tiempo** time tunnel

Túnez *m* (país) Tunisia; (ciudad) Tunis

túnica *f* (Hist) tunic; (Relig) robe

tuno -na *m,f*

A (Esp fam) (bribón) rascal (colloq)

B **tuno** *m* (Mús) *member of a* **tuna B**

tuntún *m* (fam): **al ~** ‹*elegir*› at random; **contestó al ~** he just said the first thing that came into his head

tupamaro -ra *adj/m,f* Tupamaro

tupé *m*

A (fam) (descaro) nerve

B (Esp) (peluquín) toupee; (mechón de pelo) forelock

tupido¹ -da *adj*

A ‹*follaje/vegetación*› dense; ‹*tela*› closely-woven; ‹*cejas*› bushy; ‹*niebla*› thick

B (Col, RPl) (tapado) ‹*cañería*› blocked; ‹*nariz*› blocked

tupido² *adv* (Méx) intensely

turba *f*

A (carbón) peat

B (muchedumbre) mob

turbación *f* (liter *o* period) 1 (aturdimiento, confusión) confusion 2 (agitación) concern, alarm

turbante *m* turban

turbar [A1] *vt*

A (liter *o* period) ‹*orden/silencio*› to disturb

B (liter *o* period) 1 (aturdir, confundir): **sus insistentes miradas la ~on** the way he kept looking at her embarrassed and confused her; **su presencia lo turbó** her presence made him uncomfortable 2 (preocupar) to worry, alarm

■ **turbarse** *v pron* (liter *o* period) 1 (aturdirse, confundirse): **la besó en la mejilla y se turbó** he kissed her on the cheek and she was covered with confusion (liter); **se turbó ante tantos elogios** such praise confused and embarrassed him 2 (preocuparse): **se turbó cuando oyó las noticias** he was worried when he heard the news

turbina *f* turbine

turbio -bia *adj* 1 ‹*agua*› cloudy; **el río baja ~** the waters of the river are muddy 2 ‹*visión/ojos*› blurred, misty 3 ‹*asunto/negocio*› shady, murky

turbión *m* (Meteo) (aguacero) downpour; (aluvión) flood

turbo¹ *adj inv* turbocharged

turbo² *m* (turbocompresor) turbocharger; (automóvil) turbo

turbulencia *f* 1 (de las aguas) turbulence 2 (Aviac, Meteo) turbulence 3 (confusión, disturbios) turmoil

turbulento -ta *adj* ‹*río/atmósfera*› turbulent; ‹*reunión/romance*› stormy, turbulent; ‹*época*› turbulent, troubled

turco¹ -ca *adj* (Geog) Turkish

turco² -ca *m,f*

A 1 (Geog) (persona) Turk; ***celoso como un ~*** madly jealous 2 (AmL) (árabe) *term used (often pejoratively) to refer to someone of Middle Eastern origin*

B **turco** *m* (idioma) Turkish

turf /turf/ *m* 1 (deporte): **el ~** horseracing, the turf 2 (pista) racetrack (AmE), racecourse (BrE)

turfista¹ *adj* horseracing (*before n*)

turfista² *mf* racegoer

turgente *adj*, **túrgido -da** *adj* turgid

turismo *m* (Com, Ocio) tourism; **los ingresos del ~** income from tourism *o* from the tourist industry; **dependen del ~ alemán** they rely on German tourists; **oficina de ~** tourist office; **hacer ~** to travel (around)

turista¹ *adj* tourist (*before n*); **clase ~** economy class

turista² *mf* tourist

turistear [A1] *vi* (Andes, Méx) (en país) to tour around; (en ciudad) to do some sightseeing

turístico -ca *adj* ‹*información/folleto*› tourist (*before n*); ‹*viaje*› sightseeing (*before n*); ‹*empresa*› travel (*before n*); ‹*atracción/actividad/lugar*› tourist (*before n*)

turma *f* 1 (testículo) testicle 2 (Bot, Coc) truffle

turnarse [A1] *v pron* to take turns

turnio -nia *adj* (Chi fam) ‹*persona*› cross-eyed; ‹*ojos*› squint

turno *m* 1 (horario): **trabajar por ~s** to work (in) shifts; **~ de día/noche** day/night shift; **estar de ~** to be on duty 2 (personas) shift 3 (en un orden): **pedir ~** (Esp) *to ask who is last in the line* (AmE) *o* (BrE) *queue*; **cuando te toque el ~ a ti ...** when your turn comes ...; **cuidémoslo por ~s** let's take turns looking after him; **llegó con el novio de ~** she turned up with her boyfriend of the moment

Compuesto **turno de preguntas** question-and-answer session

turquesa *adj/f* turquoise

Turquía *f* Turkey

turrón *m*: *type of candy traditionally eaten at Christmas*

turulato -ta *adj* (fam) (atontado) stunned, dazed; (pasmado) stunned (colloq), flabbergasted (colloq)

turupe *m* (Col fam) lump

tusa *f*

A (Col, Ven) corncob (*stripped of its kernels*)

B (Chi) (de un caballo) mane; ***hasta la ~*** (fam) fed up to the back teeth

tusar [A1] *vt* (Col, RPl) 1 ‹*caballo*› to clip 2 (fam) (trasquilar) to scalp (colloq)

tute *m*: *card game in which the object is to win all the kings or queens*; ***darle un ~ a algo*** to give sth a lot of use *o* wear; ***darse un ~*** (darse un golpe) to bang one's head (*o* arm *etc*); (esforzarse) to sweat blood

tutear [A1] *vt*: *to address sb using the familiar* **tú** *form*

tutela *f* 1 (Der) guardianship, tutelage 2 (protección) protection

tutelado -da *m,f* (Der) ward; (Educ) tutee, student

tutelaje *m* (AmL) ▸ **tutela**

tutelar¹ *adj* (Der) tutelary; (protector) guardian (*before n*)

tutelar² [A1] *vt* to have the charge of (frml)

tuteo *m*: *use of the familiar* **tú** *form*

tuto *m* (Chi, Per leng infantil): **hacer ~** to go bye-byes (used to or by children); **tengo ~, mamá** I'm sleepy, mommy

tutor -tora *m,f*

A (Educ) (encargado de curso) course tutor, class teacher; (en la universidad) tutor

B (Der) guardian

tutoría *f*

A (Educ) tutorship

B (Der) guardianship, tutelage

tutti frutti *m* tutti frutti

tutú *m* (Indum) tutu

tuve, tuviera, etc *see* **tener**

tuyo¹ -ya *adj* yours; **esto es ~** this is yours; **¿es amigo ~?** is he a friend of yours?; **fue idea tuya** it was your idea

tuyo² -ya *pron*: **el ~, la tuya** *etc* yours; **son parecidos a los ~s** they're similar to yours; **la música no es lo ~** music isn't your strong point *o* your forte; **los ~s** (tu familia) your family and friends

tweed /'twi(ð)/ *m* (*pl* **~**) tweed

twist /twis(t)/ *m* twist

Uu

U, u *f* (*pl* **úes**) (*read as* /u/) the letter **U, u**

u *conj* [*used instead of* **o** *before* **o-** *or* **ho-**] or; **siete u ocho** seven or eight

ubérrimo -ma *adj* (liter) bountiful (liter)

ubicación *f* 1 (esp AmL) (situación, posición) location 2 (AmL) (localización): **se hizo difícil la ~ del avión** locating the airplane was very difficult

ubicado -da *adj* 1 (esp AmL) (en lugar) located, situated; **quedé mal ~** I didn't get a good place; **una casa bien ubicada** a well-situated house; **esto está mal ~ en este lugar** (AmL) this is in the wrong place here 2 (AmL) (en empleo): **está muy bien ~** he's really well set up in his job

ubicar [A2] *vt* (AmL) 1 (colocar, situar): **me ~on a su lado** they placed me next to him; **el triunfo ubicó al equipo en segundo lugar** the victory put the team in second place; **~on las sillas para la reunión** they arranged the chairs for the meeting 2 (localizar) ‹*persona/lugar*› to find, locate; **no lo he podido ~ en todo el día** I haven't been able to get hold of him all day 3 (identificar): **lo ubico sólo de nombre** I only know him by name; **lo ubiqué por el color** I recognized it by the color; **me suena el nombre, pero no lo ubico** the name rings a bell, but I can't quite place him

■ **ubicarse** *v pron*

A (AmL) 1 (colocarse, situarse): **se ubicó en la primera fila** he sat in the front row; **nos ubicamos en un buen lugar** we got really good seats 2 (en empleo) to get oneself a good job 3 (orientarse) to find one's way around; **¿te ubicas?** have you got your bearings?

B (esp AmL) (estar situado) to be, be situated *o* located; **el equipo se ubica en primer puesto** the team is in first place

ubicuidad *f* (liter) ubiquity (frml); **no tengo el don de la ~** (hum) I can't be in two places *o* everywhere at once

ubicuo -cua *adj* (liter) ubiquitous (frml)

ubre *f* udder

UCI /'usi, 'uθi/ *f* (= **Unidad de Cuidados Intensivos**) ICU

UCP *f* (= **Unidad Central de Proceso**) CPU

ud. = **usted**

uds. = **ustedes**

UE *f* (= **Unión Europea**) EU

UEFA /'wefa/ *f* UEFA

uf *interj* (expresando — cansancio, sofocación) whew! (colloq); (— repugnancia) yuck (colloq)

ufanarse [A1] *v pron* **~ DE** *or* **CON algo** to boast ABOUT *o* OF sth

ufano -na *adj* 1 (satisfecho, orgulloso) proud; **iba muy ~ con su hija** he walked proudly along with his daughter 2 (engreído) self-satisfied, smug

ufología *f* study of UFOs, ufology

ujier *m* uniformed doorman; (en tribunales) usher

ukelele *m* ukulele

úlcera *f* ulcer

ulceración *f* ulceration

ulcerar [A1] *vt* to ulcerate

■ **ulcerarse** *v pron* to ulcerate

ulceroso -sa *adj* ulcerous

ulpo *m* (Chi) *cold drink made with roasted flour and sugar*

ulterior *adj* (frml) subsequent, later

ulteriormente *adv* (frml) later, subsequently

ultimación *f* (de preparativos) conclusion, completion; (de detalles) finalization

últimamente *adv* recently, lately

ultimar [A1] *vt*

A ‹*preparativos*› to complete; ‹*detalles*› to finalize

B (AmL frml) (matar) to kill, murder; **lo ~on a balazos** they shot him dead

ultimátum *m* (*pl* **~** *or* **-tums**) ultimatum

último[1] **-ma** *adj* (*delante del n*)

A 1 (en el tiempo) last; **hasta últimas horas de la noche** until late at night; **en el ~ momento** *or* **a última hora** at the last minute *o* moment 2 (más reciente): **¿cuándo fue la última vez que lo usaste?** when did you last use it?; **su ~ libro** his latest book; **en los ~s tiempos** recently, in recent years (*o* months *etc*)

B 1 (en una serie) last; **estar en ~ lugar** to be last; **~ aviso a los pasajeros del vuelo ...** last *o* final call for passengers on flight ...; **en el ~ puesto de la división** at the bottom of the division; **por última vez** for the last time; **como ~ recurso** as a last resort; ***ser lo ~*** (fam) (el colmo) to be the last straw *o* the limit; (lo más reciente) to be the latest thing 2 (*como adv*) (CS) ‹*salir/terminar*› last; **llegó ~ en la carrera** he finished last in the race

C (en el espacio): **el ~ piso** the top floor; **la última fila** the back row; **la última página del periódico** the back page of the newspaper; **aunque tenga que ir al ~ rincón del mundo** even if I have to go to the ends of the earth

D (definitivo): **es mi última oferta** it's my final offer; **siempre tiene que decir la última palabra** he always has to have the last word

(Compuestos)

- **Última Cena** *f* Last Supper
- **última hora** *f* late item (of news)
- **última morada** *f* (period) last resting place (frml)
- **última voluntad** *f* last wishes (*pl*)

último[2] **-ma** *m,f* last one; **era el ~ que me quedaba** it was my last one; **el ~ de la lista** the last person on the list; **es el ~ de la clase** he's bottom of the class; **¿sabes la última que me hizo?** do you know what he's done to me now?; **¿te cuento la última?** (fam) do you want to hear the latest? (colloq); **a últimos de** (Esp) toward(s) the end of; **por último** finally, lastly; **en** (Col) *or* (Ven) **de últimas** as a last resort, if the worst comes to the worst; ***a la última*** (fam): **siempre va a la última** she always wears trendy clothes; ***estar en las últimas*** (estar a punto de morir) to be at death's door; (no tener dinero) (fam) to be broke (colloq); ***tomar la última*** (fam) to have one for the road (colloq)

ultra *mf* (Esp) right-wing extremist

ultraderecha *f*: **la ~** the far *o* extreme right

ultrafino -na *adj* ultrafine, superfine

ultraizquierda *f*: **la ~** the far *o* extreme left

ultrajante *adj* (frml) ‹*acto/palabras*› offensive, insulting

ultrajar [A1] *vt* (frml) ‹*persona*› to outrage, offend ... deeply; ‹*bandera*› to insult; ‹*honor*› to offend against

ultraje *m* outrage, insult; **un ~ a la bandera** an insult to the flag

ultraligero *m* ultralite, microlight

ultramar *m*: **de ~** overseas; **los países de ~** the overseas countries; **productos de ~** foreign products

ultramarinos *m* 1 (tienda) grocery store (AmE), grocer's shop (BrE) 2 **ultramarinos** *mpl* (comestibles) groceries

ultramoderno -na *adj* ultramodern

ultranza *f* 1 **a ultranza** (*loc adj*) out-and-out, fanatical; **es nacionalista a ~** he's a fanatical nationalist 2 **a ultranza** (*loc adv*): **luchó a ~ por sus ideales** she fought tooth and nail to defend her ideals

ultrasónico -ca *adj* ultrasonic

ultrasonido *m* ultrasound

ultratumba *f*: **la vida de ~** life after death; **una voz de ~** a voice from the beyond

ultravioleta *adj* (*pl* ~ *or* **-tas**) ultraviolet

ulular [A1] *vi* «*búho*» to hoot; «*viento*» to howl; «*persona*» to wail

ululato *m* (del búho) hoot; (de persona) wail

umbilical *adj* umbilical

umbral *m* 1 (de puerta) threshold 2 (borde, frontera) *tb* **~es** threshold; **en el ~** *or* **los ~es de la muerte** at death's door; **en el ~** *or* **los ~es de la locura** on the verge of madness; **en los ~es de la civilización** at the dawn of civilization 3 (Econ, Fin) threshold

(Compuesto) **umbral de rentabilidad** break-even point

umbría *f* (liter) shady place *o* spot

umbrío -bría, **umbroso -sa** *adj* (liter) shady

un (*pl* **unos**), **una** (*pl* **unas**) *art* [*the masculine article* **un** *is also used before feminine nouns which begin with stressed* **a** *or* **ha** *e.g.* **un arma poderosa, un hambre feroz**]

A (*sing*) a; (*delante de sonido vocálico*) an; (*pl*) some; **una nueva droga** a new drug; **un asunto importante** an important matter; **hay unas cartas para ti** there are some letters for you; **los hijos son unas lumbreras** the children are very bright; **tiene unos ojos preciosos** he has lovely eyes

B (con valor ponderativo): **tú haces unas preguntas ...** you do ask some questions!; **me dio una vergüenza ...** I was so embarrassed!

C (con nombres propios) a; **es un Miró** it's a Miró

D (*sing*) (como genérico): **un geranio no necesita tanta agua** geraniums don't need so much water

E (*pl*) (expresando aproximación) about; **tiene unos 30 años** she's about 30

una *pron* (*ver tb* **un, uno**) 1 (fam) (mala pasada): **me hizo ~ gordísima** she played a really dirty trick on me (colloq) 2 (fam) (paliza, bofetada, etc): **te voy a dar ~** you're going to get a good thumping (*o* whack *etc*) (colloq) 3 (fam) (con valor ponderativo): **¡había ~ de gente ...!** there was such a crowd (colloq) 4 **a una** together 5 **a la ~, a las dos, ¡a las tres!** ready, steady, go!

unánime *adj* unanimous

unanimidad *f* unanimity; **por ~** unanimously

unción *f* unction

uncir [I4] *vt* to yoke

UNCTAD /uŋk'tað/ *f*: **la ~** UNCTAD

undécimo -ma *adj/pron* eleventh; *para ejemplos ver* **quinto**

UNESCO /u'nesko/ *f*: **la ~** UNESCO

ungir [I7] *vt* to anoint

ungüento *m* ointment

únicamente *adv* only

unicameral *adj* single-chamber (*before n*), unicameral (frml)

UNICEF /uni'sef, uni'θef/ *f*: **la ~** UNICEF

unicelular *adj* unicellular, single-cell (*before n*)

unicidad *f* (frml) (de producto, fenómeno) uniqueness

único[1] **-ca** *adj*

A (solo) only; **lo ~ que quiero** the only thing I want, all I want; **¡es lo ~ que faltaba!** that's all we needed!; **un sistema de partido ~** a single-party *o* one-party system; **soy hijo ~** I'm an only child; **un acontecimiento ~** a once-in-a-lifetime *o* a unique event; **tarifa única** flat rate; **talla única** one size

B (extraordinario) extraordinary; **¡este hombre es ~** *or* **es un caso ~!** (fam) this guy is something else! (colloq)

único[2] **-ca** *m,f*: **el ~/las únicas que tengo** the only one/ones I have

unicornio *m* unicorn

unidad *f*

A 1 (Com, Mat) unit; **~es y decenas** units and tens; **costo por ~** unit cost; **precio por ~: 20 euros** 20 euros each 2 (de ejército) unit; (de flota) vessel; (Aviac) aircraft; (de tren) carriage 3 (de magnitud) unit; **~ métrica** metric unit; **~ de peso** unit of weight 4 (en libro, texto) unit; **Primera U~** Unit One

(Compuestos)

- **unidad central de proceso** central processing unit
- **unidad de cuidados intensivos** *or* (Esp) **de vigilancia intensiva** *or* (Arg, Méx) **de terapia intensiva** *or* (Chi) **de tratamiento intensivo** intensive care unit
- **unidad monetaria** monetary unit
- **unidad móvil** outside broadcasting unit

B (unión, armonía) unity; **la ~ de estilo de la plaza** the overall style of the square

unidimensional *adj* one-dimensional

unidireccional *adj* unidirectional

unido -da *adj* 1 ‹*familia/amigos*› close 2 (sobre un tema) united

unifamiliar *adj*: **viviendas ~es** houses (*as opposed to apartments in a block*)

unificación *f* unification

unificador -dora *adj*: **una política ~a** a unifying policy

unificar [A2] *vt* ‹*país*› to unify; ‹*precios*› to standardize

uniformado -da *adj* uniformed; **iban ~s** they were in uniform

uniformar [A1] *vt* to standardize

uniforme[1] *adj* ‹*velocidad/temperaturas*› constant, uniform; ‹*superficie*› even, uniform; ‹*terreno*› even, level; ‹*paisaje/estilo*› uniform; ‹*criterios/precios*› standard, uniform

uniforme[2] *m* uniform

uniformidad *f* (del paisaje) sameness, uniformity; (de estilo, criterios, precios) uniformity; (de terreno) evenness

unilateral *adj* ‹*desarme/decisión*› unilateral; ‹*criterio/opinión*› one-sided

unión *f*

A 1 (acción): **la ~ de las dos empresas** the merger of the two companies; **la ~ de estos factores** the combination of these factors; ***la ~ hace la fuerza*** united we stand 2 (agrupación) association 3 **la Unión Americana** (Méx) (Period) (Estados Unidos) the United States

B (relación) union, relationship; (matrimonio) union, marriage

C (juntura) joint

Unión Europea *f* European Union

Unión Soviética *f* (Hist) Soviet Union

unipartidismo *m* one-party system, single-party system

unipersonal *adj* individual (*before n*)

unir [I1] *vt*

A 1 ‹*cables*› to join; (con cola, pegamento) to stick … together; ‹*esfuerzos*› to combine; **unió los trozos con un pegamento** she glued the pieces together; **los unió en matrimonio** (frml) he joined them in matrimony (frml) 2 «*sentimientos/intereses*» to unite; **unida sentimentalmente a ...** (period) romantically involved with … 3 ‹*características/cualidades/estilos*› to combine; **~ algo A algo** to combine sth WITH sth

B (comunicar) ‹*lugares*› to link

C (fusionar) ‹*empresas/organizaciones*› to merge

D ‹*salsa*› to mix

■ **unirse** *v pron*

A 1 (aliarse) «*personas/colectividades*» to join together; **se unieron para hacer un frente común** they joined forces *o* united in a common cause; **~se en matrimonio** to be joined in matrimony (frml); **se unió a nuestra causa** he joined our cause 2 «*características/cualidades*» to combine; **a su belleza se une una gran simpatía** she combines beauty and a very pleasant personality

B (juntarse) «*caminos*» to converge, meet

C (fusionarse) «*empresas/organizaciones*» to merge

unisex /'uniseks/ *adj inv* unisex

unísono[1] **-na** *adj* unisonous

unísono[2] *m* unison; **al ~** in unison

unitario[1] **-ria** *adj* ‹*política*› unitary; (Relig) Unitarian

unitario[2] **-ria** *m,f* Unitarian

U

Univ. (= **universidad**) U, Univ.

universal *adj* 1 ‹*ley/principio*› universal; **una marca de fama ~** a world-famous brand; **no tiene validez ~** it is not universally valid 2 ‹*llave/enchufe*› universal

universalidad *f* universality

universalizar [A4] *vt* to universalize

universiada *f* student games (*pl*)

universidad *f* university

Compuestos

- **universidad a distancia** *or* (Méx) **abierta** open university
- **universidad laboral** ≈ technical college (*school with emphasis on vocational training*)

universitario¹ -ria *adj* university (*before n*)

universitario² -ria *m,f* (estudiante) undergraduate, (university) student; (licenciado) (university) graduate

universo *m* universe

unívoco -ca *adj* ‹*palabra/frase*› univocal (frml)

uno¹, una *adj*

A 1 (refiriéndose al número) one; **no había ni un asiento libre** there wasn't one empty seat *o* a single empty seat; **me costó un dólar y pico** it cost me a dollar something; **treinta y un pasajeros** thirty-one passengers; **cuarenta y una mujeres** forty-one women 2 **uno** (*pospuesto al n*) one; **el capítulo/número uno** chapter/number one

B (único): **la solución es una** there's only one solution; **Dios es uno** God is one; ***ser uno y lo mismo*** *or* ***ser todo uno***: **vernos y empezar a pelear es uno y lo mismo** as soon as we see each other we start arguing

uno², una *pron*

A (numeral) one; **entraban de a uno/una** they were going in one at a time *o* one by one; **es de tres por uno** it is three meters (long) by one (wide); **uno a** *or* **por uno** one by one; **es la una** it's one o'clock; ***más de uno/una*** (fam): **más de una va a lamentar su partida** there'll be quite a few sorry to see him go (colloq); **eso le molestó a más de uno** that annoyed quite a few people *o* a number of people; ***(ni) una*** (fam) not a thing (colloq); ***no dar una*** (fam): **los meteorólogos no dan una** the weathermen just never get it right (colloq); **no doy ni una** I can't get a thing right (colloq); ***una de dos*** one thing or the other; *ver tb* **una**

B (personal) (*sing*) one; (*pl*) some; **uno es profesor y el otro estudiante** one's a teacher and the other's a student; **¿te gustaron? — unos sí, otros no** did you like them? — some I did, others I didn't; **se envidian el uno al otro** they're jealous of each other; **se ayudan los unos a los otros** they help one another; ***ser uno/una de tantos/tantas*** to be nothing special

C (fam) (alguien) (*m*) some guy (colloq); (*f*) some woman (colloq); **les pregunté a unos que estaban allí** I asked some people who were there

D (uso impersonal) 1 (como sujeto) you; **uno no sabe qué decir** you don't *o* (frml) one doesn't know what to say; **aquí se sirve uno mismo** here you serve yourself 2 (como complemento) you; **nunca le dicen nada a uno** they don't tell you anything; **los demás lo critican a uno** people like to criticize (one)

uno³ *m* (number) one; *para ejemplos ver* **cinco**; ***del uno*** (Chi fam): **pasarlo del uno** to have a great time (colloq); **estar del uno** (hablando — de persona) to be hot stuff; (— de comida) to be delicious; ***hacer del uno*** (Méx, Per fam) to have a pee (colloq)

untar [A1] *vt*

A 1 (cubrir): **~ las galletas con miel** spread honey on the cookies; **se unta el molde con mantequilla** grease the cake tin (with butter) 2 (empapar) **~ algo EN algo** to dip sth IN sth; **untó el pan en la salsa** he dipped his bread in the sauce

B (fam) (sobornar) to bribe

■ **untarse** *v pron* 1 (ensuciarse): **se untó las manos de pintura** he got paint all over his hands 2 (ponerse): **se untó los hombros con bronceador** she rubbed suntan lotion on her shoulders

unto *m* (ungüento) ointment; (Coc) lard, pig fat

untuoso -sa *adj* sticky, glutinous; ‹*voz*› sickly sweet

uña *f*

A 1 (Anat) (de la mano) nail, fingernail; (del pie) nail, toenail; ***arreglarse*** *or* ***hacerse las ~s*** (*refl*) to do one's nails; (*caus*) to have one's nails done; ***dejarse las ~s en algo*** (fam) to work very hard at sth; ***enseñar*** *or* ***mostrar*** *or* ***sacar las ~s*** to show one's teeth; ***rascarse con las propias ~s*** (Méx fam) to fend for oneself; ***ser largo de ~s*** *or* ***tener las ~s largas*** (fam) to be light-fingered (colloq); ***ser ~ y carne*** *or* ***carne y ~*** (fam) to be as thick as thieves (colloq) 2 (de oso, gato) claw; (de caballo, oveja) hoof; (de alacrán) sting; ***afilarse las ~s*** to sharpen one's claws; ***a ~ de caballo*** at top speed

B (Mec, Tec) toe; (de ancla) fluke

C (Méx, Ven) (Mús) plectrum

uñalarga *mf* (Per fam) (ladrón) thief; (carterista) pickpocket

uñero *m* (inflamación) whitlow; (uña encarnada) ingrowing nail

uñeta *f* (CS) plectrum

uperización *f* UHT treatment, sterilization

uperizado -da *adj* UHT (*before n*)

uralita® *f* asbestos

uranio *m* uranium

Compuesto **uranio enriquecido** enriched uranium

Urano *m* Uranus

urbanidad *f* courtesy, urbanity (frml); **las más elementales nociones de ~** the most basic social graces

urbanismo *m* city (AmE) *o* (BrE) town planning

urbanista *mf* city (AmE) *o* (BrE) town planner

urbanístico -ca *adj* urban development (*before n*)

urbanita *mf* urbanite, city dweller

urbanizable *adj*: **tierras ~s** building land

urbanización *f* (acción) urbanization, development; (núcleo residencial) (Esp) (housing) development

urbanizado -da *adj* built-up; **esta zona está muy poco urbanizada/muy urbanizada** this area has hardly been developed/is heavily developed; **una zona urbanizada** a built-up area

urbanizar [A4] *vt* ‹*zona, terreno*› to develop, urbanize; **una zona sin ~** an undeveloped area

urbano -na *adj* ‹*núcleo/transporte*› urban, city (*before n*); ‹*población*› urban

urbe *f* (frml) large *o* major city, metropolis

urdimbre *f* 1 (Tex) warp 2 (intriga) intrigue; **la ~ de la novela** the intricate workings of the novel

urdir [I1] *vt* 1 (en telar) to warp; ‹*puntos*› to cast on 2 ‹*plan*› to devise, hatch

urea *f* urea

uréter *m* ureter

uretra *f* urethra

urgencia *f* 1 (cualidad) urgency; **con ~** urgently; **con la máxima ~** with the utmost urgency 2 (Med) (emergencia) emergency; (caso urgente) emergency (case); **sala de ~s** casualty department *o* ward; Ⓢ **urgencias** accident and emergency; **lo operaron de ~** he had an emergency operation; **lo hospitalizaron de ~** he was rushed into hospital

urgente *adj* ‹*asunto*› pressing, urgent; ‹*mensaje*› urgent; ‹*caso/enfermo*› emergency (*before n*); ‹*carta*› express (*before n*)

urgido -da *adj* (AmL) **estar ~ DE algo**: **estaban ~s de dinero** they were in urgent need of money; **estamos ~s de tiempo** we are pressed for time

urgir [I7] *vi* (*en 3ª pers*): **urge la finalización del proyecto** the project must be finished as soon as possible; **urge acabar con el conflicto** the conflict must be brought to an end as speedily as possible; Ⓢ **urge vender piso** apartment for quick sale; (+ *me/te/le/etc*): **me urge estar allí el martes** I absolutely must be there on/by Tuesday; **le urge el préstamo** he needs the loan urgently

■ **urgir** *vt*: **urgido por la necesidad/el hambre** driven by necessity/hunger; **~ a algn A + INF/A QUE + SUBJ** to urge sb to do sth; **los urgieron a abandonar el país** they were urged to leave the country

úrico -ca *adj* uric

urinario *m* urinal

urna *f*

A (vasija) urn; (de exposición) display case; (para votar) ballot box; ***acudir a las ~s*** (period) to go to the polls (journ)

Compuesto **urna cineraria** funerary urn

B (Chi, Ven) (ataúd) coffin, wooden box (euph)

U

urogallo *m* capercaillie; (como nombre genérico) grouse
urología *f* urology
urólogo -ga *m,f* urologist
urraca *f* magpie
URSS /urs/ *f* (Hist) (= **Unión de Repúblicas Socialistas Soviéticas**) USSR
urticaria *f* nettlerash, hives
urubú *m* black vulture
Uruguay *m* 1 (país) *tb* **el ~** Uruguay 2 (río): **el (río) ~** the Uruguay River
uruguayismo *m* Uruguayan word/expression
uruguayo -ya *adj/m,f* Uruguayan
USA /'usa/ (fam) USA
usado -da *adj* 1 [SER] (de segunda mano) secondhand; Ⓢ **se venden coches usados** used cars for sale 2 [ESTAR] (gastado, viejo) worn
usanza *f* (liter): **bailes a la antigua ~** old-style dances; **vestidos a la ~ india** dressed in Indian costume
usar [A1] *vt*
A 1 (emplear, utilizar) to use; **¿cómo se usa esto?** ‹*máquina*› how does this work?; ‹*diccionario/herramienta*› how do you use this?; **~ algo/a algn** DE *or* COMO **algo** to use sth/sb AS sth 2 ‹*instalaciones/servicio*› to use 3 ‹*producto/combustible*› to use
B (llevar) ‹*alhajas/ropa*› to wear; ‹*perfume*› to use, wear; **estos zapatos están sin ~** these shoes are unworn, these shoes have never been worn
C (esp AmL) ‹*persona*› to use; **me sentí usada** I felt used
■ **usar** *vi*
A *ver* **abusar B**
B **usar de** (frml) (hacer uso de) ‹*influencia/autoridad*› to use
■ **usarse** *v pron* (*en 3ª pers*) (esp AmL) (estar de moda) ‹‹*color/ropa*›› to be in fashion; **se usan mucho las prendas de cuero** leather clothing is very popular; **ya no se usa hacer fiestas de compromiso** people don't tend to have engagement parties any more
Usía *pron pers* (arc) your Lordship (frml)
usina *f* (AmS) (fábrica) large factory; (industria) industry
(Compuesto) **usina eléctrica** (AmS) power station
uslero *m* (Chi) rolling pin
uso *m*
A (utilización) 1 (de producto, medicamento) use; (de máquina, material) use; **desgastarse con el ~** to wear out with use; **instrucciones para su ~** instructions for use; **de ~ personal** for personal use; **métodos de ~ extendido en ...** methods widely used in ...; **los trenes todavía no han entrado en ~** the trains are not in service yet; **hacer ~ de algo** to use sth; **su ~ prolongado puede producir dependencia** it can be habit-forming if taken over a long period; Ⓢ **de uso externo** (Farm) for external use only 2 (de idioma, expresión) use; **una expresión sancionada por el ~** (frml) an expression that has gained acceptance through usage 3 (de facultad, derecho): **en pleno ~ de sus facultades mentales** in full possession of his mental faculties; **hacer ~ de un derecho** to exercise a right; **hacer ~ de la palabra** (frml) to speak; ***hacer ~ y abuso de algo*** (de privilegio) to abuse sth; **se ha hecho ~ y abuso de esta metáfora** this metaphor has been used time and again
B (de prenda): **estos zapatos tienen años de ~** I've had years of wear out of these shoes; **ropa de ~ diario** everyday clothes; **los zapatos ceden con el ~** shoes give with wear
(Compuesto) **uso de razón** use of reason; **desde que tengo ~ de ~** ever since I can remember
C (utilidad, aplicación) use; **una batidora con múltiples ~s** a multi-purpose mixer
D (usanza) custom; **~s aztecas que aún sobreviven** Aztec customs which still survive
usted *pron pers* [*Polite form of address but also used in some areas, eg Colombia and Chile, instead of the familiar* **tú** *form*]
A 1 (como sujeto) you; **¿quién lo va a hacer? — ¿usted?** who's going to do it? — you (are); **lo que ~ diga** whatever you say; **tratar a algn de ~** to address sb using the **usted** form 2 (en comparaciones, con preposiciones) you; **no es tan alta como ~** she isn't as tall as you; **muchas gracias — a ~** thank you very much — thank *you*; **con/contra/para ~** with/against/for you; **son de ~** they're yours
B (uno) you, one (frml); **le dicen eso y ~ no sabe qué contestar** when they say that you just don't know *o* one just doesn't know what to say in reply
ustedes *pron pers pl* [*Polite plural form of address also used in Latin American countries as the familiar plural form*] 1 (como sujeto) you; **¿quién lo va a hacer? — ustedes** who's going to do it? — you (are); **~ mismos lo dijeron** you said so yourselves 2 (en comparaciones, con preposiciones) you; **no tienen tantos como ~** they don't have as many as you; **con/contra/para ~** with/against/for you; **son de ~** they're yours; **sabe lo de ~** she knows about you two
usual *adj* usual, normal; **no es ~ que venga tanta gente** it's unusual for there to be so many people here
usuario -ria *m,f* user
usufructo *m* usufruct
usufructuario -ria *adj/m,f* usufructuary
usura *f* usury
usurero -ra *m,f* usurer
usurpación *f* (frml) (de propiedad, título) misappropriation; (de territorio) seizure; (del poder) usurpation
usurpador -dora *m,f* usurper
usurpar [A1] *vt* (frml) ‹*propiedad/título*› to misappropriate; ‹*territorio*› to seize; ‹*poder*› to usurp
utensilio *m* (instrumento) utensil; (herramienta) tool; **~s de cocina** kitchen *o* cooking utensils; **~s de laboratorio** laboratory apparatus; **~s de pesca** fishing tackle
uterino -na *adj* uterine
útero *m* womb, uterus (tech); **alquiler de ~s** commercial surrogacy
útil *adj* useful
utilería *f* (esp AmL) (Cin, Teatr) props (*pl*)
utilero -ra *m,f* (esp AmL) (Cin, Teatr) props manager
útiles *mpl* 1 (herramientas, instrumentos) tools (*pl*), implements (*pl*); **~ de labranza** agricultural equipment; **~ de pesca** fishing tackle; **~ de jardinería** gardening tools 2 (AmL) (artículos escolares) *tb* **~ escolares** *pencils, pens, rulers, etc for school*
utilidad *f* 1 (de aparato) usefulness; **no es de mucha ~ práctica** it doesn't have much practical use; **un coche me sería de mucha ~** a car would be of great use to me 2 **utilidades** *fpl* (AmL) (ganancia, beneficio) profits (*pl*)
utilitario *m* small (economical) car
utilización *f* use, utilization (frml); **la ~ de los recursos naturales** the exploitation *o* utilization of natural resources; **la ~ de la energía solar** the harnessing of solar energy
utilizar [A4] *vt* to use, utilize (frml); **~ los recursos naturales indiscriminadamente** to make indiscriminate use of natural resources; **la están utilizando** she's being used
utillaje *m* tools (*pl*), implements (*pl*)
utopía *f* Utopia
utópico -ca *adj* Utopian
utopista *mf* Utopian
UV /u'βe/ (= **ultravioleta**) UV
uva *f* grape; ***de ~s a peras*** (fam) once in a blue moon; ***estar de mala ~*** (fam) to be in a (foul) mood (colloq); ***tener mala ~*** (fam) to be a nasty piece of work (colloq); ***tomar las ~s*** to see the New Year in (*by eating one grape on each chime of the clock*)
(Compuestos)
- **uva blanca/negra** white/black grape
- **uva de mesa** dessert grape

uve *f* (Esp) *name of the letter* **v**
(Compuesto) **uve doble** (Esp) *name of the letter* **w**
UVI /'uβi/ *f* (Esp) = **Unidad de Vigilancia Intensiva**
uxoricidio *m* uxoricide
uy *interj* (expresando — asombro) ooh! (colloq); (— malestar, disgusto) oh!; (— emoción súbita) ah!, oh!; (— dolor) ow!, ouch!

u

Vv

V, v *f* (*read as* /be/, /be 'korta/, /be 'tʃika/, /be pe'keɲa/ *or* (Esp) /'uβe/) *the letter* **V, v**

V, v
A (= **varón**) M, male
B (= **versus**) v, vs, versus
C (= **verso**) v, verse

va, vas, etc *see* **ir**

vaca *f* 1 (Zool) cow; ***estar/ponerse como una ~*** (fam) to be/get very fat; ***hacerse la ~*** (Per fam) to play hooky (esp AmE colloq), to skive off (school) (BrE colloq); ***hacer una ~*** (AmL fam) to make a collection; ***las ~s gordas/flacas*: la época de las ~s gordas/flacas** the boom/lean years 2 (Coc): **(carne de) ~** beef; **filete de ~** fillet steak

Compuestos
- **vaca lechera** dairy cow
- **vaca marina** manatee, sea cow
- **vaca sagrada** sacred cow

vacacional *adj* (frml) vacation (*before n*)

vacacionar [A1] *vi* (Méx) to spend one's vacation(s) *o* holidays

vacaciones *fpl* vacation(s) (esp AmE), holiday(s) (esp BrE); **~ de verano/Navidad** summer/Christmas vacation *o* holidays; **~ escolares** school vacation(s) *o* holidays; **irse** *or* **marcharse de ~** to go away on vacation *o* on holiday; **estamos de ~** we're on vacation *o* holiday; **tomarse unas ~** to take a vacation *o* holiday; **este año no tengo ~** I don't get any vacation *o* holiday this year

vacacionista *mf* (Méx) vacationer (AmE), holidaymaker (BrE)

vacada *f* herd of cows *o* cattle

vacante¹ *adj* ‹*puesto/plaza*› vacant; ‹*piso/asiento*› empty, unoccupied

vacante² *f* vacancy; **proveer** *or* **cubrir una ~** to fill a vacancy

vacar [A2] *vi* «*puesto*» to fall vacant; «*local*» to be left vacant

vaciado *m* 1 (de depósito, cañería) emptying 2 (Art) (acción) casting; (figura) cast, casting; **~ de yeso** plaster cast

vaciar [A17] *vt*
A 1 ‹*vaso/botella*› to empty; ‹*radiador*› to drain; ‹*bolsillo/cajón*› to empty; **me ~on la casa** they cleaned my house out (colloq) 2 ‹*contenido*› to empty (out)
B ‹*estatua*› to cast
C (ahuecar) to hollow out
■ **vaciarse** *v pron* to empty

vacilación *f* hesitation, vacillation (frml); **sin ~** without any hesitation; **tras un momento de ~** after a moment's hesitation

vacilada *f*
A (Esp fam) (timo) con (colloq); **la exposición es una ~** the exhibition is garbage (AmE) *o* (BrE) is a load of rubbish
B (Méx fam) 1 (jolgorio) merrymaking; **irse de ~** to go out on the town 2 (broma) joke

vacilante *adj* 1 (oscilante) unsteady, shaky; **entró con paso ~** he came in, walking unsteadily 2 (dubitativo) ‹*expresión*› doubtful; ‹*voz*› hesitant 3 ‹*luz*› flickering

vacilar [A1] *vi*
A 1 (dudar) to hesitate; **sin ~** without hesitating; **vaciló antes de entrar** he hesitated before going in; **vacila entre irse o quedarse** she's hesitating over whether to go or stay; **no vaciles más, hazlo** stop dithering and do it; **~ EN + INF** to hesitate TO + INF; **no vaciló en aceptar** he accepted without hesitation 2 «*fe/determinación*» to waver 3 «*luz*» to flicker
B (oscilar) «*persona*» to stagger, totter; **vacilaba al andar** he swayed from side to side as he walked
C (Esp, Méx fam) (bromear) to joke, to kid (colloq)
D (AmL exc CS fam) (divertirse) to have fun
■ **vacilar** *vt* (Esp, Méx fam) to tease

vacile *m* (fam) (tomadura de pelo) joke; **basta de ~** that's enough kidding (colloq)

vacilón -lona *m,f*
A (Esp, Méx fam) (bromista) joker (colloq), clown (colloq)
B **vacilón** *m* (AmL fam) 1 (diversión): **le encanta el ~** he loves having a good time; **la fiesta fue un ~** the party was great fun 2 (tomadura de pelo) joke; **es puro ~** it's just a joke

vacío¹ -cía *adj* 1 ‹*botella/caja*› empty; ‹*calle/ciudad*› empty, deserted; ‹*casa*› empty, unoccupied; ‹*palabras/retórica*› empty; **con el estómago ~** on an empty stomach; **los envases ~s** the empty bottles, the empties (colloq); **la despensa está vacía** there's no food in the house; ***volver de ~*** (Esp) «*camión*» to come back empty; «*persona*» to come back empty-handed 2 (frívolo) ‹*persona*› shallow; ‹*vida/frase*› empty, meaningless

vacío² *m* 1 (Fís) vacuum; **envasado al ~** vacuum-packed; ***hacerle el ~ a algn*** to give sb the cold shoulder 2 (espacio vacío) space; **mirar al ~** to gaze into space; **saltó al ~** he leapt into the void *o* into space; ***caer en el ~*** to fall on deaf ears 3 (falta, hueco) gap; **dejó un ~ en su vida** she left a gap *o* a void in his life; **una sensación de ~** a feeling of emptiness

Compuesto **vacío de poder** power vacuum

vacuidad *f* (frml) vacuity (frml)

vacuna *f* vaccine; **me tengo que poner la ~** I have to have my vaccination; **~ oral** oral vaccine

Compuestos
- **vacuna antigripal** flu vaccine
- **vacuna contra la viruela/difteria** smallpox/diphtheria vaccine

vacunación *f* vaccination

vacunar [A1] *vt* to vaccinate; **~ a algn CONTRA algo** to vaccinate sb AGAINST sth; **me ~on contra la difteria** I was vaccinated against diphtheria; **estoy vacunado contra sus insultos** I've become immune to his insults

vacuno -na *adj* bovine; **ganado ~** cattle (*pl*)

vacuo -cua *adj* (frml) vacuous (frml), inane

vadear [A1] *vt* to ford, cross, wade across

vado *m* (de río) ford; (en vías públicas) entrance, access; Ⓢ **vado permanente** no parking

vagabundear [A1] *vi* to drift (around)

vagabundeo *m* drifting

vagabundería *f* (Ven) crooked deal, dirty business; **las ~s de su marido** her husband's appalling behavior

vagabundo¹ -da *adj* ‹*perro*› stray; **niños ~s** street urchins

vagabundo² -da *m,f* tramp, vagrant

vagancia *f* 1 (pereza, holgazanería) laziness, idleness; **no lo hizo por ~** she was too lazy *o* idle to do it 2 (Der) vagrancy

vagar [A3] *vi* to wander, roam

vagido *m* cry (*of a new-born child*)

vagina *f* vagina

vaginal *adj* vaginal

vago[1] -ga *adj*

A (fam) ‹*persona*› lazy, idle

B ‹*recuerdo/idea*› vague, hazy; ‹*contorno/forma*› vague, indistinct; ‹*explicación*› vague; **un ~ parecido** a vague resemblance

vago[2] -ga *m,f* (fam) layabout, slacker (colloq); **deja ya de hacer el ~** stop lazing around (colloq)

vagón *m* (de pasajeros) coach, car (AmE), carriage (BrE)

Compuestos

- **vagón cisterna** tank car (AmE) *o* (BrE) wagon
- **vagón de carga** (abierto) freight car (AmE), goods *o* freight wagon (BrE); (cerrado) boxcar (AmE), goods van (BrE)
- **vagón de cola** caboose (AmE), guard's van (BrE)
- **vagón de ganado** stock car (AmE), cattle truck (BrE)
- **vagón de primera** first-class car (AmE) *o* (BrE) carriage
- **vagón restaurante** dining *o* (BrE) restaurant car

vagoneta *f* 1▸ (Ferr) tipping skip, dump car 2▸ (Méx) (para pasajeros) van, minibus

vaguada *f* (Geog) river bed

vaguear [A1] *vi* to laze around

vaguedad *f* (de palabras, ideas) vagueness; (expresión imprecisa) vague remark

vahído *m* dizzy spell; **le dio un ~** he had a dizzy turn

vaho *m* 1▸ (aliento) breath 2▸ (vapor) steam, vapor* 3▸ (inhalación): **hacer ~s** to inhale

vaina *f*

A (de espada) scabbard; (de navaja) sheath

B (Bot) (de habas, etc) pod; (del tallo) leaf sheath

C (Col, Per, Ven fam) 1▸ (problema, contrariedad): **¡qué ~!** what a drag *o* pain (colloq); **la ~ es que no sé cómo** the thing *o* problem is that I don't know how, **estoy metida en una ~** I'm in a spot of trouble (colloq) 2▸ (cosa, asunto) thing, thingamajig (colloq); **aquí esa ~ no existe** you won't find anything like that round here; ***echarle una ~ a algn*** (Ven fam) to shaft sb (AmE colloq), to do the dirty on sb (BrE colloq); ***echar ~*** (Ven fam) (molestar) to be a pest; (divertirse) to have a good time (colloq) 3▸ (comportamiento sospechoso): **tenían una ~** they were up to something funny; **¿qué ~ te traes tú?** what are you up to?

vainilla *f* (Bot, Coc) vanilla

vais *see* **ir**

vaivén *m* (de columpio, péndulo) swinging; (de tren) rocking; (de barco) rolling; (de mecedora) rocking; (de gente) toing and froing; **los vaivenes de la fortuna** the swings of fortune

vajilla *f* (en general) dishes (*pl*); (juego) dinner service *o* set

valdré, valdría, etc *see* **valer**

vale[1] *m*

A 1▸ (para adquirir algo) voucher; (por devolución) credit note *o* slip; **un ~ de descuento** a money-off coupon 2▸ (pagaré) IOU

B (Per) (apuesta) *tb* **~ triple** treble

vale[2] *interj*: *ver* **valer D**

valedero -ra *adj* (frml) valid; **~ hasta ...** valid until ...

valedor -dora *m,f*

A (frml) (defensor) defender, champion

B (Méx fam) (compañero) buddy, mate (BrE colloq)

valenciana *f* (Méx) cuff (AmE), turn-up (BrE)

valenciano[1] -na *adj/m,f* Valencian

valenciano[2] *m* (Ling) Valencian

> **valenciano**
>
> The variety of catalán spoken in the autonomous region of Valencia. Some people regard it as a separate language from Catalan, which enjoys official status, but it is not officially recognized as such

valentía *f* bravery, courage; **con ~** courageously

valer [E28] *vt*

A 1▸ (tener un valor de) to be worth; (costar) to cost; **no vale mucho dinero** it isn't worth much; **¿cuánto valen?** how much are they?, what do they cost? 2▸ (equivaler a): **si x vale 8 ¿cuánto vale y?** if x is 8, what is the value of y?; **¿cuánto vale un dólar en pesos?** how many pesos are there to the dollar?

B (+ *me/te/le etc*) 1▸ (ganar): **le valió una bofetada** it earned him a slap in the face; **esta obra le valió un premio** this play earned *o* won her a prize 2▸ (causar): **sus declaraciones le valieron un gran disgusto** his statement brought him a lot of trouble

■ **valer** *vi*

A 1▸ (+ *compl*) (tener cierto valor) to be worth; (costar) to cost; **vale más, pero es mejor** it costs more but it's better 2▸ (equivaler) **~ POR algo** to be worth sth; **vale por un regalo** it can be exchanged for a gift

B (tener valor no material): **ha demostrado que vale** he has shown his worth; **como profesor no vale (nada)** as a teacher he's useless; **vales tanto como él** you're as good as he is; **no valgo nada para él** I mean nothing to him; **la novela no vale gran cosa** the novel isn't much good; ***hacerse ~*** to assert oneself; ***hacer ~ algo*** ‹*derecho*› to assert sth, enforce sth; **hizo ~ su autoridad** he used *o* imposed his authority

C (servir): **ésta no vale, es muy ancha** this one's no good, it's too wide; **no ~ PARA algo** to be useless *o* no good AT sth; **¡no vales para nada!** you're completely useless; **~ DE algo** (+ *me/te/le etc*): **no le valió de nada protestar** protesting got him nowhere; **sus consejos me valieron de mucho** her advice was very useful *o* valuable to me

D **vale** (Esp fam) 1▸ (expresando acuerdo) OK; **¡~!** sure, fine, OK!; **¿~?** OK?, all right?; **que llegues tarde una vez ~, pero...** being late once is one thing, but... 2▸ (basta): **¿~ así?** is that OK *o* enough?; **ya ~ ¿no?** don't you think that's enough?

E **más vale**: **más vale que no se entere** she'd better not find out; **más vale así** it's better that way; (+ *me/te/le etc*) **más te vale ir** you'd better go; **dijo que vendría — ¡más le vale!** he said he'd come — he'd better!; ***más vale prevenir que curar*** better safe than sorry

F 1▸ (ser válido) «*entrada/pasaporte*» to be valid, «*jugada/partido*» to count; **no hay excusa que valga** I don't want to hear any excuses; **valga la comparación** if you know *o* see what I mean; **... y valga la expresión** ... for want *o* lack of a better expression; **valga la redundancia** if you'll excuse the repetition 2▸ (estar permitido): **eso no vale, estás haciendo trampa** that's not fair, you're cheating; **no vale mirar** you're not allowed to look

G (Méx fam) 1▸ (no importar) (+ *me/te/le etc*): **a mí eso me vale** I don't give a damn about that (colloq) 2▸ (no tener valor) to be useless *o* no good (colloq) 3▸) (estropearse): **mi coche ya valió** my car's had it (colloq)

■ **valerse** *v pron*

A (servirse) **~se DE algo/algn** to use sth/sb; **se valió de sus apellidos para conseguirlo** he took advantage of *o* used the family name to obtain it; **~se de mentiras** to lie

B «*anciano/enfermo*»: **~se solo** *or* **por sí mismo** to look after oneself

C (estar permitido, ser correcto): **no se vale golpear abajo del cinturón** hitting below the belt is not allowed; **¡no se vale!** that's not fair!

valeriana *f* valerian

valeroso -sa *adj* brave, courageous, valiant (liter)

valet *m* (*pl* **-lets**) (Chi, Méx) (ayuda de cámara) valet, manservant

valga, valgas, etc *see* **valer**

valía *f* worth; **un joven de gran ~** a young man of great worth; **según ~ del candidato** according to the merits of the candidate

validación *f* validation

validar [A1] *vt* to validate

validez *f* validity; **tiene ~ hasta 1996** it is valid until 1996; **sin ~** invalid; **falta de ~** invalidity; **dar ~** to validate

valido *m* (Hist) favorite*

válido -da *adj* ‹*documento/excusa/argumento*› valid; **~ por/hasta ...** valid for/until ...

valiente[1] *adj*

A ‹*persona*› brave, courageous, valiant (liter); **se las da de ~** he makes out that he's brave

B (*delante del n*) (iró) (en exclamaciones): **¡~ sinvergüenza estás hecho!** you have some nerve (AmE colloq), you've got a nerve (BrE colloq); **¡~ amigo que tienes!** some friend *he* is! (colloq & iro)

V

valiente[2] *mf* brave person; **los ∼s** the brave (frml)

valija *f* (RPl) suitcase

(Compuesto) **valija diplomática** diplomatic bag

valioso -sa *adj* ‹*joya/cuadro*› valuable; ‹*consejo/experiencia*› valuable; **un hombre ∼** a man of great worth

valla *f* 1 (cerca) fence 2 (Dep) (en atletismo) hurdle; **100 metros ∼s** 100 meters hurdles 3 (en fútbol) goal

(Compuesto) **valla publicitaria** billboard (AmE), hoarding (BrE)

vallado *m* fence

valle *m* valley

(Compuesto) **valle de lágrimas** vale of tears (liter)

vallista *mf* hurdler

valona *f*: *traditional Mexican song*

valor *m*

(Sentido I)

A 1 (Com, Fin) value; **libros por ∼ de $150** books to the value of $150; **droga por (un) ∼ de ...** drugs worth *o* with a value of ...; **objetos de ∼** valuables 2 (importancia, mérito) value; **∼ artístico** artistic merit; **∼ sentimental** sentimental value; **su palabra tiene un gran ∼ para mí** I set great store by what he says; **¿qué ∼ tiene si lo copió?** what merit is there in it if he copied it? 3 (validez) validity; **sin la firma no tiene ningún ∼** it's not valid without the signature

(Compuestos)

- **valor adquisitivo** purchasing power
- **valor alimenticio** *or* **nutritivo** nutritional value
- **valor añadido** value added, added value
- **valor catastral** *value of a property recorded in the land registry*
- **valor nominal** par *o* nominal value

B **valores** *mpl* (Econ, Fin) securities (*pl*), stocks (*pl*), shares (*pl*)

C (persona): **los ∼es del tenis** the tennis stars; **los nuevos ∼es de nuestra música** our up-and-coming musicians

D **valores** *mpl* (principios morales) values (*pl*)

(Sentido II)

A (coraje, valentía) courage; **me faltó ∼** I didn't have the courage; **hay que tener ∼ para hacer algo así** it takes courage to do a thing like that; **armarse de ∼** to pluck up courage

B (fam) (descaro, desvergüenza) nerve (colloq)

valoración *f* 1 (de bienes, joyas) valuation; (de pérdidas, daños) assessment 2 (frml) (de suceso, trabajo) assessment, appraisal (frml); **hacer una ∼ de algo** to assess *o* (frml) appraise sth

valorar [A1] *vt* 1 ‹*joya/cuadro*› to value; ‹*pérdida/daño*› to assess; **∼ algo EN algo** to value sth at sth; **la casa está valorada en ...** the house is valued at ...; **las pérdidas se valoran en varios millones de dólares** the damage is estimated at several million dollars; **eso no se puede ∼ en dinero** you cannot put a value on it 2 (frml) ‹*trabajo/actuación*› to assess; **∼ algo positivamente/negativamente** to consider sth to be positive/negative 3 ‹*amistad/lealtad*› to value; **valoraba muy poco su dedicación** he attached very little value to her dedication; Ⓢ **se valorará experiencia** experience an advantage

valorización *f* 1 (tasación) ▸**valoración 1** 2 (AmL) (aumento de valor) increase in value, appreciation

valorizar [A4] *vt* ▸**valorar 1**

■ **valorizarse** *v pron* to appreciate, increase in value

vals *m* waltz; **bailar un ∼** to waltz

valuar *vt* [A18] (AmL) to value

valva *f* (Bot, Zool) valve

válvula *f* valve

(Compuesto) **válvula de escape** (Tec) exhaust valve; (de nervios) safety valve

vamos *see* **ir**

vampiresa *f* femme fatale, vamp (dated)

vampiro *m* 1 (en historias de horror) vampire; (explotador) vampire, bloodsucker 2 (Zool) vampire (bat)

van *see* **ir**

vanagloriarse [A1] *v pron* **∼ DE algo** to boast *o* brag ABOUT sth

vandálico -ca *adj* 1 (Hist) Vandalic 2 ‹*acción/comportamiento*› vandalistic

vandalismo *m* vandalism, hooliganism

vándalo[1] **-la** *adj* (Hist) Vandal (*before n*), Vandalic

vándalo[2] **-la** *m,f* 1 (Hist) Vandal 2 (gamberro) vandal, hooligan

vanguardia *f* (Mil) vanguard; (Art, Lit) avant-garde; **teatro de ∼** avant-garde theater; **ir** *or* **estar a la ∼ (de algo)** to be in the vanguard (of sth)

vanguardismo *m* avant-gardism

vanguardista *adj* avant-garde

vanidad *f* (presunción) vanity, conceit; (en cuanto al aspecto físico) vanity; (Relig) vanity

vanidoso[1] **-sa** *adj* (presumido) vain, conceited; (en cuanto al aspecto físico) vain

vanidoso[2] **-sa** *m,f*: **es un ∼** he's so vain *o* conceited

vano[1] **-na** *adj* 1 (ineficaz) ‹*discusión/intento*› vain, futile; ‹*amenazas*› idle; ‹*esfuerzo*› futile; ‹*excusa*› pointless; **en ∼** in vain 2 (falto de realidad) vain; **ilusiones vanas** wishful thinking 3 ‹*palabra/promesa*› empty

vano[2] *m* opening, space

vapor *m* 1 (Fís, Quím) vapor*, steam; ***a todo* ∼** at full tilt *o* steam 2 (Coc): **al ∼** steamed 3 (Náut) steamer, steamship

(Compuesto) **vapor de agua** water vapor*

vaporización *f* vaporization

vaporizador *m* vaporizer

vaporizar [A4] *vt* to vaporize

■ **vaporizarse** *v pron* to vaporize

vaporoso -sa *adj* filmy, diaphanous (liter)

vapulear [A1] *vt* to beat, give ... a beating

vapuleo *m* beating

vaquería *f* (ant) dairy

vaqueriza *f* (recinto) winter enclosure; (edificio) cowshed

vaquero[1] **-ra** *adj* 1 ‹*falda/cazadora*› denim; **un pantalón ∼** a pair of jeans *o* denims 2 ‹*estilo*› cowboy (*before n*)

vaquero[2] **-ra** *m,f*

A (Agr) (*m*) cowboy, cowhand; (*f*) cowgirl, cowhand

B (Per fam) (Educ) truant, skiver (BrE colloq)

C **vaquero** *m* (Indum) *tb* **∼s**: **unos ∼s nuevos** a new pair of jeans *o* denims

vaqueta *f* (Col, RPl) calfskin, leather

vaquetón -tona *adj* (Méx fam) shameless

vaquilla *f* heifer; **corrida de ∼s** *amateur bullfight with young bulls*

vaquillona *f* (CS, Per) heifer (*of between two and three years*)

vara *f*

A 1 (palo) stick, pole; (patrón) yardstick; **depende de la ∼ con que lo midas** it depends on the standards *o* criteria you're judging it by 2 (bastón de mando) staff of office 3 (Taur) lance, pike 4 (del trombón) slide 5 (medida de longitud) *unit of length approximately equivalent to one yard*

B (Per fam) (influencia) connections (*pl*) (colloq)

varadero *m* dry dock

varado -da *adj*

A 1 (Náut) ‹*barco*› aground; **quedar ∼** to run aground; **una ballena varada** a beached whale 2 (AmL) (detenido): **quedarse ∼** to be left stranded; **se quedaron ∼s subiendo la cuesta** they had a breakdown halfway up the hill

B 1 (Col, Méx fam) (sin dinero) broke (colloq) 2 (Andes) (sin empleo) out of work

varar [A1] *vt* to beach, careen

■ **varar** *vi* to run aground

■ **vararse** *v pron* to run aground

varear [A1] *vt* ‹*almendros/olivos*› to knock down; ‹*lana*› to beat

variable[1] *adj* ‹*carácter/humor*› changeable; **tiempo ∼** unsettled *o* changeable weather

variable[2] *f* variable

variación *f*

A (cambio) change, variation; **no habrá variaciones en la temperatura** there won't be much variation in temperature

B (Mat, Mús) variation

variado -da *adj* 1▸ ‹*programa/vida/trabajo*› varied 2▸ (diverso): **ropa de colores ~s** clothes in a variety of *o* in various colors; **S aperitivos/postres variados** choice of aperitifs/desserts; **hubo opiniones variadas** there were a variety of opinions

variante *f*
A (de palabra) variant
B (carretera) turnoff; **con la nueva ~, el puerto quedará a una hora de aquí** when the new road is opened, the port will only be an hour's drive from here

variar [A17] *vi* «*precio/temperatura*» to change; **las temperaturas varían entre 20°C y 25°C** temperatures range between 20°C and 25°C; **para ~** (iró) (just) for a change (iro); **el viento varió de dirección** the wind changed direction; **~ de opinión** to change one's mind
■ **variar** *vt*
A (hacer variado) ‹*menú*› to vary; ‹*producción*› to vary, diversify
B (cambiar) to change, alter

varicela *f* chicken pox

várices, (Esp) **varices** *fpl* ▸ **variz**

varicoso -sa *adj* varicose

variedad *f* 1▸ (diversidad) variety; **~ de opiniones** variety of opinions; ***en la ~ está el gusto*** variety is the spice of life 2▸ (clase, especie) variety 3▸ **variedades** *fpl* (Espec) vaudeville (AmE), variety (BrE); **espectáculo de ~es** vaudeville *o* variety show

varilla *f* (en general) rod; (de abanico, paraguas) rib; (de jaula) bar; (de rueda de bicicleta) spoke; (para medir el aceite) dipstick

varillo *m* (Col arg) joint (colloq), spliff (sl)

vario -ria *adj*
A **~s/varias** (más de dos) several; **sucedió varias veces/hace ~s años** it happened several times/several years ago; **una o varias circunstancias atenuantes** one or more mitigating circumstances
B (variado, diverso) various; **gastos ~s** miscellaneous expenses; **asuntos ~s** various matters; (en el orden del día) (any) other business

variopinto -ta *adj*: **el público asistente era de lo más ~** there was a really mixed audience; **objetos ~s** miscellaneous objects

varios -rias *pron* several; **lo compraron entre ~s** several of them got together to buy it

varita[1] *f* wand
(Compuesto) **varita mágica** magic wand

varita[2] *mf* (RPl fam) traffic cop (colloq)

variz (*pl* **várices** *or* (Esp) **varices**) *f* varicose vein

varo *m* (Méx fam) peso; **no traigo ni un ~** I don't have a penny on me (colloq)

varón[1] *adj* ‹*heredero/descendiente*› male; **un hijo ~** a son

varón[2] *m* (niño) boy; (hombre) man, male; **es un santo ~** he's a real saint (colloq)

varonera *f* (Arg fam) tomboy

varonil *adj* 1▸ (viril) manly, masculine; **voz/aspecto ~** masculine voice/appearance 2▸ ‹*mujer*› (hombruna) mannish, masculine

vas *see* **ir**

vasallaje *m* vassalage; **rendir ~** to pay homage and fealty

vasallo *m* vassal

vasco[1] **-ca** *adj/m,f* Basque

vasco[2] *m* (idioma) Basque

> **vasco** *or* **vascuence**
> ▸ **euskera**

Vascongadas *adj*: **las (Provincias) ~** (Hist) the Basque Country

vascular *adj* vascular

vasectomía *f* vasectomy

vaselina *f* Vaseline®, petroleum jelly

vasija *f* (Arqueol) vessel (frml); **una ~ de barro** an earthenware pot

vaso *m*
A 1▸ (recipiente) glass; **un ~ de vino** a wine glass; **~ de papel** paper cup 2▸ (contenido) glass; **se bebió el ~ de un trago** he drank the whole glassful *o* glass down in one go; **añadir dos ~s de agua** ≈ add two cups of water; **un ~ de vino** a glass of wine; ***ahogarse en un ~ de agua*** (fam) to make a mountain out of a molehill 3▸ (Arqueol) vase, urn
(Compuesto) **vasos comunicantes** *mpl* communicating vessels (*pl*)
B (Anat) vessel
(Compuesto) **vaso sanguíneo** blood vessel

vástago *m*
A (Bot) shoot
B (liter) (descendiente) scion (liter), descendant, offspring; **el último ~ de su estirpe** the last (descendant) of his line
C (de copa) stem

vastedad *f* vastness, immensity

vasto -ta *adj* (*gen delante del n*) ‹*mar/llanura*› vast, immense; ‹*conocimientos/experiencia*› vast, enormous

vate *m* (liter) bard (liter)

váter *m* (Esp fam) (inodoro) toilet, lavatory; (cuarto) bathroom (esp AmE), lavatory, toilet

vaticano -na *adj* Vatican (*before n*)

Vaticano *m*: **el ~** the Vatican; **Ciudad del ~** Vatican City

vaticinar [A1] *vt* (period) ‹*victoria/fracaso*› to forecast

vaticinio *m* (period) prediction, forecast

vatio *m* watt

vaya, vayas, etc *see* **ir**

Vd. = usted

Vda. = viuda

ve[1] *f* (AmL) *tb* **~ corta** *or* **chica** *or* **pequeña** *name of the letter* **v**

ve[2] *see* **ir, ver**

VE = Vuestra Excelencia

vea, veas, etc *see* **ver**

vecinal *adj* ‹*asociación/comisión*› neighborhood* (*before n*), local (*before n*)

vecindad *f*
A (lugar, barrio) neighborhood*, area; (vecinos) residents (*pl*)
B (Méx) (edificio) tenement house

vecindario ▸ **vecindad A**

vecino[1] **-na** *adj* 1▸ (contiguo) neighboring*; **los países ~s** the neighboring countries; **~ A algo** bordering ON sth, adjoining sth 2▸ (cercano) neighboring*, nearby

vecino[2] **-na** *m,f* 1▸ (persona que vive cerca) neighbor*; **mi ~ de al lado** my next-door neighbor 2▸ (habitante — de población, municipio) inhabitant; (— de barrio, edificio) resident

veda *f* (en caza y pesca) closed (AmE) *o* (BrE) close season; **la perdiz está en ~** it is the closed *o* close season for partridge

vedado *m* reserve
(Compuesto) **vedado de caza** game reserve

vedar [A1] *vt* 1▸ ‹*caza/pesca*› to prohibit, ban (*during the closed season*); **desde mañana queda vedada la pesca** the fishing season ends today 2▸ (prohibir) to ban; **tiene la entrada vedada allí** he's been banned from there; **ese tema está vedado** that subject is taboo *o* banned; **placeres que les están vedados** pleasures which are forbidden to them

vedette /be'ðet/ *f* cabaret star

vega *f*
A (Geog) ≈ meadow (*area of low-lying fertile land*)
B (Chi) (mercado de abastos) market

vegetación *f* 1▸ (Bot) vegetation 2▸ (Med) **vegetaciones** *fpl* adenoids (*pl*)

vegetal[1] *adj* ‹*vida*› plant (*before n*); ‹*aceite*› vegetable (*before n*)

vegetal[2] *m* plant, vegetable

vegetar [A1] *vi* 1▸ (Bot) to grow 2▸ (fam) «*persona*» to vegetate (colloq & pej)

vegetarianismo *m* vegetarianism

vegetariano -na *adj/m,f* vegetarian

vegetativo -va *adj* vegetative

vehemencia *f* vehemence; **con ~** vehemently

vehemente *adj* vehement

vehicular *adj* ‹*control*› traffic (*before n*); **el movimiento ~** the traffic

V

vehículo *m* vehicle
(Compuestos)
- **vehículo automóvil** car, automobile (AmE)
- **vehículo espacial** spacecraft

veía, veíamos, etc *see* ver
veinte[1] *adj inv/pron* twenty; *para ejemplos ver* **cinco, cincuenta**; ***caer el ~*** (Méx fam): **no me cayó el ~ de que ...** it didn't dawn on me that ... (colloq)
veinte[2] *m* (number) twenty
veinteavo[1] -va *adj* [1] (partitivo): **la veinteava parte** a twentieth [2] (crit) (ordinal) twentieth; **llegó en ~ lugar** she came twentieth; **es la veinteava edición del premio** the prize is in its twentieth year; **en el ~ piso** on the twentieth floor
veinteavo[2] *m* twentieth
veintena *f*: **una ~ de personas** about 20 people
veintitantos -tas *adj/pron* twenty-odd
veintiuna *f* blackjack
veintiuno[1] -na *adj/pron* [**veintiún** *is used before masculine nouns and before feminine nouns which begin with accented* **a** *or* **ha**] twenty-one; **veintiún años/armas** twenty-one years/weapons; *para ejemplos ver tb* **cinco**
veintiuno[2] *m* (number) twenty-one
vejación *f*, **vejamen** *m* humiliation
vejar [A1] *vt* to ill-treat
vejatorio -ria *adj* humiliating, degrading
vejestorio *m* [1] (fam) (persona): **la profesora es un ~** the teacher is ancient (colloq) [2] (AmL fam) (cosa) old relic (colloq), piece of old junk (colloq)
vejete *m* (fam) old guy (colloq)
vejez *f* old age; ***a la ~, viruela(s)*** (fam) you're only as young as you feel
vejiga *f* (Anat) bladder
vejucón *m* (Ven pey) dirty old man (pej)
vejucona *f* (Ven fam) middle-aged woman
vela *f*
A (para alumbrar) candle; ***darle a algn ~ en este entierro***: **nadie te ha dado ~ en este entierro** nobody asked for your opinion; ***hasta que las ~s no ardan*** (Chi fam) forever (colloq)
B (vigilia): **pasé la noche en ~ estudiando** I was up all night studying; **estuvo en ~ hasta que llegué** he couldn't get to sleep until I arrived
C [1] (de barco) sail; ***arriar*** *or* ***recoger ~s*** (Náut) to take down the sails; (dar marcha atrás) to back down; ***a toda ~*** ‹*navegar*› under full sail; ‹*trabajar/ir*› flat out; ***estar a dos ~s*** (fam) (sin dinero) to be broke (colloq); (sin entender) to be completely lost; ***hacerse a la ~*** to set sail [2] (deporte) sailing; **hacer ~** to go sailing
(Compuesto) **vela mayor** mainsail
D (fam) (de moco): **andar con la(s) ~(s) colgando** to have a runny nose
velación *f*, **velaciones** *fpl* (a difunto) wake
velada *f* evening; **una ~ literaria** a literary evening *o* soirée
velado -da *adj* ‹*película*› fogged; ‹*amenaza/referencia*› veiled; ‹*sonido*› muffled
velador[1] *m* [1] (mesa) pedestal table [2] (AmS) (mesilla de noche) bedside table, night stand (AmE) [3] (Col, RPl, Ven) (lámpara) bedside lamp
velador[2] -dora *m,f* (Méx) (de fábrica) watchman, guard
veladora *f* [1] (Méx, RPl) (lámpara) bedside lamp [2] (Méx) (vela) candle
velamen *m* sails (*pl*)
velar [A1] *vt*
A [1] ‹*difunto*› to hold a wake over; **lo ~on en su casa** they held the wake at his home [2] ‹*enfermo*› to watch over
B ‹*película*› to fog, expose; ‹*crítica*› to mask, veil
■ **velar** *vi*
A (permanecer despierto) to stay up *o* awake
B (cuidar) **~ POR algo/algn** to watch OVER sth/sb; **un organismo que vela por los derechos de ...** an organization which safeguards *o* protects the rights of ...
■ **velarse** *v pron* «*película*» to get fogged *o* exposed
velatorio *m* [1] (acción, reunión) wake, vigil (frml) [2] (establecimiento) funeral parlor*; (sala) chapel of rest

veleidad *f* [1] (volubilidad, ligereza) flightiness, fickleness; **~es de juventud** youthful follies [2] (RPl) (aire de grandeza): **tiene unas ~es ...** she really gives herself airs
veleidoso -sa *adj* fickle, capricious; (en relaciones amorosas) flighty, fickle
velero *m* [1] (Náut) (grande) sailing ship; (pequeño) sailboat (AmE), sailing boat (BrE) [2] (Aviac) glider
veleta *f* [1] (para el viento) weather vane, weathercock [2] **veleta** *mf* (fam) (persona inconstante) fickle person
vello *m*
A (pelusa) down; (en las piernas, etc) hair
(Compuesto) **vello púbico** pubic hair
B (Bot) bloom
vellocino *m* fleece
(Compuesto) **vellocino de oro** Golden Fleece
vellón *m* (piel) sheepskin; (de lana) fleece
vellosidad *f* (con pelusa) downiness; (de las piernas, etc) hairiness
velloso -sa, velludo -da *adj* [1] (con pelusa) downy [2] ‹*piernas*› hairy
velludo -da *adj* hairy; **es muy ~** he's very hairy
velo *m* veil; **~ de novia/monja** bridal/nun's veil; ***correr*** *or* ***echar un tupido ~ sobre algo*** to draw a veil over sth; ***descorrer el ~ sobre algo*** to uncover sth; ***tomar el ~*** to take the veil
velocidad *f*
A [1] (medida, relación) speed; **¿a qué ~ iba?** how fast was he going?; **cobrar ~** to pick up *o* gather speed; **disminuir la ~** to slow down; **a toda/gran ~** at top/high speed; **de alta ~** high-speed [2] (rapidez) speed; **la ~ con que lo hizo** the speed with which he did it
(Compuestos)
- **velocidad de crucero** cruising speed
- **velocidad de subida** rate of climb
- **velocidad máxima** *or* **punta** maximum *o* top speed

B (Auto, Mec) gear; **un modelo de cinco ~es** a five-gear model; **en primera ~** in first (gear)
velocímetro *m* speedometer
velocípedo *m* velocipede
velocista *mf* sprinter
velódromo *m* cycle track, velodrome
velomotor *m* moped
velorio *m* wake
veloz *adj* ‹*corredor*› fast; ‹*movimiento*› swift, quick; **~ *como un rayo*** *or* ***relámpago*** as quick as a flash
ven *see* **venir, ver**
vena *f*
A (Anat) vein; **inyectar en ~** to inject into a vein; **cortarse las ~s** to slash *o* cut one's wrists
(Compuesto) **vena coronaria/yugular** cardiac/jugular vein
B (Geol, Min) vein, seam
C (de madera) grain; (de piedra) vein, stripe
D [1] (disposición) vein, disposition; **en ~ poética** in a poetic vein; ***darle la ~ a algn*** (fam): **le dio la ~ y dejó el trabajo** she upped and left her job on an impulse (colloq); **cuando le da la ~ de pintar ...** when he's in the mood to paint ...; ***estar en ~*** (fam) to be in the mood; ***tener ~ de algo*** to have the makings of sth [2] (talento) talent
venado *m* [1] (Zool) deer; ***pintar ~*** (Méx fam) to play hooky (esp AmE colloq), skive off (school) (BrE colloq) [2] (Coc) venison
venal *adj* (frml) venal (frml)
venalidad *f* (frml) venality (frml)
vencedor[1] -dora *adj* ‹*ejército/país*› victorious; ‹*equipo/jugador*› winning (*before n*)
vencedor[2] -dora *m,f* (en guerra) victor; (en competición) winner; **no habrá ~es ni vencidos** (frml) there will be no victors and no vanquished (frml)
vencejo *m* swift
vencer [E2] *vt* [1] ‹*enemigo*› to defeat, vanquish (liter); ‹*rival/competidor*› to defeat, beat; **no te dejes ~** don't give in [2] ‹*miedo/pesimismo/obstáculo*› to overcome [3] (dominar): **me venció el sueño/el cansancio** I was overcome by sleep/tiredness
■ **vencer** *vi*

V

A «*ejército/equipo*» to win, be victorious; **¡~emos!** we shall overcome!
B 1 «*pasaporte/garantía*» to expire; **el lunes vence el plazo** Monday is the deadline; **antes de que venza la garantía** before the guarantee runs out *o* expires 2 «*letra*» to be due for payment
■ **vencerse** *v pron*
A «*tabla/rama*» to give way, break
B (AmL) «*pasaporte/garantía*» to expire; **se me venció el carnet** my card expired *o* ran out

vencido[1] -da *adj*
A ‹*ejército/país*› defeated, vanquished (liter); ‹*equipo/jugador*› losing (*before n*), beaten; ***darse por ~*** to give up *o* in
B 1 ‹*visa/pasaporte*› expired, out-of-date; **pagar a mes ~** to pay a month in arrears; **estos antibióticos están ~s** (AmL) these antibiotics are past their expiration (AmE) *o* (BrE) expiry date 2 ‹*boleto/cheque*› out-of-date 3 ‹*letra/intereses*› due for payment
C (doblado, torcido): **la viga está vencida** the beam is weak *o* is sagging; **era ~ de espaldas** he had a stoop

vencido[2] -da *m,f*: **los ~s** the defeated, the vanquished (liter); ***jugar a las vencidas*** (Méx) to armwrestle

vencimiento *m* (de letra, pago) due date; (de carnet, licencia) expiration (AmE) *o* (BrE) expiry date

venda *f* bandage; **~ elástica** elastic bandage; ***caérsele a algn la ~ de los ojos***: **se le cayó la ~ de los ojos** the scales fell from his eyes; ***tener una ~ en los ojos*** to be blind (colloq); **tiene una ~ en los ojos y cree que es perfecto** she's blind (to his faults) and thinks he's perfect

vendaje *m* dressing; **poner un ~** to put on a dressing

vendar [A1] *vt* to bandage; **un brazo vendado** a bandaged arm

vendaval *m* gale, strong wind

vendedor -dora *m,f* 1 (en mercado) stallholder, stallkeeper (AmE); (en tienda) salesclerk (AmE), shop assistant (BrE); (viajante, representante) sales representative 2 (Der) (propietario que vende) vendor

Compuestos
- **vendedor -dora a domicilio** *m,f* door-to-door sales agent
- **vendedor -dora ambulante** *m,f* peddler, hawker
- **vendedor -dora de periódicos** *m,f* newspaper vendor *o* seller

vendepatria *mf* (fam) traitor

vender [E1] *vt*
A ‹*mercancías/casa*› to sell; **vendió la casa muy bien** she got a very good price for her house; **le vendí el reloj** I sold him the watch; **se vende muy bien/poco** it sells very well/doesn't sell very well; Ⓢ **se vende** for sale; **~ al por mayor/menor** to sell wholesale/retail; **~ algo A algo** to sell sth AT sth; **lo venden a $500 el kilo** they sell it at $500 a kilo; **~ algo EN** *or* **POR algo** to sell sth FOR sth; **vendí el cuadro en** *or* **por $20.000** I sold the painting for $20,000; **~ algo POR algo**: **se vende por kilo(s)/unidad(es)** it's sold by the kilo/unit
B 1 (traicionar) to betray 2 (delatar) to give … away; **el acento lo vende** his accent gives him away
■ **vender** *vi* «*producto*» to sell; **una escritora que vende** a best-selling author
■ **venderse** *v pron* to sell out; **se vendió por un ascenso** he sold out to get promotion

vendible *adj* salable*

vendimia *f* grape harvest, wine harvest

vendimiador -dora *m,f* grape harvester *o* picker

vendimiar [A1] *vt* to pick, harvest

vendré, vendría, etc *see* **venir**

venduta *f* (Col) public sale (*of household goods*)

Venecia *f* Venice

veneciano -na *adj/m,f* Venetian

veneno *m* 1 (sustancia tóxica) poison; (de culebra) venom; **el tabaco es un ~ para la salud** tobacco *o* smoking is very harmful to your health 2 (malevolencia) venom

venenosidad *f* toxicity

venenoso -sa *adj* ‹*sustancia/planta*› poisonous; ‹*araña/serpiente*› poisonous, venomous; ‹*palabras/mirada*› venomous

venera *f* scallop (shell)

venerable *adj/m,f* venerable

veneración *f* 1 (adoración) adoration, veneration (frml); **siente ~ por su hija** he worships his daughter 2 (Relig) veneration

venerar [A1] *vt* (adorar, reverenciar) to revere, worship; (Relig) to venerate

venéreo -rea *adj* venereal

venero *m* (yacimiento) vein, seam, lode; (manantial) (frml & liter) spring; **un ~ de datos** a mine of information

venezolanismo *m* Venezuelan word (*o* phrase *etc*), Venezuelanism

venezolano -na *adj/m,f* Venezuelan

Venezuela *f* Venezuela

venga *interj* (Esp fam) 1 (para animar) come on; ***¡~ ya!*** (fam) come off it! (colloq) 2 (para exigir algo): **~ el lápiz que me quitaste** let's have the pencil you took off me (colloq) 3 (expresando insistencia) **~ A + INF** (fam): **y ~ a protestar** and they just kept *o* went on (and on) complaining

vengador[1] -dora *adj* avenging (*before n*)

vengador[2] -dora *m,f* avenger

vengáis, vengamos, etc *see* **venir**

venganza *f* revenge, vengeance (liter); **actuó por ~** she acted out of a desire for revenge

vengar [A3] *vt* ‹*insulto/derrota*› to take revenge for, to avenge; ‹*persona*› to avenge
■ **vengarse** *v pron* to take revenge; **~se DE** *or* **POR algo** to take revenge FOR sth; **~se DE/EN algn** to take (one's) revenge ON sb

vengativo -va *adj* vindictive, vengeful (liter)

vengo *see* **venir**

venia *f*
A 1 (frml) (autorización) consent, authorization 2 (para pedir la palabra) permission, leave; **con la ~ de la sala** with the permission of the court
B 1 (Andes, RPl, Ven) (inclinación de cabeza) bow 2 (RPl) (saludo militar) salute; **hacer la ~** to salute

venial *adj* venial

venialidad *f* veniality

venida *f* 1 (llegada) arrival 2 (AmL) (vuelta): **a la** *or* **de ~** on the way back

venidero -ra *adj* future (*before n*)

venir [I31] *vi*
A 1 (a un lugar) to come; **vine en tren/avión** I came by train/plane; **¿a qué vino?** what did he come by *o* around for?; **¿ha venido el electricista?** has the electrician been?; **¡que venga el encargado!** I want to see the person in charge!; **vine dormida todo el tiempo** I slept (for) the whole journey; **~ POR** *or* (Esp) **A POR algn/algo** to come FOR sb/sth, come to pick sb/sth up; **~ A + INF** to come to + INF; **ven a ver esto** come and see this 2 (volver) to come back; **ahora vengo** I'll be back in a moment; **no vengas tarde** don't be late home *o* back 3 (salir) **~ CON algo**: **me vino con un cuento** he came up with some excuse; **no me vengas con exigencias** don't start making demands; **no me vengas con eso ahora** don't give me that (colloq); **y ahora viene con que necesita el doble** and now he says he needs double 4 (sobrevenir) (+ *me/te/le etc*): **me vino una gripe** I came *o* went down with flu; **me vinieron unas ganas de reír …** I felt like bursting out laughing
B 1 (tener lugar): **ahora viene esa escena que te conté** that scene I told you about is coming up now; **entonces vino la guerra** then the war came; **¿qué viene después de las noticias?** what's on after the news?; **ya vendrán tiempos mejores** things will get better 2 (indicando procedencia) **~ DE algo** to come FROM sth; **viene de la India** it comes from India; **le viene de familia** it runs in his family; **de ahí viene que tenga deudas** that's why he has debts; **¿a qué viene eso?** why do you say that?; **¿a qué vienen esos gritos?** what's all the shouting about? 3 (indicando presentación) to come; **viene en tres tamaños** it comes in three sizes; **el folleto viene en inglés** the brochure is available in English 4 (estar incluido): **viene en primera página** it's on the front page; **no viene nada sobre la huelga** there's nothing about the strike
C (+ *me/te/le etc*) 1 (quedar) (+ *compl*): **la camisa te viene ancha** the shirt's too big for you; **ese abrigo le viene mal** that coat doesn't suit her; **el cargo le viene grande**

V

he isn't up to the job 2 (convenir) (+ *compl*): **estas cajas me vendrían muy bien** these boxes would come in handy; **¿te viene bien a las ocho?** is eight o'clock all right *o* OK for you?; **el jueves no me viene bien** Thursday's no good for me; **me vendría bien un descanso** I could do with a rest

D (*como aux*) 1 ~ A + INF: **esto viene a confirmar mis sospechas** this confirms my suspicions; **vendrá a tener unos 30 años** she must be about 30; **el precio viene a ser el mismo** the price works out (about) the same 2 ~ + GER: **hace mucho que lo venía diciendo** I'd been saying so all along; **viene trabajando aquí desde hace muchos años** he has been working here for many years

■ **venirse** *v pron* (*enf*) 1 (a un lugar) to come; **se vinieron a pie** they came on foot; **¿te vienes al parque?** are you coming to the park?; ***~se abajo*** «*persona*» to go to pieces; «*techo*» to fall in, collapse; «*estante*» to collapse; «*ilusiones*» to go up in smoke; «*proyectos*» to fall through 2 (volver) to come back

venoso -sa *adj* ‹*sangre/enfermedades*› venous; ‹*manos/hoja*› veined

venta *f*

A (Com) sale; **se dedica a la compra y ~ de coches usados** he's in the used car business; ⓢ **prohibida su venta** not for sale; ⓢ **prohibida la venta ambulante** no hawkers; **pronto saldrá a la ~** it will be on sale soon; **de ~ en kioscos** on sale at newsstands; **estar en** *or* **a la ~** «*coche/bicicleta*» to be for sale; «*casa*» to be (up) for sale

Compuestos
- **venta al contado** cash sale
- **venta al por mayor/menor** wholesale/retail
- **venta a plazos** installment plan (AmE), hire purchase (BrE)
- **venta de garaje** garage sale
- **venta piramidal** pyramid selling
- **venta por catálogo** *or* **correo** mail order

B (posada) (arc) inn, hostelry (arch)

ventaja *f* 1 (beneficio) advantage; **tiene la ~ de que está cerca** it has the advantage of being near; **tienes ~ por tu experiencia** you have an advantage because of your experience 2 (en carrera): **lleva** *or* **tiene una ~ de diez segundos** she has a ten-second lead; **te doy una ~ de tres metros** I'll give you a three-meter head start; **sacó ~ en la curva** he pulled ahead on the bend; **estaba jugando con ~** he was at an advantage

ventajero -ra *m,f* (RPl) opportunist

ventajista[1] *adj* opportunistic, opportunist (*before n*)

ventajista[2] *mf* opportunist

ventajoso[1] **-sa** *adj* 1 ‹*negocio*› profitable; ‹*acuerdo/situación*› favorable*, advantageous 2 (Col) ‹*persona*› opportunistic

ventajoso[2] **-sa** *m,f* (Col) opportunist

ventana *f*

A 1 (Arquit, Const) window; ***tirar algo por la ~*** (literal) to throw sth out of the window; (desperdiciar) to throw sth away 2 (Inf) window

Compuestos
- **ventana de guillotina** sash window
- **ventana de socorro** emergency exit

B (de la nariz) nostril

ventanal *m* large window

ventanilla *f* 1 (de coche, tren) window; ⓢ **prohibido asomarse por la ventanilla** do not lean out of the window 2 (en oficinas) window; (en cines, teatros) box office; **horario de ~** opening hours 3 (Inf) window

ventanillo *m* small window

ventarrón *m* (fam) strong wind

ventear [A1] *vt*

A «*animal*» to sniff

B ‹*ropa*› to air

■ **ventear** *v impers*: **está venteando mucho** it's very windy

ventero -ra *m,f* innkeeper

ventilación *f* 1 (posibilidad de ventilarse) ventilation; **la única ~ era un extractor** the only means of ventilation was an extractor fan 2 (acción de ventilar) airing

ventilador *m* (aparato) fan; (abertura) ventilator, air vent

Compuesto **ventilador hélice** *or* **de aspas** ceiling fan

ventilar [A1] *vt*

A ‹*habitación*› to air, ventilate; ‹*ropa/colchón*› to air

B 1 ‹*secreto*› to spread around; **siempre ventilan sus problemas matrimoniales delante de todos** they're forever airing their marital differences in front of everyone 2 ‹*asunto/problema*› to talk about

■ **ventilarse** *v pron*

A «*habitación/ropa*» to air

B (fam) (tomar el aire) to get a breath of fresh air, get some air

ventisca *f* snowstorm; (con más viento) blizzard

ventiscar [A2], **ventisquear** [A1] *v impers*: **está ventiscando** there is a blizzard blowing

■ **ventiscar** *vi* «*nieve*» to drift

ventisquero *m* (lugar expuesto) *place exposed to blizzards*; (nevero) snowfield, icefield; (nieve) snowdrift

ventolera *f* gust of wind; ***darle a algn la ~*** (fam): **le dio la ~ de casarse** he suddenly decided that he ought to get married

ventolina *f* (viento flojo) light wind; (ráfaga) (CS) gust of wind

ventosa *f* 1 (de goma, plástico) suction pad 2 (Zool) sucker 3 (Med) cupping glass

ventosidad *f* wind, flatulence

ventoso -sa *adj* windy

ventrículo *m* ventricle

ventrílocuo -cua *m,f* ventriloquist

ventriloquismo *m* ventriloquy

ventura *f*

A (liter) 1 (suerte) fortune; **tiene la ~ de tenerlo a usted para ayudarlo** he is fortunate *o* he has the good fortune to have you to help him; **tuvo la buena ~ de que no le ocurriese nada** she was fortunate that nothing happened to her; **quiso la ~ que ...** as chance *o* luck would have it ...; ***echarle la buena ~ a algn*** to tell sb's fortune 2 (satisfacción, dicha) happiness; **le deseo la mayor de las ~s** I wish him every happiness

B (*en locs*) **a la ventura: viven a la ~** they take each day as it comes; **salieron a la ~** they set out with no fixed plan; **no había estudiado, fue a la ~** he hadn't studied, he just went along hoping for the best; **por ventura** (frml) (afortunadamente) fortunately; (acaso) perhaps

venturoso -sa *adj* (*delante del n*) (liter) happy; **ese ~ encuentro** that fortunate meeting (liter); **el ~ día en que la conocí** the happy day that I met her (liter)

ventuta *f* (Col) garage sale

venus *f* beauty, goddess

Venus 1 *m* (Astron) Venus 2 *f* (Art, Mit) Venus

veo *see* **ver** [2]

ver[1] *m*

A (aspecto): **de buen ~** good-looking, attractive; **no es de mal ~** she's not bad-looking

B (opinión): **a mi/su ~** in my/his view

ver[2] [E29] *vt*

A 1 (percibir con la vista) to see; **¿ves algo?** can you see anything?; **no se ve nada aquí** you can't see a thing in here; **tú ves visiones** you're seeing things; **es como si lo estuviera viendo** it's as if I were seeing him/it now; **~ algo/a algn + INF** to see sth/sb + INF; **la vi bailar hace años** I saw her dance years ago; **lo vi hablando con ella** I saw him talking to her; ***si te he visto no me acuerdo*** (fam) he/she doesn't/didn't want to know; **~ *venir algo*** to see sth coming 2 (mirar) ‹*programa/partido*› to watch; **~ (la) televisión** to watch television; **esa película ya la he visto** I've seen that movie before; **déjame ~** let me see; ***no poder (ni) ~ a algn***: **no puede ni ~la** *or* **no la puede ~** he can't stand her 3 (imaginar) to see, picture

B (entender, notar) to see; **¿no ves lo que está pasando?** don't *o* can't you see what's happening?; **no quiere ~ la realidad** he won't face up to reality; **sólo ve sus problemas** he's only interested in his own problems; **se te ve en la cara** I can tell by your face; **se la ve feliz/preocupada** she looks happy/worried; **ya lo veo** I can see that; ***hacerse ~*** (RPl) to show off; ***echar de ver*** (Esp) to realize

C 1 (constatar, comprobar) to see; **ve a ~ quién es** go and see who it is; **¡ya ~ás lo que pasa!** you'll see what happens; **habrá que ~ si lo hace** it remains to be seen whether he does it; **¡eso ya se ~á!** we'll see; **¡eso está por ~!** we'll see about that!; **no me olvidé ¡para que veas!** I didn't forget, see?; **le gané ¡para que veas!** I beat him, so there! **2▸** (ser testigo de) to see; **vieron confirmadas sus sospechas** they saw their suspicions confirmed; **¡nunca he visto cosa igual!** I've never seen anything like it!; **¡habráse visto semejante desfachatez!** what a nerve! (colloq); **¡si vieras lo mal que lo pasé!** you can't imagine how awful it was!; **es tan bonita, si vieras ...** she's so pretty, you should see her; **¡vieras** *or* **hubieras visto cómo se asustaron ...!** (AmL) you should have seen the fright they got!; **ya ves, aquí me tienes** well, here I am; **¡hay que ~!** would you believe it!; **¡hay que ~ lo que ha crecido!** wow *o* gosh! hasn't he grown!; **hay que ~ lo grosera que es** she's incredibly rude; ***que no veas*** (Esp fam): **me echó una bronca que no veas** you wouldn't believe the earful she gave me! (colloq); ***que no veo*** (AmL fam): **tengo un hambre que no veo** (fam) I'm absolutely starving (colloq); **tengo un sueño que no veo** I'm so tired I can hardly keep my eyes open

D **a ver**: **(vamos) a ~ ¿de qué se trata?** OK *o* all right, now, what's the problem?; **aquí está en el periódico — ¿a ~?** it's here in the newspaper — let's see; **¿a ~ qué tienes ahí?** let me see what you've got there; **apriétalo a ~ qué pasa** press it and let's see what happens; **a ~ si me entienden** (justificando) don't get me wrong; (explicando) let me make myself clear; **a ~ si estudias más** I'd think about studying harder; **a ~ si escribes pronto** make sure you write soon; **¡cállate, a ~ si alguien te oye!** shut up, somebody might hear you; **a ~ cuándo vienes a visitarnos** come and see us soon

E **1▸** (estudiar): **esto mejor que lo veas tú** you'd better have a look at this; **tengo que ~ cómo lo arreglo** I have to work out how I can fix it; **ya ~é qué hago** I'll decide what to do later; **véase el capítulo anterior** see (the) previous chapter; **no vimos ese tema en clase** we didn't cover that topic in class **2▸** ‹*médico*› (examinar) to see; **¿la ha visto un médico?** has she been seen by a doctor yet?; **se hizo ~ por un especialista** (AmS) she saw a specialist **3▸** (Der) ‹*causa*› to try, hear

F **1▸** (juzgar, considerar): **yo eso no lo veo bien** I don't think that's right; **cada uno ve las cosas a su manera** everybody sees things differently; **a mi modo** *or* **manera de ~** the way I see it **2▸** (encontrar) to see; **no le veo salida a esto** I can't see any way out of this; **no le veo la gracia** I don't think it's funny; **no le veo nada de malo** I can't see anything wrong in it

G (visitar, entrevistarse con) ‹*amigo/pariente*› to see, visit; ‹*médico/jefe*› to see; **¡cuánto tiempo sin ~te!** I haven't seen you for ages!, long time, no see (colloq); **ahora lo vemos menos** we don't see so much of him now

H **tener ... que ver**: **¿y eso qué tiene que ~?** and what does that have to do with it?; **no tengo nada que ~ con él** I have nothing to do with him; **¿tuviste algo que ~ en esto?** did you have anything to do with this?; **¿qué tiene que ~ que sea sábado?** what difference does it make that it's Saturday?; **¿tendrán algo que ~ con los Zamora?** are they related in any way to the Zamoras?

■ **ver** *vi*

A (percibir con la vista) to see; **enciende la luz que no veo** turn on the light, I can't see; **no veo bien de lejos/de cerca** I'm shortsighted/longsighted

B (constatar): **¿hay cerveza? — no sé, voy a ~** is there any beer? — I don't know, I'll have a look; **¿está Juan? — voy a ~** is Juan in? — I'll go and see; **~ás, no quería decírtelo, pero ...** look, I didn't want to tell you, but ...; **pues ~ás, todo empezó cuando ...** well you see, the whole thing began when ...; **~ *para creer*** seeing is believing

C (pensar) to see; **¿vas a decir que sí? — ya ~é** are you going to accept? — I'll see; ***estar/seguir en ~emos*** (AmL fam): **todavía está en ~emos** it isn't certain yet; **seguimos en ~emos** we still don't know anything

■ **verse** *v pron*

A (*refl*) **1▸** (percibirse) to see oneself; **se vio reflejado en el agua** he saw his reflection in the water **2▸** (imaginarse) to see oneself

B **1▸** (hallarse) (+ *compl*) to find oneself; **me vi en un aprieto** I found myself in a tight spot; **me vi obligado a despedirlo** I had no choice but to dismiss him; ***vérselas venir*** (fam): **me las veía venir** I could see it coming; ***~se venir algo*** to see sth coming **2▸** (frml) (ser): **este problema se ha visto agravado por ...** this problem has been made worse by ...; **el país se ~á beneficiado** the country will benefit

C (dejar ver) (+ *me/te/le etc*): **se te ve todo** you're showing everything

D (esp AmL) (parecer): **se ve bien con esa falda** she looks good in that skirt; **no se ve bien con ese peinado** that hairdo doesn't suit her

E (*recípr*) (encontrarse) to meet; (visitarse) to see each other; **nos vemos a las siete** I'll meet *o* see you at seven; **no nos vimos durante un tiempo** we didn't see each other for a while; **¡nos vemos!** (esp AmL) see you!; **~se con algn** to see sb; ***vérselas con algn***: **tendrá que vérselas conmigo** he'll have me to deal with

vera *f* (ant) (de río) bank; **a la ~ del camino** by the roadside

veracidad *f* veracity (frml), truthfulness; **la ~ de sus palabras** the truth of his words

veranda *f* (galería) veranda, verandah; (de vidrio) conservatory

veraneante *mf* vacationer (AmE), holidaymaker (BrE)

veranear [A1] *vi*: **solía ~ en un pueblo** she used to spend her summer vacation (AmE) *o* (BrE) holidays in a small town

veraneo *m*: **fuimos de ~ al campo** we spent our summer vacation (AmE) *o* (BrE) holidays in the country; **lugar de ~** summer resort

veraniego -ga *adj* summer (*before n*); **vas muy ~** you're looking very summery

verano *m* summer; (en la zona tropical) dry season; **en ~** in summertime; **ropa de ~** summer clothes; **en pleno ~** at the height of summer, in high summer

veras: **de ~** (*loc adv*) really; **lo siento de ~** I really am sorry; **esta vez va de ~** this time it's serious *o* (colloq) it's for real; **¡no lo dirás de ~!** you can't be serious!

veraz *adj* truthful

verbal *adj* verbal

verbalizar [A4] *vt* to verbalize, put ... into words

verbena *f*

A (Bot) verbena

B (fiesta popular) festival; (baile) open-air dance

verbenero -ra *adj* festive

verbigracia *loc adv* (frml) for example, eg

verbo *m*

A (Ling) verb

B (lenguaje) speech; **un hombre de ~ fluido** an articulate *o* eloquent man; **con dominio del ~** eloquently

C **el Verbo** (Relig) the Word

verborrea *f* verbiage, verbosity; **sufre de ~** (fam & hum) he has verbal diarrhea* (colloq & hum)

verbosidad *f* verbosity

verboso -sa *adj* verbose, wordy

verdad *f*

A **1▸** (veracidad) truth; **es la pura ~** it's the gospel truth; **a decir ~ ...** to tell you the truth ...; **me dijo la ~ a medias** she only told me half the truth; **la ~, no lo sé** I don't honestly know; **la ~ es que ...** the truth is that ...; **en honor a la ~** in all fairness; **¡eso no es ~!** that's not true!; **si bien es ~ que ...** it might well be true that ...; **faltar a la ~** to be untruthful; ***creer que se está en posesión de la ~*** to think one is always right **2▸** **de verdad** (*loc adv*) really; (*loc adj*) real; **¡de ~ que me gusta!** I really do like it!; **de ~ que lo siento** I really am sorry; **una pistola de ~** a real gun **3▸** (buscando corroboración): **¡es muy guapa ¿~?** she's very beautiful, isn't she?; **¿~ que tú me entiendes?** you understand me, don't you?

B (enunciado verdadero) truth; **eso es una gran ~** that is *so* true!; ***cantarle*** *or* ***decirle cuatro ~es a algn*** to tell sb a few home truths; ***ser una ~ como un templo*** to be self-evident; ***~es como puños***: **dice ~es como puños** he isn't afraid to tell the truth

verdaderamente *adv* **1▸** ‹*feliz/asqueroso/difícil*› really **2▸** (*indep*) honestly; **~, no sé qué hacer** I honestly *o* really don't know what to do

verdadero -ra *adj*
A 1 ‹*premisa/historia*› true; ‹*caso/nombre*› real 2 ‹*pieles/joyas*› real
B (*delante del n*) (uso enfático) real; **se portó como un ~ imbécil** he behaved like a real *o* (colloq) proper idiot; **fue un ~ padre para mí** he was like a father to me

verde[1] *adj*
A ‹*color/ojos/vestido*› green; **zapatos ~ claro/oscuro** light/dark green shoes; **ojos ~ azulado** bluish *o* (BrE) bluey green eyes; ***estar ~ de envidia*** (CS) to be green with envy
B ‹*fruta*› green, unripe; ‹*leña*› green; ***estar ~*** (fam) (no tener experiencia) to be green (colloq); (en una asignatura): **está ~ en historia** he doesn't know the first thing about history (colloq); **el plan todavía está ~** the plan is still in its very early stages
C (Pol) Green
D (fam) ‹*chiste*› dirty, blue (colloq); ▸ **viejo**[2]**A**

verde[2] *m*
A (color) green; (Bot) greenery
(Compuestos)
- **verde botella** *adj inv* bottle-green
- **verde esmeralda** *adj inv* emerald-green, emerald
- **verde oliva** *adj inv* olive-green
- **verde perico** (Col) *adj inv* bright-green

B **verde** *mf* (Pol) Green; **los ~s** the Greens

verdear [A1] *vi* (aparecer de color verde) to look green; (ponerse verde) to turn green

verdín *m* 1 (musgo) moss 2 (moho) mold*; (en el agua) slime; (en metal) verdigris

verdor *m* greenness

verdoso -sa *adj* greenish

verdugo *m*
A 1 (en ejecuciones) executioner; (en la horca) hangman 2 (persona cruel) tyrant
B (Indum) balaclava; (para el esquí) ski mask
C 1 (vástago) shoot 2 (látigo) whip, lash; (espada) rapier

verdugón *m* welt, weal

verdulería, verdurería *f* fruit and vegetable store, greengrocer's (BrE)

verdulero -ra, verdurero -ra *m,f* (persona) greengrocer; **habla como una verdulera** (fam) she talks like a real fishwife (colloq)

verdura *f* (Bot, Coc) vegetable; (verdor) (liter) greenness (liter)

vereda *f* 1 (senda) path; ***entrar en ~*** to toe the line; ***hacer entrar a algn en ~*** to make sb toe the line 2 (CS, Per) (acera) sidewalk (AmE), pavement (BrE) 3 (Col) (distrito) district

veredicto *m* (Der) verdict; (dictamen) opinion, verdict
(Compuesto) **veredicto de culpabilidad/inocencia** verdict of guilty/not guilty

verga *f*
A 1 (Náut) spar, yard 2 (varilla) rod
B (Zool) penis; (pene) (vulg) cock (vulg)

vergel *m* (liter) (huerto) orchard; (jardín) garden

verglás *m* (en roca, superficie) verglas; (en autopista, camino) black ice

vergonzante *adj* ‹*enfermedad/error*› embarrassing

vergonzoso -sa *adj*
A (tímido) shy, bashful
B ‹*asunto/comportamiento*› disgraceful, shameful

vergüenza *f*
A (turbación) embarrassment; **no lo hagas pasar ~** don't embarrass him; **se puso colorado de ~** he blushed with embarrassment; **me da ~ pedírselo otra vez** I'm embarrassed to ask him again; **sentí ~ ajena** I felt embarrassed for him/her/them
B (sentido del decoro) (sense of) shame; **¡no tienes ~!** you should be ashamed of yourself!; **¡qué falta de ~ tienes!** have you no shame?; ***perder la ~*** to lose all sense of shame
C (escándalo, motivo de oprobio) disgrace; **una ~ nacional** a national disgrace; **ser una ~ para algo/algn** to be a disgrace to sth/sb; **estos precios son una ~** these prices are outrageous; **¿perdiste otra vez? ¡qué ~!** (hum) you mean you lost again? shame on you!
D **vergüenzas** *fpl* (euf & hum) (genitales) privates (*pl*) (euph & hum)

vericuetos *mpl* (terreno abrupto) rough terrain; (vueltas) twists and turns (*pl*); **los ~s de la vida** the ups and downs of life

verídico -ca *adj* true

verificable *adj* verifiable

verificación *f* (de hechos) verification, establishment; (de resultados) checking; (de máquina) testing, checking

verificar [A2] *vt* ‹*hechos*› to establish, verify; ‹*resultado*› to check; ‹*pagos/cuentas*› to check, audit; ‹*máquina/instrumento*› to check, test
■ **verificarse** *v pron* 1 (period) «*suceso/acto*» to take place, be held 2 «*pronóstico/predicción*» to come true

verificativo *m* (Méx frml): **tener ~** to take place

verismo *m* (realismo) realism; (Art, Lit) verism

verja *f* (cerca) railings (*pl*); (puerta) wrought-iron gate; (de ventana) (wrought-iron) grille

vermut[1] /ber'mu(t)/ *m* (*pl* **-muts**) vermouth

vermut[2] /ber'mu(t)/ *f* (*pl* **-muts**) (CS) early evening performance

vernáculo -la *adj* vernacular

verónica *f* (Taur) *pass made with cape held in both hands*

verosímil *adj* ‹*excusa/versión*› plausible; **las situaciones que narra no resultan muy ~es** the situations he writes about are not very realistic *o* true to life

verosimilitud *f* (de excusa, historia) plausibility; (de versión, personaje) credibility

verraco[1] **-ca** *adj* (Col fam) 1 (estupendo) fantastic (colloq) 2 (valiente) plucky (colloq), gutsy (colloq)

verraco[2] *m* boar

verruga *f* 1 (Med) (en la mano, cara) wart; (en los pies) verruca 2 (Bot) wart

versado -da *adj* [SER] **~ EN algo**: **es ~ en la materia** he's an authority on the subject; **un hombre muy ~ en filosofía** a man who is well versed in philosophy

versalita *f* small capital

versar [A1] *vi* (liter) «*tratado/discurso*» **~ SOBRE algo** to deal with sth

versátil *adj* 1 (polifacético) versatile 2 (inconstante) fickle, changeable

versatilidad *f*
A 1 (diversidad) versatility 2 (inconstancia) fickleness, changeability
B (Zool) versatility

versículo *m* verse

versificación *f* versification

versificar [A2] *vi/vt* to versify

versión *f* 1 (de obra, suceso) version; **~ cinematográfica** movie version 2 (traducción) translation 3 (modelo) model
(Compuestos)
- **versión alfa/beta** alpha/beta version
- **versión original** *movie in its original language*

verso *m*
A (Lit) (línea) line, verse; (poema) poem; (género) verse; **en ~** in verse
(Compuesto) **verso blanco/libre** blank/free verse
B (RPl fam) (mentira): **es todo ~** it's all lies; ***hacerle el ~ a algn*** (RPl) to try to con sb (colloq)

versus *prep* versus, against

vértebra *f* vertebra

vertebrado[1] **-da** *adj* vertebrate

vertebrado[2] *m* vertebrate; **los ~s** the vertebrates

vertebral *adj* vertebral; ▸ **columna**

vertedero *m*
A (para basura) dump; **un ~ de residuos nucleares** a dumping site for nuclear waste
B (desagüe) outlet

vertedor *m* (de depósito) outlet; (de presa) spillway

verter [E31] *or* [E8] *vt*
A 1 (echar) ‹*agua/vino/trigo*› to pour; **~ residuos radiactivos** to dump radioactive waste 2 (derramar) ‹*líquido*› to spill; ‹*lágrimas/sangre*› (liter) to shed (liter)
B (period) (expresar) ‹*opiniones*› to voice, state
C (frml) 1 (traducir) **~ algo A algo** to translate *o* (frml) render sth INTO sth; **vertió el poema al francés** he translated the poem into French 2 (trasladar): **vertió sus sentimientos al papel** he put his feelings down on paper

■ **verter** *vi* to flow; **el Ebro vierte al Mediterráneo** the Ebro flows into the Mediterranean

vertical[1] *adj*
A [1] ‹*línea/madero*› vertical; **en posición ~** in an upright *o* a vertical position [2] (en crucigramas): **el tres ~** three down
B (Pol, Rels Labs) vertical

vertical[2] *f* [1] (Mat, Tec) vertical line, vertical (tech); **una caída en ~** a sheer drop [2] (Dep) handstand

vertical[3] *m* (Dep) post, upright

verticalidad *f* verticality

verticalista *adj* (AmS) vertical

vértice *m* (de ángulo, figura) vertex, apex; (coronilla) crown

vertido *m* (accidental) spilling, spillage; (deliberado) dumping

vertiente *f* [1] (de montaña, tejado) slope [2] (faceta, aspecto) aspect [3] (CS) (manantial) spring

vertiginoso -sa *adj* ‹*velocidad*› dizzy, giddy, vertiginous (frml); **una vertiginosa caída del dólar** a dramatic *o* vertiginous fall in the value of the dollar

vértigo *m* [1] (por la altura) vertigo; **padecer de/tener ~** to suffer from/have vertigo; **me da** *or* **produce ~** it makes me dizzy *o* giddy; ***de ~***: **a una velocidad de ~** at breakneck speed; **precios de ~** skyhigh prices [2] (actividad intensa) frenzy; **el ~ de la vida moderna** the frantic pace of modern life

ves *see* **ver**

vesícula *f* vesicle

(Compuesto) **vesícula biliar** gallbladder

vesicular *adj* vesicular

vespa® *f* Vespa®, scooter

vespertina *f* (Col) early evening performance

vespertino[1] **-na** *adj* evening (*before n*); **diario ~** evening newspaper

vespertino[2] *m* [1] (period) (periódico) evening newspaper [2] (Chi) (Educ) night school

vespino® *m* moped

vestal[1] *adj* vestal

vestal[2] *f* vestal virgin

vestíbulo *m* (de casa particular) hall; (de edificio público) lobby; (de teatro, cine) foyer

vestido[1] **-da** *adj* dressed; **bien/mal ~** well/badly dressed; **¿cómo iba ~?** what was he wearing?; **~ DE algo**: **iba vestida de azul** she was wearing blue; **~ de calle/uniforme** in casual clothes/uniform; **¿de qué vas a ir ~?** what are you going to go as?

vestido[2] *m* [1] (ropa) clothes (*pl*), dress; **la historia del ~** the history of costume [2] (de mujer) dress [3] (Col) (de hombre) suit

(Compuestos)
- **vestido de baño** (Col) swimsuit
- **vestido de fiesta** party dress *o* frock
- **vestido de noche** evening dress
- **vestido de novia** wedding dress *o* gown

vestidor[1] **-dora** *adj* (Andes, Méx) dressy

vestidor[2] *m* (en casa) dressing room; (en club, gimnasio) (Chi, Méx) locker room (AmE), changing room (BrE)

vestiduras *fpl* [1] (ant) (ropa, prendas) clothes (*pl*); ***rasgarse las ~*** to throw up one's hands in horror [2] (Relig) *tb* **~ sacerdotales** vestments (*pl*)

vestier *m* (Col) (en tienda) fitting room; (en club, gimnasio) locker room (AmE), changing room (BrE)

vestigio *m* trace; **no quedan ~s de aquella civilización** no trace remains of that civilization; **~s de una antigua cultura** remains of an ancient culture; **en su rostro aún quedaban ~s de su belleza** (liter) her face still bore vestiges of her beauty (liter)

vestimenta *f* clothes (*pl*); **¿dónde vas con esa ~?** (pey) where are you going in that get-up? (pej)

vestir [I14] *vt*
A [1] ‹*niño/muñeca*› to dress [2] (proporcionar ropa a) to clothe (frml); **los viste la abuela** their grandmother buys their clothes for them [3] (confeccionar ropa a) «*modisto*» to dress [4] ‹*casa/pared*› to decorate
B (liter *o* period) (llevar puesto) to wear; **viste un traje verde** she is wearing a green suit

■ **vestir** *vi*
A «*persona*» to dress, get dressed; **~ bien/mal** to dress well/badly; **~ DE algo** to wear sth; ***el mismo que viste y calza*** (fam) the very same
B (ser elegante): **no sabe ~** he has no dress sense; **el negro viste mucho** black looks very smart; **de ~** ‹*traje/zapatos*› smart

■ **vestirse** *v pron* (*refl*)
A [1] (ponerse ropa) to dress, get dressed [2] (de cierta manera): **se viste bien/mal** he dresses well/badly; **se viste a la última moda** she wears the latest styles; **~se DE algo** to wear sth; **siempre se viste de verde** she always wears green [3] (disfrazarse) **~se DE algo** to dress up AS sth
B (liter) (engalanarse): **los campos se vistieron de flores** the fields were carpeted in flowers; **la ciudad se vistió de gala** the city was all decked out
C (comprarse la ropa) to buy one's clothes

vestón *m* (CS) jacket

vestuario *m*
A (conjunto de ropa) wardrobe; (Cin, Teatr) wardrobe
B (en club, gimnasio) locker room (AmE), changing room (BrE)

veta *f*
A [1] (filón — en madera) streak; (— en mármol) vein [2] (veteado — en la madera) grain; (— en el mármol) veining [3] (en la carne) streak [4] (en la roca) vein, seam
B (inclinación) bent, leanings (*pl*)

vetar [A1] *vt* to veto

vetarro -rra (Méx fam & hum) (*m*) old codger (colloq & hum); (*f*) old biddy (colloq & hum)

veteado[1] **-da** *adj* ‹*madera*› grained; ‹*mármol*› veined; **verde ~ de gris** green with streaks of gray

veteado[2] *m* (de la madera) grain; (del mármol) veining

veteranía *f* (experiencia) experience; (antigüedad) seniority

veterano[1] **-na** *adj* veteran (*before n*); **es ~ en esas lides** he has a great deal of experience in these matters

veterano[2] **-na** *m,f* veteran

veterinaria *f* (ciencia) veterinary science *o* medicine; (clínica) veterinary surgery

veterinario[1] **-ria** *adj* ‹*clínica*› veterinary (*before n*); **médico ~** vet, veterinarian (AmE), veterinary surgeon (BrE)

veterinario[2] **-ria** *m,f* vet, veterinarian (AmE), veterinary surgeon (BrE)

veto *m* veto; **derecho de** *or* **al ~** right of veto; **poner el ~ a algo** to veto sth

vetustez *f* (liter) great age

vetusto -ta *adj* (liter) ancient, very old

vez *f*
A (ocasión) time; **una ~/dos veces** once/twice; **una ~ por semana/año** once a week/year; **me acuerdo de una/aquella ~ cuando ...** I remember once/that time when ...; **la última/primera ~ que lo vi** the last/first time I saw him; **mil veces** *or* **miles de veces** a thousand times *o* thousands of times; **alguna ~ me he sentido tentada** there have been times when I've been tempted; **algunas veces** sometimes; **¿te has arrepentido alguna ~?** have you ever regretted it?; **¡la de veces** *or* **las veces que se lo dije!** the (number of) times I told him!; **érase** *or* **había una ~** (liter) once upon a time (liter); **por primera ~** for the first time; **otra ~** again; **¿por qué no lo dejamos para otra ~?** why don't we leave it for another time *o* day?; **repetidas veces** again and again, time and again; **por esta ~ pase** we'll forget it this time; **otra ~ será** maybe next time; **una ~ más** once again *o* more; **las más de las veces** more often than not
B (*en locs*) **a la vez** at the same time; **a mi/tu/su vez** for my/your/his part; **... quien a su ~ depende del director** ... who in turn reports to the director; **a veces** sometimes; **cada vez** every *o* each time; **lo encuentro cada ~ más viejo** he looks older every time I see him; **se utiliza cada ~ más** it's being used increasingly *o* more and more; **cada ~ menos** less and less; **de una vez** (expresando impaciencia) once and for all; (simultáneamente) in one go; **de vez en cuando** from time to time, every now and then; **en vez de** instead of; **rara vez** seldom, hardly ever; **una vez** once; **una ~ que hayan terminado** once *o* when you have finished; ***hacer las veces de algo*** «*caja/libro*» to serve as sth; «*persona*» to act as sth

C (Mat): **cabe una ~ y sobran dos** it goes once and two left over

D (Esp) (turno en una cola): **¿quién tiene** *or* **me da la ~?** who's last?; **pedir la ~** to ask who's last

v.g., v.gr. eg

vi *see* **ver**

vía[1] *f*

A **1** (ruta, camino): **una ~ urbana** (frml) an urban thoroughfare (frml); **la ~ rápida** the fast route; **~ navegable** waterway; **una ~ al diálogo** a channel *o* an avenue for dialogue; **¡dejen ~ libre!** clear the way!; ***dar ~ libre a algo*** to give sth the go-ahead *o* the green light; ***tener ~ libre*** to have a free hand **2** (medio de transporte): **por ~ aérea/marítima/terrestre** by air/by sea/by land; ⓢ **vía aérea** airmail **3** (medio, procedimiento) channels (*pl*); **por la ~ diplomática/política** through diplomatic/political channels; **por la ~ de la violencia** by using violent methods *o* means **4** (Der) proceedings (*pl*)

Compuestos
- **vía de comunicación** road (*o* rail *etc*) link
- **Vía Láctea** Milky Way
- **vía marítima** sea route, seaway
- **vía pública** (frml) public highway
- **vías respiratorias/urinarias** *fpl* respiratory/urinary tract

B **en vías de**: **está en ~s de solucionarse** it's in the process of being resolved; **países en ~s de desarrollo** developing countries; **una especie en ~s de extinción** an endangered species; **el plan está en ~s de ejecución** the plan is now being carried out

C (Ferr) track; **saldrá por la ~ dos** (frml) it will depart from track (AmE) *o* (BrE) platform two (frml); **un tramo de ~ única/de doble ~** a single-track/double-track section

Compuestos
- **vía estrecha** *or* (Méx) **angosta** narrow gauge
- **vía férrea** railroad track (AmE), railway track *o* line (BrE)
- **vía muerta** siding

D (Anat, Med): **por ~ oral/venosa** orally/intravenously; **por ~ renal** by *o* through the kidneys

vía[2] *prep* via; **~ Miami** via Miami; **un enlace ~ satélite** a link via satellite

viabilidad *f* (de proyecto) viability, feasibility; (de bebé) viability

viable *adj* ‹*proyecto/plan*› viable, feasible; ‹*bebé*› viable

vía crucis *m* (*pl* ~) **1** (Relig) Stations of the Cross (*pl*) **2** (aflicción) terrible ordeal

viada *f* (Per fam) speed; **a toda ~** flat out

viaducto *m* viaduct

viajante *mf* traveling* salesman/saleswoman

viajar [A1] *vi* to travel; **~ en avión** to travel by plane; **~on hacia el norte** they traveled north; **~ en primera clase** to travel *o* go first class

viaje *m*

A (a un lugar) trip, journey; **hacer un ~** to go on a trip *o* journey; **un ~ en tren** a train journey; **hace frecuentes viajes al extranjero** he makes frequent trips abroad; **hizo el ~ en coche/bicicleta** he drove/cycled; **estar de ~** to be away; **salir de ~** to go on a trip; **en el ~ de vuelta** on the way back; **¡buen ~!** have a good trip!, bon voyage!; **hicimos un ~ por todo Chile** we traveled all around Chile; **el segundo ~ de Colón** Columbus' second voyage; **en sus ~s por Sudamérica** on her travels through South America

Compuestos
- **viaje de estado** state visit
- **viaje de negocios** business trip
- **viaje de novios** honeymoon
- **viaje de placer**: **es un ~ de ~ y no de negocios** it's a vacation *o* (BrE) holiday, not a business trip
- **viaje organizado** package tour
- **viaje relámpago** quick trip; (de trabajo) flying *o* lightning visit

B (ida y venida) trip, journey (esp BrE); **hice varios ~s para llevarlas todas** I made several trips to take them all; ***de un (solo) ~*** (Andes fam) in one go

C (con drogas) trip (colloq)

viajero[1] **-ra** *adj*: **son muy ~s** they're great travelers*, they like traveling*

viajero[2] **-ra** *m,f* traveler*; (pasajero) passenger

vial *adj* road (*before n*)

vialidad *f* highway administration

vianda *f* **1** (carne, pescado) food; **~s** food **2** (CS) (fiambrera) lunch pail (AmE) *o* (BrE) box

viandante *mf* (transeúnte) passerby; (peatón) pedestrian

viático *m*

A (Relig) viaticum

B **viáticos** *mpl* (esp AmL) (dinero) travel allowance

víbora *f* **1** (Zool) viper **2** (fam & pey) (persona): **es una ~** he has a vicious tongue

Compuesto **víbora de cascabel** (Méx) rattlesnake

vibración *f* vibration

vibrante *adj* **1** ‹*voz*› vibrant, resonant; ‹*discurso*› vibrant; **con la voz ~ de emoción** in a voice quivering *o* vibrating with emotion **2** (Ling) ‹*sonido*› trilled, rolled

vibrar [A1] *vi* «*cuerdas/cristales*» to vibrate; **~ de emoción** to quiver *o* vibrate with emotion

vibrátil *adj* vibratile

vibrato *m* vibrato

vicaría *f* vicariate; ***pasar por la ~*** (fam) to get hitched in church (colloq)

vicario -ria *m,f* (párroco) vicar; **el ~ de Dios** the Vicar of God

Compuestos
- **vicario castrense** army chaplain
- **vicario general** vicar-general

vicealmirante *m* vice admiral

vicecampeón -peona *m,f* runner-up

vicecónsul *mf* vice-consul

vicegobernador -dora *m,f* deputy governor

vicepresidencia *f* (Gob, Pol) vice presidency; (de empresa) vice presidency (AmE), deputy chairmanship (BrE)

vicepresidente -ta *m,f*, **vicepresidente** *mf* (Gob, Pol) vice president; (de empresa) vice president (AmE), deputy chairman/chairwoman (BrE)

vice versa *adv* vice versa

vichar [A1] *vi* (RPl fam) to peep (colloq)

■ **vichar** *vt* to peep at; **me vichaba a través de las cortinas** he was peeking out at me from behind the curtains

viciado -da *adj*

A ‹*atmósfera*› stuffy; **aquí dentro el aire está ~** it's very stuffy in here

B ‹*estilo/dicción*› marred

viciar [A1] *vt*

A ‹*persona*› to get ... into a bad habit; ‹*estilo/lenguaje*› to mar

B (Der) to invalidate, vitiate (frml)

■ **viciarse** *v pron* **1** «*persona*»: **~ con algo** to become addicted to sth **2** «*estilo/lenguaje*» to deteriorate

vicio *m*

A (corrupción) vice; **darse al ~** to give oneself over to vice *o* evil ways

B (hábito): **el juego es un ~ para él** he's a compulsive gambler; **tiene el ~ de la bebida** she's a heavy drinker; **el único ~ que tengo** my only vice *o* bad habit; **se queja de ~** (fam) she complains for the sake of it

C (defecto) fault, defect

D (Der) flaw, error

vicioso[1] **-sa** *adj* ‹*persona*› depraved, debauched

vicioso[2] **-sa** *m,f* dissolute person

vicisitud *f* vicissitude (liter); **llegué tras muchas ~es** I arrived after many difficulties *o* mishaps; **las ~es de la vida** life's ups and downs

víctima *f* **1** (persona perjudicada) victim; **no hubo que lamentar ~s mortales** (period) nobody was killed *o* fatally injured; **~ de algo** victim of sth; **fue ~ de una emboscada** he was the victim of an ambush; **~s del cáncer** cancer victims; **falleció ~ de un accidente** he died as a result of an accident; **el terremoto cobró miles de ~s** the earthquake claimed thousands of lives **2** (en sacrificio) victim

victimar [A1] *vt* (AmL frml) to kill

victimario -ria *m,f* (AmL period) (asesino) murderer, killer

victimismo *m* victim mentality; **tiene tendencia al ~** he tends to see himself as a victim

V

victoria *f* victory; **el equipo local se alzó con la ~** the home team won *o* was victorious; **no cantes ~ antes de tiempo** don't count your chickens before they're hatched; **conseguir ese puesto fue una gran ~ para ella** getting that job was a big achievement for her

victorioso -sa *adj* victorious

vicuña *f* vicuna

vid *f* vine

vida *f*

A [1]▸ (Biol) life; **la ~ marina** marine life; **a los tres meses de ~** at three months (old); **el derecho a la ~** the right to life; **una cuestión de ~ o muerte** a matter of life and death; **se debate entre la ~ y la muerte** she's fighting for her life; **140 personas perdieron la ~** (period) 140 people lost their lives (journ); **quitarse la ~** to take one's (own) life (frml); **eso le costó la ~** (period) that cost him his life; **como si le fuera la ~ en ello** as if his life depended on it; **salir con ~** to escape alive; **dieron la ~ por la patria** they gave *o* sacrificed their lives for their country; **la mujer que te dio la ~** the woman who brought you into this world; ***mientras hay ~ hay esperanza*** where there is life there is hope [2]▸ (viveza, vitalidad) life; **lleno de ~** full of life; **le falta ~** it's/she's/he's not very lively

B (extensión de tiempo) life; **a lo largo de su ~** throughout his life; **toda una ~** a lifetime; **en ~ de tu padre** when your father was alive; **la relación tuvo una ~ muy corta** the relationship was very short-lived; **la ~ de un coche** the life-span of a car; **un amigo de toda la ~** a lifelong friend; **el hombre de su ~** the man of her dreams; **el amor de mi ~** the love of my life; ***amargarle la ~ a algn*** to make sb's life a misery; ***amargarse la ~*** to make oneself miserable; ***complicarle la ~ a algn*** to make sb's life difficult; ***complicarse la ~*** to make life difficult for oneself; ***de por ~*** for life; ***en la/mi ~***: **¡en la** *or* **en mi ~ he visto cosa igual!** I've never seen anything like it in my life!; **¡en la** *or* **mi ~ haría una cosa así!** I'd never dream of doing something like that!; ***hacerle la ~ imposible a algn*** to make sb's life impossible; ***tener siete ~s*** to have nine lives

C [1]▸ (manera de vivir, actividades) life; **lleva una ~ muy ajetreada** she leads a very busy life; **la música es toda su ~** she lives for music; **¿qué es de tu ~?** what have you been up to?; **hace** *or* **vive su ~** he gets on with *o* lives his own life; **¡esto sí que es ~!** this is the life!; **¡(así) es la ~!** that's life, such is life; **¡qué ~ ésta!** what a life!; ***darse la gran ~*** to live the life of Riley (colloq); ***estar encantado de la ~*** to be thrilled, to be over the moon (colloq); ***estar/quedar loco de la ~*** (CS fam) to be over the moon (colloq); ***la ~ y milagros de algn*** (CS fam) sb's life story; ***pasar a mejor ~*** (hum) ‹*persona*› to kick the bucket (colloq); ‹*traje/botas*› to bite the dust (colloq); ***pegarse la ~ padre*** (fam) to live the life of Riley (colloq) [2]▸ (en determinado aspecto) life; **~ privada** private life; **su ~ sentimental** his love life [3]▸ (biografía) life

Compuestos

- **vida alegre** (euf): **una mujer de ~ ~** a woman of easy virtue
- **vida de perros** (fam) dog's life; **¡que ~ de ~!** it's a dog's life!
- **vida eterna**: **la ~ ~** eternal *o* everlasting life
- **vida social** social life; **hacer ~ ~** to socialize

D (necesidades materiales): **tiene la ~ resuelta** she's set up for life; **la ~ está carísima** the cost of living is very high; **ganarse la ~** to earn one's *o* a living; ***buscarse la ~*** (fam) to make a living

E (como apelativo) darling; **¡mi ~!** (my) darling!

vidente *mf* (que ve) sighted person; (que adivina) clairvoyant

video, (Esp) **vídeo** *m* [1]▸ (medio, sistema) video; **en ~** on video; **cinta de ~** videotape [2]▸ (cinta) videocassette, videotape, video (colloq); (grabación) video [3]▸ (aparato) video (cassette recorder), VCR

Compuestos

- **video compuesto/inverso** (Inf) composite/reverse video
- **video doméstico** video

videocámara *f* video camera, camcorder

videocassette *m*, **videocinta** *f* videocassette, videotape, video (colloq)

videoclip *m* video

videoclub *m* (*pl* **-clubs** *or* **-clubes**) videoclub

videoconsola *f* games console

videodisco *m* videodisk, videodisc

videófono *m* videophone

videograbación *f* video recording

videograbador *m*, **videograbadora** *f* video recorder

videograbar [A1] *vt* to videotape, video

videojuego *m* video game

videopiratería *f* video piracy

videoteca *f* video library

videoteléfono *m* videophone

videoterminal *f* terminal, VDU

videotex *m* videotex(t), teletext

vidorra *f* (Esp fam) easy life

vidriado¹ -da *adj* glazed

vidriado² *m* (barniz) glaze; (cerámica vidriada) piece of glazed pottery; **~s** glazed pottery

vidriar [A1] *vt* to glaze

vidriera *f* [1]▸ (puerta) glazed door; (ventana) window; (en iglesia) *tb* **~ de colores** stained glass window [2]▸ (AmL) (escaparate) shop window; **mirar ~s** to window-shop

vidriería *f* glassworks

vidrierismo *m* (AmL) window dressing

vidrierista *mf* (AmL) window dresser

vidriero *m* glazier

vidrio *m* [1]▸ (material) glass; **fábrica de ~** glassworks; **una botella de ~** a glass bottle [2]▸ (esp AmL) (objeto): **limpiar los ~s** to clean the windows; **cambié uno de los ~s** I replaced one of the panes *o* windowpanes; **me corté con un ~** I cut myself on a piece of glass; **hay ~s rotos en la calle** there is broken glass in the street [3]▸ (de reloj) crystal, glass; ***ahí nos ~s*** (Méx fam) see you around! (colloq); ***pagar los ~s rotos*** to take the responsibility *o* blame

vidrioso -sa *adj* [1]▸ ‹*material*› glassy [2]▸ ‹*ojos*› glassy; ‹*mirada*› glassy, glazed [3]▸ ‹*asunto*› delicate

vidurria *f* (RPl fam) easy life

vieira *f* (molusco) scallop; (concha) scallop shell

vieja *f* (Col, Méx, Ven fam) (mujer) broad (AmE sl), bird (BrE sl); *ver tb* **viejo²**

viejazo *m*: ***dar el ~*** (Méx fam) to age *o* grow old suddenly

viejo¹ -ja *adj*

A [SER] ‹*persona/animal*› old; ‹*coche/ropa/casa*› old; **hacerse ~** to get old; **ese peinado te hace vieja** that hairstyle makes you look old; ***ser más ~ que Matusalén*** to be as old as the hills

B [1]▸ [ESTAR] ‹*persona/animal*› (envejecido) old; **ya está ~** he's got(ten) old; **¡qué vieja estoy!** I look so old! [2]▸ [ESTAR] ‹*zapatos/pantalones*› (desgastado) old

C (*delante del n*) (antiguo) ‹*costumbre/amigo*› old; **los ~s tiempos** the old days

Compuestos

- **Viejo Continente** *m*: **el ~ ~** Europe
- **Viejo Mundo** *m*: **el ~ ~** the Old World
- **Viejo Testamento** *m* Old Testament

viejo² -ja *m,f*

A (*m*) old man; (*f*) old woman; **los ~s** old people, the elderly; **llegar a ~** to reach old age; **un ~ gruñón** a grumpy old man; **un viejecito** *or* **viejito encantador** a delightful old man; ***de viejo***: **se casó de ~** he was an old man when he got married; **se murió de ~** he died of old age

Compuestos

- **Viejo Pascuero** *m* (Chi) ▸ **Papá Noel**
- **viejo verde** *or* (Méx) **viejo rabo verde** *m* (fam) dirty old man

B (fam) (refiriéndose a los padres): **mi ~/mi vieja** my old man/lady (colloq); **tus ~s** your folks, your Mom and Dad

C (AmL) (hablándole a un niño, al cónyuge etc) darling (colloq), love (colloq); (a un amigo) buddy (AmE), mate (BrE)

D (Méx fam) (esposo) (*m*) old man (colloq); (*f*) old woman *o* lady (colloq)

Viena *f* Vienna

viendo *see* **ver**

viene, vienes, etc *see* **venir**

vienés -nesa *adj/m,f* Viennese

viento *m*
A (Meteo) wind; **correr** *or* **hacer ~** to be windy; **un ~ helado** an icy wind; **~ en contra/a favor** *or* **de cola** head/tail wind; ***a los cuatro ~s***: **lo proclamó a los cuatro ~s** she announced it to all and sundry; ***beber los ~s por algn*** to be crazy about sb (colloq); ***contra ~ y marea***: **lo haré contra ~ y marea** I'll do it come hell or high water; **luchó contra ~ y marea para salvarlo** she fought against all the odds to save it; ***correr*** *or* ***soplar malos ~s***: **corren malos ~s para la inversión** it's a bad time for investment; ***echar a algn con ~ fresco*** (fam) to throw sb out on his/her ear; ***mandar a algn a tomar ~*** (fam) to tell sb to get lost (colloq); ***tomarse los ~s*** (RPl fam) to clear off (colloq); ***~ en popa***: **con el ~ en popa** (Náut) with a following wind; **todo va ~ en popa** everything's going extremely well; ***quien siembra ~s recoge tempestades*** he who sows the wind shall reap the whirlwind
(Compuesto) **vientos alisios** *mpl* trade winds (*pl*)
B (Mús): **instrumento/cuarteto de ~** wind instrument/quartet
C (de tienda de campaña) guy (rope)

vientre *m*
A (Anat) 1 (cavidad) abdomen; **el bajo ~** the lower abdomen 2 (órganos): **hacer de ~** to have a bowel movement 3 (región exterior) stomach, belly (colloq)
B (de mujer embarazada) womb, belly (colloq)
C (de barco, vasija) belly

viera, vieras, etc *see* **ver**
viern. (= **viernes**) Fri
viernes *m* (*pl* ~) Friday; *para ejemplos ver* **lunes**
(Compuesto) **Viernes Santo** Good Friday
viese, vieses, etc *see* **ver**
Vietnam *m* Vietnam
(Compuesto) **Vietnam del Norte/Sur** North/South Vietnam
vietnamita[1] *adj/mf* Vietnamese
vietnamita[2] *m* (idioma) Vietnamese
viga *f* (de madera) joist, beam; (de metal) beam, girder
vigencia *f* 1 (de ley) validity; **entrar en ~** to come into force *o* effect; **estar en ~** to be in force 2 (de costumbre) validity; (de pasaporte, contrato) validity
vigente *adj* 1 ‹*pasaporte/contrato*› valid; **la legislación ~** the legislation currently in force, the current legislation; **estar ~** ‹*ley*› to be in force; **precios ~s** current prices 2 ‹*argumento/razón*› valid
vigésimo -ma *adj/pron* 1 (ordinal) twentieth; **~ primero/sexto** twenty-first/twenty-sixth; **el ~ aniversario** the twentieth anniversary 2 (partitivo): **la vigésima parte** a twentieth

vigía *mf*
A (persona) lookout
B **vigía** *f* (atalaya) watchtower

vigilancia *f* 1 (atención, cuidado) vigilance, watchfulness; (por guardias, la policía): **habrá que extremar la ~** security will have to be tightened up; **estar bajo ~** to be under surveillance *o* watch; **servicio de ~** security patrol; **~ policial** police surveillance 2 (servicio) security service
vigilante[1] *adj* vigilant, on the alert; **en actitud ~** on the alert
vigilante[2] *mf* (en tienda) store detective; (en banco, edificio público) security guard
(Compuesto) **vigilante jurado/nocturno** security guard/night watchman
vigilar [A1] *vt* 1 (cuidar, atender) to watch, keep an eye on 2 ‹*preso/local*› to guard, keep watch on; ‹*frontera/zona*› to guard, patrol; ‹*examen*› to proctor (AmE), to invigilate at (BrE) 3 (fam) (espiar) to watch
■ **vigilar** *vi* to keep watch

vigilia *f*
A (vela) wakefulness; **de ~** awake
B (Relig) (víspera) vigil; (abstinencia) abstinence; (tiempo de abstinencia) day/period of abstinence

vigor *m* 1 (fuerza, energía) vigor*, energy; **con ~** vigorously 2 **en vigor**: **entrar en ~** to come into effect *o* force; **estar en ~** to be in force
vigorizar [A4] *vt* to invigorate
vigoroso -sa *adj* ‹*persona/movimiento*› vigorous, energetic; ‹*esfuerzo*› strenuous
vigueta *f* tie-beam, tie
VIH *m* (= **virus de inmunodeficiencia humana**) HIV
vihuela *f* vihuela (*early form of guitar*)
vikingo[1] **-ga** *adj* Viking (*before n*)
vikingo[2] **-ga** *m,f* Viking
vil *adj* (liter) ‹*acto/persona*› vile, despicable
vileza *f* (liter) (cualidad) vileness; (acción) vile act, despicable deed
vilipendiar [A1] *vt* (frml) (insultar) to vilify (frml), to insult; (humillar) to revile (frml), to humiliate
vilipendio *m* (frml) (insultos) vilification (frml), abuse; (humillación) humiliation
vilipendioso -sa *adj* (frml) insulting

villa *f*
A (Hist) (población) town; **la V~ y Corte** Madrid
(Compuesto) **villa miseria** (Arg) shantytown
B (casa) villa; **una ~ romana** a Roman villa

Villadiego *m*: ***tomar(se) las de ~*** to clear off
villancico *m* (Christmas) carol
villano[1] **-na** *adj* 1 (ruin) villainous 2 (Hist) peasant (*before n*)
villano[2] **-na** *m,f* 1 (persona ruin) rogue, scoundrel 2 (Hist) villein, peasant
villorrio *m* dump (colloq), one-horse town (colloq)
vilo: **en ~** (*loc adv*): **la levantó en ~** he lifted her up (off the ground/floor); **se mantienen en ~ esperando el resultado** they're on tenterhooks awaiting the result
vinagre *m* vinegar

vinagrera *f*
A 1 (para vinagre) vinegar bottle 2 **vinagreras** *fpl* (para aceite y vinagre) cruet set *o* stand
B (Chi, Per fam) (acidez estomacal) indigestion

vinagreta *f* vinaigrette
vinatería *f* wineshop, liquor store (*specializing in wines*)
vinatero[1] **-ra** *adj* wine (*before n*)
vinatero[2] **-ra** *m,f* vintner (AmE), wine merchant (BrE)
vincha *f* (AmS) (elástica, rígida) hairband; (hebilla del pelo) barrette (AmE), hair slide (BrE)

vinculación *f*
A (relación) links (*pl*), connections (*pl*); **~ CON** *or* **A algo/algn** links *o* connections WITH sth/sb
B (de bienes) entailment

vincular [A1] *vt*
A 1 (conectar, relacionar): **están vinculados por lazos de amistad** they are linked by bonds *o* ties of friendship; **los vincula una pasión por el arte** they are united by a passion for art; **grupos estrechamente vinculados** closely linked groups; **~ algo/a algn A** *or* **CON algo/algn** to link sth/sb TO *o* WITH sth/sb 2 (comprometer) to bind, be binding on
B ‹*bienes*› to entail

vínculo *m*
A (unión, relación) tie, bond; **~s familiares** family ties; **el ~ matrimonial** the bond of matrimony
B (Der) entailment

vindicación *f*
A (frml) 1 (de derecho) ▸**reivindicación** 2 (de persona) vindication
B (frml) (venganza) vengeance, revenge

vindicar [A2] *vt*
A (frml) 1 ‹*derecho*› ▸**reivindicar** 2 ‹*persona/buen nombre*› to vindicate
B (frml) (vengar) to avenge

vine *see* **venir**
vinería *f* (AmL) wineshop, liquor store (*specializing in wines*)
vinero -ra *adj* (Chi, Per) wine (*before n*)
vinícola *adj* ‹*industria/producción*› wine (*before n*); ‹*región*› wine-producing, wine-growing
vinicultor -tora *m,f* wine producer, winegrower
vinicultura *f* wine production, wine growing
viniera, viniese, etc *see* **venir**
vinificación *f* vinification

vinilo, (Méx) **vinil** *m* vinyl

viniste, etc *see* **venir**

vino[1] *m*

A (bebida) wine; ~ **dulce/seco** sweet/dry wine; ***bautizar el*** ~ (fam) to water down the wine

(Compuestos)

- **vino blanco/rosado/tinto** white/rosé/red wine
- **vino de la casa** house wine
- **vino del país** local wine
- **vino de mesa** table wine
- **vino espumoso** *or* (CS) **espumante** sparkling wine

B (recepción) reception

(Compuesto) **vino de honor** reception

vino[2] *see* **venir**

vinoso -sa *adj* (aroma/sabor) of/like wine, vinous (frml); (color) like wine; **color rojo** ~ blood red, dark red

viña *f* vineyard; **de todo hay en la** ~ **del Señor** (fr hecha) it takes all sorts to make a world

viñatero[1] **-ra** *adj* (AmL) wine, wine-growing (*before n*)

viñatero[2] **-ra** *m,f* (AmL) 1 (propietario) winegrower 2 (trabajador) vineyard worker

viñedo *m* vineyard

viñeta *f* (en libro) vignette; (en periódico) cartoon; (en procesamiento de textos) bullet (point)

viola *f* 1 (instrumento) viola 2 **viola** *mf* (persona) viola player, violist (AmE)

violáceo -cea *adj* purplish

violación *f* 1 (de persona) rape 2 (de ley, acuerdo, derecho) violation; (de templo) violation

(Compuesto) **violación de domicilio** (CS, Ven) unlawful entry

violador -dora *m,f* 1 (de persona) rapist 2 (de ley, acuerdo) violator

violar [A1] *vt* 1 ‹*persona*› to rape 2 ‹*ley*› to violate, break, ‹*tratado/derecho*› to violate; ‹*templo*› to violate

violatorio -ria *adj* (frml) ~ **DE algo**: **actos** ~**s del acuerdo/de los derechos humanos** acts in violation of the agreement/of human rights

violencia *f* violence; **recurrir a la** ~ to resort to violence *o* force

(Compuesto) **violencia de género** gender violence

violentar [A1] *vt* 1 (forzar) ‹*cerradura/puerta*› to force; ‹*persona*› to rape 2 (distorsionar) ‹*texto*› to distort 3 (poner en situación embarazosa) to make … feel awkward

■ **violentarse** *v pron* to get embarrassed

violento -ta *adj*

A ‹*choque/deporte/muerte*› violent; ‹*discurso*› vehement; ‹*persona/tono/temperamento*› violent

B (incómodo) ‹*situación*› embarrassing, awkward; **le es** *or* **resulta** ~ **hablar del tema** she finds it embarrassing to talk about it; **estaba muy** ~ I felt very awkward

violeta[1] *f* violet

violeta[2] *adj inv* ‹*color/tela*› violet; **flores** ~ violet flowers

violín *m* 1 (instrumento) violin; ***pintarle*** *o* ***hacerle violines*** *or* ***un*** ~ ***a algn*** (Méx fam) ≈ to give sb the finger (AmE), to make a V sign at sb (BrE); ***tocar el*** ~ (Chi fam) to be a third wheel (AmE colloq), to play gooseberry (BrE colloq); ***yo,*** ~ ***en bolsa*** (RPl fam) I'm keeping well out of it 2 **violín** *mf* (persona) violinist

violinista *mf* violinist

violón *m* 1 (instrumento) double bass 2 **violón** *mf* (persona) double bass player

violoncelista, violonchelista *mf* cellist

violoncelo, violonchelo *m* 1 (instrumento) cello, violoncello 2 **violoncelo** *mf* (persona) cellist

vira *f* (de zapato) welt

virago *f* virago

viraje *m*

A 1 (Náut) tack, tacking maneuver* 2 (de vehículo) turn; **un** ~ **brusco** a swerve 3 (de gobierno, persona) change, switch

B (Fot) toning

viral *adj* viral

virar [A1] *vi* 1 (Náut) to tack, go about 2 «*vehículo/conductor*» to turn; **viró bruscamente** she swerved 3 «*política/partido*» to veer

■ **virar** *vt*

A 1 (Náut) to tack 2 ‹*traje/cuello*› to turn

B (Fot) to tone

virgen[1] *adj* 1 ‹*persona*›: **una mujer/un hombre** ~ a virgin; **ser** ~ to be a virgin 2 ‹*cinta*› blank; ‹*película*› unexposed 3 ‹*selva*› virgin

virgen[2] *f* 1 (persona) virgin 2 **la Virgen** (Relig) the Virgin; **la Santísima V**~ the Blessed Virgin; **¡V**~ **Santa** *or* **Santísima!** my goodness!

virginal *adj* virginal

virginidad *f* virginity

virgo *m* virginity

Virgo[1] *m* (signo) Virgo; **es (de)** ~ she's (a) Virgo, she's a Virgoan

Virgo[2], **virgo** *mf* (*pl* ~ *or* **-gos**) (persona) Virgo, Virgoan

vírico -ca *adj* viral

viril *adj* ‹*cualidades*› virile, manly

virilidad *f* virility

virología *f* virology

virreina *f* vicereine

virreinato *m* (cargo) viceroyship, viceroyalty; (territorio) viceroyalty

virrey *m* viceroy

virtual *adj* 1 (potencial) virtual; **es ya el** ~ **campeón** he is already virtually the champion 2 (tácito) implicit

virtud *f* 1 (cualidad) virtue 2 (capacidad) power; **con** ~**es curativas** with healing powers; **tiene la** ~ **de exasperarme** (iró) he has a knack of driving me up the wall; **en** ~ **de** by virtue of

virtuosismo *m* virtuosity

virtuoso[1] **-sa** *adj* virtuous

virtuoso[2] **-sa** *m,f* virtuoso

viruela *f* (enfermedad) smallpox; (marca) pockmark; **picado de** ~**s** pockmarked

virulé *f*: **a la** ~ (*loc adv*) (Chi) (desordenadamente) haphazardly; ▸**ojo**

virulencia *f* virulence

virulento -ta *adj* virulent

virus *m* (*pl* ~) virus; ~ **de inmunodeficiencia humana** human immunodeficiency virus, HIV

viruta *f* shaving

vis *f*: ~ **cómica** comic talent

visa *f*, (Esp) **visado** *m* visa

visaje *m* (funny) face; **hizo un** ~ **cómico** he pulled a funny face

visar [A1] *vt* ‹*documento*› to endorse; ‹*pasaporte*› to visa

visceral *adj* 1 (Anat) visceral 2 ‹*odio/impresión*› visceral, deep; **un sentimiento** ~ a gut feeling

vísceras *fpl* entrails (*pl*), viscera (*pl*)

visconde -desa (*m*) viscount; (*f*) viscountess

viscosa *f* viscose

viscosidad *f* viscosity

viscoso -sa *adj* viscous

visera *f* (de casco) visor; (de gorra) peak; (de jugador) eyeshade

visibilidad *f* visibility

visible *adj* 1 [SER] (que puede verse) visible 2 [SER] (manifiesto) visible, clear 3 (fam) [ESTAR] (presentable) presentable, decent

visillo *m* net curtain, lace curtain

visión *f*

A 1 (vista) vision, sight; **pérdida de** ~ loss of vision *o* sight; **perdió la** ~ **de un ojo** she lost the sight of one eye 2 (acción de ver): **la** ~ **de aquella escena lo impresionó** seeing *o* witnessing that scene shocked him 3 (aparición) vision; ***ver visiones*** to be seeing things

B (enfoque, punto de vista) view; **una** ~ **de futuro** a forward-looking approach; **una** ~ **de conjunto** an overview

visionar [A1] *vt* «*crítico*» to view; «*espectador*» to see

visionario -ria *adj/m,f* visionary

visir *m* vizier

visita *f* [1] (acción) visit; **hacer(le) una ~ (a algn)** to pay (sb) a visit; **ir de ~** to go visiting; **devolver una ~** to return a visit; **sólo estoy/vine de ~** I'm just visiting; **horario de ~** visiting hours *o* times; **~ *de médico*** (fam) flying visit [2] (visitante) visitor, caller; (invitado) guest; **tener ~** to have visitors/guests

(Compuestos)
- **visita a domicilio** house call
- **visita de cortesía** courtesy call, duty visit
- **visita de pésame** visit to offer one's condolences
- **visita guiada** (AmL) guided tour
- **visita relámpago** flying visit

visitador social, -dora social *m,f* (AmL) social worker

visitante¹ *adj* visiting (*before n*)

visitante² *mf* visitor

visitar [A1] *vt* [1] ‹*persona*› to visit, visit with (AmE) [2] ‹*lugar*› to visit

■ **visitarse** *v pron* (*recípr*) to visit each other

vislumbrar [A1] *vt* to make out, discern (frml); **a lo lejos se vislumbraba una iglesia** a church could just be made out in the distance; **lo alcancé a ~ entre los arbustos** I just managed to glimpse it amongst the bushes; **se vislumbra una solución** there is a solution in sight

vislumbre *f* [1] (resplandor) glimmer [2] (indicio) sign

viso *m*

A (Indum) petticoat, underskirt

B **visos** *mpl* [1] (apariencia): **tiene ~s de tragedia** it could have tragic consequences; **no tiene ~s de resolverse** it shows no sign of being solved; **una historia con pocos ~s de verosimilitud** a story which seems to bear little resemblance to reality [2] (refulgencia): **la piedra daba ~s de colores** the gem sparkled with different colors; **los ~s incandescentes del atardecer** (liter) the glowing rays of evening [3] (en tela) sheen; **azul con ~s verdes** blue shot with green *o* with a greenish sheen

visón *m* mink

visor *m* [1] (en cámara) viewfinder; (para diapositivas) slide viewer [2] (Arm) sight

víspera *f*

A (día anterior): **la ~** the day before, the eve (liter *o* journ); **~s de fiesta** days prior to public holidays

B **vísperas** *fpl* [1] (tiempo anterior): **en ~s de algo** days before sth, on the eve of sth (liter *o* journ) [2] (Relig) vespers (*pl*)

vista¹ *mf* customs officer *o* official

vista² *f*

A [1] (sentido) sight, eyesight; **tener buena/mala ~** to have good/bad eyesight; **ser corto de ~** to be near-sighted; **perdió la ~** he lost his sight [2] (ojos) eyes; **le hace daño a la ~** it hurts his eyes; **lo operaron de la ~** he had an eye operation [3] (perspicacia) vision

(Compuesto) **vista cansada** eyestrain

B [1] (mirada): **alzar** *or* **levantar/bajar la ~** to look up/down; **torcer la ~** to be cross-eyed, to have a squint; **fijó la ~ en el horizonte** she fixed her eyes on the horizon [2] (espectáculo) sight

C (*en locs*) **a la vista**: **¡tierra a la ~!** land ho!; **ponlo bien a la ~** put it where it can be seen easily; **estar/no estar a la ~** to be within/out of sight; **pagar al portador y a la ~** pay the bearer at sight; **cuenta corriente a la ~** sight account; **a la ~ de todos** in full view of everyone; **¿tienes algún proyecto a la ~?** do you have any projects in view?; **a primera** *or* **a simple vista** at first sight *o* glance; **se notaba a simple ~** you could tell just by looking; **con vistas a** with a view to; **de vista** by sight; **en vista**: **tener algo/a algn en ~** to have sth/sb in mind; **en vista de** in view of; **en ~ de que ...** in view of the fact that ...; **¡hasta la vista!** see you!, so long! (colloq); ***a ~ de pájaro***: **ver algo a ~ de pájaro** to get a bird's-eye view of sth; ***a ~ y paciencia de algn*** (Chi, Per fam) in front of sb; ***hacer la ~ gorda*** to turn a blind eye; ***perder algo/a algn de ~*** to lose sight of sth/sb; **al terminar la carrera los perdí de ~** I lost touch with them when we graduated; ***perderse de ~*** to disappear from view; ***saltar a la ~***: **lo primero que salta a la ~ es el color que tiene** the first thing that hits *o* strikes you is the color; **salta a la ~ que hicieron trampa** it's obvious they cheated; ***tener la ~ puesta en algo/algn*** to have one's eye on sth/sb; ***tener ~ de águila*** *or* ***lince*** to have eyes like a hawk; ***volver la ~ atrás*** to look back

D (panorama) view; **con ~ al mar** with a sea view; **~ aérea** aerial view

E (Der) hearing; **la ~ del juicio se celebrará el ...** the hearing will take place on ...

F (Com, Fin): **a 20 días ~** within 20 days

vistazo *m* look; **darle** *or* **echarle un ~ a algo** to have a look at sth; **échale un ~ rápido** just have a quick look at it

viste¹, visteis *see* **ver**

viste², visten, etc *see* **vestir**

visto¹ -ta *adj*

A [1] (claro, evidente) obvious, clear; **está/estaba ~ que ...** it is/was clear *o* obvious that ... [2] (*en locs*) **por lo visto** apparently; **visto que** given that, in view of the fact that

B [1] [ESTAR] (común, trillado): **esa blusa está muy vista** everybody's wearing blouses like that; **un truco que está muy ~** an old trick; **eso ya está muy ~** that's not very original, that's old hat [2] **nunca visto**: **la cantidad de gente que había allí, fue lo** *or* **algo nunca ~** never before had such a large number of people been seen there; **cosa nunca vista antes, nevó en Montevideo** it snowed in Montevideo, which was unheard of

C (considerado) **estar bien/mal ~**: **en ciertos círculos eso no está bien ~** in some circles that is not considered correct; **estaba mal ~ que las mujeres fumaran** it was not the done thing *o* it was frowned upon for women to smoke

visto² *m* (Esp) check (AmE), tick (BrE)

(Compuesto) **visto bueno** *m* approval; **tiene que dar el ~ ~** she has to give her approval *o* (colloq) has to give it the go ahead

visto³ *see* **vestir, ver**

vistosidad *f*: **la ~ del plumaje** the brilliant colors of the plumage; **un espectáculo de una ~ extraordinaria** an amazingly spectacular show

vistoso -sa *adj* bright and colorful•

visual¹ *adj* visual; ▸ **campo**

visual² *f* line of sight *o* vision

visualización *f* (Inf) display

visualizador *m* VDU, visual display unit

visualizar [A4] *vt* [1] (formarse una imagen) to visualize [2] (Inf) to display

vital *adj*

A (fundamental) vital; **de ~ importancia** of vital importance; **bombardearon puntos ~es** they bombarded strategic *o* key points

B [1] (Biol, Med) ‹*órgano*› vital (*before n*) [2] ‹*persona*› dynamic, full of life

vitalicio -cia *adj* ‹*miembro/presidente*› life (*before n*); **cargo ~** post held for life

vitalidad *f* vitality

vitamina *f* vitamin

vitaminado -da *adj* vitamin-enriched

vitamínico -ca *adj* vitamin (*before n*)

vitela *f* vellum

vitícola *adj* vine-growing (*before n*)

viticultivo *m* vine-growing

viticultor -tora *m,f* vine-grower

viticultura *f* vine-growing

vitivinícola *adj* wine (*before n*)

vitivinicultor -tora *m,f* grape grower and wine producer

vitivinicultura *f* grape growing and wine production

vitola *f* cigar band

vítor *m* cheer; **fue recibido entre ~es y aplausos** he was cheered and applauded

vitorear [A1] *vt* to cheer

vitral *m* stained-glass window

vitraux *m* /bi'tro/ (CS) stained-glass window

vítreo -trea *adj* ‹*porcelana*› vitreous; ‹*ojos/mirada*› glassy

vitrificar [A2] *vt* to vitrify

vitrina *f* 1 (mueble — en tienda) showcase; (— en casa) glass cabinet, display cabinet 2 (AmL) (escaparate) shop window

vitrinear [A1] *vi* (Andes fam) to window-shop

vitrinista *mf* (AmL) window dresser

vitrola *f* (AmS) phonograph (AmE), gramophone (BrE)

vituallas *fpl* (arc) provisions (*pl*), victuals (*pl*) (arch)

vituperar [A1] *vt* (frml) to vituperate against (frml)

vituperio *m* (frml) criticism, vituperation (frml); **lo llenó de ~s** she vituperated against him (frml)

viudedad *f* 1 (de mujer) widowhood; (de hombre) widowerhood 2 (pensión) widow's/widower's pension

viudez *f* ▸ **viudedad 1**

viudo[1] -da *adj* ‹*persona*›: **su madre es** *or* (Esp) **está viuda** her mother is a widow; **(se) quedó ~ a los 40 años** he lost his wife *o* he was widowed when he was 40

viudo[2] -da *m,f* (*m*) widower; (*f*) widow

(Compuesto) **viudo de verano** *m* grass widower

viva *m*: **dar ~s** to cheer; **fuera se oían ~s** cheering *o* shouts of 'viva' could be heard outside; **dar ~s al Rey** to shout 'Long live the King!'

vivacidad *f* (de persona) liveliness, vivacity; (de ojos) brightness

vivamente *adv* ‹*recordar/describir*› vividly; **le interesa ~** he is extremely *o* deeply interested; **me impresionó ~** she made a deep *o* strong impression on me

vivar[1] [A1] *vt* (AmS) to cheer

vivar[2] *m* (de conejos) warren; (de peces) hatchery

vivaracho -cha *adj* 1 ‹*ojos*› sparkling; ‹*niño*› lively 2 (AmL) (espabilado) crafty

vivaz *adj* ‹*persona*› lively, vivacious; ‹*ojos*› bright; ‹*imaginación*› vivid, lively

vivencia *f* experience

víveres *mpl* provisions (*pl*), supplies (*pl*)

vivero *m* (de plantas) nursery; (de peces) hatchery; (de moluscos) bed; **un ~ de ostras** an oyster bed *o* bank

viveza *f*

A 1 (rapidez, agilidad) liveliness; **~ de ingenio** readiness *o* sharpness of wit 2 (de recuerdo) vividness; **lo describió con gran ~** she described it very vividly 3 (de color) brightness; (de ojos, mirada) liveliness, brightness; (de emoción, deseo) strength, intensity

B (astucia) sharpness; **fue una de sus ~s** it was one of his little schemes

(Compuesto) **viveza criolla** (AmS hum & pey) native wit and cunning

vivido -da *adj* (experimentado): **los momentos ~s** the times we (*o* they *etc*) have had *o* experienced; **una experiencia vivida por el autor** an experience which the author went *o* lived through

vívido -da *adj* vivid, lively

vividor -dora *m,f* pleasure seeker

vivienda *f*: **el problema de la ~** the housing *o* accommodation problem; **la escasez de ~s** the housing shortage; **perdió su ~** she lost her home; **quedarse sin ~** to be made *o* left homeless; **un bloque de ~s** an apartment building, a block of flats (BrE); **la construcción de 50 ~s** the construction of 50 homes *o* (frml) dwellings

(Compuesto) **vivienda de protección oficial** *or* (Méx, Per) **de interés social** state-subsidized apartment (*o* house *etc*)

viviente *adj* living

vivificador, vivificante *adj* ‹*experiencia*› invigorating, revitalizing; ‹*lluvia/brisa*› refreshing; ‹*baño*› invigorating, refreshing

vivificar [A2] *vt* «*experiencia*» to revitalize; «*brisa/lluvia*» to refresh, revitalize; «*baño*» to refresh, invigorate

vivíparo[1] -ra *adj* viviparous

vivíparo[2] -ra *m,f* viviparous mammal

vivir[1] *m* (way of) life; ***de mal ~***: **una mujer de mal ~** a loose woman; **es gente de mal ~** they are all undesirable characters

vivir[2] [I1] *vi*

A (estar vivo) to be alive; **su recuerdo ~á siempre** his memory will live for ever; ***¿quién vive?*** (Mil) who goes there?

B 1 (pasar la vida): **vive ilusionada pensando que él volverá** she spends her life dreaming that he'll come back; **~ para algo/algn** to live for sth/sb; **~ en paz** to live in peace; **déjalo ~** leave him be; ***no dejar ~ a algn***: **los dolores de cabeza no la dejan ~** the headaches are making her life a misery; **este niño no me deja ~** this child doesn't give me a moment's peace; ***¡~ para ver!*** who would believe *o* credit it!; ***vive y deja ~*** live and let live 2 (gozar de la vida) to live

C (subsistir): **la pintura no da para ~** you can't make a living from painting; **~ con honradez** to make an honest living; **el sueldo no le alcanza para ~** his salary isn't enough (for him) to live on; **~ DE algo** to live ON sth; **viven de la caridad** they live on charity; **viven de la pesca** they live from *o* by fishing; **~ de ilusiones** to live on dreams *o* hopes

D (residir) to live; **vive solo** he lives alone *o* on his own; **vive con sus padres** she lives at home; **no vive nadie ahí** there's no one living there

E (*como interj*): **¡viva el Rey!** long live the King!; **¡vivan los novios!** three cheers for the bride and groom!; **¡viva!** hurray!

■ **vivir** *vt* 1 (pasar por): **~ momentos difíciles** to live in difficult times; **los que vivimos la guerra** those of us who lived through the war; **el país vive una semana de violencia** the country is experiencing a week of violence 2 ‹*personaje/música*› to live 3 ‹*vida*› to live

vivisección *f* vivisection

vivito -ta *adj*: **~ y coleando** (fam) alive and kicking (colloq)

vivo[1] -va *adj*

A 1 (con vida) alive; **no quedó nadie ~** no one was left alive; **es una leyenda viva** he is a living legend; **mantener ~ un recuerdo** to keep a memory alive; ***a lo ~*** (fam) without anesthetic*; ***en ~*** ‹*actuación/transmisión*› live 2 ‹*lengua*› living (*before n*)

B 1 ‹*persona*› (despierto, animado) vivacious, bubbly; ‹*descripción*› vivid, graphic; ‹*relato/imaginación*› lively 2 ‹*color*› bright, vivid; ‹*llama/fuego*› bright; ‹*ojos/mirada*› lively, bright 3 ‹*sentimiento/deseo*› intense, strong; ***en lo más ~***: **me hirió en lo más ~** he cut me to the quick; **me afectó en lo más ~** it affected me very deeply

C (avispado, astuto) sharp; **no seas tan ~** don't try to be clever; **esos vendedores son muy ~s** those salesmen are razor-sharp (colloq)

vivo[2] -va *m,f* (oportunista) sharp *o* smooth operator (colloq); (aprovechado) freeloader

vizcacha *f* viscacha

vizcondado *m* viscounty

vizconde -desa (*m*) viscount; (*f*) viscountess

V°B° *m* = **visto bueno**

vocablo *m* (frml) word

vocabulario *m* vocabulary; **¡qué ~!** what language!; **¡modera tu ~!** mind your language!

vocación *f* 1 (inclinación) vocation; **tiene ~ de músico/para las artes** he has a vocation for music/for the arts 2 (Relig) vocation, calling

vocacional[1] *adj* vocational

vocacional[2] *f* (Chi, Méx) *post-school vocational training*

vocal[1] *adj* vocal

vocal[2] *f*

A (Ling) vowel

B **vocal** *mf* (de consejo, tribunal) member

vocalía *f* (cargo): *position as a member of a council, court, or committee*; (local): *office of member of a council, court, or committee*

vocalista *mf* vocalist, singer

vocalizar [A4] *vi* to vocalize

voceador *m* 1 (pregonero) town crier 2 (Col, Méx) (de periódicos) newspaper vendor

vocear [A1] *vt* 1 ‹*mercancías*› to cry (dated); ‹*noticias*› to shout out 2 (hacer público) to spread 3 (corear) to shout 4 (Méx) ‹*persona*› to page

■ **vocear** *vi* to shout (out)

vocería *f* (AmL) position of spokesperson

vocerío *m* clamor*, shouting

vocero -ra (esp AmL) (*m*) spokesman, spokesperson; (*f*) spokeswoman, spokesperson

V

vociferar [A1] *vi* to shout, vociferate (frml)

vocinglero -ra *adj* ‹niños› noisy; **una mujer vocinglera** a loud *o* loudmouthed woman

vodevil *m* vaudeville (AmE), variety (BrE)

vodka *m or f* /'bo(ð)ka/ vodka

voduismo *m* (esp AmL) voodooism

vol. (= **volumen**) vol.

volada *f*
A (Col) 1 (demolición) blowing-up 2 (fam) (escapada): **pegarse una ~** ‹‹*preso*›› to escape; ‹‹*alumno*›› to play hooky (esp AmE colloq), to skive off (school) (BrE colloq)
B 1 (AmS fam): **en una ~** in no time; ***aprovechar la ~*** (RPl fam) to take one's chance 2 (Méx fam): **de ~** (*loc adv*) quickly

voladizo -za *adj* projecting

volado¹ -da *adj*
A 1 [ESTAR] (fam) (loco) crazy (colloq); (fumado) high (colloq) 2 [SER] (distraído) (Chi fam) absentminded; (irascible) (Col fam) irritable, quick-tempered
B (Col fam) (salido) protruding; **dientes ~s** protruding teeth

volado² -da *m,f*
A 1 (fam) (loco) crazy fool 2 (Chi fam) (distraído) absent-minded person
B **volado** *m* 1 (Méx fam) (con moneda): **te lo juego a un ~** I'll toss you for it; **echar un ~** to toss *o* flip a coin; ***ser un ~*** to be a gamble 2 (RPl, Ven) (en costura) flounce

volado³ -da *adv* (Esp, Méx) in a rush, in a hurry

volador¹ -dora *adj* flying (*before n*)

volador² *m*
A (pez) flying fish
B (en pirotecnia) rocket

> **voladores**
>
> A Mexican pre-Columbian ritual dance, originally an agricultural fertility rite. Four or six men are attached by ropes to a platform on top of a 60 to 90 foot (17 to 27 meter) high pole. They dance on the platform and at the end of the dance, come circling down to the ground, hanging by their feet, as the ropes attaching them unwind

voladura *f* blowing-up

volandas *fpl* 1 **en ~s**: **llevar a algn en ~s** to carry sb shoulder-high 2 (Col fam) **a las ~s** in a rush *o* hurry

volandera *f* (de molino) upper millstone, runner; (Mec) bush, bushing

volandero -ra *adj*
A (suelto) loose
B ‹pájaro› full-fledged

volanta *f* (RPl) horse-drawn carriage

volantazo *m* (Esp, Méx) swerve; **dar un ~** to swerve

volante¹ *adj* flying (*before n*)

volante² *m*
A 1 (Auto) steering wheel; **ir/ponerse al ~** to be at/to take the wheel 2 (Mec, Tec) flywheel; (para regular altura, velocidad) wheel, handwheel 3 (de reloj) balance wheel
B 1 (AmL) (de propaganda) leaflet, flier 2 (Esp) (para el médico) referral note *o* slip
C (en costura) flounce
D (Dep) shuttlecock
E **volante** *mf* (Chi) (conductor) racing driver; (en fútbol) winger

volantín *m*
A (Chi) (cometa) kite; **encumbrar un ~** to fly a kite
B (Per) (en gimnasia) somersault

volar [A10] *vi*
A ‹‹*pájaro/avión*›› to fly
B 1 ‹‹*tiempo*›› to fly; **¡cómo vuela el tiempo!** doesn't time fly!; **las malas noticias vuelan** bad news travels fast 2 **volando** *ger* ‹comer/cambiarse› in a rush, in a hurry; **se fue volando** he/she rushed off; **las entradas se acaban volando** the tickets sell out very quickly *o* in no time at all; ***quedar(se) volando*** (Méx fam) ‹‹*asunto/persona*›› to be left up in the air
C 1 (con el viento): **~on todos los papeles** my papers blew all over the place; **le voló el sombrero** his hat blew off 2 (fam) (desaparecer) to vanish, disappear; **los bombones ~on** the chocolates vanished *o* disappeared 3 (Méx fam) **a ~: niños, a ~** OK you kids, go away *o* get out of here; **toma el dinero y a ~** take the money and run; ***mandar a ~ a algn*** (Méx) to tell sb to get lost (colloq)

■ **volar** *vt*
A ‹puente/edificio› to blow up; ‹caja fuerte› to blow
B (Méx, Ven fam) (robar) to swipe (colloq), to nick (BrE colloq)

■ **volarse** *v pron*
A (AmS fam) (de rabia, fiebre): **estaba que se volaba de rabia** she was beside herself with rage *o* anger; **tiene una fiebre que se vuela** he has a really high temperature
B 1 (Col fam) ‹‹*preso*›› to escape 2 (Col, Méx fam) ‹‹*alumno*›› to play hooky (esp AmE colloq), to skive off (school) (BrE colloq)
C (Méx fam) 1 (coquetear) to flirt 2 (robar) to swipe (colloq), nick (BrE colloq); **se voló un lápiz** he swiped a pencil

volátil *adj* volatile

volatilidad *f* volatility

volatilizar [A4] *vt* to volatilize

■ **volatilizarse** *v pron* 1 (Fís, Quím) to volatilize 2 ‹‹*dinero/persona*›› to vanish into thin air

volatín *m*: **hacer volatines** to perform *o* do acrobatics

volatinero -ra *m,f* acrobat

volcado *m* (Inf) *tb* **~ de memoria** dump

volcán *m* volcano; **un ~ de pasiones** a hotbed of passion; ***estar sobre un ~*** to be sitting on a time bomb

volcánico -ca *adj* volcanic

volcar [A9] *vt*
A 1 (tumbar) to knock over 2 ‹carga› to tip, dump 3 ‹molde› to turn over 4 (vaciar) to empty (out) 5 (Inf) to dump
B (poner, depositar) **~ algo EN algn/algo: volcó todas sus esperanzas en él** she pinned all her hopes on him; **vuelca toda su energía en el trabajo** she puts all her energy into her work

■ **volcar** *vi* ‹‹*automóvil/camión*›› to overturn, turn over; ‹‹*embarcación*›› to capsize

■ **volcarse** *v pron*
A 1 ‹‹*vaso/botella*›› to get knocked *o* tipped over 2 ▸ **volcar** *vi*
B 1 (entregarse, dedicarse) **~se EN/A algo** to throw oneself INTO sth; **se ~on a la tarea** they threw themselves into the task 2 (lanzarse): **el pueblo se volcó a las calles** the people poured onto the streets
C (desvivirse) **~se PARA** *or* **POR + INF** to go out of one's way to + INF; **se vuelca por hacer que te sientas cómodo** she goes out of her way to make you feel at home; **~se CON algn: se ~on conmigo** they bent over backwards to make me feel welcome

volea *f* volley; **marcó de ~** (en fútbol) he volleyed the ball into the net; (en tenis) he won the point with a volley

volear [A1] *vt/vi* (Dep) to volley

vóleibol, voleibol *m* volleyball

voleo *m*: **a** *or* **al ~** at random; **sembrar a ~** to scatter seeds; **contesté al ~** I said the first thing that came into my head

volibol *m* (Col, Méx, Ven) volleyball

volición *f* volition

volován *m* vol-au-vent

volquete *m*, **volqueta** *f* dump truck (AmE), dumper truck (BrE)

voltaico -ca *adj* galvanic, voltaic

voltaje *m* voltage

volteada *f* (RPl) (de animales) roundup

volteado¹ -da *adj* (Col, Méx fam & pey) bent (pej), queer (pej)

volteado² -da *m,f* (Col, Méx fam & pey) (*m*) (homosexual) fag (AmE colloq & pej), bender (BrE colloq & pej); (*f*) (lesbiana) dyke (colloq & pej)

voltear [A1] *vt*
A 1 ‹mies› to winnow; ‹tierra› to turn (over) 2 (por el aire) ‹‹*toro*›› to toss; ‹‹*caballo*›› to throw
B ‹campanas› to ring
C (AmL exc CS) 1 ‹tortilla/disco› to turn over; ‹cuadro› to turn … around; ‹copa/jarrón› (poner — boca arriba) to turn … the right way up; (— boca abajo) to turn … upside down 2 ‹calcetín/manga› (poner del revés) to turn … inside out; (poner del derecho) to turn … the right way round; **el viento me volteó el paraguas** the wind blew my umbrella inside out; **~ la página** to turn the page

D (AmL exc CS) (dar la vuelta): **me volteó la espalda** she turned her back on me; **al oír su voz volteó la cara** when she heard his voice she turned her head
E (CS) (tumbar, echar abajo) ‹*bolos/botella*› to knock over; ‹*puerta*› to knock down
■ **voltear** *vi* «*campanas*» to peal, ring out
■ **voltearse** *v pron* 1 (AmL exc CS) (volverse, darse la vuelta) to turn around; (cambiar de ideas) to change one's ideas; **se ha volteado contra mí** he's turned against me 2 (Méx) «*vehículo*» to overturn, turn over

voltereta *f* somersault

voltímetro *m* voltmeter

voltio *m* volt

volubilidad *f* changeableness, fickleness

voluble *adj* (inconstante) changeable, fickle

volumen *m*
A 1 (de un cuerpo) volume; **bultos de ese ~** pieces of luggage that size 2 (magnitud, cantidad) volume; **~ de ventas** volume of sales, turnover
B (de sonido) volume; **bajar/subir el ~** to turn the volume down/up; **a todo ~** on full volume, at full blast (colloq)
C (tomo) volume

voluminoso -sa *adj* ‹*paquete*› sizeable, bulky; ‹*deuda*› massive, enormous; ‹*mangas*› voluminous; **senos ~s** ample bosom

voluntad *f*
A 1 (facultad) will 2 (deseo) wish; **por expresa ~ de los familiares** by express wish of the family; **hace su santa ~** she does whatever she likes *o* pleases; **lo hizo por (su) propia ~** he did it of his own free will *o* of his own volition; **~ DE + INF** wish to + INF; **manifestó su ~ de renunciar** he expressed his wish to resign; **por causas ajenas a su ~** for reasons beyond his control; **hágase tu ~** (Relig) Thy will be done; ***a ~***: **se puede comer a ~** you can eat to your heart's content; **la donación es a ~** donations are at one's discretion
(Compuesto) **voluntad divina** divine will, God's will
B (firmeza de intención) *tb* **fuerza de ~** willpower
(Compuesto) **voluntad de hierro** will of iron
C (disposición, intención): **con la mejor ~** with the best of intentions; **paz a los hombres de buena ~** peace to all men of goodwill; **agradezco tu buena ~** I appreciate your willingness to help; **lo dijo con mala ~** she was trying to cause trouble when she said it; ***ganarse la ~ de algn*** to win sb's favor*; ***tenerle mala ~ a algn*** to dislike sb

voluntariedad *f* 1 (cualidad de voluntario) voluntary nature 2 (Der) (intencionalidad) (wilful) intent

voluntario[1] -ria *adj* 1 ‹*acto/donación*› voluntary; **fue una elección voluntaria** I/he did it of my/his own free will 2 (*como adv*) voluntarily

voluntario[2] -ria *m,f* volunteer

voluntarioso -sa *adj* 1 (esforzado, bien intencionado) willing, keen 2 (obstinado, caprichoso) self-willed, stubborn

voluntarista *adj* 1 (con fuerza de voluntad) strong-willed 2 (obstinado) self-willed, stubborn

voluptuosidad *f* voluptuousness

voluptuoso -sa *adj* voluptuous

voluta *f* (Arquit) scroll, volute; (de humo) spiral, column

volver [E11] *vi*
A (regresar — al lugar donde se está) to come back; (— a otro lugar) to go back; **no sé a qué hora ~é** I don't know what time I'll be back; **¿cómo vas a ~?** how are you getting back?; **volvió muy cambiada** she came back *o* returned a different person; **¿cuándo piensas ~ por aquí?** when do you think you'll be *o* come back this way?; **ha vuelto con su familia** she's gone back to her family; **~ A algo** ‹*a un lugar*› to go back TO sth; ‹*a una situación/actividad*› to return TO sth; **no había vuelto a su pueblo** he hadn't been back to his home town; **~ a clases** to go back to school; **volviendo a lo que decía ...** to get *o* go back to what I was saying ...; **ya volvemos a lo de siempre** so we're back to the same problem; **~ DE algo: ¿cuándo volviste de las vacaciones?** when did you get back from your vacation?; **ha vuelto de Roma** she's back from Rome; **volvió cansado del trabajo** he was tired when he got home from work; **~ *atrás*** (literal) to go *o* turn back; (al pasado) to turn back the clock
B 1 (repetirse) «*momento*» to return 2 «*calma/paz*» to return; **~ A algo** to return TO sth
C **volver en sí** to come to *o* round
D (reconciliarse) **~ CON algn** to make up WITH sb
■ **volver** *v aux*: **~ A + INF**: **~ a empezar** to start again *o* (AmE) over; **no ~á a ocurrir** it won't happen again; **no lo volví a ver** I never saw him again; **lo tuve que ~ a llevar al taller** I had to take it back to the workshop
■ **volver** *vt*
A (dar la vuelta) 1 ‹*colchón/tortilla*› to turn (over); ‹*tierra*› to turn *o* dig over; ‹*calcetín/chaqueta*› (poner del revés) to turn ... inside out; (poner del derecho) to turn ... the right way round; ‹*cuello*› to turn; **~ la página** to turn the page 2 ‹*cabeza/mirada*›: **volvió la cabeza** she turned her head; **volvió la mirada hacia mí** he turned his gaze toward(s) me 3 ‹*esquina*› to turn
B (convertir en, poner): **la ha vuelto muy egoísta** it has made her very selfish; **me está volviendo loca** it's/he's/she's driving me mad; **lo vuelve de otro color** it turns it a different color
C (Méx) **~ el estómago** to be sick
■ **volverse** *v pron*
A (girar) to turn (around); **se volvió hacia él** she turned to face him; **no te vuelvas, que nos están siguiendo** don't look back, we're being followed; **se volvió de espaldas** he turned his back on me (*o* her *etc*); **~se boca arriba/abajo** to turn over onto one's back/stomach; ***~se atrás*** to back out; ***~se contra algn*** to turn against sb
B (convertirse en, ponerse): **se ha vuelto muy antipático** he's become very unpleasant; **se está volviendo muy quisquillosa** she's getting very fussy; **se vuelve agrio** it turns *o* goes sour; **se volvió loca** she went mad

vomitar [A1] *vi* to vomit, be sick; **tengo ganas de ~** I think I'm going to vomit *o* be sick, I feel nauseous *o* sick
■ **vomitar** *vt* 1 ‹*comida*› to bring up; **~ sangre** to cough up blood 2 ‹*fuego/lava*› to spew (out); ‹*smoke*› to belch out 3 ‹*insultos/maldiciones*› to hurl
■ **vomitarse** *v pron* (Col, Méx, Ven) to vomit, be sick

vomitivo[1] -va *adj* (Med) emetic; (repugnante) (fam) revolting, disgusting

vomitivo[2] *m* emetic

vómito *m* 1 (acción) vomiting; **¿ha tenido ~s?** have you been vomiting *o* (BrE) sick? 2 (cosa vomitada) vomit
(Compuesto) **vómito de sangre** coughing up of blood

voracidad *f* voracity

vorágine *f* (liter) (en el mar) whirlpool; (situación confusa) maelstrom (liter)

voraz *adj* ‹*persona/animal/apetito*› voracious; ‹*incendio/fuego*› fierce

vórtice *m* (remolino — de viento) whirlwind; (— de agua) whirlpool, vortex; (de un ciclón) eye, center*

vos *pron pers*
A [*Familiar form of address which is widely used instead of* **tú** *mainly in the River Plate area and parts of Central America*] 1 (como sujeto) you; **¿quién lo va a hacer? — vos** who's going to do it? — you (are); **che, ~** hey, you; **~ misma lo dijiste** you said so yourself 2 (en comparaciones, con preposiciones) you; **más/menos que ~** more/less than you; **para/sin ~** for/without you 3 (uno) you; **te dan tres opciones y ~ elegís** they give you three options and you choose
B (arc) (*sing*) thou (arch *or* dial); (con preposiciones) thee (arch *or* dial); (*pl*) ye (arch); **en V~ confío** (Relig) in Thee I trust

vosear [A1] *vt* to address sb using the **vos** form

voseo *m* use of the **vos** form instead of **tú**

vosotros -tras *pron pers pl* [*Familiar form of address not normally used in Latin America or in certain parts of Spain, where* **ustedes** *is used instead*] 1 (como sujeto) you; **¿quién lo va a hacer? — vosotros** who's going to do it? — you (are); **lo podéis hacer ~ mismos** you can do it yourselves 2 (en comparaciones, con preposiciones) you; **más/mejor que ~** more/better than you; **con/contra/para ~** with/against/for you

votación *f* (acción) voting; (método) vote; **la ~ arrojó los siguientes resultados** the voting produced the following results; **decidir por ~** to decide by ballot; **fue elegida por ~** she was elected *o* voted in; **se sometió a ~** it was put to the vote; **hagamos una ~** let's vote on it; **una ~ a mano alzada** a vote by a show of hands; **~ secreta** secret ballot *o* vote

V

votante *mf* voter
(Compuesto) **votante ausente** absentee ballot (AmE) postal voter (BrE)
votar [A1] *vi* to vote; ~ **en blanco** to spoil one's vote (*by returning a blank ballot paper*); ~ **POR algo/algn** to vote FOR sth/sb; ~ **A FAVOR DE/EN CONTRA DE algo** to vote FOR/AGAINST sth
■ **votar** *vt* ‹*candidato*› to vote for; ‹*reforma/aumento*› to approve, vote to approve
voto *m*
A **1** (de elector) vote; **el electorado emite hoy su ~** (period) the electorate will go to the polls today; **~s a favor/en contra** votes for/against **2** (votación) vote; ~ **secreto** secret ballot *o* vote; **por ~ a mano alzada** on *o* by a show of hands; ~ **de una mayoría calificada** qualified majority voting **3** (derecho) vote
(Compuestos)
- **voto de calidad** casting vote, tiebreaker (AmE)
- **voto de confianza/censura** vote of confidence/no confidence
- **voto en blanco** blank ballot paper
- **voto por correo** postal vote, absentee ballot (AmE)

B (Relig) vow; **hacer los ~s solemnes** to take vows
(Compuesto) **voto de castidad/obediencia/pobreza** vow of chastity/obedience/poverty
C (frml) (expresión de un deseo): **hacemos ~s por su pronta mejoría** we wish him a speedy recovery; **con mis mejores ~s para el futuro** with best wishes for the future
vox populi *loc adj*: **ser ~ ~** to be common knowledge
voy *see* **ir**
voyeurismo /bwaʏe'rismo, boɟer'ismo/ *m* voyeurism
voyeurista /bwaʏe'rista, boɟer'ista/ *mf* voyeur
vóytelas *interj* (Méx fam) wow (colloq)
voz *f*
A **1** (sonido) voice; **le temblaba la ~** her voice shook; **levantar la ~** to raise one's voice; **aclararse la ~** to clear one's throat; **tener la ~ tomada** to be hoarse; **hablar en ~ baja** to speak quietly; **en ~ alta** ‹*hablar*› loudly; ‹*leer*› aloud, out loud; **me lo dijo a media ~** he whispered it to me; **la ~ de la conciencia** the voice of one's conscience; ***a ~ en grito** or **cuello*** at the top of one's voice; ***de viva ~*** personally, in person **2** (capacidad de hablar) voice; **quedarse sin ~** to lose one's voice
B (opinión) voice; **la ~ del pueblo** the voice of the people; ***no tener ni ~ ni voto***: **no tiene ni ~ ni voto en esto** he has no say in the matter
C **1** **voces** *fpl* (gritos) shouting, shouts (*pl*); **a voces**: **hablar a voces** to talk in loud voices; **llamar a voces** to call out, to shout; **pedir algo a voces** to cry out for sth; ***dar la ~ de alarma*** to raise the alarm **2** (rumor) rumor*; **corre la ~ de que ...** word *o* rumor has it that ...
D (Mús) **1** (persona) voice **2** (línea melódica): **una pieza a cuatro voces** a piece for four voices, a four-part piece; **cantar a dos voces** to sing a duet; ***llevar la ~ cantante*** (fam) to call the tune *o* shots (colloq)
E (Ling) **1** (frml) (palabra) word **2** (forma verbal) voice
(Compuesto) **voz activa/pasiva** active/passive (voice)
vozarrón *m* booming voice
V.S. (Cin) = **versión subtitulada**
vudú *m* voodoo
vuela, vuelan, etc *see* **volar**
vuelco *m*
A (sobre sí mismo): **dar un ~** «*coche*» to overturn, turn over; «*embarcación*» to capsize; ***me/le dio un ~ el corazón*** my/his heart missed *o* skipped a beat
B (cambio radical): **las cosas pueden dar un ~** things could change *o* alter drastically; **el mercado dio un ~ favorable** the market registered a favorable upturn
C (Inf) dump
vuelo[1] *m*
A **1** (acción): **el ~ de las gaviotas** the seagulls' flight; **remontar el ~** to soar up; **horas de ~** (Aviac) flying time; ***agarrarlas** or **cogerlas al ~*** to be very quick on the uptake; ***alzar** or **levantar el ~*** «*pájaro*» to fly away *o* off; «*avión*» to take off; «*persona*» to fly *o* leave the nest; ***a ~ de pájaro*** (AmL): **un cálculo a ~ de pájaro** a rough estimate; **lo leí a ~ de pájaro** I just skimmed through it; ***de alto ~*** «*proyecto*» big, important; «*ejecutivo*» high-flying (*before n*); ***no se oía ni el ~ de una mosca*** you could have heard a pin drop (colloq); ***tomar ~*** to take flight **2** (trayecto, viaje) flight; **son dos horas de ~** it is a two-hour flight **3** (avión) flight
(Compuestos)
- **vuelo a vela** gliding, soaring (AmE)
- **vuelo charter/regular** charter/schedule flight
- **vuelo espacial** spaceflight
- **vuelo internacional/nacional** international/domestic *o* internal flight
- **vuelo libre** hang-gliding
- **vuelo rasante** low-level flight
- **vuelo sin motor** gliding, soaring (AmE)

B (en costura) **1** (amplitud): **la falda tiene mucho ~** it is a very full skirt **2** (Chi) (adorno) flounce
C (pluma) flight (feather)
vuelo[2] *see* **volar**
vuelta *f*
(Sentido I)
A **1** (circunvolución): **dar ~s alrededor de algo** to go around sth; **da ~s alrededor de su eje** it spins *o* turns on its axis; **dar la ~ al mundo** to go around the world; **todo/la cabeza me da ~s** everything's/my head's spinning; **dar una ~ a la manzana** to go around the block; **dar toda la ~** to go all the way around; **¡las ~s que da la vida!** isn't life strange!; **me pasé el día dando ~s tratando de encontrarlo** I spent the whole day going from pillar to post trying to find it; ***andarse con ~s*** (fam) to beat about the bush (colloq); ***buscarle las ~s a algn*** (fam) to try to catch sb out; ***buscarle la ~ a algo*** (CS fam) to try to find a way of doing sth; ***darle cien (mil) ~s a algn*** (fam) to be miles *o* heaps better than sb (colloq); ***no tener ~*** (Chi fam) to be a hopeless case **2** (Dep) (en golf) round; (en carreras) lap **3** (en carretera) bend; **el camino da muchas ~s** the road winds about a lot; **el autobús da muchas ~s** the bus takes a very roundabout route
(Compuestos)
- **vuelta al ruedo** (Taur) lap of honor
- **vuelta ciclista** cycle race, tour
- **vuelta de honor** lap of honor*

B (giro): **darle ~ a algo** ‹*llave/manivela*› to turn sth; **dale otra ~** give it another turn; ***darle ~s a algo*** to think about sth; **no le des más ~s al asunto** stop agonizing about it; ***poner a algn de ~ y media*** (fam) to tear into sb (AmE colloq), to tear sb off a strip (BrE colloq)
(Compuestos)
- **vuelta de campana**: **el coche dio una ~ de ~** the car turned (right) over
- **vuelta (de) carnero** (CS) somersault
- **vuelta en redondo** (vuelta completa) 360 degree turn, complete turn; (cambio radical) U-turn

C **1** **darle la ~ A algo** ‹*a disco/colchón*› to turn ... (over); ‹*a calcetín*› (ponerlo — del derecho) turn ... the right way out; (— del revés) turn ... inside out; ‹*a copa*› (ponerla — boca arriba) to turn ... the right way up; (— boca abajo) to turn ... upside down; **dar la ~ a la página** to turn the page, turn over; ***no hay ~ que darle*** (fam) there are no two ways about it; ***no tener ~ de hoja***: **sus argumentos no tienen ~ de hoja** you can't argue with the things she says; **eso no tiene ~ de hoja** there are no two ways about it **2** (para cambiar de dirección, posición): **dar la ~** (Auto) to turn (around); **darse la ~** to turn (around); **el paraguas se me dio la ~** my umbrella blew inside out
D (CS) **dar vuelta** ‹*disco/colchón*› to turn ... over; ‹*calcetín*› (ponerlo — del derecho) to turn ... the right way out; (— del revés) to turn ... inside out; ‹*copa*› (ponerla — boca arriba) to turn ... the right way up; (— boca abajo) to turn ... upside down; **dar ~ la página** to turn the page, turn over; **dio ~ la cara** she looked away; **¿damos ~ aquí?** (Auto) shall we turn (around) here?; **darse ~** «*persona*» to turn (around); «*vehículo*» to overturn; «*embarcación*» to capsize; **se me dio ~ el paraguas** my umbrella blew inside out
E **1** (paseo): **dar una ~** (a pie) to go for a walk; (en coche) to go for a drive; (en bicicleta) to go for a ride **2** (con un propósito): **date una ~ por la oficina** drop into the office (colloq); **a ver cuándo te das una ~ por casa** drop in and see us some time
F **1** **a la vuelta**: **escríbelo a la ~** write it on the other side *o* on the back; **vive a la ~** she lives around the corner; ***a la ~ de la esquina*** just around the corner **2** **vuelta y vuelta** (Coc) rare

V

(*Sentido* **II**)

A 1 (regreso) return; (viaje de regreso) return journey; **a la ~ paramos para almorzar** on the way back we stopped for lunch; **a la ~ se encontró con una sorpresa** when he got back he found a surprise; **¡hasta la ~!** see you when you get back!; **su ~ a las tablas** her return to the stage; ***estar de ~*** to be back; **yo ya estoy de ~ de esas cosas** I've seen it all before; **cuando tú vas yo ya estoy de ~** I'm way ahead of you 2 **a ~ de correo** by return mail (AmE), by return (of post) (BrE)

B 1 (a un estado anterior) **~ A algo** return TO sth; **la ~ a la normalidad** the return to normality 2 (fam) (indicando repetición): **¡~ con lo mismo!** there you/there they go again! (colloq)

(*Sentido* **III**) 1 (Esp) (cambio) change; **quédese con la ~** keep the change 2 **vueltas** (Col) (cambio, dinero suelto) change

(*Sentido* **IV**)

A 1 (en elecciones) round 2 (de bebidas) round; **esta ~ la pago yo** this round's on me

B (Per, RPl fam) 1 (vez) time; **esta ~ les ganamos** we'll beat them this time 2 **de vuelta** (de nuevo) again

(*Sentido* **V**)

A 1 (de collar) strand 2 (en labores de punto) row; (en costura) facing; (de pantalones) cuff (AmE), turn-up (BrE)

B (Náut) bend

vuelto[1] -ta *pp*: *see* **volver**

vuelto[2] *m* (AmL) change; **quédese con el ~** keep the change

vuelva, vuelvas, etc *see* **volver**

vuesa merced *pron pers* (arc) thou (arch)

vuestro[1] -tra *adj* 1 (Esp) (de vosotros) your; **~s libros** *or* **los libros ~s** your books; **un amigo ~** a friend of yours; **la responsabilidad es vuestra** it's your responsibility 2 (frml) your; **Vuestra Majestad/Excelencia** Your Majesty/Excellency

vuestro[2] -tra *pron* (Esp): **el ~, la vuestra,** *etc* yours; **sabe lo ~** he knows about the two of you

vulcanización *f* vulcanization

vulcanizadora *f* (Chi, Méx) tire* repairshop

vulcanizar [A4] *vt* to vulcanize

vulgar *adj* 1 (corriente, común) common; **un ~ resfriado** a common cold; **~ *y corriente*** ordinary 2 (poco refinado) vulgar, coarse 3 (no técnico) common, popular

vulgaridad *f* 1 (cualidad) vulgarity, coarseness; **la ~ de sus modales** his vulgar *o* coarse manners 2 (dicho, hecho): **no hagas/digas esas ~es** don't be so vulgar

vulgarismo *m* vulgarism

vulgarización *f* popularization, vulgarization

vulgarizar [A4] *vt* 1 (hacer popular) to popularize, vulgarize (frml) 2 (quitar refinamiento a) to vulgarize

vulgo[1] *adv* commonly known as

vulgo[2] *m*: **el ~** ordinary people (*pl*), the masses (*pl*)

vulnerabilidad *f* vulnerability

vulnerable *adj* vulnerable

vulneración *f* violation, infringement

vulnerar [A1] *vt* (frml) 1 ‹*derecho/ley*› to violate 2 ‹*dignidad*› to wound, hurt; ‹*posición*› to damage

vulva *f* vulva

vv (= **versos**) vv

Ww

W, w *f* (*read as* /'doβle βe/, /'doβle u/ *or* (Esp) /'doβle 'uβe/, /'uβe 'ðoβle/) *the letter* **W, w**

w. (= **watio**) w, watt

wachimán /ɣwatʃi'man/ *m* (AmL) watchman

wafle /'(g)wafle/ *m* (AmL) waffle

waflera *f* (AmL) waffle iron

wagneriano -na *adj* Wagnerian

walkie-talkie /'wo(l)ki 'to(l)ki/ *m* (*pl* **-kies**) walkie-talkie

walkman® *m* (*pl* **-mans**) Walkman®

warfarina *f* warfarin

wáter /'(g)water *or* (Esp) 'bater/ *m* (inodoro) toilet; (cuarto) (Esp) toilet, bathroom (esp AmE)

waterpolista *mf* water polo player

waterpolo /'(g)waterpolo/ *m* water polo

watt /bat, ɣwat/ *m* (*pl* ∼**s**) watt

WC /'be θe, 'uβe 'ðoβle θe/ *m* WC

wedge /(g)wedʒ/ *m* (Dep) wedge

weekend /'wiken/ *m* weekend

welter *m* (*pl* ∼) welterweight

western *m* (*pl* ∼ *or* **-terns**) western

whiskería *f* bar (*selling a large range of whiskies*)

whisky /'(g)wiski/ *m* (*pl* **-kies** *or* **-kys**) whiskey•

(Compuesto) **whisky americano** bourbon

Winchester® /'wintʃeste(r)/ *m* (*pl* **-ters**) Winchester® (rifle)

windsurf /'winsurf/ *m* (deporte) windsurfing; (tabla) windsurfer, sailboard

windsurfing /'winsurfin/ *m* windsurfing

windsurfista *mf* windsurfer

wolframio *m* wolfram

won (Fin) *m* won

X, x *f (read as /'ekis/) the letter* **X, x**

xenofobia *f* xenophobia

xenófobo -ba *adj* xenophobic

xenón *m* xenon

xerocopia *f* photocopy, xerox®

xerocopiar [A1] *vt* to photocopy, xerox

xerografía *f* xerography

xilema *m* xylem

xilofón, xilófono *m* xylophone

xilografía *f* (arte) xylography; (impresión) xylograph

xoconostle *m* (en Méx) *type of prickly pear*

Y, **y** *f* (*read as* /i 'ɣrjeɣa/, /je/ *or* (RPl) /ʒe/) *the letter* **Y, y**

y *conj*

A **1** (indicando conexión, añadidura) and; **habla inglés y alemán** he speaks English and German; **un cielo azul y sin nubes** a cloudless blue sky **2** (con valor adversativo) while, and; **¡yo gano el dinero y él lo gasta!** I earn the money and he spends it!

B **1** (indicando acumulación) and; **iba llegando gente y más gente** more and more people kept arriving; **habla y habla todo el día** he just talks and talks all day long **2** (introduciendo una consecuencia) and; **atrévete y verás** just you dare and you'll see!

C **1** (en preguntas): **¿y tu padre? ¿qué tal está?** and how's your father?; **¿y Mónica? ¿no viene?** what about Monica? isn't she coming?; **yo no oigo nada ¿y tú?** I can't hear anything, can you?; **a mí me regaló dinero ¿y a ti?** she gave me money, what did she give *you*?; **¿y? ¿qué resolvieron?** well? *o* so? what did you decide?; **¿cómo estás? — bien ¿y tú?** how are you? — I'm fine, and you?; **a mí me encanta ¿y a ti?** I love it, what about you? **2** (fam) (expresando indiferencia) so (colloq); **no hay trenes — ¿y?** *or* **¿y qué?** there are no trains — so what?; **¿y a mí qué?** so, what's it to me?

D (esp RPl fam) (encabezando respuestas) well; **¿y fuiste? — y sí, no tuve más remedio** and did you go? — well yes, I had no choice; **y bueno** oh well

E (en números): **cuarenta y cinco** forty-five; **doscientos treinta y tres** two hundred and thirty-three; **uno y medio** one and a half

ya¹ *adv* [*Both the simple past* **ya terminé** *and the present perfect* **ya he terminado** *are used to refer to the recent indefinite past. The former is the preferred form in Latin America while in Spain there is a tendency to use the latter*]

A **1** (en frases afirmativas o interrogativas) already; **¿~ te has gastado todo el dinero?** have you spent all the money already?; **~ terminé** I've (already) finished; **~ te dije que no** I've already said no; **¿~ ha llegado Ernesto?** has Ernesto arrived yet?, did Ernesto arrive yet? (AmE); **~ lo sé** I (already) know; **aprietas este botón ¡y ~ está!** you press this button, and that's it!; **le teníamos tanta fe y ~ ves, nos ha defraudado** we had such faith in him and look what happened, he's let us down **2** (expresando que se ha comprendido) yes, sure (colloq); **dile que venga — ~, pero ¿si no quiere?** tell her to come — yes, but what if she doesn't want to?; **me he pasado el día estudiando — ¡~, ~!** (iró) I spent the whole day studying — oh sure! (iro)

B **1** (en frases negativas) any more; **ese color ~ no se lleva** nobody wears that color any more; **~ ni siquiera me escribe** he doesn't even write (to) me any more; **estaba muy segura pero ~ no sé qué pensar** I was very sure about it, but now I don't know what to think; **creo que ~ no vienen** I don't think they'll come now **2** **no ya ... sino** not (just) ... but; **estamos hablando no ~ de cambios sino de una total reestructuración** we are not (just) talking about changes but about a total restructuring

C (enseguida, ahora) right now; **¡~ voy!** coming!; **la comida ~ va a estar** the meal's almost ready; **preparados listos ¡~!** on your mark(s), get set, go!; **~ puedes ir haciéndote a la idea** you'd better start getting used to the idea; **desde ~ te digo que no puede ser** (esp AmL) I can tell you right now that it's not possible; **~ mismo** (esp AmL) right away, straightaway (BrE)

D (con verbo en futuro): **~ te contaré** I'll tell you all about it; **~ lo entenderás** you'll understand one day

E (en comparaciones): **éste ~ no me gusta tanto** I don't like this one so much; **pintado de blanco ~ es otra cosa** it really does look much better painted white

F (uso enfático): **¡~ quisiera yo!** I should be so lucky!; **~ era hora** about time (too)!; **¡~ me tienes harta!** I'm (just about) fed up with you!; **¿te parece que allí se vive mejor? — ¡~ lo creo!** do you think people live better there? — you bet! (colloq)

G **ya que** since, as; **~ que estás aquí** since *o* as you're here; **~ que estoy, limpio éste también** while I'm at it I may as well clean this one too

ya² *conj*: **~ por tierra, ~ por mar** (liter) whether by land or by sea; **se puede solicitar ~ sea en persona o por teléfono** it can be ordered either in person or by telephone

yacaré *m* cayman

yacente *adj* (liter) reclining (*before n*), recumbent (liter)

yacer [E5] *vi* **1** (frml) (estar enterrado) to lie (frml); **aquí yacen sus restos mortales** here lie her mortal remains **2** (liter) (estar tendido) to lie; **~ con algn** (arc) to lie with sb (arch)

yacimiento *m* **1** (de mineral) deposit; **~ petrolífero** oilfield **2** (Arqueol) site

yacuzzi /ja'kusi/ *m* jacuzzi®

yagua *f* royal palm

yagual *m* padded ring (*used to carry heavy objects on the head*)

yaguareté *m* jaguar

yak *m* yak

Yakarta *f* Jakarta

yámbico -ca *adj* iambic

yambo *m*

A (Lit) iamb

B (Bot) rose apple

yámper *m* (Per) jumper (AmE), pinafore dress (BrE)

yanacón -cona *m,f* (Hist) Indian servant

yanacona *mf* (Per) sharecropper

yanqui¹ *adj* (*pl* **-quis**) (fam) Yankee (colloq)

yanqui² *mf* (*pl* **-quis**) (fam) Yank (colloq), Yankee (colloq)

Yanquilandia *f* (fam) the States (colloq)

yantar [A1] *vi* (arc) to eat

yapa *f* (CS, Per fam) *small amount of extra goods given free*, lagniappe (AmE); **dar algo de ~** to throw sth in (for free) (colloq); **me dio dos de ~** she threw in a couple extra; **te cobraron con ~** they really ripped you off (colloq)

yarará *f* pit viper

yarda *f* yard

yate *m* yacht

yaya *f* (Chi, Per fam): **tengo ~** it hurts; **hacerse ~** to hurt oneself; **estar con ~** to be sick *o* ill

yayo -ya *m,f* (fam) (*m*) grandpa (colloq), granddad (colloq); (*f*) granny (colloq), grandma (colloq)

ye *f*: *name of the letter* **y**

yedra *f* ivy

yegua *f*

A (Zool) mare

B (Chi fam) **1** (persona torpe) bonehead (colloq) **2** (puta) whore (sl)

yeguada *f* 1 (ganado caballar) horses (*pl*) 2 (caballeriza) stable, stables (*pl*) 3 (CS) (manada de yeguas) group *o* herd of mares

yeísmo *m*: *the pronunciation of 'll' in many parts of Spain and Latin America as 'y'*

yelmo *m* helmet

yema *f* 1 (de huevo) yolk 2 (dulce) *sweet made with egg yolk and sugar* 3 (del dedo) fingertip 4 (Bot) leaf bud

Yemen *m* Yemen

(Compuesto) **Yemen del Sur** South Yemen

yen *m* yen

yendo *see* **ir**

yerba *f* 1 *tb* **~ mate** maté 2 (Andes, Méx, Ven fam) (marihuana) grass (sl) 3 ▸**hierba A**

yerbatero¹ -ra *adj* maté (*before n*)

yerbatero² -ra *m,f* (Andes) (curandero) witch doctor; (que vende hierbas medicinales) herbalist

yerga, yergue *see* **erguir**

yermo¹ -ma *adj* (liter) (despoblado) uninhabited; (estéril) barren

yermo² *m* wasteland

yerno *m* son-in-law

yerra, yerras, etc *see* **errar**

yerro *m* error, mistake

yerto -ta *adj* stiff, rigid

yesca *f* (madera) punk, tinder; (piedra) flint

yesería *f* (fábrica) plaster factory, plaster works (*sing or pl*); (obra) plasterwork, plastering

yesero -ra *m,f* plasterer

yeso *m* 1 (Art, Const) plaster 2 (AmL) (Med) plaster 3 (Min) gypsum

yesquero *m* (Col, RPl, Ven) cigarette lighter

yeta *f* (RPl fam) (mala suerte) bad luck; (influencia adversa) jinx

yeti *m* yeti

ye-ye *adj* (ant) trendy (colloq)

yídish, yiddish /'ɪɪðɪʃ/ *m* Yiddish

yihad *m or f* jihad

yira *f* (RPl arg) hooker (colloq)

yirar [A1] *vi* (RPl arg) to hustle (AmE colloq), to tout for business (BrE euph)

yo¹ *pron pers* 1 (como sujeto) I; **¿quién quería verme? — ~ no** who wanted to see me? — not me *o* it wasn't me; **¿quién quiere más? — ¡~!** who wants some more? — me! *o* I do!; **soy ~** it's me; **fui ~ el que llamó** it was me *o* (frml) I who called; **¿quién, ~?** who?, me?; **~ misma** myself; **estoy cansada — ~ también** I'm tired — so am I *o* me too; **¿y ~ qué?** what about me?; **~ que tú/él** if I were you/him; **~ misma** myself 2 (en comparaciones, con ciertas preposiciones) me; **come más que ~** he eats more than me *o* more than I do; **es tan alto como ~** he's as tall as me *o* as tall as I am; **llegó después que ~** she arrived after me; **se sentó entre Isabel y ~** he sat between Isabel and me; **lo preparamos entre Charo y ~** Charo and I prepared it between us

yo² *m*: **el ~** the ego

yodo *m* iodine

yoga *m* yoga

yogui *m* yogi

yogur, yogurt *m* (*pl* **-gurts**) yogurt, yoghurt

yogurtera *f* yogurt maker

yonqui *mf* (*pl* **-quis**) (fam) junkie (colloq)

yo-yo *m* (*pl* **-yos**) yo-yo

yuca *f* (tubérculo comestible) cassava, manioc; (planta ornamental) yucca

yudo *m* judo

yudoca *mf* judoka, judoist

yugo *m* 1 (de bueyes) yoke; **mañana de vuelta al ~** (fam) it's back to the grindstone tomorrow (colloq) 2 (opresión) yoke

Yugoslavia, Yugoeslavia *f* (Hist) Yugoslavia

yugoslavo -va, yugoeslavo -va *adj/m,f* (Hist) Yugoslavian

yugular *adj/f* jugular

yuju *interj* yoo-hoo!

yungas *mpl or fpl* warm valleys (*pl*) (*in Bolivia and Peru*)

yunque *m* anvil

yunta *f* 1 (de bueyes) yoke 2 (Chi fam) (de personas): **forman una buena ~** the two of them make a good team; **hacer ~ con alguien** to join forces *o* team up with sb

yuntero -ra *m,f* plowman (AmE), ploughman (BrE)

yupi¹ *adj/mf* (*pl* **-pis**) yuppie

yupi² *interj* (fam) hooray!, yippee! (colloq), whoopee! (colloq), wahey! (colloq)

yute *m* jute

yuxtaponer [E22] *vt* to juxtapose

yuxtaposición *f* juxtaposition

yuyo *m* 1 (Per, RPl) (hierba) herb; **té de ~s** herbal tea 2 (RPl) (mala hierba) weed 3 (Per) (alga) seaweed

Zz

Z, z *f* (*read as* /'seta/ *or* (Esp) /'θeta/) *the letter* **Z, z**
zacate *m* (AmC, Méx) 1 (hierba) grass; (heno) hay 2 (esponja) sponge; (estropajo) scourer
zácatelas *interj* (Méx, RPl fam) all of a sudden (colloq)
zafacoca *f* (Chi fam) commotion
zafado¹ -da *adj* (fam) 1 (AmL) loopy (colloq), crazy (colloq) 2 (CS) (descarado) fresh (AmE colloq), cheeky (BrE colloq)
zafado² -da *m,f* (AmL fam) crazy fool
zafar [A1] *vt* 1 (Chi, Méx) ‹*brazo/dedo*› to dislocate 2 (Col, Ven) ‹*nudo*› to untie; ‹*tuerca*› to unscrew; ‹*persona/animal*› to let ... loose
■ **zafarse** *v pron* 1 (de compromiso) **~se DE algo** to get *o* wriggle OUT OF sth 2 (soltarse) «*persona/animal*» to get loose, get away 3 «*lazo/nudo*» to come undone 4 (*refl*) (Chi, Méx) (dislocarse): **~se la muñeca** to dislocate one's wrist
zafarrancho *m* (fam) 1 (caos) chaos; (alboroto) commotion; **se armó un ~ tremendo** all hell broke loose 2 (desastre) (fam): **hacer un ~** to make a mess
(Compuesto) **zafarrancho de combate** call to action *o* battle stations
zafio -fia *adj* coarse, crude
zafiro *m* sapphire
zafra *f*
A (cosecha) sugarcane harvest; (temporada) harvest time
B (Arg) (esquila) shearing
zaga *f* 1 (Dep) defense* 2 **a la zaga** ‹*ir/quedarse*› in the rear, behind; **él será grosero pero tú no te quedas a la ~** he may be rude but you're not far behind
zagal -gala *m,f* 1 (fam) (joven) (*m*) lad, boy; (*f*) girl, lass 2 (ant) (pastor) (*m*) shepherd boy; (*f*) shepherd girl
zaguán *m* hallway
zaguero -ra *m,f* (Dep) defender
zaherir [I11] *vt* to hurt, wound
zahorí *mf* dowser
zaino -na *adj* ‹*caballo*› chestnut; ‹*toro*› black
Zaire *m* (Hist): *tb* **el ~** Zaire
zalamería *f*: *tb* **~s** sweet talk, flattery; **hacerle ~s a algn** to sweet-talk sb
zalamero -ra *adj* ‹*palabras*› flattering; **¡qué ~ estás!** you're being very nice (to me)! (iro)
zalema *f* (reverencia) salaam, bow
zamaquear [A1] *vt* (Per) to rock
zamarra *f* (chaqueta) leather/sheepskin jacket; (chaleco) leather/sheepskin jerkin
zamarrear [A1] *vt* ‹*persona*› to shake ‹*presa*› to shake ... in its jaws
zamarro -rra *m,f*
A (Bol, Per) (pillo) sharp customer (colloq)
B **zamarros** *mpl* (pantalones) (Col) chaps (*pl*)
zamba *f* zamba (*South American folk dance*)
zambo¹ -ba *adj* bowlegged
zambo² -ba *m,f* (AmL) *person of mixed black and Amerindian origin*
zambomba *f*
A (Mús) *traditional drum-like instrument*
B (*como interj*) **¡~!** wow! (colloq)
zambra *f* (fiesta) gypsy festivity (*with dancing*); (jaleo, pelea) commotion
zambullida *f* (salto) dive, plunge; (baño) dip
zambullirse [I9] *v pron* (lanzarse) to dive (in); (sumergirse) to duck *o* dive underwater
zambullón *m* (AmS) ▸ **zambullida**
zampar [A1] *vt*
A (esp AmL fam) 1 (poner) to put, stick (colloq); **lo zampé en el suelo de un golpe** I floored him with one blow 2 (pegar): **~le una trompada/cachetada a algn** to thump/slap sb; **le zampó tremenda patada** she kicked him really hard
B (AmL) (decir): **así nomás le zampó que ...** she just came right *o* straight out and said that ...
■ **zampar** *vi* (Esp) to stuff one's face (colloq)
■ **zamparse** *v pron*
A (fam) ‹*comida*› to wolf down (colloq); ‹*bebida*› to knock back (colloq)
B (AmL fam) (tirarse, lanzarse) to throw oneself, to leap
zampoña *f* panpipes (*pl*)
zamuro *m* (Ven) turkey vulture
zanahoria¹ *adj* 1 (RPl fam) (tonto) stupid 2 (Ven fam) (anticuado) square (colloq)
zanahoria² *f*
A (Bot, Coc) carrot
B **zanahoria** *mf* 1 (RPl fam) (tonto) idiot, nerd (colloq) 2 (Ven fam) (mojigato) strailaced person; (anticuado) old fogey (colloq)
zanahorio -ria *adj* (Col fam) (mojigato) straitlaced; (anticuado) square (colloq)
zanca *f* leg
zancada *f* stride; **bajaba la cuesta a ~s** he came striding down the hill; ***en dos ~s*** in no time
zancadilla *f* trip; **me hizo una ~** he tripped me (up)
zancón -cona *adj* (Méx fam) ‹*falda*› short
zancos *mpl* stilts (*pl*)
zancuda *f* wader, wading bird
zancudero *m* (Col, Ven) swarm of mosquitoes
zancudo¹ -da *adj* 1 ‹*ave*› wading (*before n*) 2 (fam) ‹*persona*› long-legged
zancudo² *m* (típula) crane fly, daddy longlegs; (mosquito) (AmL) mosquito
zandunga *f*
A (baile) ▸ **sandunga C**
B (AmL) (juerga) ▸ **sandunga B**
zanganear [A1] *vi* (fam) to loaf *o* laze around (colloq)
zángano -na *m,f*
A (fam) (persona) lazybones (colloq)
B **zángano** *m* (abeja) drone
zangolotear [A1] *vt* (fam) to shake
■ **zangolotearse** *v pron* (fam): **el avión se zangoloteó mucho** the plane was buffeted (about) a lot; **deja de ~te** stop jumping up and down (colloq)
zangoloteo *m* (de tren) jolting; (de persona) shaking; **nadie pudo dormir con el ~ del avión** no one could sleep because the plane was being buffeted about
zanja *f* (para desagüe) ditch; (para cimientos, tuberías) trench; (acequia) irrigation channel
zanjar [A1] *vt* ‹*polémica/diferencias*› to settle, resolve; ‹*deuda*› to settle, pay off
zanjón *m* (Chi) gorge
zapa *f* (pala) spade; (Mil) sap

zapador *m* (Mil) sapper

zapallito *m* (CS): *tb* ~ **largo** *or* **italiano** zucchini (AmE), courgette (BrE)

zapallo *m* (CS, Per) (Bot, Coc) pumpkin

zapapico *m* pickax*

zapata *f* (Auto, Mec) brake shoe

zapatazo *m* (golpe) blow with a shoe; ***tratar a algn a ~s*** to be rude to sb

zapateado *m* (baile español) zapateado; (en baile) foot stamping (*in time to the music*)

zapatear [A1] *vi* 1 (en danza) to tap one's feet; (más fuerte) to stamp (*in time to the music*) 2 (para protestar, vitorear) to stamp (one's feet)

zapateo *m* tapping; (más fuerte) stamping

(Compuesto) **zapateo americano** (CS) tap dancing

zapatería *f* (tienda) shoe store (AmE), shoe shop (BrE); (taller — de fabricación) shoemaker's, cobbler's; (— de reparación) shoe repairer's, cobbler's

zapatero -ra *m,f* shoemaker, cobbler; ***~, a tus zapatos*** stick to what you know, let the cobbler stick to his last

(Compuesto) **zapatero remendón** cobbler

zapatilla *f* 1 (de lona) canvas shoe; (para deportes) sneaker (AmE), trainer (BrE); (alpargata) espadrille; (para ballet) ballet shoe; (pantufla) slipper 2 (Méx) (zapato de mujer) lady's shoe; **~ de piso** flat shoe

zapato *m* shoe; **~s bajos/de tacón** *or* (CS) **de taco alto** low-heeled/high-heeled shoes; ***como un niño*** *or* ***chico con ~s nuevos*** like a child with a new toy; ***cada uno sabe dónde le aprieta el ~*** each person knows where his own problems lie

(Compuestos)
- **zapato de cordón/golf** lace-up/golf shoe
- **zapato de goma** (Ven) sneaker (AmE), trainer (BrE)

zapatón *m* (para la lluvia) (Col) galosh, overshoe; (para caminar) (Chi) walking shoe

zapear [A1] *vt* (Per fam) to gawk at (colloq)

zaperoco *m* (Ven fam) riot

zapote *m* (árbol) sapodilla; (fruto) sapodilla plum, naseberry

zapoteca *adj/mf* Zapotec

zapping /'sapin, 'θapin/ *m* channel-hopping, channel-surfing (AmE); **hacer ~** to channel-hop, channel-surf (AmE)

zar *m* tsar, czar

zarabanda *f* 1 (Mús) sarabande 2 (fam) (jaleo) racket (colloq), row (colloq) 3 (Méx) (paliza) beating

zaragata *f* (pelea) fight; (ajetreo) bustle; (jaleo) hullabaloo

zaragatero[1] -ra *adj* rowdy, noisy

zaragatero[2] -ra *m,f* (jaranero) reveler*; (peleador) thug, hooligan

Zaragoza *f* Saragossa

zaranda *f* sieve

zarandajas *fpl* (Esp fam): **cotilleos y otras ~** gossip and other tittle-tattle (colloq); **lleva un montón de papeleo y demás ~** it involves filling out loads of forms and other fiddly little things (colloq)

zarandear [A1] *vt* (de un lado a otro) to shake; (para arriba y para abajo) to shake *o* jog up and down; **la vida lo ha zarandeado mucho** he has taken some hard knocks in his life

■ **zarandearse** *v pron* (esp AmL): **nos zarandeamos mucho durante el vuelo** we got shaken around *o* buffeted a lot during the flight; **¡qué manera de ~se este tren!** this train's shaking around like anything (colloq); **el barco se zarandeó mucho** the boat rocked *o* tossed about a lot

zarandeo *m* 1 (sacudida): **con tanto ~ se cayeron las maletas** all the jolting brought the suitcases down 2 (esp AmL) (trajín): **el ~ de fin de año** the end-of-year hustle and bustle; **pasó el día en ~s para acá y para allá** he spent the day rushing around from one place to another (colloq)

zarape *m* (en AmC, Méx) serape (*colorful blanket-like shawl worn esp by men*)

zarcillo *m*
A (arete) earring
B (Bot) tendril

zarco -ca *adj* light blue, azure (liter)

zarigüeya *f* opossum, possum

zarina *f* czarina

zarista *adj/mf* czarist

zarpa *f* 1 (Zool) paw 2 (fam) (mano) paw (colloq); ***echarle la ~ a algn/algo*** «*animal*» to pounce on sb/sth; «*persona*» to get one's hands on sb/sth

zarpar [A1] *vi* to set sail, weigh anchor

zarpazo *m* 1 (de gato, león) swipe; **me dio un ~** it took a swipe at me (with its paw) 2 (de persona) snatch; **se lo quitó de un ~** she snatched it from him; **los ~s de la fatalidad** (liter) fate's cruel blows (liter)

zarrapastroso[1] -sa *adj* (fam) shabby

zarrapastroso[2] -sa *m,f* (fam) scruffy person (colloq)

zarza *f* bramble, blackberry bush

zarzal *m* bramble patch

zarzamora *f* (fruto) blackberry; (arbusto) bramble, blackberry bush

zarzo *m* (Col) loft, attic; ***ser como caído del ~*** (Col fam) to be a sucker (colloq)

zarzuela *f* (Espec, Mús) *traditional Spanish operetta*

zarzuela

A musical drama consisting of alternating passages of dialogue, songs, choruses, and dancing, that originated in Spain in the seventeenth century. Its name comes from the Palacio de la Zarzuela, Madrid. It is also popular in Latin America. *Zarzuela* declined in the eighteenth century but revived in the early nineteenth century. The revived *zarzuela* dealt with more popular themes and was called *género chico*. A more serious version developed, known as *género grande*

(Palacio de) la Zarzuela

The Madrid palace where the Spanish Royal Family now lives

zas *interj* (en la mejilla) smack!

zascandil *mf* (Esp fam) good-for-nothing (colloq)

zascandilear [A1] *vi* (Esp fam) (hacer cosas sin utilidad) to mess around

zenit *m* zenith

zeppelin /sepe'lin, θepe'lin/, **zepelín** *m* zeppelin, airship

zeta[1] *f*: *name of the letter* **z**

zeta[2] *m* (Esp fam) patrol car, police car

zigoto *m* zygote

zigzag *m* (*pl* **-zags** *or* **-zagues**) zigzag

zigzaguear [A1] *vi* to zigzag

zigzagueo *m* zigzagging, zigzag movement

Zimbabwe, Zimbabue *m* Zimbabwe

zinc *m* zinc; **techo de chapa de ~** corrugated iron roof

zíngaro -ra *adj/m,f* gypsy (*especially from Central Europe*)

zíper *m* (AmC, Méx, Ven) zipper (AmE), zip (BrE)

zipizape *m* (Esp fam) commotion

zócalo *m*
A (rodapié) baseboard (AmE), skirting board (BrE)
B (de columna) base, plinth
C (Méx) (plaza) main square

zoco[1] -ca *adj* (Col fam) left-handed

zoco[2] *m* souk

zodíaco *m* zodiac

zombi *mf* zombie

zona *f*
A (área, región) area; **fue declarada ~ neutral** it was declared a neutral zone; **~ de influencia** sphere of influence; Ⓢ **zona de carga y descarga** loading and unloading only

(Compuestos)
- **zona catastrófica** *or* (Chi) **de emergencia** disaster area
- **zona cero** ground zero
- **zona comercial** commercial district
- **zona de castigo** penalty area

- **zona del euro** euro zone
- **zona de libre comercio** free-trade zone
- **zona desnuclearizada** *or* **no nuclear** nuclear-free zone
- **zona de tolerancia** red-light district
- **zona franca** duty-free zone
- **zona industrial** industrial park
- **zona parachoque** *or* **tampón** buffer zone
- **zona peatonal** pedestrian precinct
- **zona roja** (AmL) (zona de prostitución) red-light district
- **zona verde** park, green space

B (en baloncesto) free-throw lane, three-second area

zonal *adj* zonal, area (*before n*)

zoncear [A1] *vi* (AmL fam) to fool around (colloq), to mess around (colloq)

zoncera *f* **1** (AmL fam) (cualidad) stupidity **2** (RPl) ▸**sonsera** **3** (Col) (fatiga) drowsiness

zonificar [A2] *vt* to zone, divide *o* mark off into zones

zonzo¹ -za *adj* **1** (AmL fam) (tonto) silly **2** (Col, Méx fam) (atontado) dazed, stunned

zonzo² -za *m,f* (AmL fam) idiot, fool

zoo *m* zoo

zoología *f* zoology

zoológico¹ -ca *adj* zoological

zoológico² *m* zoo, zoological garden (frml)

zoólogo -ga *m,f* zoologist

zoom /sum, θum/ *m* zoom (lens); **hay un acercamiento con ~** the camera zooms in

zopenco¹ -ca *adj* (fam) stupid, idiotic

zopenco² -ca *m,f* (fam) blockhead (colloq)

zopilote *m* (AmC, Méx) turkey vulture

zoquete¹ *adj* (fam) dim, dense (colloq)

zoquete² *m*

A (CS) (Indum) sock, ankle sock

B **zoquete** *mf* (fam) (persona) dimwit (colloq), blockhead (colloq)

zorongo *m* (baile) *Andalusian dance*

zorra *f*

A (fam & pey) (prostituta) whore (colloq & pej); ***no tener ni ~ idea (de algo)*** (Esp fam): **no tengo ni ~ idea (de política)** I don't have a clue (about politics); *ver tb* **zorro²**

B **1** (carro) cart **2** (RPl) (Ferr) handcar

zorrear [A1] *vi* (fam) to be up to no good

zorrera *f* (Zool) earth

zorrería *f* (fam) (cualidad) slyness; (acto) sly trick

zorrillo *m* **1** (AmL) (mofeta) skunk **2** (Méx fam) (tonto) idiot, silly fool

zorrino *m* (CS) skunk

zorro¹ -rra *adj* (fam) sly, crafty; *ver tb* **zorra A**

zorro² -rra *m,f*

A **1** (Zool) (*m*) fox; (*f*) vixen **2** (AmC, Méx fam) (oposum) opossum **3** **zorro** *m* (piel) fox (fur); ***estar hecho unos ~s*** (Esp fam) to be dog-tired

B (fam) (persona astuta) sly *o* crafty person; *ver tb* **zorra**

zorruno -na *adj* (del zorro) fox (*before n*); (parecido al zorro) fox-like, foxy

zorzal *m* (Zool) thrush

zote¹ *adj* (fam) stupid

zote² *mf* (fam) dimwit (colloq), blockhead (colloq)

zozobra *f* anxiety; **nos llenó de ~** it made us very anxious *o* uneasy

zozobrar [A1] *vi*

A «*barco*» (hundirse) to founder; (volcar) to capsize

B «*proyecto/negocio*» to founder

zueco *m* clog

zulo *m* (Esp) cache

zulú¹ *adj/mf* Zulu

zulú² *m* (idioma) Zulu

zumaque *m* sumac, sumach

zumba *f* (AmL fam) (good) hiding (colloq)

zumbadera *f* (Col fam) (ruido molesto) noise, racket (colloq); (zumbido) buzzing, humming

zumbado -da *adj*

A [ESTAR] (Esp arg) **1** (loco) crazy **2** (despistado): **no sé lo que hago, estoy ~** I haven't (got) a clue what I'm doing, I've lost it

B [ESTAR] (Ven fam) (osado) fresh (AmE), cheeky (BrE)

zumbador *m* buzzer

zumbar [A1] *vi* **1** «*insecto*» to buzz; «*motor*» to hum, whirr; **pasar zumbando** «*bala/coche*» to whizz by; **la bala me pasó zumbando** the bullet whizzed past me; ***hacer ~ a algn*** (Chi fam) to beat sb to a pulp (colloq); ***hacer ~ algo*** (Chi, Ven fam) ‹*aparato/casa*› to wreck; ‹*plata/herencia*› to blow (colloq); ***~le a algn los oídos***: **me zumbaban los oídos** my ears were buzzing *o* ringing; **le estarán zumbando los oídos ...** his ears must be burning ... (colloq) **2** (Col fam) (molestar): **váyanse a ~ a otro lado** go and bother *o* pester someone else

■ **zumbar** *vt*

A **1** (fam) ‹*persona*› to give ... a good hiding (colloq) **2** (RPl fam) ‹*paliza/bofetada*›: **le ~on una paliza** they beat him up (colloq); **me zumbó una bofetada** she slapped me **3** ‹*pandero*› to bang

B (Ven fam) (tirar) to chuck (colloq), to throw

zumbido *m* (de insecto) buzzing, droning; (de motor) humming, whirring; **siento un ~ en los oídos** I have a buzzing *o* ringing in my ears

zumbón -bona *adj* **1** ‹*ruido*› (de motor) humming (*before n*); (de insecto) buzzing (*before n*) **2** (burlón) ‹*tono*› teasing (*before n*)

zumo *m* (esp Esp) juice

zuncho *m* metal hoop *o* band

zurcido *m* (acción) darning, mending; (arreglo) darn, mend

zurcir [I4] *vt* ‹*calcetines*› to darn, mend; ***¡que te zurzan!*** (Esp fam) get lost! (colloq)

zurda *f* (mano) left hand; (pie) left foot

zurdazo *m* (en boxeo) left; (en fútbol) shot *o* cross with the left foot

zurdo¹ -da *adj* **1** ‹*persona*› left-handed; ‹*futbolista*› left-footed; ‹*boxeador/lanzador*› southpaw (*before n*); ***no soy/es ~*** (Esp fam) I'm/he's not stupid **2** ‹*mano/pie*› left

zurdo² -da *m,f* (persona) left-handed person; (tenista) left-hander; (boxeador) southpaw

zuro *m* spike, ear

zurra *f* (fam) (good) hiding (colloq)

zurrapa *f* (posos) dregs (*pl*); (del café) grounds (*pl*)

zurrar [A1] *vt* (fam) to wallop (colloq), to give ... a (good) thrashing *o* hiding (colloq); ***~le a algn*** (Méx fam): **esas cosas me zurran** things like that really bug me (colloq); **me zurra escribir a máquina** I find typing a real pain in the neck (colloq)

zurriagazo *m* (fam) lash, stroke

zurriago *m*, **zurriaga** *f* whip

zurrón *m* (de pastor) leather bag; (de cazador) hunter's pouch

zurullo *m* (Chi fam) turd (vulg)

zutano -na *m,f* *ver* **fulano**

Guide to effective communication
Guía para la comunicación eficaz

Effective Spanish

General points

Varieties of Spanish

As in English, there are many varieties or registers of Spanish, from the very formal style of official documents to the trendy insider slang of internet blogs. It is important to be aware of this and to choose the level of language appropriate to the context in which you are writing.

Formal and literary language

As with English, formal Spanish constitutes a relatively restricted sub-group of the language. Careful writers of English generally tend to avoid over-using formal and literary terms as they can sound pompous and even unintentionally humorous. An English-speaker reading an official letter or a memo written in Spanish will often find the tone very formal. However, this tendency towards formal usage is slowly being superseded by a more straightforward style, except in specific areas such as Law. It is advisable for language learners to aim for simplicity and directness in the way they write.

Informal language

Spanish is rich in informal terms and turns of phrase that are used in almost every area of everyday life. Non-Spanish-speaking people living and working in a Spanish-speaking country are generally widely exposed to informal language through contact with their native contemporaries, friends or colleagues. This is a situation to be wary of as newcomers to the culture will not have the natural sensitivity of a native speaker when it comes to knowing what type of vocabulary to use when and where. This can easily cause offense. It is a good idea to be aware of this (a foreigner offends more easily than a native speaker) and certainly to refrain entirely from using informal Spanish when writing essays, reports, memos, etc. Conversely Spanish journalists often strive not to repeat words used in their reporting. This means that quite formal vocabulary finds its way into newspapers, with the risk that the non-native reader may assume from the context that the words are less formal than they actually are. Some examples of formal words to avoid are:

formal Spanish	**neutral Spanish**
ataviarse	vestirse
contraer matrimonio	casarse
cuita	problema
descender la montaña	bajar la montaña
ebrio	borracho
erguir	levantar
expoliar	apoderarse de
loar	alabar
mácula	mancha
morada	residencia
postrarse	arrodillarse
propincuidad	proximidad
sepultar	enterrar

Tone: personal versus impersonal

In articles, reports, and memos the tone should be as impersonal as possible. In academic articles it is still more common to find the first person plural pronoun *nosotros* used in Spanish, even when only one person is writing. A single individual writing a report on a situation in Spanish will, however, use I.

In English, the passive is often used to convey information in an objective way. The passive is much less widely used in Spanish and it is good practice to avoid it. Remember to use the impersonal pronoun *uno*, as in *cuando uno examina las cifras de cerca*, and to use the relexive form of the verb with **-se**, as in *cuando se examinan las cifras de cerca*. Both sentences mean, "when the figures are examined closely"; the first being less formal than the second.

Punctuation

Spanish punctuation conventions do not differ greatly from English. You may encounter an older style of quotation marks, «...», although nowadays the use of "..." is more frequent. Single quotation marks, '...', are not used in Spanish.

Some words are capitalized in English which are not in Spanish: names of days and months (*enero, mayo, jueves, sábado*), names and adjectives of languages or indicating nationality (*español, inglés, italiano*), and titles, even foreign ones (*el duque de Alba, lord Lucan, sir Michael Rafferty*). Note that the abbreviations '*Sr., Sra*', '*D.* and *Dña.*' are capitalized, whereas when written in full '*señor, señora*' and '*don, doña*' are not. You will often see the names of the days of the week and the months printed with capitals but that is not grammatically correct.

Spanish tends to use parentheses (...) rather than dashes – ... – , especially at the end of a sentence.

Writing in Spanish

Reports, essays, dissertations, etc. are usually less tightly structured in Spanish than in English, but you should give an introduction, a main body and a conclusion. Less attention than in English is paid, for example, to the structure of paragraphs; you will often find paragraphs that seem long or that do not keep to one main idea. However, Spanish readers

El inglés que funciona

Aspectos generales

Registros del idioma

Dentro de la lengua inglesa hay, como sucede en español, muchos registros diferentes, desde el inglés muy formal de los documentos oficiales hasta el lenguaje abreviado y muy informal con que se escribe, por ejemplo, un mensaje de SMS. Hay que tener especial cuidado de adaptar al contexto el registro en que uno se expresa en cada situación.

El vocabulario elevado o literario

Como en español, el inglés literario constituye un registro bastante restringido dentro del idioma. El empleo inapropiado de este vocabulario puede resultar pedante o ridículo, aunque no sea ésta la intención del que escribe. Es preferible, por tanto, emplear un lenguaje "natural" o neutro a la hora de escribir una redacción, un memorándum o un artículo en inglés. La tabla que se encuentra a continuación muestra ejemplos de palabras de registro culto y sus equivalentes en inglés corriente.

literario/elevado	**corriente**
to abjure	to renounce
comestible	edible
to expedite	to hasten
grandiloquent	pompous
to opine	to state an opinion
mendacious	lying
parsimonious	mean
preponderant	dominating
sojourn	stay
to vitiate	to spoil

El inglés coloquial

Si bien en el inglés escrito se prefiere, por lo general, un registro menos formal que en castellano, se ha de tener cuidado de no caer en el extremo opuesto. En la vida diaria, los castellanohablantes que viven o trabajan en un país de habla inglesa están expuestos al inglés que hablan sus amigos o compañeros de trabajo. Muchas veces éste es un idioma muy coloquial, plagado de expresiones muy informales o incluso malsonantes. Cada hablante, en su lengua materna, sabe de forma casi automática si una palabra resulta adecuada o no, dependiendo de la situación. Al hablar un idioma extranjero, es necesario tener precaución hasta que se haya desarrollado este "instinto"; de lo contrario, se corre el riesgo de usar un idioma demasiado coloquial en momentos o situaciones inadecuadas, en las que resulta ofensivo o chocante. Por esta razón, se recomienda utilizar el inglés corriente en el mundo del trabajo y, sobre todo, en la comunicación escrita, quizás con la excepción de correos electrónicos entre personas con las que se tiene confianza.

Tono personal e impersonal

En redacciones, resúmenes y cartas de negocios, se recomienda adoptar un estilo impersonal para presentar la información de manera objetiva. En ponencias o intervenciones orales sí es adecuado usar "*we*" o "*I*", aunque si se hace de forma excesiva la comunicación puede resultar demasiado coloquial.

La puntuación y el apóstrofo

En general, los signos de puntuación se usan como en español, con las siguientes excepciones:

- En inglés los signos de admiración e interrogación se usan sólo al final de la frase, y no al principio.
- Las comillas españolas ("..." o «...») son dobles, mientras que en inglés el uso varía según el país. En EEUU la norma es emplear comillas altas y dobles, mientras que en Gran Bretaña se prefieren las sencillas. En ambos sistemas se usa la versión alternativa para introducir una cita literal dentro de otra. Siguiendo el modelo norteamericano se escribiría: "*She switched the light on. He grumbled and said, 'Not again, please!', and she switched it off again.*"
- En inglés las notas a pie de página se ponen después del signo de puntuación, no antes: "... *as Freedberg maintained*"*
- En inglés, más que en español, se usan las rayas (–), sobre todo en diálogos y cumplen la misma función que los paréntesis. Si la frase entre rayas queda al final de la oración, la raya final se omite: '*All right, you can take one – if you must.*'
- En inglés se escriben con mayúscula algunas palabras que en castellano suelen ir con minúscula, como los nombres de los días de la semana y de los meses (*January*, *May*, *Thursday*), o los gentilicios y nombres de idiomas (*She is Spanish and speaks English and Italian*). Estas palabras se verán a menudo con minúscula en anuncios publicitarios, etc., pero deben escribirse con mayúscula.
- Los títulos y dignidades también se escriben con mayúscula: *Vice President Ford*, *the Duchess of Devonshire*, *Lord Lucan*, *Sir Michael Rafferty*.
- También se suelen emplear mayúsculas para escribir los sustantivos, adjetivos y verbos que forman parte de los títulos de libros, nombres de calles, etc, cuando en español sólo se usaría mayúscula en la primera palabra: *The Voyage of the Beagle*; *The Conquest of Peru*, *866 Third Avenue*.
- Cuando se usa el nombre de un cargo para hacer referencia a un personaje concreto, ese nombre va con mayúscula:

welcome precision and conciseness in writing, so aim to write short paragraphs and sentences. Write your paragraphs bearing in mind that ideally they should develop a single idea. It is also good to think of the first and last sentences in a paragraph as the introduction and conclusion, respectively, and to try to link one paragraph with the next. A simple and readable structure and mode of expression are especially necessary in a business context.

The plan

Before you start writing, it is advisable to sketch out a plan of what you are going to say. Establish what the main ideas are, and distribute them in an order that makes sense to you; then start writing a paragraph for each. It is a good idea to leave writing the conclusion, and especially the introduction, till after you have finished writing the body of your essay. Be very careful not to state your conclusion in the first paragraph.

A few tips

- Avoid long sentences as far as possible and equally avoid unnecessary 'sentence-fillers' such as '*visto lo visto*', '*huelga decir*', '*como es sabido*', '*hacer hincapié en*', '*al fin y al cabo*', etc. They may sound very Spanish, but are ultimately empty phrases.
- English speakers of Spanish have particular problems with the correct use of *ser* and *estar*, *por* and *para*. Look these words up in the dictionary as well as the grammatical note at **be**, for help in getting *ser* and *estar* right. Do not rely on guesswork as the incorrect use of ser and estar can convey a different meaning to the one you intended.
- Avoid unnecessary use of adjectives and adverbs. Make sure that you frequently establish links between the various stages of your report.

Re-read your report carefully several times. Edit out superfluous matter, particularly in the introduction, which must be clear and to the point and constructed so as to engage immediately the attention of your reader. Check carefully that the links in your argument are clearly and explicitly stated.

- Watch out for the kind of mistakes it is easy to make; for example, remember that *gente* is singular and therefore its verb is also singular. Spanish generally uses an article (*el*, *un*) with percentages: *una subida/bajada de un 20%; el 15% de los consumidores*.
- Check that adjectives agree with their nouns and that words like *diagrama*, *drama*, *programa*, *problema*, *sistema*, are masculine nouns.
- Do not assume that look-alike words in each language are spelled in a parallel way, compare:

  appropriate, *fragrance*, *responsibility*
  apropiado, *fragancia*, *reponsabilidad*

- Be aware of differences in Spanish itself: ***respeto/respecto***:

  faltarle respeto al profesor/con respecto a su petición
  to be disrespectful to the teacher/regarding *or* with respect to your request

- Do not assume that constructions and usages in one language are reflected in the other:

to pay *for* the drinks	*pagar las* bebidas
to wait *for* the arrival of ...	*esperar la* llegada de ...
to ask a question	*hacer* una pregunta
the Smiths have arrived (= the Smith family)	han llegado *los Smith*
Women in the Twenty-first Century	*La mujer* en el siglo veintiuno

Common mistakes made by Spanish native speakers

It is very easy to copy habits of speech and writing used by native speakers of Spanish, but there are some common errors which should be avoided. (Forms with an asterisk are incorrect.)

tí* as in para tí*
for **ti** which never takes an accent (unlike *mi* and *mí*)

Use of the plural form of **haber** instead of the impersonal form in sentences such as:

van* a haber dos reuniones en paralelo
for **va a haber** dos reuniones en paralelo

habían* turistas por todos lados
for **había** turistas por todos lados

Confusion of ***b*** and ***v*** in spelling because they are pronounced the same in Spanish:

un baso* de agua
for un vaso de agua

Use of capitals in names of months, days of the week, etc

The President was met by the King.

The constitution limits a president's term of office to four years.

Las formas contraídas

El apóstrofo se emplea en las contracciones, como por ejemplo *I'll, he'll, we're, don't, won't, can't, couldn't, wouldn't, haven't, hasn't*, etc. Estas contracciones se pueden usar en escritos más bien informales, como los correos electrónicos, los textos de eslóganes publicitarios, las cartas personales o los diálogos. Si utiliza estas contracciones, no se olvide de los apóstrofos. Por otra parte, nunca use formas contraídas en contextos más formales, como redacciones, resúmenes, artículos, órdenes del día, actas de reuniones, etc. En textos periodísticos, el uso de contracciones varía según la intención del periodista, que a menudo podría emplear las formas contraídas para dar un tono personal y directo a su escrito.

El guión

En términos generales se emplea el guión cada vez menos en los compuestos, que se escriben como una sola palabra o como dos palabras separadas. En ciertos casos se debe utilizar; por ejemplo, cuando una frase se emplea de forma adjetiva ante el sustantivo al que se refiere. Compare:

*This information is **out of date.***

*She gave us **out-of-date** information.*

*His politics are **well known**.*

*It's a **well-known** tactic.*

*The church was built in the **thirteenth century**.*

*The village has a **thirteenth-century** church.*

Redacción en inglés

- Evite las frases largas y complicadas y la tentación de emplear giros prescindibles, como "*as the reader already knows*", "*needless to say*", "*at this point in time*", "*in this day and age*", etc. Aunque suenan auténticos, en la realidad son frases vacías.
- Elimine adverbios y adjetivos superfluos (sobre todo en escritos académicos), p. ej. '*a very big palace*', '*quite a small difference*', etc. Sea preciso; evite expresiones como "*seems to be*" o "*may be*".
- Revise concienzudamente el texto en busca de los errores gramaticales que suele cometer más a menudo. Por ejemplo, recuerde que *people* es plural, y que *his* y *her* se usan según el género del poseedor, no de la cosa poseída.
- Verifique que se ha añadido la *-d*, o *-ed*, final de los tiempos pasados de los verbos regulares: *dived, filed, watched, wanted*, etc.
- Evite la influencia del español a la hora de usar preposiciones y verbos en inglés, por ejemplo *arrive* se usa con *at* o *in*; nunca con *to*.

Errores comunes entre los hablantes nativos

Es muy fácil copiar los errores cometidos por los hablantes nativos. He aquí algunos de los más comunes que se escucharán y verán frecuentemente en las conversaciones y en los medios de comunicación. (* = forma incorrecta)

there is/there are
El uso de *there is* + complemento plural, especialmente en la forma contraída

*There's lots of birds on the lawn.
There are/There're lots of birds on the lawn.

Confusión entre **bought** (pretérito de *buy*) y **brought** (pretérito de *bring*)

*She bought it back from Mallorca.
She brought it back from Mallorca.

participio pasado/participio presente: El uso del participio pasado en lugar del participio presente en los tiempos continuos:

*She was sat there when I arrived.
She was sitting there when I arrived.

to **lie**/to **lay**: se suele confundir *to lay* con *to lie* en los tiempos terminados en *-ing*:

*There were bodies laying everywhere.
There were bodies lying everywhere.

to **affect**/to **effect**: Confusión de *to affect* con *to effect*:

*The bank affected payment without authorization.
The bank effected payment without authorization.

less/fewer: Se debe usar *less* con sustantivos *incontables* como *coverage, prosperity*:

There is less sports coverage than before.
Less prosperity leads to less confidence in the future.

Se debe usar *fewer* con sustantivos *contables* y plurales

Fewer candidates passed this year.
Fewer people than ever stay at home for their vacations.

Difficulties in Spanish

Lexical difficulties

Many English and Spanish words have common origins. Many of these Spanish *cognates* are transparent to an English speaker, e.g. *accidente*, *enciclopedia*, *inteligencia*, *situación*. These are *true friends*; they mean the same thing. However, there are also many *false friends*. These are words that have important semantic differences. Below is a list of some false friends.

Spanish	English translation	English look-alike	Spanish translation
actual: *la situación actual*	present: the present situation	***actual:*** ***the actual cost***	*real:* *el costo/coste real*
actualmente: *actualmente viven en París*	currently: they are currently living in Paris	***actually:*** *he's actually a lot older*	*en realidad:* *en realidad es mucho mayor*
atender: *no atiende en clase*	to pay attention: he never pays attention in class	**attend:** *she didn't attend the meeting*	*asistir a:* *no asistió a la reunión*
decepción: *fue una gran decepción*	disappointment: it was such a disappointment	***deception:*** *a cruel deception*	*engaño:* *un cruel engaño*
disgustado: *está muy disgustada con lo sucedido*	upset: she's very upset about what happened	***disgusted:*** *he was disgusted at the way we'd been treated*	*indignado:* *estaba indignado por la forma en que nos habían tratado*
éxito: *la perseverancia es la clave del éxito*	success: perseverance is the key to success	***exit:*** *where's the exit?*	*salida:* *¿dónde está la salida?*
genial: *una idea genial*	brilliant, great: a great idea	***genial:*** *a genial character*	*simpático:* *una persona simpática*
gentil: *gracias, eres muy gentil*	kind: thank you, that's very kind of you	***gentle:*** *a gentle voice*	*suave:* *una voz suave*
jubilación: 1) *su inminente jubilación* 2) *cobra una buena jubilación*	1) retirement: his imminent retirement 2) pension he gets a good pension	***jubilation:*** *scenes of jubilation*	*júbilo:* *escenas de júbilo*
librería: *en venta en todas las buenas librerías*	bookstore: available from all good bookstores	***library:*** *I borrowed it from the library*	*biblioteca:* *lo saqué de la biblioteca*
pinchar: *se divertía pinchando los globos*	to burst: he was having fun bursting the balloons	***pinch:*** *don't pinch me!*	*pellizcar:* *¡no me pellizques!*
preservativo: *un paquete de preservativos*	condom: a packet of condoms	***preservative:*** *without artificial colorings or preservatives*	*conservante:* *sin colorantes ni conservantes artificiales*
pretender: *pretendía que lo hiciera yo*	to expect: she expected me to do it	***pretend*** *he pretended not to notice*	*fingir:* *fingió no darse cuenta*
sanidad: *el gasto en sanidad*	public health: spending on public health	***sanity:*** *to preserve your sanity*	*cordura:* *mantener la cordura*
sensible: *una mujer frágil y sensible*	sensitive: a fragile, sensitive woman	***sensible:*** *at your age you should be more sensible*	*sensato:* *a tu edad deberías ser más sensato*

Dificultades del inglés

Hay muchos términos ingleses de uso diario que son cognados de términos españoles, se reconocen fácilmente y tienen el mismo significado.

Inglés	Español
intelligence	inteligencia
instinct	instinto
immediate	inmediato
information	información
false	falso
minor	menor
diplomacy	diplomacia
period	período, periodo

Pasando por alto algunas diferencias ortográficas menores estos vocablos son iguales. Podrían ser verdaderos amigos. Sin embargo muchos de ellos han evolucionado semánticamente de diferentes maneras. Algunas de las diferencias más notables se incluyen a continuación. Son **falsos amigos** por lo que vale la pena ser consciente de ellos.

Inglés	Traducción española	Cognado español	Traducción inglesa
actually	de hecho	***actualmente***	*at present, currently, now*
advice	consejo	***aviso***	*warning*
assist	ayudar	***asistir a***	*to be present at*
caravan	remolque	***caravana***	*convoy*
to **collapse**	hundirse	***colapsar***	*to bring to a standstill*
compromise	acuerdo	***compromiso***	*commitment*
conductor	director de orquesta	***conductor***	*driver*
deception	engaño	***decepción***	*disappointment*
to **demand**	pedir	***demandar***	*to sue*
to **disgust**	dar asco	***degustar***	*to taste*
disgust	asco	***disgusto***	*upset*
eventually	finalmente	***eventualmente***	*possibly*
exit	salida	***éxito***	*success*
fabric	tejido	***fábrica***	*factory*
flan	tarta	***flan***	*crème caramel*
injury	herida	***injuria***	*insult*
jubilation	alegría	***jubilación***	*retirement*
journey	viaje	***jornada***	*day*
lecture	conferencia	***lectura***	*reading*
library	biblioteca	***librería***	*bookstore*
marmalade	mermelada de naranja	***mermelada***	*jam*
motorist	automovilista	***motorista***	*motor cyclist*
preservative	conservante	***preservativo***	*condom*
to **pretend**	fingir	***pretender***	*to claim*
to **rest**	descansar	***restar***	*to subtract*
to **revise**	repasar	***revisar***	*to check*
sanity	cordura, razón	***sanidad***	*health*
sensible	sensato	***sensible***	*sensitive*
sympathetic	comprensivo	***simpático***	*nice*
tremendous	enorme	***tremendo***	*dreadful, terrible*
truculent	malhumorado	***truculento***	*horrifying*

▸690

Contrast the following:

simpático: *gente simpática y cordial*	nice, pleasant: nice, friendly people
sympathetic: *his boss was sympathetic*	*comprensivo:* *su jefe se mostró comprensivo*
truculento: *la truculenta historia de su asesinato*	horrifying: the horrifying story of his murder
truculent: *the service was slow and the staff truculent*	*malhumorado y agresivo:* *el servicio era lento y los empleados malhumorados y agresivos*

There are cases where the English and Spanish words share a number of meanings but they diverge in one or more senses. These are known as *partial false friends*. The difficulty here is that often it is the meaning that does not exist in English that seems to be the most frequent or important in Spanish. Here are a few examples:

Spanish word	English look-alike	Spanish word also means		
asistir	assist	to attend	no podré asistir I won't be able to attend	no asistió a la reunión he didn't attend the meeting
agenda	agenda	diary	lo anotó en su agenda he wrote it down in his diary	
coincidir	to coincide	to agree	Coincidimos en que ya no hacía falta We agreed that it was no longer necessary	
declarar	to declare	to give evidence	*Morales declaró ante el juez durante dos horas* Morales gave evidence in court for two hours	
denunciar	to denounce	to report	denunciaron el atraco inmediatamente a la policía municipal they immediately reported the hold-up to the municipal police	
dirección	direction	address	¿tienes su dirección? have you got her address?	
embarazo	embarrassment	pregnancy	durante el embarazo during pregnancy	
exposición	exposition	exhibition	*una exposición retrospectiva de la obra de …* a retrospective exhibition of the work of …	
formidable	formidable	tremendous, great	una idea formidable a tremendous idea	
importante	important	considerable, significant	sufrieron importantes pérdidas they suffered considerable losses	
manifestación	manifestation	demonstration	una manifestación en contra de la guerra a demonstration against the war	
posibilidad	possibility	opportunity	*tuve la posibilidad de estudiar en Estados Unidos* I had the opportunity of studying in the United States	
profesor	professor	teacher	mi profesor de inglés my English teacher	
registrar	to register	to search	Registraron la casa del sospechoso The suspect's house was searched	
sugestivo	suggestive	stimulating	publicó un artículo sugestivo sobre el tema he published a stimulating article on the subject	
vital	vital	life (*before noun*)	su ciclo vital dura sólo cuatro semanas its life cycle lasts only four weeks	

Un segundo grupo de vocablos tiene otras diferencias significativas de sus cognados españoles, normalmente debido a su diferencia semántica en relación al contexto, aún cuando coincidan en algunos sentidos.

Inglés	Español	diferencia semántica en inglés
conference	conferencia	nunca en contextos de teléfono
to control	controlar	sólo en el sentido de *mantener bajo control*
direction	dirección	nunca significa domicilio
demonstration	demostración	también tiene el sentido de *manifestación*
formation	formación	nunca en el sentido educativo
important	importante	nunca se usa con *número*, *cantidad* etc
impressive	impresionante	nunca en el sentido de *horroroso*
interrogate	interrogar	con complemento: *witness*, se emplea to *question*
notorious	notorio	en inglés, siempre es peyorativo
pavilion	pabellón	sólo se usa en contextos de ferias comerciales y los deportes
possibility	posibilidad	nunca es sinónimo de oportunidad
punctual	puntual	sólo se usa referido a tiempo
real	real	sólo se usa en contextos de realidad
to register	registrar	sólo se usa en contextos de documentación
relevant	relevante	nunca es sinónimo de importante
sanitary	sanitario	nunca conceptualmente referido a la salud pública
vital	vital	normalmente significa muy importante

Espanglish que parece inglés pero no lo es

Algunos vocablos aunque pareciera que son muy ingleses, son ininteligibles o suenan muy raros para la mayoría de los hablantes nativos de inglés:

Espanglish	Inglés
mobbing	harassment
camping	camp ground (AmE), campsite (BrE)
footing	jogging
(un) piercing	(a) stud
jet	jet set
smoking	tuxedo (AmE), dinner jacket (BrE)
parking	parking lot (AmE), car park (BrE)
controller	financial controller

Se debe tener cuidado al emplear términos que se sospecha que sean espanglish, como los que terminan en *-ing* usados de manera contable (con números o el artículo definido), ya que en su mayoría no se pueden usar correctamente así en inglés.

Personal correspondence

Christmas and New Year Wishes

On a card:

Feliz Navidad **1** y Próspero Año Nuevo **2**

Feliz Navidad **1** y los mejores deseos para el Año Nuevo **3**

1 Or: *Felices Pascuas, Felices Navidades.*

2 Or: *Próspero Año 2009.*

3 Or: *para el Año 2009.*

In a letter:

- Beginning: the name on the first line is followed by a colon if the traditional indented format is used. When block style is used, the colon is omitted.

Barcelona, 18 de diciembre de 2009

Queridos Juan y Elsa:

4 Antes que nada, os* deseamos a vosotros* y a los niños **5** unas muy felices Navidades y os* enviamos nuestros mejores deseos para el año 2010. Esperamos que estéis** todos estupendamente **6**. No sabéis** cómo nos alegramos con el anuncio de vuestro* viaje para enero. Ya tenemos pensado todo lo que podemos hacer durante vuestra* estancia aquí. Os* esperamos.

Conchita hizo los exámenes del último año de su carrera y sacó muy buenas notas. Ahora tiene que hacer su trabajo de práctica. Elena está bien y muy contenta en el colegio. Tiene muchísimos amigos y es muy buena chica. Luis y yo estamos bien también y sumamente felices con la reciente noticia del próximo ascenso de Luis. En definitiva, el 2009 ha sido un buen año y no nos podemos quejar. Confiamos en que el próximo será aún mejor.

Decidnos** con antelación la fecha de vuestro* viaje para que podamos ir a esperaros* al aeropuerto.

Recibid** todo nuestro cariño y un fuerte abrazo.

Luis y Ana.

4 This is a letter to friends who are addressed as *vosotros*, the plural of the familiar form *tú*. However, Latin American Spanish uses the formal plural *ustedes* instead of this form, so would replace the words marked * in the letter as follows: *vosotros* by *ustedes*, *vuestro* and *vuestra* by *su* or *de ustedes*, *os* by *les* or *los*. The verbs, marked **, should be replaced by the formal plural form, e.g. *estéis* by *estén*.

5 Or (if the children are older): *para vosotros y los chicos* (or y *las chicas* if there are only females), *para vosotros y para toda la familia*.

6 Or: *todos muy bien*.

Correspondencia de carácter personal

Saludos de Navidad y Año Nuevo

En una tarjeta:

[Best wishes for a] Happy **1** Christmas and a Prosperous New Year

Best wishes for Christmas and the New Year

Wishing you every happiness this Christmas and in the New Year

1 O: *Merry.*

En una carta:

44 Louis Gardens
London NW6 4GM

20th December 2009

Dear Peter and Claire,

First of all, a very happy Christmas and all the best for the New Year to you and the children. **2** We hope you're all well **3** and that we'll see you again. It seems ages since we last met up.

We've had a very eventful year. Last summer Gavin came off his bike and broke his arm and collarbone. Kathy scraped through her A Levels and is now at Sussex doing European Studies.
Poor Tony lost his job in October and is still looking for a new one.

Do come and see us next time you are over this way. Just give us a ring a couple of days before so we can fix something.

All best wishes

Tony and Ann

2 O (si los hijos son mayores): *to you and your family.*

3 O (coloquial): *flourishing.*

Invitación (informal)

Madrid, 22 de abril de 2009

Querido James

Te escribo para preguntarte si te apetecería [1] pasar las vacaciones de verano con nosostros.

A Tito y a Pilar les haría mucha ilusión (y también a Juan y a mí, por supuesto) [2]. Pensamos ir al noreste del país a finales de julio o a principios de agosto. Es una región realmente hermosa y nos encantaría que tú también vinieras. Es muy probable que llevemos tiendas de campaña ¡espero que no te importe dormir en el suelo!

Te agradecería que me avisaras lo más pronto posible si puedes venir.

Un cariñoso saludo,

Ana de Salas

[1] Or (in Latin America and also in Spain): *si te gustaría*.

[2] Or (in Latin America and also in Spain): *Tito y Pilar estarían muy felices (también Juan y yo, por supuesto)*.

Invitation (formal)

Invitations to parties are usually by word of mouth, while for weddings announcements are usually sent out.

Carmen S. de Pérez y Ramón Pérez Arrate, Lucía N. de Salas y Mario Salas Moro
Participan a Ud. de la boda de sus hijos

Consuelo y Hernán

Y le invitan a la ceremonia religiosa que se efectuará en la Capilla del Sagrado Corazón, de Mirasierra, Madrid, el sábado 24 de julio de 2009 a las 7 p.m.

Y luego a una recepción en la Sala de Banquetes del Restaurante Galán en C/Los Santos 10 de Majadahonda, Madrid.

S.R.C. [3]

- In Latin America invitations to the reception are sent to relatives and close friends in a separate smaller card enclosed with the announcement.

- In Spanish-speaking countries, the answer is not usually given in writing.

[3] In Latin America: R.S.V.P.

Invitación (informal)

- La fecha también se puede escribir de la siguiente manera: *April 22, 22 April*. En el inglés norteamericano, el orden de las fechas suele ser de la siguiente manera: mes, día y año.
- La dirección del remitente va en el ángulo superior derecho de la carta y la fecha va inmediatamente debajo.

35 Winchester
Drive
Stoke Gifford
Bristol
BS34 8PD

22nd April 2009

Dear Luis,

Is there any chance of your coming to stay with us in the summer holidays? Roy and Debbie would be delighted if you could (as well as David and me, of course). We hope to go to North Wales at the end of July/beginning of August, and you'd be very welcome to come too. It's really beautiful up there. We'll probably take tents – I hope that's OK by you.

Let me know as soon as possible if you can manage it.

All best wishes

Rachel Hemmings

Invitación (formal)

Invitación a una boda con recepción:

Mr and Mrs John Horowitz
request the pleasure of your company
at the marriage of their daughter
Jennifer Heather Horowitz
to
Michael Javier Iribarne
at Grace United Church, Montecito
on Saturday July 25, 2009 at 2 p.m.
and join us afterwards at the Manzanita Hotel, Montecito

1895 Ocean View
Santa Barbara
CA93101

R.S.V.P

- En la actualidad es cada vez más corriente que la invitación se haga por los futuros contrayentes.

Writing to one's bank

Avda. de los Castros s/n.
39005 Santander.

30 de noviembre de 2009

Sr. Gerente
Banco Nacional Real
Paseo de los Infantes, 100
39005 Santander.

Número de cuenta: 00498793

Estimado señor:

Se adjunta un cheque por la cantidad de 450.00€ para ingresar en mi cuenta, en su sucursal.

También agradecería, si al recibo de esta carta, se hiciera una transferencia de mi cuenta corriente a mi cuenta de ahorros (número 55676789), por la suma de 1,200€ (mil doscientos euros).

Aprovecho esta oportunidad para solicitarle que me envíe un nuevo talonario de cheques a la dirección indicada arriba.

Ruego a Vd. me confirme, en su debido momento, que estas instrucciones se han llevado a cabo.

Le agradezco de antemano la atención prestada.

Atentamente,

J. J. Carbonell
Teléfono: 851-626-7576

Letter openings

The standard opening greeting for personal correspondence is *Querido/Querida, Queridos/Queridas*, even for close friends and family.

Affectionate variations for friends and family:

- *Mi querida María Alicia*
- *Mi querida/-o amiga/-o*
- *Mis queridos tíos/amigos*
- *Mis queridas chicas*

Useful phrases

Perdón por no haber contestado antes pero ...

Muchísimas gracias por... te/le agradezco mucho [tu/su carta, tu/su invitación, tu/su precioso regalo]

Me ha dado mucha alegría recibir tu/su carta [tu/su invitación/noticias tuyas/suyas]

Me alegro de [comunicarte/-le que, invitarte/-lo, -la a]

Estamos encantados con la noticia/de poder recibirlos/-las

Te/Le escribo para pedirte/-le si...

Siento [comunicarte/-le que.., que no será posible...]

Sentí mucho [el fallecimiento de..., que no pudieras venir...]

Estamos muy afectados con [la muerte de..., la noticia de que...]

Closures

When a formal tone is needed:

- *Lo/-Los saludo atentamente* ('*Le/Les saludo atentamente*', in Spain)
- *Me despido de usted/-ustedes atentamente,*
- *Reciba atentos saludos /un atento saludo de...*
- *Atentos saludos de...*
- *Atentamente,*
- *Un cordial saludo,*

When an informal tone is appropriate:

- *Un (fuerte) abrazo de*
- *Un cariñoso saludo,*
- *Tu amiga que te quiere/te echa de menos*
- *Tu amigo que no te olvida,*
- *Muchos besos y abrazos de*
- *Dale mis recuerdos a ...* ('*mis cariños a*' also in AmL)
- *Laura les manda sus recuerdos* ('*les manda cariños*', also in AmL)

Carta con instrucciones a un banco

23 St John's Road
London
NW12 4AA

November 30, 2009

The Manager
First National Bank
860 Thirteenth Avenue
New York
NY 10022

Account number: 00498793

Dear Sir

Please find enclosed a check for $450.00 which is to be paid into my checking account, number 00498793, at your branch.

I should also be grateful if you would transfer the sum of $1,500 (one thousand five hundred dollars) from my checking account to my savings account (number 55676789) on receipt of this letter.

While writing, could I also ask you to send me a new check book at the above address.

Please confirm in due course that these instructions have been carried out.

Yours faithfully

Jerome M. Matthews (Dr)
Daytime telephone: 0207-626-7576

Encabezamientos

La formula más usual para todo tipo de cartas es:
Dear

A los amigos cercanos y miembros de la familia:

- *My dearest Alex*
- *Darling Katie*

A una familia o grupo de personas:

- *Dear all*

Expresiones útiles

Thank you for your letter [inviting, offering, confirming]

I am very grateful to you for [letting me know, offering, writing]

It was so kind of you to [write, invite, send]

Many thanks for [sending, inviting, enclosing]

I'm writing to tell you that...

I'm writing to ask you if...

I'm delighted to announce that...

I was delighted to hear that...

I'm sorry to inform you that...

I was so sorry to hear that...

Fórmulas de despedida

Al dirigirse a conocidos o a personas que ejercen funciones oficiales:

- *Best wishes,* o *With best wishes*
- *Kindest regards*

A amigos cercanos o miembros de la familia:

- *All my love*
- *All the best*
- *Love (from)*
- *Lots of love*
- *Much love* o *With love*
- *Love from us both*
- *See you soon*
- *Once again many thanks*
- *I look forward to seeing you*
- *With love and best wishes*
- *With love to you all*
- Paul *sends his love to you both*
- *Do give my kindest regards to* Silvia

The world of work

Replying to a job advertisement

- In Spain when the full address is given it is usually written in the top left-hand corner and in Latin America in the bottom left-hand corner, beneath the signature.

- This is the most commonly used opening for a formal or business letter, or when the addressee is not personally known to you. Alternatively *Estimado Sr.* and, in Latin America, *De mi mayor consideración*, can also be used.
- When the full address is given, the name of the town or city is not repeated with the date.

David Baker
67 Whiteley Avenue
St George
Bristol
BS5 6TW

26 de septiembre de 2009

Gerente del Personal
Renos Software S.A.
Alcalá 52
28014 Madrid

Muy señor mío

Con referencia al puesto de programador anunciado recientemente en El País del 15 de septiembre del presente, les agradecería me enviaran información más detallada acerca de la plaza vacante **1**.

Actualmente estoy trabajando para una empresa de Bristol, pero mi contrato termina a finales de este mes y querría aprovechar esta oportunidad para **2** trabajar en Madrid. Como se desprende del currículum vitae que adjunto, viví durante algún tiempo en España, tengo perfecto dominio del idioma español y también las cualificaciones **3** y experiencia requeridas.

Estaré disponible para asistir a una entrevista, en cualquier momento desde el 6 de octubre, fecha a partir de la cual se me puede contactar en la siguiente dirección en Madrid:

C/ Sevilla 25
28020 Madrid
Teléf. 91 429-96-67

Sin otro particular, quedo a la espera de su respuesta, **4**

Atentamente, **5**

1 Or if you have enough details and want to apply for the job right away: *quisiera solicitar la plaza vacante.*

2 Or if you are unemployed: *Actualmente estoy buscando trabajo y quisiera ...*

3 In Latin America: *calificaciones.*

4 Or: *Agradeciendo de antemano su atención* or *En espera de su respuesta.*

5 Or: *Le* (*Lo* in Latin America) *saluda atentamente. Me despido de usted atentamente, Muy atentamente,* or *Esperando su respuesta, se despide atentamente* are also possible.

El mundo del trabajo

Respuesta a un anuncio de trabajo

C/Islas Baleares 18. 2° B
FUENCARRAL
28080 Madrid
Spain

13th February 2009

The Personnel Manager [1]
Patterson Software plc
Milton Estate
Bath BA6 8YZ

Dear Sir or Madam, [1]

I am interested in the post of programmer advertised in The Guardian of 12 February and would be very grateful if you could send me further particulars. [2]

I am currently working for the Sempo Corporation, but my contract finishes at the end of the month, and I would like [3] to come and work in Britain. As you can see from my CV (enclosed), I have an excellent command of English and also the qualifications and experience required for the job.

I will be available for interview any time after 6th March, after which date I can be contacted at the following address in the UK:

c/o Lewis
51 Dexter Road
London N7 6BW
Tel. 020 7607 5512

I look forward to hearing from you. [4]

Yours sincerely

María Luisa Márquez Blanco

Encl.

[1] Otra alternativa puede ser *Ms Angela Summers*, ..., si en el anuncio aparece *Reply to Angela Summers* o *Dear Ms Summers*, *Dear Mrs Wright*, si en el anuncio sólo se indica el apellido.

[2] O *and would like to apply for this position*, si en el anuncio se incluye suficiente información acerca del puesto.

[3] O si se encuentra desempleado: *I am currently looking for work and I would like …*

[4] También: *Thanking you in advance.*

Resumé (AmE), Curriculum Vitae (BrE)

CURRÍCULUM VITAE

Nombre y apellidos	David Baker
Fecha de nacimiento	30 de junio de 1978
Lugar	Londres
Estado civil	Soltero [1]
Domicilio actual	67 Whiteley Avenue St George Bristol BS5 6TW Gran Bretaña
Téléfono:	+44 (0)117 945 3421
Téléfono Móvil/Celular:	+44 (0)7980 08 29 28
Correo electrónico:	d.baker732@kwickestmail.com

DATOS ACADÉMICOS

1993–95	GCSE (equivalente a la ESO en España) en 7 asignaturas.
1995–97	A Levels (equivalente al Bachillerato Superior en España) en Matemáticas, Informática y Español, Croydon Sixth Form College.
1997–98	Trabajos temporales de oficina en España y estudios de Español para los negocios en clases nocturnas.
1998–2002	Universidad de Aston, Birmingham, BSc en Informática (equivalente a Licenciatura en Ciencias de la Información).

EXPERIENCIA PROFESIONAL

2002–2003 Trabajo de práctica como programador de software para IBM, desarrollo de programas para la industria, con especialidad en infografía.

2004–al presente Programador para Wondersoft plc, Bristol.

IDIOMAS

Inglés	Lengua materna.
Español	Dominio total, hablado y escrito.
Francés	Bueno.

AFICIONES

Leer, viajar, esquí, tenis.

[1] Or: *Casado* (*sin hijos* or *con un hijo/dos/tres* etc, *hijos*), *Divorciado* (*sin hijos* or *con un hijo/dos/tres* etc, *hijos*).

Currículum Vitae

RESUMÉ [1]

Name:	María Luisa Márquez Blanco
Address:	C/Islas Baleares 18. 2ºB FUENCARRAL 28080 Madrid Spain
Cell phone/ Mobile phone:	(34) (0) 726 76 53
Email:	María-Luisa.Blanco@ubercorreo.com
Nationality:	Spanish
Date of Birth: [2]	11 March 1980

EDUCATION:

1998–2002	Degree Course in Information Technology and English at Universidad Complutense of Madrid.
1994–1998	BUP (secondary education)/COU (equivalent to A levels) at the Instituto de Enseñanza Media in Fuencarral.

EMPLOYMENT:

2004–present	Program development engineer with Sempo Informática, Madrid, specializing in computer graphics.
2002–2003	Trainee programmer with Oregón-España, Madrid.

FURTHER SKILLS:

Languages:	Spanish (mother tongue), English (fluent, spoken and written), French (good).
Interests:	Travel, fashion, tennis.

[1] O: *Curriculum Vitae* (*BrE*). [2] En Estados Unidos se suele omitir la fecha de nacimiento.

Compre billetes / boletos por Internet con **Europtrains**

Billetes / Boletos | Horarios | Mapas, destinos & planificador de rutas

Desde
Seleccione estación ▼ **Vea todas las estaciones**

Hacia
Seleccione estación ▼ **Vea todas las estaciones**

Fecha de partida
17 ▼ jul ▼ 2009 ▼
Hora
A cualquier hora ▼
calendario

Fecha de regreso
(deje en blanco para billetes/boletos sólo de ida)
18 ▼ jul ▼ 2009 ▼
Hora
A cualquier hora ▼
calendario

¿Fechas flexibles? ☐

Número de pasajeros — **Adultos** ▼ **Niños** ▼ **Estudiantes** ▼ **Tercera Edad** ▼

Primera clase ☐
Segunda clase ☐

BÚSQUEDA

Oferta especial

Ahorre un 25% cuando reserve por Internet desde el 1 de julio 2009 en adelante

•

De Londres a Bruselas sólo de ida
a mitad de precio

Haga clic aquí para más información

•

De Londres a París ida y vuelta desde sólo €50

Haga clic aquí para detalles

•

Estudiantes: compren su pase y ahorren dinero al viajar

Llamar para detalles.
Se aplican condiciones.

Mi cuenta

Nombre de usuario
Contraseña

Recordar mi contraseña ☐
¿Olvidó su contraseña?
Regístrese aquí

Más opciones

Viajeros de negocios
Viajeros en grupo
Viajar con silla de ruedas
Viajar con bicicleta

Cambio de una reserva
Cancelación de una reserva
Recepción de sus billetes/boletos

Más ofertas especiales
Pases de ferrocarril
Hoteles
Seguro de viaje

Mapa del sitio | Sobre nosotros | PMF | Contáctenos

Buy tickets online with **Europtrains**

Tickets | Timetables | Maps, destinations & route planner

From
Select station ▼ See all stations

To
Select station ▼ See all stations

Departure date
Jun ▼ 17 ▼ 2009 ▼
calendar

Time
Anytime ▼

Return date
(leave blank for one-way travel)
Jun ▼ 18 ▼ 2009 ▼
calendar

Time
Anytime ▼

Flexible dates? ☐

Number of passengers — **Adults** ▼ **Children** ▼ **Students** ▼ **Seniors** ▼

First class ☐
Second class ☐

SEARCH

Special offer

Save 25%
when you book online from 1st July 2009 onwards

•

London to Brussels one way half-price

To find out more, click here

•

London to Paris round trip from just €50

Click here for details

•

Students: buy your pass card and save money on travel

Call for details. Conditions apply

My account

Username
Password

Remember my password ☐
Forgotten your password?
Register here

More options

Business travellers
Group travellers
Travelling with a wheelchair
Travelling with a bicycle

Changing a reservation
Cancelling a reservation
Receiving your tickets

More special offers
Rail passes
Hotels
Travel Insurance

site map | about us | FAQ | contact us

Banco Ejemplar en línea

Solicitud para la banca por Internet

Ponga sus detalles personales abajo y haga clic en "**Enviar**".
Los casilleros marcados con * son obligatorios.

Haga clic aquí para **Ayuda**

Vea nuestra **muestra interactiva** o lea las preguntas más frecuentes de nuestros clientes **PMF**.

Sus detalles personales

*** Título** *** Nombre** *** Primer apellido** *** Segundo apellido**

*** Fecha de nacimiento** dd mm aaaa **Número Telefónico** **Teléfono Móvil / Celular**

*** Domicilio particular** *** Código postal**

Direccíon de correo electrónico

Al Banco Ejemplar en línea y a otras compañías del Grupo Ejemplar, les gustaría mandarle información por email acerca de nuestros productos y servicios que podrían interesarle. Por favor, marque este ***casillero*** *si no desea recibir esta información.* ☐

* Detalles de la cuenta bancaria – Obligatorio

Por favor proporcione los detalles de la cuenta corriente que ya se tenga en el Banco Ejemplar, o dé el número de su tarjeta de crédito si no tiene cuenta corriente en éste

◉ **Número de sucursal / agencia** **Número de cuenta**

o

○ **Número de tarjeta de crédito** **Código de Seguridad** **¿Cuál es mi código de seguridad?**

* ¿Tiene otras cuentas en el Banco Ejemplar o en las compañías del Grupo Ejemplar? **S** ☐ **N** ☐

¿Qué es esto?

* Su contraseña/clave de acceso

Por favor proporcione los detalles de la cuenta corriente que ya se tenga en el Banco Ejemplar, o dé el número de su tarjeta de crédito si no tiene cuenta corriente en éste.

Introduzca contraseña/clave de acceso

Confirme contraseña/clave de acceso

(entre 8 a 16 caracteres – solamente minúsculas y números)

No le dé su contraseña/clave de acceso a nadie. Úsela sólo para su cuenta en el Banco Ejemplar en línea

* Condiciones Legales

☐ He leído los **términos y condiciones legales** del Banco Ejemplar en línea y confirmo que los he entendido y los acepto como obligatorios.

Exemplary Bank Online

Application for Internet banking

Fill in your details below and click **'Send'**. Boxes marked * are mandatory

Click here for **Help?**

View our **Interactive demo** or read our customers' most frequently asked questions **FAQ**.

Your details

*** Title** *** First name** *** Last name / Surname**

*** Date of birth** dd mm yyyy **Telephone number** **Mobile / Cell number**

*** Home address** *** Zip code / Postcode**

Email address

*Exemplary Bank Online, and other Exemplary Group companies, would like to email you about our products and services that may interest you. Please check this box if you do **not** want to receive this information.* ☐

* Account details – mandatory

Please provide details of the checking/current account you already have with the Exemplary Bank.

Give your credit card number if you do not have an Exemplary Bank checking/current account.

◉ **Routing number / Sort code** **Account number**

or

○ **Credit card number** **Security code** **What is my security code?**

* Do you have any other accounts with Exemplary Bank or Exemplary Bank Group companies? Y☐ N☐

What's this?

* Your password

Please enter your password for your Exemplary Bank Online internet banking service

Enter password

Confirm password

(between 8 and 16 characters – lower case letters and numbers only)

Do not reveal your password to others. Use it only for your Exemplary Bank Online **account**

* Legal conditions

☐ I have read the Exemplary Bank Online **terms and conditions** and confirm that I have understood them and agree to be bound by them.

Emails

Personal

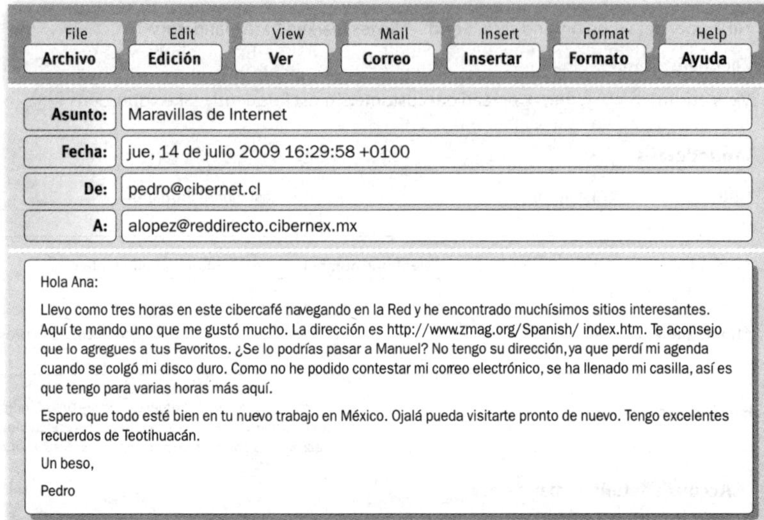

File
Archivo
Edit
Edición
View
Ver
Mail
Correo
Insert
Insertar
Format
Formato
Help
Ayuda
Asunto: Maravillas de Internet
Fecha: jue, 14 de julio 2009 16:29:58 +0100
De: pedro@cibernet.cl
A: alopez@reddirecto.cibernex.mx
Hola Ana:
Llevo como tres horas en este cibercafé navegando en la Red y he encontrado muchísimos sitios interesantes. Aquí te mando uno que me gustó mucho. La dirección es http://www.zmag.org/Spanish/ index.htm. Te aconsejo que lo agregues a tus Favoritos. ¿Se lo podrías pasar a Manuel? No tengo su dirección, ya que perdí mi agenda cuando se colgó mi disco duro. Como no he podido contestar mi correo electrónico, se ha llenado mi casilla, así es que tengo para varias horas más aquí.
Espero que todo esté bien en tu nuevo trabajo en México. Ojalá pueda visitarte pronto de nuevo. Tengo excelentes recuerdos de Teotihuacán.
Un beso,
Pedro

Business

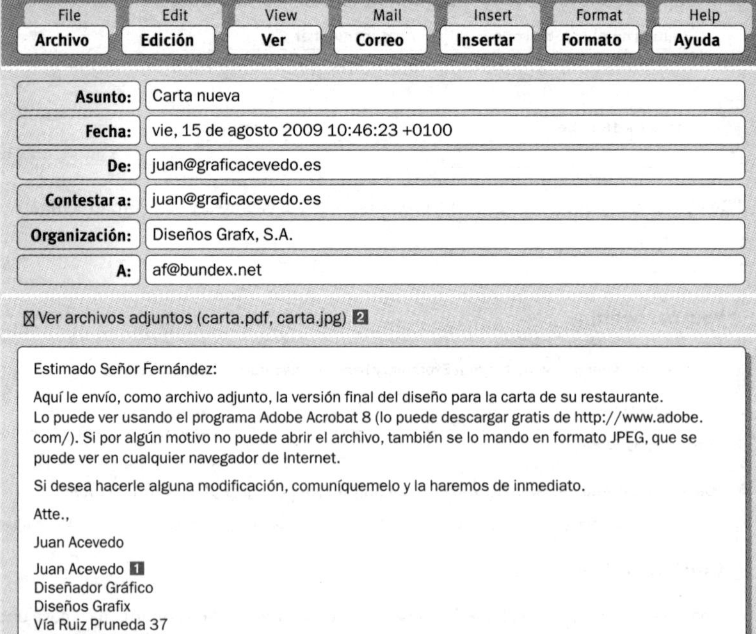

File
Archivo
Edit
Edición
View
Ver
Mail
Correo
Insert
Insertar
Format
Formato
Help
Ayuda
Asunto: Carta nueva
Fecha: vie, 15 de agosto 2009 10:46:23 +0100
De: juan@graficacevedo.es
Contestar a: juan@graficacevedo.es
Organización: Diseños Grafx, S.A.
A: af@bundex.net
☒ Ver archivos adjuntos (carta.pdf, carta.jpg) 2
Estimado Señor Fernández:
Aquí le envío, como archivo adjunto, la versión final del diseño para la carta de su restaurante.
Lo puede ver usando el programa Adobe Acrobat 8 (lo puede descargar gratis de http://www.adobe.com/). Si por algún motivo no puede abrir el archivo, también se lo mando en formato JPEG, que se puede ver en cualquier navegador de Internet.
Si desea hacerle alguna modificación, comuníquemelo y la haremos de inmediato.
Atte.,
Juan Acevedo
Juan Acevedo 1
Diseñador Gráfico
Diseños Grafix
Vía Ruiz Pruneda 37
Madrid 20
Tel. fijo: +34-1 587-5163
Tel. móvil: +34-1 726-5164
Correo-e: juan@grafic.es

1 Your email signature is *la firma*.

2 An attachment is *un adjunto* or *un anexo*.

El correo electrónico

Correo personal

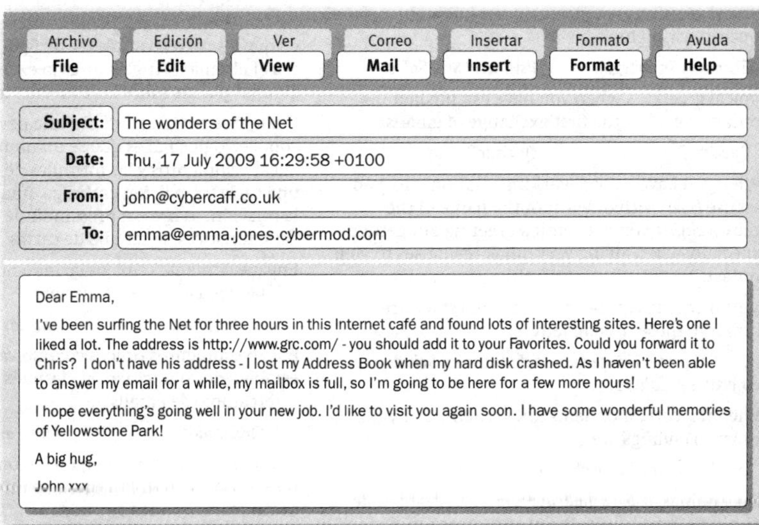

Archivo	Edición	Ver	Correo	Insertar	Formato	Ayuda
File	**Edit**	**View**	**Mail**	**Insert**	**Format**	**Help**

Subject: The wonders of the Net
Date: Thu, 17 July 2009 16:29:58 +0100
From: john@cybercaff.co.uk
To: emma@emma.jones.cybermod.com

Dear Emma,

I've been surfing the Net for three hours in this Internet café and found lots of interesting sites. Here's one I liked a lot. The address is http://www.grc.com/ - you should add it to your Favorites. Could you forward it to Chris? I don't have his address - I lost my Address Book when my hard disk crashed. As I haven't been able to answer my email for a while, my mailbox is full, so I'm going to be here for a few more hours!

I hope everything's going well in your new job. I'd like to visit you again soon. I have some wonderful memories of Yellowstone Park!

A big hug,

John xxx

Correo de negocios

Archivo	Edición	Ver	Correo	Insertar	Formato	Ayuda
File	**Edit**	**View**	**Mail**	**Insert**	**Format**	**Help**

Subject: New menu
Date: Fri, 15 Aug 2009 10:46:23 +0100
From: pdawson@metanoiagraphics.com
Reply to: pdawson@metanoiagraphics.com
Organization: Metanoia Graphics
To: joe.rutherford@padway.co.uk

▸ View attachments (menu.pdf, menu.jpg) **2**

Dear Mr Rutherford

I am attaching the final version of the new menu for your restaurant. You can view it using Adobe Acrobat 8 (which is available free at http://www.adobe.com/). If, for some reason, you cannot open the file, I have also attached a copy in JPEG format, which you can view in any web browser.

If you would like any alterations, please let me know and I'll make them immediately.

With best wishes,

Philip Dawson

Metanoia Graphics **1**
27 Goodwin Road
London N4 3QL
T 020-8974 1974
M 07960 374 917
E pdawson@metanoigraphics.com

1 Su *firma* de correo electrónico = su *signature*.

2 Éstos son los nombres de los archivos adjuntos al mensaje: *attachments* o *enclosures*.

Emails in the business context

When emailing a person one has never met, it is usual to maintain formal openings and closings as in letters, but once a relationship is established, it is common to dispense with almost all the features of the traditional formal letter.

Typical greetings when you do not know the person you are writing to:

Estimado Sr. Ortega: *Estimada Sra. Salas:*

Typical greetings when you have established contact, e.g. after the first exchange of emails:

Querido Ramón: *Querida Paula:*

When you have a good working relationship, you can use *Hola* (with or without the name of the addressee), or you may omit a greeting altogether, especially when giving very quick responses to your contact.

Typical endings in the initial, formal stage are similar to those used in letters.

Cordialmente, *Un afectuoso saludo* (or *un Saludo afectuoso*), *Saludos*

When the correspondents know each other well, common endings are:

Un abrazo, *Un fuerte abrazo*

The endings: *Lo/La saluda atentamente*, *Atentamente* are almost never used. If you are corresponding in your second language and you are in doubt about when to adopt a less formal tone, a good rule is to follow the lead of your correspondent.

Emails en correspondencia de negocios

En los últimos años los emails han reemplazado a las cartas y a los memorandums como una manera de mantener la comunicación con los contactos de negocios, dentro y fuera de una organización. Esto ha conllevado un relajamiento general en la manera en que los corresponsales se dirigen entre sí, sea cual sea el idioma. El inglés no es la excepción y he aquí algunas pautas sobre las convenciones que se usan.

Cuando se envía un email a una persona que no se conoce, lo normal es que se mantengan los encabezamientos y las fórmulas de despedida de una carta formal. Sin embargo, una vez establecida la relación, es común prescindir de casi todas las características de tal tipo de cartas.

Encabezamientos típicos cuando no se conoce a la persona a la cual se escribe:

Dear Mr Jones: *Dear Ms Smith*

Encabezamientos típicos cuando ya se ha establecido contacto, p. ej. después del primer intercambio de emails:

Dear Gerald: *Dear Paula:*

Cuando se tiene una buena relación laboral, se puede usar *Hi*, o *Hello* (seguido o no del nombre del destinatario), o bien se puede omitir totalmente el encabezamiento, en especial en el caso de una respuesta rápida al contacto.

Las fórmulas de despedida, típicas en la etapa inicial formal, son similares a las que se usan en las cartas:

With best wishes, *All the best*, o *Regards*, seguido de su nombre

Las formulas: *Sincerely*, (*GB Yours sincerely,*) o *Yours faithfully*, casi nunca se usan. Si se mantiene correspondencia en un segundo idioma y se duda acerca de cuándo se debe adoptar el tono menos formal, una buena regla a seguir, es hacer lo mismo que el corresponsal.

a

Aa

A, a /eɪ/ *n*
A [1] (letter) A, a *f*; **the A to Z of Gardening** el abecé de la jardinería; **he knows his subject from A to Z** conoce el tema perfectamente *or* de cabo a rabo; ***to get from A to B*** ir* de un sitio a otro [2] (Mus) la *m*; **A flat/sharp/natural** la bemol/sostenido/natural; **A major/minor** la mayor/menor; **the piece is in A** la pieza es en la mayor
B [1] (in house numbers) **35A** ≈ 35 bis, ≈ 35 duplicado [2] (in sizes of paper) (BrE) **A3** A3 (*420 x 297mm*); **A4** A4 (*297 x 210mm*); **A5** A5 (*210 x 148mm*) [3] (Transp) (in UK) (*before n*) **A road** ≈ carretera *f or* ruta *f* nacional

a /ə, *stressed form* eɪ/ (*before vowel* **an**) *indef art*
A un, una; **a problem/an idea** un problema/una idea; **a Mrs Smith called** llamó una tal señora Smith; **she's a lawyer** es abogada; **she's a famous lawyer** es una famosa abogada; **have you got a car?** ¿tienes coche?; **he didn't say a word** no dijo ni una palabra; **half a dozen/an hour** media docena/hora; **what a pity!** ¡qué lástima!; **what a huge dog!** ¡qué perro más enorme!, **half a cup** media taza
B (per) por; **twice a week** dos veces por semana *or* a la semana; **50 miles an hour** 50 millas por hora; **they're six dollars a pound** están a seis dólares la libra

A1 /'eɪ'wʌn/ *adj* excelente, de primera calidad

AA *n*
A (*no art*) = **Alcoholics Anonymous**
B (in US) = **Associate in Arts**
C (in UK) = **Automobile Association**

AAA *n* = **American Automobile Association**

aback /ə'bæk/ *adv see* **take aback**

abacus /'æbəkəs/ *n* (*pl* **-cuses** *or* **-ci** /-saɪ/) ábaco *m*

abandon¹ /ə'bændən/ *vt* [1] (leave behind) ‹*home/equipment*› abandonar, dejar; **to ~ ship** abandonar el barco [2] (desert) ‹*family/friend*› abandonar [3] (give up) ‹*project/idea*› renunciar a; **to ~ hope** perder* *or* abandonar las esperanzas; **the search was ~ed** se abandonó la búsqueda
■ *v refl* (liter) **to ~ oneself TO sth** abandonarse A algo; **she ~ed herself to despair** se dejó llevar por la desesperación

abandon² *n* [u]: **they were dancing with wild** *o* **gay ~** bailaban desenfrenadamente

abandoned /ə'bændənd/ *adj* (deserted) abandonado

abandonment /ə'bændənmənt/ *n* [u] (frml) abandono *m*

abase /ə'beɪs/ *v refl* **to ~ oneself** humillarse, rebajarse

abasement /ə'beɪsmənt/ *n* [u] (liter) humillación *f* (liter)

abashed /ə'bæʃt/ *adj* (*pred*) avergonzado

abate /ə'beɪt/ (frml) *vi* «*storm/wind*» amainar, calmarse; «*anger*» aplacarse*, calmarse; «*noise/violence*» disminuir*; «*pain*» calmarse, ceder
■ **abate** *vt* (calm) ‹*anger*› aplacar*; ‹*pain*› calmar, mitigar*

abatement /ə'beɪtmənt/ *n* (frml) (of wind, fever) disminución *f*; (of pain) alivio *m*; (of anger) aplacamiento *m*; (of noise, pollution) disminución *f*, reducción *f*

abattoir /'æbətwɑːr || 'æbətwɑː(r)/ *n* matadero *m*

abbess /'æbəs || 'æbes/ *n* abadesa *f*

abbey /'æbi/ *n* (*pl* **abbeys**) abadía *f*

abbot /'æbət/ *n* abad *m*

abbreviate /ə'briːvieɪt/ *vt* abreviar

abbreviation /ə'briːvi'eɪʃən/ *n* [1] [c] (shortened word) abreviatura *f* [2] [u] (shortening of word) abreviación *f*

ABC *n*
A [1] (alphabet) abecé *m* [2] (rudiments) abecé *m*
B (in US) (*no art*) (= **American Broadcasting Company**) la ABC

abdicate /'æbdɪkeɪt/ *vt* [1] ‹*throne*› abdicar* [2] (frml) ‹*responsibility*› abdicar* de (frml), no asumir
■ **abdicate** *vi* «*monarch/pope*» abdicar*

abdication /'æbdɪ'keɪʃən/ *n* [u c] abdicación *f*

abdomen /'æbdəmən/ *n* abdomen *m*, vientre *m*

abdominal /æb'dɑːmənl̩ || æb'dɒmɪnl̩/ *adj* abdominal

abdominoplasty /æb'dɑːmɪnəʊ,plæsti/ *n* [u] abdominoplastia *f*

abduct /æb'dʌkt || əb'dʌkt/ *vt* (frml) raptar, secuestrar

abduction /æb'dʌkʃən || əb'dʌkʃən/ *n* [c u] (frml) rapto *m*, secuestro *m*, plagio *m* (AmL)

abductor /æb'dʌktər || əb'dʌktə(r)/ *n* (frml) raptor, -tora *m,f*, secuestrador, -dora *m,f*

aberrant /æ'berənt || ə'berənt/ *adj* (frml) ‹*behavior*› aberrante; (in statistics) atípico, anómalo

aberration /'æbə'reɪʃən/ *n* [c u] aberración *f*, anomalía *f*

abet /ə'bet/ *vt* **-tt-** ▸**aid²**

abeyance /ə'beɪəns/ *n* [u]: **to be in ~** estar* suspendido *or* en suspenso; **to fall into ~** caer* en desuso

abhor /əb'hɔːr || əb'hɔː(r)/ *vt* **-rr-** (frml) detestar, aborrecer*

abhorrence /əb'hɔːrəns || əb'hɒrəns/ *n* [u] (frml) aversión *f*, aborrecimiento *m*

abhorrent /əb'hɔːrənt || əb'hɒrənt/ *adj* (frml) detestable, aborrecible; **the idea is ~ to me** la idea me resulta repugnante

abide /ə'baɪd/ *vt* tolerar, soportar

Phrasal verb
• **abide by** [v ▸ prep ▸ o] ‹*verdict*› acatar; ‹*rules*› acatar, atenerse* a; ‹*promise*› cumplir

abiding /ə'baɪdɪŋ/ *adj* (frml) (*before n*) ‹*interest/joy*› duradero, perdurable; ‹*fear/hatred*› pertinaz

ability /ə'bɪləti/ *n* (*pl* **-ties**) (talent) capacidad *f*, aptitud *f*; (faculty, power) capacidad *f*; **to the best of one's ~** lo mejor que uno pueda

abject /'æbdʒekt/ *adj* (frml) (*before n*) [1] ‹*slave/flattery/cowardice*› abyecto, vil (liter) [2] ‹*condition*› lamentable; **in ~ poverty** en la mayor miseria

abjure /æb'dʒʊr || əb'dʒʊə(r)/ *vt* (frml) ‹*belief*› abjurar de (frml); ‹*activity/claims*› renunciar a

ablative /'æblətɪv/ *n* ablativo *m*

ablaze /ə'bleɪz/ *adj* (*pred*): **to be ~** arder, estar* en llamas; **to set sth ~** prenderle fuego a algo; **to be ~ WITH sth**: **her eyes were ~ with indignation** tenía los ojos encendidos de indignación; **the street was ~ with color** la calle resplandecía de color

able /'eɪbəl/ *adj*
A (*pred*) **to be ~ to + INF** poder* + INF; (referring to particular skills) saber* + INF; **to be ~ to see/hear** poder* ver/oír; **to be ~ to sew/swim** saber* coser/nadar; **will you be ~ to go?** ¿podrás ir?; **those least ~ to afford it** aquellos que menos pueden permitírselo
B **abler** /'eɪblər || 'eɪblə(r)/, **ablest** /'eɪbləst || 'eɪblɪst/ (proficient) hábil, capaz

able-bodied /'eɪbəl'bɑːdid || ,eɪbəl'bɒdid/ *adj* sano, no discapacitado

ablution /ə'blu:ʃən/ *n* (Relig) (*usu pl*) ablución *f*; **to perform one's ~s** (hum) hacerse* la toilette (hum)

ably /'eɪbli/ *adv* (frml) hábilmente, con mucha habilidad

abnormal /'æb'nɔ:rməl || æb'nɔ:məl/ *adj* anómalo, anormal

abnormality /'æbnər'mæləti || ˌæbnɔ:'mæləti/ *n* [c u] (*pl* **-ties**) anomalía *f*, anormalidad *f*

abnormally /'æb'nɔ:rməli || æb'nɔ:məli/ *adv* 1 (Med) anormalmente, de modo anormal 2 (unusually) desacostumbradamente

aboard[1] /ə'bɔ:rd || ə'bɔ:d/ *adv* (on ship, aircraft) a bordo; (on train) en el tren; (on bus) en el autobús; **to go ~** subir a bordo, embarcar*, embarcarse*; **all ~!** (ship) ¡pasajeros a bordo!; (train) ¡pasajeros (suban) al tren!

aboard[2] *prep* a bordo de

abode /ə'bəʊd/ *n* 1 [c] (dwelling-place) (liter *or* hum) morada *f* (liter *o* hum) 2 [u] (Law): **place of ~** domicilio *m* (frml), residencia *f* (frml); **of no fixed ~** sin domicilio fijo

abolish /ə'bɑ:lɪʃ || ə'bɒlɪʃ/ *vt* ‹*institution/practice*› abolir*; ‹*law*› derogar*, abolir*

abolition /'æbə'lɪʃən/ *n* [u] (of institution, practice) abolición *f*, supresión *f*; (of law) derogación *f*, abolición *f*

abominable /ə'bɑ:mənəbəl || ə'bɒmɪnəbəl/ *adj* 1 (horrible) ‹*deed*› abominable 2 (awful) (colloq) ‹*weather/food*› espantoso, terrible

abominably /ə'bɑ:mənəbli || ə'bɒmɪnəbli/ *adv* ‹*behave*› de una manera abominable *or* detestable; ‹*perform/write*› pésimamente

abomination /ə'bɑ:mə'neɪʃən || əˌbɒmɪ'neɪʃən/ *n* 1 [c] (act, thing) (frml *or* hum) abominación *f* 2 [u] (disgust) (frml) abominación *f*, repugnancia *f*

aboriginal[1] /'æbə'rɪdʒənl/ *adj* 1 (indigenous) aborigen, indígena 2 **Aboriginal** (in Australia) de los aborígenes australianos

aboriginal[2] *n* 1 (indigenous inhabitant) aborigen *mf* 2 ▸ **Aborigine**

Aborigine /'æbə'rɪdʒəni/ *n* aborigen australiano, -na *m,f*

abort /ə'bɔ:rt || ə'bɔ:t/ *vt* 1 (Med) abortar 2 ‹*flight/process*› suspender, abandonar; ‹*efforts/plans*› malograr; (Comput) abortar

■ **abort** *vi*

A (Med) abortar

B 1 (abandon mission) abandonar 2 (fail) malograrse

abortifacient /əˌbɔ:rtə'feɪʃənt || əˌbɔ:tɪ'feɪʃənt/ *adj* abortivo

abortion /ə'bɔ:rʃən || ə'bɔ:ʃən/ *n* [c u] aborto *m* (*provocado*); **to have an ~** hacerse* un aborto, abortar

abortionist /ə'bɔ:rʃənəst || ə'bɔ:ʃənɪst/ *n* abortista *mf*

abortive /ə'bɔ:rtɪv || ə'bɔ:tɪv/ *adj* frustrado

abound /ə'baʊnd/ *vi* abundar; **to ~ IN** *o* **WITH sth** abundar EN algo

about[1] /ə'baʊt/ *adv*

A (approximately) más o menos, aproximadamente; **she must be ~ 60** debe (de) tener alrededor de *or* unos 60 años, debe (de) andar por los 60 (fam); **at ~ six o'clock** alrededor de *or* a eso de las seis, sobre las seis (Esp); **there were ~ 12 of us** éramos unos 12, éramos como 12; **in ~ three hours** en unas tres horas; **~ a month ago** hace cosa de un mes, hará un mes

B **to be about to + INF**: **I was ~ to say something** iba a decir algo; **we were just ~ to start** estábamos a punto de empezar; **I'm not ~ to mention it to her** no tengo la más mínima intención de mencionárselo

C (movement): **the dog followed him ~** el perro lo seguía a todas partes; **she can't get ~ very easily** le cuesta desplazarse; **he glanced ~ nervously** miraba nervioso a su alrededor

D (in the vicinity, in circulation) (esp BrE): **is Teresa ~?** ¿Teresa anda por aquí?; **there's a lot of flu ~** hay mucha gente con gripe

about[2] *prep*

A 1 (concerning) sobre, acerca de; **what's the play ~?** ¿de qué se trata la obra?; **he wants to see you about something** quiere verte acerca de *or* por algo; **~ tonight: are you coming?** (con) respecto a lo de esta noche ¿vas a venir?; **what's so unusual ~ that?** ¿qué tiene eso de raro?; **what was all that shouting ~?** ¿a qué venían todos esos gritos?; **what ~ Helen? isn't she coming?** ¿y Helen? ¿no viene?; **I don't know what to buy her — what ~ a record?** no sé qué comprarle — ¿qué te parece *or* qué tal un disco?; **she won — how ~ that!** ganó — ¡pues qué te parece! *or* ¡pues mira tú! 2 (pertaining to): **there's something ~ him that I don't like** tiene un no sé qué *or* algo que no me gusta

B (engaged in): **while you're ~ it, could you fetch my book?** ¿ya que estás me traes el libro?; **why did you take so long ~ it?** ¿por qué tardaste *or* (esp AmL) demoraste tanto (en hacerlo)?

C 1 (in, on, through) (esp BrE): **they were playing ~ the house** estaban jugando en la casa; **do you have a pencil ~ you?** ¿tienes un lápiz? 2 (encircling) (liter) alrededor de

about: **~face** /ə'baʊt'feɪs/, (BrE also) **~-turn** /-'tɜ:rn || -'tɜ:n/ *n* cambio *m* radical de postura; **to do an ~face** cambiar radicalmente de postura; **~ face**, (BrE also) **~ turn** *interj* (Mil) ¡media vuelta!

above[1] /ə'bʌv/ *prep*

A 1 (on top of, over) encima de; **the room ~ mine** la habitación encima de la mía; **~ sea level** sobre el nivel del mar; **we were flying ~ the clouds** volábamos por encima de las nubes; **her voice rose ~ the noise** su voz se elevó por encima del ruido 2 (upstream of) más allá *or* más arriba de

B (superior to) por encima de; **a lieutenant is ~ a sergeant** un teniente está por encima de un sargento; **she went ~ me and complained to my boss** me pasó por encima y se quejó a mi jefe; **she's not ~ telling a lie** es muy capaz de decir una mentira; **he's ~ suspicion** está por encima de toda sospecha; ***to get ~ oneself*** (pej) subirse a la parra

C (more than): **~ average** por encima de la media; **~ and beyond** más allá de

above[2] *adv*

A (on top, higher up, overhead) arriba; **the room ~** la habitación de arriba; **seen from ~** visto desde arriba; **orders from ~** órdenes *fpl* superiores *or* (fam) de arriba

B (in text): **as shown ~** como se demostró anteriormente *or* más arriba; **see ~, page 43** véase página 43

above[3] *adj* (frml) (*before n*): **for the ~ reasons** por dichas razones, por lo antedicho

above[4] *n* (frml) **the ~** (facts, text) lo anterior (frml)

aboveboard /ə'bʌv'bɔ:rd || əˌbʌv'bɔ:d/ *adj* (*pred*) legítimo, limpio; **open and ~** sin tapujos

abovementioned[1] /ə'bʌv'mentʃənd || əˌbʌv'menʃənd/ *adj* antedicho, citado anteriormente, susodicho (frml *o* hum)

abovementioned[2] *n* (*pl* **~**) **the ~** el antedicho, la antedicha; (*pl*) los antedichos, las antedichas

abrasion /ə'breɪʒən/ *n* [c] (Med) escoriación *f* (frml)

abrasive[1] /ə'breɪsɪv/ *adj* 1 (rough) ‹*powder*› abrasivo; ‹*surface*› áspero 2 ‹*tone/manner*› áspero, brusco

abrasive[2] *n* [c u] abrasivo *m*

abrasively /ə'breɪsɪvli/ *adv* ‹*say*› ásperamente, de modo brusco y desagradable

abreast /ə'brest/ *adv* 1 (side by side): **to march four ~** marchar en columna de cuatro en fondo 2 (up to date): **to be/keep** *o* **stay ~ of sth** estar*/mantenerse* al día en *or* al corriente de algo

abridge /ə'brɪdʒ/ *vt* ‹*book*› compendiar, condensar; **~d edition** edición *f* condensada *or* abreviada

abridgment, abridgement /ə'brɪdʒmənt/ *n* resumen *m*, compendio *m*

abroad /ə'brɔ:d/ *adv*

A (in/to other countries) ‹*live/work*› en el extranjero *or* el exterior; **to go ~** irse* al extranjero *or* al exterior; **when he's ~** cuando está fuera del país; **I've never been ~** nunca he salido del país

B (in circulation) (arch *or* liter): **there are unpleasant rumors ~** corren rumores desagradables

abrogate /'æbrəgeɪt/ *vt* (frml) (Law) abrogar* (frml), derogar*

abrogation /'æbrə'geɪʃən/ *n* [c u] (frml) (Law) abrogación *f* (frml), derogación *f*

abrupt /ə'brʌpt/ *adj* 1 (sudden) ‹*departure/conclusion*› repentino, súbito; ‹*rise/decline*› abrupto, brusco 2 (brusque) ‹*manner*› brusco, cortante

abruptly /ə'brʌptli/ *adv* 1 (suddenly) ‹*end/stop*› repentinamente, súbitamente; ‹*rise/fall*› bruscamente, abruptamente 2 (curtly) ‹*speak/act*› abruptamente, con brusquedad

abscess /'æbses/ *n* absceso *m*

abscond /æb'skɑːnd || əb'skɒnd/ *vi* (frml) fugarse*, huir*

absconder /æb'skɑːndər || əb'skɒndə(r)/ *n* evadido, -da *m,f*, fugado, -da *m,f*

abseil /'æbseɪl/ *vi* (BrE Sport) descender* en rappel

abseiling /'æbseɪlɪŋ/ *n* (BrE Sport) rappel *m*

absence /'æbsəns/ *n* 1 (of person) ausencia *f*; **~ makes the heart grow fonder** la ausencia es al amor lo que al fuego el aire: que apaga el pequeño y aviva el grande 2 (lack) **~ OF sth** falta *f* DE algo; **in the ~ of suitable alternatives** a falta de alternativas adecuadas

absent[1] /'æbsənt/ *adj* 1 (not present) ausente; **the teacher marked her ~** el profesor le puso falta *or* la anotó ausente; **to be ~ FROM sth** faltar A algo; **his sense of humor was conspicuously ~** su sentido del humor brilló por su ausencia 2 (vague) (*before n*) ‹*look*› distraído, ausente

absent[2] /æb'sent || əb'sent/ *v refl* **to ~ oneself (FROM sth)** (frml) ausentarse (DE algo) (frml)

absentee /'æbsən'tiː/ *n* (*pl* **-tees**) ausente *mf*; (*before n*) **~ ballot** (AmE) voto *m* por correo; **~ landlord** propietario, -ria *m,f* ausentista *or* (Esp) absentista

absenteeism /'æbsən'tiːɪzəm/ *n* [u] ausentismo *m or* (Esp) absentismo *m*

absently /'æbsəntli/ *adv* distraídamente

absentminded /'æbsənt'maɪndəd || ˌæbsənt'maɪndɪd/ *adj* (temporarily) distraído; (habitually) despistado, distraído

absentmindedly /'æbsənt'maɪndədli || ˌæbsənt'maɪndɪdli/ *adv* distraídamente

absinth, absinthe /'æbsɪnθ/ *n* [c u] ajenjo *m*

absolute /'æbsəluːt/ *adj*

A 1 (complete) ‹*trust/confidence*› absoluto, pleno; **the ~ truth** la pura verdad; **an ~ beginner** un principiante que no sabe absolutamente nada 2 (*as intensifier*) total; **it was an ~ disaster** fue un absoluto desastre *or* un desastre total; **~ chaos** el caos más absoluto; **he's an ~ idiot** es un tonto redomado; **a look of ~ hatred** una mirada de odio reconcentrado

B 1 (unconditional) ‹*right*› incuestionable; ‹*pardon/freedom*› incondicional; ‹*guarantee*› absoluto 2 ‹*monarch/rule*› absoluto

absolutely /'æbsə'luːtli/ *adv* 1 (completely) ‹*deny/reject*› rotundamente, terminantemente; **I'm ~ certain** estoy segurísima *or* absolutamente segura; **she's not ~ convinced** no está totalmente convencida 2 (*as intensifier*) ‹*impossible*› absolutamente; **it's ~ revolting** es de lo más asqueroso; **it's ~ true** es la pura verdad; **you're ~ right!** ¡tienes toda la razón! 3 (*as interj*): **do you agree? — oh, ~!** ¿estás de acuerdo? — ¡claro *or* por supuesto (que sí)!

absolution /'æbsə'luːʃən/ *n* [u] absolución *f*

absolve /əb'zɑːlv || əb'zɒlv/ *vt* **to ~ sb OF sth** absolver* a algn DE algo; **to ~ sb FROM sth** eximir *or* dispensar a algn DE algo

absorb /əb'sɔːrb || əb'zɔːb/ *vt* 1 ‹*light/energy*› absorber 2 ‹*impact/shock*› amortiguar* 3 ‹*information*› asimilar 4 ‹*time*› absorber, llevar

absorbed /əb'sɔːrbd || əb'zɔːbd/ *adj* ‹*expression/look*› absorto; **to be ~ IN sth** estar* absorto EN algo

absorbency /əb'sɔːrbənsi || əb'zɔːbənsi/ *n* [u] absorbencia *f*

absorbent /əb'sɔːrbənt || əb'zɔːbənt/ *adj* absorbente

absorbent cotton *n* [u] (AmE) algodón *m* (hidrófilo)

absorbing /əb'sɔːrbɪŋ || əb'zɔːbɪŋ/ *adj* absorbente

absorption /əb'sɔːrpʃən || əb'zɔːpʃən/ *n* [u]

A (being engrossed) concentración *f*, ensimismamiento *m*

B (of liquid, gas, light) absorción *f*; (of shock) absorción *f*, amortiguamiento *m*

abstain /əb'steɪn/ *vi*

A (in vote) abstenerse*

B (refrain) **to ~ (FROM sth/-ING)** abstenerse* (DE algo/+ INF)

abstainer /əb'steɪnər || əb'steɪnə(r)/ *n* 1 (non-drinker) abstemio, -mia *m,f* 2 (non-voter) abstencionista *mf*

abstemious /əb'stiːmiəs/ *adj* (frml) sobrio, frugal

abstention /əb'stentʃən || əb'stenʃən/ *n* [c u] (refusal to vote) abstención *f*

abstinence /'æbstənəns || 'æbstɪnəns/ *n* [u] abstinencia *f*

abstract[1] /'æbstrækt/ *adj* abstracto

abstract[2] /'æbstrækt/ *n* 1 (summary) resumen *m*, compendio *m* 2 (painting) cuadro *m* abstracto

abstract[3] /æb'strækt || əb'strækt/ *vt* (frml) ‹*idea*› abstraer*; ‹*substance*› extraer*

abstruse /æb'struːs || əb'struːs/ *adj* abstruso

absurd /əb'sɜːrd || əb'sɜːd/ *adj* absurdo; **don't be ~!** ¡no seas ridículo!

absurdity /əb'sɜːrdəti || əb'sɜːdəti/ *n* [c u] (*pl* **-ties**) lo absurdo, absurdez *f*

absurdly /əb'sɜːrdli || əb'sɜːdli/ *adv* ‹*behave*› de manera absurda; ‹*generous/complicated*› ridículamente, absurdamente

abundance /ə'bʌndəns/ *n* [u] abundancia *f*; **an ~ OF sth** abundancia DE algo

abundant /ə'bʌndənt/ *adj* ‹*resources*› abundante; ‹*enthusiasm*› desbordante; **she has ~ energy** tiene energías de sobra

abundantly /ə'bʌndəntli/ *adv* ‹*grow*› abundantemente, en abundancia; ‹*supplied*› con abundancia; **to be ~ clear/obvious** estar* perfectamente claro; **they made that ~ clear** no dejaron ningún lugar a dudas al respecto

abuse[1] /ə'bjuːs/ *n*

A [u] (insulting language) insultos *mpl*, improperios *mpl*; **to shout ~ at sb** insultar a algn, lanzar* improperios contra algn; **a stream of ~** una sarta de insultos; **a term of ~** un insulto *or* una grosería

B [c u] (misuse) abuso *m*; **to be open to ~** prestarse al abuso; **physical ~** malos tratos *mpl*; **sexual ~** abusos *mpl* deshonestos; (rape) violación *f*; **child ~** malos tratos *mpl* a la infancia, (sexual) abusos *mpl* deshonestos (*a un niño*); **drug ~** consumo *m* de drogas *or* (frml) estupefacientes

abuse[2] /ə'bjuːz/ *vt*

A 1 (use wrongly) ‹*power/hospitality*› abusar de 2 ‹*child/woman*› maltratar; (sexually) abusar de; **the children had been sexually ~d** los niños habían sufrido abusos deshonestos

B (insult) insultar

abuser /ə'bjuːzər || ə'bjuːzə(r)/ *n* 1 (of rights) violador -dora *m,f* 2 (of rules, norms) infractor -tora *m,f* 3 (of substance — drugs) toxicómano -na *m,f*; (— alcohol) alcohólico -ca *m,f* 4 (of child) pedófilo -la *m,f* 5 (of woman) culpable *m* de malos tratos

abusive /ə'bjuːsɪv/ *adj* insultante, grosero; **he began to use ~ language** empezó a lanzar improperios (frml); **to become ~** empezar* a soltar groserías

abut /ə'bʌt/ *vi* **-tt-** (frml) **to ~ ON sth** «*land*» lindar CON algo; **to ~ AGAINST** *o* **ON sth** «*building*» estar* contiguo A algo, colindar CON algo

abysmal /ə'bɪzməl/ *adj* pésimo, desastroso

abysmally /ə'bɪzməli/ *adv* ‹*fail*› desastrosamente (mal)

abyss /ə'bɪs/ *n* (liter) abismo *m*

a/c 1 **= air conditioning** 2 (**= account**) cta.

AC /'eɪ'siː/ 1 (**= alternating current**) CA 2 (esp AmE) **= air conditioning**

academic[1] /'ækə'demɪk/ *adj*

A 1 ‹*career/record*› académico; **~ year** (in universities) año *m* académico; (in schools) año *m* escolar 2 ‹*child/student*› intelectualmente capaz

B (abstract) ‹*question/debate*› puramente teórico; **that's ~ now** eso ya no tiene ninguna trascendencia

academic[2] *n* académico, -ca *m,f*

academy /ə'kædəmi/ *n* (*pl* **-mies**) academia *f*; **~ of art** escuela *f* de bellas artes; **~ of music** conservatorio *m*; (*before n*) **A~ Award** Oscar *m*

ACAS /'eɪkæs/ *n* (in UK) (*no art*) **= Advisory Conciliation and Arbitration Service**

accede /ək'siːd/ *vi* (frml) 1 (grant) **to ~ TO sth** ‹*to demand/request*› acceder A algo 2 (ascend): **to ~ to the throne** subir *or* acceder al trono

accelerate /ək'seləreɪt/ *vi* «*vehicle*» acelerar; «*person*» acelerar; (Auto) apretar* el acelerador; «*process/growth*» acelerarse

a

■ **accelerate** *vt* 1 ‹*process*› acelerar, apresurar 2 **accelerated** *past p* acelerado

acceleration /ək'selə'reɪʃən/ *n* [u c] aceleración *f*

accelerator /ək'seləreɪtər || ək'seləreɪtə(r)/ *n* (Auto) acelerador *m*; **to step on the ~** apretar* el acelerador

accent¹ /'æksent || 'æksent, 'æksənt/ *n*
A (pronunciation) acento *m*; **with a German/southern ~** con acento alemán/del sur
B 1 (stress) (Ling, Mus) acento *m* 2 (emphasis) énfasis *m*; **to put the ~ on sth** poner* énfasis en algo
C (symbol) (Ling) acento *m*, tilde *f*

accent² /æk'sent/ *vt* ‹*syllable/word*› acentuar*

accentuate /ək'sentʃueɪt/ *vt* 1 ‹*difference*› hacer* resaltar; ‹*fact/necessity*› subrayar, recalcar*; ‹*eyes/features*› realzar*, hacer* resaltar 2 ‹*syllable/word*› acentuar*

accept /ək'sept/ *vt* 1 ‹*gift/invitation/argument/credit card*› aceptar; ‹*evidence*› aceptar, admitir; **it is ~ed practice in this sort of case** es la práctica establecida en este tipo de casos 2 (recognize) reconocer*; **do you ~ that you were wrong?** ¿reconoces *or* admites que estabas equivocado?

acceptability /ək'septə'bɪləti/ *n* [u] aceptabilidad *f*

acceptable /ək'septəbəl/ *adj* 1 ‹*conduct*› (satisfactory) aceptable; (tolerable) admisible; **socially ~** socialmente admisible *or* aceptable; **to be ~ TO sb** resultarle aceptable A algn 2 (welcome) ‹*gift*› muy adecuado; **that would be most ~** eso me (*or* nos *etc*) resultaría muy grato

acceptably /ək'septəbli/ *adv* de forma aceptable

acceptance /ək'səptəns/ *n*
A [u c] (of offer, responsibility) aceptación *f*; **this does not imply our ~ of your terms** eso no implica que aceptemos sus condiciones
B [u] (approval) aprobación *f*; **it met with universal ~** obtuvo la aprobación de todos

access¹ /'ækses/ *n* [u]
A (to building, room) acceso *m*; **both bedrooms have direct ~ to the bathroom** ambos dormitorios tienen acceso directo al baño *or* comunican con el baño; **how did the thieves gain ~?** ¿cómo entraron los ladrones?
B (to person, information) **~ TO sb/sth** acceso *m* A algn/algo; **to grant a parent ~ to her/his children** conceder a la madre/al padre el derecho de visita; **do you have ~ to a telephone?** ¿hay algún teléfono que puedas usar?

access² *vt* (Comput) obtener* acceso a, entrar a

accessibility /ək'sesə'bɪləti/ *n* [u] 1 (of place) fácil acceso *m* 2 (openness) (frml) **~ TO sth** receptividad *f* A algo

accessible /ək'sesəbəl/ *adj* 1 (reachable) accesible; **museums should be made more ~ to disabled visitors** se debería facilitar el acceso de los minusválidos a los museos 2 (approachable) ‹*leader/politician*› accesible, asequible 3 (available) ‹*information*› accesible

accession /ək'seʃən, æk'seʃən/ *n* (frml)
A [u] (to position, office): **on the ~ of Prince Rupert** al subir al trono el príncipe Rupert
B [u c] (acquisition) adquisición *f*

accessory /ək'sesəri/ *n* (*pl* **-ries**)
A 1 (extra) accesorio *m* 2 **accessories** *pl* (Clothing) accesorios *mpl*, complementos *mpl*
B (Law) **~ (TO sth)** cómplice *mf* (EN algo)

access provider *n* (Comput) proveedor *m* de acceso

accident /'æksədənt || 'æksɪdənt/ *n* 1 [c] (mishap) accidente *m*; **to have an ~** tener* *or* sufrir un accidente; **their third child was an ~** su tercer hijo fue un descuido; **~s will happen** a cualquiera le puede pasar 2 [c u] (chance) casualidad *f*; **it is no ~ that ...** no es una casualidad *or* un hecho fortuito que ...; **by ~** (by chance) por casualidad; (unintentionally) sin querer

accidental /'æksə'dentl̩ || ,æksɪ'dentl̩/ *adj* 1 ‹*discovery/meeting*› fortuito; ‹*blow*› accidental 2 ‹*injury/damage*› producido por accidente; **~ death** muerte *f* por caso fortuito

accidentally /'æksə'dentli || ,æksɪ'dentəli/ *adv* 1 (by chance) por casualidad, de manera fortuita 2 (unintentionally) sin querer; **he did it ~ on purpose** (colloq & hum) lo hizo sin queriendo (fam & hum)

Accident and Emergency Department *n* servicio *m* de urgencias

accident-prone /'æksədəntprəʊn || 'æksɪdəntprəʊn/ *adj* propenso a los accidentes

acclaim¹ /ə'kleɪm/ *vt* 1 (praise) aclamar 2 (proclaim) (frml) aclamar, proclamar

acclaim² *n* [u] aclamación *f*, elogio *m*

acclamation /'æklə'meɪʃən/ *n* [u] aclamación *f*

acclimate /'ækləmeɪt/ *vt* (AmE) ▸**acclimatize**

acclimation /'æklə'meɪʃən/ *n* [u] (AmE) ▸**acclimatization**

acclimatization /ə'klaɪmətə'zeɪʃən || ə,klaɪmətaɪ'zeɪʃən/ *n* [u] **~ (TO sth)** aclimatación *f* (A algo)

acclimatize /ə'klaɪmətaɪz/ *vt* aclimatar; **to ~ oneself** aclimatarse; **to become ~d TO sth** aclimatarse A algo

accolade /'ækəleɪd/ *n* (praise) elogio *m*; (honor) honor *m*; (award) galardón *m*

accommodate /ə'kɑːmədeɪt || ə'kɒmədeɪt/ *vt*
A 1 (provide lodging for) ‹*guests*› alojar, hospedar 2 (have room for) tener* cabida para
B (cater to) ‹*wish*› tener* en cuenta, complacer*; ‹*need*› tener* en cuenta, satisfacer*; **I will not change the date to ~ him** no voy a cambiar la fecha para su conveniencia
C (adapt) (frml) **to ~ sth TO sth** adaptar *or* acomodar algo A algo

accommodating /ə'kɑːmədeɪtɪŋ || ə'kɒmədeɪtɪŋ/ *adj* complaciente

accommodation /ə'kɑːmə'deɪʃən || ə,kɒmə'deɪʃən/ *n*
A 1 [u] (AmE also) **accommodations** (lodgings) alojamiento *m*, hospedaje *m*; **I can provide ~ for five** puedo alojar *or* dar alojamiento a cinco personas 2 [c] (seat, berth) (AmE) plaza *f*
B [u c] (agreement, compromise) acuerdo *m*

accompaniment /ə'kʌmpənimənt/ *n* [u c] acompañamiento *m*

accompanist /ə'kʌmpənəst || ə'kʌmpənɪst/ *n* acompañante *mf*

accompany /ə'kʌmpəni/ *vt* **-nies, -nying, -nied** 1 (go with) acompañar; **she was accompanied by her family** iba acompañada de su familia; **the ~ing instructions** las instrucciones adjuntas 2 (Mus) acompañar; **she accompanies herself on the guitar/piano** se acompaña con la guitarra/al piano

accomplice /ə'kɑːmpləs || ə'kʌmplɪs/ *n* cómplice *mf*; **~ IN/TO sth** cómplice EN algo

accomplish /ə'kɑːmplɪʃ || ə'kʌmplɪʃ/ *vt* ‹*task*› llevar a cabo, realizar*; ‹*goal*› lograr, conseguir*; **mission ~ed!** ¡misión cumplida!

accomplished /ə'kɑːmplɪʃt || ə'kʌmplɪʃt/ *adj* ‹*performer*› consumado; ‹*performance*› logrado; ‹*liar/thief*› consumado, hábil; **he is a very ~ speaker** es muy buen orador

accomplishment /ə'kɑːmplɪʃmənt || ə'kʌmplɪʃmənt/ *n* 1 [u] (of aim) logro *m*, consecución *f* (frml) 2 [c] (success) logro *m* 3 [c u] (skill) habilidad *f*, destreza *f*

accord¹ /ə'kɔːrd || ə'kɔːd/ *n*
A [u] (agreement, harmony) acuerdo *m*; **to be in ~ with sb/sth** estar* de acuerdo con algn/algo; ***of one's own* ~** (de) motu proprio, voluntariamente; ***with one* ~** de común acuerdo
B [c] (treaty, understanding) acuerdo *m*

accord² *vt* (frml) ‹*honor*› conceder, otorgar*, conferir*; ‹*welcome*› dar*; ‹*priority/significance*› conceder, dar*

Phrasal verb

• **accord with** [v ▸ prep ▸ o] (frml) coincidir *or* concordar* con

accordance /ə'kɔːrdn̩s || ə'kɔːdn̩s/ *n*: **in ~ with** de acuerdo con *or* a, conforme a, según

according /ə'kɔːrdɪŋ || ə'kɔːdɪŋ/ **according to** *prep* según; **~ to you/him** según tú/él; **it all went ~ to plan** todo salió conforme a *or* según lo planeado

accordingly /ə'kɔːrdɪŋli || ə'kɔːdɪŋli/ *adv* 1 (correspondingly) en consecuencia; **you must accept the reponsibility and act ~** debe asumir la responsabilidad y obrar en consecuencia 2 (so, therefore) (*as linker*) por lo tanto, por consiguiente

accordion /ə'kɔːrdiən || ə'kɔːdiən/ *n* acordeón *m*

accost /ə'kɔːst || ə'kɒst/ *vt* abordar; **he was ~ed by a man in the street** un hombre lo abordó en la calle

account[1] /ə'kaʊnt/ *n*

(Sense I)

A (explanation) explicación *f*; (version) versión *f*; (report) informe *m*; **by his own ~** según él mismo cuenta; **by all ~s** a decir de todos, por lo que dicen todos; ***to bring*** *o* ***call sb to ~ for sth*** pedirle* cuentas a algn sobre algo; ***to give a good ~ of oneself*** dar* lo mejor de sí; ***to hold sb to ~ for sth*** responsabilizar* a algn de algo

B (consideration): **to take sth into ~** tener* algo en cuenta

C (importance) (frml): **to be of no/little ~ (to sb)**: **it's of no ~** no tiene importancia; **it is of little ~ (to me) whether he agrees or not** a mí me importa muy poco que esté o no de acuerdo

D (*in phrases*) **on account of** (*as prep*) debido a; **on ~ of his being too old** debido a que es demasiado mayor; **on this/that ~** por esta/esa razón; **on ~ of she was late** (*as conj*) (AmE colloq) debido a que llegó tarde; **on no account, not on any account** de ningún modo, de ninguna manera, bajo ningún concepto; **on one's own account** (for oneself) por cuenta propia; **on sb's account** por algn

(Sense II) (Fin)

A (with bank, at shop) cuenta *f*; **checking** *o* (BrE) **current ~** cuenta *f* corriente; **savings** *o* **deposit ~** cuenta *f* de ahorros; **put it on/charge it to my ~** cárguelo a mi cuenta; **I gave her $200 on ~** le di 200 dólares a cuenta *or* de anticipo; **to have an ~ with** *o* **at a bank** tener* una cuenta en un banco; **to keep (an) ~ of sth** llevar (la) cuenta de algo; **to settle one's ~** pagar* *or* saldar su (*or* mi *etc*) cuenta; ***to put*** *o* ***turn sth to (good) ~*** sacar* (buen) provecho de algo; ***to settle*** *o* ***square an ~ with sb*** ajustarle (las) cuentas a algn

B **accounts** 1 (Busn, Fin) (+ *pl vb*) contabilidad *f*; **to keep the ~s** llevar la contabilidad *or* las cuentas 2 (BrE) (+ *sing vb*) (department) contaduría *f*

account[2] *vt* (frml) considerar

(Phrasal verb)

- **account for** [v ▸ prep ▸ o]

A 1 (provide record of, justify) ‹*expenditure/time*› dar* cuentas de; **$500 remains to be ~ed for** aún no se han dado explicaciones sobre el destino de 500 dólares; **is everyone ~ed for?** ¿falta alguien (*or* algún pasajero *etc*)? 2 (explain) explicar*; ***there's no ~ing for taste*** sobre gustos no hay nada escrito

B (add up to): **wages ~ for 70% of the total** los sueldos representan un *or* el 70% del total

accountability /ə'kaʊntə'bɪləti/ *n* [u] responsabilidad *f*; **~ TO sb** responsabilidad *f* ANTE algn

accountable /ə'kaʊntəbəl/ *adj* (*pred*) responsable; **to be ~ TO sb (FOR sth)** ser* responsable ANTE algn (DE algo); **I'm not ~ to anybody** yo no tengo por qué darle cuentas a nadie

accountancy /ə'kaʊntn̩si/ *n* [u] contabilidad *f*

accountant /ə'kaʊntn̩t/ *n* contador, -dora *m,f* (AmL), contable *mf* (Esp)

accounting /ə'kaʊntɪŋ/ *n* [u] 1 (Busn, Fin) contabilidad *f*, teneduría *f* de libros 2 (reckoning) cálculos *mpl*, estimaciones *fpl*

accouterments /ə'ku:tərmənts/, (BrE) **accoutrements** /ə'ku:trəmənts/ *pl n* (frml) equipo *m*

accredit /ə'kredət || ə'kredɪt/ *vt* (*usu pass*) 1 acreditar 2 **accredited** *past p* ‹*representative*› acreditado; ‹*qualification*› reconocido; ‹*agent*› autorizado

accrue /ə'kru:/ *vi* (build up) acumularse

■ **accrue** *vt* ‹*interest/profits*› acumular

acct (= **account**) cta.

accumulate /ə'kju:mjəleɪt || ə'kju:mjʊleɪt/ *vt* ‹*wealth/interest*› acumular; ‹*information/evidence*› reunir*, acumular; **these ornaments just ~ dust** estos adornos no hacen más que juntar polvo

■ **accumulate** *vi* acumularse

accumulation /ə'kju:mjə'leɪʃən || ə,kju:mjʊ'leɪʃən/ *n* 1 [c] (collection, mass) montón *m* 2 [u] (growth, increase) acumulación *f*

accumulator /ə'kju:mjəleɪtər || ə'kju:mjʊleɪtə(r)/ *n* (Comput) acumulador *m*

accuracy /'ækjərəsi/ *n* [u] (of measurement, map, instrument) exactitud *f*, precisión *f*; (of weapon) precisión *f*; (of aim, blow) lo certero; (of description, prediction) exactitud *f*; (of translation) exactitud *f*, fidelidad *f*

accurate /'ækjərət/ *adj* ‹*measurement/instrument*› exacto, preciso; ‹*weapon/aim/blow*› certero; ‹*description/assessment*› exacto; ‹*translation*› exacto, fiel; **to be strictly ~, it was 2.15** para ser preciso *or* exacto, eran las 2.15

accurately /'ækjərətli/ *adv* ‹*measure/describe/aim*› con exactitud *or* precisión; ‹*copy*› fielmente; ‹*translate*› con exactitud, fielmente

accursed /ə'kɜ:rst , ə'kɜ:rsɪd || ə'kɜ:sɪd/ *adj* (liter) 1 (hateful) (*before n*) execrable (liter), detestable 2 (under a curse) maldito

accusation /'ækjə'zeɪʃən || ,ækju:'zeɪʃən/ *n* [c u] acusación *f*; **what is the ~ against him?** ¿de qué se lo acusa?

accusative /ə'kju:zətɪv/ *n* acusativo *m*

accuse /ə'kju:z/ *vt* acusar; **to ~ sb OF sth/-ING** acusar a algn DE algo/+INF; **they stand ~d of murder/robbery** se les acusa de asesinato/robo

accused /ə'kju:zd/ *n* (*pl* ~) (Law) **the ~** el acusado, la acusada; (*pl*) los acusados, las acusadas

accuser /ə'kju:zər || ə'kju:zə(r)/ *n* acusador, -dora *m,f*

accusing /ə'kju:zɪŋ/ *adj* acusador, acusatorio

accusingly /ə'kju:zɪŋli/ *adv* ‹*say*› en tono acusador *or* acusatorio; **she looked at me ~** me lanzó una mirada acusadora *or* acusatoria

accustom /ə'kʌstəm/ *vt* **to ~ sb TO sth/-ING** acostumbrar *or* habituar* a algn A algo/+INF; **to ~ oneself TO sth/-ING** acostumbrarse *or* habituarse* A algo/+ INF

accustomed /ə'kʌstəmd/ *adj* 1 (habituated) (*pred*) **to be ~ TO sth/-ING** estar* acostumbrado A algo/+ INF; **to become** *o* **get ~ TO sth/-ING** acostumbrarse *or* habituarse* A algo/+ INF 2 (usual, customary) (*before n*) acostumbrado

AC/DC /'eɪsi:'di:si:/ *adj* 1 (Elec) CA/CC 2 (bisexual) (sl) bisexual

ace[1] /eɪs/ *n* 1 (in cards, dice) as *m*; ***to be/come within an ~ of sth***: **he came within an ~ of beating the champion** estuvo a punto de ganarle al campeón; ***to have*** *o* ***hold all the ~s*** tener* todas las de ganar 2 (in tennis) ace *m* 3 (expert, champion) as *m*

ace[2] *adj* 1 (colloq) (*before n*) ‹*reporter/negotiator*› de primera, destacado; **an ~ driver/pilot** un as del volante/de la aviación 2 (BrE sl) ‹*party/bike*› bárbaro (fam), guay (Esp arg)

acerbic /ə'sɜ:rbɪk || ə'sɜ:bɪk/ *adj* mordaz, acerbo

acetate /'æsəteɪt || 'æsɪteɪt/ *n* [u] acetato *m*

acetic acid /ə'si:tɪk/ *n* [u] ácido *m* acético

acetone /'æsətəʊn || 'æsɪtəʊn/ *n* [u] acetona *f*

ache[1] /eɪk/ *vi*

A 1 (give pain) «*tooth/ear/leg*» doler*; **my back ~s** me duele la espalda; **I'm aching all over** me duele todo el cuerpo 2 **aching** *pres p* ‹*shoulders/muscles*› dolorido; **with an aching heart** con gran dolor de corazón

B (yearn) **to ~ to + INF** ansiar* + INF; **to ~ FOR sth** suspirar POR algo

ache[2] *n* dolor *m* (*sordo y continuo*); **~s and pains** achaques *mpl*

achievable /ə'tʃi:vəbəl/ *adj* ‹*target/goal*› alcanzable

achieve /ə'tʃi:v/ *vt* 1 (accomplish) lograr; **the meeting didn't ~ much** no se logró demasiado en la reunión 2 (attain) ‹*success/victory*› conseguir*, obtener*; ‹*aim*› lograr, conseguir*, alcanzar*; ‹*ambition*› hacer* realidad

achievement /ə'tʃi:vmənt/ *n* 1 [c] (feat) logro *m*; **it was quite an ~** fue toda una hazaña *or* todo un logro 2 [u] (success) éxito *m*, logro *m*; **a sense of ~** la satisfacción de haber logrado algo; **high/low ~** (Educ) buen/mal rendimiento

achiever /ə'tʃi:vər || ə'tʃi:və(r)/ *n*: **he's a high ~** siempre obtiene excelentes resultados

Achilles /ə'kɪli:z/: **~ heel** *n* talón *m* de Aquiles; **~ tendon** *n* tendón *m* de Aquiles

acid[1] /'æsəd || 'æsɪd/ *n* 1 [u c] (Chem) ácido *m* 2 [u] (LSD) (sl) ácido *m*

acid[2] *adj* 1 (Chem) ácido 2 ‹*taste*› ácido, agrio 3 (spiteful) ‹*voice/reply*› agrio, mordaz

acidic /ə'sɪdɪk/ *adj* ▸**acid**[2] **1, 2**

acidity /ə'sɪdəti/ *n* [u] acidez *f*

acidly /'æsədli || 'æsɪdli/ *adv* agriamente, mordazmente

acid: **~ paper** *n* [u] papel *m* ácido; **~ rain** *n* [u] lluvia *f* ácida; **~ test** *n* **the ~ test** la prueba de fuego

a

acknowledge /ək'nɑːlɪdʒ || ək'nɒlɪdʒ/ *vt*
A 1 (admit) ‹*mistake/failure*› admitir, reconocer* 2 (recognize) ‹*achievement/authority/right*› reconocer*; ‹*quotations/sources*› hacer* mención de; **to ~ sb AS sth** reconocer* a algn COMO algo 3 (express appreciation of) agradecer*
B ‹*letter/order*› acusar recibo de; ‹*greeting*› responder a; ‹*person*› saludar

acknowledgment, acknowledgement /ək'nɑːlɪdʒmənt || ək'nɒlɪdʒmənt/ *n* [c u] 1 (recognition) reconocimiento *m* 2 (confirmation, response): **I've had no ~ of my letter** no han acusado recibo de mi carta 3 **acknowledgments** *pl* (in book) lista *f* de menciones

ACLU *n* = **American Civil Liberties Union**

acme /'ækmi/ *n* **the ~ OF sth** el súmmum *or* el colmo DE algo

acne /'ækni/ *n* [u] acné *m or f*, acne *f*‡

acolyte /'ækəlaɪt/ *n* acólito *m*

acorn /'eɪkɔːrn || 'eɪkɔːn/ *n* bellota *f*; (*before n*) **~ squash** *calabaza pequeña de corteza verde y forma de bellota*; ▸**oak**

acoustic /ə'kuːstɪk/ *adj* acústico

acoustics /ə'kuːstɪks/ *n* 1 (Phys) (+ *sing vb*) acústica *f* 2 (of room) (+ *pl vb*) acústica *f*

acquaint /ə'kweɪnt/ *vt* **to ~ sb WITH sth** (inform of) poner* a algn al corriente DE algo; (familiarize with) familiarizar* a algn CON algo; **to ~ oneself WITH sth** familiarizarse* CON algo

acquaintance /ə'kweɪntn̩s/ *n* 1 [c] (person) conocido, -da *m,f*; **we're old ~s** nos conocemos desde hace tiempo 2 [u c] (with person) relación *f*; **to make the ~ of sb, to make sb's ~** conocer* a algn 3 [u c] (knowledge) **~ WITH sth** conocimiento *m* DE algo

acquainted /ə'kweɪntəd || ə'kweɪntɪd/ *adj* (*pred*) 1 **to be ~ WITH sb** conocer* a algn; **we need time to become** *o* **get ~** necesitamos tiempo para (llegar a) conocernos 2 **to be ~ WITH sth** (be informed of) estar* al corriente DE algo; (be familiar with) estar* familiarizado CON algo

acquiesce /,ækwi'es/ *vi* **to ~ IN sth/-ING** consentir* algo/EN + INF

acquiescence /,ækwi'esn̩s/ *n* [u] consentimiento *m*, aquiescencia *f* (frml)

acquiescent /,ækwi'esn̩t/ *adj* aquiescente (frml), conforme

acquire /ə'kwaɪr || ə'kwaɪə(r)/ *vt* ‹*collection/skill*› adquirir*; ‹*reputation*› hacerse*, adquirir*; ‹*fortune*› hacer*; ‹*territories*› hacerse* con, apoderarse de; **I've ~d a taste for ...** le he tomado el gusto a ...; **he'd ~d a British accent** se le había pegado el acento británico

acquired /ə'kwaɪrd || ə'kwaɪəd/ *adj* ‹*characteristic*› adquirido; **it's an ~ taste** es algo a lo que se le va tomando el gusto con el tiempo

acquisition /'ækwə'zɪʃən || ,ækwɪ'zɪʃən/ *n* [c u] adquisición *f*

acquisitive /ə'kwɪzətɪv/ *adj* (greedy) codicioso; (inclined to acquire): **I'm not at all ~** no tengo interés en poseer cosas materiales

acquit /ə'kwɪt/ **-tt-** *vt* **to ~ sb (OF sth)** absolver* a algn (DE algo)
■ *v refl* **to ~ oneself** desenvolverse*, desempeñarse (AmL)

acquittal /ə'kwɪtl̩/ *n* [c u] (Law) absolución *f*

acre /'eɪkər || 'eɪkə(r)/ *n* acre *m* (*0,405 hectáreas*); **we had ~s of space** teníamos muchísimo lugar *or* sitio

acrid /'ækrəd || 'ækrɪd/ *adj* acre

acrimonious /'ækrə'məʊniəs || ,ækrɪ'məʊniəs/ *adj* ‹*words*› áspero, cáustico; ‹*dispute*› enconado

acrobat /'ækrəbæt/ *n* acróbata *mf*

acrobatic /'ækrə'bætɪk/ *adj* acrobático

acrobatics /'ækrə'bætɪks/ *pl n* acrobacia *f*

acronym /'ækrənɪm/ *n* sigla *f*

across¹ /ə'krɔːs || ə'krɒs/ *adv* 1 (indicating movement): **the boatman ferried them ~** el barquero los cruzó; **seven ~** (crossword clue) siete horizontal 2 (indicating position) del otro lado; **they're already ~** ya están del otro lado; **she sat ~ from me** estaba sentada frente a mí *or* enfrente de mí 3 (in width, diameter): **it is 20m ~** tiene *or* mide 20m de ancho

across² *prep* 1 (from one side to other): **they ran ~ the road** cruzaron la calle corriendo; **he shouted to her ~ the room** le gritó desde el otro lado de la habitación; **a tree had fallen ~ the road** un árbol se había caído en mitad de la carretera 2 (on the other side of): **they live just ~ the road** viven justo enfrente

acrylic /ə'krɪlɪk/ *n* [u c] acrílico *m*; (*before n*) acrílico

act¹ /ækt/ *vi*
A 1 (take action, do sth) actuar* 2 (function, work) ‹‹*drug/chemical*›› hacer* efecto, actuar* 3 (serve) **to ~ AS sth** servir* DE algo; **she will ~ as interpreter** hará de intérprete 4 **acting** *pres p* ‹*chairman/director*› interino
B (behave) comportarse, actuar*; **just ~ as if nothing had happened** haz como si no hubiera pasado nada; **don't ~ dumb** ¡no te hagas el tonto!
C (perform) actuar*, trabajar; (as profession) ser* actor/actriz
■ **act** *vt* 1 (perform) ‹*role/part*› interpretar, hacer*; **the play was very well ~ed** la obra estuvo muy bien interpretada *or* actuada 2 (behave like, play role of) hacerse*

Phrasal verbs

- **act for** [v ▸ prep ▸ o] (represent) representar
- **act on** [v ▸ prep ▸ o] 1 (follow) ‹*advice*› seguir*; ‹*orders*› cumplir; **~ing on information received, the police ...** actuando sobre la base de información recibida, la policía ...; **she took a decision, but failed to ~ on it** tomó una decisión pero no obró en consecuencia 2 (affect) ‹‹*drug/chemical*›› actuar* sobre
- **act out** [v ▸ o ▸ adv, v ▸ adv ▸ o] representar; **the drama was ~ed out before our eyes** la tragedia ocurrió *or* se desarrolló ante nuestros propios ojos
- **act up** [v ▸ adv] (cause trouble) (colloq) ‹‹*child/machine*›› dar* guerra (fam)
- **act upon** ▸**act on**

act² *n*
A (deed) acto *m*; **an ~ of aggression/treason** una agresión/traición; **destroying the animal was an ~ of kindness** sacrificar al animal fue un acto piadoso; **the A~s of the Apostles** los Hechos de los Apóstoles; ***to catch sb in the ~*** agarrar *or* (esp Esp) coger* a algn con las manos en la masa
B (Govt) ley *f*; **an ~ of Parliament/Congress** una ley aprobada por el Parlamento/Congreso
C 1 (division of play) acto *m* 2 (routine) número *m*; ***to be a hard*** *o* ***difficult ~ to follow*** ser* difícil de igualar; ***to do a disappearing*** *o* ***vanishing ~*** esfumarse como por arte de magia; ***to get into*** *o* ***in on the ~*** meterse en el asunto; ***to get one's ~ together*** organizarse*; ***to smarten up one's ~*** enmendarse*
D (pretense): **it was all a big ~** era puro cuento *or* puro teatro (fam); ***to put on an ~*** hacer* teatro (fam), fingir*

ACT *n* = **American College Test**

ACT – American College Test

Una prueba que los estudiantes de la mayoría de los estados que forman Estados Unidos deben aprobar para ser admitidos en la universidad. Normalmente tiene lugar al final de la **high school** y cubre un número de materias principales, p.ej. inglés y matemáticas

acting /'æktɪŋ/ *n* [u] 1 (performance) interpretación *f*, actuación *f* 2 (as activity): **have you done any ~ before?** ¿has hecho teatro/cine alguna vez?; **I want to go into ~** quiero ser actor

action /'ækʃən/ *n*
A [u] 1 (practical measures): **prompt ~ by the police saved several lives** la rápida actuación de la policía salvó varias vidas; **~ is needed now** hay que actuar inmediatamente; **we demand ~!** ¡exigimos que se haga algo!; **which course of ~ do you recommend?** ¿qué medidas recomienda?; **disciplinary ~** medidas *fpl* disciplinarias; **to take ~ (against sb/sth)** tomar medidas (contra algn/algo); **~!** (Cin) ¡acción! 2 (*in phrases*) **in action** en acción; **I'm back in ~ again** (colloq) ya estoy de nuevo al pie del cañón (fam); **to go into ~** entrar en acción; **to put sth into ~** poner* algo en práctica; **out of action**: **my car is out of ~** tengo el coche averiado *or* (AmL tb) descompuesto; **he'll be out of ~ for a few weeks** va a estar fuera de circulación durante unas semanas (hum)
B [c] (deed) acto *m*; **I won't be responsible for my ~s if it happens again** si vuelve a suceder, yo no respondo de mí; ***~s speak louder than words*** obras son amores y no buenas razones

C [u] (Mil) acción *f* (de guerra); **wounded in ~** herido en combate

D [u] **1** (plot of play, movie) acción *f* **2** (exciting activity) animación *f*; ***to get a piece*** *o* ***slice of the ~*** (colloq) sacar* tajada (fam)

E **1** [c] (movement) movimiento *m* **2** [u] (operation) funcionamiento *m* **3** [u] (of drug, chemical) ~ **(ON sth)** acción *f* *or* efecto *m* (SOBRE algo)

action: **~-packed** *adj* lleno de acción; **~ replay** *n* (BrE Sport, TV) repetición *f* de la jugada; **~ stations** *pl n* (BrE) puestos *mpl* (de combate); (*as interj*) ¡a sus puestos!

activate /'æktəveɪt || 'æktɪveɪt/ *vt* **1** ‹*alarm/bomb*› activar **2** (AmE Mil) ‹*troops/unit*› movilizar*

active[1] /'æktɪv/ *adj*

A **1** (energetic, busy) ‹*person/life*› activo; **we had a very ~ holiday** pasamos unas vacaciones llenas de actividad **2** (Chem, Pharm) activo **3** ‹*volcano*› en actividad

B **1** (practising) activo; **sexually ~ teenagers** adolescentes que mantienen relaciones sexuales; **to be politically ~** militar políticamente **2** (positive, keen) ‹*member/role*› activo; **he takes an ~ interest in sport** sigue con mucho interés todo lo relacionado con el deporte **3** (Mil) (*before n*) ‹*service/duty*› activo

C (Ling) activo

active[2] *n* (Ling) **the ~** la voz activa

actively /'æktɪvli/ *adv* ‹*encourage/support*› activamente; **to be ~ involved in sth** tomar parte activa en algo

activist /'æktəvəst || 'æktɪvɪst/ *n* activista *mf*

activity /æk'tɪvəti/ *n* (*pl* **-ties**) **1** [c u] (work, doings) actividad *f*; **leisure activities** pasatiempos *mpl*; **they offer many different leisure activities** ofrecen diversas actividades para ocupar el tiempo **2** [u] (action, movement) actividad *f*, movimiento *m*; (noisy) bullicio *m*

activity holiday *n* (BrE) *vacaciones con actividades programadas*

actor /'æktər || 'æktə(r)/ *n* actor, actriz *m,f*

actress /'æktrəs/ *n* actriz *f*

actual /'æktʃuəl/ *adj* (*before n*) **1** (real) real; **he cited ~ cases** citó casos reales *or* de la vida real; **there was no ~ written agreement** no hubo un acuerdo escrito propiamente dicho; **in ~ fact** en realidad **2** (precise, very) mismo; **on the ~ day of the election** el mismo día de las elecciones; **those were her ~ words** ésas fueron sus palabras textuales

actuality /'æktʃu'æləti/ *n* [u c] (*pl* **-ties**) (frml) realidad *f*

actually /'æktʃuəli/ *adv*

A (really, in fact) en realidad; **she's ~ very bright** la verdad es que *or* en realidad es muy inteligente; **I never believed I'd ~ win** nunca creí que llegaría a ganar; **she did 20 lengths — 22, ~** se hizo 20 largos — 22, para ser exactos; **~, I'd rather not go** la verdad es que preferiría no ir

B (for emphasis): **the Queen ~ waved to me** la Reina hasta me saludó y todo; **it's ~ stopped raining!** aunque parezca mentira, ha parado de llover

actuary /'æktʃueri || 'æktʃʊəri/ *n* (*pl* **-ries**) actuario, -ria *m,f* de seguros

acumen /ə'kju:mən || 'ækju:mən/ *n* [u] sagacidad *f*, perspicacia *f*; **business ~** visión *f* para los negocios

acupuncture /'ækjə,pʌŋktʃər || 'ækjʊ,pʌŋktʃə(r)/ *n* [u] acupuntura *f*

acute /ə'kju:t/ *adj*

A **1** (Med) agudo **2** ‹*crisis/shortage*› grave

B **1** ‹*pain*› agudo; ‹*anxiety*› profundo **2** ‹*sense of smell*› fino, muy desarrollado; ‹*sight, hearing*› agudo

C (perceptive) agudo, perspicaz

D (Ling) ‹*accent*› agudo

acutely /ə'kju:tli/ *adv* **1** ‹*painful/embarrassing*› extremadamente, sumamente **2** (keenly) plenamente; **to be ~ aware of sth** ser* *or* (Chi, Méx) estar* plenamente consciente de algo

ad /æd/ *n* (colloq) ▸ **advertisement**

AD (= **Anno Domini**) después de Cristo; (written form) d. de C., d. de J.C.

adage /'ædɪdʒ/ *n* (liter) dicho *m*, adagio *m*

Adam /'ædəm/ *n* Adán; **~'s apple** nuez *f* (de Adán); ***I don't know him from ~*** no lo conozco de nada *or* para nada

adamant /'ædəmənt/ *adj* ‹*refusal*› firme, categórico; **I asked him to reconsider, but he was ~** le pedí que lo reconsiderara pero se mantuvo inflexible; **she was ~ that she wouldn't go** se mantuvo firme en su decisión de no ir

adamantly /'ædəməntli/ *adv* ‹*deny*› categóricamente; ‹*insist/say*› con firmeza

adapt /ə'dæpt/ *vt* adaptar; **to ~ oneself** adaptarse, amoldarse

■ **adapt** *vi* adaptarse; **to ~ TO sth/-ING** adaptarse A algo/+ INF

adaptability /ə'dæptə'bɪləti/ *n* [u] capacidad *f* de adaptación, adaptabilidad *f*

adaptable /ə'dæptəbəl/ *adj* adaptable

adaptation /'ædæp'teɪʃən/ *n* [u c] adaptación *f*

adapter, adaptor /ə'dæptər || ə'dæptə(r)/ *n* (Elec) (plug — with several sockets) enchufe *m* múltiple, ladrón *m*; (— for different sockets) adaptador *m*

ADC *n* = **aide-de-camp**

add /æd/ *vt*

A (put in in addition) añadir, agregar*; **this will ~ a touch of class** esto le dará un toque extra de distinción; **we were soaked, ~ed to which, it was starting to snow** estábamos empapados y por si esto fuera poco, empezaba a nevar; **at least I think so, she ~ed** —al menos eso creo —añadió *or* agregó; **there's nothing to ~** no hay más que decir

B (Math) sumar; **~ (on) 20** súmale veinte; **~ the four numbers (together)** suma los cuatro números

C **added** *past p* ‹*bonus/incentive*› adicional, extra; **with ~ed vitamins** con vitaminas; **no ~ed sugar** sin azúcar

■ **add** *vi* sumar

Phrasal verbs

• **add to** [v ▸ prep ▸ o] (increase, extend) ‹*building*› ampliar*; ‹*confusion/difficulties*› aumentar

• **add up**

A [v ▸ adv] **1** (Math) ‹‹*numbers/sum/accounts*›› cuadrar; **it seems to ~ up differently every time** cada vez que lo sumo me da (un resultado) diferente **2** (make sense) (colloq) ‹‹*facts/story*›› cuadrar; **it just doesn't ~ up** no tiene sentido

B [v ▸ o ▸ adv, v ▸ adv ▸ o] (Math) ‹*figures*› sumar; ‹*bill*› hacer*, preparar; **when you ~ it all up ...** si se tiene todo en cuenta ...

• **add up to** [v ▸ adv ▸ prep ▸ o] ‹‹*figures*›› sumar en total; ‹‹*total*›› ascender* a; **it ~s up to quite a lot of money** en total es *or* resulta una buena cantidad de dinero; **it doesn't ~ up to much** no es gran cosa

adder /'ædər || 'ædə(r)/ *n* víbora *f*

addict /'ædɪkt/ *n* adicto, -ta *m,f*; **drug ~** drogadicto, -ta *m,f*, toxicómano, -na *m,f* (frml); **I'm a real TV ~** (colloq) soy fanático de la televisión

addicted /ə'dɪktəd || ə'dɪktɪd/ *adj* **to be ~ (TO sth)** ser* adicto (A algo); **she became ~ to heroin** se hizo adicta a la heroína; **he's ~ to video games** es un adicto de los videojuegos; **I've become ~ to chocolate** (colloq) me he enviciado con el chocolate

addiction /ə'dɪkʃən/ *n* [u c] adicción *f*; **heroin ~** adicción a la heroína; **drug ~** drogadicción *f*, toxicomanía *f* (frml)

addictive /ə'dɪktɪv/ *adj* ‹*drug*› adictivo, que crea adicción *or* dependencia; ‹*activity*› que crea hábito

Addis Ababa /'ɑ:dɪs'ɑ:bəbə || 'ædɪs'æbəbə/ *n* Addis-Abeba *m*

addition /ə'dɪʃən/ *n*

A **1** [u] (Math) suma *f*, adición *f* (frml) **2** [u] (adding) adición *f*; **she recommends the ~ of brandy** recomienda que se le añada *or* que se le agregue brandy **3** (*in phrases*) **in addition** además; **in addition to** además de

B [c] (extra thing, person): **these rooms are later ~s** estas habitaciones se construyeron después; **a useful ~ to your toolkit** un práctico complemento para su caja de herramientas; **we're expecting an ~ to the family** dentro de poco aumentará la familia

additional /ə'dɪʃnəl || ə'dɪʃənl/ *adj* ‹*cost/weight*› extra, adicional; **it's an ~ reason for not telling her** es razón de más para no decírselo

additionally /ə'dɪʃnəli/ *adv* **1** (also) además **2** (even more) ‹*difficult/complicated*› aún más

additive /'ædətɪv || 'ædɪtɪv/ *n* [c u] aditivo *m*

additive-free /'ædətɪv'fri: || ,ædɪtɪv'fri:/ *adj* sin aditivos

a

addled /'ædḷd/ *adj* 1 (confused) confundido, aturullado (fam) 2 ‹*egg*› podrido

address¹ /'ædres || ə'dres/ *n*
A 1 (of house, offices etc) dirección *f*, señas *fpl*; **home ~** dirección particular; ⊜ **address** (on form) domicilio; **they're no longer at this ~** ya no viven aquí; (*before n*) **~ book** libreta *f* de direcciones 2 (Comput) dirección *f*
B [c] (speech) discurso *m*, alocución *f* (frml)
C **form of ~** tratamiento *m*

address² /ə'dres/ *vt*
A (AmE also) /'ædres/ ‹*mail*› ponerle* la dirección a; **the package was ~ed to you** el paquete estaba dirigido a ti
B 1 (speak to) ‹*person*› dirigirse* a; ‹*assembly*› pronunciar un discurso ante 2 **to ~ sb AS sth**: **they ~ her as "madam"** la llaman "madam" 3 (direct) (frml) ‹*question/remark*› dirigir*; **to ~ sth TO sb** dirigir* algo A algn
C (deal with, confront) ‹*problem/issue*› tratar
■ *v refl* 1 (speak to) **to ~ oneself TO sb** dirigirse* A algn 2 (turn one's attention to) (frml) **to ~ oneself TO sth** dedicarse* A algo

adenoids /'ædṇɔɪdz || 'ædənɔɪdz/ *pl n* vegetaciones *fpl* (adenoideas)

adept¹ /ə'dept/ *adj* experto, hábil; **to be ~ AT sth/-ING** ser* experto EN algo/+ INF

adept² /'ædept/ *n* (frml) experto, -ta *m,f*, maestro, -tra *m,f*

adeptly /ə'deptli/ *adv* con destreza *or* habilidad

adequacy /'ædɪkwəsi/ *n* 1 (of resources, facilities) suficiencia *f* 2 (of person in given capacity) aptitud *f*

adequate /'ædɪkwət/ *adj* 1 ‹*help/funding*› suficiente 2 ‹*standard/explanation*› adecuado, aceptable

adequately /'ædɪkwətli/ *adv* 1 (sufficiently) suficientemente 2 (well enough) de forma aceptable *or* adecuada

adhere /æd'hɪr || əd'hɪə(r)/ *vi* (frml) 1 (stick) **to ~ (TO sth)** adherirse* (A algo) 2 **to ~ TO sth** ‹*to principles/cause*› adherirse* A algo; ‹*to regulations*› observar algo

adherence /æd'hɪrəns || əd'hɪərəns/ *n* [u] (frml) **~ (TO sth)** ‹*to principles/customs*› adhesión *f* (A algo); ‹*to rules*› observancia *f* (DE algo)

adherent /æd'hɪrənt || əd'hɪərənt/ *n* (frml) partidario, -ria *m,f*, adepto, -ta *m,f*

adhesion /æd'hi:ʒən || əd'hi:ʒən/ *n* [u] (with glue) (frml) adhesión *f*, adherencia *f*

adhesive¹ /æd'hi:sɪv || əd'hi:sɪv/ *adj* adhesivo

adhesive² *n* [c u] adhesivo *m*, pegamento *m*

ad hoc /'æd'hɑ:k || ,æd'hɒk/ *adj* ‹*arrangement/measure*› ad hoc, a propósito para el caso; **the problems are dealt with on an ~ ~ basis** los problemas se van tratando según van surgiendo; **~ ~ committee** comisión *f* especial *or* ad hoc

adieu /ə'du: || ə'dju:/ *n* (*pl* **adieus** *or* **adieux** /-z/) (arch) adiós *m*; (*as interj*) ¡adiós!

ad infinitum /'æd,ɪnfɪ'naɪtəm/ *adv* indefinidamente

adjacent /ə'dʒeɪsṇt/ *adj* ‹*territories/fields*› adyacente, colindante; ‹*rooms/buildings*› contiguo

adjective /'ædʒɪktɪv/ *n* adjetivo *m*

adjoin /ə'dʒɔɪn/ *vt* (frml) 1 (be adjacent to) lindar con, colindar con 2 **adjoining** *pres p* ‹*houses*› contiguo, colindante; **the ~ing room** el cuarto de al lado, el cuarto contiguo

adjourn /ə'dʒɜ:rn || ə'dʒɜ:n/ *vt* ‹*talks/trial*› suspender; **the meeting was ~ed** se levantó la sesión
■ **adjourn** *vi* (stop): **the court ~ed** el tribunal levantó la sesión; **let's ~ to the garden** (frml *or* hum) pasemos al jardín

adjournment /ə'dʒɜ:rnmənt || ə'dʒɜ:nmənt/ *n* [u c] suspensión *f*

adjudicate /ə'dʒu:dɪkeɪt/ *vi* (give judgment) arbitrar
■ **adjudicate** *vt* (frml) ‹*competition*› juzgar*; ‹*claim*› decidir sobre

adjudication /ə'dʒu:dɪ'keɪʃən/ *n* [u c] (Law) laudo *m*, fallo *m*, decisión *f*; (appraisal) evaluación *f*

adjudicator /ə'dʒu:dɪkeɪtər || ə'dʒu:dɪkeɪtə(r)/ *n* (in competition) juez *mf*

adjunct /'ædʒʌŋkt/ *n* **~ (TO/OF sth)** (addition) complemento *m* (DE algo); (appendage) apéndice *m* (DE algo)

adjust /ə'dʒʌst/ *vt* 1 ‹*instrument*› ajustar, poner* a punto; ‹*volume/temperature/speed*› regular 2 (modify) ‹*prices/wages*› ajustar 3 (straighten, correct) arreglar; **he ~ed his tie** se arregló la corbata
■ **adjust** *vi* «*seat/strap*» poderse* ajustar; «*person*» **to ~ (oneself) (TO sth/-ING)** adaptarse *or* amoldarse (A algo/+ INF)

adjustable /ə'dʒʌstəbəl/ *adj* ‹*focus/temperature*› regulable, graduable; **~ wrench** *o* (BrE also) **spanner** llave *f* inglesa

adjustment /ə'dʒʌstmənt/ *n*
A [c] (to machine, instrument) ajuste *m*; (to figures) ajuste *m*, reajuste *m*; (to clothes) arreglo *m*; (to plan, system) cambio *m*, modificación *f*; **we had to make some ~s to our lifestyle** tuvimos que cambiar *or* adaptar un poco
B [u] (act, process) 1 (of machine, instrument) ajuste *m* 2 (of person) adaptación *f*

ad lib /'æd'lɪb/ *adv* improvisando

ad-lib¹ /'æd'lɪb/ *vt/i* **-bb-** improvisar

ad-lib² *adj* (*pred* **ad lib**) improvisado

Adm (title) = **Admiral**

admin /'ædmɪn/ *n* (BrE colloq) 1 [u] (activity) papeleo *m* (fam), administración *f* 2 (department) (*no art*) administración *f*

administer /əd'mɪnəstər || əd'mɪnɪstə(r)/ *vt*
A (manage) administrar
B (frml) ‹*punishment/drug*› **to ~ sth (TO sb)** administrar(le) algo (A algn) (frml)

administration /əd'mɪnə'streɪʃən || əd,mɪnɪ'streɪʃən/ *n*
A [u] (managing) (— of institution, business) administración *f*, dirección *f*; (— of estate, fund) administración *f*
B [c] (managing body) administración *f*; (Pol) gobierno *m*, administración *f*
C [u] (of justice, medicine) administración *f*

administrative /əd'mɪnəstreɪtɪv || əd'mɪnɪstrətɪv/ *adj* administrativo; **~ staff** personal *m* de administración

administrator /əd'mɪnəstreɪtər || əd'mɪnɪstreɪtə(r)/ *n* administrador, -dora *m,f*

admirable /'ædmərəbəl/ *adj* ‹*honesty/work*› digno de admiración, admirable; ‹*plan*› excelente

admirably /'ædmərəbli/ *adv* admirablemente, de forma admirable

admiral /'ædmərəl/ *n* almirante *mf*

Admiralty /'ædmərəlti/ *n* (in UK) **the ~ (Board)** el Almirantazgo, el ministerio de marina del Reino Unido

admiration /'ædmə'reɪʃən/ *n* [u] admiración *f*

admire /əd'maɪr || əd'maɪə(r)/ *vt* ‹*skill/work/scenery*› admirar; **I was just admiring your tablecloth** me estaba fijando en lo bonito que es el mantel

admirer /əd'maɪrər || əd'maɪərə(r)/ *n* admirador, -dora *m,f*

admiring /əd'maɪrɪŋ || əd'maɪərɪŋ/ *adj* (*before n*) ‹*look/tone*› de admiración, admirativo

admiringly /əd'maɪrɪŋli || əd'maɪərɪŋli/ *adv* con admiración

admissible /əd'mɪsəbəl/ *adj* (frml) ‹*conduct/language*› aceptable, admisible; **~ evidence** (Law) pruebas *fpl* admisibles

admission /əd'mɪʃən/ *n*
A 1 [u] (to building, exhibition) entrada *f*, admisión *f*; (price) (precio *m* de) entrada *f* 2 [u] (into college, society) ingreso *m*, admisión *f* 3 [c] (into hospital) ingreso *m*
B [c u] (confession) admisión *f*, reconocimiento *m*; **he was, on** *o* **by his own ~, a poor father** él mismo admitía *or* reconocía que no era un buen padre

admit /əd'mɪt/ **-tt-** *vt*
A 1 (allow entry) dejar entrar, admitir (frml); ‹*light/air*› permitir *or* dejar entrar; ⊜ **admit one** entrada individual 2 ‹*patient*› ingresar
B 1 (confess) ‹*crime/mistake*› admitir, reconocer*; **to ~ sth TO sb** confesarle* algo A algn; **I must ~ that ...** tengo que admitir *or* reconocer que ...; **he ~ted stealing the money** admitió haber robado el dinero 2 (acknowledge) ‹*truth/validity*› reconocer* 3 ▸**admit of**

Phrasal verbs

- **admit of** [v ▸ prep ▸ o] (frml) admitir
- **admit to** [v ▸ prep ▸ o] (confess) ‹*error*› admitir, reconocer*; ‹*crime*› declararse culpable de; **to ~ to -ING**: **she won't ~ to loving him** no quiere admitir *or* reconocer que lo quiere

admittance /əd'mɪtn̩s/ *n* [u] (frml) ~ **(TO sth)** acceso *m or* entrada *f* (A algo); ⊘ **no admittance** prohibida la entrada

admittedly /əd'mɪtədli || əd'mɪtɪdli/ *adv* (*indep*): ~, **it wasn't an easy task, but ...** hay que reconocer *or* admitir que no era una tarea fácil pero ...

admonish /æd'mɑːnɪʃ || əd'mɒnɪʃ/ *vt* (frml) **to ~ sb (FOR sth/-ING)** amonestar *or* reprender a algn (POR algo/+ INF)

admonition /'ædmə'nɪʃən/ *n* (frml) (scolding) amonestación *f*, admonición *f* (frml); (warning) advertencia *f*

ad nauseam /æd'nɔːziəm || ˌæd'nɔːziæm/ *adv* hasta la saciedad

ado /ə'duː/ *n* [u]: **without further** *o* **more ~** sin más (preámbulos); **much ~ about nothing** mucho ruido y pocas nueces

adolescence /'ædə'lesn̩s/ *n* [u] adolescencia *f*

adolescent¹ /'ædə'lesn̩t/ *n* adolescente *mf*

adolescent² *adj* adolescente

adopt /ə'dɑːpt || ə'dɒpt/ *vt* 1 ‹*child*› adoptar 2 ‹*idea/custom/title*› adoptar 3 ‹*recommendation*› aprobar*

adopted /ə'dɑːptəd || ə'dɒptɪd/ *adj* ‹*son/country*› adoptivo; **she's ~** es adoptada

adoption /ə'dɑːpʃən || ə'dɒpʃən/ *n* 1 [u c] (of child) adopción *f* 2 [u] (of approach, custom, title) adopción *f* 3 [u] (of report, motion) aprobación *f*

adoptive /ə'dɑːptɪv || ə'dɒptɪv/ *adj* (*before n*) adoptivo

adorable /ə'dɔːrəbəl/ *adj* ‹*house/hat*› divino, monísimo (fam); ‹*child*› adorable

adoration /'ædə'reɪʃən/ *n* [u] adoración *f*

adore /ə'dɔːr || ə'dɔː(r)/ *vt* 1 (love) adorar 2 **adoring** *pres p* ‹*gaze*› lleno de adoración; ‹*mother*› amantísimo 3 (like, enjoy): **I ~ figs** me encantan *or* me enloquecen los higos 4 (worship) adorar

adoringly /ə'dɔːrɪŋli/ *adv* con adoración

adorn /ə'dɔːrn || ə'dɔːn/ *vt* (frml *or* liter) adornar, ornar (liter)

adornment /ə'dɔːrnmənt || ə'dɔːnmənt/ *n* [uc] adorno *m*; **without ~** sin adornos *or* embellecimientos

ADP *n* [u]
A (= **adenosine diphosphate**) ADP *m*
B (= **automatic data processing**) PAD *m*

adrenaline /ə'drenl̩ən || ə'drenəlɪn/ *n* [u] adrenalina *f*

Adriatic /'eɪdri'ætɪk/ *n* **the ~ (Sea)** el (mar) Adriático

adrift /ə'drɪft/ *adj* (*pred*) (Naut) a la deriva; ***to come*** *o* ***go ~*** «*plans*» fallar, salir* mal

adroit /ə'drɔɪt/ *adj* 1 ‹*answer/speaker*› hábil; **to be ~ AT -ING** ser* hábil PARA + INF 2 ‹*movement*› ágil; ‹*player*› diestro

adroitly /ə'drɔɪtli/ *adv* 1 ‹*question*› hábilmente, con habilidad 2 ‹*move*› con agilidad, ágilmente

ADSL *n* [u] (= **Asymmetric Digital Subscriber Line**) ADSL *f*

adulation /'ædʒə'leɪʃən || ˌædjʊ'leɪʃən/ *n* [u] adulación *f*

adult¹ /ə'dʌlt, 'ædʌlt/ *n* adulto, -ta *m,f*

adult² *adj* 1 (physically mature) adulto; **all my ~ life** toda mi vida de adulto 2 (mature) ‹*behavior/approach*› maduro, adulto 3 (suitable for adults) para mayores *or* adultos

adult education *n* [u] educación *f* para adultos

adulterate /ə'dʌltəreɪt/ *vt* adulterar

adultery /ə'dʌltəri/ *n* [u] adulterio *m*

adulthood /ə'dʌlthʊd || 'ædʌlthʊd/ *n* [u] edad *f* adulta, adultez *f*

advance¹ /əd'væns || əd'vɑːns/ *vi* 1 «*person/vehicle/troops*» avanzar*; «*science/project/society*» avanzar*, progresar; **to ~ ON sb/sth** avanzar* HACIA algn/SOBRE algo 2 **advancing** *pres p*: **a man of advancing years** un hombre entrado en años

■ **advance** *vt*
A (move forward) avanzar*, adelantar; (further) ‹*knowledge*› fomentar, potenciar; ‹*interests/cause*› promover*
B (suggest) ‹*idea*› presentar, proponer*; ‹*opinion*› dar*
C 1 ‹*date/meeting*› adelantar 2 ‹*money/wages*› anticipar, adelantar

advance² *n*
A [c u] (of person, army, vehicle) avance *m*; (of civilization, science) avance *m*, progreso *m*, adelanto *m*; **with the ~ of old age** con el paso de los años, a medida que envejece (*or* envejecía *etc*)
B **advances** *pl* (overtures) insinuaciones *fpl*; **to make ~s to sb** hacerle* insinuaciones a algn, insinuársele* a algn
C [c] 1 (early payment) anticipo *m*, adelanto *m*; **~ ON sth**: **they gave me an ~ of £100 on my salary** me dieron un adelanto *or* anticipo de 100 libras a cuenta del sueldo 2 (loan) préstamo *m*
D (*in phrases*) **in advance**: **to pay in ~** pagar* por adelantado *or* por anticipado; **tickets are $10 in ~** las entradas cuestan 10 dólares si se compran por adelantado; **it was planned well in ~** se planeó con mucha antelación *or* anticipación; **thanking you in ~** agradeciéndole de antemano su atención

advance³ *adj* (*before n*) 1 (ahead of time): **the ~ publicity for a product** la promoción previa al lanzamiento de un producto; **~ booking is essential** es imprescindible hacer la reserva por anticipado *or* con anticipación; **without any ~ warning** *o* **notice** sin previo aviso; **~ payment** pago *m* anticipado *or* (por) adelantado 2 **~ man** (AmE Pol) relaciones *m* públicas; **~ man** *o* **agent** (AmE Theat) agente *m*

advanced /əd'vænst || əd'vɑːnst/ *adj* ‹*civilization/technology/course*› avanzado; ‹*student*› avanzado, adelantado; **to be ~ in years** ser* entrado en años; **the project isn't very far ~** el proyecto no está muy adelantado

Advanced level *n* (frml) ▸**A level**

Advanced Supplementary level *n* (in UK) ▸**AS Level**

advancement /əd'vænsmənt || əd'vɑːnsmənt/ *n* [u] 1 (furtherance) fomento *m* 2 (in rank) (frml) ascenso *m*

advantage /əd'væntɪdʒ || əd'vɑːntɪdʒ/ *n* 1 [c] (superior factor) ventaja *f*; **to have an ~ over sb** tener* ventaja sobre algn; ⊘ **knowledge of German an advantage** se valorarán conocimientos de alemán 2 [u] (gain): **to turn sth to (one's) ~** sacar* provecho *or* partido de algo; **this vase shows off the roses to their best ~** las rosas lucen al máximo en este florero; **to take ~ of sth** aprovechar algo, (pej) aprovecharse de algo; **to take ~ of sb** (exploit) aprovecharse de algn 3 (in tennis) (*no pl*) ventaja *f*

advantageous /ˌædvæn'teɪdʒəs || ˌædvən'teɪdʒəs/ *adj* ‹*arrangement*› ventajoso, favorable; ‹*position/situation*› de ventaja, ventajoso; **to be ~ TO sb** ser* ventajoso *or* favorable PARA algn

advent /'ædvent/ *n* 1 (arrival) llegada *f*, advenimiento *m* (frml) 2 **Advent** (Relig) Adviento *m*

adventure /əd'ventʃər || əd'ventʃə(r)/ *n* [c u] aventura *f*; **the spirit of ~** el espíritu aventurero *or* de aventura; (*before n*) ‹*story/film*› de aventuras

adventurer /əd'ventʃərər || əd'ventʃərə(r)/ *n* aventurero, -ra *m,f*

adventurous /əd'ventʃərəs/ *adj* 1 ‹*film/design*› atrevido, audaz; ‹*architect/composer*› audaz, innovador 2 ‹*traveler*› intrépido; ‹*spirit/person*› aventurero

adverb /'ædvɜːrb || 'ædvɜːb/ *n* adverbio *m*

adversary /'ædvərseri || 'ædvəsəri/ *n* (*pl* **-ries**) (frml) adversario, -ria *m,f*

adverse /'ædvɜːrs, æd'vɜːrs || 'ædvɜːs/ *adj* ‹*criticism/consequences*› adverso, desfavorable; ‹*wind*› en contra, adverso; ‹*effect*› adverso, negativo; **~ weather conditions** condiciones *fpl* climatológicas adversas

adversely /'ædvɜːrsli, æd'vɜːrsli || 'ædvɜːsli/ *adv* adversamente, negativamente, desfavorablemente

adversity /æd'vɜːrsəti || əd'vɜːsəti/ *n* [u c] (*pl* **-ties**) adversidad *f*; **in ~** en la adversidad

advert /'ædvɜːrt || 'ædvɜːt/ *n* (BrE colloq) ▸**advertisement**

advertise /'ædvərtaɪz || 'ædvətaɪz/ *vt*
A ‹*product*› hacerle* publicidad *or* propaganda a, hacerle* réclame a (AmL); **I saw it ~d on TV** lo vi anunciado en la tele; **the job was ~d in yesterday's paper** el trabajo salió anunciado en el diario de ayer
B ‹*intentions*› anunciar, revelar

■ **advertise** *vi* hacer* publicidad *or* propaganda; **to ~ FOR sb/sth**: **they're advertising for nurses/antiques** han puesto un anuncio *or* (AmL tb) aviso solicitando enfermeras/para comprar antigüedades

advertisement /'ædvər'taɪzmənt || əd'vɜːtɪsmənt/ *n* [c] (on radio, television) anuncio *m*, spot *m* (publicitario), aviso *m* (AmL); (in newspaper) anuncio *m*, aviso *m* (AmL); **she's a good ~ for vegetarianism** su salud dice mucho en favor del vegetarianismo

a

advertiser /'ædvərtaɪzər || 'ædvətaɪzə(r)/ *n* anunciante *mf*

advertising /'ædvərtaɪzɪŋ || 'ædvətaɪzɪŋ/ *n* [u] 1 (action, business) publicidad *f*; (*before n*) ‹*campaign/slot*› publicitario; **~ agency** agencia *f* de publicidad 2 (advertisements) propaganda *f*, publicidad *f*

advice /əd'vaɪs/ *n* 1 [u] (counsel) consejos *mpl*; (professional) asesoramiento *m*; **a piece of ~** un consejo; **he gave me some good ~** me dio buenos consejos, me aconsejó bien; **~ ON *o* ABOUT sth: I'd like some ~ on these contracts** quisiera que se me aconsejara *or* se me asesorara sobre estos contratos; **to give sb ~** aconsejar a algn; **to seek medical ~** consultar a un médico; **to take *o* follow sb's ~** seguir* los consejos de algn; **take my ~** hazme caso 2 [u c] (notification) aviso *m*, notificación *f*

advisable /əd'vaɪzəbəl/ *adj* aconsejable, conveniente; **it is ~ to book a seat** es aconsejable *or* se aconseja reservar un asiento

advise /əd'vaɪz/ *vt*

A 1 (recommend) aconsejar, recomendar*; **he ~d starting at once** aconsejó que se empezara inmediatamente; **to ~ sb to + INF** aconsejar(le) A algn QUE (+ *subj*); **he ~d me to wait** me aconsejó que esperara; **you would be well ~d to see a lawyer** sería aconsejable que se asesorara con un abogado; **to ~ sb AGAINST sth/-ING: they ~d him against marrying so young** le aconsejaron que no se casara tan joven; **the committee ~d them against it** el comité se lo desaconsejó 2 (give advice to) aconsejar; (professionally) asesorar

B (inform) (frml) informar; (in writing) notificar* (frml)

■ **advise** *vi* aconsejar; (professionally) asesorar; **to ~ AGAINST sth/-ING** desaconsejar algo/+ INF

advisedly /əd'vaɪzədli || əd'vaɪzɪdli/ *adv* (frml) ‹*act/say*› con conocimiento de causa; **I use the term ~** utilizo el término intencionadamente

adviser, advisor /əd'vaɪzər || əd'vaɪzə(r)/ *n* consejero, -ra *m,f*; (professional) asesor, -sora *m,f*

advisory /əd'vaɪzəri/ *adj* ‹*body/service*› consultivo; **in an ~ capacity** en calidad de asesor

advocate[1] /'ædvəkət/ *n* 1 (supporter, defender) **~ (OF sth)** defensor, -sora *m,f* (DE algo) 2 (in a court of law) abogado, -da *m,f*

advocate[2] /'ædvəkeɪt/ *vt* ‹*idea*› recomendar*, abogar* por, propugnar (frml); **to ~ -ING** recomendar* + INF

Aegean /ɪ'dʒiːən/ *n* **the ~ (Sea)** el (mar) Egeo

aegis, (AmE also) **egis** /'iːdʒəs || 'iːdʒɪs/ *n*: **under the ~ of sth/sb** (frml) bajo los auspicios de algo/algn (frml)

aeon, (AmE also) **eon** /'iːən, 'iːɑːn || 'iːən/ *n* siglo *m*

aerial[1] /'eriəl || 'eəriəl/ *adj* (*before n*) aéreo; **~ photograph** aerofoto *f*

aerial[2] *n* antena *f*

aerialist /'eriələst || 'eəriəlɪst/ *n* (AmE) (on trapeze) trapecista *mf*; (on tightrope) equilibrista *mf*, funámbulo, -la *m,f*

aerie, eyrie /'eri || 'eəri/ *n* aguilera *f*

aero- /'erəʊ || 'eərəʊ/ *pref* aero-

aerobatics /'erə'bætɪks || ,eərə'bætɪks/ *pl n* acrobacia *f* aérea

aerobic /e'rəʊbɪk, ə- || eə'rəʊbɪk/ *adj* 1 (Biol) aerobio 2 ‹*exercise*› aeróbico

aerobics /e'rəʊbɪks, ə- || eə'rəʊbɪks/ *n* (+ *sing or pl vb*) aerobic(s) *m*, aerobismo *m* (CS)

aerodynamic /'erəʊdaɪ'næmɪk || ,eərəʊdaɪ'næmɪk/ *adj* aerodinámico

aerodynamics /'erəʊdaɪ'næmɪks || ,eərəʊdaɪ'næmɪks/ *n* [u] aerodinámica *f*

aerogram, aerogramme /'erəgræm || 'eərəgræm/ *n* aerograma *m*

aeronautics /'erə'nɔːtɪks || ,eərə'nɔːtɪks/ *n* [u] aeronáutica *f*

aeroplane /'erəpleɪn || 'eərəpleɪn/ *n* (BrE) avión *m*

aerosol /'erəsɑːl || 'eərəsɒl/ *n* (can, contents) aerosol *m*, spray *m*

aerospace /'erəʊspeɪs || 'eərəʊspeɪs/ *adj* (*before n*) ‹*research/industry*› aeroespacial

aesthete, (AmE also) **esthete** /'esθiːt || 'iːsθiːt/ *n* esteta *mf*

aesthetic, (AmE also) **esthetic** /es'θetɪk || iːs'θetɪk/ *adj* estético

aesthetics, (AmE also) **esthetics** /es'θetɪks || iːs'θetɪks/ *n* [u] estética *f*

afar /ə'fɑːr || ə'fɑː(r)/ *adv* (liter) lejos

affable /'æfəbəl/ *adj* afable

affably /'æfəbli/ *adv* afablemente

affair /ə'fer || ə'feə(r)/ *n*

A 1 (case) caso *m*, affaire *m*; **the Watergate ~** el caso *or* affaire Watergate 2 (event): **the wedding was a small, family ~** la boda se celebró en la intimidad; **it was a very formal ~** fue una ocasión muy ceremoniosa; **the last outing was a very different ~** la última excursión fue muy diferente 3 (business, concern) asunto *m*; **that's my ~!** ¡eso es asunto mío! 4 **affairs** *pl* (matters) asuntos *mpl*

B (liaison) affaire *m*, aventura *f* (amorosa), lío *m* (fam); **she's having an ~** tiene un amante; **they're having an ~** tienen relaciones, tienen un lío (fam)

C (thing) (colloq): **her dress was a very elaborate ~** su vestido era un modelo super complicado (fam)

affect /ə'fekt/ *vt*

A 1 (have effect on) afectar a; **your pension will not be ~ed** su pensión no se verá afectada 2 (attack) ‹*organ/nervous system*› comprometer, afectar a 3 (move, touch) (frml) afectar a

B ‹*indifference/interest*› afectar; ‹*accent*› afectar, adoptar

affectation /'æfek'teɪʃən/ *n* [c u] afectación *f*

affected /ə'fektəd || ə'fektɪd/ *adj*

A (false) ‹*manner/person*› afectado; ‹*interest/grief*› fingido

B ‹*area/organ*› afectado

affection /ə'fekʃən/ *n* 1 [c u] (fondness) cariño *m*, afecto *m* 2 **affections** *pl* (feelings): **to trifle with sb's ~s** jugar* con los sentimientos de algn; **she has a special place in my ~s** le tengo un cariño muy especial

affectionate /ə'fekʃnət/ *adj* cariñoso, afectuoso; **your ~ son, Peter** (Corresp) tu hijo que te quiere, Peter; **to be ~ TOWARD sb** ser* cariñoso CON algn

affectionately /ə'fekʃnətli/ *adv* cariñosamente

affidavit /'æfə'deɪvət || ,æfɪ'deɪvɪt/ *n* declaración *f* jurada, affidávit *m*

affiliate /ə'fɪlieɪt/ *vt* (*often pass*) afiliar; **to be ~d TO sth** estar* afiliado A algo

■ **affiliate** *vi* afiliarse; **to ~ TO/WITH sth** afiliarse A algo

affiliation /ə'fɪli'eɪʃən/ *n* [c u] **~ (TO/WITH sth)** afiliación *f* (A algo); **her political ~s** su filiación política

affinity /ə'fɪnəti/ *n* (*pl* **-ties**) [c u] afinidad *f*

affirm /ə'fɜːrm || ə'fɜːm/ *vt* declarar

affirmation /'æfər'meɪʃən || ,æfə'meɪʃən/ *n* [c u] afirmación *f*

affirmative[1] /ə'fɜːrmətɪv || ə'fɜːmətɪv/ *adj* afirmativo; **~ action** (AmE) discriminación *f* positiva

affirmative[2] *n*: **her answer was in the ~** respondió afirmativamente

affix[1] /ə'fɪks/ *vt* (frml) ‹*stamp/seal*› poner*; ‹*notice*› fijar

affix[2] /'æfɪks/ *n* afijo *m*

afflict /ə'flɪkt/ *vt* «*disease/problem*» aquejar; **to be ~ed BY *o* WITH a disease** estar* aquejado DE una enfermedad; **don't mock the ~ed** (hum) no te burles de las desgracias de otros

affliction /ə'flɪkʃən/ *n* 1 [u] (suffering) aflicción *f* 2 [c] (cause of suffering) desgracia *f*; (ailment) mal *m*, dolencia *f* (frml)

affluence /'æfluəns/ *n* [u] prosperidad *f*, bienestar *m* económico

affluent /'æfluənt/ *adj* ‹*suburb/country*› próspero; ‹*person*› acomodado, rico; **the ~ society** la sociedad de la abundancia

afford /ə'fɔːrd || ə'fɔːd/ *vt*

A ‹*money/time*›: **I can't ~ a new car** no me alcanza el dinero para comprarme un coche nuevo; **I just can't ~ the time to do it** es que no dispongo de tiempo para hacerlo; **to ~ to + INF: I can't ~ to pay for it** no tengo con qué pagarlo, no puedo pagarlo; **you can't ~ to miss this opportunity** no puedes perderte esta oportunidad

B (frml) ‹*view/protection*› ofrecer*

affordable /ə'fɔːrdəbəl || ə'fɔːdəbəl/ *adj* asequible

afforestation /ə'fɔːrə'steɪʃən || ə,fɒrɪ'steɪʃən/ *n* [u] forestación *f*

affray /ə'freɪ/ *n* (frml) riña *f*; (Law) alteración *f* del orden público

affront /ə'frʌnt/ *n* (frml) ~ (**TO sb/sth**) afrenta *f* (A algn/algo)

Afghan¹ /'æfgæn/ *adj* afgano

Afghan² *n* afgano, -na *m,f*

Afghanistan /æf'gænəstæn || æf'gænɪstɑːn/ *n* Afganistán *m*

afield /ə'fiːld/ *adv*: **she travels as far ~ as China** viaja a lugares tan distantes como la China; **we had to look further ~ for help** tuvimos que buscar ayuda en otra parte

aflame /ə'fleɪm/ *adj* (liter) (*pred*) en llamas; **her eyes were ~ with jealousy** los celos encendían su mirada (liter)

AFL-CIO /'eɪef'el'siːaɪ'əʊ/ *n* = **American Federation of Labor and Congress of Industrial Organizations**

afloat /ə'fləʊt/ *adj* (*pred*) [1] (on water) a flote; **to stay ~** mantenerse* a flote [2] (operational) a flote; **to keep a business ~** mantener* un negocio a flote

afoot /ə'fʊt/ *adj* (*pred*): **plans are ~ to create ...** hay planes *or* proyectos de crear ...; **what's ~?** ¿qué se está tramando?

aforementioned /ə'fɔːr'mentʃənd || ə,fɔː'menʃənd/, **aforesaid** /ə'fɔːrsed || ə'fɔːsed/ *adj* (frml: used esp in legal texts) (*before n*) ‹*clause/statement*› anteriormente mencionado, antedicho (frml); **the ~ person** el susodicho, la susodicha (frml *o* hum)

afraid /ə'freɪd/ *adj* (*pred*)

A (scared): **to be ~ OF sb/sth/-ING**: **he is ~ of the dark** le tiene miedo a la oscuridad; **he's ~ of her** le tiene miedo; **there's nothing to be ~ of** no tienes nada que temer; **I was ~ of falling** tenía miedo de caerme; **I'm not ~ of hard work** a mí el trabajo no me asusta; **to be ~ to + INF**: **he's ~ to go into the cellar** le da miedo entrar en el sótano; **never be ~ to ask for help** si necesitas ayuda, no tengas miedo de pedirla; **to be ~ (THAT)** tener* miedo DE QUE (+ *subj*); **I was ~ you'd be offended** tenía miedo de que te ofendieras

B (sorry) **to be ~ (THAT)**: **I'm ~ (that) that won't be possible** (me) temo que no va a ser posible; **she's not in, I'm ~** lo siento pero no está; **is that all? — I'm ~ so** ¿eso es todo? — sí, lo siento; **I'm ~ not** me temo que no

afresh /ə'freʃ/ *adv*: **to start ~** empezar* de nuevo, volver* a empezar

Africa /'æfrɪkə/ *n* África *f*‡

African¹ /'æfrɪkən/ *adj* africano

African² *n* africano, -na *m,f*

African-American¹ /'æfrɪkənə'merɪkən/*adj* norteamericano de origen africano

African-American² *n* norteamericano, -na *m,f* de origen africano

> **African-American**
>
> El término de más amplia aceptación en Estados Unidos para referirse a norteamericanos de origen africano

Afrikaans /'æfrɪ'kɑːns/ *n* [u] afrikaans *m*

Afrikaner /'æfrɪ'kɑːnər || ,æfrɪ'kɑːnə(r)/ *n* afrikaner *mf*, afrikánder *mf*

Afro /'æfrəʊ/ *n* peinado *m* afro

Afro- /'æfrəʊ/ *pref* afro-

Afro-American¹ /'æfrəʊə'merɪkən/ *adj* afroamericano

Afro-American² *n* afroamericano, -na *m,f*

Afro-Caribbean /'æfrəʊ,kærɪ'biːən/ *adj* (BrE) afroantillano, afrocaribeño

> **Afro-Caribbean**
>
> El término de más amplia aceptación en Gran Bretaña para referirse a gente con antepasados africanos que procede del Caribe o que vive allí

aft /æft || ɑːft/ *adv* ‹*go*› a popa; ‹*sit/be*› en la popa

after¹ /'æftər || 'ɑːftə(r)/ *prep*

A (following in time) después de; **I'll be at home ~ eight o'clock** estaré en casa después de *or* a partir de las ocho; **~ a few days** después de *or* al cabo de unos días; **it's just ~ midnight** son las doce pasadas; **it's a quarter ~ two** (AmE) son las dos y cuarto; **they arrived ~ us** llegaron más tarde *or* después que nosotros; **the day ~ the party** al día siguiente de la fiesta

B (in sequence, rank) tras; **day ~ day** día tras día; **one ~ the other** uno tras otro; **do go in — ~ you!** pase — ¡primero usted!

C [1] (behind): **shut the door ~ you** cierra la puerta al salir/entrar [2] (in pursuit of) tras; **he ran ~ them** corrió tras ellos; **the police are ~ him** la policía anda tras él; **he's just ~ my money** sólo le interesa mi dinero; **I think she's ~ something** creo que anda tras algo [3] (about, concerning) por; *see also* **ask after, inquire**

D [1] (in view of, considering) después de; **~ all I've done for you?** ¿después de *or* con todo lo que he hecho por ti? [2] **after all** después de todo

E (in the style of) al estilo de, a la manera de; (in honor of) por, en honor de; ▸**heart B**

after² *conj*: **it happened ~ you left** ocurrió después de que tú te fuiste; **~ examining it** después de examinarlo; **~ he died, the house remained empty** al morir él *or* cuando él murió, la casa quedó vacía; **the day ~ we arrived** al día siguiente de nuestra llegada; **~ you've washed it, hang it out to dry** cuando *or* una vez que lo hayas lavado, tiéndelo para que se seque

after³ *adv* [1] (afterward, following) después; **soon ~** poco después; **the day ~** al día siguiente [2] (behind) detrás

after⁴ *adj* (*before n*) posterior

after: **~birth** *n* [u] placenta *f*; **~care** *n* [u] (Med) asistencia *f* post-operatoria; **~-dinner** /'æftər'dɪnər || ,ɑːftə'dɪnə(r)/ *adj* ‹*speech*› de sobremesa; **~effect** *n* (of drug) efecto *m* secundario; (of problem) secuela *f*, repercusión *f*; **~-hours** /'æftər'aʊrz || ,ɑːftə'aʊəz/ *adj/adv* después de horas, fuera de horas; **~life** *n* [u] vida *f* después de la muerte; **in the ~life** en la otra vida

aftermath /'æftərmæθ || 'ɑːftəmæθ, 'ɑːftəmɑːθ/ *n* [1] (subsequent period): **in the ~** en el período subsiguiente; **in the ~ of the riots** tras los disturbios, en el período que siguió a los disturbios [2] (consequence) repercusiones *fpl*, secuelas *fpl*

afternoon /'æftər'nuːn || ,ɑːftə'nuːn/ *n* tarde *f*; **on Friday ~** el viernes por *or* (AmL) en la tarde; **at four o'clock in the ~** a las cuatro de la tarde; **he came in the ~** vino por la tarde, vino en la tarde (AmL); **good ~!** ¡buenas tardes!; (*before n*) **~ nap** siesta *f*; **~ tea** (BrE) té *m* (de las cinco)

afters /'æftərz || 'ɑːftəz/ *n* (*pl* ~) (BrE colloq) (+ *sing or pl vb*) postre *m*

after: **~-sales service** *n* servicio *m* post-venta; **~shave (lotion)** *n* [u] loción *f* para después de afeitarse, aftershave *m*; **~taste** *n* [u] regusto *m*, dejo *m*; **~thought** *n*: **it occurred to me as an ~thought that ...** después se me ocurrió que ...; **it was added on as an ~thought** fue una idea de último momento

afterward /'æftərwərd || 'ɑːftəwəd/, (BrE also) **afterwards** /-z/ *adv* después; **you'll regret it ~** después *or* luego te vas a arrepentir; **it was only ~ that I realized** no me di cuenta hasta después

again /ə'gen, ə'geɪn/ *adv*

A (another time) otra vez, de nuevo; **I had to do it ~** tuve que hacerlo otra vez *or* de nuevo, tuve que volver a hacerlo; **I've told you time and time ~** *o* **~ and ~!** ¡te lo he dicho mil veces *or* una y otra vez!; **I'll never speak to you ~** no te vuelvo a hablar en la vida; **never ~!** ¡nunca más!, ¡(es) la última vez!; **not ~!** ¡otra vez!

B (in comparisons): **I'd like as much ~** quisiera otro tanto

C **(then** *o* **there) again** (on the other hand) (*as linker*): **they might go, but (then) ~ they might not** puede que vayan, pero también puede que no; **(there) ~, what do they know about art?** además *or* por otro lado ¿ellos qué saben de arte?

against¹ /ə'genst, ə'geɪnst/ *prep*

A (in opposition to) en contra de, contra; **personally, I've nothing ~ her** personalmente, no tengo nada contra ella *or* en contra suya *or* en contra de ella; **have you got something ~ going by train?** ¿tienes algún problema en ir en tren?; **he succeeded ~ all expectations** contrariamente a lo que se esperaba, lo logró

B (in opposite direction) contra; **~ the current** contra la corriente

C [1] (alongside) contra; **the table stood ~ the wall** la mesa

a

estaba contra la pared; **they checked the list ~ the original** cotejaron la lista con el original; **he put a cross ~ my name** puso una cruz al lado de mi nombre [2] (on, onto) contra; **to lean ~ sth** apoyarse contra algo

D [1] (in contrast to) contra; **it stands out ~ the dark background** resalta contra el fondo oscuro [2] (in relation to): **the pound dropped to a new low ~ the dollar** la libra registró un nuevo mínimo frente al dólar

E (as protection from) contra; **it's insured ~ theft** está asegurado contra robo

against² *adv* en contra

agate /'ægət/ *n* [u c] ágata *f*

age¹ /eɪdʒ/ *n*

A [c u] (of person, animal, thing) edad *f*; **what ~ was she when she died?** ¿qué edad *or* cuántos años tenía cuando murió?; **at the ~ of 17** a la edad de *or* a los 17 años; **from an early ~** desde pequeño, desde temprana edad (liter); **when you're my ~** cuando tengas mi edad *or* mis años; **I have a son your ~** tengo un hijo de tu edad; **he is six years of ~** tiene seis años; **he's starting to look his ~** se le están empezando a notar los años; **to act one's ~**: **it's time he acted his ~** ya es hora de que siente cabeza *or* de que empiece a actuar con madurez; (*before n*) **~ discrimination** discriminación *f* por razones de edad; **~ group** grupo *m* etario (frml); **the 12 to 15 ~ group** el grupo de edades comprendidas entre los 12 y los 15 años; **~ limit** límite *m* de edad

B [u] (maturity): **to be of/under ~** ser* mayor/menor de edad; **to come of ~** llegar* a la mayoría de edad

C [c] [1] (epoch, period) era *f*; **down** *o* **through the ~s** a través de los tiempos [2] (long time) (colloq): **I've been waiting ~s** *o* **an ~** llevo siglos *or* un siglo esperando (fam); **I haven't seen her for ~s** hace siglos que no la veo (fam)

age² (*pres p* **aging** *or* **ageing**; *past p* **aged** /eɪdʒd/) *vi* ⟨⟨*person*⟩⟩ envejecer*; ⟨⟨*cheese*⟩⟩ madurar; **this wine ~s well** este vino se conserva muy bien

■ **age** *vt* ⟨*person*⟩ hacer* envejecer, avejentar; ⟨*wine*⟩ añejar, criar*

aged¹ *adj*

A /'eɪdʒəd || 'eɪdʒɪd/ (elderly) anciano

B /eɪdʒd/ (*pred*): **he was ~ 20** tenía 20 años de edad; **she died ~ 60** murió a los 60 años

aged² /'eɪdʒəd || 'eɪdʒɪd/ *pl n* **the ~** los ancianos, las personas de la tercera edad (frml)

ageing *adj/n* ▸ **aging**

ageism /'eɪdʒɪzəm/ *n* [u] discriminación *f* por razones de edad

ageist /'eɪdʒɪst/ *adj* discriminatorio por motivo de edad

ageless /'eɪdʒləs || 'eɪdʒlɪs/ *adj* ⟨*man/woman*⟩ eternamente joven, por el/la que no pasan los años; ⟨*beauty*⟩ clásico

agency /'eɪdʒənsi/ *n* (*pl* **-cies**)

A [c] [1] (office) agencia *f* [2] (branch) sucursal *f*, filial *f* [3] (department) organismo *m*

B [u] (means): **through the ~ of friends** a través de *or* por medio de amigos

agenda /ə'dʒendə/ *n* orden *m* del día, agenda *f*

agent /'eɪdʒənt/ *n*

A [c] [1] (for person) agente *mf*; **you're a free ~** eres libre *or* tienes total libertad (de hacer lo que quieras) [2] (for company — person) agente *mf*, representante *mf*; (— firm) agencia *f* [3] (government officer in US) agente *mf*

B [c] (spy) agente *mf*

C [c u] (substance) agente *m*

age-old /'eɪdʒ'əʊld/ *adj* añejo, antiquísimo

agglomeration /ə'glɑːmə'reɪʃən || ə,glɒmə'reɪʃən/ *n* aglomeración *f*

aggravate /'ægrəveɪt/ *vt* [1] (make worse) agravar, empeorar [2] (annoy) (colloq) exasperar, sacar* de quicio

aggravating /'ægrəveɪtɪŋ/ *adj* (colloq) ⟨*manner/noise*⟩ enervante (fam)

aggravation /'ægrə'veɪʃən/ *n* [1] [u] (of situation, illness) empeoramiento *m* [2] [u c] (annoyance) (colloq) fastidio *m*

aggregate /'ægrɪgət/ *n* [u] (whole, total) (frml) total *m*; **to win/lose on ~** (in soccer) ganar/perder* por puntos

aggression /ə'greʃən/ *n* [1] [u] (feeling, attitude) agresividad *f* [2] [c] (unprovoked attack) agresión *f*

aggressive /ə'gresɪv/ *adj* [1] (hostile) ⟨*person/country*⟩ agresivo; ⟨*tactics/strategy*⟩ de agresión [2] (assertive, forceful) con empuje y dinamismo, agresivo

aggressively /ə'gresɪvli/ *adv* [1] ⟨*behave/react/play*⟩ agresivamente [2] ⟨*sell*⟩ con empuje y dinamismo

aggressiveness /ə'gresɪvnəs || ə'gresɪvnɪs/ *n* [u] agresividad *f*

aggressor /ə'gresər || ə'gresə(r)/ *n* agresor, -sora *m,f*

aggrieved /ə'griːvd/ *adj* ⟨*air/tone*⟩ ofendido; **to be ~ AT/ABOUT/OVER sth** sentirse* herido POR algo

aggro /'ægrəʊ/ *n* [u] (BrE sl) [1] (fighting) bronca *f* (fam) [2] (annoyance) lata *f* (fam)

aghast /ə'gæst || ə'gɑːst/ *adj* (*pred*) aterrado, horrorizado; **to be ~ AT sth**: **we were ~ at the very thought** sólo pensarlo nos aterraba *or* horrorizaba

agile /'ædʒəl || 'ædʒaɪl/ *adj* ágil

agility /ə'dʒɪləti/ *n* [u] agilidad *f*

aging¹ /'eɪdʒɪŋ/ *adj* (*before n*) ⟨*person*⟩ envejecido, avejentado

aging² *n* [u] envejecimiento *m*; (*before n*) **the ~ process** el (proceso de) envejecimiento

agitate /'ædʒəteɪt || 'ædʒɪteɪt/ *vt* [1] (disturb) ⟨*surface/liquid*⟩ agitar [2] (upset) inquietar

■ **agitate** *vi* **to ~ FOR/AGAINST sth** hacer* campaña A FAVOR DE/EN CONTRA DE algo

agitated /'ædʒəteɪtəd || 'ædʒɪteɪtɪd/ *adj* ⟨*movements/gestures*⟩ nervioso, agitado; **to become/get ~** ponerse* nervioso, inquietarse

agitation /'ædʒə'teɪʃən || ,ædʒɪ'teɪʃən/ *n* [u] agitación *f*

agitator /'ædʒəteɪtər || 'ædʒɪteɪtə(r)/ *n* (Pol) agitador, -dora *m,f*

AGM *n* (BrE) = **annual general meeting**

agnostic¹ /æg'nɑːstɪk || æg'nɒstɪk/ *n* agnóstico, -ca *m,f*

agnostic² *adj* agnóstico

ago /ə'gəʊ/ *adv*: **five days ~** hace cinco días; **a long time ~** hace mucho (tiempo); **how long ~ was it that you wrote to him?** ¿cuánto (tiempo) hace que le escribiste?; **as long ~ as 1960** ya en 1960

agog /ə'gɑːg || ə'gɒg/ *adj* (*pred*): **I was all ~** estaba que me moría de curiosidad

agonize /'ægənaɪz/ *vi*: **stop agonizing, just do it** no le des más vueltas al asunto y hazlo; **to ~ OVER sth**: **he ~d over the decision** le costó muchísimo decidirse

agonized /'ægənaɪzd/ *adj* ⟨*expression*⟩ de angustia

agonizing /'ægənaɪzɪŋ/ *adj* ⟨*experience*⟩ angustioso, desesperante; ⟨*pain*⟩ atroz, terrible; ⟨*decision*⟩ muy difícil

agonizingly /'ægənaɪzɪŋli/ *adv* ⟨*painful*⟩ terriblemente; ⟨*slow*⟩ exasperantemente

agony /'ægəni/ *n* [u c] (*pl* **-nies**) [1] (pain): **he was in ~** estaba desesperado de dolor; **these shoes are absolute ~** estos zapatos me están matando [2] (anxiety): **she's going through agonies of doubt** las dudas la están atormentando *or* martirizando; **to prolong the ~** alargar* el martirio

agoraphobia /'ægərə'fəʊbiə/ *n* agorafobia *f*

agoraphobic /'ægərə'fəʊbɪk/ *adj* agorafóbico

agree /ə'griː/ *vt*

A [1] (be in agreement over) **to ~ (THAT)** estar* de acuerdo (EN QUE); **yes, it must feel odd, he ~d** —sí, debe resultar extraño —asintió [2] (reach agreement over) decidir; **it was ~d that he should go on his own** se decidió que fuera él solo; **to ~ WHEN/WHAT/HOW** *etc* ponerse* de acuerdo EN CUÁNDO/EN QUÉ/EN CÓMO *etc*; **to ~ to + INF** quedar EN + INF; **they ~d to meet at six** quedaron en encontrarse a las seis; **let's ~ to differ** *o* **disagree, shall we?** no vale la pena discutir: ni tú me vas a convencer a mí ni yo a ti [3] (decide on) ⟨*price*⟩ acordar*

B (admit, concede) **to ~ (THAT)** reconocer* *or* admitir *or* aceptar (QUE)

■ **agree** *vi*

A (be of same opinion) estar* de acuerdo; **I couldn't ~ more** estoy completamente de acuerdo; **don't you ~?** ¿no te parece?, ¿no crees?; **to ~ ABOUT sth** estar* de acuerdo *or* coincidir EN algo; **to ~ WITH sb/sth** estar* de acuerdo CON algn/algo

B [1] (get on well) congeniar [2] (tally) ⟨⟨*statements/figures*⟩⟩ **to ~ (WITH sth)** concordar* (CON algo)

Phrasal verbs

- **agree on** [v ▸ prep ▸ o] ‹*date/details*› acordar*, ponerse* de acuerdo en; **one thing we ~ on is ...** en lo que estamos de acuerdo *or* coincidimos es en que ...
- **agree to** [v ▸ prep ▸ o] (consent to) ‹*terms/conditions*› aceptar; **they wanted to get married, but their parents wouldn't ~ to it** se querían casar, pero sus padres no lo consentían
- **agree with** [v ▸ prep ▸ o] 1 ‹‹*food/drink/climate*››: **wine doesn't ~ with him** el vino le sienta mal *or* no le sienta bien; **the heat didn't ~ with me** el calor no me sentaba 2 (approve of) estar* de acuerdo con, aprobar*

agreeable /ə'gri:əbəl/ *adj*
A (pleasant) agradable
B (*pred*) 1 (willing) **to be ~ TO sth/-ING: bring her along, if she's ~** tráela, si quiere venir; **he seemed quite ~ to coming** parecía dispuesto a venir 2 (acceptable) **to be ~ (TO sb): if that's ~ to you** si te parece bien, si no te importa

agreeably /ə'gri:əbli/ *adv* agradablemente

agreed /ə'gri:d/ *adj* 1 (in agreement) (*pred*) de acuerdo; **to be ~ ON sth: we're all ~ on that point** en eso *or* sobre ese punto estamos todos de acuerdo; **we're ~ on leaving tomorrow** quedamos en salir *or* en que saldremos mañana; **to be ~ THAT** estar* de acuerdo EN QUE 2 (prearranged)(*before n*) ‹*price/terms*› acordado; **we met at ten, as ~** nos encontramos a las diez como habíamos quedado *or* acordado

agreement /ə'gri:mənt/ *n*
A 1 [u] (shared opinion) acuerdo *m*; **to be in ~ (with sb)** estar* de acuerdo (con algn); **she nodded in ~** asintió con la cabeza 2 [c] (written arrangement) acuerdo *m*; (Busn) contrato *m*; (Lab Rel) convenio *m*, acuerdo *m*; **to come to** *o* **reach an ~ (with sb)** llegar* a un acuerdo (con algn); **to enter into an ~** aceptar los términos de un acuerdo
B [u] (consent) consentimiento *m*
C [u] (harmony, concord): **to be in ~ (with sth)** concordar* *or* estar* en concordancia (con algo)

agribusiness /'ægrə,bɪznəs || 'ægrɪ,bɪznɪs/ *n* industria *f* agropecuaria, agroindustria *f*

agrichemical /,ægrə'kemɪkəl || ,ægrɪ'kemɪkəl/ *adj* agroquímico

agricultural /'ægrɪ'kʌltʃərəl/ *adj* agrícola; **~ college** ≈ escuela *f* de agricultura *or* de agronomía

agricultural engineering *n* [u] ingeniería *f* agrícola

agriculture /'ægrɪkʌltʃər || 'ægrɪkʌltʃə(r)/ *n* [u] agricultura *f*

agrobusiness /'ægrəʊ,bɪznəs || 'ægrəʊ,bɪznɪs/ *n* [u c] ▸**agribusiness**

agronomy /ə'grɑ:nəmi || ə'grɒnəmi/ *n* [u] agronomía *f*

aground /ə'graʊnd/ *adv*: **to go** *o* **run ~ (ON sth)** encallar (EN algo)

aha /ɑ:'hɑ:/ *interj* ¡ajá!

ahead /ə'hed/ *adv*
A 1 (indicating movement): **go straight ~** siga todo recto *or* derecho; **I'll go on ~** yo iré delante *or* adelante; **full speed** *o* **steam ~!** (Naut) ¡avante a toda máquina! 2 (indicating position): **the post office is straight ~** la oficina de correos está siguiendo recto 3 (in race, competition): **our team was ~** nuestro equipo llevaba la delantera; **we're only one goal ~** vamos ganando por sólo un gol; **the Japanese are way ~ in that field** los japoneses están a la cabeza en ese campo 4 (in time): **the months ~** los meses venideros, los próximos meses; *see also* **go, think** *etc* **ahead**
B **ahead of** 1 (in front of) delante de 2 (in race, competition) por delante de 3 (before): **she got there an hour ~ of him** llegó una hora antes que él; **Athens is two hours ~ of London** Atenas va dos horas por delante de Londres

ahem /ə'hem/ *interj* ¡ejem!

ahoy /ə'hɔɪ/ *interj*: **ship ~!** ¡barco a la vista!; **~ there!** ¡ah del barco!

AI *n* [u] 1 (Comput) (= **artificial intelligence**) IA 2 (Agr) = **artificial insemination**

aid¹ /eɪd/ *n* 1 [u] (assistance, support) ayuda *f*; **to come/go to sb's ~** venir*/ir* en ayuda *or* (liter) auxilio de algn 2 [u] (monetary) ayuda *f*, asistencia *f*; **a concert in ~ of ...** un concierto a beneficio de ...; **what's all this in ~ of?** (BrE colloq) ¿a qué viene todo esto? (fam) 3 [c] (apparatus, tool): **teaching ~s** material *m* didáctico; **visual ~s** soporte *m* (de material) visual

aid² *vt* ayudar; **~ed by ...** con la ayuda de ...; **to ~ and abet sb** (Law) instigar* a algn (*en la comisión de un delito*)

aide /eɪd/ *n* asesor, -sora *m,f*

-aided /'eɪdəd || 'eɪdɪd/ *suff* 1 (assisted): **computer~** asistido por computadora 2 (funded): **state~** subvencionado por el estado

aide-de-camp /'eɪddə'kɑ:m || ,eɪddə'kɒm/ *n* (*pl* **aides-de-camp** /'eɪdz-/) ayuda *m* de campo, edecán *m*

AIDS /eɪdz/ *n* [u] (= **acquired immune deficiency syndrome**) sida *m*, SIDA *m*; (*before n*) **~ virus** virus *m* del SIDA, VIH *m*

ail /eɪl/ *vt* (arch *or* journ) aquejar (frml)

ailing /'eɪlɪŋ/ *adj* ‹*person*› enfermo; ‹*industry/economy*› renqueante, aquejado de problemas

ailment /'eɪlmənt/ *n* enfermedad *f*, dolencia *f* (frml), achaque *m* (fam)

aim¹ /eɪm/ *vt* 1 **to ~ sth (AT sb/sth): he ~ed the gun at her** le apuntó con la pistola; **their missiles are ~ed at the capital** sus misiles apuntan a la capital; **she ~ed a blow at his head** intentó darle en la cabeza 2 (*usu pass*) **to be ~ed AT sb/sth/-ING: the talks were ~ed at ending the strike** las conversaciones tenían como objetivo acabar con la huelga; **the movie is ~ed at a young audience** la película está *or* va dirigida a un público joven

■ **aim** *vi* 1 (point weapon) apuntar; **to ~ AT sth/sb** apuntar(le) A algo/algn; **to ~ FOR sth** apuntar(le) A algo 2 (aspire) aspirar; **to ~ high** aspirar a mucho; **to ~ FOR sth: we must ~ for peace** nuestro objetivo debe ser la paz 3 (intend, plan) **to ~ to + INF** querer* + INF, proponerse* + INF; **we ~ to please** nuestro objetivo es satisfacer a nuestros clientes

aim² *n* 1 [c] (goal, object) objetivo *m*, propósito *m*; **her main ~ in life is to get rich** su principal objetivo es enriquecerse; **with the ~ of -ING** con la intención *or* el propósito de + INF 2 [u] (with weapon) puntería *f*; **to take ~** hacer* puntería, apuntar

aimless /'eɪmləs || 'eɪmlɪs/ *adj* ‹*wandering*› sin rumbo (fijo); ‹*existence*› sin norte

aimlessly /'eɪmləsli || 'eɪmlɪsli/ *adv* ‹*walk*› sin rumbo (fijo); ‹*live*› sin objeto, sin norte

ain't /eɪnt/ (colloq & dial) 1 **= am not** 2 **= is not** 3 **= are not** 4 **= has not** 5 **= have not**

air¹ /er || eə(r)/ *n*
A [u] aire *m*; **to get some fresh ~** tomar el fresco; **the ~ was thick with smoke** la atmósfera estaba cargada de humo; **to take to the ~** alzar* *or* levantar el vuelo; **to go by ~** ir* en avión; ***a change of ~*** un cambio de aire(s); ***to be in the ~*** (hinted at) respirarse en el ambiente; (uncertain, undecided) estar* en el aire; **revolution was in the ~** corrían vientos de revolución; **spring is in the ~** se respiran aires primaverales; ***to be up in the ~*** ‹‹*plans*›› estar* en el aire; ***to clear the ~*** ‹‹*talk/argument*›› aclarar las cosas; (lit) ‹‹*storm*›› despejar el ambiente; ***to vanish*** *o* ***disappear into thin ~*** esfumarse, desaparecer*; ***to walk on ~*** estar* *or* sentirse* en las nubes; (*before n*) ‹*route/attack*› aéreo; **~ pressure** presión *f* atmosférica
B [u] (Rad, TV): **to be on the ~** estar* en el aire; **to come** *o* **go on the ~** salir* al aire; **we go off the ~ at 12** cerramos la emisión a las 12
C 1 [c] (manner, look, atmosphere) aire *m*; **an ~ of mystery** un aire de misterio 2 **airs** *pl* (affectations) aires *mpl*; **to put on/give oneself ~s** darse* aires; **~s and graces** afectación *f*

air² *vt*
A 1 ‹*clothes/linen*› airear, orear; ‹*bed/room*› ventilar, airear 2 ‹*opinion/grievance*› manifestar*, ventilar; ‹*knowledge*› hacer* alarde de
B (broadcast) (AmE) ‹*program*› transmitir, emitir

■ **air** *vi* ‹‹*clothes/sheets*›› airearse

air: **~ bag** *n* (Auto) bolsa *f* de aire; **~ base** *n* base *f* aérea; **~borne** *adj* 1 ‹*seeds/dust*› transportado por el aire; ‹*troops/units*› aerotransportado 2 (off the ground): **the plane is now ~borne** el avión ha despegado; **I realized we were ~borne** me di cuenta de que volábamos; **~bus** *n* aerobús *m*; **~-conditioned** /'erkən'dɪʃənd || 'eəkəndɪʃənd/ *adj* con aire acondicionado, climatizado;

~ **conditioner** *n* acondicionador *m* de aire; ~ **conditioning** *n* [u] aire *m* acondicionado; **~-cooled** /'er 'ku:ld || 'eəku:ld/ *adj* refrigerado por aire

aircraft /'erkræft || 'eəkrɑ:ft/ *n* (*pl* ~) avión *m*, aparato *m*

aircraft carrier *n* portaaviones *m*

air: **~crew** *n* tripulación *f* del avión (*or* aparato *etc*); **~drop** *n* suministro *m* por paracaídas; **~fare** *n* precio *m* del pasaje *or* (Esp tb) del billete de avión; **~fares are set to rise** van a subir las tarifas aéreas; **~field** *n* aeródromo *m*, campo *m* de aviación; **~foil** *n* (AmE) plano *m* aerodinámico; ~ **force** *n* (of nation) fuerza *f* aérea, ejército *m* del aire; (unit) (AmE) *división de la fuerza aérea estadounidense*; ~ **freshener** /'freʃnər || 'freʃnə(r)/ *n* ambientador *m*, desodorante *m* ambiental *or* de ambientes (CS); ~ **gun** *n* (revolver) pistola *f* de aire comprimido; (rifle) escopeta *f* *or* rifle *m* de aire comprimido; ~ **hostess** *n* azafata *f*, aeromoza *f* (AmL)

airily /'erəli || 'eərɪli/ *adv* sin darle importancia, con ligereza *or* displicencia

airing /'erɪŋ || 'eərɪŋ/ *n*: **to give sth an ~** ‹*clothes*› airear *or* orear algo; ‹*room*› ventilar *or* airear algo; ‹*issue*› ventilar algo

airing cupboard *n* (BrE) *armario para orear la ropa, donde suele estar el tanque de agua caliente*

airless /'erləs || 'eəlɪs/ *adj* ‹*room*› mal ventilado; **it was a hot, ~ day** hacía mucho calor y no corría nada el aire

air: ~ **letter** *n* aerograma *m*; **~lift** *n* puente *m* aéreo; **~line** *n* línea *f* aérea, aerolínea *f*, compañía *f* aérea; **~liner** *n* avión *m* (*de pasajeros*); **~lock** *n* (chamber) cámara *f* estanca; (in pipe) burbuja *f* de aire; **~mail** *n* [u] correo *m* aéreo; **to send sth (by) ~mail** mandar *or* enviar* algo por avión *or* por vía aérea; (*before n*) ‹*paper/envelope*› de avión; ~ **mile** *n* 1 (measurement) milla *f* aérea 2 (for frequent flyers) milla *f* aérea, punto *m* (aéreo) (Esp); ~ **pistol** *n* pistola *f* de aire comprimido; **~plane** *n* (AmE) avión *m*; ~ **pocket** *n* (Meteo) bache *m*, bolsa *f* de aire; **~port** *n* aeropuerto *m*; ~ **raid** *n* ataque *m* aéreo; (*before n*) **~-raid shelter** refugio *m* antiaéreo; ~ **rifle** *n* escopeta *f* *or* rifle *m* de aire comprimido; **~-sea rescue** /'er'si:/ *n* [c u] operación *f* de salvamento *or* rescate aeronaval; **~ship** *n* dirigible *m*, zepelín *m*; ~ **show** *n* demostración *f* de acrobacia aérea; ~ **shuttle** *n* puente *m* aéreo; **~sick** *adj*: **to be ~sick** estar* mareado (*en un avión*); **to get ~sick** marearse (*al viajar en avión*); **~sickness** *n* [u] mareo *m* (*al viajar en avión*); **~side¹** /'ersaɪd || 'eəsaɪd/ *n* [u] zona *f* de embarque (*en un aeropuerto*); **~side²** *adv* en la zona de embarque; **~space** *n* [u] espacio *m* aéreo; **~speed** *n* velocidad *f* relativa de vuelo; **~stream** *n* (Meteo) corriente *f* de aire; **~strip** *n* pista *f* de aterrizaje; **~tight** *adj* ‹*room/box*› hermético; ‹*alibi/argument*› a toda prueba; **~time** *n* [u] tiempo *m* de emisión *or* en antena; **~-to-air** /'ertə'er || ˌeətə'eə(r)/ *adj* ‹*missile/rocket*› aire-aire; **~-to-ground** /'ertə'graʊnd || ˌeətə 'graʊnd/ *adj* ‹*missile*› aire-superficie, aire-tierra; ~ **traffic** *n* [u] tráfico *m* aéreo; (*before n*) ~ **traffic control** control *m* del tráfico aéreo; ~ **traffic controller** controlador aéreo, controladora aérea *m,f*; **~waves** *pl n* **the ~waves** (Rad) la radio; (TV) la pequeña pantalla; **~worthy** *adj*: **to be ~worthy** estar* en condiciones de vuelo *or* de volar

airy /'eri || 'eəri/ *adj* **airier, airiest** 1 ‹*room/house*› espacioso y aireado 2 ‹*manner/reply*› displicente 3 (light, insubstantial) etéreo

aisle /aɪl/ *n* (gangway) pasillo *m*; (Archit) nave *f* lateral; **to lead sb up the ~** llevar a algn al altar; ***to be rolling in the ~s***: **the audience was rolling in the ~s** el público estaba muerto de risa *or* se desternillaba de risa

ajar /ə'dʒɑ:r || ə'dʒɑ:(r)/ *adj* (*pred*) entreabierto, entornado

AK = Alaska

aka (= also known as) alias

akimbo /ə'kɪmbəʊ/ *adj* (*after n*): **(with) arms ~** con los brazos en jarras

akin /ə'kɪn/ *adj* (*pred*) **to be ~ (TO sth)** ser* similar (A algo)

AL *n* 1 **= Alabama** 2 **(= American League)** *la liga estadounidense de béisbol*

Ala = Alabama

alabaster /'ælə,bæstər || 'ælə,bɑ:stə(r)/ *n* [u] alabastro *m*

à la carte /'ɑ:lə'kɑ:rt || ˌɑ:lɑ:'kɑ:t/ *adj/adv* a la carta

alacrity /ə'lækrəti/ *n* [u] (frml *or* liter) presteza *f* (liter), prontitud *f* (frml)

à la mode /'ælə'məʊd || ˌɑ:lɑ:'məʊd/ *adj* (*pred*) 1 (fashionable) (liter) de moda, al último grito 2 (AmE) (Culin) con helado

alarm¹ /ə'lɑ:rm || ə'lɑ:m/ *n*

A [u] (apprehension) gran preocupación *f*, gran inquietud *f*; **he fled in ~** huyó asustado

B [c] 1 (warning) alarma *f*; **to raise the ~** dar* la (voz de) alarma 2 (device) alarma *f*; (*burglar/fire* ~) alarma antirrobo/contra incendios 3 (clock) despertador *m*

alarm² *vt* (worry) alarmar, inquietar; (scare) asustar

alarm: ~ **bell** *n* alarma *f*; **her words set off ~ bells in his mind** lo que dijo lo puso en guardia; ~ **clock** *n* (reloj *m*) despertador *m*

alarmed /ə'lɑ:rmd || ə'lɑ:md/ *adj* (*pred*) 1 (apprehensive): **don't be ~** no te asustes; **I began to be ~** empecé a alarmarme *or* inquietarme 2 (fitted with alarm) ‹*fence/door*› con alarma; ‹*building/car*› dotado de sistema de alarma

alarming /ə'lɑ:rmɪŋ || ə'lɑ:mɪŋ/ *adj* alarmante, preocupante

alarmist¹ /ə'lɑ:rməst || ə'lɑ:mɪst/ *adj* alarmista

alarmist² *n* alarmista *mf*

alas /ə'læs/ *interj* (liter *or* frml) ¡ay! (liter); **~, he didn't come** lamentablemente no vino

Alaskan¹ /ə'læskən/ *adj* de Alaska, alaskeño

Alaskan² *n* habitante *mf* de Alaska, alaskeño, -ña *m,f*

Albania /æl'beɪniə/ *n* Albania *f*

Albanian¹ /æl'beɪniən/ *adj* albanés

Albanian² *n* 1 [c] (person) albanés, -nesa *m,f* 2 [u] (language) albanés *m*

albatross /'ælbətrɔ:s || 'ælbətrɒs/ *n* albatros *m*

albeit /ɔ:l'bi:ɪt/ *conj* (frml) si bien es cierto que (frml), aunque

albino /æl'baɪnəʊ || æl'bi:nəʊ/ *n* (*pl* **-nos**) albino, -na *m,f*; (*before n*) albino

album /'ælbəm/ *n* 1 (book) álbum *m*; **photograph ~** álbum de fotos 2 (Audio) álbum *m*

albumen /æl'bju:mən || 'ælbjʊmən/ *n* [u] 1 (egg white) clara *f* (de huevo) 2 (Chem) albúmina *f* 3 (Bot) albumen *m*

alchemist /'ælkəməst || 'ælkəmɪst/ *n* alquimista *mf*

alchemy /'ælkəmi/ *n* [u] alquimia *f*

alcohol /'ælkəhɔ:l || 'ælkəhɒl/ *n* [u] alcohol *m*

alcoholic¹ /'ælkə'hɔ:lɪk || ˌælkə'hɒlɪk/ *adj* alcohólico

alcoholic² *n* alcohólico, -ca *m,f*

alcoholism /'ælkəhɔ:lɪzəm / *n* [u] alcoholismo *m*

alcove /'ælkəʊv/ *n* (recess) hueco *m*; (niche) hornacina *f*, nicho *m*

alderman /'ɔ:ldərmən || 'ɔ:ldəmən/ *n* (*pl* **-men** /-mən/) 1 (in US) concejal *m* 2 (in UK) (Hist) regidor, -dora *m,f*

alderwoman /'ɔ:ldər,wʊmən || 'ɔ:ldə,wʊmən/ *n* (*pl* **-women**) (in US) concejala *f*

ale /eɪl/ *n* [u c] cerveza *f*

alert¹ /ə'lɜ:rt || ə'lɜ:t/ *adj* alerta *adj inv*; **to be ~** (vigilant) estar* alerta; (lively-minded) ser* despierto; **to stay ~** mantenerse* alerta *or* en guardia; **to be ~ TO sth** estar* atento A algo

alert² *n* alerta *f*; **to put sb on the ~** poner* a algn en guardia, alertar a algn; **be on the ~ for any suspicious visitors** estáte alerta *or* al tanto por si viene alguien sospechoso

alert³ *vt* ‹*police*› alertar, poner* sobre aviso; **to ~ sb TO sth** alertar a algn DE algo, poner* a algn sobre aviso DE algo

A level *n* (in UK) *estudios de una asignatura a nivel de bachillerato superior*

> **A level – Advanced level**
>
> Es el término genérico para referirse a los exámenes que hacen los estudiantes que desean acceder a la enseñanza superior. En el sistema reformado, el examen se divide en dos partes: *AS level* y *A2*. Por lo general los estudiantes hacen el *A2* en el último año de la enseñanza secundaria para así completar íntegramente el programa del *A level*.
>
> Las universidades u otras instituciones seleccionan a los alumnos en razón de las calificaciones que hayan obtenido, especialmente en aquellas materias que tienen relación directa con el área de estudio terciario que se ha elegido. *Ver tb* **AS level**

alfresco /æl'freskəʊ/ *adj/adv* al aire libre

alga /'ælgə/ *n* (*pl* **algae** /'ældʒiː, 'ælgiː/) alga *f*‡

algebra /'ældʒəbrə || 'ældʒɪbrə/ *n* [u] álgebra *f*‡

Algeria /æl'dʒɪriə || æl'dʒɪəriə/ *n* Argelia *f*

Algerian¹ /æl'dʒɪriən || æl'dʒɪəriən/ *adj* argelino

Algerian² *n* argelino, -na *m,f*

Algiers /æl'dʒɪrz || æl'dʒɪəz/ *n* Argel *m*

alias¹ /'eɪliəs/ *adv* alias

alias² *n* alias *m*, nombre *m* falso

alibi /'æləbaɪ || 'ælɪbaɪ/ *n* (Law) coartada *f*

alien¹ /'eɪliən/ *n* 1 (foreigner) extranjero, -ra *m,f*; **illegal ~** inmigrante *mf* ilegal 2 (in science fiction) extraterrestre *mf*

alien² *adj* 1 (strange, foreign) extraño, foráneo; **to be ~ TO sb/sth** serle* ajeno A algn/algo 2 (of foreign power) (*before n*) ‹*passport/airspace*› extranjero 3 (in science fiction) (*before n*) extraterrestre

alienate /'eɪliəneɪt/ *vt* (Pol, Psych) alienar; (estrange): **this has ~d all his friends** esto ha hecho que todos sus amigos se alejen *or* se distancien de él; **to ~ sb FROM sb/sth** alejar a algn DE algn/algo; **to ~ oneself from sb/sth** alejarse *or* distanciarse de algn/algo

alienated /'eɪliəneɪtəd || 'eɪliəneɪtɪd/ *adj* alienado

alienation /'eɪliə'neɪʃən/ *n* [u] (Pol, Psych) alienación *f*; (estrangement) **~ (FROM sb)** alejamiento *m* *or* distanciamiento *m* (DE algn)

alight¹ /ə'laɪt/ *adj* (*pred*) **to be ~** estar* ardiendo; **to set sth ~** prender(le) fuego a algo

alight² *vi* (frml) 1 (disembark) apearse (frml), descender* (frml) 2 (land) «*bird/insect*» posarse

(Phrasal verb)

- **alight on** [v ▸ prep ▸ o] (find by chance) (liter) ‹*solution/method*› dar* con, encontrar*

align /ə'laɪn/ *vt* alinear; **they ~ed themselves with the left** se alinearon con la izquierda

alignment /ə'laɪnmənt/ *n* 1 [u] (Tech) alineación *f*; **to be out of/in ~** no estar*/estar* alineado 2 [c u] (Pol) **~ (WITH sb/sth)** alineamiento *m* (CON algn/algo)

alike¹ /ə'laɪk/ *adj* (*pred*) parecido; **they don't look ~** no se parecen *or* no son parecidos; **you men are all ~!** ¡los hombres son *or* (Esp) sois todos iguales!

alike² *adv* ‹*think/act*› igual, del mismo modo; **popular with young and old ~** popular tanto entre los jóvenes como entre los mayores

alimentary /'ælə'mentəri || ˌælɪ'mentəri/ *adj* (*before n*) alimenticio; **~ canal** *o* **tract** tubo *m* digestivo

alimony /'æləməʊni || 'ælɪməni/ *n* [u] pensión *f* alimenticia

alive /ə'laɪv/ *adj* (*pred*) 1 (living) vivo; **is he still ~?** ¿todavía vive *or* está vivo?; **to stay ~** sobrevivir; **it's great to be ~!** ¡qué maravilloso es vivir!; **the richest man ~** el hombre más rico del mundo; **to bury sb ~** enterrar* vivo a algn; **~ and kicking** (colloq) vivito y coleando (fam); **they were relieved to learn that she was ~ and well** se enteraron con alivio de que estaba sana y salva 2 (animated): **the party came ~ when they arrived** la fiesta se animó cuando llegaron ellos; **the place is ~ with insects** el lugar está plagado de insectos 3 (active, in existence): **to keep sth ~** ‹*tradition/memory*› mantener* vivo algo 4 (aware) **to be ~ TO sth** ‹*to problem/possibility*› ser* sensible A algo, ser* *or* (Chi, Méx) estar* consciente DE algo

alkali /'ælkəlaɪ/ *n* (*pl* **-lis**) álcali *m*

alkaline /'ælkəlaɪn/ *adj* alcalino

all¹ /ɔːl/ *adj*

A (*before n*) todo, -da; (*pl*) todos, -das; **~ those present** todos los presentes; **~ good teachers know it** todo buen profesor lo sabe; **~ four of us went** fuimos los cuatro; **~ kinds** *o* **sorts of people** todo tipo de gente; **~ morning** toda la mañana, la mañana entera; **what's ~ this we hear about you leaving?** ¿qué es eso de que te vas?; **of ~ the stupid things to do!** ¡qué estupidez!; **I might as well not bother for ~ the notice he takes** para el caso que me hace, más vale que ni me moleste; **it isn't as bad as ~ that** no es para tanto; **he's not ~ that rich** tan rico no es; **we were dabbling in drink, drugs and ~ that** flirteábamos con la bebida, las drogas y todo eso *or* y todo lo demás; *see also* **all³ C4**

B 1 (the greatest possible): **in ~ innocence** con toda inocencia; **with ~ possible care** con el mayor cuidado posible 2 (any): **beyond ~ doubt** fuera de toda duda; **they denied ~ knowledge of it** negaron tener conocimiento alguno de ello

all² *pron*

A (everything) (+ *sing vb*) todo; **~ I can say is ...** todo lo que puedo decir es ..., lo único que puedo decir es ...; **will that be ~, madam?** ¿algo más señora?, ¿eso es todo, señora?; **they did ~ they could** hicieron todo lo que pudieron; **it was ~ I could do to stop him from hitting her** apenas pude impedir que le pegara; **~ in good time** todo a su debido tiempo, cada cosa a su tiempo; **when ~ is said and done** a fin de cuentas; **for ~ I care** por lo que a mí me importa; **for ~ I know** que yo sepa

B 1 (everyone) (+ *pl vb*) todos, -das; **~ together now** ahora todos juntos 2 (*with superl*): **she is the cleverest of ~** es la más inteligente de todos/todas; **I don't intend to tell anyone, least of ~ her!** no pienso decírselo a nadie y a ella menos todavía

C **all of**: **now that ~ of the children go to school** ahora que todos los niños van al colegio; **~ of the cheese** todo el queso; **it took ~ of 20 years to complete it** se tardó 20 años enteros en acabarlo

D (*after n, pron*) todo, -da; (*pl*) todos, -das; **she helped us ~** nos ayudó a todos; **it was ~ gone** no quedaba nada; **the unfairness of it ~** la injusticia del caso *or* del asunto; **now I've seen it ~!** ¡vivir para ver!; **that says it ~** eso ya te lo dice todo

E (*in phrases*) 1 **all in all** en general 2 **all told** en total 3 **and all** y todo; **he ate it, skin and ~** se lo comió con la cáscara y todo 4 **at all**: **they don't like him at ~** no les gusta nada; **I'm not at ~ worried** *o* **worried at ~** no estoy preocupada en absoluto, no estoy para nada preocupada; **thank you — not at ~** gracias — de nada *or* no hay de qué; **she didn't feel at ~ well** no se sentía nada bien; **it's not bad at ~, it's not at ~ bad** no está nada mal; **they'll come late, if they come at ~** vendrán tarde, si es que vienen; **if (it's) at ~ possible** si fuera posible 5 **in all** en total

all³ *adv*

A (completely): **there were flags ~ along the road** había banderas todo a lo largo del camino; **~ through the ceremony** durante toda la ceremonia; **you've gone ~ red** te has puesto todo colorado/toda colorada; **she was ~ alone** estaba completamente sola; **I got ~ wet** me mojé todo/toda; **I'm ~ ears** soy todo/toda oídos; **he won ~ the same** igual ganó; **it's ~ the same to me** a mí me da igual *or* lo mismo

B (each, apiece) (Sport): **the score was one ~** iban (empatados) uno a uno; **30 ~** 30 iguales

C (*in phrases*) 1 **all along** desde el primer momento 2 **all but** casi; **the game had ~ but finished** prácticamente *or* ya casi había terminado el partido 3 **all for**: **to be ~ for sth**: **I'm ~ for sex education** estoy totalmente a favor de la educación sexual 4 **all that** (particularly) (*usu neg*): **I don't know her ~ that well** no la conozco tan bien; **I don't care ~ that much** no me importa demasiado 5 **all the** (+ *comp*): **it is ~ the more remarkable if you consider ...** resulta aún *or* todavía más extraordinario si se tiene en cuenta ...; **~ the more reason to fire them!** ¡más razón para echarlos!; **~ the more so because ...** tanto más cuanto que ...; *see also* **all out**

all⁴ *n*: ***to give one's ~*** (make supreme effort) dar* todo de sí; (sacrifice everything) darlo* todo, dar* todo lo que se tiene

all- /ɔ:l/ *pref*: **~wool** de pura lana; **with an ~Spanish cast** con un reparto integrado exclusivamente por españoles; *see also* **all-consuming, all-important** *etc*

Allah /'ælə/ *n* Alá

all-American¹ /'ɔ:lə'merəkən || ˌɔ:lə'merɪkən/ *adj* ‹*boy/girl*› típicamente americano

all-American² *n* (Sport) atleta *mf* (*or* jugador *etc*) de clase internacional

all-around /'ɔ:lə'raʊnd/ *adj* (AmE) (*before n*) [1] (versatile) ‹*athlete/scholar*› completo [2] (comprehensive) ‹*experience/visibility*› amplio

allay /ə'leɪ/ *vt* ‹*doubt/fear*› disipar; ‹*anger*› aplacar*

all: **~-clear** /'ɔ:l'klɪr || 'ɔ:l'klɪə(r)/ *n*: **to give sb/sth the ~-clear** dar* luz verde a algn/algo; **~-consuming** /'ɔ:lkən'su:mɪŋ || 'ɔ:lkən'sju:mɪŋ/ *adj* ‹*passion*› devorador

allegation /'ælɪ'geɪʃən/ *n* acusación *f*, imputación *f* (frml); **to make an ~** hacer* una acusación

allege /ə'ledʒ/ *vt* (state) afirmar; **she is ~d to have accepted bribes** se dice que aceptó sobornos

alleged /ə'ledʒd/ *adj* (*before n*) ‹*thief/violation*› presunto

allegedly /ə'ledʒədli || ə'ledʒɪdli/ *adv* (*indep*) supuestamente, según se dice; **she ~ visited him that morning** supuestamente *or* según se dice lo habría visitado esa mañana

allegiance /ə'li:dʒəns/ *n* [u c] lealtad *f*; **political ~s** filiaciones *fpl* políticas

allegorical /'ælə'gɔ:rɪkəl || ˌælɪ'gɒrɪkəl/ *adj* alegórico

allegory /'æləgɔ:ri || 'ælɪgəri/ *n* [c u] (*pl* **-ries**) alegoría *f*

all-embracing /'ɔ:lɪm'breɪsɪŋ/ *adj* ‹*love/knowledge*› que todo lo abarca

allergen /'ælərdʒən || 'ælədʒən/ *n* alérgeno *m*

allergic /ə'lɜ:rdʒɪk || ə'lɜ:dʒɪk/ *adj* alérgico; **to be ~ TO sth** ser* alérgico A algo

allergy /'ælərdʒi || 'ælədʒi/ *n* (*pl* **-gies**) **~ (TO sth)** alergia *f* (A algo)

alleviate /ə'li:vieɪt/ *vt* ‹*pain*› aliviar, calmar; ‹*problem*› paliar

alleviation /ə'li:vi'eɪʃən/ *n* [u] (of pain) alivio *m*; (of problem) paliación *f*

alley /'æli/ *n* (*pl* **alleys**) [1] (lane) callejón *m*; ***to be right up sb's ~*** (AmE colloq): **the job was right up her ~** era un trabajo ideal para ella [2] (*bowling ~*) (lane) pista *f*; (building) bolera *f*

alley: **~ cat** *n* gato *m* callejero; **~way** *n* callejón *m*

alliance /ə'laɪəns/ *n* alianza *f*; (of political parties, countries) coalición *f*, alianza *f*; **to enter into** *o* **form an ~** aliarse*, formar una alianza

allied /'ælaɪd/ *adj*

A (combined) (*pred*) **~ WITH** *o* **TO sth** unido *or* sumado A algo

B [1] ‹*nations/groups*› aliado [2] **Allied** (of the Allies) aliado

C (related) ‹*subjects/industries*› relacionado, afín; **to be ~ TO sth** estar* relacionado CON algo, ser* afín A algo

alligator /'æləgeɪtər || 'ælɪgeɪtə(r)/ *n* [c] aligátor *m*, caimán *m*

alligator pear *n* (AmE) ▸**avocado**

all: **~-important** /'ɔ:lɪm'pɔ:rtn̩t || ˌɔ:lɪm'pɔ:tn̩t/ *adj* de suma *or* fundamental importancia, importantísimo; **~ in** *adj* (*pred*) (colloq) (*pred*) **to be ~ in** estar* molido (fam), estar* hecho polvo (fam); **~-in** /'ɔ:l'ɪn/ *adj* (esp BrE) (*before n*) [1] (Sport) **~-in wrestling** lucha *f* libre [2] (inclusive) ‹*price*› total, con todo incluido; **~-inclusive** /'ɔ:lɪn'klu:sɪv/ *adj* ‹*price*› total, con todo incluido

alliteration /ə'lɪtə'reɪʃən/ *n* [u] aliteración *f*

all-night /'ɔ:l'naɪt/ *adj* ‹*party/show*› que dura toda la noche; ‹*café/store*› que está abierto toda la noche

allocate /'æləkeɪt/ *vt* (give) ‹*seats/resources*› asignar, adjudicar*; ‹*task/duty*› asignar; (distribute) repartir, distribuir*; **within the time ~d** dentro del plazo concedido *or* establecido; **to ~ sth TO sb** asignarle algo A algn; **£3 million has been ~d for** *o* **to research** se han destinado tres millones de libras a investigación

allocation /'ælə'keɪʃən/ *n* [1] [u] (distribution) reparto *m*, distribución *f*; (assignment) asignación *f* [2] [c] (amount) asignación *f*

allot /ə'lɑ:t || ə'lɒt/ *vt* **-tt-** (distribute) repartir, distribuir*; (assign) asignar; **to ~ sth TO sb** asignarle algo A algn

allotment /ə'lɑ:tmənt || ə'lɒtmənt/ *n* [c] (in UK) (Hort) huerto *m* (*que el ayuntamiento alquila a particulares*)

all: **~out** /'ɔ:l'aʊt/ *adj* ‹*effort*› total, supremo; ‹*attack*› con todo; ‹*opposition*› acérrimo; ‹*strike*› general; ‹*war*› total; **~ out** *adv*: **they worked ~ out to finish it** trabajaron a destajo *or* a toda máquina para terminarlo; **~ over** *adv* [1] (everywhere): **I've been looking for you ~ over** te he estado buscando por todas partes; **people come from ~ over** viene gente de todas partes [2] (in every respect): **that's her ~ over** es muy típico de ella

allow /ə'laʊ/ *vt*

A [1] (permit) permitir; **smoking is not ~ed** no se permite fumar; Ⓢ **no dogs allowed** no se admiten perros; **to ~ sb to + INF** permitirle A algn + INF/QUE (+ *subj*); **they were ~ed out once a week** se les permitía salir una vez por semana; **I can't go, I'm not ~ed** no puedo ir, no me dejan [2] (give, grant) dar*; **they are ~ed an hour for lunch** les dan una hora para comer; **within the time ~ed** dentro del plazo concedido

B (plan for): **~ (yourselves) a good two hours to reach the coast** calculen *or* tengan en cuenta que les va a llevar por lo menos dos horas llegar a la costa; **~ two weeks for delivery** la entrega se hará dentro de un plazo de dos semanas; **I generally ~ about £50 for spending money** normalmente calculo unas 50 libras para gastos

C (Sport) «*referee*» ‹*goal*› dar* por bueno

Phrasal verb

• **allow for** [v ▸ prep ▸ o] ‹*contingency*› tener* en cuenta; **don't forget to ~ for leakage** no te olvides de dejar un margen para pérdidas

allowable /ə'laʊəbəl/ *adj* ‹*expense*› deducible

allowance /ə'laʊəns/ *n*

A [1] (from employer) complemento *m*, sobresueldo *m* [2] (from state) prestación *f* [3] (private) asignación *f*; (from parents) mensualidad *f*, mesada *f* (AmL)

B **to make ~(s) for sb/sth**: **you have to make ~s for him: he's very young** tienes que ser indulgente con él, es muy joven; **we've made ~(s) for delays** hemos tenido en cuenta posibles retrasos

alloy /'ælɔɪ/ *n* aleación *f*

all: **~-powerful** /'ɔ:l'paʊərfəl || ˌɔ:l'paʊəfəl/ *adj* todopoderoso, omnipotente; **~-purpose** /'ɔ:l'pɜ:rpəs || ˌɔ:l'pɜ:pəs/ *adj* ‹*knife/bag*› multiuso *adj inv*

all right¹ *adj* (*pred*)

A [1] (good enough, unobjectionable): **the weather was ~ ~** hizo buen tiempo; **the hotel looks ~ ~** el hotel no parece estar mal; **do I look ~ ~ in this dress?** ¿estoy bien con este vestido?; **the movie was all right but ...** la película no estuvo mal pero ... [2] (permissible): **I'll pay you back tomorrow: is that ~ ~?** mañana te devuelvo el dinero ¿okey? *or* (Esp) ¿vale?; **would Monday be ~ ~ (for you)?** ¿te viene bien el lunes?; **I'm sorry — that's ~ ~** lo siento — no tiene importancia; **I'll leave early today, if that's ~ ~** si no te importa, hoy me voy a ir temprano; **is it ~ ~ to swim here?** ¿se puede nadar aquí?; **to be ~ ~ WITH** *o* **BY sb**: **we'll meet on Friday, if that's ~ ~ with everybody** nos reuniremos el viernes, si nadie tiene ningún inconveniente

B [1] (well) bien; **are you ~ ~?** ¿estás bien?; **I'll be ~ ~ in a minute** enseguida se me pasa; **~ ~?** (as greeting) (colloq) ¿qué tal? (fam) [2] (in order) bien; **the brakes are ~ ~** los frenos están bien [3] (safe): **will the bikes be ~ ~ here?** ¿podemos dejar las bicis aquí? ¿no les pasará nada?; **it's ~ ~: I'm not going to hurt you** tranquilo, que no te voy a hacer daño [4] (content): **are you ~ ~ in that chair?** ¿estás bien en esa silla?; **are you ~ ~ for cash?** ¿qué tal andas de dinero? (fam); **are they ~ ~ for blankets?** ¿tienen suficientes mantas?; ▸**jack** D

all right² *adv* [1] (satisfactorily) bien; **he did ~ ~ in his exams** le fue bien en los exámenes; **we found the place ~ ~** encontramos el sitio sin problemas [2] (without a doubt) (colloq): **it's serious ~ ~** es bien grave; **yes, that's him ~ ~** sí, seguro que es él

all right³ *interj* (colloq): **I won't be home till late, ~ ~?** volveré tarde ¿okey *or* (Esp) vale? (fam); **can I come too? — all right** ¿puedo ir yo también? — bueno; **~ ~, ~ ~, I'm coming!** ¡ya voy! ¡ya voy!; **a new world record! ~ ~!** (AmE) ¡un nuevo récord mundial, sí señor!

all: **~-risk** /'ɔ:l'rɪsk/, (BrE) **~-risks** /'ɔ:l'rɪsks/ *adj* contra todo riesgo; **~-round** /'ɔ:l'raʊnd/ *adj* (esp BrE) ▸**all-**

a

around: **~-rounder** /'ɔːl'raʊndər || ˌɔːl'raʊndə(r)/ *n* (BrE Sport): **he's a good ~-rounder** juega bien en todas las posiciones; **~ Saints' Day** *n* día *m* de Todos los Santos; **~spice** *n* [u] pimienta *f* de Jamaica; **~-star** /'ɔːl'stɑːr || 'ɔːlstɑː(r)/ *adj* (*before n*): **an ~-star cast** un reparto estelar *or* de primeras figuras; **~-time** /'ɔːltaɪm/ *adj* ‹*record*› sin precedentes; ‹*favorite*› de todos los tiempos

allude /ə'luːd/ *vi* **to ~ TO sth/sb** aludir A algo/algn

allure /ə'lʊr || ə'lʊə(r)/ *n* [u] atractivo *m*, encanto *m*

alluring /ə'lʊrɪŋ || ə'lʊərɪŋ/ *adj* seductor, atrayente

allusion /ə'luːʒən/ *n* alusión *f*; **to make an ~ to sth** hacer* alusión a algo

all-weather /'ɔːl'weðər || ˌɔːl'weðə(r)/ *adj* ‹*clothing*› para todo tiempo

ally¹ /'ælaɪ/ *n* (*pl* **allies**) aliado, -da *m,f*; **the Allies** los Aliados

ally² *v refl* **allies, allying, allied**: **to ~ oneself WITH** *o* **TO sb** aliarse CON *or* A algn; *see also* **allied**

alma mater /'ælmə'mɑːtər || ˌælmə'mɑːtə(r)/ *n* (frml): **my ~ ~** mi (antigua) universidad

almanac /'ɔːlmənæk/ *n* (yearbook) anuario *m*; (calendar) almanaque *m*

almighty /ɔːl'maɪti/ *adj* **1** (all-powerful) todopoderoso; **A~ God, God A~** Dios Todopoderoso **2** (huge) ‹*bang/row*› (colloq) tremendo (fam)

Almighty *n* **the ~** el Todopoderoso

almond /'ɑːmənd/ *n* almendra *f*

almost /'ɔːlməʊst/ *adv* casi; **you ~ killed me!** ¡casi me matas!

alms /ɑːmz/ *pl n* limosnas *fpl*

aloft /ə'lɔːft || ə'lɒft/ *adv* **1** (high up) en el aire; **he held the cup ~** levantó la copa en alto **2** (Naut) en la jarcia

alone¹ /ə'ləʊn/ *adj* **1** (without others) solo; **I want to be ~ with you** quiero estar a solas contigo; **I felt all ~** me sentí muy solo **2** **to leave sth/sb ~** dejar algo/a algn en paz; ***to leave*** *o* ***let well (enough)*** **~**: **I'd leave well ~ if I were you** yo que tú no me metería (en camisa de once varas) **3** **let alone**: **I can't afford beer, let ~ champagne** no puedo comprar ni cerveza, para qué hablar de champán; **she can't sew a button on, let ~ make a dress** no sabe ni pegar un botón menos aún hacer un vestido **4** (unique) **to be ~ IN -ING**: **am I ~ in finding the novel a bore?** ¿soy la única que encuentra la novela aburrida?

alone² *adv* **1** (without others) solo; ***to go it*** **~**: **he decided to go it ~** decidió establecerse/hacerlo por su cuenta **2** (exclusively): **you and you ~ are responsible** tú eres el único responsable **3** (without addition) sólo; **their kitchen ~ is bigger than my apartment** ya sólo la cocina *or* (AmL) la cocina nomás es más grande que todo mi apartamento

along¹ /ə'lɔːŋ || ə'lɒŋ/ *adv*

A **1** (forward): **it's a bit further ~ on the right** está un poco más adelante, a mano derecha; **I was walking ~** iba caminando; *see also* **come, get, move** *etc* **along** **2** (with one): **why don't you come ~?** ¿por qué no vienes conmigo/con nosotros?; **she brought her brother ~** trajo a su hermano; **take an umbrella ~** llévate un paraguas; *see also* **sing along**

B (*in phrases*) **1** **along with** (junto) con **2** **along about** (AmE colloq): **~ about five o'clock** a eso de las cinco

along² *prep*: **we walked ~ the shore** caminamos por la playa; **all ~ the coastline** a lo largo de la costa; **a bit further ~ the road** un poco más adelante

alongside¹ /ə'lɔːŋsaɪd || ə'lɒŋsaɪd/ *prep* al lado de; **they worked ~ one another** trabajaban juntos *or* codo con codo

alongside² *adv* al costado, al lado

aloof /ə'luːf/ *adj* ‹*person/attitude*› distante

aloofness /ə'luːfnəs || ə'luːfnɪs/ *n* [u] actitud *f* distante

aloud /ə'laʊd/ *adv* en alto, en voz alta

alpaca /æl'pækə/ *n* [c u] (Tex, Zool) alpaca *f*

alpha /'ælfə/ *n* alfa *f*; (*before n*) **~ particle/ray/woman** alfa *adj inv*

alphabet /'ælfəbet/ *n* alfabeto *m*

alphabetic /'ælfə'betɪk/, **-ical** /-ɪkəl/ *adj* alfabético; **in ~ order** en *or* por orden alfabético

alphabetically /'ælfə'betɪkli/ *adv* alfabéticamente, en *or* por orden alfabético

alpine /'ælpaɪn/ *adj* **1** (of high mountains) alpino **2** **Alpine** ‹*scenery/people*› de los Alpes, alpino

Alps /ælps/ *pl n* **the ~** los Alpes

already /ɔːl'redi/ *adv* ya; **I've ~ been there, I've been there ~** ya he estado allí, ya estuve allí (AmL); **I've ~ seen** *o* (AmE also) **I ~ saw the play** ya he visto *or* (AmL tb) ya vi la obra; **they've ~ met** ya se conocen

alright /ɔːl'raɪt/ *adj/adv/interj* ▸**all right**

Alsatian /æl'seɪʃən/ *n* (esp BrE) ▸**German shepherd**

also /'ɔːlsəʊ/ *adv* **1** (as well) también **2** (moreover) (*as linker*) además

also-ran /'ɔːlsəʊˌræn/ *n* (Sport) (horse) caballo *m* no clasificado; (person) nulidad *f*

altar /'ɔːltər || 'ɔːltə(r)/ *n* altar *m*

alter /'ɔːltər || 'ɔːltə(r)/ *vt* **1** (change) ‹*text/situation*› cambiar, modificar*, alterar; ‹*garment*› arreglar **2** (castrate) (AmE colloq & euph) capar

■ **alter** *vi* cambiar

alteration /'ɔːltə'reɪʃən/ *n* [c u] (to text) cambio *m*, modificación *f*, alteración *f*; (to building) reforma *f*; (to garment) arreglo *m*; **she made major ~s to the plan** cambió radicalmente los planes

altercation /'ɔːltər'keɪʃən || ˌɔːltə'keɪʃən/ *n* altercado *m*

alter ego /'ɔːltər'iːgəʊ, -'egəʊ || ˌɔːlter'iːgəʊ, ˌæltər'egəʊ/ *n* **1** (other self) alter ego *m*, otro yo *m* **2** (intimate friend—man) amigo *m* íntimo; (— woman) amiga *f* íntima

alternate¹ /'ɔːltərnət || ɔːl'tɜːnət/ *adj* (*before n*) **1** (every second): **she works ~ Tuesdays** trabaja un martes sí y otro no; **write on ~ lines** escriba dejando un renglón por medio **2** (happening by turns) alterno **3** (AmE) ▸**alternative¹ 1**

alternate² /'ɔːltərneɪt || 'ɔːltəneɪt/ *vt* alternar

■ **alternate** *vi* alternar; **he ~d between hope and despair** oscilaba entre la esperanza y la desesperación

alternate³ /'ɔːltərnət || ɔːl'tɜːnət/ *n* (AmE) suplente *mf*

alternately /'ɔːltərnətli || ɔːl'tɜːnətli/ *adv*: **he and she take the class ~** se turnan para dar la clase

alternating /'ɔːltərneɪtɪŋ || 'ɔːltəneɪtɪŋ/ *adj* alterno

alternating current *n* [u] corriente *f* alterna

alternation /'ɔːltər'neɪʃən || ˌɔːltə'neɪʃən/ *n* [u c] alternancia *f*

alternative¹ /ɔːl'tɜːrnətɪv || ɔːl'tɜːnətɪv/ *adj* (*before n*) **1** (other): **an ~ plan/method** un plan/método diferente; **they offered her ~ accommodation** le ofrecieron alojamiento en otro sitio **2** (progressive) ‹*lifestyle/medicine*› alternativo

alternative² *n* alternativa *f*; **you have no (other) ~ but to resign** no te queda otra alternativa que dimitir; **there's no ~** no hay más remedio; **there are ~s to flying** volar no es la única forma de viajar

alternatively /ɔːl'tɜːrnətɪvli || ɔːl'tɜːnətɪvli/ *adv* (*indep*): **you can eat in the hotel or, ~, go to a restaurant** puedes comer en el hotel o bien ir a un restaurante; **~, you could stay with us** si no, te podrías quedar con nosotros

alternator /'ɔːltərneɪtər || 'ɔːl'təneɪtə(r)/ *n* alternador *m*

although /ɔːl'ðəʊ/ *conj* aunque; **~ he wasn't well, he went to work** aunque *or* a pesar de que no estaba bien, fue a trabajar

altitude /'æltətuːd || 'æltɪtjuːd/ *n* [u c] altitud *f*; (*before n*) **~ sickness** mal *m* de alturas *or* de montaña, soroche *m* (Andes)

alto¹ /'æltəʊ/ *n* (*pl* **altos**) contralto *f*

alto² *adj* alto

altogether¹ /'ɔːltə'geðər || ˌɔːltə'geðə(r)/ *adv* **1** (completely) totalmente; **that system is ~ simpler** ese sistema es mucho más sencillo; **the decision wasn't ~ wise** la decisión no fue del todo acertada **2** (*as intensifier*): **it would involve ~ too much effort** supondría un esfuerzo mayúsculo **3** (in total) en total **4** (on the whole) (*indep*) en general

altogether² *n*: ***in the*** **~** (colloq & hum) en cueros (fam & hum)

altruism /'æltruɪzəm/ *n* [u] altruismo *m*

altruistic /'æltru'ɪstɪk/ *adj* altruista

a

aluminosis /ə,lu:mə'nəʊsəs || ə,lu:mɪ'nəʊsɪs/ *n* [u] aluminosis *f*

aluminum /ə'lu:mɪnəm/, (BrE) **aluminium** /'æljə 'mɪniəm/ *n* [u] aluminio *m*

alumna /ə'lʌmnə/ *n* (*pl* **-nae** /-ni:/) (AmE) ex-alumna *f*

alumnus /ə'lʌmnəs/ *n* (*pl* **-ni** /-naɪ/) (esp AmE) ex-alumno *m*

always /'ɔ:lweɪz/ *adv* 1 (at all times, invariably) siempre 2 (alternatively) siempre, en todo caso

Alzheimer's disease /'ɑ:ltshaɪmərz || 'æltshaɪməz/ *n* [u] enfermedad *f* de Alzheimer

am¹ /æm, *weak form* əm/ *1st pers sing of* **be**

am² (before midday) a.m.; **at 7 ~** a las 7 de la mañana *or* 7 a.m.

AM *n* (Rad) (= **amplitude modulation**) AM *f*

AMA *n* = **American Medical Association**

amalgam /ə'mælgəm/ *n* [c] (combination) amalgama *f*

amalgamate /ə'mælgəmeɪt/ *vt* ‹*collections/indexes*› unir, amalgamar; ‹*companies/departments*› fusionar

■ **amalgamate** *vi* «*companies*» fusionarse

amalgamation /ə'mælgə'meɪʃən/ *n* [u c] (Busn) fusión *f*

amass /ə'mæs/ *vt* ‹*fortune*› amasar; ‹*arms/information/debts*› acumular

amateur¹ /'æmətər || 'æmətə(r)/ *n* 1 (Sport) amateur *mf* 2 (person lacking in professionalism): **a bunch of ~s** un grupo de gente sin ninguna profesionalidad

amateur² *adj* 1 (not professional) ‹*athlete/musician*› amateur; ‹*sport/competition*› para amateurs; **an ~ photographer** un aficionado a la fotografía 2 ▸**amateurish**

amateurish /'æmətərɪʃ/ *adj* (pej) de aficionados, poco serio

amaze /ə'meɪz/ *vt* asombrar

amazed /ə'meɪzd/ *adj* ‹*expression*› de asombro; **he was ~ at her reaction** su reacción lo dejó atónito *or* (fam) pasmado; **I'm ~ (at) how little you've changed** estoy asombrado de lo poco que has cambiado

amazement /ə'meɪzmənt/ *n* [u] asombro *m*; **he listened in ~** escuchó asombrado; **to his ~, she turned down the offer** rechazó la oferta, lo cual le causó gran asombro

amazing /ə'meɪzɪŋ/ *adj* increíble, asombroso, alucinante (fam)

amazingly /ə'meɪzɪŋli/ *adv* 1 (*as intensifier*) ‹*cheap/difficult*› increíblemente; **~ quickly** con una rapidez asombrosa 2 (astonishingly) (*indep*): **~ enough, I won** aunque parezca mentira, gané yo

Amazon /'æməzɑ:n || 'æməzən/ *n* 1 (Myth) amazona *f* 2 (Geog) **the ~** el Amazonas; (*before n*) **the ~ rain forest** la selva tropical amazónica

Amazonian /'æmə'zəʊniən/ *adj* amazónico

ambassador /æm'bæsədər || æm'bæsədə(r)/ *n* embajador, -dora *m,f*; **the Italian ~** el embajador de Italia

amber /'æmbər || 'æmbə(r)/ *n* [u] 1 (substance) ámbar *m* 2 (color) ámbar *m* 3 (BrE Aut) amarillo

ambiance *n* ▸**ambience**

ambidextrous /'æmbɪ'dekstrəs/ *adj* ambidiestro, ambidextro

ambience /'æmbiəns/ *n* ambiente *m*, atmósfera *f*

ambiguity /'æmbə'gju:əti || ,æmbɪ'gju:əti/ *n* [u c] (*pl* **-ties**) ambigüedad *f*

ambiguous /æm'bɪgjuəs/ *adj* ambiguo

ambit /'æmbət || 'æmbɪt/ *n* (frml) ámbito *m* (frml)

ambition /æm'bɪʃən/ *n* 1 [c u] (drive, desire) ambición *f*; **he is totally lacking in ~** no es nada ambicioso 2 [u] (energy, vitality) (AmE colloq) energía *f*

ambitious /æm'bɪʃəs/ *adj* 1 ‹*person/plan*› ambicioso; **to be ~ FOR sth/to + INF**: **she's ~ for power** tiene ambición de poder; **he's ~ to get to the top** ambiciona llegar a la cima; **you could be a bit more ~** podrías aspirar a más 2 (overadventurous) (*pred*): **aren't you being a bit ~?** ¿no estás pretendiendo hacer demasiado?

ambitiously /æm'bɪʃəsli/ *adv* (with greed) ambiciosamente; (boldly): **he tried, rather ~, to do both** intentó hacer las dos cosas, lo que quizás fue querer abarcar demasiado

ambivalence /æm'bɪvələns/ *n* [u] ambivalencia *f*

ambivalent /æm'bɪvələnt/ *adj* ambivalente; **she felt ~ toward her sister** tenía sentimientos encontrados hacia su hermana

amble /'æmbəl/ *vi*: **to ~ along** ir* tranquilamente *or* sin ninguna prisa

ambulance /'æmbjələns/ *n* ambulancia *f*

ambulanceman /'æmbjələnsmən || 'æmbjʊlənsmən/ *n* (*pl* **-men** /-mən/) (BrE) ambulanciero *m*

ambush¹ /'æmbʊʃ/ *vt* tenderle* una emboscada a

ambush² *n* emboscada *f*; **to lay an ~ (for sb/sth)** tender(le)* una emboscada (a algn/algo)

ameba /ə'mi:bə/ (AmE) ▸**amoeba**

ameliorate /ə'mi:ljəreɪt/ *vt* (frml) mejorar

amen /'ɑ:'men, 'eɪ'men/ *interj* amén, así sea

amenable /ə'mi:nəbəl/ *adj* ‹*temperament*› dócil; **if they're ~** si ellos están de acuerdo *or* si a ellos les parece bien; **to be ~ TO sth**: **they proved quite ~ to the idea** se mostraron bien dispuestos frente a la idea

amend /ə'mend/ *vt* 1 ‹*text*› corregir* 2 (Law) enmendar*

amendment /ə'mendmənt/ *n* [c] 1 (alteration) corrección *f* 2 (Law) enmienda *f*

amends /ə'mendz/ *pl n*: **to make ~ to sb** desagraviar a algn; **I tried to make ~ for the damage I had done** intenté reparar el daño que había hecho

amenity /ə'mi:nəti/ *n* (*pl* **-ties**) [c] (convenience, service) servicio *m*; **close to all amenities** cercano a todo tipo de servicios públicos

America /ə'merəkə || ə'merɪkə/ *n* (USA) Norteamérica *f*, Estados *mpl* Unidos, América *f*; (continent) América *f*

American¹ /ə'merəkən || ə'merɪkən/ *adj* (of USA) estadounidense, norteamericano, americano

American² *n* [c] (from USA) estadounidense *mf*, norteamericano, -na *m,f*, americano, -na *m,f*

the American Dream

En Estados Unidos, el sueño americano es la creencia, que cualquier persona que trabaje duro puede alcanzar el éxito económico o social. Para los inmigrantes y las minorías, este sueño también incluye libertad e igualdad de derechos

American Football

El fútbol americano se juega con dos equipos de once jugadores cada uno y con una pelota de forma ovalada. Es un deporte violento por lo que los jugadores usan cascos y almohadillas de protección. Un equipo marca 7 puntos cuando se produce un *touchdown*, es decir al llevar la pelota hacia el campo contrario y cruzar la línea de gol del equipo adversario. Se pueden marcar puntos extra si después, con un puntapié, se introduce la pelota por entre los postes de la portería

American Indian¹ *adj* amerindio, de los indios americanos

American Indian² *n* indio americano, india americana *m,f*, amerindio, -dia *m,f*

American Indian

▸**Native American**

Americanism /ə'merəkənɪzəm || ə'merɪkənɪzəm/ *n* (Ling) americanismo *m*; (characteristic) costumbre *f* (norte)americana, americanada *f* (pey)

Americanization /ə'merəkənə'zeɪʃən || ə,merɪkənaɪ 'zeɪʃən/ *n* [u] americanización *f*

Americanize /ə'merəkənaɪz || ə'merɪkənaɪz/ *vt* americanizar*, agringar* (AmL pey); **to become ~d** americanizarse*, agringarse* (AmL pey)

Amerindian¹ /'æmər'ɪndiən/ *adj* amerindio

Amerindian² *n* amerindio, -dia *m,f*

amethyst /'æməθəst || 'æməθɪst/ *n* [u c] amatista *f*

Amex /'æmeks/ (*no art*) 1 = **American Stock Exchange** 2 = **American Express®**

amiable /'eɪmiəbəl/ *adj* ‹*person/nature*› afable, amable

amiably /'eɪmiəbli/ *adv* afablemente, amablemente

amicable /'æmɪkəbəl/ *adj* ‹*person*› amigable; ‹*relations*› cordial, amistoso; ‹*agreement*› amistoso

amicably /'æmɪkəbli/ *adv* amigablemente, cordialmente

amid /ə'mɪd/, **amidst** /ə'mɪdst/ *prep* en medio de, entre

amiss¹ /ə'mɪs/ *adj (pred)*: **there was nothing ~** no había ningún problema, todo estaba bien; **there's something ~** pasa algo

amiss² *adv*: **to take sth ~** tomarse algo a mal; **a little courtesy would not come** *o* **go ~** un poco de cortesía no estaría de más

ammo /'æməʊ/ *n* [u] (colloq) munición *f*

ammonia /ə'məʊniə/ *n* [u] amoníaco *m*

ammunition /'æmjə'nɪʃən || ˌæmjʊ'nɪʃən/ *n* [u] munición *f*; **this provided further ~ for her opponents** esto proporcionó nuevos argumentos a sus contrincantes

amnesia /æm'ni:ʒə || æm'ni:ziə/ *n* [u] amnesia *f*

amnesty /'æmnəsti/ *n* (*pl* **-ties**) amnistía *f*

amoeba, (AmE also) **ameba** /ə'mi:bə/ *n* ameba *f*, amiba *f*

amok /ə'mʌk || ə'mɒk/ *adv* **to run ~** ‹‹*person*›› empezar* a comportarse como un enajenado

among /ə'mʌŋ/, **amongst** /ə'mʌŋst/ *prep* [1] (in midst of) entre; **~ other things** entre otras cosas [2] (with each other) entre; **share it ~ yourselves** repártanselo entre ustedes

amoral /'eɪ'mɔ:rəl || eɪ'mɒrəl/ *adj* amoral

amorous /'æmərəs/ *adj* ‹*look/mood*› apasionado; **to get ~** ponerse* demasiado cariñoso

amorphous /ə'mɔ:rfəs || ə'mɔ:fəs/ *adj* amorfo

amount /ə'maʊnt/ *n* [1] (quantity) cantidad *f*; **any ~ of sth** grandes cantidades de algo; **no ~ of sth**: **no ~ of arguing will change their opinions** por más que discutamos no van a cambiar de opinión [2] (sum of money) cantidad *f*, suma *f*

Phrasal verb

• **amount to** [v ▸ prep ▸ o] [1] (add up to) ‹‹*debt/assets*›› ascender* a; ***not to ~ to anything/much***: **she'll never ~ to anything** nunca llegará a nada; **what he said didn't ~ to much** no dijo gran cosa [2] (be equivalent to): **it ~s to stealing** equivale a robar; **it all ~s to the same thing** viene a ser lo mismo

amp /æmp/ *n* [1] (Elec) amperio *m* [2] (amplifier) (colloq) amplificador *m*

ampere, ampère /'æmpɪr || 'æmpeə(r)/ *n* amperio *m*

ampersand /'æmpərsænd || 'æmpəsænd/ *n*: *el signo &*

amphetamine /æm'fetəmi:n/ *n* anfetamina *f*

amphibian /æm'fɪbiən/ *n* (Zool) anfibio *m*

amphibious /æm'fɪbiəs/ *adj* anfibio

amphitheater, (BrE) **amphitheatre** /'æmfɪˌθi:ətər || 'æmfɪˌθɪətə(r)/ *n* anfiteatro *m*

ample /'æmpəl/ *adj* [1] ‹*space*› amplio; ‹*funds/resources*› abundante; ‹*helping*› generoso; **you had ~ warning** se te avisó con sobrada anticipación [2] (plenty) (*pred*) más que suficiente

amplification /'æmpləfə'keɪʃən || ˌæmplɪfɪ'keɪʃən/ *n* [u] (Audio) amplificación *f*

amplifier /'æmpləfaɪər || 'æmplɪfaɪə(r)/ *n* amplificador *m*

amplify /'æmpləfaɪ || 'æmplɪfaɪ/ *vt* **-fies, -fying, -fied** ‹*sound*› amplificar*

amplitude /'æmplətu:d || 'æmplɪtju:d/ *n* [u] (frml) amplitud *f*

amply /'æmpli/ *adv* [1] (generously): **an ~ proportioned house** una casa amplia *or* espaciosa; **her ~ proportioned figure** su figura de generosas proporciones [2] (adequately) ‹*demonstrated*› ampliamente, suficientemente

ampoule, ampule /'æmpu:l/ *n* ampolla *f*, ampolleta *f*

amputate /'æmpjəteɪt || 'æmpjʊteɪt/ *vt* amputar

amputation /'æmpjə'teɪʃən || ˌæmpjʊ'teɪʃən/ *n* [u c] amputación *f*

Amtrak /'æmtræk/ *n* (in US) Ferrocarriles *mpl* de los EEUU

amuck /ə'mʌk/ *adv* ▸**amok**

amulet /'æmjələt || 'æmjʊlɪt/ *n* amuleto *m*

amuse /ə'mju:z/ *vt* [1] (entertain) entretener*; **the game kept them ~d for a while** el juego los tuvo entretenidos un rato [2] (make laugh) divertir*, hacer* reír

■ *v refl* **to ~ oneself** entretenerse*; (have fun) divertirse*; (relax) distraerse*

amused /ə'mju:zd/ *adj* ‹*expression*› divertido; **to be ~ AT sth**: **she was ~ at the look on his face** le hizo gracia la cara que puso

amusement /ə'mju:zmənt/ *n* [1] [u] (entertainment) distracción *f*, entretenimiento *m*, entretención *f* (AmL) [2] [u] (mirth) diversión *f*; **they watched in ~** miraban divertidos; **to our great ~** *o* **much to our ~ ...** para nuestro gran regocijo ...; (*before n*) **~ arcade** sala *f* de juegos recreativos; **~ park** parque *m* de diversiones *or* (Esp) atracciones

amusing /ə'mju:zɪŋ/ *adj* divertido, gracioso, entretenido

amusingly /ə'mju:zɪŋli/ *adv* de forma muy entretenida *or* divertida

an /æn, *weak form* ən/ *indef art before vowel* ▸**a**

anabolic steroid /'ænə'bɑ:lɪk || ˌænə'bɒlɪk/ *n* esteroide *m* anabólico

anachronism /ə'nækrənɪzəm/ *n* anacronismo *m*

anachronistic /ə'nækrə'nɪstɪk/ *adj* anacrónico

anaemia *etc* (BrE) ▸**anemia** *etc*

anaesthesia *etc* (BrE) ▸**anesthesia** *etc*

anagram /'ænəgræm/ *n* anagrama *m*

anal /'eɪnl/ *adj* anal

analgesic /'ænl'dʒi:zɪk || ˌænæl'dʒi:sɪk, -zɪk/ *n* [u c] analgésico *m*

analog¹ /'ænəlɔ:g || 'ænəlɒg/ *n* (AmE) análogo *m*

analog² *adj* (Comput) analógico

analogous /ə'næləgəs/ *adj* (frml) análogo; **to be ~ TO** *o* **WITH sth** ser* análogo A algo

analogue¹ /'ænəlɔ:g || 'ænəlɒg/ *n* (frml) análogo *m*

analogue² *adj* analógico

analogy /ə'nælədʒi/ *n* [c u] (*pl* **-gies**) analogía *f*; **to draw an ~ with sth** establecer* una analogía con algo

analyse *vt* (BrE) ▸**analyze**

analysis /ə'næləsəs || ə'nælɪsɪs/ *n* (*pl* **-lyses** /-ɪsi:z/) [1] [c u] (examination) análisis *m*; **on closer ~ ...** tras haberlo analizado más detenidamente ...; **in the final ~** bien considerado, a fin de cuentas [2] [u] (Psych) psicoanálisis *m*, análisis *m*; **he's still in ~** todavía ve a un psicoanalista

analyst /'ænləst || 'ænəlɪst/ *n* [1] (of data) analista *mf* [2] (Psych) psicoanalista *mf*, analista *mf*

analytic /'ænə'lɪtɪk/, **-ical** /-ɪkəl/ *adj* analítico

analyze, (BrE) **analyse** /'ænəlaɪz/ *vt* [1] ‹*data*› analizar* [2] (Psych) psicoanalizar*, analizar*

anarchist /'ænərkəst || 'ænəkɪst/ *n* anarquista *mf*

anarchy /'ænərki || 'ænəki/ *n* [u] anarquía *f*

anathema /ə'næθəmə/ *n* (*pl* **-mas**) (*no art*) **to be ~ TO sb**: **liberal ideas are ~ to them** les repugnan *or* les resultan odiosas las ideas liberales

anatomical /'ænə'tɑ:mɪkəl || ˌænə'tɒmɪkəl/ *adj* anatómico

anatomy /ə'nætəmi/ *n* (*pl* **-mies**) [1] [u] (science) anatomía *f* [2] [c] (body) (hum) anatomía *f* (hum)

ANC *n* (= **African National Congress**) **the ~** el CNA

ancestor /'ænsestər || 'ænsestə(r)/ *n* (forefather) antepasado, -da *m,f*; (forerunner) antecesor, -sora *m,f*

ancestral /æn'sestrəl/ *adj*: **the ~ home** la casa solariega

ancestry /'ænsestri/ *n* [u] ascendencia *f*; **of noble ~** de noble linaje; **to trace one's ~** hacerse* el árbol genealógico

anchor¹ /'æŋkər || 'æŋkə(r)/ *n* [1] (Naut) ancla *f*‡; **to be** *o* **lie at ~** estar* anclado; **to cast** *o* **drop ~** echar anclas [2] (mainstay, support) sostén *m*

anchor² *vt* ‹*ship*› anclar, fondear; ‹*rope/tent*› sujetar, asegurar

anchorage /'æŋkərɪdʒ/ *n* [1] [c u] (place) fondeadero *m* [2] [u] (fee) anclaje *m*

anchor: **~man** /'æŋkərmæn || 'æŋkəmæn/ *n* (*pl* **-men** /-men/) (TV) presentador *m*; **~woman** *n* (TV) presentadora *f*

anchovy /'æntʃəʊvi || 'æntʃəvi/ *n* (*pl* **-vies** *or* **-vy**) anchoa *f*

ancient /'eɪnʃənt/ *adj* [1] ‹*civilizations/ruin*› antiguo; **A~ Greek** griego *m* clásico; **my divorce? that's all**

~ **history now** ¿mi divorcio? eso ya ha pasado a la historia 2 (colloq) (old) ‹*car*› del año de la pera (fam)

ancillary /'ænsəleri || æn'sɪləri/ *adj* (frml) 1 (supplementary) ‹*service/worker*› auxiliar 2 (subordinate) ‹*road*› secundario

and /ænd, *weak form* ənd/ *conj* [*The usual translation* **y** *becomes* **e** *when it precedes a word beginning with* **i, hi** *or* **y**]

A 1 y; **black ~ white** blanco y negro; **father ~ son** padre e hijo; **bread ~ butter** pan con mantequilla; **during June ~/or July** durante junio y/o julio 2 **and so on** etcétera; **~ so on, ~ so forth** etcétera, etcétera

B (in numbers): **one ~ a half** uno y medio; **two hundred ~ twenty** doscientos veinte

C (showing continuation, repetition): **faster ~ faster** cada vez más rápido; **he just eats ~ eats** no hace más que comer; **weeks ~ weeks passed** pasaron semanas y más semanas

D (with *inf*): **try ~ finish this today** trata de terminar esto hoy; **go ~ help your father** anda a ayudar a tu padre

Andalusia /'ændə'lu:ʒə || ,ændə'lu:siə/ *n* Andalucía *f*

Andalusian¹ /'ændə'lu:ʒən || ,ændə'lu:siən/ *adj* andaluz

Andalusian² *n* andaluz, -luza *m,f*

Andean /'ændiən/ *adj* andino

Andes /'ændi:z/ *pl n* **the ~** los Andes

Andorra /æn'dɔ:rə/ *n* Andorra *f*

androgynous /æn'drɑ:dʒənəs || æn'drɒdʒənəs/ *adj* andrógino

android /'ændrɔɪd/ *n* androide *m*

andropause /'ændrəʊ,pɔ:z/ *n* [u] andropausia *f*

anecdotal /'ænɪk'dəʊtl/ *adj* ‹*material*› anecdótico; ‹*biography/talk*› lleno de anécdotas; **~ evidence suggests that ...** los casos de los que se tiene conocimiento parecen indicar que ...

anecdote /'ænɪkdəʊt/ *n* anécdota *f*

anemia, (BrE) **anaemia** /ə'ni:miə/ *n* [u] anemia *f*

anemic, (BrE) **anaemic** /ə'ni:mɪk/ *adj* anémico

anemone /ə'neməni/ *n*

A (Bot) anémona *f*

B (*sea* ~) (Zool) anémona *f* de mar

anesthesia, (BrE) **anaesthesia** /'ænəs'θi:ʒə || ,ænɪs'θi:ziə/ *n* [u] anestesia *f*

anesthesiologist /'ænəsθi:zi'ɑ:lədʒəst || ,ænəsθi:zi'ɒlədʒɪst/ *n* (AmE) anestesiólogo, -ga *m,f*

anesthetic, (BrE) **anaesthetic** /'ænəs'θetɪk || ,ænɪs'θetɪk/ *n* [c u] anestésico *m*; **to be under ~** estar* bajo los efectos de la anestesia

anesthetist, (BrE) **anaesthetist** /ə'nesθətəst || ə'ni:sθətɪst/ *n* 1 (AmE) (other than a physician) anestesista *mf* 2 (BrE) (qualified doctor) anestesista *mf*, anestesiólogo, -ga *m,f*

anesthetize, (BrE) **anaesthetize** /ə'nesθətaɪz || ə'ni:sθətaɪz/ *vt* anestesiar

anew /ə'nu: || ə'nju:/ *adv* (liter) de nuevo, otra vez

angel /'eɪndʒəl/ *n* ángel *m*; **thanks, you're an ~** gracias, eres un ángel *or* un cielo

angelic /æn'dʒelɪk/ *adj* angelical

anger¹ /'æŋgər || 'æŋgə(r)/ *n* [u] ira *f*, enojo *m* (esp AmL), enfado *m* (esp Esp); **words spoken in ~** palabras dichas en un momento de ira

anger² *vt* (hacer*) enojar (esp AmL), (hacer*) enfadar (esp Esp)

angina (pectoris) /æn'dʒaɪnə('pektərəs) || æn'dʒaɪnə(,pektərɪs)/ *n* [u] angina *f* (de pecho)

angiogram /'ændʒiəʊgræm/ *n* angiograma *m*

angle¹ /'æŋgəl/ *n*

A 1 ángulo *m*; **at an ~: she wore her hat at an ~** llevaba el sombrero ladeado; **at an ~ to the wall** formando un ángulo con la pared 2 (corner) arista *f*

B 1 (position) ángulo *m* 2 (point of view) perspectiva *f*, punto *m* de vista; **we need a new ~ on the subject** tenemos que darle un nuevo enfoque al tema

angle² *vt* ‹*pass/shot*› sesgar*; ‹*lamp*› orientar, dirigir*

■ **angle** *vi* (fish) pescar* (con caña)

Phrasal verb

• **angle for** [v ▸ prep ▸ o] (colloq): **she's angling for an invitation** anda buscando que la inviten

angler /'æŋglər/ *n* pescador, -dora *m,f* (de caña)

Anglican¹ /'æŋglɪkən/ *n* anglicano, -na *m,f*

Anglican² *adj* anglicano; **the ~ Church** la Iglesia Anglicana

Anglicism, anglicism /'æŋglɪsɪzəm/ *n* anglicismo *m*

Anglicize, anglicize /'æŋglɪsaɪz/ *vt* anglicanizar*

angling /'æŋglɪŋ/ *n* [u] pesca *f* (con caña)

Anglo- /'æŋgləʊ/ *pref* anglo-

Anglo-Saxon¹ /'æŋgləʊ'sæksən/ *adj* anglosajón

Anglo-Saxon² *n* 1 [c] (person) anglosajón, -jona *m,f* 2 [u] (language) anglosajón *m*

Angola /æŋ'gəʊlə/ *n* Angola *f*

Angolan /æŋ'gəʊlən/ *adj* angoleño

angora /æŋ'gɔ:rə/ *n* angora *f*

angrily /'æŋgrəli || 'æŋgrɪli/ *adv* con ira, furiosamente; **no!, he shouted ~** —¡no! —gritó enojado (esp AmL) *or* (esp Esp) enfadado

angry /'æŋgri/ *adj* **angrier, angriest** 1 ‹*person*› enojado (esp AmL), enfadado (esp Esp); ‹*look*› de enojo (esp AmL), de enfado (esp Esp); ‹*animal*› furioso; ‹*silence*› cargado de ira *or* furia; **to get ~** enojarse (esp AmL), enfadarse (esp Esp); **to be ~ AT** *o* **WITH sb** estar* enojado *or* enfadado CON algn; **to be ~ ABOUT/AT sth: I'm really ~ about losing those keys** me da mucha rabia haber perdido las llaves; **I'm very ~ at the way I've been treated** estoy muy enojada *or* enfadada por cómo me han tratado 2 ‹*sea*› embravecido 3 (Med) inflamado, irritado

angst /ɑ:ŋst || æŋst/ *n* [u] angustia *f*

anguish /'æŋgwɪʃ/ *n* [u] angustia *f*; **to cause sb ~** angustiar a algn

anguished /'æŋgwɪʃt/ *adj* angustiado

angular /'æŋgjələr || 'æŋgjʊlə(r)/ *adj* ‹*shape*› angular; ‹*features*› anguloso

animal¹ /'ænəməl || 'ænɪməl/ *n* 1 (creature) animal *m*; (*before n*) **~ lover** amante *mf* de los animales 2 (brute) animal *mf*, bestia *f*

animal² *adj* ‹*desires*› carnal, de la carne; ‹*behavior*› propio de un animal

animate /'ænəmeɪt || 'ænɪmeɪt/ *vt* 1 (enliven) animar 2 (Cin) animar

animated /'ænəmeɪtəd || 'ænɪmeɪtɪd/ *adj* animado

animation /'ænə'meɪʃən || ,ænɪ'meɪʃən/ *n* [u] 1 (liveliness) animación *f*, vivacidad *f* 2 (Cin) animación *f*

animator, animater /'ænəmeɪtər || 'ænɪmeɪtə(r)/ *n* animador, -dora *m,f*

animosity /'ænə'mɑ:səti || ,ænɪ'mɒsəti/ *n* [u c] (*pl* **-ties**) animosidad *f*

aniseed /'ænəsi:d || 'ænɪsi:d/ *n* [u] anís *m*

ankle /'æŋkəl/ *n* tobillo *m*; (*before n*) **~ boot** botín *m*; **~ sock** calcetín *m* corto, soquete *m* (CS); **~ strap** tobillera *f*

ankle deep *adj*: **the street was ~ ~ in mud** el barro en la calle llegaba hasta los tobillos

anklet /'æŋklət || 'aŋklɪt/ *n* 1 (bracelet) ajorca *f*, cadenita *f* (*para el tobillo*) 2 (sock) (AmE) calcetín *m* corto

annals /'ænlz/ *pl n* (Hist) anales *mpl*, crónica *f*

annex¹ /ə'neks/ *vt* 1 ‹*territory/area*› anexar, anexarse 2 ‹*document*› adjuntar como anexo; ‹*clause*› añadir

annex², (BrE) **annexe** /'æneks/ *n* 1 (building) anexo *m*, anejo *m* 2 (to document) anexo *m*, anejo *m*, apéndice *m*

annihilate /ə'naɪəleɪt/ *vt* ‹*army/city*› aniquilar; (Sport) (colloq) darle* una paliza a

annihilation /ə'naɪə'leɪʃən/ *n* [u] aniquilación *f*

anniversary /'ænə'vɜ:rsəri || ,ænɪ'vɜ:səri/ *n* (*pl* **-ries**) aniversario *m*; **the 100th ~ of his death** el primer centenario de su muerte; **it's their 10th wedding ~** es su décimo aniversario de boda *or* de casados

annotate /'ænəteɪt/ *vt* anotar

announce /ə'naʊns/ *vt* 1 ‹*flight/guest/marriage*› anunciar; **the mayor will ~ the winner** el alcalde dará a conocer el nombre del ganador 2 (declare) anunciar 3 (AmE Rad, TV) ‹*game/race*› comentar

■ **announce** *vi* (declare candidacy) (AmE Pol) **to ~ (FOR sth)** anunciar su (*or* mi *etc*) candidatura (A algo)

announcement /ə'naʊnsmənt/ *n* anuncio *m*; **an official ~** un comunicado oficial

announcer /ə'naʊnsər || ə'naʊnsə(r)/ *n* (Rad, TV) 1 (commentator) (AmE) comentarista *mf* 2 (between programs) (BrE) locutor, -tora *m,f* de continuidad

annoy /ə'nɔɪ/ *vt* (irritate, bother) molestar, irritar, fastidiar; (anger): **it ∼s me to think that ...** me da rabia pensar que ...

annoyance /ə'nɔɪəns/ *n* 1 [u] (irritation) irritación *f*, fastidio *m*; (anger) enojo *m* (esp AmL), enfado *m* (esp Esp); **much to our ∼ they didn't turn up** no aparecieron, lo cual nos dio mucha rabia 2 [c] (cause of irritation) molestia *f*, fastidio *m*

annoyed /ə'nɔɪd/ *adj* enojado (esp AmL), enfadado (esp Esp); **to get ∼** enojarse (esp AmL), enfadarse (esp Esp); **they were ∼ at having to wait** les dio mucha rabia tener que esperar; **I was ∼ with her for not telling me** me enojé *or* enfadé con ella porque no me lo dijo

annoying /ə'nɔɪɪŋ/ *adj* ‹*person*› pesado; **it's very ∼ to have to pay** da mucha rabia tener que pagar; **he has the ∼ habit of ...** tiene la maldita costumbre de ...; **how ∼!** ¡qué rabia *or* fastidio!

annoyingly /ə'nɔɪɪŋli/ *adv* ‹*repetitive*› irritantemente

annual[1] /'ænjuəl/ *adj* (*before n*) anual

annual[2] *n*

A (plant) planta *f* anual

B (publication) anuario *m*

annual general meeting *n* (BrE) junta *f* general ordinaria annual, asamblea *f* general ordinaria anual

annually /'ænjuəli/ *adv* anualmente, cada año

annul /ə'nʌl/ *vt* **-ll-** anular

annulment /ə'nʌlmənt/ *n* [c u] anulación *f*

Annunciation /ə'nʌnsi'eɪʃən/ *n* **the ∼** la Anunciación

anodyne /'ænədaɪn/ *adj* anodino

anoint /ə'nɔɪnt/ *vt* ungir*

anomalous /ə'nɑːmələs || ə'nɒmələs/ *adj* (frml) anómalo

anomaly /ə'nɑːməli || ə'nɒməli/ *n* (*pl* **-lies**) anomalía *f*

anon[1] /ə'nɑːn || ə'nɒn/ *adv* (arch *or* liter): **(I'll) see you ∼** (colloq) te veo luego

anon[2] **= anonymous**

anonymity /'ænə'nɪməti/ *n* [u] anonimato *m*

anonymous /ə'nɑːnəməs || ə'nɒnɪməs/ *adj* anónimo; **to remain ∼** permanecer* en *or* conservar el anonimato; **∼ letter** anónimo *m*

anonymously /ə'nɑːnəməsli || ə'nɒnɪməsli/ *adv* anónimamente, de manera anónima

anorexia (nervosa) /'ænə'reksiə(nər'vəʊsə) || ,ænə'reksiə(nɜː'vəʊsə)/ *n* [u] anorexia *f* (nerviosa)

anorexic /'ænə'reksɪk/ *adj* anoréxico

another[1] /ə'nʌðər || ə'nʌðə(r)/ *adj* 1 (different, alternative) otro, otra; **I can't make it this weekend; ∼ time, perhaps?** este fin de semana no puedo, quizá(s) en otra ocasión 2 (in addition) otro, otra; (*pl*) otros, otras; **we need ∼ three chairs** nos hacen falta otras tres sillas *or* tres sillas más; **can I have ∼ one?** ¿me das otro/otra?; **he could be ∼ Picasso** podría ser otro Picasso; **only ∼ ten miles to go** sólo faltan diez millas; **it's just ∼ job** es un trabajo como cualquier otro *or* como otro cualquiera

another[2] *pron* 1 (different, alternative) otro, otra; **he says one thing and does ∼** dice una cosa y hace otra; **at one time or ∼** en algún momento 2 (in addition) otro, otra; **would you like ∼?** ¿quieres otro/otra? 3 (person) otro, otra; **I love ∼** (liter) amo a otro/a otra

ANSI /'ænsi/ *n* **= American National Standards Institute**

answer[1] /'ænsər || 'ɑːnsə(r)/ *n*

A 1 (reply) respuesta *f*, contestación *f*; **what was their ∼?** ¿qué respondieron *or* contestaron?; **there's no ∼** (to doorbell, phone) no contestan; **in ∼ to your question** para contestar tu pregunta; ***to be the ∼ to sb's prayers*** llegar* como caído del cielo; ***to know all the ∼s*** (colloq) saberlo* todo 2 (response) **∼ (TO sth)**: **her ∼ to his rudeness was to ignore it** respondió a su grosería ignorándola; **Britain's ∼ to Elvis Presley** el Elvis Presley británico 3 (plea) (Law) contestación *f*

B 1 (in exam, test, quiz) respuesta *f* 2 (solution) solución *f*; **∼ TO sth** solución DE algo

answer[2] *vt*

A 1 (reply to) ‹*person/letter*› contestar; **∼ your father!** ¡contéstale a tu padre!; **because it's too far, she ∼ed** —porque está muy lejos —contestó *or* respondió 2 ‹*telephone*› contestar, atender* (AmL), coger* (Esp); **will you ∼ the door?** ¿vas tú (a abrir)? 3 ‹*critic/criticism*› responder a

B 1 ‹*need*› satisfacer*; **their prayers were ∼ed** el cielo escuchó sus plegarias 2 (fit): **to ∼ (to) a description** responder a una descripción

■ **answer** *vi* contestar, responder; **I phoned but no one ∼ed** llamé por teléfono pero no contestaron; **if the doorbell rings, don't ∼** si tocan el timbre, no contestes/abras

Phrasal verbs

• **answer back**

A [v ▸ adv] 1 (rudely) contestar 2 (defend oneself) responder a las acusaciones (*or* a sus críticos *etc*)

B [v ▸ o ▸ adv]: **her son ∼ed her back** su hijo le contestó mal *or* de mala manera

• **answer for** [v ▸ prep ▸ o] 1 (accept responsibility for) ‹*conduct/consequences*› responder de; **his parents have a lot to ∼ for** sus padres tienen mucha culpa 2 (guarantee) ‹*truth/integrity*› garantizar*, responder de; ‹*person*› responder por

• **answer to** [v ▸ prep ▸ o] 1 (be accountable) **to ∼ to sb (FOR sth)** responder ante algn (DE algo) 2 ‹‹*dog/cat*››: **it ∼s to the name of Bob** responde al nombre de Bob 3 ▸**answer**[2] *vt* **B2**

answerable /'ænsərəbəl || 'ɑːnsərəbəl/ *adj* (*pred*) **to be ∼ (TO sb/sth) (FOR sth)**: **she said she was not ∼ for his behavior** dijo que ella no era responsable de lo que él hiciera; **I'm ∼ to no one** no tengo que rendirle cuentas a nadie

answering machine /'ænsərɪŋ || 'ɑːnsərɪŋ/ *n* contestador *m* (automático)

ant /ænt/ *n* hormiga *f*; ***he has ∼s in his pants*** (colloq) es muy inquieto

antacid /ænt'æsəd || ænt'æsɪd/ *n* [c u] antiácido *m*

antagonism /æn'tægənɪzəm/ *n* [u c] antagonismo *m*; **∼ TO/TOWARD sb/sth** antagonismo HACIA algn/algo

antagonist /æn'tægənəst || æn'tægənɪst/ *n* antagonista *mf*, contrincante *mf*

antagonistic /æn'tægə'nɪstɪk/ *adj* hostil, antagonista

antagonize /æn'tægənaɪz/ *vt* (irritate) fastidiar, hacer* enojar (esp AmL); (make hostile) suscitar el antagonismo de, antagonizar*

Antarctic[1] /ænt'ɑːrktɪk || æn'tɑːktɪk/ *adj* antártico; **the ∼ Ocean** el Océano Antártico; **the ∼ Circle** el Círculo Polar Antártico

Antarctic[2] *n* **the ∼** la región antártica

Antarctica /ænt'ɑːrktɪkə || æn'tɑːktɪkə/ *n* la Antártida

ante /'ænti/ *n* **the ∼** la apuesta inicial, la entrada (Méx); **to up** *o* **raise the ∼** subir la apuesta inicial

anteater /'ænt,iːtər || 'ænt,iːtə(r)/ *n* oso *m* hormiguero

antecedent /,æntə'siːdn̩t || ,æntɪ'siːdənt/ *n* antecedente *m*, precursor, -sora *m,f*

antechamber /'ænti,tʃeɪmbər || 'ænti,tʃeɪmbə(r)/ *n* antecámara *f*

antediluvian /'æntɪdə'luːviən || ,æntɪdɪ'luːviən/ *adj* antediluviano, antidiluviano

antelope /'æntələʊp || 'æntɪləʊp/ *n* (*pl* **∼s** *or* **∼**) antílope *m*

antenatal /'ænti'neɪtl̩/ *adj* prenatal; **∼ clinic** *consulta médica para mujeres embarazadas*

antenna /æn'tenə/ *n* 1 (*pl* **-nae** /-niː/) (Zool) antena *f* 2 (*pl* **-nas**) (Rad, TV) antena *f*

anterior /æn'tɪriər || æn'tɪəriə(r)/ *adj* anterior

anthem /'ænθəm/ *n* (song) himno *m*; **national ∼** himno nacional

anthill /'ænthɪl/ *n* hormiguero *m*

anthology /æn'θɑːlədʒi || æn'θɒlədʒi/ *n* (*pl* **-gies**) antología *f*

anthrax /'ænθræks/ *n* [u] ántrax *m*, carbunclo *m* (maligno)

anthropological /'ænθrəpə'lɑːdʒɪkəl || ,ænθrəpə'lɒdʒɪkəl/ *adj* antropológico

anthropologist /'ænθrə'pɑːlədʒəst || ,ænθrə'pɒlədʒɪst/ *n* antropólogo, -ga *m,f*

anthropology /ˌænθrəˈpɑːlədʒi || ˌænθrəˈpɒlədʒi/ *n* [u] antropología *f*

anti /ˈæntaɪ, ˈænti || ˈænti/ *prep* (colloq) en contra de

anti- /ˈæntaɪ, ˈænti || ˈænti/ *pref* anti-

anti-abortion /ˈæntaɪəˈbɔːrʃən/ *adj* antiabortista

antiaircraft /ˈæntaɪˈerkræft || ˌæntiˈeəkrɑːft/ *adj* antiaéreo

antibiotic /ˈæntɪbaɪˈɑːtɪk || ˌæntibaɪˈɒtɪk/ *n* [c u] antibiótico *m*; **he's on ~s** está tomando antibióticos

antibody /ˈæntiˌbɑːdi || ˈæntiˌbɒdi/ *n* (*pl* **-dies**) anticuerpo *m*

Antichrist /ˈæntikraɪst/ *n* **(the)** ~ el Anticristo

anticipate /ænˈtɪsəpeɪt || ænˈtɪsɪpeɪt/ *vt*

A 1 (expect) ‹*consequences*› prever*; **I don't ~ any problems** no creo que vaya a haber ningún problema; **it was more difficult than ~d** resultó más difícil de lo que se había previsto *or* de lo que se esperaba; **to ~ -ING** tener* previsto + INF 2 (look forward to) esperar

B 1 (foresee and act accordingly) ‹*movements/objections/needs*› prever*; **I ~d the blow** vi venir* el golpe 2 (preempt) anticiparse a, adelantarse a

anticipation /ænˈtɪsəˈpeɪʃən || ænˌtɪsɪˈpeɪʃən/ *n* [u] 1 (foresight) previsión *f*; **thanking you in ~** agradeciéndole de antemano su atención 2 (expectation) expectativa *f*

anticlimax /ˈæntaɪˈklaɪmæks || ˌæntiˈklaɪmæks/ *n* [c u] *suceso caracterizado por un descenso de la tensión*; (Lit) anticlímax *m*; (disappointment) decepción *f*

anticlockwise /ˈæntɪˈklɑːkwaɪz || ˌæntiˈklɒkwaɪz/ *adj/adv* (BrE) en sentido contrario a las agujas del reloj

antics /ˈæntɪks/ *pl n* (clowning) payasadas *fpl*, gracias *fpl*; (of naughty children) travesuras *fpl*

anticyclone /ˈæntɪˈsaɪkləʊn/ *n* anticiclón *m*

antidepressant /ˈæntaɪdɪˈpresn̩t || ˌæntidɪˈpresənt/ *n* antidepresivo *m*

antidote /ˈæntɪdəʊt/ *n* ~ **(TO** *o* **FOR sth)** antídoto *m* (CONTRA algo)

antifreeze /ˈæntɪfriːz/ *n* [u] anticongelante *m*

antihero /ˈæntɪˌhiːrəʊ || ˈæntiˌhɪərəʊ/ *n* (*pl* **-roes**) antihéroe *m*

antihistamine /ˈæntɪˈhɪstəmiːn || ˌæntiˈhɪstəmɪn/ *n* [c u] antihistamínico *m*

Antilles /ænˈtɪliːz/ *pl n* **the (Greater/Lesser) ~** las Antillas (Mayores/Menores)

anti-lock /ˈæntɪˈlɑːk || ˈæntilɒk/ *adj* antibloque *adj inv*; **~ brakes** frenos *mpl* antibloque

antimatter /ˈæntiˌmætər || ˈæntɪˌmætə(r)/ *n* [u] antimateria *f*

antinuclear /ˈæntɪˈnuːkliər/ *adj* antinuclear

antipathy /ænˈtɪpəθi/ *n* [c u] (*pl* **-thies**) ~ **(TO/TOWARD sb/sth)** antipatía *f or* aversión *f* (HACIA algn/algo)

antiperspirant /ˈæntɪˈpɜːrspərənt || ˌæntiˈpɜːspɪrənt/ *n* [c u] antitranspirante *m*

antipodean /ænˈtɪpəˈdiːən/ *adj* de las antípodas

antipodes /ænˈtɪpədiːz/ *pl n* **the ~** las antípodas; **the A~** (BrE) Australia y Nueva Zelanda *or* Zelandia

antiquarian¹ /ˈæntəˈkweriən || ˌæntɪˈkweəriən/ *adj* ‹*book*› antiguo; ‹*bookseller*› especializado en libros antiguos

antiquarian², antiquary /ˈæntəkweri || ˈæntɪkwəri/ *n* anticuario, -ria *m,f*

antiquated /ˈæntəkweɪtəd || ˈæntɪkweɪtɪd/ *adj* anticuado

antique¹ /ænˈtiːk/ *n* antigüedad *f*; (*before n*) **~ dealer** anticuario, -ria *m,f*; **~ shop** tienda *f* de antigüedades, anticuario *m*

antique² *adj* ‹*lace/jewelry*› antiguo; ‹*furniture*› antiguo, de época

antiquity /ænˈtɪkwəti/ *n* (*pl* **-ties**)

A [u] 1 (ancient times) antigüedad *f* 2 (age) antigüedad *f*; **of great ~** muy antiguo *or* de gran antigüedad

B antiquities *pl* antigüedades *fpl*

antiretroviral /ˈæntaɪretrəʊˈvaɪrəl/ *adj* ‹*drug/treatment*› antirretroviral

anti-Semitic /ˈæntɪsəˈmɪtɪk || ˌæntisɪˈmɪtɪk/ *adj* antisemita

anti-Semitism /ˈæntɪˈsemətɪzəm || ˌæntɪˈsemɪtɪzəm/ *n* [u] antisemitismo *m*

antiseptic¹ /ˈæntɪˈseptɪk/ *n* [c u] antiséptico *m*

antiseptic² *adj* 1 (Pharm) antiséptico 2 (sterile, lifeless) aséptico

antisocial /ˈæntɪˈsəʊʃəl/ *adj* 1 (offensive to society) antisocial 2 (unsociable) poco sociable

antistatic /ˈæntɪˈstætɪk || ˌæntiˈstætɪk/ *adj* antiestático

anti-terrorist /ˈæntaɪˈterərəst || ˌæntiˈterərɪst/ *adj* antiterrorista

antithesis /ænˈtɪθəsəs || ænˈtɪθəsɪs/ *n* (*pl* **-eses** /-əsiːz/) antítesis *f*

antitrust /ˈæntɪˈtrʌst || ˌæntiˈtrʌst/ *adj* (in US) antimonopolio *adj inv*, antitrust *adj inv*

antler /ˈæntlər || ˈæntlə(r)/ *n* cuerno *m*, asta *f*‡; **the animal's ~s** la cornamenta del animal

antonym /ˈæntənɪm/ *n* antónimo *m*

anus /ˈeɪnəs/ *n* ano *m*

anvil /ˈænvəl || ˈænvɪl/ *n* yunque *m*

anxiety /æŋˈzaɪəti/ *n* (*pl* **-ties**) 1 [u] (distress, concern) preocupación *f*, ansiedad *f* 2 [c] (problem, worry) preocupación *f* 3 [u] (Med, Psych) ansiedad *f*, angustia *f* 4 [u] (eagerness) ansias *fpl*, afán *m*

anxious /ˈæŋkʃəs/ *adj* 1 (worried) preocupado, inquieto; **to be ~ ABOUT/FOR sth** estar* preocupado POR algo 2 (worrying) ‹*time/moment*› (lleno) de preocupación 3 (eager) deseoso, ansioso; **to be ~ to + INF: he's very ~ to please** tiene mucho afán de agradar; **my parents are ~ to meet you** mis padres están ansiosos por conocerte

anxiously /ˈæŋkʃəsli/ *adv* 1 (worriedly) con preocupación *or* inquietud 2 (eagerly) ansiosamente, con ansiedad

any¹ /ˈeni/ *adj*

Sense I

A (*in questions*) 1 (+ *pl n*): **are there ~ questions?** ¿alguien tiene alguna pregunta?; **does she have ~ children?** ¿tiene hijos? 2 (+ *uncount n*): **do you need ~ help?** ¿necesitas ayuda?; **do you want ~ more coffee?** ¿quieres más café? 3 (+ *sing count n: as indef art*) algún, -guna; **is there ~ chance they'll come?** ¿existe alguna posibilidad de que vengan?

B (*in if clauses and suppositions*) 1 (+ *pl n*): **call me if there are ~ changes** llámame si hay algún cambio; **if you see ~ flowers, buy some** si ves flores, compra algunas; **report ~ accidents to me** infórmeme de cualquier accidente que ocurra 2 (+ *uncount n*): **let me know if you have ~ pain** avíseme si siente dolor; **~ rivalry between them soon disappeared** si había existido entre ellos alguna rivalidad, pronto desapareció; **take ~ money you need** toma el dinero que necesites 3 (+ *sing count n*): **if ~ lawyer can help you, she can** si hay un abogado que te pueda ayudar, es ella; **~ upset could kill him** cualquier disgusto podría matarlo; **~ act of disobedience will be punished** toda desobediencia será castigada

C (*with neg and implied neg*) 1 (+ *pl n*): **don't buy ~ more eggs** no compres más huevos; **aren't there ~ apples left?** ¿no queda ninguna manzana?, ¿no quedan manzanas? 2 (+ *uncount n*): **don't make ~ noise** no hagas ruido; **didn't he give you ~ money at all?** ¿no te dio nada de dinero?; **it doesn't make ~ sense** no tiene ningún sentido 3 (+ *sing count n*) ningún, -guna; **he didn't leave ~ telephone number** no nos dejó ningún número de teléfono; **I didn't say ~ such thing!** ¡yo no dije tal cosa!

Sense II

A 1 (no matter which): **take ~ book you want** llévate cualquier libro *or* el libro que quieras; **take ~ books you want** llévate los libros que quieras; **call me ~ time** llámame cuando quieras; **~ day now** cualquier día de éstos 2 (every, all): **in ~ large school, you'll find that ...** en cualquier *or* todo colegio grande, verás que ...

B (countless, a lot): **~ number/amount of sth** cualquier cantidad de algo

any² *pron*

A (*in questions*) 1 (*referring to pl n*) alguno, -na; **those chocolates were nice, are there ~ left?** ¡qué ricos esos bombones! ¿queda alguno? 2 (*referring to uncount n*): **we need sugar; did you buy ~?** nos hace falta azúcar ¿compraste?; **is there ~ of that cake left?** ¿queda algo de ese pastel?

B (*in if clauses and suppositions*) 1 (*referring to pl n*): **buy some**

red ones if you can find ~ compra algunas rojas si encuentras; **the advantages, if ~, are marginal** las ventajas, si (es que) las hay, son marginales; **if ~ of my friends calls, take a message** si llama alguno de mis amigos, toma el recado 2 (*referring to uncount n*): **help yourself to cake if you want ~** sírvete pastel si quieres

C (*with neg and implied neg*) 1 (*referring to pl n*): **some children were here — I didn't see ~** aquí había algunos niños — yo no vi (a) ninguno *or* no los vi; **you'll have to go without cigarettes; I forgot to buy ~** te vas a tener que arreglar sin cigarrillos porque me olvidé de comprar 2 (*referring to uncount n*): **she offered me some wine, but I didn't want ~** me ofreció vino, pero no quise; **I didn't understand ~ of that lecture** no entendí nada de esa conferencia

D (no matter which) cualquiera; **which would you like? — ~ will do** ¿cuál quieres? — cualquiera (sirve)

any[3] *adv*

A (*with comparative*): **do you feel ~ better now?** ¿te sientes (algo) mejor ahora?; **things aren't ~ better** las cosas no andan (nada) mejor; **they don't live here ~ more** ya no viven aquí

B (at all) (AmE): **have you thought about it ~ since then?** ¿has pensado en ello desde entonces?; **it doesn't seem to have affected him ~** no parece haberlo afectado en absoluto *or* (para) nada

anybody /'eni,bɑːdi || 'eni,bɒdi/ *pron*

A 1 (somebody) (*in interrog, conditional sentences*) alguien; **~ at home?** ¿hay alguien en casa?; **will ~ be seeing Emma today?** ¿alguno de ustedes va a ver a Emma hoy?; **she'll know, if ~ does** si alguien lo sabe, va a ser ella 2 (a single person) (*with neg*) nadie; **don't tell ~!** ¡no se lo digas a nadie!

B 1 (whoever, everybody): **~ that wants a ticket** quien quiera una entrada; **give it to ~ you like** dáselo a quien quieras; **~ who's been to Paris knows ...** cualquier persona *or* cualquiera que haya estado en París sabe ...; **~ interested should contact ...** los interesados pónganse en contacto con ...; **~ married to a British citizen** toda persona casada con un ciudadano británico; **before ~ could stop her** antes de que nadie pudiera detenerla 2 (no matter who) cualquiera 3 (a person of importance) alguien; **everybody who is ~ was there** toda la gente importante estaba allí

anyhow /'enihaʊ/ *adv*

A ▸**anyway**

B (haphazardly) de cualquier manera

anyone /'eniwʌn/ *pron* ▸**anybody**

anyplace /'enipleɪs/ *adv* (AmE) ▸**anywhere**[1] **A**

anything /'eniθɪŋ/ *pron*

A 1 (something) (*in interrog, conditional sentences*) algo; **do you want ~ from the shop?** ¿quieres algo de la tienda?; **have you seen ~ of Dick lately?** ¿has visto a Dick últimamente?; **have you ever heard ~ so ridiculous?** ¡habráse oído semejante ridiculez!; **if ~, he seemed slightly worse** en todo caso, parecía que estaba algo peor; **before ~ is decided** antes de decidir nada 2 (something similar) (colloq): **do you need a hammer or ~?** ¿necesitas un martillo o algo por el estilo? 3 (a single thing) (*with neg*) nada; **don't say ~!** ¡no digas nada!; **hardly ~** casi nada

B 1 (whatever): **~ you like** lo que te guste, lo que prefieras; **~ you say!** ¡lo que tú digas!; **we'll do ~ we can to help** haremos todo lo que podamos para ayudar; **don't attempt ~ too demanding** no intentes hacer nada demasiado agotador; **it lasts for ~ up to three weeks** dura hasta tres semanas 2 (no matter what): **~ is possible** todo es posible; **~ could happen** podría pasar cualquier cosa; **I'll try ~ once** estoy siempre dispuesto a probar cosas nuevas; **I'd do ~ for you** haría lo que fuera *or* cualquier cosa por ti; **he eats ~** come de todo; **I wouldn't do that for ~** no haría eso por nada del mundo

C (*used for emphasis*): **was it interesting? — ~ but!** ¿fue interesante? — ¡qué va!; **he will be ~ but pleased** no le va a hacer gracia ni mucho menos; **the portrait doesn't look ~ like her** el retrato no se parece en nada a ella

anyway /'eniweɪ/ *adv*

A 1 (in any case) de todos modos, de todas formas, igual; **who's this Jack Simmons, ~?** ¿y a todo esto, quién es el tal Jack Simmons?; **who needs dictionaries, ~?** igual *or* total ¿para qué sirven los diccionarios? 2 (at least) al menos, por lo menos; **it was a good movie; I thought so ~** la película era buena; al menos *or* por lo menos a mí me lo pareció 3 (regardless) de todos modos, igual; **I'm going ~** de todos modos *or* aún así voy a ir

B (changing the subject, moving conversation on) (*as linker*) bueno; **~, to cut a long story short, ...** bueno, en resumidas cuentas ...

anywhere[1] /'enihwer || 'eniweə(r)/ *adv*

A 1 (no matter where) en cualquier sitio *or* lugar *or* lado; **you can sit ~ you like** te puedes sentar donde quieras 2 (in, to any unspecified place): **have you seen my book ~?** ¿has visto mi libro por alguna parte *or* por algún lado?; **we never go ~ together** nunca vamos juntos a ningún lado *or* sitio; **that won't get you ~** con eso no vas a conseguir *or* lograr nada

B **anywhere near**: **is it ~ near Portland?** ¿queda cerca de Portland?; **we aren't ~ near ready yet** todavía no estamos listos ni mucho menos

anywhere[2] *pron*: **is there ~ that sells oysters?** ¿hay algún sitio *or* lugar donde vendan ostras?; **she hasn't ~ to stay** no tiene donde quedarse; **miles from ~** en un lugar muy alejado *or* apartado

AOB (= **any other business**) otros temas

aorta /eɪ'ɔːrtə || eɪ'ɔːtə/ *n* (*pl* **-tas** *or* **-tae** /-taɪ/) aorta *f*

apace /ə'peɪs/ *adv* (liter *or* journ) a paso *or* ritmo acelerado

apart /ə'pɑːrt || ə'pɑːt/ *adv*

A 1 (separated): **keep them ~** manténgalos separados; **her intelligence set her ~** se destacaba por su inteligencia; *see also* **tell apart** 2 (into pieces): *see* **come, fall, pull, take** *etc* **apart**

B (distant): **in places as far ~ as Tokyo and Paris** en lugares tan alejados el uno del otro como Tokio y París; **the first and second interviews are weeks ~** hay varias semanas entre la primera y la segunda entrevista

C (excluded) (*after n*): **these faults ~ ...** aparte de *or* fuera de estos defectos ...; **joking ~ ...** bromas aparte ...

D **apart from** (*as prep*) 1 (except for) excepto, menos, aparte de; **~ from him we're all satisfied** aparte de él *or* exceptuándolo a él, todos estamos satisfechos 2 (discounting) aparte de; **quite ~ from the time it would take, I can't afford it** aparte *or* independientemente del tiempo que me tomaría, no puedo permitírmelo 3 (separated from): **she always sits ~ from the rest of the group** siempre se sienta apartada del resto del grupo

apartheid /ə'pɑːrteɪt || ə'pɑːteɪt/ *n* [u] apartheid *m*

apartment /ə'pɑːrtmənt || ə'pɑːtmənt/ *n* (set of rooms) apartamento *m*, departamento *m* (AmL), piso *m* (Esp); (*before n*) **~ house** *o* **building** edificio *m* de apartamentos *or* (AmL tb) de departamentos; **~ hotel** (AmE) apartotel *m*

apathetic /'æpə'θetɪk/ *adj* apático

apathy /'æpəθi/ *n* [u] apatía *f*

ape[1] /eɪp/ *n* (Zool) simio *m*, mono *m*; ***to go ~*** (colloq) (lose temper) ponerse* hecho un basilisco *or* una furia (fam); (go crazy) ponerse* como loco

ape[2] *vt* remedar, imitar

aperitif, apéritif /ə'perə'tiːf || ə'perətif/ *n* aperitivo *m*

aperture /'æpərtʃər || 'æpətʃə(r)/ *n* 1 (Opt, Phot) apertura *f* 2 (hole, opening) (frml) orificio *m*; (long and narrow) rendija *f*

apex /'eɪpeks/ *n* (*pl* **apexes** *or* **apices**) 1 (Math) vértice *m* 2 (pinnacle, high point) cúspide *f*, cima *f* 3 (pointed end, tip) ápice *m*

APEX /'eɪpeks/ *adj* (= **advance purchase excursion**) (*before n*) ‹*ticket/booking*› Apex *adj inv*

aphid /'eɪfəd || 'eɪfɪd/ *n* afídido *m*, áfido *m*

aphorism /'æfərɪzəm/ *n* aforismo *m*

aphrodisiac[1] /'æfrə'dɪziæk/ *n* afrodisíaco *m*

aphrodisiac[2] *adj* afrodisíaco

apiary /'eɪpieri/ *n* (*pl* **-ries**) colmenar *m*, apiario *m* (AmL)

apices /'eɪpəsiːz || 'eɪpɪsiːz/ *pl of* **apex**

apiculture /'eɪpəkʌltʃər || 'eɪpɪkʌltʃə(r)/ *n* [u] (tech) apicultura *f*

apiece /ə'piːs/ *adv* cada uno

aplenty /ə'plenti/ *adj* (*after n*) en abundancia

aplomb /ə'plɑːm || ə'plɒm/ *n* [u] aplomo *m*

apocalypse /ə'pɑːkəlɪps || ə'pɒkəlɪps/ *n* 1 (Bib) **Apocalypse** **the A~** el Apocalipsis 2 (disaster) apocalipsis *m*

apocalyptic /ə'pɑːkə'lɪptɪk || ə,pɒkə'lɪptɪk/ *adj* apocalíptico

a

apocryphal /ə'pɑːkrəfəl || ə'pɒkrɪfəl/ *adj* ‹*text/author*› apócrifo; ‹*tale*› espurio, inventado

apogee /'æpədʒiː/ *n* apogeo *m*

apolitical /'eɪpə'lɪtɪkəl/ *adj* apolítico

apologetic /ə'pɑːlə'dʒetɪk || ə,pɒlə'dʒetɪk/ *adj* ‹*letter/look*› de disculpa; **she was very ~** se deshizo en disculpas

apologetically /ə'pɑːlə'dʒetɪkli || ə,pɒlə'dʒetɪkli/ *adv*: **I'm really tired, she said ~** —estoy muy cansada —dijo disculpándose *or* excusándose

apologize /ə'pɑːlədʒaɪz || ə'pɒlədʒaɪz/ *vi* pedir* perdón, disculparse; **to ~ (TO sb) FOR sth**: **we ~ for the delay** rogamos disculpen el retraso; **you must ~ to her for being so rude** tienes que pedirle perdón por haber sido tan grosero; **I must ~ for my son** quisiera disculparme por el comportamiento de mi hijo

apology /ə'pɑːlədʒi || ə'pɒlədʒi/ *n* (*pl* **-gies**)
A **1** (expression of regret) (*often pl*) disculpa *f*, excusa *f*; **please accept my apologies** le ruego me disculpe; **to offer one's apologies** disculparse, excusarse (frml), presentar sus (*or* mis *etc*) disculpas *or* excusas (frml); **I owe you an ~** le debo una disculpa; **to make no ~ for sth**: **I make no ~ for bringing up the subject** no tengo ningún reparo en sacar el tema a colación **2** (for not attending meeting) (BrE): **apologies from J Brown** J Brown envía sus excusas por no poder asistir
B (poor specimen) **~ FOR sth**: **it's an ~ for a team** es un remedo de equipo

apoplectic /'æpə'plektɪk/ *adj* (Med) apoplético; **she was ~ with rage** (colloq) estaba que trinaba (fam)

apoplexy /'æpəpleksi/ *n* [u] apoplejía *f*

apostle /ə'pɑːsəl || ə'pɒsəl/ *n* apóstol *m*

apostolic /'æpə'stɑːlɪk || ,æpə'stɒlɪk/ *adj* apostólico

apostrophe /ə'pɑːstrəfi || ə'pɒstrəfi/ *n* **1** [c] (Ling, Print) apóstrofo *m* **2** [u c] (Lit) apóstrofe *m or f*

apothecary /ə'pɑːθəkeri || ə'pɒθəkəri/ *n* (*pl* **-ries**) (arch) boticario, -ria *m,f* (ant)

apotheosis /ə'pɑːθi'əʊsəs || ə,pɒθi'əʊsɪs/ *n* (*pl* **-ses** /-siːz/) **1** [u] (deification) apoteosis *f* **2** [c] (extreme manifestation) (liter) súmmum *m*, quintaesencia *f*

Appalachian Mountains /'æpə'leɪtʃən/, **Appalachians** /-z/ *pl n* **the ~ ~** los (montes) Apalaches

appall, (BrE) **appal** /ə'pɔːl/ *vt* (BrE) **-ll-** horrorizar*, consternar; **I'm ~ed by their attitude** me horroriza su actitud

appalling /ə'pɔːlɪŋ/ *adj* ‹*conditions*› atroz, terrible; ‹*language/behavior*› vergonzoso; **the play is absolutely ~** la obra es pésima

appallingly /ə'pɔːlɪŋli/ *adv* ‹*bad/ignorant*› terriblemente; **to behave ~** portarse terriblemente mal

apparatus /'æpə'rætəs || ,æpə'reɪtəs/ *n* [u c] (*pl* **~**) **1** (equipment) aparatos *mpl*; **a piece of ~** un aparato **2** (Pol) aparato *m*

apparel /ə'pærəl/ *n* [u] (Clothing) **1** (finery) (liter) atavío *m* (liter) **2** (AmE Busn) ropa *f*; **intimate ~** lencería *f*

apparent /ə'pærənt/ *adj* **1** (evident): **there's no ~ difference** no se advierte *or* nota ninguna diferencia; **for no ~ reason** sin motivo aparente; **it was ~ that ...** estaba claro que ..., era evidente *or* obvio que ...; **to become ~** hacerse* patente, empezar* a verse **2** (seeming) ‹*interest/concern*› aparente

apparently /ə'pærəntli/ *adv* **1** (*indep*) al parecer, por lo visto, según parece; **is she pregnant? — apparently** ¿está embarazada? — pues eso parece *or* por lo visto sí **2** (seemingly) ‹*intelligent/happy*› aparentemente

apparition /'æpə'rɪʃən/ *n* aparición *f*

appeal¹ /ə'piːl/ *n*
A [c] (call) llamamiento *m*, llamado *m* (AmL); (request) solicitud *f*, petición *f*, pedido *m* (AmL); (plea) ruego *m*, súplica *f*; **~ (TO sb) FOR sth**: **an ~ for calm** un llamamiento *or* un llamado a la calma; **they made an urgent ~ for food** hicieron un llamamiento *or* un llamado urgente solicitando alimentos; **an ~ to reason** un llamamiento *or* un llamado a la razón
B [c] (Law) apelación *f*, recurso *m* de apelación; **to have the right of ~** tener* derecho a apelar
C [c] (fund, organization) *campaña para recaudar fondos*
D [u] (attraction) atractivo *m*

appeal² *vi*
A (call) **to ~ FOR sth** ‹*for funds*› pedir* *or* solicitar algo; **the Minister went on television to ~ for calm** el ministro apareció en televisión para hacer un llamamiento *or* (AmL tb) un llamado a la calma; **to ~ TO sb/sth**: **the police ~ed to witnesses to come forward** la policía hizo un llamamiento *or* (AmL tb) un llamado para que se presentaran testigos del hecho; **to ~ to sb's better nature** apelar a la bondad de algn
B **1** (Law) apelar **2** (Sport) recurrir *or* apelar al árbitro (*or* al juez *etc*)
C (be attractive) **to ~ TO sb** atraerle* A algn; **teaching never ~ed to me** nunca me atrajo la enseñanza; **fishing doesn't ~** pescar no tiene mucho atractivo
■ **appeal** *vt* (AmE) ‹*decision/verdict*› apelar contra *or* de

appealing /ə'piːlɪŋ/ *adj* atractivo, atrayente

appealingly /ə'piːlɪŋli/ *adv* de manera atractiva *or* atrayente

appear /ə'pɪr || ə'pɪə(r)/ *vi*
(Sense I)
A **1** (come into view) aparecer*; **he suddenly ~ed from behind the door** de pronto salió de detrás de la puerta **2** ‹‹*spirit*›› aparecerse*
B (be published) aparecer*, salir*; **to ~ in print** publicarse*
C (on television) aparecer*, salir*; (Theat) actuar*
D (Law) comparecer*; **to ~ in court** comparecer*
(Sense II) (seem) parecer*; **that's how he ~s to a lot of people** ésa es la impresión que le da a mucha gente; **so it ~s** *o* **so it would ~** eso parece; **it ~s not** *o* **it would ~ not** parecería que no; **to ~ to + INF** parecer* + INF; **she ~ed to be busy** parecía (estar) ocupada; **we ~ to be lost** parece que nos hemos perdido; **it ~s THAT**: **it ~s that she was the only one not to know** parece ser que era la única que no lo sabía

appearance /ə'pɪrəns || ə'pɪərəns/ *n*
A **1** [u c] (coming into view) aparición *f*; **he made a personal ~** apareció en persona; **she made an unexpected ~ at the party** apareció *or* se presentó inesperadamente en la fiesta; **to put in an ~** hacer* acto de presencia **2** (Law) comparecencia *f* **3** [u] (of book) aparición *f*, publicación *f*
B [u] **1** (look) aspecto *m*; **she gives the ~ of being quite contented** da la impresión de estar contenta con la vida **2** **appearances** *pl* apariencias *fpl*; **~s can be deceptive** las apariencias engañan; **to keep up ~s** guardar las apariencias; **for the sake of ~s** para salvar las apariencias

appease /ə'piːz/ *vt* ‹*person*› apaciguar*; ‹*anger*› aplacar*; ‹*hunger*› mitigar*

appeasement /ə'piːzmənt/ *n* [u] (Pol): **policy of ~** la política contemporizadora *or* de contemporización

append /ə'pend/ *vt* (frml) (add) **to ~ sth TO sth** agregar* *or* añadir algo A algo; (enclose) adjuntar *or* acompañar algo A algo

appendage /ə'pendɪdʒ/ *n* (frml) añadidura *f*, apéndice *m*

appendectomy /'æpen'dektəmi/ *n* (*pl* **-mies**) apendicectomía *f* (frml), apendectomía *f* (frml)

appendices /ə'pendəsiːz || ə'pendɪsiːz/ *pl of* **appendix**

appendicitis /ə'pendə'saɪtəs || ə,pendɪ'saɪtɪs/ *n* [u] apendicitis *f*

appendix /ə'pendɪks/ *n* (*pl* **-dixes** *or* **-dices**) **1** (Anat) apéndice *m*; **she had her ~ out** la operaron del apéndice **2** (in book) apéndice *m*

appertain /'æpər'teɪn || ,æpə'teɪn/ *vi* (frml) **to ~ TO sth** tener* relación CON algo

appetite /'æpətaɪt || 'æpɪtaɪt/ *n* [c u] apetito *m*; **the walk gave us an ~** la caminata nos abrió el apetito; **he has an enormous ~ for knowledge** tiene una enorme sed de sabiduría

appetizer /'æpətaɪzər || 'æpɪtaɪzə(r)/ *n* **1** (drink) aperitivo *m* **2** (snack) aperitivo *m*, tapa *f* (Esp), botana *f* (Méx)

appetizing /'æpətaɪzɪŋ || 'æpɪtaɪzɪŋ/ *adj* apetitoso

applaud /ə'plɔːd/ *vt* **1** ‹*person/performance*› aplaudir **2** (agree with, admire) ‹*decision/action*› aplaudir, aprobar*, celebrar
■ **applaud** *vi* aplaudir

applause /ə'plɔːz/ *n* [u] aplausos *mpl*; **let's have a round of ~ for ...** un aplauso para ...

apple /'æpəl/ *n* [c u] manzana *f*; **the Big A~** (colloq) la Gran Manzana, Nueva York; ***to be the ~ of sb's eye*** ser* la niña de los ojos de algn; (*before n*) **~ tree** manzano *m*

apple: **~cart** *n*: ***to upset the ~cart*** desbaratar los planes; **~ pie** *n* [c u] pastel *m* de manzana, pay *m* de manzana (Méx)

applet /'æplət || 'æplɪt/ *n* (Comput) applet *m*

appliance /ə'plaɪəns/ *n* (device) aparato *m*; **electrical ~s** (large) electrodomésticos *mpl*; (small) aparatos *mpl* eléctricos

applicable /'æplɪkəbəl, ə'plɪkəbəl/ *adj* (frml): **delete as ~** tache lo que no corresponda; **~ TO sb/sth**: **this part's not ~ to us** esta parte no nos atañe; **these regulations are only ~ to foreigners** estas normas se refieren *or* se aplican únicamente a los extranjeros

applicant /'æpləkənt || 'æplɪkənt/ *n* (for job) candidato, -ta *m,f*, aspirante *mf*, postulante *mf* (CS), aplicante *mf* (Ven)

application /'æplə'keɪʃən || ˌæplɪ'keɪʃən/ *n*
A [c u] (request) solicitud *f*; **~ FOR sth** ‹*for loan/grant/visa*› solicitud DE algo; **~ for bail** petición *f* de fianza; (*before n*) **~ form** (impreso *m* de) solicitud *f*
B 1▸ [c u] (use — of method, skills, theory) aplicación *f*; (— of force) uso *m*; **the machine has many ~s** la máquina tiene muchos usos 2▸ [u c] (of paint, ointment) aplicación *f*; **for external ~ only** para uso externo 3▸ [c] (Comput) aplicación *f*
C [u] (diligence) diligencia *f*, aplicación *f*

applicator /'æpləkeɪtər || 'æplɪkeɪtə(r)/ *n* aplicador *m*

applied /ə'plaɪd/ *adj* aplicado

appliqué /'æplə'keɪ || æ'pli:keɪ/ *n* [u c] (technique) *labor que consiste en hacer aplicaciones o apliques en una tela*; (decoration) aplicación *f*, aplique *m*, apliqué *m*

apply /ə'plaɪ/ **applies, applying, applied** *vt* 1▸ (put on) aplicar* 2▸ ‹*method/theory/rules*› aplicar*; **he applied his mind to the task** se concentró en la tarea; **to ~ the brakes** frenar; **to ~ pressure** usar fuerza; **she applied herself to her work** se puso a trabajar con diligencia *or* empeño

■ **apply** *vi* 1▸ (make application): **please ~ in writing to ...** diríjase por escrito a ...; **to ~ FOR sth** ‹*for loan/permission*› solicitar *or* pedir* algo; **to ~ for a job** solicitar un trabajo, presentarse para un trabajo, aplicar* a un trabajo (Ven), postular para un trabajo (CS); **to ~ TO sb FOR sth** solicitarle algo A algn; Ⓢ **apply within** infórmese aquí, razón aquí; **he applied to join the police** presentó una solicitud de ingreso en la policía 2▸ (be applicable, relevant) «*regulation/criterion*» aplicarse*

appoint /ə'pɔɪnt/ *vt*
A (name, choose) **to ~ sb (TO sth)** ‹*to post/committee*› nombrar *or* designar a algn (PARA algo); **she was ~ed director in 1987** fue nombrada directora en 1987
B (frml) ‹*date*› designar (frml), fijar; ‹*task*› asignar; **at the ~ed hour** a la hora señalada
C (BrE) **appointed** *past p*: **beautifully ~ed house** casa terminada con hermosos detalles, casa con hermoso terminado

appointment /ə'pɔɪntmənt/ *n*
A [c] (arrangement to meet) cita *f*; (with doctor, hairdresser) hora *f*, cita *f*; **I phoned the doctor's to make an ~** llamé al médico para pedir hora *or* una cita; **do you have an ~?** ¿tiene cita/hora?; **he failed to keep the ~** no acudió *or* no se presentó a la cita; **viewing by ~ only** concertar cita para visitar
B 1▸ [u c] (act of appointing) nombramiento *m*; Ⓢ **by appointment to Her Majesty Queen Elizabeth II** (in UK) proveedores de SM la reina Isabel II 2▸ [c] (post) (frml) puesto *m*; **publishing ~s** ofertas *fpl* de empleo en el campo editorial

apportion /ə'pɔ:rʃən || ə'pɔ:ʃən/ *vt* ‹*duties/time*› distribuir*; ‹*costs/sum*› prorratear, repartir; **the blame was ~ed to them both equally** se les culpó *or* se les imputó la culpa a ambos por partes iguales

apportionment /ə'pɔ:rʃənmənt || ə'pɔ:ʃənmənt/ *n* (AmE Pol) *determinación del número de escaños que corresponde proporcionar a cada estado*

apposite /'æpəzət || 'æpəzɪt/ *adj* (frml) apropiado, pertinente

appraisal /ə'preɪzəl/ *n* (of situation, employee) evaluación *f*; (of work, novel) valoración *f*, evaluación *f*; (of property) tasación *f*

appraise /ə'preɪz/ *vt* ‹*situation/employee*› evaluar*; ‹*novel/painting*› valorar; ‹*property*› tasar, avaluar* (AmL)

appreciable /ə'pri:ʃəbəl/ *adj* ‹*change/difference*› apreciable, sensible; ‹*loss/sum*› importante, considerable

appreciably /ə'pri:ʃəbli/ *adv* sensiblemente, perceptiblemente

appreciate /ə'pri:ʃieɪt/ *vt* 1▸ (value) ‹*food/novel*› apreciar; **someone who ~s good wine** una persona que aprecia *or* que sabe apreciar el buen vino; **she's not ~d here** aquí no se la valora 2▸ (be grateful for) agradecer*; **I ~ your help** (te) agradezco tu ayuda; **I'd ~ it if you could let me know** le agradecería que me avisara 3▸ (understand) ‹*danger/difficulties*› darse* cuenta de; **I (can) ~ that, but ...** te entiendo *or* lo comprendo *or* me hago cargo, pero ...

■ **appreciate** *vi* «*shares/property*» (re)valorizarse*, apreciarse (frml)

appreciation /ə'pri:ʃi'eɪʃən/ *n*
A 1▸ [u] (gratitude) agradecimiento *m*, reconocimiento *m*; **in ~ of your help** como muestra de nuestro agradecimiento por su ayuda 2▸ [u] (discriminating enjoyment): **he showed a genuine ~ of music** demostró saber apreciar la música; **art ~ classes** clases *fpl* de iniciación al arte *or* de apreciación artística 3▸ [c] (review) crítica *f*
B (Fin) (re)valorización *f*

appreciative /ə'pri:ʃətɪv/ *adj* 1▸ (grateful) ‹*smile/gesture*› de agradecimiento; **he wasn't very ~** no se mostró muy agradecido; **to be ~ OF sth** estar* agradecido POR algo 2▸ (of art, good food) apreciativo 3▸ (admiring) ‹*look*› de admiración; ‹*comment*› elogioso

appreciatively /ə'pri:ʃətɪvli/ *adv*: **she smiled at him ~** le sonrió agradecida; **the audience applauded ~** el público aplaudió en señal de apreciación

apprehend /'æprɪ'hend/ *vt* (frml) (arrest) apresar, detener*

apprehension /'æprɪ'hentʃən || ˌæprɪ'henʃən/ *n* [u]
A (anxiety) aprensión *f*, temor *m*
B (arrest) (frml) detención *f*, arresto *m*

apprehensive /'æprɪ'hensɪv/ *adj* ‹*look*› aprensivo, de aprensión; **to be ~ ABOUT sth**: **I'm rather ~ about the consequences** estoy algo inquieto *or* preocupado por lo que pueda pasar; **to grow ~** inquietarse

apprehensively /'æprɪ'hensɪvli/ *adv* con aprensión

apprentice[1] /ə'prentəs || ə'prentɪs/ *n* aprendiz, -diza *m,f*

apprentice[2] *vt*: **to be ~d TO sb** estar* de aprendiz CON algn

apprenticeship /ə'prentəsʃɪp || ə'prentɪsʃɪp/ *n* aprendizaje *m* (*de un oficio*)

apprise /ə'praɪz/ *vt* (frml) **to ~ sb OF sth** informar a algn DE algo; **he was ~d of the facts** se lo informó *or* se lo puso al tanto de los hechos

approach[1] /ə'prəʊtʃ/ *vi* acercarse*, aproximarse; **the time is fast ~ing when ...** se acerca rápidamente el momento en que ...

■ **approach** *vt* 1▸ (draw near to) aproximarse *or* acercarse* a; **he was ~ing 50** se acercaba a los 50; **something ~ing half a kilo** casi medio kilo 2▸ (talk to): **have you ~ed her about it?** ¿ya se lo ha planteado?, ¿ya ha hablado con ella del asunto?; **he ~ed me for a loan** se dirigió a mí para pedirme un préstamo; **several companies ~ed us** varias compañías se pusieron en contacto con nosotros; **to be easy/difficult to ~** ser*/no ser* muy accesible 3▸ (tackle) ‹*problem/question*› enfocar*, abordar

approach[2] *n*
A [c] (method, outlook) enfoque *m*; **~ TO sth**: **to adopt a new ~ to sth** dar un nuevo enfoque a algo; **let's try a different ~ to the problem** enfoquemos el problema de otra manera
B [c] (overture — offering sth) propuesta *f*; (— requesting sth) solicitud *f*, petición *f*, pedido *m* (AmL); **to make ~es** *o* **an ~ to sb** hacerle* una propuesta (*or* una solicitud *etc*) a algn
C [u] (drawing near): **he looked up at my ~** levantó la vista cuando me acerqué; **at the ~ of winter** al acercarse el invierno; **the pilot made his ~** el piloto efectuó las maniobras de aproximación
D [c] (means of entering) acceso *m*; (*before n*) **~ road** (BrE) camino *m* de acceso

a

approachable /ə'prəʊtʃəbəl/ *adj* 1 ‹*person*› accesible 2 ‹*place*› accesible

approaching /ə'prəʊtʃɪŋ/ *adj*: **he didn't see the ~ car** no vio el coche que se acercaba *or* se aproximaba; **he viewed his ~ retirement with concern** se acercaba el momento de su jubilación y esto lo inquietaba

approbation /'æprə'beɪʃən/ *n* [u] (frml) aprobación *f*

appropriate[1] /ə'prəʊpriət/ *adj* apropiado; **it would not be ~ for me to comment** no estaría bien que hiciera algún comentario; **take the ~ action** tome las medidas pertinentes; **delete as ~** tachar lo que no corresponda

appropriate[2] /ə'prəʊprieɪt/ *vt* 1 (take illegally) ‹*possessions*› apropiarse de 2 (set aside) ‹*money*› destinar, asignar

appropriately /ə'prəʊpriətli/ *adv* de manera apropiada, apropiadamente

appropriateness /ə'prəʊpriətnəs || ə'prəʊpriətnɪs/ *n* [u] lo apropiado

appropriation /ə'prəʊpri'eɪʃən/ *n* 1 [c u] (Govt) (in US) partida *f*, asignación *f*; (*before n*) **the House/Senate A~s Committee** el Comité de gastos de la Cámara de Representantes/del Senado 2 [u] (taking) apropiación *f* 3 [u] (of funds) asignación *f*

approval /ə'pru:vəl/ *n* [u] 1 (agreement) aprobación *f*; **to seek sb's ~ (for sth)** tratar de obtener la aprobación de algn (para algo); **I've drafted a letter for your ~** he escrito la carta en borrador para que usted le dé el visto bueno 2 **on ~** a prueba

approve /ə'pru:v/ *vi* 1 (agree): **to ~ (OF sth/sb)**: **mother seems to ~ of him** a mamá parece gustarle; **they didn't ~ of us getting married** no les pareció bien que nos casáramos; **I don't ~ of his methods** no estoy de acuerdo con sus métodos; **they don't ~ of my smoking** les parece mal que fume; **do you ~?** ¿le parece bien? 2 (agree formally) dar* su (*or* mi *etc*) aprobación *or* visto bueno

■ **approve** *vt* 1 (sanction, agree) ‹*decision/plan*› aprobar* 2 (officially recognize) ‹*institution*› acreditar; **an ~d method** un método autorizado

approving /ə'pru:vɪŋ/ *adj* ‹*smile/look*› de aprobación, aprobatorio

approvingly /ə'pru:vɪŋli/ *adv* con aprobación; **she nodded ~** asintió con la cabeza en señal de aprobación

approx /ə'prɑ:ks || ə'prɒks/ (= **approximate/approximately**) aprox.

approximate[1] /ə'prɑ:ksəmət || ə'prɒksɪmət/ *adj* aproximado

approximate[2] /ə'prɑ:ksəmeɪt || ə'prɒksɪmeɪt/ *vi* **to ~ TO sth** aproximarse A algo

approximately /ə'prɑ:ksəmətli || ə'prɒksɪmətli/ *adv* aproximadamente

approximation /ə'prɑ:ksə'meɪʃən || ə,prɒksɪ'meɪʃən/ *n* 1 (rough calculation) aproximación *f* 2 (rough equivalent): **at best it's an ~ to the truth** como mucho podría decirse que se acerca a la verdad

Apr (= **April**) abr.

APR *n* (= **annual percentage rate**) TAE

apricot /'æprəkɑ:t || 'eɪprɪkɒt/ *n* albaricoque *m* *or* (Méx) chabacano *m* *or* (CS) damasco *m*; (*before n*) **~ tree** albaricoquero *m* *or* (Méx) chabacano *m* *or* (AmS) damasco *m*

April /'eɪprəl || 'eɪprɪl/ *n* abril *m*; (*before n*) **~ fool!** ¡inocente!; **to play an ~ fool on sb** gastarle *or* hacerle* una inocentada a algn; **~ Fools' Day** ≈ el día de los (Santos) Inocentes (*en EEUU y GB se celebra el 1° de abril*); ***~ showers bring May flowers*** ≈ en abril, aguas mil; **an ~ shower** ≈ una nube *or* un chaparrón de verano; *see also* **January**

apron /'eɪprən/ *n* (for domestic use) delantal *m*, mandil *m* (Esp); (workman's) mandil *m*; ▸**string[1] A2**

apropos /'æprə'pəʊ/ *adj* 1 ‹*remark*› pertinente, acertado 2 **~ (of)** (*as prep*) a propósito de

apse /æps/ *n* ábside *m*

apt /æpt/ *adj* 1 (fitting, suitable) acertado, apropiado 2 (likely) **to be ~ to + INF** ser* propenso *or* tener* tendencia *or* tender* A + INF 3 (clever, quick) listo, capaz, despierto

aptitude /'æptətu:d || 'æptɪtju:d/ *n* [c u] **~ (FOR sth)** aptitud *f* (PARA algo); **she showed an early ~ for music** muy pronto mostró tener aptitudes musicales *or* talento para la música

aptly /'æptli/ *adv* acertadamente

aptness /'æptnəs || 'æptnɪs/ *n* [u] lo acertado

aqua /'ækwə, 'ɑ:kwə || 'ækwə/ *n* [u] (esp AmE) ▸**aquamarine 2**

Aqua-Lung® /'ækwəlʌŋ, 'ɑ:kwəlʌŋ || 'ækwəlʌŋ/ *n* escafandra *f* autónoma

aquamarine /'ækwəmə'ri:n, 'ɑ:kwəmə'ri:n || ,ækwəmə'ri:n/ *n* 1 [c u] (Min) aguamarina *f*‡ 2 [u] (color) color *m* aguamarina

aquarium /ə'kweriəm || ə'kweəriəm/ *n* (*pl* **-riums** *or* **-ria** /-riə/) acuario *m*

Aquarius /ə'kweriəs || ə'kweəriəs/ *n* 1 (sign) (*no art*) Acuario; **he was born under ~** nació bajo el signo de Acuario; **I'm ~** soy (de) Acuario 2 (person) Acuario *or* acuario *mf*, acuariano, -na *m,f*

aquatic /ə'kwætɪk, ə'kwɑ:tɪk || ə'kwætɪk/ *adj* acuático

aqueduct /'ækwədʌkt || 'ækwɪdʌkt/ *n* acueducto *m*

aquiline /'ækwəlaɪn || 'ækwɪlaɪn/ *adj* aguileño, aquilino (liter)

AR = **Arkansas**

Arab[1] /'ærəb/ *adj* árabe

Arab[2] *n* árabe *mf*

arabesque /'ærə'besk/ *n* arabesco *m*

Arabian /ə'reɪbiən/ *adj* árabe; **the ~ Nights** Las mil y una noches; **the ~ Sea** el Mar de Omán

Arabic[1] /'ærəbɪk/ *adj* árabe; **a~ numerals** números *mpl* arábigos

Arabic[2] *n* [u] árabe *m*

arable /'ærəbəl/ *adj* arable, cultivable; **~ farming** agricultura *f*; **~ land** tierras *fpl* de cultivo

Aragon /'ærəgɑ:n || 'ærəgən/ *n* Aragón *m*

arbiter /'ɑ:rbətər || 'ɑ:bɪtə(r)/ *n* árbitro, -tra *m,f*

arbitrarily /'ɑ:rbə'trerəli || 'ɑ:bɪtrərɪli/ *adv* arbitrariamente

arbitrary /'ɑ:rbə,treri || 'ɑ:bɪtrəri/ *adj* arbitrario

arbitrate /'ɑ:rbətreɪt || 'ɑ:bɪtreɪt/ *vt* ‹*dispute*› arbitrar (en)

■ **arbitrate** *vi* arbitrar

arbitration /'ɑ:rbə'treɪʃən || ,ɑ:bɪ'treɪʃən/ *n* [u] arbitraje *m*; **to go to ~** recurrir *or* someterse al arbitraje

arbitrator /'ɑ:rbətreɪtər || 'ɑ:bɪtreɪtə(r)/ *n* árbitro, -tra *m,f*

arbor, (BrE) **arbour** /'ɑ:rbər || 'ɑ:bə(r)/ *n* pérgola *f*, cenador *m*

arc /ɑ:rk || ɑ:k/ *n* (Astron, Math) arco *m*

arcade /ɑ:r'keɪd || ɑ:'keɪd/ *n* 1 (Archit) arcada *f*; (around square, along street) soportales *mpl*, recova *f* (Arg) 2 (of shops) galería *f* comercial 3 (*video ~*) sala *f* de juegos

arcane /ɑ:r'keɪn || ɑ:'keɪn/ *adj* ‹*knowledge/symbol*› arcano, misterioso; ‹*language*› críptico

arch[1] /ɑ:rtʃ || ɑ:tʃ/ *n* 1 (Archit) arco *m* 2 (of foot) arco *m*; **he has fallen ~es** tiene (los) pies planos

arch[2] *vt* ‹*eyebrows/back*› arquear

■ **arch** *vi* (form arch) formar un arco

arch[3] *adj* 1 (mischievous) ‹*remark/smile*› malicioso, pícaro 2 (superior) ‹*tone*› de superioridad

arch- /ɑ:rtʃ || ɑ:tʃ/ *pref* archi-; **~traitor** architraidor; *see also* **archbishop** *etc*

archaeological *etc* (BrE) ▸**archeological** *etc*

archaic /ɑ:r'keɪɪk || ɑ:'keɪɪk/ *adj* arcaico

archangel /'ɑ:rk,eɪndʒəl || 'ɑ:k,eɪndʒəl/ *n* arcángel *m*

archbishop /'ɑ:rtʃ'bɪʃəp || ,ɑ:tʃ'bɪʃəp/ *n* arzobispo *m*

arched /ɑ:rtʃt || 'ɑ:tʃt/ *adj* ‹*window*› en forma de arco; ‹*eyebrows/back*› arqueado

archenemy /'ɑ:rtʃ'enəmi || ,ɑ:tʃ'enəmi/ *n* (*pl* **-mies**) archienemigo, -ga *m,f*

archeological, (BrE) **archaeological** /'ɑ:rkiə'lɑ:dʒɪkəl || ,ɑ:kiə'lɒdʒɪkl/ *adj* arqueológico

archeologist, (BrE) **archaeologist** /'ɑ:rki'ɑ:lədʒəst || ,ɑ:ki'ɒlədʒɪst/ *n* arqueólogo, -ga *m,f*

archeology, (BrE) **archaeology** /'ɑ:rki'ɑ:lədʒi || ,ɑ:ki'ɒlədʒi/ *n* [u] arqueología *f*

archer /'ɑ:rtʃər || 'ɑ:tʃə(r)/ *n* arquero, -ra *m,f*

archery /'ɑːrtʃəri || 'ɑːtʃəri/ *n* [u] tiro *m* con/al arco

archetypal /'ɑːrkɪ'taɪpəl || ˌɑːkɪ'taɪpəl/ *adj* arquetípico

archetype /'ɑːrkɪtaɪp || 'ɑːkɪtaɪp/ *n* arquetipo *m*

archipelago /'ɑːrkə'peləgəʊ || ˌɑːkɪ'peləgəʊ/ *n* (*pl* **-gos** *or* **-goes**) archipiélago *m*

architect /'ɑːrkətekt || 'ɑːkɪtekt/ *n* arquitecto, -ta *m,f*; (of idea, event) artífice *mf*

architectural /'ɑːrkə'tektʃərəl || ˌɑːkɪ'tektʃərəl/ *adj* arquitectónico

architecture /'ɑːrkətektʃər || 'ɑːkɪtektʃə(r)/ *n* [u] arquitectura *f*

archive /'ɑːrkaɪv || 'ɑːkaɪv/ *n* (*often pl*) archivo *m*; **film ~(s)** filmoteca *f*

archly /'ɑːrtʃli || 'ɑːtʃli/ *adv* 1 (mischievously) maliciosamente 2 (arrogantly) con aire de superioridad

archway /'ɑːrtʃweɪ || 'ɑːtʃweɪ/ *n* (entrance) arco *m* (de entrada); (passageway) pasadizo *m* abovedado

Arctic[1] /'ɑːrktɪk || 'ɑːktɪk/ *adj* 1 ‹*flora/fauna*› ártico; **the ~ Ocean** el Océano (Glacial) Ártico, el Ártico; **the ~ Circle** el Círculo Polar Ártico 2 **arctic** ‹*temperatures/conditions*› glacial

Arctic[2] *n* **the ~** la región ártica, las tierras árticas, el Ártico

ardent /'ɑːrdnt || 'ɑːdnt/ *adj* ‹*supporter*› apasionado; ‹*lover*› apasionado, fogoso; ‹*plea/desire*› ferviente; ‹*prayer*› ferviente, fervoroso

ardently /'ɑːrdn̩tli || 'ɑːdəntli/ *adv* ardientemente, fervientemente

ardor, (BrE) **ardour** /'ɑːrdər || 'ɑːdə(r)/ *n* [u] (liter) (zeal) fervor *m*, ardor *m*; (love) pasión *f*

arduous /'ɑːrdʒuəs || 'ɑːdjuːəs/ *adj* ‹*task*› arduo; ‹*training/conditions*› duro, riguroso; ‹*march/climb*› difícil

are /ɑːr || ɑː(r), *weak form* ər/ *2nd pers sing, 1st, 2nd & 3rd pers pl pres of* **be**

area /'eriə || 'eəriə/ *n*

A 1 (geographical) zona *f*, área *f‡*, región *f*; **in the New York ~** en la zona *or* el área de Nueva York; (*before n*) ‹*manager*› regional 2 (urban) zona *f*; **the ~ we live in** el barrio en el que vivimos

B (part of room, building) zona *f*; **the library is a no-smoking ~** en la biblioteca no se puede fumar

C (expanse, patch): **the shaded ~ represents ...** el área sombreada representa ...; **apply the ointment to the affected ~s** aplicar el ungüento a las partes afectadas; **the wreckage was scattered over a wide ~** los restos del siniestro quedaron esparcidos sobre une extensa zona

D (Math) superficie *f*, área *f‡*; (of room, land) superficie *f*

E (field, sphere) terreno *m*; (of knowledge) campo *m*, terreno *m*; **to identify problem ~s** identificar* problemas

F (Sport) (*penalty* **~**) área *f‡* (de castigo)

area: **~ code** *n* (AmE) código *m* de la zona (AmL), prefijo *m* (local) (Esp); **~way** *n* (AmE) patio *m*

arena /ə'riːnə/ *n* 1 (of stadium) arena *f*, ruedo *m* 2 (scene of activity) ruedo *m*; **the political ~** el ruedo político, la arena política

aren't /ɑːrnt || ɑːnt/ 1 **= are not** 2 (*with 1st person sing*) (esp BrE) **= am not**: **~ I clever?** ¡qué lista soy! ¿no?; **I'm right, ~ I?** tengo razón ¿no?

Argentina /'ɑːrdʒən'tiːnə || ˌɑːdʒən'tiːnə/ *n* Argentina *f*

Argentine[1] /'ɑːrdʒəntaɪn || 'ɑːdʒəntaɪn/ *adj* argentino

Argentine[2] *n* (country) (dated) **the ~** (la) Argentina

Argentinian[1] /'ɑːrdʒən'tɪniən || ˌɑːdʒən'tɪniən/ *adj* argentino

Argentinian[2] *n* argentino, -na *m,f*

arguable /'ɑːrgjuəbəl || 'ɑːgjʊəbəl/ *adj* discutible; **it is ~ that ...** podría decirse que ...

arguably /'ɑːrgjuəbli || 'ɑːgjʊəbli/ *adv* (*indep*): **this is ~ his best novel** podría decirse que ésta es su mejor novela

argue /'ɑːrgjuː || 'ɑːgjuː/ *vi*

A (disagree, quarrel) discutir; (more heatedly) pelear(se), reñir* (esp Esp); **to ~ ABOUT/OVER sth** discutir *or* pelear POR algo; **don't ~ with me!** ¡no me discutas!; **$10,000 tax-free? you can't ~ with that!** ¿10.000 dólares libres de impuestos? ¡no es como para quejarse!

B (reason): **she ~s convincingly** sabe expresar su punto de vista de manera muy convincente; **to ~ FOR/AGAINST sth**: **she ~d for his reinstatement** abogó por que fuera restituido a su cargo; **he ~s against changing the law** da razones en contra de que se cambie la ley

■ **argue** *vt* 1 (put forward) ‹*case*› exponer*, presentar 2 (adduce) alegar*; (present as argument) argüir*, sostener*; **supporters of the bill ~ that ...** los partidarios del proyecto arguyen *or* sostienen que ... 3 (debate) ‹*issue*› discutir, debatir

Phrasal verb

• **argue out** [v ▸ o ▸ adv, v ▸ adv ▸ o] discutir

argument /'ɑːrgjəmənt || 'ɑːgjʊmənt/ *n*

A [c u] (quarrel, disagreement) discusión *f*; (more heated) pelea *f*, riña *f* (esp Esp); **to have an ~ with sb** tener* una discusión con algn, discutir con algn; (more heatedly) pelearse *or* (esp Esp) reñir* con algn; **I've only heard her side of the ~** sólo he oído su versión del asunto

B [u c] (debate) polémica *f*; **let's say, for the sake of ~ that ...** pongamos por caso que ...

C [c] 1 (case) razones *fpl*, argumentos *mpl*; **~ FOR/AGAINST sth** razones *or* argumentos A FAVOR/EN CONTRA DE algo; **there is a good ~ for postponing the decision** existen sobradas razones *or* sobrados motivos para postergar la decisión 2 (line of reasoning) razonamiento *m*

argumentative /'ɑːrgjə'mentətɪv || ˌɑːgjʊ'mentətɪv/ *adj* discutidor

aria /'ɑːriə/ *n* aria *f‡*

arid /'ærəd || 'ærɪd/ *adj* árido

aridity /ə'rɪdəti/ *n* [u] aridez *f*

Aries /'eriːz || 'eəriːz/ *n* 1 (sign) (*no art*) Aries 2 [c] (person) Aries *or* aries *mf*, ariano, -na *m,f*; *see also* **Aquarius**

arise /ə'raɪz/ *vi* (*past* **arose** /ə'rəʊz/; *past p* **arisen** /ə'rɪzən/)

A (occur) «*difficulty/opportunity*» surgir*, presentarse; **if the need ~s** si fuera necesario; **should the question ~** si se plantea la cuestión; **to ~ FROM *o* OUT OF sth** surgir* (a raíz) DE algo

B 1 (rise up) (liter) «*wind*» levantarse; «*cry*» alzarse* (liter) 2 (get up) (arch) levantarse

aristocracy /'ærə'stɑːkrəsi || ˌærɪ'stɒkrəsi/ *n* (*pl* **-cies**) aristocracia *f*

aristocrat /ə'rɪstəkræt || 'ærɪstəkræt/ *n* aristócrata *mf*

aristocratic /ə'rɪstə'krætɪk || ˌærɪstə'krætɪk/ *adj* aristocrático

arithmetic[1] /ə'rɪθmətɪk/ *n* [u] aritmética *f*; **I did some quick ~** hice un cálculo rápido

arithmetic[2] /'ærɪθ'metɪk/, **-ical** /-ɪkəl/ *adj* aritmético

Ariz = **Arizona**

Ark[1] = **Arkansas**

Ark[2] /ɑːrk || ɑːk/ *n* arca *f‡*; **Noah's ~** el arca de Noé; ***out of the ~*** (colloq) antediluviano *or* antidiluviano (fam)

arm[1] /ɑːrm || ɑːm/ *n*

A (Anat) brazo *m*; **they walked along ~ in ~** iban del brazo; **he had a newspaper under his ~** traía un periódico bajo el *or* debajo del brazo; **to put one's ~s around sb** abrazar* a algn; **to throw one's ~s around sb** echarle los brazos al cuello a algn; **they walked with their ~s around each other** iban abrazados; **within ~'s reach** al alcance de la mano; ***as long as your* *o* *my* ~** (colloq) más largo que un día sin pan (fam); ***the long ~ of the law*** el brazo de la ley; ***to cost an ~ and a leg*** (colloq) costar* un ojo de la cara *or* un riñón (fam); ***to keep sb at ~'s length*** guardar las distancias con algn; ***to twist sb's ~*** presionar a algn; ***to welcome sb with open ~s*** recibir a algn con (los) brazos abiertos; ▸ **tie**[2] **A2**

B 1 (of chair, crane) brazo *m* 2 (of garment) manga *f*

C (of organization) sección *f*; (Pol) brazo *m*

D **arms** *pl* (weapons) armas *fpl*; **to lay down one's ~s** deponer* las armas; ***to be up in ~s (about* *o* *over sth)***: **the locals are up in ~s about the plan** los lugareños están furiosos con el plan

arm[2] *vt* armar; **to ~ sb WITH sth** ‹*with weapons*› armar a algn DE *or* CON algo; ‹*with tools/information*› proveer* a algn DE algo; **to ~ oneself (with sth)** armarse de *or* con algo; *see also* **armed**

armada /ɑːr'mɑːdə || ɑː'mɑːdə/ *n* armada *f*, flota *f*; **the (Spanish) A~** (Hist) la Armada Invencible

Armageddon /'ɑːrmə'gedn̩ || ˌɑːmə'gedn̩/ *n* 1 (battle) el Apocalipsis 2 (place) Harmaguedón

a

armament /ˈɑːrməmənt || ˈɑːməmənt/ *n* armamento *m*

arm: ~band *n* (to denote rank, as sign of mourning etc) brazalete *m*; (for swimming) flotador *m* (*que se coloca en el brazo*), alita *f* (AmS); **~chair** *n* sillón *m*, butaca *f*; (*before n*) ‹*revolutionary*› de salón, de café

armed /ɑːrmd || ɑːmd/ *adj* ‹*resistance/struggle*› armado; **~ robbery** robo *m or* atraco *m* a mano armada; **~ WITH sth** armado DE algo; **~ with these statistics, he demanded to see the director** con estas estadísticas en mano, exigió ver al director

-armed /ˈɑːrmd || ɑːmd/ *suff*: **long~** de brazos largos; **one~** manco

Armenia /ɑːrˈmiːniə || ɑːˈmiːniə/ *n* Armenia *f*

Armenian¹ /ɑːrˈmiːniən || ɑːˈmiːniən/ *adj* armenio

Armenian² *n* 1 (person) armenio, -nia *m,f* 2 [u] (language) armenio *m*

armful /ˈɑːrmfʊl || ˈɑːmfʊl/ *n*: **an ~ of firewood** una brazada de leña; **she went into the room with an ~ of clothes** entró en la habitación con un montón de ropa

armhole /ˈɑːrmhəʊl || ˈɑːmhəʊl/ *n* sisa *f*

armistice /ˈɑːrməstəs || ˈɑːmɪstɪs/ *n* armisticio *m*; (*before n*) **A~ Day** el día del Armisticio (*día en que se conmemora el fin de la primera guerra mundial*)

armor, (BrE) **armour** /ˈɑːrmər || ˈɑːmə(r)/ *n* [u] (to protect body) armadura *f*, coraza *f*; **suit of ~** armadura *f*; **knights in ~** caballeros *mpl* con armaduras

armored, (BrE) **armoured** /ˈɑːrmərd || ˈɑːməd/ *adj* ‹*vehicle*› blindado

armor-plated, (BrE) **armour-plated** /ˈɑːrmərˈpleɪtəd || ˌɑːməˈpleɪtɪd/ *adj* blindado

armory, (BrE) **armoury** /ˈɑːrməri || ˈɑːməri/ *n* (*pl* **-ries**) 1 (stock of arms) arsenal *m* 2 (storehouse) arsenal *m* 3 (factory) (AmE) fábrica *f* de armas

armour *etc* (BrE) ▸ **armor** *etc*

arm: ~pit *n* axila *f*, sobaco *m*; **~rest** *n* (of chair, sofa) brazo *m*; (of car, airplane seat) apoyabrazos *m*; **~s dealer** *n* (legal) comerciante *mf* de armas; (illegal) traficante *mf* de armas; **~s factory** *n* fábrica *f* de armas; **~s race** *n* carrera *f* armamentista *or* de armamentos; **~ wrestling** *n* [u]: **he's very good at ~ wrestling** es muy bueno echando pulsos *or* (CS) pulseando *or* (Méx) jugando a las vencidas

army /ˈɑːrmi || ˈɑːmi/ *n* (*pl* **armies**) ejército *m*; **to be in the ~** ser* militar; **to join the ~** alistarse en el ejército; (*before n*) ‹*barracks/discipline*› militar; **~ officer** militar *mf*, oficial *mf* del ejército (de tierra)

aroma /əˈrəʊmə/ *n* aroma *m*

aromatherapy /əˈrəʊməˈθerəpi/ *n* [u] aromaterapia *f*

aromatic /ˈærəˈmætɪk/ *adj* aromático

arose /əˈrəʊz/ *past of* **arise**

around¹ /əˈraʊnd/ *adv*

A 1 (in a circle): **~ and ~ they drove** estuvieron dando vueltas y vueltas con el coche 2 (so as to face in different direction): **she glanced ~** echó un vistazo a su alrededor; *see also* **look, turn** *etc* **around** 3 (on all sides): **there's nothing for miles ~** no hay nada en millas a la redonda; **everyone crowded ~** todo el mundo se apiñó alrededor 4 (in circumference) de circunferencia; **it is 12m ~** tiene 12m de circunferencia

B 1 (in the vicinity): **is John ~?** ¿anda *or* está John por ahí?; **there's no one ~** aquí no hay nadie; **(I'll) see you ~!** (colloq) ¡nos vemos! 2 (in existence) (colloq): **computers weren't ~ in those days** en aquellos tiempos no había computadoras; **the idea had been ~ for quite a while** la idea no era nueva; **it's the best one ~** es lo mejor que hay (en plaza)

C (from one place, person to another): **the dog followed us ~** el perro nos seguía a todas partes; **she showed us ~** nos mostró *or* enseñó la casa (*or* la fábrica *etc*); **he knows his way ~** conoce la ciudad (*or* la zona *etc*); **there's a rumor going ~** corre un rumor; **I phoned ~** hice unas cuantas llamadas, llamé a varios sitios; **he's been ~** (colloq) tiene mucho mundo; **he prefers to travel ~ on his own** prefiere viajar solo

D (at, to different place): **I'll be ~ at Angela's** estaré en casa de Angela; **we had some friends ~ for a meal** invitamos a unos amigos a comer

E (approximately) más o menos, aproximadamente; **he must be ~ 35** debe (de) tener unos 35, debe (de) andar por los 35; **at ~ five thirty** alrededor de *or* a eso de *or* sobre las cinco y media; **~ two million people** unos dos millones de personas; **~ 1660** alrededor de 1660; **~ the turn of the century** hacia finales de siglo

around² *prep*

A (encircling) alrededor de; **he put his arm ~ her** la rodeó con el brazo; **they sailed ~ the world** dieron la vuelta al mundo en un velero; **the myths that have grown up ~ these events** los mitos que han surgido en torno a estos acontecimientos

B 1 (in the vicinity of) alrededor de; **do you live ~ here?** ¿vives por *or* cerca de aquí? 2 (within, through): **I had things to do ~ the house** tenía cosas que hacer en casa; **they traveled ~ Europe** viajaron por Europa; **she took them ~ the house** les mostró *or* enseñó la casa

arousal /əˈraʊzəl/ *n* [u] (awakening) despertar *m*; (sexual) excitación *f* (sexual)

arouse /əˈraʊz/ *vt* ‹*curiosity/interest/suspicion*› despertar*, suscitar; (sexually) excitar

arr 1 (Transp) = **arrives/arrival** 2 (Mus) (= **arranged by**) arr.

arrange /əˈreɪndʒ/ *vt*

A 1 (put in certain order, position) ‹*furniture*› arreglar, disponer*; ‹*flowers*› arreglar; **I ~d the cards in alphabetical order** coloqué *or* puse las fichas en orden alfabético, ordené las fichas alfabéticamente 2 (put in order) arreglar, ordenar; **to ~ one's hair/clothes** arreglarse el pelo/la ropa; **I needed time to ~ my thoughts** necesitaba tiempo para poner mis ideas en orden

B (fix up in advance) ‹*meeting/party*› organizar*; ‹*date/fee*› fijar; ‹*deal/appointment*› concertar*; ‹*loan*› tramitar; **we'll ~ your accommodation** nos encargaremos de conseguirle alojamiento; **we ~d between us who would do what** acordamos *or* arreglamos entre los dos quién se encargaría de cada cosa; **she had ~d to meet them for lunch** había quedado en encontrarse con ellos para comer, había quedado con ellos para comer (Esp)

C (Mus) arreglar

■ **arrange** *vi* **to ~ FOR sb/sth to + INF: could you ~ for the carpets to be cleaned?** ¿podría encargarse de que alguien venga a limpiar las alfombras?; **we've ~d for you to see the specialist** le hemos pedido hora *or* una cita con el especialista

arranged marriage *n*: *boda concertada por las familias de los contrayentes*

arrangement /əˈreɪndʒmənt/ *n*

A [c u] (of furniture) disposición *f*; **a flower ~** un arreglo floral

B [c] (agreement): **what's the ~ for tomorrow?** ¿cómo hemos/se ha quedado para mañana?, ¿cuál es el plan para mañana?; **we made an ~ to meet the next day** quedamos en encontrarnos al día siguiente; **I have an ~ with the bank** tengo un acuerdo *or* arreglo con el banco; **group visits by ~** se ruega concertar de antemano las visitas en grupo

C **arrangements** *pl* (plans) planes *mpl*; (for a funeral) preparativos *mpl*; **what are the sleeping ~s?** ¿cómo vamos (*or* van *etc*) a dormir?; **she made ~s for her mail to be sent on** dispuso que le reexpidieran la correspondencia; **I can't come, I've already made other ~s** no puedo venir, ya tengo otro compromiso

D [c] (Mus) arreglo *m*

arrant /ˈærənt/ *adj* (frml) (*before n, no comp*) ‹*fool/liar*› redomado; **~ nonsense** la estupidez más absoluta

array¹ /əˈreɪ/ *n* 1 [c] (range, display) selección *f*, despliegue *m* 2 [c] (Comput, Math) matriz *f* 3 [c] (Mil) formación *f*; **in battle ~** en orden de batalla

array² *vt* (liter) (spread out) exponer*, exhibir, presentar

arrears /əˈrɪrz || əˈrɪəz/ *pl n* atrasos *mpl*; **to be in ~ with the rent** estar* atrasado en el pago del alquiler; **salaries are paid monthly in ~** los sueldos se pagan mensualmente, una vez cumplido cada mes de trabajo; **to fall** *o* **get into ~ with** *o* **on sth** atrasarse *or* retrasarse en los pagos de algo

arrest¹ /əˈrest/ *n* detención *f*, arresto *m*; **to be under ~** estar* detenido *or* arrestado; **you're under ~** queda detenido *or* arrestado; **to put** *o* **place sb under ~** detener* *or* arrestar a algn

arrest² *vt*
A (detain) detener*, arrestar
B 1 ‹*progress/growth*› (hinder) dificultar, poner* freno a; (halt) detener*; ‹*decline*› atajar 2 (hold, detain) (liter) atraer*

arresting /ə'restɪŋ/ *adj* ‹*beauty/smile*› deslumbrante; ‹*image/thought*› fascinante

arrival /ə'raɪvəl/ *n*
A [u c] (coming) llegada *f*, arribo *m* (esp AmL frml); **on ~** al llegar, a su (*or* mi *etc*) llegada
B [c] (person or thing): **the latest ~s in our fashion department** las últimas novedades en nuestra sección de modas; **congratulations on your new ~** felicitaciones por el nacimiento *or* la llegada de vuestro hijo

arrive /ə'raɪv/ *vi* (come) «*person/train/letter*» llegar*; «*baby*» nacer*, llegar*; **flight 1702 arriving from Athens** el vuelo 1702 procedente de Atenas; **to ~ home** llegar* a casa; **to ~ AT/IN** llegar* A; **how did you ~ at that figure?** ¿cómo llegaste a *or* cómo obtuviste ese resultado?; **to ~ on the scene** aparecer*, llegar*

arrogance /'ærəgəns/ *n* [u] arrogancia *f*

arrogant /'ærəgənt/ *adj* arrogante

arrogantly /'ærəgəntli/ *adv* con arrogancia, arrogantemente

arrow /'ærəʊ/ *n* flecha *f*

arse /ɑːrs || ɑːs/ *n* (BrE vulg) 1 (part of body) culo *m* (fam: en algunas regiones vulg); ***he can't tell his ~ from his elbow*** no tiene ni puta idea (vulg); *see also* **ass B** 2 (idiot): **you silly ~!** ¡tonto del culo! (fam), ¡pendejo! (AmL exc CS fam)

Phrasal verb
- **arse about, arse around** [v ▸ adv] (BrE vulg) gansear (fam)

arsehole /'ɑːrshəʊl || 'ɑːshəʊl/ *n* (BrE) ▸**asshole**

arsenal /'ɑːrsn̩əl || 'ɑːsənl̩/ *n* (store) arsenal *m*

arsenic /'ɑːrsənɪk || 'ɑːsənɪk/ *n* [u] arsénico *m*

arson /'ɑːrsn̩ || 'ɑːsn/ *n* [u] incendiarismo *m*; **it was ~** el incendio fue provocado

arsonist /'ɑːrsn̩əst || 'ɑːsənɪst/ *n* incendiario, -ria *m,f*

art¹ /ɑːrt || ɑːt/ *n*
A 1 [u] (object of aesthetics) arte *m*; **~ for ~'s sake** el arte por el arte; **she's studying ~** estudia Bellas Artes; (*before n*) ‹*class*› de arte; (in school) de dibujo; **~ exhibition** exposición *f* de obras de arte; **~ gallery** (museum) museo *m* de arte; **~ school** *o* **college** escuela *f* de Bellas Artes; (for minor arts) escuela *f* de Artes y Oficios 2 [u c] (artwork) trabajos *mpl* artísticos; **~s and crafts** artesanía
B **arts** *pl* 1 **the ~s** la cultura y las artes 2 (BrE Educ) letras *fpl*
C (skill, craft) (*no pl*) arte *m*; **a dying ~** un arte que se está perdiendo; **the ~ of conversation** el arte de la conversación

art² (arch) eres; **thou ~** (tú) eres

artefact /'ɑːrtɪfækt || 'ɑːtɪfækt/ *n* (BrE) artefacto *m*

arterial /ɑːr'tɪriəl || ɑː'tɪəriəl/ *adj* (*usu before n*) ‹*blood*› arterial; ‹*river/road*› importante

artery /'ɑːrtəri || 'ɑːtəri/ *n* (*pl* **-ries**) (Anat) arteria *f*; (Transp) carretera *f* importante

artesian well /ɑːr'tiːʒən || ɑː'tiːziən/ *n* pozo *m* artesiano

art form *n* arte *m*, medio *m* de expresión artística

artful /'ɑːrtfəl || 'ɑːtfəl/ *adj* ‹*scheme*› ingenioso; ‹*person*› astuto, taimado, artero

arthritic /ɑːr'θrɪtɪk || ɑː'θrɪtɪk/ *adj* artrítico

arthritis /ɑːr'θraɪtəs || ɑː'θraɪtɪs/ *n* [u] artritis *f*

artichoke /'ɑːrtətʃəʊk || 'ɑːtɪtʃəʊk/ *n* (*globe* **~**) alcachofa *f*, alcaucil *m* (RPl); (*Jerusalem* **~**) aguaturma *f*, pataca *f*

article /'ɑːrtɪkəl || 'ɑːtɪkəl/ *n*
A (thing, item) artículo *m*, objeto *m*; **an ~ of clothing** una prenda (de vestir); **this is malt whisky, the genuine ~** esto es auténtico whisky de malta
B (in newspaper, encyclopedia) artículo *m*
C (Ling) artículo *m*
D **articles** *pl* (apprenticeship) (*no art*) aprendizaje *m*

articulate¹ /ɑːr'tɪkjəleɪt || ɑː'tɪkjʊleɪt/ *vt*
A 1 (express) ‹*idea/feeling*› expresar; ‹*policy/project*› articular 2 ‹*word/sound*› articular
B (connect by joint) articular

articulate² /ɑːr'tɪkjələt || ɑː'tɪkjʊlət/ *adj* ‹*utterance*› articulado; **he was barely ~** apenas podía articular palabra; **he's very ~** se expresa muy bien, sabe expresar sus ideas

articulated lorry /ɑːr'tɪkjəleɪtəd || ɑː'tɪkjəleɪtɪd/ *n* (BrE) camión *m* articulado, trailer *m* (Méx)

articulately /ɑːr'tɪkjələtli || ɑː'tɪkjʊlətli/ *adv* ‹*speak*› elocuentemente

articulation /ɑːr'tɪkjə'leɪʃən || ɑː,tɪkjʊ'leɪʃən/ *n* 1 [u] (of sound) articulación *f*; (of idea, feeling) expresión *f* 2 [u c] (Anat, Mech Eng) articulación *f*

artifact /'ɑːrtɪfækt/, (BrE) **artefact** *n* artefacto *m*

artifice /'ɑːrtəfəs || 'ɑːtɪfɪs/ *n* [u c] artificio *m*

artificial /'ɑːrtə'fɪʃəl || ,ɑːtɪ'fɪʃəl/ *adj* 1 ‹*cream/flowers/silk*› artificial; ‹*leather*› sintético; ‹*insemination/intelligence/respiration*› artificial; ‹*arm/leg*› ortopédico 2 (contrived) ‹*situation*› artificial; ‹*distinction/objection*› rebuscado 3 (insincere, unnatural) afectado

artificially /'ɑːrtə'fɪʃəli || ,ɑːtɪ'fɪʃəli/ *adv* 1 ‹*produce/prolong*› artificialmente 2 (in a contrived way) rebuscadamente 3 ‹*smile*› con afectación

artillery /ɑːr'tɪləri || ɑː'tɪləri/ *n* [u] artillería *f*

artisan /'ɑːrtəzən || ,ɑːtɪ'zæn/ *n* artesano, -na *m,f*

artist /'ɑːrtəst || 'ɑːtɪst/ *n* 1 (writer, musician, painter, sculptor) artista *mf*; **landscape ~** paisajista *mf*; **portrait ~** retratista *mf* 2 (performer) (Mus) intérprete *mf*; (Theat) actor, -triz *m,f*, artista *mf*

artiste /ɑːr'tiːst || ɑː'tiːst/ *n* (esp BrE) artista *mf*

artistic /ɑːr'tɪstɪk || ɑː'tɪstɪk/ *adj* artístico; **he was ~** tenía dotes artísticas

artistically /ɑːr'tɪstɪkli || ɑː'tɪstɪkli/ *adv* artísticamente; (*indep*) artísticamente, desde el punto de vista artístico

artistry /'ɑːrtəstri || 'ɑːtɪstri/ *n* [u] arte *m*

artless /'ɑːrtləs || 'ɑːtlɪs/ *adj* 1 (innocent, natural) ingenuo, sin malicia 2 (crude) (liter) tosco

artsy /'ɑːrtsi || 'ɑːtsi/ *adj* **-sier, -siest** (BrE) **arty** (colloq) ‹*book/style*› con veleidades de artístico; **she's terribly ~** se las da de artista bohemia

artwork /'ɑːrtwɜːrk || 'ɑːtwɜːk/ *n* [u] (illustrations) ilustraciones *fpl*, material *m* gráfico

arty /'ɑːrti || 'ɑːti/ *adj* **artier, artiest** (BrE) ▸**artsy**

Aryan¹ /'eriən || 'eəriən/ *adj* ario

Aryan² *n* ario, aria *m,f*

as¹ /æz, *weak form* əz/ *conj*
A 1 (when, while) cuando; **~ she was eating breakfast ...** cuando *or* mientras tomaba el desayuno ...; **~ you go toward the bank, it's the first house on the left** yendo hacia el banco, es la primera casa a mano izquierda 2 (indicating progression) a medida que; **~ (and when) we need them** a medida que *or* según los vamos necesitando; **he mellowed ~ he grew older** se fue ablandando con los años
B (because, since) como; **~ it was getting late, we decided to leave** como se hacía tarde, decidimos irnos
C (though): **try ~ he might, he could not open it** por más que trató, no pudo abrirlo; **(~) strange ~ it may seem** por extraño que parezca; **much ~ I agree with you...** aun estando de acuerdo contigo como estoy...
D 1 (expressing comparison, contrast) igual que, como; **in the 1980s, ~ in the 30s** en la década de los 80, al igual que en la de los 30 2 (in generalizations) como; **it's quite reasonable, ~ restaurants go** para como están los restaurantes, es bastante razonable 3 (in accordance with) como; **~ I was saying** como iba diciendo; **the situation, ~ we understand it, is ...** la situación, tal como nosotros la entendemos, es ...
E 1 (in the way that) como; **I love her ~ I would my own daughter** la quiero como a una hija; **do ~ you wish** haz lo que quieras *or* lo que te parezca; **do ~ I say** haz lo que te digo; **she sang ~ never before** cantó como nunca; **she arrived the next day, ~ planned/expected** llegó al día siguiente como se había planeado/como se esperaba; **use form A or B ~ appropriate** use el formulario A o B, según corresponda; **~ things stand** tal (y) como están las cosas 2 (defining): **it would be the end of civilization ~ we know it** significaría el fin de la civilización tal y como la conocemos; **I'm only interested in the changes ~ they affect me** sólo me interesan los cambios en la

medida en que me afectan a mí; **Sri Lanka, or Ceylon, ~ it used to be known** Sri Lanka, o Ceilán, como se llamaba antes **3** (*in phrases*) **as it is**: **we can't publish it ~ it is** no podemos publicarlo tal y como está, no podemos publicarlo así como está; **we've got too much work ~ it is** ya tenemos demasiado trabajo; **as it were** por así decirlo; **as was**: **our new president, our secretary ~ was** el nuevo presidente, ex secretario de nuestra organización

F (in comparisons of equal degree) **as ... as** tan ... como; **I am ~ tall ~ you (are)** soy tan alta como tú; **I left ~ soon ~ I could** me fui en cuanto pude; **there weren't ~ many people ~ (there were) last time** no había tanta gente como la última vez; **she ran ~ fast ~ she could** corrió tan rápido como pudo *or* lo más deprisa que pudo

G **as if/as though** como si (+ *subj*); **he acts ~ if** *o* **~ though he didn't care** se comporta como si no le importara; **she made ~ if to open the door** hizo como si fuera a abrir la puerta; **he looks ~ if** *o* **~ though he's had enough** tiene cara de estar harto

as² *adv*

A (equally): **it's not ~ cold today** hoy no hace tanto frío; **I can't run ~ quickly now** no puedo correr tan rápido ahora; **I have lots of stamps, but he has just ~ many/twice ~ many** yo tengo muchos sellos, pero él tiene tantos como yo/el doble (que yo); **I was disgusted and said ~ much** estaba asqueado y lo dije

B **as ... as**: **these animals grow to ~ much ~ 12ft long** estos animales llegan a medir 12 pies de largo; **~ recently ~ 1976** aún en 1976; **~ many ~ 400 people** hasta 400 personas; **~ long ago ~ 1960** ya en 1960

as³ *prep*

A **1** (in the condition, role of): **~ a child she adored dancing** de pequeña *or* cuando era pequeña le encantaba bailar; **~ a teacher ...** como maestro ...; **she was brilliant ~ Cleopatra** estuvo genial en el papel de Cleopatra; **he works ~ a clerk** trabaja de oficinista **2** (like) como; **they answered ~ one man** respondieron como un solo hombre

B (*in phrases*) **as against** frente a; **as for** en cuanto a, respecto a; **and ~ for you ...** y en cuanto a ti ..., y en lo que a ti respecta ...; **as of** *o* (BrE) **as from** desde, a partir de; **as to** en cuanto a, respecto a

ASA = American Standards Association

ASAP = as soon as possible

asbestos /æs'bestəs/ *n* [u] asbesto *m*, amianto *m*

ASBO /'æzbəʊ/ *n* (BrE) (= **antisocial behaviour order**) orden *f* judicial por comportamiento *or* conducta antisocial

ascend /ə'send/ *vi* (frml) **1** ⟪*person/rocket*⟫ ascender* (frml); **He ~ed into heaven** subió a los cielos **2** **ascending** *pres p* ‹*slope/spiral/scale*› ascendente
■ **ascend** *vt* (frml) ‹*steps*› subir; ‹*mountain*› escalar, subir a

ascendancy, ascendency /ə'sendənsi/ *n* [u] (frml) ascendiente *m* (frml)

ascendant, ascendent /ə'sendənt/ *n*: **to be in the ~** ⟪*reputation/party*⟫ estar* en alza; ⟪*star*⟫ (Astrol) estar* en su fase ascendente

ascension /ə'sentʃən || ə'senʃən/ *n* [u] **1** **the A~** (Relig) la Ascensión **2** (Astron) ascensión *f*

ascent /ə'sent/ *n* **1** [u c] (of mountain) escalada *f*, ascensión (frml) **2** [u c] (rise) ascenso *m* **3** [c] (slope) subida *f*, cuesta *f*

ascertain /'æsər'teɪn/ *vt* establecer*, determinar

ascetic¹ /ə'setɪk/ *adj* ascético

ascetic² *n* asceta *mf*

asceticism /ə'setəsɪzəm || ə'setɪsɪzəm/ *n* [u] ascetismo *m*

ASCII /'æski/ (*no art*) (= **American standard code for information interchange**) ASCII *m*

ascribe /ə'skraɪb/ *vt* **to ~ sth TO sth/sb** atribuirle* algo A algo/algn

aseptic /eɪ'septɪk/ *adj* aséptico

asexual /eɪ'sekʃuəl/ *adj* ‹*reproduction*› asexuado, asexual; ‹*person*› asexuado

ash /æʃ/ *n*

A (*often pl*) ceniza *f*; **to rise from the ~es** (liter) renacer* de las cenizas (liter); **~es to ~es, dust to dust** polvo eres y en polvo te convertirás

B **ashes** *pl* (cremated remains) cenizas *fpl*

C [c] **~ (tree)** fresno *m*

ashamed /ə'ʃeɪmd/ *adj* (*pred*) avergonzado, apenado (AmL exc CS); **to be ~ OF sth**: **she was ~ of what she'd done** estaba avergonzada de *or* (AmL exc CS) apenada por lo que había hecho; **it's nothing to be ~ of** no tienes por qué avergonzarte *or* (AmL exc CS) apenarte; **to be ~ OF sb** avergonzarse* DE algn; **you ought to be ~ of yourself** debería darte vergüenza *or* (AmL exc CS) pena; **to be ~ to + INF**: **he's ~ to ask** le da vergüenza *or* (AmL exc CS) pena preguntar

ashamedly /ə'ʃeɪmədli || ə'ʃeɪmɪdli/ *adv* con vergüenza

ash: **~-blond** /'æʃ'blɑːnd || ,æʃ'blɒnd/ *adj* rubio ceniza *adj inv*; **~can** *n* (AmE) ▸ **garbage can**

ashen /'æʃən/ *adj* lívido, ceniciento (liter)

ashore /ə'ʃɔːr/ *adv* en tierra; **to go ~** desembarcar*; **to put sb ~** desembarcar* a algn; **we swam ~** nadamos hasta la orilla

ash: **~tray** *n* cenicero *m*; **~ Wednesday** *n* miércoles *m* de Ceniza

Asia /'eɪʒə, 'eɪʃə || 'eɪʃə/ *n* Asia *f*‡; **Southeast ~** el Sudeste asiático

Asian¹ /'eɪʒən, 'eɪʃən || 'eɪʃən/ *adj* **1** (of Asia) asiático **2** (from the Indian subcontinent) (BrE) *de India, Pakistán etc*

Asian² *n* **1** (from Asia) asiático, -ca *m,f* **2** (from the Indian subcontinent) (BrE) *persona proveniente de India, Pakistán etc*

Asian American¹ *n* asiático *m* americano, asiática *f* americana

Asian American² *adj* asiático-americano

> **Asian American**
>
> El término de más amplia aceptación hoy en día para referirse a norteamericanos de origen asiático, especialmente del Extremo Oriente

Asiatic /'eɪʒi'ætɪk, 'eɪʃi'ætɪk || ,eɪʃi'ætɪk/ *adj* asiático

aside¹ /ə'saɪd/ *adv*

A a un lado; *see also* **cast aside, put aside, set aside, stand² B1, step aside, take aside**

B **aside from** (*as prep*) (esp AmE) **1** (except for) aparte de **2** (as well as) aparte de, además de

aside² *n* (line, comment) aparte *m*

asinine /'æsnaɪn || 'æsɪnaɪn/ *adj* (liter) ‹*person*› necio; **~ remark** necedad *f*

ask /æsk || ɑːsk/ *vt*

A (inquire) preguntar; (inquire of) preguntarle a; **~ your mother** pregúntale a tu madre; **to ~ a question** hacer* una pregunta; **to ~ sb sth** preguntarle algo A algn; **I ~ed him his name** le pregunté cómo se llamaba; **don't ~ me!** (colloq) ¡yo qué sé! (fam); **honestly, I ~ you!** (colloq) ¿no te parece increíble?; **I often ~ myself ...** muchas veces me pregunto ...; **to ~ sb ABOUT sth/sb/-ING**: **have you ~ed him about his trip/his mother?** ¿le has preguntado por el viaje/por su madre?; **~ her about doing overtime** pregúntale si sería posible hacer horas extras

B (request) ‹*approval/advice/favor*› pedir*; **nobody ~ed your opinion** nadie te ha pedido tu opinión; **what more can you ~?** ¿qué más se puede pedir?; **is that ~ing too much?** ¿es mucho pedir?; **to ~ sb FOR sth** pedirle* algo A algn; **I'm going to ~ him for it back** le voy a pedir que me lo devuelva; **to ~ sth OF sb**: **she ~s too much of her students** les exige demasiado a sus alumnos; **to ~ sb to + INF** pedirle* A algn QUE (+ *subj*); **they ~ed me to help out** me pidieron que les diera una mano; **I must ~ you to leave** haga el favor de irse; **I ~ed her to dance** la saqué a bailar; **to ~ to + INF**: **I ~ed to see the manager** pedí hablar con el director; **he's ~ing to be slapped** se está buscando una bofetada

C (invite) invitar; **to ~ sb (TO sth)** invitar a algn (A algo); **we'll ~ them to dinner** los invitaremos a cenar; **~ him along** invítalo *or* dile que venga: **~ them in** diles que pasen; **haven't you ~ed her out yet?** ¿todavía no la has invitado a salir?

D (demand) ‹*price*› pedir*; **to ~ sth FOR sth** pedir* algo POR algo; **how much is he ~ing for the car?** ¿cuánto pide por el coche?
■ **ask** *vi*

A (inquire) preguntar; **how are things? — don't ~!** (colloq & hum) ¿qué tal? — ¡mejor ni hablar!; **you may well ~!** ¡buena pregunta!; **to ~ ABOUT sth/sb**: **he ~ed about your health/you** preguntó por tu salud/por ti

B (request): **it's yours for the ~ing** está a tu disposición;

there's no harm in ~ing con preguntar no se pierde nada; **to ~ FOR sth**: **I ~ed for his phone number** le pedí el número de teléfono; **he ~ed for it** (colloq) se lo buscó (fam); **to ~ FOR sb** preguntar POR algn

Phrasal verbs

- **ask after** [v ▸ prep ▸ o] preguntar por; **he ~ed after your health** preguntó por ti, se interesó por tu salud
- **ask around**

A [v ▸ adv] (make inquiries): **I don't have one, but I'll ~ around** yo no tengo, pero preguntaré por ahí *or* preguntaré a ver si alguien tiene uno

B [v ▸ o ▸ adv] (invite) invitar; **I ~ed them around for a meal** los invité a comer

- **ask back** [v ▸ o ▸ adv] **1** (invite home) invitar a casa **2** (invite again) volver* a invitar **3** (reciprocate invitation) devolverle* la invitación a
- **ask round** ▸ **ask around B**

askance /ə'skæns/ *adv*: **to look ~ at sth/sb** mirar algo/a algn con recelo

askew /ə'skju:/ *adv* torcido

asleep /ə'sli:p/ *adj* (*pred*): **to be ~** estar* dormido; **fast** *o* **sound ~** profundamente dormido; **to fall ~** dormirse*; **are you ~?** ¿duermes?, ¿estás dormido *or* durmiendo?

AS level *n* (*in UK exc Scotland*)

> **AS level – Advanced Supplementary level**
>
> En el sistema reformado de *A level*, el *AS* representa la primera etapa de las dos en que se divide el programa de *A level*, *ver* **A level**. El *AS* tiene lugar en el penúltimo año de la enseñanza secundaria. Los estudiantes se examinan en más asignaturas para un *AS level* que para un *A2*, adquiriendo de esta manera, una educación más amplia antes de especializarse en las asignaturas que seleccionan para estudiar en la enseñanza superior. *Ver tb* **A level**

asp /æsp/ *n* áspid *m*

asparagus /ə'spærəgəs/ *n* [u c] espárrago *m*

ASPCA *n* = **American Society for the Prevention of Cruelty to Animals**

aspect /'æspekt/ *n*

A (feature, facet) aspecto *m*; **the security ~** la cuestión *or* el asunto de la seguridad

B (appearance) (liter) aspecto *m*

C (frml) (orientation) orientación *f*; **the room had a north-facing ~** la habitación estaba orientada al norte

aspen (tree) /'æspən/ *n* álamo *m* temblón

as per *prep* de acuerdo con, según; **~ ~ usual** (colloq) como de costumbre

aspersions /ə'spɜ:rʒənz || ə'spɜ:ʃənz/ *pl n* (*sometimes sing*): **to cast ~ on** *o* **upon sth/sb** poner* algo/a algn en entredicho

asphalt /'æsfɔ:lt || 'æsfælt/ *n* [u] asfalto *m*; (*before n*) **~ jungle** jungla *f* de asfalto

asphyxiate /æs'fɪksieɪt/ *vt* asfixiar

asphyxiation /æs'fɪksi'eɪʃən/ *n* [u] asfixia *f*

aspic /'æspɪk/ *n* [u] aspic *m*, galantina *f*

aspirant /'æspərənt, ə'spaɪərənt/ *n* (frml) aspirante *mf*

aspirate /'æspəreɪt || 'æspɪreɪt/ *vt* ‹*sound/consonant*› aspirar

aspiration /'æspə'reɪʃən || ˌæspɪ'reɪʃən/ *n*

A [c] (desire, ambition) aspiración *f*; **to have ~s TO sth** aspirar A algo, ambicionar algo

B [u] (Ling) aspiración *f*

aspire /ə'spaɪr || ə'spaɪə(r)/ *vi* **1** **to ~ TO sth/ + INF** aspirar A algo/+ INF **2** **aspiring** *pres p*: **they're aspiring artists** aspiran a ser reconocidos como artistas

aspirin /'æsprən || 'æsprɪn/ *n* [c u] (*pl* **~** *or* **-rins**) aspirina *f*

ass /æs/ *n*

A **1** (donkey) (liter) asno *m*, jumento *m* (liter) **2** (idiot) (colloq) imbécil *mf*, idiota *mf*; **you silly ~!** ¡zopenco! (fam), ¡burro! (fam); **he made an ~ of himself** quedó en ridículo

B (part of body) (AmE vulg) culo *m* (fam: en algunas regiones vulg); **get your ~ over here!** ¡ven aquí, carajo *or* coño! (vulg)

assail /ə'seɪl/ *vt* (frml) atacar*; **she was ~ed by a group of journalists** un grupo de periodistas se abalanzó sobre ella *or* la asedió; **I was ~ed by doubts** me asaltaron las dudas

assailant /ə'seɪlənt/ *n* (frml) agresor, -sora *m,f*, atacante *mf*

assassin /ə'sæsn̩ || ə'sæsɪn/ *n* asesino, -na *m,f* (*de un personaje importante*)

assassinate /ə'sæsn̩eɪt || ə'sæsɪneɪt/ *vt* asesinar (*a un personaje importante*)

assassination /ə'sæsə'neɪʃən || əˌsæsɪ'neɪʃən/ *n* [c u] asesinato *m* (*de un personaje importante*)

assault[1] /ə'sɔ:lt/ *n*

A [u c] (Law) (violence) agresión *f*; (molestation) agresión *f* sexual; (rape) violación *f*; **~ and battery** agresión con lesiones

B [c] **1** (Mil) asalto *m*, ataque *m*; **to make an ~ on sth** atacar* algo **2** (onslaught) **~ (ON sth)** ataque *m* (A algo), arremetida *f* (CONTRA algo)

assault[2] *vt* (use violence against) agredir*, atacar*; (sexually) agredir* sexualmente

assemble /ə'sembəl/ *vt* **1** (construct) montar, ensamblar; ‹*model*› armar **2** (get together) reunir* **3** (gather) ‹*facts*› recopilar, recoger*; ‹*collection*› reunir*, acumular **4** (Comput) ensamblar

■ **assemble** *vi* (gather) reunirse*, congregarse* (frml)

assembly /ə'sembli/ *n* (*pl* **-blies**)

A **1** [u] (coming together) reunión *f* **2** [c] (group) concurrencia *f* **3** [c] (Govt) asamblea *f* **4** (Educ) (*no art*) *reunión de profesores y alumnos, al iniciarse la jornada escolar*

B (Tech) [u] (process) montaje *m*, ensamblaje *m*; (*before n*) **~ line** cadena *f* de montaje; **~ plant** planta *f* de montaje

assembly: ~man /ə'semblimən/ *n* (*pl* **-men** /-mən/) (in US) miembro *m* de una asamblea legislativa; **~woman** *n* (in US) miembro *f* de una asamblea legislativa

assent[1] /ə'sent/ *n* [u] asentimiento *m*, aprobación *f*, asenso (frml); **to give one's ~ to sth** dar* su (*or* mi *etc*) conformidad a algo

assent[2] *vi* asentir*, expresar su (*or* mi etc) conformidad; **to ~ TO sth** acceder A algo, consentir* EN algo

assert /ə'sɜ:rt || ə'sɜ:t/ *vt* **1** (declare) afirmar **2** (demonstrate, enforce) ‹*superiority*› reafirmar, dejar sentado; ‹*rights/claims*› hacer* valer, reivindicar*; **to ~ one's authority** imponer* su (*or* mi *etc*) autoridad

■ *v refl* **to ~ oneself** hacerse* valer

assertion /ə'sɜ:rʃən || ə'sɜ:ʃən/ *n* **1** [c u] (declaration) afirmación *f*, aseveración *f* **2** [u] (demonstration) reafirmación *f*

assertive /ə'sɜ:rtɪv || ə'sɜ:tɪv/ *adj* ‹*tone*› autoritario; **try to be ~ without being aggressive** trata de ser firme y enérgico sin ser agresivo

assertively /ə'sɜ:rtɪvli || ə'sɜ:tɪvli/ *adv* con firmeza, con seguridad en sí mismo

assertiveness /ə'sɜ:rtɪvnəs || ə'sɜ:tɪvnɪs/ *n* [u] seguridad *f* en sí mismo; (*before n*) **~ course** cursillo *m* de reafirmación personal

assess /ə'ses/ *vt* ‹*value/amount*› calcular; ‹*student/performance*› evaluar*; ‹*situation*› aquilatar, formarse un juicio sobre; **to ~ sth AT sth**: **the value of the property was ~ed at ...** la propiedad fue tasada *or* valorada *or* (AmL tb) avaluada en ...

assessment /ə'sesmənt/ *n* [c u] (of performance, results) evaluación *f*, valoración *f*; (of amount) cálculo *m*; **what is your ~ of the situation?** ¿cómo ve usted la situación?; **continuous ~** (Educ) evaluación *f* continua (*a lo largo del curso*)

assessor /ə'sesər || ə'sesə(r)/ *n* (Educ) evaluador, -dora *m,f*

asset /'æset/ *n* **1** (valuable quality): **the city's greatest ~** el mayor atractivo de la ciudad; **her intelligence is her greatest ~** su inteligencia es su gran baza; **knowledge of French would be an ~** se valorarán conocimientos de francés; **~ TO sth/sb**: **she's an ~ to the company** es una empleada muy valiosa para la compañía; **your degree will always be an ~ to you** la carrera siempre será un punto a tu favor **2** **assets** *pl* (Fin) activo *m*

asset ~ strip *vt* vaciar*; **~ stripping** /'strɪpɪŋ/ *n* [u] vaciamiento *m*

asshole /'æshəʊl/, (BrE) **arsehole** *n* (vulg) (idiot) imbécil *mf*, pendejo, -ja *m,f* (AmL exc CS fam), gilipollas *mf* (Esp vulg), huevón, -vona *m,f* (Andes, Ven vulg), pelotudo, -da *m,f* (AmS vulg)

a

assiduous /ə'sɪdʒuəs || ə'sɪdjʊəs/ *adj* (frml) ‹*student*› diligente, aplicado

assiduously /ə'sɪdʒuəsli || ə'sɪdjʊəsli/ *adv* (frml) ‹*study*› diligentemente, aplicadamente

assign /ə'saɪn/ *vt* 1 (appoint) **to ~ sb TO sth** nombrar *or* designar a algn PARA algo, asignar a algn A algo; **a detective was ~ed to the case** se nombró a un detective para que se ocupara del caso 2 (allocate) asignar; **he was ~ed three assistants** le asignaron tres ayudantes

assignation /'æsɪg'neɪʃən/ *n* (frml) cita *f*

assignment /ə'saɪnmənt/ *n*

A [c] 1 (mission) misión *f* 2 (task) función *f*, tarea *f* 3 (schoolwork) tarea *f*, deberes *mpl*

B [u] 1 (posting) nombramiento *m* 2 (allocation) asignación *f*

assimilate /ə'sɪməleɪt || ə'sɪmɪleɪt/ *vt* asimilar

assimilation /ə'sɪmə'leɪʃən || əˌsɪmɪ'leɪʃən/ *n* [u] asimilación *f*

assist /ə'sɪst/ *vt* ayudar, asistir (frml); **to ~ sb WITH/IN sth** ayudar *or* (frml) asistir a algn EN algo; **to ~ sb IN -ING** ayudar a algn A + INF

■ **assist** *vi* (help) **to ~ WITH/IN sth** ayudar EN algo

assistance /ə'sɪstəns/ *n* [u] ayuda *f*, asistencia *f* (frml); **to give ~ to sb** prestarle ayuda *or* (frml) asistencia a algn; **they came to her ~** vinieron en su ayuda; **may I be of ~?** (frml) ¿puedo servirle en algo? (frml)

assistant[1] /ə'sɪstənt/ *n* 1 (in shop) dependiente, -ta *m,f*, empleado, -da *m,f* (AmL) 2 (subordinate, helper) ayudante *mf*; **clerical ~** auxiliar administrativo, -va *m,f* 3 (*language* ~) (BrE) (in university) ayudante *mf or* (Esp) lector, -tora *m,f*; (in school) auxiliar *mf* de lengua

assistant[2] *adj* (*before n*): **~ manager** subdirector, -tora *m,f*, director adjunto, directora adjunta *m,f*

-assisted /ə'sɪstəd || ə'sɪstɪd/ *suff* 1 (aided): **computer~** asistido por computadora 2 (funded): **government~** subvencionado por el gobierno

assizes /ə'saɪzəz || ə'saɪzɪz/ *pl n*: *sesiones que solían celebrar los tribunales superiores de los condados de Inglaterra y Gales*

assn (= **association**) Asoc.

associate[1] /ə'səʊʃieɪt, -sieɪt/ *vt* 1 (involve, connect) (*usu pass*) vincular; **he refused to be ~d with the scheme** no quiso tener nada que ver con el asunto 2 (link in mind) asociar, relacionar

■ **associate** *vi* **to ~ (WITH sb)** relacionarse (CON algn)

associate[2] /ə'səʊʃiət, -siət/ *n* 1 (in business, profession) colega *mf*; **a business ~** un asociado (*or* socio *etc*) 2 (member of professional body) colegiado, -da *m,f*

associate[3] /ə'səʊʃiət, -siət/ *adj* (*before n*) ‹*member*› no numerario; ‹*editor/professor*› (AmE) adjunto

association /ə'səʊʃi'eɪʃən, -si'eɪʃən/ *n* 1 [c] (organization) asociación *f* 2 [c u] (relationship) relación *f*; **in ~ with** (*as prep*) en asociación con 3 [c u] (mental link) asociación *f*; **what ~s does the word have for you?** ¿con qué asocias la palabra?

assorted /ə'sɔːrtəd || ə'sɔːtɪd/ *adj* (*before n*) surtido

assortment /ə'sɔːrtmənt || ə'sɔːtmənt/ *n* (Busn) surtido *m*; (collection) colección *f*; **they have an ~ of ties** tienen una variedad de corbatas

assuage /ə'sweɪdʒ/ *vt* (liter) 1 (satisfy) ‹*hunger/desire*› saciar (liter) 2 (ease) ‹*pain/grief*› aliviar, mitigar* 3 (calm) ‹*anxiety*› calmar; ‹*fear*› disipar

assume /ə'suːm || ə'sjuːm/ *vt*

A (suppose) suponer*; **let's ~ they're right** supongamos que tienen razón; **assuming that everything goes as planned** suponiendo que todo salga de acuerdo con lo previsto; **she ~s far too much** presupone demasiado

B (frml) ‹*duties/command/role/title/responsibility*› asumir; **~d name** nombre *m* ficticio

C (frml) 1 (acquire) ‹*importance*› adquirir*, cobrar 2 (feign) (liter) adoptar; **he ~d an air of cheerfulness** adoptó un aire de falsa alegría

assumption /ə'sʌmpʃən/ *n*

A [c] (supposition): **the ~ was that ...** se suponía que ...; **his reasoning is based on the ~ that ...** su razonamiento se basa en el supuesto *or* la suposición de que ...; **she agreed on the ~ that ...** accedió suponiendo que ...

B [u] (frml) (of duties, leadership, responsibility, right) asunción *f*; **~ of office** toma *f* de posesión del cargo

assurance /ə'ʃʊrəns || ə'ʃʊərəns, ə'ʃɔːrəns/ *n*

A [c] (guarantee): **she gave me her ~ that ...** me aseguró *or* me garantizó que ...

B [u] 1 (self-confidence) seguridad *f* en sí mismo 2 (certainty) convicción *f*

C [u] (insurance) (BrE) seguro *m*

assure /ə'ʃʊr || ə'ʃʊə(r), ə'ʃɔː(r)/ *vt*

A 1 (guarantee) asegurar, garantizar*; **I ~ you** se lo aseguro, se lo garantizo; **to ~ sb OF sth** garantizarle* algo a algn 2 (convince) convencer*

B (make certain) **to ~ sb (OF) sth**: **this work will ~ me (of) a regular income** este trabajo me asegurará una entrada fija

C (insure) (BrE) ‹*life*› asegurar

assured /ə'ʃʊrd || ə'ʃʊəd, ə'ʃɔːd/ *adj* 1 (certain) ‹*income*› seguro; **the play's success was ~** la obra tenía el éxito asegurado 2 (confident) ‹*person*› seguro (de sí mismo); **her ~ manner** su aplomo; **rest ~: you'll never be troubled by him again** ten la seguridad de que *or* ten por seguro que no te volverá a molestar

asterisk /'æstərɪsk/ *n* asterisco *m*

astern /ə'stɜːrn || ə'stɜːn/ *adv* 1 (backward) hacia atrás 2 **~ of** (behind) detrás de, a popa de

asteroid /'æstərɔɪd/ *n* asteroide *m*

asthma /'æzmə || 'æsmə/ *n* [u] asma *f*‡; (*before n*) **~ sufferer** asmático, -ca *m,f*

asthmatic[1] /æz'mætɪk || æs'mætɪk/ *n* asmático, -ca *m,f*

asthmatic[2] *adj* asmático

astigmatism /ə'stɪgmətɪzəm/ *n* [u c] astigmatismo *m*

astir /ə'stɜːr || ə'stɜː(r)/ *adj* (*pred*) (on the move) (liter) **to be ~** bullir*

astonish /ə'stɑːnɪʃ || ə'stɒnɪʃ/ *vt* (surprise) asombrar; (amaze) dejar helado *or* pasmado *or* estupefacto

astonished /ə'stɑːnɪʃt || ə'stɒnɪʃt/ *adj*: **the ~ look on their faces** la cara de asombro que pusieron; **I'm ~ (that) he got so far** me asombra que haya llegado tan lejos; **I was ~ to learn that...** me quedé helada *or* estupefacta *or* pasmada cuando me enteré de que...; **to be ~ AT sth**: **I was ~ at his nerve** su descaro me dejó helado *or* estupefacto *or* pasmado

astonishing /ə'stɑːnɪʃɪŋ || ə'stɒnɪʃɪŋ/ *adj* (surprising) asombroso; (amazing) pasmoso, increíble

astonishingly /ə'stɑːnɪʃɪŋli || ə'stɒnɪʃɪŋli/ *adv* ‹*good/expensive*› (surprisingly) asombrosamente; (amazingly) increíblemente; **~ enough ...** (*indep*) aunque parezca asombroso ...

astonishment /ə'stɑːnɪʃmənt || ə'stɒnɪʃmənt/ *n* [u] (surprise) asombro *m*; (amazement) estupefacción *f*; **to my ~** para mi gran asombro; **~ AT sth** asombro ANTE algo

astound /ə'staʊnd/ *vt* dejar estupefacto *or* atónito

astounded /ə'staʊndəd || ə'staʊndɪd/ *adj* atónito, pasmado; **they were ~ to learn of her resignation** se quedaron atónitos *or* pasmados al enterarse de su dimisión

astounding /ə'staʊndɪŋ/ *adj* increíble, pasmoso

astral /'æstrəl/ *adj* astral

astray /ə'streɪ/ *adv*: **to go ~** (get lost) «*letter/person*» extraviarse*, perderse*; (do wrong) (euph *or* hum) descarriarse*; **to lead sb ~** (euph *or* hum) llevar a algn por mal camino

astride /ə'straɪd/ *prep*: **he sat ~ the fence/horse** estaba sentado en la valla/montado en el caballo a horcajadas

astringent[1] /ə'strɪndʒənt/ *adj* ‹*lotion*› astringente; ‹*comment*› mordaz, cáustico

astringent[2] *n* [c u] astringente *m*

astrologer /ə'strɑːlədʒər || ə'strɒlədʒə(r)/ *n* astrólogo, -ga *m,f*

astrologist /ə'strɑːlədʒəst || ə'strɒlədʒɪst/ *n* ▸**astrologer**

astrology /ə'strɑːlədʒi || ə'strɒlədʒi/ *n* [u] astrología *f*

astronaut /'æstrənɔːt/ *n* astronauta *mf*

astronomer /ə'strɑːnəmər || ə'strɒnəmə(r)/ *n* astrónomo, -ma *m,f*

astronomical /'æstrə'nɑːmɪkəl || ˌæstrə'nɒmɪkəl/ *adj* astronómico; **of ~ proportions** de proporciones gigantescas

astronomically /'æstrə'nɑːmɪkli || ˌæstrə'nɒmɪkli/ *adv*: **they're ~ expensive** tienen unos precios astronómicos

astronomy /ə'strɑːnəmi || ə'strɒnəmi/ *n* [u] astronomía *f*

astrophysicist /ˌæstrəʊ'fɪzəsəst/ *n* astrofísico, -ca *m,f*

Asturian[1] /æ'stu:riən || æ'stjʊəriən/ *adj* asturiano

Asturian[2] *n* [1] (person) asturiano -na *m,f* [2] (language) asturiano *m*

astute /ə'stu:t || ə'stju:t/ *adj* ‹*person*› sagaz, perspicaz; ‹*decision*› inteligente; **that was very ~ of you** en eso estuviste muy listo

asunder /ə'sʌndər || ə'sʌndə(r)/ *adv* (arch *or* frml): **to be rent** *o* **torn ~** partirse por la mitad *or* en dos

asylee /əsar'li:/ *n* (AmE) asilado, -da *m,f*

asylum /ə'saɪləm/ *n* [1] [u c] (refuge) asilo *m*; **to seek political ~** pedir* *or* solicitar asilo político [2] [c] (*lunatic ~*) manicomio *m*

asymmetric /'eɪsɪ'metrɪk/, **-ical** /-ɪkəl/ *adj* asimétrico

at /æt, *weak form* ət/ *prep*

A (location) en; **~ Daniel's** en casa de Daniel, donde Daniel, en lo de Daniel (RPl); **don't call me ~ the office** no me llames a la oficina; **who was ~ the wedding?** ¿quién estuvo en la boda?; ***where it's ~*** (colloq): **Dino's is where it's ~** el lugar del momento es Dino's

B (direction): **to point ~ sth/sb** señalar algo/a algn; **she aimed the gun ~ him** le apuntó con la pistola; **he smiled ~ me** me sonrió

C (time): **~ 6 o'clock** a las seis; **~ Christmas** en Navidad, por Navidades (Esp); **~ night** por la noche, de noche; **~ that very moment** en ese mismo momento

D [1] (indicating state): **~ a disadvantage** en desventaja; **~ war/peace** en guerra/paz [2] (occupied with): **people ~ work** gente trabajando; **children ~ play** niños jugando; ***to be ~ it*** (colloq): **she's been hard ~ it studying all morning** ha estado toda la mañana dale que dale estudiando (fam); **they're ~ it again!** ¡han vuelto a empezar!; **while you're ~ it you can wipe the table** ya que estás (en ello) pásale un trapo a la mesa; ***to be ~ sth***: **she's been ~ my things** ha estado hurgando en mis cosas; **Joe's been ~ the brandy again** Joe le ha vuelto a dar al brandy (fam); ***to be (on) ~ sb*** darle* la lata a algn (fam); **she's been on ~ him to stop smoking** le ha estado dando la lata para que deje de fumar

E [1] (with measurements, numbers, rates etc): **they sell them ~ around $80** las venden a alrededor de $80; **three ~ a time** de tres en tres; **~ 80 mph** a 80 mph; **~ high temperatures** a altas temperaturas; **~ a depth of 200m** a una profundidad de 200m [2] (with superlative): **~ the latest** a más tardar; **bureaucracy ~ its most exasperating** la burocracia en su forma más exasperante; **French cooking ~ its best** lo mejor de la cocina francesa

F (because of): **he was surprised ~ the decision** le sorprendió la decisión; **they fled ~ the sound of footsteps** huyeron al oír pasos

G (concerning): **she's good ~ her job** hace bien su trabajo; **I'm bad ~ organizing things** no sirvo para organizar cosas

atavistic /'ætə'vɪstɪk/ *adj* atávico

ate /eɪt/ *past of* **eat**

atheism /'eɪθiɪzəm/ *n* [u] ateísmo *m*

atheist /'eɪθiəst || 'eɪθiɪst/ *n* ateo, atea *m,f*

Athens /'æθənz/ *n* Atenas *f*

athlete /'æθli:t/ *n* atleta *mf*

athlete's foot *n* [u] pie *m* de atleta

athletic /æθ'letɪk/ *adj* atlético

athletics /æθ'letɪks/ *n* (+ *sing or pl vb*) [1] (active sports) (AmE) deportes *mpl* [2] (track and field) (esp BrE) atletismo *m*

Atlantic[1] /ət'læntɪk/ *adj* atlántico

Atlantic[2] *n* **the ~ (Ocean)** el (océano) Atlántico

Atlantis /ət'læntəs || ət'læntɪs/ *n* Atlántida *f*

atlas /'ætləs/ *n* atlas *m*

Atlas Mountains /'ætləs/ *pl n* **the ~ ~** los Atlas

ATM *n* (= **automated teller machine**) cajero *m* automático *o* permanente

atmosphere /'ætməsfɪr || 'ætməsfɪə(r)/ *n* [1] (of planet) atmósfera *f* [2] (feeling, mood) ambiente *m*

atmospheric /'ætməs'ferɪk/ *adj* atmosférico

atmospherics /'ætməs'ferɪks/ *pl n* (Rad) interferencias *fpl*

atoll /'ætɔ:l || 'ætɒl/ *n* atolón *m*

atom /'ætəm/ *n* (Nucl Phys) átomo *m*; (tiny piece) pizca *f*

atomic /ə'tɑ:mɪk || ə'tɒmɪk/ *adj* ‹*warfare/energy*› atómico; **~ bomb** bomba *f* atómica

atomizer /'ætəmaɪzər || 'ætəmaɪzə(r)/ *n* atomizador *m*, pulverizador *m*

atone /ə'təʊn/ *vi* (frml) **to ~ FOR sth** ‹*for sins*› expiar* algo; ‹*for crime/harm*› reparar algo

atonement /ə'təʊnmənt/ *n* [u] (frml) (for sins) expiación *f*; **in ~ for his rudeness** en desagravio por su grosería

atrocious /ə'trəʊʃəs/ *adj* [1] (very bad) (colloq) ‹*spelling/manners*› espantoso (fam) [2] (horrifying) ‹*injuries/conditions*› atroz

atrociously /ə'trəʊʃəsli/ *adv* [1] (very badly) (colloq) ‹*sing/behave*› muy mal, pésimamente [2] (horrifyingly) ‹*treat/suffer*› atrozmente

atrocity /ə'trɑ:səti || ə'trɒsəti/ *n* [c u] (*pl* **-ties**) atrocidad *f*

atrophy[1] /'ætrəfi/ *vi* **-phies, -phying, -phied** atrofiarse

atrophy[2] *n* [u] atrofia *f*

at sign *n* (Comput) arroba *f*

attach /ə'tætʃ/ *vt* [1] (fasten) sujetar; (tie) atar, amarrar (AmL exc RPl); (stick) pegar*; (to letter, document) adjuntar, acompañar; **to ~ sth (TO sth)**: **it is ~ed to the wall with screws** está sujeto a la pared con tornillos; **a sports center with a restaurant ~ed** un centro deportivo con un restaurante anexo; **he ~ed a name tag to the case** le puso una etiqueta a la maleta; **please fill in the ~ed form** sírvase rellenar el formulario adjunto; **we ~ed ourselves to a group of tourists** nos unimos *or* (fam) nos pegamos a un grupo de turistas [2] (assign) (*usu pass*) **to be ~ed TO sth** estar* adscrito A algo [3] (attribute) **to ~ sth TO sth: he ~ed no importance to it** no le dio *or* concedió ninguna importancia

attaché /ˌætæ'ʃeɪ || ə'tæʃeɪ/ *n* agregado, -da *m,f*

attaché case *n* maletín *m*

attached /ə'tætʃt/ *adj* (*pred*) (fond) **to be ~ TO sb/sth** tenerle* mucho cariño *or* apego A algn/algo; **to become ~ TO sb/sth** encariñarse CON algn/algo, tomarle cariño A algn/algo

attachment /ə'tætʃmənt/ *n*

A [c] (part) accesorio *m*

B [1] [u] (fondness) **~ (TO sb/sth)** cariño *m* (POR algn/algo), apego *m* (A algn/algo) [2] [c] (relationship) relación *f*; **to form an ~** entablar una relación

attack[1] /ə'tæk/ *n*

A [1] [c u] (physical, verbal) ataque *m*; **to launch an ~** lanzar* un ataque; **terrorist ~s** atentados *mpl* terroristas; **~ ON/AGAINST sth/sb** ataque A/CONTRA algo/algn; **to come/be under ~** ser* atacado [2] [c] (Med) ataque *m*; **heart ~** infarto *m*, ataque *m* cardíaco *or* al corazón; **an anxiety ~** un ataque de ansiedad

B [u c] (part of team) (BrE Sport) delantera *f*

attack[2] *vt*

A ‹*army/target/policy*› atacar*; ‹*person*› atacar*, agredir*

B [1] (begin enthusiastically) ‹*food*› atacar*; ‹*task*› acometer [2] (deal with) ‹*problem*› combatir

■ **attack** *vi* (Mil, Sport) atacar*

attacker /ə'tækər || ə'tækə(r)/ *n* agresor, -sora *m,f*, atacante *mf*

attain /ə'teɪn/ *vt* (frml) ‹*position/goal*› alcanzar*, lograr, conseguir*; ‹*ambition*› realizar*, lograr

attainable /ə'teɪnəbəl/ *adj* alcanzable; **set yourself an ~ goal** fíjate una meta que puedas alcanzar *or* que esté a tu alcance

attainment /ə'teɪnmənt/ *n* (frml) [1] [u] (of position) logro *m*, consecución *f*; (of objective) logro *m* [2] [c] (accomplishment) logro *m*

attempt[1] /ə'tempt/ *vt* [1] (try) **to ~ to + INF/-ING** tratar DE *or* intentar + INF [2] (have a try at) ‹‹*student*›› ‹*exam question*› intentar responder a (frml); **she ~ed a smile** intentó sonreír [3] **attempted** *past p*: **~ed suicide** intento *m* de suicidio; **~ed murder/robbery** tentativa *f* de asesinato/robo; **~ed coup** intentona *f* golpista

attempt[2] *n* intento *m*; **at** *o* (esp AmE) **on the first ~** a la primera (tentativa), al primer intento; **~ to + INF**: **in my ~ to avoid the other car ...** al tratar de *or* intentar esquivar el otro coche ...; **they made no ~ to be polite** no hicieron ningún esfuerzo para ser corteses; **~ AT sth/-ING**: **I made an ~ at conversation** traté de *or* intenté

a

entablar conversación; **she had another ~ at the record** volvió a intentar batir el récord; **to make an ~ on sb's life** atentar contra la vida de algn

attend /ə'tend/ *vt*

A (frml) 1 (be present at) asistir a (frml); **the meeting was well ~ed** asistió mucha gente a la reunión 2 (go to regularly) ‹*church/school*› ir* a; ‹*classes*› ir* a, asistir a

B (take care of) ‹*patient*› atender*, ocuparse de; ‹*king/guests*› atender*

■ **attend** *vi*

A (be present) asistir

B (pay attention) **to ~ (TO sth)** atender* *or* prestar atención (A algo), poner* atención (A algo) (AmL)

Phrasal verb

• **attend to** [v ▸ prep ▸ o] 1 (look after) ‹*patient/customer*› atender*, ocuparse de 2 (deal with) ‹*correspondence/filing*› ocuparse de

attendance /ə'tendəns/ *n* 1 [u c] (presence) asistencia *f*; **to be in ~** estar* presente; (*before n*) **she has a poor ~ record** falta con frecuencia 2 [u] (service) atención *f*; **to be in ~** ‹‹*doctor*›› estar* de guardia; ***to dance ~ on sb*** estar* pendiente de algn 3 [c] (people present): **what was the ~?** ¿cuántos asistentes hubo?, ¿cuántas personas asistieron?; **to take ~** (AmE) pasar lista

attendant[1] /ə'tendənt/ *n* 1 (in museum, parking lot) guarda *m*; (in pool, toilets) encargado, -da *m,f* 2 (of royalty) miembro *m* del séquito; **the Queen and her ~s** la reina y su séquito

attendant[2] *adj* (accompanying) (frml): **parenthood and its ~ responsibilities** la paternidad y las responsabilidades que comporta *or* conlleva

attention[1] /ə'tentʃən || ə'tenʃən/ *n*

A [u] 1 (concentration) atención *f*; **(could I have your) ~, please!** ¡atención, por favor!; **to hold sb's ~** mantener* la atención de algn; **to pay ~ to sth/sb** prestarle atención a algo/algn; **he doesn't pay ~** no presta atención, no atiende; (*before n*) **~ span** capacidad *f* de concentración 2 (notice) atención *f*; **to attract ~** llamar la atención; **to attract** *o* **catch sb's ~** atraer* la atención de algn; **to be the center of ~** ser* el centro de atención; **don't pay any ~ to her, she's only teasing** no le hagas caso, te está tomando el pelo; **to bring** *o* **call sth to sb's ~** informar a algn DE algo; **it has been brought to my ~** *o* **it has come to my ~ that ...** me han informado *or* me he enterado de que ...; **I'd like to draw ~ to the fact that ...** quisiera hacerles notar que ... 3 (care) atención *f*; **he needs to show greater ~ to detail** tiene que ser más minucioso; **the engine needs ~** el motor necesita algunos ajustes *or* arreglos

B **attentions** *pl* (of admirer) atenciones *fpl*

C [u] (Mil): **to come** *o* **stand to ~** ponerse* en posición de firme(s); **to stand at ~** estar* firme(s)

attention[2] *interj* ¡atención!; (Mil) ¡firme(s)!

attentive /ə'tentɪv/ *adj* 1 (caring, considerate) atento; **to be ~ TO sb** ser* atento CON algn 2 (concentrating) atento

attentively /ə'tentɪvli/ *adv* atentamente, con atención

attenuate /ə'tenjueɪt/ *vt* atenuar*; **attenuating circumstances** circunstancias *fpl* atenuantes

attest /ə'test/ *vt* 1 (certify) ‹*fact*› atestiguar*, dar* fe de; ‹*signature*› autenticar*, autorizar* 2 (be proof of) atestiguar*, avalar

■ **attest** *vi* (be evidence) **to ~ TO sth** dar* fe DE algo, atestiguar* algo

attic /'ætɪk/ *n* desván *m*, ático *m*, altillo *m* (esp AmL)

attire[1] /ə'taɪr || ə'taɪə(r)/ *n* [u] (liter) atuendo *m* (frml), atavío *m* (liter)

attire[2] *vt* (liter) (*usu pass*) ataviar* (liter)

attitude /'ætətu:d || 'ætɪtju:d/ *n*

A (way of feeling, thinking) actitud *f*; **she takes the ~ that ...** para ella ..., ella opina *or* piensa que ...; **if you're going to take that ~** si te vas a poner así; **~ TO** *o* **TOWARD sth/sb** actitud HACIA algo/algn

B (posture) (frml) pose *f*, postura *f*; **to strike an ~** adoptar una pose

attn (= **attention**): **~ G Green** para entregar al Sr G Green

attorney /ə'tɜ:rni || ə'tɜ:ni/ *n* (*pl* **-neys**) (AmE) abogado, -da *m,f*; **prosecuting ~** fiscal *mf*; *see also* **power of attorney**

Attorney General *n* (*pl* **~ ~s** *or* **~s ~**) (in US — at national level) ≈ Ministro, -tra *m,f* de Justicia; (— at state level) ≈ Fiscal *mf* General

attract /ə'trækt/ *vt* 1 (Phys) atraer*; **I'm not very ~ed to the idea** la idea no me atrae demasiado; **I don't feel ~ed to him** no me atrae, no siento atracción por él 2 ‹*interest*› suscitar; **to ~ customers** *o* **business** atraer* clientes

attraction /ə'trækʃən/ *n* 1 [u c] (Phys) atracción *f* 2 [u] (interest): **I still feel a great ~ toward the place** todavía me atrae mucho el lugar; **babies hold no ~ for me** los bebés no me atraen; **what's the ~?** ¿qué atractivo tiene? 3 [c] (attractive feature) atractivo *m*; **tourist ~** atracción *f* turística

attractive /ə'træktɪv/ *adj* 1 (person) atractivo; ‹*personality/smile*› atractivo, atrayente 2 ‹*offer/price*› atractivo, tentador, interesante

attractively /ə'træktɪvli/ *adv* ‹*decorated/dressed*› con mucho gusto; **the products are ~ packaged** los productos vienen en envases muy atractivos

attributable /ə'trɪbjətəbəl/ *adj* (*pred*) **to be ~ TO sth** ser* atribuible *or* imputable A algo

attribute[1] /ə'trɪbjət || ə'trɪbju:t/ *vt* **to ~ sth TO sth/sb** atribuirle* algo A algo/algn

attribute[2] /'ætrəbju:t || 'ætrɪbju:t/ *n* atributo *m*

attributive /ə'trɪbjətɪv || ə'trɪbjʊtɪv/ *adj* atributivo

attrition /ə'trɪʃən/ *n* [u]

A (destruction) desgaste *m*; **war of ~** guerra *f* de desgaste

B (AmE Lab Rel) bajas *fpl* vegetativas

attune /ə'tu:n || ə'tju:n/ *vt* (*usu pass*) **to be/become ~d TO sth: he's very well ~d to her way of thinking** está muy en sintonía con su manera de pensar; **her ear soon became ~d to these sounds** su oído pronto aprendió a reconocer estos sonidos

atypical /'eɪ'tɪpɪkəl/ *adj* atípico

aubergine /'əʊbərʒi:n || 'əʊbəʒi:n/ *n* (BrE) berenjena *f*

auburn /'ɔ:bərn || 'ɔ:bən/ *adj* castaño rojizo *adj inv*, (de) color caoba

auction[1] /'ɔ:kʃən/ *n* [c u] subasta *f*, remate *m* (AmL); **to put sth up for ~** subastar *or* (AmL tb) rematar algo; (*before n*) **~ room(s)** sala(s) *f(pl)* de subasta *or* (AmL tb) de remate

auction[2] *vt* subastar, rematar (AmL)

Phrasal verb

• **auction off** [v ▸ o ▸ adv, v ▸ adv ▸ o] subastar, rematar (AmL)

auctioneer /'ɔ:kʃə'nɪr || ˌɔ:kʃə'nɪə(r)/ *n* subastador, -dora *m,f*, rematador, -dora *m,f* (AmL)

audacious /ɔ:'deɪʃəs/ *adj* 1 (daring) ‹*act/plan*› audaz, atrevido 2 (impudent) ‹*behavior/person*› atrevido, descarado

audacity /ɔ:'dæsəti/ *n* [u] 1 (daring) audacia *f* 2 (impudence) atrevimiento *m*, descaro *m*; **he had the ~ to say ...** tuvo el descaro *or* el tupé de decir ...

audible /'ɔ:dəbəl/ *adj* ‹*sigh/whisper*› audible; **it was barely ~** apenas se oía

audibly /'ɔ:dəbli/ *adv* de forma audible

audience /'ɔ:diəns/ *n*

A (at play, film) público *m*, espectadores *mpl*; (at concert, lecture) auditorio *m*, público *m*; (TV) audiencia *f*, telespectadores *mpl*; **how will American ~s react to the play?** ¿cómo reaccionará el público americano ante la obra?; **the book appealed to a wide ~** el libro era de interés para muchos tipos de lectores; (*before n*) **~ participation** participación *f* del público

B (interview) audiencia *f*

audio /'ɔ:diəʊ/ *adj* (*before n*) ‹*equipment/system*› de sonido, de audio

audio- /'ɔ:diəʊ/ *pref* audio-

audiovisual /'ɔ:diəʊ'vɪʒuəl/ *adj* audiovisual

audit[1] /'ɔ:dət || 'ɔ:dɪt/ *vt* 1 (Busn, Fin) ‹*accounts*› auditar 2 (AmE Educ) ‹*classes/course*› asistir como oyente a

audit[2] *n* [c u] (Busn, Fin) 1 (inspection) auditoría *f* 2 (report) (AmE) informe *m* de auditoría

audition[1] /ɔ:'dɪʃən/ *vi*: **to ~ (FOR sth)** dar* una audición *or* prueba (PARA algo)

■ **audition** *vt* **to ~ sb (FOR sth)** hacerle* una audición *or* prueba a algn (PARA algo)

audition² *n* ~ (FOR **sth**) audición *f or* prueba *f* (PARA algo); **to hold ~s** hacer* audiciones *or* pruebas

auditor /'ɔ:dətər || 'ɔ:dɪtə(r)/ *n* 1 (Busn, Fin) auditor, -tora *m,f* 2 (AmE Educ) oyente *mf*

auditorium /'ɔ:də'tɔ:riəm || ,ɔ:dɪ'tɔ:riəm/ *n* (*pl* **-riums** *or* **-ria** /-riə/) auditorio *m*

au fait /'əʊ'feɪ/ *adj* (*pred*) **to be ~ ~ WITH sth** estar* al tanto DE algo

Aug (= **August**) ago.

aught /ɔ:t/ *pron* (arch): **for ~ I know** que yo sepa; **for ~ I care** por mí

augment /ɔ:g'ment/ *vt* (frml) aumentar, incrementar (frml)

au gratin /əʊ'grætn̩ || ,əʊ'grætæn/ *adj* gratinado, al gratén

augur /'ɔ:gər || 'ɔ:gə(r)/ *vi*: **to ~ well/ill** ser* de buen/mal agüero; **this vote does not ~ well** *o* **~s ill for the government** esta votación no augura *or* no presagia nada bueno para el gobierno
■ **augur** *vt* (liter) augurar, presagiar

august /ɔ:'gʌst/ *adj* augusto

August /'ɔ:gəst/ *n* agosto *m*; *see also* **January**

aunt /ænt || ɑ:nt/ *n* tía *f*; **A~ Mary** tía Mary; **my ~ and uncle** mis tíos

auntie, aunty /'ænti || 'ɑ:nti/ *n* (colloq) tía *f*, tiíta *f* (fam)

au pair /'əʊ'per || ,əʊ'peə(r)/ *n* au pair *mf*; (*before n*) **~ ~ girl** chica *f* au pair

aura /'ɔ:rə/ *n* halo *m*, aura *m*

aural /'ɔ:rəl/ *adj* auditivo

aurora /ɔ:'rɔ:rə/ *n* aurora *f*; **~ australis/borealis** aurora austral/boreal

auspices /'ɔ:spəsəz || 'ɔ:spɪsɪz/ *pl n* (frml) (patronage): **under the ~ of sb/sth** bajo los auspicios de algn/algo

auspicious /ɔ:'spɪʃəs/ *adj* (frml) prometedor, auspicioso (CS); **on this ~ occasion** en esta feliz ocasión

auspiciously /ɔ:'spɪʃəsli/ *adv* con buenos auspicios, de manera prometedora

Aussie¹ /'ɔ:si || 'ɒzi/ *n* (colloq) (Australian) (BrE) australiano, -na *m,f*

Aussie² *adj* (colloq) australiano

austere /ɔ:'stɪr || ɒ'stɪə(r), ɔ:'stɪə(r)/ *adj* ‹*person/lifestyle/decor*› austero; ‹*features*› severo

austerity /ɔ:'sterəti || ɒ'sterəti, ɔ:'sterəti/ *n* [u] (of lifestyle, landscape) austeridad *f*; (of features) severidad *f*; **economic ~** austeridad económica

Australasia /'ɔ:strə'leɪʒə, -'leɪʃə || ,ɒstrə'leɪʒiə, -'leɪʃə/ *n* Australasia *f*

Australia /ɔ:'streɪliə || ɒ'streɪliə/ *n* Australia *f*

Australian¹ /ɔ:'streɪliən || ɒ'streɪliən/ *adj* australiano

Australian² *n* australiano, -na *m,f*

Austria /'ɔ:striə || 'ɒstriə/ *n* Austria *f*

Austrian¹ /'ɔ:striən || 'ɒstriən/ *adj* austriaco, austríaco

Austrian² *n* austriaco, -ca *m,f*, austríaco, -ca *m,f*

authentic /ə'θentɪk || ɔ:'θentɪk/ *adj* 1 (genuine) auténtico 2 (realistic) ‹*atmosphere*› realista, verosímil

authentically /ə'θentɪkli || ɔ:'θentɪkli/ *adv* fielmente

authenticate /ə'θentɪkeɪt || ɔ:'θentɪkeɪt/ *vt* 1 (declare genuine) autenticar*, autentificar* 2 (prove, confirm) probar*; **his story was ~d by eye-witnesses** su relato fue corroborado por testigos oculares

authenticity /'ɔ:θen'tɪsəti/ *n* [u] (of manuscript, painting) autenticidad *f*

author /'ɔ:θər || 'ɔ:θə(r)/ *n*
A (writer) escritor, -ra *m,f*; (in relation to her/his works) autor, -tora *m,f*
B (originator) autor, -tora *m,f*, creador, -dora *m,f*

authoritarian /ɔ:'θɔ:rə'teriən || ɔ:,θɒrɪ'teəriən/ *adj* autoritario

authoritative /ə'θɔ:rəteɪtɪv || ɔ:'θɒrətətɪv/ *adj*
A (reliable, respected) ‹*source*› fidedigno, autorizado; ‹*work/study*› autorizado
B (commanding) autoritario

authority /ə'θɔ:rəti || ɔ:'θɒrəti/ *n* (*pl* **-ties**)
A [u] 1 (power) autoridad *f*; **those in ~** los que tienen la autoridad, los que mandan; **I have no ~ in the matter** no tengo competencia en el asunto 2 (authorization) **~ to + INF** autorización *f* PARA + INF; **he acted without proper ~** actuó sin la debida autorización 3 (authoritativeness) autoridad *f*; **I can speak with some ~ on this subject** puedo hablar del tema con cierta autoridad
B [c] (person, body) autoridad *f*; **the proper ~** *o* **authorities** la(s) autoridad(es) competente(s); **she was detained by the Belgian authorities** fue detenida por las autoridades belgas
C [c] 1 (expert) **~ (ON sth)** autoridad *f* (EN algo); **he is an ~ on the subject** es una autoridad en la materia 2 (source) autoridad *f*; **to have sth on good ~** saber* algo de buena fuente

authorization /'ɔ:θərə'zeɪʃən || ,ɔ:θəraɪ'zeɪʃən/ *n* [u c] autorización *f*; **~ FOR sth/to + INF** autorización PARA algo/PARA + INF

authorize /'ɔ:θəraɪz/ *vt* 1 ‹*publication/demonstration/transaction*› autorizar*; ‹*funds*› aprobar* 2 (empower) **to ~ sb to + INF** autorizar* a algn PARA + INF; **you are not ~d to enter this area** usted no está autorizado *or* no tiene autorización para entrar en esta zona 3 **authorized** *past p* autorizado; **~d agent** agente *m* oficial; **~d dealer** distribuidor *m* autorizado

authorship /'ɔ:θərʃɪp || 'ɔ:θəʃɪp/ *n* [u] autoría *f*

autistic /ɔ:'tɪstɪk/ *adj* autista

auto /'ɔ:təʊ/ *n* (AmE) ▸**automobile**

auto- /'ɔ:təʊ/ *pref* (self-) auto-

autobiographical /'ɔ:tə,baɪə'græfɪkəl/ *adj* autobiográfico

autobiography /'ɔ:təbaɪ'ɑ:grəfi/ *n* [u c] (*pl* **-phies**) autobiografía *f*

autocade /'ɔ:təʊkeɪd/ *n* ▸**motorcade**

autocratic /'ɔ:tə'krætɪk/ *adj* autocrático

Autocue® /'ɔ:təʊkju:/ *n* (BrE) autocue® *m*, teleprompter *m*

autograph¹ /'ɔ:təgræf || 'ɔ:təgrɑ:f/ *n* autógrafo *m*

autograph² *vt* autografiar*

automat /'ɔ:təmæt/ *n* (in US) cafetería *f* (*donde máquinas automáticas despachan la comida*)

automata /ɔ:'tɑ:mətə || ɔ:'tɒmətə/ *pl of* **automaton**

automate /'ɔ:təmeɪt/ *vt* automatizar*; **~d teller machine** cajero *m* automático

automatic¹ /'ɔ:tə'mætɪk/ *adj*
A ‹*machine*› automático; **~ pilot** piloto *m* automático
B (inevitable): **you'll receive an ~ pay increase** recibirá automáticamente un aumento salarial

automatic² *n* (car) coche *m* automático; (pistol) automática *f*, revólver *m* automático; (washing machine) lavadora *f* automática, lavarropas *m* automático (RPl)

automatically /'ɔ:tə'mætɪkli/ *adv* automáticamente; **people ~ assume we're married** la gente da por hecho *or* por sentado que estamos casados

automatic: **~ pencil** *n* (AmE) portaminas *m*; **~ pilot** *n* [c u] piloto *m* automático

automation /'ɔ:tə'meɪʃən/ *n* [u] automatización *f*

automaton /ɔ:'tɑ:mətən || ɔ:'tɒmətən/ *n* (*pl* **automata** *or* **-tons**) autómata *m*

automobile /'ɔ:təməbi:l/ *n* (esp AmE) coche *m*, carro *m* (AmL exc CS), auto *m* (esp CS), automóvil *m* (frml); (*before n*) **~ industry** industria *f* automotriz *or* del automóvil

autonomous /ɔ:'tɑ:nəməs || ɔ:'tɒnəməs/ *adj* autónomo

autonomy /ɔ:'tɑ:nəmi || ɔ:'tɒnəmi/ *n* [u] autonomía *f*

autopilot /'ɔ:təʊ,paɪlət/ *n* piloto *m* automático

autopsy /'ɔ:tɑ:psi || 'ɔ:tɒpsi/ *n* (*pl* **-sies**) autopsia *f*; **to perform** *o* **carry out an ~ on sb** hacerle* la autopsia a algn

autoreverse /'ɔ:təʊrɪ'vɜ:rs || ,ɔ:təʊrɪ'vɜ:s/ *n* [u] rebobinado *m* automático

autumn /'ɔ:təm/ *n* (esp BrE) otoño *m*; **in (the) ~** en (el) otoño; (*before n*) ‹*day/weather*› de otoño, otoñal; **~ term** primer trimestre *m* (*del año académico*)

autumnal /ɔ:'tʌmnəl/ *adj* otoñal

auxiliary¹ /ɔ:g'zɪljəri/ *adj* auxiliar

auxiliary² *n* (*pl* **-ries**) 1 (helper, additional person) auxiliar *mf*, ayudante *mf*; **nursing ~** enfermero, -ra *m,f* auxiliar 2 **auxiliaries** *pl* (Mil) tropas *fpl* auxiliares

avail¹ /ə'veɪl/ *v refl* (frml) **to ~ oneself OF sth** aprovechar algo

a

avail² *n* [u] (liter): **to no ~** en vano; **it is of no ~** no sirve de nada, es inútil

availability /əˈveɪləˈbɪləti/ *n* [u] 1 (of funds) disponibilidad *f*; (of goods) existencias *fpl*; (of labor) oferta *f*; **subject to ~** siempre y cuando los/las tengamos en existencias 2 (being free) **~ FOR sth** disponibilidad *f* PARA algo

available /əˈveɪləbəl/ *adj* 1 (obtainable) (*pred*): **to be easily** *o* **readily ~** ser* fácil de conseguir; **cigarettes are ~ in packs of 10 or 20** los cigarrillos vienen *or* se venden en paquetes de 10 o 20; **brochures are ~ on request** hay folletos a disposición de quien los solicite; **food and drink will be ~ at the fair** en la feria habrá comida y bebida; ⓢ **available only on prescription** venta bajo receta médica 2 (at sb's disposal) ‹*resources/manpower*› disponible; **he uses every ~ minute for studying** aprovecha cada minuto que tiene para estudiar; **book me on the earliest ~ flight** consígame un billete en el primer vuelo que pueda; **to make sth ~ to sb** poner* algo a disposición de algn 3 (free, contactable) (*pred*) libre; **Mr Smith is not ~ for comment** el señor Smith no está dispuesto a formular declaraciones 4 (sexually) (euph) (*pred*) libre y dispuesto

avalanche /ˈævəlæntʃ || ˈævəlɑːnʃ/ *n* alud *m*, avalancha *f*

avant-garde¹ /ˈɑːvɑːnˈgɑːrd || ˌævɒnˈgɑːd/ *n* **the ~** la vanguardia

avant-garde² *adj* vanguardista, de vanguardia

avarice /ˈævərəs || ˈævərɪs/ *n* [u] (liter) codicia *f* (liter), avaricia *f*

avaricious /ˈævəˈrɪʃəs/ *adj* (liter) codicioso, avaro

Ave (= **Avenue**) Avda., Av.

avenge /əˈvendʒ/ *vt* vengar*

■ *v refl* **to ~ oneself (ON sb) (FOR sth)** vengarse* (EN algn) (POR algo)

avenue /ˈævənuː || ˈævənjuː/ *n*

A 1 (tree-lined walk) paseo *m* (*arbolado*) 2 (broad street) avenida *f*; **Fifth A~** la Quinta Avenida

B (means, method) vía *f*

aver /əˈvɜːr || əˈvɜː(r)/ *vt* **-rr-** (frml) afirmar, asegurar

average¹ /ˈævrɪdʒ, ˈævərɪdʒ/ *n* (Math) promedio *m*, media *f*; **$600 a week on (an) ~** un promedio *or* una media de 600 dólares a la *or* por semana; **above/below (the) ~** por encima/por debajo de la media

average² *adj* 1 (Math) ‹*time/age*› medio, promedio *adj inv*; **he is of ~ height** es de estatura mediana *or* regular 2 (typical): **that's about ~ for a man of your height** eso es lo normal en *or* para un hombre de tu estatura; **the ~ family** la familia tipo; **she's not your ~ pop singer** (colloq) no es la típica cantante pop 3 (ordinary): **how was the movie? — average** ¿qué tal la película? — normal *or* nada del otro mundo

average³ *vt* (do, get on average): **we ~d 80 miles a day** hicimos un promedio *or* una media de 80 millas al día

Phrasal verb

• **average out**

A [v ▸ o ▸ adv, v ▸ adv ▸ o] calcular el promedio *or* la media de

B [v ▸ adv] **to ~ out AT/TO sth**: **our speed ~d out at about 60mph** hicimos una media *or* un promedio de 60 millas por hora

averse /əˈvɜːrs || əˈvɜːs/ *adj* (*pred*) **to be ~ TO sth** ‹*to an idea*› ser* reacio A algo; **I'm not ~ to the occasional cigar** me gusta fumarme un puro de vez en cuando

aversion /əˈvɜːrʒən, -ʃən || əˈvɜːʃən/ *n* 1 (dislike) (*no pl*) **~ TO sth/sb** aversión *f* A algo/algn; **he has an ~ to getting up early** le tiene aversión a levantarse temprano 2 [c] (hated object): **pop music is her pet ~** aborrece la música pop

avert /əˈvɜːrt || əˈvɜːt/ *vt* 1 ‹*eyes/gaze*› **to ~ sth FROM sth** apartar algo DE algo 2 ‹*danger/suspicion*› evitar; ‹*accident/strike*› impedir*, evitar; ‹*threat*› conjurar

aviary /ˈeɪvieri/ *n* (*pl* **-ries**) pajarera *f*

aviation /ˈeɪviˈeɪʃən/ *n* [u] aviación *f*

avid /ˈævəd || ˈævɪd/ *adj* 1 (enthusiastic) (*before n*) ‹*reader/interest*› ávido; ‹*fan/follower*› ferviente 2 (greedy) (*pred*) **to be ~ FOR sth** estar* ávido DE algo

avidly /ˈævədli || ˈævɪdli/ *adv* con avidez, ávidamente

avocado /ˈævəˈkɑːdəʊ/ *n* (*pl* **-dos**) 1 [u c] **~ (pear)** aguacate *m or* (Bol, CS, Per) palta *f* 2 [c u] (tree) aguacate *m or* (Bol, CS, Per) palto *m or* palta *f or* paltero *m* 3 [u] (color) verde *m* pino

avoid /əˈvɔɪd/ *vt* ‹*obstacle/place*› evitar; ‹*topic/question*› evitar, eludir; ‹*blow*› esquivar, eludir; **why are you ~ing me?** ¿por qué me rehúyes?; **she ~ed his eyes** evitó mirarlo a los ojos; **to ~ -ING** evitar + INF

avoidable /əˈvɔɪdəbəl/ *adj* evitable

avoirdupois /ˈævərdəˈpɔɪz || ˌævədəˈpɔɪz, ˌævwɑːdjʊˈpwɑː/ *n*: *sistema de medidas de peso usado en el mundo anglosajón*

avow /əˈvaʊ/ *vt* (liter) reconocer*, confesar*

avowal /əˈvaʊəl/ *n* (liter) reconocimiento *m*, confesión *f*

avowed /əˈvaʊd/ *adj* (*before n*) declarado, confesado

avuncular /əˈvʌŋkjələr || əˈvʌŋkjələ(r)/ *adj* paternal y amistoso

aw /ɔː/ *interj* (AmE) ¡ah!

await /əˈweɪt/ *vt* 1 (wait for) esperar; **~ further instructions** espere a recibir nuevas instrucciones; **prisoners ~ing trial** detenidos a la espera de juicio; **a long ~ed event** un acontecimiento muy esperado 2 (be in store for) esperar, aguardar

awake¹ /əˈweɪk/ *adj* (*pred*) despierto; **to stay ~** no dormirse*, mantenerse* despierto; **you kept me ~ all night** no me dejaste dormir en toda la noche; **to be wide ~** estar* totalmente despierto

awake² (*past* **awoke**; *past p* **awoken**) *vi* 1 (wake up) despertar*; **I awoke to find him gone** cuando (me) desperté, él se había ido 2 (become aware) **to ~ TO sth** ‹*to danger/reality*› darse* cuenta DE algo

■ **awake** *vt* despertar*

awaken /əˈweɪkən/ *vi* ▸ **awake²**

■ **awaken** *vt* 1 (wake up) despertar* 2 (make aware) **to ~ sb TO sth** abrirle* los ojos a algn SOBRE algo

awakening /əˈweɪkənɪŋ/ *n* despertar *m*; ***a rude ~*** una sorpresa muy desagradable

award¹ /əˈwɔːrd || əˈwɔːd/ *vt* 1 ‹*prize/medal*› conceder, otorgar*; ‹*honor*› conferir*; ‹*pay increase/grant*› conceder 2 (Sport) ‹*penalty/free kick*› conceder

award² *n* 1 [c] (prize) galardón *m*, premio *m*; (medal) condecoración *f* 2 [c] (sum of money) asignación *f*, suma *f* de dinero 3 [u] (awarding — of prize, grant, pay increase) concesión *f*

award-winning /əˈwɔːrdˈwɪnɪŋ || əˈwɔːdˌwɪnɪŋ/ *adj* (*before n*) galardonado, premiado

aware /əˈwer || əˈweə(r)/ *adj* 1 (conscious) (*pred*) **to be ~ OF sth** ser* consciente DE algo, darse* cuenta DE algo; **I'm well ~ of that** soy *or* (Chi, Méx) estoy muy consciente *or* tengo plena conciencia de eso, me doy perfecta cuenta de eso; **he's not even ~ of my existence** ni siquiera sabe que existo; **as far as I'm ~** que yo sepa; **we want to make people ~ of their rights** queremos que la gente tome conciencia de sus derechos; **to be ~ THAT: is your father ~ that you drink?** ¿sabe tu padre que bebes?; **he became ~ that something was wrong** se dio cuenta de que pasaba algo 2 (alert, knowledgeable): **they are very politically ~** tienen mucha conciencia política

awareness /əˈwernəs || əˈweənɪs/ *n* [u] conciencia *f*; **~ OF sth**: **we want to increase public ~ of the dangers of smoking** queremos que haya una mayor conciencia de los peligros del tabaco

awash /əˈwɔːʃ || əˈwɒʃ/ *adj* (*pred*) (flooded) **to be ~ (WITH sth)** estar* inundado (DE algo)

away /əˈweɪ/ *adv*

A 1 (from place, person): **I looked ~** aparté la vista; **he limped ~** se alejó cojeando; **they dragged the fallen tree ~** se llevaron el árbol caído arrastrándolo 2 (indicating removal): **the bark had been stripped ~** habían quitado la corteza; *see also* **blow, take, wash, wipe** *etc* **away**

B 1 (in the distance): **it isn't far ~** no queda lejos; **a long way ~** muy lejos; **Easter is a long way ~** falta mucho para Pascua; **it's 20 miles ~** queda a 20 millas; **she lives an hour's drive ~** vive a una hora de aquí en coche 2 (absent): **she's ~ in Canada** está en Canadá; **I'll be ~ all next week** toda la semana que viene no voy a estar *or* voy a estar fuera 3 (Sport esp BrE): **to play ~** jugar* fuera (de casa)

C (on one's way): **we were ~ before sunrise** partimos *or* salimos antes del amanecer

D (continuously): **he's been painting ~ all morning** se ha pasado toda la mañana pintando; **I could hear him singing ~** lo oía cantar

E 1 (into nothing) *see* **die, fade, waste** *etc* **away** 2 (indicating use of time): **you're dreaming your life ~** se te está yendo la vida en sueños

F **away from** (*as prep*) 1 (in opposite direction to): **the hotel faces ~ from the sea** el hotel da hacia el lado opuesto al mar; **she pulled the child ~ from the cliff edge** apartó al niño del borde del acantilado 2 (at a distance, separated from) lejos de; **stand well ~ from the fire** no te acerques al fuego; **to get ~ from it all** alejarse del mundanal ruido

awe /ɔː/ *n* [u] sobrecogimiento *m*; **they were filled with ~** se sobrecogieron; **to be in ~ of sb** sentirse* intimidado por algn

awed /ɔːd/ *adj* sobrecogido, turbado; **they are somewhat ~ by their son's achievements** se sienten un tanto intimidados por los éxitos de su hijo

awe-inspiring /ˈɔːɪnˈspaɪrɪŋ || ˈɔːɪn,spaɪərɪŋ/ *adj* impresionante, imponente

awesome /ˈɔːsəm/ *adj* 1 imponente, formidable 2 (*as interj*) (AmE) ¡impresionante!

awestruck /ˈɔːstrʌk/ *adj* atemorizado

awful[1] /ˈɔːfəl/ *adj*

A (colloq) 1 ‹*journey/weather/day*› horrible, espantoso, atroz; ‹*clothes*› horroroso, espantoso; ‹*joke/movie*› malísimo, pésimo; **it smells ~** huele muy mal; **he's an ~ man** es un repugnante; **I know it sounds ~, but ...** te parecerá una barbaridad, pero ...; **I felt ~** me sentía fatal *or* muy mal; **for one ~ moment I thought he had seen me** pasé un momento horrible *or* espantoso creyendo que me había visto; **you are ~!** ¡qué malo eres!; **how ~!** ¡qué horror! 2 (*as intensifier*): **she's an ~ bore** es terriblemente aburrida; **there were an ~ lot of people there** había muchísima gente; **he doesn't eat an ~ lot** no come mucho

B (terrible) (liter) ‹*revenge/destruction*› atroz

awful[2] *adv* (AmE colloq) (*as intensifier*): **I'm ~ hot** tengo un calor espantoso; **it's an ~ long way to Tulsa** Tulsa está lejísimos

awfully /ˈɔːfli/ *adv* 1 (*as intensifier*) (colloq): **he's ~ rich** es riquísimo; **that's ~ nice of you** es muy amable de tu parte; **I'm ~ sorry** lo siento de veras *or* en el alma; **it's not ~ difficult** no es terriblemente difícil 2 (badly) espantosamente

awhile /əˈhwaɪl || əˈwaɪl/ *adv* (arch) un rato

awkward /ˈɔːkwərd || ˈɔːkwəd/ *adj*

A (clumsy) ‹*movement/person*› torpe; ‹*phrase*› poco elegante

B 1 (difficult, inconvenient) ‹*shape/angle*› incómodo, poco práctico; **it's an ~ place to get to by rail** es difícil llegar allí en tren; **you've called at a rather ~ moment, I'm afraid** me temo que llamas en mal momento; **she could make things very ~ for you** te podría hacer la vida imposible 2 (difficult to deal with) difícil; **he's at an ~ age** está en una edad difícil

C 1 (delicate, embarrassing) ‹*decision/subject*› delicado; **you've put me in a very ~ position** me has puesto en una situación muy violenta *or* embarazosa 2 (embarrassed) ‹*silence*› incómodo, violento; **I feel ~ in his company** no estoy a gusto con él

awkwardly /ˈɔːkwərdli || ˈɔːkwədli/ *adv* 1 (clumsily) ‹*move*› torpemente, con torpeza; ‹*express oneself*› con poca fluidez *or* elegancia 2 (with embarrassment): **he fidgeted ~ with his tie** violento *or* incómodo, jugueteaba con su corbata

awning /ˈɔːnɪŋ/ *n* toldo *m*

awoke /əˈwəʊk/ *past of* **awake**[2]

awoken /əˈwəʊkən/ *past p of* **awake**[2]

AWOL /ˈeɪwɔːl || ˈeɪwɒl/ *adj* (*pred*) (= **absent without leave**) ausente sin permiso; **to go ~** ausentarse sin permiso

awry /əˈraɪ/ *adj* (*pred*) torcido; **to go ~** salir* mal, fracasar

ax[1], (BrE) **axe** /æks/ *n* hacha *f*‡; ***to give sb the ~*** despedir* *or* echar a algn; **the series was given the ~** suprimieron *or* cancelaron la serie; ***to have an ~ to grind*** tener* un interés personal

ax[2], (BrE) **axe** *vt* (journ) ‹*expenditure/costs*› recortar, reducir*; ‹*project/services*› suprimir, cancelar; ‹*jobs*› suprimir, eliminar; ‹*employee*› despedir*

axiom /ˈæksiəm/ *n* axioma *m*

axiomatic /ˈæksiəˈmætɪk/ *adj* (Math, Phil) axiomático

axis /ˈæksəs || ˈæksɪs/ *n* (*pl* **axes** /ˈæksiːz/) eje *m*

axle /ˈæksəl/ *n* eje *m*

ay(e) /aɪ/ *interj* (dial) sí; **~, ~, sir** (Naut) a la orden, mi capitán (*or* almirante *etc*)

ayes /aɪz/ *pl n*: **the ~ have it** gana el sí

AZ = Arizona

Azerbaijan /ˈæzərbaɪˈdʒɑːn || ,æzəbaɪˈdʒɑːn/ *n* Azerbaiyán *m*, Azerbaiján *m*

Azerbaijani[1] /ˈæzərbaɪˈdʒɑːni || ,æzəbaɪˈdʒɑːni/ *adj* azerbaiyaní

Azerbaijani[2] *n* azerbaiyaní *mf*

Aztec[1] /ˈæztek/ *adj* azteca

Aztec[2] *n* azteca *mf*

azure[1] /ˈæʒər || ˈæzjə(r), ˈæzjʊə(r)/ *adj* (liter) azur (liter), azul celeste

azure[2] *n* [u] (liter) azur *m* (liter)

b Bb

B, b /biː/ *n*
A 1 (letter) B, b *f* 2 (Mus) si *m*; *see also* **A A2**
B 1 (in sizes of paper) (BrE) **B4** B4 (*250 x 353mm*); **B5** B5 (*176 x 250mm*) 2 (in UK) (Transp) (*before n*) **B road** carretera *f* comarcal *or* local *or* secundaria

b (= **born**) n.

BA *n* = **Bachelor of Arts**

baa /bæ || bɑː/ *vi* balar

babble¹ /ˈbæbəl/ *n* (*no pl*) (of voices) murmullo *m*; (foolish talk) parloteo *m*; (of water) susurro *m* (liter), murmullo *m* (liter)

babble² *vi* (talk foolishly) parlotear (fam); (talk unintelligibly) farfullar; ‹‹*baby*›› balbucear; **he ~d on** siguió parloteando ; **a babbling brook** (liter) un arroyo rumoroso (liter)

babe /beɪb/ *n* 1 (little child) (liter) criatura *f*; **a ~ in arms** un bebé 2 (esp AmE colloq) (*as form of address*) nena (fam), ricura (fam)

baboon /bæˈbuːn || bəˈbuːn/ *n* babuino *m*

baby¹ /ˈbeɪbi/ *n* (*pl* **babies**) 1 (infant) bebé *m*, niño, -ña *m,f*, bebe, -ba *m,f* (Per, RPl), guagua *f* (Andes); **to have a ~** tener* un hijo *or* un niño; **don't be such a ~!** ¡no seas niño!; **to leave sb holding the ~** (BrE) cargarle* el muerto a algn (fam); ***to throw the ~ out with the bathwater*** tirar las frutas frescas con las podridas *or* (Esp tb) las pochas 2 (animal) cría *f* 3 (youngest member) benjamín, -mina *m,f* 4 (pet concern) (colloq): **the campaign is her ~** la campaña es su proyecto *or* su criatura

baby² *adj* ‹*corn/car*› pequeño

baby³ *vt* **-bies, -bying, -bied** mimar, malcriar*

baby: **~-blue** /ˈbeɪbiˈbluː/ *adj* (*pred* **~ blue**) azul celeste *or* claro *adj inv*, celeste (AmL); **~ boom** *n* boom *m* de la natalidad; **~ buggy**, **~ carriage** *n* (AmE) cochecito *m* de bebé, carriola *f* (Méx); **~ face** *n* cara *f* de niño/niña; **~-faced** /ˈbeɪbiˈfeɪst/ *adj* con cara de niño/niña; **~ grand** *n* piano *m* de media cola

Babygro® /ˈbeɪbigrəʊ/ *n* (BrE) mameluco *m* (AmL), pelele *m* (Esp), enterito *m* (RPl), osito *m* (Chi)

babyhood /ˈbeɪbihʊd/ *n* [u] primera infancia *f*

babyish /ˈbeɪbiɪʃ/ *adj* infantil

Babylon /ˈbæbəlɑːn || ˈbæbɪlən/ *n* Babilonia *f*

baby: **~-sit** *vi* (*pres p* **-sitting**; *past & past p* **-sat**) cuidar niños, hacer* de canguro (Esp); **~-sitter** *n* baby sitter *mf*, canguro *mf* (Esp); **~ talk** *n* [u] *lenguaje de bebé*

bachelor /ˈbætʃələr || ˈbætʃələ(r)/ *n*
A (single man) soltero *m*; (*before n*) **~ apartment** *o* (BrE) **flat** departamento *m or* (Esp) piso *m* de soltero; **~ pad** *n* (colloq) apartamento *m* de soltero, departamento *m* de soltero (AmL), piso *m* de soltero (Esp), bulín *m* (RPl fam)
B (Educ) licenciado, -da *m,f*; **B~ of Arts/Science** (degree) licenciatura *f* en Filosofía y Letras/en Ciencias

bachelorette /ˌbætʃələˈret/ *n* (AmE) soltera *f*

back¹ /bæk/ *n*
A [c] (Anat) (of human) espalda *f*; (of animal) lomo *m*; **he was lying on his ~** estaba tumbado boca arriba; **he had his ~ to the door** estaba de espaldas a la puerta; **to break one's ~ working** deslomarse trabajando; **I was glad to see the ~ of him** me alegré de que se fuera; ***behind sb's ~***: **they laugh at him behind his ~** se ríen de él a sus espaldas; ***to be on sb's ~*** (colloq) estarle* encima a algn; **get off my ~!** déjame en paz (fam); ***to break the ~ of sth*** hacer* la parte más difícil/la mayor parte de algo; ***to get*** *o* ***put sb's ~ up*** (colloq) irritar a algn; ***to put one's ~ into sth*** poner* empeño en algo; ***to turn one's ~ on sb*** volverle* la espalda a algn; ▸**scratch²** *vt* 4
B [c] 1 (of chair) respaldo *m*; (of dress, jacket) espalda *f*; (of electrical appliance, watch) tapa *f* 2 (reverse side — of envelope, photo) dorso *m*, revés *m*; (— of head) parte *f* posterior *or* de atrás; (— of hand) dorso *m*; **read the instructions on the ~** lea las instrucciones al dorso 3 **back to front**: **your sweater is on ~ to front** te has puesto el suéter al revés; ▸**hand¹ B**
C [c u] (rear part): **the ~ of the hall** el fondo de la sala; **the ~ of the house** la parte de atrás de la casa; **at the ~ of the drawer** en el fondo del cajón; **we sat at the ~** nos sentamos al fondo; **I'll sit in the ~** (of car) yo me siento detrás *or* (en el asiento de) atrás; **there's a yard at the ~** hay un patio atrás; **we stood at the ~ of the line** nos pusimos al final de la cola; **(in) ~ of the sofa** (AmE) detrás del sofá; **he's out ~ in the yard** (AmE) está en el patio, al fondo; ***in the ~ of beyond*** quién sabe dónde, donde el diablo perdió el poncho (AmS fam), en el quinto pino (Esp fam)
D [c] (Sport) defensa *mf*, zaguero, -ra *m,f*

back² *adj* (*before n, no comp*)
A (at rear) trasero, de atrás; **the ~ row** la última fila
B (of an earlier date): **~ number** *o* **issue** número *m* atrasado; **~ pay** atrasos *mpl*

back³ *adv*
A (indicating return, repetition): **we can get there and ~ in an hour** podemos ir y volver en una hora; **the journey ~** el viaje de vuelta; **I'll be ~ tomorrow** volveré mañana; **he's ~ from Paris** ha vuelto de París; **it's ~ to work on Monday** el lunes hay que volver al trabajo; **the Democrats are ~ in power** los demócratas han vuelto al poder; **long hair is ~ (in fashion)** vuelve (a estar de moda) el pelo largo; **meanwhile, ~ at the house ...** mientras tanto, en la casa ...; **to run/fly ~** volver* corriendo/en avión; **I'll drive you ~** te llevo de vuelta en coche; **we arrived ~ in York at six** regresamos a York a las seis; **she came ~ out** volvió a salir; **he asked for the ring ~** pidió que le devolviera el anillo; **he invited me ~ for coffee** me invitó a su casa a tomar un café; **they had us ~ the following week** nos devolvieron la invitación la semana siguiente; *see also* **go, take** *etc* **back**
B (in reply, reprisal): **he slapped her and she slapped him ~** él la abofeteó y ella le devolvió la bofetada
C 1 (backward): **take two steps ~** da dos pasos atrás; **to travel ~ in time** viajar hacia atrás en el tiempo 2 (toward the rear) atrás; **we can't hear you ~ here** aquí atrás no te oímos; *see also* **hold, keep** *etc* **back**
D (in, into the past): **~ in 1972** (ya) en 1972; **a few years ~** hace unos años; **as far ~ as last June** ya en junio
E **back and forth** = **backward(s) and forward(s)**: *see* **backward² 4**

back⁴ *vt*
A 1 ‹*person/decision*› respaldar, apoyar 2 (bet money on) ‹*horse/winner*› apostar* por
B (reverse): **he ~ed the car out of the garage** sacó el coche del garaje dando marcha atrás *or* (Col, Méx) en reversa
C (lie behind): **a house ~ed by open fields** una casa cuyo fondo da a campo abierto
D (Mus) acompañar
■ **back** *vi* ‹‹*vehicle/driver*›› dar* marcha atrás, echar *or* meter reversa (Col, Méx); **he ~ed into a lamppost** se dio contra una farola al dar marcha atrás *or* al meter reversa

Phrasal verbs

- **back away** [v ▸ adv] echarse atrás; **to ~ away FROM sth** evitar algo
- **back down** [v ▸ adv] volverse* atrás, echarse para atrás
- **back off** [v ▸ adv] 1 ▸**back away** 2 (physically) (sl) retroceder
- **back on to** [v ▸ adv ▸ prep ▸ o]: **the house ~s on to the river** el fondo de la casa da al río
- **back out** [v ▸ adv] 1 (withdraw) volverse* atrás, echarse para atrás; **to ~ out OF sth: they ~ed out of the deal** no cumplieron el trato 2 (Auto) salir* dando marcha atrás
- **back up**

A [v ▸ o ▸ adv, v ▸ adv ▸ o] 1 (support) respaldar, apoyar; **her account is ~ed up by evidence** hay pruebas que respaldan *or* confirman su versión 2 (Comput) ‹*file*› hacer* una copia de seguridad de

B [v ▸ adv] 1 (reverse) dar* marcha atrás, echar *or* meter reversa (Col, Méx) 2 (form tailback): **the traffic was ~ed up as far as ...** la cola de coches se extendía hasta ...

back: ~ache *n* [u] dolor *m* de espalda; **~bencher** /'bæk'bentʃər || ˌbæk'bentʃə(r)/, **~ bench MP** *n* (in UK) diputado, -da *m,f* (*sin cargo específico en el gobierno o la oposición*); **~biting** *n* [u] murmuraciones *fpl*; **~bone** *n* (Anat) columna *f* (vertebral), espina *f* dorsal; (main strength) columna *f* vertebral, eje *m*; **~breaking** *adj* agotador; **it's ~breaking work** este trabajo te deja deslomado; **~chat** *n* [u] (colloq) impertinencia *f*, insolencia *f*; **~cloth** *n* (BrE) telón *m* de fondo; **~comb** *vt* (BrE) cardar, hacerse* crepé (Méx); **~date** /'bæk'deɪt/ *vt* ‹*wage increase*› pagar* con retroactividad *or* con efecto retroactivo; ‹*check*› ponerle* una fecha anterior a, antedatar; **an increase ~dated to April** un aumento con retroactividad desde abril; **~ door** *n* puerta *f* trasera *or* de atrás; ***through*** *o* ***by the ~ door*** a escondidas, furtivamente; **~drop** *n* telón *m* de fondo

backer /'bækər || 'bækə(r)/ *n* patrocinador, -dora *m,f*

backfire /'bækfaɪr || bæk'faɪə(r)/ *vi* 1 ‹‹*car*›› producir* detonaciones en el escape, petardear (fam) 2 (fail) fracasar, fallar, salir* mal; **his plan ~fired on him** le salió el tiro por la culata (fam)

background¹ /'bækgraʊnd/ *n* 1 (of picture, scene) fondo *m*; **against a white ~** sobre un fondo blanco; **she prefers to stay in the ~** prefiere permanecer en un segundo plano 2 (of events) **~ (TO sth)** antecedentes *mpl* (DE algo); **against a ~ of rising inflation** en un momento de creciente inflación 3 (of person — origin) origen *m*; (— education) formación *f*, currículum *m*; (— previous activities) experiencia *f*; **he comes from a working-class/a religious ~** es de clase obrera/creció en un ambiente religioso

background² *adj* (*before n*) ‹*noise/music*› de fondo; **~ reading** lecturas *fpl* preparatorias (*acerca del momento histórico, antecedentes etc*)

background³ *vt* ‹*problem/issue*› poner* en segundo plano, desenfatizar*

back: ~hand *n* revés *m*; (*before n*) **~hand shot** revés *m*; **~handed** /'bæk'hændəd || ˌbæk'hændɪd/ *adj* ‹*blow*› con el revés, de revés; **a ~handed compliment** un cumplido de esos que no sabes cómo *or* por dónde tomarlo; **~hander** /'bæk'hændər || 'bækˌhændə(r)/ *n* 1 (blow, stroke) revés *m* 2 (bribe) (BrE colloq) soborno *m*

backing /'bækɪŋ/ *n* 1 [u] (support) respaldo *m*, apoyo *m* 2 [c] (Mus) acompañamiento *m*

backlash /'bæklæʃ/ *n* [c] reacción *f* violenta; (Mech Eng) contragolpe *m*

backless /'bækləs || 'bæklɪs/ *adj* sin espalda

back: ~log *n* atraso *m*; **a ~log of work** trabajo atrasado; **~lot** /'bæklɑːt || 'bæklɒt/ *n* 1 (of house) ▸**back yard** 2 (waste ground) terreno *m* baldío; 3 (Cin) plató *m* de exteriores (*junto a un estudio*); **~ matter** *n* [u] apéndices *mpl*; **~ office** *n* (of shop) trastienda *f*; (in stock trading) back office *m* (*procesamiento administrativo y contable generado por la confirmación de una operación bursátil*); (*before n*) ‹*operations/personnel*› de back office; **~-of-the-envelope**/ˌbækəvðɪ'envələʊp/ *adj* ‹*calculation/estimates*› aproximado; **~pack** *n* mochila *f*; **~packer** *n* mochilero, -ra *m,f*; **~packing** *n* [u] *excursionismo con mochila*; **~pedal** *vi*, (BrE) **-ll-** (retreat) dar* marcha atrás, echarse atrás; **~rest** *n* respaldo *m*; **~ seat** *n* asiento *m* trasero *or* de atrás; ***to take a ~ seat*** (colloq) mantenerse* al margen, dejar que otros asuman las responsabilidades (*or* tomen las decisiones *etc*); (*before n*) **~-seat driver** *pasajero que importuna al conductor con sus indicaciones*; **~side** /'bæk'saɪd/ *n* 1 (colloq) trasero *m* (fam) 2 (reverse) (AmE) parte *f* posterior; **~slapping** /'bækˌslæpɪŋ/ *n* [u] palmaditas *fpl* en la espalda (fam); **~slash** /'bækslæʃ/ *n* barra *f* invertida, barra *f* inversa; **~sliding** *n* [u] recaída *f*, reincidencia *f*; **~stage** /'bæk'steɪdʒ/ *adj/adv* entre bastidores; **~stairs** /ˌbæk'sterz || ˌbæk'steəz/ *pl n* escalera *f* de servicio; (*before n*) ‹*deal/arrangement/lobbying*› clandestino; **~street** *n* callejuela *f*; **the ~streets** los barrios pobres; (*before n*) ‹*abortion*› clandestino, ilegal; **~stroke** *n* [u] estilo *m* espalda; **to do (the) ~stroke** nadar de espaldas *or* (Esp) a espalda *or* (Méx) de dorso; **~ talk** *n* (AmE) ▸**backchat**; **~-to-back** /'bæktə'bæk/ *adj* (*pred* **~ to ~**) 1 (consecutive) consecutivo; **the films are run ~ to ~** (*as adv*) dan las películas en sesión continua 2 **~-to-~ house** *casa adosada modesta, sin jardín trasero, de las ciudades industriales*; **~track** *vi* 1 (retrace one's steps) retroceder 2 (reverse opinion, plan) dar* marcha atrás; **~-up** *n* 1 [u] (support) respaldo *m*, apoyo *m*; (*before n*) ‹*team/equipment*› de refuerzo 2 [c] (Comput) copia *f* de seguridad; (*before n*) ‹*disk/file*› de reserva, de seguridad

backward¹ /'bækwərd || 'bækwəd/ *adj*

A (*before n*) ‹*movement*› hacia atrás; **a ~ glance** una mirada atrás

B ‹*child*› retrasado; ‹*nation*› atrasado; ***she's not exactly ~ in coming forward*** no es de las que se quedan atrás

backward², (esp BrE) **backwards** *adv* 1 (toward rear) hacia atrás; ***to bend*** *o* ***lean over ~*** hacer* lo imposible; ▸**know¹** *vt* **A1** 2 ‹*run/walk*› hacia atrás 3 (back to front, in reverse order) al revés; **you've put your sweater on ~** (AmE) te has puesto el suéter al revés 4 **backward(s) and forward(s)** para atrás y para adelante; **I've been going ~(s) and forward(s) all day between the house and the hospital** me he pasado el día de acá para allá *or* para arriba y para abajo entre la casa y el hospital; **he ran ~ and forward(s) along the clifftop** corrió de un lado para otro del acantilado

backwards /'bækwərdz || 'bækwədz/ *adv* (esp BrE) ▸**backward²**

back: ~water *n* 1 [u c] (stagnant water) agua *f*‡ estancada 2 [c] (backward place) lugar *m* atrasado; **~woods** *pl n* **the ~woods** (the countryside) el campo; (isolated, provincial place) la Cochinchina (fam); (*before n*) ‹*politician/town*› provinciano; **~woodsman** /'bækwʊdzmən/ *n* (*pl* **-men** /-mən/) (AmE) (forest dweller) *habitante de un bosque*; (rustic person) (colloq) provinciano, -na *mf*; **~ yard** *n* (paved) patio *m* trasero; (grassed) (AmE) jardín *m* trasero, fondo *m* (RPl); ***in one's own ~ yard*** (colloq) en su (*or* mi *etc*) patio trasero *or* misma puerta

bacon /'beɪkən/ *n* [u] tocino *m or* (Esp) bacon *m or* (RPl) panceta *f*; ***to save sb's ~*** (colloq) salvarle el pellejo a algn (fam)

bacteria /bæk'tɪriə || bæk'tɪəriə/ *pl of* **bacterium**

bacteriology /bæk'tɪri'ɑːlədʒi || bækˌtɪəri'ɒlədʒi/ *n* [u] bacteriología *f*

bacterium /bæk'tɪriəm || bæk'tɪəriəm/ *n* bacteria *f*

bad¹ /bæd/ *adj* (*comp* **worse**; *superl* **worst**) [*The usual translation,* **malo**, *becomes* **mal** *when it is used before a masculine singular noun*]

A 1 (of poor quality) malo; **~ example** mal ejemplo *m* 2 (unreliable, incompetent) (*pred*) **to be ~ AT sth/-ING** ser* malo PARA algo/+ INF; **I'm ~ at names** soy malo *or* no tengo cabeza para los nombres; **to be ~ ABOUT -ING: he's ~ about apologising** le cuesta pedir disculpas; **to be ~ ON sth: I'm ~ on punctuation** la puntuación no es mi fuerte

B 1 (unpleasant) malo; **I've had a ~ day** he tenido (un) mal día; **to go from ~ to worse** ir* de mal en peor; **it tastes/smells ~** sabe/huele mal 2 (unsatisfactory) malo; **you've come at a ~ moment** vienes en (un) mal momento; **that's not ~ at all!** ¡no está nada mal!; **it'll look ~ if you don't turn up** queda mal *or* feo que no vayas; **it's too ~ you can't come** es una lástima *or* una pena que no puedas venir; **if she doesn't like it, that's just too ~** (colloq) si no le gusta, peor para ella 3 (harmful) malo; **to be ~ FOR sb/sth: too much food is ~ for you** comer demasiado es malo *or* hace mal; **smoking is ~ for your health** fumar es malo *or* perjudicial para la salud

C 1 ‹*behavior/manners*› malo 2 (evil) malo; **anyone who likes children can't be all ~** si le gustan los niños no puede ser tan malo

D ‹*mistake/injury*› grave; ‹*headache*› fuerte; **he has a ~ cough** tiene mucha tos

E (rotten) ‹*egg/fruit*› podrido; **to go ~** echarse a perder

F (afflicted): **she's got a ~ knee** tiene problemas con la rodilla; **how are you? — not (too) ~!** (colloq) ¿qué tal estás? — aquí ando, tirando (fam); ***to be in a ~ way*** (colloq) estar* fatal (fam)

G (sorry): **I feel ~ about not having written to her** me da no sé qué no haberle escrito; **it's not your fault; there's no need to feel ~ about it** no es culpa tuya, no tienes por qué preocuparte

bad² *n* [u]: **all the ~ that he's done** todo el mal que ha hecho; **there's good and ~ in everybody** todos tenemos cosas buenas y malas; **you have to learn to take the ~ with the good** hay que aprender a aceptar lo bueno y lo malo

bad³ *adv* (esp AmE colloq): **to need sth real ~** necesitar algo desesperadamente; **if you want it ~ enough** si de verdad lo quieres; ***she's got it ~ for him*** está loca por él, se derrite por él (fam)

baddie, baddy /'bædi/ *n* (*pl* **-dies**) (BrE colloq) malo, -la *m,f* (de la película) (fam)

bade /bæd, beɪd/ *past of* **bid¹** *vt* **B**

badge /bædʒ/ *n* (pin-on) chapa *f*, botón *m* (AmL); (sew-on) insignia *f*; **policeman's ~** (in US) placa *f or* chapa *f* de policía

badger¹ /'bædʒər || 'bædʒə(r)/ *n* tejón *m*

badger² *vt* fastidiar, darle* la lata a (fam); **they've been ~ing me to take them to the park** me han estado dando la lata para que los lleve al parque (fam)

Badlands /'bædlændz/ *pl n* **the ~** *zona desértica de Dakota del Sur y Nebraska*

badly /'bædli/ *adv* (*comp* **worse**; *superl* **worst**)

A (poorly) ‹*play/sing*› mal; **~ organized** mal organizado; **to do ~: our team did ~** a nuestro equipo le fue mal; **we're not doing ~** vamos bastante bien

B (improperly) ‹*behave/treat*› mal

C (*as intensifier*) ‹*fail*› miserablemente, estrepitosamente; **~ injured** gravemente herido; **you're ~ mistaken** estás muy equivocado; **you ~ need a haircut** te hace mucha falta cortarte el pelo

badly off *adj* (*comp* **worse off**; *superl* **worst off**) (*pred*) mal de dinero

bad-mannered /'bæd'mænərd || ˌbæd'mænəd/ *adj* maleducado

badminton /'bædmɪntn̩/ *n* [u] bádminton *m*

badmouth /'bædmaʊθ/ *vt* (AmE sl) hablar pestes de (fam)

badness /'bædnəs || 'bædnɪs/ *n* [u] 1 (poor quality) mala calidad *f*, pobreza *f* 2 (of behavior) maldad *f*

bad-tempered /'bæd'tempərd || ˌbæd'tempəd/ *adj* ‹*reply/tone*› malhumorado; ‹*person*› (as permanent characteristic) de mal genio; (in a bad mood) de mal humor

baffle /'bæfəl/ *vt* 1 (perplex) desconcertar*; **it ~s me how they escaped** no alcanzo a entender cómo se escaparon 2 (frustrate) ‹*efforts*› frustrar

baffled /'bæfəld/ *adj* perplejo; ‹*expression*› de perplejidad

baffling /'bæflɪŋ/ *adj* ‹*problem*› desconcertante; **her disappearance is totally ~** su desaparición nos tiene perplejos

bag¹ /bæg/ *n*

A 1 (container, bagful) bolsa *f*; **a paper/plastic ~** una bolsa de papel/plástico; (*hand~*) (esp BrE) cartera *f or* (Esp) bolso *m or* (Méx) bolsa *f*; ***to leave sb holding the ~*** (AmE) cargarle* el muerto a algn; ***a mixed ~***: **today's concert is a mixed ~** en el concierto de hoy habrá un poco de todo; **my students are a very mixed ~** tengo un grupo de alumnos muy heterogéneo; ***in the ~*** (colloq): **the contract is in the ~** el contrato es un hecho; ▸**cat¹**, **nerve¹ B2** 2 (piece of luggage) maleta *f*, valija *f* (RPl), petaca *f* (Méx)

B (of skin) bolsa *f*; **to have ~s under one's eyes** (of skin) tener* bolsas en los ojos; (dark rings) tener* ojeras

C **bags** *pl* (a lot) (colloq) cantidad *f* (fam), montones *mpl* (fam), pilas *fpl* (RPl fam); **there's ~s of room** (BrE colloq) hay cantidad de lugar (fam)

D (unpleasant woman) (colloq) bruja *f* (fam)

bag² *vt* **-gg-**

A **~ (up)** (put in bag) meter en una bolsa

B ‹*pheasant/rabbit*› cazar*, cobrar

C ‹*seat*› (BrE colloq) agarrar *or* (esp Esp) coger*

bagatelle /'bægə'tel/ *n* (liter) bagatela *f*

bagel /'beɪgəl/ *n*: *bollo con forma de rosquilla*

bagful /'bægfʊl/ *n* bolsa *f*

baggage /'bægɪdʒ/ *n* [u] equipaje *m*; (*before n*) **~ allowance** límite *m* de equipaje; **~ carousel** (AmE) cinta *f* transportadora (de equipajes), banda *f* transportadora (Méx); **~ room** (AmE) consigna *f*

baggy /'bægi/ *adj* **-gier, -giest** ancho, suelto, guango (Méx)

Baghdad /'bægdæd || bæg'dæd/ *n* Bagdad *m*

bag: **~ lady** *n* vagabunda *f* (*que lleva todas sus pertenencias en bolsas*); **~man** /'bægmæn/ *n* 1 (AmE colloq) (of extortionist) cobrador *m* de extorsionadores; 2 (Austral colloq) (tramp) vagabundo *m*; **~pipes** *pl n* gaita *f*; **~-snatcher** *n* ladrón, -drona *m,f* de bolsos (*mediante el procedimiento del tirón*), tironero, -ra *m,f* (Esp)

Bahamas /bə'hɑːməz/ *pl n* **the ~** las Bahamas

bail /beɪl/ *n* [u] (Law) fianza *f*; **he was released on ~** fue puesto en libertad bajo fianza; **~ bond** *n* compromiso *m* de fianza

Phrasal verb

• **bail out**

A [v ▸ o ▸ adv, v ▸ adv ▸ o] 1 (Law): **to ~ sb out** pagarle* la fianza a algn 2 (Naut) ‹*water*› achicar*

B [v ▸ o ▸ adv, v ▸ adv ▸ o] (rescue) sacar* de apuros, echarle un cable a (fam)

C [v ▸ adv] (Aviat) tirarse en paracaídas

bailiff /'beɪləf || 'beɪlɪf/ *n* (Law) 1 (in UK) alguacil *mf* 2 (in US) *funcionario que custodia al acusado en el juzgado*

bait¹ /beɪt/ *n* [u] cebo *m*, carnada *f*; ***to rise to the ~*** picar*, morder* el anzuelo

bait² *vt*

A ‹*hook/trap*› cebar

B (persecute, torment) acosar

bake /beɪk/ *vt*: **~ in a hot oven** hornear en horno caliente; **do you fry it or ~ it?** ¿lo fríes o lo haces al horno?; **she ~s her own bread** hace el pan en casa; **~d potato** papa *f or* (Esp) patata *f* asada

■ **bake** *vi* hacer* pasteles (*or* pan *etc*)

baked beans /beɪkt/ *pl n* 1 (in can) frijoles *mpl or* (Esp) judías *fpl or* (CS) porotos *mpl* en salsa de tomate 2 (dish) (AmE) *el mismo plato preparado con cerdo*

baker /'beɪkər || 'beɪkə(r)/ *n* panadero, -ra *m,f*; **~'s (shop)** panadería *f*

bakery /'beɪkəri/ *n* (*pl* **-ries**) panadería *f*

baking¹ /'beɪkɪŋ/ *n* [u]: **we do a lot of ~** hacemos muchos pasteles (*or* pan *etc*); (*before n*) **~ dish** fuente *f* para el horno; **~ powder** polvo *m* de hornear, Royal® *m*, levadura *f* en polvo (Esp)

baking² *adj* (colloq): **I'm ~!** ¡me muero de calor! (fam), ¡me estoy asando! (fam); **it's ~ hot** (*as adv*) hace un calor achicharrante (fam)

balance¹ /'bæləns/ *n*

A [c] (apparatus) balanza *f*; ***to be o hang in the ~*** estar* en el aire; ▸**tip² B1**

B [u] 1 (physical) equilibrio *m*; **to keep/lose one's ~** mantener*/perder* el equilibrio; **the blow caught him off ~** el golpe lo agarró *or* (Esp) lo cogió desprevenido; ***to throw sb off ~*** (disconcert) desconcertar* a algn; (lit: topple) hacer* que algn pierda el equilibrio 2 [u] (equilibrium) equilibrio *m*; ***to strike a ~*** dar* con el justo medio

C [c] 1 (in accounting) balance *m*; **on ~** en general 2 (*bank ~*) saldo *m* 3 (difference, remainder) resto *m*; (of sum of money) saldo *m*

balance² *vt*

A 1 ‹*load*› equilibrar; ‹*object*› mantener* *or* sostener* en equilibrio; **he put out his arms to ~ himself** extendió los brazos para no perder el equilibrio 2 (weigh up) sopesar; **to ~ sth AGAINST sth**: **you have to ~ the risks against the likely profit** tienes que sopesar los riesgos y los posibles beneficios

B (Fin) ‹*account*› hacer* el balance de; **to ~ the books** hacer* cuadrar las cuentas

■ **balance** *vi* 1 (hold position) mantener* el equilibrio 2 (Fin) «*account*» cuadrar

Phrasal verb

• **balance out**

A [v ▸ adv] compensarse; **it all ~s out in the end** al final una cosa compensa la otra

B [v ▸ o ▸ adv, v ▸ adv ▸ o] compensar; **the losses and the gains ~ each other out** las pérdidas y las ganancias se compensan

balanced /'bælənst/ *adj* equilibrado

balancing act /'bælənsɪŋ/ *n*: **to perform a ~ ~** hacer* malabarismos

balcony /'bælkəni/ *n* (*pl* **-nies**) 1 (Archit) balcón *m*; (large) terraza *f* 2 (Theat) (in US) platea *f* alta; (in UK) galería *f*, gallinero *m* (fam)

bald /bɔːld/ *adj* **-er, -est**

A 1 ‹*man*› calvo, pelón (AmC, Méx), pelado (CS); **he's ~** es calvo (*or* pelón *etc*); **to go ~** quedarse calvo (*or* pelón *etc*); **~ patch** calva *f* 2 (worn) ‹*tire*› gastado, liso

B (plain): **the ~ truth** la verdad pura y simple

balding /'bɔːldɪŋ/ *adj*: **he's ~** se está quedando calvo

baldness /'bɔːldnəs || 'bɔːldnɪs/ *n* [u] calvicie *f*

bale /beɪl/ *n* paca *f*, fardo *m*, bala *f*

Balearic Islands /'bæli'ærɪk/ *pl n* **the ~ ~** las (Islas) Baleares

baleful /'beɪlfəl/ *adj* torvo

bale out (BrE) ▸**bail out**

balk /bɔːk/ *vt* 1 ‹*attempt/plan*› obstaculizar* 2 (avoid) (BrE) ‹*question/issue*› evitar, eludir

■ **balk** *vi* **to ~ AT -ING** mostrarse reacio A + INF; **he ~ed at the suggestion** se mostró reacio a aceptar la sugerencia

Balkan /'bɔːlkən/ *adj* balcánico; **the ~ states** los países balcánicos

Balkans /'bɔːlkənz/ *pl n* **the ~** los países balcánicos

ball /bɔːl/ *n*

A [c] 1 (in baseball, golf) pelota *f*, bola *f*; (in basketball, football) pelota *f* (esp AmL), balón *m* (esp Esp); (in billiards) bola *f*; ***the ~ is in your court*** te corresponde a ti dar el próximo paso; ***to be on the ~*** (colloq) ser* muy espabilado, tener* los ojos bien abiertos; ***to carry the ~*** (AmE) llevar la batuta *or* la voz cantante; ***to drop** o **fumble the ~*** (lit: in US football) fumblear; **you know he won't drop** *o* **fumble the ~** ya sabes que no nos va a fallar; ***to set** o **start/keep the ~ rolling*** poner*/mantener* las cosas en marcha *or* en movimiento 2 (delivery by pitcher) bola *f*

B [u] 1 **to play ~ (with sb)** (lit: play game) jugar* a la pelota (con algn); **we tried to persuade him but he wouldn't play ~** (colloq) intentamos convencerlo, pero no quiso saber de nada 2 (*base~*) (AmE) béisbol *m*

C 1 [c] (round mass) bola *f*; (of string, wool) ovillo *m*; **she was curled up in a ~** estaba hecha un ovillo; ***the whole ~ of wax*** (AmE) toda la historia (fam) 2 [c] (Anat): **the ~ of the foot** la parte anterior de la planta del pie

D **balls** *pl* (vulg) 1 (testicles) huevos *mpl* (vulg), pelotas *fpl* (vulg), cojones *mpl* (vulg), tanates *mpl* (Méx vulg) 2 (nonsense) pendejadas *fpl* *or* (Andes, Ven) huevadas *fpl* *or* (Esp) gilipolleces *fpl* *or* (Col, RPl) boludeces *fpl* (vulg)

E [c] (dance) baile *m*; ***to have a ~*** (colloq) divertirse* de lo lindo *or* como loco (fam)

Phrasal verb

• **ball up**, (BrE) **balls up** [v ▸ o ▸ adv, v ▸ adv ▸ o] (spoil) (sl) ‹*plans/task*› joder (vulg), fastidiar (fam)

ballad /'bæləd/ *n* (narrative poem, song) romance *m*; (sentimental song) balada *f*

ballast /'bæləst/ *n* [u] (Aviat, Naut) lastre *m*

ball boy *n* recogepelotas *m*, recogebolas *m* (Col, Méx), pelotero *m* (Chi)

ballerina /'bælə'riːnə/ *n* bailarina *f* (de ballet)

ballet /'bæleɪ/ *n* [u c] ballet *m*; (*before n*) **~ dancer** bailarín, -rina *m,f* de ballet

ball: **~ game** *n* juego *m* de pelota; (baseball game) (AmE) partido *m* de béisbol; (US football game) (AmE) partido *m* de fútbol *or* (AmC, Méx) futbol americano; ⊘ **no ball games** prohibido jugar a la pelota; ***it's a whole new ~ game*** (colloq) ha cambiado totalmente el panorama; **~ girl** *n* recogepelotas *f*, recogebolas *f* (Col, Méx), pelotera *f* (Chi)

ballistic /bə'lɪstɪk/ *adj* balístico; ***to go ~*** (colloq) ponerse* hecho un basilisco (fam), ponerse* hecho una furia (fam)

ballistics /bə'lɪstɪks/ *n* (+ *sing vb*) balística *f*

balloon[1] /bə'luːn/ *n* 1 (toy) globo *m*, bomba *f* (Col), chimbomba *f* (AmC) 2 (Aviat) globo *m*, aeróstato *m*; **meteorological** *o* **weather ~** globo *m* sonda; ***to go over** o* (BrE) ***down like a lead balloon*** (colloq) caer* muy mal (fam); ***when the ~ goes up*** (BrE) cuando estalle *or* (fam) reviente el asunto 3 (in comic strip) globo *m*, bocadillo *m*

balloon[2] *vi* 1 (Aviat): **to go ~ing** (ir* a) pasear en globo 2 (swell) hincharse

ballot[1] /'bælət/ *n* 1 [u] (system of voting) votación *f*; **to decide by ~** decidir por votación; (*before n*) **~ box** urna *f* 2 [c] (instance of voting) votación *f*; **to hold** *o* **take a ~ on sth** someter algo a votación 3 [c] (number of votes cast) número *m* de votos 4 [c] **~ (paper)** papeleta *f*, boleta *f* electoral (Méx, RPl)

ballot[2] *vt* ‹*members*› invitar a votar; **to ~ sb ON sth** someter algo a la votación de algn

ball: **~park** *n* (AmE Sport) estadio *m* *or* (Méx) parque *m* de béisbol; ***to be in the ~park***: **total costs will be in the 5 million ~park** el costo total será del orden de cinco millones; **several of the bids are in our ~park** varias de las ofertas están a nuestro alcance; (*before n*) **a ~park figure** una cifra aproximada; **~player** *n* (AmE) (in baseball) jugador, -dora *m,f* de béisbol, beisbolista *mf*; (in US football) jugador, -dora *m,f* de fútbol *or* (Méx) de futbol americano; (in basketball) jugador, -dora *m,f* de baloncesto, baloncestista *mf*, basquetbolista *mf* (AmL); **~point** *n* [c u] **~point (pen)** bolígrafo *m*, esfero(gráfico) *m* (Col), pluma *f* atómica (Méx), birome *f* (RPl), lápiz *m* de pasta (Chi); **~room** *n* sala *f* *or* salón *m* de baile; **~room dancing** *n* [u] baile *m* de salón; **~s-up** *n* (BrE sl) cagada *f* (vulg), despelote *m* (AmL fam); **he made a complete ~s-up of the arrangements** la cagó con la organización (vulg)

ballyhoo[1] /'bælihuː/ *n* [u] (colloq) propaganda *f*, bombo *m* (fam)

ballyhoo[2] *vt* (esp AmE colloq) ‹*event*› anunciar con bombos y platillos *or* (Esp) a bombo y platillo

balm /bɑːm/ *n* [u c] bálsamo *m*

balmy /'bɑːmi/ *adj* **-mier, -miest** 1 ‹*evening/air*› templado y agradable 2 (crazy) (esp AmE colloq) chiflado (fam), rayado (AmS fam)

baloney /bə'ləʊni/ *n* 1 [u] (nonsense) (colloq) tonterías *fpl*, chorradas *fpl* (Esp fam), macanas *fpl* (RPl fam) 2 [u c] (AmE) ▸**bologna**

Baltic[1] /'bɔːltɪk/ *adj* báltico

Baltic[2] *n* **the ~ (Sea)** el (mar) Báltico

bamboo /'bæm'buː || bæm'buː/ *n* [u c] (*pl* **-boos**) bambú *m*; (*before n*) **~ shoots** (Culin) brotes *mpl* de bambú

bamboozle /bæm'buːzəl/ *vt* (colloq) enredar (fam); **to ~ sb (INTO sth)**: **he was ~d into financing their plan** lo engatusaron para que financiara su plan

ban[1] /bæn/ *vt* **-nn-** ‹*book/smoking*› prohibir*; ‹*organization*› proscribir*; **~ the bomb!** ¡no a la bomba atómica!; **to ~ sb FROM sth/-ING**: **he was ~ned from the club** le prohibieron la entrada al club; **he was ~ned from playing for one year** (Sport) lo suspendieron por un año

ban[2] *n*

A (prohibition) prohibición *f*; **to put** *o* **impose a ~ on sth** prohibir* algo

B **bans** *pl* ▸**banns**

banal /bə'næl, 'beɪnəl || bə'nɑːl/ *adj* banal

banality /bə'næləti/ *n* [u c] (*pl* **-ties**) banalidad *f*

banana /bə'nænə || bə'nɑːnə/ *n* plátano *m*, banana *f* (Per, RPl), banano *m* (AmC, Col), cambur *m* (Ven); ***to be top/second ~*** (AmE colloq) ser* el mandamás/el segundo de a bordo (fam); (*before n*) **~ tree** (plátano *m*) bananero *m*, banano *m* (AmL), cambur *m* (Ven)

banana: **~ peel** *n* (AmE) ▸**banana skin**; **~ republic** *n* república *f* banana *or* bananera

bananas /bə'nænəz || bə'nɑːnəz/ *adj* (sl) (*pred*): **she's completely ~** está chiflada (fam); **to go ~** perder* la chaveta (fam)

banana skin *n* (esp BrE) cáscara *f* de plátano *or* (Per, RPl) de banana *or* (AmC, Col) de banano, piel *f* de plátano (Esp), concha *f* de cambur (Ven)

band /bænd/ *n*

A 1 (group) grupo *m*; (of thieves, youths) pandilla *f*, banda *f*

b

2 (Mus) (*jazz* ~) grupo *m* or conjunto *m* de jazz; (*rock* ~) grupo *m* or banda *f* de rock
B 1 (ribbon) cinta *f*; (strip — of cloth) banda *f*, tira *f*; (— for hat) cinta *f* 2 (stripe) franja *f*
C (*wave*~) (banda *f* de) frecuencia *f*
D (ring) anillo *m*; (*wedding* ~) alianza *f*, argolla *f* (AmL)
Phrasal verb
• **band together** [v ▸ adv] unirse, hacer* causa común
bandage¹ /'bændɪdʒ/ *n* venda *f*
bandage² *vt* vendar; **she ~d (up) my ankle** me vendó el tobillo
Band-Aid® /'bændeɪd/ *n* (AmE) curita® *f* or (Esp) tirita® *f*
bandanna, bandana /bæn'dænə/ *n* pañuelo *m* (*de colores*)
B & B /'biːən'biː/ *n* = **bed and breakfast**
bandit /'bændət || 'bændɪt/ *n* bandido, -da *m,f*, bandolero, -ra *m,f*
band: ~**stand** *n* quiosco *m* de música; ~**wagon** *n*: ***to jump on the ~wagon*** subirse al carro or al tren
bandy¹ /'bændi/ *adj* **-dier, -diest** arqueado, torcido
bandy² **-dies, -dying, -died** *vt* ‹*remarks/jokes*› intercambiar; ***to ~ words with sb*** discutir con algn
Phrasal verb
• **bandy about,** (AmE also) **bandy around** [v ▸ o ▸ adv]: **a phrase that's bandied about a lot nowadays** una frase que se maneja mucho hoy en día
bandy-legged /'bændi'legd/ *adj* patizambo, zambo
bane /beɪn/ *n* ruina *f*, pesadilla *f*; **to be the ~ of sb's life** *o* **existence** ser* la cruz de algn
bang¹ /bæŋ/ *n*
A 1 [c] (loud noise) estrépito *m*; (explosion) explosión *f*, estallido *m*; ***to go over*** *o* (BrE) ***off with a ~***, ***to go with a ~*** ser* todo un éxito; **she returned to politics with a ~** volvió a la política a lo grande 2 (pleasure) (AmE colloq) (*no pl*): **to get a ~ out of sth** disfrutar como loco con algo (fam)
B [c] (blow) golpe *m*, trancazo *m*, golpetazo *m*
C [c] **bangs** *pl* (AmE) (fringe) flequillo *m*, cerquillo *m* (AmL), chasquilla *f* (Chi), capul *f* (Col), fleco *m* (Méx), pollina *f* (Ven)
bang² *vt* 1 (strike) golpear; **she ~ed her forehead on the shelf** se golpeó la frente con el estante; **he was ~ing his fist on the table** golpeaba la mesa con el puño 2 (slam): **he ~ed the door** dio un portazo (fam)
■ **bang** *vi* 1 (strike) **to ~ ON sth** golpear algo; **he started ~ing on the door** empezó a aporrear la puerta; **to ~ INTO sth** darse* CONTRA algo 2 (slam) «*door*» cerrarse* de un golpe, dar* un portazo; **the gate was ~ing in the wind** la puerta daba golpes or (AmL tb) se golpeaba con el viento 3 (move noisily): **he was ~ing about the kitchen** andaba por la cocina haciendo ruido
Phrasal verbs
• **bang away** [v ▸ adv] 1 (hit hard, work hard) (colloq): **she's been ~ing away at the typewriter all day** se ha pasado todo el día dale que (te) dale con la máquina de escribir; **he was ~ing away on the piano** aporreaba el piano 2 (fire continually) «*guns*» retumbar
• **bang out** [v ▸ o ▸ adv, v ▸ adv ▸ o] 1 (play) ‹*tune*› (colloq) aporrear (fam) 2 (type) (colloq) escribir* (*a máquina*)
• **bang up** [v ▸ o ▸ adv, v ▸ adv ▸ o] (damage, injure) (AmE colloq) dejar hecho polvo (fam)
bang³ *adv*
A : **to go ~** «*gun*» dispararse, hacer* ¡bang! or ¡pum!; **~ went our holiday** (BrE colloq) nuestras vacaciones se fueron al garete or al diablo (fam)
B (*as intensifier*) (esp BrE colloq): **~ in the middle** justo or exactamente en el medio; **to be ~ up to date** estar* muy al día; **~ on time** a la hora justa or exacta; ***to be ~ on*** dar* en el blanco, acertar* de lleno
bang⁴ *interj* ¡pum!, ¡bang!; **~! ~! you're dead!** (used to or by children) ¡pum! ¡pum! ¡te maté!
banger /'bæŋər || 'bæŋə(r)/ *n* (BrE colloq) 1 (sausage) salchicha *f* 2 (firework) petardo *m* 3 (car) (*old* ~) cacharro *m* (fam)
Bangkok /'bæŋkɑːk || ˌbæŋ'kɒk/ *n* Bangkok *m*
Bangladesh /ˌbɑːŋglə'deʃ || ˌbæŋglə'deʃ/ *n* Bangladesh *m*
Bangladeshi¹ /ˌbɑːŋglə'deʃi || ˌbæŋglə'deʃi/ *adj* bangladesí
Bangladeshi² *n* bangladesí *mf*
bangle /'bæŋgəl/ *n* pulsera *f*, brazalete *m*; (thin, of gold or silver) esclava *f*, aro *m*
banish /'bænɪʃ/ *vt* 1 (exile) desterrar*; ‹*fear/doubts*› hacer* olvidar, desvanecer* (liter) 2 (prohibit) prohibir*
banister /'bænəstər || 'bænɪstə(r)/ *n* pasamanos *m*, barandal *m*
bank¹ /bæŋk/ *n*
A 1 (Fin) banco *m*; ***to laugh all the way to the ~*** morirse* de risa (fam); (*before n*) **~ balance** saldo *m*; **~ statement** estado *m* or extracto *m* de cuenta 2 (in gambling) **the ~** la banca; **to break the ~**: **one evening at the theater isn't going to break the ~** ir una noche al teatro no nos va a arruinar 3 (store, supply) banco *m*; **blood/sperm ~** banco de sangre/semen
B (edge of river) orilla *f*, ribera *f*
C **~ of earth/snow** montículo *m* de tierra/nieve; **~ of clouds** masa *f* de nubes
bank² *vt*
A (Fin) depositar or (esp Esp) ingresar (en el banco)
B (deflect) (AmE) hacer* rebotar
■ **bank** *vi*
A (Fin): **I ~ with the National** tengo la cuenta en el National
B (Aviat) ladearse
Phrasal verb
• **bank on** [v ▸ prep ▸ o] ‹*victory/help*› contar* con; **I wouldn't ~ on it** yo no me confiaría demasiado; **we were ~ing on them accepting our offer** contábamos con or confiábamos en que aceptarían nuestra oferta

> **Bank of England**
> El Banco de Inglaterra es el banco central del Reino Unido. Asesora al gobierno en asuntos financieros y actúa como banquero del gobierno y otros bancos

bank: **~ account** *n* cuenta *f* bancaria; **~book** *n* libreta *f* de ahorros; **~card** *n* (AmE) tarjeta *f* de crédito (*expedida por un banco*); (BrE) tarjeta *f* bancaria; **~ clerk** *n* (BrE) empleado, -da *m,f* de banco or banca
banker /'bæŋkər || 'bæŋkə(r)/ *n* 1 (Fin) banquero, -ra *m,f* 2 (in gambling) banca *f*
banker: **~'s draft** *n* (BrE) cheque *m* or efecto *m* bancario; **~'s order** *n* orden *f* de débito bancario (AmL), orden *m* de domiciliación bancaria (Esp)
bank holiday *n* (BrE) día *m* festivo, feriado *m* (esp AmL)

> **bank holiday**
> Día festivo de carácter oficial en el Reino Unido, en el que cierran los bancos, correos, la mayoría de las oficinas y muchas tiendas. Siempre cae en lunes

banking /'bæŋkɪŋ/ *n* [u] (business) banca *f*; (*before n*) ‹*charges/system*› bancario
bank: **~ note** *n* 1 (promissory note) (AmE) pagaré *m* 2 (paper money) (BrE) billete *m* de banco; **~ rate** *n* tasa *f* or (esp Esp) tasa *f* de interés; **~roll** *n* (AmE colloq) (funds) fondos *mpl*; (roll of money) fajo *m* de billetes
bankrupt¹ /'bæŋkrʌpt/ *adj* en quiebra, en bancarrota; **to be ~** estar* en quiebra or en bancarrota; **to go ~** quebrar*, ir* a la bancarrota; **a morally ~ country** un país en (la) bancarrota moral
bankrupt² *vt* llevar a la quiebra or a la bancarrota
bankruptcy /'bæŋkrʌptsi/ *n* [u c] (*pl* **-cies**) quiebra *f*, bancarrota *f*; **to go into ~** quebrar
banner¹ /'bænər || 'bænə(r)/ *n* (flag) estandarte *m*; (in demonstration) pancarta *f*
banner² *adj* (AmE) excepcional
banning /'bænɪŋ/ *n* prohibición *f*
bannister *n* ▸**banister**
banns /bænz/ *pl n* amonestaciones *fpl*; **to read the ~** leer* las amonestaciones
banquet /'bæŋkwət || 'bæŋkwɪt/ *n* banquete *m*
bantam /'bæntəm/ *n* gallinita *f* de Bantam
bantamweight /'bæntəmweɪt/ *n* peso *m* gallo
banter /'bæntər || 'bæntə(r)/ *n* [u] bromas *fpl*
baptism /'bæptɪzəm/ *n* [c u] bautismo *m*
Baptist¹ /'bæptəst || 'bæptɪst/ *n* baptista *mf*, bautista *mf*
Baptist² *adj* baptista, bautista
baptize /bæp'taɪz/ *vt* bautizar*

bar¹ /bɑːr || bɑː(r)/ *n*
A **1** (rod, rail) barra *f*; (— on cage, window) barrote *m*, barra *f*; (— on door) tranca *f*; **to put sb/to be behind ~s** meter a algn/estar* entre rejas **2** (of electric fire) (BrE) resistencia *f*
B **1** (Sport) (*cross~*) (in soccer) larguero *m*, travesaño *m*; (in rugby) travesaño *m*; (in high jump) barra *f* *or* (Esp) listón *m*; (*horizontal ~*) barra *f* (fija) **2** (in ballet) barra *f*
C (block) barra *f*; **~ of chocolate** barra *f* *or* tableta *f* de chocolate; **gold ~** lingote *m* de oro; **~ of soap** pastilla *f* *or* (CS) barra *f* de jabón
D **1** (establishment) bar *m*; (counter) barra *f*, mostrador *m* **2** (stall) puesto *m*; **heel ~** (BrE) *puesto de reparación rápida de calzado*
E (Law) **1** **the Bar** (legal profession) (AmE) la abogacía; (barristers) (BrE) *el conjunto de* **barristers**; **to be called to the B~** (BrE) obtener* el título de **barrister** **2** (in court) banquillo *m*; **the prisoner at the ~** el acusado, la acusada
F (Mus) compás *m*
G (impediment) **~ TO sth** obstáculo *m* *or* impedimento *m* PARA algo
H (band of light, color) franja *f*

bar² *vt* **-rr-**
A (secure) ‹*door/window*› atrancar*, trancar*
B (block) ‹*path/entrance*› bloquear; **a tree was ~ring our way** un árbol nos cortaba *or* bloqueaba *or* impedía el paso
C (prohibit) ‹*smoking/jeans*› prohibir*; **reporters were ~red from the meeting** se excluyó a los periodistas de la reunión; **his criminal record ~s him from the job** sus antecedentes penales le impiden acceder al puesto

bar³ *prep* salvo, excepto, a *or* con excepción de; **~ none** sin excepción

barb /bɑːrb || bɑːb/ *n* (of fishhook, arrow) lengüeta *f*

Barbados /bɑːr'beɪdəʊs || bɑː'beɪdɒs/ *n* Barbados *m*

barbarian¹ /bɑːr'beriən || bɑː'beəriən/ *adj* bárbaro

barbarian² *n* bárbaro, -ra *m,f*

barbaric /bɑːr'bærɪk || bɑː'bærɪk/ *adj* **1** (primitive) primitivo **2** (brutal) brutal

barbarity /bɑːr'bærəti || bɑː'bærəti/ *n* (*pl* **-ties**) **1** [u c] (brutality) brutalidad *f*; **the barbarities of the regime** las atrocidades del régimen **2** [u] (lack of cultivation) barbarie *f*

barbarous /'bɑːrbərəs || 'bɑːbərəs/ *adj* **1** ‹*tribes/rites*› bárbaro **2** ‹*punishment/captors*› brutal

barbecue¹ /'bɑːrbɪkjuː || 'bɑːbɪkjuː/ *n*
A (grid and fireplace) barbacoa *f*, parrilla *f*, asador *m* (AmL)
B (social occasion) barbacoa *f*, parrillada *f*, asado *m* (AmL)

barbecue² *vt* asar a la parrilla *or* a la brasa

barbed /bɑːrbd || bɑːbd/ *adj* mordaz

barbed wire *n* [u] alambre *m* de púas *or* (Esp tb) de espino

barber /'bɑːrbər || 'bɑːbə(r)/ *n* peluquero *m*, barbero *m* (ant); **the ~('s)** la peluquería

barbiturate /bɑːr'bɪtʃərət || bɑː'bɪtjʊrət/ *n* [u c] barbitúrico *m*

barbwire /'bɑːrb'waɪr || ˌbɑːb'waɪə(r)/ *n* [u] (AmE) ▸**barbed wire**

bar: **~ chart** *n* gráfico *m* de barras; **~ code** *n* código *m* de barras

bard /bɑːrd || bɑːd/ *n* (poet) (liter) bardo *m* (liter), vate *m* (liter)

bare¹ /ber || beə(r)/ *adj* **barer** /berər/, **barest** /berəst/
A **1** (uncovered) ‹*blade/flesh*› desnudo; ‹*head*› descubierto; ‹*foot*› descalzo; ‹*floorboards*› sin alfombrar; ‹*tree*› pelado, desnudo; ‹*wire*› pelado *or* (Esp) desnudo; **to lay sth ~** poner* *or* dejar algo al descubierto **2** ‹*walls*› desnudo; ‹*room*› con pocos muebles
B (*before n*) **1** (without details) ‹*statement*› escueto; **he gave me the ~ facts** se ciñó a los hechos **2** (mere): **the ~ essentials** lo estrictamente esencial; **they earn the ~ minimum** ganan lo justo para vivir

bare² *vt*: **to ~ one's head** descubrirse* (la cabeza); **to ~ one's chest** mostrar* el pecho; **the dog ~d its teeth** el perro enseñó *or* mostró los dientes; **he ~d his soul** *o* **heart to me** me abrió su corazón

bare: **~back** *adv* ‹*ride*› a pelo; **~-chested** /ˌber 'tʃestəd || ˌbeə'tʃestɪd/ *adj* desnudo de la cintura para arriba, sin camisa; **~faced** *adj* ‹*liar/lie*› descarado

barefoot¹ /'berfʊt || 'beəfʊt/ *adj* descalzo

barefoot² *adv*: **she ran ~** corrió descalza

bare: **~footed** /'ber'fʊtəd || ˌbeə'fʊtɪd/ *adj/adv* ▸**barefoot**; **~headed** /'ber'hedəd || ˌbeə'hedɪd/ *adj* sin sombrero, con la cabeza descubierta; **~-legged** /'ber'legd || ˌbeə'legd/ *adj* con las piernas descubiertas; (without stockings) sin medias

barely /'berli || 'beəli/ *adv* **1** (hardly) apenas **2** (scantily): **a ~ furnished room** una habitación con pocos muebles

bareness /'bernəs || 'beənɪs/ *n* [u] (of body, walls, tree) desnudez *f*; (of room) lo vacío

bargain¹ /'bɑːrgən || 'bɑːgən/ *n*
A (cheap purchase) ganga *f*; (*before n*) ‹*counter/rail*› de ofertas, de oportunidades
B (deal, agreement) trato *m*, acuerdo *m*; **it's a ~!** ¡trato hecho!; **to make a ~ with sb** hacer* un trato *or* pacto con algn; **to strike a ~** llegar a un acuerdo; ***into*** *o* (AmE also) ***in the ~*** encima, por si fuera poco; ***to drive a hard ~***: **he drives a hard ~** sabe cómo conseguir lo que quiere

bargain² *vi* **1** (haggle) **to ~ (WITH sb) (OVER sth)** regatear (CON algn) (POR algo) **2** (negotiate) negociar

Phrasal verbs
- **bargain for** [v ▸ prep ▸ o]: **we hadn't ~ed for such an eventuality** no habíamos tenido en cuenta esa posibilidad; **I got more than I had ~ed for** no me esperaba algo así
- **bargain on** ▸**bargain for**

bargain: **~ basement** *n* sección *f* de ofertas *or* oportunidades; **~ hunter** *n* cazador, -dora *m,f* de gangas; **~ hunting** *n* [u]: **to go ~ hunting** ir* en busca de gangas

bargaining /'bɑːrgənɪŋ || 'bɑːgənɪŋ/ *n* [u] **1** (haggling) regateo *m* **2** (negotiating) negociaciones *fpl*; (*before n*) ‹*strategy/position*› negociador, de negociación

barge¹ /bɑːrdʒ || bɑːdʒ/ *n* barcaza *f*, gabarra *f*

barge² *vi* (+ *adv compl*): **she ~d through the crowd** se abrió paso a empujones entre la multitud; **he ~d past (me)** me dio un empujón para pasar; **he always ~s in when we're trying to talk** siempre se entromete cuando queremos hablar; **to ~ into sb** chocar* con algn

bargepole /'bɑːrdʒpəʊl || 'bɑːdʒpəʊl/ *n* (BrE) pértiga *f*, bichero *m*; ***I wouldn't touch him/it with a ~*** (colloq) yo con él no me metería/eso no lo compraría (*or* aceptaría *etc*) ni que me pagaran

bar: **~ graph** *n* gráfico *m* de barras; **~hop** *vi* **-pp-** (AmE) ir* de bar en bar, ≈ ir* de tascas (*en Esp*)

baritone /'bærətəʊn || 'bærɪtəʊn/ *n* barítono *m*

bark¹ /bɑːrk || bɑːk/ *n*
A [u] (on tree) corteza *f*
B [c] (of dog, seal) ladrido *m*; ***her/his ~ is worse than her/his bite*** perro que ladra no muerde *or* (Esp) perro ladrador, poco mordedor

bark² *vi* ladrar; **to ~ AT sb/sth** ladrarle A algn/algo
■ **bark** *vt* (shout) ‹*instructions/question*› espetar; **to ~ (out) an order** gritar una orden, dar* una orden a gritos

barkeep /'bɑːrkiːp || 'bɑːkiːp/, **barkeeper** /-ˌkiːpər || -ˌkiːpə(r)/ *n* (AmE) (bar owner) tabernero, -ra *m,f*; (male bartender) barman *m*, camarero *m* (Esp); (female bartender) mesera *f* *or* (Esp) camarera *f* *or* (Col, CS) moza *f*

barley /'bɑːrli || 'bɑːli/ *n* [u] cebada *f*

bar: **~maid** *n* mesera *f* *or* (Esp, Ven) camarera *f* *or* (Col, RPl) moza *f*; **~man** /'bɑːrmən || 'bɑːmən/ *n* (*pl* **-men** /-mən/) (BrE) barman *m*, camarero *m* (Esp, Ven)

barmy /'bɑːrmi || 'bɑːmi/ *adj* **-ier, -iest** (BrE colloq) ▸**balmy 2**

barn /bɑːrn || bɑːn/ *n* **1** (for crops) granero *m*; (for livestock) establo *m*; ▸**door 1** **2** (for vehicles) (AmE) cochera *f*

barnacle /'bɑːrnɪkəl || 'bɑːnəkəl/ *n* percebe *m*

barn: **~ dance** *n* (dance party) *fiesta donde se baila música folclórica*; (country dance) (BrE) *baile folclórico inglés*; **~ owl** *n* lechuza *f*; **~storm** *vi* (esp AmE) *recorrer zonas rurales durante una campaña electoral*; **~storming** /'bɑːrnstɔːrmɪŋ || 'bɑːnstɔːmɪŋ/ *adj* (BrE) arrollador

barometer /bə'rɑːmətər || bə'rɒmɪtə(r)/ *n* barómetro *m*

baron /'bærən/ *n* **1** (nobleman) barón *m* **2** (magnate) magnate *m*; **press ~** magnate de la prensa

baroness /'bærə'nes, 'bærənes/ *n* baronesa *f*

baronet /'bærənet/ *n* baronet *m*

b

baroque¹ /bəˈrəʊk || bəˈrɒk/ *adj also* **Baroque** (Archit, Art, Mus) barroco

baroque², Baroque *n* **the ~** el barroco

barrack /ˈbærək/ *vt*
A ‹*soldiers*› alojar en barracones
B (jeer) (BrE) ‹*speaker/performer*› abuchear

barracking /ˈbærəkɪŋ/ *n* [u c] (BrE) abucheo *m*, silbatina *f* (AmS)

barrack room *n* (BrE) barracón *m*, barraca *f*

barracks /ˈbærəks/ *n* (*pl* ~) (+ *sing or pl vb*) cuartel *m*

barrage /bəˈrɑːʒ || ˈbærɑːʒ/ *n* 1 (Mil) (action) descarga *f*; (fire) cortina *f or* barrera *f* de fuego 2 (deluge) aluvión *m*; **a ~ of criticism** un aluvión de críticas

barred /bɑːrd || bɑːd/ *adj* ‹*windows*› con barrotes

barrel /ˈbærəl/ *n*
A (container) barril *m*, tonel *m*; ***a ~ of laughs***: **it wasn't exactly a ~ of laughs** no fue de lo más divertido; ***it's like shooting fish in a ~*** (AmE) es pan comido (fam); ***to have sb over a ~*** tener* a algn entre la espada y la pared; ***to scrape (the bottom of) the ~*** no quedarle a uno más recursos; **have you seen her new boyfriend? she's really scraping the ~!** ¿has visto con quién sale ahora? ¡tiene que estar muy desesperada!
B (of gun) cañón *m*; (of cannon) tubo *m*

Phrasal verb

- **barrel along** [v ▸ adv] (AmE) ir* disparado *or* (fam) como un bólido

barrel organ *n* organillo *m*

barren /ˈbærən/ *adj* **-er, -est** (infertile) ‹*land/soil*› estéril, yermo (liter); ‹*tree/plant/animal*› (*no comp*) estéril; ‹*woman*› (dated *or* liter) infecunda, estéril

barrette /bɑːˈret || bəˈret/ *n* (AmE) pasador *m*, broche *m* (Méx, Ur), hebilla *f* (Arg)

barricade¹ /ˈbærəkeɪd || ˌbærɪˈkeɪd/ *n* barricada *f*

barricade² *vt* cerrar* con barricadas; **they ~d themselves in the building** se atrincheraron en el edificio

barrier /ˈbæriər || ˈbæriə(r)/ *n*
A 1 (wall) barrera *f*, muro *m*; **crash ~** valla *f* protectora 2 (gate) (BrE) barrera *f*; (*ticket* ~) *punto de acceso al andén, donde hay que presentar el billete*
B 1 (obstacle) barrera *f*; **language ~** barrera idiomática 2 (crucial point) barrera *f*; **the sound ~** la barrera del sonido

Barrier Reef *n* **the Great ~ ~** el Gran Arrecife Coralino, la Gran Barrera Coral

barring /ˈbɑːrɪŋ/ *prep*: **~ accidents** a menos que suceda algo imprevisto; **he said that, ~ delays, ...** dijo que, a menos que *or* salvo que hubiera algún retraso, ...

barrio /ˈbɑːriəʊ || ˈbæriəʊ/ *n* (*pl* **-os**) (in US) *barrio de hispanohablantes en una ciudad norteamericana*

barrister /ˈbærəstər || ˈbærɪstə(r)/ *n* (BrE) abogado, -da *m,f* (*habilitado para alegar ante un tribunal superior*)

barrow /ˈbærəʊ/ *n*
A (*wheel*~) carretilla *f*
B (grave mound) (Archeol) túmulo *m*

bar: **~stool** *n* taburete *m*; **~tender** *n* (esp AmE) (male) barman *m*, camarero *m* (Esp, Ven); (female) mesera *f or* (Esp, Ven) camarera *f or* (Col, CS) moza *f*

barter¹ /ˈbɑːrtər || ˈbɑːtə(r)/ *vt* cambiar, trocar*
■ **barter** *vi* hacer* trueques

barter² *n* [u] trueque *m*, permuta *f*

base¹ /beɪs/ *n*
A 1 (of column, wall) base *f*, basa *f*; (of mountain, tree) pie *m*; (of spine, skull) base *f* 2 (of lamp) pie *m*
B (foundation, basis) base *f*
C 1 (of patrol, for excursion) base *f* 2 **~ (camp)** (for expedition) campamento *m* base 3 (of organization) sede *f*
D (Culin) (main ingredient) base *f*; **dishes with a rice ~** platos *mpl* a base de arroz
E (Chem, Math) base *f*
F (in baseball) base *f*; ***to be off ~*** (wrong) (AmE) estar* equivocado; (lit: in baseball) estar* fuera de (la) base; ***to catch sb off ~*** (by surprise) (AmE) pillar *or* (AmL) agarrar a algn desprevenido; (lit: in baseball) pillar *or* (AmL) agarrar a algn fuera de (la) base; ***to touch ~***: **I called them, just to touch ~** los llamé, para mantener el contacto

base² *vt*
A (found) **to ~ sth** ON *o* UPON **sth** ‹*opinion/conclusion*› basar *or* fundamentar algo EN algo; **the movie is ~d on a real event** la película se basa *or* está basada en una historia real
B (locate) basar; **he's/the company is ~d in Madrid** tiene/la compañía tiene su base en Madrid; **where are you ~d now?** ¿dónde estás (*or* vives *etc*) ahora?

base³ *adj* **baser, basest** 1 ‹*conduct/motive*› abyecto, innoble, vil 2 (inferior): **~ metal** metal *m* de baja ley

baseball /ˈbeɪsbɔːl/ *n* 1 [u] (game) béisbol *m*; (*before n*) **~ bat** bate *m* de béisbol 2 [c] (ball) pelota *f* de béisbol

> **baseball**
>
> El béisbol, deporte nacional de EEUU, se juega con dos equipos de nueve jugadores cada uno que corren entre tres *bases* (bolsas llenas de arenas) y un plato (*home plate*) que forman un rombo. El lanzador (*pitcher*) tira una pelota de cuero al bateador (*batter*), que debe golpearla con un bate para lanzarla fuera del alcance de los fildeadores (*fielders*), correr a las bases y volver al plato para obtener una carrera (*run*). Si la pelota, lanzada por alguno de los *fielders*, alcanza cualquiera de las bases antes de que el bateador llegue allí, éste queda fuera del juego. El torneo anual de béisbol más importante es la Serie Mundial (**World Series**)

baseboard /ˈbeɪsbɔːrd || ˈbeɪsbɔːd/ *n* (AmE) zócalo *m*, rodapié *m*

-based /beɪst/ *suff* 1 (having its base in): **London~** con sede en Londres 2 (having as basis): **acrylic~** con base de acrílico

base hit *n* sencillo *m*

baseless /ˈbeɪsləs || ˈbeɪslɪs/ *adj* infundado

base: **~line** /ˈbeɪslaɪn/ *n* 1 (starting point) línea *f* base; 2 (in tennis, volleyball) línea *f* de saque; (in baseball) línea *f* de bases; **~man** /ˈbeɪsmæn/ *n* (*pl* **-men** /-men/) (AmE): **first/second/third ~man** jugador *m* de primera/segunda/tercera base

basement /ˈbeɪsmənt/ *n* sótano *m*

base: **~ pay** *n* [u] (AmE) sueldo *m* base *or* básico; **~ rate** *n* (BrE) tasa *f or* (esp Esp) tipo *m*

bases¹ /ˈbeɪsiːz/ *pl of* **basis**

bases² /ˈbeɪsəz || ˈbeɪsɪz/ *pl of* **base¹**

bash¹ /bæʃ/ *n* (colloq)
A 1 (blow) golpe *m*, madrazo *m* (Méx fam) 2 (dent) (BrE) abolladura *f*, madrazo *m* (Méx fam)
B (party) juerga *f* (fam)
C (attempt) (BrE): **come on, have a ~!** ¡vamos, inténtalo *or* haz la prueba!; **I'll give it a ~** lo intentaré, haré la prueba

bash² *vt* (colloq) (hit) pegarle* a; **I ~ed my knee on** *o* **against the door** me golpeé *or* (fam) me reventé la rodilla contra la puerta

Phrasal verbs

- **bash around,** (BrE) **bash about** [v ▸ o ▸ adv] (colloq) tratar a golpes *or* (AmL tb fam) a las patadas
- **bash in** (colloq)

A [v ▸ o ▸ adv, v ▸ adv ▸ o] 1 ‹*door*› echar abajo 2 (dent) ‹*box/car*› abollar
B [v ▸ o ▸ adv]: **to ~ sb's head in** romperle* la cabeza *or* (fam) la crisma a algn

bashful /ˈbæʃfəl/ *adj* tímido, vergonzoso, penoso (AmL exc CS)

bashfully /ˈbæʃfəli/ *adv* con timidez

basic /ˈbeɪsɪk/ *adj*
A (fundamental) fundamental; **to be ~** TO **sth** ser* fundamental PARA algo
B (simple, rudimentary) ‹*knowledge*› básico, elemental; ‹*need*› básico, esencial; ‹*hotel/food*› sencillo
C (Econ) ‹*pay*› básico

basically /ˈbeɪsɪkli/ *adv* fundamentalmente; **I was lucky, ~** más que nada *or* fundamentalmente tuve suerte; **what went wrong? — ~, we made a mistake** ¿qué pasó? — en dos palabras: nos equivocamos

basics /ˈbeɪsɪks/ *pl n* lo básico, lo esencial; **we must get back to ~** tenemos que replantearnos todo desde cero

basil /ˈbeɪzəl || ˈbæzəl/ *n* [u] albahaca *f*

basilica /bəˈsɪlɪkə, bəˈzɪlɪkə/ *n* (*pl* **-cas**) basílica *f*

basin /ˈbeɪsn̩/ *n* 1 (for liquid, food) cuenco *m*, bol *m*, tazón *m* 2 (*hand* ~) (BrE) lavamanos *m*, lavabo *m*, pileta *f* (RPl) 3 (Geog, Geol) cuenca *f*

basis /ˈbeɪsəs || ˈbeɪsɪs/ *n* (*pl* **bases** /ˈbeɪsiːz/)
A [c u] (foundation, grounds) base *f*; **on what ~ do you make these assertions?** ¿en qué se basa usted para afirmar eso?; **on the ~ that ...** partiendo de la base de que ...
B (system, level) (*no pl*): **we meet on a regular/monthly ~** nos reunimos regularmente/mensualmente; **on a regional/national ~** a nivel regional/nacional

bask /bæsk || bɑːsk/ *vi*: **to ~ in the sun** disfrutar (del calor) del sol; **she ~ed in their adulation** se deleitaba *or* se regodeaba con su adulación

basket /ˈbæskət || ˈbɑːskɪt/ *n*
A (for shopping) canasta *f* (esp AmL), cesta *f* (esp Esp); (*before n*) **~ making** cestería *f*
B (in basketball) 1 (goal) canasta *f*, cesto *m* 2 (score) canasta *f*, enceste *m*

basketball /ˈbæskətbɔːl || ˈbɑːskɪtbɔːl/ *n* 1 [u] (game) baloncesto *m*, básquetbol *m* (AmL) 2 [c] (ball) pelota *f* de básquetbol *or* (Esp) balón *m* de baloncesto

Basque[1] /bæsk || bæsk, bɑːsk/ *adj* vasco; **the ~ Country** el País Vasco, Euskadi *m*

Basque[2] *n* 1 [c] (person) vasco, -ca *m,f* 2 [u] (language) euskera *m*, vasco *m*, vascuence *m*

bas-relief /ˈbɑːrɪˈliːf || ˈbæsrɪˌliːf/ *n* [uc] bajorrelieve *m*

bass[1] *n*
A /beɪs/ (*pl* **~es**) (Mus) 1 [u c] (voice, singer) bajo *m* 2 [c] (double bass or bass guitar) (contra)bajo *m*; (*before n*) **~ player** (contra)bajo *mf*, (contra)bajista *mf* 3 [u] (Audio) graves *mpl*
B [c] /bæs/ (*pl* ~) (*sea* ~) lubina *f*

bass[2] /beɪs/ *adj* ‹voice› de bajo; **~ clef** clave *f* de fa; **~ drum** bombo *m*; **~ guitar** contrabajo *m*

basset hound /ˈbæsət || ˈbæsɪt/ *n* basset *m*

bassinet /ˈbæsəˈnet || ˌbæsɪˈnet/ *n* (AmE) (cradle) moisés *m*

bassoon /bəˈsuːn/ *n* fagot *m*

bastard[1] /ˈbæstərd || ˈbɑːstəd/ *n*
A (illegitimate child) bastardo, -da *m,f*
B (colloq *or* vulg) cabrón *m* (fam *o* vulg), hijo *m* de puta (vulg)

bastard[2] *adj* (*before n*) ‹child/son› bastardo

bastardize /ˈbæstərdaɪz || ˈbɑːstədaɪz/ *vt* envilecer*, prostituir*

baste /beɪst/ *vt* 1 (Culin) *rociar con su jugo o con mantequilla etc durante la cocción* 2 (sew loosely) hilvanar 3 (thrash) (AmE colloq) pegarle* una paliza a

bastion /ˈbæstʃən || ˈbæstiən/ *n* 1 (Archit) bastión *m* 2 (stronghold) baluarte *m*, bastión *m*

bat[1] /bæt/ *n*
A (in baseball, cricket) bate *m*; (in table tennis) (BrE) paleta *f*, raqueta *f*; **to be at ~** (in baseball) (AmE) ser* bateador; ***off one's own ~*** (BrE) (de) motu proprio, por su (*or* mi *etc*) cuenta, por iniciativa propia; ***right off the ~*** (AmE) de buenas a primeras; ***to go to ~ for sb*** (AmE) echarle* una mano a algn
B 1 (Zool) murciélago *m*; ***like a ~ out of hell*** (colloq) como alma que lleva el diablo; ***to be (as) blind as a ~*** ser* más ciego que un topo 2 (hag) (colloq): **old ~** vieja *f*

bat[2] **-tt-** *vi* (Sport) batear
■ **bat** *vt*
A 1 (hit) ‹ball› golpear, darle* a 2 (average in baseball) tener* un promedio de
B (flutter): **to ~ one's eyelashes** *o* (BrE) **eyelids at sb** hacerle* ojitos *or* caídas de ojo a algn; ***not to ~ an eyelash*** *o* (BrE) ***an eyelid*** *o* ***an eye*** no pestañear, no inmutarse

batch /bætʃ/ *n* (of cakes) hornada *f*, tanda *f*; (of goods) (Busn) lote *m*; (of trainees, candidates) grupo *m*, tanda *f*; (of mail, paperwork) pila *f*, montón *m*; (Comput) lote *m*

batch processing *n* [u] (Comput) procesamiento *m* por lotes

bated /ˈbeɪtəd || ˈbeɪtɪd/ *adj*: **with ~ breath** con ansiedad, conteniendo la respiración

bath[1] /bæθ || bɑːθ/ *n* (*pl* **baths** /bæðz || bɑːðz/)
A 1 (wash) baño *m*; **to have** *o* (AmE also) **take a ~** bañarse, darse* un baño; **to give sb a ~** bañar a algn 2 (tub) bañera *f*, tina *f* (AmL); **I was in the ~ when you rang** me estaba bañando cuando llamaste 3 (bathwater): **to run a** *o* **the ~** preparar un baño
B **baths** *pl* 1 (*swimming* ~*s*) (BrE) piscina *f*, alberca *f* (Méx), pileta *f* (RPl) 2 (*public* ~*s*) (for washing) baños *mpl* públicos

bath[2] (BrE) *vt* bañar
■ **bath** *vi* bañarse

bathe[1] /beɪð/ *vt* 1 (wash) ‹wound/eyes› lavar; ‹baby/dog› (AmE) bañar 2 (drench) (*usu pass*) **to be ~d IN sth** ‹in tears/light› estar* bañado EN algo
■ **bathe** *vi* 1 (take bath) (AmE) bañarse 2 (go swimming) (BrE) bañarse

bathe[2] *n* (BrE colloq) (*no pl*) baño *m* (*en el mar etc*)

bather /ˈbeɪðər || ˈbeɪðə(r)/ *n* (esp BrE) bañista *mf*

bathing /ˈbeɪðɪŋ/ *n* [u] (BrE): ⊘ **bathing prohibited** prohibido bañarse; (*before n*) **~ suit** *o* (BrE also) **costume** traje *m* de baño, bañador *m* (Esp), malla *f* (de baño) (RPl), vestido *m* de baño (Col)

bathmat /ˈbæθmæt || ˈbɑːθmæt/ *n* alfombrilla *f* *or* alfrombrita *f* *or* tapete *m* *or* (Chi) piso *m* de baño

bathos /ˈbeɪθɑːs || ˈbeɪθɒs/ *n* [u] *paso repentino de lo sublime a lo prosaico y trivial*

bath: **~robe** *n* bata *f* de baño, albornoz *m* (Esp); **~room** *n* 1 (room with bath) (cuarto *m* de) baño *m* 2 (toilet) (esp AmE) baño *m*, servicio *m*; **to go to the ~room** ir* al baño *or* al servicio; **~tub** *n* bañera *f*, tina *f* (AmL), bañadera *f* (Arg)

baton /bəˈtɑːn || ˈbætən/ *n* 1 (Mus) batuta *f* 2 (truncheon) (BrE) bastón *m* 3 (in relay race) testigo *m* 4 (officer's) (BrE Mil) bastón *m* de mando 5 (drum major's) bastón *m*

batsman /ˈbætsmən/ *n* (*pl* **-men** /-mən/) bateador *m*

battalion /bəˈtæljən/ *n* batallón *m*

batten down /ˈbætn̩ˈdaʊn/ [v ▸ adv ▸ o] (Naut): **to ~ down the hatches** cerrar* las escotillas

batter[1] /ˈbætər || ˈbætə(r)/ *vt*
A (beat) ‹victim/opponent› apalear, aporrear; ‹child/wife› maltratar, pegarle* a; **boats ~ed by the storm** barcos azotados por la tormenta
B (cover with batter) rebozar*

Phrasal verbs
• **batter around**, (BrE) **batter about** [v ▸ o ▸ adv] maltratar, pegarle* a
• **batter down** [v ▸ o ▸ adv, v ▸ adv ▸ o] derribar a golpes

batter[2] *n*
A [u] (for fried fish, etc) rebozado *m*, pasta *f* para rebozar; (for pancakes) masa *f*; (for cake) (AmE) masa *f*
B [c] (in baseball) (AmE) bateador, -dora *m,f*

battered /ˈbætərd || ˈbætəd/ *adj* ‹car› abollado; ‹hat/suitcase› estropeado; ‹reputation/image› maltrecho; ‹baby/wife› maltratado, que recibe (*or* ha recibido *etc*) malos tratos; **her ~ pride** su orgullo herido

battering /ˈbætərɪŋ/ *n* paliza *f*

battering ram *n* ariete *m*

battery /ˈbætəri/ *n* (*pl* **-ries**)
A [c] (in radio, lamp) pila *f*; (in car, motorcycle) batería *f*; ***to recharge one's batteries*** cargar* las baterías, recuperar la energía; (*before n*) **~ acid** electrolito *m*; **~ charger** cargador *m* de pilas; (Auto) cargador *m* de baterías
B [c] (artillery) batería *f*
C [c] (Agr) batería *f* (*conjunto de jaulas instaladas para la explotación avícola intensiva*); (*before n*) ‹eggs/hens› de criadero, de batería; **~ farm** *n* granja *f* de cría intensiva; **~ farming** cría *f* intensiva
D [c] (array, set): **a ~ of tests** una serie de tests; **a ~ of questions** una sarta de preguntas
E [u] (Law) lesiones *fpl*

batting /ˈbætɪŋ/ *n* [u] bateo *m*

battle[1] /ˈbætl̩/ *n* [c u]
A (Mil) batalla *f*; **to do ~** luchar; (*before n*) **~ cry** grito *m* de guerra
B (struggle) lucha *f*; **a ~ of wits** una lucha de ingenio; **that's half the ~ (won)** eso ya es un gran paso adelante; **to fight a losing ~** luchar por una causa perdida

battle[2] *vi* (struggle) luchar
■ **battle** *vt* (oppose) (AmE) combatir

Phrasal verbs
• **battle on** [v ▸ adv] seguir* luchando
• **battle out** [v ▸ o ▸ adv]: ***to ~ it out*** luchar hasta el final

battle: **~-ax**, (BrE) **~-axe** *n* (weapon) hacha *f*‡ de guerra; (woman) (colloq) sargenta *f* (fam), sisebuta *f* (RPl fam); **~field**

b

n campo *m* de batalla; **~front** *n* frente *m* de batalla; **~ground** *n* campo *m* de batalla

battlements /ˈbætl̩mənts/ *pl n* almenas *fpl*

battleship /ˈbætl̩ʃɪp/ *n* acorazado *m*

batty /ˈbæti/ *adj* **-tier, -tiest** (colloq) chiflado (fam), rayado (AmS fam); **to go ~** chiflarse (fam), rayarse (AmS fam)

bauble /ˈbɔːbəl/ *n* (for decoration) chuchería *f*; (on Christmas tree) adorno *m*

baud /bɔːd/ *n* (Comput) baudio *m*; (*before n*) **~ rate** velocidad *f* media de transferencia

baulk /bɔːk/ *vt/i* (esp BrE) ▸ **balk**

bawdy /ˈbɔːdi/ *adj* **-dier, -diest** ‹*language/scene*› subido de tono; ‹*joke*› subido de tono

bawl /bɔːl/ *vi* 1 (shout) vociferar, desgañitarse; **to ~ AT sb** gritarle A algn 2 (cry noisily) berrear

■ **bawl** *vt* ‹*insults*› gritar; ‹*order*› dar* a gritos

Phrasal verb

• **bawl out** [v ▸ o ▸ adv, v ▸ adv ▸ o] 1 ‹*insults*› gritar; ‹*order*› dar* a gritos 2 (scold) (colloq) regañar, retar (CS)

bay[1] /beɪ/ *n*

A (Geog) bahía *f*

B 1 (*loading* ~) muelle *m* or plataforma *f* de carga 2 (Archit) (*before n*) **~ window** ventana *f* en saliente 3 (area, recess) espacio *m*; **parking ~** (BrE) plaza *f* de estacionamiento or (Esp) de aparcamiento

C : **at ~** acorralado; **to bring sth/sb to ~** acorralar algo/a algn; **to keep** o **hold sth/sb at ~** mantener* algo/a algn a raya, contener* algo/a algn

D **~ (tree)** laurel *m*

bay[2] *vi* «*hounds*» aullar*

bay[3] *adj* ‹*horse*› zaino, castaño

bayleaf /ˈbeɪliːf/ *n* (*pl* **-leaves**) hoja *f* de laurel

bayonet /ˈbeɪənət/ *n* bayoneta *f*

bayou /ˈbaɪuː, -əʊ/ *n* (*pl* **-ous**) pantano *m* (*en el sur de los EEUU*)

bazaar /bəˈzɑːr || bəˈzɑː(r)/ *n* 1 (oriental market) bazar *m* 2 (charity sale) venta *f* benéfica

bazooka /bəˈzuːkə/ *n* bazuka *m*

BBC *n* (= **British Broadcasting Corporation**) **the ~** la BBC; **~ English** *n* [u] inglés *m* de la BBC (*hablado por sus locutores y considerado estándar*)

> **BBC – British Broadcasting Corporation**
>
> Una de las principales cadenas emisoras británicas. La BBC transmite principalmente a través de sus dos canales de televisión, BBC 1 y BBC 2. También opera un número de canales digitales y de retransmisión vía satélite. Cuenta con cinco emisoras nacionales de radio: Radio 1 (música pop y de rock), Radio 2 (música popular, programas de entretenimiento), Radio 3 (música clásica), Radio 4 (noticias, programas informativos, drama) y Radio 5 (deportes), además de numerosas emisoras locales

BC 1 (= **before Christ**) antes de Cristo; (written form) aC, a. de C., a. de J.C. 2 = **British Columbia**

be /biː, *weak form* bi/ (*pres* **am, are, is**; *past* **was, were**; *past p* **been**) *vi* [*See notes at* **ser** *and* **estar**]

Sense I

A 1 (*followed by an adjective*): **she's French/intelligent** es francesa/inteligente; **he's worried/furious** está preocupado/furioso; **he's blind** es or (Esp tb) está ciego; **he's short and fat** es bajo y gordo; **he's so fat he can't get into his clothes any more** está tan gordo que ya no le cabe la ropa; **these shoes are new** estos zapatos son nuevos; **have you never had gazpacho? it's delicious!** ¿nunca has comido gazpacho? ¡es delicioso!; **the gazpacho is delicious, did you make it yourself?** el gazpacho está delicioso ¿lo hiciste tú?; **she was very rude to me** estuvo or fue muy grosera conmigo; **she's very rude** es muy grosera; **~ good** sé bueno; **don't ~ silly!** ¡no seas tonto! 2 (talking about marital status): **Tony is married/divorced/single** Tony está or (esp AmL) es casado/divorciado/soltero; **to ~ married to sb** estar* casado con algn; **we've been married for eight years** llevamos ocho años casados

B 1 (*followed by a noun*) ser*; **she's a lawyer** es abogada; **he's a Catholic** es católico; **she was Prime Minister for 11 years** fue Primera Ministra durante 11 años; **who was Prime Minister at the time?** ¿quién era Primer Ministro en ese momento?; **it's me/Daniel** soy yo/es Daniel; **if I were you, I'd stay** yo que tú or yo en tu lugar me quedaría 2 (play the role of) hacer* de; **I was Juliet in the school play** hice de Julieta en la obra del colegio

C 1 (talking about mental and physical states): **how are you?** ¿cómo estás?; **I'm much better** estoy or me encuentro mucho mejor; **she's pregnant/tired** está embarazada/cansada; **I'm cold/hot/hungry/thirsty/sleepy** tengo frío/calor/hambre/sed/sueño; **she has been ill** ha estado enferma; **he's dead** está muerto 2 (talking about age) tener*; **how old are you?** ¿cuántos años tienes?; **I'm 31** tengo 31 años; **Paul was four last Monday** Paul cumplió cuatro años el lunes pasado; **he's a lot older/younger** es mucho mayor/menor; **our house is over 100 years old** nuestra casa tiene más de 100 años 3 (giving cost, measurement, weight): **how much is that? — that'll ~ $15, please** ¿cuánto es? — (son) 15 dólares, por favor; **they are $15 each** cuestan or valen 15 dólares cada una; **two plus two is four** dos más dos son cuatro; **how tall/heavy is he?** ¿cuánto mide/pesa?; **Jim's over six feet (tall)** Jim mide más de seis pies

Sense II

A 1 (exist, live): **I think, therefore I am** pienso, luego existo; **to ~ or not to ~** ser o no ser; **to let sth/sb ~** dejar tranquilo or en paz algo/a algn; **her husband-to-~** su futuro marido 2 (in expressions of time): **don't ~ too long** no tardes mucho, no (te) demores mucho (esp AmL); **I'm drying my hair, I won't ~ long** me estoy secando el pelo, enseguida estoy; **how long will dinner ~?** ¿cuánto falta para la cena? 3 (take place) ser*; **the party is tomorrow** la fiesta es mañana

B (be situated, present) estar*; **where is the library?** ¿dónde está or queda la biblioteca?; **where are you?** ¿dónde estás?; **what's in that box?** ¿qué hay en esa caja?; **who's in the movie?** ¿quién actúa or trabaja en la película?; **he's here for two weeks** va a estar aquí dos semanas; **how long are you in Chicago (for)?** (colloq) ¿cuánto (tiempo) te vas a quedar en Chicago ?

C (*only in perfect tenses*) (visit) estar*; **I've never been to India** nunca he estado en la India; **have you been to the exhibition yet?** ¿ya has estado en or has ido a la exposición?

■ **be** *v impers*

A 1 (talking about physical conditions, circumstances): **it's sunny/cold/hot** hace sol/frío/calor; **it's cloudy** está nublado; **it was three degrees below zero** hacía tres grados bajo cero; **it's so noisy/quiet in here!** ¡qué ruido/silencio hay aquí!; **I have enough problems as it is, without you ...** yo ya tengo suficientes problemas sin que tú encima ... 2 (in expressions of time) ser*; **it's three o'clock** son las tres; **it's one o'clock** es la una; **it was still very early** todavía era muy temprano; **it's Wednesday today** hoy es miércoles; **hi, Joe, it's been a long time** qué tal, Joe, tanto tiempo (sin verte) 3 (talking about distance) estar*; **it's 500 miles from here to Detroit** Detroit queda or está a 500 millas de aquí

B 1 (introducing person, object) ser*; **it was me who told them** fui yo quien se lo dije or dijo, fui yo el que se lo dije or dijo 2 (*in conditional use*) ser*; **if it hadn't been** o **had it not been for Juan, we would have been killed** si no hubiera sido por Juan or de no ser por Juan, nos habríamos matado

■ **be** *v aux*

A **to ~ -ING** 1 (used to describe action in progress) estar* + GER; **what was I saying?** ¿qué estaba diciendo?; **she was leaving when ...** se iba cuando ...; **how long have you been waiting?** ¿cuánto (tiempo) hace que esperas?, ¿cuánto (tiempo) llevas esperando? 2 (with future reference): **he is** o **will ~ arriving tomorrow** llega mañana; **when are you seeing her?** ¿cuándo la vas a ver or la verás?; **she'll ~ staying at the Plaza** se va a alojar en el Plaza

B (*in the passive voice*) ser* [*The passive voice, however, is less common in Spanish than it is in English*] **it was built in 1903** fue construido en 1903, se construyó en 1903, lo construyeron en 1903; **she was told that ...** le dijeron or se le dijo que ...; **it is known that ...** se sabe que ...

C **to ~ to + INF** 1 (with future reference): **I'm to ~ met at the airport by Joe** Joe me irá a buscar al aeropuerto; **the dessert is (still) to come** todavía falta el postre; **if a solution is to ~ found ...** si se quiere encontrar or si se ha de encontrar una solución ... 2 (expressing possibility): **what are we to do?** ¿qué podemos hacer?; **he wasn't to know** no tenía cómo saberlo; **it was nowhere to ~ found** no se lo pudo encontrar por ninguna parte 3 (expressing obligation) deber* + INF, tener* que + INF, haber* de + INF; **tell her she's to stay here** dile que debe quedarse *or* tiene que quedarse aquí, dile que se quede aquí; **you are not to tell Carol!** ¡no debes decírselo a Carol!; **am I to understand that ... ?** ¿debo entender que ... ?; **I'm not to ~ disturbed!** ¡que nadie me moleste!

D (in hypotheses): **what would happen if she were** *o* **was to die?** ¿qué pasaría si ella muriera?

E 1 (*in tag questions*): **she's right, isn't she?** tiene razón, ¿no? ¿verdad? *or* ¿no es cierto?; **so that's what you think, is it?** de manera que eso es lo que piensas 2 (*in elliptical uses*): **are you disappointed? — yes, I am/no, I'm not** ¿estás desilusionado? — sí (, lo estoy)/no (, no lo estoy); **she was told the news, and so was he/but I wasn't** a ella le dieron la noticia, y también a él/pero a mí no; **I'm surprised, are/aren't you?** estoy sorprendido, ¿y tú?/¿tú no?

beach[1] /biːtʃ/ *n* playa *f*; **a day at the ~** un día en la playa; (*before n*) **~ ball** pelota *f* de playa

beach[2] *vt* ‹*boat*› arrastrar a la playa; ‹*whale*› hacer* embarrancar

beacon /ˈbiːkən/ *n* (light) faro *m*; (fire) almenara *f*

bead /biːd/ *n* 1 (on necklace, bracelet) cuenta *f*, abalorio *m* 2 (drop) gota *f*; **~s of sweat** gotas de sudor

beady /ˈbiːdi/ *adj*: **~ eyes** ojos redondos y brillantes

beagle /ˈbiːgəl/ *n* beagle *m*

beak /biːk/ *n* 1 (of bird, animal) pico *m* 2 (nose) (colloq & hum) napia(s) *f(pl)* (fam & hum)

beaker /ˈbiːkər || ˈbiːkə(r)/ *n* 1 (Chem) vaso *m* de precipitados 2 (cup) (BrE) taza *f* (*gen alta y sin asa*)

be-all and end-all /ˈbiːɔːlənˈendɔːl/ *n*: **it is the ~ ~ ~ of his life** es su razón de ser; **work isn't the ~ ~ ~** el trabajo no lo es todo

beam[1] /biːm/ *n*

A 1 (in building) viga *f*; (in ship) bao *m*; (in gymnastics) barra *f* sueca *or* de equilibrio 2 (widest part of ship) manga *f*; ***to be broad in the ~*** (colloq) ser* culón (fam), tener* un buen trasero (fam)

B (ray) rayo *m*; (broad) haz *m* de luz; **a ~ of light** un rayo de luz; **keep the headlights on high** *o* (BrE) **full** *o* **main ~** (Auto) deja las (luces) largas *or* (Chi) altas

beam[2] *vi* 1 (shine) brillar 2 (smile) sonreír* (*abiertamente*); **a ~ing smile** una sonrisa radiante

■ **beam** *vt* (broadcast) transmitir

bean[1] /biːn/ *n*

A 1 (fresh, in pod) ▸**green bean** 2 (dried) frijol *m or* (Esp) alubia *f or* judía *f or* (CS) poroto *m or* (Ven) caraota *f*; ***to be full of ~s*** (colloq) estar* lleno de vida; ***to spill the ~s*** descubrir* el pastel, levantar la liebre *or* (RPl) la perdiz 3 (*coffee ~*) grano *m* (de café)

B (colloq) 1 (scrap, trace) (esp BrE) (*with neg*): **it isn't worth a ~** no vale nada; ***not to have a ~*** (BrE) estar* pelado (fam); ***not to know ~s about sth*** (AmE) no saber* ni papa de algo (fam) 2 (head) (AmE) coco *m* (fam), mate *m* (AmS fam)

bean[2] *vt* (AmE colloq): **to ~ sb** darle* un porrazo *or* un mamporro en la cabeza a algn (fam)

bean: ~bag *n* 1 **~bag (chair)** *sillón formado por una gran bolsa rellena de cuentas de poliestireno etc* 2 (toy) *pequeño saco relleno que se arroja para que otro lo ataje*; **~ curd** *n* tofu *m*, queso *m* de soya (AmL) *or* (Esp) soja; **~pole** *n* (Hort) rodrigón *m*; (person) (colloq): **she's a ~pole** es un espárrago, es muy larguirucha; **~shoot, ~ sprout** *n* frijol *m* germinado *or* (Esp) judía *f* germinada *or* (CS) poroto *m* germinado; (of soy bean) brote *m or* germinado *m* de soya (AmL) *or* (Esp) soja

beanie, beanie cap /ˈbiːni/ *n* gorrita *f* (*que se fija en la parte de atrás de la cabeza*)

bear[1] /ber || beə(r)/ (*past* **bore**; *past p* **borne**) *vt*

A 1 (support) ‹*weight*› aguantar, resistir; ‹*cost*› correr con; ‹*responsibility*› cargar* con 2 (endure) ‹*pain/uncertainty*› soportar, aguantar; **the pain was too much to ~** el dolor se hizo insoportable 3 (put up with, stand) (colloq) (*with can*) ‹*person*› aguantar (fam), soportar; ‹*noise*› aguantar, soportar; **I can't ~ her** no la soporto, no la aguanto *or* no la puedo ver (fam); **he can't ~ being criticized** no soporta que lo critiquen; **to ~ to + INF**: **I can't ~ to watch!** no puedo mirar 4 (stand up to): **his work ~s comparison with the best** su obra puede compararse con las mejores; **her argument doesn't ~ close scrutiny** su razonamiento no resiste un análisis cuidadoso; **it doesn't ~ thinking about** da miedo sólo de pensarlo

B 1 (carry) (liter) ‹*banner/coffin*› llevar, portar (liter); **our raft was borne along by the current** la corriente arrastraba nuestra balsa; **a letter ~ing good news** una carta portadora de buenas noticias 2 (harbor): **she's not one to ~ a grudge** no es rencorosa *or* resentida; **I ~ him no ill will** no le deseo ningún mal

C (have, show) ‹*title/signature*› llevar; ‹*scars*› tener*; ‹*resemblance*› tener*, guardar; **his account ~s little relation to the truth** su versión tiene poco que ver *or* guarda poca relación con la verdad

D 1 (produce) ‹*fruit/crop*› dar*; ‹*interest*› devengar* 2 (give birth to) ‹*child*› dar* a luz; **she bore him six children** (liter) le dio seis hijos (liter); *see also* **born**[1]

■ **bear** *vi* 1 (turn) torcer*; **~ left/right** tuerza *or* doble a la izquierda/derecha 2 (weigh down) (frml) **to ~ ON sb**: **the responsibility bore heavily on her** la responsabilidad pesaba sobre sus hombros; ▸**bring B1**

■ *v refl* (frml) 1 (hold, carry): **there's something very distinguished about the way he ~s himself** tiene un porte muy distinguido 2 (behave) **to ~ oneself** comportarse, conducirse* (frml)

Phrasal verbs

- **bear down** [v ▸ adv] (in childbirth) empujar, pujar
- **bear down on** [v ▸ adv ▸ prep ▸ o]: **to ~ down on sth** hacer* presión sobre algo; **the locomotive was ~ing down on them** la locomotora se les venía encima
- **bear out** [v ▸ o ▸ adv, v ▸ adv ▸ o] ‹*theory*› confirmar; **the results seem to ~ him out** los resultados parecen confirmar que está en lo cierto
- **bear up** [v ▸ adv]: **I'm ~ing up, thanks** voy tirando *or* (Méx) ahí la llevo *or* (Col, Ven tb) ahí, llevándola, gracias (fam); **she bore up well under the strain** sobrellevó muy bien la situación
- **bear with** [v ▸ prep ▸ o] tener* paciencia con; **if you'll just ~ with me a moment, ...** (asking to wait) si tienen la bondad de esperar un momento, ...; (asking for patience) si puedo poner a prueba su paciencia, ...

bear[2] *n* oso, osa *m,f*; **he's a regular ~ in the morning** (AmE) por las mañanas está de un humor de perros; ***to be like a ~ with a sore head*** (colloq) estar* de un humor de perros (fam); ***to be loaded for ~*** (AmE colloq) estar* listo para el ataque; (*before n*) **~ cub** osezno *m*

bearable /ˈberəbəl || ˈbeərəbəl/ *adj* soportable

beard /bɪrd || bɪəd/ *n* (of person) barba *f*; **a man with a ~** un hombre con *or* de barba; **to have** *o* **wear a ~** tener* barba

bearded /ˈbɪrdəd || ˈbɪədɪd/ *adj* ‹*man*› con *or* de barba, barbado (liter)

bearer /ˈberər || ˈbeərə(r)/ *n* 1 (of news) portador, -dora *m,f* 2 (carrier, porter) portador, -dora *m,f*, porteador, -dora *m,f* 3 (holder — of check) portador, -dora *m,f*; (— of passport) titular *mf*

bear hug *n*: **he gave me a ~ ~** me estrechó fuertemente entre sus brazos

bearing /ˈberɪŋ || ˈbeərɪŋ/ *n*

A 1 [c] (Aviat, Naut) demora *f*; ***to find/get one's ~s*** orientarse; ***to lose one's ~s*** desorientarse, perderse* 2 [u c] (relevance) **~ ON sth**: **that has no ~ on the subject** eso no tiene ninguna relación con el tema

B [c] (way of standing) porte *m*

beast /biːst/ *n* 1 (animal) bestia *f*, fiera *f*; **~ of burden** bestia *or* animal *m* de carga 2 (unkind person) (BrE colloq): **don't be such a ~!** ¡no seas malo *or* asqueroso! (fam)

beastly /ˈbiːstli/ *adj* **-lier, -liest** (colloq & dated): **that ~ brother of hers** el asqueroso de su hermano (fam); **what a ~ thing to say!** ¡qué cosa más horrorosa de decir!

beat[1] /biːt/ (*past* **beat**; *past p* **beaten** /ˈbiːtn̩/) *vt*

A 1 (hit repeatedly) golpear; ‹*carpet*› sacudir; ‹*wings*› batir; **she ~ her fists against the door** aporreó la puerta con los puños 2 (inflict blows on): **he ~s his children** les pega a sus hijos, maltrata a sus hijos; **he was ~en to death** lo mataron a golpes 3 (hammer) ‹*metal*› batir 4 (Culin) batir

B 1 (defeat) ‹*opponent*› ganarle a, derrotar, vencer*; **he always ~s me at chess** siempre me gana al ajedrez; **you've got to know when you're ~en** hay que saber reconocer la derrota; **the government has ~en inflation** el gobierno ha vencido la inflación; **(it) ~s me how anyone can do such a thing!** no logro entender cómo se puede llegar a hacer una cosa así; **if you can't ~ them, join them** si no puedes con ellos, únete a ellos **2** (be better than) ‹*record*› batir, superar; **our prices can't be ~en** nuestros precios son imbatibles; **I scored 470, ~ that!** yo saqué 470 ¿a que no me ganas?; **you can't ~ home-made apple pie** no hay como el pastel de manzana casero; **it ~s working any day** (colloq) siempre es más divertido que trabajar

C (arrive before, anticipate): **if we go early we should ~ the traffic** si vamos temprano nos evitamos el tráfico; **to ~ sb TO sth**: **I ~ him to the telephone** llegué antes que él al teléfono; **I'll ~ you to the shop** te echo *or* (RPl) te juego una carrera hasta la tienda; ***to ~ sb to it*** adelantársele a algn

D (Mus) ‹*time*› marcar*

E (tread): **they had ~en a path across the field** habían dejado marcado un sendero en el campo; **~ *it!*** (colloq) ¡lárgate! (fam)

■ **beat** *vi* **1** (strike) **to ~ ON sth**: **he could hear them ~ing on the door** los oía golpear la puerta; **the sun ~ down on them** el sol caía de lleno sobre ellos **2** (pulsate) «*heart*» latir, palpitar; «*drum*» redoblar; «*wings*» batir

Phrasal verbs

- **beat back** [v ▸ o ▸ adv, v ▸ adv ▸ o] rechazar*
- **beat down** [v ▸ o ▸ adv, v ▸ adv ▸ o] **1** (when bargaining): **we ~ him down to half the original figure** conseguimos que nos lo dejara a mitad de precio **2** (flatten) ‹*door*› tirar *or* echar abajo, derribar; ‹*crop*› aplastar
- **beat in** [v ▸ o ▸ adv] (colloq): **to ~ sb's head/brains in** romperle* la cabeza *or* (fam) la crisma a algn
- **beat off** [v ▸ o ▸ adv, v ▸ adv ▸ o] rechazar*
- **beat out**

A [v ▸ o ▸ adv, v ▸ adv ▸ o] **1** ‹*rhythm*› marcar* **2** ‹*fire*› apagar* (*a golpes*)

B [v ▸ o ▸ adv] (smash) (colloq): **to ~ sb's brains out** romperle* la cabeza *or* (fam) la crisma a algn

- **beat up** [v ▸ o ▸ adv, v ▸ adv ▸ o] (colloq) darle* una paliza a (fam): **to ~ oneself up ABOUT sth**, (AmE) **to ~ up on oneself ABOUT sth** martirizarse* POR algo
- **beat up on** [v ▸ adv ▸ prep ▸ o] (AmE colloq) darle* una paliza a

beat² *n*

A (of heart) latido *m*; (of drum) golpe *m*; **his heart skipped** *o* **missed a ~** le dio un vuelco el corazón

B (Mus) (rhythmic accent) tiempo *m*; (rhythm) ritmo *m*

C (of policeman) ronda *f*; **on the ~** de ronda

beat³ *adj* (colloq) (*pred*) (exhausted) reventado (fam), molido (fam); **to be dead ~** estar* reventado *or* molido

beaten /ˈbiːtn̩/ *past p of* **beat¹**

beater /ˈbiːtər || ˈbiːtə(r)/ *n* **1** (*egg ~*) batidor *m*, batidora *f* **2** (*carpet ~*) sacudidor *m*

beating /ˈbiːtɪŋ/ *n* **1** [c] (thrashing) paliza *f* **2** [c] (defeat) paliza *f* (fam); **they gave us/we took a ~** nos dieron una paliza **3** [u] (surpassing): **to take some/a lot of ~**: **her time will take some/a lot of ~** va a ser difícil/muy difícil superar su marca

beatitude /biːˈætətuːd || biˈætɪtjuːd/ *n* [u] beatitud *f*; **the B~s** las bienaventuranzas

beat-up /ˈbiːtʌp/ *adj* (*pred* **beat up**) (AmE colloq) ‹*car/furniture*› destartalado; ‹*clothes*› andrajoso

beautician /bjuːˈtɪʃən/ *n* esteticista *mf*

beautiful /ˈbjuːtəfəl || ˈbjuːtɪfəl/ *adj* **1** ‹*scenery/poem/colors*› precioso, hermoso, bello (liter); ‹*woman/child*› precioso, guapísimo, hermoso, bello (liter); ‹*hair/voice*› precioso, hermoso, bello (liter) **2** (very good) (colloq) ‹*meal/weather*› estupendo, buenísimo; ‹*shot/serve*› magnífico; **small is ~** (set phrase) lo bueno viene en frascos pequeños *or* (AmL tb) chicos **3** (kind) (esp AmE) ‹*person*› encantador

beautifully /ˈbjuːtəfli || ˈbjuːtɪfəli/ *adv* **1** (excellently, very well) ‹*sing/dance*› maravillosamente (bien); **she was ~ dressed** iba elegantísima; **it was ~ cooked** estaba hecho a la perfección; **the children behaved ~** los niños se portaron estupendamente *or* a las mil maravillas **2** (*as intensifier*): **it was ~ quiet** había un maravilloso silencio; **the water was ~ cool** el agua estaba deliciosamente fresca

beautify /ˈbjuːtəfaɪ || ˈbjuːtɪfaɪ/ *vt* embellecer*

beauty /ˈbjuːti/ *n* (*pl* **-ties**)

A **1** [u] (quality) belleza *f*, hermosura *f*; ***~ is in the eye of the beholder*** todo es según el color del cristal con que se mira; (*before n*) **~ contest** *o* (esp AmE) **pageant** concurso *m* de belleza; **~ queen** reina *f* de la belleza **2** [c] (advantage) (colloq): **the ~ of the plan is that ...** lo bueno del plan es que ...

B [c] **1** (woman) belleza *f*, beldad *f*; **B~ and the Beast** la Bella y la Bestia **2** (fine specimen) (colloq) preciosidad *f*, preciosura *f* (AmL), maravilla *f*

beauty: **~ parlor**, (BrE) **parlour** *n* salón *m* de belleza; **~ salon** *n* salón *m* de belleza; **~ shop** *n* (AmE) salón *m* de belleza; **~ sleep** *n* [u] (colloq & hum): **I need my ~ sleep** tengo que acostarme temprano para estar guapa y fresca; **~ spot** *n* **1** (place) lugar *m* pintoresco **2** (on face) lunar *m*

beaver /ˈbiːvər || ˈbiːvə(r)/ *n* [c] (Zool) castor *m*; ***to be an eager ~*** ser* muy entusiasta y trabajador

Phrasal verb

- **beaver away** [v ▸ adv] (colloq) trabajar como una hormiguita

became /bɪˈkeɪm/ *past of* **become**

because /bəˈkɔːz, bɪˈkɒz/ *conj*

A porque; **~ he loves her, he doesn't see it** como la quiere, no se da cuenta; **but why? — because!** (colloq) ¿pero por qué? — ¡porque sí!

B **because of** (*as prep*) por, a *or* por causa de (frml); **I was late ~ of him** llegué con retraso por su culpa

beck /bek/ *n* (summons): ***to be at sb's ~ and call*** estar* siempre a entera disposición de algn

beckon /ˈbekn̩/ *vt*: **to ~ sb in/over** hacerle* señas a algn para que entre/se acerque

■ **beckon** *vi* hacer* una seña; **she ~ed and he went over to her** le hizo una seña y (él) se acercó; **she ~ed to him to follow** le hizo señas para que la siguiera

become /bɪˈkʌm/ (*past* **became**; *past p* **become**) *vi*: **to ~ arrogant/distant** volverse* arrogante/distante; **to ~ famous** hacerse* famoso; **to ~ accustomed to sth** acostumbrarse a algo; **she soon became bored/tired** pronto se aburrió/se cansó; **eating out has ~ so expensive** comer fuera se ha puesto carísimo; **the heat became unbearable** el calor se hizo insoportable; **to ~ a lawyer** hacerse* abogado; **he was later to ~ manager** más tarde llegaría a ser gerente; **they became friends** se hicieron amigos; **she's becoming a nuisance** se está poniendo muy fastidiosa; **when she became President** cuando asumió la presidencia

■ **become** *vt* **1** (befit) (frml) (*often neg*) ser* apropiado para **2** (suit) favorecer*

Phrasal verb

- **become of** (*usu interrog*) ser* de; **whatever became of that friend of yours?** ¿qué fue de (la vida de) aquella amiga tuya?; **what's to ~ of me?** ¿qué va a ser de mí?

becoming /bɪˈkʌmɪŋ/ *adj* **1** (fitting) (frml) apropiado **2** ‹*outfit/hat*› favorecedor, sentador (AmL)

bed¹ /bed/ *n*

A (for sleeping) cama *f*; **to make the ~** hacer* *or* (AmL tb) tender* la cama; **to get into ~** acostarse*, meterse en la cama; **to get out of ~** levantarse; **to go to ~** acostarse*; **he's in ~ with measles** está en cama con sarampión; **time for ~!** ¡ya es hora de acostarse *or* irse a la cama!; **you look ready for ~** tienes cara de sueño; **to take to one's ~** (frml) caer* en cama; **we put the children to ~ early** acostamos a los niños temprano; **to go to ~ with sb** (euph) acostarse* con algn (euf); ***a ~ of roses*** un lecho de rosas; ***to get up on the wrong side of the ~*** (AmE) *o* (BrE) ***to get out of ~ (on) the wrong side*** levantarse con el pie izquierdo; ***you've made your ~ and now you must lie in it*** con tu pan te lo comas; ***early to ~ and early to rise (makes a man healthy, wealthy and wise)*** a quien madruga, Dios lo ayuda

B (for plants) arriate *m*, cantero *m* (RPl)

C (of river) lecho *m*, cauce *m*; (of sea) fondo *m*

D **1** (base, support) base *f*; **on a ~ of rice** sobre arroz **2** (stratum) capa *f*

bed² **-dd-** *vt* (have sex with) (dated) llevarse a la cama

Phrasal verb

- **bed down** [v ▸ adv] acostarse*

BEd /ˈbiːˈed/ *n* (in UK) = **Bachelor of Education**

bed and breakfast /ˈbedn̩ˈbrekfəst/ *n* 1 [u] (service): **they do ~ ~ ~** dan alojamiento y desayuno 2 [c] (establishment) ≈ pensión *f*

> **bed and breakfast**
>
> Los *bed & breakfast* o *B&B* son casas privadas o pequeños hoteles que ofrecen alojamiento y desayuno a precios generalmente módicos

bedazzle /bɪˈdæzəl/ *vt* (*often pass*) deslumbrar

bed: **~bug** *n* chinche *f or m*; **~clothes** *pl n* ropa *f* de cama; **to change the ~clothes** cambiar las sábanas

bedding /ˈbedɪŋ/ *n* [u] 1 ▸**bedclothes** 2 (for animals) cama *f*

bedding plant *n* planta *f* de arriate, planta *f* parterre (Esp), planta *f* de cantero (RPl)

bedeck /bɪˈdek/ *vt* (liter) (*usu pass*): **to be ~ed with sth** estar* adornado *or* engalanado con algo

bedevil /bɪˈdevl̩/ *vt*, (BrE) **-ll-**: **the project was ~ed with** *o* **by problems** el proyecto estaba plagado de problemas

bedfellow /ˈbedˌfeləʊ/ *n*: **to make strange ~s** hacer* una extraña pareja

bedlam /ˈbedləm/ *n* [u] (colloq): **there was ~ when he announced the news** se armó la de San Quintín cuando anunció la noticia (fam); **it was ~ in there!** aquello era una locura *or* (fam) un loquero

Bedouin /ˈbedʊɪn/ *n* (*pl* **~s** *or* **~**) beduino, -na *m,f*

bedpan /ˈbedpæn/ *n* (Med) cuña *f*, chata *f*

bedraggled /bɪˈdrægəld/ *adj* desaliñado; ‹*hair*› despeinado, enmarañado

bed: **~ridden** *adj* postrado en cama; **~rock** *n* [u] lecho *m* de roca, roca *f* firme; **the ~rock of his theory** los cimientos *or* la base de su teoría; **~room** *n* dormitorio *m*, cuarto *m*, pieza *f* (esp AmL), recámara *f* (esp Méx); (*before n*) **~room slippers** pantuflas *fpl*, zapatillas *fpl*; **~side** *n*: **they sat at his ~side throughout the night** pasaron toda la noche junto a su cabecera; (*before n*) **~side manner**: **she has a nice ~side manner** tiene una forma de tratar a los pacientes muy agradable; **~side table** mesita *f* de noche, velador *m* (AmS), mesa *f* de luz (RPl); **~sit**, **~sitter** /ˈbedˌsɪtər || ˌbedˈsɪtə(r)/ *n* (BrE colloq) habitación *f* amueblada (*cuyo alquiler suele incluir el uso de baño y cocina comunes*); **~sore** *n* escara *f*, úlcera *f* de decúbito (frml) (*llaga que se produce por estar mucho tiempo en cama*); **~spread** *n* cubrecama *m*, colcha *f*; **~stead** *n* cama *f* (*sólo el armazón*), catre *m* (CS); **~time** *n* [u] hora *f* de acostarse *or* de irse a la cama; **it's way past your ~time** hace rato que deberías estar durmiendo; (*before n*) **~time story** cuento *m* (*que se cuenta a los niños cuando se van a la cama*)

bee /biː/ *n*

A (Zool) abeja *f*; **you have been a busy ~, haven't you?** ¡cómo has trabajado!; ***to have a ~ in one's bonnet about sth*** (colloq) tener* monomanía con algo, tener* algo metido entre ceja y ceja; ***to think one is the ~'s knees*** (colloq) creerse* lo máximo *or* el no va más (fam)

B (social gathering) (esp AmE) círculo *m*; **sewing ~** círculo de costura

beech /biːtʃ/ *n* **~ (tree)** haya *f*

beef[1] /biːf/ *n*

A [u] (meat) carne *f* de vaca *or* (AmC, Méx) de res, ternera *f* (Esp)

B (Agr) 1 [u] (beef cattle) ganado *m* vacuno/bovino 2 [c] (*pl* **beeves** /biːvz/) (animal) (AmE) cabeza *f* de ganado vacuno/bovino

C [c] (*pl* **beefs**) (complaint) (colloq) queja *f*

beef[2] *vi* (colloq) **to ~ (ABOUT sth)** refunfuñar (POR algo) (fam)

beef: **~burger** *n* (esp BrE) hamburguesa *f*; **~eater** *n*: *alabardero de la Torre de Londres*; **~steak** *n* [u c] ▸**steak B**

beefy /ˈbiːfi/ *adj* **-fier, -fiest** (colloq) fornido

bee: **~hive** *n* colmena *f*; **~line** *n*: ***to make a ~line for sb/sth*** (colloq) irse* derechito a algn/algo (fam)

been /bɪn || biːn/ 1 *past p of* **be** 2 *past p of* **go**[1] *vi Sense* **I B**

beep[1] /biːp/ *n* (colloq) pitido *m*

beep[2] *vt*

A ‹*horn*› (colloq) pitar; **to ~ one's horn** pitar

B (AmE Telec) ‹*person*› llamar con un buscapersonas *or* (AmL) bíper *or* beeper

■ **beep** *vi* pitar

beeper /ˈbiːpər || ˈbiːpə(r)/ *n* (colloq) buscapersonas *m*, busca *m* (Esp fam), bip *m* (Méx fam), bíper *m* (Chi)

beer /bɪr || bɪə(r)/ *n* [u c] cerveza *f*

beer: **~ belly**, **~ gut** *n* (colloq) panza *f* (fam) (*de bebedor de cerveza*); **~ garden** *n*: *jardín o patio abierto de un bar*; **~ mat** *n* posavasos *m* (*de cartón*)

beeswax /ˈbiːzwæks/ *n* [u] cera *f* de abeja

beet /biːt/ *n* 1 [u c] (*pl* **~**) (*sugar* **~**) remolacha *f* azucarera 2 [c] (*pl* **~s**) (beetroot) (AmE) remolacha *f or* (Méx) betabel *m or* (Chi) betarraga *f*; **as red as a ~** rojo *or* colorado como la grana *or* (fam) como un tomate

beetle /ˈbiːtl̩/ *n* (Zool) escarabajo *m*

beetroot /ˈbiːtruːt/ *n* [c u] (BrE) ▸**beet 2**

beeves /biːvz/ *pl of* **beef**[1] **B2**

befall /bɪˈfɔːl/ *vt* (*past* **befell** /bɪˈfel/ *past p* **befallen** /bɪˈfɔːlən/) (liter) sucederle *or* ocurrirle a

befit /bɪˈfɪt/ *vt* **-tt-** (frml): **with a magnificence ~ting the occasion** con un esplendor acorde con *or* a la ocasión; **as ~s a princess** como corresponde a una princesa

before[1] /bɪˈfɔːr || bɪˈfɔː(r)/ *prep*

A (preceding in time) antes de; **~ dinner** antes de la cena; **~ long** dentro de poco; **they arrived ~ us** llegaron antes que nosotros; **~ going in** antes de entrar; **ten minutes ~ the end of the match** diez minutos antes de que terminara el partido; **the day ~ her departure** el día anterior a su partida

B 1 (in front of) delante de, ante (frml) 2 (in rank, priority): **she puts her work ~ her family** antepone el trabajo a su familia; **safety comes ~ anything else** la seguridad (está) ante todo

before[2] *conj* 1 (earlier than) antes de que (+ *subj*), antes de (+ *inf*); **~ it gets dark** antes de que anochezca; **he died ~ he was 30** murió antes de cumplir los 30 años 2 (rather than) antes que; **she would die ~ ...** prefería morir antes que ...

before[3] *adv* (preceding) antes; **this has never happened ~** esto no había sucedido nunca antes; **the day/year ~** el día/año anterior; **have you been to Canada ~?** ¿ya has estado en el Canadá?; **not that page, the one ~** esa página no, la anterior

beforehand /bɪˈfɔːrhænd || bɪˈfɔːhænd/ *adv* (earlier) antes; (in advance) de antemano, con anticipación *or* antelación

befriend /bɪˈfrend/ *vt* hacerse* amigo de

befuddle /bɪˈfʌdl̩/ *vt* (*often pass*) aturdir, ofuscar*; **he was ~d by drink** estaba ofuscado por la bebida

beg /beg/ **-gg-** *vt*

A ‹*money/food*› pedir*, mendigar*

B (frml) 1 (entreat) ‹*person*› suplicarle* a, rogarle* a; **I ~ you!** ¡te lo suplico!, ¡te lo ruego!; **to ~ sb to + INF** suplicarle* *or* rogarle* A algn QUE (+ *subj*) 2 (ask for) ‹*forgiveness*› suplicar*, rogar*; **to ~ sth OF sb** suplicarle* algo A algn; ▸**differ** *vi* **B**

■ **beg** *vi* 1 ‹‹*beggar*›› pedir*, mendigar*; **to ~ FOR sth** mendigar* algo; **they live by ~ging** viven de la mendicidad; **she taught the dog to ~** le enseñó al perro a levantar las patitas 2 (ask) (frml) **to ~ FOR sth**: **she ~ged for more time** pidió por favor que le dieran una prórroga; **to ~ for mercy** pedir* *or* suplicar* clemencia

(Phrasal verb)

• **beg off** [v ▸ adv] dar* una excusa

began /bɪˈgæn/ *past of* **begin**

beget /bɪˈget/ *vt* (*pres p* **begetting**; *past* **begot** *or* (arch) **begat** /bɪˈgæt/; *past p* **begotten**) (liter) (father) engendrar; (give rise to) provocar*, engendrar (liter)

beggar[1] /ˈbegər || ˈbegə(r)/ *n* 1 mendigo, -ga *m,f*; ***~s can't be choosers*** a veces no se está en situación de exigir nada 2 (fellow): **you lucky ~!** (BrE colloq) ¡qué suertudo eres! (AmL fam), ¡qué potra tienes! (Esp fam)

beggar[2] *vt* arruinar, empobrecer*; (stronger) pauperizar*; **to ~ description** ser* indescriptible

begin /bɪˈgɪn/ (*pres p* **beginning**; *past* **began**; *past p* **begun**) *vt* empezar*, comenzar*; **to ~ work on sth** empezar* *or* comenzar* a trabajar en algo; **to ~ -ING/to + INF** empezar* *or* comenzar* A + INF; **he began talking** *o* **to talk about his work** empezó a hablar sobre su trabajo;

she began to cry empezó *or* se puso a llorar; **I can't ~ to thank you** no sé cómo agradecerte; **that won't even ~ to cover the cost** eso no alcanza ni remotamente para cubrir los gastos

■ **begin** *vi* 1 (start) empezar*, comenzar*, iniciarse (frml); **I don't know where to ~** no sé dónde empezar *or* comenzar; **the author ~s by describing ...** el autor empieza por describir ...; **to ~ with** para empezar 2 (originate) «*river*» nacer*; «*custom*» originarse, empezar*

beginner /bɪˈgɪnər || bɪˈgɪnə(r)/ *n* principiante *mf*; **~'s luck** la suerte del principiante

beginning /bɪˈgɪnɪŋ/ *n* 1 (in time, place) principio *m*, comienzo *m*; **the ~ of the end** (set phrase) el principio del fin; **at the ~ of the year/of June** a principios del año/de junio; **I'll start again from the ~** volveré a empezar desde el principio; **from ~ to end** de principio a fin 2 (origin, early stage) (*often pl*) comienzo *m*, inicio *m* 3 (start, debut) (*no pl*) comienzo *m*

begot /bɪˈgɑːt || bɪˈgɒt/ *past of* **beget**

begotten /bɪˈgɑːtn̩ || bɪˈgɒtn̩/ *past p of* **beget**

begrudge /bɪˈgrʌdʒ/ *vt* 1 (envy) envidiar; **I don't ~ you your success** no te envidio el éxito que tienes 2 (resent) **to ~ -ING**: **I ~ paying so much** me da rabia *or* me duele pagar tanto

beguile /bɪˈgaɪl/ *vt* 1 (deceive) **to ~ sb INTO -ING**: **he was ~d into signing the contract** lo engatusaron para que firmara el contrato 2 (charm) cautivar, seducir*

beguiling /bɪˈgaɪlɪŋ/ *adj* cautivador, seductor

begun /bɪˈgʌn/ *past p of* **begin**

behalf /bɪˈhæf || bɪˈhɑːf/ *n*: **on** *o* (AmE also) **in ~ of sb, on** *o* (AmE also) **in sb's ~**: **he argued on her ~ that ...** alegó en su defensa *or* en su favor que ...; **I'd like to thank you on ~ of the team** quisiera darle las gracias en nombre de *or* de parte de todo el equipo; **he accepted the award on her ~** aceptó el premio en su nombre; **I'm ringing on ~ of a friend** llamo de parte de un amigo; **don't worry on my ~** por mí no te preocupes

behave /bɪˈheɪv/ *vi* 1 (act) comportarse; (esp of children) portarse; **he has no idea how to ~** no sabe comportarse; **he's very badly ~d** se porta muy mal; **she ~d in a suspicious manner** actuó de forma sospechosa 2 (be good) «*child/animal*» portarse bien, comportarse 3 (function) (+ *adv compl*): **to ~ AS sth** funcionar COMO algo

■ *v refl* **to ~ oneself** portarse bien, comportarse; **~ yourself!** ¡pórtate bien!

behavior, (BrE) **behaviour** /bɪˈheɪvjər || bɪˈheɪvjə(r)/ *n* [u] (conduct) conducta *f*, comportamiento *m*; **he was on his best ~** se portó mejor que nunca; **his ~ toward his wife was disgraceful** fue vergonzoso como se portó con su mujer

behavioral, (BrE) **behavioural** /bɪˈheɪvjərəl/ *adj* de conducta, conductual; **~ science** ciencia *f* de la conducta

behead /bɪˈhed/ *vt* decapitar

beheld /bɪˈheld/ *past and past p of* **behold**

behest /bɪˈhest/ *n*: **at the ~ of sb, at sb's ~** (frml) a instancia(s) de algn (frml)

behind[1] /bɪˈhaɪnd/ *prep*

A 1 (to the rear of) detrás de, atrás de (AmL); **~ me** detrás de mí; **we're ten years ~ the Japanese in microelectronics** en microelectrónica llevamos un retraso de diez años respecto a los japoneses; **she's well ~ the rest of the class** está muy atrasada con respecto al resto de la clase 2 (on the other side of) detrás de, atrás de (AmL)

B 1 (responsible for) detrás de; **I know who's ~ this** yo sé quién está detrás de esto 2 (underlying): **the theory ~ it is that ...** la teoría sobre la que se basa es que ...; **the motives ~ his decision** los motivos que lo llevaron a esa decisión

C (in support of): **we're all ~ the police** todos respaldamos a la policía; **I'm ~ you all the way** tienes todo mi apoyo

D 1 (to one's name) a sus (*or* mis *etc*) espaldas, en su (*or* mi *etc*) haber; **she has four years' experience ~ her** tiene cuatro años de experiencia a sus espaldas *or* en su haber 2 (in time): **all that is ~ us now** todo eso ha quedado atrás; **I'm ~ schedule** voy retrasado *or* atrasado (con el trabajo *or* los preparativos *etc*)

behind[2] *adv* 1 (to the rear, following): **I want the small children here and the taller ones ~** que los niños pequeños se pongan aquí y los más altos detrás *or* (AmL tb) atrás; **I was attacked from ~** me atacaron por la espalda; **keep an eye on the car ~** no pierdas de vista al coche de atrás; *see also* **stay behind** 2 (in race, competition): **England were two goals ~** Inglaterra iba perdiendo por dos goles 3 (in arrears): **I'm ~ with my work/payments** estoy atrasada con el trabajo/en los pagos; *see also* **fall, get** *etc* **behind** 4 (in time): **Buenos Aires is five hours ~** Buenos Aires tiene cinco horas más temprano

behind[3] *n* (colloq & euph) trasero *m* (fam)

behind-the-scenes /bɪˌhaɪndðəˈsiːnz/ *adj* ‹*footage/role*› de entre bambalinas, de entre bastidores

behold /bɪˈhəʊld/ (*past and past p* **beheld**) *vt* (liter) contemplar (liter)

■ **behold** *vi* (*only in imperative*) mirar; *see also* **lo**

beholden /bɪˈhəʊldn̩/ *adj* (*pred*) **to be ~ TO sb (FOR sth)** estar* en deuda CON algn (POR algo)

beholder /bɪˈhəʊldər || bɪˈhəʊldə(r)/ *n*: *see* **beauty**

behoove /bɪˈhuːv/, (BrE) **behove** /bɪˈhəʊv/ *v impers* (frml) **it ~s sb to + INF**: **it ~s us to support him** nos corresponde apoyarlo

beige[1] /beɪʒ/ *adj* beige *adj inv*, beis *adj inv* (Esp)

beige[2] *n* [u] beige *m*, beis *m* (Esp)

Beijing /ˈbeɪˈdʒɪŋ/ *n* Beijing *m*

being /ˈbiːɪŋ/ *n* 1 [c] (person, creature) ser *m* 2 [u] (existence, life) ser *m*; **to come into ~** nacer*

bejeweled, (BrE) **bejewelled** /bɪˈdʒuːəld/ *adj* (liter) enjoyado

belabor, (BrE) **belabour** /bɪˈleɪbər || bɪˈleɪbə(r)/ *vt* (liter) fustigar* (liter)

Belarus /ˈbeləˈruːs/ *n* Bielorrusia *f*

belated /bɪˈleɪtəd || bɪˈleɪtɪd/ *adj* tardío

belatedly /bɪˈleɪtədli || bɪˈleɪtɪdli/ *adv* ‹*arrive*› con retraso; ‹*respond*› tardíamente

belch[1] /beltʃ/ *vi* 1 «*person*» eructar 2 **to ~ FROM sth**: **flames ~ed from the mouth of the cannon** la boca del cañón escupía llamas

■ **belch** *vt* **~ (out)** escupir

belch[2] *n* eructo *m*; **he gave/let out a ~** eructó

beleaguer /bɪˈliːgər || bɪˈliːgə(r)/ *vt* 1 (besiege) asediar, sitiar 2 **beleaguered** *past p* (harassed) atribulado

Belgian[1] /ˈbeldʒən/ *adj* belga

Belgian[2] *n* belga *mf*

Belgium /ˈbeldʒəm/ *n* Bélgica *f*

Belgrade /ˈbelˈgreɪd/ *n* Belgrado *m*

belie /bɪˈlaɪ/ *vt* **belies, belying, belied** 1 (disguise) no dejar traslucir, ocultar 2 (show to be false): **this ~s the notion that ...** esto demuestra que no es cierto que ...

belief /bəˈliːf || bɪˈliːf/ *n* 1 [u c] (conviction, opinion) creencia *f*; **contrary to popular ~** contrariamente a lo que comúnmente se cree; **it is my ~ that he lied** (frml) creo que mintió; **she acted in the ~ that ...** actuó convencida de que ...; **their attitude irritated me beyond ~** su actitud me irritó increíblemente *or* sobremanera 2 [u] (confidence) **~ IN sb/sth** confianza *f* *or* fe *f* EN algn/algo 3 [uc] (Relig) fe *f*

believable /bəˈliːvəbəl || bɪˈliːvəbəl/ *adj* ‹*story/account*› verosímil, creíble

believe /bəˈliːv || bɪˈliːv/ *vt* 1 ‹*statement/story*› creer*; ‹*person*› creerle* a; **I don't ~ a word she says** no le creo ni una palabra; **I don't ~ she's capable of that** no la creo capaz de eso; **~ it or not** aunque no lo creas, aunque parezca mentira; **I could hardly ~ my ears/eyes** no daba crédito a mis oídos/mis ojos; **don't you ~ it!** (colloq) ¡créetelo! (fam & iró); **would you ~ it!** (colloq) ¡habráse visto!, ¡será posible!; **I don't ~ it!** ¡no puedo creerlo!; **~ you me!** (colloq) ¡te lo juro!; **you'd better ~ it!** (esp AmE) ¡como lo oyes!; **you won't ~ who I've just seen** ¡no te imaginas a quién acabo de ver!; ***to make ~ (that)*** hacer* de cuenta que 2 (think) creer*; **I ~ so/not** creo que sí/no, tengo entendido que sí/no; **to ~ sb/sth to + INF** (*often pass*): **the police ~ him to be dangerous** la policía cree que es peligroso; **it was ~d to be harmless** se creía que era inofensivo

■ **believe** *vi* creer*; **to ~ IN sth/sb** creer* EN algo/algn; **to ~ in God** creer* en Dios; **I ~ in discipline** soy partidario de la disciplina

believer /bə'li:vər || bɪ'li:və(r)/ *n* **1** (Relig) creyente *mf* **2** **~ IN sth** partidario, -ria *m,f* DE algo

Belisha beacon /bə'li:ʃə/ *n* (in UK) *señal luminosa intermitente en un cruce peatonal*

belittle /bɪ'lɪtl/ *vt* ‹*achievements*› menospreciar; ‹*person*› denigrar, rebajar; **to ~ oneself** menospreciarse, tenerse* en menos

Belize /bə'li:z/ *n* Belice *m*

bell /bel/ *n*

A (of church, clock) campana *f*; (on cat, toy) cascabel *m*; (on door, bicycle) timbre *m*; (of telephone, timer) timbre *m*; **his voice was as clear as a ~** lo oía como si estuviera a mi lado; ***to give sb a ~*** (BrE colloq) darle* un telefonazo a algn (fam); ***to ring a ~***: **the name rings a ~** me suena el nombre; (*before n*) **~ tower** campanario *m*

B (Sport) **the ~** la campana; ***to be saved by the ~***: **he was saved by the ~** lo salvó la campana

bell: **~-bottoms** *pl n* pantalones *mpl* de pata de elefante; **~boy** *n* botones *m*

belle /bel/ *n* belleza *f*, beldad *f*; **the ~ of the ball** la reina de la fiesta

bellhop /'belhɑ:p || 'belhɒp/ *n* (AmE) botones *m*

bellicose /'belɪkəʊs/ *adj* belicoso

belligerence /bə'lɪdʒərəns/ *n* [u] agresividad *f*

belligerent /bə'lɪdʒərənt/ *adj* agresivo

belligerently /bə'lɪdʒərəntli/ *adv* agresivamente

bellow[1] /'beləʊ/ *vi* «*bull*» bramar; **to ~ AT sb** gritarle A algn

■ **bellow** *vt* bramar

bellow[2] *n* bramido *m*

bellows /'beləʊz/ *n* (*pl* ~) (for fire) fuelle *m*; **a pair of ~** un fuelle

bell pepper *n* (AmE) ▸**capsicum**

belly /'beli/ *n* (*pl* **-lies**) **1** (of person) vientre *m*, barriga *f* (fam); (of animal) panza *f*, vientre *m*; **he's got a bit of a ~** (colloq) es un poco barrigón *or* panzón *or* (Andes) guatón (fam); (*before n*) **~ button** (colloq) ombligo *m*; **~ dance** danza *f* del vientre; **to do a ~ flop** darse* un planchazo *or* (Andes) un guatazo (fam); **a ~ laugh** una sonora carcajada

bellyache[1] /'belieɪk/ *n* [c u] (colloq) dolor *m* de barriga (fam)

bellyache[2] *vi* (colloq & pej) rezongar*, refunfuñar; **to ~ ABOUT sb/sth** quejarse constantemente DE algn/algo

bellyful /'belifʊl/ *n*: **to have had a ~ (of sb/sth)** (colloq) estar* hasta la coronilla (de algn/algo) (fam)

belong /bɪ'lɔ:ŋ || bɪ'lɒŋ/ *vi*

A **1** (be property) **to ~ TO sb** ser* DE algn, pertenecerle* A algn; **it ~s to her** es suyo, es de ella, le pertenece (a ella); **does this ~ to you?** ¿esto es tuyo?; **who does that car ~ to?** ¿de quién es ese coche? **2** (be member) **to ~ TO sth** ‹*to a club*› ser* socio DE algo; ‹*to a union/political party*› estar* afiliado A algo **3** (be part) **to ~ TO sth** ser* DE algo, pertenecer* A algo

B **1** (have as usual place) ir*; **that jug ~s in the cupboard** esa jarra va en el armario; **put them back where they ~** vuélvelos a poner en su lugar **2** (in category) pertenecer*; **it ~s to the reptile family** pertenece a la familia de los reptiles **3** (be suitable): **we ~ together** estamos hechos el uno para el otro **4** (socially): **I don't feel I ~ here** no me siento a gusto aquí

belongings /bɪ'lɔ:ŋɪŋz || bɪ'lɒŋɪŋz/ *pl n* pertenencias *fpl*; **personal ~** efectos *mpl or* objetos *mpl* personales

beloved[1] /bɪ'lʌvəd || bɪ'lʌvɪd/ *adj* (*before n*) ‹*person*› querido, amado, bienamado (liter); ‹*place*› querido

beloved[2] *n* amado, -da *m,f* (liter), bienamado, -da *m,f* (liter); ▸**dearly A**

below[1] /bɪ'ləʊ/ *prep*

A (under) debajo de, abajo de (AmL); **the room directly ~ this one** la habitación justo debajo *or* (AmL tb) abajo de ésta; **500m ~ the surface** a 500m bajo la superficie *or* por debajo de la superficie

B (inferior, junior to) por debajo de

C (less than) por debajo de; **~ average** inferior a *or* por debajo de la media; **if you earn ~ $15,000 a year** si ganas menos de 15.000 dólares al año; **~ zero** bajo cero; **~ standard** por debajo del nivel exigido

below[2] *adv*

A (underneath) abajo; **put it on the shelf ~** ponlo en el estante de abajo; **down ~ we could see ...** abajo veíamos ...

B (in text) más abajo; **see diagram ~** véase el diagrama más abajo

C (of temperature): **20 (degrees) ~** 20 (grados) bajo cero

below-the-line /bɪˌləʊðə'laɪn/ *adj*

A (in bridge) por debajo de la raya, por debajo de la línea

B (in accounts) extraordinario

belt[1] /belt/ *n*

A (Clothing) cinturón *m*; ***to have sth under one's ~*** tener* algo a sus (*or* mis *etc*) espaldas, tener* algo en su (*or* mi *etc*) haber; ***to hit below the ~*** dar* un golpe bajo; **that was a bit below the ~** ¡ése fue un golpe bajo!; ***to tighten one's ~*** apretarse* el cinturón

B (Mech Eng) correa *f*

C (area): **a ~ of low pressure** un frente de bajas presiones; **the industrial ~** el cinturón industrial; **the cotton ~** la zona *or* región algodonera; ▸**Bible Belt**

belt[2] *vt* (colloq) darle* una paliza a; **he ~ed me on the ear** (AmE) *o* (BrE) **round the ear** me dio un tortazo *or* (Méx) un trancazo (fam)

■ **belt** *vi* **to ~ along/in** ir*/entrar zumbando (fam)

Phrasal verbs

- **belt down** [v ▸ o ▸ adv, v ▸ adv ▸ o] (AmE colloq): **to ~ one down** tomarse una; **he's ~ing them down** está empinando el codo (fam)
- **belt out** [v ▸ o ▸ adv, v ▸ adv ▸ o] (colloq) (sing) cantar a grito pelado (fam); (play) tocar* muy fuerte
- **belt up** [v ▸ adv] (BrE colloq) **1** (be quiet) callarse la boca, cerrar* el pico (fam) **2** (Auto) ponerse* el cinturón

belting /'beltɪŋ/ *n* (colloq) paliza *f*

beltway /'beltweɪ/ *n* (AmE) carretera *f or* ronda *f* de circunvalación, periférico *m* (AmC, Méx)

bemoan /bɪ'məʊn/ *vt* lamentarse de

bemuse /bɪ'mju:z/ *vt* **1** (puzzle) desconcertar* **2** **bemused** *past p* ‹*expression*› de desconcierto

bench[1] /bentʃ/ *n*

A [c] **1** (seat) banco *m* **2** (*work~*) mesa *f* de trabajo

B (Law) **the bench** *or* **the Bench** (judges collectively) la judicatura; (tribunal) el tribunal

C (Sport): **the ~** el banquillo *or* (AmL tb) la banca

bench[2] *vt* (esp AmE) mandar al banquillo *or* (AmL tb) a la banca

benchmark /'bentʃmɑ:rk || 'bentʃmɑ:k/ *n* **1** (in surveying) cota *f* de referencia **2** (criterion) punto *m* de referencia

bend[1] /bend/ *n* **1** (in road, river) curva *f*; **to take a ~** tomar *or* (esp Esp) coger* una curva; ***to be round the ~*** (esp BrE colloq) estar* chiflado (fam); **I'm going round the ~** me estoy volviendo loco; **that noise is driving me round the ~** ese ruido me está volviendo loco **2** **bends** *pl* **the ~s** la enfermedad del buzo

bend[2] (*past and past p* **bent**) *vt*

A ‹*wire/branch*› torcer*, curvar; ‹*back/leg*› doblar, flexionar; ⊘ **do not bend** no doblar; **he was bent double with pain** se retorcía de dolor; **~ your head back/forward** inclina *or* echa la cabeza hacia atrás/adelante

B (direct) (frml) ‹*energies/attention*› concentrar

■ **bend** *vi*

A **1** «*pipe/wire*» torcerse*; **he had to ~ to get through the door** tuvo que agacharse para pasar por la puerta; **to ~ forward/backward** inclinarse hacia adelante/atrás; ▸**backward**[2] **1** **2** «*road/river*» hacer* una curva; **the road ~s to the right** la carretera tuerce a la derecha

B (submit) ceder; **to ~ (TO sth)** ceder (A algo)

Phrasal verbs

- **bend down** [v ▸ adv] agacharse
- **bend over** [v ▸ adv] inclinarse

bender /'bendər || 'bendə(r)/ *n* (colloq) juerga *f* (fam); **to go on a ~** irse* de juerga

beneath[1] /bɪ'ni:θ/ *prep*

A (under) bajo; **the city lay spread out ~ us** la ciudad se extendía a nuestros pies

B **1** (inferior to): **those ~ him** los que están (*or* estaban *etc*) por debajo de él; **she married ~ her** no se casó bien **2** (unworthy of): **it's ~ her** es indigno de ella; **you're ~ contempt** no mereces ni desprecio

beneath[2] *adv*: **I wondered what lay ~** me preguntaba qué habría debajo *or* abajo

Benedictine /'benə'dɪktən, -ti:n|| ˌbenɪ'dɪktɪn, -ti:n/ *adj* benedictino

b

benediction /'benə'dɪkʃən || ˌbenɪ'dɪkʃən/ *n* bendición *f*

benefactor /'benəfæktər || 'benɪfæktə(r)/ *n* benefactor, -tora *m,f*

beneficial /'benə'fɪʃəl || ˌbenɪ'fɪʃəl/ *adj* beneficioso; **to be ~ TO sb/sth** ser* beneficioso PARA algn/algo

beneficiary /'benə'fɪʃieri || ˌbenɪ'fɪʃəri/ *n* (*pl* **-ries**) beneficiario, -ria *m,f*

benefit[1] /'benəfɪt || 'benɪfɪt/ *n*

A (good) beneficio *m*, bien *m*; (advantage) provecho *m*, ventaja *f*; **she is exploiting the situation for her own ~** está explotando la situación en beneficio propio *or* para su provecho; **it will be of great ~ to them** será muy beneficioso para ellos *or* les beneficiará mucho; ***to give sb the ~ of the doubt*** darle* a algn el beneficio de la duda

B 1 (Soc Adm) prestación *f*; **he's on unemployment ~s** *o* (BrE) **~** recibe subsidio de desempleo *or* (Chi) de cesantía, está cobrando el paro (Esp) 2 [c] (perk) beneficio *m or* ventaja *f* (extrasalarial)

C (concert, performance) beneficio *m*, función *f* benéfica; (*before n*) con fines benéficos

benefit[2] **-t-** *or* (AmE also) **-tt-** *vt* beneficiar

■ **benefit** *vi* beneficiarse; **to ~ FROM sth**: **he didn't ~ much from the experience** no sacó mucho (provecho) de la experiencia; **you will all ~ from the change** todos se van a beneficiar con el cambio

Benelux /'benlʌks || 'benɪlʌks/ *n* Benelux *m*

benevolence /bə'nevələns/ *n* [u] benevolencia *f*, bondad *f*

benevolent /bə'nevələnt/ *adj* 1 ‹*person/smile*› benévolo; ‹*gesture*› de benevolencia 2 ‹*society/organization*› benéfico, de beneficencia

benevolently /bə'nevələntli/ *adv* con benevolencia

Bengali[1] /beŋ'gɔ:li/ *adj* bengalí

Bengali[2] *n* 1 [c] (person) bengalí *mf* 2 [u] (language) bengalí *m*

benign /bɪ'naɪn/ *adj* 1 ‹*person/attitude*› benévolo 2 (Med) benigno

benignly /bɪ'naɪmli/ *adv* con benevolencia, benévolamente

bent[1] /bent/ *past and past p of* **bend**[2]

bent[2] *adj*

A ‹*pipe*› curvado, torcido

B (determined) **to be ~ ON doing sth** estar* empeñado EN hacer algo

C (BrE sl) 1 (corrupt) corrupto, chueco (AmL fam) 2 (homosexual): **to be ~** ser* del otro bando (fam)

bent[3] *n* (*no pl*) 1 (inclination) inclinaciones *fpl*; **people of (an) artistic ~** personas con inclinaciones artísticas 2 (aptitude) aptitud *f*

bequeath /bɪ'kwi:ð, -'kwi:θ/ *vt* **to ~ sth TO sb, to ~ sb sth** legarle* algo A algn

bequest /bɪ'kwest/ *n* legado *m*

berate /bɪ'reɪt/ *vt* (frml) **to ~ sb (FOR sth)** reprender *or* amonestar a algn (POR algo)

bereaved[1] /bɪ'ri:vd/ *adj* desconsolado, afligido (*por la muerte de un ser querido*)

bereaved[2] *n* (*pl* ~) **the ~** los deudos, la familia del difunto/de la difunta

bereavement /bɪ'ri:vmənt/ *n* [c u] dolor *m*, pesar *m* (*por la muerte de un ser querido*); **they have suffered** *o* **had a ~ in the family** han sufrido la pérdida de un familiar

bereft /bɪ'reft/ *adj* (*pred*) **to be ~ OF sth** verse* privado DE algo; **totally ~ of inspiration** desprovisto de toda inspiración

beret /bə'reɪ || 'bereɪ/ *n* boina *f*

berk /bɜ:rk || bɜ:k/ *n* (BrE sl) imbécil *mf*

Berlin /'bɜ:r'lɪn || bɜ:'lɪn/ *n* Berlín *m*

Bermuda /bər'mju:də || bə'mju:də/ *n* las (islas) Bermudas; (*before n*) **~ shorts** bermudas *fpl*; **the ~ Triangle** el triángulo de las Bermudas

Bermudas /bər'mju:dəz || bə'mju:dəz/ *pl n* bermudas *fpl*

Bern, Berne /bɜ:rn || bɜ:n/ *n* Berna *f*

berry /'beri/ *n* (*pl* **-ries**) (Bot) baya *f*; (Culin) *fresas, frambuesas, moras etc*; **as brown as a ~** negro como el carbón

berserk /bər'sɜ:rk || bə'sɜ:k/ *adj*: **to go ~** ponerse* como una fiera *or* como un loco

berth[1] /bɜ:rθ || bɜ:θ/ *n* 1 (couchette, bunk) litera *f*, cucheta *f* (RPl); (cabin) camarote *m* 2 (mooring) atracadero *m*; ***to give sb a wide ~*** eludir *or* rehuir* a algn 3 (AmE Sport) **a starting ~** un puesto de (jugador) titular

berth[2] *vt/i* atracar*

beseech /bɪ'si:tʃ/ *vt* (*past & past p* **beseeched** *or* **besought**) (liter) suplicar*, rogar*; **to ~ sb TO + INF** suplicarle* *or* rogarle* a algn QUE (+ *subj*)

beset /bɪ'set/ *vt* (*pres p* **besetting**; *past & past p* **beset**) «*anxieties/fears*» acuciar; **he was ~ by doubts** lo acosaban las dudas; **the way ahead is ~ with difficulties** tenemos (*or* tienen *etc*) muchos obstáculos por delante

beside[1] /bɪ'saɪd/ *prep* 1 (at the side of) al lado de, junto a; **she's the one ~ me in the photograph** es la que está a mi lado *or* junto a mí en la foto; ***to be ~ oneself***: **he was ~ himself with rage** estaba fuera de sí (de la rabia); **she's ~ herself with happiness** está que no cabe en sí de la alegría 2 (compared with) comparado con 3 (extraneous to): **that's ~ the point** eso no tiene nada que ver, eso no viene al caso 4 ▸**besides**[1]

beside[2] *adv* 1 (alongside) al lado 2 ▸**besides**[2]

besides[1] /bɪ'saɪdz/ *prep* 1 (in addition to) además de; **there are five others coming ~ you** además de *or* aparte de ti, vienen otros cinco 2 (apart from) excepto, aparte de, fuera de; **no one knows ~ you** nadie lo sabe excepto tú *or* aparte de ti *or* fuera de ti

besides[2] *adv* además; **and plenty more ~** y mucho más todavía

besiege /bɪ'si:dʒ/ *vt* sitiar, asediar, cercar*; **an angry crowd ~d the embassy** una muchedumbre enfurecida rodeó *or* cercó la embajada; **the village was ~d by reporters** el pueblo se vio asediado por periodistas; **they were ~d with letters of protest** los inundaron con cartas de protesta

besmirch /bɪ'smɜ:rtʃ || bɪ'smɜ:tʃ/ *vt* (frml) ensuciar, mancillar (liter)

besotted /bɪ'sɑ:təd || bɪ'sɒtɪd/ *adj* (*usu pred*) **to be ~ WITH sb**: **he's totally ~ with her** está perdidamente enamorado de ella, está loco por ella

besought /bɪ'sɔ:t/ *past & past p of* **beseech**

bespatter /bɪ'spætər || bɪ'spætə(r)/ *vt* **to ~ sth WITH sth** salpicar* algo DE algo

bespectacled /bɪ'spektɪkəld/ *adj* de anteojos *or* lentes (AmL), con gafas (esp Esp)

bespoke /bɪ'spəʊk/ *adj* (*before n*) (esp BrE) Ⓢ **bespoke tailor** trajes a medida

best[1] /best/ *adj* (*superl of* **good**[1]) mejor; **he was (the) ~** él era el mejor; **this year's carnival will be the ~ ever** el carnaval de este año estará mejor que nunca; **for the ~ part of an hour** durante casi una hora; **~ of all was the windsurfing** lo mejor de todo fue el windsurf; **the ~ things in life are free** (set phrase) los mejores placeres no cuestan dinero; **may the ~ man/team win** (set phrase) que gane el mejor; Ⓢ **best before July 29** consumir preferentemente antes del 29 de julio; **she knows what's ~ for you** ella sabe qué es lo que más te conviene; **the ~ thing (to do) is to wait** lo mejor es esperar; **she's not very tolerant at the ~ of times** la tolerancia no es precisamente una de sus características

best[2] *adv*

A (*superl of* **well**[1,2]) mejor; **which color suits me (the) ~?** ¿qué color me queda mejor?; **I like this painting (the) ~ (of all)** éste es el cuadro que más me gusta; **I did it as ~ I could** lo hice lo mejor que pude; **he's ~ remembered for his poems** se lo recuerda sobre todo por sus poesías; **it's ~ forgotten** más vale olvidarlo

B **had best** (ought): **we'd ~ leave that decision to him** lo mejor va a ser que dejemos que eso lo decida él; *see also* **better**[1,2]

best[3] *n*

A **the ~** 1 (+ *sing vb*) lo mejor; **choose ABC hotels when only the ~ will do** si usted exige lo mejor, escoja hoteles ABC; **he's in the ~ of health** está en excelente estado de salud; **I don't look my ~ in the mornings** por la mañana no es cuando me veo mejor; **to do** *o* **try one's (level) ~** hacer* todo lo posible; **it's the ~ I can do** no lo puedo hacer mejor; **to make the ~ of sth**: **we'll just have to make the ~ of what we've got** tendremos que arreglarnos con lo que tenemos; **they had to make the ~ of a**

bad job tuvieron que hacer lo que pudieron; **it all turned out for the ~ in the end** al final todo fue para bien; **he did it to the ~ of his ability** lo hizo lo mejor que pudo; **to the ~ of my knowledge** que yo sepa [2] (+ *pl vb*): **even the ~ of us are wrong sometimes** todos nos equivocamos; **she can ski with the ~ of them** (colloq) esquía tan bien como el mejor; **they're (the) ~ of friends** son de lo más amigos

B [1] **at best**: **at ~, we'll just manage to cover costs** como mucho, podremos cubrir los gastos; **at ~, she's irresponsible** lo menos que se puede decir es que es una irresponsable [2] **at/past one's best**: **she's not at her ~ in the morning** la mañana no es su mejor momento del día; **at his ~, his singing rivals that of Caruso** en sus mejores momentos puede compararse a Caruso; **it's British theater at its ~** es un magnífico exponente de lo mejor del teatro británico; **the roses were past their ~** las rosas ya no estaban en su mejor momento

C [1] (in greetings): **all the ~!** ¡buena suerte!, ¡que te (*or* les *etc*) vaya bien! [2] (Sport) récord *m*; **a personal ~ for Flynn** un récord para Flynn

best-before date /ˌbestbɪ'fɔːr || ˌbestbɪ'fɔː(r)/ *n* fecha *f* de consumo preferente

bestial /'bestʃəl || 'bestiəl/ *adj* ‹*cruelty/crime*› brutal, salvaje

bestiality /ˌbestʃi'æləti || ˌbesti'æləti/ *n* [u]
A (cruelty) brutalidad *f*, bestialidad *f*
B (sex with animals) bestialidad *f*

best man *n*: *amigo que acompaña al novio el día de la boda*, ≈ padrino *m*, testigo *m*

bestow /bɪ'stəʊ/ *vt* (frml *or* liter) **to ~ sth ON** *o* **UPON sb** ‹*title/award*› conferirle* *or* otorgarle* algo A algn (frml); **he ~ed his affections on her** la hizo depositaria de su amor (liter)

best: **~-seller** /'best'selər || ˌbest'selə(r)/ *n* (book) bestseller *m*, superventas *m*; (product) superventas *m*; (author) autor, -tora *m,f* de bestsellers; **~-selling** /'best'selɪŋ/ *adj* (*before n*): **a ~-selling book** un libro de gran éxito de ventas, un superventas; **a ~-selling writer** un escritor que tiene gran éxito de ventas

bet[1] /bet/ *n* [1] (wager) apuesta *f*; **I had** *o* **made a ~ with Charlie that Brazil would win** le aposté a Charlie que ganaría Brasil [2] (option): **your best ~ is to stay here** lo mejor que puedes hacer es quedarte aquí; **it's a pretty good** *o* **fair ~ that someone here speaks English** es casi seguro que aquí alguien habla inglés; ***to hedge one's ~s*** cubrirse*

bet[2] (*pres p* **betting**; *past & past p* **bet**) *vt* [1] (gamble) apostar*; **David ~ him £5 the Liberals would win** David le apostó cinco libras (a) que ganaban los liberales [2] (be sure) jugarse*, apostar*; **I ~ he doesn't even remember my name** apuesto (a) que ni se acuerda de mi nombre; **I had a hard time persuading him — I'll ~ you did!** me costó mucho convencerlo — ¡me lo puedo imaginar!; **I can do it! — (I) ~ (you) you can't!** ¡a que puedo hacerlo!, —¡a que no!; **I ~ you any money** *o* **anything you like, they're late** me juego *or* te apuesto lo que quieras (a) que llegan tarde; ***you can ~ your life*** *o* ***your bottom dollar*** (colloq) apuesto *or* me juego la cabeza *or* camisa (fam)

■ **bet** *vi* [1] (gamble) jugar*; **I'm not a ~ting man, but ...** yo no soy jugador, pero ...; **to ~ ON sth/sb** apostarle* A algo/algn [2] (be sure): **I wouldn't ~ on it** yo no estaría tan seguro, yo no me fiaría; **(do you) want to ~?** (colloq) ¿qué *or* cuánto (te) apuestas?, ¿quieres apostar?; **will you be there? — you ~!** (colloq) ¿irás? — ¡por supuesto!; **I ~!** (colloq & iro) sí, seguro (iró), sí, ya (iró)

beta-test /'biːtəˌtest/ *vt* ‹*product/software*› realizar* una prueba beta de, realizar* un beta test de *o* (AmL tb) un testeo beta de

bête noire /'bet'nwɑːr || ˌbet'nwɑː(r)/ *n* (*pl* **~s ~s** /'bet 'nwɑːr || ˌbet'nwɑː(r), -'nwɑːrz/) bestia *f* negra (period), bête noire *f* (period)

Bethlehem /'beθləhem || 'beθlɪhem/ *n* Belén *m*

betide /bɪ'taɪd/ *vi* (liter & arch) ▸ **woe 1**

betray /bɪ'treɪ/ *vt* [1] ‹*ally*› traicionar; **to ~ sb's trust** defraudar la confianza que algn ha puesto en uno; **he ~ed us to the enemy** nos vendió al enemigo [2] (reveal) revelar, delatar; **her voice ~ed her nervousness** su voz revelaba *or* delataba el miedo que sentía

betrayal /bɪ'treɪəl/ *n* [c u] traición *f*; (of secrets) delación *f*; **a ~ of trust** un abuso de confianza

betroth /bɪ'trəʊð/ *vt* (frml) prometer en matrimonio (frml)

betrothal /bɪ'trəʊðəl/ *n* [u c] (frml) esponsales *mpl* (frml), compromiso *m* (matrimonial)

better[1] /'betər || 'betə(r)/ *adj*
A (*comp of* **good[1]**) mejor; **he's ~ at playing the guitar than at singing** toca la guitarra mejor de lo que canta; **fruit's much ~ for you than candy** la fruta es mucho más sana que los caramelos; **things couldn't be ~** todo va de maravilla; **what do you think of the wine? — I've tasted ~** ¿qué te parece el vino? — los he probado mejores; **to get ~** mejorar; **the bigger the ~** cuanto más grande mejor; **the less said about it the ~** cuanto menos se hable del tema mejor; **the garden looks all the ~ for the rain** la lluvia le ha venido bien al jardín; **if they can both come, so much the ~** si pueden venir los dos, mucho *or* tanto mejor; **she's little ~ than a thief** es poco menos que una ladrona; **he's moved on to ~ things since then** desde entonces se ha superado mucho; **I can go one ~: I'll give you interest-free credit** yo puedo hacerle una oferta aún mejor: le doy crédito sin interés
B (*pred*) (recovered from illness) **to be ~** estar* mejor; **to get ~** recuperarse

better[2] *adv*
A (*comp of* **well[1,2]**) mejor; **she swims ~ than I do** *o* **than me** nada mejor que yo; **we get on ~ than before** nos llevamos mejor que antes; **I can see ~ from here** desde aquí veo mejor; **we'd've done ~ to wait** hubiera sido mejor esperar; **at the last moment he thought ~ of it** a último momento cambió de idea
B **had better** (ought): **hadn't you ~ phone them?** ¿no deberías llamarlos?; **I'd ~ leave before it gets dark** va a ser mejor que me vaya antes de que oscurezca; **well, I'd ~ be off** bueno, me tengo que ir; **you'd ~ do as I say** más te vale hacer lo que yo te diga; **you'd ~ not complain!** ¡más te vale no quejarte!; **you'd ~ believe it!** (colloq) sí señor
C (more) (AmE) más; **it cost me ~ than $100** me costó más de 100 dólares

better[3] *n* [1] (superior of two) **the ~ of the two** el mejor de los/las dos; **for the ~** para bien, para mejor; **things took a turn for the ~** las cosas dieron un giro positivo; ***to get the ~ of sb/sth*** ganarle la batalla a algn/algo; **my curiosity got the ~ of me** la curiosidad fue más fuerte que yo *or* pudo más que yo [2] **betters** *pl* (superiors) superiores *mpl*; **his elders and ~s** sus mayores

better[4] *vt* [1] (improve) mejorar; **to ~ oneself** superarse [2] (surpass) ‹*score/record*› mejorar, superar

betterment /'betərmənt || 'betəmənt/ *n* [u] mejoramiento *m*, mejora *f*

better-off /ˌbetər'ɔːf || ˌbetər'ɒf/ *adj* (*pred* **better off**) [1] (financially) de mejor posición económica; **he's ~ ~ than her** tiene mejor posición económica que ella, es de posición más acomodada que ella [2] (emotionally, physically) (*pred*) mejor; **I'm ~ ~ divorced** estoy mejor divorciado

betting /'betɪŋ/ *n* [u] (BrE): **what's the ~ he won't turn up?** ¿qué (te) apuestas (a) que no viene?; (*before n*) **~ shop** agencia *f* de apuestas

between[1] /bɪ'twiːn/ *prep*
A (between two points, times, numbers) entre; **~ now and Thursday** de aquí al jueves; **it is closed ~ 1 and 3** está cerrado de 1 a 3; **~ 80 and 100 guests** entre 80 y 100 invitados; **nothing can come ~ us** nada podrá separarnos
B (among) entre; **they divided** *o* **shared the money ~ them** se dividieron el dinero entre ellos; **this is strictly ~ you and me** *o* **~ ourselves** esto debe quedar entre nosotros
C [1] (jointly, in combination) entre; **we spent $250 ~ us** gastamos 250 dólares entre los dos; **~ them they managed to lift it** entre los dos consiguieron levantarlo [2] (what with) (colloq) entre; **~ working and training I've no time for reading** entre el trabajo y el entrenamiento no tengo tiempo para leer

between[2] *adv*: **the one ~** el/la de en medio; **there are very large houses and very small apartments and nothing (in) ~** hay casas muy grandes o apartamentos muy pequeños pero no hay nada intermedio

betwixt[1] /bɪ'twɪkst/ *prep* (liter & arch) entre

betwixt² *adv*: **~ and between**: **they're ~ and between, neither children nor adults** no son ni una cosa ni otra, ni niños ni adultos

bevel /ˈbevəl/ *vt*, (BrE) **-ll-** biselar; **~ed edge** borde *m* biselado

beverage /ˈbevərɪdʒ/ *n* bebida *f*

bewail /bɪˈweɪl/ *vt* ‹*lack/decline*› lamentarse de, lamentar; ‹*loss*› llorar

beware /bɪˈwer || bɪˈweə(r)/ *vi* (*only in inf and imperative*): **~!** ¡(ten) cuidado!, ¡atención!; **to ~ OF sth/sb**: Ⓢ **beware of the dog** cuidado con el perro; **he was told to ~ of pickpockets** le dijeron que se cuidara de los carteristas *or* (Méx) bolsistas; **~ of imitations** desconfíe de las imitaciones

■ **beware** *vt* guardarse *or* cuidarse de

bewilder /bɪˈwɪldər || bɪˈwɪldə(r)/ *vt* (confuse) desconcertar*, dejar perplejo; (overwhelm) apabullar

bewildered /bɪˈwɪldərd || bɪˈwɪldəd/ *adj* desconcertado, perplejo; (overwhelmed) apabullado

bewildering /bɪˈwɪldərɪŋ/ *adj* desconcertante; (overwhelming) apabullante

bewilderment /bɪˈwɪldərmənt || bɪˈwɪldəmənt/ *n* [u] perplejidad *f*, desconcierto *m*; **the child looked around in ~** el niño miraba perplejo a su alrededor

bewitch /bɪˈwɪtʃ/ *vt* (cast spell on) embrujar, hechizar*; (entrance, delight) cautivar

bewitching /bɪˈwɪtʃɪŋ/ *adj* ‹*beauty*› cautivador; ‹*smile*› hechicero, cautivador

beyond¹ /bɪˈɑːnd || bɪˈjɒnd/ *prep*

A (on other side of): **I live just ~ the station** vivo justo pasando la estación; **~ this point** de aquí en adelante, más allá

B 1 (further than): **try to think ~ the immediate future** trata de pensar más allá del futuro inmediato; **I didn't read ~ the first chapter** no pasé del primer capítulo; **this has gone ~ a joke** esto pasa de ser una broma 2 (later than): **I didn't stay ~ the opening speeches** sólo estuve para los discursos inaugurales 3 (more than, apart from): **I can't tell you anything ~ that** no te puedo decir nada más que eso

C 1 (past, no longer permitting): **it's ~ repair** ya no tiene arreglo 2 (outside reach, scope of): **~ the reach of the law** fuera del alcance de la ley; **circumstances ~ our control** circunstancias ajenas a nuestra voluntad; **his integrity is ~ question** su integridad está fuera de toda duda; **it's ~ me what she sees in him** (colloq) no puedo entender qué es lo que ve en él 3 (surpassing): **to live ~ one's means** vivir por encima de sus (*or* mis *etc*) posibilidades; **it's ~ belief** es increíble, es de no creer; **it has succeeded ~ our wildest expectations** ha tenido un éxito que ha superado en mucho nuestras expectativas más optimistas

beyond² *adv* 1 (in space) más allá 2 (in time): **we're planning for the year 2000 and ~** estamos haciendo planes para el 2000 y más allá del 2000

beyond³ *n* (liter) 1 (Occult) **the ~** el más allá 2 (unexplored territory) **the great ~** lo desconocido

bhp = brake horsepower

bi- /baɪ/ *pref* bi-

biannual /baɪˈænjuəl/ *adj* ‹*report*› semestral; ‹*event/festival*› que se celebra dos veces al año

biannually /baɪˈænjuəli/ *adv* dos veces al año

bias¹ /ˈbaɪəs/ *n*

A [u c] 1 (prejudice, unfairness) parcialidad *f*, sesgo *m*; **to be without ~** ser* imparcial, no ser* tendencioso *or* parcial; **the firm's ~ in favor of younger applicants** la preferencia de la compañía por los candidatos más jóvenes 2 (leanings, tendency): **his scientific ~** su inclinación por las ciencias; **the course has a scientific ~** el curso tiene un enfoque científico

B [u] (in sewing): **to cut sth on the ~** cortar algo al bies *or* al sesgo

bias² *vt* ‹*judgment*› influir* en, afectar

biased, biassed /ˈbaɪəst/ *adj* ‹*report/criticism*› tendencioso, parcial; ‹*judge*› parcial; **to be ~ AGAINST sth/sb** estar* predispuesto EN CONTRA DE algo/algn, tener* prejuicio EN CONTRA DE algo/algn; **to be ~ TOWARD(S) sth/sb** estar* predipuesto A FAVOR DE algo/algn

bib /bɪb/ *n* 1 (for baby) babero *m* 2 (on dungarees) peto *m*; ***to put on one's best ~ and tucker*** ponerse* sus mejores galas

Bible /ˈbaɪbəl/ *n* Biblia *f*; **the Holy ~** la Sagrada *or* Santa Biblia; **the feminist's b~** la biblia *or* el libro de cabecera de las feministas

Bible Belt *n* (in US) **the ~ ~** *zona de los EEUU donde impera un fundamentalismo protestante*

biblical /ˈbɪblɪkəl/ *adj* bíblico

bibliographic /ˈbɪbliəˈgræfɪk/, **-ical** /-ɪkəl/ *adj* bibliográfico

bibliography /ˈbɪbliˈɑːgrəfi || ˌbɪbliˈɒgrəfi/ *n* (*pl* **-phies**) bibliografía *f*

bicarbonate of soda /baɪˈkɑːrbəneɪt || baɪˈkɑːbəneɪt/ *n* [u] bicarbonato *m* de sodio *or* de soda *or* (Esp) de sosa

bicentenary /ˈbaɪsenˈtenəri || ˌbaɪsenˈtiːnəri/, **bicentennial** /ˈbaɪsenˈteniəl/ *n* bicentenario *m*

biceps /ˈbaɪseps/ *n* (*pl* ~) bíceps *m*

bicker /ˈbɪkər || ˈbɪkə(r)/ *vi* pelear, discutir

bickering /ˈbɪkərɪŋ/ *n* [u] peleas *fpl*, discusiones *fpl*

bicycle¹ /ˈbaɪsɪkəl/ *n* bicicleta *f*; **to ride a ~** andar* *or* (Esp) montar en bicicleta; (*before n*) **~ race** carrera *f* ciclista *or* de bicicletas

bicycle² *vi* ir* en bicicleta

bid¹ /bɪd/ *vt*

A (*pres p* **bidding**; *past & past p* **bid**) 1 (at auction) ofrecer*; **what am I ~ for this vase?** ¿cuánto ofrecen por este jarrón? 2 (in bridge) declarar

B (*pres p* **bidding**; *past* **bade** *or* **bid**; *past p* **bidden** *or* **bid**) (liter) 1 (wish, say): **to ~ sb welcome** darle* la bienvenida a algn; **to ~ sb farewell** despedirse* de *or* decirle* adiós a algn 2 (request) **to ~ sb (to) + INF** pedirle* a algn QUE + SUBJ

■ **bid** *vi* (*pres p* **bidding**; *past & past p* **bid**) 1 (at auction) hacer* ofertas, pujar; **to ~ FOR sth** pujar POR algo; **a woman was ~ding against me** una mujer estaba haciendo ofertas *or* pujando por el mismo lote que yo 2 (in bridge) declarar

bid² *n*

A 1 (at auction) oferta *f*, puja *f* 2 (in bridge) declaración *f*; **no ~** paso

B (attempt) intento *m*, tentativa *f*; (unsuccessful) intentona *f*, conato *m*, intento *m*, tentativa *f*; **an escape ~** un conato *or* una intentona de fuga; **~ FOR sth**: **their ~ for power** su intento de hacerse con el poder; **he made one last ~ for freedom** hizo un último intento de escapar; **~ to + INF** intento *m* DE + INF; **his ~ to topple the regime** su intento de derribar al gobierno

bidden /ˈbɪdn̩/ *past p of* **bid¹** *vt* **B**

bidder /ˈbɪdər || ˈbɪdə(r)/ *n* postor, -tora *m,f*, interesado, -da *m,f*; **the highest ~** el mejor postor

bidding /ˈbɪdɪŋ/ *n* [u]

A 1 (at auction): **who'll open the ~ at $1,000?** ¿quién ofrece 1.000 dólares para empezar?; **the ~ opened at $100** la subasta abrió con una oferta de $100; **~ was brisk** la puja estaba muy animada 2 (in bridge) declaración *f*

B (wishes): **they had servants to do their ~** tenían criados para lo que se les antojara; **at his father's ~** a petición de su padre

biddy /ˈbɪdi/ *n* (*pl* **-dies**) (colloq): **an old ~** una viejecita; (less polite) una vieja

bide /baɪd/ *vt*: ***to ~ one's time*** esperar *or* aguardar el momento oportuno

bidet /bɪˈdeɪ || ˈbiːdeɪ/ *n* bidet *m*, bidé *m*

biennial¹ /baɪˈeniəl/ *adj* bienal

biennial² *n* planta *f* bienal *or* bianual

bier /bɪr || bɪə(r)/ *n* andas *fpl*; **on a ~** en andas

biff¹ /bɪf/ *n* (colloq) puñetazo *m*

biff² *vt* (colloq) pegarle* un puñetazo a

bifocals /ˈbaɪˈfəʊkəlz/ *pl n* anteojos *mpl or* (esp Esp) gafas *fpl* bifocales

big¹ /bɪg/ *adj* **-gg-** [*the usual translation,* **grande**, *becomes* **gran** *when it is used before a singular noun*]

A 1 (in size) grande; **a ~ garden** un jardín grande, un gran jardín; **her ~ blue eyes** sus grandes ojos azules; **how ~ is the table?** ¿cómo es de grande *or* qué tamaño tiene

la mesa? [2] (in scale, intensity) grande; **a ~ explosion** una gran explosión; **a ~ hug/kiss** un abrazote/besote (fam)
B [1] (major) grande, importante; **Acme Corp is our ~gest customer** Acme Corp es nuestro cliente más importante [2] (great) grande; **I'm a ~ fan of his** soy un gran admirador suyo; ***to be ~ on sth*** (colloq) ser* entusiasta de algo
C (significant, serious) grande; **a ~ decision** una gran decisión, una decisión importante; **it was a ~ mistake** fue un gran *or* grave error; **the ~ question now is ...** el quid del asunto *or* de la cuestión ahora es ...
D (older, grown up) grande; **my ~ brother** mi hermano mayor
E (magnanimous) generoso; **it was ~ of her** fue muy generoso de su parte; **that's ~ of you!** ¡qué generoso eres!
F (boastful): **~ talk** fanfarronada *f*; ***to get too ~ for one's boots*** *o* ***breeches***: **he's getting too ~ for his boots** *o* **breeches** se le han subido los humos a la cabeza
G (popular) (colloq) (*pred*) conocido, famoso; **she's really ~ in Europe** es muy conocida *or* famosa en Europa

big[2] *adv* (colloq) [1] (ambitiously): **to think ~** ser* ambicioso, planear las cosas a lo grande [2] (boastfully): **to talk ~** darse* importancia *or* ínfulas, fanfarronear [3] (with great success): **the movie went over ~ in Europe** la película tuvo un gran éxito *or* (fam) fue un exitazo en Europa; ***to make it ~*** tener* un gran éxito

bigamist /ˈbɪgəməst || ˈbɪgəmɪst/ *n* bígamo, -ma *m,f*

bigamous /ˈbɪgəməs/ *adj* bígamo

bigamy /ˈbɪgəmi/ *n* [u] bigamia *f*

big: **~ bang** *n* **the ~ bang** el big bang, la gran explosión; **~-boned** /ˈbɪgˈbəʊnd/ *adj* de huesos grandes; **~ business** *n* [u] el gran capital; **to be ~ business** ser* un gran negocio; **~ cheese** *n* (sl) pez *m* gordo (fam); **~ dipper** *n* [1] (AmE Astron) **B~ Dipper** la Osa Mayor [2] (in amusement park) (BrE) montaña *f* rusa; **~ gun** *n* (colloq) pez *m* gordo (fam); **~head** *n* (colloq) [1] [c] (person) creído, -da *m,f* (fam), engreído, -da *m,f* [2] [u] (conceit) (AmE) engreimiento *m*, **~-headed** /ˈbɪgˈhedəd || ˌbɪgˈhedɪd/ *adj* (colloq) creído (fam), engreído; **~-hearted** /ˈbɪgˈhɑːrtəd || ˌbɪgˈhɑːtɪd/ *adj* de buen corazón, generoso; **~ hitter** *n* peso *m* pesado; **~ league** *n* (AmE) (Sport) liga *f* mayor; (top rank) los grandes; **~-league** /ˈbɪgˈliːg/ *adj* (AmE) (*before n*) ‹*baseball/player*› de las ligas mayores; ‹*business/politician*› de alto(s) vuelo(s); ‹*crook*› de marca mayor (fam); **~mouth** *n* (colloq) (boaster) fanfarrón, -rrona *m,f*; (gossip) chismoso, -sa *m,f*, cotilla *mf* (Esp fam), hocicón, -cona *m,f* (Chi, Méx fam); **~-name** /ˈbɪgˈneɪm/ *adj* (*before n*) de renombre, importante

bigot /ˈbɪgət/ *n* intolerante *mf*

bigoted /ˈbɪgətəd || ˈbɪgətɪd/ *adj* intolerante, prejuicioso

bigotry /ˈbɪgətri/ *n* [u] intolerancia *f*

big: **~-screen** /ˈbɪgˈskriːn/ *adj* (*before n*) ‹*version*› para la pantalla grande; ‹*actor*› de la pantalla grande; **~ shot** *n* (colloq) pez *m* gordo (fam); **~-ticket** /ˈbɪgˈtɪkət/ *adj* (AmE colloq) caro, costoso; **~ time** *n* (colloq) **the ~ time** el estrellato; **to make** *o* **reach** *o* **hit the ~ time** alcanzar* el estrellato, triunfar; **~ top** *n* carpa *f* de circo; **~ wheel** *n* (BrE) rueda *f* gigante *or* (Méx) de la fortuna *or* (Andes) de Chicago, noria *f* (Esp), vuelta *f* al mundo (Arg); **~wig** *n* (colloq) pez *m* gordo (fam)

bijou /ˈbiːʒuː/ *adj* (BrE) (*before n*) monísimo

bike /baɪk/ *n* (colloq) (bicycle) bici *f* (fam); (motorcycle) moto *f*

biker /ˈbaɪkər || ˈbaɪkə(r)/ *n* motociclista *mf*, motorista *mf* (Esp)

bikini /bɪˈkiːni/ *n* bikini *m or* (RPl) *f*; (*before n*) **~ bottom/top** parte *f* de abajo/arriba del bikini; **~ line** entrepierna *f*

bilateral /baɪˈlætərəl/ *adj* bilateral

bilberry /ˈbɪlˌberi || ˈbɪlbəri/ *n* (*pl* **-ries**) arándano *m*

bile /baɪl/ *n* [u] [1] (Physiol) bilis *f* [2] (bad temper) (liter) mal genio *m*

bilge /bɪldʒ/ *n*
A (Naut) [c] (part of hull) pantoque *m*
B [u] [1] **~ (water)** agua *f*‡ de pantoque [2] (nonsense) (BrE colloq) paparruchas *fpl* (fam)

bilingual /baɪˈlɪŋgwəl/ *adj* bilingüe

bilious /ˈbɪliəs/ *adj*: **to feel ~** sentirse* descompuesto; **~ attack** ataque *m* al *or* de hígado

bill[1] /bɪl/ *n*
A [1] (invoice) factura *f*, cuenta *f*; **the telephone ~** la cuenta *or* (Esp tb) el recibo del teléfono [2] (in restaurant) (esp BrE) cuenta *f*, nota *f*, adición *f* (RPl) [3] (costs) gastos *mpl*; ▸**foot**[2]
B (Fin) (banknote) (AmE) billete *m*; **a dollar ~** un billete de un dólar
C (Govt) proyecto *m* de ley; **private ~** (BrE) *proyecto de ley presentado por un diputado*
D [1] (poster) (dated) cartel *m*, anuncio *m* [2] (program) programa *m*; **to head** *o* **top the ~** encabezar* el reparto; ***to fill*** *o* (BrE also) ***fit the ~*** reunir* las condiciones, satisfacer* los requisitos
E (certificate): **~ of sale** contrato *m or* escritura *f* de venta; **a clean ~ of health** (favorable report) el visto bueno; ***to sell sb a ~ of goods*** (AmE colloq) darle* *or* (Chi) pasarle *or* (Col) meterle gato por liebre a algn (fam)
F (beak) pico *m*

bill[2] *vt*
A (invoice, charge) pasarle la cuenta *or* la factura a
B (advertise) ‹*play/performer*› anunciar
■ **bill** *vi*: ***to ~ and coo*** estar* como dos tortolitos

billboard /ˈbɪlbɔːrd || ˈbɪlbɔːd/ *n* (AmE) cartelera *f*, valla *f* (publicitaria)

billet /ˈbɪlət || ˈbɪlɪt/ *vt* alojar

billfold /ˈbɪlfəʊld/ *n* (AmE) billetera *f*, cartera *f*

billiard /ˈbɪljərd || ˈbɪljəd/ *adj* (*before n*) de billar; **a ~ ball/table** una bola/mesa de billar

billiards /ˈbɪljərdz || ˈbɪljədz/ *n* [u] (+ *sing vb*) billar *m*

billing /ˈbɪlɪŋ/ *n* [u] *orden de importancia en un reparto*; **to be given top ~** encabezar* el reparto

billion /ˈbɪljən/ *n* [1] (10^9) mil millones *mpl*, millar *m* de millones [2] (BrE) (10^{12}) billón *m*

billionaire /ˈbɪljəˈner / *n* multimillonario, -ria *m,f*

bill of rights *n* (*pl* **~s ~ ~**) declaración *f* de derechos

billow /ˈbɪləʊ/ *vi* [1] **~ (out)** «*sail/parachute*» hincharse, inflarse [2] «*smoke*»: **smoke ~ed from the window** nubes de humo salían de *or* por la ventana [3] **billowing** *pres p* ‹*sails*› hinchado, inflado; **~ing smoke** nubes *fpl* de humo

billposter /ˈbɪlˌpəʊstər || ˈbɪlˌpəʊstə(r)/, (BrE also) **billsticker** /ˈbɪlˌstɪkər/ *n*: *persona que pega carteles*

billy /ˈbɪli/ *n* (*pl* **-lies**) **~ (goat)** macho *m* cabrío

billy: **~can** *n* (BrE) cacerola *f*, cazo *m*; **~ club** *n* (AmE colloq) porra *f*, cachiporra *f*

bimbo /ˈbɪmbəʊ/ *n* (*pl* **-os**) (colloq) *joven bonita y tonta*

bimonthly[1] /ˈbaɪˈmʌnθli/ *adj* (every two months) bimestral; (twice a month) bimensual, quincenal

bimonthly[2] *adv* (every two months) bimestralmente; (twice a month) bimensualmente, quincenalmente

bin[1] /bɪn/ *n* (for kitchen refuse etc) (BrE) cubo *m or* (CS) tacho *m or* (Méx) bote *m or* (Col) caneca *f or* (Ven) tobo *m* de la basura; (wastepaper basket) (BrE) papelera *f*, papelero *m*, caneca *f* (Col); (*litter* ~) papelera *f*, basurero *m* (Chi, Méx), caneca *f* (Col)

bin[2] *vt* **-nn-** (BrE) [1] (discard) tirar a la basura, botar a la basura (AmL excl RPl) [2] ‹*proposal/project*› rechazar*

binary /ˈbaɪnəri/ *adj* binario; **~ code** código *m* binario

bin bag *n* (BrE) bolsa *f* de basura

bind[1] /baɪnd/ (*past & past p* **bound**) *vt*
A (tie, fasten) ‹*person*› atar, amarrar; **the ties that ~ us** los lazos que nos unen; ▸**bound**[4] **A1**
B [1] (wrap) envolver* [2] **~ (up)** ‹*wound*› vendar [3] (in sewing) ribetear
C (Law) obligar*
D ‹*book*› encuadernar, empastar
E (Culin) ligar*, unir

Phrasal verb

- **bind over** [v ▸ o ▸ adv, v ▸ adv ▸ o]: **the judge had him bound over to the sheriff** (AmE) quedó bajo la custodia del sheriff por disposición judicial; **they were bound over to keep the peace** (BrE) quedaron bajo apercibimiento

bind[2] *n* (colloq) [1] (difficult situation) aprieto *m*, apuro *m*; **to be in a ~** estar* en un aprieto *or* apuro, estar* metido en un lío (fam) [2] (nuisance) (BrE) lata *f* (fam), plomo *m* (fam), rollo *m* (Esp fam)

binder /ˈbaɪndər || ˈbaɪndə(r)/ *n* (file, folder) carpeta *f*

binding¹ /ˈbaɪndɪŋ/ *n* [1] [c] (book cover) tapa *f*, cubierta *f* [2] [u] (tape) ribete *m*

binding² *adj* ‹*promise/commitment*› que hay que cumplir; (Law) vinculante

bindweed /ˈbaɪndwiːd/ *n* [u] convólvulo *m*, correhuela *f*

binge¹ /bɪndʒ/ *n* (colloq): **to go on a ~** irse* de juerga *or* parranda *or* farra (fam); **she dieted for two weeks and then had a huge ~** estuvo dos semanas a régimen y después se dio tremenda comilona (fam)

binge² *vi* (colloq) darse* una comilona (fam); **to ~ ON sth** atiborrarse *or* hartarse DE algo

binge-drinking *n* [u] hábito *m* de agarrar *or* (esp Esp) coger borracheras

bingo¹ /ˈbɪŋgəʊ/ *n* [u] bingo *m*, lotería *f* (de cartones)

bingo² *interj* (describing sudden effect) ¡zas!, ¡sorpresa!

binliner /ˈbɪn,laɪnər/ *n* (BrE) bolsa *f* de la basura

binoculars /bəˈnɑːkjələrz || bɪˈnɒkjʊləz/ *pl n* binoculares *mpl*, gemelos *mpl*, prismáticos *mpl*, largavistas *m*, anteojos *fpl* de larga vista (esp AmL)

bio- /ˈbaɪəʊ/ *pref* bio-

biochemical /ˈbaɪəʊˈkemɪkəl/ *adj* bioquímico

biochemist /ˈbaɪəʊˈkeməst/ *n* bioquímico, -ca *m,f*

biochemistry /ˈbaɪəʊˈkeməstri/ *n* [u] bioquímica *f*

biodegradable /ˈbaɪəʊdɪˈgreɪdəbəl/ *adj* biodegradable

biofuel /ˈbaɪəʊfjuːəl/ *n* biocombustible *m*

biographer /baɪˈɑːgrəfər || baɪˈɒgrəfə(r)/ *n* biógrafo, -fa *m,f*

biographic /ˈbaɪəˈgræfɪk/, **-ical** /-ɪkəl/ *adj* biográfico

biography /baɪˈɑːgrəfi || baɪˈɒgrəfi/ *n* [u c] (*pl* **-phies**) biografía *f*

biological /ˈbaɪəˈlɑːdʒɪkəl || ,baɪəˈlɒdʒɪkəl/ *adj* biológico

biologist /baɪˈɑːlədʒəst || baɪˈɒlədʒɪst/ *n* biólogo, -ga *m,f*

biology /baɪˈɑːlədʒi || baɪˈɒlədʒi/ *n* [u] biología *f*

bionic /baɪˈɑːnɪk || baɪˈɒnɪk/ *adj* biónico

biophysics /ˈbaɪəʊˈfɪzɪks/ *n* (+ *sing vb*) biofísica *f*

biopsy /ˈbaɪɑːpsi || ˈbaɪɒpsi/ *n* (*pl* **-sies**) biopsia *f*

biorhythm /ˈbaɪəʊ,rɪðəm/ *n* biorritmo *m*

biotechnology /ˈbaɪəʊtekˈnɑːlədʒi/ *n* [u] [1] (in industry) biotecnología *f* [2] (ergonomics) (AmE) ergonomía *f*

bioterrorism /ˈbaɪəʊˈterərɪzəm / *n* [u] bioterrorismo *m*

bipartisan /ˈbaɪˈpɑːrtəzən || ,baɪpɑːtɪˈzæn, ,baɪˈpɑːtɪzən/ *adj* de dos partidos

bipartite /ˈbaɪˈpɑːrtaɪt || ,baɪˈpɑːtaɪt/ *adj* [1] (in two parts) dividido en dos partes, bipartido (frml) [2] (bilateral) ‹*contract/treaty*› bipartito

biped /ˈbaɪped/ *n* bípedo *m*

biplane /ˈbaɪpleɪn/ *n* biplano *m*

birch /bɜːrtʃ || bɜːtʃ/ *n* ~ **(tree)** abedul *m*

bird /bɜːrd || bɜːd/ *n*

A (small) pájaro *m*; (large) ave *f‡*; **a little ~ told me** me lo dijo un pajarito; **the ~ has flown** (set phrase) el pájaro ha volado; ***the ~s and the bees***: **he told us about the ~s and the bees** nos contó de dónde venían los niños; ***to be (strictly) for the ~s*** (colloq) no valer* nada; ***to kill two ~s with one stone*** matar dos pájaros de un tiro; ***~s of a feather flock together*** Dios los cría y ellos se juntan; **they're ~s of a feather** son tal para cual; ***a ~ in the hand is worth two in the bush*** más vale pájaro en mano que ciento volando; ***it's the early ~ that catches the worm*** a quien madruga Dios lo ayuda

B [1] (person): **he's an odd ~** es un bicho raro (fam) [2] (woman) (BrE sl) chica *f*

bird: **~brained** /ˈbɜːrdˈbreɪnd || ˈbɜːdbreɪnd/ *adj* (colloq) lelo (fam); **~cage** *n* jaula *f* de pájaros; (large) pajarera *f*; **~dog** *vt* **-gg-** (AmE colloq) controlar, vigilar; **~ dog** *n* (AmE) [1] (in hunting) perro, -rra *m,f* de caza [2] (person) (colloq) guardián, -diana *m,f*; **~ flu** *n* gripe *f* aviar

birdie /ˈbɜːrdi || ˈbɜːdi/ *n* [1] (bird) (used esp to or by children) pajarito *m* [2] (in golf) birdie *m*

bird: **~ of paradise** *n* (*pl* **~s of paradise**) ave *f‡* del Paraíso; **~ of prey** *n* (*pl* **~s of prey**) ave *f‡* rapaz *or* de rapiña *or* de presa; **~seed** *n* [u] alpiste *m*; **~'s-eye view** *n* vista *f* aérea *or* a vuelo de pájaro; **~watcher** /ˈbɜːrdˈwɑːtʃər || ˈbɜːd,wɒtʃə(r)/*n* observador, -dora *m,f* de aves; **~watching** /ˈbɜːrd,wɑːtʃɪŋ || ˈbɜːd,wɒtʃɪŋ/ *n* [u] observación *f* de las aves (*como hobby*)

Biro®, **biro** /ˈbaɪrəʊ || ˈbaɪərəʊ/ *n* (*pl* **biros**) (BrE) bolígrafo *m*, pluma *f* atómica (Méx), birome *f* (RPl), esfero *m* (Col), lápiz *m* de pasta (Chi), boli *m* (Esp fam)

birth /bɜːrθ || bɜːθ/ *n* [u c] nacimiento *m*; (childbirth) parto *m*; **at ~** al nacer; **he's Irish by ~** es irlandés de nacimiento; **date of ~** fecha *f* de nacimiento; **to be of humble/noble ~** (liter) ser* de humilde cuna/de noble linaje (liter); **to give ~** dar* a luz, parir; ***to give ~ to sth*** dar* origen a algo

birth: **~ certificate** *n* partida *f or* certificado *m or* (Méx) acta *f* de nacimiento; **~ control** *n* [u] control *m* de la natalidad

birthday /ˈbɜːrθdeɪ || ˈbɜːθdeɪ/ *n* (of person) cumpleaños *m*; (of institution etc) aniversario *m*; **it'll be his fifth ~** cumple cinco años; **happy ~!** ¡feliz cumpleaños!; (*before n*) ‹*cake/card/party*› de cumpleaños; **the ~ boy/girl** el (niño)/la (niña) del cumpleaños, el cumpleañero/la cumpleañera (AmL)

birthday suit *n*: **in one's ~ ~** (hum) tal como Dios lo trajo al mundo, tal como uno vino al mundo, en traje de Adán/Eva (hum)

birth: **~mark** *n* mancha *f or* marca *f* de nacimiento, antojo *m*; **~place** *n* (of person) lugar *m* de nacimiento; (of movement, fashion, idea) cuna *f*; **~rate** *n* (índice *m or* tasa *f* de) natalidad *f*; **~right** *n* derecho *m* de nacimiento; (of eldest child) primogenitura *f*

Biscay /ˈbɪskeɪ/ *n* **the Bay of ~** el Golfo de Vizcaya

biscuit /ˈbɪskɪt/ *n* [c] (Culin) [1] (AmE) bollo *m*, panecillo *m*, bísquet *m* (Méx) [2] (cookie, cracker) (BrE) galleta *f*, galletita *f* (RPl); ***to take the ~*** (BrE colloq) ser* el colmo *or* el acabóse (fam); «*person*» llevarse la palma

bisect /baɪˈsekt/ *vt* bisecar*

bisexual¹ /,baɪˈsekʃuəl/ *adj* bisexual

bisexual² *n* bisexual *mf*

bishop /ˈbɪʃəp/ *n* [1] (Relig) obispo *m* [2] (in chess) alfil *m*

bison /ˈbaɪsn̩/ *n* (*pl* ~) bisonte *m*

bit¹ /bɪt/ *past of* **bite¹**

bit² *n*

A [1] (fragment, scrap) pedazo *m*, trozo *m*; **in tiny ~s** en pedacitos *or* trocitos; **to smash sth to ~s** hacer* pedazos *or* añicos algo; **the critics pulled the book to ~s** los críticos destrozaron el libro; ***~s and pieces*** (assorted items) cosas *fpl*; (belongings) cosas *fpl*, bártulos *mpl* (fam); (broken fragments) pedazos *mpl*; ***to be thrilled to ~s*** (BrE colloq) estar* contentísimo, no caber* en sí de alegría [2] (small piece) (esp BrE) trocito *m*, pedacito *m*; **a ~ of paper** un trocito de papel *or* un papelito [3] (component part) (BrE) pieza *f*; **to take sth to ~s** desarmar algo

B (section, piece) parte *f*; ***to do one's ~*** (BrE) aportar *or* poner* su (*or* mi *etc*) granito de arena, hacer* lo suyo (*or* mío *etc*)

C **a bit of** [1] (some, a little) (+ *uncount noun*) un poco de; **a ~ of peace** un poco de paz; **we had a ~ of difficulty finding a hotel** nos resultó algo difícil encontrar un hotel; **it takes a ~ of getting used to** cuesta un poco acostumbrarse; **they have a fair ~** *o* **quite a ~ of work to do** tienen bastante trabajo que hacer; **whether you come or not won't make a ~ of difference** da exactamente lo mismo que vengas o no [2] (rather) (BrE): **we had a ~ of an argument** tuvimos una pequeña discusión; **she's a ~ of an expert** es casi una experta; **was he ashamed? not a ~ of it!** (also AmE) ¿que si estaba avergonzado? ¡para nada! *or* ¡en absoluto! *or* ¡ni lo más mínimo!

D **a bit** (*as adv*) [1] (somewhat) un poco; **a ~ faster** un poco más rápido; **the town's changed a ~** la ciudad ha cambiado algo *or* un poco; **I drank a ~ too much** bebí un poco más de la cuenta *or* un poco demasiado; **that must be worth a ~!** ¡eso debe de valer mucho *or* lo suyo!; **we spent quite a ~** gastamos bastante; **were you worried? — not a ~** ¿estabas preocupado? — en absoluto; **I wouldn't be a ~ surprised** no me sorprendería para nada *or* en lo más mínimo; **she hasn't changed a ~** no ha cambiado (para) nada [2] (a while) un momento *or* rato

E (*in adv phrases*) [1] **bit by bit** poco a poco, de a poco (AmL) [2] **every bit**: **I'm every ~ as disappointed as you** estoy absolutamente tan decepcionado como tú; **he looks every ~ the young executive** tiene todo el aspecto del joven ejecutivo

F [1] (in US): **two ~s** veinticinco centavos de dólar; **his**

promise isn't worth two ~s su promesa no vale ni cinco *or* (Méx) ni un quinto; **I don't care** *o* **give two ~s what she thinks** me importa un bledo *or* un comino lo que piense (fam) 2 (coin) (BrE colloq) moneda *f*; **a 50p ~** una moneda de 50 peniques
G (Comput) bit *m*
H (of bridle) freno *m*, bocado *m*; ***to champ at the ~***: **he was champing at the ~** lo consumía la impaciencia, estaba que no se podía aguantar; ***to have the ~ between one's teeth***: **she has the ~ between her teeth** está que no la para nadie (fam)

bitch¹ /bɪtʃ/ *n*
A (female dog) perra *f*
B 1 (spiteful woman) (AmE vulg, BrE sl) puta *f* (vulg), bruja *f* (fam), arpía *f* (fam) 2 (difficult, unpleasant thing) (colloq) lata *f* (fam), coñazo *m* (Esp fam), chingadera *f* (Méx arg)
C 1 (malicious talk) (colloq): **to have a good ~** chismear de lo lindo (fam) 2 (complaint) (AmE colloq) queja *f*

bitch² *vi* (colloq) 1 (complain) (AmE) quejarse, refunfuñar; **to ~ ABOUT sth/sb** quejarse DE algo/algn 2 (talk maliciously) (BrE) chismear (fam); **to ~ ABOUT sth/sb** hablar pestes DE algo/algn, criticar* algo/a algn

bitchy /'bɪtʃi/ *adj* **bitchier, bitchiest** (colloq) ‹*remark*› malicioso, incidioso, de mala leche (Esp fam); **she was really ~ about her friend** habló pestes de su amiga

bite¹ /baɪt/ (*past* **bit**; *past p* **bitten**) *vt* «*person/dog*» morder*; «*bug*» picar*; **to ~ one's nails** comerse *or* morderse* las uñas; **the dog bit his finger off** el perro le arrancó el dedo de un mordisco; ***to ~ off more than one can chew*** tratar de abarcar más de lo que se puede; ***once bitten, twice shy*** el gato escaldado del agua fría huye

■ **bite** *vi*
A 1 «*person/dog*» morder*; «*mosquito*» picar*; «*wind/frost*» cortar; **to ~ INTO sth** darle* un mordisco A algo, hincarle* el diente A algo; **to ~ ON sth** morder* algo 2 (take bait) «*fish*» picar*
B «*law/recession*» hacerse* sentir

Phrasal verb
• **bite back** [v ▸ o ▸ adv, v ▸ adv ▸ o] ‹*anger*› contener*; **he bit back his words** se mordió la lengua (fam), fue a decir algo pero se contuvo

bite² *n*
A [c] (act) mordisco *m*; (fierce) tarascada *f*; **take a ~ of this** prueba esto; ***to have*** *o* ***get two ~s at the cherry*** (BrE) tener* una segunda oportunidad
B [c] (wound — from insect) picadura *f*; (— from dog, snake) mordedura *f*
C [c] (snack) (colloq) (*no pl*) bocado *m*; **to have a ~ (to eat)** comer un bocado, comer algo
D [u] 1 (of flavor) lo fuerte 2 (sharpness) mordacidad *f*

biting /'baɪtɪŋ/ *adj* ‹*wind*› cortante, penetrante; ‹*sarcasm/criticism*› mordaz, cáustico

bit: **~map** *n* mapa *m* de bits; **~ part** *n* papel *m* pequeño

bitten /'bɪtn̩/ *past p of* **bite¹**

bitter¹ /'bɪtər || 'bɪtə(r)/ *adj*
A 1 (in taste) amargo 2 (very cold) ‹*weather*› glacial, muy frío; ‹*wind/frost*› cortante, penetrante, glacial; **it's ~** hace un frío glacial
B 1 (painful, hard) ‹*disappointment*› amargo; **they fought on to the ~ end** lucharon valientemente hasta el final 2 ‹*person*› resentido, amargado 3 ‹*enemies/hatred*› implacable, a muerte; ‹*struggle*› enconado

bitter² *n* [u] (BrE) *tipo de cerveza ligeramente amarga*

bitterly /'bɪtərli || 'bɪtəli/ *adv*
A ‹*cold*›: **it was ~ cold** hacía un frío glacial
B 1 ‹*disappointed/resentful*› tremendamente; ‹*weep/complain*› amargamente; ‹*say*› amargamente, con amargura 2 (implacably) implacablemente, a muerte

bitterness /'bɪtərnəs || 'bɪtənɪs/ *n* [u]
A (of taste) amargor *m*
B (of disappointment) amargura *f*; (of person) amargura *f*, resentimiento *m*

bittersweet /'bɪtərswi:t || ˌbɪtə'swi:t/ *adj* agridulce; ‹*chocolate*› (AmE) amargo

bitty /'bɪti/ *adj* **-tier, -tiest** 1 (disjointed, scrappy) deshilvanado, sin cohesión 2 (in texture) (BrE) granuloso 3 (tiny) (AmE colloq): **it's just a little ~ spider!** ¡es una arañita de nada! (fam)

bitumen /bɪ'tu:mən || 'bɪtjʊmən/ *n* [u] betún *m*

bivouac¹ /'bɪvuæk/ *n* vivac *m*, campamento *m*

bivouac² *vi* **-ck-** vivaquear, acampar

biweekly¹ /'baɪ'wi:kli/ *adj* (every two weeks) quincenal; (twice a week) bisemanal

biweekly² *adv* (every two weeks) quincenalmente, cada dos semanas; (twice a week) bisemanalmente, dos veces por semana

bizarre /bɪ'zɑ:r || bɪ'zɑ:(r)/ *adj* ‹*story/coincidence*› extraño; ‹*appearance/behavior*› estrambótico, estrafalario

blab /blæb/ **-bb-** *vi* (colloq) 1 (prattle) parlotear (fam) 2 (reveal secrets) descubrir* el pastel (fam)

■ **blab** *vt* **to ~ sth TO sb** soplarle algo A algn

blabbermouth /'blæbərmaʊθ || 'blæbəmaʊθ/ *n* (colloq) bocazas *mf* (fam)

black¹ /blæk/ *adj* **-er, -est**
A 1 ‹*dress/hair/ink*› negro; ‹*sky*› oscuro, negro; **~ cloud** nubarrón *m*, nube *f* negra; ***to beat sb ~ and blue*** (colloq) darle* una tremenda paliza a algn (fam) 2 (dirty) (*pred*) negro, sucísimo 3 ‹*coffee*› negro (AmL), solo (Esp), tinto (Col), puro (Chi); ‹*tea*› solo, sin leche, puro (Chi)
B *also* **Black** ‹*person/community*› negro; **a ~ man** un (hombre) negro
C (sad, hopeless) negro; **things were looking pretty ~** las cosas tomaban mal cariz *or* se estaban poniendo feas; ▸**paint²** *vt* 3
D (illegal): **the ~ economy** la economía informal *or* paralela (AmL), la economía sumergida (Esp)

black² *n*
A [u] (color) negro *m*
B [c] *also* **Black** (person) negro, -gra *m,f*
C (freedom from debt): ***to be in the ~*** no estar* en números rojos

black³ *vt* 1 (bruise): **to ~ sb's eye** ponerle* un ojo morado a algn 2 (boycott) (BrE) boicotear

Phrasal verb
• **black out**
A [v ▸ adv] (lose consciousness) perder* el conocimiento
B [v ▸ o ▸ adv, v ▸ adv ▸ o] 1 (in wartime) ‹*windows*› tapar; ‹*lights*› apagar* 2 (by accident) ‹*town/district*› dejar sin luz *or* a oscuras 3 ‹*transmission/show*› cortar

black: **~ and white** *n* (Cin, Phot, TV) blanco y negro *m*; ***in ~ and white***: **it's here in ~ and white** aquí está escrito bien claro; **she sees things in ~ and white** para ella no hay términos medios; **~-and-white** /'blækən 'hwaɪt || 'blækən'waɪt/ *adj* (*pred* **~ and white**) en blanco y negro; **~ bear** *n* oso *m* negro americano; **~ belt** *n* (belt) cinturón *m* negro, cinto *m* negro, cinta *f* negra (Méx); (person) cinturón *mf* negro, cinta *mf* negra (Méx)

blackberry¹ /'blæk,beri || 'blækbəri/ *n* (*pl* **-ries**) mora *f*; (*before n*) **~ bush** zarzamora *f*, moral *m*

blackberry² *vi* (*only in -ing form*): **to go ~ing** ir* a recoger moras

black: **~bird** *n* (European) mirlo *m*; (N American) totí *m*; **~board** *n* pizarra *f*, pizarrón *m* (AmL), tablero *m* (Col); **~ box** *n* (Aviat) caja *f* negra; **~ consciousness** *n* [u] conciencia *f* negra; **~currant** /'blæk'kɜ:rənt || ˌblæk 'kʌrənt/ *n* grosella *f* negra; **~ Death** *n* **the B~ Death** la Peste Negra

blacken /'blækən/ *vt* 1 (make black) ennegrecer* 2 (defame) ‹*person*› deshonrar, desacreditar; ‹*reputation*› manchar, mancillar (liter)

■ **blacken** *vi* ennegrecerse*

black: **~ eye** *n* 1 (bruise) ojo *m* morado, ojo *m* a la funerala (Esp fam), ojo *m* en compota (CS fam), ojo *m* en tinta (Chi fam); **to give sb a ~ eye** ponerle* un ojo morado (*or* a la funerala *etc*) a algn 2 (bad reputation) (AmE) mala fama *f*; **~ Forest** *n* **the B~ Forest** la Selva Negra; **~ Forest gateau**, **Black Forest cake** *n* pastel *m* selva negra, tarta *f* (Esp) *or* torta *f* (CS, Ven) selva negra; **~guard** /'blægərd || 'blægɑ:d/ *n* (dated) villano *m* (ant), canalla *m*; **~head** *n* espinilla *f*, punto *m* negro, comedón *m* (frml); **~ hole** *n* agujero *m* negro; **~ ice** *n* [u] *capa fina de hielo en las carreteras*; **~jack** *n* 1 [u] (Games) black-jack *m* 2 [c] (weapon) (AmE) cachiporra *f*

blacklist¹ /'blæklɪst/ *n* lista *f* negra

blacklist² *vt* poner* en la lista negra

blackmail¹ /'blækmeɪl/ *n* [u] chantaje *m*

b

blackmail² *vt* chantajear, hacerle* chantaje a; **to ~ sb INTO -ING** chantajear a algn PARA QUE (+ *subj*)

black: **~mailer** /'blæk,meɪlər || 'blæk,meɪlə(r)/ *n* chantajista *mf*; **~ Maria** /mə'raɪə/ *n* (colloq) coche *m* or furgón *m* celular, cuca *f* (Chi fam), jaula *f* (Col fam), julia *f* (Méx fam); **~ mark** *n* punto *m* en contra; **~ market** *n* mercado *m* negro

blackness /'blæknəs || 'blæknɪs/ *n* [u] 1 (black color) negrura *f* 2 (darkness) oscuridad *f*

blackout /'blækaʊt/ *n*
A (loss of consciousness) desvanecimiento *m*, desmayo *m*; **to have a ~** tener* or sufrir un desvanecimiento
B (in wartime) *oscurecimiento de la ciudad para que ésta no sea visible desde los aviones enemigos*
C 1 (power failure) apagón *m* 2 (embargo): **a news ~** un bloqueo informativo

black: **~ Sea** *n* **the B~ Sea** el Mar Negro; **~ sheep** *n* oveja *f* negra; **~smith** *n* herrero *m*; **~ tie** *n* (on invitation) traje *m* de etiqueta, smoking *m*, esmoquin *m*

blacktop¹ /'blæktɑːp || 'blæktɒp/ *n* [u] (AmE) 1 (material) asfalto *m* 2 (surface) (colloq) pista *f*

blacktop² *vt* **-pp-** (AmE) asfaltar, pavimentar

black widow *n* viuda *f* negra

bladder /'blædər || 'blædə(r)/ *n* (Anat) vejiga *f*

blade /bleɪd/ *n*
A (of knife, razor) hoja *f*
B (of propeller) pala *f*, paleta *f*
C (Bot) (of grass) brizna *f*

blag -gg- (BrE colloq) *vt* 1 (obtain by deception) conseguir* con camelos (fam), conseguir* con chamullos (Chi fam) 2 (rob with violence) atracar*, asaltar

blah¹ /blɑː/ *n* [u] 1 (nonsense) (colloq) pamplinas *fpl* (fam) 2 (*as interj*) **~, ~, ~** bla, bla, bla (fam), etcétera, etcétera 3 **blahs** *pl*: **to have the ~s** (AmE colloq) estar* con la depre (fam)

blah² *adj* (AmE colloq) pesado, plomizo (fam)

blame¹ /bleɪm/ *vt* 1 echarle la culpa a, culpar; **don't ~ me** no me eches la culpa a mí or no me culpes a mí; **to ~ sb FOR sth** culpar a algn DE algo, echarle la culpa DE algo A algn; **she ~s herself for the accident** se siente culpable del accidente; **to be to ~ for sth** tener* la culpa de algo; **no one's to ~** no es culpa de nadie, nadie tiene la culpa; **you have only yourself to ~** tú tienes toda la culpa; **to ~ sth ON sb/sth** echarle la culpa DE algo A algn/algo 2 (disagree with, criticize) (colloq): **I'm not having any more to do with him — I don't ~ you** no quiero saber nada más de él — y con toda la razón; **you can't ~ me for getting upset** es normal que me molestara ¿no?

blame² *n* [u] 1 (responsibility) culpa *f*; **it's always me that gets the ~** siempre me echan la culpa a mí; **to put** o **lay the ~ on sb** culpar a algn, echarle la culpa a algn; **to take the ~ for sth** asumir la responsabilidad de algo 2 (reproach) (frml): **without ~** libre de culpa (frml)

blameless /'bleɪmləs || 'bleɪmlɪs/ *adj* 1 (irreproachable) ‹*life*› intachable, sin tacha 2 (guiltless) ‹*victim*› inocente

blameworthy /'bleɪm,wɜːrði || 'bleɪm,wɜːði/ *adj* (frml) ‹*person*› culpable; ‹*act*› censurable

blanch /blæntʃ || blɑːntʃ/ *vt* (Culin) escaldar, blanquear
■ **blanch** *vi* «*person*» palidecer*; **he ~ed at the sight of the body** palideció al ver el cadáver

bland /blænd/ *adj* **-er, -est** 1 ‹*colors/music*› soso, insulso, desabrido; ‹*food/taste*› insípido, soso, desabrido; ‹*statement/reply*› anodino, que no dice nada; ‹*smile/manner*› insulso 2 (mild) ‹*diet/food*› suave

blandishments /'blændɪʃmənts/ *pl n* (liter) 1 (inducements) incentivos *mpl* 2 (flatteries) lisonjas *fpl* (liter)

blandly /'blændli/ *adv* ‹*smile*› de manera insulsa

blank¹ /blæŋk/ *adj* 1 (empty) ‹*page/space*› en blanco; ‹*tape*› virgen; **the screen went ~** se fue la imagen (de la pantalla); **my mind went ~** me quedé en blanco; *see also* **blank check** 2 (lifeless): **a ~ expression** un rostro carente de expresión 3 (uncomprehending): **he stared at me in ~ amazement** me miró perplejo 4 (uncompromising) ‹*refusal/rejection*› rotundo, tajante 5 (Mil) ‹*ammunition*› de fogueo

Phrasal verb
• **blank out** [v ▸ o ▸ adv, v ▸ adv ▸ o] borrar

blank² *n* 1 (empty space) espacio *m* en blanco; **can you guess the word? A, ~, ~, C, E** ¿puedes adivinar la palabra? A, raya, raya, C, E; **my mind was a complete ~** me quedé totalmente en blanco 2 ***to draw a ~*** no obtener* ningún resultado 3 (Mil) cartucho *m* de fogueo

blank check, (BrE) **cheque** *n* cheque *m* en blanco; ***to give sb a ~ ~*** darle* a algn carta blanca

blanket¹ /'blæŋkət || 'blæŋkɪt/ *n* 1 (cover) manta *f*, cobija *f* (AmL), frazada *f* (AmL) 2 (layer) manto *m*; **a ~ of snow** un manto de nieve

blanket² *adj* (*before n, no comp*) ‹*measure*› global

blanket³ *vt* cubrir*

blankly /'blæŋkli/ *adv*: **to look at sb ~** mirar a algn sin comprender

blank verse *n* [u] verso *m* blanco

blare¹ /bler || bleə(r)/ *n* estridencia *f*, estruendo *m*

blare² *vi* atronar*; **blaring horns** bocinas atronadoras

Phrasal verb
• **blare out**
A [v ▸ adv ▸ o]: **the radio was blaring out music** el radio emitía música retumbante; **to ~ out an order** dar una orden a gritos
B [v ▸ adv] «*voice*» resonar*, bramar

blarney /'blɑːrni || 'blɑːni/ *n* [u] (colloq) labia *f* (fam)

blasé /blɑː'zeɪ || 'blɑːzeɪ/ *adj* ‹*manner/remark*› displicente; **you sound very ~ about your exams** no parecen preocuparte mucho tus exámenes

blaspheme /blæs'fiːm/ *vi* blasfemar

blasphemous /'blæsfəməs/ *adj* blasfemo

blasphemy /'blæsfəmi/ *n* [u c] (*pl* **-mies**) blasfemia *f*

blast¹ /blæst || blɑːst/ *n*
A (of air, wind) ráfaga *f*; (of water) chorro *m*
B 1 (explosion) (journ) explosión *f* 2 (shock wave) onda *f* expansiva
C (of sound) toque *m*; ***(at) full ~***: **he had the TV on full ~** tenía la tele a todo lo que daba (fam)
D (enjoyable event) (AmE colloq): **it'll be a ~** será el desmadre (fam)

blast² *vt*
A 1 (blow) ‹*rock*› volar*; **they used dynamite to ~ the safe open** usaron dinamita para volar or hacer saltar la caja fuerte 2 (shoot) (journ) acribillar 3 (attack) (journ) atacar*, arremeter contra
B (expressing annoyance) (esp BrE colloq): **~ it!** ¡maldición! (fam); **~ the exam!** ¡al diablo con el examen!

Phrasal verbs
• **blast off** [v ▸ adv] despegar*
• **blast out** [v ▸ prep ▸ o] ‹*message*› emitir a todo volumen; ‹*music*› tocar* a todo lo que da (fam)

blast³ *interj* (BrE colloq) ¡maldición! (fam)

blasted /'blæstəd || 'blɑːstɪd/ *adj* (colloq) maldito (fam), condenado (fam)

blast-off /'blæstɔːf || 'blɑːstɒf/ *n* despegue *m*

blatant /'bleɪtn̩t/ *adj* 1 (unconcealed) ‹*prejudice/disrespect*› descarado, ostensible; ‹*lie*› flagrante; **to be ~ ABOUT sth**: **they're so ~ about it** lo hacen (or dicen etc) con tanto descaro or tanta desfachatez 2 (obvious) ‹*incompetence*› patente

blatantly /'bleɪtn̩tli/ *adv* 1 (openly) descaradamente, abiertamente, ostensiblemente 2 (clearly): **it's ~ untrue** está claro que no es cierto; **it's ~ obvious that ...** está clarísimo que ...

blather /'blæðər || 'blæðə(r)/ *vi* (colloq) parlotear (fam); **what are you ~ing (on) about?** ¿qué tonterías dices? (fam)

blaze¹ /bleɪz/ *n*
A 1 [c] (in grate) fuego *m*; (bonfire) fogata *f*, hoguera *f*; (flames) llamaradas *fpl* 2 [c] (dangerous fire) (journ) incendio *m*
B (dazzling display) (*no pl*): **a ~ of color** un derroche de color; **in a ~ of glory** cubierto de gloria
C **blazes** *pl* (hell) (colloq & euph): **how/what the ~s ... ?** ¿cómo/qué demonios or diablos ... ? (fam); ***like ~s*** (very fast) como un bólido (fam)

blaze² *vi* 1 «*fire*» arder; «*lights*» brillar, resplandecer*; **the sun ~d down** el sol abrasaba 2 «*eyes*» centellear; **she ~d with anger** ardía de indignación

blazer /'bleɪzər || 'bleɪzə(r)/ *n* blazer *m*

blazing /'bleɪzɪŋ/ *adj* ‹*building*› en llamas; ‹*torch*› encendido; ‹*sun*› abrasador; ‹*lights*› resplandeciente; ‹*eyes*› centelleante; ‹*row*› (colloq) violento

bleach¹ /bli:tʃ/ *n* [u c] lejía *f*, blanqueador *m* (Col, Méx), lavandina *f* (Arg), agua *f*‡ Jane® (Ur), cloro *m* (AmC, Chi)

bleach² *vt* ‹*cloth*› (in the sun) blanquear; (with bleach) poner* en lejía (*or* blanqueador *etc*)

bleachers /'bli:tʃərz || 'bli:tʃəz/ *pl n* (AmE) tribuna *f* descubierta

bleak /bli:k/ *adj* **-er, -est** **1** ‹*landscape*› inhóspito; ‹*room*› lóbrego **2** ‹*winter*› crudo; ‹*day*› gris y deprimente **3** (miserable, cheerless) ‹*prospects/news*› sombrío, funesto

bleakly /'bli:kli/ *adv* sombríamente

bleary /'blɪri || 'blɪəri/ *adj* **-rier, -riest** **her eyes were ~ with tears** tenía los ojos empañados *or* nublados de lágrimas

bleary-eyed /'blɪri'aɪd || 'blɪəri'aɪd/ *adj* con cara de sueño; **to be ~ from sleep** tener* cara de sueño

bleat¹ /bli:t/ *vi* balar

bleat² *n* balido *m*

bleed /bli:d/ (*past & past p* **bled** /bled/) *vi* sangrar; **my nose is ~ing** me sale sangre de la nariz; **he bled to death** murió desangrado; **my heart ~s for you** ¡qué lástima me das!

■ **bleed** *vt* **1** (Med) sangrar; ***to ~ sb dry*** chuparle la sangre a algn (fam) **2** ‹*brakes/radiator*› purgar*

bleeding¹ /'bli:dɪŋ/ *n* [u] hemorragia *f*

bleeding² *adj* (BrE sl) ▸**bloody¹ B**

bleeding³ *adv* (BrE sl) ▸**bloody²**

bleep¹ /bli:p/ *n* pitido *m*

bleep² *vi* (BrE) emitir un pitido

bleeper /'bli:pər || 'bli:pə(r)/ *n* (BrE buscapersonas *m*, busca *m* (Esp fam), bip *m* (Méx fam), bíper *m* (Chi)

blemish¹ /'blemɪʃ/ *n* (on skin) imperfección *f*; **a ~ on his reputation** una mancha en su reputación; **a life without ~** (liter) una vida intachable *or* sin tacha

blemish² *vt* ‹*honor/reputation*› manchar

blench /blentʃ/ *vi* **1** (recoil) estremecerse* **2** (turn pale) palidecer*

blend¹ /blend/ *n* combinación *f*, mezcla *f*

blend² *vt* ‹*ingredients/colors*› mezclar, combinar; (in blender) licuar*, pasar por la licuadora

■ **blend** *vi* **1** **~ (together)** «*flavors/colors*» armonizar* **2** (merge) **to ~ WITH/INTO sth**: **the house ~s (in) well with its surroundings** la casa forma un conjunto armonioso con su entorno; **he learned to ~ into the background** aprendió a pasar desapercibido

Phrasal verb

• **blend in**

A [v ▸ o ▸ adv, v ▸ adv ▸ o] ‹*ingredients*› añadir *or* agregar* y mezclar; ‹*make-up*› difuminar, extender*

B [v ▸ adv] (merge, harmonize) armonizar*, no desentonar

blended /'blendəd || 'blendɪd/ *adj* ‹*whisky*› de mezcla

blender /'blendər || 'blendə(r)/ *n* licuadora *f*

bless /bles/ *vt* (*past* **blessed**; *past p* **blessed** *or* (arch) **blest**) **1** (give benediction) bendecir* **2** (favor) (*usu pass*) **to be ~ed WITH sth**: **he is ~ed with good health** goza de buena salud **3** (*in interj phrases*) **~ you!** (to sb who sneezes) ¡salud! *or* (Esp) ¡Jesús!; (expressing gratitude) (colloq) muchísimas gracias; (as benediction) (que) Dios te (*or* los *etc*) bendiga; **he's done all the ironing, ~ him!** (colloq) ha planchado toda la ropa ¡qué tierno! (fam); **Jane, ~ her heart, has offered to put us up** la buena de Jane nos ha ofrecido alojamiento; **~ me/my soul!** (colloq) ¡válgame Dios! **4** (consecrate) ‹*wine/bread/marriage*› bendecir* **5** (adore) bendecir*; **~ the Lord!** ¡bendito *or* alabado sea el Señor!

blessed¹ /blest/ *past & past p of* **bless**

blessed² /'blesəd || 'blesɪd/ *adj* **1** (hallowed) bienaventurado; **the B~ Virgin (Mary)** la Santísima Virgen (María) **2** (fortunate, happy) (arch): **~ are the poor** (Bib) bienaventurados los pobres **3** (damn) (colloq) bendito (fam), dichoso (fam); **it's a ~ nuisance** es un latazo (fam)

blessing /'blesɪŋ/ *n*

A **1** (benediction) bendición *f* **2** (approval) aprobación *f*, consentimiento *m* **3** (of marriage) bendición *f*; (of bread, wine) consagración *f*

B (fortunate thing) bendición *f* (del cielo); ***a ~ in disguise***: **this may turn out to be a ~ in disguise** puede que todo sea para bien *or* para mejor; ***to be a mixed ~*** tener* sus pros y sus contras; ***you should count your ~s*** deberías dar gracias por lo que tienes

blest /blest/ (arch) *past & past pt of* **bless**

blether /'bleðər || 'bleðə(r)/ *vi* ▸**blather**

blew /blu:/ *past of* **blow²**

blight¹ /blaɪt/ *n* [u] **1** (Agr, Hort) añublo *m*; (loosely) peste *f* **2** (curse) plaga *f*, cáncer *m*

blight² *vt* **1** ‹*plant/crop*› arruinar, infestar; ‹*region*› asolar* **2** ‹*career/health*› arruinar; ‹*hopes*› malograr

blighter /'blaɪtər || 'blaɪtə(r)/ *n* (BrE colloq) tipo *m* (fam); **you lucky ~!** ¡qué suertudo eres! (AmL fam), ¡qué potra tienes! *m* (Esp fam)

blimey /'blaɪmi/ *interj* (BrE colloq) ¡caray! (fam), ¡(la) pucha! (esp AmL fam)

blind¹ /blaɪnd/ *adj*

A **1** (Med) ciego; **~ man** ciego *m*; **~ woman** ciega *f*; **to be ~ in one eye** ser* tuerto; **he's been ~ since birth** es ciego de nacimiento; **to go ~** quedarse ciego; **to be ~ TO sth** no ver* algo; **how could I have been so ~?** ¿cómo pude haber sido tan ciego? **2** (Auto) ‹*corner*› de poca visibilidad

B (lacking reason, judgment) ‹*faith/fury*› ciego

C (BrE colloq) (*as intensifier*): **nobody took a ~ bit of notice** nadie le hizo ni pizca de caso (fam)

blind² *vt* **1** (permanently) dejar ciego; **he was ~ed in an accident** perdió la vista en un accidente **2** «*ambition/passion*» cegar*, enceguecer* (AmL); «*light/wealth*» deslumbrar, encandilar; **he was ~ed by her beauty** su belleza lo deslumbró *or* encandiló; **love ~ed her to his faults** el amor le impedía ver sus defectos

blind³ *n*

A (outside window) persiana *f*; (*roller ~*) persiana *f* (de enrollar), estor *m* (Esp); (*venetian ~*) persiana *f* veneciana

B (blind people) (+ *pl vb*) **the ~** los ciegos, los invidentes (frml); ***it's a case of the ~ leading the ~*** tan poco sabe el uno como el otro

blind⁴ *adv* (BrE colloq) (*as intensifier*): **to swear ~ that ...** jurar y perjurar que ...; **to be ~ drunk** estar* más borracho que una cuba (fam)

blind date *n* cita *f* con un desconocido/una desconocida

blinders /'blaɪndərz || 'blaɪndə(r)z/ *n pl* (AmE) (on horse) anteojeras *fpl*

blindfold¹ /'blaɪndfəʊld/ *vt* vendarle los ojos a

blindfold² *n* venda *f* (*para tapar los ojos*)

blindfold³ *adv* con los ojos vendados; **I could do it ~** podría hacerlo con los ojos cerrados

blindfolded /'blaɪndfəʊldəd || 'blaɪndfəʊldɪd/ *adj* con los ojos vendados

blinding /'blaɪndɪŋ/ *adj* ‹*light*› cegador, deslumbrador, enceguecedor (AmL); ‹*headache/pain*› atroz

blindly /'blaɪndli/ *adv* **1** (without seeing) ‹*grope*› a ciegas, a tientas **2** (without reasoning) ‹*follow*› ciegamente

blind man's buff *n* [u] la gallina ciega

blindness /'blaɪndnəs || 'blaɪndnɪs/ *n* [u] ceguera *f*

bling /blɪŋ/ *n* [u] (colloq) bling bling *m* (moda que consiste en adornarse ostentando riqueza mediante joyas caras, ropa de marca, pieles, relojes, etc)

blind: **~ spot** *n* **1** (weak point) punto *m* flaco *or* débil **2** (Auto) punto *m* ciego; **~ test** *n* prueba *f* a ciegas, test *m* ciego

blink¹ /blɪŋk/ *n* parpadeo *m*, pestañeo *m*; ***to be on the ~*** (colloq) no marchar, no andar* bien (AmL); ***to go on the ~*** estropearse, descomponerse* (AmL)

blink² *vi* «*eye/person*» pestañear, parpadear; «*light*» parpadear; **if you ~, you'll miss it!** (colloq & hum) si te descuidas, te lo pierdes

■ **blink** *vt* ‹*eye*› guiñar, picar* (Col); **to ~ back tears** contener* las lágrimas

blinker /'blɪŋkər || 'blɪŋkə(r)/ *n*

A **1** (Auto colloq) intermitente *m*, direccional *f* (Col, Méx), señalizador *m* (Chi) **2** (AmE Transp) señal *f* intermitente

B **blinkers** *pl* (on horse) anteojeras *fpl*

blinkered /'blɪŋkərd || 'blɪŋkəd/ *adj* ‹*attitude*› de miras estrechas; ‹*view/outlook*› estrecho

blinking /'blɪŋkɪŋ/ *adj* **1** ‹*light*› intermitente **2** (BrE colloq): **what a ~ nerve!** ¡qué cara! (fam); **what a ~ idiot!** ¡qué tipo más imbécil! (fam)

blip /blɪp/ *n* 1 (sound) bip *m*, pitidito *m* 2 (irregularity) accidente *m*; (problem) problema *m* pasajero

bliss /blɪs/ *n* [u] dicha *f*, felicidad *f* absoluta

blissful /'blɪsfəl/ *adj* ‹*smile*› de gozo, de gran felicidad; **she babbled on, in ~ ignorance of the fact that ...** siguió parloteando tan tranquila, sin percatarse de que ...

blissfully /'blɪsfəli/ *adv* ‹*smile/sigh*› con gran felicidad; **she was ~ unaware of what was going on** ella, muy tranquila, ni cuenta se daba de lo que estaba pasando; **they were ~ happy** eran completamente felices

blister¹ /'blɪstər || 'blɪstə(r)/ *n* 1 (Med) ampolla *f*; **these shoes give me ~s** estos zapatos me hacen ampollas 2 (on paintwork) ampolla *f*, burbuja *f*

blister² *vi* «*skin/paint*» ampollarse

■ **blister** *vt* ampollar

blistering /'blɪstərɪŋ/ *adj* 1 (hot) ‹*heat/sun*› abrasador; **a ~ hot day** (colloq) un día de calor achicharrante (fam) 2 (harsh, angry) ‹*attack*› virulento

blithe /blaɪð/ *adj* 1 (unconcerned) despreocupado 2 (happy, carefree) risueño

blithely /'blaɪðli/ *adv* alegremente; **he seemed ~ unconcerned** tenía un aire risueño y despreocupado

blithering /'blɪðərɪŋ/ *adj* (colloq) (*before n*): **you ~ idiot!** ¡imbécil! (fam)

blitz¹ /blɪts/ *n* 1 (Aviat, Mil) bombardeo *m* aéreo; **the B~** *el bombardeo alemán de Londres en 1940-41* 2 (intense attack) **~ ON sth**: **this weekend we're going to have a ~ on the garden** (colloq) este fin de semana vamos a atacar el jardín 3 (in US football) carga *f* (defensiva)

blitz² *vt* 1 ‹*area*› bombardear (desde el aire) 2 (AmE Sport) ‹*quarterback*› hacerle* una carga (defensiva) a

blizzard /'blɪzərd || 'blɪzəd/ *n* ventisca *f*, tormenta *f* de nieve

bloated /'bləʊtəd || 'bləʊtɪd/ *adj* ‹*body/face*› hinchado, abotagado; **I feel ~ after all that food** me siento hinchado de tanto comer

blob /blɑːb || blɒb/ *n* 1 (drip) gota *f*, goterón *m* (fam) 2 (indistinct shape) mancha *f*, borrón *m*

bloc /blɑːk || blɒk/ *n* (Pol) bloque *m*

block¹ /blɑːk || blɒk/ *n*

A 1 (of stone, wood) bloque *m*; **the executioner's ~** el tajo del verdugo; ***to knock sb's ~ off*** (colloq) romperle* la crisma a algn (fam) 2 (*starting ~*) (Sport) taco *m* de salida; **to be first off the ~s** ser* el primero en la salida 3 (of paper) bloc *m*

B 1 (space enclosed by streets) manzana *f*; (distance between two streets): **to go for a walk around the ~** dar* una vuelta a la manzana; **it's eight ~s from here** (AmE) está a ocho cuadras (AmL) *or* (Esp) calles de aquí 2 (building): **a ~ of flats** (BrE) un edificio de apartamentos *or* de departamentos (AmL), una casa de pisos (Esp); **an office ~** un edificio de oficinas

C (section of text) sección *f*, bloque *m*

D (Comput) bloque *m*

E 1 (blockage) obstrucción *f*, bloqueo *m*; **I have a mental ~ about physics** tengo un bloqueo mental con la física 2 (obstacle) **~ TO sth** obstáculo *m* PARA algo 3 (embargo) bloqueo *m*; **to put a ~ on sth** bloquear algo

F (Sport) bloqueo *m*

block² *vt*

A 1 (obstruct) ‹*road/entrance*› bloquear; **you're ~ing my way** me estás impidiendo *or* bloqueando el paso; **that fat man is ~ing my view** ese gordo no me deja ver 2 ‹*drain/sink*› atascar*, tapar (AmL); **my nose is ~ed** tengo la nariz tapada

B 1 (prevent) ‹*progress*› obstaculizar*, impedir*; ‹*funds/sale*› congelar, bloquear 2 (Sport) bloquear

■ **block** *vi* (Sport) bloquear

Phrasal verbs

- **block in** [v ▸ o ▸ adv, v ▸ adv ▸ o] (hem in) cerrarle* el paso a
- **block off** [v ▸ o ▸ adv, v ▸ adv ▸ o] ‹*street*› cortar
- **block out** [v ▸ o ▸ adv, v ▸ adv ▸ o] 1 (shut out) ‹*thought*› ahuyentar, borrar de la mente 2 (obstruct) ‹*light*› tapar
- **block up**

A [v ▸ o ▸ adv, v ▸ adv ▸ o] 1 (seal) ‹*entrance/window*› tapiar, cerrar* 2 (cause obstruction in) ‹*drain/sink*› atascar*, tapar (AmL); **my nose is ~ed up** tengo la nariz tapada

B [v ▸ adv] (become obstructed) atascarse*, taparse (AmL)

blockade¹ /blɑː'keɪd || blɒ'keɪd/ *n* bloqueo *m*

blockade² *vt* bloquear

blockage /'blɑːkɪdʒ || 'blɒkɪdʒ/ *n* (in pipe, road) obstrucción *f*; (Med) oclusión *f*

block: **~buster** /'blɑːk,bʌstər || 'blɒk,bʌstə(r)/ *n* (movie) éxito *m* de taquilla; (book) bestseller *m*, superventas *m*; **~ capitals** *pl n* (letras *fpl*) mayúsculas *fpl* de imprenta

blocked /blɑːkt || blɒkt/ *adj* 1 ‹*pipe/artery*› obstruido; ‹*road*› bloqueado, cerrado; **I have a ~ nose** tengo la nariz tapada 2 ‹*account/currency*› bloqueado, congelado

blocked-up /'blɑːkt'ʌp || ,blɒkt'ʌp/ *adj* (*pred* **blocked up**) ‹*pipe/drain*› atascado, tapado (AmL); **to be ~ ~** «*person*» estar* congestionado

block: **~head** *n* (colloq) burro, -rra *m,f* (fam), bruto, -ta *m,f* (fam); **~ letters** *pl n* ▸**block capitals**

blog /blɑːg || blɒg/ *n* blog *m*, bitácora *f*

bloke /bləʊk/ *n* (BrE colloq) tipo *m* (fam), tío *m* (Esp fam)

blond¹ /blɑːnd || blɒnd/ *adj* (*f* **blonde**) rubio *or* (Méx) güero *or* (Col) mono *or* (Ven) catire

blond² *n* (*f* **blonde**) rubio, -bia *m,f or* (Méx) güero, -ra *m,f or* (Col) mono, -na *m,f or* (Ven) catire *mf*

blood /blʌd/ *n* [u]

A sangre *f*; **music is in his ~** lleva la música en la sangre; ***bad ~*** resentimiento *m*, animosidad *f*; **~ *and guts*** (colloq) violencia *f*; ***fresh o new o young ~*** sangre *or* savia *f* nueva; ***in cold ~*** a sangre fría; ***to be out for ~*** estar* buscando con quién desquitarse; **they're out for o after her ~** se la tienen jurada (fam); ***to draw ~*** (lit: wound) sacar* *or* hacer* salir sangre; ***to get ~ out of o from a stone*** sacar* agua de las piedras; **trying to get information from him is like trying to get ~ out of a stone** a él hay que sacarle la información con sacacorchos *or* con tirabuzón; **you can't get ~ out of a stone** no se le puede pedir peras al olmo; ***to have sb's ~ on one's hands*** tener* las manos manchadas con la sangre de algn; ***to make sb's ~ boil***: **it makes my ~ boil to think that ...** me hierve la sangre cuando pienso que ...; ***to make sb's ~ run cold***: **his laugh made my ~ run cold** su risa hizo que se me helara la sangre (en las venas); ***to sweat ~*** (colloq) (work hard) sudar sangre *or* tinta (fam); (be anxious) sudar la gota gorda (fam); (*before n*) **~ cell** *o* **corpuscle** glóbulo *m*; **~ donor** donante *mf* de sangre; **~ group** *o* **type** grupo *m* sanguíneo; **~ poisoning** septicemia *f*; **~ test** análisis *m* de sangre; **~ transfusion** transfusión *f* de sangre

B (lineage, family) sangre *f*; **of noble ~** de sangre noble; **it runs in their ~** lo llevan en la sangre; **~ *is thicker than water*** la familia siempre tira, la sangre tira; (*before n*) **we're not ~ relations** no tenemos lazos de sangre

blood: **~ bath** *n* masacre *f*; **~curdling** /'blʌd,kɜːrdlɪŋ/ *adj* espeluznante, aterrador; **~hound** *n* sabueso *m*

bloodily /'blʌdl̩i || 'blʌdɪli/ *adv*: **the rebellion was ~ suppressed** la rebelión fue sofocada de forma sangrienta

bloodless /'blʌdləs || 'blʌdlɪs/ *adj* 1 (without bloodshed) ‹*coup*› sin derramamiento de sangre 2 (lacking vitality) ‹*person*› sin sangre en las venas

blood: **~mobile** /'blʌdməbiːl/ *n* (AmE) unidad *f* móvil de extracción de sangre; **~ money** *n* [u] dinero *m* sucio (*obtenido a costa de la muerte de algn*); **~ orange** *n* naranja *f* sanguina *or* de sangre; **~ pressure** *n* [u] tensión *f or* presión *f* (arterial); **to have high/low ~ pressure** tener* la tensión *or* presión alta/baja; **~red** /'blʌd'red/ *adj* (*pred* **~ red**) ‹*sky*› teñido de rojo; ‹*rose*› encarnado; **~shed** *n* [u] derramamiento *m* de sangre; **~shot** *adj* rojo, inyectado de sangre; **~ sport** *n* deporte *m* sangriento; **~stain** *n* mancha *f* de sangre; **~-stained** *adj* manchado de sangre; **~stream** *n* **the ~stream** el torrente sanguíneo; **~sucker** *n* (Zool) hematófago *m*; (person) sanguijuela *f* (fam); **~thirsty** *adj* 1 (cruel) sanguinario 2 ‹*story/description*› sangriento; **~ vessel** *n* vaso *m* sanguíneo; ***to burst a ~ vessel*** (colloq): **she nearly burst a ~ vessel when he told her** casi le dio un ataque cuando se enteró (fam)

bloody¹ /'blʌdi/ *adj* **-dier, -diest**

A 1 ‹*hands/clothes*› ensangrentado; ‹*wound*› que sangra, sangrante 2 ‹*battle*› sangriento

B (esp BrE vulg *or* colloq) (*no comp*) (expressing annoyance, surprise, shock etc): **where's that ~ dog?** ¿dónde está ese maldito *or* puñetero *or* (Méx) pinche perro? (fam); **I didn't understand a ~ word!** no entendí ni jota (fam); **turn that ~ television off!** ¡apaga esa televisión, carajo! (vulg); **~ hell!** ¡coño! (vulg), ¡chingado! (Méx vulg), ¡hostias! (Esp vulg)

bloody² *adv* (BrE vulg *or* colloq) (*as intensifier*): **the weather was ~ awful!** ¡hizo un tiempo de mierda! (vulg); **not ~ likely!** ¡ni loco! (fam)

bloody³ *vt* **-dies, -dying, -died** manchar de sangre

bloody-minded /'blʌdi'maɪndəd || ˌblʌdi'maɪndɪd/ *adj* (esp BrE colloq) difícil, empecinado, atravesado (AmL fam)

bloody-mindedness /'blʌdi'maɪndədnəs || ˌblʌdi'maɪndɪdnɪs/ *n* [u] (esp BrE colloq) empecinamiento *m*; **he did it out of sheer ~** lo hizo sólo para fastidiar

bloom¹ /blu:m/ *n*
A 1 [c] (flower) flor *f* 2 [u] **to be in ~** estar* en flor; **to be in full ~** estar* en plena floración
B [u] (on fruits, leaves) vello *m*, pelusa *f*; ***to lose one's ~*** ajarse

bloom² *vi* ‹‹*plant/garden*›› florecer*; ‹‹*flower*›› abrirse*

bloomer /'blu:mər || 'blu:mə(r)/ *n*
A (mistake) (BrE colloq) metedura *f or* (AmL tb) metida *f* de pata
B **bloomers** *pl* (garment) bombachos *mpl*

blooming /'blu:mɪŋ/ *adj* 1 (BrE colloq) (*before n*): **I missed the ~ bus!** ¡perdí el condenado *or* maldito autobús! (fam) 2 (happy and healthy) (*pred*) radiante

blooper /'blu:pər || 'blu:pə(r)/ *n* (esp AmE) metedura *f or* (AmL tb) metida *f* de pata (fam)

blossom¹ /'blɑ:səm || 'blɒsəm/ *n* 1 [u] (mass of flowers) flores *fpl* 2 [c] (by single bloom) flor *f*

blossom² *vi* 1 (flower) ‹‹*tree*›› florecer*, dar* flor 2 (flourish) ‹‹*arts*›› florecer*; ‹‹*person/relationship*›› alcanzar* su plenitud; **to ~ INTO sth: our friendship ~ed into love** nuestra amistad se transformó en amor; **Helen has ~ed (out) into a delightful young woman** Helen se ha convertido en una chica encantadora

blot¹ /blɑ:t || blɒt/ *n* 1 (of ink) borrón *m*, manchón *m* 2 (blemish) **~ (ON sth)**: **the factory is a ~ on the landscape** la fábrica afea *or* estropea el paisaje

blot² **-tt-** *vt* 1 (stain, smear) ‹*page/word*› emborronar, borronear 2 (dry) ‹*ink*› secar* (*con papel secante*)

Phrasal verb
- **blot out** [v ▸ o ▸ adv, v ▸ adv ▸ o] ‹*word*› tachar; ‹*view*› tapar; ‹*memory*› borrar

blotch¹ /blɑ:tʃ || blɒtʃ/ *n* 1 (on skin) mancha *f* 2 (of paint) borrón *m*, manchón *m*

blotch² *vt* ‹*page*› emborronar, borronear

blotchy /'blɑ:tʃi || 'blɒtʃi/ *adj* **blotchier, blotchiest** ‹*skin*› lleno de manchas

blotter /'blɑ:tər || 'blɒtə(r)/ *n* 1 (sheet) hoja *f* de papel secante; (on desktop) carpeta *f*, cartapacio *m* 2 (record book) (AmE) registro *m*; **police ~** fichero *m* de la policía

blotting paper /'blɑ:tɪŋ || 'blɒtɪŋ/ *n* [u] papel *m* secante

blotto /'blɑ:təʊ || 'blɒtəʊ/ *adj* (colloq) (*pred*) como una cuba (fam), tomado (AmL fam)

blouse /blaʊs || blaʊz/ *n* blusa *f*

blow¹ /bləʊ/ *n*
A 1 (stroke) golpe *m*; **to come to ~s** llegar* a las manos; ***at a (single) ~*** de un golpe, a la vez 2 (shock, setback) golpe *m*; **~ TO sb** golpe PARA algn; **his death came as a ~ to us** su muerte fue un duro golpe para nosotros
B (action) soplo *m*, soplido *m*; **to give one's nose a ~** sonarse* la nariz

blow² (*past* **blew**; *past p* **blown**) *vt*
A (propel) soplar; **she blew the ash onto the floor** sopló y echó la ceniza al suelo; **stop ~ing smoke in my face!** ¡no me eches el humo a la cara!; **a gust blew the door shut** una ráfaga de viento cerró la puerta de golpe; **her umbrella was ~n away by the wind** el viento tiró lejos su paraguas; **her hat was ~n off** se le voló el sombrero; **the plane was ~n off course** el viento sacó el avión de su curso; ▸**wind¹ A**
B 1 (make by blowing): **to ~ bubbles** hacer* pompas de jabón 2 (clear): **to ~ one's nose** sonarse* la nariz 3 (play) ‹*note*› tocar*; ‹*signal*› dar*; **the referee blew the whistle** el árbitro tocó *or* hizo sonar el silbato *or* pito; ***to ~ one's own trumpet*** *o* (AmE) ***horn*** darse* bombo, tirarse flores
C 1 (smash) ‹*bridge/safe*› volar*, hacer* saltar; **the car was ~n to pieces** el coche voló en pedazos; **to ~ sb's head off** volarle* la tapa de los sesos a algn; ***to ~ sth sky high***: **this ~s his theory sky high** esto echa por tierra su teoría; **if this goes off, we'll be ~n sky high** como explote, saltamos por los aires 2 (burn out) ‹*fuse*› fundir, hacer* saltar, quemar 3 (burst) ‹*gasket*› reventar*; ***to ~ one's top*** *o* ***lid*** (colloq) explotar, ponerse* hecho una furia
D (colloq) 1 (squander) ‹*money*› despilfarrar, tirar 2 (spoil): **they were getting on well, but he blew it by starting to ...** se estaban llevando bien, pero él lo echó todo a perder cuando empezó a ...; **I blew the oral test** la pifié en el oral (fam), la regué en el oral (Méx fam)
E (*past p* **blowed**) (BrE colloq): **~ me if she didn't make the same mistake!** ¿y no va y se equivoca otra vez?; **I'll be ~ed if I'll apologize!** ¡ya pueden esperar sentados a que pida perdón! (fam)

■ **blow** *vi*
A 1 ‹‹*wind*›› soplar; ***to ~ hot and cold*** dar* una de cal y otra de arena 2 ‹‹*person*›› soplar; **she came up the stairs, puffing and ~ing** subió las escaleras bufando y resoplando
B (be driven by wind): **litter was ~ing everywhere** volaba basura por todas partes; **sand had ~n in under the door** con el viento se había colado arena por debajo de la puerta; **his hat blew off** se le voló el sombrero; **the door blew open** la puerta se abrió con el viento
C (produce sound) ‹‹*whistle*›› sonar*
D (burn out) ‹‹*fuse*›› fundirse, saltar, quemarse

Phrasal verbs
- **blow away** [v ▸ o ▸ adv] (sl) 1 (kill) liquidar (fam) 2 (have strong effect on) (AmE): **that kind of music just ~s me away** ese tipo de música me enloquece (fam); **the tragedy blew me away** la tragedia me dejó anonadado; *see also* **blow²** *vt* **A**
- **blow down**
A [v ▸ o ▸ adv, v ▸ adv ▸ o] tirar (abajo), derribar
B [v ▸ adv] caerse* (*con el viento*)
- **blow in** [v ▸ adv] (colloq) aparecer*, caer* (fam)
- **blow out**
A [v ▸ o ▸ adv, v ▸ adv ▸ o] 1 (extinguish) ‹*match/flame*› apagar* (*soplando*) 2 (shoot) (colloq): **to ~ sb's brains out** saltarle *or* volarle* la tapa de los sesos a algn (fam)
B [v ▸ adv] (become extinguished) ‹‹*candle*›› apagarse*
- **blow over** [v ▸ adv] 1 (be forgotten) ‹‹*trouble*›› caer* en el olvido 2 ‹‹*storm*›› pasar
- **blow up**
A [v ▸ adv] 1 (explode) ‹‹*bomb*›› estallar, hacer* explosión; ‹‹*car*›› saltar por los aires 2 (begin) ‹‹*wind/storm*›› levantarse; ‹‹*conflict*›› estallar; **to ~ up INTO sth**: **the affair blew up into a major scandal** el caso terminó en un gran escándalo 3 (become angry) (colloq) explotar (fam)
B [v ▸ o ▸ adv, v ▸ adv ▸ o] 1 ‹*mine/car*› volar* 2 ‹*balloon*› inflar 3 (colloq) ‹*incident*› exagerar, sacar* de quicio; **it's been ~n up out of all proportion** lo han sacado totalmente de quicio 4 ‹*photo*› ampliar*

blow-by-blow /'bləʊbaɪ'bləʊ/ *adj* (*before n*) ‹*account*› con pelos y señales (fam)

blow-dry¹ /'bləʊdraɪ/ *vt* **-dries, -drying, -dries**: **to ~ one's hair** hacerse* un brushing (*secarse el pelo con secador de mano y cepillo*)

blow-dry² *n* (*pl* **-dries**) brushing *m*

blower /'bləʊər || 'bləʊə(r)/ *n* 1 (fan) calefactor *m* 2 (telephone) (BrE colloq & dated) teléfono *m*

blow: **~gun** *n* (AmE) cerbatana *f*; **~hard** *n* (AmE colloq) fanfarrón, -rrona *m,f*

blown /bləʊn/ *past p of* **blow²**

blow: **~out** *n* 1 (feast) (colloq) comilona *f* (fam) 2 (burst tire) reventón *m*; **we had a ~out** se nos reventó un neumático; **~pipe** *n* cerbatana *f*

blowsy *adj* **-sier, -siest** ▸**blowzy**

blow: **~torch** *n* soplete *m*; **~up** *n* (colloq) (Phot) ampliación *f*

blowy /'bləʊi/ *adj* **-wier, -wiest** (colloq) ‹*day*› ventoso, de mucho viento

blowzy /'blaʊzi/ *adj* **-zier, -ziest**: **a ~ woman** una mujer con pinta de ordinaria (fam)

blubber¹ /'blʌbər || 'blʌbə(r)/ *n* [u] (whale fat) grasa *f* de ballena; (on person) (colloq) grasa *f*

blubber² *vi* (colloq & pej) lloriquear

b

bludgeon /ˈblʌdʒən/ *vt* (strike) aporrear; (bully) coaccionar

blue¹ /bluː/ *adj* **bluer, bluest**

A ‹*dress/sea/sky*› azul; **~ with cold** amoratado de frío; **she went ~ in the face** se le amorató la cara

B (pornographic) (colloq) verde, porno *adj inv*, colorado (Méx)

C (unhappy) (esp AmE) triste, deprimido

blue² *n* azul *m*; ***out of the ~*** ‹*call/arrive*› cuando menos se (*or* me *etc*) lo esperaba

blue: **~bell** *n* jacinto *m* silvestre; **~berry** /ˈbluː,beri || ˈbluːbəri/ *n* arándano *m*; **~-blooded** /ˈbluːˈblʌdəd || ,bluːˈblʌdɪd/ *adj* de sangre azul; **~bottle** *n* mosca *f* azul, moscarda *f*; **~-collar** /ˈbluːˈkɑːlər || ,bluːˈkɒlə(r)/ *adj* ‹*union*› obrero; ‹*job*› manual; **~-collar workers** los obreros; **~-eyed** *adj* de ojos azules; **~-eyed boy** niño *m* mimado; **~ grass** *n* [u] (Bot) *hierba que se usa como forraje*; **~ jay** *n* urraca *f* de América; **~ jeans** *pl n* (esp AmE) vaqueros *mpl*, (blue) jeans *mpl*, bluyines *mpl* (Andes); **~ law** *n* (AmE Law) *ley que prohíbe la realización de ciertas actividades los domingos*; **~nose** *n* (AmE colloq) puritano, -na *m,f*; **~print** *n* (of technical drawing) plano *m*, proyecto *m*; (plan of action) programa *m*; **~-ribbon** /ˈbluːˈrɪbən/ *adj* (elite) (esp AmE) ‹*group/panel*› de élite, selecto

blues /bluːz/ *pl n*

A (depression) (colloq): **the ~** la depre (fam); **to have the ~** estar* con la depre (fam)

B (Mus) blues *m*; **to play/sing (the) ~** tocar*/cantar blues

blue: **~ shark** *n* tiburón *m* azul; **~ tit** *n* alionín *m*, herrerillo *m*

bluff¹ /blʌf/ *vi* hacer* un bluff *or* (Col, Méx) blof

■ **bluff** *vt*: **he managed to ~ his way out of it** logró salir del apuro embaucándolos

bluff² *n*

A [u c] (pretense) bluff *m*, blof *m* (Col, Méx); **to call sb's ~** poner* a algn en evidencia

B [c] (cliff) risco *m*, acantilado *m*

bluff³ *adj* **-er, -est** ‹*person*› francote (fam), campechano

bluish /ˈbluːɪʃ/ *adj* azulado

blunder¹ /ˈblʌndər || ˈblʌndə(r)/ *vi*

A (move clumsily, stumble): **he ~ed into the table** se topó con el jefe en el pasillo; **he ~ed around in the dark** andaba dando tumbos en la oscuridad

B **1** (make mistake) cometer un error garrafal **2** **blundering** *pres p*: **that ~ing idiot!** ¡ese idiota perdido! (fam)

blunder² *n* (mistake) error *m* garrafal; (faux pas) metedura *f or* (AmL tb) metida *f* de pata (fam)

blunderbuss /ˈblʌndərbʌs || ˈblʌndəbʌs/ *n* trabuco *m*

blunt¹ /blʌnt/ *adj* **-er, -est** **1** (not sharp) ‹*pencil*› desafilado, que no tiene punta, mocho (esp AmL); ‹*tip/edge*› romo; ‹*knife*› (BrE) desafilado; **a ~ instrument** un objeto contundente **2** (straightforward) ‹*person/manner*› directo, franco; ‹*refusal*› rotundo, categórico

blunt² *vt* **1** ‹*pencil*› despuntar; ‹*knife/scissors*› desafilar **2** (make dull) ‹*senses/intellect*› embotar

bluntly /ˈblʌntli/ *adv* ‹*say*› sin rodeos, claramente; ‹*refuse*› rotundamente; **to put it ~, you bore me** hablando en plata, me aburres (fam)

bluntness /ˈblʌntnəs || ˈblʌntnɪs/ *n* [u] **1** (of blade) falta *f* de filo; (of point) lo poco afilado, lo mocho (esp AmL) **2** (straightforwardness) franqueza *f*

blur¹ /blɜːr || blɜː(r)/ **-rr-** *vt* ‹*outline*› desdibujar, hacer* borroso; ‹*distinction*› hacer* menos claro; ‹*memory*› hacer* borroso

■ **blur** *vi* «*outline*» desdibujarse, hacerse* borroso

blur² *n*: **everything became a ~** todo se volvió borroso; **a ~ of colors** una masa de colores indistintos

blurb /blɜːrb || blɜːb/ *n* propaganda *f*, nota *f* publicitaria (*en folleto, tapa de libro etc*)

blurred /blɜːrd || blɜːd/ *adj* ‹*outline/vision*› borroso; **the photos were ~** las fotos habían salido mal enfocadas; **I felt dizzy and then everything went ~** me mareé y empecé a verlo todo borroso; **the distinction had become ~ in her mind** ya no veía claramente la diferencia

blurry /ˈblɜːri/ *adj* borroso

blurt /blɜːrt || blɜːt/ *vt* **to ~ sth (out)** espetar algo, soltar* algo (fam)

blush¹ /blʌʃ/ *vi* ruborizarse*, ponerse* colorado *or* rojo, sonrojarse

blush² *n* (*often pl*) rubor *m*; **spare my ~es!** no me hagas pasar vergüenza, no hagas que me ruborice

blusher /ˈblʌʃər || ˈblʌʃə(r)/ *n* [u c] colorete *m*, rubor *m* (Méx, RPl)

bluster¹ /ˈblʌstər || ˈblʌstə(r)/ *vi* **1** (talk threateningly) bravuconear **2** «*wind*» rugir*, bramar

bluster² *n* [u] bravatas *fpl*, bravuconería *f*

blustery /ˈblʌstəri/ *adj* ‹*wind*› borrascoso; ‹*night*› tempestuoso

Blvd (esp AmE) (= **Boulevard**) Blvar., Br.

BMA *n* = **British Medical Association**

B-movie /ˈbiː,muːvi/ *n* película *f* de serie B *or* de bajo presupuesto

bn = **billion**

BNP *n* = **British National Party**

BO *n* [u] (colloq) (= **body odor** *or* (BrE) **odour**) olor *m* a transpiración

boa /ˈbəʊə/ *n* **1** (Zool) boa *f*; **a ~ constrictor** una boa constrictor **2** (Clothing) boa *m or f*

boar /bɔːr || bɔː(r)/ *n* (*pl* **~s** *or* **~**) **1** (male pig) cerdo *m* macho, verraco *m* **2** (*wild* **~**) jabalí *m*

board¹ /bɔːrd || bɔːd/ *n*

A [c] **1** (plank) tabla *f*, tablón *m*; (*floor~*) tabla *f* (del suelo); ***as stiff as a ~*** más tieso que un palo *or* que una tabla; ***to tread the ~s*** pisar las tablas **2** (for chopping etc) tabla *f* (de madera) **3** (*circuit* **~**) placa *f* base

B [c] **1** (*diving* **~**) trampolín *m* **2** (for surfing, windsurfing) tabla *f* (de surf) **3** (Games) tablero *m*; ***to sweep the ~*** arrasar con *or* llevarse todos los premios

C [c] **1** (*notice~*) tablero *m or* (Esp) tablón *m* de anuncios, cartelera *f* (AmL), diario *m* mural (Chi) **2** (sign) letrero *m*, cartel *m* **3** (*score~*) marcador *m* **4** (blackboard) pizarra *f*, pizarrón *m* (AmL), tablero *m* (Col)

D [c] **1** (committee) junta *f*, consejo *m* **2** (administrative body): **the Water/Gas B~** la compañía del agua/gas **3** **~ (of directors)** (Busn) junta *f* directiva, consejo *m* de administración **4** (of examiners) tribunal *m*

E [u] (provision of meals): **~ and lodging** comida y alojamiento; **full/half ~** pensión *f* completa/media pensión *f*

F [u] (*in phrases*) **across the board**: **they have promised to reduce taxation across the ~** han prometido una reducción general de impuestos; **on board** a bordo; **on ~ the ship/plane** a bordo del barco/avión; **to go on ~** embarcarse*; (*before n*) **on-board** ‹*entertainment*› de a bordo; ***to go by the ~***: **all these precautions tend to go by the ~** todas estas precauciones suelen dejarse a un lado; ***to take sth on ~*** ‹*idea*› (BrE) asumir algo

board² *vt*

A (go aboard): **to ~ a ship** embarcar(se)*, abordar (Méx)

B (accommodate) hospedar

■ **board** *vi*

A (go aboard) embarcar(se)*, abordar (Col, Méx)

B (be accommodated) **to ~ WITH sb** alojarse *or* hospedarse en casa de algn

Phrasal verb

• **board up** [v ▸ o ▸ adv, v ▸ adv ▸ o] cerrar* con tablas

boarder /ˈbɔːrdər || ˈbɔːdə(r)/ *n* **1** (lodger) huésped *mf* **2** (at boarding school) (esp BrE) interno, -na *m,f*

board game *n* juego *m* de mesa

boarding /ˈbɔːrdɪŋ || ˈbɔːdɪŋ/: **~ card** *n* ▸**~ pass**; **~ house** *n* pensión *f*, casa *f* de huéspedes; **~ pass** *n* tarjeta *f* de embarque, pase *m* de abordar (Chi, Méx); **~ school** *n* internado *m*

board: **~room** *n* sala *f or* salón *m* de juntas; **~walk** *n* (AmE) *paseo marítimo entarimado*

boast¹ /bəʊst/ *vi* presumir, fanfarronear; **to ~ ABOUT/OF sth** alardear *or* jactarse *or* vanagloriarse DE algo

■ **boast** *vt* **1** (brag): **I won, he ~ed** —gané yo —dijo vanagloriándose **2** (possess) contar* con

boast² *n* (claim) alarde *m*, fanfarronada *f* (fam); (cause of pride): **it is her proud ~ that ...** se jacta de que ...

boaster /ˈbəʊstər || ˈbəʊstə(r)/ *n* presumido, -da *m,f*

boastful /ˈbəʊstfəl/ *adj* jactancioso

boat /bəʊt/ *n* barco *m*; (small, open) bote *m*, barca *f*; **by ~** en barco; ***to be in the same ~*** estar* en la misma situación; ***to rock the ~*** hacer* olas; ▸**burn¹** *vt* **A1**, **miss²** *vt* *Sense* **IB**

boathouse /ˈbəʊthaʊs/ *n* cobertizo *m* (*para botes*)

boating /ˈbəʊtɪŋ/ *n* [u]: **to go ~** ir* a dar un paseo en bote (*or* barca *etc*)

boat: **~load** *n* cargamento *m*; **a ~load of tourists** un barco cargado de turistas; **~man** /ˈbəʊtmən/ *n* (*pl* **-men** /-mən/) barquero *m*; **~ race** *n* regata *f*; **~swain** /ˈbəʊsn̩/ *n* contramaestre *m*

bob¹ /bɑːb || bɒb/ *n*
A **1** (movement of head) inclinación *f* **2** (curtsy) reverencia *f*
B (haircut) melena *f*
C (*pl* ~) (BrE Fin colloq & dated) chelín *m*; **she's not short of a few ~** *o* **of a ~ or two** está forrada (fam)

bob² **-bb-** *vi* (move abruptly): **the cork ~bed up and down on the water** el corcho cabeceaba en el agua
■ **bob** *vt* ‹*head*› inclinar

Phrasal verb
• **bob up** [v ▸ adv] (colloq) aparecer*

Bob /bɑːb || bɒb/: **~'s *your uncle!*** (BrE colloq) ¡listo!, ¡ya está!

bobbin /ˈbɑːbən || ˈbɒbɪn/ *n* bobina *f*, carrete *m*

bobble /ˈbɑːbəl || ˈbɒbəl/ *n* **1** (on hat etc) borla *f*, pompón *m* **2** (AmE Sport) fomble *m*

bobby /ˈbɑːbi || ˈbɒbi/ *n* (*pl* **-bies**) (BrE colloq) bobby *m* (*policía británico*)

bobby: **~ pin** *n* (AmE) horquilla *f*, pasador *m* (Méx), pinche *m* (Chi); **~ socks**, (AmE also) **bobby sox** /sɑːks || sɒks/ *pl n* calcetines *mpl* cortos

bobbysoxer /ˈbɑːbiˌsɑːksər || ˈbɒbiˌsɒksə(r)/ *n* (AmE colloq) quinceañera *f* (fam), calcetinera *f* (Chi)

bobcat /ˈbɑːbkæt || ˈbɒbkæt/ *n* lince *m* rojo

bobsled /ˈbɑːbsled || ˈbɒbsled/, (BrE also) **bobsleigh** /ˈbɑːbsleɪ || ˈbɒbsleɪ/ *n* bobsleigh *m*

bod /bɑːd || bɒd/ *n* **1** (body) (AmE colloq) cuerpo *m*, figura *f* **2** (person) (BrE colloq) tipo, -pa *m,f* (fam); **an odd ~** un bicho raro (fam)

bodacious /bəʊˈdeɪʃəs/ *adj* (AmE dial & hum) ‹*appetite*› voraz; ‹*hurry*› espantoso (fam)

bode /bəʊd/ *vi* (liter): **to ~ well/ill** ser* buena/mala señal
■ **bode** *vt* presagiar, augurar

bodega /bəʊˈdeɪgə || bəˈdiːgə/ *n* (grocery store) (AmE) tienda *f* de comestibles *or* (Méx) de abarrotes, almacén *m* (CS)

bodice /ˈbɑːdəs || ˈbɒdɪs/ *n* (of dress) canesú *m*; (undergarment) corpiño *m*

-bodied /ˈbɑːdid || ˈbɒdid/ *suff*: **big~** corpulento; **green~** de cuerpo verde; *see also* **able-bodied**

bodily¹ /ˈbɑːdl̩i || ˈbɒdɪli/ *adj* (*before n*) corporal, del cuerpo; **~ functions** funciones *fpl* fisiológicas

bodily² *adv*: **they dragged him ~ into the car** lo agarraron y lo metieron en el coche a la fuerza

body /ˈbɑːdi || ˈbɒdi/ *n* (*pl* **bodies**)
A [c] **1** (of human, animal) cuerpo *m*; **~ *and soul*** en cuerpo y alma; ***to keep ~ and soul together*** subsistir, sobrevivir; (*before n*) **~ language** lenguaje *m* corporal **2** (trunk) cuerpo *m* **3** (corpse) cadáver *m*; **a dead ~** un cadáver; ***over my dead ~!*** ¡tendrán (*or* tendrá *etc*) que pasar por encima de mi cadáver!
B **1** [c] (main part — of plane) fuselaje *m*; (— of ship) casco *m*; (Auto) carrocería *f*; (*before n*) **~ shop** taller *m* de carrocería **2** (majority, bulk): **the ~ of sth** el grueso de algo
C **1** [c] (organization) organismo *m* **2** (unit) (*no pl*): **they walked out in a ~** salieron en masa *or* en bloque; **we must act together as a ~** tenemos que actuar unidos **3** [c] (collection): **a ~ of evidence** un conjunto de pruebas; **a growing ~ of opinion** una creciente corriente de opinión **4** [c] (of water) masa *f*
D [c] (object) cuerpo *m*; **foreign ~** cuerpo *m* extraño; **heavenly ~** (poet) cuerpo *m* celeste
E [u] (density — of wine) cuerpo *m*; (— of hair) volumen *m*, cuerpo *m*
F [c] (body stocking) body *m*

body: **~ builder** *n* fisiculturista *mf*; **~ building** *n* [u] fisiculturismo *m*; **~ clock** *n* reloj *m* biológico; **~guard** *n* guardaespaldas *mf*; (group) escolta *f*; **~ search** *n* cacheo *m*; **~ shirt** *n* (AmE) (blouse) blusa *f*; (leotard) body *m*, maillot *m*; **~ stocking** *n* body *m*; **~work** *n* [u] (body) carrocería *f*; (repairing) (AmE) trabajo *m* de carrocería

bog /bɔːg, bɑːg || bɒg/ *n*
A [c u] (swamp) ciénaga *f*; (*peat* ~) tremedal *m*
B [c] (lavatory) (BrE sl) retrete *m*

Phrasal verb
• **bog down**: **-gg-** [v ▸ o ▸ adv] (*usu pass*): **to be ~ged down with work** estar* inundado de trabajo; **don't get ~ged down in details** no te enredes con demasiados detalles

bogey /ˈbəʊgi/ *n* (*pl* **bogeys**)
A (evil spirit) ▸ **bogeyman**
B (nasal mucus) (BrE sl) moco *m* (seco)

bogeyman /ˈbəʊgimæn/ *n* (*pl* **-men** /-men/) coco *m* (fam), cuco *m* (CS, Per fam)

boggle /ˈbɑːgəl || ˈbɒgəl/ *vi*: **the mind ~s** (hum) uno se queda helado *or* pasmado, uno alucina (Esp, Méx fam)

boggy /ˈbɔːgi, ˈbɑːgi || bɒgi/ *adj* **-gier, -giest** cenagoso

BOGOF /ˈbɔːgɔːf || ˈbɒgɒf/ *n* (colloq) (= **buy one, get one free**) dos por uno *m*

bog-standard /ˈbɒgˈstandɑːrd/ *adj* (BrE, colloq) común y corriente *or* (AmL tb colloq) y silvestre

bogus /ˈbəʊgəs/ *adj* ‹*claim/name*› falso; ‹*argument*› falaz; **a ~ company** una empresa fantasma

boil¹ /bɔɪl/ *n*
A (Med) furúnculo *m*
B (boiling point): ***on the ~***: **the vegetables are on the ~** las verduras se están haciendo; **he has another project on the ~** tiene otro proyecto entre manos; ***to bring sth to the ~***: **bring the water to the ~** dejar que el agua rompa el hervor; **they have brought the issue back to the ~** han vuelto a poner el tema sobre el tapete; ***to go off the ~***: **interest in the affair has gone off the ~** ha decaído el interés en el asunto

boil² *vi* **1** (be at boiling point) «*water/vegetables*» hervir*; **the kettle's ~ing!** ¡hierve el agua!; **~ing water** agua hirviendo; **the rice has ~ed dry** el arroz se ha quedado sin agua **2** (be excited): **he was ~ing with rage** le hervía la sangre de rabia
■ **boil** *vt*
A (bring to boiling point) hervir*; (keep at boiling point) hervir*, dejar hervir; (cook in boiling water) ‹*vegetables*› cocer*, hervir*; **~ the eggs for three minutes** cocer *or* hervir los huevos tres minutos
B **boiled** *past p* ‹*potatoes/rice*› hervido; ‹*ham*› cocido; ‹*egg*› (soft) pasado por agua; (hard) duro; **~ed sweet** (BrE) caramelo *m* de fruta

Phrasal verbs
• **boil down** [v ▸ o ▸ adv, v ▸ adv ▸ o] ‹*stock/sauce*› reducir*
• **boil down to** [v ▸ adv ▸ prep ▸ o] reducirse* a; **what it ~s down to is this** en resumidas cuentas, lo que pasa es esto
• **boil over** [v ▸ adv] «*milk*» irse* por el fuego, salirse*; «*pan*» desbordarse; «*person*» perder* el control
• **boil up** [v ▸ adv] (colloq) estarse* preparando

boiler /ˈbɔɪlər || ˈbɔɪlə(r)/ *n* **1** (water heater) (BrE) caldera *f*, calentador *m* **2** (in steam engine) caldera *f*

boiler: **~maker** *n* (AmE colloq) *whisky con cerveza*; **~ room** *n* (BrE) sala *f* de calderas; **~ suit** *n* (BrE) mono *m*, overol *m* (AmL)

boiling /ˈbɔɪlɪŋ/ *adj* (colloq): **this coffee is ~** este café está hirviendo; **I'm ~** estoy asado (fam); **it's ~ hot today/in here** (*as adv*) hace un calor espantoso hoy/aquí

boiling point *n* punto *m* de ebullición; ***to be at/reach ~ ~*** «*situation*» estar*/ponerse* al rojo vivo

boisterous /ˈbɔɪstərəs/ *adj* ‹*game*› bullicioso, escandaloso; ‹*child*› bullicioso

bold /bəʊld/ *adj* **-er, -est**
A (daring) audaz, atrevido
B (impudent) ‹*smile/advances*› descarado, atrevido; **if I may be so ~ as to …** si me permite el atrevimiento de …; ***to make ~ with sth*** usar algo como si fuera propio
C ‹*pattern*› llamativo; ‹*color*› fuerte, vivo

bold (face) *n* [u] negrita *f*

boldly /ˈbəʊldli/ *adv* **1** (daringly) con audacia *or* atrevimiento, audazmente **2** (impudently) descaradamente

boldness /ˈbəʊldnəs || ˈbəʊldnɪs/ *n* [u] **1** (daring) audacia *f* **2** (impudence) descaro *m*, atrevimiento *m* **3** (of colors, design) fuerza *f*

Bolivia /bəˈlɪviə/ *n* Bolivia *f*

Bolivian¹ /bəˈlɪviən/ *adj* boliviano

Bolivian[2] *n* boliviano, -na *m,f*

bollard /ˈbɑːlərd || ˈbɒlɑːd/ *n* 1 (on quay) noray *m*, bolardo *m* 2 (by road) (BrE) baliza *f*

bollix /ˈbɑːlɪks || ˈbɒlɪks/ *vt* ~ **(up)** (AmE sl): **try not to ~ it up this time!** ¡esta vez intenta no cagarla! (vulg); **the numbers are all ~ed (up)** los números están todos liados (fam)

bollocking /ˈbɑːləkɪŋ || ˈbɒləkɪŋ/ *n* (BrE sl): **to give sb a ~** echarle una bronca a algn (fam)

bollocks /ˈbɑːləks || ˈbɒləks/ *pl n* (BrE vulg) 1 (testicles) huevos *mpl* (vulg), pelotas *fpl* (vulg), cojones *mpl* (vulg), tanates *mpl* (Méx vulg) 2 (nonsense) pendejadas *fpl* *or* (Esp) gilipolleces *fpl* *or* (AmS) pelotudeces *or* (Col, RPl) boludeces *fpl* *or* (Andes, Ven) huevadas *fpl* (vulg)

bologna /bəˈləʊni || bəˈləʊnjə/ *n* [u] (AmE) *tipo de salchicha ahumada*

bolognese /ˈbəʊləˈniːz || ˌbɒləˈneɪz/ *adj*: ~ **sauce** salsa *f* boloñesa, ≈ tuco *m* (RPl)

Bolshevik[1] /ˈbəʊlʃəvɪk || ˈbɒlʃəvɪk/ *n* bolchevique *mf*

Bolshevik[2] *adj* bolchevique

bolshie, bolshy /ˈbəʊlʃi || ˈbɒlʃi/ *adj* **-shier, -shiest** (BrE colloq) rebelde, díscolo

bolster[1] /ˈbəʊlstər || ˈbəʊlstə(r)/ *vt* **to ~ (up)** ‹*popularity/economy*› reforzar*; ‹*argument*› reafirmar; ‹*morale*› levantar

bolster[2] *n* cabezal *m* (*almohada de forma cilíndrica*)

bolt[1] /bəʊlt/ *n*

A (Tech) tornillo *m*, perno *m*

B 1 (on door) pestillo *m*, pasador *m*, cerrojo *m* 2 (on firearm) cerrojo *m*

C ~ **(of lightning)** relámpago *m*, rayo *m*

D (dash) **to make a ~ for sth**: **I made a ~ for the door** corrí *or* me lancé hacia la puerta

bolt[2] *vt*

A (fasten with bolt) atornillar, sujetar con un tornillo *or* perno; **the tables are ~ed to the floor** las mesas están atornilladas al suelo

B ‹*door*› echarle el pestillo *or* el pasador *or* el cerrojo a

C ~ **(down)** ‹*food/meal*› engullir*

■ **bolt** *vi* «*horse*» desbocarse*; «*person*» salir* disparado

bolt[3] *adv*: ~ **upright** muy erguido; **he suddenly sat ~ upright in bed** se irguió de repente en la cama

bomb[1] /bɑːm || bɒm/ *n*

A (Mil) (explosive device) bomba *f*; **the room looked as if a ~ had hit it** (colloq) la habitación estaba toda patas arriba (fam); (*before n*) ~ **scare** amenaza *f* de bomba; ~ **squad** (colloq) brigada *f* antiexplosivos *or* de explosivos

B (flop) (AmE colloq) desastre *m* (fam)

C (large sum) (BrE colloq) (*no pl*): ***to cost a ~*** costar* un dineral

bomb[2] *vt*

A (from air) bombardear; (plant bomb in) colocar* una bomba en

B (condemn) (AmE colloq) poner* por los suelos (fam)

■ **bomb** *vi* (colloq)

A (flop) «*play*» ser* un fracaso, tronar* (Méx fam)

B (go fast) (BrE) **to ~ along** ir* a todo lo que da (fam)

bombard /bɑːmˈbɑːrd || bɒmˈbɑːd/ *vt* 1 (Mil) bombardear 2 (assail) **to ~ sb WITH sth**: **she was ~ed with questions** la acribillaron *or* bombardearon a preguntas

bombardment /bɑːmˈbɑːrdmənt || bɒmˈbɑːdmənt/ *n* [u c] bombardeo *m*

bombastic /bɑːmˈbæstɪk || ˌbɒmˈbæstɪk/ *adj* (frml) grandilocuente, bombástico

bomb disposal *n* [u] desactivación *f* de explosivos; (*before n*) ~ ~ **expert** artificiero, -ra *m,f*

bombed /bɑːmd || bɒmd/ *adj* (AmE colloq) (*pred*): **to be ~** estar* como una cuba (fam), estar* tomado (AmL fam)

bomber /ˈbɑːmər || ˈbɒmə(r)/ *n* 1 (aircraft) bombardero *m* 2 (terrorist) terrorista *mf* (*que perpetra atentados colocando bombas*)

bomber jacket *n* chaqueta *f* *or* (Esp) cazadora *f* *or* (Méx) chamarra *f* *or* (RPl) campera *f* de aviador

bombing /ˈbɑːmɪŋ || ˈbɒmɪŋ/ *n* [c u] 1 (from aircraft) bombardeo *m* 2 (by terrorists) atentado *m* (terrorista)

bombshell /ˈbɑːmʃel || ˈbɒmʃel/ (shocking news) *n* bomba *f*; **the news of their divorce came as a ~** la noticia de su divorcio cayó como una bomba; **a blonde ~** (colloq) una rubia explosiva (fam & period)

bona fide /ˈbəʊnəfaɪd || ˌbəʊnəˈfaɪdi/ *adj* genuino, auténtico

bonanza /bəˈnænzə/ *n* 1 (piece of luck) filón *m*, mina *f* de oro 2 (plentiful supply) superabundancia *f*, gran oferta *f*

bond[1] /bɑːnd || bɒnd/ *n*

A [c] 1 (link) vínculo *m*; **the ~ between mother and child** el vínculo afectivo entre madre e hijo 2 **bonds** *pl* (fetters) cadenas *fpl*

B [u] (adhesion) adherencia *f*

C (Fin) [c] (debt certificate) bono *m*, obligación *f*; **my word is my ~** puedes fiar de *or* confiar en mi palabra

bond[2] *vi* 1 (stick) adherirse* 2 (form relationship) establecer* vínculos *or* lazos afectivos

■ **bond** *vt* (stick) **to ~ sth TO sth** adherir* *or* pegar* algo A algo

bondage /ˈbɑːndɪdʒ || ˈbɒndɪdʒ/ *n* [u] (enslavement) (liter) cautiverio *m* (liter), esclavitud *f*

bonded /ˈbɑːndəd || ˈbɒndɪd/ *adj* 1 (esp AmE) ‹*guard/salesperson*› protegido por seguro de infidelidad 2 ‹*goods*› en depósito aduanero; ~ **warehouse** (almacén *m* de) depósito *m*

bonding /ˈbɑːndɪŋ || ˈbɒndɪŋ/ *n* [u] (Psych) vinculación *f* afectiva *or* emocional

bondsman /ˈbɑːndzmən || ˈbɒndzmən/ *n* (*pl* **-men** /-mən/) (AmE Law) aval *m*, fiador *m*

bone[1] /bəʊn/ *n* 1 [c u] (Anat) hueso *m*; **I can feel it in my ~s** tengo ese presentimiento; **meat on/off the ~** carne *f* con/sin hueso; **the bare ~s (of sth)** lo básico (de algo); **he cut his finger to the ~** se cortó el dedo hasta el hueso; ***as dry as a ~*** requeteseco; ***to be a ~ of contention*** ser* la manzana de la discordia; ***to be close to the ~*** pasarse de castaño oscuro (fam); ***to have a ~ to pick with sb*** tener* que ajustar cuentas con algn; ***to make no ~s about sth***: **she makes no ~s about being an atheist** no esconde *or* no oculta que es atea 2 [c] (of fish) espina *f* 3 [c] **bones** *pl* (of dead person) restos *mpl*, huesos *mpl* (fam)

bone[2] *vt* ‹*meat*› deshuesar; ‹*fish*› quitarle las espinas a

Phrasal verb

• **bone up on** [v ▸ adv ▸ prep ▸ o] (colloq) estudiar

bone: ~ **china** *n* [u] porcelana *f* fina; **~-dry** /ˈbəʊn ˈdraɪ/ (*pred* ~ **dry**) *adj* completamente seco; **~head** *n* (colloq) estúpido, -da *m,f*; **~headed** /ˈbəʊnˈhedəd || ˈbəʊn ˈhedɪd/ *adj* (colloq) estúpido; ~ **idle** *adj* (BrE colloq) haragán, flojo (fam)

boner /ˈbəʊnər || ˈbəʊnə(r)/ *n* (AmE colloq) metedura *f* *or* (AmL tb) metida *f* de pata (fam)

bonfire /ˈbɑːnfaɪr || ˈbɒnfaɪə(r)/ *n* hoguera *f*, fogata *f*; (*before n*) ~ **night** (in UK) ▸ **Guy Fawkes Night**

Bonfire Night

Cada 5 de noviembre los británicos celebran *Bonfire Night* para conmemorar la Conspiración de la Pólvora (*the Gunpowder Plot*). En esa misma fecha en 1605, un grupo de conspiradores católicos, encabezado por Guy Fawkes, intentaron volar el Parlamento inglés cuando el rey Jaime I se encontraba en su interior. Sin embargo, fueron descubiertos y ejecutados. En la actualidad es un acontecimiento que carece de significado político o religioso. Se lanzan fuegos artificiales y se encienden hogueras en las que se quema un muñeco de trapo (*guy*) que representa a Guy Fawkes

bonhomie /ˈbɑːnəˈmiː || ˈbɒnəmiː/ *n* [u] cordialidad *f*

bonk /bɑːŋk || bɒŋk/ *vt* (hit) (colloq): **to ~ sb on the nose** pegarle* *or* darle* un golpe en la nariz a algn

■ **bonk** *vi* (BrE sl) echar(se) un polvo (fam)

bonkers /ˈbɑːŋkərz || ˈbɒŋkəz/ *adj* (BrE sl & hum) (*pred*) **to be ~** estar* chiflado (fam); **to go ~** perder* la chaveta (fam)

bonnet /ˈbɑːnət || ˈbɒnɪt/ *n*

A (Clothing) sombrero *m*; (for baby) gorrito *m*

B (BrE Auto) capó *m*, capote *m* (Méx)

bonus /ˈbəʊnəs/ *n*

A 1 (payment to employee) plus *m*, prima *f*, bonificación *f* 2 (in competition): **for a ~ of two points** para ganar dos puntos extra

B (added advantage): **(added) ~** ventaja *f*

bony /ˈbəʊni/ *adj* **bonier, boniest** 1 ‹*knee*› huesudo 2 (made of bone) óseo

boo¹ /buː/ *interj* ¡bu!; ***he/she wouldn't say ~ to a goose*** (BrE) es incapaz de matar una mosca

boo² *n* ≈ silba *f*, ≈ rechifla *f*

boo³, **boos, booing, booed** *vt* abuchear; **she was ~ed off the stage** la abuchearon y tuvo que abandonar el escenario

■ **boo** *vi* abuchear

boob /buːb/ *n* (colloq)

A (blunder) metedura *f* *or* (AmL tb) metida *f* de pata (fam); **to make a ~** meter la pata (fam)

B (breast) teta *f* (fam *o* vulg), pechuga *f* (fam & hum)

C (foolish person) (AmE) bobo, -ba *m,f* (fam)

boo-boo /ˈbuːbuː/ *n* ▸ **boob A**

booby /ˈbuːbi/: **~ hatch** *n* (AmE sl) loquero *m* (fam); **~ prize** *n* premio *m* al peor; **~ trap** *n* (Mil) trampa *f*; (bomb) bomba *f* trampa; **~-trap** *vt* **-pp-** (Mil): **his car was ~-trapped** le pusieron una bomba en el coche

booger /ˈbʊgər || ˈbuːgə(r)/ *n* (AmE colloq) moco *m* (seco)

boogey-man /ˈbʊgimæn || ˈbuːgimæn/ *n* (AmE) ▸ **bogeyman**

boogie /ˈbʊgi || buːgi/ *vi* **-gies, -gying, -gied** (colloq) bailar

boo-hoo /ˈbuːˈhuː/ *interj* ¡buuah!

booing /ˈbuːɪŋ/ *n* [u] abucheo *m*

book¹ /bʊk/ *n*

A (printed work) libro *m*; **it sounds like something out of a ~** parece de cuento; **the good B~** (frml) la Biblia; **by** *o* **according to the ~** ciñéndose a las reglas *or* normas; **to go by the ~** ceñirse* (estrictamente) a las normas *or* reglas; **in my ~** a mi modo de ver; ***to be a closed ~ to sb*** ser* un misterio para algn; ***to be an open ~*** ser* (como) un libro abierto; ***to be in sb's good/bad ~s***: (colloq) **I'm in her bad ~s now** en este momento no soy santo de su devoción; **try to get into her good ~s** trata de conquistártela; ***to bring sb to ~*** pedirle* cuentas a algn; **to be brought to ~** tener* que rendir cuentas; ***to read sb like a ~***: **don't tell me stories, I can read you like a ~** a mí no me vengas con cuentos, que yo ya te conozco; ***to throw the ~ at sb*** castigar* duramente a algn; (*before n*) **~ club** club *m* del libro, círculo *m* de lectores; **~ review** reseña *f* (*de un libro*)

B 1 (*exercise ~*) cuaderno *m* 2 (*note~*) libreta *f* *or* cuaderno *m* (de apuntes) 3 (*telephone ~*) (colloq) guía *f*, directorio *m* (AmL exc CS)

C (set — of samples) muestrario *m*; (— of matches, stamps) librito *m*

D **books** *pl* 1 (Busn, Fin): **the ~s** los libros; **to keep** *o* **do the ~s** llevar los libros *or* la contabilidad 2 (of club, agency) registro *m*; **are you on our ~s?** ¿está inscrito aquí?

E (betting) (AmE): **I'd make ~ they'll lose the game!** me apuesto *or* me juego la cabeza a que pierden el partido

book² *vt*

A 1 ‹*room/seat/flight*› reservar; ‹*appointment*› concertar*; **the hotel/flight is fully ~ed** el hotel/vuelo está completo; **we're fully ~ed until June** hasta junio no nos queda nada; **I'm ~ed (up) all this week** tengo toda la semana ocupada 2 ‹*performer*› contratar

B (record) ‹*order*› asentar*

C 1 (record charge against) multar, ponerle* una multa a 2 (in soccer) (BrE) amonestar

■ **book** *vi* hacer* una reserva

Phrasal verbs

• **book in** (esp BrE)

A [v ▸ adv] (register arrival) (BrE) inscribirse*, registrarse

B [v ▸ o ▸ adv, v ▸ adv ▸ o] (reserve room for): **she'd ~ed us in at the Hilton** nos había reservado habitación en el Hilton

• **book up** [v ▸ o ▸ adv, v ▸ adv ▸ o] (reserve) (*often pass*): **the hotels are all ~ed up** los hoteles están todos completos; **tonight's performance is ~ed up** no quedan localidades para la función de esta noche

bookable /ˈbʊkəbəl/ *adj* (BrE) 1 ‹*seat*› que se puede reservar 2 (Sport) ‹*offense*› que se sanciona con tarjeta amarilla

book: **~binding** *n* [u] encuadernación *f* (de libros); **~case** *n* biblioteca *f*, estantería *f*, librería *f* (Esp), librero *m* (Méx); **~end** *n* sujetalibros *m*

bookie /ˈbʊki/ *n* (colloq) ▸ **bookmaker**

booking /ˈbʊkɪŋ/ *n* (esp BrE) 1 [c u] (reservation) reserva *f*, reservación *f* (AmL); (*before n*) **~ fee** suplemento *m*, recargo *m* 2 [c] (engagement) compromiso *m*

booking office *n* (BrE Theat) taquilla *f*, boletería *f* (AmL)

bookish /ˈbʊkɪʃ/ *adj* ‹*style*› libresco; **one of those ~ types** un ratón de biblioteca (fam)

book: **~keeper** *n* tenedor, -dora *m,f* de libros, contable *mf* (Esp); **~keeping** *n* [u] contabilidad *f*, teneduría *f* de libros

booklet /ˈbʊklət || ˈbʊklɪt/ *n* folleto *m*

book: **~list** *n* (of bookseller, publisher) catálogo *m* de libros; (reading list) bibliografía *f*; **~maker** *n* corredor, -dora *m,f* de apuestas; **~mark** *n* señalador *m*, marcador *m*; **~mobile** /ˈbʊkməbiːl/ *n* (AmE) biblioteca *f* ambulante; **~plate** *n* ex libris *m*; **~seller** *n* librero, -ra *m,f*; **~shelf** *n* 1 (shelf) estante *m*, balda *f* (Esp) (*para libros*) 2 **~shelves** ▸ **bookcase**; **~shop** *n* librería *f*; **~stall** *n* (in station) quiosco *m* (*de prensa y libros*); **~store** *n* (AmE) librería *f*; **~ token** *n* (BrE) cheque *m* regalo *m*, vale *m* (*canjeable por libros*); **~worm** *n* ratón *m* de biblioteca (fam)

boom¹ /buːm/ *n*

A (Econ, Fin) boom *m*; (*before n*) **~ industry** industria *f* en auge

B (sound — of waves, wind) bramido *m*; (— of guns, explosion) estruendo *m*

boom² *vi*

A «*guns*» tronar*; «*voice/thunder*» retumbar

B (*usu in -ing form*) «*market/industry*» vivir un boom

Phrasal verb

• **boom out** [v ▸ adv] retumbar, resonar*

boomerang¹ /ˈbuːməræŋ/ *n* bumerang *m*

boomerang² *vi* tener* el efecto contrario al buscado

booming /ˈbuːmɪŋ/ *adj* 1 ‹*sound*› retumbante 2 ‹*industry*› en auge

boon /buːn/ *n* (blessing) gran ayuda *f*

boondocks /ˈbuːndɑːks || ˈbuːndɒks/ *pl n* (AmE colloq & hum), **boonies** /ˈbuːniːz/ *pl n* (AmE sl): **the ~** los quintos infiernos (fam)

boondoggle /ˈbuːnˌdɑːgəl || ˈbuːnˌdɒgəl/ *n* (AmE colloq) despilfarro *m*

boor /bʊr || bʊə(r), bɔː(r)/ *n* grosero, -ra *m,f*

boorish /ˈbʊrɪʃ || ˈbʊərɪʃ, ˈbɔː-/ *adj* zafio, grosero

boost¹ /buːst/ *n* [c] (uplift): **to give a ~ to sth** dar* empuje a algo, estimular algo; **it was a tremendous ~ to her confidence** le dio mucha más confianza en sí misma

boost² *vt* ‹*economy/production*› estimular; ‹*sales*› aumentar, incrementar; ‹*morale*› levantar; **to ~ sb's confidence** darle* más confianza en sí mismo a algn

booster /ˈbuːstər || ˈbuːstə(r)/ *n* 1 (Rad, Telec, TV) repetidor *m* 2 (Auto) booster *m* 3 (Med) **~ (shot)** (vacuna *f* de) refuerzo *m*

booster cable *n* (AmE) cable *m* de arranque

boot¹ /buːt/ *n*

A (Clothing) bota *f*; (short) botín *m*; **a pair of ~s** unas botas, un par de botas; ***the ~'s on the other foot now*** se ha vuelto la tortilla; ***to be as tough as an old ~*** *o* (BrE) ***old ~s*** (colloq) «*meat*» estar* como una suela de zapato; «*person*» ser* muy fuerte; ***to die with one's ~s on*** *o* ***in one's ~s*** morir* con las botas puestas; ***to lick sb's ~s*** (colloq) adular a algn, hacerle* la pelota *or* (Méx) la barba *or* (Chi) la pata a algn (fam), chuparle las medias a algn (RPl fam), lambonear a algn (Col fam); ***to put*** *o* ***stick the ~ in*** (BrE colloq) dar* patadas; ▸ **big¹ F**

B (kick) (colloq) (*no pl*) patada *f*, puntapié *m*; ***to give sb the ~*** (colloq) echar a algn, darle* la patada a algn (fam)

C (BrE Auto) maletero *m*, portamaletas *m*, cajuela *f* (Méx), baúl *m* (Col, CS, Ven), maleta *f* (Chi), maletera *f* (Per)

D **to boot** (hum) (*as linker*) para rematarla, por si fuera poco

boot² *vt* 1 (kick) (colloq) darle* un puntapié a; **he ~ed the ball into the net** metió el balón en la red de una patada 2 (Comput) **~ (up)** cargar*, hacer* el cebado de

Phrasal verb

• **boot out** [v ▸ o ▸ adv, v ▸ adv ▸ o] (colloq) echar, poner* de patitas en la calle (fam)

boot camp *n* (AmE) *campamento de entrenamiento de reclutas de Marina*

bootee, (AmE also) **bootie** /'bu:ti: || bu:'ti:/ *n* (for baby) botita *f* (*de punto*); (for woman) botín *m*

booth /bu:θ || bu:ð, bu:θ/ *n* 1 (cabin) cabina *f*; **ticket ~** taquilla *f*, boletería *f* (AmL); **photo ~** fotomatón *m* 2 (*polling ~*) cabina *f* de votación 3 (*telephone ~*) cabina *f* (de teléfono) 4 (stall — at fair) barraca *f*, caseta *f*; (— at exhibition) stand *m*

bootleg¹ /'bu:tleg/ *vt* **-gg-** ‹*liquor*› dedicarse* al contrabando de; **to ~ tapes** grabar y vender cintas piratas

bootleg² *adj* (*before n*) ‹*liquor*› de contrabando; ‹*tape*› pirata *adj inv*

bootlegger /'bu:t,legər || 'bu:t,legə(r)/ *n* contrabandista *mf*

booty /'bu:ti/ *n* [u] botín *m*

booze¹ /bu:z/ *n* [u] (colloq) bebida *f*, trago *m* (esp AmL fam)

booze² *vi* (colloq) beber, tomar (esp AmL)

boozer /'bu:zər || 'bu:zə(r)/ *n* (colloq) 1 (drinker) borrachín, -china *m,f* (fam) 2 (pub) (BrE) bar *m*

booze-up /'bu:zʌp/ *n* (BrE colloq) juerga *f* (fam)

boozy /'bu:zi/ *adj* **-zier, -ziest** (colloq) ‹*person*› borrachín (fam); **a ~ meal** una comida regada con abundante alcohol

bop¹ /bɑ:p || bɒp/ *n*
A (dance) (BrE colloq): **to go for a ~** ir* a bailar
B (blow) (colloq): **a ~ on the head** un coscorrón (fam)

bop² **-pp-** (colloq) *vi* (BrE) bailar
■ **bop** *vt* (hit): **to ~ sb** pegarle* un coscorrón a algn (fam)

bordello /bɔ:r'deləʊ || bɔ:'deləʊ/ *n* burdel *m*

border¹ /'bɔ:rdər || 'bɔ:də(r)/ *n*
A (Pol) frontera *f*; **Paraguay has ~s with three countries** Paraguay limita con tres países; (*before n*) ‹*dispute/town*› fronterizo
B 1 (edge) borde *m* 2 (edging — on fabric, plate) cenefa *f*
C (in garden) arriate *m*, cantero *m* (RPl)

border² *vt* 1 ‹*country/state*› limitar con; ‹*fields/lands*› lindar con; **~ing states** estados *mpl* limítrofes *or* fronterizos 2 (edge — with ribbon, binding) ribetear; **the plates were ~ed with a blue band** los platos tenían una cenefa azul

Phrasal verb

• **border on**, **border upon** [v ▸ prep ▸ o] 1 ‹‹*country*›› limitar con 2 (verge on) rayar en, lindar con

border: **~land** *n* [u c] zona *f* fronteriza; **~line** *adj* ‹*case/score*› dudoso; ‹*candidate*› en el límite entre el aprobado y el reprobado *or* (Esp) el suspenso; **a ~line pass** un aprobado muy justo

bore¹ /bɔ:r || bɔ:(r)/ *past of* **bear¹**

bore² *vt*
A ‹*shaft/tunnel*› hacer*, abrir*; **they ~d a hole into the rock** hicieron una perforación en la roca
B (weary) aburrir
■ **bore** *vi* perforar, taladrar; **they are boring for oil** están haciendo perforaciones en busca de petróleo

bore³ *n*
A (person) pesado, -da *m,f* (fam), pelmazo *m* (fam), plomo *m* (fam); (thing) aburrimiento *m*, pesadez *f* (fam), lata *f* (fam)
B (of cylinder, gun barrel) calibre *m*; **12-~ shotgun** (BrE) escopeta *f* de calibre 12

bored /bɔ:rd || bɔ:d/ *adj* aburrido; **to be ~ WITH sth** estar* aburrido DE algo; **to get ~** aburrirse

boredom /'bɔ:rdəm || 'bɔ:dəm/ *n* [u] aburrimiento *m*

boring /'bɔ:rɪŋ/ *adj* aburrido, aburridor (AmL)

born¹ /bɔ:rn || bɔ:n/ (*past p of* **bear¹**): **to be ~** nacer*; **when was she ~?** ¿cuándo nació?; **to be ~ lucky** nacer* con suerte; **poets are ~ not made** los poetas nacen, no se hacen; **with the confidence ~ of experience** con la confianza que da la experiencia; **to be ~ TO sth/to + INF**: **he was ~ to (a life of) luxury** nació para (ser) rico; **this is what I was ~ for** *o* **what I was ~ to do** yo he nacido para esto; **I wasn't ~ yesterday, you know!** ¡oye, que no nací ayer!; **there's one ~ every minute!** (set phrase) hay tontos para repartir

born² *adj* (*before n*) ‹*teacher/leader*› nato; **in all my ~ days** (colloq) en toda mi vida; **he's a ~ loser** siempre ha sido y será un perdedor

-born /'bɔ:rn || bɔ:n/ *suff*: **Austrian~/Dallas~** nacido en *or* oriundo de Austria/Dallas

born-again /'bɔ:rnə'gen || ,bɔ:nə'gen/ *adj* (*before n*): **~ Christian** *cristiano convertido, especialmente a una secta evangélica*

borne /bɔ:rn || bɔ:n/ *past p of* **bear¹**

borough /'bɜ:rəʊ || 'bʌrə/ *n* 1 (in New York, London) ≈ municipio *m*; **the Five B~s** la ciudad de Nueva York 2 (in US) distrito *m* municipal 3 (in UK) municipio *m* 4 (in Alaska) condado *m*

borrow /'bɑ:rəʊ || 'bɒrəʊ/ *vt*
A 1 (have on loan): **may I ~ your pencil?** ¿me prestas *or* (Esp tb) me dejas el lápiz?; **the ladder is ~ed** la escalera es prestada; **to ~ sth FROM sb** pedirle* prestado algo A algn; **I ~ed a ladder from Tim** le pedí una escalera prestada a Tim; **I ~ed $5,000 from the bank** pedí un préstamo de 5.000 dólares al banco; **he was living on ~ed time** tenía los días contados 2 (from library) sacar*
B ‹*idea*› sacar*; ‹*word*› tomar; **a term ~ed from German** un préstamo del alemán, una palabra tomada del alemán

borrower /'bɑ:rəʊər || 'bɒrəʊə(r)/ *n* 1 (Fin) prestatario, -ria *m,f* 2 (from library) usuario, -ria *m,f*

borrowing /'bɑ:rəʊɪŋ || 'bɒrəʊɪŋ/ *n* [u] (Fin) préstamos *mpl*

borstal /'bɔ:rstl̩ || 'bɔ:stəl/ *n* (formerly in UK) reformatorio *m*

Bosnia Herzegovina /'bɑ:zniə,hertsəgəʊ'vi:nə || ,bɒzniə,hɜ:tsəgəʊ'vi:nə/ *n* Bosnia Herzegovina *f*

Bosnian¹ /'bɑ:zniən || 'bɒzniən/ *adj* bosnio

Bosnian² *n* bosnio, -nia *m,f*

bosom /'bʊzəm/ *n* 1 (breast, chest) (liter) pecho *m*; (*before n*) ‹*friend*› del alma, íntimo 2 (of woman — bust) pecho *m*, busto *m*; (— breast) pecho *m*, seno *m* 3 (heart, center) (liter) seno *m*

boss /bɑ:s || bɒs/ *n* (colloq) 1 (superior) jefe, -fa *m,f*; (employer, factory owner) patrón, -trona *m,f*; **you decide, you're the ~** decídelo tú, que eres el que manda; **I want to be my own ~** quiero ser mi propio patrón 2 (leader) dirigente *mf*; **union ~es** dirigentes *mpl* sindicales; **a Mafia ~** un capo de la Mafia

Phrasal verb

• **boss around**, (BrE also) **boss about** [v ▸ o ▸ adv] (colloq) mandonear (fam)

bossily /'bɑ:sl̩i || 'bɒsɪli/ *adv* ‹*say*› en tono autoritario; ‹*behave*› de manera autoritaria

bossy /'bɑ:si || 'bɒsi/ *adj* **bossier, bossiest** (colloq) mandón (fam)

bosun /'bəʊsn̩/ *n* ▸ **boatswain**

botanic /bə'tænɪk/, **-ical** /-ɪkəl/ *adj* botánico, de botánica; **~ gardens** jardín *m* botánico

botanist /'bɑ:tn̩əst || 'bɒtənɪst/ *n* botánico, -ca *m,f*

botany /'bɑ:tn̩i || 'bɒtəni/ *n* [u] 1 (subject) botánica *f* 2 (of particular place) flora *f*

botch¹ /bɑ:tʃ || bɒtʃ/ *vt* (colloq) **~ (up)** ‹*repair*› hacer* una chapuza de (fam); ‹*plan*› estropear

botch², **botch-up** /'bɑ:tʃʌp || 'bɒtʃʌp/ *n* (colloq) chapuza *f* (fam); **to make a ~ of sth** hacer* una chapuza de algo (fam)

both¹ /bəʊθ/ *adj* ambos, -bas, los dos, las dos; **~ the girls live nearby** ambas *or* las dos chicas viven cerca; **~ their fathers were truck drivers** los padres de los dos *or* de ambos eran camioneros; **on ~ sides of the street** a ambos lados de la calle

both² *pron* 1 ambos, -bas, los dos, las dos; **~ of them wanted to go** los dos *or* ambos querían ir; **~ of my brothers can swim** mis dos hermanos saben nadar 2 (*after n, pron*): **we ~ like chess** a los dos nos gusta el ajedrez; **her parents ~ like jazz** tanto a su padre como a su madre les gusta el jazz; **the coats are ~ too big** los dos abrigos son demasiado grandes; **she sends her love to you ~** les manda recuerdos a los dos

both³ *conj* **both ... and ...**: **~ Paul and John are in Italy** tanto Paul como John están en Italia, Paul y John están los dos en Italia; **~ young and old will enjoy this movie** esta película les gustará tanto a los niños como a los mayores; **she ~ wrote and played the music** compuso y tocó la música ella misma

bother¹ /ˈbɑːðər || ˈbɒðə(r)/ *vt* [1] (irritate) molestar; (pester) molestar, fastidiar; **does my smoking ~ you?** ¿te molesta que fume?; **sorry to ~ you** perdone (que lo moleste) [2] (trouble) preocupar; **what's ~ing you?** ¿qué es lo que te preocupa?; **she's very quiet, but don't let it ~ you** es muy callada, no te inquietes por ello; **to ~ oneself about sth/sb** preocuparse por algo/algn [3] (make effort) **not to ~ -ING: don't ~ writing a long letter** no hace falta que escribas una carta larga; **I don't ~ cooking any more** ya no me molesto en cocinar; **to ~ to + INF** tomarse la molestia DE + INF, molestarse EN + INF

■ **bother** *vi* [1] (make effort) molestarse; **you shouldn't have ~ed** no debiste haberte molestado; **why ~?** ¿para qué (molestarse)?; **I don't usually ~ with lunch** normalmente no como nada al mediodía [2] (worry) **to ~ ABOUT sth/sb** preocuparse POR algo/algn

bother² *n* [1] [u] (trouble) molestia *f*; (work) trabajo *m*; (problems) problemas *mpl*; **it isn't worth the ~** no vale la pena; **a spot of ~** (BrE colloq) un problemita (fam) [2] (nuisance) (*no pl*): **if it isn't too much of a ~ for you** si no es mucho problema *or* demasiada molestia para usted

bother³ *interj* (BrE): **~ (it)!** ¡maldito sea! (fam)

bothered /ˈbɑːðərd || ˈbɒðəd/ *adj* (*pred*): **I can't be ~ to go** me da pereza ir; **she yelled at him, but he wasn't a bit ~** le pegó un berrido, pero él ni se inmutó; **I'm not ~** (I don't mind) (BrE) me da igual *or* lo mismo; ▸**hot A1**

bothersome /ˈbɑːðərsəm || ˈbɒðəsəm/ *adj* ‹*demands*› molesto; ‹*person*› pesado, fastidioso

bottle¹ /ˈbɑːtl̩ || ˈbɒtl̩/ *n*

A [c] [1] (container, contents) botella *f*; (of perfume) frasco *m*; **return empty ~s** devuelva los envases *or* (Esp tb) los cascos; **a milk ~** una botella de leche (*el envase*); **baby's** *o* **feeding ~** biberón *m*, mamadera *f* (CS, Per), tetero *m* (Col), mamila *f* (Méx); (*before n*) **~ brush** cepillo *m or* escobilla *f* para limpiar botellas; **~ opener** abrebotellas *m*, destapador *m* (AmL) [2] (alcohol) (colloq): ***to hit the ~*** darle* a la bebida *or* (esp AmL) al trago (fam)

B [u] (courage, nerve) (BrE colloq) agallas *fpl* (fam); **to lose one's ~** achicarse* (fam)

bottle² *vt* [1] ‹*wine/milk*› embotellar; **~d milk** leche *f* en *or* de botella; **~d water** agua *f*‡ embotellada [2] (BrE) ‹*fruit/vegetables*› poner* en conserva

Phrasal verbs

- **bottle out** [v ▸ adv] (BrE sl) rajarse (fam), acobardarse
- **bottle up** [v ▸ o ▸ adv, v ▸ adv ▸ o] (colloq) ‹*emotion*› reprimir; **don't ~ it all up inside you** no te lo guardes dentro

bottle: ~ bank *n* contenedor *m* de recogida de vidrio; **~feed** *vt* (*past & past p* **-fed**) alimentar *or* criar* con biberón *or* (Méx) con mamila *or* (CS, Per) con mamadera *or* (Col) con tetero; **~-green** /ˈbɑːtl̩ˈgriːn || ˌbɒtl̩ˈgriːn/ *adj* (*pred* **~ green**) verde botella *adj inv*

bottleneck¹ /ˈbɑːtl̩nek || ˈbɒtl̩nek/ *n* (narrow stretch of road) cuello *m* de botella; (hold-up) embotellamiento *m*

bottleneck² *vt* (AmE) obstaculizar*

bottom¹ /ˈbɑːtəm || ˈbɒtəm/ *n*

A [1] (of box, bottle, drawer) fondo *m*; (of hill, stairs) pie *m*; (of page) final *m*, pie *m*; (of pile) parte *f* de abajo; **at the ~ of the list** al final de la lista; **~s up!** (colloq) ¡al centro y pa'dentro! (fam); **I wonder what's/who's at the ~ of it all** me pregunto qué es lo que hay/quién está detrás de todo esto; ***from the ~ of one's heart*** de todo corazón; ***to get to the ~ of sth*** llegar* al fondo de algo [2] (underneath — of box) parte *f* de abajo; (— of ship) fondo *m*; ***the ~ has fallen out of the market*** los precios han caído en picada *or* picado; ***to knock the ~ out of sth*** echar por tierra algo [3] (of bed) pies *mpl*; (of garden) fondo *m*; (of road) final *m* [4] (of sea, river, lake) fondo *m*; ***to hit*** *o* ***touch ~*** tocar* fondo

B (of hierarchy): **he is at the ~ of the class** es el último de la clase; **the team is at the ~ of the league** el equipo está a la cola de la liga; **she started out at the ~** empezó desde abajo

C [1] (of person) trasero *m* (fam), traste *m* (CS fam); ▸**smooth¹ A1** [2] (of pyjamas, tracksuit) (*often pl*) pantalón *m*, pantalones *mpl*; (of bikini) parte *f* de abajo

D **bottoms** *pl* (river valley) (AmE) valle *m*, vega *f*

E (in baseball) parte *f* baja, segunda *f*

Phrasal verb

- **bottom out** [v ▸ adv] tocar* fondo

bottom² *adj* (*before n*) ‹*shelf/layer*› de más abajo; ‹*grade*› más bajo; ‹*part/edge/lip*› inferior, de abajo; **the ~ left-hand corner** el ángulo inferior izquierdo

bottomless /ˈbɑːtəmləs || ˈbɒtəmlɪs/ *adj* ‹*well/shaft*› sin fondo; **he's a ~ pit** tiene la solitaria (fam), es un barril sin fondo (AmL fam)

bottom line *n* (result): **the ~ ~ is that ...** en pocas palabras *or* en resumidas cuentas, esto implica que ...

botulism /ˈbɑːtʃəlɪzəm || ˈbɒtjʊlɪzəm/ *n* [u] botulismo *m*

boudoir /ˈbuːdwɑːr || ˈbuːdwɑː(r)/ *n* tocador *m*

bough /baʊ/ *n* rama *f*

bought /bɔːt/ *past & past p of* **buy¹**

boulder /ˈbəʊldər || ˈbəʊldə(r)/ *n* roca *f* (*grande, alisada por la erosión*)

boulevard /ˈbʊləvɑːrd || ˈbuːləvɑːd/ *n* bulevar *m*

bounce¹ /baʊns/ *vi* [1] «*ball/object*» rebotar, picar* (AmL), botar (Esp, Méx); **the box was bouncing around on the back seat** la caja iba dando tumbos en el asiento de atrás; **the child was bouncing up and down on the sofa** el niño saltaba *or* daba brincos en el sofá [2] (move jauntily) (+ *adv compl*): **she ~d into the room** entró a la habitación saltando *or* brincando *or* dando brincos [3] «*check*» (colloq) ser* devuelto *or* rechazado, rebotar (fam) [4] **bouncing** *pres p* ‹*baby*› sano, rozagante

■ **bounce** *vt*

A [1] ‹*ball/object*› hacer* rebotar, darle* botes a, hacer* picar (AmL), (hacer*) botar (Esp, Méx); **she ~d the child on her knee** le hacía (el) caballito al niño [2] ‹*check*› (colloq) devolver*, rechazar*

B (get rid of) (esp AmE colloq) ‹*drunk/employee*› echar, botar (AmL exc RPl fam)

Phrasal verb

- **bounce back** [v ▸ adv] (recover) (colloq) levantarse, recuperarse

bounce² *n*

A [1] [c] (action) rebote *m*, bote *m*, pique *m* (AmL); **he hit the ball on the ~** le dio a la pelota de rebote [2] [u] (springiness, vitality): **this shampoo puts the ~ back into your hair** este champú les da nueva vida a sus cabellos; **she's full of ~** es una persona llena de vida

B (dismissal) (AmE colloq): **to give sb the ~** poner* a algn de patitas en la calle (fam), botar a algn (AmE excl RPl fam)

bouncer /ˈbaʊnsər || ˈbaʊnsə(r)/ *n* (colloq) gorila *m* (fam), sacabullas *m* (Méx fam)

bouncy /ˈbaʊnsi/ *adj* **-cier, -ciest** [1] ‹*ball*› que rebota *or* (Esp, Méx) bota bien; ‹*mattress*› firme y elástico; ‹*ride*› movido [2] (lively, cheerful) ‹*person*› animado, lleno de vida; ‹*tune*› alegre

bound¹ /baʊnd/ *n*

A **bounds** *pl* (limits) límites *mpl*; **her generosity knows no ~s** su generosidad no tiene límite(s); **within the ~s of possibility** dentro de lo posible; **the shop is out of ~s to schoolchildren** los niños tienen prohibido entrar en la tienda

B (jump) salto *m*, brinco *m*

bound² *vi* [1] (leap) saltar [2] (move) (+ *adv compl*): **the dog ~ed along behind the bicycle** el perro iba dando saltos detrás de la bicicleta; **to ~ in/out/away** entrar/salir*/irse* dando saltos

■ **bound** *vt* ‹*area/country*› delimitar

bound³ *past & past p of* **bind¹**

bound⁴ *adj*

A [1] (tied up) atado, amarrado (AmL exc RPl); **my hands were ~** tenía las manos atadas *or* (AmL exc RPl) amarradas [2] (obliged) **to be ~ BY sth (to + INF)**: **you are still ~ by your promise** sigues estando obligado a cumplir lo que prometiste; **they are ~ by law to supply the goods** están obligados por ley a suministrar los artículos; **to be ~ to + INF**: **he felt ~ to tell his mother what had happened** se sintió obligado a decirle a su madre lo que había sucedido; **I'm duty/honor ~ to tell you the truth** es mi deber/obligación decirte la verdad; **~ and determined** (AmE) empeñado

B (*pred*) (certain) **to be ~ to + INF**: **it was ~ to happen sooner or later** tarde o temprano tenía que suceder; **she's ~ to be elected** seguro que sale elegida; **it was ~ to go wrong** no cabía duda de que iba a salir mal; **they're up to no good, I'll be ~** (colloq & dated) estoy seguro de que están haciendo algo que no deben

C (headed) (*pred*) ~ FOR: **a ship ~ for New York** un barco con rumbo a Nueva York; **the truck was ~ for Italy** el camión iba rumbo a Italia

-bound /baʊnd/ *suff* **1** (heading for): **passengers for the Birmingham~ train** los pasajeros con destino a Birmingham; **it crashed into the Moscow~ train** chocó con el tren que se dirigía a Moscú **2** (Publ): **leather~** encuadernado en cuero **3** (immobilized by): **snow~** paralizado por la nieve **4** (confined to): **wheelchair~** confinado a una silla de ruedas

boundary /'baʊndri, -dəri/ *n* (*pl* **-ries**) límite *m*; **the ~ between fiction and fact** la frontera *or* la línea divisoria entre la ficción y la realidad; (*before n*) **~ line** línea *f* divisoria, linde *m or f*

boundless /'baʊndləs || 'baʊndlɪs/ *adj* ‹*love/patience*› sin límites; ‹*resources*› ilimitado, inagotable; ‹*universe*› infinito

bountiful /'baʊntɪfəl/ *adj* (liter) ‹*king/nature*› munificente (liter), pródigo (liter); ‹*harvest/gifts*› copioso, abundante; ***to play Lady B~*** (BrE) hacerse* la dadivosa

bounty /'baʊnti/ *n* (*pl* **-ties**)
A [u c] (liter) (generosity) munificencia *f* (liter)
B [c] (reward) recompensa *f*; (*before n*) **~ hunter** cazador, -dora *m,f* de recompensas

bouquet /bəʊ'keɪ, buː'keɪ || bʊ'keɪ, bəʊ'keɪ/ *n*
A (of flowers) ramo *m*; (small) ramillete *m*
B (of wine) bouquet *m*, aroma *m*

bouquet garni /buː'keɪgɑːr'niː, 'bəʊkeɪ- || buː'keɪ'gɑːni/ *n* (*pl* **~s ~s** /-keɪz/) ramito *m* compuesto

bourbon /'bɜːrbən || 'bɜːbən/ *n* [u c] bourbon *m*

bourgeois[1] /'bʊrʒwɑː || 'bɔːʒwɑː, 'bʊəʒ-/ *adj* burgués

bourgeois[2] *n* burgués, -guesa *m,f*

bourgeoisie /'bʊrʒwɑː'ziː || ˌbɔːʒwɑː'ziː, ˌbʊəʒ-/ *n* [u] burguesía *f*

bout /baʊt/ *n*
A (period, spell): **I had a ~ of flu** tuve una gripe *or* (Col, Méx) una gripa muy mala; **~s of depression** frecuentes depresiones; **a ~ of activity** una racha de actividad; **a drinking ~** una borrachera *or* juerga
B (in boxing, wrestling) combate *m*, encuentro *m*

boutique /buː'tiːk/ *n* boutique *f*

bovine /'bəʊvaɪn/ *adj* bovino

bow[1] /baʊ/ *n*
A (movement) reverencia *f*; **the actress took a ~** la actriz salió a saludar al público/hizo una reverencia
B (of ship) (*often pl*) proa *f*

bow[2] /baʊ/ *vi* hacer* una reverencia; **to ~ TO sb** hacerle* una reverencia A algn, inclinarse ANTE algn; **to ~ TO sth**: **we must ~ to her experience** debemos tratarla con la deferencia que su experiencia merece; **they ~ed to government pressure** cedieron ante la presión del gobierno
■ **bow** *vt* ‹*head*› inclinar, agachar

Phrasal verbs
- **bow down** [v ▸ adv] doblegarse*; **to ~ down TO sb/sth** someterse A algn/algo
- **bow out** [v ▸ adv] retirarse

bow[3] /bəʊ/ *n*
A (knot) lazo *m*, moño *m* (esp AmL); **to tie a ~** hacer* un lazo (*or* moño *etc*); **to tie sth in a ~** hacer* un lazo (*or* moño *etc*) con algo
B (weapon) arco *m*; **~ and arrow** arco y flecha
C (Mus) arco *m*

bow[4] /bəʊ/ *vi* «*branch/plank*» arquearse, doblarse, pandearse (esp AmL)
■ **bow** *vt* ‹*branch/beam*› arquear

bowdlerize /'baʊdləraɪz/ *vt* (pej) expurgar*

bowel /'baʊəl/ *n*
A (Anat) *also* **large ~** intestino *m* grueso
B **bowels** *pl* (liter): **in the ~s of the earth** en las entrañas de la tierra

bower /baʊr || 'baʊə(r)/ *n* enramada *f*

bowl[1] /bəʊl/ *n*
A **1** (container) (Culin) bol *m*, tazón *m*, cuenco *m*; (for washing etc) palangana *f*, barreño *m*; **fruit ~** frutero *m*, frutera *f* (CS); **soup ~** sopero *m* **2** (contents) bol *m*, tazón *m* **3** (of toilet) taza *f*, inodoro *m*
B (in game of bowls) bola *f*, bocha *f*; *see also* **bowls**

bowl[2] *vi* (throw) lanzar*; **to go ~ing** *ir a jugar a los bolos, la petanca, las bochas etc*
■ **bowl** *vt* **1** ‹*ball*› lanzar* **2** (in cricket) ‹*batsman*› eliminar

Phrasal verb
- **bowl over** [v ▸ o ▸ adv, v ▸ adv ▸ o] **1** (knock down) derribar, tirar al suelo **2** (impress): **we were ~ed over by the beauty of the island** la belleza de la isla nos dejó pasmados *or* boquiabiertos

bowlegged /'bəʊ'legd/ *adj* patizambo

bowler /'bəʊlər || 'bəʊlə(r)/ *n*
A (in cricket) lanzador, -dora *m,f*; (in bowling, bowls) jugador, -dora *m,f*
B **~ (hat)** bombín *m*, sombrero *m* de hongo

bowling /'bəʊlɪŋ/ *n* [u]
A **1** (in bowling alley) bolos *mpl* **2** (on grass) ▸**bowls**
B (in cricket) lanzamiento *m*

bowling: **~ alley** *n* bolera *f*, bowling *m*; **~ green** *n*: *pista donde se juega a los* **bowls**

bowls /bəʊlz/ *n* (+ *sing vb*) *juego semejante a la petanca que se juega sobre césped*

bowser /'baʊzə(r)/ *n* tanque *m* de agua transportable

bow tie /bəʊ/ *n* corbata *f* de moño (AmL), pajarita *f* (Esp)

box[1] /bɑːks || bɒks/ *n*
A (container, contents) caja *f*; (large) cajón *m*; (for watch, pen) estuche *m*; (*ballot ~*) urna *f*; (*collection ~*) alcancía *f* (AmL), hucha *f* (Esp); (*jewelry ~*) joyero *m*, alhajero *m* (AmL); (*tool ~*) caja *f* de herramientas
B **1** (*penalty ~*) (in ice hockey) banquillo *m* (*de castigo*); (in soccer) área *f*‡ (de penalty *or* de castigo) **2** (in baseball) área *f*‡
C (on form) casilla *f*
D **1** (in theater) palco *m* **2** (booth) cabina *f*; **witness ~** estrado *m*
E (television) (esp BrE colloq): **the ~** la tele (fam); **what's on the ~?** ¿qué dan en la tele? (fam)
F (thump): **a ~ around the ears** un sopapo

box[2] *vi* boxear
■ **box** *vt*
A (put in boxes) poner* en una caja, embalar
B **1** (hit): **to ~ sb around the ear(s)** darle* un sopapo a algn **2** (fight) (Sport) boxear *or* pelear con *or* contra

Phrasal verb
- **box in** [v ▸ o ▸ adv, v ▸ adv ▸ o] **1** (restrict, surround) cerrarle* el paso a **2** (enclose) ‹*pipes*› esconder (*tapando con una tabla etc*)

boxcar /'bɑːkskɑːr || 'bɒkskɑː(r)/ *n* (AmE) vagón *m* de carga, furgón *m*

boxer /'bɑːksər || 'bɒksə(r)/ *n* **1** (person) boxeador, -dora *m,f* **2** (dog) bóxer *mf*

boxer shorts *pl n* calzoncillos *mpl*, calzones *mpl* (Méx), interiores *mpl* (Col, Ven)

boxing /'bɑːksɪŋ || 'bɒksɪŋ/ *n* [u] boxeo *m*; (*before n*) **~ ring** ring *m*, cuadrilátero *m*

Boxing Day /'bɑːksɪŋ || 'bɒksɪŋ/ *n*: *el 26 de diciembre*

> **Boxing Day**
>
> En Gran Bretaña es el 26 de diciembre, día festivo oficial en que se llevan a cabo actividades deportivas y de caza. Antiguamente era la ocasión en que se regalaban pequeñas sumas de dinero (*Christmas boxes*) a los comerciantes y a sus empleados. En Irlanda se denomina *(Saint) Stephen's Day*

box: **~ number** *n* (at post office) apartado *m* (de correos), apartado *m* postal (Méx), casilla *f* postal *or* de correo (CS); **~ office** *n* taquilla *f*, boletería *f* (AmL)

boy[1] /bɔɪ/ *n* **1** (baby, child) niño *m*, chico *m*; **is it a ~ or a girl?** ¿es niño o niña?, ¿es varón o nena? (esp AmL); **~s will be ~s** así son los chicos *or* los niños; **the little ~s' room** (AmE euph) el (cuarto de) baño, el váter (Esp fam) **2** (son) hijo *m*, chico *m*; **she has three ~s** tiene tres hijos *or* chicos *or* (esp AmL) varones; **one of the Smith ~s** uno de los hijos *or* chicos de los Smith **3** (young man) (colloq) muchacho *m*, chico *m*; **a good old ~** (AmE) un sureño típico; **a night out with the ~s** una noche de juerga con los muchachos; **jobs for the ~s** (BrE colloq) amiguismo *m*; **the ~s in blue** (BrE colloq) la policía **4** (servant) criado *m*, mozo *m*

boy[2] *interj* (esp AmE colloq) ¡vaya!

boycott[1] /'bɔɪkɑːt || 'bɔɪkɒt/ *n* boicot *m*

boycott[2] *vt* boicotear

boyfriend /'bɔɪfrend/ *n* novio *m*, pololo *m* (Chi fam)

boyhood /'bɔɪhʊd/ *n* [u c] niñez *f*

boyish /'bɔɪɪʃ/ *adj* 1 ‹*enthusiasm/smile*› de chico, de niño; **his ~ looks** su aspecto juvenil *or* de chico 2 (used of woman) de muchacho, de chico

boy: **~ racer** (colloq) *automovilista joven que conduce demasiado rápido*; **~ scout** *n* boy scout *m*, explorador *m*

bozo /'bəʊzəʊ/ *n* (*pl* **bozos**) (AmE sl & pej) sujeto *m* (pey)

BR = **British Rail**

bra /brɑː/ *n* sostén *m*, sujetador *m* (Esp), brasier *m* (Col, Méx), corpiño *m* (RPl), soutien *m* (Ur)

brace[1] /breɪs/ *n*

A (support) abrazadera *f*

B (Dent) ▸ **D2**

C (drill) berbiquí *m*; **~ and bit** berbiquí y barrena

D **braces** *pl* 1 (BrE Clothing) tirantes *mpl*, cargaderas *fpl* (Col), tiradores *mpl* (RPl), suspensores *mpl* (Chi) 2 (esp AmE Dent) aparato(s) *m(pl)*, frenos *mpl* (Méx), fierros *mpl* (Méx, Per), frenillos *mpl* (Chi)

E (*pl* ~) (pair) (BrE) par *m*

brace[2] *vt* (support) apuntalar

■ *v refl* **to ~ oneself for sth** prepararse para algo

■ **brace** *vi* (AmE) **to ~ (FOR sth)** prepararse (PARA algo)

Phrasal verb

• **brace up** [v ▸ adv] (AmE) animarse; **~ up!** ¡arriba ese ánimo!

bracelet /'breɪslət || 'breɪslɪt/ *n* pulsera *f*, brazalete *m*

bracing /'breɪsɪŋ/ *adj* vigorizante

bracken /'brækən/ *n* [u] helechos *mpl*

bracket[1] /'brækət || 'brækɪt/ *n*

A 1 (Print) (square bracket) corchete *m* 2 (parenthesis) (BrE) paréntesis *m*; **in ~s** entre paréntesis

B (category): **tax ~** ≈ banda *f* impositiva; **income ~** nivel *m* de ingresos; **the best car in this price ~** el mejor coche dentro de esta gama de precios; **the 25-30 age ~** el grupo etario de entre 25 y 30 años

C (support) soporte *m*; (for shelves) escuadra *f*

bracket[2] *vt* 1 ‹*word/phrase*› poner* entre corchetes; (in parentheses) (BrE) poner* entre paréntesis 2 (categorize) catalogar*; **you can't ~ these two cases together** no se puede equiparar estos dos casos

brackish /'brækɪʃ/ *adj* salobre

brag /bræg/ **-gg-** *vi* fanfarronear (fam); **to ~ ABOUT** *o* **OF sth/-ING** alardear *or* jactarse DE algo/+ INF; **that's nothing to ~ about** eso no es como para enorgullecerse

■ **brag** *vt* fanfarronear (fam); **to ~ THAT** hacer* alarde *or* jactarse DE QUE

braggart /'brægərt || 'brægət/ *n* fanfarrón, -rrona *m,f*, jactancioso, -sa *m,f*

braid[1] /breɪd/ *n* 1 [c] (of hair) (esp AmE) trenza *f*; **she wears her hair in ~s** lleva el pelo trenzado 2 [u] (Tex) galón *m*

braid[2] *vt* trenzar*

braille, Braille /breɪl/ *n* [u] braille *m*, Braille *m*

brain[1] /breɪn/ *n*

A (organ) cerebro *m*; (*before n*) **~ damage** lesión *f* cerebral; **~ surgeon** neurocirujano, -na *m,f*; **~ surgery** neurocirugía *f*; **~ tumor** tumor *m* cerebral

B (intellect): **she's got a good ~** es muy inteligente; ***to have sth on the ~*** (colloq) tener* algo metido en la cabeza

C (clever person) cerebro *m*; (*before n*) **the ~ drain** la fuga de cerebros; *see also* **brains**

brain[2] *vt* (colloq) romperle* la crisma a (fam)

brain: **~box** *n* (BrE colloq) cerebrito *m* (fam); **~child** *n* creación *m*; **~-dead** *adj* clínicamente muerto

brainless /'breɪnləs || 'breɪnlɪs/ *adj* (colloq) estúpido

brains /breɪnz/ *n*

A (+ *pl vb*) 1 (substance) sesos *mpl*; (Culin) sesos *mpl*; ***to blow sb's ~ out*** levantarle la tapa de los sesos a algn 2 (intelligence) inteligencia *f*; ***to pick sb's ~***: **I'd like to pick your ~ about sth** quisiera hacerte unas preguntas *or* consultas acerca de algo; ***to rack one's ~ (over sth)*** devanarse los sesos (con algo)

B (+ *sing vb*) (mastermind) cerebro *m*, autor, -tora *m,f* intelectual (AmL); **she's the ~ behind the operation** es el cerebro *or* (AmL tb) la autora intelectual de la operación; **he's the ~ of the family** es la lumbrera de la familia

brain: **~storm** *n* (colloq) 1 (confusion) (BrE): **I/he had a ~storm** se me/le cruzaron los cables (fam) 2 (AmE) ▸ **~wave**; **~teaser** /'breɪn,tiːzər || 'breɪn,tiːzə(r)/ *n* rompecabezas *m*; **~ trust** *n* (AmE) grupo *m* de expertos; **~wash** *vt* hacerle* un lavado de cerebro a, lavarle el cerebro a; **~wave** *n* (colloq) idea *f* genial *or* brillante, lamparazo *m* (Col fam)

brainy /'breɪni/ *adj* **-nier, -niest** (colloq) inteligente, listo

braise /breɪz/ *vt* estofar

brake[1] /breɪk/ *n* 1 (on vehicle) freno *m*; ***to put the ~s o a ~ on sth*** (colloq) poner* freno a algo; (*before n*) **~ lights** luces *fpl* de freno *or* de frenado 2 (*hand~*) freno *m* de mano; **to put on** *o* **apply the ~** poner* el freno de mano

brake[2] *vi/t* frenar

braking /'breɪkɪŋ/ *n* [u] frenado *m*; (*before n*) **~ distance** distancia *f* de frenado

bramble /'bræmbəl/ *n* zarza *f*; (blackberry bush) (BrE) zarzamora *f*

bran /bræn/ *n* [u] salvado *m*, afrecho *m*

branch[1] /bræntʃ || brɑːntʃ/ *n* (of tree) rama *f*; (of river, road, railway) ramal *m*; (of family, field of study) rama *f*; (of computer program) bifurcación *f*, ramificación *f*; (of company, bank) sucursal *f*; **the American ~ of the company** la división americana de la compañía; **the three ~es of the armed forces** los tres cuerpos del ejército

branch[2] *vi* ‹‹*river/family*›› ramificarse*; ‹‹*road*›› bifurcarse*; **a path ~es (off) to the right** un sendero sale a la derecha

Phrasal verb

• **branch out** [v ▸ adv] 1 (take on new activity) diversificar* sus (*or* nuestras *etc*) actividades; **to ~ out INTO sth: the company has ~ed out into publishing** la compañía ha diversificado sus actividades lanzándose al campo editorial 2 (become independent): **he has ~ed out on his own** ‹‹*business partner*›› se ha establecido por su cuenta

brand[1] /brænd/ *n*

A 1 (Busn) marca *f* 2 (type) tipo *m*; (style) estilo *m*; **her ~ of socialism** su tipo de socialismo

B (identification mark) marca *f* (*hecha a fuego*), hierro *m*

C (torch) (liter) tea *f*, hacha *f*‡ (liter)

brand[2] *vt* 1 (mark) ‹*cattle*› marcar* (*con hierro candente*) 2 (label) **to ~ sth/sb AS sth** tachar *or* tildar algo/a algn DE algo

branding iron /'brændɪŋ/ *n* hierro *m* (de marcar)

brandish /'brændɪʃ/ *vt* blandir

brand: **~ name** *n* marca *f*; **~-new** /'brænd'nuː || ,brænd'njuː/ *adj* ‹*toy/car*› nuevo, flamante

brandy /'brændi/ *n* [u c] (*pl* **-dies**) coñac *m*, brandy *m*

brash /bræʃ/ *adj* **-er, -est** excesivamente desenvuelto, de gran desparpajo

brass /bræs || brɑːs/ *n*

A [u] 1 (Metall) latón *m*; ***to be as bold as ~*** ser* muy descarado; (*before n*) ‹*button*› dorado 2 (Mus) (+ *sing or pl vb*) bronces *mpl*, metales *mpl*; (*before n*) **~ instrument** instrumento *m* de metal; **the ~ section** los bronces, los metales

B [c] (in church) *placa conmemorativa o mortuoria de latón grabada con inscripciones o figuras*

brass band *n* banda *f* de música, tambora *f* (Méx)

brassiere /brə'zɪr || 'bræziə(r)/ *n* ▸ **bra**

brass: **~ knuckles** *pl n* (AmE) nudilleras *fpl* de metal, manoplas *fpl* (AmL); **~ rubbing** *n* 1 [u] (activity) *técnica de calcar por frotación un* **brass B** 2 [c] (product) *calco por frotación de un* **brass B**

brassy /'bræsi || 'brɑːsi/ *adj* **-sier, -siest** (colloq) ordinario, chabacano

brat /bræt/ *n* (pej) (child) mocoso, -sa *m,f* (pey); (spoilt person) niño mimado, niña mimada *m,f*

bravado /brə'vɑːdəʊ/ *n* [u] bravuconadas *fpl*, bravatas *fpl*

brave[1] /breɪv/ *adj* **-ver, -vest** valiente, valeroso; **that was ~ of you!** ¡qué valiente!

brave[2] *vt* ‹*peril*› afrontar, hacer* frente a; **to ~ the weather** hacerle frente al mal tiempo

b

brave[3] *n*
A (North American Indian) guerrero *m* piel roja
B (liter) (+ *pl vb*) **the ~** los valientes

bravely /ˈbreɪvli/ *adv* valientemente, con valor

bravery /ˈbreɪvəri/ *n* [u] valentía *f*, valor *m*, coraje *m*

bravo /ˈbrɑːvəʊ || brɑːˈvəʊ/ *interj* ¡bravo!

brawl[1] /brɔːl/ *n* pelea *f*, reyerta *f*

brawl[2] *vi* pelearse, armar camorra (fam)

brawn /brɔːn/ *n* [u] (strength) músculos *mpl*

brawny /ˈbrɔːni/ *adj* **-nier, -niest** musculoso

bray /breɪ/ *vi* «*donkey*» rebuznar; «*person*» cacarear

brazen /ˈbreɪzn || ˈbreɪzən/ *adj* descarado; **the ~ hussy!** ¡esa fresca *or* descarada!

Phrasal verb
• **brazen out** [v ▸ o ▸ adv, v ▸ adv ▸ o]: **to ~ it out** negar* descaradamente lo evidente

brazier /ˈbreɪʒər, ˈbreɪziər || ˈbreɪziə(r)/ *n* brasero *m*

Brazil /brəˈzɪl/ *n* Brasil *m*

Brazilian[1] /brəˈzɪliən/ *adj* brasileño

Brazilian[2] *n* brasileño, -ña *m,f*

brazil (nut) /brəˈzɪl/ *n* coquito *m* del Brasil, castaña *f* de Pará (RPl)

breach[1] /briːtʃ/ *n*
A [c u] (of law) infracción *f*, violación *f*; **~ of contract** incumplimiento *m* de contrato; **a ~ of confidence** *o* **trust** un abuso de confianza, una infidencia; **she was arrested for ~ of the peace** la detuvieron por alterar el orden público
B [c] (gap, opening) (frml) brecha *f*; ***to step into/fill the ~*** llenar el hueco
C [c] (break) (frml) ruptura *f*

breach[2] *vt* 1 ‹*rule*› infringir*, violar; ‹*security*› poner* en peligro 2 (frml) ‹*defenses*› abrir* una brecha en

bread /bred/ *n* [u]
A (Culin) pan *m*; **sliced ~** pan de molde; **~ and butter** pan con mantequilla *or* (RPl) manteca; ***the greatest/best thing since sliced ~*** (colloq) lo mejor que hay; ***to be sb's ~ and butter***: **teaching is his ~ and butter** se gana la vida enseñando; ***to earn one's ~ (and butter)*** ganarse la vida *or* (liter) el pan; ***to know which side one's ~ is buttered (on)*** saber* lo que conviene (a uno); ***to take the ~ out of sb's mouth*** quitarle el pan de la boca a algn; ***to want one's ~ buttered on both sides*** querer* el oro y el moro; (*before n*) **~ knife** cuchillo *m* del pan
B (money) (sl) guita *f* (arg), lana *f* (AmL fam), pasta *f* (Esp fam)

bread: **~basket** *n* (container) panera *f*; **~bin** *n* (BrE) ▸ **~box**; **~board** *n* tabla *f* de cortar el pan; **~box** *n* (AmE) panera *f* (*para guardar el pan*); **~crumb** *n* miga *f* (de pan); **~crumbs** (Culin) pan *m* rallado *or* (Méx) molido; **~line** *n*: ***they're on the ~line*** (colloq) apenas tienen *or* apenas les alcanza para vivir; **~ maker** *n* máquina *f* de hacer pan, máquina *f* panificadora

breadth /bredθ/ *n* 1 [c u] (width) anchura *f*, ancho *m* 2 [u] (extent) amplitud *f*; **~ of vision** amplitud de miras

breadwinner /ˈbred,wɪnər || ˈbred,wɪnə(r)/ *n*: **she's the ~ of the family** es la que mantiene *or* sostiene a la familia; **he's the sole ~** es el único sostén de la familia

break[1] /breɪk/ (*past* **broke**; *past p* **broken**) *vt*
A ‹*window/plate*› romper*; ‹*stick*› partir, romper*, quebrar* (AmL); **I've broken my pencil** se me ha roto la punta del lápiz; **he broke his wrist** se rompió la muñeca; **she broke the chocolate into four pieces** partió el chocolate en cuatro trozos
B (render useless) ‹*machine*› romper*, descomponer* (AmL)
C (violate) ‹*rule*› infringir*, violar; ‹*promise*› no cumplir, faltar a; ‹*contract*› incumplir, romper*; ‹*strike*› romper*; ▸ **law A2, word**[1] **C**
D (end) ‹*strike*› poner* fin a; ‹*drug ring*› desarticular; ‹*impasse*› salir* de; ‹*habit*› dejar
E 1 (ruin) ‹*person/company*› arruinar a 2 (crush) ‹*person*› destrozar*, deshacer*; ▸ **heart B, spirit**[1] **C, will**[2] **A2**
F (impart) **to ~ sth (TO sb)**: **Sue broke the news to him** Sue le dio la noticia; **they broke it to her gently** se lo dijeron con mucho tacto
G (exceed) ‹*record*› batir
H 1 (interrupt) ‹*circuit*› cortar; ‹*fast/silence*› romper* 2 (disrupt) ‹*pattern/monotony*› romper*
I (breach, pierce) ‹*soil*› roturar; **I haven't broken the skin** no me he abierto la piel
J 1 (get into) ‹*safe*› forzar*; **we broke the toolbox open** abrimos la caja de herramientas forzándola 2 (escape from) (AmE) ‹*jail*› escaparse *or* fugarse* de 3 (decipher) ‹*code*› descifrar
K (tame) ‹*horse*› domar

■ **break** *vi*
A 1 «*window/plate*» romperse*; «*stick*» partirse, romperse*, quebrarse* (AmL); **my watch broke** se me rompió el reloj 2 (separate): **a splinter group which broke from the party** un grupo disidente que se escindió del partido; ▸ **loose**[1] **B**
B (give in) «*resistance*» desmoronarse, venirse* abajo; **she broke under constant interrogation** no resistió el constante interrogatorio
C 1 (begin) «*storm*» estallar; «*day*» romper*, apuntar, despuntar 2 (change) «*weather*» cambiar; **his voice is ~ing** le está cambiando *or* mudando la voz; **his voice broke** (with emotion) se le entrecortó la voz 3 (become known) «*story*» hacerse* público
D «*wave/surf*» romper*
E (adjourn) parar, hacer* una pausa; **to ~ for lunch** parar para almorzar
F (happen) (AmE colloq): **things are ~ing well for me** me están saliendo bien las cosas; ▸ **even**[2] **B**
G (in snooker, pool) abrir* el juego

Phrasal verbs
• **break away** [v ▸ adv] **to ~ away (FROM sth)** «*piece*» desprenderse (DE algo); «*faction/region*» escindirse *or* separarse (DE algo); **the boat broke away from its moorings** el barco se soltó de las amarras; **to ~ away from tradition** romper* con la tradición; **he broke away from the pack** (Sport) se adelantó al pelotón

• **break down**
Sense I [v ▸ adv]
A «*vehicle/machine*» estropearse, averiarse*, descomponerse* (AmL), quedarse en pana (Chi), quedarse varado (Col); «*system*» fallar, venirse* abajo; «*talks*» fracasar
B (lose composure) perder* el control
C (divide into components): **it ~s down as follows** el total puede desglosarse de la siguiente manera
Sense II [v ▸ o ▸ adv, v ▸ adv ▸ o]
A ‹*door/barrier*› echar abajo, derribar
B 1 (divide up) ‹*expenditure*› desglosar; ‹*sentence*› descomponer*; **the process can be broken down into three steps** el proceso puede dividirse en tres pasos 2 (Chem) descomponer*

• **break in**
A [v ▸ adv] 1 «*intruder*» entrar, meterse (*para robar etc*) 2 (interrupt) interrumpir; **I didn't mean to ~ in on your conversation** no quería interrumpirles la conversación
B [v ▸ o ▸ adv, v ▸ adv ▸ o] ‹*horse*› domar; ‹*shoes*› ablandar, domar (hum)

• **break into** [v ▸ prep ▸ o]
A 1 ‹*building*› entrar en, meterse en (*para robar etc*); **our house was broken into** nos entraron a robar 2 (start on) ‹*banknote*› cambiar; **they had to ~ into their savings** tuvieron que echar mano de sus ahorros
B (begin): **to ~ into a run** echarse a correr; **to ~ into applause** romper* *or* prorrumpir en aplausos

• **break off**
A [v ▸ o ▸ adv, v ▸ adv ▸ o] 1 (detach) partir 2 ‹*engagement/diplomatic relations*› romper*
B [v ▸ adv] 1 (snap off, come free) «*piece of ice*» desprenderse; **the handle broke off** se le rompió el asa 2 (stop talking) parar (de hablar), detenerse*

• **break out** [v ▸ adv]
A 1 (start) «*war/epidemic/rioting*» estallar 2 (appear): **a rash broke out on his face** le salió un sarpullido en la cara 3 (develop) **to ~ out (IN sth)**: **he broke out in spots** le salieron granos; **to ~ out in a sweat** empezar* a sudar; **chocolate makes me ~ out** (AmE) el chocolate me hace salir granos
B (escape) «*prisoner*» escaparse, fugarse*

• **break through**
A [v ▸ adv] (penetrate) (Mil) penetrar en las defensas enemigas; «*sun*» salir*
B [v ▸ prep ▸ o] ‹*barrier*› atravesar*, romper*; **they broke through our defenses** penetraron en nuestras defensas;

the sun broke through the clouds el sol se abrió paso entre las nubes

• **break up**

(Sense I) [v ▸ o ▸ adv, v ▸ adv ▸ o]

A 1 ‹*ship*› desguazar* 2 (divide) ‹*land*› dividir; ‹*sentence*› descomponer*; ~ **it up into four pieces** divídelo *or* rómpelo en cuatro pedazos; **it helps ~ up the long mornings** ayuda a que las mañanas no parezcan tan largas

B 1 ‹*demonstration*› disolver*; **he broke up the fight** separó a los niños (*or* hombres *etc*) que se estaban peleando; **come on, ~ it up!** ¡vamos, basta ya! 2 (wreck, ruin) ‹*home*› deshacer*; **he felt responsible for ~ing up their marriage** se sentía responsable del fracaso de su matrimonio

(Sense II) [v ▸ adv]

A 1 ‹‹*lovers/band*›› separarse; **their marriage broke up** su matrimonio fracasó; **to ~ up WITH sb** romper* *or* terminar CON algn 2 ‹‹*meeting*›› terminar; ‹‹*crowd*›› dispersarse 3 (BrE Educ): **we ~ up on the 21st** las clases terminan el 21

B ‹‹*boat/ship*›› romperse*, deshacerse*

• **break with** [v ▸ prep ▸ o] ‹*tradition*› romper* con

break² *n*

A 1 (Rad, TV) pausa *f* (comercial); (Theat) entreacto *m*, intermedio *m* 2 (rest period) descanso *m*; (at school) (BrE) recreo *m*; **we have a coffee ~ at 11** a las 11 paramos para tomar un café; **we worked without a ~** trabajamos sin parar *or* descansar 3 (short vacation) vacaciones *fpl* 4 (change, respite) cambio *m*; **I need a ~ from all this** necesito descansar de todo esto; (a holiday) necesito un cambio de aires; ***give me a ~!*** (colloq) ¡déjame en paz!, ¡no me embromes! (AmL fam)

B 1 (gap) interrupción *f* 2 (in circuit) ruptura *f*, corte *m*

C (fracture) fractura *f*, rotura *f*

D (chance, opportunity) (colloq) oportunidad *f*; **he got a ~** se le presentó una oportunidad

E (separation, rift) ruptura *f*; **to make a clean ~** cortar por lo sano; **he made a ~ with his past life** rompió *or* cortó con su pasado

F (sudden move): **he made a ~ for the door** corrió hacia la puerta

G (escape) fuga *f*, evasión *f* (frml)

H (in snooker, pool) tacada *f*, serie *f*; (in tennis) ruptura *f*, quiebre *m*

I (beginning) (liter): **at (the) ~ of day** al rayar el alba (liter)

A (discount) (AmE colloq) descuento *m*

breakable /'breɪkəbəl/ *adj* frágil

breakables /'breɪkəbəlz/ *pl n* objetos *mpl* frágiles

breakage /'breɪkɪdʒ/ *n* 1 [u] (action) rotura *f* 2 **breakages** *pl* (objects broken) roturas *fpl*

break: **~away** *n* 1 (separation) ruptura *f*, escisión *f*; (*before n*) ‹*faction*› disidente, escindido 2 (Sport) escapada *f*; **~down** *n* 1 (failure — of car, machine) avería *f*, descompostura *f* (Méx), varada *f* (Col), pana *f* (Chi); (—of service, communications) interrupción *f*; (— of negotiations) fracaso *m*, ruptura *f*; **the system suffered a complete ~down** (Comput) el sistema colapsó; **a ~down in traditional values** un desmoronamiento de los valores tradicionales; **they had a ~down on the motorway** se les estropeó el coche en la autopista; (*before n*) **~down service** servicio *m* de asistencia en carretera; **~down truck** grúa *f* 2 (*nervous ~down*) crisis *f* nerviosa; 3 (analysis): **a ~down of expenditure** un desglose de los gastos; **a complete ~down of the report** un análisis punto por punto del informe 4 (into constituent elements) descomposición *f*

breaker /'breɪkər || 'breɪkə(r)/ *n*

A (wave) gran ola *f*

B (BrE Auto) **~'s yard** cementerio *m* de automóviles

breakfast /'brekfəst/ *n* desayuno *m*; **to have ~** desayunar, tomar el desayuno; (*before n*) **~ television** televisión *f* matinal

break: **~front** *n* (AmE) *mueble con estantes en la parte superior y armarios cerrados debajo*; **~-in** *n* robo *m* (*con escalamiento*); **they had a ~-in next door** entraron a robar en la casa de al lado

breaking /'breɪkɪŋ/: **~ and entering** /'breɪkɪŋənd 'entərɪŋ/ *n* [u] allanamiento *m* de morada; **~ point** *n* [u] límite *m*; **the soldiers were at ~ point** los soldados habían llegado al límite de sus fuerzas

break: **~neck** *adj* (*before n*): **at ~neck speed** a una velocidad vertiginosa; **~out** *n* (from prison) fuga *f*, evasión *f*; **~through** *n* gran avance *m*, gran adelanto *m*; **a major ~through** un avance *or* adelanto importantísimo; **~up** *n* (of structure, family) desintegración *f*; (of empire, company) desmembramiento *m*; (of political party) disolución *f*; (of talks) fracaso *m*; **the ~up of their marriage** su separación *or* ruptura; **~water** *n* rompeolas *m*

breast /brest/ *n* 1 [c] (of woman) pecho *m*, seno *m*; (*before n*) **~ cancer** cáncer *m* de mama *or* de pecho 2 [c] (chest) (liter) pecho *m*; ***to beat one's ~*** darse* golpes de pecho; ***to make a clean ~ of sth*** confesar* algo; (*before n*) **~ pocket** bolsillo *m* superior (*de una chaqueta*) 3 [c u] (Culin) (of chicken, turkey) pechuga *f*; **~ of lamb** pecho *m* de cordero

breast: **~feed** (*past & past p* **-fed**) *vt* darle* el pecho a, darle* de mamar a, amamantar; **a ~fed baby** un niño amamantado; *vi* dar* el pecho, dar* de mamar; **~plate** *n* peto *m*; **~stroke** *n* (estilo) pecho *m* (AmL), braza *f* (Esp)

breath /breθ/ *n* [c u] (air exhaled or inhaled) aliento *m*; **to have bad ~** tener* mal aliento; **to take a ~** aspirar, inspirar; **take a deep ~** respire hondo; **just let me get my ~ back** déjame recobrar el aliento; **he gets short of ~** se queda sin aliento; **out of ~** sin aliento; ***in the same o next ~*** a continuación, a renglón seguido; ***to be a ~ of fresh air*** ser* (como) una bocanada de aire fresco; ***to draw ~*** (lit: breathe) respirar; (live) (liter) vivir; ***to draw one's last ~*** (liter) exhalar el último suspiro (liter); ***to hold one's ~*** contener* la respiración *or* el aliento; **he promised — well, don't hold your ~** (colloq & hum) lo prometió — sí, pero mejor espera sentado (fam & hum); ***to say sth under one's ~*** decir* algo entre dientes; ***to take sb's ~ away*** dejar a algn sin habla; ***to waste one's ~*** gastar saliva; ***with bated ~*** con el corazón en un puño; ▸**save¹ C1**

breathalyze /'breθəlaɪz/ *vt* (BrE) hacerle* la prueba del alcohol *or* de la alcoholemia a

Breathalyzer®, **Breathalyser®** /'breθəlaɪzər || 'breθəlaɪzə(r)/ *n* alcohómetro *m*, alcoholímetro *m*; (*before n*) **~ test** prueba *f* del alcohol *or* de la alcoholemia

breathe /bri:ð/ *vi* 1 ‹‹*person/animal*›› respirar; ***to ~ deeply*** respirar hondo; ***to ~ again/easily/freely*** respirar tranquilo 2 ‹‹*fabric/leather*›› dejar pasar el aire

■ **breathe** *vt* 1 ‹*air/fumes*› aspirar, respirar; ***to ~ one's last*** (liter) exhalar el último suspiro (liter) 2 (exhale): **she ~d garlic all over me** me echó todo su aliento a ajo 3 (instill, inspire) infundir; **to ~ new life into sth** infundirle nueva vida a algo 4 (utter) ‹*sigh*› dejar escapar; **don't ~ a word of this to anyone** no le digas una palabra de esto a nadie

(Phrasal verbs)

• **breathe in**

A [v ▸ adv] aspirar

B [v ▸ o ▸ adv, v ▸ adv ▸ o] ‹*air/fumes*› aspirar, respirar

• **breathe out**

A [v ▸ adv] espirar

B [v ▸ o ▸ adv, v ▸ adv ▸ o] ‹*smoke*› expeler; ‹*air*› exhalar, expulsar

breather /'bri:ðər || 'bri:ðə(r)/ *n* (colloq): **to have o take a ~** tomar un respiro *or* descanso

breathing /'bri:ðɪŋ/ *n* [u] respiración *f*

breathing space *n* [u] respiro *m*

breathless /'breθləs || 'breθlɪs/ *adj*: **the blow left me ~** el golpe me dejó sin aliento; **he arrived ~** llegó jadeando

breathlessly /'breθləsli || 'breθlɪsli/ *adv* entrecortadamente, jadeando

breathlessness /'breθləsnəs || 'breθlɪsnɪs/ *n* [u] dificultad *f* al respirar

breathtaking /'breθ,teɪkɪŋ/ *adj* impresionante, imponente

bred /bred/ *past & past p of* **breed²**

breech /bri:tʃ/ *adj* ‹*birth*› de nalgas

breeches /'brɪtʃəz || 'brɪtʃɪz/ *pl n* (*knee ~*) (pantalones *mpl*) bombachos *mpl*; (*riding ~*) pantalones *mpl* de montar

b

breed¹ /bri:d/ *n* (of animals) raza *f*; (of plants) variedad *f*; **a new ~ of athletes** una nueva generación de atletas; **a dying ~** una especie en vías de extinción; **a ~ apart** un mundo aparte

breed² (*past & past p* **bred**) *vt* 1 ‹*animals*› criar* 2 (raise, educate): **I'm a Londoner born and bred** nací y me crié en Londres 3 ‹*violence*› engendrar, generar; **success ~s success** el éxito llama al éxito

■ **breed** *vi* (reproduce) reproducirse*

breeder /'bri:dər || 'bri:də(r)/ *n* (of animals) criador, -dora *m,f*; (of plants) cultivador, -dora *m,f*

breeding /'bri:dɪŋ/ *n* [u] 1 (reproduction) reproducción *f* 2 (raising — of animals) cría *f*; (— of plants) cultivo *m* 3 (upbringing): **a woman of ~** una mujer de buena cuna; **politeness is a sign of good ~** la cortesía es señal de buena educación

breeding ground *n* (Zool) lugar *m* de cría; **a ~ ~ for revolutionaries** un semillero de revolucionarios; **a ~ ~ for violence** un caldo de cultivo para la violencia

breeze¹ /bri:z/ *n*

A [c u] (light wind) brisa *f*

B (sth easy) (colloq): **to be a ~** ser* pan comido (fam), ser* un bollo (RPl fam)

breeze² *vi* (colloq): **to ~ in/out** entrar/salir* tan campante *or* tan pancho (fam); **he ~d into the office** entró en la oficina como Pedro *or* Perico por su casa (fam)

Phrasal verb

• **breeze through** [v ▸ prep ▸ o] (colloq): **they ~d through the exam** el examen les resultó un paseo (fam)

breezily /'bri:zəli || 'bri:zɪli/ *adv* (cheerfully) alegremente, jovialmente

breezy /'bri:zi/ *adj* **-zier, -ziest**

A (windy) ‹*spot*› ventoso; **it was pleasantly ~** soplaba una agradable brisa; **it's a bit ~ today** hace un poco de vientecito hoy

B (lively) (colloq) ‹*person*› dinámico; ‹*smile/greeting*› alegre y simpático

brethren /'breðrən/ *pl n* (arch *or* liter) hermanos *mpl*

Breton¹ /'bretn̩/ *adj* bretón

Breton² *n* 1 [c] (person) bretón, -tona *m,f* 2 [u] (language) bretón *m*

brevity /'brevəti/ *n* [u] 1 (shortness) (frml) brevedad *f* 2 (conciseness) brevedad *f*, concisión *f*; **~ is the soul of wit** lo bueno, si breve, dos veces bueno

brew¹ /bru:/ *n* brebaje *m*

brew² *vt* ‹*beer*› fabricar*, hacer*; ‹*tea*› preparar, hacer*; ‹*mischief*› tramar, maquinar

■ **brew** *vi* 1 (make beer) fabricar* cerveza 2 «*tea*»: **the tea is ~ing** el té se está haciendo 3 «*storm*» avecinarse; «*trouble*» gestarse

brewer /'bru:ər || 'bru:ə(r)/ *n* cervecero, -ra *m,f*

brewery /'bru:əri/ *n* (*pl* **-ries**) fábrica *f* de cerveza, cervecería *f*

briar /'braɪər || 'braɪə(r)/ *n* [c] ▸ **brier**

bribe¹ /braɪb/ *n* soborno *m*; **to take** *o* **accept a ~** dejarse sobornar, aceptar un soborno

bribe² *vt* sobornar; **to ~ sb to + INF** sobornar a algn PARA QUE (+ *subj*)

bribery /'braɪbəri/ *n* [u] soborno *m*

bric-a-brac /'brɪkəbræk/ *n* [u] baratijas *fpl*, chucherías *fpl*

brick /brɪk/ *n* 1 (Const) ladrillo *m*; ***to drop a ~*** (BrE) meter* la pata (fam) 2 (toy) cubo *m*

Phrasal verb

• **brick in, brick up** [v ▸ o ▸ adv, v ▸ adv ▸ o] tabicar*, tapiar

brick: **~layer** *n* albañil *m*; **~red** /'brɪk'red/ *adj* (*pred* **~ red**) rojo teja *adj inv*, rojo ladrillo *adj inv*; **~s and mortar** *n* [u] (buildings) propiedad *f* inmobiliaria; (*before n*) ‹*investment/company*› inmobiliario; **~work** *n* [u] (bricks) enladrillado *m*, ladrillos *mpl*; (way bricks are laid) aparejo *m*

bridal /'braɪdl̩/ *adj* ‹*procession*› nupcial; ‹*shop*› para novias; **~ gown** traje *m* de novia

bride /braɪd/ *n* novia *f*; **the ~ and groom** los novios; (after ceremony) los recién casados, los novios

bride: **~groom** *n* novio *m*; **~smaid** *n* dama *f* de honor; (child) *niña que acompaña a la novia*

bridge¹ /brɪdʒ/ *n*

A [c] 1 puente *m*; ***to build ~s*** tender* un puente (de unión); ***we'll cross that ~ when we come to it*** ese problema lo resolveremos cuando llegue el momento; ▸ **burn¹** *vt* **A1**, **water¹ A** 2 (on ship) puente *m* (de mando) 3 (of nose) caballete *m*; (of glasses) puente *m*

B [c] (Dent) puente *m*

C [u] (card game) bridge *m*

bridge² *vt* ‹*river*› tender* *or* construir* un puente sobre; ‹*differences*› salvar

bridle¹ /'braɪdl̩/ *n* brida *f*

bridle² *vi* **to ~ (AT sth)** molestarse (POR algo)

■ **bridle** *vt* ‹*horse*› embridar, ponerle* la brida a

bridle path *n* camino *m* de herradura

brief¹ /bri:f/ *adj* 1 ‹*reign/interlude*› breve 2 ‹*statement/summary*› breve, sucinto; **his report was ~ and to the point** su informe era breve e iba al grano; **in ~** en resumen 3 (scanty) diminuto

brief² *n* 1 (Law) *expediente entregado por el abogado al* **barrister** 2 (instructions) instrucciones *fpl*; (area of responsibility) competencia *f*

brief³ *vt* ‹*lawyer*› instruir*; ‹*pilot/spy*› darle* instrucciones *or* órdenes a; ‹*committee*› informar; **the president had been badly ~ed for the meeting** el presidente no había sido bien preparado para la reunión

briefcase /'bri:fkeɪs/ *n* maletín *m*, portafolio(s) *m* (esp AmL)

briefing /'bri:fɪŋ/ *n* 1 (**~** *session*) sesión *f* para dar instrucciones 2 (*press* **~**) reunión *f* informativa (para la prensa)

briefly /'bri:fli/ *adv* 1 ‹*visit/rule*› por poco tiempo; **she ~ wondered what he was doing there** se preguntó por un momento qué hacía él allí 2 ‹*reply/speak*› brevemente, sucintamente 3 (*indep*) en resumen, en pocas palabras

briefs /bri:fs/ *pl n* (man's) calzoncillos *mpl*, slip *m*; (woman's) calzones *mpl* (esp AmL), bragas *fpl* (Esp), bombachas *fpl* (RPl), pantaletas *fpl* (AmC, Ven)

brier /'braɪər || 'braɪə(r)/ *n* (wild rose) rosal *m* silvestre; (thornbush) zarza *f*

brig /brɪg/ *n* (AmE) (prison) calabozo *m*

brigade /brɪ'geɪd/ *n* brigada *f*; **the brown rice ~** (colloq) los fanáticos de la cocina macrobiótica

brigadier /'brɪgə'dɪr || ,brɪgə'dɪə(r)/ *n* (in UK) general *mf* de brigada

brigadier general *n* (in US) general *mf* de brigada

bright /braɪt/ *adj* **-er, -est**

A 1 ‹*star*› brillante; ‹*light*› brillante, fuerte; ‹*room*› con mucha luz; **draw the curtains, it's too ~** corre las cortinas, hay demasiada luz; **it was a ~, sunny day** era un día de sol radiante 2 ‹*color*› fuerte, vivo, brillante; **a ~ red shirt** una camisa de un rojo fuerte *or* vivo *or* brillante

B 1 (cheerful) ‹*eyes*› lleno de vida, vivaracho; **to get up ~ and early** (colloq) levantarse tempranito (fam) 2 (hopeful) ‹*future*› prometedor; **the prospects are not very ~** las perspectivas no son muy prometedoras; **things are looking ~er now** las cosas tienen mejor cara ahora; ***to look on the ~ side of sth*** mirar *or* ver* el lado bueno de algo

C (intelligent) ‹*person*› inteligente; **whose ~ idea was it to ...?** (iro) ¿quién tuvo la brillante idea de ...? (iró)

brighten /'braɪtn̩/ *vi* 1 (become brighter) «*light*» hacerse* más brillante *or* más fuerte; **her eyes ~ed** se le iluminaron los ojos 2 **~ (up)** (become cheerful, hopeful) «*person*» animarse, alegrarse; «*situation/prospects*» mejorar; **it ~ed up in the afternoon** por la tarde salió el sol *or* aclaró; **her face ~ed (up)** se le iluminó la cara

■ **brighten** *vt* 1 (make brighter) iluminar 2 **~ (up)** ‹*room*› alegrar; ‹*occasion/party*› animar

bright-eyed /'braɪt'aɪd/ *adj* de ojos vivos *or* vivarachos; ***~ and bushy-tailed*** (hum) lleno de vida y energía

brightly /'braɪtli/ *adv* 1 ‹*shine*› intensamente, vivamente; **a ~ polished table** una mesa resplandeciente 2 ‹*say/smile*› alegremente

brightness /'braɪtnəs || 'braɪtnɪs/ *n* [u]

A (of light, star) brillo *m*, resplandor *m*; (of morning) claridad *f*, luminosidad *f*

B (cheerfulness) alegría *f*

C (intelligence) inteligencia *f*

brights /braɪts/ *pl n* (Auto) (AmE colloq) (luces *fpl*) largas *or* (Andes, Méx) altas *fpl*

bright spark *n* (BrE iro) lumbrera *f* (iró), genio *m* (iró)

brilliance /'brɪljəns/ *n* [u] **1** (brightness) resplandor *m*, fulgor *m* **2** (skill, intelligence) brillantez *f*

brilliant /'brɪljənt/ *adj* **1** ‹*light*› brillante; ‹*sunshine*› radiante; ‹*red/green*› brillante, luminoso **2** ‹*student/performance*› brillante **3** (BrE colloq) ‹*person/party*› genial (fam), fenomenal (fam); **¡~!** ¡genial! (fam)

brilliantine /'brɪljənti:n/ *n* [u] brillantina *f*

brilliantly /'brɪljəntli/ *adv* **1** ‹*shine*› intensamente **2** ‹*write*› con brillantez; ‹*funny*› extraordinariamente; **he played ~** (colloq) jugó genial *or* fenomenal (fam)

brim[1] /brɪm/ *n*

A (of hat) ala *f‡*

B (of vessel) borde *m*

brim[2] **-mm-** *vi*: **to ~ WITH sth**: **her eyes were ~ming with tears** tenía los ojos llenos de lágrimas; **to be ~ming with happiness** estar* rebosante *or* desbordante de felicidad

Phrasal verb

- **brim over** [v ▸ adv] ‹‹*cup*›› desbordarse, rebosar; **he was ~ming over with enthusiasm** estaba rebosante *or* desbordante de entusiasmo

brimful /'brɪm'fʊl/ *adj* (*pred*) **to be ~ OF sth** ‹*of ideas*› estar* repleto DE algo; ‹*of energy*› estar* rebosante *or* desbordante DE algo

brimstone /'brɪmstəʊn/ *n* [u] (arch) azufre *m*; *see also* **fire[1] A1**

brine /braɪn/ *n* [u] **1** (saltwater) salmuera *f* **2** (seawater) agua *f‡* salada *or* de mar **3** (the sea) (liter) **the ~** el piélago (liter)

bring /brɪŋ/ (*past & past p* **brought**) *vt*

A **1** (convey, carry) traer*; **~ this to the kitchen** (AmE) lleva esto a la cocina; **she's ~ing Lucy with her** va a venir con Lucy, va a traer a Lucy; **~ your passport with you** traiga el pasaporte; **that ~s me to my next point: ...** esto me lleva a lo siguiente: ...; **~ the chair inside/outside** mete (dentro) *or* (AmL) entra/saca la silla; **~ her in** hazla pasar *or* entrar **2** (attract, cause to come) atraer*; **what ~s you here?** ¿qué te trae por aquí?

B **1** (result in, produce) traer*; **it will ~ enormous benefits** va a traer *or* reportar enormes beneficios; **these benefits ~ with them certain responsibilities** estas ventajas conllevan ciertas responsabilidades; **you've brought so much happiness to those poor children** les has dado tanta alegría a esos pobres niños; **to ~ a smile to sb's face** hacer* sonreír a algn; **it brought tears to my eyes** hizo que se me llenaran los ojos de lágrimas; ***to ~ sth to bear***: **to ~ pressure to bear on sb** ejercer* presión sobre algn; **he brought his experience to bear on the problem** hizo uso de toda su experiencia para resolver el problema **2** (persuade): **I couldn't ~ myself to do it** no pude hacerlo

C (earn) ‹*profit/return*› dejar

Phrasal verbs

- **bring about** [v ▸ o ▸ adv, v ▸ adv ▸ o] (cause) ‹*downfall/crisis*› dar* lugar a, ocasionar; **to try to ~ about change in society** tratar de lograr que se produzcan cambios en la sociedad
- **bring along** [v ▸ o ▸ adv, v ▸ adv ▸ o] traer*
- **bring around**

A [v ▸ o ▸ adv, v ▸ adv ▸ o] (take along) traer*

B [v ▸ o ▸ adv] **1** (persuade) convencer*; **we finally brought her around to our point of view** finalmente conseguimos convencerla **2** (steer): **I brought the conversation around to James** llevé la conversación al tema de James **3** (restore consciousness) hacer* volver en sí

- **bring back** [v ▸ o ▸ adv, v ▸ adv ▸ o] **1** (return): **I'll ~ your book back tomorrow** te devolveré *or* (AmL exc CS) te regresaré el libro mañana; **crying won't ~ him back** con llorar no vas a conseguir que vuelva; **this ~s us back to the question of money** esto nos vuelve a llevar al tema del dinero; **to ~ sb back to life** devolverle* la vida a algn **2** ‹*gift/souvenir*› traer* **3** (reintroduce) ‹*custom*› volver* a introducir **4** (recall) recordar*; **it brought back memories** me (*or* le *etc*) trajo recuerdos
- **bring down** [v ▸ o ▸ adv, v ▸ adv ▸ o] **1** (lower) ‹*price*› reducir*, hacer* bajar; ‹*temperature*› hacer* bajar **2** (cause to fall) ‹*tree/wall*› tirar, echar abajo; ‹*player/opponent/plane*› derribar; ‹*government*› derrocar*, hacer* caer
- **bring forth** [v ▸ adv ▸ o] (arch *or* liter) ‹*fruit*› dar*; ‹*child*› dar* a luz
- **bring forward** [v ▸ o ▸ adv, v ▸ adv ▸ o] **1** ‹*witness*› hacer* comparecer; ‹*evidence/idea*› presentar **2** (to earlier time) ‹*appointment*› adelantar
- **bring home** [v ▸ o ▸ adv, v ▸ adv ▸ o]: **her letter brought home to me the seriousness of the situation** su carta me hizo dar cuenta cabal de la gravedad de la situación
- **bring in** [v ▸ o ▸ adv, v ▸ adv ▸ o]

A **1** (earn): **his job doesn't ~ in much money** no saca mucho dinero con su trabajo **2** (attract) ‹*customers*› atraer* **3** (involve, use): **they had to ~ the police in** tuvieron que hacer intervenir a la policía; **we have to ~ in extra staff in the summer** tenemos que contratar personal extra en verano

B **1** (introduce) ‹*regulation/system*› introducir*, implantar; ‹*bill*› presentar **2** (Law): **to ~ in a verdict of guilty** declarar culpable a algn

- **bring off** [v ▸ o ▸ adv, v ▸ adv ▸ o] ‹*feat/victory*› conseguir*, lograr; ‹*plan*› llevar a cabo; ‹*deal*› conseguir*
- **bring on**

A [v ▸ o ▸ adv, v ▸ adv ▸ o] **1** (cause) ‹*attack/breakdown*› provocar*; **what brought this on?** ¿esto a qué se debe? **2** (introduce) ‹*player*› hacer* salir

B [v ▸ o ▸ prep ▸ o] (cause to befall): **he brought it all on himself** él (mismo) se lo buscó

- **bring out**

A [v ▸ o ▸ adv, v ▸ adv ▸ o] **1** ‹*product/model*› sacar* (al mercado); ‹*edition/book*› publicar*, sacar* **2** (accentuate): **children ~ out the best in her** el trato con niños hace resaltar *or* pone de manifiesto sus mejores cualidades **3** (make bloom) hacer* florecer **4** (BrE) **to ~ sb out IN sth**: **it brought me out in spots** hizo que me salieran granos

B [v ▸ o ▸ adv] (make less shy): **I tried to ~ her out a bit** traté de ayudarla a vencer su timidez

- **bring round** (BrE) ▸**bring around**
- **bring together** [v ▸ o ▸ adv, v ▸ adv ▸ o]: **the conference will ~ together scientists from all over the world** el congreso reunirá *or* congregará a científicos de todo el mundo; **a tragedy like this can ~ a family together** una tragedia así puede unir a una familia; **they were brought together by chance** el destino quiso que se conocieran (*or* se encontraran *etc*)
- **bring up** [v ▸ o ▸ adv, v ▸ adv ▸ o] **1** (rear) ‹*child*› criar*; **I was brought up in India** me crié en la India; **you were badly brought up** te criaron muy mal; **they brought us up to respect authority** desde niños nos enseñaron a respetar la autoridad **2** (mention) ‹*subject*› sacar*; **did you have to ~ that up?** ¿por qué tuviste que sacar ese tema?; **I wanted to ~ up the matter of ...** quería mencionar el asunto de ... **3** (vomit) vomitar, devolver*
- **bring upon** ▸**bring on B**

brink /brɪŋk/ *n* borde *m*; **the country stood on the ~ of war** el país estaba al borde de la guerra; **to be on the ~ of -ING** estar* a punto de +INF

brinkmanship /'brɪŋkmənʃɪp/ *n* [u] política *f* arriesgada *or* suicida

briny /'braɪni/ *adj* **-nier, -niest** salobre

brisk /brɪsk/ *adj* **1** (lively, quick) ‹*pace*› rápido y enérgico, brioso; ‹*walk*› a paso ligero; **ice-cream sellers did a ~ trade** los vendedores de helados vendieron muchísimo **2** (efficient) ‹*person/manner*› enérgico *or* dinámico y eficiente **3** ‹*wind/morning*› fresco

brisket /'brɪskət || 'brɪskɪt/ *n* [u] pecho *m* (*corte de carne del cuarto delantero*)

briskly /'brɪskli/ *adv* ‹*walk*› con brío; ‹*say*› con tono de eficiencia; **it's selling ~** se está vendiendo muy bien

bristle[1] /'brɪsəl/ *n* [c u] **1** (on animal) cerda *f* **2** (on person): **his face was covered in ~(s)** tenía la barba crecida

bristle[2] *vi* **1** (stand up) ‹‹*hair*›› erizarse*, ponerse* de punta **2** (show annoyance) erizarse*; **to ~ AT sth**: **she ~d at his rudeness** su grosería la irritó **3** (have many) **to ~ WITH sth**: **the place was bristling with tourists** el lugar estaba repleto *or* (pey) plagado de turistas; **to ~ with difficulties** estar* erizado de dificultades

bristly /'brɪsli/ *adj* ‹*beard*› hirsuto; **don't kiss me, you're too ~** no me beses, que tu barba está muy rasposa

b

Brit /brɪt/ *n* (colloq) británico, -ca *m,f*
Britain /'brɪtn̩ || 'brɪtən/ *n* Gran Bretaña *f*
britches /'brɪtʃəz || 'brɪtʃɪz/ *pl n* ▸ **breeches**
British[1] /'brɪtɪʃ/ *adj* británico
British[2] *pl n* **the ~** los británicos

British Council

Una organización que corresponde en algunos aspectos al Instituto Cervantes español, financiada por el gobierno británico para promover la difusión de la lengua inglesa en el mundo y el conocimiento de la cultura, literatura y costumbres de las distintas naciones y regiones del Reino Unido. Tiene sedes en 227 ciudades en 109 países. En EEUU no existe ningún equivalente exacto del *British Council*, pero en cada embajada norteamericana existe una filial del Departamento de Estado llamada *Information Resource Center*, que desempeña algunas de las mismas funciones culturales

Britisher /'brɪtɪʃər || 'brɪtɪʃə(r)/ *n* (AmE) británico, -ca *m,f*
British: **~ Isles** *pl n* **the ~ Isles** las Islas Británicas; **~ Summer Time** *n* [u] *hora de verano en Gran Bretaña, adelantada en una hora con respecto a la hora de Greenwich*

British Isles

Las Islas Británicas comprenden Gran Bretaña (Great Britain), Irlanda (tanto Irlanda del Norte como la República de Irlanda) y las islas más pequeñas que están a su alrededor, como las Islas Shetlands (*the Shetlands*), la Isla de Man (*Isle of Man*) y las Islas Anglonormandas (*the Channel Islands*)

British Library

La Biblioteca Nacional Británica, antiguamente la biblioteca del *British Museum* (Museo Nacional Británico), existe desde 1973 como entidad independiente. Cuenta hoy con una de las colecciones más prestigiosas de libros, periódicos, revistas, mapas, partituras, grabaciones sonoras y manuscritos del mundo entero. Su modernísima nueva sede, cerca de la estación londinense de *Saint Pancras*, fue inaugurada en 1997

Briton /'brɪtn̩ || 'brɪtən/ *n* ciudadano británico, ciudadana británica *m,f*; **the ancient ~s** los antiguos britanos
Brittany /'brɪtn̩i || 'brɪtəni/ *n* Bretaña *f*
brittle /'brɪtl̩/ *adj* 1 ‹*twigs/bones*› quebradizo; ‹*peace*› frágil, precario 2 ‹*laugh/voice*› crispado
broach /brəʊtʃ/ *vt* ‹*subject*› mencionar
broad[1] /brɔ:d/ *adj*
A ‹*avenue*› ancho; ‹*valley*› grande; ‹*forehead*› despejado, amplio; ‹*grin*› de oreja a oreja; **she has ~ hips** es ancha de caderas
B 1 (extensive) ‹*syllabus*› amplio; ‹*interests*› numeroso, variado; **in its ~est sense** en su sentido más amplio 2 (general) ‹*guidelines/conclusions*› general
C 1 **a ~ hint** una indirecta muy clara *or* (hum) muy directa 2 ‹*accent*› cerrado
broad[2] *n* (woman) (AmE sl) tipa *f* (fam), vieja *f* (Col, Méx, Ven fam)
broadband[1] /'brɔ:dbænd/ *adj* de banda ancha
broadband[2] *n* [u] banda *f* ancha
broad bean *n* haba *f*
broadcast[1] /'brɔ:dkæst || 'brɔ:dkɑ:st/ (*past & past p* **broadcast**) *vt* 1 ‹*program*› transmitir, emitir; **the fight was ~ live** la pelea se transmitió *or* (Esp) se retransmitió en directo 2 (make known) difundir, divulgar*
■ **broadcast** *vi* transmitir, emitir
broadcast[2] *n* programa *m*, emisión *f* (frml)
broadcaster /'brɔ:dkæstər || 'brɔ:dkɑ:stə(r)/ *n*: *presentador, locutor etc de radio o televisión*
broadcasting /'brɔ:dkæstɪŋ || 'brɔ:dkɑ:stɪŋ/ *n* [u] (Rad) radiodifusión *f*; (TV) televisión *f*
broaden /'brɔ:dn̩/ *vt* ‹*scope/horizons/interests*› ampliar*; **travel ~s the mind** los viajes amplían los horizontes
■ **broaden** *vi* «*scope/interests*» ampliarse*; «*river*» ensancharse
broadly /'brɔ:dli/ *adv*
A (generally, approximately): **the two systems are ~ similar** en líneas generales, los dos sistemas son similares; **~ speaking** en líneas generales, hablando en términos generales
B ‹*grin*› de oreja a oreja
broad: **~minded** /'brɔ:d'maɪndəd || ,brɔ:d'maɪndɪd/ *adj* de criterio amplio; **~sheet** *n*: *periódico de formato grande*; **~-shouldered** /'brɔ:d'ʃəʊldərd || ,brɔ:d'ʃəʊldəd/ *adj* ancho de espaldas
broadside[1] /'brɔ:dsaɪd/ *n* 1 (volley) andanada *f* 2 (verbal or written attack) ataque *m*, invectiva *f*
broadside[2], **broadside on** *adv* de lado, de costado

Broadway

Una calle famosa por sus teatros que atraviesa el barrio neoyorquino de Manhattan. El término a menudo se usa para referirse al teatro y al mundo del espéctaculo de EEUU en general. Antes del surgimiento de la industria del cine, era el lugar principal donde los actores podían hacerse famosos

brocade /brəʊ'keɪd || brə'keɪd/ *n* [u] brocado *m*
broccoli /'brɑ:kəli || 'brɒkəli/ *n* [u] brócoli *m*, brécol *m*
brochure /brəʊ'ʃʊr || 'brəʊʃə(r)/ *n* folleto *m*
brogan /'brəʊgən/ *n* (AmE) ▸ **brogue**
brogue /brəʊg/ *n*
A (shoe) *zapato bajo de cuero*
B (Irish accent) (*no pl*) acento *m* irlandés
broil /brɔɪl/ (esp AmE) *vt* asar a la parrilla *or* al grill
broiler /'brɔɪlər || 'brɔɪlə(r)/ *n* (AmE) parrilla *f*, grill *m*
broke[1] /brəʊk/ *past of* **break**[1]
broke[2] *adj* (colloq) (*pred*): **to be ~** estar* pelado; **to be flat** *o* **stony** *o* (AmE) **stone ~** estar* pelado *or* (Chi) planchado *or* (Esp) sin un duro *or* (Col) en la olla
broken[1] /'brəʊkən/ *past p of* **break**[1]
broken[2] *adj*
A 1 ‹*window/vase/chair*› roto; ‹*bone*› roto, quebrado (AmL); **~ glass** vidrios *mpl or* (esp Esp) cristales *mpl* rotos; **do not apply to ~ skin** no aplicar si hay cortes, rasguños etc 2 (not working) roto
B (emotionally) ‹*voice*› quebrado, entrecortado; **she died of a ~ heart** murió de pena; **he's a ~ man** está destrozado
C 1 ‹*home/marriage*› deshecho 2 (not fulfilled) ‹*promise/contract*› roto; ‹*trust*› defraudado
D (interrupted): **she'd only had a few hours' ~ sleep** había dormido poco y mal, despertándose cada dos por tres; **a ~ line** una línea discontinua
E (irregular, rough) ‹*ground*› accidentado
F (imperfect): **in ~ English** en inglés chapurreado
broken: **~-down** /'brəʊkən'daʊn/ *adj* ‹*car/machine*› averiado, descompuesto (AmL), en pana (Chi), varado (Col); ‹*shed/gate*› destartalado; **~-hearted** /'brəʊkən'hɑ:rtəd || ,brəʊkən'hɑ:tɪd/ *adj* destrozado, deshecho
broker[1] /'brəʊkər || 'brəʊkə(r)/ *n* 1 (agent) agente *mf*; **insurance ~** agente *mf* de seguros 2 (*stock~*) corredor, -dora *m,f* de bolsa
broker[2] *vt* (AmE) ‹*bonds/commodities*› hacer* corretaje de
brolly /'brɑ:li || 'brɒli/ *n* (*pl* **-lies**) (BrE colloq) paraguas *m*
bromide /'brəʊmaɪd/ *n* [c u] bromuro *m*
bronchial /'brɑ:ŋkiəl || 'brɒŋkiəl/ *adj* bronquial; **~ tubes** bronquios *mpl*
bronchitis /brɑ:ŋ'kaɪtəs || brɒŋ'kaɪtɪs/ *n* [u] bronquitis *f*
bronco /'brɑ:ŋkəʊ || 'brɒŋkəʊ/ *n* (*pl* **-cos**) (AmE) potro *m* salvaje
bronze /brɑ:nz || brɒnz/ *n*
A 1 [u] (Metall) bronce *m*; (*before n*) **the B~ Age** la Edad de bronce 2 [c] **~ (medal)** medalla *f* de bronce
B [u] (color) color *m* bronce
bronzed /brɑ:nzd || brɒnzd/ *adj* bronceado
brooch /brəʊtʃ/ *n* prendedor *m*, broche *m*
brood[1] /bru:d/ *n* 1 (of birds) nidada *f*; (of mammals) camada *f* 2 (of children) (hum) prole *f* (fam & hum)
brood[2] *vi* (reflect): **she sat ~ing on the unfairness of life** rumiaba lo injusta que era la vida; **stop ~ing on** *o* **over it** deja de darle vueltas al asunto
broody /'bru:di/ *adj* **-dier, -diest**
A : **~ hen** gallina *f* clueca; **it makes me feel ~** (BrE colloq & hum) me despierta el instinto maternal
B (moody) meditabundo
brook[1] /brʊk/ *n* arroyo *m*

brook² *vt* (frml) (*usu with neg*) tolerar, admitir

broom /bru:m/ *n*
A [c] (brush) escoba *f*; ***a new ~ sweeps clean*** escoba nueva barre bien; (*before n*) ~ **cupboard** *o* (AmE) **closet** armario *m* de los artículos de limpieza
B [u] (plant) retama *f*, hiniesta *f*

broomstick /ˈbru:mstɪk/ *n* palo *m* de escoba; (of a witch) escoba *f*

broth /brɔ:θ || brɒθ/ *n* [u] caldo *m*

brothel /ˈbrɑ:θəl || ˈbrɒθəl/ *n* burdel *m*

brother¹ /ˈbrʌðər || ˈbrʌðə(r)/ *n* 1 (relative) hermano *m*; **do you have any ~s and sisters?** ¿tienes hermanos?; **the Jones ~s** los hermanos Jones 2 (comrade) compañero *m* 3 (*as form of address*) (AmE colloq) hermano (fam), tío (Esp fam), mano (AmL exc CS fam)

brother² *interj* (esp AmE colloq): **(oh) ~!** ¡Dios mío!

brotherhood /ˈbrʌðərhʊd || ˈbrʌðəhʊd/ *n* 1 [u] (fellowship) fraternidad *f* 2 [c] (association) hermandad *f*, (Relig) cofradía *f*

brother-in-law /ˈbrʌðərɪn,lɔ:/ *n* (*pl* **brothers-in-law**) cuñado *m*

brotherly /ˈbrʌðərli || ˈbrʌðəli/ *adj* fraternal

brought /brɔ:t/ *past & past p of* **bring**

brow /braʊ/ *n* 1 (forehead) (liter) frente *f* 2 (*eye~*) ceja *f* 3 (of hill) cima *f*

browbeat /ˈbraʊbi:t/ *vt* (*past* **browbeat**; *past p* **browbeaten** /ˈbraʊ,bi:tn̩/) intimidar; **they tried to ~ me into joining them** intentaron intimidarme para que me uniera a ellos

brown¹ /braʊn/ *adj* **-er, -est** ‹*shoe/dress/eyes*› marrón, café *adj inv* (AmC, Chi, Méx), carmelito (Col); ‹*hair*› castaño; ‹*skin/person*› (naturally) moreno; (suntanned) bronceado, moreno; **to get ~** broncearse, ponerse* moreno

brown² *n* [u] marrón *m*, café *m* (AmC, Chi, Méx), carmelito *m* (Col)

brown³ *vt* 1 (Culin) dorar 2 (tan) broncear
■ **brown** *vi* 1 (Culin) dorarse 2 (tan) broncearse, ponerse* moreno

brown: ~ **bear** *n* oso *m* pardo; ~ **bread** *n* pan *m* negro *or* (Esp) moreno

browned-off /ˈbraʊndˈɔ:f || ˌbraʊndˈɒf/ *adj* (BrE colloq) (*pred*) **to be ~** estar* harto

brownie /ˈbraʊni/ *n*
A (cake) *bizcocho de chocolate y nueces*
B (in UK) **Brownie** alita *f*; ***to earn B~ points*** (colloq) marcarse* *or* anotarse puntos

brown: **~out** *n* (AmE) apagón *m* (parcial); ~ **paper** *n* [u] papel *m* de estraza; ~ **rice** *n* arroz *m* integral; ~ **sauce** *n* [u c] 1 (thickened stock) salsa *f* (*hecha con jugo de carne*) 2 (spicy relish) (BrE) *salsa agridulce con especias*; **~stone** *n* (AmE) 1 [u] (stone) piedra *f* rojiza 2 [c] (building) casa *f* de piedra rojiza; ~ **sugar** *n* [u] azúcar *m* moreno, azúcar *f* morena

browse /braʊz/ *vi* (look) mirar (*en una tienda, catálogo etc*); **to ~ THROUGH sth**: **she was browsing through the records/a magazine** estaba echando un vistazo a los discos/hojeando una revista
■ **browse** *vt* (Comput) explorar

browser /ˈbraʊzər || ˈbraʊzə(r)/ *n*
A (Comput) navegador *m*
B (person) curioso, -sa *m,f*

bruise¹ /bru:z/ *n* moretón *m*, cardenal *m*, morado *m* (Esp, Ven)

bruise² *vt* ‹*body/arm*› contusionar (frml); ‹*fruit*› magullar, mallugar* (Méx, Ven); ‹*feelings/ego*› herir*
■ **bruise** *vi* «*fruit*» magullarse, mallugarse* (Méx, Ven); **he ~s very easily** le salen moretones (*or* cardenales *etc*) con mucha facilidad

bruiser /ˈbru:zər || ˈbru:zə(r)/ *n* (colloq) muchachote *m* (fam); (aggressive) matón *m*

bruit /bru:t/ *vt* (esp AmE liter) pregonar, divulgar*

brunch /brʌntʃ/ *n* [u c] (colloq) brunch *m* (*combinación de desayuno y almuerzo*)

brunette /bru:ˈnet/ *n* morena *f*, morocha *f* (CS)

brunt /brʌnt/ *n*: **to bear** *o* **take the ~ of sth** sufrir algo; **I had to bear the ~ of his anger** tuve que sufrir su cólera; **the city has taken the full ~ of the recession** la ciudad es la que más ha sufrido la crisis económica

brush¹ /brʌʃ/ *n*
A [c] (for cleaning) cepillo *m*; (for hair) cepillo *m*; (*paint~*) pincel *m*; (large) brocha *f*; ***to be tarred with the same ~*** (colloq) estar* cortados por la misma tijera *or* por el mismo patrón
B [c] (of fox) cola *f*
C [c] 1 (act): **I gave my hair a ~** me cepillé el pelo 2 (faint touch) roce *m* 3 (encounter) ~ **WITH sth/sb** ‹*with the law/the police*› roce *m* CON algo/algn; **she has had several ~es with death** ha visto la muerte de cerca en varias ocasiones
D [u] 1 (scrub) maleza *f* 2 (cut branches) broza *f*

brush² *vt* 1 (clean, groom) ‹*jacket/hair*› cepillar; **to ~ one's teeth** lavarse *or* cepillarse los dientes; **she ~ed his hair** le cepilló el pelo 2 (sweep): **he ~ed the crumbs off the table** quitó las migas de la mesa 3 (touch lightly) rozar*
■ **brush** *vi* **to ~ AGAINST sth/sb** rozar* algo/a algn

(Phrasal verbs)

• **brush aside** [v ▸ o ▸ adv, v ▸ adv ▸ o] ‹*person/obstacle*› apartar; ‹*objection/suggestion*› desdeñar

• **brush down** [v ▸ o ▸ adv, v ▸ adv ▸ o] (BrE) cepillar

• **brush off**
A [v ▸ o ▸ adv, v ▸ adv ▸ o] 1 ‹*mud/hair*› quitar (*cepillando*) 2 ‹*advances/suggestions*› no hacer* caso de, hacer* caso omiso de
B [v ▸ adv] «*dirt/mark*» salir*, quitarse (*al cepillarlo*)

• **brush up** 1 [v ▸ o ▸ adv, v ▸ adv ▸ o] (colloq) darle* un repaso a 2 [v ▸ adv] **to ~ up ON sth** darle* un repaso A algo

brush: **~-off** *n* (colloq): **to give sb the ~-off** darle* calabazas a algn (fam); **~stroke** *n* pincelada *f*; **~-up** *n* (BrE) (*no pl*) (grooming): **to have a wash and ~-up** lavarse y arreglarse un poco; **~wood** *n* [u] (cut branches) broza *f*, (scrub) maleza *f*; **~work** *n* [u] manejo *m* del pincel

brusque /brʌsk || brʊsk/ *adj* brusco

brusquely /ˈbrʌskli || ˈbrʊskli/ *adv* con brusquedad

Brussels /ˈbrʌsəlz/ *n* Bruselas *f*

brussels sprout, Brussels Sprout /ˈbrʌsəlz/ *n* col *f or* (AmS) repollito *m* de Bruselas

brutal /ˈbru:tl̩/ *adj* 1 (cruel, savage) ‹*killer/attack*› brutal; **a ~ sport** un deporte salvaje 2 (harsh) ‹*truth/frankness*› crudo 3 (severe) ‹*conditions*› atroz

brutality /bru:ˈtæləti/ *n* [u c] (*pl* **-ties**) brutalidad *f*; **police ~** malos tratos *mpl* por parte de la policía

brutalize /ˈbru:tl̩aɪz/ *vt* insensibilizar*, endurecer*

brutally /ˈbru:tl̩i/ *adv* 1 (cruelly) ‹*attack/treat*› brutalmente 2 (mercilessly) ‹*frank/honest*› crudamente, despiadadamente

brute¹ /bru:t/ *n* (colloq) 1 (person) animal *mf* (fam), bestia *f or mf*, bruto, -ta *m,f*; **he is a big ~ of a man** es un animal, es una *or* un bestia 2 (animal) bestia *f* (fam)

brute² *adj* (*before n*) ~ **force** fuerza *f* bruta

brutish /ˈbru:tɪʃ/ *adj* (coarse) bruto; (cruel) brutal, salvaje

BS *n* (AmE) = **Bachelor of Science**

BSc *n* (BrE) = **Bachelor of Science**

BSE (= **bovine spongiform encephalopathy**) encefalopatía *f* espongiforme bovina

BSI *n* = **British Standards Institution**

BST = **British Summer Time**

bubble¹ /ˈbʌbəl/ *n* (of air, gas) burbuja *f*; (of soap) pompa *f*; (in paintwork) ampolla *f*; **to blow ~s** hacer* pompas; **speech/thought ~** bocadillo *m*, globito *m* (*en una historieta*)

bubble² *vi*
A (form bubbles) «*lava*» bullir*; «*champagne*» burbujear
B «*person*»: **she ~s with enthusiasm** rebosa (de) *or* desborda entusiasmo, el entusiasmo le sale por los poros

(Phrasal verb)

• **bubble over** [v ▸ adv] (colloq): **she was bubbling over with enthusiasm** no cabía en sí de entusiasmo

bubble: ~ **bath** *n* [c u] baño *m* de burbujas *or* espuma; ~ **gum** *n* [u] chicle *m* (de globos), chicle *m* de bomba (Col, Ven), chicle *m* globero (Ur)

bubblejet printer /ˈbʌbəldʒet/ *n* impresora *f* de inyección (de tinta) por burbujas

b

bubbly[1] /ˈbʌbli/ *adj* **-lier, -liest** [1] ‹*person*› lleno de vida; ‹*personality*› efervescente [2] (full of bubbles) burbujeante

bubbly[2] *n* [u] (colloq) champán *m*, champaña *m or f*

bubonic plague /bu:ˈbɑ:nɪk ‖ bju:ˈbɒnɪk/ *n* [u] peste *f* bubónica

buccaneer /ˈbʌkəˈnɪr ‖ ˌbʌkəˈnɪə(r)/ *n* bucanero *m*

Bucharest /ˈbu:kərest ‖ ˌbu:kəˈrest/ *n* Bucarest *m*

buck[1] /bʌk/ *n*

A (male deer) ciervo *m* (macho); (male rabbit) conejo *m* (macho)

B (dollar) (esp AmE colloq) dólar *m*, verde *m* (AmL fam); ***to make a fast o quick ~*** hacer* dinero *or* (AmL fam tb) plata fácil

C (responsibility): ***to pass the ~*** (colloq) pasar la pelota (fam); **the ~ stops here** la responsabilidad es mía (*or* nuestra *etc*)

buck[2] *vi* [1] «*horse*» corcovear [2] (move jerkily) (AmE) «*car/deck*» dar* sacudidas [3] (resist, oppose) (esp AmE) **to ~ AGAINST sth/sb** rebelarse CONTRA algo/algn; **to ~ AGAINST *o* AT -ING** resistirse A + INF

■ **buck** *vt* ‹*trend*› resistirse *or* oponerse* a; **to ~ the system** ir* contra la corriente

Phrasal verb

• **buck up** (colloq)

A [v ▸ adv] [1] (become cheerful) levantar el ánimo; **~ up!** ¡levanta el ánimo!, ¡arriba ese ánimo! (fam) [2] (make effort) (BrE) esforzarse* [3] (hurry) (BrE) moverse* (fam), acelerar (fam)

B [v ▸ o ▸ adv, v ▸ adv ▸ o] (cheer up) ‹*person*› levantarle el ánimo a; ***to ~ one's ideas up*** (BrE) mejorar el comportamiento/ponerse* a trabajar en serio

bucket[1] /ˈbʌkət ‖ ˈbʌkɪt/ *n* balde *m or* (Esp) cubo *m or* (Méx) cubeta *f or* (Ven) tobo *m*; **a ~ of water** un balde (*or* un cubo *etc*) de agua; **to rain ~s** llover* a cántaros; **to cry ~s** llorar a lágrima viva *or* (fam) a moco tendido; ***to kick the ~*** (colloq & hum) estirar la pata (fam & hum)

bucket[2] *vi* (esp BrE colloq) **~ (down)**: **it's ~ing (down)** está lloviendo a cántaros

bucket shop *n* (BrE colloq) agencia *f* de viajes (*que vende boletos de avión a precios reducidos*)

buckle[1] /ˈbʌkəl/ *n* hebilla *f*

buckle[2] *vt*

A (fasten) abrochar

B (bend) torcer*, combar

■ **buckle** *vi* (bend, crumple) «*wheel/metal*» torcerse*, combarse; **his knees ~d beneath him** se le doblaron las rodillas

Phrasal verbs

• **buckle down** [v ▸ adv] ponerse* a trabajar en serio

• **buckle up** [v ▸ adv] (AmE) ponerse* *or* abrocharse el cinturón de seguridad

buck: **~shot** *n* [u] perdigón *m*; **~skin** *n* [u] gamuza *f*; **~teeth** /ˈbʌkˈti:θ/ *pl n*: **to have ~teeth** tener* los dientes salidos; **~wheat** *n* [u] trigo *m* rubión *or* sarraceno, alforfón *m*

bud[1] /bʌd/ *n*

A (Bot) brote *m*, yema *f*; (of flower) capullo *m*; **to be in ~** tener* brotes; ***to nip sth in the ~*** (colloq) cortar algo de raíz

B (*as form of address*) (AmE colloq) ▸ **buddy**

bud[2] *vi* **-dd-** echar brotes

Budapest /ˈbu:dəpest ‖ ˌbu:dəˈpest/ *n* Budapest *m*

Buddha /ˈbu:də ‖ ˈbʊdə/ *n* Buda *m*

Buddhism /ˈbu:dɪzəm ‖ ˈbʊdɪzəm/ *n* [u] budismo *m*

Buddhist[1] /ˈbu:dəst ‖ ˈbʊdɪst/ *n* budista *mf*

Buddhist[2] *adj* budista

budding /ˈbʌdɪŋ/ *adj* (*before n*) ‹*artist/genius*› en ciernes

buddy /ˈbʌdi/ *n* (*pl* **-dies**) (AmE colloq) amigo *m*, compinche *m* (fam), cuate *m* (Méx fam); (*as form of address*) hermano (fam), macho (Esp fam), güey (Méx fam), gallo (Chi fam)

buddy-buddy /ˈbʌdiˈbʌdi/ *adj* (esp AmE colloq) (*pred*) muy compinche *or* (Méx) cuate (fam); **to be ~ WITH sb** estar* a partir un piñón *or* (CS) a partir (de) un confite con algn (fam)

budge /bʌdʒ/ *vi* (*usu with neg*) [1] (move) moverse*; **he stood there and refused to ~** se plantificó ahí y no hubo quien lo moviera [2] (change opinion) cambiar de opinión

■ **budge** *vt* [1] (move) correr [2] (persuade) convencer*, hacer* cambiar de opinión

budgerigar /ˈbʌdʒərigɑ:r ‖ ˈbʌdʒərigɑ:(r)/ *n* periquito *m*

budget[1] /ˈbʌdʒət ‖ ˈbʌdʒɪt/ *n* presupuesto *m*; **the B~** (in UK) los presupuestos generales del Estado; **the project ran over ~** el proyecto costó más de lo presupuestado *or* excedió el presupuesto; **a big-/low-~ production** una producción con un gran presupuesto/con un presupuesto reducido; **how to eat well on a (tight) ~** cómo comer bien económicamente *or* con un presupuesto reducido

budget[2] *vi* administrarse; **to learn to ~** aprender a administrar el dinero; **to ~ FOR sth/-ING**: **I hadn't ~ed for staying in a hotel** no había contado con *or* no había previsto gastos de hotel

budgie /ˈbʌdʒi/ *n* (BrE colloq) periquito *m*

buff[1] /bʌf/ *n*

A [u] [1] **~ (leather)** gamuza *f* [2] (color) beige *m* [3] (bare skin): **in the ~** (colloq & hum) en cueros (fam & hum)

B [c] (enthusiast) (colloq) aficionado, -da *m,f*; **film ~** cinéfilo, -la *m,f*; **jazz ~** aficionado al jazz

buff[2] *adj* [1] (made of buff) (*before n*) de gamuza [2] (buff-colored) beige *adj inv*, beis *adj inv* (Esp)

buff[3] *vt* ‹*metal*› pulir; ‹*shoes*› sacar* brillo a

buffalo /ˈbʌfələʊ/ *n* (*pl* **-loes** *or* **-los**) [1] (wild ox) búfalo *m*; (*water ~*) búfalo *m* de agua, carabao *m* [2] (bison) (AmE) bisonte *m*

buffer /ˈbʌfər ‖ ˈbʌfə(r)/ *n*

A [1] (AmE Auto) parachoques *m*, paragolpes *m* (RPl) [2] (BrE Rail) (on train) tope *m*; (in station) parachoques *m*, amortiguador *m* de choques; (*before n*) **~ state** estado *m* tapón; **~ zone** zona *f* parachoques

B (Comput) memoria *f* intermedia *or* interfaz, tampón *m*

buffet[1] /bəˈfeɪ ‖ ˈbʊfeɪ, ˈbʌfeɪ/ *n*

A (meal) buffet *m*

B (BrE) [1] (in train) bar *m*; (*before n*) **~ car** (also AmE) coche *m* restaurante, coche *m* comedor, vagón *m* restaurante [2] (cafeteria) bar *m* (*en una estación*)

buffet[2] /ˈbʌfət ‖ bʌfɪt/ *vt* zarandear, sacudir

buffeting /ˈbʌfətɪŋ ‖ ˈbʌfɪtɪŋ/ *n* (*no pl*): **the ~ of the waves** el embate de las olas; **the area took a ~ during the storm** la zona fue azotada *or* castigada por la tormenta

buffoon /bəˈfu:n/ *n* payaso, -sa *m,f*, bufón, -fona *m,f*

bug[1] /bʌg/ *n*

A [1] (biting insect) chinche *f or m*; ***to be as snug as a ~ in a rug*** (colloq) estar* en la gloria (fam) [2] (any insect) (esp AmE) bicho *m*

B (germ, disease) (colloq): **he caught *o* picked up a stomach ~** se agarró algo al estómago

C (colloq) [1] (obsession): **she got the travel ~** le entró la fiebre de los viajes [2] (enthusiast) (AmE): **a movie ~** un cinéfilo, un amante del cine

D (listening device) (colloq) micrófono *m* oculto

E (fault) problema *m*

F (Comput) error *m* (de programación), bug *m*

bug[2] **-gg-** *vt* (colloq)

A ‹*room/telephone*› colocar* micrófonos ocultos en

B (bother, irritate) fastidiar; **it really ~s me when you do that** me saca de quicio que hagas eso; **what's ~ging you?** ¿qué mosca te ha picado?

■ **bug** *vi* (AmE) «*eyes*» salirse* de las órbitas

bugbear /ˈbʌgber ‖ ˈbʌgbeə(r)/ *n* pesadilla *f*

bugger[1] /ˈbʌgər ‖ ˈbʌgə(r)/ *n*

A (BrE) [1] (unpleasant person) (vulg) hijo, -ja *m,f* de puta (vulg) [2] (person) (sl): **poor ~!** ¡pobre tipo! (fam)

B (sth difficult, unpleasant) (BrE sl): **the exam was a real ~** el examen fue jodidísimo (vulg); **~ *all***: **she did ~ all** no hizo un carajo (vulg)

bugger[2] *vt*

A (BrE) [1] (*in interj phrases*) (vulg): **(I'm) ~ed if I know!** ¡no tengo ni puta idea! (vulg) [2] (ruin, spoil) (sl) joder (vulg), chingar* (Méx vulg)

B (commit buggery with) sodomizar*

Phrasal verbs

• **bugger about** (BrE vulg)

A [v ▸ adv] (act foolishly) joder (vulg)

B [v ▸ o ▸ adv, v ▸ adv ▸ o] (inconvenience) joder (vulg)

• **bugger off** [v ▸ adv] (BrE vulg): **~ off!** ¡vete a la mierda! (vulg); **he ~ed off** se largó (fam)

• **bugger up** [v ▸ o ▸ adv, v ▸ adv ▸ o] (BrE vulg) joder (vulg); **I ~ed up my exam** la cagué en el examen (vulg)

bugger[3] *interj* (BrE vulg) ¡carajo! (vulg)

buggery /'bʌgəri/ *n* [u] sodomía *f*

bugging device /'bʌgɪŋ/ *n* micrófono *m* oculto

buggy /'bʌgi/ *n* (*pl* **-gies**)
A (horse-drawn vehicle) calesa *f*
B (*baby* ~) (baby carriage) (AmE) cochecito *m*; (pushchair) (BrE) sillita *f* de paseo (*plegable*)

bugle /'bju:gəl/ *n* clarín *m*, corneta *f*

build[1] /bɪld/ (*past & past p* **built**) *vt* ‹*house*› construir*, edificar*, hacer*; ‹*bridge/road/ship*› construir*; ‹*wall*› construir*, levantar, hacer*; ‹*fire/nest*› hacer*; ‹*career*› forjarse; ‹*empire*› levantar, construir*
■ **build** *vi* 1 (erect buildings) edificar* 2 (increase) «*tension/pressure*» aumentar

Phrasal verbs
- **build on** [v ▸ prep ▸ o] ‹*extension/kitchen*› agregar*
- **build up**
A [v ▸ o ▸ adv, v ▸ adv ▸ o] 1 (make bigger, stronger) ‹*muscles*› fortalecer*; **to ~ up one's strength** fortalecerse* 2 (accumulate) ‹*supplies/experience*› acumular; ‹*reserves*› acrecentar*; **they are ~ing up their forces in the area** están intensificando su presencia militar en la zona 3 (develop) ‹*reputation*› forjarse; ‹*confidence*› desarrollar; ‹*speed*› agarrar *or* (Esp) coger*; **to ~ up one's hopes** hacerse* ilusiones; **he built the firm up from nothing** levantó la empresa de la nada 4 (praise) (colloq) poner* por las nubes (fam)
B [v ▸ adv] 1 (accumulate) «*dirt*» acumularse, juntarse; **their debts had built up** sus deudas se habían ido acumulando 2 (increase) «*pressure/noise*» ir* en aumento; **to ~ up TO sth**: **the tension ~s up to a climax** la tensión va en aumento hasta llegar a un punto culminante

build[2] *n* complexión *f*; **with a slim ~** de complexión delgada; **the ~ of a swimmer** el físico de un nadador

builder /'bɪldər || 'bɪldə(r)/ *n* albañil *mf*; (contractor) contratista *mf*

building /'bɪldɪŋ/ *n* 1 [c] (edifice) edificio *m*, inmueble *m* (frml) 2 [u] (construction) construcción *f*; (*before n*) **~ contractor** contratista *mf* (de obras); **~ site** obra *f*; **the ~ trade** la industria de la construcción

building society *n* (in UK) sociedad *f* de crédito hipotecario

buildup /'bɪldʌp/ *n* 1 (accumulation) acumulación *f*; (of tension, pressure) aumento *m*, intensificación *f*, concentración *f* 2 (of troops) concentración *f* 3 (publicity) propaganda *f*, bombo *m* (fam)

built[1] /bɪlt/ *past & past p of* **build**[1]

built[2] *adj* (*pred*) 1 (constructed): **the school is ~ around a courtyard** la escuela está construida alrededor de un patio; **to be ~ OF/OUT OF sth** estar hecho* DE algo; **to be ~ INTO sth**: **the aquarium is ~ into the wall** el acuario está empotrado en la pared 2 (physically): **he's ~ like an ox** es muy corpulento; **she's heavily ~** es de complexión robusta; **athletically ~** con físico de atleta

-built /bɪlt/ *suff* (constructed): **brick~/stone~** hecho de ladrillo/piedra; **sturdily~** de construcción sólida

built: **~ environment** *n* urbanismo *m*, planificación *f* urbana; **~-in** /'bɪlt'ɪn/ *adj* (*before n*) 1 ‹*bookcase/desk*› empotrado, encastrado; ‹*equipment*› fijo; ‹*mechanism/feature*› incorporado 2 (inherent) ‹*weakness/tendency*› intrínseco; **~-up** /'bɪlt'ʌp/ *adj* (*before n*) ‹*area*› urbanizado

bulb /bʌlb/ *n*
A (Bot, Hort) (of flower) bulbo *m*, papa *f* (Chi); (of garlic) cabeza *f*
B (*light* ~) bombilla *f* or (Méx) foco *m* or (Col, Ven) bombillo *m* or (RPl) bombita *f* or lamparita *f* or (Chi) ampolleta *f* or (AmC) bujía *f*

bulbous /'bʌlbəs/ *adj* ‹*growth*› bulboso; ‹*nose*› protuberante

Bulgaria /bʌl'geriə || bʌl'geəriə/ *n* Bulgaria *f*

Bulgarian[1] /bʌl'geriən || bʌl'geəriən/ *adj* búlgaro

Bulgarian[2] *n* 1 [c] (person) búlgaro, -ra *m,f* 2 [u] (language) búlgaro *m*

bulge[1] /bʌldʒ/ *n* bulto *m*

bulge[2] *vi* 1 (protrude) sobresalir*; **her eyes ~d at the thought** los ojos se le salían de las órbitas de sólo pensarlo; **the bag was bulging with books** la bolsa estaba repleta de libros 2 **bulging** *pres p* ‹*pocket/bag*› repleto; ‹*eyes*› saltón

bulimia (nervosa) /bju:'li:miə(nɜ:r'vəʊsə) || bju:'lɪmiə (nɜ:'vəʊsə)/ *n* [u] bulimia *f* (nerviosa)

bulimic /bju:'li:mɪk || bjʊ'lɪmɪk/ *adj* bulímico

bulk /bʌlk/ *n* [u]
A 1 (Busn) (large quantity): **in ~** en grandes cantidades 2 (large mass) mole *f*
B (largest part): **the ~ of sth** la mayor parte de algo, gran parte de algo

bulky /'bʌlki/ *adj* **-kier, -kiest** ‹*package*› voluminoso, grande; ‹*person*› corpulento; ‹*sweater*› (AmE) grueso

bull /bʊl/ *n*
A [c] 1 (male bovine) toro *m*; ***to be like a ~ in a china shop*** ser* como chivo *or* elefante en cristalería (fam); ***to take the ~ by the horns*** agarrar *or* (esp Esp) coger* al toro por los cuernos *or* las astas 2 (male of other species) macho *m*; (*before n*) macho *adj inv*
B [u] (sl) (boasting, lying) estupideces *fpl*, chorradas *fpl* (Esp fam), macanas *fpl* (RPl fam), jaladas *fpl* (Méx arg); ▸**shoot**[2] *vt* **A1**

bull: **~dog** *n* bul(l)dog *m*; **~doze** *vt* demoler*, derribar; **to ~doze sb INTO sth/-ING** forzar* a algn A algo/+ INF; **~dozer** /'bʊldəʊzər / *n* bulldozer *m*, topadora *f* (Arg)

bullet /'bʊlət || 'bʊlɪt/ *n* bala *f*

bulletin /'bʊlətn̩ || 'bʊlətɪn/ *n* (notice) anuncio *m*, comunicado *m*; (newsletter) boletín *m*; (report) (Journ) boletín *m* (informativo)

bulletin board *n* (AmE) tablero *m* or (Esp) tablón *m* de anuncios, cartelera *f* (AmL), diario *m* mural (Chi)

bulletproof /'bʊlətpru:f || 'bʊlɪtpru:f/ *adj* ‹*vest*› antibalas *adj inv*, a prueba de balas; ‹*vehicle*› blindado

bull: **~fight** *n* corrida *f* de toros; **~fighter** *n* torero, -ra *m,f*; **~fighting** *n* [u] (deporte *m* de) los toros; (art) toreo *m*, tauromaquia *f*; **~fighting is very popular here** los toros *or* las corridas de toros son muy populares aquí; **~frog** *n* rana *f* toro; **~horn** *n* (AmE) megáfono *m*

bullion /'bʊljən || 'bʊliən/ *n* [u]: **gold/silver ~** oro/plata en lingotes

bullock /'bʊlək/ *n* (castrated bull) buey *m*; (young bull) (esp AmE) novillo *m*

bull: **~pen** *n* (AmE) 1 (in baseball) (place) bull pen *m*, zona *f* de calentamiento (*en un diamante de béisbol*) 2 (pitchers) pítchers *mpl* or lanzadores *mpl* de reserva; 3 (prison cell) (colloq) calabozo *m*; **~ring** *n* plaza *f* de toros; **~ session** *n* (AmE colloq) charla *f* (fam); **~seye** *n* diana *f*; **to score a ~seye** dar* en el blanco

bullshit[1] /'bʊlʃɪt/ *n* [u] (vulg) (nonsense) sandeces *fpl* (fam), pendejadas (AmL exc CS vulg), gilipolleces *fpl* (Esp arg), huevadas *fpl* (Andes, Ven vulg), boludeces *fpl* (Col, RPl vulg), mamadas *fpl* (Méx vulg)

bullshit[2] *vi* **-tt-** (vulg) 1 (talk nonsense) decir* sandeces (*or* gilipolleces *etc*); *see* **bullshit**[1] 2 (boast, brag) tirarse un farol (fam), mandarse la(s) parte(s) (CS fam)

bull: **~shitter** /'bʊl,ʃɪtər || 'bʊl,ʃɪtə(r)/ *n* (sl) farolero, -ra *m,f* (fam), fantasma *mf* (Esp fam), mandaparte *mf* (RPl fam), hocicón, -cona *m,f* (Méx fam), mandador, -dora *m,f* de parte (Chi fam); **~ terrier** *n* bulterrier *m*

bully[1] /'bʊli/ *n* (*pl* **-lies**) 1 [c] (thug, tyrant) matón, -tona *m,f*, bravucón, -cona *m,f* 2 [c] (in field hockey) bully *m*, salida *f*

bully[2], **-lies, -lying, -lied** *vt* intimidar, matonear (AmL fam); **to ~ sb INTO sth**: **she bullied him into doing it** lo acosó hasta que lo hizo

Phrasal verb
- **bully off** [v ▸ adv] (in field hockey) sacar*

bully[3] *interj*: **~ for you/him!** (dated *or* iro) ¡bravo!

bullying /'bʊliɪŋ/ *n* 1 (in school) acoso *m* escolar, bullying *m* 2 (at work) acoso *m* laboral, mobbing *m*

bulrush /'bʊlrʌʃ/ *n* 1 [c] (cattail) (BrE) enea *f*, anea *f*, totora *f* 2 [c u] (rush) junco *m* (marinero)

bulwark /'bʊlwərk || 'bʊlwək/ *n* 1 (defense) baluarte *m* 2 **bulwarks** *pl* (Naut) macarrones *mpl*

bum[1] /bʌm/ *n* (colloq)
A 1 (worthless person) vago, -ga *m,f* (fam) 2 (vagrant) (AmE) vagabundo, -da *m,f* 3 (enthusiast) (AmE): **ski/tennis ~** loco, -ca *m,f* del esquí/tenis (fam); **he's/she's a beach ~** se pasa la vida en la playa
B (buttocks) (BrE) trasero *m* (fam), culo *m* (fam *o* vulg), traste *m* (CS fam), poto *m* (Chi, Per fam)

b

bum² **-mm-** *vt* (sl) **to ~ sth** FROM *o* OFF **sb** gorronearle *or* gorrearle algo A algn, pecharle algo A algn (CS fam)

■ **bum** *vi* 1 (drift): **to ~ around** vagabundear 2 (cadge) **to ~** OFF **sb** gorronearle *or* gorrearle *or* (RPl) garronearle *or* (CS) pecharle a algn (fam)

bum³ *adj* (sl) (*before n*) 1 ‹*job/place*› de porquería (fam) 2 (AmE): **a ~ rap** una acusación falsa; **it turned out to be a ~ deal** resultó ser un chanchullo (fam)

bumblebee /ˈbʌmbəlˌbiː/ *n* abejorro *m*

bumbling /ˈbʌmblɪŋ/ *adj* torpe, incompetente

bumf /bʌmf/ *n* [u] (BrE colloq) papelerío *m* (fam), papeles *mpl*

bummer /ˈbʌmər || ˈbʌmə(r)/ *n* (sl) latazo *m* (fam), plomo *m* (fam), plomazo *m* (fam), coñazo *m* (Esp arg)

bump¹ /bʌmp/ *n*

A 1 (blow) golpe *m*; (jolt) sacudida *f*; (collision) topetazo *m*, golpe *m*; **that brought me back to reality with a ~** eso me devolvió de golpe a la realidad 2 (sound) golpe *m*; **things that go ~ in the night** cosas que dan miedo

B (lump — in surface) bulto *m*, protuberancia *f*; (— on head) chichón *m*; (— on road) bache *m*

bump² *vt*

A (hit, knock lightly): **I ~ed my elbow on** *o* **against the door** me di en el codo con *or* contra la puerta; **I ~ed the post as I was reversing** choqué con *or* contra el poste al dar marcha atrás

B (remove, throw out) (AmE colloq) echar; **we got ~ed from the flight** nos quedamos sin plaza en el vuelo

■ **bump** *vi* (hit, knock) **to ~** (AGAINST **sth/sb)** darse* *or* chocar* (CONTRA *or* CON algo/algn)

Phrasal verbs

- **bump into** [v ▸ prep ▸ o] 1 (collide with) darse* *or* chocar* contra 2 (meet by chance) (colloq) toparse *or* tropezarse* con, encontrarse* con
- **bump off** [v ▸ o ▸ adv, v ▸ adv ▸ o] (sl) liquidar (fam)
- **bump up** [v ▸ o ▸ adv, v ▸ adv ▸ o] (colloq) aumentar

bumper¹ /ˈbʌmpər || ˈbʌmpə(r)/ *n* (Auto) parachoques *m*, paragolpes *m* (RPl); **the cars were ~ to ~** los coches iban pegados unos a otros

bumper² *adj* (*before n*) ‹*crop/year*› récord *adj inv*, extraordinario; ‹*edition*› extra; ‹*pack*› gigante

bumper car *n* coche *m* de choque, carrito *m* chocón (Méx, Ven), autito *m* chocador (RPl), carro *m* loco (Andes)

bumph /bʌmf/ *n* [u] ▸**bumf**

bumpkin /ˈbʌmpkɪn/ *n*: **(country) ~** pueblerino, -na *m,f*, paleto, -ta *m,f* (Esp fam), pajuerano, -na *m,f* (RPl fam)

bumptious /ˈbʌmpʃəs/ *adj* engreído

bumpy /ˈbʌmpi/ *adj* **-pier, -piest** 1 (uneven) ‹*surface*› desigual, con desniveles; ‹*road*› lleno de baches 2 (rough): **we had a ~ flight** el avión se movió mucho; **it was a ~ ride and she felt sick** se mareó con el traqueteo del autobús (*or* el coche *etc*)

bun /bʌn/ *n*

A 1 (sweetened) bollo *m*; **currant ~** bollo con pasas 2 (bread roll) panecillo *m*, pancito *m* (CS), bolillo *m* (Méx)

B (hairstyle) moño *m*, rodete *m* (RPl), chongo *m* (Méx)

C **buns** *pl* (AmE colloq) trasero *m* (fam), culo *m* (fam *o* vulg), traste *m* (CS fam), poto *m* (Chi, Per fam)

bunch¹ /bʌntʃ/ *n*

A 1 (of flowers) ramo *m*, bonche *m* (Méx); (small) ramillete *m*; (of bananas) racimo *m*, penca *f* (Méx), cacho *m* (RPl); (of grapes) racimo *m*; (of keys) manojo *m* 2 (group) grupo *m*; **they're a ~ of idiots** son una panda *or* (AmL) una punta de idiotas (fam); **they're an odd ~** son gente de lo más rara 3 (a lot) (AmE colloq) montón *m*, porrón *m* (Esp fam), chorro *m* (Méx fam); **thanks a ~!** (colloq & iro) ¡gracias mil! (iró)

B **bunches** *pl* (hairstyle) (BrE) coletas *fpl*

bunch² *vi* 1 **~ (together)** ‹‹*runners/cars*›› amontonarse 2 ‹‹*cloth*›› fruncirse*

bundle¹ /ˈbʌndl/ *n* 1 (of clothes) lío *m*, fardo *m*, atado *m* (AmL); (of newspapers, letters) paquete *m*; (of money) fajo *m*; (of sticks) haz *m*, atado *m* (AmL); **software ~** paquete *m* de software; **that child is a ~ of mischief** ese niño es un diablillo; **she's a ~ of nerves** es un manojo de nervios; **the play isn't exactly a ~ of laughs** la obra no es precisamente muy cómica 2 (large sum of money): **a ~** (colloq) un dineral, un platal (AmS fam), un pastón (Esp fam), un lanón (Méx fam)

bundle² *vt* 1 (make into a bundle) liar*, atar 2 (push) (+ *adv compl*): **she ~d them off to school** los despachó al colegio; **they ~d him into the car** lo metieron a empujones en el coche

Phrasal verb

- **bundle up** 1 [v ▸ adv ▸ o] ‹*clothes/papers*› liar* 2 [v ▸ adv] (AmE colloq) abrigarse*

bung¹ /bʌŋ/ *n* tapón *m*

bung² *vt* 1 (put bung in) taponar 2 (BrE colloq) (put) poner*, meter; **just ~ it out** tíralo (a la basura)

Phrasal verb

- **bung up** [v ▸ o ▸ adv, v ▸ adv ▸ o] (BrE colloq) ‹*sink/pipe*› atascar*, tapar (AmL); **I'm really ~ed up** tengo la nariz tapada

bungalow /ˈbʌŋgələʊ/ *n* casa *f* de una planta

bungee jumping /ˈbʌndʒi/ *n* banyi *m*

bungle /ˈbʌŋgəl/ *vt* echar a perder; **a ~d attempt** un intento fallido

bungling /ˈbʌŋglɪŋ/ *adj* (*before n, no comp*) torpe

bungy jumping *n* ▸**bungee jumping**

bunion /ˈbʌnjən/ *n* juanete *m*

bunk /bʌŋk/ *n*

A [c] (bed) litera *f*

B ***to do a ~*** (BrE sl) largarse* (fam)

Phrasal verb

- **bunk off** ▸**skive off**

bunk bed *n* litera *f*

bunkum /ˈbʌŋkəm/ *n* [u] (colloq) bobadas *fpl* (fam)

bunny (*pl* **-nies**), **bunny rabbit** /ˈbʌni/ *n* (used to or by children) conejito *m* (fam); **~ girl** *n* conejita *f*

bunting /ˈbʌntɪŋ/ *n* [u] (fabric) (esp AmE) *tela usada para la confección de banderas*

buoy /bɔɪ, ˈbuːi || bɔɪ/ *n* boya *f*

Phrasal verb

- **buoy up** [v ▸ o ▸ adv, v ▸ adv ▸ o] 1 ‹*boat/person*› mantener* a flote 2 (keep cheerful) animar

buoyancy /ˈbɔɪənsi/ *n* [u] 1 (ability to float) flotabilidad *f*; (of liquid) sustentación *f* hidráulica 2 (resilience) optimismo *m* 3 (Fin) (of currency) solidez *f*; (of market) tendencia *f* alcista

buoyant /ˈbɔɪənt/ *adj* 1 (able to float) flotante, boyante 2 ‹*mood/spirits*› optimista 3 (Fin) ‹*currency*› fuerte; ‹*market*› alcista

burble /ˈbɜːrbəl || ˈbɜːbəl/ *vi* 1 ‹‹*stream/spring*›› borbotar, borbotear 2 (talk meaninglessly) parlotear (fam), cotorrear (fam); (talk excitedly) hablar atropelladamente

burden¹ /ˈbɜːrdn̩ || ˈbɜːdn̩/ *n* 1 (load) (liter) carga *f* 2 (encumbrance) carga *f*; **the ~ of responsibility** el peso de la responsabilidad; **to be a ~ to** *o* **on sb** ser* una carga para algn

burden² *vt* cargar*; **to ~ sb** WITH **sth** ‹*with work*› cargarle* a algn CON algo; **I don't want to ~ you with my problems** no te quiero preocupar con mis problemas

burdensome /ˈbɜːrdn̩səm || ˈbɜːdn̩səm/ *adj* oneroso

bureau /ˈbjʊrəʊ || ˈbjʊərəʊ/ *n* (*pl* **bureaus** *or* **bureaux** /-z/)

A 1 (agency) agencia *f* 2 (government department) (AmE) departamento *m*

B 1 (chest of drawers) (AmE) cómoda *f* 2 (desk) (BrE) buró *m*, escritorio *m*

bureaucracy /bjʊˈrɑːkrəsi || bjʊəˈrɒkrəsi/ *n* [u c] (*pl* **-cies**) burocracia *f*

bureaucrat /ˈbjʊrəkræt || ˈbjʊərəkræt/ *n* burócrata *mf*

bureaucratic /ˈbjʊrəˈkrætɪk || ˌbjʊərəˈkrætɪk/ *adj* burocrático

bureau de change /ˈbjʊrəʊdəˈʃɑːnʒ || ˈbjʊərəʊdəˈʃɑ̃ʒ/ *n* (*pl* **bureaux de change**) (casa *f* de) cambio *m*

burgeon /ˈbɜːrdʒən || ˈbɜːdʒən/ *vi* 1 (grow, flourish) (liter) florecer* 2 **burgeoning** *pres p* ‹*demand*› creciente; ‹*market*› pujante, floreciente

burger /ˈbɜːrgər || ˈbɜːgə(r)/ *n* (colloq) hamburguesa *f*

burglar /ˈbɜːrglər || ˈbɜːglə(r)/ *n* ladrón, -drona *m,f*; (*before n*) **~ alarm** alarma *f* antirrobo

burglarize /ˈbɜːrgləraɪz || ˈbɜːgləraɪz/ *vt* (AmE) robar

burglary /ˈbɜːrgləri || ˈbɜːgləri/ *n* [c u] (*pl* **-ries**) robo *m* (*con allanamiento de morada o escalamiento*)

burgle /ˈbɜːrgəl || ˈbɜːgəl/ *vt* robar; **our house was/we were ~d** nos entraron ladrones en casa, nos entraron a robar

burgundy /ˈbɜːrgəndi || ˈbɜːgəndi/ *n* (color) burdeos *m or* (RPl) bordó *m or* (Chi) concho *m* de vino

burial /ˈberiəl/ *n* [c u] entierro *m*; (*before n*) **~ ground** cementerio *m*; **~ rites** ritos *mpl* funerarios

Burkina Faso /bɜːrˈkiːnəˈfæsəʊ || ˌbɜːkiːnəˈfæsəʊ/ *n* Burkina Faso *m*

burlesque /bɜːrˈlesk || bɜːˈlesk/ *n* [c u] obra *f* burlesca

burly /ˈbɜːrli || ˈbɜːli/ *adj* **-lier, -liest** fornido, corpulento

Burma /ˈbɜːrmə || ˈbɜːmə/ *n* Birmania *f*

Burmese¹ /ˈbɜːrˈmiːz || bɜːˈmiːz/ *adj* birmano

Burmese² *n* (*pl* ~) [1] [c] (person) birmano, -na *m,f* [2] [u] (language) birmano *m*

burn¹ /bɜːrn || bɜːn/ (*past & past p* **burned** *or* **burnt**) *vi*

A [1] «*fire/flame/building*» arder; «*wood/coal*» arder, quemarse; **something's ~ing!** se está quemando algo; **I can smell ~ing** huele *or* hay olor a quemado; **the smell of ~ing rubber** el olor a goma quemada *or* (Méx) hule quemado [2] «*food*» quemarse [3] (in sun) «*skin*» quemarse

B [1] (be hot) arder; **my cheeks were ~ing** me ardían las mejillas [2] (sting) «*eyes/wound*» escocer*, arder (esp AmL); **a ~ing sensation** un escozor, un ardor (esp AmL)

C (be consumed) arder; **she was ~ing with curiosity** ardía de curiosidad; **she ~ed for revenge** (liter) deseaba ardientemente vengarse

■ **burn** *vt*

A [1] ‹*letter/rubbish*› quemar; ‹*building/town*› incendiar, quemar; **I ~ed a hole in my sleeve** me quemé la manga (*con un cigarrillo etc*); ***to ~ one's boats*** *o* ***bridges*** quemar las naves [2] (overcook) quemar; **I've ~ed the cake** se me ha quemado el pastel; ▸**candle, oil¹ A4**

B [1] (injure) quemar; **to ~ oneself (ON sth)** quemarse (CON algo); **I've ~ed my tongue** me he quemado la lengua; **to be ~ed to death** morir* abrasado [2] (swindle) (AmE sl) estafar, timar (fam)

(Phrasal verbs)

- **burn down**

A [v ▸ o ▸ adv, v ▸ adv ▸ o] incendiar

B [v ▸ adv] incendiarse

- **burn off** [v ▸ o ▸ adv, v ▸ adv ▸ o] ‹*paint/varnish*› quitar (*con llama*); ‹*gas/calories*› quemar
- **burn out**

A [v ▸ adv] [1] «*fire/candle*» apagarse* [2] «*motor*» quemarse

B [v ▸ o ▸ adv]: **to ~ itself out** «*fire*» apagarse*; **he's ~t himself out** está acabado *or* (fam) quemado

- **burn up**

A [v ▸ o ▸ adv, v ▸ adv ▸ o] [1] (consume) ‹*fuel*› consumir; ‹*calories*› quemar [2] (annoy, anger) (AmE colloq) enfermar (AmL fam), poner* enfermo (Esp fam)

B [v ▸ adv] «*meteorite/rocket*» desintegrarse

burn² *n*

A (on skin, surface) quemadura *f*

B (stream) (dial *or* poet) arroyo *m*

burner /ˈbɜːrnər || ˈbɜːnə(r)/ *n* quemador *m*

burning /ˈbɜːrnɪŋ || ˈbɜːnɪŋ/ *adj* (*before n*) [1] (hot) ‹*sand*› ardiente; ‹*sun*› abrasador [2] (*as adv*): **it's ~ hot** está muy caliente, está ardiendo; **the ~ hot sand** la arena ardiente [3] (intense) ‹*desire*› ardiente; ‹*hatred*› violento [4] (urgent) ‹*question/issue*› candente

burnish /ˈbɜːrnɪʃ || ˈbɜːnɪʃ/ *vt* bruñir*

burnout /ˈbɜːrnaʊt || ˈbɜːnaʊt/ *n* [c u] (colloq) agotamiento *m*, surmenage *m*

> **Burns Night**
>
> Cada 25 de enero los escoceses en todo el mundo celebran el día del nacimiento del poeta Robert Burns, preparando una cena llamada *Burns Supper*, cuyo plato principal es *haggis* (estómago de oveja relleno con una mezcla de hígado y otras vísceras, avena, cebollas y especias). También se bebe whisky y se suelen leer poemas de Burns

burnt¹ /bɜːrnt || bɜːnt/ *past & past p of* **burn¹**

burnt² *adj* ‹*food/toast*› quemado; ‹*smell/taste*› a quemado

burnt-out /ˈbɜːrntˈaʊt || ˈbɜːntˌaʊt/ *adj* calcinado

burp¹ /bɜːrp || bɜːp/ *n* eructo *m*

burp² *vi* eructar, soltar* un eructo (fam)

burrow¹ /ˈbərəʊ || ˈbʌrəʊ/ *n* madriguera *f*; (of rabbits) conejera *f*

burrow² *vi* (in sand, soil) cavar; (in handbag, drawer) hurgar*, escarbar

bursar /ˈbɜːrsər || ˈbɜːsə(r)/ *n* administrador, -dora *m,f*

burst¹ /bɜːrst || bɜːst/ (*past & past p* **burst**) *vi*

A «*balloon/tire*» reventarse*; «*pipe*» reventar*, romperse*; «*dam*» romperse*; **to ~ open** abrirse* de golpe

B (move suddenly) (+ *adv compl*): **they ~ into the room** entraron de sopetón en la habitación; **the demonstrators ~ through the police cordon** los manifestantes rompieron el cordón policial

■ **burst** *vt* ‹*balloon/bubble*› reventar*; **the river ~ its banks** el río se desbordó *or* se salió de madre

(Phrasal verbs)

- **burst in** [v ▸ adv] entrar (de sopetón); **don't come ~ing in like that!** ¡no se entra así de sopetón, sin llamar!; **to ~ in ON sb**: **he ~ in on us** entró de sopetón donde estábamos; **they ~ in on the meeting** irrumpieron en la reunión
- **burst into** [v ▸ prep ▸ o]: **to ~ into tears** echarse *or* ponerse* *or* (liter) romper* a llorar; **to ~ into song** ponerse* a cantar; **to ~ into flames** estallar en llamas
- **burst out** [v ▸ adv] [1] (cry): **you're lying!, she ~ out suddenly** —¡estás mintiendo! —saltó de repente [2] (exit) salir* [3] (start): **he ~ out laughing** se echó a reír

burst² *n*

A [1] (short surge) (of applause) salva *f*; (of activity) arrebato *m*, arranque *m*; **a ~ of energy** un arranque de energía; **there was a ~ of laughter from the table in the corner** se oyeron carcajadas en la mesa del rincón [2] (of gunfire) ráfaga *f*

B (of pipe) rotura *f*

bursting /ˈbɜːrstɪŋ || ˈbɜːstɪŋ/ *adj* (*pred, no comp*) [1] (overflowing) **to be ~ (WITH sth)** estar* repleto (DE algo); **he was ~ with energy** rebosaba (de) energía; **I'm ~** (colloq) (have eaten too much) estoy que reviento (fam) [2] (anxious, impatient) (colloq) **to be ~ to + INF** morirse* POR + INF

bursting (point) *n*: **to be filled** *o* **full to ~ with sth** estar* (lleno) hasta los topes *or* hasta el tope de algo

burton /ˈbɜːrtn̩ || ˈbɜːtn̩/ *n*: ***to go for a ~*** (BrE colloq) «*plan*» irse* al traste *or* al diablo *or* al cuerno (fam)

bury /ˈberi/ **buries, burying, buried** *vt*

A enterrar*, sepultar (frml); **to ~ sb at sea** dar* sepultura a algn en el mar (frml); **the village was buried by the avalanche** el pueblo fue sepultado por la avalancha; **a little village buried away in the Pyrenees** un pueblecito de algún rincón de los Pirineos

B (plunge, thrust) **to ~ sth (IN sth)**: **she buried the knife in his chest** le enterró *or* le hundió *or* le clavó el cuchillo en el pecho; **he buried his head in his hands** ocultó la cabeza entre las manos

■ *v refl* [1] (immerse oneself) **to ~ oneself IN sth** ‹*in one's work/one's books*› enfrascarse* EN algo [2] (become lodged) «*bullet*» alojarse

bus¹ /bʌs/ *n* (*pl* **buses** *or* (AmE also) **busses**) (Transp) [1] (local) autobús *m*, bus *m* (AmL), camión *m* (AmC, Méx), colectivo *m* (Arg), ómnibus *m* (Per, Ur), micro *f* (Chi), guagua *f* (Cu); ***to look like*** *o* ***have a face like the back (end) of a ~*** (colloq) ser* feo con ganas (fam); (*before n*) **~ conductor** cobrador, -dora *m,f*, guarda *mf* (RPl) de autobuses; **~ driver** conductor, -tora *m,f or* chofer *mf or* (Esp) chófer *mf* de autobús, camionero, -ra *m,f* (AmC, Méx), colectivero, -ra *m,f* (Arg), microbusero, -ra *m,f* (Chi); **~ stop** parada *f or* (AmL exc RPl) paradero *m* de autobús (*or* bus *etc*); ▸**miss²** *Sense* **I B** [2] (long-distance) autobús *m*, autocar *m* (Esp), pullman *m* (CS)

bus² *vt* **-s-** *or* **-ss-** llevar *or* transportar en autobús (*or* bus *etc*); ‹*schoolchildren*› (in US) *transportar a colegios fuera de su zona para favorecer la integración racial*

busboy /ˈbʌsbɔɪ/ *n* (AmE) ayudante *m* de camarero

bush¹ /bʊʃ/ *n*

A [1] [c] (shrub) arbusto *m*, mata *f*; ***to beat about the ~*** andarse* con rodeos; **stop beating about the ~!** ¡déjate de rodeos! [2] **bushes** *pl* (thicket) matorrales *mpl*, maleza *f*; ***to beat the ~es for sth*** (AmE) buscar* algo por todas partes

B [u] (wild country) **the ~** el monte

bush[2] *adj* (AmE colloq) poco profesional

bushbaby /'bʊʃ,beɪbi/ *n* (*pl* **-bies**) gálago *m*

bushed /bʊʃt/ *adj* (colloq) (*pred*) hecho polvo (fam), agotado

bushel /'bʊʃəl/ *n* ≈ fanega *f* (*EEUU: 35,23*dm^3*, RU: 36,37*dm^3); ▸ **light**[1] A

bush league *n* (AmE) liga *f* menor

bushy /'bʊʃi/ *adj* **bushier, bushiest** ‹*beard*› poblado, espeso; ‹*eyebrows*› tupido, poblado; ‹*undergrowth*› espeso

busily /'bɪzəli || 'bɪzɪli/ *adv*: **they were all working ~** todos trabajaban afanosamente; **she was ~ writing her journal** estaba muy ocupada escribiendo en su diario

business /'bɪznəs || 'bɪznɪs/ *n*

A [u] (Busn) [1] (world of commerce, finance) negocios *mpl*; (*before n*) **~ studies** (ciencias *fpl*) empresariales *fpl*; **~ school** escuela *f* de administración *or* gestión de empresas; **a course in ~ German** un curso de alemán comercial [2] (commercial activity, trading) comercio *m*; **to be in ~**: **the firm has been in ~ for 50 years** la empresa tiene 50 años de actividad comercial; **the factory is back in ~ again** la fábrica ha reanudado sus operaciones; **to set up in ~** montar *or* poner* un negocio; **go into ~**: **they went into ~ together** montaron *or* pusieron un negocio juntos; **to go out of ~** cerrar*; **~ is good** el negocio anda *or* marcha bien; **the company lost two million dollars' worth of ~** la compañía perdió ventas (*or* contratos *etc*) por valor de dos millones de dólares; **we open for ~ at nine o'clock** abrimos al público a las nueve [3] (custom, clients): **to lose ~** perder* clientes *or* clientela

B [c] [1] (firm) negocio *m*, empresa *f* [2] (branch of commerce): **I'm in the insurance/antiques ~** trabajo en el ramo de los seguros/en la compra y venta de antigüedades; **the fashion/music ~** la industria *or* el negocio de la moda/música; **she's the best designer in the ~** es la mejor diseñadora del ramo

C [u] [1] (transactions): **it's been a pleasure to do ~ with you** ha sido un placer trabajar con usted; **she's here/away on ~** está aquí/de viaje por negocios; **to mix ~ with pleasure** mezclar el trabajo con la diversión; **unfinished ~** asuntos *mpl* pendientes; **~ *before pleasure*** antes es la obligación que la devoción, primero el deber (y después el placer); ***to get down to*** **~** ir* al grano, entrar en materia; ***to mean*** **~** decir* algo muy en serio; ***to talk*** **~** hablar de negocios; (*before n*) ‹*appointment/lunch*› de trabajo, de negocios; **~ letter** carta *f* comercial; **~ trip** viaje *m* de negocios [2] (items on agenda) asuntos *mpl*, temas *mpl*; **any other ~** otros asuntos, ≈ ruegos y preguntas [3] (rightful occupation, concern) asunto *m*, incumbencia *f*; **mind your own ~!** ¡no te metas en lo que no te importa!; **that's none of your ~** eso no es asunto tuyo, eso no te incumbe; **you had no ~ apologizing on my behalf** no te correspondía a ti disculparte de mi parte; **I shall make it my ~ to find out** yo me ocuparé *or* me encargaré de averiguarlo; ***like nobody's*** **~** (colloq): **she was getting through those chocolates like nobody's ~** les estaba dando duro a los bombones (fam); **he was dashing around like nobody's ~** estaba corriendo como un loco de aquí para allá

D (affair, situation, activity) (colloq) (*no pl*) asunto *m*; **what's all this ~ about you leaving?** ¿qué es eso de que te vas?; ***to give sb the*** **~** (AmE) (reprimand) echarle la bronca a algn (fam); (tease) tomarle el pelo a algn (fam)

business: **~-class** *adv* en clase preferente *or* business-class; **~like** *adj* ‹*person/manner*› (serious) formal, serio; (efficient) eficiente; ‹*discussion*› serio; **~man** /'bɪznəsmæn || 'bɪznɪsmən/ *n* (*pl* **-men** /-men || -mən/) empresario *m*, hombre *m* de negocios; **~-to-~** /,bɪznəstə'bɪznəs || ,bɪznɪstə'bɪznɪs/ *adj* empresa-empresa *adj inv*; **~ commerce** comercio *m* empresa-empresa; **~woman** *n* empresaria *f*, mujer *f* de negocios

busk /bʌsk/ *vi* (BrE colloq) *cantar o tocar un instrumento en la calle o en estaciones del transporte público*

busker /'bʌskər || 'bʌskə(r)/ *n* (BrE) músico *m* callejero

busload /'bʌsləʊd/ *n*: **a ~ of schoolchildren** un autobús (lleno) de escolares; **tourists were arriving by the ~/in ~s** iban llegando autocares (*or* autobuses *etc*) llenos de turistas

bust[1] /bʌst/ *vt* [1] (*past & past p* **busted** *or* (BrE also) **bust**) (break) (colloq) romper* [2] (*past & past p* **busted**) (raid) (sl) ‹*person*› agarrar (fam), trincar* (Esp fam); ‹*premises*› hacer* una redada en [3] (*past & past p* **busted**) (bankrupt) (AmE colloq) dejar sin un centavo *or* (Esp tb) sin blanca *or* (Méx tb) sin un quinto [4] (*past & past p* **busted**) (punch) (AmE colloq) darle* un puñetazo a [5] (*past & past p* **busted**) **~ (down)** (demote) (AmE sl) degradar

■ **bust** *vi* (*past & past p* **busted** *or* (BrE also) **bust**) (colloq) ‹‹*object/machine*›› romperse*, estropearse, sonar* (CS fam)

bust[2] *n*

A [1] (sculpture) busto *m* [2] (bosom) busto *m*, pecho *m*

B (collapse) (esp AmE) caída *f*, descalabro *m*

bust[3] *adj*

A [1] (bankrupt) (colloq): **to go ~** quebrar*, ir(se)* a la bancarrota, fundirse (Per, RPl fam) [2] (Games) (*pred*): **it's a gold medal or ~** o la medalla de oro o nada

B (broken) (BrE) roto, estropeado

busted /'bʌstəd || 'bʌstɪd/ *adj* (esp AmE colloq) roto, estropeado

buster /'bʌstər || 'bʌstə(r)/ *n* (AmE colloq) (*as form of address*) fulano (fam), macho (Esp fam), güey (Méx fam), gallo (Chi fam), che (RPl fam)

bustle[1] /'bʌsəl/ *vi* [1] (move busily): **I could hear her bustling along the corridor** la oía ir y venir afanosamente por el corredor; **to ~ around** ir* de aquí para allá, trajinar [2] (be crowded, lively) ‹‹*street/store*›› **to ~ (WITH sth)** bullir* (DE algo)

bustle[2] *n*

A [u] (activity) ajetreo *m*, bullicio *m* (fam)

B [c] (Clothing, Hist) polisón *m*, miriñaque *m*

bustling /'bʌslɪŋ/ *adj* ‹*street/shop*› animado, de mucho movimiento

bust-up /'bʌstʌp/ *n* [1] (breakup) ruptura *f* [2] (quarrel) (BrE colloq) pelea *f*, bronca *f* (fam)

busty /'bʌsti/ *adj* **bustier, bustiest** (colloq) pechugona (fam)

busy[1] /'bɪzi/ *adj* **busier, busiest**

A (occupied) ‹*person*› ocupado; **the children keep me very ~** los niños me tienen muy atareada *or* me dan mucho que hacer; **to get ~** ponerse* a trabajar; **I was ~ writing a letter** estaba ocupada escribiendo una carta

B ‹*street/market*› concurrido, de mucho movimiento; **I've had a ~ day** he tenido un día de mucho trabajo; **I have a ~ schedule** tengo un programa muy apretado; **a ~ road** una carretera con mucho tráfico *or* muy transitada

C (Telec) ocupado (AmL), comunicando (Esp)

busy[2] *v refl* **busies, busying, busied**: **to ~ oneself -ING** ponerse* A + INF; **to ~ oneself WITH sth** entretenerse* CON algo

busy: **~body** *n* (colloq) entrometido, -da *m,f*, metomentodo *mf* (fam), metiche *mf* (AmL fam); **~ signal** *n* (AmE) tono *m* *or* señal *f* de ocupado (AmL), señal *f* de comunicando (Esp)

but[1] /bʌt, *weak form* bət/ *conj*

A [1] (however) pero; **she was fired, ~ they were not** la despidieron a ella pero no a ellos; **everybody, ~ everybody knows that** eso no hay nadie que no lo sepa; **you're really bugging me ~ good!** (AmE colloq) ¡qué manera de darme la lata! (fam) [2] (used for introductory emphasis) pero; **~ what made you say it?** ¿pero por qué lo dijiste?; **surely he doesn't believe that? — oh, ~ he does!** no puede ser que se crea eso — pues sí que se lo cree [3] **but then** (*as linker*) (however, still) pero; (in that case) pero entonces; **~ then you never were very ambitious, were you?** pero la verdad es que tú nunca fuiste muy ambicioso ¿no?; **I don't want to, ~ then again I do** no quiero, pero a la vez *or* al mismo tiempo sí quiero

B : **not ... but ...** no ... sino ...; **it appears that she's not Greek ~ Albanian** parece que no es griega, sino albanesa; **not only did she hit him, ~ she also ...** no sólo le pegó, sino que también ...

but[2] *prep* [1] (except): **everyone ~ me** todos menos *or* excepto *or* salvo yo; **the last street ~ one** la penúltima calle; **the next street ~ one** la próxima calle no: la siguiente; **I had no alternative ~ to leave** no me quedó otra alternativa que irme; **there's nothing we can do ~ wait** no podemos hacer otra cosa sino esperar, lo único que podemos hacer es esperar [2] **but for**: **~ for them, we'd have lost everything** de no haber sido *or* si no hubiera sido por ellos, habríamos perdido todo

but[3] *adv* (frml): **we can ~ try** con intentarlo no se pierde nada; **he's ~ a child** no es más que un niño; **one can't**

help ~ admire her audacity uno no puede (por) menos que admirar su audacia

but⁴ /bʌt/ *n* pero *m*; **no ~s: come here at once!** no hay pero que valga, ¡ven aquí inmediatamente!

butane /'bju:teɪn/ *n* [u] butano *m*

butch /bʊtʃ/ *adj* (colloq) ‹*man*› machote (fam); ‹*woman*› hombruna, machota (fam)

butcher¹ /'bʊtʃər || 'bʊtʃə(r)/ *n* 1 (meat dealer) carnicero, -ra *m,f*; **~'s (shop)** carnicería *f* 2 (murderer) asesino, -na *m,f*

butcher² *vt* 1 ‹*cattle/pig*› matar, carnear (CS) 2 ‹*people*› masacrar

butchery /'bʊtʃəri/ *n* [u] matanza *f*, carnicería *f*

butler /'bʌtlər || 'bʌtlə(r)/ *n* mayordomo *m*

butt¹ /bʌt/ *n*

A 1 (of rifle) culata *f* 2 **~ (end)** (blunt end) extremo *m* 3 (of cigarette) colilla *f*, bacha *f* (Méx fam) 4 (cigarette) (AmE colloq) cigarrillo *m*, pucho *m* (AmL fam)

B (target of jokes or criticism) blanco *m*

C 1 (from goat) topetazo *m* 2 (*head* ~) cabezazo *m*, topetazo *m*

D (buttocks) (AmE colloq) trasero *m* (fam), culo *m* (fam *o* vulg), traste *m* (CS fam), poto *m* (Chi, Per fam); **to get off one's ~** ponerse* a trabajar

butt² *vt* «*goat*» topetar, darle* un topetazo a

Phrasal verb

• **butt in** [v ▸ adv] interrumpir, meter la cuchara (fam)

butter¹ /'bʌtər || 'bʌtə(r)/ *n* [u] mantequilla *f*, manteca *f* (RPl); **apple ~** (AmE) mermelada *f or* (CS tb) dulce *m* de manzana; **~ *wouldn't melt in her/his mouth*** es una mosquita muerta

butter² *vt* ‹*bread*› untar con mantequilla *or* (RPl) manteca, ponerle* mantequilla *or* (RPl) manteca a; **~ed toast** tostadas con mantequilla *or* (RPl) manteca

Phrasal verb

• **butter up** [v ▸ o ▸ adv, v ▸ adv ▸ o] (colloq) darle* jabón a (fam), hacerle* la barba a (Méx fam), hacerle* la pata a (Chi fam)

butter: **~ bean** *n* 1 (dried bean) *tipo de frijol blanco*, poroto *m* de manteca (RPl) 2 (wax bean) (AmE) *tipo de frijol fresco con vaina amarilla*; **~cup** *n* ranúnculo *m*; **~fingers** *n* (*pl* ~) (colloq) torpe *mf*, patoso, -sa *m,f* (Esp fam); **~fly** *n* 1 [c] (Zool) mariposa *f* 2 [u] (swimming stroke) estilo *m* mariposa 3 **~flies** *pl* (nervous feeling) nervios *mpl*; **to get/have ~flies (in one's stomach)** ponerse*/estar* nervioso; **~milk** *n* [u] suero *m* (de la leche); **~scotch** *n* [u] *caramelo duro hecho con azúcar y mantequilla*

buttock /'bʌtək/ *n* nalga *f*

button¹ /'bʌtn̩/ *n*

A (Clothing) botón *m*; ***on the ~*** (esp AmE): **his answer was right on the ~** dio en el clavo con su respuesta; **she arrived on the ~** llegó en punto *or* muy puntual; ***to be as bright as a ~*** ser* muy despierto, ser* más listo que el hambre (fam); (*before n*) **~ mushroom** champiñón *m* pequeño; **~ nose** nariz *f* chata y pequeña

B (switch) botón *m*

button² *vt* abotonar, abrochar

■ **button** *vi* abotonarse, abrocharse

Phrasal verb

• **button up** [v ▸ o ▸ adv, v ▸ adv ▸ o] abotonar, abrochar

button-down /'bʌtn̩daʊn/ *adj* (*before n*): **~ collar** *cuello cuyas puntas se abotonan a la camisa*

buttoned-down /'bʌtn̩ddaʊn/ *adj* (*before n*) (staid, conventional) (AmE colloq) acartonado

buttonhole /'bʌtn̩həʊl/ *n* 1 (Clothing) ojal *m* 2 (flower) (BrE) *flor que se lleva en el ojal*

buttress¹ /'bʌtrəs || 'bʌtrɪs/ *n* (Archit) contrafuerte *m*; **flying ~** arbotante *m*

buttress² *vt* 1 (Archit) ‹*wall*› reforzar* con un contrafuerte 2 (support) ‹*argument/case*› respaldar, apoyar

butty /'bʌti/ *n* (*pl* **-ties**) (BrE colloq) sandwich *m*, bocata *m* (Esp fam)

buxom /'bʌksəm/ *adj* con mucho busto *or* pecho

buy¹ /baɪ/ (*past & past p* **bought**) *vt*

A (purchase) comprar; **money can't ~ happiness** el dinero no hace la felicidad; **to ~ sb sth** comprarle algo a algn; **let me ~ you a drink** déjame invitarte a una copa; **I bought myself a hat** me compré un sombrero; **I bought this mirror for $50** compré este espejo por 50 dólares; **to ~ sth FROM sb** comprarle algo A algn; **I bought the radio from** *o* (colloq) **off a friend** le compré la radio a un amigo; **to ~ sth FOR sb** comprar algo PARA algn

B (accept, believe) (colloq) tragarse* (fam)

■ **buy** *vi* comprar; **to ~ FROM sb** comprarle A algn

Phrasal verbs

• **buy in** (BrE) [v ▸ o ▸ adv, v ▸ adv ▸ o] ‹*food/supplies*› comprar (*para abastecerse*)

• **buy into** [v ▸ prep ▸ o] ‹*company*› adquirir* participación en, comprar acciones en

• **buy off** [v ▸ o ▸ adv, v ▸ adv ▸ o] sobornar, comprar (fam)

• **buy out** [v ▸ o ▸ adv, v ▸ adv ▸ o] ‹*partner/shareholder*› comprarle su parte a

• **buy up** [v ▸ adv ▸ o] comprarse todas las existencias de

buy² *n* compra *f*

buyer /'baɪər || 'baɪə(r)/ *n* 1 (customer) comprador, -dora *m,f* 2 (buying agent) encargado, -da *m,f* de compras

buzz¹ /bʌz/ *n*

A 1 (of insect) zumbido *m* 2 (of voices) rumor *m*, murmullo *m*; **there was a ~ of excitement in the hall** hubo un murmullo de agitación en la sala 3 (as signal) zumbido *m*

B (phone call) (colloq): **to give sb a ~** darle* *or* pegarle* *or* (Méx) echarle un telefonazo a algn (fam), darle* un toque a algn (Esp fam)

C (thrill): **I get a ~ out of surfing** el surf me vuelve loco

buzz² *vi* 1 «*insect*» zumbar; **my ears were ~ing** me zumbaban los oídos 2 «*telephone/alarm clock*» sonar* 3 (be animated) (*usu in -ing form*) **to ~ WITH sth**: **the town was ~ing with rumors** la ciudad era un hervidero de rumores; **the Boston arts scene is really ~ing** hay una actividad febril en el mundo artístico de Boston

■ **buzz** *vt* 1 (call on intercom) llamar por el interfono 2 (call on phone) (AmE colloq) darle* *or* pegarle* *or* (Méx) echarle un telefonazo a (fam), darle* un toque a (Esp fam)

Phrasal verb

• **buzz off** [v ▸ adv] (colloq) (*usu in imperative*) largarse* (fam), picar* (RPl fam)

buzzard /'bʌzərd || 'bʌzəd/ *n* 1 (hawk) (esp BrE) águila *f*‡ ratonera 2 (vulture) (AmE) aura *f*‡, gallinazo *m*, zopilote *m* (AmC, Méx)

buzzer /'bʌzər || 'bʌzə(r)/ *n* timbre *m*, chicharra *f*

buzz: **~ saw** *n* (AmE) sierra *f* circular; **~word** *n* palabra *f* de moda

BVD ® /'bi:vi:'di:/ *n* (AmE) *prenda interior de hombre*

BVM *n* (= **Blessed Virgin Mary**) Ntra. Sra.

b/w = black and white

by¹ /baɪ/ *prep*

A 1 (not later than): **he told her to be home ~ 11** le dijo que volviera antes de las 11; **they should be there ~ now** ya deberían estar allí; **will it be ready ~ 5?** ¿estará listo para las 5?; **~ the time he arrived, Ann had left** cuando llegó, Ann se había ido 2 (during, at) **~ day/night** de día/noche; **Rome ~ night** Roma de noche

B 1 (at the side of, near to) al lado de, junto a; **come and sit ~ me** ven a sentarte a mi lado *or* junto a mí; **it's right ~ the door** está justo al lado de la puerta 2 (to hand) (AmE): **I always keep some money ~ me** siempre llevo algo de dinero encima

C 1 (past): **I said hello, but he walked right ~ me** lo saludé pero él pasó de largo 2 (via, through) por; **I came in ~ the back door** entré por la puerta de atrás; **~ land/sea/air** por tierra/mar/avión

D (indicating agent, cause) (*with passive verbs*) por [*The passive voice is, however, less common in Spanish than it is in English*] **she was brought up ~ her grandmother** la crió su abuela, fue criada por su abuela; **she was accompanied ~ her father** iba acompañada de su padre; **a play ~ Shakespeare** una obra de Shakespeare; **it was written ~ Pinter** fue escrita por Pinter

E 1 (indicating means, method): **made ~ hand** hecho a mano; **to travel ~ car/train** viajar en coche/tren; **to pay ~ credit card** pagar* con tarjeta de crédito; **to navigate ~ the stars** guiarse* por las estrellas; **~ moonlight** a la luz de la luna; **~ -ING: you won't get anywhere ~ shouting** no vas a conseguir nada con gritar; **I'll begin ~ introducing myself** empezaré por presentarme 2 (owing to, from): ~ **chance** por casualidad; **she is Spanish ~ birth** es española de nacimiento; **he had two children ~ his second wife** tuvo dos hijos con *or* de su segunda mujer; ~ **-ING**: ~ **specializing, she has limited her options** al especializarse, ha restringido sus posibilidades; **they have lost public support ~ being too extreme** han perdido apoyo popular por ser demasiado extremistas

F 1 (according to): ~ **that clock it's almost half past** según ese reloj son casi y media; ~ **the look of things** por lo visto *or* al parecer; **that's fine ~ me** por mí no hay problema 2 (*in oaths*): **I swear ~ Almighty God ...** juro por Dios Todopoderoso ...; ~ **God, you'll be sorry you said that!** te juro que te vas a arrepentir de haber dicho eso

G 1 (indicating rate) por; **we are paid ~ the hour** nos pagan por hora(s); **they make them ~ the thousand** hacen miles y miles de ellos 2 (indicating extent of difference): **she broke the record ~ several seconds** batió el récord en *or* por varios segundos; **we missed the train ~ seconds** perdimos el tren por unos segundos; **I'm taller than you ~ an inch or two** soy una pulgada o dos más alto que tú 3 (indicating gradual progression): **one ~ one** uno por uno; **they went in two ~ two** entraron de dos en dos; **little ~ little** poco a poco, de a poco (CS)

H (Math) por; **multiply two ~ three** multiplica dos por tres; **divide six ~ three** divide seis por *or* entre tres; **a room 20ft ~ 12ft** una habitación de 20 pies por 12

I (in compass directions): **north ~ northeast** nornor(d)este

A **by oneself** (alone, without assistance) solo; **I need to be ~ myself** necesito estar solo *or* a solas; **they do their homework ~ themselves** hacen los deberes solos

by² *adv* 1 (past): **let me ~!** ¡déjenme pasar!; **she rushed ~ without seeing me** pasó corriendo y no me vio; **they watched the parade march ~** vieron pasar el desfile 2 (aside, in reserve): **I put a little money ~ each week** ahorro un poco de dinero cada semana 3 (to sb's residence): **call** *o* **stop ~ on your way to work** pasa por casa de camino al trabajo 4 (*in phrases*) **by and by**: ~ **and ~ they came to the clearing** al poco rato llegaron al claro; **it's going to rain ~ and ~** va a llover dentro de poco; **by and large** por lo general, en general; **by the by** *see* **bye¹**

bye¹ /baɪ/ *n*: ***by the*** **~**: **he mentioned it by the ~** lo mencionó de pasada

bye², (AmE) **'bye** /baɪ/ *interj* (colloq) ¡adiós!, ¡chao *or* chau! (esp AmL fam)

bye-bye /'baɪ'baɪ/ *interj* (colloq) ¡adiós!, ¡chaucito! (AmL fam), ¡chaíto! (Chi fam)

by: **~gone** *adj* (liter) (*before n*) ‹*age/days*› de antaño (liter), pasado; ***to let ~gones be ~gones*** olvidar el pasado; **let ~gones be ~gones** lo pasado, pasado está; **~law** *n* (BrE) ordenanza *f* municipal

BYOB /ˌbiːˌwaɪˌəʊ'biː/ *n* = **bring your own bottle** *o* **booze** *o* **beer**

bypass¹ /'baɪpæs || 'baɪpɑːs/ *n* 1 (road) (BrE) carretera *f* de circunvalación, bypass *m*, libramiento *m* (Méx), carretera *f* circunvalar (Col) 2 (Med) bypass *m*

bypass² *vt* 1 (circumvent) ‹*person/difficulty*› eludir 2 (Transp) «*road*» circunvalar; «*driver*» evitar entrar en

bypath /'baɪpæθ || 'baɪpɑːθ/ *n*

A (side path, indirect route) desvío *m*

B (minor branch of a subject) subrama *f*

by: **~-product** *n* (in manufacture) subproducto *m*, producto *m* secundario, derivado *m*; (consequence) consecuencia *f*; **~road** *n* carretera *f* secundaria *or* vecinal; **~stander** /'baɪˌstændər || 'baɪˌstændə(r)/ *n*: **they opened fire, killing innocent ~standers** abrieron fuego y mataron a varias personas inocentes *or* a varios transeúntes

byte /baɪt/ *n* byte *m*, octeto *m*

by: **~way** *n* camino *m* (*apartado*); **~word** *n*: **to be a ~word FOR sth** ser* sinónimo DE algo; **~-your-leave** /'baɪjər'liːv || ˌbaɪjɔː'liːv/ *n*: ***without so much as a ~-your-leave*** sin (ni) siquiera pedir permiso

Byzantine /'bɪznṭiːn, -taɪn || bɪ'zæntaɪn, baɪ'zæntaɪn/ *adj* bizantino

Byzantium /bə'zæntiəm || bɪ'zæntiəm, baɪ-/ *n* Bizancio *m*

Cc

C, c /si:/ *n* 1 (letter) C, c *f* 2 (Mus) do *m*; *see also* **A A2**

c 1 (Corresp) (= **copy to**): **c H. Palmer** copia a H. Palmer 2 (in US) (= **cent(s)**) centavo(s) *m(pl)* 3 (= **circa**): **c. 800 B.C.** hacia el 800 aC

C (= **Celsius** *or* **centigrade**) C; **20°C** 20°C

ca = **circa**

CA, Ca = **California**

CAA *n* (in UK) = **Civil Aviation Authority**

cab /kæb/ *n*

A (taxi) taxi *m*; **to call a ~** llamar a un taxi; (*before n*) **~ driver** taxista *mf*

B (driver's compartment) cabina *f*

CAB *n*

A (in US) = **Civil Aeronautics Board**

B (in UK) = **Citizens' Advice Bureau**

cabal /kə'bæl/ *n* 1 (group) conciliábulo *m* 2 (plot) conspiración *f*

cabaret /ˌkæbə'reɪ || 'kæbəreɪ/ *n* [c u] cabaret *m*

cabbage /'kæbɪdʒ/ *n* 1 [c u] (vegetable) repollo *m*, col *f*; (*before n*) **I found her/him in the ~ patch** (AmE euph & hum) la/lo trajo la cigüeña (euf & hum) 2 [c] (person) (BrE colloq) vegetal *m* (fam)

cabby, cabbie /'kæbi/ *n* (colloq) taxista *mf*, ruletero, -ra *m,f* (Méx fam), tachero, -ra *m,f* (RPl fam)

cabin /'kæbən || 'kæbɪn/ *n*

A (hut) cabaña *f*; (in motel) bungalow *m*

B (Naut) camarote *m*

C (Aerosp, Auto, Aviat) cabina *f*

cabin: **~ boy** *n* grumete *m*; **~ cruiser** *n* yate *m* de motor

cabinet /'kæbənət || 'kæbɪnɪt/ *n*

A (cupboard) armario *m*; **(glass) ~** vitrina *f*; **medicine ~** botiquín *m*

B *also* **Cabinet** (Govt) gabinete *m* (ministerial); (*before n*) **~ minister** ≈ ministro, -tra *m,f*, ≈ secretario, -ria *m,f* de Estado

cable¹ /'keɪbəl/ *n*

A [c] (Elec, Naut) cable *m*

B [c] (Telec) cable *m*, telegrama *m*

C [u] ▸**cable television**

cable² *vt* (Telec) ‹*message/news*› cablegrafiar*, telegrafiar*; **she ~d me $2,000** me envió un giro (telegráfico) de 2.000 dólares

cable: **~ car** *n* (suspended) teleférico *m*; (funicular) funicular *m*; (streetcar) (AmE) tranvía *m*; **~gram** *n* (frml) cablegrama *m* (frml); **~ railway** *n* funicular *m*; **~ television** *n* [u] televisión *f* por cable, cablevisión *f* (esp AmL)

caboodle /kə'bu:dl/ *n*: **the whole ~** (colloq) absolutamente todo

caboose /kə'bu:s/ *n* (AmE Rail) furgón *m* de cola, cabús *m* (Méx)

cache /kæʃ/ *n*

A (of provisions) alijo *m*

B (Comput) cache *m*

cackhanded /'kæk'hændəd || ˌkæk'hændɪd/ *adj* (BrE colloq) torpe, patoso (Esp fam)

cackle¹ /'kækəl/ *vi* ‹‹*hen*›› cacarear; ‹‹*person*›› (laugh) reírse* socarronamente

cackle² *n* (of hen) cacareo *m*; (laugh) risa *f* socarrona; ***cut the ~!*** (colloq) ¡menos charla! (fam)

cacophony /kə'kɑ:fəni || kə'kɒfəni/ *n* 1 (dissonance) disonancia *f*, algarabía *f* 2 (Ling) cacofonía *f*

cactus /'kæktəs/ *n* (*pl* **-ti** /-taɪ/ *or* **-tuses**) cactus *m*

cad /kæd/ *n* (colloq & dated) canalla *m*, sinvergüenza *m*

CAD *n* [u] (= **computer-aided design**) CAD *m*

cadaver /kə'dævər || kə'dɑ:və(r)/ *n* cadáver *m*

cadaverous /kə'dævərəs/ *adj* (liter) cadavérico

caddie¹ /'kædi/ *n* caddie *mf*

caddie² *vi* **-dies, -dying, -died** hacer* de caddie; **to ~ for sb** ser* el caddie de algn

caddy¹ /'kædi/ *n* 1 ▸**tea caddy** 2 ▸**caddie¹** 3 (for shopping) (AmE) carrito *m* de la compra

caddy² *vi* ▸**caddie²**

cadence /'keɪdn̩s/ *n* cadencia *f*

cadet /kə'det/ *n* cadete *mf*

cadge /kædʒ/ (colloq) *vt* **to ~ sth FROM** *o* **OFF sb** gorronearle *or* gorrearle *or* (RPl) garronearle *or* (Chi) bolsearle algo A algn (fam)

■ **cadge** *vi* **to ~ FROM** *o* **OFF sb** gorronearle *or* gorrearle *or* (RPl) garronearle *or* (Chi) bolsearle A algn (fam)

Cadiz /kə'dɪz/ *n* Cádiz *m*

cadre /'kædri || 'kɑ:də(r)/ *n* cuadro *m*

Caesar /'si:zər || 'si:zə(r)/ *n* César

Caesarean (section) /sɪ'zæriən || sɪ'zeəriən/ *n* ▸**Cesarean (section)**

café, cafe /kæ'feɪ || 'kæfeɪ/ *n* (coffee bar) café *m*, cafetería *f*; (restaurant) *restaurante económico*

cafeteria /ˌkæfə'tɪriə || ˌkæfə'tɪəriə/ *n* (in hospital, college) cantina *f*, cafetería *f*; (restaurant) restaurante *m* autoservicio, self-service *m*

cafetière /ˌkæfə'tjer || ˌkæfə'tjeə(r)/ *n* cafetera *f* de émbolo *or* de pistón

caffeine /kæ'fi:n || 'kæfi:n/ *n* [u] cafeína *f*

cage¹ /keɪdʒ/ *n* jaula *f*; (Anat) **rib ~** caja *f* torácica; (in basketball) canasta *f*, cesta *f*; (in ice hockey) portería *f*, meta *f*, arco *m* (Col, CS)

cage² *vt* (*usu pass*) enjaular

cagey /'keɪdʒi/ *adj* **cagier, cagiest** (colloq) ‹*reply*› reservado, cauteloso

cagily /'keɪdʒəli || 'keɪdʒɪli/ *adv* ‹*reply*› cautelosamente

cagy /'keɪdʒi/ *adj* **cagier, cagiest** ▸**cagey**

cahoots /kə'hu:ts/ *n*: ***to be in ~ (with sb)*** (colloq) estar* confabulado *or* (fam) conchabado (con algn)

Cain /keɪn/ *n* Caín; ***to raise ~*** (colloq) armar la de Dios es Cristo (fam)

Cairo /'kaɪrəʊ || 'kaɪərəʊ/ *n* El Cairo

cajole /kə'dʒəʊl/ *vt* convencer* con zalamerías *or* halagos

Cajun¹ /'keɪdʒən/ *adj* cajún

Cajun² *n* 1 [c] (person) cajún *mf* (*descendiente de inmigrantes franceses en el estado norteamericano de Luisiana*) 2 [u] (Ling) *dialecto del francés hablado por los* **Cajun**

cake¹ /keɪk/ *n*

A [u c] (Culin) (large) pastel *m*, tarta *f* (Esp), torta *f* (esp CS); (small, individual) pastel *m*, masa *f* (RPl); **sponge ~** bizcocho *m*, queque *m* (AmL exc RPl), bizcochuelo *m* (CS), ponqué *m* (Col, Ven), panque *m* (Méx); ***the icing*** *o* (AmE also) ***frosting on the ~*** un extra; ***to be a piece of ~*** (colloq) ser* pan comido (fam); ***to take the ~*** (colloq) ser el colmo (fam); ‹‹*person*››

C

llevarse la palma (fam); ***to go** o **sell like hot ~s*** venderse como pan caliente *or* como rosquillas; ***to have one's ~ and eat it**: **you can't have your ~ and eat it too*** no puedes tenerlo todo, tienes que elegir

B [c] **~ of soap** pastilla *f* de jabón

cake[2] *vt* (*usu pass*) **to be ~d WITH sth**: **our shoes were ~d with mud** teníamos los zapatos cubiertos de barro endurecido

cake tin *n* (BrE) (for baking) molde *m* (para pastel); (for storage) lata *f* (*para guardar pasteles*)

cal (= calorie(s)) cal.

Cal [1] (= **Calorie(s)**) kcal [2] = **California**

CAL *n* [u] = **computer-aided learning**

calabash /'kæləbæʃ/ *n* calabaza *f*, güira *f* (AmC), totumo *m* (Col, Ven)

calabrese /'kæləbri:z/ *n* [u] brócoli *m* calabrés

calamine (lotion) /'kæləmaɪn/ *n* [u] loción *f* de calamina

calamity /kə'læməti/ *n* (*pl* **-ties**) calamidad *f*, desastre *m*

calcify /'kælsəfaɪ || 'kælsɪfaɪ/ **-fies, -fying, -fied** *vt* calcificar*

■ **calcify** *vi* calcificarse*

calcium /'kælsiəm/ *n* [u] calcio *m*

calculate /'kælkjəleɪt || 'kælkjʊleɪt/ *vt*

A (compute, estimate) calcular

B (aim) **to be ~d to + INF**: **his remarks were ~d to offend** lo dijo con la intención *or* el próposito de ofender

■ **calculate** *vi* calcular

calculated /'kælkjəleɪtəd || 'kælkjʊleɪtɪd/ *adj* (*before n*) ‹*risk*› calculado; ‹*act*› deliberado; ‹*insult*› dicho con toda intención

calculating /'kælkjəleɪtɪŋ || 'kælkjʊleɪtɪŋ/ *adj* calculador

calculation /'kælkjə'leɪʃən || ˌkælkjʊ'leɪʃən/ *n* [c u] cálculo *m*; **according to my ~(s)** según mis cálculos

calculator /'kælkjəleɪtər || 'kælkjʊleɪtə(r)/ *n* calculadora *f*; **pocket ~** calculadora *f* de bolsillo

caldron, (BrE) **cauldron** /'kɔ:ldrən/ *n* caldero *m*

calendar /'kæləndər || 'kælɪndə(r)/ *n* [c] calendario *m*, almanaque *m*; **~ of events** programa *m* de actos; **the sporting ~** el calendario deportivo; (*before n*) **~ month** mes *m* (del calendario)

calf /kæf || kɑ:f/ *n* (*pl* **calves**)

A (Zool) [1] [c] (animal) ternero, -ra *m,f*, becerro, -rra *m,f*; ***to kill the fatted ~*** (liter) celebrar una gran fiesta de bienvenida [2] [u] (leather) (piel *f* *or* cuero *m* de) becerro *m*

B (Anat) pantorrilla *f*

calfskin /'kæfskɪn || 'kɑ:fskɪn/ *n* [u] (piel *f* *or* cuero *m* de) becerro *m*

caliber, (BrE) **calibre** /'kæləbər || 'kælɪbə(r)/ *n* [1] [c] (diameter) calibre *m* [2] [u] (quality) calibre *m*; **a writer of his ~** un escritor de su calibre

calibrate /'kæləbreɪt || 'kælɪbreɪt/ *vt* calibrar

calibration /'kælə'breɪʃən || ˌkælɪ'breɪʃən/ *n* [c u] calibrado *m*

calibre *n* (BrE) ▸**caliber**

calico /'kælɪkəʊ/ *n* [u c] (*pl* **-coes** *or* **-cos**) (printed cotton) algodón *m* estampado, percal *m*; (white cotton) (BrE) lienzo *m*, percal *m*

Calif = **California**

California /'kælə'fɔ:rniə || ˌkælɪ'fɔ:niə/ *n* California *f*

Californian /'kælə'fɔ:rniən || ˌkælɪ'fɔ:niən/ *adj* californiano

calipers, (BrE) **callipers** /'kæləpərz || 'kælɪpəz/ *pl n* [1] (for measuring) calibrador *m* [2] (Med) aparato *m* ortopédico (*para la pierna*)

calisthenics, (BrE) **callisthenics** /'kæləs'θenɪks || ˌkælɪs'θenɪks/ *n* (+ *sing o pl vb*) calistenia *f*

call[1] /kɔ:l/ *n*

A (by telephone) llamada *f*; **to make a ~** hacer* una llamada (telefónica); **to give sb a ~** llamar a algn (por teléfono); **will you take the ~?** (talk to sb) ¿le paso la llamada?; (accept charges) ¿acepta la llamada?; **local/long-distance ~** llamada urbana/interurbana

B [1] (of person — cry) llamada *f*, llamado *m* (AmL); (— shout) grito *m* [2] (of animal) grito *m*; (of bird) reclamo *m*

C [1] (summons): **to be on ~** estar* de guardia; **beyond the ~ of duty** más de lo que el deber exigía (*or* exige *etc*) (frml); **to answer** *o* **obey the ~ of nature** (euph) hacer* sus (*or* mis *etc*) necesidades (euf) [2] (lure) llamada *f*, atracción *f*

D (demand) llamamiento *m*, llamado *m* (AmL); **there were ~s for his resignation** pidieron su dimisión

E (claim): **there are too many ~s on my time** muchas cosas reclaman mi atención

F (*usu with neg*) [1] (reason) motivo *m*; **he had no ~ to be rude** no tenía por qué ser grosero [2] (demand) demanda *f*; **there's not much ~ for this product** no hay mucha demanda para este producto

G (visit) visita *f*; **to pay a ~ on sb** hacerle* una visita a algn

H (Sport) decisión *f*, cobro *m* (Chi)

call[2] *vt*

A (shout) llamar; **to ~ sb's name** llamar a algn

B ‹*police/taxi/doctor*› llamar; ‹*strike*› llamar a, convocar*

C (contact — by telephone, radio) llamar; **for more information ~ us on** *o* **at 341-6920** para más información llame *or* llámenos al (teléfono) 341-6920; **don't ~ us, we'll ~ you** (set phrase) ya lo llamaremos; **~ me on my cell phone** llámame al celular (AmL) *or* móvil (Esp)

D (name, describe as) llamar; **we ~ her Betty** la llamamos *or* (esp AmL) le decimos Betty; **what are you going to ~ the baby?** ¿qué nombre le van a poner al bebé?; **what is this ~ed in Italian?** ¿cómo se llama esto en italiano?; **are you ~ing me a liar?** ¿me estás llamando mentiroso?; **he ~s himself an artist, but ...** se dice *or* se considera un artista pero ...; **what sort of time do you ~ this?** ¿éstas son horas de llegar?; **I don't ~ that difficult** yo no diría que es difícil; **shall we ~ it $30?** digamos *or* pongamos que treinta dólares

E (in poker) ver*; (in bridge) declarar

■ **call** *vi*

A «*person*» llamar; **to ~ TO sb**: **she ~ed to me for help** me llamó para que la ayudara

B (by telephone, radio) llamar; **who's ~ing, please?** ¿de parte de quién, por favor?; **Madrid ~ing** aquí Madrid

C (visit) pasar

Phrasal verbs

- **call around** [v ▸ adv] [1] (Telec) llamar (*a varias personas*) [2] (visit) pasar (por casa)
- **call at** [v ▸ prep ▸ o]: **this train ~s at all stations** este tren para en todas las estaciones; **I ~ed at your place yesterday** ayer pasé por tu casa
- **call away** [v ▸ o ▸ adv, v ▸ adv ▸ o]: **she was ~ed away from the meeting** la llamaron y tuvo que salir de la reunión; **he was ~ed away on business** tuvo que ausentarse por motivos de trabajo
- **call back**

A (Telec) [v ▸ o ▸ adv]: **can I ~ you back?** ¿puedo llamarte más tarde?

B [v ▸ adv] (Telec) volver* a llamar

- **call for** [v ▸ prep ▸ o] [1] (require) ‹*skill/courage*› requerir*, exigir*; **you won? this ~s for champagne!** ¿ganaste? ¡esto hay que celebrarlo con champán! [2] (demand) pedir* [3] (shout for) pedir* (*a gritos*) [4] (collect) ‹*goods/person*› pasar a buscar *or* a recoger
- **call forth** [v ▸ adv ▸ o] (frml) ‹*protest/criticism*› provocar*, dar* lugar a; ‹*emotion*› inspirar
- **call in**

A [v ▸ o ▸ adv, v ▸ adv ▸ o] [1] (summon) ‹*expert/doctor*› llamar [2] (withdraw) retirar de circulación

B [v ▸ adv] [1] (visit) **to ~ in (ON sb)**: **I'll ~ in later** me paso luego (fam); **shall we ~ in on the Rowsons?** ¿por qué no pasamos a ver a los Rowson? [2] (telephone) llamar

- **call off** [v ▸ o ▸ adv, v ▸ adv ▸ o] [1] (cancel) suspender; **if that's how you feel, let's ~ the whole thing off** mira, si eso es lo que piensas mejor olvidémoslo [2] (order to stop) ‹*men*› retirar; ‹*dog*› llamar
- **call on** [v ▸ prep ▸ o] [1] (visit) pasar a ver *or* a visitar a, visitar [2] ▸**call upon**
- **call out** [v ▸ o ▸ adv, v ▸ adv ▸ o] [1] (summon) ‹*fire brigade*› llamar; ‹*army*› hacer* intervenir a; ‹*doctor*› llamar, hacer* venir [2] (on strike) (BrE) llamar a la huelga [3] (utter): **he ~ed out her name** la llamó, pronunció su nombre (liter)
- **call round** [v ▸ adv] [1] (visit) (BrE) pasar [2] (Telec) (esp BrE) llamar (*a varias personas*)
- **call up** [v ▸ o ▸ adv, v ▸ adv ▸ o] [1] (cause to return) ‹*memory/image*› traer* a la memoria, evocar* (liter); ‹*spirits*› invocar*,

llamar 2▸ (telephone) (esp AmE) llamar 3▸ (Mil) (*often pass*) llamar (a filas)
• **call upon** [v ▸ prep ▸ o] 1▸ (invite): **to ~ upon sb to speak** dar* la palabra a algn 2▸ (appeal to) apelar a
call box *n* (BrE) cabina *f* telefónica
caller /'kɔːlər || 'kɔːlə(r)/ *n*: **we didn't have many ~s** no vino mucha gente; (Telec) no tuvimos *or* no hubo muchas llamadas; **the ~ didn't leave her name** la persona que llamó no dejó su nombre
callgirl /'kɔːlgɜːrl || 'kɔːlgɜːl/ *n* (colloq) call-girl *f* (*prostituta que da citas por teléfono*)
calligraphy /kə'lɪgrəfi/ *n* [u] caligrafía *f*
call-in /'kɔːlɪn/ *n* (AmE) *programa de radio o TV en el que el público participa por teléfono*
calling /'kɔːlɪŋ/ *n* (vocation) vocación *f*
calling card *n* (AmE) tarjeta *f* de visita
callipers *pl n* (BrE) ▸ **calipers**
callisthenics *n* (BrE) ▸ **calisthenics**
callous /'kæləs/ *adj* insensible, cruel
callously /'kæləsli/ *adv* cruelmente
call-out /'kɔːlaʊt/ *adj* (BrE) ‹*charge/fee*› por desplazamiento; ‹*service*› a domicilio
callow /'kæləʊ/ *adj* inmaduro, inexperto
callus /'kæləs/ *n* (*pl* **-luses**) (Med) callo *m*, callosidad *f*
calm¹ /kɑːm/ *adj* **-er, -est** ‹*sea*› en calma, tranquilo, calmo (esp AmL); ‹*person/voice*› tranquilo, calmado, calmo (esp AmL); **keep ~!** ¡tranquilo!, ¡calma!
calm² *vt* tranquilizar*, calmar; **I had a drink to ~ my nerves** me tomé una copa para tranquilizarme *or* calmarme
(Phrasal verb)
• **calm down**
A [v ▸ o ▸ adv, v ▸ adv ▸ o] tranquilizar*, calmar
B [v ▸ adv] tranquilizarse*; **~ down!** ¡tranquilízate!, ¡tranquilo!
calm³ *n* 1▸ (stillness) (*no pl*) calma *f*; **the ~ before the storm** la calma que precede a la tormenta 2▸ [u] (peace, tranquillity) calma *f*, tranquilidad *f*
calming /'kɑːmɪŋ/ *adj* tranquilizante
calmly /'kɑːmli/ *adv* con calma
calmness /'kɑːmnəs || 'kɑːmnɪs/ *n* [u] 1▸ (of person) calma *f*, tranquilidad *f* 2▸ (of sea, wind) calma *f*
Calor Gas® /'kælər || 'kælə(r)/ *n* [u] (BrE) (gas *m*) butano *m*, supergás® *m* (RPl)
calorie /'kæləri/ *n* 1▸ (Phys) caloría *f* 2▸ *also* **Calorie** (Culin) (kilo)caloría *f*; (*before n*) **a ~-controlled diet** una dieta *or* un régimen bajo en calorías
calorific /ˌkælə'rɪfɪk/ *adj* calorífico; **~ value** (of food) contenido *m* calórico
calumny /'kæləmni/ *n* [c u] (*pl* **-nies**) (frml) calumnia *f*
calves /kævz || kɑːvz/ *pl of* **calf**
Calvinist /'kælvənəst || 'kælvɪnɪst/ *n* calvinista *mf*
calypso /kə'lɪpsəʊ/ *n* (*pl* **-soes** *or* (BrE) **-sos**) (Mus) calipso *m*
camaraderie /ˌkɑːmə'rɑːdəri || ˌkæmə'rɑːdəri/ *n* [u] camaradería *f*, compañerismo *m*
camcorder /'kæmˌkɔːrdər || 'kæmˌkɔːdə(r)/ *n* videocámara *f*, camcórder *m*
came /keɪm/ *past of* **come**
camel /'kæməl/ *n*
A [c] (Zool) camello *m*
B [u] (color) beige *m*
cameo /'kæmiəʊ/ *n*
A (jewelry) camafeo *m*
B (Cin, TV) actuación *f* especial; (*before n*) **a ~ performance** una actuación especial
camera /'kæmərə/ *n* (Phot) cámara *f* (fotográfica), máquina *f* fotográfica *or* de fotos; (Cin, TV) cámara *f*
camera: **~man** /'kæmərəmæn/ *n* (*pl* **-men** /-men/) camarógrafo, -fa *m,f*, cameraman *mf* (esp AmL), cámara *mf* (Esp); **~ phone** *n* (teléfono *m*) celular *f* (AmL) *or* (Esp) móvil *m* cámara; **~ work** *n* [u] fotografía *f*
Cameroon /'kæmə'ruːn/ *n* Camerún *m*
camisole /'kæməsəʊl || 'kæmɪsəʊl/ *n* camisola *f*
camomile /'kæməmaɪl/ *n* ▸ **chamomile**

camouflage¹ /'kæməflɑːʒ/ *n* [c u] camuflaje *m*
camouflage² *vt* camuflar, camuflajear (AmL)
camp¹ /kæmp/ *n*
A [c] (collection of tents, huts) campamento *m*; **(summer) ~** (in US) campamento *m* de verano, colonia *f* de vacaciones *or* verano; **army ~** campamento *m* militar
B [c] (group, position) bando *m*
C [u] (affected behavior, style) amaneramiento *m*, afectación *f*
camp² *vi* acampar; **to go ~ing** ir* de camping *or* de campamento *or* de acampada
(Phrasal verbs)
• **camp out** [v ▸ adv] acampar
• **camp up** (*v + o + adv*): ***to ~ it up*** actuar* amaneradamente *or* con afectación
camp³ *adj* 1▸ (effeminate) amanerado, afeminado 2▸ ‹*performance*› afectado, exagerado
campaign¹ /kæm'peɪn/ *n* campaña *f*
campaign² *vi* (Pol, Sociol) **to ~ FOR/AGAINST sth** hacer* una campaña A FAVOR DE/EN CONTRA DE algo
campaigner /kæm'peɪnər || kæm'peɪnə(r)/ *n* (Pol, Sociol) defensor, -sora *m,f*; **an old ~** un veterano
camper /'kæmpər || 'kæmpə(r)/ *n*
A (in tent) campista *mf*, acampante *mf*
B (Transp) cámper *f*
camp: **~fire** *n* fogata *f*, hoguera *f*, fogón *m* (AmL); **~ follower** *n* (sympathizer) simpatizante *mf*; (Mil) (prostitute) prostituta *f*; **~ground** *n* (AmE) camping *m*
camphor /'kæmfər || 'kæmfə(r)/ *n* [u] alcanfor *m*
camping /'kæmpɪŋ/ *n* [u]: **I like ~** me gusta ir de camping *or* de campamento *or* de acampada; **Ⓢ no camping** prohibido acampar
campsite /'kæmpsaɪt/ *n* camping *m*
campus /'kæmpəs/ *n* (*pl* **-puses**) campus *m*
can¹ /kæn/ *n*
A 1▸ (container) lata *f*, bote *m* (Esp), tarro *m* (Chi); ***a ~ of worms*** (colloq) un problema complicado; (*before n*) **~ opener** abrelatas *m* 2▸ (for petrol, water) bidón *m*; (for garbage) (AmE) cubo *m or* (CS) tacho *m or* (Col) caneca *f or* (Méx) bote *m or* (Ven) tobo *m* de la basura; ***to carry the ~*** (BrE colloq) pagar* el pato (fam)
B (AmE sl) 1▸ (prison) cárcel *f*, cana *f* (AmS arg), bote *m* (Méx, Ven arg), trullo *m* (Esp arg); **to be in the ~** estar* a la sombra (fam) 2▸ (toilet) trono *m* (fam) 3▸ (buttocks) culo *m* (fam *o* vulg), trasero *m* (fam)
can² *vt* **-nn-**
A (put in cans) enlatar; (bottle) (AmE) ‹*fruit*› preparar conservas de
B (AmE colloq) (dismiss) echar (fam), correr (fam); (stop) (*usu in impera*): **~ it!** ¡basta ya!
can³ /kæn, *weak form* kən/ *v mod* (*past* **could**)
A (indicating ability) poder*; (referring to particular skills) saber*; **she couldn't answer the question** no pudo contestar la pregunta; **we ~ but try** con intentarlo no se pierde nada; **~ you swim/speak German?** ¿sabes nadar/(hablar) alemán?
B 1▸ (with verbs of perception): **I ~'t see very well** no veo muy bien; **~ you hear me?** ¿me oyes? 2▸ (with verbs of mental activity): **I ~'t understand it** no lo entiendo, no logro *or* no puedo entenderlo; **~'t you tell he's lying?** ¿no te das cuenta de que está mintiendo?
C 1▸ (indicating, asking etc permission) poder*; **~ I come with you?** ¿puedo ir contigo?; **you ~ stay as long as you like** te puedes quedar todo el tiempo *or* todo lo que quieras 2▸ (in requests) poder*; **~ you turn that music down, please?** ¿puedes bajar esa música, por favor?; **~ I have two salads, please?** ¿me trae dos ensaladas, por favor? 3▸ (in offers): **~ I help you?** ¿me permite?; (in shop) ¿lo/la atienden?, ¿qué desea?; **~ I carry that for you?** ¿quieres que (te) lleve eso?
D 1▸ (allow oneself to) (*with neg or interrog*) poder*; **you ~'t blame her** no puedes echarle la culpa; **I couldn't very well tell him just then** no se lo podía decir justo en ese momento; **how *could* you?** pero ¿cómo se te ocurrió hacer (*or* decir *etc*) una cosa así?, pero ¿cómo pudiste hacer (*or* decir *etc*) una cosa así? 2▸ (in suggestions, advice): **~'t you give it another try?** ¿por qué no lo vuelves a intentar? 3▸ (in orders): **for a start, you ~ clean all this up** puedes empezar por limpiar todo esto
E 1▸ (indicating possibility) poder*; **anything ~ happen now**

ahora puede pasar cualquier cosa; **what *can* she be doing in there?** ¿qué estará haciendo ahí?, ¿qué puede estar haciendo ahí?; **it ~'t be true!** ¡no puede ser!, ¡no es posible!; **you ~'t be serious!** ¡no lo dirás en serio! 2 (indicating characteristic): **she ~ be charming when she wants to** es encantadora cuando quiere *or* cuando se lo propone; **she's as happy as ~ be** está contentísima, está de lo más contenta; *see also* **could**

C

Canada /'kænədə/ *n* (el) Canadá *m*

Canadian¹ /kə'neɪdiən/ *adj* canadiense

Canadian² *n* canadiense *mf*

canal /kə'næl/ *n* (for transport, irrigation) canal *m*; (Anat) canal *m*

Canaries /kə'neriz || kə'neəriz/ *pl n* **the ~** (las) Canarias

canary /kə'neri || kə'neəri/ *n* (*pl* **-ries**) 1 (bird) canario *m* 2 (informer) (AmE sl) soplón, -plona *m,f* (fam), chivato, -ta *m,f* (Esp fam)

canary: **~ Islands** *pl n* **the C~ Islands** las Islas Canarias; **~-yellow** /kə'neri'jeləʊ || kə'neəri'jeləʊ/ *adj* (*pred* **~ yellow**) amarillo canario *or* (AmL tb) patito *adj inv*

cancel /'kænsəl/, (BrE) **-ll-** *vt*

A ‹*meeting/subscription/flight*› cancelar; ‹*command/decree/check*› anular

B (Math) eliminar

■ **cancel** *vi* (call off): **he ~ed at the last minute** a último momento canceló la cita (*or* el viaje *etc*)

Phrasal verb

• **cancel out** [v ▸ o ▸ adv, v ▸ adv ▸ o] 1 (Math) anular 2 (offset) ‹*deficit/loss*› compensar; ‹*debt*› cancelar; **those advantages are ~ed out by the practical difficulties** las dificultades de orden práctico anulan esas ventajas

cancellation /'kænsə'leɪʃən/ *n* [u c] cancelación *f*; (Theat) **there may be some ~s on the night** quizás haya alguna devolución esa misma noche

cancer /'kænsər || 'kænsə(r)/ *n*

A [u c] (disease) (Med) cáncer *m*

B **Cancer** (Astrol) 1 (sign) (*no art*) Cáncer 2 [c] (person) Cáncer *or* cáncer *mf*, canceriano, -na *m,f*; *see also* **Aquarius**

cancerous /'kænsərəs/ *adj* canceroso

candelabra /'kændə'lɑːbrə/ *n* (*pl* **-bras**) candelabro *m*

candid /'kændəd || 'kændɪd/ *adj* (frank) franco, sincero

candidacy /'kændədəsi || 'kændɪdəsi/ *n* (*pl* **-cies**) candidatura *f*

candidate /'kændədeɪt || 'kændɪdət/ *n* candidato, -ta *m,f*

candied /'kændid/ *adj* confitado, abrillantado (RPl)

candle /'kændl̩/ *n* (for domestic use) vela *f*; (for altar) cirio *m*; ***to burn the ~ at both ends*** tratar de abarcar demasiado, hacer* de la noche día; ***to hold a ~ to sb***: **she can't** *o* **doesn't hold a ~ to her sister** no le llega ni a la suela del zapato a la hermana; (*before n*) **~ holder** palmatoria *f*; (for birthday cakes *etc*) portavela *m*

candle: **~light** *n* [u]: **by ~light** a la luz de una vela/de las velas; **~lit** *adj* ‹*room/restaurant*› alumbrado con velas; **a ~lit dinner** una cena íntima a la luz de las velas; **~stick** *n* candelero *m*; (flat) palmatoria *f*; **~wick** *n* [u] (Tex) chenilla *f*

candor, (BrE) **candour** /'kændər || 'kændə(r)/ *n* [u] franqueza *f*

C & W /'siːən'dʌbəljuː/ *n* [u] **= country and western**

candy /'kændi/ *n* (*pl* **-dies**) (AmE) 1 [u] (confectionery) golosinas *fpl*, dulces *mpl* (AmL exc RPl); (*before n*) **~ bar** *golosina en barra* 2 [c] (individual piece) caramelo *m*, dulce *m* (AmL exc RPl)

candy: **~ apple** *n* (AmE) manzana *f* acaramelada; **~floss** *n* [u] (BrE) algodón *m* (de azúcar); **~striped** *adj* (Tex) a *or* de rayas

cane¹ /keɪn/ *n*

A 1 [c] (of bamboo) caña *f* 2 [c] (*sugar ~*) caña *f* de azúcar 3 [u] (for wickerwork) mimbre *m*

B [c] (walking stick) bastón *m*; (for punishment) palmeta *f*; (for supporting plants) rodrigón *m*, tutor *m*; **he got the ~** le dieron con la palmeta

cane² *vt* castigar* con la palmeta

canine¹ /'keɪnaɪn/ *n*

A (Zool) canino *m*, cánido *m*

B **~ (tooth)** (diente *m*) canino *m*, colmillo *m*

canine² *adj* canino

caning /'keɪnɪŋ/ *n*: **to give sb a ~** castigar* a algn con la palmeta

canister /'kænəstər || 'kænɪstə(r)/ *n* 1 (for tea, coffee) lata *f*, bote *m* (Esp) 2 (Mil) bote *m* (*de humo, metralla etc*)

canker /'kæŋkər || 'kæŋkə(r)/ *n* [u c] (*before n*) **~ sore** (AmE) afta *f*‡

cannabis /'kænəbəs || 'kænəbɪs/ *n* [u] (drug) hachís *m*, cannabis *m*; (*before n*) **~ plant** cáñamo *m* índico

canned /kænd/ *adj* 1 ‹*food*› enlatado, en *or* de lata, en conserva 2 (pre-recorded) (colloq) ‹*music*› enlatado (fam); ‹*laughter*› grabado

cannelloni /,kænə'ləʊni/ *n* [u c] canelones *mpl*

cannery /'kænəri/ *n* (*pl* **-ries**) fábrica *f* de conservas *or* enlatados

cannibal /'kænəbəl || 'kænɪbəl/ *n* caníbal *mf*, antropófago, -ga *m,f*

cannibalism /'kænəbəlɪzəm || 'kænɪbəlɪzəm/ *n* [u] canibalismo *m*, antropofagia *f*

cannibalize /'kænəbəlaɪz || 'kænɪbəlaɪz/ *vt* ‹*machine/car*› canibalizar*; ‹*material*› fusilarse (fam), plagiar

cannon /'kænən/ *n* (*pl also* ~) cañón *m*; (*before n*) **~ fodder** carne *f* de cañón

cannonball /'kænənbɔːl/ *n* (Mil) bala *f* de cañón

cannot /'kænɑːt || 'kænɒt/ **= can not**

canny /'kæni/ *adj* **-nier, -niest** (shrewd) astuto

canoe¹ /kə'nuː/ *n* canoa *f*, piragua *f*

canoe² *vi* **-noes, -noeing, -noed** ir* en canoa *or* piragua

canoeing /kə'nuːɪŋ/ *n* [u] piragüismo *m*, canotaje *m*

canoeist /kə'nuːəst || kə'nuːɪst/ *n* piragüista *mf*, remero, -ra *m,f* de canoas, canoero, -ra *m,f*

canon /'kænən/ *n*

A 1 (church decree) canon *m*; (*before n*) **~ law** derecho *m* canónico 2 (standard, criterion) (frml) canon *m*

B (clergyman) canónigo *m*

canonize /'kænənaɪz/ *vt* canonizar*

canoodle /kə'nuːdl̩/ *vi* (colloq) besuquearse (fam)

canopy /'kænəpi/ *n* (*pl* **-pies**) (over bed, throne) dosel *m*, baldaquín *m*, baldaquino *m*; (over person) palio *m*, dosel *m*

canst /kænst/ (arch) *2nd pers sing pres of* **can³**

cant /kænt/ *n* [u] 1 (insincere talk) hipocresía *f* 2 (jargon) jerga *f*

can't /kænt || kɑːnt/ **= can not**

cantankerous /kæn'tæŋkərəs/ *adj* cascarrabias *adj inv*

canteen /kæn'tiːn/ *n*

A (dining hall) (BrE) cantina *f*, comedor *m*, casino *m* (Chi) (*en un lugar de trabajo, colegio etc*)

B (water bottle) cantimplora *f*

C (for cutlery) (BrE) *estuche para guardar un juego de cubiertos*; **~ of cutlery** juego *m* de cubiertos, cubertería *f*

canter¹ /'kæntər || 'kæntə(r)/ *n* medio galope *m*

canter² *vi* ir* a medio galope

cantilever /'kæntl̩iːvər || 'kæntɪliːvə(r)/ *n* viga *f* voladiza; (*before n*) **~ bridge** puente *m* voladizo

Canuck /kə'nʌk, kə'nək/ *n* (AmE sl & often pej) canadiense *mf*

canvas /'kænvəs/ *n*

A [u] (cloth) lona *f*; **under ~** (in a tent) en una tienda de campaña *or* (AmL) en una carpa

B (Art) 1 [c u] (for painting) lienzo *m*, tela *f* 2 [c] (painting) cuadro *m*, lienzo *m* (frml), tela *f* (frml)

canvass /'kænvəs/ *vt*

A 1 (Pol): **to ~ voters in an area** hacer* campaña entre los votantes de una zona 2 ‹*opinion*› sondear, hacer* un sondeo de

B (scrutinize) (AmE): **to ~ the votes** hacer* el escrutinio de los votos

■ **canvass** *vi* (Pol) hacer* campaña, hacer* propaganda electoral; **to ~ FOR sb** hacer* campaña A *or* EN FAVOR DE algn

canvasser /'kænvəsər || 'kænvəsə(r)/ *n* (Pol) *persona que solicita votos durante una campaña electoral*

canvassing /'kænvəsɪŋ/ *n* [u] (Pol) solicitación *f* de votos

canyon /'kænjən/ *n* cañón *m*

canyoning /'kænjənɪŋ/ *n* [u] barranquismo *m*, cañonismo *m*

cap¹ /kæp/ *n*

A (hat) gorra *f*; **swimming ~** gorro *m or* (esp AmL) gorra *f* de baño; **baseball/golf ~** gorra de béisbol/golf; **~ and gown** (Educ) toga *f* y birrete *m*; ***if the ~ fits wear it*** al que le caiga *or* le venga el sayo *or* saco, que se lo ponga (AmL), el que se pica ajos come (Esp); ***to put one's thinking ~ on*** (colloq) usar la materia gris (fam); ▸**hand¹ B**

B 1▸ (of bottle) tapa *f*, tapón *m*; (metal) chapa *f*, tapa *f*; (of pen) capuchón *m*, tapa *f*; **gas** *o* (BrE) **petrol ~** tapa *f* del depósito *or* tanque de gasolina 2▸ (diaphragm) (BrE) diafragma *m*

C (for toy gun) fulminante *m*

D (upper limit) tope *m*; **to put a ~ on sth** poner* un tope a algo

cap² *vt* **-pp-**

A ‹*bottle/tube*› tapar

B 1▸ (outdo): **they were always trying to ~ each other's jokes** estaban siempre tratando de contar un chiste mejor que el del otro 2▸ (crown, complete) rematar, coronar; **to ~ it all off** *o* (BrE) **to ~ it all ...** para colmo (de desgracias *or* de males) ..., para rematarla ... (fam)

C (set upper limit) ‹*expenditure*› poner* un tope a, limitar

D (Dentistry): **to have a tooth ~ped** ponerse* una funda *or* una corona

cap³ (= **capital city**) Cap.

CAP *n* (= **Common Agricultural Policy**) PAC *f*

capability /'keɪpə'bɪləti/ *n* (*pl* **-ties**) 1▸ [u] (ability) capacidad *f*; **~ to + INF** capacidad PARA + INF 2▸ **capabilities** *pl* (potential) aptitudes *fpl*

capable /'keɪpəbəl/ *adj*

A (competent) capaz, competente; **I'll leave you in the ~ hands of Mr Smith** lo dejo con el Sr Smith que lo ayudará en todo lo que necesite

B (*pred*) (able) **to be ~ OF -ING** ser* capaz DE + INF

capably /'keɪpəbli/ *adv* competentemente

capacity /kə'pæsəti/ *n* (*pl* **-ties**)

A [u c] 1▸ (maximum content) capacidad *f*; (*before n*) **a ~ crowd** un lleno completo *or* total 2▸ (output) capacidad *f*; **to operate at full ~** funcionar al límite de capacidad *or* a pleno rendimiento

B [u] (ability) capacidad *f*; **~ FOR sth** capacidad DE algo; **~ to + INF** capacidad PARA + INF; **the job was beyond her ~** el trabajo estaba por encima de su capacidad

C [c] (role) calidad *f*; **in his ~ as union delegate** en su calidad de delegado del sindicato

cape /keɪp/ *n*

A (Clothing) capa *f*

B (Geog) cabo *m*

cape: **~ Horn** *n* el Cabo de Hornos; **~ of Good Hope** *n* **the C~ of Good Hope** el Cabo de Buena Esperanza

caper¹ /'keɪpər || 'keɪpə(r)/ *n*

A (jump) salto *m*

B (prank) travesura *f*, broma *f*

C (Bot, Culin) alcaparra *f*

caper² *vi* correr y brincar*, dar* saltos *or* brincos

Cape Town *n* Ciudad *f* del Cabo

capful /'kæpfʊl/ *n* contenido *m* de una tapa (*or* un tapón *etc*)

capillary¹ /'kæpəleri || kə'pɪləri/ *adj* (*before n*) capilar

capillary² *n* (*pl* **-ries**) (vaso *m*) capilar *m*

capital¹ /'kæpətl̩ || 'kæpɪtl/ *n*

A [c] (city) capital *f*

B [c] (letter) mayúscula *f*

C [u] (Fin) capital *m*; **to make ~ (out) of sth** sacar* provecho *or* partido de algo; (*before n*) **~ expenditure/investment** gasto *m*/inversión *f* de capital; **~ gains tax** impuesto *m* sobre la plusvalía

capital² *adj*

A (Law) ‹*offense*› que está sancionado con la pena de muerte; **~ punishment** pena *f* capital *or* de muerte

B 1▸ (major) primordial 2▸ (Geog, Pol): **~ city** capital *f*

C (Print) ‹*letter*› mayúscula; **he's into art with a ~ A** (iro) le interesa el Arte con mayúscula

capitalism /'kæpətl̩ɪzəm || 'kæpɪtəlɪzəm/ *n* [u] capitalismo *m*

capitalist¹ /'kæpətl̩əst || 'kæpɪtəlɪst/ *n* capitalista *mf*

capitalist² *adj* capitalista

capitalize /'kæpətl̩aɪz || 'kæpɪtəlaɪz/ *vt*

A (Fin) capitalizar*

B (Print) *imprimir o escribir con mayúsculas*

(Phrasal verb)

• **capitalize on** [v ▸ prep ▸ o] sacar* provecho *or* partido de, capitalizar*

Capitol /'kæpətl̩ || 'kæpɪtl̩/ *n* **the ~** el Capitolio

> **Capitol – The Capitol**
>
> El Capitolio o sede del Congreso (Congress) de Estados Unidos, en Washington DC. Situado en *Capitol Hill*, a menudo la prensa emplea este nombre para hacer referencia al Congreso de EEUU

Capitol Hill /'kæpətl̩ || 'kæpɪtl̩/ *n* (in US) *el Congreso de los EEUU*

capitulate /kə'pɪtʃəleɪt || kə'pɪtjʊleɪt/ *vi* capitular

capitulation /kə'pɪtʃə'leɪʃən || kə,pɪtjʊleɪʃən/ *n* [u] capitulación *f*

Caplet® /'kæplət/ *n* (AmE) comprimido *m* (*de forma ovalada*)

capo /'keɪpəʊ || 'kæpəʊ/ *n* (*pl* **-pos**) (for guitar) capotasto *m*, ceja *f*

capon /'keɪpən/ *n* capón *m*

cappuccino /,kæpə'tʃi:nəʊ/ *n* (*pl* **-nos**) capuchino *m*

caprice /kə'pri:s/ *n* [c u] capricho *m*

capricious /kə'prɪʃəs/ *adj* ‹*person*› caprichoso; ‹*weather*› variable

Capricorn /'kæprɪkɔ:rn || 'kæprɪkɔ:n/ *n* 1▸ (sign) (*no art*) Capricornio 2▸ [c] (person) Capricornio *or* capricornio *mf*, capricorniano, -na *m,f*; *see also* **Aquarius**

caps = capital letters

capsicum /'kæpsɪkəm/ *n* pimiento *m*, pimentón *m* (AmS exc RPl), ají *m* (RPl)

capsize /'kæpsaɪz || kæp'saɪz/ *vi* volcarse*; (right over) dar* una vuelta de campana

■ **capsize** *vt* hacer* volcar; (right over) hacer* dar una vuelta de campana

capsule /'kæpsəl || 'kæpsju:l/ *n* 1▸ (Pharm) cápsula *f* 2▸ (*space* ~) cápsula *f* espacial

Capt (title) = **Captain**

captain¹ /'kæptən || 'kæptɪn/ *n* 1▸ (rank) capitán *m* 2▸ (person in command) capitán, -tana *m,f*; (of airline plane) comandante *mf* 3▸ (headwaiter) (AmE) maître *m*, jefe *m* de comedor, capitán *m* de meseros (Méx)

captain² *vt* (Naut, Sport) capitanear

captaincy /'kæptənsi || 'kæptɪnsi/ *n* [u c] (*pl* **-cies**) capitanía *f*

caption /'kæpʃən/ *n* (under picture) leyenda *f*, pie *m* de foto (*or* ilustración *etc*); (headline) título *m*

captivate /'kæptəveɪt || 'kæptɪveɪt/ *vt* cautivar

captivating /'kæptəveɪtɪŋ || 'kæptɪveɪtɪŋ/ *adj* encantador, cautivador

captive¹ /'kæptɪv/ *n* (liter) cautivo, -va *m,f*

captive² *adj*: **to hold sb ~** mantener* cautivo *or* prisionero a algn; **to have a ~ audience** tener* un público que no tiene más remedio que escuchar

captivity /kæp'tɪvəti/ *n* [u] cautiverio *m*, cautividad *f*

captor /'kæptər || 'kæptə(r)/ *n* (of person) captor, -tora *m,f*

capture¹ /'kæptʃər || 'kæptʃə(r)/ *vt*

A (seize by force) ‹*person/animal*› capturar; ‹*ship*› apresar; ‹*city*› tomar

B 1▸ (attract, hold) ‹*attention/interest*› captar, atraer* 2▸ (preserve, record) ‹*mood/atmosphere*› captar, reproducir*

capture² *n* [u] (of person, animal) captura *f*; (of city) conquista *f*, toma *f*; (of ship) apresamiento *m*

car /kɑ:r || kɑ:(r)/ *n* 1▸ (Auto) coche *m*, automóvil *m* (frml), carro *m* (AmL exc CS), auto *m* (esp CS); **to go by ~** ir* en coche (*or* carro *etc*); (*before n*) **~ bomb** coche *m* bomba; **~ seat** (part of car) asiento *m* del coche; (for infant) asiento *m* de bebé (*para el coche*) 2▸ (Rail, Transp) vagón *m*, coche *m* 3▸ (of elevator) cabina *f*

carafe /kə'ræf/ *n* (for wine) garrafa *f*; (for water) *botella de boca ancha*

caramel /'kɑ:rml̩ || 'kærəmel, -mel/ *n* 1▸ [u] (burnt sugar) caramelo *m*; (*before n*) **~ sauce** caramelo *m* 2▸ [c u] (confectionery) *caramelo hecho a base de leche y azúcar*

C

carat /ˈkærət/ *n* 1 (for gold) (AmE also **karat**) quilate *m*; **18-~ gold** oro *m* de 18 quilates 2 (for precious stones) quilate *m*

caravan /ˈkærəvæn/ *n* 1 (group) caravana *f* 2 (vehicle) (BrE) caravana *f*, rulot *f* (Esp), casa *f* rodante (CS), tráiler *m* (Andes, Méx); **gypsy ~** carromato *m* de gitanos; (*before n*) **~ park** *o* **site** camping *m* para caravanas

caraway /ˈkærəweɪ/ *n* alcaravea *f*; (*before n*) **~ seed** carvi *m*

carbohydrate /ˈkɑːrbəʊˈhaɪdreɪt || ˌkɑːbəˈhaɪdreɪt/ *n* [c u] hidrato *m* de carbono, carbohidrato *m*

carbon /ˈkɑːrbən || ˈkɑːbən/ *n*
A [u] (Chem) carbono *m*
B [c] 1 (paper) ▸**carbon paper** 2 (copy) ▸**carbon copy**

carbonate /ˈkɑːrbəneɪt || ˈkɑːbəneɪt/ *n* carbonato *m*

carbonated /ˈkɑːrbəneɪtəd || ˈkɑːbəneɪtɪd/ *adj* ‹*water*› carbonatado; ‹*drink*› gaseoso

carbon: **~ copy** *n* copia *f* (*hecha con papel carbón*); ***to be a ~ copy of sb/sth*** ser* un calco de algn/algo; **~-date** /ˌkɑːrbənˈdeɪt || ˌkɑːbənˈdeɪt/ *vt* datar mediante la técnica del carbono; **~ dating** /ˈdeɪtɪŋ/ *n* [u] *datación mediante el método del carbono 14*; **~ dioxide** *n* [u] anhídrido *m* carbónico, bióxido *m* or dióxido *m* de carbono; **~ emissions** *pl n* emisiones *fpl* de carbono; (*before n*) **~ ~ trading** comercio *m* de derechos de emisión de gases de efecto invernadero; **~ footprint** *n* impacto *m* de carbono, huella *f* de carbono

carbonize /ˈkɑːrbənaɪz || ˈkɑːbənaɪz/ *vt* carbonizar*

carbon: **~ monoxide** /məˈnɑːksaɪd || məˈnɒksaɪd/ *n* [u] monóxido *m* de carbono; **~ paper** *n* papel *m* carbón, papel *m* de calco, papel *m* carbónico (RPl)

car boot sale *n* (BrE): *mercadillo improvisado en el que particulares venden o intercambian objetos que ya no usan y que colocan en el maletero del coche para que puedan ser vistos*

carbuncle /ˈkɑːrbʌŋkəl || ˈkɑːbʌŋkəl/ *n* (Med) forúnculo *m*, furúnculo *m*, carbunco *m*

carburetor, (BrE) **carburettor** /ˌkɑːrbəˈreɪtər || ˌkɑːbəˈretə(r)/ *n* carburador *m*

carcass, (BrE also) **carcase** /ˈkɑːrkəs || ˈkɑːkəs/ *n* (dead animal) *cuerpo de animal muerto*; (for meat) res *f* (*muerta*); (of poultry) huesos *mpl*

carcinogenic /ˈkɑːrsṇəˈdʒenɪk || ˌkɑːsɪnəˈdʒenɪk/ *adj* cancerígeno, carcinógeno

carcinoma /ˈkɑːrsəˈnəʊmə/ *n* carcinoma *m*

card¹ /kɑːrd || kɑːd/ *n*
A [c] 1 (for identification, access) tarjeta *f*; (*business* **~**) tarjeta (de visita); (*credit* **~**) tarjeta (de crédito); ***to give sb their ~s*** (BrE colloq) echar a algn, darle* la patada a algn (fam) 2 (*greeting* **~**) tarjeta *f* (de felicitación); **birthday ~** tarjeta de cumpleaños; **Christmas ~** tarjeta de Navidad, tarjeta de Pascua (Chi, Per), crismas *m* (Esp) 3 (*index* **~**) ficha *f*; (*before n*) **~ catalog/index** fichero *m* 4 (*post***~**) (tarjeta *f*) postal *f* 5 (for collecting) cromo *m*, estampa *f* (Méx), lámina *f* (Andes), figurita *f* (RPl)
B [u] (thin cardboard) cartulina *f*
C [c] (playing card) carta *f*, naipe *m*, baraja *f* (AmC, Col, Méx, RPl); **a deck** *o* (BrE) **pack of ~s** una baraja, un mazo (esp AmL); ***to be in*** *o* (BrE) ***on the ~s***: **it was in** *o* **on the ~s that something like this would happen** se veía venir *or* era seguro que iba a pasar algo así; **to play ~s** jugar* a las cartas *or* (Col) jugar* cartas; ***to lay*** *o* ***put one's ~s on the table*** poner* las cartas boca arriba *or* sobre la mesa; ***to play one's ~s right*** jugar* bien sus (*or* mis *etc*) cartas; ▸**chest A**

card² *vt* (Tex) cardar

cardamom /ˈkɑːrdəməm/ *n* [u] cardamomo *m*

cardboard /ˈkɑːrdbɔːrd || ˈkɑːdbɔːd/ *n* [u] (stiff) cartón *m*; (thin) cartulina *f*; (*before n*) **~ box** caja *f* de cartón

card: **~carrying** *adj*: **he's a ~carrying member of the party** está afiliado al partido, es un miembro activo del partido; **~holder** *n* titular *mf* (*de una tarjeta de crédito*), tarjetahabiente *mf* (Méx, Ven)

cardiac /ˈkɑːrdiæk || ˈkɑːdiæk/ *adj* ‹*condition*› cardíaco; **~ arrest** paro *m* cardíaco

cardigan /ˈkɑːrdɪgən/ *n* cárdigan *m*, chaqueta *f* de punto, rebeca *f* (esp Esp), saco *m* (tejido) (RPl), chaleca *f* (Chi)

cardinal¹ /ˈkɑːrdṇəl || ˈkɑːdɪnḷ/ *n*
A (Relig) cardenal *m*
B **~ (number)** número *m* cardinal

cardinal² *adj* ‹*rule/idea*› fundamental, esencial; **~ sin** pecado *m* capital; **~ virtue** virtud *f* cardinal; **~ point** punto *m* cardinal

cardiologist /ˈkɑːrdiˈɑːlədʒəst/ *n* cardiólogo, -ga *m,f*

cardiology /ˈkɑːrdiˈɑːlədʒi || ˌkɑːdiˈɒlədʒi/ *n* [u] cardiología *f*

card: **~phone** *n* (BrE) *teléfono público que funciona mediante tarjetas prepagadas y/o de crédito*; **~sharp**, (AmE also) **~shark** *n* tahúr *mf*, tramposo, -sa *m,f*, fulero, -ra *m,f* (Esp fam)

care¹ /ker || keə(r)/ *n*
A [u] (attention, carefulness) cuidado *m*, atención *f*; ❺ **handle with care** frágil; **to take ~** tener* cuidado; **take ~!** ¡ten cuidado!; **to take ~ over** *o* **with sth** poner* cuidado en algo, cuidar algo; **he took ~ that all the figures were correct** se aseguró de que todas las cifras eran las correctas
B [u] (of people): **medical ~** asistencia *f* médica; (of animals, things) cuidado *m*; **her children were taken into ~** (BrE Soc Admin) le quitaron la patria potestad; **in ~ of** (AmE), **~ of** (BrE) (on letters) en casa de
C **to take ~ of sb/sth** 1 (look after) ‹*of patient*› atender* a algn, cuidar de algn; ‹*of children*› cuidar a *or* de algn, ocuparse *or* encargarse* de algn; ‹*of pet/plant/machine*› cuidar algo; **take ~!** (saying goodbye) ¡cuídate!, ¡que estés bien!; (as a warning) ¡ten cuidado!; **I can take ~ of myself** yo sé cuidarme 2 (deal with) ocuparse *or* encargarse* de algn/algo; **that takes ~ of that!** ¡listo!, ¡eso ya está!
D [c u] (worry) preocupación *f*

care² *vi* **to ~ (ABOUT sth/sb)** preocuparse (POR algo/algn); **all he ~s about is sport** lo único que le interesa es el deporte; **I don't ~** no me importa, me es *or* me da igual; **who ~s!** ¡y a mí qué!; **see if I ~!** ¡me da igual!
■ **care** *vt* 1 (feel concern) (*usu neg, interrog*): **I couldn't ~ less what he does** me tiene *or* me trae sin cuidado lo que haga, no me importa en absoluto lo que haga; **who ~s what she thinks?** ¿y a quién le importa lo que ella piense? 2 (wish) (frml) **to ~ to + INF**: **would you ~ to join us for dinner?** ¿le gustaría cenar con nosotros?; **he needs her more than he ~s to admit** la necesita más de lo que está dispuesto a reconocer

Phrasal verb
• **care for** [v ▸ prep ▸ o] 1 (look after) ‹*patient*› cuidar (de), atender*; ‹*house/garden*› cuidar, ocuparse *or* encargarse* de; **well ~d for** bien cuidado 2 (be fond of) querer*, sentir* afecto *or* cariño por 3 (like) (*usu neg*): **the house was lovely, but I didn't ~ for the furniture** la casa era preciosa, pero los muebles no me gustaron *or* no eran de mi gusto 4 (in offers) (frml): **would you ~ for a cigar?** ¿puedo ofrecerle un puro?

careen /kəˈriːn/ *vi* (AmE) ir* a toda velocidad

career¹ /kəˈrɪr || kəˈrɪə(r)/ *n* carrera *f*; **he made a ~ for himself as a journalist** se forjó una carrera como periodista; (*before n*) **~ girl/woman** mujer *f* de carrera

career² *vi* ir* a toda velocidad

carefree /ˈkerfriː || ˈkeəfriː/ *adj* despreocupado

careful /ˈkerfəl || ˈkeəfəl/ *adj*
A (cautious) cuidadoso, prudente; **you should be more ~ in future** tendrías que tener más cuidado en el futuro; **you can't be too ~** toda prudencia es poca; **(be) ~** (ten) cuidado; **(be) ~ you don't fall!** ¡cuidado, no vayas a caerte!; **be ~ what you say** (ten) cuidado con lo que dices; **to be ~ OF sb/sth** tener* cuidado CON algn/algo; **to be ~ to + INF** procurar + INF; **to be ~ WITH sth** tener* cuidado CON algo
B (painstaking) ‹*planning*› cuidadoso; ‹*work*› cuidado, esmerado, bien hecho; ‹*worker*› meticuloso; **after ~ consideration of all the options** después de considerar detenidamente todas las opciones

carefully /ˈkerfli || ˈkeəfəli/ *adv* ‹*handle/drive*› con cuidado; ‹*plan/examine*› cuidadosamente, detenidamente; ‹*designed/chosen*› con esmero; **think it over ~** piénsatelo bien; **listen ~** presta atención

careless /ˈkerləs || ˈkeəlɪs/ *adj* 1 (inattentive, negligent) ‹*person*› descuidado, poco cuidadoso; ‹*work*› poco cuidado; ‹*driving*› negligente; **you made some ~ mistakes** cometiste errores por descuido 2 (indifferent) **to be ~ OF**

sth: **she seems ~ of the danger** no parece importarle *or* preocuparle el peligro

carelessly /'kerləsli || 'keəlɪsli/ *adv* 1 (inattentively) sin la debida atención 2 (casually) de manera despreocupada

carelessness /'kerləsnəs || 'keəlɪsnɪs/ *n* [u] falta *f* de atención *or* de cuidado

carer /'kerər || 'keərə(r)/ *n*: *persona que tiene a su cuidado a un anciano o a un incapacitado sin recibir por ello remuneración*

caress[1] /kə'res/ *n* caricia *f*

caress[2] *vt* acariciar

care: **~taker** *n* conserje *mf*; (*before n*) ‹*government*› provisional; **~worn** *adj* agobiado por las preocupaciones

carfare /'kɑ:rfer || 'kɑ:feə(r)/ *n* (AmE) precio *m* del boleto *or* (Esp) del billete

carful /'kɑ:rfʊl || 'kɑ:fʊl/ *n* ▸**carload 1**

cargo /'kɑ:rgəʊ || 'kɑ:gəʊ/ *n* (*pl* **-goes** *or* **-gos**) 1 [c] (load) cargamento *m* 2 [u] (goods) carga *f*; (*before n*) **~ ship** carguero *m*, barco *m* de carga

carhop /'kɑ:rhɑ:p || 'kɑ:hɒp/ *n* (in US) (in drive-in restaurants) *persona que atiende a los clientes en sus coches*

Caribbean[1] /ˌkærə'bi:ən, kə'rɪbiən || ˌkærɪ'bi:ən/ *adj* caribeño, del Caribe

Caribbean[2] *n* **the ~ (Sea)** el (mar) Caribe; **the ~** (region) el Caribe, las Antillas

caribou /'kærəbu: || 'kærɪbu:/ *n* (*pl* ~) caribú *m*

caricature[1] /'kærɪkətʃʊr || 'kærɪkətʃʊə(r)/ *n* caricatura *f*

caricature[2] *vt* caricaturizar*

caring /'kerɪŋ || 'keərɪŋ/ *adj* ‹*society/approach*› humanitario; ‹*person*› (kindly) bondadoso, generoso; (sympathetic) comprensivo; **in the ~ professions** en las profesiones de vocación social

carload /'kɑ:rləʊd || 'kɑ:ləʊd/ *n* 1 (Auto): **we were driving with a ~ of children** íbamos con el coche lleno de niños 2 (AmE Rail): **a ~ of oranges** un vagón lleno *or* cargado de naranjas

carnage /'kɑ:rnɪdʒ || 'kɑ:nɪdʒ/ *n* [u] carnicería *f*

carnal /'kɑ:rnl̩ || 'kɑ:nl̩/ *adj* carnal

carnation /kɑ:r'neɪʃən || kɑ:'neɪʃən/ *n* clavel *m*

carnival /'kɑ:rnəvəl || 'kɑ:nɪvəl/ *n* 1 (festival) carnaval *m* 2 (traveling fair) (AmE) feria *f* ambulante

carnivore /'kɑ:rnəvɔ:r || 'kɑ:nɪvɔ:(r)/ *n* carnívoro, -ra *m,f*

carnivorous /kɑ:r'nɪvərəs || kɑ:'nɪvərəs/ *adj* carnívoro

carol /'kærəl/ *n* villancico *m*

carom /'kærəm/ *vi* (AmE) (in billiards) hacer* carambola; **the car ~ed off the fence into a tree** el coche rebotó contra la valla y dio contra un árbol

carouse /kə'raʊz/ *vi* (liter *or* hum) estar* de juerga *or* jarana (fam)

carousel /'kærə'sel/ *n* 1 (AmE) ▸**merry-go-round 1** 2 (for baggage) cinta *f or* correa *f* transportadora, carrusel *m* (Esp) 3 (in shops) (AmE) expositor *m* giratorio

carp[1] /kɑ:rp || kɑ:p/ *n* (*pl* ~ *or* ~**s**) carpa *f*

carp[2] *vi* (find fault) criticar* por criticar; (complain) quejarse

car park *n* (BrE) (open space) ▸**parking lot**; (building) ▸**parking garage**

Carpathians /kɑ:r'peɪθiənz || kɑ:'peɪθiənz/ *pl n* **the ~** los (montes) Cárpatos

carpenter /'kɑ:rpəntər || 'kɑ:pəntə(r)/ *n* carpintero, -ra *m,f*

carpentry /'kɑ:rpəntri || 'kɑ:pəntri/ *n* [u] carpintería *f*

carpet[1] /'kɑ:rpət || 'kɑ:pɪt/ *n* 1 [c] (rug) alfombra *f*, tapete *m* (Col, Méx, Ven); (*before n*) **~ beater** sacudidor *m* (de alfombras); ▸**pull**[1] *vt* **A2**, **sweep**[2] *vt* **A2** 2 [u c] (wall-to-wall) alfombra *f*, moqueta *f* (Esp), moquette *f* (RPl) 3 [c] (of flowers, leaves, moss) (liter) alfombra *f* (liter)

carpet[2] *vt* ‹*floor/room*› alfombrar, enmoquetar (Esp)

carpet: **~bagger** /'kɑ:rpət,bægər || 'kɑ:pɪt,bægə(r)/ *n*: *político oportunista que logra o pretende representar a una localidad que no es la suya*; **~ bombing** *n* bombardeo *m* por *or* de saturación

carpeting /'kɑ:rpətɪŋ || 'kɑ:pɪtɪŋ/ *n* [u] alfombras *fpl*, alfombrado *m*

carpet: **~ slipper** *n* zapatilla *f or* pantufla *f* de felpa; **~ sweeper** *n* cepillo *m* mecánico (*para barrer alfombras*); **~ tile** *n* loseta *f* de alfombra *or* (Esp) de moqueta

carphone /'kɑ:rfəʊn || 'kɑ:fəʊn/ *n* teléfono *m* de automóvil

carping /'kɑ:rpɪŋ || 'kɑ:pɪŋ/ *adj* criticón

car: **~ pool** *n*: *acuerdo entre varias personas que se trasladan juntas al lugar de trabajo etc utilizando por turnos el coche de cada una*; **~-pool** *vi* (AmE) *organizar o formar un* **~ pool**

carriage /'kærɪdʒ/ *n*

A [c] 1 (horse-drawn) carruaje *m*, coche *m* 2 (BrE Rail) vagón *m* 3 (*baby* ~) (AmE) cochecito *m*, carriola *f* (Méx)

B [u] (transport) transporte *m*, porte *m*

C [u] (bearing) (frml) porte *m*

carrier /'kæriər || 'kæriə(r)/ *n*

A (company) compañía *f or* empresa *f* de transportes; (Aviat) línea *f* aérea

B (of disease, gene) portador, -dora *m,f*

C **~ (bag)** (BrE) bolsa *f* (de plástico *or* papel)

carrier pigeon *n* paloma *f* mensajera

carrion /'kæriən/ *n* [u] carroña *f*

carrot /'kærət/ *n* 1 [c u] (Bot, Culin) zanahoria *f* 2 [c] (incentive) incentivo *m*; **a ~-and-stick policy** una política de incentivos y amenazas

carry /'kæri/ **-ries, -rying, -ried** *vt*

A 1 (bear, take) llevar; **I can't ~ this, it's too heavy** no puedo cargar con esto, pesa demasiado; **she was ~ing her baby in her arms** llevaba a su hijo en brazos 2 (have with one) llevar encima 3 (be provided with) ‹*guarantee*› tener*; **every pack carries the logo of the company** todos los paquetes vienen con *or* traen el logotipo de la compañía 4 (be pregnant with) estar* embarazada *or* encinta de

B 1 (convey) ‹*goods/passengers*› llevar, transportar, acarrear; **the car can ~ four people** el coche tiene cabida para cuatro personas, en el coche caben cuatro personas; **she was carried along by the crowd** fue arrastrada por la multitud; **as fast as his legs would ~ him** tan rápido como pudo 2 (channel, transmit) ‹*oil/water/sewage*› llevar; **the wind carried her voice to him** el viento le hizo llegar su voz 3 ‹*disease*› ser* portador de

C 1 (support) ‹*weight*› soportar, resistir 2 (take responsibility for) ‹*cost/blame*› cargar* con 3 (sustain): **the lead actress carried the play** la protagonista sacó la obra adelante

D (involve, entail) ‹*responsibility*› conllevar; ‹*consequences/penalty*› acarrear, traer* aparejado

E (extend, continue): **the fighting was carried over the border** la lucha se extendió más allá de la frontera; **never ~ a diet too far** no hay que exagerar con los regímenes

F 1 (gain support for) ‹*bill/motion*› aprobar* 2 (Pol) (win) ‹*constituency/city*› hacerse* con; ***to ~ all before one*** arrasar con todo

G 1 (stock) ‹*model*› tener*, vender 2 (include) (Journ) traer*, publicar*

■ *v refl* **to ~ oneself** 1 (in bearing): **she carries herself well** tiene buen porte 2 (behave) comportarse, actuar*

■ **carry** *vi*: **sound carries further in the mountains** en la montaña los sonidos llegan más lejos; **her voice carries well** su voz tiene mucha proyección

Phrasal verbs

- **carry away** [v ▸ o ▸ adv, v ▸ adv ▸ o] (*usu pass*): **they were carried away by the excitement of the occasion** se dejaron llevar por lo emocionante de la ocasión; **I got carried away and painted the window as well** me entusiasmé y pinté la ventana también; **there's no need to get carried away** no te pases
- **carry forward** [v ▸ o ▸ adv, v ▸ adv ▸ o] ‹*total*› llevar (*a la columna o página siguiente*); Ⓢ **carried forward** suma y sigue
- **carry off** [v ▸ o ▸ adv, v ▸ adv ▸ o]

A (abduct) ‹*victim/hostage*› llevarse; (kill) «*disease*» (dated) llevarse

B 1 (win) ‹*trophy/cup*› llevarse, hacerse* con; **she carried off all the prizes** barrió *or* arrasó con todos los premios 2 (succeed with): **she carried the interview off very well** salió muy airosa *or* muy bien parada de la entrevista; **she tried to appear disinterested but failed to ~ it off** intentó aparentar desinterés pero no lo logró *or* consiguió

- **carry on**

A 1 [v ▸ o ▸ adv, v ▸ adv ▸ o] ‹*practice*› seguir* *or* continuar* con 2 [v ▸ adv ▸ o] ‹*conversation/correspondence*› mantener*

B [v ▸ adv] 1 (continue) seguir*, continuar*; **to ~ on -ING** seguir* + GER; **to ~ on WITH sth** seguir* CON algo 2 (make a fuss) (colloq): **what a way to ~ on!** ¡qué manera de hacer escándalo, por favor!; **there's no need to ~ on about it!** ¡no hay necesidad de seguir dale que dale con el asunto! (fam) 3 (have affair) (colloq): **they'd been ~ing on for years** hacía años que tenían un enredo (fam)

- **carry out** [v ▸ o ▸ adv, v ▸ adv ▸ o] ‹*work/repairs*› llevar a cabo, realizar*, hacer*; ‹*order*› cumplir; ‹*duty*› cumplir con
- **carry over** [v ▸ o ▸ adv, v ▸ adv ▸ o] ‹*business*› postergar*, posponer*; ‹*surplus/debt*› transferir*
- **carry through**

A [v ▸ o ▸ adv] [v ▸ o ▸ prep ▸ o] (enable to survive): **enough supplies to ~ them through the winter** suficientes provisiones que les permitan sobrevivir el invierno; **his determination carried him through** su resolución lo alentó a seguir

B [v ▸ o ▸ adv, v ▸ adv ▸ o] (bring to completion) ‹*plan*› llevar a cabo *or* a término, ejecutar; ‹*reform*› realizar*, llevar a cabo *or* a término; ‹*idea*› poner* en práctica

carry: **~all** *n* (AmE) bolso *m* de viaje, bolsón *m* (RPl); **~cot** *n* (BrE) cuna *f* portátil, capazo *m*

carryings-on /ˈkæriɪŋzˈɑːn || ˈkæriɪŋzˈɒn/ *pl n* (colloq) enredos *mpl* (fam), líos *mpl* (fam)

carry-on[1] /ˈkæriɑːn || ˈkæriɒn/ *n* [u] (BrE colloq) lío *m* (fam), jaleo *m* (fam), follón *m* (Esp fam)

carry-on[2] *adj* (AmE) (*before n*) ‹*bag/baggage*› de mano

carryout /ˈkæriaʊt/ *n*: *comida preparada o bebida que se vende para consumir fuera del lugar de venta*

carsick /ˈkɑːrsɪk || ˈkɑːsɪk/ *adj* mareado; **I get ~** me mareo (cuando viajo) en coche

cart[1] /kɑːrt || kɑːt/ *n* 1 (waggon) carro *m*, carreta *f*; ***to put the ~ before the horse*** empezar* la casa por el tejado 2 (*hand~*) carretilla *f* 3 (in supermarket, airport) (AmE) carrito *m*

cart[2] *vt* (colloq): **I had to ~ the books around all day** tuve que cargar con los libros todo el día; **they were ~ed off to prison** se los llevaron a la cárcel

carte blanche /ˈkɑːrtˈblɑːnʃ || ˌkɑːtˈblɑːnʃ/ *n* [u]: **to give sb/have ~ ~** darle* a algn/tener* carta blanca

cartel /kɑːrˈtel || kɑːˈtel/ *n* cártel *m*

carthorse /ˈkɑːrthɔːrs || ˈkɑːthɔːs/ *n* caballo *m* de tiro

cartilage /ˈkɑːrtlɪdʒ || ˈkɑːtɪlɪdʒ/ *n* [u c] cartílago *m*

cartographer /kɑːrˈtɑːgrəfər || kɑːˈtɒgrəfə(r)/ *n* cartógrafo, -fa *m,f*

cartography /kɑːrˈtɑːgrəfi || kɑːˈtɒgrəfi/ *n* [u] cartografía *f*

carton /ˈkɑːrtn̩ || ˈkɑːtn̩/ *n* (of milk, fruit juice, eggs) (envase *m* de) cartón *m*; (of cigarettes) cartón *m*

cartoon /kɑːrˈtuːn || kɑːˈtuːn/ *n* 1 (humorous drawing) chiste *m* (*gráfico*), viñeta *f* (Esp), mono *m* (Chi) 2 (Cin) dibujos *mpl* animados 3 (*strip ~*) (BrE) historieta *f*, tira *f* cómica, monitos *mpl* (Chi, Méx)

cartridge /ˈkɑːrtrɪdʒ || ˈkɑːtrɪdʒ/ *n* (for gun, pen) cartucho *m*; (*before n*) **~ belt** cartuchera *f*

cartwheel /ˈkɑːrthwiːl || ˈkɑːtwiːl/ *n* (in gymnastics) voltereta *f* lateral, rueda *f*, vuelta *f* de carro (Méx), rueda *f* de carro (Ur), medialuna *f* (Arg)

carve /kɑːrv || kɑːv/ *vt*

A (Art) ‹*wood/stone*› tallar; ‹*figure/bust*› esculpir, tallar; ‹*initials*› grabar

B (Culin) ‹*meat*› cortar, trinchar

■ **carve** *vi* (Culin) cortar *or* trinchar la carne (*or* el pollo *etc*)

(Phrasal verbs)

- **carve out** [v ▸ o ▸ adv, v ▸ adv ▸ o] ‹*reputation*› forjarse; ‹*name*› hacerse*
- **carve up** [v ▸ o ▸ adv, v ▸ adv ▸ o] (divide) (colloq & pej) ‹*country/company*› dividir, repartir

carving /ˈkɑːrvɪŋ || ˈkɑːvɪŋ/ *n* talla *f*, escultura *f*

carving knife *n* trinchante *m*, cuchillo *m* de trinchar

car wash *n* túnel *m* *or* tren *m* de lavado

Casanova /ˈkæzəˈnəʊvə || ˌkæsəˈnəʊvə/ *n* Casanova; **he's a real ~** (colloq) es un casanova *or* un Don Juan

cascade[1] /kæsˈkeɪd/ *n* cascada *f*

cascade[2] *vi* caer* en cascada

case[1] /keɪs/ *n*

A (matter) caso *m*; **the Greene ~** el caso Greene; **to lose/win a ~** perder*/ganar un pleito *or* juicio; ***an open-and-shut ~*** un caso claro; ***to be on sb's ~*** (AmE) estar* encima de algn; **get off my ~!** ¡déjame tranquilo *or* en paz!; ***to make a federal ~ out of sth*** (AmE colloq) hacer* un drama de algo

B 1 (Med, Soc Adm) caso *m*; **a hopeless ~** (colloq) un caso perdido 2 (eccentric) (colloq) caso *m* (fam)

C (instance, situation) caso *m*; **it was a ~ of doing what we were told** era cuestión de hacer lo que se nos mandara; **a ~ in point** un ejemplo que viene al caso, un buen ejemplo; **as the ~ may be** según (sea) el caso; **he won't go — in that ~, neither will I** no quiere ir — (pues) en ese caso, yo tampoco; **that is the ~** así es, esa es la cuestión; **if that's the ~** si es así; **in that ~, I'm not interested** en ese caso, no me interesa

D (*in phrases*) **in any case** de todas maneras *or* formas, en cualquier caso, de cualquier modo; **in case** (*as conj*): **make a note in ~ you forget** apúntalo por si te olvidas, apúntalo en caso de que se te olvide; **just in case** por si acaso; **in case of** en caso de

E (argument): **the ~ for the prosecution/defense** la acusación/la defensa; **she has a good/strong ~** sus argumentos son buenos/poderosos; **there is a ~ for doing nothing** hay razones para no hacer nada; **to make (out) a ~ for sth/-ING** exponer* los argumentos a favor de algo/para + INF; **to put/state one's ~** dar*/exponer* sus (*or* mis *etc*) razones; ***I rest my ~*** a las pruebas me remito

F 1 (*suit~*) maleta *f*, petaca *f* (Méx), valija *f* (RPl) 2 (*attaché ~*) maletín *m* 3 (crate) caja *f*, cajón *m*, jaba *f* (Chi, Per); (of wine, liquor) *caja de 12 botellas* 4 (hard container — for small objects) estuche *f*; (— for large objects) caja *f*; (soft container) funda *f*

case[2] *vt* (sl): **to ~ the joint** reconocer* el terreno (*antes de cometer un delito*)

case: **~book** *n* registro *m*; **~ history** *n* (Med) historial *m* clínico *or* médico, historia *f* clínica (AmL); **~ load** *n* número *m* de casos (*atendidos por un médico, abogado etc*)

casement /ˈkeɪsmənt/ *n* marco *m* (*de ventana con bisagras*); (*before n*) **~ window** *ventana cuya hoja u hojas se abren por medio de bisagras*

case: **~ notes** *pl n* notas *fpl* sobre el caso

case-sensitive /ˌkeɪsˈsensətɪv/ *adj* (Comput) 1 (of a program, function) sensible a las mayúsculas y minúsculas, que distingue las mayúsculas de las minúsculas 2 (of input) que trata de forma diferente a las mayúsculas y a las minúsculas

case: **~ study** *n* estudio *m*, monografía *f*, trabajo *m*; **~work** *n* [u] *trabajo de asistencia social individual*; **~worker** *n* asistente *mf* social

cash[1] /kæʃ/ *n* [u] 1 (notes and coins) dinero *m* (en) efectivo; **we pay ~ for gold** compramos oro al contado; **(in) ~** en efectivo, en metálico; **~ on delivery** entrega *f* contra reembolso; **~ in hand** (saldo *m* de) caja *f*; ***~ on the barrelhead*** (AmE colloq) dinero contante y sonante (fam), dinero en mano (fam); (*before n*) ‹*payment*› en efectivo; ‹*refund*› al contado; **a ~ sale** una venta pagada en efectivo 2 (funds) (colloq) dinero *m*, lana *f* (AmL fam), plata *f* (AmL fam), tela *f* (Esp fam)

cash[2] *vt* ‹*check*› cobrar

(Phrasal verb)

- **cash in**

A [v ▸ o ▸ adv, v ▸ adv ▸ o] (exchange for money) canjear, cobrar

B [v ▸ adv] (profit) **to ~ in (ON sth)** aprovecharse *or* sacar* provecho (DE algo), sacar* tajada (DE algo) (fam)

cash: **~ and carry** *n*: *tienda de venta al por mayor*; **~book** *n* libro *m* de caja; **~box** *n* caja *f* (*del dinero*); **~card** *n* (BrE) tarjeta *f* del cajero automático; **~ crop** *n* cultivo *m* industrial *or* comercial; **~ desk** *n* (BrE) caja *f*; **~ dispenser** *n* cajero *m* automático *o* permanente

cashew (nut) /ˈkæʃuː/ *n* anacardo *m*, castaña *f* de cajú (CS, Ven), nuez *f* de la India (Méx)

cash flow *n* flujo *m* de caja, cash-flow *m*; (*before n*) **~ ~ problem** problema *m* de liquidez

cashier /kæˈʃɪr || kæˈʃɪə(r)/ *n* cajero, -ra *m,f*

cashier's check *n* (AmE) cheque *m* bancario *or* de caja *or* de gerencia

cash machine *n* cajero *m* automático *or* permanente

cashmere /'kæʒmɪr || ˌkæʃ'mɪə(r)/ *n* [u] cachemir *m*, cachemira *f*

cash: **~point** *n* (BrE) cajero *m* automático *or* permanente; **~ register** *n* caja *f* registradora

casing /'keɪsɪŋ/ *n* (cover) cubierta *f*; (case) caja *f*

casino /kə'si:nəʊ/ *n* (*pl* **-nos**) casino *m*

cask /kæsk || kɑ:sk/ *n* barril *m*, tonel *m*

casket /'kæskət || 'kɑ:skɪt/ *n* 1 (for jewels) cofre *m* 2 (coffin) (AmE) ataúd *m*

Caspian Sea /'kæspiən/ *n* **the ~ ~** el mar Caspio

cassava /kə'sɑ:və/ *n* [u] mandioca *f*

casserole /'kæsərəʊl/ *n* 1 [c] (dish) cazuela *f*, fuente *f* de horno (*con tapa*) 2 [c u] (food) guiso *m*, guisado *m* (Méx)

cassette /kə'set/ *n* 1 (Audio) cassette *f* *or* *m*; (*before n*) **~ deck** platina *f*, pletina *f*; **~ player** pasacintas *m*, cassette *m* (Esp), pasacassettes *m* (RPl), tocacassettes *m* (Chi); **~ recorder** grabadora *f* *or* grabador *m* (de cassettes), cassette *m* (Esp) 2 (Video) videocassette *m*, (cinta *f* de) video *m* *or* (Esp) vídeo *m*, videocinta *f*

cassock /'kæsək/ *n* (of priest) sotana *f*

cast[1] /kæst || kɑ:st/ *n*
A 1 (molded object) (Art) vaciado *m*; (Metall) pieza *f* fundida; **a plaster ~ of the footprint** un molde de yeso de la huella 2 (mold) molde *m* 3 (for broken limb) yeso *m* *or* (Esp) escayola *f*
B (Cin, Theat) (+ *sing or pl vb*) reparto *m*, elenco *m* (esp AmL); **she met the ~** le presentaron a los actores (*or* bailarines etc)

cast[2] (*past & past p* **cast**) *vt*
A 1 ‹*stone*› arrojar, lanzar*, tirar; ‹*line*› lanzar*; ‹*net*› echar 2 ‹*shadow/light*› proyectar; **to ~ doubt on sth** poner* algo en duda; **~ your eye over this** échale una mirada *or* una ojeada *or* un vistazo a esto 3 ‹*vote*› emitir
B (shed) ‹‹*snake*›› ‹*skin*› mudar de, mudar; **the horse ~ a shoe** al caballo se le salió una herradura
C (mold) (Art) vaciar*; (Metall) fundir
D (Cin, Theat) ‹*role*› asignar; **she was ~ as the princess** le dieron el papel de la princesa; **he's well ~ as Iago** está bien elegido para el papel de Yago
■ **cast** *vi* (in angling) lanzar*

Phrasal verbs

- **cast about for** [v ▸ adv ▸ prep ▸ o] ‹*for idea/excuse*› tratar de encontrar, buscar*
- **cast aside** [v ▸ o ▸ adv, v ▸ adv ▸ o] (abandon) ‹*person*› hacer* a un lado, dejar de lado; ‹*doubts/worries*› desechar, apartar de sí
- **cast away** [v ▸ o ▸ adv]: **they were ~ away on a desert island** llegaron a una isla desierta tras naufragar
- **cast back** [v ▸ o ▸ adv]: **~ your mind back** trata de recordar, rememora (liter)
- **cast off**
A [v ▸ adv] 1 (in knitting) cerrar* 2 (Naut) soltar* amarras
B [v ▸ o ▸ adv, v ▸ adv ▸ o] 1 (in knitting) ‹*stitch*› cerrar* 2 (abandon) ‹*friend/lover*› dejar, abandonar
- **cast on**
A [v ▸ adv] (in knitting) poner* *or* montar los puntos
B [v ▸ o ▸ adv, v ▸ adv ▸ o] ‹*stitch*› montar, poner*
- **cast out** [v ▸ o ▸ adv, v ▸ adv ▸ o] (expel) (liter) expulsar

castanets /ˌkæstə'nets/ *pl n* castañuelas *fpl*

castaway /'kæstəweɪ || 'kɑ:stəweɪ/ *n* náufrago, -ga *m,f*

caste /kæst || kɑ:st/ *n* [c u] casta *f*

caster /'kæstər || 'kɑ:stə(r)/ *n* (wheel) ruedecita *f*, ruedita *f* (esp AmL)

caster sugar *n* (BrE) *azúcar blanca de granulado muy fino*

castigate /'kæstəgeɪt || 'kæstɪgeɪt/ *vt* (frml) ‹*pupil*› reprender; ‹*government*› fustigar* (liter), criticar* severamente

Castile /kæs'ti:l || kæ'sti:l/ *n* Castilla *f*

Castilian[1] /kæs'tɪljən || kə'stɪliən/ *adj* castellano

Castilian[2] *n* 1 [c] (person) castellano, -na *m,f* 2 [u] (language) castellano *m*

casting vote /'kæstɪŋ || 'kɑ:stɪŋ/ *n* voto *m* de calidad

cast: **~ iron** *n* [u] hierro *m* fundido *or* colado; **~-iron** *adj* (*before n*) (Metall) de hierro fundido *or* colado; ‹*guarantee*› sólido; ‹*will*› férreo; ‹*evidence*› irrefutable; ‹*alibi*› a toda prueba; **a ~-iron constitution** una salud de hierro

castle /'kæsəl || 'kɑ:səl/ *n*
A (Archit) castillo *m*; ***(to build) ~s in the air*** *o* ***in Spain*** (construir*) castillos en el aire
B (in chess) torre *f*

castoff /'kæstɔ:f || 'kɑ:stɒf/ *n*: **she gave me her ~s** me dio la ropa que ya no quería

castor /'kæstər || 'kɑ:stə(r)/ *n* ▸ **caster**

castor oil *n* [u] aceite *m* de ricino *or* (CS tb) (de) castor

castrate /'kæstreɪt || kæ'streɪt/ *vt* castrar

casual /'kæʒuəl/ *adj*
A 1 (superficial) (*before n*) ‹*inspection*› superficial; **a ~ acquaintance** un conocido, una conocida; **~ sex** relaciones *fpl* sexuales promiscuas 2 (chance) (*before n*) ‹*visit/caller/reader*› ocasional 3 (informal) ‹*chat*› informal; ‹*clothes*› de sport, informal
B (unconcerned) ‹*attitude/tone*› despreocupado; ‹*remark*› hecho al pasar; **she seemed very ~ about the whole thing** parecía como si no tuviera nada que ver con ella
C (not regular) ‹*employment/labor*› eventual, ocasional; **~ worker** (on farm) jornalero, -ra *m,f*; (in factory) obrero, -ra *m,f* eventual

casually /'kæʒuəli/ *adv*
A (informally) ‹*dressed*› de manera informal, informalmente; ‹*chat*› informalmente
B (with indifference) con indiferencia

casuals /'kæʒuəlz/ *pl n* (Clothing) ropa *f* de sport

casualty /kæʒuəlti/ *n* (*pl* **-ties**)
A (injured person) herido, -da *m,f*; (dead person) víctima *f*; (Mil) baja *f*
B (hospital department) (BrE) (*no art*) urgencias *fpl*

casuistry /'kæʒuəstri || 'kæzjʊɪstri, -ʒʊɪ-/ *n* [u] casuística *f*

cat /kæt/ *n* (domestic animal) gato, -ta *m,f*; (lion, tiger) felino *m*; **the big ~s** los felinos mayores; ***has the ~ got your tongue?*** (colloq) ¿te comieron la lengua los ratones? (fam); ***he thinks he's the ~'s whiskers*** *o* ***pajamas*** se cree el súmmum; ***you look like something the ~ dragged in*** ¡parece que vinieras de la guerra!; ***not to have a ~ in hell's chance*** (BrE colloq) no tener* la más mínima posibilidad; ***there's not enough*** *o* ***no room to swing a ~*** (colloq) no cabe ni un alfiler (fam); ***to fight like ~ and dog*** andar* como (el) perro y (el) gato; ***to grin like a Cheshire ~*** sonreír* de oreja a oreja; ***to let the ~ out of the bag*** descubrir* el pastel, levantar la liebre *or* (RPl) la perdiz; ***to play ~ and mouse (with sb)*** jugar* al gato y al ratón (con algn); ***to rain ~s and dogs*** llover* a cántaros *or* a mares; ***to set*** *o* ***put the ~ among the pigeons*** levantar un revuelo

cataclysm /'kætəklɪzəm/ *n* cataclismo *m*

catacombs /'kætəkəʊmz || 'kætəku:mz/ *pl n* catacumbas *fpl*

Catalan[1] /'kætḷæn || 'kætəlæn/ *adj* catalán

Catalan[2] *n* 1 [c] (person) catalán, -lana *m,f* 2 [u] (language) catalán *m*

catalog[1], **catalogue** /'kætḷɔ:g || 'kætəlɒg/ *n* (list, book) catálogo *m*; **a ~ of disasters** un desastre detrás de otro

catalog[2], **catalogue** *vt* catalogar*

Catalonia /ˌkætḷ'əʊniə || ˌkætə'ləʊniə/ *n* Cataluña *f*

Catalonian /ˌkætḷ'əʊniən || ˌkætə'ləʊniən/ *adj* catalán

catalyst /'kætḷəst || 'kætəlɪst/ *n* catalizador *m*

catalytic converter /ˌkætḷ'ɪtɪk || ˌkætə'lɪtɪk/ *n* catalizador *m*

catamaran /ˌkætəmə'ræn/ *n* catamarán *m*

catapult[1] /'kætəpʊlt || 'kætəpʌlt/ *n* (Aviat, Mil) catapulta *f*; (used by children) (BrE) tirachinas *m*, honda *f* (CS, Per), resortera *f* (Méx), cauchera *f* (Col), china *f* (Ven)

catapult[2] *vt* catapultar; **the crash ~ed her through the windshield** el choque la hizo salir disparada por el parabrisas

cataract /'kætərækt/ *n*
A (over a precipice) catarata *f*; (in a river) rápido *m*
B (Med) catarata *f*

catarrh /kə'tɑ:r || kə'tɑ:(r)/ *n* [u] catarro *m*

catastrophe /kə'tæstrəfi/ *n* catástrofe *f*

catastrophic /ˌkætə'strɑ:fɪk || ˌkætə'strɒfɪk/ *adj* catastrófico

catatonic /ˈkætəˈtɑːnɪk || ˌkætəˈtɒnɪk/ *adj* catatónico

cat: **~ burglar** *n* ladrón, -drona *m,f* (*que escala paredes para entrar a un edificio*); **~call** *n* silbido *m*; **~calls** abucheo *m*, silbatina *f* (AmS)

catch¹ /kætʃ/ (*past & past p* **caught**) *vt*

A ‹*ball/object*› agarrar, coger* (esp Esp); **he caught her by the arm** la agarró *or* (esp Esp) cogió del brazo

B (capture) ‹*mouse/lion*› atrapar, coger* (esp Esp); ‹*fish*› pescar*, coger* (esp Esp); ‹*thief*› atrapar

C 1 (take by surprise) agarrar, pillar (fam), pescar* (fam); **to ~ sb in the act** agarrar (*or* pillar *etc*) a algn infraganti *or* con las manos en la masa; **she caught him reading her mail** lo pilló leyendo sus cartas (fam); **you won't ~ me going there again!** (colloq) ¡a mí no me vuelven a ver el pelo por ahí! (fam); **we got caught in the rain** nos sorprendió *or* (fam) nos pilló *or* pescó la lluvia 2 (intercept) ‹*person*› alcanzar*; **~ you later** (AmE colloq) nos vemos

D 1 ‹*train/plane*› (take) tomar, coger* (esp Esp); (be in time for) alcanzar*; **I only just caught it** lo alcancé con el tiempo justo, por poco lo pierdo 2 (manage to see, hear): **we'll just ~ the end of the game** todavía podemos pescar el final del partido (fam); **we could ~ a movie before dinner** (AmE) podríamos ir al cine antes de cenar

E (entangle, trap): **I caught my skirt on a nail** se me enganchó *or* (Méx tb) se me atoró *or* (Chi) se me pescó la falda en un clavo; **I caught my finger in the drawer** me pillé *or* (AmL tb) me agarré el dedo en el cajón; **I got caught in a traffic jam** me agarró *or* (esp Esp) me cogió un atasco

F 1 (attract): **try to ~ his attention** trata de atraer su atención; **the dress caught her fancy** se encaprichó con el vestido 2 (hear or understand clearly): **did you ~ what she said?** ¿oíste *or* entendiste lo que dijo? 3 ‹*mood/likeness*› captar, reflejar

G (become infected with) ‹*disease*› contagiarse de; **to ~ a cold** resfriarse*, agarrar *or* (esp Esp) coger* *or* (fam) pescar* *or* pillar un resfriado; **I caught (the) measles from him** me contagió *or* (fam) me pegó el sarampión

H (hit): **he caught his head on the beam** se dio en la cabeza con la viga; ***to ~ it*** *o* (AmE also) **~ *hell*** (colloq): **you'll really ~ it if he sees you!** ¡si te ve, te mata!

I 1 (hold back): **he caught his breath in surprise** se le cortó la respiración de sorpresa 2 (restrain): **to ~ oneself** contenerse*

■ **catch** *vi*

A 1 (grasp) agarrar, coger* (esp Esp), cachar (Méx) 2 (bite, take hold) «*mechanism*» engranar 3 (become hooked) engancharse

B (ignite) «*fire*» prender, agarrar (AmL)

Phrasal verbs

• **catch on** [v ▸ adv] (colloq) 1 (become popular) «*fashion/idea*» imponerse*; «*game/style*» ponerse* de moda 2 (understand) caer* (fam); **to ~ on TO sth** darse* cuenta DE algo, entender* algo

• **catch out** [v ▸ o ▸ adv, v ▸ adv ▸ o] 1 **to ~ sb out** pillar *or* agarrar a algn desprevenido 2 (trick) pillar (fam), agarrar (CS fam)

• **catch up**

A [v ▸ adv] (draw level): **I missed three weeks' classes, and it was a struggle to ~ up** perdí tres semanas de clase y me costó ponerme al día; **to ~ up WITH sb/sth** (physically) alcanzar* a algn/algo; ‹*on gossip/news*› ponerse* al corriente DE algo; **she had to ~ up with** *o* **on the rest of the class/the work she'd missed** tuvo que ponerse al nivel del resto de la clase/al día con el trabajo; **all those late nights eventually caught up on** *o* **with me** todas esas trasnochadas finalmente pudieron más que yo

B 1 [v ▸ o ▸ adv] (draw level with) (BrE) alcanzar* 2 [v ▸ o ▸ adv, v ▸ adv ▸ o] (pick up) recoger*

C (trap, involve) **to be/get caught up in sth** ‹*in barbed wire/thorns*› estar*/quedar enganchado/atrapado en algo; ‹*in scandal/dispute*› verse* envuelto en algo; ‹*in thoughts*› estar* absorto *or* ensimismado en algo; ‹*in excitement/enthusiasm*› contagiarse de algo; **I got caught up in the traffic** me agarró *or* (esp Esp) me cogió el tráfico

catch² *n*

A 1 (Sport) atrapada *f*, parada *f*, atajada *f* (CS) 2 (potential partner): **he's/she's a good ~** (colloq) es un buen partido 3 (of fish) pesca *f*

B (fastening device — on door) pestillo *m*, pasador *m* (AmL); (— on window, box, necklace) cierre *m*; **safety ~** seguro *m*

C (hidden drawback) trampa *f*; **I knew there'd be a ~ in** *o* **to it somewhere** ya sabía yo que tenía que haber gato encerrado; **it's a C~-22 situation** es una situación sin salida

D (in voice) temblor *m*; **with a ~ in her voice** con la voz entrecortada *or* temblorosa

catchall /ˈkætʃɔːl/ *n* cajón *m* de sastre; (*before n*) ‹*clause/phrase/term*› comodín *adj inv*

catcher /ˈkætʃər || ˈkætʃə(r)/ *n* (in baseball) receptor, -tora *m,f*, catcher *mf*

catching /ˈkætʃɪŋ/ *adj* (*pred*) contagioso

catchment area /ˈkætʃmənt/ *n* (of hospital, school) zona *f* de captación (*distrito que corresponde a un hospital, colegio etc*)

catch: **~phrase** *n* (of person) latiguillo *m*; (of political party) eslogan *m*; **~word** *n* 1 (slogan) eslogan *m* 2 ▸ **~phrase**

catchy /ˈkætʃi/ *adj* **catchier, catchiest** pegadizo, pegajoso (AmL exc RPl)

catechism /ˈkætəkɪzəm/ *n* 1 [u] (instruction) catequesis *f* 2 [c] (book) catecismo *m*

categoric /ˈkætəˈgɔːrɪk || ˌkætəˈgɒrɪk/, **-ical** /-ɪkəl/ *adj* categórico, terminante; ‹*refusal*› rotundo

categorically /ˈkætəˈgɔːrɪkli || ˌkætəˈgɒrɪkli/ *adv* ‹*state/say*› categóricamente; ‹*refuse/deny*› rotundamente

categorize /ˈkætəgəraɪz/ *vt* ‹*things*› clasificar*; ‹*people*› catalogar*, calificar*

category /ˈkætəgɔːri || ˈkætəgəri/ *n* (*pl* **-ries**) categoría *f*

cater /ˈkeɪtər || ˈkeɪtə(r)/ *vi* (Culin) *encargarse del servicio de comida y bebida para fiestas, cafeterías etc*

■ **cater** *vt* (AmE) encargarse* del buffet de

Phrasal verb

• **cater to**, (BrE) **cater for** [v ▸ prep ▸ o]: **to ~ to** *o* **for people of all ages** ofrecer* servicios para gente de todas las edades; **we try to ~ to** *o* **for all needs** tratamos de satisfacer todas las necesidades

cater-corner /ˈkætərˌkɔːrnər || ˈkætəˌkɔːnə(r)/, **cater-cornered** /-ˌkɔːrnərd || -ˌkɔːnəd/ *adj* (AmE) diagonal

caterer /ˈkeɪtərər || ˈkeɪtərə(r)/ *n*: *persona o firma que se encarga del servicio de comida y bebida para fiestas, cafeterías etc*

catering /ˈkeɪtərɪŋ/ *n* [u] 1 (provision of food): **to do the ~** encargarse* del servicio de comida y bebida (*or* del buffet *etc*) 2 (trade, department) restauración *f*

caterpillar /ˈkætərpɪlər || ˈkætəpɪlə(r)/ *n*

A (Zool) oruga *f*, azotador *m* (Méx), cuncuna *f* (Chi)

B **C~® (track)** (Mil, Transp) oruga *f*

caterwaul /ˈkætərwɔːl || ˈkætəwɔːl/ *vi* «*cat*» maullar*; «*person*» aullar*, dar* aullidos

cat: **~fish** *n* (*pl* **~fish** *or* **~fishes**) siluro *m*, bagre *m*; **~flap** *n* gatera *f*

catharsis /kəˈθɑːrsəs || kəˈθɑːsɪs/ *n* [u c] (*pl* **catharses** /-siːz/) catarsis *f*

cathedral /kəˈθiːdrəl/ *n* catedral *f*

catherine wheel /ˈkæθrən || ˈkæθrɪn/ *n* (BrE) rueda *f* (*de fuegos artificiales*), girándula *f*

catheter /ˈkæθətər || ˈkæθɪtə(r)/ *n* catéter *m*

cathode /ˈkæθəʊd/ *n* cátodo *m*

cathode ray *n* rayo *m* catódico

Catholic¹ /ˈkæθəlɪk/ *n* católico, -ca *m,f*

Catholic² *adj*

A (Relig) católico; **the Roman ~ Church** la iglesia católica (apostólica romana)

B **catholic** ‹*tastes/interests*› variado

Catholicism /kəˈθɑːləsɪzəm || kəˈθɒlɪsɪzəm/ *n* [u] catolicismo *m*

catkin /ˈkætkən || ˈkætkɪn/ *n* amento *m*, candelilla *f*

cat: **~nap** *n* siestecita *f*, cabezada *f*; **to have** *o* **take a ~nap** echarse una siestecita *or* cabezada; **~nip** *n* [u] nébeda *f*; **~-o'-nine-tails** /ˈkætəˈnaɪnteɪlz/ *n* (*pl* **~**) (+ *sing vb*) azote *m* (*de tiras con nueve nudos*); **~'s cradle** *n* [u]: **to play ~'s cradle** (jugar* a) hacer* cunitas; **~'s-eye®** *n* (Transp) catafaros *m*, ojo *m* de gato (CS), estoperol *m* (Col); **~ suit** *n* (BrE) malla *f* (entera)

catsup /ˈkætsəp/ *n* [u c] (AmE) ▸ **ketchup**

cattail /ˈkætteɪl/ *n* (AmE) enea *f*, totora *f*

cattle /ˈkætl̩/ *pl n* ganado *m*, reses *fpl*; (*before n*) **~ breeder** ganadero, -ra *m,f*; **~ breeding** ganadería *f*; **~ guard** *o* (BrE)

grid *rejilla en la carretera que permite pasar a los vehículos pero no al ganado*

cattle: **~ car** *n* (AmE Rail) vagón *m* de ganado; **~ market** *n* feria *f* de ganado; **~ truck** *n* (AmE Transp) camión *m* de ganado; (BrE Rail) vagón *m* de ganado

catty /'kæti/ *adj* **-tier, -tiest** (colloq) malicioso, venenoso

catwalk /'kætwɔːk/ *n* (for models, on scaffolding) pasarela *f*

Caucasian[1] /kɔː'keɪʒən/ *adj* (Geog, Ling) caucasiano, caucásico; (Anthrop) caucásico

Caucasian[2] *n* (Anthrop) caucásico, -ca *m,f*; **the suspect is a male ~** el sospechoso es un hombre de raza blanca

Caucasus /'kɔːkəsəs/ *n* **the ~ (Mountains)** el Cáucaso

caught /kɔːt/ *past & past p of* **catch**[1]

cauldron *n* (BrE) ▸**caldron**

cauliflower /'kɑːlɪflaʊər || 'kɒlɪflaʊə(r)/ *n* [c u] coliflor *f*; (*before n*) **~ cheese** (BrE) *coliflor gratinada con queso*; **to have a ~ ear** tener* la oreja deformada (por golpes)

causal /'kɔːzəl/ *adj* causal

causality /kɔː'zæləti/ *n* [u] causalidad *f*

cause[1] /kɔːz/ *n*

A **1** [c] (of accident, event, death) causa *f*; **~ and effect** causa y efecto **2** [u] (reason, grounds) motivo *m*, razón *f*; **there's some ~ for concern** existen motivos *or* razones para preocuparse; **there's no ~ for concern** no hay por qué preocuparse; **without (good) ~** sin causa (justificada) *or* motivo (justificado)

B [c] (ideal, movement) causa *f*; **to fight/die for the ~** luchar/morir* por la causa; **it's a good ~** es una buena causa; **they fought in the ~ of freedom** lucharon en pro de la libertad

cause[2] *vt* causar; **to ~ sb problems** causarle *or* ocasionarle problemas a algn; **to ~ sb/sth TO + INF** hacer* que algn/algo (+ *subj*)

cause célèbre /'kəʊzsə'lebrə || ˌkɔːzse'lebrə/ *n* (*pl* **~s ~s** /'kəʊzsə'lebrə || 'kɔːzsəlebrə/) caso *m* famoso *or* célebre; **the strike became a ~ ~** la huelga dio mucho que hablar

causeway /'kɔːzweɪ/ *n* (path) paso *m* elevado; (road) carretera *f* elevada

caustic /'kɔːstɪk/ *adj* (Chem) cáustico; ‹*wit/remark*› cáustico, mordaz

cauterize /'kɔːtəraɪz/ *vt* cauterizar*

caution[1] /'kɔːʃən/ *n* **1** [u] (care, prudence) cautela *f*, prudencia *f*; **to use** *o* **exercise ~** tener* mucho cuidado; ***to throw ~ to the wind(s)*** echar la precaución por la borda **2** [c] (warning) advertencia *f*, aviso *m*; (Law, Sport) amonestación *f*

caution[2] *vt* **1** (warn) advertir* **2** (inform of rights) informar de sus derechos **3** (reprimand) **to ~ sb ABOUT sth** llamarle la atención a algn POR algo; **to ~ sb FOR -ING** (Law, Sport) amonestar a algn POR + INF

cautionary /'kɔːʃəneri || 'kɔːʃənəri/ *adj*: **~ words** *o* **remarks** advertencias *fpl*; **~ tale** cuento *m* con moraleja

cautious /'kɔːʃəs/ *adj* cauteloso, cauto; **the senator was ~ about committing himself** el senador se cuidó de comprometerse

cautiously /'kɔːʃəsli/ *adv* cautelosamente; **I'm ~ optimistic** soy prudentemente optimista

cavalcade /'kævəlkeɪd/ *n* cabalgata *f*

cavalier[1] /'kævə'lɪr || ˌkævə'lɪə(r)/ *n* (liter) caballero *m*

cavalier[2] *adj* displicente

cavalry /'kævəlri/ *n* [u] caballería *f*

cave /keɪv/ *n* cueva *f*; (*before n*) **~ dweller** (prehistoric) cavernícola *mf*, troglodita *mf*; (modern) habitante *mf* de las cuevas; **~ painting** pintura *f* rupestre

Phrasal verb

• **cave in** [v ▸ adv] **1** (collapse) «*roof/tunnel*» derrumbarse, hundirse **2** (yield) (colloq) «*person*» ceder

caveat /'kɑːviɑːt || 'kæviæt/ *n* (warning) (frml) advertencia *f*; **with the ~ that ...** con la salvedad de que ...

caveman /'keɪvmæn/ *n* (*pl* **-men** /-men/) (prehistoric) hombre *m* de las cavernas

cavern /'kævərn || 'kævən/ *n* caverna *f*

cavernous /'kævərnəs || 'kævənəs/ *adj* ‹*building/hall*› grande y tenebroso; ‹*pit*› profundo y oscuro, como la boca de un lobo

caviar, caviare /'kæviɑːr || 'kæviɑː(r)/ *n* [u] caviar *m*

cavil /'kævəl || 'kævɪl/ *vi*, (BrE) **-ll-**: **to ~ AT** *o* **ABOUT sth** ponerle* reparos A algo

caving /'keɪvɪŋ/ *n* [u] espeleología *f*

cavity /'kævəti/ *n* (*pl* **-ties**) cavidad *f*; (Dent) caries *f*

cavort /kə'vɔːrt || kə'vɔːt/ *vi* retozar*; **he's ~ing with his secretary** está tonteando con su secretaria (fam)

caw[1] /kɔː/ *vi* graznar

caw[2] *n* graznido *m*

cayenne (pepper) /keɪ'en/ *n* [u] (pimienta *f* de) cayena *f*

CB *n* [u c] = **citizens' band**

CBE *n* (in UK) = **Commander of the British Empire** (*condecoración*)

CBI *n* (in UK) = **Confederation of British Industry**

CBS *n* (in US) (*no art*) (= **Columbia Broadcasting System**) la CBS

cc **1** (= **cubic centimeter** *o* (BrE) **centimetre**) c.c. **2** (Corresp) (= **copies to**): **~ H. Palmer, T. Rees** copias a H. Palmer y T. Rees

CCTV *n* = **closed circuit television**

CD *n* (= **compact disc** *or* (AmE also) **disk**) CD *m*; (*before n*) **~ burner** quemador *m* de CDs; **~ changer** cambiador *m* de CDs; **~ writer** (Comput) grabadora *f* de CDs

cease /siːs/ *vt* **1** **to ~ to + INF/ to ~ -ING** dejar DE + INF; **his naiveté never ~s to amaze me** no me explico cómo puede ser tan ingenuo **2** ‹*production/publication*› interrumpir, suspender

▪ **cease** *vi* «*noise*» cesar; «*production*» interrumpirse; «*work*» detenerse*

cease-fire /'siːs'faɪr || 'siːsfaɪə(r)/ *n* alto *m* el fuego, cese *m* del fuego (AmL)

ceaseless /'siːsləs || 'siːslɪs/ *adj* incesante

cedar /'siːdər || 'siːdə(r)/ *n* (tree) cedro *m*

cede /siːd/ *vt* **to ~ sth (TO sb)** ceder(le) algo (A algn)

ceilidh /'keɪli/ *n*: *fiesta tradicional escocesa o irlandesa con música y baile*

ceiling /'siːlɪŋ/ *n* (Const) techo *m*, cielo *m* raso; (upper limit) límite *m*, tope *m*

celebrate /'seləbreɪt || 'selɪbreɪt/ *vt* **1** ‹*birthday/success*› celebrar, festejar **2** (praise) (frml) ‹*virtues/deeds*› celebrar (liter), loar (liter)

▪ **celebrate** *vi*: **we won: let's ~!** ¡ganamos, vamos a celebrarlo *or* festejarlo!

celebrated /'seləbreɪtəd || 'selɪbreɪtɪd/ *adj* célebre, famoso

celebration /'selə'breɪʃən || ˌselɪ'breɪʃən/ *n* **1** [c u] (event) fiesta *f*; **he attended the ~s** asistió a los festejos *or* las festividades; **we ought to have a little ~** deberíamos celebrarlo *or* festejarlo **2** [u] (praise) celebración *f* (liter), loa *f* (liter); **the play is a ~ of life** la obra es un canto *or* (liter) una loa a la vida

celebratory /sə'lebrətɔːri/ *adj*: **we had a ~ drink** nos tomamos una copa para celebrarlo *or* festejarlo

celebrity /sə'lebrəti || sɪ'lebrəti/ *n* (*pl* **-ties**) (person) famoso, -sa *m,f*, celebridad *mf*

celery /'seləri/ *n* [u] apio *m*; **a stick/head of ~** una rama/mata de apio

celestial /sə'lestʃəl || sɪ'lestiəl/ *adj* (Astron) celeste; (liter) celestial (liter)

celibacy /'seləbəsi || 'selɪbəsi/ *n* [u] celibato *m*

celibate /'seləbət || 'selɪbət/ *adj* célibe

cell /sel/ *n*

A (in prison, monastery, honeycomb) celda *f*

B (Biol) célula *f*; (*before n*) ‹*division/wall*› celular

C (Elec) célula *f*; (in battery) elemento *m*, pila *f*

cellar /'selər || 'selə(r)/ *n* sótano *m*; (for coal) carbonera *f*; (for wine) bodega *f*; ***to be/finish in the ~*** (AmE colloq) estar*/llegar* en el último lugar

cellist /'tʃeləst || 'tʃelɪst/ *n* violoncelista *mf*, violonchelista *mf*, chelista *mf*

cello /'tʃeləʊ/ *n* (*pl* **-los**) violoncelo *m*, violonchelo *m*, chelo *m*

cellophane, (BrE) **Cellophane**® /'seləfeɪn/ *n* [u] celofán *m*

cellphone /'selfəʊn/ *n* teléfono *m* celular

cellular /'seljələr || 'seljʊlə(r)/ *adj* celular
cellulite /'seljəlaɪt || 'seljʊlaɪt/ *n* [u] celulitis *f*
celluloid /'seljəlɔɪd || 'seljʊlɔɪd/ *n* [u] celuloide *m*
cellulose /'seljələʊs || 'seljʊləʊs/ *n* [u] celulosa *f*
celly /'seli/ *n* (*pl* **-lies**) (AmE colloq) [1] (cell mate) compañero, -ra *m,f* de celda [2] (cell phone) celular *m* (AmL), móvil *m* (Esp)
Celsius /'selsiəs/ *adj*: **20 degrees ~** 20 grados centígrados *or* Celsio(s)
Celt /kelt/ *n* celta *mf*
Celtic /'keltɪk/ *adj* celta
cement[1] /sɪ'ment/ *n* [u] cemento *m*
cement[2] *vt* [1] (Const) unir con cemento; **to ~ sth (over)** revestir* algo de cemento, cementar algo (AmL) [2] (make firm) ‹*friendship/alliance*› consolidar, fortalecer*
cement mixer *n* hormigonera *f*
cemetery /'seməteri || 'semətri/ *n* (*pl* **-ries**) cementerio *m*
cenotaph /'senətæf || 'senətɑ:f/ *n* cenotafio *m*
censor[1] /'sensər || 'sensə(r)/ *n* censor, -sora *m,f*
censor[2] *vt* censurar
censorship /'sensərʃɪp || 'sensəʃɪp/ *n* [u] censura *f*
censure[1] /'sentʃər || 'sensjə(r)/ *vt* censurar
censure[2] *n* [u] censura *f*
census /'sensəs/ *n* (*pl* **-suses**) censo *m*
cent /sent/ *n* (of euro) céntimo *m*; (of dollar) centavo *m*; ***I don't have/it isn't worth a red ~*** (AmE colloq) no tengo/no vale ni un céntimo *or* centavo; ***to put in one's two ~s' worth*** (AmE colloq) meter baza *or* (fam *o* pey) cuchara, dar* su (*or* mi *etc*) opinión
centenarian /'sentn̩'eriən/ *n* centenario, -ria *m,f*
centenary /sen'tenəri/ *n* (*pl* **-ries**) centenario *m*
centennial[1] /sen'teniəl/ *adj* del centenario
centennial[2] *n* (esp AmE) centenario *m*
center[1], (BrE) **centre** /'sentər || 'sentə(r)/ *n*
A [1] (middle point, area) centro *m*; **to be the ~ of attention** ser* el centro de atención [2] (Pol) centro *m*; **he's left of ~** es de centro izquierda [3] (filling) relleno *m*
B (site of activity) centro *m*; **community ~** centro cívico
C (Sport) (in US football, rugby) centro *mf*; (in basketball) pivot *mf*, pivote *mf* (AmL)
center[2], (BrE) **centre** *vt*
A [1] (position) centrar [2] (Sport) ‹*ball*› lanzar* un centro con
B [1] (concentrate, focus) **to ~ sth ON sth/sb** centrar algo EN algo/algn [2] (base around): **the major industries are ~ed on Chicago** las principales industrias están concentradas en Chicago y sus alrededores
■ **center** *vi* [1] (focus on) **to ~ ON** *o* **UPON sth/sb** centrarse EN algo/algn; **his hopes ~ed on being promoted** cifraba todas sus esperanzas en que lo ascendieran [2] (revolve around) **to ~ ON** *o* **AROUND sth/sb** girar ALREDEDOR DE *or* EN TORNO A algo/algn
center: **~ field** *n* (AmE) (in baseball) (area) jardín *m* central, centro *m* campo; **~ fielder** *n* (AmE) (in baseball) jardinero *mf* centro, centro *mf* campo; **~fold** *n* póster *m or* encarte *m* central; **~ forward** *n* delantero *mf* centro; **~ half** (*pl* **halfs** *or* **halves**) *n* medio *mf* centro; **~ of gravity** *n* centro *m* de gravedad; **~piece** *n* (decoration) centro *m* (de mesa); (main feature) eje *m*
centi- /'senti/ *pref* centi-
centigrade /'sentɪgreɪd/ *adj* centígrado; **20 degrees ~** 20 grados centígrados
centiliter, (BrE) **centilitre** /'sentə,li:tər || 'sentɪ,li:tə(r)/ *n* centilitro *m*
centimeter, (BrE) **centimetre** /'sentə,mi:tər || 'sentɪ,mi:tə(r)/ *n* centímetro *m*
centipede /'sentəpi:d || 'sentɪpi:d/ *n* ciempiés *m*
central /'sentrəl/ *adj*
A (main) central; ‹*problem*› fundamental, principal; **to be ~ TO sth**: **this is ~ to the success of the project** esto es fundamental para que el proyecto sea un éxito
B (in the center) ‹*area/street*› céntrico; **our office is very ~** nuestra oficina está en una zona céntrica *or* en un lugar muy céntrico; **in ~ Chicago** en el centro de Chicago
central: **~ African Republic** *n* **the C~ African Republic** la República Centroafricana; **~ America** *n* Centroamérica *f*, América *f* Central
Central American[1] *adj* centroamericano, de (la) América Central
Central American[2] *n* centroamericano, -na *m,f*
Central Europe *n* Europa *f* Central
Central European[1] *adj* centroeuropeo, de (la) Europa Central
Central European[2] *n* centroeuropeo, -pea *m,f*
central heating *n* [u] calefacción *f* central
centrally /'sentrəli/ *adv*: **~ heated** con calefacción central; **it's ~ located** está en una zona céntrica *or* en un lugar céntrico
central: **~ reservation** *n* (BrE) mediana *f*, bandejón *m* (central) (Chi), camellón *m* (Méx); **~ Standard Time** *n* [u] horario *m* de la zona central
centre *etc* (BrE) ▸ **center** *etc*
centrifugal /sen'trɪfjəgəl || ,sentrɪ'fju:gəl, ,sen'trɪfjʊgəl/ *adj* centrífugo
centrifuge /'sentrəfju:dʒ || 'sentrɪfju:dʒ/ *n* centrifugador *m*
century /'sentʃəri/ *n* (*pl* **-ries**) [1] (100 years) siglo *m*; **in the 19th ~** en el siglo XIX; **a centuries-old tradition** una tradición secular *or* de siglos [2] (in cricket) centena *f*
CEO *n* (esp AmE) = **chief executive officer**
ceramic /sə'ræmɪk || sɪ'ræmɪk/ *adj* ‹*pot*› de cerámica; **~ tile** (for walls) azulejo *m*; (for floors) baldosa *f* (de cerámica)
ceramics /sə'ræmɪks || sɪ'ræmɪks/ *n* [1] (art, process) (+ *sing vb*) cerámica *f* [2] (objects) (+ *pl vb*) objetos *mpl* de cerámica, cerámicas *fpl*
cereal /'sɪriəl || 'sɪəriəl/ *n* [c u] [1] (plant, grain) cereal *m* [2] (*breakfast ~*) cereales *mpl*
cerebral /sə'ri:brəl || 'serɪbrəl/ *adj* cerebral
cerebral palsy *n* [u] parálisis *f* cerebral
ceremonial /,serə'məʊniəl || ,serɪ'məʊniəl/ *adj* ‹*robes*› ceremonial; ‹*occasion*› solemne
ceremonious /,serə'məʊniəs || ,serɪ'məʊniəs/ *adj* ceremonioso
ceremony /'serəməʊni || 'serɪməni/ *n* [c u] (*pl* **-nies**) ceremonia *f*; ***to stand on ~*** ser* muy ceremonioso; **don't stand on ~** déjate de ceremonias
cerise /sə'ri:s, -ri:z/ *n* [u] color *m* guinda; (*before n*) color guinda *adj inv*
cert /sɜ:rt || sɜ:t/ *n* (BrE sl): **she's a dead ~ to win an award** seguro que se lleva un premio
certain[1] /'sɜ:rtn̩ || 'sɜ:tn̩/ *adj*
A [1] (definite) seguro; **they were heading for ~ death** iban a una muerte segura; **she made ~ of a good seat by arriving early** llegó temprano para asegurarse una buena localidad; **it's not ~ (that) they'll approve of the idea** no es seguro que aprueben la idea; **one thing** *o* **this much is ~ ...** de lo que no cabe la menor duda es de que ...; **to be ~ to + INF**: **it's ~ to rain** seguro que llueve; **for ~** con certeza; **I can't say for ~** no lo puedo decir a ciencia cierta; **she won't do that again, that's (for) ~** no volverá a hacerlo, eso es seguro *or* de eso no cabe duda [2] (convinced) (*pred*) **to be ~ (OF sth)** estar* seguro (DE algo); **I feel ~ (that) it was a mistake** tengo la seguridad *or* la certeza de que fue un error; **I checked the list to make ~ (that) ...** revisé la lista para asegurarme de que ...
B (particular) (*before n*) cierto; **it's only open on ~ days** está abierto solamente ciertos días; **he has a ~ something** tiene un no sé qué *or* (un) algo especial; **a ~ person refused to go** cierta persona se negó a ir, alguien que yo conozco se negó a ir; **a ~ Jill Brown** una tal Jill Brown
certain[2] *pron* (frml) (+ *pl vb*): **~ of his colleagues/her works** ciertos colegas suyos/ciertas obras suyas
certainly /'sɜ:rtn̩li || 'sɜ:tn̩li/ *adv* [1] (definitely): **we're almost ~ going to win** es casi seguro que vamos a ganar; **do you see what I mean? — certainly** ¿te das cuenta de lo que quiero decir? — desde luego; **he's ~ intelligent, but ...** no hay duda de que es inteligente, pero ..., es cierto que es inteligente, pero ... [2] (emphatic): **I ~ won't be buying anything there again!** por cierto que *or* por supuesto que no voy a volver a comprar nada allí; **he may be rich, but he ~ isn't generous** será rico, pero de generoso no tiene nada; **it's cold today — it ~ is!** hoy

hace frío — ¡ya lo creo! 3 (responding to request): **~, sir** por supuesto *or* cómo no, señor; **~ not!** ¡de ninguna manera!, ¡por supuesto que no!

certainty /'sɜ:rtn̩ti || 'sɜ:tn̩ti/ *n* (*pl* **-ties**) 1 [u c] (belief, conviction) certeza *f*, seguridad *f* 2 [c] (certain event): **defeat is now a ~** la derrota es algo seguro *or* es cosa segura

certifiable /'sɜ:rtəfaɪəbəl || 'sɜ:tɪfaɪəbəl/ *adj* demente

certificate /sər'tɪfɪkət || sə'tɪfɪkət/ *n* certificado *m*

certification /,sɜ:rtəfə'keɪʃən || ,sɜ:tɪfɪ'keɪʃən/ *n* [u] certificación *f*

certify /'sɜ:rtəfaɪ || 'sɜ:tɪfaɪ/ *vt* **-fies, -fying, -fied** 1 ‹*facts/claim/death*› certificar*; **this is to ~ that ...** por la presente certifico que *or* doy fe de que ... 2 (declare insane) (*usu pass*) declarar demente 3 (license) (AmE): **he isn't certified to teach in this state** no está habilitado para ejercer la docencia en este estado 4 **certified** *past p* (AmE) certificado; **certified milk** leche *f* con garantía sanitaria; **certified public accountant** contador público, contadora pública *m,f* (AmL), censor jurado, censora jurada *m,f* de cuentas (Esp)

cervical /'sɜ:rvɪkəl || 'sɜ:vɪkəl, sɜ:'vaɪkəl/ *adj* del cuello del útero; **~ smear** (BrE) citología *f*, Papanicolau *m* (AmL)

cervix /'sɜ:rvɪks || 'sɜ:vɪks/ *n* (*pl* **-vixes** *or* **-vices** /-vəsi:z/) cuello *m* del útero

Cesarean (section), Cesarian (section) /sɪ'zæriən || sɪ'zeəriən/ *n* (AmE) cesárea *f*

cessation /se'seɪʃən/ *n* [u c] (frml) cese *m*, cesación *f*

cesspit /'sespɪt/, **cesspool** /-pu:l/ *n* pozo *m* negro *or* séptico *or* ciego

Ceylon /sɪ'lɑ:n || sɪ'lɒn/ *n* (Hist) Ceilán *m*

cf (compare) cf.

CFC *n* **= chlorofluorocarbon**

ch *n* (*pl* **chs**) (**= chapter**) c.

chad /tʃæd/ *n*: *trocito redondo de papel que se desprende al usar una perforadora*

chafe /tʃeɪf/ *vt* rozar*

■ **chafe** *vi* 1 (rub) rozar* 2 (be frustrated) irritarse; **he ~d at the restrictions** lo irritaban las trabas

chaff /tʃæf || tʃɑ:f/ *n* [u] (husks) barcia *f*, ahechaduras *fpl*, granzas *fpl*; (worthless material) paja *f*, broza *f*

chaffinch /'tʃæfɪntʃ/ *n* pinzón *m*

chagrin /ʃə'grɪn || 'ʃægrɪn/ *n* [u] (liter) disgusto *m*, desilusión *f*; **to my/his ~** para mi/su disgusto

chain¹ /tʃeɪn/ *n* 1 cadena *f*; **to be in ~s** estar* encadenado; **~ of office** *collar que es atributo de un cargo oficial* 2 (series) cadena *f*; **a ~ of events** una cadena *or* (frml) concatenación de acontecimientos; **mountain ~** cadena montañosa *or* de montañas 3 (Busn) cadena *f*

chain² *vt* **to ~ sth/sb TO sth** encadenar algo/a algn A algo

Phrasal verb

• **chain up** [v ▸ o ▸ adv, v ▸ adv ▸ o] encadenar

chain: **~ gang** *n* cuerda *f* *or* cadena *f* de presos; **~ letter** *n* carta *f* (*de una cadena*); **~ mail** *n* [u] cota *f* de malla; **~ reaction** *n* reacción *f* en cadena; **~saw** *n* motosierra *f*, sierra *f* de cadena; **~smoke** *vi* fumar un cigarrillo tras otro; **~smoker** *n*: *persona que fuma un cigarrillo tras otro*; **~ store** *n* tienda *f* de una cadena

chair¹ /tʃer || tʃeə(r)/ *n*

A 1 (seat) silla *f*; (*arm~*) sillón *m*, butaca *f* (esp Esp) 2 (*electric ~*) (AmE colloq): **the ~** la silla eléctrica

B 1 (at university) cátedra *f* 2 (in meeting) presidencia *f*; **to be in/take the ~** presidir 3 (person) presidente, -ta *m,f*

chair² *vt* ‹*meeting/committee*› presidir

chair: **~lift** *n* telesilla *f* *or* (Esp) telesquí *m*; **~man** /'tʃermən || 'tʃeəmən/ *n* (*pl* **-men** /-mən/) presidente, -ta *m,f*; **~person** *n* (*pl* **-persons**) presidente, -ta *m,f*; **~woman** *n* presidenta *f*

chalet /'ʃæleɪ/ *n* 1 (cabin) chalet *m* (*de montaña*) 2 (in motel) (BrE) bungalow *m*

chalice /'tʃæləs || 'tʃælɪs/ *n* cáliz *m*

chalk¹ /tʃɔ:k/ *n*

A [u] (Geol) creta *f*, caliza *f*; ***to be as different as ~ and cheese*** (BrE) ser* (como) la noche y el día *or* (como) el día y la noche

B [c u] (for writing) tiza *f*, gis *m* (Méx); **a piece of ~** una tiza, un gis (Méx); ***not by a long ~*** (BrE colloq) ni mucho menos

chalk² *vt* (write with chalk) escribir* con tiza *or* (Méx) gis

Phrasal verb

• **chalk up**

A [v ▸ adv ▸ o] 1 (write on blackboard) escribir*, anotar 2 ‹*win/success*› apuntarse, anotarse

B [v ▸ o ▸ adv] (charge) (colloq) **to ~ sth up TO sb** anotar algo en la cuenta de algn

chalkboard /'tʃɔ:kbɔ:rd || 'tʃɔ:kbɔ:d/ *n* (AmE) ▸ **blackboard**

chalky /'tʃɔ:ki/ *adj* **-kier, -kiest** (containing chalk) calcáreo; (like chalk) terroso; (covered in chalk) lleno de tiza *or* (Méx) de gis

challenge¹ /'tʃæləndʒ || 'tʃælɪndʒ/ *vt*

A 1 (summon) desafiar*, retar; **to ~ sb to + INF** desafiar* a algn A QUE (+ *subj*) 2 (offer competition to): **no one can ~ the leaders now** nadie puede hacer peligrar la posición de los líderes 3 (question) ‹*authority/findings*› cuestionar; ‹*assumption/theory*› cuestionar, poner* en entredicho *or* en duda *or* en tela de juicio

B (stimulate) «*job*» suponer* *or* constituir* un reto *or* un desafío para

C (stop) (Mil) darle* el alto a

challenge² *n*

A [c] 1 (to duel, race) desafío *m*, reto *m*; **to issue a ~ to sb** desafiar* *or* retar a algn 2 (competition) rival *m*

B [c u] (stimulation) reto *m*, desafío *m*

C [c] (by policeman, sentry) alto *m*

challenger /'tʃæləndʒər || 'tʃælɪndʒə(r)/ *n* contendiente *mf*, rival *mf*; **the ~ for the title** el/la aspirante al título

challenging /'tʃæləndʒɪŋ || 'tʃælɪndʒɪŋ/ *adj* 1 ‹*movie/book*› que da que pensar, que cuestiona ideas establecidas 2 ‹*task*› que supone *or* constituye un reto *or* un desafío 3 ‹*look/tone*› desafiante, retador

chamber /'tʃeɪmbər || 'tʃeɪmbə(r)/ *n*

A (room) (arch) cámara *f* (arc)

B (of gun) recámara *f*

chamberlain /'tʃeɪmbərlən || 'tʃeɪmbəlɪn/ *n* chambelán *m*

chamber: **~maid** *n* camarera *f* (*en un hotel*); **~ music** *n* [u] música *f* de cámara; **~ of commerce** *n* cámara *f* de comercio; **~ pot** *n* orinal *m* *or* (AmL exc RPl) bacinilla *f* *or* (CS) escupidera *f*

chameleon /kə'mi:liən/ *n* camaleón *m*

chamois 1 /'ʃæmi, 'ʃæmwɑ: || 'ʃæmwɑ:/ *n* (Zool) gamuza *f* 2 **~ (leather)** /'ʃæmi/ gamuza *f*

chamomile /'kæməmaɪl/ *n* manzanilla *f*, camomila *f*; **~ tea** manzanilla *f*

champ¹ /tʃæmp/ *vi* (chew) masticar*, mascar*; ▸ **bit²** H

champ² *n* (colloq) campeón, -peona *m,f*

champagne /ʃæm'peɪn/ *n* 1 [u c] (Culin) champán *m*, champaña *f* *or* *m* 2 [u] (color) color *m* champán *or* champaña

champion¹ /'tʃæmpiən/ *n*

A (Sport) campeón, -peona *m,f*

B (Hist) paladín *m*, campeón *m*; **she's a ~ of lost causes** es una defensora de pleitos perdidos *or* de causas perdidas

champion² *vt* abogar* por, defender*

championship /'tʃæmpiənʃɪp/ *n* [c] (Sport) (*often pl*) campeonato *m*

chance¹ /tʃæns || tʃɑ:ns/ *n*

A [u] (fate) casualidad *f*, azar *m*; **it was pure ~ that we met** nos encontramos de *or* por pura casualidad; **to leave nothing to ~** no dejar nada (librado) al azar; **by ~** por *or* de casualidad; **have you seen my hat, by any ~?** ¿has visto mi sombrero por casualidad?; (*before n*) ‹*meeting/occurrence*› casual, fortuito

B [c] (risk) riesgo *m*; **don't take any ~s** no te arriesgues, no corras riesgos

C [c] 1 (opportunity) oportunidad *f*, ocasión *f*; **to jump** *o* **leap at the ~** aprovechar *or* no dejar escapar la oportunidad *or* ocasión; **the ~ of a lifetime** la oportunidad de su (*or* mi *etc*) vida; **finished yet? — give me a ~!** ¿has acabado ya? — ¡espera un poco!; **give them half a ~ and they'll fleece you** en cuanto te descuidas te despluman 2 (raffle ticket) (AmE) número *m*, boleto *m*

D [c] (likelihood) posibilidad *f*, chance *f* *or* *m* (esp AmL); **they don't stand much of a ~** lo tienen (bien) difícil; **not a** *o* **no ~!** (colloq) ¡ni de casualidad *or* ni en broma! (fam); **it's a million-to-one ~** *o* **a ~ in a million** las posibilidades son muy remotas; **(the) ~s are (that) ...** (colloq) lo más probable es que ...; ***to be in with a ~*** (BrE) tener* posibilidades *or* chances

chance² *vt* 1 (risk): **to ~ it** arriesgarse*, correr el riesgo 2 (happen) **to ~ to + INF**: **I just ~d to be passing your office** pasaba por tu oficina por casualidad

Phrasal verb

- **chance on, chance upon** [v ▸ prep ▸ o] ‹*object*› encontrar* por casualidad; ‹*person*› encontrarse* por casualidad con

C

chancellor /'tʃænsḷər || 'tʃɑːnsələ(r)/ *n* 1 **Chancellor (of the Exchequer)** (in UK) ≈ ministro, -tra *m,f* de Economía/Hacienda 2 (premier) canciller *mf* 3 (of university) rector, -tora *m,f*

chancery /'tʃænsəri || 'tʃɑːnsəri/ *n* (*pl* **-ries**) (in US) *tribunal de justicia que conoce de casos no contemplados por el derecho consuetudinario o el escrito*

chancy, chancey /'tʃænsi || 'tʃɑːnsi/ *adj* **-cier, -ciest** (colloq) arriesgado

chandelier /'ʃændə'lɪr || ˌʃændə'lɪə(r)/ *n* araña *f* (*de luces*)

change¹ /tʃeɪndʒ/ *n*

A 1 [u c] (alteration) cambio *m*; **a ~ in temperature** un cambio de temperatura; **there's been a ~ in the weather** ha cambiado el tiempo; **to make ~s to sth** hacerle* cambios a algo; **a ~ for the better/worse** un cambio para mejor/para peor; **the ~ (of life)** (euph) la menopausia 2 [c] (replacement) cambio *m*; **a ~ of address** un cambio de dirección; ***to have a ~ of heart*** cambiar de idea 3 (of clothes) muda *f* 4 [c] (sth different from usual) cambio *m*; **at least it's** *o* **it makes a ~ from chicken** por lo menos no es pollo; **for a ~** para variar; ***to ring the ~s*** introducir* variaciones; ***a ~ is as good as a rest*** con un cambio de actividad se renuevan las energías

B [u] 1 (coins) cambio *m*, monedas *fpl*, sencillo *m* (AmL), feria *f* (Méx fam), menudo *m* (Col); **one dollar in ~** un dólar en monedas 2 (money returned) cambio *m*, vuelto *m* (AmL), vuelta *f* (Esp), vueltas *fpl* (Col); **keep the ~** quédese con el cambio (*or* vuelto *etc*); **you won't get much ~ from** *o* **out of $1,000** no te costará mucho menos de 1.000 dólares

change² *vt*

A 1 ‹*appearance/rules/situation*› cambiar; **the sorcerer ~d her into a stone** el mago la convirtió en una piedra 2 ‹*tire/oil/sheets*› cambiar; **to ~ one's address/doctor** cambiar de dirección/médico; **to ~ one's clothes** cambiarse de ropa; **to ~ color** cambiar de color; **let's ~ the subject** cambiemos de tema; **she ~d her name from Bronowski to Brown** se cambió el apellido de Bronowski a Brown 3 (exchange) cambiar(se) de; **I wouldn't want to ~ places with her** no quisiera estar *or* verme en su lugar; **he ~d it for a red one** lo cambió por uno rojo 4 ‹*baby*› cambiar

B ‹*money*› 1 (into smaller denominations) cambiar; **can anyone ~ $20?** ¿alguien me puede cambiar 20 dólares? 2 (into foreign currency) **to ~ sth (INTO sth)** cambiar algo (A *or* (Esp tb) EN algo)

C (Transp): **you have to ~ train(s) at Nice** tienes que hacer transbordo *or* cambiar (de trenes) en Niza

■ **change** *vi*

A 1 (become different) cambiar; **I can't believe how much she's ~d** me parece increíble lo mucho que ha cambiado; **to ~ INTO sth** convertirse* *or* transformarse EN algo 2 (from one thing to another) cambiar; **the scene ~s to wartime Rome** la escena pasa *or* se traslada a Roma durante la guerra 3 **changing** *pres p* ‹*needs/role/moods*› cambiante

B 1 (put on different clothes) cambiarse; **she ~d into a black dress** se cambió y se puso un vestido negro; **I'm going to ~ into something more comfortable** me voy a poner algo más cómodo; **to get ~d** cambiarse 2 (Transp) cambiar, hacer* transbordo

Phrasal verbs

- **change around**

A [v ▸ o ▸ adv, v ▸ adv ▸ o] (rearrange) cambiar de sitio *or* de lugar

B [v ▸ adv] cambiar

- **change over** [v ▸ adv] (change function, system) cambiar; **to ~ over TO sth** cambiar A algo, adoptar algo
- **change round** (esp BrE) ▸ **change around**

changeable /'tʃeɪndʒəbəl/ *adj* cambiante, variable

changeling /'tʃeɪndʒlɪŋ/ *n*: *niño sustituido por otro al nacer*

change: **~over** *n* (transition) **~ (FROM sth)(TO sth)** cambio *m* (DE algo) (A algo); **~ purse** *n* (AmE) monedero *m*, portamonedas *m*

changing room /'tʃeɪndʒɪŋ/ *n* (BrE) 1 (Sport) vestuario *m*, vestidor *m* (Chi, Méx) 2 (in shop) probador *m*

channel¹ /'tʃænl/ *n*

A (strait) canal *m*; (course of river) cauce *m*; (navigable course) canal *m*; **the (English) C~** el Canal de la Mancha

B (for irrigation) canal *m*, acequia *f*

C (system, method) vía *f*; **through diplomatic ~s** por la vía diplomática; **you must go through the official ~s** tiene que hacer el trámite por los conductos *or* las vías oficiales; **distribution ~s** canales *mpl* de distribución

D (Comput, TV) canal *m*

channel² *vt*, (BrE) **-ll-** canalizar*, encauzar*, dirigir*

channel: **~ Islands** *pl n* **the C~ Islands** las Islas Anglonormandas, las islas del Canal de la Mancha; **~-surf** *vi* (TV) hacer* zapping; **~ Tunnel** *n* **the C~ Tunnel** el Eurotúnel, el túnel del Canal de la Mancha

chant¹ /tʃænt || tʃɑːnt/ *n* (of demonstrators) consigna *f*; (of sports fans) alirón *m*, canción *f*

chant² *vt/i* 1 (Mus, Relig) salmodiar 2 «*crowd*» gritar

Chanukah /'hɑːnəkə/ *n* ▸ **Hanukkah**

chaos /'keɪɑːs || 'keɪɒs/ *n* [u] caos *m*

chaotic /keɪ'ɑːtɪk || keɪ'ɒtɪk/ *adj* caótico

chap /tʃæp/ *n*

A (man) (colloq) tipo *m* (fam); **the poor little ~!** ¡pobrecito!

B (Med) grieta *f*

chap. *n* (*pl* **chaps**) (= **chapter**) c., cap.

chaparral /'tʃæpə'ræl, 'ʃæ-/ *n* (AmE) chaparral *m*

chapel /'tʃæpəl/ *n* (Relig) (building, area in church) capilla *f*; (Nonconformist church) templo *m*

chaperon¹, **chaperone** /'ʃæpərəʊn/ *n* (of young lady) acompañante *f*, chaperona *f*; (for children) (AmE) acompañante *mf*

chaperon², **chaperone** *vt* acompañar

chaplain /'tʃæplən || 'tʃæplɪn/ *n* capellán *m*

chapped /tʃæpt/ *adj* ‹*lips*› agrietado, partido

chaps /tʃæps/ *pl n* zahones *mpl*, chaparreras *fpl* (Méx), p(i)erneras *fpl* (CS), zamarros *mpl* (Col)

chapter /'tʃæptər || 'tʃæptə(r)/ *n* (of book) capítulo *m*; **to quote ~ and verse** citar textualmente *or* palabra por palabra

char¹ /tʃɑːr || tʃɑː(r)/ *vt* **-rr-** carbonizar*

char² *n* (BrE) (cleaner) mujer *f* de la limpieza, asistenta *f* (Esp)

character /'kærəktər || 'kærəktə(r)/ *n*

A (of person) 1 (temperament, nature) carácter *m*; **to be in/out of ~** ser*/no ser* típico; **she's a good judge of ~** es buena psicóloga 2 (*good* ~) reputación *f*; (*before n*) **~ assassination** (public slander) difamación *f*; **~ reference** referencias *fpl* 3 (strength of personality) carácter *m*

B (of place, thing) carácter *m*; **her face is full of ~** tiene una cara con mucha personalidad

C [c] 1 (in novel, play, movie) personaje *m*, carácter *m* (Col, Méx); **he doesn't react in ~** su reacción no es la que cabría esperar de su personaje 2 (person) tipo *m* (fam); **he's a nasty ~** es un mal tipo (fam) 3 (eccentric person) caso *m*

D [c] (symbol) carácter *m*

characteristic¹ /'kærəktə'rɪstɪk/ *n* característica *f*

characteristic² *adj* característico

characterize /'kærəktəraɪz/ *vt* 1 (be typical of) caracterizar* 2 (describe) calificar*; **to ~ sth/sb AS sth** calificar* algo/a algn DE algo

characterless /'kærəktərləs || 'kærəktəlɪs/ *adj* ‹*restaurant/town*› sin carácter

charade /ʃə'reɪd || ʃə'rɑːd/ *n* (farse) farsa *f*, payasada *f*; **~s** (+ *sing vb*) (game) charada *f*

charbroiled /'tʃɑːrbrɔɪld || 'tʃɑːbrɔɪld/ *adj* (AmE) (hecho) a la brasa *or* a las brasas

charcoal /'tʃɑːrkəʊl || 'tʃɑːkəʊl/ *n* [u] carbón *m* (vegetal); (Art) carboncillo *m*, carbonilla *f* (RPl)

charge¹ /tʃɑːrdʒ || tʃɑːdʒ/ *n*

A [c] (Law) cargo *m*, acusación *f*; **he's being tried on a ~ of**

murder se lo juzga por homicidio; **to bring** *o* **press ~s against sb** formular *or* presentar cargos contra algn; **to drop ~s** retirar la acusación *or* los cargos

B [c] (price) precio *m*; (fee) honorario *m*; **there is no ~ for the service** no se cobra por el servicio, el servicio es gratis; **free of** *o* **without ~** gratuitamente, gratis, sin cargo; **at no extra ~** sin cargo adicional; **electricity ~s are going up again** las tarifas eléctricas vuelven a subir

C 1 [c] (command, commission) orden *f*, instrucción *f* 2 (responsibility): **who is in ~?** ¿quién es el/la responsable?; **I left Paul in ~** dejé a Paul a cargo; **to be in ~ of sth/sb** tener* algo/a algn a su (*or* mi *etc*) cargo; **in the ~ of sb, in sb's ~** a cargo de algn; **to take ~ of sb/sth/-ING**: **she took ~ of the situation** se hizo cargo de la situación; **Sarah took ~ of the guests/of buying the food** Sarah se encargó de los invitados/de comprar la comida 3 [c] (sb entrusted): **a nanny with her young ~s** una niñera con los niños a su cargo *or* cuidado

D [c u] (Elec, Phys) carga *f*

E [c] (of explosive) carga *f*

F [c] 1 (attack) carga *f* 2 (in US football) ofensiva *f* (*en la que se gana mucho terreno*)

charge[2] *vt*

A (accuse) **to ~ sb WITH sth/-ING** acusar a algn DE algo/+ INF

B (ask payment) cobrar; **they ~d him $15 for a haircut** le cobraron 15 dólares por el corte de pelo

C (obtain on credit): **she never carries cash, she just ~s everything** (AmE) nunca lleva dinero, lo compra todo con tarjeta (de crédito)/lo carga todo a su cuenta; **to ~ sth TO sb** cargar* algo a la cuenta de algn

D 1 (entrust) (frml) **to ~ sb WITH sth/-ING** encomendarle* A algn algo/QUE (+ *subj*) 2 (command) (liter) **to ~ sb to + INF** ordenarle A algn + INF *or* QUE (+ *subj*) 3 (allege) (AmE) aducir*

E (attack) (Mil) cargar* contra; ‹‹*animal*›› embestir* *or* arremeter contra

F (Elec) ‹*battery*› cargar*

■ **charge** *vi* 1 **to ~ (AT sth/sb)** (Mil) cargar* (CONTRA algo/algn); ‹‹*animal*›› arremeter *or* embestir* (CONTRA algo/algn); **~!** ¡al ataque!, ¡a la carga! 2 (rush) (colloq) (+ *adv compl*): **he ~d straight into me** se abalanzó hacia mí; **don't all ~ off at the end of the lesson** no salgan en estampida al acabar la clase

charge: **~ account** *n* cuenta *f* de crédito; **~ card** *n* tarjeta *f* de pago

charged /tʃɑːrdʒd || tʃɑːdʒd/ *adj* cargado; **a voice ~ with emotion** una voz cargada de emoción

chargé d'affaires /ʃɑːrˈʒeɪdəˈfer || ˌʃɑːdʒeɪdæˈfeə(r)/ *n* (*pl* **chargés d'affaires** /-z/) encargado, -da *m,f* de negocios

charger /ˈtʃɑːrdʒər || ˈtʃɑːdʒə(r)/ *n*

A (*battery* ~) cargador *m*

B (horse) (liter) caballo *m* (de batalla), corcel *m* (liter)

chariot /ˈtʃæriət/ *n* carro *m* (de guerra)

charioteer /tʃærɪəˈtɪr || ˌtʃærɪəˈtɪə(r)/ *n* auriga *m*

charisma /kəˈrɪzmə/ *n* [u] carisma *m*

charismatic /ˈkærəzˈmætɪk || ˌkærɪzˈmætɪk/ *adj* carismático

charitable /ˈtʃærətəbəl || ˈtʃærɪtəbəl/ *adj* 1 (generous, giving) caritativo 2 (kind) ‹*person*› bueno; ‹*interpretation*› benévolo, generoso 3 (for charity): **a ~ organization** una organización de beneficencia, una obra benéfica

charitably /ˈtʃærətəbli || ˈtʃærɪtəbli/ *adv* caritativamente, con caridad *or* generosidad

charity /ˈtʃærəti/ *n* (*pl* **-ties**)

A 1 [c] (organization) organización *f* benéfica *or* de beneficencia, obra *f* benéfica 2 [u] (relief) obras *fpl* de beneficencia; **to raise money for ~** recaudar dinero para un fin benéfico; (*before n*) ‹*work*› de beneficencia, benéfico; **a ~ performance** una función benéfica *or* de beneficencia, un beneficio

B [u] (generosity, kindness) caridad *f*, amor *m* al prójimo; **~ *begins at home*** la caridad bien entendida empieza por casa *or* (Esp) por uno mismo

charlady /ˈtʃɑːrˌleɪdi || ˈtʃɑːˌleɪdi/ *n* (*pl* **-ladies**) (BrE) mujer *f* de la limpieza

charlatan /ˈʃɑːrlətən || ˈʃɑːlətən/ *n* charlatán, -tana *m,f*

charley horse /ˈtʃɑːrli || ˈtʃɑːli/ *n* (AmE colloq) calambre *m*

charm[1] /tʃɑːrm || tʃɑːm/ *n*

A 1 [u] (attractiveness) encanto *m*, atractivo *m*; **to turn on the ~** ponerse* encantador 2 [c] (attractive quality, feature) encanto *m*

B [c] (spell) hechizo *m*; ***to work/go like a ~*** funcionar/ir* *or* andar* a las mil maravillas

C [c] (amulet) amuleto *m*, fetiche *m*; (on bracelet) dije *m*

charm[2] *vt*

A (delight) cautivar, embelesar; **he can ~ the birds off** *o* **out of the trees** es capaz de convencer a cualquiera con sus encantos

B 1 (bewitch) ‹*snake*› encantar 2 **charmed** *past p*: **to lead a ~ed life** tener* mucha suerte en la vida

charmer /ˈtʃɑːrmər || ˈtʃɑːmə(r)/ *n* persona *f* encantadora, encanto *m*

charming /ˈtʃɑːrmɪŋ || ˈtʃɑːmɪŋ/ *adj* ‹*person*› encantador; ‹*room/house*› precioso, encantador

charm school *n* (AmE) *escuela para señoritas donde se enseña a comportarse en sociedad*

chart[1] /tʃɑːrt || tʃɑːt/ *n*

A (Aviat, Naut) carta *f* de navegación; (Meteo) mapa *m*, carta *f*; (diagram, graph) gráfico *m*; (table) tabla *f*

B **charts** *pl* (best-selling records) **the ~s** la lista de éxitos, el hit parade

chart[2] *vt* 1 (make map of) trazar* el mapa de 2 (plan, plot) trazar* 3 ‹*progress/changes*› (follow closely) seguir* atentamente; (record) registrar gráficamente

charter[1] /ˈtʃɑːrtər || ˈtʃɑːtə(r)/ *n*

A [c] 1 (of university) estatutos *mpl*; (of city) fuero *m*; (of company) escritura *f* de constitución; **by royal ~** por cédula real 2 (constitution) carta *f* 3 (guarantee of rights) fuero *m*, privilegio *m*

B [u] (hire) (Transp) (contrato *m* de) fletamento *m*; (*before n*) ‹*flight/plane*› chárter *adj inv*

charter[2] *vt*

A 1 (grant charter to) aprobar* los estatutos de 2 (BrE) **chartered** *past p* ‹*engineer/surveyor*› colegiado; **~ed accountant** contador público, contadora pública *m,f* (AmL), censor jurado, censora jurada *m,f* de cuentas (Esp)

B (hire) ‹*plane/ship/bus*› fletar, alquilar

charwoman /ˈtʃɑːrwʊmən || ˈtʃɑːwʊmən/ *n* (*pl* **-women**) (BrE) mujer *f* de la limpieza

chary /ˈtʃeri || ˈtʃeəri/ *adj* **charier, chariest** (*pred*) **to be ~ OF -ING**: **she's ~ of making commitments** es reacia a contraer compromisos

chase[1] /tʃeɪs/ *n* 1 (pursuit) persecución *f*; **car ~** persecución en coche; **to give ~** salir* en persecución de algn/algo, ir* tras algn/algo, darle* caza a algn/algo 2 (hunting) **the ~** la caza

chase[2] *vt* (follow, pursue) ‹*thief*› perseguir*, darle* caza a; **they're both chasing the same woman** (colloq) ambos andan detrás de la misma mujer

■ **chase** *vi*: **we ~d after the thief** fuimos *or* salimos tras el ladrón; **to ~ after girls** ir* *or* andar* detrás de las chicas

Phrasal verb

• **chase up** [v ▸ o ▸ adv, v ▸ adv ▸ o] (colloq): **~ up this order for me, please** averíguame qué pasó con este pedido, por favor; **I'll have to ~ him up about the report** voy a tener que recordarle lo del informe

chaser /ˈtʃeɪsər || ˈtʃeɪsə(r)/ *n*: *bebida de bajo contenido en alcohol que se toma después de otra más fuerte*

chasm /ˈkæzəm/ *n* sima *f*, abismo *m*

chassis /ˈtʃæsi || ˈʃæsi/ *n* (*pl* **chassis** /ˈtʃæsiz || ˈʃæ-/) (Auto) chasis *m*, bastidor *m* (Esp)

chaste /ˈtʃeɪst/ *adj* **chaster, chastest** casto

chasten /ˈtʃeɪsn̩/ *vt* hacer* escarmentar

chastise /tʃæsˈtaɪz/ *vt* (frml) (verbally) reprender, reprobar*; (physically) castigar*

chastity /ˈtʃæstəti/ *n* [u] castidad *f*; (*before n*) **~ belt** cinturón *m* de castidad

chat[1] /tʃæt/ *n* charla *f*, conversación *f* (esp AmL), plática *f* (AmC, Méx); **to have a ~ with sb** charlar *or* hablar *or* (esp AmL) conversar *or* (AmC, Méx) platicar* con algn

chat[2] **-tt-** *vi* 1 (talk) **to ~ (TO** *o* **WITH sb)** charlar *or* hablar *or* (esp AmL) conversar *or* (AmC, Méx) platicar* (CON algn) 2 (on Internet) **to ~ (TO** *or* **WITH) sb** chatear (CON algn)

C

(Phrasal verb)

- **chat up** [v ▸ o ▸ adv, v ▸ adv ▸ o] (BrE colloq) tratar de ligar con (fam), llevarle la carga a (RPl fam)

chat show *n* (BrE) programa *m* de entrevistas

chatter¹ /ˈtʃætər || ˈtʃætə(r)/ *vi* «*person*» charlar, chacharear (fam), parlotear (fam), cotorrear (fam); «*monkeys*» parlotear; «*birds*» cotorrear; **his teeth are ~ing** le castañetean los dientes

chatter² *n* [u] (idle talk) cháchara *f* (fam), parloteo *m* (fam)

chatterbox /ˈtʃætərbɑːks || ˈtʃætəbɒks/ *n* charlatán, -tana *m,f*, cotorra *f* (fam)

chatty /ˈtʃæti/ *adj* **-tier, -tiest** ‹*person*› conversador, hablador; ‹*style*› informal, llano; ‹*letter*› simpático y lleno de noticias

chauffeur¹ /ˈʃəʊfər || ˈʃəʊfə(r)/ *n* chofer *mf or* (Esp) chófer *mf*; **a ~-driven limousine** una limusina con chofer *or* (Esp) con chófer

chauffeur² *vt* 1 ‹*person*› hacer* de chofer *or* (Esp) de chófer para 2 (AmE): **a ~ed car** un coche con chofer *or* (Esp) con chófer

chauvinism /ˈʃəʊvənɪzəm || ˈʃəʊvɪnɪzəm/ *n* [u] 1 (jingoism) chovinismo *m*, patriotería *f* 2 (sexism): **male ~** machismo *m*

chauvinist /ˈʃəʊvənəst || ˈʃəʊvɪnɪst/ *n* 1 (jingoist) chovinista *mf*, patriotero, -ra *m,f* 2 (sexist): **(male) ~** machista *m*

chav /tʃæv/ *n* (BrE colloq, pej) chav *mf*, ≈ bakala *mf* (Esp)

cheap¹ /tʃiːp/ *adj* **-er, -est**

A 1 (inexpensive) barato; ‹*restaurant/hotel*› económico; ‹*fare/ticket*› (BrE) económico, de precio reducido; **it's ~ at the price** a ese precio es barato, a ese precio resulta económico; **~ and cheerful** bonito y barato; ***on the* ~** gastando lo menos posible 2 (shoddy) ‹*merchandise/jewelry*› ordinario, de baratillo; ‹*mechanic/electrician*› (AmE) chapucero

B 1 (vulgar, contemptible) ‹*joke/gimmick*› de mal gusto; ‹*trick/tactics*› bajo, rastrero; ‹*liar/crook*› vil 2 (worthless) ‹*flattery/promises*› fácil; **words are ~** es fácil hablar 3 (stingy) (AmE colloq) agarrado (fam), apretado (fam)

cheap² *adv* **-er, -est the house was going ~** la casa se vendía barata

cheapen /ˈtʃiːpən/ *vt* quitarle valor a, degradar; **to ~ oneself** rebajarse, degradarse

cheaply /ˈtʃiːpli/ *adv* ‹*buy/sell/get*› barato, a bajo precio; ‹*dress/eat/live*› con poco dinero, económicamente

cheap: **~ shot** *n* (AmE) golpe *m* bajo; **~skate** *n* (colloq) agarrado, -da *m,f* (fam), apretado, -da *m,f* (fam)

cheat¹ /tʃiːt/ *vt* 1 (deceive) estafar, engañar, timar; **to ~ sb (OUT) OF sth**: **they were ~ed (out) of their land** los estafaron *or* engañaron *or* timaron quitándoles las tierras 2 (avoid) burlar; **he ~ed death** (liter) burló a la muerte (liter)

■ **cheat** *vi* 1 (act deceitfully) hacer* trampas 2 (be unfaithful) **to ~ ON sb** engañar a algn

cheat² *n* 1 (AmE also) **cheater** /ˈtʃiːtər || ˈtʃiːtə(r)/ (swindler) estafador, -dora *m,f*; (at cards) tramposo, -sa *m,f*, fulero, -ra *m,f* (Esp fam); (in exam) tramposo, -sa *m,f* (fam) 2 (trick, fraud) trampa *f*, estafa *f*

check¹ /tʃek/ *n*

A [c] (stop, restraint) control *m*, freno *m*; **to keep** *o* **hold sth/sb in ~** controlar *or* contener* algo/a algn; **to put a ~ to sth** (AmE) impedir* algo

B [c] 1 (inspection — of passport, documents) control *m*, revisión *f*; (— of work) examen *m*, revisión *f*; (— of machine, product) inspección *f*; **to keep a ~ on sth/sb** controlar *or* vigilar algo/a algn 2 (of facts) verificación *f*

C [c u] (cloth) tela *f* a *or* de cuadros; (*before n*) ‹*jacket/shirt*› a *or* de cuadros

D [u] (in chess) jaque *m*

E (Fin), (BrE) **cheque** cheque *m*, talón *m* (Esp); **to pay by ~** pagar* con cheque *or* (Esp) con talón; **a ~ for $50** un cheque de 50 dólares *or* por valor de 50 dólares

F [c] (restaurant bill) (AmE) cuenta *f*, adición *f* (RPl)

G [c] (tick) marca *f*, tic *m*, visto *m* (Esp), palomita *f* (Méx fam)

check² *vt*

A (restrain) ‹*enemy advance*› frenar; ‹*anger/impulse*› contener*

B 1 (inspect) ‹*passport/ticket*› revisar, controlar, checar* (Méx); ‹*machine/product*› inspeccionar; ‹*quality*› controlar; ‹*temperature/pressure/volume*› comprobar*, chequear, checar* (Méx) 2 (verify) ‹*facts/information*› comprobar*, verificar*, chequear, checar* (Méx); ‹*accounts/bill*› revisar, comprobar*; **to ~ sth AGAINST sth** cotejar *or* chequear algo CON algo; **~ that it's closed** asegúrate de que *or* comprueba que esté cerrado

C (AmE) 1 (deposit — in cloakroom) dejar en el guardarropa; (— in baggage office) dejar *or* (frml) depositar en consigna 2 (register) (Aviat) ‹*baggage*› facturar, chequear (AmL)

D (tick) (AmE) marcar*, hacer* un tic *or* (Méx fam) una palomita en, poner* un visto en (Esp)

■ **check** *vi* 1 (verify, make sure) comprobar*, verificar*, chequear, checar* (Méx); **just ~ing!** sólo me quería asegurar 2 (tally) (AmE) **to ~ WITH sth** coincidir *or* concordar* CON algo

(Phrasal verbs)

- **check in**

A [v ▸ adv] 1 (register) (at airport) facturar *or* (AmL tb) chequear el equipaje; (at hotel) registrarse 2 (make routine contact) (AmE): **he usually ~s in after lunch** generalmente llama/pasa después de comer

B [v ▸ o ▸ adv, v ▸ adv ▸ o] 1 (register) ‹*luggage*› facturar, chequear (AmL); **the girl who ~ed us in** la chica que nos atendió (*or* nos facturó el equipaje *etc*) 2 (return) (AmE) ‹*book/equipment*› devolver*

- **check off** [v ▸ o ▸ adv, v ▸ adv ▸ o] ‹*items/details*› ir* marcando

- **check out**

A [v ▸ adv (▸ prep ▸ o)] (leave): **he ~ed out (of the hotel) this morning** dejó el hotel esta mañana (*habiendo pasado la factura etc*)

B [v ▸ adv] (tally) (AmE) «*story*» cuadrar

C [v ▸ o ▸ adv, v ▸ adv ▸ o] 1 ‹*facts/story*› verificar*, comprobar*, chequear, checar* (Méx); **we must ~ out the new film** (colloq) tenemos que ir a ver qué tal es la nueva película 2 (esp AmE) ‹*shopping*› «*customer*» pagar*; «*cashier*» cobrar

- **check up** [v ▸ adv]: **to ~ up (ON sb/sth)**: **have you been ~ing up on me?** ¿me has estado vigilando *or* espiando?; **we ~ed up and found out he was lying** hicimos averiguaciones y comprobamos que mentía; **can you ~ up on that?** ¿puedes comprobarlo *or* confirmarlo?

check³ *interj* 1 (in chess) ¡jaque! 2 (expressing confirmation) (AmE colloq) ¡sí, señor!

checkbook, (BrE) **chequebook** /ˈtʃekbʊk/ *n* chequera *f*, talonario *m* de cheques (esp Esp)

checked /tʃekt/ *adj* (*no comp*) ‹*material/shirt*› a *or* de cuadros

checker /ˈtʃekər || ˈtʃekə(r)/ *n* (AmE) (cashier) cajero, -ra *m,f*

checkerboard /ˈtʃekərbɔːrd || ˈtʃekəbɔːd/ *n* (AmE) tablero *m* de ajedrez/damas

checkered, (BrE) **chequered** /ˈtʃekərd || ˈtʃekəd/ *adj* 1 ‹*career/history*› accidentado, con altibajos 2 ‹*pattern/design*› a *or* de cuadros

checkers /ˈtʃekərz || ˈtʃekəz/ *n* (AmE) (+ *sing vb*) damas *fpl*

check-in /ˈtʃekɪn/ *n* (at airport) (place & act) facturación *f* de equipajes; (*before n*) **~ desk** *o* **counter** (at airport) mostrador *m* de facturación; (in hotel) (AmE) recepción *f*; **~ time** hora *f* de facturación

checking account /ˈtʃekɪŋ/ *n* (AmE) cuenta *f* corriente

check: **~list** *n* lista *f* de control; **~mate** *n* [c u] (jaque *m*) mate *m*; **~out** *n* 1 (in supermarket) caja *f*; (*before n*) **~out counter** caja *f*; **~out girl** cajera *f* 2 (in hotel) (*before n*) **~out time** *hora en que se debe dejar libre la habitación*; **~point** *n* control *m*; **~room** *n* (AmE) guardarropa *m*; **~up** *n* 1 (Med) chequeo *m*, revisión *f*, reconocimiento *m* (médico) (frml); **to have a ~up** hacerse* un chequeo 2 (Dent) chequeo *m*, revisión *f* 3 (AmE Auto) revisión *f*, servicio *m* (AmL)

cheddar /ˈtʃedər || ˈtʃedə(r)/ *n* [u] queso *m* (de) Cheddar

cheek /tʃiːk/ *n*

A [c] (Anat) 1 (of the face) mejilla *f*, cachete *m* (AmL fam); ***~ by jowl with sb*** uno junto al otro; ***to turn the other* ~** dar* la otra mejilla 2 (buttock) (colloq) nalga *f*, cachete *m* (CS fam)

B [u] (colloq) (impudence) descaro *m*, frescura *f*, cara *f* (fam); **what (a) ~!** ¡qué cara (más dura)! (fam), ¡qué caradura es! (fam)

cheekbone /'tʃi:kbəʊn/ *n* pómulo *m*

cheekily /'tʃi:kəli || 'tʃi:kɪli/ *adv* descaradamente

cheeky /'tʃi:ki/ *adj* **-kier, -kiest** ‹*boy/girl*› fresco, atrevido, descarado; ‹*grin*› pícaro; ‹*remark*› impertinente

cheep¹ /tʃi:p/ *vi* piar*

cheep² *n* piada *f*, piído *m*

cheer¹ /tʃɪr || tʃɪə(r)/ *n*

A [c] 1 (of encouragement, approval) ovación *f*, aclamación *f*; **to give three ~s for sb** vitorear *or* (AmS tb) vivar a algn; **three ~s for Fred!** ¡viva Fred! 2 (cheerleaders' routine) (AmE) hurra *m*

B **cheers** *pl* (*as interj*) 1 (drinking toast) ¡salud! 2 (thanks) (BrE colloq) gracias

C [u] (cheerfulness) (liter) alegría *f*, animación *f*; **be of good ~** ¡ánimo!, ¡levanta el ánimo!

cheer² *vt*

A 1 (shout in approval) aclamar, vitorear 2 **~ (on)** (shout encouragement at) animar, darle* ánimos a

B (gladden, comfort) alegrar, reconfortar

■ **cheer** *vi* aplaudir, gritar entusiasmadamente

Phrasal verb

• **cheer up**

A [v ▸ adv] animarse

B [v ▸ o ▸ adv, v ▸ adv ▸ o] ‹*person*› animar, levantarle el ánimo a; **some bright curtains would ~ the room up** unas cortinas en colores vivos alegrarían el cuarto

cheerful /'tʃɪrfəl || 'tʃɪəfəl/ *adj* alegre; ‹*news/prospect*› alentador

cheerfully /'tʃɪrfəli || 'tʃɪəfəli/ *adv* alegremente; **I could have ~ murdered him** lo hubiera matado

cheerily /'tʃɪrəli || 'tʃɪərɪli/ *adv* con alegría

cheering¹ /'tʃɪrɪŋ || 'tʃɪərɪŋ/ *adj* alentador

cheering² *n* ovaciones *fpl*, aplausos *mpl*, vítores *mpl*

cheerio /'tʃɪri'əʊ || ˌtʃɪəri'əʊ/ *interj* (BrE colloq) (goodbye) hasta luego, chao *or* chau (esp AmL fam)

cheerleader /'tʃɪrˌli:dər || 'tʃɪəˌli:də(r)/ *n* animador, -dora *m,f* (*en encuentros deportivos, mitines políticos*), porrista *mf* (Col, Méx)

cheerless /'tʃɪrləs || 'tʃɪəlɪs/ *adj* ‹*room/house*› triste, sin alegría; ‹*day/landscape*› triste

cheery /'tʃɪri || 'tʃɪəri/ *adj* **-rier, -riest** ‹*smile*› de felicidad, alegre; ‹*greeting*› lleno de alegría; ‹*manner*› risueño y optimista

cheese /tʃi:z/ *n* [u c] queso *m*; **say ~!** (Phot) ¡sonría (*or* sonrían *etc*)!; ***hard ~*** mala pata (fam)

Phrasal verb

• **cheese off** [v ▸ o ▸ adv, v ▸ adv ▸ o] (BrE colloq) (*usu pass*): **to be ~d off** estar* mosqueado (fam)

cheese: **~board** *n* (course) tabla *f* de quesos; **~burger** *n* hamburguesa *f* con queso; **~cake** *n* [u c] (Culin) tarta *f* de queso; **~cloth** *n* [u] estopilla *f*, bambula *f*

cheeseparing /'tʃi:zˌperɪŋ || 'tʃi:zˌpeərɪŋ/ *adj* tacaño (fam)

cheesy /'tʃi:zi/ *adj* **-sier, -siest** 1 ‹*smell/taste*› (como) a queso 2 (shoddy) (AmE sl) de mala calidad, rasca (CS fam)

cheetah /'tʃi:tə/ *n* guepardo *m*, chita *f*

chef /ʃef/ *n* chef *m*, jefe, -fa *m,f* de cocina

chemical¹ /'kemɪkəl/ *n* [c u] sustancia *f* química, producto *m* químico

chemical² *adj* químico

chemist /'kemәst || 'kemɪst/ *n* 1 (scientist) químico, -ca *m,f* 2 (pharmacist) (BrE) farmacéutico, -ca *m,f*; **dispensing ~** farmacéutico, -ca *m,f*; **at the ~'s** en la farmacia

chemistry /'kemәstri || 'kemɪstri/ *n* [u] 1 (science) química *f* 2 (interaction) sintonía *f*, vibraciones *fpl*; **good/bad ~** buena/mala sintonía

chemotherapy /'ki:məʊ'θerәpi/ *n* [u] quimioterapia *f*

cheque /tʃek/ *n* (BrE) ▸**check¹** E; (*before n*) **~ (guarantee) card** tarjeta *f* bancaria

chequebook /'tʃekbʊk/ *n* (BrE) ▸**checkbook**

chequered /'tʃekərd || 'tʃekəd/ *adj* (BrE) ▸**checkered**

cherish /'tʃerɪʃ/ *vt* 1 (care for, value) apreciar, valorar 2 (cling to) ‹*memory/hope*› conservar, mantener*; ‹*illusion/dream*› abrigar*, acariciar 3 **cherished** *past p* preciado; **a long ~ed ambition** una ambición albergada durante largo tiempo

cheroot /ʃə'ru:t/ *n* puro *m* (*cortado en ambos extremos*)

cherry /'tʃeri/ *n* (*pl* **-ries**) 1 (fruit) cereza *f*; **black ~** guinda *f*; (*before n*) **~ brandy** aguardiente *m* de cerezas 2 (tree) cerezo *m*; (*before n*) **~ blossom** flor *f* de cerezo; **~ orchard** cerezal *m*

cherry-pick /'tʃeriˌpɪk/ *vt* ‹*candidates/students/proposals*› elegir* los mejores

cherry-red /'tʃeri'red/ *adj* (*pred* **cherry red**) rojo cereza *adj inv*, color guinda *adj inv*

cherub /'tʃerəb/ *n* querubín *m*

chess /tʃes/ *n* [u] ajedrez *m*

chessboard /'tʃesbɔ:rd/ *n* tablero *m* de ajedrez

chest /tʃest/ *n*

A (Anat) pecho *m*; ***to get sth off one's ~*** desahogarse* contando/confesando algo; ***to play o keep one's cards close to one's ~*** no soltar* prenda (fam)

B (box) arcón *m*

C (AmE) (treasury) tesorería *f*; (funds) fondos *mpl*

chestnut¹ /'tʃesnʌt/ *n*

A [c] 1 (nut) castaña *f* 2 **~ (tree)** castaño *m* 3 (old story) (colloq): **an old ~** una historia muy vieja *or* pasada

B [u] (color) castaño *m*

chestnut² *adj* ‹*horse*› castaño, zaino; ‹*hair*› castaño

chest of drawers *n* (*pl* **~s ~ ~**) cómoda *f*

chesty /'tʃesti/ *adj* **-tier, -tiest** (BrE Med) ‹*cough/cold*› de pecho

chew /tʃu:/ *vt* ‹*food*› mascar*, masticar*; ‹*nails/pencil*› morder*; ‹*tobacco/gum*› mascar*; ***to ~ the fat o rag*** (colloq) charlar *or* (esp AmL) conversar *or* (AmC, Méx) platicar*

■ **chew** *vi* **to ~ AT/ON sth** mordiscar* algo, mordisquear algo

Phrasal verbs

• **chew out** [v ▸ o ▸ adv, v ▸ adv ▸ o] (scold, reprimand) (AmE colloq) regañar, reñir* (Esp, Méx), retar (CS fam)

• **chew over** [v ▸ o ▸ adv, v ▸ adv ▸ o] (colloq) ‹*suggestion/offer*› considerar; ‹*problem*› darle* vueltas a

• **chew up** [v ▸ o ▸ adv, v ▸ adv ▸ o] (when eating) masticar* *or* mascar* bien; **the dog had ~ed up the carpet** el perro había destrozado la alfombra a mordiscos

chewing gum /'tʃu:ɪŋ/ *n* [u] chicle *m*

chewy /'tʃu:i/ *adj* **chewier, chewiest** ‹*meat*› duro, correoso, latigudo (Chi fam); ‹*candy*› masticable

chic /ʃi:k/ *adj* **-er, -est** chic

chicane /ʃɪ'keɪn/ *n* chicane *f*

chicanery /ʃɪ'keɪnəri/ *n* [u c] (*pl* **-eries**) (liter) argucia *f*

Chicano /tʃɪ'kɑ:nəʊ/ *n* (*pl* **-nos**) chicano *m*

> **Chicano**
>
> Estadounidense de origen mexicano. En un principio el término se usaba como insulto, pero en la actualidad ha dejado de serlo e incluso los propios mexicoamericanos lo prefieren

chick /tʃɪk/ *n* 1 (young bird) polluelo, -la *m,f*, pichón, -chona *m,f*; (young chicken) pollito, -ta *m,f* 2 (young woman) (sl) muchacha *f*, chavala *f* (Esp fam), pebeta *f* (RPl fam), cabra *f* (Chi fam)

chickadee /'tʃɪkədi:/ *n* (AmE) paro *m*, herrerillo *m*

chicken¹ /'tʃɪkən || 'tʃɪkɪn/ *n* 1 [c] (hen) gallina *f*; (as generic term) pollo *m*; **to play ~** jugar* a ver quién es más gallito; ***don't count your ~s (before they're hatched)*** no cantes victoria antes de tiempo; ***she's no (spring) ~*** no es ninguna niña *or* nena; ▸**roost²** 2 [u] (Culin) pollo *m*; (hen) gallina *f*

Phrasal verb

• **chicken out** [v ▸ adv (▸ prep ▸ o)] (colloq) acobardarse, achicarse* (fam), rajarse (fam); **to ~ out OF sth**: **she ~ed out of telling him** no se atrevió a decírselo

chicken² *adj* (colloq) (*pred*) gallina (fam)

chicken: **~ feed** *n* [u] (colloq) una miseria (fam), calderilla *f* (fam); **~hearted** /'tʃɪkən'hɑ:rtəd || ˌtʃɪkɪn'hɑ:tɪd/ *adj* cobarde, miedoso; **~pox** /'tʃɪkənpɑ:ks || 'tʃɪkɪnpɒks/ *n* [u] varicela *f*, peste *f* cristal (Chi); **~ wire** *n* [u] alambrera *f*

chick: **~ lit** /tʃɪk lɪt/ *n* [u] (colloq) chick lit *f*, literatura *f* para la mujer moderna; **~pea** /'tʃɪkpi:/ *n* garbanzo *m*

chicory /'tʃɪkəri/ *n* [u] (Bot) endivia *f*; (in coffee) achicoria *f*

C

chide /tʃaɪd/ *vt* (*past* **chided** *or* **chid** /tʃɪd/; *past p* **chided** *or* **chid** *or* **chidden** /'tʃɪdn̩/) (frml *or* lit in BrE) **to ~ sb (FOR sth/-ING)** reprender *or* censurar a algn (POR algo/+ INF)

chief[1] /tʃi:f/ *n* (head) jefe, -fa *m,f*, líder *mf*; **~ of police** jefe de policía

chief[2] *adj* (*before n, no comp*) (main) principal; (highest in rank): **~ constable** jefe, -fa *m,f* de policía

chief justice *n* (in US) presidente, -ta *m,f* del tribunal

chiefly /'tʃi:fli/ *adv* principalmente

chieftain /'tʃi:ftən/ *n* (of tribe) cacique *m*

chiffon /ʃɪ'fɑ:n || 'ʃɪfɒn/ *n* [u] chiffón *m*

chilblain /'tʃɪlbleɪn/ *n* sabañón *m*

child /tʃaɪld/ *n* (*pl* **children** /'tʃɪldrən/) 1 (boy) niño *m*; (girl) niña *f*; ***to be ~'s play*** ser* un juego de niños; (*before n*) ‹*psychology*› infantil; **~ benefit** (in UK) *prestación que se recibe del Estado por cada hijo independientemente del ingreso de los padres*, ≈ asignación *f* familiar (*en CS*); **~ labor** trabajo *m* de menores; *see also* **abuse**[1] **B** 2 (son) hijo *m*; (daughter) hija *f*; **have you any ~ren?** ¿tiene hijos?; **to be with ~** (liter) estar* encinta

child: **~bearing** *n* [u] maternidad *f*; (*before n*) **to be of ~bearing age** estar* en edad fértil; **~birth** *n* [u] parto *m*, alumbramiento *m* (frml); **she died in ~birth** murió de parto; **~care** *n* cuidado *m* de los niños, puericultura *f*

childhood /'tʃaɪldhʊd/ *n* [u c] niñez *f*, infancia *f*

childish /'tʃaɪldɪʃ/ *adj* (immature) infantil, pueril; (typical of a child) infantil

childishly /'tʃaɪldɪʃli/ *adv* de una manera infantil

childless /'tʃaɪldləs || 'tʃaɪldlɪs/ *adj* sin hijos

child: **~like** *adj* ingenuo, de niño; **~minder** *n* (BrE) ≈ niñero, -ra *m,f* (*que cuida a un niño mientras sus padres trabajan*), madre *f* del día (Esp); **~ molester** /mə'lestər || mə'lestə(r)/ *n*: *persona que somete a un niño a abusos deshonestos*; **~proof** *adj* a prueba de niños

children /'tʃɪldrən/ *pl of* **child**

Chile /'tʃɪli/ *n* Chile *m*

Chilean[1] /'tʃɪliən/ *adj* chileno

Chilean[2] *n* chileno, -na *m,f*

chili, chilli /'tʃɪli/ *n* (*pl* **-lies**) ají *m*, chile *m*; (*before n*) **~ powder** ají *or* chile en polvo

chill[1] /tʃɪl/ *n* 1 [u] (coldness — of weather) frío *m*, fresco *m*; **to take the ~ off/out of sth** templar *or* calentar* algo 2 [c] (Med) enfriamiento *m*, resfriado *m*; **to catch a ~** resfriarse*

chill[2] *vt* enfriar*; ‹*wine/food*› poner* a enfriar; ❸ **serve chilled** sírvase frío; **we were ~ed to the bone** estábamos congelados (de frío)

(Phrasal verb)

• **chill out** [v ▸ adv] (colloq) 1 (calm down) tranquilizarse; **come on man, ~ out!** ¡vamos hombre, tú tranqui! (fam) 2 (pass time) pasar el tiempo

chiller /'tʃɪlər || 'tʃɪlə(r)/ *n*

A (refrigerator) refrigerador *m*

B (colloq) película *f* de suspenso *or* (Esp) de suspense y terror

chill factor *n* [u] sensación *f* térmica (*por efecto de la exposición al viento*)

chilli *n* (*pl* **-lies**) ▸**chili**

chilling /'tʃɪlɪŋ/ *adj* escalofriante, espeluznante

chill-out /'tʃɪl,aʊt/ *adj* (colloq) ‹*area/room*› de descanso, de chill-out (fam)

chilly /'tʃɪli/ *adj* **-lier, -liest** 1 ‹*room/weather*› frío; **~ today, isn't it?** hace fresquito hoy ¿no? 2 ‹*greeting*› frío

chime[1] /tʃaɪm/ *n* 1 (sound — of bells) repique *m*; (— of clock) campanada *f*; (— of doorbell) campanilla *f* 2 (device) (*usu pl*) carillón *m*

chime[2] *vt* ‹*tune*› tocar*

■ **chime** *vi* «*bell*» sonar*, repicar*; «*clock*» dar* la hora

(Phrasal verb)

• **chime in** [v ▸ adv] (colloq) meter (la) cuchara (fam)

chimera /kaɪ'mɪrə || kaɪ'mɪərə/ *n* quimera *f*

chimney /'tʃɪmni/ *n* chimenea *f*; ***to smoke like a ~*** (colloq) fumar como un carretero *or* una chimenea (fam)

chimney sweep *n* deshollinador, -dora *m,f*

chimp /tʃɪmp/ *n* (colloq) chimpancé *m*

chimpanzee /'tʃɪmpæn'zi:/ *n* chimpancé *m*

chin /tʃɪn/ *n* barbilla *f*, mentón *m*, pera *f* (CS fam); ***to keep one's ~ up*** no perder* el ánimo; **~ up!** (colloq) ¡ánimo! (fam); ***to take it on the ~*** (AmE) sufrir las consecuencias, pagar* el pato (fam); ***to take sth on the ~*** (suffer stoically) (BrE) aguantar algo con resignación

china /'tʃaɪnə/ *n* [u] (ceramic ware) loza *f*; (fine) porcelana *f*

China /'tʃaɪnə/ *n* China *f*

Chinese[1] /tʃaɪ'ni:z/ *adj* chino

Chinese[2] *n* (*pl* ~) 1 [c] (person) chino, -na *m,f* 2 [u] (language) chino *m*

Chinese whispers *n* (+ *sing vb*) juego *m* del teléfono

chink[1] /tʃɪŋk/ *n*

A (crack — in fence, wall) grieta *f*, abertura *f*; (— of door) rendija *f*, resquicio *m*; **a ~ of light entered through the shutters** la luz entraba por las rendijas de la persiana

B ***a ~ in sb's armor***: **they found a ~ in his armor** le encontraron un punto flaco *or* débil

C (of coins, glasses) tintineo *m*

chink[2] *vt* ‹*glasses*› hacer* tintinear; ‹*coins*› hacer* sonar

■ **chink** *vi* «*glasses*» tintinear; «*coins*» sonar*

chino /'tʃi:nəʊ/ *n*

A (Tex) *gabardina de algodón de color caqui*

B **chinos** *pl* (Clothing) pantalones *mpl* chinos

chintzy /'tʃɪntsi/ *adj* **-zier, -ziest** 1 (shoddy, cheap) (AmE colloq) barato, ordinario 2 (flowery, pretty) (BrE) ‹*decor/furnishings*› coquetón (fam)

chinwag /'tʃɪnwæg/ *n* (colloq) (*no pl*) cháchara *f* (fam); **to have a ~** chacharear (fam)

chip[1] /tʃɪp/ *n*

A 1 (of wood) astilla *f*; (of stone) esquirla *f*; ***he's/she's a ~ off the old block*** de tal palo tal astilla; ***to have a ~ on one's shoulder*** ser* un resentido 2 (crack, break) desportilladura *f*, muesca *f*

B (Culin) 1 (thin, crisp slice): **(potato) ~s** (AmE) papas *fpl* *or* (Esp) patatas *fpl* fritas, patatas *fpl* a la inglesa (Esp), papas *fpl* chip (Ur) 2 (French fry) (BrE) papa *f* *or* (Esp) patata *f* frita; (*before n*) **~ shop** pescadería *f* (*donde se vende pescado frito y papas fritas*)

C (counter) (Games) ficha *f*; ***to be in the ~s*** (AmE) estar* rico *or* boyante; ***to have had one's ~s*** (BrE colloq): **I thought I'd had my ~s** creí que me había llegado la hora; ***when the ~s are down*** (colloq) a la hora de la verdad

D (Comput, Electron) chip *m*; **silicon ~** pastilla *f* de silicio

chip[2] **-pp-** *vt*

A 1 (damage) ‹*crockery*› desportillar, cascar* (RPl), saltar (Chi); ‹*tooth*› romper* un trocito de 2 (cut, break) ‹*hole*› hacer*, abrir*; **I ~ped off the old plaster** quité el yeso viejo quebrándolo *or* rompiéndolo

B (slice) (Culin) cortar; **~ped beef** (AmE) *carne de vaca ahumada y cortada en rodajas finas*

C (in golf, tennis, soccer) *levantar la pelota mediante un golpe corto y preciso*

■ **chip** *vi* «*china/cup*» desportillarse, cascarse* (RPl), saltarse (Chi); «*paint/varnish*» saltarse, desconcharse

(Phrasal verb)

• **chip in** [v ▸ adv] (colloq) 1 (speak) meter (la) cuchara (fam) 2 (contribute) contribuir*

chipboard /'tʃɪpbɔ:rd || 'tʃɪpbɔ:d/ *n* [u] 1 (of wood) madera *f* prensada *or* aglomerada, aglomerado *m* 2 (of paper) (AmE) cartón *m* prensado

chipmunk /'tʃɪpmʌŋk/ *n* ardilla *f* listada

chippings /'tʃɪpɪŋz/ *pl n* (BrE) gravilla *f*, cascajo *m*

chiropodist /kə'rɑ:pədəst || kɪ'rɒpədɪst/ *n* pedicuro, -ra *m,f*, podólogo, -ga *m,f*, callista *mf*

chiropody /kə'rɑ:pədi || kɪ'rɒpədi/ *n* [u] podología *m*

chirp[1] /tʃɜ:rp || tʃɜ:p/ *vi* «*bird*» piar*

■ **chirp** *vt* decir* alegremente

chirp[2] *n* [c u] (of bird) piada *f*, piído *m*

chirpy /'tʃɜ:rpi/ *adj* **-pier, -piest** (BrE colloq) alegre

chirrup /'tʃɪrəp/ *n/vi/t* ▸**chirp**[1,2]

chisel[1] /'tʃɪzəl/ *n* (for stone) cincel *m*; (for wood) formón *m*, escoplo *m*

chisel[2] *vt*, (BrE) **-ll-** 1 ‹*stone*› cincelar; ‹*wood*› labrar, tallar 2 **chiseled** *past p*: **his finely ~ed features** sus finamente cincelados *or* dibujados rasgos

chit /tʃɪt/ *n* (receipt) recibo *m*, resguardo *m*; (note) nota *f*; (to exchange for sth) vale *m*

chitchat /'tʃɪttʃæt/ *n* [u] (colloq) cháchara *f* (fam)

chivalrous /'ʃɪvəlrəs/ *adj* cortés, caballeroso

chivalry /ˈʃɪvəlri/ *n* [u] (in conduct) caballerosidad *f*, cortesía *f*; (Hist) caballería *f*

chives /tʃaɪvz/ *pl n* cebollinos *mpl*, cebolletas *fpl*

chivvy /ˈtʃɪvi/ *vt* **chivvies, chivvying, chivvied** ▸**chivy**

chivy /ˈtʃɪvi/ *vt* **chivies, chivying, chivied** (colloq) ‹*person*› meterle prisa a, apurar (AmL); **she had to ~ me into applying** me tuvo que empujar para que hiciera la solicitud

chlorinate /ˈklɔːrəneɪt || ˈklɔːrɪneɪt/ *vt* clorar, tratar con cloro

chlorine /ˈklɔːriːn/ *n* [u] cloro *m*

chlorofluorocarbon /ˈklɔːrəʊˈflʊrəʊˈkɑːrbən || ˌklɔːrəʊˌflʊərəʊˈkɑːbən, -flɔːrə-/ *n* clorofluorocarbono *m*

chloroform /ˈklɔːrəfɔːrm || ˈklɒrəfɔːm/ *n* [u] cloroformo *m*

chlorophyl, (BrE) **chlorophyll** /ˈklɔːrəfɪl || ˈklɒrəfɪl/ *n* [u] clorofila *f*

choc-ice /ˈtʃɑːkaɪs || ˈtʃɒkaɪs/ *n* (BrE) bombón *m* helado

chock-a-block /ˈtʃɑːkəˈblɑːk || ˌtʃɒkəˈblɒk/ *adj* (colloq) (*pred*) **to be ~ (WITH sth/sb)** estar* hasta los topes (DE algo/algn) (fam)

chock-full /ˈtʃɑːkˈfʊl || ˌtʃɒkˈfʊl/ *adj* (*pred*) **to be ~ OF** *o* **WITH sth/sb** estar* hasta los topes DE algo/algn (fam)

chocolate¹ /ˈtʃɑːklət || ˈtʃɒklət/ *n*

A **1** [u c] chocolate *m*; (candy, sweet) bombón *m*; **milk/dark** *o* (BrE) **plain ~** chocolate con/sin leche; (*before n*) ‹*egg/cake*› de chocolate; **~ bar** chocolatina *f*, chocolatín *m* (RPl); **~-chip cookie** *galleta con pedacitos de chocolate*; **~ liqueur** bombón de licor **2** [u] (*drinking ~*) chocolate *m* en polvo; **a cup of hot ~** una taza de chocolate

B [u] (color) color *m* chocolate, marrón *m* *or* (Chi, Méx) café *m* *or* (Col) carmelito *m* oscuro

chocolate² *adj* (in color) color chocolate *adj inv*, marrón *or* (Chi, Méx) café *or* (Col) carmelito oscuro *adj inv*

choice¹ /tʃɔɪs/ *n*

A [c u] (act, option) elección *f*; **I had no ~ but to obey** no tuve más remedio *or* alternativa que obedecer; **to make one's ~** elegir*, escoger*; **I'm single by ~** no me he casado porque no he querido *or* por decisión propia; **you can take any two books of your ~** puede llevarse dos libros a elección

B **1** [c] (person, thing chosen): **she's a possible ~ for the job** es una de las candidatas posibles para el puesto; **it was an unfortunate ~ of words** no fue la mejor manera de decirlo **2** (variety) (*no pl*) surtido *m*, selección *f*; **to be spoiled for ~** (BrE) tener* mucho de donde elegir

choice² *adj* **choicer, choicest**

A (high-quality) ‹*fruit/vegetables/wine*› selecto, escogido; ‹*beef/veal*› (in US) de primera

B ‹*language/phrase*› (liter) exquisito; **he used some ~ language when he found out** (iro) soltó unas perlitas cuando se enteró (iró)

choir /kwaɪr || ˈkwaɪə(r)/ *n* coro *m*

choirboy /ˈkwaɪrbɔɪ || ˈkwaɪəbɔɪ/ *n*: *niño que canta en un coro de iglesia*

choke¹ /tʃəʊk/ *vt*

A (stifle) estrangular, ahogar*, asfixiar; **a voice ~d by sobs** una voz ahogada en llanto

B (overwhelm): **the garden is ~d with weeds** el jardín está invadido de malezas

■ **choke** *vi* ahogarse*, asfixiarse; **to ~ ON sth** atragantarse *or* (AmL tb) atorarse CON algo

(Phrasal verbs)

• **choke back** [v ▸ adv ▸ o] ‹*tears*› contener*, tragarse*; **I ~d back my anger** me contuve

• **choke up**

A [v ▸ o ▸ adv, v ▸ adv ▸ o] (block) ‹*drain/pipe*› obstruir*, atascar*, tapar (AmL)

B [v ▸ adv] (colloq) (fail) (AmE) fallar

choke² *n* [c u] (Auto) choke *m*, estárter *m*, cebador *m* (RPl), chupete *m* (Chi)

choked /tʃəʊkt/ *adj* (husky): **goodbye, he said in a ~ voice** —adiós —dijo, con la voz entrecortada por la emoción

choker /ˈtʃəʊkər || ˈtʃəʊkə(r)/ *n* (necklace) gargantilla *f*

cholera /ˈkɑːlərə || ˈkɒlərə/ *n* [u] cólera *m*

cholesterol /kəˈlestərəʊl || kəˈlestərɒl/ *n* [u] colesterol *m*

chomp /tʃɑːmp || tʃɒmp/ *vt/i* mascar*, masticar*

choose /tʃuːz/ (*past* **chose**; *past p* **chosen**) *vt* **1** (select) elegir*, escoger*; ‹*candidate*› elegir* **2** (decide) **to ~ to + INF** decidir + INF, optar POR + INF

■ **choose** *vi* elegir*, escoger*; **you can ~ from this range** puede elegir *or* escoger dentro de esta gama; **there's little** *o* **not much to ~ between them** no hay gran diferencia entre ellos

choosy /ˈtʃuːzi/ *adj* **-sier, -siest** (colloq) exigente, difícil de contentar

chop¹ /tʃɑːp || tʃɒp/ *n*

A **1** (with ax, cleaver) hachazo *m*; (with hand) manotazo *m*; (Sport) golpe *m* cortado; (in karate) golpe *m* **2** (dismissal, cancellation) (BrE colloq): **to give sb the ~** echar a algn; **they all got the ~** los echaron a todos

B (Culin) chuleta *f*, costilla *f* (AmS)

C **chops** *pl* (colloq) (of person) boca *f*, jeta *f* (fam), morro *m* (fam); **to lick** *o* **smack one's ~s** relamerse; **to bust sb's ~s** (AmE sl) arremeter contra algn

chop² **-pp-** *vt* **1** (cut) ‹*wood*› cortar; ‹*meat/apple*› cortar (*en trozos pequeños*); ‹*parsley/onion*› picar* **2** **chopped** *past p* ‹*onions/herbs*› picado; ‹*meat*› (AmE) molido *or* (Esp, RPl) picado

■ **chop** *vi* (strike) golpear, cortar; **to ~ and change** (BrE colloq) cambiar continuamente

(Phrasal verbs)

• **chop down** [v ▸ o ▸ adv, v ▸ adv ▸ o] ‹*tree*› cortar, talar; ‹*branch/pole*› cortar

• **chop off** [v ▸ o ▸ adv, v ▸ adv ▸ o] ‹*branch*› cortar; ‹*finger*› cortar, cercenar

• **chop up** [v ▸ o ▸ adv, v ▸ adv ▸ o] ‹*onion/parsley*› picar*; ‹*meat/apple*› cortar (*en trozos pequeños*)

chopper /ˈtʃɑːpər || ˈtʃɒpə(r)/ *n*

A (hatchet) hacha *f*‡ pequeña

B (helicopter) (colloq) helicóptero *m*

C **choppers** *pl* (colloq) dientes *mpl* postizos, comedor *m* (fam & hum)

chopping board /ˈtʃɑːpɪŋ || ˈtʃɒpɪŋ/ *n* tabla *f* de picar

choppy /ˈtʃɑːpi || ˈtʃɒpi/ *adj* **-pier, -piest** ‹*sea*› picado

chopstick /ˈtʃɑːpstɪk || ˈtʃɒpstɪk/ *n* palillo *m* (*para comer comida oriental*)

choral /ˈkɔːrəl/ *adj* coral

chord /kɔːrd || kɔːd/ *n* (Mus) acorde *m*; ***to strike a ~***: **that struck a ~ with her** eso le tocó la fibra sensible; **his speech struck the right ~ with the audience** su discurso estuvo en perfecta sintonía con el sentir del público

chore /tʃɔːr || tʃɔː(r)/ *n* (routine task) tarea *f*; (tedious task) lata *f* (fam)

choreographer /ˈkɔːriˈɑːgrəfər || ˌkɒriˈɒgrəfə(r)/ *n* coreógrafo, -fa *m,f*

choreography /ˈkɔːriˈɑːgrəfi || ˌkɒriˈɒgrəfi/ *n* [u] coreografía *f*

chortle¹ /ˈtʃɔːrtl || ˈtʃɔːtl/ *vi* **to ~ (OVER sth)** reírse* (DE algo) (*con satisfacción*)

chortle² *n* risa *f* (*de satisfacción*)

chorus /ˈkɔːrəs/ *n*

A (+ *sing o pl vb*) (in musical, opera, tragedy) coro *m*; (*before n*) **~ girl** corista *f*; **~ line** coro *m*

B **1** (refrain) estribillo *m*; (choral piece) coral *m* **2** (outburst) coro *m*; **a ~ of protest** un coro de protestas

chose /tʃəʊz/ *past of* **choose**

chosen¹ /ˈtʃəʊzən/ *past p of* **choose**

chosen² *adj* (*before n*): **only a ~ few were invited to attend** sólo invitaron a una selecta minoría; **God's ~ people** el pueblo elegido

chow /tʃaʊ/ *n* [u] (food) (sl) comida *f*

chowder /ˈtʃaudər || ˈtʃaudə(r)/ *n* [u] *sopa o guiso de pescado*

Chrissake /ˈkraɪsseɪk/ *interj*: **for ~** (sl) ¡por Dios!, ¡por favor!

Christ /kraɪst/ *n* **1** (Relig) Cristo **2** (*as interj*) (colloq) ¡Jesús! (fam); **for ~'s sake!** ¡por amor de Dios!

christen /ˈkrɪsn/ *vt* **1** (baptize) bautizar* **2** (use for first time) (esp BrE colloq) estrenar

Christendom /ˈkrɪsndəm/ *n* (frml) la Cristiandad

C

christening /ˈkrɪsn̩ɪŋ/ *n* [u c] bautismo *m*, bautizo *m*

Christian¹ /ˈkrɪstʃən/ *n* cristiano, -na *m,f*

Christian² *adj* cristiano

Christian Democrat *n* cristiano, -na *m,f* demócrata

Christianity /ˈkrɪstiˈænəti, ˈkrɪstʃi- ‖ ˌkrɪstiˈænətɪ/ *n* [u] (faith) cristianismo *m*; (believers) los cristianos, el cristianismo

Christian: ~ **name** *n* nombre *m* de pila; ~ **Scientist** *n* Cientista Cristiano, -na *m,f*, Científico Cristiano, Científica Cristiana *m,f*

Christmas /ˈkrɪsməs/ *n* Navidad *f*, Pascua *f* (Chi, Per); (~*time*) las Navidades, la Navidad, la Pascua (Chi, Per); **merry** *o* (BrE also) **happy** ~! ¡Feliz Navidad!, ¡Felices Pascuas!; (*before n*) ~ **cake** pastel *m* de Navidad (*pastel de frutas cubierto de mazapán y azúcar glaseado*); ~ **card** tarjeta *f* de Navidad, tarjeta *f* de Pascua (Chi, Per), crismas *m* (Esp); ~ **carol** villancico *m*; ~ **cracker** (BrE) *sorpresa que se abre durante la comida de Navidad*; ~ **Day** día *m* de Navidad *or* (Chi, Per tb) de Pascua; ~ **dinner** comida *f* de Navidad; ~ **Eve** (day) la víspera de Navidad; (evening) Nochebuena *f*; ~ **present** *o* (esp AmE) **gift** regalo *m* de Navidad *or* (Chi, Per tb) de Pascua; ~ **pudding** (esp BrE) pudding *m* de Navidad (*hecho a base de frutas confitadas y coñac*), plum pudding *m*; ~ **tree** árbol *m* de Navidad *or* (Chi, Per tb) de Pascua

chrome /krəʊm/ *n* [u] cromo *m*

chromium /ˈkrəʊmiəm/ *n* [u] cromo *m*; (*before n*) ~ **plating** cromado *m*

chromosome /ˈkrəʊməsəʊm/ *n* cromosoma *m*

chronic /ˈkrɑːnɪk ‖ ˈkrɒnɪk/ *adj* 1 (Med) crónico; ‹*unemployment/shortages*› crónico; ‹*smoker/liar*› empedernido; ~ **fatigue syndrome** [u] síndrome *m* de fatiga crónica, SFC *m* 2 (terrible) (BrE colloq) pésimo, terrible

chronicle /ˈkrɑːnɪkəl ‖ ˈkrɒnɪkəl/ *n* crónica *f*

chronological /ˈkrɑːnəˈlɑːdʒɪkəl ‖ ˌkrɒnəˈlɒdʒɪkəl/ *adj* cronológico; **in** ~ **order** en *or* por orden cronológico

chronology /krəˈnɑːlədʒi ‖ krəˈnɒlədʒi/ *n* [u c] (*pl* **-gies**) cronología *f*

chronometer /krəˈnɑːmətər ‖ krəˈnɒmɪtə(r)/ *n* cronómetro *m*

chrysalis /ˈkrɪsələs ‖ ˈkrɪsəlɪs/ *n* crisálida *f*

chrysanthemum /krɪˈsænθəməm/ *n* crisantemo *m*

chubby /ˈtʃʌbi/ *adj* **-bier, -biest** (colloq) ‹*legs/cheeks/face*› regordete (fam); ‹*person*› gordinflón (fam), regordete (fam); **~-cheeked** mofletudo

chuck¹ /tʃʌk/ *vt*

A (colloq) 1 (throw) tirar, aventar* (Col, Méx, Per) 2 (throw away) tirar, botar (AmL exc RPl) 3 (give up) (colloq) ‹*job*› dejar, plantar (fam); ‹*boyfriend/girlfriend*› plantar (fam), botar (AmC, Chi fam), largar* (RPl fam)

B **to ~ sb under the chin** darle* una palmadita en la barbilla a algn

Phrasal verbs

- **chuck away** [v ▸ o ▸ adv, v ▸ adv ▸ o] 1 (squander, waste) (colloq) ‹*money*› derrochar, despilfarrar, tirar; ‹*opportunity*› desperdiciar 2 ▸**chuck out A 1**
- **chuck in** [v ▸ o ▸ adv, v ▸ adv ▸ o] ‹*job/studies*› (BrE colloq) dejar, mandar al diablo (fam)
- **chuck out** (colloq)

A [v ▸ o ▸ adv, v ▸ adv ▸ o] 1 (get rid of) ‹*rubbish*› tirar, botar (AmL exc RPl) 2 (reject) (BrE) ‹*plan/suggestion*› rechazar*

B [v ▸ o ▸ adv, v ▸ adv ▸ o] (expel) echar

- **chuck up** [v ▸ adv] (vomit) (sl) lanzar* (fam), guacarear (Méx fam), buitrear (Chi, Per fam)

chuck² *n* [u] *corte de carne vacuna del cuarto delantero*

chuckle¹ /ˈtʃʌkəl/ *vi* reírse*

chuckle² *n* risita *f*; **they had a ~ over** *o* **about that** se estuvieron riendo de eso

chuck wagon *n* (AmE) *furgón en el que se transportan víveres y utensilios de cocina*

chuffed /tʃʌft/ *adj* (BrE colloq) (*pred*) contento

chug /tʃʌg/ *vi* **-gg-** (+ *adv compl*): **the engine ~ged up the hill** la locomotora subió la cuesta dando resoplidos; **the project is ~ging along** el proyecto sigue marchando

chugalug /ˈtʃʌgəlʌg/ *vt* **-gg-** (AmE colloq) beberse *or* tomarse de un trago

chum /tʃʌm/ *n*

A [c] (friend) (colloq) amigo, -ga *m,f*, compinche *mf* (fam), cuate *m* (Méx fam), pata *m* (Per fam), pana *mf* (Ven fam)

B [u] (bait) (AmE) carnada *f*, cebo *m*

chunk /tʃʌŋk/ *n* (of bread, meat) pedazo *m*, trozo *m*, cacho *m* (fam)

chunky /ˈtʃʌŋki/ *adj* **-kier, -kiest** 1 ‹*person*› fornido, macizo; ‹*sweater*› grueso, gordo (fam) 2 ‹*marmalade*› con trozos grandes de cáscara

Chunnel /ˈtʃʌnl̩/ *n* (colloq) **the** ~ el Eurotúnel, el túnel del Canal de la Mancha

chunter on /ˈtʃʌntər ‖ ˈtʃʌntə(r)/[v ▸ adv ▸ prep ▸ o] (BrE colloq): **to ~ on about sth** darle* al tema de (fam)

church /tʃɜːrtʃ ‖ tʃɜːtʃ/ *n* (building) iglesia *f*; **the C~** (as organization) la Iglesia; **the C~ of England/Scotland** la Iglesia Anglicana/Presbiteriana Escocesa; **to go to ~** ir* a la iglesia, ≈ ir* a misa; (*before n*) **a ~ service** un oficio religioso; **he wants a ~ wedding** quiere casarse por la Iglesia *or* (Bol, Per, RPl) por iglesia

Church of England

La Iglesia Anglicana, protestante, es la Iglesia oficial de Inglaterra. Fue creada en 1534, bajo el reinado de Enrique VIII, por una ley suprema (*Act of Supremacy*) mediante la cual el rey reemplazó al Papa como jefe de la Iglesia en Inglaterra. En la actualidad el monarca lo sigue siendo, pero sus obispos y arzobispos son designados a propuesta del Primer Ministro (*Prime Minister*). El jefe espiritual de la Iglesia es el Arzobispo de Canterbury. Inglaterra está dividida en 44 diócesis y 13.000 parroquias (*parishes*) cada una de las cuales está a cargo de un párroco (*vicar*). En 1992, el *General Synod* u organismo rector de la Iglesia, permitió a las mujeres ser párrocos. En muchos países del mundo donde existen comunidades miembros de la *Anglican Communion*, como EEUU o Escocia, los anglicanos se autodenominan *Episcopalians*

Church of Scotland

La Iglesia Presbiteriana Escocesa es la Iglesia oficial de Escocia. Tuvo sus inicios en 1560, encabezada por John Knox y Andrew Melville y fue aceptada oficialmente en 1690. No tiene obispos y los miembros de su clero se denominan *ministers* o pastores en lugar de sacerdotes. Tanto los hombres como las mujeres pueden ser *ministers*

churchgoer /ˈtʃɜːrtʃˌgəʊər ‖ ˈtʃɜːtʃˌgəʊə(r)/ *n* practicante *mf*

churlish /ˈtʃɜːrlɪʃ ‖ ˈtʃɜːlɪʃ/ *adj* grosero, maleducado

churn¹ /tʃɜːrn ‖ tʃɜːn/ *n* (for making butter) mantequera *f*

churn² *vt* 1 ‹*milk*› batir; ‹*butter*› hacer*; ‹*water/mud*› agitar, revolver* 2 (Fin) ‹*account/portfolio*› hacer* rotar en exceso (*para incrementar comisiones*)

■ **churn** *vi* ‹‹*water*›› arremolinarse; **my stomach was ~ing** (with nerves) tenía un nudo en el estómago; (with nausea) tenía el estómago revuelto

Phrasal verbs

- **churn out** [v ▸ o ▸ adv, v ▸ adv ▸ o] (colloq) producir* como salchichas (fam)
- **churn up** [v ▸ o ▸ adv, v ▸ adv ▸ o] revolver*

chute /ʃuːt/ *n* tolva *f*, vertedor *m*; (in swimming pool, amusement park) tobogán *m*, rodadero *m* (Col)

chutes and ladders *n* (AmE) juego *m* de la oca, serpientes y escaleras *fpl*

chutney /ˈtʃʌtni/ *n* [u] chutney *m* (*conserva agridulce que se come con carnes, queso etc*)

CIA *n* (= **Central Intelligence Agency**) CIA *f*

CID *n* (in UK) = **Criminal Investigation Department**

cider /ˈsaɪdər ‖ ˈsaɪdə(r)/ *n* [u c] 1 (alcoholic) sidra *f*; **hard ~** (AmE) sidra fermentada 2 (non-alcoholic) (AmE): **(sweet) ~** jugo *m* *or* (Esp) zumo *m* de manzana

cigar /sɪˈgɑːr ‖ sɪˈgɑː(r)/ *n* cigarro *m*, puro *m*, tabaco *m* (Col)

cigarette /ˈsɪgəˈret/ *n* cigarrillo *m*; (*before n*) **~ butt** *o* **end** colilla *f*; **~ holder** boquilla *f*; **~ lighter** encendedor *m*, mechero *m* (Esp)

cinch¹ /sɪntʃ/ *n* (colloq) (*no pl*) 1 (easy task): **it's a ~** es pan comido (fam), es tirado (Esp fam), es una papa *or* un bollo (RPl fam), es botado (Chi fam) 2 (certainty) (AmE): **it's a**

~ **that she'll get the part** (de) fijo que le dan el papel (fam)

cinch² *vt* (AmE) (make sure of) (colloq) asegurar

cinder /'sɪndər || 'sɪndə(r)/ *n* 1▸ [c] (ember) carbonilla *f*, carboncillo *m*; **the dinner was burnt to a ~** la cena estaba carbonizada 2▸ **cinders** *pl* (ashes) ceniza *f*, rescoldo *m*

Cinderella /'sɪndə'relə/ *n* (Lit) (la) Cenicienta

cinder track *n* pista *f* de ceniza

cinecamera /'sɪni,kæmərə/ *n* (BrE) filmadora *f* (AmL), tomavistas *m* (Esp); (large, professional) cámara *f* cinematográfica

cinema /'sɪnəmə || 'sɪnəmɑː/ *n* 1▸ [c] (building) (BrE) cine *m*; **what's on at the ~?** ¿qué dan en el cine? 2▸ [u] (films) cine *m*; **French ~** el cine francés

cinemagoer /'sɪnəmə,gəʊər || 'sɪnəmə,gəʊə(r)/ *n*: **he's a keen ~** es muy aficionado al cine

cinnamon /'sɪnəmən/ *n* [u] 1▸ (Culin) canela *f*; (*before n*) ~ **stick** trozo *m* de canela en rama 2▸ (color) canela *m*

cipher /'saɪfər || 'saɪfə(r)/ *n* [c u] (code) clave *f*, cifra *f*

circa /'sɜːrkə || 'sɜːkə/ *prep* alrededor de, hacia

circle¹ /'sɜːrkəl || 'sɜːkəl/ *n*

A 1▸ (shape) círculo *m*; ***to come/go full*** ~ volver* al punto de partida; ***to go around in ~s***: **the negotiations seem to be going around in ~s** las negociaciones están estancadas *or* en un (*or* una) impasse; ***to run around in ~s***: **I was running around in ~s trying to get everything ready** estaba (dando vueltas) como loco tratando de tenerlo todo listo 2▸ (of trees, houses) círculo *m*, cinturón *m* 3▸ (around eye) ojera *f*

B (BrE Theat): **dress ~** primer piso *m*, platea *f* alta; **upper ~** segundo piso *m*

C (group) círculo *m*; **their ~ of friends** su círculo de amigos; **in business ~s** en el mundo de los negocios

circle² *vt*

A (move around) dar* vueltas alrededor de; (be around) rodear, cercar*; **we ~d the landing site** sobrevolamos en círculo el lugar de aterrizaje

B (draw circle around) trazar* un círculo alrededor de

■ **circle** *vi* dar* vueltas; «*aircraft/bird*» volar* en círculos, circunvolar* (frml); **to ~ AROUND sth** dar* vueltas ALREDEDOR DE algo

circuit /'sɜːrkət || 'sɜːkɪt/ *n*

A (passage around) recorrido *m*, vuelta *f*; **the athlete ran six ~s of the track** el atleta dio seis vueltas a la pista

B (Elec) circuito *m*

C (motor racing track) autódromo *m*, pista *f*

circuit board *n* placa *f* base

circuitous /sər'kjuːətəs || sɜː'kjuːɪtəs/ *adj* (frml) ‹*route*› poco directo; ‹*argument*› que no conduce a nada

circuitry /'sɜːrkətri || 'sɜːkɪtrɪ/ *n* [u] sistema *m* de circuitos

circuit training *n* [u] tabla *f* (de gimnasia)

circular¹ /'sɜːrkjələr || 'sɜːkjʊlə(r)/ *adj* 1▸ (round) circular, redondo 2▸ (making a circuit) ‹*route*› de circunvalación; **a ~ tour** un circuito 3▸ ‹*argument*› viciado

circular² *n* circular *f*

circular saw *n* sierra *f* circular

circulate /'sɜːrkjəleɪt || 'sɜːkjʊleɪt/ *vi* circular

■ **circulate** *vt* (disseminate) ‹*report/news*› hacer* circular, divulgar*

circulation /'sɜːrkjə'leɪʃən || ,sɜːkjʊ'leɪʃən/ *n* [u] circulación *f*; **to be in/out of ~** estar* en/fuera de circulación

circumcise /'sɜːrkəmsaɪz || 'sɜːkəmsaɪz/ *vt* circuncidar

circumcision /'sɜːrkəm'sɪʒən || ,sɜːkəm'sɪʒən/ *n* [c u] circuncisión *f*

circumference /sər'kʌmfərəns || sə'kʌmfərəns/ *n* circunferencia *f*

circumflex (accent) /'sɜːrkəmfleks || 'sɜːkəmfleks/ *n* (acento *m*) circunflejo *m*

circumnavigate /'sɜːrkəm'nævəgeɪt || ,sɜːkəm'nævɪgeɪt/ *vt* circunnavegar*

circumscribe /'sɜːrkəmskraɪb || 'sɜːkəmskraɪb/ *vt* (frml) limitar, restringir*

circumspect /'sɜːrkəmspekt || 'sɜːkəmspekt/ *adj* (frml) circunspecto (frml), cauto

circumstance /'sɜːrkəmstæns || 'sɜːkəmstəns/ *n*

A (condition, fact) circunstancia *f*; **~s beyond our control** circunstancias ajenas a nuestra voluntad; **in** *o* **under the ~s** dadas las circunstancias; **in** *o* **under no ~s** bajo ningún concepto, bajo ninguna circunstancia

B **circumstances** *pl* (financial position): **a person in my ~s** una persona en mi situación *or* posición económica

circumstantial /'sɜːrkəm'stæntʃəl || ,sɜːkəm'stænʃəl/ *adj* ‹*evidence*› circunstancial

circumvent /'sɜːrkəm'vent || ,sɜːkəm'vent/ *vt* ‹*law/rule*› burlar; ‹*difficulty/obstacle*› sortear, salvar

circus /'sɜːrkəs || 'sɜːkəs/ *n* (Theat) circo *m*

cirrhosis /sə'rəʊsəs || sɪ'rəʊsɪs/ *n* [u] cirrosis *f*; **~ of the liver** cirrosis hepática

cirrus /'sɪrəs/ *n* (*pl* **cirri** /'sɪraɪ/) cirro *m*

CIS *n* (= **Commonwealth of Independent States**) CEI *f*

cissy /'sɪsi/ *n* (*pl* **-sies**) (BrE) ▸**sissy**

cistern /'sɪstərn || 'sɪstən/ *n* (water tank) cisterna *f*, tanque *m* del agua; (of lavatory) (BrE) cisterna *f*

citadel /'sɪtədl̩, -del/ *n* ciudadela *f*

citation /saɪ'teɪʃən/ *n* 1▸ [c u] (quotation) cita *f* 2▸ [c] (commendation) mención *f*

cite /saɪt/ *vt* (quote) citar, mencionar

citizen /'sɪtəzən || 'sɪtɪzən/ *n* 1▸ (of country) ciudadano, -na *m,f* 2▸ (of town, city): **the ~s of Cuenca** los habitantes *or* vecinos de Cuenca, los conquenses

citizen: **~'s arrest** *n*: *detención llevada a cabo por un ciudadano común*; **~s' band** *n* (Rad) banda *f* ciudadana

citizenship /'sɪtəzənʃɪp || 'sɪtɪzənʃɪp/ *n* [u] ciudadanía *f*

citric acid /'sɪtrɪk/ *n* [u] ácido *m* cítrico

citrus /'sɪtrəs/ *adj* (*before n*) cítrico

city /'sɪti/ *n* (*pl* **cities**) 1▸ ciudad *f*; (*before n*) **~ center** centro *m* de la ciudad; **~ council** ayuntamiento *m*, municipio *m*; **~ planner** (AmE) urbanista *mf*; **~ planning** (AmE) urbanismo *m* 2▸ **City** (in UK) **the C~** la City (de Londres) (*el centro financiero londinense*)

> **City – The City**
>
> Es el área que se encuentra dentro de los límites de la antigua ciudad de Londres. Hoy en día es el centro financiero y de negocios de la capital. Allí tienen sus sedes centrales muchos bancos e instituciones financieras. A menudo, cuando se habla de *The City*, se está refiriendo a estas instituciones y no a la zona propiamente dicha

city: **~ fathers** *pl n* concejales *mpl* y mandatarios *mpl* municipales; **~ hall** *n* (AmE) ayuntamiento *m*, municipio *m*; **~ slicker** *n* (colloq) urbanita *mf* (hum), futre *mf* (Chi fam); **~-state** /'sɪti'steɪt/ *n* ciudad *f* estado

citywide /'sɪtiwaɪd/ *adj* ‹*network*› que abarca toda la ciudad

civet /'sɪvət || 'sɪvɪt/ *n* [c] **~ (cat)** civeta *f*, gato *m* de algalia

civic /'sɪvɪk/ *adj* ‹*authorities*› civil; ‹*leader*› de la ciudad; ‹*duty/virtues*› cívico; **~ center** edificios *mpl* municipales

civies *pl n* ▸**civvies**

civil /'sɪvəl || 'sɪvl̩/ *adj*

A 1▸ (of society, citizens) civil; **~ unrest** malestar *m* social 2▸ (not military) civil 3▸ (Law) civil

B (polite) cortés; **that's very ~ of you** es muy gentil de su parte

> **Civil War (en Estados Unidos)**
>
> La Guerra de Secesión (1861-1865), entre los estados del norte y los del sur de EEUU, se inició principalmente a raíz del problema de los esclavos. Abraham Lincoln, elegido presidente en 1860, se oponía a la esclavitud, pero sostenía que no le pondría fin. Once estados del sur, donde la economía agrícola dependía del trabajo de los esclavos, no lo creyeron así y en 1861 formaron la **Confederate States of America**, a menudo llamada *The Confederacy* (La Confederación) para separarse de la Unión. La Guerra estalló el 12 de abril. Al rendirse la Confederación el 9 de abril de 1865 habían muerto 620.000 personas. Lincoln fue asesinado cinco días más tarde. Se abolió la esclavitud y en 1870, posteriores enmiendas a la Constitución otorgaron a los negros, al menos en teoría, los mismos derechos de los blancos

C

Civil War (en Inglaterra)

Muchas de las causas que provocaron la guerra civil (1642-1651) entre los *Royalists* (monárquicos) o *Cavaliers* (partidarios del rey Carlos I) y las fuerzas parlamentarias (apodadas *Roundheads*), encabezadas por Oliver Cromwell, tenían que ver con los problemas religiosos y económicos de la época. Desde tiempos del rey Enrique VIII el parlamento había luchado por conseguir más poder frente al monarca, y el intento de Carlos I de arrestar a los miembros del cuerpo legislativo, al negarle éste los fondos necesarios para seguir gobernando como autócrata, fue lo que desencadenó el conflicto militar. Vencido en las batallas de Marston Moor (1644) y Naseby (1645), el rey se entregó al ejército escocés un año más tarde. Condenado a muerte por una comisión parlamentaria bajo Cromwell, fue ajusticiado en 1649. Durante los años de la *Commonwealth* que siguieron, el *Protector* (Cromwell) se mostró tan intolerante como su predecesor. Disolvió el Parlamento en varias ocasiones y gobernó durante varios años como dictador. La monarquía fue restaurada en 1660 bajo Carlos II, hijo de Carlos I

civil: ~ **defense**, (BrE) **defence** *n* [u] defensa *f* civil; ~ **engineer** *n* ingeniero, -ra *m,f* civil *or* (Esp tb) de caminos

civilian¹ /sə'vɪljən || sɪ'vɪljən/ *n* civil *mf*

civilian² *adj* ‹*casualties*› entre la población civil; **in ~ dress** (Mil) vestido de civil *or* de paisano

civility /sə'vɪləti || sɪ'vɪləti/ *n* (*pl* **-ties**) 1 [u] (courtesy) educación *f*, cortesía *f*, urbanidad *f* 2 [c] (act, utterance) cortesía *f*, cumplido *m*

civilization /'sɪvələ'zeɪʃən || ˌsɪvəlaɪ'zeɪʃən/ *n* [u c] civilización *f*

civilize /'sɪvəlaɪz/ *vt* civilizar*

civilized /'sɪvəlaɪzd/ *adj* ‹*society*› civilizado; ‹*person*› educado; **please call back at a more ~ hour** por favor llame a una hora más decente

civil: ~ **liberties** *pl n* derechos *mpl* civiles; ~ **list** *n* **the ~ list** (in UK) *presupuesto anual asignado por el Parlamento a la familia real*; ~ **partnership** *n* (in UK) unión *f* civil; ~ **rights** *pl n* derechos *mpl* civiles; ~ **servant** *n* funcionario, -ria *m,f* (del Estado); ~ **service** *n* **the ~ service** la administración pública; (employees) el funcionariado (del Estado); ~ **war** *n* [u c] guerra *f* civil; **the C~ War** la guerra civil; (in US) la guerra de Secesión

civvies /'sɪviz/ *pl n* (colloq): **in ~** de civil, de paisano

CJD *n* [u] (= **Creutzfeld-Jakob disease**) ECJ *f*

cl (= **centiliter(s)** *or* (BrE) **centilitre(s)**) cl.

clack /klæk/ *vi* tabletear; «*high heels*» taconear

clad¹ /klæd/ (arch *or* liter) *past and past p of* **clothe 2**

clad² *adj* (liter *or* hum) vestido; **scantily ~** ligero de ropa (hum); ~ **IN sth** vestido DE algo

-clad /klæd/ *suff*: **leather~** con ropa de cuero

claim¹ /kleɪm/ *n*

A (demand): **wage** *o* **pay ~** reivindicación *f* salarial, demanda *f* de aumento salarial; **insurance ~** reclamación *f* al seguro; **~ FOR sth**: **to put in a ~ for expenses** presentar una solicitud de reembolso de gastos; **she makes enormous ~s on my time** me quita muchísimo tiempo

B (to right, title) **~ (TO sth)** derecho *m* (A algo); **that's her only ~ to fame** eso es lo único por lo que se destaca; **to lay ~ to sth** reivindicar* algo

C (allegation) afirmación *f*

D (piece of land) concesión *f*; *see also* **stake² B 1**

claim² *vt*

A 1 (assert title to) ‹*throne/inheritance/land*› reclamar; ‹*right*› reivindicar*; **to ~ diplomatic immunity** alegar* inmunidad diplomática 2 (demand as being one's own) ‹*lost property*› reclamar; **the earthquake ~ed many lives** el terremoto se cobró muchas vidas 3 ‹*social security/benefits*› (apply for) solicitar; (receive) cobrar; **he's going to ~ compensation** va a exigir que se lo indemnice, va a reclamar una indemnización; **you can ~ your expenses back** puedes pedir que te reembolsen los gastos

B (allege, profess): **no one has ~ed responsibility for the attack** nadie ha reivindicado el atentado; **no one can yet ~ victory** nadie puede cantar victoria todavía; **he ~ed (that) he knew nothing about it** aseguraba *or* afirmaba no saber nada de ello; **to ~ to + INF**: **they ~ to have found the cure** dicen *or* aseguran haber encontrado la cura; **I can't ~ to be an intellectual** no pretendo ser un intelectual

C ‹*attention/interest*› reclamar

■ **claim** *vi* presentar una reclamación; **to ~ FOR sth** reclamar algo; **to ~ ON**: **you can ~ on the insurance** puedes reclamar al seguro

claimant /'kleɪmənt/ *n* 1 (Soc Adm) solicitante *mf* 2 (to throne) pretendiente, -ta *m,f*

clairvoyant /kler'vɔɪənt || kleə'vɔɪənt/ *n* clarividente *mf*

clam /klæm/ *n* almeja *f*; ***to shut up like a ~*** (colloq) quedarse como una tumba (fam)

Phrasal verb

• **clam up**: **-mm-** [v ▸ adv] (colloq) ponerse* muy poco comunicativo

clambake /'klæmbeɪk/ *n* (in US) *picnic en la playa en el que se cuecen almejas*

clamber /'klæmbər || 'klæmbə(r)/ *vi* trepar; **they ~ed over the wall** treparon *or* se encaramaron al muro y saltaron

clammy /'klæmi/ *adj* **-mier, -miest** ‹*handshake*› húmedo; ‹*weather*› bochornoso, pegajoso (fam)

clamor¹, (BrE) **clamour** /'klæmər || 'klæmə(r)/ *n* [u] clamor *m*

clamor², (BrE) **clamour** *vi* gritar; **to ~ FOR sth**: **to ~ for justice** clamar por justicia

clamp¹ /klæmp/ *n* 1 (Const) abrazadera *f*; (in carpentry) tornillo *m* de banco 2 (Med) pinza *f*, clamp *m* 3 (*wheel ~*) (BrE) cepo *m*

clamp² *vt* 1 (join, fasten) sujetar con abrazaderas 2 (BrE Auto colloq) **to ~ a car** ponerle* el cepo a un coche

Phrasal verb

• **clamp down** [v ▸ adv] **to ~ down ON sth/sb** tomar medidas drásticas CONTRA algo/algn

clampdown /'klæmpdaʊn/ *n* (colloq) **~ ON sth/sb**: **a ~ on illegal immigrants** medidas *fpl* drásticas contra los inmigrantes ilegales; **there's been a ~ on loans** se ha restringido severamente la concesión de créditos

clan /klæn/ *n* clan *m*

clandestine /klæn'destən || klæn'destɪn/ *adj* clandestino

clang¹ /klæŋ/ *vi* «*bells*» sonar*, repicar*; **the gate ~ed shut** la verja se cerró con gran estruendo

■ **clang** *vt* hacer* sonar, tocar*

clang² *n* [u c] sonido *m* metálico (*fuerte*)

clanger /'klæŋər || 'klæŋə(r)/ *n* (BrE colloq) metedura *f or* (AmL tb) metida *f* de pata; ***to drop a ~*** meter la pata (fam)

clank¹ /klæŋk/ *vi* hacer* ruido

■ **clank** *vt* hacer* sonar

clank² *n* [u c] ruido *m* metálico (*de cadenas etc*)

clap¹ /klæp/ *n* 1 (applause): **to give sb a ~** aplaudir a algn 2 (slap) palmada *f* 3 (noise): **a ~ of thunder** un trueno

clap² **-pp-** *vt*

A 1 (applaud) aplaudir 2 (slap): **he ~ped me on the back** me dio una palmada en la espalda; **she ~ped her hands (together)** batió palmas *or* dio una palmada de alegría (*or* satisfacción *etc*)

B (put, place) (colloq): **he was ~ped in prison** lo metieron en la cárcel; **he ~ped his hand over my eyes** me tapó los ojos con la mano; ▸ **eye¹ A2**

■ **clap** *vi* 1 (applaud) aplaudir 2 (strike hands together) dar* una palmada

clapped-out /'klæpt'aʊt/ *adj* (*pred* **clapped out**) (BrE colloq) ‹*machine*› destartalado (fam); **a ~ car** un cacharro (fam), una carcacha (Chi, Méx fam), una tartana (Esp fam); **to be/feel ~ ~** estar* reventado *or* hecho polvo (fam)

clapper /'klæpər || 'klæpə(r)/ *n* (of bell) badajo *m*; ***like the ~s*** (BrE colloq): **it was going like the ~s** iba como una bala *or* como un bólido (fam)

clapperboard /'klæpərbɔːrd || 'klæpəbɔːd/ *n* claqueta *f*

clapping /'klæpɪŋ/ *n* [u] aplausos *mpl*

claptrap /'klæptræp/ *n* [u] (colloq) paparruchas *fpl* (fam)

claret /'klærət/ *n* 1 [u c] (wine) burdeos *m*, clarete *m* 2 [u] (color) granate *m*

clarification /'klærəfə'keɪʃən || ˌklærɪfɪ'keɪʃən/ *n* [u] (explanation) aclaración *f*

clarify /'klærəfaɪ || 'klærɪfaɪ/ **-fies, -fying, -fied** *vt* 1 (explain, make clear) aclarar 2 (purify) ‹*fat/wine*› clarificar*

clarinet /'klærə'net/ *n* clarinete *m*

clarity /'klærəti/ *n* [u] (of thought, expression) claridad *f*

clash¹ /klæʃ/ *n*
A [c] (of interests) conflicto *m*; (of cultures, personalities) choque *m*; (of opinions, views) disparidad *f*; **I missed the lecture because of a timetable ~** me perdí la conferencia porque tenía otra cosa a la misma hora *or* por un problema de coincidencia de horarios
B [c] (between armies, factions) enfrentamiento *m*, choque *m*
C (noise): **the ~ of swords** el sonido del choque de espadas; **the ~ of the cymbals** el sonido de los platillos

clash² *vi*
A 1 «*aims/interests*» estar* en conflicto *or* en pugna; «*personalities*» chocar* 2 «*colors/patterns*» desentonar
B «*armies/factions/leaders*» chocar*; **to ~ WITH sb (OVER sth)** chocar* con algn (ACERCA DE algo); **police ~ed with demonstrators** hubo choques entre la policía y los manifestantes
C «*dates*» coincidir; **the concert ~es with the film tonight** el concierto y la película de esta noche son a la misma hora
D 1 (make noise) «*cymbals/swords*» sonar* (*al entrechocarse*) 2 (collide) chocar*
■ **clash** *vt* ‹*cymbals*› tocar*; ‹*weapons*› entrechocar*

clasp¹ /klæsp || klɑ:sp/ *n* (fastening) broche *m*, cierre *m*

clasp² *vt* (grip, embrace): **she ~ed her bag firmly** sujetó *or* agarró firmemente el bolso; **they ~ed hands** se dieron un fuerte apretón de manos; **he ~ed her in his arms** la estrechó entre sus brazos

class¹ /klæs || klɑ:s/ *n*
A [c u] (social stratum) clase *f*; (*before n*) **the ~ struggle** la lucha de clases
B [c] (group of students) clase *f*; (lesson) clase *f*; **the ~ of '86** la promoción del 86
C [c] (group, type) clase *f*; **to be in a ~ of one's/its own** ser* único *or* inigualable; **they're not in the same ~ as their opponents** no están a la altura de sus contrincantes
D [u] 1 (Transp) clase *f* 2 (in UK) (Post): **send the letter first/second ~** manda la carta por correo preferente/normal 3 (in UK) (Educ) *tipo de título que se concede según las calificaciones obtenidas durante la carrera y/o exámenes finales*; (*before n*) **he got a first ~ degree** ≈ se recibió con la nota más alta (*en AmL*), ≈ sacó matrícula de honor en la carrera (*en Esp*)
E [u] (style) (colloq) clase *f*, estilo *m*

class² *vt* catalogar*

class-conscious /'klæs'kɑ:ntʃəs || ,klɑ:s'kɒnʃəs/ *adj* (Pol, Sociol) con conciencia de clase; (classist) clasista, consciente de las distinciones sociales

classic¹ /'klæsɪk/ *adj* clásico; ‹*scene/line*› memorable

classic² *n* 1 (play, film, book) clásico *m*; *see also* **classics** 2 (Clothing) prenda *f* clásica

classical /'klæsɪkəl/ *adj* 1 (of Greece, Rome) clásico; **a ~ scholar** un humanista especializado en lenguas clásicas 2 (traditional) clásico; **~ music** música *f* clásica

classics /'klæsɪks/ *n* [u] (+ *sing vb*) clásicas *fpl*

classification /'klæsəfə'keɪʃən || ,klæsɪfɪ'keɪʃən/ *n* [c u] clasificación *f*

classified /'klæsəfaɪd || 'klæsɪfaɪd/ *adj* 1 (categorized) clasificado; **~ advertising** anuncios *mpl* por palabras, avisos *mpl* clasificados (AmL) 2 (secret) ‹*information*› secreto, confidencial

classify /'klæsəfaɪ || 'klæsɪfaɪ/ *vt* **-fies, -fying, -fied** (categorize) ‹*books/data*› clasificar*

classist /'klæsist || 'klɑ:sɪst/ *adj* clasista

classless /'klæsləs || 'klɑ:slɪs/ *adj* ‹*society*› sin clases

class: ~mate *n* compañero, -ra *m,f* de clase; **~room** *n* aula *f*‡, clase *f*, sala *f* *or* salón *m* de clase (frml)

classy /'klæsi || 'klɑ:sɪ/ *adj* **-sier, -siest** (colloq) con estilo *or* clase

clatter¹ /'klætər || 'klætə(r)/ *vi* «*pans*» hacer* ruido; «*hooves*» chacolotear, hacer* ruido; «*typewriter*» repiquetear
■ **clatter** *vt* ‹*pans/cutlery*› hacer* ruido con

clatter² *n* [u] (of trains) traqueteo *m*; (of typewriters) repiqueteo *m*; (of hooves) chacoloteo *m*

clause /klɔ:z/ *n* 1 (in contract) cláusula *f* 2 (Ling) oración *f*, cláusula *f*

claustrophobia /'klɔ:strə'fəʊbiə || ,klɒstrə'fəʊbiə/ *n* [u] claustrofobia *f*

claustrophobic /'klɔ:strə'fəʊbɪk || ,klɒstrə'fəʊbɪk/ *adj* claustrofóbico

claw¹ /klɔ:/ *n* (of tiger, lion) zarpa *f*, garra *f*; (of eagle) garra *f*; (of crab, lobster) pinza *f*; ***to get one's ~s into sb*** (colloq): **he won't stand a chance if she gets her ~s into him** es hombre muerto si cae en sus garras

claw² *vt*: **the cat had ~ed the rug to shreds** el gato había destrozado la alfombra con las uñas; ***to ~ one's way***: **they ~ed their way through the rubble** se abrieron camino como pudieron entre los escombros; **he ~ed his way to the top** no reparó en medios para llegar a la cima
■ **claw** *vi* arañar; **to ~ AT sth** arañar algo

Phrasal verb

• **claw back** [v ▸ o ▸ adv, v ▸ adv ▸ o] (esp BrE) ‹*money/revenue*› recuperar

clay /kleɪ/ *n* [u c] arcilla *f*; (for children) (AmE) plastilina® *f*, plasticina® *f* (CS); (*before n*) **~ court** (Sport) cancha *f* de arcilla (AmL), pista *f* de tierra batida (Esp); **~ pipe** pipa *f* de cerámica *or* barro

clay pigeon *n* plato *m* (*de tiro*); (*before n*) **~ ~ shooting** tiro *m* al plato

clean¹ /kli:n/ *adj* **-er, -est**
A 1 (not soiled) limpio; **are your hands ~?** ¿tienes las manos limpias?; **she wiped the table ~** limpió la mesa 2 (not used) ‹*clothes/towel*› limpio; **use a ~ sheet of paper** usa una hoja de papel nueva 3 (pure, non-polluting) ‹*air/water*› limpio, puro; ‹*smell*› a limpio; ‹*taste*› refrescante
B 1 (morally) ‹*joke*› inocente; **keep it ~** no te pases 2 (fair) ‹*game/player*› limpio
C (unblemished) ‹*driver's license*› donde no constan infracciones; **to come ~ about sth** (colloq) confesar* algo
D (well defined) ‹*stroke/features*› bien definido, nítido; **a ~ break** una fractura limpia; **she made a ~ break with the past** cortó radicalmente con el pasado

clean² *adv* (colloq) 1 (completely): **I ~ forgot about it** se me olvidó por completo; **they got ~ away** se escaparon sin dejar ni rastro 2 (fairly) ‹*fight/play*› limpio, limpiamente

clean³ *vt* 1 (remove dirt from) limpiar; ‹*blackboard*› borrar, limpiar; **to ~ one's teeth** lavarse los dientes; **to ~ sth OFF sth**: **he ~ed the splashes off the windows** limpió las salpicaduras que había en las ventanas 2 (dry-clean) limpiar en seco, llevar a la tintorería 3 ‹*fish/chicken*› limpiar
■ **clean** *vi* (remove dirt) «*substance/device*» limpiar

Phrasal verbs

• **clean out**
A [v ▸ o ▸ adv, v ▸ adv ▸ o] (clean thoroughly) vaciar* y limpiar (*a fondo*)
B [v ▸ o ▸ adv, v ▸ adv ▸ o] (colloq) (leave with no money) dejar pelado; (steal everything from) desplumar

• **clean up**
A [v ▸ o ▸ adv, v ▸ adv ▸ o] 1 (make clean) ‹*room/garden*› limpiar; **I'll just ~ myself up a bit** voy a arreglarme *or* lavarme un poco 2 (morally) limpiar
B [v ▸ adv] (make clean) limpiar; **I'm tired of ~ing up after you** estoy harto de limpiar lo que tú ensucias

clean⁴ *n* (colloq) (*no pl*) limpieza *f*; **just give it a quick ~** dale una repasadita (fam)

clean-cut /'kli:n'kʌt/ *adj* ‹*outline*› bien definido, nítido; ‹*appearance*› muy cuidado

cleaner /'kli:nər || 'kli:nə(r)/ *n* 1 (person) limpiador, -dora *m,f* 2 (substance) producto *m* de limpieza 3 (*dry ~*) tintorero, -ra *m,f*; **take it to the ~'s** *o* **~s** llévalo a la tintorería; ***to take sb to the ~s*** *o* ***~'s*** (colloq) dejar limpio *or* pelado *or* (CS tb) pato a algn (fam)

cleaning /'kli:nɪŋ/ *n* [u] limpieza *f*; (*before n*) **~ fluid** líquido *m* limpiador; **the ~ lady** *o* **woman** la señora *or* mujer de la limpieza

cleanliness /'klenlinəs || 'klenlinɪs/ *n* [u] (bodily hygiene) aseo *m*; (of surroundings) limpieza *f*; **personal ~** el aseo personal

C

clean-living /'kliːn'lɪvɪŋ/ *adj* sin vicios, de vida sana

cleanly /'kliːnli/ *adv*
A (evenly) ‹*cut/snap*› limpiamente
B (fairly) ‹*fight/play*› limpio, limpiamente, con limpieza

cleanness /'kliːnnəs || 'kliːnnɪs/ *n* [u] **1** (absence of dirt) limpieza *f* **2** (of air, water) pureza *f*

cleanse /klenz/ *vt* limpiar

cleanser /'klenzər || 'klenzə(r)/ *n* [c u] (for household use) producto *m* de limpieza; (for skin) leche *f* (*or* crema *f etc*) limpiadora *or* de limpieza

clean-shaven /'kliːn'ʃeɪvən/ *adj* ‹*face*› bien afeitado *or* (esp Méx) rasurado; **a ~ man** un hombre sin barba ni bigote

cleansing[1] /'klenzɪŋ/ *adj* limpiador; **~ lotion** loción *f* limpiadora *or* de limpieza

cleansing[2] *n* limpieza *f*

cleanup /'kliːnʌp/ *n* (*no pl*) **1** (clean) limpieza *f* **2** (large profit) (AmE colloq) tajada *f* (fam)

clear[1] /klɪr || klɪə(r)/ *adj* **-er, -est**
A ‹*sky*› despejado, claro; ‹*day*› despejado; ‹*liquid/glass*› transparente; **~ soup** consomé *m*; **to have a ~ conscience** tener* la conciencia tranquila *or* limpia; **she has very ~ skin** tiene muy buen cutis; **to keep a ~ head** mantener* la mente despejada
B (distinct) ‹*outline/picture*› nítido, claro; ‹*voice*› claro
C **1** (plain, evident): **it's a ~ case of suicide** es un caso evidente *or* claro de suicidio; **the Bears are ~ favorites** los Bears son, sin lugar a dudas, el equipo favorito; **it became ~ that ...** se hizo evidente *or* patente que ... **2** ‹*explanation/instructions*› claro; **is that ~?** ¿está *or* queda claro?; **let's get this ~** entendámonos bien; **do I make myself ~?** ¿me explico?, ¿está claro?
D (free, unobstructed) ‹*space/road*› despejado; **S keep clear** no obstruya el paso; **all ~!** ¡el campo está libre!
E (entire): **we've got two ~ days** tenemos dos días enteros; **he makes a ~ $450 a week** saca 450 dólares netos *or* limpios a la semana
F ***to be in the*** **~** (free — from danger) estar* fuera de peligro; (— from debt) estar* libre de deudas; (— from suspicion) estar* libre de toda sospecha
G (in showjumping) ‹*round*› sin faltas

clear[2] *adv*
A (beyond, outside): **once you're ~ of the town** una vez que hayas salido de la ciudad; **stand ~ of the doors** manténganse alejados de las puertas; **he leapt ~ of the oncoming car** se apartó de un salto del coche que venía; **the curtains should hang ~ of the radiators** las cortinas no deben tocar los radiadores
B (as intensifier): **the cargo sank ~ to the bottom** la carga se fue a pique hasta el fondo; **he fell ~ through the ceiling** se cayó y atravesó el techo
C **to keep/stay/steer ~ (of sth)** (lit) mantenerse* alejado (de algo); **keep ~!** ¡no se acerquen!; **I advised her to steer ~ of him** le aconsejé que no tuviera nada que ver con él
D (distinctly) ▸**loud**[2]

clear[3] *vt*
A **1** (make free, unobstructed) ‹*room*› vaciar*; ‹*surface*› despejar; ‹*drain/pipe*› desatascar*, destapar (AmL); ‹*building*› desalojar; ‹*land*› despoblar de árboles, desmontar; **to ~ the table** levantar *or* (Esp tb) quitar la mesa; **to ~ one's throat** carraspear, aclararse la voz; **to ~ a space for sth** hacer* sitio *or* lugar para algo; **an agreement that ~s the way for increased trade** un acuerdo que abre camino para un mayor intercambio comercial; **police ~ed the area** la policía evacuó la zona; **let's ~ all this paper off the desk** quitemos todos estos papeles del escritorio; ▸**air**[1] A **2** (Comput) ‹*screen*› despejar; ‹*data*› borrar
B ‹*fence/ditch*› salvar, saltar por encima de; **the plane just ~ed the trees** el avión pasó casi rozando los árboles; **to ~ customs** pasar por la aduana
C (free from suspicion): **he was ~ed of all charges** lo absolvieron de todos los cargos; **she is determined to ~ her name** está decidida a limpiar su nombre
D **1** (authorize) autorizar*, darle* el visto bueno a; **you'll have to ~ that with Tom** tendrás que obtener autorización *or* el visto bueno de Tom **2** (Fin) compensar
E **1** (settle) ‹*debt/account*› liquidar, saldar **2** (earn) sacar* **3** (sell off) ‹*stock*› liquidar; **S reduced to clear** (BrE) rebajas por liquidación
F (Sport) ‹*ball/puck*› despejar

■ **clear** *vi*
A **1** «*sky/weather*» despejarse; «*water*» aclararse; **her head began to ~** se le empezó a despejar la cabeza **2** (disperse) «*fog/smoke*» levantarse, disiparse; «*traffic/congestion*» despejarse
B (Fin) «*check*» ser* compensado

Phrasal verbs

• **clear off**
A [v ▸ adv] (go away) (colloq) largarse* (fam)
B [v ▸ o ▸ adv, v ▸ adv ▸ o] **1** (pay) ‹*debt*› liquidar **2** (remove) echar de

• **clear out**
A [v ▸ o ▸ adv, v ▸ adv ▸ o] ‹*cupboard/drawer*› vaciar* y ordenar
B [v ▸ adv] (leave) (colloq) largarse* (fam)

• **clear up**
A [v ▸ o ▸ adv, v ▸ adv ▸ o] **1** (resolve) ‹*crime*› esclarecer*, resolver*; ‹*misunderstanding/doubts*› aclarar **2** (tidy) ‹*rubbish*› recoger*; **can you ~ up this mess?** ¿puedes ordenar todo esto?
B [v ▸ adv] **1** (tidy) ordenar **2** «*weather*» despejar **3** (get better) «*cough/cold*» mejorarse, irse*; **the rash has ~ed up** se le (*or* me *etc*) ha ido el sarpullido

clearance /'klɪrəns || 'klɪərəns/ *n* [u]
A (authorization) autorización *f*; (from customs) despacho *m* de aduana
B (free space) espacio *m* (libre)
C (of building land) desmonte *m*, despeje *m*
D (of stock) liquidación *f*
E (of check) compensación *f*

clear: **~-cut** /'klɪr'kʌt || ˌklɪə'kʌt/ *adj* claro, bien *or* netamente definido; **~-headed** /'klɪr'hedəd || ˌklɪə'hedɪd/ *adj* lúcido

clearing /'klɪrɪŋ || 'klɪərɪŋ/ *n* (in forest) claro *m*

clearing: **~ bank** *n* (in UK) banco *m* de compensación; **~ house** *n* (Fin) cámara *f* de compensación

clearly /'klɪrli || 'klɪəli/ *adv*
A **1** (distinctly) ‹*visible/marked*› claramente; ‹*speak/write/think*› con claridad, claramente **2** (without ambiguity) ‹*speak/show*› claramente
B (obviously): **it's ~ impossible** es a todas luces imposible, está claro que es imposible; **~, this must stop** (*indep*) evidentemente *or* desde luego, esto se tiene que terminar

clear: **~-out** *n* (BrE colloq) limpieza *f* (*deshaciéndose de trastos etc*); **~-sighted** /'klɪr'saɪtəd || 'klɪə'saɪtɪd/ *adj* de gran lucidez, perspicaz; **~way** *n* (in UK) *tramo de carretera en el que está prohibido detenerse*

cleavage /'kliːvɪdʒ/ *n* [c u] (bosom) escote *m*

cleave /kliːv/ *vt* (*past* **cleaved** *or* **cleft** *or* (arch) **clove**; *past p* **cleaved** *or* **cleft** *or* (arch) **cloven**) (arch *or* liter) hender* (liter), partir

■ **cleave** *vi* (*past & past p* **cleaved**)
A (cut through): **to ~ through sth** ‹*crowd/enemy*› abrirse* camino a través de algo; ‹*waves*› surcar*
B (be faithful) (liter) **to ~ TO sb/sth** serle* fiel A algn/algo

cleaver /'kliːvər || 'kliːvə(r)/ *n* cuchilla *f* de carnicero

clef /klef/ *n* clave *f*

cleft[1] /kleft/ *past & past p of* **cleave** *vt*

cleft[2] *adj* ‹*chin*› partido; **~ palate** paladar *m* hendido, fisura *f* del paladar

cleft[3] *n* hendidura *f*, grieta *f*

clematis /'klemətəs || 'klemətɪs/ *n* [u c] clemátide *f*

clemency /'klemənsi/ *n* [u] **1** (mercy) clemencia *f* **2** (of weather) benignidad *f*

clementine /'kleməntiːn || 'kleməntaɪn/ *n* (BrE) clementina *f*

clench /klentʃ/ *vt* **1** (close) ‹*fist/jaw*› apretar*; **he spoke through ~ed teeth** masculló algo, dijo algo entre dientes **2** (grip) apretar*, agarrar

clergy /'klɜːrdʒi || 'klɜːdʒi/ *n* (+ *sing or pl vb*) clero *m*

clergyman /'klɜːrdʒimən || 'klɜːdʒimən/ *n* (*pl* **-men** /-mən/) clérigo *m*

cleric /'klerɪk/ *n* clérigo, -ga *m,f*, eclesiástico, -ca *m,f*

clerical /'klerɪkəl/ *adj*
A (Relig) clerical
B (of a clerk) ‹*job/work*› de oficina; **~ assistant** oficinista *mf*,

empleado, -da *m,f*; ~ **staff** personal *m* administrativo

clerk¹ /klɜːrk || klɑːk/ *n* (in office) empleado (administrativo), empleada (administrativa) *m,f*, oficinista *mf*; (in bank) empleado, -da *m,f*, bancario, -ria *m,f* (CS); (*sales*~) (AmE) vendedor, -dora *m,f*, dependiente, -ta *m,f*; (*desk* ~) (AmE) recepcionista *mf*

clerk² *vi* (AmE colloq) trabajar de dependiente (*or* de oficinista, *etc*)

clever /ˈklevər || ˈklevə(r)/ *adj* **-verer, -verest** 1 (intelligent) inteligente, listo 2 (artful) (pej) listo; **don't try to be ~ with me** no te hagas el listo conmigo 3 (skillful, adept) ‹*player/politician*› hábil; ‹*invention/solution*› ingenioso; **to be ~ AT sth** ser* bueno PARA algo; **she's ~ with her hands** es hábil con las manos

clever dick, **clever Dick** *n* (BrE colloq) sabelotodo *mf*, sabihondo, -da *m,f*

cleverly /ˈklevərli/ *adv* hábilmente, ingeniosamente

cleverness /ˈklevərnəs || ˈklevənɪs/ *n* [u] 1 (of design, plan) lo ingenioso 2 (of person — intelligence) inteligencia *f*; (— skill) habilidad *f*

cliché /kliːˈʃeɪ || ˈkliːʃeɪ/ *n* [c u] lugar *m* común, cliché *m*, tópico *m*

clichéd /kliːˈʃeɪd || ˈkliːʃeɪd/ *adj* estereotipado

click¹ /klɪk/ *vt* ‹*fingers*› chasquear, tronar* (Méx); ‹*tongue*› chasquear; **to ~ one's heels** dar* un taconazo

■ **click** *vi*

A (make clicking sound) hacer* un ruidito seco, hacer* 'clic'; **it ~s into place** encaja en su lugar haciendo 'clic'

B (colloq) 1 (strike home): **it suddenly ~ed: ...** de repente caí en la cuenta *or* lo vi todo claro: ... 2 (relate well) congeniar; **we just ~ed** congeniamos *or* nos entendimos desde un principio 3 (succeed) (esp AmE) tener* éxito

click² *n* (sound — of fingers, tongue) chasquido *m*; (— of heels) taconazo *m*; (— of camera, switch) clic *m*

client /ˈklaɪənt/ *n* cliente, -ta *m,f*

clientele /ˌklaɪənˈtel || ˌkliːɒnˈtel, ˌkliːənˈtel/ *n* (+ *sing or pl vb*) clientela *f*

cliff /klɪf/ *n* acantilado *m*; (not by sea) precipicio *m*

cliffhanger /ˈklɪfˌhæŋər || ˈklɪfˌhæŋə(r)/ *n* (at end of episode) situación *f* de suspenso *or* (Esp) de suspense

climate /ˈklaɪmət || ˈklaɪmɪt/ *n* clima *m*

climate change *n* [u] cambio *m* climático

climate control *n* [u] 1 (of car) climatizador *m* 2 (of the environment) control *m* del clima 3 (of micro-environment) climatización *f*

climatic /klaɪˈmætɪk/ *adj* climático, climatológico

climax /ˈklaɪmæks/ *n* (*pl* **-maxes**) clímax *m*, punto *m* culminante; (orgasm) orgasmo *m*

climb¹ /klaɪm/ *vt* ‹*mountain*› escalar, subir a; ‹*tree*› trepar a, subirse a, treparse a (esp AmL); ‹*stairs*› subir

■ **climb** *vi* 1 (clamber) trepar, treparse; **to go ~ing** (Sport) hacer* alpinismo *or* (AmL tb) andinismo, ir* a escalar *or* de escalada; **she ~ed onto the table** se subió a la mesa, trepó *or* se trepó a la mesa; **to ~ into/out of bed** meterse en/levantarse de la cama; **he ~ed into his pajamas** se puso el pijama 2 (rise) subir, ascender* (frml)

Phrasal verbs

• **climb down**

A [v ▸ prep ▸ o] (descend) ‹*rope*› bajarse por; ‹*tree*› bajarse de

B [v ▸ adv] 1 (descend) bajar(se), descender* (frml) 2 (withdraw, concede) (colloq) ceder

• **climb up**

A [v ▸ prep ▸ o] ‹*tree*› trepar a, treparse a (esp AmL); ‹*hill*› subir; ‹*rockface*› escalar; ‹*rope*› subir *or* trepar por

B [v ▸ adv] subir

climb² *n* 1 (ascent) subida *f*; (Sport) escalada *f* 2 (gradient) ascenso *m*, subida *f* 3 (Aviat) ascenso *m*

climb-down /ˈklaɪmdaʊn/ *n* (BrE) marcha *f* *or* vuelta *f* atrás

climber /ˈklaɪmər || ˈklaɪmə(r)/ *n* 1 (*rock* ~) escalador, -dora *m,f*; (mountaineer) alpinista *mf*, andinista *mf* (AmL) 2 (Hort) enredadera *f*, trepadora *f* 3 (*social* ~) (pej) arribista *mf*, trepador, -dora *m,f*

climbing¹ /ˈklaɪmɪŋ/ *adj* trepador

climbing² *n* [u] (Sport) alpinismo *m*, montañismo *m*, andinismo *m* (AmL)

clinch¹ /klɪntʃ/ *vt* ‹*deal*› cerrar*; ‹*title*› ganar, hacerse* con; **this ~ed the argument** esto resolvió la discusión de forma contundente

■ **clinch** *vi* (assure victory) (AmE) ganar

clinch² *n* (in boxing) clinch *m*; (embrace) (colloq) abrazo *m*, achuchón *m* (Esp fam), apercolle *m* (Col fam), apapacho *m* (Méx fam)

cling /klɪŋ/ *vi* (*past & past p* **clung**)

A 1 (hold fast) **to ~ TO sth/sb** estar* aferrado A algo/algn; **she still ~s to that hope/belief** sigue aferrada a esa esperanza/creencia; **the boy clung on to her hand** el niño no le soltaba la mano 2 (be dependent) (pej) **to ~ (TO sb)** pegársele* A algn

B (stick) **to ~ (TO sth)** pegarse* *or* adherirse* (A algo)

clingfilm /ˈklɪŋfɪlm/ *n* [u] (BrE) film *m* transparente (*para envolver alimentos*)

clinging /ˈklɪŋɪŋ/ *adj* 1 ‹*child*› poco independiente; ‹*person*› (pej) pegajoso, pesado 2 ‹*dress*› que se pega *or* se ciñe al cuerpo

clinic /ˈklɪnɪk/ *n* (in state hospital) consultorio *m*; (private hospital) clínica *f*

clinical /ˈklɪnɪkəl/ *adj* 1 (Med) (*before n*) clínico 2 (unemotional) ‹*manner/detachment*› frío

clink¹ /klɪŋk/ *vt* hacer* tintinear; **we ~ed glasses** entrechocamos los vasos

■ **clink** *vi* tintinear

clink² *n*

A (sound) (*no pl*) tintineo *m*

B [c] (prison) (sl) cárcel *f*, trullo *m* (Esp arg), bote *m* (Méx arg), cana *f* (AmS arg)

clinker /ˈklɪŋkər || ˈklɪŋkə(r)/ *n* [c] (AmE sl) 1 (gaffe) metedura *f* *or* (AmL tb) metida *f* de pata (fam), pifia *f* (fam), pifiada *f* (fam) 2 (bad product) porquería *f* (fam), basura *f*

clip¹ /klɪp/ *n*

A (device) clip *m*, gancho *m*; *see also* **hairclip, paperclip**

B (from film) fragmento *m*, clip *m*

C (foul) (AmE) bloqueo *m* por la espalda (*fuera de la zona legal*)

D (blow): ***to give sb a ~ on o round the ear*** (colloq) darle* una torta *or* un tortazo a algn (fam)

E (item): **a ~** (AmE colloq) cada uno

clip² **-pp-** *vt*

A 1 (cut) ‹*hair/nails/grass/hedge*› cortar; ‹*sheep*› trasquilar, esquilar; ‹*dog*› recortarle el pelo a 2 (punch) ‹*ticket*› picar*, perforar

B (cut out) (AmE) recortar

C (hit) golpear; **to ~ sb round the ear** (BrE colloq) darle* una torta *or* un tortazo a algn (fam)

D (attach) sujetar (*con un clip*)

■ **clip** *vi*: **the lid ~s on** la tapa se ajusta con unos ganchos

clip: **~board** *n* tablilla *f* con sujetapapeles; **~-clop** /ˈklɪpˈklɑːp || ˈklɪpˌklɒp/ *n* (*no pl*) ruido *m* de cascos; **~-on** *adj* (*before n*) ‹*brooch/sunglasses*› que se engancha; ‹*earrings*› de clip

clipped /klɪpt/ *adj* ‹*accent/speech*› cortado

clippers /ˈklɪpərz || ˈklɪpəz/ *pl n* (for nails) cortaúñas *m*; (for hair) maquinilla *f* (*para cortar el pelo*); (for hedge, lawn) podadera *f*, tijeras *fpl* de podar

clipping /ˈklɪpɪŋ/ *n* 1 (*press* ~) recorte *m* de prensa 2 **clippings** *pl* (clipped pieces) recortes *mpl*, pedazos *mpl*; **grass ~s** hierba *f* cortada; **nail ~s** pedazos *mpl* de uñas

clique /kliːk/ *n* camarilla *f*

clitoris /ˈklɪtərəs || ˈklɪtərɪs/ *n* clítoris *m*

cloak¹ /kləʊk/ *n* (Clothing) capa *f*; (disguise) tapadera *f*

cloak² *vt* ‹*purpose/activities*› encubrir*; **to be ~ed IN sth** (in darkness, mist) estar* envuelto EN algo; **the whole affair was ~ed in secrecy** todo el asunto estuvo rodeado de un velo *or* un manto de secreto

cloakroom /ˈkləʊkruːm, -rʊm/ *n* 1 (for coats) guardarropa *m* 2 (lavatory) (BrE) lavabo *m*, baño *m* (de las visitas) (AmL)

clobber¹ /ˈklɑːbər || ˈklɒbə(r)/ *vt* (colloq) darle* una paliza a, cascar* (fam); (defeat heavily) darle* una paliza a (fam)

clobber² *n* [u] (BrE colloq) bártulos *mpl* (fam)

clock¹ /klɑːk || klɒk/ *n* 1 (timepiece) reloj *m*; **to work around *o* round the ~** trabajar las veinticuatro horas del día, trabajar día y noche; **around-the-~** *o* **round-**

C

the-~ surveillance vigilancia *f* las veinticuatro horas del día; **to put the ~s back/forward** atrasar/adelantar los relojes; ***to turn*** *o* ***put the ~ back*** volver* atrás [2] (*time* ~) reloj *m* registrador *or* (Méx) checador [3] (Auto) (odometer) (colloq) cuentakilómetros *m*; (speedometer) velocímetro *m* [4] (in taxi) (colloq) taxímetro *m*

clock² *vt* (colloq) [1] (achieve, reach) ‹*speed/time*› registrar, hacer* [2] (time) ‹*athlete/race*› cronometrar

C

Phrasal verbs

- **clock in**, (BrE) **clock on** [v ▸ adv] [1] (register time of arrival) fichar, marcar* *or* (Méx) checar* tarjeta (*al entrar al trabajo*) [2] (arrive at work) entrar (al trabajo)
- **clock out**, (BrE) **clock off** [v ▸ adv] [1] (register time of departure) fichar, marcar* *or* (Méx) checar* tarjeta (*al salir del trabajo*) [2] (leave work) salir* del trabajo
- **clock up** [v ▸ adv ▸ o] (accumulate) (colloq) ‹*miles/hours*› hacer*; ‹*successes*› apuntarse, anotarse (AmL)

clock: ~ **radio** *n* radiodespertador *f or m*; ~ **speed** *n* [u] velocidad *f* operativa; ~**tower** *n* torre *f* de(l) reloj

clockwise¹ /ˈklɑːkwaɪz || ˈklɒkwaɪz/ *adj* ‹*direction*› de las agujas del reloj

clockwise² *adv* en el sentido de las agujas del reloj

clockwork /ˈklɑːkwɜːrk || ˈklɒkwɜːk/ *n* [u] mecanismo *m* de relojería; **the organization runs like ~** la organización funciona como un reloj; ***as regular as ~*** (colloq) como un reloj (fam); (*before n*) ~ **toy** (esp BrE) juguete *m* de cuerda

clod /klɑːd || klɒd/ *n* [1] (of earth) terrón *m* [2] (oaf) (colloq) zoquete *mf* (fam), zopenco, -ca *m,f* (fam)

clodhopper /ˈklɑːdˌhɑːpər || ˈklɒdhɒpə(r)/ *n* (colloq) [1] (yokel) patán *m* [2] (heavy shoe) zapatón *m* (fam)

clog¹ /klɑːg || klɒg/ *n* zueco *m*

clog² **-gg-** ~ **(up)** *vt* ‹*pipe/filter*› obstruir*, atascar*; ‹*wheels*› atascar*

■ **clog** *vi* «*pipe*» obstruirse*, atascarse*; «*wheel*» atascarse*

cloister /ˈklɔɪstər || ˈklɔɪstə(r)/ *n* (*often pl*) claustro *m*

cloistered /ˈklɔɪstərd || ˈklɔɪstəd/ *adj* (Archit) (*before n*) enclaustrado; **he had led a ~ existence** había vivido muy enclaustrado

clone¹ /kləʊn/ *n* clon *m*

clone² *vt* clonar

close¹ /kləʊs/ *adj* **closer, closest**

A [1] (near) próximo, cercano; **at ~ range** *o* **quarters** de cerca; ~ **TO sth/sb** próximo *or* cercano A algo/algn, cerca DE algo/algn [2] ‹*shave*› al ras, apurado; ***that was a ~ shave*** *o* ***call*** (colloq) se salvó (*or* me salvé *etc*) por un pelo *or* por los pelos (fam)

B ‹*link/connection*› estrecho; ‹*contact*› directo; ‹*relative*› cercano; **they are ~ friends** son muy amigos, son amigos íntimos; **they've always been very ~** siempre han sido *or* (Esp) estado muy unidos; **sources ~ to the government** fuentes allegadas *or* cercanas al gobierno

C (in similarity): **it's not the same color but it's a ~ match** no es el mismo color pero es casi igual; **he bears a ~ resemblance to his brother** tiene un gran parecido a *or* con su hermano, se parece mucho a su hermano; **that's the ~st thing to a hammer I've got** esto es lo más parecido a un martillo que tengo

D ‹*fit*› ajustado, ceñido

E (strictly guarded): **it was kept a ~ secret** se mantuvo en el más absoluto *or* riguroso secreto

F (careful) ‹*examination*› detenido, detallado; **to pay ~ attention to sth** prestar mucha atención a algo; **to keep a ~ watch on sth/sb** vigilar algo/a algn de cerca

G ‹*contest/finish*› reñido; **he finished a ~ second** llegó en segundo lugar, muy cerca del ganador

H ‹*weather/atmosphere*› pesado, bochornoso

close² /kləʊs/ *adv* **closer, closest**

A (in position) cerca; **to draw/get/come ~** acercarse*; ~ **TO sth/sb** cerca DE algo/algn; **to hold sb ~** abrazar* a algn; **they're following ~ behind** nos siguen de cerca; **phew, that was ~!** ¡uf, nos salvamos por poco *or* por los pelos!

B (in intimacy): **the tragedy brought them ~r together** *o* **to each other** la tragedia los acercó *or* unió más

C (in approximation): **it's not my favorite, but it comes pretty ~** no es mi favorito pero casi; ~ **TO sth**: **the temperature is ~ to ...** la temperatura es de casi ...; **he must be ~ to 50** debe tener cerca de *or* casi 50 años; **that's the ~st to an apology you'll get** eso es lo más parecido a una disculpa que vas a recibir; **he was ~ to tears** estaba a punto de llorar

D (*in phrases*) **close by** cerca; **close on**: **there were ~ on 10,000 present** había cerca de *or* casi 10.000 asistentes; **close together** (physically) juntos; **our birthdays are ~ together** nuestros cumpleaños caen por las mismas fechas *or* muy cerca; **close up** de cerca

close³ *n*

Sense I /kləʊz/ (conclusion, end) fin *m*; **to come/draw to a ~** llegar*/acercarse* a su fin; **to bring sth to a ~** poner* *or* dar* fin a algo; **at the ~ of day** (liter) al caer el día (liter)

Sense II /kləʊs/ (in residential area) (BrE) calle *f* (*sin salida*)

close⁴ /kləʊz/ *vt*

A ‹*window/book/valve*› cerrar*; **he ~d his mouth/eyes** cerró la boca/los ojos

B (block) ‹*road*› cerrar*

C (terminate, wind up) ‹*branch/file/account*› cerrar*

D (conclude) ‹*deal*› cerrar*; ‹*debate/meeting*› cerrar*, poner* fin a

■ **close** *vi*

A «*door/window*» cerrar(se)*; «*gap/wound*» cerrarse*; **her eyes ~d and she fell asleep** se le cerraron los ojos y se quedó dormida

B «*shop/library/museum*» cerrar*

C [1] (finish, end) «*lecture/book*» terminar, concluir* [2] **closing** *pres p* último

D (get closer) acercarse*; **to ~ ON sth/sb** acercarse* A algo/algn

Phrasal verbs

- **close down**

A [v ▸ o ▸ adv, v ▸ adv ▸ o] ‹*shop/factory*› cerrar*

B [v ▸ adv] (cease operations) «*shop/factory*» cerrar*

- **close in** [v ▸ adv] [1] «*pursuers/enemy*» acercarse*, aproximarse; **to ~ in ON sth/sb** cercar* algo/a algn [2] «*winter*» acercarse*; **night was closing in** estaba oscureciendo *or* anocheciendo, caía la noche (liter) [3] (get shorter) «*days*» acortarse
- **close off** [v ▸ o ▸ adv, v ▸ adv ▸ o] clausurar, cerrar*

Phrasal verbs

- **close out** [v ▸ o ▸ adv, v ▸ adv ▸ o] (AmE) liquidar
- **close up**

A [v ▸ adv] «*shop/museum*» cerrar*; «*wound/gash*» cerrarse*, cicatrizar*; **come on, everybody, ~ up a bit!** ¡vamos, pónganse un poco más juntos!

B [v ▸ o ▸ adv, v ▸ adv ▸ o] ‹*shop/museum*› cerrar*

- **close with** [v ▸ prep ▸ o] (engage) ‹*enemy*› enfrentarse a

closecropped /ˈkləʊsˈkrɑːpt || ˌkləʊsˈkrɒpt/ *adj* ‹*grass*› muy corto; **to have ~ hair, to be ~** llevar el pelo (cortado) al rape

closed /kləʊzd/ *adj*

A ‹*door/book/flower*› cerrado; **his eyes were ~** tenía los ojos cerrados

B (not operating, trading) cerrado

C ‹*road*› cerrado; ‹*meeting*› a puerta(s) cerrada(s)

D ‹*case/matter*› cerrado

closed: ~ **circuit** *n* circuito *m* cerrado; (*before n*) ~**-circuit television** televisión *f* en circuito cerrado; ~**-door** *adj* (AmE) ‹*meeting/briefing*› a puerta(s) cerrada(s)

close-down /ˈkləʊzdaʊn/ *n* (of factory) cierre *m*

closed shop *n*: *empresa que tiene un convenio con un sindicato determinado por el cual todo empleado debe estar afiliado a éste*

close /kləʊs/: ~**-fisted** /ˈkləʊsˈfɪstəd || ˌkləʊsˈfɪstɪd/ *adj* tacaño, agarrado (fam), amarrete (AmS fam); ~**-fitting** *adj* ajustado, ceñido; ~**-knit** *adj* unido

closely /ˈkləʊsli/ *adv*

A ‹*connected/associated*› estrechamente; **we are ~ related** somos parientes cercanos; **they worked ~ with the French** trabajaron en estrecha colaboración con los franceses

B [1] (at a short distance) ‹*follow/mark*› de cerca [2] (carefully) ‹*study/examine*› detenidamente; ‹*watch*› de cerca, atentamente; ‹*question*› a fondo; **a ~ guarded secret** un secreto muy bien guardado

C [1] (in approximation): **somebody who resembled her ~** alguien que se le parecía mucho [2] (nearly equally): **a ~ fought** *o* **contested game** un partido muy reñido

closeout /ˈkləʊzaʊt/ *n* (AmE) liquidación *f*

close: **~-run** /'kləʊs'rʌn/ *adj* ‹*race*› muy reñido; **~-set** /'kləʊs'set/ *adj* ‹*eyes*› junto

closet[1] /'klɑ:zət || 'klɒzɪt/ *n* (AmE) (cupboard) armario *m*, placard *m* (RPl); (for clothes) armario *m*, closet *m* (AmL exc RPl), placard *m* (RPl); ***to come out of the ~*** (colloq) destaparse (fam), declararse abiertamente homosexual

closet[2] *adj* ‹*gay/racist*› encubierto, de closet (Méx fam), de tapadillo (Esp fam)

closet[3] *vt* (*usu pass*): **to be ~ed (WITH sb)** estar* encerrado (CON algn)

close-up /'kləʊsʌp/ *n* primer plano *m*

closing /'kləʊzɪŋ/: **~ date** *n* fecha *f* límite, fecha *f* tope; **~ time** *n* hora *f* de cierre

closure /'kləʊʒər || 'kləʊʒə(r)/ *n* [u c] (of factory, hospital, road) cierre *m*

clot[1] /klɑ:t || klɒt/ *n*
A (of blood) coágulo *m*
B (idiot) (BrE colloq) bobalicón, -cona *m,f* (fam)

clot[2] *vi* **-tt-** «*blood*» coagularse

cloth /klɔ:θ || klɒθ/ *n*
A 1 [u] (fabric) tela *f*, género *m*; (thick, woolen) paño *m*; ***to be made (up) out of whole ~*** (AmE) ser* pura invención *or* puro invento; ▸**coat**[1] **A1** 2 [c] (for cleaning) trapo *m* 3 [c] (*table~*) mantel *m*
B (Relig): **the ~** el clero; **a man of the ~** un clérigo

clothe /kləʊð/ *vt* 1 (provide clothes for) vestir* 2 (*past & past p* **clothed** *or* **clad**) (dress) (liter) vestir*, ataviar* (liter); *see also* **clad**[2]

cloth-eared /'klɔ:θ'ɪrd || ˌklɒθ'ɪəd/ *adj* (colloq) sordo (como una tapia)

clothes /kləʊðz/ *pl n* ropa *f*; **to put on/take off one's ~** ponerse*/quitarse la ropa; **she jumped in with her ~ on** se metió vestida; **he had no ~ on** estaba desnudo; (*before n*) **~ brush** cepillo *m* para *or* de la ropa, escobilla *f* de ropa (Chi); **~ horse** tendedero *m* (*plegable*); **~ line** cuerda *f* de tender; **~ pin** *o* (BrE) **peg** pinza *f or* (Arg) broche *m or* (Chi) perrito *m or* (Col, Ven) gancho *or* (Ur) palillo *m* (de tender la ropa); **~ shop** tienda *f or* casa *f* de modas; **~ tree** (AmE) perchero *m*

clothing /'kləʊðɪŋ/ *n* [u] ropa *f*; (*before n*) **the ~ industry** la industria de la confección

clotted cream /'klɑ:təd || 'klɒtɪd/ *n* [u] *crema muy espesa, típica del sudoeste de Inglaterra*

cloud[1] /klaʊd/ *n* 1 [c u] (Meteo) (single) nube *f*; (mass) nubes *fpl*, nubosidad *f*; **there's not a ~ in the sky** está totalmente despejado; **the only ~ on the horizon is my exam** la única nube en el horizonte *or* el único nubarrón es mi examen; ***to be on ~ nine*** (colloq) estar* en el séptimo cielo *or* en la gloria; ***under a ~*** en circunstancias sospechosas *or* poco claras; ***every ~ has a silver lining*** no hay mal que por bien no venga 2 [c] (of gas, smoke, dust) nube *f*; (of suspicion, ambiguity) halo *m*, nube *f*

cloud[2] *vt* 1 (dim, blur) ‹*view/vision*› nublar; **emotion ~ed his judgment** la emoción lo ofuscaba, estaba obnubilado por la emoción; **to ~ the issue** embrollar el asunto, crear confusión 2 (spoil, mar) ‹*enjoyment/relationship*› empañar

Phrasal verb

- **cloud over** [v ▸ adv] nublarse

cloud: **~burst** *n* chaparrón *m*, aguacero *m*; **~-cuckoo-land** /'klaʊd'ku:ku:lænd || ˌklaʊd'kʊku:lænd/ *n*: **she lives in ~-cuckoo-land** vive en las nubes *or* en otro mundo

cloudless /'klaʊdləs || 'klaʊdlɪs/ *adj* totalmente despejado, sin una nube

cloudy /'klaʊdi/ *adj* **-dier, -diest** 1 (Meteo) ‹*day*› nublado; ‹*sky*› nublado, nuboso 2 ‹*liquid*› turbio; ‹*memory*› poco claro

clout[1] /klaʊt/ *n* (colloq)
A [c] (blow) tortazo *m* (fam)
B [u] (power, influence) peso *m*, influencia *f*

clout[2] *vt* (colloq): **to ~ sb** darle* un tortazo a algn (fam)

clove[1] /kləʊv/ *n* 1 (spice) clavo *m* (de olor) 2 (of garlic) diente *m*

clove[2] (arch) *past of* **cleave** *vt*

cloven /'kləʊvən/ (arch) *past p of* **cleave** *vt*

cloven hoof *n* pezuña *f* partida *or* hendida

clover /'kləʊvər || 'kləʊvə(r)/ *n* [u c] trébol *m*; **four-leaf** *o* **four-leaved ~** trébol de cuatro hojas; ***to be*** *o* ***live in ~*** vivir a lo grande, darse* la gran vida

clown[1] /klaʊn/ *n* payaso, -sa *m,f*

clown[2] *vi* **~ (around** *o* **about)** hacer* payasadas, payasear (AmL fam), hacer* el payaso (Esp)

cloy /klɔɪ/ *vi* empalagar*

cloying /'klɔɪɪŋ/ *adj* empalagoso

cloze test /kləʊz/ *n* prueba *f* cloze, ejercicio *m* de comprensión (*en el que hay que rellenar blancos*)

club[1] /klʌb/ *n*
A 1 (cudgel) garrote *m*, cachiporra *f* 2 (*golf ~*) palo *m* de golf
B (society, association) club *m*; **sports ~** club deportivo; **to join a ~** hacerse* socio de un club; **I'm fed up — join the ~!** estoy harto — ¡no eres el único! *or* ¡ya somos dos!
C 1 (Games) **clubs** *pl* (suit) (+ *sing or pl vb*) tréboles *mpl*; (in Spanish pack) bastos *mpl* 2 (for dancing) discoteca *f*

club[2] **-bb-** *vt* aporrear, darle* garrotazos a
■ **club** *vi* (visit dancing venues): **to go clubbing** ir* de discotecа, ir* de marcha (Esp fam), carretear (Chi fam)

Phrasal verb

- **club together** [v ▸ adv] (contribute money) (BrE): **they ~bed together to buy her a present** le compraron un regalo entre todos

clubber /'klʌbər || 'klʌbə(r)/ *n* discotequero, -ra *m,f*, clubero, -ra *m,f* (AmL), marchoso, -sa *m,f* (Esp fam), carretero, -ra *m,f* (Chi fam)

club: **~foot** /'klʌb'fʊt/ *n* pie *m* deforme; **~house** *n* (building for club) casa *f* club; (of grandstand, stadium) (AmE) club *m* de tribuna; **~ sandwich** *n* sandwich *m* club *or* de dos pisos

cluck[1] /klʌk/ *vi* «*hen*» cloquear; «*person*» chascar* *or* chasquear la lengua

cluck[2] *n*
A (of hen) cloqueo *m*; (of person) chasquido *m* (de la lengua)
B (fool) (AmE colloq) idiota *mf* (fam)

clue /klu:/ *n* (indication) pista *f*; (in crosswords) clave *f*; ***not to have a ~*** (colloq) (not know, be incompetent) no tener* ni (la más mínima *or* la menor) idea (fam)

clued-up /'klu:d'ʌp/ *adj* (*pred* **clued up**) (colloq) ‹*person*› bien informado; **to be ~ ~ ABOUT sth** estar* muy al tanto DE algo

clueless /'klu:ləs || 'klu:lɪs/ *adj* 1 (not having found clue) (AmE journ) sin pistas 2 (incompetent) (BrE colloq) negado (fam)

clump[1] /klʌmp/ *n* 1 (of trees) grupo *m*; (of flowers) macizo *m* 2 (of earth) terrón *m*

clump[2] *vi* (walk heavily) (colloq) caminar pisando fuerte

clumsily /'klʌmzəli || 'klʌmzɪli/ *adv* 1 ‹*handle/apologize*› torpemente, con torpeza 2 ‹*made*› toscamente; ‹*written*› con poca fluidez

clumsiness /'klʌmzinəs || 'klʌmzɪnɪs/ *n* [u] 1 (of movement, words) torpeza *f* 2 (of construction, design) tosquedad *f*

clumsy /'klʌmzi/ *adj* **-sier, -siest** 1 ‹*person/movement*› torpe, patoso (Esp fam) 2 ‹*tool/shape*› tosco; ‹*translation/forgery*› burdo; ‹*writing*› falto de fluidez

clung /klʌŋ/ *past & past p of* **cling**

clunk[1] /klʌŋk/ *vi* golpetear

clunk[2] *n* golpetazo *m* (metálico)

clunky /'klʌŋki/ *adj* 1 (out of date) anticuado 2 (clumsy, awkward) tosco y pesado

cluster[1] /'klʌstər || 'klʌstə(r)/ *n* (of people, buildings) grupo *m*; (of berries, bananas) racimo *m*; (of stars) grupo *m*

cluster[2] *vi* (bunch) apiñarse, agruparse
■ **cluster** *vt*: **all the hotels are ~ed around the station** todos los hoteles están agrupados *or* concentrados alrededor de la estación

clutch[1] /klʌtʃ/ *n*
A 1 **clutches** *pl* garras *fpl*; **to be in/fall into sb's/sth's ~es** estar*/caer* en las garras de algn/algo 2 (difficult, crucial situation) (AmE): **in the ~** (colloq) en las emergencias; (*before n*) **~ situation** situación *f* de emergencia
B 1 (device) embrague *m*, clutch *m* (AmC, Col, Méx, Ven) 2 **~ (pedal)** (pedal *m* del) embrague *m*, clutch *m* (AmC, Col, Méx, Ven); **to let out the ~** desembragar*, soltar* el embrague
C 1 (of eggs) nidada *f* 2 (group, bunch) puñado *m*

clutch[2] *vt* tener* firmemente agarrado; **she ~ed the child to her breast** estrechó *or* apretó al niño contra su pecho
■ **clutch** *vi* **to ~ AT sth** tratar de agarrarse DE algo
clutch bag *n: bolso sin asas,* sobre *m* (AmL)
clutter[1] /'klʌtər || 'klʌtə(r)/ *n* [u]: **the room was full of ~** la habitación estaba abarrotada *or* atestada de cosas; **a ~ of books and papers** un revoltijo de libros y papeles
clutter[2] *vt* **~ (up)** abarrotar; **to ~ sth WITH sth** abarrotar algo DE algo; **don't ~ your essay with unnecessary detail** no recargues el trabajo con detalles superfluos
cluttered /'klʌtərd || 'klʌtəd/ *adj* abarrotado *or* atestado de cosas
cm (= **centimeter(s)** *or* (BrE) **centimetre(s)**) cm.
Cmdr (title) = **Commander**
CND *n* (in UK) (= **Campaign for Nuclear Disarmament**) Campaña *f* pro Desarme Nuclear
co- /'kəʊ/ *pref* co-
c/o (= **in care of** *or* (BrE) **care of**): **John Smith, c/o Ana Mas** John Smith, en casa de Ana Mas, Ana Mas, para entregar a John Smith
Co 1 /kəʊ/ (= **company**) Cía. 2 (Geog) = **County**
CO
A (Geog) = **Colorado**
B (Mil) = **Commanding Officer**
coach[1] /kəʊtʃ/ *n*
A 1 (horse-drawn carriage) coche *m* (de caballos), carruaje *m*; (*stage* ~) diligencia *f* 2 (long-distance bus) (BrE) autobús *m*, autocar *m* (Esp), pullman *m* (CS)
B (Rail) 1 (AmE) vagón *m* de tercera (clase); (*before n*) ‹*fare/passenger*› de tercera 2 (BrE) vagón *m*
C 1 (tutor) profesor, -sora *m,f* particular 2 (team manager) entrenador, -dora *m,f*, director técnico, directora técnica *mf* (AmL)
coach[2] *vt* ‹*team/player*› entrenar; ‹*pupil/student/singer*› preparar, darle* clases a
coaching /'kəʊtʃɪŋ/ *n* [u] 1 (training) entrenamiento *m* 2 (tutoring) preparación *f*, clases *fpl* 3 (prompting) (AmE colloq) ayuda *f*
coachload /'kəʊtʃləʊd/ *n* (BrE) ▸ **busload**
coagulate /kəʊ'ægjəleɪt || kəʊ'ægjʊleɪt/ *vi* «*blood*» coagularse
coal /kəʊl/ *n* [u c] carbón *m*; ***to carry ~s to Newcastle*** llevar leña al monte, ir* a vendimiar y llevar uvas de postre; ***to haul sb over the ~s*** reprender severamente a algn, poner* a algn como chupa de dómine; (*before n*) **~ bin** *o* (BrE) **bunker** carbonera *f*; **~ cellar** carbonera *f*; **~ dust** carbonilla *f*; **~ fire** fuego *m* de *or* a carbón; **~ mine** mina *f* de carbón; **~ miner** minero, -ra *m,f* del carbón; **~ shed** carbonera *f*
coal: **~-black** /'kəʊl'blæk/ *adj* (*pred* **~ black**) negro como el carbón; **~face** *n* tajo *m*, frente *m* de explotación del carbón; **~field** *n* yacimiento *m* de carbón; (area of working mines) área *f*‡ *or* zona *f* de minas de carbón
coalition /'kəʊə'lɪʃən/ *n* [u c] coalición *f*
coal: **~man** /'kəʊlmæn/ *n* (*pl* **-men** /-men/) carbonero *m*; **~ mining** *n* [u] explotación *f* hullera *or* de las minas de carbón; (*before n*) **~-mining area** zona *f* minera; **~ scuttle** /'kəʊl,skʌtl/ *n* cubo *m* del carbón; **~ tar** *n* alquitrán *m* de hulla; (*before n*) **~ tar soap** jabón *m* de brea
coarse /kɔːrs || kɔːs/ *adj* **coarser, coarsest** 1 ‹*sand/filter*› grueso; ‹*cloth*› basto, ordinario, burdo; ‹*bread*› basto; ‹*features*› tosco 2 ‹*person*› basto, ordinario, burdo; ‹*manners*› ordinario, basto, tosco; ‹*language/joke*› ordinario, basto, grosero
coarsely /'kɔːrsli || 'kɔːsli/ *adv* 1 ‹*chop*› en trozos grandes; ‹*weave*› toscamente 2 ‹*speak/behave*› de manera ordinaria, con ordinariez
coarsen /'kɔːrsn || 'kɔːsən/ *vt* 1 ‹*skin*› poner* áspero 2 ‹*person/manners*› volver* ordinario *or* tosco *or* basto
■ **coarsen** *vi* 1 «*skin*» volverse* áspero 2 «*person/language*» volverse* más ordinario *or* basto
coast[1] /kəʊst/ *n* 1 (shoreline) costa *f*; ***the ~ is clear*** no hay moros en la costa 2 (region) costa *f*, litoral *m*; **from ~ to ~** de costa a costa
coast[2] *vi* 1 (freewheel) «*car*» deslizarse* (*sin llevar el motor en marcha*) 2 (proceed effortlessly): **she ~ed through her exams** superó fácilmente los exámenes
coastal /'kəʊstl/ *adj* (*before n*) costero
coaster /'kəʊstər || 'kəʊstə(r)/ *n* 1 (ship) barco *m* de cabotaje 2 (drink mat) posavasos *m*
coast: **~guard** *n* 1 (organization) **the C~guard** los guardacostas 2 [c] (person) guardacostas *mf*; **~guardsman** /'kəʊstgɑːrdzmən || 'kəʊstgɑːdzmən/ *n* (*pl* **-men** /-mən/) (AmE) ▸ **~guard 2**; **~line** *n* [u c] costa *f*, litoral *m*; **~ to coast** *adv* (AmE) a lo largo y ancho del país; **~-to-coast** /'kəʊsttə'kəʊst/ *adj* (AmE) de costa a costa
coat[1] /kəʊt/ *n*
A (Clothing) 1 (*over*~) (for men) abrigo *m* *or* (RPl) sobretodo *m*; (for women) abrigo *m* *or* (RPl) tapado *m*; **white ~** (doctor's etc) bata *f* blanca; ***to cut one's ~ according to one's cloth*** (BrE) vivir según sus (*or* mis *etc*) posibilidades, adaptarse a las circunstancias; (*before n*) **~ hanger** percha *f*; **~ stand** perchero *m* 2 (jacket) chaqueta *f*; (heavier) chaquetón *m*
B (of animals) pelaje *m*
C (layer) capa *f*; (of paint) capa *f*, mano *f*
coat[2] *vt* cubrir*
-coated /'kəʊtəd || 'kəʊtɪd/ *suff* (Culin): **sugar~** cubierto de azúcar; **chocolate~** cubierto de chocolate, bañado en chocolate
coating /'kəʊtɪŋ/ *n* (of dust, grease) capa *f*; (Culin) capa *f*, baño *m*; **protective ~** revestimiento *m* de protección
coat of arms *n* (*pl* **~s ~ ~**) escudo *m* de armas
coax /kəʊks/ *vt* **to ~ sb/sth INTO -ING**: **I ~ed the child into going to bed** convencí al niño para que se acostara; **I ~ed the animal into the cage** con paciencia logré que el animal se metiera en la jaula; **to ~ sb TO + INF**: **she ~ed them to eat** con paciencia intentó que comieran; **to ~ sth FROM *o* OUT OF sb** sonsacarle* algo A algn; **a ~ing voice** una voz persuasiva
coaxing /'kəʊksɪŋ/ *n* [u] persuasión *f*, mano *f* izquierda
cob /kɑːb || kɒb/ *n* (*corn*~) mazorca *f* (de maíz), choclo *m* (AmS), elote *m* (AmC, Méx)
cobalt /'kəʊbɔːlt/ *n* [u] cobalto *m*
cobble /'kɑːbəl || 'kɒbəl/ *vt* 1 ‹*shoe*› arreglar 2 **cobbled** *past p* ‹*street*› adoquinado

Phrasal verb
• **cobble together** [v ▸ o ▸ adv, v ▸ adv ▸ o] (colloq) ‹*meal*› improvisar; ‹*essay/speech*› redactar a las carreras (fam)

cobbler /'kɑːblər || 'kɒblə(r)/ *n*
A (shoe repairer) zapatero *m* (remendón)
B **cobblers** *pl* (nonsense) (BrE sl) estupideces *fpl*
cobblestone /'kɑːbəlstəʊn || 'kɒbəlstəʊn/ *n* adoquín *m*
cobra /'kəʊbrə/ *n* cobra *f*
cobweb /'kɑːbweb || 'kɒbweb/ *n* telaraña *f*
cocaine /kəʊ'keɪn/ *n* [u] cocaína *f*
coccyx /'kɑːksɪks || 'kɒksɪks/ *n* (*pl* **coccyges** /'kɑːksədʒiːz || 'kɒksɪdʒiːz/ *or* **coccyxes**) coxis *m*, cóccix *m*
cochineal /'kɑːtʃəniːl || ,kɒtʃɪ'niːl/ *n* [u] cochinilla *f*
cock[1] /kɑːk || kɒk/ *n*
A [c] (male fowl) gallo *m*; (male bird) macho *m*
B [c] (penis) (vulg) verga *f*, pija *f* (RPl vulg), polla *f* (Esp vulg), pico *m* (Chi vulg)
cock[2] *vt*
A ‹*gun*› montar, amartillar
B ‹*head*› ladear; ‹*ears*› levantar, parar (AmL); **the dog ~ed its leg at each tree** el perro levantaba la pata en cada árbol

Phrasal verb
• **cock up** [v ▸ o ▸ adv, v ▸ adv ▸ o] (BrE sl) fastidiar (fam), joder (vulg)

cock-a-doodle-doo /'kɑːkə'duːdl̩'duː || ,kɒkə,duːdl̩'duː/ *interj* ¡quiquiriquí!
cock-a-hoop /'kɑːkə'huːp || ,kɒkə'huːp/ *adj* (exultant) (*usu pred*) **to be ~ ABOUT sth** estar* contentísimo *or* como unas castañuelas CON algo
cockamamy /'kɑːkə'meɪmi || ,kɒkə'mæmi/ *adj* (AmE colloq) absurdo, disparatado
cock-and-bull /'kɑːkən'bʊl || ,kɒkən'bʊl/ *adj* (colloq): **~ story** *o* **tale** cuento *m* (chino) (fam), camelo *m* (fam)
cockatoo /'kɑːkətuː || ,kɒkə'tuː/ *n* (*pl* **-toos**) cacatúa *f*
cocked hat *n*: ***to knock sb/sth into a ~ ~*** darle* cien *or* cien mil vueltas a algn/algo (fam), ser* muchísimo mejor que algn/algo

cockerel /ˈkɑːkrəl || ˈkɒkərəl/ *n* gallito *m*

cocker spaniel /ˈkɑːkər || ˈkɒkə(r)/ *n* cocker *mf* (spaniel)

cockeyed /ˈkɑːkaɪd || ˈkɒkaɪd/ *adj* 1 (ridiculous) disparatado 2 (askew) torcido, chueco (AmL)

cock: ~**fight** *n* pelea *f* de gallos, riña *f* de gallos (AmS); ~**fighting** *n* [u] peleas *fpl* de gallos, riñas *fpl* de gallos (AmS)

cockle /ˈkɑːkəl || ˈkɒkəl/ *n* (Zool) berberecho *m*; ***to warm the ~s of sb's heart*** enternecer* a algn

Cockney, cockney /ˈkɑːkni || ˈkɒkni/ *n* (*pl* **-neys**) cockney *mf* (*persona nacida en el East End de Londres*)

cockpit /ˈkɑːkpɪt || ˈkɒkpɪt/ *n*
A (Aviat) cabina *f* de mando; (Naut) puente *m* de mando; (in racing car) cabina *f*
B (for cockfights) gallera *f*, reñidero *m*, palenque *m* (Méx)

cockroach /ˈkɑːkrəʊtʃ || ˈkɒkrəʊtʃ/ *n* cucaracha *f*

cocksure /ˈkɑːkˈʃʊr || kɒkˈʃʊə(r), ˌkɒkˈʃɔː(r)/ *adj* (colloq) creído (fam), petulante, engreído

cocktail /ˈkɑːkteɪl || ˈkɒkteɪl/ *n* 1 [c] (drink) cóctel *m*, coctel *m*, combinado *m*; (*before n*) ~ **bar** bar *m*, coctelería *f*; ~ **cabinet** mueble-bar *m*; ~ **party** cóctel *m*, coctel *m*; ~ **stick** palillo *m*, mondadientes *m*, escarbadientes *m* 2 [c u] (food): **shrimp** *o* (BrE) **prawn** ~ cóctel *m* de camarones *or* (Esp) de gambas *or* (CS) de langostinos, langostinos *mpl* con salsa golf (RPl)

cock-up /ˈkɑːkʌp || ˈkɒkʌp/ *n* (BrE colloq) lío *m*, follón *m* (Esp fam); **I made a ~ of it** la fastidié (fam), la embarré (AmS fam)

cocky /ˈkɑːki || ˈkɒkɪ/ *adj* **cockier, cockiest** (colloq) gallito (fam), chulo (Esp fam)

cocoa /ˈkəʊkəʊ/ *n* [u c] (powder) cacao *m*, cocoa *f* (AmL); (drink) chocolate *m*, cocoa *f* (AmL)

coconut /ˈkəʊkənʌt/ *n* [c u] coco *m*

coconut: ~ **milk** *n* agua *f*‡ de coco; ~ **palm** *n* cocotero *m*, palma *f* de coco (Col); ~ **shy** *n* (in UK) tiro *m* al coco; ~ **tree** *n* ▸ ~ **palm**

cocoon¹ /kəˈkuːn/ *n* (Zool) capullo *m*

cocoon² *vt* **to ~ sb IN sth** arrebujar *or* arropar a algn EN *or* CON algo

cod /kɑːd || ˈkɒd/ *n* [c u] (*pl* ~ *or* ~**s**) bacalao *m*

COD *adv* (= **cash** *or* (AmE also) **collect on delivery**) contra reembolso

coddle /ˈkɑːdl̩ || ˈkɒdl̩/ *vt* mimar

code¹ /kəʊd/ *n*
A 1 [c u] (cipher) clave *f*, código *m*; **in ~** en clave, cifrado 2 [c] (for identification) código *m* 3 [u] (Comput) código *m* 4 [c] (Telec) código *m*, prefijo *m*
B [c] 1 (social, moral) código *m*; ~ **of practice** código de práctica 2 (Law) código *m*

code² *vt* 1 (encipher) cifrar, poner* en clave 2 (give identifying number, mark) codificar*; (Comput) codificar*

codeine /ˈkəʊdiːn/ *n* [u] codeína *f*

codger /ˈkɑːdʒər || ˈkɒdʒə(r)/ *n* (colloq): **old ~** vejete *m* (fam)

coding /ˈkəʊdɪŋ/ *n* [u c] 1 (use of ciphers) cifrado *m*, notación *f* en clave 2 (Comput) codificación *f*

cod-liver oil /ˈkɑːdˌlɪvər || ˈkɒdˌlɪvə(r)/ *n* [u] aceite *m* de hígado de bacalao

co-driver /ˈkəʊˈdraɪvər || ˈkəʊˌdraɪvə(r)/ *n* copiloto *mf*

codswallop /ˈkɑːdzwɑːləp || ˈkɒdzwɒləp/ *n* [u] (BrE colloq) paparruchas *fpl* (fam)

coed /ˈkəʊed/, **coeducational** /kəʊˈedʒəˈkeɪʃn̩əl || ˌkəʊˌedjʊˈkeɪʃənəl/ *adj* mixto

coefficient /ˈkəʊəˈfɪʃənt || ˌkəʊɪˈfɪʃənt/ *n* coeficiente *m*

coeliac disease /ˈsiːljæk/ *n* [u] enfermedad *f* celiaca

coerce /kəʊˈɜːrs || kəʊˈɜːs/ *vt* **to ~ sb (INTO -ING)** coaccionar a algn (PARA QUE (+ *subj*)), compeler a algn (A + INF) (frml)

coercion /kəʊˈɜːrʒən || kəʊˈɜːʃən/ *n* [u] coacción *f*

coexist /ˈkəʊɪgˈzɪst/ *vi* **to ~ (WITH sb/sth)** coexistir *or* convivir (CON algn/algo)

coexistence /ˈkəʊɪgˈzɪstəns/ *n* [u] coexistencia *f*, convivencia *f*

C of E *adj* (BrE colloq) (= **Church of England**) anglicano

coffee /ˈkɔːfi || ˈkɒfi/ *n*
A [u] (beans, granules, drink) café *m*; **black ~** café negro *or* (Esp) solo *or* (Chi) puro *or* (Col) tinto; **white ~** (BrE) café con leche; (*before n*) ~ **break** pausa *f* del café; ~ **mill** *o* **grinder** molinillo *m* de café; ~ **percolator** cafetera *f* de filtro
B (color) (color *m*) café *m* con leche

coffee: ~ **bar** *n* (BrE) café *m*, cafetería *f*; ~ **cake** *n* [u c] (in US) *bizcocho con fruta seca*; (in UK) pastel *m* de café; ~ **house** *n* café *m*, cafetería *f*; ~ **klatsch** /klætʃ, klɑːtʃ / *n* (AmE) tertulia *f*; ~ **maker** *n* cafetera *f*, máquina *f* para preparar café; ~**pot** *n* cafetera *f*; ~ **table** *n* mesa *f* de centro, mesa *f* ratona (RPl); (*before n*) ~**-table book** *libro ilustrado de gran formato*

coffer /ˈkɔːfər || ˈkɒfə(r)/ *n* 1 (chest) cofre *m* 2 **coffers** *pl* (funds) fondos *mpl*

coffin /ˈkɔːfən || ˈkɒfɪn/ *n* ataúd *m*, féretro *m*, cajón *m* (AmL)

cog /kɑːg || kɒg/ *n* 1 (tooth) diente *m* 2 (wheel) piñón *m*, rueda *f* dentada; **to be a ~ in the machine** ser* una pieza más en el engranaje del organismo (*or* del partido *etc*)

cogent /ˈkəʊdʒənt/ *adj* convincente, contundente

cogitate /ˈkɑːdʒəteɪt || ˈkɒdʒɪteɪt/ *vi* **to ~ (ON** *o* **UPON sth)** cavilar *or* meditar (SOBRE algo)

cogitation /ˈkɑːdʒəˈteɪʃən || ˌkɒdʒɪˈteɪʃən/ *n* [u] (frml) (*often pl*) cavilación *f*, meditación *f*

cognac /ˈkɑːnjæk || ˈkɒnjæk/ *n* [u c] coñac *m*, coñá *m*

cognitive /ˈkɑːgnətɪv || ˈkɒgnɪtɪv/ *adj* cognoscitivo

cohabit /kəʊˈhæbət || kəʊˈhæbɪt/ *vi* (frml) **to ~ (WITH sb)** cohabitar (CON algn) (frml)

cohere /kəʊˈhɪr || kəʊˈhɪə(r)/ *vi* 1 (form unit) formar una unidad 2 (be consistent) **to ~ (WITH sth)** ser* coherente *or* congruente (CON algo)

coherence /kəʊˈhɪrəns || kəʊˈhɪərəns/, **coherency** /-si/ *n* [u] 1 (logical connection) coherencia *f*, congruencia *f* 2 (of group) cohesión *f*

coherent /kəʊˈhɪrənt || kəʊˈhɪərənt/ *adj* coherente, congruente

cohesion /kəʊˈhiːʒən/ *n* [u] cohesión *f*

cohesive /kəʊˈhiːsɪv/ *adj* ‹*group*› unido

cohort /ˈkəʊhɔːrt || ˈkəʊhɔːt/ *n* 1 (Hist, Mil) cohorte *f* 2 (follower) (AmE) seguidor, -dora *m,f*

coiffure /kwɑːˈfjʊr || kwɑːˈfjʊə(r)/ *n* peinado *m*

coil¹ /kɔɪl/ *n*
A 1 (series of loops — of rope, wire) rollo *m*; (— of smoke) espiral *f*, volutas *fpl*; (— of hair) moño *m*, chongo *m* (Méx), rodete *m* (RPl) 2 (single loop) lazada *f*, vuelta *f*
B (contraceptive) (BrE) espiral *f*

coil² *vt* ‹*rope/wire*› enrollar; **to ~ sth/oneself AROUND sth** enrollar algo/enrollarse *or* enroscarse* ALREDEDOR DE algo
■ **coil** *vi*: **smoke ~ed into the air** el humo se alzaba en volutas *or* en espiral

coin¹ /kɔɪn/ *n* [c] moneda *f*; ***the other side of the ~*** la otra cara de la moneda

coin² *vt* 1 (invent) ‹*word/expression*› acuñar; **to ~ a phrase** (set phrase) como se suele decir 2 (mint) acuñar

coinage /ˈkɔɪnɪdʒ/ *n*
A [u] (system) sistema *m* monetario
B [c] (invented word, phrase) palabra *f* (*or* frase *f etc*) de nuevo cuño

coin box *n* depósito *m* de monedas

coincide /ˈkəʊənˈsaɪd || ˌkəʊɪnˈsaɪd/ *vi* **to ~ (WITH sth)** coincidir (CON algo)

coincidence /kəʊˈɪnsədəns || kəʊˈɪnsɪdəns/ *n* [c u] casualidad *f*, coincidencia *f*; **by ~ he was there** dio la casualidad de que estaba allí

coincidental /kəʊˈɪnsəˈdentl̩ || kəʊˈɪnsɪdentl̩/ *adj* casual, fortuito

coincidentally /kəʊˈɪnsəˈdentl̩i || kəʊˌɪnsɪˈdentəli/ *adv* por casualidad, casualmente

coin-operated /ˈkɔɪnˈɑːpəreɪtəd || ˈkɔɪnˌɒpəreɪtɪd/ *adj* que funciona con monedas

coitus /ˈkəʊətəs || ˈkəʊɪtəs/, **coition** /kəʊˈɪʃn̩/ *n* [u] (frml) coito *m* (frml)

coke /kəʊk/ *n* [u]
A (fuel) (carbón *m* de) coque *m*
B (cocaine) (colloq) coca *f* (fam)

C

C **Coke**® (colloq) Coca-Cola® *f*

Col (title) (= **Colonel**) Cnel.

colander /'kʌləndər || 'kʌləndə(r)/ *n* colador *m*, escurridor *m* (*de pasta, verduras*)

cold¹ /kəʊld/ *adj*

A ‹*water/weather/drink*› frío; **I'm ~** tengo frío; **my feet are ~** tengo los pies fríos, tengo frío en los pies; **it's ~ today/in here** hoy/aquí hace frío; **the soup is ~** la sopa está fría; **I'm getting ~** me está entrando frío; **it's getting ~** está empezando a hacer frío; **the engine starts straight from ~** el motor arranca en frío; **no, you're still ~, getting ~er** (in game) no, frío, más frío; **the trail had gone ~** se habían borrado las huellas; ▸**blow²** *vi* **A1**

B 1 (unfriendly, unenthusiastic) frío; **I got a very ~ reception** me recibieron con mucha frialdad *or* muy fríamente; **to be ~ TO** *o* **WITH sb** tratar a algn con frialdad, estar*/ser* frío con algn; ***to leave sb ~***: **that leaves me ~** (colloq) (eso) me deja frío *or* tal cual (fam), (eso) no me da ni frío ni calor (fam) 2 (impersonal) ‹*logic*› frío

C (unconscious) ▸**out² A2**

D (without preparation) sin ninguna preparación; **I came to the job ~** empecé el trabajo sin ninguna preparación

cold² *n*

A [u] (low temperature) frío *m*; **to shiver with ~** temblar* de frío; **to feel the ~** ser* friolento *or* (Esp) friolero, sentir* el frío; ***to leave sb/be left out in the ~*** dejar a algn/quedarse al margen

B [c] (Med) resfriado *m*, catarro *m*, constipado *m* (Esp), resfrío *m* (CS); **to have a ~** estar* resfriado; **to catch a ~** resfriarse*, coger* un resfriado (Esp), agarrarse un resfrío (CS)

cold³ *adv* (*as intensifier*): **I've got the part down ~ now** (AmE) ahora me sé el papel perfectamente *or* (fam) de pe a pa

cold: **~-blooded** /'kəʊld'blʌdəd || ˌkəʊld'blʌdɪd/ *adj* 1 ‹*murder*› a sangre fría; ‹*killer*› despiadado, cruel, desalmado 2 (Zool) de sangre fría; **~ calling** *n* [u] venta *f* en frío; **~ cream** *n* [u] crema *f* limpiadora *or* de limpieza, cold cream *f*; **~ cuts** *pl n* (AmE) fiambres *mpl*; **~-hearted** /'kəʊld'hɑːrtəd || ˌkəʊld'hɑːtɪd/ *adj* frío, insensible

coldly /'kəʊldli/ *adv* con frialdad, fríamente

coldness /'kəʊldnəs || 'kəʊldnɪs/ *n* [u] 1 (of person, attitude) frialdad *f* 2 (temperature) frío *m*

cold: **~-shoulder** /'kəʊld'ʃəʊldər || ˌkəʊld'ʃəʊldə(r)/ *vt* (colloq) hacerle* el vacío a; **~ sore** *n* herpes *m* (labial), boquera *f*, fuego *m* (AmL), pupa *f* (Esp fam); **~ storage** *n* [u] almacenamiento *m* en cámaras frigoríficas; **~ turkey** *adv* (sl): **to go ~ turkey** estar* con el mono (arg); **~ war** *n* guerra *f* fría

coleslaw /'kəʊlslɔː/ *n* [u] *ensalada de repollo, zanahoria y cebolla con mayonesa*

colic /'kɑːlɪk || 'kɒlɪk/ *n* [u] cólico *m*

collaborate /kə'læbəreɪt/ *vi* colaborar

collaboration /kə'læbə'reɪʃən/ *n* [u] (cooperation) colaboración *f*; (with enemy) colaboracionismo *m*; **in ~ with** en colaboración con

collaborator /kə'læbəreɪtər || kə'læbəreɪtə(r)/ *n* (partner) colaborador, -dora *m,f*; (with enemy) colaboracionista *mf*

collage /kə'lɑːʒ || 'kɒlɑːʒ/ *n* [c u] collage *m*

collapse¹ /kə'læps/ *vi*

A (fall down) «*building*» derrumbarse, desmoronarse, desplomarse

B 1 (fall) «*person*» desplomarse; **we ~d with laughter** nos desternillamos de risa 2 (Med) «*person*» sufrir un colapso

C (fail) fracasar, venirse* abajo

D 1 (fold up) «*table/chair*» plegarse* 2 **collapsing** *pres p* ‹*table/chair*› plegable

collapse² *n* [c u] 1 (of building) derrumbe *m*, desmoronamiento *m* 2 (Med) colapso *m* 3 (of plan) fracaso *m*; (of company) quiebra *f*

collapsible /kə'læpsəbəl/ *adj* ‹*table/bed*› plegable

collar¹ /'kɑːlər || 'kɒlə(r)/ *n* 1 (Clothing) cuello *m*; (Med) collarín *m*, cuello *m* ortopédico; ***to get hot under the ~*** sulfurarse, ponerse* hecho una furia 2 (for animal) collar *m*

collar² *vt* (colloq): **he ~ed me as I was leaving** me agarró *or* me pescó cuando salía (fam)

collarbone /'kɑːlərbəʊn || 'kɒləbəʊn/ *n* clavícula *f*

collate /kɑː'leɪt || kə'leɪt/ *vt* 1 (assemble) reunir*, recopilar 2 (order) poner* en orden, compaginar

collateral /kə'lætərəl/ *n* [u] (Fin) garantía *f*, fianza *f*

collateral damage *n* [u] daños *mpl* colaterales

colleague /'kɑːliːg || 'kɒliːg/ *n* colega *mf*, compañero, -ra *m,f* (de trabajo)

collect¹ /kə'lekt/ *vt*

A 1 (gather together) ‹*information/evidence/data*› reunir*, recopilar; **we're ~ing old clothes for charity** estamos juntando ropa usada para una obra benéfica; **we ~ed (up) our belongings** recogimos nuestras cosas 2 (attract, accumulate) ‹*dust*› acumular, juntar 3 (earn) (colloq) sacar(se)* (fam), ganarse

B (as hobby) coleccionar, juntar (esp AmL)

C (fetch, pick up) recoger*; **they ~ the garbage every Monday** todos los lunes pasan a recoger la basura; **she ~s her from school every day** la recoge del colegio *or* la va a buscar al colegio todos los días

D (obtain payment) ‹*rent/fine/subscription*› cobrar; ‹*taxes*› recaudar

E (put in order): **give me some time to ~ my thoughts** déjame pensar un momento; ***to ~ oneself*** recobrar la calma, serenarse

■ **collect** *vi*

A 1 (gather, assemble) «*people*» reunirse*, congregarse* 2 (accumulate) «*dust/water*» acumularse, juntarse

B (solicit contributions) recaudar dinero, hacer* una colecta

collect² *adj* (AmE) ‹*call/cable*› a cobro revertido, por cobrar (Chi, Méx)

collect³ *adv* (AmE) ‹*call*› a cobro revertido, por cobrar (Chi, Méx)

collected /kə'lektəd || kə'lektɪd/ *adj* 1 (composed) sereno, compuesto 2 (Lit): **the ~ works of Jane Austen** las obras completas de Jane Austen

collectible, collectable *n* 1 (publication) coleccionable *m* 2 (antique) objeto *m* coleccionable

collection /kə'lekʃən/ *n*

A 1 [u] (of evidence) recopilación *f*; (of rent, debts) cobro *m*; (of taxes) recaudación *f*; (*before n*) **a debt ~ agency** una agencia de cobro a morosos 2 [u] (act of fetching): **the goods are ready for ~** puede recoger *or* pasar a buscar las mercancías 3 [c] (of mail, refuse) recogida *f*

B [c] (of money) colecta *f*; **to make** *o* **hold a ~ for sth** hacer* una colecta para algo; (*before n*) **~ box** alcancía *f* (AmL), hucha *f* (Esp); **~ plate** (Relig) bandeja *f*, cepillo *m*

C [c] (group — of objects) colección *f*; (— of people) grupo *m*

collective¹ /kə'lektɪv/ *adj* (*usu before n*) colectivo

collective² *n* (Econ) colectivo *m*, cooperativa *f*

collector /kə'lektər || kə'lektə(r)/ *n* 1 coleccionista *mf*; **a ~'s item** *o* **piece** una pieza de colección 2 (official) cobrador, -dora *m,f*; **tax ~** recaudador, -dora *m,f* de impuestos

college /'kɑːlɪdʒ || 'kɒlɪdʒ/ *n* 1 (university) (esp AmE) universidad *f*; (*before n*) ‹*education/life/lecturer*› universitario 2 (for vocational training) escuela *f*, instituto *m*; *see also* **teachers college** 3 (department of university) facultad *f*, departamento *m*; (in Britain) colegio *m* universitario

collegiate /kə'liːdʒət, -dʒiət/ *adj* (esp AmE) universitario

collide /kə'laɪd/ *vi* 1 (crash) «*vehicle*» chocar*, colisionar (frml); **to ~ WITH sth/sb** chocar* CON algo/algn 2 (disagree) **to ~ (WITH sb/sth) (OVER sth)** tener* un enfrentamiento (CON algn/algo) (SOBRE *or* ACERCA DE algo)

collie /'kɑːli || 'kɒli/ *n* collie *mf*, pastor escocés, pastora escocesa *m,f*

collier /'kɑːljər || 'kɒliə(r)/ *n* minero, -ra *m,f* (*de carbón*)

colliery /'kɑːljəri || 'kɒlɪəri/ *n* (*pl* **-ries**) mina *f* de carbón

collision /kə'lɪʒən/ *n* [c u] 1 (crash — of cars, trains) choque *m*, colisión *f* (frml); (— of boats) abordaje *m*, colisión *f* (frml); **to be in ~ with sth** chocar* *or* (frml) colisionar CON algo; (*before n*) **the two ships were on a ~ course** los dos barcos llevaban rumbo de colisión 2 (disagreement) enfrentamiento *m*, confrontación *f*

colloquial /kə'ləʊkwiəl/ *adj* coloquial

colloquialism /kə'ləʊkwiəlɪzəm/ *n* palabra *f*/expresión *f* coloquial

colloquially /kə'ləʊkwiəli/ *adv* coloquialmente

collusion /kəˈluːʒən/ *n* [u] colusión *f*, connivencia *f*; **to be in ~ with sb** estar* coludido con algn, estar* en colusión *or* connivencia con algn

collywobbles /ˈkɑːliˈwɑːbəlz || ˈkɒlɪwɒblz/ *pl n* (nerves) (colloq): **to have the ~** estar* nerviosísimo, tener* canguelo (Esp fam), tener* culillo (Col, Ven fam), tener* ñáñaras (Méx fam)

Colo = **Colorado**

cologne /kəˈləʊn/ *n* [u c] (*eau de ~*) colonia *f*

Colombia /kəˈlʌmbiə/ *n* Colombia *f*

Colombian[1] /kəˈlʌmbiən/ *adj* colombiano

Colombian[2] *n* colombiano, -na *m,f*

colon /ˈkəʊlən/ *n*

A (Anat) colon *m*

B (in punctuation) dos puntos *mpl*

colonel /ˈkɜːrnl̩ || ˈkɜːnl̩/ *n* coronel, -nela *m,f*

colonial /kəˈləʊniəl/ *adj* colonial

colonialism /kəˈləʊniəlɪzəm/ *n* [u] colonialismo *m*

colonist /ˈkɑːlənəst || ˈkɒlənɪst/ *n* colono, -na *m,f*

colonize /ˈkɑːlənaɪz || ˈkɒlənaɪz/ *vt* colonizar*

colony /ˈkɑːləni || ˈkɒləni/ *n* (*pl* **-nies**) colonia *f*

color[1], (BrE) **colour** /ˈkʌlər || ˈkʌlə(r)/ *n*

A 1 [c u] (shade) color *m*; **what ~ is the ball?** ¿de qué color es la pelota?; **her hair is reddish-brown in ~** tiene el pelo (de color) castaño-rojizo 2 [u] (not monochrome) color *m*; **in full ~** a todo color; (*before n*) ‹*photograph*› en colores *or* (Esp) en color; ‹*television*› en colores *or* (Esp) en color *or* (Andes, Ven) a color; **~ supplement** suplemento *m* a todo color *or* en color 3 [u] (vividness) color *m*, colorido *m*; **local ~** el color local

B [u] (racial feature) color *m*; (*before n*) **~ prejudice** prejuicio *m* racial

C [u] (complexion) color *m*; **to bring the ~ back to sb's cheeks** devolverle* el color *or* los colores a algn; *see also* **off-color**

D **colors** *pl* 1 (flag) bandera *f*; **the ~s of the regiment** el estandarte del regimiento; ***one's true ~s***: **she showed her true ~s** se mostró tal cual era en realidad; ***with flying ~s***: **he passed his exams with flying ~s** le fue estupendamente en los exámenes; **she passed the test with flying ~s** pasó airosa la prueba 2 (BrE Sport): **the team ~s** los colores del equipo

color[2], (BrE) **colour** *vt* 1 (Art) pintar, colorear; **to ~ sth blue** colorear algo de azul 2 (dye) teñir* 3 (influence, bias) ‹*atmosphere*› empañar; **you shouldn't let that ~ your judgment** no deberías dejar que eso influya en tu opinión

■ **color** *vi* (flush) ruborizarse*, sonrojarse, ponerse* colorado

Phrasal verb

• **color in** [v ▸ o ▸ adv, v ▸ adv ▸ o] colorear

Colorado beetle /ˈkɑːləˈrɑːdəʊ || ˌkɒləˈrɑːdəʊ/ *n* escarabajo *m* de la papa *or* (Esp) patata

color: **~-blind** *adj* daltónico, daltoniano; **~-coded** /ˈkʌlərˈkəʊdəd || ˌkʌləˈkəʊdɪd/ *adj* codificado con colores; **~-coordinated** /ˈkʌlərkəʊˈɔːrdn̩eɪtəd || ˈkʌləkəʊˈɔːdɪneɪtɪd/ *adj* haciendo juego, con colores coordinados

colored[1], (BrE) **coloured** /ˈkʌlərd || ˈkʌləd/ *adj*

A ‹*walls/blouse*› de color

B (non-white) (often offensive) de color; (in S Africa) mestizo

C (biased) parcial

colored[2], (BrE) **coloured** /ˈkʌlərd || ˈkʌləd/ *n*

A *also* **Colored** (non-white) (often offensive) persona *f* de color; (*Cape C~*) (in S Africa) persona *f* de color (*hijo de padres de distinta raza*)

B **coloreds** *pl* ropa *f* de color

-colored, (BrE) **-coloured** /ˌkʌlərd || ˈkʌləd/ *suff*: **slate~/coral~** de color pizarra/coral; **a dark~ hat** un sombrero de (un) color oscuro

colorfast, (BrE) **colourfast** /ˈkʌlərfæst || ˈkʌləfɑːst/ *adj* que no destiñe, de colores sólidos *or* inalterables

colorful, (BrE) **colourful** /ˈkʌlərfəl || ˈkʌləfəl/ *adj* ‹*clothes/plumage*› de colores muy vivos *or* vistosos; ‹*parade*› lleno de color *or* de colorido, vistoso; ‹*description*› lleno de color *or* de colorido; **he's a very ~ character** es un hombre de lo más pintoresco *or* original

colorfully, (BrE) **colourfully** /ˈkʌlərfəli || ˈkʌləfəli/ *adv* (with bright colors) vistosamente, con colores vivos *or* brillantes; (in vivid terms) con gran colorido

coloring, (BrE) **colouring** /ˈkʌlərɪŋ/ *n* [u]

A (of picture) colorido *m*; (*before n*) **~ book** libro *m* de *or* para colorear

B (of skin) color *m*, tono *m*; (of fur, plumage) colorido *m*

C (*food ~*) colorante *m*

colorless, (BrE) **colourless** /ˈkʌlərləs || ˈkʌləlɪs/ *adj* incoloro, sin color; (dull) ‹*person/life*› anodino, gris

color scheme, (BrE) **colour scheme** *n* (combinación *f* de) colores *mpl*

colossal /kəˈlɑːsəl || kəˈlɒsəl/ *adj* (colloq) colosal, descomunal

colossus /kəˈlɑːsəs || kəˈlɒsəs/ *n* (*pl* **-suses** *or* **-si** /-saɪ/) coloso *m*

colour *etc* (BrE) ▸ **color** *etc*

colt /kəʊlt/ *n* (Equ) potro *m*

Columbus /kəˈlʌmbəs/ *n* **(Christopher** /krɪstəfər/**) ~** (Cristóbal) Colón

Columbus Day *n* (in US) el día de la Raza *or* de la Hispanidad

column /ˈkɑːləm || ˈkɒləm/ *n* 1 (Archit) columna *f* 2 (on grid, chart, screen) columna *f* 3 (Journ, Print) columna *f*; **he writes a ~ for 'The Globe'** es columnista de 'The Globe' 4 (Mil) columna *f*

columnist /ˈkɑːləmnəst, ˈkɑːləməst || ˈkɒləmnɪst, ˈkɒləmɪst/ *n* columnista *mf*, articulista *mf*

coma /ˈkəʊmə/ *n* (*pl* **~s**) (Med) coma *m*; **to be in/to go into a ~** estar*/entrar *or* caer* en coma

comatose /ˈkəʊmətəʊs/ *adj* (Med) comatoso

comb[1] /kəʊm/ *n*

A (for hair) peine *m*, peinilla *f* (AmL), peineta *f* (Chi); (worn in hair) peineta *f*; ***to go over sth with a fine-tooth(ed) ~*** examinar *or* revisar algo minuciosamente *or* con lupa

B (act) (*no pl*): **your hair needs a ~** tienes que peinarte

comb[2] *vt*

A (pass a comb through): **to ~ sb's hair** peinar a algn; **to ~ one's hair** peinarse

B (search) ‹*area/field*› peinar, rastrear; ‹*files/archives*› rebuscar* en; **to ~ sth FOR sth**: **they ~ed the area for survivors** peinaron *or* rastrearon la zona en busca de supervivientes

combat[1] /kəmˈbæt || ˈkɒmbæt/ *vt*, (BrE) **-tt-** combatir, luchar contra

combat[2] /ˈkɑːmbæt || ˈkɒmbæt/ *n* [c u] combate *m*; (*before n*) **~ jacket** guerrera *f*

combatant /kəmˈbætn̩t || ˈkɒmbətənt/ *n* combatiente *mf*

combination /ˈkɑːmbəˈneɪʃən || ˌkɒmbɪˈneɪʃən/ *n*

A [c u] (mixture) combinación *f*

B [c] (of lock) combinación *f*; (*before n*) **~ lock** cerradura *f* de combinación

combine[1] /kəmˈbaɪn/ *vt* ‹*elements*› combinar; ‹*ingredients*› (Culin) mezclar; ‹*efforts*› aunar*; **she ~s charm and intelligence** reúne encanto e inteligencia; **this, ~d with the fact that ...** esto, unido *or* sumado al hecho de que ...

■ **combine** *vi* «*elements*» combinarse; «*ingredients*» mezclarse; «*teams/forces*» unirse

combine[2] /ˈkɑːmbaɪn || ˈkɒmbaɪn/ *n*

A **~ (harvester)** (Agr) cosechadora *f*

B (coalition) (AmE) alianza *f*, coalición *f*

combined /kəmˈbaɪnd/ *adj* conjunto; **our ~ efforts led to success** la suma de nuestros esfuerzos nos condujo al éxito; **it's a pen, watch and calculator ~** es bolígrafo, reloj y calculadora a la vez

combustible /kəmˈbʌstəbəl/ *adj* combustible, inflamable

combustion /kəmˈbʌstʃən/ *n* [u] combustión *f*; (*before n*) **~ engine** motor *m* de combustión

come /kʌm/ *vi* (*past* **came**; *past p* **come**)

A 1 (advance, approach, travel) venir*; **~ here** ven (aquí); **have you ~ far?** ¿vienes de lejos?; **as I was coming up/down the stairs** cuando subía/bajaba (por) las escaleras; **we've ~ a long way since ...** (made much progress) hemos avanzado mucho desde que ...; (many things have happened) ha llovido mucho desde que ...; **he came running into the room** entró corriendo en la habitación; **~ (and) look at this** ven a ver esto; **~ and get it!** (colloq) ¡a comer! 2 (be present, visit, accompany) venir*; **can I ~ with you?** ¿puedo ir contigo?, ¿te puedo acompañar?; **to ~ AS sth**: **Sue's**

C

coming as a clown Sue va a venir (vestida) de payaso
B 1 (arrive): **what time are you coming?** ¿a qué hora vas a venir?; **after a while, you'll ~ to a crossroads** al cabo de un rato, llegarás a un cruce; **I'm coming, I won't be a moment** enseguida voy; **to ~ ABOUT sth** venir* POR algo; **to ~ FOR sth/sb** venir* a buscar algo/a algn, venir* A POR algo/algn (Esp) 2 **to come and go** ir* y venir*; **you can ~ and go as you please** puedes salir y entrar a tu antojo; **she doesn't know whether she's coming or going** está hecha un lío (fam); **Presidents ~ and go, the problems remain the same** los presidentes cambian pero los problemas son siempre los mismos; **three o'clock came and went and he still hadn't arrived** pasaron las tres y no llegaba
C 1 (occur in time, context): **Christmas ~s but once a year** sólo es Navidad una vez al año; **Christmas is coming** ya llega la Navidad; **this coming Friday** este viernes que viene; **it came as a complete surprise** fue una sorpresa total; **to take life as it ~s** aceptar la vida tal (y) como se presenta; **~ what may** pase lo que pase; **he had it coming (to him)** se lo tenía merecido 2 (*as prep*) para; **I'll be tired out ~ Friday** estaré agotado para el viernes 3 **to come** (in the future) (*as adv*): **in years to ~** en años venideros, en el futuro; **a taste of things to ~** una muestra de lo que nos espera; **the best is yet to ~** todavía nos queda lo mejor
D (extend, reach) (+ *adv compl*) llegar*; **the water only came up to our knees** el agua sólo nos llegaba a las rodillas
E (be gained): **it'll ~, just keep practicing** ya te va a salir *or* lo vas a lograr; sigue practicando; **driving didn't ~ easily to me** aprender a manejar *or* (Esp) conducir no me fue *or* no me resultó fácil
F (be available, obtainable) (+ *adv compl*) venir*; **sugar ~s in half-pound bags** el azúcar viene en paquetes de media libra; **to ~ WITH sth**: **the car ~s with the job** el coche te lo dan con el trabajo; **it ~s with instructions** viene con *or* trae instrucciones; **these watches don't ~ cheap** estos relojes no son nada baratos; **he's as silly as they ~** es de lo más tonto que hay
G (+ *adv compl*) 1 (in sequence, list, structure): **Cancer ~s between Gemini and Leo** Cáncer está entre Géminis y Leo 2 (in race, competition) llegar*; **to ~ first** (in a race) llegar* el primero; (in an exam) quedar *or* salir* el primero 3 (be ranked) estar*; **my children ~ first** primero están mis hijos
H 1 (become) (+ *adj compl*): **it's ~ loose** se ha aflojado; **my dream has ~ true** mi sueño se ha hecho realidad 2 (reach certain state) **to ~ to + INF** llegar* a + INF; **how do you ~ to be here?** ¿cómo es que estás aquí?; **I could have done it yesterday, ~ to think of it** lo podría haber hecho ayer, ahora que lo pienso
I (have orgasm) (colloq) venirse* *or* (Esp) correrse *or* (AmS) acabar (arg)
A (*in phrases*) **come, come!** ¡vamos, vamos!, ¡dale! (CS fam); **come again?** (colloq) ¿qué? *or* (AmL fam) ¿qué qué?; **how come?** (colloq) ¿cómo?; **how ~ you didn't know?** ¿cómo es que no sabías?
■ **come** *vt* (BrE): **don't ~ the victim with me!** no te hagas la víctima conmigo

Phrasal verbs

• **come about** [v ▸ adv] (happen) ocurrir, suceder; **how does it ~ about that... ?** ¿cómo es que ...?
• **come across**
A [v ▸ prep ▸ o] (find) encontrar(se)*; (meet) ‹*person*› encontrarse* con; **I'd never ~ across the word before** era la primera vez que oía/leía la palabra
B [v ▸ adv] (communicate, be communicated) «*meaning*» ser* comprendido; «*feelings*» transmitirse; **he came across very well in the interview** hizo muy buena impresión en la entrevista
• **come after** [v ▸ prep ▸ o] seguir*
• **come along** [v ▸ adv]
A (*in imperative*) 1 (hurry up): **~ along, children** ¡vamos, niños!, ¡de prisa, niños!, ¡apúrense, niños! (AmL), ¡órale, niños! (Méx fam) 2 (as encouragement, rebuke) **~ along!** ¡vamos!
B 1 (accompany): **we're going to the exhibition — can I ~ along?** vamos a la exposición — ¿puedo ir (yo) también?; **~ along with me** ven conmigo, acompáñame 2 (arrive): **you came along just at the right time** llegaste justo en el momento adecuado; **grab the first taxi that ~s along** toma el primer taxi que pase *or* venga
C (progress) ir*, marchar
• **come apart** [v ▸ adv] 1 (fall apart) deshacerse* 2 (have detachable parts) desmontarse, desarmarse
• **come around**, (BrE also) **come round**
A [v ▸ prep ▸ o] (turn) ‹*bend*› tomar; ‹*corner*› doblar
B [v ▸ adv] 1 (visit) (esp BrE) venir* 2 (recover consciousness) volver* en sí 3 (change mind): **he'll ~ around eventually** ya se va a convencer; **to ~ around to sb's point of view** aceptar el punto de vista de algn 4 (occur): **winter is coming around again** ya vuelve el invierno
• **come away** [v ▸ adv]
A (leave, depart) **to ~ away (FROM sth)** ‹*from meeting/stadium*› salir* (DE algo); **I came away with the impression that ...** me quedé con la impresión de que ...; **~ away from there!** ¡apártate de ahí!, ¡no te acerques ahí!
B (become detached) «*handle*» salirse*; «*wallpaper*» despegarse*
• **come back** [v ▸ adv]
A 1 (return) volver*; **would you like to ~ back to my place for a drink?** ¿quieres venir a casa a tomar algo? 2 (be remembered) **to ~ back (TO sb)**: **it's all coming back (to me)** estoy volviendo a recordarlo todo
B (with reply, comment): **I'll ~ back to you with the results** ya le comunicaré los resultados
• **come between** [v ▸ prep ▸ o] interponerse* entre, separar
• **come by** [v ▸ prep ▸ o] (get, acquire) conseguir*, hacerse* con; **to be easy/hard to ~ by** ser* fácil/difícil de conseguir
• **come down** [v ▸ adv]
A 1 (descend) bajar 2 (reach) llegar*; **her hair came down to her waist** el pelo le llegaba hasta *or* a la cintura 3 (collapse) «*ceiling/wall*» caerse*, venirse* abajo 4 «*plane*» aterrizar*; (in accident) caer*
B (decrease) «*price*» bajar; **she's ~ down in my estimation** ha bajado en mi estima; **they've ~ down in the world** (se) han venido a menos
C (from the north) venir*
D (decide) **to ~ down against/in favor of sth/sb** «*judge/court*» fallar en contra/a favor de algo/algn
E (be passed down, inherited): **the ring came down to her from her mother** heredó el anillo de su madre
F (deal with) **to ~ down ON sb/sth**: **the firm ~s down severely on absenteeism** la empresa trata el ausentismo con mano dura
• **come down to** [v ▸ adv ▸ prep ▸ o] (be a question of) (*impers*) ser* cuestión de
• **come down with** [v ▸ adv ▸ prep ▸ o] (become ill with) caer* enfermo de
• **come forward** [v ▸ adv] «*witness*» presentarse; «*volunteer*» ofrecerse*, presentarse; «*culprit*» darse* a conocer, presentarse; **to ~ forward with a solution** ofrecer* *or* sugerir* una solución
• **come from** [v ▸ prep ▸ o]
A (originate from) venir* de; «*person*» ser* de; **where do you ~ from?** ¿de dónde eres?; ***I want to know where you're coming from on this*** (AmE colloq) quiero saber qué te propones con esto
B (result from) resultar de, surgir* de
• **come home to** [v ▸ adv ▸ prep ▸ o] (strike, convince): **it suddenly came home to him that ...** de pronto se dio cuenta de que ...
• **come in** [v ▸ adv]
A (enter) entrar; **~ in!** ¡adelante!, ¡pase!
B 1 (arrive) «*boat*» llegar* 2 «*tide*» subir 3 (to work) venir* 4 (in race) llegar*; **she came in last** llegó la última
C 1 (be received) «*signal*» recibirse; «*applications/reports/donations*» llegar* 2 (as income) «*revenue*» entrar, recibirse; **they have $600 coming in each month** les entran 600 dólares al mes
D 1 (be implemented) «*law*» entrar en vigor; «*regulations*» entrar en vigencia 2 (become fashionable) ponerse* de moda
E 1 (join in) intervenir*; **they came in on the deal** participaron en el negocio 2 (play useful role): **where do I ~ in?** ¿cuál es mi papel?; **that's where these boxes ~ in** para eso están estas cajas; **to ~ in handy** venir* bien, resultar útil
F (come to power) (Govt) subir al poder

- **come in for** [v ▸ adv ▸ prep ▸ o] (be subject to) ‹*criticism*› ser* objeto de
- **come into** [v ▸ prep ▸ o] 1 (enter into) entrar en, entrar a (AmL) 2 (inherit) heredar 3 (be, become relevant): **principles don't ~ into it** no es cuestión de principios; **I want to know where I ~ into this** quiero saber cuál es mi papel en todo esto
- **come of** [v ▸ prep ▸ o] (result): **it was a good idea, but nothing came of it** era una buena idea, pero todo quedó en la nada; **no good can ~ of it** nada bueno puede salir de ello
- **come off**

A 1 [v ▸ adv] (detach itself) «*handle*» soltarse*; «*button*» desprenderse, caerse*; «*wallpaper*» despegarse*; «*dirt/grease*» quitarse, salir* 2 [v ▸ prep ▸ o] (fall off) ‹*horse/motorcycle*› caerse* de

B [v ▸ adv] 1 (take place) suceder 2 (succeed) tener* éxito 3 (fare, acquit oneself): **to ~ off badly** salir* mal parado; **he always ~s off worst** siempre sale perdiendo 4 (appear, seem) (AmE colloq) **to ~ off AS sth**: **she doesn't ~ off as very bright** no da la impresión de ser muy inteligente

C [v ▸ prep ▸ o] 1 (stop taking) ‹*drug*› dejar de tomar 2 (be serious): **~ *off it!*** (colloq) ¡anda! ¡no digas tonterías! (fam)

- **come on** [v ▸ adv]

A 1 (urging sb) (*only in imperative*): **~ on!** ¡vamos! ¡date prisa! *or* (AmL tb) ¡apúrate!, ¡órale! (Méx fam); **~ on! you can do it!** ¡vamos, que lo puedes hacer! 2 (inviting sb) (*usu in imperative*): **hi! ~ on in/up** hola, pasa/sube 3 (advance) avanzar*

B 1 (begin) «*night/winter*» entrar, empezar*; **I can feel a headache coming on** me está empezando un dolor de cabeza 2 (begin to operate) «*heating/appliance*» encenderse*, ponerse* en funcionamiento; «*light*» encenderse*

C (progress) avanzar*

D 1 «*actor/perfomer*» aparecer*, salir* a escena 2 (Rad, TV) «*program/show*» empezar*, salir* al aire 3 (Sport) «*player*» entrar

- **come on to** [v ▸ adv ▸ prep ▸ o] pasar a
- **come out**

(*Sense I*) [v ▸ adv (▸ prep ▸ o)]

A 1 (from inside, indoors) salir*; **to ~ out OF sth** salir* DE algo; **if you take this route, you ~ out at Park Lane** por este camino se sale a Park Lane 2 (from prison, hospital) salir*

B «*tooth/hair*» caerse*; «*stain*» salir*

(*Sense II*) [v ▸ adv]

A (appear) «*sun/stars*» salir*; «*flowers*» florecer*, salir*

B 1 (be said, spoken) salir*; **I tried to say it in French but it came out all wrong** quise decirlo en francés pero me salió mal; **I didn't mean to say it, it just came out** no lo dije a propósito, se me escapó 2 (be revealed, emphasized) «*secret/truth*» revelarse, salir* a la luz

C 1 (declare oneself) declararse; **to ~ out (on strike)** declararse en huelga, ir* a la huelga 2 (as being gay) destaparse (fam), declararse abiertamente homosexual

D (be published, become available) «*newspaper/record/product*» salir*

E 1 (have as outcome, total) salir*; **everything came out right in the end** al final todo salió bien 2 (fare, acquit oneself): **to ~ out well/badly** salir* bien/mal parado

F (Phot) salir*

- **come out in** [v ▸ adv ▸ prep ▸ o]: **I/she came out in spots** me/le salieron granos; **he came out in a cold sweat** le entró un sudor frío
- **come out with** [v ▸ adv ▸ prep ▸ o] (say) ‹*excuse/allegation*› salir* con
- **come over**

A [v ▸ adv] 1 (to sb's home): **telephone me or, better still, ~ over** llámame o, mejor aún, pásate por casa *or* ven a casa 2 (from overseas) venir* 3 (change sides, opinions): **she came over to our side** se pasó a nuestro bando 4 (have sudden feeling): **he came over all shivery** de repente le dieron escalofríos 5 ▸ **come across B**

B [v ▸ prep ▸ o] (affect, afflict): **a feeling of nausea came over her** le dieron náuseas; **I don't know what came over me** no sé qué me pasó

- **come round** (BrE) ▸ **come around**
- **come through**

A [v ▸ adv] 1 (into room, office etc) (BrE) pasar 2 (be received) «*message/news/supplies*» llegar*; **you're coming through loud and clear** te recibimos *or* oímos muy bien 3 (not fail) (AmE): **in the end they came through with the money** al final pusieron el dinero; **when the chips were down, you came through for me** a la hora de la verdad, tú no me fallaste

B [v ▸ adv] (penetrate) «*water/light*» penetrar, entrar; «*sound/noise*» oírse*

C [v ▸ prep ▸ o] (survive) ‹*ordeal/illness*› salir* de; ‹*war*› sobrevivir; **he came through the ordeal greatly scarred** salió de la experiencia muy marcado

- **come to**

(*Sense I*) [v ▸ prep ▸ o]

A 1 (reach) llegar* a; **what's the world coming to!** ¡hasta dónde vamos a llegar!, ¡adónde vamos a ir a parar! 2 (occur) «*idea/answer/name*» ocurrirse; **it came to me in a flash** se me ocurrió de repente 3 (be a question of): **when it ~s to ...** cuando se trata de ...; **or you could do it yourself, ~ to that** o lo podrías hacer tú misma ¿por qué no?

B (amount to) «*total*» ascender* a (frml); **it ~s to $15 exactly** son 15 dólares justos; **the plan never came to anything** el plan nunca llegó a nada; **it ~s to the same thing** viene a ser lo mismo

(*Sense II*) [v ▸ adv] (recover consciousness) volver* en sí, recobrar el conocimiento

- **come together** [v ▸ adv] 1 «*group/people*» reunirse* 2 «*plan/idea*» cuajar
- **come under** [v ▸ prep ▸ o] 1 ‹*domination/spell*› caer* bajo 2 (be classified under) ir* bajo
- **come up** [v ▸ adv]

A 1 (ascend, rise) «*person*» subir; «*sun/moon*» salir* 2 (approach) acercarse*; **to ~ up TO sb** acercársele* A algn

B 1 (grow) «*seed/plant*» crecer* 2 (after cleaning) quedar; **the sheets have ~ up beautifully** las sábanas han quedado muy bien 3 (swell) (BrE) hincharse

C 1 (occur, arise) «*problem*» surgir*, presentarse; **something important has just ~ up** acaba de surgir algo importante; **two hamburgers, coming up** dos hamburguesas, marchando *or* marchan dos hamburguesas 2 (be raised, mentioned) «*subject/point*» surgir*; «*name*» ser* mencionado 3 (Law): **my case ~s up next Wednesday** mi caso se ve el próximo miércoles

- **come up against** [v ▸ adv ▸ prep ▸ o] ‹*opposition/prejudice*› enfrentarse a, toparse *or* tropezarse* con
- **come up for** [v ▸ adv ▸ prep ▸ o]: **the car is coming up for its annual service** dentro de poco hay que hacerle la revisión anual al coche; **I should ~ up for promotion next year** me deberían considerar para un ascenso el año que viene; **to ~ up for re-election** presentarse a la re-elección
- **come upon** [v ▸ prep ▸ o] (arch *or* liter) (encounter, reach) encontrarse* con
- **come up to** [v ▸ adv ▸ prep ▸ o] 1 (reach as far as) llegar* a *or* hasta; **the water came up to my chest** el agua me llegaba al pecho 2 (attain) ‹*standard*› alcanzar*, llegar* a; **her performance didn't ~ up to expectations** su actuación no estuvo a la altura de lo que se esperaba 3 (be nearly): **it's coming up to four o'clock** son cerca de las cuatro; **we're coming up to the end of this stage** nos estamos acercando al final de esta etapa
- **come up with** [v ▸ adv ▸ prep ▸ o] (find) ‹*plan/scheme*› idear; ‹*proposal*› presentar, plantear; ‹*money*› conseguir*; **if you can ~ up with a better idea** si a ti se te ocurre algo mejor

comeback /ˈkʌmbæk/ *n*

A (return, revival) vuelta *f*, retorno *m*; **he made** *o* **staged a ~ at 60** volvió a la escena (*or* a la política *etc*) a los 60 (años); **70s fashion is making a ~** vuelve la moda de los años 70

B (redress) (*no pl*): **the trouble is (that) you have no ~ at all** el problema es que no puedes hacer ninguna reclamación *or* no puedes exigir reparación

C (retort) respuesta *f*, réplica *f*

comedian /kəˈmiːdiən/ *n* humorista *mf*, cómico, -ca *m,f*

comedienne /kəˈmiːdiˈen/ *n* 1 (comic) humorista *f*, cómica *f* 2 (actress) actriz *f* cómica

comedown /ˈkʌmdaʊn/ *n* degradación *f*, humillación *f*

comedy /ˈkɑːmədi ‖ ˈkɒmədi/ *n* [c u] (*pl* **-dies**) 1 (play, film) comedia *f* 2 (comic entertainment) humorismo *m*; (*before n*) ‹*show/program*› humorístico, de humor 3 (of situation) comicidad *f*, lo cómico

C

comely /ˈkʌmli/ *adj* **-lier, -liest** (liter) bonito, lindo

come-on /ˈkʌmɑːn || ˈkʌmɒn/ *n* (sexual) (colloq): **to give sb the ~** insinuársele* a algn, tirarle los tejos a algn (Esp fam)

comer /ˈkʌmər || ˈkʌmə(r)/ *n* 1 **all ~s: the contest is open to all ~s** el certamen está abierto al público en general *or* a todos los que quieran participar 2 (promising person, thing) (AmE colloq): **she/he/it looks like a ~** parece que tiene posibilidades *or* futuro, parece prometedora/prometedor

comet /ˈkɑːmət || ˈkɒmɪt/ *n* cometa *m*

come-uppance /ˈkʌmˈʌpəns/ *n* [u] (colloq): **to get one's ~** recibir *or* llevarse su (*or* mi *etc*) merecido

comfort[1] /ˈkʌmfərt || ˈkʌmfət/ *n*

A 1 [u] (physical, material) comodidad *f*, confort *m*; **to live in ~** vivir desahogadamente *or* con holgura 2 [c] (sth pleasant, luxury) comodidad *f*; ▸ **home**[3] **1**

B [u] (mental) consuelo *m*; **he was a great ~ to me** me sirvió de mucho consuelo; **to give aid and ~ to terrorists** (in US) cooperar con terroristas; **to take ~ from sth** consolarse* con algo; **too close for ~** peligrosamente cerca; ***to be cold ~*** no servir* de consuelo

comfort[2] *vt* ‹*child*› consolar*; ‹*bereaved person*› consolar*, confortar; **I was ~ed by the knowledge that you'd be there** me reconfortó saber que estarías allí

comfortable /ˈkʌmftərbəl || ˈkʌmftəbəl/ *adj*

A 1 ‹*chair/clothes*› cómodo; ‹*house/room*› confortable, cómodo; **I'm not very ~ in this dress** no estoy muy cómoda con este vestido; **make yourself ~!** ¡ponte cómodo! 2 (Med) estable 3 (at ease) (*pred*) cómodo; **to feel ~ with sb** sentirse* cómodo *or* a gusto con algn

B ‹*income*› bueno; **a ~ lifestyle** una vida desahogada

C ‹*margin/majority*› amplio, holgado

comfortably /ˈkʌmftərbli || ˈkʌmftəbli/ *adv* 1 ‹*lie/sit*› cómodamente, confortablemente 2 ‹*live*› holgadamente, con holgura; **to be ~ off** vivir holgadamente, tener* una posición desahogada 3 ‹*win*› holgadamente, sin problemas

comforter /ˈkʌmfərtər || ˈkʌmfətə(r)/ *n* 1 (bedcover) (AmE) edredón *m* 2 (for baby) (BrE) ▸ **pacifier**

comforting /ˈkʌmfərtɪŋ || ˈkʌmfətɪŋ/ *adj* ‹*words*› de consuelo, reconfortante; **it's a ~ thought** es reconfortante *or* es un consuelo pensarlo

comfort station *n* (AmE euph) baño *m* (público), servicios *mpl* (públicos) (Esp)

comfy /ˈkʌmfi/ *adj* **-fier, -fiest** (colloq) cómodo

comic[1] /ˈkɑːmɪk || ˈkɒmɪk/ *adj* ‹*actor/scene*› cómico; ‹*writer*› humorístico; **~ opera** ópera *f* bufa *or* cómica; **~ relief** toque *m* de humor

comic[2] *n*

A (comedian) cómico, -ca *m,f*, humorista *mf*

B 1 (BrE) (book) comic *m*, libro *m* de historietas; (magazine) ▸ **comic book** 2 **comics** *pl* (comic strips) (AmE) tiras *fpl* cómicas, historietas *fpl*, monitos *mpl* (Andes, Méx)

comical /ˈkɑːmɪkəl || ˈkɒmɪkəl/ *adj* cómico

comic: **~ book** *n* (AmE) revista *f* de historietas, tebeo *m* (Esp), revista *f* de chistes (RPl); (for adults) comic *m*; **~ strip** *n* tira *f* cómica, historieta *f*

coming[1] /ˈkʌmɪŋ/ *adj* (*before n*) (approaching) ‹*week/year*› próximo, entrante; **this ~ Monday** este lunes, el lunes que viene, el lunes próximo; **the ~ election** las próximas elecciones

coming[2] *n* [u c] llegada *f*; (Relig) advenimiento *m*; **there was a lot of ~ and going** había mucho ir y venir de gente, había mucho movimiento

coming: **~-of-age** /ˈkʌmɪŋəvˈeɪdʒ/ *n* mayoría *f* de edad; **~-out** /ˈkʌmɪŋˈaʊt/ *n* (of debutante) presentación *f* en sociedad, puesta *f* de largo

comma /ˈkɑːmə || ˈkɒmə/ *n* coma *f*

command[1] /kəˈmænd || kəˈmɑːnd/ *vt*

A 1 (order) **to ~ sb to + INF** ordenarle A algn QUE (+ *subj*) 2 ‹*army/ship*› estar* al *or* tener* el mando de, comandar

B ‹*wealth/resources*› contar* con, disponer* de

C ‹*respect*› imponer*, infundir, inspirar; ‹*fee*› exigir*; ‹*price*› alcanzar*

command[2] *n*

A 1 [c] (order) orden *f* 2 [u] (authority) mando *m*; **to be at sb's ~** estar* a las órdenes de algn; **who's in ~ on this ship?** ¿quién está al mando de este barco?, ¿quién manda en este barco?; **she's in ~ of the situation** es dueña de la situación; **under sb's ~** bajo las órdenes de algn 3 [c] (leadership) (+ *sing or pl vb*) mando *m*; (*before n*) **~ post** puesto *m* de mando

B [u] (mastery) dominio *m*

C [c] (Comput) orden *f*, comando *m*

commandant /ˈkɑːməndænt || ˈkɒməndænt/ *n* comandante *mf*

commandeer /ˈkɑːmənˈdɪr || ˌkɒmənˈdɪə(r)/ *vt* 1 (Mil) ‹*vehicle/building/supplies*› requisar; ‹*personnel*› reclutar (*por la fuerza*) 2 (take arbitrarily) apropiarse (de)

commander /kəˈmændər || kəˈmɑːndə(r)/ *n* 1 (officer in command) comandante *mf* 2 (navy rank) ≈ capitán *m* de fragata

commander-in-chief /kəˈmændərənˈtʃiːf || kəˈmɑːndərɪnˈtʃiːf/ *n* (*pl* **commanders-in-chief**) comandante *mf* en jefe

commanding /kəˈmændɪŋ || kəˈmɑːndɪŋ/ *adj* 1 (dominant) ‹*position*› de superioridad, dominante; ‹*lead*› considerable 2 (authoritative) ‹*presence*› que impone; ‹*tone*› autoritario, imperioso 3 (overlooking) ‹*position*› prominente

commanding officer *n* oficial *mf* al mando

commandment /kəˈmændmənt || kəˈmɑːndmənt/ *n* precepto *m*; **the Ten C~s** los diez mandamientos

commando /kəˈmændəʊ || kəˈmɑːndəʊ/ *n* (*pl* **-dos** *or* **-does**) (unit, soldier) comando *m*

commemorate /kəˈmeməreɪt/ *vt* conmemorar

commemoration /kəˈmeməˈreɪʃən/ *n* [c u] conmemoración *f*

commemorative /kəˈmemərətɪv/ *adj* conmemorativo

commence /kəˈmens/ *vi* (frml) ‹‹*session/celebration*›› dar* comienzo (frml), iniciarse; ‹‹*person*›› comenzar*

■ **commence** *vt* (frml) ‹*work/discussion*› dar* comienzo a (frml), iniciar (frml), comenzar*; **to ~ + -ING** comenzar* A + INF

commencement /kəˈmensmənt/ *n* [u c] 1 (beginning) (frml) inicio *m*, comienzo *m* 2 (graduation) (AmE) (ceremonia *f* de) graduación *f*

commend /kəˈmend/ *vt*

A 1 (praise) elogiar; **to ~ sb FOR sth** elogiar a algn POR algo; ⓢ **highly commended** mención de honor, accésit 2 (recommend) recomendar*; **it has little/much to ~ it** tiene pocos/muchos méritos; **to ~ sth TO sb** recomendar(le)* algo A algn

B (frml) (entrust) **to ~ sb/sth TO sb** encomendar(le)* algn/algo A algn

commendable /kəˈmendəbəl/ *adj* loable, encomiable

commendation /ˈkɑːmənˈdeɪʃən || ˌkɒmenˈdeɪʃən/ *n* 1 [u c] (praise) (frml) encomio *m* (frml), elogios *mpl* 2 [c] (award) mención *f* de honor, accésit *m*

commensurate /kəˈmensərət || kəˈmenʃərət, -sjə-/ *adj* (frml) acorde; **~ WITH sth** acorde *or* en proporción CON algo

comment[1] /ˈkɑːment || ˈkɒment/ *n* 1 [c] (remark) comentario *m*, observación *f*; **~ ON sth**: **the film is a ~ on modern society** la película es una reflexión sobre la sociedad actual 2 [u] (reaction) comentarios *mpl*; **to pass ~ on sth** hacer* comentarios sobre algo; **the minister is unavailable for ~** (journ) el ministro no desea hacer ningún comentario; **no ~** sin comentarios

comment[2] *vi* **to ~ (ON sth)** hacer* comentarios (SOBRE algo)

■ **comment** *vt* comentar, observar

commentary /ˈkɑːmənteri || ˈkɒməntəri, -tri/ *n* (*pl* **-ries**) 1 (Rad, Sport, TV) comentarios *mpl*, crónica *f* 2 (analysis) comentario *m*

commentate /ˈkɑːmənteɪt || ˈkɒmənteɪt/ *vi* **to ~ (ON sth)** hacer* los comentarios *or* la crónica (DE algo)

commentator /ˈkɑːmənteɪtər || ˈkɒmənteɪtə(r)/ *n* comentarista *mf*

commerce /ˈkɑːmərs || ˈkɒmɜːs/ *n* [u] 1 (trade) comercio *m* 2 **Commerce** (in US) (Govt colloq) (*no art*) departamento *m* de Comercio

commercial[1] /kəˈmɜːrʃəl || kəˈmɜːʃəl/ *adj* comercial; **~ law** derecho *m* mercantil *or* comercial

commercial² *n* (Rad, TV) spot *m* publicitario, anuncio *m*, aviso *m* (AmL), comercial *m* (AmL)

commercialism /kə'mɜːrʃəlɪzəm || kə'mɜːʃəlɪzəm/ *n* [u] comercialismo *m*

commercialize /kə'mɜːrʃəlaɪz || kə'mɜːʃəlaɪz/ *vt* comercializar*

commercially /kə'mɜːrʃəli || kə'mɜːʃəli/ *adv* ‹*manufacture/sell*› comercialmente; **~ viable** rentable

commercial: **~ paper** *n* [u] (AmE) efectos *mpl* negociables, papel *m* comercial; **~ traveller** *n* (BrE) viajante *mf* de comercio, corredor, -dora *m,f* (RPl)

Commie, commie /'kɑːmi || 'kɒmi/ *n* (sl & pej) rojo, -ja *m,f* (fam & pey), comunista *mf*

commiserate /kə'mɪzəreɪt/ *vi*: **I ~d with him about losing his job** le dije cuánto sentía que se hubiera quedado sin trabajo

commiseration /kə'mɪzə'reɪʃən/ *n* [u] (*often pl*) conmiseración *f*

commission¹ /kə'mɪʃən/ *n*

A [c] (group) comisión *f*; **the European C~** la Comisión Europea *or* de las Comunidades Europeas

B [c u] (for sales) comisión *f*; **to sell sth on ~** vender algo a comisión

C [c] **1** (for music, painting, building) encargo *m*, comisión *f* (esp AmL) **2** (office) (Govt) cargo *m*

D [u] (use) servicio *m*; **to be out of ~** «*ship*» estar* fuera de servicio; «*machine*» no funcionar

commission² *vt*

A **1** **to ~ sb to + INF** ‹*artist/writer/researcher*› encargarle* a algn que (+ *subj*) **2** ‹*painting/novel/study*› encargar*, comisionar (esp AmL)

B **1** (Mil) nombrar oficial; **~ed officer** oficial *mf* (del ejército) (*con grado de teniente o superior a teniente*) **2** (Naut) ‹*ship*› poner* en servicio

commissionaire /kə'mɪʃə'ner || kə,mɪʃə'neə(r)/ *n* (BrE) conserje *m*, portero *m*

commissioner /kə'mɪʃənər || kə'mɪʃənə(r)/ *n* **1** (commission member) comisionado, -da *m,f*, miembro *mf* de la comisión; **EC C~** comisario, -ria *m,f* de la CE **2** (of police) (BrE) inspector, -tora *m,f* jefe **3** (AmE Sport) presidente, -ta *m,f* (*de una federación deportiva*)

commit /kə'mɪt/ **-tt-** *vt*

A (perpetrate) ‹*crime/error/sin*› cometer; **to ~ suicide** suicidarse

B (assign) ‹*funds/time/resources*› asignar, consignar (frml); **to ~ sth to sb's care** confiar* algo al cuidado de algn; **to ~ sth to memory** memorizar* algo; **to ~ sth to paper** *o* **writing** poner* *or* (frml) consignar algo por escrito

C (send): **to ~ sb to an asylum** internar a algn en un manicomio; **she was ~ted to trial** se dictó auto de procesamiento *or* (en Méx) auto de sujeción a proceso contra ella

D (bind) comprometer, obligar*; **to ~ sb TO -ING/+ INF** comprometer *or* obligar* a algn A + INF

■ *v refl* **to ~ oneself** **1** (bind) comprometerse; **to ~ oneself TO -ING/+ INF** comprometerse A + INF **2** (state views) comprometerse; **he wouldn't ~ himself** no quiso comprometerse

commitment /kə'mɪtmənt/ *n*

A [c] **1** (responsibility) responsabilidad *f*; (obligation) obligación *f*; **family ~s** obligaciones *fpl* *or* cargas *fpl* familiares; **there's no ~ to join** no hay (ninguna) obligación de afiliarse **2** (engagement) compromiso *m*

B [u] (dedication) **~ (TO sth)** dedicación *f* *or* entrega *f* (A algo)

committed /kə'mɪtəd || kə'mɪtɪd/ *adj* **1** (dedicated) ‹*Christian/Communist/feminist*› comprometido; ‹*teacher/worker*› entregado a su trabajo, dedicado **2** (under obligation, pledged) comprometido; **I am ~ to helping her** me he comprometido a ayudarla

committee /kə'mɪti/ *n* (of club, society) comité *m*, comisión *f*; (of parliament) comisión *f*; **to be on a ~** ser* miembro de un comité *or* una comisión; (*before n*) ‹*meeting/member*› del comité *or* de la comisión

committee: **~man** /kə'mɪtimən/ *n* (*pl* **-men** /-mən/) (AmE) miembro *m* de una comisión *or* de un comité; **~woman** *n* (AmE) miembro *f* de una comisión *or* de un comité

commode /kə'məʊd/ *n* **1** (chest of drawers) cómoda *f* **2** (for invalid) *silla con orinal* **3** (toilet) (AmE) inodoro *m*, taza *f*

commodious /kə'məʊdiəs/ *adj* (frml) espacioso, amplio

commodity /kə'mɑːdəti || kə'mɒdəti/ *n* (*pl* **-ties**) **1** (product) artículo *m*, producto *m*, mercancía *f*, mercadería *f* (AmS) **2** (Fin) materia *f* prima

common¹ /'kɑːmən || 'kɒmən/ *adj*

A **1** (widespread, prevalent) común, corriente; **the ~ cold** el resfriado común; **(to be) in ~ use** (ser*) de uso corriente **2** (average, normal) ‹*soldier*› raso; **the ~ man** el hombre medio *or* de la calle; **the ~ people** la gente común y corriente; **I was treated like a ~ criminal** me trataron como a un vulgar delincuente; **it's ~ decency** es una cuestión de elemental (buena) educación **3** (low class, vulgar) ordinario

B **1** (shared, mutual) común; **~ ground** puntos *mpl* en común *or* de coincidencia; **to be ~ TO sth** ser* común A algo **2** (public): **it's ~ knowledge** todo el mundo lo sabe; **by ~ consent he's the best** todos coinciden en que es el mejor; **the ~ good** el bien común *or* de todos

common² *n*

A [u] (*in phrases*) **in common** en común; **to have sth in ~ (with sb)** tener* algo en común (con algn); **in common with** (*as prep*) al igual que; *see also* **Commons**

B [c] (in UK) *terreno perteneciente al municipio*

commoner /'kɑːmənər || 'kɒmənə(r)/ *n* plebeyo, -ya *m,f*

common law *n* [u] derecho *m* consuetudinario; (*before n*) **common-law wife** concubina *f*, conviviente *f* (Chi)

commonly /'kɑːmənli || 'kɒmənli/ *adv* comúnmente; **a ~ held belief** una creencia muy generalizada *or* extendida

Common Market *n* **the ~ ~** el Mercado Común

commonness /'kɑːmənnəs || 'kɒmənnɪs/ *n* [u] **1** (frequency) frecuencia *f* **2** (vulgarity) ordinariez *f*

common-or-garden /'kɑːmənɔːr'gɑːrdn̩ || 'kɒmənɔː'gɑːdn̩/ *adj* (BrE colloq) vulgar *or* común y corriente

commonplace¹ /'kɑːmənpleɪs || 'kɒmənpleɪs/ *adj* **1** (ordinary) común, corriente **2** (trite) banal, trillado

commonplace² *n* **1** (common occurrence) cosa *f* frecuente *or* común *or* corriente **2** (platitude) lugar *m* común, tópico *m*

Commons /'kɑːmənz || 'kɒmənz/ *n* (in UK) (+ *sing or pl vb*) **the ~** la Cámara de los Comunes

common: **~sense** /'kɑːmən'sens || ,kɒmən'sens/ *adj* (*before n*) lleno de sentido común; **he has a ~sense attitude to things** ve las cosas con mucho sentido común; **~ sense** *n* [u] sentido *m* común

Commonwealth /'kɑːmənwelθ || 'kɒmənwelθ/ *n* **the (British) ~** la *or* el Commonwealth

> **Commonwealth**
>
> La *Commonwealth* o Comunidad Británica de Naciones, creada en 1931, es una asociación de estados independientes, en su mayoría ex colonias, más algunas dependencias británicas, tales como Las Bermudas, Las Islas Malvinas y Gibraltar. Los miembros trabajan juntos para lograr ciertos fines como la paz mundial, fomento del comercio y la defensa de la democracia. Cada dos años se celebra una reunión de todos los jefes de gobierno de la Comunidad (*the Commonwealth Conference*), para debatir asuntos de carácter político y económico. Cada cuatro años se celebran los *Commonwealth Games*, competencia deportiva en el que uno de los miembros es el anfitrión

commotion /kə'məʊʃən/ *n* (*no pl*) **1** (outrage) conmoción *f*; **to cause (a) ~** producir* *or* causar una conmoción **2** (noise) alboroto *m*, jaleo *m* (fam)

communal /kə'mjuːnl̩ || 'kɒmjʊnl̩, kə'mjuːnl̩/ *adj* **1** (shared) ‹*land/ownership*› comunal; ‹*kitchen/bathroom*› común **2** (in community) ‹*life*› comunitario **3** (between groups) ‹*violence*› interno, intestino (frml)

communally /kə'mjuːnl̩i || 'kɒmjʊnəli, kə'mjuːnəli/ *adv* en comunidad

commune¹ /'kɑːmjuːn || 'kɒmjuːn/ *n* comuna *f*

commune² /kə'mjuːn/ *vi* (liter): **to ~ with God/nature** estar* en íntima comunión con Dios/la naturaleza

communicable /kə'mjuːnɪkəbəl/ *adj* comunicable; (Med) transmisible

communicate /kə'mjuːnɪkeɪt/ *vi*

A «*person/aircraft*» comunicarse*

B 1 (connect) ⟨⟨*room*⟩⟩ **to ~ (WITH sth)** comunicar(se)* (CON algo) 2 **communicating** *pres p* ⟨*rooms*⟩ que se comunican; ⟨*doors*⟩ de comunicación

■ **communicate** *vt* 1 (make known) **to ~ sth (TO sb)** ⟨*knowledge/idea*⟩ comunicar(le)* algo (A algn) 2 (transmit) **to ~ sth TO sb** ⟨*feeling*⟩ transmitirle *or* comunicarle* algo A algn

communication /kə'mju:nə'keɪʃən || kə,mju:nɪ'keɪʃən/ *n*

A [u] (act) comunicación *f*; **to be in/get into ~ (with sb)** estar*/ponerse* en comunicación *or* en contacto (con algn); (*before n*) **~ skills** (Educ) aptitud *f* para comunicarse

B **communications** *pl* (means of communicating) comunicaciones *fpl*; (*before n*) **~s satellite** satélite *m* de telecomunicaciones

communicative /kə'mju:nəkeɪtɪv || kə'mju:nɪkətɪv/ *adj* comunicativo

communion /kə'mju:njən/ *n*

A (Relig) [u] **Communion**: **Holy C~** la Santa *or* Sagrada Comunión; **to take C~** recibir la comunión *or* la eucaristía, comulgar*

B [u] (exchange of ideas, fellowship) (frml) comunión *f*

communiqué /kə'mju:nəkeɪ || kə'mju:nɪkeɪ/ *n* comunicado *m*

communism, Communism /'kɑ:mjənɪzəm || 'kɒmjʊnɪzəm/ *n* [u] comunismo *m*

communist¹, Communist /'kɑ:mjənəst || 'kɒmjʊnɪst/ *adj* comunista

communist², Communist *n* comunista *mf*

community /kə'mju:nəti/ *n* (*pl* **-ties**)

A 1 (people in a locality) comunidad *f* 2 (society at large) **the ~** la comunidad; (*before n*) **~ service** trabajo *m* comunitario (*prestado en lugar de cumplir una pena de prisión*); **~ spirit** espíritu *m* de comunidad

B 1 (large grouping) comunidad *f*, colectividad *f*; **the city's black ~** la población *or* comunidad negra de la ciudad 2 (people living together) comuna *f*

community: **~ center**, (BrE) **~ centre** *n* centro *m* social; **~ chest** *n* (in US) *fondos reunidos voluntariamente por la comunidad, destinados a beneficencia y bienestar social*; **~ college** *n* (in US) *establecimiento donde se imparten cursos de nivel terciario de dos años de duración*; **~ property** *n* (in US) bien *m* ganancial

commutation /'kɑ:mjə'teɪʃən || ,kɒmju:'teɪʃən/ *n* [c u] conmutación *f*

commutation ticket *n* abono *m* de viaje

commute /kə'mju:t/ *vi* viajar todos los días (*entre el lugar de residencia y el de trabajo*)

■ **commute** *vt* ⟨*sentence/punishment*⟩ conmutar; **to ~ sth TO sth** conmutar algo POR algo

commuter /kə'mju:tər || kə'mju:tə(r)/ *n*: *persona que viaja diariamente una distancia considerable entre su lugar de residencia y el de trabajo*; (*before n*) **the ~ belt** los barrios periféricos

compact¹ /kəm'pækt/ *adj* 1 (small and neat) compacto 2 (tightly packed) ⟨*soil*⟩ compacto 3 (concise) ⟨*style of writing*⟩ conciso

compact² /'kɑ:mpækt || 'kɒmpækt/ *n*

A **(powder) ~** polvera *f*

B **~ (car)** (AmE) coche *m* compacto

C (agreement) (frml) pacto *m*, acuerdo *m*

compact³ /kəm'pækt/ *vt* (*usu pass*) ⟨*soil/snow*⟩ compactar, comprimir

compact disc, compact disk /'kɑ:mpækt || 'kɒmpækt/ *n* disco *m* compacto, compact-disc *m*; (*before n*) **~ ~ player** (reproductor *m* de) compact-disc *m*

companion /kəm'pænjən/ *n*

A 1 (associate, comrade) compañero, -ra *m,f*; **a traveling ~** un compañero de viaje 2 (employee) dama *f* de compañía, señorita *f*/señora *f* de compañía

B (accompanying item) compañero *m*, pareja *f*

C (guide) guía *f*, manual *m*

companionable /kəm'pænjənəbəl/ *adj* sociable, amigable

companionship /kəm'pænjənʃɪp/ *n* [u] 1 (fellowship) camaradería *f*, compañerismo *m* 2 (company of others) compañía *f*

company /'kʌmpəni/ (*pl* **-nies**) *n*

A [u] 1 (companionship) compañía *f*; **in sb's ~** en compañía de algn; **to keep sb ~** hacerle* compañía a algn; **to keep ~ with sb** andar* en compañía de algn; **to part ~ (with sb/sth)** separarse (de algn/algo) 2 (companion, companions): **the dog will be ~ for her** el perro le hará compañía; **she's excellent ~** es muy agradable (*or* divertido *etc*) estar con ella; **to keep bad ~** andar* en malas compañías; **present ~ excepted** exceptuando a los presentes, mejorando lo presente 3 (guests) visita *f*; **we've got ~** tenemos visita

B [c] (Busn) compañía *f*, empresa *f*; (*before n*) ⟨*car*⟩ de la compañía *or* empresa

C [c] 1 (Theat) compañía *f* 2 (Mil) compañía *f* 3 (Naut): **ship's ~** tripulación *f*, dotación *f*

comparable /'kɑ:mpərəbəl || 'kɒmpərəbəl/ *adj* comparable, equiparable; **~ WITH *o* TO sth** comparable *or* equiparable A algo

comparably /'kɑ:mpərəbli || 'kɒmpərəbli/ *adv* de modo análogo *or* similar

comparative¹ /kəm'pærətɪv/ *adj* 1 (relative) relativo 2 ⟨*literature/linguistics*⟩ comparado; ⟨*analysis/study*⟩ comparativo, comparado 3 (Ling) comparativo

comparative² *n* (Ling) comparativo *m*

comparatively /kəm'pærətɪvli/ *adv* relativamente

compare¹ /kəm'per || kəm'peə(r)/ *vt* 1 (make comparison between) comparar; **to ~ sth/sb TO *o* WITH sth/sb** comparar algo/a algn CON algo/algn; **it's tiny ~d to your house** es pequeñísima comparada con tu casa *or* en comparación con tu casa 2 (liken) **to ~ sth/sb TO sth/sb** comparar algo/a algn CON *or* A algo/algn

■ **compare** *vi*: **how do the two models ~ for speed?** en cuanto a velocidad ¿qué diferencia hay entre los dos modelos?; **to ~ WITH sth**: **nothing ~s with good home cooking** la comida casera no se puede comparar con nada; **it ~s favorably with your previous efforts** este trabajo está mejor que los anteriores

compare² *n* [u] (liter): **beyond ~** sin comparación, incomparable

comparison /kəm'pærəsən || kəm'pærɪsən/ *n* [u c] comparación *f*; **there is no ~ between them** no tienen comparación, no hay (ni punto de) comparación entre ellos; **by/in ~ (with sth/sb)** en comparación (con algo/algn)

compartment /kəm'pɑ:rtmənt || kəm'pɑ:tmənt/ *n* 1 (of bag, desk, refrigerator) compartimento *m*, compartimiento *m* 2 (in train) (BrE Rail) compartimento *m*, compartimiento *m*

compartmentalize /kəm,pɑ:rt'mentḷaɪz || ,kɒmpɑ:t'mentəlaɪz/ *vt* compartimentar

compass /'kʌmpəs/ *n*

A [c] (*magnetic* ~) brújula *f*; **the points of the ~** los puntos cardinales

B [c] (Math) (*often pl*) compás *m*; **a pair of ~es** un compás

C [u] (limits, scope) (frml) alcance *m*; **it falls within the ~ of the board** cae dentro de la competencia de la junta

compassion /kəm'pæʃən/ *n* [u] compasión *f*, piedad *f*; **~ TOWARD sb** compasión CON algn

compassionate /kəm'pæʃənət/ *adj* compasivo; **~ leave** (BrE) permiso *m* por motivos familiares

compatibility /kəm'pætə'bɪləti/ *n* [u] compatibilidad *f*

compatible /kəm'pætəbəl/ *adj* 1 ⟨*people/ideas/principles*⟩ compatible; **to be ~ WITH sb/sth** ser* compatible CON algn/algo 2 (Comput) compatible; **an IBM ~ computer** una computadora *or* (Esp tb) un ordenador compatible con IBM

compatriot /kəm'peɪtriət || kəm'pætriət/ *n* compatriota *mf*

compel /kəm'pel/ *vt* **-ll-** 1 (force) **to ~ sb to + INF** obligar* *or* forzar* a algn A + INF; **I feel ~led to warn you that ...** me veo en la obligación de advertirle que ... 2 (command) (frml) ⟨*obedience/respect*⟩ imponer*

compelling /kəm'pelɪŋ/ *adj* ⟨*argument/evidence*⟩ convincente, persuasivo; ⟨*book*⟩ absorbente; ⟨*need*⟩ imperioso

compendium /kəm'pendiəm/ *n* (*pl* **-diums** *or* **-dia** /-dɪə/) (BrE) 1 (book) compendio *m* 2 (of games) juegos *mpl* reunidos

compensate /'kɑ:mpənseɪt || 'kɒmpenseɪt/ *vt* (indemnify) indemnizar*, compensar; **to ~ sb FOR sth** indemnizar* *or* compensar a algn POR algo, resarcir* a algn DE algo

■ **compensate** *vi* **to ~ FOR sth** compensar algo

compensation /ˈkɑːmpənˈseɪʃən || ˌkɒmpenˈseɪʃən/ *n* [1] [u c] (recompense) **~ (FOR sth)** indemnización *f or* compensación *f* (POR algo); **I received $20,000 as** *o* **in ~ for the damage** me dieron 20.000 dólares de indemnización *or* en compensación por los daños [2] [u] (remuneration) (AmE) remuneración *f*, retribución *f*; (*before n*) **~ package** paquete *m* salarial

compere¹, **compère** /ˈkɑːmper || ˈkɒmpeə(r)/ *n* (BrE) presentador, -dora *m,f*, animador, -dora *m,f*

compere², **compère** *vt* (BrE) presentar, animar

compete /kəmˈpiːt/ *vi* competir*, participar; **to ~ FOR sth** competir* POR algo, disputarse algo; **to ~ AGAINST sb/sth** competir* CONTRA algn/algo; **we can't ~ with the big firms** no podemos competir con las grandes firmas, no podemos hacerles la competencia a las grandes firmas

competence /ˈkɑːmpətəns || ˈkɒmpɪtəns/ *n* [u] [1] (ability) competencia *f*, capacidad *f*; **level of ~ in French** nivel *m* (de conocimientos) de francés [2] (jurisdiction) (Law) competencia *f*

competent /ˈkɑːmpətənt || ˈkɒmpɪtənt/ *adj* [1] ‹*person*› competente, capaz; **to be ~ to + INF** estar* capacitado PARA + INF [2] (adequate) aceptable [3] (Law) ‹*court*› competente; ‹*witness*› hábil

competently /ˈkɑːmpətəntli || ˈkɒmpɪtəntli/ *adv* competentemente

competition /ˈkɑːmpəˈtɪʃən || ˌkɒmpəˈtɪʃən/ *n*
A [u] [1] (competing) competencia *f*; **to be in ~ with sb/sth** competir* con algn/algo [2] (opposition) competencia *f*
B [c] (contest) concurso *m*; (literary) certamen *m*, concurso *m*; (Sport) competencia *f* (AmL), competición *f* (Esp)

competitive /kəmˈpetətɪv || kəmˈpetɪtɪv/ *adj* competitivo; **~ examination** concurso *m* de *or* por oposición, oposición *f* (Esp)

competitively /kəmˈpetətɪvli || kəmˈpetɪtɪvli/ *adv* [1] ‹*play*› con espíritu competitivo [2] (Busn): **~ priced** a precios competitivos

competitor /kəmˈpetətər || kəmˈpetɪtə(r)/ *n* [1] (contestant) participante *mf*, concursante *mf* [2] (rival) (Busn) competidor, -dora *m,f*, rival *mf*; (Sport) contrincante *mf*, rival *mf*

compilation /ˈkɑːmpəˈleɪʃən || ˌkɒmpɪˈleɪʃən/ *n* [1] [u] (of list) compilación *f*; (of information) recopilación *f* [2] [c] (collection) recopilación *f*

compile /kəmˈpaɪl/ *vt* [1] ‹*dictionary/index*› compilar [2] ‹*information*› recopilar, reunir*, recabar [3] (Comput) ‹*program*› compilar

complacency /kəmˈpleɪsn̩si/ *n* [u] autocomplacencia *f*

complacent /kəmˈpleɪsn̩t/ *adj* ‹*person*› satisfecho de sí mismo; ‹*attitude*› displicente

complacently /kəmˈpleɪsn̩tli/ *adv* ‹*smile*› con suficiencia

complain /kəmˈpleɪn/ *vi* quejarse, reclamar; **to ~ TO sb ABOUT sth** quejarse A algn POR algo; **I can't ~** no me puedo quejar; **to ~ OF sth** quejarse DE algo

■ **complain** *vt*: **you're hurting me, she ~ed** —me haces daño —protestó *or* se quejó; **he ~ed that …** se quejó de que …

complaint /kəmˈpleɪnt/ *n* [1] (grievance) queja *f*, reclamo *m* (AmL); **to make a ~** quejarse, reclamar; **to lodge a ~** presentar una queja, hacer* una reclamación *or* (AmL tb) presentar un reclamo; **cause/grounds for ~** motivo *m* de queja [2] (ailment) dolencia *f* (frml)

complement¹ /ˈkɑːmpləmənt || ˈkɒmplɪmənt/ *n*
A **~ (TO sth)** complemento *m* (DE algo)
B (full number): **the orchestra had the full ~ of strings** la orquesta contaba con una sección de cuerdas completa; **the ship's ~** (Naut) la tripulación *or* dotación completa

complement² *vt* complementar; **those colors ~ each other** esos colores se complementan (entre sí)

complementary /ˈkɑːmpləˈmentri || ˌkɒmplɪˈmentri/ *adj* complementario

complete¹ /kəmˈpliːt/ *adj*
A [1] (entire) ‹*set/edition*› completo; **it comes ~ with batteries** viene con las pilas incluidas [2] (finished) terminado, concluido
B (thorough, absolute) (*as intensifier*) total, completo; **it came as a ~ surprise** fue una auténtica sorpresa; **a ~ waste of time** una pérdida de tiempo total y absoluta

complete² *vt* [1] (finish) ‹*building/education*› acabar, terminar; ‹*sentence*› cumplir; ‹*investigations*› completar, concluir* [2] (make whole) ‹*set/collection*› completar [3] (fill in) (frml) ‹*form*› llenar, rellenar

completely /kəmˈpliːtli/ *adv* completamente, totalmente; **I ~ forgot** me olvidé completamente

completion /kəmˈpliːʃən/ *n* [u] finalización *f*, terminación *f*; **to bring sth to ~** terminar algo, llevar algo a término (frml); **the building is nearing ~** falta poco para terminar el edificio

complex¹ /ˈkɑːmpleks || ˈkɒmpleks/ *adj* [1] (complicated) ‹*person/issue/situation*› complejo, complicado [2] (intricate) ‹*system/pattern/design*› complejo

complex² *n*
A (buildings) complejo *m*
B (Psych) complejo *m*

complexion /kəmˈplekʃən/ *n* [1] (skin type) cutis *m*; (in terms of color) tez *f* [2] (aspect) cariz *m*; **to put a different/new ~ on sth** darle* otro/un nuevo cariz a algo

complexity /kəmˈpleksəti/ *n* [u c] (*pl* **-ties**) complejidad *f*

compliance /kəmˈplaɪəns/ *n* [u] [1] (acquiescence) conformidad *f*; **in ~ with your wishes …** conforme a *or* en conformidad con sus deseos … [2] (submissiveness) docilidad *f*

compliant /kəmˈplaɪənt/ *adj* ‹*person*› dispuesto a acatar los deseos de otros

complicate /ˈkɑːmpləkeɪt || ˈkɒmplɪkeɪt/ *vt* complicar*

complicated /ˈkɑːmpləkeɪtəd || ˈkɒmplɪkeɪtɪd/ *adj* complicado

complication /ˈkɑːmpləˈkeɪʃən || ˌkɒmplɪˈkeɪʃən/ *n* complicación *f*; **~s set in** (Med) surgieron complicaciones

complicity /kəmˈplɪsəti/ *n* [u] **~ (IN sth)** complicidad *f* (EN algo)

compliment¹ /ˈkɑːmpləmənt || ˈkɒmplɪmənt/ *n* [1] (expression of praise) cumplido *m*, halago *m*; **to pay sb a ~** hacerle* un cumplido a algn, halagar* a algn; **she returned the ~** me devolvió el cumplido; **my ~s to the chef** felicitaciones al cocinero [2] **compliments** *pl* (best wishes) saludos *mpl*; **with the ~s of the management** gentileza *or* cortesía de la casa, con los mejores deseos de la dirección; (*before n*) **~s slip** ≈ tarjeta *f*

compliment² *vt* **to ~ sb (ON sth)** felicitar a algn (POR algo); **she ~ed him on his new suit** le alabó el traje nuevo

complimentary /ˈkɑːmpləˈmentəri || ˌkɒmplɪˈmentri/ *adj* [1] (flattering) ‹*remark/review*› elogioso, halagüeño; **she wasn't very ~ about her teacher** no habló muy bien de su profesora [2] (free) ‹*copy*› de obsequio *or* regalo; **~ ticket** invitación *f*

comply /kəmˈplaɪ/ *vi* **-plies, -plying, -plied to ~ WITH sth**: **to ~ with a request** acceder a una solicitud; **to ~ with an order** cumplir una orden; **to ~ with the law** acatar la ley; **all machinery must ~ with safety regulations** toda la maquinaria debe cumplir con *or* llenar los requisitos de seguridad

component¹ /kəmˈpəʊnənt/ *n* [1] (constituent part) componente *m* [2] (Auto) pieza *f*; (Electron) componente *m*

component² *adj* componente; ‹*element*› constituyente; **~ part** componente *m*, parte *f* integrante

comportment /kəmˈpɔːrtmənt || kəmˈpɔːtmənt/ *n* [u] (frml) conducta *f*, comportamiento *m*

compose /kəmˈpəʊz/ *vt*
A (constitute) (*usu pass*) **to be ~d OF sth** estar* compuesto DE algo, componerse* DE algo
B ‹*music*› componer*; ‹*letter*› redactar
C (calm, control) (liter): **to ~ one's thoughts** poner* en orden sus (*or* mis *etc*) ideas; **to ~ oneself** serenarse, recobrar la compostura

composed /kəmˈpəʊzd/ *adj* sereno, tranquilo

composer /kəmˈpəʊzər || kəmˈpəʊzə(r)/ *n* compositor, -tora *m,f*

composition /ˈkɑːmpəˈzɪʃən || ˌkɒmpəˈzɪʃən/ *n* [u c] composición *f*

compos mentis /ˈkɑːmpəsˈmentəs || ˌkɒmpəsˈmentɪs/ *adj* (frml) (*pred*) en plena posesión de sus (*or* mis *etc*) facultades (mentales) (frml)

C

compost /'kɑːmpəʊst || 'kɒmpɒst/ *n* [u] abono *m* orgánico *or* vegetal; (*before n*) **~ heap** *lugar donde se amontonan desechos para preparar abono*

composure /kəm'pəʊʒər || kəm'pəʊʒə(r)/ *n* [u] compostura *f*, calma *f*, serenidad *f*; **to lose/regain one's ~** perder*/recobrar la compostura (*or* la calma *etc*)

compound[1] /'kɑːmpaʊnd || 'kɒmpaʊnd/ *adj* ‹*number/interest/leaf*› compuesto

compound[2] /'kɑːmpaʊnd || 'kɒmpaʊnd/ *n*
A 1 (Chem) compuesto *m* 2 (word) palabra *f* compuesta
B (residence) complejo *m* habitacional; (for prisoners etc) barracones *mpl*

compound[3] /kɑːm'paʊnd || kəm'paʊnd/ *vt*
A (make worse) ‹*problem*› agravar, exacerbar; ‹*risk/difficulties*› acrecentar*, aumentar
B (*usu pass*) (combine) (liter) **to be ~ed WITH sth** ir* acompañado DE algo

comprehend /'kɑːmprɪ'hend || ˌkɒmprɪ'hend/ *vt*
A (understand) comprender
B (include) (frml) abarcar*, comprender

comprehensible /'kɑːmprɪ'hensəbəl || ˌkɒmprɪ'hensəbəl/ *adj* comprensible

comprehension /'kɑːmprɪ'hentʃən || ˌkɒmprɪ'henʃən/ *n* 1 [u] (understanding) comprensión *f*; **it's beyond my ~** me resulta incomprensible 2 [c u] (school exercise) (BrE) ejercicio *m* de comprensión

comprehensive /'kɑːmprɪ'hensɪv || ˌkɒmprɪ'hensɪv/ *adj* 1 ‹*survey/report*› exhaustivo, global; ‹*view*› integral, de conjunto; ‹*list/range*› completo; ‹*insurance/cover*› contra todo riesgo 2 (Educ) (in UK) *relativo al sistema educativo en el cual no se separa a los alumnos según su nivel de aptitud*

comprehensives /ˌkɑːmprɪ'hensɪvz || ˌkɒmprɪ'hensɪvz/ *pl n* (in US) exámenes *mpl* finales (*en asignaturas de todo el curso o la carrera*)

comprehensive (school) *n* (in UK) *instituto de segunda enseñanza para alumnos de cualquier nivel de aptitud*

compress[1] /kəm'pres/ *vt* comprimir; **~ed air** aire *m* comprimido

compress[2] /'kɑːmpres || 'kɒmpres/ *n* compresa *f*

compression /kəm'preʃən/ *n* [u] compresión *f*

comprise /kəm'praɪz/ *vt* 1 (consist of) comprender, constar de 2 (constitute, make up) componer*

compromise[1] /'kɑːmprəmaɪz || 'kɒmprəmaɪz/ *n* [c u] (agreement) acuerdo *m* mutuo, arreglo *m*, compromiso *m*; **to come to** *o* **reach a ~** llegar* a un acuerdo mutuo

compromise[2] *vi* 1 (make concessions) transigir*, transar (AmL) 2 (give way): **we cannot ~ on this point** en este punto no podemos ceder *or* transigir
■ **compromise** *vt* 1 (discredit) ‹*person/organization/reputation*› comprometer; **to ~ oneself** ponerse* en una situación comprometida 2 (endanger) comprometer, poner* en peligro

compromising /'kɑːmprəmaɪzɪŋ || 'kɒmprəmaɪzɪŋ/ *adj* ‹*evidence*› comprometedor; ‹*situation*› comprometido

comptroller /kən'trəʊlər || kən'trəʊlə(r)/ *n* (frml) interventor, -tora *m,f*, contralor, -lora *m,f* (AmL)

compulsion /kəm'pʌlʃən/ *n* 1 [u] (force, duress) coacción *f* 2 [c] (obsession) compulsión *f*

compulsive /kəm'pʌlsɪv/ *adj* 1 (compelling): **the book is ~ reading** es uno de esos libros que se empiezan y no se pueden dejar; **the film is ~ viewing** es una película que no hay que perderse 2 (obsessive) ‹*behavior*› compulsivo; **he's a ~ eater/liar** come/miente por compulsión; **a ~ gambler** un jugador *m* empedernido

compulsory /kəm'pʌlsəri/ *adj* ‹*attendance*› obligatorio; ‹*retirement*› forzoso

compulsory purchase *n* (BrE) expropiación *f*

compunction /kəm'pʌŋkʃən/ *n* [u] reparo *m*; **to have no ~ about -ING** no tener* ningún reparo en + INF

computation /'kɑːmpju'teɪʃən || ˌkɒmpjuː'teɪʃən/ *n* [u c] cálculo *m*, cómputo *m*

compute /kəm'pjuːt/ *vt* calcular, computar

computer /kəm'pjuːtər || kəm'pjuːtə(r)/ *n* computadora *f* (esp AmL), computador *m* (esp AmL), ordenador *m* (Esp); **all the data is on ~** todos los datos están computarizados *or* computerizados; (*before n*) ‹*society/age/revolution*› de la informática; ‹*program/game*› de computadora (*or* ordenador *etc*); ‹*graphics/animation*› por computadora (*or* ordenador *etc*); **~ programmer** programador, -dora *m,f*; **~ programming** programación *f*; **~ science** informática *f*; **~ studies** informática *f*, computación *f*

computer: **~-aided** /kəm'pjuːtər'eɪdəd || kəmˌpjuːtər'eɪdɪd /, **~-assisted** /-ə'sɪstəd || -ə'sɪstɪd/ *adj* ‹*learning/design*› asistido por computadora (*or* ordenador *etc*); **~-friendly** /kəmˌpjuːtər'frendli || kəmˌpjuːtə'frendli/ *adj* 1 (compatible with IT) ‹*systems/methods*› compatible con computadoras (*or* ordenadores *etc*) 2 (able to use IT) ‹*employee/work force*› con conocimientos de informática

computerization /kəm'pjuːtərə'zeɪʃən || kəmˌpjuːtəraɪ'zeɪʃən/ *n* [u] (of data) computarización *f*, computerización *f*; (of business) informatización *f*

computerize /kəm'pjuːtəraɪz/ *vt* computarizar*, computerizar*; ‹*company/department*› informatizar*

computer: **~-literate** /kəmˌpjuːtər'lɪtərət || kəmˌpjuːtə'lɪtərət/ *adj* con conocimientos de informática *or* de computación, con competencia en informática *or* en computación; **~-operated** /kəm'pjuːtər'ɑːpəreɪtəd || kəmˌpjuːtər'ɒpəreɪtɪd/ *adj* operado por computadora (*or* ordenador *etc*), computarizado, computerizado; **~ virus** *n* virus *m* informático

computing /kəm'pjuːtɪŋ/ *n* [u] informática *f*, computación *f*; (*before n*) **~ skills** competencia *f* en el uso de computadoras (*or* ordenadores *etc*)

comrade /'kɑːmræd || 'kɒmreɪd/ *n* compañero, -ra *m,f*, camarada *mf*

comradeship /'kɑːmrædʃɪp || 'kɒmreɪdʃɪp/ *n* [u] camaradería *f*

con[1] /kɑːn || kɒn/ *n*
A (fraud) (colloq) timo *m* (fam), estafa *f*
B (prisoner, convict) (sl) preso, -sa *m,f*
C (colloq) (objection) contra *m*; *see also* **pro**[1] **B**

con[2] *vt* **-nn-** (colloq) (deceive) timar (fam), estafar; (sweet-talk) engatusar, embaucar*, camelar (fam); **to ~ sb INTO/OUT OF sth**: **I was ~ned into it** me embaucaron *or* (fam) me camelaron para que lo hiciera (*or* para que fuera *etc*); **I was ~ned into thinking that ...** me engatusaron haciéndome creer que ...; **he ~ned the old ladies out of their savings** embaucó a las ancianas y les quitó los ahorros

concave /'kɑːnkeɪv || 'kɒŋkeɪv/ *adj* cóncavo

conceal /kən'siːl/ *vt* 1 ‹*object/facts/truth*› ocultar; ‹*emotions*› disimular, ocultar; **with barely ~ed hatred** con mal disimulado odio; **to ~ sth FROM sb** ocultar(le) algo A algn 2 **concealed** *past p* ‹*door/camera*› oculto; ‹*lighting*› indirecto

concede /kən'siːd/ *vt* 1 (admit) reconocer*; **to ~ defeat** admitir la derrota, darse* por vencido 2 (allow) ‹*right/privilege*› conceder 3 (give away) ‹*game/penalty*› conceder
■ **concede** *vi* (admit defeat) admitir la derrota, darse* por vencido

conceit /kən'siːt/ *n* engreimiento *m*, presunción *f*

conceited /kən'siːtəd || kən'siːtɪd/ *adj* engreído, presuntuoso, creído (fam)

conceivable /kən'siːvəbəl/ *adj* imaginable; **every ~ means** todos los medios imaginables; **it's just ~ that he forgot** cabe la posibilidad de que se haya olvidado

conceivably /kən'siːvəbli/ *adv* (*indep*): **they may ~ have decided to sell it** cabe la posibilidad de que hayan decidido venderlo

conceive /kən'siːv/ *vt*
A 1 (devise) ‹*plan*› concebir* 2 (imagine) imaginar, pensar*; (consider) considerar; **I can't ~ why you did it** no concibo *or* no me cabe en la cabeza por qué lo hiciste
B ‹*child*› concebir*
■ **conceive** *vi* (become pregnant) concebir*

Phrasal verb

• **conceive of** [v ▸ prep ▸ o] (frml) imaginar, concebir*

concentrate[1] /'kɑːnsəntreɪt || 'kɒnsəntreɪt/ *vt*
A ‹*energies/attention*› **to ~ sth (ON sth)** concentrar algo (EN algo)
B (gather, bring together) **to ~ sth IN/INTO sth** concentrar algo EN algo
■ **concentrate** *vi*
A (focus attention) «*person*» concentrarse; «*talks*» centrarse; **~ on getting this finished** concéntrate en terminar esto
B (converge) «*people*» concentrarse

concentrate² *n* [u] concentrado *m*

concentrated /ˈkɑːnsəntreɪtəd || ˈkɒnsəntreɪtɪd/ *adj* 1 ‹*effort*› intenso y continuado 2 ‹*solution/juice*› concentrado

concentration /ˈkɑːnsənˈtreɪʃən || ˌkɒnsənˈtreɪʃən/ *n* [c u] concentración *f*

concentration camp *n* campo *m* de concentración

concept /ˈkɑːnsept || ˈkɒnsept/ *n* concepto *m*

conception /kənˈsepʃən/ *n*
A [c u] (idea) noción *f*, concepción *f*; **they have no ~ of ...** no tienen noción *or* idea de ...
B [u] (of baby, plan) concepción *f*

concern¹ /kənˈsɜːrn || kənˈsɜːn/ *n*
A [c] (business, affair) asunto *m*; **that's no ~ of yours** eso no es asunto tuyo
B [u] 1 (anxiety) preocupación *f*, inquietud *f*; **cause for ~** motivos *mpl* de preocupación *or* para preocuparse 2 (interest) **~ FOR sb/sth** interés *m* POR algn/algo; **to be of ~ to sb** importarle *or* preocuparle a algn; **it's of no great ~ to me what he does** no me importa *or* no me preocupa mucho lo que haga
C [c] (firm) empresa *f*, negocio *m*; ▸ **going²**

concern² *vt*
A (affect, involve) concernir*, incumbir; **the people ~ed** la gente en cuestión; **those ~ed know who they are** los interesados ya saben quiénes son; **to be ~ed WITH sth** ocuparse DE algo; **where money is ~ed ...** en lo que respecta al dinero ...; **as far as I'm ~ed** en lo que a mí respecta, por mi parte; **to whom it may ~** (frml) a quien corresponda (frml)
B 1 (interest) interesar; **I'm more ~ed with quality than quantity** me interesa más la calidad que la cantidad 2 (worry, bother) preocupar, inquietar
C (relate to): **my fears ~ing her health were unfounded** mis temores en cuanto a *or* respecto a su salud eran infundados; **item one ~s the new office** el primer punto trata de la nueva oficina
■ *v refl* **to ~ oneself (ABOUT sb/sth)** preocuparse (POR algn/algo); **to ~ oneself WITH sth** (be busy with sth) ocuparse DE algo; (interest) **I don't ~ myself with their affairs** yo no me inmiscuyo en sus asuntos

concerned /kənˈsɜːrnd || kənˈsɜːnd/ *adj* ‹*person*› preocupado; ‹*look*› de preocupación; **to be ~ ABOUT/FOR sb/sth** estar* preocupado POR algn/algo; *see also* **concern²**

concerning /kənˈsɜːrnɪŋ || kənˈsɜːnɪŋ/ *prep* sobre, acerca de, con respecto a

concert¹ /ˈkɑːnsərt || ˈkɒnsət/ *n* 1 (performance) concierto *m*; (*before n*) **~ hall** sala *f* de conciertos, auditorio *m*; **~ pianist** concertista *mf* de *or* en piano 2 **in concert** (performing live) en vivo, en concierto

concert² /kənˈsɜːrt || kənˈsɜːt/ *vt* (frml) concertar*, coordinar; **we made a ~ed effort to ...** coordinamos *or* concertamos nuestros esfuerzos para ...

concertina¹ /ˈkɑːnsərˈtiːnə || ˌkɒnsəˈtiːnə/ *n* concertina *f*

concertina² *vi* aplastarse como un acordeón

concertmaster /ˈkɑːnsərtˌmæstər || ˈkɒnsətˌmɑːstə(r)/ *n* (AmE) primer violín *mf*, concertino *mf*

concerto /kənˈtʃertəʊ || kənˈtʃɜːtəʊ, kənˈtʃeətəʊ/ *n* (*pl* **-tos** *or* **-ti**) concierto *m*; **violin ~** concierto para violín

concession /kənˈseʃən/ *n* [c u] concesión *f*; Ⓢ **admission £3; concessions £2** (BrE) entrada £3; estudiantes, jubilados *etc* £2

concessionary /kənˈseʃəneri || kənˈseʃənəri/ *adj* ‹*fare/ticket*› a precio reducido, con descuento

conch (shell) /kɑːŋk, kɑːntʃ || kɒŋk, kɒntʃ/ *n* caracola *f*

conciliate /kənˈsɪlieɪt/ *vt* conciliar

conciliation /kənˈsɪliˈeɪʃən/ *n* [u] conciliación *f*

conciliatory /kənˈsɪliətɔːri || kənˈsɪliətəri/ *adj* conciliador, conciliatorio

concise /kənˈsaɪs/ *adj* ‹*instructions/writing*› conciso; **~ dictionary** diccionario *m* abreviado

conclude /kənˈkluːd/ *vt*
A 1 (end) concluir* (frml), finalizar* 2 (settle) ‹*deal*› cerrar*; ‹*agreement*› llegar* a; ‹*treaty*› firmar; ‹*alliance*› pactar
B (infer) concluir* (frml)
■ **conclude** *vi* 1 (come to an end) concluir* (frml), terminar; **to ~, I would like to ...** para concluir, querría ... 2 **concluding** *pres p* ‹*remarks/chapter*› final

conclusion /kənˈkluːʒən/ *n*
A [c] (end) conclusión *f*; **in ~** (*as linker*) para concluir, como conclusión
B [c] (decision, judgment) conclusión *f*; **to come to** *o* **reach a ~** llegar* a una conclusión; **I've come to the ~ that ...** he llegado a la conclusión de que ...; **to draw a ~** sacar* una conclusión; ***to jump to ~s*** precipitarse (a sacar conclusiones)

conclusive /kənˈkluːsɪv/ *adj* ‹*evidence/argument*› concluyente; ‹*victory*› decisivo, contundente

conclusively /kənˈkluːsɪvli/ *adv* de manera concluyente, concluyentemente

concoct /kənˈkɑːkt || kənˈkɒkt/ *vt* ‹*meal/drink*› preparar; ‹*excuse/story*› inventarse; ‹*plan*› tramar

concoction /kənˈkɑːkʃən || kənˈkɒkʃən/ *n* [c u] (food, drink): **I'm not eating/drinking that ~** (pej) yo no me como ese mejunje/bebo ese brebaje (pey); **one of Pierre's delicious ~s** una de las exquisitas creaciones de Pierre

concord /ˈkɑːnkɔːrd || ˈkɒŋkɔːd/ *n* [u c] (harmony) (frml) concordia *f*

concordance /kənˈkɔːrdn̩s || kənˈkɔːdn̩s/ *n* concordancia *f*; (index) concordancias *fpl*

concourse /ˈkɑːnkɔːrs || ˈkɒŋkɔːs/ *n*
A (large hall) explanada *f*
B (gathering) (liter) concurrencia *f*

concrete¹ /kɑːnˈkriːt, ˈkɑːnkriːt || ˈkɒnkriːt/ *adj* concreto

concrete² /ˈkɑːnkriːt || ˈkɒnkriːt/ *n* [u] hormigón *m*, concreto *m* (AmL); (in loose usage) cemento *m*; (*before n*) ‹*building*› de hormigón *or* (AmL tb) concreto

concrete³ /ˈkɑːnkriːt || ˈkɒnkriːt/ *vt* ‹*path*› pavimentar con hormigón *or* (AmL tb) con concreto

concubine /ˈkɑːŋkjʊbaɪn || ˈkɒŋkjʊbaɪn/ *n* concubina *f*

concur /kənˈkɜːr || kənˈkɜː(r)/ *vi* **-rr-** (frml) (agree) **to ~ (WITH sb/sth)** coincidir (CON algn/algo), estar* de acuerdo (CON algn/algo)

concurrent /kənˈkɜːrənt || kənˈkʌrənt/ *adj* (frml) ‹*event*› concurrente (frml), simultáneo

concurrently /kənˈkɜːrəntli || kənˈkʌrəntli/ *adv* (frml) simultáneamente

concuss /kənˈkʌs/ *vt* (*usu pass*): **to be ~ed** sufrir una conmoción (cerebral) *or* una concusión

concussion /kənˈkʌʃən/ *n* [u] conmoción *f* cerebral, concusión *f*

condemn /kənˈdem/ *vt*
A 1 (sentence) condenar; **he was ~ed to death** lo condenaron *or* fue condenado a muerte; **the ~ed man** el condenado a muerte 2 (censure) condenar
B 1 (declare unusable) ‹*building*› declarar ruinoso 2 (in US: convert to public use) ‹*building*› expropiar (*por causa de utilidad pública*)

condemnation /ˈkɑːndemˈneɪʃən || ˌkɒndemˈneɪʃən/ *n* [u] condena *f*, repulsa *f*

condemnatory /kənˈdemnətɔːri || ˌkɒndemˈneɪtərɪ/ *adj* condenatorio

condensation /ˈkɑːndenˈseɪʃən || ˌkɒndenˈseɪʃən/ *n* [u]
A 1 (process) condensación *f* 2 (on windows etc) vapor *m*, vaho *m*
B (abridgment) condensación *f*

condense /kənˈdens/ *vt*
A (abridge) ‹*book/article*› condensar, compendiar, resumir
B (Chem) condensar
■ **condense** *vi* (Chem) condensarse

condensed /kənˈdensd/ *adj* condensado, resumido; **~ milk** leche *f* condensada; **~ soup** sopa *f* concentrada

condescend /ˈkɑːndɪˈsend || ˌkɒndɪˈsend/ *vi* 1 (deign) **to ~ to + INF** dignarse *or* condescender* A + INF 2 (patronize) **to ~ TO sb** tratar a algn con condescendencia

condescending /ˈkɑːndɪˈsendɪŋ || ˌkɒndɪˈsendɪŋ/ *adj* ‹*tone/smile*› condescendiente; **to be ~ TO** *o* **TOWARD(S) sb** tratar a algn con condescendencia

condescension /ˈkɑːndɪˈsentʃən || ˌkɒndɪˈsenʃən/ *n* [u] condescendencia *f*

condiment /ˈkɑːndəmənt || ˈkɒndɪmənt/ *n* (seasoning) condimento *m*, aliño *m*; (relish) salsa *f* (*para condimentar*)

condition[1] /kən'dɪʃən/ *n*
A (stipulation, requirement) condición *f*; **on one ~** con una condición; **on ~ that** con la condición de que, a condición de que
B 1 (state) (*no pl*) estado *m*, condiciones *fpl*; **to be in no ~ to + INF** no estar* en condiciones de + INF 2 (state of fitness): **to be in/out of ~** estar*/no estar* en forma 3 (Med) afección *f* (frml), enfermedad *f*; **a heart/liver ~** una afección cardíaca/hepática (frml)
C **conditions** *pl* 1 (circumstances) condiciones *fpl*; **working/housing ~s** condiciones de trabajo/vivienda 2 (Meteo): **weather ~s are good** el estado del tiempo es bueno

condition[2] *vt*
A (influence, determine) condicionar; **to ~ sb to + INF** condicionar a algn A + INF
B (make healthy) ‹*hair*› acondicionar

conditional /kən'dɪʃn̩əl || kən'dɪʃənl̩/ *adj* 1 (provisional) ‹*agreement/acceptance*› condicional, con condiciones; **to be ~ ON** *o* **UPON sth** estar* condicionado *or* supeditado A algo 2 (Ling) condicional

conditioner /kən'dɪʃn̩ər || kən'dɪʃn̩ə(r)/ *n* (*hair ~*) acondicionador *m*, enjuague *m* (AmL), suavizante *m* (Esp), bálsamo *m* (Chi); (*fabric ~*) suavizante *m*

conditioning /kən'dɪʃn̩ɪŋ/ *n* [u] (Psych) condicionamiento *m*

condo /'kɑːndəʊ || 'kɒndəʊ/ *n* (AmE colloq) ▸ **condominium**

condolence /kən'dəʊləns/ *n* (frml) 1 [u] (sympathy): **letter of ~** carta *f* de condolencia (frml) 2 **condolences** *pl* condolencias *fpl* (frml), pésame *m*; **he offered/sent his ~s to the widow** le dio/envió el pésame *or* (frml) sus condolencias a la viuda

condom /'kɑːndəm || 'kɒndɒm/ *n* preservativo *m*, condón *m*

condominium /'kɑːndə'mɪniəm || ˌkɒndə'mɪniəm/ *n* (*pl* ~s) (AmE) 1 [u] (ownership) régimen de propiedad horizontal 2 [c] (building) condominio *m* (AmL), bloque *m* de pisos (Esp) 3 [c] (apartment) apartamento *m*, piso *m* (Esp) (*en régimen de propiedad horizontal*)

condone /kən'dəʊn/ *vt* ‹*violence/conduct*› aprobar*

conducive /kən'duːsɪv || kən'djuːsɪv/ *adj* (*pred*) **to be ~ TO sth** ser* propicio PARA algo

conduct[1] /'kɑːndʌkt || 'kɒndʌkt/ *n* [u] 1 (behavior) conducta *f*, comportamiento *m* 2 (management): **her ~ of the investigation** la manera *or* el modo en que condujo la investigación

conduct[2] /kən'dʌkt/ *vt*
A ‹*inquiry/experiment*› llevar a cabo, realizar*; ‹*conversation*› mantener*; **to ~ business** llevar a cabo actividades comerciales
B (Mus) dirigir*
C ‹*visitor/tour/party*› guiar*
D ‹*heat/electricity*› conducir*
■ *v refl* **to ~ oneself** conducirse* (frml), comportarse
■ **conduct** *vi* (Mus) dirigir*

conduction /kən'dʌkʃən/ *n* [u] conducción *f*

conductor /kən'dʌktər || kən'dʌktə(r)/ *n*
A (Mus) director, -tora *m,f* (de orquesta)
B 1 (on bus) cobrador, -dora *m,f*, guarda *mf* (RPl) 2 (on train) (AmE) cobrador, -dora *m,f*
C (Elec, Phys) conductor *m*

conductress /kən'dʌktrəs || kən'dʌktrɪs/ *n* 1 (on bus) cobradora *f*, guarda *f* (RPl) 2 (on train) (AmE) cobradora *f*

conduit /'kɑːnduːət || 'kɒndjuɪt/ *n* conducto *m*

cone /kəʊn/ *n*
A (Auto, Math) cono *m*; **~-shaped** cónico
B (*ice-cream ~*) cucurucho *m or* barquillo *m or* (Ven) barquilla *f or* (Col) cono *m*

confab /'kɑːnfæb || 'kɒnfæb/ *n* (colloq) charla *f*

confectioner /kən'fekʃn̩ər || kən'fekʃənə(r)/ *n* pastelero, -ra *m,f*, confitero, -ra *m,f*

confectionery /kən'fekʃəneri || kən'fekʃənəri/ *n* [u] productos *mpl* de confitería

confederacy /kən'fedərəsi/ *n* confederación *f*

confederate[1] /kən'fedərət/ *adj* confederado

confederate[2] *n* 1 (state) confederado *m* 2 (accomplice) (liter) cómplice *mf*

> **Confederate States of America**
>
> Los once estados norteamericanos, Carolina del Norte y del Sur, Misisipí, Florida, Georgia, Luisiana, Alabama, Tejas, Virginia, Arkansas, Tennessee, que se apartaron de la Unión en 1861, provocando el comienzo de la Guerra de Secesión (Civil War)

confederation /kən'fedə'reɪʃən/ *n* confederación *f*

confer /kən'fɜːr || kən'fɜː(r)/ **-rr-** *vt* (bestow) conceder, conferir* (frml); **to ~ sth ON** *o* **UPON sb/sth** concederle *or* (frml) conferirle* algo A algn/algo
■ **confer** *vi* (discuss) consultar; **to ~ WITH sb (ABOUT sth)** consultar (algo) CON algn

conference /'kɑːnfrəns || 'kɒnfərəns/ *n* 1 [c] (large assembly, convention) congreso *m*, conferencia *f*; (*before n*) **~ center** *o* (BrE) **centre** centro *m* de conferencias 2 [c u] (meeting, discussion) conferencia *f*; **to be in ~ with sb** estar* reunido *or* en reunión *or* (frml) en conferencia con algn; (*before n*) **~ room** sala *f* de juntas *or* reuniones; **at the ~ table** en la mesa de las negociaciones 3 (esp AmE Sport) liga *f*

confess /kən'fes/ *vt* confesar*
■ **confess** *vi*
A 1 (admit) confesar*; **he ~ed to five murders** confesó haber cometido cinco asesinatos 2 **confessed** *past p* ‹*thief/liar*› declarado
B (Relig) confesarse*

confession /kən'feʃən/ *n*
A [c] (statement) confesión *f*; **to make a ~** confesar*, hacer* una confesión; **a signed ~** una confesión por escrito
B [c u] (of sins) confesión *f*; **to go to ~** ir* a confesarse

confessional /kən'feʃn̩əl/ *n* confesionario *m*, confesonario *m*

confessor /kən'fesər || kən'fesə(r)/ *n* confesor *m*

confetti /kən'feti/ *n* [u] confeti *m or* (Chi) chaya *f or* (RPl) papel *m* picado *or* (Ven) papelillos *mpl*

confidant /'kɑːnfədænt || 'kɒnfɪˌdænt/ *n* confidente *m*

confidante /'kɑːnfədænt || ˌkɒnfɪ'dænt/ *n* confidente *f*

confide /kən'faɪd/ *vi* 1 (tell secrets) **to ~ IN sb** confiarse* A algn 2 (trust) (liter) **to ~ IN sb/sth** confiar* EN algn/algo
■ **confide** *vt* **to ~ sth TO sb** confiarle* algo A algn

confidence /'kɑːnfədəns || 'kɒnfɪdəns/ *n*
A [u] 1 (trust, faith) confianza *f*; **~ IN sb/sth** confianza EN algn/algo 2 (self-confidence) confianza *f* en sí mismo, seguridad *f* en sí mismo
B 1 [u] (confidentiality): **he took her into his ~** se confió a ella; **in ~** en confianza; **in strict ~** con absoluta reserva 2 [c] (secret) confidencia *f*; **they exchanged ~s** se hicieron confidencias

confidence game *n* (AmE), **confidence trick** *n* estafa *f*, timo *m* (fam)

confident /'kɑːnfədənt || 'kɒnfɪdənt/ *adj* 1 (sure) ‹*statement/forecast*› hecho con confianza *or* seguridad; **I am ~ that she won't disappoint us** tengo (la) plena confianza de que no nos defraudará; **to be ~ OF sth** confiar* EN algo 2 (self-confident) ‹*person*› seguro de sí mismo

confidential /'kɑːnfə'dentʃəl || ˌkɒnfɪ'denʃəl/ *adj* 1 (secret) ‹*information*› confidencial 2 (private) (*before n*) ‹*secretary*› de confianza 3 (intimate) ‹*tone*› confidencial

confidentiality /'kɑːnfə'dentʃi'æləti || ˌkɒnfɪdenʃɪ'æləti/ *n* [u] confidencialidad *f*

confidentially /'kɑːnfə'dentʃəli || ˌkɒnfɪ'denʃəli/ *adv* confidencialmente

confidently /'kɑːnfədəntli || 'kɒnfɪdəntli/ *adv* con seguridad *or* confianza

configuration /kən'fɪgjə'reɪʃən || kənˌfɪgə'reɪʃən/ *n* configuración *f*

confine /kən'faɪn/ *vt* 1 (limit, restrict) **to ~ sth TO sth** limitar *or* restringir* algo A algo; **drug addiction is not ~d to large cities** la drogadicción no afecta únicamente a las grandes ciudades; **the fire was ~d to the basement** el incendio sólo afectó al sótano 2 (shut in, imprison) ‹*person*› confinar, recluir*; ‹*animal*› encerrar*; **he was ~d to bed for several months** tuvo que guardar cama varios meses

confined /kən'faɪnd/ *adj* ‹*space*› limitado, reducido

confinement /kən'faɪnmənt/ *n* 1 [u] (act, state) reclusión *f*, confinamiento *m* 2 [u c] (in childbirth) parto *m*

confines /'kɑːnfaɪnz || 'kɒnfaɪnz/ *pl n* confines *mpl*, límites *mpl*

confirm /kən'fɜːrm || kən'fɜːm/ *vt*

A **1** (substantiate) ‹*report/reservation*› confirmar **2** (ratify) (frml) ‹*treaty/agreement*› ratificar* **3** **confirmed** *past p* ‹*bachelor/liar*› empedernido

B (Relig) confirmar

confirmation /'kɑːnfər'meɪʃən || ,kɒnfə'meɪʃən/ *n*

A [u] **1** (substantiation) confirmación *f* **2** (ratification) (frml) ratificación *f*

B [u c] (Relig) confirmación *f*

confiscate /'kɑːnfəskeɪt || 'kɒnfɪskeɪt/ *vt* confiscar*, decomisar; **to ~ sth FROM sb** confiscarle* *or* decomisarle algo A algn

confiscation /'kɑːnfə'skeɪʃən || ,kɒnfɪ'skeɪʃən/ *n* [u c] confiscación *f*, decomiso *m*

conflate /kən'fleɪt/ *vt* refundir, combinar

conflict[1] /'kɑːnflɪkt || 'kɒnflɪkt/ *n* [c u] conflicto *m*; **to come into ~ with sth/sb** entrar en conflicto con algo/algn; **a ~ of interests** un conflicto de intereses

conflict[2] /kən'flɪkt/ *vi* discrepar, estar* reñido

conflicting /kən'flɪktɪŋ/ *adj* ‹*interests*› opuesto, encontrado; ‹*views/accounts/emotions*› contradictorio

conform /kən'fɔːrm || kən'fɔːm/ *vi* **1** (be in accordance) **to ~ TO** *o* **WITH sth** ajustarse A *or* cumplir CON algo **2** (act in a conformist way) ser* conformista; **to ~ TO sth**: **he usually ~s to their wishes** por lo general se aviene a sus deseos

conformist[1] /kən'fɔːrməst/ *adj* conformista

conformist[2] *n* conformista *mf*

conformity /kən'fɔːrməti || kən'fɔːməti/ *n* [u] conformidad *f*; **in ~ with** (frml) conforme a, en conformidad con (frml)

confound /kən'faʊnd/ *vt* **1** (perplex) ‹*person*› confundir, desconcertar* **2** (thwart) ‹*attempt*› frustrar; ‹*plan*› echar por tierra **3** (damn) (colloq & dated): **~ it!** ¡maldita sea!

confounded /kən'faʊndəd || kən'faʊndɪd/ *adj* (*before n*) (colloq & dated) maldito, condenado

confront /kən'frʌnt/ *vt* **1** (come face to face with) ‹*danger/problem*› afrontar, enfrentar, hacer* frente a; **police were ~ed by a group of demonstrators** la policía se vio enfrentada a un grupo de manifestantes **2** (face up to) ‹*enemy/fear/crisis*› hacer* frente a, enfrentarse a; **I decided to ~ him on the matter** decidí plantearle la cuestión cara a cara; **to ~ sb WITH sth**: **I intend to ~ him with it tomorrow** pienso encararme con él mañana y decírselo

confrontation /'kɑːnfrʌn'teɪʃən || ,kɒnfrʌn'teɪʃən/ *n* **1** [c u] (conflict) enfrentamiento *m*, confrontación *f* **2** [c] (encounter) confrontación *f*

confuse /kən'fjuːz/ *vt*

A **1** (bewilder) confundir, desconcertar* **2** (blur) ‹*situation*› complicar*, enredar

B (mix up, be unable to distinguish) ‹*ideas/sounds*› confundir; **to ~ sth/sb WITH sth/sb** confundir algo/a algn CON algo/algn

confused /kən'fjuːzd/ *adj* **1** (perplexed) confundido; **to get ~** confundirse; **what are you ~ about?** ¿qué es lo que te tiene confundido? **2** (unclear) ‹*argument*› confuso

confusing /kən'fjuːzɪŋ/ *adj* confuso, poco claro

confusion /kən'fjuːʒən/ *n* [u]

A **1** (turmoil) confusión *f*; **the meeting ended in ~** la reunión terminó en medio de la confusión general **2** (disorder) desorden *m*

B **1** (perplexity) confusión *f*, desconcierto *m* **2** (embarrassment) turbación *f*; **her presence threw him into ~** su presencia lo turbó

con game *n* (AmE) timo *m* (fam), estafa *f*

congeal /kən'dʒiːl/ *vi* «*fat*» solidificarse*, cuajar; **~ed blood** sangre *f* coagulada

congenial /kən'dʒiːniəl/ *adj* ‹*person*› simpático, agradable; **a ~ atmosphere** un ambiente amigable

congenital /kən'dʒenɪtl̩/ *adj* congénito

congested /kən'dʒestəd || kən'dʒestɪd/ *adj* **1** (with traffic) congestionado; (with people) abarrotado *or* repleto de gente **2** (Med) congestionado

congestion /kən'dʒestʃən/ *n* [u] **1** (with traffic) congestión *f*; (with people) abarrotamiento *m* **2** (Med) congestión *f*

congestion charge *n pago en concepto de peaje que se cobra por conducir en el centro de Londres dentro de cierto horario*

conglomerate /kən'glɑːmərət || kən'glɒmərət/ *n* (Busn) conglomerado *m* (de empresas)

conglomeration /kən'glɑːmə'reɪʃən || kən,glɒmə'reɪʃən/ *n* acumulación *f*, conglomerado *m*

Congo /'kɑːŋgəʊ || 'kɒŋgəʊ/ *n* el Congo

congratulate /kən'grætʃəleɪt || kən'grætjʊleɪt/ *vt* felicitar; **to ~ sb ON sth/-ING** felicitar *or* darle* la enhorabuena a algn POR algo/+ INF

■ *v refl* **to ~ oneself ON sth** felicitarse POR *or* DE algo, congratularse POR *or* DE algo (frml)

congratulation /kən'grætʃə'leɪʃən || kən,grætjʊ'leɪʃən/ *n* **1** [u] (praise) felicitación *f* **2** **congratulations** *pl* enhorabuena *f*, felicitaciones *fpl*; (*as interj*) **(my) ~s!** ¡enhorabuena!, ¡felicitaciones! (AmL)

congratulatory /kən'grætʃələtɔːri || kən'grætjʊlətəri/ *adj* (frml) de enhorabuena *or* felicitación

congregate /'kɑːŋgrɪgeɪt || 'kɒŋgrɪgeɪt/ *vi* congregarse*

congregation /'kɑːŋgrɪ'geɪʃən || ,kɒŋgrɪ'geɪʃən/ *n* (Relig) (attending service) fieles *mpl*; (parishioners) feligreses *mpl*

congress /'kɑːŋgrəs || 'kɒŋgres/ *n* **1** (conference) congreso *m* **2** **Congress** (in US) el Congreso (de los Estados Unidos)

Congress

El Congreso es el organismo nacional legislativo de Estados Unidos. Se reúne en el Capitolio (**Capitol**) y está compuesto por dos cámaras: el Senado (**Senate**) y la Cámara de Representantes (**House of Representatives**). Se renueva cada dos años y su función es elaborar leyes. Toda nueva ley debe ser aprobada primero por las dos cámaras y posteriormente por el Presidente

congressional /kən'greʃn̩l || kən'greʃənl̩/ *adj* (in US) ‹*committee*› del Congreso; **~ district** distrito *m* electoral; **~ elections** elecciones *fpl* parlamentarias; **the C~ Record** las Actas del Congreso (de los EEUU)

congress: **~man** /'kɑːŋgrəsmən || 'kɒŋgresmən/ *n* (*pl* **-men** /-mən/) (in US) miembro *m* del Congreso; **~woman** *n* (in US) miembro *f* del Congreso

conical /'kɑːnɪkəl || 'kɒnɪkəl/ *adj* cónico

conifer /'kɑːnəfər || 'kɒnɪfə(r)/ *n* conífera *f*

coniferous /kəʊ'nɪfərəs || kə'nɪfərəs/ *adj* conífero; ‹*forest*› de coníferas; **a ~ tree** una conífera

conjecture[1] /kən'dʒektʃər || kən'dʒektʃə(r)/ *n* **1** [u] (guesswork): **it's pure ~** no son más que conjeturas *or* suposiciones **2** [c] (guess) (frml) conjetura *f*

conjecture[2] *vt/i* (frml) conjeturar

conjugal /'kɑːndʒəgəl || 'kɒndʒʊgəl/ *adj* (frml) conyugal

conjugate /'kɑːndʒəgeɪt || 'kɒndʒʊgeɪt/ *vt* conjugar*

■ **conjugate** *vi* «*verb*» conjugarse*

conjugation /'kɑːndʒə'geɪʃən || ,kɒndʒʊ'geɪʃən/ *n* [c u] (Ling) conjugación *f*

conjunction /kən'dʒʌŋkʃən/ *n* **1** [c] (Ling) conjunción *f* **2** [c u] (combination) conjunción *f*

conjunctivitis /kən'dʒʌŋktɪ'vaɪtəs || kən,dʒʌŋktɪ'vaɪtɪs/ *n* [u] conjuntivitis *f*

conjure /'kɑːndʒər || 'kʌndʒə(r)/ *vt*: **to ~ sth out of thin air** hacer* aparecer algo como por arte de magia

■ **conjure** *vi* (perform tricks) hacer* magia

Phrasal verb

• **conjure up** [v ▸ o ▸ adv, v ▸ adv ▸ o] (evoke) evocar*, traer* a la memoria; **it ~s up images of ...** hace pensar en ...

conjurer /'kɑːndʒərər || 'kʌndʒərə(r)/ *n* prestidigitador, -dora *m,f*, mago, -ga *m,f*

conjuring /'kɑːndʒərɪŋ || 'kʌndʒərɪŋ/ *n* [u] prestidigitación *f*, magia *f*; (*before n*) **~ trick** truco *m* de magia

conjuror *n* ▸**conjurer**

conker /'kɑːŋkər || 'kɒŋkə(r)/ *n* (BrE colloq) castaña *f* (de Indias)

conk out /kɑːŋk || kɒŋk/*vi* (colloq) «*engine/car*» averiarse*, descomponerse* (AmL)

con man *n* estafador *m*, timador *m*

Conn = **Connecticut**

connect /kə'nekt/ *vt*

A **1** (attach) **to ~ sth (TO sth)** conectar algo (A algo) **2** (link

C

together) ‹*rooms/buildings*› comunicar*; ‹*towns*› conectar 3▸ (Telec): **I'm trying to ~ you** un momento que lo comunico *or* (Esp) le pongo con el número 4▸ ‹*phone/gas*› conectar

B (associate) ‹*people/ideas/events*› relacionar, asociar

■ **connect** *vi*

A 1▸ (be joined together) «*rooms*» comunicarse*; «*pipes*» empalmar 2▸ (be fitted) **to ~ (TO sth)** estar* conectado (a algo)

B (Transp) **to ~ WITH sth** «*train/flight*» enlazar* CON algo, conectar CON algo (AmL)

Phrasal verb

• **connect up**

A [v ▸ o ▸ adv, v ▸ adv ▸ o] ‹*wires/apparatus*› conectar

B [v ▸ adv] «*wires*» conectarse; **it all ~s up** todo está relacionado

connected /kə'nektəd || kə'nektɪd/ *adj* ‹*ideas/events*› relacionado; **the two firms are in no way ~** las dos empresas no tienen conexión *or* relación alguna; **she's very well ~** está muy bien relacionada *or* conectada, tiene muy buenas conexiones (AmL); **to be ~ed WITH sth** estar* relacionado *or* conectado CON algo

connecting /kə'nektɪŋ/ *adj* (*before n*): **~ rooms** habitaciones *fpl* que se comunican (entre sí); **the ~ door was locked** la puerta que comunicaba las dos habitaciones estaba cerrada con llave; **~ flight** vuelo *m* de enlace

connection /kə'nekʃən/ *n*

A [c] 1▸ (link) **~ (WITH sth)** enlace *m or* conexión *f* (CON algo) 2▸ (Elec) conexión *f*

B [c] (Transp) **~ (WITH sth)** conexión *f or* enlace *m* (CON algo); **I missed my ~** perdí la combinación *or* conexión

C [c u] 1▸ (relation) relación *f or* conexión *f*; **she is wanted in ~ with the killing** se la busca en relación *or* en conexión con el asesinato 2▸ (relationship) conexión *f*

D **connections** *pl* 1▸ (links, ties) lazos *mpl* 2▸ (influential people) contactos *mpl*, conexiones *fpl* (AmL) 3▸ (relations) familiares *mpl*, parientes *mpl*

connexion /kə'nekʃən/ *n* [c u] (esp BrE) ▸ **connection**

connivance /kə'naɪvəns/ *n* [u] complicidad *f*, connivencia *f* (frml)

connive /kə'naɪv/ *vi* 1▸ (plot) **to ~ (WITH sb)** actuar* en complicidad *or* (frml) en connivencia (CON algn) 2▸ (cooperate) **to ~ AT sth** ser* cómplice EN algo

conniving /kə'naɪvɪŋ/ *adj* maniobrero, maquinador

connoisseur /'kɑːnə'sɜːr || ˌkɒnə'sɜː(r)/ *n* entendido, -da *m,f*

connotation /'kɑːnə'teɪʃən || ˌkɒnə'teɪʃən/ *n* [u c] connotación *f*

conquer /'kɑːŋkər || 'kɒŋkə(r)/ *vt* ‹*country/mountain*› conquistar; ‹*enemy*› vencer*; ‹*fear*› vencer, superar; **the ~ing army** el ejército victorioso

conqueror /'kɑːŋkərər || 'kɒŋkərə(r)/ *n* conquistador, -dora *m,f*

conquest /'kɑːŋkwest || 'kɒŋkwest/ *n* [c u] conquista *f*

conquistador /kɔːŋ'kiːstədɔːr || kɒn'kwɪstədɔː(r)/ *n* (*pl* **-dors** *or* **-dores** /-'dɔːriːz || -'dɔːrez/) conquistador *m*

conscience /'kɑːntʃəns || 'kɒnʃəns/ *n* [c u] conciencia *f*; **to have a clear ~** tener* la conciencia tranquila *or* limpia; **she has a guilty ~** no tiene la conciencia tranquila, le remuerde la conciencia; **her ~ was troubling her** le remordía la conciencia; **I don't want that on my ~** no quiero tener ese cargo de conciencia

conscientious /'kɑːntʃi'entʃəs || ˌkɒnʃi'enʃəs/ *adj* ‹*work*› concienzudo, serio; ‹*student*› aplicado, serio

conscientiously /'kɑːntʃi'entʃəsli || ˌkɒnʃi'enʃəsli/ *adv* a conciencia, concienzudamente

conscientious objector *n* objetor, -tora *m,f* de conciencia

conscious /'kɑːntʃəs || 'kɒnʃəs/ *adj*

A 1▸ (awake, alert) (*no comp*) consciente 2▸ (aware) (*pred*) **to be ~ OF sth** ser* *or* (Chi, Méx) estar* consciente DE algo, tener* conciencia DE algo; **to become ~ of sth** tomar conciencia de algo

B (deliberate) ‹*decision*› deliberado; **she made a ~ effort to be nice** se esforzó por ser amable

-conscious /ˌkɑːntʃəs || ˌkɒnʃəs/ *suff*: **safety~** preocupado por la seguridad; **a fashion~ girl** una chica que sigue *or* siempre va a la última moda; *see also* **class-conscious**

consciously /'kɑːntʃəsli || 'kɒnʃəsli/ *adv* ‹*choose/avoid*› deliberadamente

consciousness /'kɑːntʃəsnəs || 'kɒnʃəsnɪs/ *n* [u]

A (state of being awake, alert) conocimiento *m*; **to lose/regain ~** perder*/recobrar el conocimiento *or* el sentido

B (awareness) conciencia *f*; **to raise sb's ~** concientizar* *or* (Esp) concienciar a algn

consciousness-raising /'kɑːntʃəsnəsˌreɪzɪŋ || 'kɒnʃəsnɪsˌreɪzɪŋ/ *n* [u] concientización *f* (AmL), concienciación *f* (Esp)

conscript[1] /'kɑːnskrɪpt || 'kɒnskrɪpt/ *n* recluta *mf*, conscripto, -ta *m,f* (AmL)

conscript[2] /kən'skrɪpt/ *vt* ‹*soldiers/army*› reclutar; **he was ~ed into the army** lo llamaron a filas; (for national service) lo llamaron a cumplir el servicio militar

conscription /kən'skrɪpʃən/ *n* [u] conscripción *f* (esp AmL), reclutamiento *m* (*para el servicio militar obligatorio en casos de guerra*)

consecrate /'kɑːnsəkreɪt || 'kɒnsɪkreɪt/ *vt* consagrar

consecration /'kɑːnsə'kreɪʃən || ˌkɒnsɪ'kreɪʃən/ *n* [u c] consagración *f*

consecutive /kən'sekjətɪv || kən'sekjʊtɪv/ *adj* (successive) ‹*numbers*› consecutivo; **he was absent on three ~ days** faltó tres días seguidos

consensus /kən'sensəs/ *n* [c u] 1▸ (agreement) consenso *m* 2▸ (opinion) opinión *f* general; **the ~ (of opinion) is that ...** la opinión general *or* más generalizada es que ...

consent[1] /kən'sent/ *vi* acceder; **to ~ TO sth** acceder A *or* consentir* EN algo; **~ing adult** (Law) *adulto que realiza un acto por su propia y libre voluntad*

consent[2] *n* [u] consentimiento *m*; **by mutual ~** de común acuerdo; **he gave his ~ to their marriage** dio su consentimiento para que se casaran; **age of ~** (Law) *edad a partir de la cual es válido el consentimiento que se da para tener relaciones sexuales*

consequence /'kɑːnsəkwens || 'kɒnsɪkwəns/ *n*

A [c] (result) consecuencia *f*; **to be a ~ of sth** ser* consecuencia *or* resultado de algo; **to have ~s** tener* *or* traer* consecuencias; **to take the ~s** atenerse* a *or* aceptar las consecuencias; **he neglected the business, with the ~ that ...** descuidó el negocio y a consecuencia de ello ...

B [u] (importance) trascendencia *f*, importancia *f*; **to be of ~ to sb** tener* trascendencia *or* ser* de importancia para algn; **that's of no ~** eso no tiene importancia

consequent /'kɑːnsəkwənt || 'kɒnsɪkwənt/ *adj* consiguiente

consequential /'kɑːnsə'kwentʃəl || ˌkɒnsɪ'kwenʃəl/ *adj* 1▸ (resultant) consiguiente, resultante 2▸ (important) (frml) trascendental, importante

consequently /'kɑːnsəkwentli || 'kɒnsɪkwentli/ *adv* consiguientemente, por consiguiente

conservation /'kɑːnsər'veɪʃən || ˌkɒnsə'veɪʃən/ *n* [u] (Ecol) protección *f or* conservación *f* del medio ambiente; (*before n*) ‹*group/scheme*› conservacionista; **~ area** (BrE) zona *f* protegida (*por su interés ecológico o arquitectónico*)

conservationist /'kɑːnsər'veɪʃənəst || ˌkɒnsə'veɪʃənɪst/ *n* conservacionista *mf*

conservatism /kən'sɜːrvətɪzəm || kən'sɜːvətɪzəm/ *n* [u] conservadurismo *m*

conservative[1] /kən'sɜːrvətɪv || kən'sɜːvətɪv/ *adj* 1▸ (traditional) conservador 2▸ **Conservative** (in UK) (*before n*) conservador; **the C~ (and Unionist) Party** el Partido Conservador 3▸ (cautious) cauteloso, prudente; **at a ~ estimate** calculando por lo bajo

conservative[2] *n* 1▸ (traditionalist) conservador, -dora *m,f* 2▸ **Conservative** (in UK) conservador, -dora *m,f*; **the C~s** los conservadores, el Partido Conservador

Conservative Party

El Partido Conservador es uno de los principales partidos políticos británicos. Se sitúa a la derecha del espectro político que apoya el sistema capitalista, la libre empresa y la privatización de la industria y los servicios públicos. Surgió alrededor de 1830 como resultado de la evolución del *Tory Party* y a menudo se le denomina aún por este nombre

conservatory /kən'sɜːrvətɔːri || kən'sɜːvətri/ *n* (*pl* **-ries**)
A (greenhouse) jardín *m* de invierno
B (school of music) conservatorio *m*

conserve¹ /kən'sɜːrv || kən'sɜːv/ *vt* 1 (preserve) ‹*wildlife/rivers*› proteger*, conservar 2 (save) ‹*energy/resources*› conservar; **to ~ one's strength** ahorrar energías

conserve² /'kɑːnsɜːrv || 'kɒnsɜːv/ *n* [u c] conserva *f*; (jam) confitura *f*

consider /kən'sɪdər || kən'sɪdə(r)/ *vt* 1 (examine) ‹*advantages/offer*› considerar; **it is my ~ed opinion that ...** lo he pensado mucho y considero *or* opino que ... 2 (contemplate) ‹*possibility*› considerar, plantearse, contemplar; **I wouldn't even ~ it!** ¡yo ni me lo plantearía!; **we're ~ing Ann for the job** estamos pensando en Ann para el puesto; **to ~ + -ING**: **we're ~ing moving house** estamos pensando en mudarnos; **would you ~ selling it if ... ?** ¿le interesaría venderlo si ... ? 3 (take into account) tener* en cuenta, considerar; **all things ~ed, I think that ...** bien considerado *or* bien mirado, creo que ... 4 (regard as) considerar; **they ~ themselves (to be) above such things** consideran que están por encima de ese tipo de cosas; **what do you ~ a lot of money?** ¿tú qué entiendes por mucho dinero?; **~ it done!** ¡dalo por hecho!; **~ yourself lucky** puedes darte por afortunado; **it's ~ed to be the best of its class** está considerado como el mejor de su clase; *see also* **considering**

considerable /kən'sɪdərəbəl/ *adj* ‹*achievement/risk*› considerable; ‹*sum*› importante, considerable; **with ~ difficulty** con bastante dificultad; **to a ~ extent** en gran parte

considerably /kən'sɪdərəbli/ *adv* bastante, considerablemente

considerate /kən'sɪdərət/ *adj* atento, considerado

consideration /kən'sɪdə'reɪʃən/ *n*
A 1 [u] (attention, thought): **their case has been given careful ~** su caso ha sido estudiado *or* considerado detenidamente; **to take sth into ~** tener* algo en cuenta, considerar algo; **the report is under ~** el informe está siendo estudiado; **in ~ of** (frml) en consideración a 2 [c] (factor): **a major ~ is the cost** un factor muy a tener en cuenta es el costo
B (thoughtfulness) consideración *f*
C (importance): **of little/no ~** de poca/ninguna importancia *or* trascendencia
D (payment): **for a small ~** por una módica suma *or* cantidad

considering¹ /kən'sɪdərɪŋ/ *prep* teniendo en cuenta

considering² *conj*: **~ (that) she's only two years old** teniendo en cuenta que tiene sólo dos años

considering³ *adv* (colloq): **it's not too bad ~** no está tan mal, si te pones a pensar *or* después de todo

consign /kən'saɪn/ *vt* 1 (hand over) (frml) **to ~ sb TO sth**: **the boy was ~ed to the care of his aunt** el niño fue encomendado a su tía, el niño fue confiado al cuidado de su tía 2 (send) ‹*goods*› consignar

consignment /kən'saɪnmənt/ *n* 1 [c] (goods sent) envío *m*, remesa *f* 2 [u] (sending) envío *m*

consist /kən'sɪst/ *vi* **to ~ OF sth** constar DE algo, estar* compuesto DE algo

consistency /kən'sɪstənsi/ *n* (*pl* **-cies**) 1 [u] (regularity) regularidad *f* 2 [u c] (of mixture) consistencia *f* 3 [u] (coherence) coherencia *f*

consistent /kən'sɪstənt/ *adj* 1 (compatible) **to be ~ (WITH sth)** ‹‹*statements/beliefs*›› concordar* (CON algo) 2 (constant) ‹*excellence/failure*› constante; ‹*denial*› sistemático, constante; **we have to be ~ in our approach** tenemos que ser coherentes *or* consecuentes en el enfoque

consistently /kən'sɪstəntli/ *adv* 1 (without change) ‹*argue*› coherentemente; ‹*behave*› consecuentemente, coherentemente 2 (constantly) ‹*claim/refuse*› sistemáticamente, constantemente

consolation /'kɑːnsə'leɪʃən || ˌkɒnsə'leɪʃən/ *n* [c u] consuelo *m*; **if it's any ~ to you** si te sirve de consuelo; (*before n*) **~ prize** premio *m* de consolación, premio *m* (de) consuelo (CS)

consolatory /kən'səʊlətɔːri || kən'sɒlətri/ *adj* (frml) de consuelo

console¹ /'kɑːnsəʊl || 'kɒnsəʊl/ *n* (control panel) consola *f*

console² /kən'səʊl/ *vt* consolar*; **I ~d myself with the thought that ...** me consolé pensando que ...

consolidate /kən'sɑːlədeɪt || kən'sɒlɪdeɪt/ *vt* 1 (reinforce) ‹*support/position*› consolidar 2 (combine) ‹*companies*› fusionar; ‹*debts*› consolidar

consolidation /kənˌsɑːlə'deɪʃən || kənˌsɒlɪ'deɪʃən/ *n* 1 [u] (reinforcement) consolidación *f* 2 [u c] (merging of companies) fusión *f*

consoling /kən'səʊlɪŋ/ *adj* ‹*words*› de consuelo

consommé /'kɑːnsə'meɪ || kən'sɒmeɪ/ *n* [u c] consomé *m*

consonant /'kɑːnsənənt || 'kɒnsənənt/ *n* consonante *f*

consort /'kɑːnsɔːrt || 'kɒnsɔːt/ *n* (spouse) (frml) consorte *mf* (frml); **prince ~** príncipe *m* consorte

Phrasal verb

• **consort with** /kən'sɔːrt || kən'sɔːt/ [v ▸ prep ▸ o] (frml) (associate with) tener* trato con; **to ~ with the enemy** confraternizar* con el enemigo

consortium /kən'sɔːrʃəm || kən'sɔːtiəm/ *n* (*pl* **-tia** /-tiə/ *or* **-tiums**) consorcio *m*

conspicuous /kən'spɪkjuəs/ *adj* ‹*hat/badge*› llamativo; ‹*differences/omissions*› manifiesto, evidente; **to make oneself ~** llamar la atención; **to be ~ by one's absence** brillar por su (*or* mi *etc*) ausencia; **to be ~ FOR sth** ‹*for bravery/loyalty*› destacar(se)* POR algo

conspicuously /kən'spɪkjuəsli/ *adv*: **she was ~ dressed** iba vestida de forma muy llamativa

conspiracy /kən'spɪrəsi/ *n* [c u] (*pl* **-cies**) conspiración *f*; **~ to + INF** conspiración PARA + INF

conspirator /kən'spɪrətər || kən'spɪrətə(r)/ *n* conspirador, -dora *m,f*

conspiratorial /kən'spɪrə'tɔːriəl/ *adj* de complicidad

conspire /kən'spaɪr || kən'spaɪə(r)/ *vi* (plot) conspirar; **to ~ to + INF** conspirar PARA + INF; **to ~ AGAINST sb** conspirar CONTRA algn

constable /'kɑːnstəbəl || 'kʌnstəbəl/ *n* (BrE) agente *mf* de policía

constabulary /kən'stæbjəleri/ *n* (*pl* **-ries**) (BrE) policía *f*

constancy /'kɑːnstənsi || 'kɒnstənsi/ *n* [u] 1 (steadfastness) constancia *f* 2 (fidelity) (liter) fidelidad *f*, lealtad *f*

constant¹ /'kɑːnstənt || 'kɒnstənt/ *adj* 1 (continual) ‹*pain/complaints*› constante, continuo; **it is in ~ use** se usa continuamente 2 (unchanging) ‹*temperature/speed*› constante 3 (loyal) (liter) fiel, leal

constant² *n* constante *f*

constantly /'kɑːnstəntli || 'kɒnstəntli/ *adv* constantemente; **a ~ changing world** un mundo en constante cambio

constellation /'kɑːnstə'leɪʃən || ˌkɒnstə'leɪʃən/ *n* constelación *f*

consternation /'kɑːnstər'neɪʃən || ˌkɒnstə'neɪʃən/ *n* [u] consternación *f*

constipated /'kɑːnstəpeɪtəd || 'kɒnstɪpeɪtɪd/ *adj* estreñido

constipation /ˌkɑːnstə'peɪʃən || ˌkɒnstɪ'peɪʃən/ *n* [u] estreñimiento *m*

constituency /kən'stɪtʃuənsi || kən'stɪtjʊənsi/ *n* (*pl* **-cies**) 1 (area) circunscripción *f* *or* distrito *m* electoral 2 (supporters) electores *mpl* potenciales (*de una circunscripción electoral*)

constituent¹ /kən'stɪtʃuənt || kən'stɪtjʊənt/ *n*
A (Pol) elector, -tora *m,f*
B (component) (frml) componente *m*, elemento *m* constitutivo *or* constituyente

constituent² *adj* (*before n*) ‹*part/element*› constituyente, constitutivo

constitute /'kɑːnstətuːt || 'kɒnstɪtjuːt/ *vt* (frml)
A 1 (represent) constituir* (frml) 2 (compose, make up) constituir* (frml), formar
B (establish) (*often pass*) constituir* (frml)

constitution /'kɑːnstə'tuːʃən || ˌkɒnstɪ'tjuːʃən/ *n*
A 1 (of country) constitución *f* 2 (of association, party) estatutos *mpl*
B (of person) constitución *f*, complexión *f*

constitutional¹ /'kɑːnstə'tuːʃn̩əl || ˌkɒnstɪ'tjuːʃənl/ *adj* constitucional

C

constitutional[2] *n* (dated *or* hum) paseo *m*

constrain /kən'streɪn/ *vt* (compel) (*often pass*) obligar*, constreñir* (frml); **she felt ~ed to be polite** se sintió obligada a ser cortés

constraint /kən'streɪnt/ *n* 1 [u] (compulsion) coacción *f* 2 [u c] (restriction) (*often pl*) restricción *f*, limitación *f*; **without ~** sin restricciones *or* limitaciones

constrict /kən'strɪkt/ *vt* ‹*opening/channel*› estrechar; ‹*flow/breathing*› dificultar; ‹*freedom*› coartar, restringir*

constricted /kən'strɪktəd || kən'strɪktɪd/ *adj* 1 ‹*opening/channel*› estrecho, angosto 2 (inhibited) coartado

constriction /kən'strɪkʃən/ *n* 1 [c] (narrow part) estrechamiento *m* 2 [u] (tightness) opresión *f*; (Med) constricción *f* 3 [u c] (limitation, hampering) restricción *f*, limitación *f*

construct /kən'strʌkt/ *vt* 1 (build) (frml) construir* 2 (put together) ‹*model*› armar, montar

construction /kən'ʃtrʌkʃən/ *n*
A [u] 1 (of building) construcción *f*; (*before n*) ‹*industry/worker*› de la construcción 2 (Ling, Math) construcción *f*
B [c] (structure) estructura *f*, construcción *f*
C [c] (interpretation) interpretación *f*

constructive /kən'strʌktɪv/ *adj* ‹*criticism/suggestion*› constructivo

construe /kən'stru:/ *vt* interpretar

consul /'kɑ:nsəl || 'kɒnsəl/ *n* cónsul *mf*

consulate /'kɑ:nsələt || 'kɒnsjʊlət/ *n* consulado *m*

consult /kən'sʌlt/ *vt* consultar; **we were not ~ed about the office move** no se nos consultó (sobre) el traslado de la oficina
■ **consult** *vi*: **they ~ed and decided to leave** se consultaron entre sí y decidieron irse; **I ought to ~ with my wife first** primero debería consultárselo a *or* consultarlo con mi mujer

consultancy /kən'sʌltənsi/ *n* [c u] (*pl* **-cies**) (Busn) asesoría *f*, consultoría *f*; (*before n*) **~ fees** honorarios *mpl* por asesoría

consultant /kən'sʌltənt/ *n*
A (adviser) asesor, -sora *m,f*, consultor, -tora *m,f*
B (BrE Med) especialista *mf*

consultation /'kɑ:nsəl'teɪʃən || ˌkɒnsəl'teɪʃən/ *n* [u c] 1 (with doctor, lawyer) consulta *f* 2 (of dictionary, notes) consulta *f* 3 (discussion): **there was no ~ with the tenants** no se consultó a los inquilinos; **in ~ with sb** en conferencia con algn

consultative /kən'sʌltətɪv/ *adj* consultivo

consulting /kən'sʌltɪŋ/ *adj* (*before n*) (Med): **~ hours** horario *m or* horas *fpl* de consulta; **~ room** consultorio *m*, consulta *f*

consume /kən'su:m || kən'sju:m/ *vt* 1 (eat, drink) (frml) consumir 2 (use up) ‹*electricity/energy/resources*› consumir 3 (Econ) ‹*commodity/product*› consumir 4 (destroy) ‹‹*fire*›› reducir* a cenizas; **he was ~d by** *o* **with jealousy** lo consumían los celos

consumer /kən'su:mər || kən'sju:mə(r)/ *n* consumidor, -dora *m,f*; (*before n*) **~ demand** demanda *f* de consumo; **~ goods** artículos *mpl or* bienes *mpl* de consumo; **~ research** estudio *m* de mercado; **~ rights** derechos *mpl* del consumidor; **~ survey** encuesta *f* del *o* al consumidor; **the ~ society** la sociedad de consumo

Consumer Price Index *n* índice *m* de precios al consumo *or* al consumidor

consuming /kən'su:mɪŋ || kən'sju:mɪŋ/ *adj* (*before n*) ‹*passion*› devorador; ‹*interest*› arrollador, absorbente

consummate[1] /'kɑ:nˌsəmət || 'kɒnsəmət/ *adj* (frml) (*before n*) ‹*actor/liar*› consumado

consummate[2] /'kɑ:nsəmeɪt || 'kɒnsəmeɪt/ *vt* consumar

consumption /kən'sʌmpʃən/ *n* [u]
A 1 (eating, drinking) consumo *m*; **it is fit/unfit for human ~** es/no es apto para el consumo 2 (use) consumo *m*; **water ~** consumo de agua
B (tuberculosis) (dated) tisis *f* (ant), consunción *f* (ant)

consumptive /kən'sʌmptɪv/ *adj* (dated) tísico (ant)

cont (= **continued**) sigue

contact[1] /'kɑ:ntækt || 'kɒntækt/ *n*
A 1 [u] (physical) contacto *m*; **to come in/into ~ with sth** hacer* contacto con algo; **the plane's wheels made ~ with the ground** las ruedas del avión tocaron tierra; **point of ~** punto *m* de contacto; (*before n*) **~ sport** deporte *m* de choque 2 [u c] (communication) contacto *m*; **to come in/into ~ with sb** tratar a algn; **to be/get in ~ with sb** estar*/ponerse* en contacto con algn; **to lose ~ with sb** perder* (el) contacto con algn
B (Elec) [u c] contacto *m*
C [c] (influential person) contacto *m*

contact[2] *vt* ponerse* en contacto con, contactar (con)

contact: **~ lens** *n* lente *f or* (AmL) lente *m* de contacto, lentilla *f* (Esp); **~ print** *n* contacto *m*

contagious /kən'teɪdʒəs/ *adj* contagioso

contain /kən'teɪn/ *vt*
A (hold) contener*
B 1 ‹*enemy/fire/epidemic*› contener* 2 ‹*anger/laughter*› contener*; **to ~ oneself** contenerse*, aguantarse

container /kən'teɪnər || kən'teɪnə(r)/ *n* 1 (receptacle) recipiente *m*; (as packaging) envase *m* 2 (Transp) contenedor *m*, contáiner *m*; (*before n*) **~ ship** buque *m* portacontenedores

containment /kən'teɪnmənt/ *n* [u] contención *f*

contaminate /kən'tæməneɪt || kən'tæmɪneɪt/ *vt* contaminar; **to become ~d** contaminarse

contamination /kən'tæmə'neɪʃən || kənˌtæmɪ'neɪʃən/ *n* [u] contaminación *f*

contd (= **continued**) sigue

contemplate /'kɑ:ntəmpleɪt || 'kɒntəmpleɪt/ *vt* 1 (look at) contemplar 2 (ponder) ‹*position/alternatives*› contemplar, considerar 3 (consider possibility of) **to ~ sth/-ING**: **she is contemplating a trip to China** está pensando *or* proyectando hacer un viaje a la China; **I ~d phoning her** pensé (en) llamarla

contemplation /'kɑ:ntəm'pleɪʃən || ˌkɒntem'pleɪʃən/ *n* 1 [u c] (reflection) reflexión *f*, meditación *f* 2 [u] (observation) contemplación *f*

contemplative /kən'templətɪv/ *adj* pensativo, meditabundo

contemporary[1] /kən'tempəreri || kən'tempərəri/ *adj* 1 (of the same period) ‹*person*› contemporáneo, coetáneo; ‹*object*› de la época; **to be ~ WITH sb/sth** ser* contemporáneo *or* coetáneo DE algn/algo 2 (present-day) contemporáneo, actual

contemporary[2] *n* (*pl* **-ries**) 1 (sb living at same time) contemporáneo, -nea *m,f*, coetáneo, -nea *m,f* 2 (sb of same age): **he looks older than his contemporaries** parece mayor que la gente de su edad *or* generación

contempt /kən'tempt/ *n* [u]
A (scorn) desprecio *m*, desdén *m*; **to hold sth/sb in ~** despreciar *or* desdeñar algo/a algn; **to be beneath ~** ser* despreciable *or* deleznable
B **~ (of court)** (Law) desacato *m* al tribunal

contemptible /kən'temptəbəl/ *adj* despreciable, deleznable

contemptuous /kən'temptʃuəs || kən'temptjʊəs/ *adj* despectivo, desdeñoso; **to be ~ OF sth/sb** despreciar *or* desdeñar algo/a algn

contemptuously /kən'temptʃuəsli || kən'temptjʊəsli/ *adv* con desdén, desdeñosamente

contend /kən'tend/ *vi* 1 (compete) **to ~ (WITH sb) (FOR sth)** competir* (CON algn) (POR algo) 2 (face) **to ~ WITH sth** lidiar CON *or* enfrentarse A algo 3 **contending** *pres p* ‹*teams*› contrario, rival; ‹*interests*› en pugna, antagónico, opuesto
■ **contend** *vt* argüir*, sostener*

contender /kən'tendər || kən'tendə(r)/ *n* **~ (FOR sth)** aspirante *mf* (A algo)

content[1] /'kɑ:ntent || 'kɒntent/ *n*
A **contents** *pl* (of box, bottle, book) contenido *m*; **she read the ~s of the letter** leyó la carta; **(table of) ~s** (of book) índice *m* de materias, sumario *m*; (in magazine) sumario *m*
B [u] 1 (amount contained) contenido *m*; **sugar ~** contenido de azúcar 2 (substance) contenido *m*
C [u] /kən'tent/ (contentment) (liter) contento *m* (liter)

content[2] /kən'tent/ *adj* (*pred*) contento; **to be ~ WITH sth** estar* contento CON algo; **not ~ with raising taxes ...** no contentos con subir los impuestos ...

content³ /kən'tent/ *vt* contentar, satisfacer*

■ *v refl* **to ~ oneself** WITH **sth**/-ING contentarse *or* conformarse CON algo/+ INF

contented /kən'tentəd || kən'tentɪd/ *adj* ‹*sigh/purr*› de satisfacción; ‹*person/workforce*› satisfecho; **to be ~** WITH **sth** contentarse *or* conformarse CON algo

contentedly /kən'tentədli || kən'tentɪdli/ *adv* con satisfacción

contention /kən'tentʃən || kən'tenʃən/ *n*

A (dispute): **there is considerable ~ over ...** existe un gran desacuerdo sobre ...

B [c] (assertion) opinión *f*; **it is her ~ that ...** ella sostiene que ...

C [u] (competition): **all three cyclists are in ~ for the title** los tres ciclistas compiten por el título

contentious /kən'tentʃəs || kən'tenʃəs/ *adj* [1] ‹*issue/decision*› polémico, muy discutido [2] ‹*person*› discutidor

contentment /kən'tentmənt/ *n* [u] satisfacción *f*

contest¹ /'kɑːntest || 'kɒntest/ *n* [1] (competition) (Games) concurso *m*; (Sport) competencia *f*, competición *f* (Esp); (in boxing) combate *m* [2] (struggle) lucha *f*, contienda *f*

contest² /kən'test/ *vt* [1] ‹*allegation*› refutar; ‹*will*› impugnar; ‹*decision*› protestar contra [2] ‹*election*› presentarse como candidato a

contestant /kən'testənt/ *n* concursante *mf*

context /'kɑːntekst || 'kɒntekst/ *n* [u c] contexto *m*; **out of ~** fuera de contexto

continent /'kɑːntṇənt || 'kɒntɪnənt/ *n*

A (land mass) continente *m*

B the Continent Europa *f* (continental)

continental /'kɑːntṇ'entḷ || ˌkɒntɪ'nentl/ *adj*

A (Geog) continental

B Continental (European) de Europa (continental)

continental: **~ breakfast** *n* [u] desayuno *m* continental (*desayuno de café o té y bollos con mantequilla y mermelada*); **~ quilt** *n* (BrE) ▸ **duvet**

contingency /kən'tɪndʒənsi/ *n* [c] (*pl* **-cies**) (eventuality) contingencia *f*, eventualidad *f*; (*before n*) ‹*fund*› (para casos) de emergencia, para imprevistos; **we've made ~ plans** hemos tomado medidas previendo cualquier contingencia *or* eventualidad

contingent¹ /kən'tɪndʒənt/ *n* contingente *m*

contingent² *adj* (dependent) **to be ~** ON **sth** estar* supeditado A algo, depender DE algo

continua /kən'tɪnjuə/ *pl of* **continuum**

continual /kən'tɪnjuəl/ *adj* continuo, constante

continually /kən'tɪnjuəli/ *adv* continuamente, constantemente

continuation /kən'tɪnju'eɪʃən/ *n* [1] [u] (maintenance) mantenimiento *m* [2] [c] (resumption) reanudación *f*, continuación *f* [3] [c] (extension — of street, canal) prolongación *f*, continuación *f*; (— of story, film) continuación *f*

continue /kən'tɪnjuː/ *vi* [1] (carry on) continuar*, seguir*; **we ~d on our way** reanudamos el camino [2] (resume) continuar*, seguir*, proseguir* (frml) [3] (go, extend) ‹‹*road/canal*›› continuar*, seguir*

■ **continue** *vt* [1] (keep on) continuar*, seguir* con; **to ~** -ING/**to** + INF continuar* *or* seguir* + GER; **her health ~s to improve** su salud continúa *or* sigue mejorando [2] (resume) continuar*, seguir* con, proseguir* (frml); **to be ~d** continuará; **~d on p 96** continúa en la pág 96 [3] (extend, prolong) prolongar*

continued /kən'tɪnjuːd/ *adj* (*before n*) ‹*success*› ininterrumpido; ‹*support*› constante

continuing /kən'tɪnjuɪŋ/ *adj* (*before n*) continuado

continuity /'kɑːntṇ'uːəti || ˌkɒntɪ'njuːɪti/ *n* [u] continuidad *f*

continuous¹ /kən'tɪnjuəs/ *adj*

A ‹*line*› continuo; **~ assessment** evaluación *f* continua; **~ performance** (Cin) función *f* continua (AmL exc CS), sesión *f* continua (Esp), función *f* continuada (CS)

B (Ling) continuo

continuous² *n* (Ling) **the ~** el continuo

continuously /kən'tɪnjuəsli/ *adv* continuamente, sin interrupción

continuum /kən'tɪnjuəm/ *n* (*pl* **~s** *or* **-nua** /-njuə/) continuo *m*

contort /kən'tɔːrt || kən'tɔːt/ *vt* ‹*face*› contraer*, crispar; **to ~ one's body** contorsionarse; *see also* **contorted**

■ **contort** *vi* crisparse, contraerse*; **his face ~ed with pain** se le crispó *or* se le contrajo el rostro de dolor

contorted /kən'tɔːrtəd || kən'tɔːtɪd/ *adj* (twisted): **his face was ~ with pain** tenía el rostro contraído *or* crispado de dolor

contortion /kən'tɔːrʃən || kən'tɔːʃən/ *n* contorsión *f*

contortionist /kən'tɔːrʃənəst || kən'tɔːʃənɪst/ *n* contorsionista *mf*

contour /'kɑːntʊr || 'kɒntʊə(r)/ *n* [1] (outline) contorno *m* [2] **contours** *pl* (curves) curvas *fpl* [3] **~ (line)** curva *f* de nivel, cota *f*; (*before n*) **~ map** mapa *m* acotado *or* topográfico

contraband /'kɑːntrəbænd || 'kɒntrəbænd/ *n* [u] contrabando *m*

contraception /'kɑːntrə'sepʃən || ˌkɒntrə'sepʃən/ *n* [u] anticoncepción *f*, contracepción *f*

contraceptive /'kɑːntrə'septɪv || ˌkɒntrə'septɪv/ *n* anticonceptivo *m*, contraconceptivo *m*

contract¹ /'kɑːntrækt || 'kɒntrækt/ *n*

A [c] (agreement, document) contrato *m*; (for public works, services) contrata *f*; **to be under ~ to sb/sth** estar* bajo contrato con algn/algo; **to put sth out to ~** otorgar* la contrata de *or* para algo; **to exchange ~s** (in UK: on property deal) suscribir* el contrato de compraventa; (*before n*) **~ law** derecho *m* contractual; **to sign a ~** firmar *or* (frml) suscribir* un contrato

B (for murder) (sl): **to put out a ~ on sb** ponerle* precio a la cabeza de algn; (*before n*) **~ killer** asesino, -na *m,f* a sueldo, sicario, -ria *m,f*

contract² /kən'trækt/ *vt also* /'kɑːntrækt/ (place under contract) ‹*person*› contratar; ‹*debt*› contraer* (frml); ‹*disease*› contraer* (frml); ‹*muscle*› contraer*

■ **contract** *vi*

A *also* /'kɑːntrækt/ (enter into an agreement) **to ~ (**WITH **sb)** FOR **sth** celebrar un contrato (CON algn) PARA algo

B (become smaller) contraerse*

(Phrasal verb)

• **contract out** /'kɑːntrækt || 'kɒntrækt/ [v ▸ o ▸ adv, v ▸ adv ▸ o] ‹*job/work*› subcontratar

contraction /kən'trækʃən/ *n* [c u] contracción *f*

contractor /kən'træktər || kən'træktə(r)/ *n* contratista *mf*; **a firm of building ~s** una empresa de construcciones

contradict /'kɑːntrə'dɪkt || ˌkɒntrə'dɪkt/ *vt* [1] (assert the opposite of) ‹*statement/person*› contradecir*; **to ~ oneself** contradecirse* [2] (be inconsistent with) ‹*principles/spirit*› contradecirse* con

contradiction /'kɑːntrə'dɪkʃən || ˌkɒntrə'dɪkʃən/ *n* [c u] contradicción *f*; **a ~ in terms** un contrasentido

contradictory /'kɑːntrə'dɪktəri || ˌkɒntrə'dɪktəri/ *adj* contradictorio

contralto /kən'træltəʊ/ *n* (*pl* **~s**) contralto *f*

contraption /kən'træpʃən/ *n* (colloq) artilugio *m*, artefacto *m*

contrarian *n* inversor, -ra *mf* que va contra corriente

contrarily /'kɑːntrerəli || kən'treərɪli/ *adv*: **she behaves so ~** hace todo lo contrario de lo que se le dice

contrary¹ *adj*

A /'kɑːntreri || 'kɒntrəri/ [1] (opposed, opposite) contrario; **to be ~** TO **sth** ir* en contra DE algo [2] **contrary to** (*as prep*) contrariamente a, al contrario de

B /'kɑːntreri, kən'treri || kən'treəri/ ‹*person/child*›: **he's so ~** siempre tiene que llevar la contraria

contrary² /'kɑːntreri || 'kɒntrəri/ *n* (*pl* **-ries**) [1] (opposite) **the ~** lo contrario; **unless you hear to the ~ ...** a menos de que se les informe lo contrario ...; **despite his assertions to the ~ ...** a pesar de sus declaraciones en sentido contrario ... [2] **on the contrary** (*as linker*) al contrario, todo lo contrario, por el contrario

contrast¹ /'kɑːntræst || 'kɒntrɑːst/ *n*

A [1] [c] (difference) contraste *m* [2] [u] (Art, Cin, Phot) contraste *m*

B [1] [c] (different person, thing) **to be a ~** TO **sb/sth** contrastar CON algn/algo [2] [u c] (comparison) comparación *f*

C (*in phrases*) **by contrast** (*as linker*) por contraste, en comparación; **in contrast to** *o* **with** (*as prep*) en contraste con, a diferencia de

contrast² /kən'træst || kən'trɑːst/ *vt* contrastar, comparar; **to ~ sth/sb WITH sth/sb** comparar algo/a algn CON algo/algn

■ **contrast** *vi* 1 (differ) contrastar 2 **contrasting** *pres p* ‹*opinions/approaches*› contrastante, opuesto

contravene /ˈkɑːntrəˈviːn || ˌkɒntrəˈviːn/ *vt* contravenir*, infringir*, violar

contravention /ˈkɑːntrəˈventʃən || ˌkɒntrəˈvenʃən/ *n* [u c] contravención *f*, infracción *f*

contretemps /ˈkɑːntrətɑːn || ˈkɒntrətɑ̃/ *n* (*pl* ~) contratiempo *m*

contribute /kənˈtrɪbjət, -bjuːt/ *vt* 1 ‹*money/time*› contribuir* con, aportar, hacer* una aportación *or* (esp AmL) un aporte de; ‹*suggestions/ideas*› aportar 2 ‹*article/poem/paper*› escribir*

■ **contribute** *vi* 1 (play significant part) **to ~ (TO sth)** contribuir* (A algo) 2 (give money) contribuir*; **to ~ TO sth**: **they all ~d to his present** todos contribuyeron con dinero para su regalo 3 (participate) **to ~ TO sth** participar EN algo 4 (Journ) **to ~ TO sth** escribir* PARA algo

contribution /ˈkɑːntrəˈbjuːʃən || ˌkɒntrɪˈbjuːʃən/ *n* 1 [c] (participation, part played) contribución *f*; **to make a ~ to sth** hacer* una contribución a algo; **his ~ to the debate** su intervención en el debate 2 [c u] (payment, donation) contribución *f*; (to a fund) aportación *f*, aporte *m* (esp AmL)

contributor /kənˈtrɪbjətər || kənˈtrɪbjʊtə(r)/ *n* 1 (writer) colaborador, -dora *m,f*; **he is a regular ~ to the local paper** escribe regularmente para el periódico local 2 (donor) donante *mf*

contributory /kənˈtrɪbjətɔːri || kənˈtrɪbjʊtəri/ *adj* 1 ‹*factor/circumstance*› que contribuye 2 ‹*pension plan*› de aportación obligatoria por parte del empleado

con trick *n* (colloq) timo *m* (fam), estafa *f*

contrite /ˈkɑːntraɪt || ˈkɒntraɪt, kənˈtraɪt/ *adj* arrepentido, contrito (liter)

contrition /kənˈtrɪʃən/ *n* [u] arrepentimiento *m*, contrición *f* (liter)

contrivance /kənˈtraɪvəns/ *n* 1 [c] (device) artilugio *m*, aparato *m* 2 [c u] (stratagem) artimaña *f*, treta *f*

contrive /kənˈtraɪv/ *vt* 1 (manage) **to ~ to + INF** lograr + INF/QUE (+ *subj*), ingeniárselas *or* arreglárselas PARA + INF/PARA QUE (+ *subj*) 2 (create) ‹*method/device*› idear; ‹*meeting*› arreglar

contrived /kənˈtraɪvd/ *adj* artificioso; **her reaction seemed a little ~** su reacción pareció un poco afectada

control¹ /kənˈtrəʊl/ *vt* -ll-

A 1 (command) ‹*country/people*› controlar, ejercer* control sobre 2 (regulate) ‹*temperature/flow*› controlar, regular; ‹*traffic*› dirigir*; ‹*inflation/growth*› controlar

B 1 (curb, hold in check) ‹*animal/fire*› controlar; ‹*emotion*› controlar, dominar; **to ~ oneself** controlarse, dominarse 2 (manage, steer) ‹*vehicle/boat*› controlar; ‹*horse*› controlar, dominar

control² *n*

A [u] 1 (command) control *m*; **who's in ~ here?** ¿quién manda aquí?; **to be in ~ of sth** dominar *or* controlar algo; **to gain/take ~ of sth** hacerse* con el control de algo; **to have/lose ~ of sth** tener*/perder* el control de algo; **the zone was under Arab ~** la zona estaba bajo el control *or* el dominio de los árabes 2 (ability to control, restrain) control *m*; (authority) autoridad *f*; **to be beyond sb's ~** estar* fuera del control de algn; **circumstances beyond our ~** circunstancias ajenas a nuestra voluntad; **to be out of ~** estar* fuera de control; **to get out of ~** descontrolarse; **the epidemic is under ~** la epidemia está bajo control; **he lost ~ of the car** perdió el control del coche

B [u c] (regulation, restriction) **~(s) ON/OF sth** control *m* DE algo; **price ~(s)** control *m* de precios

C 1 [u] (knob, switch) botón *m* de control, control *m* 2 **controls** *pl* (of vehicle) mandos *mpl*

D 1 (headquarters) (*no art*) control *m* 2 [c] (checkpoint) control *m*

E [c] (in experiment) patrón *m* (de comparación); (*before n*) **~ group** grupo *m* de control

F [u] (skill, mastery) dominio *m*

control: **~ column** *n* palanca *f* de mando; **~ key** *n* tecla *f* de control

controlled /kənˈtrəʊld/ *adj* 1 (contained) ‹*voice/emotion*› contenido; ‹*response*› mesurado 2 (regulated) ‹*conditions/experiment*› controlado

controller /kənˈtrəʊlər || kənˈtrəʊlə(r)/ *n* 1 (director) director, -tora *m,f* 2 (device) controlador *m*

controlling /kənˈtrəʊlɪŋ/ *adj* (*before n*): **~ interest** participación *f* mayoritaria *or* de control

control: **~ room** *n* (Mil, Naut) centro *m* de operaciones; (Audio, Rad, TV) sala *f* de control; **~ tower** *n* torre *f* de control

controversial /ˈkɑːntrəˈvɜːrʃəl || ˌkɒntrəˈvɜːʃəl/ *adj* controvertido, polémico

controversy /ˈkɑːntrəvɜːrsi || ˈkɒntrevɜːsi, kənˈtrɒvəsi/ *n* [u c] (*pl* **-sies**) controversia *f*, polémica *f*

conundrum /kəˈnʌndrəm/ *n* adivinanza *f*, acertijo *m*

conurbation /ˈkɑːnɜːrˈbeɪʃən || ˌkɒnɜːˈbeɪʃən/ *n* conurbación *f*

convalesce /ˈkɑːnvəˈles || ˌkɒnvəˈles/ *vi* recuperarse, convalecer*; **to ~ AFTER** *o* **FROM sth** convalecer* *or* recuperarse DE algo

convalescence /ˈkɑːnvəˈlesn̩s || ˌkɒnvəˈlesn̩s/ *n* [u] convalecencia *f*

convalescent¹ /ˈkɑːnvəˈlesn̩t || ˌkɒnvəˈlesn̩t/ *n* convaleciente *mf*; (*before n*) **~ home** clínica *f* de reposo

convalescent² *adj* (*no comp, pred*) convaleciente

convection /kənˈvekʃən/ *n* [u] convección *f*; (*before n*) **~ heater** estufa *f or* calentador *m* de convección

convector /kənˈvektər || kənˈvektə(r)/ *n* estufa *f or* calentador *m* de convección

convene /kənˈviːn/ *vt* convocar*

■ **convene** *vi* reunirse*

convenience /kənˈviːniəns/ *n* 1 [u] (comfort, practicality) conveniencia *f*, comodidad *f*; **at your ~** cuando le resulte conveniente; **at your earliest ~** (Corresp) a la mayor brevedad posible, a la brevedad 2 [c] (amenity, appliance): **with every modern ~** con todas las comodidades modernas

convenience food *n* [c u] comida *f* de preparación rápida

convenient /kənˈviːniənt/ *adj* 1 (opportune, suitable) conveniente; **would it be ~ for me to call tomorrow?** ¿estaría bien que pasara mañana?; **his resignation was most ~ for the firm** su dimisión fue muy oportuna para la empresa 2 (neat, practical) práctico, cómodo 3 (handy, close): **it's very ~ having the school so near** resulta muy práctico tener la escuela tan cerca

conveniently /kənˈviːniəntli/ *adv* 1 (handily) convenientemente; **it's ~ situated** está convenientemente situada 2 (expediently): **the government ~ forgets its election promises** le resulta muy cómodo al gobierno olvidarse de sus promesas electorales; **~ for him, the banks were closed** le vino muy bien *or* le convino que los bancos estuvieran cerrados

convent /ˈkɑːnvənt || ˈkɒnvənt/ *n* convento *m*; (*before n*) **~ school** colegio *m* de monjas

convention /kənˈventʃən || kənˈvenʃən/ *n*

A 1 [u] (social code) convenciónes *fpl*, convencionalismos *mpl*; **~ dictates that one should wear black on such occasions** es costumbre vestir de negro en tales ocasiones 2 [c] (established practice) convención *f*; **literary ~** convención literaria

B [c] (agreement) convención *f*

C [c] (conference) convención *f*, congreso *m*

conventional /kənˈventʃnəl || kənˈvenʃənl̩/ *adj* ‹*behavior/method/arms*› convencional; ‹*design/style*› tradicional, clásico

conventionally /kənˈventʃn̩əli || kənˈvenʃn̩əli/ *adv* ‹*dress/behave*› de manera convencional; ‹*built/designed*› de manera tradicional *or* clásica

converge /kənˈvɜːrdʒ || kənˈvɜːdʒ/ *vi* «*lines/roads*» converger*, convergir*; «*crowd/armies*» reunirse*; **they all ~d on the square** todos se reunieron en la plaza

conversant /kənˈvɜːrsn̩t || kənˈvɜːsn̩t/ *adj* (*pred*) **to be ~ WITH sth** ser* versado EN algo

conversation /ˈkɑːnvərˈseɪʃən || ˌkɒnvəˈseɪʃən/ *n* [u c] conversación *f*; **they were deep in ~** estaban en plena conversación; **to make polite ~** conversar como un gesto de amabilidad; **to have a ~ (about sth)** hablar de *or* conversar sobre algo; (*before n*) ~ **piece** tema *m* de conversación; **his remark was a real ~ stopper** (colloq) su comentario los (*or* nos *etc*) dejó a todos callados

conversational /ˈkɑːnvərˈseɪʃn̩əl || ˌkɒnvəˈseɪʃənl/ *adj* ‹*manner/tone*› familiar, coloquial

conversationalist /ˈkɑːnvərˈseɪʃn̩ələst || ˌkɒnvəˈseɪʃn̩əlɪst/ *n* conversador, -dora *m,f*; **he's not much of a ~** no es muy buen conversador

converse¹ /kənˈvɜːrs || kənˈvɜːs/ *vi* **to ~ (ON** *o* **ABOUT sth)** conversar (SOBRE *or* ACERCA DE algo)

converse² /ˈkɑːnvɜːrs || ˈkɒnvɜːs/ *n*: **the ~** lo contrario *or* lo opuesto

converse³ /kənˈvɜːrs, ˈkɑːnvɜːrs || ˈkɒnvɜːs/ *adj* (*before n*) contrario, inverso

conversely /kənˈvɜːrsli, ˈkɑːnvɜːrsli || ˈkɒnvɜːsli/ *adv* (*as linker*) a la inversa

conversion /kənˈvɜːrʒən || kənˈvɜːʃən/ *n* [u c] 1 (transformation) ~ **(INTO/TO sth)** conversión *f* *or* transformación *f* (EN algo); (*before n*) ~ **table** tabla *f* de conversión *or* de equivalencias 2 (change, switch) ~ **(FROM sth TO sth)** conversión *f* (DE algo A algo) 3 (Relig) conversión *f*

convert¹ /ˈkɑːnvɜːrt || ˈkɒnvɜːt/ *n* converso, -sa *m,f*

convert² /kənˈvɜːrt || kənˈvɜːt/ *vt*

A ‹*building*› remodelar, reformar; ‹*vehicle*› transformar; **to ~ sth INTO sth** convertir* *or* transformar algo EN algo; **a ~ed barn** un granero convertido en vivienda; **to ~ pounds into** *o* **to kilos** convertir* libras a *or* en kilos

B (cause to change view) convertir*; **to ~ sb TO sth** convertir* a algn A algo; **a ~ed Jew** un judío converso

C (Sport) transformar, convertir*

■ **convert** *vi*

A (change into) **to ~ INTO** *o* **TO sth** convertirse* *or* transformarse EN algo

B (Pol, Relig) **to ~ TO sth** convertirse* A algo

converter /kənˈvɜːrtər || kənˈvɜːtə(r)/ *n* convertidor *m*

convertible¹ /kənˈvɜːrtəbəl || kənˈvɜːtəbəl/ *adj* convertible

convertible² *n* 1 (Auto) descapotable *m*, convertible (AmL) *m* 2 (sofa bed) (AmE) sofá-cama *m*

convex /ˈkɑːnveks || ˈkɒnveks/ *adj* convexo

convey /kənˈveɪ/ *vt* ‹*goods/people/electricity*› transportar, conducir*; ‹*sound*› transmitir, llevar; ‹*opinion/feeling*› expresar, transmitir; ‹*thanks*› hacer* llegar, transmitir; **try to ~ to him that ...** trata de hacerle ver que ...

conveyance /kənˈveɪəns/ *n* 1 [u] (transport) transporte *m* 2 [c] (vehicle) vehículo *m*, medio *m* de transporte

conveyor (belt) /kənˈveɪər || kənˈveɪə(r)/ *n* cinta *f* *or* correa *f* transportadora, banda *f* transportadora (Méx)

convict¹ /ˈkɑːnvɪkt || ˈkɒnvɪkt/ *n* recluso, -sa *m,f*, presidiario, -ria *m,f*

convict² /kənˈvɪkt/ *vt* (*often pass*) declarar culpable, condenar; **a ~ed murderer** un asesino convicto; **to be ~ed OF sth** ser* condenado POR algo

conviction /kənˈvɪkʃən/ *n* [u c]

A (Law) ~ **(FOR sth)** condena *f* (POR algo)

B (certainty, strong belief) convicción *f*; **to speak without ~** hablar sin convicción; **their claims carry little ~** lo que sostienen es poco convincente

convince /kənˈvɪns/ *vt* convencer*; **to ~ sb OF sth** convencer* a algn DE algo; **to ~ sb THAT** convencer* a algn DE QUE; **to ~ sb to + INF** convencer* a algn PARA QUE (+ *subj*)

convinced /kənˈvɪnst/ *adj* (persuaded) (*pred*): **to be ~ OF sth** estar* convencido DE algo; **to be ~ THAT** estar* convencido DE QUE

convincing /kənˈvɪnsɪŋ/ *adj* convincente

convincingly /kənˈvɪnsɪŋli/ *adv* convincentemente

convivial /kənˈvɪviəl/ *adj* ‹*atmosphere*› cordial, de camaradería; ‹*person*› simpático, sociable

convoke /kənˈvəʊk/ *vt* (frml) convocar*

convoluted /ˈkɑːnvəluːtəd || ˈkɒnvəluːtɪd/ *adj* ‹*story/argument*› intrincado, enrevesado

convoy /ˈkɑːnvɔɪ || ˈkɒnvɔɪ/ *n* (of ships, vehicles) convoy *m*

convulse /kənˈvʌls/ *vt* 1 (contort) (*usu pass*): **he was ~d with pain** se retorcía del dolor; **their antics ~d the audience** el público se desternillaba (de risa) con sus payasadas (fam) 2 (shake, rock) convulsionar, sacudir

convulsion /kənˈvʌlʃən/ *n* (spasm) convulsión *f*; **their antics had us in ~s** (colloq) nos desternillamos de risa con sus payasadas (fam)

convulsive /kənˈvʌlsɪv/ *adj* convulsivo; **he collapsed into ~ laughter** le dio un ataque de risa

coo /kuː/ *vi* «*dove/pigeon*» arrullar, zurear; **everyone was ~ing over the baby** todos estaban bobos con el bebé (fam)

■ **coo** *vt* susurrar

cook¹ /kʊk/ *n* cocinero, -ra *m,f*; **he's a good ~** cocina muy bien, es muy buen cocinero; ***too many ~s spoil the broth*** muchas manos en un plato hacen mucho garabato

cook² *vt* 1 ‹*food/meal*› hacer*, preparar 2 (falsify) (colloq) ‹*books/accounts*› amañar (fam)

■ **cook** *vi* 1 (prepare food) cocinar, guisar 2 (become ready) «*food*» hacerse*

Phrasal verb

- **cook up** [v ▸ o ▸ adv, v ▸ adv ▸ o] (colloq) ‹*excuse/alibi*› inventarse; ‹*scheme*› tramar

cookbook /ˈkʊkbʊk/ *n* libro *m* de cocina *or* de recetas, recetario *m*

cooked /kʊkt/ *adj* ‹*ham*› cocido; ‹*meal/breakfast*› caliente; **it's not quite ~ yet** le falta un poco todavía; ~ **meats** fiambres *mpl*

cooker /ˈkʊkər || ˈkʊkə(r)/ *n* (BrE) (stove) cocina *f* *or* (Col, Méx) estufa *f*

cookery /ˈkʊkəri/ *n* [u] cocina *f*; (*before n*) ~ **book** (BrE) ▸ **cookbook**

cookie /ˈkʊki/ *n* 1 (biscuit) (AmE Culin) galleta *f*, galletita *f* (RPl); ***that's the way the ~ crumbles*** ¡qué se le va a hacer!, ¡así es la vida!; (*before n*) ***to be caught with one's hand in the ~ jar***: **he was caught with his hand in the ~ jar** lo agarraron *or* lo pillaron con las manos en la masa (fam) 2 (person) (colloq): **she's a smart ~** es más lista que el hambre (fam); **he's a tough ~** es un tipo durísimo (fam); 3 (Comput) cookie *f* *or* *m*, galleta *f*

cooking /ˈkʊkɪŋ/ *n* [u]: **to do the ~** cocinar; **it is used in ~** se usa para cocinar *or* en cocina; **home ~** la comida casera; **his ~ is awful** cocina muy mal; **Spanish ~** la cocina *or* la gastronomía española; (*before n*) ‹*oil*› comestible; ‹*sherry/apple*› para cocinar; ‹*utensils*› de cocina

cookout /ˈkʊkaʊt/ *n* (AmE) comida *f* al aire libre

cooky *n* ▸ **cookie**

cool¹ /kuːl/ *adj* **-er, -est**

A (cold) ‹*climate/air/clothes*› fresco; ‹*drink*› fresco, frío; **it's ~ outside** hace *or* está fresco (a)fuera

B (reserved, hostile) ‹*reception/behavior*› frío; **to be ~ TO** *o* **TOWARD sb** estar* frío CON algn

C 1 (calm) sereno, tranquilo; **keep ~!** ¡tranquilo!, no te pongas nervioso; **~, calm and collected** (set phrase) tranquilo y sereno; ***to play it ~*** (colloq) tomarse las cosas con calma 2 (unperturbed) impasible; **he's a very ~ customer** tiene una sangre fría impresionante

D (sl) (trendy, laid-back): **he's really ~** es muy en la onda (fam)

E (sl) (acceptable, all right): **he's ~** es un tipo bien (fam), es un tío legal (Esp fam); **I'm coming. —cool!** ya voy. —¡fenomenal *o* (fam) — ¡bárbaro!

F (with numbers) (colloq): **a ~ one million dollars** la friolera de un millón de dólares (fam)

cool² *n*

A (low temperature): **let's stay here in the ~** quedémonos aquí al fresco; **in the ~ of the evening** por la tarde cuando está *or* hace fresco

B [u] (composure) calma *f*; **to keep/lose one's ~** mantener*/perder* la calma

cool³ *vt* ‹*air/room*› refrigerar; ‹*engine/food/enthusiasm*› enfriar*; **to ~ sb's temper** apaciguar* a algn; ***to ~ it*** (colloq): **~ it, you two! we don't want any fights in here** ya está bien, que aquí no queremos peleas; **~ it! he's watching us!** (AmE) disimula, que nos está mirando

■ **cool** *vi* «*air/room*» refrigerarse; «*engine/food/enthusiasm*» enfriarse*; **to ~ TOWARD sb/sth** (AmE) perder* el entusiasmo POR algn/algo

Phrasal verbs

- **cool down**

A [v ▸ adv] 1 (become cooler) «*food/iron*» enfriarse*; «*person*» refrescarse* 2 (become calmer) «*temper/person*» calmarse

B [v ▸ o ▸ adv, v ▸ adv ▸ o] 1 (make cooler) ‹*food*› enfriar*; ‹*person*› refrescar* 2 (make calmer) ‹*person*› calmar

- **cool off** [v ▸ adv] 1 (become cooler) «*person*» refrescarse*

C

2 (become calmer) calmarse 3 (lose enthusiasm, passion) enfriarse*

coolant /'ku:lənt/ *n* [c u] (líquido *m*) refrigerante *m*

-cooled /ku:ld/ *suff* **air/water~** enfriado por aire/por agua; **gas~ reactor** reactor *m* enfriado por gas

cooler /'ku:lər || 'ku:lə(r)/ *n*
A (container, device) (Tech) refrigerador *m*
B (sl): **in the ~** (in jail) a la sombra (fam); (in a cell) en el calabozo

cool-headed /'ku:l'hedəd || ˌku:l'hedɪd/ *adj* sereno

cooling /'ku:lɪŋ/ *adj* ‹*drink/swim*› refrescante

cooling: **~-off** /'ku:lɪŋ'ɔ:f || ˌku:lɪŋ'ɒf/ *n* (*no pl*) enfriamiento *m*; (*before n*) **~-off period** período *m* de reflexión; **~ tower** *n* torre *f* de refrigeración

coolly /'ku:lli/ *adv* 1 (calmly) con serenidad *or* calma 2 (boldly) descaradamente, con la mayor frescura 3 (with reserve, hostility) fríamente, con frialdad

coolness /'ku:lnəs || 'ku:lnɪs/ *n* [u]
A (in temperature) frescor *m*, frescura *f*
B 1 (calmness) serenidad *f*, sangre *f* fría 2 (boldness) descaro *m*, frescura *f*
C (reserve, hostility) frialdad *f*

coop /ku:p/ *n*: **chicken/hen ~** gallinero *m*

Phrasal verb
• **coop up** [v ▸ o ▸ adv, v ▸ adv ▸ o] (*usu passive*) encerrar*

co-op /'kəʊɑ:p || 'kəʊɒp/ *n* cooperativa *f*

cooperate /kəʊ'ɑ:pəreɪt || kəʊ'ɒpəreɪt/ *vi* cooperar, colaborar

cooperation /kəʊ'ɑ:pə'reɪʃən || kəʊˌɒpə'reɪʃən/ *n* [u] cooperación *f*, colaboración *f*

cooperative[1] /kəʊ'ɑ:pərətɪv || kəʊ'ɒpərətɪv/ *adj* 1 (obliging) ‹*attitude*› de colaboración, cooperativo; **he was very ~** se mostró muy dispuesto a cooperar *or* a colaborar 2 ‹*effort/venture*› conjunto 3 (collective) ‹*farm*› en régimen de cooperativa; **~ society/store** cooperativa *f*

cooperative[2] *n* cooperativa *f*

co-opt /kəʊ'ɑ:pt || kəʊ'ɒpt/ *vt*: **to ~ sb onto a committee** invitar a algn a formar parte de una comisión

coordinate[1] /kəʊ'ɔ:rdneɪt || ˌkəʊ'ɔ:dɪmeɪt/ *vt*
A (make function together) coordinar
B ‹*clothes*› combinar, coordinar

coordinate[2] /kəʊ'ɔ:rdṇət || kəʊ'ɔ:dɪmət/ *n*
A (Math) coordenada *f*
B **coordinates** *pl* prendas *fpl* para combinar, coordinados *mpl*

coordination /kəʊ'ɔ:rdṇ'eɪʃən || kəʊˌɔ:dɪ'neɪʃən/ *n* [u] coordinación *f*

coordinator /kəʊ'ɔ:rdneɪtər || kəʊ'ɔ:dɪneɪtə(r)/ *n* coordinador, -dora *m,f*

coot /ku:t/ *n* (*pl* **~s** *or* **~**) focha *f*, fúlica *f*

cootie /'ku:ti/ *n* (AmE sl) (louse) piojo *m*

cop[1] /kɑ:p || kɒp/ *n* (colloq)
A (police officer) poli *mf* (fam), tira *mf* (Méx fam), cana *mf* (RPl arg), cachaco, -ca *m,f* (Per fam), paco, -ca *m,f* (Chi fam); **to play ~s and robbers** jugar* a policías y ladrones
B (good, use) (BrE): **to be not much ~** no ser* nada del otro mundo *or* del otro jueves (fam)

cop[2] **-pp-** *vt* 1 (win) (AmE journ) ‹*medal/prize*› llevarse 2 (get) (esp BrE colloq): **~ (a load of) this/him/her!** ¡no te lo/la pierdas! (fam); ***to ~ it*** (BrE): **you'll ~ it if they find out** como se enteren, estás arreglado *or* te vas a llevar una buena (fam) 3 (catch, seize) (BrE colloq) ‹*person*› agarrar, pillar (fam), pescar* (fam)

Phrasal verb
• **cop out** [v ▸ adv] (sl) rajarse (fam), evadirse; **to ~ out OF sth** ‹*of responsibility/task*› escabullirse* DE algo, sacarle* el cuerpo A algo (fam)

cope /kəʊp/ *vi* **to ~ (WITH sth/sb)**: **to ~ with stress** saber* sobrellevar el estrés; **I can't ~ with all this work** no doy abasto *or* no puedo con tanto trabajo; **how do you ~ without a washing machine?** ¿cómo te las arreglas sin lavadora?; **I just can't ~ any more** ya no puedo más; **how is he coping on his own?** ¿qué tal se las arregla *or* se defiende solo?; **these are some of the problems they have to ~ with** éstos son algunos de los problemas a los que tienen que enfrentarse

Copenhagen /'kəʊpən'heɪgən/ *n* Copenhague *m*

copier /'kɑ:piər || 'kɒpiə(r)/ *n* fotocopiadora *f*

copilot /'kəʊˌpaɪlət/ *n* copiloto *mf*

copious /'kəʊpiəs/ *adj* copioso, abundante

cop-out /'kɑ:paʊt || 'kɒpaʊt/ *n* (colloq): **that's just a ~** eso es evadirse

copper /'kɑ:pər || 'kɒpə(r)/ *n*
A 1 [u] (metal) cobre *m* 2 **coppers** *pl* (coins) (colloq) peniques *mpl*, perras *fpl* (Esp fam), quintos *mpl* (Méx fam), chauchas *fpl* (Chi fam), vintenes *mpl* (Ur fam) 3 (color) color *m* cobre; (*before n*) cobrizo
B (police officer) (colloq) ▸**cop**[1] **A**

copperplate /'kɑ:pərpleɪt || 'kɒpəpleɪt/ *n* [u] **~ (handwriting)** letra *f* de caligrafía

coppice /'kɑ:pəs || 'kɒpɪs/, **copse** /kɑ:ps || kɒps/ *n* bosquecillo *m*

copulate /'kɑ:pjəleɪt || 'kɒpjʊleɪt/ *vi* copular

copy[1] /'kɑ:pi || 'kɒpi/ *n* (*pl* **copies**)
A [c] (of painting, document) copia *f*
B [c] (of newspaper, book) ejemplar *m*; **back ~** número *m* atrasado
C [u] 1 (text): **good news doesn't make good ~** las buenas noticias no se venden bien 2 (unprinted matter) manuscrito *m*

copy[2] **copies, copying, copied** *vt*
A 1 (reproduce, transcribe) copiar; **to ~ sth FROM *o* OFF sb** copiarle algo A algn; **to ~ sth FROM *o* OUT OF sth** copiar algo DE algo 2 (photocopy) fotocopiar
B (imitate) ‹*painter/singer*› copiarle a; ‹*style/behavior*› copiar
■ **copy** *vi* copiar

copy: **~book** *n* cuaderno *m*; ***to blot one's ~book*** (BrE) manchar su (*or* mi *etc*) reputación; **~cat** *n* (colloq) copión, -piona *m,f* (fam), imitamonos *mf* (Méx fam); (*before n*) ‹*murder*› (journ) inspirado en otros; **~right** *n* [u] copyright *m*, derechos *mpl* de reproducción; (*before n*) **~right law** ley *f* de propiedad intelectual; **~right library** biblioteca *f* de depósito legal; **~writer** *n* redactor publicitario, redactora publicitaria *m,f*

coquettish /kəʊ'ketɪʃ || kɒ'ketɪʃ/ *adj* (liter) coqueto

coral /'kɔ:rəl || 'kɒrəl/ *n* [u] 1 (substance) coral *m*; (*before n*) **~ reef** arrecife *m* de coral, barrera *f* coralina 2 (color) (color *m*) coral *m*

cord /kɔ:rd || kɔ:d/ *n*
A [c u] 1 (string, rope) cuerda *f*; (of pajamas, curtains) cordón *m* 2 (AmE Elec) cordón *m*, cable *m* 3 (Anat) ▸**spinal cord, umbilical cord, vocal cords**
B 1 [u] (Tex) pana *f*, corderoy *m* (AmS), cotelé *m* (Chi) 2 **cords** *pl* (Clothing) pantalones *mpl* de pana (*or* corderoy *etc*)

cordial[1] /'kɔ:rdʒəl || 'kɔ:diəl/ *adj* cordial

cordial[2] *n* [c u] (soft drink) refresco *m* (*concentrado*)

cordially /'kɔ:rdʒəli || 'kɔ:diəli/ *adv* cordialmente

cordless /'kɔ:rdləs || 'kɔ:dlɪs/ *adj* inalámbrico

cordon /'kɔ:rdṇ || 'kɔ:dṇ/ *n* cordón *m*

Phrasal verb
• **cordon off** [v ▸ o ▸ adv, v ▸ adv ▸ o] acordonar

corduroy /'kɔ:rdərɔɪ || 'kɔ:dərɔɪ/ *n* 1 [u] (Tex) pana *f*, corderoy *m* (AmS), cotelé *m* (Chi) 2 **corduroys** *pl* (Clothing) pantalones *mpl* de pana (*or* corderoy *etc*)

core[1] /kɔ:r || kɔ:(r)/ *n* 1 (of apple, pear) corazón *m*, centro *m*; (of Earth) centro *m*, núcleo *m*; (of nuclear reactor) núcleo *m*; ***to the ~***: **the organization is rotten to the ~** la organización está totalmente corrompida 2 (central, essential part) núcleo *m*; (of problem) meollo *m*; **a hard ~ of resistance** un foco de resistencia férrea; **to be ~ (to sth)** ser* un factor clave (para algo); (*before n*) ‹*subject/vocabulary*› (Educ) básico; ‹*supplier/currency/values*› clave; **~ curriculum** plan *m* de estudios común 3 (Comput) núcleo *m* magnético; (*before n*) **~ memory** memoria *f* central 4 (of electric cable) alma *f*‡

core[2] *vt* ‹*apple*› quitarle el corazón *or* el centro a

coriander /'kɔ:riændər/ *n* cilantro *m*, culantro *m*

cork[1] /kɔ:rk || kɔ:k/ *n* [u c] corcho *m*

cork[2] *vt* ‹*bottle*› ponerle* un (tapón de) corcho a

corkage /'kɔ:rkɪdʒ || 'kɔ:kɪdʒ/ *n* [u] *precio que cobra un restaurante por abrir botellas que el cliente trae consigo*

corkscrew /'kɔ:rkskru: || 'kɔ:kskru:/ *n* sacacorchos *m*, tirabuzón *m*

corm /kɔːrm || kɔːm/ *n* bulbo *m*

cormorant /'kɔːrmərənt || 'kɔːmərənt/ *n* cormorán *m*

corn /kɔːrn || kɔːn/ *n*

A [u] **1** (cereal crop — in general) grano *m*; (maize) (AmE) maíz *m*; (wheat) (BrE) trigo *m*; (oats) (BrE) avena *f* **2** (foodstuff) maíz *m*, choclo *m* (AmS); **~ on the cob** mazorca *f* de maíz *or* (AmS) de choclo, elote *m* (AmC, Méx); (*before n*) ‹*oil*› de maíz; **~ meal** harina *f* de maíz

B [c] (on toe) callo *m*

corncob /'kɔːrnkɑːb || 'kɔːnkɒb/ *n* mazorca *f* de maíz *or* (AmS) de choclo, elote *m* (AmC, Méx)

cornea /'kɔːrniə || 'kɔːniə/ *n* córnea *f*

corned beef /kɔːrnd || kɔːnd/ *n* [u] corned beef *m* (*carne en conserva*)

corner[1] /'kɔːrnər || 'kɔːnə(r)/ *n*

A **1** (inside angle — of room, cupboard) rincón *m*; (— of field) esquina *f*; (— of mouth) comisura *f*; **in the top righthand ~ of the page** en el ángulo superior derecho de la página; **a quiet ~ of Hampshire** un tranquilo rincón de Hampshire; **out of the ~ of one's eye** con el rabillo del ojo; ***from all** o **the four ~s of the earth** o **world*** de todas partes (del mundo); ***to be in a (tight) ~*** estar* en un aprieto; ***to drive/force sb into a ~*** acorralar a algn **2** (outside angle — of street, page) esquina *f*; (— of table) esquina *f*, punta *f*; (bend in road) curva *f*; **he took the ~ too fast** tomó la curva demasiado rápido; ***around the ~*** a la vuelta de la esquina; ***to cut ~s***: **we could produce a cheaper article, but only by cutting ~s** podríamos producir un artículo más barato, pero sólo si cuidáramos menos los detalles; (*before n*) **~ shop** (BrE) tienda *f* de la esquina; (local shop) tienda *f* de barrio

B (in soccer) (**~** *kick*) córner *m*, tiro *m or* saque *m* de esquina

C (in boxing) esquina *f*

corner[2] *vt*

A (trap) acorralar; **I ~ed her in the corridor** la abordé en el pasillo

B (monopolize) acaparar

■ **corner** *vi* tomar una curva; **this car ~s well** este coche tiene buen agarre en las curvas

cornerstone /'kɔːrnərstəʊn || 'kɔːnəstəʊn/ *n* piedra *f* angular

cornet /kɔːr'net || 'kɔːnɪt/ *n* **1** (Mus) corneta *f* **2** (BrE Culin) cucurucho *m*, barquillo *m*

corn: **~field** *n* (in US) maizal *m*; (in UK — of wheat) trigal *m*; (— of oats) avenal *m*; **~flakes** *pl n* copos *mpl or* hojuelas *fpl* de maíz; **~flour** *n* [u] (BrE) maizena® *f*; **~flower** *n* aciano *m*

Cornish[1] /'kɔːrnɪʃ || 'kɔːnɪʃ/ *adj* de Cornualles

Cornish[2] *n* [u] córnico *m*

cornstarch /'kɔːrnstɑːrtʃ || 'kɔːnstɑːtʃ/ *n* [u] (AmE) maizena® *f*

cornucopia /'kɔːrnə'kəʊpiə || ˌkɔːnjʊ'kəʊpiə/ *n* cornucopia *f*, cuerno *m* de la abundancia

Cornwall /'kɔːrnwɔːl || 'kɔːnwɔːl/ *n* Cornualles *m*

corny /'kɔːrni || 'kɔːni/ *adj* **-nier, -niest** (colloq) **1** ‹*song/movie*› cursi, sensiblero **2** (BrE) ‹*joke*› malo

corollary /'kɔːrəleri || kə'rɒləri/ *n* (*pl* **-ries**) **~ (OF** *o* **TO sth)** corolario *m* (DE algo)

coronary[1] /'kɔːrəneri || 'kɒrənri/ *adj* coronario

coronary[2] *n* (*pl* **-ries**) infarto *m* (de miocardio)

coronation /'kɔːrə'neɪʃən || ˌkɒrə'neɪʃən/ *n* [u c] coronación *f*

coroner /'kɔːrənər || 'kɒrənə(r)/ *n*: *funcionario encargado de investigar las causas de muertes violentas, repentinas o sospechosas*, ≈ juez *mf* de instrucción

coronet /'kɔːrə'net || 'kɒrənet/ *n* **1** (small crown) corona *f* (*de príncipe, duque etc*) **2** (tiara) diadema *f*

corp = corporation

corporal /'kɔːrprəl || 'kɔːpərəl/ *n* cabo *m*

corporal punishment *n* [u] castigos *mpl* corporales

corporate /'kɔːrpərət || 'kɔːpərət/ *adj*

A **1** (of a company) ‹*headquarters/lawyer*› de la empresa *or* compañía; **the ~ image** la imagen de la empresa *or* compañía **2** ‹*mentality/jargon*› empresarial

B (joint, collective) ‹*action/decision*› colectivo

corporate raider *n* tiburón *m* (empresarial)

corporation /'kɔːrpə'reɪʃən || ˌkɔːpə'reɪʃən/ *n*

A (company — in US) sociedad *f* anónima; (— in UK) compañía *f*, empresa *f*, corporación *f*

B (municipal council) (BrE) corporación *f* (municipal), municipio *m*, ayuntamiento *m*

corps /kɔːr || kɔː(r)/ *n* (*pl* **~** /-z/) (+ *sing or pl vb*) cuerpo *m*

corpse /kɔːrps || kɔːps/ *n* cadáver *m*

corpulent /'kɔːrpjələnt || 'kɔːpjʊlənt/ *adj* corpulento

corpuscle /'kɔːrpʌsəl || 'kɔːpʌsəl/ *n* corpúsculo *m*

corral /kə'ræl || kɒ'rɑːl/ *n* corral *m*

correct[1] /kə'rekt/ *vt* corregir*; **~ me if I'm wrong, but ...** perdón, pero yo creo que ...; **I stand ~ed** (frml *or* hum) reconozco mi error

correct[2] *adj* **1** ‹*answer/time/figures*› correcto **2** (proper) ‹*manners/dress*› correcto

correction /kə'rekʃən/ *n* [u c] corrección *f*; **~ fluid** (líquido *m*) corrector *m*

correctional /kə'rekʃn̩əl || kə'rekʃənl̩/ *adj* (AmE): **~ institution** correccional *m or f*; **~ regime** sistema *m* penitenciario

correctly /kə'rektli/ *adv* correctamente

correlate /'kɔːrəleɪt || 'kɒ-/ *vt* correlacionar, establecer* una correlación entre

■ **correlate** *vi* **to ~ (WITH sth)** estar* correlacionado (CON algo), guardar correlación (CON algo)

correlation /ˌkɔːrə'leɪʃən || ˌkɒrə'leɪʃən/ *n* [c u] correlación *f* (frml)

correspond /'kɔːrə'spɑːnd || ˌkɒrə'spɒnd/ *vi*

A **1** (tally) **to ~ (WITH sth)** corresponderse *or* concordar* (CON algo) **2** (be equivalent) **to ~ (TO sth)** equivaler* *or* corresponder (A algo)

B (communicate by letter) **to ~ (WITH sb)** mantener* correspondencia (CON algn)

correspondence /'kɔːrə'spɑːndəns || ˌkɒrə'spɒndəns/ *n*

A [u c] (agreement) correspondencia *f*

B [u] (letters, letter-writing) correspondencia *f*; **to be in ~ with sb** escribirse* *or* cartearse con algn

correspondence course *n* curso *m* por correspondencia

correspondent /'kɔːrə'spɑːndənt || ˌkɒrə'spɒndənt/ *n* **1** (letter writer) corresponsal *mf* **2** (Journ) corresponsal *mf*

corresponding /'kɔːrə'spɑːndɪŋ || ˌkɒrə'spɒndɪŋ/ *adj* (*before n*) correspondiente

correspondingly /'kɔːrə'spɑːndɪŋli || ˌkɒrə'spɒndɪŋli/ *adv* (proportionately) en proporción, en la misma medida; (as a result) en consecuencia

corridor /'kɔːrədər || 'kɒrɪdɔː(r)/ *n* pasillo *m*, corredor *m*

corroborate /kə'rɑːbəreɪt || kə'rɒbəreɪt/ *vt* corroborar

corroboration /kə'rɑːbə'reɪʃən || kəˌrɒbə'reɪʃən/ *n* [u] corroboración *f*

corrode /kə'rəʊd/ *vt* corroer*

■ **corrode** *vi* corroerse*

corrosion /kə'rəʊʒən/ *n* [u] **1** (action) corrosión *f* **2** (substance) herrumbre *f*, orín *m*

corrosive /kə'rəʊsɪv/ *adj* corrosivo

corrugated /'kɔːrəgeɪtəd || 'kɒrəgeɪtɪd/ *adj* ondulado; **~ cardboard** cartón *m* corrugado; **~ iron** chapa *f* de zinc, calamina *f* (Chi, Per)

corrupt[1] /kə'rʌpt/ *vt* (deprave) corromper; (bribe) sobornar; ‹*text*› viciar; (Comput) corromper

corrupt[2] *adj* ‹*person/government*› corrompido, corrupto; ‹*text*› viciado; **~ practices** (Govt, Law) corrupción *f*, corruptela *f* (fam)

corruptible /kə'rʌptəbəl/ *adj* corruptible

corruption /kə'rʌpʃən/ *n* [u c] (of morals, language) corrupción *f*; (of text) deformación *f*

corset /'kɔːrsət || 'kɔːsɪt/ *n* (*often pl*) corsé *m*

Corsica /'kɔːrsɪkə || 'kɔːsɪkə/ *n* Córcega *f*

cortege, cortège /kɔːr'teʒ || kɔː'teɪʒ/ *n* cortejo *m*

cortex /'kɔːrteks || 'kɔːteks/ *n* (*pl* **-tices** /-təsiːz/) corteza *f*

cortisone /'kɔːrtəzəʊn || 'kɔːtɪzəʊn/ *n* [u] (Pharm, Physiol) cortisona *f*

cosh¹ /kɑːʃ || kɒʃ/ *n* (BrE) porra *f*, cachiporra *f*, macana *f* (AmL)

cosh² *vt* (BrE): **to ~ sb over the head** aporrear a algn en la cabeza

cosignatory /ˈkəʊˈsɪgnətɔːri || ˌkəʊˈsɪgnətəri/ *n* (*pl* **-ries**) **~ (OF *o* TO sth)** cosignatario, -ria *m,f* (DE algo)

cosmetic /kɑːzˈmetɪk || kɒzˈmetɪk/ *adj* 1 (beautifying) (*before n*) ‹*powder/cream*› cosmético; **~ surgery** cirugía *f* estética 2 (superficial) ‹*reforms/changes*› superficial

cosmetics /kɑːzˈmetɪks || kɒzˈmetɪks/ *pl n* cosméticos *mpl*, productos *mpl* de belleza

cosmic /ˈkɑːzmɪk || ˈkɒzmɪk/ *adj* cósmico

cosmology /kɑːzˈmɑːlədʒi || kɒzˈmɒlədʒi/ *n* [u] cosmología *f*

cosmonaut /ˈkɑːzmənɔːt || ˈkɒzmənɔːt/ *n* cosmonauta *mf*

cosmopolitan /ˈkɑːzməˈpɑːlətn̩ || ˌkɒzməˈpɒlɪtn̩/ *adj* cosmopolita

cosmos /ˈkɑːzməʊs || ˈkɒzmɒs/ *n* **the ~** el cosmos

cosset /ˈkɑːsət || ˈkɒsɪt/ *vt* mimar

cost¹ /kɔːst || kɒst/ *n*

A 1 (expense) (*often pl*) costo *m* (esp AmL), coste *m* (Esp); **at no additional *o* extra ~** sin cargo adicional; **he has no idea of the ~ of running a car** no tiene idea de cuánto cuesta mantener un coche; **to cover/cut ~s** cubrir*/reducir* los gastos; (*before n*) **~ accounting** contabilidad *f* analítica de costos *or* (Esp) costes 2 **costs** *pl* (Law) costas *fpl*; **to pay ~s** pagar* las costas 3 [u] (price) costo *m*, coste *m* (Esp); **at ~** (Busn) a precio de costo *or* (Esp) coste, al costo (AmL)

B [u] (loss, sacrifice): **at the ~ of sth** a costa *or* a expensas de algo; **she helped me out, at great ~ to herself** sacrificó mucho al ayudarme; **he did it without stopping to count the ~** lo hizo sin detenerse a pensar en sí mismo; **at all ~s** a toda costa, a cualquier precio

cost² *vt*

A (*past & past p* **cost**) 1 ‹‹*article/service*›› costar*; **how much did it ~ you?** ¿cuánto te costó?; **how much does it ~?** ¿cuánto cuesta?, ¿cuánto vale?; **it'll ~ you!** (colloq) ¡mira que te va a salir caro! 2 (cause to lose) costar*; **one slip ~ him the title** un error le costó el título

B (*past & past p* **costed**) 1 (calculate cost of) calcular el costo *or* (Esp) coste de; **she ~ed the project** hizo un presupuesto para el proyecto 2 (find out price of) averiguar* el precio de

co-star¹ /ˈkəʊstɑːr || ˈkəʊstɑː(r)/ *n* coprotagonista *mf*

co-star² **-rr-** *vt*: **~ring Peter Lorre** con Peter Lorre (*en un papel secundario*)

■ **co-star** *vi* **to ~ (WITH sb)** actuar* (CON algn)

Costa Rica /ˈkɔːstəˈriːkə || ˌkɒstəˈriːkə/ *n* Costa Rica *f*

Costa Rican¹ /ˈkɔːstəˈriːkən || ˌkɒstəˈriːkən/ *adj* costarricense

Costa Rican² *n* costarricense *mf*, tico, -ca *m,f* (fam)

cost-effective /ˈkɔːstɪˈfektɪv || ˌkɒstɪˈfektɪv/, **cost-efficient** /-ɪˈfɪʃənt/ *adj* rentable, económico

costing /ˈkɔːstɪŋ || ˈkɒstɪŋ/ *n* [u c] presupuesto *m*, cálculo *m* de costos *or* (Esp) costes

costly /ˈkɔːstli || ˈkɒstli/ *adj* **-lier, -liest** costoso

cost: **~ of living** *n*: **the ~ of living** el costo *or* (Esp) coste de (la) vida; **~ price** *n* precio *m* de costo *or* (Esp) de coste

costume /ˈkɑːstuːm || ˈkɒstjuːm/ *n* 1 [u] (style of dress) traje *m*; (for parties, disguise) disfraz *m*; **in ~** disfrazado 2 [c] (wardrobe) (Theat) vestuario *m*; (individual outfit) traje *m* 3 [c] (*swimming ~*) traje *m* de baño

costume jewelry, (BrE) **costume jewellery** *n* [u] bisutería *f*, alhajas *fpl* de fantasía

cosy¹ /ˈkəʊzi/ *adj* **cosier, cosiest** (BrE) ▸**cozy¹**

cosy² *n* (*pl* **cosies**) (BrE) ▸**cozy²**

cot /kɑːt || kɒt/ *n* 1 (campbed) (AmE) catre *m* 2 (for child) (BrE) cuna *f*, cama *f* (*con barandas*)

cot death *n* [u c] (BrE) muerte *f* de cuna, muerte *f* súbita (infantil)

coterie /ˈkəʊtəri/ *n* círculo *m*

cottage /ˈkɑːtɪdʒ || ˈkɒtɪdʒ/ *n* casita *f*

cottage: **~ cheese** *n* [u] requesón *m*; **~ industry** *n* industria *f* artesanal

cotton /ˈkɑːtn̩ || ˈkɒtn̩/ *n* [u]

A 1 (cloth) algodón *m*; (*before n*) ‹*dress/sheet/print*› de algodón 2 (thread) (BrE) hilo *m* (de coser) 3 (*absorbent ~*) (AmE) algodón *m* (hidrófilo *or* en rama)

B (plant, fiber) algodón *m*; (*before n*) **~ gin** almarrá *m*; **~ mill** fábrica *f* de tejidos (*de algodón*)

Phrasal verbs

- **cotton on** [v ▸ adv] (colloq) **to ~ on (TO sth)** darse* cuenta (DE algo), caer* en la cuenta (DE algo)
- **cotton to** [v ▸ prep ▸ o] (AmE) 1 (take a liking to) (colloq) simpatizar* con 2 (realize, understand) ‹*implications/dangers*› darse* cuenta de, caer* en la cuenta de

cotton: **~ bud** *n* (BrE) bastoncillo *m*, cotonete *m* (Méx); **~ candy** *n* [u] (AmE) algodón *m* de azúcar; **~-picking** *adj* (AmE colloq) (*as intensifier*) maldito (fam), condenado (fam); **~ swab** *n* (BrE) bastoncillo *m*, cotonete *m* (Méx); **~ wool** *n* [u] (BrE) algodón *m* (hidrófilo *or* en rama)

couch¹ /kaʊtʃ/ *n* (sofa) sofá *m*; (doctor's, psychoanalyst's) diván *m*

couch² *vt* expresar, formular

couchette /kuːˈʃet/ *n* (BrE) litera *f*

couch: **~grass** /ˈkaʊtʃgræs, ˈkuːtʃ- || ˈkaʊtʃgrɑːs, ˈkuːtʃ-/ *n* [u] grama *f*; **~ potato** *n* (colloq) teleadicto, -ta *m,f* (fam)

cougar /ˈkuːgər || ˈkuːgə(r)/ *n* puma *m*

cough¹ /kɔːf || kɒf/ *n* tos *f*; **to have a ~** tener* tos; **he gave a loud ~** tosió ruidosamente; (*before n*) **~ drop** pastilla *f* para la tos; **~ mixture *o* syrup** jarabe *m* para la tos; **~ sweet** (BrE) caramelo *m* para la tos

cough² *vi* toser

■ **cough** *vt* **~ (up)** expectorar, esputar

Phrasal verb

- **cough up**

A [v ▸ adv ▸ o] (pay) (colloq) ‹*money*› soltar* (fam), aflojar (fam)

B [v ▸ adv] (pay) soltar* la plata (AmS fam) *or* (Esp) la pasta *or* (AmL tb) la lana (fam)

could /kʊd/ *v mod*

A *past of* **can³**

B (indicating possibility) poder*; **if I took a taxi, I ~ get there on time** si tomara un taxi, podría llegar a tiempo; **I would help you if I ~** te ayudaría si pudiera; **you ~ have killed us all!** ¡podrías *or* podías habernos matado a todos!; **you ~ be right** puede (ser) que tengas razón; **she ~n't have got there before six even if she'd tried** no podría haber llegado antes de las seis aunque lo hubiera intentado; **they ~n't be happier** están contentos a más no poder

C 1 (asking permission): **~ I use your bathroom?** ¿podría *or* me permitiría pasar al baño? 2 (in requests): **~ you sign here please?** ¿quiere firmar aquí, por favor?

D 1 (in suggestions) poder*; **you ~ try doing it this way** podrías tratar de hacerlo de esta manera; **you ~ at least apologize!** ¡al menos podrías pedir perdón! 2 (indicating strong desire) poder*; **I ~ have killed her** la hubiera matado, la podría *or* podía haber matado

couldn't /ˈkʊdn̩t/ **= could not**

coulee /ˈkuːliː/ *n* (AmE) barranco *m*, quebrada *f*

council /ˈkaʊnsəl/ *n* 1 (advisory group) consejo *m* 2 (Govt) ayuntamiento *m*, municipio *m*; **~ housing** (BrE) *viviendas de alquiler subvencionadas por el ayuntamiento*

councillor *n* (BrE) ▸**councilor**

council: **~man** /ˈkaʊnsəlmən/ *n* (*pl* **-men** /-mən/) (AmE) concejal *m*; **~ of Europe** *n* **the C~ of Europe** el Consejo de Europa

councilor, (BrE) **councillor** /ˈkaʊnsələr || ˈkaʊnsələ(r)/ *n* concejal, -jala *m,f*

council: **~ tax** *n* (in UK) ≈ contribución *f* (municipal *or* inmobiliaria); **~woman** *n* (AmE) concejala *f*

counsel¹ /ˈkaʊnsəl/ *n* 1 [u c] (advice) (frml *or* liter) consejo *m*; **to hold/take ~ with sb** asesorarse *or* aconsejarse con algn; ***to keep one's own ~*** reservarse la opinión 2 (*pl* **~**) (*no art*) (Law) abogado, -da *m,f*; **~ for the defense** abogado defensor, abogada defensora *m,f*; **~ for the prosecution** fiscal *mf*

counsel² *vt*, (BrE) **-ll-** (frml) aconsejar, recomendar*; **to ~ sb to + INF** aconsejarle a algn QUE (+ *subj*)

counseling, (BrE) **counselling** /ˈkaʊnsəlɪŋ/ *n* [u] (Educ, Psych) orientación *f* psicopedagógica

counselor, (BrE) **counsellor** /'kaʊnsələr || 'kaʊnsələ(r)/ *n* 1 (Educ, Psych) consejero, -ra *m,f*, orientador, -dora *m,f* 2 (AmE Law) abogado, -da *m,f*

counselor-at-law /'kaʊnsələrət'lɔː/ *n* (*pl* **counselors-at-law**) (AmE) abogado, -da *m,f*

count[1] /kaʊnt/ *n*

A 1 (act of counting) recuento *m*, cómputo *m*; (of votes) escrutinio *m*, recuento *m*, cómputo *m*, conteo *m* (Andes, Ven); (in boxing) cuenta *f*, conteo *m* (Andes, Ven); **to make** *o* (colloq) **do a ~ of sth** hacer* un recuento de algo; **at the last ~** en el último recuento; **we'll begin on the ~ of four** a los cuatro empezamos; **to keep/lose ~ of sth** llevar/perder* la cuenta de algo; ***to be out for the ~*** estar* fuera de combate 2 (total) total *m*; **the final ~** (of votes) el recuento *or* cómputo final

B (point): **to be found guilty on all ~s** (Law) ser* declarado culpable de todos los cargos; **it's been criticized on several ~s** ha sido criticado por varios motivos

C (rank) conde *m*

count[2] *vt*

A (enumerate, add up) contar*; **I'm ~ing the hours till he arrives** no veo la hora de que llegue

B (include) contar*; **not ~ing the driver** sin contar al conductor; **there'll be fourteen of us, ~ing you and me** seremos catorce, tú y yo incluidos

C (consider) considerar; **to ~ oneself lucky** darse* por afortunado; **to ~ sb among one's friends** contar* a algn entre sus (*or* mis *etc*) amigos

■ **count** *vi*

A (enumerate) contar*

B (be valid, matter) contar*; **that doesn't ~** eso no cuenta *or* no vale; **every minute ~s** cada minuto cuenta

(Phrasal verbs)

- **count against** [v ▸ prep ▸ o] perjudicar*; **his age ~ed against him** su edad fue un factor negativo *or* lo perjudicó
- **count for** [v ▸ prep ▸ o] contar*; **your opinion ~s for a great deal/won't ~ for much** tu opinión importa mucho/no va a contar mucho
- **count in** [v ▸ o ▸ adv] incluir*; **you can ~ me in** yo me apunto (fam), yo me anoto (CS fam), cuenten conmigo
- **count on** [v ▸ prep ▸ o] 1 (rely on) ‹*friend/help*› contar* con; **I wouldn't ~ on it** yo que tú no me confiaría; **we were ~ing on her for support** contábamos con que nos apoyaría 2 (expect) esperar; **we hadn't ~ed on that happening** no esperábamos que fuera a pasar eso
- **count out**

A [v ▸ o ▸ adv]: **you can ~ me out** a mí no me incluyan, no cuenten conmigo

B [v ▸ o ▸ adv, v ▸ adv ▸ o] ‹*money/objects*› contar* (*uno por uno*)

- **count toward**, (BrE) **count towards** [v ▸ adv ▸ o] contar* para

countable /'kaʊntəbəl/ *adj* (Ling) numerable

countdown /'kaʊntdaʊn/ *n* cuenta *f* atrás *or* regresiva, conteo *m* regresivo (Andes, Ven); **in the ~ to the Olympic Games** en los días que precedieron (*or* preceden *etc*) al inicio de los Juegos Olímpicos

countenance[1] /'kaʊntṇəns || 'kaʊntənəns/ *n* [c] (face, expression) (liter) semblante *m* (liter), rostro *m* (liter)

countenance[2] *vt* (frml) (*usu neg*) tolerar, aceptar

counter[1] /'kaʊntər || 'kaʊntə(r)/ *n*

A (in shop) mostrador *m*; (in café) barra *f*; (in bank, post office) ventanilla *f*; (in kitchen) (AmE) encimera *f*; **that drug is not available over the ~** esa medicina no se puede comprar sin receta

B (Games) ficha *f*

counter[2] *vt* 1 (oppose) ‹*deficiency/trend*› contrarrestar 2 (in debate) ‹*idea/statement*› rebatir, refutar; **to ~** THAT responder *or* replicar* QUE

counter[3] *adv* **~ TO sth**: **to run** *o* **go ~ to sth** ser* contrario a *or* oponerse* a algo

counter- /'kaʊntər || 'kaʊntə(r)/ *pref* contra-

counteract /'kaʊntər'ækt/ *vt* contrarrestar

counterattack[1] /'kaʊntərə'tæk/ *n* contraataque *m*

counterattack[2] *vi* contraatacar*

counterbalance[1] /'kaʊntər'bæləns || 'kaʊntə,bæləns/ *n* contrapeso *m*

counterbalance[2] *vt* contrapesar, servir* de contrapeso a

counter: **~ clerk** *n* (in post office) empleado, -da *m,f*; (in bank) (BrE) cajero, -ra *m,f*; **~clockwise** /'kaʊntər'klɑːkwaɪz || ,kaʊntə'klɒkwaɪz/ *adj/adv* (AmE) en sentido contrario a las agujas del reloj

counterespionage /'kaʊntər'espiənɑːʒ/ *n* [u] contraespionaje *m*

counterfeit[1] /'kaʊntərfɪt || 'kaʊntəfɪt/ *n* falsificación *f*

counterfeit[2] *vt* ‹*money*› falsificar*

counterfeit[3] *adj* ‹*money*› falso

counterfeiter /'kaʊntərfɪtər || 'kaʊntəfɪtə(r)/ *n* falsificador, -dora *m,f*

counter: **~foil** *n* talón *m* (AmL), matriz *f* (Esp); **~intelligence** /'kaʊntərɪn'telədʒəns || ,kaʊntərɪn'telɪdʒəns/ *n* [u] contraespionaje *m*; **~part** *n* (person) homólogo, -ga *m,f*; (thing) equivalente *m*; **~point** *n* [u c] (Mus) contrapunto *m*; **~productive** /'kaʊntərprə'dʌktɪv || ,kaʊntəprə'dʌktɪv/ *adj* contraproducente; **~revolution** /'kaʊntərrevə'luːʃən || ,kaʊntə,revə'luːʃən/ *n* contrarrevolución *f*; **~revolutionary** /'kaʊntərrevə'luːʃənəri || ,kaʊntə,revə'luːʃənəri/ *adj* contrarrevolucionario; **~sign** *vt* ‹*document*› refrendar; **~terrorism** /'kaʊntər,terərɪzəm || 'kaʊntə,terərɪzəm/ *n* [u] contraterrorismo *m*; (*before n*) ‹*coordinator/expert*› en contraterrorismo; **~top** *n* (AmE) encimera *f*

countess /'kaʊntəs || 'kaʊntes/ *n* condesa *f*

countless /'kaʊntləs || 'kaʊntlɪs/ *adj* ‹*stars/hours*› incontables, innumerables

countrified /'kʌntrɪfaɪd/ *adj* rústico, rural

country /'kʌntri/ *n* (*pl* **-tries**)

A [c] (nation) país *m*; (people) pueblo *m*; (native land) patria *f*

B [u] (rural area) **the ~** el campo; (*before n*) ‹*life/lane*› rural; ‹*people*› del campo; ‹*cottage*› de campo

C [u] (region) terreno *m*, territorio *m*; **cattle-farming ~** región *f* ganadera

D [u] (Mus) (música *f*) country *m*

country: **~-and-western** /'kʌntriən'westərn || ,kʌntriən'westən/ *n* [u] (música *f*) country *m*; **~ bumpkin** *n* pueblerino, -na *m,f*, paleto, -ta *m,f* (Esp), pajuerano, -na *m,f* (RPl fam); **~ cousin** *n* pueblerino, -na *m,f*; **~ dancing** *n* [u] (esp BrE) danzas *fpl* folklóricas; **~ house** *n* casa *f* solariega; **~man** /'kʌntrimən/ *n* (*pl* **-men** /-mən/) (compatriot) (liter) compatriota *m*; **~ mile** *n* (AmE colloq): ***to miss sth by a ~ mile*** errar* por mucho *or* por una legua, errarle* feo (RPl fam); **~side** *n* [u] campiña *f*, campo *m*; **~ store** *n* (AmE) tienda *f* de pueblo (*en la que se vende de todo*); **~wide** /'kʌntri'waɪd/ *adj/adv* a escala nacional; **~woman** *n* (*pl* **-women**) (compatriot) (liter) compatriota *f*

county /'kaʊnti/ *n* (*pl* **-ties**) 1 (in US) condado *m*; (*before n*) **~ line** límite *m* del condado; **~ seat** cabeza *f* de partido 2 (in UK) condado *m*; (*before n*) **~ town** capital *f* del condado

> **county**
>
> Región administrativa de Gran Bretaña que agrupa un número de distritos (*districts*). Los condados son las principales unidades administrativas de Gran Bretaña y muchos tienen demarcaciones que se remontan a muchos años atrás. Sin embargo, en las últimas décadas, éstas y sus nombres han cambiado mucho, y el término *county* a menudo ya no se usa. La mayoría de los estados en EEUU también están divididos en condados. Hay alrededor de 3.000 condados en EEUU

county: **~ council** *n* (in UK) *corporación de gobierno a nivel de condado*; **~ court** *n* (in US) juzgado *m* comarcal; (in UK) juzgado *m* comarcal (*que conoce de causas de derecho civil*)

coup /kuː/ *n* (*pl* **~s** /kuːz/)

A (successful action) golpe *m* maestro

B **~ (d'état)** /deɪtɑː/(Pol) golpe *m* (de estado)

coup de grâce /'kuːdə'grɑːs/ *n* (*pl* **~s ~ ~**) golpe *m* de gracia

couple[1] /'kʌpəl/ *n*

A (two people) (+ *sing o pl vb*) pareja *f*; **a married ~** un matrimonio; **the happy ~** los recién casados, los novios

B (two or small number): **a ~ (of sth)** (+ *pl vb*) un par (de algo); **I think he'd had a ~** (colloq & euph) creo que tenía unas copas de más (fam & euf); **a ~ hundred books** (AmE colloq) unos doscientos libros

C

couple[2] *vt* [1] (connect) (Rail) enganchar; ‹*theories/events*› asociar; **to ~ sth/sb** WITH **sth/sb** asociar algo/a algn CON algo/algn [2] (combine) (*often pass*): **the fall in demand, ~d with competition from abroad** el descenso de la demanda, unido a la competencia extranjera

(Phrasal verb)

- **couple up** [v ▸ o ▸ adv, v ▸ adv ▸ o] enganchar

couplet /ˈkʌplət || ˈkʌplɪt/ *n* pareado *m*, dístico *m*

coupon /ˈkuːpɑːn || ˈkuːpɒn/ *n* [1] (voucher — for discount) vale *m*; (— in rationing) cupón *m* de racionamiento [2] (form — in advertisement) cupón *m*; (— for competition) boleto *m*

courage /ˈkərɪdʒ || ˈkʌrɪdʒ/ *n* [u] valor *m*, coraje *m*; **to have/lack the ~ of one's convictions** ser*/no ser* fiel a sus (*or* mis *etc*) convicciones; **to lose (one's) ~** acobardarse; **he took ~ from her smile** su sonrisa le dio ánimo; ***to pluck up ~ (to + INF)*** armarse de valor *or* de coraje (para + INF); ***to take one's ~ in both hands*** hacer* de tripas corazón (fam)

courageous /kəˈreɪdʒəs/ *adj* ‹*person*› valiente, corajudo; ‹*words*› valiente; ‹*act*› valeroso, de valor *or* de valentía

courageously /kəˈreɪdʒəsli/ *adv* con valor *or* valentía

courgette /kʊrˈʒet || kɔːˈʒet/ *n* [c u] (BrE) ▸ **zucchini**

courier /ˈkʊriər || ˈkʊriə(r)/ *n* [1] (guide) guía *mf* [2] (messenger) (BrE) mensajero, -ra *m,f*, correo *mf*, rutero, -ra *m,f*; (*before n*) **~ service** servicio *m* de mensajero

course[1] /kɔːrs || kɔːs/ *n*

A [1] (of river) curso *m*; (of road) recorrido *m* [2] (way of proceeding): **the only ~ open to us** el único camino que tenemos, nuestra única opción [3] (progress) (*no pl*): **in the normal ~ of events** normalmente, en circunstancias normales; **in due ~** a su debido tiempo; **in the ~ of time** con el tiempo; **in** *o* **during the ~ of our conversation** en el curso *or* transcurso de nuestra conversación; **it changed the ~ of history** cambió el curso de la historia; ***to run*** *o* ***take its ~*** seguir* su curso

B **of course** claro, desde luego, por supuesto; **am I invited? — of ~ you are!** ¿estoy invitado? — ¡claro *or* desde luego *or* por supuesto que sí!; **of ~ not** claro que no; **I'm not always right, of ~** claro que no siempre tengo razón

C (Aviat, Naut) rumbo *m*; **to set ~ for** poner* rumbo a; **to go off ~** desviarse* de rumbo; **to change ~** cambiar de rumbo

D [1] (Educ) curso *m*; **a short ~** un cursillo; **~ IN/ON sth** curso DE/SOBRE algo; **to take** *o* (BrE also) **do a ~** hacer* un curso; **to go on a ~** ir* a hacer un curso; (*before n*) **~work** trabajo *m* [2] (Med): **a ~ of treatment** un tratamiento

E (part of a meal) plato *m*; **main ~** plato principal *or* fuerte *or* (Ven) central; **as a** *o* **for the first ~** de primer plato, de entrada; **a three-~ meal** una comida de dos platos y postre

F (Sport) (*race~*) hipódromo *m*, pista *f* (de carreras); (*golf ~*) campo *m or* (CS tb) cancha *f* (de golf); ***to last*** *o* ***stay the ~*** (persist to the end) aguantar hasta el final

course[2] *vi* (flow swiftly) (liter): **he felt the blood coursing through his veins** sentía correr la sangre por sus venas (liter)

court[1] /kɔːrt || kɔːt/ *n*

A (Law) [1] (tribunal) tribunal *m*; **to appear in ~** comparecer* ante el tribunal *or* los tribunales; **I'll see you in ~!** ¡te voy a demandar!; **to settle out of ~** transigir* extrajudicialmente, llegar* a una transacción extrajudicial; **to go to ~** acudir a los tribunales; **to take sb to ~** demandar a algn, llevar a algn a juicio; **the ~ is adjourned** se levanta la sesión; ***to laugh sb/sth out of ~*** reírse* de algn/algo; (*before n*) **~ case** causa *f*, juicio *m*; **~ order** orden *f* judicial [2] (building) juzgado *m*

B [1] (of sovereign) corte *f* [2] (palace) palacio *m*

C (Sport) cancha *f* (AmL), pista *f* (Esp)

D (courtyard) patio *m*

court[2] *vt* [1] ‹*girl*› (dated) cortejar (ant), hacerle* la corte a (ant) [2] (seek) ‹*danger/favor*› buscar*; ‹*disaster*› exponerse* a

■ **court** *vi* «*couple*» (dated) estar* de novios, noviar (AmL fam), pololear (Chi fam)

courteous /ˈkɜːrtiəs || ˈkɜːtiəs/ *adj* ‹*person/behavior*› cortés, educado, fino; ‹*reply/letter*› cortés

courteously /ˈkɜːrtiəsli || ˈkɜːtiəsli/ *adv* cortésmente, con cortesía

courtesan /ˈkɔːrtəzən || ˌkɔːtɪˈzæn/ *n* (liter) cortesana *f*

courtesy /ˈkɜːrtəsi || ˈkɜːtəsi/ *n* (*pl* **-sies**) [1] [u] (politeness) cortesía *f*; **it is common ~** es de (simple) cortesía *or* de buena educación; **you could have had the ~ to inform us** podría haber tenido la gentileza de avisarnos [2] [c] (greeting): **they exchanged courtesies** se saludaron con las cortesías de rigor [3] [c] (favor) atención *f*, gentileza *f*; **by ~ of** por atención *or* gentileza de

courthouse /ˈkɔːrthaʊs || ˈkɔːthaʊs/ *n* juzgado *m*

courtier /ˈkɔːrtiər || ˈkɔːtiə(r)/ *n* cortesano, -na *m,f*

courtly /ˈkɔːrtli || ˈkɔːtli/ *adj* **-lier, -liest** distinguido, fino; **~ love** (Lit) (el) amor cortés

court-martial[1] /ˈkɔːrtˈmɑːrʃəl || ˌkɔːtˈmɑːʃəl/ *n* (*pl* **courts-martial** /ˈkɔːrts-/) consejo *m* de guerra

court-martial[2] *vt*, (BrE) **-ll-** ‹*soldier*› formarle consejo de guerra a

courtroom /ˈkɔːrtruːm, -rʊm || ˈkɔːtruːm, -rʊm/ *n* sala *f* (*de un tribunal*)

courtship /ˈkɔːrtʃɪp || ˈkɔːtʃɪp/ *n*

A (of people) noviazgo *m*

B (Zool) cortejo *m*

court: **~ shoe** *n* (BrE) zapato *m* (de) salón; **~yard** *n* patio *m*

cousin /ˈkʌzn̩/ *n* primo, -ma *m,f*; **first ~** primo hermano *or* carnal, prima hermana *or* carnal; **second ~** primo segundo, prima segunda

cove /kəʊv/ *n* (Geog) cala *f*, caleta *f*

coven /ˈkʌvn̩/ *n* aquelarre *m*

covenant /ˈkʌvənənt/ *n* [1] (contract) pacto *m*, cláusula *f* [2] (Bib) alianza *f*

Coventry /ˈkʌvəntri || ˈkɒvəntri/ *n*: ***to send sb to ~*** hacerle* el vacío a algn

cover[1] /ˈkʌvər || ˈkʌvə(r)/ *n*

A [c] [1] (lid, casing) tapa *f*, cubierta *f*; (for cushion, sofa, typewriter) funda *f*; (for book) forro *m*; (*bed ~*) cubrecama *m*, colcha *f* [2] **covers** *pl* (bedclothes) **the ~s** las mantas, las cobijas (AmL), las frazadas (AmL)

B [c] [1] (of book) tapa *f*, cubierta *f*; (of magazine) portada *f*, carátula *f* (Andes); (*front ~*) portada *f*; **back ~** contraportada *f*; **to read sth from ~ to ~** leer* algo de cabo a rabo [2] (envelope): **under separate ~** por separado

C [1] [u] (shelter, protection): **to take ~** guarecerse*, ponerse* a cubierto; **to run for ~** correr a guarecerse *or* a ponerse a cubierto; **under ~ of darkness** *o* **night** al abrigo *or* amparo de la oscuridad *or* de la noche [2] [c u] (front, pretense) tapadera *f*, pantalla *f*; **to blow** *o* **break sb's ~** desenmascarar a algn

D [u] (insurance) (BrE) cobertura *f*

E [c] **~ (charge)** (in restaurant) cubierto *m*; (in nightclub) (AmE) ≈ consumición *f* mínima

cover[2] *vt*

A [1] (overlay) cubrir*; **to be ~ed IN sth** estar* cubierto DE algo [2] ‹*hole/saucepan*› tapar [3] ‹*cushion*› ponerle* una funda a; ‹*book*› forrar; ‹*sofa*› tapizar*, recubrir* [4] ‹*passage/terrace*› techar, cubrir*

B [1] (extend over) ‹*area/floor*› cubrir*; ‹*page*› llenar [2] (travel) ‹*distance*› recorrer, cubrir*

C [1] (deal with) ‹*syllabus*› cubrir*; ‹*topic*› tratar; ‹*eventuality*› contemplar [2] (report on) (Journ) cubrir*

D [1] (hide) tapar; **she ~ed her eyes** se tapó los ojos; **to ~ one's head** cubrirse* (la cabeza) [2] (mask) ‹*surprise/ignorance*› disimular; ‹*mistake*› ocultar, tapar (fam)

E [1] (guard, protect) cubrir*; **I'll keep you ~ed** yo te cubro [2] (point gun at) apuntarle a; **we've got you ~ed!** ¡te estamos apuntando! [3] (Sport) ‹*opponent*› marcar*; ‹*shot/base*› cubrir*

F (Fin) [1] ‹*costs/expenses*› cubrir*; ‹*liabilities*› hacer* frente a; **will $100 ~ it?** ¿alcanzará con 100 dólares? [2] (insurance) cubrir*, asegurar

■ **cover** *vi* [1] (deputize) **to ~ FOR sb** sustituir* *or* suplir a algn [2] (conceal truth) **to ~ FOR sb** encubrir* a algn

■ *v refl* **to ~ oneself** cubrirse* las espaldas

(Phrasal verbs)

- **cover over** [v ▸ o ▸ adv, v ▸ adv ▸ o] [1] (roof) techar, cubrir* [2] (conceal) tapar, cubrir*
- **cover up**

A [v ▸ o ▸ adv, v ▸ adv ▸ o] [1] (cover completely) cubrir*, tapar [2] (conceal) ‹*facts/truth*› ocultar, tapar (fam); ‹*mistake*› disimular

B [v ▸ adv] (conceal error) disimular; (conceal truth) **to ~ up FOR sb** encubrir* a algn

coverage /ˈkʌvərɪdʒ/ *n* [u] cobertura *f*; **press/television/news ~** cobertura periodística/televisiva/informativa; **there will be live ~ of the game** el partido será transmitido *or* (Esp) retransmitido en directo

cover: **~-alls** /ˈkʌvərɔːlz/ *pl n* (AmE) overol *m* (AmL), mono *m* (de trabajo) (Esp); **~ girl** *n* modelo *f* de portada

covering /ˈkʌvərɪŋ/ *n*: **use it as a ~ for the floor** úsalo para cubrir *or* tapar el suelo; **a ~ of dust** una capa de polvo

covering letter *n* carta *f* adjunta

coverlet /ˈkʌvərlət || ˈkʌvəlɪt/ *n* cobertor *m*

cover story *n* (in magazine) tema *m* de portada; (in newspaper) noticia *f* de primera plana

covert /ˈkəʊvərt || ˈkʌvət, ˈkəʊ-/ *adj* encubierto

covertly /ˈkəʊvərtli || ˈkʌvətli, ˈkəʊ-/ *adv* encubiertamente

cover-up /ˈkʌvərʌp/ *n* (of crime) encubrimiento *m*; **there has been a ~** ha habido una maniobra para encubrir el asunto

covet /ˈkʌvət/ *vt* codiciar

coveted /ˈkʌvətəd || ˈkʌvətɪd/ *adj* codiciado

covetous /ˈkʌvətəs/ *adj* codicioso; **to be ~ OF sth** (frml) codiciar algo

cow[1] /kaʊ/ *n* [1] (Agr) vaca *f*; ***till*** *o* ***until the ~s come home*** (colloq) hasta el día del juicio final [2] (female whale, elephant, seal) hembra *f* [3] (woman) (BrE colloq & pej): **stupid ~!** ¡imbécil! (fam)

cow[2] *vt* intimidar; **he wasn't ~ed by their threats** no se dejó acobardar *or* intimidar por sus amenazas; **a ~ed look** una mirada acobardada

coward /ˈkaʊərd || ˈkaʊəd/ *n* cobarde *mf*

cowardice /ˈkaʊərdəs || ˈkaʊədɪs/ *n* [u] cobardía *f*

cowardly /ˈkaʊərdli || ˈkaʊədli/ *adj* cobarde

cowboy /ˈkaʊbɔɪ/ *n* [1] (in Western US) vaquero *m*; (in Wild West) vaquero *m*, cowboy *m*; **to play ~s and Indians** jugar* a indios y vaqueros; (*before n*) ‹*hat*› de vaquero, de cowboy; **~ boots** botas *fpl* camperas *or* tejanas [2] (unscrupulous trader) (BrE colloq) pillo, -lla *m,f* (fam), pirata *mf* (fam)

cower /ˈkaʊər || ˈkaʊə(r)/ *vi* encogerse* (de miedo)

cow: **~girl** *n* vaquera *f*; **~hand** *n* peón *m* (de campo); **~herd** *n* vaquero, -ra *m,f*; **~hide** *n* [c u] cuero *m or* (Esp tb) piel *f* de vaca

cowl /kaʊl/ *n* (monk's cloak) hábito *m* (*con capucha*)

cow: **~lick** *n* (AmE) remolino *m*; **~man** /ˈkaʊmən/ *n* (*pl* **-men** /-mən/) (in US) (ranch owner) ganadero *m*; (ranch worker) vaquero *m*, peón *m*

coworker /ˈkəʊˈwɜːrkər || kəʊˈwɜːkə(r)/ *n* (esp AmE) (workmate) colega *mf*, compañero, -ra *m,f* de trabajo; (collaborator) colaborador, -dora *m,f*

cow: **~pat** *n* boñiga *f*, bosta *f* (esp AmL) (*de vaca*); **~poke** *n* (AmE colloq) vaquero *m*; **~puncher** /ˈkaʊpʌntʃər || ˈkaʊpʌntʃə(r)/ *n* (AmE colloq) vaquero *m*, cowboy *m*; **~shed** *n* establo *m* (de las vacas); **~slip** *n* prímula *f*

coxswain /ˈkɑːksən || ˈkɒksən/ *n* (Naut) timonel *m*

coy /kɔɪ/ *adj* **coyer, coyest** (shy) tímido; (evasive) evasivo; **a ~ little smile** una sonrisita tímida y coqueta

coyly /ˈkɔɪli/ *adv* con (coqueta) timidez

coyote /kaɪˈəʊti || kɔɪˈəʊti/ *n* (*pl* **-otes** *or* **-ote**) coyote *m*

coypu /ˈkɔɪpuː/ *n* coipo *m*

cozy[1], (BrE) **cosy** /ˈkəʊzi/ *adj* **cozier, coziest** [1] ‹*room*› acogedor; **in her ~ bed** en su cama cómoda y calentita [2] ‹*chat*› íntimo y agradable [3] (convenient) (pej) de lo más conveniente (pey)

cozy[2], (BrE) **cosy** *n* (*pl* **-ies**): **tea ~** cubreteteras *m*

Phrasal verb

- **cozy up to**: **cozies, cozying, cozied** [v ▸ adv ▸ prep ▸ o] (AmE) adular, tratar de quedar bien con

CPA *n* (in US) **= Certified Public Accountant**

Cpl (title) **= Corporal**

CPU *n* (**= central processing unit**) CPU *f*

crab /kræb/ *n*

A [c u] (animal, meat) cangrejo *m*, jaiba *f* (AmL)

B **crabs** *pl* (pubic lice) (colloq) ladillas *fpl*

crab apple *n* (fruit) manzana *f* silvestre; (tree) manzano *m* silvestre

crabby /ˈkræbi/ *adj* **-bier, -biest** (colloq) rezongón (fam), refunfuñón (fam)

crack[1] /kræk/ *n*

A [c] [1] (in ice, wall, pavement) grieta *f*; (in glass, china) rajadura *f*; ***to paper*** *o* ***paste over the ~s*** ponerle* parches al problema (*or* a la situación *etc*) [2] (chink, slit) rendija *f*

B [c] (sound — of whip, twig) chasquido *m*; (— of rifle shot) estallido *m*; (— of thunder) estruendo *m*; (— of bones) crujido *m*; ***to give sb a fair ~ of the whip*** (BrE) darle* todas las oportunidades a algn

C [c] (blow) golpe *m*

D (instant): **at the ~ of dawn** al amanecer, al despuntar el día (liter)

E [c] (attempt) (colloq) intento *m*; **to have a ~ at sth** intentar algo

F (colloq) (wisecrack) comentario *m* socarrón

G [u] (drug) crack *m*

crack[2] *adj* (*before n*) ‹*shot/troops*› de primera

crack[3] *vt*

A ‹*cup/glass*› rajar; ‹*ground/earth*› agrietar, resquebrajar; ‹*skin*› agrietar; **he ~ed a rib** se fracturó una costilla

B [1] (break open) ‹*egg*› cascar*, romper*; ‹*nut*› cascar*, partir; ‹*safe*› forzar*; ‹*drugs ring/spy ring*› desmantelar, desarticular; ***to ~ a book*** (AmE colloq) abrir* un libro; ***to ~ open a bottle*** (colloq) abrir* *or* descorchar una botella; ***to ~ a smile*** sonreír* [2] (decipher, solve) ‹*code*› descifrar, dar* con; ‹*problem*› resolver*; **I've ~ed it!** (colloq) ¡ya lo tengo!

C (make cracking sound with) ‹*whip*› (hacer*) chasquear *or* restallar; ‹*finger/knuckle*› hacer* crujir; ▸**whip**[1]

D (hit sharply) pegar*

E ‹*joke*› (colloq) contar*

■ **crack** *vi*

A [1] «*cup/glass*» rajarse; «*rock/paint/skin*» agrietarse [2] (make cracking sound) «*whip*» chasquear, restallar; «*bones/twigs*» crujir [3] «*voice*» quebrarse* [4] (break down): **she ~ed under the strain** sufrió una crisis nerviosa a causa de la tensión

B (be active, busy): **to get ~ing** (colloq) poner(se)* manos a la obra; **come on, get ~ing!** ¡vamos, muévete! (fam)

Phrasal verbs

- **crack down** [v ▸ adv] **to ~ down ON sb/sth** tomar medidas enérgicas CONTRA algn/algo
- **crack up**

A [v ▸ adv] [1] (break down) (colloq) «*person*» sufrir un ataque de nervios, sucumbir a la presión [2] (burst out laughing) (colloq) soltar* una carcajada

B [v ▸ o ▸ adv] (colloq) (make laugh) matar de la risa (fam)

C [v ▸ o ▸ adv] (praise) (colloq) (*usu pass*): **it isn't all it's ~ed up to be** no es tan bueno como lo pintan (fam)

crackdown /ˈkrækdaʊn/ *n* **~** (**ON sth/sb**) ofensiva *f or* campaña *f* (CONTRA algo/algn), medidas *fpl* enérgicas (CONTRA algo/algn)

cracked /krækt/ *adj* [1] ‹*cup/glass*› rajado; ‹*rib*› fracturado; ‹*wall/ceiling*› con grietas, resquebrajado; ‹*lips*› partido, agrietado; ‹*skin*› agrietado [2] (crazy) (colloq) ‹*person*› loco, chiflado (fam) [3] ‹*voice*› cascado

cracker /ˈkrækər || ˈkrækə(r)/ *n*

A (biscuit) cracker *f*, galleta *f* (*salada*)

B [1] (*fire~*) petardo *m* [2] (BrE) sorpresa *f* (*que estalla al abrirla*)

cracker: **~-barrel** *adj* (AmE) ‹*humor/philosopher*› sin sofisticaciones; **~jack** *n* (AmE colloq) as *m* (fam); (*before n*) ‹*person/idea/car*› fuera de serie (fam)

crackers /ˈkrækərz || ˈkrækəz/ *adj* (BrE colloq) (*pred*) (crazy) chiflado (fam)

cracking /ˈkrækɪŋ/ *adj* (colloq): **at a ~ pace** a toda pastilla (fam), a un ritmo endemoniado (fam); *see also* **crack**[3] *vi* **B**

crackle[1] /ˈkrækəl/ *vi* «*fire*» crepitar, chisporrotear; «*twigs/paper*» crujir; **the line's crackling a lot** hay mucho ruido en la línea

crackle[2] *n* [u] (of twigs, paper) crujido *m*; (of fire) chisporroteo *m*

crackling /ˈkræklɪŋ/ *n*

A [u] (noise — of paper) crujido *m*; (— of fire) chisporroteo *m*

B (Culin) [1] [u] (crisp pork rind) *piel crujiente y tostada del cerdo asado* [2] **cracklings** *pl* (AmE) chicharrones *mpl*

C

C

crack: **~pot** *n* (colloq) chiflado, -da *m,f* (fam), chalado, -da *m,f* (fam); (*before n*) **a ~pot idea** una idea descabellada; **~up** *n* (colloq) 1 (mental breakdown) crisis *f* nerviosa 2 (collision) (AmE) choque *m*

cradle¹ /ˈkreɪdl/ *n*
A (for baby) cuna *f*
B (for telephone receiver) horquilla *f*

cradle² *vt* ‹*baby*› acunar, mecer*; ‹*guitar*› sostener* contra el pecho

cradle robber /ˈkreɪdl̩ˌrɑːbər/ *n* (AmE colloq), **cradle-snatcher** /ˈkreɪdl̩ˌsnætʃər/ *n* (BrE colloq) corruptor, -tora *m,f* de menores (hum), asaltacunas *mf* (Méx fam)

craft¹ /kræft || krɑːft/ *n*
A 1 [u c] (trade) oficio *m*; (skill) arte *m*; (*before n*) **~ fair** feria *f* artesanal *or* de artesanía 2 **crafts** *pl* artesanía *f*; *see also* **art¹ A2**
B [u] (guile, deceit) (liter) artimañas *fpl*
C [c] (*pl* ~) (Naut) embarcación *f*; (Aerosp, Aviat) nave *f*

craft² *vt* trabajar

craftily /ˈkræftəli/ *adv* ‹*act*› con astucia, astutamente

craftsman /ˈkræftsmən/ *n* (*pl* **-men** /mən/) artesano *m*, artífice *m*

craftsmanship /ˈkræftsmənʃɪp || ˈkrɑːftsmənʃɪp/ *n* [u] 1 (skill) destreza *f* 2 (workmanship) trabajo *m*

crafty /ˈkræfti || ˈkrɑːfti/ *adj* **-tier, -tiest** ‹*person*› astuto, zorro (fam); ‹*methods/tactics*› hábil, artero

crag /kræg/ *n* peñasco *m*, risco *m*

craggy /ˈkrægi/ *adj* **-gier, -giest** ‹*rocks/mountains*› escarpado; **he had a ~, weather-beaten face** tenía un rostro curtido y de facciones bien marcadas

cram /kræm/ **-mm-** *vt* (stuff) meter; **I ~med all my things into a case** metí *or* embutí todas mis cosas en una maleta; **the room was ~med with people/books** la habitación estaba abarrotada *or* atiborrada de gente/libros; **to ~ oneself with food** atiborrarse de comida

■ **cram** *vi*
A (for exam) empollar (Esp fam), zambutir (Méx), tragar* (RPl fam), matearse (Chi fam), empacarse* (Col fam)
B (get in) meterse; **we all ~med into the room** nos metimos todos en la habitación

cramp¹ /kræmp/ *n* [u c] calambre *m*, rampa *f* (Esp); **I've got (a) ~ in my leg** me ha dado un calambre *or* (Esp tb) (una) rampa en la pierna; **(stomach) ~s** retorcijones *mpl or* (Esp) retortijones *mpl* en el estómago

cramp² *vt* (limit) ‹*work/progress*› entorpecer*; ***to ~ sb's style*** cortarle los vuelos a algn

cramped /kræmpt/ *adj* ‹*handwriting*› apretado; **I'm ~ (for space)** tengo poco sitio *or* lugar; **they work in ~ conditions** están muy estrechos en el trabajo; **we were a bit ~ in the car** íbamos algo apretujados *or* apretados en el coche

cranberry /ˈkrænˌberi || ˈkrænbəri/ *n* (*pl* **-ries**) arándano *m* (*rojo y agrio*)

crane¹ /kreɪn/ *n*
A (for lifting) grúa *f*
B (Zool) grulla *f*

crane² *vt*: **to ~ one's neck** estirar el cuello

■ **crane** *vi* estirarse

cranefly /ˈkreɪnflaɪ/ *n* (*pl* **-flies**) típula *f*

cranium /ˈkreɪniəm/ *n* (*pl* **-nia** /-nɪə/) cráneo *m*

crank¹ /kræŋk/ *n*
A 1 (Mech Eng) cigüeñal *m* 2 **~ (handle)** (Auto) manivela *f* (de arranque)
B (colloq) 1 (eccentric) maniático, -ca *m,f*, raro, -ra *m,f* 2 (bad-tempered person) (AmE) cascarrabias *mf*

crank² *vt* ‹*car*› (hacer*) arrancar* con la manivela

crankshaft /ˈkræŋkʃæft || ˈkræŋkʃɑːft/ *n* (eje *m or* árbol *m* del) cigüeñal *m*

cranky /ˈkræŋki/ *adj* **-kier, -kiest** (colloq) 1 (eccentric) maniático, raro; ‹*idea*› estrafalario, raro 2 (bad-tempered) (AmE) malhumorado

cranny /ˈkræni/ *n* (*pl* **-nies**) ranura *f*; ▸ **nook**

crap /kræp/ *n* [u] 1 (excrement) (vulg) mierda *f* (vulg) 2 (nonsense) (sl) estupideces *fpl*, gilipolleces *fpl* (Esp fam *o* vulg), pendejadas *fpl* (AmL exc CS fam), huevadas *fpl* (Andes, Ven vulg), boludeces *fpl* (Col, RPl vulg)

crap game *n* (AmE) ▸ **craps**

crappy /ˈkræpi/ *adj* **-pier, -piest** (sl) malo, de porquería (fam), de mierda (vulg)

craps /kræps/ *n* (AmE) (+ *sing vb*) crap *m* (*juego de azar que se juega con dos dados*); **to shoot ~** jugar* al crap

crash¹ /kræʃ/ *n* 1 (loud noise) estrépito *m*; **the ~ of the waves** el estruendo de las olas al romper 2 (collision, accident) accidente *m*, choque *m*; **plane/car ~** accidente aéreo/de automóvil 3 (financial failure) crac *m*, crack *m*

crash² *vt*
A (smash): **he ~ed the car** tuvo un accidente con el coche, chocó
B (colloq) **to ~ a party** colarse* en una fiesta (fam)

■ **crash** *vi*
A 1 (collide) **to ~ (INTO sth)** estrellarse *or* chocar* (CONTRA algo) 2 (make loud noise) «*thunder*» retumbar; **the dishes ~ed to the floor** los platos se cayeron al suelo estrepitosamente 3 (Fin) «*shares*» caer* a pique, colapsar
B (spend the night) (esp AmE colloq) quedarse a dormir
C (Comput) fallar

Phrasal verb

• **crash out** [v ▸ adv]
1 (colloq) (to go to sleep) quedarse dormido; **we ~ed out on the floor** nos tiramos a dormir en el suelo 2 (in competitions) quedar eliminado

crash³ *adj* (*before n*) ‹*program/course*› intensivo; **~ diet** régimen *m* muy estricto

crash: **~ barrier** *n* barrera *f* de protección; **~ helmet** *n* casco *m* (protector); **~-landing** /ˈkræʃ ˈlændɪŋ/ *n* aterrizaje *m* forzoso *or* de emergencia

crash pad *n*
A (shock-absorbing material) material *m* amortiguador
B (place to sleep) (colloq) lugar *m* donde quedarse a dormir (*sólo una noche*)

crass /kræs/ *adj* **-er, -est** 1 ‹*joke*› burdo; ‹*remark*› grosero, de muy poco gusto (*or* tacto *etc*) 2 ‹*ignorance*› craso, supino; ‹*stupidity*› extremo

crate /kreɪt/ *n* 1 (container) cajón *m* (de embalaje), jaula *f*, jaba *f* (Chi) 2 (old plane, car) (sl) cascajo *m* (fam), cacharro *m* (fam)

crater /ˈkreɪtər || ˈkreɪtə(r)/ *n* cráter *m*

cravat /krəˈvæt/ *n* pañuelo *m* de cuello (de caballero)

crave /kreɪv/ *vt* ‹*admiration/flattery*› ansiar*; ‹*affection*› tener* ansias de; ‹*food/drink*› morirse* por (fam)

craving /ˈkreɪvɪŋ/ *n* [u c] 1 (strong desire) ansias *fpl*, ansia *f*‡, sed *f* (liter) 2 (in pregnancy) antojo *m*

crawfish /ˈkrɔːfɪʃ/ *n* (*pl* **-fish** *or* **-fishes**) ▸ **crayfish**

crawl¹ /krɔːl/ *vi*
A 1 (creep) arrastrarse; «*baby*» gatear, ir* a gatas; «*insect*» andar*; ▸ **flesh 1** 2 (go slowly) «*traffic/train*» avanzar* muy lentamente
B (teem): **the beach was ~ing with tourists** la playa estaba plagada de turistas, la playa hervía de turistas
C (demean oneself) (colloq) arrastrarse, rebajarse; **to ~ TO sb** arrastrarse *or* rebajarse ANTE algn

crawl² *n*
A (slow pace) (*no pl*): **to go at a ~** avanzar* muy lentamente, ir* a paso de tortuga (fam)
B (swimming stroke) crol *m*

crawler /ˈkrɔːlər || ˈkrɔːlə(r)/ *n* (person) (colloq) pelota *mf* (Esp fam), chupamedias *mf* (CS, Ven fam), lambiscón, -cona *m,f* (Méx fam), lambón, -bona *m,f* (Col fam)

crayfish /ˈkreɪfɪʃ/ *n* (*pl* **-fish** *or* **-fishes**) 1 (freshwater) ástaco *m*, cangrejo *m* de río 2 (marine) langosta *f* (*pequeña*), cigala *f*

crayon /ˈkreɪɑːn || ˈkreɪən/ *n* (pencil) lápiz *m* de color; (wax ~) crayola® *f*, crayón *m* (Méx, RPl), lápiz *m* de cera (Chi)

craze /kreɪz/ *n* (fashion) moda *f*; (fad) manía *f*

crazed /kreɪzd/ *adj* ‹*expression*› de loco; ‹*person*› enloquecido

crazy /ˈkreɪzi/ *adj* **-zier, -ziest** 1 (mad, foolish) loco; **that's ~** es una locura; **to go ~** volverse* loco, enloquecerse*; **to drive sb ~** volver* loco a algn; **like ~** como (un) loco 2 (very enthusiastic) (colloq) (*pred*) **to be ~ ABOUT** *o* (AmE) **FOR** *o* (AmE) **OVER sb** estar* loco POR algn (fam); **I'm not ~ about the idea** la idea no me enloquece *or* no me vuelve loco

crazy: **~ paving** *n* [u] (BrE) *enlosado de diseño irregular*; **~ quilt** *n* (AmE) colcha *f* de retazos, centón *m*

creak[1] /kriːk/ *vi* «*door*» chirriar*; «*bedsprings/floorboards/joints*» crujir

creak[2] *n* (of door) chirrido *m*; (of bedsprings, floorboards, joints) crujido *m*

creaky /'kriːki/ *adj* **-kier, -kiest** ‹*door*› que chirría, chirriante; ‹*stairs*› que cruje

cream[1] /kriːm/ *n*
A (Culin) crema *f* (de leche) (esp AmL), nata *f* (Esp); **light** *o* (BrE) **single ~** crema líquida (AmL), nata líquida (Esp); **heavy** *o* (BrE) **double ~** crema doble (AmL), doble crema (Méx), nata para montar (Esp); **whipped ~** crema batida (AmL), nata montada (Esp); **~ of mushroom soup** crema *f* de champiñones; (*before n*) **~ tea** (in UK) *té servido con* **scones**, *mermelada y crema batida*
B [c u] (lotion) crema *f*; **face ~** crema para la cara
C [u] (elite) **the ~ of society** la flor y nata *or* la crema de la sociedad
D (color) color *m* crema

cream[2] *adj* color crema *adj inv*

cream[3] *vt* ‹*butter/sugar*› batir (*hasta obtener una consistencia cremosa*); **~ed potatoes** puré *m* de papas *or* (Esp) patatas

Phrasal verb
- **cream off** [v ▸ o ▸ adv, v ▸ adv ▸ o] (BrE colloq) ‹*profits*› llevarse, quedarse con

cream: **~ cake** *n* 1 [c u] (gateau) tarta *f* or (CS) torta *f* con crema *or* (Esp) con nata 2 [c] (individual) pastel *m or* bollo *m* de crema *or* (Esp) de nata, masa *f* de crema (RPl); **~ cheese** *n* [u] queso *m* crema (AmL), queso *m* para untar (Esp); **~ cracker** *n* (BrE) galleta *f* (*salada*), cracker *f*

creamer /'kriːmər || 'kriːmə(r)/ *n*
A [c] (jug) (AmE) jarrita *f* para crema
B [u] (powder) leche *f* en polvo

cream soda *n* [u] *gaseosa con sabor a vainilla*

creamy /'kriːmi/ *adj* **-mier, -miest** 1 (containing cream) con crema 2 (smooth) cremoso

crease[1] /kriːs/ *n* (in paper, clothes) arruga *f*; (in trousers) raya *f*, pliegue *m* (Méx, Ven)

crease[2] *vi* arrugarse*
■ **crease** *vt* ‹*clothes*› arrugar*; ‹*paper*› doblar, plegar*

Phrasal verb
- **crease up** (BrE colloq) [v ▸ adv] (laugh) desternillarse *or* partirse de risa

create /kri'eɪt/ *vt* 1 (bring into existence) crear; **to ~ jobs** crear *or* generar empleo 2 (cause) ‹*problem/confusion*› crear; ‹*impression*› producir*, causar
■ **create** *vi* (make a fuss) (BrE colloq) armar jaleo (fam)

creation /kri'eɪʃən/ *n* [u c] creación *f*

creative /kri'eɪtɪv/ *adj* creativo; **~ writing** creación *f* literaria

creativity /'krieɪ'tɪvəti/ *n* [u] creatividad *f*

creator /kri'eɪtər || kri'eɪtə(r)/ *n* creador, -dora *m,f*

creature /'kriːtʃər || 'kriːtʃə(r)/ *n* 1 (animate being) criatura *f*; **sea ~** animal *m* marino; (*before n*) **~ comforts** las comodidades 2 (person) ser *m*, criatura *f*

creche, crèche /kreʃ/ *n*
A 1 (hospital for foundlings) (AmE) orfanato *m*, orfelinato *m*, orfanatorio *m* 2 (day nursery) (BrE) guardería *f* (infantil) (*puede ser en el lugar de trabajo para los empleados etc*)
B (Nativity scene) (AmE) nacimiento *m*, pesebre *m*, belén *m* (Esp)

credence /'kriːdṇs/ *n* [u] (frml): **to give** *o* **lend ~ to sth** dar* crédito a algo

credentials /krɪ'dentʃəlz || krɪ'denʃəlz/ *pl n* (of ambassador) cartas *fpl* credenciales; (references) referencias *fpl*; (identifying papers) documentos *mpl* (de identidad)

credibility /'kredə'bɪləti/ *n* [u] credibilidad *f*

credible /'kredəbəl/ *adj* creíble

credit[1] /'kredət || 'kredɪt/ *n*
A (Fin) 1 [u] (in store) crédito *m*; **on ~** a crédito; (*before n*) **~ account** (BrE) credicuenta *f*, cuenta *f* de *or* a crédito 2 [u] (in banking): **if your account is in ~ ...** si está en números negros ..., si tiene fondos en su cuenta ...; **to keep one's account in ~** mantener* un saldo positivo; (*before n*) **~ balance** saldo *m* positivo; **~ limit** límite *m* de crédito; **~ memorandum** *o* (BrE) **note** (given by store) vale *m* de devolución; **~ rating** calificación *f* crediticia 3 [c] (on balance sheet) saldo *m* acreedor *or* a favor
B [u] (honor, recognition) mérito *m*; **she deserves some ~ for trying** merece que se le reconozca el mérito de haberlo intentado; **he's brighter than I gave him ~ for** es más listo de lo que yo lo creía; **Jim must take the ~ for the excellent organization** la excelente organización es obra de Jim; **your children are a ~ to you** puedes estar orgulloso de tus hijos; **to her ~, she's very modest** dicho sea en su honor, es muy modesta; **the results do ~ to the school** los resultados hablan muy bien del colegio *or* (le) hacen honor al colegio; **~ where it's due, she's a good cook** en honor a la verdad, hay que reconocer que cocina muy bien
C [c] (Educ) 1 (for study) crédito *m* (*unidad de valor de una asignatura dentro de un programa de estudios*) 2 (grade) ≈ notable *m*
D **credits** *pl* (Cin, TV, Video) créditos *mpl*, rótulos *mpl* (de crédito)

credit[2] *vt*
A ‹*sum/funds*› **to ~ sth TO sth** abonar *or* ingresar algo EN algo
B 1 (ascribe to) **to ~ sb WITH sth/-ING**: **I'd ~ed you with more common sense** te creía con más sentido común; **please, ~ me with *some* intelligence** reconóceme algo de inteligencia, por favor; **they are ~ed with having invented the game** se les atribuye la invención del juego 2 (believe) creer*, dar* crédito a; **can you ~ it?** ¿te lo puedes creer?, ¿no te parece increíble?

creditable /'kredətəbəl || 'kredɪtəbəl/ *adj* encomiable, meritorio

credit card *n* tarjeta *f* de crédito

creditor /'kredətər || 'kredɪtə(r)/ *n* acreedor, -dora *m,f*

creditworthy /'kredət,wɜːrði || 'kredɪt,wɜːði/ *adj* con capacidad de pago, solvente (*para que se le conceda un crédito*)

credulity /krɪ'duːləti || krɪ'djuːləti/ *n* [u] credulidad *f*

credulous /'kredʒələs || 'kredjʊləs/ *adj* crédulo

creed /kriːd/ *n* credo *m*

creek /kriːk/ *n* 1 (stream) (AmE) arroyo *m*, riachuelo *m*; ***to be up the ~*** estar* mal, estar* equivocado; ***to be up the ~*** (colloq) *o* (vulg) ***up shit ~ (without a paddle)*** (in difficulty) estar* en aprietos *or* en apuros, estar* jodido (vulg) 2 (inlet) (BrE) cala *f*

creep[1] /kriːp/ (*past & past p* **crept**) *vi*
A (+ *adv compl*) 1 (crawl) arrastrarse 2 (move stealthily): **to ~ into a room** entrar en un cuarto sigilosamente; **a note of suspicion crept into his voice** se empezó a notar un elemento de sospecha en su voz; **several mistakes have crept in** se han deslizado varios errores 3 (move slowly): **the water crept higher** el agua iba subiendo poco a poco; **~ing inflation/unrest** creciente inflación/malestar 4 «*plant/vine*» trepar
B (ingratiate oneself) (BrE colloq) **to ~ TO sb** adular a algn, hacerle* la pelota a algn (Esp fam), hacerle* la pata a algn (Chi fam), chuparle las medias a algn (RPl fam); ▸ **flesh 1**

Phrasal verb
- **creep up on** (*past & past p* **crept**) [v ▸ adv ▸ prep ▸ o]: **they crept up on him** se le acercaron sigilosamente; **old age ~s up on you** vas envejeciendo sin darte cuenta

creep[2] *n*
A [c] (colloq) 1 (unpleasant person) asqueroso, -sa *m,f* 2 (favor-seeking person) adulador, -dora *m,f*, pelota *mf* (Esp fam), chupamedias *mf* (CS, Ven fam), lambiscón, -cona *m,f* (Méx fam), lambón, -bona *m,f* (Col fam)
B **creeps** *pl* (colloq): ***to give sb the ~s*** ponerle* los pelos de punta a algn (fam), darle* escalofríos a algn

creeper /'kriːpər || 'kriːpə(r)/ *n* (plant) planta *f* trepadora, enredadera *f*

creepy /'kriːpi/ *adj* **-pier, -piest** (colloq) 1 ‹*story/film*› escalofriante, espeluznante 2 ‹*person*› repulsivo, asqueroso

C

creepy-crawly /'kri:pi'krɔ:li/ *n* (*pl* **-lies**) (colloq) bicho *m* (fam)

cremate /'kri:meɪt || krɪ'meɪt/ *vt* incinerar, cremar

cremation /krɪ'meɪʃən/ *n* [c u] incineración *f*, cremación *f*

crematorium /'kri:mə'tɔ:riəm || ˌkremə'tɔ:riəm/ *n* (*pl* **-riums** *or* **-ria** /-riə/) crematorio *m*

crème /krem/: **~ caramel** *n* flan *m*; **~ de la crème** /'kremdəlɑ:'krem/ *n* **the ~ de la ~** la flor y nata, la crema, la crème de la crème; **~ de menthe** /'kremdə'menθ || 'kremdə'mɒnθ/ *n* [u] crema *f* de menta

Creole¹ /'kri:əʊl/ *adj* criollo

Creole² *n* 1 (person) criollo, -lla *m,f* 2 **creole** (Ling) criollo *m*

creosote /'kri:əsəʊt/ *n* [u] creosota *f*

crepe, crêpe /kreɪp/ *n*
A [u] (fabric) crep *m*, crepé *m*
B [u] **~ (rubber)** crep *m*, crepé *m*
C [c] (pancake) (Culin) crep *m*, crêpe *f*, panqueque *m* (AmC, CS), crepa *f* (Méx)

crepe paper *n* [u] papel *m* crepé *or* crep

crept /krept/ *past & past p of* **creep¹**

crescendo /krə'ʃendəʊ || krɪ'ʃendəʊ/ *n* (*pl* **-dos**) (Mus) crescendo *m*; (climax) punto *m* culminante

crescent¹ /'kresn̩t/ *n*
A (moon) creciente *m*
B 1 (shape) media luna *f* 2 (street) *calle en forma de media luna*

crescent² *adj* creciente

cress /kres/ *n* [u] mastuerzo *m*; (*water~*) berro *m*

crest /krest/ *n*
A (Zool) (of skin) cresta *f*; (of feathers) penacho *m*
B (in heraldry) emblema *m*, divisa *f*
C (of wave) cresta *f*; (of mountain) cima *f*; ***to be on** o **ride (on) the ~ of a wave*** estar* en la cresta de la ola

crested /'krestəd || 'krestɪd/ *adj*
A ‹*notepaper*› con emblema *or* escudo
B (Zool) con cresta

crestfallen /'krest,fɔ:lən/ *adj* alicaído

cretin /'kri:tn̩ || 'kretɪn/ *n* 1 (stupid person) estúpido, -da *m,f*, imbécil *mf* 2 (Med) cretino, -na *m,f*

crevasse /krə'væs/ *n* grieta *f* (*en un glaciar*)

crevice /'krevəs || 'krevɪs/ *n* grieta *f*

crew /kru:/ *n* 1 (Aviat, Naut) tripulación *f*; **cabin/flight/ground ~** personal *m* de cabina/vuelo/tierra; (*before n*) **~ member** miembro *mf* de la tripulación, tripulante *mf* 2 (team) equipo *m*; **film ~** (Cin) equipo *m* de rodaje *or* filmación 3 (gang, band) banda *f*, pandilla *f*

crew: **~ cut** *n* pelo *m* cortado al rape; **~ neck** *n* cuello *m* redondo

crib¹ /krɪb/ *n*
A 1 (child's bed) (AmE) cuna *f* 2 (Nativity scene) nacimiento *m*, pesebre *m*, belén *m* (Esp)
B (Agr) 1 (manger) pesebre *m* 2 (for storing grain) (AmE) granero *m*
C (colloq) 1 (for cheating in exam) chuleta *f or* (Méx) acordeón *m or* (Chi) torpedo *m* (fam) 2 (plagiarism) refrito *m* (fam), plagio *m* 3 (translation) traducción *f*

crib² **-bb-** *vt* (colloq) ‹*answer*› copiar
■ **crib** *vi* copiar

cribbage /'krɪbɪdʒ/ *n* [u] *juego de naipes*

crib death *n* (AmE) muerte *f* de cuna, muerte *f* súbita (infantil)

crick¹ /krɪk/ *n* calambre *m*; **I've got a ~ in my neck** me ha dado tortícolis

crick² *vt*: **to ~ one's neck** hacer* un mal movimiento con el cuello

cricket /'krɪkət || 'krɪkɪt/ *n*
A [c] (Zool) grillo *m*
B [u] (game) (Sport) críquet *m*; ***that's not ~*** (BrE colloq) eso no es jugar limpio; (*before n*) ‹*ball/match/bat*› de críquet

> **cricket**
>
> El críquet se juega principalmente en Gran Bretaña y los países de la **Commonwealth**. Se juega en un campo de césped, entre dos equipos de once jugadores cada uno. Se emplean bates (*bats*) y una pelota de cuero. Cada equipo batea en una entrada (*innings*) para marcar carreras (*runs*). Los jugadores del equipo contrario (*bowlers*) lanzan (*bowl*) la pelota al bateador y fildean (*field*), es decir interceptan la pelota, con el objetivo, si lo logran, de dejar al bateador fuera del juego (*out*) o que obtenga el menor número de carreras posibles. Hay dos bateadores (*batsmen*) a la vez en el campo, cada uno defendiendo un *wicket*, que son de tres palos verticales (*stumps*) que sostienen a su vez dos palos cortos (*bails*). Los *wickets* se encuentran uno frente al otro y están separados por una distancia de 22 yardas (20,1 metros aproximadamente). Las carreras se marcan cuando los bateadores corren de un wicket a otro

cricketer /'krɪkətər || 'krɪkɪtə(r)/ *n* jugador, -dora *m,f* de críquet

crikey /'kraɪki/ *interj* (BrE colloq & dated) ¡caramba! (fam)

crime /kraɪm/ *n* 1 [c] (wrongful act) delito *m*; (murder) crimen *m*; **it's a ~ to waste such talent** (colloq) es un crimen *or* un pecado desperdiciar un talento así 2 [u] (criminal activity) delincuencia *f*; **~ doesn't pay** (set phrase) no hay crimen sin castigo (fr hecha); (*before n*) ‹*rate/figures*› de criminalidad; **~ wave** ola *f* delictiva

criminal¹ /'krɪmənl̩ || 'krɪmɪnl̩/ *n* delincuente *mf*; (serious offender) criminal *mf*

criminal² *adj* 1 (of crime) (Law) ‹*act*› delictivo; ‹*organization/mind*› criminal; **~ court** juzgado *m* en lo penal; **~ law** derecho *m* penal; **~ lawyer** abogado, -da *m,f* criminalista *or* penalista; **~ negligence** negligencia *f* criminal; **~ offense** delito *m*; **to start ~ proceedings against sb** iniciar proceso penal *or* enjuiciamiento contra algn 2 (shameful) (colloq) vergonzoso (fam)

criminally /'krɪmənl̩i || 'krɪmɪnəli/ *adv*: **an institution for the ~ insane** una institución penitenciaria para delincuentes psicóticos

criminal record *n* antecedentes *mpl* penales, prontuario *m* (CS)

criminology /'krɪmə'nɑ:lədʒi || ˌkrɪmɪ'nɒlədʒi/ *n* [u] criminología *f*

crimp¹ /krɪmp/ *vt* ‹*hair*› rizar*, ondular (*con tenacillas*)

crimp² *n*: ***to put a ~ in sth*** (AmE colloq) obstaculizar* *or* dificultar algo

crimson¹ /'krɪmzən/ *n* [u] carmesí *m*

crimson² *adj* carmesí *adj inv*; **to turn** *o* **flush ~** ponerse* colorado *or* rojo

cringe /krɪndʒ/ *vi* 1 (shrink, cower) encogerse*; **I ~d at his jokes** sus chistes me hacían sentir vergüenza ajena 2 (grovel) arrastrarse

crinkle¹ /'krɪŋkəl/ *n* arruga *f*

crinkle² **~ (up)** *vt* arrugar*
■ **crinkle** *vi* arrugarse*

crinkly /'krɪŋkli/ *adj* **-klier, -kliest** ‹*material/face*› arrugado; ‹*hair*› rizado

crinoline /'krɪnl̩ən || 'krɪnəlɪn/ *n* crinolina *f*, miriñaque *m*

cripple¹ /'krɪpəl/ *n* lisiado, -da *m,f*, tullido, -da m,f

cripple² *vt* 1 (lame, disable): **he was ~d for life** quedó lisiado de por vida; **he's ~d with arthritis** la artritis lo tiene casi inmovilizado; **a ~d arm** un brazo tullido 2 (make inactive, ineffective) ‹*ship/plane*› inutilizar*; ‹*industry*› paralizar*

crippling /'krɪplɪŋ/ *adj* ‹*costs/debts*› agobiante; ‹*losses/strike*› de consecuencias catastróficas; ‹*pain*› atroz

crisis /'kraɪsəs || 'kraɪsɪs/ *n* (*pl* **-ses** /-si:z/) crisis *f*; **an identity ~** una crisis de identidad; **she's good in a ~** reacciona bien en los momentos difíciles; (*before n*) **to reach ~ point** hacer* crisis

crisp¹ /krɪsp/ *adj* **-er, -est**
A 1 (brittle) ‹*toast/bacon*› crujiente, crocante (RPl) 2 (fresh) ‹*lettuce*› fresco; ‹*apple/snow*› crujiente; ‹*sheets*› limpio y almidonado 3 (cold) ‹*air*› frío y vigorizante
B (brisk, concise) ‹*manner*› seco; ‹*style*› escueto

crisp[2] *n* (*potato* ~) (BrE) papa *f or* (Esp) patata *f* frita (*de bolsa*), papa *f* chip (Ur); ***to burn sth to a*** ~ achicharrar algo

crispbread /'krɪspbred/ *n* [u] *galleta delgada y crujiente, generalmente de centeno*

crisscross[1] /'krɪskrɔːs || 'krɪskrɒs/ *adj* entrecruzado

crisscross[2] *vt* entrecruzar*

criterion /kraɪ'tɪriən || kraɪ'tɪəriən/ *n* (*pl* **-ria** /-riə/) criterio *m*

critic /'krɪtɪk/ *n* 1 (Art, Theat, Lit) crítico, -ca *m,f* 2 (detractor) detractor, -tora *m,f*

critical /'krɪtɪkəl/ *adj*

A 1 (censorious) ‹*remark/report*› crítico; **to be ~ OF sth/sb** criticar* algo/a algn 2 (journalistic, academic) crítico

B 1 (very serious) ‹*condition/shortage*› crítico 2 (decisive, crucial) ‹*period*› crítico; ‹*decision*› de importancia fundamental

critically /'krɪtɪkli/ *adv*

A ‹*ill*› gravemente

B 1 (as a critic): **she looked ~ at her reflection** miró con ojo crítico la imagen que le devolvía el espejo 2 (censoriously): **she spoke rather ~ of him** habló de él en tono de crítica

critical: ~ **mass** *n* [u] masa *f* crítica; **to achieve ~ mass** alcanzar* la masa crítica; ~ **path analysis** *n* [u] análisis *m* del camino crítico

criticism /'krɪtəsɪzəm || 'krɪtɪsɪzəm/ *n* [c u] crítica *f*

criticize /'krɪtəsaɪz || 'krɪtɪsaɪz/ *vt* (censure) criticar*

critique /krɪ'tiːk/ *n* crítica *f*

critter /'krɪtər || 'krɪtə(r)/ *n* (AmE sl) bicho *m* (fam)

croak[1] /krəʊk/ *n* (of frog) croar *m*, canto *m*; (of raven) graznido *m*; (of person) voz *f* ronca, graznido *m*

croak[2] *vi*

A «*frog*» croar; «*raven*» graznar; «*person*» hablar con voz ronca

B (die) (sl) estirar la pata (fam)

■ **croak** *vt* (utter) decir* con voz ronca

Croat /'krəʊæt/ *n* croata *mf*

Croatia /krəʊ'eɪʃə/ *n* Croacia *f*

Croatian[1] /krəʊ'eɪʃən/ *adj* croata

Croatian[2] *n* croata *mf*

crochet[1] /krəʊ'ʃeɪ || 'krəʊʃeɪ/ *vt* tejer a crochet *or* a ganchillo

■ **crochet** *vi* hacer* crochet *or* ganchillo, tejer a crochet

crochet[2] *n* [u] crochet *m*, ganchillo *m*

crock /krɑːk || krɒk/ *n*

A (earthen vessel) vasija *f* de barro

B 1 (nonsense) (AmE sl): **ain't that a ~!** (set phrase) ¡qué estupidez! (fam) 2 (decrepit thing) antigualla *f* (fam), cacharro *m* (fam); (decrepit person) (esp BrE colloq) vejestorio *m* (fam)

crockery /'krɑːkəri || 'krɒkəri/ *n* [u] vajilla *f*, loza *f*

crocodile /'krɑːkədaɪl || 'krɒkədaɪl/ *n* cocodrilo *m*; (*before n*) ***(to shed o weep)*** ~ ***tears*** (derramar *or* llorar) lágrimas de cocodrilo

crocus /'krəʊkəs/ *n* (*pl* **-cuses**) azafrán *m* de primavera

croissant /krwɑː'sɑːn || 'krwʌsɒŋ/ *n* croissant *m*, medialuna *f* (Arg), cachito *m* (Ven), cuernito *m* (Méx)

crone /krəʊn/ *n* vieja *f* bruja

crony /'krəʊni/ *n* (*pl* **-nies**) (colloq) compinche *mf* (fam), amigote, -ta *m,f* (fam)

crook[1] /krʊk/ *n*

A (criminal) sinvergüenza *mf*, pillo, -lla *m,f* (fam)

B (of the arm) *parte interior del codo*

crook[2] *vt* ‹*finger/arm*› doblar

crooked /'krʊkəd || 'krʊkɪd/ *adj* 1 ‹*line/legs*› torcido, chueco (AmL); ‹*back*› encorvado; ‹*path*› sinuoso, lleno de curvas; ‹*smile*› torcido; **she gave me a ~ grin** me hizo una mueca 2 (dishonest) (colloq) ‹*person/deal*› deshonesto, chueco (Chi, Méx fam)

croon /kruːn/ *vi* cantar con voz suave

■ **croon** *vt* cantar suavemente

crooner /'kruːnər || 'kruːnə(r)/ *n* cantante melódico, -ca *m,f*

crop[1] /krɑːp || krɒp/ *n*

A 1 (quantity of produce) cosecha *f* 2 (type of produce) cultivo *m*; (*before n*) ~ **rotation** rotación *f* de cultivos 3 (batch) (colloq) tanda *f* (fam)

B (haircut) corte *m* de pelo muy corto

C (*riding* ~) fusta *f*, fuete *m* (AmL exc CS)

crop[2] **-pp-** *vt* (cut) ‹*hair*› cortar muy corto; **to ~ grass** pastar, pacer*

Phrasal verb

- **crop up** [v ▸ adv] (occur, present itself) (colloq) surgir*; **something must have ~ped up at work** debe haber surgido algún problema en el trabajo; **one phrase that ~s up again and again** una frase que se repite constantemente

cropper /'krɑːpər || 'krɒpə(r)/ *n*: ***to come a*** ~ (colloq) (fall) darse* *or* pegarse* un porrazo (fam); (suffer defeat, disaster) fracasar por completo

croquet /krəʊ'keɪ || 'krəʊkeɪ/ *n* [u] croquet *m*

croquette /krəʊ'ket/ *n* (*potato* ~) *rollito de puré de papa envuelto en pan rallado y frito*

cross[1] /krɔːs || krɒs/ *n*

A 1 (Relig) cruz *f*; **to make the sign of the ~** hacer* la señal de la cruz; (cross oneself) persignarse, santiguarse*, hacerse* la señal de la cruz; **we all have our ~ to bear** todos cargamos con *or* llevamos nuestra cruz 2 (mark, sign) cruz *f*

B (hybrid) (Biol) cruce *m*, cruza *f* (AmL); **a ~ between anger and disbelief** una mezcla de ira e incredulidad

C (Sport) 1 (in soccer) pase *m* cruzado 2 (in boxing) cruzado *m*, cross *m*

cross[2] *vt*

A (go across) ‹*road*› cruzar*; ‹*river/desert*› cruzar*, atravesar*; **it ~ed my mind that ...** se me ocurrió que ..., me pasó por la cabeza que ...

B ‹*arms/legs*› cruzar*; **we have a ~ed line** (Telec) se han cruzado las líneas, está ligado (Arg, Ven); ***to have one's lines o wires ~ed*** (colloq): **I think maybe we've got our wires ~ed** me parece que no hablamos de lo mismo

C (put line through): **to ~ the t** ponerle* el palito a la t

D (BrE Fin) ‹*cheque*› cruzar*

E ‹*plants/breeds*› cruzar*; **to ~ sth WITH sth** cruzar* algo CON algo

F (go against) ‹*person*› contrariar*; ‹*plans*› frustrar

G (Sport) ‹*ball*› cruzar*, tirar cruzado

■ **cross** *vi* 1 (walk across road) cruzar*; **to ~ over (the road)** cruzar* (la calle) 2 «*paths/roads*» cruzarse*; «*letters*» cruzarse*

■ *v refl* **to ~ oneself** persignarse, santiguarse*, hacerse* la señal de la cruz

Phrasal verbs

- **cross off** [v ▸ o ▸ adv, v ▸ adv ▸ o, v ▸ o ▸ prep ▸ o] ‹*name/item*› tachar; **she ~ed it off the list** lo tachó de la lista
- **cross out** [v ▸ o ▸ adv, v ▸ adv ▸ o] ‹*name/item*› tachar

cross[3] *adj* **-er, -est** (esp BrE) enojado (esp AmL), enfadado (esp Esp); **to get ~** enojarse (esp AmL), enfadarse (esp Esp); **it makes me ~** me da rabia; **to be ~ ABOUT sth** estar* enojado *or* (esp Esp) enfadado POR algo

cross: **~bar** *n* (on bicycle) barra *f*; (of goal) larguero *m*, travesaño *m*, horizontal *m* (Andes); (in pole vaulting, high jump) listón *m*; **~bones** *pl n*: *see* **skull**; **~bow** /'krɔːsbəʊ || 'krɒsbəʊ/ *n* ballesta *f*; **~bred** *adj* cruzado

crossbreed[1] /'krɔːsbriːd || 'krɒsbriːd/ *n* cruce *m*, cruza *f* (AmL)

crossbreed[2] *vt* (*past & past p* **-bred**) cruzar*

cross-Channel /'krɔːs'tʃænḷ || ˌkrɒs'tʃænḷ/ *adj* (*before n*) ‹*ferry/traffic*› que cruza el Canal de la Mancha

cross-check[1] /'krɔːs'tʃek || ˌkrɒs'tʃek/ *vt* ‹*facts/references*› verificar* (*consultando otras fuentes*); **to ~ sth AGAINST sth** cotejar algo CON algo

■ **cross-check** *vi* hacer* una comprobación *or* verificación

cross-check[2] *n* comprobación *f*, verificación *f*

cross-country[1] /'krɔːs'kʌntri || krɒs'kʌntri/ *adj* (across countryside) ‹*route/drive*› campo a través, a campo traviesa, a campo través; ‹*skiing*› de fondo; **~ race** cross *m*

cross-country[2] *adv* (across countryside) ‹*travel/drive*› campo a través, a campo traviesa, a campo través

cross: **~-cultural** /'krɔːs'kʌltʃərəl || ˌkrɒs'kʌltʃərəl/ *adj* intercultural, transcultural; **~-examination** /'krɔːsɪgˌzæmə'neɪʃən || ˌkrɒsɪgˌzæmɪ'neɪʃən/ *n* [c u] repreguntas *fpl*, contrainterrogación *f* (Chi); **~-examine** /'krɔːsɪg'zæmən || 'krɒsɪg'zæmɪn/ *vt* ‹*witness*› repreguntar; **~-eyed** /'krɔːs'aɪd || 'krɒsaɪd/ *adj* bizco; **to be/go**

~-eyed ser*/ponerse* bizco; **~fire** *n* [u] fuego *m* cruzado

crossing /'krɔːsɪŋ || 'krɒsɪŋ/ *n*
A (across sea) travesía *f*, cruce *m* (AmS)
B (for pedestrians) cruce *m* peatonal *or* de peatones

cross-legged /'krɔːs'legd|| ˌkrɒs'legd/ *adv* con las piernas cruzadas (*en el suelo*)

crossly /'krɔːsli || 'krɒsli/ *adv*: **no, she said ~** —no— dijo enojada (esp AmL) *or* (esp Esp) enfadada

cross: **~-purposes** /'krɔːs'pɜːrpəsəz/ *pl n*: **we're (talking) at ~-purposes** estamos hablando de cosas distintas; **~-question** /'krɔːs'kwestʃən/ *vt* interrogar*; **~-rate** /'krɔːsreɪt/ *n* tipo *m* de cambio cruzado; **~-reference** /'krɔːs'refrəns/ *n* remisión *f*; **~roads** *n* (*pl* **~roads**) cruce *m*, encrucijada *f* (liter); ***to be at a*** *o* ***the ~roads*** estar* en una encrucijada; **~ section**, (BrE) **~-section** /'krɔːs'sekʃən/ *n* [c u] (Biol, Eng) sección *f*, corte *m* transversal; **a ~ section of society** una muestra representativa de los distintos estratos sociales; **~town** /'krɔːs'taʊn/ *adj* (AmE) que cruza *or* atraviesa la ciudad; **~walk** *n* (AmE) cruce *m or* (Esp) paso *m* de peatones

crossways /'krɔːsweɪz || 'krɒsweɪz/ *adv*, **crosswise** /'krɔːswaɪz || 'krɒswaɪz/ *adv* transversalmente, en diagonal

crossword (puzzle) /'krɔːswɜːrd || 'krɒswɜːd/ *n* crucigrama *f*, palabras *fpl* cruzadas (CS)

crotch /krɑːtʃ || krɒtʃ/ *n* entrepierna *f*

crotchet /'krɑːtʃət || 'krɒtʃɪt/ *n*
A (idiosyncrasy) (AmE): **it/he has its/his little ~s!** ¡tiene sus mañas!
B (BrE Mus) negra *f*

crotchety /'krɑːtʃəti || 'krɒtʃɪti/ *adj* (colloq) cascarrabias *adj inv*, malhumorado

crouch /kraʊtʃ/ *vi* «*person*» agacharse, ponerse* en cuclillas; **to ~ down** agacharse

croup /kruːp/ *n* [u] (Med) crup *m*

croupier /'kruːpiər || 'kruːpiə(r)/ *n* crupier *mf*, croupier *mf*

crouton /'kruːtɑːn || 'kruːtɒn/ *n* crutón *m*, picatoste *m* (Esp)

crow¹ /krəʊ/ *n*
A (Zool) cuervo *m*; ***as the ~ flies*** en línea recta; ▸ **eat** *vt* **A**, **stone²**
B (cry — of rooster) cacareo *m*

crow² *vi* **1** «*cock*» cacarear **2** (exult) alardear, pavonearse; **to ~ ABOUT/OVER sth** alardear *or* jactarse DE algo
■ **crow** *vt* alardear

crowbar /'krəʊbɑːr || 'krəʊbɑː(r)/ *n* palanca *f*

crowd¹ /kraʊd/ *n* **1** (gathering of people) muchedumbre *f*, multitud *f*, gentío *m*; **the game attracted a good ~** el partido atrajo mucho público; **there was quite a ~** había mucha gente; **~s of shoppers** multitud de clientes **2** (masses, average folk) (pej): ***to go with*** *o* ***follow the ~*** seguir* (a) la manada, dejarse arrastrar *or* llevar por la corriente; ***to stand out from/rise above the ~*** destacar(se)* **3** (group, set) (colloq): **they are a nice ~** son gente simpática; **I thought she was one of Jane's ~** creí que era de la pandilla *or* del grupo de Jane **4** (large number) (colloq) (*no pl*) montón *m*

crowd² *vi* aglomerarse; **they ~ed around him** se aglomeraron a su alrededor; **they ~ed into the hall** entraron en tropel a la sala
■ **crowd** *vt* «*people*» ‹*hall/entrance*› llenar, abarrotar; **don't try to ~ everything onto one page** no trates de meter todo en una página; *see also* **crowded**

crowded /'kraʊdəd || 'kraʊdɪd/ *adj* ‹*street/room/bus*› abarrotado, atestado, lleno de gente; **the beach gets very ~** la playa se llena de gente

crowd-puller /'kraʊdˌpʊlər || 'kraʊdˌpʊlə(r)/ *n* (colloq) gran atracción *f* (*espectáculo o persona que atrae mucho público*)

crown¹ /kraʊn/ *n*
A **1** [c] (of monarch) corona *f* **2** (Govt, Law) **the C~** la corona
B [c] (top — of hill) cima *f*; (— of tree) copa *f*; (— of tooth) corona *f*; (— of head) coronilla *f*; (— of hat) copa *f*; (— of road) centro *m*
C [c] (Fin) corona *f*

crown² *vt*
A (make monarch) coronar
B **1** (surmount) coronar, rematar **2** (be culmination of) coronar; **to ~ it all, I lost my wallet** y para rematarla, perdí la billetera
C (Dent) ‹*tooth*› poner* una corona en
D (hit) (colloq) darle* un coscorrón a (fam)

crown court *n* (in UK) juzgado *m* (*que conoce de causas de derecho penal*)

crowning /'kraʊnɪŋ/ *adj* (*before n*) ‹*success/achievement*› supremo, mayor

crown: **~ jewels** *pl n* joyas *fpl* de la corona; **~ prince** *n* príncipe *m* heredero; **~ princess** *n* princesa *f* heredera

crow: **~'s feet** *pl n* patas *fpl* de gallo; **~'s nest** *n* cofa *f*

crucial /'kruːʃəl/ *adj* crucial, decisivo

crucifix /'kruːsəfɪks || 'kruːsɪfɪks/ *n* crucifijo *m*

crucifixion /'kruːsə'fɪkʃən || ˌkruːsɪ'fɪkʃən/ *n* [u c] crucifixión *f*

crucify /'kruːsəfaɪ || 'kruːsɪfaɪ/ (*past & past p* **-fied**) *vt* **1** (execute) crucificar* **2** (treat severely) (colloq): **they were crucified in the press** la prensa los destrozó; **the other team crucified us** los del otro equipo nos dieron una paliza (fam)

crud /krʌd/ *n* [u] (impurities) porquería *f*

crude¹ /kruːd/ *adj* **-der, -dest** **1** (vulgar) ordinario, grosero **2** (unsophisticated) rudimentario, burdo **3** (containing impurities) (*before n*) ‹*oil*› crudo

crude² *n* [u c] crudo *m*

crudely /'kruːdli/ *adv* **1** (vulgarly) groseramente; **to put it ~** hablando en plata (fam) **2** (roughly) de un modo rudimentario

cruel /'kruːəl/ *adj* **crueller, cruellest** cruel; ‹*winter*› crudo; ‹*blow*› duro; **to be ~ TO sb** ser* cruel CON algn; ***to be ~ to be kind*** hacer* sufrir a algn para hacerle un bien

cruelly /'kruːəli/ *adv* cruelmente

cruelty /'kruːəlti/ *n* [u c] (*pl* **-ties**) crueldad *f*; **~ TO sb** crueldad CON algn

cruet /'kruːət || 'kruːɪt/ *n* (Culin) vinagrera *f*, aceitera *f*, alcuza *f* (Chi)

cruise¹ /kruːz/ *vi*
A **1** (Naut) hacer* un crucero, navegar* **2** «*police car*» patrullar
B (travel at steady speed) «*plane*» volar*, desplazarse*; «*car*» ir* (*a una velocidad constante*); **cruising speed** velocidad *f* de crucero

cruise² *n* crucero *m*; **to go on a ~** hacer* un crucero

cruise missile *n* misil *m* de crucero

cruiser /'kruːzər || 'kruːzə(r)/ *n* **1** (warship) crucero *m* **2** (*cabin* **~**) lancha *f*, barco *m*

crumb /krʌm/ *n* [c] (of bread, cake) miga *f*; **a ~ of comfort** unas migajas algo de consuelo

crumble /'krʌmbəl/ *vi* «*cake/soil*» desmenuzarse*; «*wall*» desmoronarse; «*democracy/resolve*» desmoronarse, derrumbarse
■ **crumble** *vt* ‹*earth/cake*› desmenuzar*; ‹*bread*› desmigajar

crummy /'krʌmi/ *adj* **-mier, -miest** (colloq) malo, horrible

crumpet /'krʌmpət || 'krʌmpɪt/ *n* (Culin) *panecillo de levadura que se come tostado*

crumple /'krʌmpəl/ *vt* ‹*paper/clothes*› arrugar*; ‹*metal*› abollar; **she ~d the sheet of paper into a ball** hizo una bola estrujando la hoja de papel; **to ~ sth up** arrugar* algo
■ **crumple** *vi* (become creased) «*fabric/shirt*» arrugarse*

crunch¹ /krʌntʃ/ *vt* **1** (eat noisily) mascar*, ronchar, ronzar* **2** (crush) aplastar (*haciendo crujir*); **to ~ sth up** triturar algo
■ **crunch** *vi* **1** (eat noisily) mascar*, ronchar, ronzar* **2** (make grinding sound): **our footsteps ~ed on the gravel** nuestros pasos hacían crujir la grava

crunch² *n*
A (noise) crujido *m*

B (crisis): **when it comes/came to the ~** a la hora de la verdad

crunchy /'krʌntʃi/ *adj* **-chier, -chiest** crujiente

crusade[1] /kru:'seɪd/ *n* [1] (Hist) *also* **Crusade** cruzada *f* [2] (campaign) cruzada *f*, campaña *f*

crusade[2] *vi* **to ~ (against/for sth)** hacer* una cruzada *or* campaña (contra algo/a favor de algo)

crusader /kru:'seɪdər || kru:'seɪdə(r)/ *n* [1] (Hist) *also* **Crusader** cruzado *m* [2] (campaigner) defensor, -sora *m,f*

crush[1] /krʌʃ/ *vt*

A [1] (squash) ‹*box/car/person/fingers*› aplastar; ‹*garlic*› machacar*; ‹*grapes*› prensar, pisar; ‹*dress/suit*› arrugar* [2] **~ (up)** (pound, pulverize) triturar; **~ed ice** hielo *m* picado *or* (Méx) frappé

B (subdue) ‹*resistance/enemy*› aplastar

■ **crush** *vi* «*fabric*» arrugarse*

crush[2] *n*

A (crowd) (*no pl*) aglomeración *f*; **three people were injured in the ~** tres personas resultaron heridas en el tumulto

B [c] (infatuation) (colloq) enamoramiento *m*; **to have a ~ on sb** estar* chiflado por algn (fam)

C [u c] (drink) (BrE): **orange ~** naranjada *f*; **lemon ~** limonada *f*

crush barrier *n* valla *f* de protección *or* de contención

crushing /'krʌʃɪŋ/ *adj* ‹*defeat*› aplastante; ‹*reply/contempt*› apabullante

crust /krʌst/ *n* [1] (on bread) corteza *f*; **a ~ of bread** un mendrugo; ***to earn a*** *o* ***one's ~*** (colloq) ganarse el pan *or* (fam) los garbanzos [2] (on pie) tapa *f* de masa [3] (thin outer layer) costra *f*, corteza *f*; **the earth's ~** la corteza terrestre

crustacean /krʌ'steɪʃən/ *n* crustáceo *m*

crusty /'krʌsti/ *adj* **-tier, -tiest** [1] (crispy) ‹*bread*› crujiente [2] (irascible) malhumorado

crutch /krʌtʃ/ *n*

A [1] (walking aid) muleta *f*; **to be/walk on ~es** andar* con muletas [2] (support) muleta *f*, apoyo *m*

B (BrE) ▸**crotch**

crux /krʌks/ *n* (*no pl*) quid *m*; **the ~ of the matter** el quid de la cuestión

cry[1] /kraɪ/ *n* (*pl* **cries**)

A [c] [1] (exclamation) grito *m*; **to give/let out a ~** dar*/soltar* un grito; **she heard cries for help** oyó gritos de socorro; ***to be a far ~ from sth*** ser* muy distinto de *or* a algo [2] (of street vendor) pregón *m* [3] (*no pl*) (call — of seagull) chillido *m*

B (weep) (colloq) (*no pl*) llanto *m*; **to have a ~** llorar

C (slogan) lema *m*, slogan *m*

cry[2] **cries, crying, cried** *vi*

A (weep) llorar

B (call) «*bird*» chillar; «*person*» gritar; ***for ~ing out loud!*** (colloq) ¡por el amor de Dios!

■ **cry** *vt*

A (weep) llorar; **he cried himself to sleep** lloró hasta quedarse dormido

B (call) gritar

Phrasal verbs

- **cry off** [v ▸ adv] (esp BrE) echarse atrás; **several of the guests cried off at the last minute** a último momento varios de los invitados dijeron que no podían venir
- **cry out** [v ▸ adv] [1] (call out) gritar [2] (need) **to ~ out FOR sth** pedir* algo a gritos

crybaby /'kraɪ,beɪbi/ *n* (*pl* **-babies**) (colloq) llorón, -rona *m,f* (fam), lloretas *mf* (Col fam), chillón, -llona *m,f* (Méx)

crying /'kraɪɪŋ/ *adj* (*before n*) ‹*need/urgency*› apremiante; **it's a ~ shame!** es una verdadera pena *or* lástima

cryogenic /,kraɪə'dʒenɪk/ *adj* criogenético

cryosurgery /,kraɪəʊ'sɜ:rdʒəri || ,kraɪəʊ'sɜ:dʒəri/ *n* [u] criocirugía *f*

crypt /krɪpt/ *n* cripta *f*

cryptic /'krɪptɪk/ *adj* ‹*remark/reference*› enigmático, críptico; ‹*crossword*› críptico

crystal[1] /'krɪstl/ *n*

A [c] (Chem) cristal *m*

B [u] **~ (glass)** cristal *m*

crystal[2] *adj* (liter) (*before n*) cristalino

crystal: **~ ball** *n* bola *f* de cristal; **~-clear** /'krɪstḷ'klɪr || ,krɪstḷ'klɪə(r)/ *adj* ‹*water*› (liter) cristalino; ‹*sound/image*› nítido, claro; **it is ~-clear that ...** está clarísimo que ..., está más claro que el agua que ...

crystallize /'krɪstəlaɪz/ *vi* cristalizarse*

■ **crystallize** *vt* [1] (Chem, Geol) cristalizar* [2] ‹*idea/plan*› materializar* [3] (Culin) ‹*fruit*› confitar, escarchar, abrillantar (RPl), cristalizar* (Méx)

CS gas /'si:'es/ *n* [u] gas *m* lacrimógeno

CST (in US) = **Central Standard Time**

CT = **Connecticut**

cu = **cubic**

cub /kʌb/ *n* [1] (young animal) cachorro *m* [2] **Cub (Scout)** lobato *m*

Cuba /'kju:bə/ *n* Cuba *f*

Cuban[1] /'kju:bən/ *adj* cubano

Cuban[2] *n* cubano, -na *m,f*

cubbyhole /'kʌbihəʊl/ *n* (for storage) cuchitril *m*

cube[1] /kju:b/ *n* (solid, shape) cubo *m*; (of meat, cheese) dado *m*, cubito *m*; (of sugar) terrón *m*

cube[2] *vt*

A (cut into cubes) cortar en dados *or* cubitos

B (Math) elevar al cubo, cubicar*

cube root *n* raíz *f* cúbica

cubic /'kju:bɪk/ *adj* (of measure, shape) cúbico; **~ capacity** volumen *m*; (of engine) cilindrada *f*, cubicaje *m*

cubicle /'kju:bɪkəl/ *n* (in dormitory, toilets) cubículo *m*; (booth) cabina *f*; (in store) probador *m*

cubism, Cubism /'kju:bɪzəm/ *n* [u] cubismo *m*

cubist, Cubist /'kju:bəst || 'kju:bɪst/ *adj* cubista

cuckold[1] /'kʌkəʊld/ *n* cornudo *m*

cuckold[2] *vt* ponerle* los cuernos a

cuckoo[1] /'ku:ku: || 'kʊku:/ *n* (*pl* **cuckoos**) [1] (bird) cuco *m*, cucú *m*, cuclillo *m*; ***a ~ in the nest*** un usurpador [2] (call) cucú *m*

cuckoo[2] *adj* (colloq) chiflado (fam), chalado (fam)

cuckoo clock *n* reloj *m* de cuco *or* cucú

cucumber /'kju:kʌmbər || 'kju:kʌmbə(r)/ *n* [c u] pepino *m*; ***(as) cool as a ~*** tan fresco *or* pancho (fam)

cud /kʌd/ *n* [u]: ***to chew the ~*** (lit) «*cow*» rumiar; «*person*» rumiar el asunto

cuddle[1] /'kʌdḷ/ *vt* abrazar*

■ **cuddle** *vi* abrazarse*; **to ~ up TO sb** acurrucarse* CONTRA algn

cuddle[2] *n* abrazo *m*

cuddly /'kʌdli/ *adj* **-dlier, -dliest** ‹*baby/person*› adorable; **~ toy** muñeco *m* de peluche

cudgel /'kʌdʒəl/ *n* garrote *m*, porra *f*

cue[1] /kju:/ *n*

A (Mus) entrada *f*; (Theat) pie *m*; **to miss one's ~** no salir* a escena en el momento debido; **right on ~** en el momento justo; ***to take one's ~ from sb*** seguir* el ejemplo de algn

B (in snooker, billiards) taco *m*; (*before n*) **~ ball** bola *f* blanca

cue[2] **cues, cuing, cued** *vt* ‹*actor*› darle* el pie a; ‹*musician*› darle* la entrada a

cuff[1] /kʌf/ *n*

A [1] (of sleeve) puño *m*; (of pants) (AmE) vuelta *f or* (Chi) bastilla *f or* (Méx) valenciana *f or* (RPl) botamanga *f* [2] (*in phrases*) **off the cuff** (*as adv*): **he spoke off the ~** habló improvisando; (*as adj*): **an off-the-~ speech** un discurso improvisado; **on the cuff** (AmE): **he let me have the beer on the ~** me fió la cerveza [3] **cuffs** *pl* (handcuffs) (colloq) esposas *fpl*, pulseras *fpl* (arg)

B (blow — on face) cachete *m*, bofetón *m*, cachetada *f* (AmL); (— on head) coscorrón *m*; **a ~ on** *o* (BrE) **round the ear** un bofetón

cuff[2] *vt* (strike) darle* un cachete (*or* coscorrón *etc*) a

cuff link *n* gemelo *m or* (Col) mancorna *f or* (Chi) collera *f or* (Méx) mancuernilla *or* mancuerna *f*

cuisine /kwɪ'zi:n/ *n* [u c] cocina *f*

cul-de-sac /'kʌldɪsæk/ *n* calle *f* sin salida *or* (Col) ciega *or* (RPl) cortada

culinary /'kʌləneri || 'kʌlɪnəri/ *adj* culinario

cull /kʌl/ *vt* [1] ‹*seals/deer*› *sacrificar de forma selectiva* [2] ‹*facts/information*› seleccionar

culminate /'kʌlməneɪt || 'kʌlmɪneɪt/ *vi* (reach peak) **to ~ IN sth** culminar EN algo

C

C

■ **culminate** *vt* (AmE) ser* la culminación de

culmination /ˈkʌlməˈneɪʃən || ˌkʌlmɪˈneɪʃən/ *n* [u] (of events, efforts) culminación *f*, punto *m* culminante

culottes /ˈkuːlɑːts || ˈkjuːlɒts/ *pl n* falda *f* pantalón, pollera *f* pantalón (CS, Per)

culpable /ˈkʌlpəbəl/ *adj* (frml) ‹*person*› culpable; ‹*action*› culposo

culprit /ˈkʌlprət || ˈkʌlprɪt/ *n* culpable *mf*

cult /kʌlt/ *n* 1 (belief, worship) culto *m* 2 (sect) secta *f* 3 (craze) culto *m*; **personality ~** el culto a la personalidad; (*before n*) **~ figure** ídolo *m*; **~ movie** película *f* de culto

cultivate /ˈkʌltəveɪt / *vt* cultivar; **she ~d an air of indifference** adoptaba un estudiado aire de indiferencia

cultivated /ˈkʌltəveɪtəd || ˈkʌltɪveɪtɪd/ *adj* cultivado

cultivation /ˌkʌltəˈveɪʃən || ˌkʌltɪˈveɪʃən/ *n* [u] 1 (Agr, Hort) cultivo *m*; **under ~** en cultivo 2 (of friendship) cultivo *m* 3 (refinement) refinamiento *m*

cultural /ˈkʌltʃərəl/ *adj* cultural

culture¹ /ˈkʌltʃər || ˈkʌltʃə(r)/ *n*

A [c u] (civilization) cultura *f*; (*before n*) **~ shock** choque *m* cultural *or* de culturas

B [u] (intellectual activity) cultura *f*

C [c u] (Agr, Biol) cultivo *m*

culture² *vt* cultivar

cultured /ˈkʌltʃərd || ˈkʌltʃəd/ *adj* 1 ‹*person/mind*› culto; ‹*tastes*› refinado, propio de una persona culta 2 (Agr, Biol) de cultivo; **~ pearls** perlas *fpl* cultivadas *or* de cultivo

culture vulture *n* (colloq & hum) devorador, -dora *m,f* de cultura

cum /kʌm/ *prep*: **a study-~-library** un estudio-biblioteca; **my secretary-~-assistant** mi secretaria y ayudante a la vez

cumbersome /ˈkʌmbərsəm || ˈkʌmbəsəm/ *adj* ‹*movements/gait*› pesado y torpe

cumin /ˈkʌmən || ˈkʌmɪn/ *n* [u] comino *m*

cum laude /kʊmˈlaʊdə / *adv* (AmE) cum laude

cummerbund /ˈkʌmərbʌnd / *n* faja *f* (*de smoking*)

cumulative /ˈkjuːmjələtɪv / *adj* acumulativo

cumulus /ˈkjuːmjələs / *n* (*pl* **-li** /-laɪ/) cúmulo *m*

cunning¹ /ˈkʌnɪŋ/ *adj*

A 1 (clever, sly) astuto; ‹*smile*› malicioso 2 (ingenious) ‹*device*› ingenioso

B (cute, attractive) (AmE): **a ~ guy** un tipo guapo *or* (esp AmL) buen mozo

cunning² *n* [u] astucia *f*

cunt /kʌnt/ *n* (vulg) coño *m* (vulg), concha *f* (AmS vulg), pucha *f* (Méx vulg)

cup¹ /kʌp/ *n*

A [c] 1 (container, contents, cupful) taza *f*; **paper ~** vaso *m* de papel; ***to be sb's ~ of tea***: **he isn't my ~ of tea** no es santo de mi devoción; **this might be more your ~ of tea** quizás esto te guste más *or* esto sea más de tu gusto 2 (goblet) copa *f*

B [c] (trophy) copa *f*; (*before n*): **the ~ final** la final de copa

cup² *vt* **-pp-**: **to ~ one's hands** (to drink) ahuecar* las manos; (to shout) hacer* bocina (con las manos)

cupboard /ˈkʌbərd || ˈkʌbəd/ *n* 1 (cabinet) armario *m*; (in dining-room) aparador *m* 2 (full-length, built-in) (BrE) armario *m or* (AmL exc RPl) clóset *m or* (RPl) placard *m*

cupboard love *n* [u] (BrE) cariño *m* interesado

cupcake /ˈkʌpkeɪk/ *n* ≈ magdalena *f*

cupful /ˈkʌpfʊl/ *n* (*pl* **cupfuls** *or* **cupsful** /ˈkʌpsfʊl/) taza *f*

Cupid /ˈkjuːpəd || ˈkjuːpɪd/ *n* Cupido

cuppa /ˈkʌpə/ *n* (BrE colloq) (taza *f* de) té *m*

cur /kɜːr || kɜː(r)/ *n* (liter & dated) 1 (dog) (pej) perro *m* callejero 2 (despicable man) bellaco *m*

curable /ˈkjʊrəbəl / *adj* curable, que tiene cura

curate /ˈkjʊrət || ˈkjʊərət/ *n* coadjutor *m*

curator /kjʊˈreɪtər || kjʊəˈreɪtə(r)/ *n* (of museum, art gallery) conservador, -dora *m,f*; (of exhibition) comisario, -ria *m,f*

curb¹ /kɜːrb || kɜːb/ *n*

A (restraint) freno *m*; **to put a ~ on sth** poner* freno *or* coto a algo

B **curb**, (BrE) **kerb** (in street) bordillo *m* (de la acera), borde *m* de la banqueta (Méx), cuneta *f* (Chi), sardinel *m* (Col), cordón *m* de la vereda (RPl)

curb² *vt* (control) ‹*anger*› dominar, refrenar; ‹*spending/prices*› poner* freno a, frenar; ❸ **curb your dog** (AmE) controle a su perro

curd /kɜːrd || kɜːd/ *n* [u] 1 (from milk) (*often pl*) cuajada *f* 2 (paste) (esp BrE): **bean ~** tofu *m*, queso *m* de soya (AmL) *or* (Esp) soja ; **lemon ~** crema *f* de limón

curdle /ˈkɜːrdl || ˈkɜːdl/ *vi* 1 (go bad, separate) «*milk/sauce*» cortarse 2 (form curds) «*milk*» cuajarse

■ **curdle** *vt* 1 (cause to go bad, separate) cortar 2 (cause to form curds) cuajar

cure¹ /kjʊr || ˈkjʊə(r)/ *vt*

A 1 (Med) curar; **to ~ sb OF sth** ‹*of illness/shyness*› curar a algn DE algo; ‹*of habit/idea*› quitarle algo A algn 2 ‹*problem*› remediar, poner* remedio a

B 1 ‹*meat*› curar 2 ‹*rubber*› vulcanizar*

cure² *n* 1 (remedy — for disease) cura *f*; (— for problem) remedio *m* 2 (return to health) restablecimiento *m*, curación *f*

cure-all /ˈkjʊrɔːl || ˈkjʊərɔːl/ *n* panacea *f*

curfew /ˈkɜːrfjuː || ˈkɜːfjuː/ *n* toque *m* de queda

curio /ˈkjʊriəʊ || ˈkjʊəriəʊ/ *n* (*pl* **-os**) curiosidad *f*

curiosity /ˈkjʊriˈɑːsəti || ˌkjʊəriˈɒsəti/ *n* (*pl* **-ties**)

A [u] (inquisitive interest) curiosidad *f*; ***~ killed the cat*** por querer saber, la zorra perdió la cola

B [c] (novelty) curiosidad *f*; (*before n*) **~ value** valor *m* de pieza rara

curious /ˈkjʊriəs || ˈkjʊəriəs/ *adj* 1 (inquisitive) curioso; **why do you ask? — oh, I'm just ~** ¿por qué lo preguntas? — sólo por curiosidad; **to be ~ to + INF** tener* curiosidad POR + INF 2 (strange) curioso, extraño

curiously /ˈkjʊriəsli || ˈkjʊəriəsli/ *adv* 1 (with curiosity) con curiosidad 2 (strangely) curiosamente; **~ enough, ...** (*indep*) curiosamente, ..., aunque parezca mentira, ...

curl¹ /kɜːrl || kɜːl/ *n* 1 (of hair) rizo *m*, rulo *m* (CS), chino *m* (Méx); (ringlet) bucle *m*, tirabuzón *m* 2 (of smoke) voluta *f*

curl² *vt* 1 ‹*hair*› rizar*, encrespar (CS), enchinar (Méx), enrular (RPl) 2 (twist, bend): **to ~ one's lip** hacer* una mueca, torcer* el gesto; **the snake ~ed itself around the branch** la serpiente se enroscó en la rama

■ **curl** *vi* 1 «*hair*» rizarse*, ensortijarse (liter), encresparse (CS), enchinarse (Méx), enrularse (RPl) 2 «*paper/leaf/edge*» ondularse, rizarse* 3 «*smoke*» formar *or* hacer* volutas, subir en espirales

Phrasal verb

• **curl up** [v ▸ adv] (twist) «*leaf/pages*» ondularse, rizarse*; **the cat ~ed up in front of the fire** el gato se hizo un ovillo frente a la chimenea; **to ~ up in a chair** acurrucarse* en un sillón; **I just wanted to ~ up and die** (colloq) quería que la tierra me tragara

curler /ˈkɜːrlər || ˈkɜːlə(r)/ *n* (for hair) rulo *m*, rulero *m* (RPl), marrón *m* (Col), tubo *m* (Chi, Méx)

curling /ˈkɜːrlɪŋ || ˈkɜːlɪŋ/ *n* [u] (Sport) curling *m*

curling irons, **curling tongs** *pl n* tenacillas *fpl* (*para rizar el pelo*)

curly /ˈkɜːrli || ˈkɜːli/ *adj* **-lier, -liest** ‹*hair*› rizado, ensortijado (liter), crespo (CS), chino (Méx); ‹*tail*› enroscado

currant /ˈkɜːrənt || ˈkʌrənt/ *n* pasa *f* de Corinto

currency /ˈkɜːrənsi || ˈkʌrənsi/ *n* (*pl* **-cies**)

A (Fin) [c u] (type of money) moneda *f*; **foreign ~** moneda *f* extranjera, divisas *fpl*

B (prevalence) difusión *f*; **to gain ~** «*view/fashion*» extenderse*, ganar adeptos

current¹ /ˈkɜːrənt || ˈkʌrənt/ *adj*

A (*before n*) 1 (existing) ‹*situation/prices*› actual; ‹*year*› en curso 2 (most recent) ‹*issue*› último

B 1 (valid) ‹*license/membership*› vigente 2 (prevailing) ‹*opinion/practice*› corriente, común, habitual

current² *n*

A [c] 1 (flow of water, air) corriente *f*; **against the ~** contra la corriente; **with the ~** en el sentido de la corriente 2 (general trend) corriente *f*; **to go with the ~** dejarse llevar por la corriente

B [c u] (Elec) corriente *f*; **to run off household ~** (AmE) funcionar con electricidad

current: **~ account** *n* (BrE) cuenta *f* corriente; **~ affairs** *pl n* sucesos *mpl* de actualidad; **~ events**

pl n sucesos *mpl or* acontecimientos *mpl* de actualidad

currently /'kɜːrəntli || 'kʌrəntli/ *adv* [1] (at present) actualmente [2] (commonly) comúnmente

curriculum /kə'rɪkjələm || kə'rɪkjʊləm/ *n* (*pl* **-lums** *or* **-la** /-lə/) [1] (range of courses) plan *m* de estudios [2] (for single course) programa *m* (de estudio), currículo *m*

curriculum vitae /'viːtaɪ/ *n* (*pl* **curricula vitae**) (BrE) currículum *m* (vitae), historial *m* personal

curry¹ /'kɜːri || 'kʌri/ *n* (*pl* **curries**) [1] [c u] (dish) curry *m* [2] [u] ~ **(powder)** curry *m*

curry² *vt* **-ries, -rying, -ried**
A (Culin) preparar al curry; **curried chicken** pollo *m* al curry
B ▸**favor¹ A1**

curse¹ /kɜːrs || kɜːs/ *n* [1] (evil spell) maldición *f*; **to put a ~ on sb** echarle una maldición a algn [2] (oath) maldición *f*, palabrota *f* [3] (burden) maldición *f*; **the ~ of unemployment** la lacra del desempleo [4] (menstruation) (colloq & euph) **the ~** la regla

curse² *vt* [1] (put spell on) maldecir* [2] (express annoyance at) maldecir*; **~ her!** ¡maldita sea! [3] (swear at) insultar [4] (afflict) (*usu pass*) **to be ~d WITH sth** estar* aquejado DE algo, padecer* DE algo
■ **curse** *vi* maldecir*, soltar* palabrotas

cursor /'kɜːrsər || 'kɜːsə(r)/ *n* cursor *m*

cursory /'kɜːrsəri || 'kɜːsəri/ *adj* ‹*glance*› rápido; ‹*description*› somero; ‹*interest*› superficial

curt /kɜːrt || kɜːt/ *adj* cortante, seco

curtail /kɜːr'teɪl || kɜː'teɪl/ *vt* [1] (cut short) abreviar, acortar [2] (restrict) restringir*; (reduce) reducir*

curtailment /kɜːr'teɪlmənt || kɜː'teɪlmənt/ *n* [u] [1] (cutting short) acortamiento *m* [2] (of freedom) restricción *f*; (of spending) reducción *f*

curtain /'kɜːrtn̩ || 'kɜːtn̩/ *n* [1] (at window) cortina *f*; **a pair of ~s** unas cortinas [2] (Theat) telón *m*; ***it's ~s for you*** (colloq) estás acabado [3] (of rain) cortina *f*; (of fog) manto *m*; (of mystery, secrecy) halo *m*, velo *m*

Phrasal verb
• **curtain off** [v ▸ o ▸ adv, v ▸ adv ▸ o] separar con una cortina

curtain call *n* salida *f* a escena *or* al escenario (*para saludar*), telón *m* (Méx)

curtly /'kɜːrtli || 'kɜːtli/ *adv* de manera cortante

curtsey¹ *n* (*pl* **-seys**) (esp BrE) ▸**curtsy¹**

curtsey² *vi* **-seys, -seying, -seyed** (BrE) ▸**curtsy²**

curtsy¹ /'kɜːrtsi || 'kɜːtsi/ *n* (*pl* **-sies**) reverencia *f* (*que hacen las mujeres agachándose*)

curtsy² *vi* **-sies, -sying, -sied** hacer* una reverencia

curvaceous /kɜːr'veɪʃəs / *adj* curvilíneo, escultural

curvature /'kɜːrvətʃʊr || 'kɜːvətʃə(r)/ *n* [u] curvatura *f*; **~ of the spine** desviación *f* de columna

curve¹ /kɜːrv || kɜːv/ *n* curva *f*; ***to throw sb a ~*** (AmE) agarrar *or* (esp Esp) coger* a algn desprevenido

curve² *vi* [1] «*surface*» estar* curvado *or* combado [2] «*river/ball*» describir* una curva; **the path ~s down to the sea** el sendero tuerce y baja hacia el mar

curved /kɜːrvd || kɜːvd/ *adj* curvo

curvy /'kɜːrvi || 'kɜːvi/ *adj* **-vier, -viest** ‹*line*› curvo; ‹*figure*› curvilíneo

cushion¹ /'kʊʃən/ *n* [1] (on chair) almohadón *m*, cojín *m*; (*before n*) **~ cover** funda *f* de almohadón *or* cojín [2] (padding) colchón *m*

cushion² *vt* [1] ‹*blow*› amortiguar* [2] (protect) **to ~ sth/sb AGAINST sth** proteger* algo/a algn CONTRA algo

cushy /'kʊʃi/ *adj* **cushier, cushiest** (colloq) cómodo, fácil

cusp /kʌsp/ *n*: ***to be on the ~ of sth*** estar* a las puertas *or* al borde de algo

cuspidor /'kʌspədɔːr || 'kʌspɪdɔː(r)/ *n* (AmE) escupidera *f*

cuss¹ /kʌs/ *n* (esp AmE colloq) [1] (curse) palabrota *f*, mala palabra *f* (esp AmL), taco *m* (Esp fam); ***not to give*** *o* ***care a ~***: **I don't give** *o* **care a ~** me importa un comino (fam) [2] (person) tipo, -pa *m,f* (fam)

cuss² (esp AmE colloq) *vt*: **she ~ed us for being late** nos puso de vuelta y media por llegar tarde (fam)
■ **cuss** *vi* [1] (complain) despotricar* [2] (swear) maldecir*, soltar* palabrotas

cuss word *n* (AmE colloq) palabrota *f*, mala palabra *f* (esp AmL), taco *m* (Esp fam)

custard /'kʌstərd || 'kʌstəd/ *n* [1] (sauce) (BrE) crema *f*; (cold, set) ≈ natillas *fpl* [2] (*egg ~*) *especie de flan*; (*before n*) **~ tart** tarta *f* de crema

custodian /kʌ'stəʊdiən/ *n* conservador, -dora *m,f*

custody /'kʌstədi/ *n* [u]
A (detention): **to be in (police) ~** estar* detenido; **to take sb into ~** detener* a algn
B [1] (of child) custodia *f* [2] (safekeeping) (frml) custodia *f*, cuidado *m*

custom¹ /'kʌstəm/ *n*
A [c u] (convention, tradition, habit) costumbre *f*; **he broke with ~** rompió con la tradición
B [u] (patronage) (esp BrE): **if they value our ~** si no nos quieren perder como clientes; **I'll take my ~ elsewhere** dejaré de ser su cliente
C **customs** *pl* [1] (organization, place) aduana *f*; **to go through ~s** pasar por la aduana; (*before n*) **~s officer** *o* **official** agente *mf or* oficial *mf* de aduanas [2] (tax) derechos *mpl* arancelarios *or* de aduana

custom² *adj* (*before n*) (esp AmE) ‹*tailor*› que trabaja por encargo; ‹*suit*› a (la) medida; ‹*car*› (hecho) de encargo

customarily /'kʌstə'merəli / *adv* habitualmente

customary /'kʌstəməri/ *adj* [1] (traditional) tradicional; **it is ~ to + INF** es la costumbre + INF [2] (habitual) habitual, acostumbrado, de costumbre

custom-built /'kʌstəm'bɪlt/ *adj* hecho de encargo

customer /'kʌstəmər || 'kʌstəmə(r)/ *n* [1] (client) cliente, -ta *m,f*; (*before n*) ⓢ **customer services** información y reclamaciones [2] (fellow) (colloq) tipo, -pa *m,f* (fam), tío, -tia *m,f* (Esp fam)

customize /'kʌstəmaɪz/ *vt* ‹*car/program*› hacer* (*or* adaptar *etc*) según los requisitos del cliente

custom-made /'kʌstəm'meɪd/ *adj* ‹*furnishings/furniture*› hecho de encargo; ‹*suit/shoes*› a la medida

cut¹ /kʌt/ *n*
A [1] (wound) tajo *m*, corte *m* [2] (incision) corte *m*
B [1] (reduction): **a wage ~** un recorte salarial; **to make ~s in essential services** hacer* recortes en los servicios esenciales; **to take a ~ in salary** aceptar un sueldo más bajo [2] (in text, film) corte *m* [3] (*power ~*) apagón *m*
C [1] (*hair~*) corte *m* de pelo [2] (of suit) corte *m*; ***to be a ~ above sb/sth*** (colloq): **he thinks himself a ~ above the rest** se cree superior a los demás; **this hotel is a ~ above the Ambassador** este hotel es de mayor categoría que el Ambassador
D (of meat — type) corte *m*; (— piece) trozo *m*
E (share) (colloq) tajada *f* (fam), parte *f*
F (blow — with knife) cuchillada *f*; **~ *and thrust*: the ~ and thrust of politics** el toma y daca de la vida política

cut² (*pres p* **cutting**; *past & past p* **cut**) *vt*
A ‹*wood/paper/wire/rope*› cortar; **to ~ sth/sb loose** soltar* algo/a algn; **~ the top off it** córtale la parte de arriba; **they ~ a path through the undergrowth** abrieron un camino a través de la maleza; ***to ~ it fine*** (colloq) calcular muy justo, dejar poco margen; **to ~ sth in half** cortar algo por la mitad; **I ~ my finger** me corté el dedo; *see also* **short² A**
B [1] (trim) ‹*hair/nails*› cortar; ‹*grass/corn*› cortar, segar*; **to get one's hair ~** cortarse el pelo [2] (shape) ‹*glass/stone*› tallar; ‹*key*› hacer*
C (excavate) **to ~ sth (INTO sth)**: **a tunnel ~ into the mountain** un túnel excavado en la montaña
D (reduce) ‹*level/number*› reducir*; ‹*budget*› recortar; ‹*price/rate*› rebajar, reducir*; ‹*service/workforce*› hacer* recortes en
E [1] (shorten) ‹*text*› acortar [2] (remove) ‹*scene*› cortar [3] ‹*film*› (edit) editar; «*censors*» hacer* cortes en
F (in cards) ‹*deck*› cortar
G (colloq) (ignore): ***to ~ sb dead*** dejar a algn con el saludo en la boca
H (colloq) [1] (cease): **~ the sob story!** ¡deja ya de dar pena!; **~ the wisecracks!** ¡basta ya de bromas! [2] (switch off) ‹*engine/lights*› apagar*
■ **cut** *vi*
A [1] «*knife/scissors*» cortar; **to ~ INTO sth**: **the rope ~ into her wrists** la cuerda le estaba cortando *or* lastimando las muñecas; ***to ~ loose*** (colloq) (break free) romper* las ataduras; (lose restraint) (esp AmE): **he ~ loose with a string of**

C

insults soltó una sarta de insultos 2 «*words*» herir*; **her remarks ~ deep** sus palabras lo (*or* la *etc*) hirieron en lo más vivo 3 (be cuttable): **it ~s easily** se corta fácilmente
B (Cin, Rad): **~!** ¡corte(n)!
C (in cards) cortar

(Phrasal verbs)

• **cut across** [v ▸ prep ▸ o] 1 (take shortcut across) cortar por, tomar un atajo a través de 2 (cross boundaries of) trascender*

• **cut back**
A [v ▸ o ▸ adv, v ▸ adv ▸ o] 1 (prune) ‹*hedge*› podar, recortar 2 (reduce) ‹*spending*› recortar, reducir*
B [v ▸ adv] (make reductions) hacer* economías, constreñirse*; **to ~ back ON sth** reducir* algo

• **cut down**
A [v ▸ o ▸ adv, v ▸ adv ▸ o] 1 (fell) ‹*tree*› cortar, talar 2 (kill) matar; **he was ~ down in his prime** (liter) su vida fue segada en flor (liter) 3 (reduce) ‹*expenditure*› reducir*, recortar; ‹*consumption*› reducir*, disminuir*
B [v ▸ adv] (make reductions): **cigarette? — no, thanks, I'm trying to ~ down** ¿un cigarrillo? — no, gracias, estoy tratando de fumar menos; **to ~ down ON sth: you should ~ down on carbohydrates** debería reducir el consumo de hidratos de carbono

• **cut in** [v ▸ adv] 1 (interrupt) interrumpir 2 (Auto) atravesarse*

• **cut off**
A [v ▸ o ▸ adv, v ▸ adv ▸ o] (sever) ‹*branch/limb*› cortar
B [v ▸ o ▸ adv, v ▸ adv ▸ o] (interrupt, block) ‹*supply/route*› cortar
C [v ▸ o ▸ adv] 1 (separate, isolate) aislar*; **to feel ~ off** sentirse* aislado; **the town was ~ off** la ciudad quedó sin comunicaciones 2 (on telephone): **we were ~ off** se cortó la comunicación

• **cut out**
A [v ▸ o ▸ adv, v ▸ adv ▸ o] ‹*article/photograph*› recortar
B [v ▸ o ▸ adv, v ▸ adv ▸ o] 1 ‹*dress/cookies*› cortar 2 (exclude) ‹*noise/carbohydrates*› eliminar, suprimir; **he ~ me out of his will** me excluyó de su testamento; **~ it out!** (colloq) ¡basta ya!; ▸**work¹ A**
C (suit): **to be ~ out FOR sth** estar* hecho para algo; **I'm not ~ out to be a teacher** no estoy hecho para la enseñanza
D [v ▸ adv] 1 (stop working) «*engine*» pararse, calarse 2 (switch off) apagarse*

• **cut through** [v ▸ prep ▸ o] 1 (overcome) abrirse* camino por entre 2 (take shortcut) cortar camino por, atajar por

• **cut up**
A [v ▸ o ▸ adv, v ▸ adv ▸ o] ‹*vegetables/wood*› cortar en pedazos
B (upset) (colloq): **to be ~ up about sth** estar* disgustado por algo

cut³ *adj* (*before n*) ‹*flowers*› cortado; ‹*glass*› tallado

cut: ~-and-dried /ˈkʌtn̩ˈdraɪd/ *adj* (*pred* **~ and dried**) ‹*arrangements*› preparado de antemano; ‹*opinions*› preconcebido; **her election isn't ~ and dried** no se puede dar por sentado que vaya a salir elegida; **~-and-paste** /ˌkʌtən(d)ˈpeɪst/ *vt* cortar y pegar; **~back** *n* (reduction) recorte *m*, reducción *f*

cute /kjuːt/ *adj* **cuter, cutest** 1 (sweet) ‹*baby/face*› mono (fam), cuco (fam), rico (CS fam) 2 (attractive) (AmE) guapo 3 (clever) (AmE) ‹*person*› listo, vivo (AmL fam) 4 (contrived) (AmE) afectado, efectista

cutesy /ˈkjuːtsi/ *adj* **-sier, -siest** (AmE) cursi

cut-glass /ˈkʌtˈglæs || kʌtˈglɑːs/ *adj* de cristal tallado

cuticle /ˈkjuːtɪkəl/ *n* cutícula *f*

cutie /ˈkjuːti/ *n* (esp AmE colloq) (woman) bombón *m* (fam), churro *m* (AmS fam); **she's/he's a little ~** (child) es una monada (fam)

cutlery /ˈkʌtləri/ *n* [u] cubiertos *mpl*, cubertería *f*, cuchillería *f* (Chi)

cutlet /ˈkʌtlət || ˈkʌtlɪt/ *n* (chop) chuleta *f* (*pequeña*)

cut: ~off *n* 1 **~off (point)** límite *m*; (*before n*) **~off date** fecha *f* límite *or* tope; 2 (shortcut) (AmE) atajo *m*; 3 **~offs** *pl* shorts *mpl* vaqueros; **~out** *n* (image, silhouette) recortable *m*, figura *f* para recortar; **~-price** /ˈkʌt ˈpraɪs/ (BrE), **~-rate** /ˈkʌtˈreɪt/ (AmE) *adj* ‹*goods/travel*› a precio rebajado; ‹*shop*› de ocasión

cutter /ˈkʌtər || ˈkʌtə(r)/ *n*
A (tool — for wire) tenazas *fpl*
B (worker) cortador, -dora *m,f*

cutthroat¹ /ˈkʌtθrəʊt/ *n* 1 (murderer) (liter) degollador, -dora *m,f*, asesino, -na *m,f* 2 **~ (razor)** (BrE) navaja *f*

cutthroat² *adj* ‹*competition*› feroz, salvaje

cutting¹ /ˈkʌtɪŋ/ *n*
A [c] 1 (from newspaper) (BrE) recorte *m* 2 (from plant) esqueje *m*
B [c] (for road, railway) (BrE) zanja *f*
C [u] (Cin, Rad, TV) montaje *m*, edición *f*

cutting² *adj* 1 (*before n*) ‹*tool/blade*› cortante; ***the ~ edge*: at the ~ edge of technology** a la vanguardia de la tecnología 2 (cold) ‹*wind*› cortante 3 (hurtful) ‹*remark*› hiriente

cuttlefish /ˈkʌtlfɪʃ/ *n* (*pl* **-fishes** *or* **-fish**) jibia *f*, sepia *f*

CV *n* = **curriculum vitae**

cwt *n* = **hundredweight**

cyanide /ˈsaɪənaɪd/ *n* [u] cianuro *m*

cybercafé /ˈsaɪbərˌkæfeɪ || ˈsaɪbəˌkæfeɪ/ *n* cibercafé *m*

cybernaut /ˈsaɪbərnɔːt || ˈsaɪbənɔːt/ *n* 1 (person who wears sensory devices) usuario, -ria de casco de realidad virtual 2 (Internet user) cibernauta *mf*, internauta *mf*

cybernetics /ˈsaɪbərˈnetɪks || ˌsaɪbəˈnetɪks/ *n* (+ *sing vb*) cibernética *f*

cyberspace /ˈsaɪbərspeɪs / *n* [u] ciberespacio *m*

cycle¹ /ˈsaɪkəl/ *n*
A 1 (process) ciclo *m*; **the life ~** el ciclo de la vida 2 (of washing machine) programa *m*
B (Elec, Comput) ciclo *m*
C (bicycle) bicicleta *f*

cycle² *vi* «*person*» ir* en bicicleta

cycling /ˈsaɪklɪŋ/ *n* [u] ciclismo *m*; **to go ~** salir* en bicicleta, ir* a andar en bicicleta (AmL)

cyclist /ˈsaɪkləst || ˈsaɪklɪst/ *n* ciclista *mf*

cyclo-cross /ˈsaɪkləʊkrɔːs || ˈsaɪkləʊkrɒs/ *n* [u] ciclo-cross *m*

cyclone /ˈsaɪkləʊn/ *n* 1 (storm) ciclón *m* 2 (low-pressure area) zona *f* de bajas presiones

cygnet /ˈsɪgnət || ˈsɪgnɪt/ *n* pollo *m* de cisne

cylinder /ˈsɪləndər || ˈsɪlɪndə(r)/ *n*
A (Math) cilindro *m*
B 1 (of engine) cilindro *m* 2 (container — for liquid gas) tanque *m* *or* (Esp) bombona *f* *or* (RPl) garrafa *f* *or* (Chi) balón *m* 3 (component — of gun) tambor *m*

cylindrical /səˈlɪndrɪkəl || sɪˈlɪndrɪkəl/ *adj* cilíndrico

cymbal /ˈsɪmbəl/ *n* platillo *m*, címbalo *m*

cynic /ˈsɪnɪk/ *n* cínico, -ca

cynical /ˈsɪnɪkəl/ *adj* cínico

cynically /ˈsɪnɪkli/ *adv* cínicamente

cynicism /ˈsɪnəsɪzəm/ *n* [u] cinismo *m*

cypher *n* (esp BrE) ▸**cipher**

cypress /ˈsaɪprəs/ *n* ciprés *m*

Cypriot¹ /ˈsɪpriət/ *n* chipriota *mf*; **Greek/Turkish ~** greco-/turco-chipriota *mf*

Cypriot² *adj* chipriota

Cyprus /ˈsaɪprəs/ *n* Chipre *f*

Cyrillic /səˈrɪlɪk || sɪˈrɪlɪk/ *adj* cirílico

cyst /sɪst/ *n* quiste *m*

cystic fibrosis /ˈsɪstɪkfaɪˈbrəʊsəs || ˌsɪstɪkfaɪˈbrəʊsɪs/ *n* [u] fibrosis *f* cística *or* pancreática

cystitis /sɪˈstaɪtəs || sɪˈstaɪtɪs/ *n* [u] cistitis *f*

czar /zɑːr || zɑː(r)/ *n* (esp AmE) ▸**tsar**

Czech¹ /tʃek/ *adj* checo

Czech² *n* 1 [c] (person) checo, -ca *m,f* 2 [u] (language) checo *m*

Czechoslovakia /ˈtʃekəsləˈvɑːkiə || ˌtʃekəsləˈvækiə/ *n* (Hist) Checoslovaquia *f*

Czechoslovakian /ˈtʃekəsləˈvɑːkiən || ˌtʃekəsləˈvækiən/ *adj* (Hist) checoslovaco

Czech Republic *n* **the ~ ~** la República Checa

Dd

D, **d** /diː/ *n* 1 (letter) D, d *f* 2 (Mus) re *m*; *see also* **A A2** 3 (AmE Pol) = **Democrat**

d (= **died**) m., fallecido en

d' = **do**; **d'you go there often?** ¿vas ahí a menudo?

'd /d/ 1 = **had** 2 = **would** 3 = **did**

DA *n* (in US) = **district attorney**

dab¹ /dæb/ *n* 1 (small amount — of cream, paint) toque *m* 2 (pat): **he gave his tie a ~ with a damp cloth** se frotó un poco la corbata con un trapo húmedo

dab² **-bb-** *vt*: **~ the stain with a damp cloth** frote suavemente la mancha con un trapo húmedo; **~ antiseptic on the cut** dése unos toques de antiséptico en la herida

dabble /'dæbəl/ *vt*: **we ~d our hands/feet in the river** chapoteamos en el río

■ **dabble** *vi* **to ~ IN sth**: **to ~ in politics/journalism** tener* escarceos con la política/el periodismo

dabbler /'dæblər/ *n* diletante *mf*

dab hand *n* (BrE colloq): **to be a ~ ~ at sth** tener* (buena) mano para algo

dachshund /'dɑːksʊnt || 'dækshʊnd/ *n* teckel *mf*, perro, -rra *m,f* salchicha (fam)

Dacron® /'deɪkrɑːn || 'dækrɒn, 'deɪkrɒn/ *n* [u] (AmE) Dacrón® *m*

dad /dæd/ *n* (colloq) papá *m* (fam)

daddy /'dædi/ *n* papi *m* (fam)

daddy longlegs /'lɔːŋlegz || 'lɒŋlegz/ *n* (*pl* ~ ~) (colloq) 1 (harvestman) (AmE) segador *m*, falangio *m* 2 (cranefly) (BrE) típula *f*

daffodil /'dæfədɪl/ *n* narciso *m*

daft /dæft || dɑːft/ *adj* **-er, -est** (esp BrE colloq) tonto, bobo (fam); **that was a ~ thing to do/say** hiciste una tontería/decir eso fue una tontería

dagger /'dægər || 'dægə(r)/ *n* daga *f*, puñal *m*; ***to be at ~s drawn with sb*** (BrE) estar* a matar con algn; ***to look ~s at sb*** lanzarle* una mirada asesina a algn

dahlia /'dæljə || 'deɪliə/ *n* dalia *f*

daily¹ /'deɪli/ *adj* (*before n*) ‹*newspaper/prayers*› diario; ‹*walk/visit*› diario, cotidiano; **employed/paid on a ~ basis** contratado/pagado por día(s)

daily² *adv* a diario, diariamente

daily³ *n* (*pl* **-lies**) diario *m*, periódico *m*

daintily /'deɪntḷi || 'deɪntɪli/ *adv* con delicadeza, delicadamente

dainty /'deɪnti/ *adj* **-tier, -tiest** 1 (delicate) ‹*flowers/vase*› delicado; ‹*appearance*› delicado, refinado; ‹*physique*› delicado 2 (delicious) exquisito

dairy /'deri || 'deəri/ *n* (*pl* **-ries**) 1 (on farm) lechería *f*; (*before n*) ‹*produce*› lácteo; ‹*butter/cream*› de granja; ‹*cow/industry*› lechero; **~ farm** granja *f* lechera, tambo *m* (RPl) 2 (shop) lechería *f*; (company) central *f* lechera

dais /'daɪəs || 'deɪɪs/ *n* (*pl* **daises**) tarima *f*; (rostrum) estrado *m*

daisy /'deɪzi/ *n* (*pl* **-sies**) (cultivated) margarita *f*; (wild) margarita *f* de los prados, maya *f*; ***as fresh as a ~*** tan fresco como una lechuga; ***to be pushing up (the) daisies*** (colloq & hum) estar* criando malvas; (*before n*) **~ chain** guirnalda *f* de margaritas

daisy wheel *n* margarita *f*; (*before n*) **daisy-wheel printer** impresora *f* de margarita

dale /deɪl/ *n* (liter) valle *m*

dalliance /'dæliəns/ *n* [u] (liter) devaneo *m* (liter), escarceos *mpl*

dally /'dæli/ *vi* **-lies, -lying, -lied** perder* el tiempo

Dalmatian /dæl'meɪʃən/ *n* dálmata *mf*

dam¹ /dæm/ *n* dique *m*, presa *f*, represa *f* (AmS)

dam² *vt* **-mm-** construir* una presa *or* (AmS) una represa en

Phrasal verb

• **dam up** [v ▸ o ▸ adv, v ▸ adv ▸ o] ▸ **dam²**

damage¹ /'dæmɪdʒ/ *n*

A [u] (to object) daño *m*; (to reputation, cause) daño *m*, perjuicio *m*; **storm/fire ~** daños ocasionados por una tormenta/un incendio; **the ~ is done** el daño ya está hecho; ***what's the ~?*** (sl) ¿cuánto se debe?

B **damages** *pl* (Law) daños y perjuicios *mpl*

damage² *vt* 1 ‹*building/vehicle*› dañar; ‹*health*› perjudicar*, ser* perjudicial para; ‹*reputation/cause*› perjudicar*, dañar 2 **damaged** *past p* ‹*stock*› dañado, averiado

damage limitation *n* [u] (*before n*) **~ ~ exercise** (for accidents, fires) acción *f* para minimizar los daños; (in public relations) operación *f* de lavado de imagen

damaging /'dæmɪdʒɪŋ/ *adj* perjudicial; **to be ~ TO sb/sth** ser* perjudicial PARA algn/algo

Damascus /də'mæskəs/ *n* Damasco *m*

damask /'dæməsk/ *n* [u] damasco *m*

dame /deɪm/ *n*

A **Dame** (title in UK) Dame (*título honorífico*)

B (woman) (AmE sl) tipa *f* (fam), tía *f* (Esp fam)

dammit /'dæmɪt/ *interj* (colloq) ¡caray! (fam & euf); ***as near as ~*** (BrE colloq) poco más o menos

damn¹ /dæm/ *vt*

A 1 (Relig) condenar 2 (condemn) condenar

B (colloq) (*in interj phrases*): **(God) ~ it!** ¡caray! (fam & euf), ¡maldita sea! (fam); **well, I'll be ~ed!** ¡vaya! (fam)

damn² *n* (colloq) (*no pl*): ***not to give a ~***: **I don't give a ~ what they think** me importa un bledo *or* un pito *or* un comino lo que piensen (fam)

damn³ *interj* (colloq) ¡caray! (fam & euf)

damn⁴ *adj* (colloq) (*before n*) (*as intensifier*) condenado (fam), maldito (fam), pinche (Méx fam)

damn⁵ *adv* (colloq) (*as intensifier*): **you know ~ well what I mean!** ¡sabes de sobra lo que quiero decir!

damnation /dæm'neɪʃən/ *n* [u] condenación *f*

damned¹ /dæmd/ *pl n* **the ~** los condenados

damned² /dæmnd/ *adj* 1 ‹*souls*› condenado 2 ▸ **damn⁴**

damned³ *adv* ▸ **damn⁵**

damnedest /'dæmdəst || 'dæmdɪst/ *n* (colloq): ***to do one's ~***: **she did her ~ to stop it** hizo todo lo que pudo para impedirlo

damning /'dæmɪŋ/ *adj* 1 (condemnatory) ‹*evidence*› condenatorio 2 (critical) ‹*appraisal*› crítico

damp¹ /dæmp/ *adj* **-er, -est** húmedo; **there are ~ patches on the ceiling** hay manchas de humedad en el techo; **to smell ~** oler* a humedad

damp² *n* [u] humedad *f*

damp³ *vt* **~ (down)** ‹*fire*› sofocar*; ‹*enthusiasm/excitement*› apagar*, enfriar*

damp course *n* membrana *f* aislante

dampen /ˈdæmpən/ *vt*
A (moisten) humedecer*, mojar
B (discourage) ‹*hopes*› hacer* perder; ‹*enthusiasm*› hacer* perder, apagar*; **to ~ sb's spirits** desanimar *or* desalentar* a algn

damper /ˈdæmpər || ˈdæmpə(r)/ *n* (of piano) sordina *f*; ***to put a ~ on sth*** (colloq): **the bad news put a ~ on the celebrations** la mala noticia estropeó las fiestas

damp: **~-proof** *vt* proteger* contra la humedad; **~-proof course** *n* ▸**damp course**

d

damsel /ˈdæmzəl/ *n* (arch *or* poet) damisela *f* (arc *o* liter), doncella *f* (arc *o* liter); **a ~ in distress** (hum) una señorita en apuros (hum)

damson /ˈdæmzən/ *n* ciruela *f* damascena

dance¹ /dæns || dɑːns/ *n*
A 1 [c] (act) baile *m*; ***to lead sb a merry ~*** (BrE) darle* quebraderos de cabeza a algn 2 [c] (set of steps) baile *m*, danza *f* 3 [u] (art form) danza *f*, baile *m*
B (occasion) baile *m*; (*before n*) ‹*music*› de baile, bailable

dance² *vi*
A 1 (to music) bailar 2 (skip) dar* saltos
B «*eyes/flames*» (liter) bailar, danzar* (liter);
■ **dance** *vt* ‹*waltz/tango*› bailar; **they ~d the night away** bailaron durante toda la noche; ▸**attendance 2**

dancer /ˈdænsər || ˈdɑːnsə(r)/ *n* bailarín, -rina *m,f*

dancing /ˈdænsɪŋ || ˈdɑːnsɪŋ/ *n* [u] baile *m*; **he loves ~** le encanta bailar; (*before n*) ‹*lesson/shoes*› de baile

dandelion /ˈdændəlaɪən || ˈdændɪlaɪən/ *n* diente *m* de león

dandle /ˈdændl̩/ *vt* ‹*baby*› mecer* (*sobre las rodillas*)

dandruff /ˈdændrʌf/ *n* [u] caspa *f*; (*before n*) **~ shampoo** champú *m* anti-caspa

dandy¹ /ˈdændi/ *n* dandi *m*, dandy *m*

dandy² *adj* **-dier, -diest** (AmE colloq) súper (fam), chulo (Esp fam)

Dane /deɪn/ *n* danés, -nesa *m,f*, dinamarqués, -quesa *m,f*

danger /ˈdeɪndʒər || ˈdeɪndʒə(r)/ *n* [u c] peligro *m*; **there's no ~ of that** no hay peligro de que eso suceda; **in ~** en peligro *or* en riesgo; **out of ~** fuera de peligro; **to be in ~ of -ING** correr peligro *or* riesgo de + INF; **~ TO sb/sth** peligro PARA algn/algo; (*before n*) **to be on/off the ~ list** encontrarse* en estado grave/estar* fuera de peligro; **~ signal/zone** señal *f*/zona *f* de peligro

danger money *n* [u] (esp BrE) plus *m or* prima *f* de peligrosidad

dangerous /ˈdeɪndʒərəs/ *adj* peligroso; **~ driving** conducción *f* con imprudencia temeraria

dangerously /ˈdeɪndʒərəsli/ *adv* peligrosamente; **to live ~** llevar una vida arriesgada; **she came ~ close to losing her life** estuvo a un paso de la muerte

dangle /ˈdæŋgəl/ *vi* colgar*, pender
■ **dangle** *vt* hacer* oscilar; **he ~d the possibility of promotion in front of her** quiso tentarla con la posibilidad de un ascenso

Danish¹ /ˈdeɪnɪʃ/ *adj* danés, dinamarqués

Danish² *n* [u] danés *m*

Danish: **~ blue** *n* [u] *tipo de queso azul*; **~ (pastry)** *n*: *bollo cubierto de azúcar glaseado*

dank /dæŋk/ *adj* frío y húmedo

Danube /ˈdænjuːb/ *n* **the ~** el Danubio

dapper /ˈdæpər || ˈdæpə(r)/ *adj* atildado, pulcro

dappled /ˈdæpəld/ *adj* ‹*horse*› rodado, pinto; ‹*pattern*› veteado

dapple-gray, (BrE) **dapple-grey** /ˈdæpl̩ˈgreɪ/ *adj* (*pred* **dapple gray**) tordo rodado, tordillo, tordo

dare¹ /der || deə(r)/ *n* reto *m*, desafío *m*; **she did it on** *o* (BrE) **for a ~** lo hizo porque la retaron *or* la desafiaron

dare² *v mod* atreverse a, osar (liter); **just you ~!** ¡atrévete y verás!; **don't you ~ go in there!** ¡ni se te ocurra entrar ahí!; **how ~ you!** ¡cómo te atreves!; **I ~n't tell her** (esp BrE) no me atrevo *or* no me animo a decírselo; **I ~ say you've had enough** estarás harto(, me imagino)
■ **dare** *vt*
A (be so bold) **to ~ to + INF** atreverse a + INF, osar + INF (liter)
B (challenge) **to ~ sb to + INF** retar *or* desafiar* a algn a + INF *or* A QUE (+ *subj*); **go on, dive in, I ~ you!** ¡anda, tírate! ¿a que no te atreves *or* a que no eres capaz?

daredevil /ˈderˌdevl̩ || ˈdeəˌdevl̩/ *n* corajudo, -da *m,f* (fam); (*before n*) ‹*feat/exploit*› temerario

daring¹ /ˈderɪŋ || ˈdeərɪŋ/ *adj* 1 ‹*explorer/pilot*› osado, temerario; ‹*plan*› audaz 2 ‹*dress/film*› atrevido

daring² *n* [u] 1 (courage) arrojo *m*, coraje *m* 2 (audacity) audacia *f*

dark¹ /dɑːrk || dɑːk/ *adj* **-er, -est**
A (unlit) ‹*room/night*› oscuro; **it's getting ~** está oscureciendo, se está haciendo de noche; **the ~ side of the moon** el lado oculto de la luna
B 1 (in color) oscuro; **~ chocolate** chocolate *m* sin leche; **~ glasses** anteojos *mpl* oscuros (esp AmL), gafas *fpl* negras (Esp) 2 (in complexion) moreno
C 1 (evil, sinister) (liter) ‹*deeds/threats*› oscuro; **there's a ~ side to his nature/his activities** hay algo (de) siniestro en él/sus actividades 2 (somber) ‹*thoughts*› sombrío 3 (mysterious, obscure) ‹*allusion*› oscuro; ***to keep sth ~*** mantener* algo en secreto

dark² *n* [u] 1 (absence of light) **the ~** la oscuridad; ***to keep sb in the ~ about sth*** ocultarle algo a algn; **to be in the ~ about sth** estar* a oscuras sobre algo 2 (nightfall): **to wait until ~** esperar hasta que anochezca; **before ~** antes de que anochezca; **after ~** de noche

Dark Ages *pl n* **the ~ ~** la Alta Edad Media, la Edad de las tinieblas; **they're living in the ~ ~** viven en la prehistoria

darken /ˈdɑːrkən || ˈdɑːkən/ *vt* 1 (make dark) oscurecer*; ▸**door 1** 2 (make somber) ensombrecer*
■ **darken** *vi* 1 (grow dark) «*room/color*» oscurecerse*; «*sky*» oscurecerse*, nublarse 2 (grow somber) ensombrecerse*

dark horse *n* 1 (surprise victor) (AmE) ganador, -dora *m,f* sorpresa 2 (unknown quantity) enigma *m*

darkly /ˈdɑːrkli || ˈdɑːkli/ *adv* ‹*hint*› misteriosamente

darkness /ˈdɑːrknəs || ˈdɑːknɪs/ *n* [u] 1 (of night, room) oscuridad *f*; **the building was in complete** *o* **total ~** el edificio estaba totalmente a oscuras; **when ~ falls** al caer la noche 2 (evil) tinieblas *fpl*; **the powers of ~** los poderes del mal

dark: **~room** *n* cuarto *m* oscuro; **~-skinned** /ˈdɑːrk ˈskɪnd || ˌdɑːkˈskɪnd/ *adj* de piel oscura

darling¹ /ˈdɑːrlɪŋ || ˈdɑːlɪŋ/ *n* (*as form of address*) cariño; **she was the ~ of the public** era la niña mimada del público

darling² *adj* 1 (beloved) (*before n*) querido 2 (delightful) (dated) mono (fam)

darn¹ /dɑːrn || dɑːn/ *vt*
A (mend) zurcir*
B (colloq & euph) (*in interj phrases*): **~ it!** ¡caray! (fam & euf)

darn² *n* zurcido *m*

darn³ *interj* ¡caray! (fam & euf)

darn⁴, **darned** /dɑːrnd || dɑːnd/ *adj* (colloq & euph) (*as intensifier*) maldito (fam); **I can't see a ~ thing** no veo ni medio (fam)

darn⁵, **darned** *adv* (colloq & euph) (*as intensifier*): **he's too ~ clever** se pasa de listo

darning /ˈdɑːrnɪŋ || ˈdɑːnɪŋ/ *n* [u] 1 (action) zurcido *m* 2 (things to be darned) ropa *f* para zurcir

dart¹ /dɑːrt || dɑːt/ *n* 1 (weapon) dardo *m* 2 (Games) dardo *m* 3 (Clothing) pinza *f*

dart² *vi*: **to ~ into/out of a room** entrar como una flecha en/salir* como una flecha de una habitación
■ **dart** *vt* ‹*look*› lanzar*

dartboard /ˈdɑːrtbɔːrd || ˈdɑːtbɔːd/ *n* diana *f*

darts /dɑːrts || dɑːts/ *n* (+ *sing vb*) dardos *mpl*

dash¹ /dæʃ/ *n*
A (sudden movement) (*no pl*): **to make a ~ for safety/shelter** correrse a ponerse a salvo/a cobijarse; ***to make a ~ for it*** (colloq) salir* a toda mecha (fam)
B [c] (small amount) poquito *m*; **a ~ of milk/salt** un chorrito de leche/una pizca de sal
C [c] 1 (punctuation mark) guión *m* 2 (in Morse code) raya *f*
D [u] (spirit, nerve) brío *m*
E [c] (Sport): **the 100 m ~** los 100m planos *or* (Esp) lisos *or* (RPl) llanos

dash² *vt*
A (hurl) tirar; **she ~ed the plate to pieces** hizo añicos *or* trizas el plato; **the ship was ~ed against the rocks** el barco se estrelló contra las rocas
B (disappoint) ‹*hopes*› (*usu pass*) defraudar
■ **dash** *vi*
A (rush): **I ~ed to the rescue** me lancé al rescate; **she ~ed out** salió disparada; **I must ~** (colloq) tengo que irme corriendo
B (crash) «*waves*» romper*

Phrasal verb
• **dash off**
A [v ▸ o ▸ adv, v ▸ adv ▸ o] (write hurriedly) escribir* corriendo
B [v ▸ adv] (leave hastily) irse* corriendo

dashboard /ˈdæʃbɔːrd || ˈdæʃbɔːd/ *n* tablero *m* de mandos, salpicadero *m* (Esp)

dashing /ˈdæʃɪŋ/ *adj* 1 (lively) gallardo 2 (smart) elegante

dastardly /ˈdæstərdli || ˈdæstədli/ *adj* (liter *or* hum) ‹*deed*› ruin (liter)

data /ˈdeɪtə/ *n* (*pl of* **datum**)
A (facts, information) (+ *pl vb*) datos *mpl*, información *f*
B (Comput) (+ *sing vb*) datos *mpl*; **a piece of ~** un dato; (*before n*) **~ bank** banco *m* de datos; **~ capture** toma *f* de datos; **~ file** archivo *m* de datos; **~ input** introducción *f* de datos; **~ processing** procesamiento *m or* proceso *m* de datos; **~ protection** protección *f* de datos *or* de la información; **~ retrieval** rescate *m* de datos

database /ˈdeɪtəbeɪs/ *n* base *f* de datos; **~ management system** sistema *m* de gestión *or* (AmL tb) de manejo de bases de datos

date¹ /deɪt/ *n*
A (of appointment, battle) fecha *f*; **what's the ~ today?** ¿a qué fecha estamos?; **to ~** hasta la fecha, hasta el momento
B (colloq) 1 (appointment) cita *f*; **Greg has a ~ with Ana on Sunday** Greg sale con Ana el domingo 2 (person) (esp AmE): **he's my regular ~** estoy saliendo con él 3 (booking): **he's playing three ~s in London** va a actuar tres veces en Londres
C (fruit) dátil *m*

date² *vt*
A 1 (mark with date) fechar 2 (give date to) ‹*remains/pottery/fossil*› datar, determinar la antigüedad de
B (betray age) (colloq): **that song really ~s you** eso delata tu edad, eso demuestra lo viejo que eres
C (go out with) (esp AmE colloq) salir* con (fam)
■ **date** *vi*
A (originate in) datar; **it ~s from the 14th century** data del siglo XIV; **his title ~s back to the 14th century** los orígines de su título se remontan al siglo XIV
B (become old-fashioned) pasar de moda
C (go on dates) (esp AmE colloq) salir* con chicas/chicos *or* (AmL tb) a noviar, pololear (Chi fam)

dated /ˈdeɪtəd || ˈdeɪtɪd/ *adj* ‹*fashion/word*› anticuado; **his plays are ~** sus obras han perdido actualidad

date: **~line** *n* (Journ) data *f* (*línea de un texto periodístico en la que constan fecha y lugar de origen del mismo*); **~ Line** *n* **the (International) D~ Line** línea *f* del cambio de fecha; **~ rape** *n* violación *f* (*cometida durante una cita*); **~ stamp** *n* (instrument) fechador *m*; (date) fecha *f*; **~-stamp** *vt* fechar

dating agency /ˈdeɪtɪŋ/ *n* agencia *f* matrimonial *or* de contactos

dative /ˈdeɪtɪv/ *n* dativo *m*

datum /ˈdeɪtəm/ *n* (*pl* **data**) (frml) dato *m*; *see also* **data**

daub¹ /dɔːb/ *vt* (smear) **to ~ sth WITH sth** embadurnar algo DE algo

daub² *n* (smear) mancha *f*; *see also* **wattle**

daughter /ˈdɔːtər || ˈdɔːtə(r)/ *n* hija *f*

daughter-in-law /ˈdɔːtərɪnlɔː/ *n* (*pl* **daughters-in-law**) nuera *f*

daunt /dɔːnt/ *vt* (*usu pass*) amilanar, intimidar; **nothing ~ed, we carried on** (liter) impertérritos, seguimos adelante

daunting /ˈdɔːntɪŋ/ *adj* ‹*prospect*› desalentador, sobrecogedor; ‹*task*› de enormes proporciones

dauntless /ˈdɔːntləs || ˈdɔːntlɪs/ *adj* (liter) intrépido

davenport /ˈdævənpɔːrt || ˈdævənpɔːt/ *n* (AmE) sofá *m* (*grande*)

dawdle /ˈdɔːdl/ *vi* entretenerse*; **to ~ OVER sth**: **she ~d over her meal** comió con gran parsimonia

dawdler /ˈdɔːdlər || ˈdɔːdlə(r)/ *n* persona *f* lenta *or* (fam) cachazuda, lerdo, -da *m,f*

dawn¹ /dɔːn/ *n* [u c] (daybreak) amanecer *m*; **at ~** al amanecer, al alba (liter); **from ~ till dusk** de sol a sol, de la mañana a la noche; **since the ~ of civilization** desde los albores de la civilización; (*before n*) ‹*patrol/start*› de madrugada

dawn² *vi* (liter) «*day*» amanecer*, clarear, alborear (liter); «*new age*» alborear (liter), nacer*

Phrasal verb
• **dawn on** [v ▸ prep ▸ o]: **it gradually ~ed on me that ...** fui cayendo en la cuenta de que ...

dawn chorus *n* **the ~ ~** el trino de los pájaros al amanecer

day /deɪ/ *n*
A (unit of time) día *m*; **twice a ~** dos veces al día; **a three-~-old chick** un pollito de tres días; **he's arriving in two ~s** *o* **in two ~s' time** llega dentro de dos días; **he's forty if he's a ~** tiene cuarenta años como poco; ***a nine ~s' wonder***: **the case was a nine ~s' wonder** el interés en el caso duró lo que un suspiro; ***from ~ one*** desde el primer momento
B (daylight hours) día *m*; **all ~** todo el día; **we went to the beach for the ~** fuimos a pasar el día a la playa; **~ and night** día y noche; ▸ **happy A1, light¹ A**
C 1 (point in time) día *m*; **what ~ is (it) today?** ¿qué día es hoy?; **every ~** todos los días; **every other ~** un día sí y un día no, día por medio (CS, Per); **the ~ before** el día anterior; **(on) the following ~** al día siguiente; **the ~ before yesterday** anteayer, antes de ayer; **the ~ after tomorrow** pasado mañana; **any ~ (now)** cualquier día de éstos; **one ~** un día; **one of these ~s** un día de éstos; **~ after ~** día tras día; **~ by ~** día a día, de día en día; **~ in, ~ out** todos los días; **from ~ to ~** de día en día, día a día; **from one ~ to the next** de un día para (el) otro; **from this ~ on(ward)** de hoy *or* de ahora en adelante; **it's 12 years to the ~ since we met** hoy hace exactamente 12 años que nos conocimos; **to this ~** hasta el día de hoy; **it's not my/his ~** no es mi/su día; **that'll be the ~** (colloq & iro) cuando las ranas críen cola; **did you have a good/bad ~?** ¿te fue *or* te ha ido bien/mal hoy?; **have a good** *o* **nice ~!** (esp AmE) ¡que le vaya bien!; ***any ~*** (colloq): **caviar? I'd rather have a hamburger any ~** ¿caviar? prefiero mil veces una hamburguesa; ***at the end of the ~*** a *or* en fin de cuentas, al fin y al cabo; ***to call it a ~*** (temporarily) dejarlo para otro día; (permanently) dejar de trabajar (*or* estudiar *etc*); ***to make sb's ~*** (colloq) alegrarle la vida a algn; ***to save for a rainy ~*** ahorrar para cuando lleguen las vacas flacas 2 (specified day, date) día *m*; **it's her ~ for doing the washing** hoy le toca lavar (la ropa) *or* (Esp) hacer la colada 3 (working day) jornada *f*, día *m*; **to take a ~ off (from) work** tomarse un día libre
D 1 (period of time) día *m*; **up to the present ~** hasta el día de hoy; **the burning issues of the ~** los temas candentes del día; **in ~s gone by** (liter) antaño (liter); **in ~s to come** (liter) en días venideros (liter); **in ~s of old, in olden ~s** (liter) antaño (liter); **in the old ~s** antiguamente; **the good old ~s** los viejos tiempos; **in this ~ and age** hoy (en) día, el día de hoy; **in those ~s** en aquellos tiempos, en aquella época; **these ~s** hoy (en) día; **those were the ~s!** ¡qué tiempos aquéllos!; ***it's early ~s yet*** (BrE) aún es pronto; ***to have seen*** *o* ***known better ~s*** haber* visto tiempos mejores 2 (period of youth, success) (*no pl*) día *m*; **your ~ will come** ya te llegará el día; **he was the leading politician of his ~** en su día fue el político de mayor influencia; ***to have had one's ~***: **the steam engine has had its ~** la locomotora de *or* a vapor ha pasado a la historia 3 **days** *pl n* (lifetime) días *mpl*; **to end one's ~s** acabar mis (*or* sus *etc*) días; ***his ~s are numbered*** tiene los días contados
E (contest): ***to carry*** *o* ***win the ~*** prevalecer*; ***to save the ~***: **her quick thinking saved the ~** su rapidez mental nos (*or* los *etc*) sacó del apuro
F **days** (*as adv*): **to work ~s** trabajar durante el día

day: **~break** *n* [u] alba *f*‡ (liter), amanecer *m*; **at ~break** al alba (liter), al amanecer; **~ care** *n* [u] (for children) (AmE) servicio *m* de guardería infantil; (for old/disabled people) (BrE) *atención prestada durante el día a ancianos, minusválidos etc*; **~-care center** *n* (AmE) guardería *f* infantil; **~ centre** *n* (BrE) *centro diurno para ancianos minusválidos etc*

daydream¹ /'deɪdri:m/ *n* ensueño *m*, ensoñación *f*

daydream² *vi* soñar* despierto, fantasear

day: **~ laborer**, (BrE) **labourer** *n* jornalero, -ra *m,f*; **~light** *n* [u] luz *f* (del día); **in broad ~light** a plena luz del día; **before ~light** antes de que amanezca; ***to beat/scare the (living) ~lights out of sb*** (colloq): **that dog scares the (living) ~lights out of me** ese perro me da pánico *or* terror; **he beat the (living) ~lights out of him** le dio una paliza tremenda; ▸**robbery**; **~light (saving) time** *n* [u] (AmE) hora *f* de verano; **~ patient** *n* paciente ambulatorio, -ria *mf*, paciente externo, -na *mf*; **~ release** *n* [u] (in UK) *sistema que permite a un empleado ausentarse regularmente de su trabajo para seguir estudios relacionados con el mismo*; **~room** *n*: *sala de estar comunal en hospitales, prisiones etc*; **~time** *n*: **in** *o* **during the ~time** de día *or* durante el día; **~-to-day** /'deɪtə'deɪ/ *adj* (*before n*) ‹*occurrence*› cotidiano, diario; ‹*chores/difficulties*› de cada día; ‹*existence*› diario; **~ trip** *n* excursión *f* de un día; **~-tripper** *n* excursionista *mf*

daze¹ /deɪz/ *n* (*no pl*) aturdimiento *m*; **to go about in a ~** estar* en las nubes

daze² *vt* (*usu pass*) aturdir

dazed /deɪzd/ *adj* aturdido

dazzle¹ /'dæzəl/ *vt* «*light*» deslumbrar, encandilar; «*beauty/wit*» deslumbrar

dazzle² *n* [u] (of lights) resplandor *m*, brillo *m*; (of publicity) hechizo *m*

dazzling /'dæzlɪŋ/ *adj* (bright) ‹*light/glare*› deslumbrante, resplandeciente, que encandila; (impressive) ‹*wit/looks*› deslumbrante, deslumbrador

db, dB (= **decibel**) dB

DBE *n* (in UK) = **Dame of the British Empire**

DC **1** (= **direct current**) CC **2** = **District of Columbia**

D-day /'di:deɪ/ *n* **1** (in World War II) día *m* D (*día del desembarco aliado en Normandía*) **2** (important day) el día señalado

DE = **Delaware**

DEA *n* (= **Drug Enforcement Administration**) DEA *f*

deacon /'di:kən/ *n* diácono *m*

deaconess /'di:kənəs || ˌdi:kə'nes, 'di:kənɪs/ *n* diaconisa *f*

deactivate /di:'æktəveɪt || di:'æktɪveɪt/ *vt* desactivar

dead¹ /ded/ *adj*

A (no longer alive) muerto; **he's ~** está muerto; **she has been ~ for 50 years** hace 50 años que murió; **~ body** cadáver *m*, cuerpo *m* sin vida; **he was ~ on arrival at the hospital** cuando llegó al hospital ya había muerto, ingresó cadáver (Esp); **to drop ~** caerse* muerto; **drop ~!** ¡vete al demonio *or* al diablo!; ***as ~ as a dodo*** *o* ***doornail*** requetemuerto (fam); **~ *and gone***: **when I'm ~ and gone** cuando yo me muera; ***not to be seen*** *o* ***caught ~*** (colloq): **I wouldn't be seen** *o* **caught ~ in that dress** yo no me pondría ese vestido ni muerta *or* ni loca; ▸**body A3**

B **1** (numb) (*usu pred*) dormido; **to go ~** «*limb*» dormirse* **2** (unresponsive) **to be ~ TO sth** ser* sordo A algo

C (very tired, ill) (colloq) muerto (fam)

D **1** (obsolete) ‹*language*› muerto; ‹*custom*› en desuso **2** (past, finished with) ‹*issue*› pasado

E **1** (not functioning) ‹*wire/circuit*› desconectado; ‹*telephone*› desconectado, cortado; ‹*battery*› descargado; **the line went ~** se cortó (la comunicación) **2** (not alight) ‹*fire/match*› apagado **3** (not busy) ‹*town/hotel/party*› muerto

F (*as intensifier*): **in ~ silence** en un silencio absoluto *or* total; **a ~ calm** una calma chicha

dead² *adv*

A **1** (exactly) justo; **she was ~ on time** (esp BrE) llegó puntualísima **2** (directly) justo, directamente; **~ ahead** justo delante **3** (suddenly): **to stop ~** parar en seco

B **1** (absolutely) (colloq) ‹*straight/level*› completamente; **~ slow** lentísimo; **~ tired** muerto (de cansancio) (fam), cansadísimo; **you're ~ right** tienes toda la razón; **to be ~ certain** *o* **sure** estar* totalmente seguro **2** (*as intensifier*) (sl): **it was ~ easy** estuvo regalado *or* tirado (fam); **~ boring/expensive** aburridísimo/carísimo

dead³ *n*

A (+ *pl vb*) **the ~** los muertos

B (depth): **in the** *o* (BrE also) **at ~ of night** a altas horas de la noche *or* de la madrugada

deadbeat /'dedbi:t/ *n* (colloq) **1** (lazy person) vago, -ga *m,f*, bueno, -na *m,f* para nada, flojo, -ja *m,f* (fam) **2** (scrounger) (AmE) aprovechado, -da *m,f*, gorrón, -rrona *m,f* (Esp fam), aprovechador, -dora *m,f* (CS fam)

deaden /'dedn̩/ *vt* ‹*impact*› amortiguar; ‹*noise/vibration*› reducir*; ‹*pain*› atenuar*, aliviar; ‹*nerve*› insensibilizar*; ‹*faculties*› entorpecer*

dead: **~ end** *n* callejón *m* sin salida; **~-end** /'ded'end/ *adj* ‹*street*› sin salida, ciego (Andes, Ven); **a ~-end job** (colloq) un trabajo sin porvenir *or* futuro; **~head** *n* (AmE colloq) pánfilo, -la *m,f* (fam); **~ heat** *n* empate *m*; **~ letter** *n* (Law) letra *f* muerta; (undelivered letter) carta *f* no reclamada; (*before n*) **~-letter office** departamento *m* de cartas no reclamadas; **~line** *n* fecha *f* tope *or* límite, plazo *m* de entrega; **to meet a ~line** entregar* un trabajo dentro del plazo previsto; **~lock** *n* (*no pl*) punto *m* muerto, impasse *m*

deadly¹ /'dedli/ *adj* **-lier, -liest**

A **1** (fatal) ‹*disease/poison*› mortal; ‹*weapon*› mortífero **2** (*as intensifier*) ‹*seriousness*› enorme; ‹*enemy/rival*› a muerte; **a ~ silence** un silencio sepulcral

B (dull) (colloq) aburridísimo, terriblemente aburridor (AmL)

deadly² *adv* (*as intensifier*) ‹*dull*› terriblemente; **I'm ~ serious** lo digo muy en serio

deadly nightshade /'naɪtʃeɪd/ *n* [c u] belladona *f*

dead: **~pan** *adj* ‹*expression*› de póquer *or* (fam) de palo; ‹*voice/delivery*› deliberadamente inexpresivo; **~ Sea** *n* **the D~ Sea** el Mar Muerto; **~ weight** *n* peso *m* muerto; **~ wood**, (AmE also) **~wood** *n* [u] (dead branches) ramas *fpl* secas; **to get rid of the ~ wood among the staff** sacarse* de encima al personal inútil

deaf¹ /def/ *adj* **1** sordo; **to go ~** quedarse sordo; **~ and dumb** sordomudo **2** (unwilling to hear) **to be ~ TO sth** hacer* oídos sordos A algo

deaf² *pl n* **the ~** los sordos

deaf-aid /'defeɪd/ *n* (BrE) audífono *m*

deafen /'defən/ *vt* ensordecer*

deafening /'defənɪŋ/ *adj* ensordecedor

deaf-mute /'def'mju:t/ *n* sordomudo, -da *m,f*

deafness /'defnəs || 'defnɪs/ *n* [u] sordera *f*

deal¹ /di:l/ *n*

A **1** (indicating amount): **it makes a great/good** *o* **fair ~ of difference** cambia mucho/bastante las cosas; **I've given it a great ~ of thought** he reflexionado mucho sobre el asunto; **a great ~ of money** mucho dinero **2** **a great/good ~** (*as adv*): **we've seen a great ~ of her lately** la hemos visto mucho *or* muy a menudo últimamente

B [c] **1** (agreement) trato *m*, acuerdo *m*; **it's a ~!** ¡trato hecho!; **to do** *o* **make a ~ with sb** llegar* a un acuerdo con algn, hacer* un trato *or* un pacto con algn; **what's the ~?** (AmE colloq) ¿qué pasa?; ***to make a big ~ out of sth***: **she made such a big ~ out of choosing a hat** hizo tantos aspavientos para elegir un sombrero; **it's no big ~** no es nada del otro mundo **2** (financial arrangement) acuerdo *m*; **she got a very good ~ when she left the company** llegó a un buen arreglo económico al dejar la compañía **3** (bargain): **you'll get a better ~ if you shop around** lo conseguirás más barato si vas a otras tiendas

C (treatment) trato *m*; **she's had a raw ~ in life** la vida la ha tratado muy mal

D (Games) (*no pl*) reparto *m* (*de las cartas*); **it's my ~** me toca a mí dar *or* repartir, doy *or* reparto yo

deal² (*past & past p* **dealt**) *vt*

A ‹*cards*› dar*, repartir

B **to ~ sb/sth a blow** asestarle un golpe a algn/algo

■ **deal** *vi* (Games) dar*, repartir

Phrasal verbs

- **deal in** [v ▸ prep ▸ o] (Busn) dedicarse* a la compra y venta de, comerciar en
- **deal out** [v ▸ o ▸ adv, v ▸ adv ▸ o] ‹*gifts/money*› repartir, distribuir*; **the punishment that was ~t out to them** el castigo que se les aplicó *or* impuso
- **deal with** [v ▸ prep ▸ o]

A **1** (do business with) ‹*company*› tener* relaciones comerciales con; **I prefer to ~ with her** yo prefiero tratar con ella

2 (behave): **to ~ fairly with sb** tratar a algn con justicia
B 1 (tackle, handle) ‹*complaint*› ocuparse de, atender*; ‹*situation*› manejar; **the problem must be ~t with now** hay que ocuparse del *or* hay que resolver el problema ahora mismo; **I don't know how to ~ with this problem** no sé qué hacer con *or* no sé cómo atacar este problema; **I know how to ~ with him** yo sé cómo tratarlo; **let me ~ with her** yo me encargo de ella 2 (be responsible for) ocuparse *or* encargarse* de 3 (punish): **your mother will ~ with you** ya te las verás con tu madre; **the judge ~t with her severely** el juez fue severo con ella
C ‹*issue*› (discuss, treat) tratar; (have as subject) tratar de

dealer /'di:lər || 'di:lə(r)/ *n*
A 1 (trader): **a ~ in livestock** un consignatario *or* tratante de ganado; **she's a car ~** se dedica a la compra-venta de coches; **visit your local Ford/Hoover ~** visite a su concesionario Ford/representante Hoover más próximo; **drug ~** traficante *mf* de drogas 2 (Fin) corredor, -dora *m,f* de bolsa *or* de valores
B (Games): **the ~** el que da *or* reparte las cartas

dealership /'di:lərʃɪp || 'di:ləʃɪp/ *n* concesión *f*, representación *f*

dealing /'di:lɪŋ/ *n*
A 1 [u] (business methods): **the company has a reputation for honest/shady ~** la empresa tiene fama de honradez en los negocios/de hacer negocios turbios 2 **dealings** *pl* (contacts, relations) relaciones *fpl*, trato *m*; **the company has ~s with the Far East** la compañía tiene negocios con el Lejano Oriente
B [u] 1 (trafficking) tráfico *m* 2 (on stock exchange) (BrE) transacciones *fpl*

dealt /delt/ *past & past p of* **deal²**

dean /di:n/ *n*
A (Relig) deán *m*
B 1 (in university) decano, -na *m,f* 2 (in college, secondary school) (AmE) *docente a cargo del asesoramiento y de la disciplina de los estudiantes*

dear¹ /dɪr, || dɪə(r)/ *adj* **dearer, dearest**
A (loved) querido; **~ (old) Jane** la buena de Jane; **his ~est wish/possession** su mayor deseo/su bien más preciado; **to be ~ TO sb**: **memories that are very ~ to him** recuerdos que le son muy caros *or* que significan mucho para él; **to hold sb ~** (frml) tener* a algn en mucha estima
B (in direct address) 1 (in speech): **my ~ Mrs Harper, I can assure you that ...** mi buena señora (Harper), le aseguro que ... 2 (in letter-writing): **D~ Mr Jones** Estimado Sr. Jones; **D~ Jimmy** Querido Jimmy; **D~ Sir or Madam** Estimado/a Señor(a), Muy señor mío/señora mía
C (lovable) adorable; **he's such a ~ little thing!** ¡es una ricura *or* monada (de niño)!
D (expensive) caro; **was it very ~?** ¿te costó muy caro?

dear² *interj*: **oh ~!** ¡ay!, ¡qué cosa!

dear³ *n*
A (*as form of address*) querido, -da, cariño
B (nice person) (colloq): **he's/she's such a ~** es un ángel *or* un cielo; **(you) poor ~!** ¡pobre ángel!, ¡pobrecito!

dear⁴ *adv* caro

dearly /'dɪrli || 'dɪəli/ *adv*
A (*as intensifier*): **I love him ~** lo quiero mucho *or* de verdad; **I should ~ like to get my revenge** ¡cómo me gustaría vengarme!; **~ beloved** (frml) (*as form of address*) (Relig) (amados) hermanos
B (at great cost) caro *adj*; **he paid ~ for his generosity** pagó cara su generosidad

dearth /dɜ:rθ || dɜ:θ/ *n* (lack) (*no pl*) **a ~ (OF sth)** escasez *f* (DE algo)

death /deθ/ *n* [u c] muerte *f*, fallecimiento *m* (frml); **he died a horrible ~** tuvo una muerte horrible; **to put sb to ~** ejecutar a algn; **he was beaten to ~** lo mataron a golpes; **that was the ~ of my ambitions** eso acabó con mis ambiciones; **to ~** (*as intensifier*) (colloq): **to be scared to ~** estar* muerto de miedo; **to be worried to ~** estar* preocupadísimo; ***at ~'s door*** a las puertas de la muerte; ***to be the ~ of sb*** acabar con algn; ***to catch one's ~ (of cold)*** agarrarse *or* (Esp) coger* una pulmonía doble; ***to do sth to ~***: **that play has been done to ~** esa obra está muy trillada; ***to hang on like grim ~*** aferrarse con todas sus fuerzas; **you look like ~ warmed over** *o* (BrE) **up** (hum) ¡tienes muy mala cara!

death: **~bed** *n* lecho *m* de muerte; (*before n*) ‹*confession*› in extremis, in artículo mortis; **~ benefit** *n* [u c] indemnización *f* por muerte *or* fallecimiento, compensación *f* por muerte *or* fallecimiento; **~ blow** *n* golpe *m* mortal; **~ cell** *n* celda *f* de la muerte, celda *f* de los condenados a muerte; **~ certificate** *n* certificado *m* de defunción; **~-dealing** *adj* (liter) mortífero; **~ duties** *pl n* (BrE) impuesto *m* sobre sucesiones *or* a la herencia

deathly¹ /'deθli/ *adj* ‹*silence*› de muerte, sepulcral; ‹*pallor*› cadavérico

deathly² *adv*: **she looked ~ white** *o* **pale** estaba blanca como el *or* un papel, estaba lívida

death: **~ penalty** *n* **the ~ penalty** la pena de muerte; **~ row** /rəʊ/ *n* (*no art*) pabellón *m* de los condenados a muerte, corredor *m* de la muerte; **~ sentence** *n*: **the ~ sentence** la pena de muerte; **~ squad** *n* escuadrón *m* de la muerte; **~ throes** *pl n* agonía *f*; **to be in one's ~ throes** agonizar*; **~ toll** *n* número *m* de víctimas (mortales) *or* de muertos; **~ trap** *n*: *edificio, vehículo etc muy poco seguro*; **~ warrant** *n* sentencia *f* de muerte; **~watch beetle** *n* carcoma *f*; **~ wish** *n* (*no pl*) (Psych) pulsión *f* de muerte

deb /deb/ *n* (colloq) debutante *f*

debacle, débâcle /deɪ'bɑ:kəl/ *n* debacle *f*, descalabro *m*

debar /dɪ'bɑ:r || dɪ'bɑ:(r)/ *vt* **-rr-** (frml) **to ~ sb FROM sth/-ING**: **the fact that she didn't have a degree ~red her from promotion** el hecho de no tener un título universitario le impedía ascender; **he was ~red from taking his final exam** se le prohibió rendir el examen final

debase /dɪ'beɪs/ *vt* 1 (devalue) ‹*ideal/principle*› degradar, envilecer*; ‹*language*› corromper, viciar 2 (demean) ‹*person*› degradar, rebajar

debatable /dɪ'beɪtəbəl/ *adj* discutible

debate¹ /dɪ'beɪt/ *n* 1 [u] (public, parliamentary) debate *m* 2 [u] (discussion) debate *m*, discusión *f*

debate² *vt* 1 ‹*question/topic/motion*› debatir, discutir 2 (weigh up) ‹*idea/possibility*› darle* vueltas a, considerar

debating /dɪ'beɪtɪŋ/ *n* [u] discusión *f*; (*before n*) **~ society** círculo *m* de debate y discusión

debauch /dɪ'bɔ:tʃ/ *vt* (liter) pervertir*, corromper

debauched /dɪ'bɔ:tʃt/ *adj* vicioso, libertino

debauchery /dɪ'bɔ:tʃəri/ *n* [u] disipación *f*, libertinaje *m*; **to lead a life of ~** llevar una vida disipada *or* disoluta

debenture /dɪ'bentʃər || dɪ'bentʃə(r)/ *n* **~ (bond)** (Fin) obligación *f*, bono *m*

debilitate /dɪ'bɪləteɪt || dɪ'bɪlɪteɪt/ *vt* (*often pass*) debilitar

debilitating /dɪ'bɪləteɪtɪŋ || dɪ'bɪlɪteɪtɪŋ/ *adj* ‹*disease*› debilitante; ‹*climate*› extenuante; **her ~ shyness** su timidez enfermiza

debility /dɪ'bɪləti/ *n* [u] debilidad *f*

debit¹ /'debət || 'debɪt/ *n* débito *m*, cargo *m*; (*before n*) **~ balance** saldo *m* deudor; **~ card** tarjeta *f* de cobro automático; **~ note** nota *f* de cargo

debit² *vt* (Fin) debitar, cargar*

debonair /ˌdebə'ner || ˌdebə'neə(r)/ *adj* (suave) elegante y desenvuelto; (courteous) cortés, afable

debrief /'di:'bri:f/ *vt*: **he was ~ed by his captain** rindió informe *or* dio parte de su misión al capitán

debriefing /'di:'bri:fɪŋ/ *n* [u c]: **they were sent for ~** los llamaron para que rindiesen informe *or* diesen parte de su misión

debris /də'bri: || 'debri:, 'deɪbri:/ *n* [u] 1 (rubble) escombros *mpl*; (of plane, ship) restos *mpl*; (rubbish) desechos *mpl* 2 (Geol) detritos *mpl*

debt /det/ *n* 1 [u] (indebtedness) endeudamiento *m*; **I'm $200 in ~** debo 200 dólares, tengo deudas por 200 dólares; **to be in sb's ~** *o* **in ~ to sb** (frml) estarle* en deuda a algn, estar* en deuda con algn; **to get** *o* **run into ~** endeudarse, llenarse *or* cargarse* de deudas; **to get/be out of ~** salir* de/no tener* deudas 2 [c] (money owing) deuda *f*; **foreign ~** deuda externa; **a ~ of honor** una deuda de honor; **bad ~s** deudas incobrables

debt collector *n* cobrador, -dora *m,f* de deudas *or* de morosos

debtor /'detər || 'detə(r)/ *n* deudor, -dora *m,f*

d

debug /ˈdiːˈbʌg/ *vt* **-gg-**
A (Comput) depurar
B ‹*room/building*› localizar* y retirar los micrófonos ocultos de

debunk /ˈdiːˈbʌŋk/ *vt* (colloq) desacreditar

debut, début /ˈdeɪbjuː, ˈde-/ (*pl* **-buts** /-bjuːz/) *n* debut *m*; **to make one's ~** (on stage etc) debutar, hacer* su (*or* mi *etc*) debut

debutante /ˈdebjuːtɑːnt, ˈdeɪ-/ *n* debutante *f*

Dec (= **December**) dic.

decade /ˈdekeɪd/ *n* década *f*

decadence /ˈdekədəns/ *n* [u] decadencia *f*

decadent /ˈdekədənt/ *adj* decadente

decaffeinated /ˈdiːˈkæfəneɪtəd ‖ ˌdiːˈkæfɪneɪtɪd/ *adj* descafeinado

decal /ˈdiːkæl/ *n* (AmE) calcomanía *f*

decamp /dɪˈkæmp/ *vi* 1 (abscond) (hum) esfumarse (fam), hacerse* humo (AmL fam) 2 (Mil frml) levantar campamento

decant /dɪˈkænt/ *vt* ‹*wine*› decantar

decanter /dɪˈkæntər ‖ dɪˈkæntə(r)/ *n* licorera *f*

decapitate /dɪˈkæpɪteɪt/ *vt* decapitar

decathlon /dɪˈkæθlən/ *n* decatlón *m*

decay[1] /dɪˈkeɪ/ *vi*
A (rot) «*foodstuffs/corpse*» descomponerse*, pudrirse*; «*wood*» pudrirse*; «*tooth*» cariarse, picarse*
B (deteriorate) «*building/machine*» deteriorarse; «*empire/culture/civilization*» decaer*, declinar
■ **decay** *vt* (rot) ‹*food/corpse*› descomponer*; ‹*wood*› pudrir*; ‹*tooth*› picar*, cariar

decay[2] *n* [u]
A (of organic matter) descomposición *f*; (*tooth* ~) caries *f*
B (of building) deterioro *m*; (of culture) decadencia *f*

deceased[1] /dɪˈsiːst/ *n* (*pl* ~) (frml) **the ~** el difunto, la difunta; (*pl*) los difuntos, las difuntas (frml)

deceased[2] *adj* (frml) difunto; **her ~ husband** su difunto marido; **William Jones, ~** el difunto William Jones

deceit /dɪˈsiːt/ *n* [u c] engaño *m*

deceitful /dɪˈsiːtfəl/ *adj* ‹*person*› falso, embustero; ‹*action*› engañoso

deceive /dɪˈsiːv/ *vt* engañar; **he was ~d by her story** se dejó engañar por lo que le contó; **to ~ sb INTO -ING** engañar a algn PARA QUE (+ *subj*); **to ~ oneself** engañarse

deceiver /dɪˈsiːvər ‖ dɪˈsiːvə(r)/ *n* impostor, -tora *m,f*

decelerate /ˈdiːˈseləreɪt/ *vi* (frml) «*vehicle/driver*» reducir* *or* aminorar la velocidad

December /dɪˈsembər ‖ dɪˈsembə(r)/ *n* diciembre *m*; *see also* **January**

decency /ˈdiːsn̩si/ *n* 1 [u] (of dress, conduct) decencia *f*, decoro *m* 2 [u] (propriety) buena educación *f*, consideración *f*; **she didn't even have the ~ to ask me** ni siquiera tuvo la consideración de preguntarme 3 **decencies** *pl* (proper conduct) (frml): **to observe the decencies** guardar las formas

decent /ˈdiːsn̩t/ *adj*
A 1 (appropriate) ‹*language/conduct/dress*› decente, decoroso; **are you ~?** ¿estás presentable?; **to do the ~ thing** hacer* lo que corresponde *or* es correcto 2 (respectable) decente
B (acceptable) ‹*person*› pasable, aceptable; ‹*meal/housing*› decente, como es debido
C (kind) amable; **he's being very ~ about it all** se está portando muy bien

decently /ˈdiːsn̩tli/ *adv*
A 1 (respectably) ‹*dress/behave*› decentemente, con decencia 2 (reasonably): **we couldn't ~ refuse** hubiera sido descortés *or* una descortesía el no aceptar
B (acceptably) ‹*perform/cook*› bastante bien
C (kindly) amablemente

decentralization /diːˈsentrələˈzeɪʃən ‖ diːˌsentrəlaɪˈzeɪʃən/ *n* [u] descentralización *f*

decentralize /diːˈsentrəlaɪz/ *vt* descentralizar*

deception /dɪˈsepʃən/ *n* [u c] engaño *m*; **to obtain sth by ~** obtener* algo mediante *or* valiéndose de engaños

deceptive /dɪˈseptɪv/ *adj* engañoso; **appearances can be ~** las apariencias engañan

deceptively /dɪˈseptɪvli/ *adv*: **it's ~ simple** es aparentemente simple

decibel /ˈdesəbel ‖ ˈdesɪbel/ *n* decibelio *m*, decibel *m*

decide /dɪˈsaɪd/ *vt*
A (make up one's mind) decidir; **I can't ~ which I prefer** no puedo decidir cuál prefiero, no sé por cuál decidirme; **to ~ to + INF** decidir *or* resolver + INF; **what finally ~d me was the price** lo que me decidió *or* me hizo decidir fue el precio
B (settle) ‹*question/issue*› decidir; ‹*outcome*› determinar
■ **decide** *vi* decidirse; **to ~ IN FAVOR OF/AGAINST sth/sb: we ~d in favor of the cheaper one** nos decidimos por el más barato; **the judge ~d in favor of/against the plaintiff** el juez resolvió a favor/en contra del demandante; **she ~d against buying** decidió no comprarlo

Phrasal verb

• **decide on, decide upon** [v ▸ prep ▸ o] ‹*date/venue*› decidir; ‹*candidate*› decidirse por

decided /dɪˈsaɪdəd ‖ dɪˈsaɪdɪd/ *adj* 1 (definite) (*before n*) ‹*improvement/advantage*› claro, marcado 2 (determined) ‹*character/tone*› decidido

decidedly /dɪˈsaɪdədli ‖ dɪˈsaɪdɪdli/ *adv* 1 (definitely) decididamente 2 (determinedly) ‹*speak/act*› con decisión

decider /dɪˈsaɪdər ‖ dɪˈsaɪdə(r)/ *n* (Sport) **the ~** (match) el (partido de) desempate; (point, goal) el tanto (*or* el set *etc*) decisivo

deciding /dɪˈsaɪdɪŋ/ *adj* ‹*factor*› decisivo

deciduous /dɪˈsɪdʒuəs ‖ dɪˈsɪdjʊəs/ *adj* de hoja caduca, caducifolio (téc)

decimal[1] /ˈdesəməl ‖ ˈdesɪməl/ *adj* decimal; **accurate to three ~ places** exacto hasta la tercera cifra decimal

decimal[2] *n* decimal *m*

decimalization /desəmələˈzeɪʃən ‖ ˌdesɪməlaɪˈzeɪʃən/ *n* decimalización *f*, conversión *f* al sistema decimal

decimalize /ˈdesəməlaɪz ‖ ˈdesɪməlaɪz/ *vt* decimalizar*, convertir* al sistema decimal

decimal point *n* ≈ coma *f* (*decimal o de los decimales*), punto *m* decimal

decimate /ˈdesəmeɪt ‖ ˈdesɪmeɪt/ *vt* diezmar

decipher /dɪˈsaɪfər ‖ dɪˈsaɪfə(r)/ *vt* descifrar

decision /dɪˈsɪʒən/ *n* [c u] decisión *f*; **to make** *o* (BrE also) **take a ~** tomar una decisión; **on** *o* **by a ~** (in boxing) por puntos, por decisión (AmL)

decision-making /dɪˈsɪʒənˌmeɪkɪŋ/ *n* [u] toma *f* de decisiones; (*before n*) ‹*body/process*› decisorio

decisive /dɪˈsaɪsɪv/ *adj*
A (conclusive) ‹*battle/factor*› decisivo; ‹*victory*› contundente
B (purposeful) ‹*person*› decidido, resuelto; ‹*leadership/answer*› firme

decisively /dɪˈsaɪsɪvli/ *adv* 1 (convincingly) ‹*beat/win*› contundentemente 2 (purposefully) ‹*speak/act*› con decisión

deck[1] /dek/ *n*
A 1 (Naut) cubierta *f*; **below ~(s)** bajo cubierta; **to go up on ~** salir* a cubierta; ***to be on ~*** (AmE) (in baseball) estar* esperando turno, estar* en el círculo de espera; (ready, to hand) estar* a mano; ***to clear the ~(s)***: **let's clear the ~s before we start the new project** despejemos el camino antes de embarcarnos en el nuevo proyecto 2 (of stadium) (AmE) nivel *m* 3 (*sun* ~) terraza *f* 4 (of bus) (BrE) piso *m*
B (ground) (sl): ***to hit the ~*** (fall flat) caerse* al suelo
C (Audio) deck *m* (AmL), pletina *f* (Esp)
D 1 (AmE Games) ~ **(of cards)** baraja *f*, mazo *m* (esp AmL) 2 (Comput) lote *m*, paquete *m*

deck[2] *vt*
A (adorn) **to ~ sth (out) WITH sth** engalanar *or* adornar algo CON algo; **he was all ~ed out in his Sunday best** iba muy endomingado, iba de punta en blanco
B (knock down) (AmE colloq) tumbar (fam)

deck: **~chair** *n* silla *f* de playa, perezosa *f* (Col, Per), reposera *f* (RPl); ***to rearrange the ~chairs on the Titanic*** tocar* el violín mientras el barco se hunde; **~hand** *n* marinero *m*

decking /ˈdekɪŋ/ *n* [u] 1 (of ship) material *m* de cubierta 2 (material for floors, doors etc) tablones *mpl* 3 (embellishment) embellecimiento *m*

declaim /dɪˈkleɪm/ *vt/i* declamar

declaration /ˈdekləˈreɪʃən/ *n*
A (statement) declaración *f*; **a customs ~** una declaración de aduanas
B (Law) (finding) pronunciamiento *m* (oficial); (statement) declaración *f*

declare /dɪ'kler || dɪ'kleə(r)/ *vt* 1 (state, announce) ‹*intention*› declarar; ‹*opinion*› manifestar*; **to ~ war** declarar la guerra; **to ~ war on** *o* **against sb/sth** declararle la guerra a algn/algo; **the museum was officially ~d open** el museo fue inaugurado oficialmente 2 (Tax) ‹*goods/income*› declarar; **nothing to ~** nada que declarar

■ **declare** *vi*

A (AmE Pol) 1 (announce candidacy) anunciar su (*or* mi *etc*) candidatura 2 (take sides) **to ~ FOR/AGAINST sb/sth** declararse *or* pronunciarse A FAVOR/EN CONTRA DE algn/algo

B (*as interj*) (dated): **well, I (do) ~!** ¡válgame Dios! (ant)

declared /dɪ'klerd || dɪ'kleəd/ *adj* (*before n*) ‹*aim/motive*› declarado

declassify /'di':klæsəfaɪ || ˌdi:'klæsɪfaɪ/ *vt* **-fies, -fying, -fied**: **the information has been declassified** el público tiene ahora libre acceso a la información

declension /dɪ'klenʃən/ *n* [c u] (Ling) declinación *f*

decline[1] /dɪ'klaɪn/ *n* (*no pl*) 1 (decrease) descenso *m*, disminución *f* 2 (downward trend) declive *m*, decadencia *f*, deterioro *m*; **to be in ~** estar* en declive *or* en decadencia; **to fall into ~** entrar en decadencia; **to go into a ~** entrar en decadencia; (Med) empezar* a empeorar

decline[2] *vi*

A 1 (decrease) «*production/strength*» disminuir*, decrecer*; «*interest*» disminuir*, decaer*; **to ~ in importance** perder* importancia 2 (deteriorate) «*health*» deteriorarse; «*industry/region/standards*» decaer* 3 **declining** *pres p* ‹*industry/region/standards*› en declive, en decadencia; **in his declining years** en sus últimos años

B (refuse): **I invited him, but he ~d** lo invité, pero rehusó *or* declinó mi invitación

■ **decline** *vt*

A (refuse) ‹*offer/invitation*› rehusar, declinar; **he ~d to comment** declinó hacer declaraciones

B (Ling) declinar

declutch /'di:'klʌtʃ/ *vi* desembragar*, sacar* el clutch (Col, Méx)

decode /'di:'kəʊd/ *vt* ‹*signal*› descodificar*; ‹*message*› descifrar

decoder /'di:'kəʊdər || ˌdi:'kəʊdə(r)/ *n* descodificador *m*

decolonize /di:'kɑ:lənaɪz || di:'kɒlənaɪz/ *vt* descolonizar*

decommission /ˌdi:kə'mɪʃən/ *vt* 1 (take out of service) ‹*ship*› retirar del servicio a 2 (make safe, dismantle) ‹*weapons/nuclear reactor*› desmantelar

decompose /'di:kəm'pəʊz/ *vi* descomponerse*, pudrirse*

decomposition /'di:kɑ:mpə'zɪʃən || ˌdi:kɒmpə'zɪʃən/ *n* [u] descomposición *f*

decompress /ˌdi:kəm'pres/ *vt*

A ‹*diver*› someter a descompresión

B ‹*data*› descomprimir*

decompression /'di:kəm'preʃən/ *n* [u]

A (Naut) descompresión *f*; (*before n*) **~ chamber** cámara *f* de descompresión

B (expansion of compressed data) descompresión *f*

decongestant /'di:kən'dʒestənt/ *n* [u c] descongestionante *m*, anticongestivo *m*

deconstructivism /'di:kəns'trʌktɪvɪzm/ *n* [u] deconstructivismo *m*

decor, décor /deɪ'kɔ:r || 'deɪkɔ:(r)/ *n* [u c] 1 (furnishings) decoración *f* 2 (Theat) decorado *m*, escenografía *f*

decorate /'dekəreɪt/ *vt*

A 1 ‹*room/house*› (with paint) pintar; (with wallpaper) empapelar 2 ‹*Christmas tree*› adornar, decorar (AmL); ‹*cake*› decorar

B (award medal to) (*usu pass*) **to ~ sb (FOR sth)** condecorar a algn (POR algo)

■ **decorate** *vi* (paint) pintar; (hang wallpaper) empapelar

decorating /'dekəreɪtɪŋ/ *n* [u]: **he helped me with the ~** me ayudó a decorar la casa (*or* la habitación *etc*)

decoration /'dekə'reɪʃən/ *n*

A 1 [u] (act) decoración *f* 2 [u] (ornamentation) decoración *f*; **for ~** de adorno 3 [c] (ornament) adorno *m*

B [u c] (Mil) condecoración *f*

decorative /'dekərətɪv/ *adj* ‹*object*› ornamental, de adorno; **the ~ arts** las artes decorativas

decorator /'dekəreɪtər || 'dekəreɪtə(r)/ *n* 1 (painter) pintor, -tora *m,f*; (paperhanger) empapelador, -dora *m,f* 2 (designer) decorador, -dora *m,f*, interiorista *mf*

decorous /'dekərəs/ *adj* (frml) decoroso

decorum /dɪ'kɔ:rəm/ *n* [u] decoro *m*

decoy /'di:kɔɪ/ *n* (lure) señuelo *m*; (in hunting) señuelo *m*, reclamo *m*

decrease[1] /dɪ'kri:s, 'di:kri:s/ *vi* 1 (in quantity) «*amount/numbers*» disminuir*, decrecer*; «*prices*» bajar; «*speed*» disminuir* 2 (in intensity) «*quality*» disminuir*, bajar; «*power/effectiveness*» disminuir*, decrecer*; «*interest*» disminuir*, decaer*

■ **decrease** *vt* disminuir*, reducir*

decrease[2] /'di:kri:s, dɪ'kri:s/ *n* [c u] disminución *f*, descenso *m*; **crime is on the ~** la delincuencia está disminuyendo

decreasing /dɪ'kri:sɪŋ/ *adj* decreciente

decree[1] /dɪ'kri:/ *n* 1 (command) decreto *m* 2 (Law): **~ nisi/absolute** sentencia *f* provisional/definitiva (*en un juicio de divorcio*)

decree[2] *vt* decretar

decrepit /dɪ'krepət || dɪ'krepɪt/ *adj* 1 (dilapidated) ‹*bus/furniture*› destartalado; ‹*house*› deteriorado, viejo y en mal estado 2 (infirm) ‹*person/animal*› decrépito

decrepitude /dɪ'krepətu:d || dɪ'krepɪtju:d/ *n* [u] 1 (dilapidation) deterioro *m* 2 (infirmity) decrepitud *f*

decriminalize /'di:'krɪmɪnəlaɪz/ *vt* despenalizar*

decry /dɪ'kraɪ/ *vt* **decries, decrying, decried** (condemn) condenar, censurar; (disparage) menospreciar

decryption /di:'krɪpʃən/ *n* desciframiento *m*, descodificación *f*

dedicate /'dedɪkeɪt/ *vt*

A 1 (devote) **to ~ sth TO sth/-ING** dedicar* algo A algo/+ INF 2 ‹*poem/book*› dedicar*; **to ~ sth TO sb** dedicarle* algo A algn

B 1 (consecrate) ‹*church/shrine/memorial*› dedicar* 2 (declare open) (AmE) ‹*building/fair*› inaugurar

dedicated /'dedɪkeɪtəd || 'dedɪkeɪtɪd/ *adj*

A ‹*musician/nurse/teacher*› de gran dedicación, dedicado *or* entregado a su (*or* mi *etc*) trabajo; **to be ~ TO sth** estar* dedicado *or* entregado A algo

B (Comput) (*before n*) dedicado

dedication /'dedɪ'keɪʃən/ *n*

A [u] (devotion) **~ (TO sth)** dedicación *f* *or* entrega *f* (A algo)

B [c] (written message) dedicatoria *f*

C [u] 1 (consecration) dedicación *f* 2 (opening) (AmE) inauguración *f*

deduce /dɪ'du:s || dɪ'dju:s/ *vt*: **to ~ sth FROM sth** deducir* *or* inferir* algo DE algo

deduct /dɪ'dʌkt/ *vt* **to ~ sth (FROM sth)** deducir* *or* descontar* algo (DE algo)

deductible[1] /dɪ'dʌktəbəl/ *adj* deducible; (*tax-~*) desgravable

deductible[2] *n* (AmE) franquicia *f*

deduction /dɪ'dʌkʃən/ *n*

A [u c] (subtraction) deducción *f*, descuento *m*; **he gets $260 a week after ~s** gana 260 dólares semanales netos

B [u c] (reasoning, conclusion) deducción *f*

deed[1] /di:d/ *n*

A (action) hecho *m*; **~s, not words** hechos y no palabras; **good ~s** buenas acciones *fpl*, buenas obras *fpl*; **in word and in ~** de palabra y obra

B (Law) escritura *f*; **the ~** *o* **~s to the house** la escritura de la casa

deed[2] *vt* (AmE) ceder, transferir*

deed poll *n* (BrE): **to change one's name by ~ ~** ≈ cambiarse el apellido oficialmente

deejay /'di:ˌdʒeɪ/ *n* (colloq) disc-jockey *mf*, pinchadiscos *mf* (Esp fam)

deem /di:m/ *vt* (frml) considerar, juzgar*

deep[1] /di:p/ *adj* **-er, -est**

A 1 ‹*water*› profundo; ‹*hole/pit*› profundo, hondo; ‹*gash*› profundo; ‹*dish*› hondo; ‹*pan*› alto; **the ditch is 6 ft ~** la zanja tiene 6 pies de profundidad; *see also* **deep end** 2 (horizontally) ‹*shelf*› profundo; **the soldiers were standing 12 ~** los soldados formaban columnas de 12 en fondo 3 (broad) ‹*edge*› ancho

B ‹*sigh/groan*› profundo, hondo; **take a ~ breath** respire hondo

C 1 ‹*voice*› profundo, grave; ‹*note*› grave 2 ‹*color*› intenso, subido

d

D 1 (intense) ‹*sleep/love/impression*› profundo; **it is with ~ regret that ...** es con gran *or* profundo pesar que ...; **to be in ~ trouble** estar* en un serio apuro *or* (fam) en un buen lío 2 ‹*thoughts*› profundo 3 ‹*mystery/secret*› profundo; **she's a ~ one** (colloq) es un enigma

deep² *adv* **-er, -est**

A 1 (of penetration): **to dig ~** cavar hondo; **he thrust his hands ~ in(to) his pockets** hundió las manos en los bolsillos; **feelings run very ~ among the population** hay un sentir muy fuerte entre la población; **he looked ~ into her eyes** la miró fijamente a los ojos 2 (thoroughly): **to go ~er (into sth)** ahondar *or* profundizar* más (en algo)

B 1 (situated far from edge): **~ in the forest** en lo profundo del bosque; **~ down you know I'm right** en el fondo sabes que tengo razón 2 (greatly involved) **to be ~ IN sth**: **I found her ~ in her book** la encontré absorta *or* ensimismada en su libro; **you're in this too ~** (colloq) estás metido en esto hasta el cuello (fam)

C (extensively): **to drink ~ of sth** (liter) embeberse de *or* en algo

deep³ *n* (liter) (*no pl*) (sea) **the ~** el piélago (liter)

deepen /'di:pən/ *vt*

A ‹*canal/well*› hacer* más profundo *or* hondo

B ‹*knowledge*› profundizar* *or* ahondar en; ‹*concern*› aumentar; ‹*friendship*› estrechar

■ **deepen** *vi*

A «*gorge/river*» hacerse* *or* volverse* más hondo *or* profundo

B «*concern/love*» hacerse* más profundo, aumentar; «*friendship*» estrecharse; «*mystery*» crecer*, aumentar; «*crisis*» acentuarse*; «*darkness*» hacerse* más profundo

deep end *n* **the ~ ~** (of swimming pool) la parte honda, lo hondo (fam); ***to go*** *o* ***jump off the ~ ~*** (colloq) ponerse* hecho una furia (fam); ***to throw sb in (at) the ~ ~*** meter a algn de lleno en lo más difícil

deepening /'di:pənɪŋ/ *adj* ‹*waters/darkness/mystery*› cada vez más profundo; ‹*dismay/crisis*› creciente, cada vez mayor

deep: ~ freeze *n* 1 [c] (in shop, home) congelador *m*, freezer *f* (AmL); 2 [u] (state): **the proposal is in ~ freeze** la propuesta ha sido congelada; **~-freeze** /'di:p'fri:z/ *vt* (*past* **-froze**; *past p* **-frozen**) congelar; (commercially) ultracongelar; **~-frozen cod** bacalao *m* ultracongelado; **~ freezer** *n* ▸ **~ freeze A**; **~-fry** /'di:p'fraɪ/ *vt* **-fries, -frying, -fried** freír* (*en abundante aceite*); **~ fryer** *n* freidora *f*

deeply /'di:pli/ *adv*

A ‹*sigh*› profundamente; **to breathe ~** respirar hondo; **he cut ~ into the wood** hizo un corte profundo en la madera

B ‹*think*› a fondo; ‹*concerned*› profundamente; ‹*interested*› sumamente; **I was ~ offended by his remarks** me sentí muy ofendida por sus comentarios

deep: ~-rooted /'di:p'ru:təd || ˌdi:p'ru:tɪd/ *adj* ‹*belief*› profundamente arraigado; **~-sea** /'di:p'si:/ *adj* (*before n*) **~-sea diving** buceo *m* de altura *or* en alta mar; **~-sea fishing** pesca *f* de altura; **~-seated** /'di:p'si:təd || ˌdi:p'si:tɪd/ *adj* ‹*prejudice/conviction*› profundamente arraigado; ‹*problem*› de raíces profundas; **~-set** /'di:p'set/ *adj* ‹*eyes*› hundido; **~ South** *n* **the D~ South** *el sureste de Estados Unidos, Carolina del Sur, Georgia, Alabama, Misisipí y Luisiana*; **~ space** *n* [u] espacio *m* interplanetario; **~-vein thrombosis** /'di:p'veɪn/ *n* trombosis *f* venosa profunda, TVP *f*

deer /dɪr || dɪə(r)/ *n* (*pl* ~) ciervo *m*, venado *m*

deerstalker /'dɪrˌstɔ:kər || 'dɪəˌstɔ:kə(r)/ *n* gorra *f* de cazador

de-escalate /'di:'eskəleɪt/ *vt* ‹*bombing*› desescalar, reducir*; ‹*crisis*› desacelerar

■ **de-escalate** *vi* «*violence*» disminuir*, reducirse*; «*situation*» mejorar

deface /dɪ'feɪs/ *vt* ‹*wall/notice*› pintarrajear

de facto /deɪ'fæktəʊ/ *adj/adv* (frml) de facto

defamation /'defə'meɪʃən/ *n* [u] (frml) difamación *f*

defamatory /dɪ'fæmətɔ:ri || dɪ'fæmətri/ *adj* difamatorio

defame /dɪ'feɪm/ *vt* (frml) difamar

default¹ /dɪ'fɔ:lt/ *n* [u]

A (omission) omisión *f*; (on payments) mora *f*; (failure to appear) incomparecencia *f*; (Law) rebeldía *f*; **she won by ~** (Sport) ganó por incomparecencia de su rival

B (lack) falta *f*; **he was elected by ~** fue elegido por ausencia de otros candidatos; (*before n*) **~ option** (Comput) opción *f* por defecto

default² *vi* 1 (Fin) **to ~ (ON sth)** no pagar* (algo) 2 (Law) estar* en rebeldía 3 (Sport) no presentarse

defaulter /dɪ'fɔ:ltər || dɪ'fɔ:ltə(r)/ *n* 1 (Fin) moroso, -sa *m,f* 2 (Law) rebelde *mf*

defeat¹ /dɪ'fi:t/ *n* [u c] 1 (by opponent) derrota *f*; **to accept** *o* **admit ~** darse* por vencido 2 (of motion, bill) (Adm, Govt) rechazo *m*

defeat² *vt*

A ‹*opponent*› derrotar, vencer*

B ‹*hopes/plans*› frustrar; **that would ~ the object of the exercise** eso iría en contra de lo que se pretende lograr

C (Adm, Govt) ‹*opposition*› derrotar; ‹*bill/motion*› rechazar*

D (baffle) (colloq): **it ~s me** no alcanzo a comprenderlo

defeatism /dɪ'fi:tɪzəm/ *n* [u] derrotismo *m*

defeatist¹ /dɪ'fi:təst || dɪ'fi:tɪst/ *adj* derrotista

defeatist² *n* derrotista *mf*

defecate /'defɪkeɪt || 'defəkeɪt/ *vi* (frml) defecar* (frml)

defect¹ /'di:fekt/ *n* defecto *m*; **a speech/birth ~** un defecto en el habla/de nacimiento

defect² /dɪ'fekt/ *vi* (Pol) desertar*, defeccionar (period); **their key man has ~ed to a rival team** su mejor hombre se ha pasado a un equipo rival

defection /dɪ'fekʃən/ *n* [u c] deserción *f*; (Pol) defección *f*

defective /dɪ'fektɪv/ *adj*

A (imperfect) defectuoso

B (Ling) defectivo

defector /dɪ'fektər || dɪ'fektə(r)/ *n* desertor, -tora *m,f*

defence *etc* (BrE) ▸ **defense** *etc*

defend /dɪ'fend/ *vt* defender*; **to ~ oneself** defenderse*; **to ~ sth/sb FROM/AGAINST sth/sb** defender* algo/a algn DE algo/algn

■ **defend** *vi*

A (Law) actuar* por la defensa

B (Sport): **he's better at ~ing** juega mejor como defensa

defendant /dɪ'fendənt/ *n* (Law) (in civil case) demandado, -da *m,f*; (in criminal case) acusado, -da *m,f*

defender /dɪ'fendər || dɪ'fendə(r)/ *n* 1 (of cause, course of action, opinion) defensor, -sora *m,f* 2 (Sport) defensa *mf*

defending /dɪ'fendɪŋ/ *adj*: **the ~ champion** el actual campeón (*que defiende su título*); **~ counsel** (Law) abogado defensor, abogada defensora *m,f*

defense, (BrE) **defence** /dɪ'fens, 'di:fens || dɪ'fens/ *n*

A [u] 1 (Mil) defensa *f*; **Secretary of D~** (in US) Ministro, -tra *m,f* *or* (Méx) Secretario, -ria *m,f* de Defensa; (*before n*) **Defence Minister** (in UK) Ministro, -tra *m,f* *or* (Méx) Secretario, -ria *m,f* de Defensa 2 (on personal level) defensa *f*; **to come to sb's ~** salir* *or* acudir en defensa de algn

B [c] 1 (protection) defensa *f*, protección *f* 2 (apologia) defensa *f*

C **defenses** *pl* (Mil, Med, Psych) defensas *fpl*; **to lower** *o* **drop one's ~s** bajar la guardia

D [c] (Law) defensa *f*; (*before n*) **~ counsel** abogado defensor, abogada defensora *m,f*

E 1 [u] (Sport) defensa *f* 2 [c] (in chess) defensa *f*

defenseless, (BrE) **defenceless** /dɪ'fensləs || dɪ'fenslɪs/ *adj* indefenso

defense mechanism, (BrE) **defence mechanism** *n* (Physiol, Psych) mecanismo *m* de defensa

defensible /dɪ'fensəbəl/ *adj* 1 (Mil) defendible 2 ‹*theory/conduct*› defendible, justificable

defensive /dɪ'fensɪv/ *adj* defensivo; **to get ~** ponerse* a la defensiva; ***to be on the ~*** (Mil, Psych) estar* a la defensiva

defer /dɪ'fɜ:r || dɪ'fɜ:(r)/ **-rr-** *vt* 1 (postpone) (frml) diferir* (frml), aplazar*, postergar* (esp AmL) 2 **deferred** *past p* ‹*charges/taxation*› (Fin) diferido; ‹*shares*› (Fin) de dividendo diferido; ‹*sentence*› (Law) aplazado 3 (AmE Mil): **he was ~red on medical grounds** le concedieron una prórroga por razones médicas

Phrasal verb

• **defer to** [v ▸ prep ▸ o] (frml) deferir* a (frml)

deference /'defərəns/ *n* [u] (frml) deferencia *f*; **in/out of ~ to sb/sth** por deferencia a algn/algo

deferential /'defə'rentʃəl || ˌdefə'renʃəl/ *adj* deferente; **to be ~ TO sb** ser* deferente (PARA) CON algn

deferment /dɪ'fɜ:rmənt || dɪ'fɜ:mənt/ *n* [u c] [1] (of decision, payment) (frml) aplazamiento *m* [2] (AmE Mil) prórroga *f*

defiance /dɪ'faɪəns/ *n* [u]: **an act of ~** un desafío, un acto de rebeldía; **in ~ of her orders** haciendo caso omiso de sus órdenes

defiant /dɪ'faɪənt/ *adj* ‹*attitude/tone*› desafiante; ‹*person*› rebelde

defiantly /dɪ'faɪəntli/ *adv* con actitud desafiante

defibrillator /di:'fɪbrəleɪtər || di:'fɪbrɪleɪtə(r)/ *n* desfibrilador *m*

deficiency /dɪ'fɪʃənsi/ *n* (*pl* **-cies**)
A [c u] [1] (Med) deficiencia *f* [2] (shortage) escasez *f*, déficit *m*
B [c] (shortcoming) deficiencia *f*

deficient /dɪ'fɪʃənt/ *adj* (frml) deficiente, insuficiente; **~ IN sth**: **foods ~ in vitamins** alimentos de bajo contenido vitamínico; **a plan ~ in imagination** un plan carente de imaginación

deficit /'defəsɪt || 'defɪsɪt/ *n* déficit *m*

defile /dɪ'faɪl/ *vt* [1] (Relig) profanar [2] (liter) ‹*mind/spirit*› envilecer* (liter), corromper*; ‹*memory*› profanar; ‹*woman*› deshonrar (liter)

definable /dɪ'faɪnəbəl/ *adj* definible

define /dɪ'faɪn/ *vt*
A [1] (state meaning of, describe) ‹*word/position*› definir [2] ‹*powers/duties*› delimitar [3] (characterize) distinguir*
B (outline) (*usu pass*) definir

definite /'defənət, 'defnət || 'defɪnɪt/ *adj*
A [1] (final) ‹*date/price/offer*› definitivo, en firme [2] (certain) seguro, confirmado [3] (firm, categorical) ‹*tone*› firme, terminante; **she was very ~ about wanting to come** dijo categóricamente que quería venir [4] (distinct): **it's a ~ advantage/possibility** es, sin duda, una ventaja/posibilidad
B (Ling): **~ article** artículo *m* determinado *or* definido

definitely /'defənətli, 'defnətli || 'defɪnɪtli/ *adv* [1] (without doubt): **it's ~ true/an improvement** es indudablemente cierto/una mejora; **he ~ said we should meet here** seguro que dijo que nos encontráramos aquí [2] (definitively) ‹*arrange/agree*› definitivamente [3] (firmly) ‹*speak/say*› terminantemente, categóricamente; ‹*act*› con firmeza

definition /'defə'nɪʃən || ˌdefɪ'nɪʃən/ *n*
A [c u] [1] (statement of meaning) definición *f*; **what's your ~ of good music?** ¿tú qué entiendes por buena música?; **by ~** por definición [2] (categorization) definición *f*, delimitación *f*
B [u] [1] (focus): **the plot lacked ~** la trama argumental no estaba bien definida [2] (Cin, Phot, TV) nitidez *f*, definición *f*

definitive /dɪ'fɪnətɪv/ *adj* (*no comp*) [1] (final) ‹*verdict/victory*› definitivo [2] (authoritative) ‹*biography/study*› de mayor autoridad

definitively /dɪ'fɪnətɪvli/ *adv* definitivamente

deflate /dɪ'fleɪt/ *vt*
A [1] ‹*balloon/tire*› desinflar [2] (humble): **to ~ sb** *o* **sb's ego** bajarle los humos a algn [3] (depress) deprimir; **I felt ~d** me sentí por los suelos
B (Econ) deflactar
■ **deflate** *vi* «*balloon/tire*» desinflarse

deflation /dɪ'fleɪʃən/ *n* [u] deflación *f*

deflationary /dɪ'fleɪʃəneri || dɪ'fleɪʃənəri/ *adj* deflacionario

deflect /dɪ'flekt/ *vt* **to ~ sth (FROM sth)** desviar* algo (DE algo)
■ **deflect** *vi* desviarse*

deflection /dɪ'flekʃən/ *n* [u c] (of ball, bullet) desviación *f*; (of light) refracción *f*; (of particle) deflexión *f*

deflower /'di:'flaʊər || ˌdi:'flaʊə(r)/ *vt* (liter) desflorar (liter), desvirgar*

defog /'di:'fɔ:g || ˌdi:'fɒg/ *vt* **-gg-** (AmE) desempañar

defogger /'di:'fɔ:gər || ˌdi:'fɒgə(r)/ *n* (AmE) desempañador *m*

defoliate /'di:'fəʊlieɪt/ *vt* defoliar

defoliation /'di:'fəʊli'eɪʃən/ *n* [u] defoliación *f*

deforestation /'di:'fɔ:rə'steɪʃən || ˌdi:fɒrɪ'steɪʃən/ *n* [u] deforestación *f*, despoblación *f* forestal (Esp)

deform /dɪ'fɔ:rm || dɪ'fɔ:m/ *vt* deformar

deformation /'di:fɔ:r'meɪʃən || ˌdi:fɔ:'meɪʃən/ *n* [u c] deformación *f*

deformed /dɪ'fɔ:rmd || dɪ'fɔ:md/ *adj* deforme

deformity /dɪ'fɔ:rməti || dɪ'fɔ:məti/ *n* [u c] (*pl* **-ties**) [1] (disfigurement, malformation) deformidad *f* [2] (of mind, character) deformación *f*

defraud /dɪ'frɔ:d/ *vt* ‹*person*› estafar; **to ~ the state** defraudar al estado; **to ~ sb OF sth** estafarle algo A algn

defray /dɪ'freɪ/ *vt* (frml) ‹*cost*› sufragar* (frml), costear

defrock /'di:'frɑ:k || ˌdi:'frɒk/ *vt* (Relig): **he was ~ed** lo apartaron del sacerdocio

defrost /'di:'frɔ:st || ˌdi:'frɒst/ *vt* [1] ‹*food*› descongelar; ‹*refrigerator*› deshelar*, descongelar [2] (AmE) ‹*windshield*› desempañar
■ **defrost** *vi* «*meat*» descongelarse; «*refrigerator*» deshelarse*, descongelarse

deft /deft/ *adj* **-er, -est** ‹*movement*› hábil, diestro; **to be ~ AT sth/-ING** ser* hábil PARA algo/+ INF

deftly /'deftli/ *adv* hábilmente, con destreza

defunct /dɪ'fʌŋkt/ *adj* [1] (extinct) ‹*idea/theory*› caduco; ‹*institution*› desaparecido, extinto, fenecido (frml) [2] (dead) (frml) difunto (frml)

defuse /'di:'fju:z/ *vt* ‹*bomb*› desactivar; ‹*situation*› distender*; ‹*crisis*› calmar

defy /dɪ'faɪ/ *vt* **defies, defying, defied**
A [1] (disobey) ‹*order/authority*› desacatar, desobedecer* [2] (resist): **to ~ understanding/description** ser* incomprensible/indescriptible; **to ~ all logic** *o* **reason** no tener* ninguna lógica, ir* en contra de toda lógica [3] (ignore) ‹*danger/death*› desafiar*
B (challenge) **to ~ sb to + INF** desafiar* a algn A QUE (+ *subj*)

degenerate[1] /dɪ'dʒenəreɪt/ *vi* degenerar; «*health*» deteriorarse; **to ~ INTO sth** degenerar EN algo

degenerate[2] /dɪ'dʒenərət/ *adj* degenerado

degenerate[3] /dɪ'dʒenərət/ *n* (frml) degenerado, -da *m,f*

degeneration /dɪ'dʒenə'reɪʃən/ *n* [u] [1] (deterioration) degeneración *f*, deterioro *m* [2] (Med) (of tissue, organs) degeneración *f*

degenerative /dɪ'dʒenərətɪv/ *adj* degenerativo

degradation /'degrə'deɪʃən/ *n* [u] degradación *f*

degrade /dɪ'greɪd/ *vt* degradar; **to ~ oneself** degradarse, rebajarse

degrading /dɪ'greɪdɪŋ/ *adj* degradante

degree /dɪ'gri:/ *n*
A (level, amount) grado *m*, nivel *m*; **it's a matter** *o* **question of ~** es cuestión de grados; **there's a ~ of truth in what she says** hay cierta verdad en lo que dice; **to a certain** *o* **limited ~** hasta cierto punto; **to a high ~** en alto grado; ***to a ~*** (extremely) en grado sumo; (to some extent) hasta cierto punto
B (grade, step) grado *m*; **first/third ~ burns** quemaduras *fpl* de primer/tercer grado; **first/second ~ murder** (in US) homicidio *m* en primer/segundo grado; ***by ~s*** gradualmente, paulatinamente; *see also* **third degree**
C (Math, Geog, Meteo, Phys) grado *m*; **it was 40 ~s in the shade** hacía 40 grados a la sombra; **12 ~s below zero** 12 grados bajo cero; **this wine is 12 ~s proof** este vino es de *or* tiene 12 grados
D (Educ) título *m*; **first ~** licenciatura *f*; **he has** *o* (frml) **holds a ~ in chemistry** es licenciado en química; **to take a philosophy ~** hacer* la carrera de filosofía, licenciarse en filosofía; (*before n*) **~ course** licenciatura *f*

dehumanize /'di:'hju:mənaɪz/ *vt* deshumanizar*

dehydrate /'di:'haɪdreɪt/ *vt* deshidratar

dehydrated /'di:haɪ'dreɪtəd || ˌdi:haɪ'dreɪtɪd/ *adj* deshidratado; **to become ~** deshidratarse

dehydration /'di:haɪ'dreɪʃən/ *n* [u] deshidratación *f*

deice /'di:'aɪs/ *vt* deshelar*

deicer /'di:'aɪsər || ˌdi:'aɪsə(r)/ *n* [c u] descongelante *m*

deify /'di:əfaɪ || 'di:ɪfaɪ/ *vt* **-fies, -fying, -fied** deificar*

deign /deɪn/ *vi* **to ~ to + INF** dignarse (A) + INF

deity /'di:əti/ *n* (*pl* **-ties**) deidad *f*; **the D~** Dios

d

d

déjà vu /ˈdeɪʒɑːˈvuː/ *n* [u] déjà vu *m*

dejected /dɪˈdʒektəd || dɪˈdʒektɪd/ *adj* abatido, desalentado

dejectedly /dɪˈdʒektədli || dɪˈdʒektɪdli/ *adv* con desaliento *or* desánimo

dejection /dɪˈdʒekʃən/ *n* [u] abatimiento *m*, desánimo *m*

de jure *adj/adv* de jure

Del = Delaware

delay¹ /dɪˈleɪ/ *vt*

A 1 (make late, hold up) retrasar, demorar (esp AmL); **I don't want to ~ you** no quiero entretenerte 2 **delaying** *pres p* ‹*action/tactics*› dilatorio

B 1 (defer) ‹*decision/payment*› retrasar, demorar (esp AmL); **to ~ -ING: we ~ed signing the contract** retrasamos *or* (AmL tb) demoramos la firma del contrato 2 **delayed** *past p* ‹*action/effect/reaction*› retardado

■ **delay** *vi* tardar, demorar (esp AmL); **there's no point in ~ing any longer** no tiene sentido esperar más tiempo

delay² *n*

A 1 [u] (waiting) tardanza *f*, dilación *f*, demora *f* (esp AmL); **and now, without further ~ ...** y ahora, sin más preámbulos ... 2 [c] (holdup) retraso *m*, demora *f* (esp AmL); **~s can be expected on major roads** se puede esperar embotellamientos en las principales carreteras

B [c] 1 (extra time) (Law) aplazamiento *m*, prórroga *f* 2 (interval) lapso *m*, intervalo *m*

delayed action /dɪˈleɪd/ *n* [u] acción *f* retardada; (*before n*) **delayed-action mechanism** mecanismo *m* de accion retardada

delectable /dɪˈlektəbəl/ *adj* 1 (delicious) delicioso, exquisito 2 (delightful) delicioso, encantador

delectation /ˈdiːlekˈteɪʃən/ *n* [u] (liter) deleite *m*, delectación *f* (frml)

delegate¹ /ˈdelɪgeɪt/ *vt* 1 ‹*duties/powers/responsibility*› **to ~ sth (TO sb)** delegar* algo (EN algn) 2 (depute) **to ~ sb to + INF** delegar* a algn PARA QUE (+ *subj*)

■ **delegate** *vi* delegar*

delegate² /ˈdelɪgət/ *n* delegado, -da *m,f*

delegation /ˈdelɪˈgeɪʃən/ *n*

A [c] 1 (deputation) delegación *f* 2 (in US) (Govt) *grupo de representantes de un estado en el Congreso*

B [u] (act of delegating) delegación *f*

delete /dɪˈliːt/ *vt* suprimir, eliminar; (by crossing out) tachar

deleterious /ˈdeləˈtɪriəs || ˌdelɪˈtɪəriəs/ *adj* (frml) nocivo, perjudicial

deletion /dɪˈliːʃən/ *n* [u c] supresión *f*

deli /ˈdeli/ *n* (colloq) ▸**delicatessen**

deliberate¹ /dɪˈlɪbərət, -brət/ *adj*

A (intentional) ‹*act/attempt*› deliberado, intencionado; **it was a ~ insult** lo dijo (*or* hizo *etc*) con (la) intención de insultar

B 1 (considered) reflexivo 2 (unhurried) pausado, lento

deliberate² /dɪˈlɪbəreɪt/ *vi* (frml) **to ~ (ABOUT/ON sth)** deliberar (SOBRE algo)

■ **deliberate** *vt* (frml) deliberar sobre

deliberately /dɪˈlɪbərətli, -brətli/ *adv*

A (intentionally) adrede, a propósito

B (unhurriedly) pausadamente, con parsimonia

deliberation /dɪˈlɪbəˈreɪʃən/ *n* (frml)

A 1 [u] (consideration) deliberación *f*; **after long ~** tras largas deliberaciones *or* una larga deliberación 2 **deliberations** *pl* (decision-making) deliberaciones *fpl*

B [u] (unhurried manner) parsimonia *f*, calma *f*

delicacy /ˈdelɪkəsi/ *n* (*pl* **-cies**)

A [u] 1 (fineness, intricacy) delicadeza *f*, lo delicado; (fragility) fragilidad *f*, lo delicado 2 (tact) delicadeza *f* 3 (subtleness) lo delicado

B [c] (choice food) manjar *m*, exquisitez *f*

delicate /ˈdelɪkət/ *adj*

A 1 (fine, intricate) ‹*lace/features*› delicado; ‹*workmanship*› fino, esmerado 2 (fragile, needing care) delicado; **a ~ child** un niño delicado (de salud)

B 1 (needing skill) delicado 2 (needing tact) delicado 3 (tactful) delicado, discreto

C (subtle) ‹*shade/taste*› delicado

delicately /ˈdelɪkətli/ *adv*

A ‹*carve/paint*› con delicadeza, delicadamente

B ‹*behave/treat*› con delicadeza

C ‹*patterned/perfumed*› delicadamente

delicatessen /ˈdelɪkəˈtesən/ *n* charcutería *f*, rotisería *f* (CS), salsamentaria *f* (Col), salchichonería *f* (Méx)

delicious /dɪˈlɪʃəs/ *adj* 1 ‹*food/smell*› delicioso, exquisito, riquísimo; **it tastes** *o* **it's ~** está delicioso *or* exquisito *or* riquísimo 2 (delightful) ‹*breeze/feeling*› delicioso

deliciously /dɪˈlɪʃəsli/ *adv* deliciosamente

delight¹ /dɪˈlaɪt/ *n* 1 [u] (joy) placer *m*, deleite *m*; **to take ~ in sth** disfrutar *or* gozar* con algo 2 [c] (source of joy) placer *m*; **her happiness was a ~ to see** era un placer *or* daba gusto verla tan feliz

delight² *vt* 1 (make very happy) llenar de alegría; **his success ~ed them** su éxito los llenó de alegría 2 (give pleasure to) deleitar; **the clown ~ed the children** el payaso hizo las delicias de *or* deleitó a los niños

■ **delight** *vi* **to ~ IN -ING** deleitarse + GER

delighted /dɪˈlaɪtəd || dɪˈlaɪtɪd/ *adj* ‹*grin/look*› de alegría; **to be ~: I told him the news and he was ~** le di la noticia y se alegró muchísimo; **I'm ~ (that) you can come** me alegra mucho que puedas venir; **to be ~ AT sth: we were ~ at the news** la noticia nos causó una enorme alegría *or* nos llenó de alegría; **to be ~ WITH sth/sb** estar* encantado CON algo/algn; **to be ~ to + INF: I am ~ to hear it** no sabes cuánto *or* cómo me alegro; **will you come? — (I should be) ~ (to)** ¿vendrá? — con mucho gusto

delightful /dɪˈlaɪtfəl/ *adj* ‹*weather/evening*› muy agradable, delicioso; ‹*person*› encantador; ‹*dress*› precioso

delightfully /dɪˈlaɪtfəli/ *adv* ‹*sing/paint*› divinamente, de maravilla

delimit /ˈdiːˈlɪmət, dɪ- || diˈlɪmɪt/ *vt* delimitar

delineate /dɪˈlɪnieɪt/ *vt* (frml) 1 (draw) trazar*, delinear 2 (describe) ‹*problem*› definir

delinquency /dɪˈlɪŋkwənsi/ *n* [u] (Law, Sociol) delincuencia *f*

delinquent¹ /dɪˈlɪŋkwənt/ *n* delincuente *mf*

delinquent² *adj* ‹*youth*› delincuente; ‹*activities*› delictivo

delirious /dɪˈlɪriəs/ *adj* 1 (Med) delirante; **to be ~** delirar, desvariar* 2 (wildly excited, happy) (colloq) loco de alegría (fam)

deliriously /dɪˈlɪriəsli/ *adv* 1 ‹*mutter*› delirantemente 2 (colloq): **she was ~ happy** estaba loca de alegría (fam)

delirium /dɪˈlɪriəm/ *n* [u] (Med) delirio *m*, desvarío *m*

delirium tremens /ˈtriːmənz/ *n* delírium tremens *m*

deliver /dɪˈlɪvər || dɪˈlɪvə(r)/ *vt*

A 1 (hand over) entregar*; *see also* **good² C1** 2 (distribute) repartir (*a domicilio*); **we have our paper ~ed every day** nos traen el periódico a casa todos los días

B (save) (liter) librar; **to ~ sb FROM sth** librar a algn DE algo

C 1 (administer) ‹*blow/punch*› propinar, asestar 2 (issue) ‹*ultimatum/lecture/sermon*› dar*; ‹*warning*› hacer*; ‹*speech*› pronunciar; ‹*judgment*› dictar, pronunciar, emitir 3 (produce, provide): **he promised much, but ~ed little** cumplió muy poco de lo mucho que había prometido 4 (Sport) ‹*ball*› lanzar* 5 (in elections) (AmE) ‹*state*› ganar

D (Med): **her husband ~ed the baby** su marido la asistió en el parto

■ **deliver** *vi*

A (Busn): **we ~ free of charge** hacemos reparto(s) a domicilio gratuitamente

B (produce the necessary) (colloq) cumplir

deliverance /dɪˈlɪvərəns/ *n* [u] (liter) liberación *f*

delivery /dɪˈlɪvəri/ *n* (*pl* **-ries**)

A 1 [u] (act) entrega *f*; **how much do you charge for ~?** ¿cuánto cobran por el envío *or* transporte?; **cash on ~** entrega contra reembolso; **to take ~ of sth** recibir algo; (*before n*) **~ charges** gastos *mpl* de envío *or* transporte; **~ man** repartidor *m*; **~ note** (esp BrE) nota *f* de entrega, albarán *m* (de entrega) (Esp); **~ period** plazo *m* de entrega; **~ service** servicio *m* de reparto a domicilio; **~ truck** *o* (BrE) **van** camioneta *f* *or* furgoneta *f* de los repartos 2 [c] (occasion) reparto *m*; **is there a ~ on Saturdays?** ¿hay reparto los sábados? 3 [c] (consignment) partida *f*, remesa *f*

B [u] (freeing) (liter) liberación *f*

C [c] (of baby) parto *m*, alumbramiento *m* (frml); (*before n*) **~ room** sala *f* de partos

D [u] (manner of speaking) expresión *f* oral

B (Sport) **1** [c] (throw) lanzamiento *m* **2** [u] (manner of throwing) (AmE) estilo *m* de lanzamiento

dell /del/ *n* (poet) hondonada *f*

delouse /'di:'laʊs/ *vt* despiojar

delta /'deltə/ *n* delta *m*

delude /dɪ'lu:d/ *vt* engañar; **to ~ sb INTO -ING**: **they ~d him into believing that he had talent** le hicieron creer que tenía talento
■ *v refl* **to ~ oneself** engañarse

deluded /dɪ'lu:dəd || dɪ'lu:dɪd/ *adj* engañado

deluge[1] /'delju:dʒ/ *n*
A **1** (flood) inundación *f*; **the D~** el diluvio (universal) **2** (downpour) diluvio *m*
B (of protests, questions, letters) aluvión *m*, avalancha *f*

deluge[2] *vt*
A (overwhelm): **they were ~d with protests/letters** recibieron un aluvión de protestas/cartas; **he was ~d with offers** le llovieron las ofertas
B (flood) inundar

delusion /dɪ'lu:ʒən/ *n* **1** (mistaken idea) error *m*; (vain hope) falsa ilusión *f* **2** (Psych) idea *f* delirante; **he has ~s of grandeur** tiene delirios de grandeza

deluxe /də'lʊks/ *adj* de lujo

delve /delv/ *vi* **1** (research) (liter) **to ~ INTO sth** ahondar EN algo; **to ~ into the past** hurgar* en el pasado **2** (rummage) hurgar*, escarbar

Dem (in US) = **Democrat**

demagog, (BrE) **demagogue** /'deməgɑ:g || 'deməgɒg/ *n* demagogo, -ga *m,f*

demagogue, (AmE) **demagog** /'deməgɑ:g || 'deməgɒg/ *n* demagogo, -ga *m,f*

demand[1] /dɪ'mænd || dɪ'mɑ:nd/ *vt*
A ‹‹*person*›› (call for, insist on) exigir*; **the unions are ~ing better conditions** los sindicatos reclaman mejores condiciones; **what have I done? he ~ed** —¿qué he hecho yo? —preguntó; **to ~ to + INF** exigir* + INF *or* QUE (+ *subj*); **she ~ed to know the reason** quiso saber el porqué, exigió que se le dijera por qué; **to ~ sth OF sb** exigirle* algo A algn
B (require) ‹*determination/perseverance*› exigir*, requerir*

demand[2] *n*
A [c] (claim) exigencia *f*; (Lab Rel, Pol) reivindicación *f*, reclamo *m*; (request) petición *f*, pedido *m* (AmL); **by popular ~** a petición *or* (AmL tb) pedido del público; **the ~s of the job** las exigencias del trabajo; **abortion on ~** libre aborto *m*; **payable on ~** pagadero a la vista
B [u] (requirement) demanda *f*; **these shoes are much in ~** estos zapatos tienen gran demanda *or* se venden mucho; **he's in great ~** está muy solicitado, es popular

demanding /dɪ'mændɪŋ || dɪ'mɑ:ndɪŋ/ *adj* ‹*job*› que exige mucho; ‹*book/music*› difícil; ‹*teacher*› exigente; **she's a very ~ child** es una niña que exige mucha atención; **it's physically ~** es agotador

demarcate /'di:mɑ:rkeɪt || 'di:mɑ:keɪt/ *vt* (frml) ‹*frontier/area/limit*› demarcar*; ‹*concept*› delimitar

demarcation /'di:mɑ:r'keɪʃən || ˌdi:mɑ:'keɪʃən/ *n* [u] **1** (delimitation) demarcación *f*; (*before n*) **~ line** línea *f* de demarcación **2** (BrE Lab Rel) delimitación *f* de atribuciones

demean /dɪ'mi:n/ *vt* (frml) degradar; **to ~ oneself** rebajarse, degradarse

demeaning /dɪ'mi:nɪŋ/ *adj* degradante

demeanor, (BrE) **demeanour** /dɪ'mi:nər || dɪ'mi:nə(r)/ *n* [u] (frml) **1** (behavior) comportamiento *m*, conducta *f* **2** (bearing) porte *m*

demented /dɪ'mentəd || dɪ'mentɪd/ *adj* **1** (insane) ‹*person*› demente; ‹*screams/mutterings*› enloquecido, de demente **2** (very worried, irritated) (colloq) histérico (fam)

dementia /dɪ'mentʃə || dɪ'menʃə/ *n* [u] demencia *f*

demerara (sugar) /'demə'rɑ:rə || ˌdemə'reərə/ *n* [u] (BrE) azúcar *f* morena, azúcar *m* moreno

demerge /di:'mɜ:rdʒ || di:'mɜ:dʒ/ *vt* (BrE) escindir

demerger /di:'mɜ:rdʒər || di:'mɜ:dʒə(r)/ *n* escisión *f*

demerit /di:'merət || di:'merɪt/ *n* **1** (fault) (frml) demérito *m* (frml) **2** (black mark) (AmE) sanción *f*

demigod /'demɪgɑ:d || 'demɪgɒd/ *n* semidiós *m*

demilitarize /'di:'mɪlɪtəraɪz/ *vt* desmilitarizar*; **~d zone** zona *f* desmilitarizada

demise /dɪ'maɪz/ *n* (*no pl*) (frml) **1** (death) fallecimiento *m* (frml), deceso *m* (AmL frml) **2** (end) desaparición *f*

demist /'di:'mɪst/ *vt* (BrE) desempañar

demister /'di:'mɪstər || ˌdi:'mɪstə(r)/ *n* (BrE) desempañador *m*

demo /'deməʊ/ *n* (*pl* **demos**)
A (Mus) demostración *f*; (*before n*) **~ tape** cinta *f* de demostración
B (protest) (BrE colloq) manifestación *f*

demob /'di:'mɑ:b || ˌdi:'mɒb/ *vt* **-bb-** (BrE) desmovilizar*

demobilization /dɪ'məʊbələ'zeɪʃən || di:ˌməʊbɪlaɪ'zeɪʃən/ *n* [u] desmovilización *f*

demobilize /'dɪ'məʊbəlaɪz || di:'məʊbɪlaɪz/ *vt* desmovilizar*

democracy /dɪ'mɑ:krəsi || dɪ'mɒkrəsi/ *n* [u c] (*pl* **-cies**) democracia *f*

democrat /'deməkræt/ *n* **1** (believer in democracy) demócrata *mf* **2** **Democrat** (in US) demócrata *mf*

democratic /'demə'krætɪk/ *adj* **1** ‹*country/election*› democrático **2** **Democratic** (in US) demócrata

> **Democratic Party**
>
> El Partido Demócrata, creado en 1792, es uno de los dos principales partidos políticos de Estados Unidos. El otro es el Partido Republicano (**Republican Party**). El Partido Demócrata está considerado como el propulsor de políticas más liberales, especialmente referidas a temas que afectan a la sociedad. Por esta razón, consigue el apoyo de sindicatos y grupos minoritarios

democratically /'demə'krætɪkli/ *adv* democráticamente

democratization /dɪ'mɑ:krətə'zeɪʃən || dɪˌmɒkrətaɪ'zeɪʃən/ *n* [u] democratización *f*

democratize /dɪ'mɑ:krətaɪz || dɪ'mɒkrətaɪz/ *vt* democratizar*

demographer /dɪ'mɑ:grəfər || dɪ'mɒgrəfə(r)/ *n* demógrafo, -fa *m,f*

demographic /'demə'græfɪk/ *adj* demográfico

demography /dɪ'mɑ:grəfi || dɪ'mɒgrəfi/ *n* [u] demografía *f*

demolish /dɪ'mɑ:lɪʃ || dɪ'mɒlɪʃ/ *vt*
A ‹*structure/building*› demoler*, derribar, echar abajo; ‹*argument/theory*› demoler*, echar por tierra
B (colloq) **1** (defeat) hacer* polvo (fam) **2** (eat up) zamparse (fam)

demolition /'demə'lɪʃən/ *n* [u c] (of building) demolición *f*, derribo *m*; (of theory) demolición *f*, destrucción *f*

demon /'di:mən/ *n* demonio *m*; **she worked like a ~ all week** (colloq) trabajó como una bestia toda la semana (fam)

demonstrably /dɪ'mɑ:nstrəbli || 'demɒnstrəbli/ *adv* (frml): **a ~ true/false statement** una afirmación cuya verdad/falsedad es demostrable

demonstrate /'demənstreɪt/ *vt* **1** (show) ‹*need/ability*› demostrar* **2** (Marketing) hacer* una demostración de
■ **demonstrate** *vi* (Pol) manifestarse*

demonstration /'demən'streɪʃən/ *n*
A **1** (expression) muestra *f*, demostración *f* **2** (display) demostración *f*
B (Pol) manifestación *f*

demonstrative /dɪ'mɑ:nstrətɪv || dɪ'mɒnstrətɪv/ *adj*
A (expressive) efusivo, expresivo, demostrativo (AmL)
B (Ling) demostrativo

demonstrator /'demənstreɪtər || 'demənstreɪtə(r)/ *n*
A (Pol) manifestante *mf*
B (Marketing) demostrador, -dora *m,f*

demoralize /dɪ'mɔ:rəlaɪz || dɪ'mɒrəlaɪz/ *vt* desmoralizar*

demoralizing /dɪ'mɔ:rəlaɪzɪŋ || dɪ'mɒrəlaɪzɪŋ/ *adj* desalentador, desmoralizante

demote /dɪ'məʊt, 'di:-/ *vt* (in organization) bajar de categoría; (Mil) degradar

demotion /dɪ'məʊʃən, di:-/ *n* [u c] (in organization) descenso *m* de categoría; (Mil) degradación *f*

demotivate /di:'məʊtɪveɪt/ *vt* desmotivar

d

demur¹ /dɪˈmɜːr || dɪˈmɜː(r)/ *vi* **-rr-** (frml) objetar; **to ~ AT sth** poner*(le) objeciones *or* reparos A algo

demur² *n* (frml): **without ~** sin poner objeciones *or* reparos

demure /dɪˈmjʊr || dɪˈmjʊə(r)/ *adj* recatado

demurely /dɪˈmjʊrli || dɪˈmjʊəli/ *adv* recatadamente, con recato

demystify /ˈdiːˈmɪstəfaɪ || ˌdiːˈmɪstɪfaɪ/ *vt* **-fies, -fying, -fied** desmitificar*

den /den/ *n* 1▸ (lair) guarida *f*, cubil *m*; (of thieves) guarida *f*; **a ~ of iniquity** un antro de perdición 2▸ (room) (colloq) cuarto *m* de estar; (for study, work) estudio *m*, gabinete *m*

denationalize /ˈdiːˈnæʃnəlaɪz/ *vt* desnacionalizar*

denatured alcohol /ˈdiːˈneɪtʃərd || ˌdiːˈneɪtʃəd/ *n* [u] alcohol *m* desnaturalizado

denial /dɪˈnaɪəl/ *n*
A [u c] (of accusation, fact): **to issue a ~ of sth** desmentir* algo
B [u c] (of request, rights) denegación *f*
C [u c] (repudiation) negación *f*, rechazo *m*; **to be in ~** negarse* a *or* ser* incapaz de aceptar la realidad
D [u] (abstinence) renuncia *f*, abnegación *f*

denier /ˈdenjər || ˈdenɪə(r)/ *n* denier *m*

denigrate /ˈdenɪgreɪt/ *vt* (frml) 1▸ ‹*character/person*› denigrar 2▸ ‹*effort*› menospreciar

denim /ˈdenəm || ˈdenɪm/ *n*
A [u] (Tex) tela *f* vaquera *or* de jeans, mezclilla *f* (Chi, Méx); (*before n*) ‹*jacket/skirt*› vaquero, tejano (Esp), de mezclilla (Chi, Méx)
B **denims** *pl* (colloq) 1▸ (jeans) vaqueros *mpl*, jeans *mpl*, bluyines *mpl* (Andes) 2▸ (overalls) (AmE) pantalón *m* de peto, mono *m*, overol *m* (AmL)

denizen /ˈdenəzən || ˈdenɪzən/ *n* (liter *or* hum) morador, -dora *m,f*, habitante *mf*

Denmark /ˈdenmɑːrk || ˈdenmɑːk/ *n* Dinamarca *f*

denominate /dɪˈnɑːməneɪt/ *vt* (frml) denominar

denomination /dɪˈnɑːməˈneɪʃən || dɪˌnɒmɪˈneɪʃən/ *n*
A (Relig) confesión *f*
B (of currency) valor *m*, denominación *f* (AmL); **bills in $10 and $20 ~s** billetes de 10 y 20 dólares

denominational /dɪˈnɑːmɪˈneɪʃn̩əl || dɪˌnɒmɪˈneɪʃənl̩/ *adj* confesional

denominator /dɪˈnɑːməneɪtər || dɪˈnɒmɪneɪtə(r)/ *n* (Math) denominador *m*; *see also* **lowest common denominator**

denote /dɪˈnəʊt/ *vt* denotar

denouement, dénouement /ˈdeɪnuːˈmɑːn || deɪˈnuːmɒŋ/ *n* desenlace *m*

denounce /dɪˈnaʊns/ *vt* denunciar

dense /dens/ *adj* **denser, densest**
A 1▸ (closely spaced) ‹*forest/jungle*› espeso; ‹*population/traffic*› denso; ‹*crowd*› compacto, apretado 2▸ (thick) ‹*fog/mist/smoke*› denso, espeso 3▸ (Phys) denso 4▸ (complicated) ‹*prose/article*› denso
B (stupid) (colloq) burro (fam), duro de entendederas (fam)

densely /ˈdensli/ *adv* ‹*populated/forested*› densamente; ‹*packed*› apretadamente

density /ˈdensəti/ *n* [u c] (*pl* **-ties**) densidad *f*; (of fog) lo espeso, densidad *f*

dent¹ /dent/ *n* (in metal) abolladura *f*, abollón *m*; (in wood) marca *f*; **it's made a big ~ in our savings** (colloq) se ha llevado *or* se ha comido una buena parte de nuestros ahorros (fam)

dent² *vt* ‹*metal*› abollar; ‹*wood*› hacer* una marca en; ‹*popularity*› afectar; ‹*pride*› hacer* mella en
■ **dent** *vi* ‹‹*metal*›› abollarse

dental /ˈdentl̩/ *adj* dental; ‹*school*› de odontología

dental: **~ floss** *n* [u] hilo *m* *or* seda *f* dental; **~ surgeon** *n* (frml) cirujano, -na *m,f* dentista

dentist /ˈdentəst || ˈdentɪst/ *n* dentista *mf*, odontólogo, -ga *m,f* (frml); **to go to the ~('s)** ir* al dentista

dentistry /ˈdentəstri || ˈdentɪstri/ *n* [u] odontología *f*

denture /ˈdentʃər || ˈdentʃə(r)/ *n* 1▸ (dental plate) (frml) prótesis *f* dental (frml) 2▸ **dentures** *pl* dentadura *f* postiza; **a set of ~s** una dentadura postiza

denude /dɪˈnuːd || dɪˈnjuːd/ *vt* 1▸ (Geog) ‹*land*› denudar 2▸ (strip) (liter) **to ~ sth/sb OF sth** despojar algo/a algn DE algo (liter)

denunciation /dɪˈnʌnsiˈeɪʃən/ *n* [u c] denuncia *f*

deny /dɪˈnaɪ/ *vt* **denies, denying, denied**
A ‹*accusation/fact*› negar*; ‹*rumors*› desmentir*; **there's no ~ing that ...** es innegable *or* no se puede negar que ...; **he denied (that) other people had been present** negó que hubiera habido alguien más presente; **to ~ -ING**: **she denied stealing** *o* **having stolen it** negó haberlo robado
B (refuse) ‹*request*› denegar*; **to ~ sb sth** negarle* algo a algn; ***to ~ oneself*** sacrificarse*
C (disavow) (liter) ‹*faith/country*› renegar* de

deodorant /diːˈəʊdərənt/ *n* [c u] desodorante *m*

deodorize /diːˈəʊdəraɪz/ *n* desodorizar*

dep = **departs/departure**

depart /dɪˈpɑːrt || dɪˈpɑːt/ *vi*
A (leave) (Transp) salir*, partir (frml); ‹‹*person*›› (frml) partir (frml), salir*
B (deviate) (frml) **to ~ FROM sth** apartarse DE algo; **his version ~s from the truth at several points** su versión se aparta *or* se aleja de la verdad en varios puntos
■ **depart** *vt* (liter): **she ~ed this life** *o* **world at the age of 87** (euph) dejó de existir a los 87 años de edad (frml)

departed¹ /dɪˈpɑːrtəd || dɪˈpɑːtɪd/ *adj* 1▸ (dead) (frml & euph) difunto (frml) 2▸ (past) (liter) ‹*happiness/joys/youth*› perdido

departed² *n* (*pl* ~) (frml & euph) **the ~** el difunto, la difunta; (*pl*) los difuntos, las difuntas (frml)

department /dɪˈpɑːrtmənt || dɪˈpɑːtmənt/ *n*
A (of store) sección *f*; (of company) departamento *m*, sección *f*
B 1▸ (Govt) ministerio *m*, secretaría *f* (Méx); **the D~ of Education** el Ministerio de Educación 2▸ (AmE Adm): **the police/fire ~** el cuerpo de policía/bomberos
C (Educ) departamento *m*
D (area of competence, responsibility) (colloq): **cooking is my husband's ~** la cocina es cosa de mi marido (fam)

departmental /ˈdiːpɑːrtˈmentl̩ || ˌdiːpɑːtˈmentl̩/ *adj* departamental

department store *n* (grandes) almacenes *mpl*, tienda *f* de departamentos (Méx)

departure /dɪˈpɑːrtʃər || dɪˈpɑːtʃə(r)/ *n*
A 1▸ [u c] (Transp) salida *f*, partida *f* (frml); **point of ~** punto *m* de partida; (*before n*) **~ time** hora *f* de salida; **~ gate/lounge** puerta *f*/sala *f* de embarque 2▸ [u] (of person) (frml) partida *f* (frml), ida *f*
B (deviation) (*no pl*): **a ~ from the norm** una desviación de la norma; **it is a new ~ for this government** es una nueva orientación de este gobierno

depend /dɪˈpend/ *vi*
A 1▸ (rely, be dependent) **to ~ ON sb/sth** depender DE algn/algo 2▸ (be determined by) **to ~ ON sth** depender DE algo; **are you going to the cinema tonight? — it ~s** ¿vas a ir al cine esta noche? —depende
B (count on) **to ~ ON** *o* **UPON sb/sth** contar* CON algn/algo; **you can't ~ on him to tell the truth** no puedes estar seguro de que va a decir la verdad

dependable /dɪˈpendəbəl/ *adj* ‹*person*› formal, digno de confianza; ‹*ally/workman*› digno de confianza, con el que se puede contar

dependant, (AmE also) **dependent** /dɪˈpendənt/ *n*: **your children and other ~s** sus hijos y otras personas a su cargo *or* y otras cargas familiares

dependence /dɪˈpendəns/ *n* [u] 1▸ (reliance) dependencia *f* 2▸ (addiction) (Med) dependencia *f*; **drug ~** drogodependencia *f* (frml)

dependency /dɪˈpendənsi/ *n* (*pl* **-cies**) (Govt) dependencia *f*, dominio *m*

dependent¹ /dɪˈpendənt/ *adj* 1▸ (reliant) (*pred*) **to be ~ ON sth/sb** depender DE algo/algn 2▸ (Soc Adm) (*before n*): **~ relative** carga *f* familiar, familiar *mf* a su (*or* mi *etc*) cargo 3▸ (Govt) (*usu before n*) ‹*territory*› dependiente 4▸ (Ling) subordinado 5▸ (conditional) (*pred*) **to be ~ ON sth** depender DE algo

dependent² *n* (AmE) ▸ **dependant**

depersonalize /ˈdiːˈpɜːrsn̩əlaɪz || ˌdiːˈpɜːsn̩əlaɪz/ *vt* despersonalizar*

depict /dɪˈpɪkt/ *vt* (frml) 1▸ (portray) representar 2▸ (describe) describir*, pintar

depiction /dɪ'pɪkʃən/ *n* [u c] (frml) 1 (representation) representación *f* 2 (description) descripción *f*

depilate /'depəleɪt || 'depɪleɪt/ *vt* depilar

depilatory[1] /dɪ'pɪlətɔ:ri || dɪ'pɪlətri/ *adj* depilatorio

depilatory[2] *n* [c u] (*pl* **-ries**) depilatorio *m*

deplane /'di:'pleɪn/ *vi* (AmE) desembarcar*, descender* del avión (frml)

deplete /dɪ'pli:t/ *vt* (reduce) ‹*supply/stock*› reducir*; (exhaust) ‹*energy source*› agotar

depletion /dɪ'pli:ʃən/ *n* [c u] (reduction) reducción *f*, disminución *f*; (exhaustion) agotamiento *m*

deplorable /dɪ'plɔ:rəbəl/ *adj* 1 (disgraceful) deplorable, vergonzoso 2 (regrettable) lamentable

deplore /dɪ'plɔ:r || dɪ'plɔ:(r)/ *vt* (frml) 1 (condemn) deplorar, condenar 2 (regret) deplorar, lamentar

deploy /dɪ'plɔɪ/ *vt*
A (position) (Mil) desplegar*
B (distribute, use) (frml) utilizar*, hacer* uso de

deployment /dɪ'plɔɪmənt/ *n* [u c]
A (Mil) despliegue *m*
B (distribution, use) (frml) utilización *f*

depopulate /'di:'pɑ:pjəleɪt || ˌdi:'pɒpjʊleɪt/ *vt* despoblar*

depopulation /'di:'pɑ:pjə'leɪʃən || di:ˌpɒpjʊ'leɪʃən/ *n* [u] despoblación *f*

deport /dɪ'pɔ:rt || dɪ'pɔ:t/ *vt* deportar

deportation /'di:pɔ:r'teɪʃən || ˌdi:pɔ:'teɪʃən/ *n* [u c] deportación *f*

deportment /dɪ'pɔ:rtmənt || dɪ'pɔ:tmənt/ *n* [u] (frml) 1 (carriage) porte *m* 2 (conduct) conducta *f*

depose /dɪ'pəʊz/ *vt*
A (overthrow, unseat) ‹*dictator/ruler*› deponer*, derrocar*; ‹*champion/king*› destronar
B (Law) declarar, deponer* (frml)

deposit[1] /dɪ'pɑ:zət || dɪ'pɒzɪt/ *vt*
A 1 (set down) depositar, poner* 2 (Geol) ‹*silt*› depositar
B 1 (leave) depositar; **I ~ed the will with my lawyer** dejé el testamento en manos de mi abogado 2 ‹*money*› depositar, ingresar (Esp)

deposit[2] *n*
A 1 (payment into account) depósito *m*, ingreso *m* (Esp); (*before n*) **~ slip** comprobante *m* *or* (RPl) boleta *f* de depósito, resguardo *m* de ingreso (Esp) 2 (down payment — on large amounts) depósito *m*, entrega *f* inicial; (— on small amounts) depósito *m*, señal *f*, seña *f* (RPl) 3 (security) depósito *m*, fianza *f*; **is there a ~ on this bottle?** ¿cobran el envase *or* (Esp, Méx) casco?
B (accumulation — of silt, mud) depósito *m*; (— of dust) capa *f*
C (Min) (of gas) depósito *m*; (of gold, copper) yacimiento *m*

deposit account *n* (BrE) cuenta *f* de ahorro(s)

deposition /'depə'zɪʃən/ *n*
A [c u] (Law) deposición *f* (frml), declaración *f*
B [u] (of leader) destitución *f*; (of king) destronamiento *m*

depositor /dɪ'pɑ:zətər || dɪ'pɒzɪtə(r)/ *n* inversionista *mf*, ahorrista *mf* (RPl), ahorrante *mf* (Chi)

depot /'di:pəʊ || 'depəʊ/ *n*
A 1 (storehouse) depósito *m*, almacén *m* 2 (Mil) depósito *m*
B (esp AmE) (bus station) terminal *f* *or* (Chi) *m*, estación *f* de autobuses; (train station) estación *f*
C (esp BrE) (storage area) 1 (for buses) garage *m* (esp AmL), cochera *f* (Esp), depósito *m* (Chi) 2 (for trains) depósito *m* de locomotoras

depraved /dɪ'preɪvd/ *adj* depravado

depravity /dɪ'prævəti/ *n* [u] depravación *f*

deprecate /'deprɪkeɪt/ *vt* (frml) 1 (express disapproval of) reprobar*, criticar* 2 (belittle) menospreciar, despreciar

deprecating /'deprɪkeɪtɪŋ/ *adj* (frml) 1 (disapproving) ‹*remark*› de desaprobación, reprobatorio 2 (belittling) ‹*smile/laugh*› de desprecio

deprecatory /'deprəkətɔ:ri || 'deprəkət(ə)ri, 'deprəkeɪt(ə)ri/ *adj*
A (disapproving) de desaprobación, reprobatorio
B (apologetic) de disculpa

depreciate /dɪ'pri:ʃieɪt/ *vt* (Fin) depreciar
■ **depreciate** *vi* (Fin) depreciarse

depreciation /dɪ'pri:ʃi'eɪʃən/ *n* [c u] (Fin) depreciación *f*

depress /dɪ'pres/ *vt*
A (sadden) deprimir, abatir
B (press down) (frml) ‹*lever*› bajar; ‹*button*› pulsar (frml)
C (Econ) ‹*market*› deprimir; ‹*prices/wages*› reducir*, hacer* bajar

depressant /dɪ'presənt/ *n* [c u] (Pharm) depresivo *m*

depressed /dɪ'prest/ *adj*
A (dejected) deprimido, abatido; **to get/become ~** deprimirse, dejarse abatir
B (Econ) ‹*economy/market*› deprimido, en crisis; ‹*area*› deprimido, de gran desempleo
C (substandard) (AmE) ‹*stock*› de calidad inferior; **his reading skills are ~** en lectura está por debajo de lo normal

depressing /dɪ'presɪŋ/ *adj* deprimente

depressingly /dɪ'presɪŋli/ *adv*: **the crime rate is ~ high** el índice de criminalidad ha alcanzado unos niveles deprimentes

depression /dɪ'preʃən/ *n*
A [u] (despondency) depresión *f*, abatimiento *m*; **to suffer from ~** sufrir depresiones
B [c] (in flat surface) depresión *f*
C [c] (Econ) depresión *f*, crisis *f*
D [c] (Meteo) depresión *f* atmosférica, borrasca *f*

depressive /dɪ'presɪv/ *adj* depresivo

depressurize /'di:'preʃəraɪz/ *vt* despresurizar*

deprivation /'deprə'veɪʃən || ˌdeprɪ'veɪʃən/ *n* [u c] (lack, loss) privación *f*; (hardship) privaciones *fpl*, penurias *fpl*; **to suffer ~(s)** pasar *or* sufrir privaciones *or* penurias

deprive /dɪ'praɪv/ *vt*: **to ~ sb OF sth** privar a algn DE algo
■ *v refl* **to ~ oneself of sth** privarse de algo

deprived /dɪ'praɪvd/ *adj* ‹*child*› carenciado, desventajado; ‹*region*› carenciado

deprogram, (BrE) **deprogramme** /'di:'prəʊgræm/ *vt* desprogramar

dept (= **department**) Dpto.

depth /depθ/ *n*
A [u c] 1 (of hole, water) profundidad *f*; ***out of one's ~***: **when it comes to computers I'm out of my ~** estoy muy flojo en informática; **don't go out of your ~** (in water) no vayas donde no haces pie *or* no tocas fondo 2 (of shelf, cupboard) profundidad *f*, fondo *m*; (of hem) ancho *m* 3 (of shot) (Sport) alcance *m*
B [u c] (of emotion, knowledge) profundidad *f*; **to study sth in ~** estudiar algo a fondo *or* en profundidad
C (of voice) profundidad *f*; (of sound) intensidad *f*
D **depths** *pl n*: **in the ~s of the ocean/forest** en las profundidades del océano/la espesura del bosque; **in the ~s of despair** en lo más hondo de la desesperación; ***to plumb the ~s***: **to plumb the ~s of despair** (liter) hundirse en la desesperación (liter); **he has sunk to such ~s that ...** ha caído tan bajo que ...

depth charge *n* carga *f* de profundidad

deputation /'depjə'teɪʃən || ˌdepjʊ'teɪʃən/ *n* delegación *f*

depute /'dɪpju:t || dɪ'pju:t/ *vt* **to ~ sb TO sth** encomendarle* algo A algn, comisionar a algn PARA algo

deputize /'depjətaɪz || 'depjʊtaɪz/ *vi* **to ~ FOR sb** desempeñar las funciones de algn
■ **deputize** *vt* (AmE) 1 ▸**depute** 2 (appoint as deputy) (Law) nombrar como segundo

deputy /'depjəti/ *n* (*pl* **-ties**)
A 1 (second-in-command) segundo, -da *m,f*; (substitute) suplente *mf*, reemplazo *mf*; (*before n*) **~ director** subdirector, -tora *m,f*, director adjunto, directora adjunta *m,f* 2 **~ (sheriff)** (AmE Law) ayudante *mf* del sheriff
B (Govt) diputado, -da *m,f*

derail /dɪ'reɪl/ *vt* 1 ‹*train*› hacer* descarrilar 2 (upset) ‹*plan*› desbaratar
■ **derail** *vi* descarrilarse

derailment /dɪ'reɪlmənt/ *n* [c u] descarrilamiento *m*

deranged /dɪ'reɪndʒd/ *adj* trastornado, desquiciado

derby /'dɜ:rbi || 'dɑ:bi/ *n* (*pl* **derbies**)
A (Sport): **the D~** (in UK) el Derby, el clásico de Epsom; **the Kentucky D~** el Derby de Kentucky; **a local ~** (in soccer) (BrE) *enfrentamiento de dos equipos vecinos a nivel nacional*
B (hat) (AmE) bombín *m*, hongo *m*, sombrero *m* (de) hongo

deregulate /'di:'regjəleɪt || ˌdi:'regjʊleɪt/ *vt* desregular, liberalizar*

deregulation /'di:'regjə'leɪʃən || di:ˌregjʊ'leɪʃən/ *n* [u] desregulación *f*, liberalización *f*

derelict¹ /'derəlɪkt/ *adj* abandonado y en ruinas

derelict² *n* (vagrant) marginado, -da *m,f*

dereliction /'derə'lɪkʃən/ *n* [u]
A (of property, area) abandono *m*
B (neglect) (frml): ~ **of duty** negligencia *f* en el cumplimiento del deber

deride /dɪ'raɪd/ *vt* ridiculizar*, burlarse *or* reírse* de

de rigueur /dəri:'gɜ:r || dərɪ'gɜ:(r)/ *adj* (*pred*) **to be ~ ~** ser* de rigor

d

derision /dɪ'rɪʒən/ *n* [u] escarnio *m* (frml), irrisión *f* (frml); **to make sth/sb the** *o* **an object of ~** ridiculizar* algo/a algn

derisive /dɪ'raɪsɪv/ *adj* ‹*smile/laughter*› burlón; ‹*attitude/remark*› desdeñoso y burlón

derisively /dɪ'raɪsɪvli/ *adv* burlonamente, con sorna

derisory /dɪ'raɪzəri/ *adj* ‹*sum/offer*› irrisorio

derivation /'derə'veɪʃən || ˌderɪ'veɪʃən/ *n* [u c] (Ling) (process) derivación *f*; (origin) origen *m*

derivative¹ /dɪ'rɪvətɪv/ *adj* (unoriginal) ‹*novel*› carente de originalidad; ‹*plot/theme*› manido, trillado; ‹*artist/writer*› adocenado

derivative² *n* 1 (in industry) derivado *m* 2 (Ling) (word) derivado *m*; (language) lengua *f* derivada 2 (Fin) derivado *m*, derivada *f*

derive /dɪ'raɪv/ *vt* **to ~ sth FROM sth**: **children can ~ great enjoyment from the simplest things** las cosas más simples pueden dar enorme placer a un niño; **penicillin is ~d from mold** la penicilina se obtiene (a partir) del moho; **the name is ~d from the Greek** el nombre viene *or* deriva del griego
■ **derive** *vi*
A (stem from) **to ~ FROM sth** «*attitude/problem*» provenir* DE algo; «*idea*» tener* su origen EN algo
B (Ling) **to ~ FROM sth** derivar(se) DE algo

dermatitis /'dɜ:rmə'taɪtəs || ˌdɜ:mə'taɪtɪs/ *n* [u] dermatitis *f*

dermatologist /ˌdɜ:rmə'tɑ:lədʒəst || ˌdɜ:mə'tɒlədʒɪst/ *n* dermatólogo, -ga *m,f*

dermatology /ˌdɜ:rmə'tɑ:lədʒi || ˌdɜ:mə'tɒlədʒi/ *n* [u] dermatología *f*

derogatory /dɪ'rɑ:gətɔ:ri || dɪ'rɒgətri/ *adj* despectivo, peyorativo

derrick /'derɪk/ *n* 1 (over oil well) torre *f* de perforación, derrick *m* 2 ~ **(crane)** (Naut) grúa *f*

dervish /'dɜ:rvɪʃ || 'dɜ:vɪʃ/ *n* derviche *mf*

descale /'di:'skeɪl/ *vt* (BrE) quitarle el sarro a

descant /'deskænt/ *n* contrapunto *m*

descend /dɪ'send/ *vi*
A (move downwards) descender* (frml), bajar
B **descending** *pres p* descendente; **in ~ing order of importance** en orden decreciente *or* descendente de importancia
C (set in) «*mist*» descender* (frml); «*rain*» caer*; «*silence/gloom*» abatirse (liter)
D (stoop) **to ~ TO sth/-ING** rebajarse A algo/+ INF; **don't ~ to his level** no te pongas a su nivel
E (be descended) **to ~ FROM sb** descender* DE algn, ser* descendiente de algn
■ **descend** *vt* descender* (frml), bajar

Phrasal verb
• **descend on, descend upon** [v ▸ prep ▸ o] 1 (attack) lanzarse *or* caer* sobre; **a plague ~ed on the town** una plaga se abatió sobre la ciudad (liter) 2 (invade) invadir; **the whole family will be ~ing on us at Christmas** (hum) nos va a invadir *or* nos va a caer toda la familia para Navidad (fam)

descendant, (AmE also) **descendent** /dɪ'sendənt/ *n* descendiente *mf*

descended /dɪ'sendəd || dɪ'sendɪd/ *adj* (*pred*) **to be ~ FROM sb** ser* descendiente DE algn, descender* DE algn

descendent *n* (AmE) ▸ **descendant**

descent /dɪ'sent/ *n*
A [u c] 1 (by climbers, plane) descenso *m*, bajada *f* 2 (in terrain) pendiente *f*, bajada *f*
B [u] (decline) caída *f*
C [u] (lineage) ascendencia *f*

descramble /'di:'skræmbəl/ *vt* descodificar*

descrambler /'di:'skræmblər || ˌdi:'skræmblə(r)/ *n* descodificador *m*

describe /dɪ'skraɪb/ *vt*
A (put into words) describir*
B (characterize) **to ~ sb/sth (AS sth)**: **he ~s himself as a socialist** se define como socialista; **I would ~ the book as dull and repetitive** yo diría que es un libro soso y repetitivo
C 1 (draw) (Math) trazar* 2 (move in shape of) (frml) ‹*curve/arc*› describir* (frml)

description /dɪ'skrɪpʃən/ *n* [c u] descripción *f*; **powers of ~** talento *m* para describir; **her beauty was beyond ~** su belleza era indescriptible; **of every ~, of all ~s** de todo tipo, de toda clase; **we don't have anything of that ~** no tenemos nada de ese tipo

descriptive /dɪ'skrɪptɪv/ *adj* ‹*passage/powers*› descriptivo; ‹*adjective*› calificativo

desecrate /'desɪkreɪt/ *vt* profanar

desecration /'desɪ'kreɪʃən/ *n* [u c] profanación *f*

desegregation /'di:segrɪ'geɪʃən/ *n* [u] abolición *f* de la segregación racial

deselect /'di:sə'lekt/ *vt* (BrE) no reelegir* como candidato a diputado

desensitize /'di:'sensətaɪz || ˌdi:'sensɪtaɪz/ *vt* **to ~ sb TO sth** insensibilizar* a algn A algo, hacer* a algn insensible A algo

desert¹ /'dezərt || 'dezət/ *n* (Geog) desierto *m*; (*before n*) ‹*region/climate*› desértico; ‹*tribe/sand*› del desierto

desert² /dɪ'zɜ:rt || dɪ'zɜ:t/ *vt* 1 (frml) ‹*place*› abandonar, huir* de 2 ‹*family*› abandonar; ‹*cause*› desertar de; **his courage ~ed him** su valor lo abandonó
■ **desert** *vi* (Mil) desertar

desert boots *pl n*: *botas bajas de ante*

deserted /dɪ'zɜ:rtəd || dɪ'zɜ:tɪd/ *adj* 1 ‹*streets/village*› desierto 2 ‹*husband/wife*› abandonado

deserter /dɪ'zɜ:rtər || dɪ'zɜ:tə(r)/ *n* desertor, -tora *m,f*

desertion /dɪ'zɜ:rʃən || dɪ'zɜ:ʃən/ *n* [u] 1 (Mil) deserción *f* 2 (of family, place) abandono *m*

desert island *n* isla *f* desierta

deserts /dɪ'zɜ:rts || dɪ'zɜ:ts/ *pl n*: ***to get one's just ~*** recibir su (*or* tu *etc*) merecido

deserve /dɪ'zɜ:rv || dɪ'zɜ:v/ *vt* 1 ‹*success/praise/criticism*› merecer(se)*; **they ~ each other** son tal para cual; **they got what they ~d** se llevaron su merecido; **to ~ to + INF** merecer* + INF 2 ‹*attention/investigation*› merecer*, ser* digno de
■ **deserve** *vi*: **they ~d better of us all** merecían que los tratáramos mejor

deservedly /dɪ'zɜ:rvədli || dɪ'zɜ:vɪdli/ *adv* merecidamente

deserving /dɪ'zɜ:rvɪŋ || dɪ'zɜ:vɪŋ/ *adj* ‹*cause/case*› meritorio; **the ~ poor** los pobres dignos de ayuda; **to be ~ OF sth** (frml) ser* merecedor *or* digno DE algo

desiccated /'desɪkeɪtəd || 'desɪkeɪtɪd/ *adj* seco; **~ coconut** coco *m* rallado

design¹ /dɪ'zaɪn/ *n*
A [c u] 1 (of product, car, machine) diseño *m*; (drawing) diseño *m*, boceto *m*; (*before n*) **a ~ fault** un defecto de diseño; **it's still at the ~ stage** todavía lo estan diseñando 2 (pattern, decoration) diseño *m*, motivo *m*, dibujo *m* 3 (product, model) modelo *m*
B [u] 1 (Art) diseño *m* 2 (style) estilo *m*, líneas *fpl*
C 1 [c] (plan) (liter) plan *m*; **by ~** deliberadamente; **more by accident than ~** por casualidad más que porque se hubiera planeado 2 **designs** *pl n* (intentions) propósitos *mpl*, designios *mpl* (liter); ***to have ~s on sth/sb*** tener* los ojos puestos en algo/algn

design² *vt*
A (devise) ‹*house/garden*› diseñar, proyectar; ‹*dress/product*› diseñar; ‹*course/program*› planear, estructurar
B **designed** *past p* 1 (created) diseñado; **a well-~ed chair/machine** una silla/máquina bien diseñada *or* de buen diseño 2 (meant): **a statement ~ed to reassure the public** una declaración destinada a tranquilizar al público

designate¹ /ˈdezɪgneɪt/ *vt*

A (name officially) nombrar, designar; **the area was ~d a national park** la zona fue declarada parque nacional

B (call) (frml) designar

C (indicate) (frml) indicar*

designate² /ˈdezɪgneɪt, -nət || ˈdezɪgnət/ *adj* (*after n*): **the governor ~** quien ha sido nombrado gobernador

designation /ˌdezɪgˈneɪʃən/ *n*

A 1 [u] (naming) designación *f* 2 [c] (name) (frml) denominación *f* (frml), nombre *m*

B [c u] (appointment) nombramiento *m*, designación *f*

designer /dɪˈzaɪnər || dɪˈzaɪnə(r)/ *n* diseñador, -dora *m,f*; **a fashion/furniture ~** un diseñador de modas/muebles; (*before n*) ‹*clothes/jeans*› de diseño exclusivo; ‹*furniture/pen*› de diseño

desirability /dɪˈzaɪrəˈbɪləti || dɪˌzaɪərəˈbɪlɪti/ *n* [u] 1 (of action, idea) conveniencia *f* 2 (of person) atractivo *m*

desirable /dɪˈzaɪrəbəl || dɪˈzaɪərəbəl/ *adj* 1 ‹*property/location*› atractivo 2 (sexually) ‹*man/woman*› atractivo, deseable, apetecible 3 ‹*outcome*› deseable, conveniente; ‹*option*› conveniente, aconsejable

desire¹ /dɪˈzaɪr || dɪˈzaɪə(r)/ *n*

A [c] (wish) deseo *m*, anhelo *m* (liter); **a ~ FOR sth** deseos *mpl* DE algo; **he expressed a ~ to see his family** dijo que deseaba ver a su familia

B [u] (lust) deseo *m*

desire² *vt* 1 (want) ‹*happiness/success*› desear; **to leave much/a lot to be ~d** dejar mucho/bastante que desear 2 (lust after) ‹*person*› desear 3 **desired** *past p* deseado; **to have the ~d effect** surtir el efecto deseado

desirous /dɪˈzaɪrəs || dɪˈzaɪərəs/ *adj* (frml) (*pred*) **to be ~ OF sth**: **we are ~ of your success** le deseamos éxito

desist /dɪˈzɪst/ *vi* (frml) **to ~ (FROM sth/-ING)** (cease) desistir (DE algo/+ INF); (abstain) abstenerse* (DE algo/+ INF)

desk /desk/ *n* 1 (table) escritorio *m*, mesa *f* de trabajo; (in school) pupitre *m*, (*before n*) ‹*lamp*› de escritorio, de (sobre) mesa; **~ diary** agenda *f* de escritorio; **a ~ job** un trabajo de oficina 2 (service counter) mostrador *m*; **information ~** (mostrador *m* de) información *f*, **reception ~** recepción *f* 3 (Journ) sección *f*

desk: **~bound** *adj* sedentario; **~ clerk** *n* recepcionista *mf*; **~top** *adj* (*before n*) ‹*calculator/computer*› de escritorio, de (sobre)mesa; **~top publishing** autoedición *f*, edición *f* electrónica

desolate /ˈdesələt/ *adj*

A (deserted) ‹*place/landscape*› desierto, desolado

B ‹*person*› desconsolado, desolado; ‹*outlook/existence*› sombrío, lúgubre

desolation /ˈdesəˈleɪʃən/ *n* [u]

A (of land, area) desolación *f*

B (misery) desolación *f*, desconsuelo *m*

despair¹ /dɪˈsper || dɪˈspeə(r)/ *n* [u] desesperación *f*; **to be in ~** estar* desesperado

despair² *vi* perder* las esperanzas, desesperar(se); **to ~ OF sb/sth/-ING**: **she ~ed of ever seeing her family again** perdió las esperanzas de volver a ver a su familia; **honestly, I ~ of you!** ¡francamente, eres un caso perdido!

despairing /dɪˈsperɪŋ || dɪˈspeərɪŋ/ *adj* ‹*look/cry*› de desesperación; **his ~ mother** su desconsolada madre

despairingly /dɪˈsperɪŋli || dɪˈspeərɪŋli/ *adv* con desesperación, desesperadamente

despatch /dɪˈspætʃ/ *vt/n* ▸ **dispatch¹,²**

desperado /ˈdespəˈrɑːdəʊ/ *n* (*pl* **-does** *or* **-dos**) forajido, -da *m,f*

desperate /ˈdespərət/ *adj*

A 1 (frantic, reckless) ‹*person/attempt*› desesperado; **to be ~** estar* desesperado; **these are ~ measures** éstas son medidas tomadas en la desesperación 2 (in urgent need) (colloq): **where's the bathroom? I'm ~!** ¿dónde está el baño? estoy que no (me) aguanto más (fam); **~ FOR sth**: **she's ~ for work** está desesperada por conseguir trabajo; **~ to + INF**: **I'm ~ to get home** estoy que me muero por llegar a casa (fam)

B (critical) ‹*state/situation*› grave, desesperado; ‹*need*› apremiante

desperately /ˈdespərətli/ *adv* 1 ‹*struggle*› desesperadamente 2 ‹*need*› urgentemente, con urgencia 3 (*as intensifier*): **she's ~ ill** está gravemente enferma, está gravísima; **we're not ~ busy at the moment** (colloq) no estamos lo que se dice ocupadísimos

desperation /ˈdespəˈreɪʃən/ *n* [u] desesperación *f*; **in ~** en la desesperación

despicable /dɪˈspɪkəbəl/ *adj* vil, despreciable

despise /dɪˈspaɪz/ *vt* despreciar (profundamente)

despite /dɪˈspaɪt/ *prep* a pesar de

despoil /dɪˈspɔɪl/ *vt* (liter) saquear

despondency /dɪˈspɑːndənsi || dɪˈspɒndənsi/ *n* [u] desaliento *m*, abatimiento *m*

despondent /dɪˈspɑːndənt || dɪˈspɒndənt/ *adj* abatido, descorazonado

despot /ˈdespɑːt || ˈdespɒt/ *n* déspota *mf*

despotic /deˈspɑːtɪk || deˈspɒtɪk/ *adj* despótico

despotism /ˈdespətɪzəm/ *n* [u] despotismo *m*

dessert /dɪˈzɜːrt || dɪˈzɜːt/ *n* [c u] postre *m*

dessert: **~spoon** *n* cuchara *f* de postre; **~spoonful** *n* (*pl* **-spoonfuls** *or* **-spoonsful**) (BrE) cucharada *f* de postre

destabilize /ˈdiːˈsteɪbəlaɪz/ *vt* desestabilizar*

destination /ˈdestəˈneɪʃən || ˌdestɪˈneɪʃən/ *n* 1 (end of journey) destino *m* 2 (purpose) meta *f*

destined /ˈdestənd || ˈdestɪnd/ *adj* (*pred*)

A (fated) **to be ~ to + INF** estar* (pre)destinado A + INF; **it was ~ to fail** estaba condenado al fracaso

B 1 (intended) **~ FOR sth** destinado A algo 2 (bound, on way): **~ for the West Indies** con destino al Caribe

destiny /ˈdestəni || ˈdestɪni/ *n* [c u] (*pl* **-nies**) destino *m*, sino *m* (liter)

destitute /ˈdestətuːt || ˈdestɪtjuːt/ *adj* indigente; **she was left ~** quedó en la indigencia *or* miseria

destock /diːˈstɑːk || diːˈstɒk/ *vi* (BrE) liquidar las existencias

destroy /dɪˈstrɔɪ/ *vt*

A 1 (ruin, wreck) ‹*building/forest*› destruir*; ‹*reputation/confidence*› acabar con; ‹*life*› arruinar, destrozar* 2 ‹*animal*› sacrificar* (euf)

B (colloq) 1 (defeat) ‹*opposition*› aplastar, darle* una paliza a (fam) 2 (disappoint) (AmE) (*usu pass*) decepcionar

destroyer /dɪˈstrɔɪər || dɪˈstrɔɪə(r)/ *n* destructor *m*

destruct /dɪˈstrʌkt/ *n* (Aerosp, Mil) (auto)destrucción *f*; (*before n*) ‹*mechanism/system*› de (auto)destrucción

destruction /dɪˈstrʌkʃən/ *n* [u]

A (of city, books, forest) destrucción *f*; (of reputation, civilization) ruina *f*, destrucción *f*; (slaughter) exterminación *f*

B (cause of downfall) (frml) ruina *f*, perdición *f*

C (damage) destrucción *f*, estragos *mpl*, destrozos *mpl*

destructive /dɪˈstrʌktɪv/ *adj* ‹*storm/weapon*› destructor; ‹*tendency*› destructivo; ‹*child*› destrozón; ‹*criticism*› destructivo, negativo

desultory /ˈdesəltɔːri || ˈdezəltəri/ *adj* ‹*effort/attempt*› desganado; **in a ~ fashion** sin entusiasmo, con desgana *or* (esp AmL) desgano

detach /dɪˈtætʃ/ *vt* (separate) separar, quitar; (unstick) despegar*; **the headrest can be ~ed** el apoyacabezas se puede desmontar *or* quitar; **to ~ oneself from sth** distanciarse de algo

detachable /dɪˈtætʃəbəl/ *adj* ‹*cover*› de quita y pon, de quitar y poner; ‹*lining*› desmontable

detached /dɪˈtætʃt/ *adj*

A ‹*person/manner*› (aloof) distante, indiferente; (objective) objetivo, imparcial

B (BrE) ‹*house*› no adosado

detachment /dɪˈtætʃmənt/ *n*

A [u] (aloofness) distancia *f*, indiferencia *f*; (objectivity) objetividad *f*, imparcialidad *f*

B [u] (act of detaching) (frml) desprendimiento *m*

C [c] (Mil) destacamento *m*

detail¹ /dɪˈteɪl, ˈdiːteɪl || ˈdiːteɪl/ *n*

A [c] 1 (particular) detalle *m*, pormenor *m*; **he asked for further ~s** pidió más información *or* información más detallada 2 (embellishment) detalle *m* 3 (insignificant matter) minucia *f*, detalle *m* (sin importancia)

B [u] (minutiae) detalles *mpl*; **to go into ~** entrar en detalles *or* pormenores; **to describe/explain sth in ~** describir*/explicar* algo detalladamente *or* minuciosamente

d

C [c] (Mil) destacamento *m*, cuadrilla *f*

detail² *vt*
A (describe) exponer* en detalle, detallar
B (Mil) destacar*; **to ~ sb to + INF** destacar* a algn A *or* PARA + INF

detailed /ˈdiːteɪld/ *adj* ‹*description*› detallado, minucioso, pormenorizado; ‹*examination*› minucioso, detenido

detain /dɪˈteɪn/ *vt* 1 (delay) (frml): **don't let me ~ you** no quiero entretenerlo *or* demorarlo 2 (in custody) detener*

detainee /ˈdiːteɪˈniː/ *n* detenido, -da *m,f*

detect /dɪˈtekt/ *vt* ‹*object/substance*› detectar; **I ~ed a note of sarcasm in his voice** noté cierto tonillo sarcástico en su voz

detectable /dɪˈtektəbəl/ *adj* perceptible, detectable

detection /dɪˈtekʃən/ *n* [u]
A (of error) descubrimiento *m*; (of act, crime, criminal): **to escape ~** pasar desapercibido *or* inadvertido
B (of substance) detección *f*

detective /dɪˈtektɪv/ *n* (private) detective *mf*; (in police force) agente *mf*, oficial *mf*; (*before n*) **~ story** novela *f* policíaca *or* policial; **~ work** pesquisas *fpl*, investigaciones *fpl*

detector /dɪˈtektər || dɪˈtektə(r)/ *n* detector *m*

detente /deɪˈtɑːnt/ *n* [u] (Pol) distensión *f*

detention /dɪˈtentʃən || dɪˈtenʃən/ *n* [u]
A (in custody) detención *f*; (*before n*) **~ order** orden *f* de arresto
B (Educ): **to be in ~** estar* castigado

detention home, (BrE) **detention centre** *n* reformatorio *m*, correccional *m or f* de menores

deter /dɪˈtɜːr || dɪˈtɜː(r)/ *vt* **-rr-** ‹*person*› disuadir, hacer* disuadir; ‹*crime/war*› impedir*; **to ~ sb FROM sth/-ING** disuadir a algn DE algo/ + INF

detergent /dɪˈtɜːrdʒənt || dɪˈtɜːdʒənt/ *n* [u c] (Chem) detergente *m*; (for clothes) detergente *m*; (for dishes) lavavajillas *m*

deteriorate /dɪˈtɪriəreɪt || dɪˈtɪəriereɪt/ *vi* «*health/relationship/material*» deteriorarse; «*weather/work*» empeorar; **to ~ INTO sth** degenerar EN algo

deterioration /dɪˈtɪriəˈreɪʃən || dɪˌtɪəriəˈreɪʃən/ *n* [u] deterioro *m*

determination /dɪˈtɜːrməˈneɪʃən || dɪˌtɜːmɪˈneɪʃən/ *n* [u] (resoluteness) determinación *f*, resolución *f*; **with an air of ~** con aire resuelto *or* decidido

determine /dɪˈtɜːrmən || dɪˈtɜːmɪn/ *vt*
A (ascertain) establecer*, determinar
B 1 (influence) determinar, condicionar; **determining factor** factor *m* determinante 2 (mark) ‹*boundary/limit*› definir, demarcar*
C (liter) (resolve) decidir; **to ~ to + INF** decidir + INF, tomar la determinación DE + INF

Phrasal verb
• **determine on**, **determine upon** [v ▸ prep ▸ o] (frml) decidirse por

determined /dɪˈtɜːrmənd || dɪˈtɜːmɪnd/ *adj* ‹*mood/person*› decidido, resuelto; **we must make a ~ effort to prevent it** debemos poner todo nuestro empeño en impedirlo; **to be ~ to + INF** estar* decidido A + INF, estar* empeñado EN + INF; **to be ~ THAT** estar* resuelto *or* decidido A QUE (+ *subj*)

determinism /dɪˈtɜːrmənɪzəm || dɪˈtɜːmɪnɪzəm/ *n* [u] determinismo *m*

deterrent /dɪˈterənt/ *n*: **it may act as a ~ to thieves** puede servir para disuadir a los ladrones; **the nuclear ~** las armas nucleares como fuerza disuasoria

detest /dɪˈtest/ *vt* detestar, odiar; **to ~ -ING** detestar *or* odiar + INF

detestable /dɪˈtestəbəl/ *adj* detestable, odioso

dethrone /dɪˈθrəʊn/ *vt* destronar

detonate /ˈdetəneɪt/ *vt* hacer* detonar
■ **detonate** *vi* detonar, explotar, estallar

detonator /ˈdetəneɪtər || ˈdetəneɪtə(r)/ *n* detonador *m*

detour¹ /ˈdiːtʊr || ˈdiːtʊə(r)/ *n* 1 (deviation) rodeo *m*, vuelta *f*; **to make a ~** dar* un rodeo, desviarse* 2 (AmE Transp) desvío *m*, desviación *f*

detour² *vt* (AmE) ‹*traffic*› desviar*

detoxification /ˈdiːˈtɑːksəfəˈkeɪʃən || ˌdiːˌtɒksɪfɪˈkeɪʃən/ *n* [u] (of addict) desintoxicación *f*; (of substance) eliminación *f* de la toxicidad

detoxify /ˈdiːˈtɑːksəfaɪ || ˌdiːˈtɒksɪfaɪ/ *vt* **-fies, -fying, -fied** ‹*addict/alcoholic*› desintoxicar*; ‹*substance/material*› eliminar la toxicidad de

detract /dɪˈtrækt/ *vi* **to ~ FROM sth**: **I didn't wish to ~ from her achievement** no quise quitarle méritos *or* restarle valor a su logro; **it ~s from the beauty of the painting** desmerece la belleza del cuadro

detractor /dɪˈtræktər || dɪˈtræktə(r)/ *n* detractor, -tora *m,f*

detriment /ˈdetrəmənt || ˈdetrɪmənt/ *n* [u] (frml) detrimento *m*, perjuicio *m*; **to the ~ of sb/sth** en detrimento *or* perjuicio de algn/algo

detrimental /ˈdetrəˈmentḷ || ˌdetrɪˈmentḷ/ *adj* (frml) **~ (TO sb/sth)** perjudicial (PARA algn/algo)

detritus /dɪˈtraɪtəs/ *n* [u] 1 (debris) desechos *mpl* 2 (Geol) detrito *m*, detritus *m*

deuce /duːs || djuːs/ *n* [u c]
A (in tennis) deuce *m*, cuarenta *mpl* iguales
B (Games) dos *m*

deutschmark /ˈdɔɪtʃmɑːrk || ˈdɔɪtʃmɑːk/ *n* (Hist) marco *m* (alemán)

devaluation /ˈdiːˈvæljuˈeɪʃən/ *n* [u c] (Fin) devaluación *f*

devalue /ˈdiːˈvæljuː/ *vt* (Fin) devaluar*

devastate /ˈdevəsteɪt/ *vt* 1 (lay waste) devastar, asolar 2 (overwhelm) ‹*opposition/argument*› aplastar, demoler*; **I was ~d when I heard** quedé deshecho *or* anonadado cuando me enteré

devastating /ˈdevəsteɪtɪŋ/ *adj* 1 ‹*punch/shock*› devastador; **the news was ~** la noticia fue un golpe tremendo 2 ‹*accuracy/logic*› abrumador, apabullante; ‹*reply/defeat*› demoledor, aplastante; ‹*beauty*› irresistible

devastatingly /ˈdevəsteɪtɪŋli/ *adv* ‹*frank/witty*› tremendamente; ‹*beautiful/funny*› irresistiblemente

devastation /ˈdevəˈsteɪʃən/ *n* [u] devastación *f*

develop /dɪˈveləp/ *vt*
A 1 (elaborate, devise) ‹*theory/plan*› desarrollar, elaborar; ‹*idea*› desarrollar; ‹*method*› idear, desarrollar; ‹*plot/story/character*› desarrollar 2 (improve) ‹*skill/ability/quality*› desarrollar 3 (exploit) ‹*land/area*› urbanizar* 4 (expand) ‹*business/range*› ampliar* 5 (create) ‹*drug/engine*› crear
B (acquire) ‹*immunity/resistance*› desarrollar; ‹*disease*› contraer* (frml); **the machine ~ed a fault** la máquina empezó a funcionar mal; **I've ~ed a taste for ...** le he tomado (el) gusto a ...
C (Phot) revelar
■ **develop** *vi*
A 1 (grow) «*person/industry*» desarrollarse; «*interest*» crecer*, aumentar 2 (evolve) **to ~ INTO sth** convertirse* *or* transformarse EN algo 3 (Econ) «*nation/region*» desarrollarse, progresar 4 (unfold) «*plot/novel*» desarrollarse
B (appear) «*problem/complication*» surgir*, aparecer*; «*crisis*» producirse*

developed /dɪˈveləpt/ *adj* ‹*nation/region*› desarrollado

developer /dɪˈveləpər || dɪˈveləpə(r)/ *n*
A [c] (of land, property) promotor inmobiliario, promotora inmobiliaria *m,f*
B [u] (Phot) revelador *m*
C [c] (Psych): **a slow/late ~** un individuo de desarrollo lento/tardío

developing /dɪˈveləpɪŋ/ *adj* ‹*country*› en vías de desarrollo

development /dɪˈveləpmənt/ *n*
A [u] 1 (physical, mental) desarrollo *m* 2 (of argument, idea, plot) desarrollo *m*; (of situation, events) desarrollo *m*, evolución *f*
B [u] (of drug, engine) creación *f*
C [u] (of land, area) urbanización *f*
D [c] (*housing ~*) complejo *m* habitacional, fraccionamiento *m* (Méx), urbanización *f* (Esp)
E [u] (Econ) desarrollo *m*
F [c] 1 (happening, event) acontecimiento *m*, suceso *m*; **we are awaiting further ~s** estamos a la espera de novedades *or* de nuevos acontecimientos

developmental /dɪˈveləpˈmentḷ/ *adj* del desarrollo

deviance /ˈdiːviəns/ *n* 1 [u] (Psych) desviación *f* 2 [c] (idiosyncracy) anomalía *f*

deviancy /'di:viənsi/ *n* [u c] ▸**deviance**

deviant /'di:viənt/ *adj* ‹*practices/conduct*› desviado, que se aparta de la norma; ‹*person/personality*› anormal

deviate /'di:vieɪt/ *vi* **to ~ FROM sth** ‹*from course*› desviarse* DE algo; ‹*from truth/norm*› apartarse DE algo

deviation /'di:vi'eɪʃən/ *n* [u c] desviación *f*

device /dɪ'vaɪs/ *n*

A (gadget, tool) artefacto *m*, dispositivo *m*, aparato *m*; (mechanism) dispositivo *m*, mecanismo *m*

B (stratagem) recurso *m*, estratagema *f*; ***to leave sb to her/his own ~s*** dejar que algn se las arregle solo

devil /'devḷ/ *n*

A **1** (Relig) diablo *m*, demonio *m*; ***the ~ finds work for idle hands (to do)*** el ocio es la madre de todos los vicios; ***better the ~ you know (than the ~ you don't)*** más vale malo conocido que bueno por conocer; ***speak*** *o* ***talk of the ~ ...*** hablando del rey de Roma ...; ***(the) ~ take the hindmost*** ¡sálvese quien pueda!; ***to be (caught) between the ~ and the deep blue sea*** estar* entre la espada y la pared **2** (evil spirit) demonio *m*

B (colloq) (*in intensifying phrases*): **who/what/where the ~ ...?** ¿quién/qué/dónde demonios *or* diablos ... ? (fam)

C (colloq) (person): **he's a little ~!** ¡es un diablillo!; **go on, be a ~, have another one!** (BrE) ¡anda, cómete otro, no seas tonto!; **poor ~!** ¡pobre diablo!

devilish /'devḷɪʃ/ *adj* (dated) diabólico

devil: **~-may-care** /'devḷmer'ker || ,devḷmer'keə(r)/ *adj* (colloq) (*before n*) despreocupado; **~'s advocate** *n* abogado *m* del diablo

devious /'di:viəs/ *adj* **1** (underhand) ‹*person*› taimado, artero; **by ~ means** con artimañas, con tejemanejes **2** (roundabout) ‹*route/path*› tortuoso, sinuoso

deviously /'di:viəsli/ *adv* arteramente

deviousness /'di:viəsnəs || 'di:viəsnɪs/ *n* [u] artería *f*

devise /dɪ'vaɪz/ *vt* ‹*plan/system*› idear, crear, concebir*; ‹*machine/tool*› inventar

devoid /dɪ'vɔɪd/ *adj* (*pred*) (frml) **to be ~ OF sth** carecer* DE algo

devolution /'devə'lu:ʃən || ,di:və'lu:ʃən/ *n* [u]

A **1** (delegation) delegación *f*, transferencia *f* **2** (BrE Govt) *transferencia de competencias del gobierno central a un gobierno regional*

B (Law) cesión *f*

devolve /dɪ'vɑ:lv || dɪ'vɒlv/ *vi* **1** (frml) **to ~ TO** *o* **(UP)ON sb** «*duties/responsibilities*» recaer* SOBRE *or* EN algn; «*authority/power*» pasar A algn **2** «*property*» **to ~ TO** *o* **ON sb** pasar A algn

■ **devolve** *vt* (frml) ‹*power*› delegar*, transferir*; ‹*privilege/right*› conceder

devote /dɪ'vəʊt/ *vt* **to ~ sth TO sth/-ING** dedicar* algo A algo/ + INF; **the chapter is ~d to medical matters** el capítulo está dedicado a tratar asuntos de medicina

■ *v refl* **to ~ oneself TO sth/-ING** dedicarse* A algo/+ INF

devoted /dɪ'vəʊtəd || dɪ'vəʊtɪd/ *adj* **1** (loving) ‹*couple/family*› unido; **to be ~ TO sb** sentir* devoción POR algn **2** (dedicated) (*before n*) ‹*follower/admirer*› ferviente, devoto; ‹*service/friendship*› leal

devotee /'devə'ti:/ *n* (Relig) devoto, -ta *m,f*; (fan) adepto, -ta *m,f*, partidario, -ria *m,f*

devotion /dɪ'vəʊʃən/ *n*

A [u] (love) devoción *f*; (loyalty) lealtad *f*; **~ TO sb/sth**: **they showed great ~ to their king** demostraron gran devoción por/lealtad a su rey; **her ~ to the cause** su dedicación *or* entrega a la causa

B [u] (of money, time, space) dedicación *f*

C [c] (Relig) oración *f*, rezo *m*

devotional /dɪ'vəʊʃṇəl || dɪ'vəʊʃənl/ *adj* piadoso, devoto

devour /dɪ'vaʊr || dɪ'vaʊə(r)/ *vt* **1** (consume) ‹*food/book*› devorar **2** (torment) (*usu pass*) devorar; **he was ~ed by jealousy** lo consumían los celos

devout /dɪ'vaʊt/ *adj* **1** (Relig) devoto, piadoso; **she is a ~ Catholic** es muy católica **2** (earnest) (frml) (*before n*) ‹*supporter*› ferviente

devoutly /dɪ'vaʊtli/ *adv* ‹*pray*› con devoción; ‹*hope*› fervientemente

dew /du: || dju:/ *n* [u] rocío *m*

dewdrop /'du:drɑ:p || 'dju:drɒp/ *n* gota *f* de rocío

dewy /'du:i || 'dju:i/ *adj* **dewier, dewiest** **1** ‹*grass/lawn*› cubierto de rocío **2** (liter) ‹*eyes*› húmedo

dewy-eyed /'du:i'aɪd || ,dju:i'aɪd/ *adj* (innocent) ingenuo

dexterity /dek'sterəti/ *n* [u] (manual) destreza *f*, habilidad *f*; (skill) habilidad *f*

dexterous, dextrous /'dekstrəs/ *adj* (frml) diestro, hábil

diabetes /'daɪə'bi:ti:z/ *n* [u] diabetes *f*

diabetic[1] /'daɪə'betɪk/ *adj* diabético; ‹*jam/chocolate*› para diabéticos

diabetic[2] *n* diabético, -ca *m,f*

diabolical /'daɪə'bɑ:lɪkəl || ,daɪə'bɒlɪkəl/ *adj* **1** (fiendish) ‹*machinations*› diabólico, satánico; ‹*cruelty*› perverso, satánico **2** (very bad) (BrE colloq) espantoso, atroz

diabolically /'daɪə'bɑ:lɪkli || ,daɪə'bɒlɪkli/ *adv* **1** (fiendishly) ‹*laugh*› diabólicamente, perversamente; ‹*clever/difficult*› endemoniadamente **2** (very badly) (BrE colloq): **he sings ~** canta pésimo

diadem /'daɪədem/ *n* diadema *f*

diaeresis /daɪ'erəsɪs/ *n* [c u] (*pl* **-ses** /-si:z/) diéresis *f*, crema *f*

diagnose /'daɪəgnəʊs, -əʊz || 'daɪəgnəʊz/ *vt* **1** (Med) ‹*illness*› diagnosticar*; **the doctor ~d her as epileptic** el médico le diagnosticó epilepsia **2** ‹*cause/fault*› determinar, establecer*

diagnosis /'daɪəg'nəʊsəs || ,daɪəg'nəʊsɪs/ *n* (*pl* **-ses** /-si:z/) diagnóstico *m*; **to make/give a ~** hacer*/dar* un diagnóstico

diagnostic /'daɪəg'nɑ:stɪk || ,daɪəg'nɒstɪk/ *adj* (*before n*) diagnóstico

diagonal[1] /daɪ'ægənḷ/ *adj* ‹*line*› diagonal; ‹*path*› en diagonal

diagonal[2] *n* diagonal *f*

diagonally /daɪ'ægənḷi/ *adv* diagonalmente, en diagonal

diagram /'daɪəgræm/ *n* diagrama *m*, esquema *m*, gráfico *m*

diagrammatic /'daɪəgrə'mætɪk/ *adj* esquemático, gráfico

dial[1] /'daɪl || 'daɪəl/ *n* (on clock, watch) esfera *f*; (on measuring instrument) cuadrante *m*; (of telephone) disco *m*; (on radio) dial *m*

dial[2], (BrE) **-ll-** *vt* (Telec) marcar*, discar* (AmL)

■ **dial** *vi* (Telec) marcar*, discar* (AmL)

dialect /'daɪəlekt/ *n* dialecto *m*; (*before n*) **a ~ word** un vocablo dialectal, un dialectalismo

dialectic /'daɪə'lektɪk/ *n*, **dialectics** /-tɪks/ (+ *sing vb*) *n* dialéctica *f*

dialling code /'daɪlɪŋ || 'daɪəlɪŋ/ *n* (BrE) prefijo *m* *or* (AmL tb) código *m* de acceso (telefónico)

dialling tone /'daɪlɪŋ || 'daɪəlɪŋ/ *n* (BrE) ▸**dial tone**

dialogue, (AmE also) **dialog** /'daɪələ:g || 'daɪəlɒg/ *n* [c u] diálogo *m*

dial tone *n* tono *m* de marcar *or* (AmL) de discado

dialysis /daɪ'æləsəs || ,daɪ'æləsɪs/ *n* [u] diálisis *f*

diameter /daɪ'æmətər || daɪ'æmɪtə(r)/ *n* diámetro *m*

diametrically /'daɪə'metrɪkli/ *adv* diametralmente; **~ opposed views** opiniones *fpl* diametralmente opuestas

diamond /'daɪəmənd/ *n*

A [c u] (Min) diamante *m*; (cut) brillante *m*, diamante *m*; **he's a ~ in the rough** *o* (BrE) **a rough ~** no es muy pulido, pero tiene buenas cualidades; (*before n*) **~ ring** anillo *m* *or* sortija *f* de brillantes *or* diamantes

B (shape) rombo *m*

C (Games) **diamonds** (suit) (+ *sing or pl vb*) diamantes *mpl*

D (in baseball) **1** (area inside bases) diamante *m*, cuadro *m* **2** (entire field) campo *m* (de béisbol)

diaper /'daɪpər || 'daɪəpə(r)/ *n* (AmE) pañal *m*; (*before n*) **she has ~ rash** está escaldada *or* (Méx) rozada

diaphanous /daɪ'æfənəs/ *adj* diáfano, transparente

diaphragm /'daɪəfræm/ *n*

A (Anat) diafragma *m*

B (contraceptive) diafragma *m*

diarrhea, (BrE) **diarrhoea** /'daɪə'ri:ə || ,daɪə'rɪə/ *n* [u] diarrea *f*; **verbal ~** verborrea *f*, diarrea *f* verbal (hum)

d

diary /'daɪəri/ *n* (*pl* **-ries**)
A (personal record) diario *m*
B (book for appointments) agenda *f*
diatribe /'daɪətraɪb/ *n* diatriba *f*, invectiva *f*
dice[1] /daɪs/ *n* (*pl* ~) dado *m*
dice[2] *pl of* **die**[2] *and of* **dice**[1]
dice[3] *vt* (Culin) cortar en dados *or* cubitos
■ **dice** *vi*: ***to ~ with death*** jugar* con la muerte
dicey /'daɪsi/ *adj* **dicier, diciest** (colloq) (risky) arriesgado, riesgoso (AmL); (uncertain) dudoso, incierto
dichotomy /daɪ'kɑːtəmi || daɪ'kɒtəmi/ *n* dicotomía *f*
dick /dɪk/ *n* (vulg) verga *f* (vulg), pija *f* (RPl vulg), polla *f* (Esp vulg), pico *m* (Chi vulg)
dickhead /'dɪkhed/ *n* (vulg) huevón, -vona *m,f* (Andes, Ven vulg), pelotudo, -da *m,f* (AmS vulg), pendejo, -ja *m,f* (AmL exc CS fam *o* vulg), gilipollas *mf* (Esp fam *o* vulg)
dicky /'dɪki/ *adj* (BrE colloq): **he's got a ~ heart** tiene problemas cardíacos
Dictaphone® /'dɪktəfəʊn/ *n* dictáfono® *m*
dictate[1] /'dɪkteɪt || dɪk'teɪt/ *vt*
A (read out) dictar
B (prescribe, lay down) «*law*» establecer*, dictar; «*common sense*» dictar; **to ~ terms** imponer* condiciones
■ **dictate** *vi* dictar
Phrasal verb
• **dictate to** [v ▸ prep ▸ o] mandar, darle* órdenes a
dictate[2] /'dɪkteɪt/ *n* mandato *m*; **to follow the ~s of one's conscience** seguir* los dictados de la conciencia
dictation /dɪk'teɪʃən/ *n* **1** [u] (Corresp) dictado *m*; **she asked her secretary to take ~** llamó a la secretaria para dictarle una carta (*or* un informe *etc*) **2** [c u] (Educ) dictado *m*
dictator /'dɪkteɪtər || dɪk'teɪtə(r)/ *n* dictador, -dora *m,f*
dictatorial /'dɪktə'tɔːriəl/ *adj* dictatorial
dictatorship /dɪk'teɪtərʃɪp || dɪk'teɪtəʃɪp/ *n* [c u] dictadura *f*
diction /'dɪkʃən/ *n* [u] dicción *f*
dictionary /'dɪkʃəneri || 'dɪkʃənri, 'dɪkʃənəri/ *n* (*pl* **-ries**) diccionario *m*
did /dɪd/ *past of* **do**[1]
didactic /daɪ'dæktɪk/ *adj* didáctico
diddle /'dɪdl̩/ *vt* (colloq) estafar, timar (fam); **to ~ sb OUT OF sth**: **he ~d me out of 50 dollars** me sacó *or* me estafó 50 dólares
didn't /'dɪdn̩t/ = **did not**
die[1] /daɪ/ **dies, dying, died** *vi*
A **1** (stop living) morir*; (violently) matarse, morir*; **he ~d of cancer** (se) murió de cáncer **2** (be overcome) (colloq) morirse*; **to ~ laughing** morirse* de risa; **I nearly ~d!** casi me muero **3** (want very much) (colloq) **to be dying FOR sth** morirse* POR algo; **to be dying to + INF** morirse* POR + INF, morirse* de ganas de + INF
B **1** (cease to exist) «*love/hatred*» morir*; **old habits ~ hard** las viejas costumbres no se pierden fácilmente **2** (be extinguished) «*fire*» extinguirse*, apagarse*; «*light*» extinguirse* **3** (stop functioning) «*engine/motor*» apagarse*, dejar de funcionar
C (colloq) (in baseball) quedarse embasado, ser* dejado en base
■ **die** *vt*: **to ~ a natural death** morir* de muerte natural; **to ~ a violent death** tener* *or* sufrir una muerte violenta; ***to ~ a death*** (BrE colloq) quedar en la nada
Phrasal verbs
• **die away** [v ▸ adv] «*storm/wind*» amainar; «*anger*» pasar; **her voice ~d away** su voz se fue apagando *or* (liter) extinguiendo
• **die down** [v ▸ adv] «*fire/noise*» irse* apagando; «*storm/wind*» amainar; «*anger/excitement*» calmarse
• **die off** [v ▸ adv] ir* muriendo
• **die out** [v ▸ adv] «*race/species*» extinguirse*; «*custom*» morir*, caer* en desuso
die[2] *n* (*pl* **dice** /daɪs/) (Games) dado *m*; **the ~ is cast** la suerte está echada; ***as straight as a ~*** derecho hasta decir basta, honrado como él sólo; ***no dice!*** (AmE) ¡ni hablar!, ¡ni lo sueñes!
diehard /'daɪhɑːrd || 'daɪhɑːd/ *n* intransigente *mf*; (*before n*) intransigente, acérrimo

dieresis /daɪ'erəsɪs/ *n* [c u] (*pl* **-ses** /-siːz/) (AmE) ▸ **diaeresis**
diesel[1] /'diːzəl/ *n* **1** [c] (vehicle) coche *m* (*or* camión *m etc*) diesel, diesel *m* **2** [u] (fuel) diesel *m*, gasóleo *m*, gas-oil *m*
diesel[2] *adj* (*before n*) diesel *adj inv*
diet[1] /'daɪət/ *n* **1** (special food) régimen *m*, dieta *f*; **to be/go on a ~** estar*/ponerse* a régimen *or* a dieta; (*before n*) ‹*cola*› light *adj inv* **2** (nourishment) alimentación *f*, dieta *f* (alimenticia); **they live on a ~ of rice and fish** se alimentan de arroz y pescado
diet[2] *vi* hacer* régimen *or* dieta
dietary /'daɪəteri || 'daɪətri/ *adj* ‹*habits*› alimenticio; ‹*fiber*› dietético
dietician, dietitian /'daɪə'tɪʃən/ *n* dietista *mf*, experto, -ta *m,f* en dietética
differ /'dɪfər || 'dɪfə(r)/ *vi*
A **1** (be at variance) diferir*; **how do they ~?** ¿en qué difieren? **2** (be unlike) ser* distinto *or* diferente; **to ~ FROM sb/sth** diferenciarse *or* diferir* DE algn/algo
B (disagree) discrepar, diferir* (frml); **I beg to ~ but ...** lamento discrepar (de su opinión) pero ...
difference /'dɪfrəns/ *n*
A [c u] **1** (dissimilarity) diferencia *f*; **to tell the ~** notar *or* ver* la diferencia; **a vacation with a ~** unas vacaciones diferentes **2** **to make a/no ~**: **it could make a ~ in** *o* (BrE) **to the outcome** podría influir en el resultado; **it will make no ~ to you** a ti no te va a afectar; **it makes a ~ having a computer** las cosas son muy distintas con una computadora; **what ~ does it make? — it makes all the ~ in the world** ¿qué importa? — importa muchísimo **3** (Math) diferencia *f*; ***to split the ~*** dividirse la diferencia (a partes iguales)
B [c] (disagreement) (often euph) diferencia *f*; **to settle** *o* **resolve one's ~s** saldar *or* resolver* sus (*or* nuestras *etc*) diferencias
different /'dɪfrənt/ *adj* **1** (not the same) distinto, diferente; **~ FROM** *o* **TO** *o* (AmE also) **THAN sth/sb** distinto *or* diferente DE *or* A algo/algn **2** (unusual) diferente, original
differential[1] /'dɪfə'rentʃəl || ˌdɪfə'renʃəl/ *adj* (Fin, Math) diferencial
differential[2] *n* diferencial *m*
differentiate /'dɪfə'rentʃieɪt || ˌdɪfə'renʃieɪt/ *vi* distinguir*
■ **differentiate** *vt* (frml): **to ~ sth (FROM sth)** diferenciar *or* distinguir* algo (DE algo)
differently /'dɪfrəntli/ *adv*: **they think ~** no piensan igual *or* del mismo modo; **I view things ~** yo veo las cosas de otra forma *or* otro modo
difficult /'dɪfɪkəlt/ *adj* difícil; **the ~ bit** *o* **part is ...** lo difícil es ..., la dificultad está en ...; **we'll make things very ~ for him** le haremos la vida imposible; **he's ~ to live with** es difícil convivir con él
difficulty /'dɪfɪkəlti/ *n* (*pl* **-ties**) **1** [u] (of situation, task) dificultad *f*; **he has ~ (in) understanding English** tiene dificultad para entender el inglés; **she had great ~ walking** caminaba con mucha dificultad **2** [c] (problem) dificultad *f*, problema *m*; **to be in difficulties** estar* en apuros; **to get into difficulties** meterse en líos; **to make difficulties** crear problemas
diffidence /'dɪfədəns || 'dɪfɪdəns/ *n* [u] falta *f* de seguridad en sí mismo, retraimiento *m*
diffident /'dɪfədənt || 'dɪfɪdənt/ *adj* ‹*person*› poco seguro de sí mismo; ‹*smile*› tímido
diffraction /dɪ'frækʃən/ *n* [u] difracción *f*
diffuse[1] /dɪ'fjuːz/ *vt* ‹*heat*› difundir, esparcir*; ‹*light*› tamizar*, difuminar; ‹*knowledge*› (frml) difundir
■ **diffuse** *vi* difundirse
diffuse[2] /dɪ'fjuːs/ *adj* difuso
diffusion /dɪ'fjuːʒən/ *n* [u] difusión *f*
dig[1] /dɪg/ (*pres p* **digging**; *past & past p* **dug**) *vt*
A **1** ‹*ground*› cavar; ‹*hole/trench*› (by hand) cavar; (by machine) excavar; **to ~ the garden** cavar en el jardín **2** ‹*potatoes*› sacar* **3** (Archeol) excavar
B (jab, thrust) **to ~ sth INTO sth** clavar algo EN algo; **to ~ sb in the ribs** darle* *or* (fam) pegarle* un codazo en las costillas a algn
■ **dig** *vi*
A **1** (excavate — by hand) cavar; (— by machine) excavar; «*dog*»

escarbar; **to ~ for oil** hacer* prospecciones petrolíferas 2 (Archeol) hacer* excavaciones, excavar
B (search) buscar*; **she dug in her pockets for the key** buscó la llave en los bolsillos

Phrasal verbs
- **dig around** [v ▸ adv] (colloq) revolver*, escarbar (*buscando algo*)
- **dig in** [v ▸ adv] 1 (Mil) atrincherarse 2 (start eating) (colloq): **~ in!** ¡al ataque! (fam), ¡ataquen! (fam)
- **dig into** [v ▸ prep ▸ o] (colloq) 1 (start eating) atacar* (fam) 2 (investigate) investigar* 3 ‹*resources/reserves*› echar mano de
- **dig out** [v ▸ o ▸ adv, v ▸ adv ▸ o] 1 (remove) sacar* (*de entre los escombros, la nieve etc*); (from soil) desenterrar* 2 (find) (colloq) sacar*, desempolvar
- **dig up** [v ▸ o ▸ adv, v ▸ adv ▸ o] 1 ‹*lawn*› levantar; ‹*weeds/tree*› arrancar* 2 ‹*body/treasure*› desenterrar* 3 ‹*facts*› (colloq) sacar* a la luz

dig[2] *n*
A (Archeol) excavación *f*
B (jab — with elbow) codazo *m*; (— with pin) pinchazo *m*; **to give sb a ~ in the ribs** darle* un codazo en las costillas a algn
C (critical remark) (colloq) pulla *f*; (hint) indirecta *f*; **to have a ~ at sb/sth** meterse con algn/algo
D **digs** *pl n* (lodgings) (BrE): **to live in ~s** *vivir en una habitación alquilada, una pensión etc*

digest[1] /daɪˈdʒest, -də- || daɪˈdʒest, dɪ-/ *vt* ‹*food*› digerir*; (assimilate mentally) asimilar, digerir* (fam)
digest[2] /ˈdaɪdʒest/ *n* (summary) compendio *m*; (journal) boletín *m*, revista *f*
digestible /daɪˈdʒestəbəl, də- || daɪˈdʒestəbəl, dɪ-/ *adj* (Physiol) digerible; (comprehensible) fácil de asimilar *or* (fam) digerir; **easily ~** fácil de digerir
digestion /daɪˈdʒestʃən, də- || daɪˈdʒestʃən, dɪ-/ *n* [u] digestión *f*
digestive /daɪˈdʒestɪv, də- || daɪˈdʒestɪv, dɪ-/ *adj* digestivo; **the ~ system** el aparato digestivo
digestive biscuit *n* (BrE) galleta *f* integral
digger /ˈdɪgər || ˈdɪgə(r)/ *n*
A (machine) excavadora *f*; (person) excavador, -dora *m,f*
B (Austral, colloq) (an Australian) australiano, -na *m,f*
digicam /ˈdɪdʒɪˈkæm/ *n* cámara *f* digital
digit /ˈdɪdʒət || ˈdɪdʒɪt/ *n*
A (Math) dígito *m* (frml)
B (Anat) dedo *m*
digital /ˈdɪdʒətəl || ˈdɪdʒɪtl/ *adj* digital; **~ camera** cámara *f* (fotográfica) digital; **~ image** imagen *f* digital; **~ image processing** procesamiento *m* *or* tratamiento *m* de imágenes digitales; **~ television** [c] (**~** TV set) televisor *m* digital; [u] (system) televisión *f* digital; **~ video disc** videodisco *m* digital
dignified /ˈdɪgnəfaɪd || ˈdɪgnɪfaɪd/ *adj* 1 ‹*person/reply*› digno, circunspecto; ‹*silence/attitude*› digno; **it's not very ~** no es muy decoroso 2 (stately) majestuoso
dignify /ˈdɪgnəfaɪ || ˈdɪgnɪfaɪ/ *vt* **-fies, -fying, -fied** 1 (grace) dignificar* 2 (make respectable) darle* categoría a; **I would not ~ that question with an answer** esa pregunta no es digna de respuesta
dignitary /ˈdɪgnəˈteri/ *n* (*pl* **-ries**) dignatario, -ria *m,f*
dignity /ˈdɪgnəti/ *n* [u]
A (dignified air) 1 (of person) dignidad *f*; ***to stand on one's ~*** mantener* las distancias 2 (of occasion) solemnidad *f*
B (status, worth) dignidad *f*, categoría *f*; **she considers it to be beneath her ~** lo considera una degradación
digress /daɪˈgres/ *vi*: **if I may ~ for a moment** si me permiten hacer un breve inciso *or* paréntesis; **but I ~** pero estoy divagando; **to ~ FROM sth** apartarse DE algo
digression /daɪˈgreʃən/ *n* [c u] digresión *f*; **by way of (a) ~** a modo de inciso *or* paréntesis
dike /daɪk/ *n*
A 1 (to keep out water) dique *m* 2 (causeway) terraplén *m* 3 (ditch) acequia *f*
B ▸**dyke B**
dilapidated /dəˈlæpədeɪtəd || dɪˈlæpɪdeɪtɪd/ *adj* ‹*building*› ruinoso; ‹*car*› destartalado, desvencijado
dilapidation /dəˈlæpəˈdeɪʃən || dɪˌlæpɪˈdeɪʃən/ *n* [u] (frml) deterioro *m* (frml)
dilate /daɪˈleɪt/ *vi* dilatarse
■ **dilate** *vt* dilatar
dilated /daɪˈleɪtəd || daɪˈleɪtɪd/ *adj* (*usu pred*) dilatado; **his pupils were ~** tenía las pupilas dilatadas
dilation /daɪˈleɪʃən/, **dilatation** /ˈdaɪləˈteɪʃən/ *n* [u] dilatación *f*; **~ and curettage** (Med) dilatación y legrado
dilatory /ˈdɪlətɔːri || ˈdɪlətəri/ *adj* (frml) 1 (causing delay) dilatorio 2 (not prompt) tardío
dilemma /dəˈlemə, daɪ- || dɪˈlemə, daɪ-/ *n* dilema *m*
dilettante /ˈdɪləˈtɑːnt || ˌdɪlɪˈtænti/ *n* (*pl* **-tes** *or* **-ti** /-ti/) diletante *mf*
diligence /ˈdɪlədʒəns || ˈdɪlɪdʒəns/ *n* [u] diligencia *f*
diligent /ˈdɪlədʒənt || ˈdɪlɪdʒənt/ *adj* ‹*worker*› diligente, cumplidor; ‹*student*› aplicado, diligente; ‹*work/study*› esmerado, concienzudo
diligently /ˈdɪlədʒəntli || ˈdɪlɪdʒəntli/ *adv* con diligencia, diligentemente
dill /dɪl/ *n* [u] (Culin) 1 (herb) eneldo *m* 2 **~ (pickle)** (AmE) pepinillos *mpl* (al vinagre de eneldo)
dilly-dally /ˈdɪliˈdæli/ *vi* **-dallies, -dallying, -dallied** (colloq) perder* el tiempo
dilute[1] /daɪˈluːt || daɪˈljuːt/ *vt* diluir*
dilute[2] *adj* diluido
dilution /daɪˈluːʃən || daɪˈljuːʃən/ *n* [u] dilución *f*
dim[1] /dɪm/ *adj* **-mm-**
A 1 (dark) ‹*room*› oscuro, poco iluminado; ‹*light*› débil, tenue 2 (indistinct) ‹*memory/shape*› borroso; ‹*idea*› vago; **in the ~ and distant past** en el pasado remoto 3 (gloomy) ‹*prospects*› nada halagüeño, nada prometedor; ▸**view**[1] **C**
B (stupid) (colloq) corto (de luces) (fam), tonto (fam)
dim[2] **-mm-** *vt* 1 ‹*lights*› atenuar*; **to ~ one's headlights** (AmE) poner* las (luces) cortas *or* de cruce *or* (AmL tb) las (luces) bajas 2 ‹*eyesight*› ir* debilitando; ‹*memory*› ir* borrando
■ **dim** *vi* 1 «*light*» irse* atenuando 2 «*memory*» irse* borrando; «*sight*» irse* debilitando
dime /daɪm/ *n* (AmE colloq) *moneda de diez centavos*; **it's not worth a ~** no vale nada; ***to be a ~ a dozen*: they are a ~ a dozen** (very cheap) son baratísimos; (very common) los hay a patadas *or* a montones (fam)
dimension /deˈmentʃən, daɪ- || dɪˈmenʃən, daɪ-/ *n* dimensión *f*; **a problem of enormous ~s** un problema de enormes dimensiones
dime store *n* (AmE) *tienda que vende artículos de bajo precio*, ≈ baratillo *m*
diminish /dəˈmɪnɪʃ || dɪˈmɪnɪʃ/ *vi* 1 «*cost/number*» disminuir*, reducirse*; «*enthusiasm*» disminuir*, apagarse*; **to ~ in value** disminuir* de valor, depreciarse 2 **diminishing** *pres p* ‹*amount/importance*› cada vez menor; **the law of ~ing returns** (Econ) la ley de los rendimientos decrecientes
■ **diminish** *vt* ‹*size/cost*› reducir*, disminuir*; ‹*enthusiasm*› disminuir*
diminished /dəˈmɪnɪʃt || dɪˈmɪnɪʃt/ *adj* ‹*expectations*› más limitado; **to plead ~ responsibility** alegar* una atenuante de responsabilidad
diminutive[1] /dəˈmɪnjətɪv || dɪˈmɪnjʊtɪv/ *adj* diminuto, minúsculo
diminutive[2] *n* (Ling) diminutivo *m*
dimly /ˈdɪmli/ *adv* ‹*shine*› débilmente; **a ~ lit room** una habitación poco iluminada *or* iluminada por una luz tenue
dimmer /ˈdɪmər || ˈdɪmə(r)/ *n* potenciómetro *m*, dimmer *m*; (*before n*) **~ switch** (Elec) potenciómetro *m*, dimmer *m*; (AmE Auto) conmutador *m* de las luces
dimple /ˈdɪmpəl/ *n* (in cheeks, chin) hoyuelo *m*
dim: **~wit** *n* (colloq) tarado, -da (mental) *m,f* (fam); **~-witted** /ˈdɪmˈwɪtəd || ˌdɪmˈwɪtɪd/ *adj* (colloq) tonto (fam), idiota
din /dɪn/ *n* [u] (colloq) (*no pl*) (of conversation, voices) barullo *m* (fam), bulla *f* (fam); (of drill, traffic) estruendo *m*, ruido *m*
dine /daɪn/ *vi* (frml) cenar; **to ~ ON *o* OFF sth** cenar algo

Phrasal verb
- **dine out** [v ▸ adv] cenar (a)fuera; ***to ~ out on sth*: you'll be dining out on that for years** te va a dar tema de

conversación para quién sabe cuántas ocasiones

diner /'daɪnər || 'daɪnə(r)/ *n*
A (person) comensal *mf*
B 1 (restaurant) (AmE) cafetería *f* 2 ▸ **dining car**

dinette /daɪ'net/ *n* ~ **(set)** (AmE) juego *m* de comedor diario

ding-dong /'dɪŋdɔːŋ || 'dɪŋdɒŋ/ *n* [u] talán, talán *m*

dinghy /'dɪŋgi, 'dɪŋi/ *n* (*pl* **-ghies**) (sailing boat) bote *m*; (*inflatable o rubber* ~) bote *m* neumático

dingo /'dɪŋgəʊ/ *n* (*pl* **-goes**) dingo *m*

dingy /'dɪndʒi/ *adj* **-gier, -giest** ‹*building/room*› lúgubre, deprimente; ‹*furnishings*› deslucido; (dirty) sucio

dining /'daɪnɪŋ/: ~ **car** *n* coche *m* comedor, vagón *m* restaurante; ~ **hall** *n* refectorio *m*; ~ **room** *n* comedor *m*; ~ **table** *n* mesa *f* (de comedor)

dinky /'dɪŋki/ *adj* **-kier, -kiest** 1 (AmE colloq) ‹*town*› de mala muerte (fam); **a ~ apartment/room** un cuchitril (fam) 2 (cute) (BrE colloq) mono (fam), lindo (AmL)

dinner /'dɪnər || 'dɪnə(r)/ *n* [u c] 1 (in evening) cena *f*, comida *f* (AmL); **to eat** *o* **have ~** cenar, comer (AmL); **to go out to ~** salir* a cenar fuera 2 (formal) cena *f* (de gala) 3 (at midday) almuerzo *m*, comida *f* (esp Esp, Méx); **to eat** *o* (BrE) **have ~** almorzar*, comer (esp Esp, Méx); **he's had more girlfriends than you've had hot ~s** (colloq) ¡cambia de novia como de camisa! (fam)

dinner: ~ **dance** *n* cena *f* con baile, comida *f* bailable (esp AmL), cena-baile *f* (Méx); ~ **jacket** *n* (esp BrE) esmoquin *m*, smoking *m*; ~ **party** *n* cena *f*, comida *f* (AmL); ~ **plate** *n* plato *m* llano *or* (Méx) plano *or* (RPl tb) playo *or* (Chi) bajo; ~ **service**, ~ **set** *n* vajilla *f*; ~ **table** *n* mesa *f*; ~**time** *n* [u c] (in evening) hora *f* de cenar *or* (esp AmL) de comer; (at midday) hora *f* de almorzar *or* (esp Esp, Méx) de comer

dinosaur /'daɪnəsɔːr || 'daɪnəsɔː(r)/ *n* dinosaurio *m*; (outdated thing) pieza *f* de museo

dint /dɪnt/ *n*
A: **by ~ of sth** a fuerza de algo
B (AmE) ▸ **dent**[1]

diocese /'daɪəsəs || 'daɪəsɪs/ *n* diócesis *f*

diode /'daɪəʊd/ *n* diodo *m*

dioxide /daɪ'ɑːksaɪd || daɪ'ɒksaɪd/ *n* [c u] dióxido *m*, bióxido *m*

dioxin /daɪ'ɑːksən || daɪ'ɒksɪn/ *n* [u] dioxina *f*

dip[1] /dɪp/ **-pp-** *vt*
A **to ~ sth IN(TO) sth** meter algo EN algo; (into liquid) mojar algo EN algo; **~ it in flour** páselo por harina, enharínelo
B (Agr) ‹*sheep*› desinfectar (*haciendo pasar por un baño*)
C 1 (lower) ‹*head*› agachar, bajar 2 (BrE Auto): **to ~ one's headlights** poner* las (luces) cortas *or* de cruce *or* (AmL tb) las (luces) bajas
■ **dip** *vi* 1 (decrease) «*sales/prices*» bajar 2 (move downward) «*aircraft/bird*» bajar en picada *or* (Esp) en picado; **the sun ~ped below the horizon** (liter) el sol desapareció *or* se escondió tras el horizonte 3 (slope) «*land*» descender*, bajar

Phrasal verb
• **dip into** [v ▸ prep ▸ o] 1 ‹*reserves/savings*› echar mano de 2 ‹*book*› hojear, leer* por encima

dip[2] *n*
A (swim) (colloq) (*no pl*) chapuzón *m* (fam); **to take a ~** darse* un chapuzón (fam)
B (Agr) baño *m* desinfectante
C (depression, hollow) hondonada *f*
D (in sales, production) caída *f*, descenso *m*
E [u c] (Culin) *salsa en la que se mojan diferentes bocaditos (en una fiesta etc)*

diphtheria /dɪf'θɪriə || dɪf'θɪəriə/ *n* [u] difteria *f*

diphthong /'dɪfθɔːŋ || 'dɪfθɒŋ/ *n* diptongo *m*

diploma /də'pləʊmə || dɪ'pləʊmə/ *n* diploma *m*; **to have** *o* **hold a ~ in sth** ser* diplomado en algo

diplomacy /də'pləʊməsi || dɪ'pləʊməsi/ *n* [u] diplomacia *f*

diplomat /'dɪpləmæt/ *n* diplomático, -ca *m,f*

diplomatic /'dɪplə'mætɪk/ *adj* 1 (Govt) (*before n*) diplomático; ~ **bag** (BrE) *o* (AmE) **pouch** valija *f* diplomática; **the ~ corps** el cuerpo diplomático; ~ **immunity** inmunidad *f* diplomática; **to establish/break off ~ relations** establecer* relaciones diplomáticas/romper* (las) relaciones diplomáticas 2 (tactful) diplomático

dipper /'dɪpər || 'dɪpə(r)/ *n*
A (Zool) tordo *m* de agua
B (ladle) (AmE) cucharón *m*, cazo *m*

dipsomaniac /'dɪpsəʊ'meɪniæk/ *n* dipsómano, -na *m,f*

dip: ~**stick** *n* varilla *f* (medidora) del aceite; ~ **switch** *n* (BrE) conmutador *m* (de las luces)

dire /daɪr || 'daɪə(r)/ *adj* **direr, direst**
A 1 ‹*news/consequences*› funesto, nefasto; **to be in ~ straits** estar* en una situación desesperada 2 (very bad) (BrE colloq) espantoso (fam), atroz
B (ominous) ‹*warning*› serio, grave
C (desperate) ‹*need/misery*› extremo

direct[1] /də'rekt, daɪ- || daɪ'rekt, dɪ-/ *adj*
A 1 ‹*route/flight*› directo; ‹*contact*› directo; ‹*cause/consequence*› directo; ~ **dialing** *o* (BrE) **dialling** (Telec) servicio *m* automático, discado *m* directo *or* automático (AmL); ~ **taxation** tributación *f* directa 2 (in genealogy): **he's a ~ descendant of the duke** desciende del duque por línea directa 3 (exact) ‹*equivalent/quotation*› exacto; **to score a ~ hit** dar* en el blanco 4 (Ling) (*before n*) ‹*question/command*› en estilo directo; ~ **discourse** *o* (BrE) **speech** estilo *m* directo
B (frank, straightforward) ‹*person/manner*› franco, directo; ‹*question*› directo

direct[2] *adv*
A ‹*write/phone*› directamente; ‹*go/travel*› (BrE) directo, directamente; **to dial ~** (Telec) marcar* *or* (AmL tb) discar* directamente el número
B (straight) directamente; ~ **from Paris** (Rad, TV) en directo desde París
C (straightforwardly) (esp AmE colloq) directamente, sin rodeos

direct[3] *vt*
A 1 (give directions to) indicarle* el camino a 2 (address) ‹*letter/parcel*› mandar, dirigir*
B (aim) dirigir*; **it was ~ed at us** iba dirigido a nosotros
C ‹*play/orchestra/traffic*› dirigir*
D (order) (frml) ordenar; **to ~ sb to + INF** ordenarle A algn QUE (+ *subj*)
■ **direct** *vi* (Cin, Theat) dirigir*

direct: ~ **access** *n* [u] acceso *m* directo; ~ **action** *n* [u] acción *f* directa; ~ **billing** *n* [u c] (AmE) débito *m* bancario *or* (Esp) domiciliación *f* de pagos; ~ **current** *n* [u] corriente *f* continua; ~ **debit** *n* [u c] ▸ ~ **billing**

direction /də'rekʃən, daɪ- || daɪ'rekʃən, dɪ-/ *n*
A [c] (course, compass point) dirección *f*; **sense of ~** sentido *m* de (la) orientación; **it's a step in the right ~** es un paso positivo; **in the ~ of** en dirección a
B [u] (purpose): **he lacks ~** no tiene un norte
C [u] (supervision) dirección *f*
D **directions** *pl* (for route) indicaciones *fpl*; (for task, use, assembly) instrucciones *fpl*, indicaciones *fpl*

direction finder *n* radiogoniómetro *m*

directive /də'rektɪv, daɪ- || daɪ'rektɪv, dɪ-/ *n* directriz *f*, directiva *f* (esp AmL)

directly /də'rektli, daɪ- || daɪ'rektli, dɪ-/ *adv*
A 1 (without stopping) ‹*go/drive/fly*› directamente, directo 2 (without intermediaries) ‹*report/deal*› directamente; **he's ~ responsible** es el responsable directo 3 (exactly) ‹*opposite/above*› justo 4 (in genealogy) ‹*related/descended*› por línea directa
B (frankly, straightforwardly) ‹*ask*› directamente; ‹*speak*› con franqueza
C (now, at once) inmediatamente, ahora mismo

direct mail *n* [u] publicidad *f* por correo

directness /də'rektnəs, daɪ- || daɪ'rektnɪs, dɪ-/ *n* [u] 1 (of character, remark) franqueza *f* 2 (of aim, attack) lo directo

director /də'rektər, daɪ- || daɪ'rektə(r), dɪ-/ *n*
A (of company) directivo, -tiva *m,f*; (of department, project) director, -tora *m,f*; *see also* **managing director**
B (Cin, Theat) director, -tora *m,f*; (esp AmE Mus) director, -tora *m,f*

directorate /də'rektərət, daɪ- || daɪ'rektərət, dɪ-/ *n* (+ *sing o pl vb*) dirección *f*, (junta *f*) directiva *f*

director general *n* director, -tora *m,f* general

directorial /'dərek'tɔːriəl, 'daɪ- || ˌdaɪrek'tɔːriəl, ˌdɪ-/ *adj* ‹*techniques/tricks*› de dirección; ‹*experience*› en dirección, como director; ‹*debut*› como director

directorship /də'rektərʃɪp, daɪ- || daɪ'rektəʃɪp, dɪ-/ *n* dirección *f*, cargo *m* de director

directory /də'rektəri, daɪ- || daɪ'rektəri, dɪ-/ *n* (*pl* **-ries**) 1 (*telephone* ~) guía *f* telefónica *or* de teléfonos, directorio *m* telefónico (Col, Méx); (*before n*) ~ **assistance** *o* (BrE) **enquiries** servicio *m* de información telefónica, información *f* (de teléfonos) 2 (index, yearbook) directorio *m*, guía *f*; **a street** *o* (AmE) **city** ~ una guía de calles, un callejero

dirge /dɜːrdʒ || dɜːdʒ/ *n* canto *m* fúnebre

dirt /dɜːrt || dɜːt/ *n* [u]

A (unclean substance) suciedad *f*, mugre *f*

B 1 (scandal): **to dig up** ~ **on** *o* **about sb** sacarle* los trapos sucios a relucir *or* al sol a algn 2 (obscenity) (esp BrE colloq) inmundicia *f*

C (earth, soil) (esp AmE) tierra *f*; **to hit the** ~ (sl) caerse* al suelo; (*before n*) ‹*road/track*› de tierra

dirt: ~ **cheap** *adj* (*before n* ~**-cheap**) (colloq) baratísimo, regalado (fam), tirado (fam); ~ **farmer** *n* (AmE) *agricultor que trabaja su propia tierra*

dirtily /'dɜːrtḷi || 'dɜːtɪli/ *adv* ‹*laugh/leer*› lascivamente; ‹*eat*› sin modales

dirty¹ /'dɜːrti || 'dɜːti/ *adj* **-tier, -tiest**

A (soiled) sucio; **the floor is** ~ el suelo está sucio; **my hands are** ~ tengo las manos sucias; **to get** ~ ensuciarse; ***to get one's hands*** ~ ensuciarse *or* mancharse las manos

B 1 (obscene) ‹*story/book*› cochino (fam), guarro (Esp fam); ‹*leer/grin*› lascivo; ‹*joke*› verde *or* (Méx) colorado; ‹*magazine*› porno *adj inv*; **to have a** ~ **mind** tener* una mente de cloaca 2 (shameful) ‹*job/work*› sucio; ~ **money** dinero *m* sucio *or* negro; **to do sb's** ~ **work** hacerle* el trabajo sucio a algn 3 (despicable) (colloq): **he played a** ~ **trick on me** me jugó una mala pasada; ***to do the*** ~ ***on sb*** (BrE) jugársela* a algn 4 (unfair) ‹*tactics*› sucio; **he's a** ~ **player** juega sucio

C (angry, accusing): **a** ~ **look** una mirada asesina

dirty² *vt* **dirties, dirtying, dirtied** ensuciar; ‹*reputation*› manchar

dirty³ *adv* (colloq)

A 1 (unfairly) ‹*fight/play*› sucio 2 (indecently): **to talk** ~ decir* cochinadas

B (BrE sl) (*as intensifier*): ~ **great** tremendo

dirty: ~ **old man** *n* (colloq) viejo *m* verde (fam); ~ **tricks** *pl n* chanchullos *mpl*; ~ **weekend** *n* (BrE colloq): **to go on a** ~ **weekend with sb** irse* de fin de semana con un/una amante; ~ **word** *n* palabrota *f*, mala palabra *f* (AmL)

disability /'dɪsə'bɪləti/ *n* (*pl* **-ties**) 1 [u] (state) invalidez *f*, discapacidad *f*; (*before n*) ‹*pension/allowance*› por invalidez 2 [c] (particular handicap) problema *m*

disable /dɪs'eɪbəl/ *vt* 1 «*illness/accident/injury*» dejar inválido (*or* lisiado *or* ciego *etc*) 2 ‹*machine/weapon*› (Mil) inutilizar*

disabled¹ /dɪs'eɪbəld/ *adj* discapacitado, minusválido

disabled² *pl n* **the** ~ los discapacitados, los minusválidos

disabuse /'dɪsə'bjuːz/ *vt* (frml) desengañar; **to** ~ **sb OF sth**: **I tried to** ~ **him of the notion that ...** intenté sacarlo del error de que ...

disadvantage /'dɪsəd'væntɪdʒ || ˌdɪsəd'vɑːntɪdʒ/ *n* (hindrance, drawback) desventaja *f*, inconveniente *m*; **to be at a** ~ estar* en desventaja; **this puts them at a** ~ esto los pone en desventaja; **to sb's/sth's** ~, **to the** ~ **of sb/sth** en perjuicio de algn/algo

disadvantaged /'dɪsəd'væntɪdʒd || ˌdɪsəd'vɑːntɪdʒd/ *adj* ‹*children/area*› desfavorecido, carenciado

disadvantageous /dɪs'ædvæn'teɪdʒəs || dɪsˌædvən'teɪdʒəs/ *adj* desventajoso, desfavorable

disaffected /'dɪsə'fektəd || ˌdɪsə'fektɪd/ *adj* desafecto

disaffection /'dɪsə'fekʃən/ *n* [u] desafección *f*

disagree /'dɪsə'griː/ *vi*

A 1 (differ in opinion) **to** ~ **(WITH sb/sth)** no estar* de acuerdo (CON algn/algo), discrepar (DE algn/algo) (frml) 2 (quarrel) **to** ~ **(WITH sb)** discutir (CON algn) 3 (conflict) «*figures/accounts*» no coincidir, discrepar; **to** ~ **WITH sth** no coincidir CON algo

B (cause discomfort) «*food*» **to** ~ **WITH sb** sentarle* *or* caerle* mal A algn; **onions** ~ **with her** las cebollas le sientan *or* le caen mal

disagreeable /'dɪsə'griːəbəl/ *adj* ‹*smell/experience/person*› desagradable; ‹*task/job*› ingrato, desagradable

disagreeably /'dɪsə'griːəbli/ *adv* ‹*look/say*› de mala manera, de manera desagradable; **it was** ~ **hot** hacía un calor desagradable

disagreement /'dɪsə'griːmənt/ *n* 1 [u] (difference of opinion) desacuerdo *m*, disconformidad *f*; **to be in** ~ **(with sb/sth)** estar* en desacuerdo (con algn/algo) 2 [c] (quarrel) discusión *f* 3 [u c] (disparity) discrepancia *f*

disallow /'dɪsə'laʊ/ *vt* (frml) ‹*claim/evidence*› (Law) rechazar*, desestimar; ‹*goal*› anular

disappear /'dɪsə'pɪr || ˌdɪsə'pɪə(r)/ *vi* 1 (become invisible) desaparecer*; **the ship** ~**ed over the horizon** el barco desapareció *or* se perdió en el horizonte; ▸ **act² C2** 2 (go away) «*pain/problems*» desaparecer*, irse*; «*worries/fears*» desvanecerse*

disappearance /'dɪsə'pɪrəns || ˌdɪsə'pɪərəns/ *n* desaparición *f*

disappoint /'dɪsə'pɔɪnt/ *vt* ‹*person*› decepcionar; ‹*hopes/desires*› defraudar

disappointed /'dɪsə'pɔɪntəd || ˌdɪsə'pɔɪntɪd/ *adj* 1 (*pred*) **to be** ~ estar* desilusionado *or* decepcionado; **to be** ~ **AT -ING**: **she was** ~ **at losing the match** se llevó una desilusión al perder el partido; **to be** ~ **WITH sth**: **I'm** ~ **with the results** los resultados me han decepcionado; **to be** ~ **IN sth/sb**: **she was** ~ **in love** tuvo un desengaño amoroso; **I'm** ~ **in you** me has decepcionado *or* defraudado 2 ‹*look/sigh*› de desilusión

disappointing /'dɪsə'pɔɪntɪŋ/ *adj* decepcionante

disappointingly /'dɪsə'pɔɪntɪŋli/ *adv* ‹*perform/react*› de manera decepcionante; **it's** ~ **short** es tan corto que resulta decepcionante

disappointment /'dɪsə'pɔɪntmənt/ *n* 1 [u] (emotion) desilusión *f*, decepción *f*; **much to my** ~ para mi gran desilusión 2 [c] (letdown) decepción *f*, chasco *m*

disapproval /'dɪsə'pruːvəl/ *n* [u]

A (dislike) desaprobación *f*; **to voice** *o* **express one's** ~ **of sb/sth** mostrar* *or* expresar su (*or* mi *etc*) desaprobación respecto de algn/algo

B (rejection) (AmE) (of bill) no aprobación *f*; (of grant) denegación *f*

disapprove /'dɪsə'pruːv/ *vi* **to** ~ **(OF sth/sb)**: **she wants to be a singer but her parents** ~ quiere ser cantante pero a sus padres no les parece bien *or* (frml) sus padres desaprueban la idea; **he** ~**s of smoking** está en contra del tabaco *or* del cigarrillo; **she** ~**s of her son's fiancée** no tiene buen concepto de la novia de su hijo

■ **disapprove** *vt* (AmE) ‹*plan/expenditure*› rechazar*, no aprobar*

disapproving /'dɪsə'pruːvɪŋ/ *adj* ‹*tone/look*› de reproche

disapprovingly /'dɪsə'pruːvɪŋli/ *adv* con desaprobación

disarm /dɪs'ɑːrm || dɪs'ɑːm/ *vt*

A ‹*troops/opposition*› desarmar; ‹*bomb/mine*› desactivar; ‹*criticism*› desbaratar

B (win confidence of) desarmar

■ **disarm** *vi* desarmarse

disarmament /dɪs'ɑːrməmənt || dɪs'ɑːməmənt/ *n* [u] desarme *m*

disarming /dɪs'ɑːrmɪŋ || dɪs'ɑːmɪŋ/ *adj* que desarma

disarmingly /dɪs'ɑːrmɪŋli || dɪs'ɑːmɪŋli/ *adv*: **she's** ~ **frank** es de una franqueza que desarma

disarray /'dɪsə'reɪ/ *n* [u] (of political party) desorganización *f*; (of appearance) desaliño *m*; **the troops were in** ~ entre las tropas reinaba la confusión *or* el caos; **her papers were in total** ~ sus papeles estaban completamente desordenados

disassociate /'dɪsə'səʊʃieɪt, -sieɪt/ *vt* ▸ **dissociate**

disassociation /'dɪsə'səʊʃɪ'eɪʃən, -sɪ'eɪʃən/ *n* [u] ▸ **dissociation**

disaster /dɪ'zæstər || dɪ'zɑːstə(r)/ *n*

A [c] (flood, earthquake) catástrofe *f*, desastre *m*; (crash, sinking) siniestro *m*, desastre *m*; (*before n*) ~ **fund** fondo *m* para los damnificados

B [c] 1 (fiasco) desastre *m* 2 (hopeless person) (colloq) desastre *m* (fam)

C [u] (misfortune): **~ struck** ocurrió *or* se produjo una catástrofe

disaster area *n* zona *f* siniestrada, zona *f* de desastre; **my room is a real ~ ~** (colloq & hum) mi habitación está hecha un desastre (fam)

disastrous /dɪ'zæstrəs || dɪ'zɑːstrəs/ *adj* desastroso, catastrófico

disastrously /dɪ'zæstrəsli || dɪ'zɑːstrəsli/ *adv* desastrosamente

disband /dɪs'bænd/ *vt* ‹*organization*› disolver*; ‹*army*› licenciar

■ **disband** *vi* «*organization*» disolverse*; «*group*» desbandarse

disbelief /'dɪsbə'liːf/ *n* [u] incredulidad *f*; **she looked at me in ~** me miró incrédula *or* sin dar crédito a lo que veía (*or* oía *etc*)

disbelieve /'dɪsbə'liːv/ *vt* (frml) ‹*statement*› no creer*; ‹*person*› no creerle* a

disbelieving /'dɪsbə'liːvɪŋ/ *adj* (*before n*) incrédulo

disburse /dɪs'bɜːrs || dɪs'bɜːs/ *vt* (frml) desembolsar

disbursement /dɪs'bɜːrsmənt || dɪs'bɜːsmənt/ *n* [u c] (frml) **1** (payment) desembolso *m* **2** **disbursements** *pl* (expenses) gastos *mpl*

disc /dɪsk/ *n*

A (esp BrE) ▸**disk**

B (*parking* ~) (BrE Transp) disco *m* (de estacionamiento)

discard /dɪs'kɑːrd || dɪs'kɑːd/ *vt* **1** (dispose of) desechar, deshacerse* de **2** ‹*idea/belief*› desechar **3** (shed) ‹*skin/leaves*› mudar **4** (take off) ‹*clothing*› desembarazarse* de

disc brake *n* freno *m* de disco

discern /dɪ'sɜːrn || dɪ'sɜːn/ *vt* (frml) distinguir*, percibir

discernible /dɪ'sɜːrnəbəl || dɪ'sɜːnəbəl/ *adj* (frml) ‹*likeness/change*› apreciable, ostensible; ‹*fault/drawback*› perceptible

discerning /dɪ'sɜːrnɪŋ || dɪ'sɜːnɪŋ/ *adj* ‹*reader/customer*› exigente, con criterio; ‹*palate/taste*› exigente, fino; ‹*ear/eye*› educado

discharge¹ /dɪs'tʃɑːrdʒ || dɪs'tʃɑːdʒ/ *vt*

A **1** (release) ‹*prisoner*› liberar, poner* en libertad; ‹*patient*› dar* de alta; ‹*juror*› dispensar; ‹*bankrupt*› rehabilitar; **I ~d myself from hospital** me di de alta yo mismo del hospital; **he was ~d from the army** fue dado de baja del ejército **2** (dismiss) (frml) despedir*

B **1** (send out) ‹*fumes*› despedir*; ‹*electricity*› descargar*; ‹*sewage/waste*› verter*; **to ~ pus** supurar **2** (unload) ‹*cargo*› descargar* **3** (shoot) ‹*volley/broadside*› descargar*

C **1** ‹*duty*› cumplir con **2** ‹*debt*› saldar, liquidar

■ **discharge** *vi* **1** «*river*» desembocar*, descargar* (téc) **2** «*battery*» descargarse*

discharge² /'dɪstʃɑːrdʒ || 'dɪstʃɑːdʒ/ *n*

A [u c] (release — from army) baja *f*; (— from hospital) alta *f*‡; (— from prison) puesta *f* en libertad; **conditional ~** (Law) libertad *f* condicional

B **1** [c] (Med) secreción *f*; (*vaginal* ~) flujo *m* (vaginal) **2** [c u] (of toxic fumes, gases) emisión *f*; (of sewage, waste) vertido *m* **3** [c u] (Elec) descarga *f*

C [u] (of debt, liabilities) liquidación *f*, pago *m*; (of duty) (frml) cumplimiento *m*

disciple /dɪ'saɪpəl/ *n* (Relig) discípulo, -la *m,f*; (adherent) seguidor, -dora *m,f*

disciplinarian /'dɪsəplə'neriən || ˌdɪsɪplɪ'neəriən/ *n*: **he is a strict ~** impone una disciplina férrea

disciplinary /'dɪsəpləneri || ˌdɪsɪ'plɪnəri/ *adj* disciplinario

discipline¹ /'dɪsəplən || 'dɪsɪplɪn/ *n* [u c] disciplina *f*

discipline² *vt* **1** (control) ‹*child/pupils*› disciplinar; ‹*emotions*› controlar **2** (punish) ‹*employee*› sancionar **3** (train) ‹*body/mind*› disciplinar

■ *v refl* **to ~ oneself to + INF** imponerse* la disciplina de + INF, obligarse* A + INF

disciplined /'dɪsəplənd || 'dɪsɪplɪnd/ *adj* disciplinado

disc jockey *n* disc(-)jockey *mf*, pinchadiscos *mf* (Esp fam)

disclaim /dɪs'kleɪm/ *vt* (deny): **she ~ed all knowledge of his whereabouts** negó conocer su paradero; **he ~ed any connection with him** negó tener ninguna relación con él

disclaimer /dɪs'kleɪmər || dɪs'kleɪmə(r)/ *n* (Law) descargo *m* de responsabilidad

disclose /dɪs'kləʊz/ *vt* revelar

disclosure /dɪs'kləʊʒər || dɪs'kləʊʒə(r)/ *n* [u c] revelación *f*

disco /'dɪskəʊ/ *n* (*pl* **-cos**) discoteca *f*, disco *f* (fam)

discolor, (BrE) **discolour** /dɪs'kʌlər || dɪs'kʌlə(r)/ *vt* (fade) decolorar; (stain) dejar amarillento, manchar

■ **discolor** *vi* (lose color) decolorarse; (become stained) volverse* amarillento

discoloration /dɪs'kʌlə'reɪʃən/ *n* [u c] (fading) decoloración *f*; (stain) mancha *f*

discolour *vt/vi* (BrE) ▸**discolor**

discomfit /dɪs'kʌmfət || dɪs'kʌmfɪt/ *vt* (frml) desconcertar*

discomfiture /dɪs'kʌmfətʃʊr || dɪs'kʌmfɪtʃə(r)/ *n* [u] (frml) turbación *f*

discomfort¹ /dɪs'kʌmfərt || dɪs'kʌmfət/ *n* **1** [u c] (lack of comfort) incomodidad *f*; (pain) molestia(s) *f(pl)*, malestar *m*; **to be in ~** tener* molestias **2** [u] (emotional, mental) inquietud *f*, desasosiego *m*

discomfort² *vt* (esp AmE) molestar, incomodar

disconcert /'dɪskən'sɜːrt || ˌdɪskən'sɜːt/ *vt* desconcertar*

disconcerting /'dɪskən'sɜːrtɪŋ || ˌdɪskən'sɜːtɪŋ/ *adj* desconcertante

disconnect /'dɪskə'nekt/ *vt* desconectar; **I didn't pay my bills, so I was ~ed** me cortaron el teléfono (*or* el gas *etc*) por no pagar

disconnected /'dɪskə'nektəd || ˌdɪskə'nektɪd/ *adj* ‹*remarks/thoughts*› inconexo, sin ilación

disconsolate /dɪs'kɑːnsələt || dɪs'kɒnsələt/ *adj* desconsolado

discontent /'dɪskən'tent/ *n* **1** [u] (dissatisfaction) descontento *m* **2** **discontents** *pl* (grievances) (frml) quejas *fpl*

discontented /'dɪskən'tentəd || ˌdɪskən'tentɪd/ *adj* descontento; **to be ~ WITH sth** estar* descontento CON algo

discontentment /'dɪskən'tentmənt/ *n* [u] descontento *m*

discontinue /'dɪskən'tɪnjuː/ *vt* ‹*production*› suspender; ‹*model*› discontinuar*, descontinuar*; ‹*action/suit*› (Law) desistir de

discord /'dɪskɔːrd || 'dɪskɔːd/ *n*

A [u] (conflict) discordia *f*

B (Mus) **1** [u] (lack of harmony) discordancia *f*, disonancia *f* **2** [c] (chord) acorde *m* disonante

discordant /dɪs'kɔːrdn̩t || dɪ'skɔːdn̩t/ *adj* ‹*music/colors*› discordante; ‹*atmosphere*› de discordia

discotheque /'dɪskətek/ *n* ▸**disco**

discount¹ /'dɪskaʊnt/ *n* descuento *m*; **I got a 10% ~** *o* **a ~ of 10%** me hicieron un 10% de descuento *or* un descuento del 10%; **cash ~** descuento por pago en efectivo *or* al contado; **at a ~** ‹*sell*› con descuento, a precio reducido; (*before n*) ‹*store*› de saldos; ‹*goods*› de saldo

discount² /'dɪskaʊnt, dɪs'kaʊnt || dɪs'kaʊnt/ *vt*

A (Busn) **1** ‹*amount*› descontar* **2** ‹*goods*› rebajar **3** ‹*price*› reducir*

B (disregard) ‹*possibility*› descartar; ‹*claim/criticism*› pasar por alto, no tener* en cuenta

discount rate *n* (Fin) tasa *f* *or* (esp Esp) tipo *m* de descuento

discourage /dɪs'kɜːrɪdʒ || dɪs'kʌrɪdʒ/ *vt* **1** (depress) desalentar*, desanimar; **to become ~d** desanimarse **2** (deter) ‹*crime/speculation*› poner* freno a; ‹*burglar*› ahuyentar, disuadir **3** (dissuade) **to ~ sb FROM -ING**: **she ~d me from taking the exam** trató de convencerme de que no me presentara al examen

discouragement /dɪs'kɜːrɪdʒmənt || dɪs'kʌrɪdʒmənt/ *n* **1** [u] (dejection) desánimo *m*, desaliento *m* **2** [c] (deterrent) freno *m*; (obstacle) impedimento *m*

discouraging /dɪs'kɜːrɪdʒɪŋ || dɪs'kʌrɪdʒɪŋ/ *adj* ‹*news/result*› desalentador, descorazonador

discourse /'dɪskɔːrs || 'dɪskɔːs/ *n* (frml) **1** [c] (dissertation) disertación *f* **2** [u] (talk) conversación *f*

discourteous /dɪs'kɜːrtiəs/ *adj* descortés

discourtesy /dɪs'kɜːrtəsi || dɪs'kɜːtəsi/ *n* [u c] (*pl* **-sies**) (frml) descortesía *f*

discover /dɪs'kʌvər || dɪs'kʌvə(r)/ *vt* **1** (find) ‹*planet/cure*› descubrir*; ‹*error*› descubrir*, darse* cuenta de **2** (find out) ‹*reason/solution/culprit*› descubrir*, hallar **3** ‹*talent/star*› descubrir*

discoverer /dɪs'kʌvərər || dɪs'kʌvərə(r)/ *n* descubridor, -dora *m,f*

discovery /dɪs'kʌvəri/ *n* [u c] (*pl* **-ries**) descubrimiento *m*; **she's Hollywood's newest ~** es el último descubrimiento *or* la última revelación de Hollywood

discredit¹ /dɪs'kredət || dɪs'kredɪt/ *vt* desacreditar

discredit² *n* [u] descrédito *m*; **to bring ~ on** *o* **upon sb/sth** traer* el descrédito a algn/algo

discreet /dɪs'kri:t/ *adj* 1 (tactful) ‹*person/inquiries*› discreto; **I followed at a ~ distance** seguí a una distancia prudencial 2 (restrained) ‹*elegance/colors*› discreto, sobrio

discreetly /dɪs'kri:tli/ *adv* discretamente, con discreción

discrepancy /dɪs'krepənsi/ *n* [c u] (*pl* **-cies**) discrepancia *f*

discrete /dɪs'kri:t/ *adj* (frml) ‹*events/units*› diferenciado

discretion /dɪs'kreʃən/ *n* [u]
A (tact) discreción *f*
B (judgment) criterio *m*; **use your ~** usa tu criterio, haz lo que mejor te parezca; **at the committee's ~** a criterio *or* a discreción de la comisión; **~ *is the better part of valor*** la prudencia es la madre de la ciencia

discretionary /dɪs'kreʃəneri || dɪs'kreʃənəri, -ənri/ *adj* discrecional

discriminate /dɪs'krɪməneɪt || dɪ'skrɪmɪneɪt/ *vi*
A (act with prejudice) hacer* discriminaciones, discriminar; **to ~ AGAINST sb** discriminar a algn; **to ~ IN FAVOR OF sb** favorecer* a algn
B 1 (distinguish) distinguir*, discriminar 2 (be discerning) discernir*, utilizar* el sentido crítico

discriminating /dɪs'krɪməneɪtɪŋ || dɪ'skrɪmɪneɪtɪŋ/ *adj* (discerning) ‹*critic/customer*› exigente; ‹*judgment*› sagaz; ‹*taste*› refinado, educado, que sabe distinguir

discrimination /dɪs'krɪmə'neɪʃən || dɪ,skrɪmɪ'neɪʃən/ *n* [u]
A (unfair treatment) discriminación *f*; **racial/sexual ~** discriminación racial/sexual
B (discernment) criterio *m*, discernimiento *m*

discus /'dɪskəs/ *n* (*pl* **-cuses**) disco *m*

discuss /dɪs'kʌs/ *vt* (talk about) ‹*person*› hablar de; ‹*topic*› hablar de, tratar; (debate) debatir; ‹*plan/problem*› discutir

discussion /dɪs'kʌʃən/ *n* [c u] discusión *f*, debate *m*; **it's still under ~** todavía se está discutiendo *or* estudiando; **she suggested a topic for ~** sugirió un tema para debatir; (*before n*) **~ document** documento *m* base *or* de consulta; **~ group** (in general) coloquio *m*, grupo *m* de debate *or* discusión; (Internet) foro *m*

disdain¹ /dɪs'deɪn/ *n* [u] desdén *m*

disdain² *vt* desdeñar; **to ~ to + INF** (frml) no dignarse A + INF

disdainful /dɪs'deɪnfəl/ *adj* ‹*manner/tone*› despectivo, desdeñoso; **to be ~ TOWARD** *o* **OF sth** despreciar *or* desdeñar algo

disdainfully /dɪs'deɪnfəli/ *adv* con desdén, desdeñosamente

disease /dɪ'zi:z/ *n* enfermedad *f*, dolencia *f* (frml)

diseased /dɪ'zi:zd/ *adj* 1 ‹*organ/tissue*› afectado; ‹*plant/animal*› enfermo 2 (abnormal) ‹*mind*› enfermizo, morboso; ‹*society*› enfermo

disembark /'dɪsəm'bɑ:rk || ,dɪsɪm'bɑ:k/ *vi* **to ~ (FROM sth)** desembarcar* (DE algo)

disembarkation /dɪs'embɑ:r'keɪʃən || dɪs,embɑ:'keɪʃən/ *n* [u] (of people) desembarco *m*; (of cargo) desembarque *m*

disembodied /'dɪsəm'bɑ:did || ,dɪsɪm'bɒdid/ *adj* incorpóreo

disembowel /'dɪsəm'baʊəl || ,dɪsɪm'baʊəl/ *vt*, (BrE) **-ll-** destripar

disenchanted /'dɪsn̩'tʃæntəd || ,dɪsɪn'tʃɑ:ntɪd/ *adj* **to be ~ WITH sb/sth** estar* desilusionado CON *or* DE algn/DE algo

disenchantment /'dɪsn̩'tʃæntmənt || ,dɪsɪn'tʃɑ:ntmənt/ *n* [u] desencanto *m*, desilusión *f*

disenfranchise /'dɪsn̩'frænt∫aɪz || ,dɪsɪn'frænt∫aɪz/ *vt* ‹*person*› privar del derecho al voto; ‹*place*› privar del derecho de representación

disengage /'dɪsn̩'geɪdʒ || ,dɪsɪn'geɪdʒ/ *vt*
A 1 (extricate) **to ~ sth (FROM sth)** soltar* algo (DE algo); **he ~d his hand from hers** se soltó de su mano 2 (Mil) ‹*troops/forces*› retirar
B (Tech) ‹*gears/mechanism*› desconectar; **to ~ the clutch** desembragar*, soltar* el embrague
■ **disengage** *vi* (Tech) «*gears/mechanism*» desconectarse

disentangle /'dɪsn̩'tæŋgəl || ,dɪsɪn'tæŋgəl/ *vt* ‹*rope/hair/wool*› desenredar, desenmarañar; ‹*mystery*› esclarecer*, desentrañar

disfavor, (BrE) **disfavour** /dɪs'feɪvər || dɪs'feɪvə(r)/ *n* [u] (frml) desaprobación *f*; **to view** *o* **look on sth with ~** desaprobar* algo (frml), no ver* algo con buenos ojos; **to fall into ~** «*person*» caer* en desgracia

disfigure /dɪs'fɪgjər || dɪs'fɪgə(r)/ *vt* ‹*face/person*› desfigurar; ‹*landscape/building*› afear, estropear

disfigurement /dɪs'fɪgjərmənt || dɪs'fɪgəmənt/ *n* [u] (of person) desfiguración *f*; (of scenery, building) afeamiento *m*

disgrace¹ /dɪs'greɪs/ *n* [u c] 1 (shame) vergüenza *f*; **it's a ~** es una vergüenza, es un escándalo; **he brought ~ on his family** trajo la deshonra a su familia; **she was sent upstairs in ~** la mandaron arriba castigada 2 (sb, sth shameful) (*no pl*) vergüenza *f*; **to be a ~ (TO sb/sth)** ser* una vergüenza (PARA algn/algo)

disgrace² *vt* 1 (bring shame on) ‹*person/family/school*› deshonrar; **I ~d myself by getting drunk** hice un papelón emborrachándome (fam) 2 (destroy reputation of) ‹*enemy/politician*› desacreditar

disgraceful /dɪs'greɪsfəl/ *adj* vergonzoso

disgracefully /dɪs'greɪsfəli/ *adv* vergonzosamente

disgruntled /dɪs'grʌntl̩d/ *adj* ‹*child/look*› contrariado; ‹*employee*› descontento

disguise¹ /dɪs'gaɪz/ *vt* 1 ‹*person*› disfrazar*; ‹*voice*› cambiar; **to ~ oneself (AS sth)** disfrazarse* (DE algo) 2 (conceal) ‹*mistake*› ocultar; ‹*disapproval/contempt*› disimular

disguise² *n* [c u] disfraz *m*; **in ~** disfrazado

disgust¹ /dɪs'gʌst/ *vt* darle* asco a

disgust² *n* [u] (revulsion) indignación *f*; (physical, stronger) asco *m*, repugnancia *f*; **much to my ~, they ate it raw** se lo comieron crudo, lo cual me dio un asco espantoso; **she stormed out of the meeting in ~** salió indignada *or* furiosa de la reunión

disgusted /dɪs'gʌstəd || dɪs'gʌstɪd/ *adj* indignado; (stronger) asqueado; **~ AT** *o* **WITH sb/oneself**: **she's ~ with him/herself** está indignada *or* furiosa con él/furiosa consigo misma

disgusting /dɪs'gʌstɪŋ/ *adj* 1 ‹*smell/taste/food*› asqueroso, repugnante; **how ~!** ¡qué asco! 2 ‹*conduct/attitude*› vergonzoso

disgustingly /dɪs'gʌstɪŋli/ *adv* (*as intensifier*) ‹*dirty*› asquerosamente; **he's ~ rich** (hum) está podrido de dinero, está podrido en plata (AmL fam)

dish /dɪʃ/ *n*
A 1 (plate) plato *m*; (*serving ~*) fuente *f* 2 (amount) plato *m* 3 **dishes** *pl n* (crockery): **to wash** *o* **do the ~es** lavar los platos
B (Culin) plato *m*
C (Telec, TV) antena *f* parabólica

Phrasal verbs

- **dish out** [v ▸ o ▸ adv, v ▸ adv ▸ o] 1 (Culin) servir* 2 (distribute) (colloq) repartir; ‹*advice*› dar*
- **dish up** [v ▸ o ▸ adv, v ▸ adv ▸ o] [v ▸ adv] (Culin) servir*

dishcloth /'dɪʃklɔ:θ || 'dɪʃklɒθ/ *n* 1 (for drying) paño *m* de cocina, repasador *m* (RPl), limpión *m* (Col) 2 (BrE) ▸**dishrag**

dishearten /dɪs'hɑ:rtn̩ || dɪs'hɑ:tn̩/ *vt* desanimar, descorazonar, desalentar*

disheartening /dɪs'hɑ:rtn̩ɪŋ || dɪs'hɑ:tn̩ɪŋ/ *adj* descorazonador, desalentador

disheveled, (BrE) **dishevelled** /dɪ'ʃevəld/ *adj* despeinado

dishonest /dɪs'ɑ:nəst || dɪs'ɒnɪst/ *adj* ‹*person/answer*› deshonesto; ‹*dealings/means*› fraudulento, deshonesto

dishonestly /dɪs'ɑ:nəstli || dɪs'ɒnɪstli/ *adv* deshonestamente, con deshonestidad

dishonesty /dɪs'ɑ:nəsti || dɪs'ɒnɪsti/ *n* [u] deshonestidad *f*, falta *f* de honradez; (of statement) falsedad *f*; (of dealings) fraudulencia *f*

dishonor¹, (BrE) **dishonour** /dɪs'ɑ:nər || dɪs'ɒnə(r)/ *n* [u] (disgrace) deshonra *f*, deshonor *m*; **to bring ~ on** *o* **upon**

d

sb/sth traer* la deshonra a algn/algo

dishonor², (BrE) **dishonour** *vt*
A (bring disgrace on) deshonrar
B (renege on) ‹*agreement/treaty*› no respetar; ‹*promise*› no cumplir, faltar a

dishonorable, (BrE) **dishonourable** /dɪs'ɑːnərəbəl || dɪs'ɒnərəbəl/ *adj* deshonroso

dishonorably, (BrE) **dishonourably** /dɪs'ɑːnərəbli || dɪs'ɒnərəbli/ *adv* de manera deshonrosa; **to be ~ discharged** ser* dado de baja con deshonor

dish: **~pan** *n* (AmE) palangana *f* (*para lavar los platos*); (*before n*) **~pan hands** manos *fpl* de fregona; **~rag** *n* (AmE) trapo *m*, bayeta *f*, fregón *m* (RPl); **~ soap** *n* [u] (AmE) lavavajillas *m*, detergente *m*; **~towel** *n* ▸ **dishcloth 1**; **~washer** /'dɪʃ'wɔːʃər || 'dɪs,wɒʃə(r)/ *n* (machine) lavaplatos *m*, lavavajillas *m*; **~washing liquid** /'dɪʃ,wɔːʃɪŋ || 'diʃ,wɒʃiŋ/ *n* [u] (AmE) ▸ **~ soap**; **~water** *n* [u] agua *f*‡ de fregar *or* de lavar los platos

disillusion /'dɪsə'luːʒən || ,dɪsɪ'luːʒən/ *vt* desilusionar

disillusionment /'dɪsə'luːʒənmənt || ,dɪsɪ'luːʒənmənt/ *n* [u] desilusión *f*

disincentive /'dɪsn̩'sentɪv || ,dɪsɪn'sentɪv/ *n* [u c] falta *f* de incentivos; **it is a ~ to savers** no fomenta el ahorro

disinclined /'dɪsn̩'klaɪnd || ,dɪsɪn'klaɪnd/ *adj* (frml) (*pred*) **~ to + INF**: **she was ~d to listen to him** no se sentía inclinada a escucharlo

disinfect /'dɪsn̩'fekt || ,dɪsɪn'fekt/ *vt* desinfectar

disinfectant /'dɪsn̩'fektənt || ,dɪsɪn'fektənt/ *n* [u c] desinfectante *m*

disinflation /'dɪsn̩'fleɪʃən || ,dɪsɪn'fleɪʃən/ *n* [u] desinflación *f*

disinformation /'dɪsɪnfər'meɪʃən || ,dɪsɪnfə'meɪʃən/ *n* [u] desinformación *f*

disingenuous /'dɪsn̩'dʒenjuəs || ,dɪsɪn'dʒenjʊəs/ *adj* insincero, falso

disinherit /'dɪsn̩'herət || ,dɪsɪn'herɪt/ *vt* **1** ‹*heir*› desheredar **2** (deprive) **to ~ sb OF *o* FROM sth** despojar a algn DE algo

disintegrate /dɪs'ɪntəgreɪt || dɪs'ɪntɪgreɪt/ *vi* (fragment) desintegrarse
■ **disintegrate** *vt* desintegrar

disintegration /dɪs'ɪntə'greɪʃən || dɪs,ɪntɪ'greɪʃən/ *n* desintegración *f*

disinter /'dɪsɪn'tɜːr || ,dɪsɪn'tɜː(r)/ *vt* **-rr-** (frml) desenterrar*, exhumar (frml)

disinterested /dɪs'ɪntrəstəd || dɪs'ɪntrəstɪd/ *adj* ‹*decision/advice*› imparcial; ‹*action*› desinteresado

disinvestment /,dɪsɪn'vestmənt/ *n* [u] desinversión *f*

disjointed /dɪs'dʒɔɪntəd || dɪs'dʒɔɪntɪd/ *adj* inconexo, deshilvanado

disk /dɪsk/ *n* **1** (flat, circular object) disco *m* **2** (Comput, Audio, Anat) disco *m*

disk drive *n* unidad *f* de disco

diskette /dɪs'ket/ *n* disquete *m*

dislike¹ /dɪs'laɪk/ *vt*: **I ~ dogs** no me gustan los perros; **he ~d her intensely** no la podía ver, le tenía verdadera aversión; **to ~ -ING**: **he ~s wearing a tie** le desagrada *or* no le gusta llevar corbata

dislike² *n* **1** [u] (emotion) (*no pl*): **I have a strong ~ of dogs** no me gustan nada los perros, (les) tengo aversión a los perros; **to take a ~ to sb** tomarle antipatía a algn **2** [c] (sth disliked): **you'll have to tell us all your likes and ~s** tendrás que decirnos lo que te gusta y lo que no te gusta

dislocate /'dɪsləkeɪt/ *vt* (Med) dislocarse*

dislocation /'dɪslə'keɪʃən/ *n* [u] (Med) dislocación *f*

dislodge /dɪs'lɑːdʒ || dɪs'lɒdʒ/ *vt* **1** (shift, remove) sacar*; **the wind ~d some tiles** el viento causó que se soltaran varias tejas **2** (drive out) **to ~ sb (FROM sth)** desplazar* a algn (DE algo)

disloyal /dɪs'lɔɪəl/ *adj* desleal; **to be ~ TO sb/sth** ser* desleal CON *or* A algn/A algo

disloyalty /dɪs'lɔɪəlti/ *n* [u] **~ TO sb/sth** deslealtad *f* CON *or* A algn/A algo

dismal /'dɪzməl/ *adj* **1** (gloomy) ‹*place/tone*› sombrío, deprimente, lúgubre **2** (very bad) ‹*news/prophecy*› funesto; ‹*future*› muy negro; ‹*weather*› malísimo; ‹*results/performance*› pésimo

dismantle /dɪs'mæntl̩/ *vt* ‹*machinery/furniture*› desmontar; ‹*organization*› desmantelar

dismay¹ /dɪs'meɪ/ *n* [u] consternación *f*; **they looked at him in *o* with ~** lo miraron consternados; **much to my/his ~** para mi/su desgracia

dismay² *vt* consternar; **I was ~ed at her reaction** su reacción me dejó consternado

dismember /dɪs'membər || dɪs'membə(r)/ *vt* ‹*animal*› descuartizar*; ‹*corpse*› desmembrar*

dismiss /dɪs'mɪs/ *vt*
A **1** ‹*employee*› despedir*; ‹*executive, minister*› destituir* **2** (send away) ‹*class*› dejar salir; **class ~ed!** pueden retirarse
B ‹*possibility/suggestion*› descartar, desechar; ‹*request/petition/claim*› desestimar, rechazar*
C (Law) ‹*charge/appeal*› desestimar; **to ~ a case** sobreseer* una causa
■ **dismiss** *vi* (Mil): **~!** ¡rompan filas!

dismissal /dɪs'mɪsəl/ *n* [u c] **1** (of employee) despido *m*; (of executive, minister) destitución *f* **2** (sending away) autorización *f* para retirarse **3** (of theory, request) rechazo *m* **4** (Law) desestimación *f*

dismissive /dɪs'mɪsɪv/ *adj* ‹*attitude/smile*› desdeñoso; ‹*tone*› displicente

dismount /dɪs'maʊnt/ *vi* desmontar

disobedience /'dɪsə'biːdiəns/ *n* [u] desobediencia *f*

disobedient /'dɪsə'biːdiənt/ *adj* desobediente

disobey /'dɪsə'beɪ/ *vt/i* desobedecer*

disorder /dɪs'ɔːrdər || dɪs'ɔːdə(r)/ *n*
A [u] **1** (confusion) desorden *m* **2** (unrest) desórdenes *mpl*, disturbios *mpl*
B [c] (Med) afección *f* (frml), problema *m*

disordered /dɪs'ɔːrdərd || dɪs'ɔːdəd/ *adj* desordenado

disorderly /dɪs'ɔːrdərli || dɪs'ɔːdəli/ *adj* **1** (untidy) desordenado **2** (unruly) ‹*crowd*› alborotado; ‹*person*› revoltoso; **~ conduct** alteración *f* del orden público

disorganization /dɪs'ɔːrgənə'zeɪʃən || dɪs,ɔːgənaɪ'zeɪʃən/ *n* [u] desorganización *f*

disorganized /dɪs'ɔːrgənaɪzd || dɪs'ɔːgənaɪzd/ *adj* desorganizado

disorient /dɪs'ɔːrient/ *vt* desorientar; **to become ~ed** desorientarse

disorientate /dɪs'ɔːrɪənteɪt/ *vt* ▸ **disorient**

disorientation /dɪs'ɔːrien'teɪʃən/ *n* [u] desorientación *f*

disown /dɪs'əʊn/ *vt* **1** (repudiate) renegar* de, repudiar **2** (deny responsibility for) no reconocer* como propio

disparage /dɪs'pærɪdʒ/ *vt* menospreciar

disparaging /dɪs'pærədʒɪŋ/ *adj* desdeñoso, despreciativo; **she was very ~ about their efforts** habló de sus intentos en tono desdeñoso *or* despreciativo

disparagingly /dɪs'pærədʒɪŋli/ *adv* en tono desdeñoso *or* despreciativo

disparate /dɪs'pærət, 'dɪspərət || 'dɪspərət/ *adj* (frml) **1** (varied) dispar **2** (distinct, separate) distinto

disparity /dɪs'pærəti/ *n* [c u] (inequality) disparidad *f*; (difference) discrepancia *f*

dispassionate /dɪs'pæʃənət/ *adj* ‹*account*› desapasionado, objetivo; ‹*adjudication/onlooker*› imparcial

dispassionately /dɪs'pæʃənətli/ *adv* sin apasionamiento

dispatch¹ /dɪ'spætʃ/ *vt*
A (send) despachar, enviar*
B **1** (carry out) (frml) ‹*task/duty*› despachar **2** (kill) (euph) ‹*person/animal*› despachar (euf) **3** (consume) (hum) ‹*food/drink*› despacharse (hum)

dispatch² *n*
A [c] (message) despacho *m*; (Mil) parte *m*
B [u] (sending) despacho *m*, envío *m*, expedición *f*; **to be mentioned in ~es** (BrE) recibir una mención de honor

dispatch: **~ case** *n* portafolio(s) *m*; **~ rider** *n* (on motorcycle) (BrE) mensajero, -ra *m,f*

dispel /dɪ'spel/ *vt* **-ll-** **1** ‹*doubts/fear*› disipar, hacer* desvanecer **2** ‹*fog*› disipar

dispensable /dɪ'spensəbəl/ *adj* prescindible

dispensary /dɪ'spensəri/ *n* (*pl* **-ries**) (in hospital) dispensario *m*, farmacia *f*; (in school) enfermería *f*

dispensation /'dɪspən'seɪʃən/ *n*
A [c] [1] (exemption) exención *f*; **he was granted a ~ from military service** lo declararon exento del servicio militar [2] (Relig) dispensa *f*
B [u] (of justice) administración *f*

dispense /dɪ'spens/ *vt*
A [1] ‹*grants/alms*› dar*; ‹*advice*› ofrecer*, dar*; ‹*favors*› conceder* [2] ‹‹*machine*›› ‹*coffee/soap*› expender
B ‹*drugs/prescription*› despachar, preparar
C (administer) ‹*justice*› administrar

Phrasal verb
• **dispense with** [v ▸ prep ▸ o] prescindir de

dispenser /dɪ'spensər || dɪ'spensə(r)/ *n*
A (device): **a cash ~** un cajero automático; **a soap ~** un dispositivo que suministra jabón
B (pharmacist) (BrE) farmacéutico, -ca *m,f*

dispersal /dɪ'spɜ:rsəl || dɪ'spɜ:səl/ *n* [u] dispersión *f*

disperse /dɪ'spɜ:rs || dɪ'spɜ:s/ *vt* dispersar
■ **disperse** *vi* dispersarse

dispirited /dɪ'spɪrətəd || dɪ'spɪrɪtɪd/ *adj* ‹*person*› desanimado, abatido; **to become ~** desanimarse

dispiriting /dɪ'spɪrətɪŋ || dɪ'spɪrɪtɪŋ/ *adj* desalentador, descorazonador

displace /dɪs'pleɪs/ *vt* [1] (Phys) ‹*liquid/volume*› desplazar* [2] (replace) reemplazar* [3] (force from home) ‹*refugees/workers*› desplazar*

displaced person /dɪs'pleɪst/ *n* desplazado, -da *m,f*

displacement /dɪs'pleɪsmənt/ *n* [u] [1] (replacement) sustitución *f*, reemplazo *m* [2] (of refugees) desplazamiento *m*

display[1] /dɪ'spleɪ/ *vt* [1] (put on show) ‹*exhibit*› exponer*; ‹*data/figures*› (Comput) visualizar*; **the shopkeeper ~ed his wares** el tendero colocó los artículos en el escaparate (*or* la estantería *etc*) [2] (flaunt) ‹*finery/erudition*› hacer* despliegue *or* gala de; ‹*muscles*› lucir*, hacer* alarde de [3] (reveal) ‹*anger/interest*› demostrar*, manifestar*; ‹*feelings*› exteriorizar*, demostrar*; ‹*tendencies/symptoms*› presentar; ‹*skill/courage*› demostrar*, dar* prueba de

display[2] *n*
A [1] (exhibition) exposición *f*, muestra *f*; (show) show *m*; **firework ~** fuegos *mpl* artificiales; **to be on ~** ‹‹*painting/wares*›› estar* expuesto; **to put sth on ~** exponer* algo [2] (arrangement): **a ~ of flowers** un arreglo floral; (*before n*) **~ cabinet** vitrina *f*; **~ stand** expositor *m* [3] (of feeling) exteriorización *f*, demostración *f*; (of courage, strength, knowledge) despliegue *m*; (of ignorance) demostración *f*; **he made (a) great ~ of his experience in those matters** hizo gran alarde de su experiencia en ese campo
B (Comput, Electron) display *m*, visualizador *m*; **digital/analog ~** visualizador digital/analógico; (*before n*) ‹*screen/panel*› de visualización (de datos)
C (Journ, Print) (*before n*) **~ advertising** anuncios *mpl* destacados

displease /dɪs'pli:z/ *vt* desagradar, contrariar*; **to be ~d WITH sb** estar* disgustado CON algn

displeasing /dɪs'pli:zɪŋ/ *adj* desagradable

displeasure /dɪs'pleʒər || dɪs'pleʒə(r)/ *n* [u] desagrado *m*; **he incurred the king's ~** contrarió al rey

disposable /dɪ'spəʊzəbəl/ *adj*
A ‹*cup/razor/pen*› desechable, de usar y tirar
B ‹*income*› disponible

disposal /dɪ'spəʊzəl/ *n*
A [1] (removal, riddance): **the problem of the ~ of waste** el problema de cómo deshacerse de residuos; **arrangements were made for the ~ of the body** se hicieron arreglos para que el cadáver fuera inhumado (*or* trasladado al crematorio *etc*) [2] (Fin) enajenación *f* [3] (of bomb) desactivación *f*
B (of troops) despliegue *m*
C (power to use) disposición *f*; **to have sth at one's ~** disponer* de algo, tener* algo a su (*or* mi *etc*) disposición; **to put sth/oneself at sb's ~** *o* **the ~ of sb** poner* algo/ponerse* a disposición de algn

dispose /dɪ'spəʊz/ *vt* (frml)
A (incline) predisponer*
B (arrange) disponer* (frml), colocar*

Phrasal verb
• **dispose of** [v ▸ prep ▸ o]
A [1] (get rid of) ‹*refuse/evidence*› deshacerse* de; ‹*rival/opponent*› deshacerse* de, liquidar (fam) [2] (sell) ‹*house/car/land*› vender, enajenar (frml) [3] (deal with) ‹*problem/question/objection*› despachar
B (have use of) (frml) ‹*funds/resources*› disponer* de

disposed /dɪ'spəʊzd/ *adj* (*pred*) [1] (inclined) **to be ~ to + INF** estar* dispuesto A + INF; **I don't feel ~ to help him** no me siento inclinada a ayudarlo; **to be favorably/unfavorably ~ to** *o* **toward sb** estar* bien/mal dispuesto hacia algn [2] (liable) (frml) **to be ~ TO sth** ser* propenso A algo, tener* propensión A algo

disposition /'dɪspə'zɪʃən/ *n*
A [1] [c] (personality) manera *f or* modo *m* de ser, temperamento *m* [2] (inclination) (*no pl*) (frml) **~ TO sth** predisposición *f* A algo
B [u c] (arrangement) disposición *f*

dispossess /'dɪspə'zes/ *vt* (frml) **to ~ sb OF sth** desposeer* *or* despojar a algn DE algo (frml)

dispossessed /'dɪspə'zest/ *pl n* (frml) **the ~** los desposeídos (frml)

disproportionate /'dɪsprə'pɔ:rʃnət || ˌdɪsprə'pɔ:ʃənət/ *adj* ‹*number/size*› desproporcionado; **a ~ amount of money is spent on advertising** lo que se gasta en propaganda es desmesurado

disproportionately /'dɪsprə'pɔ:rʃnətli || ˌdɪsprə'pɔ:ʃənətli/ *adv* desproporcionadamente

disprove /dɪs'pru:v/ *vt* ‹*claim/assertion/charge*› desmentir*; ‹*doctrine/theory*› rebatir, refutar

dispute[1] /dɪ'spju:t/ *n* [1] [c] (controversy, clash) polémica *f*, controversia *f* [2] [u] (debate) discusión *f*; (quarrel) disputa *f*; **the territory in** *o* **under ~** el territorio en litigio; **the matter is still in** *o* **under ~** aún no se ha llegado a un acuerdo sobre el asunto [3] [c] (Lab Rel) conflicto *m* (laboral); **an industrial ~** un conflicto laboral

dispute[2] *vt*
A [1] (contest) discutir, cuestionar; **I don't ~ (the fact) that it was a mistake** no discuto que fue un error; **it cannot be ~d that ...** no se puede negar *or* hay que reconocer que ... [2] ‹*will/decision*› impugnar [3] (argue) ‹*point/question*› debatir, discutir [4] **disputed** *past p* ‹*decision*› discutido, polémico; ‹*territory*› en litigio
B (fight for) ‹*possession/victory/territory*› disputarse

disqualification /dɪs'kwɑ:ləfə'keɪʃən || dɪsˌkwɒlɪfɪ'keɪʃən/ *n* [u c] (from exam, competition) descalificación *f*; (from office, service) inhabilitación *f*; **a three-year ~ from driving** (BrE) la inhabilitación para manejar *or* (Esp) conducir por tres años

disqualify /dɪs'kwɑ:ləfaɪ || dɪs'kwɒlɪfaɪ/ *vt* **-fies, -fying, -fied** [1] (make ineligible): **as a professional she was disqualified from entering the Olympics** el hecho de ser profesional le impedía participar en las Olimpíadas; **a criminal record disqualifies you from jury service** tener antecedentes penales inhabilita para ser miembro de un jurado [2] (debar) (Sport) descalificar*

disquiet /dɪs'kwaɪət/ *n* [u] (frml) inquietud *f*, intranquilidad *f*, desasosiego *m*

disquieting /dɪs'kwaɪətɪŋ/ *adj* (frml) inquietante, intranquilizante

disregard[1] /'dɪsrɪ'gɑ:rd || ˌdɪsrɪ'gɑ:d/ *vt* ‹*danger/difficulty*› ignorar, despreciar; ‹*advice*› hacer* caso omiso de, no prestar atención a; ‹*feelings/wishes*› no tener* en cuenta

disregard[2] *n* [u] **~ FOR sth/sb** indiferencia *f* HACIA algo/algn; **with complete ~ for her own safety** sin ni siquiera considerar su propia seguridad

disrepair /'dɪsrɪ'per || ˌdɪsrɪ'peə(r)/ *n* [u] mal estado *m*; **to be in/fall into (a state of) ~** estar* en mal estado/deteriorarse

disreputable /dɪs'repjətəbəl || dɪs'repjʊtəbəl/ *adj* ‹*person/firm*› de dudosa reputación, de mala fama; ‹*nightclub/district*› de mala fama; ‹*conduct/action*› vergonzoso

disrepute /'dɪsrɪ'pju:t/ *n* [u] (frml): **to fall into ~** caer* en descrédito; **to bring sth into ~** desacreditar algo

disrespect /'dɪsrɪ'spekt/ *n* [u] **~ (FOR sth)** falta *f* de respeto (HACIA algo); **I meant no ~** no fue mi intención ofenderlo, no quise faltarle al *or* (CS) el respeto

disrespectful /ˈdɪsrɪˈspektfəl/ *adj* ‹*person*› irrespetuoso; ‹*attitude*› irreverente; **to be ~ TO** *o* **TOWARD sb** ser* irrespetuoso PARA CON algn, faltarle al *or* (CS) el respeto A algn

disrupt /dɪsˈrʌpt/ *vt* ‹*meeting/class*› perturbar el desarrollo de; ‹*traffic/communications*› crear problemas de, afectar a; ‹*plans*› desbaratar, trastocar*

disruption /dɪsˈrʌpʃən/ *n* [u c] trastorno *m*; **~ TO sth**: **this caused serious ~ to our schedules** esto desbarató nuestro calendario de trabajo, esto ocasionó graves trastornos en nuestro calendario de trabajo

disruptive /dɪsˈrʌptɪv/ *adj* ‹*influence*› perjudicial, negativo; **a ~ pupil** un alumno problema

dissatisfaction /ˈdɪsˈsætəsˈfækʃən || dɪsˌsætɪsˈfækʃən/ *n* [u] descontento *m*, insatisfacción *f*

dissatisfied /ˈdɪsˈsætəsfaɪd || dɪˈsætɪsfaɪd/ *adj* ‹*customer*› descontento, insatisfecho; **to be ~ WITH sth/sb** estar* descontento *or* insatisfecho CON algo/algn

dissect /dɪˈsekt, daɪ-/ *vt* 1 (cut up) ‹*animal/body*› diseccionar, hacer* la disección de 2 (analyze) ‹*theory/book*› analizar* minuciosamente, diseccionar

dissemble /dɪˈsembəl/ *vt* (frml) ‹*truth/motive*› ocultar; ‹*emotions*› disimular

■ **dissemble** *vi* (frml) fingir*

disseminate /dɪˈsemənett || dɪˈsemɪneɪt/ *vt* (frml) ‹*virus/spores*› diseminar; ‹*idea/information*› difundir, diseminar

dissension /dɪˈsentʃən || dɪˈsenʃən/ *n* [u c] disensión *f* (frml), desacuerdo *m*

dissent¹ /dɪˈsent/ *vi* (frml) 1 **to ~ (FROM sth)** discrepar *or* (frml) disentir* (DE algo) 2 **dissenting** *pres p* discrepante

dissent² *n* [u] (frml) desacuerdo *m*, disconformidad *f*

dissenter /dɪˈsentər || dɪˈsentə(r)/ *n* (frml) disidente *mf*

dissertation /ˈdɪsərˈteɪʃən || ˌdɪsəˈteɪʃən/ *n* (in US: for PhD) tesis *f* (doctoral); (in UK: for lower degree) tesis *f*, tesina *f*

disservice /ˈdɪsˈsɜːrvəs || dɪsˈsɜːvɪs/ *n* [u] (frml): **to do sb a ~**: **this report does him a ~** este informe no le hace justicia

dissidence /ˈdɪsədəns || ˈdɪsɪdəns/ *n* [u] disidencia *f*

dissident¹ /ˈdɪsədənt || ˈdɪsɪdənt/ *n* disidente *mf*

dissident² *adj* disidente

dissimilar /ˈdɪˈsɪmələr || dɪˈsɪmɪlə(r)/ *adj* distinto, diferente; **to be ~ TO sth** (*usu neg*) ser* distinto DE *or* A algo

dissimilarity /ˈdɪsɪməˈlærəti || ˌdɪsɪmɪˈlærəti/ *n* [u c] (*pl* **-ties**) diferencia *f*, disimilitud *f* (frml)

dissimulate /dɪˈsɪmjəleɪt || dɪˈsɪmjʊleɪt/ *vt* (liter) ‹*feelings/intention*› disimular, encubrir*

dissipate /ˈdɪsəpeɪt || ˈdɪsɪpeɪt/ *vt* (frml) 1 (squander) ‹*inheritance*› disipar, dilapidar; ‹*energy/talents*› desperdiciar 2 (dispel) ‹*anxiety*› disipar, hacer* desvanecer

■ **dissipate** *vi* (frml) ‹‹*anger/doubts*›› disiparse, desvanecerse*

dissipated /ˈdɪsəpeɪtəd || ˈdɪsɪpeɪtɪd/ *adj* disipado, disoluto

dissipation /ˈdɪsəˈpeɪʃən || ˌdɪsɪˈpeɪʃən/ *n* [u] disipación *f*, libertinaje *m*

dissociate /dɪˈsəʊʃieɪt, -sieɪt/ *vt* 1 (separate) **to ~ sth/sb (FROM sth)** disociar algo/a algn (DE algo) 2 (distance) **to ~ oneself FROM sb/sth** desvincularse DE algn/algo

dissociation /dɪˈsəʊʃiˈeɪʃən, -sieɪʃən/ *n* [u] (from opinion, act) desvinculación *f*

dissolute /ˈdɪsəluːt/ *adj* disoluto

dissolution /ˈdɪsəˈluːʃən/ *n* [u] disolución *f*; (of empire) desintegración *f*

dissolve /dɪˈzɑːlv || dɪˈzɒlv/ *vt*

A (in liquid) disolver*

B 1 (dismiss) ‹*assembly/parliament*› disolver* 2 (break up) ‹*company/marriage*› disolver*

■ **dissolve** *vi*

A (in liquid) disolverse*

B 1 (vanish) (liter) desvanecerse* 2 (emotionally): **to ~ into tears** deshacerse* en lágrimas

dissonance /ˈdɪsənəns/ *n* 1 [c u] (Mus) disonancia *f* 2 [u] (lack of agreement) discordancia *f*

dissonant /ˈdɪsənənt/ *adj* 1 (discordant) ‹*music*› disonante 2 (dissenting) ‹*opinions/beliefs*› discrepante 3 (clashing) ‹*colors/characteristics*› discordante

dissuade /dɪˈsweɪd/ *vt* **to ~ sb (FROM sth)** disuadir a algn (DE algo); **to ~ sb FROM -ING**: **I managed to ~ her from leaving** logré convencerla de que no se fuera

distaff /ˈdɪstæf || ˈdɪstɑːf/ *n* rueca *f*; (*before n*) **on the ~ side** por línea materna, por parte de madre

distance¹ /ˈdɪstəns/ *n* [c u]

A 1 (space between two points) distancia *f*; **what's the ~ between ... ?** ¿qué distancia hay entre ... ?; **stopping ~** (Auto) distancia de parada; **within easy walking ~** a poca distancia a pie; **from a ~ of 12 miles** a una distancia de 12 millas; **I can't walk long ~s** no puedo caminar mucho; ***to be within striking ~ (of sth)*** estar* cerca (de algo) 2 (faraway point): **in the (far) ~** en la distancia *or* lejanía, a lo lejos; **at** *o* **from a ~ he looked like a young man** de lejos parecía joven 3 (in time) distancia *f*; **from a ~ of ten years** a diez años de distancia, después de diez años

B (emotional) distanciamiento *m*; ***to keep one's ~*** (remain aloof) guardar las distancias; (lit: keep away) no acercarse*; ***to keep sb at a ~*** guardar las distancias con algn

C (Sport) distancia *f*; ***to go the ~***: **the fight went the ~** la pelea duró hasta el último round; **she started the project enthusiastically, but I'm not sure if she'll go the ~** empezó con mucho entusiasmo pero no sé si llevará el proyecto a buen término; (*before n*) **~ runner** corredor, -dora *m,f* de fondo

distance² *v refl* **to ~ oneself (FROM sb/sth)** (emotionally) distanciarse (DE algn/algo); (deny involvement) desvincularse DE algn/algo

distance learning *n* [u] enseñanza *f* a distancia

distant /ˈdɪstənt/ *adj*

A 1 (in space) ‹*spot/country*› distante, lejano; **I could hear the ~ sound of bells** oía campanas a lo lejos 2 (in time): **in the ~ past/future** en el pasado remoto/en un futuro lejano

B (*pred*) (in space): **cities 50 miles ~ (from each other)** ciudades que distan 50 millas (la una de la otra)

C ‹*relative*› lejano; ‹*resemblance/connection*› remoto

D 1 (aloof) distante, frío 2 (absentminded) ‹*expression/tone*› ausente, ido

distantly /ˈdɪstəntli/ *adv* 1 (in the distance) ‹*hear/see*› en la lejanía 2 (loosely): **we are ~ related** somos parientes lejanos; **a ~ remembered episode** un incidente que recordaba (*or* recordaban *etc*) vagamente 3 (coldly) ‹*nod/greet*› con frialdad 4 (absentmindedly): **yes, she replied ~** —sí —respondió distante

distaste /dɪsˈteɪst/ *n* [u] desagrado *m*

distasteful /dɪsˈteɪstfəl/ *adj* 1 (unpleasant) ‹*task/chore*› desagradable 2 (offensive) ‹*remark/picture*› de mal gusto

distemper /dɪsˈtempər || dɪˈstempə(r)/ *n* [u]

A (Vet Sci) moquillo *m*

B (paint) (BrE) pintura *f* al temple

distend /dɪˈstend/ *vt* dilatar, hinchar

■ **distend** *vi* dilatarse, hincharse

distension, (AmE also) **distention** /dɪˈstentʃən || dɪˈstenʃən/ *n* [u] dilatación *f*

distill, (BrE) **distil** *vt* **-ll-** /dɪˈstɪl/ 1 ‹*liquid/spirits*› destilar; **~ed water** agua *f*‡ destilada 2 ‹*information/ideas*› extraer*

distillation /ˈdɪstəˈleɪʃən || ˌdɪstɪˈleɪʃən/ *n*

A 1 [u] (process) destilación *f* 2 [c] (product) destilado *m*

B [c] (of facts, experiences) síntesis *f*

distiller /dɪˈstɪlər || dɪˈstɪlə(r)/ *n* destilador, -dora *m,f*

distillery /dɪˈstɪləri/ *n* (*pl* **-ries**) destilería *f*

distinct /dɪˈstɪŋkt/ *adj*

A ‹*shape/outline*› definido, claro, nítido; ‹*likeness*› obvio, marcado; ‹*improvement*› decidido, marcado; ‹*possibility*› nada desdeñable

B 1 (different, separate) distinto, bien diferenciado; **to be ~ FROM sth** ser* distinto *or* diferente DE *or* A algo; **we are talking about English people as ~ from British people** nos referimos a los ingleses en particular y no a los británicos 2 (unmistakable) (*pred*) inconfundible

distinction /dɪˈstɪŋkʃən/ *n*

A 1 [c] (difference) distinción *f*; **we must make** *o* **draw a ~ between ...** debemos distinguir entre ... 2 [u] (act of differentiating) distinción *f*; **without ~ of race or creed** sin distinción de raza o credo

B 1 [u] (merit, excellence): **a writer of ~** un distinguido *or*

destacado escritor; **a car of ~** un coche de categoría [2] [u] (distinguished appearance) distinción *f*; **he has an air of ~** tiene un aire distinguido *or* de distinción [3] [c u] (mark of recognition) honor *m*, distinción *f* [4] [u c] (BrE Educ) mención *f* especial

distinctive /dɪ'stɪŋktɪv/ *adj* ‹*marking/plumage*› distintivo, característico; ‹*gesture/laugh*› personal, inconfundible; ‹*decor/dress*› particular

distinctively /dɪ'stɪŋktɪvli/ *adv* ‹*dress/behave*› de manera muy particular *or* personal; ‹*dressed/furnished*› con personalidad

distinctly /dɪ'stɪŋktli/ *adv* [1] ‹*speak/enunciate*› con claridad [2] ‹*hear*› perfectamente, claramente; **I ~ remember telling you** me acuerdo perfectamente *or* muy bien de que te lo dije [3] (decidedly): **he sounded ~ Scottish** tenía un inconfundible acento escocés

distinguish /dɪ'stɪŋgwɪʃ/ *vt*
A [1] (differentiate) distinguir*, diferenciar; **to ~ sth/sb FROM sth/sb** distinguir* *or* diferenciar algo/a algn DE algo/algn [2] **distinguishing** *pres p* ‹*feature/mark*› distintivo, característico
B (make out) distinguir*
■ **distinguish** *vi* distinguir*; **he can't ~ between green and blue** no distingue entre el verde y el azul, no distingue el verde del azul
■ *v refl* **to ~ oneself** distinguirse*, destacarse*

distinguishable /dɪ'stɪŋgwɪʃəbəl/ *adj* [1] (recognizable as different) **to be ~ (FROM sth/sb)** distinguirse* (DE algo/algn) [2] (discernible): **to be ~** distinguirse*

distinguished /dɪ'stɪŋgwɪʃt/ *adj* distinguido

distort /dɪ'stɔːrt || dɪ'stɔːt/ *vt* [1] (deform) ‹*metal/object*› deformar; **his face was ~ed by** *o* **with pain** tenía el rostro crispado del dolor [2] (Opt) ‹*image/reflection*› deformar, distorsionar [3] (Electron) ‹*signal/sound*› distorsionar [4] (misrepresent) ‹*facts/statement*› tergiversar, distorsionar

distortion /dɪ'stɔːrʃən || dɪ'stɔːʃən/ *n* [1] [u] (of metal, object) deformación *f*; (of features) distorsión *f* [2] (Opt) deformación *f*, distorsión *f* [3] [u c] (of facts, news) tergiversación *f*, distorsión *f*

distract /dɪ'strækt/ *vt* [1] (divert) ‹*person*› distraer*; **to ~ sb FROM sth** distraer* a algn DE algo [2] (amuse) entretener*, distraer*

distracted /dɪ'stræktəd || dɪ'stræktɪd/ *adj* ‹*person*› trastornado; ‹*look*› enajenado

distractedly /dɪ'stræktədli || dɪ'stræktɪdli/ *adv* como un loco

distraction /dɪ'strækʃən/ *n*
A [1] [c u] (interruption) distracción *f* [2] [c] (entertainment) (frml) entretenimiento *m*, distracción *f*
B [u] (madness): **to drive sb to ~** sacar* a algn de quicio; **to love sb to ~** estar* perdidamente enamorado de algn

distraught /dɪ'strɔːt/ *adj* ‹*voice/person*› consternado, angustiado; **to be ~ with grief/worry** estar* consternado por el dolor/por la preocupación; **she's utterly ~** está deshecha *or* destrozada

distress¹ /dɪ'stres/ *n* [u] [1] (mental) angustia *f*, aflicción *f*; **he was in great ~** sufría mucho [2] (physical): **respiratory ~** dificultades *fpl* respiratorias; **he showed signs of ~ during the race** tuvo síntomas de agotamiento durante la carrera [3] (danger) **in ~** en peligro; (*before n*) ‹*call/signal*› de socorro

distress² *vt* (upset) afligir*; (grieve) consternar; **please don't ~ yourself** por favor, no se aflija

distressed /dɪ'strest/ *adj* [1] (upset) afligido [2] (poor) (euph): **to be in ~ circumstances** pasar estrecheces [3] ‹*leather/wood*› envejecido

distressing /dɪ'stresɪŋ/ *adj* ‹*news/circumstance*› penoso, angustiante; **it was ~ to see him like that** angustiaba verlo así

distribute /dɪ'strɪbjət, -bjuːt || dɪ'strɪbjuːt/ *vt* [1] (hand out) ‹*leaflets/food*› distribuir*, repartir [2] (share out) ‹*profits*› repartir; ‹*tasks/responsibilities*› distribuir* [3] (supply) (Busn) distribuir* [4] (spread out) distribuir*; **the weight must be evenly ~d** el peso debe estar bien distribuido

distribution /'dɪstrɪ'bjuːʃən/ *n* [u c] distribución *f*, reparto *m*; (of dividends) reparto *m*; (*before n*) **~ network** red *f* de distribuidores

distributive /dɪ'strɪbjətɪv || dɪ'strɪbjʊtɪv/ *adj* (Busn): **the ~ trades** el sector de (la) distribución

distributor /dɪ'strɪbjətər || dɪ'strɪbjʊtə(r)/ *n*
A (Busn) distribuidor *m*; (Cin) distribuidora *f*
B (Auto, Elec) distribuidor *m* (del encendido)

district /'dɪstrɪkt/ *n*
A [1] (region) zona *f*, región *f* [2] (locality) barrio *m*; **financial ~** distrito *m* financiero; **the Federal D~** el distrito federal
B (Govt) (in US: of state, city) distrito *m*

district: **~ attorney** *n* (in US) fiscal *mf* del distrito; **~ court** *n* (in US) tribunal *m* de distrito; **~ nurse** *n* (in UK) *enfermero que tiene a su cuidado a los pacientes de un distrito*

distrust¹ /dɪs'trʌst/ *vt* desconfiar* de, no fiarse* de

distrust² *n* [u] desconfianza *f*, recelo *m*; **~ OF sth/sb** falta *f* de confianza EN algo/algn

distrustful /dɪs'trʌstfəl/ *adj* desconfiado, receloso; **to be ~ OF sb** desconfiar* *or* recelar DE algn

disturb /dɪ'stɜːrb || dɪ'stɜːb/ *vt*
A [1] (interrupt): **the noise ~ed my concentration** el ruido me hizo perder la concentración; **the calm was ~ed by the arrival of the tourists** la llegada de los turistas vino a perturbar la calma; **he was arrested for ~ing the peace** lo detuvieron por alterar el orden público [2] (inconvenience) molestar; **I'm sorry to ~ you, but ...** perdone que lo moleste, pero ... [3] (burst in upon) ‹*thief*› sorprender
B (disarrange): **she found that her papers had been ~ed** notó que alguien había tocado sus papeles
C (trouble) perturbar, inquietar, llenar de inquietud

disturbance /dɪ'stɜːrbəns || dɪ'stɜːbəns/ *n*
A [u c] [1] (noisy disruption): **to cause/create a ~** provocar*/armar un alboroto; **the aircraft are a continual ~** los aviones son una molestia constante [2] (interruption) interrupción *f*
B [u c] (of routine) alteración *f*
C [c] (riot) disturbio *m*

disturbed /dɪ'stɜːrbd || dɪ'stɜːbd/ *adj*
A [1] (Psych) ‹*person/mind*› trastornado; **she is emotionally ~** tiene problemas emocionales [2] (perturbed) (*pred*): **I was greatly ~ to hear of his misfortune** la noticia de su desgracia me impresionó *or* afectó muchísimo
B (restless) ‹*sleep*› agitado, inquieto; **I had a ~ night** dormí muy mal

disturbing /dɪ'stɜːrbɪŋ || dɪ'stɜːbɪŋ/ *adj* (worrying, upsetting) inquietante, perturbador; (alarming) alarmante

disunity /dɪʃ'uːnəti || dɪs'juːnəti/ *n* [u] desunión *f*

disuse /dɪʃ'uːs || dɪs'juːs/ *n* [u] desuso *m*; **to fall into ~** «*words/customs*» caer* en desuso; «*building/port*» dejar de utilizarse

disused /dɪʃ'uːzd || dɪs'juːzd/ *adj* ‹*factory/quarry*› abandonado; ‹*machinery*› en desuso

ditch¹ /dɪtʃ/ *n* zanja *f*; (at roadside) cuneta *f*; (for irrigation) acequia *f*

ditch² *vt*
A (abandon) (colloq) ‹*girlfriend/boyfriend*› plantar (fam), botar (AmC, Chi fam); ‹*object*› deshacerse* de, botar (AmL exc RPl), tirar (Esp, RPl); ‹*plan*› abandonar, desechar
B (Aviat): **to ~ a plane** hacer* un amaraje *or* amarizaje *or* amerizaje (forzoso)

dither /'dɪðər || 'dɪðə(r)/ *vi* (colloq) [1] (become agitated) (AmE) ponerse* muy nervioso [2] (be indecisive) titubear, vacilar; **I was ~ing over whether to go or not** no sabía si ir o no ir

ditto¹ /'dɪtəʊ/ *adv* (colloq): **I'm fed up — ditto!** estoy harto — ¡y yo ídem de ídem! (fam)

ditto² *n* (*pl* **-tos**) ídem *m*

ditty /'dɪti/ *n* (*pl* **-ties**) *cancioncilla o poema simple*

diuretic¹ /'daɪjə'retɪk || daɪjʊ'retɪk/ *n* diurético *m*

diuretic² *adj* diurético

diva /'diːvə/ *n* (*pl* **-vas** *or* (AmE also) **-ve** /-veɪ/) diva *f*

divan /dɪ'væn/ *n* [1] (sofa) diván *m*, canapé *m* [2] **~ (bed)** cama *f* turca

dive¹ /daɪv/ (*past* **dived** *or* (AmE also) **dove**; *past p* **dived**) *vi*
A [1] (from height) zambullirse*, tirarse (al agua), tirarse *or* echarse un clavado (AmL); **she ~d into the water** se zambulló, se tiró al agua [2] (from surface) «*person/whale*» sumergirse*, zambullirse*; «*submarine*» sumergirse*; **to ~ for treasure** bucear buscando tesoros; **to go diving** ir*

d

a hacer submarinismo *or* a bucear [3] (swoop) ⟪*plane/bird*⟫ bajar en picada *or* (Esp) en picado
B (lunge, move suddenly): **he ~d for cover under the table** se tiró *or* se metió debajo de la mesa para protegerse
C (drop sharply) (journ) ⟪*currency/sales*⟫ caer* en picada *or* (Esp) en picado, pegar* un bajón (fam)

(Phrasal verb)

• **dive in** [v ▸ adv] (colloq) (into water) tirarse de cabeza al agua, tirarse *or* echarse un clavado (AmL)

dive² *n*
A [1] (into water) zambullida *f*, clavado *m* (AmL); (Sport) salto *m* (de trampolín), clavado *m* (AmL) [2] (of submarine, whale) inmersión *f* [3] (swoop) descenso *m* en picada *or* (Esp) en picado
B (lunge, sudden movement) (colloq): **he made a ~ for the gun** se abalanzó sobre la pistola; **(full-length) ~** (in soccer) estirada *f*
C (disreputable club, bar) (colloq) antro *m*

dive-bomb /'daɪvbɑ:m || 'daɪvbɒm/ *vt* bombardear en picada *or* (Esp) en picado

diver /'daɪvər || 'daɪvə(r)/ *n* [1] (from diving board *etc*) saltador, -dora *m,f*, clavadista *mf* [2] (deep-sea) buzo *mf*, submarinista *mf*

diverge /də'vɜ:rdʒ || daɪ'vɜ:dʒ/ *vi* [1] ⟪*lines/paths*⟫ separarse, divergir* (frml) [2] ⟪*opinions/explanations*⟫ divergir*; **to ~ FROM sth** discrepar DE algo

divergence /də'vɜ:rdʒəns || daɪ'vɜ:dʒəns/ *n* [u] divergencia *f*

divergent /də'vɜ:rdʒənt || daɪ'vɜ:dʒənt/ *adj* divergente

divers /'daɪvərz || 'daɪvəz/ *adj* (arch) (*before n*) diversos

diverse /daɪ'vɜ:rs || daɪ'vɜ:s/ *adj* [1] (varied) ⟨*interests/tastes*⟩ diversos, variados; **plant life in the area is extremely ~** la vegetación en la zona es muy variada [2] (unlike) diferentes, distintos

diversification /də'vɜ:rsəfə'keɪʃən || daɪˌvɜ:sɪfɪ'keɪʃən/ *n* [u] variedad *f*; (Busn) diversificación *f*

diversify /də'vɜ:rsəfaɪ || daɪ'vɜ:sɪfaɪ/, **-fies, -fying, -fied** *vt* diversificar*
■ **diversify** *vi* (Busn) diversificarse*; **to ~ INTO sth**: **they diversified into sportswear** diversificaron su producción introduciéndose en el mercado de ropa de deporte

diversion /də'vɜ:rʒən || daɪ'vɜ:ʃən/ *n*
A [1] [u] (of river) desviación *f* [2] [u] (of funds) malversación *f* [3] [c] (BrE Transp) desvío *m*, desviación *f*
B [c] (distraction) (Mil) diversión *f*, divertimiento *m* estratégico; **you create a ~ and I'll make my escape** tú los distraes mientras yo me escapo
C [c u] (amusement) (frml) diversión *f*, entretenimiento *m*

diversity /də'vɜ:rsəti || daɪ'vɜ:səti/ *n* diversidad *f*

divert /də'vɜ:rt || daɪ'vɜ:t/ *vt*
A [1] (redirect) ⟨*stream/flow*⟩ desviar*; ⟨*traffic*⟩ (BrE) desviar*; **I tried to ~ the conversation away from the topic** intenté desviar la conversación hacia otro tema [2] (ward off) ⟨*blow/attack*⟩ eludir, esquivar
B (distract) ⟨*attention/thoughts*⟩ distraer*
C (amuse) (frml) divertir*, entretener*

divest /daɪ'vest/ *vt*
A (deprive): **to ~ sb/sth OF sth** despojar a algn/algo DE algo
B (sell off) ⟨*asset/operation/stake*⟩ deshacerse* de *v refl* **to ~ oneself OF sth** deshacerse* DE algo

divide /də'vaɪd || dɪ'vaɪd/ *vt*
A [1] (split up) dividir; **to ~ sth INTO sth** dividir algo EN algo [2] (separate) **to ~ sth FROM sth** separar algo DE algo [3] **dividing** *pres p* ⟨*wall/barrier*⟩ divisorio [4] (share) ⟨*cake/money/work*⟩ repartir; **I ~ my time between England and Italy** paso parte del tiempo en Inglaterra y parte en Italia
B (cause to disagree) dividir
C (Math) dividir; **to ~ 10 by 5** dividir 10 entre *or* por 5; **10 ~d by 5 is 2** 10 dividido entre *or* por 5 es (igual a) 2
■ **divide** *vi*
A [1] (fork) ⟪*road/river*⟫ dividirse [2] (split) ⟪*group/particles/cells*⟫ dividirse [3] (vote) (BrE Govt) votar
B (Math) dividir

(Phrasal verbs)

• **divide off** [v ▸ o ▸ adv, v ▸ adv ▸ o] separar
• **divide up**
A [v ▸ o ▸ adv, v ▸ adv ▸ o] dividir
B [v ▸ adv] dividirse

divided /də'vaɪdəd || dɪ'vaɪdɪd/ *adj* ⟨*opinion*⟩ dividido; **they are ~ on the issue** sus opiniones al respecto están muy divididas

divided: **~ highway** *n* (AmE) autovía *f*; **~ skirt** *n* falda *f* pantalón, pollera *f* pantalón (CS)

dividend /'dɪvədend || 'dɪvɪdend/ *n* dividendo *m*; ***to pay ~s*** dar* dividendos, reportar beneficios

divider /də'vaɪdər || dɪ'vaɪdə(r)/ *n* [1] (screen) mampara *f*; (in filing system) separador *m* [2] **dividers** *pl* (Math) **(pair of) ~s** compás *m* de puntas fijas

dividing line /də'vaɪdɪŋ || dɪ'vaɪdɪŋ/ *n* línea *f* divisoria

divine¹ /də'vaɪn || dɪ'vaɪn/ *adj*
A (*before n*) ⟨*intervention/inspiration*⟩ divino; **it was ~ justice** fue un castigo de Dios
B (wonderful) divino, precioso

divine² *vt* [1] (discover, guess) (liter) adivinar [2] ⟨*water/minerals*⟩ descubrir* (*con una varita de zahorí*)

divine right *n* derecho *m* divino

diving /'daɪvɪŋ/ *n* [u] [1] (from height) saltos *mpl* de trampolín, clavados *mpl* (AmL) [2] (under water) submarinismo *m*, buceo *m*

diving: **~ board** *n* trampolín *m*; **~ suit** *n* escafandra *f*, traje *m* de buzo

divining rod /də'vaɪnɪŋ || dɪ'vaɪnɪŋ/ *n* varita *f* de zahorí

divinity /də'vɪnəti || dɪ'vɪnəti/ *n* (*pl* **-ties**) (frml) [1] [u c] (divine nature, being) divinidad *f* [2] [u] (theology) teología *f*

divisible /də'vɪzəbəl || dɪ'vɪzəbəl/ *adj* (*pred*) divisible; **21 is ~ by 3** 21 es divisible entre *or* por 3

division /də'vɪʒən || dɪ'vɪʒən/ *n*
A [1] [u c] (distribution) reparto *m*, división *f*; **the ~ of labor** (Econ) la división del trabajo [2] [c] (boundary) división *f*; **linguistic/class ~s** divisiones lingüísticas/de clase [3] [c] (part) división *f*
B [u] (disagreement) desacuerdo *m*
C [c] (department) división *f*, sección *f*
D [c] (Mil) división *f*
E [c] (Sport) [1] (in boxing) categoría *f* [2] (in US: area) zona *f* [3] (in UK: by standard) división *f*
F [u c] (Math) división *f*; **long ~** división larga *or* desarrollada
G [c] (BrE Govt) votación *f*

divisive /də'vaɪsɪv || dɪ'vaɪsɪv/ *adj* divisivo

divorce¹ /də'vɔ:rs || dɪ'vɔ:s/ *n* [c u] divorcio *m*; **to get a ~ (from sb)** conseguir* el divorcio (de algn); (*before n*) **~ proceedings** trámites *mpl* de divorcio

divorce² *vt*
A (Law) divorciarse de; **to get ~d** divorciarse
B (separate) **to ~ sth (FROM sth)** divorciar algo (DE algo)
■ **divorce** *vi* divorciarse

divorced /də'vɔ:rst || dɪ'vɔ:st/ *adj* [1] (Law) divorciado [2] (detached) **to be ~ FROM sth** estar* divorciado DE algo

divorcee /də'vɔ:r'seɪ || dɪˌvɔ:'si:/ *n* divorciado, -da *m,f*

divulge /daɪ'vʌldʒ/ *vt* divulgar*; **to ~ sth TO sb** revelarle algo A algn

Dixie /'dɪksi/ *n* [u] (colloq) (AmE) *los estados del sur en EEUU*

DIY *n* [u] (BrE) (= **do-it-yourself**) bricolaje *m*

dizziness /'dɪzinəs || 'dɪzinɪs/ *n* [u] mareo *m*, vahído *m*

dizzy /'dɪzi/ *adj* **-zier, -ziest** [1] (giddy) ⟨*sensation*⟩ de mareo; **I had a ~ spell** me dio un mareo; **to feel ~** estar* mareado [2] (causing dizziness) ⟨*speed*⟩ vertiginoso; ⟨*height*⟩ de vértigo [3] (scatterbrained) (colloq) tarambana (fam)

DJ *n* = **disc jockey**

DNA *n* [u] (= **deoxyribonucleic acid**) ADN *m*, DNA *m*; **~ profile** perfil *m* genético *or* de ADN; **~ profiling** /'prəʊfaɪlɪŋ/ *n* [u] análisis *m* de muestras de ADN

do¹ /du:, *weak form* dʊ, də/ (*3rd pers sing pres* **does**; *pres* **doing**; *past* **did**; *past p* **done**) *vt*
A hacer*; **~ something!** ¡haz algo!; **are you ~ing anything this evening?** ¿vas a hacer algo esta noche?; **to have something/nothing to ~** tener* algo/no tener* nada que hacer; **it was a silly thing to ~** fue una estupidez; **can I ~ anything to help?** ¿puedo ayudar en algo?; **he does a lot for charity** trabaja mucho para obras de caridad; **what have you done to your hair?** ¿qué te has hecho en el pelo?; **I don't know what I'm going to ~ with you!** ¡no sé qué voy a hacer contigo!; *see also* **do with**
B (carry out) ⟨*job/task*⟩ hacer*; **to ~ one's homework** hacer*

los deberes; **to ~ the cooking** cocinar; **let me ~ the talking** déjame hablar a mí; **well done!** ¡muy bien!

C (as job): **what do you ~?** ¿usted qué hace *or* a qué se dedica?; **what does he ~ for a living?** ¿en qué trabaja?

D (achieve, bring about): **she's done it: it's a new world record** lo ha logrado: es una nueva marca mundial; **it was climbing those stairs that did it** fue por subir esa escalera; **now you've done it!** ¡ahora sí que la has hecho buena! (iró); **he's late again: that does it!** vuelve a llegar tarde ¡esto ya es la gota que colma el vaso!; **to ~ sth FOR sb/sth**: **that mustache really does something for him** la verdad es que le queda muy bien el bigote; **what has EC membership done for Greece?** ¿en qué ha beneficiado a Grecia ser miembro de la CE?

E [1] (fix, arrange, repair): **I have to ~ my nails** me tengo que arreglar las uñas; **she had her hair done** se hizo peinar [2] (clean) ‹*dishes*› lavar; ‹*brass/windows*› limpiar

F (make, produce) [1] ‹*meal*› preparar, hacer*; **would you ~ the carrots?** ¿me preparas (*or* pelas *etc*) las zanahorias? [2] ‹*drawing/translation*› hacer*; **he doesn't ~ live concerts any more** ya no da más conciertos en vivo

G (BrE) (offer): **they ~ a set meal for £12** tienen un menú de 12 libras

H (suffice for, suit): **two shirts will ~ me** con dos camisas me alcanza *or* tengo suficiente

I (travel): **he was ~ing 100 mph** iba a 100 millas por hora; **the car has only done 4,000 miles** el coche sólo tiene 4.000 millas

A [1] (study) estudiar; **we're ~ing Balzac** estamos estudiando Balzac [2] (visit) (colloq) ‹*sights/museum*› visitar; **we did Europe last year** el año pasado recorrimos Europa

A (Theat) [1] (play role of) hacer* el papel de [2] (take part in) ‹*play*› actuar* en [3] (impersonate) imitar

A (colloq) (serve in prison) cumplir; **he's ~ing eight years for armed robbery** está cumpliendo ocho años por atraco a mano armada

A (BrE colloq) [1] (catch, prosecute) agarrar; **he was done for speeding** le encajaron una multa por exceso de velocidad (fam) [2] (cheat) estafar, timar; **I've been done!** ¡me han estafado *or* timado!

A (use) (sl): **to ~ drugs** drogarse*, consumir drogas

A (colloq) (finish) terminar; **are** *o* (esp BrE) **have you done complaining?** ¿has terminado de quejarte?

■ **do** *vi*

A (act, behave) hacer*; **~ as you're told!** ¡haz lo que se te dice!

B (get along, manage): **how are you ~ing?** ¿qué tal estás *or* andas *or* te va?; **how do you ~?** (as greeting) mucho gusto, encantado; **how ~?** (colloq & dial) ¿qué tal?; **how are we ~ing for time/cash?** ¿cómo *or* qué tal vamos *or* andamos de tiempo/dinero?; **she did well/badly in her exams** le fue bien/mal en los exámenes; **he's done well for himself** ha sabido abrirse camino; **to ~ well/badly out of sth** salir* bien/mal parado de algo

C (go on, happen) (colloq) (*in -ing form*): **there's nothing ~ing in town** no pasa nada en el pueblo; **nothing ~ing!** ¡ni hablar!, ¡ni lo sueñes!

D [1] (be suitable, acceptable): **look, this won't ~!** ¡mira, esto no puede ser!; **it's not ideal, but it'll ~** no es lo ideal, pero sirve; **I'm not going to cook, bread and cheese will ~ for them!** no pienso cocinar, se tendrán que conformar con pan y queso; **it doesn't ~ to get emotional** no hay que ponerse sentimental [2] **to ~ FOR** *o* **AS sth**: **this box will ~ for** *o* **as a table** esta caja nos servirá de mesa

E (be enough) ser* suficiente, alcanzar*, bastar; **one bottle will ~** con una botella basta *or* es suficiente; **one egg will ~ for me** un huevo es suficiente para mí; **that'll ~! shut up!** ¡basta! ¡cállate la boca!

F (finish) (*in past p*) terminar; **I'm not** *o* (BrE) **I haven't done yet!** no he terminado todavía

G : **his concern to ~ well by his son** su preocupación por hacer todo lo posible por su hijo; ***do as you would be done by*** trata a los demás como tú quisieras ser tratado

■ **do** *v aux* [*El verbo auxiliar* **do** *se usa para formar el negativo* (*Sense* **I A**) *y el interrogativo* (*Sense* **I B**), *para agregar énfasis* (*Sense* **I C**) *o para sustituir a un verbo usado anteriormente* (*Sense* **II**)]

Sense **I**

A [1] (*used to form negative*): **I ~ not** *o* **don't know** no sé; **I did not** *o* **didn't see her** no la vi; Ⓢ **do not touch!** no tocar [2] (*with inversion after negative adv*): **not once did he apologize** no se disculpó ni siquiera una vez; **not only does it cost more, it also ...** no sólo cuesta más, sino que también ...

B [1] (*used to form interrogative*): **does this belong to you?** ¿esto es tuyo?; **did I frighten you?** ¿te asusté? [2] (*in exclamations*): **doesn't it make you sick!** ¡dime si no es asqueante!; **boy, ~ you need a bath!** ¡Dios mío! ¡qué falta te hace un baño!

C [1] (emphasizing): **you ~ exaggerate!** ¡cómo exageras!; **you must admit, she did look ill** tienes que reconocer que tenía mala cara; **~ be quiet!** ¿te quieres callar?; **~ please help yourself** sírvete por favor [2] (expressing alternatives): **I haven't decided, but if I ~ accept ...** todavía no lo he decidido, pero si aceptara ... [3] (in legal formulae): **I, Charles Brown, ~ solemnly swear that ...** yo, Charles Brown, juro solemnemente que ...

Sense **II**

A (*in elliptical uses*): **~ you live here? — yes, I ~/no, I don't** ¿vives aquí? — sí/no; **she wanted to come, but he didn't** ella quería venir, pero él no; **she found it in your drawer — oh, *did* she?** lo encontró en tu cajón — ¿ah, sí?; **I don't need a haircut — yes, you ~!** no necesito cortarme el pelo — ¡cómo que no!; **she says she understands, but she doesn't** dice que comprende, pero no es así; **I play the guitar — so ~ I** toco la guitarra — yo también; **I don't like her music — I ~** no me gusta su música — a mí sí

B (*in tag questions*): **you know Bob, don't you?** conoces a Bob, ¿no? *or* ¿verdad? *or* ¿no es cierto?; **I told you, didn't I?** te lo dije ¿no? *or* ¿no es cierto?

Phrasal verbs

- **do away with** [v ▸ adv ▸ prep ▸ o] [1] (abolish) ‹*privilege/tax*› abolir*, suprimir; ‹*need*› eliminar, acabar con [2] (kill) (colloq) eliminar, liquidar (fam)
- **do down** [v ▸ o ▸ adv, v ▸ adv ▸ o] (BrE) menospreciar, hacer* de menos
- **do for** [v ▸ prep ▸ o] (BrE) (cause collapse of): **to be done for** (also AmE): **they've spotted us, we're done for!** ¡nos han visto, estamos perdidos!; **we've been walking for hours, I'm absolutely done for!** (colloq) hemos caminado horas, estoy molido *or* hecho polvo (fam)
- **do in** [v ▸ o ▸ adv, v ▸ adv ▸ o] (colloq) [1] (kill) eliminar, liquidar (fam) [2] (tire out) agotar, reventar* (fam); **to be done in** estar* reventado *or* molido *or* hecho polvo (fam) [3] (injure, ruin) (BrE) ‹*back/shoulder*› hacerse* daño en, embromarse (AmS fam); ‹*engine*› estropear, arruinar (CS), cargarse* (Esp fam)
- **do out** [v ▸ o ▸ adv, v ▸ adv ▸ o] [1] (clean out) (BrE) ‹*room*› hacer* una limpieza a fondo de [2] (decorate) (esp BrE): **the bedroom was done out in pink** el dormitorio estaba pintado de/empapelado en rosa
- **do out of** [v ▸ o ▸ adv ▸ prep ▸ o] (colloq) quitar, birlar; **he was done out of his share** le quitaron *or* le birlaron su parte
- **do over**

A [v ▸ o ▸ adv, v ▸ adv ▸ o] (beat up) (BrE sl) darle* una paliza a, sacarle* la mugre a (AmL fam)

B [v ▸ o ▸ adv] (do again) (AmE) volver* a hacer

- **do up** [v ▸ o ▸ adv, v ▸ adv ▸ o] [1] (fasten) ‹*coat/necklace/button*› abrochar; ‹*zipper*› subir; **to ~ up one's shoes** atarse los cordones *or* (Méx) las agujetas *or* (Per) los pasadores (de los zapatos); **~ up your tie** hazte el nudo de la corbata [2] (wrap up) ‹*parcel*› envolver* [3] (dress up) (colloq): **she was all done up** estaba muy elegante [4] (colloq) ‹*house*› arreglar (*pintando, empapelando etc*)
- **do with** [v ▸ prep ▸ o]

A (benefit from) (*with can, could*): **that door could ~ with a coat of paint** no le vendría mal una mano de pintura a esa puerta; **you could ~ with a change** te hace falta *or* te vendría bien un cambio

B (expressing connection) **to have/be sth to ~ with sth/sb**: **I don't want to have anything to ~ with him/this business** yo no quiero tener nada que ver con él/este asunto; **what's that got to ~ with it?** ¿y eso qué tiene que ver?; **it's to ~ with your son** se trata de su hijo; **it's nothing to ~ with you!** no es nada que te concierna *or* que te importe a ti; **I've had nothing to ~ with my family for years** hace años que no tengo ningún contacto con mi familia

- **do without**

A [v ▸ prep ▸ o]: **to ~ without sth/sb** prescindir de *or*

arreglárselas sin algo/algn; **her coming to stay is something I can ~ without!** ¡ni falta que me hace que ella se venga a quedar!; **you really think you could ~ without me?** ¿te las puedes arreglar sin mí?, ¿te las puedes arreglar solo?
B [v ▸ adv] arreglárselas; **you'll just have to ~ without, like everyone else** te las tendrás que arreglar, como todos los demás

do² /du:/ *n* (*pl* **dos**)
A [c] (party, gathering) (colloq) fiesta *f*, reunión *f*
B (state of affairs) (colloq) (*no pl*): ***fair ~s*** (BrE colloq): **fair ~s all round** a partes iguales para todos; (*as interj*) ¡seamos justos!
C **do's and don'ts** (rules) normas *fpl*; **the ~'s and don'ts of foreign travel** qué hacer y qué evitar cuando se viaja al extranjero

do³ /dəʊ/ *n* (*pl* **dos**) (Mus) do *m*

DOA *adj* (AmE) (*pred*) = **dead on arrival**

DOB *n* (esp AmE) = **date of birth**

doc /dɑ:k || dɒk/ *n* (colloq) doctor, -tora *m,f*

docile /'dɑ:səl || 'dəʊsaɪl/ *adj* dócil, sumiso

dock¹ /dɑ:k || dɒk/ *n*
A (Naut) 1 [c] (wharf, quay) muelle *m*; (for cargo ships) dársena *f*; **to be in ~** «*ship*» estar* en puerto; (*before n*) ‹*worker/strike*› portuario 2 **docks** *pl* puerto *m*
B (Law) (*no pl*) **the ~** el banquillo de los acusados
C [u] (Bot) acedera *f*

dock² *vt*
A 1 ‹*tail*› cortar 2 ‹*wages*› descontar* dinero de
B ‹*vessel/ship*› fondear, atracar*
■ **dock** *vi* 1 (Naut) «*ship/vessel*» atracar*, fondear 2 (Aerosp) acoplarse

docker /'dɑ:kər || 'dɒkə(r)/ *n* (BrE) estibador, -dora *m,f*

docket /'dɑ:kət || 'dɒkɪt/ *n*
A (AmE Law) lista *f* de casos
B (BrE Busn) (label) etiqueta *f*, rótulo *m*; (delivery note) resguardo *m* de entrega

docking /'dɑ:kɪŋ || 'dɒkɪŋ/ *n* [u] (Aerosp) acoplamiento *m*

dock: **~land** *n* (BrE) (*often pl*) zona *f* portuaria; **~yard** *n* (*often pl*) astillero *m*

doctor¹ /'dɑ:ktər || 'dɒktə(r)/ *n*
A (Med) médico, -ca *m,f*, doctor, -tora *m,f*, facultativo, -va *m,f* (frml); **D~ Jones** el doctor Jones; ***just what the ~ ordered*** (colloq) justo lo que hace falta (fam)
B (Educ) doctor, -tora *m,f*; **D~ of Philosophy/Law** doctor en filosofía/derecho

doctor² *vt*
A (pej) 1 ‹*food/drink*› adulterar 2 ‹*text*› arreglar 3 ‹*results/evidence*› falsificar*, amañar
B (neuter) (BrE euph) ‹*cat/dog*› operar (euf)

doctoral /'dɑ:ktərəl || 'dɒktərəl/ *adj* ‹*thesis/dissertation*› doctoral

doctorate /'dɑ:ktərət || 'dɒktərət/ *n* doctorado *m*

doctrinaire /'dɑ:ktrə'ner || ,dɒktrɪ'neə(r)/ *adj* doctrinario

doctrinal /'dɑ:ktrənḷ || dɒk'traɪnḷ/ *adj* doctrinal

doctrine /'dɑ:ktrən || 'dɒktrɪn/ *n* [u c] doctrina *f*

document¹ /'dɑ:kjəmənt || 'dɒkjʊmənt/ *n* documento *m*; **are your ~s in order?** ¿tiene los documentos *or* (fam) papeles en regla?

document² *vt* /'dɑ:kjəment || 'dɒkjʊment/ documentar

documentary¹ /'dɑ:kjə'mentəri || ,dɒkjʊ'mentri/ *adj* documental

documentary² *n* (*pl* **-ries**) documental *m*

documentation /'dɑ:kjəmen'teɪʃən || ,dɒkjʊmen'teɪʃən/ *n* [u] documentación *f*

dodder /'dɑ:dər || 'dɒdə(r)/ *vi* (colloq) 1 (totter) andar* tambaleándose *or* con paso inseguro 2 **doddering** *pres p* (pej) chocho (fam)

doddery /'dɑ:dəri || 'dɒdəri/ *adj* (colloq) temblequeante

doddle /'dɑ:dḷ || 'dɒdḷ/ *n* (BrE): **it's a ~** está tirado (fam), está regalado (Chi, Méx, Ven fam)

dodge¹ /dɑ:dʒ || dɒdʒ/ *vt* 1 ‹*blow*› esquivar; ‹*pursuer*› eludir 2 ‹*question*› esquivar, soslayar; ‹*problem/issue*› soslayar; ‹*work/responsibility*› eludir; ‹*tax*› evadir; **we ~d our fare** viajamos sin pagar
■ **dodge** *vi* echarse a un lado, apartarse; **she ~d behind the car** se escondío rápidamente detrás del coche

dodge² *n*
A (trick) (colloq) treta *f*, truco *m*, artimaña *f*
B (sidestep) esquive *m*

dodgem (car) /'dɑ:dʒəm || 'dɒdʒəm/ *n* ▸ **bumper car**

dodger /'dɑ:dʒər || 'dɒdʒə(r)/ *n*: **tax ~** evasor, -sora *m,f* de impuestos; **fare ~** *persona que intenta viajar sin pagar en un medio de transporte público*

dodgy /'dɑ:dʒi || 'dɒdʒi/ *adj* **dodgier, dodgiest** (BrE colloq) 1 (unreliable, dubious): **the brakes are a bit ~** los frenos no andan muy bien; **he's a ~ character** no es un tipo de fiar (fam) 2 (risky) arriesgado, riesgoso (AmL)

dodo /'dəʊdəʊ/ *n* (*pl* **dodos** *or* **dodoes**) dodo *m*

doe /dəʊ/ *n* (of deer) hembra *f* de gamo, gama *f*; (of rabbit) coneja *f*

doer /'du:ər || 'du:ə(r)/ *n* (colloq) (active person) persona *f* emprendedora *or* dinámica

does /dʌz, *weak form* dəz/ *3rd pers sing pres of* **do¹**

doesn't /'dʌzṇt/ = **does not**

doff /dɑ:f || dɒf/ *vt*: **to ~ one's hat to sb** quitarse el sombrero *or* descubrirse* ante algn

dog¹ /dɔ:g || dɒg/ *n* (Zool) perro, -rra *m,f*; (male canine) macho *m*; ***a ~'s life*** una vida de perros; ***dressed* o *done up like a ~'s dinner*** (BrE) todo emperifollado (fam); ***it's (a case of) ~ eat ~*** hay una competencia brutal; ***not to have* o *stand a ~'s chance*** no tener* ni la más remota posibilidad; ***to go to the ~s*** venirse* abajo; **the country's going to the ~s** el país se viene abajo; ***to treat sb like a ~*** tratar a algn como a un perro; ***every ~ has its day*** a todos les llega su momento de gloria; ***give a ~ a bad name (and hang it)*** (BrE) por un perro que maté, mataperros me llamaron; ***let sleeping ~s lie*** mejor no revolver el asunto; ***you can't teach an old ~ new tricks*** loro viejo no aprende a hablar; (*before n*) **~ show** exposición *f* canina

dog² *vt* **-gg-** 1 (trouble) (*often pass*) perseguir*; **we've been ~ged by bad luck from the beginning** la mala suerte nos ha perseguido desde el principio 2 (follow closely) perseguir*; **to ~ sb's footsteps** *o* **heels** pisarle los talones a algn

dog: **~ collar** *n* (clerical collar) (colloq *or* hum) alzacuello *m*, clergyman *m*; **~ days** *pl n* **the ~ days** la canícula (liter); **~-eared** /'dɔ:gɪrd || 'dɒgɪəd/ *adj* sobado y con las esquinas dobladas; **~-end** *n* (BrE colloq) colilla *f*, pucho *m* (AmL fam); **~fight** *n* (Aviat) combate *m* aéreo; (between dogs) pelea *f* de perros

dogged /'dɔ:gəd || 'dɒgɪd/ *adj* obstinado, emperrado (fam)

doggedly /'dɔ:gədli || 'dɒgɪdli/ *adv* obstinadamente

doggerel /'dɔ:gərəl || 'dɒgərəl/ *n* [u] ripios *mpl*

doggie *n* ▸ **doggy**

doggo /'dɔ:gəʊ || 'dɒgəʊ/ *adv*: ***to lie ~*** (BrE colloq) quedarse escondido (*sin hacer ruido*)

doggone /'dɑ:g'gɑ:n || 'dɒgɒn/ *adj* (AmE colloq & euph) (*before n*) maldito (fam)

doggy /'dɔ:gi || 'dɒgi/ *n* (*pl* **-gies**) (used to or by children) guauguau *m* (leng infantil), perrito *m*

doggy: **~ bag** *n*: *bolsita que proporcionan en algunos restaurantes para llevarse las sobras a casa*; **~ paddle** *n* [u] (used to or by children) ▸ **dog paddle**

dog: **~house** *n* (AmE) casa *f or* casilla *f or* (Esp) caseta *f or* (Chi) casucha *f* del perro, perrera *f* (Col); ***to be in the ~house*** (also BrE colloq) haber* caído en desgracia; **~ in the manger** *n*: **don't be a ~ in the manger** no seas como el perro del hortelano (que ni come ni deja comer)

dogma /'dɔ:gmə || 'dɒgmə/ *n* dogma *m*

dogmatic /dɔ:g'mætɪk || dɒg'mætɪk/ *adj* dogmático

do-gooder /'du:,gʊdər || du:'gʊdə(r)/ *n* (pej) hacedor, -dora *m,f* de buenas obras (hum)

dog: **~ paddle** *n* [u] estilo *m* perro *or* perrito; **~sbody** *n* (esp BrE colloq): **I'm just the general ~sbody around here** yo aquí no soy más que el botones; **I'm fed up with being his ~sbody** estoy harta de ser su sirvienta; **~ tag** *n* (Mil) placa *f* de identificación; **~-tired** *adj* (*pred*) (colloq) muerto de cansancio, hecho polvo (fam)

doh /dəʊ/ *n* (Mus) do *m*

doily /'dɔɪli/ *n* (*pl* **-lies**) 1 (on plate) blonda *f* 2 (under plate, ornament) tapete *m*, pañito *m*, carpeta *f* (Col, CS)

doing /ˈduːɪŋ/ *n*
A [u] (action): **it'll take a bit/lot of ~** va a dar un poco de/mucho trabajo; **that takes some ~** eso no es nada fácil; **it was none of our ~** nosotros no tuvimos nada que ver
B **doings** *pl* (activities, events) actividades *fpl*

do-it-yourself /ˈduːətʃərˈself || ˌduːɪtjəːˈself/ *n* [u] bricolaje *m*; (*before n*) **~ enthusiast** aficionado, -da *m,f* al bricolaje, bricolero, -ra *m,f*

doldrums /ˈdəʊldrəmz, ˈdɑːl- || ˈdɒldrəmz/ *pl n*: ***to be in the ~*** estar* de capa caída

dole /dəʊl/ *n* (BrE) **the ~** el subsidio de desempleo, el paro (Esp), la cesantía (Chi); **to be on the ~** estar* cobrando subsidio de desempleo *or* (Chi tb) de cesantía, estar* en el paro (Esp); (*before n*) **to join the ~ queue** pasar a engrosar el número del desempleo *or* (Esp tb) del paro

Phrasal verb

• **dole out** [v ▸ o ▸ adv, v ▸ adv ▸ o] ‹*food/money*› dar*, repartir

doleful /ˈdəʊlfəl/ *adj* ‹*face/look*› compungido, triste; ‹*sound/voice*› plañidero, lúgubre

doll /dɑːl || dɒl/ *n*
A (toy) muñeca *f*
B [1] (pretty little girl) muñeca *f*; (attractive woman) (AmE) muñeca *f* [2] (pleasant person) (AmE colloq) encanto *m* (fam)

Phrasal verb

• **doll up** [v ▸ o ▸ adv] (colloq): **to get (all) ~ed up** *o* **to ~ oneself up** emperifollarse (fam)

dollar /ˈdɑːlər || ˈdɒlə(r)/ *n* dólar *m*; ***~s to doughnuts*** (AmE colloq): **it's ~s to doughnuts they'll come** te apuesto *or* juego lo que quieras (a) que vienen; ***to be (as) sound as a ~*** (AmE colloq) «*heart/engine*» funcionar *or* marchar como un reloj; «*person*» estar* (fuerte) como un toro; ***to feel/look like a million ~s***: **he made me feel like a million ~s** me hizo sentir en el séptimo cielo *or* a las mil maravillas; **she looked like a million ~s** estaba despampanante; ***top ~*** (AmE colloq) el mejor precio (*or* sueldo *etc*); ***you can bet your bottom ~*** (colloq) puedes estar seguro, te lo doy firmado (fam); (*before n*) **~ bill** billete *m* de un dólar; **~ sign** signo *m* *or* símbolo *m* del dólar

dollarization /ˌdɑːlərəˈzeɪʃən || ˌdɒləraɪˈzeɪʃən/ *n* [u] dolarización *f*

dollhouse /ˈdɑːlhaus || ˈdɒlhaʊs/ (AmE) *n* casa *f* de muñecas

dollop /ˈdɑːləp || ˈdɒləp/ *n* (colloq) (served with a spoon) cucharada *f*; (serving, measure) porción *f*

doll's house *n* (BrE) casa *f* de muñecas

dolly /ˈdɑːli || ˈdɒli/ *n* (*pl* **-lies**) (used to or by children) muñequita *f*

dolphin /ˈdɑːlfən || ˈdɒlfɪn/ *n* (*pl* **~s** *or* **~**) delfín *m*

dolt /dəʊlt/ *n* imbécil *mf*

domain /dəˈmeɪn, dəʊ-/ *n* (sphere of influence, activity) campo *m*, esfera *f*; **in the public ~** de(l) dominio público

dome /dəʊm/ *n* (Archit) cúpula *f*

domed /dəʊmd/ *adj* ‹*building*› con cúpula; ‹*roof*› abovedado

domestic[1] /dəˈmestɪk/ *adj*
A [1] (of the home) ‹*life/problems*› doméstico; **they live in ~ bliss** la felicidad de su hogar es perfecta; **~ violence** violencia *f* en el hogar; **~ staff** personal *m* doméstico *or* de servicio [2] (home-loving) casero, hogareño
B ‹*animal*› doméstico
C (Econ, Pol) ‹*affairs/policy/market*› interno; ‹*produce*› nacional; **~ flight** vuelo *m* nacional

domestic[2] *n* (frml) empleado doméstico, empleada doméstica *m,f*, doméstico, -ca *m,f*

domesticate /dəˈmestɪkeɪt/ *vt* domesticar*

domesticated /dəˈmestɪkeɪtəd || dəˈmestɪkeɪtɪd/ *adj*
A ‹*animal/species*› domesticado
B (of person) (*pred*) (hum): **he's not very ~** no es un hombre muy de su casa

domesticity /ˈdəʊmesˈtɪsəti || ˌdɒmesˈtɪsəti, dəʊ-/ *n* [u] (frml *or* hum) domesticidad *f*

domestic science *n* [u] economía *f* doméstica, hogar *m* (Esp)

domicile /ˈdɑːməsaɪl || ˈdɒmɪsaɪl/ *n* (frml) domicilio *m* (frml); **to have ~ in England** estar* domiciliado en Inglaterra (frml)

dominance /ˈdɑːmənəns || ˈdɒmɪnəns/ *n* [u] [1] (supremacy) dominio *m*, dominación *f* [2] (predominance) predominio *m*, preponderancia *f*

dominant /ˈdɑːmənənt/ *adj* [1] (more powerful) ‹*nation/influence*› dominante [2] (predominant) ‹*crop/industry*› predominante, preponderante [3] (Biol, Ecol) dominante

dominate /ˈdɑːməneɪt || ˈdɒmɪneɪt/ *vt* dominar
■ **dominate** *vi* [1] (have control) dominar [2] (predominate) **to ~ (OVER sth)** predominar (SOBRE algo)

domination /ˈdɑːməˈneɪʃən/ *n* [u] dominación *f*

domineer /ˈdɑːməˈnɪr || ˌdɒmɪˈnɪə(r)/ *vi* avasallar

domineering /ˈdɑːməˈnɪrɪŋ/ *adj* dominante

Dominican /dəˈmɪnɪkən/ *adj*
A (Relig) dominico, domínico
B (from the Dominican Republic) dominicano

Dominican Republic /dəˈmɪnɪkən/ *n* **the ~ ~** la República Dominicana

dominion /dəˈmɪnjən/ *n* [u c] (power) (liter) dominio *m*; **to have** *o* **hold ~ over sth/sb** tener* *or* mantener* algo/a algn bajo dominio

domino /ˈdɑːmənəʊ || ˈdɒmɪnəʊ/ *n* (*pl* **-noes**) [1] (counter) ficha *f* de dominó; (*before n*) **~ effect** efecto *m* dominó [2] **dominoes** (+ *sing vb*) dominó *m*

don[1] /dɑːn || dɒn/ *n* (BrE) profesor universitario, profesora universitaria *m,f* (*esp en Oxford y Cambridge*)

don[2] *vt* **-nn-** (put on) (liter) ponerse*

donate /ˈdəʊneɪt, dəʊˈneɪt/ *vt* donar

donation /dəʊˈneɪʃən/ *n* [1] [c] (gift) donativo *m*, donación *f* [2] [u] (act) donación *f*

done[1] /dʌn/ *past p of* **do**[1]

done[2] *adj* (*no comp*)
A (*pred*) [1] (finished) hecho; **I must have this ~ by five o'clock** tengo que tener esto hecho *or* terminado para las cinco; **I'm ~** he terminado; **have** *o* **are you ~ with the iron?** ¿has terminado con la plancha?; **why don't you tell the truth and have** *o* **be ~ with it?** ¿por qué no dices la verdad y acabamos de una vez?; **I'd like to get this over and ~ with as quickly as possible** quisiera quitar esto de en medio cuanto antes [2] (cooked) cocido; ***~ and dusted*** asunto concluido, oleado y sacramentado (Andes)
B (accepted): **it's not ~** *o* **not the ~ thing** no está bien visto

done[3] *interj* ¡trato hecho!, ¡vale! (Esp)

donkey /ˈdɑːŋki || ˈdɒŋki/ *n* (*pl* **-keys**) burro *m*, asno *m*; ***~'s years*** (colloq) siglos *mpl* (fam)

donkey: **~ jacket** *n* (BrE) *chaquetón de trabajo con un refuerzo impermeable en los hombros*; **~ work** *n* (colloq) trabajo *m* pesado

donor /ˈdəʊnər || ˈdəʊnə(r)/ *n* donante *mf*; (*before n*) **~ card** tarjeta *f* de donante

don't[1] /dəʊnt/ **= do not**

don't[2] *n* ▸ **do**[2] **C**

donut /ˈdəʊnʌt/ *n* ▸ **doughnut**

doodad /ˈduːdæd/ *n* (AmE colloq) cosa *f*, chisme *m* (Esp, Méx fam), coso *m* (AmS fam), vaina *f* (Col, Per, Ven fam)

doodah /ˈduːdɑː/ *n* (BrE) ▸ **doodad**

doodle[1] /ˈduːdl/ *vi/t* garabatear, garrapatear

doodle[2] *n* garabato *m*

doom[1] /duːm/ *vt* [1] (fate) (*usu pass*) condenar; **the project was ~ed from the start** el proyecto estaba condenado al fracaso desde el principio [2] **doomed** *past p* ‹*man*› condenado, sentenciado; **~ed to failure** predestinado *or* condenado al fracaso

doom[2] *n* [u] [1] (fate) sino *m* (liter); (death) muerte *f* [2] (ruin) fatalidad *f*; **the prophets of ~** los catastrofistas *or* agoreros

doomsday /ˈduːmzdeɪ/ *n* (arch) día *m* del Juicio Final

door /dɔːr || dɔː(r)/ *n* [1] puerta *f*; **front/back ~** puerta principal/trasera; **double ~s** puerta de dos hojas; **she was at the ~** estaba en la puerta; **the meeting went on behind closed ~s** la reunión se celebró a puerta(s) cerrada(s); **the things people get up to behind closed ~s** lo que hace la gente en la intimidad; **Ⓢ doors open at six** entrada a partir de las seis; **there's someone at the ~** llaman a la puerta; **to answer the ~** abrir* la puerta; ***to darken sb's ~*** poner* los pies en casa de algn; ***to lay sth at sb's ~*** echarle la culpa de algo a algn; ***to lock the***

d

barn* ~ *after the horse is stolen *o* (BrE) ***to lock the stable* ~ *after the horse has bolted*** tomar precauciones cuando ya es tarde *or* asno muerto, la cebada al rabo; ***to show sb the*** ~ mostrarle* *or* enseñarle la puerta a algn, echar a algn 2▸ (doorway, entrance) puerta *f*, entrada *f*; **tickets are available at the** ~ se pueden comprar las localidades en la puerta *or* a la entrada; ***by*** *o* ***through the back*** ~ por la puerta trasera 3▸ (room, building) puerta *f*; **to go from** ~ **to** ~ ir* de puerta en puerta; **out of** ~**s: he's not allowed out of** ~**s** no le permiten salir; **I like having breakfast out of** ~**s** me gusta desayunar al aire libre 4▸ (means of access) puerta *f*; ***when one* ~ *shuts, another opens*** donde una puerta se cierra, otra se abre

d

door: ~**bell** *n* timbre *m*; ~**frame** *n* marco *m* de la puerta; ~**keeper** *n* ▸ ~**man**; ~ **knob** *n* pomo *m* (de la puerta); ~ **knocker** *n* aldaba *f*, llamador *m*; ~**man** /'dɔːrmən / *n* (*pl* **-men** /-mən/) portero *m*; ~**mat** *n* felpudo *m*; **I'm fed up with being a** ~**mat** estoy harta de que me pisoteen; ~**step** *n* umbral *m*; **he turned up on my** ~**step** apareció en mi puerta; ***on the/one's*** ~***step*** a la vuelta de la esquina; ~**stop** *n* cuña *f* (*para mantener la puerta abierta*); ~**-to-door** /'dɔːrtə 'dɔːr / *adj* ‹*delivery/service*› de puerta a puerta, a domicilio; **a** ~**-to-**~ **salesman** un vendedor ambulante (*que va de puerta a puerta*); ~**way** *n* entrada *f*; **the** ~**way to fulfillment** (frml) la senda *or* el camino que lleva a la realización

dope[1] /dəʊp/ *n*
A 1▸ [u] (drugs) (sl) droga *f*, pichicata *f* (CS, Per fam); (cannabis) hachís *m*, chocolate *m* (Esp arg) 2▸ [u] (Sport) estimulante *m*, droga *f*, doping *m*; (*before n*) ‹*test*› antidoping *adj inv*
B [u] (information) (sl) información *f*; **so what's the** ~ **on Brian?** ¿qué hay de Brian? (fam)
C [c] (stupid person) (colloq) imbécil *mf*, tarugo *mf* (fam)

dope[2] *vt* (colloq) ‹*person/racehorse*› dopar (fam), drogar*; ‹*food/drink*› poner* droga en

dopehead /'dəʊphed/ *n* (AmE sl) drogata *mf* (Esp arg), pichicatero, -ra *m,f* (CS, Per fam), grifo, -fa *m,f* (Méx fam)

dopey, dopy /'dəʊpi/ *adj* **dopier, dopiest** (colloq) 1▸ (stupid) lelo (fam), bobo (fam) 2▸ (befuddled) atontado, grogui (fam)

dorm /dɔːrm || dɔːm/ *n* (colloq) ▸ **dormitory**

dormant /'dɔːrmənt || 'dɔːmənt/ *adj*
A 1▸ ‹*animal/plant*› aletargado 2▸ ‹*volcano*› inactivo
B (frml) ‹*idea/emotion*› latente

dormer (window) /'dɔːrmər / *n* buhardilla *f*

dormice /'dɔːrmaɪs || 'dɔːmaɪs/ *pl of* **dormouse**

dormitory /'dɔːrmətɔːri || 'dɔːmɪtri/ *n* (*pl* **-ries**) 1▸ (in school, hostel) dormitorio *m*; (*before n*) ~ **town/suburb** (BrE) ciudad *f*/barrio *m* dormitorio 2▸ (students' residence) (AmE) residencia *f* de estudiantes

Dormobile®, dormobile /'dɔːrməbiːl || 'dɔːməbiːl/ *n* (BrE) cámper *m*

dormouse /'dɔːrmaʊs / *n* (*pl* **-mice** /-maɪs/) lirón *m*

dorsal /'dɔːrsəl || 'dɔːsəl/ *adj* dorsal

DOS /dɑːs || dɒs/ *n* (= **disc-operating system**) DOS *m*

dosage /'dəʊsɪdʒ/ *n* [c u] dosis *f*; ⓢ **dosage: one every three hours** posología: uno cada tres horas

dose[1] /dəʊs/ *n*
A (of medication) dosis *f*; **he's fine in small** ~**s** (hum) se lo puede aguantar en pequeñas dosis; ***like a* ~ *of salts*** (colloq) en menos que canta un gallo (fam)
B (portion, amount) (colloq): **a bad** ~ **of flu** una gripe *or* (Col, Méx) una gripa muy mala

dose[2] *vt*: **I'm all** ~**d up with painkillers** me he tomado no sé cuántos analgésicos

dosh /dɑːʃ || dɒʃ/ *n* (BrE sl) ▸ **dough B**

doss /dɑːs || dɒs/ *vi* (BrE colloq) 1▸ (sleep) dormir* 2▸ (be lazy) haraganear, rascarse* (fam), flojear (fam)

dosser /'dɑːsər || 'dɒsə(r)/ *n* (BrE colloq) 1▸ (tramp) vagabundo, -da *m,f* 2▸ (idler) vago, -ga *m,f*, flojo, -ja *m,f* (fam), manta *mf* (Esp fam)

dosshouse /'dɑːshaʊs || 'dɒshaʊs/ *n* (BrE colloq) albergue *m* (*para vagabundos o pobres*)

dossier /'dɔːsieɪ / *n* dossier *m*, expediente *m*

dost /dʌst/ (arch) *2nd pers sing pres of* **do**[1]

dot[1] /dɑːt || dɒt/ *n* 1▸ (spot) punto *m*; ~ ~ ~ puntos suspensivos; ***on the*** ~ en punto; ***the year*** ~ (BrE) (fam): **since the year** ~ hace (mil) años 2▸ (in Morse code) punto *m*

dot[2] *vt* **-tt-**
A (add dot) puntuar*
B **dotted** *past p* 1▸ ‹*line*› de puntos; **to sign on the** ~**ted line** firmar la línea punteada *or* de puntos 2▸ (Mus) ‹*note*› con puntillo
C (scatter) (*usu pass*) salpicar*; **her family is** ~**ted about all over Europe** su familia está desperdigada por toda Europa

dotage /'dəʊtɪdʒ/ *n* [u] (frml *or* hum): **to be in one's** ~ estar* chocho (fam), chochear (fam)

dot com, dot-com /'dɑːt 'kɑːm || ˌdɒt 'kɒm/ *n* 1▸ (Internet site) sitio *m* web 2▸ (Internet company) puntocom *f*, punto com *f*; (*before n*) ~ **millionaire** millonario *m* puntocom *or* punto com; ~ **revolution** revolución de las puntocom *or* punto com

dote /dəʊt/ *vi* **to** ~ **ON sb** adorar a algn

doth /dʌθ/ (arch) *3rd pers sing pres of* **do**[1]

doting /'dəʊtɪŋ/ *adj*: **his** ~ **mother** su madre, que lo adora

dot matrix *n* matriz *f* de puntos; (*before n*) **dot-matrix printer** impresora *f* matricial

dotty /'dɑːti || 'dɒti/ *adj* **-tier, -tiest** (colloq) ‹*person*› chiflado (fam); ‹*idea*› descabellado

double[1] /'dʌbəl/ *adj*
A 1▸ (twice as much) ‹*amount/portion*› doble; **a** ~ **brandy** un coñac doble; **it's** ~ **that** es el doble de eso; **we get** ~ **pay on Sundays** los domingos nos pagan el doble *or* nos dan paga doble 2▸ (in pair) ‹*consonant*› doble; **my number is** ~ **three seven** ~ **four eight** (esp BrE) mi número es tres tres siete, cuatro cuatro ocho; **it's spelled with a** ~ **'t'** se escribe con dos tes; ~ **bend** curva *f* en S (*read as: curva en ese*); **a** ~**-page spread** un artículo a doble página; **inflation reached** ~ **figures** *o* **digits** la inflación alcanzó/rebasó el 10% 3▸ (for two) ‹*room*› doble; ‹*bed*› de matrimonio, de dos plazas (AmL) 4▸ (folded) doble; **to fold sth** ~ doblar algo por la mitad; **he was bent** ~ **with the pain** se retorcía del dolor
B 1▸ (dual) doble; **a** ~ **purpose** un doble propósito 2▸ (false): **to lead a** ~ **life** llevar una doble vida

double[2] *adv* 1▸ (twice as much) ‹*pay/earn/cost*› el doble; **she spends** ~ **what she earns** gasta el doble de lo que gana 2▸ (two together): **to see** ~ ver* doble

double[3] *n*
A 1▸ (hotel room) doble *f* 2▸ (of spirits): **I'll have a** ~ (deme) uno doble
B (lookalike) doble *mf*
C 1▸ (in bridge, dice, dominoes, darts) doble *m* 2▸ (in baseball) doble *m*, doblete *m* 3▸ (Sport) (double win) doblete *m*
D (pace): **at** *o* **on the** ~ (Mil) a paso ligero; **come here at the** ~**!** ¡ven aquí inmediatamente!

double[4] *vt* 1▸ (increase twofold) ‹*earnings/profits*› doblar, duplicar*; ‹*efforts*› redoblar; **I'd** ~ **the amount of sugar** yo le pondría el doble de azúcar; **I'll** ~ **that offer** yo ofrezco el doble 2▸ (Games) ‹*stake/call/bid*› doblar

■ **double** *vi*
A (increase twofold) ‹‹*price/amount*›› duplicarse*, doblarse
B (have dual role): **the table** ~**s as a desk** la mesa también se usa como escritorio; **somebody** ~**d for him in the dangerous scenes** alguien lo doblaba en las escenas peligrosas

Phrasal verbs

- **double back** [v ▸ adv] ‹‹*person/animal*›› volver* sobre sus pasos; **the path** ~**d back on itself** el camino doblaba sobre sí mismo
- **double up** [v ▸ adv (▸ o)] 1▸ (bend): **to** ~ **up with laughter** morirse* *or* desternillarse de risa; **he was** ~**d up with pain** se retorcía de dolor 2▸ (redouble) (AmE) doblar

double: ~ **act** *n*: **they do/are a** ~ **act** actúan en pareja; ~ **agent** *n* doble agente *mf*; ~**-barreled**, (BrE) ~**-barrelled** /'dʌbəl'bærəld/ *adj* 1▸ ‹*shotgun*› de dos cañones 2▸ (BrE) ‹*surname*› compuesto; ~ **bass** /beɪs/ *n* contrabajo *m*; ~ **bill** *n* programa *m* doble; ~**-book** /'dʌbəl'bʊk/ *vt* (BrE): **the room had been** ~**-booked** la habitación había sido reservada para dos personas distintas; ~ **booking** *n* [u c] (BrE) doble reserva *f*; **we have a** ~ **booking for the 27**th nos hemos comprometido con dos personas a la vez para el 27; ~**-breasted** /'dʌbəl 'brestəd || ˌdʌbəl'brestɪd/ *adj* cruzado; ~**-check** /'dʌbəl-

'tʃek/ *vi* volver* a mirar, verificar* dos veces; **~-check** *vt* ‹*facts/information*› volver* a revisar; **~ chin** *n* papada *f*; **~-click** /'dʌbəl'klɪk/ *vt* ‹*icon/open/close*› hacer* doble clic en, pinchar dos veces en; **~-click** *vi* hacer* doble clic, pinchar dos veces; **to ~-click ON sth** hacer doble clic EN algo, pinchar dos veces EN algo; **~-clutch** /'dʌbəl 'klʌtʃ/ *vi* hacer* un doble embrague; **~ cream** *n* (BrE) crema *f* doble, nata *f* para montar (Esp), doble crema *f* (Méx); **~-cross** /'dʌbəl'krɔːs || ˌdʌbəl'krɒs/ *vt* traicionar

double-dealing[1] /'dʌbəl'diːlɪŋ/ *n* [u] doble juego *m*

double-dealing[2] *adj* (*before n*) maniobrero

double: **~-decker** /'dʌbəl'dekər || ˌdʌbəl'dekə(r)/ *n* **~-decker (bus)** (esp BrE) autobús *m* de dos pisos; **~-decker (sandwich)** sandwich *m* doble *or* de dos pisos; **~-declutch** /'dʌbəldiː'klʌtʃ/ *vi* ▸**double-clutch**; **~ Dutch** *n* [u] (colloq) chino *m* (fam); **~-edged** /'dʌbəl'edʒd/ *adj* ‹*knife/blade/scheme*› de doble filo; ‹*remark/comment*› de doble sentido

double entendre /'duːblɑːn'tɑːndr/ *n* doble sentido *m*

double: **~-entry bookkeeping** /'dʌbəl'entri/ *n* [u] contabilidad *f* por partida doble; **~ feature** *n* programa *m* doble; **~-glaze** /'dʌbəl'gleɪz/ *vt* (BrE) instalar doble ventana en; **~ glazing** *n* [u] (BrE) doble ventana *f*; **~-header** /'dʌbəl'hedər / *n* (AmE) *dos encuentros consecutivos entre los mismos equipos*; **~-jointed** /'dʌbəl'dʒɔɪntəd / *adj*: **he's ~-jointed** tiene articulaciones dobles; **~-lock** /'dʌbəl'lɑːk / *vt* cerrar* con doble llave; **~ meaning** *n* doble sentido *m*; **~-page spread** /'dʌbəl'peɪdʒ/ *n* doble página *f*; **~-parked** *adj* estacionado *or* aparcado en doble fila; **~-quick** *adv* (colloq) volando (fam)

doubles /'dʌbəlz/ *pl n* dobles *mpl*; **the women's/men's/mixed ~** los dobles femeninos *or* damas/masculinos *or* caballeros/mixtos

double: **~ standard** *n*: **to apply** *o* **have ~ standards** aplicar* una ley para unos y otra para otros; **~ whammy** /'hwæmi || 'wæmi/ *n* (colloq) doble palo (fam), doble revés *m*; **we face the ~ whammy of deflation and tax increases** nos enfrentamos al doble palo *or* revés de la deflación y el aumento de los impuestos

doublet /'dʌblət || 'dʌblɪt/ *n* (Clothing) jubón *m*

double: **~-take** /'dʌbəl'teɪk/ *n*: **to do a ~-take** reaccionar (tardíamente); **~-talk** *n* [u] ambigüedades *fpl*; **~think** *n* [u] *aceptación de principios contradictorios*; **~ time** *n* [u] (Busn) paga *f* doble; **on Sundays we're on ~ time** los domingos nos pagan el doble

doubly /'dʌbli/ *adv* ‹*difficult/dangerous/interesting*› doblemente; **make ~ sure you lock the door** asegúrate bien de cerrar la puerta; **it's an awful road, ~ so when it's raining** es una carretera pésima y es dos veces peor cuando llueve

doubt[1] /daʊt/ *n* **1** [u] (uncertainty) duda *f*, incertidumbre *f*; **no ~ she will phone** con seguridad que llama, seguro que llama; **she is, without (a) ~, the best** es, sin duda alguna *or* sin la menor duda *or* indudablemente, la mejor; **his integrity is not in ~** su integridad no está en duda *or* en tela de juicio; **beyond reasonable ~** (Law) más allá de toda duda fundada; **when in ~** en caso de duda; **if in ~, don't go** si estás en (la) duda, no vayas; **to cast ~ on sth** poner* algo en duda **2** [c] (reservation) duda *f*; **I have my ~s** tengo mis dudas

doubt[2] *vt* **1** ‹*fact/truth*› dudar de; **I ~ed my own eyes** no daba crédito a mis (propios) ojos; **there was no ~ing his enthusiasm** no se podía dudar de su entusiasmo **2** (consider unlikely) dudar; **I very much ~ it** lo dudo mucho; **to ~ (THAT)** *o* **if** *o* **whether** dudar QUE (+ *subj*); **I ~ he'll agree** dudo que vaya a acceder

doubter /'daʊtər || 'daʊtə(r)/ *n* escéptico, -ca *m,f*

doubtful /'daʊtfəl/ *adj*

A **1** (full of doubt) ‹*expression/tone*› de indecisión *or* duda, dubitativo; **to be ~ ABOUT** *o* **AS TO sth**: **I am ~ as to its value** tengo mis dudas acerca de su valor **2** (in doubt) dudoso; **the outcome remains ~** el resultado sigue siendo dudoso *or* incierto; **it is ~ THAT** no es seguro que (+ *subj*)

B (questionable) dudoso; **a man of ~ character** un hombre de moral dudosa

doubtfully /'daʊtfəli/ *adv* ‹*say*› sin convicción; ‹*agree*› con reserva

doubting Thomas /'daʊtɪŋ'tɑːməs || ˌdaʊtɪŋ'tɒməs/ *n* escéptico, -ca *m,f*

doubtless /'daʊtləs || 'daʊtlɪs/, **doubtlessly** /-li/ *adv* sin duda, indudablemente

douche /duːʃ/ *n* (jet of liquid) irrigación *f or* ducha *f* vaginal; (syringe) irrigador *m* vaginal

dough /dəʊ/ *n* [u]

A (Culin) masa *f*

B (money) (sl) guita *f* (arg), lana *f* (AmL fam), plata *f* (AmL fam), pasta *f* (Esp fam)

doughnut /'dəʊnʌt/ *n* donut *m*, rosquilla *f*

dour /daʊr, dʊr || dʊə(r)/ *adj* adusto

douse /daʊs/ *vt* ‹*flames*› sofocar*; **he ~d himself with petrol** se roció con gasolina

dove[1] /dʌv/ *n* paloma *f*

dove[2] /dəʊv/ (AmE) *past of* **dive**[1]

dove /dʌv/: **~cote** /'dʌvkɑːt || 'dʌvkɒt/, **~cot** *n* palomar *m*; **~-gray**, (BrE) **~-grey** /'dʌv'greɪ/ *adj* (*pred* **~ gray**) gris perla *adj inv*

dovetail[1] /'dʌvteɪl/ *n* **~ (joint)** (ensambladura *f* a) cola *f* de milano

dovetail[2] *vi* **to ~ (INTO/WITH sth)** encajar (EN/CON algo)

dowager /'daʊədʒər || 'daʊədʒə(r)/ *n*: *viuda de un noble*; (*before n*) **the ~ Duchess of Devon** la duquesa viuda de Devon

dowdy /'daʊdi/ *adj* **-dier, -diest** ‹*woman*› sin gracia, sin estilo; **she wears ~ clothes** se viste con poca gracia

Dow Jones (Index) /'daʊ'dʒəʊnz/ *n* **the ~ ~ (~)** el índice de Dow Jones

> **Dow Jones Average**
>
> También conocido como *Dow Jones Index* (Índice Dow Jones), es un índice que expresado en puntos indica la evolución de la oferta y la demanda de las acciones cotizadas en la Bolsa de Nueva York. Se basa en el precio promedio de ciertas acciones seleccionadas. Se emplea para medir la fuerza del mercado bursátil de EEUU. Se dan cuatro índices, el más importante de los cuales es el *Dow Jones Industrial Average - DJIA* (Índice Dow Jones de Valores Industriales) que refleja la actividad de 30 valores

down[1] /daʊn/ *adv*

A **1** (in downward direction): **to go ~** bajar; **to look ~** mirar (hacia *or* para) abajo; **I ran all the way ~ to the bottom** corrí hasta abajo; **to help sb ~** ayudar a algn a bajar; **from the waist ~** desde la cintura para abajo; **~, boy!** ¡abajo!; **~ with tyranny!** ¡abajo la tiranía! **2** (downstairs): **can you come ~?** ¿puedes bajar?

B **1** (of position) abajo; **~ in the valley** abajo en el valle; **two floors ~** dos pisos más abajo; **~ here/there** aquí/allí (abajo); **~ *under*** (colloq) en Australia **2** (downstairs): **I'm ~ in the cellar** estoy aquí abajo, en el sótano **3** (lowered, pointing downward) bajado; **with the blinds ~** con las persianas bajadas; **face ~** boca abajo **4** (in position): **the carpet isn't ~ yet** aún no han puesto *or* colocado la alfombra **5** (prostrate): **I was ~ with flu all last week** estuve con gripe toda la semana pasada

C (of numbers, volume, intensity): **with the volume ~ low** con el volumen al mínimo; **my temperature is ~ to 38° C** la fiebre me ha bajado a 38° C; **circulation is ~** la circulación ha bajado; **they were two goals ~** iban perdiendo por dos goles; **from the president ~** desde el presidente para abajo

D **1** (in, toward the south): **to go/come ~ south/to London** ir*/venir* al sur/a Londres **2** (at, to another place) (esp BrE): **~ on the farm** en la granja; **I'm going ~ to the library** voy a la biblioteca

E **1** (dismantled, removed): **the room looks bare with the pictures ~** la habitación queda desnuda sin los cuadros; **once this wall is ~** una vez que hayan derribado esta pared; *see also* **burn, cut, fall** *etc* **down** **2** (out of action): **the telephone lines are ~** las líneas de teléfono están cortadas; **the system is ~** (Comput) el sistema no funciona **3** (deflated): **one of your tires is ~** tienes un neumático desinflado

F (in writing): **he's ~ for tomorrow at ten** está apuntado *or* anotado para mañana a las diez; **she's ~ as unemployed** consta *or* figura como desempleada

G (hostile): **to be ~ on sb** (colloq): **my teacher's ~ on me at**

the moment la maestra me tiene ojeriza, la maestra la ha agarrado conmigo (AmL fam)

H **down to** 1 (as far as) hasta; **from the roof ~ to the foundations** desde el tejado hasta los cimientos; **right ~ to the present day** hasta nuestros días 2 (reduced to): **we're ~ to our last tin of tomatoes** nos queda sólo una lata de tomates 3 (to be done by): **the rest is ~ to you** el resto depende de ti

down² *prep*

A 1 (in downward direction): **we ran ~ the slope** corrimos cuesta abajo; **to come ~ the stairs** bajar por la escalera; **it fell ~ a hole** se cayó por un agujero; **you've spilled wine ~ your shirt** te has manchado la camisa de vino 2 (at lower level): **halfway ~ the page** hacia la mitad de la página

B 1 (along): **we drove on ~ the coast/the Mississippi** seguimos por la costa/a lo largo del Misisipí 2 (further along): **the library is just ~ the street** la biblioteca está un poco más allá *or* más adelante 3 (to, in) (BrE colloq): **I saw her ~ the pub yesterday** ayer la vi en el bar

C (through): **~ the centuries** a través de los siglos

down³ *adj*

A (*before n*) (going downward): **the ~ escalator** la escalera mecánica de bajada *or* para bajar

B (depressed) (colloq) (*pred*) deprimido

down⁴ *n*

A [u] 1 (on bird) plumón *m* 2 (on face, body) vello *m*, pelusilla *f* 3 (on plant, fruit) pelusa *f*

B **downs** *pl* (esp BrE Geog) colinas *fpl*

down⁵ *vt* 1 (drink) beberse *or* tomarse rápidamente 2 (knock down) ‹*person*› tumbar, derribar

down: **~ and out** *adj* (colloq) (*pred*): **to be ~ and out** estar* en la miseria; **~-and-out** /'daʊnən'aʊt/, (AmE also) **~-and-outer** /-ər || -ə(r)/ *n* vagabundo, -da *m,f*; **~-at-heel** /'daʊnət'hiːl/ *adj* (esp BrE) (*pred* **~ at heel**) ‹*shoe*› con el tacón *or* (CS, Per) el taco gastado; ‹*person*› desastrado; ‹*place*› venido abajo *or* a menos; **a ~-at-heel cafe** un café de mala muerte; **~beat** *adj* (low-key) relajado; **~cast** *adj* 1 (dejected) alicaído, abatido 2 (directed downward): **with ~cast eyes** con la mirada baja

downer /'daʊnər || 'daʊnə(r)/ *n* (sl) 1 (barbiturate) sedante *m* 2 (depressing experience) (*no pl*) palo *m* (fam); ***to be on a ~*** estar* con la depre (fam)

downfall /'daʊnfɔːl/ *n* (of person) perdición *f*, ruina *f*; (of king, dictator) caída *f*

downgrade¹ /'daʊngreɪd/ *vt* ‹*employee/hotel*› bajar de categoría

downgrade² *n* (AmE) bajada *f*; **a ~ of 1 in 40** una pendiente del 2,5%; ***to be on the ~*** ir* cuesta abajo, ir* de mal en peor

downhearted /'daʊn'hɑːrtəd || ˌdaʊn'hɑːtɪd/ *adj* desanimado, desmoralizado

downhill¹ /'daʊn'hɪl/ *adv* ‹*walk/run*› cuesta abajo; ***to go ~*** ir* cuesta abajo, ir* de mal en peor

downhill² /'daʊnhɪl/ *adj*

A 1 (downward) ‹*path*› cuesta abajo; **a ~ slope** una bajada, una pendiente 2 (in skiing) de descenso contra-reloj

B (easy, pleasant) (*pred*): **it's all ~ from here** de aquí en adelante todo va a marchar sobre ruedas *or* todo va a ser coser y cantar

downhill³ /'daʊnhɪl/ *n* (in skiing) **the ~** el descenso contra-reloj

down-home /'daʊn'həʊm/ *adj* (AmE) ‹*entertainment/sound*› sureño, del sur (*de los EEUU*); ‹*cooking*› casero; ‹*appearance*› rústico; ‹*appeal*› de las cosas sencillas

Downing Street /'daʊnɪŋ/ *n* Downing Street (*calle de Londres donde se encuentra la residencia oficial del primer ministro británico*)

> **Downing Street**
>
> Una calle del céntrico barrio londinense de Westminster. El número 10 es la residencia oficial del Primer Ministro y el número 11 la del *Chancellor of the Exchequer* (equivalente al cargo del Ministro de Economía y Hacienda). Los periodistas utilizan a menudo las expresiones *Downing Street* o *Number 10* para referirse al despacho del Primer Ministro

download /'daʊn'ləʊd/ *vt* (Comput) trasvasar

downloadable /ˌdaʊn'ləʊdəbəl/ *adj* descargable

downmarket¹ /'daʊn'mɑːrkət / *adv*: **the paper has gone ~** el diario ha perdido categoría; (deliberately) el diario se dirige ahora a un sector más popular del público

downmarket² *adj* ‹*newspaper*› popular; ‹*store*› barato

down: **~ payment** *n* cuota *f or* entrega *f* inicial, entrada *f* (Esp), pie *m* (Chi); **~pipe** /'daʊnpaɪp/ *n* (BrE) bajante *m*; **~pour** *n* aguacero *m*, chaparrón *m*

downright¹ /'daʊnraɪt/ *adj* ‹*lie/insolence*› descarado; ‹*crook/liar/rogue*› redomado, de tomo y lomo (fam); ‹*madness*› total y absoluto

downright² *adv*: **it was ~ dangerous!** ¡fue peligrosísimo!; **he was ~ rude!** ¡estuvo de lo más grosero!

down: **~river** /'daʊn'rɪvər || ˌdaʊn'rɪvə(r)/ *adv* río abajo; **~side** *n* inconveniente *m*, desventaja *f*; **on the ~side, it is expensive** tiene el inconveniente de ser caro

downshift *vi* (AmE)

A (change to lower gear) cambiar a una velocidad inferior

B (slow down) ralentizar*

downsize /'daʊnsaɪz/ *vt* (AmE) 1 ‹*design*› reducir* el tamaño de; ‹*dimensions*› reducir* 2 ‹*staff/head-count*› recortar, reducir*

■ **downsize** *vi* hacer* recortes del personal, hacer* recortes en la planilla *or* (Esp) plantilla

Down's syndrome /daʊnz/ *n* [u] síndrome *m* de Down; (*before n*) ‹*child*› afectado por el síndrome de Down

downstairs¹ /'daʊn'sterz || ˌdaʊn'steəz/ *adv* abajo; **the kitchen's ~** la cocina está abajo *or* en el piso de abajo; **he went ~ to open the door** bajó a abrir la puerta; **he fell ~** se cayó por las escaleras

downstairs² *n* planta *f* baja; (*before n*) ‹*neighbor/toilet*› (del piso) de abajo

down: **~state** /'daʊn'steɪt/ *adv* (AmE): **she lives ~state** vive en el sur del estado; **~stream** /'daʊn'striːm/ *adv* río abajo; **~time** *n* [u] tiempo *m* de inactividad; **~-to-earth** /'daʊntu'ɜːrθ || ˌdaʊntə'ɜːθ/ *adj* (*pred* **~ to earth**) realista, práctico

downtown¹ /'daʊn'taʊn/ *n* [u] (AmE) centro *m* (*de la ciudad*); (*before n*) **~ New York** el centro de Nueva York; **a ~ restaurant** un restaurante céntrico *or* del centro

downtown² *adv* (AmE): **to go/live ~** ir* al/vivir en el centro

down: **~trodden** /'daʊn'trɑːdn̩ || 'daʊnˌtrɒdn̩/ *adj* oprimido; **~turn** *n* (Econ): **the economy has taken a ~turn** la situación económica ha empeorado

downward¹ /'daʊnwərd || 'daʊnwəd/ *adj* ‹*direction/pressure*› hacia abajo; ‹*movement/spiral*› descendente; ‹*tendency*› (Fin) a la baja; **a ~ path** un camino en bajada *or* cuesta abajo

downward² /'daʊnwərd || 'daʊnwəd/, (esp BrE) **downwards** /-z/ *adv* hacia abajo

downwind /'daʊn'wɪnd/ *adv* en la dirección del viento

dowry /'daʊəri/ *n* (*pl* **-ries**) dote *f*

doyen /'dɔɪən/ *n* decano, -na *m,f*

doyenne /dɔɪ'en/ *n* decana *f*, gran dama *f*

doz /dʌz/ **= dozen**

doze /dəʊz/ *vi* dormitar

Phrasal verb

• **doze off** [v ▸ adv] quedarse dormido, dormirse*

dozen¹ /'dʌzn̩/ *n* (*pl* **~** *or* **~s**) docena *f*; **four dollars a** *o* **per ~** cuatro dólares la docena; **I got ~s of cards** recibí montones de tarjetas (fam); **I've told him ~s of times** se lo he dicho miles de veces; **baker's ~** docena del fraile

dozen² *adj* docena *f* de; **a ~/two ~ eggs** una docena/dos docenas de huevos

dozy /'dəʊzi/ *adj* **dozier, doziest** 1 (sleepy) amodorrado, adormilado 2 (quiet) dormido; **a ~ village** un pueblecito dormido 3 (stupid) (BrE colloq) tonto, abombado (AmL fam)

DPhil /'diː'fɪl/ *n* (BrE) (**= Doctor of Philosophy**) ▸**PhD**

Dr /'dɑːktər || 'dɒktə(r)/ (title) (**= Doctor**) Dr., Dra.

drab /dræb/ *adj* 1 (dull) ‹*clothing/decor/appearance*› soso, sin gracia; **a ~ green** un verde apagado 2 (humdrum) ‹*life/occupation*› gris, monótono

draft¹ /dræft || drɑːft/ *n*

A [c] (BrE) **draught** (cold air) corriente *f* de aire

B [c] (formulation) versión *f*; **the final ~ of my speech** la ver-

sión final de mi discurso; **a rough ~** un borrador; (*before n*) **~ bill** anteproyecto *m* de ley
C (Fin) cheque *m or* efecto *m* bancario
D (AmE) **the ~** (Mil) el llamamiento *or* (AmL tb) llamado a filas

draft² *vt*
A (formulate) ‹*document/contract/letter*› redactar el borrador de; ‹*speech*› preparar
B (conscript) (AmE) reclutar, llamar a filas

draft: **~ dodger** *n* (AmE) prófugo, -ga *m,f*, insumiso *m* (Esp), remiso *m* (Andes); **~proof** *adj* hermético

draftsman, (BrE) **draughtsman** /'dræftsmən || 'drɑ:ftsmən/ *n* (*pl* **-men** /-mən/) dibujante *mf*

drafty, (BrE) **draughty** /'dræfti || 'drɑ:fti/ *adj* **-tier, -tiest** con corrientes de aire

drag¹ /dræg/ **-gg-** *vt*
A [1] (haul) arrastrar, llevar a rastras; ***to ~ sb's name*** *o* ***reputation through the mud*** *o* ***dirt*** cubrir* de fango *or* manchar el buen nombre de algn [2] (force) (colloq): **I ~ged myself out of bed** me forcé a salir de la cama; **how did I get ~ged into this ridiculous plan?** ¿cómo me dejé meter en un plan tan absurdo?; **I couldn't ~ myself away** no tenía fuerzas para irme
B (allow to trail) ‹*tail/garment/anchor*› arrastrar; **I don't want to ~ the kids around with me all day** no quiero andar con los niños a cuestas todo el día; ***to ~ one's feet*** *o* ***heels*** dar(le)* largas al asunto
C (dredge) ‹*river/lake*› dragar*
■ **drag** *vi*
A [1] (trail) «*anchor*» garrar; «*coat*» arrastrar [2] (lag) rezagarse*
B (go on slowly) «*work/conversation*» hacerse* pesado; «*film/play*» hacerse* largo
C (race cars) (AmE colloq) echarse un pique (fam)

Phrasal verbs
• **drag down** [v ▸ o ▸ adv, v ▸ adv ▸ o] (morally) arrastrar; **he tries to ~ everyone down to his level** quiere arrastrar a los demás a su nivel
• **drag in** [v ▸ o ▸ adv, v ▸ adv ▸ o] ‹*subject/topic*› sacar* a colación
• **drag on** [v ▸ adv] alargarse* (*interminablemente*)
• **drag out** [v ▸ o ▸ adv, v ▸ adv ▸ o] alargar*
• **drag up** [v ▸ o ▸ adv, v ▸ adv ▸ o] [1] (recall) sacar* a relucir [2] ‹*child*› (BrE hum) criar*

drag² *n* (*no pl*)
A (tiresome thing): **what a ~!** ¡qué lata! (fam)
B [u] (resistant force) resistencia *f* al avance
C [c] (on cigarette) (colloq) pitada *f* (AmL), calada *f* (Esp)
D [u] (women's clothes): **in ~** vestido de mujer; (*before n*) ‹*act/show*› de travestis *or* transformistas; **~ queen** reinona *f* (arg)
E (street) (AmE sl): **the main ~** la calle principal

dragnet /'drægnet/ *n*
A (police operation) operación *f or* (AmL tb) operativo *m* policial de captura
B (large net) red *f* barredera

dragon /'drægən/ *n* (Myth) dragón *m*

dragonfly /'drægənflaɪ/ *n* (*pl* **-flies**) libélula *f*, caballito *m* del diablo, matapiojos *m* (Andes)

dragoon¹ /drə'gu:n/ *n* dragón *m*

dragoon² *vt* **to ~ sb** INTO **-ING** presionar a algn PARA QUE (+ *subj*)

drain¹ /dreɪn/ *n*
A [1] (pipe) sumidero *m*, resumidero *m* (AmL); **the ~s** (of town) el alcantarillado; (of building) las tuberías de desagüe [2] (grid) (BrE) sumidero *m*, resumidero *m* (AmL)
B (plughole) desagüe *m*; ***that's money down the ~*** eso es tirar el dinero
C (*no pl*) [1] (cause of depletion) **a ~** ON **sth**: **a ~ on the country's resources** una sangría para el país; **the extra work is an enormous ~ on my energy** el trabajo extra me está agotando [2] (outflow, loss) fuga *f*

drain² *vt*
A [1] ‹*container/tank*› vaciar*; ‹*land/swamp*› drenar, avenar; ‹*blood*› drenar; ‹*sap/water*› extraer* [2] (Culin) ‹*vegetables/pasta*› escurrir, colar* [3] (Med) drenar
B (drink up) ‹*glass/cup*› vaciar*, apurar
C (consume, exhaust) ‹*resources/strength*› agotar, consumir
■ **drain** *vi* [1] (dry) «*dishes*» escurrir(se) [2] (disappear): **all the strength seemed to ~ from my limbs** los brazos y las piernas se me quedaron como sin fuerzas [3] (discharge) «*pipes/river*» desaguar*

Phrasal verbs
• **drain away** [v ▸ adv] [1] «*liquid*»: **the bathwater takes ages to ~ away** la bañera tarda mucho en vaciarse; **the rain gradually ~s away into the soil** la lluvia se va filtrando en la tierra [2] «*strength/resources*» irse* agotando
• **drain off**
A [v ▸ adv] «*rainwater*» escurrirse
B [v ▸ o ▸ adv, v ▸ adv ▸ o] [1] (Culin) escurrir [2] (Tech) extraer*

drainage /'dreɪnɪdʒ/ *n* [u] [1] (of household waste) desagüe *m* (de aguas residuales); (of rainwater) canalización *f* (de agua de lluvia); (*before n*) **~ system** (red *f* de) alcantarillado *m* [2] (of fields, marshes) drenaje *m*, avenamiento *m*

drainboard /'dreɪnbɔ:rd / *n* (AmE) escurridero *m*

drained /dreɪnd/ *adj* agotado, exhausto

draining board /'dreɪnɪŋ/ *n* (BrE) escurridero *m*

drainpipe /'dreɪnpaɪp/ *n* tubo *m or* caño *m* del desagüe, bajante *f*; (*before n*) **~ trousers** (BrE) pantalón *m* pitillo

drake /dreɪk/ *n* pato *m* (macho)

dram /dræm/ *n* [1] (of Scotch, spirits) (esp Scot) copita *f* [2] (fluid measure) *medida de capacidad equivalente a 1,77cc*

drama /'drɑ:mə/ *n* (*pl* **-mas**)
A (Theat) [1] [c] (play) obra *f* dramática, drama *m* [2] [u] (plays collectively) teatro *m*, drama *m*; (dramatic art) arte *m* dramático
B [1] [u] (excitement) dramatismo *m* [2] [c] (exciting event, story) (journ): **hijack ~ continues** continúan los dramáticos sucesos en torno al secuestro

dramatic /drə'mætɪk/ *adj*
A [1] (Theat) (*before n*) dramático, teatral [2] (exaggerated) ‹*pause/entrance*› dramático, histriónico
D [1] (striking) ‹*change/improvement*› espectacular, drástico; (increase) espectacular [2] (momentous) ‹*events/development*› dramático

dramatically /drə'mætɪkli/ *adv* [1] (exaggeratedly) ‹*pause/announce*› dramáticamente, de manera teatral *or* histriónica [2] (strikingly) ‹*change/improve/increase*› de manera espectacular

dramatics /drə'mætɪks/ *n* [1] (Theat) (+ *sing vb*): **amateur ~** teatro *m* amateur *or* de aficionados [2] (histrionics) (+ *pl vb*): **his ~ are very wearing** hace tanto teatro *or* es tan teatral que uno llega a cansarse

dramatis personae /'dræmətəspər'səʊni: / *pl n* personajes *mpl* (*de una obra teatral*)

dramatist /'dræmətɪst/ *n* dramaturgo, -ga *m,f*

dramatization /'dræmətə'zeɪʃən || ˌdræmətaɪ'zeɪʃən/ *n* [u c] (Theat) dramatización *f*, adaptación *f* teatral

dramatize /'dræmətaɪz/ *vt*
A ‹*story/novel*› (Theat) dramatizar*, hacer* una adaptación teatral de; (Cin) llevar al cine
B (exaggerate) ‹*situation/event*› dramatizar*, exagerar

drank /dræŋk/ *past of* **drink²**

drape /dreɪp/ *vt* [1] (arrange): **they ~d a flag over the tomb** colocaron una bandera formando pliegues sobre la tumba; **she ~d herself over the sofa** se tendió sobre el sofá [2] (cover) cubrir*

drapery /'dreɪpəri/ *n* (*pl* **-ries**)
A (BrE) [1] [u] (merchandise) mercería *f* [2] [c] (shop) mercería *f*, pañería *f* (ant)
B [u] (covering) (*often pl*) colgaduras *fpl*

drapes /dreɪps/ *pl n* (AmE) cortinas *fpl*

drastic /'dræstɪk/ *adj* [1] (radical) ‹*solution/measure*› drástico, radical [2] (striking) ‹*change/effect*› radical, drástico, espectacular

drastically /'dræstɪkli/ *adv* drásticamente

drat /dræt/ *interj* (colloq): **~ (it)!** ¡caray! (fam)

draught /dræft || drɑ:ft/ *n*
A [u] (storage under pressure): **beer on ~** cerveza *f* de barril; (*before n*) ‹*beer/cider*› de barril
B [c] (liter) [1] (of water, beer) trago *m* [2] (of drug): **a sleeping ~** una pócima para dormir
C (BrE) ▸ **draft¹ A**

draught: **~ excluder** /ɪk'sklu:dər || ɪk'sklu:də(r)/ *n* (BrE) burlete *m*; **~proof** *adj* ▸ **draftproof**

draughts /dræfts || drɑːfts/ *n* (BrE) (+ *sing vb*) damas *fpl*

draughtsman /'dræftsmən / *n* (BrE) ▸**draftsman**

draughty /'dræfti || 'drɑːfti/ *adj* ▸**drafty**

draw¹ /drɔː/ (*past* **drew**; *past p* **drawn**) *vt*

A [1] (move by pulling) ‹*curtains/bolt*› (open) descorrer; (shut) correr; ‹*bow*› tensar [2] (in specified direction): **he drew her aside** *o* **to one side** la llevó a un lado, la llevó aparte; **to ∼ one's chair up** acerar* *or* arrimar la silla a la mesa [3] (pull along) ‹*cart/sled*› tirar de, arrastrar

B [1] (pull out) ‹*tooth/cork*› sacar*, extraer* (frml); ‹*gun*› desenfundar, sacar*; ‹*sword*› desenvainar, sacar* [2] (cause to flow) sacar*; **to ∼ blood** sacar* sangre, hacer* sangrar; **to ∼ breath** respirar; **to ∼ water from a well** sacar* agua de un pozo [3] (Games) ‹*card/domino*› sacar*, robar [4] (in contest, tournament): **Italy has been ∼n to play France** a Italia le ha tocado en el sorteo jugar contra Francia

C [1] (Fin) ‹*salary/pension*› cobrar, percibir (frml); ‹*check*› girar, librar; **to ∼ money from** *o* **out of the bank** retirar *or* sacar* dinero del banco [2] (derive) ‹*strength/lesson*› sacar*; **she drew comfort from the fact that ...** se consoló pensando que ...

D (establish) ‹*distinction/parallel*› establecer*

E [1] (attract) ‹*customers/crowd*› atraer*; **to be ∼n to sb/sth** sentirse* atraído por algn/algo [2] (elicit) ‹*praise*› conseguir*; ‹*criticism/protest*› provocar*, suscitar; **to ∼ tears/a smile from sb** hacer* llorar/hacer* sonreír a algn; **I asked him about it, but he wouldn't be ∼n** se lo pregunté, pero se negó a decir nada

F (sketch) ‹*flower/picture*› dibujar; ‹*line*› trazar*

G (BrE Games, Sport) empatar

■ **draw** *vi*

A (move): **to ∼ close to** *o* **near (to) sth/sb** acercarse* a algo/algn; **to ∼ to an end** *o* **a close** terminar, finalizar* (frml); **the train drew out of/into the station** el tren salió de/entró en la estación; **to ∼ ahead of sb/sth** adelantarse a algn/algo

B (Art) dibujar

C (BrE Games, Sport) empatar; (in chess game) hacer* tablas

D (take in air) «*chimney/cigar*» tirar

(Phrasal verbs)

• **draw away** [v ▸ adv] [1] (move off) **to ∼ away FROM sth** alejarse DE algo [2] (in competition, race) **to ∼ away FROM sb** alejarse *or* distanciarse DE algn, dejar atrás a algn [3] (recoil) **to ∼ away (FROM sb/sth)** apartarse (DE algn/algo)

• **draw back** [v ▸ adv] [1] (retreat) retirarse [2] (recoil) retroceder

• **draw down** [v ▸ o ▸ adv, v ▸ adv ▸ o] ‹*blind*› bajar

• **draw in**

A [v ▸ o ▸ adv, v ▸ adv ▸ o] [1] (retract) ‹*claws*› esconder, retraer* [2] (into quarrel, war) involucrar; (into conversation) darle* participación a

B [v ▸ adv] [1] (arrive) «*train*» llegar* [2] «*days/nights*» hacerse* más corto

• **draw off** [v ▸ o ▸ adv, v ▸ adv ▸ o] [1] (drain) ‹*beer/sap*› sacar*, extraer* (frml) [2] (divert) ‹*pursuers*› confundir [3] (remove) ‹*glove/stocking*› quitarse

• **draw on**

A [v ▸ o ▸ adv, v ▸ adv ▸ o] ‹*glove/stocking*› ponerse*

B [v ▸ prep ▸ o] (make use of) ‹*resources/reserves*› recurrir a, hacer* uso de; **she drew on her own experiences** se inspiró en sus propias experiencias

C [v ▸ adv] (approach, advance): **night is ∼ing on** está anocheciendo

• **draw out**

A [v ▸ adv] [1] (depart) «*train*» salir* [2] (become longer) hacerse* más largo

B [v ▸ o ▸ adv, v ▸ adv ▸ o] [1] (prolong) alargar*, estirar [2] (extract, remove) ‹*tooth/thorn*› sacar*, extraer* (frml); ‹*wallet/handkerchief*› sacar*; ‹*information*› sacar*, sonsacar*; ‹*confession*› arrancar* [3] (withdraw) ‹*money*› sacar*

C [v ▸ o ▸ adv (▸ prep ▸ o)] (persuade to talk): **see if you can ∼ him out of himself** a ver si logras que se muestre un poco más comunicativo

• **draw together**

A [v ▸ o ▸ adv, v ▸ adv ▸ o] reunir, juntar

B [v ▸ adv] unirse, acercarse*

• **draw up**

A [v ▸ adv] «*car*» detenerse*, parar

B [v ▸ o ▸ adv, v ▸ adv ▸ o] [1] (prepare, draft) ‹*contract/treaty*› redactar, preparar; ‹*list*› hacer* [2] (arrange in formation) ‹*troops/competitors*› alinear, formar [3] (bring near) ‹*chair*› acercar*, arrimar

C [v ▸ o ▸ adv] (straighten oneself): **to ∼ oneself up** erguirse*

draw² *n*

A (raffle) sorteo *m*; **a prize ∼** un sorteo de premios

B (tie) (Games, Sport) empate *m*; **the game ended in a ∼** el partido acabó en empate

C (attraction) (colloq) gancho *m* (fam), atracción *f*

D (of handgun): **the fastest ∼ in Texas** el pistolero más rápido de Texas; ***to be quick on the ∼*** (with gun) ser* rápido en desenfundar; (with reply) pescarlas* al vuelo (fam)

draw: **∼back** *n* inconveniente *m*, desventaja *f*; **∼bridge** *n* puente *m* levadizo

drawee /drɔː'iː/ *n* librado, -da *m,f*, girado, -da *m,f*

drawer *n*

A /drɔːr || 'drɔː(r)/ (in furniture) cajón *m*, gaveta *f* (esp AmC, Méx); *see also* **top drawer**

B /'drɔːər / (of check) librador, -dora *m,f*, girador, -dora *m,f*

C /'drɔːər || 'drɔːə(r)/ (Art) dibujante *mf*

D **drawers** /drɔːrz || drɔːz/ *pl* (Clothing) calzones *mpl*

drawing /'drɔːɪŋ/ *n* [c u] dibujo *m*

drawing: **∼ board** *n* tablero *m*, mesa *f* de dibujo; ***back to the ∼ board!*** ¡vuelta a empezar!; **∼ pin** *n* (BrE) ▸**thumbtack**; **∼ room** *n* sala *f*, salón *m*

drawl¹ /drɔːl/ *vi* hablar arrastrando las palabras

■ **drawl** *vt* decir* arrastrando las palabras

drawl² *n*: *acento caracterizado por la longitud de las vocales*; **a Southern ∼** un acento sureño

drawn¹ /drɔːn/ *past p of* **draw¹**

drawn² *adj* ‹*features/face*› demacrado

drawn-out /'drɔːn'aʊt/ *adj* larguísimo, interminable

drawstring /'drɔːstrɪŋ/ *n* cordón *m* (*del que se tira para cerrar algo*); (*before n*) ‹*bag/waist*› fruncido con un cordón o una cinta

dray /dreɪ/ *n* carro *m* fuerte

dread¹ /dred/ *vt* tenerle* terror *or* pavor a; **I ∼ to think what might have happened** no quiero ni pensar en lo que podría haber pasado

dread² *n* [u] terror *m*; **∼ OF sth**: **we lived in constant ∼ of being discovered** vivíamos temiendo constantemente que nos descubrieran

dreadful /'dredfəl/ *adj* ‹*news/experience/weather*› espantoso, terrible; **how ∼ for you!** ¡qué horror! ¡pobrecito!; **I feel ∼** me siento pésimo *or* (fam) fatal; **I feel ∼ about not having helped** me siento muy mal por no haber ayudado; **you look ∼** tienes muy mala cara

dreadfully /'dredfəli/ *adv* ‹*upset/late*› terriblemente, enormemente; ‹*write/sing*› espantosamente (mal); **I'm ∼ sorry** lo siento muchísimo *or* en el alma

dreadlocks /'dredlɑːks || 'dredlɒks/ *pl n*: *rizos al estilo de los rastafaris*

dream¹ /driːm/ *n*

A [1] (while sleeping) sueño *m*; **to have a ∼ about sth/sb** soñar* con algo/algn; **a bad ∼** una pesadilla; **sweet ∼s!** ¡que duermas bien!, ¡que sueñes con los angelitos! (hum) [2] (daydream) sueño *m*, ensueño *m*; **he goes around in a ∼** vive en las nubes

B (fantasy, ideal, aspiration) sueño *m*; **it was beyond my wildest ∼s** ni en sueños lo hubiera imaginado; **a ∼ come true** un sueño hecho realidad; **I had ∼s of being famous** soñaba con la fama *or* con hacerme famoso; (*before n*) **he lives in a ∼ world** vive de ilusiones, vive en las nubes; **your ∼ home** la casa de sus sueños

C (sth wonderful) (colloq) sueño *m*; ***to go like a ∼*** «*event*» salir* a las mil maravillas; «*car*» funcionar de maravilla

dream² (*past & past p* **dreamed** *or* (BrE also) **dreamt** /dremt/) *vi*

A [1] (in sleep) soñar*; **to ∼ ABOUT** *o* **OF sth/sb** soñar* CON algo/algn [2] (daydream) soñar* (despierto), estar* en las nubes

B [1] (imagine) **to ∼ OF sth** soñar* CON algo; **I ∼ed of going to live in the country** soñaba con irme a vivir al campo [2] (contemplate) **(not) to ∼ OF sth/-ING**: **would you do that? — I wouldn't ∼ of it!** ¿harías eso? — ¡ni pensarlo! *or* ¡ni en sueños!; **I wouldn't ∼ of borrowing money** ni se me ocurriría pedir dinero prestado

■ **dream** *vt*

A (in sleep) soñar*; **I ~ed (that) I was drowning** soñé que me ahogaba
B (imagine) (*usu neg*) imaginarse; **I never ~ed he'd be so rude** nunca (me) imaginé que iba a ser tan grosero

Phrasal verbs
- **dream away** [v ▸ o ▸ adv, v ▸ adv ▸ o] pasarse soñando
- **dream up** [v ▸ o ▸ adv, v ▸ adv ▸ o] ‹*plan*› idear

dreamer /ˈdri:mər || ˈdri:mə(r)/ *n* soñador, -dora *m,f*
dreamless /ˈdri:mləs || ˈdri:mlɪs/ *adj* ‹*sleep*› tranquilo
dreamt /dremt/ (BrE) *past & past p of* **dream²**
dreamy /ˈdri:mi/ *adj* **-mier, -miest** 1 (abstracted) ‹*person*› soñador, fantasioso; ‹*gaze*› distraído 2 ‹*music*› etéreo, sutil
dreary /ˈdrɪri || ˈdrɪəri/ *adj* **-rier, -riest** 1 ‹*room/landscape*› deprimente, lóbrego, sombrío; ‹*weather*› gris, deprimente 2 ‹*work/routine*› monótono, aburrido, aburridor (AmL)
dredge /dredʒ/ *vt* dragar*

Phrasal verb
- **dredge up** [v ▸ o ▸ adv, v ▸ adv ▸ o] ‹*mud/sand*› dragar*; ‹*story/scandal*› desenterrar*, sacar* a relucir

dredger /ˈdredʒər || ˈdredʒə(r)/ *n* (machine) draga *f*; (vessel) dragador *m*, draga *f*
dregs /dregz/ *pl n* (sediment) posos *mpl*, cunchos *mpl* (Col), conchos *mpl* (Chi); **the ~ of society** la escoria de la sociedad
drench /drentʃ/ *vt* (*usu pass*) empapar; **to get ~ed** empaparse
drenching /ˈdrentʃɪŋ/ *n* (*no p*): **to get a ~** empaparse
dress¹ /dres/ *n*
A [c] (for woman, girl) vestido *m*
B [u] (clothing, style of dressing): **they arrived in formal ~** llegaron vestidos de etiqueta; **they adopted Western ~** adoptaron el modo de vestir *or* la vestimenta occidental; (*before n*) **she has no ~ sense** tiene mal gusto para vestirse
dress² *vt*
A (put clothes on) vestir*; **to get ~ed** vestirse*; **I'm not ~ed** no estoy vestido; **he was ~ed in white** iba (vestido) de blanco
B (Culin) 1 (prepare) ‹*chicken/fish*› preparar; **~ed crab** cangrejo *m* preparado 2 (season) ‹*salad*› aliñar
C (Med) ‹*wound*› vendar
■ **dress** *vi* 1 (put on, wear clothes) vestirse*; **he always ~es in black** siempre (se) viste de negro; **she ~es very well** (se) viste muy bien 2 (dress formally): **to ~ for dinner** cambiarse para cenar

Phrasal verb
- **dress up**
A [v ▸ adv] 1 (dress smartly) ponerse* elegante; ***all ~ed up and no place*** *o* (BrE) ***nowhere to go*** compuesta y sin novio 2 (in fancy dress) disfrazarse*; **to ~ up AS sth** disfrazarse* DE algo
B [v ▸ o ▸ adv, v ▸ adv ▸ o] ‹*idea/plan*› disfrazar*; **criticism ~ed up as advice** críticas disfrazadas de consejos

dressage /drəˈsɑ:ʒ || ˈdresɑ:ʒ/ *n* [u] *método de adiestramiento de caballos para que ejecuten ciertas maniobras*
dress circle *n* platea *f* alta
dress-down /ˈdresˈdaʊn/ *n* ropa *f* informal; (*before n*) ‹*day*› de ropa informal
dresser /ˈdresər || ˈdresə(r)/ *n*
A 1 (person): **he's a sloppy/stylish ~** (se) viste con mucho descuido/estilo 2 (Theat) ayudante, -ta *m,f* de camerino
B 1 (in bedroom) (AmE) tocador *m* 2 (in kitchen) (BrE) aparador *m*
dressing /ˈdresɪŋ/ *n*
A [c] (Med) apósito *m*, gasa *f*; (bandage) vendaje *m*
B [u c] (Culin) (for salad) aliño *m*, aderezo *m*; (stuffing) (AmE) relleno *m*
dressing: **~-down** /ˈdresɪŋˈdaʊn/ *n* (*no pl*) reprimenda *f*; **~ gown** *n* bata *f*, salto *m* de cama (CS); (of toweling) albornoz *m*, salida *f* de baño; **~ room** *n* (Theat) camerino *m*; (in house) vestidor *m*; **~ table** *n* tocador *m*
dress: **~maker** *n* modista *mf*; (designer) modisto, -ta *m,f*; **~making** *n* [u] costura *f*; (*before n*) **~making course** curso *m* de corte y confección; **~ rehearsal** *n* ensayo *m* general; **~ shirt** *n* camisa *f* de etiqueta; **~ suit** *n* traje *m* de etiqueta; **~ uniform** *n* [u c] uniforme *m* de gala

dressy /ˈdresi/ *adj* **-sier, -siest** elegante
drew /dru:/ *past of* **draw¹**
dribble¹ /ˈdrɪbəl/ *vi*
A (drool) babear; **he ~s** se le cae la baba, babea
B (Sport) driblar, driblear
■ **dribble** *vt*
A : **to ~ saliva** babear
B (Sport): **he ~d the ball past** *o* **around a defender** dribló *or* dribleó *or* regateó a un defensa
dribble² *n* [u] (saliva) baba *f*
dribs and drabs /ˈdrɪbzənˈdræbz/ *pl n*: **in ~ ~ ~** poquito a poco
dried¹ /draɪd/ *past & past p of* **dry²**
dried² *adj* ‹*figs/flowers*› seco; ‹*fish*› salado, seco; ‹*milk/eggs*› en polvo
drier /ˈdraɪər || ˈdraɪə(r)/ *n* ▸ **dryer**
drift¹ /drɪft/ *vi*
A 1 (on water) *moverse empujado por la corriente* 2 (be adrift) ‹‹*boat/person*›› ir* a la deriva; **the boat ~ed off course** el barco se desvió de su rumbo 3 (in air) ‹‹*balloon*›› *moverse empujado por el viento*
B (proceed aimlessly): **he ~ed from job to job** iba sin rumbo de un trabajo a otro; **the crowd began to ~ away** la muchedumbre comenzó a dispersarse; **to ~ apart** ‹‹*couple/friends*›› distanciarse
C (pile up) ‹‹*sand/snow*›› amontonarse
drift² *n*
A [c] (of sand) montón *m*; (of snow) ventisquero *m*
B (meaning) (*no pl*) sentido *m*; **I didn't quite catch your ~** no entendí *or* capté muy bien lo que querías decir; **if you get my ~** tú ya me entiendes
C (movement): **the ~ from the land** el éxodo rural; **the ~ of public opinion** el cambio en la opinión pública
drifter /ˈdrɪftər || ˈdrɪftə(r)/ *n*
A (person): **he's a ~** va dando tumbos por la vida
B (boat) trainera *f*
driftwood /ˈdrɪftwʊd/ *n* [u] *madera, tablas etc que flotan en el mar a la deriva o que arrastra el mar hasta la playa*
drill¹ /drɪl/ *n*
A [c] (*electric o power ~*) taladradora *f*, taladro *m*; (*hand ~*) taladro *m* (manual); (Dent) torno *m*, fresa *f*; (Eng, Min) perforadora *f*, barreno *m*; (drill head) broca *f*
B 1 [u] (Mil) instrucción *f* 2 [c] (Educ) ejercicio *m* 3 [u c] (rehearsal): **fire ~** simulacro *m* de incendio 4 [u] (correct procedure) (BrE colloq): **what's the ~?** ¿qué se hace?
C [u] (Tex) dril *m*
drill² *vt*
A ‹*hole*› hacer*, perforar; ‹*wood/metal*› taladrar, perforar, barrenar; ‹*tooth*› trabajar *or* limpiar con la fresa
B 1 (Mil) ‹*soldiers*› instruir* 2 **to ~ sth INTO sb** inculcarle* algo A algn
■ **drill** *vi* perforar, hacer* perforaciones; **to ~ for oil/water** perforar en busca de petróleo/agua
drilling platform /ˈdrɪlɪŋ/ *n* plataforma *f* de perforación
drily /ˈdraɪli/ *adv* secamente, con sequedad
drink¹ /drɪŋk/ *n*
A [u] 1 (any liquid) bebida *f* 2 (alcohol) bebida *f*; **to drive sb/to take to ~** llevar a algn/darse* a la bebida
B [c] 1 (amount drunk, served, sold): **have a ~ of water/milk** bebe *or* (esp AmL) toma un poco de agua/leche 2 (alcoholic) copa *f*, trago *m* (fam); **to have a ~** tomar una copa; **the ~s are on me!** ¡yo invito!
drink² (*past* **drank**; *past p* **drunk**) *vt* beber, tomar (esp AmL); **give me something to ~** dame algo de beber *or* (esp AmL) para tomar
■ *v refl*: **he drank himself to death** lo mató la bebida
■ **drink** *vi*
A (swallow) beber, tomar (esp AmL)
B 1 (consume alcohol) beber, tomar (AmL); **I don't ~** no bebo, no tomo (alcohol) (AmL) 2 (toast) **to ~ TO sb** brindar POR algn; **I'll ~ to that!** ¡brindo por que así sea!

Phrasal verbs
- **drink in** [v ▸ o ▸ adv, v ▸ adv ▸ o] ‹*scenery*› empaparse de; **plants ~ in water through their roots** las plantas absorben el agua a través de sus raíces; **we drank in the fresh air** respiramos el aire puro
- **drink up**

d

A [v ▸ adv] bebérselo *or* (esp AmL) tomárselo todo, terminar su (*or* mi *etc*) copa (*or* leche *etc*)
B [v ▸ o ▸ adv, v ▸ adv ▸ o] beberse, tomarse (esp AmL)

drinkable /'drɪŋkəbəl/ *adj* ‹water› potable; **this is not ~!** ¡esto no se puede beber!

drink-driving /'drɪŋk'draɪvɪŋ/ *n* (BrE) ▸**drunk driving**

drinker /'drɪŋkər || 'drɪŋkə(r)/ *n*: **he's a heavy ~** es un gran bebedor *or* un bebedor empedernido; **I'm a beer ~ myself** yo prefiero la cerveza

drinking /'drɪŋkɪŋ/ *n* [u] **1** (of liquid) beber **2** (of alcohol): **his ~ is causing concern** lo mucho que bebe está causando preocupación

drinking: **~ chocolate** *n* [u] chocolate *m* en polvo; **~ fountain** *n* fuente *f* (*de agua potable*), bebedero *m* (CS, Méx); **~ water** *n* [u] agua *f*‡ potable

drip[1] /drɪp/ **-pp-** *vi* **1** (fall in drops): **water was ~ping from the ceiling** el techo goteaba, caían gotas del techo; **he had blood ~ping from his nose** le goteaba sangre de la nariz **2** (let drops fall) «*washing/hair*» chorrear, gotear; «*faucet/tap*» gotear; **I'm ~ping with sweat** estoy chorreando de sudor **3** (display) **to ~ WITH sth**: **she was ~ping with diamonds** iba cubierta de brillantes
■ **drip** *vt*: **you're ~ping coffee down your shirt** te estás manchando la camisa de café, te estás chorreando la camisa con el café (AmL)

drip[2] *n*
A (of rainwater, tap) (*no pl*) goteo *m*; **the steady ~, ~ of the rain** el continuo gotear de la lluvia
B (Med) suero *m*, gota a gota *m*; **he's on a ~** le han puesto suero *or* el gota a gota
C (ineffectual person) (colloq) soso, -sa *m,f* (fam)

drip-dry /'drɪp'draɪ/ *adj* ‹*fabric/garment*› de lava y pon, de lavar y poner

dripping[1] /'drɪpɪŋ/ *n* [u] (BrE) *grasa de carne asada que se usa para cocinar y untar en el pan*

dripping[2] *adj* (colloq) empapado; (*as intensifier*) **to be ~ wet** estar* chorreando *or* empapado

drive[1] /draɪv/ (*past* **drove**; *past p* **driven**) *vt*
A (Transp) **1** ‹*car/bus/train*› manejar *or* (Esp) conducir*; ‹*racing car/power boat*› pilotar, pilotear; **she ~s a Renault** tiene un Renault **2** (convey in vehicle) llevar en coche; **she drove me home** me llevó en coche a casa
B **1** (cause to move) (+ *adv compl*): **the Indians were ~n off their land** los indios fueron expulsados de sus tierras; **we drove them away with sticks** los ahuyentamos con palos; **he drove his cattle south** condujo su ganado hacia el sur **2** (Sport) ‹*ball*› mandar, lanzar* **3** (provide power for, operate) hacer* funcionar, mover*
C **1** (make penetrate) ‹*nail*› clavar; ‹*stake*› hincar*; **he drove the nail through the plank** atravesó la tabla con el clavo; **to ~ sth INTO sth** clavar/hincar* algo EN algo **2** (open up) ‹*tunnel/shaft*› perforar, abrir*
D **1** (cause to become) volver*; **imprisonment drove him insane** la prisión lo volvió loco *or* lo llevó a la locura; **he ~s me crazy** *o* **mad with his incessant chatter** me saca de quicio con su constante cháchara; **she ~s me wild!** (colloq) ¡me vuelve loco! (fam) **2** (compel to act) **to ~ sb to + INF** llevar *or* empujar a algn A + INF; **we were ~n to it by fear** fue el miedo lo que nos llevó a hacerlo; **she is ~n by ambition** la impulsa *or* motiva la ambición **3** (overwork): **he drove them mercilessly** los hizo trabajar como esclavos; **she ~s herself too hard** se exige demasiado a sí misma
■ **drive** *vi* manejar *or* (Esp) conducir*; **to ~ on the right/left** manejar *or* (Esp) conducir* por la derecha/izquierda; **she ~s to work** va a trabajar en coche; **we drove all night** viajamos toda la noche

Phrasal verbs

• **drive at** [v ▸ prep ▸ o] (*only in -ing form*) querer* decir, insinuar*; **what are you driving at?** ¿qué quieres decir?, ¿qué (es lo que) estás insinuando?

• **drive off**
A [v ▸ adv] **1** «*car/driver*» irse*, partir **2** (in golf) salir*
B [v ▸ o ▸ adv, v ▸ adv ▸ o] (repel) ahuyentar

• **drive on**
A [v ▸ o ▸ adv] (incite) empujar
B [v ▸ adv] seguir* (adelante)

• **drive out** [v ▸ o ▸ adv, v ▸ adv ▸ o] expulsar

• **drive up**
A [v ▸ adv] «*vehicle/driver*» llegar*
B [v ▸ o ▸ adv, v ▸ adv ▸ o] ‹*prices/demand*› hacer* subir

drive[2] *n*
A [c] (in vehicle): **to go for a ~** ir* a dar un paseo *or* una vuelta en coche; **it's a three-hour ~** es un viaje de tres horas en coche
B [c] **1** (leading to house) camino *m*, avenida *f* (*que lleva hasta una casa*) **2** (in front of house) entrada *f* (*para coches*)
C [c] (in golf, tennis) golpe *m* fuerte
D **1** [u] (energy) empuje *m*, dinamismo *m* **2** [c] (compulsion) (Psych) impulso *m*, instinto *m*; **the sex ~** el apetito sexual
E [c] **1** (organized effort) campaña *f*; **a sales ~** una campaña de ventas **2** (attacking move) (Mil) ofensiva *f*, avanzada *f* **3** (in US football) ataque *m*
F **1** [u c] (propulsion system) transmisión *f*, propulsión *f* **2** [u] (Auto): **front-wheel/rear-wheel ~** tracción *f* delantera/trasera; **four-wheel ~** tracción en las cuatro ruedas; **right-/left-hand ~** con el volante a la derecha/a la izquierda

drive-in[1] /'draɪvɪn/ *adj* (AmE): **~ bank** autobanco *m*

drive-in[2] *n* (AmE) (cinema) autocine *m*; (restaurant) drive in *m* (*restaurante que sirve a los clientes en el propio automóvil*)

drivel[1] /'drɪvəl/ *n* [u] tonterías *fpl*, estupideces *fpl*

drivel[2] *vi*, (BrE) **-ll-** decir* tonterías

driven /'drɪvən/ *past p of* **drive**[1]

driver /'draɪvər || 'draɪvə(r)/ *n* (of car, truck, bus) conductor, -ra *m,f*, chofer *m or* (Esp) chófer *mf*; (of racing car) piloto *mf*; **~s are asked to avoid this area** se ruega a los automovilistas que eviten circular por esta zona; **she's a good ~** maneja *or* (Esp) conduce bien

driver: **~'s license** *n* (AmE) licencia *f or* (Esp) permiso *m* de conducción; (less formally) carné *m or* permiso *m* (de conducir) (Esp), carné *m* (Chi) *or* (Ur) libreta *f or* (AmC, Méx, Ven) licencia *f or* (Col) pase *m* (de manejar), registro *m* (Arg), brevete *m* (Per); **~'s seat** *n* asiento *m* del conductor; ***to be in the ~'s seat*** estar* al frente, llevar las riendas

driveway /'draɪvweɪ/ *n* ▸**drive**[2] **B2**

driving[1] /'draɪvɪŋ/ *n* [u] (Auto) conducción *f* (frml); **I don't think much of his ~** no me gusta mucho como maneja *or* (Esp) conduce

driving[2] *adj* **1** ‹*rain*› torrencial; ‹*wind*› azotador **2** (dynamic): **she's the ~ force behind the project** es el alma-máter *or* la impulsora del proyecto

driving: **~ instructor** *n* instructor, -tora *m,f* de autoescuela; **~ licence** *n* (BrE) ▸**driver's license**; **~ mirror** *n* (BrE) (espejo *m*) retrovisor *m*; **~ range** *n*: *campo de golf diseñado para practicar tiros de salida*; **~ school** *n* autoescuela *f*, escuela *f* de conductores *or* de choferes (AmL), escuela *f* de manejo (Méx); **~ seat** *n* ▸**driver's seat**; **~ test** *n* examen *m* de conducir *or* (AmL tb) de manejar; **~ wheel** *n* rueda *f* motriz

drizzle[1] /'drɪzəl/ *n* llovizna *f*, garúa *f* (AmL)

drizzle[2] *v impers* lloviznar, garuar* (AmL)

droll /drəʊl/ *adj* **1** (comic) gracioso, con chispa **2** (quaint, curious) curioso

dromedary /'drɑːməderi / *n* (*pl* **-ries**) dromedario *m*

drone[1] /drəʊn/ *n*
A [c] (bee) zángano *m*
B [u] (sound — of bees, traffic, aircraft) zumbido *m*; (of voice) cantinela *f* (fam), sonsonete *m*

drone[2] *vi* «*bee/engine/plane*» zumbar

Phrasal verb

• **drone on** [v ▸ adv]: **she ~d (on) for hours** estuvo horas con la misma perorata (fam)

drool[1] /druːl/ *vi* «*dog/baby*» babear; **we ~ed at the sight of the cakes** se nos hizo agua la boca *or* (Esp) la boca agua al ver los pasteles; **he ~s over you** se le cae la baba por ti (fam)

drool[2] *n* [u] (AmE) **1** (dribble) babas *fpl*, baba *f* **2** (drivel) (sl) bobadas *fpl* (fam)

droop /druːp/ *vi* **1** (sag) «*flowers*» ponerse* mustio; **his shoulders ~ed** se encorvó; **her eyelids began to ~** se le empezaron a cerrar los ojos **2** (flag) «*spirits*» flaquear, decaer*; «*person*» desfallecer*, decaer* **3** **drooping** *pres p* ‹*head*› gacho; ‹*flowers*› mustio

drop[1] /drɑːp || drɒp/ *n*
A **1** (of liquid) gota *f*; **we haven't had a ~ of rain for six weeks** no ha caído una gota de agua en seis semanas **2** (small amount) gota *f*; **can I have a ~?** ¿me das una gotita?; **she's had a ~ too much** ha bebido más de la

cuenta; ***a ~ in the ocean*** un grano de arena en el desierto, una insignificancia 3 **drops** *pl* (Med) gotas *fpl*; **ear/nose ~s** gotas para los oídos/la nariz; **eye ~s** colirio *m* 4 (candy): **acid ~s** caramelos *mpl* ácidos; **chocolate ~s** pastillas *fpl* de chocolate
B 1 (fall) (*no pl*) (in temperature) descenso *m*; (in prices) caída *f*, baja *f*; **she had to take a ~ in salary** tuvo que aceptar un sueldo más bajo; **a ~ of 30%** *o* **a 30% ~ in sales** un descenso del 30% en las ventas; ***at the ~ of a hat*** en cualquier momento 2 (difference in height) caída *f*; **a sheer ~** una caída a plomo
C (of supplies) lanzamiento *m*
D (AmE) 1 (letter box) buzón *m* 2 (collection point) punto *m* de recogida

drop² **-pp-** *vt*
A 1 (accidentally): **I/you/he ~ped the cup** se me/te/le cayó la taza; **don't ~ it!** ¡que no se te caiga!; **this is your big chance, so don't ~ the ball** (AmE) es tu gran oportunidad, así que no vayas a meter la pata (fam); **I've ~ped a stitch** se me ha escapado un punto 2 (deliberately) ‹*cup/vase*› dejar caer, tirar; ‹*bomb/supplies*› lanzar*; **~ that gun!** ¡suelta ese revólver!; ***to ~ a brick*** *o* (BrE) ***a clanger*** meter la pata (fam); ***to ~ sb/sth like a hot potato*** no querer* saber nada más de algn/algo
B (lower) ‹*hem*› alargar*, bajar; ‹*eyes/voice*› bajar
C 1 (set down) ‹*passenger/cargo*› dejar 2 (deliver) pasar a dejar; **I can ~ them there on my way home** puedo pasar por allí a dejarlos de camino a casa
D (send) (colloq) ‹*card/letter*› mandar; **~ me a line** a ver si me mandas *or* me escribes unas líneas
E (utter) ‹*hint/remark*› soltar*, dejar caer; **to let it ~ that ...** (inadvertently) dejar escapar que ...; (deliberately) dejar caer que ...
F 1 (omit) ‹*letter/syllable/word*› omitir; **to ~ sth (FROM sth)** ‹*chapter/scene/article*› suprimir algo (DE algo); **to ~ sb from a team** sacar* a algn de un equipo 2 (give up, abandon) ‹*case*› abandonar; ‹*charges*› retirar; ‹*plan/idea*› abandonar, renunciar a; ‹*friend/associate*› dejar de ver a; **let's ~ the subject** cambiemos de tema; **just ~ everything and come** déjalo todo y vente
■ **drop** *vi*
A 1 (fall) «*object*» caer(se)*; «*plane*» bajar, descender*; **he ~ped to the ground** (deliberately) se tiró al suelo; (fell) cayó de un golpe 2 (collapse) desplomarse; **to be ready to ~** estar* cayéndose; **to ~ (down) dead** caerse* muerto; **~ dead!** (colloq) ¡vete al demonio! (fam)
B 1 (decrease) «*wind*» amainar; «*temperature*» bajar, descender*; «*prices*» bajar, experimentar un descenso (frml); «*voice*» bajar 2 (in height) «*terrain*» caer*

Phrasal verbs
- **drop away** [v ▸ adv] «*ground*» caer*; «*support/interest*» disminuir*
- **drop back** [v ▸ adv] rezagarse*, quedarse atrás; **she ~ped back to third place** se rezagó, quedando en el tercer puesto
- **drop behind** 1 [v ▸ adv] rezagarse*, quedarse atrás 2 [v ▸ prep ▸ o] ‹*competitors/classmates*› quedar atrás *or* rezagarse* con respecto a
- **drop by** 1 [v ▸ adv] (colloq) pasar; **why don't you ~ by for a cup of coffee sometime?** ¿por qué no pasas un día a tomar un café? 2 [v ▸ prep ▸ o] pasar por; **I have to ~ by the office** tengo que pasar por la oficina
- **drop in** [v ▸ adv] (colloq) pasar; **I'll ~ in sometime tomorrow** pasaré mañana en algún momento; **to ~ in ON sb** pasar a ver a algn, caerle* a algn (fam)
- **drop off**
A [v ▸ adv] 1 (fall off) caerse* 2 (fall asleep): **to ~ off (to sleep)** dormirse*, quedarse dormido 3 (decrease) «*sales/numbers*» disminuir*
B [v ▸ o ▸ adv] ‹*person/goods*› dejar
- **drop out** [v ▸ adv] **to ~ out (OF sth)**: **to ~ out of school** abandonar los estudios; **to ~ out of a course** dejar de asistir a un curso; **to ~ out (of a competition/race)** (before event) no presentarse (a un concurso/una carrera); (during event) abandonar (un curso/una carrera); **to ~ out of politics** abandonar *or* dejar la política; **to ~ out (of society)** marginarse, convertirse* en un marginado
- **drop over**, **drop round** [v ▸ adv] (BrE colloq) pasar; **I'll ~ over to her house** pasaré por su casa

drop: **~cloth** *n* (AmE) cubierta *f* (*para proteger muebles y suelos mientras se pinta*); **~-dead** /'drɑːp'ded|| 'drɒp'ded/ *adj* (colloq) ‹*beauty/elegance*› que es de morirse (fam), que te caes de espaldas (fam); **he's ~-dead gorgeous** es para morirse de guapo (fam), es que te caes de espaldas de guapo (fam), está como un tren (Esp fam); **~ kick** *n* (in rugby) botepronto *m*; (in wrestling) patada *f* voladora

droplet /'drɑːplət || 'drɒplɪt/ *n* gotita *f*

dropout /'drɑːpaʊt || 'drɒpaʊt/ *n* marginado, -da *m,f*

dropper /'drɑːpər || 'drɒpə(r)/ *n* cuentagotas *m*, gotero *m*

droppings /'drɑːpɪŋz / *pl n* (of bird, flies) excremento *m* (frml), cagadas *fpl* (fam); (of rabbit, sheep) cagarrutas *fpl*

drop shot *n* dejada *f*

dropsy /'drɑːpsi || 'drɒpsi/ *n* [u] hidropesía *f*

drop zone *n* (esp AmE) zona *f* de lanzamiento

dross /drɑːs / *n* [u] 1 (waste) basura *f* 2 (Metall) escoria *f*

drought /draʊt/ *n* [c u] sequía *f*

drove¹ /drəʊv/ *past of* **drive¹**

drove² *n* 1 (of animals) manada *f* 2 **droves** *pl* (of people) hordas *fpl*, manadas *fpl*; **they came in ~s** vino gente a montones (fam)

drown /draʊn/ *vt*
A 1 ‹*person/animal*› ahogar*; **to be ~ed** ahogarse*, morir* ahogado 2 ‹*landscape/fields*› anegar*, cubrir*; **he ~ed his meal in gravy** se puso un montonazo de salsa en la comida (fam)
B **~ (out)** (make inaudible) ‹*noise/cries/screams*› ahogar*
■ **drown** *vi* ahogarse*, morir* ahogado

drowse /draʊz/ *vi* dormitar

drowsy /'draʊzi/ *adj* **-sier, -siest** 1 (sleepy) ‹*person/look*› somnoliento, adormilado; **wine makes me ~** el vino me da sueño *or* me amodorra 2 (peaceful, inactive) ‹*atmosphere/afternoon*› somnoliento, perezoso

drubbing /'drʌbɪŋ/ *n*: **to give sb a ~** darle* una paliza a algn

drudge /drʌdʒ/ *n* esclavo, -va *m,f*

drudgery /'drʌdʒəri/ *n* [u]: **this job is sheer ~** este trabajo es una pesadez

drug¹ /drʌg/ *n* 1 (narcotic) droga *f*, estupefaciente *m* (frml); **to be on ~s** drogarse*; **I don't do ~s** (sl) yo no me drogo; (*before n*) **~ dependence** drogodependencia *f* (frml); **~ pusher** (colloq) camello *mf* (arg), conecte *mf* (Méx arg), jíbaro *mf* (Col, Ven arg) 2 (medication) medicamento *m*, medicina *f*, fármaco *m* (frml)

drug² *vt* **-gg-** 1 ‹*person/animal*› drogar* 2 **drugged** *past p* drogado; **a ~ged sleep** un sueño pesado 3 (add drugs to) ‹*food/wine*› adulterar con drogas

drug: **~ abuse** *n* [u] consumo *m* de drogas *or* (frml) estupefacientes; **~ addict** *n* drogadicto, -ta *m,f*, toxicómano, -na *m,f* (frml); **~ addiction** *n* [u] drogadicción *f*; **~ baron** *n* capo, -pa *m,f* de la droga

druggist /'drʌgɪst/ *n* (AmE) farmacéutico, -ca *m,f*

drug: **~store** *n* (AmE) *establecimiento que vende medicamentos, cosméticos, periódicos y una gran variedad de artículos*; **~-taking** *n* [u] consumo *m* de drogas; **~ test** *n* control *m* antidóping

drum¹ /drʌm/ *n*
A (Mus) 1 tambor *m* 2 **drums** *pl* (in band) batería *f*
B 1 (container) bidón *m* 2 (machine part) tambor *m*; **a revolving ~** un tambor giratorio 3 (spool) tambor *m*

drum² **-mm-** *vt* ‹*table/floor*› golpetear; **to ~ one's fingers** tamborilear con los dedos
■ **drum** *vi* 1 (Mus) tocar* el tambor 2 (beat, tap) «*person*» dar* golpecitos, tamborilear; «*rain/hooves*» repiquetear

Phrasal verbs
- **drum into** [v ▸ o ▸ prep ▸ o]: **to ~ sth into sb** *o* **sb's head** hacerle* aprender algo a algn a fuerza de repetírselo *or* (fam) de machacárselo
- **drum out of** [v ▸ o ▸ adv ▸ prep ▸ o] ‹*army*› expulsar de
- **drum up** [v ▸ adv ▸ o] ‹*support*› conseguir*, obtener*

drum: **~beat** *n* son *m* del tambor; **~ brake** *n* freno *m* de tambor; **~kit** *n* batería *f*

drummer /'drʌmər || 'drʌmə(r)/ *n* (pop, jazz) batería *mf*, baterista *mf* (AmL); (military) tambor *m*; ***to hear*** *o* ***move to*** *o* ***march to a different ~*** (AmE) ir* contra la corriente

drumstick /'drʌmstɪk/ *n*
A palillo *m* (de tambor), baqueta *f*
B (Culin) muslo *m*, pata *f*

drunk¹ /drʌŋk/ *past p of* **drink²**

drunk² *adj* 1 (*pred*) (intoxicated) borracho; **to be ~** estar* borracho; **to get ~ (on beer/wine)** emborracharse (con cerveza/vino); **~ and disorderly** (Law) en estado de embriaguez y alterando el orden público (frml); **~ driver** conductor, -tora *m,f* en estado de embriaguez (frml) 2 (elated) **to be ~ WITH sth** estar* ebrio *or* borracho DE algo; **~ with success/power** ebrio *or* borracho de poder

drunk³ *n* borracho, -cha *m,f*

drunkard /'drʌŋkərd || 'drʌŋkəd/ *n* (frml & pej) borracho, -cha *m,f*, beodo, -da *m,f* (frml)

drunk: **~ driver** /ˌdrʌŋk'draɪvər || ˌdrʌŋk'draɪvə(r)/ *n* conductor bebido, conductora bebida *m,f*; **~ driving** *n* (AmE) delito *m* de conducir bajo la influencia del alcohol

d

drunken /'drʌŋken/ *adj* (*before n*) ‹*person/mob*› borracho; ‹*orgy/brawl*› de borrachos; **in a ~ stupor** en un sopor etílico (frml *o* hum)

drunkenness /'drʌŋkənnəs || 'drʌŋkənnɪs/ *n* [u] 1 (state) borrachera *f*, embriaguez *f* (frml) 2 (alcoholism) alcoholismo *m*

dry¹ /draɪ/ *adj* **drier, driest**

A 1 (not wet) ‹*ground/washing*› seco 2 (lacking natural moisture) ‹*leaves/skin/hair*› seco; ‹*cough*› seco; **there wasn't a ~ eye in the house** (set phrase) no hubo quien no llorara 3 (dried-up) ‹*well/river*› seco; **to run ~** «*river/well*» secarse* 4 (not rainy, not humid) ‹*climate/weather/heat*› seco; **tomorrow will be ~** mañana no lloverá 5 (using no fluid) ‹*cell*› seco; **a piece of ~ bread** una rebanada de pan sin mantequilla; **he had a ~ shave** se afeitó en seco

B (prohibiting sale of alcohol) ‹*state/county*› seco, donde está prohibida la venta de bebidas alcohólicas

C (not sweet) ‹*wine/sherry*› seco; ‹*champagne*› brut, seco

D 1 (ironic) ‹*humor/wit*› mordaz, cáustico 2 (lacking warmth) ‹*laugh/style*› seco

E (dull, boring) ‹*lecture/book*› árido

dry² **dries, drying, dried** *vt* 1 ‹*clothes/crockery*› secar*; **to ~ oneself** secarse*; **to ~ one's eyes/tears** secarse* *or* (liter) enjugarse* las lágrimas 2 (preserve) ‹*fish/fruit/meat*› secar*

■ **dry** *vi* «*washing/dishes/paint*» secarse*; **you wash and I'll ~** tú lavas y yo seco

Phrasal verbs

• **dry off** [v ▸ adv] secarse*

• **dry out**

A [v ▸ adv] 1 «*soil/clothes*» secarse* 2 (colloq) «*alcoholic*», hacerse* una cura de desintoxicación

B [v ▸ o ▸ adv, v ▸ adv ▸ o] ‹*soil/clothes*› secar*

• **dry up**

A [v ▸ adv] 1 «*stream/pond*» secarse* (*completamente*) 2 «*funds/resources/inspiration*» agotarse 3 (colloq) «*actor*» quedarse en blanco 4 (dry dishes) (BrE) secar* los platos

B [v ▸ o ▸ adv, v ▸ adv ▸ o] 1 ‹*well/stream*› secar* (*completamente*) 2 ‹*dishes*› (BrE) secar*

dry: **~ clean** *vt* limpiar en seco; **I had my coat ~ cleaned** mandé el abrigo a la tintorería; **~ cleaner('s)** *n* tintorería *f*; **~ cleaning** *n* [u] (action) limpieza *f* en seco; (clothes): **I collected my ~ cleaning** recogí mi ropa de la tintorería; **~ dock** *n* dique *m* seco

dryer /'draɪər || 'draɪə(r)/ *n* 1 (for clothes — machine) secadora *f*; (— rack) tendedor *m*, tendedero *m*; (*spin* ~) secadora *f* (centrífuga); (*tumble* ~) secadora *f* (de aire caliente) 2 ▸**hairdrier**

dry: **~-eyed** /'draɪ'aɪd/ *adv* sereno, sin una lágrima; **~ goods** *pl n* 1 (clothing) (AmE) artículos *mpl* *or* prendas *fpl* de confección; (*before n*) **~ goods store** tienda *f* de confecciones 2 (groceries) (BrE) comestibles *mpl* no perecederos; **~ ice** *n* [u] hielo *m* seco

drying-up /'draɪɪŋ'ʌp/ *n* (BrE): **to do the ~** secar* los platos

dryly *adv* ▸**drily**

dryness /'draɪnəs || 'draɪnɪs/ *n* [u]

A (of ground, hair, skin, climate) sequedad *f*

B (of wine, sherry) lo seco

C (of manner) sequedad *f*; (of humor, wit) lo mordaz *or* cáustico

dry: **~ rot** *n* [u] *putrefacción de la madera producida por un hongo*; **~ run** *n* simulacro *m*; **~ shampoo** *n* [u c] champú *m* seco; **~ wall**, (BrE) **~-stone wall** *n* muro *m* de mampostería sin mortero

DTs /'di:'ti:z/ *pl n* (colloq) = **delirium tremens**

dual /'du:əl || 'dju:əl/ *adj* (*before n*) 1 (double) ‹*role/function*› doble; ‹*nationality*› doble; **~ personality** doble personalidad *f* 2 (joint) ‹*ownership/interest*› compartido

dual: **~ carriageway** /'kærɪdʒweɪ/ *n* (BrE) autovía *f*, carretera *f* de doble pista; **~-control** /'du:əlkən'trəʊl / *adj* ‹*car/brakes*› de doble mando *or* control

duality /du:'æləti || dju:'æləti/ *n* [u c] (*pl* **-ties**) dualidad *f*

dual-purpose /'du:əl'pɜ:rpəs || ˌdju:əl'pɜ:pəs/ *adj* ‹*utensil*› de doble uso; ‹*cleaner*› de doble acción; ‹*furniture*› de doble función *or* uso

dub /dʌb/ *vt* **-bb-**

A 1 (nickname) apodar 2 **to ~ sb (a) knight** armar a algn caballero

B 1 (Cin) ‹*film*› doblar 2 (Audio) mezclar

dubbing /'dʌbɪŋ/ *n* [u] 1 (Cin) doblaje *m* 2 (Audio) mezcla *f*

dubious /'du:biəs || 'dju:biəs/ *adj* 1 (questionable) ‹*honor/achievement*› dudoso, discutible; ‹*past*› turbio; ‹*motives/person*› sospechoso; **he seems a rather ~ character to me** no me parece una persona de fiar 2 (doubtful) **to be ~ (ABOUT sth/sb)** tener* reservas *or* dudas (SOBRE *or* ACERCA DE algo/algn)

dubiously /'du:biəsli || 'dju:biəsli/ *adv* 1 (doubtfully) ‹*look/say*› con recelo *or* desconfianza 2 (suspiciously) ‹*behave*› sospechosamente

duchess /'dʌtʃəs || 'dʌtʃɪs/ *n* duquesa *f*

duchy /'dʌtʃi/ *n* (*pl* **duchies**) ducado *m*

duck¹ /dʌk/ *n* pato, -ta *m,f*; ***a dead ~*** un asunto acabado; ***to take to sth like a ~ to water***: **he took to skiing like a ~ to water** empezó a esquiar como si lo hubiera hecho toda la vida; ▸**water¹ A**

duck² *vi* (bow down) agacharse; (hide): **I ~ed behind a pillar** me escondí rápidamente detrás de una columna

■ **duck** *vt*

A (lower) ‹*head*› agachar, bajar

B (submerge) hundir

C (dodge) ‹*question*› eludir, esquivar; ‹*responsibility*› evadir, eludir

Phrasal verb

• **duck out** [v ▸ adv] **to ~ out OF sth** escabullirse* DE algo, eludir algo

duck-billed platypus /'dʌkbɪld/ *n* ornitorrinco *m*

ducking /'dʌkɪŋ/ *n* chapuzón *m*

duckling /'dʌklɪŋ/ *n* 1 [c] (Zool) patito *m*, anadón *m* 2 [u] (Culin) pato *m* (*joven*)

duct /dʌkt/ *n* (Tech, Anat) conducto *m*

ductile /'dʌktḷ || 'dʌktaɪl/ *adj* dúctil

dud¹ /dʌd/ *n* (colloq) 1 (useless thing) birria *f* (fam), porquería *f* (fam) 2 (useless person) calamidad *f*, inútil *mf*

dud² *adj* (colloq) 1 (useless, valueless) ‹*note/coin*› falso; ‹*check*› sin fondos; **a ~ battery** una pila gastada *or* que no funciona 2 (Mil) ‹*shell/bomb*› que no estalla

dude /du:d || dju:d/ *n* (AmE sl) tipo *m* (fam), tío *m* (Esp fam)

dudgeon /'dʌdʒən/ *n*: **in high ~** indignadísimo, lleno de indignación

due¹ /du: || dju:/ *adj*

A (*pred*) 1 (payable): **the rent is ~** hay que pagar el alquiler; **the payment becomes** *o* **falls ~ on the 5th** hay que hacer efectivo el pago el día 5 2 (owed): **~ TO sb/sth**: **the respect ~ to one's elders** el respeto que se les debe a los mayores; **the money ~ to them** el dinero que se les debe *or* (frml) se les adeuda; **it's all ~ to you** todo gracias a ti, te lo debemos todo a ti; **it was ~ to a technical problem** se debió a un problema técnico 3 **due to** (*as prep*) (crit) debido a; **all flights were canceled ~ to bad weather** se cancelaron todos los vuelos debido al mal tiempo 4 (scheduled): **when is the next train/flight ~?** ¿cuándo llega el próximo tren/vuelo?; **when is the baby ~?** ¿para cuándo espera *or* tiene fecha?; **she's ~ back tomorrow** vuelve mañana, su regreso está previsto para mañana; **she is ~ for promotion** le corresponde un ascenso

B (*before n*) 1 (proper) ‹*consideration/regard*› debido; **without ~ cause** sin causa justificada; **with all ~ respect** con el debido respeto, con todo el respeto que se merece; **in ~ course** en su debido momento, a su debido tiempo 2 (deserved) ‹*reward*› merecido

due² *adv*: **the fort is ~ west of the town** el fuerte está justo *or* exactamente al oeste del pueblo; **we headed ~ north** nos dirigimos derecho hacia el norte

due³ *n*
A **to give him his ~, he is efficient** tienes que reconocer que es eficiente
B **dues** *pl n* (subscription) cuota *f*

due date *n* **1** (Fin) fecha *f* de vencimiento **2** (of birth): **when's your ~ ~?** ¿para cuándo esperas *or* tienes fecha?

duel /ˈduːəl / *n* duelo *m*; **to fight a ~** batirse en *or* a duelo

duet /duːˈet || djuːˈet/ *n* dúo *m*; **a violin ~** un dúo de violín; **a piano ~** una pieza para piano a cuatro manos

duff¹ /dʌf/ *adj* (BrE colloq) malo, chafa (Méx fam)

Phrasal verb
• **duff up** [v ▸ o ▸ adv, v ▸ adv ▸ o] (BrE colloq) darle* una paliza a

duff² *n* (AmE sl) trasero *m* (fam), culo *m* (fam: en algunas regiones vulg)

duffel /ˈdʌfəl/ **1** [u] (Tex) *tela gruesa de lana* **2** [c] **~ (coat)** trenca *f*, montgomery *m* (CS)

duffel bag *n* talego *m*, bolso *m* marinero (RPl)

duffer /ˈdʌfər || ˈdʌfə(r)/ *n* (colloq) inútil *mf*, zoquete *mf* (fam), chambón, -bona *m,f* (AmL fam)

duffle /ˈdʌfəl/ *n* ▸ **duffel**

dug /dʌg/ *past & past p of* **dig¹**

dugout /ˈdʌgaʊt/ *n*
A (Mil) refugio *m* subterráneo
B **~ (canoe)** piragua *f*
C (in baseball) dogaut *m*, caseta *f*

duke /duːk || djuːk/ *n* duque *m*

dukedom /ˈduːkdəm || ˈdjuːkdəm/ *n* ducado *m*

dulcet /ˈdʌlsət || ˈdʌlsɪt/ *adj* (liter *or* iro) dulce; **I could hear her ~ tones** (iro) oía su dulce voz (iró)

dull¹ /dʌl/ *adj*
A **1** (not bright) ‹*color*› apagado; ‹*light/glow*› pálido; ‹*eyes/complexion*› sin brillo **2** (not shiny) ‹*finish*› mate; ‹*hair*› sin brillo **3** (overcast) ‹*day/morning*› gris, feo; **it's rather ~ out today** hoy está bastante nublado
B (boring) ‹*speech/person*› aburrido
C **1** ‹*faculties*› torpe, lerdo; ‹*pain/ache*› sordo; ‹*sound*› sordo, amortiguado **2** ‹*edge/blade*› romo, embotado

dull² *vt* **1** (make less bright) ‹*color/surface*› quitar el brillo a, opacar* **2** (make less sharp) ‹*pain*› aliviar, calmar; ‹*senses*› entorpecer*, embotar

dullard /ˈdʌlərd / *n* (arch *o* liter) zopenco, -ca *m,f* (fam)

dully /ˈdʌlli/ *adv* **1** (dimly) ‹*glow/shine*› débilmente, pálidamente **2** (boringly) ‹*talk/write*› de manera aburrida

duly /ˈduːli || ˈdjuːli/ *adv* **1** (as expected, planned): **permission was ~ granted** el permiso fue concedido, como era de esperar; **he ~ arrived at four** llegó a las cuatro, como estaba previsto **2** (correctly, properly) debidamente; **your comments have been ~ noted** se ha tomado debida nota de sus observaciones

dumb /dʌm/ *adj*
A **1** (unable to speak) mudo; **she's deaf and ~** es sordomuda; **~ animals** los animales **2** (temporarily silent): **to be struck ~** quedarse mudo *or* sin habla
B (stupid) (colloq) bobo (fam); **to act ~** hacerse* el tonto

dumb: **~bell** *n* pesa *f*, mancuerna *f*; **~found** /ˈdʌm ˈfaʊnd/ *vt* (*usu pass*) anonadar; **we were ~founded at the news** la noticia nos dejó anonadadas; **~struck** *adj* estupefacto; **~waiter** /ˈdʌmˈweɪtər || ˌdʌmˈweɪtə(r)/ *n* (elevator) montaplatos *m*; (table) mesita *f* rodante

dummy¹ /ˈdʌmi/ *n*
A **1** (in window display, for dressmaker) maniquí *m* **2** (in tests, stunts) muñeco *m*; **ventriloquist's ~** muñeco de ventrílocuo **3** (in US football) domi *m*
B (for baby) (BrE) ▸ **pacifier**
C (fool) (colloq) bobo, -ba *m,f* (fam)
D (in bridge, whist) mano *f* del muerto; (player) muerto *m*

dummy² *adj* **1** (imitation) ‹*gun/telephone*› de juguete; **a ~ package** un paquete vacío **2** (Busn) ‹*shareholder*› que actúa como testaferro; **a ~ firm** una empresa fantasma

dummy run *n* (BrE colloq) ensayo *m*, prueba *f*

dump¹ /dʌmp/ *n*
A (place for waste) vertedero *m* (de basura), basural *m* (AmL), tiradero *m* (Méx)
B (temporary store) (Mil) depósito *m*
C (unpleasant place) (colloq) lugar *m* de mala muerte
D **dumps** *pl n* (colloq): ***to be (down) in the ~s*** estar* *or* andar* con la depre (fam)

dump² *vt*
A **1** (get rid of) ‹*waste/refuse*› tirar, botar (AmL exc RPl) **2** (Busn) **to ~ goods/products** inundar el mercado con mercancías/productos a bajo precio **3** ‹*boyfriend/girlfriend*› (colloq) plantar (fam), botar (AmS exc RPl fam), largar* (RPl fam)
B **1** (set on ground) ‹*load/sand*› descargar*, verter*; **he ~ed the bags (down) beside the car** plantó las maletas junto al coche (fam); **where can I ~ my things?** (colloq) ¿dónde puedo dejar *or* poner mis cosas? **2** (Comput) ‹*data/disks*› volcar*
■ **dump** *vi* (Comput) volcar*

dumper (truck) /ˈdʌmpər || ˈdʌmpə(r)/ *n* ▸ **dump truck**

dumping /ˈdʌmpɪŋ/ *n* [u]
A (of waste): ⊘ **no dumping** prohibido arrojar *or* tirar basura; **the ~ of nuclear waste** el vertido de residuos nucleares
B (Busn) dumping *m*

dumping ground *n* vertedero *m*, basural *m* (AmL), tiradero *m* (Méx)

dumpling /ˈdʌmplɪŋ/ *n*: *bola de masa que se come en sopas o guisos*; **apple ~** *manzana al horno, envuelta en masa*

Dumpster® /ˈdʌmpstər || ˈdʌmpstə(r)/ *n* (AmE) contenedor *m* (*para escombros*)

dump truck *n* volquete *m*, camión *m* volteador (RPl) *or* (Méx) de volteo, volqueta *f* (Col)

dumpy /ˈdʌmpi/ *adj* **-pier, -piest** regordete

dun /dʌn/ *adj* pardo

dunce /dʌns/ *n* (pej) burro, -rra *m,f*

dunce cap, (BrE) **dunce's cap** *n* capirote *m*, orejas *fpl* de burro

dune /duːn || djuːn/ *n* duna *f*

dung /dʌŋ/ *n* [u] **1** (feces) boñiga *f*, bosta *f* **2** (manure) (esp BrE) estiércol *m*

dungarees /ˈdʌŋgəˈriːz/ *pl n* (workman's) overol *m*; (fashion) pantalón *m* de peto

dungeon /ˈdʌndʒən/ *n* mazmorra *f*, calabozo *m*

dungheap /ˈdʌŋhiːp/, **dunghill** /-hɪl/ *n* estercolero *m*

dunk /dʌŋk/ *vt* ‹*cake/cracker*› (re)mojar

dunno /dəˈnəʊ/ (colloq): **(I) ~** no sé, ni idea (fam)

duo /ˈduːəʊ || ˈdjuːəʊ/ *n* (*pl* **-os**) dúo *m*

duodenal /ˈduːəˈdiːnl̩ || ˌdjuːəˈdiːnl̩/ *adj* duodenal

duodenum /ˈduːəˈdiːnəm / *n* duodeno *m*

dupe¹ /duːp || djuːp/ *vt* **to ~ sb (INTO -ING)** engañar *or* embaucar* a algn (PARA QUE + *subj*)

dupe² *n* inocentón, -tona *m,f*, primo, -ma *m,f* (Esp fam)

duplex /ˈduːpleks || ˈdjuːpleks/ *n* (AmE) **~ (apartment)** dúplex *m*; **~ (house)** *casa de dos viviendas adosadas*

duplicate¹ /ˈduːplɪkət || ˈdjuːplɪkət/ *adj* (*before n*): **a ~ copy** un duplicado; **a ~ key** un duplicado *or* una copia de una llave

duplicate² /ˈduːplɪkət || ˈdjuːplɪkət/ *n* duplicado *m*, copia *f*; **in ~** por duplicado

duplicate³ /ˈduːplɪkeɪt || ˈdjuːplɪkeɪt/ *vt* **1** (copy) ‹*letter/document*› hacer* copias de **2** (repeat) ‹*work/efforts*› repetir* (*en forma innecesaria*)

duplicating machine /ˈduːplɪkeɪtɪŋ || ˈdjuːplɪkeɪtɪŋ/ *n* mimeógrafo *m*, multicopista *f*

duplication /ˈduːplɪˈkeɪʃən || ˌdjuːplɪˈkeɪʃən/ *n* [u] **1** (of document) copia *f*, duplicación *f* **2** (of effort, work) repetición *f* (innecesaria)

duplicator /ˈduːplɪkeɪtər / *n* ▸ **duplicating machine**

duplicity /dʊˈplɪsəti || djuːˈplɪsəti/ *n* [u] (frml) duplicidad *f*

durability /ˈdʊrəˈbɪləti || ˌdjʊərəˈbɪləti/ *n* [u] durabilidad *f*

durable /ˈdʊrəbəl || ˈdjʊərəbəl/ *adj* durable; **~ goods** (Busn) bienes *mpl* (de consumo) duraderos

durables /ˈdʊrəbəlz || ˈdjʊərəbəlz/ *pl n* bienes *mpl* (de consumo) duraderos

duration /dʊˈreɪʃən || ˈdjʊəˈreɪʃən/ *n* [u] duración *f*; **for the ~ of the conference** mientras dure la conferencia; **for the ~** (Mil) mientras dure la guerra

d

duress /dʊ'res || djʊə'res/ *n* [u]: **under ~** bajo coacción

Durex® /'djʊreks || 'djʊəreks/ *n*
A [c] (condom) (BrE) preservativo *m*, condón *m*
B [u] (Austral) ▸**Scotch tape**®

during /'dʊrɪŋ || 'djʊərɪŋ/ *prep* durante; **you never see them ~ the day** nunca se los ve durante el día *or* de día; **~ his lifetime he was relatively unknown** en vida no fue muy conocido; **she'll call ~ the week** llamará durante la semana

dusk /dʌsk/ *n* [u] anochecer *m*; **at ~** al anochecer

dusky /'dʌski/ *adj* **-kier, -kiest** ‹*complexion*› moreno; ‹*pink*› oscuro

dust¹ /dʌst/ *n*
A [u] (particles of matter) polvo *m*; **gold ~** oro *m* en polvo; **the horses raised a cloud of ~** los caballos levantaron una polvareda; **ashes to ashes, ~ to ~** (liter) polvo eres y en polvo te convertirás; **to gather ~** llenarse de polvo; ***as dry as ~*** árido; ***to bite the ~*** «*person*» morder* el polvo; «*project/plan*» irse* a pique; ***not to see sb for ~*** (colloq): **mention work and you won't see him for ~** basta hablarle de trabajo para que ponga los pies en polvorosa; ***when the ~ has settled*** cuando haya pasado la tormenta; ***to shake the ~ off one's feet*** largarse* hecho una furia
B (dusting) (*no pl*): **to give sth a ~** sacarle* *or* limpiarle el polvo a algo

dust² *vt*
A (remove dust from): **to ~ the furniture** quitarles el polvo a los muebles, sacudir los muebles (CS, Méx)
B (sprinkle) **to ~ sth (WITH sth)** espolvorear algo (CON algo); **she ~ed her feet with talcum powder** se echó *or* se puso talco en los pies

Phrasal verbs
- **dust down** [v ▸ o ▸ adv] sacudirle el polvo a
- **dust off** [v ▸ o ▸ adv, v ▸ adv ▸ o] **1** ‹*table/shelf*› quitarle el polvo a, sacudir (CS, Méx); ‹*dirt*› quitar **2** (revive) desempolvar

dust: **~bin** /'dʌstbɪn, 'dʌsbɪn/ *n* (BrE) cubo *m* *or* (CS, Per) tacho *m* *or* (Méx) tambo *m* *or* (Col) caneca *f* *or* (Ven) tobo *m* de la basura; **~bin man** *n* (BrE) ▸**dustman**; **~ bowl** *n*: *terreno semidesértico expuesto a la erosión causada por el viento*; **~cart** /'dʌstkɑːrt, 'dʌskɑːrt || 'dʌstkɑːt, dʌskɑːt/ *n* (BrE) camión *m* de la basura; **~ cloth** *n* (AmE) trapo *m* del polvo, trapo *m* de sacudir (CS, Méx), sacudidor *m* (Méx); **~ cover** *n* **1** (for furniture) funda *f* (*para proteger del polvo*) **2** (hard cover) tapa *f*; (flexible cover) funda *f* **3** (dust jacket) sobrecubierta *f*

duster /'dʌstər || 'dʌstə(r)/ *n*
A (Clothing) (housecoat) (AmE) guardapolvo *m*
B (BrE) **1** (for blackboard) borrador *m* **2** ▸**dust cloth**

dust: **~ jacket** *n* sobrecubierta *f*; **~man** /'dʌstmən, 'dʌsmən/ *n* (*pl* **-men** /-mən/) (BrE) basurero *m*; **~pan** /'dʌstpæn, 'dʌspæn/ *n* pala *f*, recogedor *m*; **~ rag** *n* ▸**dust cloth**; **~sheet** /'dʌstʃiːt, 'dʌsʃiːt/ *n* (BrE) ▸**dust cover 1**; **~ storm** *n* tormenta *f* de polvo; **~up** *n* (colloq) pelea *f*; **to have a ~up** pelearse

dusty /'dʌsti/ *adj* **-tier, -tiest** ‹*furniture*› cubierto de polvo; ‹*road/plain*› polvoriento; **to get ~** llenarse de polvo, empolvarse

Dutch¹ /dʌtʃ/ *adj* holandés; ***to go ~*** pagar* a escote (fam), pagar* *or* ir* a la americana (AmL), pagar* *or* ir* a la inglesa (Chi fam)

Dutch² *n* **1** [u] (language) holandés *m* **2** (people) (+ *pl vb*) **the ~** los holandeses

Dutch: **~ cap** *n* (BrE) diafragma *m*; **~ courage** *n* [u] (colloq) *valentía o arrojo que se debe a la ingestión de una bebida alcohólica*; **~ elm disease** *n* [u] grafiosis *f* del olmo; **~man** /'dʌtʃmən/ *n* (*pl* **-men** /-mən/) holandés *m*; **~woman** *n* holandesa *f*

dutiable /'duːtiəbəl/ *adj* sujeto a derechos arancelarios

dutiful /'duːtifəl / *adj* consciente de sus deberes

dutifully /'duːtifəli || 'djuːtifəli/ *adv* diligentemente

duty /'duːti || 'djuːti/ *n* (*pl* **duties**)
A [c u] (obligation) deber *m*, obligación *f*; **to do one's ~ (by sb)** cumplir con su (*or* mi *etc*) deber *or* obligación (para con algn); **she made it her ~ to ...** se impuso la obligación de ...; (*before n*) **~ call** *o* **visit** visita *f* de cumplido
B [u] **1** (service) servicio *m*; **to do night ~** hacer* el turno nocturno; **to do ~ as sth** hacer* las veces de algo, servir* de algo **2** (in phrases) **to be on/off ~** «*nurse/doctor*» estar*/no estar* de turno *or* guardia; «*policeman/fireman*» estar*/no estar* de servicio; (*before n*) **~ officer** oficial *mf* de servicio; **~ roster** lista *f* de guardias **3** **duties** *pl n* (responsibilities) (frml) funciones *fpl*, responsabilidades *fpl*
C [c u] (Tax) (*often pl*) impuesto *m*; **to pay ~ on sth** pagar* impuestos sobre algo

duty-free¹ /'duːti'friː || ˌdjuːti'friː/ *adj* libre de impuestos

duty-free² *adv* sin pagar impuestos

duty-free shop *n* tienda *f* libre de impuestos

duvet /'duːveɪ/ *n* (BrE) edredón *m* (nórdico); (*before n*) **~ cover** funda *f* de edredón

DVD *n* **1** = **digital versatile disc** **2** = **digital video disc**

DVD: **~ burner** *n* quemador *m* de DVD; **~ player** *n* lector *m* DVD; **~ recorder** *n* grabadora *f* de DVD, grabador *m* de DVD; **~ writer** *n* quemador *m* de DVD

'd've /dəv/ = **would have**

dwarf¹ /dwɔːrf || dwɔːf/ *n* (*pl* **~s** *or* **dwarves** /dwɔːrvz/) enano, -na *m,f*; (*before n*) ‹*tree/species*› enano

dwarf² *vt* ‹*building*› hacer* parecer pequeño; **her achievements ~ those of her rivals** sus logros eclipsan los de sus rivales

dwell /dwel/ (*past & past p* **dwelt** *or* **dwelled**) *vi* (liter) morar (liter), vivir

Phrasal verb
- **dwell on** [v ▸ prep ▸ o]: **try not to ~ on the past** trata de no pensar en el pasado; **the documentary ~s too much on ...** el documental se detiene demasiado en ...

-dweller /ˌdwelər || ˌdwelə(r)/ *suff*: **city~s** la gente que vive en la ciudad

dwelling /'dwelɪŋ/ *n* **1** (habitation) (liter) morada *f* (liter) **2** (house) (frml) vivienda *f*

dwelt /dwelt/ *past & past p of* **dwell**

dwindle /'dwɪndl̩/ *vi* **1** «*numbers/population*» disminuir*, menguar*, reducirse*; **to ~ away to nothing** irse* reduciendo hasta quedar en la nada **2** **dwindling** *pres p*: **dwindling resources** recursos cada vez más limitados

dye¹ /daɪ/ *n* tintura *f*, tinte *m*

dye² **dyes, dyeing, dyed** *vt* ‹*clothes*› teñir*; **she ~s her hair blonde** se tiñe el pelo de rubio

dyed-in-the-wool /'daɪdɪnðə'wʊl/ *adj* (*before n*) recalcitrante

dyer /'daɪər || 'daɪə(r)/ *n* tintorero, -ra *m,f*

dying¹ /'daɪɪŋ/ *adj* (*before n*) **1** (near death, extinction) ‹*person/animal*› moribundo, agonizante; ‹*race/art*› en vías de extinción **2** (related to time of death) ‹*wish/words/breath*› último, postrero (liter); **to my/his ~ day** hasta el fin de mis/sus días

dying² *pl n* **the ~** los moribundos

dyke /daɪk/ *n*
A ▸**dike A**
B (lesbian) (sl & often pej) tortillera *f* (arg)

dynamic /daɪ'næmɪk/ *adj* dinámico

dynamics /daɪ'næmɪks/ *n*
A (+ *sing vb*) (Phys) dinámica *f*
B (+ *pl vb*) (forces for change) dinámica *f*

dynamism /'daɪnəmɪzəm/ *n* [u] dinamismo *m*

dynamite¹ /'daɪnəmaɪt/ *n* dinamita *f*; **these latest disclosures are political ~** estas nuevas revelaciones son políticamente explosivas

dynamite² *vt* dinamitar, volar* con dinamita

dynamo /'daɪnəməʊ/ *n* (*pl* **-mos**) dínamo *m* *or* dinamo *m* (AmL), dinamo *f* *or* dínamo *f* (Esp)

dynasty /'daɪnəsti || 'dɪnəsti/ *n* (*pl* **-ties**) dinastía *f*

dysentery /'dɪsn̩teri || 'dɪsəntri/ *n* [u] disentería *f*

dysfunction /dɪs'fʌŋkʃən/ *n* [u c] disfunción *f*

dysfunctional /dɪs'fʌŋkʃn̩əl / *adj* disfuncional

dyslexia /dɪs'leksiə/ *n* [u] dislexia *f*

dyslexic /dɪs'leksɪk/ *adj* disléxico

dyspepsia /dɪs'pepsiə/ *n* [u] dispepsia *f*

Ee

E, e /iː/ *n* **1** (letter) E, e *f* **2** (Mus) mi *m*; *see also* **A A2**

E (= **east**) E

each¹ /iːtʃ/ *adj* cada *adj inv*; **~ one of us/them** cada uno de nosotros/ellos; **~ child received a gift** cada niño recibió un regalo

each² *pron*

A **1** cada uno, cada una; **I'll have a little of ~, please** sírveme un poco de cada uno, por favor **2** **each of**: **~ of the houses is slightly different** cada una de las casas es ligeramente diferente; **he questioned ~ of them in turn** les preguntó uno por uno **3** (*after n, pron*): **they ~ received a gift** cada uno recibió un regalo

B **each other**: **they hate ~ other** se odian; **they are always criticizing ~ other** siempre se están criticando el uno al otro; (if more than two people) siempre se están criticando unos a otros; **their respect/contempt for ~ other** su mutuo respeto/desprecio, el respeto/desprecio que sienten el uno por el otro; **we read ~ other's books** cada uno lee los libros del otro

each³ *adv*: **we were paid $10 ~** nos pagaron 10 dólares a cada uno; **the apples are 20 cents ~** las manzanas valen 20 centavos por pieza *or* cada una

eager /ˈiːgər || ˈiːgə(r)/ *adj* (excited, impatient) impaciente, ansioso; (keen) entusiasta; **she looked at their ~ faces** miró sus caras llenas de ilusión; **she's ~ to learn** tiene muchos deseos *or* muchas ganas de aprender; **he's ~ to please** está deseoso de complacer; **to be ~ FOR sth**: **she is ~ for change** tiene muchos deseos de cambio

eagerly /ˈiːgərli || ˈiːgəli/ *adv* ‹*accept/agree*› con entusiasmo; ‹*await*› ansiosamente, con ansiedad e impaciencia; ‹*listen/read*› con avidez

eagerness /ˈiːgərnəs || ˈiːgənɪs/ *n* [u] entusiasmo *m*; (impatience) impaciencia *f*; **~ to + INF**: **her ~ to please** su afán de agrado

eagle /ˈiːgəl/ *n* (Zool) águila *f*‡

eagle: **~ eye** *n* mirada *f* escrutadora, ojo *m* de lince; **~-eyed** /ˈiːgəlˈaɪd/ *adj* con ojos de lince

ear /ɪr || ɪə(r)/ *n*

A **1** (Anat) oreja *f*; (organ) oído *m*; **the inner/middle/outer ~** el oído interno/medio/externo; ***her ~s must be burning*** le deben estar ardiendo las orejas *or* zumbando los oídos; ***to be all ~s*** ser* todo oídos; ***to be wet behind the ~s*** estar* verde, no tener* experiencia; ***to fall down about*** *o* ***around one's ~s***: **the house is falling down around our ~s** la casa se nos está viniendo abajo *or* cayendo a pedazos; ***to fall on deaf ~s*** caer* en oídos sordos; ***to give sb a thick ~*** (colloq) darle* una torta *or* un moquete a algn (fam); ***to go in one ~ and out the other*** (colloq): **it just goes in one ~ and out the other** me/te/le entra por un oído y me/te/le sale por el otro; ***to have/keep one's ~ to the ground*** mantenerse* atento; ***to lend an ~ to sb*** prestarle atención a algn; ***to prick up one's ~s*** ‹‹*person*›› aguzar* el oído, parar la(s) oreja(s) (AmL fam); (lit) ‹‹*dog/horse*›› levantar *or* (AmL) parar las orejas; ***to set sth on its ~*** (AmE) causar revuelo en algo, revolucionar algo; ***to turn a deaf ~ to sb/sth*** hacer* oídos sordos a algn/algo **2** (sense of hearing) (*no pl*) oído *m*; **to have a good ~ for music/languages** tener* oído para la música/los idiomas; **to play sth by ~** tocar* algo de oído; ***to play it by ~***: **I don't know what I'm going to say, I'll just have to play it by ~** no sé que voy a decir, ya veré llegado el momento *or* sobre la marcha

B (of corn) espiga *f*

ear: **~ache** *n* [u c] dolor *m* de oído; **~drops** *pl n* gotas *fpl* para los oídos; **~drum** *n* tímpano *m*

earful /ˈɪrfʊl || ˈɪəfʊl/ *n* (colloq): **my mother gave me an ~** mi madre me echó un rapapolvo *or* (RPl) me cafeteó (fam)

earl /ɜːrl || ɜːl/ *n* conde *m*

earlobe /ˈɪrləʊb || ˈɪələʊb/ *n* lóbulo *m* de la oreja

early¹ /ˈɜːrli || ˈɜːli/ *adj* **-lier, -liest**

A (before expected time) ‹*arrival/elections*› anticipado; **to be ~** ‹‹*person*›› llegar* temprano; ‹‹*baby*›› adelantarse; **we were 20 minutes ~** llegamos con 20 minutos de adelanto; **the bus was ~** el autobús pasó (*or* salió *etc*) antes de la hora

B **1** (before normal time): **to have an ~ night/lunch** acostarse*/comer temprano; **~ retirement** jubilación *f* anticipada **2** ‹*crop/variety*› temprano, tempranero

C (far back in time): **~ man** el hombre primitivo; **his earliest memories** sus primeros recuerdos

D (toward beginning of period): **it's too ~ to tell** es demasiado pronto para saber; **at an ~ stage** en una etapa temprana; **in the ~ hours of the morning** en las primeras horas de la mañana, de madrugada; **in ~ June** a principios *or* a comienzos de junio; **in ~ childhood** en la primera infancia; **from an ~ age** desde pequeño, desde temprana edad (liter); **he was in his ~ twenties** tenía poco más de veinte años; **we caught an earlier train** tomamos un tren que salía más temprano

E (in near future) pronto; **at the earliest possible moment** lo antes *or* lo más pronto posible

early² *adv* **-lier, -liest**

A (before expected time) temprano; **the baby arrived two weeks ~** el niño se adelantó dos semanas

B (before usual time) temprano, pronto (Esp)

C (long ago): **it was known as ~ as 200 BC** ya se sabía en el año 200 A.C.

D (toward beginning of period): **~ in the morning/afternoon** por la mañana/tarde temprano; **~ in the week/year** a principios de semana/año; **~ (on) in her career** en los comienzos de su carrera; **book ~** haga su reserva cuanto antes

E (soon) pronto; **they won't be here till nine at the earliest** por temprano que lleguen no estarán aquí antes de las nueve

ear: **~mark** *vt* ‹*money/funds*› destinar; **~muffs** *pl n* orejeras *fpl*

earn /ɜːrn || ɜːn/ *vt*

A ‹*money/wages*› ganar; ‹*interest*› dar*, devengar* (frml)

B ‹*respect/gratitude*› ganarse; ‹*promotion*› ganar

■ **earn** *vi* (esp BrE) trabajar, ganar dinero

earned income /ɜːrnd || ɜːnd/ *n* ingresos *mpl* en concepto de salario *or* sueldo, ingresos *mpl* por trabajo personal (Esp)

earner /ˈɜːrnər || ˈɜːnə(r)/ *n* **1** (person): **she's the major/sole ~ in the family** es la que más dinero gana de la familia/es la única que gana dinero en la familia **2** (source of income) (BrE colloq): **it's a nice little ~** ese negocio me/te/le gana un buen dinerito (fam)

earnest¹ /ˈɜːrnəst || ˈɜːnɪst/ *adj* **1** (sincere) (frml) ‹*effort/attempt*› serio, concienzudo; ‹*wish*› ferviente **2** (serious) serio; **he's terribly ~** se lo toma todo muy en serio

earnest² *n* **in ~** en serio; **work has begun in ~** el trabajo ha empezado en serio *or* de verdad

earnestly /'ɜːrnəstli || 'ɜːnɪstli/ *adv* ‹*speak/look*› con seriedad; ‹*desire/believe*› (frml) de todo corazón

earnings /'ɜːrnɪŋz || 'ɜːnɪŋz/ *pl n* ingresos *mpl*

earnings-related /'ɜːrnɪŋzrɪ'leɪtəd || ˌɜːnɪŋzrɪ'leɪtɪd/ *adj* (BrE) proporcional al sueldo

ear: **~phone** *n* audífono *m*; **~piece** *n* (of phone) auricular *m*, tubo *m* (RPl); **~piercing** *n* [u] *perforación del lóbulo de la oreja*; **~plug** *n* tapón *m* para el oído; **~ring** *n* arete *m* (AmL), aro *m* (CS), pendiente *m* (Esp), caravana *f* (Ur); **~shot** *n*: **to be within/out of ~shot** estar*/no estar* lo suficientemente cerca como para oír; **~splitting** /'ɪːrˌsplɪtɪŋ || 'ɪəˌsplɪtɪŋ/ *adj* ‹*scream*› estridente, que rompe los tímpanos; ‹*noise*› ensordecedor

earth¹ /ɜːrθ || ɜːθ/ *n*
A [u] **1** (Astron, Relig) tierra *f*; **the ~** *o* **E~** la Tierra; **nothing on ~ would make me do it** no lo haría por nada del mundo; **you look like nothing on ~ with that new hairdo** (colloq) ese peinado te queda espantoso; ***to cost the ~*** (BrE colloq) costar* un ojo de la cara (fam); ***to promise the ~*** prometer el oro y el moro **2** (*as intensifier*): **why on ~ didn't you warn me?** ¿por qué diablos *or* demonios no me avisaste?; **who on ~ would do that?** ¿a quién puede ocurrírsele hacer eso?
B [u] **1** (land, the ground) tierra *f*; ***to bring sb (back) down to ~*** hacer* bajar de las nubes a algn; ***to come down to ~*** bajar de las nubes, poner* los pies sobre la tierra **2** (soil) tierra *f*
C [u] (BrE Elec) tierra *f*
D [c] (burrow, hole) madriguera *f*; ***to go to ~*** «*person*» esconderse; ***to run sb/sth to ~*** dar* con algn/algo

earth² *vt* (BrE Elec) conectar a tierra

earthenware /'ɜːrθənwer || 'ɜːθənweə(r)/ *n* [u] (material) barro *m* (cocido); (dishes) vajilla *f* de barro (cocido)

earthly¹ /'ɜːrθli || 'ɜːθli/ *adj* **1** (worldly) ‹*life*› terrenal, terreno; **all her ~ possessions** todo lo que poseía (*or* posee *etc*) en este mundo **2** (*as intensifier*) (colloq): **it's no ~ use asking her** es inútil preguntarle

earthly² *n* (BrE colloq) **1** (chance): **you don't have** *o* **stand an ~ against her** no tienes ni la más remota posibilidad de ganarle **2** (idea): **I haven't got an ~** no tengo ni la menor *or* ni la más remota idea

earth: **~-moving equipment** /'ɜːrθmuːvɪŋ || 'ɜːθmuːvɪŋ/ *n* maquinaria *f* excavadora; **~quake** *n* terremoto *m*; **~shaking** /'ɜːrθˌʃeɪkɪŋ || 'ɜːθˌʃeɪkɪŋ/, **~-shattering** *adj* ‹*event/news*› que causa conmoción; **~work** *n* (*usu pl*) (bank) terraplén *m*; **~worm** *n* lombriz *f* (de tierra)

earthy /'ɜːrθi || 'ɜːθi/ *adj* **-thier, -thiest** **1** ‹*shade*› terroso; ‹*taste/smell*› a tierra **2** ‹*person*› llano, campechano; ‹*humor*› desenfadado, directo

earwax /'ɪrwæks || 'ɪəwæks/ *n* [u] cerilla *f*, cerumen *m*

earwig /'ɪrwɪg || 'ɪəwɪg/ *n* tijereta *f*, cortapicos *m*

ease¹ /iːz || iːz/ *n* [u]
A (facility) facilidad *f*; **~ of operation/reference** facilidad de manejo/consulta; **for ~ of access** para facilitar el acceso; **with ~** fácilmente, con facilidad
B **1** (freedom from constraint): **at ~** a gusto; **I don't feel at ~ with her** con ella no me siento a gusto; **to put sb at his/her ~** hacer* que algn se sienta a gusto *or* se relaje; **to put/set sb's mind at ~** tranquilizar* a algn **2** (Mil): **(stand) at ~!** ¡descansen!
C (leisure): **a life of ~** una vida desahogada

ease² *vt*
A **1** (relieve) ‹*pain*› calmar, aliviar; ‹*tension*› hacer* disminuir, aliviar; ‹*burden*› aligerar; **to ~ sb's mind** tranquilizar* a algn; **he did it to ~ his conscience** lo hizo para descargarse la conciencia **2** (make easier) ‹*situation*› paliar, mejorar; ‹*transition*› facilitar; **to ~ the way for sth** preparar el terreno para algo
B **1** ‹*rules/restrictions*› relajar **2** ‹*belt/rope*› aflojar
C (move with care) (+ *adv compl*): **they ~d him into the wheelchair** lo sentaron con cuidado en la silla de ruedas; **he ~d the key into the lock** introdujo la llave en la cerradura con cuidado *or* cuidadosamente

■ **ease** *vi* «*pain*» aliviarse, calmarse; «*tension*» disminuir*, decrecer*

Phrasal verbs

- **ease off** [v ▸ adv] «*rain*» amainar; «*pain*» aliviarse, calmarse; «*pressure/traffic*» disminuir*
- **ease up** [v ▸ adv] (slacken pace — of life) tomarse las cosas con más calma; (— of work, activity) bajar el ritmo

easel /'iːzəl/ *n* caballete *m*

easily /'iːzəli || 'iːzɪli/ *adv*
A **1** (without difficulty) fácilmente, con facilidad; **he's ~ fooled** es fácil de engañar; **it's ~ obtainable** se consigue sin problemas; **it's ~ done** es fácil que suceda eso; **languages come ~ to him** tiene facilidad para los idiomas **2** (readily) ‹*break/stain/cry*› con facilidad; **you gave up too ~** te diste por vencido demasiado pronto
B **1** (by far) con mucho, fácil (fam), (de) lejos (AmL fam); **there's ~ enough for everybody** hay de sobra para todos **2** (at least) por lo menos, fácil (fam); **it must have cost ~ $100** debe de haber costado por lo menos $100
C (very conceivably) perfectamente, fácilmente

easiness /'iːzinəs || 'iːzɪnɪs/ *n* [u] **1** (of task) lo fácil, facilidad *f* **2** (of manner, movement) soltura *f*, naturalidad *f*

easing /'iːzɪŋ/ *n*: **an ~ of tension between the two countries** un relajamiento de la tensión entre los dos países; **the ~ of traffic congestion** la descongestión del tráfico

east¹ /iːst/ *n* [u]
A **1** (point of the compass, direction) este *m*; **the ~, the E~** el este, el Este; **to the ~ of the city** al este de la ciudad; **~-north~** estenoreste **2** (region) **the ~, the E~** el este; **a town in the ~ of England** una ciudad del este *or* en el este de Inglaterra
B **the East** (the Orient) (el) Oriente; (the Communist bloc) (Hist, Pol) el Este
C **East** (in bridge) Este *m*

east² *adj* (*before n*) este *adj inv*, oriental; ‹*wind*› del este

east³ *adv* al este; **~ OF sth** al este DE algo; **it is ~ of Dallas** está al este de Dallas; **back ~** (in US) en el este, en los estados del Este

east: **~bound** *adj* que va (*or* iba *etc*) en dirección este *or* hacia el este; **~ End** *n* (in UK) **the E~ End (of London)** *barrio del este de Londres de tradición obrera*; **~ender** /'iːst 'endər || ˌiːst'endə(r)/ *n* (in UK) *persona que vive o ha nacido en el* **E~ End**

Easter /'iːstər || 'iːstə(r)/ *n* Pascua *f* (de Resurrección); (*before n*) **~ Day** *o* **Sunday** (el) Domingo de Pascua *or* Resurrección; **~ egg** huevo *m* de Pascua; **~ Monday** (el) lunes de Pascua; **~ week** Semana *f* Santa; **the ~ vacation** las vacaciones de Semana Santa

easterly /'iːstərli || 'iːstəli/ *adj* ‹*wind*› del este; **in an ~ direction** hacia el este *or* en dirección este

eastern /'iːstərn || 'iːstən/ *adj* **1** (Geog) (*before n*) oriental, este *adj inv*; **the ~ areas of the country** las zonas orientales *or* este del país; **heavy rain over ~ England** fuertes lluvias en *or* sobre el este de Inglaterra; **the ~ states** los estados del este; **E~ Europe** Europa Oriental *or* del Este **2** (oriental) ‹*appearance/custom*› oriental

Easterner, easterner /'iːstərnər || 'iːstənə(r)/ *n*: *nativo o habitante del este del país o de la región*

easternmost /'iːstərnməʊst || 'iːstənməʊst/ *adj* (*before n*) ‹*town/island*› más al este; **the ~ tip of the island** el extremo este *or* oriental de la isla

eastward¹ /'iːstwərd || 'iːstwəd/, **eastwardly** /-li/ *adj* (*before n*): **in an ~ direction** en dirección este, hacia el este

eastward², (BrE) **eastwards** /-z/ *adv* ‹*travel/turn*› hacia el este; **~ OF sth** al este DE algo

easy¹ /'iːzi/ *adj* **easier, easiest**
A (not difficult) fácil; **it's very ~ to do** es muy fácil de hacer; **it's ~ to see that ...** es fácil ver que ...; **~ money** dinero *m* fácil, plata *f* (AmS fam) fácil *or* dulce (AmL fam); **to take the ~ way out** optar por el camino fácil; **that's ~ for you to say** se dice muy fácil, es fácil hablar; **she was an ~ winner** ganó sin problemas
B (undemanding) ‹*life*› fácil, desahogado; **~ terms** (Busn) facilidades de pago; **to be ~ on the eye/ear** ser* agradable a la vista/al oído
C **1** (lenient): **to be ~ ON sb** ser* poco exigente *or* severo CON

algn 2 (without strong opinion) (esp BrE colloq) (*pred*): **I'm ~** me da igual *or* lo mismo

easy² *adv*

A (without difficulty): **love/money doesn't come ~** el amor/dinero no es fácil de conseguir; **~ *come,* ~ *go*** así como viene se va

B 1 (slowly, calmly) despacio, con calma; **~ does it** despacito; **to take it/things ~** tomárselo/tomarse las cosas con calma 2 (sparingly): **go ~ on** *o* **with the sugar** no te pases *or* (Méx) llévatela suave con el azúcar (fam) 3 (leniently): **go ~ on him** no seas muy duro con él

easy: **~ chair** *n* sillón *m*, poltrona *f*, butaca *f*; **~going** /ˈi:ziˈgəʊɪŋ/ *adj*: **she's very ~going** es una persona de trato fácil *or* sin complicaciones; **the new teacher is fairly ~going** el profesor nuevo no es muy exigente *or* (Méx sl) es bastante barco; **~-peasy** /ˌi:ziˈpi:zi/ *adj* (BrE colloq: used to or by children) super fácil (fam), regalado (Chi, Méx, Ven fam), chupado (Esp fam), chiche (AmC fam), botado (Andes fam)

eat /i:t/ (*past* **ate**; *past p* **eaten**) *vt*

A ‹*meal/food*› comer; **I won't ~ you!** (colloq) ¡no te voy a comer!; ***to ~ humble pie*** *o* ***eat dirt*** *o* (AmE) ***crow*** morder* el polvo (fam), tragarse* el orgullo

B (upset, bother) (sl): **what's ~ing her?** ¿a ésta qué le pica *or* qué bicho la picó? (fam)

■ **eat** *vi* comer; **to ~ in/out** comer en casa/(a)fuera; **we usually ~ at 7** solemos cenar a las siete; **~, *drink and be merry*** a beber y a tragar

Phrasal verbs

- **eat away** [v ▸ o ▸ adv, v ▸ adv ▸ o] «*rats/mice*» roer*; «*moths*» picar*, comerse; «*acid*» corroer*
- **eat away at** [v ▸ adv ▸ prep ▸ o] «*rats/mice*» roer*; «*moths*» picar*, comerse; «*acid*» corroer*; ‹*savings*› comerse
- **eat into** [v ▸ prep ▸ o] «*acid/rust*» corroer*; ‹*profits/savings*› comerse
- **eat up**

A [v ▸ o ▸ adv, v ▸ adv ▸ o] (finish) ‹*meal/food*› comerse; **~ it all up now!** ¡cómetelo todo!

B [v ▸ adv] (finish meal) terminar (de comer)

C [v ▸ adv ▸ o] (consume) ‹*fuel/electricity*› consumir, gastar

D [v ▸ o ▸ adv] «*curiosity/ambition*» consumir; **she's ~en up with envy** la envidia la carcome, la consume la envidia

eatable /ˈi:təbəl/ *adj* pasable, comible

eaten /ˈi:tn̩/ *past p of* **eat**

eater /ˈi:tər || ˈi:tə(r)/ *n*: **he's a big ~** come mucho, es muy comelón *or* (CS, Esp) comilón (fam); **we're big meat ~s** comemos mucha carne

eatery /ˈi:təri/ *n* (*pl* **-ries**) (AmE colloq) restaurante *m*

eating /ˈi:tɪŋ/ *n* [u] (el) comer; **it is/makes very good ~** es muy sabroso; (*before n*) ‹*apple*› de mesa

eats /i:ts/ *pl n* (colloq) comida *f*, manduca *f* (fam)

eau de Cologne /ˈəʊdəkəˈləʊn/ *n* [u] agua *f*‡ de colonia, colonia *f*

eaves /i:vz/ *pl n* alero *m*

eavesdrop /ˈivzdrɑ:p || ˈi:vzdrɒp/ *vi* **-pp- to ~ (ON sth/sb)** escuchar (algo/a algn) a escondidas

eavesdropper /ˈi:vzˌdrɑ:pər || ˈi:vzˌdrɒpə(r)/ *n*: *persona que escucha las conversaciones de otros*

ebb¹ /eb/ *n* reflujo *m*; **the ~ and flow of the tide** el flujo y reflujo de la marea; **the tide was on the ~** la marea estaba bajando; ***to be at a low ~*** «*person*» estar* decaído; «*diplomatic relations*» estar* en un punto bajo; **his fortunes were at a low ~** atravesaba un mal momento

ebb² *vi* 1 «*tide*» bajar, retroceder; **to ~ and flow** fluir* y refluir*, ir* y venir* 2 (dwindle) decaer*, disminuir*

Phrasal verb

- **ebb away** [v ▸ adv]: **his life was ~ing away** se consumía poco a poco; **I felt my strength ~ing away** sentí que me abandonaban las fuerzas

ebb tide *n* reflujo *m*

ebitda *n* = **earnings before interest, taxes, depreciation and amortization** ebitda *m*

Ebonics /eˈbɑ:nɪks || eˈbɒnɪks/ *n* (+ *sing vb*): *variante del inglés hablada por la población negra norteamericana*

Ebonics

Es una especie de inglés que hablan muchos afroamericanos. Su nombre oficial es *African American Vernacular English (AAVE)*. En 1996 en Oakland, California, fue reconocido como una lengua especial y fue aceptado en los trabajos escritos de los estudiantes. Lo mismo hicieron otros colegios, hasta que en 1998 se abandonó esta práctica ante la insistencia en que los estudiantes hablaran el inglés estándar con el fin de conseguir mejores empleos

ebony /ˈebəni/ *n* [u] 1 (wood) ébano *m* 2 (color) color *m* (de) ébano; (*before n*) ‹*hair/skin*› negro como el ébano

ebullient /ɪˈbʌljənt, ɪˈbʊljənt/ *adj* ‹*person*› vivaz, lleno de vida; **he was in an ~ mood** estaba lleno de energía

e-business /ˈi:ˌbɪznəs || ˈi:ˌbɪznɪs/ *n* 1 [u] (world of electronic commerce) e-business *m*, negocios *mpl* electrónicos 2 [c] (firm) e-business *m*

EC *n* (= **European Community**) CE *f*

eccentric¹ /ɪkˈsentrɪk, ek-/ *adj* excéntrico

eccentric² *n* excéntrico, -ca *m,f*

eccentricity /ˈeksenˈtrɪsəti/ *n* [u c] (*pl* **-ties**) excentricidad *f*

ecclesiastic /ɪˈkli:ziˈæstɪk/, **-ical** /-ɪkəl/ *adj* eclesiástico

echelon /ˈeʃəlɑ:n || ˈeʃəlɒn/ *n*

A [c u] (Mil) escalón *m*

B [c] **echelons** *pl* (levels): **the upper ~s of the civil service** los niveles más altos del funcionariado (público)

echo¹ /ˈekəʊ/ *n* (*pl* **-oes**) eco *m*

echo² *vi* «*footsteps/voices*» hacer* eco, resonar*; **the room ~ed with** *o* **to the sound of laughter** la sala resonaba *or* retumbaba con risas

■ **echo** *vt* 1 (repeat): **to ~ sb's words** repetir* las palabras de algn 2 (express agreement with) ‹*opinion/criticism*› hacerse* eco de

echo sounder /ˈsaʊndər || ˈsaʊndə(r)/ *n* sonda *f* acústica *or* por eco

eclair /eɪˈkleə(r), ɪˈkleə(r)/ *n*: *pastel individual relleno de crema*

eclampsia /ɪˈklæmpsiə/ *n* [u] eclampsia *f*

eclectic /eˈklektɪk || ɪˈklektɪk/ *adj* ecléctico

eclipse¹ /ɪˈklɪps/ *n* eclipse *m*

eclipse² *vt* eclipsar

eco-friendly /ˌi:kəʊˈfrendli/ *adj* ecológico

ecological /ˈi:kəˈlɑ:dʒəkəl || ˌi:kəˈlɒdʒɪkəl/ *adj* ecológico

ecologically /ˈi:kəˈlɑ:dʒɪkli || ˌi:kəˈlɒdʒɪkli/ *adv* ecológicamente; (*indep*) desde el punto de vista ecológico, ecológicamente hablando

ecologist /ɪˈkɑ:lədʒəst || i:ˈkɒlədʒɪst/ *n* (student of ecology) ecólogo, -ga *m,f*; (conservationist) ecologista *mf*

ecology /ɪˈkɑ:lədʒi || ɪˈkɒlədʒi/ *n* [u] ecología *f*

e-commerce /i:ˈkɑ:mərs || i:ˈkɒmɜ:s/ *n* comercio *m* electrónico, e-comercio *m*

economic /ˈekəˈnɑ:mɪk, ˈi:k- || ˌi:kəˈnɒmɪk, ˌek-/ *adj* 1 ‹*development/growth/policy*› económico 2 (profitable) (BrE) ‹*rent*› rentable

economical /ˈekəˈnɑ:mɪkəl, ˈi:k- || ˌi:kəˈnɒmɪkəl, ˌek-/ *adj* económico

economically /ˈekəˈnɑ:mɪkli, ˈi:k- || ˌi:kəˈnɒmɪkli, ˌek-/ *adv* 1 ‹*sound/secure*› económicamente; (*indep*) desde el punto de vista económico 2 (thriftily) ‹*use*› de manera económica

economics /ˈekəˈnɑ:mɪks, ˈi:k- || ˌi:kəˈnɒmɪks, ˌek-/ *n* 1 (+ *sing vb*) economía *f* 2 (financial aspect) (+ *pl vb*) aspecto *m* económico

economist /ɪˈkɑ:nəməst || ɪˈkɒnəmɪst/ *n* economista *mf*

economize /ɪˈkɑ:nəmaɪz || ɪˈkɒnəmaɪz/ *vi* economizar*; **to ~ ON sth** economizar* *or* ahorrar algo

■ **economize** *vt* economizar*, ahorrar

economy /ɪˈkɑ:nəmi, i:- || ɪˈkɒnəmi/ *n* (*pl* **-mies**)

A [c] (economic state or system of country) economía *f*; **a mixed/market ~** una economía mixta/de mercado

B 1 [c] (saving): **to make economies** economizar*, hacer* economía(s); **economies of scale** economías *fpl* de escala 2 [u] (thrift) economía *f*; (*before n*) ‹*pack/size*› familiar; **~ class** clase *f* turista; **~ class syndrome** /ɪˈkɑ:nəmi

ˌklæs || ɪ'kɒnəmiˌklɑːs/ *n* [u] síndrome *m* de la clase turista; **we're on an ~ drive** estamos tratando de economizar

eco: **~system** /'iːkəʊˌsɪstəm/ *n* ecosistema *m*; **~tourism** /'iːkəʊˌtʊrɪzəm || 'iːkəʊˌtʊərɪzəm, -ˌtɔːr-/ *n* ecoturismo *m*, turismo *m* ecológico

ecru /'eɪkruː/ *n* [u] color *m* crudo

ecstasy /'ekstəsi/ *n* (*pl* **-sies**) 1 [u c] (state) éxtasis *m*; **she was in ~** *o* (BrE also) **ecstasies over Jane's new baby** estaba embelesada con el bebé de Jane 2 [u] (drug) éxtasis *m*

ecstatic /ɪk'stætɪk/ *adj* ‹*look/expression*› extasiado, extático; ‹*applause*› clamoroso, frenético

ecstatically /ɪk'stætɪkli/ *adv* ‹*applaud*› con gran entusiasmo; **~ happy** extático de felicidad

ectopic pregnancy /ek'tɑːpɪk || ek'tɒpɪk/ *n* embarazo *m* ectópico *or* extrauterino

Ecuador /'ekwədɔːr || 'ekwədɔː(r)/ *n* Ecuador *m*

Ecuadorean¹ /'ekwə'dɔːriən/ *adj* ecuatoriano

Ecuadorean² *n* ecuatoriano, -na *m,f*

ecumenical /'ekjə'menɪkəl || ˌiːkjuː'menɪkəl, 'ek-/ *adj* ecuménico

eczema /ɪg'ziːmə, 'egzəmə || 'eksɪmə/ *n* [u] eczema *m*

ed /ed/ 1 **= editor/edited by** 2 **(= edition)** Ed.

eddy¹ /'edi/ *n* (*pl* **eddies**) remolino *m*, torbellino *m*

eddy² *vi* **eddies, eddying, eddied** «*water*» formar remolinos; «*smoke/dust*» arremolinarse

edema, (BrE) **oedema** /ɪ'diːmə/ *n* (*pl* **-mata** /-mətə/) edema *m*

Eden /'iːdn̩/ *n* Edén *m*; **the Garden of ~** el Paraíso Terrenal, el (jardín del) Edén

edge¹ /edʒ/ *n*

A 1 (*no pl*) (border, brink — of town) afueras *fpl*; (— of forest) lindero *m*, borde *m*; (— of river, lake) orilla *f*, margen *m*; (— of cliff) borde *m*; **at the water's ~** a la orilla del agua 2 (of plate, table, chair) borde *m*; (of coin) canto *m*; (of page) margen *m*; **frayed at the ~s** deshilachado en los bordes; **it kept us on the ~ of our seats until the end** nos tuvo en vilo *or* en tensión hasta el final

B (cutting part) filo *m*; **to put an ~ on sth** afilar algo; ***to be on ~*** estar* nervioso, tener* los nervios de punta (fam); **this will take the ~ off your appetite** esto te calmará un poco el hambre; **his voice had a menacing ~ to it** su voz tenía un tono amenazante

C (advantage) ventaja *f*; **we have the ~ over our competitors** estamos en una posición de ventaja con respecto a nuestros competidores

edge² *vt*

A (border): **the collar was ~d with fur** el cuello estaba ribeteado de piel; **the paper was ~d in black** el papel tenía un borde negro

B (move cautiously): **he ~d his chair closer to hers** fue acercando su silla a la de ella; **she ~d her way along the ledge** fue avanzando poco a poco por la cornisa

C (AmE) ▸ **edge out**

■ **edge** *vi* (+ *adv compl*): **to ~ forward/closer/away** ir* avanzando/acercándose/alejándose (poco a poco); **the child ~d closer to his mother** el niño se fue arrimando a su madre

Phrasal verb

• **edge out** [v ▸ o ▸ adv, v ▸ adv ▸ o] ‹*rival/opponent*› ganarle por la mano a *or* (CS) de *or* la mano a

edgeways /'edʒweɪz/, (esp AmE) **edgewise** /'edʒwaɪz/ *adv* de lado

edging /'edʒɪŋ/ *n* borde *m*; **the collar had an ~ of lace** el cuello tenía puntilla alrededor

edgy /'edʒi/ *adj* tenso, con los nervios de punta

edible /'edəbəl/ *adj* (safe to eat) comestible; (eatable) pasable, comible

edict /'iːdɪkt/ *n* (Hist) edicto *m*; (order) mandato *m*, orden *f*

edification /'edəfə'keɪʃən || ˌedɪfɪ'keɪʃən/ *n* [u] (frml) edificación *f* del espíritu (frml); **here's a copy of the boss's memo for your ~** (iro) aquí tienes una copia del memorándum del jefe para que te instruyas (iró)

edifice /'edəfəs || 'edɪfɪs/ *n* (frml) edificio *m*

edify /'edəfaɪ || 'edɪfaɪ/ *vt* **-fies, -fying, -fied** (frml) edificar*

edifying /'edəfaɪɪŋ || 'edɪfaɪɪŋ/ *adj* edificante

Edinburgh /'edn̩ˌbɜːrə, -rəʊ || 'edɪnbrə/ *n* Edimburgo *m*

> **Edinburgh Festival**
>
> Un festival internacional de tres semanas de música, teatro, danza etc., que se viene celebrando cada agosto en Edimburgo desde 1947. Muchos turistas vienen a ver las actuaciones y los conciertos, incluida la gran cantidad que no forma parte oficial del festival y que se conoce como *Edinburgh Fringe*. En la actualidad, éste se considera tan importante como el festival mismo por la originalidad y nivel de su contenido

edit /'edət || 'edɪt/ *vt*

A ‹*manuscript*› (correct) corregir*, editar; (cut) recortar, editar

B ‹*movie/tape*› editar

C (manage) ‹*newspaper/magazine*› dirigir*

Phrasal verb

• **edit out** [v ▸ o ▸ adv, v ▸ adv ▸ o] suprimir, eliminar

editing /'edətɪŋ || 'edɪtɪŋ/ *n* [u]

A (Publ) 1 (managing) redacción *f*, dirección *f* 2 (correction) corrección *f*, revisión *f*, edición *f*; (cutting) recorte *m*

B (Cin, TV, Audio) edición *f*

edition /ɪ'dɪʃən/ *n* edición *f*

editor /'edətər || 'edɪtə(r)/ *n*

A (of text) redactor, -tora *m,f*, editor, -tora *m,f*; (of collected works, series) editor, -tora *m,f*

B (of newspaper, magazine) director, -tora *m,f*, redactor, -tora *m,f* responsable

C (of movie, radio show) editor, -tora *m,f*

editorial¹ /'edə'tɔːriəl || ˌedɪ'tɔːriəl/ *adj* 1 (Publ) ‹*assistant/director*› de redacción 2 (Journ) ‹*comment/decision/freedom*› editorial

editorial² *n* editorial *m*

editorship /'edətərʃɪp || 'edɪtəʃɪp/ *n* dirección *f*

EDP *n* **(= electronic data processing)** PED *m*

EDT (in US) **= Eastern Daylight Time**

educate /'edʒəkeɪt || 'edjʊkeɪt/ *vt* 1 (teach, school) educar*; **she was ~d in France** se educó en Francia 2 (make aware) concientizar* *or* (Esp) concienciar

educated /'edʒəkeɪtəd || 'edjʊkeɪtɪd/ *adj* ‹*person*› culto; **to make an ~ guess** hacer* una conjetura hecha con cierta base

education /'edʒə'keɪʃən || ˌedjʊ'keɪʃən/ *n*

A (schooling, instruction) educación *f*; **primary/higher ~** enseñanza *f* primaria/superior; **he didn't have a university ~** no tuvo *or* (frml) no cursó estudios universitarios; **health ~** clases *fpl* de higiene; (*before n*) ‹*system/policy*› educativo

B [u] (academic subject) pedagogía *f*, (teoría *f* de la) educación *f*

C [u] (knowledge, culture) cultura *f*

educational /'edʒə'keɪʃn̩əl || ˌedjʊ'keɪʃənl/ *adj* 1 ‹*establishment*› docente, de enseñanza; ‹*toy*› educativo, instructivo 2 (instructive) instructivo

educationalist /'edʒə'keɪʃn̩ələst || ˌedjʊ'keɪʃn̩əlɪst/ *n* pedagogo, -ga *m,f*

educationally /'edʒə'keɪʃn̩əli || ˌedjʊ'keɪʃn̩əli/ *adv*: **such methods are ~ unsound** tales métodos carecen de una sólida base pedagógica; **~ subnormal** con dificultades de aprendizaje; **~, it makes no sense** (*indep*) desde un punto de vista pedagógico, no tiene sentido

educationist /'edʒə'keɪʃənəst || ˌedjʊ'keɪʃənɪst/ *n* ▸ **educationalist**

educator /'edʒəkeɪtər || 'edjʊkeɪtə(r)/ *n* educador, -dora *m,f*

Edwardian /ed'wɔːrdiən || ed'wɔːdiən/ *adj* eduardiano

EEA *n* 1 **(= European Economic Area)** AEE *f* 2 **(= European Environment Agency)** AEMA *f*

eel /iːl/ *n* anguila *f*; ***as slippery as an ~*** escurridizo como una anguila

e'er /er || eə(r)/ *adv* (poet & arch) ▸ **ever**

eerie /'ɪri || 'ɪəri/ *adj* **eerier, eeriest** ‹*atmosphere/silence/cry*› inquietante, espeluznante; ‹*glow/place*› fantasmagórico; ‹*resemblance*› inquietante, sobrecogedor

eff /ef/ *vi* ***to ~ and blind*** (BrE sl) decir* palabrotas, soltar* tacos (Esp fam)

efface /ɪ'feɪs/ *vt* (frml) borrar

effect¹ /ɪ'fekt/ *n*

A 1 (consequence) efecto *m*; **to take ~** surtir efecto; **the**

warnings had no ~ on him at all las advertencias no hicieron mella en él; **it had the ~ of increasing output** tuvo como resultado un aumento de la producción; **to be of little/no ~** (frml) dar* poco/no dar* resultado 2 **in effect** de hecho, realmente 3 (phenomenon) efecto *m*; **the Doppler ~** el efecto de Doppler

B (impression) impresión *f*; **he only did it for ~** lo hizo sólo para llamar la atención

C (applicability, operation): **to come into ~, to take ~** entrar en vigor *or* en vigencia; **with ~ from June 15, it will be compulsory** a partir del 15 de junio será obligatorio; **to put sth into ~** poner* en práctica algo

D (meaning): **a statement was issued to the ~ that ...** (frml) se hizo público un comunicado anunciando que ...; **he said it wasn't true, or words to that ~** dijo que no era verdad o algo de ese tenor

E **effects** *pl* 1 (*special ~s*) (Cin, TV) efectos *mpl* especiales 2 (belongings) (frml) efectos *mpl* (frml); **personal ~s** efectos personales

effect² *vt* (frml) ‹*reconciliation/cure*› lograr; ‹*escape*› llevar a cabo; ‹*repairs*› efectuar* (frml); ‹*payment*› efectuar* (frml)

effective /ɪ'fektɪv/ *adj* 1 (producing the desired result) ‹*method/treatment*› eficaz, efectivo 2 (striking) ‹*design/contrast*› de mucho *or* gran efecto 3 (real) (*before n*) ‹*control/leader*› efectivo, real

effectively /ɪ'fektɪvli/ *adv* 1 ‹*manage/spend*› con eficacia, eficazmente; **the cure worked extremely ~** el tratamiento logró muy buenos resultados 2 ‹*contrast/decorate*› con mucho *or* gran efecto; ‹*speak*› convincentemente 3 (in effect) (*indep*) de hecho, realmente

effectiveness /ɪ'fektɪvnəs || ɪ'fektɪvnɪs/ *n* [u] 1 (of plan) eficacia *f*; (of cure, treatment) eficacia *f*, efectividad *f* 2 (of color scheme, display) gran efecto *m*

effeminate /ə'femənət || ɪ'femɪnət/ *adj* afeminado

effervesce /'efər'ves || ˌefə'ves/ *vi* «*liquid*» estar* en efervescencia, burbujear; «*person*» estar* eufórico

effervescent /'efər'vesənt || ˌefə'vesənt/ *adj* ‹*liquid/personality*› efervescente; **to be ~** «*person*» estar* eufórico

effete /ɪ'fi:t/ *adj* 1 ‹*manners/person*› amanerado, afectado 2 ‹*civilization/institution*› decadente

efficacious /'efə'keɪʃəs || ˌefɪ'keɪʃəs/ *adj* (frml) eficaz, efectivo

efficacy /'efɪkəsi/ *n* [u] (frml) eficacia *f*

efficiency /ɪ'fɪʃənsi/ *n* (*pl* **-cies**)

A [u] (of person, system) eficiencia *f*; (Mech Eng, Phys) rendimiento *m*

B [c] **~ (apartment)** (AmE) apartamento *m* pequeño (*gen amueblado*)

efficient /ɪ'fɪʃənt/ *adj* ‹*person/system*› eficiente; ‹*machine/engine*› de buen rendimiento

efficiently /ɪ'fɪʃəntli/ *adv* eficientemente, de manera eficiente

effigy /'efədʒi || 'efɪdʒi/ *n* (*pl* **-gies**) efigie *f*

effluent /'efluənt/ *n* [u c] (liquid waste) vertidos *mpl*; (sewage) aguas *fpl* residuales

effort /'efərt || 'efət/ *n*

A 1 [c u] (attempt) esfuerzo *m*; **to make an ~** hacer* un esfuerzo, esforzarse*; **she made no ~ to hide her displeasure** no hizo ningún esfuerzo por disimular su descontento 2 [u] (exertion, strain) esfuerzo *m*; **they've put a lot of ~ into it** han trabajado *or* se han esforzado mucho en ello; **it's not worth the ~** no merece *or* vale la pena

B 1 [c] (*no pl*) (initiative): **the war ~** *campaña solidaria de la población civil durante una guerra* 2 [c] (achievement) (colloq): **what do you think of my latest ~?** ¿qué te parece mi última obra *or* creación?; **for an amateur, that's not a bad ~** para un aficionado, no está nada mal

effortless /'efərtləs || 'efətlɪs/ *adj* ‹*grace*› natural; ‹*prose/style*› fluido

effortlessly /'efərtləsli || 'efətlɪsli/ *adv* ‹*move/accomplish*› sin esfuerzo; (gracefully) con gracia *or* donaire

effrontery /ɪ'frʌntəri/ *n* [u] (frml) desfachatez *f*, descaro *m*

effusive /ɪ'fju:sɪv/ *adj* efusivo

effusively /ɪ'fju:sɪvli/ *adv* efusivamente

effusiveness /ɪ'fju:sɪvnəs || ɪ'fju:sɪvnɪs/ *n* [u] efusividad *f*

EFL *n* [u] (= **English as a foreign language**) inglés *m* para extranjeros

e.g., eg (for example) p. ej. *or* vg. *or* e.g.; (in speech) por ejemplo

egalitarian /ɪ'gælə'teriən/ *adj* igualitario

egg /eg/ *n* huevo *m*; ***a good ~*** (colloq & dated): **he's a good ~** es buena gente (AmL), es un tipo bien (Esp fam); ***to be left with ~ on one's face*** quedar mal; ***to put all one's ~s in one basket*** jugárselo* todo a una carta

Phrasal verb

• **egg on** [v ▸ o ▸ adv, v ▸ adv ▸ o] incitar, azuzar*; **to ~ sb on to + INF** incitar a algn A + INF, azuzar* a algn PARA QUE (+ *subj*)

egg: **~cup** *n* huevera *f*; **~ custard** *n* [u c] natillas *fpl*; **~head** *n* (colloq) cerebro *m* (fam); **~nog** /'egnɑ:g || 'egnɒg/ *n* [u c] ponche *m* de huevo, rompope *m* (AmC, Méx), candeal *m* (RPl), cola *f* de mono (Chi); **~plant** *n* [c u] (AmE) berenjena *f*; **~ roll** *n* (AmE) rollito *m* (de) primavera; **~shell** *n* [c u] cáscara *f* de huevo; **~ timer** *n* (with sand) reloj *m* de arena (*de tres minutos*); (clockwork) avisador *m*; **~ white** *n* [c u] clara *f* de huevo; **~ yolk** *n* [c u] yema *f* de huevo

egis /'i:dʒəs || 'i:dʒɪs/ *n* (AmE) ▸**aegis**

EGM *n* = **extraordinary general meeting**

ego /'i:gəʊ, 'egəʊ/ *n* (*pl* **egos**) 1 (Psych) **the ~** el yo, el ego 2 (self-regard) amor *m* propio, ego *m*; **to boost sb's ~** alimentar el ego de algn

egocentric /'i:gəʊ'sentrɪk, 'eg-/ *adj* egocéntrico

egoism /'i:gəʊɪzəm, 'eg-/ *n* [u] 1 (selfishness) egoísmo *m* 2 ▸**egotism 1**

egoist /'i:gəʊəst, 'eg-/ *n* 1 (selfish person) egoísta *mf* 2 ▸**egotist 1**

egoistic /'i:gəʊ'ɪstɪk, 'eg-/, **-tical** /-tɪkəl/ *adj* 1 (selfish) egoísta 2 ▸**egotistic 1**

egotism /'i:gətɪzəm, 'eg-/ *n* [u] 1 (self importance) egotismo *m* 2 ▸**egoism 1**

egotist /'i:gətəst, 'eg-/ *n* 1 (self-important person) egotista *mf* 2 ▸**egoist 1**

egotistic /'i:gə'tɪstɪk, 'egə-/, **-tical** /-tɪkəl/ *adj* 1 (self-important) egotista 2 ▸**egoistic 1**

ego trip *n* (colloq): **his autobiography is simply an ~ ~** su autobiografía es un regodeo ególatra

egregious /ɪ'gri:dʒəs/ *adj* (frml) mayúsculo, atroz

egret /'i:gret || 'i:grɪt/ *n* garceta *f*

Egypt /'i:dʒəpt || 'i:dʒɪpt/ *n* Egipto *m*

Egyptian¹ /ɪ'dʒɪpʃən/ *adj* egipcio

Egyptian² *n* egipcio, -cia *m,f*

eh /ei/ *interj* 1 (expressing interest): **so you went to Paris, ~?** ah, ¿así que fuiste a París? 2 (inviting agreement) ¿eh?, ¿no? 3 (inviting repetition) ¿eh?, ¿qué?, ¿cómo?

EHIC *n* (= **European Health Certificate**) TSE *f*

eiderdown /'aɪdərdaʊn || 'aɪdədaʊn/ *n* edredón *m*

eider (duck) /'aɪdər || 'aɪdə(r)/ *n* eider *m*

eight¹ /eɪt/ *n* ocho *m*; ***to have had one over the ~*** (colloq) haber* bebido de más; *see also* **four¹**

eight² *adj* ocho *adj inv*; *see also* **four²**

eighteen /'eɪ'ti:n/ *adj/n* dieciocho *adj inv/m*

eighteenth¹ /'eɪ'ti:nθ/ *adj* decimoctavo; *see also* **fifth¹**

eighteenth² *adv* en decimoctavo lugar; *see also* **fifth²**

eighteenth³ *n* 1 (Math) dieciochoavo *m* 2 (part) dieciochoava parte *f* 3 (birthday): **it's her ~ today** hoy cumple dieciocho años

eightfold /'eɪtfəʊld/ *adj/adv see* **-fold**

eighth¹ /eɪtθ/ *adj* octavo; *see also* **fifth¹**

eighth² *adv* en octavo lugar; *see also* **fifth²**

eighth³ *n* 1 (Math) octavo *m* 2 (part) octava parte *f*

eighth note *n* (AmE) corchea *f*

eight hundred number *n* (AmE Telec) *número de teléfono de llamada gratuita*

eightieth¹ /'eɪtiəθ/ *adj* octogésimo; *see also* **fifth¹**

eightieth² *adv* en octogésimo lugar; *see also* **fifth²**

eightieth³ *n* 1 (Math) ochentavo *m* 2 (part) ochentava *or* octogésima parte *f*

eighty /'eɪti/ *adj/n* ochenta *adj inv/m*; *see also* **seventy**

Eire /'erə || 'eərə/ *n* Eire *m*, Irlanda *f*

eisteddfod /aɪ'steðvɔ:d || aɪ'stedvəd, aɪ'steðvɒd/ *n*: *festival galés de música y poesía*

Eisteddfod

Los *eisteddfodau* son festivales tradicionales en Gales, de uno o dos días de duración, durante los cuales individuos y grupos en representación de aldeas, iglesias, colegios o condados rivales compiten entre sí en la composición e interpretación de poesía, prosa y piezas musicales. El primer *eisteddfod* a nivel nacional se celebró en el castillo de Aberteifi-Cardigan en el año 1176. Desde 1880 el *National Eisteddfod of Wales* que dura más de una semana viene celebrándose cada agosto en una localidad distinta de Gales. Todos los eventos se celebran en galés (Welsh)

either[1] /'i:ðər, 'aɪðər || 'i:ðə(r), 'aɪðə(r)/ *conj* **either ... or ...** o ... o ... [o *becomes* u *when it precedes a word beginning with* o *or* ho]; **you can have ~ tea or coffee** puedes tomar (o) té o café; **he can't speak ~ Spanish or Italian** no sabe hablar (ni) español ni italiano; **~ your work improves or you're fired!** ¡o mejora tu trabajo o estás despedido!

either[2] *adj* 1 (one or the other): **you can take ~ route** puedes tomar cualquiera de las dos rutas; **the key wasn't in ~ drawer** la llave no estaba en ninguno de los dos cajones 2 (each): **on ~ side of the path** a ambos lados *or* a cada lado del camino

either[3] *pron* (esp BrE) cualquiera; (*with neg*) ninguno, -na; (*in questions*) alguno, -na; **~ (one) would be suitable** cualquiera (de los dos) serviría; **I couldn't wear ~ of those dresses** no podría ponerme ninguno de esos vestidos

either[4] *adv* (*with neg*) tampoco; **she can't cook and he can't ~** ella no sabe cocinar y él tampoco; **and I don't have to pay a penny ~** y ni siquiera tengo que pagar nada

ejaculate /ɪ'dʒækjəleɪt || ɪ'dʒækjʊleɪt/ *vi* (Physiol) eyacular

■ **ejaculate** *vt* (cry out) (frml) exclamar

eject /ɪ'dʒekt/ *vt* ‹*troublemaker/cassette*› expulsar

■ **eject** *vi* (Aviat) eyectarse

ejection /ɪ'dʒekʃən/ *n* [u] (of troublemaker) expulsión *f*; (by pilot) eyección *f*

ejection seat, (BrE) **ejector seat** /ɪ'dʒektər || ɪ'dʒektə(r)/ *n* asiento *m* de eyección

eke out /i:k/ [v ▸ adv ▸ o, v ▸ o ▸ adv] 1 (make last) ‹*resources/funds*› estirar, hacer* alcanzar 2 (barely obtain): **to ~ out a living** ganarse la vida a duras penas

el /el/ *n* [u c] (AmE colloq) = **elevated railroad**

elaborate[1] /ɪ'læbərət/ *adj* ‹*decoration/design/hairstyle*› complicado, intrincado, muy elaborado; ‹*meal*› de mucho trabajo; ‹*plan/arrangements*› minucioso, detallado; **in ~ detail** con todo detalle, muy minuciosamente

elaborate[2] /ɪ'læbəreɪt/ *vt* elaborar, idear

■ **elaborate** *vi* dar* (más) detalles, entrar en detalles *or* explicaciones; **to ~ ON** *o* **UPON sth** ampliar* algo, explicar* algo en mayor detalle

elaborately /ɪ'læbərətli/ *adv* ‹*planned*› minuciosamente, detalladamente; ‹*decorated*› muy elaboradamente

elaboration /ɪ'læbə'reɪʃən/ *n* [u] (of a theory, plan) elaboración *f*

élan /eɪ'lɑ:n/ *n* [u] (liter) ímpetu *m*, brío *m*, elán *m* (liter)

elapse /ɪ'læps/ *vi* transcurrir, pasar

elastic[1] /ɪ'læstɪk/ *n* 1 [u] (Tex) elástico *m* 2 [c] (garter) (AmE) liga *f* 3 [c] (AmE) ▸ **elastic band**

elastic[2] *adj* ‹*waistband/garter*› de elástico, elástico; ‹*stocking*› elastizado, elástico; ‹*fiber/properties*› elástico; ‹*rule/definition*› elástico

elasticated /ɪ'læstəkeɪtəd || ɪ'læstɪkeɪtɪd/ *adj* (BrE) con elástico

elastic band *n* (esp BrE) goma *f* (elástica), gomita *f* (RPl), liga *f* (Méx), caucho *m* (Col), elástico *m* (Chi), banda *f* elástica (Ven)

elasticity /ɪ,læs'tɪsəti/ *n* [u] (of fiber, substance) elasticidad *f*; (of rule, definition) flexibilidad *f*

elasticized /ɪ'læstəsaɪzd || ɪ'læstɪsaɪzd/ *adj* (AmE) con elástico

elated /ɪ'leɪtəd || ɪ'leɪtɪd/ *adj* eufórico

elation /ɪ'leɪʃən/ *n* [u] euforia *f*, júbilo *m* (liter)

elbow[1] /'elbəʊ/ *n* (of person, in pipe) codo *m*; (on river, road) recodo *m*; **my sweater is going at the ~s** se me están gastando los codos del suéter; ***to give sb the ~*** (BrE colloq) deshacerse* de algn

elbow[2] *vt* darle* un codazo a; **they ~ed us out of the way** nos apartaron a empujones

elbow: **~ grease** *n* [u] (colloq): **put some ~ grease into it!** ¡dale con más fuerza! (fam); **~ room** *n* [u] espacio *m*

elder[1] /'eldər || 'eldə(r)/ *adj* ‹*brother/sister/child*› mayor; **Pliny the E~** Plinio el Viejo

elder[2] *n*

A 1 (older person): **she's my ~ by two years** me lleva dos años, es dos años mayor que yo 2 (senior person): **the village/tribal ~s** los ancianos del pueblo/de la tribu 3 (Relig) miembro *m* del consejo

B (Bot) saúco *m*

elderberry /'eldər,beri || 'eldəberi/ *n* (*pl* **-ries**) baya *f* del saúco

elderly[1] /'eldərli || 'eldəli/ *adj* mayor, de edad, anciano; **an ~ lady** una señora mayor *or* de edad, una anciana

elderly[2] *pl n* **the ~** los ancianos

elder statesman *n* veterano *m* de la política

eldest /'eldəst || 'eldɪst/ *adj* (*before n*) ‹*brother/sister/child*› mayor; **the ~** (*as pron*) el/la mayor, el/la de más edad

elect[1] /ɪ'lekt/ *vt*

A (Adm, Govt) elegir*; **he was ~ed president** lo eligieron *or* fue elegido presidente

B (choose) (frml) **to ~ to + INF** optar POR + INF

elect[2] *adj* (*after n*): **the president ~** el presidente electo, la presidenta electa

election /ɪ'lekʃən/ *n* 1 [c] (event) elecciones *fpl*; **to call/hold an ~** convocar*/celebrar elecciones; (*before n*) ‹*campaign/speech*› electoral; ‹*day/results*› de las elecciones 2 [u] (act) elección *f*

electioneer /ɪ'lekʃə'nɪr || ɪ,lekʃə'nɪə(r)/ *vi* hacer* campaña *or* propaganda electoral

electioneering /ɪ'lekʃə'nɪrɪŋ || ɪ,lekʃə'nɪərɪŋ/ *n* [u] campaña *f* electoral

elective[1] /ɪ'lektɪv/ *adj*

A ‹*post/assembly*› electivo

B (optional) ‹*course/subject*› optativo

elective[2] *n* optativa *f*

elector /ɪ'lektər || ɪ'lektə(r)/ *n* elector, -tora *m,f*

electoral /ɪ'lektərəl/ *adj* (*usu before n*) ‹*system/reform*› electoral; **~ college** colegio *m* electoral; **~ register** *o* **roll** padrón *m* (AmL) *or* (Esp) censo *m or* (Chi, Ven) registro *m or* (Col) planilla *f* electoral

Electoral College

Es el sistema adoptado por los EEUU para elegir Presidente y Vicepresidente, mediante el cual los votantes de cada estado eligen a compromisarios (*electors*) que conforman los colegios electorales, los que a su vez se comprometen a votar por un determinado candidato. Todos los votos de un estado van a un candidato. Sólo se necesitan 270 votos (*electoral college votes*) para obtener la victoria, lo que significa que el Presidente puede ser elegido sin obtener la mayoría del voto popular

electorate /ɪ'lektərət/ *n* (+ *sing or pl vb*) electorado *m*

electric /ɪ'lektrɪk/ *adj* eléctrico; ‹*fence*› electrificado; ‹*performance/atmosphere*› electrizante; **~ bill** (AmE) cuenta *f or* recibo *m* de la electricidad *or* (fam) de (la) luz

electrical /ɪ'lektrɪkəl/ *adj* eléctrico

electrical: **~ engineer** *n* técnico, -ca *m,f* electricista; (with university degree) ingeniero electrotécnico, ingeniera electrotécnica *m,f*; **~ storm** *n* tormenta *f* eléctrica

electric: **~ blanket** *n* manta *f or* (AmL exc CS) cobija *f or* (CS) frazada *f* eléctrica; **~-blue** /ɪ'lektrɪk'blu:/ *adj* (*pred* **~ blue**) azul eléctrico *adj inv*; **~ chair** *n* silla *f* eléctrica

electrician /ɪ,lek'trɪʃən/ *n* electricista *mf*

electricity /ɪ,lek'trɪsəti/ *n* [u] electricidad *f*; **it runs on ~** funciona con *or* a electricidad; **is the ~ (turned) off/on?** ¿está desconectada/conectada la corriente?; (*before n*) **~ bill** (BrE) cuenta *f or* recibo *m* de la electricidad

electric shock *n* [c u] descarga *f* eléctrica
electrification /ɪˈlektrəfəˈkeɪʃən || ɪˌlektrɪfɪˈkeɪʃən/ *n* [u] electrificación *f*
electrify /ɪˈlektrəfaɪ || ɪˈlektrɪfaɪ/ *vt* **-fies, -fying, -fied** electrificar*; (excite, thrill) electrizar*
electrifying /ɪˈlektrəfaɪɪŋ || ɪˈlektrɪfaɪɪŋ/ *adj* electrizante
electrocute /ɪˈlektrəkjuːt/ *vt* electrocutar
electrocution /ɪˈlektrəˈkjuːʃən/ *n* [u c] electrocución *f*
electrode /ɪˈlektrəʊd/ *n* electrodo *m*
electrolysis /ɪˈlekˈtrɑːləsɪs || ˌɪlekˈtrɒləsɪs/ *n* [u] electrólisis *f*
electrolyte /ɪˈlektrəlaɪt/ *n* [c u] electrolito *m*
electromagnet /ɪˈlektrəʊˈmægnət || ɪˌlektrəʊˈmægnɪt/ *n* electroimán *m*
electromagnetic /ɪˈlektrəʊmægˈnetɪk/ *adj* electromagnético
electron /ɪˈlektrɑːn || ɪˈlektrɒn/ *n* electrón *m*
electronic /ɪˈlekˈtrɑːnɪk || ˌɪlekˈtrɒnɪk/ *adj* electrónico; **~ data processing** procesamiento *m* electrónico de datos; **~ publishing** edición *f* electrónica; **~ tag** etiqueta *f* de control electrónico
electronic: **~ cash** *n* [u] dinero *m* electrónico; **~ engineer** *n* ingeniero electrónico, ingeniera electrónica *m,f*; **~ mail** *n* [u] correo *m* electrónico
electronics /ɪˈlekˈtrɑːnɪks || ˌɪlekˈtrɒnɪks/ *n* 1 (subject) (+ *sing vb*) electrónica *f*; (*before n*) ‹*industry*› electrónico 2 (circuitry) (+ *sing or pl vb*) sistema *m* electrónico
electron microscope *n* microscopio *m* electrónico
electroplate /ɪˈlektrəpleɪt/ *vt* (with silver) galvanoplatear, platear mediante electrólisis; (with gold) electrodorar, dorar mediante electrólisis
elegance /ˈelɪgəns/ *n* [u] elegancia *f*
elegant /ˈelɪgənt/ *adj* elegante
elegantly /ˈelɪgəntli/ *adv* con elegancia, elegantemente
elegiac /ˈeləˈdʒaɪək || ˌelɪˈdʒaɪək/ *adj* (Lit) elegíaco
elegy /ˈelədʒi/ *n* (*pl* **-gies**) elegía *f*
element /ˈeləmənt || ˈelɪmənt/ *n*
A 1 (component part) elemento *m*; **the ~ of surprise** el factor sorpresa 2 (small amount): **an ~ of chance/doubt** algo de suerte/duda 3 (distinct group of people) elemento *m*, grupo *m*; **extremist ~s in society** elementos *mpl* extremistas de la sociedad 4 **elements** *pl* (rudiments): **the basic ~s of self-defense** los principios elementales de la defensa personal
B (Chem) elemento *m*
C **elements** *pl* (weather) (liter) **the ~s** los elementos
D (preferred environment) elemento *m*; **to be in one's ~** estar* en su (*or* mi *etc*) elemento, estar* como pez en el agua
E (of kettle, heater) resistencia *f*, elemento *m* (CS)
elemental /ˈeləˈmentl̩ || ˌelɪˈmentl̩/ *adj* (*usu before n*) ‹*forces*› de la naturaleza; ‹*feelings/fears*› primario
elementary /ˈeləˈmentəri/ *adj* elemental, básico
elementary: **~ school** *n* (in US) escuela *f* (de enseñanza) primaria; **~ teacher** *n* (in US) maestro, -tra *m,f* de enseñanza primaria
elephant /ˈeləfənt || ˈelɪfənt/ *n* 1 elefante, -ta *m,f*; ***the ~ in the room*** el problema importante y obvio que nadie quiere mencionar 2 (in US) (Pol) **the ~** *símbolo del partido republicano de los EEUU*
elevate /ˈeləveɪt || ˈelɪveɪt/ *vt* 1 (promote) **to ~ sb TO sth**: **to ~ sb to the peerage** concederle a algn el título de lord/lady; **he's been ~d to the position of manager** (hum) lo han ascendido a director 2 (frml) ‹*spirit*› elevar 3 ‹*load/platform*› elevar (frml), subir
elevated /ˈeləveɪtəd || ˈelɪveɪtɪd/ *adj* elevado
elevated railroad *n* [u c] (AmE) ferrocarril *m* elevado
elevation /ˈeləˈveɪʃən || ˌelɪˈveɪʃən/ *n*
A [u] (promotion) elevación *f*
B [c] (angle) elevación *f*; **the angle of ~** el ángulo de elevación
C [c] 1 (altitude) altura *f*, altitud *f* 2 (high place, hill) (frml) elevación *f* (del terreno)
D [c] (scale drawing) alzado *m*; **the front ~ of the house** la fachada de la casa
elevator /ˈeləveɪtər || ˈelɪveɪtə(r)/ *n* 1 (for passengers) (AmE) ascensor *m*, elevador *m* (Méx) 2 (for goods) elevador *m*, montacargas *m*(for goods) elevador *m*, montacargas *m*
eleven[1] /ɪˈlevən/ *n* 1 (number) once *m* 2 (in soccer, field hockey) equipo *m*, once *m* (period)
eleven[2] *adj* once *adj inv*
elevenses /ɪˈlevənzəz || ɪˈlevənzɪz/ *n* [u] (BrE colloq) (+ *sing or pl vb*) *tentempié de media mañana*, mediasnueves *fpl* (Col), almuerzo *m* (Esp, Méx)
eleventh[1] /ɪˈlevənθ/ *adj* undécimo; *see also* **fifth**[1]
eleventh[2] *adv* en undécimo lugar; *see also* **fifth**[2]
eleventh[3] *n* 1 (Math) onceavo *m* 2 (part) onceava parte *f*
eleventh hour *n*: **at the ~ ~** en el *or* a último momento; (*before n*) **eleventh-hour attempt** intento *m* de última hora
elf /elf/ *n* (*pl* **elves**) geniecillo *m*, elfo *m*
elicit /ɪˈlɪsət || ɪˈlɪsɪt/ *vt* ‹*laughter/smile*› provocar*; **to ~ sth (FROM sb)** ‹*explanation/reply*› obtener* algo (DE algn)
elide /ɪˈlaɪd/ *vt* (Ling) elidir
eligibility /ˈelədʒəˈbɪləti || ˌelɪdʒəˈbɪləti/ *n* [u] 1 (right, qualification): **the rules governing ~ for benefits** el reglamento que establece los requisitos necesarios para tener derecho a las prestaciones 2 (suitability for job, rank) idoneidad *f*
eligible /ˈelədʒəbəl || ˈelɪdʒəbəl/ *adj* 1 (qualified, suitable) ‹*applicant/candidate*› que reúne los requisitos necesarios; **to be ~ FOR sth: he's ~ for a grant** tiene derecho a solicitar una beca; **she's eminently ~ for promotion** es firme candidata a un ascenso; **~ to + INF: he is not ~ to compete** no reúne los requisitos necesarios para competir 2 (marriageable): **an ~ bachelor** un buen partido
eliminate /ɪˈlɪməneɪt || ɪˈlɪmɪneɪt/ *vt* eliminar; ‹*possibility/alternative/suspect*› descartar; **to ~ sth FROM sth** eliminar algo DE algo
elimination /ɪˈlɪməˈneɪʃən || ɪˌlɪmɪˈneɪʃən/ *n* [u] (getting rid of) eliminación *f*; (ruling out) descarte *m*; **by a process of ~** por (un proceso de) eliminación *or* descarte
elision /ɪˈlɪʒən/ *n* [u c] (Ling) elisión *f*
elite[1] /eɪˈliːt, ɪ-/ *n* (+ *sing or pl vb*) elite *f*, élite *f*
elite[2] *adj* (*before n*) selecto, de elite *or* élite
elitism /eɪˈliːtɪzəm, ɪ-/ *n* [u] elitismo *m*
elitist /eɪˈliːtɪst, ɪ-/ *adj* elitista
elixir /ɪˈlɪksər || ɪˈlɪksə(r)/ *n* elixir *m*
Elizabethan /ɪˈlɪzəˈbiːθən/ *adj* isabelino
elk /elk/ *n* (*pl* **~s** *or* **~**) (European animal) alce *m*; (American animal) uapití *m*
ellipse /ɪˈlɪps/ *n* elipse *f*
ellipsis /ɪˈlɪpsəs || ɪˈlɪpsɪs/ *n* (*pl* **-ses** /-siːz/) 1 [u c] (Ling) (omission) elipsis *f* 2 [c] (in punctuation) puntos *mpl* suspensivos
elliptical /ɪˈlɪptɪkəl/ *adj* elíptico

Ellis Island

Una pequeña isla en la bahía de Nueva York. Fue el lugar de entrada oficial a EEUU para la mayoría de los inmigrantes entre 1891 y 1943. Alrededor de 20 millones de personas ingresaron por allí

elm /elm/ *n* 1 [c] **~ (tree)** olmo *m* 2 [u] (wood) (madera *f* de) olmo *m*
elocution /ˈeləˈkjuːʃən/ *n* [u] dicción *f*, elocución *f*
elongate /ɪˈlɔːŋgeɪt || ˈiːlɒŋgeɪt/ *vt* alargar*
elongated /ɪˈlɔːŋgeɪtəd || ˈiːlɒŋgeɪtɪd/ *adj* alargado
elope /ɪˈləʊp/ *vi* fugarse* (*con un amante, novio para casarse*)
elopement /ɪˈləʊpmənt/ *n* [u] fuga *f* (*con un amante, novio para casarse*)
eloquence /ˈeləkwəns/ *n* [u] elocuencia *f*
eloquent /ˈeləkwənt/ *adj* elocuente
eloquently /ˈeləkwəntli/ *adv* con elocuencia, elocuentemente
El Salvador /elˈsælvədɔːr || ˌelˈsælvədɔː(r)/ *n* El Salvador
else /els/ *adv*
A (*after pron*): **somebody** *o* **someone ~** otra persona; **everybody** *o* **everyone ~** todos los demás; **everything ~** todo lo demás; **if all ~ fails** si todo lo demás falla, como último recurso; **there's little ~** *o* **not much ~ we can do**

no podemos hacer mucho más; **nobody** *o* **no one ~** nadie más; **there's nothing ~ to do** no nos queda otro remedio; **they have nowhere ~ to go** no tienen ningún otro sitio *or* lugar adonde ir; **was there anybody** *o* **anyone ~ there?** ¿estaba alguien más?; **anything ~?** ¿algo más?; **I never drink anything ~** nunca bebo otra cosa; **I can't think of anything ~** no se me ocurre nada más

B (with interrog): **what/who ~?** ¿qué/quién más?; **what ~ can you expect from her?** ¿qué otra cosa se puede esperar de ella?; **why ~ do you think he did it?** ¿y por qué (te) crees que lo hizo (si no por eso)?

C **or else** (*as conj*) si no; **do as I tell you or ~ ...!** ¡o haces lo que te digo o vas a ver!, ¡haz lo que te digo porque si no ...!

elsewhere /'elshwer || ˌels'weə(r)/ *adv*: **to go/look ~** ir* a/mirar en otro sitio *or* lugar; **~ in Europe** en otras partes *or* otros lugares de Europa

elucidate /ɪ'lu:sədeɪt || ɪ'lu:sɪdeɪt/ *vt* ‹*theory/point*› dilucidar, aclarar; ‹*mystery/incident*› esclarecer*

■ **elucidate** *vi*: **allow me to ~** permítame aclararlo

elucidation /ɪ'lu:sə'deɪʃən || ˌɪlu:sɪdeɪʃən/ *n* [u] (of theory, point) dilucidación *f*, aclaración *f*; (of mystery) esclarecimiento *m*

elude /i:'lu:d || ɪ'lu:d/ *vt* (avoid) eludir; (escape from) escaparse de; **success ~d him** el éxito le era esquivo; **the title ~s me** no puedo recordar el título

elusive /i:'lu:sɪv || i'lu:sɪv/ *adj* ‹*enemy/prey*› escurridizo, difícil de aprehender; ‹*goal/agreement*› difícil de alcanzar; **you're an ~ man** no hay quien te pille (fam), eres difícil de localizar

elver /'elvər || 'elvə(r)/ *n* angula *f*

elves /elvz/ *pl of* **elf**

emaciated /ɪ'meɪʃieɪtəd || ɪ'meɪsieɪtɪd/ *adj* ‹*person/animal*› escuálido; ‹*body/face*› consumido, descarnado

e-mail[1] /'i:meɪl/ *n* **1** [u] (system) correo *m* electrónico, email *m*; **to be on/have ~** tener* correo electrónico, tener* email; (*before n*) **~ address** dirección *f* de correo electrónico *or* de email **2** [c] (message) correo *m* electrónico, email m, emilio *m* (fam)

e-mail[2] *vt* **1** ‹*message*› enviar por correo electrónico, emailear (fam); **I'll ~ it to you** te lo mandaré por correo electrónico, te lo emailearé (fam) **2** ‹*person*›: **I'll ~ him right away** le mandaré un correo electrónico *or* un email *or* (hum) emilio enseguida, lo emailearé enseguida (fam)

emanate /'eməneɪt/ *vi* **to ~ FROM sth** «*gas/light/sound*» emanar DE algo; «*ideas/suggestions*» provenir* *or* proceder DE algo

emancipate /ɪ'mænsəpeɪt || ɪ'mænsɪpeɪt/ *vt* (frml) **to ~ sb (FROM sth)** emancipar a algn (DE algo)

emancipated /ɪ'mænsəpeɪtəd || ɪ'mænsɪpeɪtɪd/ *adj* emancipado; ‹*viewpoint/lifestyle*› independiente y progresista; **to become ~** emanciparse

emancipation /ɪ'mænsə'peɪʃən || ɪˌmænsɪ'peɪʃən/ *n* [u] (frml) emancipación *f*

emasculate /ɪ'mæskjəleɪt || ɪ'mæskjʊleɪt/ *vt* **1** (castrate) (frml) castrar, emascular (frml) **2** (weaken) ‹*legislation/political party*› debilitar; **he felt ~d** se sentía anulado

embalm /ɪm'bɑ:m/ *vt* embalsamar

embankment /ɪm'bæŋkmənt/ *n* (for road, railroad) terraplén *m*; (as protection) muro *m* de contención

embargo /ɪm'bɑ:rgəʊ || ɪm'bɑ:gəʊ/ *n* (*pl* **-goes**) **1** (trade sanctions) embargo *m*, prohibición *f*; **~ ON sth** embargo *or* prohibición DE algo; **a trade ~** un embargo comercial; **to lay** *o* **place** *o* **put an ~ on sth** imponer* un embargo sobre algo; **to lift** *o* **raise** *o* **remove an ~** levantar un embargo **2** (prohibition) **~ ON sth** prohibición *f* DE algo; **to put an ~ on sth** prohibir* algo

embark /ɪm'bɑ:rk || ɪm'bɑ:k/ *vi* **1** (on ship, plane) embarcar(se)* **2** (start) **to ~ ON** *o* **UPON sth** ‹*on career/new life*› emprender algo; ‹*on adventure/undertaking*› embarcarse* EN algo

embarkation /ˌembɑ:r'keɪʃən || ˌembɑ:'keɪʃən/ *n* [u] embarque *m*

embarrass /ɪm'bærəs/ *vt* hacerle* pasar vergüenza a, avergonzar*

embarrassed /ɪm'bærəst/ *adj*: **an ~ silence** un silencio violento *or* embarazoso; **I'm ~** me da vergüenza, me da pena (AmL exc CS); **to be ~ ABOUT -ING**: **she felt ~ about telling me** le daba vergüenza *or* (AmL exc CS) pena contármelo (fam); **to be ~ to + INF**: **I was ~ to ask any more questions** me dio vergüenza *or* apuro seguir preguntando

embarrassing /ɪm'bærəsɪŋ/ *adj* ‹*situation/question*› embarazoso; ‹*attempt/performance*› penoso, lamentable; **how ~!** ¡qué vergüenza *or* (AmL exc CS) pena!

embarrassingly /ɪm'bærəsɪŋli/ *adv*: **she was ~ close to tears** estaba a punto de llorar, lo cual era muy violento

embarrassment /ɪm'bærəsmənt/ *n* **1** [u] (shame) bochorno *m*, vergüenza *f*, pena *f* (AmL exc CS) **2** [c] (cause of shame): **this meal is an ~!** ¡esta comida es una vergüenza!; **he's an ~ to his friends** les hace pasar vergüenza a sus amigos

embassy /'embəsi/ *n* (*pl* **-sies**) embajada *f*

embattled /ɪm'bætḷd/ *adj* ‹*city*› asediado; ‹*troops*› en combate; ‹*politician*› acuciado por problemas

embed /ɪm'bed/ *vt* **-dd-** (in rock, wood) enterrar*, incrustar; **the bullet was ~ded in his arm** la bala quedó alojada en el brazo; **the incident is ~ded in my memory** el incidente está grabado en mi memoria

embellish /ɪm'belɪʃ/ *vt* adornar

embellishment /ɪm'belɪʃmənt/ *n* [c u] adorno *m*

ember /'embər || 'embə(r)/ *n* brasa *f*, ascua *f*

embezzle /ɪm'bezəl/ *vt* desfalcar*, malversar

embezzlement /ɪm'bezəlmənt/ *n* [u] desfalco *m*, malversación *f* (de fondos)

embezzler /ɪm'bezlər || ɪm'bezlə(r)/ *n* desfalcador, -dora *m,f*

embitter /ɪm'bɪtər || ɪm'bɪtə(r)/ *vt* ‹*person*› amargar*; ‹*relations*› agriar*

embittered /ɪm'bɪtərd || ɪm'bɪtəd/ *adj* ‹*person*› amargado; ‹*fighting/rivalry*› enconado; **to be/feel ~ about sth** estar*/sentirse* resentido por algo

emblazon /ɪm'bleɪzṇ/ *vt* (*usu pass*) estampar

emblem /'embləm/ *n* emblema *m*, símbolo *m*

embodiment /ɪm'bɑ:dɪmənt || ɪm'bɒdɪmənt/ *n* (personification, expression) encarnación *f*, personificación *f*

embody /ɪm'bɑ:di || ɪm'bɒdi/ *vt* **-dies, -dying, -died** **1** (personify) encarnar, personificar* **2** (express) ‹*thought/idea*› plasmar, expresar

embolden /ɪm'bəʊldṇ/ *vt* (liter) envalentonar

embolism /'embəlɪzəm/ *n* embolia *f*

emboss /ɪm'bɑ:s, ɪm'bɔ:s || ɪm'bɒs/ *vt* **1** ‹*leather/metal*› repujar **2** **embossed** *past p* ‹*stationery*› con membrete en relieve; ‹*wallpaper*› estampado en relieve

embrace[1] /ɪm'breɪs/ *vt* **1** (hug) abrazar* **2** ‹*idea/principle*› abrazar*; ‹*lifestyle/religion*› adoptar, abrazar* **3** (include) ‹*range/elements*› abarcar*, comprender

■ **embrace** *vi* «*couple/friends*» abrazarse*

embrace[2] *n* abrazo *m*

embrocation /ˌembrə'keɪʃən/ *n* [u c] linimento *m*, embrocación *f* (ant)

embroider /ɪm'brɔɪdər || ɪm'brɔɪdə(r)/ *vt* ‹*cloth/design*› bordar; ‹*story*› adornar

■ **embroider** *vi* bordar

embroidery /ɪm'brɔɪdəri/ *n* [u c] (*pl* **-ries**) bordado *m*

embroil /ɪm'brɔɪl/ *vt* **to ~ sb IN sth** envolver* *or* enredar *or* embrollar a algn EN algo; **to be/become ~ed in sth** estar*/verse* envuelto *or* enredado en algo

embryo /'embriəʊ/ *n* (*pl* **-os**) embrión *m*

embryonic /ˌembri'ɑ:nɪk || ˌembri'ɒnɪk/ *adj* (Biol) embrionario; ‹*plan/policy*› en estado embrionario

emcee /'em'si:/ *n* (colloq) (of program) presentador, -dora *m,f*; (of function) maestro, -tra *m,f* de ceremonias

emend /i:'mend || ɪ'mend/ *vt* (frml) enmendar*, corregir*

emendation /'i:men'deɪʃən/ *n* [u c] (frml) enmienda *f*

emerald /'emərəld/ *n* **1** [c u] (gem) esmeralda *f* **2** [u] (color) verde *m* esmeralda

emerald-green /'emərəld'gri:n/ *adj* (*pred* **emerald green**) verde esmeralda *adj inv*

emerge /ɪ'mɜ:rdʒ || ɪ'mɜ:dʒ/ *vi*

A **1** (come out) salir*, aparecer*; **to ~ FROM sth** salir* DE algo **2** (become evident, known) «*problem*» surgir*, aparecer*;

«*pattern*» dibujarse; «*truth*» revelarse; «*facts*» salir* a la luz
B [1] (come into being, evolve) «*idea/system*» surgir* [2] **emerging** *pres p* ‹*nation*› emergente, joven; ‹*industries*› naciente, incipiente

emergence /ɪ'mɜːrdʒəns || ɪ'mɜːdʒəns/ *n* (coming out) salida *f*, aparición *f*; (of movement, trend) aparición *f*, surgimiento *m*

emergency /ɪ'mɜːrdʒənsi || ɪ'mɜːdʒənsi/ *n* [c u] (*pl* **-cies**) [1] (serious situation) emergencia *f*; **it's an ~** es una situación de emergencia; **in an ~** *o* **in case of ~** en una emergencia *or* en caso de emergencia [2] (Med) urgencia *f*; (*before n*) ‹*case/operation*› de urgencia [3] (Govt): **a state of ~ was declared** se declaró el estado de excepción

emergency: **~ exit** *n* salida *f* de emergencia; **~ landing** *n* aterrizaje *m* forzoso; **~ room** *n* (AmE) sala *f* de urgencias *or* de guardia; **~ stop** *n* parada *f* de emergencia

emergent /ɪ'mɜːrdʒənt || ɪ'mɜːdʒənt/ *adj* (*usu before n*) ‹*nation*› joven, emergente; (developing) en vías de desarrollo; ‹*subculture/technology*› incipiente, emergente

emeritus /ɪ'merətəs || ɪ'merɪtəs/ *adj* emérito; **professor ~** *o* **~ professor** profesor emérito, profesora emérita *m,f*

emery /'eməri/: **~ board** *n* lima *f* de esmeril; **~ paper** *n* [u] papel *m* de lija

emetic /ɪ'metɪk/ *n* vomitivo *m*, emético *m*

emigrant /'eməgrənt || 'emɪgrənt/ *n* emigrante *mf*

emigrate /'eməgreɪt || 'emɪgreɪt/ *vi* emigrar

emigration /'emə'greɪʃən || ˌemɪ'greɪʃən/ *n* [u c] emigración *f*

émigré /'emɪgreɪ, ˌemɪ'greɪ || 'emɪgreɪ/ *n* (*f also* **-grée**) exiliado, -da *m,f*

eminence /'emənəns || 'emɪnəns/ *n*
A [u] (fame) prestigio *m*, renombre *m*
B [c] **Eminence** (title of cardinal) Eminencia

eminent /'emənənt || 'emɪnənt/ *adj* eminente, ilustre

eminently /'emənəntli || 'emɪnəntli/ *adv* (*as intensifier*) sumamente

emir /ə'mɪr || e'mɪə(r)/ *n* emir *m*

emirate /ə'mɪrət || 'emɪərət/ *n* emirato *m*

emissary /'eməseri || 'emɪsəri/ *n* (*pl* **-ries**) emisario, -ria *m,f*

emission /iː'mɪʃən || ɪ'mɪʃən/ *n* [u c] emisión *f*

emit /iː'mɪt || i'mɪt/ *vt* **-tt-** ‹*gas/smell/vapor*› despedir*; ‹*heat/light/radiation/sound*› emitir

> **Emmy**
>
> Los *Emmies* son el equivalente televisivo de los *Academy Awards* (Oscar awards), otorgados anualmente en Los Ángeles por la *National Academy of Television Arts and Sciences* a programas de televisión y sus realizadores en varias categorías

emoticon /ɪ'məʊtəkɑːn || ɪ'mɒtɪkɒn/ *n* emoticono *m*

emotion /ɪ'məʊʃən/ *n* [1] [c] (feeling) sentimiento *m* [2] [u] (strength of feeling) emoción *f*

emotional /ɪ'məʊʃnəl || ɪ'məʊʃənl/ *adj* [1] ‹*disorder*› emocional, afectivo; **~ blackmail** chantaje *m* afectivo [2] (sensitive) ‹*person/nature*› emotivo [3] (upset) emocionado; **to get ~** emocionarse [4] (moving) ‹*speech/experience/scene*› emotivo, conmovedor

emotionally /ɪ'məʊʃnəli/ *adv* [1] (Psych) ‹*mature*› emocionalmente; **~ deprived** con carencias afectivas *or* emocionales [2] ‹*behave/react/speak*› con gran emotividad

emotive /ɪ'məʊtɪv/ *adj* emotivo, cargado de emotividad

empathize /'empəθaɪz/ *vi* **to ~ WITH sb** identificarse* CON algn

empathy /'empəθi/ *n* [u] empatía *f*

emperor /'empərər || 'empərə(r)/ *n* emperador *m*

emphasis /'emfəsəs || 'emfəsɪs/ *n* (*pl* **-ses** /-siːz/) énfasis *m*; **to lay** *o* **place** *o* **put ~ on sth** hacer* hincapié *or* poner* énfasis en la importancia de algo

emphasize /'emfəsaɪz/ *vt* ‹*phrase/word*› enfatizar*, poner* énfasis en; ‹*fact/point/warning*› recalcar*, hacer* hincapié en; ‹*fault/value*› poner* de relieve; ‹*shape/feature*› resaltar, hacer* resaltar

emphatic /ɪm'fætɪk/ *adj* ‹*gesture/tone*› enérgico, enfático; ‹*assertion/refusal*› categórico

emphatically /ɪm'fætɪkli/ *adv* ‹*say/declare*› enérgicamente; ‹*deny*› categóricamente, rotundamente

emphysema /'emfə'ziːmə, -'siː- || ˌemfɪ'siːmə/ *n* [u] enfisema *m*

empire /'empaɪr || 'empaɪə(r)/ *n* [u c] imperio *m*

empirical /em'pɪrɪkəl, ɪm- || em'pɪrɪkəl, ɪm-/ *adj* empírico

empiricism /em'pɪrəsɪzəm, ɪm- || em'pɪrɪsɪzəm, ɪm-/ *n* [u] empirismo *m*

employ[1] /ɪm'plɔɪ/ *vt* [1] ‹*person*› (take on) contratar, emplear; (have working) emplear, dar* empleo a; **he's ~ed as a nightwatchman** trabaja de vigilante nocturno [2] ‹*method/tactics/tool*› emplear, valerse* de

employ[2] *n* (frml): **to be in sb's ~** *o* **in the ~ of sb** trabajar para algn

employable /ɪm'plɔɪəbəl/ *adj*: **he is no longer ~** ya nadie le va a dar trabajo

employee, (AmE also) **employe** /ɪm'plɔɪ'iː/ *n* empleado, -da *m,f*

employer /ɪm'plɔɪər || ɪm'plɔɪə(r)/ *n* empleador, -dora *m,f*; (of domestic worker etc) patrón, -trona *m,f*; **unions and ~s** los sindicatos y la patronal *or* los empresarios; **list your three most recent ~s** indique las tres últimas empresas para las que ha trabajado

employment /ɪm'plɔɪmənt/ *n* [u] [1] (work) trabajo *m*; **to be in ~** tener* trabajo; (*before n*) **~ agency** agencia *f* de trabajo *or* colocación [2] (availability of work) empleo *m*; **full ~** pleno empleo *m*; (*before n*) ‹*legislation*› laboral [3] (hiring, taking on) contratación *f*

emporium /em'pɔːriəm || ɪm'pɔːriəm/ *n* (*pl* **-riums** *or* **-ria** /-riə/) emporio *m* (comercial)

empower /ɪm'paʊər || ɪm'paʊə(r)/ *vt* [1] (authorize) conferirle* *or* otorgarle* poderes a; **she is ~ed to sign the contract on my behalf** está autorizada a *or* para firmar el contrato en mi nombre [2] (Pol, Sociol): **to ~ sb/oneself** investir* de poder a algn/investirse* de poder

empress /'emprəs || 'emprɪs/ *n* emperatriz *f*

emptiness /'emptinəs || 'emptinɪs/ *n* [u] (of landscape, region) *ausencia de vegetación, habitantes etc*; (meaninglessness) lo vacío, vacuidad *f* (frml)

empty[1] /'empti/ *adj* **-tier, -tiest** ‹*container/table*› vacío; ‹*words/gesture/life*› vacío; ‹*threat/promise*› vano

empty[2] **-ties, -tying, -tied** *vt* [1] ‹*container/warehouse*› vaciar* [2] (take or pour out): **she emptied the water down the sink** tiró el agua por el fregadero; **she emptied the contents all over the floor** vació la caja (*or* el bolso *etc*) en el suelo
■ **empty** *vi* «*room/street*» vaciarse*; «*river/stream*» **to ~ INTO sth** desaguar* EN algo

Phrasal verb

• **empty out** [v ▸ o ▸ adv, v ▸ adv ▸ o] ‹*bag/drawer/pockets*› vaciar*; ‹*garbage*› tirar, botar (AmL exc RPl)

empty[3] *n* (*pl* **-ties**) (colloq) (bottle) envase *m* (vacío), casco *m* (Esp, Méx)

empty: **~-handed** /'empti'hændəd || ˌempti'hændɪd/ *adv* con las manos vacías; **~-headed** /'empti'hedəd || ˌempti'hedɪd/ *adj*: **she's so ~-headed** es una cabeza hueca

EMS *n* (= **European Monetary System**) SME *m*

emu /'iːmjuː/ *n* emú *m*

emulate /'emjəleɪt || 'emjʊleɪt/ *vt* emular

emulation /'emjə'leɪʃən || ˌemjʊ'leɪʃən/ *n* emulación *f*

emulsifier /ɪ'mʌlsəfaɪər || ɪ'mʌlsɪfaɪə(r)/ *n* [u c] emulsionante *m*, emulsivo *m*

emulsion /ɪ'mʌlʃən/ *n* **~ (paint)** pintura *f* al agua

enable /ɪn'eɪbəl/ *vt* [1] (provide means for) **to ~ sb to + INF** permitir(le) A algn + INF [2] (make possible) posibilitar, permitir

enact /ɪn'ækt/ *vt*
A (Govt, Law) ‹*law*› promulgar*
B ‹*play/role*› representar; **the scene being ~ed before us** la escena que se desarrollaba ante nosotros

enamel[1] /ɪ'næməl/ *n* [u] esmalte *m*

enamel[2] *vt*, (BrE) **-ll-** esmaltar

e

enamored, (BrE) **enamoured** /ɪ'næmərd || ɪ'næməd/ *adj* (frml) **to be ~ OF sb** estar* enamorado *or* (frml *o* hum) prendado DE algn; **I'm not very ~ of** *o* **with the idea** no estoy muy entusiasmado con la idea

enc (= **enclosed**) anexo

encampment /ɪn'kæmpmənt/ *n* campamento *m*

encapsulate /ɪn'kæpsəleɪt || ɪn'kæpsjʊleɪt/ *vt* ‹*story/problem*› condensar, compendiar

encase /ɪn'keɪs/ *vt* revestir*, recubrir*; **~d IN sth** revestido *or* recubierto DE algo

encash /ɪn'kæʃ/ *vt* (BrE frml) hacer* efectivo (frml), cobrar

encephalitis /ɪn'sefə'laɪtəs || en,sefə'laɪtɪs/ *n* [u] encefalitis *f*

enchant /ɪn'tʃænt || ɪn'tʃɑːnt/ *vt* (delight, charm) cautivar; (Occult) hechizar*, encantar

enchanted /ɪn'tʃæntəd || ɪn'tʃɑːntɪd/ *adj* (under a spell) encantado; (delighted) **~ WITH/AT sth** encantado CON algo

enchanter /ɪn'tʃæntər || ɪn'tʃɑːntə(r)/ *n* mago, -ga *m,f*

enchanting /ɪn'tʃæntɪŋ || ɪn'tʃɑːntɪŋ/ *adj* encantador

enchantment /ɪn'tʃæntmənt || ɪn'tʃɑːntmənt/ *n* 1 [c u] (charm) encanto *m*, hechizo *m* (liter) 2 [u] (delight) embeleso *m* 3 [c] (spell) encantamiento *m*, hechizo *m*

enchantress /ɪn'tʃæntrəs || ɪn'tʃɑːntrɪs/ *n* maga *f*, hechicera *f*

encircle /ɪn'sɜːrkəl || ɪn'sɜːkəl/ *vt* ‹*camp/house*› rodear; ‹*waist/wrist*› ceñir*

enclave /'enkleɪv/ *n* enclave *m*

enclose /ɪn'kləʊz/ *vt*
A 1 (surround) encerrar*; (fence in) cercar*; **a valley ~d by high mountains** un valle circundado *or* rodeado de altas montañas 2 **enclosed** *past p* ‹*area/space*› cerrado
B (in letter) adjuntar, acompañar; **please find ~d ...** se adjunta *or* se acompaña ...

enclosure /ɪn'kləʊʒər || ɪn'kləʊʒə(r)/ *n*
A [c] 1 (enclosed space) recinto *m*; **a fenced ~** un cercado 2 (for spectators) (BrE Sport) recinto *m*
B [u] (of land) cercamiento *m*

encode /ɪn'kəʊd, en-/ *vt* codificar*, cifrar

encompass /ɪn'kʌmpəs/ *vt* (frml) abarcar*, englobar

encore /'ɑːnkɔːr || 'ɒŋkɔː(r)/ *n* bis *m*; (*as interj*) ¡otra!

encounter¹ /ɪn'kaʊntər || ɪn'kaʊntə(r)/ *vt* 1 (be faced with) ‹*danger/difficulty/opposition*› encontrar*, encontrarse* con 2 (come across) tropezar* *or* toparse con

encounter² *n* encuentro *m*; **his first ~ with the law** su primer tropiezo con la ley

encourage /ɪn'kɜːrɪdʒ || ɪn'kʌrɪdʒ/ *vt* 1 (give hope, courage to) animar, alentar* 2 (stimulate, inspire) **to ~ sb to + INF**: **she/it ~d me to carry on** me animó a seguir adelante; **to ~ sb IN sth**: **don't ~ him in bad habits** no le fomentes las malas costumbres 3 ‹*industry/competition/bad habit*› fomentar; ‹*growth*› fomentar, estimular; ‹*speculation*› intensificar*

encouragement /ɪn'kɜːrɪdʒmənt || ɪn'kʌrɪdʒmənt/ *n* [u c] (heartening) ánimo *m*; **she doesn't need any ~** no (le) hace falta que la animen a hacerlo

encouraging /ɪn'kɜːrɪdʒɪŋ || ɪn'kʌrɪdʒɪŋ/ *adj* ‹*news/progress*› alentador, esperanzador; **she's very ~** me (*or* nos *etc*) alienta mucho *or* me da muchos ánimos

encroach /ɪn'krəʊtʃ/ *vi* **to ~ ON** *o* **UPON sth** ‹*on land*› invadir algo; ‹*on rights*› cercenar algo

encroachment /ɪn'krəʊtʃmənt/ *n* [u c] (on land) invasión *f*; (on rights) cercenamiento *m* (frml)

encrust /ɪn'krʌst/ *vt* recubrir*; **~ed WITH sth**: **~ed with mud** con una costra de barro; **~ed with jewels** con incrustaciones de pedrería

encumber /ɪn'kʌmbər || ɪn'kʌmbə(r)/ *vt* 1 (burden) cargar*; **to be ~ed WITH sth** ‹*with debt/responsibility*› estar* cargado *or* agobiado DE algo 2 (hamper) estorbar

encumbrance /ɪn'kʌmbrəns/ *n* (burden, hindrance) estorbo *m*; **an ~ TO sb** un estorbo PARA algn

encyclical (letter) /en'sɪklɪkəl/ *n* encíclica *f*

encyclopedia, (BrE also) **encyclopaedia** /ɪn'saɪklə'piːdiə/ *n* enciclopedia *f*

encyclopedic, (BrE also) **encyclopaedic** /ɪn'saɪklə'piːdɪk/ *adj* enciclopédico

end¹ /end/ *n*
A 1 (extremity — of rope, stick) extremo *m*, punta *f*; (— of nose) punta *f*; (— of street) final *m*; **at the other/far ~ of the garden** al otro extremo/al fondo del jardín; **from one ~ of the country to the other** de punta a punta *or* de un extremo a otro del país; **the top ~ of the range** lo mejor de la gama; **to stand sth on (its) ~** poner* algo vertical, parar algo (AmL); **for weeks on ~** durante semanas y semanas, durante semanas enteras; **it measured five feet (from) ~ to ~** medía cinco pies de un lado al otro *or* de punta a punta; ***not to know/be able to tell one ~ of sth from the other*** no tener* ni idea de algo (fam); ***to be at the ~ of one's rope*** *o* (BrE) ***tether***: **I'm at the ~ of my rope** ya no puedo más *or* ya no aguanto más; ***to go off at the deep ~*** (colloq) ponerse* como una fiera; ***to make ~s meet*** llegar* a fin de mes; *see also* **deep end** 2 (part, side) (colloq) parte *f* (fam); **are there any problems at your ~?** ¿hay algún problema por tu lado? 3 (remaining part) final *m*, resto *m*
B 1 (finish, close) fin *m*, final *m*; Ⓢ **the end** fin; **at the ~ of the month** a fin de mes; **she read it to the very ~** lo leyó hasta el fin *or* final; **just give him the money and let that be an ~ of** *o* **to it** dale el dinero y que no se hable más; **that was the ~ of the story** ahí (se) acabó *or* terminó la historia; **we'll never hear the ~ of this** nunca nos va a dejar olvidar esto; **in the ~** al final; **to put an ~ to sth** poner* fin *or* poner* punto final a algo; ***at the ~ of the day*** (finally) al fin y al cabo, a fin de cuentas; (lit) al acabar *or* terminar el día 2 (death, destruction) final *m*, fin *m*; **they met a violent ~** tuvieron un final *or* fin violento; **to come to a sticky ~** (BrE) acabar *or* terminar mal 3 (outcome) final *m* 4 ***no ~*** (BrE colloq): **there were no ~ of people there** había la mar *or* la tira de gente (fam); **we enjoyed ourselves no ~** nos divertimos a más no poder (fam)
C (purpose) fin *m*; **an ~ in itself** un fin en sí mismo; **to use sth for one's own ~s** usar algo para sus (*or* mis *etc*) propios fines; **to this ~** (frml) con *or* a este fin (frml)

end² *vt* 1 (stop) ‹*argument/discussion/fight*› terminar, dar* *or* poner* fin a; ‹*gossip/speculation*› acabar *or* terminar con 2 (conclude) terminar, concluir* (frml)

■ **end** *vi* acabar, terminar; **it will all ~ in tears** va a acabar *or* terminar mal; **a word ~ing in 'x'** una palabra que termina en 'x'

Phrasal verb

• **end up** [v ▸ adv] terminar, acabar; **I ~ed up doing it myself** terminé *or* acabé haciéndolo yo mismo

endanger /ɪn'deɪndʒər || ɪn'deɪndʒə(r)/ *vt* 1 ‹*life*› poner* en peligro; ‹*chances/reputation*› hacer* peligrar 2 **endangered** *past p* ‹*species/wildlife*› en peligro *or* en vías de extinción

endear /ɪn'dɪr || ɪn'dɪə(r)/ *vt* **to ~ oneself TO sb** granjearse el cariño de algn

endearing /ɪn'dɪrɪŋ || ɪn'dɪərɪŋ/ *adj* atractivo

endearment /ɪn'dɪrmənt || ɪn'dɪəmənt/ *n* [c u] expresión *f* de cariño; **terms/words of ~** palabras *fpl* cariñosas *or* de cariño

endeavor¹, (BrE) **endeavour** /ɪn'devər || ɪn'devə(r)/ *n* (frml) (attempt) esfuerzo *m*, intento *m*; **he made every ~ to help** intentó ayudar por todos los medios

endeavor², (BrE) **endeavour** *vt* (frml) **to ~ to + INF** intentar por todos los medios + INF, esforzarse* POR + INF

endemic /en'demɪk/ *adj* endémico

ending /'endɪŋ/ *n* 1 (conclusion) final *m*, desenlace *m*; **the story has a happy ~** la historia tiene un final feliz 2 (Ling) desinencia *f*, terminación *f*; **verb ~s** desinencias verbales

endive /'endaɪv, -dɪv/ *n* (AmE) endivia *f*, endibia *f*; (BrE) escarola *f*

endless /'endləs || 'endlɪs/ *adj* 1 ‹*journey/meeting*› interminable; ‹*plain/patience*› sin límites, infinito; ‹*chatter/complaining*› continuo, incesante 2 (innumerable) innumerable; **the possibilities are ~** las posibilidades son infinitas

endlessly /'endləsli || 'endlɪsli/ *adv* 1 (infinitely): **the plain/road stretched out ~ before us** la llanura/carretera se extendía interminable ante nosotros 2 (incessantly) ‹*talk/chatter*› constantemente, incesantemente, sin parar 3 (time and time again) ‹*try/argue*› hasta la saciedad

endocrine /'endəkrən || 'endəʊkraɪn, -krɪn/ *adj* endocrino

end-of-term /'endəv'tɜːrm || ˌendəv'tɜːm/ *adj* (BrE) (*before n*) de final de trimestre

endorse /ɪn'dɔːrs || ɪn'dɔːs/ *vt*
A 1 (approve) ‹*statement/decision*› aprobar*, refrendar; **I fully ~ that opinion** comparto totalmente esa opinión 2 (Pol) refrendar 3 ‹*product*› promocionar
B (sign) ‹*check/bill*› endosar
C (BrE Auto, Law) *anotar los detalles de una infracción de tráfico en el permiso de conducir*

endorsement /ɪn'dɔːrsmənt || ɪn'dɔːsmənt/ *n* [c u]
A 1 (approval) aval *m*, aprobación *f* 2 (Pol) refrendo *m* 3 (Marketing) promoción *f*
B (on driving licence) (BrE) anotación *f* (*de una infracción de tráfico*)

endow /ɪn'daʊ/ *vt* 1 (provide) (*usu pass*) **~ed WITH sth** dotado DE algo 2 (provide income for) ‹*college/school/hospital*› dotar (de fondos) a

endowment /ɪn'daʊmənt/ *n*
A [c u] (Fin) donación *f*, legado *m*; (*before n*) **~ mortgage** (BrE) hipoteca *f* de inversión
B (attribute) (frml) atributo *m* (frml), dote *f*

end: **~ product** *n* producto *m* final; **~ result** *n* resultado *m* final

endurable /ɪn'dʊrəbəl || ɪn'djʊərəbəl/ *adj* (*usu neg*) soportable, tolerable

endurance /ɪn'dʊrəns || ɪn'djʊərəns/ *n* [u] (physical) resistencia *f*, aguante *m*; (mental) entereza *f*, fortaleza *f*; **powers of ~** capacidad *f* de aguante; (*before n*) **~ test** prueba *f* de resistencia

endure /ɪn'dʊr || ɪn'djʊə(r)/ *vt* soportar
■ **endure** *vi* «*fame/friendship/memories*» perdurar

enduring /ɪn'dʊrɪŋ || ɪn'djʊərɪŋ/ *adj* ‹*fame/memory*› imperecedero, perdurable; ‹*peace/change*› duradero

end user *n* destinatario *m* final, usuario *m*

endways /'endweɪz/, (AmE also) **endwise** /-waɪz/ *adv* (with end forward) de canto, de lado, (end to end) a lo largo

ENE (= **east-northeast**) ENE

enema /'enəmə/ *n* enema *m*

enemy /'enəmi/ *n* (*pl* **-mies**) 1 (adversary) enemigo, -ga *m,f*; **she's her own worst ~** su peor enemigo es ella misma 2 (opponent in war) (+ *sing o pl vb*) **the ~** el enemigo; (*before n*) ‹*action/forces/territory*› enemigo

energetic /ˌenər'dʒetɪk || ˌenə'dʒetɪk/ *adj* 1 ‹*person*› lleno de energía; ‹*exercise*› enérgico; ‹*vacation/day*› muy activo 2 (forceful) ‹*denial/protest*› enérgico

energetically /ˌenər'dʒetɪkli || ˌenə'dʒetɪkli/ *adv* 1 ‹*work/dance*› con energía 2 ‹*argue/deny*› enérgicamente

energy /'enərdʒi || 'enədʒi/ *n* [u] energía *f*; (power, effort) energías *fpl*; (*before n*) **~ crisis** crisis *f* energética

energy: **~-efficient** /ˌenərdʒiɪ'fɪʃənt || ˌenədʒiɪ'fɪʃənt/ *adj* energéticamente eficiente; **~-saving** /'enərdʒi ˌseɪvɪŋ || 'enədʒiˌseɪvɪŋ/ *adj* de ahorro energético

enervating /'enərveɪtɪŋ || 'enəveɪtɪŋ/ *adj* (frml) debilitante

enfant terrible /ˌɑːnfɑːnte'riːblə || ˌɒnfɒnte'riːblə/ *n* (*pl* **enfants terribles** /ˌɑːnfɑːnte'riːblə || ˌɒnfənte'riːblə/) enfant terrible *mf*

enfold /ɪn'fəʊld/ *vt* (liter) envolver*

enforce /ɪn'fɔːrs || ɪn'fɔːs/ *vt* 1 ‹*law/regulation*› hacer* respetar *or* cumplir; ‹*claim/right*› hacer* valer 2 **enforced** *past p* ‹*leisure/silence*› forzoso, impuesto

enforcement /ɪn'fɔːrsmənt || ɪn'fɔːsmənt/ *n* [u]: **they are responsible for the ~ of the law** son responsables de hacer cumplir *or* respetar la ley; (*before n*) **~ agencies** (AmE) departamentos *mpl* de seguridad del estado; **~ officers** (AmE) agentes *mfpl* de la ley

engage /ɪn'geɪdʒ/ *vt*
A ‹*attention/interest*› captar, atraer*; **to ~ sb in conversation** entablar una conversación con algn
B ‹*cog/wheel*› engranar con; ‹*gear*› engranar, meter (fam); **to ~ the clutch** embragar*, apretar* el embrague
C (hire) ‹*staff/performer*› contratar
■ **engage** *vi*
A (take part) **to ~ IN sth**: **to ~ in politics** dedicarse* a la política
B «*cog/wheel*» engranar

engaged /ɪn'geɪdʒd/ *adj*
A (betrothed) prometido, comprometido (AmL); **to be ~ TO sb** estar* prometido A algn, estar* comprometido CON algn (AmL); **to get ~** prometerse, comprometerse (AmL)
B (*pred*) 1 (occupied) (frml) ocupado; **I'm otherwise ~** tengo otro compromiso; **~ IN** *o* **ON**: **they are ~ in a new business venture** tienen un nuevo negocio entre manos; **the work we are ~ on** el trabajo que nos ocupa 2 (BrE) ‹*toilet*› ocupado 3 (BrE Telec) ocupado, comunicando (Esp); **the ~ tone** *o* **signal** la señal de ocupado *or* (Esp) de comunicando

engagement /ɪn'geɪdʒmənt/ *n*
A (pledge to marry) compromiso *m*; (period) noviazgo *m*; **they have broken off their ~** han roto su compromiso; (*before n*) **~ ring** anillo *m* de compromiso
B (appointment) compromiso *m*

engaging /ɪn'geɪdʒɪŋ/ *adj* atractivo, encantador; **she's very ~** es muy simpática

engender /ɪn'dʒendər || ɪn'dʒendə(r)/ *vt* (frml) engendrar (frml)

engine /'endʒən || 'endʒɪn/ *n* 1 (motor) motor *m*; **the ship's ~s** las máquinas del barco; (*before n*) **to have ~ trouble** tener* problemas con el motor 2 (locomotive) locomotora *f*, máquina *f*

engine driver *n* (BrE) maquinista *mf*

engineer¹ /ˌendʒə'nɪr || ˌendʒɪ'nɪə(r)/ *n*
A 1 (graduate) ingeniero, -ra *m,f* 2 (in factory) (BrE) oficial, -ciala *m,f* 3 (for maintenance) (BrE) técnico *mf*, ingeniero, -ra *m,f* (Méx)
B (AmE Rail) maquinista *mf*

engineer² *vt* ‹*plan*› urdir, tramar; ‹*defeat/downfall*› fraguar*; **genetically ~ed** creado por la ingeniería genética

engineering /ˌendʒə'nɪrɪŋ || ˌendʒɪ'nɪərɪŋ/ *n* [u] ingeniería *f*

engine room *n* (Naut) cuarto *m or* sala *f* de máquinas

England /'ɪŋglənd/ *n* Inglaterra *f*; (*before n*) ‹*squad/team/player*› (BrE) inglés

English¹ /'ɪŋglɪʃ/ *adj* inglés

English² *n* 1 [u] (language) inglés *m*; **British/American ~** inglés británico/americano; (*before n*) ‹*lesson/teacher*› de inglés 2 (people) (+ *pl vb*) **the ~** los ingleses

English: **~man** /'ɪŋglɪʃmən/ *n* (*pl* **-men** /-mən/) inglés *m*; ***an ~man's home is his castle*** *frase que señala la importancia que el inglés atribuye a la privacidad del hogar*; **~-speaking** *adj* de habla inglesa; **~woman** *n* inglesa *f*

engrave /ɪn'greɪv/ *vt* grabar; **to ~ sth WITH sth**: **he had the bracelet ~d with her name** hizo grabar su nombre en la pulsera; **to ~ sth ON sth** grabar algo EN algo

engraver /ɪn'greɪvər || ɪn'greɪvə(r)/ *n* grabador, -dora *m,f*

engraving /ɪn'greɪvɪŋ/ *n* [c u] grabado *m*

engross /ɪn'grəʊs/ *vt* absorber*; **to be ~ed IN sth** estar* absorto *or* enfrascado EN algo

engrossing /ɪn'grəʊsɪŋ/ *adj* fascinante, apasionante

engulf /ɪn'gʌlf/ *vt* «*flames/fire/waves*» envolver*; «*lava*» sepultar; «*feeling*» asaltar; **war ~ed the country** el país se sumió en la guerra

enhance /ɪn'hæns || ɪn'hɑːns/ *vt* ‹*beauty/taste*› realzar*, dar* realce a; ‹*value*› aumentar; ‹*reputation/performance*› mejorar

enhancement /ɪn'hænsmənt || ɪn'hɑːnsmənt/ *n* [u] (of quality, performance) mejora *f*; (of flavor, beauty) realce *m*; (of value) aumento *m*

enigma /ɪ'nɪgmə/ *n* (*pl* **-mas**) enigma *m*

enigmatic /ˌenɪg'mætɪk/ *adj* enigmático

enjoin /ɪn'dʒɔɪn/ *vt* (frml)
A (strongly urge) **to ~ sth ON sb** encarecerle* algo a algn; **to ~ sb to + INF** encarecerle* a algn QUE (+ *subj*)
B (prohibit) (AmE Law) **to ~ sb FROM -ING** prohibirle* a algn QUE (+ *subj*)

enjoy /ɪn'dʒɔɪ/ *vt*
A (like): **I ~ed the book** me gustó mucho el libro; **I ~ wine/music** me gusta el vino/la música; **I ~ed the party** lo pasé bien en la fiesta; **to ~ each moment to the full** disfrutar al máximo de cada momento; **I ~ traveling** me gusta viajar, disfruto viajando
B (have, experience) ‹*good health*› disfrutar de, gozar* de

■ **enjoy** *vi* (on serving food) **~!** ¡buen provecho!
■ *v refl* **to ~ oneself** divertirse*, pasarlo *or* pasarla bien

enjoyable /ɪn'dʒɔɪəbəl/ *adj* ‹*day/meal/vacation*› agradable, placentero (frml); **an ~ book** un libro de lectura muy amena

enjoyment /ɪn'dʒɔɪmənt/ *n* [u c] (pleasure) placer *m*; **she gets a lot of ~ from** *o* **out of reading** disfruta mucho leyendo, le encanta leer

enlarge /ɪn'lɑːrdʒ || ɪn'lɑːdʒ/ *vt* ‹*hole/area*› agrandar; ‹*gland/heart*› dilatar; ‹*room/office*› ampliar*; ‹*print/photograph*› ampliar*
■ **enlarge** *vi* (frml) **to ~ (ON** *o* **UPON sth)** extenderse* (SOBRE algo)

enlargement /ɪn'lɑːrdʒmənt || ɪn'lɑːdʒmənt/ *n* [1] [u] (of gland, heart) dilatación *f* [2] [u] (of building) ampliación *f* [3] [u c] (Phot) ampliación *f*

enlarger /ɪn'lɑːrdʒər || ɪn'lɑːdʒə(r)/ *n* ampliadora *f*

enlighten /ɪn'laɪtn̩/ *vt* ‹*people/population*› ilustrar (frml); **would you care to ~ me?** ¿te importaría explicarme?

enlightened /ɪn'laɪtn̩d/ *adj* ‹*person/view*› progresista; ‹*decision*› inteligente

enlightening /ɪn'laɪtn̩ɪŋ/ *adj* esclarecedor, instructivo

enlightenment /ɪn'laɪtn̩mənt/ *n* [u] [1] (explanation): **I turned to her for ~** recurrí a ella en busca de una explicación *or* de una aclaración [2] (Hist) **the (Age of) E~** la Ilustración, el Siglo de las Luces

enlist /ɪn'lɪst/ *vi* alistarse; **to ~ IN sth** alistarse EN algo
■ **enlist** *vt* ‹*soldiers/helpers/members*› reclutar, alistar; ‹*sailors*› enrolar; ‹*support/aid*› conseguir*; **to ~ sb IN sth** conseguir* el apoyo de algn EN algo

enlisted man /ɪn'lɪstəd || ɪn'lɪstɪd/ *n* (AmE) soldado *m* raso

enlistment /ɪn'lɪstmənt/ *n* [u] (Mil) alistamiento *m*, reclutamiento *m*

enliven /ɪn'laɪvən/ *vt* ‹*conversation/person*› animar; ‹*room/place*› darle* vida *or* alegría a, alegrar

en masse /ɑːn'mæs || ɒn'mæs/ *adv* en masa, en bloque

enmesh /ɪn'meʃ/ *vt* **to be ~ed IN sth** estar* enredado EN algo

enmity /'enməti/ *n* [u c] (*pl* **-ties**) (frml) enemistad *f*

ennui /'ɑː'nwiː || ɒn'wiː/ *n* [u] (liter) hastío *m*

enormity /ɪ'nɔːrməti || ɪ'nɔːməti/ *n* [u] enormidad *f*

enormous /ɪ'nɔːrməs || ɪ'nɔːməs/ *adj* enorme, inmenso; ‹*strength/courage*› enorme

enormously /ɪ'nɔːrməsli || ɪ'nɔːməsli/ *adv* ‹*enjoy/benefit*› enormemente; **he's ~ fat/rich** es gordísimo/riquísimo

enough[1] /ɪ'nʌf/ *adj* bastante, suficiente; (*pl*) bastantes, suficientes; **I don't have ~ money to buy it** no me alcanza el dinero para comprarlo; **I didn't get ~ sleep** no dormí bastante *or* lo suficiente; **they had more than ~ time** tuvieron tiempo de sobra

enough[2] *pron*: **do you need any more chairs/paper? — no, I have ~** ¿necesitas más sillas/papel? — no, tengo suficientes *or* bastantes/suficiente *or* bastante; **they don't pay us ~** no nos pagan bastante *or* lo suficiente; **that's ~ for me, thank you** (es) suficiente, gracias; **you've had more than ~ to drink** ya has bebido más que suficiente; **~ is ~!** ¡ya basta!; **I've had ~!** ¡ya estoy harto!

enough[3] *adv*
A (sufficiently): **you don't go out ~** no sales lo suficiente; **make sure it's big/heavy ~** asegúrate de que sea lo suficientemente grande/pesado; **that's not good ~** eso no me satisface, con eso no alcanza; **I was foolish ~ to give him my phone number** fui tan idiota, que le di el número de teléfono; **their house is more than big ~ for three people** su casa basta y sobra para tres personas; **would you be kind ~ to open the window?** ¿sería tan amable de abrir la ventana?
B [1] (*as intensifier*): **the threat was plain ~** la amenaza fue muy clara; **curiously ~** curiosamente *or* aunque parezca curioso [2] (quite, very): **it's natural ~ that he should want to see her** es muy normal que la quiera ver; **he seemed willing ~ to help** parecía muy dispuesto a ayudar [3] (tolerably, passably): **I like my job well ~ but ...** mi trabajo me gusta pero ...; **it's a nice ~ city** como ciudad no está mal

enquire /ɪn'kwaɪr || ɪn'kwaɪə(r)/ *vt/i* ▸ **inquire**

enquiring /ɪn'kwaɪrɪŋ || ɪn'kwaɪərɪŋ/ *adj* ▸ **inquiring**

enquiry /'ɪnkwairi, 'ɪnkwəri || ɪn'kwaɪəri/ *n* ▸ **inquiry**

enrage /ɪn'reɪdʒ/ *vt* enfurecer*, encolerizar*

enraged /ɪn'reɪdʒd/ *adj* enfurecido; **he was ~ when he found out** cuando se enteró se puso furioso *or* se enfureció

enrich /ɪn'rɪtʃ/ *vt* enriquecer*

enrichment /ɪn'rɪtʃmənt/ *n* [u] enriquecimiento *m*

enroll, (BrE) **enrol -ll-** /ɪn'rəʊl/ *vi* matricularse, inscribirse*
■ **enroll** *vt* «*parents*» matricular, inscribir*; **the club ~ed 20 new members last year** el año pasado 20 personas se hicieron socias del club

enrollment, (BrE) **enrolment** /ɪn'rəʊlmənt/ *n* [u c] inscripción *f*, matrícula *f*

en route /ɑːn'ruːt || ɒn'ruːt/ *adv* por el camino, de camino; **we were ~ ~ to** *o* **for Cambridge** íbamos camino a Cambridge

ensconce /ɪn'skɑːns || ɪn'skɒns/ *vt*: **I was comfortably ~d in an armchair** estaba cómodamente arrellanado *or* instalado en un sillón
■ *v refl* **to ~ oneself** instalarse

ensemble /ɑːn'sɑːmbəl || ɒn'sɒmbəl/ *n*
A (group of performers) conjunto *m*
B (Clothing) conjunto *m*
C (whole) conjunto *m*

enshrine /ɪn'ʃraɪn/ *vt* (preserve) consagrar; **these principles are ~d in the constitution** la constitución consagra estos principios

ensign /'ensaɪn, 'ensən/ *n*
A (flag) enseña *f*, pabellón *m*
B (in US navy) alférez *mf*

enslave /ɪn'sleɪv/ *vt* esclavizar*

ensnare /ɪn'sner || ɪn'sneə(r)/ *vt* atrapar

ensue /ɪn'suː || ɪn'sjuː/ *vi* seguir*; **in the ensuing days** en los días que siguieron; **in the ensuing fight** en la pelea que tuvo lugar a continuación

en suite /ˌɑːn'swiːt || ˌɒn'swiːt/ *adj* adjunto, en suite

ensure /ɪn'ʃʊr || ɪn'ʃʊə(r), ɪn'ʃɔː(r)/ *vt* asegurar, garantizar*; **please ~ that ...** por favor asegúrese de que ...

entail /ɪn'teɪl/ *vt* ‹*risk*› implicar*, suponer*, conllevar; ‹*expense*› acarrear, implicar*, suponer*; **the position ~s a lot of responsibility** el cargo implica *or* conlleva mucha responsabilidad

entangle /ɪn'tæŋgəl/ *vt* enredar; **to become ~d in sth** (physically) enredarse en algo; (in scheme, lie) verse* envuelto *or* involucrado en algo

entanglement /ɪn'tæŋgəlmənt/ *n* [c u] enredo *m*

enter[1] /'entər || 'entə(r)/ *vt*
A [1] ‹*room/house/country*› entrar en, entrar a (esp AmL); **to ~ port** «*ship*» tomar puerto; **it never ~ed my head** ni se me pasó por la mente *or* la cabeza [2] (penetrate) entrar en
B (begin) ‹*period/phase*› entrar en
C [1] (join) ‹*army*› alistarse en, entrar en; ‹*firm/organization*› entrar en, incorporarse a; **to ~ the priesthood** hacerse* sacerdote [2] (begin to take part in) ‹*war/negotiations*› entrar en; ‹*debate/dispute*› sumarse a [3] ‹*student/candidate*› presentar; **12 horses have been ~ed in the race** se han inscrito 12 caballos para tomar parte en la carrera [4] ‹*race*› inscribirse* (para tomar parte) en; **to ~ a competition** presentarse a un concurso
D [1] (record — in register) inscribir*; (— in ledger, book) anotar, dar* entrada a [2] (Comput) dar* entrada a, introducir*
E (Law): **to ~ a plea of guilty/not guilty** declararse culpable/inocente
■ **enter** *vi*
A entrar; **~!** ¡adelante! *or* ¡pase!
B **to ~ (FOR sth)** ‹*for competition/race*› inscribirse* (EN algo); ‹*for examination*› presentarse (A algo)

Phrasal verb

• **enter up** [v ▸ o ▸ adv, v ▸ adv ▸ o] (BrE) ‹*transaction*› anotar, registrar

enter[2] *n* (Comput) intro *m*

enteritis /'entə'raɪtəs || ˌentə'raɪtɪs/ *n* [u] enteritis *f*

enterprise /'entərpraɪz || 'entəpraɪz/ *n*
A [1] [c] (project) empresa *f* [2] [u] (initiative, daring) empuje *m*, iniciativa *f*
B [1] [c] (company) empresa *f* [2] [u] (business activity): **free ~** la

libre empresa; **private ~** la iniciativa privada; (sector) el sector privado

enterprising /'entərpraɪzɪŋ || 'entəpraɪzɪŋ/ *adj* ‹*person*› emprendedor, con iniciativa; ‹*plan/venture*› que demuestra iniciativa

entertain /'entər'teɪn || ˌentə'teɪn/ *vt*
A (amuse) ‹*audience*› entretener*; **to keep sb ~ed** entretener* *or* tener* entretenido a algn
B (give hospitality to): **we enjoy ~ing friends** nos gusta recibir (a los amigos) en casa *or* invitar a los amigos
C (frml) ‹*idea/suggestion*› contemplar, considerar; ‹*doubt/suspicions*› abrigar* (frml), albergar* (frml)
■ **entertain** *vi*
A (provide entertainment) entretener*
B (have guests) recibir

entertainer /'entər'teɪnər || ˌentə'teɪnə(r)/ *n* artista *mf* (*del mundo del espectáculo*); (presenter of program) (Rad, TV) animador, -dora *m,f*

entertaining[1] /'entər'teɪnɪŋ || ˌentə'teɪnɪŋ/ *adj* ‹*book/movie/anecdote*› entretenido, ameno; ‹*person*› divertido

entertaining[2] *n*: **they do a lot of ~** reciben mucho *or* a menudo

entertainment /'entər'teɪnmənt || ˌentə'teɪnmənt/ *n*
A 1 [u] (amusement) entretenimiento *m* 2 [c] (show) espectáculo *m*
B [u] (hospitality) (*before n*) ‹*allowance/expenses*› de representación

enthrall, (BrE) **enthral** /ɪn'θrɔːl/ *vt* **-ll-** cautivar, embelesar

enthralling /ɪn'θrɔːlɪŋ/ *adj* fascinante, apasionante

enthrone /ɪn'θrəʊn/ *vt* ‹*king/queen*› entronizar*, exaltar al trono

enthuse /ɪn'θuːz || ɪn'θjuːz/ *vi* **to ~ ABOUT/OVER sth** mostrarse* muy entusiasmado CON algo
■ **enthuse** *vt* (colloq) entusiasmar

enthusiasm /ɪn'θuːziæzəm || ɪn'θjuːziæzəm/ *n* [u c] entusiasmo *m*

enthusiast /ɪn'θuːziæst || ɪn'θjuːziæst/ *n* entusiasta *mf*

enthusiastic /ɪn'θuːzi'æstɪk || ɪnˌθjuːzi'æstɪk/ *adj* entusiasta; **to be ~ about sth** estar* entusiasmado con algo

enthusiastically /ɪn'θuːzi'æstɪkli || ɪnˌθjuːzi'æstɪkli/ *adv* con entusiasmo

entice /ɪn'taɪs/ *vt* atraer*; **to ~ people into the shops** para atraer a la gente a las tiendas; **they ~d him away with the offer of a higher salary** se lo llevaron prometiéndole un sueldo más alto

enticement /ɪn'taɪsmənt/ *n* 1 [u] (act of enticing) incentivación *f* 2 [c] (thing that entices) señuelo *m*, incentivo *m*

enticing /ɪn'taɪsɪŋ/ *adj* tentador, apetecible, atractivo

entire /ɪn'taɪr || ɪn'taɪə(r)/ *adj* 1 (whole) (*before n*) entero 2 (intact) (*pred*) intacto

entirely /ɪn'taɪrli || ɪn'taɪəli/ *adv* totalmente, completamente; **I'm not ~ surprised** no me sorprende del todo; **it's ~ up to you** como tú quieras

entirety /ɪn'taɪrəti || ɪn'taɪərəti/ *n* [u]: **in its ~** íntegramente, en su totalidad

entitle /ɪn'taɪtḷ/ *vt*
A (give right) **to ~ sb TO sth** darle* a algn derecho A algo; **to be ~d TO sth** tener* derecho A algo
B (name) (frml) (*often pass*) titular, poner* por título, darle* el título de; **a poem ~d 'Laura'** un poema titulado *or* que lleva por título 'Laura'

entitlement /ɪn'taɪtḷmənt/ *n* [u c] **~ (TO sth)** derecho (A algo); (*before n*) ‹*program*› (AmE) de ayuda social

entity /'entəti/ *n* (*pl* **-ties**) entidad *f*

entomology /'entə'mɑːlədʒi || ˌentə'mɒlədʒi/ *n* [u] entomología *f*

entourage /'ɑːntʊ'rɑːʒ || ˌɒntʊ'rɑːʒ/ *n* séquito *m*

entrails /'entreɪlz/ *pl n* (of person) entrañas *fpl*; (of animal) vísceras *fpl*

entrance[1] /'entrəns/ *n*
A 1 [c] (way in) entrada *f*; **at the ~ to the building** en *or* a la entrada del edificio 2 [c] (foyer) hall *m*; (*before n*) **~ hall** hall *m*, vestíbulo *m* 3 [u] (access) (frml) entrada *f*; **to gain ~** entrar
B [u] (admission — to club, museum) entrada *f*; (— to school, university) ingreso *m*; (*before n*) **~ fee** (for entry) (precio *m* de) entrada *f*; (to join club) cuota *f* de ingreso *or* inscripción; (for exam, competition) cuota *f or* tasa *f* de inscripción; **there is an ~ charge** se cobra la entrada
C [c] 1 (act of entering) entrada *f*; **to make one's ~** hacer* su (*or* mi *etc*) entrada 2 (Theat) entrada *f* en escena

entrance[2] /ɪn'træns || ɪn'trɑːns/ *vt* embelesar, extasiar*

entrancing /ɪn'trænsɪŋ || ɪn'trɑːnsɪŋ/ *adj* fascinante

entrant /'entrənt/ *n* (in competition) participante *mf*; (for exam) candidato, -ta *m,f*

entreat /ɪn'triːt/ *vt* (liter) suplicar*, rogar*; **to ~ sb to + INF** suplicarle* *or* rogarle* a algn QUE (+ *subj*)

entreaty /ɪn'triːti/ *n* (*pl* **-ties**) (liter) súplica *f*, ruego *m*

entrée, entree /'ɑːntreɪ || 'ɒntreɪ/ *n* [c] 1 (main dish) (esp AmE) plato *m* fuerte *or* principal, segundo plato *m* 2 (first course) (BrE) entrada *f*, entrante *m* (Esp)

entrenched /ɪn'trentʃt/ *adj* ‹*position*› afianzado; **deeply ~ prejudices** prejuicios *mpl* muy arraigados

entrepreneur /'ɑːntrəprə'nɜːr || ˌɒntrəprə'nɜː(r)/ *n* empresario, -ria *m,f*

entrepreneurial /'ɑːntrəprə'nɜːriəl || ˌɒntrəprə'nɜːriəl/ *adj* (*usu before n*) ‹*spirit*› emprendedor (*en los negocios*); ‹*abilities/talents*› para los negocios

entrust /ɪn'trʌst/ *vt* **to ~ sth TO sb** encomendarle* *or* confiarle* algo A algn; **I ~ my son to your care** te encomiendo a mi hijo, te confío el cuidado de mi hijo; **to ~ sb WITH sth** confiarle* algo A algn

entry /'entri/ *n* (*pl* **entries**)
A [u] (coming, going in) entrada *f*; **~ INTO sth** entrada EN *or* (esp AmL) A algo
B [u] (access) entrada *f*, acceso *m*; ⊘ **no entry** (on door) prohibida la entrada; (on road sign) prohibido el paso; **to refuse sb ~** negarle* la entrada *or* la admisión a algn
C [c u] 1 (in accounts) entrada *f*, asiento *m* 2 (in diary) anotación *f*, entrada *f* 3 (in dictionary — headword) entrada *f*; (in encyclopedia — article) artículo *m*
D [c] (in contest) (person entered) participante *mf*; (thing entered): **the winning ~ in the painting competition** el ejemplar ganador del concurso de pintura; **there were 20 entries** hubo 20 inscripciones
E [c] (door, gate) (AmE) entrada *f*

entry: **~-level** /'entrilevəl/ *adj* 1 (suitable for beginners) ‹*computing/course*› para principiantes 2 (basic) ‹*computer*› básico; 3 (AmE) ‹*job/worker*› de la categoría más baja; **~phone** *n* (BrE) portero *m* eléctrico *or* (Esp) automático, interfón *m* (Méx), intercomunicador *m* (Ven); **~way** *n* (AmE) entrada *f*

entwine /ɪn'twaɪn/ *vt* (liter) 1 (twist together) entrelazar* 2 (twist around): **the ivy ~d itself** *o* **was ~d around the tree** la hiedra se enroscaba en el árbol

E-number /'iːˌnʌmbər || 'iːˌnʌmbə(r)/ número *m* E (*aditivo alimentario*)

enumerate /ɪ'nuːməreɪt || ɪ'njuːməreɪt/ *vt* enumerar

enunciate /ɪ'nʌnsieɪt/ *vt* (frml) 1 (pronounce) ‹*syllable/word*› articular 2 (state) ‹*idea/theory*› enunciar

enunciation /ɪ'nʌnsi'eɪʃən/ *n* [u] (frml) (diction) dicción *f*; (articulation) articulación *f*

envelop /ɪn'veləp/ *vt* envolver*; **(to be) ~ed IN sth** (estar*) envuelto EN algo

envelope /'envələʊp/ *n* sobre *m*

enviable /'enviəbəl/ *adj* envidiable

envious /'enviəs/ *adj* envidioso; ‹*expression*› (lleno) de envidia; **to be ~ OF sth/sb** envidiar algo/a algn

enviously /'enviəsli/ *adv* con envidia; **she looked at me ~** me miró envidiosa *or* con envidia

environment /ɪn'vaɪrənmənt || ɪn'vaɪərənmənt/ *n* 1 (Ecol) **the ~** el medio ambiente; **the Department of the E~** (in UK) el Ministerio del Medio Ambiente, ≈ la Secretaría de Desarrollo Urbano y Ecología (*en Méx*) 2 (surroundings): **a hostile ~ for man** un medio hostil al hombre; **she's studying gorillas in their natural ~** estudia a las gorilas en su entorno *or* hábitat natural; **the work/home ~** el ambiente de trabajo/del hogar

environmental /ɪn'vaɪrən'mentḷ || ɪnˌvaɪərən'mentḷ/ *adj* 1 (Ecol) ‹*factor*› ambiental, medioambiental; ‹*damage*› al medio ambiente, medioambiental; **~ groups** grupos *mpl* ecologistas 2 (of surroundings) ‹*factor*› ambiental; ‹*influence*› del ambiente *or* entorno *or* medio

e

environmentalist /ɪn'vaɪrən'mentḷəst || ɪn,vaɪərən'mentəlɪst/ *n* ecologista *mf*; (*before n*) ‹*group/movement*› ecologista

environmentally /ɪn'vaɪrən'mentḷi || ɪn,vaɪərən'mentəli/ *adv* 1▸ **~-friendly products** productos *mpl* ecológicos, productos *mpl* que no dañan al medio ambiente 2▸ (*indep*) desde el punto de vista ecológico

environs /ɪn'vaɪrənz || ɪn'vaɪərənz/ *pl n* alrededores *mpl*, entorno *m*

envisage /ɪn'vɪzɪdʒ/ *vt* 1▸ (foresee) prever*; **we don't ~ staying for long** no tenemos pensado quedarnos mucho tiempo 2▸ (visualise) imaginarse, concebir*

envision /ɪn'vɪʒən/ *vt* (AmE) prever*

envoy /'envɔɪ/ *n* enviado, -da *m,f*

envy¹ /'envi/ *n* [u] envidia *f*; **you'll be the ~ of the whole school** serás la envidia de toda la escuela

envy² *vt* **envies, envying, envied** envidiar; **to ~ sb sth** envidiarle algo a algn

enzyme /'enzaɪm/ *n* enzima *f*

eon /'iːɑːn, 'iːən || 'iːən, 'iːɒn/ *n* (Geol) eón *m*; **~s ago** (liter) hace millones de años

EP *n* (= **extended-play record**) (disco *m*) EP *m*

EPA *n* (in US) = **Environmental Protection Agency**

epaulette, (AmE also) **epaulet** /'epəlet/ *n* (on dress uniform) charretera *f*; (on trenchcoat) trabilla *f*

epee, épée /'epeɪ || 'eɪpeɪ/ *n* espada *f* (*de esgrima*)

ephemera /ɪ'femərə/ *pl n*: *objetos coleccionables que no tienen valor intrínseco, como programas de teatro etc*

ephemeral /ɪ'femərəl/ *adj* efímero

epic¹ /'epɪk/ *adj* (*usu before n*) ‹*poem/poetry/film*› épico; ‹*achievement/struggle*› colosal, de epopeya; **on an ~ scale** a *or* en gran escala

epic² *n* (poem) poema *m* épico; (film) superproducción *f*; (novel) epopeya *f*

epicenter, (BrE) **epicentre** /'epəsentər || 'epɪsentə(r)/ *n* (Geol) epicentro *m*

epicure /'epəkjʊr || 'epɪkjʊə(r)/ *n* (frml) sibarita *mf*

epidemic¹ /'epə'demɪk || ,epɪ'demɪk/ *n* epidemia *f*

epidemic² *adj* epidémico; **the crisis has reached ~ proportions** la crisis afecta ya a toda la región (*or* el país *etc*)

epidermis /'epə'dɜːrməs || ,epɪ'dɜːmɪs/ *n* [u] epidermis *f*

epidural /'epɪ'dʊrəl || ,epɪ'djʊərəl/ *n* anestesia *f* epidural *or* peridural

epiglottis /'epə'glɑːtəs || ,epɪ'glɒtɪs/ *n* epiglotis *f*

epigram /'epəgræm || 'epɪgræm/ *n* epigrama *m*

epilepsy /'epəlepsi || 'epɪlepsi/ *n* [u] epilepsia *f*

epileptic¹ /'epə'leptɪk || ,epɪ'leptɪk/ *adj* ‹*fit/attack*› epiléptico, de epilepsia; **she's ~** es epiléptica

epileptic² *n* epiléptico, -ca *m,f*

epilogue, (AmE also) **epilog** /'epəlɔːg || 'epɪlɒg/ *n* epílogo *m*

Epiphany /ɪ'pɪfəni/ *n* **the ~** la Epifanía (del Señor)

episcopal /ɪ'pɪskəpəl/ *adj* episcopal; **the E~ Church** (in Scotland and US) la Iglesia Episcopaliana *or* Episcopal

Episcopalian /ɪ'pɪskə'peɪliən/ *adj* episcopaliano

episode /'epəsəʊd || 'epɪsəʊd/ *n* episodio *m*

episodic /'epə'sɑːdɪk || ,epɪ'sɒdɪk/ *adj* (made up of episodes) en episodios; (intermittent) episódico

epistle /ɪ'pɪsəl/ *n* 1▸ **Epistle** (Relig) epístola *f*; **the E~s** las Epístolas 2▸ (letter) (hum) epístola *f* (hum)

epitaph /'epətæf || 'epɪtɑːf/ *n* epitafio *m*

epithet /'epəθet || 'epɪθet/ *n* (descriptive word, phrase) epíteto *m*; (descriptive title) apelativo *m*, sobrenombre *m*

epitome /ɪ'pɪtəmi/ *n* (embodiment) personificación *f*; (typical example) arquetipo *m*; **she is the ~ of kindness** es la bondad personificada *or* la personificación de la bondad

epitomize /ɪ'pɪtəmaɪz/ *vt* tipificar*; ‹‹*person*›› ser* la personificación de

epoch /'epək || 'iːpɒk/ *n* era *f*, época *f*

epoch-making /'epək,meɪkɪŋ || 'iːpɒk,meɪkɪŋ/ *adj* (*before n*) que hace época, que marca un hito

eponymous /ɪ'pɑːnəməs || ɪ'pɒnɪməs/ *adj* epónimo

EPOS /'iːpɑːs || 'iːpɒs/ (= **electronic point of sale**) terminal *m* punto de venta

Epsom salts /'epsəm/ *pl n* sulfato *m* de magnesia (*usado como purgante*)

equable /'ekwəbəl/ *adj* ‹*character*› sereno, ecuánime; ‹*climate*› constante

equal¹ /'iːkwəl/ *adj*

A 1▸ (in size, amount, ability) igual; **five miles is ~ to eight kilometers** cinco millas equivalen a *or* son iguales a ocho kilómetros; **the windows are ~ in size** las ventanas son de igual tamaño *or* son iguales de tamaño; **all (other) things being ~** si no intervienen otros factores 2▸ (in privilege, status) igual; **everyone is ~ before the law** todos somos iguales ante la ley; **~ opportunities/rights** igualdad *f* de oportunidades/derechos; **we are an ~ opportunities** *o* **opportunity employer** practicamos una política de igualdad de oportunidades (*sin discriminar por razones de sexo, raza, credo, orientación sexual etc*)

B (capable, adequate) **~ TO sth**: **he isn't/doesn't feel ~ to the task** no es/no se siente capaz de hacerlo

equal² *n* igual *mf*; **my boss treats me as an ~** mi jefe me trata como a su igual *or* de igual a igual

equal³ *vt*, (BrE) **-ll-**

A (Math) ser* igual a; **three times three ~s nine** tres por tres son nueve *or* es igual a nueve; **his ignorance is ~ed only by his stupidity** su ignorancia sólo puede compararse a su estupidez

B ‹*record/time*› igualar

Phrasal verb

• **equal out** (esp AmE colloq) ▸**even out**

equality /ɪ'kwɑːləti || ɪ'kwɒləti/ *n* [u] igualdad *f*

equalize /'iːkwəlaɪz/ *vt* ‹*pressure/weight*› igualar; ‹*incomes*› equiparar

■ **equalize** *vi* (Sport) empatar, igualar el marcador

equalizer /'iːkwəlaɪzər || 'iːkwəlaɪzə(r)/ *n* (Sport) gol *m* de la igualada *or* del empate

equally /'iːkwəli/ *adv*

A 1▸ (in equal amounts) ‹*divide/share*› por igual, equitativamente 2▸ (without bias) ‹*treat*› de la misma manera *or* forma, (por) igual

B (to an equal degree) igualmente; **~ easily/comfortably** con igual *or* con la misma facilidad/comodidad

C (*indep*) 1▸ (just as possibly) **~ (well)** de igual modo 2▸ (at the same time) (*as linker*) al mismo tiempo

equal sign, (BrE) **equals sign** *n* igual *m*, signo *m* de igual

equanimity /'ekwə'nɪməti/ *n* [u] (frml) ecuanimidad *f*

equate /ɪ'kweɪt/ *vt* (compare) equiparar; (identify) identificar*; **to ~ sth WITH sth** equiparar/identificar* algo CON algo

■ **equate** *vi* **to ~ WITH sth** corresponder A algo

equation /ɪ'kweɪʒən/ *n* ecuación *f*; **a simple/quadratic ~** una ecuación de primer/segundo grado

equator /ɪ'kweɪtər || ɪ'kweɪtə(r)/ *n* **the ~** *o* **E~** el ecuador

equatorial /'ekwə'tɔːriəl/ *adj* ecuatorial

equestrian /ɪ'kwestriən/ *adj* ‹*skills*› ecuestre; ‹*sports*› hípico

equidistant /'iːkwə'dɪstənt || ,iːkwɪ'dɪstənt/ *adj* equidistante; **to be ~ FROM sth** equidistar *or* ser* equidistante DE algo

equilateral /'iːkwə'lætərəl || ,iːkwɪ'lætərəl/ *adj* equilátero

equilibrium /'iːkwə'lɪbriəm || ,iːkwɪ'lɪbriəm/ *n* [u] (*pl* **-riums** *or* **-ria** /-riə/) (balance) equilibrio *m*; (poise) calma *f*

equine /'ekwaɪn/ *adj* (frml) equino

equinox /'iːkwənɑːks, 'ek- || 'iːkwɪnɒks, 'ek-/ *n* equinoccio *m*

equip /ɪ'kwɪp/ *vt* **-pp-** 1▸ (furnish, supply) ‹*troops/laboratory*› equipar; **to ~ sth/sb WITH sth** proveer* algo/a algn DE algo 2▸ (prepare, make capable) preparar; **to ~ sb TO + INF** preparar a algn PARA + INF

equipment /ɪ'kwɪpmənt/ *n* [u] equipo *m*; **office ~** *mobiliario, máquinas y material de oficina*; **sports ~** artículos *mpl* deportivos

equitable /'ekwətəbəl || 'ekwɪtəbəl/ *adj* (frml) equitativo

equitably /'ekwətəbli || 'ekwɪtəbli/ *adv* equitativamente

equity /'ekwəti/ *n*

A [u] (fairness) (frml) equidad *f* (frml)

B (Busn, Fin) **1** [u] (shareholders' interest in company) patrimonio *m* neto; (*before n*) ~ **capital** capital *m* propio **2** **equities** *pl n* (shares) valores *mpl* de renta variable

equivalent¹ /ɪ'kwɪvələnt/ *adj* **1** (equal) ‹*size/value*› equivalente; **to be ~ TO sth/-ING** equivaler A algo/+ INF **2** (corresponding) ‹*position/term*› equivalente; **to be ~ TO sth** ser* el equivalente DE algo

equivalent² *n* equivalente *m*

equivocal /ɪ'kwɪvəkəl/ *adj* ‹*reply/result*› equívoco, ambiguo; ‹*attitude*› ambiguo

equivocate /ɪ'kwɪvəkeɪt/ *vi* hablar con evasivas

equivocation /ɪ'kwɪvə'keɪʃən/ *n* [c u] evasiva *f*, subterfugio *m*

er /ɜːr/ *interj* este, esto (Esp)

era /'ɪrə, 'erə || 'ɪərə/ *n* era *f*, época *f*

ERA
A (in US) (Law) = **Equal Rights Amendment**
B (in baseball) = **Earned Run Average**

eradicate /ɪ'rædəkeɪt || ɪ'rædɪkeɪt/ *vt* ‹*corruption/disease*› erradicar*

erase /ɪ'reɪs || ɪ'reɪz/ *vt* borrar; ‹*blackboard*› (AmE) borrar

eraser /ɪ'reɪsər || ɪ'reɪzə(r)/ *n* goma *f* (de borrar); **a blackboard ~** (AmE) un borrador

ere¹ /er || eə(r)/ *prep* (arch *or* poet) antes de; **~ long** dentro de poco

ere² *conj* (arch *or* poet) antes de que

erect¹ /ɪ'rekt/ *adj*
A ‹*bearing/posture*› erguido, derecho
B (Physiol) erecto

erect² *vt* ‹*altar/monument*› erigir* (frml), levantar; ‹*barricade/wall*› levantar; ‹*tent*› armar, montar, levantar

erection /ɪ'rekʃən/ *n*
A (frml) **1** [u] (of building, monument) construcción *f*; (of barricade) levantamiento *m* **2** [c] (building) construcción *f*
B [c] (Physiol) erección *f*

ergonomics /'ɜːrgə'nɑːmɪks || ˌɜːgə'nɒmɪks/ *n* (field of study) (+ *sing vb*) ergonomía *f*

Eritrea /'erə'treɪə || ˌerɪ'treɪə/ *n* Eritrea *f*

ERM *n* = **Exchange Rate Mechanism**

ermine /'ɜːrmən || 'ɜːmɪn/ *n* [u c] armiño *m*

erode /ɪ'rəʊd/ *vt* «*water/wind/waves*» erosionar; «*acid*» corroer*; ‹*confidence/faith*› minar, socavar

erogenous zone /ɪ'rɑːdʒənəs/ *n* zona *f* erógena

erosion /ɪ'rəʊʒən/ *n* [u] (by water, wind, waves) erosión *f*; (by acid) corrosión *f*; (of confidence, power, rights) menoscabo *m*, deterioro *m*

erotic /ɪ'rɑːtɪk || ɪ'rɒtɪk/ *adj* erótico

erotica /ɪ'rɑːtɪkə || ɪ'rɒtɪkə/ *n* (+ *sing or pl vb*) (literature) literatura *f* erótica; (art) arte *m* erótico

eroticism /ɪ'rɑːtəsɪzəm || ɪ'rɒtɪsɪzəm/ *n* [u] erotismo *m*

err /er || ɜː(r)/ *vi* (frml): **to ~ IN sth/-ING** equivocarse* *or* errar* EN algo/AL + INF; **to ~ on the side of caution** pecar* de cauteloso *or* por exceso de precaución

errand /'erənd/ *n* **1** (short mission) mandado *m* (esp AmL), recado *m* (Esp); **to run an ~ for sb** hacerle* un mandado *or* (Esp) recado a algn; (*before n*) **~ boy** mandadero *m*, chico *m* de los mandados *or* (Esp) recados **2** (task) (liter) misión *f*; **an ~ of mercy** una misión de caridad *or* auxilio

errant /'erənt/ *adj* (liter) ‹*child*› descarriado; ‹*husband*› infiel

errata /e'rɑːtə/ *pl of* **erratum**

erratic /ɪ'rætɪk/ *adj* ‹*performance/work*› desigual, irregular; ‹*person/moods*› imprevisible; ‹*course*› errático

erratum /e'rɑːtəm/ *n* (*pl* **-ta**) errata *f*; **S errata** fe de erratas

erroneous /ɪ'rəʊniəs/ *adj* erróneo

erroneously /ɪ'rəʊniəsli/ *adv* erróneamente

error /'erər || 'erə(r)/ *n* [c u] error *m*; **a clerical/printer's ~** un error administrativo/de imprenta; **to make an ~** cometer un error; **in ~** por equivocación, por error; **to be in ~** estar* en un error; ***to see the ~ of one's ways*** darse* cuenta de que se ha actuado mal; (*before n*) **~ message** (Comput) mensaje *m* de error

ersatz /'ersɑːts || 'ɜːzæts, 'eə-/ *adj* (*before n*) (pej): **~ fur** imitación *f* piel, piel *f* sintética; **~ coffee** sucedáneo *m or* sustituto *m* del café

erstwhile /'ɜːrsthwaɪl || 'ɜːstwaɪl/ *adj* (liter) antiguo

erudite /'erjədaɪt || 'eruːdaɪt/ *adj* (frml) erudito

erudition /'erjə'dɪʃən || ˌeruː'dɪʃən/ *n* [u] (frml) erudición *f*

erupt /ɪ'rʌpt/ *vi* **1** «*volcano/geyser*» entrar en erupción, hacer* erupción **2** «*water*» salir* *or* manar a chorros **3** (break out) «*violence/fighting*» estallar; **he ~ed with anger at the news** estalló en cólera al oír la noticia

eruption /ɪ'rʌpʃən/ *n* [c u] **1** (of volcano) erupción *f* **2** (of violence) brote *m*; (of anger) estallido *m*

escalate /'eskəleɪt/ *vi* **1** «*fighting/violence/dispute*» intensificarse*; «*prices/claims*» aumentar; **the scuffles ~d into a riot** las refriegas terminaron en serios disturbios callejeros **2** **escalating** *pres p* ‹*dispute/tension*› creciente; **escalating wages/prices** sueldos/precios en continuo aumento *or* que van en escalada
■ **escalate** *vt* ‹*fighting/tension*› intensificar*; ‹*demands*› aumentar

escalation /'eskə'leɪʃən/ *n* [u c] (of war, violence) escalada *f*; (of dispute) intensificación *f*; (of prices) aumento *m*, escalada *f*

escalator /'eskəleɪtər || 'eskəleɪtə(r)/ *n* escalera *f* mecánica

escapade /'eskəpeɪd/ *n* aventura *f*

escape¹ /ɪ'skeɪp/ *vi*
A **1** (flee) escaparse; «*prisoner*» fugarse*, escapar(se); **to ~ FROM sth** ‹*from prison*› fugarse* *or* escapar(se) DE algo; ‹*from cage/zoo*› escaparse DE algo; ‹*from danger/routine*› escapar DE algo **2** **escaped** *past p* ‹*animal*› escapado; **an ~d convict** un preso que se ha fugado de la cárcel **3** «*air/gas/water*» escaparse
B (from accident, danger) salvarse; **she ~d with minor injuries** sólo sufrió heridas leves
■ **escape** *vt* ‹*pursuer/police*› escaparse *or* librarse de; ‹*capture*› salvarse de, escapar a; ‹*responsibilities/consequences*› librarse de; **they ~d punishment/prosecution** se libraron de ser castigados/juzgados; **that detail had ~d my notice** se me había escapado ese detalle; **the name ~s me** no puedo recordar el nombre

escape² *n* **1** [c u] (from prison) fuga *f*, huida *f*; **to make one's ~** escaparse; (*before n*) **~ attempt** intento *m* de fuga; **our ~ route was blocked** el camino por donde pensábamos fugarnos estaba cortado **2** [c u] (from accident, danger): **to have a narrow/miraculous ~** salvarse *or* escaparse por muy poco/milagrosamente; **there's no ~** no hay escapatoria posible **3** [c] (of gas, air, water) escape *m*, fuga *f* **4** [c u] (from reality) evasión *f* **5** [c u] (Comput): **press ~** pulse *or* oprima la tecla de escape; (*before n*) ‹*key/routine*› de escape

escape: **~ artist** *n* escapista *mf*; **~ clause** *n* cláusula *f* de escape *or* de evasión

escapee /ˌɪskeɪ'piː/ *n* fugitivo, -va *m,f*

escapism /ɪ'skeɪpɪzəm/ *n* [u] escapismo *m*

escapist /ɪ'skeɪpəst || ɪ'skeɪpɪst/ *adj* escapista

escapologist /ɪ'skeɪ'pɑːlədʒəst || ˌeskə'pɒlədʒɪst/ *n* escapista *mf*

escarpment /ɪ'skɑːrpmənt || ɪ'skɑːpmənt/ *n* escarpa *f*, escarpadura *f*

eschew /ɪs'tʃuː/ *vt* (frml) evitar, abstenerse* de (frml)

escort¹ /'eskɔːrt || 'eskɔːt/ *n*
A (guard) escolta *f*; **under police/naval ~** escoltado por la policía/la armada; (*before n*) ‹*vessel/carrier/fighter*› de escolta
B (companion) acompañante *mf*; (male companion) (frml) acompañante *m*, caballero *m*; (hired companion — woman) señorita *f* de compañía; (— man) acompañante *m*; (*before n*) **~ agency** agencia *f* de acompañantes, agencia *f* de edecanes (Méx)

escort² /ɪ'skɔːrt || ɪ'skɔːt/ *vt* **1** (accompany) acompañar; ‹*prisoner/intruder*› llevar, conducir* **2** (for protection) ‹*politician/procession/ship*› escoltar

escudo /ɪ'ʃkuːdəʊ || e'skjuːdəʊ/ *n* (*pl* **-dos**) escudo *m*

ESE (= **east southeast**) ESE

Eskimo¹ /'eskəməʊ || 'eskɪməʊ/ *adj* esquimal

Eskimo² *n* (*pl* **-mos**) **1** [c] (person) esquimal *mf* **2** [u] (Ling) (aleuto)esquimal *m*

ESOL /'iːsɑːl || 'iːsɒl/ *n* = **English for speakers of other languages**

esophagus, (BrE) **oesophagus** /ɪ'sɑːfəgəs || iː'sɒfəgəs/ *n* esófago *m*

esoteric /'esə'terɪk || ˌiːsəʊ'terɪk, ˌesəʊ-/ *adj* esotérico

ESP *n* [u] = **extrasensory perception**

espadrille /ˌespə'drɪl/ *n* alpargata *f*

especial /ɪ'speʃəl/ *adj* (*before n*) especial, particular

especially /ɪ'speʃli/ *adv* especialmente, particularmente; **why did you choose that one ~?** ¿por qué escogió ése precisamente *or* en particular?; **everyone was bored, ~ me** estaba todo el mundo aburrido, sobre todo *or* especialmente yo

e

Esperanto /ˌespə'ræntəʊ/ *n* [u] esperanto *m*

espionage /'espiənɑːʒ/ *n* [u] espionaje *m*; **industrial ~** espionaje industrial

esplanade /'esplənɑːd || ˌesplə'neɪd/ *n* paseo *m* marítimo, malecón *m* (AmL), costanera *f* (CS)

espouse /ɪ'spaʊz/ *vt* apoyar, propugnar

espresso /e'spresəʊ/ *n* (*pl* **-sos**) café *m* exprés, expreso *m* (CS)

Esq (title) (esp BrE) = **Esquire**

Esquire /ɪ'skwaɪr || ɪ'skwaɪə(r)/ *n* (as title): **Frederick Saunders, ~** Sr. Frederick Saunders, Sr Don Frederick Saunders (esp Esp)

essay /'eseɪ/ *n* (literary composition) ensayo *m*; (academic composition) trabajo *m*, ensayo *m*; (language exercise) composición *f*, redacción *f*

essayist /'eseɪəst || 'eseɪɪst/ *n* ensayista *mf*

essence /'esn̩s/ *n*

A [u] **1** (central feature, quality) esencia *f*; **in ~** en esencia; **of the ~** de fundamental importancia **2** (personification) personificación *f*; **he's the very ~ of a diplomat** es la diplomacia personificada, es la personificación de la diplomacia

B [c u] (Culin): **vanilla ~** *o* **~ of vanilla** esencia *f* de vainilla

essential¹ /ɪ'sentʃəl || ɪ'senʃəl/ *adj* esencial; **the ~ thing** lo esencial; **to be ~ TO sth/sb** ser* esencial *or* imprescindible PARA algo/algn

essential² *n* **1** (sth indispensable) imperativo *m*, elemento *m* esencial; **she brought only the bare ~s** trajo sólo lo imprescindible **2** **essentials** *pl n* (fundamental features) puntos *mpl* esenciales *or* fundamentales

essentially /ɪ'sentʃəli || ɪ'senʃəli/ *adv* esencialmente, fundamentalmente; (*indep*) en lo esencial, esencialmente

est (= **estimated**) est.

EST (in US) = **Eastern Standard Time**

establish /ɪ'stæblɪʃ/ *vt* **1** ‹*colony/community/company*› establecer*, fundar; ‹*committee/fund*› instituir*, crear **2** ‹*criteria/procedure/diplomatic relations*› establecer* **3** (prove) ‹*guilt/innocence*› establecer*; (ascertain) ‹*motive/fact/identity*› establecer*

■ *v refl* **to ~ oneself** «*person*» establecerse*

established /ɪ'stæblɪʃt/ *adj*

A ‹*expert/company*› de reconocido prestigio; ‹*star*› de renombre; ‹*reputation*› sólido; ‹*practice*› establecido; ‹*fact*› comprobado

B ‹*church/religion*› oficial

establishment /ɪ'stæblɪʃmənt/ *n*

A [u] **1** (of colony, business) fundación *f*; (of committee) creación *f* **2** (of criteria, relations) establecimiento *m*

B [c] (club, hotel, shop) establecimiento *m*; **research ~** centro *m* de investigación

C **1** **the Establishment** la clase dirigente, el establishment **2** (ruling group): **the literary ~** las figuras consagradas del mundo literario; **the medical ~** el establishment dentro de la profesión médica

estate /ɪ'steɪt/ *n*

A **1** (land, property) finca *f*, propiedad *f* **2** (group of buildings): **a private ~** un complejo habitacional, una urbanización (Esp), un fraccionamiento (Méx)

B (Law) patrimonio *m*; (of deceased person) sucesión *f*

C **~ (car)** (BrE) ▸ **station wagon**

estate agent *n* (BrE) agente *mf* de la propiedad inmobiliaria

esteem¹ /ɪ'stiːm/ *n* [u] estima *f*, aprecio *m*; **I hold him in high** *o* **great ~** lo aprecio mucho, lo tengo en gran estima; **he's gone down in my ~ since that incident** desde que pasó aquello no le tengo la misma estima

esteem² *vt* (frml) ‹*person*› tener* en gran estima (frml), apreciar; ‹*quality*› valorar, estimar

esteemed /ɪ'stiːmd/ *adj* (frml *or* hum) estimado (frml)

esthete /'esθiːt || 'iːsθiːt/ *etc*: *see* **aesthete** *etc*

estimate¹ /'estəmeɪt || 'estɪmeɪt/ *vt* **1** (calculate approximately) ‹*price/number/age*› calcular; **to ~ sth AT sth**: **the company ~s its losses at 7 million** la compañía calcula que ha sufrido pérdidas del orden de 7 millones **2** **estimated** *past p* ‹*cost/speed*› aproximado; **~d time of arrival** hora *f* de llegada prevista **3** (form judgment of) ‹*outcome/ability*› juzgar*, valorar

estimate² /'estəmət || 'estɪmət/ *n* **1** (rough calculation) cálculo *m* aproximado; **at a rough ~** haciendo un cálculo aproximado **2** (of costs) (Busn) presupuesto *m*

estimation /'estə'meɪʃən || ˌestɪ'meɪʃən/ *n* **1** [c] (judgment, opinion) juicio *m*, valoración *f*; **in my ~** a mi juicio **2** [u] (esteem): **to go up/down in sb's ~** ganarse/perder* la estima de algn

Estonia /es'təʊniə/ *n* Estonia *f*

Estonian¹ /es'təʊniən/ *adj* estonio

Estonian² *n* **1** [c] (person) estonio, -nia *m,f* **2** [u] (language) estonio *m*

estrange /ɪ'streɪndʒ/ *vt*: **she is ~d from her husband** vive *or* está separada de su marido; **his ~d wife** su mujer, de quien está separado

estrangement /ɪ'streɪndʒmənt/ *n* [u c] alejamiento *m*, distanciamiento *m*

estrogen, (BrE) **oestrogen** /'estrədʒən || 'iːstrədʒən/ *n* [u] estrógeno *m*

estuary /'estʃueri || 'estjʊəri/ *n* (*pl* **-ries**) estuario *m*

ETA *n*

A (Transp) = **estimated time of arrival**

B (Basque separatist organization) /'etə/ ETA *f*

et al /et'æl/ (and others) et al.

etc (= **et cetera**) etc.

et cetera /ɪt'setrə/ *adv* etcétera

etch /etʃ/ *vt* (Art, Print) grabar; **to be ~ed on sb's mind** *o* **memory** (liter) estar* grabado en la memoria de algn

etching /'etʃɪŋ/ *n* [c u] grabado *m*

eternal /ɪ'tɜːrnl̩ || ɪ'tɜːnl̩/ *adj* eterno; (colloq) ‹*noise/complaints*› constante

eternally /ɪ'tɜːrnl̩i || ɪ'tɜːnəli/ *adv* (forever) para siempre, eternamente; (colloq) (continually) ‹*complain*› permanentemente, constantemente

eternity /ɪ'tɜːrnəti || ɪ'tɜːnəti/ *n* [u c] (*pl* **-ties**) eternidad *f*

eternity ring *n* anillo *m* *or* aro *m* de brillantes (*como símbolo de amor eterno*)

ether /'iːθər || 'iːθə(r)/ *n* [u] (Chem) éter *m*

ethereal /ɪ'θɪriəl || ɪ'θɪəriəl/ *adj* (liter) etéreo (liter)

ethic /'eθɪk/ *n* ética *f*

ethical /'eθɪkəl/ *adj* ‹*dilemma*› ético; ‹*code*› de conducta; **~ banking** banca *f* ética

ethics /'eθɪks/ *n*

A (Phil) (+ *sing vb*) ética *f*

B (+ *pl vb*) (morality) ética *f*; **professional ~** ética *f* profesional

Ethiopia /ˌiːθi'əʊpiə/ *n* Etiopía *f*

Ethiopian /ˌiːθi'əʊpiən/ *adj* etíope

ethnic /'eθnɪk/ *adj* ‹*origin/group*› étnico; ‹*culture/art/vote*› de las minorías étnicas; **an ~ minority** una minoría étnica; **~ cleansing** limpieza *f* étnica

ethnicity /eθ'nɪsəti/ *n* [u c] (*pl* **-ties**) (origin) origen *m* étnico; (identity) identidad *f* étnica

ethnocentric /ˌeθnəʊ'sentrɪk/ *adj* etnocéntrico

ethos /'iːθɑːs || 'iːθɒs/ *n*: **the middle class ~** los valores y las actitudes de la clase media; **the ~ of free enterprise** el espíritu de la libre empresa

etiolated /'iːtiəleɪtəd || 'iːtiəʊleɪtɪd/ *adj* (Bot) decolorado

etiquette /'etɪket/ *n* [u] etiqueta *f*, protocolo *m*; **it is medical/professional ~** es de protocolo *or* es lo acostumbrado entre los médicos/en la profesión

etymological /'etəmə'lɑːdʒɪkəl/ *adj* etimológico

etymologist /'etə'mɑːlədʒəst || ˌetɪ'mɒlədʒɪst/ *n* etimólogo, -ga *m,f*, etimologista *mf*

etymology /'etə'mɑːlədʒi || ˌetɪ'mɒlədʒi/ *n* [u c] (*pl* **-gies**) etimología *f*

EU *n* = European Union

eucalyptus /'juːkə'lɪptəs/ *n* (*pl* **-tuses**) 1 [c] (tree) eucalipto *m* 2 [u] ~ **(oil)** (bálsamo *m* de) eucalipto *m*

Eucharist /'juːkərəst || 'juːkərɪst/ *n* Eucaristía *f*

eugenics /juː'dʒenɪks/ *n* (+ *sing vb*) eugenesia *f*

eulogize /'juːlədʒaɪz/ *vt* elogiar, ensalzar*

eulogy /'juːlədʒi/ *n* (*pl* **-gies**) (liter) elogio *m*, loa *f* (liter)

eunuch /'juːnək/ *n* eunuco *m*

euphemism /'juːfəmɪzəm/ *n* [c u] eufemismo *m*

euphemistic /'juːfə'mɪstɪk/ *adj* eufemístico

euphoria /juː'fɔːriə/ *n* [u] euforia *f*

euphoric /juː'fɔːrɪk || juː'fɒrɪk/ *adj* eufórico

Eurasia /jʊ'reɪʒə || jʊə'reɪʒə/ *n* Eurasia *f*

Eurasian /jʊ'reɪʒən || jʊə'reɪʒən/ *adj* eurasiático

euro /'jʊrəʊ || 'jʊərəʊ/ *n* euro *m*

Euro- /'jʊrəʊ || 'jʊərəʊ/ *pref* euro-

eurocheque /'jʊrəʊtʃek || 'jʊərəʊtʃek/ *n* eurocheque *m*

Eurodollar /'jʊrəʊˌdɑːlər/ *n* eurodólar *m*

euro-MP /'jʊrəʊˌempiː/ *n* eurodiputado, -da *m,f*

Europe /'jʊrəp || 'jʊərəp/ *n* 1 (Geog) Europa *f* 2 (the EC) (BrE) Europa *f*

European¹ /'jʊrə'piːən || ˌjʊərə'piən/ *adj* europeo

European² *n* europeo, -pea *m,f*

European: ~ **Commission** *n* Comisión *f* Europea, Comisión *f* de las Comunidades Europeas; ~ **Economic Area** *n* Área *f* Económica Europea; ~ **Health Insurance Certificate** *n* tarjeta *f* sanitaria europea; ~ **Union** *n* Unión *f* Europea

Euro: ~**phile** *n* europeísta *mf*; ~**phobe** /'jʊrəfəʊb/ *n* eurófobo, -ba *m,f*; ~**vision** /'jʊrəʊ'vɪʒən/ *n* [u] Eurovisión *f*; (*before n*) **the ~vision Song Contest** el Festival de Eurovisión; ~**zone** *n* zona *f* euro

euthanasia /'juːθə'neɪʒə || ˌjuːθə'neɪziə/ *n* [u] eutanasia *f*

evacuate /ɪ'vækjueɪt/ *vt* ‹*building/area*› evacuar*, desalojar; ‹*residents/population*› evacuar*

evacuation /ɪ'vækju'eɪʃən/ *n* [u c] evacuación *f*, desalojo *m*

evacuee /ɪ'vækjuː'iː/ *n* evacuado, -da *m,f*

evade /ɪ'veɪd/ *vt* ‹*arrest/enemy/responsibility*› eludir, evadir; ‹*question/issue*› eludir; ‹*regulations/military service*› eludir; ‹*taxes*› evadir

evaluate /ɪ'væljueɪt/ *vt* 1 ‹*ability/data*› evaluar* 2 (value) (AmE) valorar, tasar, avaluar* (AmL)

evaluation /ɪ'vælju'eɪʃən/ *n* [u c] 1 (of data) evaluación *f* 2 (of monetary value) (AmE) tasación *f*, valoración *f*

evangelical /'iːvæn'dʒelɪkəl/ *adj* evangélico

evangelism /ɪ'vændʒəlɪzəm/ *n* [u] evangelismo *m*

evangelist /ɪ'vændʒələst || ɪ'vændʒəlɪst/ *n*
A 1 (preacher) predicador, -dora *m,f* 2 (member of an evangelical church) evangelista *mf*
B (Bib): **the four E~s** los cuatro evangelistas

evaporate /ɪ'væpəreɪt/ *vi* «*liquid*» evaporarse; «*hope/fear*» desvanecerse*; «*support/opposition*» evaporarse, esfumarse; «*confidence*» esfumarse
■ **evaporate** *vt* hacer* evaporar, evaporar

evaporated milk /ɪ'væpəreɪtəd || ɪ'væpəreɪtɪd/ *n* [u] leche *f* evaporada, leche *f* condensada (*sin azúcar*)

evaporation /ɪ'væpə'reɪʃən/ *n* [u] evaporación *f*; (of support, confidence) desaparición *f*, desvanecimiento *m*

evasion /ɪ'veɪʒən/ *n* 1 [u] (of responsibility) evasión *f* 2 [c] (evasive statement) evasiva *f*

evasive /ɪ'veɪsɪv/ *adj* 1 (equivocal) ‹*reply*› evasivo 2 (Mil): **to take ~ action** realizar* maniobras para eludir un ataque

eve /iːv/ *n* (day, night before) (liter *or* journ) víspera *f*; **on the ~ of the battle** la víspera de la batalla

Eve /iːv/ *n* Eva

even¹ /'iːvən/ *adv*
A 1 hasta, incluso; ~ **a child could do it** hasta un niño lo podría hacer; ~ **now, five years later** incluso ahora, cuando ya han pasado cinco años; **it would be madness ~ to attempt it** intentarlo ya sería una locura 2 (*with neg*): **he can't ~ sew a button on** no sabe ni pegar un botón; **you're not ~ trying** ni siquiera lo estás intentando 3 (*with comparative*) aún, todavía; **the next day was ~ colder** al día siguiente hizo aún *or* todavía más frío
B (*in phrases*) **even if** aunque (+ *subj*); **we'll do it ~ if it takes months** lo haremos aunque lleve meses; ~ **if I knew, I wouldn't tell you** aunque lo supiera, no te lo diría; **even so** aun así; **even then** aun así; **even though** aun cuando, a pesar de que

even² *adj*
A 1 (flat, smooth) ‹*ground/surface*› plano; ‹*coat of paint*› uniforme; **the floor isn't ~** el suelo no está nivelado 2 (regular, uniform) ‹*color/lighting*› uniforme, parejo (AmL); ‹*breathing*› acompasado, regular; ‹*temperature*› constante
B (equal) ‹*distribution*› equitativo, igual; **after four rounds they're ~** tras cuatro vueltas están *or* van igualados *or* empatados; **so now we're ~** *o* **so that makes us ~** así que estamos en paz *or* (AmL tb) a mano; **to break ~** recuperar los gastos, no tener* ni pérdidas ni beneficios; ***to get ~*** desquitarse, vengarse*; **I'll get ~ with her** me las pagará
C (divisible by two) ‹*number*› par

even³ *vt*
A (level) ‹*surface*› allanar, nivelar
B (make equal) ‹*score*› igualar; ‹*contest/situation*› equilibrar

Phrasal verbs

• **even out**
A [v ▸ o ▸ adv, v ▸ adv ▸ o] compensar, nivelar
B [v ▸ adv] compensarse, nivelarse

• **even up**
A [v ▸ o ▸ adv, v ▸ adv ▸ o] (balance) ‹*numbers/amounts*› equilibrar
B [v ▸ adv] (repay) (AmE colloq) **to ~ up WITH sb** arreglar cuentas CON algn

even-handed /'iːvən'hændəd/ *adj* imparcial

evening /'iːvnɪŋ/ *n*
A 1 (after dark) noche *f*; (before dark) tarde *f*; **at 10 in the ~** a las 10 de la noche; **at 6 in the ~** a las 6 de la tarde; **he came in the ~** (before dark) vino por la tarde, vino en la tarde (AmL), vino a la tarde *or* de tarde (RPl); (after dark) vino por la noche, vino de noche, vino en la noche (AmL); **every Tuesday ~** todos los martes por la tarde/noche (*or* en la tarde *etc*); **good ~** (early on) buenas tardes; (later) buenas noches; (*before n*) ~ **meal** cena *f*; ~ **paper** periódico *m* de la tarde, vespertino *m* (period) 2 (period of entertainment) velada *f* (frml), noche *f*
B **evenings** (*as adv*) (before dark) por la tarde, en la tarde (AmL), a la tarde *or* de tarde (RPl); (after dark) por la noche, de noche, en la noche (AmL)

evening: ~ **class** *n* clase *f* nocturna *or* vespertina; ~ **dress** *n* 1 [c] (for woman) traje *m* de noche 2 [u] (formal wear) traje *m* de etiqueta

evenly /'iːvənli/ *adv*
A (equally) ‹*distribute/divide*› equitativamente, en *or* a partes iguales; ‹*spread*› uniformemente
B 1 (calmly) ‹*say/speak*› sin alterar la voz 2 (steadily) ‹*breathe*› con regularidad

evens /'iːvənz/ *adj* ‹*favorite/bet*› *que paga la misma cantidad que se apuesta*

event /ɪ'vent/ *n*
A 1 (happening, incident) acontecimiento *m*; **in the normal course of ~s** en circunstancias normales 2 (Sport) prueba *f*
B (*in phrases*) **in the event**: **she was afraid he might be rude, but in the ~ ...** tenía miedo de que se portara groseramente, pero llegado el momento ...; **in the ~ of the reactor becoming overheated** en caso de que el reactor se recalentara; **in any/either event** en todo/cualquier caso; **at all events** de cualquier modo; **after the event** a posteriori

even-tempered /'iːvən'tempərd / *adj* ecuánime

eventful /ɪ'ventfəl/ *adj* 1 ‹*week*› lleno de incidentes; ‹*life*› rico en experiencias 2 (momentous) (AmE) crucial

eventual /ɪ'ventʃuəl/ *adj* (*before n*) (final): **the ~ outcome was ...** lo que sucedió finalmente fue ...; **the ~ winners** el equipo que acabó alzándose con la victoria

eventuality /ɪ'ventʃu'æləti/ *n* (*pl* **-ties**) eventualidad *f*

eventually /ɪ'ventʃuəli/ *adv* finalmente, al final; ~ **people became used to the idea** con el tiempo, la gente se acostumbró a la idea

ever /'evər || 'evə(r)/ *adv*
A 1 (at any time): **have you ~ visited London?** ¿has estado

en Londres (alguna vez)?; **will we ~ get there?** ¿llegaremos algún día?; **don't you ~ listen?** ¿es que nunca escuchas?; **nobody ~ comes to see me** nunca viene nadie a verme; **hardly ~** casi nunca; **I seldom, if ~, eat meat** muy rara vez como carne **2** (expressing incredulity, indignation): **did you ~ see such a thing!** ¡habráse visto cosa igual!; **as if he'd ~ do such a terrible thing!** ¡como si fuera capaz de hacer semejante cosa!

B (*after comp or superl*): **these are our worst ~ results** éstos son los peores resultados que hemos tenido hasta ahora; **the situation is worse than ~** la situación está peor que nunca

C (always, constantly) **1** (*in phrases*) **as ever** como siempre; **they lived happily ~ after** (in fairy tales) vivieron felices y comieron perdices; **ever since**: **~ since we first saw her** desde que la vimos por primera vez; **we've been friends ~ since** somos amigos desde entonces; **for ever** para siempre **2** (*before pres p and adj*): **the ~ growing threat of war** la creciente amenaza de la guerra; **~ helpful, he offered to drive me there** gentil como siempre, se ofreció a llevarme en coche

D (*as intensifier*) **1** (*in wh- questions*): **when will you ~ learn?** ¿cuándo vas a aprender?; **why ~ did you tell him?** ¿por qué diablos se lo dijiste? (fam); **what ~ can have happened?** ¿qué podrá haber pasado? **2** (esp BrE colloq): **thanks ~ so** *o* **~ so much** *o* **~ such a lot** muchísimas gracias; **it's ~ so cold in here** hace muchísimo frío aquí

evergreen¹ /'evərgri:n || 'evəgri:n/ *adj* ‹*tree/shrub*› de hoja perenne; (*before n*) ‹*story/song*› favorito; ‹*subject of conversation*› eterno, perenne

evergreen² *n* (plant) planta *f* de hoja perenne; (tree) árbol *m* de hoja perenne

everlasting /'evər'læstɪŋ || ˌevə'lɑ:stɪŋ/ *adj* **1** (eternal) ‹*peace/love/gratitude*› eterno; ‹*fame/glory*› imperecedero (liter) **2** (constant) (colloq) continuo, eterno

evermore /'evər'mɔ:r || ˌevə'mɔ:(r)/ *adv* (liter) eternamente (liter); **for ~** por siempre jamás (liter)

every /'evri/ *adj*

A (each): **~ room was searched** se registraron todas las habitaciones, se registró cada una de las habitaciones; **she wins ~ time** siempre gana; **~ day/minute is precious** cada día/minuto es precioso; **she comes ~ month** viene todos los meses; **~ one of you** todos y cada uno de ustedes

B (indicating recurrence) cada; **~ three days, ~ third day** cada tres días; **he comes ~ other day** viene un día sí, otro no *or* (CS, Per) viene día por medio; **~ now and then** *o* **again** de tanto en tanto; **~ so often** cada tanto, de vez en cuando

C (very great, all possible): **they have ~ confidence in us** confían plenamente en nosotros; **I wished them ~ happiness** les deseé toda la felicidad del mundo; **she made ~ effort to satisfy him** hizo lo indecible *or* todo lo posible por satisfacerlo

everybody /'evrɪˌbɑ:di || 'evrɪˌbɒdi/ *pron* todos; **is that ~?** ¿están todos?, ¿está todo el mundo?

everyday /'evri'deɪ/ *adj* (*before n*) ‹*occurrence/problems/activities*› de todos los días, cotidiano; ‹*suit/clothes*› de diario; ‹*expression*› corriente, de todos los días; **~ life** la vida diaria *or* cotidiana; **in ~ use** de uso diario

everyone /'evriwʌn/ *pron* ▸**everybody**

everyplace /'evripleɪs/ *adv* (AmE) ▸**everywhere**

everything /'evriθɪŋ/ *pron* todo; **~ possible has been done** se ha hecho todo lo posible; **she's ~ to me** (ella) lo es todo para mí

everywhere /'evrihwer/ *adv*: **I've looked ~ for it** lo he buscado por todas partes *or* por todos lados; **they go ~ by car** van a todos lados *or* a todas partes en coche

evict /ɪ'vɪkt/ *vt* ‹*tenant/squatter*› desahuciar, desalojar; ‹*demonstrators*› desalojar

eviction /ɪ'vɪkʃən/ *n* [u c] (of tenant, squatter) desalojo *m*, desahucio *m*; (*before n*) **~ order** orden *f* de desalojo

evidence /'evədəns || 'evɪdəns/ *n* [u]

A (Law) **1** (proof) pruebas *fpl*; **what ~ is there that ... ?** ¿qué prueba(s) hay de que ... ? **2** (testimony) testimonio *m*; **on the ~ of those present** según (el testimonio de) los que estaban presentes; **the ~ for the defense/prosecution** el descargo de la defensa/el capítulo de cargos; **to give ~** declarar *or* prestar declaración **3** (objects) pruebas *fpl*

B (sign, indication) indicio *m*, señal *f*; **in ~**: **he isn't much in ~ these days** últimamente no se lo ve mucho

evident /'evədənt || 'evɪdənt/ *adj* evidente, manifiesto

evidently /'evədəntli || 'evɪdəntli/ *adv* **1** ‹*embarrassed/unsuitable*› claramente, obviamente **2** (*indep*) aparentemente, según parece; **is she coming too? — evidently** ¿ella también viene? — eso parece *or* según parece

evil¹ /'i:vəl/ *adj* **1** (wicked) ‹*demon/wizard*› malvado, maligno; ‹*deeds/thoughts/character*› de gran maldad; ‹*influence*› maléfico, funesto; ‹*plan/suggestion*› diabólico, maléfico; **an ~ spirit** un espíritu maligno *or* maléfico **2** (unpleasant) ‹*smell*› asqueroso; **to put off the ~ day/hour** retrasar *or* posponer* el día/momento fatídico *or* funesto

evil² *n* [u c] (sin, wrong-doing) mal *m*; **the lesser of two ~s** el menor de dos males

evil: **~doer** /'i:vəl'du:ər || 'i:vəlˌdu:ə(r)/ *n* malhechor, -chora *m,f*; **~doing** /'i:vəl'du:ɪŋ/ *n* [u] maldad *f*; **~ eye** *n*: **the ~ eye** el mal de ojo; **to put the ~ eye on sb** echarle *or* (RPl) hacerle* mal de ojo a algn; **~-smelling** /'i:vəl'smelɪŋ/ *adj* hediondo; **~-tempered** /'i:vəl'tempərd || ˌi:vəl'tempəd/ *adj* con un humor de perros

evince /ɪ'vɪns/ *vt* (frml) ‹*desire/astonishment*› mostrar*, manifestar*; ‹*talent/qualities*› dar* prueba de, poner* de manifiesto

evocation /'i:vəʊ'keɪʃən/ *n* [c u] evocación *f*

evocative /ɪ'vɑ:kətɪv || ɪ'vɒkətɪv/ *adj* evocador; **to be ~ OF sth** evocar* algo

evoke /ɪ'vəʊk/ *vt* ‹*response/admiration/sympathy*› provocar*, suscitar (frml); ‹*memories/associations*› evocar*

evolution /'evə'lu:ʃən || ˌi:və'lu:ʃən/ *n* [u] evolución *f*

evolutionary /'evə'lu:ʃəneri || ˌi:və'lu:ʃənəri/ *adj* ‹*theory*› evolucionista; ‹*development/process*› evolutivo

evolve /ɪ'vɑ:lv || ɪ'vɒlv/ *vi* evolucionar; «*idea/system*» evolucionar, desarrollarse

■ **evolve** *vt* ‹*system/theory*› desarrollar

ewe /ju:/ *n* oveja *f* (*hembra*)

ewer /'ju:ər || 'ju:ə(r)/ *n* aguamanil *m*

ex /eks/ *n* (colloq) ex *mf* (fam); **his/my ~** su/mi ex (fam)

ex- /'eks/ *pref* ex(-); **~wife** ex(-)esposa

exacerbate /ɪg'zæsərbeɪt || ɪg'zæsəbeɪt/ *vt* exacerbar (frml), agravar

exact¹ /ɪg'zækt/ *adj* **1** (precise) ‹*number/size/time/date*› exacto; **23, to be ~** 23, para ser exactos; **those were her ~ words** ésas fueron sus palabras textuales **2** (accurate) ‹*description/definition*› preciso

exact² *vt* ‹*promise*› arrancar*; **the price they ~ed from us** el precio que nos hicieron pagar; **he ~ed his revenge** se vengó

exacting /ɪg'zæktɪŋ/ *adj* ‹*work/job*› que exige mucho; ‹*supervisor/employer*› exigente; ‹*standards*› riguroso

exactitude /ɪg'zæktətu:d || ɪg'zæktɪtju:d/ *n* [u] (frml) exactitud *f*, precisión *f*

exactly /ɪg'zæktli/ *adv* ‹*measure/calculate*› exactamente, con precisión; **at six-thirty ~** *o* **at ~ six-thirty** a las seis y media en punto; **~ how/where did you do it?** ¿cómo/dónde lo hizo exactamente?; **they weren't ~ pleased to see us** (iro) no es que estuvieran precisamente encantados de vernos (iró)

exactness /ɪg'zæktnəs || ɪg'zæktnɪs/ *n* [u] exactitud *f*, precisión *f*

exaggerate /ɪg'zædʒəreɪt/ *vi/t* exagerar

exaggerated /ɪg'zædʒəreɪtəd/ *adj* exagerado

exaggeration /ɪg'zædʒə'reɪʃən/ *n* [c u] exageración *f*

exalt /ɪg'zɔ:lt/ *vt* (frml) **1** (elevate) exaltar (frml), elevar **2** (praise) ensalzar*, exaltar (frml)

exaltation /'egzɔ:l'teɪʃən/ *n* [u] (liter) júbilo *m* (liter)

exalted /ɪg'zɔ:ltəd || ɪg'zɔ:ltɪd/ *adj* ‹*position/person*› elevado, exaltado (frml)

exam /ɪg'zæm/ *n* ▸**examination A**

examination /ɪg'zæmə'neɪʃən || ɪgˌzæmɪ'neɪʃən/ *n*

A [c] (frml Educ) examen *m*; **to take** *o* (BrE also) **sit an ~** dar* *or* hacer* *or* (CS) rendir* *or* (Méx) tomar un examen, examinarse (Esp); **to pass an ~** aprobar* *or* pasar un examen; **to fail an ~** reprobar* *or* (Esp) suspender *or* (Ur) perder* un examen

B [c u] **1** (inspection — of accounts) revisión *f*, inspección *f*; (— of

passports) control *m*; (— by doctor) reconocimiento *m*, examen *m*, revisación *f* (RPl) 2 (study, investigation) examen *m*; **on closer ~** al examinarlo más de cerca
C [c] (of witness) interrogatorio *m*

examine /ɪɡ'zæmən || ɪɡ'zæmɪn/ *vt*
A 1 (inspect) examinar; ‹*accounts*› inspeccionar, revisar; ‹*baggage*› registrar, revisar (AmL); ‹*document/dossier*› examinar, estudiar 2 (Med, Dent) examinar, revisar (AmL) 3 (study, investigate) examinar, estudiar
B 1 (Educ) examinar; **to ~ sb ON sth** examinar a algn SOBRE *or* DE algo; **to ~ sb IN sth** (esp BrE) examinar a algn DE algo 2 (Law) ‹*witness/accused*› interrogar*

examinee /ɪɡ'zæmə'niː || ɪɡ,zæmɪ'niː/ *n* (Educ) examinando, -da *m,f* (frml), alumno, -na *m,f*; (for professional exam) candidato, -ta *m,f*, aspirante *mf*

examiner /ɪɡ'zæmənər/ *n* examinador, -dora *m,f*

example /ɪɡ'zæmpəl || ɪɡ'zɑːmpəl/ *n*
A (specimen, sample) ejemplo *m*; **for ~** por ejemplo
B 1 (model) ejemplo *m*; **to set sb an ~, to set an ~ for** *o* (BrE also) **to sb** darle* (el) ejemplo a algn; **to follow sb's ~** seguir* el ejemplo de algn 2 (warning): **to make an ~ of sb** darle* un castigo ejemplar a algn

exasperate /ɪɡ'zæspəreɪt/ *vt* exasperar, sacar* de quicio

exasperated /ɪɡ'zæspəreɪtəd || ɪɡ'zæspəreɪtɪd/ *adj* exasperado; **to get** *o* **become ~** exasperarse

exasperating /ɪɡ'zæspəreɪtɪŋ/ *adj* exasperante

exasperation /ɪɡ'zæspə'reɪʃən/ *n* [u] exasperación *f*; **leave me alone! she cried in ~** —¡déjame en paz! —gritó exasperada

excavate /'ekskəveɪt/ *vt/i* excavar

excavation /'ekskə'veɪʃən/ *n* [u c] excavación *f*

excavator /'ekskəveɪtər || 'ekskəveɪtə(r)/ *n* (machine) excavadora *f*; (person) excavador, -dora *m,f*

exceed /ɪk'siːd/ *vt* 1 (be greater than) exceder de, sobrepasar 2 (go beyond) ‹*limit/minimum*› rebasar, sobrepasar; ‹*expectations/fears/hopes*› superar; ‹*powers*› (frml) excederse en

exceedingly /ɪk'siːdɪŋli/ *adv* (frml) (*as intensifier*) sumamente, extremadamente

excel /ɪk'sel/ **-ll-** *vi* **to ~ AT/IN sth** destacar* EN algo
■ *v refl* **to ~ oneself** lucirse*

excellence /'eksələns/ *n* [u] excelencia *f*

Excellency /'eksələnsi/ *n* (*pl* **-cies**): **His/Her ~** Su Excelencia; (*as form of address*) **(Your) ~** (Vuestra *or* Su) Excelencia

excellent /'eksələnt/ *adj* 1 excelente; (Educ) sobresaliente 2 (*as interj*) ¡estupendo!, ¡excelente!

except[1] /ɪk'sept/ *prep* 1 (apart from): **~ (for)** menos, excepto, salvo 2 **~ for** (if it weren't for) si no fuera por

except[2] *conj* **~ that** *o* (colloq) **~** (if it weren't that) pero

except[3] *vt* 1 (exclude) (frml) **to ~ sb FROM sth** eximir a algn DE algo (frml); **to ~ sth FROM sth** excluir* algo DE algo 2 **excepted** *past p* (*after n: as prep*) excepto, con *or* a excepción de

excepting /ɪk'septɪŋ/ *prep* 1 (except) excepto, salvo, a excepción de 2 (excluding): **we must invite everyone, not ~ Sam** tenemos que invitarlos a todos, incluso a Sam

exception /ɪk'sepʃən/ *n*
A [c u] excepción *f*; **with the ~ of sth/sb** con *or* a excepción de algo/algn; **without ~** sin excepción; **to make an ~** hacer* una excepción
B (offense): **to take ~ to sth** ofenderse por algo

exceptional /ɪk'sepʃn̩əl || ɪk'sepʃənl̩/ *adj* excepcional

exceptionally /ɪk'sepʃn̩əli/ *adv* excepcionalmente

excerpt /'eksɜːrpt || 'eksɜːpt/ *n* pasaje *m*

excess[1] /ɪk'ses/ *n*
A 1 (*no pl*) exceso *m*; **an ~ of caution** un exceso de precaución; **to eat and drink to ~** comer y beber en exceso; **to carry sth to ~** llevar algo a la exageración 2 **excesses** *pl* excesos *mpl*, desafueros *mpl*
B [u] (surplus) excedente *m*; **in ~ of** superior a, por encima de

excess[2] /ɪk'ses || 'ekses/ *adj*: **~ weight/profits** exceso *m* de peso/beneficios

excess /ɪk'ses || 'ekses/: **~ baggage** *n* [u] exceso *m* de equipaje; **~ fare** *n* (BrE) suplemento *m* (*pagado en el transporte público*)

excessive /ɪk'sesɪv/ *adj* ‹*price/charges*› excesivo, abusivo; ‹*demands/pressure*› exagerado; ‹*interest/ambition*› exagerado, desmesurado

excessively /ɪk'sesɪvli/ *adv* ‹*worry/praise*› en exceso, demasiado; ‹*concerned/severe*› excesivamente

exchange[1] /ɪks'tʃeɪndʒ/ *n*
A 1 [c u] (of information, greetings, insults) intercambio *m*; (of prisoners, hostages) canje *m*; **in ~ for sth** a cambio de algo 2 [c] (of students) intercambio *m*; (*before n*) **~ student** *estudiante que hace un intercambio* 3 [c] (dialogue) intercambio *m* de palabras 4 [u] (of currency) cambio *m*
B [c] (Telec) (*telephone* **~**) central *f* telefónica

exchange[2] *vt* 1 (give in place of) **to ~ sth FOR sth** cambiar algo POR algo; **to ~ dollars for pesos** cambiar dólares a *or* (Esp) en pesos 2 ‹*information/addresses*› intercambiar(se); ‹*blows*› darse*; ‹*insults*› intercambiar; ‹*prisoners/hostages*› canjear; **we ~d a few words** cruzamos unas palabras; **to ~ sth WITH sb**: **I ~d seats with him** cambié de asiento con él, le cambié el asiento; **we ~d greetings (with them)** nos saludamos

exchange: **~ rate** *n* tasa *f or* (esp Esp) tipo *m* de cambio, paridad *f*; **~ Rate Mechanism** *n* mecanismo *m* de paridades *or* de cambio

Exchequer /'ekstʃekər || ɪks'tʃekə(r)/ *n* (in UK) **the ~** el tesoro público, el erario público; *see also* **chancellor 1**

excise[1] /ɪk'saɪz/ *vt* (frml) (Med) extirpar; (delete) suprimir, eliminar

excise[2] /'eksaɪz/ *n* impuestos *mpl* internos; **Customs and Excise** (in UK) el servicio de aduanas

excise duty /'eksaɪz/ *n* [u] impuesto *m* interno *or* de consumo

excitable /ɪk'saɪtəbəl/ *adj* excitable, nervioso

excite /ɪk'saɪt/ *vt*
A 1 (make happy, enthusiastic) entusiasmar; (make impatient, boisterous) ‹*children*› alborotar 2 (sexually) excitar
B ‹*interest/admiration*› despertar*, suscitar; ‹*envy/curiosity*› provocar*

excited /ɪk'saɪtəd || ɪk'saɪtɪd/ *adj* 1 (happy, enthusiastic) ‹*person*› entusiasmado, excitado; ‹*shouts*› de excitación *or* entusiasmo; **to be ~ about sth** estar* entusiasmado con algo; **to get ~** entusiasmarse; **don't get too ~** no te hagas demasiadas ilusiones 2 (nervous, worried) ‹*person*› excitado, agitado; ‹*voice/gesture*› vehemente, ansioso, nervioso; **don't get ~** no te agites, no te pongas nervioso 3 (impatient, boisterous) ‹*children*› excitado, alborotado, revolucionado 4 (sexually) excitado

excitedly /ɪk'saɪtədli || ɪk'saɪtɪdli/ *adv* con excitación

excitement /ɪk'saɪtmənt/ *n* [u] (enthusiasm, happiness) excitación *f*, entusiasmo *m*; (agitation) agitación *f*, alboroto *m*

exciting /ɪk'saɪtɪŋ/ *adj* ‹*events/experience*› emocionante; ‹*film/story*› apasionante; ‹*performer*› fascinante

excl *prep* (= **excluding** *o* **exclusive of**): **$80, ~ postage** 80 dólares, franqueo no incluido

exclaim /ɪk'skleɪm/ *vi* exclamar; **to ~ AT sth** (frml) (indignantly) manifestar* su (*or* mi *etc*) indignación POR algo; (admiringly) prorrumpir en exclamaciones de admiración ANTE algo (frml)
■ **exclaim** *vt* exclamar

exclamation /'eksklə'meɪʃən/ *n* exclamación *f*

exclamation point, (BrE) **exclamation mark** *n* signo *m* de admiración

exclamatory /ɪk'sklæmətɔːri/ *adj* exclamativo

exclude /ɪk'skluːd/ *vt* 1 (leave out) excluir*; **to ~ sth/sb FROM sth** excluir* algo/a algn DE algo 2 (debar): **women were ~d from membership** a las mujeres no se las admitía como socias 3 ‹*sunlight/air*› no dejar entrar

excluding /ɪk'skluːdɪŋ/ *prep* sin incluir, excluyendo

exclusion /ɪk'skluːʒən/ *n* [u] exclusión *f*; **she concentrated on tennis to the ~ of everything else** se concentró exclusivamente en el tenis; (*before n*) **~ order** (in UK) orden *f* de exclusión

exclusive[1] /ɪk'skluːsɪv/ *adj*
A ‹*rights/ownership/privileges*› exclusivo; ‹*story/interview*› en exclusiva
B ‹*club/gathering*› selecto, exclusivo
C (sole) único
D (excluding): **the two proposals are mutually ~** las dos pro-

puestas se excluyen mutuamente; ~ OF **sth** sin incluir algo, excluyendo algo

exclusive² *n* (Journ) exclusiva *f*

exclusively /ɪk'sklu:sɪvli/ *adv* exclusivamente, únicamente

exclusivity /ˌeksklu:'sɪvəti/ *n* [u] exclusividad *f*: (*before n*) ~ **clause** cláusula *f* de exclusividad

excommunicate /'ekskə'mju:nəkeɪt/ *vt* excomulgar*

excommunication /'ekskə'mju:nə'keɪʃən || ˌekskə ˌmju:nɪ'keɪʃən/ *n* [u c] excomunión *f*

ex-convict /'eks'kɑ:nvɪkt || ˌeks'kɒnvɪkt/ *n* ex presidiario, -ria *m,f*, ex convicto, -ta *m,f* (frml)

excrement /'ekskrəmənt/ *n* [u] (frml) excremento *m* (frml)

excreta /ɪk'skri:tə/ *pl n* (frml) excrementos *mpl* (frml)

excrete /ɪk'skri:t/ *vt* (frml) excretar (frml)

excruciating /ɪk'skru:ʃieɪtɪŋ/ *adj* ‹*pain*› atroz, espantoso; ‹*boredom/embarrassment*› espantoso, terrible

excruciatingly /ɪk'skru:ʃieɪtɪŋli/ *adv* ‹*painful*› terriblemente; ‹*boring*› espantosamente, terriblemente

exculpate /'ekskʌlpeɪt/ *vt* (frml) exculpar (frml)

excursion /ɪk'skɜ:rʒən || ɪk'skɜ:ʃən/ *n* excursión *f*; **to go on an** ~ ir* de excursión

excusable /ɪk'skju:zəbəl/ *adj* perdonable, disculpable

excuse¹ /ɪk'skju:z/ *vt*

A **1** (forgive) ‹*mistake/misconduct*› disculpar, perdonar; ~ **my interrupting** *o* ~ **me for interrupting, but ...** perdóneme la interrupción, pero ..., perdone que le interrumpa, pero ...; ~ **me!** (attracting attention) ¡perdón!, ¡perdone (usted)! (frml); (apologizing) perdón, perdóneme (*or* perdóname *etc*); ~ **me, please** (con) permiso, ¿me permite, por favor? **2** (justify) ‹*conduct/rudeness*› excusar, justificar*

B (release from obligation) disculpar; **please may I be ~d?** (used by schoolchildren) señorita (*or* profesor *etc*) ¿puedo ir al baño *or* (Esp) al servicio?; **to** ~ **sb** (FROM) **sth** dispensar *or* eximir a algn DE algo

■ *v refl* **to** ~ **oneself** **1** (on leaving) excusarse **2** (offer excuse) excusarse, disculparse

excuse² /ɪk'skju:s/ *n* **1** (justification) excusa *f*; **there's no** ~ **for rudeness** la mala educación no tiene excusa **2** (pretext) excusa *f*, pretexto *m*; **to make ~s** poner* excusas **3** **excuses** *pl* excusas *fpl*; **to make one's ~s** excusarse

ex-directory /'eksdaɪ'rektəri/ *adj* (BrE Telec) que no figura en la guía telefónica, privado (Méx)

execrable /'eksɪkrəbəl/ *adj* (frml) execrable (frml), deplorable

execute /'eksɪkju:t/ *vt*

A (carry out, perform) ejecutar; ‹*duties*› desempeñar, ejercer*

B (put to death) ejecutar

execution /'eksɪ'kju:ʃən/ *n*

A [u] (of order, plan) ejecución *f*; (of duties) desempeño *m*; **to put a plan into** ~ ejecutar un plan

B [u c] (putting to death) ejecución *f*

executioner /'eksɪ'kju:ʃn̩ər/ *n* verdugo *m*

executive¹ /ɪg'zekjətɪv || ɪg'zekjʊtɪv/ *adj*

A (Adm, Busn) (managerial) ejecutivo; ‹*washroom/suite/jet*› para ejecutivos; ‹*car/briefcase*› de ejecutivo

B (Govt) ‹*powers/branch*› ejecutivo; ~ **privilege** (in US) *inmunidad de los miembros del ejecutivo*

executive² *n*

A (manager) ejecutivo, -va *m,f*

B **1** (branch of government) **the** ~ el (poder) ejecutivo **2** (~ *committee*) (esp BrE) comisión *f* directiva, comité *m* ejecutivo

executor /ɪg'zekjətər || ɪg'zekjʊtə(r)/ *n* albacea *mf*, testamentario, -ria *m,f*

exemplary /ɪg'zempləri/ *adj* ejemplar

exemplify /ɪg'zempləfaɪ || ɪg'zemplɪfaɪ/ *vt* **-fies, -fying, -fied** **1** (give example of) ejemplificar*, ilustrar **2** (be example of) demostrar*

exempt¹ /ɪg'zempt/ *vt* **to** ~ **sb** FROM **sth** eximir a algn DE algo

exempt² *adj*: **to be** ~ FROM **sth** estar* exento DE algo; **to be** ~ FROM **-ING** estar* eximido DE + INF; ~ **from tax** exento *or* libre de impuestos

exemption /ɪg'zempʃən/ *n* **1** [u c] ~ FROM **sth** exención *f* *or* exoneración *f* DE algo **2** [c] (AmE) ▸ **tax exemption**

exercise¹ /'eksərsaɪz || 'eksəsaɪz/ *n*

A [u] (physical) ejercicio *m*; **to take** ~ hacer* ejercicio; (*before n*) ~ **bicycle** bicicleta *f* de ejercicio

B [c] (Sport, Educ) ejercicio *m*; (Mil) ejercicios *mpl*, maniobras *fpl*

C [c] (undertaking): **a public relations** ~ una operación de relaciones públicas; **the object of the** ~ **is to ...** lo que se persigue con esto es ...

D [u] (use — of rights, power) (frml) ejercicio *m*; (— of caution, patience) uso *m*

exercise² *vt*

A ‹*body*› ejercitar; ‹*dog*› pasear; ‹*horse*› ejercitar, trabajar

B ‹*power/control/right*› ejercer*; ‹*patience/tact*› hacer* uso de; **to** ~ **great care** proceder con sumo cuidado

■ **exercise** *vi* hacer* ejercicio

exercise book *n* cuaderno *m*

exert /ɪg'zɜ:rt || ɪg'zɜ:t/ *vt* ejercer*; ‹*force*› emplear

■ *v refl* **to** ~ **oneself** hacer* un (gran) esfuerzo

exertion /ɪg'zɜ:rʃən/ *n* [u] (effort) (*often pl*) esfuerzo *m*

exeunt /'eksiʌnt/ salen

ex-gratia /'eks'greɪʃə/ *adj* (frml): **an** ~ **payment** un pago discrecional

exhale /eks'heɪl/ *vt* (breathe out) espirar, exhalar

■ **exhale** *vi* espirar

exhaust¹ /ɪg'zɔ:st/ *n* **1** [c] (~ *pipe*) tubo *m* *or* (RPl) caño *m* de escape, mofle *m* (AmC, Méx), exhosto *m* (Col) **2** [c] (system) escape *m*, exhosto *m* (Col) **3** [u] (fumes) gases *mpl* del tubo de escape

exhaust² *vt*

A (tire) agotar

B **1** (use up) agotar **2** (cover thoroughly) ‹*subject*› agotar

exhausted /ɪg'zɔ:stəd || ɪg'zɔ:stɪd/ *adj* agotado, exhausto

exhaustible /ɪg'zɔ:stəbəl/ *adj* limitado

exhausting /ɪg'zɔ:stɪŋ/ *adj* agotador

exhaustion /ɪg'zɔ:stʃən/ *n* [u] agotamiento *m*

exhaustive /ɪg'zɔ:stɪv/ *adj* (frml) exhaustivo

exhibit¹ /ɪg'zɪbət || ɪg'zɪbɪt/ *vt*

A ‹*goods/paintings*› exponer*

B (frml) ‹*skill/dexterity*› demostrar*, poner* de manifiesto; ‹*fear/courage*› mostrar*; ‹*symptoms*› presentar

exhibit² *n* **1** (in gallery, museum) *objeto en exposición*; **the paintings on** ~ las pinturas expuestas **2** (Law) *documento u objeto que se exhibe en un juicio como prueba* **3** (exhibition) (AmE) exposición *f*

exhibition /'eksə'bɪʃən || ˌeksɪ'bɪʃən/ *n* [c u]

A (of paintings, goods) exposición *f*; **to be on** ~ estar* expuesto; (*before n*) ~ **hall** sala *f* *or* salón *m* de exposiciones

B (of trait, quality) muestra *f*; **to make an** ~ **of oneself** dar* un espectáculo, hacer* el ridículo

exhibitionism /'eksə'bɪʃənɪzəm || ˌeksɪ'bɪʃənɪzəm/ *n* [u] exhibicionismo *m*

exhibitionist /'eksə'bɪʃn̩əst/ *n* exhibicionista *mf*

exhibitor /ɪg'zɪbətər || ɪg'zɪbɪtə(r)/ *n* expositor, -tora *m,f*

exhilarate /ɪg'zɪləreɪt/ *vt* **1** (make happy) llenar de júbilo; **we were ~d by the news** las noticias nos llenaron de júbilo **2** (stimulate) tonificar*, estimular

exhilarating /ɪg'zɪləreɪtɪŋ/ *adj* ‹*experience*› excitante; ‹*climate*› tonificante, estimulante

exhilaration /ɪg'zɪlə'reɪʃən/ *n* [u] (excitement) euforia *f*, excitación *f*; (joy) júbilo *m*

exhort /ɪg'zɔ:rt || ɪg'zɔ:t/ *vt* (frml) **to** ~ **sb to** + INF exhortar a algn A + INF, exhortar a algn A QUE (+ *subj*)

exhortation /'egzɔ:r'teɪʃən || ˌegzɔ:'teɪʃən/ *n* [c u] (frml) exhortación *f* (frml)

exhume /ɪg'zu:m/ *vt* (frml) exhumar (frml), desenterrar*

exile¹ /'eksaɪl/ *n* **1** [c] (person — voluntary) exiliado, -da *m,f*, exilado, -da *m,f*; (— expelled) desterrado, -da *m,f*, exiliado, -da *m,f*, exilado, -da *m,f* **2** [u] (state) exilio *m*, destierro *m*; **to be in** ~ estar* exiliado *or* en el exilio; **to go into** ~ exiliarse, exilarse; **to be sent into** ~ ser* desterrado *or* enviado al exilio

exile² *vt* desterrar*, exiliar, exilar

exist /ɪg'zɪst/ *vi*

A (be real) existir

B (survive) subsistir, vivir; **to** ~ ON **sth**: **we ~ed on bread**

and butter estábamos a base de pan y mantequilla

existence /ɪɡ'zɪstəns/ *n*

A [u] (being) existencia *f*; **this is the only copy in ~** éste es el único ejemplar existente; **to come into ~** «*republic/country*» nacer*; «*organization/party*» crearse, fundarse

B [c] (life) vida *f*, existencia *f*

existentialism /'egzɪs'tentʃəlɪzəm || ,egzɪ'stenʃəlɪzəm/ *n* [u] existencialismo *m*

existentialist /'egzɪs'tentʃələst/ *adj* existencialista

existing /ɪɡ'zɪstɪŋ/ *adj* existente, actual

exit¹ /'egzət || 'eksɪt/ *n* (from building, aircraft, freeway) salida *f*; **to make one's ~** salir*, irse*, retirarse; (*before n*) ‹*visa/permit*› de salida

exit² *vi* salir*

exodus /'eksədəs/ *n* (*no pl*) éxodo *m*

ex officio /'eksə'fɪʃiəʊ/ *adj* (*before n*) ex oficio, en virtud del cargo

exonerate /ɪɡ'zɑːnəreɪt || ɪɡ'zɒnəreɪt/ *vt* (frml) **to ~ sb (FROM sth)** exonerar a algn (DE algo) (frml)

exorbitant /ɪɡ'zɔːrbətənt || ɪɡ'zɔːbɪtənt/ *adj* (frml) ‹*price/rent*› exorbitante, desorbitado

exorcism /'eksɔːrsɪzəm/ *n* [u c] exorcismo *m*

exorcist /'eksɔːrsəst || 'eksɔːsɪst/ *n* exorcista *mf*

exorcize /'eksɔːrsaɪz || 'eksɔːsaɪz/ *vt* (Relig) exorcizar*; ‹*memory*› borrar, conjurar

exotic /ɪɡ'zɑːtɪk || ɪɡ'zɒtɪk/ *adj* exótico

expand /ɪk'spænd/ *vt*

A (enlarge) expandir; ‹*lungs*› ensanchar, dilatar; ‹*chest*› desarrollar; ‹*horizons*› ampliar*, ensanchar; ‹*influence/role*› extender*

B ‹*story/summary*› ampliar*; **I ~ed my notes into an article** escribí un artículo ampliando mis notas

■ **expand** *vi*

A 1 «*metal/gas*» expandirse; «*elastic/rubber band*» estirarse 2 **expanding** *pres p* ‹*industry/market*› en expansión

B (give further information) **to ~ ON sth** extenderse* SOBRE *or* EN algo

expanse /ɪk'spæns/ *n* [c u] extensión *f*

expansion /ɪk'spæntʃən || ɪk'spænʃən/ *n* 1 [u] expansión *f*; (*before n*) **~ card** (Comput) tarjeta *f* de expansión *or* de ampliación 2 [c] (of summary) ampliación *f*

expansionism /ɪk'spæntʃənɪzəm || ɪk'spænʃənɪzəm/ *n* [u] expansionismo *m*

expansive /ɪk'spænsɪv/ *adj* expansivo, comunicativo

expat /'eks'pæt/ *n* (BrE colloq) expatriado, -da *m,f*

expatriate¹ /eks'peɪtriət/ *n* expatriado, -da *m,f*

expatriate² *adj* expatriado

expect /ɪk'spekt/ *vt*

A (anticipate) esperar; **I ~ed as much** ya me lo esperaba; **is he coming tonight? — I ~ so** ¿va a venir esta noche? — supongo que sí; **we're not ~ing any trouble** no creemos que vaya a haber problemas; **to ~ to + INF**: **she ~s to win the match** espera ganar el partido; **you can ~ to pay £20 a head** calcule que le va a costar unas 20 libras por persona; **to ~ sb/sth to + INF**: **I ~ed her to complain** pensé *or* creí que iba a protestar; **don't ~ the situation to improve/change** no esperes que la situación mejore/cambie; **now we know what to ~** ahora sabemos a qué atenernos

B (imagine) suponer*, imaginarse; **I ~ (that) you're tired** supongo *or* me imagino que estarás cansado

C (await) esperar; **I'll ~ you at eight** te espero a las ocho; **to be ~ing a baby** esperar un bebé

D (require) **to ~ sb to + INF**: **I'm ~ed to do it without help** (se supone que) lo tengo que hacer solo; **I ~ you to be there** espero que *or* cuento con que estés allí; **he ~ed me to pay** esperaba *or* pretendía que yo pagara; **to ~ sth (FROM sb)**: **do they ~ a tip (from us)?** ¿tenemos que dejarles propina?; **that's the least you'd ~** es lo menos que se puede esperar

■ **expect** *vi* (colloq): **she's ~ing** está esperando (familia), está en estado

expectancy /ɪk'spektənsi/ *n* [u] expectación *f*; **a look/an air of ~** una mirada/un aire expectante *or* de expectación; **life ~** esperanza *f* de vida

expectant /ɪk'spektənt/ *adj* ‹*air/crowd*› expectante; **~ mother** futura mamá *f*

expectantly /ɪk'spektəntli/ *adv* con expectación

expectation /'ekspek'teɪʃən/ *n*

A 1 [u] (anticipation): **in ~ of victory** previendo la victoria; **an atmosphere of great ~** un ambiente de gran expectación 2 [u c] (preconceived idea) (*often pl*) expectativa *f*; **the performance came up to/fell short of our ~(s)** la actuación estuvo/no estuvo a la altura de lo que esperábamos

B **expectations** *pl* (of inheritance, promotion) expectativas *fpl*

expectorant /ek'spektərənt/ *n* [u c] expectorante *m*

expediency /ɪk'spiːdiənsi/, **expedience** /-əns/ *n* [u] conveniencia *f*

expedient¹ /ɪk'spiːdiənt/ *adj* (frml) (*usu pred*) conveniente, oportuno

expedient² *n* (frml) recurso *m*, expediente *m* (frml)

expedition /'ekspə'dɪʃən || ,ekspɪ'dɪʃən/ *n* expedición *f*; **to go/set out on an ~** ir*/salir* de expedición

expeditionary force /'ekspə'dɪʃəneri || ,ekspə'dɪʃənəri/ *n* cuerpo *m* expedicionario

expel /ɪk'spel/ *vt* **-ll-** ‹*person*› expulsar; ‹*air/liquid/smoke*› expulsar, expeler (frml)

expend /ɪk'spend/ *vt* (frml) ‹*money*› gastar; ‹*time*› dedicar*

expendable /ɪk'spendəbəl/ *adj* (dispensable) prescindible

expenditure /ɪk'spendɪtʃər || ɪk'spendɪtʃə(r)/ *n* [u] (amount) gastos *mpl*; (spending) gasto *m*

expense /ɪk'spens/ *n*

A [u] (cost, outlay) gasto *m*; **to go to the ~ of buying sth** meterse en el gasto de comprar algo; **at very little ~** por muy poco dinero; **at the company's ~** a cargo *or* a cuenta de la compañía; **they had a good laugh at my ~** se partieron de risa a costa mía *or* a mi costa; **at the ~ of sth/sb** a expensas de algo/algn

B **expenses** *pl* (Busn) (incidental costs) gastos *mpl*; **all ~s paid** con todos los gastos pagados; **to put sth on ~s** cargar* algo a la cuenta de la compañía

expense account *n* cuenta *f* de gastos de representación

expensive /ɪk'spensɪv/ *adj* caro; **an error like that could prove ~** un error así podría costar *or* salir caro

expensively /ɪk'spensɪvli/ *adv* ‹*dine/live*› sin reparar en gastos, por todo lo alto; ‹*dress*› con ropa muy cara

experience¹ /ɪk'spɪriəns/ *n* [u c] experiencia *f*; **to know sth by** *o* **from ~** saber* algo por experiencia; **work ~** experiencia laboral; **S previous experience essential** imprescindible tener experiencia previa

experience² *vt* ‹*loss/setback/delays*› sufrir; ‹*difficulty*› tener*, encontrarse* con; ‹*change/improvement*› experimentar; ‹*pleasure/pain/relief*› experimentar, sentir*

experienced /ɪk'spɪriənst || ɪk'spɪəriənst/ *adj* ‹*secretary/chef*› con experiencia; ‹*driver*› experimentado; **~ IN sth** con experiencia EN algo

experiment¹ /ɪk'sperəmənt || ɪk'sperɪmənt/ *n* experimento *m*; **as an ~, by way of ~** como experimento

experiment² *vi* **to ~ ON sth/sb** experimentar CON algo/algn; **to ~ WITH sth** experimentar CON algo

experimental /ɪk'sperə'mentl̩/ *adj* experimental

experimentation /ɪk'sperəmən'teɪʃən || ɪk,sperɪmen'teɪʃən/ *n* [u] experimentación *f*

expert¹ /'ekspɜːrt || 'ekspɜːt/ *n* experto, -ta *m,f*; **a medical/financial ~** un experto en medicina/finanzas; **~ AT sth/-ING** experto EN algo/+ INF; **~ ON/IN sth** experto EN algo; **I'm no ~** no soy ningún experto

expert² *adj* experto; **to seek ~ advice** asesorarse *or* consultar con un experto; **~ witness** perito, -ta *m,f*; **~ AT sth/-ING** experto EN algo/+ INF

expertise /'ekspɜːr'tiːz || ,ekspɜː'tiːz/ *n* [u] pericia *f*

expertly /'ekspɜːrtli || 'ekspɜːtli/ *adv* expertamente

expiate /'ekspieɪt/ *vt* (liter) expiar* (liter)

expire /ɪk'spaɪr || ɪk'spaɪə(r)/ *vi*

A (run out) «*visa/passport/ticket*» caducar*, vencer*; «*lease/contract*» vencer*

B (die) (liter) expirar (liter)

expiry /ɪk'spaɪri/ *n* [u] vencimiento *m*, caducidad *f*; (*before n*) **~ date** fecha *f* de vencimiento *or* de caducidad

explain /ɪk'spleɪn/ *vt* explicar*; **to ~ sth TO sb** explicarle* algo A algn; **that ~s everything!** eso lo explica *or* aclara todo

■ *v refl* **to ~ oneself** explicarse*

e

■ **explain** *vi*: **will you ~?** ¿me lo explicas?; **he's got some ~ing to do** nos debe una explicación

(Phrasal verb)

• **explain away** [v ▸ o ▸ adv, v ▸ adv ▸ o] ‹*fact/result*› encontrar* una explicación convincente para; **how are you going to ~ that away?** ¿cómo te las vas a arreglar para explicar eso?

explanation /'eksplə'neɪʃən/ *n* [c u] explicación *f*; **by way of ~** como explicación *or* aclaración; **~ FOR sth**: **there must be an ~ for this** esto tiene que tener una explicación

explanatory /ɪk'splænətɔːri/ *adj* explicativo

expletive /'eksplətɪv/ *n* (frml) improperio *m*, palabrota *f*

explicit /ɪk'splɪsət || ɪk'splɪsɪt/ *adj* explícito; ‹*denial/refutation*› categórico, rotundo; **sexually ~** sexualmente explícito; **she was quite ~ on this point** fue muy explícita *or* categórica en cuanto a ese punto

explicitly /ɪk'splɪsətli || ɪk'splɪsɪtli/ *adv* ‹*state*› explícitamente; ‹*identify/define*› claramente

explode /ɪk'spləʊd/ *vi* 1 «*gunpowder/bomb*» estallar, hacer* explosión, explotar; «*vehicle*» hacer* explosión; (with emotion) explotar, estallar; **he ~d with anger** estalló de rabia 2 «*population/costs*» dispararse

■ **explode** *vt*

A ‹*bomb/dynamite*› explosionar, hacer* explotar *or* estallar

B (discredit) ‹*theory*› rebatir, refutar; ‹*myth*› destruir*

exploit¹ /ɪk'splɔɪt/ *vt* explotar; ‹*situation/relationship*› aprovecharse de, explotar

exploit² /'eksplɔɪt/ *n* hazaña *f*, proeza *f*

exploitation /'eksplɔɪ'teɪʃən/ *n* [u] explotación *f*

exploitative /ɪk'splɔɪtətɪv/ *adj* ‹*person*› explotador; ‹*system/company*› que explota

exploiter /ɪk'splɔɪtər/ *n* explotador, -dora *m,f*

exploration /'eksplə'reɪʃən/ *n* [u c] exploración *f*

exploratory /ɪk'splɔːrətɔːri || ɪk'splɒrətəri/ *adj* ‹*talks*› preliminar, preparatorio; ‹*surgery*› exploratorio

explore /ɪk'splɔːr || ɪk'splɔː(r)/ *vt* ‹*territory/town*› explorar; ‹*topic/possibility*› investigar*, examinar

■ **explore** *vi* explorar

explorer /ɪk'splɔːrər || ɪk'splɔːrə(r)/ *n* 1 (traveler) explorador, -dora *m,f* 2 **Explorer** (in US) boy scout *m* (*mayor de 14 años*)

explosion /ɪk'spləʊʒən/ *n* 1 (of bomb, gas) explosión *f*, estallido *m* 2 (of anger) estallido *m*, explosión *f* 3 (increase): **a population ~** una explosión demográfica; **there has been a price ~** los precios se han disparado

explosive¹ /ɪk'spləʊsɪv/ *adj* explosivo

explosive² *n* [c u] explosivo *m*

exponent /ɪk'spəʊnənt/ *n* (of idea, theory) defensor, -sora *m,f*, partidario, -ria *m,f*; (of art style) exponente *mf*

export¹ /ek'spɔːrt || ɪk'spɔːt/ *vt* exportar

export² /'ekspɔːrt || 'ekspɔːt/ *n* 1 [c] (item exported) artículo *m or* producto *m* de exportación 2 [u] (act of exporting) exportación *f*; (*before n*) **~ credit** crédito *m* a la exportación; **~ duties** aranceles *mpl* de exportación

exportation /'ekspɔːr'teɪʃən/ *n* [u] exportación *f*

exporter /ek'spɔːrtər/ *n* exportador, -dora *m,f*

expose /ɪk'spəʊz/ *vt*

A 1 (lay bare) ‹*nerve/wire/wound*› exponer* 2 (subject) **to ~ sth/sb TO sth** exponer* algo/a algn A algo; **to ~ oneself to criticism** exponerse* a las críticas

B (uncover) ‹*secret/scandal*› poner* al descubierto, sacar* a la luz; ‹*inefficiency/weaknesses*› poner* en evidencia; ‹*criminal*› desenmascarar

C (Phot) exponer*

■ *v refl* **to ~ oneself** hacer* exhibicionismo

exposé /'ekspəʊ'zeɪ || ek'spəʊzeɪ/ *n* revelación *f*

exposed /ɪk'spəʊzd/ *adj* 1 ‹*nerve/wire*› expuesto 2 ‹*hillside/plateau*› expuesto, desprotegido

exposition /'ekspə'zɪʃən/ *n* [u c] exposición *f*

expostulate /ɪk'spɑːstʃəleɪt || ɪk'spɒstjʊleɪt/ *vi* (frml) objetar, protestar; **to ~ WITH sb ABOUT/ON sth** reconvenir* a algn SOBRE algo (frml)

■ **expostulate** *vt* (frml) protestar

expostulations /ɪk'spɑːstʃə'leɪʃənz/ *pl n* (frml) objeciones *fpl*

exposure /ɪk'spəʊʒər || ɪk'spəʊʒə(r)/ *n*

A [u] 1 (contact) **~ TO sth** exposición *f* A algo 2 **indecent ~** exhibicionismo *m* 3 (Med) congelación *f*; **to be suffering from ~** tener* síntomas de congelación; **to die from ~** morir* de frío

B [u] 1 (unmasking): **she was threatened with public ~** amenazaron con ponerla al descubierto 2 (publicity) publicidad *f*

C (Phot) exposición *f*

expound /ɪk'spaʊnd/ *vt* (frml) exponer*

■ **expound** *vi* (frml) hablar

express¹ /ɪk'spres/ *vt* expresar

■ *v refl* **to ~ oneself** expresarse

express² *n* [c] (train) expreso *m*, rápido *m*; (bus) directo *m*

express³ *adj*

A (fast) ‹*train*› expreso, rápido; ‹*bus*› directo; ‹*delivery/letter*› exprés *adj inv*, urgente

B (specific) (frml) ‹*intention/wish*› expreso, explícito

express⁴ *adv* por correo exprés *or* expreso

expression /ɪk'spreʃən/ *n*

A 1 (of feelings) expresión *f*; **to give ~ to sth** expresar algo; **to find ~ in sth** expresarse a través de algo; **freedom of ~** libertad *f* de expresión 2 (of face) expresión *f*

B (Ling) expresión *f*

expressionism /ɪk'spreʃənɪzəm/ *n* [u] expresionismo *m*

expressionist /ɪk'spreʃənəst/ *adj* expresionista

expressionless /ɪk'spreʃənləs/ *adj* inexpresivo

expressive /ɪk'spresɪv/ *adj* expresivo

expressly /ɪk'spresli/ *adv* (frml) expresamente

expressway /ɪk'spresweɪ/ *n* (AmE) autopista *f*; (urban) vía *f* rápida

expropriate /eks'prəʊprieɪt/ *vt* expropiar

expropriation /eks'prəʊpri'eɪʃən/ *n* [u c] expropiación *f*

expulsion /ɪk'spʌlʃən/ *n* [u c] expulsión *f*

expunge /ɪk'spʌndʒ/ *vt* (frml) suprimir, eliminar

expurgate /'ekspərgeɪt || 'ekspəgeɪt/ *vt* expurgar*

exquisite /ek'skwɪzət || 'ekskwɪzɪt/ *adj* 1 ‹*dress/meal/taste*› exquisito; ‹*carving/brooch*› de exquisita factura; ‹*work/workmanship*› intrincado 2 ‹*pleasure*› infinito

exquisitely /ek'skwɪzətli || ek'skwɪzɪtli/ *adv* 1 (superbly) ‹*made*› de manera exquisita, exquisitamente; ‹*dressed*› con un gusto exquisito 2 ‹*polite/painful*› sumamente

ex-serviceman /'eks'sɜːrvəsmən || ,eks'sɜːvɪsmən/ *n* (*pl* **-men** /-mən/) soldado (*or* marinero *etc*) *m* retirado

ext (= **extension**) Ext., extensión *f*, interno *m* (RPl), anexo *m* (Chi)

extant /ek'stænt/ *adj* (frml) existente

extemporize /ɪk'stempəraɪz/ *vt/i* (frml) improvisar

extend /ɪk'stend/ *vt*

A 1 (stretch out) ‹*limbs/wings/telescope*› extender*; ‹*rope/wire*› tender* 2 (lengthen) ‹*road/line/visit*› prolongar*; ‹*lease/contract*› prorrogar*; ‹*deadline*› prorrogar*, extender* 3 (enlarge) ‹*house/room*› ampliar*; ‹*range/scope/influence*› extender*, ampliar*; **to ~ sth TO sth** extender* algo A algo

B (offer) (frml): **to ~ an invitation to sb** invitar a algn; (of written invitations) cursarle invitación a algn (frml); **to ~ a warm welcome to sb** darle* una calurosa bienvenida a algn

C (stretch mentally): **this job does not ~ me** este trabajo no me exige lo que podría rendir

■ **extend** *vi* 1 (stretch) «*fence/property/jurisdiction/influence*» extenderse* 2 (in time) «*talks/negotiations*» prolongarse* 3 (become extended) «*ladder/rod/antenna*» extenderse* 4 **extending** *pres p* ‹*table/leg/ladder*› extensible

extended /ɪk'stendəd || ɪk'stendɪd/ *adj* 1 ‹*warranty/guarantee*› extendido; ‹*period/stay*› prolongado, largo; ‹*version*› ampliado, más extenso; **the ~ family** el clan familiar, la familia extensa 2 (stretched out) extendido; **with arms ~** con los brazos extendidos

extension /ɪk'stentʃən || ɪk'stenʃən/ *n*

A 1 [u] (of power, meaning) extensión *f*, ampliación *f*; **by ~** por extensión 2 [u c] (lengthening) prolongación *f*; (of deadline) prórroga *f*, extensión *f*

B [c] (to building) ampliación *f*

C [c] (Telec) **1** (line) extensión *f*, interno *m* (RPl), anexo *m* (Chi) **2** (telephone) supletorio *m*
D [u] (Educ) (*before n*) ‹*course*› de extensión universitaria

extension cord, (BrE) **extension lead** *n* extensión *f*, alargador *m*, alargue *m* (RPl)

extensive /ɪk'stensɪv/ *adj* ‹*area/field*› extenso; ‹*knowledge*› vasto, extenso, amplio; ‹*experience/coverage*› amplio; ‹*search/inquiries*› exhaustivo; ‹*damage/repairs*› de consideración, importante; **to make ~ use of sth** hacer* abundante uso de algo

extensively /ɪk'stensɪvli/ *adv* **1** (widely): **he's traveled ~** ha viajado por todas partes, ha viajado mucho; **this technique is used ~** esta técnica es de uso extendido **2** (thoroughly, at length) ‹*research/investigate*› exhaustivamente; **she has written ~ on the subject** ha escrito mucho sobre el tema

extent /ɪk'stent/ *n* [u]
A (size, area) extensión *f*; **to its fullest ~** en toda su extensión
B **1** (range, degree — of knowledge) amplitud *f*, vastedad *f*; (— of problem) alcance *m*; **the ~ of the damage** la importancia *or* el alcance de los daños; (in monetary terms) la cuantía de los daños **2** (*in phrases*) **to some extent, to a certain extent** hasta cierto punto, en cierta medida; **to a large extent** en gran parte, en buena medida; **to a greater/lesser extent** en mayor/menor medida, en mayor/menor grado; **to that extent** hasta ese punto; **to what extent** en qué medida, hasta qué punto

extenuate /ɪk'stenjueɪt/ *vt* (frml) atenuar*; **extenuating circumstances** circunstancias *fpl* atenuantes

exterior[1] /ek'stɪriər || ɪk'stɪəriə(r)/ *adj* **1** (external) ‹*wall/surface*› exterior **2** (Cin) ‹*shot/scene*› de exteriores **3** (for use outside) ‹*paint/plaster*› para exteriores

exterior[2] *n* exterior *m*

exterminate /ɪk'stɜːrməneɪt || ɪk'stɜːmɪneɪt/ *vt* exterminar

external /ek'stɜːrnl̩ || ɪk'stɜːnl/ *adj* **1** (exterior) ‹*appearance/sign*› externo, exterior; ‹*wall*› exterior; ‹*wound/treatment*› externo; ⓢ **for external use only** uso tópico, de uso externo **2** ‹*aid/influence*› del exterior; ‹*pressure/evidence*› externo **3** (foreign) ‹*affairs/trade/policy*› exterior

externally /ek'stɜːrnl̩i || ɪk'stɜːnəli/ *adv*
A (on the outside) exteriormente, por fuera
B (by outside agency) ‹*vetted*› independientemente, por un tercero

extinct /ɪk'stɪŋkt/ *adj* ‹*animal/species*› extinto, desaparecido; ‹*volcano*› extinto, apagado; **to become ~** extinguirse*

extinction /ɪk'stɪŋkʃən/ *n* [u] extinción *f*

extinguish /ɪk'stɪŋgwɪʃ/ *vt* **1** ‹*fire*› extinguir*; ‹*candle/cigar*› apagar* **2** (liter) ‹*hope/memory*› apagar* (liter); ‹*passion/life*› extinguir* (liter)

extinguisher /ɪk'stɪŋgwɪʃər || ɪk'stɪŋgwɪʃə(r)/ *n* (*fire ~*) extinguidor *m* (AmL), extintor *m* (Esp)

extol, (AmE also) **extoll** /ɪk'stəʊl/ *vt* **-ll-** (frml) ensalzar* (frml)

extort /ɪk'stɔːrt || ɪk'stɔːt/ *vt*: **to ~ money from sb** extorsionar a algn; **to ~ a confession/promise from sb** arrancarle* a algn *or* obtener* de algn una confesión/promesa

extortion /ɪk'stɔːrʃən || ɪk'stɔːʃən/ *n* [u] (Law) extorsión *f*; **that's sheer ~!** ¡eso es un robo!

extortionate /ɪk'stɔːrʃənət || ɪk'stɔːʃənət/ *adj* ‹*fee/price*› abusivo, exorbitante; ‹*demand*› excesivo, desmesurado

extortionist /ɪk'stɔːrʃənəst || ɪk'stɔːʃənɪst/ *n* extorsionador, dora *m,f*, extorsionista *mf* (AmL)

extra[1] /'ekstrə/ *adj* **1** (additional) (*before n*) de más; **do some ~ copies** haz unas copias de más; **we need ~ sheets/staff** necesitamos más sábanas/personal; **it costs an ~ $15** cuesta 15 dólares más; **they organized three ~ flights** organizaron tres vuelos adicionales; **~ time** (in soccer) prórroga *f*, tiempo *m* suplementario, tiempos *mpl* extra (Méx) **2** (especial) (*before n*) ‹*care/caution*› especial **3** (subject to additional charge) (*after n*): **a shower is $2 ~** con ducha cuesta dos dólares más; **postage and handling ~** gastos de envío no incluidos

extra[2] *adv* **1** (*as intensifier*): **~ fine/long** extrafino/extralargo; **I worked ~ hard** trabajé más que nunca **2** (more): **to charge ~ for sth** cobrar algo aparte; **you have to pay a little ~ for that** para eso hay que pagar un poco más

extra[3] *n*
A (additional payment or expense) extra *m*; **optional ~s** (Auto) equipamiento *m* opcional, extras *mpl*
B (Cin) extra *mf*
C (Journ) número *m* extra

extract[1] /ɪk'strækt/ *vt*
A ‹*tooth/juice*› extraer*; ‹*iron/gold*› extraer*
B **1** (obtain) ‹*information*› extraer*, sacar* **2** ‹*passage/quotation*› extraer*, sacar*

extract[2] /'ekstrækt/ *n*
A [c] (excerpt) fragmento *m*, trozo *m*
B [u c] (concentrate) extracto *m*; **beef/yeast ~** extracto de carne/levadura

extraction /ɪk'strækʃən/ *n*
A **1** [c u] (Dent) extracción *f* **2** [u] (of mineral, juice) extracción *f*
B [u] (ancestry) extracción *f*; **of Polish ~** de extracción polaca

extractor fan /ɪk'stræktər || ɪk'stræktə(r)/ *n* (BrE) extractor *m* (de aire)

extracurricular /'ekstrəkə'rɪkjələr/ *adj* extracurricular

extradite /'ekstrədaɪt/ *vt* extraditar

extradition /'ekstrə'dɪʃən/ *n* [u] extradición *f*; (*before n*) ‹*order/treaty*› de extradición

extramarital /'ekstrə'mærətl̩/ *adj* extramatrimonial

extramural /'ekstrə'mjʊrəl || ˌekstrə'mjʊərəl/ *adj* (Educ) ‹*course*› de extensión; ‹*student*› externo, libre

extraneous /ek'streɪniəs/ *adj* (frml) ‹*argument/detail/decoration*› superfluo; ‹*influence*› externo; **to be ~ to sth** no tener* relación CON algo, ser* extrínseco A algo (frml)

extraordinarily /ɪk'strɔːrdn̩'erəli || ɪk'strɔːdn̩rəli/ *adv* (*as intensifier*) ‹*kind/handsome*› extraordinariamente

extraordinary /ɪk'strɔːrdn̩eri || ɪk'strɔːdn̩ri/ *adj*
A (exceptional) extraordinario; (very odd) ‹*sight/appearance*› insólito; (incredible) increíble, insólito; **how ~!** ¡qué increíble!
B (frml Adm, Govt) ‹*powers/meeting*› extraordinario

extrapolate /ɪk'stræpəleɪt/ *vt* (frml) extrapolar
■ **extrapolate** *vi* (frml) **to ~ FROM sth** hacer* una extrapolación DE algo

extrapolation /ɪk'stræpə'leɪʃən/ *n* [c u] (frml) extrapolación *f*

extrasensory /'ekstrə'sensəri/ *adj* extrasensorial; **~ perception** percepción *f* extrasensorial

extraterrestrial /'ekstrətə'restriəl/ *adj* ‹*life*› extraterrestre; ‹*exploration*› del espacio

extravagance /ɪk'strævəgəns/ *n*
A **1** [u] (lavishness, wastefulness) despilfarro *m*, derroche *m* **2** [c] (luxury) lujo *m*
B [u] (of gestures, dress) extravagancia *f*; (of claim, story) lo insólito

extravagant /ɪk'strævəgənt/ *adj* **1** (lavish, wasteful) ‹*person*› derrochador, despilfarrador; ‹*lifestyle*› de lujo **2** ‹*claim/notions*› insólito; ‹*praise/compliments*› exagerado, desmesurado; ‹*behavior/dress/gesture*› extravagante

extravagantly /ɪk'strævəgəntli/ *adv* **1** (lavishly, wastefully) ‹*live/celebrate*› a lo grande; **to spend ~** derrochar (el dinero) **2** ‹*dress/behave*› de manera extravagante; ‹*praise*› exageradamente, desmesuradamente

extravaganza /ɪk'strævə'gænzə/ *n* gran espectáculo *m* (*realizado con alarde de color, fantasía y dinero*)

extreme[1] /ɪk'striːm/ *adj* **1** (very great) ‹*poverty/caution/urgency*› extremo; ‹*annoyance/relief*› enorme; ‹*heat*› extremado, intensísimo; **with ~ care** con sumo cuidado **2** (not moderate) ‹*action/measure*› extremo, extremado; ‹*opinion*› extremista; **the ~ left/right** (Pol) la extrema izquierda/derecha **3** (outermost) (*before n*): **in the ~ north/south** en la zona más septentrional/meridional

extreme[2] *n* extremo *m*; **~s of temperature** temperaturas *fpl* extremas; **to go from one ~ to the other** ir* de un extremo al *or* a otro; **she carries things to ~s** es una extremada

extremely /ɪk'striːmli/ *adv* (*as intensifier*) sumamente; **it's ~ interesting/difficult** es interesantísimo/dificilísimo, es sumamente interesante/difícil; **it's ~ unlikely** es muy poco probable

e

extremist¹ /ɪk'stri:məst || ɪk'stri:mɪst/ *adj* extremista

extremist² *n* extremista *mf*

extremity /ɪk'streməti/ *n* (*pl* **-ties**)
A 1 [c] (farthest point) extremo *m* 2 **extremities** *pl* (Anat) extremidades *fpl*
B [u c] (critical degree, situation) (frml) extremo *m*

extricate /'ekstrəkeɪt || 'ekstrɪkeɪt/ *vt* **to ~ sth/sb FROM sth** sacar* algo/a algn DE algo (*con dificultad*); **I ~d myself from her embrace** conseguí soltarme de su abrazo

extrovert¹ /'ekstrəvɜ:rt || 'ekstrəvɜ:t/ *adj* extrovertido

extrovert² *n* extrovertido, -da *m,f*

extrude /ɪk'stru:d/ *vt* extrudir

exuberant /ɪg'zu:bərənt || ɪg'zju:bərənt/ *adj* 1 (lively) ‹*person/character*› desbordante de vida y entusiasmo 2 (vigorous, profuse) ‹*style/foliage*› exuberante

exude /ɪg'zu:d || ɪg'zju:d/ *vi* «*resin*» rezumar
■ **exude** *vt* ‹*resin/fluid*› exudar; ‹*charm/confidence*› emanar, irradiar; **the wound ~d yellow pus** de la herida salía un pus amarillo

exult /ɪg'zʌlt/ *vi* (frml) exultar (frml), regocijarse; **to ~ IN sth** regocijarse CON algo

exultant /ɪg'zʌltn̩t/ *adj* (frml) ‹*person/crowd*› jubiloso, exultante (de alegría) (frml); ‹*cry/shout*› de júbilo

exultation /'egzʌl'teɪʃən/ *n* [u] (frml) exultación *f* (frml), júbilo *m* (liter)

eye¹ /aɪ/ *n*
A 1 (Anat) ojo *m*; **he has blue ~s** tiene los ojos azules; **to have sharp ~s** tener* (una) vista de lince, tener* ojo de águila; **as far as the ~ can/could see** hasta donde alcanza/alcanzaba la vista; **in the twinkling of an ~** en un abrir y cerrar de ojos; **I can't believe my ~s** si no lo veo, no lo creo, no doy crédito a mis ojos; ***to be all ~s*** mirar lleno de curiosidad; ***to close*** *o* ***shut one's ~s to sth*** cerrar* los ojos a algo; ***to cry one's ~s out*** llorar a lágrima viva *or* a mares; **I went into it with my ~s wide open** me metí sabiendo muy bien lo que hacía; ***to have ~s in the back of one's head*** tener* ojos en la nuca; ***to keep one's ~s open*** (to avoid danger, problems) andarse* *or* ir* con cuidado; (looking for sth): **keep your ~s open for a restaurant** vete mirando *or* fíjate bien a ver si ves un restaurante; ***to keep one's ~s peeled*** *o* ***skinned*** (colloq) (to avoid danger, problems) andarse* *or* ir* con mucho ojo (fam); (looking for sth) estar(se)* ojo avizor (fam); ***to make ~s at sb*** hacerle* ojitos a algn; ***to open sb's ~s*** abrirle* los ojos a algn; ***to open sb's ~s to sth*** hacerle* ver algo a algn; ***to see ~ to ~ with sb*** (*usu with neg*) estar* de acuerdo con algn, coincidir con algn; ***with one's ~s shut*** *o* ***closed*** con los ojos cerrados; ***to be up to one's eyes in sth*** estar* hasta aquí de algo (fam); **I'm up to my ~s in work** estoy agobiada *or* (fam) hasta aquí de trabajo; **we're up to our ~s in debt** estamos cargados de deudas, debemos hasta la camisa (fam); (*before n*) **~ contact**: **to make/avoid ~ contact with sb** mirar/evitar mirar a algn a los ojos; **at ~ level** a la altura de la vista 2 (look, gaze) mirada *f*; **under the watchful ~(s) of the teacher** bajo la atenta mirada del profesor; **to cast** *o* **run one's ~ over sth** recorrer algo con la vista; **before my very ~s** ante mis propios ojos; **nothing caught my ~ in the store** no vi nada que me llamara la atención en la tienda; **I tried to catch his ~** intenté llamar su atención; **these colors really catch the ~** estos colores son verdaderamente llamativos; **to have one's ~s on sb/sth** no quitarle los ojos de encima a algn/algo; **in Mary's ~s he's perfect** para Mary *or* a ojos de Mary es perfecto; **in the ~s of the Law** ante la ley; **to keep one's ~(s) on sth/sb**: **keep your ~s on the road!** ¡no apartes la vista de la carretera!; **keep your ~s on him** no lo pierdas de vista; **to look sb straight in the ~** mirar a algn directamente a los ojos; **she won't look me in the ~** no se atreve a mirarme a la cara; **he couldn't take his ~s off her** no podía quitarle los ojos de encima; ***easy on the ~*** (colloq) agradable a la vista; ***to keep an ~ on sth/sb*** vigilar *or* cuidar algo/a algn; **keep an ~ on those two** no pierdas de vista a esos dos, vigila a esos dos; ***to lay*** *o* ***set*** *o* (colloq) ***clap ~s on sb/sth***: **from the moment I laid** *o* **set** *o* (colloq) **clapped ~s on him/it** desde el primer momento que lo vi; ***to turn a blind ~ (to sth)*** hacer* la vista gorda (frente a *or* ante algo) 3 (attention): **the ~s of the world will be on her** todo el mundo tendrá la vista puesta en ella; **the company has been in the public ~ a lot recently** últimamente se ha hablado mucho de la compañía; ***to have one's ~ on sth*** echarle el ojo a algo (fam); **with an ~ to sth** con miras a algo 4 (ability to judge) ojo *m*; **to have an ~ for design** tener* ojo *or* idea para el diseño; **to have an ~ for detail** ser* detallista
B 1 (of needle) ojo *m* 2 (of hurricane, storm) ojo *m* 3 (in potato) ojo *m*

eye² *vt* (*pres p* **eying** *or* (BrE) **eyeing**) 1 (observe) mirar, observar; **to ~ sb up and down** mirar a algn de arriba abajo; **to ~ sth suspiciously** observar algo con sospecha 2 (ogle) mirar, pasarle revista a (fam)

eyeball¹ /'aɪbɔ:l/ *n* (Anat) globo *m* ocular; ***to meet ~ to ~ with sb*** (colloq) enfrentarse cara a cara con algn; ***to be up to one's ~s in sth*** estar* hasta aquí de algo (fam)

eyeball² *vt* (AmE colloq) mirar de arriba a abajo

eye: **~bath** *n* (BrE) (cup) lavaojos *m*; (procedure) baño *m* ocular *or* de ojos; **~brow** *n* ceja *f*; **to raise one's ~brows** arquear *or* enarcar* las cejas; ***to raise one's ~brows at sth*** asombrarse ante algo; (*before n*) **~brow pencil** lápiz *m* de cejas; **~-catching** *adj* llamativo, vistoso; **~ cup** *n* (AmE) lavaojos *m*

-eyed /aɪd/ *suff*: **green~/almond~** de ojos verdes/almendrados

eyedrops /'aɪdrɑ:ps || 'aɪdrɒps/ *pl n* colirio *m*, gotas *fpl* para los ojos

eyeful /'aɪfʊl/ *n*: **I got an ~ of dust** se me llenó el ojo de polvo; **quick, get an ~ of this** (colloq) ven a ver esto, no te lo pierdas

eye: **~glass** *n* (monocle) monóculo *m*; **~glasses** *pl n* (AmE) gafas *fpl*, anteojos *mpl* (esp AmL), lentes *mpl* (esp AmL); **~lash** *n* pestaña *f*; **a pair of false ~lashes** unas pestañas postizas

eyelet /'aɪlət || 'aɪlɪt/ *n* ojete *m*

eye: **~lid** *n* párpado *m*; **~liner** *n* [u] delineador *m* (de ojos); **~-opener** *n* (colloq) (*no pl*) revelación *f*; **it was a real ~-opener** me (*or* nos *etc*) hizo abrir los ojos; **~patch** *n* parche *m*; **~piece** *n* ocular *m*; **~shade** *n* visera *f*; **~ shadow** *n* [u c] sombra *f* de ojos; **~sight** *n* [u] vista *f*; **to have good/poor ~sight** tener* buena/mala vista; **~sore** *n* monstruosidad *f*, adefesio *m*; **~strain** *n* [u] fatiga *f* visual, vista *f* cansada; **~tooth** /'aɪ'tu:θ/ *n* colmillo *m*; ***to give one's ~teeth for sth***: **I'd give my ~teeth for that ring/to go** no sé qué daría *or* daría cualquier cosa por ese anillo/por ir; **~wash** *n* [u] colirio *m*, solución *f* oftálmica; **it's a lot of ~wash** (colloq) es un cuento chino (fam); **~witness** /'aɪ'wɪtnəs || 'aɪwɪtnɪs/ *n* testigo *mf* ocular *or* presencial

eyrie /'aɪri/ *n* ▸ **aerie**

F, f /ef/ *n* [1] (letter) F, f *f* [2] (Mus) fa *m*; *see also* **A A2**

f [1] (= **female**) de sexo femenino [2] (Ling) (= **feminine**) f

F (= **Fahrenheit**) F; **70°F** 70°F

fa /fɑː/ *n* (Mus) fa *m*

FA *n* (in UK) = **Football Association**

fable /ˈfeɪbəl/ *n* [c u] fábula *f*

fabled /ˈfeɪbəld/ *adj* (liter *or* journ) legendario, fabuloso

fabric /ˈfæbrɪk/ *n*
A [u c] (Tex) tela *f*, tejido *m*, género *m*
B [u] (of building, society) estructura *f*

fabricate /ˈfæbrɪkeɪt/ *vt* [1] (invent) inventar(se) [2] (manufacture) (Tech) fabricar*

fabrication /ˈfæbrɪˈkeɪʃən/ *n* [1] [c u] (lie) invención *f*, mentira *f* [2] [u] (manufacture) (Tech) fabricación *f*

fabulous /ˈfæbjələs || ˈfæbjʊləs/ *adj* [1] ‹*sum/price*› astronómico, exorbitante; ‹*wealth*› fabuloso [2] (wonderful) (colloq) magnífico, fabuloso; **you look absolutely ~!** ¡estás fantástica *or* fenomenal! [3] (imaginary) fabuloso

fabulously /ˈfæbjələsli || ˈfæbjʊləsli/ *adv* (*as intensifier*) fabulosamente

facade, façade /fəˈsɑːd/ *n* fachada *f*

face¹ /feɪs/ *n*
A [c] [1] (of person, animal) cara *f*, rostro *m*; **if your ~ doesn't fit ...** si no le/les caes bien ...; **I'm not just a pretty ~, you know!** (set phrase) no te creas que soy tan tonta; **I must put my ~ on** *o* **do my ~** (hum) tengo que maquillarme *or* pintarme; **she put on a brave ~ for the funeral** se mantuvo compuesta para el funeral; **to feed** *o* **stuff one's ~** (colloq) atiborrarse de comida, ponerse* morado (Esp fam); **in the ~ of stiff opposition** en medio de *or* ante una fuerte oposición; ***to argue/shout until one is blue in the ~*** discutir/gritar hasta cansarse; ***to blow up in sb's ~*** salir* mal; ***to fall flat on one's ~*** caerse* de bruces; (blunder) darse* de narices; ***to fly in the ~ of sth*** hacer* caso omiso de algo; ***to laugh on the other side of one's ~***: **you'll laugh on the other side of your ~ when you're fired!** ¡se te van a acabar las ganas de reír(te) cuando te despidan!; ***to sb's ~*** a *or* en la cara; ***to show one's ~*** aparecer*; ***to stare sb in the ~***: **the solution was staring me in the ~** tenía la solución delante de las narices [2] (person) cara *f*; **a new ~** una cara nueva [3] (expression) cara *f*; ***to keep a straight ~***: **I could hardly keep a straight ~** casi no podía aguantarme (de) la risa; ***to make*** *o* (BrE also) ***pull a ~*** poner* mala cara; **the children were making ~s at each other** los niños se hacían muecas; ***to put a brave ~ on it*** poner(le)* al mal tiempo buena cara
B [1] (appearance, nature) (*no pl*) fisonomía *f*; ***on the ~ of it*** aparentemente [2] [c] (aspect) aspecto *m* [3] [u] (dignity): **to lose ~** desprestigiarse, quedar mal; **to save ~** guardar las apariencias; **loss of ~** desprestigio *m*
C [c] (of coin, medal, solid) cara *f*; (of clock, watch) esfera *f*, carátula *f* (Méx)
D [c] (of cliff) pared *f*; ***to disappear off the ~ of the earth*** desaparecer* de la faz de la tierra

face² *vt*
A (be opposite): **she turned to ~ him/the wall** se volvió hacia él/la pared; **he was sitting facing the wall** estaba sentado en frente de la pared; **the hotel ~s the sea** el hotel está frente al mar
B (confront) enfrentarse a; **I don't know how I'll ~ him when he finds out** no sé cómo le podré dar la cara cuando se entere; **to be ~d with sth** estar* *or* verse* frente a *or* ante algo; **let's ~ it, we have no alternative** seamos realistas, no nos queda otra alternativa
C [1] (be presented with) ‹*problem/increase*› enfrentarse a; **I ~ that problem every day** todos los días me encuentro con *or* me enfrento a un problema así [2] (bear): **I can't ~ going through all that again** no podría volver a pasar por todo eso; **I can't ~ food first thing in the morning** no puedo ni oler la comida temprano por la mañana [3] (lie ahead of): **several problems ~ us** se nos presentan *or* se nos plantean varios problemas
D (Const) ‹*wall/surface*› recubrir*
■ **face** *vi*: **the house ~s north** la casa está orientada *or* da al norte; **I was facing the other way** miraba para el otro lado

Phrasal verbs
• **face down** [v ▸ o ▸ adv, v ▸ adv ▸ o] hacerle* frente a
• **face up to** [v ▸ adv ▸ prep ▸ o] ‹*reality/responsibility*› afrontar, hacer* frente a; **we have to ~ up to the fact that ...** tenemos que aceptar *or* reconocer que ...

face: **~ card** *n* (AmE) figura *f*; **~cloth**, (BrE also) **~ flannel** *n* toallita *f* (*para lavarse*), ≈ manopla *f*

faceless /ˈfeɪsləs || ˈfeɪslɪs/ *adj* (pej) ‹*bureaucrat*› anónimo

face: **~ lift** *n* (Med) lifting *m*, estiramiento *m* (facial); (renovation): **the building was given a ~ lift** remozaron el edificio; **~ mask** *n* [1] (for diving) máscara *f* [2] (in US football — piece of equipment) barra *f* del casco; (— foul) barra *f* [3] (as beauty treatment) mascarilla *f* (*de belleza*); **~-off** *n* [1] (in ice hockey) salida *f*, saque *m* [2] (showdown) (AmE) confrontación *f*; **~ pack** *n* mascarilla *f* (*de belleza*); **~-saving** /ˈfeɪs ˈseɪvɪŋ/ *adj* (*before n*) ‹*measures*› para guardar *or* cubrir las apariencias

facet /ˈfæsət || ˈfæsɪt/ *n* faceta *f*

facetious /fəˈsiːʃəs/ *adj* burlón, gracioso (iró)

facetiously /fəˈsiːʃəsli/ *adv* ‹*talk/write*› en tono de burla

face: **~ to face** *adv* cara a cara, frente a frente; **we were brought ~ to ~ with reality** tuvimos que enfrentarnos a la realidad; **~-to-face** /ˈfeɪstəˈfeɪs/ *adj* cara a cara, frente a frente; **~ value** *n* [u] (of money) valor *m* nominal; ***to take sth/sb at ~ value***: **I took her/what she said at ~ value** me fié de ella/yo me creí lo que dijo

facial¹ /ˈfeɪʃəl/ *adj* facial, de la cara

facial² *n* limpieza *f* de cutis

facile /ˈfæsəl || ˈfæsaɪl/ *adj* superficial, simplista

facilitate /fəˈsɪləteɪt || fəˈsɪlɪteɪt/ *vt* (frml) facilitar

facilitator /fəˈsɪləteɪtər || fəˈsɪlɪteɪtə(r)/ *n* facilitador, -dora *m,f*

facility /fəˈsɪləti/ *n* (*pl* **-ties**)
A **facilities** *pl* [1] (amenities): **sports facilities** instalaciones *fpl* deportivas; **facilities for the disabled** instalaciones *fpl* para minusválidos; **the hotel has conference facilities** el hotel dispone de sala(s) de conferencia [2] (Fin): **credit facilities** crédito *m*, facilidades *fpl* de pago
B (building) (AmE) complejo *m*, centro *m*
C [u] (ability) (frml) facilidad *f*

facing /ˈfeɪsɪŋ/ *n* [c u]
A (Clothing) entretela *f*
B (Const) revestimiento *m*

-facing /ˈfeɪsɪŋ/ *suff*: **north/south~** que da al norte/sur

facsimile /fæk'sɪməli/ n 1 (copy) facsímil m, facsímile m; (before n) ‹edition› facsimilar 2 (Telec) facsímil(e) m

fact /fækt/ n
A [c] (sth true) hecho m; **he twisted the ~s** distorsionó los hechos; **she got her ~s right/wrong** su información era correcta/incorrecta; **hard ~s** datos mpl concretos; **give me all the ~s and figures** dame toda la información; **if it wasn't for the ~ that he's my son ...** si no fuera porque es mi hijo ...; **I know for a ~ that ...** sé a ciencia cierta que ...; **it's a well-known ~** todo el mundo lo sabe; ***to face (the) ~s*** aceptar la realidad
B 1 [u] (truth, reality): **this novel is based on ~** esta novela está basada en hechos reales; **in ~** de hecho, en realidad; **as a matter of ~: I do know her, as a matter of ~ she's one of my best friends** sí que la conozco, (de hecho) es muy amiga mía; **in point of ~** de hecho; **the ~ of the matter is (that) ...** el hecho es que ... 2 [c] (criminal event) (Law): **after the ~** después de los hechos

fact-finding /'fækt,faɪndɪŋ/ adj (before n) de investigación, investigador

faction /'fækʃən/ n (group) facción f

factional /'fækʃn̩əl || 'fækʃənl/ adj de/entre facciones

fact of life n
A (unpleasant truth) (triste or dura) realidad f (de la vida)
B **the ~s of life** (euph): **his father told him the ~s ~ ~** su padre le explicó cómo se reproducen los seres humanos

factor[1] /'fæktər || 'fæktə(r)/ n factor m; **the time ~** el factor tiempo

factor[2] vt (Busn) hacer* factoring de

(Phrasal verbs)
- **factor in** [v ▸ o ▸ adv, v ▸ adv ▸ o] ‹prices/costs› tener* or tomar en consideración, tener* en cuenta
- **factor out** [v ▸ o ▸ adv, v ▸ adv ▸ o] ‹prices/costs› no tener* or tomar en consideración, no tener en cuenta

factory /'fæktri, -təri/ n (pl **-ries**) fábrica f; (before n) ‹inspector› industrial; **~ worker** obrero, -ra m,f (de fábrica)

factory: **~ farm** n: *establecimiento ganadero de producción intensiva*; **~ farming** n [u] (BrE) cría f intensiva; **~ ship** n buque m factoría

factotum /fæk'təʊtəm/ n (frml or hum) factótum m (frml o hum)

fact sheet n hoja f informativa

factual /'fæktʃuəl/ adj ‹account› que se atiene a los hechos, objetivo; **a ~ error** un error de hecho

factually /'fæktʃuəli/ adv en cuanto a los hechos

faculty /'fækəlti/ n (pl **-ties**)
A (sense) facultad f
B (Educ) 1 (of university, college) facultad f 2 (academic personnel) (AmE) cuerpo m docente, profesorado m (*de una facultad etc*)

fad /fæd/ n moda f pasajera

fade /feɪd/ vi
A ‹‹color›› apagarse*, perder* intensidad; ‹‹fabric›› perder* color, desteñirse*; **the light was beginning to ~** empezaba a oscurecer or a irse la luz
B 1 (disappear) ‹‹hope/memories›› desvanecerse*; ‹‹beauty›› marchitarse; ‹‹interest›› decaer*; **his smile ~d** se le desvaneció la sonrisa; **her strength was beginning to ~** sus fuerzas empezaban a debilitarse 2 ‹‹flower/plant›› ajarse; ‹‹elderly person/patient››: **she's fading fast** se está apagando or consumiendo rápidamente
C ‹‹sound›› debilitarse, perderse*
D (Sport) 1 (veer) ‹‹baseball/golfball›› desviarse* 2 (in US football) retroceder
E (Cin, TV) fundir
■ **fade** vt ‹fabric› desteñir*, hacer* perder el color a

(Phrasal verbs)
- **fade away** [v ▸ adv] ‹‹love/grief/sound›› irse* apagando; ‹‹chances/memory›› desvanecerse*; **he ~d away into obscurity** fue cayendo poco a poco en el olvido; **you must eat something or you'll ~ away** si no comes algo te vas a consumir
- **fade in**
A [v ▸ adv] ‹‹song›› empezar* a oírse (poco a poco)
B [v ▸ o ▸ adv] ‹song› subir gradualmente el volumen de; ‹image› fundir
- **fade out**
A [v ▸ adv] ‹‹music››: **the music ~d out** el volumen de la música fue bajando gradualmente
B [v ▸ o ▸ adv] ‹song› bajar gradualmente el volumen de; ‹image› fundir

faded /'feɪdəd || 'feɪdɪd/ adj ‹color› apagado, desvaído; ‹fabric› desteñido, descolorido

fade: **~-in** n fundido m; **~-out** n fundido m

faeces /'fi:si:z/ pl n (BrE frml) ▸ **feces**

Faeroe Islands /'ferəʊ || 'feərəʊ/, **Faeroes** /'ferəʊz || 'feərəʊz/ pl n **the ~ ~** las Islas Feroe

faff about, faff around /fæf/ [v ▸ adv] (BrE colloq) dar* vueltas (perdiendo el tiempo)

fag /fæg/ n
A (male homosexual) (AmE sl & pej) maricón m (fam & pey)
B (chore) (no pl) (BrE colloq): **to be a ~** ser* una pesadez or una lata (fam)
C (cigarette) (BrE colloq) cigarrillo m, pitillo m (fam)
D (schoolboy) (BrE) *alumno que está al servicio de un alumno mayor*

(Phrasal verb)
- **fag out** [v ▸ o ▸ adv] (colloq): **to be ~ged out** estar* reventado or hecho polvo (fam)

fag end n (esp BrE colloq) colilla f

faggot /'fægət/ n
A (AmE also) **fagot** (bundle of sticks) (liter) haz m de leña
B (AmE sl & pej) maricón m (fam & pey)
C (meatball) (BrE) albóndiga f de hígado

fah /fɑ:/ n (BrE Mus) fa m

Fahrenheit /'færənhaɪt/ adj Fahrenheit adj inv; **84 degrees ~** 84 grados Fahrenheit

fail[1] /feɪl/ vi
A 1 (not do) **to ~ to + INF**: **he ~ed to live up to our expectations** no dio todo lo que se esperaba de él; **the engine ~ed to start** el motor no arrancó; **you ~ed to mention the crucial point** no mencionaste el punto esencial; **it never ~s to amaze me how many people ...** nunca deja de asombrarme cuánta gente ...; **he ~ed in his obligations** faltó a or no cumplió sus obligaciones 2 (not succeed) ‹‹marriage/business›› fracasar; ‹‹plan›› fallar, fracasar; **if all else ~s** como último recurso 3 **failed** past p ‹businessman/writer› fracasado
B 1 ‹‹brakes/lights›› fallar 2 ‹‹crop›› perderse*, malograrse 3 **failing** pres p: **he could no longer read because of his ~ing eyesight** la vista se le había deteriorado tanto que ya no podía leer; **he retired because of ~ing health** se retiró porque su salud se había deteriorado mucho
C (in exam) ser* reprobado (AmL), suspender (Esp)
■ **fail** vt
A 1 ‹exam› no pasar, ser* reprobado en (AmL), suspender (Esp), reprobar* (Méx), perder* (Col, Ur), salir* mal en (Chi) 2 ‹student› reprobar* or (Esp) suspender
B (let down): **his courage/memory ~ed him** le faltó valor/le falló la memoria; **you have ~ed him** le has fallado, lo has decepcionado; **words ~ me!** ¡es el colmo!; **in describing his genius, words ~ me** me no encuentro palabras para describir su genio

fail[2] n
A [c] (in exam, test) (BrE) reprobado m or (Esp) suspenso m or (RPl) aplazo m
B [u] **without ~** sin falta

failing[1] /'feɪlɪŋ/ n defecto m

failing[2] prep: **~ that, try bleach** si eso no resulta, prueba con lejía

fail-safe /'feɪlseɪf/ adj ‹mechanism› de seguridad

failure /'feɪljər || 'feɪljə(r)/ n
A 1 [u] (of marriage, talks) fracaso m 2 [c] (unsuccessful thing, attempt) fracaso m; (insolvency) quiebra f; (before n) **~ rate** (Busn) proporción f de quiebras; (Educ) índice m de fracaso escolar 3 [c] (person) fracaso m 4 [c u] (breakdown): **engine ~** falla f mecánica or (Esp) fallo m mecánico; **power ~** apagón m; **heart/kidney ~** insuficiencia f cardíaca/renal
B (expressing negation) **~ to + INF**: **~ to carry out orders** el incumplimiento de las órdenes; **her ~ to understand** el (hecho de) que no entendiera/entienda

fain /feɪn/ adv (arch or poet) de buen grado

faint[1] /feɪnt/ adj **-er, -est**
A ‹line› apenas visible; ‹light› débil, tenue; ‹noise› apenas perceptible, débil; ‹hope/smile› ligero, leve; ‹recollection› vago; **what's going on? — I haven't the ~est (idea)**

(colloq) ¿qué pasa? — no tengo la más mínima idea
B (weak) (*pred*): **to be ~ with hunger** estar* desfallecido de hambre; **I feel ~** estoy mareado

faint² *vi* desmayarse

faint³ *n* desmayo *m*; **she collapsed in a dead ~** cayó desvanecida, se desmayó

faint-hearted¹ /'feɪnt'hɑ:rtəd || ,feɪnt'hɑ:tɪd/ *adj* ‹*person*› pusilánime, timorato; ‹*attempt*› tímido

faint-hearted² *pl n* **the ~** los pusilánimes

faintly /'feɪntli/ *adv* [1] (barely perceptibly) ‹*see/hear*› apenas; ‹*shine/sound*› débilmente [2] (slightly) ‹*interested/amused*› ligeramente; ‹*amusing/ridiculous*› algo

fair¹ /fer || feə(r)/ *adj* **-er, -est**
A (just) ‹*person/decision*› justo, imparcial; ‹*contest/election*› limpio; **come on, now: ~'s ~** vamos, seamos justos *or* lo justo es justo; **by ~ means or foul** por las buenas o por las malas; **~ enough** bueno, está bien; **I've had my ~ share of problems recently** ya he tenido bastantes problemas últimamente; **to be ~ ON** *o* **TO sb**: **it's not ~ to her to expect her to do it** no es justo pretender que lo haga ella; **that wouldn't be ~ on the others** eso no sería justo para los demás; **~ *and square***: **he won ~ and square** ganó en buena ley *or* con todas las de la ley; ***all's ~ in love and war*** en el amor y en la guerra todo vale
B ‹*hair*› rubio, güero (Méx), mono (Col), catire (Ven); ‹*skin*› blanco
C (beautiful) (liter) hermoso, bello; **the ~ sex** (hum) el bello sexo (hum); **with my own ~ hands** (esp BrE hum) con estas dos manitas
D [1] (quite good) ‹*work/essay*› pasable, aceptable; **we have a ~ chance of winning** tenemos bastantes posibilidades de ganar; **doctors say her condition is ~** los médicos opinan que su estado es satisfactorio; **~ *to middling*** (colloq & hum): **how are you? — ~ to middling** ¿qué tal estás? — voy tirando *or* (Méx) ahí la llevo *or* (Col, Ven) ahí, llevándola (fam) [2] (considerable) (*before n*) ‹*number/amount*› bueno
E (Meteo) (of weather): **the weather tomorrow will be ~** mañana va a hacer buen tiempo

fair² *adv* (impartially) ‹*play*› limpio, limpiamente

fair³ *n*
A (market) feria *f*; (*trade ~*) feria *f or* exposición *f* industrial/comercial; (bazaar) feria *f* (*con fines benéficos*)
B (funfair) (BrE) feria *f*

fair: **~ground** *n* (funfair) (BrE) feria *f*; (permanent) parque *m* de diversiones *or* (Esp) atracciones; **~-haired** /'fer'herd || ,feə'heəd/ *adj*: **she's ~-haired** (BrE) es rubia *or* (Méx) güera *or* (Col) mona *or* (Ven) catira; **the boss's ~-haired boy** (AmE colloq) el niño mimado *or* el favorito del jefe

fairing /'ferɪŋ || 'feərɪŋ/ *n* (Auto) carenado *m*

fairly /'ferli || 'feəli/ *adv*
A (justly, honestly) ‹*play*› limpio; ‹*judge*› con imparcialidad; ‹*divide*› equitativamente; ‹*obtain*› limpiamente, en buena lid *or* ley
B (moderately) bastante; **I'm ~ sure** estoy casi segura

fair-minded /'fer'maɪndəd || ,feə'maɪndɪd/ *adj* justo, imparcial

fairness /'fernəs || 'feənɪs/ *n* [u] (impartiality) imparcialidad *f*, justicia *f*; **in (all) ~ to her** para ser justos con ella; **in all ~** sinceramente, francamente

fair: **~ play** *n* [u] juego *m* limpio; **~-sized** /'fer'saɪzd || ,feə'saɪzd/ *adj* (*before n*) bastante grande; **~ trade** *n* comercio *m* justo; **~way** *n* (in golf) calle *f*, fairway *m*; **~-weather friend** /'fer'weðər || ,feə'weðə(r)/ *n* amigo, -ga *m,f* sólo cuando las cosas marchan bien

fairy /'feri || 'feəri/ *n* (*pl* **-ries**)
A (Myth) hada *f*‡
B (male homosexual) (colloq: pej & dated) mariquita *m* (fam & pey)

fairy: **~ godmother** *n* hada *f*‡ madrina; **~land** *n* el país de las hadas; **~ lights** *pl n* (BrE) luces *fpl or* bombillas *fpl* de colores; **~ story**, **~ tale** *n* (Lit) cuento *m* de hadas; (fabricated story) (pej) cuento *m* (chino) (pey); **~tale** *adj* (*before n*) ‹*romance/wedding*› de cuento

fait accompli /'feɪtəkɑ:m'pli: || ,feɪtə'kɒmpli:/ *n* (*pl* **~s ~s**) hecho *m* consumado

faith /feɪθ/ *n*
A [u] (trust) confianza *f*; **to have ~ IN sb/sth** tener* confianza *or* fe EN algn/algo, tenerle* a algn/algo confianza *or* fe; **to put one's ~ in sb/sth** confiar* en algn/algo; ***to act in good/bad ~*** actuar* de buena/mala fe
B (Relig) [u c] fe *f*

faithful¹ /'feɪθfəl/ *adj* ‹*follower*› fiel; ‹*translation*› fiel; **to be ~ TO sb/sth** serle* fiel A algn/ser* fiel a algo

faithful² *pl n* **the ~** (Relig) los fieles; (loyal followers): **the party ~** los incondicionales, los seguidores más fieles

faithfully /'feɪθfəli/ *adv* [1] (in letters): **yours ~** (esp BrE) (le saluda) atentamente [2] ‹*serve/record*› fielmente [3] ‹*attend*› religiosamente

faithfulness /'feɪθfəlnəs || 'feɪθfəlnɪs/ *n* [u] fidelidad *f*

faith healer *n* curandero, -ra *m,f*, santero, -ra *m,f*

faithless /'feɪθləs || 'feɪθlɪs/ *adj* (liter) (disloyal) desleal

fake¹ /feɪk/ *n* [1] (object) falsificación *f*, imitación *f*; **this passport is a ~** este pasaporte es falso [2] (person) farsante *mf*, impostor, -tora *m,f*

fake² *adj* ‹*jewel/document*› falso; ‹*fur*› sintético

fake³ *vt* [1] (forge) ‹*document/signature*› falsificar*; ‹*results/evidence*› falsear, amañar [2] (AmE Sport) amagar* [3] (feign) ‹*illness/enthusiasm*› fingir*
■ **fake** *vi* [1] (pretend) fingir* [2] (in US football) hacer* un engaño

fakir /fə'kɪr || 'feɪkɪə(r)/ *n* faquir *m*

falcon /'fælkən || 'fɔ:lkən/ *n* halcón *m*

falconer /'fælkənər || 'fɔ:lkənə(r)/ *n* halconero, -ra *m,f*

falconry /'fælkənri || 'fɔ:lkənri/ *n* [u] cetrería *f*

Falkland Islands, Falklands /'fɔ:lkləndz/ *pl n* **the ~ ~** las (Islas) Malvinas

fall¹ /fɔ:l/ *n*
A (tumble, descent) caída *f*; ***to be heading*** *o* (esp AmE) ***riding for a ~*** ir* camino al desastre; **the tree broke my ~** el árbol frenó mi caída
B (autumn) (AmE) otoño *m*
C (decrease): **a ~ in temperature** un descenso de (las) temperaturas *or* de la temperatura; **a ~ in prices** una bajada *or* caída de precios
D (defeat, collapse) caída *f*
E (of snow) nevada *f*; (of rocks) desprendimiento *m*, derrumbe *m*
F **falls** *pl* (waterfall) cascada *f*, caída *f* de agua; (higher) catarata *f*

fall² (*past* **fell**; *past p* **fallen**) *vi*
A [1] (tumble) caerse*; **he fell into bed** se dejó caer en la cama; **I fell over a piece of wood** tropecé con un trozo de madera; **to let sth ~** dejar caer algo; **I fell down the stairs** me caí por la escalera; **he fell down the well** se cayó al pozo; **he fell off his horse** se cayó del caballo; ***to ~ foul of sb/sth***: **he fell foul of the law/his boss** tuvo problemas con la ley/su jefe [2] (descend) «*night/rain*» caer*; **a sudden hush fell over the crowd** de repente se hizo el silencio entre la multitud
B «*temperature*» bajar, descender* (frml); «*price*» bajar, caer*; «*wind*» amainar; **his face fell** puso cara larga
C (be captured, defeated) **to ~ (TO sb)** «*city/country*» caer* (en manos *or* en poder de algn)
D [1] (pass into specified state): **to ~ ill** *o* (esp AmE) **sick** caer* *or* (Esp tb) ponerse* enfermo, enfermarse (AmL); **to ~ silent** callarse, quedarse callado; **to ~ into decay/disrepute** irse* deteriorando/desprestigiarse; **she fell on hard times** las cosas le empezaron a ir mal [2] (enter): **to ~ into a trance/coma** entrar en trance/coma; **to ~ into a trap** caer* en una trampa; **she fell into a deep sleep** se durmió profundamente; *see also* **prey, victim**
E [1] (land): **Christmas ~s on a Thursday this year** este año Navidad cae en (un) jueves; **the stress ~s on the first syllable** el acento cae *or* recae sobre la primera sílaba; **the burden will ~ on the poor** los pobres serán los que sufrirán la carga [2] (into category): **the problems ~ into three categories** los problemas se pueden clasificar en tres tipos diferentes
F (be slain) (frml) caer* (frml)

Phrasal verbs

- **fall about** [v ▸ adv] (BrE colloq) morirse* de risa (fam)
- **fall apart** [v ▸ adv] «*clothing*» deshacerse*; «*system*» venirse* abajo, desmoronarse; «*relationship*» irse* a pique, fracasar
- **fall away** [v ▸ adv] [1] (slope down) «*ground*» caer* en declive [2] (decline) «*attendance/production*» decaer*; **to ~ away sharply** irse* a pique [3] (disappear) «*doubt*» disiparse, desvanecerse*

f

f

- **fall back** [v ▸ adv] ⟪*troops*⟫ replegarse*
- **fall back on** [v ▸ adv ▸ prep ▸ o] ⟨*one's parents*⟩ recurrir a; ⟨*resources*⟩ echar mano de; **if this doesn't work you've always got your degree to ~ back on** si esto no te funciona siempre tienes la carrera hecha
- **fall behind** [v ▸ adv] [v ▸ prep ▸ o] (in class, race) rezagarse*, quedarse atrás; **to ~ behind WITH sth** ⟨*with payments*⟩ atrasarse EN algo; **I'm ~ing behind with my work** tengo el trabajo muy atrasado
- **fall down** [v ▸ adv] 1 (to the ground) ⟪*person/tree*⟫ caerse*; ⟪*house/wall*⟫ venirse* abajo, derrumbarse 2 (fail) ⟪*plan*⟫ fracasar, fallar; **to ~ down ON sth** (BrE) fallar EN algo
- **fall for** [v ▸ prep ▸ o] 1 (be attracted to) ⟨*man/woman*⟩ enamorarse de, quedar prendado de 2 (be deceived by) ⟨*trick/story*⟩ tragarse* (fam)
- **fall in** [v ▸ adv] 1 (tumble in) caerse* (*a un pozo, al agua etc*) 2 (collapse) ⟪*roof*⟫ venirse* abajo, hundirse 3 (form ranks) (Mil) formar filas
- **fall in with** [v ▸ adv ▸ prep ▸ o] 1 (meet and join) juntarse con 2 (agree with) ⟨*plan*⟩ aceptar
- **fall off** [v ▸ adv] 1 (tumble down) caerse* (*de una bicicleta, un caballo etc*) 2 (break off) ⟪*button/handle*⟫ caerse* 3 (decline) ⟪*production/attendance*⟫ decaer*
- **fall on** [v ▸ prep ▸ o] ⟨*enemy/victim*⟩ caer* sobre; **they fell on the food** se abalanzaron sobre la comida
- **fall out** [v ▸ adv] 1 (drop out) caerse* 2 (break ranks) (Mil) romper* filas 3 (quarrel) ⟪*friends*⟫ pelearse, reñir*; **to ~ out WITH sb** pelearse *or* reñir CON algn
- **fall over** [v ▸ adv] ⟪*person/object*⟫ caerse*; ***to ~ over oneself/each other to do sth***: **they were ~ing over themselves to help** se desvivían por ayudar; **they are ~ing over each other to get the contract** están desesperados por conseguir el contrato
- **fall through** [v ▸ adv] (fail) no salir* adelante
- **fall to**

A [v ▸ adv] (begin working enthusiastically) poner(se*) manos a la obra

B [v ▸ prep ▸ o] 1 (begin) **to ~ TO -ING** ponerse* *or* empezar* A + INF 2 (be sb's responsibility) ⟪*duty*⟫ corresponderle a; **the task fell to Mr Lennox** le tocó al señor Lennox hacerlo

- **fall upon** ▸**fall on**

fallacious /fə'leɪʃəs/ *adj* (frml) 1 (illogical) ⟨*reasoning*⟩ erróneo, falaz 2 (misleading) ⟨*claim*⟩ engañoso, falaz

fallacy /'fæləsi/ *n* [c u] (*pl* **-cies**) falacia *f*

fallback /'fɔːlbæk/ *n*: **I've always got my secretarial skills as a ~** siempre puedo trabajar como secretaria si fuera necesario

fallen¹ /'fɔːlən/ *adj*: **~ arches** pies *mpl* planos; **a ~ woman** (arch & euph) una mujer perdida (arc & euf)

fallen² *past p of* **fall²**

fallen³ *pl n* **the ~** los caídos

fall guy *n* (colloq) cabeza *f* de turco, chivo *m* expiatorio *or* emisario

fallibility /'fælə'bɪləti/ *n* [u] falibilidad *f*

fallible /'fæləbəl/ *adj* falible

falling /'fɔːlɪŋ/ *adj*: **the ~ price of tin** la caída *or* baja en el precio del estaño

falling: **~-off** /'fɔːlɪŋ'ɔːf || ˌfɔːlɪŋ'ɒf/ *n* ▸**falloff**; **~-out** /'fɔːlɪŋ'aʊt/ *n* (AmE) pelea *f*

falloff /'fɔːlɔːf || 'fɔːlɒf/ *n* (*no pl*) (in speed) disminución *f*, reducción *f*; **there has been a ~ in interest** ha decaído el interés

Fallopian tube /fə'ləʊpiən/ *n* trompa *f* de Falopio

fallout /'fɔːlaʊt/ *n* [u] (Nucl Phys) lluvia *f or* precipitación *f* radiactiva; (*before n*) **~ shelter** refugio *m* antinuclear *or* antiatómico

fallow /'fæləʊ/ *adj* ⟨*land*⟩ en barbecho; **to lie ~** estar* en barbecho

fallow deer *n* gamo *m*

false /fɔːls/ *adj*

A 1 (untrue) ⟨*statement/rumor*⟩ falso 2 (incorrect) ⟨*belief*⟩ erróneo; **true or ~?** ¿verdadero o falso?, ¿verdad o mentira?; **one ~ move and you're dead!** ¡un movimento en falso y te mato! 3 (misplaced) ⟨*modesty/pride*⟩ falso

B (not genuine) ⟨*eyelashes/fingernails*⟩ postizo; ⟨*name/passport*⟩ falso; **the case had a ~ bottom** la maleta era de doble fondo

C (disloyal) (arch *or* liter) ⟨*friend/spouse*⟩ infiel

false: **~ alarm** *n* falsa alarma *f*; **~ ceiling** *n* cieloraso *m* suspendido; **~ hem** *n* dobladillo *m* falso

falsehood /'fɔːlshʊd/ *n* [c u] (frml) falsedad *f*

falsely /'fɔːlsli/ *adv* (wrongly) ⟨*accuse*⟩ falsamente

false: **~ start** *n* (Sport) salida *f* en falso; (to career, speech) intento *m* fallido; **~ teeth** *pl n* dentadura *f* postiza

falsetto /fɔːl'setəʊ/ *n* (*pl* **-tos**) falsete *m*

falsify /'fɔːlsəfaɪ || 'fɔːlsɪfaɪ/ *vt* **-fies, -fying, -fied** ⟨*accounts/evidence*⟩ falsificar*; ⟨*truth/situation*⟩ falsear

falter /'fɔːltər || 'fɔːltə(r)/ *vi* 1 (speak hesitantly) titubear, balbucear 2 ⟪*enthusiasm/interest*⟫ decaer*; ⟪*courage/resolve*⟫ flaquear 3 (move unsteadily) tambalearse 4 **faltering** *pres p* ⟨*voice*⟩ titubeante; ⟨*step*⟩ tambaleante

fame /feɪm/ *n* [u] fama *f*; **Arthur C. Clarke of** *2001* **~** Arthur C. Clarke, famoso por *2001*

famed /feɪmd/ *adj* célebre, famoso; **to be ~ FOR sth** ser* famoso POR algo

familiar¹ /fə'mɪljər || fə'mɪlɪə(r)/ *adj*

A (well-known) ⟨*sound/face*⟩ familiar, conocido; ⟨*excuse*⟩ consabido; **the name sounds ~** el nombre me suena; **these violent scenes are becoming all too ~** nos estamos acostumbrando demasiado a estas escenas violentas

B (having knowledge of) (*pred*) **to be ~ WITH sth/sb** estar* familiarizado CON algo/algn

C 1 (informal): **I'm not on ~ terms with the neighbors** todavía no conozco bien a los vecinos 2 (too informal) que se toma demasiadas confianzas *or* libertades, confianzudo (esp AmL); **he's too ~ with his students** trata a sus alumnos con demasiada confianza

familiar² *n* (Occult) *espíritu con forma animal que supuestamente ayuda a magos y brujos*

familiarity /fə'mɪli'ærəti/ *n* (*pl* **-ties**)

A 1 (knowledge) **~ WITH sth**: **she claimed extensive ~ with the method** dijo estar muy familiarizada con el método; **some ~ with computers would be an asset** se valorará la experiencia previa con computadoras 2 (of person, book, landscape) familiaridad *f*; ***~ breeds contempt*** lo que se tiene no se aprecia

B (overintimacy) exceso *m* de confianza

familiarize /fə'mɪljəraɪz || fə'mɪlɪəraɪz/ *vt* **to ~ sb/oneself WITH sth** familiarizar* a algn/familiarizarse* CON algo

familiarly /fə'mɪljərli || fə'mɪlɪəli/ *adv* 1 (usually) comúnmente 2 (informally) ⟨*speak/treat*⟩ sin ceremonias

family /'fæmli, 'fæməli || 'fæmɪli, 'fæmli/ *n* [c u] (*pl* **-lies**) 1 (relatives) familia *f*; **the Smith ~** la familia Smith; **it runs in the ~** es cosa de familia *or* le (*or* me/les *etc*) viene de familia; (*before n*) ⟨*business*⟩ familiar; ⟨*fortune*⟩ de la familia; **a ~ show** un espectáculo para familias 2 (children) hijos *mpl*

family: **~ allowance** *n* [u] (BrE) ▸**child benefit**, *see* **child**; **~-friendly** /ˌfæmli'frendli || ˌfæməli'frendli/ *adj* pensado para familias; **~ name** *n* apellido *m*; **~ planning** *n* [u] planificación *f* familiar; **~ practice** *n* (AmE) 1 [u] (general medicine) medicina *f* general 2 [c] (medical practice) consultorio *m*, consulta *f*; **~ room** *n* 1 (in house) sala *f* de estar 2 (in hotel) habitación *f* familiar; **~ tree** *n* árbol *m* genealógico

famine /'fæmən || 'fæmɪn/ *n* [c u] hambruna *f*, hambre *f*‡

famished /'fæmɪʃt/ *adj* famélico, hambriento; **I'm ~!** (colloq) ¡estoy muerto de hambre! (fam)

famous /'feɪməs/ *adj* famoso

famously /'feɪməsli/ *adv* (BrE): **they got on ~** se llevaron divinamente *or* a las mil maravillas

fan¹ /fæn/ *n*

A 1 (hand-held) abanico *m* 2 (mechanical) ventilador *m*

B (devotee — of group, actor) fan *mf*, admirador, -dora *m,f*; (— of football team) hincha *mf*; (*before n*) **~ mail** cartas *fpl* de admiradores *or* de fans

fan² **-nn-** *vt*

A 1 (direct air at): **to ~ sb/oneself** abanicar* a algn/abanicarse*; **he ~ned the fire with a magazine** le echó aire al fuego con una revista 2 (intensify) ⟨*interest/curiosity*⟩ avivar; ***to ~ the flames*** (of controversy) echar leña al fuego

B (in baseball) ⟨*hitter*⟩ ponchar; ⟨*pitch*⟩ abanicar*

(Phrasal verb)

- **fan out**

A [v ▸ adv] ⟨⟨*searchers*⟩⟩ abrirse* en abanico
B [v ▸ o ▸ adv, v ▸ adv ▸ o] ⟨*cards*⟩ abrir* en abanico

fanatic /fəˈnætɪk/ *n* fanático, -ca *m,f*

fanatical /fəˈnætɪkəl/ *adj* ⟨*believer*⟩ fanático; ⟨*belief*⟩ ciego

fanatically /fəˈnætɪkli/ *adv* fanáticamente

fanaticism /fəˈnætəsɪzəm || fəˈnætɪsɪzəm/ *n* [u] fanatismo *m*

fan belt *n* correa *f or* (Méx) banda *f* del ventilador

fanciful /ˈfænsɪfəl/ *adj* 1 (impractical) ⟨*idea*⟩ extravagante, descabellado 2 (elaborate) ⟨*design*⟩ imaginativo

fan club *n* club *m* de fans *or* de admiradores

fancy¹ /ˈfænsi/ **fancies, fancying, fancied** *vt* (esp BrE)
A (expressing surprise) (*in interj*): **(just) ~ that!** ¡pues mira tú!, ¡imagínate!; **~ saying a thing like that!** ¡cómo se te (*or* le etc) ocurre decir una cosa así!; **~ meeting them here!** ¡qué casualidad encontrarnos con ellos aquí!
B (feel urge, desire for) (colloq) **to ~ sth/-ING**: **I really ~ an ice-cream** ¡qué ganas de tomarme un helado!; **do you ~ going to see a movie?** ¿tienes ganas de *or* te gustaría *or* (esp Esp) te apetece ir al cine?
C (be physically attracted to) (colloq) **to ~ sb**: **I ~ her/him** me gusta mucho
D (rate highly): **I don't ~ his chances** no creo que tenga muchas posibilidades
E (imagine) (frml) **to ~ (THAT)**: **she fancied she saw his face in the crowd** creyó ver su cara entre la multitud
■ *v refl* **to ~ oneself** (colloq) ser* (un) creído; **to ~ oneself AS sth**: **he fancies himself as an actor** se las da de actor

fancy² *adj* **-cier, -ciest** 1 (elaborate) elaborado 2 (superior) (pej) ⟨*hotel*⟩ de campanillas; ⟨*car*⟩ lujoso; ⟨*ideas*⟩ extravagante, estrambótico; **they gave us some ~ foreign dish** nos sirvieron un plato extranjero de ésos raros; **nothing ~, just a sandwich will do** nada complicado, con un sandwich basta 3 (of foodstuffs) (AmE): **US Grade F~** ≈ extra, ≈ de primera calidad

fancy³ *n* (*pl* **-cies**)
A 1 (liking) (*no pl*): **to take a ~ to sb/sth**: **they took a real ~ to each other** quedaron prendados el uno del otro; **she seems to have taken a ~ to you** parece que le has caído en gracia; **he's taken a ~ to that book** se ha encaprichado con ese libro; **to take** *o* **catch sb's ~**: **the ring quite took** *o* **caught my ~** el anillo me encantó *or* me dejó fascinada; **buy whatever takes your ~** compra lo que te apetezca; ***to tickle sb's ~***: **the idea rather tickled my ~** la idea me resultó atractiva 2 [c] (whim) capricho *m*, antojo *m*
B [c u] 1 (unfounded idea) (liter) fantasía *f* 2 (imagination) imaginación *f*, fantasía *f*

fancy: ~ dress *n* [u] (BrE) disfraz *m*; (*before n*) **~-dress party/ball** fiesta *f*/baile *m* de disfraces; **~-free** /ˈfænsi ˈfriː/ *adj see* **footloose**; **~ goods** *pl n* (Busn) artículos *mpl* para regalo; **~ man** *n* (colloq & pej) amiguito *m* (fam & pey); **~ woman** *n* (colloq & pej) 1 (prostitute) (AmE) puta *f* (vulg) 2 (lover) (BrE) amiguita *f* (fam & pey), querida *f*

fanfare /ˈfænfer || ˈfænfeə(r)/ *n* fanfarria *f*

fang /fæŋ/ *n* (of dog) colmillo *m*; (of snake) diente *m*

fan: ~ heater *n* electroconvector *m*, ventiloconvector *m*; **~light** *n* 1 (decorative) montante *m* (*en forma de abanico*) 2 (small, top window) tragaluz *m*

fanny /ˈfæni/ *n* (*pl* **-nies**)
A (buttocks) (AmE sl) culo *m* (fam: en algunas regiones vulg), traste *m* (CS fam), poto *m* (Chi, Per fam)
B (BrE sl) ▸ **pussy 2**

fantasist /ˈfæntəsəst || ˈfæntəsɪst/ *n* 1 (person who fantasizes) fantasioso, -sa *m,f* 2 (writer of fantasies) escritor, -ra *m,f* de literatura fantástica

fantasize /ˈfæntəsaɪz/ *vi* fantasear; **to ~ ABOUT sth** fantasear CON (la idea de) algo

fantastic /fænˈtæstɪk/ *adj*
A 1 (wonderful) (colloq) fantástico, estupendo 2 (enormous) fabuloso, fantástico
B 1 (incredible) ⟨*story*⟩ absurdo, increíble 2 (unrealistic) ⟨*plan*⟩ descabellado
C (based on fantasy) ⟨*literature*⟩ fantástico

fantastical /fænˈtæstɪkəl/ *adj* ▸ **fantastic B**

fantastically /fænˈtæstɪkli/ *adv* (*as intensifier*) ⟨*cheap/lucky*⟩ increíblemente; ⟨*rich*⟩ fabulosamente; **we all get on ~ (well)** nos llevamos todos a las mil maravillas

fantasy /ˈfæntəsi/ *n* (*pl* **-sies**)
A 1 [u c] (unreality) fantasía *f*; **the story is (a) complete ~** la historia es pura invención; (*before n*) **he lives in a ~ world** vive en un mundo de fantasía 2 [c] (daydream) sueño *m*; **sexual fantasies** fantasías *fpl* sexuales
B [u] (Lit) literatura *f* fantástica

fanzine /ˈfænziːn/ *n* fanzine *m* (*revista para fans*)

FAO *n* (= **Food and Agriculture Organization**) FAO *f*

FAQ *n* = **frequently asked questions**

far¹ /fɑːr || fɑː(r)/ *adv*
A (*comp* **further** *or* **farther**; *superl* **furthest** *or* **farthest**) 1 (in distance) lejos; **how ~ can you swim?** ¿qué distancia puedes hacer a nado?; **how ~ is it?** ¿a qué distancia está?; **how ~ is it from New York to Seattle?** ¿qué distancia hay de Nueva York a Seattle?; **it's not ~ (to go) now** ya falta *or* queda poco; **go as ~ as that tree** camina hasta ese árbol; **~ away in the distance** a lo lejos 2 (in progress): **the plans are now quite ~ advanced** los planes están ya muy avanzados; **that girl will go ~** esa chica va a llegar lejos; **£20 doesn't go ~ these days** hoy no se hace nada con 20 libras 3 (in time): **Christmas isn't ~ away** *o* **off now** ya falta *or* queda poco para Navidad; **I can't remember that ~ back** no recuerdo cosas tan lejanas; **I haven't planned that ~ ahead** no he hecho planes tan a largo plazo 4 (in extent, degree): **the new legislation doesn't go ~ enough** la nueva legislación no tiene el alcance necesario; **this has gone ~ enough!** esto ya pasa de castaño oscuro; **I wouldn't go so ~ as to say that** yo no diría tanto como eso; **our estimates weren't too ~ out** *o* **off** no nos equivocamos mucho en los cálculos; **his jokes went a bit too ~** se pasó un poco con esos chistes
B (very much): **~ superior** muy superior; **~ better** mucho mejor; **the advantages ~ outweigh the disadvantages** las ventajas superan ampliamente *or* con mucho las desventajas
C (*in phrases*) **as** *o* **so far as**: **as** *o* **so ~ as I know** que yo sepa; **as** *o* **so ~ as I'm concerned ...** en lo que a mí respecta *or* por mí ...; **by far**: **she's better than the rest by ~** es muchísimo mejor que el resto; **their team was by ~ the worst** su equipo fue con mucho el peor; **far and away**: **he's ~ and away the best player** es sin lugar a dudas *or* con mucho el mejor jugador; **far and near** *o* **wide** (liter): **they searched ~ and near** *o* **wide** buscaron por todas partes; **from ~ and near** *o* **wide** de todas partes; **far from**: **the matter is ~ from over** el asunto no está terminado ni mucho menos; **it is ~ from satisfactory** dista mucho de ser satisfactorio; **she's not rich: ~ from it!** no es rica ¡todo lo contrario!; **~ be it from me to interfere, but ...** no es que yo quiera entrometerme ni mucho menos, pero ...; **so far**: **so ~, everything has gone according to plan** hasta ahora *or* hasta este momento todo ha salido de acuerdo a lo planeado; **is the plan working? — yes, so ~, so good** ¿funciona el plan? — por el momento, sí

far² *adj* (*comp* **farther**; *superl* **farthest**) 1 (distant) lejano; **in the ~ distance** a lo lejos 2 (most distant, extreme) (*before n, no comp*): **at the ~ end of the room** en el otro extremo de la habitación; **she's on the ~ right of the party** está en la extrema derecha del partido

faraway /ˈfɑːrəˈweɪ/ *adj* (*before n*) ⟨*lands*⟩ lejano, remoto; ⟨*look*⟩ ausente, perdido

farce /fɑːrs || fɑːs/ *n* [c u] farsa *f*

farcical /ˈfɑːrsɪkəl || ˈfɑːsɪkəl/ *adj* ridículo, absurdo

fare¹ /fer || feə(r)/ *n*
A 1 [c] (cost of travel — by air) pasaje *m or* (Esp) billete *m*; (— by bus) boleto *m or* (esp Esp) billete *m*; **how much** *o* **what is the ~ to Athens?** cuánto cuesta el boleto *or* (Esp) billete a Atenas?; **she'd lost her bus ~** había perdido el dinero para el autobús; **~s will rise again next year** las tarifas subirán de nuevo en el próximo año; **S exact fare only** no se da cambio 2 [c] (passenger) pasajero, -ra *m,f*
B [u] (food and drink) comida *f*, platos *mpl*

fare² *vi* (liter *or* journ): **how did she ~ in her exams?** ¿cómo le fue en los exámenes?; **the poor have ~d badly under this government** los pobres han salido mal parados bajo este gobierno

f

Far East *n* **the ~ ~** el Lejano *or* Extremo Oriente

farewell¹ /ˈferˈwel ‖ ˌfeəˈwel/ *n* despedida *f*; **to say ~ to sb/sth** despedirse* de algn/algo, decirle* adiós a algn/algo; (*before n*) ‹*dinner/party*› de despedida

farewell² *interj* (liter) adiós

far: **~-fetched** /ˈfɑːrˈfetʃt ‖ ˌfɑːˈfetʃt/ *adj* exagerado, rocambolesco; **~-flung** /ˈfɑːrˈflʌŋ ‖ ˌfɑːˈflʌŋ/ *adj* (distant) (liter *or* journ) remoto, lejano; (widespread) extendido

farm¹ /fɑːrm ‖ fɑːm/ *n* (small) granja *f*, chacra *f* (CS, Per); (large) hacienda *f*, cortijo *m* (Esp), rancho *m* (Méx), estancia *f* (RPl), fundo *m* (Chi); (*before n*) ‹*machinery/worker*› agrícola

farm² *vi* ser* agricultor (*or* ganadero)

■ **farm** *vt* ‹*land*› cultivar, labrar

Phrasal verb

• **farm out** [v ▸ o ▸ adv, v ▸ adv ▸ o] 1▸ ‹*work*› encargar* (*a terceros*) 2▸ ‹*children*›: **they had to ~ the children out to friends** tenían que pedirle a algún amigo que les cuidara a los niños

farmer /ˈfɑːrmər ‖ ˈfɑːmə(r)/ *n* agricultor, -tora *m,f*, granjero, -ra *m,f*, chacarero, -ra *m,f* (CS, Per); (owner of large farm) hacendado, -da *m,f*, ranchero, -ra *m,f* (Méx), estanciero, -ra *m,f* (RPl), dueño, -ña *m,f* de fundo (Chi); **cattle ~** ganadero, -ra *m,f*

farmers' market *n* (in UK) mercado *m* de los agricultores locales

farm: **~hand** *n* peón *m or* (Esp) mozo *m* de labranza; **~house** *n* casa *f* de labranza, alquería *f* (*en Esp*), ≈ casco *m* de la estancia (*en RPl*)

farming /ˈfɑːrmɪŋ ‖ ˈfɑːmɪŋ/ *n* [u] (of land) labranza *f*, cultivo *m*; (of animals) crianza *f*, cría *f*; **to go into ~** dedicarse* a la agricultura; (*before n*) ‹*community*› agrícola; ‹*methods*› de labranza, de cultivo

farm: **~land** *n* [u] tierras *fpl* de labranza; **~yard** *n* corral *m*

Faroe Islands /ˈferəʊ ‖ ˈfeərəʊ/, **Faroes** /ˈferəʊz ‖ ˈfeərəʊz/ *pl n* **the ~ ~** las Islas Feroe

far: **~-off** /ˈfɑːrˈɔːf ‖ ˈfɑːrɒf/ *adj* (*pred* **~ off**) (in space) remoto, lejano; (in time) distante; **~-out** /ˈfɑːrˈaʊt/ *adj* (*pred* **~ out**) (sl & dated) 1▸ (unconventional) extravagante 2▸ (wonderful) genial, bárbaro (fam); **~-reaching** /ˈfɑːrˈriːtʃɪŋ ‖ ˌfɑːˈriːtʃɪŋ/ *adj* de gran alcance, trascendental; **~-sighted** /ˈfɑːrˈsaɪtəd ‖ ˌfɑːˈsaɪtɪd/ *adj* 1▸ (showing foresight) ‹*person*› con visión de futuro, clarividente; ‹*decision*› con visión de futuro 2▸ (AmE Med) hipermétrope

fart¹ /fɑːrt ‖ fɑːt/ *n* (vulg) pedo *m* (fam)

fart² *vi* (vulg) tirarse *or* echarse un pedo (fam)

Phrasal verb

• **fart around**, (esp BrE) **fart about** [v ▸ adv] (sl) perder* el tiempo

farther¹ /ˈfɑːrðər ‖ ˈfɑːðə(r)/ *adv comp of* **far¹**

farther² *adj comp of* **far²**

farthest¹ /ˈfɑːrðəst ‖ ˈfɑːðɪst/ *adv superl of* **far¹ A**

farthest² *adj superl of* **far²**

farthing /ˈfɑːrðɪŋ ‖ ˈfɑːðɪŋ/ *n* (formerly in UK) cuarto *m* de penique

fascinate /ˈfæsn̩eɪt ‖ ˈfæsɪneɪt/ *vt* fascinar

fascinated /ˈfæsn̩eɪtəd ‖ ˈfæsɪneɪtɪd/ *adj* fascinado

fascinating /ˈfæsn̩eɪtɪŋ ‖ ˈfæsɪneɪtɪŋ/ *adj* fascinante

fascination /ˈfæsn̩ˈeɪʃən ‖ ˌfæsɪˈneɪʃən/ *n* [u] fascinación *f*; **we watched in ~** miramos fascinados

fascism /ˈfæʃɪzəm/ *n* [u] fascismo *m*

fascist¹ /ˈfæʃəst ‖ ˈfæʃɪst/ *n* fascista *mf*

fascist² *adj* fascista

fashion¹ /ˈfæʃən/ *n*

A 1▸ [c u] (vogue) moda *f*; **to be in ~** estar* de moda; **to be out of ~** estar* pasado de moda; **to come into/go out of ~** ponerse*/pasar de moda 2▸ [c u] (Clothing) moda *f*; **the latest Paris ~s** la última moda parisiense; (*before n*) **~ accessories** accesorios *mpl*; **~ designer** diseñador, -dora *m,f* de modas; **~ victim** esclavo, -va *m,f* de la moda

B [u] (custom) costumbre *f*

C [u] (manner) manera *f*, modo *m*; **in her own inimitable ~** como sólo ella puede hacerlo; **in the French ~** a la francesa; ***after a ~***: **can you swim? — well, after a ~** ¿sabes nadar? — bueno, a mi manera *or* si se le puede llamar nadar …

fashion² *vt* ‹*object*› crear

-fashion /ˌfæʃən/ *suff*: **cowboy~** a la manera *or* al estilo de los vaqueros

fashionable /ˈfæʃn̩əbəl/ *adj* ‹*clothes/designs*› a la moda, moderno; ‹*restaurant/people/idea*› de moda

fashionably /ˈfæʃn̩əbli/ *adv* a la moda

fashion: **~ parade** *n* (BrE) desfile *m* de modas *or* de modelos; **~ show** *n* desfile *m* de modas *or* de modelos

fast¹ /fæst ‖ fɑːst/ *adj* **-er, -est**

A 1▸ (speedy) rápido; **it's her ~est time over this distance** es su mejor tiempo en esta distancia; **she's a ~ learner** aprende muy rápido; ***to pull a ~ one on sb*** (colloq) jugarle* una mala pasada a algn, hacerle* una jugarreta a algn 2▸ (*pred*): **my watch is five minutes ~** mi reloj (se) adelanta cinco minutos, tengo el reloj cinco minutos adelantado

B (permanent) ‹*color*› inalterable

fast² *adv*

A (quickly) rápidamente, rápido, deprisa; **not so ~!** ¡más despacio!; **how ~ were you going?** ¿a qué velocidad ibas?

B (firmly): **to hold ~ to sth** agarrarse fuerte a *or* de algo; **to stand ~** mantenerse* firme; **the car was stuck ~ in the mud** el coche estaba atascado en el barro completamente; **to be ~ asleep** estar* profundamente dormido

fast³ *vi* ayunar

fast⁴ *n* ayuno *m*

fast breeder (reactor) *n* (reactor *m*) reproductor *m* rápido

fasten /ˈfæsn̩ ‖ ˈfɑːsn̩/ *vt*

A 1▸ (attach) sujetar; (tie) atar 2▸ (do up, close) ‹*case*› cerrar*; ‹*coat*› abrochar; ‹*laces*› atar, amarrar (AmL exc RPl); **~ the door** échale el cerrojo a la puerta; **~ your seat belt** abróchate el cinturón de seguridad

B (fix) ‹*eyes*› clavar, fijar; **to ~ the blame on sb** echarle la culpa a algn

■ **fasten** *vi* «*suitcase*» cerrar*; «*skirt/necklace*» abrocharse; **this belt won't ~** este cinturón no se abrocha bien

Phrasal verb

• **fasten on, fasten onto** [v ▸ prep ▸ o]: **to ~ onto an idea** aceptar *or* acoger una idea; **he had ~ed on(to) poor Anna** se le había pegado a la pobre Anna (fam)

fastener /ˈfæsn̩ər ‖ ˈfɑːsn̩ə(r)/, **fastening** /ˈfæsn̩ɪŋ ‖ ˈfɑːsn̩ɪŋ/ *n* cierre *m*

fast: **~ food** *n* [c u] comida *f* rápida; (*before n*) **fast-food restaurant** *n* restaurante *m* de comida rápida; **~-forward** /ˈfæstˈfɔːrwərd ‖ ˌfɑːstˈfɔːwəd/ *vt/i* avanzar*; **~ forward (button)** *n* botón *m* de avance rápido

fastidious /fæsˈtɪdiəs/ *adj* 1▸ (demanding) muy exigente 2▸ (fussy) maniático, mañoso (AmL)

fast reactor *n* reactor *m* rápido

fat¹ /fæt/ *adj* **-tt-**

A 1▸ (obese) gordo; **to get/grow ~** engordar; ***to grow ~ on sth*** enriquecerse* con algo 2▸ (BrE) ‹*pork/lamb*› que tiene mucha grasa 3▸ (thick) ‹*book/cigar*› grueso, gordo

B 1▸ (lucrative) ‹*contract*› lucrativo, jugoso (fam) 2▸ (large) ‹*salary*› muy alto; **a ~ check** un cheque por mucho dinero

C (very little) (colloq & iro): **(a) ~ chance you've got of winning!** ¡muchas posibilidades tienes tú de ganar! (iró); **will he pass? — ~ chance** ¿aprobará? — ni soñarlo; **a ~ lot of good that'll do!** ¡para lo que va a servir!; **a ~ lot you know about it!** ¡no tienes la más mínima idea!

fat² *n* [u c] grasa *f*; **to run to ~** echar carnes (fam); ***the ~ is in the fire*** se va a armar la gorda (fam); ***to live off the ~ of the land*** (pej) vivir de (las) rentas; ▸**chew** *vt*

fatal /ˈfeɪtl̩/ *adj* 1▸ (causing death) mortal 2▸ (disastrous) ‹*decision/mistake*› fatídico, de funestas consecuencias

fatalism /ˈfeɪtl̩ɪzəm ‖ ˈfeɪtəlɪzəm/ *n* [u] fatalismo *m*

fatalist /ˈfeɪtl̩əst ‖ ˈfeɪtəlɪst/ *n* fatalista *mf*

fatalistic /ˈfeɪtl̩ˈɪstɪk ‖ ˌfeɪtəˈlɪstɪk/ *adj* fatalista

fatality /feɪˈtæləti ‖ fəˈtæləti/ *n* [c] (*pl* **-ties**) (person killed) muerto *m*, víctima *f* mortal

fatally /ˈfeɪtl̩i ‖ ˈfeɪtəli/ *adv* mortalmente, de muerte

fat cat *n* (colloq) potentado, -da *m,f*

fate /feɪt/ *n* 1▸ [u] (destiny) destino *m*; ▸**tempt 1** 2▸ (*no pl*) (one's lot, end) suerte *f*; ***a ~ worse than death*** (hum): **having to move to the country would be a ~ worse than death** preferiría morirme *or* (fam) pegarme un tiro antes que tener que mudarme al campo

fated /'feɪtəd || 'feɪtɪd/ *adj* (destined) **to be ~ to + INF** (liter) estar* predestinado A + INF

fateful /'feɪtfəl/ *adj* [1] (momentous) ‹*day/decision*› fatídico, funesto [2] (prophetic) ‹*words*› profético

fat-free /'fæt'fri:/ *adj* ‹*food*› sin grasa; ‹*diet*› sin grasas

fat: **~head** *n* (colloq) imbécil *mf*, estúpido, -da *m,f*; **~headed** /'fæt'hedəd || ,fæt'hedɪd/ *adj* (colloq) imbécil, estúpido

father¹ /'fɑ:ðər || 'fɑ:ðə(r)/ *n*

A (parent, originator) padre *m*; **his mother and ~** sus padres; **the F~ of English poetry** el padre de la poesía inglesa; ***like ~, like son*** de tal palo tal astilla, hijo de tigre sale pintado (AmL)

B (Relig) [1] **Father** (God) Padre *m*; **in the name of the F~, the Son and the Holy Ghost** en el nombre del Padre, del Hijo y del Espíritu Santo [2] (priest) padre *m*; **F~ Brown** el padre Brown

father² *vt* ‹*child*› engendrar, tener*

father: **~ Christmas** *n* (BrE) Papá *m* Noel, viejo *m* Pascuero (Chi); **~ figure** *n* figura *f or* imagen *f* paterna

fatherhood /'fɑ:ðərhʊd || 'fɑ:ðəhʊd/ *n* [u] paternidad *f*

father: **~-in-law** *n* (*pl* **~s-in-law**) suegro *m*; **~land** *n* patria *f*

fatherless /'fɑ:ðərləs || 'fɑ:ðəlɪs/ *adj* huérfano de padre, sin padre

fatherly /'fɑ:ðərli || 'fɑ:ðəli/ *adj* paternal

Father's Day *n* el día del Padre (*en EEUU y GB el tercer domingo de junio*)

fathom¹ /'fæðəm/ *n* braza *f*

fathom² *vt* **~ (out)** entender*, comprender

fatigue¹ /fə'ti:g/ *n*

A [u] (tiredness) fatiga *f*, cansancio *m*

B [c] (Mil) [1] (menial work) (*usu pl*) faena *f* [2] **fatigues** *pl* (clothing) ropa *f or* uniforme *m* de faena

fatigue² *vt* (tire) fatigar*, cansar

fatless /'fætləs || 'fætlɪs/ *adj* sin grasa

fatness /'fætnəs || 'fætnɪs/ *n* [u] [1] (of person, animal) gordura *f* [2] (of wad, book) grosor *m*

fatso /'fætsəʊ/ *n* (sl) gordo, -da *m,f*

fatten /'fætn̩/ *vt* **~ (up)** ‹*animal*› cebar, engordar

fattening /'fætn̩ɪŋ/ *adj* que engorda; **cakes are extremely ~** los pasteles engordan muchísimo

fatty¹ /'fæti/ *adj* **-tier, -tiest** ‹*food/substance*› graso, grasoso (AmL); (Physiol) ‹*tissue*› adiposo

fatty² *n* (*pl* **-ties**) (colloq) gordito, -ta *m,f* (fam)

fatuous /'fætʃuəs || 'fætjuəs/ *adj* necio

faucet /'fɔ:sət/ *n* (AmE) llave *f or* (Esp) grifo *m or* (RPl) canilla *f or* (Per) caño *m or* (AmC) paja *f*; **to turn the ~ on/off** abrir*/cerrar* la llave (*or* el grifo *etc*)

fault¹ /fɔ:lt/ *n*

A [u] (responsibility, blame) culpa *f*; **it's your ~** tú tienes la culpa, la culpa es tuya; **she was at ~** la culpa fue suya; **he lost his job through no ~ of his own** no fue culpa suya el perder el trabajo; **my memory could be at ~** puede que me esté fallando la memoria; **they're always finding ~ with me** todo lo que hago les parece mal, siempre me están criticando

B [c] [1] (failing, flaw) defecto *m*, falta *f*; **she is generous to a ~** es generosa en extremo [2] (in machine) avería *f*; (in goods) defecto *m*, falla *f* [3] (error) error *m*, falta *f*

C [c] (Geol) falla *f*

D [c] (in tennis, show jumping) falta *f*

fault² *vt* encontrarle* defectos a; **his behavior cannot be ~ed** su comportamiento es intachable *or* impecable

faultfinder /'fɔ:lt,faɪndər || 'fɔ:lt,faɪndə(r)/ *n* criticón, -ona *m,f*, sacafaltas *mf* (Esp fam)

faultfinding¹ /'fɔ:lt,faɪndɪŋ/ *n* [u]: **I'm tired of his ~** estoy harta de que a todo le encuentre defectos

faultfinding² *adj* (*before n*) criticón (fam)

faultless /'fɔ:ltləs || 'fɔ:ltlɪs/ *adj* impecable, sin tacha

faulty /'fɔ:lti/ *adj* **-tier, -tiest** [1] ‹*goods/design*› defectuoso; ‹*motor*› defectuoso, que falla; ‹*workmanship*› imperfecto [2] ‹*grammar/logic*› incorrecto

faun /fɔ:n/ *n* fauno *m*

fauna /'fɔ:nə/ *n* (*pl* **-nas** *or* **-nae** /-ni:/) fauna *f*

faux pas /'fəʊ'pɑ:/ *n* (*pl* **~ ~** /-z/) metedura *f or* (AmL tb) metida *f* de pata (fam)

favor¹, (BrE) **favour** /'feɪvər || 'feɪvə(r)/ *n*

A [u] [1] (approval): **to find ~ with sb** (frml) ser* bien recibido por algn, tener* buena acogida por parte de algn (frml); **to gain/lose ~** ganar/perder* aceptación; **to fall from** *o* **out of ~**: **that idea has fallen out of ~ with them** esa idea ha perdido popularidad entre ellos; **she's fallen from ~ with his family** ha caído en desgracia con su familia; ***to curry ~ with sb*** tratar de congraciarse con algn, tratar de ganarse el favor de algn [2] (partiality) favoritismo *m*; **to show ~ to sb** favorecer* a algn

B **in ~** a favor; **to speak in ~ of sb** *o* **in sb's ~** hablar a *or* en favor de algn; **to be/speak in ~ of sth/-ING** estar*/hablar a favor de algo/+ INF; **the judge found in the plaintiff's ~** el juez se pronunció a *or* en favor del demandante; **the wind is in our ~** llevamos *or* tenemos el viento a nuestro favor

C [c] (act of kindness) favor *m*; **can I ask you a ~** *o* **ask a ~ of you?** ¿puedo pedirte un favor?; **to do sb a ~** hacerle* un favor a algn

favor², (BrE) **favour** *vt* [1] (be in favor of) ‹*proposal*› estar* a favor de, ser* partidario de, apoyar; **a spot ~ed by anglers** un lugar que goza de popularidad entre los pescadores [2] (benefit) favorecer* [3] (treat preferentially) favorecer*, tratar con favoritismo [4] **favored** *past p*: **most ~ed nation** nación *f* más favorecida; **the** *o* **a ~ed few** una minoría selecta

favorable, (BrE) **favourable** /'feɪvrəbəl/ *adj* [1] ‹*report/answer*› favorable [2] ‹*weather*› favorable; ‹*deal/exchange rate*› favorable, ventajoso; **to be ~ TO sth** ‹*to expansion, investment*› favorecer* algo

favorably, (BrE) **favourably** /'feɪvrəbli/ *adv* favorablemente; **he spoke very ~ of her** habló muy bien de ella; **to be ~ disposed to(ward) sb/sth** estar* bien dispuesto hacia algn/algo

favorite¹, (BrE) **favourite** /'feɪvrət || 'feɪvərɪt/ *adj* preferido, predilecto

favorite², (BrE) **favourite** *n*

A [1] (person, thing) preferido, -da *m,f*, favorito, -ta *m,f*; **chocolate ice cream! my ~!** ¡helado de chocolate! ¡lo que más me gusta! [2] (of teacher, ruler) favorito, -ta *m,f*

B (Sport) favorito, -ta *m,f*

favoritism, (BrE) **favouritism** /'feɪvrətɪzəm || 'feɪvərɪtɪzəm/ *n* [u] favoritismo *m*

favour *etc* (BrE) ▸ **favor** *etc*

fawn¹ /fɔ:n/ *n*

A [c] (young deer) cervato *m*

B [u] (color) beige *m*, beis *m* (Esp); (*before n*) ‹*sweater/coat*› beige *adj inv*, beis *adj inv* (Esp)

fawn² *vi* [1] (flatter) **to ~ ON sb** ‹‹*person*›› (pej) adular *or* lisonjear a algn [2] **fawning** *pres p* adulador

fax¹ /fæks/ *n* fax *m*, telefax *m*; (*before n*) **~ machine/message** fax *m*; **~ number** número *m* de fax

fax² *vt* faxear

faze /feɪz/ *vt* (colloq) perturbar, desconcertar*; **he wasn't at all ~d by the question** ni se inmutó cuando le hicieron la pregunta

FBI *n* (in US) (= **Federal Bureau of Investigation**) FBI *m*

FC *n* = **Football Club**

FCC *n* (in US) = **Federal Communications Commission**

FD *n* (in US) = **Fire Department**

FDA *n* (in US) = **Food and Drug Administration**

> **FDA – Food and Drug Administration**
>
> Un organismo del gobierno de EEUU que establece los niveles de calidad para los alimentos y las medicinas y verifica que se puedan ingerir sin peligro

FDIC *n* (in US) = **Federal Deposit Insurance Corporation**

fear¹ /fɪr || fɪə(r)/ *n*

A [u c] (apprehension) miedo *m*, temor *m*; **~ of death/heights** miedo a la muerte/las alturas; **~ FOR sb/sth**: **there are ~s for the passengers' safety** se teme por la seguridad de los pasajeros; **to go** *o* **be in ~ of sb/sth** (frml) vivir atemorizado por algn/algo; **to be in ~ of one's life** temer por su (*or* mi *etc*) vida; **in ~ and trembling** (liter) atemorizado, lleno de miedo; **she wouldn't touch it for ~ of breaking it** no quería tocarlo por miedo a romperlo;

have no ~ (arch *or* hum) pierde (*or* pierda *etc*) cuidado; ***to put the ~ of God into sb*** asustar muchísimo a algn

B [u] (risk, chance, likelihood): **there's no ~ of that happening** no hay peligro de que eso ocurra; **no ~!** (*as interj*) (colloq) ¡ni loco! *or* ¡ni muerto!

fear² *vt* **1** (dread) temer, tenerle* miedo a; **to ~ the worst** temer(se) lo peor; **to ~ (THAT)** temer QUE **2** (suspect) **to ~ (THAT)** temerse QUE

■ **fear** *vi* temer; **to ~ FOR sb/sth** temer POR algn/algo

fearful /'fɪrfəl || 'fɪəfəl/ *adj*

A **1** (frightening) aterrador **2** (dreadful) (colloq) ‹*cold/mess*› espantoso, horrible; ‹*liar*› tremendo, terrible

B (timid) miedoso, temeroso; **to be ~ of -ING** temer + INF

fearfully /'fɪrfəlɪ || 'fɪəfəli/ *adv* (in, with fear) con temor

fearless /'fɪrləs || 'fɪəlɪs/ *adj* intrépido, audaz; **he is utterly ~** no le tiene miedo a nada; **~ of the consequences ...** sin temor a las consecuencias ...

fearlessly /'fɪrləsli || 'fɪəlɪsli/ *adv* sin temor

fearlessness /'fɪrləsnəs || 'fɪəlɪsnɪs/ *n* [u] audacia *f*

fearsome /'fɪrsəm || 'fɪəsəm/ *adj* ‹*enemy*› aterrador; ‹*task*› tremendo

feasibility /'fi:zə'bɪləti/ *n* [u] (of a plan) viabilidad *f*; (*before n*) **~ study** estudio *m* de viabilidad

feasible /'fi:zəbəl/ *adj* **1** (practicable) ‹*plan/proposal*› viable; (possible) posible, factible **2** (plausible) (crit) ‹*story/excuse*› verosímil

feast¹ /fi:st/ *n*

A (banquet) banquete *m*, festín *m*; **a ~ of colors/entertainment** un derroche de color(es)/un sinfín de diversiones

B (Relig) fiesta *f*; (*before n*) **~ day** día *m* festivo

feast² *vi* festejar; **to ~ ON sth** darse* un festín DE algo

■ **feast** *vt*: **to ~ one's eyes (ON sth)** regalarse los ojos *or* la vista (CON algo)

feat /fi:t/ *n* hazaña *f*, proeza *f*

feather¹ /'feðər || 'feðə(r)/ *n* pluma *f*; ***a ~ in one's cap*** un triunfo personal; ***as light as a ~*** ligero *or* (esp AmL) liviano como una pluma; ***to ruffle sb's ~s*** hacer* enojar *or* (esp Esp) enfadar a algn; ***you could have knocked me down with a ~*** (colloq) casi me caigo de espaldas; (*before n*) **~ bed** colchón *m* de plumas; **~ duster** plumero *m*

feather² *vt* ▸**nest¹ A**

featherbrained /'feðər,breɪnd || 'feðə,breɪnd/ *adj*: **a ~ idea** una idea disparatada

feathered /'feðərd || 'feðəd/ *adj* con plumas, emplumado; **our ~ friends** nuestras amigas las aves

featherweight *n* peso *m* pluma

feathery /'feðəri/ *adj* **-rier, -riest** como pluma

feature¹ /'fi:tʃər || 'fi:tʃə(r)/ *n*

A **1** (of face) rasgo *m*; **~s** rasgos, facciones *fpl*; **a smile lit up his ~s** una sonrisa le iluminó el rostro **2** (of character, landscape, style) característica *f*, rasgo *m* (distintivo); **the house has many original ~s** la casa conserva muchos detalles arquitectónicos de época; **his legs are his best ~** lo mejor que tiene son las piernas; **to make a ~ of sth** destacar* algo, hacer* resaltar algo **3** (of machine, book) característica *f*

B **1** **~ (film)** película *f*; **full-length ~** largometraje *m* **2** (Journ) artículo *m*; (*before n*) **~ writer** *n* articulista *mf* **3** (Rad, TV) documental *m*

C (incentive to buy) (AmE) oferta *f*

feature² *vt*

A **1** (Journ): **he was ~d in 'The Globe' recently** 'The Globe' publicó un artículo sobre él hace poco; **the state visit was ~d on the television news** se destacó la visita de estado en las noticias de la televisión **2** (Cin): **the film ~s her as ...** en la película aparece en el papel de ...; **featuring John Ball** con la actuación de John Ball

B **1** (have as feature) ‹‹*hotel/house*›› ofrecer* **2** (depict) mostrar*

■ **feature** *vi* **1** (appear) figurar; **rice ~s prominently in their diet** el arroz ocupa un lugar importante en su alimentación **2** (Cin) aparecer*, actuar*

feature-length /'fi:tʃər'leŋθ || ,fi:tʃə'leŋθ/ *adj* **1** (Cin) de largometraje **2** (Journ) ‹*article*› especial

featureless /'fi:tʃərləs || 'fi:tʃəlɪs/ *adj* monótono, sin ninguna característica especial

Feb (= **February**) feb

febrile /'febraɪl || 'fi:braɪl/ *adj* (liter) febril

February /'februeri || 'februəri/ *n* febrero *m*; *see also* **January**

feces, (BrE) **faeces** /'fi:si:z/ *pl n* (frml) heces *fpl* (frml), excrementos *mpl* (frml)

feckless /'fekləs || 'feklɪs/ *adj* (irresponsible) irresponsable; (lacking purpose) sin objetivos

fecund /'fekənd, 'fi:kənd/ *adj* (liter) fecundo

fecundity /fɪ'kʌndəti/ *n* [u] (liter) fecundidad *f*

fed¹ /fed/ *past & past p of* **feed¹**

fed² *n* (AmE colloq) **1** **feds** *pl* (Law) **the ~s** *los agentes del FBI u otro organismo estatal de los EEUU* **2** = **Federal Reserve Board** *o* **System**

federal /'fedərəl/ *adj* **1** ‹*republic/government*› federal; ‹*taxes/law*› nacional, federal **2** **Federal** (in US history) federal, nordista

Federal /'fedərəl/ *n* (in US history) federal *mf*, nordista *mf*

> **Federal Reserve System**
>
> También llamado *the Fed*, es la autoridad bancaria estadounidense que desempeña las funciones de un banco central y que controla el volumen de la masa monetaria en circulación, poniendo a disposición de los bancos un sistema nacional de encaje

federalism /'fedərəlɪzəm/ *n* [u] federalismo *m*

federalist /'fedərələst || 'fedərəlɪst/ *n* **1** (Pol) federalista *mf* **2** **Federalist** (US history) federalista *mf*, federal *mf*, nordista *mf*

federal: **~ Republic of Germany** *n* **the F~ Republic of Germany** la República Federal de Alemania; **~ Reserve Board** *n* (in US) la Junta de Gobernadores de la Reserva Federal

federate¹ /'fedəreɪt/ *vt* federar

■ **federate** *vi* federarse

federate² /'fedərət/ *adj* federado

federation /'fedə'reɪʃən/ *n* [c u] federación *f*

fed up *adj* (colloq) (*usu pred*) **1** (exasperated) **~ ~ (WITH sb/sth/-ING)** harto (DE algn/algo/+ INF); **to be/get ~ ~** estar* harto/hartarse **2** (depressed) (BrE): **I'm generally ~ ~ today** hoy estoy algo deprimido *or* alicaído

fee /fi:/ *n* **1** (payment — to doctor, lawyer) honorarios *mpl*; (— to actor, singer) caché *m*, cachet *m* **2** (charge) (*often pl*): **on payment of a small ~** por una módica suma; **entrance ~** (precio *m* de) entrada *f*; **membership ~(s)** cuota *f* (de socio); **registration/course ~(s)** matrícula *f*, inscripción *f*; **all his salary goes in school ~s** todo el salario se le va en pagar el colegio

feeble /'fi:bəl/ *adj* **-bler** /-blər || -blə(r)/, **-blest** /-bləst || -blɪst/ **1** (weak) débil **2** (poor) ‹*joke*› flojo, malo; ‹*excuse*› pobre, poco convincente

feeble-minded /'fi:bəl'maɪndəd || ,fi:bəl'maɪndɪd/ *adj* **1** (foolish) imbécil, tonto **2** (mentally deficient) (dated) débil mental

feebleness /'fi:bəlnəs || 'fi:bəlnɪs/ *n* [u] **1** (of person, voice) debilidad *f* **2** (of excuse) lo flojo, lo poco convincente

feebly /'fi:bli/ *adv* **1** (weakly) débilmente **2** (unconvincingly) sin energía

feed¹ /fi:d/ (*past & past p* **fed**) *vt*

A **1** (give food to) dar* de comer a; **the patient had to be fed intravenously** hubo que alimentar al paciente por vía intravenosa; **to ~ sb ON sth** darle* de comer algo a algn **2** ‹*baby*› (breastfeed) darle* el pecho a, darle* de mamar a; (with a bottle) darle* el biberón *or* (CS, Per) la mamadera *or* (Col) el tetero a **3** (provide food for) alimentar; **there's enough food here to ~ an army** hay suficiente comida como para alimentar a un batallón **4** (give as food) **to ~ sth TO sb** dar* algo (de comer) A algn; **we fed the leftovers to the dog** le dimos las sobras al perro

B **1** (supply): **to ~ information to sb** pasarle información a algn; **it ~s the industry with raw material** provee *or* alimenta a la industria de materia prima; **blood ~s the brain cells with oxygen** la sangre lleva oxígeno a las neuronas; **two streams ~ the river** dos riachuelos vierten sus aguas en el río **2** (insert) **to ~ sth INTO sth** ‹*into a machine*› introducir* algo EN algo; **I have to ~ the meter** tengo que echar más monedas en el parquímetro

C (sustain) ‹*imagination/rumor*› avivar; ‹*hope*› alimentar; ‹*fire*› alimentar

■ **feed** *vi* comer, alimentarse; **to ~ ON sth** alimentarse DE algo, comer algo; **fear ~s on ignorance** el miedo se ceba en la ignorancia

Phrasal verbs

- **feed off** [v ▸ prep ▸ o] 1 (use as food) alimentarse de 2 (prey on) cebarse en
- **feed up** [v ▸ o ▸ adv, v ▸ adv ▸ o] (BrE) ‹*animal*› engordar, cebar; **you need ~ing up** habrá que darte bien de comer

feed² *n*
A 1 [c] (act of feeding): **it's time for the baby's ~** es hora de darle de comer al niño 2 [u] (food) alimento *m*; (for cattle) pienso *m*; **to be off one's ~** (AmE sl) estar* desganado *or* inapetente
B [c] (on machine) alimentador *m*
C [c] (AmE Rad, TV) material *m* (*de programación*)

feed: **~back** *n* [u] (reaction) reacción *f*; (Audio, Electron) retroalimentación *f*; **~bag** *n* (AmE) morral *m*

feeding /'fi:dɪŋ/: **~ bottle** *n* (BrE) biberón *m*, mamadera *f* (CS, Per), tetero *m* (Col, Ven); **~ frenzy** *n* 1 (of sharks, piranhas) frenético festín *m* 2 (involving media) frenesí *m* de los medios de comunicación; **~ time** *n* [c u] hora *f* de comer *or* de la comida

feel¹ /fi:l/ (*past & past p* **felt**) *vi*
A (physically) sentirse*, encontrarse*; **how do you ~** *o* **how are you ~ing?** ¿cómo *or* qué tal te encuentras *or* te sientes?; **I ~ fine** me encuentro *or* estoy *or* me siento bien; **to ~ hot/cold/hungry/thirsty** tener* calor/frío/hambre/sed; **I'm not ~ing quite myself today** hoy no me siento del todo bien; **my arm ~s stiff** tengo el brazo entumecido
B (emotionally, mentally) sentirse*; **to ~ sad** sentirse* *or* estar* triste; **I ~ (like) a complete idiot** me siento como un perfecto imbécil; **how do you ~ about your parents' divorce?** ¿cómo has tomado el divorcio de tus padres?; **it ~s wonderful to be back** es maravilloso estar de vuelta; **I ~ bad about not having asked her** me da no sé qué no haberla invitado; **how does it ~, what does it ~ like?** ¿qué se siente?
C (have opinion): **I ~ that …** me parece que …, opino *or* creo que …; **it's something I ~ strongly about** es algo que me parece muy importante; **how do you ~ about these changes?** ¿qué opinas de *or* qué te parecen estos cambios?
D **to feel like sth** (to be in the mood for sth): **I ~ like a cup of tea** tengo ganas de tomar una taza de té, me apetece una taza de té (esp Esp); **to ~ like -ING** tener* ganas DE + INF; **come tomorrow if you ~ like it** ven mañana si tienes ganas *or* (esp Esp) si te apetece
E (seem, give impression of being): **your hands ~ cold** tienes las manos frías; **the water ~s very chilly at first** el agua parece muy fría al principio; **how does that ~? — it's still too tight** ¿cómo lo sientes? — todavía me queda apretado
F (search, grope) **to ~ FOR sth** buscar* algo a tientas; **he felt in his pocket for his lighter** se llevó la mano al bolsillo buscando el mechero

■ **feel** *vt*
A (touch) ‹*surface/body*› tocar*, palpar; ***to ~ one's way*** ir* a tientas
B (perceive, experience) ‹*sensation/movement/indignation/shame*› sentir*; **I couldn't ~ my fingers** no sentía los dedos; **he felt the bed move** sintió moverse la cama *or* que la cama se movía; **the consequences will be felt for a long time to come** las consecuencias se sentirán *or* se notarán durante mucho tiempo
C (consider) considerar; **I ~ it important to warn you** creo *or* considero que es importante advertirte; **he felt himself to be a burden on his family** se sentía una carga para su familia

Phrasal verbs

- **feel for** [v ▸ prep ▸ o] compadecer*; **I really ~ for you, having to work for her …** de verdad te compadezco, tener que trabajar para ella …; *see also* **feel** *vi* **F**
- **feel out** [v ▸ o ▸ adv, v ▸ adv ▸ o] ‹*person/situation*› tantear
- **feel up** [v ▸ o ▸ adv, v ▸ adv ▸ o] (colloq) meterle mano a (fam), manosear
- **feel up to** [v ▸ adv ▸ prep ▸ o]: **to ~ up to doing sth** sentirse* con ánimo como para hacer algo; **do you ~ up to it?** ¿te sientes con ánimo?

feel² *n* (*no pl*)
A 1 (sensation) sensación *f*; **I love the ~ of the wind on my face** me encanta sentir el viento en la cara 2 (act of touching): **to have a ~ of sth** tocar* algo 3 (sense of touch) tacto *m*; **it's smooth to the ~** es suave (al tacto)
B 1 (atmosphere — of house, room) ambiente *m*; **the music had a baroque ~ to it** la música tenía un aire barroco 2 (instinct): **to have a ~ for sth** tener* sensibilidad para algo; **to get the ~ of sth** acostumbrarse a algo, familiarizarse* con algo

feeler /'fi:lər || 'fi:lə(r)/ *n* 1 (Zool) (antenna) antena *f*; (tentacle) tentáculo *m* 2 (tentative approach): **to put out ~s** tantear el terreno

feelgood /'fi:lgʊd/ *adj* ‹*movie/experience*› que hace sentir bien; **the ~ factor** la sensación de bienestar

feeling /'fi:lɪŋ/ *n*
A 1 [u] (physical sensitivity) sensibilidad *f* 2 [c] (physical, emotional sensation) sensación *f*
B 1 [u] (sincere emotion) sentimiento *m*; **bad** *o* **ill ~** resentimiento *m* 2 **feelings** *pl* (sensitivity) sentimientos *mpl*; **to hurt sb's ~s** herir* los sentimientos de algn; ***no hard ~s***: **one of us had to win; no hard ~s, eh?** uno de los dos tenía que ganar; no nos guardemos rencor ¿eh?
C [c u] (opinion) opinión *f*; **what are your ~s on the matter?** ¿tú que opinas del asunto?
D (*no pl*) 1 (sensitivity, appreciation): **(to have) a ~ for sth** tener* sensibilidad para algo, saber* apreciar algo 2 (intuition, impression) impresión *f*, sensación *f*; **I've a ~ that he knows already** tengo *or* me da la sensación *or* la impresión de que ya lo sabe

fee-paying /'fi:'peɪɪŋ/ *adj* (esp BrE) ‹*student*› que paga cuotas *or* (Méx) colegiatura; **~ school** colegio *m* particular

feet /fi:t/ *n pl of* **foot¹**

feign /feɪn/ *vt* (fake) ‹*ignorance/enthusiasm*› fingir*, simular; **he ~ed illness** fingió estar enfermo

feint¹ /feɪnt/ *n*
A [c] (Sport) finta *f*
B [u] (on paper): **narrow ~** renglones *mpl* estrechos

feint² *vi* (Sport) fintar, fintear (AmL)

feisty /'faɪsti/ *adj* **-stier, -stiest** (colloq) batallador

felicitous /fɪ'lɪsətəs || fə'lɪsɪtəs/ *adj* (frml) oportuno, acertado, feliz

felicity /fɪ'lɪsəti || fə'lɪsəti/ *n* [u] (*pl* **-ties**) (liter) júbilo *m* (liter), dicha *f*

feline¹ /'fi:laɪn/ *adj* felino

feline² *n* felino *m*

fell¹ /fel/ *past of* **fall²**

fell² *vt* ‹*tree*› talar; ‹*person*› derribar

fella, (AmE also) **fellah** /'felə/ *n* (colloq) tipo *m* (fam)

fellow¹ /'feləʊ/ *n*
A (man) tipo *m* (fam), hombre *m*, sujeto *m*; (*as term of address*): **my dear ~** amigo mío, mi buen *or* querido amigo; **now listen to me, young ~** óigame bien, jovencito
B (member — of college) *miembro del cuerpo docente y de la junta rectora de una universidad*; (— of learned society) miembro *mf* de número

fellow² *adj* (*before n*): **~ student/worker/traveler** compañero, -ra *m,f* de estudios/trabajo/viaje; **~ citizen** conciudadano, -na *m,f*; **~ countryman** compatriota *mf*; **he has no love for his ~ men** no le tiene amor al prójimo

fellow feeling *n* [u] camaradería *f*, compañerismo *m*

fellowship /'feləʊʃɪp/ *n*
A [c] (Educ) 1 (at university) título *m* de **fellow¹ B** 2 (endowment) beca *f* de investigación
B [u] 1 (companionship) (liter) hermandad *f* (liter), compañerismo *m* 2 (Relig) comunión *f* 3 (fraternity, association) fraternidad *f*

fellow traveler, (BrE) **traveller** *n* 1 (on journey) compañero, -ra *m,f* de viaje 2 (Pol) compañero, -ra *m,f* de viaje, simpatizante *mf* (*del partido comunista*)

felon /'felən/ *n* (in US law) delincuente *mf* (*que ha cometido un delito grave*)

felony /'feləni/ *n* [c u] (*pl* **-nies**) (in US Law) delito *m* grave

felt¹ /felt/ *n* [u] fieltro *m*

felt² *past & past p of* **feel¹**

felt pen, **felt-tip (pen)** /'felttɪp/ *n* rotulador *m*, marcador *m* (AmL)

f

female[1] /ˈfi:meɪl/ *adj*
A 1 (Biol, Bot, Zool) ‹*sex*› femenino; ‹*animal/plant*› hembra; **a ~ elephant** un elefante hembra, una hembra de elefante 2 (of women) ‹*ward/prison*› de mujeres; **~ employees** empleadas *fpl*; **the victim was ~** la víctima era una mujer
B (Tech) ‹*thread/socket/coupling*› hembra *adj inv*

female[2] *n*
A (Bot, Zool) hembra *f*
B (woman, girl) mujer *f*

feminine[1] /ˈfemənən || ˈfemɪnɪn/ *adj* femenino

feminine[2] *n* (Ling): **(in) the ~** (en) el femenino

femininity /ˌfeməˈnɪnəti || ˌfemɪˈnɪnəti/ *n* [u] femineidad *f*, feminidad *f*

feminism /ˈfemənəzəm || ˈfemɪnɪzəm/ *n* [u] feminismo *m*

feminist[1] /ˈfemənəst || ˈfemɪnɪst/ *n* feminista *mf*

feminist[2] *adj* feminista

feminization /ˌfemənəˈzeɪʃən || ˌfemɪnaɪˈzeɪʃən/ *n* [u] feminización *f*

femme fatale /ˈfæmfəˈtæl || ˌfæmfæˈtɑ:l/ *n* (*pl* **~s ~s** /-fəˈtælz || -fæˈtɑ:lz/) mujer *f* fatal

femur /ˈfi:mər || ˈfi:mə(r)/ *n* (*pl* **femurs** *or* **femora** /ˈfemərə/) fémur *m*

fen /fen/ *n* terreno *m* pantanoso, pantano *m*

fence[1] /fens/ *n*
A 1 (barrier) cerca *f*, valla *f*, cerco *m* (AmL); **wire ~** alambrada *f*, alambrado *m* (AmL); ***to sit on the ~*** nadar entre dos aguas, no definirse 2 (in showjumping) valla *f*
B (receiver of stolen goods) (colloq) *persona que comercia con objetos robados*, reducidor, -dora *m,f* (AmS)

fence[2] *vt* ‹*garden/field*› cercar*, vallar
■ **fence** *vi* (Sport) practicar* la esgrima, hacer* esgrima
Phrasal verbs
• **fence in** [v ▸ adv ▸ o, v ▸ o ▸ adv] cercar*, vallar
• **fence off** [v ▸ adv ▸ o, v ▸ o ▸ adv] separar con una cerca

fencepost /ˈfenspəʊst/ *n* poste *m*

fencer /ˈfensər || ˈfensə(r)/ *n* esgrimista *mf*, esgrimidor, -dora *m,f*

fencing /ˈfensɪŋ/ *n* [u]
A (Sport) esgrima *f*
B 1 (material) *materiales para cercos o vallas* 2 (fence) cerca *f*, cerco *m*, valla *f*; **wire ~** alambrada *f*, alambrado *m* (AmL)

fend /fend/ *vi*: **to ~ for oneself** valerse* por sí mismo, arreglárselas solo
Phrasal verb
• **fend off** [v ▸ o ▸ adv, v ▸ adv ▸ o] ‹*attack/enemy*› rechazar*; ‹*blow*› esquivar, desviar*; ‹*questions*› eludir, esquivar

fender /ˈfendər || ˈfendə(r)/ *n*
A (around fireplace) rejilla *f*
B (on car) (AmE) guardabarros *m* *or* (Méx) salpicadera *f* *or* (Chi, Per) tapabarro(s) *m*; (on boat) defensa *f*; (on train) quitapiedras *m*

fennel /ˈfenl/ *n* [u] hinojo *m*

fenugreek /ˈfenu:gri:k, ˈfenjə- || ˈfenjʊgri:k/ *n* [c] fenogreco *m*, alholva *f*

feral /ˈferəl/ *adj* asilvestrado

ferment[1] /fərˈment || fəˈment/ *vt* (Chem, Culin) (hacer*) fermentar; ‹*trouble/unrest*› fomentar
■ **ferment** *vi* ‹‹*wine/beer*›› fermentar

ferment[2] /ˈfɜ:rment || ˈfɜ:ment/ *n* [u] (turmoil) agitación *f*; **to be in ~** estar* agitado *or* conmocionado

fermentation /ˈfɜ:rmenˈteɪʃən || ˌfɜ:menˈteɪʃən/ *n* [u] fermentación *f*

fern /fɜ:rn || fɜ:n/ *n* [c u] helecho *m*

ferocious /fəˈrəʊʃəs/ *adj* ‹*animal*› feroz, fiero; ‹*appearance*› feroz; ‹*argument*› violento

ferociously /fəˈrəʊʃəsli/ *adv* 1 (like a wild beast) con ferocidad 2 (intensely) ‹*quarrel*› violentamente, ferozmente; **the sun beat down ~** el sol caía a plomo

ferocity /fəˈrɑ:səti || fəˈrɒsəti/, **ferociousness** /fəˈrəʊʃəsnəs || fəˈrəʊʃəsnɪs/ *n* [u] (of animal) ferocidad *f*; (of wind, sea) furia *f*; (of anger) ferocidad *f*, violencia *f*

ferret[1] /ˈferət || ˈferɪt/ *n* hurón *m*

ferret[2] *vi* (Sport): **to go ~ing** huronear, cazar* con hurones
Phrasal verbs
• **ferret around**, **ferret about** [v ▸ adv] husmear, hurgar*
• **ferret out** [v ▸ o ▸ adv, v ▸ adv ▸ o] (colloq) ‹*secret*› descubrir*; **to ~ sth out OF sb** sonsacarle* algo a algn

ferric /ˈferɪk/ *adj* férrico

Ferris wheel /ˈferəs || ˈferɪs/ *n* ▸ **big wheel 2**

ferrous /ˈferəs/ *adj* ferroso

ferrule /ˈferəl || ˈferu:l/ *n* regatón *m*, contera *f*

ferry[1] /ˈferi/ *n* (*pl* **-ries**) (boat) transbordador *m*, ferry *m*; (smaller) balsa *f*, barca *f*

ferry[2] *vt* **-ries, -rying, -ried** llevar, transportar; **to ~ sth/sb across** *o* **over a river** llevar algo/a algn al otro lado de un río; **we ~ the children to and from school in the car** llevamos a los niños al colegio y los vamos a buscar en coche

ferry: **~boat** *n* ▸ **ferry**[1]; **~man** /ˈferimən/ (*pl* **-men** /-mən/) *n* barquero *m*

fertile /ˈfɜ:rtl || ˈfɜ:taɪl/ *adj* 1 (fruitful) ‹*soil*› fértil 2 (capable of reproducing) ‹*woman/animal/plant*› fértil; ‹*seed/egg*› fecundado 3 (inventive) ‹*imagination*› fértil, fecundo

fertility /fərˈtɪləti || fəˈtɪləti/ *n* [u] fertilidad *f*; (*before n*) ‹*drug/clinic*› para el tratamiento de la infertilidad

fertilize /ˈfɜ:rtḷaɪz || ˈfɜ:tɪlaɪz/ *vt* 1 (Biol) ‹*egg/plant/cell*› fecundar 2 (Agr, Hort) ‹*soil/crop*› abonar, fertilizar*

fertilizer /ˈfɜ:rtḷaɪzər || ˈfɜ:tɪlaɪzə(r)/ *n* [u c] fertilizante *m*, abono *m*

fervent /ˈfɜ:rvənt || ˈfɜ:vənt/ *adj* ferviente

fervently /ˈfɜ:rvəntli || ˈfɜ:vəntli/ *adv* ‹*hope*› fervientemente; ‹*speak*› con fervor

fervor, (BrE) **fervour** /ˈfɜ:rvər || ˈfɜ:və(r)/ *n* [u] fervor *m*, ardor *m*

fester /ˈfestər || ˈfestə(r)/ *vi* ‹‹*wound/feeling of resentment*›› enconarse; **a ~ing sore** una llaga purulenta

festival /ˈfestəvəl || ˈfestɪvəl/ *n* 1 (Relig) fiesta *f*, festividad *f* 2 (Cin, Mus, Theat) festival *m*; **a pop ~** un festival de música pop 3 (celebration) fiesta *f*

festive /ˈfestɪv/ *adj* festivo, alegre; **the ~ season** (set phrase) las Navidades, las fiestas (de fin de año); **we were in (a) ~ mood** estábamos muy alegres

festivity /fesˈtɪvəti/ *n* 1 [c] (celebration) (*usu pl*) celebración *f*, festividad *f* 2 [u] (merriment) fiesta *f*

festoon /feˈstu:n/ *vt* **to ~ sth/sb (WITH sth)** adornar *or* engalanar algo/a algn (CON algo)

fetal, (BrE) **foetal** /ˈfi:tl/ *adj* fetal

fetch /fetʃ/ *vt*
A (bring) ‹*person/thing*› traer*, ir* a buscar, ir* a por (Esp); **go and ~ help!** ¡ve a buscar ayuda!; **~ (it)!** (to dog) ¡busca, busca!; **you'd better ~ the washing in** va a ser mejor que entres la ropa; **to ~ sb from the station** recoger* *or* ir* a buscar a algn a la estación
B (sell for) (colloq): **the car ~ed $4,000** el coche se vendió en 4.000 dólares, sacaron 4.000 dólares por el coche
C (colloq) (deal): **to ~ sb a blow** darle* *or* asestarle un golpe a algn
■ **fetch** *vi*: ***to ~ and carry*** ser* el recadero/la recadera
Phrasal verb
• **fetch up** (BrE colloq) [v ▸ adv] acabar, ir* a parar

fetching /ˈfetʃɪŋ/ *adj* ‹*smile*› atractivo; ‹*dress/hat*› sentador, que sienta bien (Esp); **you look very ~ in that hat** ese sombrero te queda muy bien

fete[1], **fête** /feɪt/ *n* 1 (fund-raising event) (BrE) feria *f* (*benéfica*), kermesse *f* (CS, Méx), bazar *m* (Col) 2 (party) (AmE) fiesta *f* (*en un jardín*)

fete[2], **fête** *vt* ‹*person*› agasajar; ‹*book/work*› celebrar

fetid /ˈfetəd || ˈfetɪd/ *adj* fétido

fetish /ˈfetɪʃ/ *n* fetiche *m*

fetishism /ˈfetɪʃɪzəm/ *n* [u] fetichismo *m*

fetishist /ˈfetɪʃəst || ˈfetɪʃɪst/ *n* fetichista *mf*

fetlock /ˈfetlɑ:k || ˈfetlɒk/ *n* espolón *m*

fetter /ˈfetər || ˈfetə(r)/ *vt* (liter) ‹*prisoner*› encadenar, ponerle* grillos a; **he felt ~ed by convention** se sentía prisionero de los convencionalismos

fetters /ˈfetərz || ˈfetəz/ *pl n* (liter) grillos *mpl*

fettle /ˈfetḷ/ *n*: ***to be in fine ~*** estar* en (buena) forma

fetus, (BrE) **foetus** /ˈfi:təs/ *n* feto *m*

feud[1] /fjuːd/ *n* contienda *f* (frml), enemistad *f*

feud[2] *vi* contender* (frml), pelear

feudal /'fjuːdl̩/ *adj* feudal

feudalism /'fjuːdlɪzəm/ *n* [u] feudalismo *m*

fever /'fiːvər || 'fiːvə(r)/ *n*

A (Med) 1▸ [c u] (temperature) fiebre *f*, calentura *f*; **she has a ~ of 102** ≈ tiene 39 de fiebre; **to run a ~** tener* fiebre *or* calentura 2▸ [u] (disease): **scarlet ~** escarlatina *f*; **yellow ~** fiebre *f* amarilla

B (agitated state) (*no pl*): **the town was in a ~ over the visit** la ciudad estaba revolucionada con la visita; **election/gold ~** fiebre *f* electoral/del oro

fever blister *n* (AmE) ▸ **cold sore**

feverish /'fiːvərɪʃ/ *adj* 1▸ (Med) con fiebre, afiebrado; **to be ~** estar* afiebrado, tener* fiebre *or* calentura 2▸ (frantic) febril

fever pitch *n*: ***to be at ~ ~*** estar* al rojo vivo; ***to rise to o reach ~ ~*** llegar* al paroxismo

few[1] /fjuː/ *adj* **-er, -est** 1▸ (not many) pocos, -cas; **~ people know about this** lo sabe poca gente, lo saben pocos; **the** *o* **what ~ chances I had** las pocas posibilidades que tenía; **there were six books too ~** faltaban seis libros; **every ~ days** cada pocos días; **the last ~ days have been difficult** estos últimos días han sido difíciles; **there were ~er people than usual** había menos gente que de costumbre; **~er and ~er trains stop here** cada vez paran menos trenes aquí 2▸ **a few** (some): **a ~ people complained** algunos se quejaron/bastante gente se quejó; **I've been there a ~ times** he estado allí unas cuantas veces; **there are quite a ~ mistakes** hay bastantes faltas

few[2] *pron* **-er, -est** 1▸ (not many) pocos, -cas; **we have too ~ to go around** no tenemos suficientes para todos; **the privileged ~** la minoría privilegiada; **as ~ as 30% pass first time** tan sólo un 30% aprueba a la primera; **~er than 200 tickets have been sold** se han vendido menos de 200 entradas; ***to be ~ and far between***: **good beaches are ~ and far between** las playas buenas son contadísimas 2▸ **a few** (some): **a ~ objected** algunos se opusieron; **all but a ~** casi todos; **a good ~** *o* **quite a ~ already know** ya lo saben bastantes; **there are still quite a ~ left** todavía quedan unos cuantos; **a ~ of us complained** algunos (de nosotros) nos quejamos; **he's had a ~ (too many)** (colloq) se ha tomado unas cuantas

ff (= **and (those) following**) y sig.

FHA *n* (in US) = **Federal Housing Administration**

fiancé /'fiːɑːn'seɪ, fiː'ɑːnseɪ || fiː'ɒnseɪ/ *n* prometido *m*, novio *m*

fiancée /'fiːɑːn'seɪ, fiː'ɑːnseɪ || fiː'ɒnseɪ/ *n* prometida *f*, novia *f*

fiasco /fi'æskəʊ/ *n* (*pl* **-cos** *or* **-coes**) fracaso *m*, fiasco *m*

fiat /'fiːæt, 'faɪæt/ *n* (frml) orden *m* (*oficial*), decreto *m*

fib[1] /fɪb/ *n* (colloq) mentirilla *f*, bola *f* (fam)

fib[2] *vi* **-bb-** (colloq) mentir*, decir* mentirillas *or* (fam) bolas

fibber /'fɪbər || 'fɪbə(r)/ *n* (colloq) cuentista *mf*, cuentero, -ra *m,f* (Méx, RPl), mojonero, -ra *m,f* (Ven fam)

fiber, (BrE) **fibre** /'faɪbər || 'faɪbə(r)/ *n*

A 1▸ [c] (thread) fibra *f* 2▸ [c] (cloth) fibra *f* (textil)

B 1▸ [c] (Anat) fibra *f*; **with every ~ of her being** (liter) con todo su ser 2▸ [u] (firmness) fibra *f*, carácter *m*; **he has no (moral) ~** no tiene fibra *or* carácter

C [u] (Bot) fibra *f*; **a high ~ diet** una dieta rica en fibra

fiber: **~glass** *n* [u] fibra *f* de vidrio; **~ optics** *n* [u] (+ *sing vb*) transmisión *f* por fibra óptica

fibroid /'faɪbrɔɪd/ *n* fibroma *f*

fibrositis /'faɪbrə'saɪtəs || ˌfaɪbrə'saɪtɪs/ *n* [u] fibrositis *f*

fibrous /'faɪbrəs/ *adj* fibroso

fiche /fiːʃ/ *n* microficha *f*

fickle /'fɪkəl/ *adj* veleidoso, inconstante

fiction /'fɪkʃən/ *n* 1▸ [u] (Lit) ficción *f*, narrativa *f* 2▸ [u c] (invention) ficción *f*

fictional /'fɪkʃn̩əl || 'fɪkʃənl̩/ *adj* ficticio, imaginario

fictionalize /'fɪkʃn̩əlaɪz/ *vt* llevar a la ficción, novelar

fictitious /fɪk'tɪʃəs/ *adj* 1▸ (false) ‹*name*› ficticio, falso 2▸ (imaginary) imaginario, ficticio

fiddle[1] /'fɪdl̩/ *n*

A (violin) violín *m*; ***as fit as a ~*** rebosante de salud; ***to play second ~*** desempeñar un papel secundario

B (cheat) (BrE colloq) chanchullo *m* (fam); **she's on the ~** está metida en un chanchullo (fam)

C (tricky operation) (colloq): **it's a ~ to get this in** meter esto tiene sus vueltas *or* (Méx) su chiste

fiddle[2] *vt* (BrE colloq) ‹*accounts*› hacer* chanchullos con (fam); ‹*results*› amañar

■ **fiddle** *vi* (fidget) **to ~ WITH sth**: **stop fiddling with the typewriter!** deja de jugar con *or* de toquetear la máquina de escribir; **he ~d nervously with his tie** jugueteaba nerviosamente con la corbata

Phrasal verb

• **fiddle around**, (BrE) **fiddle about** [v ▸ adv]

A (touch) **to ~ around WITH sth** ‹*with pencil/ruler*› juguetear CON algo; **I don't want you fiddling around with my things** no quiero que andes toqueteando mis cosas (fam)

B (do little jobs) hacer* un poco de esto y un poco de aquello

fiddler /'fɪdlər || 'fɪdlə(r)/ *n* (violinist) violinista *mf*

fiddling[1] /'fɪdlɪŋ/ *adj* (colloq) tonto (fam), trivial

fiddling[2] *n* [u] (BrE colloq) chanchullos *mpl* (fam)

fiddly /'fɪdli/ *adj* **-dlier, -dliest** (BrE colloq) ‹*task*› complicado, difícil; ‹*object*› complicado *or* difícil de usar

fidelity /fə'deləti || fɪ'deləti/ *n* [u] fidelidad *f*

fidget[1] /'fɪdʒət || 'fɪdʒɪt/ *vi*: **stop ~ing** ¡estáte quieto!; **to ~ WITH sth** juguetear CON algo

fidget[2] *n* 1▸ (person) persona *f* inquieta; **don't be such a ~** no seas tan inquieto 2▸ **fidgets** *pl*: **to get the ~s** ponerse* inquieto

fidgety /'fɪdʒəti || 'fɪdʒɪti/ *adj* inquieto

fiduciary /fɪ'duːʃəri || fɪ'djuːʃəri/ *adj* fiduciario

fief /fiːf/, **fiefdom** /'fiːfdəm/ *n* feudo *m*

field[1] /fiːld/ *n*

A (Agr) (for crops) campo *m*; (for grazing) campo *m*, prado *m*, potrero *m* (AmL); **a ~ of corn/wheat** un maizal/trigal

B (Sport) 1▸ (area of play) campo *m*, cancha *f* (AmL) 2▸ (competitors) (+ *sing o pl vb*): **Brown was leading the ~** Brown iba a la cabeza de los participantes (*or* corredores *etc*), Brown llevaba la delantera; **our products lead the ~** nuestros productos son los líderes del mercado; ***to play the ~*** (colloq) tantear el terreno (fam)

C (Mil) *also* **~ of battle** campo *m* de batalla

D 1▸ (of study, work) campo *m*; (of activities) esfera *f*; **my ~ is 20th century poetry** mi especialidad es la poesía del siglo XX 2▸ (of practical operations) campo *m*; **it has been tested in the ~** se ha probado sobre el terreno; (*before n*) ‹*research/survey*› de campo

E (Opt, Phot, Phys) campo *m*; **~ of vision** campo visual; **magnetic ~** campo magnético

field[2] *vt*

A 1▸ (Sport) ‹*ball*› fildear, interceptar y devolver* 2▸ ‹*question*› sortear

B 1▸ (Sport) ‹*team*› alinear 2▸ ‹*candidates*› presentar

■ **field** *vi* (in baseball, cricket) fildear, interceptar y devolver* la pelota

field day *n*: ***to have a ~ ~*** ‹‹*thieves/vendors*›› hacer* su agosto; **the press have had a ~ ~ with the scandal** el escándalo ha sido un verdadero festín para la prensa

fielder /'fiːldər || 'fiːldə(r)/ *n* (in cricket, baseball) fildeador, -dora *m,f*

field: **~ event** *n* prueba *f* de atletismo; **~ glasses** *pl n* gemelos *mpl*, prismáticos *mpl*, largavistas *m*; **~ goal** *n* (in basketball) canasta *f* (*de dos puntos*); (in US football) gol *m* de campo; **~ hockey** *n* [u] (AmE) hockey *m* (sobre hierba); **~ marshal** *n* mariscal *m* de campo; **~mouse** *n* (in Europe) ratón *m* silvestre *or* de campo; (in US) campañol *m*; **~sman** /'fiːldzmən/ *n* (*pl* **-men** /-mən/) (BrE) fildeador *m* (*jugador que no batea*); **~ sports** *pl n*: *la caza y la pesca*; **~ study** *n* estudio *m* de campo; **~ test**, **~ trial** *n* prueba *f* sobre el terreno; **~-test** *vt* probar* sobre el terreno; **~ trip** *n* viaje *m* de estudio; **~work** *n* [u] (research) trabajo *m* de campo

fiend /fiːnd/ *n*

A 1▸ (demon) demonio *m* 2▸ (cruel person) (journ *or* hum) desalmado, -da *m,f*; **sex ~** maníaco *m* sexual

B (fan) (colloq & hum): **he's a golf ~** es un fanático del golf

fiendish /'fiːndɪʃ/ *adj* 1▸ (wicked) diabólico; **to take a ~ delight in sth** regodearse *or* refocilarse con algo 2▸ (very difficult) (colloq) endemoniado (fam), endiablado (fam)

f

fiendishly /'fi:ndɪʃli/ *adv* 1 ‹*cruel*› diabólicamente 2 (colloq) ‹*clever/difficult*› endemoniadamente (fam), endiabladamente (fam)

fierce /fɪrs || 'fɪəs/ *adj* **fiercer, fiercest** 1 ‹*dog/lion*› fiero, feroz; ‹*glance*› feroz, furibundo; ‹*temper*› feroz, temible 2 ‹*hatred/love*› intenso, violento; ‹*fighting*› encarnizado; ‹*criticism/opposition*› violento, virulento; ‹*defender/opponent*› acérrimo; **they are ~ enemies** son enemigos encarnizados 3 ‹*storm*› violento; ‹*wind*› fortísimo; **the ~ tropical sun** el implacable sol del trópico

fiercely /'fɪrsli || 'fɪəsli/ *adv* 1 ‹*growl*› con ferocidad, ferozmente 2 ‹*fight*› con fiereza; ‹*criticize*› duramente, virulentamente; ‹*competitive/independent*› extremadamente; **she was ~ protective of them** los protegía con uñas y dientes 3 ‹*burn/blow*› violentamente; **the sun shone ~ down** el sol caía implacable

fiery /'faɪri || 'faɪəri/ *adj* **-rier, -riest** ‹*glow*› ardiente; ‹*red*› encendido; ‹*heat/sun*› abrasador; ‹*liquor*› muy fuerte; ‹*temper*› exaltado; ‹*speech*› fogoso

FIFA /'fi:fə/ *n* (*no art*) la FIFA

fife /faɪf/ *n* pífano *m*

fifteen /'fɪf'ti:n/ *adj/n* quince *adj inv/m*

fifteenth[1] /'fɪf'ti:nθ/ *adj* decimoquinto; *see also* **fifth**[1]

fifteenth[2] *adv* en decimoquinto lugar; *see also* **fifth**[2]

fifteenth[3] *n* 1 (Math) quinceavo *m* 2 (part) quinceava parte *f*

fifth[1] /fɪfθ/ *adj*

A 1 quinto; **you're the ~ person to ask me that** eres la quinta persona que me pregunta eso; **Henry V** *(léase: Henry the Fifth)* Enrique V *(read as: Enrique quinto)*; **it's his ~ birthday** cumple cinco años; **it's their ~ wedding anniversary** cumplen cinco años de casados, es su quinto aniversario de boda; **I was ~ on the list** yo era el quinto/la quinta de la lista; **~ part/share** quinta parte *f*, quinto *m* 2 (in seniority, standing) quinto

B (elliptical use): **Paradise Boy fell at the ~** Paradise Boy cayó en la quinta valla; **he'll be arriving on the ~ (of the month)** llegará el (día) cinco; **Uncle Ben is the ~ from the right** el tío Ben es el quinto de derecha a izquierda; **we'll arrive (on) the ~ of May** *o* **May ~** *o* (BrE) **May the ~** llegaremos el cinco de mayo

fifth[2] *adv* 1 (in position, time, order) en quinto lugar; **Goodwill finished ~** Goodwill llegó el quinto *or* en quinto lugar 2 (with superl): **the ~ highest mountain in the world** la quinta montaña más alta del mundo

fifth[3] *n*

A 1 (Math) quinto *m*; **one ~ of ten is two** un quinto *or* la quinta parte de diez es dos 2 (part) quinta parte *f*, quinto *m* 3 (Mus) quinta *f* 4 (measure) (AmE) *medida equivalente a 0,757 litros* 5 (in competition): **he finished a disappointing ~** llegó en un deslucido quinto lugar *or* puesto

B **~ (gear)** (*no art*) quinta *f*

fiftieth[1] /'fɪftiəθ/ *adj* quincuagésimo; *see also* **fifth**[1]

fiftieth[2] *adv* en quincuagésimo lugar; *see also* **fifth**[2]

fiftieth[3] *n* 1 (Math) cincuentavo *m* 2 (part) cincuentava *or* quincuagésima parte *f*

fifty /'fɪfti/ *adj/n* cincuenta *adj inv/m*; *see also* **seventy**

fifty-fifty[1] /'fɪfti'fɪfti/ *adv* (colloq) a medias; **to go ~ with sb/on sth** ir* a medias con algn/en algo; **we split the takings ~** nos repartimos lo recaudado mitad y mitad *or* por partes iguales

fifty-fifty[2] *adj* (colloq): **a ~ chance** un 50% de posibilidades; **on a ~ basis** a medias, por partes iguales

fig /fɪg/ *n* higo *m*; **~ tree** higuera *f*; **I don't care** *o* **give a ~!** ¡me importa un bledo!

fight[1] /faɪt/ (*past & past p* **fought**) *vi* 1 ‹‹*army/country*›› luchar, combatir; ‹‹*person*›› pelear, luchar; ‹‹*animal*›› luchar; **to ~ AGAINST sb/sth** luchar CONTRA algn/algo; **to ~ FOR sb/sth** ‹*for country/cause*› luchar POR algn/algo; ‹*for aim/policy*› luchar por conseguir *or* lograr algo; **she was ~ing for her life** se debatía entre la vida y la muerte; **to go down ~ing** luchar hasta el final; **he had to ~ for breath** le costaba muchísimo respirar; ***to ~ shy of sth***: **he tends to ~ shy of emotional commitments** tiende a eludir *or* evitar los compromisos afectivos 2 (quarrel) **to ~ OVER/ABOUT sth** pelearse POR algo 3 **fighting** *pres p* ‹*troops/units*› de combate

■ **fight** *vt*

A 1 ‹*army/country*› luchar *or* combatir contra; **if you want it, you'll have to ~ me for it** si lo quieres vas a tener que vértelas conmigo; **Frazier fought Ali for the world title** Frazier peleó contra Ali *or* se enfrentó a Ali por el título mundial; **I had to ~ my way into the hall** tuve que abrirme camino *or* paso a la fuerza para entrar en la sala 2 (oppose) ‹*fire/disease*› combatir; ‹*measure/proposal*› combatir, oponerse* a; **we'll ~ them all the way** no les vamos a dar cuartel

B 1 (conduct): **to ~ a battle** librar una batalla; **they fought a long war against the rebels** lucharon contra los rebeldes durante largo tiempo 2 (contest) ‹*election*› presentarse a; **we intend to ~ the case** (Law) pensamos llevar el caso a los tribunales (*or* defendernos *etc*)

Phrasal verbs

- **fight back**

A [v ▸ adv] defenderse*; **to ~ back AGAINST sb/sth** luchar CONTRA algn/algo

B [v ▸ o ▸ adv, v ▸ adv ▸ o] ‹*tears*› contener*; ‹*anger*› reprimir

- **fight down** [v ▸ o ▸ adv, v ▸ adv ▸ o] ‹*fear*› vencer*; ‹*anger*› reprimir; ‹*tears*› contener*
- **fight off** [v ▸ o ▸ adv, v ▸ adv ▸ o] ‹*attack/enemy*› rechazar*; ‹*cold*› combatir; **she struggled to ~ off sleep** trató de que no la venciera el sueño
- **fight on** [v ▸ adv] seguir* luchando
- **fight out** [v ▸ o ▸ adv]: **they are ~ing it out for second place** están compitiendo por el segundo puesto; **you'll have to ~ it out among yourselves** tendrán que resolverlo *or* (frml) dirimirlo entre ustedes

fight[2] *n*

A [c] 1 (between persons) pelea *f*; (between armies, companies) lucha *f*, contienda *f*; **to put up a good ~** ofrecer* *or* oponer* resistencia; **they're looking for a ~** están buscando camorra *or* bronca 2 (boxing match) pelea *f*, combate *m*

B [c] 1 (struggle) lucha *f* 2 (quarrel) pelea *f*

C [u] (fighting spirit): **he was still full of ~** aún seguía con ganas de pelear; **there's no ~ left in him** no le quedan ánimos para luchar

fighter /'faɪtər || 'faɪtə(r)/ *n*

A 1 (person) luchador, -dora *m,f* 2 (boxer) boxeador, -dora *m,f*, púgil *mf*, pugilista *mf*

B (plane) caza *m*, avión *m* de combate; (*before n*) **~ pilot** piloto *m* de caza

fighter-bomber /'faɪtər'bɑ:mər || ,faɪtə'bɒmə(r)/ *n* cazabombardero *m*

fighting[1] /'faɪtɪŋ/ *n* [u] (Mil) enfrentamientos *mpl*; (brawling, arguing) peleas *fpl*

fighting[2] *adj* (*before n*): **~ chance**: ***to be in with*** *o* ***have a ~ chance*** tener* posibilidades de ganar; ***to give sb a ~ chance*** darle* a algn una oportunidad; **~ fit** (colloq) en plena forma; **~ strength** (Mil) capacidad *f* ofensiva; **~ talk** (BrE colloq): **that's ~ talk!** ¡así se habla!

figment /'fɪgmənt/ *n*: **a ~ of the imagination** (un) producto de la imaginación

figurative /'fɪgjərətɪv || 'fɪgərətɪv/ *adj* ‹*meaning*› figurado, metafórico

figuratively /'fɪgjərətɪvli || 'fɪgərətɪvli/ *adv* ‹*speak/write*› de manera figurada *or* metafórica; **~ speaking** metafóricamente hablando

figure[1] /'fɪgjər || 'fɪgə(r)/ *n*

A 1 (digit) cifra *f*; **inflation is now into double ~s** la inflación pasa del 10% 2 (piece of data) dato *m*; **recent ~s show that ...** estadísticas *or* datos recientes muestran que ... 3 (amount, price) cifra *f*; **I wouldn't like to put a ~ on it** no quisiera darle una cifra exacta; **she's good at ~s** es buena para las matemáticas, se le dan bien los números

B 1 (person) figura *f*; **a public ~** un personaje público; **a ~ of fun** un hazmerreír 2 (body shape) figura *f*, tipo *m*; **she's a fine ~ of a woman** es una mujer de buena planta

C (Art, Math, Mus) figura *f*

D (diagram) figura *f*

figure[2] *vi*

A (feature) figurar; **to ~ prominently** destacarse*

B (make sense) (colloq): **it just doesn't ~** no me lo explico

■ **figure** *vt* (reckon) (AmE colloq) calcular

Phrasal verbs

- **figure in** [v ▸ adv ▸ o] (AmE) incluir* (*en los cálculos*), contar*
- **figure on** [v ▸ prep ▸ o] (AmE colloq) contar* con

- **figure out** [v ▸ o ▸ adv, v ▸ adv ▸ o] 1 (understand) entender* 2 (calculate) ‹*sum/result*› calcular; ‹*problem*› resolver*
- **figure up** [v ▸ adv ▸ o] (AmE) sumar

figure: **~head** *n* (Naut) mascarón *m* de proa; **he's merely a ~head** no es más que una figura decorativa; **~ of eight**, (AmE also) **figure eight** *n* ocho *m*; **~ of speech** *n* (Ling, Lit) figura *f* retórica; **it's just a ~ of speech** es (sólo) un decir *or* una forma de hablar; **~ skating** *n* [u] patinaje *m* artístico

figurine /ˌfɪgjəˈriːn || ˌfɪgəˈriːn/ *n* figura *f*, estatuilla *f*

Fiji /ˈfiːdʒiː/ *n* Fiji

filament /ˈfɪləmənt/ *n* filamento *m*

filch /fɪltʃ/ *vt* (colloq) birlar (fam), afanar (arg)

file[1] /faɪl/ *n*

A (tool) lima *f*

B 1 (folder) carpeta *f*; (*box* ~) clasificador *m*, archivador *m*; (for card index) fichero *m* 2 (collection of documents) archivo *m*; (of a particular case) expediente *m*, dossier *m*; **they were keeping a ~ on him** lo tenían fichado; **to put sth on ~** archivar algo; **to be on ~** «*information*» estar* archivado 3 (Comput) archivo *m*; (*before n*) ‹*copy/extension/name*› de archivo *or* fichero

file[2] *vt*

A (sort) ‹*papers*› archivar

B ‹*application/complaint*› presentar; **to ~ a suit** presentar *or* entablar una demanda

C (Tech) ‹*metal*› limar; **to ~ one's nails** limarse las uñas

■ **file** *vi*

A (walk in line) (+ *adv compl*): **they ~d out of/into the room** salieron de/entraron en la habitación en fila; **the crowd ~d past the tomb** la multitud desfiló ante la tumba

B (Law): **to ~ for divorce** presentar una demanda de divorcio

file: **~ card** *n* (AmE) ficha *f*; **~ clerk** *n* (AmE) administrativo, -va *m,f* (*encargado de archivar*)

filibuster[1] /ˈfɪləbʌstər || ˈfɪlɪbʌstə(r)/ *vi* practicar* el obstruccionismo

filibuster[2] *n*: *intervención parlamentaria hecha con el propósito de impedir que un asunto se someta a votación*

filigree /ˈfɪləgriː || ˈfɪlɪgriː/ *n* [u] filigrana *f*; (*before n*) ‹*brooch*› de filigrana; ‹*decoration*› afiligranado

filing /ˈfaɪlɪŋ/ *n*: **there's a lot of ~ to do** hay mucho que archivar

filing: **~ cabinet** /ˈfaɪlɪŋ/ *n* archivador *m*, kárdex *m*; **~ clerk** *n* (BrE) ▸**file clerk**

filings /ˈfaɪlɪŋz/ *pl n* limaduras *fpl*

Filipino[1] /ˈfɪləˈpiːnəʊ || ˌfɪlɪˈpiːnəʊ/ *adj* filipino

Filipino[2] *n* (*pl* **-nos**) filipino, -na *m,f*

fill[1] /fɪl/ *vt*

A 1 (make full) **to ~ sth (WITH sth)** ‹*glass/room*› llenar algo (DE algo); ‹*cake/sandwich*› rellenar algo (DE algo); **he ~ed the tank with water** llenó el tanque de agua; **the wind ~ed the sails** el viento hinchó las velas; **the news ~ed us with anger** la noticia nos llenó de ira 2 ‹*area*› ocupar, llenar 3 (plug) ‹*hole/crack*› rellenar, tapar; ‹*tooth*› empastar, tapar (Andes), emplomar (RPl), calzar* (Col)

B ‹*need*› satisfacer*

C ‹*vacancy*› cubrir*, llenar

■ **fill** *vi* «*bath/auditorium*» **to ~ (WITH sth)** llenarse (DE algo); «*sails*» hincharse

(Phrasal verbs)

- **fill in**

A [v ▸ o ▸ adv, v ▸ adv ▸ o] 1 ‹*hole/outline*› rellenar 2 ‹*form*› rellenar, llenar 3 (write in) ‹*name/age*› poner*

B [v ▸ o ▸ adv] (inform) (colloq) **to ~ sb in (ON sth)** poner* a algn al corriente (DE algo)

C [v ▸ adv] (deputize) **to ~ in FOR sb** sustituir* *or* reemplazar* a algn

- **fill out**

A [v ▸ o ▸ adv, v ▸ adv ▸ o] ‹*form*› rellenar, llenar

B [v ▸ adv] 1 «*person*» engordar; **her face has ~ed out** se le ha llenado la cara, tiene la cara más llenita 2 «*sail*» hincharse

- **fill up**

A [v ▸ o ▸ adv, v ▸ adv ▸ o] (make full) llenar; **they give us bread to ~ us up** nos dan pan para llenarnos; **~ her up!** (Auto) ¡llénelo!, lleno, por favor; **to ~ sth up WITH sth** llenar algo DE algo

B [v ▸ adv] 1 (become full) llenarse 2 (buy fuel) echar *or* poner* gasolina

fill[2] *n*: **to eat/drink one's ~ of sth** (liter) comer/beber algo hasta saciarse; **to have had one's ~ of sth** estar* harto de algo

filler /ˈfɪlər || ˈfɪlə(r)/ *n*

A [u c] (for cracks) masilla *f*

B [c] (Journ) artículo *m* de relleno

fillet[1] /ˈfɪlət || ˈfɪlɪt/ *n* [u c] (Culin) (of beef) filete *m*, solomillo *m* (Esp), lomo *m* (AmS); (of pork) lomo *m*; (of fish) filete *m*; (*before n*) **a ~ steak** un filete, un solomillo de ternera (Esp), un bife de lomo (RPl)

fillet[2] *vt* ‹*meat*› cortar en filetes; ‹*fish*› quitarle la espina a

filling[1] /ˈfɪlɪŋ/ *n*

A [c] (Dent) empaste *m*, tapadura *f* (Chi, Méx), emplomadura *f* (RPl), calza *f* (Col)

B [u c] (Culin) relleno *m*

filling[2] *adj*: **pasta's very ~** la pasta llena mucho

filling station *n* ▸**gas station**

fillip /ˈfɪləp || ˈfɪlɪp/ *n* (*no pl*) estímulo *m*; **to give sth/sb a ~** estimular algo/a algn

filly /ˈfɪli/ (*pl* **-lies**) *n* potra *f*

film[1] /fɪlm/ *n*

A 1 [c u] (Phot) película *f* (fotográfica); **a (roll of) ~** un rollo *or* un carrete (de fotos), una película 2 [c] (movie) película *f*, film(e) *m* (period); (*before n*) **~ buff** cinéfilo, -la *m,f*; **~ festival** festival *m* cinematográfico *or* de cine; **the ~ industry** la industria cinematográfica; **~ star** estrella *f* de cine 3 [u] (cinematic art) cine *m*

B 1 [c] (thin covering) película *f* 2 [u] (wrap) film *m* *or* envoltura *f* transparente

film[2] *vt* ‹*scene*› filmar; ‹*novel/play*› llevar al cine

■ **film** *vi* rodar*, filmar; **~ing starts tomorrow** el rodaje *or* la filmación empieza mañana

> **film rating (US), film certificate (UK)**
>
> Una calificación que se otorga a las películas y videos. Establece la clase de público autorizado para verlos. En EEUU pueden tener seis calificaciones: G (*general audiences*) para todos los públicos; PG (*parental guidance*) es decir que los padres deciden si sus hijos pueden verlos; PH-13 (*parental guidance for children under 13*); R (*restricted*) es decir que los menores de 17 años sólo pueden verlos si están acompañados de uno de los padres o de su tutor; NC-17 (*no children-17*) que están prohibidos para menores de 17 años; X que sólo los pueden ver los mayores de 17 años. En Gran Bretaña las películas y los videos pueden tener 5 calificaciones: U, para todo público; PG, pueden verlos los niños si están acompañados de un adulto; 12, sólo para mayores de 12 años; 15, sólo para mayores de 15 años; 18, sólo para mayores de 18 años

filmstrip /ˈfɪlmstrɪp/ *n*: *película o serie de filminas para proyección fija*

Filofax® /ˈfaɪləfæks/ *n* filofax® *m*

filter[1] /ˈfɪltər || ˈfɪltə(r)/ *n*

A (device) filtro *m*; (*before n*) **~ coffee** café *m* americano

B (BrE Transp) flecha *f* (*que autoriza el giro a derecha o izquierda en algunos semáforos*); (*before n*) **~ lane** carril *m* de giro

filter[2] *vt* filtrar

■ **filter** *vi* (penetrate) «*gas/light/sound*» filtrarse; **the news finally ~ed through to us** al final nos llegó la noticia

(Phrasal verb)

- **filter out**

A [v ▸ adv] «*news*» filtrarse

B [v ▸ o ▸ adv, v ▸ adv ▸ o]: **the system ~s out the dust** el sistema elimina el polvo por un proceso de filtrado

filter-tipped /ˈfɪltərˈtɪpt || ˌfɪltəˈtɪpt/ *adj* con filtro

filth /fɪlθ/ *n* [u] 1 (dirt) mugre *f*, roña *f* 2 (obscene language, literature): **I've never heard/seen such ~!** ¡nunca he oído/visto una porquería *or* indecencia igual!

filthy[1] /ˈfɪlθi/ *adj* **-thier, -thiest** 1 (dirty) mugriento, roñoso 2 (obscene) ‹*books*› indecente; ‹*joke*› verde *or* picante *or* (Méx) colorado 3 (unpleasant) (BrE colloq) ‹*weather/habit*› asqueroso (fam)

f

filthy² *adv* (colloq) (*as intensifier*): **he's ~ rich** está podrido de dinero (fam), está podrido en plata (AmL fam); **it's ~ dirty** está mugriento *or* roñoso

filtration /fɪl'treɪʃən/ *n* [u] filtración *f*

fin /fɪn/ *n* aleta *f*

finagle /fɪ'neɪgəl/ *vt* (AmE colloq) ‹*deal/invitation*› arreglárselas para conseguir (fam)

final¹ /'faɪnl̩/ *adj*

A (last) (*before n*) último; **a ~ demand (for payment)** (Busn) un último aviso de pago; **I'd like to make one ~ point: ...** por último quisiera señalar que ...

B (definitive) final; **and that's my ~ word on the subject** y no se hable más del asunto; **you can't go and that's ~** no puedes ir y no hay más que hablar; **the judges' decision is ~** (frml) la decisión del jurado es inapelable

final² *n*

A (Games, Sport) (*often pl*) final *f*; **to go through to the ~s** pasar a la(s) final(es)

B finals *pl* (Educ) exámenes *mpl* finales

finale /fə'næli || fɪ'nɑːli/ *n* 1 (Mus) final *m* 2 (Theat) apoteosis *f*; (grand finish) apoteosis *f*, final *m* triunfal

finalist /'faɪnl̩əst || 'faɪnəlɪst/ *n* finalista *mf*

finality /faɪ'næləti/ *n* [u] (of decision) irrevocabilidad *f*, carácter *m* definitivo

finalize /'faɪnl̩aɪz || 'faɪnəlaɪz/ *vt* ‹*plans*› ultimar, concluir*; ‹*date*› fijar, concretar

finally /'faɪnl̩i || 'faɪnəli/ *adv* 1 (lastly) (*indep*) por último, finalmente 2 (at last) por fin, finalmente

finance¹ /fə'næns, faɪ- || 'faɪnæns, faɪ'næns/ *n* 1 [u] (banking, business) finanzas *fpl*; **high ~** altas finanzas 2 **finances** *pl* recursos *mpl* financieros, situación *f* financiera *or* económica 3 [u] (funding) financiación *f*, financiamiento *m* (esp AmL)

finance² *vt* ‹*project/trip*› financiar

finance: **~ Bill** *n* (Govt) proyecto *m* de ley presupuestaria; **~ company**, (BrE also) **~ house** *n* compañía *f* de crédito comercial, (sociedad *f* *or* casa *f*) financiera *f*

financial /fə'næntʃəl || faɪ'nænʃəl/ *adj* ‹*system/risk*› financiero; ‹*difficulties/independence*› económico; ‹*news*› (Journ) de economía, de negocios; **~ advice** asesoría *f* económica; **~ management** gestión *f* financiera

> **Financial Times Indices**
>
> Son listas que se publican diariamente en el *Financial Times* y que contienen los índices de los precios de las acciones en la Bolsa de Valores de Londres (*London Stock Exchange*). Sirven para mostrar la tendencia general de los mercados financieros de Gran Bretaña. El más conocido es el *FTSE 100 Share Index* y se calcula tomando como base el valor de las acciones de las 100 empresas más grandes de Gran Bretaña

financially /fə'næntʃəli || faɪ'nænʃəli/ *adv* ‹*independent/viable*› económicamente

financial: **~ statement** *n* estado *m* contable, estado *m* financiero; **~ year** *n* (BrE) (of company) ejercicio *m*; (of government) año *m* fiscal

financier /'fɪnən'sɪr || faɪ'nænsɪə(r)/ *n* financiero, -ra *m,f*

financing /fə'nænsɪŋ || faɪ'nænsɪŋ/ *n* financiación *f*

finch /fɪntʃ/ *n* pinzón *m*

find¹ /faɪnd/ (*past & past p* **found**) *vt*

A (sth lost or hidden) encontrar*; **I can't ~ it** no lo encuentro; ***to ~ one's way***: **it's difficult to ~ one's way around this town** es difícil orientarse en esta ciudad; **you'll soon ~ your way around the office** en poco tiempo te familiarizarás con la oficina; **can you ~ your way there?** ¿sabes ir?

B (come across) encontrar*; **I found the door wide open** encontré la puerta abierta de par en par; **there were no cherries to be found** no había cerezas por ninguna parte; **I hope this letter ~s you well** espero que al recibir esta carta te encuentres bien; **this species is found all over Europe** esta especie se encuentra en toda Europa

C 1 (discover) ‹*cause/answer*› encontrar*; **he was found to have AIDS** descubrieron que tenía el sida; **I found (that) it was easier to do it this way** descubrí que era más fácil hacerlo así; **I think you'll ~ (that) I'm right** ya verás como tengo razón 2 (Law): **to ~ sb guilty/not guilty** declarar *or* hallar a algn culpable/inocente; **how do you ~ the accused?** ¿cuál es su veredicto?

D (experience as) encontrar*; **she ~s him attractive** lo encuentra atractivo; **I ~ it difficult to concentrate** me es *or* me resulta difícil concentrarme; **I ~ that hard to believe!** ¡me cuesta creerlo!

E (acquire) encontrar*; **how are we going to ~ $20,000?** ¿cómo vamos a conseguir *or* de dónde vamos a sacar 20.000 dólares?

■ *v refl* **to ~ oneself** 1 (discover) (+ *adv compl*) encontrarse*; **I now ~ myself in a position to ...** ahora me encuentro en posición de ...; **I found myself unable to answer** fui *or* me vi incapaz de responder 2 (discover identity, vocation) encontrarse* a sí (*or* mí *etc*) mismo

■ **find** *vi* (Law) **to ~ FOR/AGAINST sb** fallar A FAVOR DE/CONTRA algn; **the judge found in the plaintiff's favor** el juez se pronunció a *or* en favor del demandante

Phrasal verb

• **find out**

A [v ▸ o ▸ adv, v ▸ adv ▸ o] (discover) ‹*truth*› descubrir*; ‹*information*› (by making enquiries) averiguar*; **I was afraid of being found out** tenía miedo de que me descubrieran; **to ~ sth out FROM sb**: **we're hoping to ~ out more from Robert** esperamos que Robert nos dé más información

B [v ▸ adv] 1 (learn) enterarse; **to ~ out ABOUT sth** enterarse DE algo 2 (make inquiries) averiguar*; **to ~ out ABOUT sth** informarse SOBRE algo

find² *n* hallazgo *m*; **to be a real ~** ser* todo un hallazgo

finder /'faɪndər || 'faɪndə(r)/ *n* (of treasure) descubridor, -dora *m,f*; **~s keepers: found it, it's mine! ~s keepers!** yo me lo encontré, así que me lo quedo

findings /'faɪndɪŋz/ *pl n* conclusiones *fpl*

fine¹ /faɪn/ *adj* **finer, finest**

A (*usu before n*) 1 (excellent) ‹*house/speech/example*› magnífico, excelente; ‹*wine/ingredients*› de primera calidad, selecto; **goods of the ~st quality** artículos *mpl* de la mejor calidad; **the country's ~st minds** los cerebros más brillantes del país 2 (iro): **a ~ friend you are!** ¡menudo *or* valiente amigo eres tú! (iró); **you've picked a ~ time to tell me!** ¡en buen momento me lo dices! (iró); **you're a ~ one to talk!** ¡mira quién habla! 3 (fair) ‹*weather*› bueno; **I hope it stays** *o* **keeps ~** espero que siga haciendo buen tiempo 4 (elegant) ‹*manners/gentleman/lady*› fino, refinado

B (colloq) (*pred*) 1 (in good health) muy bien 2 (OK) bien; (perfect) perfecto; **more wine? — no thanks; I'm ~** ¿más vino? — no, gracias, tengo suficiente; **that's ~ by me** por mí no hay problema

C 1 (thin) ‹*hair/thread*› fino, delgado; ‹*china*› fino 2 ‹*point/blade/rain/particles*› fino; ***to cut it/things ~*** no dejarse ningún margen de tiempo 3 ‹*workmanship*› fino, delicado; ‹*adjustment*› preciso

D (subtle) ‹*distinction/nuance*› sutil; ‹*judgment*› certero; ‹*balance*› delicado; **the ~r points of poetry** los matices más sutiles de la poesía; **there's a very ~ line between eccentricity and madness** la línea divisoria entre la excentricidad y la locura es muy tenue *or* sutil

fine² *adv* (adequately) bien; (very well) muy bien

fine³ *n* multa *f*

fine⁴ *vt* multar, ponerle* *or* aplicarle* una multa a

fine art *n* [u c] arte *m*; **the ~ ~s** las bellas artes; ***to have (got) sth down to a ~ ~*** hacer* algo a la perfección

finely /'faɪnli/ *adv* 1 (in small pieces): **to chop/dice sth ~** picar*/cortar algo muy fino *or* menudo 2 (subtly) ‹*adjust*› con precisión; **~ wrought** delicadamente trabajado

fine print *n* (AmE) **the ~ ~** la letra pequeña *or* menuda, la letra chica (AmL)

finery /'faɪnəri/ *n* [u]: **in all their ~** con sus mejores galas

finesse /fə'nes || fɪ'nes/ *n* [u] 1 (refinement) finura *f*, refinamiento *m* 2 (tact) diplomacia *f*

fine: **~-tooth(ed) comb** /'faɪn'tu:θ(t)/ *n* peine *m* de dientes finos *or* púas finas; ***to go over*** *o* ***through sth with a ~-tooth(ed) comb*** mirar algo con lupa; **~-tune** /'faɪn'tu:n || ˌfaɪn'tju:n/ *vt* ‹*engine*› ajustar, poner* a punto; ‹*receiver*› ajustar; ‹*plan*› afinar, poner* a punto

finger¹ /'fɪŋgər || 'fɪŋgə(r)/ *n* (of hand, glove) dedo *m*; **first** *o* **index ~** (dedo) índice *m*; **middle ~** (dedo) corazón *m* *or* medio *m*; **third** *o* **ring ~** (dedo) anular *m*; **fourth** *o* **little ~** (dedo) meñique *m*; **you can count on the ~s of one**

hand the number of times ... se pueden contar con los dedos de una mano las veces ...; ***not to lift*** *o* ***raise a ∼*** no mover* un dedo; ***to be all ∼s and thumbs*** (esp BrE) ser* torpe; ***to burn one's ∼s*** *o* ***get one's ∼s burned*** pillarse los dedos; ***to cross one's ∼s***: **well, here goes, ∼s crossed** bueno, ahí va ¡a ver si hay suerte!; **I'll keep my ∼s crossed for you** ojalá (que) tengas suerte; ***to have a ∼ in every pie*** estar* metido en todo; ***to have sticky ∼s*** tener* la mano larga; ***to lay a ∼ on sb***: **if you so much as lay a ∼ on her ...** si le llegas a poner la mano encima ...; ***not to lift a ∼ to do sth*** no levantar un dedo para hacer algo; ***to point the ∼ at sb*** culpar a algn; ***to pull*** *o* ***get one's ∼ out*** (BrE sl) (d)espabilarse (fam); ***to put one's ∼ on sth***: **there's something about him, I can't quite put my ∼ on it** tiene algo, no sabría decir concretamente qué es; ***to slip through sb's ∼s*** escapársele a algn de las manos; ***to snap one's ∼s*** chasquear *or* (Méx) tronar* los dedos; ***to work one's ∼s to the bone*** deslomarse trabajando

finger² *vt* (handle) toquetear, tentalear (Méx)

fingering /ˈfɪŋgərɪŋ/ *n* [u] (Mus) digitación *f*

finger: **∼mark** *n* marca *f*, huella *f*; **∼nail** *n* uña *f*; **∼print** *n* huella *f* digital *or* dactilar, impresión *f* digital; **∼tip** *n* yema *f* del dedo; ***to have sth at one's ∼tips*** saberse* algo al dedillo

finicky /ˈfɪnɪki/ *adj* (colloq) 1 (choosy) maniático, mañoso (AmL) 2 (overelaborate) recargado

finish¹ /ˈfɪnɪʃ/ *vt*

A 1 (complete) terminar, acabar; **we ∼ school/work at four o'clock today** hoy salimos a las cuatro; **to ∼ -ING** terminar *or* acabar DE + INF 2 (consume) ‹*drink/rations*› terminar, acabar

B (create surface texture on) ‹*cloth/porcelain*› terminar; ‹*wood*› pulir

C (destroy) (colloq) acabar con

■ **finish** *vi* terminar, acabar; **she ∼ed by summarizing the main points** concluyó resumiendo los puntos principales; **if you've quite ∼ed, may I get a word in?** (iró) si has acabado ya ¿me dejas meter baza? (iró); **to ∼ first/last** terminar en primer/último lugar

Phrasal verbs

• **finish off**

A [v ▸ o ▸ adv, v ▸ adv ▸ o] 1 (complete) terminar, acabar 2 (exhaust) dejar agotado *or* (fam) hecho polvo 3 (consume) terminar, acabar 4 (kill) matar, acabar con, liquidar (fam)

B [v ▸ adv] (conclude) terminar, acabar, concluir* (frml)

• **finish up**

A [v ▸ o ▸ adv, v ▸ adv ▸ o] ‹*food/paint*› terminar

B [v ▸ adv] (end up) acabar; **I knew he'd ∼ up crying** yo sabía que iba a terminar *or* acabar llorando

finish² *n*

A (*no pl*) 1 (end) fin *m*, final *m*; **a fight to the ∼** una lucha a muerte 2 (of race) llegada *f*; **it was a very close ∼** llegaron a la meta casi a la par

B (surface texture) acabado *m*; **a matt ∼** un acabado mate

finished /ˈfɪnɪʃt/ *adj*

A (*pred*) 1 (complete, achieved): **to get sth ∼** terminar *or* acabar algo; **to be ∼ WITH sth/sb**: **I'm ∼ with you!** tú y yo hemos acabado; **I'm ∼ with the scissors** no necesito más la tijera 2 (ruined) acabado; **he's ∼ as an actor** está acabado como actor 3 (exhausted) (colloq) muerto (fam)

B ‹*article*› terminado; **these clothes are very badly ∼** esta ropa está muy mal terminada *or* acabada

finishing /ˈfɪnɪʃɪŋ/: **∼ line** *n* (BrE) ▸**finish line**; **∼ school** *n*: *colegio privado para señoritas donde se aprende a comportarse en sociedad*; **∼ touch** *n*: **to add/put the ∼ touch(es) to sth** darle* los últimos toques a algo

finish line, (BrE) **finishing line** *n* meta *f*, línea *f* de llegada

finite /ˈfaɪnaɪt/ *adj*

A ‹*number/amount*› finito; **our resources are ∼** nuestros recursos son limitados

B (Ling) conjugado

fink¹ /fɪŋk/ *n* (AmE sl) 1 (contemptible person) mequetrefe *mf* (fam) 2 (informer) soplón, -plona *m,f* (fam) 3 (strike breaker) (pej) rompehuelgas *mf* (pey), esquirol, -rola *m,f* (Esp fam & pey), carnero, -ra (RPl fam & pey)

fink² *vi* (inform) (AmE sl) **to ∼ ON sb** delatar a algn, ir* con el soplo sobre algn

Phrasal verb

• **fink out** [v ▸ adv] (AmE sl) rajarse (arg), echarse atrás

Finland /ˈfɪnlənd/ *n* Finlandia *f*

Finn /fɪn/ *n* finlandés, -desa *m,f*, finés, -nesa *m,f*

Finnish¹ /ˈfɪnɪʃ/ *adj* finlandés, finés

Finnish² *n* [u] finlandés *m*

fiord /fiˈɔːrd || fiˈɔːd/ *n* fiordo *m*

fir /fɜːr || fɜː(r)/ *n* abeto *m*; (*before n*) **∼ cone** (BrE) piña *f*

fire¹ /faɪr || ˈfaɪə(r)/ *n*

A 1 [u] (flames) fuego *m*; **to be on ∼** estar* en llamas, estar* ardiendo; **to set sth on ∼** *o* **to set ∼ to sth** prenderle fuego a algo; **to catch ∼** prender fuego; «*twigs*» prender; **∼ and brimstone** el fuego eterno, los tormentos del infierno; ***to fight ∼ with ∼*** pagar* con la misma moneda; ***to play with ∼*** jugar* con fuego; ***to set the world on ∼*** comerse el mundo 2 [c] (outdoors) hoguera *f*, fogata *f*; **wood ∼** fuego *m* de leña 3 [c] (in hearth) fuego *m*, lumbre *f* (liter)

B [c] (blaze which destroys a building) incendio *m*; (*as interj*) **∼!** ¡fuego!; (*before n*) **∼ curtain** telón *m* contra incendios; **this is a ∼ hazard** esto podría causar un incendio

C [c] (heater) (BrE) estufa *f*, calentador *m*

D [u] (of guns) fuego *m*; **to open ∼ on sb/sth** abrir* fuego sobre algn/algo; **to exchange ∼** tirotearse; **to come under ∼** «*troops*» entrar en la línea de fuego; «*politician*» ser* el blanco de las críticas; ***to hang ∼*** esperar, aguantarse (AmS)

fire² *vt*

A 1 ‹*gun/shot*› disparar; ‹*rocket*› lanzar* 2 (direct) **to ∼ questions at sb** hacerle* *or* lanzarle* preguntas a algn

B (dismiss) (colloq) echar, despedir*; **she was ∼d** la echaron, la despidieron; **you're ∼d!** ¡queda usted despedido!

C (stimulate) ‹*imagination*› avivar; **to ∼ sb with enthusiasm** llenar de entusiasmo a algn

D ‹*pottery*› cocer*

■ **fire** *vi* (shoot) disparar, hacer* fuego; **to ∼ AT sb/sth** disparar CONTRA algn/algo, dispararle A algn/algo; **to ∼ ON sb** disparar SOBRE algn; **ready, aim** *o* (BrE) **take aim, ∼!** apunten ¡fuego!

Phrasal verbs

• **fire away** [v ▸ adv] (colloq) (*usu in imperative*): **there are some questions I'd like to ask you — ∼ away!** quisiera hacerte unas preguntas — ¡adelante! *or* (AmL tb) ¡pregunta nomás!

• **fire off** [v ▸ o ▸ adv, v ▸ adv ▸ o] ‹*round of bullets*› disparar; ‹*questions*› lanzar*

fire: **∼ alarm** *n* (apparatus) alarma *f* contra incendios; (signal) alarma *f*; **∼arm** *n* arma *f*‡ de fuego; **∼ball** *n* (in nuclear explosion) bola *f* de fuego

firebomb¹ /ˈfaɪrbɑːm || ˈfaɪəbɒm/ *n* bomba *f* incendiaria

firebomb² *vt* bombardear (*con bombas incendiarias*)

fire: **∼brand** *n* (person) activista *mf*, agitador, -dora *m,f*; **∼ brigade** *n* (esp BrE) cuerpo *m* de bomberos; **∼ company** *n* (AmE) equipo *m* *or* (Esp) retén *m* *or* (Chi) compañía *f* de bomberos; **∼cracker** *n* petardo *m*

-fired /ˌfaɪrd || ˌfaɪəd/ *suff*: **oil∼/coal∼ heating** calefacción *f* a gas-oil/carbón

fire: **∼ department** *n* (AmE) cuerpo *m* de bomberos; **∼ door** *n* puerta *f* contra incendios, puerta *f* cortafuegos; **∼ drill** *n* simulacro *m* de incendio; **∼-eater** *n* tragafuegos *m*; **∼ engine** *n* (BrE) ▸**∼ truck**; **∼ escape** *n* escalera *f* de incendios; **∼ exit** *n* salida *f* de incendios; **∼ extinguisher** *n* extinguidor *m* (de incendios) (AmL), extintor *m* (Esp); **∼fighter** *n* bombero *mf*; **∼fly** *n* luciérnaga *f*; **∼ guard** *n* rejilla *f* (*de chimenea*); **∼ hydrant** *n* boca *f* de incendios *or* (Esp) de riego, hidrante *m* de incendios (AmC, Col), grifo *m* (Chi); **∼ irons** *pl n* accesorios *mpl* para la chimenea; **∼light** *n* [u] luz *f* de la lumbre *or* del hogar; **∼lighter** *n*: *líquido o pastilla utilizados para facilitar el encendido del fuego de leña o carbón*; **∼man** /ˈfaɪrmən || ˈfaɪəmən/ (*pl* **-men** /-mən/) *n* 1 (firefighter) bombero *mf*; 2 (Rail) fogonero *m*; **∼place** *n* chimenea *f*, hogar *m*; **∼plug** *n* (AmE) ▸**∼ hydrant**; **∼power** *n* [u] potencia *f* de fuego; **∼proof** *adj* ‹*material*› ignífugo, incombustible; **∼-resistant** /ˈfaɪrrɪˈzɪstənt || ˈfaɪərɪˌzɪstənt/ *adj* incombustible, ignífugo; **∼ screen** *n* pantalla *f* (*de chimenea*); **∼side** *n* [u] hogar *m*; **we sat by the ∼side** nos

sentamos al calor del fuego, nos sentamos junto a la chimenea *or* junto al hogar; **~ station** *n* estación *f* *or* (Esp) parque *m* *or* (RPl) cuartel *m* de bomberos, bomba *f* (Chi); **~trap** *n*: *edificio peligroso en caso de incendio*; **~ truck** *n* (AmE) carro *m* *or* (Esp) coche *m* de bomberos, autobomba *m* (RPl), bomba *f* (Chi); **~wall** /'faɪrwɔːl || 'faɪəwɔːl/ *n*
A (in building) muro *m* cortafuego(s);
B (Comput) fire wall *f*, *barrera de control de accesos*; **~wood** *n* [u] leña *f*; **~work** *n* dispositivo *m* pirotécnico (frml); **~works** fuegos *mpl* artificiales *or* de artificio; (*before n*) **~work(s) display** fuegos *mpl* artificiales *or* de artificio

firing /'faɪrɪŋ || 'faɪərɪŋ/ *n* [u] (shots) disparos *mpl*

firing: **~ line** *n*: ***to be on*** *o* (BrE) ***in the ~ line*** (exposed to criticism) estar* expuesto a las críticas; (Mil) estar* en la línea de combate *or* de fuego; **~ squad** *n* pelotón *m* de fusilamiento

firm¹ /fɜːrm || fɜːm/ *adj*
A 1 (secure) ‹*grasp*› firme; **he has a ~ handshake** da la mano con fuerza 2 (not yielding) ‹*surface/muscles*› firme; ‹*mattress*› duro; ‹*foundation*› sólido 3 (not declining) ‹*currency/market*› firme, fuerte; **the dollar remained ~ against other currencies** el dólar se mantuvo frente a otras monedas
B 1 (steadfast) ‹*friendship*› sólido; ‹*support*› firme; **he is ~ favorite to win the race** es el gran favorito de la carrera; **she is ~ in her convictions** se mantiene firme en sus convicciones 2 (strict) estricto, firme; **to take a ~ line** *o* **stand on sth** ponerse* firme sobre algo
C (definite) ‹*offer/date*› en firme

firm² *n* empresa *f*, firma *f*, compañía *f*

firm³ *vt* **~ (up)** ‹*muscles*› endurecer*

Phrasal verb

• **firm up** [v ▸ adv ▸ o] ‹*price/date/deal*› concretar, confirmar

firmament /'fɜːrməmənt || 'fɜːməmənt/ *n* (liter) firmamento *m* (liter)

firmly /'fɜːrmli || 'fɜːmli/ *adv* ‹*grasp/believe*› con firmeza, firmemente; ‹*fixed/supported/committed*› firmemente

first¹ /fɜːrst || fɜːst/ *adj*
A 1 (initial) primero [**primero** *becomes* **primer** *when it precedes a masculine singular noun*] **the ~ president of the USA** el primer presidente de los EE UU; **Henry I** *(léase: Henry the First)* Enrique I *(read as: Enrique primero)*; **who's going to be ~?** ¿quién va a ser el primero?; **our horse was ~** nuestro caballo llegó en primer lugar *or* el primero; **~ things ~** primero lo más importante 2 (in seniority, standing) primero; **the ~ eleven/fifteen** (BrE) el equipo titular; **she's ~ in line to the throne** está primera *or* es la primera en la línea de sucesión al trono
B (elliptical use): **he'll be arriving on the ~ (of the month)** llegará el primero *or* (Esp tb) el uno (del mes); **he fell at the ~** cayó en la primera valla (*or* el primer obstáculo *etc*); **he/she was the ~ to arrive** fue el primero/la primera en llegar; **he came in an easy ~** ganó fácilmente; **the ~ she knew about it was when ...** la primera noticia que tuvo de ello fue cuando ...
C (*in phrases*) **at first** al principio; **from the first** desde el principio, desde el primer momento; **from first to last** de(l) principio a(l) fin

first² *adv*
A 1 (ahead of others) primero; **he came ~ in the exam** sacó la mejor nota en el examen; **which comes ~, your family or your career?** ¿para ti qué está primero, tu familia o tu carrera?; **I always put my children ~** para mí antes que nada *or* primero están mis hijos; **ladies ~** primero las damas; ***~ come, ~ served***: **tickets will be available on a ~ come, ~ served basis** se adjudicará(n) las entradas por riguroso orden de solicitud (*or* llegada *etc*) 2 (before other actions, events) primero, en primer lugar; **~, I want to thank everyone for coming** en primer lugar *or* primero quiero agradecerles a todos que hayan venido 3 (beforehand) antes, primero 4 (for the first time) por primera vez; **when I ~ met him** cuando lo conocí 5 (rather) antes; **form a coalition? I'd resign ~** ¿formar una coalición? ¡antes (que eso) renuncio!
B (*in phrases*) **first and foremost** ante todo; **first and last** por encima de todo; **first of all** en primer lugar, antes que nada

first³ *n* 1 **~ (gear)** (Auto) (*no art*) primera *f* 2 (original idea, accomplishment) primicia *f*; **another ~ for Acme Corp** otra primicia de Acme Corp 3 (BrE Educ) *nota más alta de la escala de calificaciones de un título universitario*

first: **~ aid** *n* [u] primeros auxilios *mpl*; **to give ~ aid** prestar los primeros auxilios; (*before n*) **~-aid kit** botiquín *m* (de primeros auxilios); **~-aid station** *o* (BrE) **post** puesto *m* de primeros auxilios; **~ base** *n* [u] (AmE Sport) primera base *f*, inicial *f*; ***not to reach*** *o* ***get to ~ base*** (colloq) quedar(se) en agua de borrajas *or* en nada; **~ baseman** /'beɪsmən/ *n* (*pl* **-men** /-mən/) (AmE) primera base *m*, inicialista *m*; **~-born** *adj* (frml) (*before n*) ‹*child*› primogénito; **~ class** *adv* ‹*travel*› en primera (clase); **~-class** /'fɜːrst'klæs || ,fɜːst'klɑːs/ *adj* (*pred* **~ class**) 1 (of highest grade) ‹*hotel/ticket*› de primera clase; ‹*travel*› en primera (clase); **she has a ~-class degree** (BrE) ≈ se recibió con la nota más alta (*en AmL*), ≈ sacó la carrera con matrícula de honor (*en Esp*) 2 (excellent) de primera, de primer orden 3 (BrE Corresp) **~-class mail** *o* **post** *correspondencia enviada a una tarifa superior, que garantiza una rápida entrega*; **~-day cover** /'fɜːrst'deɪ || 'fɜːstdeɪ/ *n* sobre *m* del primer día; **~ edition** *n* [u c] primera edición *f*, edición *f* príncipe; **~ grade** *n* (AmE) primer año (*de la escuela primaria*), ≈ primero *m* de EGB (*en Esp*)

first-hand¹ /'fɜːrst'hænd || ,fɜːst'hænd/ *adj* ‹*news*› de primera mano

first-hand² *adv* directamente

first: **~ lady** *n* primera dama *f*; **~ light** *n* madrugada *f*; **at ~ light** al alba, de madrugada

firstly /'fɜːrstli || 'fɜːstli/ *adv* (*as linker*) en primer lugar, primeramente

first: **~ mate** *n* primer, -mera oficial *m,f*, segundo, -da de a bordo *m,f*; **~ name** *n* nombre *m* de pila; (*before n*) **to be on ~-name terms (with sb)** ≈ tutearse *or* tratarse de tú con algn; **~ officer** *n* ▸ **~ mate**; **~ person** *n* **the ~ person singular/plural** la primera persona del singular/plural; **~-rate** /'fɜːrst'reɪt || ,fɜːst'reɪt/ *adj* de primera, de primer orden; **~-time** *adj* (*before n*): **~-time buyer** *persona que compra algo, gen una vivienda, por primera vez*

firth /fɜːrθ || fɜːθ/ *n* (in Scotland) estuario *m*

fiscal /'fɪskəl/ *adj* ‹*policy*› fiscal; ‹*restraint*› monetario

fiscal year *n* (AmE) año *m* fiscal

fish¹ /fɪʃ/ *n* (*pl* **fish** *or* **fishes**) 1 [c] (Zool) pez *m*; ***like a ~ out of water*** (in unusual situation) como gallina en corral ajeno (fam); ***there are plenty more ~ in the sea*** hay mucho más donde elegir; ***to be a big ~ in a little pond*** ser* un pez gordo (*en un lugar pequeño*); ***to drink like a ~*** beber como un cosaco (fam), chupar como una esponja (fam); ***to have other ~ to fry*** tener* cosas mejores *or* más importantes que hacer; ***to swim like a ~*** nadar como un pez; (*before n*) **~ market** mercado *m* de pescado; **~ pond** estanque *m*; **~ tank** pecera *f* 2 [u] (Culin) pescado *m*; **wet ~** (BrE) pescado *m* fresco; **~ and chips** (esp BrE) pescado *m* frito con papas *or* (Esp) patatas fritas; ***neither ~, flesh, nor fowl*** ni chicha ni limonada *or* limoná (fam) 3 (person) (colloq): **he's a queer ~** es un tipo raro; **he's rather a cold ~** es un tipo seco

fish² *vi* 1 pescar*; **to go ~ing** ir* de pesca, ir* a pescar; **to ~ FOR sth** ‹*for trout*› pescar* algo; ‹*for compliments/information*› andar* a la caza de algo 2 (search) rebuscar*; **to ~ (around) in one's pockets/bag** rebuscar* en los bolsillos/la bolsa

■ **fish** *vt* 1 ‹*cod/mackerel*› pescar* 2 ‹*river/lake*› pescar* en

Phrasal verb

• **fish out** [v ▸ o ▸ adv, v ▸ adv ▸ o] sacar*; **to ~ sth out OF sth** sacar* algo DE algo

fish: **~bone** *n* espina *f* (*de pez*); **~cake** *n* ≈ croqueta *f* (*de pescado y papas*)

fisherman /'fɪʃərmən || 'fɪʃəmən/ *n* (*pl* **-men** /-mən/) pescador *m*

fishery /'fɪʃəri/ *n* (*pl* **-eries**)
A ▸ **fish farm**
B **fisheries** *pl* 1 (industry) industria *f* pesquera, pesca *f* 2 (area) pesquería *f*

fish: **~ farm** *n* piscifactoría *f*; **~ farming** *n* [u] piscicultura *f*; **~ finger** *n* (BrE) ▸ **fish stick**; **~hook** *n* anzuelo *m*

fishing /ˈfɪʃɪŋ/ *n* [u] 1 (professional) pesca *f*; (*before n*) ‹*industry/port*› pesquero 2 (amateur) pesca *f*; (*before n*) ‹*club/season*› de pesca; **~ tackle** aparejos *mpl* de pesca

fishing: **~ boat** *n* lancha *f or* barca *f* pesquera *or* de pesca, bote *m* pesquero *or* de pesca; **~ net** *n* red *f* de pesca; **~ pole** (AmE), **~ rod** *n* caña *f* de pescar

fish: **~monger** /ˈfɪʃˌmɑːŋgər || ˈfɪʃˌmʌŋgə(r)/ *n* (BrE) pescadero, -ra *m,f*; **at the ~monger('s)** en la pescadería; **~net** *n* 1 [c] (AmE) ▸**fishing net** 2 [u] (Tex) red *f*; (*before n*) ‹*stockings*› de malla gruesa *or* de red; **~ slice** *n* (BrE) espumadera *f*, espátula *f* (*para fritos*); **~ stick** *n* (AmE) palito *m* de bacalao (*or* merluza *etc*) (*trozo de pescado rebozado y frito*); **~tail** *vi* (AmE) colear; **~wife** *n* (colloq & pej) verdulera *f* (fam & pey)

fishy /ˈfɪʃi/ *adj* **-fishier, -fishiest**
A (of fish) ‹*smell/taste*› a pescado
B (suspicious) (colloq) ‹*story*› sospechoso; **it sounds a bit ~ to me** me huele mal *or* (Esp) me huele a chamusquina (fam)

fission /ˈfɪʃən/ *n* [u] fisión *f*

fissure /ˈfɪʃər || ˈfɪʃə(r)/ *n* (frml) (in rock) fisura *f*

fist /fɪst/ *n* puño *m*; **to clench one's ~** cerrar* el puño; **to shake one's ~ at sb** amenazar* a algn con el puño

fistfight /ˈfɪstfaɪt/ *n* pelea *f* (*a puñetazos*)

fistful /ˈfɪstfʊl/ *n* puñado *m*

fit¹ /fɪt/ *adj* **-tt-**
A 1 (healthy) en forma, sano; **to get/keep ~** ponerse*/mantenerse* en forma; **to be ~ FOR sth**: **the soldiers were passed ~ for duty** los soldados fueron declarados aptos (para el servicio); **I feel ~ for anything today** hoy me siento capaz de cualquier cosa; **to be ~ to + INF** ‹*to play/travel*› estar* en condiciones DE + INF 2 (colloq) (good-looking) guapo, de buena pinta, buen mozo (esp AmL)
B 1 (suitable) ‹*person/conduct*› adecuado, apropiado; **to be ~ FOR sth/sb**: **this book is not ~ for children** este libro no es apto *or* apropriado para niños; **this car is only ~ for the scrapheap** este coche es pura chatarra; **a feast ~ for a king** un banquete digno de reyes; **to be ~ to + INF**: **this isn't ~ to eat** (harmful) esto no está en buenas condiciones; (unappetizing) esto está incomible; **he's not ~ to be a father** no es digno de ser padre; **you're not ~ to be seen** estás impresentable 2 (right) (*pred*) **to see ~ to + INF**: **he did not see ~ to reply to our letter** ni se dignó contestar a nuestra carta; **to think ~ TO + INF** estimar conveniente + INF, creer* apropiado + INF
C (ready) **to be ~ to + INF**: **I felt ~ to drop** me sentía a punto de caer* agotada; **to laugh ~ to burst** desternillarse de risa; ▸**tie²** *vt* **A2**

fit² **-tt-** *vt*
A 1 (Clothing): **the dress ~s you perfectly** el vestido te queda perfecto; **the jacket doesn't ~ me** la chaqueta no me queda bien 2 (be right size, shape for) ‹*socket*› encajar en 3 (correspond to) ‹*theory*› concordar* con; **we have nobody ~ting that description** no tenemos a nadie que responda a esa descripción; **the punishment must ~ the crime** el castigo debe ser acorde con el delito
B (install) (esp BrE) ‹*carpet/lock*› poner*, colocar*; ‹*double glazing*› instalar; **he ~ted the two halves together** unió *or* encajó las dos mitades; **to ~ sth WITH sth** equipar algo CON algo; **a kitchen ~ted with the latest appliances** una cocina equipada con los últimos electrodomésticos; **the car is ~ted with leather upholstery** el coche está tapizado en cuero; **he's been ~ted with a pacemaker** le han colocado *or* puesto un marcapasos
C 1 (accommodate) **to ~ sth INTO sth** meter algo EN algo; **they managed to ~ everybody into one small room** lograron meter a todo el mundo en una habitación pequeña 2 (adjust) **to ~ sth TO sth** adecuar* algo A algo 3 (make suitable) **to ~ sb FOR sth/-ING** capacitar a algn PARA algo/INF
D (Clothing) ‹*dress/suit*› **to ~ sb FOR sth** tomarle medidas a algn PARA algo
■ **fit** *vi* 1 (Clothing): **these shoes don't ~** estos zapatos no me quedan bien; **to make sth ~** ajustar algo; ***if the shoe*** *o* (BrE) ***cap ~s wear it*** al que le caiga *or* venga el sayo que se lo ponga (AmL), quien se pica ajos come (Esp) 2 (be right size, shape) «*lid*» ajustar; «*key/peg*» encajar; **to make sth ~** hacer* ajustar/encajar algo 3 (correspond) «*facts/description*» encajar, cuadrar; **those jeans don't ~ with your smart image** esos vaqueros no van con tu imagen de hombre elegante

Phrasal verbs

• **fit in**
A [v ▸ adv] 1 (have enough room) caber* 2 (go) ir*; **the battery ~s in there** la pila va allí 3 (accord) «*detail/event*» concordar*, cuadrar; **to ~ in WITH sth** concordar* *or* cuadrar CON algo 4 (belong): **she doesn't ~ in here** esto no es para ella, ella no encaja aquí 5 (adjust, conform to) **to ~ in WITH sb/sth**: **he'll have to ~ in with our plans** tendrá que amoldarse a nuestros planes; **she never ~ted in with the rest** nunca se integró con los demás
B [v ▸ o ▸ adv, v ▸ adv ▸ o] 1 (find space for) acomodar 2 (fix in place) colocar* 3 (find time for): **I can ~ you in at ten o'clock** puedo atenderla *or* hacerle un hueco a las diez; **she hoped to ~ in some sightseeing** esperaba tener un poco de tiempo para salir a conocer el lugar; **I don't know how you ~ it all in** no sé cómo te las arreglas para encontrar tiempo para todo

• **fit out** [v ▸ o ▸ adv, v ▸ adv ▸ o] equipar; **to ~ sb out WITH sth** ‹*with boots/equipment*› equipar a algn CON algo; ‹*with uniform*› proveer* a algn DE algo

• **fit up** [v ▸ o ▸ adv, v ▸ adv ▸ o] (equip) (BrE) **to ~ sb up WITH sth** proveer* a algn DE algo; **to ~ sth up AS sth**: **we can ~ the garage up as a studio** podemos acondicionar el garaje para usarlo como estudio

fit³ *n*
A 1 (attack) ataque *m*; **epileptic ~** ataque epiléptico; **fainting ~** síncope *m*; ***to give sb a ~*** (colloq) darle* a algn un soponcio (fam); ***to have*** *o* ***throw a ~*** (colloq): **I nearly had a ~** casi me da un ataque *or* un síncope (fam) 2 (short burst): **a ~ of coughing** un acceso de tos; **a ~ of laughter** un ataque de risa; **a ~ of jealousy** un arrebato *or* arranque de celos; ***to have sb in ~s*** (colloq) hacer* partirse de risa a algn (fam); **we were in ~s** nos estábamos muriendo de risa; ***by*** *o* ***in ~s and starts*** a los tropezones, a trancas y barrancas
B (of size, shape) (*no pl*): **my new jacket is a good/bad ~** la chaqueta nueva me queda bien/mal; **I prefer a looser ~** prefiero la ropa más holgada; **it's a tight ~** (clothes) es muy entallado; (in confined space) **can we all get in? — it'll be a tight ~** ¿cabemos todos? — vamos a estar muy apretados

fitful /ˈfɪtfəl/ *adj* ‹*progress/sunshine*› intermitente, irregular; ‹*sleep*› irregular

fitfully /ˈfɪtfəli/ *adv* ‹*sleep/work*› de manera irregular

fitment /ˈfɪtmənt/ *n* 1 (esp BrE Const) *elemento del mobiliario o instalaciones* 2 (fitting) accesorio *m*

fitness /ˈfɪtnəs || ˈfɪtnɪs/ *n* [u]
A (healthiness) salud *f*; **(physical) ~** (buena) forma *f* física, (buen) estado *m* físico
B (suitability) aptitud *f*, capacidad *f*

fitted /ˈfɪtəd || ˈfɪtɪd/ *adj* 1 ‹*cupboard*› empotrado; ‹*shelves*› hecho a medida; ‹*sheet*› ajustable, de cajón (Méx); **~ carpet** (esp BrE) alfombra *f* de pared a pared, moqueta *f* (Esp) 2 ‹*kitchen*› integral, con armarios empotrados 3 (Clothing) ‹*jacket/waist*› entallado

fitter /ˈfɪtər || ˈfɪtə(r)/ *n*
A (Clothing) probador, -dora *m,f*
B (Tech) (mechanic — in garage) mecánico, -ca *m,f*; (— in car industry, shipbuilding) operario, -ria *m,f*

fitting¹ /ˈfɪtɪŋ/ *adj* ‹*conclusion*› adecuado; ‹*tribute*› digno; **it is ~ that he should be buried there** lo que corresponde es que se lo entierre allí

fitting² *n*
A (Clothing) 1 (trying on) prueba *f* 2 (BrE) (size — of clothes) medida *f*; (— of shoe) horma *f*
B 1 (accessory) accesorio *m* 2 **fittings** *pl* (esp BrE Const) accesorios *mpl*; **electrical ~s** instalaciones *fpl* eléctricas; **bathroom ~s** grifería *f* y accesorios *mpl* de baño

fitting room *n* probador *m*

five¹ /faɪv/ *n* cinco *m*; *see also* **four¹**

five² *adj* cinco *adj inv*; *see also* **four²**

five: **~-and-dime** /ˈfaɪvənˈdaɪm/, **~-and-ten** /-ˈten/ *n* (AmE) baratillo *m*; **~-a-side** /ˈfaɪvəˈsaɪd/ *n* [u] (Sport) *also* **~-a-side football** (BrE) fútbol *m* sala, futbito *m* (Esp), futbolito *m* (Chi, Col); **~fold** *adj/adv see* **-fold**

fiver /ˈfaɪvər || ˈfaɪvə(r)/ *n* 1 ($5) (AmE sl) cinco dólares *mpl or* (AmL fam) verdes *mpl* 2 (£5) (BrE colloq) cinco libras *fpl*

fix¹ /fɪks/ *vt*

(Sense I)

A 1 (secure) ‹*plank/shelf*› sujetar, asegurar; **to ~ a notice on a door** poner* un anuncio en una puerta; **to ~ sth TO sth** sujetar algo A algo 2 (implant): **to ~ sth in one's memory** grabar algo en la memoria

B 1 (direct steadily): **his eyes were ~ed on the road ahead** tenía la mirada fija en la carretera 2 (look at): **he ~ed her with a stony gaze** clavó en ella una mirada glacial

(Sense II)

A 1 (establish) ‹*date/time/price*› fijar; ‹*details*› concretar 2 (organize) arreglar; **how are you ~ed for next weekend?** ¿qué planes tienes para el fin de semana?

B (repair) (colloq) ‹*car/clock/kettle*› arreglar

C (esp AmE) 1 (prepare) (colloq) preparar 2 (make presentable): **to ~ one's hair/face** arreglarse el pelo/pintarse

D (colloq) ‹*election/contest*› amañar (fam), arreglar (fam)

■ **fix** *vi* (make plans, intend) (AmE): **we're ~ing to go fishing on Sunday** estamos planeando ir de pesca el domingo; **we've ~ed to meet them at one** hemos quedado (en encontrarnos) con ellos a la una

(Phrasal verbs)

- **fix on** [v ▸ prep ▸ o] decidirse por
- **fix up**

A [v ▸ o ▸ adv, v ▸ adv ▸ o] 1 (provide for): **I need somewhere to stay: can you ~ me up?** necesito alojamiento ¿me lo puedes arreglar?; **she ~ed me up with a job** me encontró *or* consiguió un trabajo 2 (organize) organizar*; **I'll ~ things up with her** lo arreglaré con ella 3 (repair) ‹*house/room*› (AmE) arreglar

B [v ▸ adv] (make arrangements) (BrE colloq) arreglar

- **fix upon** ▸ **fix on**

fix² *n*

A (predicament) (colloq) aprieto *m*, apuro *m*

B (of drug) (sl) dosis *f*; (shot) pinchazo *m*

C (Aviat, Naut) posición *f*; **to get a ~ on sth** ‹‹*sailor/airman*›› establecer* la posición de algo

fixation /fɪk'seɪʃən/ *n* [c] obsesión *f*, fijación *f*

fixative /'fɪksətɪv/ *n* [u c] 1 (adhesive) adhesivo *m* 2 (varnish) (BrE) fijador *m*

fixed /fɪkst/ *adj*

A 1 (unchanging) ‹*price/rate/ideas*› fijo; ‹*principles/position*› rígido 2 (prearranged) ‹*date/time*› fijado; **a ~-term contract** un contrato a plazo fijo

B (steady) ‹*gaze*› fijo; ‹*smile*› petrificado

C (provided with) (colloq): **how are you ~ for money/time?** ¿qué tal andas *or* estás de dinero/tiempo? (fam)

fixed: **~ assets** *pl n* activo *m* fijo; **~ capital** *n* capital *m* fijo *or* permanente; **~-interest** /'fɪkst'ɪntrəst/ *adj* a interés fijo; **~-rate** /'fɪkst'reɪt/ *adj* a una tasa de interés fija *or* (esp Esp) a tipo de interés fijo

fixings /'fɪksɪŋz/ *pl n* (AmE colloq) guarnición *f*, acompañamiento *m*

fixture /'fɪkstʃər || 'fɪkstʃə(r)/ *n*

A 1 (in building) *elemento de la instalación, como los artefactos del baño, cocina etc* 2 (permanent feature) parte *f* integrante; **she's become a ~ here** (hum) ya forma parte del mobiliario (hum)

B (BrE Sport) encuentro *m*; (*before n*) **~ list** programa *m* de encuentros

fizz¹ /fɪz/ *vi* 1 (hiss) silbar 2 ‹‹*champagne/cola*›› burbujear, hacer* burbujas

fizz² *n* [u] 1 (of champagne, soda water) burbujeo *m*, efervescencia *f* 2 (liveliness) chispa *f*

fizzle /'fɪzəl/ *vi* (fail) (AmE) fracasar

(Phrasal verb)

- **fizzle out** [v ▸ adv] ‹‹*fire/firework*›› apagarse*; ‹‹*excitement*›› esfumarse, quedar en nada

fizzy /'fɪzi/ *adj* **-zier, -ziest** gaseoso, efervescente, con gas

fjord /fi'ɔ:rd || fi'ɔ:d/ *n* fiordo *m*

FL, Fla = **Florida**

flab /flæb/ *n* [u] (colloq) gordura *f* (*fofa*)

flabbergasted /'flæbər,gæstəd || 'flæbə,gɑ:stɪd/ *adj* estupefacto, atónito, pasmado (fam)

flabby /'flæbi/ *adj* **-bier, -biest** ‹*stomach*› fofo, bofo (Mex fam); ‹*muscle*› flojo, blando

flaccid /'flæsəd, 'flæksəd || 'flæsɪd, 'flæksɪd/ *adj* (frml) fláccido

flag¹ /flæg/ *n*

A 1 (of nation, organization) bandera *f*, pabellón *m* (frml); (pennant) banderín *m*; **to sail under the Panamanian ~** navegar* con bandera panameña *or* (frml) con pabellón panameño; ***to keep the ~ flying*** (maintain traditions) mantener* las tradiciones de la patria; ***to put the ~s out*** celebrar algo por todo lo alto; ***to show*** *o* ***fly the ~*** hacer* patria, dejar bien puesta la bandera 2 (as marker, signal) bandera *f*; **to fly** *o* **wave the white ~** enarbolar la bandera blanca

B (on chart) banderita *f*

C (Comput) indicador *m*, bandera *f*

D (AmE) 1 (in taxi) bandera *f* 2 (on mailbox) *banderita metálica que indica que hay correo para recoger*

E **~(stone)** (on pavement) losa *f*, piedra *f*

flag² **-gg-** *vi* 1 ‹‹*person/animal*›› desfallecer*, flaquear 2 ‹‹*interest/conversation/spirits*›› decaer*; ‹‹*attendance*›› disminuir*, bajar; **their strength ~ged** les fallaron *or* les flaquearon las fuerzas 3 **flagging** *pres p* ‹*enthusiasm/interest/confidence*› cada vez menor

■ **flag** *vt* 1 (mark with flags) marcar* *or* señalar con banderas 2 (mark for special attention) marcar*

(Phrasal verb)

- **flag down** [v ▸ o ▸ adv, v ▸ adv ▸ o] ‹*car/motorist*› parar (*haciendo señas*)

flag day *n* 1 **Flag Day** (AmE) (el) Día de la Bandera 2 (BrE) *día en que se lleva a cabo una colecta callejera para una obra benéfica*

Flag Day

Es el día de la bandera en EEUU. Se celebra el 14 de junio para conmemorar el día, en 1777, en que **Stars and Stripes** pasó a ser el emblema oficial del país

flagellate /'flædʒəleɪt/ *vt* flagelar

flagon /'flægən/ *n* 1 (large jug) jarra *f* 2 (large bottle) botellón *m*

flagpole /'flægpəʊl/ *n* asta *f*‡ de (la) bandera, mástil *m*

flagrant /'fleɪgrənt/ *adj* flagrante

flag: **~ship** *n* (Naut) buque *m* insignia; (showpiece) producto *m* (*or* programa *m etc*) bandera; **~stone** *n* losa *f*, piedra *f*

flail¹ /fleɪl/ *n* mayal *m*

flail² *vi*: **with arms/legs ~ing** con los brazos como aspas de molino/sacudiendo las piernas; **she ~ed about on the ice, unable to get up** se debatía en el hielo sin conseguir levantarse

flair /fler || 'fleə(r)/ *n* 1 (natural aptitude) (*no pl*): **a ~ for languages/business** facilidad *f* para los idiomas/olfato *m* para los negocios 2 [u] (stylishness) estilo *m*

flak /flæk/ *n* [u] 1 (Aviat, Mil) fuego *m* antiaéreo 2 (criticism) críticas *fpl*; **to come in for** *o* **take a lot of ~** ser* muy criticado

flake¹ /fleɪk/ *n*

A (of snow, cereals) copo *m*; (of paint, rust) escama *f*, laminilla *f*; (of wood, bone) astilla *f*; (of skin) escama *f*, pellejo *m* (fam)

B (eccentric person) (AmE sl & pej) bicho *m* raro (fam)

flake² *vi* ‹‹*paint/plaster*›› descascararse, pelarse

(Phrasal verb)

- **flake out** (BrE colloq) [v ▸ adv] (slump) desplomarse, caer* redondo *or* rendido

flakey *adj* ▸ **flaky**

flak jacket, (AmE also) **flak vest** *n* chaleco *m* antibala(s)

flaky, flakey /'fleɪki/ *adj* **-kier, -kiest** ‹*piecrust*› hojaldrado; ‹*paint/plaster*› que se desconcha *or* descascara; **~ pastry** *masa tipo hojaldre*

flambé /'flæmbeɪ || 'flɒmbeɪ/ *vt* flamear

flamboyant /flæm'bɔɪənt/ *adj* 1 (dashing) ‹*style/person*› exuberante, extravagante; ‹*gesture*› ampuloso 2 (brilliant) ‹*color*› vistoso; ‹*hat/dress*› llamativo

flame¹ /fleɪm/ *n* [c u] 1 llama *f*; **to be in ~s** estar* (envuelto) en llamas; **to go up in ~s** incendiarse; ***to be shot down in ~s***: **his plan was shot down in ~s by his boss** su jefe demolió su plan; **the plane/pilot was shot down in ~s** el avión/piloto cayó envuelto en llamas 2 (lover): **he's an old ~ of mine** es un antiguo enamorado mío

flame² *vi* 1 (blaze) «*light/jewel*» refulgir*; «*fire*» arder; **her anger ~d (up) again as she reread the letter** volvió a montar *or* a arder en cólera al releer la carta 2 (glow) «*sun*» encenderse*, enrojecer*; **her cheeks ~d with anger** se le encendieron las mejillas de (la) ira

flamenco /flə'meŋkəʊ/ *n* [u c] (*pl* **-cos**) flamenco *m*

flame: **~out** /'fleɪmaʊt/ *n* 1 (of engine) pérdida *f* total de combustión 2 (failure) (AmE colloq) fracaso *m*; **~proof** *adj* ‹*fabric*› ininflamable; ‹*dish*› resistente al fuego; **~-red** /'fleɪm'red/ *adj* (*pred* **~ red**) ‹*dress/paint*› rojo fuego *adj inv*; **~-resistant** /'fleɪmrɪ'zɪstənt/ *adj* ignífugo; **~-retardant** /'fleɪmrɪ'tɑːrdənt || 'fleɪmrɪˌtɑːdənt/ *adj* de combustión lenta; **~thrower** /'fleɪm'θrəʊər || 'fleɪmˌθrəʊə(r)/*n* lanzallamas *m*

flaming /'fleɪmɪŋ/ *adj*

A ‹*logs/coals*› llameante

B (furious) ‹*quarrel*› violento; **she was in a ~ temper** *o* **rage** estaba furibunda

C (BrE colloq) (*as intensifier*) maldito (fam), condenado (fam)

flamingo /flə'mɪŋgəʊ/ *n* (*pl* **-gos** *or* **-goes**) flamenco *m*

flammable /'flæməbəl/ *adj* inflamable, flamable (Méx)

flan /flæn/ *n* [c u] (sweet) tarta *f*, kuchen *m* (Chi); (individual) tartaleta *f*, tarteleta *f* (RPl); **cheese ~** quiche *f* de queso

Flanders /'flændərz || 'flɑːndəz/ *n* Flandes *m*

flange /flændʒ/ *n* 1 (Rail) (on wheel) pestaña *f*; (on rail) cabeza *f* 2 (Const, Tech) (on pipe) reborde *m*; (on girder) ala *f*‡

flank¹ /flæŋk/ *n* 1 (of animal) ijada *f*, ijar *m*; (of person) costado *m* 2 (of hill) (liter) falda *f* 3 (Mil, Sport) flanco *m*

flank² *vt* (*often pass*) flanquear; **he was ~ed by two detectives** iba escoltado por dos detectives

flanker /'flæŋkər || 'flæŋkə(r)/ *n* 1 (in US football) corredor *m* de bola 2 (in rugby) ala *m*

flannel /'flænḷ/ *n*

A 1 [u] (fabric) franela *f*; (*before n*) ‹*shirt/nightgown*› de franela 2 **flannels** *pl* (trousers) pantalón *m* de franela

B [c] (*face* **~**) (BrE) toallita *f* (*para lavarse*), ≈ manopla *f*

C [u] (evasive talk) (BrE colloq) cuentos *mpl*

flannelette /'flænḷ'et || ˌflænə'let/ *n* [u] franela *f* (de algodón)

flap¹ /flæp/ *n*

A 1 (cover) tapa *f*; (of pocket, envelope) solapa *f*; (of table) hoja *f*; (of jacket, coat) faldón *m*; (of tent) portezuela *f*; (*ear* **~**) orejera *f*; **a cat ~** una gatera 2 (Aviat) alerón *m*

B (motion) aletazo *m*; **the eagle flew off with a ~ of its wings** el águila echó a volar con un batir de alas

C (commotion, agitation) (colloq): **to be in/get into a ~** estar*/ponerse* como loco (fam)

flap² **-pp-** *vi*

A «*sail/curtain*» agitarse, sacudirse; «*flag*» ondear, agitarse; **the bird ~ped off** el pájaro echó a volar batiendo las alas; ***her ears were ~ping*** (BrE colloq) tenía las antenas conectadas *or* (AmL tb) paradas (fam)

B (panic) (BrE colloq) agitarse, ponerse* como loco (fam)

■ **flap** *vt* ‹*wings*› batir; ‹*arms*› agitar

flapjack /'flæpdʒæk/ *n*

A (pancake) (esp AmE) *crepe o panqueque pequeño y grueso*

B (cookie) (BrE) *tipo de galleta dulce de avena*

flare¹ /fler || fleə(r)/ *n*

A 1 (marker light) bengala *f*; (on runway, road) baliza *f*; **safety ~s** (AmE Auto) luces *fpl* de emergencia 2 (sudden light) destello *m*; (flame) llamarada *f*

B (Clothing) 1 (on jacket) vuelo *m* 2 **flares** (BrE) pantalones *mpl* acampanados *or* de pata de elefante

flare² *vi* «*candle/fire*» llamear; «*torch/light*» brillar; «*violence*» estallar; **tempers ~d** los ánimos se enardecieron

■ **flare** *vt*: **he ~d his nostrils angrily** bufó *or* resopló enfadado

Phrasal verb

• **flare up** [v ▸ adv] 1 «*fire*» llamear; «*fighting*» estallar 2 «*infection/disease*» recrudecer*, empeorar 3 (lose temper) explotar, montar en cólera; **to ~ up** AT **sb** ponerse* furioso CON algn

flared /flerd || fleəd/ *adj* ‹*skirt*› con mucho vuelo, evasé (RPl); ‹*trousers*› acampanado

flare-up /'flerʌp || 'fleərʌp/ *n* (of violence) brote *m*, estallido *m*

flash¹ /flæʃ/ *n*

A [c] 1 (of light) destello *m*; (from explosion) fogonazo *m*; **a ~ of lightning** un relámpago; ***a ~ in the pan*** flor *f* de un día; ***(as) quick as a ~*** como un rayo; ***in a ~***: **it came to me in a ~** de repente lo vi claro 2 (burst): **a ~ of inspiration** un ramalazo de inspiración 3 (Phot) flash *m*

B [c] (*news* **~**) avance *m* informativo, flash *m*

flash² *vt*

A 1 (direct): **they ~ed a light in my face** me enfocaron la cara con una luz; **to ~ one's headlights at sb** hacerle* una señal con los faros a algn; **to ~ sb a smile** sonreírle a algn 2 (communicate) ‹*news*› transmitir rápidamente; **a message was ~ed on the screen** apareció un mensaje en pantalla

B (show) ‹*money/card*› mostrar*, enseñar (esp Esp); **she loves ~ing her money around** le encanta ir por ahí haciendo ostentación de su dinero

■ **flash** *vi*

A 1 (emit sudden light) destellar, brillar; **the lightning ~ed** relampagueó, hubo un relámpago 2 (Auto) hacer* una señal con los faros 3 **flashing** *pres p* ‹*sign/light*› intermitente; ‹*eyes/smile*› brillante

B (expose oneself) (sl) exhibirse en público

C (move fast) (+ *adv compl*): **a message ~ed across the screen** un mensaje apareció fugazmente en la pantalla; **it ~ed through my mind that ...** se me ocurrió de repente que ...; **to ~ by** *o* **past** «*train/car/person*» pasar como una bala *or* un rayo *or* un bólido; **to ~ by** «*time/vacation*» pasar volando, volar*

flash³ *adj* (ostentatious) (BrE colloq) ostentoso

flash: **~back** *n* (Cin, Lit) flashback *m*, escena *f* retrospectiva; **~bulb** *n* (Phot) lámpara *f* *or* bombilla *f* de flash; **~ card** *n* tarjeta *f* (*de ayuda pedagógica*); **~cube** *n* (Phot) cubo *m* (de) flash, flash *m* desechable; **~ drive** *n* memoria *f* flash

flasher /'flæʃər || 'flæʃə(r)/ *n*

A (Auto) (indicator) (BrE colloq) intermitente *m*, direccional *f* (Col, Méx), señalizador *m* (de viraje) (Chi)

B (man who exposes himself) (sl) exhibicionista *m*

flash: **~ flood** *n* riada *f*; **~ gun** *n* flash *m* electrónico

flashing /'flæʃɪŋ/ *n* [u] (Const) tapajuntas *m*

flash: **~light** *n* (esp AmE) linterna *f*; **~ stick** *n* tarjeta *f* de memoria

flashy /'flæʃi/ *adj* **-shier, -shiest** llamativo, ostentoso

flask /flæsk || flɑːsk/ *n* (bottle) frasco *m*; (in laboratory) matraz *m*, redoma *f*; (*hip* **~**) petaca *f*, nalguera *f* (Méx); (*vacuum* **~**) (BrE) termo *m*

flat¹ /flæt/ *adj* **-tt-**

A 1 ‹*surface*› plano; ‹*countryside*› llano; **~ feet** pies *mpl* planos; **houses with ~ roofs** casas *fpl* con techos planos *or* con azoteas; **I was ~ on my back for two months** (me) pasé dos meses en cama; **to fold sth ~** doblar bien algo; **he laid the map down ~ on the table** extendió el mapa sobre la mesa; **I lay down ~ and tried to relax** me tumbé *or* me tendí e intenté relajarme; ▸**face¹ A1** 2 ‹*dish*› llano, bajo (Chi), playo (RPl); **~ shoes** zapatos *mpl* bajos, zapatillas *fpl* de piso (Méx); **~ cap** *o* **hat** (BrE) gorra *f* (*de lana con visera*) 3 (deflated) ‹*ball*› desinflado, ponchado (Méx); **you have a ~ tire** *o* (BrE) **tyre** tienes un neumático desinflado *or* una rueda desinflada *or* (Méx) una llanta ponchada

B 1 ‹*lemonade/beer*› sin efervescencia, sin gas 2 ‹*battery*› descargado; **switch off or you'll get a ~ battery** apaga o se te va a descargar la batería

C (dull, uninteresting) ‹*conversation/party*› soso (fam); ‹*joke*› sin gracia; ‹*voice*› monótono; **she felt a bit ~** estaba un tanto alicaída *or* baja de moral; ***to fall ~*** «*play/project*» fracasar*, no ser* bien recibido; **the joke fell very ~** el chiste no hizo ni pizca de gracia

D (total, firm) ‹*denial/refusal*› rotundo, categórico; **they've said they won't do it and that's ~** han dicho que no lo harán y no hay vuelta de hoja (fam)

E (Mus) 1 (referring to key) bemol; **A ~** la *m* bemol 2 (too low): **you're ~** estás desafinando (*por cantar demasiado bajo*)

F (fixed) (*before n*) ‹*rate*› fijo, uniforme

G (broke) (AmE colloq) (*pred*): **to be ~** estar* pelado (fam)

flat² *adv*

A 1 ‹*refuse/turn down*› de plano, categóricamente 2 (exactly): **it took him two hours ~** tardó dos horas

f

justas *or* exactas 3▸ (AmE colloq) (*as intensifier*) completamente; *see also* **broke**[2]

B (Mus) demasiado bajo

flat[3] *n*

A (apartment) (BrE) apartamento *m*, departamento *m* (AmL), piso *m* (Esp)

B 1▸ (surface — of sword) cara *f* de la hoja; (— of hand) palma *f* 2▸ (level ground) llano *m*, terreno *m* llano

C (Mus) bemol *m*

D (Theat) bastidor *m*

E **flats** *pl* 1▸ (low-lying ground) llano *m*; **mud ~s** marismas *fpl* 2▸ (shoes) (esp AmE) zapatos *mpl* bajos, zapatillas *fpl* de piso (Méx)

flat: **~-chested** /'flæt'tʃəstəd || ˌflæt'tʃestɪd/ *adj*: **she's very ~-chested** no tiene nada de busto, es una tabla (fam); **~-footed** /'flæt'fʊtəd || ˌflæt'fʊtɪd/ *adj*: **he's ~-footed** tiene (los) pies planos

flatlet /'flætlət || 'flætlɪt/ *n* (BrE) apartamento *m* pequeño

flatline *vi* (die) (colloq) morirse*

■ **flatline** *vt* (AmE) ‹*costs/expenditure*› congelar

flatly /'flætli/ *adv* de plano, rotundamente

flatmate /'flætmeɪt/ *n* (BrE) compañero, -ra *m,f* de apartamento *or* (Esp) de piso

flat out[1] *adj* (colloq) (*pred*) 1▸ (prostrate) tirado 2▸ (exhausted) (BrE): **to be ~ ~** estar* hecho polvo (fam)

flat out[2] *adv* (at full speed) (colloq) a toda máquina

flat: **~ racing** *n* (BrE) carreras *fpl* lisas *or* (AmL) planas; **~-rate** /'flæt'reɪt/ *adj* (BrE) a una tasa de interés fija *or* (esp Esp) a tipo de interés fijo

flatten /'flætn̩/ *vt* 1▸ (make flat) ‹*surface/metal*› aplanar; ‹*path/lawn*› allanar, aplanar; **he ~ed himself against the wall** se pegó bien a la pared 2▸ (knock down) ‹*trees*› tumbar, echar *or* tirar abajo; ‹*city*› arrasar; **he ~ed his opponent with a single blow** tumbó a su contrincante de un solo golpe

flatter /'flætər || 'flætə(r)/ *vt* 1▸ (gratify) halagar* 2▸ (overpraise) adular 3▸ (show to advantage) favorecer*; **the photo doesn't ~ her** no ha salido favorecida *or* bien en la foto

■ *v refl* **to ~ oneself** 1▸ (like to think): **I ~ myself on being a good singer** me considero un buen cantante, considero que canto bien 2▸ (delude oneself): **don't ~ yourself** no te hagas ilusiones

flatterer /'flætərər || 'flætərə(r)/ *n* adulador, -dora *m,f*

flattering /'flætərɪŋ/ *adj* 1▸ ‹*words/speech*› halagador, halagüeño; (sycophantic) adulador; **it's a ~ portrait of him** en el retrato sale muy favorecido 2▸ ‹*clothes/hairstyle*› favorecedor

flattery /'flætəri/ *n* [u] halagos *mpl*; (sycophantic) adulación *f*; **~ will get you nowhere** con halagos no vas a conseguir nada

flatulence /'flætʃələns || 'flætjʊləns/ *n* [u] flatulencia *f*, gases *mpl*

flatworm /'flætwɜːrm || 'flætwɜːm/ *n* gusano *m* platelminto

flaunt /flɔːnt/ *vt* ‹*possessions*› hacer* ostentación *or* alarde de; ‹*knowledge*› alardear de, hacer* alarde de; **to ~ oneself** exhibirse

flautist /'flɔːtəst || 'flɔːtɪst/ *n* (BrE) flautista *mf*

flavor[1], (BrE) **flavour** /'fleɪvər || 'fleɪvə(r)/ *n* [c u] sabor *m*, gusto *m*; **a strong/meaty ~** un sabor fuerte/a carne; **chocolate-~** con sabor *or* gusto a chocolate; **a novel with a romantic ~** una novela de sabor romántico

flavor[2], (BrE) **flavour** *vt* ‹*food/drink*› sazonar

flavoring, (BrE) **flavouring** /'fleɪvərɪŋ/ *n* [c u] (Culin) condimento *m*, sazón *f*; (in industry) aromatizante *m*; (essence) esencia *f*

flaw /flɔː/ *n* (in material, glass) defecto *m*, imperfección *f*, falla *f*; (in argument) error *m*; (in character) defecto *m*

flawed /flɔːd/ *adj* ‹*china/glass*› con imperfecciones; ‹*argument/logic*› viciado; **the proposal is fundamentally ~** la propuesta falla por su base

flawless /'flɔːləs || 'flɔːlɪs/ *adj* ‹*performance/logic*› impecable; ‹*conduct*› intachable, impecable; ‹*complexion/gem/plan*› perfecto

flawlessly /'flɔːləsli || 'flɔːlɪsli/ *adv* impecablemente, perfectamente

flax /flæks/ *n* [u] (Bot, Tex) lino *m*

flaxen /'flæksən/ *adj* (liter) blondo (liter), rubísimo; **a ~-haired girl** una chica rubísima

flay /fleɪ/ *vt* 1▸ (remove skin) desollar*, despellejar 2▸ (beat) (colloq): **I'll ~ him (alive)** ¡lo voy a desollar vivo! (fam), ¡le voy a arrancar la piel a tiras! (fam)

flea /fliː/ *n* pulga *f*; ***to send sb away*** *o* ***off with a ~ in her/his ear*** echar a algn con cajas destempladas; (*before n*) ‹*collar/powder*› antipulgas *adj inv*

flea: **~bag** *n* (sl) 1▸ (cheap hotel) (AmE) hotel *m* de mala muerte; 2▸ (dirty person) (BrE) piojoso, -sa *m,f* (fam & pey), piojento, -ta *m,f* (fam & pey); (dog) pulgoso, -sa *m,f*, pulguiento, -ta *m,f* (CS); **~-bitten** /'fliː'bɪtn̩/ *adj* ‹*cat/dog*› pulgoso, pulguiento (CS); **~ market** *n* mercado *m* de las pulgas *or* (CS) de pulgas, rastro *m* (Esp); **~pit** *n* (BrE colloq) (cinema) cine *m* de mala muerte

fleck[1] /flek/ *n* (of dust) mota *f*; (of paint, mud) salpicadura *f*; **the fabric was blue with a green ~** *o* **~s of green** la tela era azul moteada de verde *or* con motas verdes

fleck[2] *vt* 1▸ (with mud) salpicar*; **beige ~ed with brown** beige moteado de marrón 2▸ **flecked** *past p* ‹*fabric/yarn*› moteado, jaspeado

fled /fled/ *past & past p of* **flee**

fledgling, fledgeling /'fledʒlɪŋ/ *n* (bird) polluelo *m*, volantón *m* (téc); (*before n*) **a ~ democracy** una democracia en ciernes

flee /fliː/ (*past & past p* **fled**) *vi* huir*, escapar; **to ~ FROM sb/sth** huir* *or* escapar DE algn/algo; **the little girl fled to her mother** la niña corrió hacia su madre; **to ~ TO sth**: **they fled to safety/shelter** corrieron a ponerse a salvo/a refugiarse

■ **flee** *vt* huir* de; **to ~ the country** huir* del país

fleece[1] /fliːs/ *n* [c u] (on sheep) lana *f*; (from sheep) vellón *m*; **the Golden F~** el vellocino de oro

fleece[2] *vt* (defraud) (colloq) desplumar (fam)

fleecy /'fliːsi/ *adj* **-cier, -ciest** 1▸ ‹*lining/blanket*› afelpado 2▸ ‹*clouds*› algodonoso, aborregado

fleet[1] /fliːt/ *n* 1▸ (naval unit, body of shipping) flota *f* 2▸ (navy) armada *f* 3▸ (of cars) parque *m* móvil, flota *f*

fleet[2] *adj* (liter) veloz, raudo (liter); **~ of foot** de pies ligeros (liter)

fleeting /'fliːtɪŋ/ *adj* (*usu before n*) fugaz, breve; **we caught a ~ glimpse of the sea** divisamos fugazmente el mar

fleetingly /'fliːtɪŋli/ *adv* fugazmente, momentáneamente

Fleet Street /fliːt/ *n* (in UK) Fleet Street (*calle londinense donde solían tener sus oficinas muchos periódicos*)

Flemish[1] /'flemɪʃ/ *adj* flamenco

Flemish[2] *n* 1▸ [u] (language) flamenco *m* 2▸ (people) (+ *pl vb*) **the ~** los flamencos

flesh /fleʃ/ *n* [u] 1▸ (human, animal) carne *f*; **in the ~** en persona, en carne y hueso; ***~ and blood***: **after all, I'm only ~ and blood** después de todo, soy de carne y hueso *or* soy humano; **they're my own ~ and blood** son de mi propia sangre; ***to make sb's ~ creep*** *o* ***crawl*** ponerle* los pelos de punta *or* la piel de gallina a algn; (*before n*) ‹*wound*› superficial 2▸ (of fruit) pulpa *f*

Phrasal verb

• **flesh out** [v ▸ o ▸ adv, v ▸ adv ▸ o] ‹*story*› desarrollar; ‹*character*› darle* cuerpo a

flesh: **~-eating** /'fleʃ'iːtɪŋ/ *adj* carnívoro; **~pots** *pl n* (hum) antros *mpl* de perdición

fleshy /'fleʃi/ *adj* **-shier, -shiest** *adj* ‹*arms/person*› rollizo, gordo; ‹*plant/leaf/stem*› carnoso

flew /fluː/ *past of* **fly**[2]

flex[1] /fleks/ *vt* ‹*arm/knees/body*› doblar, flexionar; **to ~ one's muscles** (to warm up) hacer* ejercicios de calentamiento; (in body building) mostrar* *or* sacar* los músculos; «*regime*» mostrar* su poderío

flex[2] *n* [u c] (BrE) cable *m* (eléctrico)

flexibility /'fleksə'bɪləti/ *n* [u] flexibilidad *f*

flexible /'fleksəbəl/ *adj* flexible

flextime /'flekstaɪm/, (BrE) **flexitime** /'fleksɪtaɪm/ *n* [u] horario *m* flexible

flick[1] /flɪk/ *vt* 1▸ (strike lightly): **she ~ed a piece of bread at me** me tiró un pedazo de pan 2▸ (remove): **he ~ed the ash off his lapel** se sacudió la ceniza de la solapa; **to**

~ **the hair out of one's eyes** apartarse *or* quitarse el pelo de los ojos

■ **flick** *vi*: **the lizard's tongue ~ed in and out** el lagarto sacaba y metía la lengua

(Phrasal verb)

• **flick through** [v ▸ prep ▸ o] ‹*book*› hojear; ‹*pages*› pasar

flick[2] *n*

A (of tail) coletazo *m*; (of wrist) giro *m*; **she gave the furniture a quick ~ with a duster** les dio una pasada rápida a los muebles con el trapo; **at the ~ of a switch** con sólo tocar *or* apretar un botón

B (colloq & dated) **flicks** *pl* **the ~s** el cine

flicker[1] /'flɪkər || 'flɪkə(r)/ *vi* «*candle/flame/TV picture*» parpadear; «*light*» parpadear, titilar; «*needle on dial*» oscilar; **his eyelids ~ed** parpadeó; **the shadows ~ed on the wall** las sombras bailaban en la pared

flicker[2] *n* [u c] [1] (of flame, eyelids) parpadeo *m*; (of light) parpadeo *m*, titileo *m*; (of needle on dial) oscilación *f* [2] (faint sensation): **a ~ of hope** un rayo de esperanza

flick knife *n* (BrE) navaja *f* automática, navaja *f* de resorte

flier /'flaɪər || 'flaɪə(r)/ *n*

A [1] (pilot) aviador, -dora *m,f* [2] (passenger) usuario -ria *m,f* (regular) del avion; **I'm not a good ~** no me gusta nada volar

B (handbill) folleto *m* (publicitario), volante *m* (AmL)

flight /flaɪt/ *n*

A [1] [u] (of bird, aircraft) vuelo *m*; (of ball, projectile) trayectoria *f*; **in ~** en vuelo, volando [2] [c] (air journey) vuelo *m*; **F~ YZ321 to/from Paris** el vuelo YZ321 con destino a/procedente de París; (*before n*) **~ path** ruta *f*; **~ recorder** caja *f* negra [3] [c] (mental): **it was just a ~ of fancy** no fue más que una fantasía

B [c] (group — of birds) bandada *f*; (— of aircraft) escuadrilla *f*

C [c] (of stairs) tramo *m*; **we had to climb six ~s of stairs** tuvimos que subir seis pisos por la escalera

D [u] [1] (act of fleeing) huida *f*; **to put sb to ~** hacer* huir a algn; **to take ~** darse* a la fuga [2] (Fin) fuga *f*

flight ~ attendant *n* auxiliar *mf* de vuelo, sobrecargo *mf*; **~ bag** *n* bolso *f* de mano; **~ deck** *n* (on plane) cabina *f* de mando; (on aircraft carrier) cubierta *f* de vuelo

flightless /'flaɪtləs || 'flaɪtlɪs/ *adj* no volador

flight test *n* vuelo *m* de prueba

flighty /'flaɪti/ *adj* **-tier, -tiest** veleidoso, inconstante

flimsy /'flɪmzi/ *adj* **-sier, -siest** [1] ‹*material/garment*› ligerísimo, muy delgado *or* fino [2] ‹*construction/object*› endeble, poco sólido [3] ‹*excuse*› pobre; ‹*argument/evidence*› poco sólido

flinch /flɪntʃ/ *vi* (wince) estremecerse*; **she bore the pain without ~ing** aguantó el dolor sin (re)chistar

fling[1] /flɪŋ/ (*past & past p* **flung**) *vt* [1] (throw violently) lanzar*, tirar, arrojar, aventar* (Col, Méx, Per); **he flung the window open** abrió la ventana de un golpe; **we flung ourselves (down) on the ground** nos tiramos *or* echamos al suelo; **he flung his arms around her neck** le echó los brazos al cuello; **the protesters were flung into a cell** echaron a los manifestantes en una celda; **he flung himself down into an armchair** se dejó caer en un sillón [2] ‹*glance/insult*› lanzar*; **to ~ sth in sb's face** ‹*past/mistake*› echarle algo en cara a algn

(Phrasal verbs)

• **fling away** [v ▸ o ▸ adv, v ▸ adv ▸ o] ‹*paper/garbage*› tirar, botar (AmS excl RPl); ‹*chance*› tirar por la ventana

• **fling out** [v ▸ o ▸ adv, v ▸ adv ▸ o] [1] (throw away) tirar, botar (AmS exc RPl) [2] (extend) ‹*arms*› abrir*, extender*

• **fling up** [v ▸ o ▸ adv, v ▸ adv ▸ o] [1] (throw upward) tirar *or* lanzar* al aire, aventar* (Col, Méx, Per) [2] (raise) ‹*arms*› levantar; **she flung up her hands in horror** se horrorizó

fling[2] *n*

A (colloq) [1] (love affair) aventura *f* [2] (wild time) juerga *f* (fam); **to have a final ~ before settling down** echarse una cana al aire antes de sentar cabeza

B (throw) lanzamiento *m*

C (*Highland ~*) *baile escocés*

flint /flɪnt/ *n* [1] [u c] (Geol) sílex *m*, pedernal *m*; (piece of stone) pedernal *m* [2] [c] (for cigarette lighter) piedra *f*

flip[1] /flɪp/ **-pp-** *vt* tirar, aventar* (Col, Méx, Per); **we'll ~ a coin to decide** vamos a echarlo a cara o cruz *or* (Andes, Ven) a cara o sello *or* (Arg) a cara o ceca, vamos a echar un volado (Méx); **to ~ one's lid** (sl) poner* el grito en el cielo (fam)

■ **flip** *vi* (sl) **~ (out)** (lose self-control) perder* la chaveta (fam)

(Phrasal verbs)

• **flip over**

A [v ▸ o ▸ adv] ‹*record/pancake/page*› darle* la vuelta a, voltear (AmL exc CS), dar* vuelta (CS)

B [v ▸ adv] «*car*» volcar*, voltearse (Méx), darse* vuelta (CS)

• **flip through** [v ▸ prep ▸ o] hojear

flip[2] *n*

A (blow) golpecito *m*

B (somersault) salto *m* mortal, voltereta *f* (en el aire)

flip[3] *adj* **-pp-** (colloq) burlón

flip[4] *interj* (BrE colloq) ¡caray! (fam)

flip-flop /'flɪpflɑ:p || 'flɪpflɒp/ *n* (BrE) ▸**thong 2**

flippancy /'flɪpənsi/ *n* [u] (of remarks) poca seriedad *f*, ligereza *f*; (of attitude) displicencia *f*, indiferencia *f*

flippant /'flɪpənt/ *adj* ‹*remark*› frívolo, poco serio; ‹*attitude*› displicente, indiferente

flippantly /'flɪpəntli/ *adv* ‹*talk*› con ligereza; ‹*behave*› displicentemente

flipper /'flɪpər || 'flɪpə(r)/ *n* aleta *f*

flip side *n* **the ~ ~** (Audio) la cara B; (of a situation) (colloq) la otra cara de la moneda (fam)

flirt[1] /flɜ:rt || flɜ:t/ *vi* **to ~ (WITH sb)** flirtear *or* coquetear (CON algn); **to ~ with an idea** dar* vueltas a una idea

flirt[2] *n*: **he/she is a terrible ~** le encanta flirtear

flirtation /flɜ:r'teɪʃən || ˌflɜ:'teɪʃən/ *n* [1] [c] (relationship) flirt *m*, devaneo *m*; **after a brief ~ with politics** tras un breve coqueteo *or* devaneo con la política [2] [u] (coquetry) flirteo *m*, coqueteo *m*

flirtatious /flɜ:r'teɪʃəs || ˌflɜ:'teɪʃəs/ *adj* ‹*glance/remark*› insinuante; **a ~ girl** una chica coqueta

flit[1] /flɪt/ *vi* **-tt-** «*bird/butterfly/bat*» revolotear; **she ~ted from room to room** iba y venía de una habitación a otra; **he continually ~s from one topic to the next** salta continuamente de un tema a otro

flit[2] *n* (BrE): **to do a (moonlight) ~** (colloq) largarse*

float[1] /fləʊt/ *vi*

A [1] (on water) flotar; **to ~ up (to the surface)** salir* a flote; **to ~ (on one's back)** hacer la plancha; **the canoe ~ed away on the tide** la marea se llevó la canoa [2] «*cloud/smoke*» flotar en el aire [3] (move lightly) «*idea/image*» vagar*

B (Fin) «*currency*» flotar

■ **float** *vt*

A ‹*ship/boat*› poner* *or* sacar* a flote; ‹*raft/logs*› llevar, arrastrar

B (Fin) [1] (establish): **to ~ a company** introducir* una compañía en Bolsa [2] (offer for sale) ‹*shares/stock*› emitir [3] (allow to fluctuate) ‹*currency*› dejar flotar

C (circulate) ‹*idea*› presentar

float[2] *n*

A [1] (for fishing, for buoyancy) flotador *m* [2] (in cistern, carburetor) flotador *m*, boya *f* [3] (raft, platform) plataforma *f* (flotante)

B [1] (in parade) carroza *f*, carro *m* alegórico (CS, Méx) [2] (*milk ~*) (BrE) furgoneta *f* (*del reparto de leche*)

C (ready cash) caja *f* chica; (Busn, Fin) fondo *m* fijo; (to provide change): **a ~ of £20** 20 libras en cambio *or* en monedas

D (AmE) *refresco o batido con helado*

floater /'fləʊtər || 'fləʊtə(r)/ *n*

A (AmE colloq) (employee) trabajador, -dora *m,f* eventual

B (AmE) (multiple voter) votante *mf* múltiple

C (undecided voter) (BrE) votante *mf* indeciso

D (drifter) (AmE colloq) vagabundo, -da *m,f*

E (in eyeball) partícula *f* flotante

F (insurance policy) (AmE) póliza *f* flotante

G (in fishing) flotador *m*

floating /'fləʊtɪŋ/ *adj* (*before n*)

A ‹*harbor/restaurant*› flotante

B (Fin) ‹*currency/exchange rate*› flotante; ‹*assets*› circulante; **~ capital** activo *m* circulante

C ‹*population*› flotante; ‹*voter*› (BrE) indeciso

flock[1] /flɑ:k || flɒk/ *n*

A [c] (+ *sing or pl vb*) [1] (of sheep) rebaño *m*; (of birds) bandada *f* [2] (of people) (*often pl*) tropel *m*, multitud *f* [3] (Relig) feligreses *mpl*, grey *f*

B [u] (stuffing) borra *f*; (*before n*) ~ **(wall)paper** *papel pintado con relieve de terciopelo*

flock² *vi* acudir (*en gran número, en masa*); **to ~ together** congregarse*, reunirse; **customers have been ~ing in** ha venido un gran número de clientes

floe /fləʊ/ *n* témpano *m* de hielo

flog /flɑːg || flɒg/ *vt* **-gg-**
A (beat) azotar; ***to ~ sth to death*** (BrE colloq) repetir* algo hasta la saciedad
B (sell) (BrE sl) vender

flogging /'flɑːgɪŋ || 'flɒgɪŋ/ *n* [c u]: **to give sb a ~** azotar a algn

flood¹ /flʌd/ *n* **1** (of water) (*often pl*) inundación *f*; (caused by river) inundación *f*, riada *f*; **the F~** (Bib) el Diluvio (Universal); **the river was in ~** el río estaba crecido; **to be in full ~** «*river*» estar* desbordado; «*speaker*» estar* en pleno discurso *or* (pey) en plena perorata; (*before n*) **the ~ damage** los daños causados por inundaciones **2** (of complaints, calls, letters) avalancha *f*, diluvio *m*; (of people) avalancha *f*, riada *f*; **she was in ~s of tears** estaba hecha un mar de lágrimas

flood² *vt* **1** ‹*field/town*› inundar, anegar*; **the kitchen was ~ed** se inundó la cocina **2** (Auto) ‹*engine*› ahogar* **3** (overwhelm) inundar; **we've been ~ed with applications** nos han inundado de solicitudes, nos han llovido las solicitudes; **to ~ the market with imports** (Busn) inundar el mercado de productos importados

■ **flood** *vi* **1** «*river/sewers*» desbordarse; «*mine/basement*» inundarse **2** (Auto) ahogarse* **3** (+ *adv compl*) «*people/crowd*»: **the crowd ~ed into the stadium** la multitud entró en tropel al estadio; **to ~ in** «*sunshine/light*» entrar a raudales; **donations came ~ing in** llovieron los donativos **4** «*emotion*»: **memories came ~ing back** los recuerdos se agolparon en su (*or* mi *etc*) memoria

Phrasal verb

• **flood out**
A [v ▸ adv] (pour out) «*water*» salir* a raudales; «*people*» salir* en tropel
B [v ▸ o ▸ adv, v ▸ adv ▸ o] **1** (inundate) ‹*building*› inundar **2** ‹*people*›: **thousands have been ~ed out** las inundaciones han obligado a miles de personas a evacuar sus casas

floodgate /'flʌdgeɪt/ *n* compuerta *f*, esclusa *f*; ***to open the ~s to sth*** abrirle* las puertas a algo

flooding /'flʌdɪŋ/ *n* [u] inundación *f*

floodlight¹ /'flʌdlaɪt/ *n* [c u] reflector *m*, foco *m*; **under ~s, by ~** con luz artificial

floodlight² *vt* (*past & past p* **floodlit** /'flʌdlɪt/) **1** iluminar (*con reflectores o focos*) **2** **floodlit** *past p* ‹*arena/building*› iluminado; ‹*game*› que se juega con luz artificial

flood: **~lighting** /'flʌdlaɪtɪŋ/ *n* [u] iluminación *f* (*con reflectores o focos*); **~ plain** *n*: *tierras que quedan inundadas durante la crecida de un río*; **~ tide** *n* pleamar *f*; **~water** *n* [u] (*often pl*) crecida *f*

floor¹ /flɔːr || flɔː(r)/ *n*
A **1** (of room, vehicle) suelo *m*, piso *m* (AmL); ***to wipe up*** *o* (BrE) ***wipe the ~ with sb*** hacer* trizas a algn **2** (for dancing) pista *f* (de baile); **to take the ~** salir* a bailar *or* a la pista **3** (of ocean, valley, forest) fondo *m*
B (storey) piso *m*; **we live on the first/second ~** (AmE) vivimos en la planta baja/el primer piso *or* (Chi) en el primer/segundo piso; (BrE) vivimos en el primer/segundo piso *or* (Chi) en el segundo/tercer piso
C **the ~** **1** (of debating chamber) el hemiciclo, la sala; **to gain/have the ~** obtener*/tener* (el uso de) la palabra **2** (audience at debate): **a question from the ~** una pregunta de uno de los asistentes **3** (of stock exchange) el parqué *or* parquet
D (for wages, prices) (Econ) mínimo *m*

floor² *vt*
A (Const): **the room is ~ed with parquet** el suelo de la habitación es de *or* está recubierto de parquet
B **1** (knock down) derribar, tirar al suelo **2** (nonplus) (colloq) «*news*» dejar helado *or* de una pieza (fam)

floorboard /'flɔːrbɔːrd || 'flɔːbɔːd/ *n* **1** (Const) tabla *f* del suelo, duela *f* (Méx) **2** (AmE Auto) suelo *m*, piso *m* (AmL)

flooring /'flɔːrɪŋ/ *n* [u] revestimiento *m* para suelos

floor: **~ lamp** *n* lámpara *f* de pie; **~ manager** *n* (Cin, TV) regidor, -dora *m,f*; (in department store) jefe, -fa *m,f* de planta; **~ show** *n* espectáculo *m* (*de cabaret*); **~walker** *n* jefe, -fa *m,f* de vendedores

floozy, floozie /'fluːzi/ *n* (*pl* **-zies**) (colloq & pej) fulana *f* (fam)

flop¹ /flɑːp || flɒp/ *vi* **-pp-**
A **1** (fall, move slackly) (+ *adv compl*): **she ~ped down into a chair** se dejó caer en un sillón; **he ~ped down exhausted onto the bed** se desplomó en la cama muerto de cansancio **2** (sleep) (AmE colloq) dormir*, apolillar (RPl fam)
B (fail) (colloq) fracasar estrepitosamente

flop² *n*
A (sound, movement) (*no pl*) golpetazo *m*, golpe *m* seco
B (failure) (colloq) fracaso *m*

flophouse /'flɑːphaʊs || 'flɒphaʊs/ *n* (AmE sl) albergue *m* para vagabundos

floppy¹ /'flɑːpi || 'flɒpi/ *adj* ‹*hat/bag*› flexible, blando; ‹*ears/tail*› caído

floppy² *n* (*pl* **-pies**) (colloq) ▸ **floppy disk**

floppy disk *n* disquete *m*, floppy (disk) *m*, disco *m* flexible *or* blando

flora /'flɔːrə/ *n* (Bot) flora *f*

floral /'flɔːrəl/ *adj* ‹*fabric/dress*› floreado; **a ~ print** un estampado de flores; **~ tribute** (frml) ofrenda *f* floral, corona *f* de flores

Florence /'flɔːrəns || 'flɒrəns/ *n* Florencia *f*

floret /'flɔːrət || 'flɒrɪt/ *n* cabezuela *f*, cogollito *m*

florid /'flɔːrəd || 'flɒrɪd/ *adj* **1** (red) ‹*complexion/cheeks*› rubicundo **2** (ornate) ‹*decoration/style*› recargado; ‹*language*› florido

florist /'flɔːrəst || 'flɒrɪst/ *n* (person) florista *mf*; **is there a ~'s near here?** ¿hay una floristería *or* (AmL tb) florería cerca de aquí?

floss¹ /flɑːs || flɒs/ *n* [u] (*dental ~*) hilo *m or* seda *f* dental

floss² *vt* limpiar con hilo *or* seda dental

flotation /fləʊ'teɪʃən/ *n*
A [c] (of company) salida *f* a Bolsa, admisión *f* a cotización en Bolsa; (of shares) emisión *f*
B [u] (Naut) flotación *f*

flotilla /fləʊ'tɪlə || flə'tɪlə/ *n* flotilla *f*

flotsam /'flɑːtsəm || 'flɒtsəm/ *n* [u] restos *mpl* flotantes (*de un naufragio*); **~ and jetsam** desechos *mpl*, restos *mpl*

flounce¹ /flaʊns/ *vi* (+ *adv compl*): **to ~ in/out** entrar/salir* indignado (*or* airado *etc*)

flounce² *n* (ruffle) volante *m*, elán *m* (Méx), volado *m* (RPl), vuelo *m* (Chi)

flounder¹ /'flaʊndər || 'flaʊndə(r)/ *vi* **1** (in water) luchar para mantenerse a flote; **the oxen ~ed through the mud** los bueyes avanzaban dando resbalones en el barro **2** «*speaker*» quedarse sin saber qué decir; **he was ~ing after only two questions** a la tercera pregunta empezó a fallar *or* a perder pie

flounder² *n* platija *f*

flour /flaʊər || 'flaʊə(r)/ *n* [u] harina *f*

flourish¹ /'flɜːrɪʃ || 'flʌrɪʃ/ *vi* «*arts/trade*» florecer*; «*business*» prosperar; «*plant*» darse* *or* crecer* bien

■ **flourish** *vt* ‹*stick/letter*› blandir, agitar

flourish² *n* **1** (showy gesture) floreo *m*, floritura *f* **2** (embellishment) floritura *f*, firulete *m* (AmL); (in signature) rúbrica *f* **3** (Mus) (fanfare) fanfarria *f*

flourishing /'flɜːrɪʃɪŋ || 'flʌrɪʃɪŋ/ *adj* ‹*business*› próspero, floreciente; **they're ~** están estupendamente, les va de maravilla

floury /flaʊri || 'flaʊəri/ *adj* ‹*hands/apron*› lleno de harina

flout /flaʊt/ *vt* desobedecer* *or* desacatar abiertamente

flow¹ /fləʊ/ *vi*
A **1** «*liquid/electric current*» fluir*; «*tide*» subir, crecer*; «*blood*» correr; (from wound) manar, salir*; **the Seine ~s through Paris** el Sena pasa por *or* atraviesa París; **the river ~s into the sea** el río desemboca *or* desagua en el mar; **tears ~ed down her cheeks** las lágrimas le corrían por las mejillas **2** (run smoothly, continuously) «*traffic*» circular con fluidez; «*music/words*» fluir*
B (be plentiful) correr como agua; **a land ~ing with milk and honey** (Bib) una tierra que mana (en) leche y miel

flow² *n*
A [u] **1** (of liquid, current) flujo *m*, circulación *f* **2** (of traffic, information) circulación *f*; (of capital, money) movimiento *m*; **he was interrupted in full ~** lo interrumpieron en pleno discurso; **it interrupted her ~ of thought** interrumpió el hilo de sus ideas; ***to go with the ~*** colloq) dejarse arrastrar *or* llevar por la corriente
B [c] (stream — of water, lava) corriente *f*
C [u] (of narrative) fluidez *f*

flow chart, flow diagram *n* organigrama *m*

flower¹ /ˈflaʊər || ˈflaʊə(r)/ *n*
A [c] (plant, blossom) flor *f*; **to be in ~**[u] estar* en flor; (*before n*) **~ arrangement** arreglo *m* floral
B [u] (finest part) (liter): **the ~ of the nation's youth** la flor y nata de la juventud del país

flower² *vi* **1** (Bot) florecer*, florear (Chi, Méx) **2** **flowering** *pres p* ‹*plant/shrub/tree*› que da flores

flowerbed /ˈflaʊrbed || ˈflaʊəbed/ *n* arriate *m* (Esp, Méx), parterre *m* (Esp), cantero *m* (Cu, RPl)

flowering /ˈflaʊrɪŋ || ˈflaʊərɪŋ/ *n* [u c] (of plant) floración *f*; (of culture, art) florecimiento *m*

flowerpot /ˈflaʊrpɑːt || ˈflaʊəpɒt/ *n* maceta *f*, tiesto *m* (Esp), macetero *m* (AmS)

flowery /ˈflaʊri || ˈflaʊəri/ *adj* ‹*fabric/pattern*› floreado, de flores; ‹*meadow/hillside*› florido; ‹*style/prose*› florido

flowing /ˈfləʊɪŋ/ *adj* **1** ‹*beard/robe*› largo y suelto **2** ‹*handwriting/movement*› fluido

flown /fləʊn/ *past p of* **fly²**

fl oz = fluid ounce(s)

flu /fluː/ *n* [u] gripe *f*, gripa *f* (Col, Méx)

flub /flʌb/ (AmE colloq) **-bb-** *vt* ‹*stroke*› fallar; ‹*chance*› echar a perder; **I ~bed the exam** la pifié en el examen (fam), troné el examen (Méx)

fluctuate /ˈflʌktʃueɪt || ˈflʌktjʊeɪt/ *vi* fluctuar*

fluctuation /ˈflʌktʃuˈeɪʃən || ˌflʌktjʊˈeɪʃən/ *n* [u c] fluctuación *f*

flue /fluː/ *n* (of chimney) tiro *m*; (of stove, boiler) tiro *m*

fluency /ˈfluːənsi/ *n* [u] fluidez *f*, soltura *f*

fluent /ˈfluːənt/ *adj* **1** (in languages): **to be ~ in Italian** *o* **to speak ~ Italian** hablar italiano con fluidez *or* soltura **2** ‹*style/delivery*› fluido; ‹*speaker*› desenvuelto

fluently /ˈfluːəntli/ *adv* con fluidez *or* soltura

fluff¹ /flʌf/ *n* [u] pelusa *f*

fluff² *vt*
A (bungle) (colloq) ‹*exam*› pifiarla en (fam); ‹*chance*› echar a perder; **she ~ed her lines** se equivocó en su parlamento
B **~ (up)** ‹*feathers*› ahuecar*

fluffy /ˈflʌfi/ *adj* **-fier, -fiest** ‹*fabric/garment*› suave y esponjoso; ‹*fur/hair*› suave y sedoso; **a ~ toy** (BrE) un juguete de peluche

fluid¹ /ˈfluːəd || ˈfluːɪd/ *n* [u c] **1** (Phys, Tech) fluido *m*; **hydraulic/brake ~** líquido *m* hidráulico/de frenos **2** (in body) líquido *m*, fluido *m*; **he's on ~s** está tomando sólo líquidos

fluid² *adj*
A ‹*substance/style*› fluido
B (not stable or fixed): **our plans are still very ~** aún no hemos concretado nuestros planes

fluid ounce *n* (in USA) *unidad de capacidad; equivalente a 29,57 mililitros*; (in UK) *unidad de capacidad equivalente a 28,42 mililitros*

fluke /fluːk/ *n* (stroke of luck) (colloq) chiripa *f* (fam), casualidad *f*

flummox /ˈflʌməks/ *vt* (colloq) desconcertar*, dejar cortado (fam)

flung /flʌŋ/ *past & past p of* **fling¹**

flunk /flʌŋk/ *vt* (colloq AmE) ‹*student*› reprobar*, rajar (Andes fam), catear (Esp), tronar* (Méx fam), bochar (RPl fam), jalar (Per arg); **I was ~ed in French** *o* (BrE also) **I ~ed French** me reprobaron (*or* me rajaron *etc*) en francés
■ **flunk** *vi* **~ (out)** (colloq AmE) salir* reprobado *or* (Esp) suspendido

flunkey /ˈflʌŋki/ *n* (*pl* **-keys** *or* **-kies**) **1** (footman) (pej) lacayo *m* **2** (henchman) (pej) esbirro *m* (pey)

flunky /ˈflʌŋki/ *n* (*pl* **-kies**) ▸ **flunkey**

fluorescence /ˈflʊˈresəns || flʊəˈresəns, flɔː-/ *n* [u] fluorescencia *f*

fluorescent /ˈflʊˈresənt || flʊəˈresənt, flɔː-/ *adj* fluorescente; **~ light** *o* **tube** tubo *m* fluorescente, tubolux® *m* (RPl)

fluoridation /ˈflʊrəˈdeɪʃən || ˌflɔːrɪˈdeɪʃən/ *n* [u] fluoración *f*, fluorización *f*

fluoride /ˈflʊraɪd || ˈflɔːraɪd/ *n* [c u] (Chem) fluoruro *m*; (Dent) flúor *m*; (*before n*) **~ toothpaste** dentífrico *m* con flúor

fluorine /ˈflʊriːn || ˈflʊəriːn, ˈflɔːriːn/ *n* [u] flúor *m*

flurry /ˈflɜːri || ˈflʌri/ *n* (*pl* **-ries**)
A (of snow, wind) ráfaga *f*; (of rain) chaparrón *m*
B **1** (sudden burst): **a ~ of excitement/activity** una oleada de emoción/un frenesí de actividad; **there was a ~ of activity when she arrived** hubo mucho trajín cuando ella llegó **2** (agitated state): **to be in a ~** estar* nervioso

flush¹ /flʌʃ/ *n*
A **1** (blush) rubor *m*; **the first pink ~ of dawn in the sky** (liter) el primer arrebol del alba en el cielo (liter) **2** (of anger, passion) arrebato *m*; **in the first ~ of success** con la euforia del triunfo
B (toilet mechanism) cisterna *f*; (action): **give the toilet another ~** tira otra vez de la cadena, jálale (a la cadena) otra vez (AmL exc CS)
C (in cards) flor *f*; **royal/straight ~** escalera *f* real/de color

flush² *vt*
A ‹*toilet*›: **to ~ the toilet** tirar de la cadena, jalarle (a la cadena) (AmL exc CS); **to ~ sth down the toilet** *o* **away** tirar algo al *or* echar algo por el wáter
B (drive out) **~ (out)** ‹*person/criminal*› hacer* salir
■ **flush** *vi*
A «*toilet*» funcionar
B (blush) «*person/face*» (with anger) enrojecer*, ponerse* rojo; (with embarrassment) ruborizarse*, sonrojarse; **her cheeks ~ed crimson** sus mejillas se encendieron

flush³ *adj*
A (level) alineado; **~ against the wall** pegado a la pared
B (having money) (colloq): **to be ~** andar* bien de dinero

flushed /flʌʃt/ *adj* ‹*cheeks*› colorado, rojo; **~ with success** exaltado por el éxito

fluster¹ /ˈflʌstər || ˈflʌstə(r)/ *vt* poner* nervioso, aturullar; **to get ~ed** ponerse* nervioso, aturullarse

fluster² *n* (*no pl*): **to be/get in a ~** estar*/ponerse* nervioso

flute /fluːt/ *n* flauta *f*

fluted /ˈfluːtəd || ˈfluːtɪd/ *adj* ‹*border/edge*› ondulado

flutist /ˈfluːtəst || ˈfluːtɪst/ *n* (AmE) flautista *mf*

flutter¹ /ˈflʌtər || ˈflʌtə(r)/ *vi* **1** «*bird/butterfly*» revolotear; **the bird ~ed away** el pájaro se alejó aleteando **2** «*flag*» ondear, agitarse; «*leaves*» agitarse **3** «*heart*» latir *or* palpitar con fuerza
■ **flutter** *vt* ‹*wings*› batir, sacudir; **to ~ one's eyelashes at sb** hacerle* ojitos *or* caídas de ojo a algn

flutter² *n*
A **~ (of wings)** (*no pl*) aleteo *m*, revoloteo *m* (de alas)
B (thrill) (*no pl*) revuelo *m*; **I was (all) in a ~ when I heard the news** cuando oí la noticia me puse nervioso
C (bet) (BrE colloq) (*usu sing*): **to have a ~ on the horses** probar* suerte en las carreras (de caballos)

flux /flʌks/ *n* [u] (constant change): **to be in (a state of) ~** estar* en un estado de cambio, cambiar continuamente

fly¹ /flaɪ/ *n* (*pl* **flies**)
A **1** (insect) mosca *f*; ***he/she wouldn't hurt a ~*** es incapaz de matar una mosca; ***the ~ in the ointment*** el único problema, la única pega (Esp fam); ***there are no flies on her/him*** no tiene un pelo de tonta/tonto; ***to be a ~ on the wall*:** **I'd like to have been a ~ on the wall when he told her** me habría gustado estar allí *or* ver su reacción cuando se lo dijo; ***to die/drop like flies*** morir*/caer* como moscas **2** (in angling) mosca *f*; (*before n*) **~ fishing** pesca *f* con mosca
B (on trousers) (*often pl in BrE*) bragueta *f*, marrueco *m* (Chi)
C **flies** *pl* (Theat) bambalinas *fpl*

fly² (*3rd pers sing pres* **flies**; *pres p* **flying**; *past* **flew**; *past p* **flown**) *vi*
A **1** «*bird/bee*» volar*; **to ~ away/in/out** irse*/entrar/salir* volando **2** «*plane/pilot*» volar*; «*passenger*» ir* en avión; **to ~ in** llegar* (*en avión*); **we will be ~ing into Orly** aterrizaremos en Orly; **to ~ out** salir* (*en avión*); **we ~ on**

f

to Denver tomorrow mañana volamos *a or* salimos en avión para Denver; ***to be ~ing high*** estar* volando alto 3 «*flag*» ondear, flamear; **with her hair/coat ~ing in the wind** con el pelo/abrigo ondeando al viento

B 1 (rush) «*person*» correr, ir* (*or* salir* *etc*) volando 2 **to ~ AT sb** lanzarse* SOBRE algn; **to ~ into a temper** *o* **rage** ponerse* hecho una furia *or* un basilisco, montar en cólera 3 (move, be thrown) volar*; **the ball flew past me** la pelota pasó volando por mi lado; **I tripped and went ~ing** tropecé y salí volando *or* disparado; ***to let ~ at sb*** emprenderla *or* arremeter contra algn; **he let ~ with a stream of abuse** soltó una sarta de insultos; ***to make the feathers*** *o* ***fur*** *o* ***sparks ~*** armar un gran lío (fam) 4 (pass quickly) «*time*» pasar volando, volar*

■ **fly** *vt*

A 1 (control) ‹*plane/glider/balloon*› pilotar; ‹*kite*› hacer* volar *or* encumbrar (Andes), remontar (RPl) 2 (carry) ‹*cargo*› transportar (*en avión*); ‹*person*› llevar (*en avión*); **the wounded were flown out by helicopter** los heridos fueron evacuados en helicóptero; **they had the equipment flown in** les mandaron el equipo por avión 3 (travel over) ‹*distance*› recorrer (*en avión*); **they ~ this route daily** tienen vuelos diarios en esta ruta 4 (travel by) ‹*airline*› volar* con

B ‹*flag*› izar*, enarbolar; **the ship was ~ing the Panamanian flag** el barco llevaba bandera panameña *or* pabellón panameño

fly³ *adj* (BrE colloq) vivo (fam), espabilado

fly: **~away** /'flaɪə'weɪ/ *adj* suelto; **~blown** *adj* 1 ‹*meat*› lleno de huevos de mosca 2 (shabby, old) ‹*café/hotel*› de mala muerte; **~by** *n* (AmE) (Aviat) desfile *m* aéreo; **~-by-night** *adj* ‹*dealer/firm*› pirata, que no inspira confianza

flyer /'flaɪər || 'flaɪə(r)/ *n* ▸ **flier**

fly half *n* medio *m* apertura

flying¹ /'flaɪɪŋ/ *adj* (*before n*) 1 (hurried): **a ~ visit** una visita relámpago 2 ‹*glass/debris*› que vuela (por los aires); **she took a ~ leap and crossed it** tomó impulso y lo cruzó de un salto; **a ~ tackle** (Sport) un placaje en el aire

flying² *n* [u] 1 (as pilot) pilotaje *m*; (*before n*) ‹*time/hours/lesson*› de vuelo; ‹*helmet/jacket*› de piloto 2 (as passenger): **I like/hate ~** me gusta/odio viajar en avión

flying: **~ boat** *n* hidroavión *m*; **~ fish** *n* pez *m* volador; **~ picket** *n* piquete *m* móvil *or* volante; **~ saucer** *n* platillo *m* volador *or* (Esp) volante; **~ squad** *n* (of UK police) brigada *f* móvil *or* volante; **~ squirrel** *n* ardilla *f* voladora; **~ start** *n* salida *f* lanzada; ***to get off to a ~ start*** «*person/business*» empezar* con muy buen pie *or* con el pie derecho

fly: **~leaf** *n* guarda *f*; **~over** *n* (BrE Transp) paso *m* elevado, paso *m* a desnivel (Méx); (AmE Aviat) desfile *m* aéreo; **~paper** *n* [u c] tira *f* matamoscas; **~past** *n* (BrE) desfile *m* aéreo; **~sheet** *n* (BrE) toldo *m* impermeable (*de una tienda de campaña*); **~ spray** *n* [u c] insecticida *m* (*en aerosol*); **~swatter** /'flaɪ,swɑːtər || 'flaɪ,swɒtə(r)/ *n* matamoscas *m*; **~weight** *n* peso *m* mosca; **~wheel** *n* volante *m*

fly-on-the-wall /,flaɪɑːnðə'wɔːl || ,flaɪɒnðə'wɔːl/ *adj* (TV): *en que las cámaras capturan fielmente la realidad con intervención mínima del director*

FM *n* (= **frequency modulation**) FM *f*

foal¹ /fəʊl/ *n* (male) potro *m*, potrillo *m*; (female) potranca *f*, potra *f*

foal² *vi* parir

foam¹ /fəʊm/ *n* [u c] espuma *f*

foam² *vi* «*sea/waves*» hacer* espuma; **to ~ at the mouth** «*animal*» echar espuma por la boca

foam rubber *n* [u] goma espuma *f*, hule *m* espuma (Méx)

fob /fɑːb || fɒb/ *n* (watchchain) leontina *f*; (*before n*) **~ watch** reloj *m* de bolsillo

Phrasal verb

• **fob off** [v ▸ o ▸ adv] 1 (placate) **to ~ sb off (WITH sth)** engatusar a algn (CON algo) 2 (dispose of) **to ~ sth off ONTO sb** encajarle *or* (AmL tb) enjaretarle algo a algn (fam)

focal /'fəʊkəl/ *adj* (*before n*) 1 (Opt) focal 2 ‹*issue*› central

focal point *n* 1 (Opt) foco *m* 2 (of attention, activity) centro *m*, foco *m*

focus¹ /'fəʊkəs/ *n* (*pl* **-cuses** *or* **foci** /'fəʊsaɪ/)

A [u] (Opt, Phot) foco *m*; **to be in ~** estar* enfocado; **to be out of ~** estar* desenfocado; **to bring** *o* **get sth into ~** enfocar* algo; **to come into ~** «*picture*» entrar en foco; **his life lacks ~** no tiene un norte en su vida

B [c] (central point) centro *m*; **to be the ~ of attention** ser* el centro de atención

C [c] (Phys, Math) foco *m*

focus² **-s-** *or* **-ss-** *vt* 1 (Opt, Phot) enfocar*; **to ~ sth ON sth/sb**: **she ~ed her binoculars on the yacht** enfocó el yate con los prismáticos 2 (concentrate) **to ~ sth (ON sth)** ‹*light/radiation*› concentrar algo (EN algo); ‹*attention*› centrar algo (EN algo)

■ **focus** *vi* 1 «*camera/eyes*» enfocar*; **to ~ ON sth/sb**: **his eyes were unable to ~ on the small print** no podía fijar la vista en la letra pequeña; **the spotlight ~ed on the singer** el reflector enfocó al cantante; **try to ~ on the tree** trata de enfocar el árbol 2 «*lecturer/chapter/attention*» **to ~ ON sth/sb** centrarse EN algo/algn

fodder /'fɑːdər || 'fɒdə(r)/ *n* [u] forraje *m*, pienso *m*; *see also* **cannon¹**

foe /fəʊ/ *n* (liter) enemigo, -ga *m,f*

foetal /'fiːtl̩/ *adj* (BrE) ▸ **fetal**

foetus /'fiːtəs/ *n* (BrE) ▸ **fetus**

fog¹ /fɔːg || fɒg/ *n* [u c] (Meteo) niebla *f*

fog² *vi* **-gg-** **~ (up** *o* **over)** «*glasses/mirror*» empañarse

fogbound /'fɔːgbaʊnd || 'fɒgbaʊnd/ *adj* ‹*airport/road*› afectado por la niebla; ‹*plane/ferry*› retenido a causa de la niebla

fogey *n* (*pl* **fogeys**) ▸ **fogy**

foggy /'fɔːgi || 'fɒgi/ *adj* **-gier, -giest** 1 ‹*day*› de niebla; ‹*weather*› nebuloso; **it's ~** hay niebla 2 (confused) confuso; ***not to have the foggiest (idea)*** no tener* ni la más remota *or* ni la más mínima idea

fog: **~horn** *n* sirena *f* (*de niebla*); **to have a voice like a ~horn** tener* un vozarrón (fam); **~ light**, (BrE) **~ lamp** *n* faro *m* antiniebla, exploradora *f* (Col fam)

fogy /'fəʊgi/ *n* (*pl* **fogies**) (colloq & pej): **an old ~** un/una carca (fam & pey)

foible /'fɔɪbəl/ *n* debilidad *f*, flaqueza *f* (liter)

foil¹ /fɔɪl/ *n*

A [u] 1 (metal sheet) lámina *f* de metal 2 (Culin) (*kitchen ~*) papel *m* de aluminio *or* de plata

B [c] (contrast) **to be a ~ FOR/TO sth**: **they are the perfect ~ for each other** se complementan perfectamente

C (sword) florete *m*

foil² *vt* ‹*plan/attempt*› frustrar; **~ed again!** (hum) ¡otro intento frustrado!

foist /fɔɪst/ *vt* **to ~ sth (OFF) ON** *o* **ONTO sb** ‹*shoddy goods/responsibility*› endilgarle* algo a algn, encajarle algo a algn (fam); **to ~ oneself on sb** pegársele* a algn (fam)

fold¹ /fəʊld/ *vt*

A 1 (bend over) ‹*paper/sheet*› doblar; **to ~ sth in half** *o* **in two** doblar algo por la mitad 2 (bring together): **the butterfly ~ed its wings** la mariposa plegó las alas; **to ~ one's arms** cruzar* los brazos

B (mix) (Culin) **to ~ sth INTO sth** incorporar algo A algo

■ **fold** *vi*

A 1 «*chair/table*» plegarse*; «*map/poster*» doblarse, plegarse* 2 **folding** *pres p* ‹*chair/table*› plegable, abatible; ‹*doors*› plegable; **~ing money** (AmE colloq) billetes *mpl*

B (fail) «*project/campaign*» venirse* abajo, fracasar; «*play*» bajar de cartel; «*business/shop*» cerrar* (sus puertas), quebrar*

Phrasal verbs

• **fold away**

A [v ▸ o ▸ adv, v ▸ adv ▸ o] ‹*clothes*› doblar y guardar; ‹*chairs*› plegar* y guardar

B [v ▸ adv]: **the chairs ~ away neatly** las sillas se pueden plegar y guardar cómodamente

• **fold up**

A [v ▸ o ▸ adv, v ▸ adv ▸ o] ‹*sheet/newspaper*› doblar; ‹*chair/table*› plegar*

B [v ▸ adv] «*map*» doblarse, plegarse*; «*chair*» plegarse*

fold² *n*

A 1 (crease) doblez *m*, pliegue *m* 2 (Geol) pliegue *m*

B (sheep pen) redil *m*, aprisco *m*

-fold /fəʊld/ *suff*: **his income increased fivefold** sus ingresos se multiplicaron por cinco *or* se quintuplicaron; **the problem is threefold** el problema tiene tres aspectos

foldaway /ˈfəʊldəweɪ/ *adj* (*before n*) plegable, plegadizo (Méx)

folder /ˈfəʊldər || ˈfəʊldə(r)/ *n* carpeta *f*

foliage /ˈfəʊliɪdʒ/ *n* [u] follaje *m*; (*before n*) **a ~ plant** (AmE) una planta decorativa

folio /ˈfəʊliəʊ/ *n* (*pl* **folios**) 1 (sheet) pliego *m* 2 (numbered leaf) folio *m* 3 (volume) libro *m* en folio, infolio *m*

folk /fəʊk/ *n*

A 1 *also* **folks** *pl* (people) (colloq) gente *f*; **young/city ~(s)** gente joven/de la ciudad; **hi ~s!** hola ¿qué tal? (fam) 2 **folks** *pl* (esp AmE colloq) (relatives) familia *f*; (parents) padres *mpl*, viejos *mpl* (fam)

B (+ *pl vb*) (Anthrop) pueblo *m*; (*before n*) ‹*art/medicine/legend*› popular; ‹*dancing*› folklórico, tradicional

C [u] (Mus) folk *m*

folk: **~lore** *n* [u] folklore *m*; **~ music** *n* [u] (traditional) música *f* folklórica; (modern) música *f* folk; **~ singer** *n* (traditional) cantante *mf* de música folklórica; (modern) cantante *mf* (de música) folk; **~ song** *n* [c u] (traditional) canción *f* popular *or* tradicional; (modern) canción *f* folk; **~ways** *pl n* (AmE) cultura *f* popular

follicle /ˈfɑːlɪkəl || ˈfɒlɪkəl/ *n* (*hair* ~) folículo *m* (piloso)

follow /ˈfɑːləʊ || ˈfɒləʊ/ *vt*

A 1 (go, come after, pursue) seguir*; **the King entered, ~ed by the Queen** el rey entró, seguido por *or* de la reina; **she ~ed him into the library** entró en la biblioteca tras él 2 (succeed, happen after): **July ~s June** después de junio viene julio; **the lecture was ~ed by a discussion** después de la conferencia hubo un debate 3 (repeat, improve on) ‹*success/achievement*› igualar

B 1 (keep to) ‹*road*› seguir* (por); ‹*trail*› seguir* 2 (obey) ‹*instructions/advice*› seguir*; ‹*order*› cumplir 3 (conform to, imitate) ‹*fashion*› seguir*; **~ her example** sigue su ejemplo, haz como ella

C 1 (pay close attention to) ‹*movement/progress*› seguir* de cerca; **to ~ sth/sb with one's eyes** seguir* algo/a algn con la mirada 2 (take interest in) ‹*news*› mantenerse* al tanto de; ‹*TV serial*› seguir*

D ‹*argument/reasoning*› entender*; **do you ~ me?** ¿(me) entiendes?

■ **follow** *vi*

A (come after): **you go first, and I'll ~** tú ve delante que yo te sigo; **a news bulletin ~s in five minutes** dentro de cinco minutos habrá un boletín de noticias; **we'll start with the soup, and have chicken to ~** para empezar tomaremos sopa y después pollo; **the winners were as ~s ...** los ganadores fueron ...

B (be logical consequence) deducirse*, seguirse*; **that doesn't necessarily ~** una cosa no implica la otra

C (understand) entender*

Phrasal verbs

- **follow on** [v ▸ adv] **to ~ on FROM sth**: **this ~s on from what we said yesterday** esto tiene relación con lo que decíamos ayer
- **follow through**

A [v ▸ o ▸ adv, v ▸ adv ▸ o] (pursue): **they lack the finance to ~ the program through** no disponen de recursos para seguir adelante con el programa; **if you ~ that line of argument through ...** con esa lógica ...

B [v ▸ adv] (Sport) acompañar el golpe

- **follow up** [v ▸ o ▸ adv, v ▸ adv ▸ o] ‹*case*› seguir*, darle* seguimiento a; **he promised to ~ the matter up** me prometió que investigaría el asunto

follower /ˈfɑːləʊər || ˈfɒləʊə(r)/ *n* seguidor, -dora *m,f*

following[1] /ˈfɑːləʊɪŋ || ˈfɒləʊɪŋ/ *adj* (*before n*) (next) siguiente; **(on) the ~ day** al día siguiente

following[2] *n*

A (followers) seguidores *mpl*; (admirers) admiradores *mpl*; **he has a large ~** tiene muchos seguidores/admiradores

B (what, who comes next) **the ~**: **the ~ are to play in tomorrow's game ...** los siguientes jugarán en el partido de mañana ...; **the letter said the ~ ...** la carta decía lo siguiente ...

follow: **~-on** /ˈfɑːləʊˈɑːn || ˌfɒləʊˈɒn/ *n* (BrE) continuación *f*; **by way of a ~-on** para continuar; **~-the-leader** /ˈfɑːləʊðəˈliːdər || ˌfɒləʊðəˈliːdə(r)/ *n* [u]: **to play ~-the-leader** jugar* a lo que haga el rey, jugar* a lo que hace la mano, hace la tras (Méx), jugar* al mono mayor (Chi); **~-up** *n* [c] (sequel) continuación *f*; (*before n*): **she sent a ~-up letter** mandó una segunda (*or* tercera *etc*) carta

folly /ˈfɑːli || ˈfɒli/ *n* (*pl* **-lies**)

A [u c] (foolishness, recklessness) locura *f*; **it was sheer ~** fue una auténtica locura

B (BrE Archit) capricho *m*

foment /fəʊˈment/ *vt* (frml) fomentar, instigar* a

fond /fɑːnd || fɒnd/ *adj* **-er, -est**

A (*pred*) **~ OF sb/sth/-ING**: **she's very ~ of Sue** le tiene mucho cariño a Sue, quiere mucho a Sue; **he was ~ of chocolate** le gustaba el chocolate; **he's a bit too ~ of criticizing other people** es demasiado aficionado a criticar a los demás; **to grow ~ of sb** tomarle cariño a algn, encariñarse con algn

B (*before n*) 1 (loving) ‹*gesture/look*› cariñoso; **with ~est regards** con mi más sincero afecto 2 (indulgent) ‹*parent/husband*› indulgente 3 (delusive, vain) ‹*hope/illusion*› vano

fondant /ˈfɑːndənt || ˈfɒndənt/ *n* fondant *m*

fondle /ˈfɑːndl || ˈfɒndl/ *vt* acariciar

fondly /ˈfɑːndli || ˈfɒndli/ *adv* 1 (lovingly) cariñosamente; ‹*remember*› con cariño 2 (foolishly) ingenuamente

fondness /ˈfɑːndnəs || ˈfɒndnɪs/ *n* [u] (love) cariño *m*; (liking) afición *f*; **her ~ for chocolate** su afición por el chocolate

font /fɑːnt || fɒnt/ *n*

A (baptismal) pila *f* bautismal

B (Print) fuente *f*

food /fuːd/ *n* 1 [u] (in general) comida *f*; **we gave him some ~** le dimos algo de comer; **to be off one's ~** estar* desganado *or* inapetente; **to go off one's ~** perder* el apetito; ***~ for thought***: **his father's words gave him ~ for thought** las palabras de su padre lo hicieron reflexionar; (*before n*) ‹*shortage/exports*› de alimentos 2 [c] (specific kind) alimento *m*

food: **~ chain** *n* cadena *f* alimenticia *or* trófica; **~ poisoning** *n* [u] intoxicación *f* (*por alimentos*); **~ processor** *n* robot *m* de cocina, procesador *m* de alimentos; **~stuffs** *pl n* productos *mpl* alimenticios, comestibles *mpl*

fool[1] /fuːl/ *n*

A [c] 1 (stupid person) idiota *mf*, tonto, -ta *m,f*; **to make a ~ of oneself** hacer* el ridículo; **to make sb look a ~** dejar a algn en ridículo; **well, more ~ you** pues peor para ti; ***he's no o nobody's ~*** no tiene un pelo de tonto, nadie le toma el pelo; ***not to suffer ~s gladly*** tener* muy poca paciencia con las estupideces de la gente; ***to act o play the ~*** hacer* payasadas; ***to live in a ~'s paradise*** vivir engañado; ***~s rush in (where angels fear to tread)*** el necio es atrevido y el sabio comedido 2 (jester) bufón *m*

B [c u] (esp BrE Culin) *postre a base de puré de frutas y crema*

fool[2] *vt* engañar; **you had me completely ~ed** me tenías absolutamente convencida; **to ~ sb INTO -ING**: **I ~ed him into thinking that ...** le hice creer que ...

■ **fool** *vi* 1 ▸**fool around** 2 (joke) bromear

Phrasal verbs

- **fool about** (esp BrE) ▸**fool around 1**
- **fool around** [v ▸ adv] 1 (act foolishly) hacer* payasadas, hacer* el tonto (Esp); **children shouldn't ~ around with electricity** los niños no deben jugar con la electricidad 2 (be sexually involved): **he was ~ing around with other women** tenía enredos *or* andaba con otras

fool[3] *adj* (*before n*) (AmE) tonto

foolhardy /ˈfuːlˈhɑːrdi || ˈfuːlhɑːdi/ *adj* imprudente, insensato

foolish /ˈfuːlɪʃ/ *adj* 1 (silly) ‹*person/prank*› tonto, idiota; ‹*look/grin*› de tonto *or* idiota; **~ remarks** tonterías *fpl*; **to make sb look ~** dejar a algn en ridículo 2 (unwise) ‹*decision/plan*› insensato, estúpido; **I know it was ~** ya sé que fue una estupidez

foolishly /ˈfuːlɪʃli/ *adv* tontamente, como un tonto/una tonta

foolishness /ˈfuːlɪʃnəs || ˈfuːlɪʃnɪs/ *n* [u] insensatez *f*, estupidez *f*

fool: **~proof** *adj* ‹*idea/plan/method*› infalible; ‹*machine/controls*› sencillo de manejar; **~scap** /ˈfuːlskæp/ *n* [u] *pliego de aprox 43 x 35 cm*

foot[1] /fʊt/ *n* (*pl* **feet**)

A [c] (of person) pie *m*; (of animal) pata *f*; (on sewing machine) pie *m*;

f

to be on one's feet estar* de pie, estar* parado (AmL); **to get back on one's feet** (after illness) recuperarse; **they got the company back on its feet** volvieron a levantar la compañía; **to get** *o* **rise to one's feet** ponerse* de pie, levantarse, pararse (AmL); **go home and put your feet up** vete a casa a descansar; **he had never set ~ in a church before** nunca había pisado una iglesia *or* entrado en una iglesia antes; **to go/come on ~** ir*/venir* a pie *or* caminando *or* andando; ***a ~ in the door***: **it's a way of getting your ~ in the door** es una manera de introducirte *or* de meterte en la empresa (*or* la profesión *etc*); ***my ~!*** (colloq): **delicate condition my ~!** ¡estado delicado mi *or* tu abuela! (fam); ***not to put a ~ wrong*** no dar* un paso en falso, no cometer ni un error; ***the shoe's*** *o* (BrE) ***boot's on the other ~*** se ha dado vuelta la tortilla; ***to be able to think on one's feet*** ser* capaz de pensar con rapidez; ***to be dead*** *o* ***asleep on one's feet*** no poder* tenerse en pie; ***to be rushed*** *o* ***run off one's feet*** estar* agobiado de trabajo; ***to fall*** *o* ***land on one's feet***: **she always seems to land on her feet** siempre le sale todo redondo; ***to find one's feet***: **it didn't take him long to find his feet in his new school** no tardó en habituarse a la nueva escuela; ***to get cold feet (about sth)***: **she got cold feet** le entró miedo y se echó atrás; ***to get off on the wrong ~*** empezar* con el pie izquierdo *or* con mal pie; ***to have itchy feet*** ser* inquieto; ***to have one's feet on the ground*** tener* los pies sobre la tierra; ***to put one's best ~ forward*** (hurry) apretar* el paso; (do one's best) esmerarse para causar la mejor impresión; ***to put one's ~ down*** (be firm) imponerse*, no ceder; (accelerate vehicle) (colloq) meterle (AmL fam), apretar* el acelerador; ***to put one's ~ in it*** (colloq) meter la pata (fam); ***to stand on one's own two feet*** valerse* por sí (*or* mí *etc*) mismo; ***to sweep sb off her/his feet***: **she was swept off her feet by an older man** se enamoró perdidamente de un hombre mayor que ella; ***under sb's feet***: **the cat keeps getting under my feet** el gato siempre me anda alrededor *or* siempre se me está atravesando; ▸ **hand**[1] **B**

B (bottom, lower end) (*no pl*) pie *m*; **the ~ of the bed** los pies de la cama

C [c] (measure) (*pl* **foot** *or* **feet**) pie *m*; **he is six ~** *o* **feet tall** mide seis pies

D [u] (infantry) (esp BrE dated) (*before n*) **~ soldier** soldado *mf* de infantería *or* de a pie

foot[2] *vt*: **to ~ the bill** pagar*

footage /ˈfʊtɪdʒ/ *n* [u] (Cin) secuencias *fpl* (filmadas)

foot-and-mouth (disease) /ˈfʊtn̩ˈmaʊθ/ *n* [u] fiebre *f* aftosa, glosopeda *f*

football /ˈfʊtbɔːl/ *n*

A [u] **1** (*American* **~**) fútbol *m* *or* (AmC, Méx) futbol *m* americano **2** (soccer) fútbol *m* *or* (AmC, Méx) futbol *m*; (*before n*) **~ match** partido *m* de fútbol *or* (AmC, Méx) futbol; **~ player** ▸ **footballer**

B [c] (ball) balón *m* *or* (esp AmL) pelota *f* de fútbol *or* (AmC, Méx) futbol

> **football**
>
> Es el deporte más popular de Gran Bretaña. Por lo general los clubes del fútbol (o *soccer*) profesional representan a grandes ciudades, especialmente en el norte de Inglaterra. En 1992, el fútbol fue reorganizado de manera que los 22 mejores equipos de Gales e Inglaterra jueguen en la *Premier League*, mientras que el resto juegue en tres *divisions*. Al final de cada temporada, los mejores equipos de cada división son ascendidos (*promoted*) y los que están al último son relegados (*relegated*). La afición inglesa tiene muy mala fama en el extranjero. (American Football)

footballer /ˈfʊtbɔːlər || ˈfʊtbɔːlə(r)/ *n* (BrE) futbolista *mf*, jugador, -dora *m,f* de fútbol *or* (AmC, Méx) futbol

football: **~ pool** *n* (AmE) apuesta *f* colectiva, polla *f* (AmL); **~ pools** *pl n* (BrE) **the ~ pools** *juego de apuestas en que se trata de acertar los resultados de los partidos de la liga de fútbol*, ≈ el pronóstico deportivo (Méx), ≈ las quinielas (*en Esp*), ≈ el prode (*en Arg*), ≈ el totogol (*en Col*), ≈ la pollagol (*en Chi*), ≈ la polla (*en Per*)

footbridge /ˈfʊtbrɪdʒ/ *n* pasarela *f*, puente *m* peatonal

-footed /ˈfʊtəd || ˈfʊtɪd/ *suff*: **four~** de cuatro patas; **light~** ligero de pies

foot: **~fall** *n* (liter) pisada *f*; **~hills** *pl n* estribaciones *fpl*; **~hold** *n* punto *m* de apoyo (*para el pie*); **to get** *o* **gain a ~hold** «*ideology*» prender*, afianzarse*; **the company gained a ~hold in the Japanese market** la compañía logró introducirse en el mercado japonés

footing /ˈfʊtɪŋ/ *n* (*no pl*)

A (balance) equilibrio *m*; **to lose** *o* **miss one's ~** resbalar, perder* el equilibrio

B (basis): **on an equal ~** en igualdad de condiciones, en situación equiparable

foot: **~lights** *pl n* candilejas *fpl*; **~loose** *adj* libre y sin compromiso; **~loose and fancy-free** libre como el viento; **~man** /ˈfʊtmən/ *n* (*pl* **-men** /-mən/) lacayo *m*; **~note** *n* nota *f* a pie de página; **~ passenger** *n* pasajero, -ra *m,f* de a pie *or* sin coche; **~path** *n* (path) sendero *m*; (pavement) (BrE) acera *f*, banqueta *f* (Méx), vereda *f* (CS, Per); **~print** *n* huella *f*; **social ~** impacto *m* social, huella *f* social; **~rest** *n* apoyapiés *m*, reposapiés *m*

footsie /ˈfʊtsi/ *n*: **to play ~ under the table** flirtear jugueteando con los pies por debajo de la mesa

foot: **~step** *n* paso *m*; ***to follow in sb's ~steps*** seguirle* los pasos a algn; **~stool** *n* escabel *m*, banqueta *f* *or* (Méx) banquito *m* para los pies; **~wear** *n* [u] calzado *m*; **~work** *n* [u] juego *m* de piernas *or* de pies

fop /fɑːp || fɒp/ *n* (dated) petimetre *m* (ant), lechuguino *m* (ant)

for[1] /fɔːr || fɔː(r), *weak form* fər || fə(r)/ *prep*

(Sense I)

A **1** (intended for) para; **is there a letter ~ me?** ¿hay carta para mí?; **my love ~ her** mi amor por ella; **clothes ~ men/women** ropa de hombre/mujer; **is it ~ sale?** ¿está en venta?, ¿se vende? **2** (on behalf of) por; **I did it ~ you** lo hice por ti; **he plays ~ England** forma parte de *or* juega en la selección inglesa; **they are agents ~ Ford** son concesionarios (de) Ford **3** (in favor of) a favor de

B (indicating purpose): **what's that ~?** ¿para qué es eso?, ¿eso para qué sirve?; **it's ~ trimming hedges** es *or* sirve para recortar setos; **it's ~ decoration** es de adorno; **I ran ~ cover** corrí a guarecerme; **an operation ~ a stomach ulcer** una operación de úlcera de estómago; **it's ~ your own good!** ¡es por tu (propio) bien!; **to go out ~ a meal** salir* a comer fuera; **I've come ~ my son** vengo a buscar a mi hijo; ***to be ~ it*** (colloq): **here comes Dad, we're ~ it now!** ahí viene papá ¡ahora sí que estamos listos *or* (Col tb) hechos *or* (CS tb) fritos! (fam)

C **1** (as): **we're having chicken ~ dinner** vamos a cenar pollo *or* hay pollo para cenar; **what's ~ dessert?** ¿qué hay de postre?; **I can now see him ~ what he is** ahora me doy cuenta de cómo es en realidad **2** (representing): **D ~ David** D de David; **what's (the) German ~ "ice cream"?** ¿cómo se dice "helado" en alemán? **3** (instead of) por; **could you call him ~ me?** ¿podrías llamarlo tú?, ¿me harías el favor de llamarlo?

D (giving reason) por; **~ that reason** por esa razón; **if it weren't ~ Joe ...** si no fuera por Joe ...; **~ one thing it's too costly and ~ another we don't need it** para empezar es muy caro y además no lo necesitamos

E **1** (in exchange for) por; **I bought the book ~ $10** compré el libro por 10 dólares; **not ~ anything in the world** por nada del mundo; **she left him ~ somebody else** lo dejó por otro **2** (indicating proportion) por; **~ every one we find, there are 20 that get away** por cada uno que encontramos, se nos escapan 20

F **1** (as concerns) para; **it's too cold ~ me here** aquí hace demasiado frío para mí; **that's men ~ you!** ¡todos los hombres son iguales! **2** (expressing appropriateness): **it's not ~ me to decide** no me corresponde a mí decidir

G **1** (in spite of): **~ all her faults, she's been very kind to us** tendrá sus defectos, pero con nosotros ha sido muy buena **2** (*with infinitive clause*): **it's unusual ~ me to forget a name** es raro que se me olvide un nombre; **is there time ~ us to have a cup of coffee?** ¿tenemos tiempo de tomar un café?

H (in exclamations): **oh, ~ some peace and quiet** ¡qué (no) daría yo por un poco de paz y tranquilidad!

(Sense II)

A (in the direction of) para; **the plane/bus ~ New York** el avión/autobús para *or* de Nueva York

B **1** (indicating duration): **he spoke ~ half an hour** habló (durante) media hora; **I've only been here ~ a day** sólo

llevo un día aquí, hace sólo un día que estoy aquí; **I've known him ~ years** lo conozco desde hace años, hace años que lo conozco; **I'll be away ~ a week** voy a estar fuera una semana; **how long are you going ~?** ¿por cuánto tiempo vas?, ¿cuánto tiempo te vas a quedar?; **we've enough food ~ six weeks** tenemos comida suficiente para seis semanas **2** (on the occasion of) para; **he gave it to me ~ my birthday** me lo regaló para mi cumpleaños **3** (by, before) para; **we have to be there ~ six o'clock** tenemos que estar allí a las seis
C (indicating distance): **we drove ~ 20 miles** hicimos 20 millas; **we could see ~ miles** se podía ver hasta muy lejos

for² *conj* (liter) pues (liter), puesto que (frml), porque

forage¹ /'fɔːrɪdʒ || 'fɒrɪdʒ/ *n* [u] (feed) forraje *m*

forage² *vi* **1** «*animal*» forrajear **2** (for supplies) **to ~ FOR sth** buscar* algo

foray /'fɔːreɪ || 'fɒreɪ/ *n* (Mil) incursión *f*

forbad(e) /fər'bæd, fə'beɪd/ *past of* **forbid**

forbear /fɔːr'ber || fɔː'beə(r)/ *vi* (*past* **forbore**; *past p* **forborne**) (frml) abstenerse*; **to ~ to + INF** abstenerse DE + INF

forbearance /fɔːr'berəns || fɔː'beərəns/ *n* [u] paciencia *f*, tolerancia *f*

forbid /fər'bɪd || fə'bɪd/ *vt* (*past* **forbad(e)**; *past p* **forbidden**)
A (not allow) prohibir*; **to ~ sb to + INF** prohibirle* A algn + INF, prohibirle* A algn QUE (+ *subj*)
B (prevent) impedir*; **God/heaven ~!** ¡Dios nos libre!

forbidden¹ /fər'bɪdn̩ || fə'bɪdn/ *past p of* **forbid**

forbidden² *adj* ‹*territory*› prohibido, vedado; ‹*topic*› tabú *adj inv*

forbidding /fər'bɪdɪŋ || fə'bɪdɪŋ/ *adj* ‹*person/look*› adusto, severo, que intimida; ‹*landscape*› imponente

forbore /fɔːr'bɔːr || fɔː'bɔː(r)/ *past of* **forbear**

forborne /fɔːr'bɔːrn || fɔː'bɔːn/ *past p of* **forbear**

force¹ /fɔːrs || fɔːs/ *n*
A [c u] (strength, coercion) fuerza *f*; **a ~ eight gale** vientos de fuerza ocho; **the police were out in ~** había una gran presencia policial; **through ~ of circumstances the plans had to be changed** razones de fuerza mayor nos hicieron cambiar de planes; **to take sth by ~** apoderarse de algo por la fuerza; **to use/resort to ~** hacer* uso de/recurrir a la fuerza
B [c] (influential thing, person) fuerza *f*; **she's a ~ to be reckoned with** no se puede menos que tenerla en cuenta; **to join ~s with sb** unirse a algn, hacer* causa común con algn
C [c] (group of people) fuerza *f*; **the (armed) ~s** las fuerzas armadas; **the (police) ~** la policía; **our sales ~** nuestro personal de ventas, nuestro equipo de vendedores
D [u] (validity) fuerza *f*; **to come into ~** entrar en vigor *or* vigencia; **to be in ~** estar* en vigor *or* vigencia

force² *vt*
A (compel) **to ~ sb to + INF** obligar* *or* forzar* a algn A + INF; **I had to ~ myself to eat** tuve que obligarme a comer; **they were ~d to sell/into selling** se vieron obligados *or* forzados a vender
B **1** (bring about, obtain) ‹*action/change*› provocar* **2** (extort) **to ~ sth OUT OF** *o* **FROM sb** ‹*secret/confession*› arrancarle* algo a la fuerza a algn
C (impose) **to ~ sth ON sb**: **the decision was ~d on us by events** los acontecimientos nos obligaron a tomar esa decisión; **I didn't want to take the money, but she ~d it on me** yo no quería el dinero pero me obligó a aceptarlo; **to ~ oneself on sb** (sexually) violar a algn
D (exert pressure, push, drive) ‹*knob/handle/door/link*› forzar*; **to ~ a door open** forzar* una puerta; **he ~d the lid off** le sacó la tapa a la fuerza; **they ~d their way in** entraron por la fuerza; **to ~ an entry** entrar por la fuerza

Phrasal verbs
- **force down** [v ▸ o ▸ adv, v ▸ adv ▸ o] **1** ‹*aircraft/pilot*› obligar* a aterrizar **2** ‹*food*› tragar* (*a duras penas*) **3** ‹*prices*› hacer* bajar
- **force up** [v ▸ o ▸ adv, v ▸ adv ▸ o] ‹*prices*› hacer* subir

forced /fɔːrst || fɔːst/ *adj* (*before n*) ‹*labor/smile/gesture*› forzado; ‹*landing/stopover*› forzoso

force-feed /'fɔːrs'fiːd || 'fɔːsfiːd/ *vt* (*past & past p* **-fed**) alimentar por la fuerza

forceful /'fɔːrsfəl || 'fɔːsfəl/ *adj* **1** (vigorous) ‹*person*› con carácter; ‹*personality*› fuerte; ‹*speech/gesture*› contundente; ‹*manner*› enérgico **2** (persuasive) ‹*words/argument*› convincente, contundente

forcefully /'fɔːrsfəli || 'fɔːsfəli/ *adv* **1** ‹*speak/write*› convincentemente **2** ‹*act/respond*› con energía

forcemeat /'fɔːrsmiːt || 'fɔːsmiːt/ *n* [u] relleno *m* (*de carne*)

forceps /'fɔːrsəps || 'fɔːseps/ *pl n* fórceps *m*

forcible /'fɔːrsəbəl || 'fɔːsəbəl/ *adj* (using force) forzoso; **~ entry** (Law) allanamiento *m* de morada

forcibly /'fɔːrsəbli || 'fɔːsəbli/ *adv* por la fuerza

ford¹ /fɔːrd || fɔːd/ *n* vado *m*

ford² *vt* vadear

fore /fɔːr || fɔː(r)/ *n*: **to come to the ~** «*issue*» saltar a primera plana

forearm /'fɔːrɑːrm || 'fɔːrɑːm/ *n* antebrazo *m*

forebear /'fɔːrber || 'fɔːbeə(r)/ *n* (frml) antepasado, -da *m,f*

forebode /fɔːr'bəʊd || fɔː'bəʊd/ *vt* (liter) augurar, presagiar

foreboding /fɔːr'bəʊdɪŋ || fɔː'bəʊdɪŋ/ *n* **1** [u] (apprehension) aprensión *f* **2** [c] (presentiment) premonición *f*

forecast¹ /'fɔːrkæst || 'fɔːkɑːst/ *n* (*weather ~*) pronóstico *m* del tiempo, parte *m* meteorológico; (prediction) previsión *f*

forecast² *vt* (*past & past p* **forecast** *or* **forecasted**) ‹*weather*› pronosticar*; ‹*result/trend*› prever*

forecaster /'fɔːrkæstər || 'fɔːkɑːstə(r)/ *n* (*weather ~*) meteorólogo, -ga *m,f*

foreclose /fɔːr'kləʊz || fɔː'kləʊz/ *vt* ‹*loan/mortgage*› ejecutar

■ **foreclose** *vi* **to ~ (ON sth)** ‹*on loan/mortgage*› ejecutar algo

foreclosure /fɔːr'kləʊʒər || fɔː'kləʊʒə(r)/ *n* ejecución *f*

forecourt /'fɔːrkɔːrt || 'fɔːkɔːt/ *n* (of garage, hotel) patio *m* delantero

foredeck /fɔːrdek || 'fɔːdek/ *n* cubierta *f* de proa

forefathers /'fɔːrˌfɑːðərz || 'fɔːfɑːðəz/ *pl n* (liter) antepasados *mpl*

forefinger /'fɔːrˌfɪŋgər || 'fɔːˌfɪŋgə(r)/ *n* índice *m*

forefoot /'fɔːrfʊt || 'fɔːfʊt/ *n* (*pl* **-feet**) pata *f* delantera

forefront /'fɔːrfrʌnt || 'fɔːfrʌnt/ *n*: **in** *o* **at the ~ of sth** al frente de algo; (in the vanguard) a la vanguardia de algo

forego /fɔːr'gəʊ || fɔː'gəʊ/ *vt* (*3rd pers sing pres* **-goes**; *pres p* **-going**; *past* **-went**; *past p* **-gone**) ▸ **forgo**

foregoing /fɔːr'gəʊɪŋ || 'fɔːgəʊɪŋ/ *adj* (frml) (*before n*) precedente, anterior

foregone¹ /fɔːr'gɑːn || fɔː'gɒn/ *past p of* **forego**

foregone² /'fɔːrgɑːn || 'fɔːgɒn/ *adj*: **the result was a ~ conclusion** el resultado era de prever *or* (fam) estaba cantado

foreground /'fɔːrgraʊnd || 'fɔːgraʊnd/ *n* **the ~** el primer plano; **in the ~** en primer plano

forehand /'fɔːrhænd || 'fɔːhænd/ *n* golpe *m* de derecho

forehead /'fɑːrəd, 'fɔːrhed || 'fɒrɪd, 'fɔːhed/ *n* frente *f*

foreign /'fɔːrən, 'fɑː- || 'fɒrən/ *adj*
A **1** ‹*custom/country/language*› extranjero **2** ‹*policy/trade/relations*› exterior; **~ debt** deuda *f* externa
B (alien) **to be ~ TO sth/sb** ser* ajeno A algo/algn
C (Med) extraño; **a ~ body** un cuerpo extraño

foreign affairs *pl n* relaciones *fpl or* (Esp) asuntos *mpl* exteriores

foreigner /'fɔːrənər, 'fɑː- || 'fɒrənə(r)/ *n* extranjero, -ra *m,f*

foreign: **~ exchange** *n* [u] divisas *fpl*; **~ minister** *n* ministro, -tra *or* (Méx) secretario, -ria *m,f* de relaciones *or* (Esp) asuntos exteriores, canciller *mf* (AmS); **~ Office** *n* (in UK) **the F~ Office** el Foreign Office, el ministerio de relaciones exteriores de Gran Bretaña; **~ Secretary** *n* (in UK) ▸ **F~ minister**

forelady /'fɔːr'leɪdi || 'fɔːˌleɪdi/ *n* (*pl* **-ladies**) (AmE) capataz *f*, capataza *f* (AmL)

foreleg /'fɔːrleg || 'fɔːleg/ *n* pata *f* delantera

forelock /'fɔːrlɑːk || 'fɔːlɒk/ *n*: ***to touch*** *o* ***tug one's ~ to sb*** saludar a algn con una reverencia, inclinarse ante algn

foreman /ˈfɔːrmən || ˈfɔːmən/ *n* (*pl* **-men** /-mən/) 1 (supervisor) capataz *m* 2 (of jury) presidente *m* del jurado

foremost¹ /ˈfɔːrməʊst || ˈfɔːməʊst/ *adj* 1 (preeminent) ‹*figure/opponent*› más importante *or* destacado; **the welfare of her family was ~ in her mind** el bienestar de su familia era su mayor preocupación 2 (first) primero

foremost² *adv* en primer lugar

forename /ˈfɔːrneɪm || ˈfɔːneɪm/ *n* nombre *m* (de pila)

forensic /fəˈrensɪk/ *adj* (*before n*) ‹*expert*› forense; **~ medicine** medicina *f* legal *or* forense

foreplay /ˈfɔːrpleɪ || ˈfɔːpleɪ/ *n* [u] *estimulación erótica previa al acto sexual*

forerunner /ˈfɔːrˌrʌnər || ˈfɔːˌrʌnə(r)/ *n* precursor, -sora *m,f*

foresee /fɔːrˈsiː || fɔːˈsiː/ *vt* (*past* **foresaw**; *past p* **foreseen**) prever*

foreseeable /fɔːrˈsiːəbəl || fɔːˈsiːəbəl/ *adj* previsible; **in the ~ future** en el futuro inmediato

foreshadow /fɔːrˈʃædəʊ || fɔːˈʃædəʊ/ *vt* prefigurar, anunciar

foreshore /ˈfɔːrʃɔːr || ˈfɔːʃɔː(r)/ *n*: *parte de la playa entre la pleamar y la bajamar*

foreshorten /fɔːrˈʃɔːrtn || fɔːˈʃɔːtn/ *vt* escorzar*

foresight /ˈfɔːrsaɪt || ˈfɔːsaɪt/ *n* [u] previsión *f*

foreskin /ˈfɔːrskɪn || ˈfɔːskɪn/ *n* prepucio *m*

forest /ˈfɔːrəst || ˈfɒrɪst/ *n* [u c] (wood) bosque *m*; (tropical) selva *f*; (*before n*) forestal

forestall /fɔːrˈstɔːl || fɔːˈstɔːl/ *vt* 1 (prevent) prevenir*, impedir* 2 (preempt) adelantarse *or* anticiparse a

forested /ˈfɔːrəstəd || ˈfɒrɪstɪd/ *adj* forestal

forester /ˈfɔːrəstər || ˈfɒrɪstə(r)/ *n* (forestry expert) silvicultor, -tora *m,f*; (ranger) guarda *mf* forestal

forest ranger *n* (esp AmE) guardabosque(s) *mf*

forestry /ˈfɔːrəstri || ˈfɒrɪstri/ *n* [u] silvicultura *f*, ingeniería *f* forestal

foretaste /ˈfɔːrteɪst || ˈfɔːteɪst/ *n* anticipo *m*

foretell /fɔːrˈtel || fɔːˈtel/ *vt* (*past & past p* **foretold**) predecir*, pronosticar*

forethought /ˈfɔːrθɔːt || ˈfɔːθɔːt/ *n* [u] previsión *f*, reflexión *f* previa

forever /fəˈrevər || fəˈrevə(r)/ *adv* 1 (for all time): **those days are gone ~** esos días no volverán; **nothing lasts ~** nada dura eternamente 2 (a long time): **to take ~** tardar una eternidad *or* un siglo 3 (continually) siempre, constantemente

forewarn /fɔːrˈwɔːrn || fɔːˈwɔːn/ *vt* **to ~ sb OF sth** advertir* A algn DE algo; ***~ed is forearmed*** hombre prevenido vale por dos

forewent *past of* **forego**

forewoman /ˈfɔːrˌwʊmən || ˈfɔːˌwʊmən/ *n* (*pl* **-women**) 1 (supervisor) capataz *f*, capataza *f* 2 (of jury) presidenta *f* del jurado

foreword /ˈfɔːrwɜːrd || ˈfɔːwɜːd/ *n* prólogo *m*

forfeit¹ /ˈfɔːrfət || ˈfɔːfɪt/ *vt* ‹*property*› perder* el derecho a; ‹*rights/respect/game*› perder*

forfeit² *n* 1 (penalty) multa *f*; **to pay a ~** pagar* una multa 2 (Games) prenda *f*

forfeiture /ˈfɔːrfətʃʊr || ˈfɔːfɪtʃə(r)/ *n* [u] (loss) pérdida *f*; (confiscation) confiscación *f*

forgave /fərˈgeɪv || fəˈgeɪv/ *past of* **forgive**

forge¹ /fɔːrdʒ || fɔːdʒ/ *vt*

A 1 (Metall) forjar 2 (create) ‹*bond*› forjar

B (counterfeit) falsificar*

Phrasal verb

- **forge ahead** [v ▸ adv] 1 (surpass rivals) escalar posiciones; **to ~ ahead OF sb** tomarle la delantera a algn 2 (make progress) seguir* adelante

forge² *n* 1 (smithy) forja *f* 2 (furnace) fragua *f*, forja *f*

forger /ˈfɔːrdʒər || ˈfɔːdʒə(r)/ *n* falsificador, -dora *m,f*

forgery /ˈfɔːrdʒəri || ˈfɔːdʒəri/ *n* [u c] (*pl* **-ries**) falsificación *f*

forget /fərˈget || fəˈget/ (*pres p* **forgetting**; *past* **forgot**; *past p* **forgotten**) *vt* 1 (fail to remember) ‹*name/fact/person/object*› olvidarse de, olvidar; **I was ~ting (that) you don't speak German** se me olvidaba que *or* me olvidaba de que no hablas alemán; **have you forgotten your manners?** ¿qué modales son ésos?; **she never lets you ~ (that) her son is a professor** está siempre recordándote que su hijo es catedrático; **I'm your father and don't you ~ it!** ¡soy tu padre, que no se te olvide!; **to ~ to + INF**: **don't ~ to phone** no te olvides de llamar, que no se te olvide llamar 2 (put out of one's mind) ‹*person/disappointment/differences*› olvidar, olvidarse de; **I'm sorry — ~ it!** perdóname — no es nada *or* no te preocupes; **if it's money you want, (you can) ~ it!** si es dinero lo que quieres, ya te puedes ir despidiendo de la idea 3 **forgotten** *past p* ‹*land/tribe*› olvidado

■ **forget** *vi*: **where does she live? — I ~** ¿dónde vive? — no me acuerdo *or* se me ha olvidado; **to ~ ABOUT sth** olvidarse *or* no acordarse* DE algo; **I'd ~ about it if I were you** yo que tú lo olvidaría *or* me olvidaría de ello

■ *v refl* **to ~ oneself** perder* el control

forgetful /fərˈgetfəl || fəˈgetfəl/ *adj* (absentminded) olvidadizo, desmemoriado

forget-me-not /fərˈgetmiˈnɑːt || fəˈgetminɒt/ *n* nomeolvides *f*

forgettable /fərˈgetəbəl || fəˈgetəbəl/ *adj* (pej) poco memorable

forgivable /fərˈgɪvəbəl || fəˈgɪvəbəl/ *adj* perdonable

forgive /fərˈgɪv || fəˈgɪv/ *vt* (*past* **forgave**; *past p* **forgiven**) ‹*person/insult*› perdonar; **to ~ sb FOR sth** perdonarle algo a algn; **to ~ sb FOR -ING**: **~ me for interrupting but ...** perdona que interrumpa pero ...; **one could be ~n for thinking that ...** no sería disparatado deducir que ...

forgiveness /fərˈgɪvnəs || fəˈgɪvnɪs/ *n* [u] (quality) clemencia *f*; **to ask/beg sb's ~ for sth** pedirle*/implorarle perdón a algn por algo

forgiving /fərˈgɪvɪŋ || fəˈgɪvɪŋ/ *adj* indulgente, comprensivo

forgo /fɔːrˈgəʊ || fɔːˈgəʊ/ *vt* (*3rd pers sing pres* **-goes**; *pres p* **-going**; *past* **-went**; *past p* **-gone**) (frml) privarse de, renunciar a

forgot /fərˈgɑːt || fəˈgɒt/ *past of* **forget**

forgotten /fərˈgɑːtn || fəˈgɒtn/ *past p of* **forget**

fork¹ /fɔːrk || fɔːk/ *n*

A (Culin) tenedor *m*; (for gardening) horca *f*, bieldo *m*, horqueta *f*

B (in road, river) bifurcación *f*; **to take the left/right ~** tomar el desvío a la izquierda/derecha

fork² *vi* 1 (split) «*branch/road/river*» bifurcarse* 2 (turn): **to ~ (to the) right/left** desviarse* a la derecha/izquierda

Phrasal verb

- **fork out** [v ▸ adv ▸ o] (colloq) desembolsar, aflojar (fam)

forked /fɔːrkt || fɔːkt/ *adj* ‹*stick/branch*› ahorquillado; ‹*tongue*› bífido; ‹*lightning*› en zigzag

forklift (truck) /ˈfɔːrkˈlɪft || ˈfɔːklɪft/ *n* carretilla *f* elevadora (*de horquilla*)

forlorn /fərˈlɔːrn || fəˈlɔːn/ *adj* 1 (wretched) ‹*glance/smile*› triste; ‹*appearance*› (of person) de tristeza y desamparo; (of house, place) de abandono 2 (desperate) ‹*attempt*› desesperado; **in the ~ hope of ...** con la vana esperanza de ...

forlornly /fərˈlɔːrnli || fəˈlɔːnli/ *adv* 1 (miserably) con tristeza 2 (half-heartedly) ‹*try/hope*› sin demasiado entusiasmo

form¹ /fɔːrm || fɔːm/ *n*

A [c u] (shape, manner) forma *f*; **what ~ should our protest take?** ¿cómo deberíamos manifestar nuestra protesta?

B 1 [c u] (type, kind) tipo; **they require some ~ of explanation** necesitan algún tipo de explicación; **other ~s of life** otras formas de vida; **birds are a higher ~ of life than insects** las aves son una especie superior a los insectos 2 [c u] (style) forma *f*; **~ and content** forma y contenido *or* fondo

C [u] (fitness, ability) forma *f*; **to be on/off ~** estar* en forma/en baja forma; **on past ~ it seems unlikely that ...** conociendo su historial, no parece probable que ...

D [u] (etiquette): **as a matter of ~** por educación *or* cortesía; **to be bad/good ~** (esp BrE) ser* de mala/buena educación

E [c] (document) formulario *m*, impreso *m*, forma *f* (Méx)

F [c] (BrE Educ) (class) clase *f*; (year) curso *m*, año *m*

form² *vt*

A 1 (shape, mold) formar; ‹*character*› formar, moldear

2 (take shape of) ‹*line/circle*› formar
B (develop) ‹*opinion*› formarse; ‹*habit*› adquirir*
C (constitute) ‹*basis/part*› formar, constituir*
D (set up, establish) ‹*committee/government/company*› formar
■ **form** *vi* «*idea/plan*» tomar forma; «*ice/fog*» formarse

formal /'fɔːrməl || 'fɔːməl/ *adj*
A (ceremonial) ‹*reception/dinner*› formal; **~ dress** traje *m* de etiqueta; **a ~ call** una visita oficial *or* de protocolo
B (official, conventional) formal; **he hasn't any ~ education** no tiene formación académica
C 1 ‹*manner/person*› ceremonioso; ‹*style/language*› formal 2 (symmetrical) ‹*garden*› de diseño formal

formaldehyde /fɔːr'mældəhaɪd || fɔː'mældɪhaɪd/ *n* [u] formaldehído *m*

formalin /'fɔːrməlin || 'fɔːməlɪn/ *n* [u] formalina *f*

formality /fɔːr'mæləti || fɔː'mæləti/ *n* (*pl* **-ties**)
A [u] (formal quality) ceremonia *f*, formalidad *f*
B [c] (convention) formalidad *f*

formalize /'fɔːrməlaɪz || 'fɔːməlaɪz/ *vt* ‹*agreement/plan*› formalizar*, dar* carácter oficial a

formally /'fɔːrməli || 'fɔːməli/ *adv* 1 (with ceremony) ceremoniosamente 2 (officially) formalmente

format¹ /'fɔːrmæt || 'fɔːmæt/ *n* [c u]
A (Comput, Print) formato *m*
B (arrangement) formato *m*, presentación *f*

format² *vt* **-tt-** formatear

formation /fɔːr'meɪʃən || fɔː'meɪʃən/ *n* [u c] formación *f*; **to fly in ~** volar* en formación

formative /'fɔːrmətɪv || 'fɔːmətɪv/ *adj* ‹*process/years*› de formación; ‹*experience/influence*› formativo

formatting /'fɔːrmætɪŋ || 'fɔːmætɪŋ/ *n* [u] formateo *m*

former¹ /'fɔːrmər || 'fɔːmə(r)/ *adj*
A (earlier, previous) antiguo; **my ~ wife/husband** mi ex-esposa/ex-esposo; **in ~ days** *o* **times** antes, en otros tiempos, antiguamente
B (first-mentioned) primero

former² *n* **the ~** el primero, la primera; (*pl*) los primeros, las primeras

formerly /'fɔːrmərli || 'fɔːməli/ *adv* antes, anteriormente

Formica ® /fɔːr'maɪkə || fɔː'maɪkə/ *n* [u] formica® *f*, fórmica® *f* (AmS), cármica® *f* (Ur)

formic acid /'fɔːrmɪk || 'fɔːmɪk/ *n* [u] ácido *m* formico

formidable /'fɔːrmədəbəl || 'fɔːmɪdəbəl, fɔː'mɪdəbəl/ *adj* ‹*task*› imponente; ‹*problem/obstacle*› tremendo; ‹*achievement/courage*› extraordinario, monumental, formidable; ‹*opponent*› temible

formidably /'fɔːrmədəbli || 'fɔːmɪdəbli, fɔː'mɪdəbli/ *adv* tremendamente

formless /'fɔːrmləs || 'fɔːmlɪs/ *adj* (liter) amorfo, informe

formula /'fɔːrmjələ || 'fɔːmjʊlə/ *n* (*pl* **-las** *o* (frml) **-lae** /-liː/)
A (Chem, Math, Phys) fórmula *f*; **a sure ~ for success** una receta infalible para tener éxito; (*before n*) ‹*comedy/drama/painting*› (AmE) sin originalidad, adocenado
B (motor racing): **~ one** fórmula uno

formulate /'fɔːrmjəleɪt || 'fɔːmjʊleɪt/ *vt* formular

formulation /'fɔːrmjə'leɪʃən || ˌfɔːmjʊ'leɪʃən/ *n* [c u] formulación *f*

fornicate /'fɔːrnəkeɪt || 'fɔːnɪkeɪt/ *vi* (frml) fornicar* (frml)

fornication /'fɔːrnə'keɪʃən || ˌfɔːnɪ'keɪʃən/ *n* [u] (frml) fornicación *f* (frml)

for-profit /fər'prɑːfət || fə'prɒfɪt/ *adj* comercial, con fines de lucro

forsake /fər'seɪk || fə'seɪk/ *vt* (*past* **forsook**; *past p* **forsaken**) (liter) 1 (abandon) abandonar 2 (relinquish) ‹*pleasure/habits*› renunciar a

forsaken /fər'seɪkən || fə'seɪkən/ *adj* abandonado, desamparado

forsook /fər'sʊk || fə'sʊk/ *past of* **forsake**

forsooth /fər'suːθ || fə'suːθ/ *interj* (arch) en verdad

forswear /fɔːr'swer || fɔː'sweə(r)/ *vt* (*past* **forswore** /fɔːr'swɔːr || fɔː'swɔː(r)/; *past p* **forsworn** /fɔːr'swɔːrn || fɔː'swɔːn/) (liter) ‹*pleasure/claim*› renunciar a

fort /fɔːrt || fɔːt/ *n* fuerte *m*; (small) fortín *m*; ***to hold the ~*** quedarse al cargo (de algo/algn)

forte /'fɔːrteɪ || 'fɔːteɪ/ *n* (strong point) fuerte *m*

forth /fɔːrθ || fɔːθ/ *adv* (liter) 1 (out): **~ he went to battle with his enemy** marchó *or* fue a luchar con su enemigo; *see also* **bring** *etc* **forth** 2 (in time): **from this day ~** de hoy *or* ahora en adelante; **from that time ~** a partir de ese momento; ***and (so on and) so ~*** etcétera, etcétera

forthcoming /'fɔːrθ'kʌmɪŋ || ˌfɔːθ'kʌmɪŋ/ *adj*
A 1 (approaching) (*usu before n*) ‹*event*› próximo; **his daughter's ~ wedding** la boda de su hija, que tendrá (*or* tendría *etc*) lugar pronto 2 (about to appear) ‹*article/record*› de próxima aparición; ‹*film*› a estrenarse próximamente
B (available) (*pred*): **no explanation was ~** no dieron (*or* dio *etc*) ninguna explicación
C (open, helpful): **he was not very ~** no estuvo muy comunicativo

forthright /'fɔːrθraɪt || 'fɔːθraɪt/ *adj* directo, franco

forthwith /'fɔːrθ'wɪð || fɔːθ'wɪθ/ *adv* (frml *or* liter) inmediatamente

fortieth¹ /'fɔːrtiəθ || 'fɔːtiəθ/ *adj* cuadragésimo; *see also* **fifth¹**

fortieth² *adv* en cuadragésimo lugar; *see also* **fifth²**

fortieth³ *n* 1 (Math) cuarentavo *m* 2 (part) cuarentava *or* cuadragésima parte *f*

fortification /'fɔːrtəfə'keɪʃən || ˌfɔːtɪfɪ'keɪʃən/ *n* [c u] (Mil) fortificación *f*

fortify /'fɔːrtəfaɪ || 'fɔːtɪfaɪ/ *vt* **-fies, -fying, -fied**
A (Mil) ‹*town/building*› fortificar*
B (strengthen) ‹*person/determination*› fortalecer*, fortificar*; ‹*argument*› reforzar*
C ‹*wine*› fortificar*, encabezar*; **fortified wine** vino *m* fortificado

fortitude /'fɔːrtətuːd || 'fɔːtɪtjuːd/ *n* [u] fortaleza *f*

Fort Knox /nɑːks || 'nɒks/ *n*: *edificio que alberga las reservas de oro estadounidenses*

fortnight /'fɔːrtnaɪt || 'fɔːtnaɪt/ *n* (esp BrE) quince días, dos semanas; (Busn) quincena *f*

fortnightly¹ /'fɔːrtnaɪtli || 'fɔːtnaɪtli/ *adv* (esp BrE) cada dos semanas

fortnightly² *adj* (esp BrE) quincenal

fortress /'fɔːrtrəs || 'fɔːtrɪs/ *n* fortaleza *f*

fortuitous /fɔːr'tuːɪtəs || fɔː'tjuːɪtəs/ *adj* ‹*occurrence/encounter*› fortuito, casual

fortuitously /fɔːr'tuːɪtəsli || fɔː'tjuːɪtəsli/ *adv* fortuitamente, por casualidad

fortunate /'fɔːrtʃṇət || 'fɔːtʃənət/ *adj* ‹*occurrence/coincidence*› afortunado, feliz; **he was very ~ to find a job** tuvo mucha suerte al encontrar trabajo; **it was ~ that he came** fue una suerte que viniera

fortunately /'fɔːrtʃṇətli || 'fɔːtʃənətli/ *adv* (*indep*) afortunadamente, por suerte

fortune /'fɔːrtʃən || 'fɔːtʃən, 'fɔːtʃuːn/ *n*
A [c] (money, prosperity) fortuna *f*; (a lot of money) (colloq) (*no pl*) dineral *m*, platal *m* (AmS fam), pastón *m* (Esp fam)
B 1 [c] (fate): **I followed his ~(s) with interest** seguí su trayectoria *or* sus peripecias con interés; **to tell/read sb's ~** decirle*/leerle la buenaventura a algn 2 [u] (destiny) destino *m*, sino *m* (liter)
C [u] (luck) **good ~** suerte *f*, fortuna *f*

fortune: **~ cookie** *n* (AmE) *galletita china que contiene una predicción del porvenir*; **~ hunter** *n* (colloq & pej) cazafortunas *mf*; **~-teller** *n* adivino, -na *m,f*

forty /'fɔːrti || 'fɔːti/ *adj/n* cuarenta *adj inv/m*; *see also* **seventy**

forum /'fɔːrəm/ *n* foro *m*

forward¹ /'fɔːrwərd || 'fɔːwəd/, (esp BrE) **forwards** /-z/ *adv* 1 (toward the front) ‹*bend/slope/lean*› hacia adelante; **she rushed ~ to greet him** corrió a saludarlo; **let's sit further ~** sentémonos más adelante; *see also* **come forward, step forward** 2 (in time) (frml) en adelante; **from this day ~** desde hoy en adelante; *see also* **bring, carry** *etc* **forward**

forward² *adj*
A (*before n*) (in direction) ‹*movement/motion*› hacia adelante; **~ pass** (Sport) pase *m* adelantado; **~ slash** *n* barra *f* (oblicua)
B (advance): **~ thinking** previsión *f*; **~ planning** planificación *f*
C (assertive, pushy) atrevido, descarado

f

forward[3] *vt* (send) (Busn) enviar, remitir; (to a different address) enviar*, mandar; ⓢ **please forward** hacer* seguir

forward[4] *n* (Sport) delantero *mf*

forwarding /ˈfɔːrwərdɪŋ || ˈfɔːwədɪŋ/ *n* [u] (to a different address) envío *m*; (*before n*) ~ **address** dirección *f* (*a la cual ha de remitirse la correspondencia que se recibe para algn*)

forward: ~**-looking** /ˈfɔːrwərdˈlʊkɪŋ || ˈfɔːwəd,lʊkɪŋ/ *adj* progresista, de amplias miras; ~ **roll** *n* voltereta *f* (*hacia adelante*), maroma *f* (Méx)

forwards /ˈfɔːrwərdz || ˈfɔːwədz/ *adv* ▸ **forward**[1]

forwent /fɔːrˈwent || fɔːˈwent/ *past of* **forgo**

fossil /ˈfɑːsəl || ˈfɒsəl/ *n* (Geol) fósil *m*; (*before n*) ‹*shell/leaf*› fosilizado

fossil fuel *n* [c u] combustible *m* fósil

fossilized /ˈfɑːsəlaɪzd || ˈfɒsəlaɪzd/ *adj* fosilizado, fósil

foster[1] /ˈfɔːstər || ˈfɒstə(r)/ *vt*

A ‹*child*› (BrE) *acoger en el hogar sin adoptarlo legalmente*

B **1** (promote) ‹*suspicion/talent*› fomentar; ‹*reconciliation/understanding*› promover* **2** (feel) ‹*hatred*› alimentar; ‹*respect*› sentir*; ‹*hope*› abrigar*

foster[2] *adj* ‹*child*› ≈ adoptivo; ~ **family** familia *f* de acogida; ~ **home** casa *f* de acogida de menores

fought /fɔːt/ *past & past p of* **fight**[1]

foul[1] /faʊl/ *adj* **-er, -est**

A (offensive) ‹*smell*› nauseabundo, fétido; ‹*taste*› repugnante, asqueroso; ‹*air*› viciado; ‹*water*› infecto

B **1** (horrible) (colloq) ‹*person*› asqueroso (fam); ‹*weather*› pésimo; **to be in a ~ mood** estar* de un humor de perros (fam) **2** (wicked) (liter) ‹*deed/crime*› vil (liter), abyecto

C (obscene) ‹*language/gesture*› ordinario, grosero

D (Sport) (invalid) ‹*shot/serve/ball*› nulo

foul[2] *n* falta *f*, faul *m* or foul *m* (AmL)

foul[3] *vt*

A (pollute) ‹*water/air*› contaminar

B **1** (block) ‹*drain/chimney*› obstruir* **2** (entangle) ‹*rope/chain*› enredar

C (Sport) cometer una falta *or* (AmL tb) un foul *or* faul contra, faulear (AmL)

■ **foul** *vi*

A (Sport) cometer* faltas *or* (AmL tb) fauls *or* fouls, faulear (AmL)

B (become entangled) «*rope/chain*» enredarse

(Phrasal verb)

• **foul up** [v ▸ o ▸ adv, v ▸ adv ▸ o] **1** (spoil) ‹*plan*› estropear, arruinar **2** (bungle) (colloq) fastidiar (fam)

foul: ~**-mouthed** /ˈfaʊlˈmaʊðd/ *adj* malhablado; ~ **play** *n* [u] **1** (Law): **they suspect ~ play** sospechan que se trata de un crimen **2** (Sport) juego *m* sucio; ~**-smelling** /ˈfaʊlˈsmelɪŋ/ *adj* hediondo; ~**-tempered** /ˈfaʊlˈtempərd || ,faʊlˈtempəd/ *adj* con un humor de perros (fam); ~**-up** *n* (colloq) desastre *m*

found[1] /faʊnd/ *past & past p of* **find**[1]

found[2] *vt*

A **1** (establish) ‹*society/company/town/settlement*› fundar **2** **founding** *pres p* fundador

B (base) **to ~ sth ON sth** fundar algo EN algo; **his suspicions were well-/ill-~ed** sus sospechas estaban bien fundadas/eran infundadas

foundation /faʊnˈdeɪʃən/ *n*

A **1** [u] (establishing) fundación *f* **2** [c] (institution) fundación *f*

B [c] (*often pl*) **1** (Const) cimientos *mpl* **2** (groundwork, basis) fundamentos *mpl*, base *f*; (*before n*) ~ **course** curso *m* preparatorio

C [u] (grounds) fundamento *m*; **the suspicion is without ~** la sospecha es infundada *or* carece de fundamento

D [c u] **1** (cosmetic) base *f* de maquillaje **2** ~ **(cream)** (crema *f*) base *f* **3** (of painting) base *f*, apresto *m*

foundation: ~ **garment** *n* (esp AmE) prenda *f* de corsetería; ~ **stone** *n* piedra *f* fundamental

founder[1] /ˈfaʊndər || ˈfaʊndə(r)/ *n* fundador, -dora *m,f*; (*before n*) ~ **member** (BrE) (socio *m*) fundador *m*, (socia *f*) fundadora *f*

founder[2] *vi* «*ship*» hundirse, zozobrar, irse* a pique; «*plan/project*» irse* a pique, zozobrar

founding father /ˈfaʊndɪŋ/ *n* fundador *m*; **the F~ F~s** (in US history) los fundadores de la nación americana

> **Founding Fathers – the Founding Fathers**
>
> Aquellos norteamericanos que sentaron las bases del gobierno de EEUU en la *Federal Constitution Convention* en 1787, ocasión en que se redactó y firmó la Constitución. Los más conocidos son George Washington, Thomas Jefferson, Benjamin Franklin, Alexander Hamilton, John Adams y James Madison

foundling /ˈfaʊndlɪŋ/ *n* (liter) expósito, -ta *m,f*

foundry /ˈfaʊndri/ *n* (*pl* **-ries**) fundición *f*

fount /faʊnt/ *n* (poet) fuente *f*

fountain /ˈfaʊntn || ˈfaʊntɪn/ *n*

A **1** (ornamental) fuente *f* **2** (spray, jet) chorro *m* **3** (*drinking* ~) fuente *f*, bebedero *m* (CS, Méx)

B (source) (liter) manantial *m* (liter), fuente *f*

C (AmE) ▸ **soda fountain**

fountain pen *n* pluma *f* (estilográfica), pluma *f* fuente (AmL), estilográfica *f*, lapicera *f* fuente (CS)

four[1] /fɔːr || fɔː(r)/ *n* cuatro *m*; **six from ten leaves ~** diez menos seis es igual a cuatro; **three ~s are twelve** tres por cuatro (son) doce; **on page ~** en la página cuatro; **he's nearly ~** tiene casi cuatro años; **at the age of ~** a los cuatro años (de edad); **it's nearly ~** son casi las cuatro; **they are sold in ~s** los venden de a cuatro *or* (Esp) de cuatro en cuatro; **the ~ of us/them** nosotros/ellos cuatro; **there were ~ of us/them** éramos/eran cuatro; **divide it into ~** divídelo en cuatro; ***on all ~s*** en *or* a cuatro patas, a gatas

four[2] *adj* cuatro *adj inv*; **it comes to ~ dollars exactly** son cuatro dólares justos; **one tablet ~ times a day** una pastilla cuatro veces al día

four: ~**-by-~** /,fɔːrbaɪˈfɔːr || ,fɔːbaɪˈfɔː(r)/ *n* (vehículo *m*) cuatro por cuatro *m*, vehículo *m* con tracción integral *or* en las cuatro ruedas; ~**-cycle** /ˈfɔːrˈsaɪkəl || fɔːˈsaɪkəl/ *adj* (AmE) de cuatro tiempos; ~**-door** /ˈfɔːrˈdɔːr || ˈfɔː,dɔː(r)/ *adj* (*before n*) de cuatro puertas; ~**fold** *adj/adv see* **-fold**; ~**-letter word** /ˈfɔːr,letər || ˈfɔː,letə/ *n* palabrota *f* (fam), taco *m* (Esp fam); ~**-ply** *adj* (*before n*) ‹*yarn*› de cuatro hebras; ~**-poster (bed)** /ˈfɔːrˈpəʊstər || ,fɔːˈpəʊstə(r)/ *n*: *cama con cuatro columnas, gen con dosel*; ~**-seater** /ˈfɔːrˈsiːtər || ˈfɔː,siːtə(r)/ *n* coche *m*/avión *m* de cuatro plazas

foursome /ˈfɔːrsəm || ˈfɔːsɒm/ *n*: *grupo de cuatro personas*

four: ~**square** /ˈfɔːrˈskwer || ,fɔːˈskweə(r)/ *adv* (squarely) firmemente; (resolutely) decididamente; ~**-stroke** *adj* (BrE) de cuatro tiempos

fourteen /ˈfɔːrˈtiːn || ,fɔːˈtiːn/ *adj/n* catorce *adj inv/m*

fourteenth[1] /ˈfɔːrˈtiːnθ || ,fɔːˈtiːnθ/ *adj* decimocuarto; *see also* **fifth**[1]

fourteenth[2] *adv* en decimocuarto lugar; *see also* **fifth**[2]

fourteenth[3] *n* **1** (Math) catorceavo *m* **2** (part) catorceava parte *f*

fourth[1] /fɔːrθ || fɔːθ/ *adj* cuarto; *see also* **fifth**[1]

fourth[2] *adv* **1** (in position, time, order) en cuarto lugar **2** (fourthly) en cuarto lugar; *see also* **fifth**[2]

fourth[3] *n*

A (part) cuarto *m*

B ~ **(gear)** (Auto) (*no art*) cuarta *f*

fourth estate *n* **the ~ ~** el cuarto poder

fourthly /ˈfɔːrθli || ˈfɔːθli/ *adv* (*indep*) en cuarto lugar

four-wheel drive /ˈfɔːrhwiːl || ˈfɔːwiːl/ *n* [u] tracción *f* integral, tracción *f* a cuatro ruedas

fowl /faʊl/ *n* (*pl* ~**s** *or* ~)

A **1** [c] (farmyard bird) ave *f*‡ (de corral) **2** [u] (meat) ave *f*‡

B (bird) (arch) ave *f*‡

fox[1] /fɑːks || fɒks/ *n* zorro *m*; (*before n*) ~ **cub** cachorro *m* de zorro

fox[2] *vt* (perplex) (colloq) confundir, dejar perplejo

fox: ~**glove** *n* [c u] dedalera *f*, digital *f*; ~**hound** *n* perro *m* raposero; ~**-hunting** *n* [u] caza *f* del zorro; **to go ~-hunting** ir* a cazar zorros; ~**trot** *n* foxtrot *m*

foyer /ˈfɔɪeɪ/ *n* (of theatre) foyer *m*, vestíbulo *m*; (of hotel) vestíbulo *m*

Fr (title) (Relig) (= **Father**) P.

fracas /ˈfreɪkəs, ˈfrækəs || ˈfrækɑː/ *n* (*pl* **fracases** *or* (BrE) **fracas** /-z/) (liter) altercado *m*

fraction /'frækʃən/ *n* [1] (Math) fracción *f*, quebrado *m* [2] (small amount) (*no pl*): **at a ~ of the cost** por un porcentaje mínimo del costo; **a ~ of a second** un instante, una fracción de segundo; **a ~ higher/lower** ligeramente superior/inferior

fractionally /'frækʃn̩əli/ *adv* levemente, un poco

fractious /'frækʃəs/ *adj* (irritable) ‹*child*› quisquilloso; ‹*old man*› cascarrabias *adj inv* (fam)

fracture¹ /'fræktʃər || 'fræktʃə(r)/ *n* [1] (Med) fractura *f* [2] (crack) fisura *f*, grieta *f*

fracture² *vt* (Med) ‹*bone*› fracturar; **she ~d her arm** se fracturó el brazo

■ **fracture** *vi* (Med) «*bone*» fracturarse

fragile /'frædʒəl || 'frædʒaɪl/ *adj* [1] ‹*object/china/glass*› frágil; ‹*relationship/link/agreement*› precario, frágil; Ⓢ **fragile, handle with care** cuidado, frágil [2] ‹*person*› débil; ‹*health*› delicado, precario

fragility /frə'dʒɪləti/ *n* [u] [1] (of object, material) fragilidad *f* [2] (of happiness, link) fragilidad *f*, precariedad *f* [3] (of person) debilidad *f*; (of health) precariedad *f*, lo delicado

fragment¹ /'frægmənt/ *n* fragmento *m*

fragment² /'frægment, fræg'ment || fræg'ment/ *vi* «*glass/china*» hacerse* añicos *or* pedazos, romperse*; «*society/group*» fragmentarse

fragmentary /'frægmənteri || 'frægməntəri/ *adj* fragmentario, incompleto

fragmentation /'frægmən'teɪʃən/ *n* [u] fragmentación *f*

fragmented /'frægmentəd || fræg'mentɪd/ *adj* [1] (broken) hecho añicos *or* pedazos [2] (disjointed) fragmentado

fragrance /'freɪɡrəns/ *n* (smell) fragancia *f*, aroma *m*; (perfume) perfume *m*, fragancia *f*

fragrant /'freɪɡrənt/ *adj* fragante, aromático

frail /freɪl/ *adj* **-er, -est** [1] (physically delicate) ‹*person*› débil, delicado; ‹*health*› delicado [2] (morally weak) débil [3] (fragile) ‹*table/boat*› precario, endeble

frailty /'freɪlti/ *n* (*pl* **-ties**) [1] [u] (of construction) precariedad *f*, endeblez *f* [2] [u] (of person) debilidad *f*; (of health) lo delicado [3] [u c] (of character) debilidad *f*, flaqueza *f*; **human ~** la flaqueza humana

frame¹ /freɪm/ *n*

A [1] (structure — of building, ship, plane) armazón *m or f*; (— of car, motorcycle, bed, door) bastidor *m*; (— of bicycle) cuadro *m*, marco *m* (Chi, Col) [2] (edge — of picture, window, door) marco *m* [3] **frames** *pl* (for spectacles) montura *f*, armazón *m or f*

B (body) cuerpo *m*

C [1] (Cin) fotograma *m*; (Phot) fotografía *f* [2] (TV) cuadro *m*

D (Sport) (unit of play in snooker) set *m*, chico *m* (Col)

frame² *vt*

A ‹*picture/photograph*› enmarcar*; ‹*face/scene*› enmarcar*, encuadrar

B [1] (compose, draft) ‹*plan/policy*› formular, elaborar; ‹*question/reply*› formular [2] (mouth) ‹*words*› formar

C (incriminate unjustly) (colloq): **I was ~d** me tendieron una trampa para incriminarme

frame: **~ of mind** *n* (*pl* **~s of mind**) estado *m* de ánimo; **to be in the right/wrong ~ of mind for sth** estar*/no estar* de humor para algo; **~-up** *n* (colloq) trampa *f* (*para incriminar a alguien*); **~work** *n* (basis) marco *m*; (plan) esquema *m*; (Eng) armazón *m or f*

franc /fræŋk/ *n* franco *m*

France /fræns || frɑ:ns/ *n* Francia *f*

franchise¹ /'fræntʃaɪz/ *n*

A (Busn) [1] [u c] (right — to operate retail outlet) franquicia *f*, licencia *f*; (— to market product, service) concesión *f* [2] [c] (retail outlet) franquicia *f*, tienda *f* bajo licencia

B (Pol frml) **the ~** el derecho de *or* al voto, el sufragio

franchise² *vt* ‹*retail outlet*› conceder en franquicia; ‹*product/service*› adjudicar* *or* dar* la concesión de

franchisee /ˌfræntʃaɪ'zi:/ *n* franquiciado, -da *m,f*

franchiser, franchisor /'fræntʃaɪzər || 'fræntʃaɪzə(r)/ *n* franquiciador, -dora *m,f*

Franciscan /fræn'sɪskən/ *n* franciscano, -na *m,f*

Franco- /'fræŋkəʊ/ *pref* franco-

franglais, Franglais /frɑ:n'gleɪ || 'frɒŋgleɪ/ *n* [u] (hum) franglés *m* (hum)

frank¹ /fræŋk/ *adj* **-er, -est** [1] (honest, candid) sincero, franco; **to be perfectly ~ ...** sinceramente *or* francamente *or* para serte franco ... [2] (direct, outspoken) franco [3] (undisguised) ‹*desire/dislike*› manifiesto

frank² *vt* [1] ‹*letter/parcel/envelope*› franquear [2] (postmark) ‹*stamp/letter*› matasellar, timbrar

frank³ *n*

A (AmE colloq) ▸ **frankfurter**

B (esp BrE Post) franqueo *m*

frankfurter /'fræŋkfɜ:rtər || 'fræŋkfɜ:tə(r)/ *n* salchicha *f* de Frankfurt *or* (Arg, Col) de Viena, frankfurter *m* (Ur), vienesa *f* (Chi), salchicha *f* alemana (Ven)

frankincense /'fræŋkənsens || 'fræŋkɪnsens/ *n* [u] incienso *m*

franking machine /'fræŋkɪŋ/ *n* (BrE) máquina *f* franqueadora, estampilladora *f* (AmL)

frankly /'fræŋkli/ *adv* francamente, con toda sinceridad *or* franqueza; (*indep*) francamente, sinceramente, para serte (*or* serle *etc*) franco

frankness /'fræŋknəs || 'fræŋknɪs/ *n* [u] franqueza *f*

frantic /'fræntɪk/ *adj* [1] (very worried, desperate) desesperado [2] (frenzied, hectic) ‹*activity*› frenético

frantically /'fræntɪkli/ *adv* [1] ‹*try/search*› desesperadamente; ‹*dash/run*› frenéticamente [2] (*as intensifier*): **I'm ~ busy** estoy agobiado de trabajo

frat /fræt/ *n* (AmE colloq)

A (building) ≈ residencia *f* universitaria, ≈ colegio *m* mayor (Esp)

B (student) ≈ residente *m* de colegio mayor, ≈ colegial *m* (Esp)

fraternal /frə'tɜ:rnl̩ || frə'tɜ:nl̩/ *adj* [1] (friendly) ‹*visit*› de camaradería, cordial; ‹*greeting*› cordial [2] (of brothers) ‹*love*› fraternal, fraterno; ‹*jealousy*› entre hermanos

fraternity /frə'tɜ:rnəti || frə'tɜ:nəti/ *n* (*pl* **-ties**)

A [u] (virtue of brotherhood) fraternidad *f*

B [c] [1] (Relig) hermandad *f*, cofradía *f* [2] (university club) asociación *f* estudiantil [3] (community): **the criminal ~** el (mundo del) hampa; **the legal ~** los abogados

> **fraternity**
>
> Una hermandad de varones en muchos establecimientos de la enseñanza superior en EEUU. Por lo general, sus miembros viven juntos en una *fraternity* house. Cada *fraternity* lleva como nombre el de dos o tres letras griegas, como por ejemplo *Lambda Delta Chi*. Hacen obras de caridad y a algunas de ellas les interesa el éxito académico. Han recibido críticas de elitistas y discriminatorias, pero en la actualidad vuelven a tener aceptación ya que su sistema comunitario reduce el costo de la vida para los estudiantes en una época en que la educación es cada vez más cara. *Ver tb* sorority

fraternization /'frætərnə'zeɪʃən || ˌfrætənaɪ'zeɪʃən/ *n* [u] confraternización *f*

fraternize /'frætərnaɪz || 'frætənaɪz/ *vi* confraternizar*, fraternizar*

fratricide /'frætrəsaɪd || 'frætrɪsaɪd/ *n* [u c] (crime) fratricidio *m*

fraud /frɔ:d/ *n*

A [u c] (deception) fraude *m*, estafa *f*

B [c] [1] (person) farsante *mf*, impostor, -tora *m,f* [2] (fraudulent thing) engaño *m*

fraudster /'frɔ:dstər || 'frɔ:dstə(r)/ *n* autor, -tora *m,f* de fraude, defraudador, -dora *m,f*

fraudulent /'frɔ:dʒələnt || 'frɔ:djʊlənt/ *adj* fraudulento

fraught /frɔ:t/ *adj* [1] (*pred*) **to be ~ WITH sth** ‹*with danger/problems*› estar* lleno DE algo [2] (tense) ‹*atmosphere/relationship*› tirante, tenso

fray¹ /freɪ/ *vi* [1] «*cloth/collar/rope*» deshilacharse; «*wire*» pelarse [2] (become strained): **tempers were ~ing** se estaban exaltando los ánimos

■ **fray** *vt* [1] ‹*rope/wire*› desgastar; ‹*cloth*› (through use) desgastar, raer*; (deliberately) deshilachar [2] ‹*nerves*› crispar

fray² *n* refriega *f*, lucha *f*; **he's ready for the ~** está listo para entrar en la refriega; **she returned to the ~** volvió al ataque

frayed /freɪd/ *adj* [1] ‹*collar/cloth*› deshilachado, raído; ‹*rope/wire*› desgastado, pelado [2] ‹*nerves*› crispado; **tempers were getting ~** se estaban exaltando los ánimos

frazzle[1] /'fræzəl/ *n* (colloq) (*no pl*): **to be burned to a ~** quedar carbonizado; **I was worn to a ~** quedé reventada *or* hecha polvo (fam)

frazzle[2] *vi* (AmE colloq): **in this kind of heat, tempers can easily ~** con este calor la gente anda muy irritable *or* con los nervios de punta

frazzled /'fræzəld/ *adj* (colloq) rendido *or* (fam) hecho polvo y con los nervios crispados

freak[1] /fri:k/ *n*

A 1 (abnormal specimen) fenómeno *m*, ejemplar *m* anormal; (monster) monstruo *m* 2 (unnatural event) fenómeno *m*, hecho *m* insólito 3 (peculiar person) (colloq) bicho *m* raro (fam)

B (fanatic) (colloq): **jazz ~** fanático, -ca *m,f* del jazz (fam)

freak[2] *adj* (*before n*) ‹*weather*› inusitado; ‹*happening*› inesperado, insólito

freak[3] *vi* (sl & dated): **she'll ~ when I tell her** le va a dar un ataque cuando se lo diga

Phrasal verb

- **freak out** (sl)

A [v ▸ adv] flipar (arg), friquear(se) (Méx arg)

B [v ▸ o ▸ adv] alucinar (fam), friquear (Méx arg)

freakish /'fri:kɪʃ/ *adj* 1 (unpredictable, unusual) extraño, imprevisible 2 (weird) extraño, raro, estrafalario

freckle /'frekəl/ *n* peca *f*

freckled /'frekəld/ *adj* ‹*skin/face*› pecoso, lleno de pecas

free[1] /fri:/ *adj* **freer** /'fri:ər || 'fri:ə(r)/, **freest** /'fri:əst || 'fri:ɪst/

A 1 (at liberty) (*usu pred*) libre; **to be ~** ser* libre; **to set sb ~** dejar *or* poner* a algn en libertad, soltar* a algn; **~ to + INF**: **you're ~ to do what you think best** eres dueño *or* libre de hacer lo que te parezca; **please feel ~ to help yourself** sírvete con confianza, sírvete nomás (AmL) 2 ‹*country/people/press*› libre; **the right of ~ speech** la libertad *f* de expresión 3 (loose) suelto; **to come/work ~** soltarse*

B (*pred*) 1 (without, rid of) **~ FROM** *o* **OF sth** libre DE algo; **at last we're ~ of her** por fin nos hemos librado de ella; **~ of** *o* **from additives/preservatives** sin aditivos/conservantes 2 (exempt): **~ of tax** libre de impuestos; **~ of charge** gratis

C (costing nothing) ‹*ticket/sample*› gratis *adj inv*, gratuito; ‹*schooling/health care*› gratuito; **you get a ~ gift with every purchase** te hacen un regalo con cada compra; **Ⓢ admission free** entrada gratuita *or* libre; **~ on board** (Busn) franco a bordo

D (not occupied) ‹*table/chair*› libre, desocupado; ‹*time/hands*› libre; **is this table ~?** ¿está libre esta mesa?; **I have no ~ time at all** no tengo ni un momento libre, no tengo nada de tiempo libre; **are you ~ tomorrow?** ¿estás libre mañana?, ¿tienes algún compromiso mañana?

E (lavish) generoso; **to be ~ WITH sth** ser* generoso CON algo; **she's too ~ with her advice** reparte consejos a diestra y siniestra *or* (Esp) a diestro y siniestro

free[2] *adv* 1 (without payment) gratuitamente, gratis; **I got in for ~** (colloq) entré gratis *or* sin pagar *or* de balde 2 (without restriction) ‹*roam/run*› a su (*or* mi *etc*) antojo

free[3] *vt*

A 1 (liberate) ‹*prisoner/hostage*› poner* *or* dejar en libertad, soltar*; ‹*animal*› soltar*; ‹*nation/people/slave*› liberar; **to ~ sb FROM sth** liberar a algn DE algo; **to ~ sb to + INF** permitirle A algn + INF 2 (relieve, rid) **to ~ sth OF sth**: **he promised to ~ the country of corruption** prometió acabar *or* terminar con la corrupción en el país

B 1 (untie, release) ‹*bound person*› soltar*, dejar libre; ‹*trapped person*› rescatar 2 (loose, clear) ‹*sth stuck or caught*› desenganchar, soltar*

Phrasal verb

- **free up** [v ▸ adv ▸ o] (AmE) ‹*resources*› liberar; ‹*time*› dejar libre; ‹*knot*› deshacer*

-free /'fri:/ *suff* **trouble~** sin problemas; **tax~** libre de impuestos; **maintenance~** que no necesita mantenimiento; **nuclear~ zone** zona *f* desnuclearizada

free: **~ agent** *n*: **you're a ~ agent** eres muy libre *or* dueño de hacer lo que quieras; **~-and-easy** /'fri:ən'i:zi/ *adj* (*pred* **~ and easy**) (tolerant) tolerante

freebie /'fri:bi/ *n* (sl) regalo *m*

freedom /'fri:dəm/ *n*

A [u c] libertad *f*; **~ of speech/expression** libertad de expresión; **journalists had complete editorial ~** los periodistas tenían carta blanca en materia editorial; **~ FROM sth**: **the plan guarantees ~ from financial worries** el plan le garantiza un futuro libre de preocupaciones económicas

B [u] (frankness) libertad *f*, desenvoltura *f*; **to speak with complete ~** hablar con toda *or* plena libertad

C [u] (rights of use or access): **~ of information** *libre acceso del ciudadano a la información contenida en los archivos gubernamentales*; **he was given the ~ of the city** le entregaron las llaves de la ciudad

freedom fighter *n* guerrillero, -ra *m,f*

free enterprise *n* [u] libre empresa *f*

free: **~-for-all** /'fri:fər'ɔ:l/ *n* gresca *f*, pelea *f*; **~hand** *adj/adv* a mano alzada *or* libre; **~ hit** *n* golpe *m* franco, tiro *m* libre

freehold[1] /'fri:həʊld/ *adj* (esp BrE): **~ property** bien *m* raíz (*que se compra o vende en plena propiedad junto con el suelo sobre el que está edificado*)

freehold[2] *n* (esp BrE) plena propiedad *f* (*de un bien raíz y del suelo*)

free: **~holder** *n* (BrE) titular *mf* de la plena propriedad; **~ kick** *n* (Sport) (in soccer) tiro *m* libre; (in rugby) patada *f* libre

freelance[1] /'fri:læns || 'fri:lɑ:ns/ *adj* por cuenta propia, freelance *adj inv*, por libre (Esp)

freelance[2] *adv* por cuenta propia, freelance, por libre (Esp)

freelance[3] *vi* trabajar por cuenta propia, trabajar freelance *or* (Esp tb) por libre

freelancer /'fri:'lænsər || 'fri:,lɑ:nsə(r)/ *n* trabajador, -dora *m,f* que trabaja por cuenta propia, freelance *mf*

freeloader /'fri:'ləʊdər || 'fri:,ləʊdə(r)/ *n* (colloq) gorrón, -rrona *m,f* *or* (AmL) gorrero, -ra *m,f* *or* (RPl) garronero, -ra *m,f* *or* (Chi) bolsero, -ra *m,f* (fam)

freely /'fri:li/ *adv*

A 1 (without restriction) libremente; **the animals roam ~ in the park** los animales andan sueltos por el parque 2 (openly) ‹*speak/write*› con libertad *or* franqueza 3 (willingly) ‹*sacrifice*› voluntariamente; ‹*offer*› de buen grado

B 1 (generously) ‹*spend/give*› a manos llenas 2 (copiously) ‹*flow/pour*› profusamente, copiosamente

free: **~ market** *n* mercado *m* libre; **~mason** /'fri:'meɪsən || 'fri:meɪsən/ *n* masón, -sona *m,f*, francmasón, -sona *m,f*; **~post** *n* [u] (BrE) franqueo *m* pagado por el destinatario; **~-range** /'fri:'reɪndʒ/ *adj* ‹*chicken/eggs*› de granja; **~standing** /'fri:'stændɪŋ/ *adj* ‹*cupboard/stove*› no empotrado; ‹*clothes rack/towel rail*› de pie; **~style** *n* estilo *m* libre; **~thinker** /'fri:'θɪŋkər || ,fri:'θɪŋkə(r)/ *n* librepensador, -dora *m,f*; **~ throw** *n* tiro *m* libre; **~ trade** *n* [u] libre comercio *m*, librecambio *m*; **~way** *n* [c u] (AmE) autopista *f* (*sin peaje*); **~wheel** /'fri:'hwi:l || ,fri:'wi:l/ *vi*: **he ~wheeled down the hill** (on bike) bajó la cuesta sin pedalear; (in car) bajó la cuesta en punto muerto; **~ will** *n* [u]: **of one's own ~ will** por su (*or* mi *etc*) propia voluntad, (de) motu proprio

free-to-air /'fri:tə'er || -'eə(r)/ *adj* ‹*channel/digital TV*› emitido en abierto

freeze[1] /fri:z/ (*past* **froze**; *past p* **frozen**) *vi*

A «*pipe/lock/ground/person*» helarse*, congelarse; **to ~ to death** morir* congelado; **I'm freezing!** ¡estoy helado!, ¡me estoy muriendo de frío!

B (stand still) quedarse inmóvil, paralizarse*; **¡~!** ¡alto *or* quieto ahí!; **the remark froze on his lips** se quedó con el comentario en la boca

C (Culin): **some fruits don't ~ well** algunas frutas no se prestan para ser congeladas

■ **freeze** *vt*

A 1 (turn to ice) ‹*water/stream*› helar*, congelar 2 (ice up) ‹*pipe/mechanism*› helar*

B 1 (preserve in freezer) congelar 2 (anesthetize) anestesiar

C (Fin) ‹*assets/account/prices*› congelar

■ **freeze** *v impers* helar*, haber* helada

Phrasal verbs

- **freeze out** [v ▸ o ▸ adv, v ▸ adv ▸ o] (colloq) excluir*, dejar fuera
- **freeze over** [v ▸ adv] helarse*, congelarse
- **freeze up** [v ▸ adv] helarse*, congelarse

freeze[2] *n* (limitation, stoppage) congelación *f*; **a wage/price ~** una congelación salarial/de precios

freeze-dried /ˈfriːzˈdraɪd/ *adj* liofilizado

freezer /ˈfriːzər || ˈfriːzə(r)/ *n* (deep freeze) freezer *m*, congelador *m*; (freezing compartment) congelador *m*

freeze-up /ˈfriːzʌp/ *n* (AmE) período *m* de temperaturas bajo cero, ola *f* de grandes fríos

freezing¹ /ˈfriːzɪŋ/ *adj* ‹*temperatures*› bajo cero; ‹*weather*› con temperaturas bajo cero; ‹*hands/feet*› helado, congelado; **~ fog** niebla *f* helada; **it's ~ (cold) in here** aquí hace un frío que pela (fam)

freezing² *n* [u]

A **~ (point)** punto *m* de congelación; **three degrees above/below ~** tres grados sobre/bajo cero

B (process) congelación *f*; ❸ **suitable for freezing** se puede congelar

freight¹ /freɪt/ *n* 1 [u] (goods transported) carga *f*, mercancías *fpl*, mercaderías *fpl* 2 [u] (transportation) transporte *m*, porte *m*, flete *m* (AmL); **~ free** franco de porte; **~ paid** porte pagado

freight² *vt* (esp AmE) enviar* *or* mandar como carga

freightage /ˈfreɪtɪdʒ/ *n* porte *m*, flete *m* (AmL)

freight car *n* (AmE) vagón *m* de carga

freighter /ˈfreɪtər || ˈfreɪtə(r)/ *n* (Naut) buque *m* de carga, carguero *m*

freight train *n* tren *m* de carga

French¹ /frentʃ/ *adj* francés

French² *n* 1 [u] (language) francés *m* 2 (people) (+ *pl vb*) **the ~** los franceses

French: **~ bean** *pl n* (BrE) ▸**green bean**; **~-Canadian** /ˈfrentʃkəˈneɪdiən/ *adj* francocanadiense; **~ doors** *pl n* (AmE) ▸**~ windows**; **~ dressing** *n* [u] *aliño para ensaladas a base de aceite, vinagre y mostaza*; (AmE) *aderezo (para ensaladas) a base de aceite, vinagre y tomate*; **~ fries** *pl n* papas *fpl or* (Esp) patatas *fpl* fritas, papas *fpl* a la francesa (Col, Méx); **~ horn** *n* trompa *f* (de pistones); **~ kiss** *n* beso *m* en la boca (*con la lengua*); **~man** /ˈfrentʃmən/ *n* (*pl* **-men** /-mən/) francés *m*; **~ polish** *n* [u] barniz *m* copal *or* de muñeca; **~ toast** *n* [u] (fried) torrija *f or* (AmL tb) torreja *f*; **~ windows** *pl n* puerta *f* ventana, cristalera *f* (Esp); **~woman** *n* francesa *f*

frenetic /frəˈnetɪk/ *adj* ‹*activity*› frenético; ‹*attempt*› desesperado

frenetically /frəˈnetɪkli/ *adv* frenéticamente

frenzied /ˈfrenzid/ *adj* frenético, desenfrenado

frenzy /ˈfrenzi/ *n* (*no pl*) frenesí *m*; **he dashed about in a ~** iba de un lado a otro como histérico; **a ~ of activity** una actividad febril; **to work oneself up into a ~** ponerse* frenético

frequency /ˈfriːkwənsi/ *n* [u c] (*pl* **-cies**) frecuencia *f*; (*before n*) **~ modulation** frecuencia *f* modulada

frequent¹ /ˈfriːkwənt/ *adj* ‹*attempts/journeys*› frecuente; ‹*visitor*› asiduo; **this is quite a ~ occurrence** esto sucede con bastante frecuencia

frequent² /friːˈkwent/ *vt* frecuentar

frequently /ˈfriːkwəntli/ *adv* con frecuencia, a menudo, frecuentemente

fresco /ˈfreskəʊ/ *n* [c] (*pl* **-cos** *or* **-coes**) fresco *m*

fresh¹ /freʃ/ *adj* **-er, -est**

A 1 (not stale, frozen or canned) ‹*food*› fresco; **we went out for a breath of ~ air** salimos a tomar un poco de aire (fresco) 2 (vigorous, not tired) ‹*complexion/face/appearance*› fresco, lozano; **it was still ~ in his memory** *o* **mind** lo tenía fresco en la memoria 3 (newly arrived, produced) (*pred*): **~ off the press/production line** recién salido de la imprenta/la línea de montaje

B (not salty): **~ water** agua *f‡ dulce*

C 1 (new, clean) ‹*clothes/linen*› limpio; **it needs a ~ coat of paint** necesita una nueva mano de pintura 2 (new, additional) ‹*supplies/initiative/evidence*› nuevo; **to make a ~ start** volver* a empezar, empezar* de nuevo

D 1 ‹*winds*› fuerte 2 (cool) fresco

E 1 (taking liberties) (colloq & dated) fresco; **to get ~ with sb** propasarse con algn 2 (cheeky) (AmE) descarado, impertinente

fresh² *adv*: **~ ground coffee** café *m* recién molido; **we're ~ out of tomatoes** (esp AmE colloq) acabamos de vender los últimos tomates

freshen /ˈfreʃən/ *vt* refrescar*

(Phrasal verb)

- **freshen up** 1 [v ▸ adv] (wash) lavarse, arreglarse 2 [v ▸ o ▸ adv, v ▸ adv ▸ o] (refill glass): **let me ~ that up for you** deja que te sirva otro

fresher /ˈfreʃər || ˈfreʃə(r)/ *n* (BrE colloq: used by students) estudiante *mf* de primer año, mechón, -chona *m,f* (Chi fam)

fresh-faced /ˌfreʃˈfeɪst/ *adj* 1 (youthful) sin experiencia 2 (healthy) saludable, lozano

freshly /ˈfreʃli/ *adv* recién

freshman /ˈfreʃmən/ *n* (*pl* **-men** /-mən/) 1 (Educ) estudiante *mf* de primer año, mechón, -chona *m,f* (Chi fam) 2 (newcomer) (AmE) novato, -ta *m,f*; (*before n*) ‹*senator/quarterback/manager*› novel, nuevo, bisoño

freshness /ˈfreʃnəs || ˈfreʃnɪs/ *n* [u]

A (of food) frescura *f*; (of taste) frescor *m*

B (of complexion) lozanía *f*, frescura *f*

C (newness) frescura *f*, originalidad *f*

D (coolness) frescor *m*, frescura *f*

freshwater /ˈfreʃˈwɔːtər || ˈfreʃˌwɔːtə(r)/ *adj* (*before n*) de agua dulce

fret¹ /fret/ *vi* **-tt-** 1 (worry) preocuparse, inquietarse 2 (become restless, agitated) **to ~ FOR sb/sth** inquietarse POR algn/algo; **don't ~!** ¡tranquilízate!

fret² *n* (Mus) traste *m*

fretful /ˈfretfəl/ *adj* 1 (querulous) ‹*child/tone*› quejoso, fastidioso 2 (anxious) ‹*person*› inquieto, preocupado

fretfully /ˈfretfəli/ *adv* 1 ‹*complain*› fastidiosamente 2 ‹*look*› con ansiedad

fret: **~saw** *n* sierra *f* de calar; **~work** *n* [u] calado *m*

Freudian slip /ˈfrɔɪdiən/ *n* lapsus *m* linguae

FRG *n* (= **Federal Republic of Germany**) RFA *f*

Fri (= **Friday**) viern.

friar /ˈfraɪər || ˈfraɪə(r)/ *n* fraile *m*; **F~ Tuck** Fray Tuck

friary /ˈfraɪəri/ *n* (*pl* **-ries**) monasterio *m*

fricassee /ˈfrɪkəsiː/ *n* [c u] fricasé *m*, fricandó *m*

fricative /ˈfrɪkətɪv/ *n* fricativa *f*

friction /ˈfrɪkʃən/ *n* [u]

A (Phys, Tech) rozamiento *m*, fricción *f*

B (discord) tirantez *f*, roces *mpl*

friction tape *n* [u] (AmE) cinta *f* aislante *or* aisladora

Friday /ˈfraɪdeɪ, -di/ *n* viernes *m*; **girl ~** chica *f* para todo (*en una oficina*); *see also* **Monday**

fridge /frɪdʒ/ *n* (colloq) nevera *f*, refrigerador *m*, frigorífico *m* (Esp), heladera *f* (RPl), refrigeradora *f* (Col, Per)

fried /fraɪd/ *adj* frito; **a ~ egg** un huevo frito *or* (Méx) estrellado; **~ foods** frituras *fpl*

friend /frend/ *n*

A (close acquaintance) amigo, -ga *m,f*; **he soon made ~s with her** en poco tiempo se hizo amigo suyo; **with ~s like that, who needs enemies?** (set phrase) con amigos así ¿quién necesita enemigos? (fr hecha); **that's what ~s are for** para eso están los amigos; **any ~ of yours is a ~ of mine** tus amigos son mis amigos; **who goes there: ~ or foe?** ¿quién vive?; ***a ~ in need is a ~ indeed*** en las malas se conoce a los amigos

B (Relig): **the Society of F~s** la Sociedad de los Amigos

friendless /ˈfrendləs || ˈfrendlɪs/ *adj* sin amigos

friendliness /ˈfrendlinəs || ˈfrendlɪnɪs/ *n* [u] simpatía *f*

friendly¹ /ˈfrendli/ *adj* **-lier, -liest** 1 ‹*person/pet*› simpático; ‹*place/atmosphere*› agradable; ‹*welcome*› cordial; **I'll give you some ~ advice** te voy a dar un consejo de amigo; **to be ~ TO sb** estar* simpático *or* ser* amable CON algn; **to be ~ WITH sb** ser* amigo, -ga DE algn; **environmentally ~ products** productos *mpl* inocuos para el medio ambiente 2 (good-natured) ‹*rivalry/game/match*› amistoso, amigable 3 (of one's own side) ‹*ship/aircraft/troops*› amigo; **~ fire** fuego amigo

friendly² *n* (*pl* **-lies**) (BrE) partido *m* amistoso

friendly society *n* (BrE) mutualidad *f*, sociedad *f* de socorros mutuos

friendship /ˈfrendʃɪp/ *n* [u c] amistad *f*

frier /ˈfraɪər || ˈfraɪə(r)/ *n* ▸**fryer**

Friesian /ˈfriːʒən/ *n* **~ (cow)** (BrE) vaca *f* holandesa

frieze /fri:z/ *n* (on building, wall) friso *m*; (on wallpaper) greca *f*, guarda *f* (*de papel pintado*)

frigate /'frɪgət || 'frɪgɪt/ *n* fragata *f*

frigate bird *n* (ave *m*) fragata *f*

fright /fraɪt/ *n* 1 [u] (fear) miedo *m*, susto *m*; **to take ~ at sth** asustarse por algo 2 [c] (shock) susto *m*; **she had the ~ of her life** se llevó un susto de muerte; **to give sb a ~** darle* *or* pegarle* un susto a algn 3 [c] (person) (colloq) espantajo *m*

frighten /'fraɪtn̩/ *vt* 1 (scare) asustar 2 (intimidate) asustar, amedrentar; **to ~ sb INTO -ING** meterle miedo a algn para que haga algo

Phrasal verb

• **frighten away, frighten off** [v ▸ o ▸ adv, v ▸ adv ▸ o] espantar, ahuyentar

frightened /'fraɪtnd/ *adj* ‹*person/animal*› asustado; **to be ~ OF sb/sth** tenerle* miedo A algn/algo; **to be ~ OF -ING/ to + INF**: **he was ~ of crossing the road** le daba miedo cruzar la calle; **I was ~ to tell him** tenía miedo de decírselo, me daba miedo decírselo; **to be ~ (THAT)**: **she was ~ (that) she would miss her train** tenía miedo de perder el tren; **to be ~ to death** *o* **out of one's wits** estar* muerto de miedo; **don't be ~** no tengas miedo, no te asustes

frightening /'fraɪtn̩ɪŋ/ *adj* ‹*experience*› espantoso; (stronger) aterrador

frightful /'fraɪtfəl/ *adj*

A (horrific) aterrador

B (BrE colloq) 1 (very unpleasant) horroroso, horrendo 2 (*as intensifier*) ‹*thirst/mess*› espantoso; **it's a ~ nuisance** es un latazo (fam)

frightfully /'fraɪtfəli/ *adv* (BrE) (*as intensifier*) ‹*nice/amusing/silly*› terriblemente, tremendamente; **I'm ~ sorry** lo siento muchísimo

frigid /'frɪdʒəd || 'frɪdʒɪd/ *adj* frígido; ‹*welcome/smile*› frío, glacial

frill /frɪl/ *n*

A (of fabric) volante *m* *or* (RPl) volado *m* *or* (Méx) olán *m* *or* (Chi) vuelo *m*

B (colloq) 1 (pretension) floritura *f*; **a ceremony with no ~s** una ceremonia sencilla 2 (refinement) detalle *m*

frilly /'frɪli/ *adj* **-lier, -liest** ‹*dress/petticoat*› de volantes *or* (RPl) de volados *or* (Méx) de olanes *or* (Chi) de vuelos

fringe[1] /frɪndʒ/ *n*

A 1 (on shawl, carpet, tablecloth) fleco *m* 2 (of trees, houses) hilera *f*

B (of hair) (BrE) flequillo *m*, cerquillo *m* (AmL), fleco *m* (Méx), chasquilla *f* (Chi), capul *m* (Col), pollina *f* (Ven)

C (periphery) (*often pl*): **to live on the ~(s) of society** vivir al margen de la sociedad; (*before n*) ‹*area/group*› marginal; ‹*music/medicine*› alternativo

fringe[2] *vt* 1 (decorate with fringe) ‹*scarf/rug*› ponerle* un fleco a 2 (border) bordear; **~d with fur** con una orla de piel

fringe benefit *n* 1 (Lab Rel) incentivo *m*, complemento, extra *m* 2 (incidental advantage) ventaja *f* adicional

frippery /'frɪpəri/ *n* (*pl* **-ries**) fruslería *f*

Frisbee® /'frɪzbi/ *n* Frisbee® *m*

Frisco /'frɪskəʊ/ *n* (AmE colloq) San Francisco

frisk /frɪsk/ *vi* retozar*, juguetear

■ **frisk** *vt* cachear, registrar, catear (Méx)

frisky /'frɪski/ *adj* **-kier, -kiest** retozón, juguetón

frisson /fri:'səʊn || 'fri:sɒn/ *n* escalofrío *m*

fritter /'frɪtər || 'frɪtə(r)/ *n* buñuelo *m*, fruta *f* de sartén (Esp)

Phrasal verb

• **fritter away** [v ▸ o ▸ adv, v ▸ adv ▸ o] ‹*money*› malgastar, derrochar; ‹*fortune*› dilapidar; ‹*time*› desperdiciar

frivolity /frɪ'vɑːləti || frɪ'vɒləti/ *n* [u c] (*pl* **-ties**) (pej) frivolidad *f*

frivolous /'frɪvələs/ *adj* frívolo

frizzle up /'frɪzəl/ [v ▸ adv] ‹‹*meat*›› achicharrarse

frizzy /'frɪzi/ *adj* **-zier, -ziest** crespo, chino (Méx), como mota (CS)

frock /frɑːk || frɒk/ *n* 1 (woman's) vestido *m* 2 (monk's) hábito *m*

frock coat *n* levita *f*

frog /frɔːg || frɒg/ *n*

A (Zool) rana *f*; **~s' legs** ancas *fpl* de rana; ***(to have) a ~ in the*** *o* ***one's throat*** tener* carraspera

B (French person) (sl & offensive) franchute *mf* (fam, a veces pey), gabacho, -cha *m,f* (Chi, Esp fam & pey)

frog: **~man** /'frɔːgmən || 'frɒgmən/ *n* (*pl* **-men** /-mən/) hombre *m* rana, submarinista *m*; **~march** *vt* (BrE): **they ~marched him out/in** lo hicieron salir/entrar por la fuerza (*sujetándole los brazos*); **~spawn** *n* [u] (BrE) huevos *mpl* de rana

frolic /'frɑːlɪk || 'frɒlɪk/ *vi* **-ck-** retozar*, juguetear

from /frɑːm || frɒm, *weak form* frəm/ *prep*

A 1 (indicating starting point) desde; (indicating origin) de; **~ the beginning** desde el principio; **the flight ~ Madrid** el vuelo procedente de Madrid; **I'm ~ Texas** soy de Texas; **~ here you can see the river** desde aquí se puede ver el río; **T-shirts ~ $15** camisetas desde *or* a partir de $15 2 (indicating distance): **2cm ~ the edge** a 2cm del borde; **we're still three hours ~ Tulsa** todavía faltan tres horas para llegar a Tulsa

B 1 (after): **~ today** a partir de hoy, desde hoy; **~ the moment we met** desde el momento en que nos conocimos; **50 years/an hour ~ now** dentro de 50 años/una hora 2 (before): **we are only minutes ~ takeoff!** ¡estamos a pocos minutos del despegue!

C (indicating source) de; **a letter ~ my lawyer** una carta de mi abogado; **that's enough ~ you!** ¡basta!, ¡cállate!; **you can tell him that ~ me!** ¡puedes decírselo de mi parte!; **have you heard ~ her?** ¿has tenido noticias suyas?; **we heard ~ Sam that …** nos enteramos por Sam de que …; **a drawing ~ life** un dibujo del natural

D **from … to …**; **they flew ~ New York to Lima** volaron de Nueva York a Lima; **they stretch ~ Derbyshire to the borders of Scotland** se extienden desde el condado de Derbyshire hasta el sur de Escocia; **~ door to door** de puerta en puerta; **we work ~ nine to five** trabajamos de nueve a cinco; **I'll be in Europe ~ June 20 to 29** voy a estar en Europa desde el 20 hasta el 29 de junio; **~ $50 to $100** entre 50 y 100 dólares

E (as a result of) de; **his eyes were red ~ crying** tenía los ojos rojos de tanto llorar; **~ experience I would say that …** según mi experiencia diría que …

F 1 (out of, off) de; **~ the cupboard/shelf** del armario/estante 2 (Math): **5 ~ 10 is 5** 10 menos 5 es 5; **if you take 5 ~ 10** si le restas 5 a 10

G (with preps & advs): **~ above/below** desde arriba/abajo; **he crawled out ~ under the table** salió gateando de debajo de la mesa; **the lady ~ across the street** la señora de enfrente

frond /frɑːnd || frɒnd/ *n* (of fern) fronda *f*; (of palm) hoja *f*

front[1] /frʌnt/ *n*

A 1 (of building) frente *m*, fachada *f*; (of dress) delantera *f*; **the skirt fastens at the ~** la falda se abrocha por delante *or* (esp AmL) por adelante 2 (forward part) frente *m*, parte *f* delantera *or* de delante *or* (esp AmL) de adelante; **he was called to the ~ of the class** lo hicieron pasar al frente de la clase

B (*in phrases*) **in front** (*as adv*) delante, adelante (esp AmL); **Midnight Orchid is out in ~** Midnight Orchid va en cabeza *or* lleva la delantera; **in front of sb/sth** delante *or* (esp AmL) adelante de algn/algo; (facing) enfrente de algn/algo; **we've got a big task in ~ of us** tenemos una gran tarea por delante

C (Meteo, Mil, Pol) frente *m*; **progress was made on all ~s** hubo avances en todos los frentes; **there is good news on the job ~** hay noticias alentadoras en el plano laboral

D 1 (outward show) fachada *f* 2 (for illegal activity) pantalla *f* 3 (of organization, party) (AmE) cabeza *f* visible

E (overlooking sea) paseo *m* marítimo, malecón *m* (AmL), rambla *f* (RPl)

front[2] *adj* (at front) ‹*seat/wheel/leg*› delantero, de delante *or* (esp AmL) de adelante; **the ~ cover** la portada; **the ~ door** la puerta de (la) calle; **the ~ yard** *o* (BrE) **garden** el jardín del frente; **a seat in the ~ row, a ~-row seat** un asiento en primera fila; *see also* **front bench, front page** *etc*

front[3] *vt* (present, head) ‹*campaign*› dirigir*; ‹*group*› liderar; ‹*show*› presentar

frontage /'frʌntɪdʒ/ *n* 1 (façade) fachada *f*, frente *m* 2 (along street, river) frente *m*

frontal /'frʌntl̩/ *adj*
A (from, at front) ‹*collision*/*attack*› frontal, de frente
B (Meteo) ‹*system*› frontal

front: **~ bench** *n* (BrE Govt) *escaños ocupados por ministros del gobierno o jefes de la oposición*; **~bencher** /'frʌnt 'bentʃər || ,frʌnt'bentʃə(r)/ *n* (BrE) *diputado con cargo ministerial en el gobierno o en el gabinete fantasma*

frontier /frʌn'tɪr || 'frʌntɪə(r)/ *n*
A 1 (between countries) frontera *f*; (*before n*) ‹*guard*/*zone*› fronterizo 2 (in US history) **the F~** la frontera (del oeste) (*el límite de los territorios colonizados*)
B **frontiers** *pl* (of knowledge, science) confines *mpl*

frontispiece /'frʌntɪspi:s/ *n* frontispicio *m*

front: **~ line** *n* (Mil) primera línea *f*; **~-loader** /'frʌnt 'ləʊdər || ,frʌnt'ləʊdə(r)/ *n* lavadora *f* de carga frontal; **~ man** *n* 1 (for dubious activity) testaferro *m* 2 (TV) presentador *m*; **~ page** *n* (Journ) primera plana *f*; **to hit** *o* **make the ~ page** aparecer* *or* salir* en primera plana; **~ room** *n* salón *m*, living *m* (esp AmL); **~-wheel drive** *n* [u] tracción *f* delantera

frost¹ /frɔ:st || frɒst/ *n* 1 [u c] (sub-zero temperature) helada *f* 2 [u] (frozen dew) escarcha *f*

frost² *vt*
A (Meteo) helar*; ‹*plant*› quemar
B (Culin) 1 ‹*cake*› (AmE) bañar 2 (cover with sugar) escarchar

Phrasal verb
• **frost over, frost up** [v ▸ adv] «*window*» helarse*, cubrirse* de escarcha

frost: **~bite** *n* [u] congelación *f*; **~bitten** *adj* 1 (Med) congelado 2 (Bot) quemado

frosted glass /'frɔ:stəd || 'frɒstɪd/ *n* [u] vidrio *m* *or* (Esp) cristal *m* esmerilado

frostily /'frɔ:stəli || 'frɒstɪli/ *adv* con frialdad

frosting /'frɔ:stɪŋ || 'frɒstɪŋ/ *n* [u] (Culin) 1 (on cake) (AmE) baño *m*; ▸ **cake¹** A 2 (of sugar) (BrE) glaseado *m*

frosty /'frɔ:sti || 'frɒsti/ *adj* **-tier, -tiest** ‹*weather*/*air*› helado; ‹*night*› de helada; ‹*manner*/*reception*› glacial, frío

froth¹ /frɔ:θ || frɒθ/ *n* [u] (foam) espuma *f*

froth² *vi* «*liquid*» hacer* espuma

frothy /'frɔ:θi || 'frɒθi/ *adj* **frothier, frothiest** ‹*liquid*› espumoso

frown¹ /fraʊn/ *vi* fruncir* el ceño *or* el entrecejo; **to ~ AT sb** mirar a algn con el ceño fruncido; **to ~ AT sth** torcer* el gesto por algo

Phrasal verb
• **frown on, frown upon** [v ▸ prep ▸ o]: **that sort of thing is ~ed upon** eso está muy mal visto

frown² *n* ceño *m* fruncido; **he wore a ~** (liter) tenía el ceño fruncido

froze /frəʊz/ *past of* **freeze¹**

frozen¹ /'frəʊzn̩/ *past p of* **freeze¹**

frozen² *adj*
A 1 (solid) ‹*water*/*pipe*/*lock*› congelado 2 (referring to a region) helado 3 (extremely cold) (colloq): **my feet are ~** tengo los pies helados *or* congelados; **I was ~ stiff** estaba congelado *or* como un témpano 4 (Culin) ‹*vegetables*/*meat*› congelado 5 (motionless): **I stood there ~ (to the spot) with horror** me quedé allí clavado, paralizado por el terror
B (Fin) ‹*prices*/*incomes*› congelado; ‹*capital*/*credits*› bloqueado

frugal /'fru:gəl/ *adj* frugal

fruit /fru:t/ *n*
A 1 [u] (collectively) fruta *f*; **a piece of ~** una (pieza de) fruta; **dried ~** (BrE) fruta *f* seca; (*before n*) **~ bowl** frutero *m*, frutera *f* (CS); **~ juice** jugo *m* *or* (Esp) zumo *m* de frutas; **~ tree** árbol *m* frutal 2 [c] (type — as food) fruta *f*; (Bot) fruto *m*
B [u c] (product) fruto *m*; **the ~(s) of his labors** el fruto de su trabajo; ***to bear ~*** dar* (su) fruto

fruit: **~cake** *n* [u c] plum-cake *m*, ponqué *m* de frutas (Col), fruit cake *m* (Méx), budín *m* inglés (RPl); ***as nutty as a ~cake*** (colloq & hum) más loco que una cabra (fam), chiflado (fam); **~ cocktail** *n* [u c] (dish) ensalada *f* *or* macedonia *f* *or* cóctel *m* de frutas; **~ cup** *n* [u c] 1 (AmE) ▸ **~ cocktail** 2 (drink) (BrE) ≈ sangría *f*, ≈ clericó *m*

fruiterer /'fru:tərə(r)/ *n* (BrE): **the ~'s** la frutería

fruit fly *n* mosca *f* de la fruta

fruitful /'fru:tfəl/ *adj* provechoso, fructífero

fruition /fru:'ɪʃən/ *n* [u] (frml): **to bring sth to ~** llevar algo a buen término; **their plan never came to** *o* **reached ~** su plan nunca cristalizó *or* se concretó

fruitless /'fru:tləs || 'fru:tlɪs/ *adj* infructuoso, inútil

fruit: **~ machine** *n* (BrE) máquina *f* tragamonedas *or* (Esp tb) tragaperras; **~ salad** *n* [u c] 1 (AmE) *ensalada de frutas, gen en gelatina* 2 (BrE) ▸ **fruit cocktail**

fruity /'fru:ti/ *adj* **-tier, -tiest** (like fruit) ‹*taste*/*smell*› a fruta(s); ‹*wine*/*bouquet*› afrutado

frump /frʌmp/ *n* (colloq) antigualla *f* (fam & pey)

frumpish /'frʌmpɪʃ/ *adj* anticuado y sin gracia

frumpy /'frʌmpi/ **-pier, -piest** ▸ **frumpish**

frustrate /'frʌstreɪt || frʌs'treɪt/ *vt* frustrar

frustrated /'frʌstreɪtəd || frʌs'treɪtɪd/ *adj* 1 (thwarted) frustrado 2 (dissatisfied) descontento; **(sexually) ~** sexualmente frustrado

frustrating /'frʌstreɪtɪŋ || frʌs'treɪtɪŋ/ *adj* frustrante

frustration /frʌs'treɪʃən/ *n* [u c] frustración *f*

fry¹ /fraɪ/ **fries, frying, fried** *vt* freír*
■ **fry** *vi* freírse*

Phrasal verb
• **fry up** [v ▸ o ▸ adv, v ▸ adv ▸ o] freír*

fry² *n* (*pl* **fries**)
A 1 [c] (cookout) (AmE) *comida al aire libre* 2 **fries** *pl* (*French fries*) papas *or* (Esp) patatas fritas, papas *fpl* a la francesa (Col, Méx)
B [u] 1 (+ *pl vb*) (Zool) alevines *mpl*, majuga *f* (Ur) 2 (people): **small ~** gente *f* de poca monta

fryer /'fraɪər || 'fraɪə(r)/ *n* (pan) sartén *f*, sartén *m* *or* *f* (AmL); **deep (fat) ~** freidora *f*

frying pan /'fraɪɪŋ/, (AmE also) **fry pan** *n* sartén *f*, sartén *m* *or* *f* (AmL); ***out of the ~ ~ into the fire***: **he jumped out of the ~ ~ into the fire** salió de Guatemala para meterse en Guatepeor (fam & hum)

fry-up /'fraɪʌp/ *n* (BrE colloq) fritada *f*, fritanga *f*

FSA *n* (in UK) 1 = **Food Standards Agency** 2 = **Financial Services Authority**

ft = **foot**/**feet**

Ft = **Fort**

FTSE 100-Share Index
▸ **Financial Times Indices**

fuchsia /'fju:ʃə/ *n* [c u] (Bot) fucsia *f*, aljaba *f* (RPl)

fuck¹ /fʌk/ *vt* (vulg) (copulate with) joder (vulg), tirarse (vulg), follarse (Esp vulg), coger* (Méx, RPl, Ven vulg)
■ **fuck** *vi* (vulg) joder (vulg), tirar (vulg), coger* (Méx, RPl, Ven vulg), follar (Esp vulg), cachar (Chi, Per vulg)

Phrasal verbs
• **fuck off** [v ▸ adv] (vulg): **~ off!** ¡vete a la mierda! (vulg), ¡vete a tomar por (el) culo! (Esp vulg), ¡vete a la chingada! (Méx vulg), ¡andá a cagar! (RPl vulg)
• **fuck up** (vulg)
A [v ▸ o ▸ adv, v ▸ adv ▸ o] 1 (spoil) ‹*plan*/*equipment*› joder (vulg), chingar* (Méx vulg) 2 (bungle) cagar* (vulg)
B [v ▸ adv] (bungle) cagarla* (vulg)

fuck² *n* (vulg)
A 1 (act) polvo *m* (arg), cogida *f* (Méx, RPl, Ven vulg); **to have a ~** echar(se) un polvo (fam) 2 (person): **she/he's a good ~** ¡tiene un polvo …! (arg), coge rico (Méx, RPl, Ven vulg)
B (*as intensifier*) **what/who/where the ~ …?** ¿qué/quién/dónde carajo *or* coño *or* (Méx) chingados …? (vulg); ***not to give a ~***: **I don't give a ~** me importa un carajo (vulg), me vale madres (Méx vulg)

fuck³ *interj* (vulg) ¡carajo! (vulg), ¡coño! (vulg), ¡chingada! (Méx vulg)

fuck-all /'fʌk'ɔ:l/ *n* (BrE vulg): **he knows ~ about it** no tiene ni puta idea (vulg), no sabe una chingada (Méx vulg)

fucking /'fʌkɪŋ/ *adj* (vulg) (*before n*): **this ~ car/hammer** este coche/martillo de mierda (vulg); **you ~ idiot!** ¡idiota de mierda! (vulg), ¡gilipollas! (Esp vulg); **~ hell!** ¡puta madre! (vulg), ¡coño! (vulg), ¡carajo! (vulg)

fuck-up /'fʌkʌp/ *n* (vulg) (disaster) cagada *f* (vulg)

fuddled /'fʌdl̩d/ *adj* ‹*mind*/*thoughts*› confuso, embotado

fuddy-duddy /'fʌdi,dʌdi/ *n* (*pl* **-dies**) (colloq) antigualla *mf* (fam), carca *mf* (fam), ruco, -ca (Méx fam)

fudge[1] /fʌdʒ/ *n* [u] (Culin) *especie de caramelo de dulce de leche*

fudge[2] *vt* (colloq) 1 (falsify) ‹*figures*› amañar 2 (evade) ‹*issue*› esquivar

■ **fudge** *vi* (colloq): **stop fudging and get to the point** deja de dar rodeos y ve al grano

fuel[1] /'fju:əl/ *n* [u c] (for heating, lighting) combustible *m*; (for engines) combustible *m*, carburante *m*; ***to add ~ to the flames*** *o* ***fire*** echar leña al fuego

fuel[2] *vt* (BrE) **-ll-**

A (provide fuel for) ‹*ship/plane*› abastecer* de combustible; ‹*stove/furnace*› alimentar

B (stimulate) ‹*hope/passion*› alimentar; ‹*debate*› avivar; ‹*fear*› exacerbar

fuel oil *n* [u] fuel-oil *m*

fug /fʌg/ *n* (esp BrE colloq) (*no pl*) atmósfera *f* viciada

fugitive[1] /'fju:dʒətɪv/ *n* fugitivo, -va *m,f*

fugitive[2] *adj* (*before n*) (runaway) fugitivo

fugue /fju:g/ *n* fuga *f*

> **Fulbright Scholarships**
>
> Las Becas Fulbright, otorgadas por el gobierno de EEUU, permiten a individuos norteamericanos ir al extranjero y a ciudadanos de otros países viajar a EEUU para estudiar, enseñar y realizar investigaciones académicas. Más de 114 mil extranjeros y 61 mil estadounidenses han aprovechado la oportunidad que ofrece el Programa Fulbright desde su fundación por el senador Democrático William Fulbright en 1946

fulcrum /'fʊlkrəm/ *n* (*pl* **-crums** *or* **-cra** /-krə/) fulcro *m*

fulfill, (BrE) **fulfil** /fʊl'fɪl/ **-ll-** *vt*

A 1 (carry out) ‹*duty*› cumplir con; ‹*task*› llevar a cabo, realizar* 2 (obey, keep) ‹*order/promise/contract*› cumplir 3 (serve) ‹*need*› satisfacer* 4 (meet) ‹*requirements*› satisfacer*, llenar

B (realize) ‹*ambition*› hacer* realidad; ‹*potential*› alcanzar*

C (make content) ‹*person*› satisfacer*

■ *v refl* **to ~ oneself** realizarse*

fulfilled /fʊl'fɪld/ *adj* (*usu pred*) realizado

fulfilling /fʊl'fɪlɪŋ/ *adj* ‹*life*› pleno; **I don't find my work ~** mi trabajo no me satisface *or* no me hace sentirme realizado

fulfillment, (BrE) **fulfilment** /fʊl'fɪlmənt/ *n* [u] 1 (of duty, promise) cumplimiento *m* 2 (realization) cumplimiento *m*; **to bring sth to ~** llevar algo a cabo 3 (satisfaction): **her family gave her a sense of ~** su familia la hacía sentirse realizada

full[1] /fʊl/ *adj* **-er, -est**

A 1 (filled) lleno; **don't speak with your mouth ~** no hables con la boca llena; **I'm ~ (up)** estoy lleno; **~ OF sth** lleno DE algo; **she's ~ of fun** es muy divertida; **they were ~ of praise for your work** elogiaron mucho tu trabajo; ***to be ~ of it*** (AmE colloq & euph) decir* puras tonterías *or* sandeces 2 (crowded) ‹*room/train*› lleno; ‹*hotel*› lleno, completo; **you've got a very ~ day ahead of you** tienes un día muy ocupado por delante

B 1 (complete) ‹*report/description*› detallado; ‹*name/answer*› completo; **to pay the ~ price** pagar* el precio íntegro; **you have my ~ support** tienes todo mi apoyo; **in ~ bloom** en plena floración; **to lead a very ~ life** llevar una vida muy activa; **a ~ week's holiday** una semana entera de vacaciones 2 (maximum): **at ~ speed** a toda velocidad; **~ employment** (Econ) pleno empleo *m*

C 1 (rounded) ‹*figure*› regordete, llenito (fam); **clothes for the ~er figure** (euph) tallas *or* (RPl) talles grandes 2 (Clothing) ‹*skirt/sleeve*› amplio

D (absorbed) **~ OF sth: they were ~ of the latest scandal** no hacían más que hablar del último escándalo; ***to be ~ of oneself*** *o* ***of one's own importance*** ser* muy creído (fam), tenérselo muy creído (fam)

full[2] *adv*

A (*as intensifier*) **~ well** muy bien; **you know ~ well that ...** sabes perfectamente *or* muy bien que ...

B (directly): **the sun shone ~ in my face** el sol me daba de lleno en la cara; **I looked him ~ in the face** lo miré directamente a la cara

C (*in phrases*) **full on: the car's headlights were ~ on** el coche llevaba las luces largas; **the heating is ~ on** la calefacción está al máximo *or* (fam) a tope; **full out** a toda máquina; **in full: write your name in ~** escriba su nombre completo; **it will be paid in ~** será pagado en su totalidad; **to the full** al máximo

full: **~back** *n* (in US football) fulbac *mf*, corredor, -dora *m,f* de poder; (in rugby) zaguero, -ra *m,f*; (in soccer) defensa *mf*, zaguero, -ra; **~-blooded** /'fʊl'blʌdəd ‖ ˌfʊl'blʌdɪd/ *adj* 1 (pure-bred) ‹*stallion*› de pura sangre 2 (lusty) apasionado 3 (forceful) ‹*argument*› vehemente; **~-blown** /'fʊl 'bləʊn/ *adj* (*before n*) ‹*riot/scandal*› verdadero, auténtico; **~-bodied** /'fʊl'bɑ:did ‖ ˌfʊl'bɒdid/ *adj* ‹*taste/aroma*› intenso; ‹*wine/port*› con cuerpo

fuller's earth /'fʊlərz ‖ ˌfʊləz/ *n* [u] tierra *f* de batán

full: **~-fledged** /'fʊl'fledʒd/ *adj* (AmE) 1 ‹*nestling/chick*› capaz de volar; 2 ‹*lawyer/nurse*› hecho y derecho; **~-frontal** /'fʊl'frʌntl/ *adj* (*before n*): **~-frontal nudity** desnudo *m* integral; **~-grown** /'fʊl'grəʊn/ *adj* (*before n*) totalmente desarrollado, adulto; **~ house** *n* 1 (Cin, Theat) lleno *m*; 2 (in poker) full *m*; (in bingo) cartón *m*

full-length[1] /'fʊl'leŋθ/ *adj* ‹*portrait/photograph/mirror*› de cuerpo entero; ‹*dress/skirt*› largo; **a ~ feature film** un largometraje

full-length[2] *adv*: **he lay ~ on the floor** estaba tendido en el piso cuan largo era

fullness /'fʊlnəs ‖ 'fʊlnɪs/ *n* [u]

A (repletion) plenitud *f*

B (completeness) lo completo; ***in the ~ of time*** con el tiempo

full: **~-page** /'fʊl'peɪdʒ/ *adj* a toda página; **~-scale** /'fʊl'skeɪl/ *adj* 1 (actual size) a escala natural; 2 (major) ‹*work*› de envergadura, importante; ‹*investigation*› a fondo; ‹*test*› a escala real; ‹*war*› declarado; **~-size** /'fʊl 'saɪz/, **~-sized** /-d/ *adj* 1 (life-size) de tamaño natural 2 (of adult size) ‹*bicycle/bed*› de adulto; **~ stop** *n* (BrE) punto *m*

full time *n* (BrE Sport) final *m* del partido *or* del tiempo reglamentario

full: **~-time**[1] /'fʊl'taɪm/ *adj* ‹*student/soldier*› de tiempo completo; ‹*employment/post*› de jornada completa, de tiempo completo; **~-time**[2] *adv* a tiempo completo; **to work full-~** trabajar a tiempo completo; **~-timer** /'fʊl 'taɪmər ‖ ˌfʊl'taɪmə(r)/ *n* trabajador, -dora *m,f* de tiempo completo

fully /'fʊli/ *adv*

A 1 (completely): **I don't ~ understand** no entiendo del todo, no acabo de entender; **she's a ~ trained nurse** es una enfermera diplomada; **~ comprehensive insurance** (Fin) seguro contra todo riesgo 2 (in full) enteramente 3 (in detail) en detalle

B (at least) por lo menos, como poco

fully-fledged /'fʊli'fledʒd/ *adj* (BrE) ▸ **full-fledged**

fulminate /'fʊlməneɪt ‖ 'fʊlmɪneɪt, 'fʌl-/ *vi* (frml) despotricar*

fulsome /'fʊlsəm/ *adj* ‹*praise*› empalagoso, exagerado; ‹*manner*› excesivamente efusivo

fumble[1] /'fʌmbəl/ *vi* (grope): **he was fumbling (around** *o* **about) in the dark** buscaba algo a tientas en la oscuridad; **she ~d in her pockets** revolvió *or* hurgó en sus bolsillos; **to ~ FOR sth: she ~d for the keyhole** buscó a tientas la cerradura; **he ~d for the right words** tartamudeó, tratando de encontrar las palabras adecuadas; **to ~ WITH sth: she ~d with her buttons** intentó torpemente abrocharse/desabrocharse

■ **fumble** *vt* ‹*ball*› dejar caer; (in US football) fumblear

fumble[2] *n* (in US football) fumble *m*

fumbling /'fʌmblɪŋ/ *adj* (*usu before n*) ‹*apology*› titubeante; ‹*attempt*› torpe

fume /fju:m/ *vi*

A (smoke) (Chem) despedir* gases

B (be angry) (colloq): **she was absolutely fuming** estaba que echaba humo *or* chispas

fumes /fju:mz/ *pl n* gases *mpl*

fumigate /'fju:məgeɪt ‖ 'fju:mɪgeɪt/ *vt* fumigar*

fun[1] /fʌn/ *n* [u] diversión *f*; **this is ~!** ¡qué divertido (es esto)!; **to have ~** divertirse*, pasarlo *or* pasársela bien; **have ~** pásatelo bien, que te diviertas; **it's not my idea of ~** no es lo que yo entiendo por pasarlo *or* pasarla bien;

he's good ~ es muy divertido; **to do sth for ~** *o* **for the ~ of it** hacer* algo por gusto; **to do/say sth in ~** hacer*/decir* algo en broma; **~ *and games*: we had some ~ and games with the baby last night** ayer pasamos una noche de perros con el bebé; **we had some ~ and games putting it together again** fue toda una odisea volver a armarlo; ***to make* ~ *of sb/sth*** reírse* de algn/algo; ***to poke* ~ *at sb/sth*** burlarse de algn/algo

fun² *adj (before n)* ‹*party*› (colloq) divertido; **he's a ~ person** es un tipo divertido; **~ run** maratón *m or f* popular

function¹ /'fʌŋkʃən/ *n*
A 1 (of tool, machine, organ) función *f*; **to carry out/perform a ~** cumplir/desempeñar una función 2 (role, duty) función *f*; **it's his only useful ~** es para lo único que sirve
B (reception, party) recepción *f*, reunión *f* social
C (Comput, Math) función *f*; (*before n*) **~ key** tecla *f* de función

function² *vi* 1 (operate) ‹‹*machine/organ*›› funcionar 2 (serve) **to ~ AS sth** ‹‹*object/building*›› hacer* (las veces) DE algo

functional /'fʌŋkʃnəl || 'fʌŋkʃənl/ *adj* 1 (functioning) ‹*machine/part*› en buen estado (de funcionamiento); ‹*law/principle*› vigente 2 (practical) ‹*furniture/design*› funcional

functionary /'fʌŋkʃəneri || 'fʌŋkʃənəri/ *n (pl* **-ries**) funcionario, -ria *m,f*

fund¹ /fʌnd/ *n* 1 (money reserve) fondo *m* 2 (store, supply) caudal *m*, cúmulo *m*; **an endless ~ of jokes** un arsenal *or* una colección inagotable de chistes 3 **funds** *pl* (resources, money) fondos *mpl*; **party ~s** fondos del partido

fund² *vt* 1 (finance) ‹*research/organization*› financiar 2 (Fin) ‹*debt*› consolidar

fund of funds *n* fondo *m* de fondos

fundamental /'fʌndə'mentl/ *adj* 1 (basic) ‹*principle/error*› fundamental, básico; **to be ~ TO sth/-ING** ser* fundamental *or* básico para algo/+ INF 2 (essential) ‹*skill/constituent*› esencial 3 (intrinsic, innate) ‹*absurdity/truth*› intrínseco; ‹*optimism*› innato

fundamentalism /'fʌndə'mentəlɪzəm/ *n* [u] integrismo *m*, fundamentalismo *m*

fundamentalist /'fʌndə'mentləst || ˌfʌndə'mentəlɪst/ *n* integrista *mf*, fundamentalista *mf*

fundamentally /'fʌndə'mentli || ˌfʌndə'mentəli/ *adv* 1 (radically) ‹*different/mistaken*› fundamentalmente 2 (in essence) ‹*correct/justified*› esencialmente, básicamente

fundamentals /'fʌndə'mentlz/ *pl n* fundamentos *mpl*

funding /'fʌndɪŋ/ *n* [u] (act) financiación *f*, financiamiento *m*; (resources) fondos *mpl*, recursos *mpl*

fund: ~-raiser /'fʌnd'reɪzər || 'fʌndˌreɪzə(r)/ *n* 1 (person) recaudador, -dora *m,f* de fondos 2 (event) *función, comida etc para recaudar fondos*; **~-raising** /'fʌnd 'reɪzɪŋ || 'fʌndˌreɪzɪŋ/ *n* [u] recaudación *f* de fondos

funeral /'fju:nərəl/ *n* funerales *mpl*, funeral *m*; (burial) entierro *m*; ***that's your ~*** (colloq) allá tú (fam), con tu pan te lo comas (fam); (*before n*) ‹*pyre/customs*› funerario; **~ service** funeral *f*, exequias *fpl* (frml)

funeral: ~ director *n* (frml) director, -tora *m,f* de una funeraria *or* de pompas fúnebres; **~ home** (AmE), **~ parlour** (BrE) *n* funeraria *f*, casa *f* de pompas fúnebres

funereal /fju:'nɪriəl || 'fju:nɪəriəl/ *adj* fúnebre

funfair /'fʌnfer || 'fʌnfeə(r)/ *n* (BrE) (traveling) feria *f*; (permanent) parque *m* de diversiones *or* (Esp) de atracciones

fungal /'fʌŋgəl/ *adj* de hongos; (Med) micótico

fungi /'fʌŋgaɪ/ *pl of* **fungus**

fungicide /'fʌndʒəsaɪd || 'fʌndʒɪsaɪd/ *n* [u c] fungicida *m*

fungus /'fʌŋgəs/ *n* [c u] (*pl* **fungi**) hongo *m*

funicular (railway) /fjʊ'nɪkjələr/ *n* funicular *m*

funk /fʌŋk/ *n* [u] (Mus) música *f* funk

funky /'fʌŋki/ *adj* **-kier, -kiest** (colloq) 1 (Mus) funky *adj inv* 2 (stylish) (esp AmE) ‹*person/party*› en la onda (fam), enrollado (Esp fam); ‹*style*› original

fun-loving /'fʌn'lʌvɪŋ/ *adj* amante de las diversiones, gozador (Chi), gozón (Col fam)

funnel /'fʌnl/ *n* (for pouring) embudo *m*; (on steamship, steam engine) (BrE) chimenea *f*; (ventilation shaft) (AmE) conducto *m* de ventilación

funnily /'fʌnli || 'fʌnɪli/ *adv* 1 (strangely) (esp BrE) de modo extraño *or* raro 2 **~ enough** (*indep*) casualmente

funny¹ /'fʌni/ *adj* **-nier, -niest**
A (amusing) ‹*joke*› gracioso, cómico; ‹*person*› divertido, gracioso; **it's not ~, you know!** ¡te advierto que no me hace ninguna gracia!
B 1 (strange) raro, extraño; **(it's) ~ (that) you should mention it** es curioso que lo menciones; **to taste/smell ~** saber*/oler* raro 2 (deceitful) (colloq): **don't try anything ~!** nada de trucos ¿eh?
C (colloq) 1 (unwell): **I felt a bit ~ on the journey** me sentí medio mal *or* (Col fam) maluco *or* (Chi fam) malón durante el viaje 2 (slightly mad) tocado (fam), rayado (AmS fam); **he's a bit ~ in the head** está medio tocado (del ala) (fam)

funny² *n (pl* **-nies**) **funnies** *pl* (comic strips) (AmE colloq) tiras *fpl* cómicas, sección *f* de historietas

funny³ *adv* (colloq) raro (fam)

funny: ~ bone *n* (colloq) hueso *m* del codo; **~ farm** *n* (colloq & hum) loquero *m* (fam), casa *f* de orates; **~ man** *n* cómico *m*; **~ money** *n* [u] (colloq) dinero *m* que no vale nada

fur /fɜ:r || fɜ:(r)/ *n* 1 [u] (of animal) (Zool) pelo *m*, pelaje *m*; (Clothing) piel *f*; **fake** *o* **fun ~** piel *f* sintética; (*before n*) **~ coat** abrigo *m* de piel *or* (Esp tb) de pieles 2 [c] (pelt) piel *f* 3 [u] (limescale) (esp BrE) sarro *m*

furbish /'fɜ:rbɪʃ || 'fɜ:bɪʃ/ *vt* 1 (polish) limpiar 2 **~ (up)** ▸**refurbish**

furious /'fjʊriəs || 'fjʊəriəs/ *adj* 1 (angry) furioso; **he was ~ with me** estaba furioso conmigo; **she'll be ~ if we're late** se va a poner furiosa *or* se va a enfurecer si llegamos tarde 2 (violent, intense) ‹*struggle*› feroz; ‹*speed*› vertiginoso; ‹*storm*› violento; ‹*activity*› febril, frenético

furiously /'fjʊriəsli || 'fjʊəriəsli/ *adv* 1 (angrily) con furia, furiosamente 2 (violently, intensely) frenéticamente

furlong /'fɜ:rlɔ:ŋ || 'fɜ:lɒŋ/ *n* estadio *m* (*medida de longitud equivalente a 201,2m*)

furlough /'fɜ:rləʊ || 'fɜ:ləʊ/ *n* [u c] (AmE) permiso *m*, licencia *f*; **on ~** de permiso, con licencia

furnace /'fɜ:rnəs || 'fɜ:nɪs/ *n* (in industry) horno *m*; (for heating) caldera *f*

furnish /'fɜ:rnɪʃ || 'fɜ:nɪʃ/ *vt*
A 1 ‹*house/room*› amueblar, amoblar* (AmL) 2 **furnished** *past p* ‹*room/apartment*› amueblado, amoblado (AmL); **the house is being let fully ~ed** la casa se alquila con mobiliario completo
B (supply) (frml) proporcionar; **to ~ sb WITH sth** ‹*with information/details*› proporcionarle *or* facilitarle algo a algn; ‹*with food/weapons*› proveer* a algn DE algo

furnishings /'fɜ:rnɪʃɪŋz || 'fɜ:nɪʃɪŋz/ *pl n*: *mobiliario, cortinas, alfombras, etc*

furniture /'fɜ:rnɪtʃər || 'fɜ:nɪtʃə(r)/ *n* [u] (in home, office) muebles *mpl*, mobiliario *m*; **a piece of ~** un mueble; ***to be/become part of the ~*** formar/pasar a formar parte del decorado; (*before n*) **~ mover** *o* (BrE) **remover** empresa *f* de mudanzas; **~ polish** cera *f* para muebles; **~ store** *o* (BrE) **shop** mueblería *f*; **~ van** (BrE) camión *m* de mudanzas *or* (Col) de trasteos

furor /'fjʊrɔ:r || 'fjʊərɔ:(r)/, (BrE) **furore** /fjʊ'rɔ:ri || fjʊə'rɔ:ri/ *n* escándalo *m*; **to cause a ~** provocar* un escándalo

furrier /'fɜ:riər || 'fʌriə(r)/ *n* peletero, -ra *m,f*

furrow¹ /'fɜ:rəʊ || 'fʌrəʊ/ *n*
A (Agr) surco *m*
B (wrinkle) surco *m*, arruga *f*

furrow² *vt* (Agr) surcar*; **she ~ed her brow in disapproval** frunció el ceño en señal de desaprobación

furry /'fɜ:ri/ *adj* **-rier, -riest** ‹*animal*› peludo; ‹*toy*› de peluche; ‹*covering/lining*› afelpado

further¹ /'fɜ:rðər || 'fɜ:ðə(r)/ *adv*
A *comp of* **far¹ A** 1 (in distance): **they live even ~ away** ellos viven aún más lejos; **how much ~ is it?** ¿cuánto camino nos queda por hacer?; **we went a little ~ and came to a bridge** avanzamos un poco más y llegamos a un puente; **let's sit a little ~ back** sentémonos un poco más atrás; **you'll need to push it ~ in** tendrás que meterlo más adentro; **~ on, there's another set of traffic lights** más adelante, hay otro semáforo; **(you need) look no ~!** ¡no busques más! 2 (in progress): **the legislation should have gone ~** la legislación debería haber ido más lejos; **have you got any ~ with that essay?** ¿has adelantado ese

trabajo? 3 (in time): **we must look back even ~** tenemos que retroceder aún más en el tiempo; **this vase dates back even ~** este jarrón es aún más antiguo *or* data de una época aún anterior 4 (in extent, degree): **I'll look ~ into that possibility** voy a estudiar esa posibilidad más a fondo; **the situation is ~ complicated by her absence** el hecho de que ella no esté complica aún más la situación

B **further to** (Corresp) (*as prep*): **~ to your letter of June 6, ...** con relación a *or* en relación con su carta del 6 de junio, ...

C (furthermore) (*as linker*) además

further² *adj* más; **have you any ~ questions?** ¿tienen más preguntas *or* alguna otra pregunta?; **please send me ~ details** le ruego (que) me envíe más información; **I have nothing ~ to say** no tengo nada que agregar; **until ~ notice** hasta nuevo aviso

further³ *vt* ‹*cause/aims*› promover*, fomentar; ‹*career/interests*› favorecer*

furtherance /'fɜ:rðərəns || 'fɜ:ðərəns/ *n* [u] (frml) promoción *f*, fomento *m*; **in ~ of his claim** en apoyo *or* respaldo de su demanda

further education *n* [u] (BrE) *programa de cursos de extensión cultural para adultos*

furthermore /'fɜ:rðərmɔ:r || ˌfɜ:ðə'mɔ:(r)/ *adv* además

furthest /'fɜ:rðəst || 'fɜ:ðɪst/ *adv superl of* **far¹ A**

furtive /'fɜ:rtɪv || 'fɜ:tɪv/ *adj* 1 (stealthy) ‹*movement/look*› furtivo; ‹*persona*› solapado 2 (suspicious, shifty) ‹*appearance*› sospechoso; ‹*manner*› solapado

furtively /'fɜ:rtɪvli || 'fɜ:tɪvli/ *adv* ‹*creep*› sigilosamente, furtivamente; ‹*peep/listen*› a hurtadillas

fury /'fjʊri || 'fjʊəri/ *n* [u c] (*pl* **furies**) (rage) ira *f*, furia *f*; **she came home in a ~** volvió a casa furiosa *or* hecha una furia; **they worked/ran like ~** trabajaron/corrieron como locos

fuse¹ /fju:z/ *n*

A (Elec) fusible *m*, plomo *m* (Esp), tapón *m* (CS); **the ~s blew** *o* **went** saltaron los fusibles *or* (CS) los tapones, se fundieron los plomos (Esp); ***to blow a ~*** «*person*» (hum) explotar (fam), estallar

B (for explosives) 1 (of powder) mecha *f*; (detonator) espoleta *f* 2 (wick) mecha *f*; ***to have a short ~*** tener pocas *or* malas pulgas, ser* una polvorilla

fuse² *vt*

A (Elec) 1 (short-circuit) (BrE): **to ~ the lights** hacer* saltar los fusibles *or* (CS tb) los tapones, fundir los plomos (Esp) 2 **fused** *past p* con fusible

B 1 (melt together) alear, fundir 2 (merge) fusionar

■ **fuse** *vi*

A (BrE Elec) fundirse; **the lights have ~d** se han fundido los fusibles *or* (Esp tb) los plomos, han saltado los fusibles *or* (CS tb) los tapones

B 1 «*metals*» fundirse; «*atoms*» fusionarse 2 (unite) fusionarse, amalgamarse

fuse box *n* caja *f* de fusibles *or* (Esp tb) de plomos *or* (CS tb) de tapones

fuselage /'fju:zəlɑ:ʒ/ *n* fuselaje *m*

fuse wire *n* (in UK) alambre *m* de fusible

fusilier /'fju:zə'lɪr || ˌfju:zə'lɪə(r)/ *n* (BrE) fusilero *m*

fusillade /'fju:səleɪd || ˌfju:zə'leɪd/ *n* descarga *f* cerrada *or* de fusilería

fusion /'fju:ʒən/ *n* [u c] fusión *f*

fuss¹ /fʌs/ *n* [u] alboroto *m*, escándalo *m*; **it was a lot of ~ about nothing** fue mucho ruido y pocas nueces, fue una tormenta en un vaso de agua; ***to kick up a ~*** armar un lío *or* un escándalo, montar un número (Esp fam); ***to make a ~ of*** *o* (AmE also) ***over sb*** mimar *or* consentir* a algn; ***to make*** *o* (AmE also) ***raise a ~*** hacer* un escándalo

fuss² *vi* (be agitated, worry) preocuparse, inquietarse; **to ~ ABOUT** *o* **OVER sth** preocuparse *or* inquietarse POR *or* CON algo

Phrasal verbs

- **fuss around, fuss about** [v ▸ adv] estar* de aquí para allá
- **fuss over** [v ▸ prep ▸ o] ‹*invalid/pet*› mimar

fussbudget /'fʌs'bʌdʒɪt/ *n* (AmE) maniático, -ca *m,f*, mañoso, -sa *m,f* (AmL)

fussily /'fʌsəli || 'fʌsɪli/ *adv* 1 (fastidiously) remilgadamente, melindrosamente 2 (elaborately) ‹*furnished/dressed*› de manera recargada

fusspot /'fʌspɑ:t || 'fʌspɒt/ *n* (esp BrE) ▸ **fussbudget**

fussy /'fʌsi/ *adj* **-sier, -siest** 1 (fastidious) exigente, quisquilloso; **I'm a ~ eater** soy muy maniático *or* (AmL tb) mañoso para comer; **to be ~ ABOUT sth** ser* exigente *or* quisquilloso CON algo; **what would you like to drink? — I'm not ~** (colloq) ¿qué quieres tomar? — cualquier cosa *or* me da lo mismo 2 (elaborate) ‹*detail/pattern*› recargado

fustian /'fʌstʃən || 'fʌstiən/ *n* [u] fustán *m*, bombasí *m*

fusty /'fʌsti/ *adj* ‹*room*› que huele a cerrado; ‹*old clothes*› que huele a húmedo

futile /'fju:tl || 'fju:taɪl/ *adj* ‹*attempt*› inútil, vano; ‹*suggestion/question*› trivial, fútil

futility /fjʊ'tɪləti/ *n* [u] inutilidad *f*

future¹ /'fju:tʃər || 'fju:tʃə(r)/ *n*

A (time ahead) **the ~** el futuro; **in the ~** en el futuro; **in the near/distant ~** en un futuro próximo/lejano; **in the not too distant ~** en un futuro no muy lejano; **in ~** de ahora en adelante

B [c u] (prospects) futuro *m*, porvenir *m*; **a job with a ~** un trabajo con futuro

C (Ling) futuro *m*

D **futures** *pl* (Fin) futuros *mpl*

future² *adj* (*before n*) 1 ‹*husband/home*› futuro 2 (Ling): **the ~ tense** el futuro

futurist /'fju:tʃərəst || 'fju:tʃərɪst/ *n* futurista *mf*

futuristic /'fju:tʃə'rɪstɪk/ *adj* futurista

fuze /fju:z/ *n* (AmE) ▸ **fuse¹ B1**

fuzz /fʌz/ *n*

A [u] (*no pl*) 1 (fine hair) pelusa *f* 2 (frizzy hair) pelo *m* crespo *or* muy rizado

B (sl) (police) (+ *pl vb*) **the ~** la pasma (Esp arg), la tomba (Col fam), la tira (Méx arg), la cana (RPl arg), los pacos (Chi fam)

fuzzy /'fʌzi/ *adj* **-zier, -ziest**

A 1 (frizzy) ‹*hair*› muy rizado, crespo; ‹*beard*› enmarañado 2 (downy) ‹*skin*› velloso, velludo 3 (furry) (AmE) ‹*bear*› peludo

B (blurred) ‹*sound*› confuso; ‹*picture/outline*› borroso

G, g /dʒiː/ *n* 1 (letter) G, g *f* 2 (Mus) sol *m*; *see also* **A A2**

g (= **gram(s)**) g., gr.

G 1 (= **gravity/gravities**) G 2 (in US) (Cin) (= **general**) apta para todo público *or* para todos los públicos

GA, Ga = Georgia

gab /gæb/ *vi* **-bb-** (colloq) charlar (fam), cotorrear (fam)

gabardine, gaberdine /'gæbərdiːn || 'gæbədiːn/ *n* [u c] gabardina *f*

gabble /'gæbəl/ *vi* (speak incoherently) hablar atropelladamente *or* confusamente, farfullar; (speak quickly) parlotear (fam); **they ~d away in Italian** parlotearon en italiano

■ **gabble** *vt* farfullar

gaberdine *n* [u c] ▶**gabardine**

gable /'geɪbəl/ *n* gablete *m*; **~ (end)** hastial *m*

Gabon /gæ'bəʊn || gə'bɒn/ *n* Gabón *m*

gad /gæd/ *vi* **-dd-** (colloq): **to ~ about** *o* **around** callejear (fam), dar* vueltas por ahí (fam)

gadfly /'gædflaɪ/ *n* (*pl* **-flies**) tábano *m*

gadget /'gædʒət || 'gædʒɪt/ *n* (colloq) aparato *m*, artilugio *m*, chisme *m* (Esp fam)

gadgetry /'gædʒətri || 'gædʒɪtri/ *n* [u] (colloq) aparatos *mpl*, artilugios *mpl*

Gaelic /'geɪlɪk/ *n* [u] gaélico *m*

> **Gaelic**
>
> Así se denominan varias lenguas de origen celta habladas en distintas regiones de las Islas Británicas. El *Scots Gaelic* es hablado por unas 50.000 personas que viven en las Highlands y en las islas del oeste de Escocia. En cuanto al *Irish* o *Irish Gaelic*, aunque casi 1,5 millones de personas afirman dominarlo, se calcula que apenas la mitad lo habla diariamente. En la Isla autónoma de Man, varios centenares de personas hablan hoy el *Manx Gaelic*

gaff /gæf/ *n*: ***to blow the ~*** (BrE colloq) descubrir* el pastel (fam), levantar la liebre *or* (RPl) la perdiz (fam)

gaffe /gæf/ *n* metedura *f* de pata, metida *f* de pata (AmL fam), gaffe *f or m*; **to make a ~** meter la pata (fam), cometer una *or* un gaffe

gaffer /'gæfər || 'gæfə(r)/ *n*
A (Cin, TV) electricista *mf*
B (BrE colloq) 1 (boss) patrón *m*, jefe *m* 2 (old man) vejete *m* (fam)

gag[1] /gæg/ *n*
A (for mouth, restraint) mordaza *f*; **to put a ~ on sb** amordazar* a algn
B (joke) (colloq) chiste *m*, gag *m*

gag[2] **-gg-** *vt*
A 1 (physically) amordazar* 2 (censor) ‹*journalist/press*› silenciar, amordazar*
B (nauseate) (AmE) producirle* náuseas a
■ **gag** *vi* hacer* arcadas

gaga /'gɑːgɑː/ *adj*: **to be ~** chochear (fam), estar* chocho (fam); **to go ~** empezar* a chochear (fam), volverse* gagá (fam)

gage /geɪdʒ/ *vt/n* (AmE) ▶**gauge**[1,2]

gaggle /'gægəl/ *n* (of geese) bandada *f*; (of people) grupo *m*, pandilla *f*

gaiety /'geɪəti/ *n* [u] alegría *f*, regocijo *m*

gaily /'geɪli/ *adv* alegremente

gain[1] /geɪn/ *vt*
A (acquire) ‹*control*› conseguir*, obtener*; ‹*experience*› adquirir*; ‹*recognition*› obtener*, ganarse; ‹*qualifications*› (BrE) obtener*; **I succeeded in ~ing their attention** logré atraer *or* captar su atención; **there's a lot to be ~ed from this** esto ofrece muchas ventajas
B (increase) ‹*strength/speed*› ganar, cobrar; **the shares ~ed 5 points** las acciones subieron 5 enteros
C ‹*time*› ganar; **my watch is ~ing ten minutes a day** mi reloj (se) adelanta diez minutos por día
■ **gain** *vi*
A 1 (improve) **to ~ IN sth**: **the shares have ~ed in value** las acciones han subido *or* aumentado de valor; **she's gradually ~ing in confidence** poco a poco va adquiriendo confianza en sí misma 2 (benefit) beneficiarse, sacar* provecho
B 1 (go fast) «*clock/watch*» adelantar(se) 2 (move nearer) **to ~ ON sb** acortar (las) distancias con respecto a algn

gain[2] *n*
A [u c] (profit) (Busn) ganancia *f*, beneficio *m*; **their loss is our ~** nosotros nos beneficiamos *or* salimos ganando con su pérdida
B [c u] (increase) aumento *m*; **the ~ in efficiency** el aumento de eficiencia
C [c] (Pol) triunfo *m*, victoria *f*

gainer /'geɪnər || 'geɪnə(r)/ *n*: **we're all ~s if we adopt this plan** salimos todos ganando *or* beneficiados si adoptamos este plan; **the biggest ~ was France** la gran beneficiada fue Francia

gainful /'geɪnfəl/ *adj* retribuido, remunerado

gainfully /'geɪnfəli/ *adv*: **to be ~ employed** tener* un trabajo retribuido *or* remunerado

gainsay /'geɪn'seɪ/ *vt* (*past & past p* **gainsaid** /'geɪn'seɪd, 'geɪn'sed || ˌgeɪn'sed/) (frml) (*usu neg*) refutar (frml)

gait /geɪt/ *n* (*no pl*) modo *m* de andar

gaiters /'geɪtərz || 'geɪtəz/ *pl n* polainas *fpl*

gal[1] /gæl/ *n* (colloq) chica *f*, muchacha *f*

gal[2] **= gallon**

gala /'gælə, 'geɪlə || 'gɑːlə/ *n* (festival) fiesta *f*; **swimming ~** (BrE) festival *m* de natación; (*before n*) **~ performance** (función *f* de) gala *f*

Galapagos Islands /gə'lɑːpəgəs || gə'læpəgəs/ *pl n* **the ~ ~** las Islas Galápagos

galaxy /'gæləksi/ *n* (*pl* **-xies**) galaxia *f*

gale /geɪl/ *n* (Meteo) (wind) vendaval *m*, viento *m* fuerte; (storm) temporal *m*, tormenta *f*; **~s of laughter** estallidos *mpl* de risa; (*before n*) **~-force winds** vientos *mpl* huracanados; **~ warning** aviso *m* de temporal

Galicia /gə'lɪʃiə, gə'lɪsiə/ *n* Galicia *f*

Galician[1] /gə'lɪʃiən, gə'lɪsiən/ *n* 1 [c] (person) gallego, -ga *m,f* 2 [u] (language) gallego *m*

Galician[2] *adj* gallego

Galilee /'gæləliː || 'gælɪliː/ *n* Galilea *f*; **the Sea of ~** el lago Tiberíades, el mar de Galilea

gall[1] /gɔːl/ *n* [u]
A (effrontery) (colloq): **to have the ~ to + INF** tener* el descaro *or* la desfachatez DE + INF
B (bitterness) (liter) hiel *f* (liter)

gall[2] *vt* irritar, darle* rabia a

gallant *adj* 1 /ˈgælənt/ (brave) (liter) ‹*warrior*› aguerrido (liter), gallardo (liter); ‹*deed*› valiente 2 /gəˈlænt/ (chivalrous) galante, cortés

gallantly /ˈgæləntli/ *adv* 1 (bravely) valerosamente, con gallardía 2 (chivalrously) galantemente

gallantry /ˈgæləntri/ *n* (*pl* **-ries**) 1 [u] (bravery) valor *m*, gallardía *f* (liter) 2 [u c] (chivalry) galantería *f*, cortesía *f*

gallbladder /ˈgɔːlˌblædər || ˈgɔːlˌblædə(r)/ *n* vesícula *f* (biliar)

galleon /ˈgæliən/ *n* galeón *m*

gallery /ˈgæləri/ *n* (*pl* **-ries**)
A (Art) museo *m* (de Bellas Artes); (commercial) galería *f* (de arte)
B (Archit) 1 (balcony) galería *f*; (for press, spectators) tribuna *f*; (BrE Theat) galería *f*, gallinero *m* (fam); ***to play to the*** ~ actuar* para la galería 2 (colonnade) galería *f*
C (*shooting* ~) tiro *m* al blanco

galley /ˈgæli/ *n*
A (ship) galera *f*
B (kitchen on boat, plane) cocina *f*

galley slave *n* galeote *m*

Gallic /ˈgælɪk/ *adj* galo, (típicamente) francés

Gallicism, gallicism /ˈgæləsɪzəm || ˈgælɪsɪzəm/ *n* galicismo *m*

galling /ˈgɔːlɪŋ/ *adj* mortificante

gallivant /ˈgæləvænt || ˈgælɪvænt/ *vi* dar* vueltas, callejear (fam)

gallon /ˈgælən/ *n* galón *m* (*EEUU: 3,78 litros, RU: 4,55 litros*)

gallop[1] /ˈgæləp/ *n* galope *m*; **to break into a** ~ echarse a galopar; **at a** ~ al galope; **at full** ~ a galope tendido, a todo galope

gallop[2] *vi* galopar

galloping /ˈgæləpɪŋ/ *adj* (*before n*) ‹*inflation*› galopante

gallows /ˈgæləuz/ *n* (*pl* ~) (+ *sing o pl vb*) horca *f*

gallstone /ˈgɔːlstəun/ *n* cálculo *m* biliar

galore /gəˈlɔːr || gəˈlɔː(r)/ *adj* (*after n*) en abundancia; **apples** ~ muchísimas manzanas, manzanas en abundancia

galosh /gəˈlɑːʃ || gəˈlɒʃ/ *n* chanclo *m* (de goma), galocha *f*

galvanize /ˈgælvənaɪz/ *vt*
A (rouse) **to** ~ **sb (INTO sth/-ING)** impulsar a algn (A algo /+ INF)
B 1 (Metall) galvanizar* 2 **galvanized** *past p* ‹*iron/steel*› galvanizado

Gambia /ˈgæmbiə/ *n* **(the)** ~ Gambia *f*

gambit /ˈgæmbət || ˈgæmbɪt/ *n* (stratagem) táctica *f*; (in chess) gambito *m*

gamble[1] /ˈgæmbəl/ *vi* 1 (lay wager) jugar*; **to** ~ **ON sth: will he come? — I wouldn't** ~ **on it** ¿vendrá? — no me fiaría yo 2 (take risk) jugar*; **to** ~ **on the Stock Exchange** especular en la Bolsa, jugar* a la Bolsa; **to** ~ **ON sth: I** ~**d on her being in** decidí correr el riesgo de que no estuviera en casa
■ **gamble** *vt* jugarse*

Phrasal verb
• **gamble away** [v ▸ prep ▸ o] perder* jugando

gamble[2] *n* (*no pl*) 1 (bet) apuesta *f* 2 (risk): **to take a** ~ arriesgarse*; **the** ~ **paid off** valió la pena arriesgarse

gambler /ˈgæmblər || ˈgæmblə(r)/ *n* jugador, -dora *m,f*

gambling /ˈgæmblɪŋ/ *n* [u] juego *m*; (*before n*) ~ **debts** deudas *fpl* de juego

gambol /ˈgæmbəl/ *vi*, (BrE) **-ll-** retozar*

game[1] /geɪm/ *n*
A [c] 1 (amusement) juego *m*; ***it's all in the*** ~ todo es parte del juego; ***to play the*** ~ jugar* limpio 2 (type of sport) deporte *m*
B [c] 1 (complete match) (Sport) partido *m*; (in board games, cards) partida *f* 2 **games** *pl* (competition) juegos *mpl*; **the Olympic G**~**s** los Juegos Olímpicos, las Olimpiadas *or* Olimpiadas 3 **games** (BrE Educ) (+ *sing vb*) deportes *mpl*, ≈ educación *f* física
C [c] (part — of tennis, squash match) juego *m*; (— of bridge rubber) manga *f*
D [c] (underhand scheme, ploy) juego *m*; **the** ~**'s up** se acabó el juego; **what's your** ~**?** ¿qué es lo que pretendes?; ***to be ahead of the*** ~ llevar la delantera; ***to beat sb at her/his own*** ~ ganarle *or* vencer* a algn con sus propias armas; ***to give the*** ~ ***away*** ‹‹*person*›› descubrir* el pastel (fam); **her blushes gave the** ~ **away** el sonrojarse la delató; ***two can play at that*** ~ donde las dan las toman
E ***to be on the*** ~ (BrE sl) hacer* la calle (fam)
F [u] (in hunting) caza *f*; **big** ~ caza mayor; ***to be fair*** ~ ser* blanco legítimo; (*before n*) ~ **birds** aves *fpl* de caza
G [u] (Culin) caza *f*

game[2] *adj* **to be** ~ **(FOR sth): we're going swimming, are you** ~**?** vamos a nadar ¿te apuntas?; **I'm** ~ **if you are** si tú te animas, yo también; **she's** ~ **for anything** se apunta a todo

game: ~**keeper** *n* guardabosque(s) *mf*; ~ **plan** *n* (Sport) plan *m* de juego; (long-term plan) estrategia *f*; ~**s console** *n* consola *f* de videojuegos; ~ **show** *n* programa *m* concurso

gamer /ˈgeɪmə(r)/ *n* 1 (player) videojugador, -dora *m,f*, jugón, -gona *m,f* (Esp colloq) 2 (enthusiast) aficionado, -da *m,f*

gamesmanship /ˈgeɪmzmənʃɪp/ *n* [u] (pej) *arte de jugar astutamente*

gaming /ˈgeɪmɪŋ/ *n* [u] (*before n*) ~ **laws** legislación *f* que rige los juegos de azar

gamma ray /ˈgæmə/ *n* rayo *m* gamma

gammon /ˈgæmən/ *n* [u] (esp BrE) jamón *m* fresco

gammy /ˈgæmi/ *adj* (BrE) (*before n*) (colloq): ~ **leg** pata *f* coja (fam)

gamut /ˈgæmət/ *n* gama *f*, espectro *m*; **to run the (whole)** ~ **of sth** cubrir* toda la gama *or* todo el espectro de algo

gander /ˈgændər || ˈgændə(r)/ *n*
A (Zool) ganso *m* (*macho*)
B (look) (colloq) (*no pl*): **to have** *o* **take a** ~ **at sth** echarle un vistazo *or* una ojeada a algo

gang /gæŋ/ *n* 1 (of criminals) banda *f*, pandilla *f*; (of youths, children) pandilla *f* 2 (of workmen) cuadrilla *f* 3 (clique) (colloq) grupo *m*

Phrasal verb
• **gang up** [v ▸ adv] (unite in opposition) (colloq) **to** ~ **up AGAINST** *o* **ON sb** ponerse*/estar* en contra de algn

gangland /ˈgæŋlænd, -lənd/ *n* (journ) hampa *f*‡, mundo *m* del crimen organizado; (*before n*) ~ **murder** asesinato *m* del mundo del hampa

ganglia *pl of* **ganglion**

gangling /ˈgaŋglɪŋ/ *adj* larguirucho (fam), desgarbado

ganglion /ˈgæŋgliən/ *n* (*pl* **-glia** /-gliə/ *or* **-glions** /-gliənz/) ganglio *m*

gangly /ˈgæŋgli/ *adj* **-glier, -gliest** ▸ **gangling**

gangplank /ˈgæŋplæŋk/ *n* plancha *f*

gangrene /ˈgæŋgriːn/ *n* [u] gangrena *f*

gangrenous /ˈgæŋgrɪnəs/ *adj* ‹*wound*› gangrenoso

gangster /ˈgæŋstər || ˈgæŋstə(r)/ *n* gángster *mf*

gangway /ˈgæŋweɪ/ *n*
A (walkway) pasarela *f*
B (between rows of seats) (BrE) pasillo *m*

gannet /ˈgænət || ˈgænɪt/ *n* (Zool) alcatraz *m*

gantlet /ˈgɔːntlət/ *n* (AmE) ▸ **gauntlet**

gantry /ˈgæntri/ *n* (*pl* **-tries**)
A (Transp) castillete *m* de señalización
B (support — for crane) pórtico *m*, puente *m*; (— for space rocket) torre *f* de lanzamiento

gaol /dʒeɪl/ *n/vt* (esp BrE) ▸ **jail**[1,2]

gap /gæp/ *n*
A (space) espacio *m*; (in fence, hedge) hueco *m*; **I looked through the** ~ **in the curtains** miré por entre las cortinas; **she has a** ~ **between her front teeth** tiene los dientes de adelante separados
B 1 (in knowledge) laguna *f* 2 (in time) intervalo *m*, interrupción *f* 3 (disparity) distancia *f*, brecha *f*; **the** ~ **between rich and poor** la desigualdad entre ricos y pobres; **to bridge the** ~ salvar la distancia 4 (void) vacío *m*; **to fill** *o* **plug a** ~ **in the market** llenar un vacío *or* un hueco en el mercado

gape /geɪp/ *vi*
A (react with astonishment) quedarse boquiabierto *or* con la boca abierta; (stare) mirar boquiabierto
B (be open) estar* abierto

gaping /ˈgeɪpɪŋ/ *adj* ‹*wound*› abierto; ‹*hole*› enorme

gap year *n* (BrE) ≈ año *m* libre (*antes de entrar a la universidad*)

garage /gəˈrɑːʒ || ˈgærɑːdʒ, -ɪdʒ/ *n*
A (for parking) garaje *m*, garage *m* (esp AmL)

B 1 (for repairs) taller *m* (mecánico), garaje *m*, garage *m* (esp AmL); (*before n*) ~ **mechanic** mecánico, -ca *m,f* 2 (for fuel) (BrE) ▸**gas station**

garage sale *n*: *venta de objetos usados en casa de su propietario*, venta *f* de garage (Méx), feria *f* americana (RPl), venta *f* (Col)

garb /gɑːrb || gɑːb/ *n* [u] (liter *or* hum) atuendo *m* (liter *o* hum)

garbage /'gɑːrbɪdʒ || 'gɑːbɪdʒ/ *n* [u] 1 (AmE) (refuse) basura *f*; (*before n*) ~ **disposal unit** triturador *m* de basura; ~ **dump** vertedero *m* (de basuras), basurero *m*, basural *m* (AmL) 2 (junk) (colloq) trastos *mpl*, cachivaches *mpl* (fam), porquerías *fpl* (fam); **this book is absolute** ~ este libro es una auténtica porquería

garbage: ~ **bag** *n* (AmE) bolsa *f* de la basura; ~ **can** *n* (AmE) cubo *m* or (CS) tacho *m* or (Col) caneca *f* or (Méx) bote *m* or (Ven) tobo *m* de la basura; ~**man** /'gɑːrbɪdʒ'mæn/ *n* (*pl* **-men** /-men/) (AmE) basurero *m*; ~ **sack** *n* (AmE) bolsa *f* de la basura; ~ **truck** *n* (AmE) camión *m* de la basura

garble /'gɑːrbəl || 'gɑːbəl/ *vt* 1 ‹*message/instructions*› tergiversar, embrollar 2 **garbled** *past p* ‹*account*› confuso, embrollado; ‹*message*› incomprensible, indescifrable

garden¹ /'gɑːrdn̩ || 'gɑːdn̩/ *n*

A (for ornamental plants) jardín *m*; (for vegetables) huerta *f*, huerto *m*; **rose** ~ rosedal *m*, rosaleda *f*; ***everything in the ~ is lovely*** *o* ***rosy*** (BrE) todo marcha a las mil maravillas

B **gardens** *pl* (public, on private estate) jardines *mpl*, parque *m*

garden² *vi* trabajar en el jardín

garden: ~ **apartment** *n* (AmE) *apartamento con jardín o terraza privados*; ~ **center**, (BrE) ~ **centre** *n* vivero *m*, centro *m* de jardinería

gardener /'gɑːrdnər || 'gɑːdnə(r)/ *n* 1 (as job) jardinero, -ra *m,f* 2 (as hobby) amante *mf* de la jardinería

garden flat *n* (BrE) *apartamento en el sótano o planta baja con jardín*

gardening /'gɑːrdnɪŋ || 'gɑːdnɪŋ/ *n* [u] jardinería *f*, (vegetable growing) horticultura *f*; **he does the** ~ él se encarga del jardín

garden: ~ **party** *n* recepción *f* al aire libre; ~ **path** *n* sendero *m* (*en un jardín*); ***to lead sb up the ~ path*** engañar *or* embaucar* a algn; ~**-variety** *adj* (AmE colloq) (*before n*) vulgar *or* común y corriente

gargantuan /gɑːr'gæntʃuən || gɑː'gæntjʊən/ *adj* ‹*appetite*› pantagruélico; ‹*effort*› titánico

gargle /'gɑːrgəl || 'gɑːgəl/ *vi* hacer* gárgaras, gargarizar*

gargoyle /'gɑːrgɔɪl || 'gɑːgɔɪl/ *n* gárgola *f*

garish /'gerɪʃ || 'geərɪʃ/ *adj* ‹*color*› chillón, estridente, charro (AmL fam); ‹*garment*› estridente, chabacano, charro (AmL fam)

garland¹ /'gɑːrlənd || 'gɑːlənd/ *n* guirnalda *f*

garland² *vt* engalanar, enguirnaldar

garlic /'gɑːrlɪk || 'gɑːlɪk/ *n* [u] ajo *m*; **a clove of** ~ un diente de ajo; (*before n*) ~ **bread** pan *m* con mantequilla y ajo; ~ **sausage** salchichón *m* de ajo

garlicky /'gɑːrlɪki || 'gɑːlɪki/ *adj* ‹*taste/smell*› a ajo

garment /'gɑːrmənt || 'gɑːmənt/ *n* prenda *f* (de ropa); (*before n*) **the** ~ **industry** (AmE) la industria de la confección *or* del vestido

garner /'gɑːrnər || 'gɑːnə(r)/ *vt* ‹*ideas/information*› recoger*; ‹*praise*› cosechar

garnet /'gɑːrnət || 'gɑːnɪt/ *n* [u c] granate *m*

garnish¹ /'gɑːrnɪʃ || 'gɑːnɪʃ/ *vt* adornar, decorar; **the fish comes ~ed with parsley/cucumber slices** el pescado viene decorado con perejil/con una guarnición de rodajas de pepino

garnish² *n* [c u] adorno *m*, aderezo *m*; (more substantial) guarnición *f*

garret /'gærət/ *n* buhardilla *f*

garrison¹ /'gærəsən || 'gærɪsən/ *n* 1 (place) plaza *f* fuerte *or* de armas 2 (troops) guarnición *f*

garrison² *vt* ‹*troops*› acuartelar

garrote¹, (BrE) **garrotte** /gə'rɑːt || gə'rɒt/ *vt* ejecutar con garrote, agarrotar

garrote², (BrE) **garrotte** *n* garrote *m*

garrulous /'gærələs/ *adj* charlatán, parlanchín

garter /'gɑːrtər || 'gɑːtə(r)/ *n* liga *f*

gas¹ /gæs/ *n* (*pl* **gases** *or* **gasses**)

A [u c] (Phys) gas *m*

B [u] 1 (fuel) gas *m*; **natural** ~ gas natural; **bottled** ~ gas de bombona *or* (RPl) de garrafa *or* (Méx) de tanque *or* (Chi) de balón; (*before n*) ‹*ring/heater*› de *or* a gas 2 (Mil) gas *m* 3 (anesthetic) gas *m*

C [u] (gasoline) (AmE) gasolina *f*, nafta *f* (RPl), bencina *f* (Andes); ***to step on the ~*** (colloq) acelerar (a fondo), meterle (AmL fam), pisar a fondo (Esp fam); (*before n*) ~ **truck** (AmE) camión *m* cisterna

D [u] (flatulence) (AmE) gases *mpl*, flatulencia *f*

E (gossip session) (BrE) (*no pl*) (colloq & dated): **to have a** ~ chismear (fam)

gas² **-ss-** *vt* (Mil) gasear; (kill) asfixiar con gas; (in gas chamber) ejecutar en la cámara de gas

■ **gas** *vi* (colloq) cotorrear (fam)

gas: ~**bag** *n* (colloq) cotorra *f* (fam); ~ **chamber** *n* cámara *f* de gas

gaseous /'gæsiəs/ *adj* gaseoso

gas: ~**-fired** /'gæs'faɪrd || ˌgæs'faɪəd/ *adj* a *or* de gas; ~ **guzzler** /'gʌzlər || 'gʌzlə(r)/ *n* (sl) esponja *f* (fam) (*coche que consume mucha gasolina*)

gash¹ /gæʃ/ *n* tajo *m*, corte *m* profundo

gash² *vt* hacer* un tajo en, cortar (*profundamente*)

gasket /'gæskət || 'gæskɪt/ *n* junta *f*; ***to blow a ~*** (get angry) (colloq) explotar (fam), ponerse* furioso

gas: ~**light** /'gæslaɪt/ *n* 1 [c] (light fitting) lámpara *f* de gas 2 [u] (illumination) luz *f* de gas; ~**man** /'gæsmæn/ *n* (*pl* **-men** /-men/) técnico *m* de la compañía del gas, el hombre del gas (fam); ~ **mask** *n* máscara *f* antigás; ~ **oil** *n* [u] gasoil *m*, gasóleo *m*

gasoline /'gæsəliːn/ *n* [u] (AmE) gasolina *f*, nafta *f* (RPl), bencina *f* (Andes)

gasp¹ /gæsp || gɑːsp/ *vi* 1 (inhale sharply) dar* un grito ahogado 2 (pant) respirar entrecortadamente, jadear; **she was ~ing for breath** respiraba con dificultad; (when dying) daba boqueadas; **I was ~ing for a cigarette** me moría por un cigarillo

■ **gasp** *vt* decir* jadeando

gasp² *n* exclamación *f*, grito *m* (*entrecortado o ahogado*); **to be at one's last** ~ (dying) estar* dando boqueadas; (exhausted) estar* hecho polvo (fam); **the old heater's at its last** ~ la estufa vieja está en las últimas (fam)

gas: ~ **pedal** *n* (esp AmE) acelerador *m*; ~**-permeable** /ˌgæs'pɜːrmiəbəl || ˌgæs'pɜːmiəbəl/ *adj* (Opt) gas permeable, permeable al oxígeno; ~ **pump** *n* [c] (AmE) (in service station) surtidor *m*, bomba *f* bencinera (Chi); (in car) bomba *f* de combustible; ~ **station** *n* (AmE) estación *f* de servicio *or* (RPl tb) de nafta, gasolinera *f*, bomba *f* (Andes, Ven), grifo *m* (Per)

gassy /'gæsi/ *adj* **-sier, -siest** (Culin)

A (flatulent) (AmE): **lentils make me** ~ las lentejas me producen gases

B (esp BrE) efervescente, con gas

gas tank *n* [c] (AmE) depósito *m or* tanque *m* de gasolina *or* (RPl) de nafta *or* (Andes) de bencina

gastric /'gæstrɪk/ *adj* gástrico

gastritis /gæ'straɪtəs || gæ'straɪtɪs/ *n* [u] gastritis *f*

gastroenteritis /'gæstrəʊˌentə'raɪtəs || ˌgæstrəʊˌentə'raɪtɪs/ *n* [u] gastroenteritis *f*

gastronomic /'gæstrə'nɑːmɪk || ˌgæstrə'nɒmɪk/ *adj* gastronómico

gastropub /'gæstrəʊ'pʌb/ *n* (BrE) *pub que se especializa en comida de calidad*

gasworks /'gæswɜːrks || 'gæswɜːks/ *n* (*pl* ~) (+ *sing o pl vb*) fábrica *f* de gas

gate /geɪt/ *n*

A 1 (to garden — wooden) puerta *f* (del jardín); (— wrought-iron) verja *f*, cancela *f* (Esp); (to field) tranquera *f* (AmL), portillo *m* (Esp) 2 (to castle, city) (*usu pl*) puerta *f* 3 (controlling admission) entrada *f* 4 (at airport) puerta *f* (de embarque)

B (*starting* ~) (in horse racing) cajón *m* de salida

gâteau, gateau /'gætəʊ/ *n* [u c] (*pl* **gâteaux** *or* **gateaus** /-z/) (BrE) pastel *m*, torta *f* (AmL), tarta *f* (Esp)

gate: ~**crash** *vt* colarse* en

■ **gate** *vi* colarse*; ~**crasher** /'geɪtˌkræʃər || 'geɪtˌkræʃə(r)/ *n*: **he must be a ~crasher** seguro que se ha colado; ~**house** *n* casa *f* del guarda *or* guardián; (in castle) torre *f* de entrada; ~**keeper** *n* guardián, -diana

g

m,f, guarda *mf*; **~post** *n* poste *m*, pilar *m* (*de una verja*); ***between you, me and the ~post*** (esp BrE) que no salga de estas cuatro paredes; **~way** *n* (Archit) verja *f*, portalón *m*; **Bombay, ~way to India** Bombay, puerta de entrada a la India; **she saw this as the ~way to stardom** pensó que esto le abriría las puertas al estrellato

gather[1] /'gæðər || 'gæðə(r)/ *vi* ⟪*crowd*⟫ congregarse*, reunirse*, juntarse; **they ~ed round the table** se reunieron *or* se agruparon en torno a la mesa; **the storm clouds were ~ing** se avecinaba la tormenta

■ **gather** *vt*

A 1 (collect) ‹*wood/berries*› recoger*, coger* (esp Esp); ‹*information*› reunir*, juntar; ‹*people*› reunir*; **to ~ dust** juntar *or* acumular polvo 2 ‹*thoughts*› poner* en orden; ‹*strength*› juntar, hacer* acopio de 3 (gain gradually) ‹*speed*› ir* adquiriendo

B (conclude) deducir*; **you don't agree, I ~** según parece no estás de acuerdo; **I ~ you're moving** tengo entendido que te mudas (de casa)

C (wrap): **she ~ed the shawl around her shoulders** se envolvió con el chal

D (by sewing) fruncir*

(Phrasal verbs)

- **gather in** [v ▸ o ▸ adv, v ▸ adv ▸ o] recoger*
- **gather up** [v ▸ o ▸ adv, v ▸ adv ▸ o] recoger*

gather[2] *n* fruncido *m*, frunce *m*

gathering[1] /'gæðərɪŋ/ *n* (meeting) reunión *f*; (group of people) concurrencia *f*

gathering[2] *adj* (*before n*) creciente, en aumento; **the ~ storm** la tormenta que se avecinaba

GATT /gæt/ *n* (= **General Agreement on Tariffs and Trade**) GATT *m*

gauche /gəʊʃ/ *adj* torpe, falto de aplomo

gaudy /'gɔːdi/ *adj* chillón, charro (AmL fam)

gauge[1], (AmE also) **gage** /geɪdʒ/ *vt* 1 (estimate) ‹*size*› calcular 2 (judge) ‹*effects*› evaluar* 3 (measure) medir*

gauge[2], (AmE also) **gage** *n*

A (instrument) indicador *m*; **oil/fuel ~** indicador (del nivel) del aceite/de la gasolina

B (measure, indication) indicio *m*

C (Rail): **narrow ~** vía *f* estrecha, trocha *f* angosta (CS)

Gaul /gɔːl/ *n* 1 (region) Galia *f* 2 (person) galo, -la *m,f*

gaunt /gɔːnt/ *adj* ‹*person*› descarnado, delgado y adusto; (from illness, tiredness) demacrado

gauntlet /'gɔːntlət || 'gɔːntlɪt/ *n* guante *m* (*con el puño largo*); (of suit of armor) guantelete *m*, manopla *f*; ***to pick up the ~*** recoger* el guante, aceptar el reto; ***to run the ~***: **she had to run the ~ of press photographers** tuvo que aguantar el acoso de los fotógrafos; ***to throw down the ~*** arrojar el guante

gauze /gɔːz/ *n* [u] (Tex, Med) gasa *f*; (fine mesh) malla *f*

gave /geɪv/ *past of* **give**[1]

gavel /'gævəl/ *n* mazo *m* *or* martillo *m* (*usado por jueces, subastadores etc*)

gawk /gɔːk/ *vi* (colloq) papar moscas (fam); **to ~ AT sth** mirar algo boquiabierto *or* embobado (fam)

gawky /'gɔːki/ *adj* **-kier, -kiest** ‹*adolescent*› desgarbado

gawp /gɔːp/ *vi* (BrE colloq) ▸ **gawk**

gay[1] /geɪ/ *adj*

A (homosexual) gay *adj inv*, homosexual

B (dated) (merry) alegre

gay[2] *n* gay *mf*, homosexual *mf*

Gaza Strip /'gɑːzə/ *n* **the ~ ~** (la franja *or* la faja *or* el corredor de) Gaza *f*

gaze[1] /geɪz/ *vi* mirar (larga y fijamente); **to ~ AT sth/sb** mirar algo/a algn; **she ~d out of the window/into space** miraba por la ventana/al vacío

gaze[2] *n* mirada *f* (*larga y fija*)

gazebo /gə'ziːbəʊ/ *n* (*pl* **-bos** *or* **-boes**) glorieta *f*, cenador *m*

gazelle /gə'zel/ *n* (*pl* **~s** *or* **~**) gacela *f*

gazette /gə'zet/ *n* 1 (in newspaper names) gaceta *f* 2 (official newsletter) (BrE) boletín *m*

gazetteer /'gæzə'tɪr || ˌgæzə'tɪə(r)/ *n* índice *m* geográfico

gazump /gə'zʌmp/ *vt/i* (BrE) *vender un inmueble a un mejor postor rompiendo un compromiso previo de venta*; **they were ~ed** se lo vendieron a alguien que ofreció más que ellos

GB = **Great Britain**

GC *n* (in UK) = **George Cross**

GCSE *n* [c u] (in UK) = **General Certificate of Secondary Education** ≈ bachillerato *m* elemental (*exámenes que se toman en diferentes asignaturas alrededor de los 16 años*)

GDP *n* (= **gross domestic product**) PNB *m*, PBI *m* (RPl), PIB *m* (Esp)

GDR *n* (Hist) (= **German Democratic Republic**) RDA *f*

gear[1] /gɪr || gɪə(r)/ *n*

A (Mech Eng) engranaje *m*; (Auto) marcha *f*, velocidad *f*, cambio *m*; **to shift** *o* (BrE) **change ~** cambiar de marcha, cambiar de velocidad, hacer* un cambio

B [u] 1 (equipment) equipo *m*; (tools) herramientas *fpl*; (*fishing ~*) aparejo(s) *m(pl)* de pesca 2 (miscellaneous items) (colloq) cosas *fpl*, bártulos *mpl* (fam) 3 (Clothing) (colloq) ropa *f*

gear[2] *vt* 1 (orient) orientar; **(to be) ~ed TO/TOWARD sth/sb** (estar*) dirigido A algo/algn; **our policy is ~ed to** *o* **toward achieving this aim** nuestra política está dirigida *or* encaminada a lograr este objetivo; **materials ~ed to the needs of different students** materiales orientados/dirigidos a las necesidades de diferentes alumnos 2 (prepare) **to ~ sth/sb FOR sth** preparar algo/a algn PARA algo

(Phrasal verb)

- **gear up**

A [v ▸ adv] (prepare) prepararse

B [v ▸ o ▸ adv, v ▸ adv ▸ o] preparar; **to ~ oneself up for sth** prepararse para algo

gear: **~box** *n* (Auto) caja *f* de cambios *or* velocidades; **~ change** *n* (BrE) 1 (action) cambio *m* de marcha *or* de velocidad 2 ▸ **~shift**; **~ lever** *n* (BrE) ▸ **~shift**; **~shift** *n* (AmE) palanca *f* de cambio *or* (Méx) de velocidades; **~ stick** *n* (BrE) ▸ **~shift**

gee /dʒiː/ *interj* 1 (AmE colloq): **~, I'm sorry to hear that** oye, lo siento; **~, thanks!** ¡pero ... gracias! 2 (directing a horse): **gee up!** ¡arre!

gee-gee /'dʒiːdʒiː/ *n* (BrE colloq: used by or to children) caballito *m* (fam), tro tro *m* (Esp leng infantil), hico hico *m* (RPl leng infantil)

geek /giːk/ *n* (AmE colloq) 1 (socially inept person) ganso, -sa (fam), pazguato, -ta *m,f* 2 (obsessive enthusiast) obseso, -sa *m,f*; **computer ~** obseso, -sa *m,f* de la informática

geese /giːs/ *pl of* **goose**

gee-string /'dʒiːstrɪŋ/ *n* ▸ **G-string**

gee whiz *interj* (AmE colloq & dated) ¡recórcholis! (fam & ant)

geezer /'giːzər || 'giːzə(r)/ *n* 1 (old man) (AmE colloq) viejo *m* (fam), vejete *m* (fam), viejales *m* (Esp fam) 2 (man) (BrE sl) tipo *m* (fam), tío *m* (Esp fam)

gel[1] /dʒel/ *n* [u] gel *m*; **hair ~** gel (para el pelo)

gel[2] *vi* **-ll-** 1 ⟪*liquid*⟫ gelificarse* 2 (BrE) ⟪*plans/ideas*⟫ cuajar

gelatin /'dʒelətn̩ || 'dʒelətɪn/, **gelatine** /'dʒelətiːn/ *n* [u] gelatina *f*

geld /geld/ *vt* castrar

gelding /'geldɪŋ/ *n* caballo *m* castrado

gelignite /'dʒelɪgnaɪt/ *n* [u] gelignita *f*

gem /dʒem/ *n* 1 (stone) gema *f*, piedra *f* preciosa/semipreciosa; (jewel) joya *f*, alhaja *f* 2 (person) (colloq) tesoro *m* (fam), joya *f* (fam), joyita *f* (fam) 3 (wonderful example) joya *f*; **she came out with some real ~s** dijo cosas de antología

Gemini /'dʒemənaɪ, -niː || 'dʒemɪnaɪ, -niː/ *n* 1 (sign) (*no art*) Géminis 2 [c] (person) Géminis *or* géminis *mf*, geminiano, -na *m,f*; *see also* **Aquarius**

gemstone /'dʒemstəʊn/ *n* piedra *f* semipreciosa/preciosa, gema *f* (*en bruto*)

Gen (= **General**) Gral.

gender /'dʒendər || 'dʒendə(r)/ *n* 1 [u c] (Ling) género *m* 2 [u] (sex) sexo *m*

gene /dʒiːn/ *n* gen *m*, gene *m*

genealogical /'dʒiːniə'lɑːdʒɪkəl || ˌdʒiːniə'lɒdʒɪkəl/ *adj* genealógico

genealogy /'dʒiːni'ælədʒi/ *n* [u] genealogía *f*

genera /'dʒenərə/ *pl of* **genus**

general[1] /'dʒenrəl/ *adj*

A 1 (not detailed or specific) general; **I get the ~ picture** me

hago una idea (general); **speaking in ~ terms, you are right** hablando en general *or* en líneas generales, tiene razón; **a ~ term** un término genérico *or* general; **in ~** en general 2 (not specialized) ‹*information*› general; ‹*laborer*› no especializado; **a guide book for the ~ reader** una guía para el gran público
B 1 (applicable to all) general; **the ~ good** el bien general *or* de todos 2 (widespread) ‹*tendency*› generalizado
C (usual) general; **as a ~ rule we don't allow it** por lo general *or* por regla general no lo permitimos
D (chief) ‹*manager*› general; **G~ Assembly** Asamblea *f* General
E (Med) ‹*anesthetic*› general

general² *n* (Mil) general *mf*

general: **~ delivery** *n* [u] (AmE) lista *f* de correos, poste *f* restante (AmL); **~ election** *n* elecciones *fpl* generales; **~ hospital** *n* centro *m* hospitalario, hospital *m* (*no especializado*)

generality /ˈdʒenəˈræləti/ *n* [u c] (*pl* **-ties**) generalidad *f*

generalization /ˈdʒenrələˈzeɪʃən || ˌdʒenrəlaɪˈzeɪʃən/ *n* generalización *f*

generalize /ˈdʒenrəlaɪz/ *vi/t* generalizar*

general knowledge *n* [u] cultura *f* general

generally /ˈdʒenrəli/ *adv* 1 (usually, as a rule) generalmente, por lo general, en general 2 (broadly) (*indep*) **~ (speaking)** por lo general, en general, por regla general 3 (as a whole) en general 4 (by everyone): **it is ~ admitted that ...** en general se reconoce que ...

general: **~ practise**, (BrE) **~ practice** *n* 1 [u] (speciality) medicina *f* general 2 [c] (clinic) consulta *f* *or* consultorio *m* de medicina general; **~ practitioner** *n* médico, -ca *m,f* de medicina general; **~ public** *n* **the ~ public** el público en general, el gran público; **~-purpose** *adj* ‹*tool*› para todo uso; ‹*dictionary*› de uso general; **~ store** *n* (AmE) tienda *f* (*que vende todo tipo de artículos en una comunidad pequeña*), almacén *m* (CS); **~ strike** *n* huelga *f* general, paro *m* general (AmL)

generate /ˈdʒenəreɪt/ *vt* generar

generating station /ˈdʒenəreɪtɪŋ/ *n* ▸**power station**

generation /ˈdʒenəˈreɪʃən/ *n*
A [c] 1 (people of similar age) generación *f*; **the older ~** la gente de más edad 2 (in families) generación *f* 3 (type) generación *f*; **first-/fifth-~ computers** computadoras *fpl* *or* (Esp tb) ordenadores *mpl* de primera/quinta generación 4 (length of time) generación *f*
B [u] (act of generating) generación *f*

generation gap *n* brecha *f* generacional

generator /ˈdʒenəreɪtər || ˈdʒenəreɪtə(r)/ *n* (Elec) generador *m*, grupo *m* electrógeno; (of bicycle, car) (AmE) dínamo *or* dinamo *m* (AmL), dinamo *or* dínamo *f* (Esp)

generic /dʒəˈnerɪk/ *adj* 1 ‹*term*› genérico 2 ‹*product*› no de marca

generosity /ˈdʒenəˈrɑːsəti || ˌdʒenəˈrɒsəti/ *n* [u] generosidad *f*

generous /ˈdʒenrəs || ˈdʒenərəs/ *adj*
A (open-handed) ‹*person*› generoso, dadivoso; ‹*contribution*› generoso; ‹*nature*› generoso; **to be ~ WITH sth**: **she is ~ with her money** es muy generosa *or* desprendida con el dinero
B (ample, large) abundante, generoso; **a ~ cup of flour** una taza bien colmada de harina

generously /ˈdʒenrəsli || ˈdʒenerəsli/ *adv* 1 (open-handedly) generosamente, con generosidad; **please give ~** por favor, sean generosos 2 (amply) generosamente; **a ~ proportioned room** una habitación de amplias proporciones

genesis /ˈdʒenəsəs || ˈdʒenəsɪs/ *n* (*pl* **-ses** /-siːz/) 1 (origin) (frml) génesis *f* (frml), origen *m* 2 (Bib) Génesis *f*

genetic /dʒəˈnetɪk || dʒɪˈnetɪk/ *adj* genético

genetically /dʒəˈnetɪkli || dʒɪˈnetɪkli/ *adv* genéticamente; **~ modified foods** alimentos *mpl* transgénicos

genetic: **~ engineering** *n* [u] ingeniería *f* genética; **~ fingerprinting** /ˈfɪŋgərˌprɪntɪŋ || ˈfɪŋgəˌprɪntɪŋ/ *n* [u] identificación *f* genética (*técnica de identificación por medio del análisis del ADN*)

geneticist /dʒəˈnetəsəst || dʒɪˈnetɪsɪst/ *n* genetista *mf*, especialista *mf* en genética

genetics /dʒəˈnetɪks || dʒɪˈnetɪks/ *n* (+ *sing vb*) genética *f*

Geneva /dʒəˈniːvə || dʒɪˈniːvə/ *n* Ginebra *f*; **Lake ~** el Lago Lemán

genial /ˈdʒiːnjəl || ˈdʒiːniəl/ *adj* ‹*person*› simpático, jovial; ‹*welcome/smile*› cordial, amistoso

genie /ˈdʒiːni/ *n* genio *m*

genital /ˈdʒenətl̩ || ˈdʒenɪtl̩/ *adj* genital

genitalia /ˈdʒenəˈteɪljə || ˌdʒenɪˈteɪliə/ *pl n* (frml) genitales *mpl*

genitals /ˈdʒenətl̩z || ˈdʒenɪtl̩z/ *pl n* genitales *mpl*

genitive /ˈdʒenətɪv/ *n* genitivo *m*

genius /ˈdʒiːniəs/ *n*
A [c] (clever person) genio *m*
B [u] 1 (brilliance) genialidad *f*; **work of ~** una obra maestra 2 (gift): **she has a ~ for music** tiene talento para la música; **he has a ~ for saying the wrong thing** tiene la habilidad *or* el don de meter la pata (fam)
C (influence): ***to be sb's evil ~*** ejercer* una influencia maligna sobre algn

genocide /ˈdʒenəsaɪd/ *n* [u] genocidio *m*

genome /ˈdʒiːnəʊm/ *n* genoma *m*

genotype /ˈdʒenətaɪp/ *n* genotipo *m*

genre /ˈʒɑːnrə/ *n* género *m*

gent /dʒent/ *n* (BrE colloq) caballero *m*; Ⓢ **Gents** Caballeros; **where's the G~s?** ¿dónde está el baño *or* (Esp) el servicio de caballeros?

genteel /dʒenˈtiːl/ *adj* refinado, elegante

gentile /ˈdʒentaɪl/ *n* gentil *mf*

gentle /ˈdʒentl̩/ *adj* **gentler** /dʒentlər || ˈdʒentlə(r)/, **gentlest** /ˈdʒentləst || ˈdʒentlɪst/
A 1 ‹*person*› dulce; ‹*character*› suave 2 (of voice): **in a ~ voice** en un tono suave *or* dulce 3 ‹*dog/horse*› manso
B ‹*murmur*› suave; ‹*heat/breeze*› suave, ligero; ‹*exercise*› moderado, ‹*slope*› poco empinado, ‹*curve*› (in road) suave, (of graph) pequeño; ‹*reminder*› discreto, diplomático; **a ~ tap** un golpecito suave

gentleman /ˈdʒentl̩mən/ *n* (*pl* **-men** /-mən/) 1 (man) caballero *m*, señor *m*; Ⓢ **Gentlemen** Caballeros; **this ~ would like ...** este señor querría ... 2 (well-bred man) caballero *m*

gentleness /ˈdʒentl̩nəs || ˈdʒentl̩nɪs/ *n* [u]
A (of nature, disposition) dulzura *f*; (of animal) mansedumbre *f*
B (in handling, touching) cuidado *m*, delicadeza *f*; (tenderness) ternura *f*

gently /ˈdʒentli/ *adv* 1 (not roughly or violently) ‹*handle*› con cuidado, cuidadosamente; ‹*tap*› ligeramente, suavemente; ‹*hint*› con tacto *or* discreción; **~ (does it)!** hay que *or* es mejor hacerlo con cuidado/poco a poco 2 (tenderly) dulcemente, con dulzura; (tactfully, kindly) con delicadeza

gentrify /ˈdʒentrəfaɪ || ˈdʒentrɪfaɪ/ *vt* aburguesar

gentry /ˈdʒentri/ *n* (+ *sing o pl vb*) alta burguesía *f*, pequeña nobleza *f*

genuflect /ˈdʒenjəflekt || ˈdʒenjuːflekt/ *vi* hacer* una genuflexión

genuflection, (BrE also) **genuflexion** /ˈdʒenjəˈflekʃən || ˌdʒenjuːˈflekʃən/ *n* [u c] genuflexión *f*

genuine /ˈdʒenjuən || ˈdʒenjʊɪn/ *adj* 1 ‹*interest*› sincero, genuino; ‹*inquiry/buyer/mistake*› serio; **she is a very ~ person** es una persona íntegra; **it was a ~ mistake** fue realmente un error; **in ~ astonishment** verdaderamente asombrado (*or* asombrados *etc*) 2 ‹*antique*› auténtico; ‹*leather*› legítimo, auténtico

genuinely /ˈdʒenjuənli || ˈdʒenjʊɪnli/ *adv* 1 (sincerely) sinceramente 2 (really) realmente; **he's ~ sorry** está realmente arrepentido, está arrepentido de veras

genus /ˈdʒiːnəs/ *n* (*pl* **genera** *or* **~es**) género *m*

geographer /dʒiˈɑːgrəfər || dʒɪˈɒgrəfə(r)/ *n* geógrafo, -fa *m,f*

geographical /ˈdʒiːəˈgræfɪkəl/, **geographic** /-ˈgræfɪk/ *adj* geográfico

geography /dʒiˈɑːgrəfi || dʒɪˈɒgrəfi/ *n* [u] geografía *f*

geological /ˈdʒiːəˈlɑːdʒɪkəl || ˌdʒiəˈlɒdʒɪkəl/ *adj* geológico

geologist /dʒiˈɑːlədʒəst || dʒiˈɒlədʒɪst/ *n* geólogo, -ga *m,f*

geology /dʒiˈɑːlədʒi || dʒiˈɒlədʒi/ *n* [u] geología *f*

geometric /'dʒi:ə'metrɪk || ˌdʒiə'metrɪk/, **geometrical** /-rɪkəl/ *adj* geométrico

geometry /dʒi:'ɑ:mətri || dʒi'ɒmətri/ *n* [u] geometría *f*

geophysics /'dʒi:ə'fɪzɪks || ˌdʒi:əʊ'fɪzɪks/ *n* (+ *sing vb*) geofísica *f*

geopolitical /'dʒi:əʊpə'lɪtɪkəl/ *adj* geopolítico

Geordie /'dʒɔ:rdi || 'dʒɔ:di/ *n* (BrE colloq) *persona oriunda de Tyneside*

George /dʒɔ:rdʒ || dʒɔ:dʒ/ *n*: **by ~!** (dated) ¡diantre! (ant)

Georgia /'dʒɔ:rdʒə || 'dʒɔ:dʒə/ *n* [1] (republic in the Caucasus) Georgia *f* [2] (US state) Georgia *f*

Georgian[1] /'dʒɔ:rdʒən || 'dʒɔ:dʒən/ *adj* [1] (of Georgia in the Caucasus) georgiano [2] (of Georgia in USA) georgiano [3] (in architecture, UK history) georgiano

Georgian[2] *n* [1] [c] (from the Caucasus) georgiano, -na *m,f* [2] [u] (language) georgiano *m* [3] [c] (from USA) georgiano, -na *m,f*

geranium /dʒə'reɪniəm/ *n* geranio *m*, malvón *m* (Méx, RPl)

gerbil /'dʒɜ:rbəl || 'dʒɜ:bɪl/ *n* jerbo *m*, gerbo *m*

geriatric /'dʒeri'ætrɪk/ *adj* (Med) ‹*patient*› anciano; ‹*ward*› de geriatría

geriatrics /'dʒeri'ætrɪks/ *n* (+ *sing vb*) geriatría *f*

germ /dʒɜ:rm || dʒɜ:m/ *n*
A (Med) microbio *m*, germen *m*
B (Biol, Bot) germen *m*

German[1] /'dʒɜ:rmən || 'dʒɜ:mən/ *adj* alemán

German[2] *n* [1] [u] (language) alemán *m* [2] [c] (person) alemán, -mana *m,f*

German Democratic Republic *n* (Hist) **the ~ ~ ~** la República Democrática Alemana

germane /dʒɜ:r'meɪn || dʒɜ:'meɪn/ *adj* (frml) **to be ~ TO sth** guardar relación CON algo (frml)

Germanic /dʒɜ:r'mænɪk || dʒɜ:'mænɪk/ *adj* ‹*tribes/folklore*› germánico; ‹*features*› germano

German: **~ measles** *n* [u] (+ *sing vb*) rubéola *f*, rubeola *f*; **~ shepherd (dog)** *n* pastor *m or* (CS) ovejero *m* alemán

Germany /'dʒɜ:rməni || 'dʒɜ:məni/ *n* Alemania *f*

germicidal /ˌdʒɜ:rmə'saɪdḷ || ˌdʒɜ:mɪ'saɪdḷ/ *adj* germicida

germicide /'dʒɜ:rməsaɪd || 'dʒɜ:mɪsaɪd/ *n* [u c] germicida *m*

germinate /'dʒɜ:rməneɪt || 'dʒɜ:mɪneɪt/ *vi* «*seed*» germinar
■ **germinate** *vt* ‹*seed*› hacer* germinar

germination /ˌdʒɜ:rmə'neɪʃən || ˌdʒɜ:mɪ'neɪʃən/ *n* [u] germinación *f*

gerrymandering /'dʒeriˌmændərɪŋ/ *n* [u] manipulaciones *fpl* (pey), maniobras *fpl* (pey)

gerund /'dʒerənd/ *n* gerundio *m*

gestate /'dʒesteɪt || dʒe'steɪt/ *vi* (Biol) estar* en período de gestación

gestation /dʒe'steɪʃən/ *n* [u] gestación *f*; (*before n*) **~ period** período *m* de gestación

gesticulate /dʒe'stɪkjəleɪt || dʒe'stɪkjʊleɪt/ *vi* gesticular

gesticulation /dʒe'stɪkjə'leɪʃən || dʒeˌstɪkjʊ'leɪʃən/ *n* [u c] gesticulación *f*

gesture[1] /'dʒestʃər || 'dʒestʃə(r)/ *n* [1] (of body) gesto *m*, ademán *m* [2] (token, expression) gesto *m*; **the card arrived late, but it was a nice ~** la tarjeta llegó tarde, pero fue todo un detalle

gesture[2] *vi* hacer* gestos; **I ~d to them to be quiet** les hice señas para que se callaran

get /get/ (*pres p* **getting**; *past* **got**; *past p* **got** *or* (AmE also) **gotten**) *vt*

Sense I

A [1] (obtain) ‹*money/information*› conseguir*, obtener*; ‹*job/staff*› conseguir*; ‹*authorization/loan*› conseguir*, obtener*; ‹*idea*› sacar*; **where did you ~ that beautiful rug?** ¿dónde conseguiste *or* encontraste esa alfombra tan preciosa?; **these pears are as good as you'll ~, I'm afraid** estas peras son de lo mejorcito que hay (fam); **the public can't ~ enough of her** el público no se cansa de ella; **to ~ sth FROM sb/sth**: **we ~ our information from official sources** sacamos la información de fuentes oficiales; **you can ~ any information from my secretary** mi secretaria le podrá dar toda la información que necesite [2] (buy) comprar; **to ~ sth FROM sb/sth**: **I ~ my bread from the local baker** le compro el pan al panadero del barrio; **I got it from Harrods** lo compré en Harrods; **we ~ them from Italy** (they supply our business) los traen de Italia [3] (achieve, win) ‹*prize/grade*› sacar*, obtener* (frml); ‹*majority*› obtener* (frml), conseguir*; **he ~s results** consigue *or* logra lo que se propone [4] (by calculation): **divide 27 by 3 and you ~ 9** si divides 27 por 3 te dará 9; **got it!** ¡ya sé! [5] (on the telephone) ‹*person*› lograr comunicarse con; **I got the wrong number** me equivoqué de número; (having dialled correctly) me salió un número equivocado

B [1] (receive) ‹*letter/reward/reprimand*› recibir; **I got a stereo for my birthday** me regalaron un estéreo para mi cumpleaños; **do I ~ a kiss, then?** ¿entonces me das un beso?; **he got 12 years for armed robbery** lo condenaron a *or* (fam) le cayeron 12 años por robo a mano armada; **to ~ sth FROM sb**: **all I ever ~ from you is criticism** lo único que haces es criticarme; **she got a warm reception from the audience** el público le dio una cálida bienvenida; **I do all the work and she ~s all the credit** yo hago todo el trabajo y ella se lleva la fama; **I seldom ~ the chance** rara vez se me presenta la oportunidad; **the kitchen doesn't ~ much sun** en la cocina no da mucho el sol [2] (Rad, TV) ‹*station*› captar, recibir, coger* (esp Esp fam), agarrar (CS fam) [3] (be paid) ‹*salary/pay*› ganar; **I got £200 for the piano** me dieron 200 libras por el piano [4] (experience) ‹*shock/surprise*› llevarse; **I ~ the feeling that ...** tengo *or* me da la sensación de que ... [5] (suffer): **how did you ~ that bump on your head?** ¿cómo te hiciste ese chichón en la cabeza?; **she got a splinter in her finger** se clavó una astilla en el dedo; **he got the full force of the blast** recibió todo el impacto de la explosión

C (find, have) (colloq): **you don't ~ elephants in America** en América no hay elefantes; **we ~ mainly students in here** nuestros clientes (*or* visitantes *etc*) son mayormente estudiantes

D (fetch) ‹*hammer/scissors*› traer*, ir* a buscar; ‹*doctor/plumber*› llamar; **~ your coat** anda *or* vete a buscar tu abrigo; **she got herself a cup of coffee** se sirvió (*or* se hizo *etc*) una taza de café

E [1] (reach) alcanzar* [2] (take hold of) agarrar, coger* (esp Esp) [3] (catch, trap) pillar (fam), agarrar (AmL), coger* (esp Esp) [4] (assault, kill) (colloq): **I'll ~ you yet!** ¡ya me las vas a pagar! (fam); **the sharks must have got him** se lo deben de haber comido los tiburones (fam)

F (contract) ‹*cold/flu*› agarrar, pescar* (fam), pillar (fam), coger* (esp Esp); **she got chickenpox from her sister** la hermana le contagió *or* (fam) le pegó la varicela

G (catch) ‹*bus/train*› tomar, coger* (Esp)

H (colloq) [1] (irritate) fastidiar [2] (arouse pity): **it ~s you right there** (set phrase) te conmueve, te da mucha lástima [3] (puzzle): **what ~s me is how ...** lo que no entiendo es cómo ...

I [1] (understand) (colloq) entender*; **don't ~ me wrong** no me malentiendas *or* malinterpretes; **~ it?** ¿entiendes?, ¿agarras *or* (Esp) coges la onda? (fam) [2] (hear, take note of) oír*; **I didn't ~ your name** no entendí tu nombre; **did you ~ the number?** ¿tomaste nota del número?

J (answer) (colloq) ‹*phone*› contestar, atender*, coger* (Esp); ‹*door*› abrir*

K (possess) **to have got** *see* **have** *vt*

Sense II

A (bring, move, put) (+ *adv compl*): **we'll ~ it there by two o'clock** lo tendremos allí antes de las dos; **just wait till I ~ you home!** ¡ya vas a ver cuando lleguemos a casa!; **they couldn't ~ it up the stairs** no lo pudieron subir por las escaleras; *see also* **get across, get in** *etc*

B (cause to be) (+ *adj compl*): **he got the children ready** preparó a los niños; **I can't ~ the window open/shut** no puedo abrir/cerrar la ventana; **they got their feet wet/dirty** se mojaron/se ensuciaron los pies

C **to ~ sb/sth + pp** [1] (with action carried out by subject): **we must ~ some work done** tenemos que trabajar un poco; **it's about time they got themselves organized** ya va siendo hora de que se organicen [2] (with action carried out by somebody else): **he got the house painted** hizo pintar la casa; **I must ~ this watch fixed** tengo que llevar a *or* (AmL tb) mandar (a) arreglar este reloj

D (arrange, persuade, force) **to ~ sb/sth to + INF**: **I'll ~ him to help you** (order) le diré que te ayude; (ask) le pediré que te ayude; (persuade) lo convenceré de que te ayude; **she could never ~ him to understand** no podría hacérselo entender; **you'll never ~ them to agree to that** no vas a lograr que acepten eso; **I can't ~ it to work** no puedo hacerlo funcionar

E (cause to start) **to ~ sb/sth -ING**: **it's the sort of record that ~s everybody dancing** es el tipo de disco que hace bailar a todo el mundo *or* que hace que todo el mundo baile; **can you ~ the pump working?** ¿puedes hacer funcionar la bomba?

■ **get** *vi*

A (reach) (+ *adv compl*) llegar*; **I got here yesterday** llegué ayer; **can you ~ there by train?** ¿se puede ir en tren?; **how do you ~ to work?** ¿cómo vas al trabajo?; **can anyone remember where we'd got to?** ¿alguien se acuerda de dónde habíamos quedado?; ***to ~ nowhere, not to ~ anywhere*** *see* **nowhere**[1] **A**, **anywhere**[1] **A2**; ***to ~ somewhere*** avanzar*, adelantar; **we're finally ~ting somewhere!** ¡por fin estamos sacando algo en limpio!; ***to ~ there***: **it's not perfect, but we're ~ting there** perfecto no es, pero poco a poco ...

B 1▸ (become): **to ~ married** casarse; **to ~ dressed** vestirse*; **your dinner's ~ting cold** se te está enfriando la cena; **he got very angry** se puso furioso; **they ~ tired easily** se cansan con facilidad 2▸ (be) (colloq): **she ~s invited to lots of parties** la invitan a muchas fiestas; **her bike got stolen** le robaron la bicicleta

C **to ~ to + INF** 1▸ (come to) llegar* a + INF; **I never really got to know him** nunca llegué a conocerlo de verdad; **you'll ~ to like it eventually** vas a ver como termina por gustarte 2▸ (have opportunity to): **in this job you ~ to meet many interesting people** en este trabajo uno tiene la oportunidad de conocer a mucha gente interesante; **when do we ~ to open the presents?** ¿cuándo podemos abrir los regalos?

D (start) **to ~ -ING** empezar* a + INF, ponerse* a + INF; **right, let's ~ moving!** bueno, ¡pongámonos en acción (*or* en marcha *oto*)!

(Phrasal verbs)

• **get about** [v ▸ adv] [v ▸ prep ▸ o] (BrE) ▸**get around** *Sense* **I A**

• **get above** [v ▸ prep ▸ o]: ***to ~ above oneself*** llenarse de ínfulas

• **get across**

A [v ▸ prep ▸ o] [v ▸ adv] (cross) ‹*river*› atravesar*, cruzar*; ‹*road*› cruzar*

B [v ▸ o ▸ adv] (take across) ‹*passengers/supplies*› pasar *or* llevar al otro lado

C [v ▸ o ▸ adv, v ▸ adv ▸ o] ‹*meaning/concept*› hacer* entender

D [v ▸ adv] (be understood) «*teacher/speaker*» hacerse* entender; **the message seems to be ~ing across** parece que van captando la idea

• **get ahead** [v ▸ adv] 1▸ (get in front) «*horse/runner*» tomar la delantera; «*student/worker*» adelantar 2▸ (progress, succeed) progresar

• **get along** [v ▸ adv]

A (be on one's way): **I must be ~ting along now** me tengo que ir, tengo que ponerme en camino

B (manage, cope): **the firm couldn't ~ along without her** la compañía no podría funcionar sin ella; **we got along for years without a computer** nos las arreglamos durante años sin computadora

C (progress) «*work/patient*» marchar, andar*; **he's ~ting along just fine at school** le va muy bien en el colegio

D (be on good terms) **to ~ along (WITH sb)** llevarse bien (CON algn); **we ~ along fine** nos llevamos bien

• **get around**

(*Sense* **I**) [v ▸ adv] [v ▸ prep ▸ o]

A 1▸ (walk, move about) caminar, andar*; (using transport, car) desplazarse* 2▸ (travel) viajar; **you certainly ~ around in your job** tu sí que viajas con tu trabajo 3▸ (circulate): **it** *o* **word soon got around that he was having an affair** pronto corrió el rumor de que estaba teniendo una aventura

B (gather in circle): **we can't all ~ around this table** no cabemos todos alrededor de esta mesa

(*Sense* **II**) [v ▸ prep ▸ o] 1▸ (avoid, circumvent) ‹*difficulty/obstacle*› sortear, evitar; ‹*rule/law*› eludir el cumplimiento de; **there's no ~ting around it: it was a terrible mistake** hay que reconocerlo: fue un error garrafal 2▸ (persuade) ‹*person*› engatusar

(*Sense* **III**) [v ▸ o ▸ adv] (cause to come, go) ‹*plumber/police*› llamar; **I'll ~ the boxes around to you this evening** te haré llegar las cajas esta noche

(*Sense* **IV**) [v ▸ adv] (go) ir*; (come) venir*; **~ around to the hospital as quickly as possible** vayan al hospital lo más pronto posible

• **get around to** [v ▸ adv ▸ prep ▸ o]: **I don't know whether the doctor will ~ around to you this afternoon** no sé si el doctor alcanzará a verlo esta tarde; **I meant to write to you, I just never got around to it** tenía intenciones de escribirte pero nunca encontré el momento; **to ~ around to -ING**: **we never got around to discussing the price** nunca llegamos a discutir el precio; **I must ~ around to writing those letters** debo ponerme a escribir esas cartas

• **get at** [v ▸ prep ▸ o]

A 1▸ (reach) ‹*pipe/wire*› llegar* a; **he can't ~ at the money until he's 18** no puede disponer del dinero *or* (fam) tocar el dinero hasta que cumpla 18 años 2▸ (ascertain) ‹*facts/truth*› establecer*

B (work on) «*rust/damp*» atacar*; **moths had got at the jacket** las polillas habían picado la chaqueta

C (nag, criticize) (colloq): **you're always ~ting at him** siempre te estás metiendo con él (fam), siempre (te) la estás agarrando con él (AmL fam)

D (hint at, mean) (colloq): **what are you ~ting at?** ¿qué quieres decir?

• **get away**

(*Sense* **I**) [v ▸ adv]

A (escape) escaparse; **there's no ~ting away from the fact that ...** hay que reconocer *or* es un hecho insoslayable que ...

B 1▸ (leave) salir*; **I got away from work early** salí *or* me escapé pronto del trabajo 2▸ (go on vacation) irse* *or* salir* de vacaciones; ***to ~ away from it all*** alejarse del mundanal ruido

C (expressing incredulity) (BrE colloq): **~ away (with you)!** ¡dale! (fam), ¡anda (ya)! (esp Esp fam)

(*Sense* **II**) [v ▸ o ▸ adv] (remove, take away): **~ that dog away from my petunias!** ¡quita *or* saca a ese perro de mis petunias!; **we got the knife away from him** le quitamos el cuchillo

• **get away with** [v ▸ adv ▸ prep ▸ o]

A (make off with) llevarse, escaparse con

B 1▸ (go unpunished for): **you won't ~ away with this** esto no va a quedar así; **don't let them ~ away with it** no dejes que se salgan con la suya; **do you think I could ~ away with wearing the dark blue dress?** ¿te parece que pasaría si me pusiera el vestido azul oscuro? 2▸ (be let off with) ‹*fine/warning*› escaparse *or* librarse con

• **get back**

A [v ▸ adv] 1▸ (return) volver*, regresar; (arrive home) llegar* (a casa); **OK, ~ back to work everybody** bueno, todo el mundo a trabajar otra vez; **to ~ back to what I was saying, ...** volviendo a lo que decía, ... 2▸ (retreat): **~ back!** ¡atrás!, ¡retrocedan!

B [v ▸ o ▸ adv, v ▸ adv ▸ o] (regain possession of) ‹*property*› recuperar; ‹*health*› recobrar, recuperar; **we never got our money back** nos devolvieron el dinero

C [v ▸ o ▸ adv] 1▸ (return) ‹*borrowed item*› devolver*; **can you ~ the children back here by eleven?** ¿puedes traer a los niños de vuelta antes de las once? 2▸ (put back): **to ~ sth back in/out** volver* a poner/a sacar algo

• **get back at** [v ▸ adv ▸ prep ▸ o] vengarse de, desquitarse con

• **get back to** [v ▸ adv ▸ prep ▸ o]: **I'll ~ back to you when I have the details** volveré a ponerme en contacto con usted (*or* lo llamaré *etc*) cuando tenga los detalles

• **get behind**

A [v ▸ adv] (fall behind) **to ~ behind (WITH sth)** atrasarse (CON algo)

B [v ▸ prep ▸ o] (move to rear of) ponerse* detrás de; (fall behind) rezagarse*, quedarse atrás

• **get by**

A [v ▸ adv] 1▸ (manage) arreglárselas; **we earn just enough to ~ by** ganamos justo lo necesario para sobrevivir *or* arreglárnoslas; **I speak enough French to ~ by** me defiendo *or* me manejo en francés; **to ~ by ON sth** arreglárselas CON algo; **she ~s by on just a few dollars a week** se las arregla con unos pocos dólares a la semana; **I can ~ by on six hours sleep a night** puedo pasar con seis horas de sueño al día; **to ~ by WITH sth** arreglárselas CON algo [2] ▸**get past A**

B [v ▸ prep ▸ o] ▸**get past B1**

• **get down**

A [v ▸ adv] [1] (descend) bajar; **~ down from there this minute!** ¡bájate de ahí inmediatamente! [2] (crouch) agacharse; **to ~ down on one's knees** arrodillarse, ponerse* de rodillas

B [v ▸ o ▸ adv, v ▸ adv ▸ o] [1] (take, lift, bring down) bajar [2] (write down) ‹*message/details*› anotar, tomar nota de; **first ~ it down on paper, then we'll discuss it** primero ponlo por escrito y luego lo discutiremos

C [v ▸ o ▸ adv] [1] (reduce) ‹*costs/inflation*› reducir*; ‹*blood pressure*› bajar; **I got my weight down to 100 lbs** adelgacé hasta pesar 100 libras [2] (depress) deprimir

D [v ▸ prep ▸ o] (descend) ‹*stairs*› bajar; ‹*ladder*› bajarse de; ‹*rope*› bajar por

• **get down to** [v ▸ adv ▸ prep ▸ o] (start work on) ponerse* a; **let's ~ down to business** (let's start working) pongamos manos a la obra; (let's get to the point) vayamos al grano; ▸**tack¹ A1**

• **get in**

A [v ▸ adv] [v ▸ prep ▸ o] (enter) entrar; **~ in the car** súbete al coche; **I was just ~ting in the bath** justo me estaba metiendo en la bañera

B [v ▸ adv] [1] (arrive) ‹‹*person/train*›› llegar* [2] (gain admission to, be selected for) entrar, ser* admitido [3] (be elected) (Pol) ganar, resultar *or* salir* elegido [4] (intervene): **I was about to say something but she got in first** *o* **before me** yo estaba a punto de decir algo pero ella se me adelantó

C [v ▸ o ▸ adv] [v ▸ o ▸ prep ▸ o] (put in) meter; ‹*seedlings*› plantar

D [v ▸ o ▸ adv] [1] (hand in) ‹*essay*› entregar*; ‹*bid*› presentar [2] (cause to be accepted, elected): **35% of the vote is not enough to ~ them in** el 35% de los votos no es suficiente para que resulten elegidos

E [v ▸ o ▸ adv, v ▸ adv ▸ o] [1] (bring in, collect up) ‹*washing/tools/chairs*› entrar, meter (dentro); ‹*harvest*› recoger* [2] (buy, obtain) (BrE) ‹*wood/coal*› aprovisionarse de; **did you remember to ~ more candles in?** ¿te acordaste de comprar más velas? [3] (summon, call out) ‹*doctor/plumber*› llamar [4] (interpose) ‹*blow/kick*› dar*; ‹*remark*› hacer*; **I couldn't ~ a word in** no me dejaron decir ni una palabra

• **get in on** (colloq)

A [v ▸ adv ▸ prep ▸ o] (take part, have share in) meterse en

B [v ▸ o ▸ adv ▸ prep ▸ o] (involve): **I want to ~ the marketing people in on the project from the start** quiero darle participación en el proyecto a la gente de marketing desde el principio

• **get into**

A [v ▸ prep ▸ o] [1] (enter) ‹*house*› entrar en *or* (AmL tb) a; ‹*car*› subir a; ‹*hole/cranny*› meterse en [2] (arrive at) ‹*station/office*› llegar* a [3] (be selected for, elected to) ‹*college/club/Congress*› entrar en *or* (AmL tb) a [4] (fit into) ‹*coat/robe*› ponerse*; **I can't ~ into this dress any more** este vestido ya no me entra *or* no me cabe [5] (into a given state): **to ~ into a rage** ponerse* furioso; **to ~ into a mess** meterse en un lío [6] (become accustomed to) ‹*job/method*› acostumbrarse a; ‹*book/subject*› meterse en [7] (affect): **what's got into her?** ¿qué le pasa?; **I don't know what's got into him lately** no sé qué le pasa últimamente

B [v ▸ o ▸ prep ▸ o] [1] (bring, take, put in) meter; **I want to ~ Diana into the picture as well** quiero que Diana también salga en la foto [2] (cause to be admitted to, elected to): **she got me into the club** consiguió que me aceptaran *or* admitieran en el club; **the Hispanic vote got him into Congress** salió elegido gracias al voto hispánico [3] (involve): **you got me into this** tú me metiste en esto

• **get in with** [v ▸ adv ▸ prep ▸ o] [1] (associate with): **he got in with a bad crowd** empezó a andar en malas compañías [2] (ingratiate oneself with) congraciarse con

• **get off**

A [v ▸ adv] [v ▸ prep ▸ o] [1] (alight, dismount) bajarse; **to ~ off the train/horse/bicycle** bajarse del tren/del caballo/de la bicicleta [2] (remove oneself from) ‹*flowerbed/lawn*› salir* de; **~ off (me)!** ¡quítateme de encima!; ***to tell sb where to ~ off*** (colloq) cantarle las cuarenta a algn (fam) [3] (finish) ‹*work/school*› salir* de

B [v ▸ adv] [1] (leave) ‹‹*person/letter*›› salir* [2] (go to sleep) (BrE) dormirse* [3] (escape unpunished, unscathed): **give me the names I want and I'll make sure you ~ off** dame los nombres que quiero y yo me encargo de que no te pase nada; **to ~ off lightly** *o* (AmE also) **easy**: **I consider I got off lightly with just a broken collar bone** creo que tuve suerte al romperme sólo la clavícula; **he got off lightly** (with little punishment) no recibió el castigo que se merecía; **to ~ off WITH sth**: **he got off with a fine** se escapó con sólo una multa

C [v ▸ prep ▸ o] [1] (get up from) ‹*floor*› levantarse de [2] (deviate from) ‹*track/tourist routes*› salir* *or* alejarse de; ‹*point*› desviarse* *or* irse* de; **I tried to ~ him off the subject** intenté hacerlo cambiar de tema; **~ off it!** (AmE colloq) ¡basta ya! [3] (evade) ‹*duty*› librarse *or* salvarse de

D [v ▸ o ▸ adv] [v ▸ o ▸ prep ▸ o] (remove) ‹*lid/top/stain*› quitar; **we tried to ~ them off our land** intentamos echarlos *or* sacarlos de nuestras tierras

E [v ▸ o ▸ adv] [1] (send, see off): **we got the children off to school** mandamos a los niños a la escuela [2] (to sleep) (BrE) ‹*children*› (hacer*) dormir* [3] (save from punishment) salvar

F [v ▸ o ▸ prep ▸ o] [1] (obtain from) (colloq): **I got these playing cards off Peter** estas cartas me las dio Peter; **~ his gun off him first** quítale la pistola primero [2] (wean from): **they're trying to ~ him off drugs** están tratando de que deje la droga

• **get off on** [v ▸ adv ▸ prep ▸ o] (sl): **he really ~s off on putting people down** disfruta de humillar a la gente

• **get off with** (BrE colloq) ligar* con (fam), levantarse a (AmS fam)

• **get on**

(Sense I) [v ▸ adv]

A [1] (move on, make progress) seguir* adelante; **I want to ~ on** quiero progresar; **I can't stand here talking, I must ~ on** no puedo quedarme aquí de charla, tengo mucho que hacer; **to ~ on TO sth** pasar A algo; *see also* **get onto** [2] (continue after interruption) **to ~ on WITH sth**: **~ on with what you're doing** sigue con lo que estás haciendo; **~ on with it!** (colloq) (hurry) dáte prisa (fam), apúrate (AmL fam)

B [1] (fare): **how's Joe ~ting on nowadays?** ¿qué tal anda Joe?; **how did he ~ on at the interview?** ¿cómo le fue en la entrevista?; **we're ~ting on very well without him** nos arreglamos muy bien sin él [2] (succeed) tener* éxito

C (be friends, agree) **to ~ on (WITH sb)** llevarse bien (CON algn); **he's very difficult to ~ on with** es muy difícil de tratar

D (*in -ing form*) [1] (in time) **it's ~ting on** *o* **time is ~ting on** se está haciendo tarde [2] (in age): **she's ~ting on (in years)** está vieja, ya no es joven; *see also* **get on for**

(Sense II) [v ▸ adv] [v ▸ prep ▸ o] (climb on, board) subirse, montarse; **to ~ on the bus/a horse** subirse al autobús/subirse a *or* montarse en un caballo

(Sense III) [v ▸ o ▸ adv] [v ▸ o ▸ prep ▸ o] (place, fix on) poner; **I can't ~ the top on (it)** no puedo ponerle la tapa

(Sense IV) [v ▸ o ▸ adv] (put on) ‹*clothes*› ponerse*; **I can't ~ it on** no me entra *or* no me cabe

• **get on for** [v ▸ adv ▸ prep ▸ o] (approach) (BrE) (*usu in -ing form*): **it's ~ting on for six o'clock** van a ser las seis; **he must be ~ting on for 40** debe (de) andar rondando los 40, debe (de) andar cerca de los 40; **it must be ~ting on for two years since ...** debe (de) hacer casi dos años desde que ...

• **get onto**

(Sense I) [v ▸ prep ▸ o]

A [1] (contact) ‹*person/department*› ponerse* en contacto con [2] (begin discussing) ‹*subject*› empezar* a hablar de

B (mount, board) ‹*table/bus/train*› subirse a; ‹*horse/bicycle*› montarse en, subirse a

(Sense II) [v ▸ o ▸ prep ▸ o] (BrE) [1] (send to deal with): **I'll ~ some more people onto this job** pondré *or* mandaré más gente a trabajar en esto [2] (cause to start discussing): **don't ~ him onto morality!** ¡no le des pie para que empiece a hablar de moral!

• **get out**

(Sense I) [v ▸ adv]

A [1] (of car, bus, train) bajar(se); (of hole, trench) salir*; (of bath) salir*; **to ~ out of bed** levantarse (de la cama) [2] (of room, country) salir*; **~ out!** ¡fuera (de aquí)! [3] (socially) salir* [4] (give up, quit): **I'm ~ting out of teaching** voy a dejar la enseñanza; **they're ~ting out of the German market** se van a retirar del mercado alemán

B [1] (escape) ‹‹*animal/prisoner*›› escaparse [2] (be released, finish work) ‹‹*prisoner/worker*›› salir* [3] (become known)

‹‹*news/truth*›› saberse*, hacerse* público (frml)

Sense II [v ▸ o ▸ adv, v ▸ adv ▸ o] 1 (remove, extract) ‹*cork/stopper/nail*› sacar*; ‹*stain*› quitar, sacar* (esp AmL) 2 (take out) ‹*knife/map*› sacar* 3 (withdraw) ‹*money*› sacar* 4 (borrow) ‹*library book*› sacar*

Sense III [v ▸ o ▸ adv, v ▸ adv ▸ o] (publish, produce, put on market) ‹*book*› publicar*, sacar*; ‹*product/new model*› sacar*, lanzar*

Sense IV [v ▸ o ▸ adv]

A 1 (remove) ‹*tenant*› echar; **~ that dog out of here!** ¡saquen (a) ese perro de aquí! 2 (release): **my lawyer will ~ you out** mi abogado hará que te suelten; **I can't ~ you out of this mess** no te puedo sacar de este lío

B (send for) ‹*doctor/repairman*› llamar

Sense V (colloq) [v ▸ prep ▸ o] (leave by, escape by) salir* por

• **get out of**

A [v ▸ adv ▸ prep ▸ o] 1 (avoid) ‹*obligation*› librarse *or* salvarse de; **he signed the contract so he can't ~ out of it** firmó el contrato, así que no tiene escapatoria; **to ~ out of -ING** librarse *or* salvarse de + INF 2 (give up): **you must ~ out of that bad habit** tienes que sacarte esa mala costumbre; **I'd got(ten) out of the habit of setting my alarm clock** había perdido la costumbre de poner el despertador

B [v ▸ o ▸ adv ▸ prep ▸ o] 1 (extract) ‹*information/truth*› sonsacar*, sacar* 2 (derive, gain) ‹*money/profit*› sacar*; **she tries to ~ the best out of her pupils** se esfuerza por que sus alumnos den lo mejor de sí; **but what do we ~ out of this deal?** ¿pero nosotros qué ganamos con *or* qué sacamos de este negocio?; **they ~ a lot of fun out of their toys** se divierten mucho con sus juguetes

• **get over**

A [v ▸ prep ▸ o] ‹*river/chasm*› cruzar*; ‹*wall/fence*› pasar por encima de; ‹*obstacle*› superar; ‹*hill/ridge*› atravesar*

B [v ▸ adv] (come, go): **~ over here at once** ven aquí enseguida

C [v ▸ prep ▸ o] 1 (recover from) ‹*loss/tragedy*› superar, consolarse* de; ‹*illness/shock*› reponerse* *or* recuperarse de; **he's very disappointed — he'll ~ over it** ha quedado muy decepcionado — ya se le pasará; **she never really got over him** nunca lo olvidó; **she actually gave him the money! I can't ~ over it!** ¡fue y le prestó el dinero! ¡no lo puedo creer! *or* ¡no salgo de mi asombro! 2 (overcome) ‹*difficulty/problem*› superar

D [v ▸ o ▸ prep ▸ o] [v ▸ o ▸ adv] (take across): **how are we going to ~ the supplies over the river?** ¿cómo vamos a pasar las provisiones al otro lado del río?

E [v ▸ o ▸ adv] (cause to come, take): **~ those documents over to Wall Street right away** manda esos documentos a Wall Street enseguida; ***to ~ sth over with***: **I'd like to ~ it over with as quickly as possible** quisiera salir de eso *or* quitarme eso de encima lo más pronto posible

F [v ▸ o ▸ adv] (communicate) ‹*feeling/emotion*› comunicar*, transmitir; **how can I ~ it over to him that ... ?** ¿cómo puedo hacerle entender que ... ?

• **get past**

A [v ▸ adv] (move past) pasar

B [v ▸ prep ▸ o] 1 (move past) ‹*vehicle*› pasar, adelantarse a; ‹*opponent/attacker*› eludir; **they got past the guards unnoticed** eludieron la vigilancia de los guardias 2 (pass undetected): **to ~ past the censors** pasar la censura 3 (get beyond) ‹*obstacle*› superar; ‹*semifinals*› pasar; **he never got past fifth grade** no pasó del quinto año

C [v ▸ o ▸ prep ▸ o]: **to ~ sth past the censor** conseguir* que algo pase la censura

• **get round** (esp BrE) ▸ **get around**

• **get through**

Sense I [v ▸ prep ▸ o] [v ▸ adv] 1 (pass through) ‹*gap/hole*› pasar por; **the tractors will never ~ through** los tractores no van a poder pasar 2 ‹*ordeal*› superar; ‹*winter/difficult time*› pasar 3 (Sport) ‹*heat*› pasar 4 (pass) (BrE) ‹*examination/test*› aprobar*, pasar

Sense II [v ▸ adv]

A 1 (reach destination) ‹‹*supplies/messenger*›› llegar* a destino; ‹‹*news/report*›› llegar* 2 (on the telephone) **to ~ through (TO sb/sth)** comunicarse* (CON algn/algo) 3 (make understand) **to ~ through (TO sb)**: **am I ~ting through to you?** ¿me entiendes?, ¿me explico?; **I can't ~ through to him** no logro hacerme entender *or* comunicarme con él

B (finish) (AmE) terminar, acabar

Sense III [v ▸ prep ▸ o] 1 (use up) (BrE) ‹*money*› gastarse; ‹*materials*› usar; ‹*shoes*› destrozar* 2 (deal with): **I've only got ten more pages to ~ through** me quedan sólo diez páginas por leer (*or* estudiar *etc*); **I have to ~ through all these applications before 5 o'clock** tengo que leer todas estas solicitudes antes de las cinco

Sense IV [v ▸ o ▸ adv] [v ▸ o ▸ prep ▸ o] (bring through) pasar; **to ~ sth through customs** pasar algo por la aduana; **it was his will power that got him through** fue su fuerza de voluntad lo que lo salvó (*or* ayudó a superar la crisis *etc*)

Sense V [v ▸ o ▸ adv] 1 (send) ‹*supplies/message*› hacer* llegar 2 (make understood) hacer* entender; **I can't ~ it through to him that ...** no logro hacerle entender que ...

• **get to** [v ▸ prep ▸ o] (annoy, upset): **don't let their comments ~ to you** no dejes que te afecten sus comentarios, no te aflijas por lo que dicen; **her behavior's really beginning to ~ to me** su comportamiento me está empezando a molestar

• **get together**

A [v ▸ adv] 1 (meet up) reunirse*, quedar (Esp); (have a family reunion) juntarse, reunirse* 2 (join forces) ‹‹*nations/unions*›› unirse; **why don't we ~ together to buy her a present?** ¿por qué no le regalamos algo juntos? 3 (become couple, team) (colloq) juntarse; **to ~ back together (again)** volverse* a juntar, reconciliarse

B [v ▸ o ▸ adv, v ▸ adv ▸ o] (assemble) ‹*people/money*› reunir*; **~ your things together, we're going** junta *or* recoge tus cosas que nos vamos

C [v ▸ o ▸ adv] 1 (reconcile) ‹*people/couple*› reconciliar 2 (sort out, make effective) (colloq) ‹*life*› poner* en orden; **they seem to have got themselves together at last** parece que por fin se han organizado; ***to ~ it together***: **I can't ~ it together to organize the vacation** no consigo organizarme para arreglar lo de las vacaciones; **he just can't seem to ~ it together** es una nulidad

• **get up**

A [v ▸ prep ▸ o] [v ▸ adv] (climb up) subir; **to ~ up ON sth** subir(se) A algo

B [v ▸ adv] 1 (out of bed) levantarse 2 (stand up) levantarse

C [v ▸ o ▸ adv] 1 (out of bed) ‹*children*› levantar 2 (raise, lift) ‹*person*› levantar 3 (erect, put up) ‹*tent*› montar, armar; ‹*curtains*› colgar*, poner* 4 (decorate) ‹*hall/restaurant*› decorar 5 (dress up) **to ~ oneself up AS sth** disfrazarse* DE algo

D [v ▸ o ▸ adv, v ▸ adv ▸ o] 1 (develop, arouse) ‹*appetite/enthusiasm*› despertar*; ‹*speed*› agarrar, coger* (esp Esp); **she didn't want to ~ their hopes up** no quería esperanzarlos *or* que se hicieran ilusiones 2 (organize) ‹*petition/team*› organizar*

• **get up to** [v ▸ adv ▸ prep ▸ o]

A (reach): **when he got up to them ...** cuando los alcanzó ...; **we got up to page 161** llegamos hasta la página 161; **he won't ~ up to the required standard in time** no alcanzará el nivel requerido a tiempo

B (be involved in) (colloq) hacer*; **to ~ up to mischief** hacer* travesuras *or* de las suyas

get: **~away** *n* (quick departure) huida *f*, fuga *f*; **to make one's ~away** escaparse, huir*; **~out clause** *n* (colloq) cláusula *f* de escape; **~-together** *n* (colloq) reunión *f*; **~up** *n* (colloq) vestimenta *f*, atuendo *m* (frml o hum), indumentaria *f* (frml o hum)

geyser /ˈgaɪzər || ˈgiːzə(r)/ *n*

A (Geog) géiser *m*

B (water heater) (BrE) calentador *m* de agua

G-force /ˈdʒiːfɔːrs || ˈdʒiːfɔːs/ *n* = **force of gravity**

Ghana /ˈgɑːnə/ *n* Ghana *f*

Ghanaian /gɑːˈneɪən/ *adj* ghanés

ghastly /ˈgæstli || ˈgɑːstli/ *adj* 1 (very bad, awful) (colloq) ‹*situation*› espantoso, horrendo (fam) 2 (horrible, hideous) ‹*accident/tale*› horrible, espantoso 3 (deathly) (liter) ‹*pallor*› cadavérico, mortal; ‹*light*› espectral (liter)

gherkin /ˈgɜːrkən || ˈgɜːkɪn/ *n* pepinillo *m*

ghetto /ˈgetəʊ/ *n* (*pl* **-tos** *or* **-toes**) gueto *m*

ghettoblaster /ˈgetəʊˌblæstər || ˈgetəʊˌblɑːstə(r)/ *n* (colloq) grabadora *f* portátil, gabacha *f* (Méx arg), loro *m* (Esp arg)

ghost[1] /gəʊst/ *n* 1 (phantom) fantasma *m*, espíritu *m*; ***to lay the ~ of sth/sb (to rest)*** enterrar el recuerdo de algo/algn; **~ ship/town** buque *m*/pueblo *m* fantasma

g

2 (hint, trace): **they do not have the** *o* **a ~ of a chance** no tienen ni la más remota posibilidad 3 ***to give up the ~*** ‹‹*person*›› (colloq) pasar a mejor vida (fam), sonar* (CS fam); ‹‹*TV*›› no dar* para más (fam), sonar (CS fam), escoñarse (Esp fam)

ghost² *vt*: **to ~ sb's speech/book** escribir* el discurso/libro de algn

ghostly /ˈgəʊstli/ *adj* **-lier, -liest** fantasmal, fantasmagórico

ghost ~ train *n* (BrE) tren *m* fantasma, tren *m* de la bruja (Esp); **~writer** *n* negro, -gra *m,f* (period) (*persona que escribe un libro firmado por otro*)

ghoul /guːl/ *n* 1 (person) morboso, -sa *m,f* 2 (evil spirit) demonio *m* necrófago

ghoulish /ˈguːlɪʃ/ *adj* ‹*person*› morboso; ‹*laugh*› macabro

GI *n* (colloq) soldado *m* estadounidense

giant¹ /ˈdʒaɪənt/ *n* gigante, -ta *m,f*; **he was a ~ of a man** era un gigantón (fam); **an intellectual ~** una lumbrera

giant² *adj* (*before n*) ‹*organization*› gigantesco; ‹*insect*› gigante, gigantesco; ‹*stride*› gigantesco, enorme

giant-sized /ˈdʒaɪəntsaɪzd/, (BrE also) **giant-size** /ˈdʒaɪəntsaɪz/ *adj* ‹*packet*› (de tamaño) gigante

gibber /ˈdʒɪbər || ˈdʒɪbə(r)/ *vi* farfullar, hablar atropelladamente; **you ~ing idiot!** ¡imbécil!

gibberish /ˈdʒɪbərɪʃ/ *n* [u]: **how am I expected to understand this ~?** ¿cómo quieres que entienda este galimatías?; **to talk ~** decir* sandeces (fam)

gibbet /ˈdʒɪbət || ˈdʒɪbɪt/ *n* horca *f*

gibbon /ˈgɪbən/ *n* gibón *m*

gibe¹ /dʒaɪb/ *n* pulla *f*, burla *f*

gibe² *vi* **to ~ AT sb/sth** burlarse *or* mofarse DE algn/algo

giblets /ˈdʒɪbləts || ˈdʒɪblɪts/ *pl n* menudillos *mpl*, menudos *mpl*

Gibraltar /dʒəˈbrɔːltər || dʒɪˈbrɔːltə(r)/ *n* Gibraltar; **the Rock/Strait(s) of ~** el Peñón/el Estrecho de Gibraltar

Gibraltarian /dʒəˌbrɔːlˈteriən || ˌdʒɪbrɔːlˈteəriən/ *n* gibraltareño, -ña *m,f*

giddiness /ˈgɪdinəs || ˈgɪdinɪs/ *n* [u] (sensation) mareo *m*, vértigo *m*

giddy /ˈgɪdi/ *adj* **-dier, -diest** ‹*sensation*› de mareo *or* aturdimiento; **he felt ~** se sentía mareado, la cabeza le daba vueltas; **don't look down, it'll make you ~** no mires hacia abajo que te va a dar vértigo

giddy up *interj* ¡arre!

gift /gɪft/ *n*

A (present) regalo *m*, obsequio *m* (frml); **it was a ~** me lo regalaron, es un regalo; **it's a ~ at that price** a ese precio es una ganga *or* un regalo (fam); ***a ~ from the gods*** un regalo del cielo; ***never look a ~ horse in the mouth*** a caballo regalado no le mires el diente *or* no se le miran los dientes; (*before n*) ‹*shop*› de novedades, de artículos para regalo

B (talent) don *m*; **to have a ~ for sth/-ING: she has a ~ for poetry** tiene talento para la poesía; **he has a ~ for making people laugh** tiene el don de saber hacer reír a la gente; ***to have the ~ of the gab*** *o* (AmE also) ***the ~ of gab*** (colloq) tener* mucha labia (fam), tener* un pico de oro (fam)

gift certificate *n* (AmE) vale *m* (*canjeable por artículos en una tienda*), cheque regalo *m*

gifted /ˈgɪftəd || ˈgɪftɪd/ *adj* ‹*person*› de talento, talentoso; **~ children** (Educ) niños *mpl* superdotados

gift ~ token, ~ voucher *n* (BrE) ▸**gift certificate**; **~ wrap, ~ wrapping** *n* [u c] papel *m* para regalo; **~-wrap** *vt* **-pp-** envolver* para regalo *or* (frml) obsequio

gig /gɪg/ *n* (jazz, rock concert) (sl) actuación *f*; **to do** *o* **play a ~** tener* una actuación

gigantic /dʒaɪˈgæntɪk/ *adj* ‹*wave*› gigantesco; ‹*success/appetite*› enorme, colosal; ‹*effort*› titánico, enorme

giggle¹ /ˈgɪgəl/ *vi* reírse* tontamente

giggle² *n* [c] risita *f*; **they got the ~s** *o* **had a fit of the ~s** les dio un ataque de risa

giggly /ˈgɪgli/ *adj* **-glier, -gliest** dado a reírse tontamente

gild /gɪld/ *vt* dorar

gill *n*

A /dʒɪl/ *medida para líquidos equivalente a la cuarta parte de una pinta o 0,142 l*

B /gɪl/ (Zool) agalla *f*, branquia *f*; ***to go green about the ~s*** ponerse* (blanco) como un *or* el papel

gilt /gɪlt/ *n* [u] dorado *m*; (*before n*) ‹*finish*› dorado

gilt-edged /ˈgɪltˈedʒd/ *adj*

A (gilded) ‹*paper*› de bordes dorados

B (Fin): **~ securities** (in US) valores *mpl* de primer orden *or* de primera clase; (in UK) papel *m* del estado

gimcrack /ˈdʒɪmkræk/ *adj* de pacotilla; **a ~ bracelet/ornament** una baratija

gimlet /ˈgɪmlət || ˈgɪmlɪt/ *n* barrena *f*

gimme /ˈgɪmi/ (sl) **= give me**

gimmick /ˈgɪmɪk/ *n* 1 (ingenious idea, device) truco *m*, ardid *m* 2 (catch, snag) (AmE) trampa *f* 3 ▸**gadget**

gimmicky /ˈgɪmɪki/ *adj* efectista

gin /dʒɪn/ *n* [u] ginebra *f*, gin *m*; **~ and tonic** gin tonic *m*

ginger¹ /ˈdʒɪndʒər || ˈdʒɪndʒə(r)/ *n* [u]

A (Culin) jengibre *m*

B (color) rojo *m* anaranjado

ginger² *adj* ‹*hair*› color zanahoria; ‹*cat*› rojizo

ginger: ~ ale *n* [u c] ginger ale *m*, refresco *m* de jengibre; **~ beer** *n* [u c] cerveza *f* de jengibre; **~bread** *n* [u] (cake) pan *m* de jengibre; (cookie) galleta *f* de jengibre

gingerly /ˈdʒɪndʒərli || ˈdʒɪndʒəli/ *adv* ‹*touch/handle*› con cuidado *or* cautela

ginseng /ˈdʒɪnseŋ/ *n* [u] ginseng *m*

gipsy, Gipsy /ˈdʒɪpsi/ *n* ▸**gypsy**

giraffe /dʒəˈræf || dʒɪˈrɑːf/ *n* jirafa *f*

gird /gɜːrd || gɜːd/ (*past & past p* **girded** *or* **girt**) *vt* (liter *or* arch) ceñir* (liter)

■ *v refl* **to ~ oneself up FOR sth/to + INF** (liter *or* hum) prepararse PARA algo/ + INF

girder /ˈgɜːrdər || ˈgɜːdə(r)/ *n* viga *f* (*de metal*)

girdle /ˈgɜːrdl̩ || ˈgɜːdl/ *n* faja *f*

girl /gɜːrl || gɜːl/ *n*

A 1 (baby, child) niña *f*, nena *f* (esp RPl) 2 (young woman) chica *f*, muchacha *f*

B 1 (daughter) hija *f*, niña *f* 2 (girlfriend) (colloq) novia *f*, chica *f* 3 (employee) chica *f*, muchacha *f*; **the ~s at the office** las chicas de la oficina

girl: ~friend *n* 1 (of man) novia *f* 2 (of woman) (esp AmE) amiga *f*; (in lesbian couple) compañera *f*; **~ guide** (BrE) ▸**girl scout**

girlie /ˈgɜːrli || ˈgɜːli/ *adj* (*before n*) ‹*magazine*› sólo para hombres; ‹*movie/show*› (AmE) de desnudos, de destape (Esp)

girlish /ˈgɜːrlɪʃ || ˈgɜːlɪʃ/ *adj* de niña; **his ~ looks** su aspecto afeminado

girl scout *n* (AmE) guía *f* (*de los scouts*), exploradora *f*

giro /ˈdʒaɪrəʊ/ *n* (*pl* **-ros**) (in UK) (system) transferencia *f*, giro *m*; **to pay by ~** hacer* una transferencia crediticia

girt /gɜːrt || gɜːt/ *past & past p of* **gird**

girth /gɜːrθ || gɜːθ/ *n*

A [c u] (of person, object) circunferencia *f*; **his ample ~** (hum) su contorno voluminoso (hum)

B [c] (Equ) cincha *f*

gist /dʒɪst/ *n* lo esencial, lo fundamental; **to get the ~ of sth** captar *or* comprender lo esencial *or* lo fundamental de algo

git¹ /gɪt/ *n* (BrE sl) imbécil *m*

git² *vi* (AmE colloq) (*only in imperative*) ¡largo (de aquí)!

give¹ /gɪv/ (*past* **gave**; *past p* **given**) *vt*

Sense I

A 1 (hand, pass) dar*; **~ her/me/them a glass of water** dale/dame/dales un vaso de agua 2 (as gift) regalar, obsequiar (frml); **to ~ sb a present** hacerle* un regalo a algn, regalarle algo a algn 3 (donate) dar*, donar; **they have ~n $100,000 for/toward a new music room** han dado *or* donado $100.000/han contribuido con $100.000 para una nueva sala de música 4 (dedicate, devote) ‹*love/affection*› dar*; ‹*attention*› prestar; **I'll ~ it some thought** lo pensaré; ***to ~ it all one's got*** dar* lo mejor de sí 5 (sacrifice)

⟨*life*⟩ dar*, entregar* **6** ⟨*injection/sedative*⟩ dar*, administrar (frml)

B **1** (supply, grant) ⟨*protection*⟩ dar*; ⟨*help*⟩ dar*, brindar; ⟨*idea*⟩ dar*; **~ her something to do** dale algo que *or* para hacer **2** (allow, concede) ⟨*opportunity/permission*⟩ dar*, conceder (frml); **~n the choice, I'd ...** si me dieran a elegir, yo ...; **he's a good worker, I'll ~ him that, but ...** es muy trabajador, hay que reconocerlo, pero ...; **the doctors only ~ him three months** los médicos le dan sólo tres meses; **it would take us 15 months, ~ or take a week or two** nos llevaría unos 15 meses, semana más, semana menos

C **1** (cause) ⟨*pleasure/shock*⟩ dar*; ⟨*cough*⟩ dar*; **don't ~ us your germs/cold!** ¡no nos pegues tus microbios/tu resfriado! (fam) **2** (yield) ⟨*results/fruit*⟩ dar*

D **1** (award, allot) ⟨*title/degree*⟩ dar*, otorgar* (frml), conferir* (frml); ⟨*authority/right*⟩ dar*, otorgar* (frml), conceder (frml); ⟨*contract*⟩ dar*, adjudicar*; ⟨*mark*⟩ dar*, poner*; **the judge gave her five years** el juez le dio cinco años *or* la condenó a cinco años **2** (entrust) ⟨*task/responsibility*⟩ dar*, confiar*; **she's ~n me her car to fix** me ha dejado el coche para que se lo arregle

E (pay, exchange) dar*; **I'd ~ anything for a cigarette** no sé qué daría por un cigarrillo

F (care) (colloq): **I don't ~ a damn** me importa un bledo *or* un comino *or* un pepino (fam)

(Sense II)

A **1** (convey) ⟨*apologies/news*⟩ dar*; **please ~ my regards to your mother** dale recuerdos *or* (AmL tb) cariños a tu madre; **she gave me to understand that ...** me dio a entender que ... **2** (state, reveal) ⟨*information*⟩ dar*; **she gave a detailed description of the place** describió el lugar detalladamente; **the judge has ~n his verdict** el juez ha dictado sentencia

B (make sound, movement) ⟨*cry/jump*⟩ dar*, pegar* (fam); ⟨*laugh*⟩ soltar*; **to ~ sb a kiss/a wink** darle* un beso a algn/hacerle* un guiño a algn; **why not ~ it a try?** ¿por qué no pruebas *or* lo intentas?

C (indicate) ⟨*speed/temperature*⟩ señalar, marcar*

D **1** (hold) ⟨*party/dinner*⟩ dar*, ofrecer* (frml) **2** ⟨*concert*⟩ dar*; ⟨*speech*⟩ decir*, pronunciar

■ **give** *vi*

A **1** (yield under pressure) ceder, dar* de sí; **they won't ~ an inch** no cederán un ápice **2** (break, give way) ⟨⟨*planks/branch*⟩⟩ romperse*

B (make gift) dar*; **to ~ to charity** dar* dinero a organizaciones de caridad; **please ~ generously** contribuyan generosamente por favor

(Phrasal verbs)

• **give away** [v ▸ o ▸ adv, v ▸ adv ▸ o]

A **1** (free of charge) regalar, obsequiar (frml) **2** ⟨*prizes*⟩ hacer* entrega de

B **1** (disclose) revelar, descubrir*; **he didn't ~ anything away** no dejó entrever nada **2** (betray) delatar, vender (fam); **to ~ oneself away** delatarse, descubrirse*, venderse (fam)

C ⟨*bride*⟩ entregar* en matrimonio; **she was ~n away by her father** ≈ su padre fue el padrino de la boda

• **give back** [v ▸ o ▸ adv, v ▸ adv ▸ o] devolver*

• **give in**

A [v ▸ adv] (surrender, succumb) ceder; (in guessing games) rendirse*, darse* por vencido; **to ~ in TO sth/sb**: **I gave in to temptation** caí en la tentación; **we will not ~ in to terrorists** no vamos a ceder frente a los terroristas

B (hand in) (esp BrE) [v ▸ o ▸ adv, v ▸ adv ▸ o] ⟨*keys/documents*⟩ entregar*; ⟨*notice*⟩ presentar

• **give off** [v ▸ adv ▸ o] ⟨*smell/fumes*⟩ despedir*, soltar* (fam), largar* (RPl fam); ⟨*heat*⟩ dar*; ⟨*radiation*⟩ emitir

• **give onto** [v ▸ prep ▸ o] (esp BrE) dar* a

• **give out**

A [v ▸ o ▸ adv, v ▸ adv ▸ o] ⟨*leaflets*⟩ repartir, distribuir*

B [v ▸ adv ▸ o] **1** (let out) ⟨*cry/yell*⟩ dar*, pegar* (fam) **2** (emit) ⟨*heat*⟩ dar*; ⟨*signal*⟩ emitir

• **give over**

A [v ▸ o ▸ adv] (devote) (*usu pass*) dedicar*; **the rest of the afternoon was ~n over to ...** el resto de la tarde se dedicó a ...; **this part of the house is ~n over to ...** esta parte de la casa está destinada a ...

B [v ▸ adv] (BrE colloq): **oh, ~ over!** (stop complaining/talking etc) ¡anda ya! (fam), ¡dale! (fam)

• **give up**

(Sense I) [v ▸ o ▸ adv, v ▸ adv ▸ o]

A **1** (renounce, cease from) ⟨*alcohol*⟩ dejar; ⟨*pleasures/title*⟩ renunciar a; ⟨*job/project*⟩ dejar, renunciar a; ⟨*principle/fight*⟩ abandonar; **to ~ up hope** perder* las esperanzas; **to ~ up -ING** dejar DE + INF; **I've ~n up smoking** he dejado de fumar **2** (relinquish, hand over) ⟨*territory/position*⟩ ceder, renunciar a; ⟨*ticket/keys*⟩ entregar*; **to ~ up one's seat to** *o* **for sb** cederle *or* darle* el asiento a algn

B (surrender): **to ~ oneself up** entregarse*

C (devote, sacrifice) ⟨*time*⟩ dedicar*

(Sense II) [v ▸ adv] **1** (cease fighting, trying) rendirse*; **the campaign is in its sixth week, you can't ~ up now!** estamos en la sexta semana de la campaña ¡no vas a abandonar la lucha ahora!; **all right, I ~ up** (in guessing games etc) está bien, me rindo *or* me doy por vencido; **to ~ up ON sb**: **I've ~n up on them, they're hopeless** yo con ellos no insisto más *or* no pierdo más tiempo, son un caso perdido **2** (stop doing sth) dejar

(Sense III) [v ▸ o ▸ adv] (abandon hope for): **to ~ sb up for lost** dar* a algn por desaparecido

give² *n* [u] elasticidad *f*; **this fabric doesn't have much ~ in it** esta tela no da mucho de sí

give: **~-and-take** /ˈgɪvənˈteɪk/ *n* [u] concesiones *fpl* mutuas, toma y daca *m*; **~away** *n* **1** (evidence): **her accent is a real ~away** el acento la delata *or* (fam) la vende; **2** (free gift) regalo *m*; (*before n*) **at ~away prices** a precio de regalo **3** (sth easily done, obtained): **the last question was a ~away** la última pregunta estaba regalada *or* tirada (fam)

given¹ /ˈgɪvən/ *past p of* **give¹**

given² *adj*

A (specified) ⟨*amount/time*⟩ determinado, dado; **at a ~ time and place** a una hora y en un lugar determinados; **at any ~ moment** en cualquier momento

B (disposed) **to be ~ TO sth/-ING** ser* dado A algo/+ INF

given³ *prep*

A (in view of) dado; **~ their reputation ...** dada su reputación ...

B (*as conj*) **~ (THAT)** dado que

given name *n* (AmE) nombre *m* de pila

giver /ˈgɪvər ‖ ˈgɪvə(r)/ *n* persona *f* generosa; **she's always been a ~** siempre ha sido una persona generosa; **if you wish to return a present to the ~ ...** si usted quiere devolver un obsequio a quien se lo ha regalado ...

give-way sign /ˈgɪvˈweɪ/ *n* (BrE) señal *f* de ceda el paso

gizmo /ˈgɪzməʊ/ *n* (*pl* **-mos**) (AmE colloq) aparatito *m* (fam), cuestión *f* (fam)

glacé /glæˈseɪ ‖ ˈglæseɪ/ *adj* (*before n*) glaseado; **~ fruits** fruta(s) *f(pl)* confitada(s)

glacial /ˈgleɪʃəl/ *adj* glacial

glacier /ˈgleɪʃər ‖ ˈglæsɪə(r), ˈgleɪsɪə(r)/ *n* glaciar *m*

glad /glæd/ *adj* **-dd-** **1** (happy, pleased) (*pred*) **to be ~ (ABOUT sth)** alegrarse DE algo; **to be ~ (THAT)** alegrarse DE QUE (+ *subj*); **to be ~ to + INF**: **I'm only too ~ to help** es un placer poder ser útil; **you'll be ~ to hear that ...** te alegrará saber que ... **2** (grateful) (*pred*) **to be ~ OF sth** (BrE): **I'd be very ~ of your help** agradecería mucho tu ayuda **3** (showing happiness) (*before n*) ⟨*smile/expression*⟩ de alegría *or* felicidad

gladden /ˈglædn̩/ *vt* (liter) llenar de alegría *or* (liter) de gozo

glade /gleɪd/ *n* (liter) claro *m*

gladiator /ˈglædieɪtər ‖ ˈglædieɪtə(r)/ *n* gladiador *m*

gladly /ˈglædli/ *adv* con mucho gusto

gladness /ˈglædnəs ‖ ˈglædnɪs/ *n* [u] (liter) alegría *f*, gozo *m* (liter)

glad rags /ˈglædræɡz/ *pl n* (colloq & hum): **she put on her ~ ~** se puso sus mejores galas *or* trapos (hum), se puso de tiros largos (hum)

glamor /ˈglæmər ‖ ˈglæmə(r)/ *n* (AmE) ▸ **glamour**

glamorous /ˈglæmərəs/ *adj* ⟨*person*⟩ glamoroso; ⟨*dress*⟩ glamoroso, seductor; ⟨*lifestyle*⟩ sofisticado; ⟨*job*⟩ rodeado de glamour

glamour, (AmE also) **glamor** /ˈglæmər ‖ ˈglæmə(r)/ *n* [u] glamour *m*

glance¹ /glæns ‖ glɑːns/ *n* mirada *f*; **to take/cast a ~ at sth** echarle *or* darle* un vistazo a algo, echarle una ojeada a algo; **at first ~** a primera vista; **I could tell at a ~ that ...** con sólo echar un vistazo me di cuenta de que ...

glance² *vi* mirar; **she ~d from the one to the other** su mirada iba de uno a otro; **to ~ AT sth** echarle una ojeada A algo, echarle *or* darle* un vistazo A algo; **to ~ AT sb** echarle una mirada A algn

glancing /'glænsɪŋ || 'glɑːnsɪŋ/ *adj* (*before n*): **to strike sth/sb a ~ blow** pegarle* a algo/a algn de refilón

gland /glænd/ *n* 1 (organ) glándula *f* 2 (lymph node) ganglio *m*

glandular /'glændjələr || 'glændjʊlə(r)/ *adj* glandular

glandular fever *n* [u] mononucleosis *f* (infecciosa)

glare¹ /gler || gleə(r)/ *n*

A [c] (stare) mirada *f* (*hostil, feroz, de odio etc*)

B [u] (light) resplandor *m*, luz *f* deslumbradora; **the ~ of publicity** las luces *or* los focos de la publicidad

glare² *vi*

A (stare) **to ~ AT sb** fulminar a algn con la mirada

B (shine) ⟨⟨*headlights*⟩⟩ brillar, relumbrar

glaring /'glerɪŋ || 'gleərɪŋ/ *adj* 1 ⟨*light*⟩ deslumbrante, cegador 2 (flagrant) (*before n*) ⟨*error*⟩ mayúsculo, que salta a la vista; ⟨*injustice/abuses*⟩ palmario, flagrante

glaringly /'glerɪŋli || 'gleərɪŋli/ *adv*: **it's ~ obvious** salta a la vista

glass /glæs || glɑːs/ *n*

A [u] 1 (material) vidrio *m*, cristal *m* (Esp); (crystal) cristal *m*; **a pane of ~** un vidrio, un cristal (Esp); **broken ~** vidrio roto, cristales rotos (Esp); (*before n*) ⟨*door/roof*⟩ de vidrio, de cristal (Esp); **a ~ case** una vitrina 2 (glassware) cristalería *f*, cristal *m*

B [c] (vessel) vaso *m*; (with stem) copa *f*; **a ~ of wine** una copa de vino; **a champagne ~** una copa de champán

C **glasses** *pl* 1 (spectacles) gafas *fpl*, lentes *mpl* (esp AmL), anteojos *mpl* (esp AmL) 2 (*field ~es*) prismáticos *mpl*, largavistas *m*

D [c] (*magnifying ~*) lupa *f*, lente *f* de aumento

glass: **~blowing** /'glæs,bləʊɪŋ || 'glɑːs,bləʊɪŋ/ *n* [u] soplado *m* del vidrio; **~ ceiling** *n* techo *m* de cristal, tope *m*; **~ fiber**, (BrE) **~ fibre** *n* [u] fibra *f* de vidrio

glassful /'glæsfʊl || 'glɑːsfʊl/ *n* vaso *m*

glass: **~house** *n* (BrE) invernadero *m*; **~paper** *n* [u] (BrE) papel *m* de vidrio; **~ware** /'glæswer || 'glɑːsweə(r)/ *n* [u] cristalería *f*; **~works** *n* (*pl* ~) (+ *sing or pl vb*) fábrica *f* de vidrio, cristalería *f*

glassy /'glæsi || 'glɑːsi/ *adj* 1 (like glass) vítreo 2 (dull, lifeless) ⟨*stare*⟩ vidrioso

Glaswegian¹ /glæz'wiːdʒən/ *adj* de Glasgow

Glaswegian² *n*: *habitante o persona oriunda de Glasgow*

glaucoma /glɔː'kəʊmə/ *n* [u] glaucoma *m*

glaze¹ /gleɪz/ *n* [c u] 1 (on pottery) vidriado *m* 2 (Culin) glaseado *m*

glaze² *vt*

A (fit with glass) ⟨*window/door*⟩ acristalar; **to ~ a window** ponerle* vidrio(s) *or* (Esp) cristal(es) a

B (make shiny, glossy) 1 ⟨*pottery*⟩ vidriar 2 (Culin) glasear

■ **glaze** *vi* **~ (over)** ⟨⟨*eyes*⟩⟩ vidriarse

glazed /gleɪzd/ *adj*

A (fitted with glass) ⟨*window/door*⟩ con vidrio *or* (Esp) cristal

B 1 (Culin, Print, Tex) glaseado 2 (glassy-eyed) ⟨*expression*⟩ vidrioso

glazier /'gleɪʒər || 'gleɪziə(r)/ *n* vidriero, -ra *m,f*, cristalero, -ra *m,f* (Esp)

glazing /'gleɪzɪŋ/ *n* [u] 1 (glass) vidrios *mpl*, cristales *mpl* (Esp) 2 (act, job) acristalamiento *m*, acristalación *f*

gleam¹ /gliːm/ *vi* ⟨⟨*metal*⟩⟩ relucir*, brillar; ⟨⟨*hair*⟩⟩ brillar

gleam² *n* (on metal, water) reflejo *m*, brillo *m*; **he had a wicked ~ in his eyes** sus ojos despedían un destello maleficioso; **a ~ of pride** una mirada orgullosa

gleaming /'gliːmɪŋ/ *adj* reluciente, brillante

glean /gliːn/ *vt* ⟨*information*⟩ recoger*, cosechar; **to ~ sth FROM sth/sb**: **figures ~ed from the official year book** cifras extraídas del anuario oficial; **I ~ed from her that ...** de lo que dijo deduje que ...

glee /gliː/ *n* [u] (delight) regocijo *m*, júbilo *m* (liter); **to laugh/shout with ~** reírse*/gritar de alegría *or* con regocijo

gleeful /'gliːfəl/ *adj* ⟨*laugh/shout*⟩ lleno de alegría *or* (liter) júbilo

gleefully /'gliːfəli/ *adv* ⟨*laugh/shout*⟩ con regocijo, alegremente; **he rubbed his hands ~** se frotó las manos regodeándose (con la idea)

glen /glen/ *n* cañada *f*

glib /glɪb/ *adj* **-bb-** ⟨*generalization/remark/answer*⟩ simplista, fácil; ⟨*salesman/politician*⟩ con mucha labia

glibly /'glɪbli/ *adv* con mucha labia *or* palabrería

glide /glaɪd/ *vi*

A (move smoothly over a surface) ⟨⟨*person/dancer/door*⟩⟩ deslizarse*

B 1 ⟨⟨*bird/plane*⟩⟩ planear 2 (pilot a glider) volar* sin motor

glider /'glaɪdər || 'glaɪdə(r)/ *n* planeador *m*

glimmer¹ /'glɪmər || 'glɪmə(r)/ *vi* brillar con luz trémula

glimmer² *n* 1 (of candle, light) luz *f* débil *or* tenue y trémula 2 (of understanding) atisbo *m*; **there's a ~ of hope** hay un rayo *or* un rayito de esperanza

glimpse¹ /glɪmps/ *n*: **I caught a ~ of the room** pude ver brevemente la habitación; **a ~ of life in rural England** una visión de la vida en la Inglaterra rural

glimpse² *vt* alcanzar* a ver, atisbar

glint¹ /glɪnt/ *vi* destellar, brillar

glint² *n* (of metal) destello *m*; (of light) destello *m*, reflejo *m*; (in eye) (*no pl*) chispa *f*, brillo *m*

glisten /'glɪsən/ *vi* brillar, refulgir* (liter)

glitch /glɪtʃ/ *n* (esp AmE sl) problema *m* técnico

glitter¹ /'glɪtər || 'glɪtə(r)/ *vi* relumbrar, relucir*

glitter² *n* 1 (sparkle) (*no pl*) destello *m*, brillo *m* 2 [u] (superficial attractiveness) oropel *m* 3 [u] (decoration) purpurina *f*, brillantes *mpl* (Arg), brillantina *f* (Ur, Ven), brillo *m* (Chi)

glittering /'glɪtərɪŋ/ *adj* 1 (sparkling) ⟨*jewels*⟩ centelleante; ⟨*stars*⟩ parpadeante, titilante 2 (brilliant, showy) ⟨*career/occasion*⟩ fastuoso, rutilante

glitz /glɪts/ *n* [u] (AmE colloq) oropel *m*

glitzy /'glɪtsi/ *adj* **-zier, -ziest** (AmE colloq) glamoroso, deslumbrante

gloat /gləʊt/ *vi* **to ~ (OVER sth)** regodearse *or* refocilarse (CON algo)

global /'gləʊbəl/ *adj* 1 (worldwide) a escala mundial, global; **the ~ village** la aldea mundial; **~ warming** calentamiento *m* global *or* del planeta 2 (overall, comprehensive) global

globalism /'gləʊbəlɪzəm/ *n* [u] globalismo *m*

globalization /,gləʊbələ'zeɪʃən || ,gləʊbəlaɪ'zeɪʃən/ *n* [u] globalización *f*, mundialización *f*

globally /'gləʊbəli/ *adv* 1 (on a world scale) a escala mundial 2 (on an overall view) globalmente

globe /gləʊb/ *n* 1 (world) **the ~** el globo 2 (model) globo *m* terráqueo

globe: **~ artichoke** *n* alcachofa *f*, alcaucil *m* (RPl); **~trotter** /'gləʊb,trɑːtər || 'gləʊb,trɒtə(r)/ *n* trotamundos *mf*; **~trotting** /'gləʊb,trɑːtɪŋ || 'gləʊb,trɒtɪŋ/ *n* [u]: **aren't you tired of all that ~trotting?** ¿no estás cansado de tanto trotar mundos?

globule /'glɑːbjuːl || 'glɒbjuːl/ *n* glóbulo *m*

gloom /gluːm/ *n* [u] 1 (darkness) penumbra *f*, oscuridad *f* 2 (melancholy) melancolía *f*; **he's always full of ~ and doom** siempre lo ve todo negro

gloomily /'gluːməli || 'gluːmɪli/ *adv* ⟨*sigh/stare*⟩ tristemente, con melancolía; ⟨*look forward/predict*⟩ con pesimismo

gloomy /'gluːmi/ *adj* **-mier, -miest** 1 (dark) ⟨*day*⟩ sombrío; ⟨*place*⟩ sombrío, lúgubre 2 (dismal) ⟨*person*⟩ lúgubre, fúnebre; ⟨*prospect*⟩ nada halagüeño; ⟨*prediction*⟩ pesimista, negativo; **she takes a ~ view of everything** todo lo ve negro

glorified /'glɔːrəfaɪd || 'glɔːrɪfaɪd/ *adj* (colloq & hum) (*before n*) con pretensiones (hum)

glorify /'glɔːrəfaɪ || 'glɔːrɪfaɪ/ *vt* **-fies, -fying, -fied** ⟨*person*⟩ ensalzar*, glorificar*; ⟨*violence/war*⟩ exaltar

glorious /'glɔːriəs/ *adj* 1 (deserving glory) ⟨*victory/deed*⟩ glorioso 2 (wonderful) ⟨*view/weather*⟩ maravilloso, espléndido, soberbio

glory¹ /'glɔːri/ *n* (*pl* **-ries**) 1 [u] (fame) gloria *f*; ***to cover oneself with*** *o* (BrE also) ***in ~*** cubrirse* de gloria 2 [u c] (beauty, magnificence) esplendor *m*, gloria *f*; **the glories of**

g

imperial China el esplendor de la China Imperial; **the ~ of the system is that ...** lo espléndido *or* lo maravilloso del sistema está en que ... **3** [u] (Relig) gloria *f*; **~ to God in the highest** gloria a Dios en las alturas; ***to be in one's* ~** estar* en la gloria

glory² *vi* **-ries, -rying, -ried**: **to ~ IN sth** (take pleasure) disfrutar DE algo; (in unpleasant way) regodearse CON algo

gloss /glɑːs || glɒs/ *n*

A **1** [u] (shine) brillo *m*, lustre *m*; ***to take the ~ off sth*** quitarle la gracia a algo; (*before n*) **~ finish** acabado *m* brillante **2** [u] **~ (paint)** (pintura *f* al *or* de) esmalte *m* **3** (attractive appearance, semblance) (*no pl*) barniz *m*; **to put a ~ on sth** disimular algo

B [c] (explanatory note) glosa *f*

Phrasal verb

• **gloss over** [v ▸ adv ▸ o] (make light of) quitarle importancia a, minimizar* la importancia de; (ignore) pasar por alto

glossary /ˈglɑːsəri || ˈglɒsəri/ *n* (*pl* **-ries**) glosario *m*

glossy¹ /ˈglɑːsi || ˈglɒsi/ *adj* **-sier, -siest** ‹*coat of animal*› brillante, lustroso; ‹*hair*› brillante, brilloso (AmL); ‹*photograph*› brillante

glossy² *n* (*pl* **-sies**) **~ (magazine)** revista *f* ilustrada (*impresa en papel satinado*)

glove /glʌv/ *n* guante *m*; ***to fit like a ~*** quedar como un guante; ***to handle* o *treat sb with kid ~s*** tratar a algn con guantes de seda *or* (CS tb) con guante blanco

glove compartment *n* guantera *f*

gloved /glʌvd/ *adj* enguantado

glove puppet *n* (BrE) títere *m* (*de guante*), polichinela *m*

glow¹ /gləʊ/ *vi* «*fire*» brillar, resplandecer*; «*metal*» estar* al rojo vivo; **to ~ with health** rebosar (de) *or* irradiar salud; **to be ~ing with happiness** estar* radiante de felicidad

glow² *n* (*no pl*) **1** (light) brillo *m*, resplandor *m* **2** (feeling): **he felt a ~ of pride/satisfaction** sintió una oleada de orgullo/satisfacción

glower /ˈglaʊər || ˈglaʊə(r)/ *vi* tener* el ceño fruncido; **to ~ AT sb** lanzarle* miradas fulminantes/una mirada fulminante A algn

glowing /ˈgləʊɪŋ/ *adj* **1** (shining) (*before n*) ‹*cheeks*› encendido; **the ~ embers** las brasas **2** (expressing praise) ‹*report*› elogioso, lleno de alabanzas; **in ~ terms** en términos elogiosos *or* (AmL tb) encomiosos

glowworm /ˈgləʊwɜːrm || ˈgləʊwɜːm/ *n* luciérnaga *f* (*larva o hembra*), gusano *m* de luz (Esp, Méx), bicho *m* de luz (RPl)

glucose /ˈgluːkəʊs, -kəʊz/ *n* [u] glucosa *f*

glue¹ /gluː/ *n* [u c] goma *f* de pegar, pegamento *m*; (*before n*) **~ sniffing** inhalación *f* de pegamento *or* (Chi) de neoprén

glue² *vt* **glues, glueing, glued** **1** (stick) pegar*; (in carpentry) encolar **2** (fix): **keep your eyes ~d on the road** no apartes la vista de la carretera; **he was ~d to the television** estaba pegado a la televisión

glum /glʌm/ *adj* **-mm-** apesadumbrado, apenado

glumly /ˈglʌmli/ *adv* con tristeza *or* pena

glut¹ /glʌt/ *n* superabundancia *f*

glut² *vt* **-tt-** saturar; **the market is being ~ted with apples** el mercado se está saturando de manzanas

glutinous /ˈgluːtn̩əs || ˈgluːtɪnəs/ *adj* pegajoso, glutinoso (frml)

glutton /ˈglʌtn̩/ *n* glotón, -tona *m,f*; ***to be a ~ for punishment*** ser* un masoquista

gluttonous /ˈglʌtn̩əs || ˈglʌtənəs/ *adj* ‹*person*› glotón

gluttony /ˈglʌtn̩i || ˈglʌtəni/ *n* [u] glotonería *f*, gula *f*; (deadly sin) gula *f*

glycerin /ˈglɪsərən || ˈglɪsərɪn/, **glycerine** /ˈglɪsərən || ˈglɪsəriːn/ *n* [u] glicerina *f*

GMB *n* (in UK) *sindicato general de trabajadores*

GMT (= **Greenwich Mean Time**) GMT

gnarled /nɑːrld || nɑːld/ *adj* ‹*wood/fingers*› nudoso; ‹*tree*› retorcido

gnash /næʃ/ *vt*: **to ~ one's teeth** hacer* rechinar los dientes

gnat /næt/ *n* jején *m*; (general usage) mosquito *m*

gnaw /nɔː/ *vt* «*animal*» roer*

■ **gnaw** *vi* **to ~ AT sth** «*animal*» roer* algo; **he ~ed at his fingernails** se comía las uñas; **her conscience kept ~ing at her** no dejaba de remorderle la conciencia

gnawing /ˈnɔːɪŋ/ *adj* ‹*pain*› lacerante, persistente; ‹*hunger*› persistente; ‹*doubt*› que atormenta, que corroe por dentro

gnome /nəʊm/ *n* (Myth) gnomo *m*; **garden ~** enanito *m*

GNP *n* (= **gross national product**) PNB *m*, PBI *m* (RPl), PIB *m* (esp Esp)

go¹ /gəʊ/ (*3rd pers sing pres* **goes**; *past* **went**; *past p* **gone**) *vi*

Sense I

A **1** (move, travel) ir*; **there she ~es** allá va; **who ~es there?** (Mil) ¿quién va?; **are you ~ing my way?** ¿vas hacia el mismo sitio que yo?; **we can discuss it as we ~** podemos hablarlo en el camino; **where do we ~ from here?** ¿y ahora qué hacemos? **2** (start moving, acting): **~ when the lights turn green** avanza *or* (fam) dale cuando el semáforo se ponga verde; **ready, (get) set, ~!** preparados *or* en sus marcas, listos ¡ya!; **let's ~!** ¡vamos!; **here ~es!** ¡allá vamos (*or* voy *etc*)!; **there you ~** (colloq) (handing sth over) toma *or* aquí tienes; (sth is ready) ya está *or* listo; **don't ~ telling everybody** (colloq) no vayas a contárselo a todo el mundo

B (*past p* **gone/been**) **1** (travel to) ir*; **she's gone to France** se ha ido a Francia; **I have never been abroad** no he estado nunca en el extranjero; **where are you ~ing?** ¿adónde vas?; **to ~ by car/bus/plane** ir* en coche/autobús/avión; **to ~ on foot/horseback** ir* a pie/a caballo; **to ~ for a walk/drive** ir* a dar un paseo/una vuelta en coche; **to ~ to + INF** ir* A + INF; **they've gone to see the exhibition** (se) han ido a ver la exposición; **they've been to see the exhibition** han visitado la exposición, han estado en la exposición; **to ~ AND + INF** ir* A + INF; **~ and see what she wants** anda *or* vete a ver qué quiere **2** (attend) ir*; **to ~ on a training course** hacer* un curso de capacitación; **to ~ on a diet** ponerse* a régimen; **to ~ -ING** ir* A + INF; **to ~ swimming/hunting** ir* a nadar/cazar

C (attempt, make as if to) **to ~ to + INF** ir* A + INF

Sense II

A (leave, depart) «*visitor*» irse*, marcharse (esp Esp); «*bus/train*» salir*; **well, I must be ~ing** bueno, me tengo que ir ya; **to leave ~** soltar*; ▸ **let²** *vt* **A3**

B **1** (pass) «*time*» pasar; **those days have gone** ya han pasado aquellos días; **it's just gone nine o'clock** (BrE) son las nueve pasadas; **the time ~es quickly** el tiempo pasa volando *or* rápidamente **2** (disappear) «*headache/fear*» pasarse *or* irse* (+ *me/te/le etc*); «*energy/confidence*» desaparecer*; **has the pain gone?** ¿se te (*or* le *etc*) ha pasado *or* ido el dolor? **3** «*money/food*» (be spent) irse*; (be used up) acabarse; **what do you spend it all on? — I don't know, it just ~es** ¿en qué te lo gastas? — no sé, se (me) va como el agua; **the money/cream has all gone** se ha acabado el dinero/la crema; **to ~ ON sth**: **half his salary ~es on drink** la mitad del sueldo se le va en bebida

C **1** (be disposed of): **that sofa will have to ~** nos vamos (*or* se van *etc*) a tener que deshacer de ese sofá; **either the cats ~ or I ~** o se van los gatos o me voy yo **2** (be sold) venderse; **the bread has all gone** no queda pan, el pan se ha vendido todo; **the painting went for £1,000** el cuadro se vendió en 1.000 libras; **~ing, ~ing, gone** a la una, a las dos, vendido

D **1** (cease to function, wear out) «*bulb/fuse*» fundirse; «*thermostat/fan/exhaust*» estropearse; **her memory/eyesight is ~ing** está fallándole *or* está perdiendo la memoria/la vista; **the brakes went as we ...** los frenos fallaron cuando ...; **the brakes have gone** los frenos no funcionan; **my legs went (from under me)** me fallaron las piernas **2** (die) (colloq) morir*

E **to go** **1** (remaining): **only two weeks to ~ till he comes** sólo faltan dos semanas para que llegue; **I still have 50 pages to ~** todavía me faltan *or* me quedan 50 páginas **2** (take away) (AmE): **two burgers to ~** dos hamburguesas para llevar

Sense III

A **1** (lead) «*path/road*» ir*, llevar **2** (extend, range) «*road/railway line*» ir*; **it only ~es as far as Croydon** sólo va *or* llega hasta Croydon; **to ~ from ... to ...** «*prices/ages/period*» ir* de ... a ... *or* desde ... hasta ...; **the belt won't**

~ around my waist el cinturón no me da para la cintura

B [1] (have place) ir*; (fit) caber*; *see also* **go in, go into** [2] (be divisible): **5 into 11 won't** *o* **doesn't ~** 11 no es divisible por 5; **8 into 32 ~es 4 (times)** 32 entre 8 cabe a 4

(Sense IV)

A [1] (become): **to ~ blind/deaf** quedarse ciego/sordo; **to ~ crazy** volverse* loco; **to ~ mouldy** (BrE) enmohecerse*; **to ~ sour** agriarse, ponerse* agrio; **her face went red** se puso colorada; **everything went quiet** se hizo un silencio total [2] (be, remain): **to ~ barefoot/naked** ir* *or* andar* descalzo/desnudo; **they went hungry** pasaron hambre

B (turn out, proceed, progress) ir*; **how are things ~ing?** ¿cómo van *or* andan las cosas?; **so it ~es** así son las cosas

C [1] (be available) (*only in -ing form*): **I'll take any job that's ~ing** estoy dispuesto a aceptar el trabajo que sea *or* cualquier trabajo que me ofrezcan; **is there any coffee ~ing?** (BrE) ¿hay café? [2] (be in general): **it's not expensive as dishwashers ~** no es caro, para lo que cuestan los lavavajillas

(Sense V)

A [1] (function, work) «*heater/engine/clock*» funcionar; **the radio was ~ing full blast** la radio estaba puesta a todo lo que daba; ***to have a lot ~ing for one*** tener* muchos puntos a favor; ***to have a good thing ~ing***: **we've got a good thing ~ing here** esto marcha muy bien [2] **to get going**: **the car's OK once it gets ~ing** el coche marcha bien una vez que arranca; **I find it hard to get ~ing in the mornings** me cuesta mucho entrar en acción por la mañana; **it's late, we'd better get ~ing** es tarde, más vale que nos vayamos; **to get sth ~ing**: **we tried to get a fire ~ing** tratamos de hacer fuego; **we need some music to get the party ~ing** hace falta un poco de música para animar la fiesta; ***to get sb ~ing***: **all this stupid nonsense really gets me ~ing** estas estupideces me sacan de quicio [3] **to keep going** (continue to function) aguantar; (not stop) seguir*; **to keep a project ~ing** mantener* a flote un proyecto

B (continue, last out) seguir*; **the club's been ~ing for 12 years now** el club lleva 12 años funcionando; **how long can you ~ before you need a break?** ¿cuánto aguantas sin descansar?; **we can ~ for weeks without seeing a soul** podemos estar *or* pasar semanas enteras sin ver un alma

C [1] (sound) «*bell/siren*» sonar* [2] (make sound, movement) hacer*

D [1] (contribute) **to ~ to + INF**: **everything that ~es to make a good school** todo lo que contribuye a que una escuela sea buena; **that just ~es to prove my point** eso confirma lo que yo decía *or* prueba que tengo razón; **it just ~es to show: we can't leave them on their own** está visto que no los podemos dejar solos [2] (be used) **to ~ TOWARD sth/to + INF**: **all their savings are ~ing toward the trip** van a gastar todos sus ahorros en el viaje; **the money will ~ to pay the workmen** el dinero se usará para pagar a los obreros

E (run, be worded) «*poem/prayer*» decir*; **how does the song ~?** ¿cómo es la (letra/música de la) canción?

F [1] (be permitted): **anything ~es** todo vale, cualquier cosa está bien [2] (be necessarily obeyed, believed): **what the boss says ~es** lo que dice el jefe, va a misa [3] (match, suit) pegar*, ir*; **that shirt and that tie don't really ~** esa camisa no pega *or* no va *or* no queda bien con esa corbata; *see also* **go together, go with**

G (have turn) (Games) ir*, jugar*

■ **go** *vt* (say) (colloq) ir* y decir* (fam); **that's enough of that, he ~es** —ya está bueno —va y dice

■ **go** *v aux* (*only in -ing form*) **to be ~ing to + INF** [1] (expressing intention) ir* A + INF; **I was just ~ing to make some coffee** iba a *or* estaba por hacer café; **don't deny it! — I wasn't ~ing to** ¡no lo niegues! — no pensaba hacerlo [2] (expressing near future, prediction) ir* A + INF; **I'm ~ing to be sick** voy a devolver

(Phrasal verbs)

• **go about** [v ▸ prep ▸ o] [1] (tackle, deal with) ‹*task*› acometer, emprender; **you'll be able to persuade them if you ~ about it the right way** los vas a poder convencer si encaras las cosas bien; **what's the best way to ~ about it?** ¿cuál es la mejor forma de hacerlo?; **to ~ about -ING**: **how would you ~ about solving this equation?** ¿cómo harías para resolver esta ecuación? [2] (occupy oneself with): **to ~ about one's business** ocuparse de sus (*or* mis *etc*) cosas

• **go after** [v ▸ prep ▸ o] (pursue, chase) perseguir*, dar* caza a

• **go against** [v ▸ prep ▸ o] ‹*instructions/policy/person*› oponerse* a, ir* en contra de, ir* contra

• **go ahead** [v ▸ adv] (proceed, begin) **to ~ ahead (WITH sth)** seguir* adelante (CON algo); **may I ask you a question? — ~ ahead!** ¿le puedo hacer una pregunta? — por supuesto *or* (AmL tb) pregunte nomás

• **go along** [v ▸ adv] [1] (accompany, be present) ir*; **I'll ~ along there with you** te acompaño, voy contigo [2] (proceed, progress) ir*; **he whistled as he went along** iba silbando; **I usually make corrections as I ~ along** normalmente hago correcciones sobre la marcha [3] (acquiesce): **to ~ along with a proposal** secundar una propuesta; **I'll ~ along with that** estoy de acuerdo con eso

• **go around**, (BrE also) **go round**

(Sense I) [v ▸ prep ▸ o]

A [1] (turn) ‹*corner*› doblar, dar* la vuelta a, dar* vuelta (CS); ‹*bend*› tomar [2] (make detour) ‹*obstacle*› rodear, sortear

B (visit, move through) ‹*country/city*› recorrer; ‹*museum/castle*› visitar; **to ~ around the world** dar* la vuelta al mundo

(Sense II) [v ▸ adv]

A [1] (move, travel, be outdoors) andar*; **she ~es around in a Cadillac** anda por ahí en un Cadillac; **to ~ around WITH sb** andar* CON algn; **to ~ around -ING** ir* por ahí + GER [2] (circulate) «*joke/rumor*» correr, circular; **it's a bug that's ~ing around** es un virus que anda por ahí [3] (be sufficient for everybody): **there aren't enough to ~ round** no alcanzan, no hay suficientes

B (revolve) «*wheel/world*» dar* vueltas

C (visit) ir*; **I'll ~ around and see him** iré a verlo

• **go at** [v ▸ prep ▸ o] (undertake vigorously): **he went at it as if his life depended on it** acometió la tarea como si le fuera la vida en ello

• **go away** [v ▸ adv] [1] (depart, leave) irse* [2] (from home): **I'm ~ing away this weekend** me voy por ahí *or* voy a salir este fin de semana; **to ~ away on vacation** irse* *or* salir* de vacaciones; **a ~ing-away party/present** una fiesta/un regalo de despedida [3] (disappear, fade away) «*smell*» irse*; «*pain*» pasarse *or* irse* (+ *me/te/le etc*)

• **go back** [v ▸ adv]

A [1] (return) volver*; **~ back!** ¡vuelve atrás!, ¡retrocede!; **there's no ~ing back now** ya no se puede (*or* no nos podemos *etc*) volver atrás [2] (in lecture, text) volver*; **to ~ back to what I was saying earlier ...** volviendo a lo que decía antes ... [3] (be returned): **this dress'll have to ~ back** voy (*or* vas *etc*) a tener que devolver ese vestido

B [1] (date, originate) «*tradition/dynasty*» remontarse; **we ~ back a long way** (colloq) nos conocemos desde hace mucho [2] (return in time, revert) volver*; **we went back to the old system** volvimos al antiguo sistema [3] «*clocks*» atrasarse

• **go back on** [v ▸ adv ▸ prep ▸ o] ‹*one's promise*› dejar de cumplir; ‹*one's word*› faltar a

• **go before**

A [v ▸ prep ▸ o] (appear before) ‹*court/committee*› presentarse ante

B [v ▸ adv] [v ▸ prep ▸ o] (happen or live previously) (liter): **everything that had gone before** todo lo que había sucedido antes; **those who have gone before us** aquellos que nos precedieron (liter)

• **go below** [v ▸ adv] (Naut) bajar

• **go by**

A [v ▸ adv] [1] (move past) pasar; **to let an opportunity ~ by** dejar pasar una oportunidad [2] (elapse) «*days/years*» pasar, transcurrir (frml); **as the years went by, he began to ...** con el paso de los años *or* (frml) con el transcurrir de los años, empezó a ...; **as time goes by** con el tiempo, con el paso del tiempo

B [v ▸ prep ▸ o] [1] (be guided by) ‹*instinct*› dejarse llevar por; ‹*rules*› seguir* [2] (base judgment on): **if previous experience is anything to ~ by** a juzgar por lo que ha sucedido en otras ocasiones; **to ~ by appearances** guiarse* *or* dejarse llevar por las apariencias

• **go down** [v ▸ adv]

A [1] (descend) «*person*» bajar; «*sun*» ponerse*; «*curtain*» (Theat) caer*, bajar; **to ~ down on one's knees/hands and knees** ponerse* de rodillas/a gatas [2] (fall) «*boxer/horse*» caerse*; «*plane*» caer*, estrellarse [3] (sink) «*ship*» hundirse 4 «*computer*» dejar de funcionar, descomponerse* (AmL) 5 (be defeated) (Sport) perder*; **to ~ down (TO sb)**: **Italy went down 2-1 to Uruguay** Italia perdió 2 a 1 frente a Uruguay; **to ~ down fighting** caer* luchando, morir* con las botas puestas

B 1 (decrease) «*temperature/exchange rate*» bajar; «*population/unemployment*» disminuir*; **to ~ down in price** bajar de precio; **to ~ down in value** perder* valor; **I went down to 110 pounds** adelgacé hasta pesar 110 libras 2 (decline) «*standard/quality*» empeorar; **she's gone down in my estimation** ha perdido *or* bajado mucho en mi estima 3 (abate, subside) «*wind/storm*» amainar; «*floods/swelling*» bajar; **his temperature's gone down** le ha bajado la fiebre 4 (deflate) «*tire*» perder* aire, desinflarse

C (extend) **to ~ down TO sth**: **this road ~es down to the beach** este camino baja a *or* hasta la playa; **the skirt ~es down to her ankles** la falda le llega a los tobillos

D 1 (toward the south) ir* (*hacia el sur*); **I'm ~ing down to Atlanta for a few days** voy a ir a pasar unos días a Atlanta 2 (to another place) (BrE) ir*; **I'm ~ing down to the shops** voy a las tiendas

E 1 (be swallowed): **it just won't ~ down** no me pasa, no lo puedo tragar; **a coffee would ~ down nicely** un café me caería de maravilla; **it went down the wrong way** se me ha ido por el otro camino 2 «*present/proposal/remarks*»: **how did the announcement ~ down?** ¿qué tipo de acogida tuvo el anuncio?, ¿cómo recibieron el anuncio?; **that won't ~ down too well with your father** eso no le va a caer muy bien a tu padre

F (be recorded, written): **all these absences will ~ down on your record** va a quedar constancia de estas faltas en tu ficha; **to ~ down in history as sb/sth** pasar a la historia como algn/algo

• **go down with** [v ▸ adv ▸ prep ▸ o] (BrE): **to ~ down with flu/hepatitis** caer* en cama con gripe/caer* enfermo de hepatitis

• **go for** [v ▸ prep ▸ o]

A 1 (head toward, reach for): **he went for the finish line** se lanzó a la meta *or* (Esp) a por la meta; **he went for his gun** fue a echar mano de la pistola 2 (attack): **he went for Bill** se le echó encima a Bill

B 1 (aim at) ir* tras, ir* a por (Esp); **~ for it!** ¡haz la tentativa!, ¡a por ello! (Esp) 2 (like, prefer): **I don't really ~ for Chinese food** a mí no me gusta mucho *or* no me entusiasma la comida china 3 (choose) decidirse *or* optar por

C (be applicable to): **and that ~es for you too** y eso va también por *or* para ti

• **go forward** [v ▸ adv] 1 (progress) «*work/negotiations*» progresar, avanzar*; **the winners ~ forward to the final** los ganadores pasan a la final 2 (be proposed, passed on) «*motion*» ser* presentado; **I allowed my name to ~ forward** permití que se me propusiera como canditata

• **go in** [v ▸ adv]

A 1 (enter) entrar 2 «*screw/key*» entrar; **the big case won't ~ in** la maleta grande no cabe 3 (go to work) ir* a trabajar 4 (Mil) atacar*; **the police went in to break up the demonstration** la policía intervino para dispersar a los manifestantes 5 (be learned, accepted) «*idea/lesson/warning*» entrar (en la cabeza)

B (be obscured) «*sun/moon*» ocultarse, esconderse

• **go in for** [v ▸ adv ▸ prep ▸ o] 1 (enter) ‹*competition*› participar en, tomar parte en; ‹*exam/test*› presentarse a 2 (take up, practice): **is she ~ing in for arts or sciences?** ¿va a estudiar *or* ha elegido letras o ciencias?; **he'd thought of ~ing in for teaching** había pensado dedicarse a la enseñanza; **we don't ~ in for that sort of thing here** ese tipo de cosa no tiene cabida aquí

• **go into** [v ▸ prep ▸ o]

A 1 (enter) ‹*room/building*› entrar en, entrar a (AmL) 2 (crash into) ‹*car/wall*› chocar* contra 3 (fit into) entrar en 4 (be divisible into): **5 goes into 20 4 times** 20 dividido por 5 da 4; **5 into 11 doesn't ~** 11 no es divisible por 5

B 1 (start, embark on) ‹*phase/era*› entrar en, empezar* 2 (enter certain state) ‹*coma/trance*› entrar en; **he went into hysterics** le dio un ataque de histeria 3 (enter profession) ‹*television/Parliament*› entrar en; **she wants to ~ into publishing** quiere meterse en el mundo editorial

C 1 (discuss, explain) entrar en; **I don't want to ~ into that** no quiero entrar en ese tema; **she refused to ~ into why she resigned** se negó a explicar por qué había dimitido 2 (investigate, analyze) ‹*problem/motives*› analizar*, estudiar

D (be devoted to): **after all the money/work that has gone into this!** ¡después de todo el dinero/trabajo que se ha metido en esto!; **so much time and energy ~es into keeping the place tidy** lleva mucho tiempo y esfuerzo mantenerlo todo ordenado

• **go off**

Sense I [v ▸ adv]

A 1 (depart) irse*, marcharse (esp Esp); **to ~ off WITH sth** llevarse algo; **she's gone off with my husband** se ha largado con mi marido (fam) 2 (end work, duty) salir*

B (become sour, rotten) «*milk/meat/fish*» echarse a perder, pasarse

C 1 (make explosion) «*bomb/firework*» estallar; «*gun*» dispararse 2 (make noise) «*alarm*» sonar*

D (turn out) salir*; **the party went off very well** la fiesta salió muy bien

E (stop operating) «*heating/lights*» apagarse*

F (go to sleep) dormirse*, quedarse dormido

Sense II [v ▸ prep ▸ o] (lose liking for) (BrE): **I've gone off beer** ya no me gusta la cerveza, me ha dejado de gustar la cerveza; **I've gone off him** ya no me gusta, ya no me cae bien; **I've gone off the idea** ya no me atrae la idea

• **go on**

Sense I [v ▸ adv]

A 1 (go further — without stopping) seguir*; (— after stopping) seguir*, proseguir* (frml); **I can't ~ on, I'm too tired** no puedo más, estoy muy cansado 2 (go ahead): **you ~ on, we'll follow** tú vete que nosotros ya iremos; **he went on ahead to look for a hotel** él fue antes *or* delante para buscar hotel

B (last, continue): **the discussion went on for hours** la discusión duró horas; **the fight ~es on** la lucha continúa; **the meeting just went on and on** la reunión se alargó interminablemente; **we can't ~ on like this** no podemos seguir así; **to ~ on -ING** seguir* + GER; **to ~ on to + INF**: **he went on to become President** llegó a ser presidente; **to ~ on TO sth**: **let us ~ on to victory** sigamos hasta triunfar; **to ~ on WITH sth** seguir* CON algo; **that's enough to be ~ing on with** (BrE) eso alcanza por el momento; **~ on!** (encouraging, urging) ¡dale!, ¡vamos!, ¡ándale! (Méx), ¡ándele! (Col), ¡venga! (Esp)

C 1 (continue speaking) seguir*, continuar*, proseguir* (frml) 2 (talk irritatingly) (pej): **he went on and on** siguió dale que dale *or* (Esp tb) dale que te pego (fam); **to ~ on ABOUT sth** hablar DE algo

D (happen): **what's ~ing on?** ¿qué pasa?; **there's an argument ~ing on next door** en la casa de al lado están discutiendo; **is there anything ~ing on between you two?** ¿hay algo entre ustedes *or* (Esp) vosotros dos?; **how long has this been ~ing on?** ¿desde cuándo viene sucediendo esto?

E 1 (pass, elapse): **the weather deteriorated as the morning went on** el tiempo empeoró a medida que avanzaba la mañana 2 (progress) marchar

F 1 (onto stage) salir* a escena; (onto field of play) salir* al campo 2 (fit, be placed): **the lid won't ~ on** no le puedo (*or* podemos *etc*) poner *or* colocar la tapa; **my gloves wouldn't ~ on** no me entraban los guantes 3 (be switched on) encenderse*, prenderse (AmL)

Sense II [v ▸ prep ▸ o]

A (approach) ir*; **he's ~ing on 80** va para los 80; **she's 16 ~ing on 17** tiene 16 para 17, está por cumplir 17; **it's ~ing on 11 o'clock** van a ser las 11, son casi las 11

B (base inquiries on): **all we have to ~ on is a phone number** lo único que tenemos es un número de teléfono; **we don't have much to ~ on** no tenemos muchos datos (*or* muchas pistas *etc*) en que basarnos

• **go out** [v ▸ adv]

A 1 (leave, exit) salir*; **some of the old spirit has gone out of him** ha perdido un poco del empuje que tenía; **to ~ out hunting/shopping** salir* de caza/de compras; **to ~ out to work** trabajar fuera 2 (socially, for entertainment) salir*; **to ~ out for a meal** salir* a comer fuera 3 (as boyfriend, girlfriend) **to ~ out (WITH sb)** salir* (CON algn)

B 1 (be broadcast) «*TV, radio program*» emitirse 2 (be issued, distributed): **a warrant has gone out for her arrest** se ha ordenado su detención; **the invitations have already gone out** ya se han mandado las invitaciones

C (be extinguished) «*fire/cigarette/light*» apagarse*

D «*tide*» bajar

E (become outmoded) «*clothes/style*» pasar de moda

- **go out to** [v ▸ adv ▸ prep ▸ o]: **my heart ∼es out to you (in sympathy)** lo lamento muchísimo; (on sb's death) te acompaño en el sentimiento
- **go over**

(Sense I) [v ▸ prep ▸ o]

A 1 (check) ‹*text/figures/work*› revisar, examinar; ‹*car*› revisar; ‹*house/premises*› inspeccionar 2 (dust, clean): **I'll just ∼ over the bedroom with a duster** voy a darle una pasada *or* un repaso al dormitorio con un trapo

B (revise, review) ‹*notes/chapter*› repasar; **I'd like to ∼ over your essay with you** quisiera que viéramos *or* analizáramos tu trabajo juntos; **I don't want to ∼ over all that again** no quiero volver otra vez sobre eso

(Sense II) [v ▸ adv]

A 1 (make one's way, travel) ir*; **she went over to Jack and took his hand** se acercó a Jack y le tomó la mano 2 (Rad, TV) pasar; **we're ∼ing over to our New York correspondent** conectamos ahora con nuestro corresponsal en Nueva York

B (change sides) pasarse; **to ∼ over to the other side/the competition** pasarse al otro bando/a la competencia

- **go past** [v ▸ adv] [v ▸ prep ▸ o] pasar; **the bus went right past (me) without stopping** el autobús pasó de largo
- **go round** (BrE) ▸ **go around**
- **go through**

(Sense I) [v ▸ prep ▸ o]

A 1 (pass through) ‹*process/stage*› pasar por; **he went through school without passing a single exam** terminó el colegio sin aprobar ni un examen; **we had to ∼ through the courts** tuvimos que acudir a *or* recurrir a los tribunales 2 (undergo) ‹*test/interview*› pasar, ser* sometido a (frml) 3 (perform): **let's ∼ through the procedure once more** repitamos otra vez todos los pasos del procedimiento 4 (endure) ‹*ordeal/hard times*› pasar por; **I've been through a great deal on your behalf** lo he pasado muy mal por tu culpa

B 1 (search) ‹*attic/suitcase*› registrar, revisar (AmL); ‹*drawers/desk*› hurgar* en; **to ∼ through sb's mail** abrirle* las cartas a algn; **have you gone** *o* (esp BrE) **been through all your pockets?** ¿(te) has mirado en todos los bolsillos? 2 ▸ **go over** *Sense* I **B**

C (consume, use up): **she went through a month's salary in two days** se gastó *or* (fam) se liquidó el sueldo de un mes en dos días; **he ∼es through ten shirts a week** ensucia diez camisas por semana

(Sense II) [v ▸ adv] 1 (be carried out) «*changes/legislation*» ser* aprobado; «*business deal*» llevarse a cabo, concretarse; **when his divorce ∼es through** cuando obtenga el divorcio 2 (Sport): **to ∼ through to the final/next round** pasar a la final/a la siguiente etapa

- **go through with** [v ▸ adv ▸ prep ▸ o] ‹*threat*› llevar a cabo, cumplir; ‹*plans*› llevar a cabo; **we went through with it for appearances' sake** lo hicimos por el qué dirán
- **go to** [v ▸ prep ▸ o]

A (see, consult) ‹*police*› ir* a; ‹*courts*› acudir a; **I want to ∼ to a specialist** quiero ir a ver a un especialista

B (be awarded to) ser* para; **... and the prize ∼es to ...** ... y el premio se lo lleva ...

- **go together** [v ▸ adv] 1 (be compatible) «*colors/patterns*» combinar, pegar* (fam); **lamb and mint sauce ∼ well together** el cordero queda muy bien con salsa de menta 2 (be normally associated): **love and marriage do not necessarily ∼ together** el amor y el matrimonio no van siempre de la mano
- **go under** [v ▸ adv] 1 (sink) «*ship*» hundirse; «*submarine/diver*» sumergirse* 2 (fail, go bankrupt) hundirse, irse* a pique
- **go up** [v ▸ adv]

A 1 (ascend) «*person*» subir; «*balloon/plane*» subir, ascender* (frml); «*curtain*» (Theat) levantarse 2 (approach) **to ∼ up (TO sb/sth)** acercarse* (A algn/algo) 3 (toward the north) ir* 4 (to another place) (esp BrE) ir*; **I'm ∼ing up to London** voy a Londres

B 1 (increase) «*temperature/price/cost*» subir, aumentar; «*population/unemployment*» aumentar; **to ∼ up in price** subir *or* aumentar de precio; **I went up to 140 lbs** engordé hasta llegar a pesar 140 libras 2 (improve) «*standard*» mejorar; **she's gone up in my estimation** ha ganado en mi estima

C 1 (be built, erected): **a church has gone up on that site** se ha levantado una iglesia en aquel terreno 2 (be put up): **a notice has gone up in the hall** han puesto un anuncio en el hall

D (burst into flames) prenderse fuego; (explode) estallar; **to ∼ up in flames** incendiarse

- **go with** [v ▸ prep ▸ o]

A 1 (be compatible with): **this sauce ∼es well with hamburgers** esta salsa queda muy bien con hamburguesas; **choose a tie to ∼ with your shirt** elija una corbata que quede bien *or* que combine con su camisa 2 (accompany, be associated with): **the house ∼es with the job** la casa va con el puesto; **the problems that ∼ with owning a car** los problemas que trae tener coche

B (have attachment) (colloq) salir* con

- **go without** 1 [v ▸ prep ▸ o] (do without) pasar sin; **she often went without food** a menudo pasaba sin comer; **they went without food/sleep for days** (not by choice) no comieron nada/no durmieron durante días 2 [v ▸ adv]: **in order to feed her children she herself often went without** para darles de comer a los niños a menudo pasaba privaciones; **there's no coffee left, you'll just have to ∼ without** no queda café, así que tendrás que pasar *or* arreglártelas sin él

go² *n* (*pl* **goes**)

A [c] 1 (attempt): **he emptied the bottle at** *o* **in one ∼** vació la botella de un tirón *or* de una sentada (fam); **she succeeded in lifting it at the third ∼** consiguió levantarlo al tercer intento; **∼ AT sth/-ING**: **it's my first ∼ at writing for radio** es la primera vez que escribo para la radio; **I want to have a ∼ at learning Arabic** quiero intentar aprender árabe; **have a ∼** prueba a ver, inténtalo; **I've had a good ∼ at the kitchen** le he dado una buena pasada *or* un buen repaso a la cocina; ***it's no ∼*** es imposible; ***to give sth a ∼*** (BrE) intentar algo; ***to have a ∼ at sb*** (colloq): **she had a ∼ at me for not having told her** se la agarró conmigo por no habérselo dicho (fam); ***to make a ∼ of sth*** sacar* algo adelante 2 (turn): **whose ∼ is it?** ¿a quién le toca?; **it's my ∼** me toca a mí 3 (chance to use): **can I have a ∼ on your typewriter?** ¿me dejas probar tu máquina de escribir?

B [u] (energy, drive) empuje *m*, dinamismo *m*; ***(to be) on the ∼***: **I've been on the ∼ all morning** no he parado en toda la mañana; **he's got three jobs on the ∼** (BrE) está haciendo tres trabajos a la vez

go³ *adj* (*pred*): **all systems ∼** todo listo *or* luz verde para despegar

goad /gəʊd/ *vt* ‹*person*› acosar; ‹*animal*› aguijonear; **to ∼ sb INTO sth/-ING**: **she was ∼ed into doing it** tanto la acosaron que lo hizo

(Phrasal verb)

- **goad on** [v ▸ o ▸ adv] (spur, incite) empujar, incitar

go-ahead /ˈgəʊəhed/ *n*: **to give sb/sth the ∼** darle* luz verde *or* el visto bueno a algn/algo

goal /gəʊl/ *n*

A (Sport) 1 (structure) portería *f*, arco *m* (AmL); **to shoot at ∼** tirar al arco *or* (Esp) a puerta; **to be in** *o* **play in** *o* **keep ∼** jugar* de guardameta *or* de portero *or* (AmL tb) de arquero; (*before n*) **∼ area** área *f*‡ chica *or* de portería *or* de meta; **∼ kick** saque *m* de puerta *or* de portería *or* (CS) de valla 2 (point) gol *m*; (*before n*) **∼ scorer** goleador, -dora *m,f*

B (aim) meta *f*, objetivo *m*; **to reach** *o* **achieve one's ∼** lograr *or* alcanzar* su (*or* mi *etc*) objetivo

goalie /ˈgəʊli/ *n* (colloq) ▸ **goalkeeper**

goal: **∼keeper** *n* portero, -ra *m,f*, guardameta *mf*, arquero, -ra *m,f* (AmL); **∼post** *n* poste *m* de la portería *or* (AmL tb) del arco; ***to move the ∼posts*** (BrE) (change rules) cambiar las reglas de juego; (change target) cambiar de planes; **∼tender** *n* (AmE) ▸ **∼keeper**

goat /gəʊt/ *n* 1 [c] (Zool) cabra *f*; **billy ∼** macho *m* cabrío; **nanny ∼** cabra *f*; ***to get sb's ∼*** exasperar *or* (fam) cabrear a algn, sacar* a algn de quicio 2 [u] (Culin) cabrito *m* 3 [c] (AmE) ▸ **scapegoat**

goatee (beard) /gəʊˈtiː/ *n* barbita *f* de chivo, perilla *f*, chiva *f* (AmL)

goatherd /ˈgəʊthɜːrd || ˈgəʊthɜːd/ *n* cabrero, -ra *m,f*

gob /gɑːb || gɒb/ *n*

A (AmE sl) **gobs** *pl* (large amount): **they have ∼s of money** tienen un montón de lana (AmL fam)

B (BrE sl) 1 (mouth) bocaza *f* (fam), jeta *f* (AmL fam) 2 (spittle) escupitajo *m* (fam), escupo *m* (Chi, Ven fam)

gobbet /ˈɡɑːbət || ˈɡɒbɪt/ *n* (colloq) (chunk — of food) cacho *m* (fam), pedazo *m*; (— of poetry, prose) trozo *m*

gobble /ˈɡɑːbəl || ˈɡɒbəl/ *vt* ‹*food/meal*› engullirse*, zamparse (fam)

▪ **gobble** *vi* «*turkey*» gluglutear

Phrasal verb

• **gobble up** [v ▸ o ▸ adv, v ▸ adv ▸ o] tragarse*, engullirse*

gobbledegook, gobbledygook /ˈɡɑːbəldiˈɡuːk || ˈɡɒbəldi,ɡuːk/ *n* [u] (colloq & pej) jerigonza *f*

gobbler /ˈɡɑːblə(r) || ˈɡɒblə(r)/ *n* (colloq) pavo *m*

go-between /ˈɡəʊbɪtwiːn/ *n* (intermediary) intermediario, -ria *m,f*, mediador, -dora *m,f*; (messenger) mensajero, -ra *m,f*

goblet /ˈɡɑːblət || ˈɡɒblɪt/ *n* copa *f*

goblin /ˈɡɑːblən || ˈɡɒblɪn/ *n* duende *m* travieso, trasgo *m*

gobsmacked /ˈɡɑːbsmækt || ˈɡɒbsmækt/ *adj* (BrE sl): **I was ~** me quedé patidifuso *or* patitieso (fam)

gobstopper /ˈɡɑːb,stɑːpər || ˈɡɒb,stɒpə(r)/ *n* (BrE) *caramelo grande*

god /ɡɑːd || ɡɒd/ *n*

A **God** **1** Dios *m*; **G~ bless (you)** que Dios te bendiga; **G~ willing** si Dios quiere, Dios mediante; ***G~ helps those who o as help themselves*** a Dios rogando y con el mazo dando, ayúdate que Dios te ayudará (AmL) **2** (*in interj phrases*) **G~!** ¡Dios (santo)!; **G~ Almighty!** ¡bendito sea Dios!; **oh, G~, *I* don't know!** ¡y yo qué sé!; **good G~, is that the time?** ¡uy Dios!, ¿ya es tan tarde?; **what will you do next? — G~ knows!** ¿y ahora qué vas a hacer? — ¡ni idea! *or* ¡(y) qué sé yo! *or* ¡sabe Dios!; **G~ only knows what they're doing in there!** ¡quién sabe qué estarán haciendo ahí dentro!; **I wish to G~ I hadn't come** ojalá no hubiera venido

B (deity, idol) dios *m*

C **gods** *pl* (Theat BrE) **the ~s** el gallinero, la galería

god: **~awful** /ˈɡɑːdˈɔːfəl || ˈɡɒd,ɔːfəl/ *adj* (colloq) espantoso, terrible; **~child** *n* ahijado, -da *m,f*

goddam¹, goddamn /ˈɡɑːdæm || ˈɡɒddæm/ *adj* (AmE sl) (*before n*) condenado (fam), maldito (fam)

goddam² *interj* (AmE sl) ¡maldición! (fam), ¡carajo! (vulg), ¡caray! (fam & euf)

goddaughter /ˈɡɑːdˈdɔːtər || ˈɡɒd,dɔːtə(r)/ *n* ahijada *f*

goddess /ˈɡɑːdəs || ˈɡɒdɪs/ *n* diosa *f*

god: **~father** /ˈɡɑːdˈfɑːðər || ˈɡɒd,fɑːðə(r)/ *n* padrino *m*; **~forsaken** /ˈɡɑːdfərˈseɪkən || ˈɡɒdfə,seɪkən/ *adj* (colloq) ‹*region/people*› dejado de la mano de Dios; ‹*town*› de mala muerte (fam); **~head** *n* (God) (liter) **the G~head** el Altísimo

godless /ˈɡɑːdləs || ˈɡɒdlɪs/ *adj* impío (frml)

godly /ˈɡɑːdli || ˈɡɒdli/ *adj* **-lier, -liest** piadoso, devoto

god: **~mother** /ˈɡɑːdˈmʌðər || ˈɡɒd,mʌðə(r)/ *n* madrina *f*; **~parent** /ˈɡɑːdˈperənt || ˈɡɒd,peərənt/ *n* (man) padrino *m*; (woman) madrina *f*; **my ~parents** mis padrinos; **~send** *n* bendición *f* (del cielo); **the check was a ~send** el cheque me (*or* nos *etc*) vino como caído del cielo; **~son** *n* ahijado *m*

-goer /,ɡəʊər || ,ɡəʊə(r)/ *suff*: **opera~s** los aficionados a *or* (CS tb) habitués de la ópera; *see also* **moviegoer, theatergoer**

gofer /ˈɡəʊfər || ˈɡəʊfə(r)/ *n* (AmE colloq) recadero, -ra *m,f*, mandadero, -ra *m,f* (AmL), milusos *mf* (Méx fam)

go-getter /ˈɡəʊˈɡetər || ,ɡəʊˈɡetə(r)/ *n* (colloq): **she's a real ~** es de las que consiguen lo que se proponen

goggle /ˈɡɑːɡəl || ˈɡɒɡəl/ *vi* (pej) **to ~ AT sth/sb** mirar algo/a algn con los ojos desorbitados

goggle-eyed /ˈɡɑːɡəlˈaɪd || ˈɡɒɡəlˈaɪd/ *adj* (colloq): **he looked at me ~** me miró con los ojos abiertos como platos (fam)

goggles /ˈɡɑːɡəlz || ˈɡɒɡəlz/ *pl n* (Sport) gafas *fpl or* anteojos *mpl* (esp AmL) de esquí (*or* natación *etc*); (for welders) gafas *fpl* protectoras, anteojos *mpl* protectores (esp AmL)

go-go /ˈɡəʊɡəʊ/ *adj* (colloq) (*before n*)

A ‹*bar/dancer*› (a) gogó

B (dynamic) ‹*economy/plan*› que promete rápidos beneficios

going¹ /ˈɡəʊɪŋ/ *n* (*no pl*)

A **1** (effort in walking, climbing): **once at the top, the ~ was easier** una vez en la cima, la marcha fue más fácil **2** (situation) situación *f*; **if I were you, I'd buy it while the ~ is good** yo que tú lo compraría ahora, aprovechando el buen momento; **when the ~ got rough** cuando las cosas se pusieron difíciles *or* (fam) feas **3** (progress): **that's pretty good ~** no está nada mal; **I found that lecture hard ~** me resultó difícil seguir la conferencia; **the novel was heavy ~** la novela era pesada

B (departure) partida *f*, marcha *f*

going² *adj* (*before n*) **1** (in operation) en marcha; **a ~ concern** (Busn) un negocio *or* una empresa en marcha **2** (present, current): **to pay above/below the ~ rate** pagar* por encima/debajo de lo normal; **that's the ~ rate** es lo que se suele cobrar/pagar

going: **~-over** /ˈɡəʊɪŋˈəʊvər || ,ɡəʊɪŋˈəʊvə(r)/ *n* (*pl* **~s-over**) **1** (examination, check) revisión *f*; **the police gave the house a thorough ~-over** la policía registró la casa de arriba a abajo **2** (cleaning) limpieza *f*; (superficial) pasada *f* (fam) **3** (beating up) (sl) paliza *f*, repaso *m* (Esp fam); **~s-on** /ˈɡəʊɪŋzˈɑːn || ,ɡəʊɪŋzˈɒn/ *pl n* (colloq) **1** (dubious conduct) tejemanejes *mpl* (fam) **2** (happenings) sucesos *mpl*; **there were strange ~s-on at the mansion** estaban pasando cosas raras en la mansión

goiter, (BrE) **goitre** /ˈɡɔɪtər || ˈɡɔɪtə(r)/ *n* [u c] bocio *m*

go-kart /ˈɡəʊkɑːrt || ˈɡəʊkɑːt/ *n* (esp BrE) ▸**kart¹**

go-karting /ˈɡəʊkɑːrtɪŋ || ˈɡəʊkɑːtɪŋ/ *n* [u] karting *m*

gold /ɡəʊld/ *n*

A **1** [u] oro *m*; (money) (monedas *fpl* de) oro *m*; ***as good as ~***: **they've been as good as ~** se han portado muy bien *or* como unos santos; ***to strike ~*** dar* con una mina de oro; ***all that glitters o glisters is not ~*** no es oro todo lo que reluce, no todo lo que brilla es oro; (*before n*) ‹*ring/medal*› de oro **2** [c u] (medal) (colloq) medalla *f* de oro

B [u] (color) dorado *m*, color *m* (de) oro

gold: **~brick** *vt* (AmE colloq) timar (fam), estafar; **~digger** *n* **1** (woman) (colloq & pej) cazafortunas *f* (fam & pey) **2** (Min) buscador, -dora *m,f* de oro; **~ dust** *n* [u] oro *m* en polvo, polvo *m* de oro; ***to be like ~ dust*** (esp BrE) ser* dificilísimo de conseguir

golden /ˈɡəʊldən/ *adj*

A **1** (made of gold) de oro **2** (in color) dorado

B **1** (happy, prosperous) ‹*years*› dorado **2** (excellent): **a ~ opportunity** una excelente oportunidad

golden: **~ age** *n* época *f* dorada, edad *f* de oro; **the G~ Age of Spanish literature** el Siglo de Oro; **~ eagle** *n* águila *f*‡ real; **~ handshake** *n* (BrE) gratificación *f* (*por fin de servicio*); **~ jubilee** *n* cincuentenario *m*; **~ oldie** /ˈəʊldi/ *n* (colloq & hum) viejo éxito *m*; **~ rule** *n* regla *f* de oro; **~ syrup** *n* (BrE) miel *f or* melaza *f* de caña (*usada en repostería*); **~ wedding (anniversary)** *n* bodas *fpl* de oro

gold: **~field** *n* yacimiento *m* de oro; **~finch** *n* (in Europe) jilguero *m*; (in North America) lugano *m*; **~fish** *n* (*pl* **-fish** *or* **-fishes**) pececito *m* (rojo); (plural) peces *mpl* de colores; **~fish bowl** *n* pecera *f* (*redonda*); **~ leaf** *n* [u] oro *m* batido, pan *m* de oro; **~ mine** *n* mina *f* de oro; **~ plate** *n* [u] (coating) baño *m* de oro; **~-plated** /ˈɡəʊldˈpleɪtəd || ,ɡəʊldˈpleɪtɪd/ *adj* chapado *or* enchapado *or* bañado en oro; **~ rush** *n* fiebre *f* del oro; **~smith** *n* orfebre *mf*

golf /ɡɑːlf || ɡɒlf/ *n* [u] golf *m*

golf: **~ ball** *n* **1** (Sport) pelota *f* de golf **2** (on typewriter) (BrE) bola *f or* esfera *f* de impresión; **~ club** *n* **1** (stick) palo *m* de golf **2** (place) club *m* de golf; **~ course** *n* campo *m or* (AmL tb) cancha *f* de golf

golfer /ˈɡɑːlfər || ˈɡɒlfə(r)/ *n* golfista *mf*

golfing /ˈɡɑːlfɪŋ || ˈɡɒlfɪŋ/ *adj* (*before n*) del (deporte del) golf; **he went on a ~ vacation** se fue de vacaciones a un lugar especial para jugar al golf

golly /ˈɡɑːli || ˈɡɒli/ *interj* (colloq & dated) ¡caray! (fam & euf), ¡recórcholis! (fam & ant)

gondola /ˈɡɑːndələ || ˈɡɒndələ/ *n* góndola *f*

gone¹ /ɡɔːn || ɡɒn/ *past p of* **go¹**

gone² *adj* (*pred*)

A **1** (not here): **my briefcase is ~!** ¡se me ha desaparecido la cartera!; **how long has she been ~?** ¿cuánto hace que se fue? **2** (past): **those days are (long) ~** de eso hace ya mucho, ha llovido mucho desde entonces; **~ are the days when one could ...** ya no se puede ... **3** (used up): **the money is all ~** se ha acabado el dinero, no queda nada de dinero **4** **far gone**: **he was too far ~ for us to**

g

be able to revive him era ya demasiado tarde para poder salvarlo; **things are too far ~ to avoid a strike** las cosas han llegado demasiado lejos, no se puede evitar la huelga; **he was pretty far ~** (drunk) (colloq) había bebido bastante más de la cuenta

B (pregnant) (colloq): **she's six months ~** está de seis meses (fam)

gone³ *prep* (BrE): **it's just ~ five** acaban de dar las cinco

goner /'gɔːnər || 'gɒnə(r)/ *n* (sl): **if you move, you're a ~** si te mueves, eres hombre muerto (fam)

gong /gɑːŋ || gɒŋ/ *n* gong *m*

gonna /gənə || 'gɒnə/ (colloq) (**= going to**) *see* **go¹** *v aux*

gonorrhea, (BrE) **gonorrhoea** /'gɑːnə'riːə || ˌgɒnə'riə/ *n* [u] gonorrea *f*

goo /guː/ *n* [u] (colloq) mugre *f*, porquería *f*; **the baby has got ~ all over his face** el niño tiene toda la cara pringada *or* (esp AmL) chorreada

good¹ /gʊd/ *adj* (*comp* **better**; *superl* **best**) [*The usual translation,* **bueno**, *becomes* **buen** *when it is used before a masculine singular noun*]

Sense I

A ‹*food/quality/book*› bueno; **it smells ~** huele bien, tiene rico *or* buen olor (AmL); **it looks ~** tiene buen aspecto; **her French is very ~** habla muy bien (el) francés; **in ~ condition** en buen estado; **this hotel is as ~ as any you'll find here** este hotel es de los mejores que hay por aquí; ***to make ~ sth***: **they undertook to make ~ the damage to the car** se comprometieron a hacerse cargo de la reparación del coche; **our losses were made ~ by the company** la compañía nos compensó las pérdidas; **to make ~ one's escape** lograr huir

B (creditable) ‹*work/progress/results*› bueno; **they've made a very ~ start** han empezado muy bien; **at least he had a ~ try** por lo menos lo intentó

C (opportune, favorable) ‹*moment/day/opportunity*› bueno; **is this a ~ time to phone?** ¿es buena hora para llamar?; **it's a ~ job nobody was listening** (colloq) menos mal que nadie estaba escuchando

D (advantageous, useful) ‹*deal/offer/advice*› bueno; **she's a ~ person to have around** es una persona que conviene tener cerca; **burn it; that's all it's ~ for** quémalo, no sirve para otra cosa; **it's a ~ idea to let them know in advance** convendría *or* no sería mala idea avisarles de antemano; **~ idea!, ~ thinking!** ¡buena idea!

E (pleasant) bueno; **to be in a ~ mood** estar* de buen humor; **I hope you have a ~ time in London** espero que te diviertas *or* que lo pases bien en Londres; **did you have a ~ flight?** ¿qué tal el vuelo?; **it's ~ to be back home** ¡qué alegría estar otra vez en casa!

F (healthy, wholesome) ‹*diet/habit/exercise*› bueno; **he is in ~ health** está bien de salud; **I'm not feeling too ~** (colloq) no me siento *or* no me encuentro muy bien; **spinach is ~ for you** las espinacas son buenas para la salud *or* son muy sanas; **he drinks more than is ~ for him** bebe demasiado *or* más de la cuenta; **she has been ~ for him** ella le ha hecho mucho bien

G (attractive): **she's got a ~ figure** tiene buena figura *or* buen tipo; **that dress looks really ~ on her** ese vestido le queda *or* le sienta muy bien

H 1 (in greetings): **~ morning** buenos días, buen día (RPl); **~ afternoon** buenas tardes; **how are you? —I'm ~** (colloq) ¿cómo estás? —estoy bien 2 (in interj phrases): **~! now to the next question** bien, pasemos ahora a la siguiente pregunta; **~ for you!** bien hecho; **~ God!** ¡Dios mío!; **~ heavens!** ¡Santo Cielo!; **~ grief/gracious!** ¡por favor!; **very ~, sir/madam** (frml) lo que mande el señor/la señora (frml) 3 (for emphasis) (colloq): **I'll do it when I'm ~ and ready** lo haré cuando me parezca; **the water's ~ and hot** el agua está bien caliente 4 **as good as**: **it's as ~ as new** está como nuevo; **he as ~ as admitted it** prácticamente lo admitió

Sense II

A (skilled, competent) bueno; **he's no ~ in emergencies** en situaciones de emergencia no sabe qué hacer; **she's very ~ in the kitchen** cocina muy bien; **to be ~ AT sth/-ING**: **to be ~ at languages** tener* facilidad para los idiomas; **he's ~ at ironing** plancha muy bien; **he is ~ with dogs/children** tiene buena mano con *or* sabe cómo tratar a los perros/los niños; **she is ~ with her hands** es muy habilidosa *or* mañosa

B (devoted, committed) bueno; **a ~ Catholic/socialist** un buen católico/socialista

C 1 (virtuous, upright) bueno; **the G~ Book** la Santa Biblia 2 (well-behaved) bueno; **be ~** sé bueno, pórtate bien; **~ boy!** ¡muy bien!

D (kind) bueno; **to be ~ TO sb**: **she was very ~ to me** fue muy amable conmigo, se portó muy bien conmigo; **it was very ~ of you to come** muchas gracias por venir; **~ old Pete** el bueno de Pete

E (decent, acceptable) bueno; **~ manners** buenos modales *mpl*; **to have a ~ reputation** tener* buena reputación

F (sound) ‹*customer/payer*› bueno; **this ticket is ~ for another week** este billete vale para una semana más; **this car's ~ for a few years yet** a este coche todavía le quedan unos cuantos años por delante

G (valid) ‹*argument/excuse*› bueno; **it's not ~ enough to say you can't do it** no basta con decir que no puedes hacerlo; **it's simply not ~ enough!** ¡esto no puede ser!, ¡esto es intolerable!

Sense III

A (substantial, considerable) ‹*meal/salary/distance*› bueno; **she's making ~ money** está haciendo mucho dinero; **there were a ~ many people there** había bastante gente *or* un buen número de personas allí

B (not less than): **it'll take a ~ hour** va a llevar su buena hora *or* una hora larga; **a ~ half of all the people interviewed** más de la mitad de los entrevistados

C (thorough, intense) ‹*rest/scolding*› bueno; **I had a ~ night's sleep** dormí bien

good² *n*

A 1 [u] (moral right) bien *m*; **to do ~** hacer* el bien; **there is some ~ in everyone** todos tenemos algo bueno; **to be up to no ~** (colloq) estar* tramando algo, traerse* algo entre manos 2 (people) **the ~** (+ *pl vb*) los buenos

B [u] 1 (benefit) bien *m*; **for the ~ of sb/sth** por el bien de algn/algo; **no ~ will come of it** nada bueno saldrá de ello; **to do sb/sth ~** hacerle* bien a algn/algo; **lying won't do you any ~ at all** mentir no te llevará a ninguna parte, no ganarás *or* no sacarás nada con mentir 2 (use): **this knife is no ~ (at all)** este cuchillo no sirve (para nada); **are you any ~ at drawing?** ¿sabes dibujar?; **this book is no ~** este libro no vale nada 3 (in phrases): **for good** para siempre

C goods *pl* 1 (merchandise) artículos *mpl*, mercancías *fpl*, mercaderías *fpl* (AmS); **manufactured ~s** productos *mpl* manufacturados, manufacturas *fpl*; ***to come up with*** *o* ***deliver the ~s*** (colloq) cumplir con lo prometido; (*before n*) ‹*train/wagon*› (BrE) de carga; ‹*depot*› de mercancías, de mercaderías (AmS) 2 (property) (frml) bienes *mpl*; **all his worldly ~s** todas sus posesiones

good³ *adv*

A (*as intensifier*): **it's been a ~ long while since ...** ha pasado su buen tiempo desde ...; **you messed that up ~ and proper, didn't you?** (BrE colloq) metiste bien la pata, ¿no? (fam)

B (AmE colloq) (well, thoroughly) bien

goodbye¹, (AmE also) **goodby** /gʊd'baɪ/ *interj* ¡adiós!, ¡chao! *or* ¡chau! (esp AmL)

goodbye², (AmE also) **goodby** *n*: **to say ~ to sb** decirle* adiós a algn; **they waved us ~** nos hicieron adiós con la mano; **they kissed me ~** me despidieron con un beso; **to say one's ~s** despedirse*; ***to say*** *o* ***kiss ~ to sth*** decirle* adiós a algo, despedirse* de algo

good-for-nothing¹ /'gʊdfər'nʌθɪŋ || 'gʊdfəˌnʌθɪŋ/ *n* inútil *mf*, gandul, gandula *m,f*

good-for-nothing² *adj* que no sirve para nada, inútil

good: **~ Friday** *n* Viernes *m* Santo; **~-humored**, (BrE) **~-humoured** /'gʊd'hjuːmərd || ˌgʊd'hjuːməd/ *adj* ‹*person*› (permanent characteristic) alegre, jovial; (in good mood) de buen humor; ‹*joke*› sin mala intención; **~-looking** /'gʊd'lʊkɪŋ/ *adj* ‹*man*› buen mozo (esp AmL), guapo (esp Esp); **a ~looking woman** una mujer bonita *or* (esp Esp) guapa; **~-luck** /'gʊd'lʌk/ *adj*: **~-luck charm** amuleto *m*, talismán *m* (*de la buena suerte*); **~-natured** /'gʊd 'neɪtʃərd || ˌgʊd'neɪtʃəd/ *adj* (as permanent characteristic) bueno, de natural bondadoso; **he was remarkably ~-natured about it** se lo tomó muy bien

goodness /'gʊdnəs || 'gʊdnɪs/ *n* [u]

A 1 (moral worth) bondad *f*; **he did it out of the ~ of his**

heart lo hizo de lo bondadoso *or* bueno que es 2 (of food) valor *m* nutritivo

B (*in interj phrases, as intensifier*): **(my) ~!** ¡Dios (mío)!; **~ me/ gracious!** ¡Dios mío!, ¡válgame Dios!; **I hope to ~ he'll be all right** ojalá *or* Dios quiera que no le pase nada; ▸**sake 3, thank 3**

good: **~night** /'gʊd'naɪt/ *n* buenas noches *fpl*; **~ practice** *n* [u] prácticas *fpl* recomendables; **it's ~ practice** es una práctica recomendable; **~ Samaritan** *n* buen samaritano, buena samaritana *m,f*; **~-sized** /'gʊd 'saɪzd/ *adj* grande, de buen tamaño; **~will** /'gʊd'wɪl/ *n* [u] 1 (benevolence) buena voluntad *f*; (*before n*) ‹*mission/ gesture*› conciliador 2 (Busn, Fin) fondo *m* de comercio, llave *f* (CS)

goody¹ /'gʊdi/ *n* (*pl* **-dies**) (colloq)

A **goodies** *pl* (food) cosas *fpl* ricas

B (hero) bueno, -na *m,f* (fam)

goody² *interj* (used esp by children) ¡viva! (fam), ¡yupi! (fam)

goody-goody /'gʊdi,gʊdi/ *n* (*pl* **goody-goodies**) (colloq & pej) santito, -ta *m,f* (fam y pey)

gooey /'gu:i/ *adj* **gooier, gooiest** (colloq) (sticky) pegajoso; (sentimental) empalagoso, sensiblero

goof¹ /gu:f/ *n* (sl) (blunder) pifia *f* (fam), embarrada *f* (AmS fam)

goof² *vi* (sl) pifiarla (fam), embarrarla (AmS fam), regarla* (Méx fam)

Phrasal verbs

- **goof around** [v ▸ adv] (AmE colloq) gansear (fam)
- **goof off** [v ▸ adv] (AmE colloq) holgazanear, flojear
- **goof up** [v ▸ o ▸ adv, v ▸ adv ▸ o] (esp AmE colloq) arruinar, fastidiar (Esp fam)

goofball /'gu:fbɔ:l/ *n* (AmE sl) memo, -ma *m,f* (fam)

goof-up /'gu:fʌp/ *n* (AmE colloq) metedura *f or* (AmL) metida *f* de pata

goofy /'gu:fi/ *adj* **-fier, -fiest** (sl) (AmE) (stupid) ‹*person*› memo (fam), tontorrón (fam); ‹*smile*› bobalicón (fam)

Google® *vt* (colloq) googlear (fam)

■ /'gu:gl/ *vi* **~ FOR sth** googlear PARA algo

goon /gu:n/ *n* (colloq)

A (silly person) ganso, -sa *m,f* (fam)

B (AmE) (thug) matón *m*, guarura *m* (Méx)

goose /gu:s/ *n* (*pl* **geese**) 1 [c] (Zool) oca *f*, ganso *m*; ***to cook sb's ~***: **that's cooked his ~** eso le servirá de lección; ***to kill the ~ that lays the golden egg(s)*** matar la gallina de los huevos de oro 2 [u] (Culin) ganso *m*

goose: **~berry** /'gu:s,beri || 'gʊzbəri/ *n* (Bot) 1 (berry) grosella *f* espinosa, uva *f* espina 2 **~berry (bush)** grosellero *m* espinoso; **I found him/her under a ~berry bush** (BrE euph *or* hum) lo/la trajo la cigüeña (euf *o* hum); 3 (unwanted third person) (BrE colloq) carabina *f* (fam), chaperón, -rona *m,f*, violinista *mf* (Chi fam); **to play ~berry** hacer* de carabina (Esp fam), tocar* el violín (Chi fam); **~ bumps** *pl n* (AmE colloq), **~flesh** *n*, **~ pimples** *pl n* carne *f* de gallina

gopher /'gəʊfər || 'gəʊfə(r)/ *n*

A (Zool) 1 (rodent) taltuza *f* 2 (ground squirrel) ardilla *f* de tierra

B (AmE) ▸**gofer**

gore¹ /gɔ:r || gɔ:(r)/ *n* [u] (blood) sangre *f* (*derramada*)

gore² *vt* cornear

gorge¹ /gɔ:rdʒ || gɔ:dʒ/ *n*

A (ravine) (Geog) desfiladero *m*, cañón *m*

B (throat) (arch): ***to make sb's ~ rise*** (liter) producirle* náuseas a algn

gorge² *v refl* **to ~ oneself** atiborrarse *or* (fam) atracarse* de comida; **to ~ oneself ON** *o* **WITH sth** atiborrarse DE algo, pegarse* un atracón DE algo (fam)

gorgeous /'gɔ:rdʒəs || 'gɔ:dʒəs/ *adj* 1 (lovely) (colloq) ‹*girl*› precioso, guapísimo; ‹*dress*› precioso, divino; ‹*day*› maravilloso, espléndido 2 (splendid) ‹*color*› magnífico

gorgeously /'gɔ:rdʒəsli || 'gɔ:dʒəsli/ *adv* (sumptuously) ‹*arrayed*› magníficamente, suntuosamente

gorgon /'gɔ:rgən || 'gɔ:gən/ *n* 1 **Gorgon** (Myth) gorgona *f* 2 (fierce woman) arpía *f*

gorilla /gə'rɪlə/ *n* gorila *m*

gormless /'gɔ:rmləs || 'gɔ:mlɪs/ *adj* (BrE colloq) idiota, corto (de entendederas) (fam)

gorse /gɔ:rs || 'gɔ:s/ *n* [u] aulaga *f*, tojo *m*

gory /'gɔ:ri/ *adj* **gorier, goriest** (sensational, violent) (colloq) ‹*scene*› sangriento; **I won't go into all the ~ details** no voy a entrar en detalles morbosos

gosh /gɑ:ʃ || gɒʃ/ *interj* (colloq) ¡(mi) Dios!, ¡Dios mío!

goshawk /'gɑ:shɔ:k || 'gɒshɔ:k/ *n* azor *m*

gosling /'gɑ:zlɪŋ || 'gɒzlɪŋ/ *n* ansarino *m* (*cría de la oca*)

go-slow /'gəʊsləʊ/ *n* (BrE) huelga *f* pasiva, trabajo *m* a reglamento (CS), huelga *f* de celo (Esp)

gospel /'gɑ:spəl || 'gɒspəl/ *n*

A [c] **Gospel** (Bib, Relig) (in New Testament) evangelio *m*

B 1 (Christian teaching) (*no pl*) Evangelio *m*; **to preach/ spread the ~** predicar*/difundir el Evangelio; (*before n*) ‹*temple/minister*› (in US) evangelista 2 [c] (doctrine) doctrina *f*, evangelio *m* 3 [u] **~ (truth)** (colloq): **he takes everything she says as ~ (truth)** para él, todo lo que dice ella es santa palabra; **it's ~ (truth)** es la pura verdad

C [u] **~ (music)** (Mus) gospel *m*

gossamer /'gɑ:səmər || 'gɒsəmə(r)/ *n* [u] (liter) telaraña *f*; (*before n*) ‹*threads*› tenue, sutil

gossip¹ /'gɑ:səp || 'gɒsɪp/ *n* 1 [u] (speculation, scandal) chismorreo *m* (fam), cotilleo *m* (Esp fam); **it's just idle ~** sólo son habladurías; **an interesting piece of ~** un chisme interesante; (*before n*) **~ column** crónica *f* de sociedad; **~ columnist** cronista *mf* de sociedad 2 [c u] (chat): **to have a ~ with sb** chismorrear (fam) *or* (Esp tb) cotillear con algn 3 [c] (person) chismoso, -sa *m,f* (fam), cotilla *mf* (Esp fam)

gossip² *vi* 1 (chatter) chismorrear (fam), cotillear (Esp fam) 2 (spread tales) contar* chismes

gossipy /'gɑ:səpi || 'gɒsɪpɪ/ *adj* 1 ‹*magazine*› de chismografía (fam); **a ~ letter** una carta llena de chismes 2 ‹*person*› chismoso (fam)

got /gɑ:t || gɒt/

A *past & past p of* **get**

B (crit) *pres of* **have**

Goth /gɑ:θ || gɒθ/ *n* godo, -da *m,f*

Gothic /'gɑ:θɪk || 'gɒθɪk/ *adj* (Archit, Lit) gótico

gotta /'gɑ:tə || 'gɒtə/ (sl) (**= have got to**): **I ~ go** me tengo que ir

gotten /'gɑ:tn̩ || 'gɒtn̩/ (AmE) *past p of* **get**

gouge /gaʊdʒ/ *vt* (cut out) ‹*hole*› abrir*, hacer*

Phrasal verb

- **gouge out** [v ▸ o ▸ adv, v ▸ adv ▸ o] sacar*, arrancar*

gourd /gʊrd, gɔ:rd || gʊəd/ *n* (Bot) calabaza *f*, jícaro *m* (AmC, Col, Méx)

gourmand /'gʊrmɑ:nd || 'gʊəmənd/ *n* (frml) 1 (heavy eater) glotón, -tona *m,f* 2 ▸**gourmet**

gourmet /'gʊrmeɪ || 'gʊəmeɪ/ *n* gourmet *mf*, gastrónomo, -ma *m,f*

gout /gaʊt/ *n* [u] gota *f*

Gov (US title) **= Governor**

govern /'gʌvərn || 'gʌvən/ *vt*

A 1 (rule) gobernar* 2 (determine) determinar; **the laws ~ing trade practices** las leyes que regulan la práctica comercial 3 **governing** *pres p* ‹*party*› de gobierno; ‹*principle*› rector; **~ing body** organismo *m* rector

B (Ling) ‹*case*› regir*

■ **govern** *vi* gobernar*

governess /'gʌvərnəs/ *n* institutriz *f*, gobernanta *f*

government /'gʌvərnmənt || 'gʌvənmənt/ *n* 1 [u] (permanent structure) gobierno *m*, estado *m*; **to be in ~** (BrE) estar* en el poder 2 [u c] (administration) gobierno *m*, régimen *m*; **~ owned** estatal, del Estado, público; (*before n*) **~ department** ministerio *m or* (Méx) secretaría *f*; **~ policy** política *f* gubernamental

governmental /'gʌvərn'mentl̩ || ,gʌvən'mentl̩/ *adj* 1 (of government) ‹*system*› de gobierno 2 (by government) ‹*interference*› gubernamental, estatal

government issue *adj* (esp AmE) ‹*equipment*› de dotación estatal; ‹*stock*› del Estado, del Tesoro

governor /'gʌvənər || 'gʌvənə(r)/ *n*

A (of state, province, colony) gobernador, -dora *m,f*

B (of institution): **prison ~** (BrE) director, -tora *m,f* (*de una cárcel*); **school ~** (BrE) *miembro de un consejo escolar*

Governor General *n* 1 (in British Commonwealth) Gobernador, -dora *m,f* General 2 (chief administrator) (BrE) director, -tora *m,f* general

govt = government

gown /gaʊn/ *n*

A 1 (dress) vestido *m*; **evening/wedding ~** traje *m* de fiesta/novia 2 (*night~*) (AmE) camisón *m*

B 1 (Educ, Law) toga *f* 2 (Med) bata *f*

GP *n* (= **general practitioner**) médico, -ca *m,f* de medicina general; **my/his ~** mi/su médico de cabecera

GPO *n* 1 (in US) = **Government Printing Office** 2 (in US, formerly in UK) = **General Post Office**

gr (= **gram(s)**) gr., g.

grab¹ /græb/ **-bb-** *vt* 1 (seize) ‹*rope/hand*› agarrar; ‹*chance*› aprovechar; **he ~bed me by the arm** me agarró del brazo 2 (appropriate) ‹*land*› apropiarse de, apoderarse de; ‹*money*› llevarse 3 (eat, take hurriedly) (colloq): **I'll just ~ a hamburger somewhere** me comeré una hamburguesa en algún sitio por ahí; **~ a seat** agárrate un asiento (AmL fam), coge asiento (Esp) 4 (appeal to) (colloq) «*idea*» atraer*; **how does that ~ you?** ¿qué te parece?

■ **grab** *vi*: **don't ~, wait your turn** no arrebates, espera que te toque a ti; **to ~ AT sth**: **she ~bed at the rope** trató de agarrar la cuerda

grab² *n* (snatch): **to make a ~ for sth** tratar de agarrar algo; ***up for ~s*** (colloq): **the job is up for ~s** el puesto está vacante *or* libre

grace¹ /greɪs/ *n*

A [u] (elegance — of movement) gracia *f*, garbo *m*; (— of expression, form) elegancia *f*

B 1 [u] (courtesy) cortesía *f*, gentileza *f* 2 [u] (good nature): **to do sth with (a) good/bad ~** hacer* algo de buen talante/a regañadientes; **in good ~** (AmE) con la conciencia tranquila 3 [c] (good quality): **her saving ~ is her sense of humor** lo que la salva es que tiene sentido del humor; **social ~s** modales *mpl*

C [u] (Relig) 1 (mercy) gracia *f*; **by the ~ of God ...** gracias a Dios ...; ***to fall from ~*** (lose favor) caer* en desgracia, (Relig) perder* la gracia divina 2 (prayer): **to say ~** (before a meal) bendecir* la mesa; (after a meal) dar* las gracias por la comida

D [u] (respite) gracia *f*; **16 days' ~, 16 days of ~** (BrE Law) 16 días de gracia

E [c] (as title): **his G~ the Archbishop of York** Su Eminencia el Arzobispo de York; **Your G~** (to duke etc) Excelencia; (to bishop) Ilustrísima

grace² *vt* (liter) adornar; **she ~d the event with her presence** honró el acto con su presencia

graceful /'greɪsfəl/ *adj* 1 ‹*dancer/movement*› lleno de gracia, grácil (liter); ‹*style*› elegante 2 ‹*apology*› digno

gracefully /'greɪsfəli/ *adv* ‹*move/dance*› con gracia *or* garbo, con gracilidad (liter)

gracefulness /'greɪsfəlnəs || 'greɪsfəlnɪs/ *n* [u] (of movement) gracia *f*, gracilidad *f* (liter)

graceless /'greɪsləs || 'greɪslɪs/ *adj* 1 (ill-mannered) tosco, descortés 2 (inelegant) desgarbado, poco elegante

gracious¹ /'greɪʃəs/ *adj*

A 1 ‹*smile/act*› gentil, cortés 2 (merciful) misericordioso

B ‹*lifestyle*› refinado, elegante

gracious² *interj*: **(good** *o* **goodness) ~!** ¡Dios Santo!, ¡válgame Dios!

graciously /'greɪʃəsli/ *adv*

A 1 ‹*smile/apologize*› gentilmente 2 (generously) (frml): **His Royal Highness has ~ agreed to ...** Su Alteza ha tenido la deferencia de acceder a ...

B ‹*live*› con elegancia

grad /græd/ *n* (AmE colloq) ▸ **graduate²**

gradation /greɪ'deɪʃən || grə'deɪʃən/ *n* [c u] (frml) gradación *f*

grade¹ /greɪd/ *n*

A 1 (quality) calidad *f*; (degree, level): **it divides hotels into four ~s** divide a los hoteles en cuatro categorías; **~ A** *o* **~ 1 tomatoes** tomates *mpl* de la mejor calidad *or* de primera 2 (in seniority) grado *m* (*del escalafón*); (Mil) rango *m*; ***to make the ~*** (colloq) (reach required level) alcanzar* el nivel requerido/necesario; (succeed) tener* éxito, triunfar

B (Educ) 1 (class) (AmE) grado *m*, año *m*, curso *m* 2 (in exam) nota *f*, calificación *f*

C (gradient) (AmE) cuesta *f*

grade² *vt*

A 1 (classify) clasificar* 2 (order in ascending scale) ‹*exercise/questions*› ordenar por grado de dificultad 3 (mark) (AmE) ‹*test/exercise*› corregir* y calificar*; **I've ~d her B** le puse una B 4 **graded** *past p* ‹*produce*› clasificado; ‹*tests/exercises*› (BrE) escalonados por grado de dificultad

B (make more level) ‹*surface/soil*› (AmE) nivelar

grade crossing *n* (AmE) paso *m* a nivel, crucero *m* (Méx)

grader /'greɪdər || 'greɪdə(r)/ *n* (student) (AmE): **a sixth ~** un alumno de sexto grado *or* año

grade school *n* (AmE) escuela *f* primaria

gradient /'greɪdiənt/ *n* 1 (slope) pendiente *f*, gradiente *f* (AmL) 2 (Math, Phys) gradiente *m*

grading /'greɪdɪŋ/ *n* 1 [c u] (classification) clasificación *f* 2 [u] (AmE Educ) calificación *f*

gradual /'grædʒuəl/ *adj* ‹*improvement*› gradual, paulatino; ‹*slope*› no muy empinado

gradually /'grædʒuəli/ *adv* ‹*improve*› gradualmente, paulatinamente, poco a poco; ‹*rise/slope*› suavemente

graduate¹ /'grædʒueɪt/ *vi*

A (Educ) 1 (from a college, university) terminar la carrera, recibirse (AmL), graduarse*; (obtain bachelor's degree) licenciarse; **she ~d from Cambridge in 1974** se licenció en *or* (Esp) por la Universidad de Cambridge en 1974 2 (from high school) (AmE) terminar el bachillerato, recibirse de bachiller (AmL)

B (progress) **to ~ (FROM sth) TO sth** pasar (DE algo) A algo

■ **graduate** *vt*

A 1 ‹*flask/test tube*› (frml) graduar* 2 ‹*payments/contributions*› escalonar

B (Educ) (AmE) ‹*student*› conferirle* el título a

graduate² /'grædʒuət/ *n* 1 (from higher education) *persona con título universitario*; (with a bachelor's degree) licenciado, -da *m,f*; (*before n*) ‹*course/student*› de posgrado *or* postgrado; **he went to ~ school** (AmE) hizo un curso de posgrado 2 (from high school) (AmE) bachiller *mf*

graduated /'grædʒueɪtəd || 'grædʒueɪtɪd/ *adj* 1 (progressive) ‹*scale*› graduado; ‹*payments*› escalonado 2 (calibrated) ‹*flask/test tube*› graduado

graduation /'grædʒu'eɪʃən/ *n* [u] (Educ) (graduating) graduación *f*; (ceremony) graduación *f*, ceremonia *f* de graduación *or* de entrega de títulos; (from high school) (AmE) graduación *f* (*ceremonia celebrada al finalizar el bachillerato en EEUU*)

graffiti /grə'fi:ti/ *n* (+ *sing o pl vb*) graffiti *mpl*

graft¹ /græft || grɑ:ft/ *vt* (Hort) injertar

■ **graft** *vi* (work hard) (BrE colloq) reventarse* trabajando (fam), currar (Esp fam), camellar (Col fam), laburar como loco (RPl arg), chambearle duro (Méx fam)

graft² *n*

A [c] (Hort, Med) injerto *m*

B [u] (bribery, corruption) (AmE colloq) chanchullos *mpl* (fam)

C [u] (hard work) (BrE colloq): **it's been hard ~** ha sido mucho trabajo, ha habido que currar *or* (Col) camellar un montón (fam), hubo que chambearle duro (Méx fam), fue un laburo bárbaro (RPl arg), ha sido mucha pega (Andes fam)

grafter /'græftər || 'grɑ:ftə(r)/ *n*

A (corrupt person) (AmE colloq) chanchullero *m* (fam)

B (hard worker) (BrE colloq) persona *f* trabajadora

graham cracker /'greɪəm/ *n* (AmE) galleta *f* integral, Granola® *f* (Esp)

grail /greɪl/ *n* (*holy ~*) (santo) grial *m*

grain /greɪn/ *n*

A [c] (of cereal, salt, sugar, sand) grano *m*; **there's not a ~ of truth in what he says** no hay ni pizca de verdad en lo que dice; ▸ **salt¹ 1**

B [u] (Agr) grano *m*, cereal *m*

C [u] (of wood — pattern) veta *f*, veteado *m*; (— texture) grano *m*; **against the ~** (in carpentry) contra el hilo; ***to go against the ~***: **it goes against the ~ for me to support them** apoyarlos va en contra de mis principios

grainy /'greɪni/ *adj* **-nier, -niest** 1 ‹*surface/wood*› veteado 2 ‹*photograph*› en que se nota mucho el grano

gram, (BrE also) **gramme** /græm/ *n* gramo *m*

grammar /'græmər || 'græmə(r)/ *n* 1 [u] gramática *f* 2 [c] **~ (book)** gramática *f*

grammarian /grə'meriən || grə'meəriən/ *n* gramático, -ca *m,f*

grammar school *n* 1 (in US) ▸ **elementary school** 2 (in UK) *colegio de enseñanza secundaria para ingresar al cual hay que aprobar un examen de aptitud*

g

grammatical /grə'mætɪkəl/ *adj* 1 (of grammar) gramatical 2 (correct) gramaticalmente correcto

grammatically /grə'mætɪkli/ *adv* 1 ‹*correct*› gramaticalmente 2 (correctly) ‹*speak/write*› correctamente

gramme /græm/ *n* (BrE) ▸ **gram**

gramophone /'græməfəʊn/ *n* (BrE dated) gramófono *m* (ant)

gramps /græmps/ *n* (AmE colloq) abuelo *m*

gran /græn/ *n* (BrE colloq) abuela *f*, nana *f*, yaya *f* (esp Esp)

granary /'greɪnəri, 'grænəri || 'grænəri/ *n* (*pl* **-ries**) granero *m*

Granary® *adj* ‹*bread/flour*› *con granos de trigo malteado*

grand[1] /grænd/ *adj* **-er, -est**

A 1 (impressive) magnífico, espléndido; **on a ~ scale** en gran escala 2 (ostentatious) ‹*gesture*› grandilocuente; ‹*entrance*› triunfal 3 (ambitious, lofty) ‹*vision*› grandioso; ‹*ideal*› elevado 4 (overall) (*before n, no comp*) global; **the ~ total** el total

B 1 (formal, ceremonial) ‹*opening/occasion*› solemne 2 (socially important) (*sing*) gran (*delante del n*); (*pl*) grandes (*delante del n*)

C (very good) (colloq) ‹*day/weather*› espléndido, fabuloso

grand[2] *n*

A (piano) piano *m* de cola; **baby ~** piano *m* de media cola

B (*pl* **grand**) (1000 dollars, pounds) (sl): **he paid six ~ for the car** el coche le costó seis mil

grandad /'grændæd/ *n* abuelo *m*

grand: **~ Canyon** *n* **the G~ Canyon** el Cañón del Colorado; **~child** /'græntʃaɪld/ *n* nieto, -ta *m,f*; **~dad** /'grændæd/ *n* abuelo *m*; **~daddy** /'græn,dædi/ *n* 1 (grandfather) (colloq) abuelito *m* (fam) 2 (first example) (hum): **the ~daddy of sth** el padre de algo; **~daughter** /'græn,dɔːtər || 'græn,dɔːtə(r)/ *n* nieta *f*

grandeur /'grændʒər || 'grændʒə(r)/ *n* [u] grandiosidad *f*, esplendor *m*

grandfather /'græn,fɑːðər || 'græn,fɑːðə(r)/ *n* abuelo *m*; (*before n*) **~ clock** reloj *m* de pie

grandiloquent /græn'dɪləkwənt/ *adj* (frml) grandilocuente

grandiose /'grændiəʊs/ *adj* ‹*claim/scheme/notion*› fatuo, presuntuoso; ‹*speech*› altisonante, grandilocuente

grand jury *n* (in US) jurado *m* de acusación (*jurado que decide si hay suficientes pruebas para procesar*)

grandly /'grændli/ *adv* 1 (impressively) ‹*conceived/planned*› grandiosamente 2 (self-importantly, pompously) ‹*walk/announce*› presuntuosamente

grand: **~ma** /'grænmɑː/ *n* (colloq) abuela *f*; **~mother** /'græn,mʌðər || 'græn,mʌðə(r)/ *n* abuela *f*; ***to teach one's ~mother to suck eggs*** (colloq): **don't teach your ~mother to suck eggs** ¿le estás queriendo enseñar a tu papá a ser hijo? (fam), ¡a mí me lo vas a decir!; **~pa** /'grænpɑː/ *n* abuelo *m*; **~parent** /'græn,perənt || 'græn,peərənt/ *n* abuelo, -la *m,f*; **my ~parents** mis abuelos; **~ piano** *n* piano *m* de cola; **~ Prix** /'grɑːn'priː/ *n* (*pl* **G~ Prix** *or* (AmE also) **G~s Prix** /-z/) Grand Prix *m*, Gran Premio *m*; **~ slam** *n* 1 (in bridge, golf, tennis) gran slam *m* 2 (in baseball) ▸ **grandslammer**; **~slammer** /'grænd'slæmər || ,grænd'slæmə(r)/ *n* jonrón *m* con casa llena, jonrón *m* barrebases; **~son** /'grænsʌn/ *n* nieto *m*

grandstand[1] /'grænstænd/ *n* tribuna *f*; (*before n*) ‹*ticket/seat*› de tribuna

grandstand[2] *vi* (AmE colloq) pavonearse (fam), fardar (Esp fam)

granite /'grænət || 'grænɪt/ *n* [u] granito *m*

granny, grannie /'græni/ *n* (*pl* **-nies**) abuelita *f* (fam)

grant[1] /grænt || grɑːnt/ *vt*

A 1 ‹*desire/request*› conceder 2 ‹*interview/asylum*› conceder 3 ‹*land/pension*› otorgar*, conceder

B (admit) reconocer*

C **granted** *past p* (admittedly): **~ed, it's very expensive, but ...** de acuerdo, es muy caro, pero ...; ***to take sth for ~ed*** dar* algo por sentado *or* por descontado

grant[2] *n* (subsidy — to body, individual) subvención *f*, subsidio *m* (AmL); (— to student) (esp BrE) beca *f*

granular /'grænjələr || 'grænjʊlə(r)/ *adj* granular

granulated /'grænjəleɪtəd || 'grænjʊleɪtɪd/ *adj*: **~ sugar** azúcar *f* granulada, azúcar *m* granulado

granule /'grænjuːl/ *n* gránulo *m*

grape /greɪp/ *n* (fruit) uva *f*; **it's sour ~s** (set phrase) las uvas están verdes (fr hecha); (*before n*) **the ~ harvest** la vendimia

grape: **~fruit** *n* (*pl* **-fruit** *or* **-fruits**) toronja *f* (AmL exc CS), pomelo *m* (CS, Esp); **~shot** *n* [u] metralla *f*; **~vine** *n* 1 (Agr, Bot) parra *f* 2 (source of information) (colloq): **I heard it on** *o* **through the ~vine** me lo dijo un pajarito (fam), lo he escuchado en radio macuto (Esp fam)

graph /græf || grɑːf/ *n* gráfico *m*, gráfica *f*

graphic /'græfɪk/ *adj*

A (vivid) ‹*account/description*› muy gráfico, vívido; **in ~ detail** con todo lujo de detalles

B (Art) gráfico; **~ design** diseño *m* gráfico

graphically /'græfɪkli/ *adv* ‹*describe*› gráficamente

graphic equalizer *n* ecualizador *m* gráfico

graphics /'græfɪks/ *pl n*

A (graphic design) (+ *pl vb*) diseño *m* gráfico

B (Comput) gráficos *mpl*; (*before n*) **~ card** tarjeta *f* gráfica

graphite /'græfaɪt/ *n* [u] grafito *m*

graph paper *n* [u] papel *m* milimetrado *or* (Méx) cuadriculado

grapple /'græpl/ *vi* **to ~ (WITH sb/sth)** (physically) forcejear (CON algn/algo); (mentally) luchar *or* lidiar CON algo; **to ~ with one's conscience** tener* escrúpulos de conciencia

grasp[1] /græsp || grɑːsp/ *vt*

A 1 (seize) ‹*object/person*› agarrar; ‹*opportunity/offer*› aprovechar 2 (hold tightly) tener* agarrado

B (understand) ‹*concept*› captar

■ **grasp** *vi* **to ~ AT sth** tratar de agarrar algo; **to ~ at an opportunity** aprovechar una oportunidad

grasp[2] *n* (*no pl*)

A 1 (grip): **his ~ on my arm tightened, he tightened his ~ on my arm** me apretó más el brazo 2 (reach) alcance *m*; **victory is (with)in our ~** la victoria está a nuestro alcance

B (understanding) comprensión *f*; (knowledge) conocimientos *mpl*; **she has a good ~ of the subject** tiene conocimientos sólidos del tema

grasping /'græspɪŋ || 'grɑːspɪŋ/ *adj* avaricioso, codicioso

grass[1] /græs || grɑːs/ *n*

A 1 [u] (as pasture) pasto *m*, zacate *m* (Méx); (lawn) césped *m*, hierba *f*, pasto *m* (AmL), grama (AmC, Ven); **to cut the ~** cortar el césped *or* la hierba *or* (AmL tb) el pasto *or* (AmC, Ven) la grama; ***to allow the ~ to grow under one's feet*** (*usu neg*) quedarse dormido; ***the ~ is always greener on the other side*** nadie está contento con su suerte; (*before n*) **~ court** cancha *f* de pasto (AmL), pista *f* de hierba (Esp) 2 [c u] (Bot) hierba *f* 3 [u] (dried) paja *f*

B [u] (marijuana) (sl) hierba *f* (arg), maría *f* (arg), monte *m* (AmC, Col, Ven arg), mota *f* (Méx arg)

C [c] (informer) (BrE colloq) soplón, -plona *m,f* (fam)

grass[2] *vi* (BrE colloq) soplar (fam), chivarse (Esp fam); **to ~ ON sb** delatar a algn

grass: **~hopper** /'græs,hɑːpər || 'grɑːs,hɒpə(r)/ *n* saltamontes *m*; **~ roots** *pl n* (ordinary members) **the ~ roots** las bases; (*before n*) ‹*support/opinion*› de las bases; **at ~ roots level** a nivel de las bases; **~ widow** *n* viuda *f* de verano

grassy /'græsi || 'grɑːsi/ *adj* **-sier, -siest** cubierto de hierba

grate[1] /greɪt/ *vt* (Culin) rallar; **~d cheese** queso *m* rallado

■ **grate** *vi* 1 (irritate) ser* crispante; **to ~ ON sth**: **his voice ~s on the ear** su voz hace daño al oído; **his laugh really ~s on my nerves** su risa me crispa los nervios 2 (make harsh noise) chirriar*

grate[2] *n* (fireplace) chimenea *f*; (metal frame in fireplace) rejilla *f*

grateful /'greɪtfəl/ *adj* agradecido; ‹*smile*› de gratitud *or* agradecimiento, agradecido; **to be ~ (TO sb) (FOR sth/-ING)**: **I'm very ~ to you for your advice** le agradezco mucho sus consejos, le estoy muy agradecido por sus consejos; **just be ~ for what you've got!** ¡da gracias (a Dios) por lo que tienes!

gratefully /'greɪtfəli/ *adv* ‹*accept*› con gratitud; **he smiled ~** sonrió agradecido

grater /'greɪtər || 'greɪtə(r)/ *n* rallador *m*

gratification /ˈgrætəfəˈkeɪʃən || ˌgrætɪfɪˈkeɪʃən/ *n* [u] gratificación *f*, satisfacción *f*

gratified /ˈgrætəfaɪd || ˈgrætɪfaɪd/ *adj* **to be ~ AT** *o* **BY sth** estar* satisfecho CON algo

gratify /ˈgrætəfaɪ || ˈgrætɪfaɪ/ *vt* **-fies, -fying, -fied** [1] (fulfill) satisfacer* [2] (give satisfaction) complacer*

gratifying /ˈgrætəfaɪɪŋ || ˈgrætɪfaɪɪŋ/ *adj* ‹*sight/feeling*› grato; ‹*task*› gratificante, gratificador (AmL)

grating¹ /ˈgreɪtɪŋ/ *adj* [1] (harsh) ‹*noise/sound*› chirriante [2] (irritating) crispante

grating² *n* rejilla *f*

gratitude /ˈgrætətuːd || ˈgrætɪtjuːd/ *n* [u] gratitud *f*, agradecimiento *m*

gratuitous /grəˈtuːətəs || grəˈtjuːɪtəs/ *adj* (pej) gratuito

gratuity /grəˈtuːəti || grəˈtjuːəti/ *n* (*pl* **-ties**) (frml) [1] (tip) propina *f* [2] (payment for long service) (esp BrE) gratificación *f*

grave¹ /greɪv/ *adj* **graver, gravest**
[A] ‹*error/danger/voice*› grave; **you do me a ~ injustice** estás cometiendo una grave injusticia conmigo
[B] /grɑːv/ (Ling) ‹*accent*› grave

grave² *n* tumba *f*, sepultura *f*; ***as quiet*** *o* ***silent as the ~*** como una tumba; ***to dig one's own ~*** cavarse su (*or* mi *etc*) propia tumba; ***to turn in one's ~***: **your father must be turning in his ~** si tu padre levantara la cabeza ...

gravedigger /ˈgreɪvˌdɪgər || ˈgreɪvˌdɪgə(r)/ *n* sepulturero, -ra *m,f*, enterrador, -dora *m,f*

gravel /ˈgrævəl/ *n* [u] (stone chips — coarse) grava *f*; (— fine) gravilla *f*; (*before n*) **~ pit** gravera *f*

gravelly /ˈgrævəli/ *adj* ‹*beach*› de grava; ‹*soil*› pedregoso; ‹*voice*› bronco, áspero

gravely /ˈgreɪvli/ *adv* [1] (seriously) gravemente; **he is ~ ill** está gravemente enfermo, está grave; **you are ~ mistaken** estás muy equivocado, cometes un grave error [2] (solemnly) con gravedad

graven /ˈgreɪvən/ *adj* (arch *or* liter) tallado, esculpido

grave: **~side** *n*: **prayers were read at the ~side** se leyeron oraciones junto a la tumba; **~stone** *n* lápida *f*; **~yard** *n* cementerio *m*, panteón *m* (Méx)

gravitate /ˈgrævəteɪt || ˈgrævɪteɪt/ *vi* **to ~ TOWARD** *o* **TO sth/sb**: **young people tend to ~ toward the big cities** las grandes ciudades son un polo de atracción para los jóvenes; **people of similar interests naturally ~ toward each other** uno tiende a acercarse a gente con intereses afines

gravitation /ˈgrævəˈteɪʃən || ˌgrævɪˈteɪʃən/ *n* [u] (Phys) gravitación *f*; **the ~ of the rural population toward the cities** la tendencia de la población rural a desplazarse hacia las ciudades

gravitational /ˈgrævəˈteɪʃn̩əl || ˌgrævɪˈteɪʃənl̩/ *adj* gravitacional

gravity /ˈgrævəti/ *n* [u]
[A] (Phys) gravedad *f*; **the force of ~** la fuerza de la gravedad
[B] (seriousness) gravedad *f*

gravy /ˈgreɪvi/ *n* [u] (Culin) *salsa hecha con el jugo de la carne asada*; (*before n*) **~ boat** salsera *f*

gravy train *n* (colloq): **to get on the ~ ~** aprovechar la ocasión, aprovecharse del chollo (Esp fam), aprovechar la bolada (RPl fam)

gray¹, (BrE) **grey** /greɪ/ *adj* **-er, -est** [1] ‹*suit/day*› gris; ‹*outlook/future*› poco prometedor; ‹*personality*› gris [2] ‹*beard*› canoso, cano (liter); **a ~ hair** una cana; **she has ~ hair** es canosa, tiene el pelo canoso; **she went ~ overnight** le salieron canas *or* se quedó canosa de la noche a la mañana [3] ‹*horse*› rucio, gris

gray², (BrE) **grey** *n* [u] gris *m*; **there were patches of ~ in his hair** tenía mechones de canas

gray: **~ area** *n* (unclear, undefined area) zona *f* gris, terreno *m* poco definido; **~-haired** /ˈgreɪˈherd || ˌgreɪˈheəd/ *adj* canoso

graying, (BrE) **greying** /ˈgreɪɪŋ/ *adj* ‹*hair*› canoso; **he's slightly ~** le están saliendo canas, tiene algunas canas

gray matter, (BrE) **grey matter** *n* [u] materia *f* gris

graze¹ /greɪz/ *vt*
[A] [1] (cut, injure) rasguñarse, rasparse [2] (touch, brush) rozar*
[B] (Agr) [1] ‹*sheep/cattle*› apacentar*, pastorear [2] ‹*field/meadow*› usar para pastoreo

■ **graze** *vi* (Agr) pastar, pacer*

graze² *n* rasguño *m*

grazing /ˈgreɪzɪŋ/ *n* [u] pastoreo *m*

grease¹ /griːs/ *n* [u] [1] (Mech Eng) grasa *f* [2] (fat) grasa *f* [3] (secreted by body) grasa *f* [4] (hair oil) brillantina *f*, gomina *f*

grease² *vt* [1] (lubricate) ‹*machinery/hinge*› engrasar [2] (Culin) ‹*dish/baking tray*›: **to ~ (with butter)** enmantequillar, untar con mantequilla, enmantecar* (RPl); **to ~ (with oil)** aceitar [3] (with hair oil): **to ~ one's hair back** llevar el pelo peinado hacia atrás con brillantina *or* gomina

grease: **~ gun** *n* pistola *f* de engrase; **~paint** *n* [u] maquillaje *m* teatral; **~proof** *adj*: **~proof paper** (BrE) papel *m* encerado *or* de cera *or* (Esp tb) parafinado *or* (RPl) (de) manteca *or* (Chi) (de) mantequilla

greasy /ˈgriːsi/ *adj* **-sier, -siest**
[A] [1] (soiled) ‹*hands*› grasiento; ‹*overalls*› cubierto *or* lleno de grasa [2] (containing grease) ‹*food*› graso; (pej) grasiento [3] ‹*hair/skin*› graso, grasoso (esp AmL)
[B] (unctuous) (colloq) ‹*person/smile*› adulador

great¹ /greɪt/ *adj*
[A] (*before n*) [1] (large in size) (*sing*) gran (*delante del n*); (*pl*) grandes (*delante del n*); **the G~ Lakes** los Grandes Lagos [2] ‹*number/quantity*› (*sing*) gran (*delante del n*); (*pl*) grandes (*delante del n*); **a ~ many people** muchísima gente; **a ~ deal of criticism** muchas críticas; **we discussed it in ~ detail** lo discutimos muy minuciosamente *or* punto por punto; **there's a dirty ~ hole in my sock** (BrE colloq) tengo un agujerazo en el calcetín (fam)
[B] (*before n*) [1] (important) ‹*landowner/occasion*› (*sing*) gran (*delante del n*); (*pl*) grandes (*delante del n*); **Catherine the G~** Catalina la Grande [2] (genuine, real) (*before n*) ‹*friend/rival*› (*sing*) gran (*delante del n*); (*pl*) grandes (*delante del n*); **I'm in no ~ hurry** no tengo mucha prisa, no estoy muy apurado (AmL); **you're a ~ help!** (colloq & iro) ¡valiente ayuda la tuya! (iró); **she's leaving — it's no ~ loss** se va — no se pierde mucho; **he's a ~ one for starting arguments** (colloq) ¡es único para empezar discusiones!, para empezar discusiones es (como) mandado a hacer (CS fam)
[C] (excellent) (colloq) ‹*goal/movie/meal*› sensacional, fabuloso; **we had a really ~ time** lo pasamos fenomenal (fam); **the ~ thing is that you don't need to clean it** lo mejor de todo es que no hay que limpiarlo; **he's a really ~ guy** es un tipo *or* (Esp tb) tío sensacional (fam); **to be ~ AT sth**: **she's ~ at organizing things/getting people together** para organizar las cosas/juntar a la gente, no hay nadie como ella; **he's ~ at mending things** se da mucha maña para hacer arreglos; (*as interj*) **(that's) ~!** ¡qué bien!, ¡fenomenal!, ¡bárbaro! (fam), ¡estupendo! (fam)

great² *n* (outstanding person) (colloq) estrella *f*, grande *mf*

great³ *adv* (esp AmE colloq) fenomenal (fam)

great: **~-aunt** /ˈgreɪtˈænt || ˌgreɪtˈɑːnt/ *n* tía *f* abuela; **~ Britain** *n* Gran Bretaña *f*; **~coat** *n* (esp BrE) sobretodo *m*; **~ Dane** *n* gran danés *m*

> **Great Britain**
>
> Gran Bretaña es la más grande de la Islas Británicas (**British Isles**). Incluye Inglaterra, Escocia y Gales. A menudo el término "Britain" se emplea erróneamente para hacer referencia al Reino Unido (**United Kingdom**) o a Inglaterra

greater /ˈgreɪtər || ˈgreɪtə(r)/ *adj* [1] *comp of* **great¹** [2] (in place names) **G~ London** el gran Londres (*Londres incluyendo la periferia*) [3] (in animal and plant names) mayor

greatest /ˈgreɪtəst || ˈgreɪtɪst/ *adj* (*superl of* **great¹**): **I'm the ~est!** ¡soy el mejor!; **with the ~ of difficulty/ease** con suma dificultad/una facilidad asombrosa

great: **~-grandchild** /ˈgreɪtˈgræntʃaɪld/ *n* bisnieto, -ta *m,f*, biznieto, -ta *m,f*; **~-granddaughter** /ˈgreɪtˈgrænˌdɔːtər || ˌgreɪtˈgrænˌdɔːtə(r)/ *n* bisnieta *f*, biznieta *f*; **~-grandfather** /ˈgreɪtˈgrænˌfɑːðer || ˌgreɪtˈgrænˌfɑːðə(r)/ *n* bisabuelo *m*; **~-grandmother** /ˈgreɪtˈgrænˌmʌðər || ˌgreɪtˈgrænˌmʌðə(r)/ *n* bisabuela *f*; **~-grandson** /ˈgreɪtˈgrænsʌn/ *n* bisnieto *m*, biznieto *m*

greatly /ˈgreɪtli/ *adv* (*as intensifier*) ‹*admire/improve/increase*› enormemente, mucho; **~ concerned** profundamente preocupado

great-nephew /ˈgreɪtˈnefjuː/ *n* sobrino *m* nieto

greatness /ˈgreɪtnəs || ˈgreɪtnɪs/ *n* [u] 1 (of person, achievement, occasion) grandeza *f* 2 (of interest, difficulty, pleasure) enormidad *f*

great: **~-niece** /ˈgreɪtˈniːs/ *n* sobrina *f* nieta; **~-uncle** /ˈgreɪtˈʌŋkəl/ *n* tío *m* abuelo

Grecian /ˈgriːʃən/ *adj* griego

Greece /griːs/ *n* Grecia *f*

greed /griːd/ *n* [u] 1 (for food) gula *f*, glotonería *f*, angurria *f* (CS) 2 (for power, money) codicia *f*, avaricia *f*

greedily /ˈgriːdl̩i || ˈgriːdɪli/ *adv* 1 ‹*eat*› con gula *or* glotonería 2 (avariciously) con avaricia

greedy /ˈgriːdi/ *adj* **-dier, -diest** 1 (for food, drink) glotón, angurriento (CS); **you ~ pig!** ¡mira que eres glotón *or* (CS tb) angurriento! 2 (for power, wealth) **to be ~ FOR sth** tener* ansias *or* estar* ávido DE algo

Greek¹ /griːk/ *adj* griego

Greek² *n* 1 [u] (language) griego *m*; ***it's all ~ to me*** (colloq) para mí es chino (fam) 2 [c] (person) griego, -ga *m,f*

green¹ /griːn/ *adj* **-er, -est**

A ‹*paint/eyes*› verde; **he was ~ with envy** se moría de envidia; **~ spaces** zonas *fpl or* espacios *mpl* verdes; **~ vegetables** verdura(s) *f(pl)* de hoja; ***to have a ~ thumb*** *o* (BrE) **~ *fingers*** tener* mano para las plantas

B 1 (unripe) verde 2 (colloq) (*pred*) (inexperienced) verde (fam); (naive) ingenuo

C (Pol) verde, ecologista; **the G~ Party** los verdes

green² *n*

A [u] (color) verde *m*; **the lights were at ~** el semáforo estaba (en) verde

B [c] (in village, town) ≈ plaza *f* (*con césped*)

C **greens** *pl* (vegetables) verdura *f* (*de hoja verde*)

D [c] **Green** (Pol) verde *mf*, ecologista *mf*

green: **~back** *n* (AmE colloq) dólar *m*, verde *m* (esp AmL fam); **~ bean** *n* habichuela *f or* (Esp) judía *f* verde *or* (Méx) ejote *m or* (RPl) chaucha *f or* (Chi) poroto *m* verde *or* (Ven) vainita *f*; **~ belt** *n* (esp BrE) zona *f* verde; **~ card** *n* 1 (in US) permiso *m* de residencia y trabajo 2 (in Europe) (Transp) carta *f* verde

> **green card**
>
> En EEUU, es un documento oficial que cualquier persona que no sea ciudadana americana debe obtener para tener el derecho a residir y trabajar en Estados Unidos. En el Reino Unido, es un documento que el conductor o dueño de un automóvil debe conseguir de la compañía de seguros al llevarlo al extranjero para que siga vigente la cobertura de la póliza

greenery /ˈgriːnəri/ *n* [u] (green vegetation): **the garden needs more ~** el jardín necesita más verde *or* más vegetación; **the lush ~** la exuberante vegetación

green: **~-eyed** /ˈgriːnˈaɪd/ *adj* ‹*person/cat*› de ojos verdes; **the ~-eyed monster** los celos; **~fly** *n* (*pl* **-flies** *or* **-fly**) (BrE) pulgón *m*; **my roses have got ~fly** mis rosales tienen pulgón *or* pulgones; **~grocer** *n* (BrE) verdulero, -ra *m,f*; **the ~grocer('s)** la verdulería; **~horn** *n* (colloq) novato, -ta *m,f*, pardillo, -lla *m,f* (Esp fam); **~house** *n* invernadero *m*; (*before n*) **the ~house effect** (Ecol) el efecto invernadero; **~house gas** gas *m* invernadero

greenish /ˈgriːnɪʃ/ *adj* verdoso

Greenland /ˈgriːnlənd/ *n* Groenlandia *f*

greenness /ˈgriːnnəs || ˈgriːnnɪs/ *n* [u] (of landscape, vegetation) verdor *m*

green onion *n* (AmE) cebolleta *f*, cebollino *m*, cebolla *f* de verdeo (RPl), cebollín *m* (Chi)

green: **~ paper** *n* (in UK) libro *m* verde (*documento de consulta que precede a la elaboración de un libro blanco*); **~ pepper** *n* (vegetable) *see* **pepper¹** B; **~stuff** *n* [u] (AmE sl) (money) guita *f* (arg), pasta *f* (Esp arg), lana *f* (AmL fam); **~way** /ˈgriːnweɪ/ *n* (AmE) zona *f* verde

Greenwich Mean Time /ˈgrenɪdʒ, ˈgrenɪtʃ/ *n* [u] hora *f* de Greenwich

greeny /ˈgriːni/ *adj* ▸ **greenish**

greet /griːt/ *vt*

A 1 (welcome, receive) ‹*guest/client*› recibir, darle* la bienvenida a 2 (say hello to) saludar

B (react to) acoger*, recibir

C (meet): **a strange sight ~ed our eyes** un extraño espectáculo se ofreció a nuestra vista; **the sound of violins ~ed her ears** oyó música de violines

greeting /ˈgriːtɪŋ/ *n* 1 (spoken) saludo *m*; (*as interj*) **~s!** (arch *or* hum) ¡buenas! (fam) 2 (message) (*usu pl*): **she sends you her ~s** te manda saludos, me dio recuerdos para ti; ⓢ **birthday/Christmas greetings** feliz cumpleaños/Navidad; (*before n*) **a ~** *o* (BrE also) **~s card** una tarjeta de felicitación

gregarious /grɪˈgeriəs || grɪˈgeəriəs/ *adj* 1 ‹*person/personality*› sociable 2 (Zool) gregario

gremlin /ˈgremlən || ˈgremlɪn/ *n* (hum) duendecillo *m*, diablillo *m*

Grenada /grəˈneɪdə/ *n* Granada *f*

grenade /grəˈneɪd/ *n* granada *f*

grenadier /ˈgrenəˈdɪr || ˌgrenəˈdɪə(r)/ *n* granadero *m*

grew /gruː/ *past of* **grow**

grey *adj/n* (BrE) ▸ **gray¹,²**

greyhound /ˈgreɪhaʊnd/ *n* galgo *m*

grid /grɪd/ *n*

A (grating over opening) rejilla *f*

B 1 (on map) (Geog) cuadriculado *m*; (*before n*) **~ reference** coordenadas *fpl* cartográficas 2 (pattern) cuadrícula *f*

C (network) (Elec esp BrE) red *f*; **the national ~** (in UK) la red de suministro de electricidad nacional

D ▸ **gridiron B**

griddle /ˈgrɪdl̩/ *n* plancha *f*

grid: **~iron** /ˈgrɪdˈaɪərn || ˈgrɪdaɪən/ *n* 1 (Culin) parrilla *f*; 2 (in US football) campo *m*, cancha *f* (AmL), emparrillado *m* (Méx); **~lock** *n* [u] (esp AmE) paralización *f* total del tráfico; **~locked** /ˈgrɪdlɑːkt || ˈgrɪdlɒkt/ *adj* 1 ‹*traffic/street*› colapsado 2 ‹*economy*› estancado, paralizado; ‹*negotiations*› en impasse, en punto muerto, paralizado

grief /griːf/ *n* [u] 1 (sorrow) dolor *m*, profunda pena *f*; ***to come to ~*** «*plans*» fracasar, irse* al traste (fam); «*driver/rider*» sufrir un accidente; **he'll come to ~ one day** va a acabar mal 2 (*in interj*): **good ~!** ¡Jesús!, ¡por Dios!

grief-stricken /ˈgriːfˌstrɪkən/ *adj* (liter) ‹*person*› consternado (liter), acongojado (liter), desconsolado; ‹*voice/expression*› acongojado (liter), apesadumbrado

grievance /ˈgriːvəns/ *n* 1 [c] (ground for complaint) motivo *m* de queja; **he seemed to have a ~ against his father** parecía estar resentido con su padre por algo; **to air one's ~s** quejarse 2 [u] (injustice): **to be filled with a sense of ~** sentirse* agraviado, sentirse* víctima de una injusticia 3 [c] (Lab Rel) queja *f* formal; (*before n*) **~ procedure** procedimiento *m* conciliatorio

grieve /griːv/ *vi* sufrir; **to ~ FOR sb** llorar a algn, llorar la muerte de algn; **to ~ OVER sth** lamentar algo

■ **grieve** *vt* apenar, entristecer*

grievous /ˈgriːvəs/ *adj* (liter) ‹*loss*› doloroso; ‹*wound/injury*› de extrema gravedad; **~ bodily harm** (Law) lesiones *fpl* (corporales) graves

grievously /ˈgriːvəsli/ *adv* (liter) ‹*disappoint*› profundamente; ‹*injure*› de gravedad, gravemente; **to be ~ mistaken** estar* en un grave error

grill¹ /grɪl/ *vt*

A (BrE Culin) (in electric, gas grill) hacer* al grill; (over hot fire) hacer* *or* asar a la parrilla *or* a las brasas; **~ed sardines** sardinas *fpl* a la parrilla *or* a la(s) brasa(s)

B (interrogate) interrogar*

grill² *n* 1 (on stove) (esp BrE) grill *m*, gratinador *m* 2 (on barbecue) parrilla *f* 3 (dish): **mixed ~** *plato de carne a la parrilla (p. ej. chuletas, hígado) con tomates y champiñones* 4 (restaurant) grill *m*

grille /grɪl/ *n* 1 (partition) reja *f*, enrejado *m* 2 (protective covering) (Tech) rejilla *f*; (Auto) calandra *f*, parrilla *f*

grilling /ˈgrɪlɪŋ/ *n* (colloq) interrogatorio *m*; **to give sb a ~** someter a algn a un interrogatorio

grim /grɪm/ *adj* **-mm-** 1 (stern) ‹*person/expression*› adusto 2 (gloomy) ‹*outlook/situation*› nefasto, desalentador; ‹*landscape*› sombrío, lúgubre; ‹*weather*› deprimente 3 (unyielding) ‹*struggle*› denodado; **she carried on with ~ determination** siguió adelante, resuelta a no dejarse vencer; **with a ~ smile** sonriendo a pesar de todo 4 (below par) (colloq): **I feel pretty ~** me siento *or* me encuentro fatal (fam)

grimace[1] /ˈgrɪməs, grɪˈmeɪs/ *n* mueca *f*
grimace[2] *vi* hacer* una mueca
grime /graɪm/ *n* [u] mugre *f*, suciedad *f*
grimly /ˈgrɪmli/ *adv* ‹*say*› con gravedad, en tono grave; ‹*laugh/smile*› forzadamente
grimy /ˈgraɪmi/ *adj* **-mier, -miest** mugriento, sucio
grin[1] /grɪn/ *vi* **-nn-** sonreír* (*abiertamente o burlonamente*); **she was ~ning from ear to ear** sonreía de oreja a oreja; ***to ~ and bear it*** aguantarse
grin[2] *n* sonrisa *f*; **and you can take** *o* **wipe that ~ off your face!** ¡y no te rías!
grind[1] /graɪnd/ (*past & past p* **ground**) *vt* 1 ‹*coffee/wheat*› moler*; (in mortar) machacar*; ‹*meat*› (AmE) moler* *or* (Esp, RPl) picar*; ‹*crystals/ore*› triturar 2 (rub together): **he ~s his teeth in his sleep** le rechinan los dientes cuando duerme; **to ~ sth INTO sth**: **he ground the cigarette end into the carpet** incrustó *or* aplastó la colilla en la alfombra
■ **grind** *vi* (move with friction) rechinar, chirriar*; **the wheels of bureaucracy ~ very slowly** las cosas de palacio van despacio; ***to ~ to a halt*** *o* ***standstill***: **the truck ground to a halt** el camión se detuvo con gran chirrido de frenos; **the negotiations have ground to a halt** las negociaciones han llegado a un punto muerto *or* se han estancado
Phrasal verbs
• **grind down** [v ▸ o ▸ adv, v ▸ adv ▸ o] 1 (polish) pulir 2 (oppress) oprimir; **don't let them ~ you down!** ¡no te dejes avasallar!
• **grind on** [v ▸ adv] continuar*
• **grind out** [v ▸ o ▸ adv, v ▸ adv ▸ o] (pej) tocar* (*mecánicamente*)
grind[2] *n* 1 (drudgery) (colloq) (*no pl*) trabajo *m* pesado, paliza *f* (fam); **the daily ~** el monótono trajín diario; **back to the ~!** ¡de vuelta al yugo! 2 (over-conscientious worker) (AmE colloq): **she's the office ~** es la niña aplicada de la oficina (iró)
grinder /ˈgraɪndər || ˈgraɪndə(r)/ *n* 1 (machine) molinillo *m*; **a coffee ~** un molinillo de café 2 (person): **a knife ~** un afilador
grinding /ˈgraɪndɪŋ/ *adj*
A (*before n*): **~ noise** chirrido *m*; **to come to a ~ halt** *o* **stop** ‹‹*vehicle*›› pararse *or* detenerse* con un chirrido; ‹‹*plan/negotiations*›› estancarse*, llegar* a un punto muerto
B (desperate): **~ poverty** miseria *f* absoluta
C (strenuous) (AmE colloq) agotador
grindstone /ˈgraɪnstəʊn, ˈgraɪndstəʊn || ˈgraɪndstəʊn/ *n* 1 (Tech) muela *f*, piedra *f* de afilar 2 (millstone) muela *f*, piedra *f* *or* rueda *f* de molino
gringo /ˈgrɪŋgəʊ/ *n* (*pl* **-gos**) (AmE pej) gringo, -ga *m,f* (pey)
grip[1] /grɪp/ *n*
A 1 (hold): **she held his arm in a strong ~** lo tenía agarrado *or* asido fuertemente del brazo; **~ ON sth**: **keep a good/firm ~ on the bar** agárrate bien de la barra; **he kept a firm ~ on expenses** llevaba un rígido control de los gastos; **he tightened his ~ on her neck** le apretó más el cuello; **get a ~ on yourself!** ¡contrólate!; **he lost his ~ on the rope** se le escapó la cuerda; **he has lost his ~ on reality** ha perdido contacto con la realidad; **the region is in the ~ of an epidemic** una epidemia asola la región; ***to come to ~s with sth*** ‹*idea/situation*› aceptar *or* asumir algo; ***to get to ~s with sth*** ‹*subject*› entender* algo; **he soon got to ~s with the new system** enseguida aprendió el nuevo sistema; **I never managed to get to ~s with the subject** nunca llegué a entender del todo el tema 2 (of tires) adherencia *f*, agarre *m*
B (on handle) empuñadura *f*
C (*hair ~*) (BrE) horquilla *f*, pinche *m* (Chi), pasador *m* (Méx)
D (bag) (dated) bolsa *f* de viaje
grip[2] **-pp-** *vt*
A (take hold of) agarrar; (have hold of) tener* agarrado, sujetar; **these tires ~ the road well** estos neumáticos tienen buena adherencia *or* buen agarre; **he was ~ped by panic** el pánico se apoderó de él, fue presa del pánico
B (of feelings, attention): **the audience was ~ped by the play** la obra captó la atención del público
■ **grip** *vi* adherirse*
gripe[1] /graɪp/ *n* (complaint) (colloq) queja *f*
gripe[2] *vi* (colloq) refunfuñar (fam), renegar*
gripping /ˈgrɪpɪŋ/ *adj* apasionante
grisly /ˈgrɪzli/ *adj* **-lier, -liest** truculento, espeluznante
grist /grɪst/ *n* [u]: ***to be ~ to the mill***: **it's all ~ to the mill** todo ayuda, todo es útil
gristle /ˈgrɪsəl/ *n* [u] cartílago *m*
gristly /ˈgrɪsli/ *adj* **gristlier, gristliest** con mucho cartílago
grit[1] /grɪt/ *n* [u]
A 1 (dirt) polvo *m*; **I got a piece of ~ in my eye** se me metió una basurita (AmL) *or* (Esp) brizna en el ojo 2 (gravel) arenilla *f*
B (courage) (colloq) agallas *fpl* (fam)
C **grits** *pl* (*hominy ~s*) (AmE Culin) sémola *f* de maíz
grit[2] *vt* **-tt-** 1 (BrE) ‹*road*› echar arenilla en 2 ▸**tooth 1**
gritty /ˈgrɪti/ *adj* **-tier, -tiest**
A (with grit in) ‹*flour/powder*› arenoso; ‹*towel/mussels*› lleno de arena
B 1 (resilient) ‹*performance/resistance*› enérgico 2 (uncompromising) descarnado
grizzle /ˈgrɪzəl/ *vi* (esp BrE colloq) lloriquear (fam)
grizzled /ˈgrɪzəld/ *adj* entrecano
grizzly /ˈgrɪzli/ *n* (*pl* **-lies**), **grizzly bear** oso *m* pardo
groan[1] /grəʊn/ *vi*
A 1 (with pain, suffering) gemir*, quejarse 2 (with dismay) gruñir* 3 (creak) ‹‹*door/timber*›› crujir
B (grumble) (colloq) refunfuñar (fam), rezongar*
groan[2] *n* 1 (of pain, suffering) quejido *m*, gemido *m*; **to let out a ~** dejar escapar un quejido *or* gemido 2 (of dismay) gruñido *m* 3 (creak) crujido *m*
grocer /ˈgrəʊsər || ˈgrəʊsə(r)/ *n* tendero, -ra *m,f*, almacenero, -ra *m,f* (esp CS); **the ~'s** (BrE) la tienda de comestibles *or* de ultramarinos, la bodega (Cu, Per, Ven), la tienda de abarrotes (AmC, Andes, Méx), el almacén (esp CS)
grocery /ˈgrəʊsəri/ *n* (*pl* **-ries**) 1 (shop) tienda *f* de comestibles *or* de ultramarinos, bodega *f* (Cu, Per, Ven), tienda *f* de abarrotes (AmC, Andes, Méx), almacén *m* (esp CS) 2 **groceries** *pl* (provisions) comestibles *mpl*, provisiones *fpl*
groggy /ˈgrɑːgi || ˈgrɒgi/ *adj* **-gier, -giest** (colloq) grogui (fam)
groin /grɔɪn/ *n* (Anat) ingle *f*
groom[1] /gruːm/ *vt* 1 ‹*dog*› cepillar; ‹*horse*› cepillar, almohazar* 2 (make neat, attractive) (*usu pass*) arreglar; (excessively) acicalar; **a well ~ed person** una persona bien arreglada 3 (prepare) preparar; **to ~ sb for sth** preparar a algn para algo
groom[2] *n*
A (Equ) mozo *m* de cuadra
B (*bride~*) novio *m*; **the bride and ~** los novios
groove /gruːv/ *n* 1 (in screw) ranura *f*, muesca *f*; (for sliding door) guía *f*; (for pulley) garganta *f*, hendidura *f* 2 (Audio) surco *m*
grope /grəʊp/ *vi* andar* a tientas; **to ~ FOR sth** buscar* algo a tientas; **they were groping for** *o* **after a solution** estaban dando palos de ciego, tratando de hallar una solución; **to ~ around** *o* **about** tantear
■ **grope** *vt* ‹*person*› (colloq) manosear, meterle mano a (fam)
gross[1] /grəʊs/ *adj*
A (extreme, flagrant) (*before n*) ‹*disregard/injustice*› flagrante; ‹*exaggeration*› burdo; **~ ignorance** ignorancia *f* crasa *or* supina; **~ negligence** (Law) culpa *f* grave; **~ indecency** (Law) ultraje *m* contra la moral pública
B (total) ‹*weight/profit/income*› bruto; **~ national product** (Econ) producto *m* nacional bruto
C 1 (fat) obeso, gordísimo 2 (disgusting) ‹*person*› asqueroso; ‹*language/joke*› soez
gross[2] *vt* ‹‹*worker/earner*›› tener* una entrada bruta de; **their profits ~ed 2 million** tuvieron beneficios brutos de 2 millones
Phrasal verb
• **gross out** [v ▸ o ▸ adv, v ▸ adv ▸ o] (disgust) (AmE sl) asquear, darle* asco a
gross[3] *n*
A (*pl ~*) (144) gruesa *f*, doce docenas *fpl*
B (*pl* **grosses**) (gross profit) (AmE) ingresos *mpl* brutos
grossly /ˈgrəʊsli/ *adv* 1 (extremely) ‹*exaggerated/unfair*› terriblemente, extremadamente; **he's ~ overweight** está

gordísimo *or* obeso [2] (crudely) ‹*behave*› groseramente

gross-out /ˈgrəʊs,aʊt/ *n* (AmE colloq) [1] (person) asqueroso, -sa *m,f*, guarro, -rra *m,f* (Esp fam) [2] (situation) situación *f* repugnante

grotesque /grəʊˈtesk/ *adj* grotesco

grotesquely /grəʊˈteskli/ *adv* de forma grotesca; **~ ugly** monstruoso

grotto /ˈgrɑːtəʊ || ˈgrɒtəʊ/ *n* (*pl* **-toes** *or* **-tos**) gruta *f*

grotty /grɑːti || ˈgrɒti/ *adj* **-tier, -tiest** (BrE colloq) ‹*place/street*› de mala muerte (fam); ‹*meal*› asqueroso (fam); **I feel really ~** no me siento nada bien, estoy chungo (Esp fam)

grouch[1] /graʊtʃ/ *n* (colloq) [1] (complaint) queja *f*, protesta *f*; **to have a ~ about sth** rezongar* por algo [2] (person) gruñón, -ñona *m,f* (fam), cascarrabias *mf* (fam)

grouch[2] *vi* (colloq) refunfuñar (fam), rezongar*

grouchy /ˈgraʊtʃi/ **-chier, -chiest** *adj* (colloq) ‹*person*› protestón (fam), cascarrabias (fam), rezongón (fam)

ground[1] /graʊnd/ *n*

A [u] (land, terrain) terreno *m*; **a patch of ~** un área de terreno; ***to be on dangerous*** *o* ***slippery ~*** pisar terreno peligroso; ***to be on safe*** *o* ***firm*** *o* ***solid ~*** pisar terreno firme; ***to be sure of one's ~*** saber* qué terreno se pisa; ***to change*** *o* ***shift one's ~*** cambiar de postura; ***to fall on stony ~*** caer* en saco roto; ***to gain/lose ~*** ganar/perder* terreno; ***to stand/hold one's ~*** (in argument) mantenerse* firme, no ceder terreno; (in battle) no ceder terreno

B **grounds** *pl* (premises) terreno *m*; (gardens) jardines *mpl*, parque *m*

C [u] (surface of the earth) suelo *m*; (soil) tierra *f*; **the rail link runs below ~** el enlace ferroviario es subterráneo; **as soon as we got above ~** en cuanto salimos a la superficie; **to fall/drop to the ~** caer* al suelo; ***thin on the ~*** (BrE colloq): **orders have been very thin on the ~ recently** últimamente han escaseado mucho los pedidos *or* ha habido muy pocos pedidos; ***to break new*** *o* ***fresh ~*** abrir* nuevos caminos; ***to cut the ~ from under sb/sb's feet***: **his evidence cut the ~ from under the prosecuting lawyer's feet** su testimonio echó por tierra el argumento del fiscal; **his sudden change of mind cut the ~ from under me** su inesperado cambio de opinión echó por tierra todos mis planes; ***to get off the ~*** «*plan/project*» llegar* a concretarse; «*talks*» empezar* a encaminarse; ***to get sth off the ~*** «*project*» poner* algo en marcha; ***to go to ~*** (BrE) «*fugitive*» esconderse; (lit) «*fox*» meterse en la madriguera; ***to prepare the ~ for sth*** preparar el terreno para algo; ***to run*** *o* ***work oneself into the ~***: **you're working yourself into the ~** te estás dejando el pellejo en el trabajo (fam); ***to suit sb down to the ~*** (colloq) «*arrangement*» venirle* de perlas a algn (fam); «*hat*» quedarle que ni pintado a algn (fam); ***to worship the ~ sb walks on*** besar la tierra que pisa algn; (*before n*) ‹*conditions*› del terreno; ‹*personnel/support*› de tierra; **~ frost** helada *f* (*con escarcha sobre el suelo*)

D [u] (matter, subject): **we covered a lot of ~ in our discussions** tratamos muchos puntos en nuestras conversaciones; **we keep going over the same ~** no hacemos más que volver sobre lo mismo

E [c] (outdoor site): **football ~** (BrE) campo *m* de fútbol, cancha *f* de fútbol (AmL); **recreation ~** parque *m* (*donde se practican deportes*)

F [u] (AmE Elec) tierra *f*

G (justification) (*usu pl*) motivo *m*; **~s for divorce** causal *f* de divorcio; **on financial ~s** por motivos económicos, por razones económicas; **on ~s of ill health** por motivos de salud; **they refused to do it, on the ~s that ...** se negaron a hacerlo, alegando *or* aduciendo que ...

H **grounds** *pl* (dregs): **coffee ~s** posos *mpl* de café

ground[2] *vt*

A (*usu pass*) [1] (base) ‹*argument/theory*› fundar, cimentar* [2] (instruct): **he is well ~ed in German** tiene una sólida base en alemán

B [1] ‹*plane*› retirar del servicio; **all flights are ~ed on account of fog** debido a la niebla no despegará ningún vuelo [2] ‹*child/teenager*› (esp AmE colloq): **I can't go out tonight; I'm ~ed** no puedo salir esta noche, estoy castigado *or* no me dejan

C (Naut) ‹*ship*› hacer* encallar

D (Sport) (in US football, rugby) ‹*ball*› poner* en tierra; (in baseball) ‹*ball*› hacer* rodar

E (AmE Elec) conectar a tierra

■ **ground** *vi* (Naut) encallar, varar

ground[3] *past & past p of* **grind**[1]

ground[4] *adj* ‹*coffee/pepper*› molido; **~ beef** (AmE) carne *f* molida *or* (Esp, RPl) picada

ground: **~-breaking** /ˈgraʊndˈbreɪkɪŋ/ *adj* pionero, innovador; **~cloth**, (BrE) **~sheet** *n* suelo *m* impermeable (*de una tienda de campaña*); **~ control** *n* [u] control *m* de tierra; **~ crew** *n* [1] (Aerosp, Aviat) personal *m* de tierra [2] (AmE Sport) personal *m* de mantenimiento; **~ floor** *n* (BrE) **the ~ floor** la planta baja, el primer piso (Chi); **~hog** *n* marmota *f* de América

> **Groundhog Day**
>
> En muchos lugares de EEUU, la gente está atenta a la aparición de la *groundhog* (marmota) el 2 de febrero o *Groundhog Day*. Según la tradición, la pequeña marmota sale de su madriguera en este día, después de su hibernación. Si hace sol y ve su propia sombra, el animal se asusta y regresa a su madriguera, por lo que habrá seis semanas más de tiempo invernal. Si no ve su sombra, indica que la primavera comenzará temprano

grounding /ˈgraʊndɪŋ/ *n* (*no pl*) base *f*

groundkeeper /ˈgraʊnd,kiːpər || ˈgraʊnd,kiːpə(r)/ *n* encargado, -da *m,f* (*del mantenimiento del campo de juego*)

groundless /ˈgraʊndləs || ˈgraʊndlɪs/ *adj* infundado

ground: **~ level** *n* [u]: **at ~ level** a ras del suelo; **above ~ level** sobre el nivel del suelo; **below ~ level** bajo tierra; **~nut** *n* (BrE) maní *m* *or* (Esp) cacahuete *m*

ground rule *n* [1] (guiding principle) directriz *f*; [2] (AmE Sport) regla *f* de terreno *or* de campo, regla local (Ven); **~sheet** *n* (BrE) ▸ **groundcloth**; **~skeeper** *n* (AmE) encargado, -da *m,f* (*de un parque, cementerio, campo de deportes*); **~sman** /ˈgraʊndzmən/ *n* (*pl* **-men** /-mən/) (BrE) encargado *m* (*del mantenimiento del campo de juego*); **~ staff** *n* (BrE) (+ *sing o pl vb*) [1] (Sport) personal *m* de mantenimiento [2] (Aviat) personal *m* de tierra; **~swell** *n* [1] (Meteo, Naut) mar *f* de fondo *or* de leva [2] (of opinion interest) corriente *f*, oleada *f*; **~swoman** *n* (BrE) encargada *f* (*del mantenimiento del campo de juego*); **~-to-air** /ˈgraʊndtəˈer/ *adj* (*usu before n*) ‹*missile/rocket/attack*› tierra-aire *adj inv*; **~-to-~** /,graʊndtəˈgraʊnd/ *adj* de tierra a tierra; **~work** *n* [u] trabajo *m* preliminar

ground zero *n*

A (in atomic warfare) hipocentro *m*;

B (Hist) (in New York) **G~ Z~** zona *f* cero;

C (starting point) punto *m* de partida

group[1] /gruːp/ *n*

A (+ *sing o pl vb*) [1] (of people) grupo *m*; **to form a ~** (physically) agruparse; (found a group) formar un grupo *or* una asociación; **a consumers'/women's ~** una asociación *or* agrupación de consumidores/mujeres; **a feminist/gay ~** un colectivo *or* una agrupación feminista/gay; **G~ of Eight** Grupo *m* de los Ocho; (*before n*) ‹*discussion/visit*› en grupo; ‹*portrait*› de conjunto [2] (Mus) grupo *m*, conjunto *m*

B (*usu + sing vb*) [1] (of things) grupo *m* [2] (class, division) grupo *m*

C (Busn, Math) grupo *m*

D (Chem) [1] (of elements) grupo *m* [2] (radical) grupo *m*

group[2] *vt* agrupar; **these cases can be ~ed together** estos casos pueden ponerse en un mismo grupo

■ **group** *vi*: **to ~ together** agruparse

groupie /ˈgruːpi/ *n* (colloq) grupi *mf* (arg) (*fan que sigue a un cantante o grupo a todos sus conciertos etc*)

grouping /ˈgruːpɪŋ/ *n* [u c] (arrangement) colocación *f*, modo *m* de agrupar

group practice *n*: *consultorio atendido por un grupo de médicos*

grouse[1] /graʊs/ *n*

A [c] (*pl* **~**) (bird) urogallo *m*

B [c] (*pl* **~s**) (complaint) (colloq) queja *f*; **to have a ~ about sb/sth** (esp BrE) quejarse de algn/algo

grouse[2] *vi* (colloq) gruñir* (fam), refunfuñar (fam); **to ~ ABOUT sb/sth** quejarse DE algn/algo

grout[1] /graʊt/ *n* [u] (in tiling) lechada *f*

grout[2] *vt* ‹*tiles*› enlechar

grove /grəʊv/ *n* (of trees) bosquecillo *m*, arboleda *f*; **an olive ~** un olivar; **an orange ~** un naranjal

grovel /ˈgrɑːvəl || ˈgrɒvəl/ *vi*, (BrE) **-ll-** (physically) postrarse; (abase oneself): **you'll have to ~ before he'll give you a**

g

pay increase tendrás que arrastrarte a sus pies para que te dé un aumento

grow /grəʊ/ (*past* **grew**; *past p* **grown**) *vi*

A (get bigger) ‹‹*plant/person*›› crecer*; (develop emotionally) madurar; (expand, increase) ‹‹*city/company*›› crecer*; ‹‹*quantity/population/membership*›› aumentar; ‹‹*suspicion/influence*›› crecer*, aumentar; **his hair has ~n** le creció el pelo; **his nails have ~n** le crecieron las uñas; **how you've ~n!** ¡qué grande estás!, ¡cómo has crecido!; **the economy is ~ing again** la economía vuelve a experimentar un período de crecimiento *or* expansión; **to ~ in popularity** crecer* *or* aumentar en popularidad

B 1 (become): **to ~ careless** volverse* descuidado; **to ~ dark** oscurecerse*; (at dusk) oscurecer*, anochecer*; **to ~ old** envejecer*, volverse* viejo; **the weather grew worse towards the end of the month** el tiempo empeoró hacia finales de mes 2 (get) **to ~ to + INF**: **she grew to love him** llegó a quererlo, se fue enamorando de él; **she'd grown to expect that of him** se había acostumbrado a esperar eso de él

■ **grow** *vt* 1 (cultivate) ‹*flowers/plants/crops*› cultivar 2 **to ~ a beard/mustache** dejarse (crecer) la barba/el bigote; **to ~ one's hair (long)** dejarse crecer el pelo

Phrasal verbs

- **grow apart** [v ▸ adv] ‹‹*friends*›› distanciarse; ‹‹*couple*››: **they were ~ing apart** su relación se estaba enfriando
- **grow away from** [v ▸ adv ▸ prep ▸ o] distanciarse de
- **grow into** [v ▸ prep ▸ o] 1 (become) convertirse* en 2 (grow to fit): **she will soon ~ into these dresses** pronto podrá usar *or* le quedarán bien estos vestidos
- **grow on** [v ▸ prep ▸ o] (colloq): **the kind of music that ~s on you** el tipo de música que llega a gustar con el tiempo
- **grow out**

A [v ▸ adv]: **to wait till a perm ~s out** esperar hasta que el pelo crezca y se pueda cortar la permanente

B [v ▸ o ▸ adv, v ▸ adv ▸ o]: **to ~ a perm out** dejarse crecer el pelo hasta poder cortarse la permanente

- **grow out of** [v ▸ adv ▸ prep ▸ o] 1 ‹*habit*› perder*, quitarse (*con el tiempo o la edad*); **it's just a phase, she'll ~ out of it** son cosas de la edad, ya se le pasará 2 ‹*clothes*›: **she's ~n out of those shoes already** esos zapatos ya le quedan chicos *or* (Esp) le están pequeños
- **grow up** [v ▸ adv] 1 (spend childhood) criarse* 2 (become adult) hacerse* mayor; **when I ~ up** cuando sea grande *or* mayor ...; **~ up!** ¡no seas infantil!; **to ~ up INTO sth** convertirse* EN algo, llegar* a ser algo 3 (arise) ‹‹*friendship/custom/feeling*›› surgir*, nacer* (liter); **a small township grew up around the mine** un pequeño poblado se desarrolló alrededor de la mina

grower /'grəʊər || 'grəʊə(r)/ *n* (farmer) cultivador, -dora *m,f*

growing /'grəʊɪŋ/ *adj* (*before n*) 1 ‹*quantity*› cada vez mayor, en aumento; ‹*reputation*› cada vez mayor; ‹*influence*› creciente, cada vez mayor; **~ numbers of people** un número cada vez mayor de personas; **there was a mood of ~ pessimism among farmers** el pesimismo iba creciendo entre los agricultores 2 ‹*child*›: **you need a lot to eat; you're a ~ boy** tienes que comer mucho, estás creciendo 3 ‹*plant/stem/vegetable*› que está creciendo

growing pains *pl n* (Physiol) dolores *mpl* del crecimiento; (initial problems) dificultades *fpl* iniciales

growl¹ /graʊl/ *vi* gruñir*; **to ~ AT sb** gruñirle* A algn

■ **growl** *vt*: **where have you been? he ~ed** —¿dónde has estado? —gruñó

growl² *n* (of dog, person) gruñido *m*; (of bear) rugido *m*

grown¹ /grəʊn/ *past p of* **grow**

grown² *adj*: **he's a ~ man now** ya es un hombre hecho y derecho, ya es un adulto hecho y derecho; **all our children are ~ now** nuestros hijos ya son mayores; **when the young are fully ~** (Zool) cuando las crías han alcanzado su pleno desarrollo

grown-up¹ /'grəʊnʌp/ *n* persona *f* mayor

grown-up² *adj* 1 (adult) mayor 2 (mature) (colloq) maduro, adulto

growth /grəʊθ/ *n*

A [u] (of animals, plants, humans) crecimiento *m*

B [u c] (of population, city) crecimiento *m*; (of quantity, profits) aumento *m*; (of industry, business) crecimiento *m*, desarrollo *m*, expansión *f*; **~ in popularity** aumento de popularidad

C 1 [u] (what grows): **prune away the dead branches to make way for new ~** pode las ramas secas para dejar crecer los brotes nuevos; **several days' ~ of beard** una barba de varios días 2 [c] (Med) bulto *m*, tumor *m*

growth rate *n* [u c] 1 (of plants, animals) tasa *f* de crecimiento 2 (Econ) tasa *f or* índice *m* de crecimiento

grub¹ /grʌb/ *n*

A [c] (Zool) larva *f*

B [u] (food) (colloq) comida *f*, papeo *m* (Esp arg), morfe *m* (CS arg)

grub² *vi* **-bb-** escarbar; **to ~ FOR sth** escarbar en busca de algo

grubby /'grʌbi/ *adj* **-bier, -biest** (dirty) mugriento, sucio

grudge¹ /grʌdʒ/ *n* rencilla *f*; **to bear sb a ~, to have** *o* **hold** *o* **bear a ~ against sb** tenerle* *or* guardarle rencor a algn

grudge² *vt* ▸ **begrudge**

grudging /'grʌdʒɪŋ/ *adj* ‹*admission*› hecho a regañadientes; **he is ~ in his praise** le cuesta mucho hacer elogios

grudgingly /'grʌdʒɪŋli/ *adv* de mala gana, a regañadientes

gruel /'gru:əl/ *n* [u] gachas *fpl*

grueling, (BrE) **gruelling** /'gru:əlɪŋ/ *adj* ‹*journey*› extenuante, agotador; ‹*experience/ordeal*› penoso, duro

gruesome /'gru:səm/ *adj* truculento, horripilante

gruff /grʌf/ *adj* **-er, -est** ‹*voice*› áspero, bronco; ‹*manner/reply*› brusco

gruffly /'grʌfli/ *adv* ásperamente, con brusquedad

grumble¹ /'grʌmbəl/ *vi* 1 (complain) refunfuñar (fam), rezongar*; **can't** *o* **mustn't ~** (colloq) no puedo quejarme; **to ~ ABOUT sth/sb** quejarse DE algo/algn 2 (rumble) ‹‹*thunder*›› retumbar; **my stomach's grumbling** las tripas me están haciendo ruido (fam)

grumble² *n* queja *f*

grumbler /'grʌmblər || 'grʌmblə(r)/ *n* rezongón, -gona *m,f*, gruñón, -ñona *m,f*

grumbling /'grʌmblɪŋ/ *adj* ‹*voice*› quejoso; ‹*person*› gruñón, refunfuñón

grumpily /'grʌmpəli || 'grʌmpɪli/ *adv* malhumoradamente, de mal humor

grumpy /'grʌmpi/ *adj* **-pier, -piest** ‹*remark/voice*› malhumorado; **he's always ~ in the mornings** siempre está gruñón *or* de mal humor por la mañana

grungy /'grʌndʒi/ *adj* **-gier, -giest** (AmE colloq) asqueroso

grunt¹ /grʌnt/ *vi* 1 ‹‹*pig*›› gruñir* 2 ‹‹*person*›› gruñir*, dar* *or* lanzar* un gruñido; (with effort) resoplar

■ **grunt** *vt* gruñir*

grunt² *n* 1 (of pig) gruñido *m* 2 (of person) gruñido *m*; (with effort) resoplido *m*

G-string /'dʒi:strɪŋ/ *n*

A (Mus) cuerda *f* de sol

B (Clothing) tanga *f*, sunga *f* (RPl)

Gt (in place names) (BrE) = **Great**

guarantee¹ /'gærən'ti:/ *n*

A 1 (on consumer goods) garantía *f*; **manufacturer's ~** garantía de fábrica 2 (assurance) garantía *f*; **there's no ~ that he'll come back** no hay ninguna garantía de que vuelva

B (Law) (document) garantía *f*; (article) garantía *f*, prenda *f*

guarantee² *vt*

A 1 (Comm) garantizar*; **to ~ sth AGAINST sth** garantizar* algo CONTRA algo 2 (Law) ‹*debt/treaty*› avalar, garantizar*

B (promise, assure of) garantizar*; **to ~ (THAT)** garantizar* QUE, dar* seguridad DE QUE

guaranteed /'gærən'ti:d/ *adj* garantizado

guarantor /'gærən'tɔ:r || ˌgærən'tɔ:(r)/ *n* garante *mf*, fiador, -dora *m,f*; **to stand ~ for sb** avalar a algn, salir* garante *or* fiador de algn

guaranty /'gærənti/ *n* ▸ **guarantee¹ B**

guard¹ /gɑ:rd || gɑ:d/ *vt* 1 (watch over) ‹*building/vehicle/prisoner*› vigilar, custodiar; ‹*person/reputation*› proteger*; ‹*secret*› guardar; **to ~ sth/sb AGAINST sth/sb** *o* **FROM sth** proteger* algo/a algn DE *or* CONTRA algn/algo 2 (AmE Sport) marcar*

Phrasal verb

- **guard against** [v ▸ prep ▸ o] ‹*injury/temptation*› evitar; ‹*risk*› protegerse* *or* precaverse contra; **we must ~ against that happening** tenemos que intentar *or* evitar que eso no ocurra

guard² *n*
A [1] [c] (sentry, soldier) guardia *mf*; **the G~s** (in UK) regimiento *m* de la Guardia Real; **bank/security ~** guarda *mf* jurado/de seguridad; **prison ~** (AmE) carcelero, -ra *m,f*, oficial *mf* de prisiones [2] (squad) (*no pl*) guardia *f* [3] [c] (Sport) (in US football) defensa *mf*; (in basketball) escolta *mf*
B [u] (surveillance) guardia *f*; **to be on ~** estar* de guardia; (*before n*) **~ duty** guardia *f*, posta *f* (AmC)
C [u] (in boxing, fencing) guardia *f*; ***to be on/off (one's) ~*** estar* alerta *or* en guardia/estar* desprevenido; ***to lower** o **drop one's ~*** bajar la guardia
D [c] [1] (*fire* ~) guardallama(s) *m* [2] (on machinery) cubierta *f* (*or* dispositivo *m etc*) de seguridad
E [c] (BrE Rail) jefe, -fa *m,f* de tren

guard dog *n* perro *m* guardián

guarded /'gɑ:rdəd || 'gɑ:dɪd/ *adj* ‹*reply/admission*› cauteloso; ‹*optimism*› cauto, comedido

guardedly /'gɑ:rdədli || 'gɑ:dɪdli/ *adv* ‹*optimistic/confident*› mesuradamente, cautamente; ‹*comment/reply*› cautelosamente, con cautela

guardhouse /'gɑ:rdhaʊs || 'gɑ:dhaʊs/ *n* [1] (guards' quarters) cuartel *m* [2] (prison) cárcel *f* militar

guardian /'gɑ:rdiən || 'gɑ:diən/ *n* [1] (of child) tutor, -tora *m,f* [2] (protector) ~ **(OF sth)** defensor, -sora *m,f* *or* custodio, -dia *m,f* (DE algo)

guardian angel *n* ángel *m* de la guarda, ángel *m* custodio

guard: **~rail** *n* [1] (in staircase) barandilla *f*, barandal *m*; (in roads etc) barrera *f* de seguridad *or* de protección; [2] (BrE Rail) contracarril *m*; **~room** *n* [1] (for guards) cuarto *m* de guardia [2] (for prisoners) calabozo *m*; **~sman** /'gɑ:rdzmən || gɑ:dzmən/*n* (*pl* **-men** /-mən/) [1] (in US) soldado *m* de la Guardia Nacional [2] (in UK) miembro *m* de la Guardia Real; **~'s van** *n* (BrE Rail) furgón *m* de cola

Guatemala /'gwɑ:tə'mɑ:lə/ *n* Guatemala *f*

Guatemalan¹ /'gwɑ:tə'mɑ:lən/ *adj* guatemalteco

Guatemalan² *n* guatemalteco, -ca *m,f*

guava /'gwɑ:və/ *n* [1] (fruit) guayaba *f* [2] ~ **(tree)** guayabo *m*

Guernsey /'gɜ:rnzi || 'gɜ:nzi/ *n* (*pl* **-seys**) [1] (Geog) Guernesey [2] *also* **guernsey** (cow) vaca *f* de Guernesey

guerrilla, guerilla /gə'rɪlə/ *n* guerrillero, -ra *m,f*; (*before n*) ‹*tactics/leader*› guerrillero; **~ war** guerra *f* de guerrillas; **~ warfare** guerrilla *f*

guess¹ /ges/ *n*: **have a ~!** ¡a ver si adivinas!; **you're allowed three ~es** tienes tres oportunidades de adivinar(lo); **it was just a wild ~** fue lo primero que (se) me vino a la cabeza; **to make a lucky ~** acertar* *or* (Méx) atinar(le) por *or* de casualidad; **your ~ is as good as mine** quién sabe, vete tú a saber

guess² *vt* [1] (conjecture, estimate) adivinar; **~ who!** adivina quién soy, ¿a que no sabes quién soy?; **~ what!** ¿sabes qué?; **you'll never ~ what he said** no te puedes imaginar lo que dijo; **I ~ed that he weighed about 150 pounds** calculé que pesaría unas 150 libras [2] (suppose) (esp AmE colloq) suponer*; **I ~ so** supongo (que sí), eso creo

■ **guess** *vi*: **how did you ~?** ¿cómo adivinaste? *or* (Esp) ¿cómo lo has adivinado?; **to ~ right** acertar*, adivinar, atinar(le) (Méx); **to ~ wrong** equivocarse*; **he kept people ~ing about his plans** los tenía a todos en suspenso *or* en la incertidumbre acerca de sus planes; **to ~ AT sth**: **we can only ~ at her motives** sólo podemos hacer conjeturas sobre cuáles fueron sus motivos

guessing game /'gesɪŋ/ *n* juego *m* de adivinanzas; **to play ~ ~s** jugar* a las adivinanzas

guesstimate /'gestəmət || 'gestɪmət/ *n* (colloq) presupuesto *m* *or* cálculo *m* aproximado

guesswork /'geswɜ:rk || 'geswɜ:k/ *n* [u] conjeturas *fpl*

guest /gest/ *n*
A (visitor) invitado, -da *m,f*; (staying overnight) invitado, -da *m,f*, huésped *mf*, alojado, -da *m,f* (Chi); (in hotel) huésped *mf*, cliente, -ta *m,f*; **we had ~s** teníamos invitados, teníamos visita(s); ***be my ~!***: **may I borrow your pen? — be my ~!** ¿me prestas el bolígrafo? — ¡por supuesto! *or* ¡(no) faltaba *or* faltaría más!; (*before n*) **~ list** lista *f* de invitados
B (non-member) invitado, -da *m,f*; (*before n*) **~ speaker** conferenciante invitado, -da *m,f*, orador invitado, oradora invitada *m,f*
C (Rad, TV) invitado, -da *m,f*; (*before n*) **~ appearance** aparición *f* especial; **~ star** estrella *f* invitada

guesthouse /'gesthaʊs/ *n* [1] (in US, attached to mansion) pabellón *m* de huéspedes [2] (Tourism) (in UK) casa *f* de huéspedes, pensión *f*

guestimate *n* ▸**guesstimate**

guestroom /'gestru:m, -rʊm/ *n* cuarto *m* de huéspedes *or* (Chi) de alojados

guffaw¹ /gʌ'fɔ:/ *n* risotada *f*, carcajada *f*

guffaw² *vi* reírse* a carcajadas, carcajearse (fam)

guidance /'gaɪdṇs/ *n* [u] orientación *f*; **he needs ~** necesita que lo orienten *or* lo aconsejen; **to seek ~ from sb** pedir* consejo a algn; (*before n*) **~ counselor** (AmE) orientador, -dora *m,f* vocacional

guide¹ /gaɪd/ *n*
A [1] (Tourism) (person) guía *mf*; (publication) guía *f* [2] (adviser) consejero, -ra *m,f*
B **Guide** (BrE) exploradora *f*, guía *f*
C (indicator) guía *f*; **to use** o **take sth as a ~** guiarse* por algo

guide² *vt* [1] ‹*tourist/stranger*› guiar*; **a priest ~d them round the cathedral** un sacerdote les hizo de guía en la catedral [2] (help, advise) guiar*, aconsejar [3] (steer, manipulate) (+ *adv compl*): **the captain ~d the ship between the rocks** el capitán condujo *or* guió el barco por entre las rocas [4] **guiding** *pres p*: **they need a guiding hand** necesitan una mano que los guíe; **guiding light** norte *m*; **guiding principle** principio *m* rector

guide: **~book** *n* guía *f*; **~ dog** *n* perro *m* guía, perro *m* lazarillo

guided tour /'gaɪdəd || 'gaɪdɪd/ *n* visita *f* guiada

guideline /'gaɪdlaɪn/ *n* pauta *f*, directriz *f*; **to lay down/issue ~s** establecer* pautas *or* directrices

guild /gɪld/ *n* [1] (of workers) gremio *m* [2] (club, society) asociación *f*, agrupación *f*

guildhall /'gɪldhɔ:l/ *n* (in UK) *antigua sede de uno o varios gremios que en la actualidad se utiliza como ayuntamiento en algunas ciudades*

guile /gaɪl/ *n* [u] astucia *f*

guileless /'gaɪlləs || 'gaɪllɪs/ *adj* (liter) cándido, sin malicia

guillotine¹ /'gɪləti:n/ *n* (for executions, cutting paper) guillotina *f*

guillotine² *vt* ‹*person/paper*› guillotinar

guilt /gɪlt/ *n* [u] [1] (blame) culpa *f*; (Law) culpabilidad *f* [2] (Psych) culpa *f*

guiltily /'gɪltəli || 'gɪltɪli/ *adv* con aire de culpabilidad

guilty /'gɪlti/ *adj* **-tier, -tiest** [1] (Law) (*no comp*) culpable; **how do you plead? — not ~** ¿cómo se declara? — inocente; **he was the ~ party** él era el culpable; **to find sb ~/not ~** declarar a algn culpable/inocente; **to be ~ OF sth** ser* culpable DE algo [2] (ashamed, remorseful) culpable [3] (shameful) (*before n*) ‹*secret/desires*› vergonzoso

guinea /'gɪni/ *n* guinea *f*

guinea pig *n* [1] (Zool) cobayo *m*, cobaya *f*, conejillo *m* de Indias, cuy *m* (AmS) [2] (person) conejillo *m* de Indias

guise /gaɪz/ *n*: **under the ~ of friendship** bajo una apariencia de amistad, aparentando amistad; **in many different ~s** de muchas formas distintas

guitar /gə'tɑ:r || gɪ'tɑ:(r)/ *n* guitarra *f*

guitarist /gə'tɑ:rəst || gɪ'tɑ:rɪst/ *n* guitarrista *mf*

Gujarati¹, **Gujerati** /'gʊdʒə'rɑ:ti/ *adj* gujaratí

Gujarati², **Gujerati** *n* [1] [u] (language) gujaratí *m*, gujerati *m* [2] [c] (person) gujaratí *mf*

gulf /gʌlf/ *n* [1] (Geog) golfo *m*; **the G~ of Mexico** el Golfo de México; (*before n*) **the G~ War** la guerra del Golfo [2] (gap) abismo *m*

gulf: **~ States** *pl n* **the G~ States** [1] (in Middle East) los países del Golfo Pérsico *or* del Golfo [2] (in US) (AmE) *los estados que bordean el Golfo de México*; **~ Stream** *n* **the G~ Stream** la corriente del Golfo; **~ War** *n* **the G~ War** la guerra del Golfo; **G~ War syndrome** síndrome *m* de la guerra del Golfo

gull /gʌl/ *n* (Zool) gaviota *f*
gullet /ˈgʌlət || ˈgʌlɪt/ *n* garganta *f*, gaznate *m* (fam); ▸**stick²** *vi* **B**
gulley /ˈgʌli/ *n* (*pl* **-leys**) ▸**gully**
gullible /ˈgʌləbəl/ *adj* crédulo
gully /ˈgʌli/ *n* (*pl* **-lies**) 1 (small valley) barranco *m* 2 (channel) surco *m*, cauce *m*
gulp¹ /gʌlp/ *vi* tragar* saliva
■ **gulp** *vt* ~ **(down)** ‹*food*› engullir*; ‹*drink/medicine*› beberse *or* tomarse de un trago
Phrasal verb
• **gulp back** [v ▸ adv ▸ o] tragarse*
gulp² *n* (of liquid) trago *m*; (of air) bocanada *f*: **he finished off the beer in one** ~ se terminó la cerveza de un trago
gum¹ /gʌm/ *n*
A [c] (Anat) encía *f*
B [u] (*chewing* ~) chicle *m*, goma *f* de mascar
C 1 [u] (glue) (BrE) goma *f* de pegar 2 [u] (from plant) resina *f*
gum² *vt* **-mm-** pegar*
gum: ~**ball** *n* (AmE) chicle *m* en forma de bola; ~**boil** *n* flemón *m*; ~**boot** *n* (BrE) bota *f* de goma *or* de agua
gumption /ˈgʌmpʃən/ *n* [u] (colloq) 1 (common sense) sentido *m* común 2 (initiative, guts) agallas *fpl* (fam)
gumtree /ˈgʌmtriː/ *n* árbol *m* del caucho; ***to be up a*** ~ (BrE) estar* en un aprieto, estar* metido en un lío (fam)
gun¹ /gʌn/ *n*
A (pistol) pistola *f*, revólver *m*; (shotgun, rifle) escopeta *f*, fusil *m*, rifle *m*; (artillery piece) cañón *m*; ***to go great*** ~***s*** (colloq) ir* viento en popa *or* a las mil maravillas; ***to spike sb's*** ~***s*** (BrE) echar por tierra los planes de algn; ***to stick to one's*** ~***s*** mantenerse* *or* seguir* en sus (*or* mis *etc*) trece
B (*starting* ~) pistola *f* (*que da el disparo de salida*); ***to jump the*** ~ adelantarse a los acontecimientos
gun² **-nn-** *vt* (AmE colloq) ‹*car/engine*› acelerar
Phrasal verbs
• **gun down** [v ▸ o ▸ adv, v ▸ adv ▸ o] (shoot) abatir a tiros
• **gun for** [v ▸ prep ▸ o] (colloq) (*only in -ing form*) andar* a la caza de (fam)
gun: ~**boat** *n* (lancha *f*) cañonera *f*; ~**dog** *n* perro *m* de caza; ~**fight** *n* tiroteo *m*, balacera *f* (AmL); ~**fire** *n* [u] disparos *mpl*; (from heavy artillery) cañoneo *m*, cañonazos *mpl*
gunge /gʌndʒ/ *n* [u] (BrE colloq) porquería *f* (fam)
gung-ho /ˈgʌŋˈhəʊ/ *adj* (colloq & pej) exaltado, fanático
gunk /gʌŋk/ *n* [u] (colloq) porquería *f* (fam)
gun: ~ **law** *n* 1 [u] (lawlessness) la ley del revólver 2 [c] *legislación para el control de armas*; ~ **license** *n* licencia *f* de armas; ~**man** /ˈgʌnmən/ *n* (*pl* **-men** /-mən/) pistolero *m*, gatillero *m* (Méx)
gunner /ˈgʌnər || ˈgʌnə(r)/ *n* artillero, -ra *m,f*; (in UK) soldado *m* de artillería
gun: ~**point** *n*: **at** ~**point** a punta de pistola; ~**powder** *n* [u] pólvora *f*; (*before n*) **the G~powder Plot** la Conspiración de la Pólvora; ~**running** *n* [u] tráfico *m* de armas; ~**shot** *n* disparo *m*, tiro *m*; (*before n*) ~**shot wound** herida *f* de bala; ~**smith** *n* armero, -ra *m,f*
gurgle¹ /ˈgɜːrgəl || ˈgɜːgəl/ *vi* «*water/brook*» borbotar, gorgotear; «*baby*» gorjear
gurgle² *n* 1 (of water, liquid) borboteo *m*, gorgoteo *m* 2 (of delight) gorjeo *m*
guru /ˈgʊruː/ *n* gurú *mf*, guru *mf*
gush¹ /gʌʃ/ *vi* 1 «*liquid*» salir* a borbotones *or* a chorros 2 (be effusive) (pej): **she tends to** ~ habla de todo con un entusiasmo exagerado
■ **gush** *vt* chorrear, derramar
gush² *n* borbotón *m*, chorro *m*
gushing /ˈgʌʃɪŋ/ *adj* (pej) demasiado efusivo
gusset /ˈgʌsət || ˈgʌsɪt/ *n* entretela *f*
gust /gʌst/ *n* ráfaga *f*
gusto /ˈgʌstəʊ/ *n* [u] entusiasmo *m*; **with** ~ ‹*eat*› con ganas; ‹*sing/play*› con brío
gusty /ˈgʌsti/ *adj* **-tier, -tiest** ‹*wind*› racheado; ‹*weather/day*› ventoso
gut¹ /gʌt/ *n* 1 [c] (intestine) intestino *m* 2 [c] (belly) (colloq) barriga *f* (fam), panza *f* (fam); ***to bust a*** ~ (laugh a lot) (AmE) desternillarse *or* (Méx) doblarse de risa; (make great effort) (BrE) herniarse (fam), echar los bofes (fam); (*before n*) ‹*reaction*› instintivo; *see also* **guts**
gut² *vt* **-tt-** 1 ‹*fish*› limpiar, vaciar*; ‹*chicken/rabbit*› limpiar, destripar 2 ‹*building*› destruir* el interior de
gutless /ˈgʌtləs || ˈgʌtlɪs/ *adj* cobarde
guts /gʌts/ *n*
A (+ *pl vb*) (colloq) (bowels) tripas *fpl* (fam); ***to hate sb's*** ~ no poder* ver a algn, odiar a algn a muerte; ***to have sb's*** ~ ***for garters*** (BrE) romperle* la cabeza *or* las costillas a algn, sacarle* las tripas a algn (fam); ***to work*** *o* (BrE also) ***slog one's*** ~ ***out*** echar los bofes (fam), deslomarse (trabajando) (fam)
B (+ *sing o pl vb*) (courage) (colloq) agallas *fpl* (fam)
gutsy /ˈgʌtsi/ *adj* **-sier, -siest** (colloq) ‹*person*› con agallas (fam), agalludo (AmL fam)
gutted /ˈgʌtɪd/ *adj* (pred) (BrE sl): **to be/feel** ~ estar* destrozado *or* hecho pedazos
gutter¹ /ˈgʌtər || ˈgʌtə(r)/ *n* 1 (on roof) canaleta *f*, canalón *m* (Esp) 2 (in street) alcantarilla *f* 3 (lowest section of society) **the** ~ el arroyo; **he picked her up out of the** ~ la sacó del arroyo; (*before n*) **the** ~ **press** la prensa sensacionalista *or* amarilla *or* amarillista
gutter² *vi* «*candle*» arder con luz parpadeante
guttering /ˈgʌtərɪŋ/ *n* [u] canaletas *fpl*, canalones *mpl* (Esp)
guttural /ˈgʌtərəl/ *adj* ‹*voice/language*› gutural
guv /gʌv/ *n* (BrE sl) (*as form of address*) jefe (fam), patrón (CS fam)
guy /gaɪ/ *n* (colloq)
A 1 (man) tipo *m* (fam), tío *m* (Esp fam), chavo *m* (Méx fam); **my/her** ~ (boyfriend) mi/su novio, mi/su chavo (Méx fam), mi/su pololo (Chi) 2 **guys** *pl* (people) (AmE) gente *f*; **do you** ~**s want breakfast?** ¿quieren *or* (Esp) queréis desayunar?
B (in UK) *efigie de Guy Fawkes que se quema en una hoguera la noche del 5 de noviembre*
Guyana /gaɪˈænə/ *n* Guyana *f*, Guayana *f*
Guyanese /ˌgaɪəˈniːz/ *adj* guyanés, guayanés
Guy Fawkes Night ▸**Bonfire Night** /ˈgaɪfɔːks/ *n* (in UK) la noche del 5 de noviembre (*aniversario de la Conspiración de la Pólvora*)
guzzle /ˈgʌzəl/ *vt* 1 (drink greedily) chupar (fam) 2 (eat greedily) (BrE) engullirse*, tragarse*
■ **guzzle** *vi* 1 (drink) chupar (fam) 2 (eat) (BrE) engullir*
guzzler /ˈgʌzlər || ˈgʌzlə(r)/ *n* 1 (person) tragón, -gona *m,f* (fam) 2 (appliance): *aparato que consume mucha energía*; **this car is a real** ~ este coche traga mucha gasolina *or* (RPL) nafta *or* (Chi) bencina
gym /dʒɪm/ *n* 1 [c] (gymnasium) gimnasio *m* 2 [u] (gymnastics) gimnasia *f*
gymkhana /dʒɪmˈkɑːnə/ *n* 1 (Equ) gincana *f* (*competición ecuestre*) 2 (in motor racing) (AmE) *competición automovilística*
gymnasium /dʒɪmˈneɪziəm/ *n* (*pl* **-siums** *or* **-sia** /-ziə/) gimnasio *m*
gymnast /ˈdʒɪmnæst/ *n* gimnasta *mf*
gymnastics /dʒɪmˈnæstɪks/ *n* 1 (activity) (+ *sing vb*) gimnasia *f* 2 (exercises) (+ *pl vb*) gimnasia *f*
gymslip /ˈdʒɪmslɪp/ *n* (BrE) jumper *m or* (Esp) pichi *m* (*de uniforme colegial*)
gynecological, (BrE) **gynaecological** /ˈgaɪnəkəˈlɑːdʒɪkəl || ˌgaɪnəkəˈlɒdʒɪkəl/ *adj* ginecológico
gynecologist, (BrE) **gynaecologist** /ˈgaɪnəˈkɑːlədʒəst || ˌgaɪnəˈkɒlədʒɪst/ *n* ginecólogo, -ga *m,f*
gynecology, (BrE) **gynaecology** /ˈgaɪnəˈkɑːlədʒi || ˌgaɪnəˈkɒlədʒi/ *n* [u] ginecología *f*
gyp¹ /dʒɪp/ *n* (colloq)
A [c] (swindle) timo *m* (fam), afano *m* (RPl arg)
B [u] (pain, trouble) (BrE): **my back's been giving me** ~ la espalda me ha estado fastidiando *or* jorobando (fam)
gyp² *vt* **-pp-** (colloq) timar, transar (Méx fam)
gypsum /ˈdʒɪpsəm/ *n* [u] yeso *m*
gypsy, Gypsy /ˈdʒɪpsi/ *n* (*pl* **-sies**) gitano, -na *m,f*
gyrate /ˈdʒaɪreɪt || dʒaɪˈreɪt/ *vi* girar
gyration /dʒaɪˈreɪʃən/ *n* [c u] (rotation) giro *m*, rotación *f*

Hh

H, h /eɪtʃ/ *n* H, h *f*

ha¹ /hɑː/ *interj* ¡ajá!

ha² (= **hectare**) Ha.

habeas corpus /'heɪbiəs'kɔːrpəs || ,heɪbiəs'kɔːpəs/ *n* [u] hábeas corpus *m*

haberdashery /'hæbər,dæʃəri || 'hæbə,dæʃəri/ *n* (*pl* **-ries**)

A [c] **1** (clothes store) (AmE) tienda *f* de ropa y accesorios para caballeros **2** (sewing materials shop) (BrE) mercería *f*

B [u] **1** (clothes) (AmE) ropa *f* y accesorios *mpl* para caballeros **2** (sewing materials) (BrE) (artículos *mpl* de) mercería *f*

habit /'hæbət || 'hæbɪt/ *n*

A **1** [c] (usual piece of behavior) costumbre *f*, hábito *m*; (bad) vicio *m*, mala costumbre *f*, mal hábito *m*; **to break a ~** perder* *or* quitarse una (mala) costumbre; **to be in the ~ of -ING** acostumbrar + INF, tener* por costumbre + INF; **to make a ~ of -ING** adoptar la costumbre de + INF; **don't make a ~ of it** que no se repita; **to get out of/into the ~ of doing sth** perder*/tomar la costumbre de hacer algo; **to have a ~ of -ING** tener* la manía de + INF **2** [u] (customary behavior) costumbre *f*; **force of ~** fuerza *f* de la costumbre **3** [u] (dependence on nicotine, drugs): **to break** *o* **kick the ~** dejar el vicio; **he now has a $100-a-day ~** ahora el vicio le cuesta 100 dólares diarios

B [c] (Clothing) hábito *m*

habitable /'hæbətəbəl || 'hæbɪtəbəl/ *adj* habitable

habitat /'hæbətæt || 'hæbɪtæt/ *n* hábitat *m*

habitation /'hæbə'teɪʃən || ,hæbɪ'teɪʃən/ *n* (frml): **unfit for human ~** inhabitable

habit-forming /'hæbət,fɔːrmɪŋ || 'hæbɪt,fɔːmɪŋ/ *adj* que crea hábito *or* dependencia

habitual /hə'bɪtʃuəl/ *adj* **1** (usual) habitual, acostumbrado **2** (compulsive) ‹*liar/gambler*› empedernido

habitually /hə'bɪtʃuəli/ *adv* por lo general, normalmente

habituate /hə'bɪtʃueɪt/ *vt* **to ~ sb/oneself TO sth/-ING** habituar* a algn/habituarse* A algo/+ INF

habitué /hə'bɪtʃueɪ/ *n* asiduo, -dua *m,f*, habitué *mf* (CS)

hacienda /'hɑːsi'endə, 'hæ- || ,hæsi'endə/ *n* (AmE) hacienda *f*

hack¹ /hæk/ *vt* cortar a tajos, tajear (Andes); **to ~ sth to bits** *o* **pieces** hacer* algo trizas

■ **hack** *vi*

A (to cut) hacer* tajos; **he was ~ing at the tree with a machete** estaba dando machetazos al árbol

B (Comput colloq) **to ~ (into)** ‹*system*› piratear

hack² *n*

A (pej *or* hum) (writer) escritorzuelo, -la *m,f* (pey); (journalist) gacetillero, -ra *m,f* (pey)

B (horse — for hire) caballo *m* de alquiler; (— worn-out) jaco *m*, jamelgo *m*

C (AmE colloq) **1** (taxi driver) taxista *mf*, tachero, -ra *m,f* (RPl fam), ruletero, -ra *m,f* (Méx fam) **2** (taxi) taxi *m*, tacho *m* (RPl fam)

hacker /'hækər || 'hækə(r)/ *n* (Comput colloq) pirata informático, -ca *m,f*

hacking¹ /'hækɪŋ/ *n* (Comput colloq) piratería *f* informática

hacking² *adj* ‹*cough*› áspero

hackles /'hækəlz/ *pl n* (on dogs) *pelo erizado del lomo*; **to have one's ~ up** ‹‹*dog*›› estar* erizado; ‹‹*person*›› estar* furioso; **her/his ~ rose** se enfureció, se indignó

hackneyed /'hæknid/ *adj* manido, trillado

hacksaw /'hæksɔː/ *n* sierra *f* de arco (*para metales*)

had /hæd, *weak form* həd, əd/ *past & past p of* **have**

haddock /'hædək/ *n* (*pl* ~) **1** [c] (Zool) eglefino *m* **2** [u] (Culin) abadejo *m*

hadn't /'hædn̩t/ = **had not**

haem- *etc* (BrE) ▶ **hem-** *etc*

hag /hæg/ *n* **1** (ugly old woman) bruja *f*, arpía *f* **2** (witch) (arch) bruja *f*, hechicera *f*

haggard /'hægərd || 'hægəd/ *adj* demacrado

haggis /'hægəs || 'hægɪs/ *n* [c u] (*pl* **-gis** *or* **-gises**) *plato escocés hecho con vísceras de cordero y avena; see also* **Burns Night**

haggle /'hægəl/ *vi* regatear; **to ~ over the price** regatear

hagiography /'hægi'ɑːgrəfi || ,hægi'ɒgrəfi/ *n* [c u] (*pl* **-phies**) hagiografía *f*

Hague /heɪg/ *n* **The ~** La Haya

hah /hɑː/ *interj* ¡ajá!

ha-ha /hɑː'hɑː/ *interj* ¡ja, ja!

hail¹ /heɪl/ *n* **1** [u] (Meteo) granizo *m*, pedrisco *m* **2** (of bullets, insults) (*no pl*) lluvia *f*

hail² *v impers* (Meteo) granizar*

■ **hail** *vt*

A (call to) ‹*person*› llamar; ‹*ship*› saludar; ‹*taxi*› hacerle* señas a; **he was within ~ing distance** desde donde estaba me podía oír

B (acclaim, welcome) ‹*king/leader*› aclamar; **it was ~ed as a major breakthrough** fue acogido como un importantísimo avance

■ **hail** *vi* **to ~ FROM** ‹‹*person*›› ser* DE

Phrasal verb

• **hail down** [v ▸ adv] ‹‹*stones/insults/blows*›› llover*

hail³ *interj* (arch *or* poet): **~ Caesar!** ¡Ave César! (arc)

hail: **~ Mary** *n* Avemaría *m*; **say three H~ Marys** rece tres Avemarías; **~stone** *n* granizo *m*, piedra *f* (de granizo); **~storm** *n* granizada *f*

hair /her || heə(r)/ , ▶ **Colors** *n*

A [u] (on human head) pelo *m*, cabello *m* (frml *o* liter); **a girl with long ~** una chica de pelo largo; **to have** *o* **get one's ~ cut** cortarse el pelo; **to do one's ~** arreglarse el pelo, peinarse; **to have one's ~ done** peinarse (*en la peluquería*); **to lose one's ~** perder* el pelo; ***to get in sb's ~*** (colloq) molestar a algn; ***keep your ~ on!*** (BrE colloq) ¡no te sulfures! (fam); ***to let one's ~ down*** (relax) soltarse* la melena (fam); (lit) soltarse* el pelo; ***to make sb's ~ stand on end*** (colloq) ponerle* los pelos de punta a algn (fam); ***to tear one's ~ (out)*** (colloq) subirse por las paredes (fam); (*before n*) ‹*gel/lacquer/oil*› para el pelo; **~ transplant** trasplante *m* capilar

B [u] **1** (on human body) vello *m*; (*before n*) **~ remover** depilatorio *m* **2** (on animal, plant) pelo *m*

C [c] (single strand) pelo *m*; **with not a ~ out of place** impecable; ***not to harm a ~ of sb's head*** no tocarle* un pelo a algn; ***not to turn a ~*** no inmutarse, quedarse como si nada *or* como si tal (fam); ***to split ~s*** buscarle* tres *or* cinco pies al gato; *see also* **hair's breadth**

hair: **~band** *n* (elastic) cinta *f*, huincha *f* (Bol, Chi, Per), balaca *f* (Col), banda *f* (Méx), vincha *f* (RPl, Ven); (rigid) diadema *f*, cintillo *m*, vincha *f* (RPl, Ven); **~brush** *n* cepillo *m* (*del pelo*); **~clip** *n* (BrE) horquilla *f*, pinche *m* (Chi), pasador *m* (Méx); **~cut** *n* corte *m* de pelo; **to have** *o* **get a ~cut** cortarse el pelo; **~do** *n* (colloq) peinado *m*; **~dresser** *n* peluquero, -ra *m,f*; **to go to the ~dresser's** ir* a la peluquería; **~drier**, **~dryer** *n* 1 (hand-held) secador *m* or (Méx) secadora *f* (de mano) 2 (hood) secador *m* or (Méx) secadora *f* (de pie)

-haired /herd || heəd/ *suff*: **long~/curly~** de pelo largo/rizado; **red~** pelirrojo

hairgrip /'hergrɪp || 'heəgrɪp/ *n* (BrE) horquilla *f*, pinche *m* (Chi), pasador *m* (Méx)

hairless /'herləs || 'heəlɪs/ *adj* ‹*head*› sin pelo, calvo, pelón (AmC, Méx), pelado (CS); ‹*body*› sin vello

hair: **~line** *n* 1 (where hair begins) nacimiento *m* del pelo 2 (fine line) línea *f* delgada; (*before n*) **a ~line fracture** una pequeña fisura; **~net** *n* redecilla *f*; **~piece** *n* postizo *m*; **~pin** *n* horquilla *f* (de moño); (*before n*) **~pin turn** *o* (BrE) **bend** curva *f* muy cerrada; **~-raising** /'her,reɪzɪŋ || 'heə,reɪzɪŋ/ *adj* espeluznante; **~'s breadth**, **~sbreadth** *n* (*no pl*): **by a ~'s breadth** por un pelo (fam); **~slide** *n* (BrE) ▸ **barrette**; **~spray** *n* laca *f*, fijador *m* (*para el pelo*); **~style** *n* peinado *m*, corte *m* de pelo; **~stylist** *n* peluquero, -ra *m,f*, estilista *mf*, peinador, -dora *m,f* (Méx)

hairy /'heri || 'heəri/ *adj* **-rier, -riest**

A ‹*legs/chest*› peludo, velludo

B (sl) (frightening, dangerous) espeluznante, horripilante

Haiti /'heɪti/ *n* Haití *m*

Haitian /'heɪʃən/ *adj* haitiano

hake /heɪk/ *n* [c u] (*pl* ~) merluza *f*

halal /hɑː'lɑːl/ *adj* (Culin) ‹*meat*› de animales faenados *or* (Esp) sacrificados según la ley musulmana

halcyon /'hælsiən/ *adj* (poet) (*before n*) ‹*weather*› paradisíaco (liter); **in those ~ days** en aquellos idílicos tiempos (liter)

hale /heɪl/ *adj* (liter): **~ and hearty** (fuerte) como un roble

half[1] /hæf || hɑːf/ *n* (*pl* **halves**)

A 1 (part) mitad *f*; **~ of the sugar** la mitad del azúcar; **the upper ~ of the body** la parte superior del cuerpo; **to break/divide sth in ~** romper*/dividir algo por la mitad *or* en dos; **how the other ~ lives** cómo viven los demás; ***not to do things by halves*** (colloq) no hacer* las cosas a medias; ***to go halves*** (colloq) pagar* a medias; ***my/his better/other ~*** (colloq & hum) mi/su media naranja; ***too ... by ~*** (BrE colloq): **she's too clever by ~** se pasa de lista (fam) 2 (Math) medio *m* 3 (elliptical use): **an hour and a ~** una hora y media; **it's ~ past ten** son las diez y media; **the train leaves at ~ past** el tren sale a y media; ***... and a ~!*** (colloq): **that was a party and a ~!** ¡eso sí que fue una fiesta!

B (Sport) 1 (period) tiempo *m*; **the first/second ~** el primer/segundo tiempo 2 (of pitch) campo *m* 3 (interval) (AmE) descanso *m*, medio tiempo *m* (AmL)

C (of beer) (BrE) (colloq) media pinta *f* (*de cerveza*)

D (fare) (BrE): **one and two halves** un adulto y dos niños

half[2] *pron* la mitad; **I only want ~** sólo quiero la mitad; ***the ~ of it*** (colloq): **you haven't heard the ~ of it** y eso no es nada

half[3] *adj* medio, -dia; **~ a pint of milk** media pinta de leche; **one and a ~ hours** una hora y media; **~ my salary goes on the mortgage** la mitad del sueldo se me va en la hipoteca; **she's going out with a man ~ her age** sale con un hombre al que dobla en edad; **she isn't ~ the player/singer she used to be** (colloq) no es ni con mucho la jugadora/cantante que era

half[4] *adv* medio; **the work is only ~ done** el trabajo está a medio hacer; **she was ~ asleep** estaba medio dormida *or* semidormida; **I ~ expected to find him here** en cierto modo esperaba encontrármelo aquí; **she is ~ Italian, ~ Greek** es hija de italianos y griegos; **they are paid ~ as much as we are** les pagan la mitad que a nosotros; **the movie isn't ~ as good as the book** (colloq) la película no es ni la mitad de buena que el libro; ***not ~*** (BrE colloq) (*as intensifier*): **do you like it? — not ~!** ¿te gusta? — no me gusta, me encanta

half- /hæf || hɑːf/ *pref*: **~closed/~open** entreabierto; **~starved** medio muerto de hambre

half: **~ a dozen** *n* (*no pl*) 1 (six) media docena *f*; **~ a dozen eggs** media docena de huevos 2 (several): **~ a dozen reasons/countries** unas cuantas razones/unos cuantos países; **~-and-half** /'hæfən'hæf || 'hɑːfən'hɑːf/ *n* [u] (AmE) *mezcla de crema y leche*; **~ an hour** *n* [u] media hora *f*; **~-assed** /'hæf'æst || 'hɑːf,ɑːst/ *adj* (AmE sl) ‹*person*› papanatas (fam), chambón (AmL fam); ‹*attempt*› torpe; **~back** *n* (in US football) half back *mf*; (in rugby) medio *m*; **~-baked** /'hæf'beɪkt || ,hɑːf'beɪkt/ *adj* (colloq) ‹*scheme*› mal concebido; **~ birthday** *n día seis meses antes o después de la fecha en que cae un cumpleaños*; **~-bottle** /'hæfbɑːtḷ || 'hɑːfbɒtḷ/ *n* media (botella) *f*; **~-breed** *n* (animal) híbrido *m*, mestizo, -za *m,f*; (person) (pej) mestizo, -za *m,f*; **~ brother** *n* hermanastro *m*, medio hermano *m*; **~-caste** *n* (often offensive) mestizo, -za *m,f*; **~ cock** *n*: **at ~ cock** (of gun) con el seguro echado; **~-cocked** /'hæf'kɑːkt || ,hɑːf'kɒkt/ *adj*: ***to go off ~-cocked*** (AmE) hacer* algo a la ligera; **~-day** /'hæf'deɪ || 'hɑːf,deɪ/ *n* [u] media jornada *f*; **~-dead** /'hæf'ded || ,hɑːf'ded/ *adj* (*no comp*) (colloq) medio muerto (fam); **~-dollar** /'hæf'dɑːlər || ,hɑːf'dɒlə(r)/ *n* (in US) medio dólar *m*; **~-empty** /,hæf'empti || ,hɑːf'empti/ *adj* medio vacío; **~-full** /'hæf'fʊl || 'hɑːf'fʊl/ *adj* ‹*glass/bottle*› medio lleno, mediado; ‹*theater*› lleno a medias; **~hearted** /'hæf'hɑːrtəd || ,hɑːf'hɑːtɪd/ *adj* poco entusiasta; **he made a ~hearted effort to ...** hizo un intento desganado de ...; **~heartedly** /'hæf'hɑːrtədli || ,hɑːf'hɑːtɪdli/ *adv* sin ganas, con poco entusiasmo; **~-hour** /'hæf'aʊr || ,hɑːf'aʊə(r)/ *n* media hora *f*

half-hourly[1] /'hæf'aʊrli || ,hɑːf'aʊəli/ *adj*: **there's a ~ service** hay un tren (*or* autobús *etc*) cada media hora; **at ~ intervals** cada media hora

half-hourly[2] *adv* cada media hora

half: **~-life** *n* (Chem, Nucl Phys) media vida *f*; **~-light** *n* [u] penumbra *f*; **~-mast** /'hæf'mæst || ,hɑːf'mɑːst/ *n* [u]: **at ~-mast** a media asta; **~ measures** *pl n* medias tintas *fpl*; **I want no ~ measures** no quiero medias tintas; **~-moon** /'hæf'muːn || ,hɑːf'muːn/ *n* media luna *f*; **~-naked** /'hæf'neɪkəd || ,hɑːf'neɪkɪd/ *adj* ‹*figure/model*› semidesnudo; (insufficiently clothed) (colloq) medio desnudo, casi en cueros (fam); **~ nelson** /'hæf'nelsən || ,hɑːf 'nelsən/ *n* llave *f* de cuello; **~ note** *n* (AmE) blanca *f*; **~penny** /'heɪpni/ *n* (Hist) 1 (*pl* **-pennies**) (coin) medio penique *m* 2 (*pl* **-pence** /'heɪpəns/) (value) medio penique *m*; **fivepence ~penny** cinco peniques y medio; ▸ **rub**[1] *vt* 1; **~ price** *n* [u] mitad *f* de precio; **to get sth (at** *o* **for) ~ price** conseguir* algo a mitad de precio; **~ sister** *n* hermanastra *f*, media hermana *f*; **~-size** /'hæf'saɪz || 'hɑːfsaɪz/ *n* 1 (of shoes) medio número *m* 2 (of woman's dress) (AmE) talla *f* or (RPl) talle *m* especial (*para mujeres gruesas*); **~-staff** *n* (AmE) ▸ **~-mast**; **~ term** *n* (in UK) vacaciones *fpl* de mitad de trimestre; (*before n*) **~-term holiday** vacaciones *fpl* de mitad de trimestre; **~-time** *n* [u] 1 (Sport) (stage of game) descanso *m*, medio tiempo *m* (AmL); **the score was 2-0 at ~-time** a mitad de tiempo iban 2 a 0; 2 (Busn, Lab Rel) media jornada *f*; **to be on ~-time** trabajar media jornada; **~-truth** *n* [c u] verdad *f* a medias

half-way[1] /'hæf'weɪ || ,hɑːf'weɪ/ *adv* 1 (at, to mid point) a mitad de camino; **we stopped ~** paramos a mitad de camino; **~ down the path** en medio del camino; **I'm about ~ through** voy por la mitad; **you're ~ there!** ya llevas la mitad del camino recorrido; ***to meet sb ~*** (compromise) llegar* a una solución intermedia *or* a un compromiso con algn; (lit: on journey) encontrarse* con algn a mitad de camino 2 (reasonably) (colloq) ‹*decent/satisfactory*› medio, semi-

half-way[2] *adj* (*before n*) ‹*point*› medio; **the ~ mark** el punto medio, la mitad; **to reach the ~ stage** llegar* a la etapa intermedia

half: **~way house** /'hæf'weɪ || ,hɑːfweɪ'/ *n* 1 (for drug addict, criminal, mental patient) centro *m* de reinserción social 2 (compromise, mid point) término *m* medio; **~-wit** *n* tonto, -ta *m,f*, imbécil *mf*; **~-witted** /'hæf'wɪtəd || ,hɑːf 'wɪtɪd/ *adj* ‹*person*› imbécil; ‹*plan*› estúpido

half-yearly[1] /'hæf'jɪrli || ,hɑːf'jɪəli/ *adj* semestral

half-yearly[2] *adv* semestralmente, dos veces al año

halibut /'hæləbət || 'hælɪbət/ *n* [c u] (*pl* ~ *or* **~s**) hipogloso *m*, halibut *m*

hall /hɔːl/ *n*
A 1 (vestibule) vestíbulo *m*, entrada *f* 2 (corridor) (AmE) pasillo *m*, corredor *m*
B 1 (for gatherings) salón *m*; **the village/school ~** el salón (de actos) del pueblo/del colegio; **the church ~** ≈ el salón parroquial 2 (in castle, mansion) sala *f*
C (BrE) 1 (student residence) residencia *f* universitaria, colegio *m* mayor (Esp) 2 (college dining room) comedor *m*, casino *m* (Chi)
D (large country house) (BrE) casa *f* solariega

hallelujah /ˈhæləˈluːjə || ˌhælɪˈluːjə/ *interj* ¡aleluya!

hallmark /ˈhɔːlmɑːrk || ˈhɔːlmɑːk/ *n*
A (on gold, silver) contraste *m*, sello *m* (de contraste)
B (distinguishing characteristic) distintivo *m*, sello *m*; **it bore all the ~s of a crime of passion** tenía todas las características de un crimen pasional

hallo /həˈləʊ/ *interj* ▸**hello**

hall: ~ of fame *n* (*pl* **~s of fame**) 1 *also* **H~ of Fame** (room, building) galería *f* de personajes famosos 2 (ranks of famous people): **this feat will ensure her place in athletics' ~ of fame** esta hazaña le garantiza un puesto entre las estrellas *or* en los anales del atletismo; **~ of residence** *n* (*pl* **~s of residence**) (BrE) ▸**hall C1**

hallow /ˈhæləʊ/ *vt* (Relig) santificar*, consagrar; **~ed be Thy name** santificado sea tu nombre; **~ed ground** terreno *m* sagrado

Halloween, Hallowe'en /ˈhæləʊˈiːn/ *n* víspera *f* del día de Todos los Santos

> **Halloween**
>
> El 31 de octubre (víspera del día de Todos los Santos), oportunidad en que se mezclaba la religión con antiguas creencias paganas. En las Islas Británicas precristianas se pensaba que era la ocasión en que las almas de los difuntos y otros poderes sobrenaturales se volvían activos. En la actualidad, es el momento en que los niños tienen fiestas, se disfrazan de fantasmas, brujas etc., y llevando una calabaza hueca iluminada por dentro con una vela, van de casa en casa diciendo las palabras "*trick or treat*" lo que significa que harán una broma pesada a menos que se les dé "*a treat*", es decir caramelos, fruta o dinero

hall porter *n* portero, -ra *m,f*

hallucinate /həˈluːsn̩eɪt || həˈluːsɪneɪt/ *vi* alucinar

hallucination /həˈluːsn̩ˈeɪʃən || həˈluːsɪˈneɪʃən/ *n* [u c] alucinación *f*

hallucinogen /həˈluːsn̩ədʒən || həˈluːsɪnədʒən/ *n* alucinógeno *m*

hallucinogenic /həˈluːsn̩əˈdʒenɪk || həˌluːsɪnəˈdʒenɪk/ *adj* alucinógeno

hallway /ˈhɔːlweɪ/ *n* ▸**hall A**

halo /ˈheɪləʊ/ *n* (*pl* **-los** *or* **-loes**) 1 (Art, Relig) aureola *f*, halo *m* 2 (Astron, Opt) halo *m*

halogen /ˈhælədʒən/ *n* halógeno *m*

halt¹ /hɔːlt || hɒlt, hɔːlt/ *n*: **to come to a ~** pararse, detenerse*; ***to call a ~ to sth*** ponerle* fin a algo

halt² *vi* detenerse* (frml); **~!** (Mil) ¡alto!
■ **halt** *vt* ‹*vehicle/troops*› detener* (frml); ‹*process*› atajar, detener* (frml); ‹*work/production*› interrumpir

halter /ˈhɔːltər || ˈhɒltə(r), ˈhɔː-/ *n* cabestro *m*, ronzal *m*

halter-neck /ˈhɔːltərnek || ˈhɒltənek, ˈhɔː-/ *n* (*before n*) ‹*dress/top*› sin espalda

halting /ˈhɔːltɪŋ || ˈhɒltɪŋ, ˈhɔː-/ *adj* ‹*voice/speech*› titubeante, vacilante; (through emotion) entrecortado

haltingly /ˈhɔːltɪŋli || ˈhɒltɪŋli, ˈhɔːl-/ *adv* ‹*speak/read*› titubeando; (through emotion) con voz entrecortada

halve /hæv || hɑːv/ *vt* 1 (reduce by half) ‹*expense/time/length*› reducir* a la mitad *or* en un 50%; ‹*number*› dividir por dos 2 (divide into halves) partir por la mitad
■ **halve** *vi* reducirse* a la mitad *or* en un 50%

halves /hævz || hɑːvz/ *pl of* **half¹**

ham /hæm/ *n*
A (Culin) (cured) jamón *m* (crudo), jamón *m* serrano (Esp); (cooked) jamón *m* (cocido), jamón *m* (de) York (Esp)
B **~ (actor)** (Theat) *actor extravagantemente histriónico*
C (*radio* **~**) radioaficionado, -da *m,f*

Phrasal verb
• **ham up** [v ▸ o ▸ adv, v ▸ adv ▸ o] ‹*part/scene*› interpretar sobreactuando; ***to ~ it up*** actuar* con afectación *or* amaneramiento

hamburger /ˈhæmbɜːrgər || ˈhæmbɜːɡə(r)/ *n* 1 [c] (patty of meat) hamburguesa *f* 2 [u] (ground beef) (AmE) carne *f* molida *or* (Esp, RPl) picada

ham-fisted /ˈhæmˈfɪstəd || ˌhæmˈfɪstɪd/, **ham-handed** /ˈhæmˈhændəd || ˌhæmˈhændɪd/ *adj* ‹*person*› torpe, patoso (Esp fam); ‹*action*› desmañado, torpe

hamlet /ˈhæmlət || ˈhæmlɪt/ *n* aldea *f*, caserío *m*

hammer¹ /ˈhæmər || ˈhæmə(r)/ *n* 1 (tool) martillo *m*; **the ~ and sickle** la hoz y el martillo; ***to go at it ~ and tongs*** (fight) luchar a brazo partido; (argue) discutir acaloradamente; (work) trabajar a toda máquina 2 (auctioneer's gavel) mazo *m*, martillo *m*; **to come under the ~** venderse en subasta

hammer² *vt* 1 ‹*nail*› clavar (*con un martillo*); ‹*metal*› martillar, batir; **she tried to ~ the rules into them** intentó meterles las reglas en la cabeza 2 (hit): **he ~ed the ball into the net** clavó el balón en la red 3 (defeat) (colloq) darle* una paliza a (fam); **they were** *o* **got ~ed** les dieron una paliza 4 (criticize) (colloq) triturar, criticar*
■ **hammer** *vi* (strike) dar* golpes; (with hammer) dar* martillazos; **to ~ AT sth** golpear algo, darle* golpes/martillazos A algo; **to ~ ON sth** golpear algo

Phrasal verbs
• **hammer home** [v ▸ o ▸ adv, v ▸ adv ▸ o] 1 ‹*nail*› remachar 2 ‹*point*› recalcar*, machacar*
• **hammer out** [v ▸ o ▸ adv, v ▸ adv ▸ o] 1 (make smooth) ‹*metal/dent*› alisar a martillazos 2 ‹*compromise/deal*› negociar (*con mucho toma y daca*)

hammering /ˈhæmərɪŋ/ *n*
A [u] (striking) golpeteo *m*, martilleo *m*; (with hammer) martillazos *mpl*
B [c] (colloq) 1 (severe defeat) paliza *f* (fam); **to give sb a ~** darle* una paliza a algn (fam) 2 (severe criticism) duras críticas *fpl*

hammock /ˈhæmək/ *n* hamaca *f*, hamaca *f* paraguaya (RPl); (Naut) coy *m*

hamper¹ /ˈhæmpər || ˈhæmpə(r)/ *vt* dificultar

hamper² *n* cesta *f*, canasta *f*

hamster /ˈhæmstər || ˈhæmstə(r)/ *n* hámster *m*

hamstring¹ /ˈhæmstrɪŋ/ *n* (of person) ligamento *m* de la corva; (of horse) tendón *m* del corvejón *or* jarrete

hamstring² *vt* (*past & past p* **-strung** /ˈhæmstrʌŋ/) (render powerless) (*usu pass*): **I was hamstrung: I couldn't help them** estaba atado de pies y manos: no podía ayudarlos; **the project was hamstrung by lack of funds** el proyecto se vio frustrado por falta de fondos

hand¹ /hænd/ *n*
A (Anat) mano *f*; **you couldn't see your ~ in front of your face** no se veía nada; **to be good** *o* **clever with one's ~s** ser* hábil con las manos, ser* mañoso; **he killed it with his bare ~s** lo mató con sus propias manos; **to give sb one's ~** darle* la mano a algn; **they were holding ~s when they arrived** llegaron tomados *or* agarrados *or* (esp Esp) cogidos de la mano; **we were all on our ~s and knees, looking for the ring** estábamos todos a gatas, buscando el anillo; **he wouldn't give it to me even if I went down on my ~s and knees** no me lo daría ni aunque se lo pidiera de rodillas; **to have/hold sth in one's ~s** tener*/llevar algo en la mano; **look, no ~s!** mira ¡sin manos!; **to hold out one's ~ to sb** tenderle* la mano a algn; **to join ~s** darse* la(s) mano(s); **~s off!** ¡quita las manos de ahí!, ¡no toques!; **~s off our schools!** ¡dejen en paz nuestros colegios!; **can you put (your) ~ on (your) heart and say it isn't true?** ¿puedes decir que no es verdad con la mano en el corazón?; **to put one's ~ up** *o* **to raise one's ~** levantar la mano; **~s up all those in favor** que levanten la mano los que estén a favor; **~s up!** ¡manos arriba!, ¡arriba las manos!; **to raise one's ~ to** *o* **against sb** levantarle la mano a algn; **from ~ to ~** de mano en mano
B (in phrases) **at hand**: **help was at ~** la ayuda estaba en camino; **to learn about sth at first ~** enterarse de algo directamente *or* personalmente *or* de primera mano; **to learn about sth at second/third ~** enterarse de algo a través de *or* por terceros; **by hand**: **made/written by ~**

h

hecho/escrito a mano; **it must be washed by ~** hay que lavarlo a mano; **he delivered the letter by ~** entregó la carta en mano; **hand in hand** (tomados *or* agarrados *or* (esp Esp) cogidos) de la mano; **poverty and disease go ~ in ~** la pobreza y la enfermedad van de la mano; **in hand**: **glass/hat in ~** con el vaso/sombrero en la mano, vaso/sombrero en mano; **to pay cash in ~** pagar* en metálico *or* en efectivo; **let's get back to the matter in** *o* (AmE also) **at ~** volvamos a lo que nos ocupa; **to have sth (well) in ~** tener* algo controlado *or* bajo control; **that boy needs taking in ~** a ese chico va a haber que meterlo en cintura; **on hand**: **we're always on ~ when you need us** si nos necesitas, aquí estamos; **the police were on ~** la policía estaba cerca; **to have sth on ~** tener* algo a mano; **out of hand**: **to get out of ~** ‹‹*child*›› descontrolarse; **the situation is getting out of ~** la situación se les (*or* nos *etc*) va de las manos; **to reject sth out of ~** rechazar* algo de plano; **to hand** (BrE) (within reach) al alcance de la mano, a (la) mano; (available) disponible; **she grabbed the first thing that came to ~** agarró lo primero que encontró; ***~ in glove*** *o* (esp AmE) ***~ and glove***: **he was ~ in glove with the enemy** estaba confabulado con el enemigo; ***~ over fist*** a manos llenas, a espuertas (esp Esp); ***her/his left ~ doesn't know what her/his right ~ is doing*** borra con el codo lo que escribe con la mano; ***not to do a ~'s turn*** (colloq) no mover* un dedo (fam), no dar* golpe (Esp, Méx fam); ***to ask for sb's ~ (in marriage)*** (frml) pedir* la mano de algn (en matrimonio); ***to beat sb/win ~s down*** ganarle a algn/ganar sin problemas; ***to bind sb ~ and foot*** atar *or* (AmL exc RPl) amarrar a algn de pies y manos; ***to bite the ~ that feeds one*** ser* un desagradecido; ***to dirty*** *o* ***sully one's ~s*** (in criminal activity) ensuciarse las manos; **she wouldn't dirty her ~s with typing** no se rebajaría a hacer de mecanógrafa: se le caerían los anillos; ***to force sb's ~***: **I didn't want to, but you forced my ~** no quería hacerlo, pero no me dejaste otra salida; ***to gain/have the upper ~***: **she gained the upper ~ over her rival** se impuso a su rival; **she's always had the upper ~ in their relationship** siempre ha dominado ella en su relación; ***to get one's ~s on sb/sth***: **just wait till I get my ~s on him!** ¡vas a ver cuando lo agarre!; **she can't wait to get her ~s on the new computer** se muere por usar la computadora nueva; ***to give sb/have a free ~*** darle* a algn/tener* carta blanca; ***to give sb the glad ~*** (AmE) saludar a algn efusivamente; ***to go hat*** *o* (BrE) ***cap in ~ (to sb)***: **we had to go to them hat in ~ asking for more money** tuvimos que ir a mendigarles más dinero; ***to grab*** *o* ***grasp*** *o* ***seize sth with both ~s***: **it was a wonderful opportunity and she grabbed it with both ~s** era una oportunidad fantástica y no dejó que se le escapara de las manos; ***to have one's ~s full*** estar* ocupadísimo, no dar* para más; ***to have one's ~s tied*** tener* las manos atadas *or* (AmL exc RPl) amarradas; ***to have sb eating out of one's ~*** hacer* con algn lo que se quiere; ***to keep one's ~ in*** no perder* la práctica; ***to know a place like the back of one's ~*** conocer* un sitio al dedillo *or* como la palma de la mano; ***to live (from) ~ to mouth*** vivir al día; ***to put*** *o* ***dip one's ~ in one's pocket*** contribuir* con dinero; ***to put*** *o* ***lay one's ~(s) on sth*** dar* con algo; ***to try one's ~ (at sth)*** probar* (a hacer algo); ***to turn one's ~ to sth***: **he can turn his ~ to anything** es capaz de hacer cualquier tipo de trabajo; ***to wait on sb ~ and foot*** hacerle* de sirviente/sirvienta a algn; ***to wash one's ~s of sth*** lavarse las manos de algo; ***many ~s make light work*** el trabajo compartido es más llevadero

C 1 (agency) mano *f*; **the ~ of God** la mano de Dios; **to die by one's own ~** (frml) quitarse la vida; **to have a ~ in sth** tener* parte en algo; **the town had suffered at the ~s of invaders** la ciudad había sufrido a manos de los invasores; **that child needs a firm ~** ese niño necesita (una) mano firme; **to rule with a heavy ~** gobernar* con mano dura 2 (assistance) (colloq): **to give** *o* **lend sb a (helping) ~** echarle *or* darle* una mano a algn; **if you need a ~** si necesitas ayuda 3 **hands** *pl* (possession, control, care): **to change ~s** cambiar de dueño *or* manos; **in good/capable ~s** en buenas manos; **my life is in your ~s** mi vida depende de ti; **how did it come into your ~s?** ¿cómo llegó a tus manos?; **he/it fell into the ~s of the enemy** *o* **into enemy ~s** cayó en manos del enemigo; **to put oneself in sb's ~s** ponerse* en manos de algn; **to get sth/sb off one's ~s** (colloq) quitarse algo/a algn de encima (fam); **on sb's ~s**: **she has the children on her ~s all day long** tiene a los niños a su cuidado todo el día; **we've got a problem on our ~s** tenemos *or* se nos presenta un problema; **out of sb's ~s**: **the matter is out of my ~s** el asunto no está en mis manos; ***to play into sb's ~s*** hacerle* el juego a algn

D (side): **on sb's right/left ~** a la derecha/izquierda de algn; **on the one ~ ... on the other (~) ...** por un lado ... por otro (lado) ...

E (Games) 1 (set of cards) mano *f*, cartas *fpl*; ***to show*** *o* ***reveal one's ~*** mostrar* *or* enseñar las cartas, mostrar* el juego; ***to strengthen sb's ~*** afianzar* la posición de algn; ***to tip one's ~*** (AmE colloq) dejar ver sus (*or* mis *etc*) intenciones 2 (round of card game) mano *f*

F 1 (worker) obrero, -ra *m,f*; (*farm ~*) peón *m* 2 (Naut) marinero *m*; **all ~s on deck** ¡todos a cubierta! 3 (experienced person): **an old ~** un veterano, una veterana

G (applause) (colloq) (*no pl*): **a big ~ for ...** un gran aplauso para ...

H (handwriting) (liter) letra *f*; **the letter was in her own ~** la carta era de su puño y letra

I (on clock) manecilla *f*, aguja *f*; **the hour ~** la manecilla *or* la aguja de las horas, el horario, el puntero (Andes); **the minute ~** el minutero, la manecilla *or* la aguja de los minutos; **the second ~** el segundero, la manecilla *or* la aguja de los segundos

J (measurement) (Equ) palmo *m*

hand² *vt* **to ~ sb sth, to ~ sth TO sb** pasarle algo A algn; **he was ~ed a stiff sentence** (AmE) le impusieron una pena severa; ***to ~ it to sb***: **you have to ~ it to her; she knows her subject** hay que reconocérselo, conoce muy bien el tema

Phrasal verbs

- **hand around,** (BrE also) **hand round** [v ▸ o ▸ adv, v ▸ adv ▸ o] (distribute) repartir, distribuir*; (offer round) ‹*cakes*› ofrecer*
- **hand down** [v ▸ o ▸ adv, v ▸ adv ▸ o] 1 (pass down) ‹*custom/heirloom/story*› transmitir; ‹*clothes*› pasar 2 (AmE Law): **to ~ down a ruling** pronunciarse, dictar sentencia
- **hand in** [v ▸ o ▸ adv, v ▸ adv ▸ o] ‹*homework/form/ticket*› entregar*; **to ~ in one's resignation** presentar su (*or* mi *etc*) dimisión *or* renuncia
- **hand off** [v ▸ o ▸ adv, v ▸ adv ▸ o] (in US football) ‹‹*quarterback*›› ‹*ball*› ceder
- **hand on** [v ▸ o ▸ adv, v ▸ adv ▸ o] ‹*skills/knowledge*› transmitir, pasar; ‹*object/photograph*› pasar
- **hand out** [v ▸ o ▸ adv, v ▸ adv ▸ o] ‹*leaflets/food*› repartir, distribuir*; ‹*advice*› dar*
- **hand over**

A [v ▸ o ▸ adv, v ▸ adv ▸ o] 1 (relinquish) entregar* 2 (on telephone) **to hand sb over TO sb** pasarle a algn CON algn 3 (transfer) transferir*

B [v ▸ adv]: **when he finally ~s over to his son** cuando finalmente le ceda el puesto a su hijo; **I'll now ~ over to our reporter in Boston** vamos a escuchar ahora a nuestro corresponsal en Boston

- **hand round** (BrE) ▸ **hand around**

hand: **~bag** *n* (used by women) cartera *f or* (Esp) bolso *m or* (Méx) bolsa *f*; (small suitcase) (AmE) maletín *m*; **~ baggage**, (BrE) **luggage** *n* [u] equipaje *m* de mano; **~ball** *n* 1 [u] (game — in US) frontón *m*, pelota *f*; (— in Europe) balonmano *m*, handball *m* (AmL) 2 [c] (ball — in US) pelota *f* de frontón; (— in Europe) pelota *f* de balonmano *or* (AmL tb) de handball 3 [u c] (in soccer) mano *f*; **~bill** *n* volante *m*, folleto *m*; **~book** *n* manual *m*; **~brake** *n* (on bicycle) (AmE) freno *m* (de pastilla); (BrE Auto) freno *m* de mano; **~cart** *n* carretilla *f*; **~clap** /ˈhændklæp/ *n* palmada *f*; **to give sb a slow ~clap** darle* a algn palmas de tango

handcraft¹ /ˈhændkræft || ˈhændkrɑːft/ *vt* (*usu pass*) hacer* a mano; **~ed products** productos *mpl* artesanales

handcraft² *n* ▸ **handicraft**

hand: **~ cream** *n* [u c] crema *f* de manos *or* para las manos; **~cuff** *vt* esposar, ponerle* esposas a; **~cuffs** *pl n* esposas *fpl*; **a pair of ~cuffs** unas esposas

handful /ˈhændfʊl/ *n* 1 (amount) puñado *m*; **his hair was coming out by the ~** el pelo se le caía a mechones *or* manojos 2 (small number) (+ *sing o pl vb*) puñado *m*; **only a ~ of people were there** sólo había unas cuantas personas 3 (troublesome person or people) (*no pl*): **that child is a real ~** ese niño da mucho trabajo

hand: **~ grenade** *n* granada *f* (de mano); **~gun** *n* pistola *f*, revólver *m*; **~-held** /'hænd'held/ *adj* de mano; **~hold** *n*: *lugar de donde asirse*

handicap[1] /'hændɪkæp/ *n*
A 1 (disability): **physical ~** impedimento *m* físico; **mental ~** retraso *m* mental 2 (disadvantage) desventaja *f*
B (Sport) 1 (in golf, polo) hándicap *m*; (penalty) desventaja *f* 2 (event) hándicap *m*

handicap[2] *vt* **-pp-**
A ‹*person/chances*› perjudicar*
B (Sport) 1 ‹*person/horse*› asignar un hándicap a 2 (AmE) ‹*contestant*› evaluar* las posibilidades de

handicapped[1] /'hændɪkæpt/ *adj* disminuido, discapacitado, minusválido; **mentally/physically ~** disminuido *or* discapacitado *or* minusválido psíquico/físico

handicapped[2] *pl n* **the ~** los disminuidos *or* discapacitados *or* minusválidos

handicraft /'hændɪkræft || 'hændɪkrɑːft/, **handcraft** *n* 1 [u] (skill) artesanía *f*, trabajo *m* artesanal 2 [c] (product) producto *m* de artesanía

handily /'hændəli || 'hændɪli/ *adv*
A (colloq) (coveniently) ‹*placed/situated*› convenientemente
B (easily) (AmE) con facilidad, fácilmente

handiwork /'hændiwɜːrk || 'hændiwɜːk/ *n* [u] 1 (craftsmanship) trabajo *m* 2 (product) artesanías *fpl*, objetos *mpl* artesanales 3 (doing) (pej) obra *f*; **it looks like Laura's ~ to me** a mí me parece obra de Laura

hand: **~kerchief** /'hæŋkərtʃəf, -tʃiːf || 'hæŋkətʃɪf, -tʃiːf/ *n* (*pl* **-chieves** /-tʃiːvz/ *or* **-chiefs**) pañuelo *m*; **~-knitted** /'hænd'nɪtəd || ,hænd'nɪtɪd/ *adj* hecho a mano, tejido a mano

handle[1] /'hændḷ/ *n* (of cup, jug) asa *f*‡; (of door) picaporte *m*; (knob) pomo *m*; (of drawer) tirador *m*, manija *f*; (of broom, knife, spade) mango *m*; (of bag, basket) asa *f*‡; (of wheelbarrow, stretcher) brazo *m*; (of pump) manivela *f*; ***to fly off the ~*** perder* los estribos

handle[2] *vt*
A 1 (touch): **please do not ~ the goods** se ruega no tocar la mercancía; Ⓢ **handle with care** frágil 2 (manipulate, manage) ‹*vehicle/weapon*› manejar; ‹*chemicals*› manipular
B (deal with) ‹*people*› tratar; ‹*situation/affair*› manejar; **I'll ~ this** yo me encargo de esto; **he can't ~ the job** (colloq) no puede con el trabajo; **I can't tell him the truth; he couldn't ~ it** (colloq) no puedo decirle la verdad; lo destrozaría
C 1 (be responsible for) ‹*business/financial matters*› encargarse* *or* ocuparse de, llevar 2 (do business in) ‹*goods/commodities*› comerciar con; **to ~ stolen goods** comerciar con objetos robados 3 (process): **the dockers refused to ~ the cargo** los estibadores se negaron a tocar el cargamento; **the airport ~s 300 flights a day** el aeropuerto tiene un tráfico de 300 vuelos diarios 4 «*computer*» ‹*data*› procesar
■ **handle** *vi* responder; **this car ~s well on bends** este coche responde bien en las curvas
■ *v refl* **to ~ oneself** desenvolverse*

handlebar /'hændḷbɑːr || 'hændḷbɑː(r)/ *n* (*often pl*) **~(s)** manillar *m*, manubrio *m* (AmL)

handler /'hændlər || 'hændlə(r)/ *n*: *persona que adiestra o está a cargo de animales*

handling /'hændlɪŋ/ *n* [u]
A (treatment — of situation) manejo *m*; (— of subject) tratamiento *m*
B 1 (holding, touching): **it had become worn as a result of constant ~** se había gastado de tanto tocarlo/usarlo 2 (Busn) porte *m* 3 (Aviat) handling *m* 4 (Auto) manejo *m*

hand: **~ luggage** *n* [u] (BrE) equipaje *m* de mano; **~made** /'hænd'meɪd/ *adj* hecho a mano; **~maiden**, **~maid** *n* (arch) sierva *f*; **~-me-down** *n*: *prenda usada o heredada*; **~off** *n* (in US football) transferencia *f* (de balón); **~out** *n* 1 (of money, food) dádiva *f* 2 (advertising leaflet) folleto *m* 3 (at lecture, in class) notas *fpl* (*que se distribuyen a los asistentes*); **~over** /'hændəʊvər || 'hændəʊvə(r)/ *n* (BrE) entrega *f*; **~-painted** /'hænd 'peɪntəd || ,hænd'peɪntɪd/ *adj* pintado a mano; **~-picked** /'hænd'pɪkt/ *adj* cuidadosamente seleccionado; **~rail** *n* (on stairs, slope) pasamanos *m*; (on bridge, ship) baranda *f*, barandilla *f*; **~-rear** /'hænd'rɪr || 'hænd,rɪə(r)/ *vt* criar* como animal doméstico; **~saw** *n* serrucho *m*, sierra *f* (*manual*); **~set** *n* auricular *m*, tubo *m* (RPl); **~shake** *n* apretón *m* de manos; *see also* **golden handshake**; **~ signal** *n* (Auto) seña *f* (*hecha con la mano*); (by referee, coach) (AmE) señal *f*; **~s-off** /'hændz'ɔːf || 'hændz,ɒf/ *adj* (*before n*) 1 (Pol) ‹*approach/policy*› de no intervención *or* interferencia 2 (Comput) ‹*operation/running*› automático

handsome /'hænsəm/ **handsomer, handsomest** *adj*
A (attractive) ‹*man*› apuesto, buen mozo (AmL), guapo (esp Esp, Méx); **she's a ~ woman** es una mujer apuesta, es muy buena moza (AmL)
B ‹*gift/offer*› generoso, espléndido; **he got a ~ return on his investment** obtuvo un excelente beneficio de su inversión
C (well rendered) (AmE) ‹*performance*› muy logrado

handsomely /'hænsəmli/ *adv*
A ‹*illustrated/bound*› magníficamente
B ‹*contribute/reward*› con generosidad *or* esplendidez; ‹*profit*› enormemente
C (with skill) (AmE) ‹*perform*› hábilmente

hand: **~s-on** /'hændz'ɑːn || 'hændz,ɒn/ *adj* (*before n*) 1 ‹*instruction/experience*› práctico 2 (Comput) ‹*operation/running*› manual; **~spring** *n* voltereta *f*, vuelta *f* de manos (Méx); **~stand** *n*: **to do a ~stand** hacer* la vertical *or* (Esp) el pino, pararse de manos (AmL); **~-to-hand** /'hændtə'hænd/ *adj* (*before n*) ‹*fighting*› cuerpo a cuerpo; **~-to-mouth** /'hændtə'maʊθ/ *adj* pobre, precario; **to lead a ~-to-mouth existence** tener* una existencia precaria; **~-wash** /'hænd'wɔːʃ || 'hænd,wɒʃ/ *vt* lavar a mano; **~writing** *n* [u] letra *f*; **~written** /'hænd'rɪtṇ/ *adj* manuscrito, escrito a mano

handy /'hændi/ *adj* **-dier, -diest** (colloq)
A (*pred*) 1 (readily accessible) a mano 2 (conveniently situated) cerca, a mano; **we're very ~ for the airport** el aeropuerto nos queda muy a mano *or* muy cerca
B (useful) práctico; **to come in ~** venir* muy bien
C ‹*cook/gardener*› hábil, habilidoso

handyman /'hændimæn/ *n* (*pl* **-men** /-men/) *hombre habilidoso para trabajos de carpintería, albañilería etc*

hang[1] /hæŋ/ *vt*
A (*past & past p* **hung**) 1 (suspend) ‹*coat/picture*› colgar*; **the streets were hung with flags** las calles estaban adornadas con banderas 2 (put in position) ‹*door/gate*› colocar*, montar; **to ~ wallpaper** empapelar 3 (Culin) ‹*game*› manir 4 **to ~ one's head** bajar *or* inclinar la cabeza
B (*past & past p* **hanged** *or* **hung**) (execute) ahorcar*, colgar*
■ **hang** *vi*
A (*past p* **hung**) 1 (be suspended) colgar*, pender (liter), estar* colgado; **to ~ BY/FROM/ON sth** colgar* DE algo; **it's ~ing on the wall** está colgado en la pared; **they were ~ing on his every word** estaban totalmente pendientes de lo que decía *or* de sus palabras; **~ *loose!*** (esp AmE sl) ¡tranquilo!; ***to ~ tough on sth*** (AmE) mantenerse* firme en algo 2 (hover) «*fog/smoke*» flotar; «*bird*» planear, cernerse*; **to ~ OVER sth**: **the mist hung over the marshes** la bruma flotaba sobre las marismas; **I still have that essay ~ing over me** todavía tengo ese ensayo pendiente 3 «*clothing/fabric*» caer*; **that skirt ~s very well** esa falda tiene muy buena caída *or* cae muy bien
B (*past & past p* **hanged** *or* **hung**) (be executed): **his murderers should ~ for their crime** sus asesinos deberían ir a la horca por este crimen

Phrasal verbs

- **hang about** [v ▸ adv] 1 ▸ **hang around A** 2 (stop, wait) (BrE colloq) (*only in imperative*): **~ about: that can't be right!** ¡(espera) un momento! ¡no puede ser!
- **hang around** (colloq)
A [v ▸ adv] 1 (wait) esperar 2 (stay) quedarse; **I hung around to see what would happen** me quedé por ahí para ver qué pasaba 3 (spend time idly): **they just ~ around on street corners** pasan el tiempo en la calle, holgazaneando; **to ~ around WITH sb** andar* *or* juntarse CON algn
B [v ▸ prep ▸ o]: **we hung around the town for a few days** nos quedamos unos días más por la ciudad
- **hang back** [v ▸ adv] (physically) quedarse atrás; **she hung back, waiting for the best moment to speak** se contuvo, esperando el mejor momento para hablar
- **hang in** (colloq) seguir* adelante; **~ in there!** ¡(sigue) adelante!, ¡persevera!

• **hang on**
A [v ▸ adv] **1** (wait) esperar; **can you ~ on (for) a minute?** (espera) un momentito; **to keep sb ~ing on** hacer* esperar a algn **2** (keep hold) **to ~ on (TO sth)**: **~ on tight!** ¡agárrate fuerte!; **you ~ on to this end of the rope** tú sostén esta punta de la cuerda **3** **to ~ on TO sth** (colloq) conservar *or* guardar algo **4** (in a crisis) aguantar, resistir
B [v ▸ prep ▸ o] (depend on) depender de
• **hang out**
A [v ▸ o ▸ adv, v ▸ adv ▸ o] ‹*washing*› tender*, colgar*; ‹*flag*› poner*
B [v ▸ adv] **1** (dangle) «*wires*» estar* suelto; **with his shirt/tongue ~ing out** con la camisa/la lengua afuera; **let it all ~ out!** (sl & dated) ¡suéltate la melena! (fam) **2** (colloq) (live) vivir; (spend time) andar*, moverse* (fam); **to ~ out WITH sb** andar* CON algn **3** (pass time) (AmE sl): **what've you been up to? — just ~ing out** ¿qué has estado haciendo? — nada, por ahí con los chicos (*or* mis amigos *etc*)
• **hang together** [v ▸ adv]: **the story doesn't ~ together** al cuento le falta coherencia
• **hang up**
A [v ▸ adv] (put down receiver) colgar*, cortar (CS); **to ~ up ON sb** colgarle* a algn
B [v ▸ o ▸ adv, v ▸ adv ▸ o] ‹*coat*› colgar*
• **hang upon** ▸ **hang on B**

hang² *n* (*no pl*) (of garment) caída *f*; ***to get the ~ of sth*** (colloq) agarrarle la onda a algo (AmL fam), cogerle* el tranquillo a algo (Esp fam), agarrarle la mano a algo (CS fam)

hangar /'hæŋər || 'hæŋə(r)/ *n* hangar *m*

hangdog /'hæŋdɔːg || 'hæŋdɒg/ *adj* (*before n*) ‹*expression*› (downcast) abatido; (ashamed) avergonzado

hanger /'hæŋər || 'hæŋə(r)/ *n* (*clothes or coat ~*) percha *f*, gancho *m* (para la ropa) (AmL)

hanger-on /'hæŋər'ɑːn || ˌhæŋgər'ɒn/ *n* (*pl* **hangers-on**) (colloq & pej) parásito *m*, adlátere *mf*

hang: **~ glider** *n* ala *f*‡ delta, deslizador *m* (Méx); **~ gliding** /'glaɪdɪŋ/ *n* [u] vuelo *m* con ala delta *or* (Méx) en deslizador

hanging¹ /'hæŋɪŋ/ *n*
A **1** [u] (penalty) la horca, la pena de muerte en la horca **2** [c] (execution) ejecución *f* (*en la horca*)
B [c] (*wall ~*) tapiz *m*

hanging² *adj* (*before n*) colgante, pendiente

hanging basket *n*: *cesto colgante para plantas*

hang: **~man** *n* (*pl* **-men** /-mən/) **1** (Law) verdugo *m* **2** (Games) (*no pl*) ahorcado *m*; **~nail** *n* padrastro *m*; **~out** *n* (colloq): **we went to all his usual ~outs** fuimos a todos los sitios que solía frecuentar; **~over** *n* **1** (from drinking) resaca *f*, cruda *f* (AmC, Méx fam), guayabo *m* (Col fam), ratón *m* (Ven fam) **2** (something surviving) vestigio *m*, reliquia *f*; **~-up** *n* (colloq) complejo *m*, trauma *m*

hank /hæŋk/ *n* (of wool) madeja *f*

hanker /'hæŋkər || 'hæŋkə(r)/ *vi* **to ~ AFTER** *o* **FOR sth** anhelar *or* ansiar* algo

hankering /'hæŋkərɪŋ/ *n* anhelo *m*, ansia *f*‡; **to have a ~ FOR sth/to + INF** anhelar *or* ansiar* algo/+ INF

hanky, hankie /'hæŋki/ *n* (*pl* **-kies**) (colloq) pañuelo *m*

hanky-panky /'hæŋki'pæŋki/ *n* [u] (colloq & hum) **1** (malpractice) tejemanejes *mpl* (fam) **2** (sexual play) juegos *mpl* de manos **3** (bad behavior) travesuras *fpl*

hansom (cab) /'hænsəm/ *n* coche *m* de caballos

Hanukkah, Hanukah /'hɑːnəkə/ *n* Janucá *m*, Hanukkah *m* (*fiesta judía de la dedicación del Templo*)

ha'penny /'heɪpni/ *n* (BrE) **1** (*pl* **-pennies**) ▸ **halfpenny 1** **2** (*pl* **-pence**) ▸ **halfpenny 2**

haphazard /'hæp'hæzərd || ˌhæp'hæzəd/ *adj* **1** (random): **they promote people in a very ~ way** ascienden a la gente caprichosamente *or* al azar **2** (without order): **his approach is very ~** no es coherente en su enfoque

haphazardly /'hæp'hæzərdli || hæp'hæzədli/ *adv* caprichosamente

hapless /'hæpləs || 'hæplɪs/ *adj* (*before n*) (liter *or* journ) desafortunado, desventurado (liter)

happen /'hæpən/ *vi*
A **1** (occur) pasar, suceder, ocurrir; **don't let it ~ again** que no vuelva a pasar *or* suceder *or* ocurrir; **she acted as though nothing had ~ed** hizo como si nada hubiera pasado; **whatever ~s, we'll stand by you** pase lo que pase, te apoyaremos; **these things ~** son cosas que pasan; **hi, what's ~ing?** (AmE colloq) hola ¿qué tal? ¿qué es de tu vida? (fam) **2** (befall, become of) **to ~ TO sb** pasarle A algn; **a strange thing ~ed to me this morning** esta mañana me pasó *or* sucedió *or* ocurrió una cosa extraña
B **to ~ to + INF**: **she ~ed to be there** dio la casualidad de que estaba ahí; **if you ~ to see her ...** si por casualidad la ves ...; **you don't ~ to know the time of the next train, do you?** ¿usted no sabrá (por casualidad) a qué hora sale el próximo tren?; **who's that fat guy over there? — he ~s to be my brother** ¿quién es ese gordo de ahí? — pues da la casualidad de que es mi hermano
■ **happen** *v impers*: **it (just) so ~s that ...** da la casualidad de que ...; **as it ~s, I'm going that way myself** da la casualidad de que yo también voy hacia allí

Phrasal verb
• **happen on, happen upon** [v ▸ prep ▸ o] ‹*acquaintance*› encontrarse* *or* toparse con; ‹*object*› encontrarse*

happening /'hæpənɪŋ/ *n* suceso *m*

happenstance /'hæpənstæns/ *n* [u c] (AmE) casualidad *f*; **by ~** por casualidad

happily /'hæpəli || 'hæpɪli/ *adv*
A **1** ‹*smile/laugh*› alegremente; **... and they lived ~ ever after** (set phrase) ... y vivieron felices y comieron perdices (fr hecha); **it all ended ~** tuvo un final feliz; **to be ~ married** ser* feliz en el matrimonio **2** (willingly, gladly) (*usu before vb*) ‹*help*› con mucho gusto; **he'll quite ~ eat six eggs for breakfast** es muy capaz de comerse seis huevos en el desayuno
B (fortunately) (*indep*) por suerte, afortunadamente

happiness /'hæpines || 'hæpinɪs/ *n* [u] felicidad *f*, dicha *f*; **I wish you every ~** que seas muy feliz

happy /'hæpi/ *adj* **-pier, -piest**
A **1** (joyful, content) ‹*person/home*› feliz; ‹*smile*› de felicidad, alegre; ‹*disposition*› alegre; **I hope you'll both be very ~** que sean *or* (Esp) que seáis muy felices; **to make sb ~** hacer* feliz a algn; **he is ~ in his work** está contento con su trabajo; **I'd be happier if you weren't going alone** me quedaría más tranquilo si no fueras solo; ***as ~ as a sandboy/as a lark/as the day (is long)/as Larry*** (esp BrE) como unas pascuas, contentísimo **2** (pleased) (*pred*) **to be ~** alegrarse; **we're so ~ you're back** nos alegramos tanto *or* estamos tan contentos de que hayas vuelto; **I'm so ~ for you** me alegro mucho por ti, ¡cuánto me alegro!; **she'd be only too ~ to help** ella ayudaría encantada *or* con mucho gusto **3** (satisfied) (*pred*) **to be ~** estar* contento **4** (fortunate) (*before n*) ‹*coincidence*› feliz; ‹*position*› privilegiado, afortunado
B ‹*days/occasion*› feliz; **the happiest days of your life** la época más feliz de la vida; **~ birthday** feliz cumpleaños; **H~ New Year** Feliz Año Nuevo

happy-go-lucky /'hæpigəʊ'lʌki/ *adj* despreocupado

harangue¹ /hə'ræŋ/ *vt* arengar*

harangue² *n* arenga *f*

harass /'hærəs, hə'ræs/ *vt* **1** (persistently annoy) acosar **2** (Mil) hostigar*

harassed /'hærəst, hə'ræst/ *adj* nervioso, tenso, abrumado *or* agobiado por el trabajo (*or* los problemas *etc*)

harassment /'hærəsmənt, hə'ræs-/ *n* [u] **1** (pestering) acoso *m*; **racial ~** hostilidad *f* racial; **sexual ~** acoso *m* sexual; **police ~** acoso *m* por parte de la policía **2** (Mil) hostigamiento *m*

harbinger /'hɑːrbəndʒər || 'hɑːbɪndʒə(r)/ *n* (liter) (thing) presagio *m*; (person) precursor *m*, heraldo *m*

harbor¹, (BrE) **harbour** /'hɑːrbər || 'hɑːbə(r)/ *n* (Naut) puerto *m*; (*before n*) **~ wall** malecón *m*, espolón *m*

harbor², (BrE) **harbour** *vt* **1** (shelter) ‹*fugitive*› albergar*, dar* refugio a **2** ‹*desire/suspicion*› albergar* (liter); ‹*hopes*› abrigar* (liter); **to ~ a grudge** guardar rencor

harbor master, (BrE) **harbour master** /'hɑːrbər 'mæstər || 'hɑːbəˌmɑːstə(r)/ *n* capitán *m* de puerto

hard¹ /hɑːrd || hɑːd/ *adj* **-er, -est**
A **1** (firm, solid) ‹*object/surface*› duro; **to set ~** endurecerse*; **to freeze ~** helarse* **2** (forceful) ‹*push/knock*› fuerte
B **1** (difficult) ‹*question/subject*› difícil; ‹*task*› arduo; **~ to come by** difícil de conseguir; **he's ~ to please** es difícil de complacer, es exigente; **I find that ~ to believe** me cuesta creerlo; **to learn sth the ~ way** aprender algo a base de cometer errores **2** (severe) ‹*winter/climate/master*›

duro, severo; **to give sb a ~ time** hacérselas* pasar mal a algn; **these are ~ times we're living in** vivimos tiempos difíciles; **don't be too ~ on him** no seas demasiado duro con él; **~ luck** mala suerte [3] (tough, cynical) ‹*person/attitude*› duro, insensible

C (concentrated, strenuous): **to take a long ~ look at sth** analizar* seriamente algo; **children are very ~ work** los niños dan mucho trabajo; **he's a ~ worker** es muy trabajador

D (definite) ‹*evidence*› concluyente

E (sharp, harsh) ‹*light/voice*› fuerte; ‹*expression*› duro

F [1] (in strongest forms): **~ drugs** drogas *fpl* duras; **~ liquor** bebidas *fpl* (alcohólicas) fuertes; **~ porn** porno *m* duro [2] (Fin): **~ cash** dinero *m* contante y sonante, efectivo *m*; **~ currency** divisa *f* *or* moneda *f* fuerte [3] ‹*water*› duro [4] (Ling) ‹*sound/consonant*› fuerte

hard² *adv* **-er, -est**

A [1] (with force) ‹*pull/push*› con fuerza; ‹*hit*› fuerte [2] (strenuously) ‹*work*› mucho, duro, duramente; **I was ~ at work** estaba concentrado en mi trabajo; **he works his students very ~** hace trabajar mucho a sus alumnos; **no matter how ~ I try** por más que me esfuerzo; **think ~ before you decide** piénsalo muy bien antes de decidir; ***to be ~ put*** *o* (BrE also) ***pushed to* + INF**: **you'd be ~ put (to it) to find a better doctor** sería difícil encontrar un médico mejor [3] (intently) ‹*listen*› atentamente, con atención

B (heavily) ‹*rain/snow*› fuerte, mucho; ‹*pant/breathe*› pesadamente

C (severely): **the southern states have been ~est hit** los estados del sur han sido los más afectados; **her death hit him very ~** su muerte fue un duro golpe para él; **to take sth ~** tomarse algo muy mal; ***to be/feel ~ done by***: **she thinks she has been** *o* **she feels ~ done by** piensa que la han tratado injustamente

hard: **~-and-fast** /ˈhɑːrdn̩ˈfæst || ˈhɑːdənˈfɑːst/ *adj* (*no comp, usu before n*) absoluto, que se puede aplicar a rajatabla; **~back** *n* [1] [c] (book) libro *m* de tapa dura *or* en cartoné [2] [u] (cover): **in ~back** con tapa dura, en cartoné; **~ball** *n* [u] (AmE) béisbol *m*; ***to play ~ball*** (colloq) ser* implacable *or* despiadado (fam); **~-bitten** /ˈhɑːrdˈbɪtn̩ || ˌhɑːdˈbɪtn̩/ *adj* endurecido; **~board** *n* [u] cartón *m* madera; **~-boiled** /ˈhɑːrdˈbɔɪld || ˌhɑːdˈbɔɪld/ *adj* [1] ‹*egg*› duro [2] (unsentimental) endurecido; **~ candy** *n* [u c] (AmE) barra *f* de caramelo; **~ copy** *n* [u] impresión *f*; **~-core** /ˈhɑːrdˈkɔːr || ˈhɑːdˌkɔː(r)/ *adj*: **~-core pornography** pornografía *f* dura; **~cover** /ˈhɑːrdˈkʌvər || ˌhɑːdˈkʌvə(r)/ *n* ► **~back 2**; **~ disk** *n* disco *m* duro; **~-earned** /ˈhɑːrdˈɜːrnd || ˈhɑːdˌɜːnd/ *adj* (*usu before n*) ‹*cash*› ganado con el sudor de la frente; ‹*rest*› bien merecido

harden /ˈhɑːrdn̩ || ˈhɑːdn̩/ *vt* [1] (make hard) ‹*clay/cement*› endurecer*; ‹*skin*› endurecer*, curtir; ‹*steel/glass*› templar [2] (make tough, unfeeling) ‹*person*› endurecer*; **to ~ sb TO sth** acostumbrar a algn A algo; **to ~ one's heart**: **you must ~ your heart and tell him to go** tienes que hacerte fuerte y decirle que se vaya [3] (make firm) ‹*resolve*› afianzar*

■ **harden** *vi* [1] (become hard, rigid) endurecerse* [2] (become inflexible) «*attitude*» volverse* inflexible

hardened /ˈhɑːrdn̩d || ˈhɑːdn̩d/ *adj*

A [1] (seasoned) ‹*troops/veterans*› curtido (en el combate); **to be ~ TO sth** estar* acostumbrado *or* hecho A algo [2] (inveterate) (*before n*) ‹*sinner/drinker*› empedernido; ‹*criminal*› habitual

B (Metall) ‹*steel*› templado

hardening /ˈhɑːrdnɪŋ || ˈhɑːdnɪŋ/ *n* [u] [1] (of material) endurecimiento *m*; **~ of the arteries** endurecimiento de las arterias, arteriosclerosis *f* [2] (of attitude, position) radicalización *f*

hard: **~-fought** /ˈhɑːrdˈfɔːt || ˌhɑːdˈfɔːt/ *adj* muy reñido; **~ goods** *pl n* (AmE) productos *mpl* no perecederos; **~ hat** *n* [1] (Clothing, Const) casco *m* [2] (construction worker) (AmE colloq) albañil *m* [3] (conservative) (AmE sl) reaccionario, -ria *m,f* (*de clase obrera*); **~-hat** *adj* (AmE) (*before n*) [1] (conservative) (sl) reaccionario [2] (blue-collar) ‹*bar*› de obreros; ‹*attitude*› de clase obrera; **~-headed** /ˈhɑːrdˈhedəd || ˌhɑːdˈhedɪd/ *adj* [1] (practical, realistic) práctico, realista [2] (stubborn) (AmE) testarudo, cabezota (fam); **~-hearted** /ˈhɑːrdˈhɑːrtəd || ˌhɑːdˈhɑːtɪd/ *adj* duro de corazón, despiadado; **~-hitting** /ˈhɑːrdˈhɪtɪŋ || ˌhɑːdˈhɪtɪŋ/ *adj* implacable, feroz; **~ labor**, (BrE) **~ labour** *n* [u] trabajos *mpl* forzados; **~-line** /ˈhɑːrdˈlaɪn || ˌhɑːdˈlaɪn/ *adj* de línea dura; **~-liner** /ˈhɑːrdˈlaɪnər || ˌhɑːdˈlaɪnə(r)/ *n* partidario, -ria *m,f* de la línea dura; **~-luck story** /ˈhɑːrdˈlʌk || ˌhɑːdˈlʌk/ *n*: **he came to me with another ~-luck story** me vino otra vez con el cuento de sus penurias

hardly /ˈhɑːrdli || ˈhɑːdli/ *adv* [1] (scarcely): **~ anyone/anything** casi nadie/nada; **~ ever** casi nunca; **I could ~ believe my eyes** apenas podía dar crédito a mis ojos, casi no podía dar crédito a mis ojos; **he ~ knew her** apenas la conocía [2] (surely not): **it's ~ what you'd call a masterpiece** no es precisamente una obra maestra; **will they appoint him? — hardly!** ¿le darán el cargo? — ¡lo veo difícil!; **I could ~ say no** no me podía negar; **I need ~ remind you that ...** ni falta hace que les recuerde que ...; **that's ~ surprising!** ¡no es de extrañarse!

hardness /ˈhɑːrdnəs || ˈhɑːdnɪs/ *n* [u] dureza *f*

hard: **~-nosed** /ˈhɑːrdˈnəʊzd || ˌhɑːdˈnəʊzd/ *adj* (tough-minded) duro; (stubborn) terco, cerril; **~ of hearing** *adj* duro de oído; **~-on** *n* (sl) erección *f*; **to have a ~-on** tenerla* dura *or* (AmL tb) parada (arg), estar* empalmado (Esp arg); **~-pressed** /ˈhɑːrdˈprest || ˌhɑːdˈprest/ *adj* (*pred* **~ pressed**) ‹*industry/nation/staff*› en apuros; **to be ~ pressed to + INF** verse* en apuros PARA + INF; **~ sauce** *n* (AmE) *mantequilla azucarada con coñac o ron*; **~ sell** *n* (*no pl*): **the ~ sell** la venta agresiva; **he gave me the ~ sell** me presionó para que comprara

hardship /ˈhɑːrdʃɪp || ˈhɑːdʃɪp/ *n* [u c]: **to experience** *o* **suffer great ~** pasar muchos apuros *or* muchas dificultades *or* privaciones; **financial ~** penuria *f* (económica); **surely it's no great ~ for you to go** no es mucho pedir que vayas, creo yo

hard: **~ shoulder** *n* (BrE) arcén *m*, acotamiento *m* (Méx), berma *f* (Andes), banquina *f* (RPl), hombrillo *m* (Ven); **~standing** /hɑːrdˈstændɪŋ || hɑːdˈstændɪŋ/ *n* [u] área *f* asfaltada para estacionar; **~top** *n* (AmE) (car) coche *m* no descapotable; **~ up** *adj* (colloq) (*pred*) [1] (short of money) **to be ~ up** estar* mal de dinero [2] (poorly provided): **to be ~ up FOR sth** andar* escaso DE algo; **~ware** /ˈhɑːrdwer || ˈhɑːdweə(r)/*n* [u] [1] (ironmongery) ferretería *f*, (*before n*) **~ware store** ferretería *f*, mercería *f* (Chi) [2] (equipment) equipo *m*, maquinaria *f*; **military ~ware** armamento *m* [3] (Comput) hardware *m*, soporte *m* físico, equipo *m*; **~-wearing** /ˈhɑːrdˈwerɪŋ || ˌhɑːdˈweərɪŋ/ *adj* (BrE) resistente, duradero; **~-won** /ˈhɑːrdˈwʌn || ˌhɑːdˈwʌn/ *adj* ganado con esfuerzo; **~wood** *n* [u c] madera *f* dura *or* noble; **~-working** /ˈhɑːrdˈwɜːrkɪŋ || ˌhɑːdˈwɜːkɪŋ/ *adj* trabajador

hardy /ˈhɑːrdi || ˈhɑːdi/ *adj* **-dier, -diest** ‹*person/animal*› fuerte; ‹*plant*› resistente (*a las heladas etc*)

hare¹ /her || heə(r)/ *n* liebre *f*; ***(as) mad as a March ~*** más loco que una cabra

hare² *vi* (BrE colloq): **to ~ in/out/up/down** entrar/salir*/subir/bajar a la carrera *or* como un bólido (fam)

hare: **~brained** /ˈherˈbreɪnd || ˈheəˌbreɪnd/ *adj* descabellado, disparatado; **~lip** /ˈherˈlɪp || ˈheəlɪp/ *n* labio *m* leporino

harem /ˈhɑːrəm, ˈherəm || ˈhɑːriːm, hɑːˈriːm/ *n* harén *m*

haricot (bean) /ˈhærɪkəʊ/ *n* frijol *m* *or* (Esp) alubia *f* *or* judía *f* *or* (CS) poroto *m* (*de color blanco*)

hark /hɑːrk || hɑːk/ *vi* (listen) (*only in imperative*) [1] (poet) escuchar [2] (BrE iro): **~ who's talking!** ¡mira quién habla!; **~ at him!** ¡habráse visto!

Phrasal verb

• **hark back** [v ► adv] **to ~ back TO sth** «*person*» rememorar algo; **this custom ~s back to the 18th century** esta costumbre tiene su origen en el siglo XVIII

harlequin /ˈhɑːrlɪkwən || ˈhɑːlɪkwɪn/ *n* arlequín *m*

harlot /ˈhɑːrlət || ˈhɑːlət/ *n* (liter) ramera *f*

harm¹ /hɑːrm || hɑːm/ *n* [u] daño *m*; **to do ~ to sb/sth** hacerle* daño a algn/algo; **to do more ~ than good** hacer* más mal *or* daño que bien; **don't worry, there's no ~ done** no se preocupe, no es nada; **there's no ~ in asking** con preguntar no se pierde nada; **where's/what's the ~ in that?** ¿y qué tiene (eso) de malo?; **he'll come to no ~, he won't come to any ~** no le va a pasar nada; **I didn't mean him any ~** no quería hacerle daño; ***to be out of ~'s way*** estar* a salvo; ***to get sb out of ~'s way*** poner* a algn a salvo

harm² *vt* ‹*person/object*› hacerle* daño a; ‹*reputation/career*› perjudicar*

harmful /ˈhɑːrmfəl || ˈhɑːmfəl/ *adj* ‹*substance*› nocivo; ‹*influence*› pernicioso, dañino; ‹*effect*› perjudicial

harmless /ˈhɑːrmləs || ˈhɑːmlɪs/ *adj* ‹*animal/person*› inofensivo; ‹*substance*› inocuo; ‹*joke/suggestion/fun*› inocente

harmlessly /ˈhɑːrmləsli || ˈhɑːmlɪsli/ *adv* sin hacer *or* causar daño

harmonica /hɑːrˈmɑːnɪkə || hɑːˈmɒnɪkə/ *n* armónica *f*

harmonious /hɑːrˈməʊniəs || hɑːˈməʊniəs/ *adj* armonioso

harmoniously /hɑːrˈməʊniəsli || hɑːˈməʊniəsli/ *adv* ‹*sing/play*› armoniosamente; ‹*live*› en armonía

harmonium /hɑːrˈməʊniəm || hɑːˈməʊniəm/ *n* armonio *m*

harmonize /ˈhɑːrmənaɪz || ˈhɑːmənaɪz/ *vi* [1] (Mus) cantar en armonía [2] (be in accord) «*colors/ideas*» armonizar*

■ **harmonize** *vt* ‹*policies/plans*› armonizar*, poner* en armonía

harmony /ˈhɑːrməni || ˈhɑːməni/ *n* [u c] (*pl* **-nies**) (Mus) armonía *f*; **to sing/play in ~** cantar/tocar* en armonía; **they live together in perfect ~** viven juntos en perfecta armonía

harness¹ /ˈhɑːrnəs || ˈhɑːnɪs/ *n* [1] [c u] (for horse) arnés *m*, arreos *mpl* [2] [c] (for baby, on parachute) arnés *m* [3] [c] (*safety* ~) arnés *m* de seguridad

harness² *vt* [1] (put harness on) ‹*horse*› enjaezar*, ponerle* los arreos *or* el arnés a [2] (utilize) ‹*energy/resources*› aprovechar, utilizar*

harp /hɑːrp || hɑːp/ *n* arpa *f*‡

Phrasal verb

- **harp on** [v ▸ adv] (colloq) **to ~ on ABOUT sth** insistir SOBRE algo

harpist /ˈhɑːrpəst || ˈhɑːpɪst/ *n* arpista *mf*

harpoon¹ /hɑːrˈpuːn || hɑːˈpuːn/ *n* arpón *m*

harpoon² *vt* arponear

harpsichord /ˈhɑːrpsɪkɔːrd || ˈhɑːpsɪkɔːd/ *n* clavicémbalo *m*

harpy /ˈhɑːrpi || ˈhɑːpi/ *n* (*pl* **-pies**) arpía *f*

harridan /ˈhærədn̩ || ˈhærɪdən/ *n* (liter) vieja *f* bruja

harrow /ˈhærəʊ/ *n* escarificador *m*, rastra *f*

harrowing /ˈhærəʊɪŋ/ *adj* ‹*tale*› desgarrador; ‹*experience*› angustioso, terrible

harry /ˈhæri/ *vt* **-ries, -rying, -ried** [1] (raid) ‹*enemy*› hostilizar* [2] (pester, bother) hostigar*, acosar

harsh /hɑːrʃ || hɑːʃ/ *adj* ‹*punishment*› duro, severo; ‹*words/conditions*› duro; ‹*light*› fuerte; ‹*climate*› riguroso; ‹*contrast*› violento; ‹*color*› chillón; ‹*sound*› discordante; ‹*tone/texture*› áspero; **the ~ realities of life** la cruel realidad (de la vida)

harshly /ˈhɑːrʃli || ˈhɑːʃli/ *adv* ‹*judge/punish/speak*› severamente, con severidad *or* rigor *or* dureza; **the painting was ~ lit** el cuadro tenía una iluminación muy cruda

harshness /ˈhɑːrʃnəs || ˈhɑːʃnɪs/ *n* [u] (of treatment) severidad *f*; (of words) dureza *f*; (of climate) rigor *m*, lo riguroso; (of sound) estridencia *f*; (of texture) aspereza *f*

hart /hɑːrt || hɑːt/ *n* (liter) venado *m*

harvest¹ /ˈhɑːrvəst || ˈhɑːvɪst/ *n* [c u] (yield) cosecha *f*; (of grain) cosecha *f*, siega *f*; (of fruit, vegetables) cosecha *f*, recolección *f*; (of grapes) vendimia *f*

harvest² *vt* ‹*crop/wheat*› cosechar; ‹*grapes*› vendimiar; ‹*field*› realizar* la cosecha en

harvester /ˈhɑːrvəstər || ˈhɑːvɪstə(r)/ *n* [1] (machine) cosechadora *f* [2] (person) segador, -dora *m,f*

harvest: **~ festival** *n* (BrE) fiesta *f* de la cosecha; **~ moon** *n* luna *f* llena *or* de otoño

has /hæz, *weak form* həz, əz/ *3rd pers sing pres of* **have**

has-been /ˈhæzbɪn || ˈhæzbiːn/ *n* (colloq & pej) nombre *m* del pasado

hash /hæʃ/ *n*

A [1] [u c] (Culin) *plato de carne y verduras picadas y doradas* [2] [c] (muddle): **to make a ~ of sth** (colloq) ‹*exam*› hacer* algo muy mal; **the carpenter made a complete ~ of the job** el carpintero hizo una verdadera chapuza

B [u] (drug) (sl) hachís *m*, chocolate *m* (Esp arg)

Phrasal verbs

- **hash out** [v ▸ o ▸ adv, v ▸ adv ▸ o] (AmE colloq) discutir
- **hash over** [v ▸ o ▸ adv, v ▸ adv ▸ o] (AmE colloq): **to ~ over sth** *o* **~ sth over** darle muchas vueltas a algo (fam)

hash: **~ browns** *pl n* (AmE colloq) *papas y cebolla doradas en la sartén*; **~ code** *n*: *número usado para codificar datos*; **~ house** *n* (AmE sl) restaurante *m* barato, fonda *f* (esp AmL), taguara *f* (Ven)

hashish /ˈhæʃiːʃ/ *n* [u] hachís *m*

hash key *n* tecla *f* (del signo) del número, tecla *f* numeral, tecla *f* de almohadilla (Esp)

hash mark *n*

A (Comput, Print) *símbolo (#), utilizado delante de un número*

B (service stripe) (AmE sl) galón *m*

C (in US football) *cada una de las marcas que señalan los límites de la banda central del campo de juego*

hasn't /ˈhæznt/ **= has not**

hasp /hæsp || hɑːsp/ *n* (for door) picaporte *m*; (for book cover, purse) cierre *m*, broche *m*

Hassidic /həˈsɪdɪk, ˈhæ-/ *adj* hasídico

hassle¹ /ˈhæsəl/ *n* [c u] (colloq) lío *m* (fam), rollo *m* (fam); **don't give me any ~** no me fastidies; **legal ~s** problemas *mpl or* dificultades *fpl* legales

hassle² *vt* (colloq) fastidiar, jorobar (fam)

hassock /ˈhæsək/ *n* [1] (in church) *cojín para arrodillarse* [2] (footstool) (AmE) escabel *m*

hast /hæst/ (arch) *2nd pers sing pres of* **have**

haste /heɪst/ *n* [u] prisa *f*, apuro *m* (AmL); **to do sth in ~** hacer* algo apresuradamente; **to make ~** darse* prisa, apurarse (AmL); ***more ~, less speed*** *o* (AmE also) ***~ makes waste*** vísteme despacio, que tengo prisa

hasten /ˈheɪsn̩/ *vt* ‹*process*› acelerar; ‹*defeat/death*› adelantar

■ **hasten** *vi* apresurarse, apurarse (AmL); **to ~ to + INF** apresurarse A + INF; **not that I've got anything against her, I ~ to add** no es que tenga nada contra ella, que conste

hastily /ˈheɪstəli || ˈheɪstɪli/ *adv* [1] (quickly) ‹*built/thought up*› a toda prisa, apresuradamente [2] (rashly) ‹*speak/act*› con precipitación, precipitadamente

hasty /ˈheɪsti/ *adj* **-tier, -tiest** [1] (quick) ‹*glance/meal*› rápido; **she made a ~ exit** salió apresuradamente *or* a toda prisa [2] (rash) ‹*move/decision/judgment*› precipitado; **I think you're being rather ~** creo que te precipitas

hat /hæt/ *n* [1] (Clothing) sombrero *m*; ***I'll eat my ~*** (colloq): **if they finish before Friday, I'll eat my ~** si acaban antes del viernes, yo soy Napoleón (fam); ***to be old ~*** no ser* nada nuevo *or* ninguna novedad; ***to keep sth under one's ~***: **keep it under your ~** de esto no digas palabra *or* (fam) ni pío; ***to pass the ~ around*** pasar la gorra; ***to pull sth out of the ~*** sacarse* algo de la manga; ***to raise*** *o* ***take off one's ~ to sb***: **you have to take your ~ off to her** hay que quitarse el sombrero, hay que sacarle *or* quitarle el sombrero (AmL); ***to talk through one's ~*** hablar por hablar, hablar sin ton ni son; ▸ **hand¹ B** [2] (indicating role, capacity): **he spoke wearing his politician's ~** habló en calidad de político

hat: **~band** *n* cinta *f* del sombrero; **~box** *n* sombrerera *f*

hatch¹ /hætʃ/ *vt* [1] ‹*egg*› incubar [2] **~ (out)** ‹*chick*› empollar [3] (devise) (pej) ‹*plot/scheme*› tramar, urdir

■ **hatch** *vi* [1] «*egg*» romperse* [2] **~ (out)** «*chick*» salir* del cascarón, nacer*

hatch² *n* [1] (opening, cover) trampilla *f*; (Aviat, Naut) escotilla *f*; ***down the ~!*** (colloq) ¡salud! [2] (*serving* ~) ventanilla *f* (*que comunica cocina y comedor*)

hatchback /ˈhætʃbæk/ *n* (car) coche *m* con tres/cinco puertas; (door) puerta *f* trasera

hatcheck /ˈhættʃek/ *adj* (*before n*) (AmE): **~ room** guardarropa *m*; **~ girl** (chica *f* del) guardarropa *f*

hatchet /ˈhætʃət || ˈhætʃɪt/ *n* hacha *f*‡, hachuela *f*; ***to bury the ~*** enterrar* el hacha de guerra, hacer* las paces

hatchet: **~ job** *n* (colloq) crítica *f* feroz; **~ man** *n* (colloq) [1] (ruthless operator) *persona contratada para ejecutar tareas o tomar decisiones desagradables* [2] (hired killer) (AmE) sicario *m*, asesino *m* a sueldo

hatchway /ˈhætʃweɪ/ *n* (opening, cover) trampilla *f*; (Aviat, Naut) escotilla *f*

hate¹ /heɪt/ *vt* odiar, aborrecer*, detestar; **to ~ sb FOR sth/-ING** odiar a algn POR algo/+ INF; **I ~ people with loud voices** no soporto a la gente que habla a gritos; **I ~ ironing** detesto *or* odio planchar; **I ~ to disturb you, but ...** perdona que te moleste, pero ...

hate² *n* 1 [u] (hatred) **~ (FOR sb/sth)** odio *m* (A *or* HACIA algn/A algo); (*before n*) **~ mail** cartas *fpl* llenas de insultos y amenazas 2 [c] (object of hatred) ▸**pet² 2**

hated /'heɪtəd || 'heɪtɪd/ *adj* odiado, aborrecido

hateful /'heɪtfəl/ *adj* odioso, aborrecible

hath /hæθ/ (arch) *3rd pers sing pres of* **have**

hatpin /'hætpɪn/ *n* alfiler *m* de sombrero

hatred /'heɪtrəd || 'heɪtrɪd/ *n* [u] **~ (FOR** *o* **OF sb/sth)** odio *m* (A *or* HACIA algn/A algo)

hatstand /'hætstænd/ *n* colgador *m* para sombreros

hatter /'hætər || 'hætə(r)/ *n* sombrerero, -ra *m,f*; ***to be as mad as a ~*** estar* como una cabra (fam)

hat trick *n*: **to score a ~ ~** marcar* tres goles (*or* tantos *etc*) en un partido; **a ~ ~ of wins** tres victorias consecutivas

haughtily /'hɔːtḷi || 'hɔːtɪli/ *adv* con altivez *or* altanería altivamente

haughty /'hɔːti/ *adj* **-tier, -tiest** altivo, altanero

haul¹ /hɔːl/ *vt* 1 (drag): **the fishermen ~ed in their nets** los pescadores cobraron *or* recogieron las redes; **a tractor ~ed the car out of the ditch** un tractor sacó el coche de la cuneta; **she was ~ed out of bed at midnight** la sacaron de la cama a medianoche 2 (Transp) transportar

Phrasal verbs

- **haul off** [v ▸ adv] (AmE colloq) armarse de valor
- **haul up** [v ▸ o ▸ adv, v ▸ adv ▸ o] (summon): **she was ~ed up before her boss** tuvo que ir a rendirle cuentas al jefe; **he was ~ed up on a fraud charge** le entablaron juicio por fraude

haul² *n*

A (distance) (Transp) recorrido *m*, trayecto *m*; ***a long ~*** (to success, victory) un camino largo y difícil; (lit: long journey) un trayecto largo; ***in*** *o* ***over the long/short ~*** (AmE) a largo/corto plazo

B (catch — of fish) redada *f*; (— of stolen goods) botín *m*

haulage /'hɔːlɪdʒ/ *n* [u] 1 (activity) transporte *m*; (*before n*) **~ contractor** transportista *mf* 2 (charge) (gastos *mpl* de) transporte *m*

hauler /'hɔːlər || 'hɔːlə(r)/, (BrE) **haulier** /'hɔːljə(r)/ *n* 1 (person) transportista *mf* 2 (business) empresa *f* de transportes

haunch /hɔːntʃ/ *n* (*usu pl*) (of animal) anca *f*‡; (of horse) grupa *f*, anca *f*‡; (of person) cadera *f*; **to squat down on one's ~es** ponerse* en cuclillas

haunt¹ /hɔːnt/ *vt* «*ghost*» rondar; «*memory/idea*» perseguir*; **he was ~ed by the fear of death** vivía obsesionado por el miedo a la muerte

haunt² *n*: **this bar is his usual/favorite ~** éste es el bar al que va siempre/es su bar favorito *or* predilecto; **we went to all her old ~s** fuimos a todos los sitios a los que solía ir *or* los sitios que frecuentaba; **a favorite ~ of artists** un lugar favorito entre los artistas

haunted /'hɔːntəd || 'hɔːntɪd/ *adj* ‹*house/room*› embrujado; ‹*look/expression*› angustiado, obsesionado

haunting /'hɔːntɪŋ/ *adj* evocador e inquietante

haute couture /ˌəʊtkuː'tʊr || ˌəʊtkuː'tjʊə(r)/ *n* (*no pl*) alta costura *f*

haute cuisine /ˌəʊtkwɪ'ziːn/ *n* [u] alta cocina *f*

Havana /hə'vænə/ *n* La Habana

have /hæv, *weak forms* həv, əv/ (*3rd pers sing pres* **has**; *past & past p* **had**) *vt*

Sense **I**

A (possess) tener*; **I ~** *o* (esp BrE) **I've got two cats** tengo dos gatos; **I don't ~** *o* (esp BrE) **~n't got any money** no tengo dinero; **do you ~ a car? — no, I don't** *o* (esp BrE) **~ you got a car? — no, I ~n't** ¿tienes coche? — no (, no tengo)

B (hold, have at one's disposal) tener*: **look out, he's got a gun!** ¡cuidado! ¡tiene una pistola *or* está armado!; **how much money do you ~** *o* (esp BrE) **~ you got on you?** ¿cuánto dinero tienes *or* llevas encima?; **I had him by the arm** lo tenía agarrado del brazo; **can I ~ a sheet of paper?** ¿me das una hoja de papel?; **may I ~ your name?** ¿me dice su nombre?; **could I ~ your Sales Department, please?** (on phone) ¿me comunica *or* (Esp tb) me pone *or* (CS tb) me da con el departamento de ventas, por favor?; **I ~ it!, I've got it!** ¡ya lo tengo!, ¡ya está, ya está!; **all right: ~ it your own way!** ¡está bien! ¡haz lo que quieras!; **what ~ we here?** ¿y esto?; **to ~ sth to + INF** tener* algo QUE + INF; **I've (got) a lot to do** tengo mucho que hacer

C 1 (receive) ‹*letter/news*› tener*, recibir; **could we ~ some silence, please?** (hagan) silencio, por favor; **we ~ it on the best authority that ...** sabemos de buena fuente que ...; **rumor/tradition has it that ...** corre el rumor de que .../según la tradición ...; ***to ~ had it*** (colloq): **I've had it** (I'm in trouble) estoy frito (AmL), me la he cargado (Esp fam); (I've lost my chance) la he fastidiado (fam); **your umbrella's had it** tu paraguas no da para más (fam); **I've had it up to here with your complaining** estoy hasta la coronilla *or* hasta las narices de tus quejas (fam); ***to ~ it in for sb*** (colloq) tenerle* manía *or* tirria a algn (fam); ***to let sb ~ it*** (sl) (attack — physically) darle* su merecido a algn; (— verbally) cantarle las cuarenta a algn (fam), poner* a algn verde (Esp fam) 2 (obtain) conseguir*; **they were the best/only seats to be had** eran los mejores/únicos asientos que había; **I'll ~ a kilo of tomatoes, please** ¿me da *or* (Esp) me pone un kilo de tomates, por favor?

D (consume) ‹*steak/spaghetti*› comer, tomar (Esp); ‹*champagne/beer*› tomar; **to ~ sth to eat/drink** comer/beber algo; **to ~ breakfast/dinner** desayunar/cenar, comer (AmL); **to ~ lunch** almorzar* *or* (esp Esp, Méx) comer; **what are we having for dinner?** ¿qué hay de cena?; **to ~ a cigarette** fumarse un cigarrillo; **~ some more sauce** sírvete más salsa; **we had too much to drink** bebimos *or* (AmL tb) tomamos demasiado

E 1 (experience, undergo) ‹*accident*› tener*; **to ~ a setback** sufrir un revés; **did you ~ good weather?** ¿te (*or* les *etc*) hizo buen tiempo?; **~ a nice day!** ¡adiós! ¡que le (*or* te *etc*) vaya bien!; **we had a very pleasant evening** pasamos una noche muy agradable; **I had an injection** me pusieron *or* me dieron una inyección; **he had a heart transplant/an X ray** le hicieron un trasplante de corazón/una radiografía; **she had a heart attack** le dio un ataque al corazón *or* un infarto; **they ~ it easy** lo tienen (todo) muy fácil 2 (organize) ‹*party*› hacer*, dar*; **they had a meeting to discuss the issue** tuvieron una reunión para discutir el tema 3 (suffer from) ‹*cancer/diabetes/flu*› tener*; **to ~ a cold** estar* resfriado; **he's got a headache/sore throat** le duele la cabeza/la garganta, tiene dolor de cabeza/garganta

F (look after) tener*; **they ~ visitors** tienen visita; **my mother offered to ~ the children** mi madre se ofreció a cuidar a los niños

G (give birth to) ‹*baby*› tener*

H (colloq) 1 (catch, get the better of): **they almost had him, but he managed to escape** casi lo agarran *or* atrapan, pero logró escaparse; **I'll ~ them for that** ya me las pagarán 2 (swindle) timar; (dupe) engañar; **you've been had!** ¡te han timado *or* engañado!

Sense **II**

A (*causative use*): **we'll ~ it clean in no time** enseguida lo limpiamos *or* lo dejamos limpio; **he had them all laughing/in tears** los hizo reír/llorar a todos; **you had me worried** me tenías preocupado; **to ~ sb + INF**: **I'll ~ her call you back as soon as she arrives** le diré *or* pediré que lo llame en cuanto llegue; **I'll ~ you know, young man, that I ...** para que sepa, jovencito, yo ...; **to ~ sth + PAST P**: **we had it repaired** lo hicimos arreglar, lo mandamos (a) arreglar (AmL); **to ~ one's hair cut** cortarse el pelo

B (indicating what happens to sb): **I ~ people coming for dinner tonight** esta noche tengo gente a cenar; **to have sth + INF/+ PAST P**: **I've had three lambs die this week** se me han muerto tres corderos esta semana; **he had his bicycle stolen** le robaron la bicicleta

C 1 (allow) (*with neg*) tolerar, consentir*; **I won't ~ it!** ¡no lo consentiré *or* toleraré!; **I won't ~ him interfering** no pienso tolerar que se inmiscuya 2 (accept, believe) aceptar, creer*; **she wouldn't ~ it** no lo quiso aceptar *or* creer

D (indicating state, position) tener*; **I had the radio on** tenía la radio puesta; **you ~** *o* (BrE) **you've got your belt twisted** tienes el cinturón torcido

■ **have** *v aux*

h

(Sense I)

A (*used to form perfect tenses*) haber*; **I ~/had seen her** la he/había visto; **I ~/had just seen her** la acabo/acababa de ver, recién la vi/la había visto (AmL); **~ you been waiting long?** ¿hace mucho que esperas?, ¿llevas mucho rato esperando?; **you *have* been busy** ¡cómo has trabajado!; **had I known that** *o* **if I'd known that ...** si hubiera sabido que ..., de haber sabido que ...; **when he had finished, she ...** cuando terminó *or* (liter) cuando hubo terminado, ella ...

B [1] (in tags): **you've been told, ~n't you?** te lo han dicho ¿no? *or* ¿no es cierto? *or* ¿no es verdad?; **you ~n't lost the key, ~ you?** ¡no habrás perdido la llave ...! [2] (elliptical use): **you may ~ forgiven him, but I ~n't** puede que tú lo hayas perdonado, pero yo no; **the clock has stopped — so it has!** el reloj se ha parado — ¡es verdad! *or* ¡es cierto!; **you've forgotten something — ~ I?** te has olvidado de algo — ¿sí?; **I've told her — you ~n't!** se lo he dicho — ¡no! ¿en serio?

(Sense II)

A (expressing obligation): **to ~ to + INF** tener* QUE + INF; **I ~** *o* **I've got to admit that ...** tengo que reconocer que ...; **you don't ~ to be an expert to realize that** no hay que *or* no se necesita ser un experto para darse cuenta de eso; **don't go out unless you ~ to** no salgas a menos que tengas que hacerlo

B (expressing certainty): **to ~ to + INF** tener* QUE + INF; **it had to happen** tenía que ocurrir; **you have to** *o* **you've got to be kidding!** ¡lo dices en broma *or* en chiste!

(Phrasal verbs)

- **have around** [v ▸ o ▸ adv] (have at one's disposal): **a useful gadget to ~ around** un aparato útil de tener a mano; **she's nice to ~ around** su compañía es agradable
- **have away** (BrE) *see* ▸**have off B2**
- **have back**

A [v ▸ o ▸ adv, v ▸ adv ▸ o] (receive back): **can I ~ the ring back?** ¿me devuelves el anillo?

B [v ▸ o ▸ adv] [1] ‹*guests*› **to ~ sb back** (invite again) volver* a invitar a algn; (reciprocate invitation) devolverle* a algn una invitación [2] (allow to return): **do you think she'll ~ him back?** ¿crees que lo aceptará de nuevo?

- **have down** [v ▸ o ▸ adv]

A (dismantle) ‹*scaffolding/shelves*› quitar; (demolish) ‹*wall/building*› tirar, echar abajo

B (AmE) (know by heart) ‹*list/poem*› saber* de memoria

- **have in** [v ▸ o ▸ adv]

A (put in, install) instalar; **they soon had the new boiler in** enseguida instalaron la nueva caldera; ***to ~ it in for sb*** tenerla* tomada con algn

B [1] ‹*workmen*›: **we ~ the decorators in** estamos con los pintores en casa [2] ‹*guests*› invitar

- **have off** [v ▸ o ▸ adv] [v ▸ o ▸ prep ▸ o]

A (from work, school): **we had a week off (from) school because of the strike** estuvimos una semana sin clase por la huelga; **I'm having two days off next week** (BrE) me voy a tomar dos días libres la semana que viene

B (remove) (esp BrE) [1] ‹*lid/paint*› quitar; **the wind nearly had our roof off** el viento casi se llevó *or* nos arrancó el tejado [2] **to ~ it off** *o* **away** (BrE sl) echarse un polvo (arg), tirar (vulg), follar (Esp vulg), coger* (Méx, RPl, Ven vulg), culear (Chi vulg)

- **have on**

A [v ▸ o ▸ adv] [v ▸ o ▸ prep ▸ o] (put on) ‹*cover/roof*› colocar*, poner*; **they soon had all the books on the shelves** pronto colocaron todos los libros en los estantes

B [v ▸ o ▸ adv, v ▸ adv ▸ o] (be wearing) llevar *or* tener* puesto; **I had nothing on** estaba desnudo

C [v ▸ o ▸ adv] (BrE) [1] (have arranged) tener*; **~ you anything on this evening?** ¿haces algo esta noche? [2] (have in progress): **the library has an exhibition on** en la biblioteca hay una exposición

D [v ▸ o ▸ adv] (tease) (colloq) **to ~ sb on** tomarle el pelo a algn (fam)

- **have out** [v ▸ o ▸ adv] [1] (have removed): **to ~ a tooth out** sacarse* una muela; **she had her tonsils out** la operaron de las amígdalas [2] (discuss forcefully) **to ~ it out WITH sb** ponerle* las cosas claras A algn
- **have over,** (BrE also) **have round** [v ▸ o ▸ adv] ‹*guests*› invitar
- **have up** [v ▸ o ▸ adv] [1] (put up) ‹*shelves*› colocar*; ‹*flag*› izar* [2] (bring before court) (BrE colloq) (*often pass*): **he was had up for speeding** lo agarraron por exceso de velocidad (fam) (*y tuvo que comparecer ante el juez*)

haven /ˈheɪvən/ *n* [1] (refuge) refugio *m*; **a ~ of tranquillity** un remanso de paz [2] (port) (liter) puerto *m*

have-nots /ˈhævˈnɑːts || ˌhævˈnɒts/ *pl n* **the ~** los pobres, los desposeídos; *see also* **haves**

haven't /ˈhævənt/ **= have not**

haversack /ˈhævərsæk || ˈhævəsæk/ *n* mochila *f*, morral *m*

haves /hævz/ *pl n* **the ~** los ricos; **the ~ and the have-nots** los ricos y los pobres *or* los desposeídos

havoc /ˈhævək/ *n* [u]: **the accident caused ~** el accidente creó gran confusión; **the children created ~** los niños armaron un lío tremendo (fam); **to play ~ with sth** trastocar* *or* desbaratar algo; **to wreak ~** causar estragos

haw /hɔː/ *n* (Bot) baya *f* del espino

Hawaii /həˈwaiː/ *n* Hawai *m*

Hawaiian /həˈwaɪən/ *adj* hawaiano

hawk¹ /hɔːk/ *n* halcón *m*; ***to watch sb like a ~*** no quitarle los ojos de encima a algn

hawk² *vt* ‹*goods/wares*› vocear, pregonar

■ **hawk** *vi* carraspear

hawker /ˈhɔːkər || ˈhɔːkə(r)/ *n* vendedor, -dora *m,f* ambulante

hawser /ˈhɔːzər || ˈhɔːzə(r)/ *n* cabo *m* grueso

hawthorn /ˈhɔːθɔːrn || ˈhɔːθɔːn/ *n* [c u] espino *m*

hay /heɪ/ *n* [u] heno *m*; ***to make ~*** (gain advantage) (AmE) sacar* tajada; (lit) segar* y secar* el heno *or* los pastos; ***make ~ while the sun shines*** a la ocasión la pintan calva; ▸**hit¹** *vt* **A1**

hay: **~ fever** *n* [u] fiebre *f* del heno, alergia *f* al polen; **~making** *n* [u] siega *f* (y recolección *f*) del heno; **~rick** /ˈheɪrɪk/ *n* almiar *m*; **~seed** *n* (AmE sl) ▸**yokel**; **~stack** *n* almiar *m*; **~wire** *adj* (colloq) (*pred*): **to go ~wire** «*person*» perder* la chaveta (fam), volverse* loco; «*machine*» estropearse, descomponerse* (AmL fam)

hazard¹ /ˈhæzərd || ˈhæzəd/ *n* peligro *m*, riesgo *m*; **a health ~** un riesgo *or* un peligro para la salud

hazard² *vt* (frml) ‹*remark/question*› aventurar, arriesgar*; **to ~ a guess** aventurar una respuesta

hazard lights, (BrE also) **hazard warning lights** *pl n* (Auto) luces *fpl* de emergencia

hazardous /ˈhæzərdəs || ˈhæzədəs/ *adj* peligroso, arriesgado

haze¹ /heɪz/ *n* (*no pl*) (due to humidity) neblina *f*, bruma *f*; (due to heat) calima *f*; **a ~ of dust/smoke** una nube de polvo/humo

haze² *vt* (AmE) hacerle* novatadas *or* (RPl fam) cargadas a

hazel /ˈheɪzəl/ *n* [1] [c] (plant) avellano *m* [2] [u] (wood) (madera *f* de) avellano *m* [3] [u] (color) color *m* avellana; (*before n*) ‹*eyes*› color avellana *adj inv*

hazelnut /ˈheɪzəlnʌt/ *n* avellana *f*

hazing /ˈheɪzɪŋ/ *n* [u] (AmE) novatadas *fpl*, cargadas *fpl* (RPl fam)

hazy /ˈheɪzi/ *adj* **hazier, haziest** [1] ‹*day*› (due to humidity) neblinoso, brumoso; (due to heat) de calima [2] ‹*memory/idea/distinction*› vago, confuso; **I'm a bit ~ about what happened** no sé muy bien qué pasó

he /hiː, *weak form* i/ *pron* él; **~'s a painter** es pintor; **~ didn't say it, I did** no fue él quien lo dijo, sino yo; **Ted Post? who's ~?** ¿Ted Post? ¿quién es Ted Post?; **~ who hesitates** (liter) quien vacila ...; **could I speak to Steve, please? — this is ~** (AmE) ¿podría hablar con Steve, por favor? — habla con él; **I'm as tall as ~ is** soy tan alto como él

head¹ /hed/ *n*

A (Anat) cabeza *f*; **a fine ~ of hair** una buena cabellera; **to stand on one's ~** pararse de cabeza (AmL), hacer* el pino (Esp); **from ~ to foot** *o* **toe** de pies a cabeza, de arriba (a) abajo; **he's a ~ taller than his brother** le lleva *or* le saca la cabeza a su hermano; **~ *over heels***: **she tripped and went ~ over heels down the steps** tropezó y cayó rodando escaleras abajo; **to be ~ over heels in love** estar* locamente *or* perdidamente enamorado; ***~s up!*** (AmE colloq) ¡ojo! (fam), ¡cuidado!; ***on your/his (own) ~ be it*** la responsabilidad es tuya/suya; ***to bang one's ~ against a (brick) wall*** darse* (con) la cabeza contra la pared; ***to be***

able to do sth standing on one's ~ poder* hacer algo con los ojos cerrados; ***to bite*** *o* ***snap sb's ~ off*** echarle una bronca a algn (fam); ***to bury one's ~ in the sand*** hacer* como el avestruz; ***to get one's ~ down*** (colloq) (work hard) ponerse* a trabajar en serio; (settle for sleep) (BrE) irse* a dormir; ***to go over sb's ~*** (bypassing hierarchy) pasar por encima de algn; (exceeding comprehension): **his lecture went straight over my ~** no entendí nada de su conferencia; ***to go to sb's ~*** subírsele a la cabeza a algn; ***to have a big*** *o* ***swelled*** *o* (BrE) ***swollen ~*** ser* un creído; **he's getting a swelled** *o* (BrE) **swollen ~** se le están subiendo los humos a la cabeza; ***to have one's ~ in the clouds*** tener* la cabeza llena de pájaros; ***to hold one's ~ up*** *o* ***high*** *o* ***up high*** ir* con la cabeza bien alta; ***to keep one's ~ above water*** mantenerse* a flote; ***to keep one's ~ down*** (avoid attention) mantenerse* al margen; (work hard) no levantar la cabeza; (lit: keep head lowered) no levantar la cabeza; ***to knock sth on the ~*** (colloq) dar* al traste con algo; ***to laugh one's ~ off*** reírse* a mandíbula batiente, desternillarse de (la) risa; **to scream/shout one's ~ off** gritar a voz en cuello; ***to make ~ or tail*** *o* (AmE also) ***~s or tails of sth*** entender* algo; **I can't make ~ or tail of it** para mí esto no tiene ni pies ni cabeza; ***to rear one's ugly ~***: **racism/fascism reared its ugly ~ again** volvió a aparecer el fantasma del racismo/fascismo; ***to stand/be ~ and shoulders above sb*** (be superior) darle* cien vueltas a algn, estar* muy por encima de algn; ***to stand*** *o* ***turn sth on its ~*** darle* la vuelta a algo, poner* algo patas arriba (fam), dar* vuelta algo (CS); ***to turn sb's ~***: **the sort of good looks that turn ~s** el tipo de belleza que llama la atención *or* que hace que la gente se vuelva a mirar; (*before n*) **~ injury** lesión *f* en la cabeza

B (mind, brain) cabeza *f*; **I said the first thing that came into my ~** dije lo primero que se me ocurrió *or* que me vino a la cabeza; **she added it up in her ~** hizo la suma mentalmente; **he needs his ~ examined** está *or* anda mal de la cabeza; **he has an old ~ on young shoulders** es muy maduro para su edad; **she has a good ~ for business/figures** tiene cabeza para los negocios/los números; **I've no ~ for heights** sufro de vértigo; **I need to keep a clear ~ for the interview** tengo que estar despejado para la entrevista; **use your ~!** ¡usa la cabeza!, ¡piensa un poco!; **if we put our ~s together, we'll be able to think of something** si lo pensamos juntos, algo se nos ocurrirá; **it never entered my ~ that ...** ni se me pasó por la cabeza *or* jamás pensé que ...; **to get sth into sb's ~** meterle* algo en la cabeza a algn; ***to be off one's ~*** (colloq) estar* chiflado (fam), estar* *or* andar* mal de la cabeza; ***to be out of one's ~*** (sl) (on drugs) estar* flipado *or* volado *or* (Col) volando *or* (Méx) hasta atrás (arg); (drunk) estar* como una cuba (fam); ***to be soft*** *o* ***weak in the ~*** estar* mal de la cabeza; ***to get one's ~ (a)round sth***: **I can't get my ~ (a)round this new system** no me entra este nuevo sistema; ***to have one's ~ screwed on (right*** *o* ***the right way)*** (colloq) tener* la cabeza bien puesta *or* sentada; ***to keep/lose one's ~*** mantener*/perder* la calma; ***two ~s are better than one*** cuatro ojos ven más que dos

C 1 (of celery) cabeza *f*; (of nail, tack, pin) cabeza *f*; (of spear, arrow) punta *f*; (of hammer) cabeza *f*, cotillo *m*; (of pimple) punta *f*, cabeza *f*; (on beer) espuma *f*; (of river) cabecera *f* 2 (top end — of bed, table) cabecera *f*; (— of page, letter) encabezamiento *m*; (— of procession, line) cabeza *f*

D 1 (chief) director, -tora *m,f*; **~ of state/government** jefe, -fa *m,f* de Estado/de Gobierno; **the ~ of the household** el/la cabeza de familia; (*before n*) **~ buyer** jefe, -fa *m,f* de compras; **~ girl/boy** (BrE Educ) *alumno elegido para representar al alumnado de un colegio*; **~ waiter** maître *m*, capitán *m* de meseros (Méx) 2 (**~** *teacher*) (esp BrE) director, -tora *m,f* (de colegio)

E 1 (person): **$15 per ~** 15 dólares por cabeza *or* persona 2 *pl* **head** (Agr): **700 ~ of cattle** 700 cabezas de ganado vacuno

F (crisis): **to come to a ~** hacer* crisis, llegar* a un punto crítico; **his arrival brought the conflict to a ~** su llegada hizo estallar el conflicto

G 1 (magnetic device) (Audio, Comput) cabeza *f*, cabezal *m* 2 (of drill) cabezal *m* 3 (*cylinder* **~**) culata *f*

H (Geog) cabo *m*

head² *vt*

A 1 ‹*march/procession*› encabezar*, ir* a la cabeza de; ‹*list*› encabezar* 2 ‹*revolt*› acaudillar, ser* el cabecilla de; ‹*team*› capitanear; ‹*expedition/department*› dirigir*, estar* al frente de

B (direct) (+ *adv compl*) ‹*vehicle/ship*› dirigir*; **which way are you ~ed?** ¿hacia *or* para dónde vas?

C (in soccer) ‹*ball*› cabecear

D ‹*page/chapter*› encabezar*

■ **head** *vi*: **the car was ~ing west** el coche iba en dirección oeste; **where are you ~ing?** ¿hacia *or* para dónde vas?; **it's time we were ~ing back** ya va siendo hora de que volvamos *or* regresemos

(Phrasal verbs)

• **head for** [v ▸ prep ▸ o] 1 (go toward) «*ship*» ir* con rumbo a; **the car was ~ing straight for me** el coche venía derecho hacia mí; **to ~ for home** ponerse* en camino a casa 2 (be in danger of): **to be ~ed** *o* **~ing for sth** ir* camino de algo

• **head off**

A [v ▸ adv] (set out) salir*

B [v ▸ o ▸ adv, v ▸ adv ▸ o] 1 (get in front of) atajar, cortarle el paso a, interceptar 2 (prevent, forestall) ‹*criticism/threat*› prevenir*

• **head up** [v ▸ adv ▸ o] dirigir*, estar* a la cabeza de

head: **~ache** *n* 1 (Med) dolor *m* de cabeza; **I've got a ~ache** tengo dolor de cabeza, me duele la cabeza 2 (problem) (colloq) quebradero *m* de cabeza, dolor *m* de cabeza; **~band** *n* cinta *f* del pelo, vincha *f* (AmS), huincha *f* (Bol, Chi, Per); **~board** *n* cabecera *f*; **~ case** *n* (BrE colloq) loco, -ca *m,f*, chiflado, -da *m,f* (fam); **~ cold** *n* resfriado *m*; **~-count** *n* recuento *m* (*de personas*); **~dress** *n* tocado *m*

headed /'hedəd || 'hedɪd/ *adj* ‹*notepaper*› con membrete, membretado, membreteado (Andes)

header /'hedər || 'hedə(r)/ *n* (in soccer) cabezazo *m*

head: **~first** /'hed'fɜːrst || ˌhed'fɜːst/ *adv* 1 (with head foremost) de cabeza; **he fell ~first into the river** se cayó de cabeza al río 2 (over-hastily) precipitadamente; **~gear** *n* [u]: **to wear the correct ~gear** llevar el sombrero (*or* casco *or* gorro *etc*) indicado; **~hunt** *vt* ofrecerle* un puesto a; **~hunter** *n* (Anthrop) cazador *m* de cabezas; (Busn) cazatalentos *m*, cazador *m* de cabezas *or* de talentos

heading /'hedɪŋ/ *n* (title) encabezamiento *m*, título *m*, acápite *m* (AmL); (letterhead) membrete *m*

head: **~lamp** *n* faro *m*; **~land** /'hedlənd/ *n* cabo *m*

headless /'hedləs || 'hedlɪs/ *adj* sin cabeza

head: **~light** *n* faro *m*; **~line** *n* titular *m*; **to hit the ~lines** aparecer* *or* salir* en primera plana; **to make ~lines** ser* noticia; **the (news) ~lines** el resumen informativo *or* de noticias; (*before n*) **~line news** noticia *f* de primera plana; **~liner** *n* (AmE) primera figura *f*, estrella *f*; **~long** *adv* 1 (hastily) precipitadamente; **she rushed ~long into it** se lanzó precipitadamente a hacerlo 2 (with head foremost) de cabeza; **~man** /'hedmæn/ *n* (*pl* **-men** /-men/) cacique *m*; **~master** /'hed'mæstər || ˌhed'mɑːstə(r)/ *n* director *m* (de colegio); **~mistress** /'hed'mɪstrəs || ˌhed'mɪstrɪs/ *n* directora *f* (de colegio); **~ office** *n* (oficina *f*) central *f*, casa *f* matriz

head-on¹ /'hed'ɑːn || ˌhed'ɒn/ *adj* ‹*crash/collision*› frontal, de frente

head-on² *adv* ‹*crash/collide*› frontalmente, de frente

head: **~phones** *pl n* auriculares *mpl*, cascos *mpl*; **~piece** /'hedpiːs/ *n* 1 (head decoration) prenda *f* de cabeza 2 (in book) viñeta *f* 3 (of bridle) cabezada *f*, cabezal *m*; **~quarters** /'hed'kwɔːrtərz || ˌhed'kwɔːtəz/ *n* (*pl* **~quarters**) (+ *sing or pl vb*) oficina *f* central; (Mil) cuartel *m* general; **police ~quarters** jefatura *f* de policía; **~rest** *n* reposacabezas *m*, apoyacabezas *m*; **~room** *n* [u] altura *f*: Ⓢ **(max) headroom 12ft 6in** circulación prohibida a vehículos de altura superior a 12 pies 6 pulgadas

heads /hedz/ *adv* (on coin) cara *f*; **~ or tails?** ¿cara o cruz?, ¿águila o sol? (Méx), ¿cara o sello? (Andes, Ven), ¿cara o ceca? (Arg)

head: **~scarf** *n* pañuelo *m* (de cabeza); **~set** *n* auriculares *mpl*, cascos *mpl*; **~shrinker** /'hedʃrɪŋkər || 'hedʃrɪŋkə(r)/ *n* (AmE colloq) loquero, -ra *m,f* (fam); **~stand** *n*: **to do a ~stand** pararse de cabeza (AmL), hacer* el pino (Esp); **~ start** *n* ventaja *f*; **to have a ~ start (on/over sb)** llevar(le) ventaja (a algn); **~stone**

n lápida *f*; **~strong** *adj* testarudo, obstinado; **~teacher** /'hed'ti:tʃər || ˌhed'ti:tʃə(r)/ *n* (BrE) director, -tora *m,f* (de colegio); **~-to-head** /'hedtə'hed/ *adj/adv* (AmE) cara a cara, frente a frente; **~waters** *pl n* cabecera *f*; **~way** *n* [u]: **to make ~way** hacer* progresos, avanzar*; **~wind** *n* viento *m* contrario *or* en contra; (Naut) viento *m* de proa; **~word** *n* lema *m*

heads-up¹ /'hedzʌp/ *adj* (AmE) (*before n*) despierto, espabilado, despabilado

heads-up² *n* [u] (colloq) dato *m*; **to give sb the ~ on sth**; poner a alguien al corriente *or* al tanto de algo; **thanks for the ~** gracias por la información

heady /'hedi/ *adj* **-dier, -diest** ‹*scent*› embriagador; ‹*wine*› que se sube a la cabeza; **these are ~ days for the country** el país vive momentos emocionantes

heal /hi:l/ *vt* [1] ‹*wound/cut*› curar; **he tried to ~ the rift within the party** intentó cerrar la brecha que había en el partido [2] ‹*person*› (frml) **to ~ sb (OF sth)** curar a algn (DE algo)

■ **heal** *vi* cicatrizar*, cerrarse*

(Phrasal verbs)

• **heal over** [v ▸ adv] ‹‹*wound/cut*›› cicatrizar*, cerrarse*

• **heal up**

A [v ▸ adv] cicatrizar*, cerrarse*

B [v ▸ o ▸ adv, v ▸ adv ▸ o] cicatrizar*

healer /'hi:lər || 'hi:lə(r)/ *n* curandero, -ra *m,f*; **time is a** *o* **the great ~** el tiempo todo lo cura

health /helθ/ *n* [u] salud *f*; **to be in good/poor ~** estar* bien/mal de salud; **(your) good ~!** (proposing a toast) ¡salud!; (*before n*) ‹*policy/services*› sanitario, de salud pública; ‹*inspector/regulations*› de sanidad

health: **~ care** *n* [u] asistencia *f* sanitaria *or* médica; **~ centre** *n* (BrE) centro *m* médico *or* de salud; **~ club** *n* gimnasio *m*; **~ farm** *n* clínica *f* de adelgazamiento; **~ food** *n* [u c] alimentos *mpl* naturales; (*before n*) **~-food shop** tienda *f* de alimentos naturales, herbolario *m*

healthful /'helθfəl/ *adj* ▸ **healthy**

healthily /'helθəli || 'helθɪli/ *adv* de forma sana

health: **~ insurance** *n* [u] seguro *m* de enfermedad; **~ service** *n* (in UK) ▸ **National Health (Service)**; **~ visitor** *n* (in UK) *enfermera de la Seguridad Social que hace visitas a domicilio*; **~ warning** *n* advertencia *f* sanitaria

healthy /'helθi/ *adj* **-thier, -thiest**

A [1] (in good health) ‹*person/animal*› sano; ‹*skin/complexion*› sano, saludable; **she has a ~ appetite** tiene buen apetito [2] (promoting good health) ‹*diet/living/environment*› sano, saludable [3] (sound) ‹*respect*› sano; ‹*debate*› abierto y sin trabas

B ‹*society/democracy*› que goza de buena salud; ‹*economy/finances*› próspero; ‹*profit*› sustancial

heap¹ /hi:p/ *n*

A [1] (pile) montón *m*, pila *f*; **to fall** *o* **collapse/lie in a ~** caer*/yacer* desplomado [2] (car) (colloq) cacharro *m* (fam)

B (colloq) (a lot): **~s** *o* (AmE also) **a ~ of sth** montones *or* un montón de algo (fam); **it's ~s** *o* (AmE) **a ~ better** es muchísimo mejor *or* (fam) requetemejor

heap² *vt* [1] (make pile) amontonar, apilar [2] (supply liberally): **she ~ed food onto his plate** *o* **~ed his plate with food** le llenó el plato de comida; **to ~ praise on sb** colmar a algn de alabanzas; **to ~ blame on sb** echarle todas las culpas a algn; **a ~ing** (AmE) *o* (BrE) **~ed spoonful** (Culin) una cucharada colmada

(Phrasal verb)

• **heap up** [v ▸ o ▸ adv, v ▸ adv ▸ o] [1] (amass) ‹*wealth*› acumular, amasar [2] (make into pile) amontonar, apilar

hear /hɪr || hɪə(r)/ (*past & past p* **heard** /hɜ:rd || hɜ:d/) *vt*

A ‹*sound*› oír*; **stop it! do you ~?** ¡basta! ¿me oyes?; **now ~ this** (AmE) presten atención; **to ~ her (talk), you'd think ...** cualquiera que la oyera creería que ...; **I must be ~ing things** (colloq) debo de habérmelo imaginado; **let's ~ it for George!** (AmE colloq) ¡un aplauso para George!

B (get to know) oír*; **I've ~d so much about you** me han hablado tanto de ti, he oído hablar tanto de ti; **have you ~d the latest?** ¿sabes la última?; **I've ~d it all before** ya conozco la historia; **he's very ill, I ~** me han dicho que está muy enfermo

C (listen to) [1] ‹*lecture/broadcast/views*› escuchar, oír*; **I ~ you** (AmE) ya veo, ya te entiendo; **to ~ mass** oír* misa [2] (Law) ‹*case*› ver*; ‹*charge*› oír*

■ **hear** *vi*

A (perceive) oír*; **~, ~!** ¡eso, eso!, ¡bien dicho!

B (get news) tener* noticias; **to ~ ABOUT sth** enterarse DE algo; **to ~ FROM sb**: **I haven't ~d from them for months** hace meses que no sé nada de ellos *or* que no tengo noticias suyas; **you'll be ~ing from us in a couple of weeks** dentro de unas semanas nos pondremos en contacto con usted

(Phrasal verbs)

• **hear of**

A [v ▸ prep ▸ o] [1] (encounter, come to know of): **I've ~d of him** he oído hablar de él; **if you ~ of anything interesting, let me know** si te enteras de algo interesante, me lo dices; **did you ever ~ of such a thing!** ¡habráse visto cosa igual! [2] (have news of) tener* noticias *or* saber* de [3] (allow): **I won't ~ of it!** ¡ni hablar!, ¡ni se te (*or* le *etc*) ocurra!

B [v ▸ o ▸ prep ▸ o] (have news of): **I've ~d nothing of them since they moved away** no he sabido nada *or* no he tenido noticias de ellos desde que se mudaron; **I warn you: you haven't ~d the last of this!** ¡te advierto que esto no va a quedar así!

• **hear out** [v ▸ o ▸ adv, v ▸ adv ▸ o] escuchar (*hasta el final*)

hearing /'hɪrɪŋ || 'hɪərɪŋ/ *n*

A [u] (sense) oído *m*; **my ~ is getting worse** cada vez oigo peor; (*before n*) **~ difficulties** problemas *mpl* auditivos *or* de audición

B [c] [1] (consideration) consideración *f*, atención *f*; **to give sth/sb a ~** escuchar algo/a algn; **she didn't get a fair ~** no le permitieron explicarse [2] (trial) vista *f* [3] (session) sesión *f*

hearing aid *n* audífono *m*

hearsay /'hɪrseɪ || 'hɪəseɪ/ *n* [u] habladurías *fpl*, rumores *mpl*; (*before n*) **~ evidence** testimonio *m* de oídas

hearse /hɜ:rs || hɜ:s/ *n* coche *m* fúnebre; (horse-drawn) carroza *f* fúnebre

heart /hɑ:rt || hɑ:t/ *n*

A (Anat) corazón *m*; ***cross my ~ (and hope to die)!*** ¡te lo juro!, ¡que me muera ahora mismo si no es verdad!; (*before n*) ‹*disease*› del corazón, cardíaco; ‹*operation*› de(l) corazón; **~ rate** ritmo *m* cardíaco

B (seat of emotions): **to have a good/kind ~** tener* buen corazón, ser* de buen corazón; **to have a cold ~** ser* duro de corazón; **his ~ rules his head** se deja llevar por el corazón; **at ~** en el fondo; **to have sb's interests at ~** preocuparse por algn; **in one's ~ of ~s** en lo más profundo de su (*or* mi *etc*) corazón, en su (*or* mi *etc*) fuero interno; **you've no ~!** ¡no tienes corazón!; **have a ~!** (colloq) ¡no seas malo! (fam), ¡ten compasión! (hum); **to be all ~** ser* todo corazón; **his ~ went out to the orphans** le daban mucha lástima los huérfanos; **to be close** *o* **near** *o* **dear to sb's ~** significar* mucho para algn; ***after sb's own ~***: **he's a man/writer after my own ~** es un hombre/escritor con el que me identifico; ***to break sb's ~***: **it breaks my ~ to see her cry** me parte el alma verla llorar; **to die of a broken ~** morirse* de pena; ***to cry one's ~ out*** llorar a lágrima viva; ***to eat one's ~ out*** morirse* de envidia; ***to find it in one's ~ to*** **+ INF**: **can you find it in your ~ to forgive me?** ¿podrás perdonarme?; ***to have a ~ of gold*** tener* un corazón de oro, ser* todo corazón; ***her/his ~ is in the right place*** es de buen corazón, es una buena persona; ***to learn/know sth by ~*** aprender/saber* algo de memoria; ***my/her/his ~ wasn't in it*** lo hacía sin ganas *or* sin poner entusiasmo; ***to one's ~'s content***: **here you can eat/swim to your ~'s content** aquí puedes comer/nadar todo lo que quieras; ***to open one's ~ to sb*** abrirle* el corazón a algn; ***to set one's ~ on sth***: **she's set her ~ on being chosen for the team** su mayor ilusión es que la elijan para formar parte del equipo; **he has his ~ set on a new bike** lo que más quiere es una bicicleta nueva; ***to take sth to ~*** tomarse algo a pecho; ***to wear one's ~ on one's sleeve*** demostrar* sus (*or* mis *etc*) sentimientos; ***with all one's ~, with one's whole ~*** de todo corazón; ***to win sb's ~*** ganarse *or* conquistarse a algn

C (courage, morale) ánimos *mpl*; **to lose ~** descorazonarse, desanimarse; **to take ~** animarse; ***my ~ was in my mouth*** tenía el corazón en un puño *or* en la boca, tenía el alma en vilo; ***my/her ~ sank*** se me/le cayó el alma a los pies; ***not to have the ~ to do sth***: **I didn't have the ~ to**

tell him no tuve valor para decírselo; ***to be in good ~*** tener* la moral muy alta; ***to do sb's ~ good*** alegrarle el corazón a algn

D 1 (central part): **the ~ of the city/country** el corazón *or* centro de la ciudad/del país; **the ~ of the matter** el meollo *or* el quid del asunto 2 (of cabbage, lettuce) cogollo *m*; **artichoke ~s** corazones *mpl* de alcachofas *or* (RPl) de alcauciles

E (heart-shaped object) corazón *m*

F (Games) **hearts** (suit) (+ *sing or pl vb*) corazones *mpl*

heart: **~ache** *n* [u] pena *f*, dolor *m*; **~ attack** *n* ataque *m* al corazón, infarto *m*; **he had a ~ attack** tuvo *or* le dio *or* (frml) sufrió un infarto; **~beat** *n* latido *m* (del corazón); **~break** *n* 1 [u] (grief) congoja *f*, sufrimiento *m* 2 [c] (cause of grief) desengaño *m*; **~breaking** *adj* desgarrador; **~broken** *adj* ‹*look/sobs*› desconsolado; **she was ~broken when he died** su muerte la dejó destrozada; **~burn** *n* [u] ardor *m* de estómago, acidez *f* (de estómago)

-hearted /ˈhɑːrtəd || ˈhɑːtɪd/ *suff*: **big~/good~** de gran/buen corazón

hearten /ˈhɑːrtn̩ || ˈhɑːtn̩/ *vt* alentar*, animar

heartfelt /ˈhɑːrtfelt || ˈhɑːtfelt/ *adj* sincero, sentido

hearth /hɑːrθ || hɑːθ/ *n* chimenea *f*, hogar *m*

heartily /ˈhɑːrtl̩i || ˈhɑːtɪli/ *adv* 1 (warmly) ‹*congratulate/greet*› efusivamente 2 (with enthusiasm) ‹*laugh/eat*› con ganas 3 (totally): **I ~ agree** estoy totalmente *or* completamente de acuerdo; **to be ~ sick of sth** (colloq) estar* hasta la coronilla *or* hasta las narices de algo (fam)

heartland /ˈhɑːrtlænd || ˈhɑːtlənd/ *n* centro *m*; **the industrial ~s of Europe** el centro industrial de Europa; **in the Tory ~s** (BrE) en el corazón del área conservadora

heartless /ˈhɑːrtləs || ˈhɑːtlɪs/ *adj* ‹*person*› sin corazón; ‹*refusal*› cruel

heart: **~-rending** /ˈhɑːrtˈrendɪŋ || ˈhɑːtˌrendɪŋ/ *adj* ‹*cry/sobs*› estremecedor, desgarrador; ‹*plight/account*› conmovedor; **~-searching** *n* [u] reflexión *f*; **~-shaped** *adj* ‹*card/cake*› con forma de corazón; ‹*face*› en forma de corazón; **~strings** *pl n*: ***to pull*** *o* ***tug at sb's ~strings*** tocarle* la fibra sensible a algn; **~ surgeon** *n* cardiocirujano, -na *m,f*, cirujano cardíaco, cirujana cardíaca *m,f*; **~throb** *n* (colloq) ídolo *m*

heart-to-heart[1] /ˈhɑːrttəˈhɑːrt || ˌhɑːttəˈhɑːt/ *adj* íntimo y franco

heart-to-heart[2] *n* (colloq) charla *f* íntima

heart-warming /ˈhɑːrtˌwɔːrmɪŋ || ˈhɑːtˌwɔːmɪŋ/ *adj* alentador, reconfortante

hearty /ˈhɑːrti || ˈhɑːti/ *adj* **-tier, -tiest** ‹*person*› campechano, bullanguero; ‹*laughter*› sonoro, desbordante; ‹*welcome*› caluroso; ‹*meal*› abundante; ‹*appetite*› bueno

heat[1] /hiːt/ *n*

A [u] 1 (warmth) calor *m*; **in the ~ of the day** cuando el sol aprieta, en las horas de más calor; ***if you can't stand the ~, get out of the kitchen*** si es demasiado para ti, quítate de en medio 2 (for cooking) fuego *m*; **on/over/at a low ~** a fuego lento

B [u] 1 (excitement, passion) calor *m*, acaloramiento *m*; **in the ~ of the moment** en un momento de enojo (*or* exaltación *etc*) 2 (pressure) (colloq): **to put the ~ on sb** apretarle* las clavijas a algn (fam); **to take the ~ off sb** darle* un respiro a algn; **the ~ is off** ya ha pasado lo peor (fam)

C [u] (estrus) celo *m*; **to come into** *o* (BrE) **on ~** ponerse* en celo; **to be in** *o* (BrE) **on ~** ‹‹*animal*›› estar* en celo

D [c] (Sport) (prueba) eliminatoria *f*

heat[2] *vt* calentar*; ‹*house*› calentar*, calefaccionar (CS)

■ **heat** *vi* calentarse*

(Phrasal verbs)

• **heat through**

A [v ▸ adv] calentarse*

B [v ▸ o ▸ adv, v ▸ adv ▸ o] calentar*

• **heat up**

A [v ▸ adv] ‹‹*food/room/air*›› calentarse*; ‹‹*game*›› animarse; ‹‹*argument/discussion*›› acalorarse

B [v ▸ o ▸ adv, v ▸ adv ▸ o] ‹*food/room*› calentar*

heated /ˈhiːtəd || ˈhiːtɪd/ *adj* 1 (warmed) ‹*pool*› climatizado; ‹*seat/rear window*› térmico 2 (impassioned) ‹*argument*› acalorado; **to get ~** acalorarse

heatedly /ˈhiːtədli || ˈhiːtɪdli/ *adv* acaloradamente

heater /ˈhiːtər || ˈhiːtə(r)/ *n* calentador *m*, estufa *f*; **(water) ~** calentador *m*

heath /hiːθ/ *n* [c u] (moorland) brezal *m*, monte *m*; (park) parque *m* (*agreste*)

heathen[1] /ˈhiːðən/ *n* pagano, -na *m,f*

heathen[2] *adj* pagano

heather /ˈheðər || ˈheðə(r)/ *n* [u] brezo *m*

heating /ˈhiːtɪŋ/ *n* [u] calefacción *f*

heat: **~-proof** *adj* refractario; **~ rash** *n* [u c] sarpullido *m* (*causado por el calor*); **~-resistant** *adj* resistente al calor; **~-seeking** /ˈhiːtˈsiːkɪŋ/ *adj* termodirigido; **~stroke** *n* [u] insolación *f*; **~ treatment** *n* [u] (Med, Metall) tratamiento *m* térmico; **~ wave** *n* ola *f* de calor

heave[1] /hiːv/ *vt*

A 1 (move with effort): **we ~d the box onto the shelf** con esfuerzo logramos subir la caja al estante 2 (throw) (colloq) tirar

B (utter): **to ~ a sigh** suspirar; **he ~d a sigh of relief** suspiró aliviado

■ **heave** *vi*

A (pull) tirar, jalar (AmL exc CS); **~!** ¡dale!; **to ~ AT sth** tirar DE algo

B 1 (rise and fall): **his chest ~d** respiraba agitadamente 2 **heaving** *pres p* ‹*chest/bosom*› palpitante; ‹*sobs*› convulsivo

C (retch) (colloq) hacer* arcadas

heave[2] *n* (pull) tirón *m*, jalón *m* (AmL exc CS); (push) empujón *m*; (effort) esfuerzo *m* (*para mover algo*)

heave-ho[1] /ˈhiːvˈhəʊ/ *n*: ***to give sth/sb the ~*** rechazar* algo/ a algn; **she gave him the ~** lo rechazó, le dio calabazas

heave-ho[2] *interj* ¡ahora!

heaven /ˈhevən/ *n*

A (place) cielo *m*; ***to be in seventh ~*** estar* en el séptimo cielo; ***to move ~ and earth*** remover* (el) cielo y (la) tierra

B (sky) (*usu pl*) cielo *m*; **the ~s opened** empezó a llover torrencialmente; ***to stink to high ~*** (colloq) oler* que apesta (fam)

C (*in interj phrases, as intensifier*) **(good) ~s!** ¡Dios mío!, ¡santo cielo!; **did you vote for him? — (good) ~s, no!** ¿votaste por él? — ¿estás loca?; **thank ~** gracias a Dios; **~s to Betsy!** (AmE hum) ¡cielo santo!; **they gave *her* the job, ~ knows why** le dieron el trabajo a ella, vete a saber porqué; ▸**forbid B, name**[1] **A, sake 3**

D (bliss) (colloq): **how was your vacation? — it was ~** ¿qué tal las vacaciones? — divinas *or* sensacionales (fam)

heavenly /ˈhevənli/ *adj* 1 (Relig) celestial 2 (Astron) celeste 3 (superb) (colloq) divino (fam)

heaven-sent /ˈhevənsent/ *adj* caído del cielo

heavenward /ˈhevənwərd || ˈhevənwəd/, **heavenwards** /-z/ *adv* hacia el cielo *or* las alturas

heavily /ˈhevəli || ˈhevɪli/ *adv*

A 1 ‹*tread/fall*› pesadamente; **a ~ laden truck** un camión con una carga muy pesada; **he was ~ built** era corpulento *or* de aspecto fornido; **to breathe ~** jadear 2 (thickly) ‹*underlined*› con trazo grueso; **she was ~ made-up** iba muy maquillada

B 1 (copiously) ‹*rain/snow*› mucho 2 (immoderately) ‹*drink/smoke*› en exceso, más de la cuenta (fam); ‹*gamble*› fuerte 3 (to a great extent) ‹*outweigh*› con mucho; **to be ~ in debt** estar* muy endeudado, tener* muchas deudas; **to be ~ subsidized** recibir cuantiosas subvenciones; **to borrow ~** contraer* considerables deudas; **a style ~ influenced by romanticism** un estilo con marcada *or* profunda influencia romántica; **they depend ~ on these imports** dependen en alto grado de estas importaciones; **~ pregnant** en avanzado estado de gravidez (frml) *or* (period) de gestación

heavy[1] /ˈhevi/ *adj* **-vier, -viest**

A 1 (weighty) ‹*load/suitcase/weight*› pesado; ‹*fabric/garment*› grueso, pesado; ‹*saucepan*› de fondo grueso; ‹*boots*› fuerte; **it's very ~** es muy pesado, pesa mucho; **~ goods vehicle** vehículo *m* (de carga) de gran tonelaje; **~ work** trabajo *m* pesado 2 (large-scale) (*before n*) ‹*artillery/machinery*› pesado

B 1 (ponderous) ‹*tread/footstep/fall*› pesado; ‹*thud*› sordo

h

2 ‹*features*› tosco, poco delicado; ‹*eyelids*› caído; ‹*sarcasm/irony*› poco sutil; **a man of ~ build** un hombre fornido; **a ~ hint** una indirecta muy directa (hum)

C 1 (oppressive) ‹*clouds/sky*› pesado; **a ~ silence** un silencio violento *or* embarazoso; **with a ~ heart** apesadumbrado, acongojado 2 (loud) ‹*sigh*› profundo; **~ breathing** (with exertion) resoplidos *mpl*; (with passion) jadeos *mpl*

D 1 (bigger than usual) ‹*expenditure*› cuantioso; ‹*crop*› abundante 2 (intense) ‹*book/treatment*› pesado, denso; ‹*rain*› fuerte; ‹*traffic*› denso; ‹*schedule*› apretado; **to be a ~ drinker/smoker** beber/fumar mucho; **he's a ~ sleeper** tiene el sueño pesado, duerme muy profundamente; **I've got a ~ cold** tengo un resfriado muy fuerte, estoy muy resfriado 3 (severe) ‹*sentence/penalty*› severo; ‹*casualties*› numeroso; ‹*blow*› duro, fuerte; **~ losses** grandes *or* cuantiosas pérdidas *fpl* 4 (violent) (sl) bruto; **the ~ mob moved in** entraron los matones

heavy² *adv*: **to lie/hang/weigh ~ on sb/sth** (liter) pesar sobre algn/algo (liter)

heavy³ *n* [c] (*pl* **-vies**) (colloq) matón *m* (fam), gorila *m* (fam)

heavy: **~ cream** *n* (AmE) crema *f* doble, nata *f* para montar (Esp), doble crema *f* (Méx); **~-duty** /ˈheviˈduːti || ˌheviˈdjuːti/ *adj* ‹*material/sacks*› muy resistente; ‹*machine*› para uso industrial; ‹*clothing/overalls*› de trabajo; **~-handed** /ˈheviˈhændəd || ˌheviˈhændɪd/ *adj* torpe; **~ industry** *n* [u c] industria *f* pesada; **~ metal** *n* 1 [c] (Chem) metal *m* pesado 2 [u] (Mus) heavy *m* (metal), rock *m* duro

heavyweight¹ /ˈheviweɪt/ *n* (Sport) peso *mf* pesado; **a political ~** un peso pesado de la política

heavyweight² *adj* 1 (Sport) (*before n*) ‹*boxer/wrestler*› de la categoría de los pesos pesados; ‹*title*› de los pesos pesados 2 (Tex) ‹*cotton/denim*› grueso y resistente

Hebrew¹ /ˈhiːbruː/ *adj* hebreo

Hebrew² *n* [u] hebreo *m*

Hebrides /ˈhebrədiːz || ˈhebrɪdiːz/ *pl n* **the ~** las (islas) Hébridas

heck /hek/ *n* (colloq & euph): **~!** ¡caray! (fam & euf); **what the ~!** ¡qué diablos! (fam); **~, no!** (AmE) ¡ni hablar!; **she's one ~ of a girl** es una chica fenomenal; **like** *o* **the ~ he did!** ¡y un cuerno que lo hizo! (fam); **he did it on his own — did he ~!** (BrE) lo hizo solo — ¡qué lo va a hacer solo!

heckle /ˈhekl̩/ *vt* interrumpir (*con preguntas o comentarios molestos*)

heckler /ˈheklər || ˈheklə(r)/ *n*: *persona que interrumpe a un orador para molestar*

heckling /ˈheklɪŋ/ *n* [u] interrupciones *fpl* (*a un orador*)

hectare /ˈhekter || ˈhekteə(r)/ *n* hectárea *f*

hectic /ˈhektɪk/ *adj* ‹*day/week*› ajetreado, agitado; ‹*journey/pace*› agotador; ‹*activity*› frenético, febril; ‹*trading*› intenso; **it was very ~ at the office today** hoy estuvimos muy agobiados de trabajo en la oficina

hectoring /ˈhektərɪŋ/ *adj* intimidante, autoritario

he'd /hiːd/ 1 = **he had** 2 = **he would**

hedge¹ /hedʒ/ *n* seto *m* (verde *or* vivo); ***you look as if you've been dragged through a ~ backwards*** parece que vinieras de la guerra

hedge² *vt* ‹*field/garden*› cercar* (*con seto*); ▸**bet¹** 2

■ **hedge** *vi* (evade the issue) dar* rodeos, tratar de escaparse por la tangente

Phrasal verb

• **hedge about** [v ▸ o ▸ adv] (*usu pass*) **to be ~d about WITH sth** estar* erizado *or* plagado DE algo

hedge fund *n* fondo *m* de inversión libre, hedge fund *m*

hedgehog /ˈhedʒhɔːg || ˈhedʒhɒg/ *n* erizo *m*

hedgerow /ˈhedʒrəʊ/ *n* [c u] seto *m* (verde *or* vivo)

hedonism /ˈhiːdn̩ɪzəm || ˈhiːdənɪzəm/ *n* [u] hedonismo *m*

hedonist /ˈhiːdn̩əst || ˈhiːdənɪst/ *n* hedonista *mf*

heed¹ /hiːd/ *n* [u]: **to take ~** tener* cuidado; **to take ~ of** *o* **pay ~ to sb** prestarle atención *or* hacerle* caso a algn

heed² *vt* prestar atención a, hacer* caso de

heedless /ˈhiːdləs || ˈhiːdlɪs/ *adj* (frml) **~ OF sth**: **~ of the danger ...** haciendo caso omiso del peligro ...

heedlessly /ˈhiːdləsli || ˈhiːdlɪsli/ *adv* (obliviously) sin prestar atención; (unthinkingly) descuidadamente; (recklessly) irresponsablemente

heel¹ /hiːl/ *n*

A 1 (Anat) talón *m*; **to turn on one's ~** dar(se)* media vuelta; ***to be (close/hard/hot) on the ~s of sb*** ir* pisándole los talones a algn; ***to bring sb to ~*** hacer* entrar en vereda a algn; **~!** (to dog) ¡ven aquí!; ***to cool*** *o* (BrE also) ***kick one's ~s*** esperar con impaciencia; ***to dig one's ~s in*** cerrarse* en banda; ***to take to one's ~s*** salir* corriendo *or* (fam) pitando; ▸**drag¹** *vt* **B** 2 (of shoe) tacón *m*, taco *m* (CS); **high/low ~s** tacones *or* (CS) tacos altos/bajos; ***to be down at ~*** (BrE) andar* desaliñado *or* mal arreglado 3 (of hosiery) talón *m*

B (contemptible person) (colloq) canalla *m*

heel² *vt* ‹*shoes*› ponerles* tacones *or* (CS) tacos nuevos a; ‹*high-heeled shoes*› ponerles* tapas *or* (Chi) tapillas a

heelbar /ˈhiːlbɑːr || ˈhiːlbɑː(r)/ *n* (BrE) taller *m* de reparación de calzado en el acto

heft¹ /heft/ *vt* (AmE colloq) 1 (heave up) levantar (*con esfuerzo*) 2 (gauge weight of) sopesar, calcular el peso de

heft² *n* [u] (AmE colloq) peso *m*

hefty /ˈhefti/ *adj* **-tier, -tiest** (colloq) 1 (large and heavy) ‹*person*› robusto, fornido, corpulento; ‹*load/case*› pesado 2 (strong) ‹*blow/pull*› fuerte; ‹*person*› fuerte 3 (substantial) ‹*price/salary*› alto; ‹*fine*› considerable

heifer /ˈhefər || ˈhefə(r)/ *n* vaquilla *f*, novilla *f*

heigh-ho /ˈheɪˈhəʊ/ *interj* ¡en fin!, ¡vaya!

height /haɪt/ *n*

A [u c] (tallness — of object) altura *f*; (— of person) estatura *f*, talla *f*; **what ~ are you?** ¿cuánto mides?; **she drew herself up to her full ~** se irguió cuan alta era; **to gain/lose ~** (Aviat) ganar/perder* altura; **at a ~ of 2,000 m above sea level** a una altura de 2.000 m sobre el nivel del mar

B (peak) (*no pl*): **to be at the ~ of one's power** estar* en la cima *or* en la cumbre *or* en la cúspide de su (*or* mi etc) poder; **when the storm was at its ~** en plena tormenta; **the ~ of fashion** el último grito (de la moda); **it's the ~ of madness** es el colmo de la locura

C **heights** *pl* 1 (high ground) cerros *mpl*, cumbres *fpl* 2 (high places, buildings) alturas *fpl*; **to be afraid of ~s** sufrir de vértigo 3 (highest level): **speculation rose to new** *o* **fresh ~s** la especulación alcanzó nuevas cotas

heighten /ˈhaɪtn̩/ *vt* ‹*effect/impression*› destacar*, realzar*; ‹*expectation/suspense*› aumentar, agudizar*; ‹*admiration/respect*› aumentar

■ **heighten** *vi*: **a period of ~ing tension** un período de creciente tensión *or* de tensión cada vez mayor

heinous /ˈheɪnəs/ *adj* (frml) atroz, abyecto

heir /er || eə(r)/ *n* heredero, -ra *m,f*; **~ TO sth** (to fortune, title) heredero DE algo; **the ~ to the throne** el heredero al trono

heiress /ˈerəs || ˈeəres/ *n* heredera *f*

heirloom /ˈerluːm || ˈeəluːm/ *n* reliquia *f*

heist¹ /haɪst/ *n* (AmE colloq) golpe *m* (fam), atraco *m*; **to pull a ~** dar* un golpe (fam)

heist² *vt* (AmE colloq) (steal) afanar (arg); (rob) atracar*

held /held/ *past and past p of* **hold¹**

helicopter /ˈheləkɑːptər || ˈhelɪkɒptə(r)/ *n* helicóptero *m*

helipad /ˈheləpæd || ˈhelɪpæd/ *n* pista *f* de aterrizaje para helicópteros

heliport /ˈheləpɔːrt || ˈhelɪpɔːt/ *n* helipuerto *m*

helium /ˈhiːliəm/ *n* helio *m*

helix /ˈhiːlɪks/ *n* (*pl* **helixes** *or* **helices** /ˈheləsiːz/) hélice *f*

hell /hel/ *n*

A 1 (Relig) infierno *m*; ***all ~ broke loose*** *o* ***out*** se armó la gorda *or* la de Dios es Cristo (fam); ***come ~ or high water*** sea como sea, pase lo que pase; ***~ for leather*** como alma que lleva el diablo (fam); ***just for the ~ of it*** sólo por divertirse*; ***there'll be ~ to pay*** (colloq) se va a armar la gorda *or* la de Dios es Cristo (fam); ***to knock ~*** *o* ***beat (the) ~ out of sb*** sacudir a algn de lo lindo (fam), sacarle* la mugre a algn (AmL fam); ***to play ~*** *o* (BrE also) ***merry ~ with sth*** hacer* estragos en algo; ***to raise ~*** (make trouble) montar un número (fam); (have rowdy fun) (AmE) armar jarana (fam) 2 (suffering, confusion): **a living ~** un auténtico infierno; **three months of sheer ~** tres meses infernales; **I went through ~ after his death** sufrí muchísimo cuando murió; ***to give sb ~*** (colloq): **those children really give her ~** esos niños le hacen pasar las de Caín (fam);

this tooth's giving me ~ esta muela me está haciendo ver las estrellas (fam); ***to make sb's life ~*** (colloq) hacerle* la vida imposible a algn

B (colloq) (*as intensifier*): **how the ~ ...?** ¿cómo demonios *or* diablos ...? (fam); **what the ~!** ¿y qué?; **why the ~ ...?** ¿por qué diablos ...? (fam); **he's a** *o* **one ~ of a guy** es un tipo sensacional (fam); **that's one ~ of a problem you've got there** ahí tienes un problema de padre y señor mío (fam); **to run like ~** correr como un loco (fam); **it hurts like ~** duele una barbaridad; **like** *o* **the ~ he will/can/did/has!** ¡y un cuerno! (fam); **get the ~ out of here!** ¡lárgate de aquí! (fam)

C (colloq) (*in interj phrases*): **go to ~!** ¡vete al cuerno *or* al diablo! (fam); **~, that's some car!** (AmE) ¡caray, qué cochazo! (fam & euf); **oh ~!** ¡caray! (fam & euf), ¡carajo *or* coño *or* mierda! (vulg); **to ~ with waiting: I'm off!** ¡qué esperar ni qué ocho cuartos! yo me voy (fam); **oh, well, what the ~!** bueno ¿qué importa? *or* ¿y qué? (fam)

he'll /hiːl/ **1** = **he will** **2** = **he shall**

hell: **~bent** *adj* empeñado; **to be ~bent ON sth/-ING** estar* empeñado EN algo/+ INF; **~fire** /'hel'faɪr || 'hel ˌfaɪə(r)/ *n* [u] el fuego eterno *or* del infierno; **~hole** *n* (colloq) lugar *m* horrible

hellion /'heljən/ *n* (AmE sl) demonio *m* (fam)

hellish /'helɪʃ/ *adj* (colloq) ‹*problem/difficulty*› de mil demonios (fam); ‹*experience*› horroroso

hello /hə'ləʊ/ *interj* **1** (greeting) ¡hola! **2** (answering the telephone) sí, aló (AmS), diga *or* dígame (Esp), bueno (Méx), olá (RPl) **3** (attracting attention) ¡oiga! **4** (expressing surprise, puzzlement) (esp BrE) ¡pero bueno!; **~! what's this doing on my desk?** ¿qué hace esto en mi escritorio?

hell: **~raiser** /'hel,reɪzər || 'hel,reɪzə(r)/ *n* (esp AmE colloq) camorrista *mf*; **~'s Angel** *n* ángel *m* del infierno

helluva /'heləvə/ *n* (esp AmE sl) (**= hell of a**) *see* **hell B**

helm /helm/ *n* (Naut) timón *m*

helmet /'helmət || 'helmɪt/ *n* (headgear) casco *m*; (armor) yelmo *m*

helm: **~sman** /'helmzmən/ *n* (*pl* **-men** /-mən/) timonel *m*; **~swoman** *n* timonel *f*

help¹ /help/ *vt*

A (assist) ayudar; **can I ~ you?** (in shop) ¿qué desea?; **so ~ me God** (frml) y que Dios me asista (frml); **to ~ sb (to) + INF** ayudar a algn A + INF; **she ~ed the old lady across the road** ayudó a la anciana a cruzar la calle; *see also* **help out**

B (avoid, prevent) (*usu neg or interrog*): **I can't ~ it** no lo puedo remediar; **I can't ~ the way I look** si soy así ¿qué (le) voy a hacer?; **they can't ~ being poor** no tienen la culpa de ser pobres; **I can't ~ thinking that ...** no puedo menos que pensar que ...; **are you going to visit them? — not if I can ~ it** ¿los vas a ir a ver? — no si lo puedo evitar; **oh, well, it can't be ~ed** bueno, paciencia *or* ¿qué se le va a hacer?

C (serve food, goods) **to ~ sb TO sth** servirle* algo A algn

■ **help** *vi* «*person/remark*» ayudar; «*tool*» servir*; **I was only trying to ~!** sólo quería ayudar; **calling her a liar didn't ~ much either** llamarla mentirosa tampoco sirvió de mucho; **every little bit** (AmE) *o* (BrE) **every little ~s** muchos pocos hacen un mucho; **to ~ to + INF** ayudar A + INF

■ *v refl* **to ~ oneself**

A (assist) ayudarse (a sí mismo)

B (resist impulse) (*usu neg*) controlarse; **I can't ~ myself** no me puedo controlar

C (take) **to ~ oneself (TO sth)** ‹*to food/a drink*› servirse* (algo); **can I use your phone? — ~ yourself** ¿puedo llamar por teléfono? — estás en tu casa; **~ yourself to any books you want** agarra *or* toma *or* (Esp) coge los libros que quieras; **he ~ed himself to $10 from the till** se agenció 10 dólares de la caja (fam)

(Phrasal verb)

• **help out**

A [v ▸ o ▸ adv, v ▸ adv ▸ o] ayudar, darle* *or* echarle una mano a

B [v ▸ adv] ayudar

help² *n*

A [u] **1** (rescue) ayuda *f*; **don't panic: ~ is on the** *o* **its way** calma, que ya vienen a ayudarnos; (*as interj*) **~!** ¡socorro!, ¡auxilio!; **to go for ~** ir* a buscar ayuda, ir* a por ayuda (Esp); **to call for/send for ~** pedir*/mandar a buscar ayuda **2** (assistance) ayuda *f*; **thanks for your ~ with the dishes** gracias por ayudarme con los platos; **was that book any ~?** ¿te sirvió de algo el libro?; **can I be of (any) ~ to you?** ¿la/lo puedo ayudar (en algo)?; **that's a great ~!** (iro) ¡pues vaya ayuda! (iró); (*before n*) ‹*file/button*› (Comput) de ayuda

B [u] (staff) personal *m*; (domestic) servicio *m* doméstico

helper /'helpər || 'helpə(r)/ *n* ayudante, -ta *m,f*; **painter's/electrician's ~** (AmE) aprendiz, -diza *m,f* de pintor/electricista

helpful /'helpfəl/ *adj* **1** (obliging) ‹*person/attitude*› servicial, amable; **thank you, you've been most ~** gracias, es usted muy amable; **I was only trying to be ~** sólo quería ayudar **2** (useful) ‹*advice/explanation*› útil

helpfully /'helpfəli/ *adv* ‹*offer/suggest*› amablemente

helping /'helpɪŋ/ *n* porción *f* (esp AmL), ración *f* (esp Esp); **are there second ~s?** ¿se puede repetir?

helpless /'helpləs || 'helplɪs/ *adj* **1** (incapacitated): **to leave/render sb ~** dejar a algn sin recursos; **the accident left him a ~ invalid** el accidente lo dejó totalmente imposibilitado; **~ with laughter** muerto de risa (fam) **2** (defenseless) ‹*prey/victim*› indefenso **3** (powerless) ‹*look/expression*› de impotencia; **to be ~ to + INF** ser* incapaz DE + INF

helplessly /'helpləsli || 'helplɪsli/ *adv* ‹*look on/stand by*› sin poder hacer nada; ‹*struggle/try*› en vano, inútilmente; ‹*laugh/giggle*› sin poder contenerse

helplessness /'helpləsnəs || 'helplɪsnɪs/ *n* [u] (powerlessness) impotencia *f*; (defenselessness) indefensión *f*

helpline /'helplaɪn/ *n* línea *f* (telefónica) de ayuda *or* de asistencia

helter-skelter¹ /'heltər'skeltər || ˌheltə'skeltə(r)/ *adv* atropelladamente, a la desbandada

helter-skelter² *n* (BrE) tobogán *m* (*en espiral*)

hem¹ /hem/ *n* dobladillo *m*, basta *f* (Chi)

hem² -mm- *vt* hacerle* el dobladillo *or* (Chi tb) la basta a

(Phrasal verb)

• **hem in** [v ▸ o ▸ adv, v ▸ adv ▸ o] encerrar*

he-man /'hiːmæn/ *n* (*pl* **-men** /-men/) (colloq) machote *m* (fam), super-macho *m* (fam)

hematologist, (BrE) **haematologist** *n* hematólogo, -ga *m,f*

hematology, (BrE) **haematology** /ˌhiːmə'tɑːlədʒi || ˌhiːmə'tɒlədʒi/ *n* [u] hematología *f*

hemisphere /'heməsfɪr || 'hemɪsfɪə(r)/ *n* **1** (Geog) hemisferio *m* **2** (Math) semiesfera *f*

hemline /'hemlaɪn/ *n* bajo *m*, ruedo *m*; **~s will rise again this year** las faldas se van a volver a llevar más cortas este año

hemlock /'hemlɑːk || 'hemlɒk/ *n* [c u] cicuta *f*

hemoglobin, (BrE) **haemoglobin** /'hiːməˌgləʊbən || ˌhiːmə'gləʊbɪn/ *n* [u] hemoglobina *f*

hemophilia, (BrE) **haemophilia** /ˌhiːmə'fɪliə/ *n* [u] hemofilia *f*

hemophiliac, (BrE) **haemophiliac** /ˌhiːmə'fɪliæk/ *n* hemofílico, -ca *m,f*

hemorrhage¹, (BrE) **haemorrhage** /'hemərɪdʒ/ *n* (Med) hemorragia *f*

hemorrhage², (BrE) **haemorrhage** *vi* «*patient*» tener* *or* (frml) sufrir una hemorragia; «*wound/blood vessel*» sangrar mucho

hemorrhoids, (BrE) **haemorrhoids** /'hemərɔɪdz/ *pl n* hemorroides *fpl*, almorranas *fpl*

hemp /hemp/ *n* [u] (fiber) cáñamo *m*; (drug) marihuana *f*, cannabis *m*; (plant) cannabis *m*, cáñamo *m* índico *or* de la India

hen /hen/ *n* (chicken) gallina *f*; (female bird) hembra *f*

hence /hens/ *adv*

A **1** (that is the reason for) de ahí; **~ my surprise** de ahí mi sorpresa, de ahí que me sorprendiera **2** (therefore) por lo tanto, por consiguiente

B (from now) (frml): **a few hours/years ~** dentro de algunas horas/algunos años

henceforth /'hens'fɔːrθ || ˌhens'fɔːθ/, **henceforward** /-'fɔːrwərd || -'fɔːwəd/ *adv* (liter) a partir de ahora, de ahora en adelante, en lo sucesivo

henchman /'hentʃmən/ *n* (*pl* **-men** /-mən/) secuaz *m*, esbirro *m*

henhouse /'henhaʊs/ *n* gallinero *m*

henna¹ /'henə/ *n* henna *f*

henna² *vt* **-nas, -naing, -naed**: **to ~ one's hair** ponerse* henna en el pelo

hen: **~ night** *n*: *noche de juerga sólo para mujeres*; (before wedding) despedida *f* de soltera; **~ party** *n* fiesta *f* de mujeres; (before wedding) despedida *f* de soltera; **~pecked** /'henpekt/ *adj* (colloq): **a ~pecked husband** un marido dominado por su mujer, un mandilón (Méx fam), un calzonazos (Esp fam)

hepatitis /'hepə'taɪtəs || ˌhepə'taɪtɪs/ *n* [u] hepatitis *f*

her¹ /hɜːr || hɜː(r), *weak form* ər || ə(r)/ *pron*

A 1 (as direct object) la; **I can't stand ~** no la soporto; **call ~** llámala 2 (as indirect object) le; (with direct object pronoun present) se; **I wrote ~ a letter** le escribí una carta; **give ~ the book** dale el libro; **give it to ~** dáselo; **I gave it to ~** se lo di 3 (after preposition) ella; **with/for ~** con/para ella

B (emphatic use) ella; **it's ~** es ella

C (for herself) (AmE colloq *or* dial): **she'd better get ~ a new job** es mejor que se busque otro trabajo

her² *adj* (*sing*) su; (*pl*) sus; **it's *her* house, not his** es la casa de ella, no de él; **she took ~ hat off** se quitó el sombrero

herald¹ /'herəld/ *n* (Hist) heraldo *m*

herald² *vt* anunciar

heraldic /he'rældɪk/ *adj* heráldico

heraldry /'herəldri/ *n* [u] heráldica *f*

herb /ɜːrb, hɜːrb || hɜːb/ *n* hierba *f*, yuyo *m* (Per, RPl); (*before n*) **~ garden** herbario *m*

herbaceous /ɜːr'beɪʃəs, hɜːr- || hɜː'beɪʃəs/ *adj* ‹*plant*› herbáceo; **~ border** (esp BrE) arriate *m or* (CS) cantero *m* de plantas perennes

herbal /'ɜːrbəl, 'hɜːrbəl|| 'hɜːbəl/ *adj* ‹*shampoo*› de hierbas; **~ tea** (esp BrE) ▸**herb tea**

herbalist /'ɜːrbələst, 'hɜːr- || 'hɜːbəlɪst/ *n* herborista *mf*, herbolario, -ria *m,f*

herbivore /'ɜːrbəvɔːr, 'hɜːr- || 'hɜːbɪvɔː(r)/ *n* herbívoro *m*

herbivorous /ɜːr'bɪvərəs, hɜːr- || hɜː'bɪvərəs/ *adj* herbívoro

herb tea *n* infusión *f*, agua *f*‡ (AmC, Andes), té *m* de yuyos (Per, RPl)

herd¹ /hɜːrd || hɜːd/ *n* 1 (of cattle) manada *f*, vacada *f*; (of goats) rebaño *m*; (of pigs) piara *f*, manada *f*; (of wild animals) manada *f*; (*before n*) **the ~ instinct** el instinto gregario; ***to ride ~ on sth/sb*** (AmE) cuidar de algo/algn 2 (of people) (pej) tropel *m*; **the (common) ~** la masa, el vulgo; **to follow the ~** seguir* a la masa *or* al rebaño

herd² *vt* ‹*animals*› arrear, arriar (RPl); **the refugees were ~ed into trucks** metieron a los refugiados en camiones como si fueran ganado

herdsman /'hɜːrdzmən || 'hɜːdzmən/ *n* (*pl* **-men** /-mən/) (of cattle) vaquero *m*, tropero *m* (CS); (of sheep) pastor *m*

here /hɪr || hɪə(r)/ *adv*

A 1 (at, to this place) aquí, acá (esp AmL); (less precise) acá; **right ~** aquí mismo; **the shops around ~** las tiendas de por aquí *or* (esp AmL) de por acá; ***to be neither ~ nor there*** no venir* al caso 2 (*in phrases*) **here and now** (right now) ahora mismo, en este mismo momento; **the ~ and now** (this life) esta vida; (the present) el presente, el momento; **here and there** aquí y allá; **here, there and everywhere** por todas partes

B (calling attention to sth, sb): **~'s £20** toma 20 libras; **~'s what you should do** esto es lo que debes hacer; **~ comes Philip/the bus** aquí está Philip/el autobús; **~ goes: wish me luck!** ¡allá voy, deséame suerte!; **~ we go again!** (expressing exasperation) ¡ya estamos *or* ya empezamos otra vez!; **~'s to the bride and groom** (proposing a toast) brindemos por los novios

C 1 (present): **were you ~ last week?** ¿viniste la semana pasada?; **he isn't ~ today** hoy no está; **Smith? — here!** (in roll call) ¿Smith? — ¡presente! 2 (arrived): **they're ~!** ¡ya llegaron!, ¡ya están aquí!; **winter'll be ~ before long** pronto llegará *or* empezará el invierno 3 (available): **help yourself, that's what it's ~ for** sírvete, para eso está

D 1 (at this moment) entonces; **~ she hesitated** entonces *or* en ese momento titubeó 2 (on this point): **~ I disagree** ahí no estoy de acuerdo

E (*as interj*): **~, let me do it** trae, deja que lo haga yo

hereabouts /'hɪrəbaʊts || ˌhɪərə'baʊts/, **hereabout** /-'baʊt/ *adv* por aquí, por acá

hereafter¹ /ˌhɪr'æftər || ˌhɪər'ɑːftə(r)/ *adv* (frml: used esp in legal texts) (from now on) de aquí en adelante; (in the future) en el futuro, en lo sucesivo

hereafter² *n* **the ~** el más allá, la otra vida

hereby /'hɪr'baɪ || hɪə'baɪ/ *adv* (frml) (Law) (in will) por el presente testamento; **I ~ pronounce you man and wife** los declaro marido y mujer (frml); **we, the undersigned, do ~ renounce ...** los abajo firmantes venimos en renunciar a ... (frml)

hereditary /hə'redəteri || hɪ'redɪtri/ *adj* hereditario

heredity /hə'redəti || hɪ'redəti/ *n* [u] herencia *f*

herein /hɪr'ɪn || hɪər'ɪn/ *adv* (frml) aquí

heresy /'herəsi/ *n* [u c] (*pl* **-sies**) herejía *f*

heretic /'herətɪk/ *n* hereje *mf*

heretical /hə'retɪkəl/ *adj* herético

herewith /hɪr'wɪθ || hɪə'wɪð/ *adv* (Corresp) adjunto

heritage /'herətɪdʒ || 'herɪtɪdʒ/ *n* (*no pl*) patrimonio *m*

hermaphrodite /hɜːr'mæfrədaɪt || hɜː'mæfrədaɪt/ *n* hermafrodita *mf*

hermetic /hɜːr'metɪk || hɜː'metɪk/ *adj* hermético

hermetically /hɜːr'metɪkli || hɜː'metɪkli/ *adv*: **~ sealed** herméticamente cerrado

hermit /'hɜːrmət || 'hɜːmɪt/ *n* ermitaño, -ña *m,f*, eremita *mf*

hermitage /'hɜːrmətɪdʒ || 'hɜːmɪtɪdʒ/ *n* ermita *f*

hermit crab *n* ermitaño *m*, paguro *m*

hernia /'hɜːrniə || 'hɜːniə/ *n* hernia *f*

hero /'hiːrəʊ || 'hɪərəʊ/ *n* (*pl* **heroes**) (brave, admirable person) héroe *m*; (personal idol) héroe *m*, ídolo *m*; (of novel, film) protagonista *mf*

heroic /hɪ'rəʊɪk/ *adj* heroico

heroics /hɪ'rəʊɪks/ *pl n* actos *mpl* heroicos; **don't try any ~** no intentes hacer ninguna heroicidad

heroin /'herəʊɪn/ *n* [u] heroína *f*; (*before n*) **~ addict** heroinómano, -na *m,f*

heroine /'herəʊɪn/ *n* (brave, admirable woman) heroína *f*; (of novel, film) protagonista *f*

heroism /'herəʊɪzəm/ *n* [u] heroísmo *m*

heron /'herən/ *n* garza *f* (real)

hero: **~ sandwich** *n* (AmE) *sándwich hecho con una barra entera de pan*; **~ worship** *n* [u] adoración *f* (*de alguien a quien se tiene como ídolo*)

herpes /'hɜːrpiːz || 'hɜːpiːz/ *n* [u] herpes *m*, herpe *f*

herring /'herɪŋ/ *n* [c u] (*pl* **herrings** *or* **herring**) arenque *m*; *see also* **red herring**

herringbone /'herɪŋbəʊn/ *n* (pattern) 1 (Archit) espina *f* de pez *or* de pescado 2 (Tex) espiga *f*, espiguilla *f*

hers /hɜːrz || hɜːz/ *pron* (*sing*) suyo, -ya; (*pl*) suyos, -yas; **~ is blue** el suyo/la suya es azul, el/la de ella es azul; **a friend of ~** un amigo suyo *or* de ella

herself /hər'self || hə'self/ *pron* 1 (reflexive): **she cut/hurt ~** se cortó/lastimó; **she bought ~ a hat** se compró un sombrero; **she only thinks of ~** sólo piensa en sí misma; **she was by ~** estaba sola; **she did it by ~** lo hizo ella sola; **she was talking to ~** estaba hablando sola; **something's not right, she thought to ~** —pasa algo —pensó para sí *or* para sus adentros 2 (emphatic use) ella misma; **she told me so ~** me lo dijo ella misma 3 (normal self): **she's not ~** no es la de siempre

hertz /hɜːrts || hɜːts/ *n* (*pl* ~) hercio *m*

he's /hiːz/ 1 = **he is** 2 = **he has**

hesitant /'hezətənt || 'hezɪtənt/ *adj* ‹*speech*› titubeante, vacilante; ‹*manner*› inseguro; ‹*steps*› vacilante; **he seemed a little ~** parecía dudar, parecía un poco indeciso; **to be ~ ABOUT -ING**: **I'm ~ about accepting the offer** no me decido *or* no estoy totalmente decidido a aceptar la oferta

hesitantly /'hezətəntli || 'hezɪtəntli/ *adv*: **she moved ~ towards the door** vacilante, se fue acercando a la puerta; **I suppose so, she replied ~** —supongo —replicó, no muy convencida

hesitate /ˈhezəteɪt || ˈhezɪteɪt/ *vi* vacilar, titubear; **I ~d before going in** dudé *or* vacilé antes de entrar; **to ~ to + INF** dudar en + INF; **please don't ~ to call me** no dudes en *or* dejes de llamarme; ***he who ~s is lost*** la ocasión la pintan calva

hesitation /ˈhezəˈteɪʃən || ˌhezɪˈteɪʃən/ *n* [u c] vacilación *f*; **she answered without the slightest ~** contestó sin titubear *or* sin la menor vacilación; **I have no ~ in recommending him** lo recomiendo sin reservas

hessian /ˈheʃən || ˈhesiən/ *n* [u] arpillera *f*

heterogeneous /ˈhetərəʊˈdʒiːniəs/ *adj* (frml) heterogéneo (frml)

heterosexual¹ /ˈhetərəʊˈsekʃuəl/ *adj* heterosexual

heterosexual² *n* heterosexual *mf*

heterosexuality /ˈhetərəʊˈsekʃuˈæləti/ *n* [u] heterosexualidad *f*

het up /ˈhetˈʌp/ *adj* (colloq) (*pred*): **to be/get (all) ~ ~ (about/over sth)** estar*/ponerse* como loco (por algo) (fam)

hew /hjuː/ *vt* (*past* **hewed**; *past p* **hewed** *or* **hewn** /hjuːn/) (extract) extraer*; (fashion) ‹*stone*› labrar, tallar

hex¹ /heks/ *n* (AmE) maleficio *m*; **to put a ~ on sb/sth** hacerle* un maleficio a algn/echar una maldición sobre algo

hex² *vt* (AmE) ‹*person*› hacerle* un maleficio a

hexagon /ˈheksəgɑːn || ˈheksəgən/ *n* hexágono *m*

hey /heɪ/ *interj* 1 (calling attention) ¡eh!; **~, mister!** ¡eh *or* oiga, señor! 2 (expressing dismay, protest, indignation) ¡oye!, ¡oiga(n)!; (expressing surprise, appreciation): **I've got a job — ~, that's really great!** conseguí trabajo — ¡pero qué bien!; **~ presto!** (BrE) ¡listo!, ¡voilá!

heyday /ˈheɪdeɪ/ *n* apogeo *m*, auge *m*; **in his ~** en sus buenos tiempos

HGV *n* (BrE) (= **heavy goods vehicle**) vehículo *m* pesado

HHS *n* (in US) = **Department of Health and Human Services**

hi /haɪ/ *interj* (colloq) hola (fam); **say ~ to your folks for me** dale recuerdos *or* saludos a tu familia de mi parte

HI = Hawaii

hiatus /haɪˈeɪtəs/ *n* (*pl* **-tuses**) (frml) paréntesis *m* (frml), pausa *f*

hibernate /ˈhaɪbərneɪt || ˈhaɪbəneɪt/ *vi* hibernar, invernar

hibernation /ˈhaɪbərˈneɪʃən || ˌhaɪbəˈneɪʃən/ *n* [u] hibernación *f*; **to go into ~** entrar en estado de hibernación

hic /hɪk/ *interj* ¡hip!

hiccough /ˈhɪkʌp/ *n/vi* ▸ **hiccup¹·²**

hiccup¹ /ˈhɪkʌp/ *n* 1 hipo *m*; **to have (the) ~s** tener* hipo; **she got the ~s** le dio hipo 2 (brief interruption) dificultad *f*, tropiezo *m* 3 (small problem) (BrE) pequeño problema *m*

hiccup² *vi*, (BrE also) **-pp-** hipar

hick¹ /hɪk/ *n* (AmE colloq & pej) pueblerino, -na *m,f*, paleto, -ta *m,f* (Esp fam & pey), pajuerano, -na *m,f* (RPl fam & pey)

hick² *adj* (AmE colloq & pej) (*before n*) pueblerino, paleto (Esp fam & pey), pajuerano (RPl fam & pey)

hickey /ˈhɪki/ *n* (*pl* **-eys**) (AmE colloq) 1 (love bite) chupón *m* (fam) (*marca dejada por un beso*) 2 (pimple) grano *m*

hickory /ˈhɪkəri/ *n* (*pl* **-ries**) 1 [c] (tree) nogal *m* americano, caria *f* 2 [u] (wood) nogal *m* americano; ***as tough as ~*** (AmE) fuerte como un roble 3 [c] **~ (stick)** palmeta *f*

hid /hɪd/ 1 *past of* **hide¹** 2 (arch) *past p of* **hide¹**

hidden¹ /ˈhɪdn̩/ *adj* ‹*entrance/camera/reserves*› oculto; ‹*cost*› no aparente; Ⓢ **no hidden extras** todo incluido

hidden² *past p of* **hide¹**

hide¹ /haɪd/ (*past* **hid** /hɪd/; *past p* **hidden**) *or* (arch) **hid**) *vt* 1 (conceal) esconder; **to ~ sth FROM sb**: **she hid the money from the police** escondió el dinero para que no lo encontrara la policía; **to ~ oneself** esconderse 2 (keep secret) ‹*feelings/thoughts*› ocultar; **to ~ sth FROM sb** ocultarle algo A algn 3 (mask, screen) tapar; **she hid her face in her hands** se tapó la cara con las manos; **some trees hid the house from view** unos árboles no dejaban ver la casa

■ **hide** *vi* esconderse; **where've you been hiding all these weeks?** ¿dónde has estado metido todas estas semanas?

(Phrasal verbs)

• **hide away**

A [v ▸ adv] esconderse

B [v ▸ o ▸ adv, v ▸ adv ▸ o] esconder

• **hide out,** (AmE also) **hide up** [v ▸ adv] (colloq) esconderse

hide² *n*

A [c u] (of animal — raw) piel *f*; (— tanned) cuero *m*; ***not to see ~ nor hair of sb*** (colloq) no verle* el pelo a algn (fam); ***to tan sb's ~*** (colloq) curtir a algn a palos (fam)

B [c] (in bird-watching, hunting) (BrE) paranza *f*, puesto *m*

hide: **~-and-seek** /ˈhaɪdn̩ˈsiːk/, (AmE & Scot also) **~-and-go-seek** /ˈhaɪdn̩gəʊˈsiːk/ *n* [u]: **to play ~-and-seek** jugar* al escondite, jugar* a las escondidas (AmL); **~away** *n* 1 (hiding place) (AmE) escondite *m*, escondrijo *m* 2 (secluded spot) rincón *m*; **~bound** *adj* ‹*attitudes/person/institution*› retrógrado; ‹*conservatism*› rígido; **~bound by tradition** encerrado en *or* apegado a la tradición

hideous /ˈhɪdiəs/ *adj* ‹*face/monster/sight*› horroroso, horrible; ‹*crime/fate*› espantoso; ‹*color/clothes/furniture*› (colloq) horrendo, espantoso

hideout /ˈhaɪdaʊt/ *n* guarida *f*

hiding /ˈhaɪdɪŋ/ *n*

A [u] (concealment): **to be in ~/go into ~ (from sb)** estar* escondido/esconderse (de algn); **to come out of ~** salir* de su (*or* mi *etc*) escondite; (*before n*) **~ place** escondite *m*, escondrijo *m*

B [c] (beating) (colloq) paliza *f*, tunda *f*; **to give sb a good ~** darle* a algn una buena paliza *or* tunda; ***to be on a ~ to nothing*** (BrE) llevar todas las de perder (fam)

hierarchy /ˈhaɪərɑːrki || ˈhaɪərɑːki/ *n* (*pl* **-chies**) jerarquía *f*

hieroglyph /ˈhaɪərəglɪf/ *n* jeroglífico *m*

hieroglyphics /ˈhaɪərəˈglɪfɪks/ *pl n* jeroglíficos *mpl*

hi-fi /ˈhaɪfaɪ/ *n* 1 [u] (equipment) alta fidelidad *f* 2 [c] (set) equipo *m* de alta fidelidad, hi-fi *m*

higgledy-piggledy /ˈhɪgəldiˈpɪgəldi/ *adv* (colloq) sin orden ni concierto, de cualquier manera

high¹ /haɪ/ *adj* **-er, -est**

A 1 (tall) ‹*building/wall/mountain*› alto; **how ~ is it?** ¿qué altura tiene?; **the tower is 40 m ~** la torre tiene 40 m de alto *or* de altura; **a 12 ft ~ wall** un muro de 12 pies de alto *or* de altura 2 (high up) ‹*window/balcony*› alto; ‹*plateau*› elevado; **at a ~ altitude** a gran altitud; **the river is very ~** el río está muy alto *or* crecido; **a ~ forehead** una frente amplia; **~ cheekbones** pómulos *mpl* salientes 3 (in status) ‹*office/rank/officials*› alto; **he has friends in ~ places** tiene amigos muy bien situados; **the ~ life** la gran vida; **~ society** la alta sociedad 4 (morally, ethically) ‹*ideals/principles/aims*› elevado 5 (in pitch) ‹*voice*› agudo; ‹*note*› alto; **the speech ended on a ~ note** el discurso terminó con una nota de optimismo

B 1 (considerable, greater than usual) ‹*temperature/speed/pressure*› alto; ‹*wind*› fuerte; **the temperature was in the ~ eighties** la temperatura rondaba los noventa grados; **to have a ~ color** (permanently) ser* rubicundo; (because of a fever) estar* muy colorado *or* rojo; **the death toll could rise as ~ as 20** el número de muertos podría elevarse a 20; **unemployment is very ~** hay mucho desempleo; **to pay a ~ price for sth** pagar* algo muy caro; **my hopes were ~ as I set out** tenía grandes esperanzas al partir; **to be ~ in vitamins/proteins** ser* rico en vitaminas/proteínas 2 (good, favorable): **he has a ~ regard for you** tiene muy buen concepto de ti

C 1 (Lit, Theat): **a moment of ~ comedy/drama** un momento comiquísimo/muy dramático 2 (climactic) culminante; **the ~ point** el punto culminante

D 1 (happy, excited): **she was in ~ spirits** estaba muy animada; **we had a ~ old time** (colloq) lo pasamos estupendamente 2 (intoxicated) (colloq) drogado, colocado (Esp fam); **to be/get ~ on sth** estar* drogado *or* (Esp tb) colocado/drogarse* *or* (Esp tb) colocarse* con algo (fam)

E (of time): **~ noon** mediodía *m*; **in ~ summer** en pleno verano; **~ days and holidays** las grandes ocasiones

F ‹*meat*› pasado; ‹*game*› que tiene un olor fuerte

high² *adv* **-er, -est** 1 ‹*fly*› alto; **the mountain towered ~ above us** la montaña se elevaba dominante sobre nosotros; **~ in the sky** en lo alto del cielo; **~ overhead** en

h

las alturas; **~ up** arriba, en lo alto; **it's pretty ~ (up) on the agenda** es uno de los asuntos más importantes; **feelings are running ~** los ánimos están exaltados; **to aim ~** ‹‹*marksman*›› apuntar alto; ‹‹*ambitious person*›› picar* alto; ***to leave sb ~ and dry*** dejar a algn en la estacada, dejar a algn tirado (fam); ***to search** o **hunt** o **look ~ and low (for sth)*** remover* cielo y tierra (para encontrar algo) **2** (in pitch) ‹*sing*› alto **3** (in amount, degree): **how ~ are you prepared to bid?** ¿hasta cuánto estás dispuesto a pujar *or* ofrecer?

high³ *n*

A **1** [c] (level) récord *m* **2** [u] **on high** (in heaven) en las alturas; (high above) en lo alto

B [c] (Meteo) (anticyclone) zona *f* de altas presiones; (high temperature) máxima *f*

C [c] (euphoria) (colloq) (from drugs) viaje *m* (fam), colocón *m* (Esp fam); (for other reasons): **I'm on a real ~ at the moment** las cosas me están yendo de maravilla

D [u] (top gear) (AmE Auto) (*no art*) directa *f*

E [c] (high school) (AmE colloq) cole *m* (fam) (*secundario*)

high- /'haɪ/ *pref*: **~income** de altos ingresos; **~quality** de alta calidad, de gran calidad; **~speed** ‹*train*› de alta velocidad; ‹*film*› de alta sensibilidad

high: **~ altar** *n* altar *m* mayor; **~-and-mighty** /'haɪən'maɪti/ *adj* altanero, arrogante

highball¹ /'haɪbɔːl/ *n* **1** (drink) highball *m*, jaibol *m* (Méx) (*whisky con soda*) **2** (drinking glass) vaso *m* de whisky, vaso *m* de jaibol (Méx)

highball² (AmE colloq) *vi* ir* a toda máquina *or* a todo lo que da

■ **highball** *vt*: ***to ~ it*** salir* a toda máquina *or* a todo lo que da

high: **~boy** *n* (AmE) cómoda *f* alta; **~brow** *adj* (colloq) ‹*tastes*› de intelectual; ‹*art/music*› para intelectuales; **~chair** *n* silla *f* alta (*para niño*)

High Church¹ *n*: *sector de la Iglesia Anglicana más cercano a la liturgia y ritos católicos*

High Church² *adj*: *relativo a la* **High Church¹**

high: **~-class** /'haɪ'klæs || ˌhaɪ'klɑːs/ *adj* ‹*restaurant/hotel*› de lujo; ‹*merchandise*› de primera calidad; **a ~-class prostitute** una prostituta de lujo; **~ command** *n* [u] alto mando *m*; **~ Commission**, **~ commission** *n* (international) Alto Comisionado *m*, Alto Comisariado *m*; (embassy) embajada *f* (*de un país del Commonwealth en otro*); **~ Commissioner**, **~ commissioner** *n* (international) alto comisario, alta comisaria *m,f*; (ambassador) embajador, -dora *m,f* (*de un país del Commonwealth en otro*); **~ Court** *n* (in England and Wales) *una de las dos ramas del Tribunal Supremo, con competencia para conocer de causas civiles cuyo coste excede cierta cuantía*; **~-definition** /ˌhaɪdefə'nɪʃən || ˌhaɪdefɪ'nɪʃən/ *adj* de alta definición; **~-definition television** televisión *f* de alta definición; **~-density** /ˌhaɪ'densəti/ *adj* **1** (Comput) ‹*disk*› de alta densidad; **2** ‹*urban area*› de alta densidad de población; **~-density housing area** zona *f* de alta densidad habitacional; **~-energy** /'haɪ'enərdʒi || ˌhaɪ'enədʒi/ *adj* ‹*particle/physics/reaction*› hiperenergético, de alta energía; ‹*snack*› de alto contenido calórico, de alto valor energético

higher /'haɪər || 'haɪə(r)/ *adj* **1** *comp of* **high¹** **2** (*before n*) ‹*mammals/organs*› superior

higher education *n* [u] enseñanza *f* superior

high: **~ explosive** *n* [c u] explosivo *m* de alta potencia; **~falutin** /'haɪfə'luːtn/, **~faluting** /-tɪŋ/ *adj* (colloq) pomposo, rimbombante; **~ fidelity** *n* [u] alta fidelidad *f*; **~ finance** *n* [u] altas finanzas *fpl*; **~flier**, **~flyer** /'haɪ'flaɪər || ˌhaɪ'flaɪə(r)/ *n*: **he's one of the company's/college's ~fliers** es uno de los empleados/estudiantes más prometedores *or* con más futuro de la compañía/del colegio; **~flown** *adj* altisonante, rimbombante; **~-flying** /'haɪ'flaɪɪŋ/ *adj* (*before n*) muy prometedor, con gran futuro; **~-frequency** /'haɪ'friːkwənsi/ *adj* de alta frecuencia; **~-grade** *adj* de calidad superior, de alta calidad; **~-handed** /'haɪ'hændəd || ˌhaɪ'hændɪd/ *adj* arbitrario, prepotente; **~-hat** /'haɪ'hæt/ *adj* (AmE colloq) esnob, pituco (CS, Per fam), popoff (Méx fam); **~-heeled** /'haɪ'hiːld/ *adj* de tacón *or* (CS) de taco alto; **~ jinks** *pl n* (colloq) francachela *f* (fam & ant), jarana *f* (fam); **~ jump** *n* salto *m* de altura, salto *m* alto (AmL); ***to be for the ~ jump*** (BrE colloq): **you're for the ~ jump if you don't mend your ways** te va a caer una buena, si no cambias de actitud (fam); **~lander** /'haɪləndər || 'haɪləndə(r)/ *n* **1** (uplander) montañés, -ñesa *m,f* **2** **H~lander** (in Scotland) *habitante o persona oriunda de las Highlands o las tierras altas de Escocia*; **~lands** /'haɪləndz/ *pl n* **1** (uplands) tierras *fpl* altas, altiplanicie *f* **2** (in Scotland) **the H~lands** las *or* los Highlands, las tierras altas; **~-level** /'haɪ'levəl/ *adj* **1** ‹*talks/delegation*› de alto nivel **2** ‹*bridge/road*› elevado **3** (Comput) de alto nivel **4** ‹*waste*› de alta radiactividad

highlight¹ /'haɪlaɪt/ *vt* (*past & past p* **-lighted**)

A (call attention to) ‹*problem/question*› destacar*, poner* de relieve

B **1** (Art, Phot) realzar*, dar* realce a **2** **to ~ one's hair** ponerse* *or* darse* reflejos (en el pelo), hacerse* claritos (RPl), hacerse* rayitos (en el pelo) (Chi), hacerse* luces (en el pelo) (Méx), hacerse* mechones (Col)

highlight² *n*

A (most memorable part) lo más destacado; **her performance was the ~ of the evening** su actuación fue el plato fuerte de la velada; **~s of the game** las jugadas más importantes del partido

B **1** (Art, Phot) toque *m* de luz **2** **highlights** *pl* (in hair) reflejos *mpl*, claritos *mpl* (RPl), visos *mpl* (Chi), luces *fpl* (Méx), mechones *mpl* (Col)

highlighter /'haɪlaɪtər || 'haɪlaɪtə(r)/ *n* [u c] **1** (makeup) sombra *f* clara de ojos **2** (pen) rotulador *m*, marcador *m* (AmL)

highly /'haɪli/ *adv* **1** (to a high degree): **~ probable/unlikely** muy/muy poco probable; **~ intelligent** inteligentísimo, sumamente inteligente; **~ trained/skilled** altamente capacitado/calificado; **he's ~ respected** lo respetan mucho **2** (favorably): **his boss speaks/thinks very ~ of him** su jefe habla muy bien/tiene muy buena opinión de él; **I recommend it ~** te lo recomiendo sin reserva **3** (at a high rate): **a ~ paid job** un trabajo muy bien pagado *or* remunerado

highly: **~-charged** /'haɪli'tʃɑːrdʒd || ˌhaɪli'tʃɑːdʒd/ *adj* muy tenso, lleno de tensión; **~-strung** /'haɪli'strʌŋ/ *adj* (BrE) ▸ **high-strung**

high: **~-minded** /'haɪ'maɪndəd || ˌhaɪ'maɪndɪd/ *adj* altruista; **~-necked** /'haɪ'nekt/ *adj* de cuello alto

Highness /'haɪnəs || 'haɪnɪs/ *n*: **Her/His/Your (Royal) ~** Su Alteza (Real)

high: **~-pitched** /'haɪ'pɪtʃt/ *adj* ‹*voice/sound*› agudo; ‹*instrument*› de tono agudo *or* alto; **~-powered** /'haɪ'paʊərd || ˌhaɪ'paʊəd/ *adj* ‹*car/machine*› muy potente, de gran potencia; ‹*executive/campaign*› dinámico, enérgico; ‹*job*› de alto(s) vuelo(s); **~-pressure** /'haɪ'preʃər || ˌhaɪ'preʃə(r)/ *adj* (*before n*) **1** (Meteo) ‹*area/zone*› de altas presiones **2** ‹*selling*› agresivo; ‹*job*› de mucho estrés; **~ priest** *n* sumo sacerdote *m*; **~ priestess** *n* suma sacerdotisa *f*; **~-profile** /'haɪ'prəʊfaɪl/ *adj* prominente; **~-ranking** /'haɪ'ræŋkɪŋ/ *adj* ‹*officer*› de alto rango; ‹*official*› alto, de alta jerarquía; **~ rise** *n* (esp AmE) torre *f* (de apartamentos *or* (Esp) pisos); **~-rise** /'haɪ'raɪz/ *adj* (*before n*) ‹*building/block*› alto, de muchas plantas; ‹*apartment*› de una torre, de un edificio alto; **~-risk** /'haɪ'rɪsk/ *adj* ‹*business/investment*› de alto riesgo; ‹*occupation*› expuesto, riesgoso (AmL); ‹*category/patient*› de alto riesgo; **~road** *n* carretera *f*; **~ roller** *n* (AmE colloq) (gambler) jugador empedernido, jugadora empedernida *m,f*; (big spender) derrochón, -chona *m,f*; **~ school** *n* colegio *m* secundario, ≈ instituto *m* (*en Esp*), ≈ liceo *m* (*en CS, Ven*); **~ season** *n* [u] temporada *f* alta; **~-sided vehicle** /'haɪsaɪdɪd/ *n* vehículo *m* de laterales altos; **~-spirited** /'haɪ'spɪrətəd || ˌhaɪ'spɪrɪtɪd/ *adj* lleno de vida, brioso; **~ spot** *n* **1** (main feature) punto *m* culminante **2** (exciting place) (AmE) atracción *f*; **~ street** *n* (BrE) calle *f* principal, calle *f* mayor (Esp); **the ~ street** (Econ) el comercio minorista; (*before n*) **the ~-street banks** los grandes bancos (*con muchas sucursales*); **~-strung** /'haɪ'strʌŋ/, (BrE) **highly-strung** *adj* ‹*person*› nervioso; ‹*dog/horse*› muy excitable; **~tail** *vt*: ***to ~tail it*** (leave in a hurry) (AmE sl) irse* volando, abrirse* (Esp arg), tomarse los vientos (RPl fam), mandarse a cambiar (Andes fam); **~ tea** *n* (esp BrE) *comida entre merienda y cena que generalmente se toma acompañada de té*; **~ tech** /'haɪ'tek/ *n* [u] (technology) alta tecnología *f*, (design) high tech *m*; **~-tech** /'haɪ'tek/ *adj* de alta tecnología; ‹*era*› high tech *adj inv*; **~ technology** *n* [u] alta tecnología *f*; **~ treason** *n* [u] alta traición *f*; **~-up** *n* (esp AmE colloq) gerifalte *mf*, capo, -pa *m,f* (fam); **~-water mark** /'haɪ'wɔːtər || ˌhaɪ'wɔːtə/ *n* (of tide) línea *f* de pleamar; (highest point) cénit *m*, apogeo *m*; **~way** *n* (main road) carretera *f*; (public way) vía *f* pública; **the ~ways and byways** (of region) las carreteras y los caminos; (*before n*) ‹*patrol/patrolman*› (AmE) de carretera; **~way Code** *n* (in UK) Código *m* de la Circulación; **~wayman** /'haɪweɪmən/ *n* (*pl* **-men** /-mən/) salteador *m* de caminos, bandolero *m*; **~way robbery** *n* (Hist) asalto *m* (*en un camino*), salteamiento *m*; **~ wire** *n* cuerda *f* floja

> **high school**
>
> En Estados Unidos, el último ciclo del colegio secundario, generalmente para alumnos cuyas edades están comprendidas entre los 14 y los 18 años. En Gran Bretaña, algunos colegios secundarios también se llaman *high schools*

hijack[1] *vt* /'haɪdʒæk/ secuestrar

hijack[2] *n* secuestro *m*

hijacker /'haɪdʒækər || 'haɪdʒækə(r)/ *n* secuestrador, -dora *m,f*; (of planes) pirata aéreo, -rea *m,f*

hike[1] /haɪk/ *n*

A (long walk) caminata *f*, excursión *f*; **it's a bit of a ~ to the station** hay un buen trecho hasta la estación; ***to take a ~*** (AmE colloq): **take a ~** vete a paseo (fam), vete por un tubo (Méx fam), andá a pasear (RPl fam)

B (increase) subida *f*; **~ IN sth** subida DE algo

hike[2] *vi* (walk) ir* de caminata *or* de excursión

Phrasal verb

- **hike up** [v ▸ o ▸ adv, v ▸ adv ▸ o] (pull up) (AmE) ‹*prices*› subir, aumentar; ‹*socks*› subirse, levantarse

hiker /'haɪkər || 'haɪkə(r)/ *n* excursionista *mf*, caminante *mf*

hiking /'haɪkɪŋ/ *n* excursionismo *m*; (*before n*) **~ boot** borceguí *m*

hilarious /hɪ'leriəs || hɪ'leəriəs/ *adj* divertidísimo, comiquísimo

hilarity /hɪ'lærəti/ *n* [u] (frml) hilaridad *f*

hill /hɪl/ *n* (low) colina *f*, cerro *m*, collado *m*; (higher) montaña *f*; (slope, incline) cuesta *f*; **on a ~** (on the top) en (lo alto de) una colina; (on a slope) en una ladera; **to walk up/down a ~** subir/bajir una colina (andando); ***as old as the ~s*** más viejo que Matusalén (fam), más viejo que andar a pie (CS fam); ***not to amount to a ~ of beans*** (AmE) no valer* nada; ***to be over the ~*** (colloq) estar* para el arrastre *or* (RPl) para el deje (fam); (*before n*) **~ country** territorio *m* montañoso, región *f* montañosa

hillbilly /'hɪlˌbɪli/ *n* (*pl* **-lies**) (AmE colloq) rústico, -ca *m,f*, paleto, -ta *m,f* (Esp fam & pey), pajuerano, -na *m,f* (RPl fam & pey); (*before n*) **~ music** música *f* country

hillock /'hɪlək/ *n* (small hill) loma *f*, altozano *m*; (mound of earth) montículo *m*

hill: **~side** *n* ladera *f*; **~ start** *n* (Auto) arranque *m* en cuesta; **~top** *n* cima *f*, cumbre *f*

hilly /'hɪli/ *adj* **-lier, -liest** accidentado

hilt /hɪlt/ *n* empuñadura *f*, puño *m*; ***(up) to the ~***: **they were mortgaged up to the ~** estaban hipotecados hasta el cuello (fam); **to back sb (up) to the ~** respaldar a algn incondicionalmente

him /hɪm, *weak form* ɪm/ *pron*

A 1 (as direct object) lo, le (Esp); **I saw ~** lo *or* (Esp tb) le vi; **call ~** llámalo, llámale (Esp) 2 (as indirect object) le; (with direct object pronoun present) se; **I sent ~ a card** le mandé una tarjeta; **I sent it to ~** se la mandé; **give ~ the book** dale el libro; **give it to ~** dáselo; **I gave it to ~** se lo di 3 (after preposition) él; **near/in front of ~** cerca/delante de él

B (emphatic use) él; **it's ~** es él

C (for himself) (AmE colloq *or* dial): **he went and got ~ a wife** fue y se buscó una mujer

Himalayas /'hɪmə'leɪəz/ *pl n* **the ~** el Himalaya

himself /hɪm'self/ *pron* 1 (reflexive): **he cut/hurt ~** se cortó/lastimó; **he bought ~ a hat** se compró un sombrero; **he only thinks of ~** sólo piensa en sí mismo; **he was by ~** estaba solo; **he did it by ~** lo hizo él solo; **very strange, he thought to ~** —muy raro —pensó para sí *or* para sus adentros; **he was talking to ~** estaba hablando solo 2 (emphatic use) él mismo; **he told me so ~** me lo dijo él mismo 3 (normal self): **he's not ~** no es el de siempre

hind[1] /haɪnd/ *adj* (*before n, no comp*) trasero; **~ legs** patas *fpl* traseras

hind[2] *n* cierva *f*

hinder /'hɪndər || 'hɪndə(r)/ *vt* dificultar

Hindi /'hɪndi/ *n* [u] indi *m*, hindi *m*

hindquarters /'haɪndˌkwɔːrtərz || ˌhaɪnd'kwɔːtəz/ *pl n* cuartos *mpl* traseros

hindrance /'hɪndrəns/ *n* [c] (impediment) estorbo *m*, obstáculo *m*; **he's more of a ~ than a help** más que ayudar, estorba

hindsight /'haɪndsaɪt/ *n* [u]: **with (the benefit of) ~** a posteriori, en retrospectiva

Hindu[1] /'hɪnduː/ *n* hindú *mf*

Hindu[2] *adj* hindú

Hinduism /'hɪnduːɪzəm/ *n* [u] hinduismo *m*

Hindustani /'hɪnduː'stɑːni || ˌhɪndʊ'stɑːni/ *n* [u] indostaní *m*, indostánico *m*

hinge[1] /hɪndʒ/ *n* (of door, window, gate) bisagra *f*, gozne *m*; (of box, lid) bisagra *f*

hinge[2] **hinges, hinging, hinged** *vi* **to ~ ON sth** (turn) girar SOBRE algo; (be fixed) ir* asegurado con bisagras A algo; (depend) depender DE algo

hinged /hɪndʒd/ *adj* de *or* con bisagras

hint[1] /hɪnt/ *n*

A 1 (oblique reference) insinuación *f*, indirecta *f*; (clue) pista *f*; **a gentle/broad ~** una pequeña/clara indirecta; **to drop a ~ to sb** lanzarle* una indirecta a algn; **to take the ~** captar *or* (Esp tb) coger* la indirecta; **OK, I can take a ~** está bien, ya entiendo *or* no me lo tienes que repetir 2 (trace): **just a ~ of bitterness/sadness** un ligero dejo amargo/de tristeza; **it's white with just a ~ of yellow** es blanco con apenas un toque de amarillo; **there was a ~ of garlic/lemon in the dish** el plato tenía un dejo *or* gusto a ajo/limón

B (tip) consejo *m*

hint[2] *vt* insinuar*, dar* a entender

■ **hint** *vi* lanzar* indirectas; **to ~ AT sth** insinuar* *or* dar* a entender algo; **he ~ed at the possibility of fresh talks** dio a entender que podría haber nuevas negociaciones

hinterland /'hɪntərlænd || 'hɪntəlænd/ *n* interior *m*

hip[1] /hɪp/ *n* 1 cadera *f*; **with one's hands on one's ~s** con los brazos en jarras; (*before n*) **~ flask** petaca *f*, botella *f* de bolsillo; **~ pocket** bolsillo *m* trasero (del pantalón) 2 (joint) cadera *f*

hip[2] *interj*: **~, ~, hooray** *o* **hurrah!** ¡hurra!, ¡viva!

hip[3] *adj* **-pp-** (sl & dated) 'in' *adj inv* (fam & ant), en la onda (fam)

hippie /'hɪpi/ *n* ▸**hippy**[1]

hippo /'hɪpəʊ/ *n* (*pl* **-pos**) (colloq) hipopótamo *m*

hippopotamus /'hɪpə'pɑːtəməs || ˌhɪpə'pɒtəməs/ *n* (*pl* **-muses** *or* **-mi** /-maɪ/) hipopótamo *m*

hippy[1], **hippie** /'hɪpi/ *n* (*pl* **-pies**) hippy *mf*

hippy[2] *adj* **-pier, -piest** (with prominent hips) (AmE) caderudo (fam)

hire[1] /haɪr || 'haɪə(r)/ *vt*

A 1 ‹*hall/boat/suit*› alquilar, arrendar* 2 (Busn, Lab Rel) ‹*staff/person*› contratar 3 **hired** *past p*: **~d hand** jornalero, -ra *m,f*; **~d killer** *o* **assassin** asesino, -na *m,f* a sueldo, sicario, -ria *m,f*; **a ~d car** un coche alquilado

B ▸**hire out A**

Phrasal verb

- **hire out**

A [v ▸ o ▸ adv, v ▸ adv ▸ o] (BrE) alquilar, arrendar*; **they ~ bikes out to tourists** les alquilan bicicletas a los turistas

B [v ▸ adv] (offer services) (AmE) **to ~ out AS sth** ofrecerse* COMO algo

hire[2] *n* [u]

A (of hall/car/suit) alquiler *m*, arriendo *m*; **have you any bikes for ~?** ¿alquilan *or* arriendan bicicletas?; **S for hire** se alquila *or* se arrienda; (on taxis) libre; (*before n*) (esp BrE) **~ car** coche *m* de alquiler; **~ charge** alquiler *m*, arriendo *m*

B (payment) alquiler *m*, arriendo *m*

h

hireling /ˈhaɪrlɪŋ || ˈhaɪəlɪŋ/ *n* (frml & pej) mercenario, -ria *m,f*, asalariado, -da *m,f*

hire purchase *n* [u] (BrE) plan *m* de financiación; **to buy sth on ~ ~** comprar algo a plazos, comprar algo en cuotas (esp AmL)

hirsute /ˈhɜːrsuːt || ˈhɜːsjuːt/ *adj* (frml) hirsuto (frml)

his¹ /hɪz, *weak form* ɪz/ *adj* (*sing*) su; (*pl*) sus; **it's *his* house, not hers** es la casa de él, no la de ella; **he broke ~ arm** se rompió el brazo

his² *pron* (*sing*) suyo, -ya; (*pl*) suyos, -yas; **~ is blue** el suyo/la suya es azul, el/la de él es azul; **~ and hers** para él y para ella; **a friend of ~** un amigo suyo *or* de él

Hispanic¹ /hɪˈspænɪk/ *adj* hispánico, hispano; ‹*community/voter*› (in US) hispano

Hispanic² *n* (esp AmE) hispano, -na *m,f*

hiss¹ /hɪs/ *vi* silbar; «*cat*» bufar; **the audience booed and ~ed** el público le silbó y abucheó a la obra (*or* al jugador *etc*)

■ **hiss** *vt* decir* entre dientes

hiss² *n* (of snake, audience) silbido *m*; (of cat) bufido *m*

histogram /ˈhɪstəgræm/ *n* histograma *m*

historian /hɪˈstɔːriən/ *n* historiador, -dora *m,f*

historic /hɪˈstɔːrɪk || hɪˈstɒrɪk/ *adj*

A **1** (momentous) ‹*event/moment*› memorable **2** (old) ‹*house/building*› histórico **3** (crit) ‹*fact*› histórico

B (Ling) ‹*tense*› histórico

historical /hɪˈstɔːrɪkəl || hɪˈstɒrɪkəl/ *adj* **1** (relating to history) histórico **2** (crit) ▸**historic A1, 2**

historically /hɪˈstɔːrɪkli || hɪˈstɒrɪkli/ *adv* históricamente; (*indep*) desde el punto de vista histórico

history /ˈhɪstəri/ *n* (*pl* **-ries**)

A [u c] historia *f*; **the worst earthquake in ~** el peor terremoto de la historia; **to make/go down in ~** hacer* historia/pasar a la historia; **this case made legal ~** este caso pasó a integrar los anales del derecho; **... and the rest is ~** y el resto ya es cosa sabida

B [c] (record, background) historial *m*; **he has a ~ of heart trouble** ha tenido problemas cardíacos en el pasado

histrionic /ˈhɪstriˈɑːnɪk || ˌhɪstriˈɒnɪk/ *adj* histriónico

histrionics /ˈhɪstriˈɑːnɪks || ˌhɪstriˈɒnɪks/ *pl n* histrionismo *m*

hit¹ /hɪt/ (*pres p* **hitting**; *past & past p* **hit**) *vt*

A **1** (deal blow to) ‹*door/table*› dar* un golpe en, golpear; ‹*person*› pegarle* a; **she ~ him with her handbag** le pegó *or* le dio un golpe con el bolso; **he ~ her across the face** le cruzó la cara; **he ~ the table with his fist** dio un puñetazo en la mesa; ***(let's)* ~ *it!*** (AmE) ¡dale!, ¡rápido!; ***to* ~ *the road* o *the trail*** ponerse* en marcha; ***to* ~ *the sack* o *the hay*** irse* al sobre *or* (Esp tb) a la piltra (fam) **2** (strike) golpear; **passers-by were ~ by flying glass** los transeúntes fueron alcanzados por trozos de cristal; **the truck ~ a tree** el camión chocó con *or* contra un árbol; **the house was ~ by a bomb** una bomba cayó sobre la casa; **the bullet ~ him in the leg** la bala le dio *or* lo alcanzó en la pierna; **I've been ~!** ¡me han dado!; **to ~ one's head/arm on** *o* **against sth** darse* un golpe en la cabeza/el brazo contra algo, darse* con la cabeza/el brazo contra algo; ***to* ~ *the ceiling* o *the roof*** poner* el grito en el cielo

B **1** (strike accurately) ‹*target*› dar* en **2** (attack) ‹*opponent/enemy*› atacar*; **thieves have ~ many stores in the area** (AmE) ha habido robos en muchas tiendas de la zona **3** (score) (Sport) anotarse, marcar*; **to ~ a home run** hacer* un cuadrangular *or* (AmL) un jonrón

C (affect adversely) afectar (a)

D **1** (meet with, run into) ‹*difficulty/problem*› toparse con **2** (reach) llegar* a, alcanzar*; **we're bound to ~ the main road sooner or later** tarde o temprano tenemos que salir a la carretera principal; **to ~ town** (colloq) llegar* a la ciudad; **to ~ the big time** llegar* a la fama

E (occur to): **suddenly it ~ me: why not ... ?** de repente se me ocurrió: ¿por qué no ... ?

■ **hit** *vi* (deal blow) pegar*, golpear

Phrasal verbs

• **hit back** **1** [v ▸ adv] (strike in return) devolver* el golpe; **to ~ back AT sb**: **she ~ back at her critics** arremetió contra sus detractores **2** [v ▸ o ▸ adv] devolverle* el golpe a

• **hit off** [v ▸ o ▸ adv]: ***to* ~ *it off with sb*** congeniar con algn; **Pete and Sue ~ it off immediately** Pete y Sue se cayeron bien desde el principio

• **hit on** [v ▸ prep ▸ o] **1** (think of) ‹*solution*› dar* con; **he ~ on the idea of ...** se le ocurrió la idea de ... **2** (make sexual advances to) (AmE sl) intentar ligar con *or* ligarse a (fam), tirarse un lance con *or* a (CS fam), afanar (Per fam) **3** (ask for) (AmE sl) **to ~ on sb FOR sth** pedirle* *or* (fam) sablearle *or* (RPl arg) manguearle algo A algn

• **hit out** [v ▸ adv] **1** (strike) **to ~ out (AT sth/sb)** pegarle* (A algo/algn) **2** (attack verbally) **to ~ out AT** *o* **AGAINST sth/sb** atacar* algo/a algn, arremeter CONTRA algo/algn

• **hit upon** ▸**hit on 1**

hit² *n*

A **1** (blow, stroke) (Sport) golpe *m* **2** (in shooting) blanco *m*; (in archery) blanco *m*, diana *f*; (of artillery) impacto *m*

B (success) (colloq) éxito *m*; **he's a big ~ with young people** es muy popular entre los jóvenes; **you made a big ~ with my mother** le caíste muy bien a mi madre, mi madre quedó impactada contigo; (*before n*) ‹*song/show*› de gran éxito

hit-and-miss /ˈhɪtənˈmɪs/ *adj* (*pred* **hit and miss**) ▸**hit-or-miss**

hit-and-run¹ /ˈhɪtənˈrʌn/ *adj* (*before n*) ‹*driver*› *que se da a la fuga tras atropellar a algn*

hit-and-run² *n*: *accidente en el que el conductor atropella a algn y se da a la fuga*

hitch¹ /hɪtʃ/ *n*

A (difficulty) complicación *f*, problema *m*, pega *f* (Esp fam); **it went off without a ~** todo salió a pedir de boca (fam), todo marchó sobre ruedas; **a technical ~** un problema técnico

B (limp) (AmE) cojera *f*, renguera *f* (AmL); **to walk with a ~** cojear, renquear, renguear (AmL)

C (period of service) (AmE colloq): **he did a three-year ~ in the navy** pasó tres años enganchado en la marina (fam)

hitch² *vt*

A (attach) **to ~ sth TO sth** enganchar algo A algo; ***to get* ~*ed*** (colloq) casarse, matrimoniarse (fam & hum)

B (thumb) (colloq): **to ~ a ride** *o* (BrE also) **a lift** hacer* dedo (fam), hacer* autostop, ir* de aventón (Col, Méx fam), pedir* cola (Ven fam); **he ~ed a ride on a truck** lo recogió *or* le paró un camión

■ **hitch** *vi* ▸**hitchhike**

Phrasal verb

• **hitch up** [v ▸ o ▸ adv, v ▸ adv ▸ o] **1** ‹*trousers/petticoat*› remangarse*, subirse, levantarse **2** ‹*horses/cart*› enganchar

hitch: **~hike** *vi* hacer* autostop, hacer* dedo (fam), ir* de aventón (Méx fam), pedir* cola (Ven fam); **we ~hiked to Rome** fuimos a dedo *or* (Col, Méx) de aventón *or* (Ven) en cola hasta Roma (fam); **~hiker** *n* autoestopista *mf*; **~hiking** /ˈhɪtʃhaɪkɪŋ/ *n* [u] autostop *m*; **I've never done ~** nunca he hecho autostop *or* (fam) dedo; nunca he ido de aventón (Col, Méx fam)

hi-tech /ˈhaɪˈtek/ *adj* ▸**high-tech**

hither /ˈhɪðər || ˈhɪðə(r)/ *adv* (arch) aquí, acá; **~ and thither** de acá para allá

hitherto /ˈhɪðərˈtuː || ˌhɪðəˈtuː/ *adv* (frml) hasta ahora, hasta la fecha

hit: **~ list** *n* (colloq) (murder list) lista *f* de sentenciados; (blacklist) lista *f* negra; **~ man** *n* (colloq) (assassin) asesino *m* a sueldo, sicario *m*; **~-or-miss** /ˈhɪtərˈmɪs || ˌhɪtɔːˈmɪs/ *adj* (*pred* **~ or miss**) ‹*method/approach*› poco científico, que deja mucho librado al azar

hitter /ˈhɪtər || ˈhɪtə(r)/ *n* (in baseball) bateador, -dora *m,f*; (in US football) liniero, -ra *m,f*

HIV *n* (= **Human Immunodeficiency Virus**) VIH *m*, virus *m* del sida; **he's ~ (positive)** es seropositivo, es portador del virus VIH *or* del virus del sida

hive /haɪv/ *n* (home of bees) colmena *f*; (bee colony) enjambre *m*; **the workshop was a ~ of activity** el taller bullía de actividad

Phrasal verb

• **hive off** [v ▸ o ▸ adv, v ▸ adv ▸ o] (make separate) escindir; (sell off) vender, enajenar

hives /haɪvz/ *n* (Med) urticaria *f*

hiya /ˈhaɪjə/ *interj* (colloq) ¡hola!

h

HM [1] (title) (= **Her/His Majesty**) S.M. [2] (= **Her/His Majesty's**); ~ **Government** el Gobierno de Su Majestad Británica

HMO *n* (in US) = **health maintenance organization**

HMRC *n* (in UK) = **Her Majesty's Revenue & Customs**

HMS (in UK) = **Her/His Majesty's Ship**

HNC *n* (in UK) = **Higher National Certificate** (*título académico para disciplinas técnicas*)

HND *n* (in UK) = **Higher National Diploma** (*título académico para disciplinas técnicas*)

ho /həʊ/ *interj* (deep-voiced laughter) **~, ~!** ¡jo, jo!

hoagie /'həʊgi/ *n* (*pl* **-gies**) (AmE): *sándwich hecho de un trozo alargado de pan blando relleno de carne, queso y ensalada*

hoard¹ /hɔːrd || hɔːd/ *n* (of food) reserva *f*; **a ~ of treasure** un tesoro escondido

hoard² *vt* acumular, juntar; (anticipating a shortage) acaparar
■ **hoard** *vi* acaparar

hoarding /'hɔːrdɪŋ || 'hɔːdɪŋ/ *n*
[A] [u] (anticipating a shortage) acaparamiento *m*
[B] [c] (billboard) (BrE) valla *f* publicitaria, barda *f* de anuncios (Méx)

hoarfrost /'hɔːrfrɔːst || 'hɔːfrɒst/ *n* [u] escarcha *f*

hoarse /hɔːrs || hɔːs/ *adj* **hoarser, hoarsest** ronco

hoarsely /'hɔːrsli || 'hɔːsli/ *adv* con voz ronca; (from emotion) con voz quebrada

hoary /'hɔːri/ *adj* **-rier, -riest** [1] (very old) ‹*joke/myth*› (hum) antediluviano (hum) [2] (white-haired) (liter) ‹*head*› cano (liter), canoso

hoax¹ /həʊks/ *n* (deception) engaño *m*; (joke) broma *f*; (tall story) patraña *f*

hoax² *vt* engañar

hoaxer /'həʊksər || 'həʊksə(r)/ *n* embaucador, -dora *m,f*; (practical joker) bromista *mf*

hob /hɑːb || hɒb/ *n* [1] (beside open fire) placa *f* [2] (of cooker) (BrE) hornillas *fpl* (AmL exc CS), hornillos *mpl* (Esp), hornallas *fpl* (RPl), platos *mpl* (Chi)

hobble /'hɑːbəl || 'hɒbəl/ *vi* cojear, renguear (AmL)
■ **hobble** *vt* ‹*horse*› manear

hobby /'hɑːbi || 'hɒbi/ *n* (*pl* **-bies**) hobby *m*, pasatiempo *m*, afición *f*

hobbyhorse /'hɑːbihɔːrs || 'hɒbihɔːs/ *n*
[A] (toy) caballito *m* (*palo con cabeza de caballo*)
[B] (favorite topic) caballo *m* de batalla; **she's (off) on her ~ again** ya empieza otra vez con la misma cantinela (fam)

hob: **~goblin** /'hɑːb'gɑːblən || 'hɒbgɒblɪn/ *n* duende *m*; **~nailed** /'hɑːbneɪld || 'hɒbneɪld/ *adj* con tachuelas; **~nob** /'hɑːbnɑːb || 'hɒbnɒb/ *vi* **-bb- to ~nob WITH sb** codearse CON algn

hobo /'həʊbəʊ/ *n* (*pl* **-boes** *or* **-bos**) (AmE colloq) vagabundo, -da *m,f*, linyera *mf* (CS fam)

Hobson's choice /'hɑːbsənz || 'hɒbsənz/ *n*: **it's ~ ~** no hay posibilidad de elegir

hock¹ /hɑːk || hɒk/ *n*
[A] [c] (Vet Sci) corvejón *m*, jarrete *m*
[B] [u] (colloq) [1] (pawn): **my watch is in ~** tengo el reloj empeñado; **to get sth out of ~** desempeñar algo [2] (debt): **I'm in ~ to the bank for $5,000** le debo $5.000 al banco
[C] [u c] (wine) (BrE) hock *m* (*vino blanco del Rhin*)

hock² *vt* (pawn) (colloq) empeñar

hockey /'hɑːki || 'hɒki/ *n* [1] (*ice ~*) (AmE) hockey *m* sobre hielo [2] (played on grass) (BrE) hockey *m* (sobre hierba)

hocus-pocus /'həʊkəs'pəʊkəs/ *n* [u] (deception) (colloq) trampa *f*; (verbal) galimatías *m*

hod /hɑːd || hɒd/ *n* (for bricks) capacho *m* (*para acarrear ladrillos*); (*before n*) **~ carrier** peón *m* de albañil

hodgepodge /'hɑːdʒpɑːdʒ || 'hɒdʒpɒdʒ/ *n* (esp AmE) batiburrillo *m* (fam), mezcolanza *f* (fam)

hoe¹ /həʊ/ *n* azada *f*, azadón *m*

hoe² *vt* azadonar, pasar la azada por

hoedown /'həʊdaʊn/ *n* (AmE) [1] (social gathering): *reunión social donde se baila danzas folklóricas* [2] (square dance) cuadrilla *f*

hog¹ /hɔːg || hɒg/ *n* (AmE Agr, Zool) cerdo, -da *m,f*, puerco, -ca *m,f*, chancho, -cha *m,f* (AmL); (person) (colloq) tragón, -gona *m,f* (fam), angurriento, -ta *m,f* (CS fam); ***to go the whole ~***: **let's go the whole ~ and have champagne** mira, de perdidos, al río: pidamos champán; ***to live high on o off the ~*** (AmE colloq) vivir a todo tren (fam)

hog² *vt* **-gg-** (colloq) ‹*food/bathroom/limelight*› acaparar; ‹*discussion*› monopolizar*

Hogmanay /'hɑːgmәneɪ || 'hɒgmәneɪ/ *n* (Scot) Nochevieja *f*, noche *f* de fin de año

hogtie /'hɔːgtaɪ || 'hɒgtaɪ/ *vt* **-ties, -tying, -tied** (AmE) atar de pies y manos

hoi polloi /'hɔɪpə'lɔɪ/ *n* (hum) **the ~ ~** el vulgo, la plebe

hoist¹ /hɔɪst/ *vt* (lift) levantar, alzar*; ‹*sail*› izar*; ‹*flag*› izar*, enarbolar; **he ~ed the sack onto his shoulder** se echó el saco al hombro

hoist² *n* (elevator) montacargas *m*; (crane, derrick) grúa *f*

hoity-toity /'hɔɪti'tɔɪti/ *adj* estirado, engreído

hokey /'həʊki/ *adj* (AmE sl) malo

hokum /'həʊkəm/ *n* (colloq) [1] (nonsense) paparruchas *fpl* (fam) [2] (corny material) (AmE) *recursos efectistas de tipo melodramático o cómico*

hold¹ /həʊld/ (*past & past p* **held**) *vt*
[A] [1] (have in one's hand(s)) tener*; **she was ~ing a newspaper** tenía un periódico en la mano; **will you ~ this for me?** ¿me puedes tener *or* (esp AmL) agarrar esto por favor? [2] (clasp): **~ it with both hands** sujétalo *or* (esp AmL) agárralo con las dos manos; **he was ~ing her hand** la tenía agarrada *or* (esp Esp) cogida de la mano; **~ me tight** abrázame fuerte; ▸ **own³** [3] (grip) (Auto) agarrar, adherirse*; **vehicles which ~ the road well** vehículos de buen agarre *or* que se agarran bien a la carretera
[B] [1] (support, bear) sostener*, aguantar; **to ~ oneself erect** mantenerse* erguido [2] (have room for) «*cup/jug*» tener* una capacidad de; «*stadium*» tener* capacidad *or* cabida para [3] (contain) contener*; ***to ~ one's liquor o*** (BrE) ***drink*** ser* de buen beber, aguantar bien la bebida *or* (fam) el trago [4] (have in store) deparar; **who knows what the future ~s** quién sabe qué nos deparará el futuro
[C] [1] (keep in position) sujetar, sostener*; **raise your legs off the floor and ~ them there** levanta las piernas del suelo y manténlas levantadas [2] (maintain) ‹*attention/interest*› mantener*; **she held the lead throughout the race** se mantuvo a la cabeza durante toda la carrera; **if Labour ~s these seats** si los laboristas retienen estos escaños *or* (RPl) estas bancas
[D] [1] (keep) ‹*tickets/room*› reservar, guardar; **I will ~ the money until ...** yo me quedaré con el dinero hasta ...; **she asked her secretary to ~ all her calls** le dijo a su secretaria que no le pasara ninguna llamada [2] (detain, imprison): **she is being held at the police station for questioning** está detenida en la comisaría para ser interrogada [3] (restrain) detener*; **once she decides to do something, there's no ~ing her** una vez que decide hacer algo, no hay nada que la detenga [4] (control) «*troops/rebels*» ocupar
[E] [1] (have) ‹*passport/ticket/permit*› tener*, estar* en posesión de (frml); ‹*degree/shares/property*› tener*; ‹*record*› ostentar, tener*; ‹*post/position*› tener*, ocupar; **he ~s the view that ...** sostiene que *or* mantiene que ..., es de la opinión de que ... [2] (consider) considerar; (assert) sostener*, mantener*; **this is held to be the case** se considera que es así; **principles which he ~s dear** principios que le son caros; **to ~ sb in high esteem** tener* a algn en mucha *or* gran estima; **to ~ sb responsible for sth** responsabilizar* a algn de algo [3] (conduct) ‹*meeting/elections*› celebrar, llevar a cabo; ‹*demonstration*› hacer*; ‹*party*› dar*; ‹*conversation*› mantener*; **interviews will be held in London** las entrevistas tendrán lugar en Londres
[F] [1] (stop): **~ it!** ¡espera!; **~ it right there or I'll shoot!** ¡quieto o disparo!; **~ your fire!** ¡alto al fuego! [2] (omit) (AmE): **I'll have a hamburger, but ~ the mustard** para mí una hamburguesa, pero sin mostaza
■ **hold** *vi*
[A] (clasp, grip): **~ tight!** ¡agárrate fuerte!
[B] [1] (stay firm) «*rope/door*» aguantar, resistir [2] (continue) «*weather*» seguir* *or* continuar* bueno, mantenerse*; **share prices have held** los precios de las acciones se han mantenido; **if our luck ~s** si nos sigue acompañando la suerte
[C] (be true) «*idea/analogy*» ser* válido; **my promise still ~s good** mi promesa sigue en pie

h

(Phrasal verbs)

- **hold against** [v ▸ o ▸ prep ▸ o]: **I won't ~ that against him** no se lo voy a tomar *or* tener en cuenta, no le voy a guardar rencor por eso
- **hold back**

A [v ▸ o ▸ adv, v ▸ adv ▸ o] **1** (restrain) ‹*crowds/water/tears*› contener* **2** (withhold, delay) ‹*information*› no revelar; ‹*payment*› retrasar; **he's ~ing something back from me** me está ocultando algo

B [v ▸ adv] (restrain oneself) contenerse*, frenarse; **she held back from telling them** se contuvo y no les dijo nada

- **hold down** [v ▸ o ▸ adv, v ▸ adv ▸ o] **1** (force, press down) ‹*lid/papers*› sujetar **2** ‹*job*›: **he can't ~ down a job** es incapaz de tener un trabajo y cumplir con él **3** (limit) ‹*price/increase*› moderar, contener*; **~ that noise down!** (AmE) ¡baja ese ruido!
- **hold forth** [v ▸ adv]: **to ~ forth on** *o* **about sth** pontificar* *or* perorar sobre algo
- **hold in** [v ▸ o ▸ adv, v ▸ adv ▸ o] ‹*stomach*› meter; ‹*feelings*› contener*; ‹*laughter*› contener*, aguantar
- **hold off**

A [v ▸ o ▸ adv, v ▸ adv ▸ o] **1** (resist) ‹*attack/enemy*› resistir, rechazar* **2** (defeat) ‹*challenger/rival*› derrotar

B [v ▸ adv] **1** (be delayed): **if the rain ~s off** si no empieza a llover, si la lluvia se aguanta (fam) **2** (keep one's distance, show restraint): **I've made my point, so I plan to ~ off for a while** yo ya he dicho lo que pensaba, así que ahora me voy a callar la boca

- **hold on**

A [v ▸ adv] **1** (wait) esperar; **~ on, please** un momentito, por favor **2** (survive) resistir, aguantar **3** (clasp, grip) agarrarse; **~ on tight** agárrate fuerte; **to ~ on TO sth/sb** agarrarse A *or* DE algo/algn; **he held on to this belief** se mantuvo firme en esta creencia **4** (keep) **to ~ on TO sth** conservar *or* guardar algo

B [v ▸ o ▸ adv, v ▸ adv ▸ o] (fasten) sujetar

- **hold out**

A [v ▸ o ▸ adv, v ▸ adv ▸ o] (extend) ‹*hands/arms*› tender*, alargar*

B [v ▸ adv ▸ o] **1** (offer) ‹*prospect/possibility*› ofrecer*; ‹*hope*› dar* **2** (represent) (*usu pass*) presentar **3** (have, retain) ‹*hope*› tener*; **I don't ~ out much hope of getting the job** no tengo muchas esperanzas de que me den el trabajo

C [v ▸ adv] **1** (survive, last) «*person*» aguantar; «*food/shoes*» durar **2** (resist, make a stand) «*army/town*» resistir; **the strikers are ~ing out for 5%** los huelguistas se mantienen firmes en su reivindicación de un 5% de aumento **3** (withhold information) (colloq): **after two days of questioning he's still ~ing out on them** ya van dos días de interrogatorios y todavía no ha cantado (fam)

- **hold over** [v ▸ o ▸ adv, v ▸ adv ▸ o] **1** (postpone) ‹*meeting/decision*› aplazar*, postergar* (esp AmL) **2** (extend) (AmE Cin, Theat): **held over by popular demand** continúa a petición *or* (AmL tb) a pedido del público
- **hold together**

A [v ▸ adv] «*arguments*» tener* lógica *or* solidez; «*people*» mantenerse* unidos

B [v ▸ o ▸ adv] (keep united) ‹*family/group*› mantener* unido

- **hold up**

A [v ▸ o ▸ adv, v ▸ adv ▸ o] **1** (raise) ‹*hand/banner*› levantar; ‹*head*› mantener* erguido; **she held the cloth up to the light** puso la tela a contraluz **2** (support) ‹*roof/walls*› sostener* **3** (delay) ‹*person/arrival*› retrasar; ‹*progress*› entorpecer*; **he was held up at the office** algo lo detuvo *or* retuvo en la oficina **4** (rob) atracar*, asaltar **5** (expose, present): **to ~ sth/sb up to ridicule** poner* algo/a algn en ridículo, ridiculizar* algo/a algn; **to ~ sth/sb up as an example** poner* algo/a algn como ejemplo

B [v ▸ adv] **1** (remain strong): **the dollar held up well against other currencies** el dólar se mantuvo firme frente a otras monedas; **he held up under the pressure** soportó *or* aguantó la presión **2** «*theory/argument*» resultar válido

- **hold with** [v ▸ prep ▸ o] estar* de acuerdo con

hold² *n*

A [u] **1** (grip, grasp): **to catch** *o* **grab** *o* **take ~ (of sth)** agarrar (algo), coger* (algo) (esp Esp); (so as not to fall etc) agarrarse *or* asirse (de *or* a algo); **he had a firm ~ on the rope** tenía la cuerda bien agarrada *or* sujeta; **to keep ~ of sth** no soltar* algo; **you keep ~ of him** que no se te escape; **to get ~ of sb** localizar* *or* (AmL tb) ubicar* a algn; **to get ~ of sth** (manage to get) conseguir* algo; **where did you get ~ of the idea that ... ?** ¿de dónde has sacado la idea de que ... ?; **the fire took ~** el fuego prendió **2** (control): **to keep a firm ~ on sth** mantener* algo bajo riguroso control; **to get a ~ of** *o* **on oneself** controlarse; **the ~ they have over the members of the sect** el dominio que ejercen sobre los miembros de la secta **3** (TV): **horizontal/vertical ~** control *m* de imagen horizontal/vertical

B [c] **1** (in wrestling, judo) llave *f*; ***with no ~s barred*** sin ningún tipo de restricciones **2** (in mountaineering) asidero *m*

C [c] (delay, pause) demora *f*; **to be on ~** «*negotiations*» estar* en compás de espera; «*project*» estar* aparcado *or* en suspenso; **I've got Mr Brown on ~** el Sr Brown está esperando para hablar con usted; **to put sth on ~** ‹*project*› dejar algo aparcado *or* en suspenso

D [c] (of ship, aircraft) bodega *f*

holdall /'həʊldɔːl/ *n* (BrE) (for travel) bolso *m* *or* (esp Esp) bolsa *f* de viaje, bolsón *m* (RPl); (for sports gear) bolsa *f* (de deportes)

holder /'həʊldər || 'həʊldə(r)/ *n*

A (of permit, passport, job) titular *mf*; (of ticket) poseedor, -dora *m,f*; (of bonds etc) titular *mf*, tenedor, -dora *m,f*; (of title, cup) poseedor, -dora *m,f*

B (wallet) funda *f*

holding /'həʊldɪŋ/ *n* [c] (Fin) **1** (of stocks): **a majority/minority ~** una participación mayoritaria/minoritaria **2** ▸**holding company** **3** **holdings** *pl* (land) tierras *fpl*, propiedades *fpl*

holding company *n* holding *m*, sociedad *f* de cartera

hold: **~out** *n* (AmE): **three of them are still ~outs** tres de ellos se siguen negando *or* mantienen su negativa; **~over** *n* (AmE) **1** (relic) vestigio *m*, reliquia *f* **2** (Cin, Theat): **'The Sting' is a ~over from last week** 'El Golpe' continúa en cartel desde la semana pasada; **~up** *n* **1** (delay) demora *f*, retraso *m*; (in traffic) atasco *m*, embotellamiento *m* **2** (armed robbery) atraco *m*

hole¹ /həʊl/ *n*

A **1** (in belt, material, clothing) agujero *m*; (in ground) hoyo *m*, agujero *m*; (in road) bache *m*; (in wall) boquete *m*; (in defenses) brecha *f*; **to make a ~ in sth** hacer* un agujero en algo, agujerear algo; **that made a ~ in their savings** eso se llevó *or* se comió buena parte de sus ahorros; ***in the ~*** (AmE): **we're $10,000 in the ~ to the bank** le debemos 10.000 dólares al banco; ***money just burns a ~ in his/her pocket*** el dinero le quema las manos; ***to need sth like a ~ in the head***: **I need a visit from him like I need a ~ in the head** ¡lo único que me faltaba! ¡que él viniera a verme! **2** (in argument, proposal) punto *m* débil; ***to pick ~s in sth*** encontrarle* defectos *or* faltas a algo **3** (of animal) madriguera *f*

B (Sport) **1** (in golf) hoyo *m* **2** (in US football) hueco *m*

C **1** (unpleasant place) (colloq): **this town is a real ~!** ¡qué pueblo de mala muerte! (fam) **2** (awkward situation) (colloq): ***to be in a ~*** estar* en un apuro *or* aprieto; ***to get sb out of a ~*** sacar* a algn de un apuro *or* aprieto

hole² *vt*

A (in golf) ‹*ball*› embocar*; ‹*putt/shot*› transformar

B ‹*ship*› abrir* una brecha en

(Phrasal verb)

- **hole up** [v ▸ adv] (colloq) esconderse, refugiarse

hole in the heart *n* (Med) comunicación *f* interventricular congénita

holiday¹ /'hɑːlədeɪ || 'hɒlədeɪ/ *n* **1** (day) fiesta *f*, día *m* festivo, (día *m*) feriado *m* (AmL) **2** (period away from work) (esp BrE) (*often pl*) vacaciones *fpl*, licencia *f* (Col, Méx, RPl); **to go on ~** *o* **one's ~s** irse* de vacaciones; **to be on ~** estar* de vacaciones; **where do you spend your summer ~s?** ¿dónde veraneas?; (*before n*) ‹*mood/feeling/spirit*› festivo; ‹*cottage/trip*› de vacaciones; **~ home** casa *f* de veraneo *or* de campo; **the ~ season** la temporada de vacaciones; (Christmas etc) las Navidades, las fiestas de fin de año (AmL) **3** (BrE Educ) (*often pl*) vacaciones *fpl*

holiday² *vi* (esp BrE) pasar las vacaciones, vacacionar (Méx); (in summer) veranear

holiday: **~ camp** *n* (BrE) colonia *f* de vacaciones; **~maker** *n* (BrE) turista *mf*; (on summer holidays) veraneante *mf*; **~ resort** *n* centro *m* turístico

holier-than-thou /'həʊliərðən'ðaʊ || ,həʊliəðən'ðaʊ/ *adj* ‹*attitude*› de superioridad moral

holiness /'həʊlinəs || 'həʊlinɪs/ *n* [u] santidad *f*

holistic /həʊ'lɪstɪk/ *adj* holístico

Holland /'hɑːlənd || 'hɒlənd/ *n* Holanda *f*

hollandaise sauce /'hɑːlən'deɪz || ,hɒlən'deɪz/ *n* [u c] salsa *f* holandesa

holler[1] /'hɑːlər || 'hɒlə(r)/ (AmE colloq) *vt/i* gritar

holler[2] *n* (AmE colloq) (shout, cry) grito *m*

hollow[1] /'hɑːləʊ || 'hɒləʊ/ *adj*

A ‹*tree/tooth/wall*› hueco; ‹*sound*› hueco; ‹*voice*› apagado, ahogado; ‹*cheeks/eyes*› hundido

B 1 ‹*success/triumph*› vacío 2 ‹*person*› vacío, vacuo; ‹*promises/threats*› vano, falso; ‹*words*› hueco, vacío; **she gave a ~ laugh** soltó una risa sardónica

Phrasal verb

• **hollow out** [v ▸ o ▸ adv, v ▸ adv ▸ o] vaciar*, ahuecar*

hollow[2] *n* 1 (empty space) hueco *m*; (depression) hoyo *m*, depresión *f*; **the ~ of one's hand** el cuenco *or* (Méx) la cuenca de la mano 2 (dell, valley) hondonada *f*

hollow[3] *adv*: **to beat sb all ~** *o* (BrE) **beat sb ~** (colloq) darle* una paliza a algn

holly /'hɑːli || 'hɒli/ *n* 1 [c] **~ (bush/tree)** acebo *m* 2 [u] (foliage) acebo *m*

hollyhock /'hɑːlihɑːk || 'hɒlihɒk/ *n* malvarrosa *f*, malva *f* real *or* loca

Hollywood

Barrio de la ciudad de Los Ángeles (California) donde se inauguró la industria cinematográfica norteamericana en 1911. Desde entonces esta localidad, apodada *the dream factory* (la fábrica de sueños), se ha convertido por antonomasia en la capital mundial del cine

holocaust /'həʊləkɔːst, 'hɑː- || 'hɒləkɔːst/ *n* hecatombe *f*, desastre *m*; **a/the nuclear ~** un/el holocausto nuclear; **the H~** el Holocausto

hologram /'həʊləgræm, 'hɑː- || 'hɒləgræm/ *n* holograma *m*

Holstein /'həʊlstiːn || 'hɒlstaɪn/ *n* (AmE) (cow) vaca *f* holandesa

holster /'həʊlstər || 'həʊlstə(r)/ *n* pistolera *f*, funda *f* de pistola (*or* revólver *etc*)

holy /'həʊli/ *adj* **-lier, -liest** ‹*ground/place*› sagrado, santo; ‹*day*› de precepto, de guardar; ‹*water*› bendito; ‹*person/life/virtue*› santo; **the H~ Bible** la Sagrada *or* Santa Biblia; **~ orders** órdenes *fpl* sagradas; **to take ~ orders** ordenarse sacerdote; **H~ Week** Semana Santa; **~ cow!** (colloq) ¡rayos y centellas!, ¡Dios bendito!

holy: **~ Communion** *n* Santa *or* Sagrada Comunión *f*; **~ Ghost** *n* **the H~ Ghost** el Espíritu Santo; **~ Land** *n* **the H~ Land** (la) Tierra Santa; **~ man** *n* santo varón *m*; **~ of holies** *n* sanctasanctórum *m*; **~ Spirit** *n* **the H~ Spirit** el Espíritu Santo

homage /'hɑːmɪdʒ || 'hɒmɪdʒ/ *n* [u] (frml) homenaje *m*; **to pay ~ to sb/sth** rendir* homenaje a algn/algo

hombre /'ɑːmbreɪ || 'ɒmbreɪ/ *n* (AmE sl) tipo *m* (fam), tío *m* (Esp fam)

homburg /'hɑːmbɜːrg || 'hɒmbɜːg/ *n* sombrero *m* de fieltro

home[1] /həʊm/ *n*

A [u c] (of person) 1 (dwelling) casa *f*; **to own one's own ~** tener* casa propia; **marital ~** domicilio *m* conyugal; *see also* **at home, home**[1] **C**; (*before n*) **~ loan** préstamo *m or* crédito *m* hipotecario, crédito *m* vivienda 2 (in wider sense): **New York's been my ~ since I was 12** he vivido en Nueva York desde que tenía 12 años; **they made their ~ in Germany** se establecieron en Alemania, fijaron su residencia en Alemania (frml); **I still think of England as ~** para mí Inglaterra sigue siendo mi patria; **~ sweet ~** hogar dulce hogar; **there's no place like ~** como en casa no se está en ningún sitio; **to leave ~** irse* de casa; **those remarks were uncomfortably close to ~** esos comentarios me (*or* le *etc*) tocaban muy de cerca; ***a ~ away from ~*** *o* (BrE) ***a ~ from ~*** una segunda casa; ***~ is where the heart is*** el verdadero hogar está donde uno tiene a los suyos 3 (family environment) hogar *m*; **she comes from a good ~** es de buena familia

B [c] 1 (of object, group, institution): **Spain is the ~ of flamenco** España es la tierra del flamenco; **the ~ of the microchip industry** el centro de la industria de los microchips; **can you find a ~ for these files somewhere?** (colloq) a ver si encuentras dónde guardar estos archivos 2 (of animal, plant) (Bot, Zool) hábitat *m*

C **at home** 1 (in house) en casa; **tell him I'm not at ~** dile que no estoy (en casa); **he's got problems at ~** tiene problemas familiares; ***what's that when it's at ~?*** (colloq) ¿y eso con qué se come? (fam) 2 (at ease): **make yourself at ~** ponte cómodo, estás en tu casa; **he's entirely at ~ in Spanish** habla español con total fluidez 3 (not abroad): **at ~ and abroad** dentro y fuera del país 4 (Sport) en casa; **to be/play at ~** jugar* en casa; **Spain is at ~ to France** España juega en casa contra Francia

D [c] (institution) (*children's ~*) asilo *m* (AmL), orfanatorio *m* (Méx), centro *m* de acogida de menores (Esp); (*old people's ~*) residencia *f* de ancianos; **dogs' ~** (BrE) perrera *f*

E (Sport) 1 [u] (the finish) meta *f* 2 [c] (in baseball) ▸**home plate**

Phrasal verb

• **home in** [v ▸ adv] **to ~ in ON sth** ‹*on target*› localizar* y dirigirse* HACIA algo; **she ~d in on his lack of experience** hizo hincapié en su falta de experiencia

home[2] *adv*

A 1 (where one lives) ‹*come/arrive*› a casa; **I'll be ~ at five** estaré en casa a las cinco; **to see sb ~** acompañar a algn a casa; ***nothing to write ~ about*** nada del otro mundo *or* (fam) del otro jueves 2 (from abroad): **we've already booked our passage ~** ya hemos reservado nuestro pasaje de vuelta; **the folks back ~** (AmE) la familia

B (Sport): **the first horse/runner ~** el primer caballo/corredor en llegar a la meta; ***to be ~ free*** *o* (BrE) ***~ and dry*** tener* la victoria asegurada

C (to desired place): **there was a clunk as the bolt went ~** se oyó un golpe sordo al encajar el cerrojo en su sitio; **to get sth ~ to sb** hacerle* entender algo a algn; ***to drive sth ~ (to sb)*** hacer(le)* entender algo (a algn); **try to drive it ~ to him that ...** hazle entender que ...; *see also* **strike** *etc* **home**

home[3] *adj* (*before n*) 1 ‹*address/telephone number*› particular; ‹*background/environment*› familiar; ‹*cooking/perm*› casero; **~ comforts** comodidades *fpl*; **~ delivery** (of purchases) entrega *f* a domicilio; **~ visit** (by doctor) (BrE) visita *f* a domicilio 2 (of origin): **~ port** (Naut) puerto *m* de matrícula; **~ state** (in US) estado *m* natal *or* de procedencia 3 (not foreign) ‹*affairs/market*› nacional 4 (Sport) ‹*team*› de casa, local; ‹*game*› en casa

home: **~ base** *n* (AmE) 1 (Busn, Mil) base *f* de operaciones 2 (in baseball) ▸**home plate**; **~body** *n* (colloq) ▸**homelover**; **~boy** *n* (AmE sl) compinche *m* (fam), cuate *m* (Méx fam); **~ brew** *n* [u] *cerveza hecha en casa*; **~coming** *n* 1 (return home) regreso *m*, vuelta *f* (*a casa, a la patria etc*) 2 (at school, college) (AmE) *fiesta estudiantil al comienzo del año académico con asistencia de ex-alumnos*; **~ computer** *n* computadora *f* doméstica, ordenador *m* doméstico (Esp); **~ Counties** *pl n* (in UK) **the H~ Counties** *los condados de los alrededores de Londres*; **~ economics** *n* (+ *sing vb*) economía *f* doméstica; **~-grown** /'həʊm'grəʊn/ *adj* 1 ‹*fruit/vegetables*› (from one's own garden) de la huerta propia; (not foreign) del país, local, nacional 2 (local, indigenous) ‹*artist/politician*› local; **~ help** *n* (BrE) auxiliar *mf*; **~ improvements** *pl n* reformas *fpl*, mejoras *fpl* (*en la vivienda*); **~land** *n* 1 (country of origin) patria *f*, tierra *f* natal 2 (in South Africa) homeland *m*

homeless[1] /'həʊmləs || 'həʊmlɪs/ *adj* sin hogar, sin techo

homeless[2] *pl n* **the ~** la gente sin hogar *or* sin techo

homelessness /'həʊmləsnəs || 'həʊmlɪsnɪs/ *n* [u] (el problema de) la falta de vivienda

home: **~like** *adj* (AmE) familiar, hogareño; **~lover** *n* persona *f* hogareña *or* casera; **he's a real ~lover** es muy casero, es muy de su casa; **~loving** *adj* hogareño, casero

homely /'həʊmli/ *adj* **-lier, -liest** 1 (characteristic of home) ‹*meal/food*› casero; ‹*atmosphere/room*› acogedor, hogareño 2 (plain) (AmE) feo 3 (unaffected) (esp BrE) sencillo

home: **~-made** /'həʊm'meɪd/ *adj* ‹*clothes*› hecho en casa; ‹*food*› casero; **~-maker** *n* ama *f*‡ de casa; **~ movie** *n* película *f* casera; **~ office** *n* (AmE) oficina *f* central; ~ **Office** *n* (in UK) **the H~ Office** el Home Office, el Ministerio del Interior británico

homeopath, (BrE) **homoeopath** /'həʊmiəpæθ/ *n* homeópata *mf*

homeopathic, (BrE) **homoeopathic** /'həʊmiə'pæθɪk/ *adj* homeopático

homeopathy, (BrE) **homoeopathy** /'həʊmi'ɑːpəθi || ˌhəʊmi'ɒpəθi/ *n* [u] homeopatía *f*

home: ~ **owner** *n* propietario, -ria *m,f* (*de una vivienda*); ~ **ownership** *n* [u]: **the increase in ~ ownership** el aumento del número de propietarios de viviendas; ~ **page** *n* portada *f or* página *f* de inicio, página *f* inicial; ~ **plate** *n* home *m*, pentágono *m* (Méx)

homer[1] /'həʊmər || 'həʊmə(r)/ *n* (AmE colloq) ▸ **home run**

homer[2] *vi* (AmE colloq) pegar* un cuadrangular, jonronear (AmL)

home: ~**room** *n* (AmE Educ) clase *f or* aula *f*‡ del curso; (*before n*) ~**room teacher** ≈ tutor, -tora *m,f* de curso; ~ **rule** *n* [u] autogobierno *m*; ~ **run** *n* cuadrangular *m*, jonrón *m* (AmL); ~ **Secretary** *n* (in UK) ministro, -tra *m,f* del Interior; ~**sick** *adj*: **I am** *o* **feel ~sick** echo de menos *or* (AmL tb) extraño a mi familia (*or* mi país *etc*); ~**sickness** *n* [u] añoranza *f*, morriña *f*; ~**spun** *adj* ‹*philosophy*› de andar por casa, popular; ‹*wisdom*› popular; ‹*virtue/folks*› sencillo

homestead /'həʊmsted/ *n* (AmE) [1] (building) casa *f* (*en una granja, hacienda etc*) [2] (Hist) *terreno cedido por el estado a los colonos con la condición de que lo trabajasen*

homesteader /'həʊmstedər || 'həʊmstedə(r)/ *n* (AmE) colono *m*

home: ~ **straight**, ~ **stretch** *n* (Sport) recta *f* final *or* de llegada; ~**town** /'həʊm'taʊn/ *n* ciudad *f*/pueblo *m* natal; (*before n*) (AmE) **he's a real ~town boy** es un chico sencillo; ~ **truth** *n* (*usu pl*) verdad *f* (*desagradable*); **to tell sb a few ~ truths** decirle* a algn unas cuantas verdades

homeward[1] /'həʊmwərd || 'həʊmwəd/ [1] (BrE also) **homewards** /-z/ *adv* ‹*travel/journey/sail*› de vuelta a casa [2] **to be ~ bound** ir* de camino *or* de vuelta a casa

homeward[2] *adj* (*before n*) ‹*journey*› de vuelta *or* de regreso

homework /'həʊmwɜːrk || 'həʊmwɜːk/ *n* [u] deberes *mpl*, tarea *f*; **to do one's ~** (for school) hacer* los deberes, hacer* la tarea; (for job, speech) prepararse, documentarse

homeworking /'həʊmwɜːrkɪŋ || 'həʊmwɜːkɪŋ/ *n* [u] trabajo *m* desde casa

homey /'həʊmi/ *adj* **homier, homiest** (AmE colloq) ‹*atmosphere/place*› hogareño, acogedor; ‹*manner*› campechano

homicidal /ˈhɑːmə'saɪdḷ || ˌhɒmɪ'saɪdḷ/ *adj* ‹*tendency*› homicida; ‹*rage*› asesino

homicide /'hɑːməsaɪd || 'hɒmɪsaɪd/ *n* [1] [u c] (crime, act) homicidio *m*; (*before n*) ‹*investigation*› de un homicidio; ‹*trial*› por homicidio [2] [c] (murderer) (frml) homicida *mf* [3] [u] (police squad) (AmE colloq) homicidios *m*

homily /'hɑːməli || 'hɒmɪli/ *n* (*pl* **-lies**) (Relig) homilía *f*, sermón *m*; (speech) sermón *m*

homing /'həʊmɪŋ/ *adj* (*before n*) ‹*instinct*› de volver al hogar; ‹*device/missile*› buscador; ~ **pigeon** paloma *f* mensajera

hominy /'hɑːməni/ *n* [u] (AmE) maíz *m* descascarillado

homoeo- *etc* (BrE) ▸ **homeo-** *etc*

homogeneous /ˈhəʊmə'dʒiːniəs || ˌhɒmə'dʒiːniəs/ *adj* homogéneo

homogenize /həʊ'mɑːdʒənaɪz, hə-|| hə'mɒdʒɪnaɪz/ *vt* homogeneizar*

homograph /'hɑːməgræf || 'hɒməgrɑːf/ *n* homógrafo *m*

homonym /'hɑːmənɪm || 'hɒmənɪm/ *n* homónimo *m*

homophobia /'həʊmə'fəʊbiə || ˌhəʊmə'fəʊbiə, ˌhɒmə-/ *n* [u] homofobia *f*

homophobic /'həʊmə'fəʊbɪk || ˌhəʊmə'fəʊbɪk, ˌhɒmə-/ *adj* homofóbico

homophone /'hɑːməfəʊn || 'hɒməfəʊn/ *n* homófono *m*

homosexual[1] /'həʊmə'sekʃuəl || ˌhəʊmə'sekʃʊəl, ˌhɒmə-/ *adj* homosexual

homosexual[2] *n* homosexual *mf*

homosexuality /'həʊmə'sekʃu'æləti || ˌhəʊməsekʃʊ'æləti, ˌhɒmə-/ *n* [u] homosexualidad *f*

Hon /ɑːn || ɒn/ (in UK) = **Honourable**

honcho /'hɑːntʃəʊ || 'hɒntʃəʊ/ *n* (*pl* ~**s**) (colloq) mandamás *mf* (fam), mero mero, mera mera *m,f* (Méx fam)

Honduran[1] /hɑːn'dʊrən || hɒn'djʊərən/ *adj* hondureño

Honduran[2] *n* hondureño, -ña *m,f*

Honduras /hɑːn'dʊrəs || hɒn'djʊərəs/ *n* Honduras *f*

hone /həʊn/ *vt* ‹*blade/edge*› afilar; ‹*style/skill*› afinar, poner* a punto

honest /'ɑːnəst || 'ɒnɪst/ *adj* [1] (trustworthy, upright) ‹*person/action*› honrado, honesto; ‹*face*› de persona honrada *or* honesta; **to make an ~ living** ganarse la vida honradamente; **he made an ~ woman of her** (hum) cumplió y se casó con ella [2] (sincere) ‹*appraisal*› sincero, franco; ‹*opinion/attempt*› sincero; **to be ~ with you ...** si quieres que te diga la verdad *or* que te sea sincero ... [3] (*as interj*) (colloq) de veras

honestly /'ɑːnəstli || 'ɒnɪstli/ *adv* [1] (sincerely) ‹*answer/say/think*› sinceramente, francamente; **I don't know and I ~ don't care** no lo sé y la verdad es que no me importa [2] (*indep*) en serio, de verdad; **I don't mind, ~** en serio *or* en verdad (que) no me importa [3] (*as interj*) (expressing exasperation) ¡por favor! [4] (legitimately) ‹*act/earn*› con honradez, honradamente

honest-to-God /'ɑːnəsttə'gɑːd || 'ɒnɪsttə'gɒd/, **honest-to-goodness** /-'gʊdnəs || -'gʊdnɪs/ *adj* (colloq) (*before n*) como es debido, como Dios manda

honesty /'ɑːnəsti || 'ɒnɪsti/ *n* [u] [1] (probity) honradez *f*, honestidad *f*, rectitud *f* [2] (truthfulness) franqueza *f*, sinceridad *f*; **in all ~ ...** para ser sincero ...; ~ ***is the best policy*** lo mejor es ser honesto

honey /'hʌni/ *n* (*pl* **honeys**)

A [u] miel *f*

B [c] [1] (*as form of address*) (colloq) cariño (fam) [2] (wonderful person) cielo *m*, encanto *m*

honey: ~**bee** *n* abeja *f*; ~**comb** *n* [c u] panal *m*

honeyed /'hʌnid/ *adj* (liter) meloso, melifluo (liter)

honeymoon[1] /'hʌnimuːn/ *n* (after wedding) luna *f* de miel; (*before n*) **the ~ couple** la pareja de recién casados; ~ **period** (of a new government) luna de miel

honeymoon[2] *vi* pasar la luna de miel

honeysuckle /'hʌniˌsʌkəl/ *n* [c u] madreselva *f*

Hong Kong /'hɑːŋ'kɑːŋ || ˌhɒŋ'kɒŋ/ *n* Hong-Kong

honk[1] /hɑːŋk || hɒŋk/ *n* (of goose) graznido *m*; (of car) bocinazo *m*

honk[2] *vi* (hoot) «*goose*» graznar; «*driver*» tocar* el claxon, pitar

■ **honk** *vt*: **he ~ed his horn a couple of times** tocó el claxon *or* pitó un par de veces, pegó un par de bocinazos

honor[1], (BrE) **honour** /'ɑːnər || 'ɒnə(r)/ *n*

A [u] [1] (good name) honor *m*; **a man of ~** un hombre de honor *or* de palabra; **to be (in) ~ bound to + INF** estar* moralmente obligado a + INF [2] (chastity) (arch *or* hum) honra *f*

B [c u] (privilege, mark of distinction) honor *m*; **it is a great ~ for me ...** es para mí un gran honor ...; **to have the ~ to + INF** *o* **of -ING** (frml) tener* el honor DE + INF (frml); **to do sb the ~ of -ING** (frml) hacerle* *or* (frml) concederle a algn el honor DE + INF; **a reception in ~ of the delegates** una recepción en honor de *or* en homenaje a los delegados; **in ~ of her visit** para celebrar su visita; ***to do the ~s*** (colloq) hacer* los honores (frml *o* hum)

C **Honor** (as title) **Your/His/Her H~** Su Señoría

D **honors** *pl* [1] (special mention) (*before n*) ~**s list** (AmE) cuadro *m* de honor [2] (Educ): **to graduate with ~s** licenciarse con matrícula (de honor) *or* con honores; (*before n*) **honours graduate** (BrE) ≈ licenciado, -da *m,f*; **an honours degree** (BrE) ≈ una licenciatura

honor[2], (BrE) **honour** *vt*

A (show respect) honrar; **would you escort me in to dinner? — I'd be ~ed (to)** ¿me acompaña al comedor? — será un honor para mí

B [1] (keep to) ‹*agreement/obligation*› cumplir (con) [2] (Fin) ‹*bill/debt*› satisfacer* (frml), pagar*; ‹*check/draft*› pagar*, aceptar

honorable, (BrE) **honourable** /'ɑːnərəbəl || 'ɒnərəbəl/ *adj*

A [1] (honest, respectable) ‹*person/action*› honorable; **he did**

the ~ thing and resigned hizo lo que correspondía: dimitió 2 (creditable) ‹*peace/settlement*› honroso
B Honourable (in UK) *tratamiento dado a representantes parlamentarios y a hijos de vizcondes, barones y condes*

honorary /'ɑːnəreri || 'ɒnərəri/ *adj* honorario; **an ~ doctorate** un doctorado honoris causa

honour *etc* (BrE) ▸**honor** *etc*

Honours List *n* (in UK): **the Birthday/New Year ~ ~** *lista de títulos honoríficos otorgados por el monarca el día de su cumpleaños oficial/el día de año nuevo*

hooch /huːtʃ/ *n* [u] (AmE sl) *bebida alcohólica de mala calidad*

hood /hʊd/ *n*
A (on coat, jacket) capucha *f*; (pointed) capirote *m*; (of monk) capucha *f*, capuchón *m*; (on ceremonial robes) muceta *f* (*con capillo*)
B 1 (on chimney, cooker) campana *f*; (on machine) cubierta *f* 2 (AmE Auto) capó *m* 3 (folding cover) (BrE) capota *f*
C (gangster) (AmE sl) matón, -tona *m,f* (fam)

hooded /'hʊdəd || 'hʊdɪd/ *adj* ‹*person*› encapuchado; ‹*garment*› con capucha

hoodie, hoody /'hʊdi/ *n* 1 (Clothing) hoodie *m*, sudadera *f* con capucha 2 (BrE) (aggressive youth) vándalo, -la *m,f*, gámberro, -rra *m,f*

hoodlum /'huːdləm/ *n* 1 (thug) (AmE) matón, -tona *m,f* (fam), gorila *mf* 2 (rowdy youth) vándalo, -la *m,f*, gamberro, -rra *m,f* (Esp)

hoodwink /'hʊdwɪŋk/ *vt* engañar; **to ~ sb INTO -ING** engañar a algn PARA QUE (+ *subj*)

hooey /'huːi/ *n* [u] (esp AmE colloq): **that's a load of ~!** ¡son puras tonterías!, ¡son puras macanas! (RPl fam)

hoof[1] /hʊf || huːf/ *n* (*pl* **hoofs** *or* **hooves**) (Zool) (of horse) casco *m*, vaso *m* (RPl), pezuña *f* (Méx); (of cow) pezuña *f*

hoof[2] *vt*: ***to ~ it*** (colloq) ir* a pata (fam)

hoof-and-mouth disease /'hʊfən'maʊθ || ˌhuːfən'maʊθ/ *n* [u] (AmE) fiebre *f* aftosa, glosopeda *f* (téc)

hoo-ha /'huːhɑː/ *n* [c u] (colloq) alboroto *m*, jaleo *m* (fam): **there was a great ~** se armó tremendo jaleo

hook[1] /hʊk/ *n*
A 1 gancho *m*; (for hanging clothes) percha *f*, gancho *m*; (for fishing) anzuelo *m*; **to take the phone off the ~** descolgar* el teléfono; ***by ~ or by crook*** sea como sea, por las buenas o por las malas; ***~, line and sinker***: **I swallowed the story ~, line and sinker** mordí *or* me tragué el anzuelo; ***to get/let sb off the ~*** sacar*/dejar salir a algn del atolladero; **he's off the ~** se ha librado; ***to sling one's ~*** (BrE sl) largarse* (fam) 2 (Clothing) corchete *m*, ganchito *m*; **~s and eyes** corchetes (*macho y hembra*)
B (in boxing) gancho *m*

hook[2] *vt*
A (grasp, secure) enganchar
B (Sport) ‹*ball*› (in golf) golpear (*hacia la izquierda*); (in rugby) talonar; (in boxing) enganchar, pegarle* un gancho a
■ **hook** *vi* (join with hook) «*dress*» abrocharse

Phrasal verb
• **hook up**
A [v ▸ o ▸ adv, v ▸ adv ▸ o] 1 (fasten) ‹*dress/bra*› abrochar 2 (connect, link) enganchar
B [v ▸ adv] 1 (Rad, TV) conectarse, transmitir en cadena 2 (fasten) «*dress*» abrocharse 3 (become associated) (AmE) engancharse

hookah /'hʊkə/ *n* narguile *m*

hook and ladder (truck) *n* (AmE) carro *m or* (Esp) coche *m* de bomberos, autobomba *m* (RPl), bomba *f* (Chi)

hooked /hʊkt/ *adj*
A (hook-shaped) ‹*tool*› en forma de gancho; ‹*beak*› ganchudo; ‹*nose*› aguileño
B (addicted) (colloq) **to be/get ~ ON sth** ‹*on drug/video games*› estar* enviciado/enviciarse CON algo, estar enganchado/engancharse A algo (Esp); **she's completely ~ on the idea of going skiing** está entusiasmadísima con la idea de ir a esquiar

hooker /'hʊkər || 'hʊkə(r)/ *n*
A (prostitute) (esp AmE colloq) prostituta *f*, puta *f* (vulg)
B (in rugby) talonador, -dora *m,f*

hookup /'hʊkʌp/ *n*
A (Rad, TV): **a nationwide ~** una cadena nacional
B (connection) (AmE) conexión *f*

hooky /'hʊki/ *n*: **to play ~** (esp AmE colloq) faltar a clase, hacer* novillos *or* (Méx) irse* de pinta *or* (RPl) hacerse* la rata *or* la rabona *or* (Per) la vaca *or* (Chi) hacer* la cimarra *or* (Col) capar clase *or* (Ven) jubilarse (fam)

hooligan /'huːlɪgən/ *n* vándalo, -la *m,f*, gamberro, -rra *m,f*

hooliganism /'huːlɪgənɪzəm/ *n* [u] vandalismo *m*, gamberrismo *m* (Esp)

hoop /huːp/ *n* aro *m*

hoop-la /'huːplɑː/ *n* [u]
A *also* **hoopla** (ballyhoo) (AmE colloq): **they launched their new product with a tremendous amount of ~** lanzaron su nuevo producto con bombos y platillos *or* (Esp) a bombo y platillo
B (BrE Games) juego *m* de los aros

hooray /hʊ'reɪ/ *interj* ¡hurra!; **hip hip ~!** ¡hip, hip, hurra!

hoosegow /'huːsgaʊ/ *n* (AmE sl) cárcel *f*, cana *f* (AmS arg), bote *m* (Méx, Ven arg), trullo *m* (Esp arg)

hoot[1] /huːt/ *n* (of owl) grito *m*, ululato *m*; **~s of laughter** risotadas *fpl*, carcajadas *fpl*; ***not to give*** *o* ***care a ~*** *o* ***two ~s*** (colloq): **I don't give a ~ about it** me importa un rábano *or* un comino *or* un pito (fam); ***to be a ~*** (colloq) ser* para morirse de risa, ser* un relajo (Méx fam), ser* un plato (AmS fam)

hoot[2] *vi* «*owl*» ulular; «*car/driver*» tocar* el claxon, pitar; **to ~ with laughter** morirse* *or* matarse de (la) risa
■ **hoot** *vt* (BrE Auto): **he ~ed his horn** tocó el claxon *or* la bocina, pitó

hooter /'huːtər || 'huːtə(r)/ *n* (BrE)
A 1 (siren) sirena *f* 2 (horn) claxon *m*, bocina *f*
B (nose) (colloq & hum) napias *fpl* (fam), naso *m* (RPl fam)

hoover /'huːvər || 'huːvə(r)/ (BrE) *vt* pasar la aspiradora *or* el aspirador por, aspirar (AmL)
■ **hoover** *vi* pasar la aspiradora *or* el aspirador, aspirar (AmL)

Hoover®, hoover /'huːvər || 'huːvə(r)/ *n* (BrE) aspiradora *f*, aspirador *m*

hooves /hʊvz || huːvz/ *pl of* **hoof**[1]

hop[1] /hɑːp || hɒp/ *n*
A 1 (jump — of person) salto *m* a la pata coja, brinco *m* de cojito (Méx); (— of rabbit) salto *m*, brinco *m*; (— of bird) saltito *m*; ***to catch sb on the ~*** (BrE colloq) pillar *or* (esp Esp) coger* a algn desprevenido *or* descuidado 2 (Aviat): **a short ~** un vuelo corto
B (dance) (colloq & dated) baile *m*, bailongo *m* (fam)
C (Bot, Culin) (*usu pl*) lúpulo *m*

hop[2] **-pp-** *vi* 1 «*frog/rabbit*» brincar*, saltar; «*bird*» dar* saltitos 2 «*person/child*» saltar a la pata coja *or* con un solo pie, brincar* de cojito (Méx) 3 (move quickly) (colloq): **~ in, I'll take you to the station** súbete, que te llevo a la estación; **to ~ off/on a train/bus** bajarse de/tomarse un tren/autobús
■ **hop** *vt*
A (AmE colloq) ‹*flight/train*› tomar, pillar (fam)
B ***to ~ it*** (BrE colloq): **~ it!** ¡lárgate! (fam)

hope[1] /həʊp/ *n* [u c] esperanza *f*; **the doctor told us she was beyond ~** el médico nos dijo que lo suyo no tenía cura; **don't get your ~s up too much** no te hagas demasiadas ilusiones; **to give up ~** perder* la(s) esperanza(s); **we have high ~s of him/his getting a gold medal** tenemos muchas esperanzas de que obtenga una medalla de oro; **she did it in the ~ of a reward** lo hizo con la esperanza de obtener una recompensa; **to build up** *o* **raise one's ~s** hacerse* *or* forjarse ilusiones; **to raise false ~s** crear falsas expectativas; **to pin one's ~s on sth/sb** cifrar *or* depositar las esperanzas en algo/algn; **we haven't got a ~ in hell** (colloq) no tenemos ni la más remota posibilidad; **not a ~!** (colloq) ¡ni lo sueñes!; **some ~!** (iro) ¡sí, espérate sentado! (fam & iró)

hope[2] *vi* esperar; **I ~ so/not** espero que sí/que no; **to ~ FOR sth**: **we're hoping for good weather** esperamos tener buen tiempo; **to ~ for the best** esperar que todo resulte (bien) *or* salga bien; ***to ~ against hope that ...*** esperar contra todo pronóstico que ...
■ **hope** *vt* **to ~ (THAT)** esperar QUE (+ *subj*); **to ~ to + INF** esperar + INF

hope chest *n* (AmE) baúl *m or* arcón *m* del ajuar

hoped-for /'həʊptfɔːr || 'həʊptfɔː(r)/ *adj* (*before n*) esperado, ansiado

hopeful[1] /'həʊpfəl/ *adj* 1 ‹*person*› esperanzado, optimista; **don't be/get too ~** no te hagas demasiadas ilusiones;

h

to be ~ OF -ING tener* esperanzas DE + INF [2] (promising) esperanzador, prometedor

hopeful² *n* aspirante *mf*, candidato, -ta *m,f*

hopefully /ˈhəʊpfəli/ *adv* [1] (in hopeful way): **can you pay me in dollars? she asked ~** —¿puedes pagarme en dólares? —preguntó esperanzada [2] (crit) (*indep*): **when do you leave? — ~, on Friday** ¿cuándo te vas? — el viernes, espero *or* si Dios quiere

hopeless /ˈhəʊpləs || ˈhəʊplɪs/ *adj*
A (allowing no hope) ‹*situation*› desesperado; ‹*love*› sin esperanzas, imposible; ‹*task*› imposible; **he's a ~ case** ‹‹*pupil*›› no tiene remedio; ‹‹*patient*›› está desahuciado
B (incompetent, inadequate) (colloq): **you're ~!** ¡eres un inútil!; **as an interviewer, she's absolutely ~** como entrevistadora, es una nulidad; **the train service on this line is ~** el servicio de trenes en esta línea es desastroso *or* es un desastre; **to be ~ AT sth** ser* negado PARA algo

hopelessly /ˈhəʊpləsli/ *adv* [1] (irredeemably) (*as intensifier*): **to be ~ lost/in love** estar* completamente perdido/perdidamente enamorado [2] (without hope) sin esperanzas

hopelessness /ˈhəʊpləsnəs || ˈhəʊplɪsnɪs/ *n* [u] [1] (of situation) lo desesperado [2] (despair) desesperanza *f*

hopping /ˈhɑːpɪŋ/ *adj*: ***to be ~ mad*** (colloq) estar* furioso

hopscotch /ˈhɑːpskɑːtʃ || ˈhɒpskɒtʃ/ *n* [u]: **to play ~** jugar* al tejo *or* (Méx) al avión *or* (RPl) a la rayuela *or* (Col) a la golosa *or* (Chi) al luche

horde /hɔːrd/ *n* (of people, tourists) (colloq) multitud *f*, horda *f*; **there were ~s of people** había miles de personas

horizon /həˈraɪzən/ *n* [1] (Geog) **the ~** el horizonte [2] **horizons** *pl* (scope, opportunities) horizontes *mpl*

horizontal¹ /ˈhɔːrəˈzɑːntl̩ || ˌhɒrɪˈzɒntl̩/ *adj* horizontal

horizontal² *n* horizontal *f*

horizontally /ˈhɔːrəˈzɑːntl̩i/ *adv* horizontalmente

hormonal /hɔːrˈməʊnl̩ || hɔːˈməʊnl̩/ *adj* hormonal

hormone /ˈhɔːrməʊn || ˈhɔːməʊn/ *n* hormona *f*; (*before n*) **~ replacement therapy** terapia *f* hormonal sustitutiva

horn /hɔːrn || hɔːn/ *n*
A [c u] (Zool) (of animal) cuerno *m*, asta *f*‡, cacho *m* (AmS), guampa *f* (CS)
B [c] (Mus) [1] (wind instrument) cuerno *m* [2] (*French ~*) trompa *f*
C [c] (Auto) claxon *m*, bocina *f*; (Naut) sirena *f*

horned /hɔːrnd/ *adj* con cuernos, con cachos (AmS)

hornet /ˈhɔːrnət || ˈhɔːnɪt/ *n* avispón *m*; ***to stir up a ~'s nest*** armar mucho revuelo, alborotar el avispero *or* el gallinero (fam)

horn-rimmed /ˈhɔːrnrɪmd || ˈhɔːnrɪmd/ *adj* ‹*spectacles*› (con montura) de carey *or* de concha

horny /ˈhɔːrni || ˈhɔːni/ *adj* **-nier, -niest**
A (hard) ‹*hand*› calloso
B (sexually excited) (sl) caliente (fam), cachondo (Esp, Méx fam)

horoscope /ˈhɔːrəskəʊp || ˈhɒrəskəʊp/ *n* horóscopo *m*

horrendous /hɔːˈrendəs || hɒˈrendəs/ *adj* [1] (horrifying) ‹*crime/account*› horrendo, horroroso [2] (dreadful) (colloq) ‹*price/mistake*› terrible

horrible /ˈhɔːrəbəl/ *adj* ‹*crime/sight/feeling*› horrible, horroroso; **he was ~ to her** fue muy malo con ella

horribly /ˈhɔːrəbli || ˈhɒrɪbli/ *adv* [1] (horrifyingly) de una forma *or* manera horrible [2] (colloq) (*as intensifier*) ‹*late/rude*› terriblemente

horrid /ˈhɔːrəd || ˈhɒrɪd/ *adj* [1] (horrible) (esp BrE colloq) ‹*weather/taste*› horroroso [2] (horrifying) (liter) horrible

horrific /hɔːˈrɪfɪk/ *adj* horroroso, espantoso

horrify /ˈhɔːrəfaɪ || ˈhɒrɪfaɪ/ *vt* **-fies, -fying, -fied** horrorizar*; **she was horrified to find out that ...** se horrorizó al enterarse de que ...

horrifying /ˈhɔːrəfaɪɪŋ/ *adj* horroroso, horrendo

horror /ˈhɔːrər || ˈhɒrə(r)/ *n*
A [1] [u] (emotion) horror *m*; **I cried out in ~** grité horrorizada; **to have a ~ of sth/-ING**: **he has a ~ of spiders** les tiene horror *or* terror a las arañas; **I have a ~ of being alone** me aterra *or* me da pavor estar sola; (*before n*) ‹*movie/story*› de terror [2] [c] (experience, event): **the ~s of nuclear warfare** los horrores de la guerra atómica [3] [c] (person, thing) (colloq) monstruo *m*
B **horrors** *pl* (colloq): **spiders give me the ~s** las arañas me ponen los pelos de punta (fam)

horror-struck /ˈhɔːrərstrʌk/ *adj* horrorizado

hors d'oeuvre /ɔːrˈdɜːrv/ *n* (*pl* **hors d'oeuvres** /-ˈdɜːrv/) entremés *m*, botana *f* (Méx)

horse /hɔːrs || hɔːs/ *n*
A [c] (Zool) caballo *m*; ***from the ~'s mouth*** (colloq): **I heard it straight from the ~'s mouth** me lo dijo él mismo/ella misma; ***his/her high ~***: **when he gets on his high ~ ...** cuando se pone a pontificar ...; ***hold your ~s*** (colloq) ¡un momentito!; ***I could eat a ~*** tengo un hambre canina; ***to beat*** *o* (BrE) ***flog a dead ~*** (colloq) pedirle* peras al olmo; ***to change ~s in midstream*** cambiar de parecer (*or* de política *etc*) a mitad de camino; ***to eat like a ~*** comer como un sabañón *or* como una lima (nueva); ***wild ~s***: **wild ~s wouldn't drag me back to that job** por nada del mundo volvería a ese trabajo; ***you can lead*** *o* ***take a ~ to water but you can't make it drink*** puedes darle un consejo a alguien, pero no puedes obligarlo a que lo siga; (*before n*) **~ riding** (BrE) equitación *f*
B [c] (vaulting-block) potro *m*, caballo *m* (Méx)
C [u] (heroin) (sl) caballo *m* (arg)

Phrasal verb
• **horse around** [v ▸ adv] (colloq) alborotar

horse: **~back** *n*: **on ~back** a caballo; (*before n*) **~back riding** (AmE) equitación *f*; **to go ~back riding** (AmE) salir* a montar *or* (CS, Méx tb) a andar a caballo; **~box** *n* (BrE) ▸ **~car 2**; **~car** *n* (AmE) [1] (drawn by horses) *tranvía tirado por caballos* [2] (for transporting horses) remolque *m* *or* trailer *m* (*para transportar caballos*); **~ chestnut** *n* [1] **~ chestnut (tree)** castaño *m* de Indias [2] (fruit) castaña *f* de Indias; **~-drawn** *adj* tirado por caballos; **~feathers** *pl n* (AmE sl) tonterías *fpl*, bobadas *fpl* (fam); **~flesh** *n* [u] (meat) carne *f* de caballo; (horses) caballos *mpl*; **~fly** *n* tábano *m*; **~hair** *n* [u] crin *f*; **~man** /ˈhɔːrsmən || ˈhɔːsmən/ *n* (*pl* **-men** /-mən/) jinete *m*

horsemanship /ˈhɔːrsmənʃɪp || ˈhɔːsmənʃɪp/ *n* [u] habilidad *f* en el manejo del caballo

horse: **~meat** *n* [u] carne *f* de caballo; **~play** *n* [u] jugueteo *m*; **~power** *n* [u] caballo *m* (de fuerza); **~ racing** *n* [u] carreras *fpl* de caballos, hípica *f*; **~radish** /ˈhɔːrsˈrædɪʃ || ˈhɔːsrædɪʃ/ *n* [c u] rábano *m* picante; **~ sense** *n* [u] (colloq) sentido *m* común, tino *m*; **~shit** *n* [u] (AmE sl) ▸ **bullshit¹**; **~shoe** *n* herradura *f*; **~ show** *n* concurso *m* hípico

horsewhip¹ /ˈhɔːrshwɪp/ *n* látigo *m*, fuete *m* (AmL exc CS)

horsewhip² *vt* **-pp-** darle* latigazos *or* (AmL exc CS) fuetazos a

horsewoman /ˈhɔːrsˌwʊmən || ˈhɔːsˌwʊmən/ *n* (*pl* **-women**) amazona *f*

horsy, horsey /ˈhɔːrsi || ˈhɔːsi/ *adj* **-sier, -siest** [1] (fond of horses) aficionado a los caballos [2] (resembling horse) ‹*face*› caballuno, de caballo

horticultural /ˈhɔːrtəˈkʌltʃərəl || ˌhɔːtɪˈkʌltʃərəl/ *adj* hortícola, de horticultura

horticulture /ˈhɔːrtəˌkʌltʃər/ *n* [u] horticultura *f*

hose /həʊz/ *n*
A [c u] (*~pipe*) manguera *f*, manga *f*; (Auto) manguito *m*
B (Clothing) (+ *pl vb*) [1] (socks) (dated) calcetines *mpl*, medias *fpl* (AmL) [2] (tights) (Hist, Theat) calzas *fpl*, malla *f* [3] (AmE) ▸ **pantyhose**

Phrasal verb
• **hose down** [v ▸ o ▸ adv, v ▸ adv ▸ o] lavar (*con manguera*)

hosepipe /ˈhəʊzpaɪp/ *n* (esp BrE) ▸ **hose A**

hosiery /ˈhəʊʒəri/ *n* [u] (frml) calcetería *f*, medias *fpl*

hospice /ˈhɑːspəs || ˈhɒspɪs/ *n* (for the dying) *residencia para enfermos desahuciados*

hospitable /hɑːˈspɪtəbəl || hɒˈspɪtəbəl/ *adj* ‹*person*› hospitalario; ‹*atmosphere*› acogedor

hospital /ˈhɑːspɪtl̩ || ˈhɒspɪtl̩/ *n* hospital *m*; **to be in the ~** (AmE) *o* (BrE) **in ~** estar* en el hospital, estar* hospitalizado, estar* internado (CS, Méx); **he went into the ~** (AmE) *o* (BrE) **into ~** ingresó en el hospital, se hospitalizó *or* (CS, Méx tb) internó; (*before n*) ‹*treatment*› hospitalario

hospital trust *n* (in UK) *hospital de la seguridad social administrado por una fundación*

hospitality /ˈhɑːspəˈtæləti || ˌhɒspɪˈtæləti/ *n* [u] hospitalidad *f*; (*before n*) ‹*suite/lounge*› (BrE) de recepción

hospitalize /ˈhɑːspɪtl̩aɪz || ˈhɒspɪtl̩aɪz/ *vt* hospitalizar*, internar (CS, Méx)

host¹ /həʊst/ *n*

A 1 (person dispensing hospitality) anfitrión, -triona *m,f*; **Barcelona played ~ to the Olympic Games** Barcelona fue la sede de las Olimpiadas; (*before n*) ‹*country/government*› anfitrión 2 (Rad, TV) presentador, -dora *m,f*

B (of parasite) huésped *m*

C (multitude) gran cantidad *f*

D **the Host** (Relig) la (Sagrada) Hostia *or* Forma, la Eucaristía

host² *vt* 1 (be the venue for) ‹*conference/event*› ser la sede de 2 (Rad, TV) ‹*program*› presentar 3 ‹*party/function*› ofrecer*

hostage /ˈhɑːstɪdʒ || ˈhɒstɪdʒ/ *n* rehén *m*; **to take/hold sb ~** tomar/tener* a algn como rehén

hostel /ˈhɑːstl̩ || ˈhɒstl̩/ *n* 1 (*youth ~*) albergue *m* juvenil *or* de juventud 2 (for students) (BrE) residencia *f*; (for the homeless, for battered wives etc) hogar *m*

hostess /ˈhəʊstəs || ˈhəʊstes/ *n* 1 (in private capacity) anfitriona *f* 2 (*air ~*) (esp BrE) ▸**stewardess 2** 3 (at exhibitions, fairs) azafata *f*; (in nightclub) cabaretera *f*, chica *f* de alterne (Esp), copera *f* (AmS); (on TV show) (presenter) presentadora *f*; (assistant) azafata *f*

hostile /ˈhɑːstl̩ || ˈhɒstaɪl/ *adj* hostil; **to be ~ TO sth** ser* hostil A algo; **to be ~ TO *o* TOWARD sb** ser* hostil CON *or* HACIA algn

hostility /hɑːˈstɪləti || hɒˈstɪləti/ *n*

A [u] **~ (TO *o* TOWARD sb/sth)** hostilidad *f* (HACIA algn/algo)

B **hostilities** *pl* (Mil frml) hostilidades *fpl* (frml)

hot /hɑːt || hɒt/ *adj* **-tt-**

A 1 ‹*food/water*› caliente; ‹*weather/day/country*› caluroso; ‹*climate*› cálido; **don't touch it, it's ~** no lo toques, está caliente; **it's ~ today/in here** hoy/aquí hace calor; **I'm/he's ~** tengo/tiene calor; **to get ~** «*oven/iron/radiator*» calentarse*; **I got really ~ in that shop/playing tennis** me dio mucho calor en esa tienda/me acaloré mucho jugando tenis (AmL) *or* jugando al tenis (Esp, RPl); **to get/be all ~ and bothered about sth** sulfurarse/estar* sulfurado por algo; **to have a ~ temper** tener* mal genio; ▸**blow²** *vi* **A1** 2 (spicy) picante, picoso (Méx)

B (dangerous) (colloq) peligroso; **to make things ~ for sb** hacerle* la vida muy difícil a algn; **the situation was too ~ to handle** la situación entrañaba demasiados riesgos *or* era demasiado comprometedora

C 1 (fresh) ‹*news/scent*› reciente, fresco; **news ~ off the press** una noticia de último momento 2 (current) ‹*story/issue*› de plena actualidad 3 (popular, in demand) ‹*product*› de gran aceptación; ‹*play/movie*› taquillero

D (colloq) 1 (expert) **to be ~ AT/ON sth**: **she's very ~ at physics** es un hacha *or* es muy buena en física; **he's very ~ on current affairs** está muy al tanto en temas de actualidad 2 (keen) **to be ~ ON sth**: **she's ~ on punctuality** le da mucha importancia a la puntualidad 3 (satisfactory) (*pred, with neg*): **how are things? — not so ~** ¿qué tal? — regular *or* más o menos

E (stolen) (sl) robado, afanado (arg)

F (in gambling): **the ~ favorite** el gran favorito; **a ~ tip** un soplo

Phrasal verb

• **hot up**: **-tt-** (esp BrE colloq) [v ▸ adv] «*competition*» ponerse* reñido; «*pace*» acelerarse; «*party*» animarse

hot: **~ air** *n* [u] palabrería *f*; **~-air balloon** /ˈhɑːtˈer || ˌhɒtˈeə/ *n* globo *m* de aire caliente; **~bed** *n* (of crime, unrest) semillero *m*, caldo *m* de cultivo; **~-blooded** /ˈhɑːtˈblʌdəd || ˌhɒtˈblʌdɪd/ *adj* apasionado, ardiente

hotchpotch /ˈhɑːtʃpɑːtʃ || ˈhɒtʃpɒtʃ/ *n* (BrE) ▸**hodgepodge**

hot: **~ cross bun** *n*: *bollo de pasas marcado con una cruz, que tradicionalmente se come el Viernes Santo*; **~dog** *vi* **-gg-** (AmE colloq) 1 (show off) fanfarronear (fam) 2 (perform acrobatics) hacer* acrobacias; **~ dog** *n* 1 (Culin) perro *m* *or* perrito *m* caliente, pancho *m* (RPl) 2 (show-off) (AmE colloq) fanfarrón, -rrona *m,f* (fam)

hotel /həʊˈtel/ *n* hotel *m*; (*before n*) **the ~ industry** la industria hotelera

hotelier /həʊˈteljər || həʊˈteliə(r)/ *n* hotelero, -ra *m,f*

hot flush, (AmE) **hot flash** *n* sofoco *m*, bochorno *m*, calor *m* (RPl fam)

hotfoot¹ /ˈhɑːtfʊt/ *adv* a toda prisa, rápidamente

hotfoot² *vt*: ***to ~ it*** (colloq) ir* volando *or* corriendo

hot: **~head** *n* exaltado, -da *m,f*; **~headed** /ˈhɑːtˈhedəd || ˌhɒtˈhedɪd/ *adj* exaltado; **~house** *n* invernadero *m*; (*before n*) ‹*plant/flowers*› de invernadero; ‹*atmosphere*› enrarecido; **~ line** *n* (Pol) teléfono *m* rojo; (for public) línea *f* directa; **~ link** *n* (Comput) 1 (connection) enlace *m* activo 2 (hypertext link) enlace *m* de hipertexto

hotly /ˈhɑːtli/ *adv* ‹*dispute/deny*› con vehemencia; ‹*debated*› acaloradamente; **she finished first, ~ pursued by Klotz** llegó en primer lugar, seguida muy de cerca por Klotz

hot: **~ pants** *pl n* minishorts *mpl*, hot pants *mpl*; **~ pepper** *n* [u c] (AmE) pimiento *m* picante, ají *m* picante (AmS), chile *m* (Méx); **~plate** *n* (for cooking) placa *f*, hornilla *f* (AmL exc CS), hornalla *f* (RPl), plato *m* (Chi); (for keeping food warm) calientaplatos *m*; **~pot** *n* [u c] estofado *m*, guiso *m*; **~ potato** *n* (colloq) asunto *m* candente; ▸**drop²** *vt* **A2**; **~ rod** *n* (colloq) coche *m* arreglado

hots /hɑːts || hɒts/ *pl n* (sl): ***to have the ~ for sb***: **she's really got the ~ for Joe** está loca por Joe (fam)

hot: **~ seat** *n* (colloq): **to be in the ~ seat** estar* en la línea de fuego; **~shot** *n* personaje *m*; (*before n*) ‹*scientist*› célebre; **a ~shot golfer** un as del golf; **~ spot** *n* (colloq) 1 (Pol) punto *m* conflictivo 2 (night club) club *m* nocturno; **~ spring** *n* fuente *f* termal; **~ stuff** *n* [u] (colloq): **it's ~ stuff** (very good) es sensacional *or* fantástico; (controversial) es controvertido *or* polémico; **he's really ~ stuff** (physically) está muy bien (fam), está buenísimo (fam); **~-tempered** /ˈhɑːtˈtempərd || ˌhɒtˈtempəd/ *adj* irascible; **~-water bottle** /ˈhɑːtˈwɔːtər || ˌhɒtˈwɔːtə/ *n* bolsa *f* de agua caliente

hottie ˈhɔːti || ˈhɒti/ *n* (colloq)

A (sexually attractive – man) monumento *m* (*fam*), cuerazo *m* (Méx, Chi fam); (– woman) bombón *m*

B (BrE) (hot-water bottle) bolsa *f* de agua caliente, guatero *m* (Chi)

hound¹ /haʊnd/ *n* perro *m* de caza, sabueso *m*

hound² *vt* acosar; **he is being ~ed by the press** está siendo perseguido y acosado por la prensa

hour /aʊr || aʊə(r)/ *n*

A 1 (60 minutes) hora *f*; **a quarter of an ~** un cuarto de hora; **to be paid by the ~** cobrar por horas 2 (time of day) hora *f*; **the clock struck the ~** el reloj dio la hora; **on the ~** a la hora en punto; **at twenty past the ~** a (las) y veinte; **at 1600 ~s** a las 16:00 horas; **to be up till all ~s** estar* levantado hasta las tantas (fam); **in the early ~s of yesterday morning** ayer de madrugada, en la madrugada de ayer; **in the wee** *o* (BrE) **small ~s** a altas horas (de la noche) 3 (particular moment) momento *m*; **her/his/their finest ~** su mejor momento; **in my ~ of need they all deserted me** todos me abandonaron cuando más los necesitaba

B **hours** *pl* 1 (long time) horas *fpl* 2 (fixed period): **during office/business ~s** en horas de oficina/trabajo; **what ~s are you open?** ¿qué horario tienen?; **doctors work long ~s** los médicos tienen un día de trabajo muy largo; **to work after ~s** trabajar después de hora; **to keep late/irregular ~s** llevar una vida noctámbula/desordenada

hourglass /ˈaʊrglæs/ *n* reloj *m* de arena; (*before n*) **~ figure** cuerpo *m* en forma de guitarra *or* de ánfora

hourly¹ /ˈaʊrli || ˈaʊəli/ *adj* ‹*rate/wage*› por hora

hourly² *adv* 1 (every hour) ‹*run/broadcast*› cada hora 2 (all the time) a cada momento 3 (at any time) (liter) ‹*expect*› en cualquier momento 4 (by the hour) ‹*pay/charge*› por hora(s)

house¹ /haʊs/ *n* (*pl* **houses** /ˈhaʊzəz/)

A 1 (dwelling, household) casa *f*; **he's useless around the ~** es un inútil para la casa; ***a ~ of cards*** un castillo de naipes; ***as safe as ~s*** (BrE) totalmente seguro; ***to clean ~*** (AmE) (restore order) poner* la casa en orden; (lit: spring-clean) hacer* (una) limpieza general; ***to eat sb out of ~ and home*** dejarle la despensa vacía a algn; ***to get along like a ~ afire*** *o* (BrE) ***on fire*** (colloq) hacer* buenas migas, llevarse muy bien; ***to keep open ~*** tener* la puerta siempre abierta; ***to put one's (own) ~ in order*** poner* sus (*or* mis *etc*) asuntos en orden, ordenar sus (*or* mis *etc*) asuntos; ***to set up ~*** poner* casa; (*before n*) **~ prices** el precio de la vivienda 2 (dynasty) casa *f*, familia *f*

B (Govt) Cámara *f*; **the H~ of Representatives** (in US) la Cámara de Representantes *or* de Diputados; **the H~ of Commons/of Lords** (in UK) la Cámara de los Comunes/de

los Lores; **the H~s of Parliament** (in UK) el Parlamento
C (Busn) casa *f*, empresa *f*; **publishing ~** editorial *f*; **drinks are on the ~** invita la casa; (*before n*) **~ wine** vino *m* de la casa
D (Theat) **1** (auditorium) sala *f*; ⓢ **house full** agotadas las localidades; ***to bring the ~ down*** (colloq): **that scene brought the ~ down** el teatro casi se viene abajo con los aplausos que siguieron a esa escena **2** (audience) público *m* **3** (performance) función *f*

house² /haʊz/ *vt* **1** (accommodate) ‹*person/family*› alojar, darle* alojamiento a **2** (contain) ‹*office/museum*› albergar* **3** (store) almacenar

house³ /haʊs/ *interj* (BrE) ¡cartón! (AmL), ¡bingo! (Esp)

House of Commons

La Cámara de los Comunes es la cámara baja del Parlamento británico o *Houses of Parliament*. Los parlamentarios elegidos para reunirse aquí se denominan *Members of Parliament*. (House of Lords)

house /haʊs/: **~ agent** *n* (BrE) agente *mf* inmobiliario; **~ arrest** *n* arresto *m* domiciliario; **~boat** *n* casa *f* flotante; **~bound** *adj*: **she's 85 and completely ~bound** tiene 85 años y está completamente confinado a su casa; **~break** *vt* (AmE) ‹*pet*› educar*; **~breaker** *n* ladrón, -drona *m,f* (*que desvalija viviendas*); **~broken** *adj* (AmE) ‹*pet*› enseñado; **~ call** *n* visita *f* a domicilio; **~coat** *n* bata *f* (*de casa*); **~fly** *n* mosca *f* común *or* doméstica; **~guest** *n* huésped *mf*, invitado, -da *m,f*

House of Lords

La Cámara de los Lores es la cámara alta del Parlamento británico. Su función es discutir y posteriormente aprobar o sugerir cambios a la legislación que haya sido aprobada en la Cámara de los Comunes (House of Commons). Sus miembros son nombrados en su mayoría por los partidos políticos

House of Representatives

La Cámara de Representantes es la cámara baja del Congreso (Congress) de Estados Unidos. Está formada por 435 representantes (*Representatives*) que son elegidos cada dos años. Cada estado de EEUU tiene un número de representantes proporcional a su población. Esta cámara es la encargada de introducir nueva legislación, por lo que toda nueva ley debe ser aprobada por ella

household /'haʊshəʊld/ *n* casa *f*; **~s with more than one wage earner** las familias *or* (frml) los hogares donde trabajan dos o más personas; (*before n*) **the ~ chores** las tareas domésticas; **a ~ name** un nombre muy conocido

householder /'haʊshəʊldər/ *n* dueño, -ña *m,f* de casa

house /haʊs/: **~-hunt** *vi* (*usu in -ing form*) buscar* casa (*para comprar o alquilar*); **~-hunter** /'haʊs,hʌntər/ *n*: *persona que busca una casa para comprar o alquilar*; **~husband** *n* (hum) *hombre que se ocupa de la casa mientras su mujer sale a trabajar*, amo *m* de casa (hum); **~keeper** *n* (woman) ama *f*‡ de llaves; (in hotel) gobernanta *f*; (man) encargado *m* de la casa; **she's a good ~keeper** es muy buena administradora; **~keeping** *n* [u] **1** (running of home) gobierno *m* de la casa **2** **~keeping (money)** dinero *m* (para los gastos) de la casa **3** (Comput) tareas *fpl* de reorganización de los ficheros; **~ lights** *pl n* (Theat, Cin) luces *fpl* de la sala; **~maid** *n* criada *f*, mucama *f* (AmL); **~man** *n* (*pl* **-men**) (BrE Med) interno, -na *m,f*; **~ martin** *n* avión *m* común; **~plant** *n* planta *f* de interior; **~-proud** *adj* (esp BrE) muy meticuloso (*en la limpieza y el arreglo de la casa*); **~room** *n* [u] (BrE) sitio *m or* espacio *m* (en casa); **I wouldn't give him/it ~room** no lo tendría en casa por nada; **~-sit** *vi* (*pres p* **-sitting** *past & past p* **-sat** /-sæt/) cuidar una casa (*mientras el dueño está ausente*); **~ surgeon** *n* (BrE) cirujano, -na *m,f* residente; **~-to-house** *adj* ‹*inquiries/search*› puerta a puerta; **~ trailer** *n* (AmE) casa *f* rodante (AmL), roulotte *f* (Esp); **~-train** *vt* (BrE) ‹*pet*› educar*; **~-trained** *adj* (BrE) ‹*pet*› enseñado; **~warming (party)** /'haʊs,wɔːrmɪŋ/ *n*: *fiesta de inauguración de una casa*; **~wife** *n* ama *f*‡ de casa; **~work** *n* [u] tareas *fpl* domésticas, trabajo *m* de la casa; **he doesn't do any ~work** no hace nada en la casa

housing /'haʊzɪŋ/ *n*
A [u] **1** (dwellings) viviendas *fpl*; (*before n*) **poor ~ conditions** viviendas inadecuadas; **~ shortage** escasez *f* de viviendas **2** (provision of houses): **the government's policy on ~** la política del gobierno en cuanto al problema de la vivienda
B [c] (cover) caja *f* protectora

housing: **~ association** *n* (in UK) *asociación que construye o renueva viviendas para alquilarlas a precios módicos*; **~ development** *n* (AmE) complejo *m* habitacional, urbanización *f* (Esp), fraccionamiento *m* (Méx); **~ estate** *n* (BrE) **1** (council estate) *urbanización de viviendas de alquiler subvencionadas por el ayuntamiento* **2** (privately owned) ▸ **~ development**; **~ project** *n* (in US) complejo *m* de viviendas subvencionadas

hovel /'hʌvəl || 'hɒvəl/ *n* casucha *f*, rancho *m* (RPl)

hover /'hʌvər || 'hɒvə(r)/ *vi* «*helicopter*» sostenerse* en el aire (*sin avanzar*); «*bird*» cernerse*; **to ~ OVER** *o* **ABOVE sth/sb** «*hawk/threat*» cernerse* SOBRE algo/algn; **a smile/question ~ed on her lips** sus labios esbozaron una sonrisa/una pregunta; **they were ~ing on the brink of disaster** estaban casi al borde del desastre; **the temperature ~ed around 20°** la temperatura rondaba los 20°; **the waiter ~ed around, waiting for a tip** el mesero estuvo rondando la mesa, esperando una propina

hovercraft /'hʌvərkræft || 'hɒvəkrɑːft/ *n* (*pl* **-craft** *or* **-crafts**) aerodeslizador *m*

how /haʊ/ *adv*
A (in questions, indirect questions) cómo; **~ are you?** ¿cómo estás?; **~'s the new job?** ¿cómo marcha el nuevo trabajo?; **~'s your French?** ¿qué tal es tu francés?; **~ do I look?** ¿cómo *or* qué tal estoy?; **~ would Monday suit you?** ¿te viene bien el lunes?; **I asked him ~ he knew** le pregunté cómo lo sabía; **~ will you vote?** ¿a *or* por quién vas a votar?
B (*with adjs, advs*) **1** (in questions, indirect questions): **~ wide is it?** ¿cuánto mide *or* tiene de ancho?, ¿qué tan ancho es? (AmL exc CS); **~ heavy is it?** ¿cuánto pesa?; **~ high can you jump?** ¿hasta dónde puedes saltar?; **~ often do you meet?** ¿con qué frecuencia se reúnen?; **~ bad is the damage?** ¿de qué gravedad son los daños?, ¿qué tan graves son los daños? (AmL exc CS); **~ old are you?** ¿cuántos años tienes?; **I can't tell you ~ grateful I am!** ¡no puedo decirte lo agradecido que estoy *or* (liter) cuán agradecido estoy! **2** (in exclamations) qué; **~ strange/rude!** ¡qué raro/grosero!; **~ right you are!** ¡cuánta razón tienes!
C (*in phrases*) **how about** *o* (colloq) **how's about sth**: **~ about a drink?** ¿nos tomamos una copa?; **Thursday's no good; ~ about Friday?** el jueves no puede ser ¿qué te parece el viernes?; **I'd love to go; ~ about you?** me encantaría ir ¿y a ti?; **10 out of 10! ~ about that?** 10 sobre 10 ¿qué te parece?; **how come** (colloq): **~ come the door's locked?** ¿cómo es que la puerta está cerrada con llave?; **and how!** (colloq) ¡y cómo!

howdy /'haʊdi/ *interj* (AmE colloq & dial) ¡hola!

however¹ /haʊ'evər || haʊ'evə(r)/ *adv*
A (*as linker*) sin embargo, no obstante (frml)
B (*used before adj or adv*) (no matter how): **~ hard she tried ...** por más que trataba ...; **locks, ~ strong, can be broken** las cerraduras, por fuertes que sean, se pueden romper
C (interrog) cómo; **~ did you manage that?** ¿cómo te las arreglaste para conseguir eso?

however² *conj*: **arrange the furniture ~ you like** pon los muebles como quieras; **it's been a disaster, ~ you look at it** ha sido un desastre, lo mires por donde lo mires

howl¹ /haʊl/ *vi* **1** «*dog/wolf*» aullar*; «*person*» dar* alaridos; «*wind/gale*» aullar*, bramar; **to ~ (with laughter)** reírse* a carcajadas; **to ~ AT sb** gritarle A algn **2** (weep noisily) (colloq) berrear (fam)
■ **howl** *vt* bramar, gritar

howl² *n* **1** [c] (of dog, wolf) aullido *m*; (of person) alarido *m*, aullido *m*; (of baby) berrido *m*; **~s of laughter** carcajadas *fpl*, risotadas *fpl* **2** [c] (something hilarious) (AmE colloq): **it really was a ~** fue para morirse de risa (fam), fue un plato (AmL) *or* (Méx) un relajo (fam)

howler /'haʊlər || 'haʊlə(r)/ *n* (colloq) barbaridad *f*, error *m* garrafal

howling /'haʊlɪŋ/ *adj* (*before n*)
A ‹*gale/storm*› huracanado
B (colloq) (*as intensifier*): **it was a ~ success** tuvo un éxito clamoroso

hp (= **horsepower**) CV, HP

HP *n* [u] (BrE) (= **hire purchase**): **to buy sth on ~** comprar algo a plazos

HQ *n* = **headquarters**

hr (= **hour**) h.

HRH (in UK) (= **Her/His Royal Highness**) S.A.R.

HRT *n* = **hormone replacement therapy**

hub /ˈhʌb/ *n* 1▸ (of wheel) cubo *m* 2▸ (focal point) centro *m*

hubbub /ˈhʌbʌb/ *n* (*no pl*) alboroto *m*, barullo *m*

hub cap *n* tapacubos *m*, taza *f* (RPl)

huckleberry /ˈhʌkəlˌberi || ˈhʌklbəri/ *n* (*pl* **-ries**) arándano *m*, ráspano *m*

huckster /ˈhʌkstər || ˈhʌkstə(r)/ *n* 1▸ (salesman, promoter) (pej) charlatán, -tana *m,f*, mercachifle *mf* 2▸ (ad writer) (AmE colloq & pej) publicitario, -ria *m,f*

HUD /hʌd/ *n* (in US) = **Department of Housing and Urban Development**

huddle¹ /ˈhʌdl/ *vi* 1▸ **~ (up)** (crowd together) apiñarse; **she ~d against her mother** se arrimó a su madre 2▸ **~ (up)** (curl up) acurrucarse* 3▸ (in US football) hacer* un timbac *or* un jol

huddle² *n* (tight group) grupo *m*, corrillo *m*; (in US football) timbac *m*, jol *m*; **to go into a ~ (with sb)** hacer* grupo aparte (con algn) (*para discutir algo*)

huddled /ˈhʌdld/ *adj* (*pred*) (crowded together) amontonado, apiñado; (curled up) acurrucado

hue /hjuː/ *n* (liter) (color) color *m*; (shade) tono *m*

hue and cry *n* (*no pl*) revuelo *m*

huff¹ /hʌf/ *n* (*no pl*): **to be/go off in a ~** estar*/salir* enfurruñado, estar*/salir* con mufa (RPl fam); **to get in** *o* **go into a ~** enfurruñarse

huff² *vi*: **to ~ and puff** (wheeze, pant) jadear, resoplar; (bluster) vociferar

huffy /ˈhʌfi/ *adj* **-fier, -fiest** enfurruñado; **to get ~ (ABOUT sth)** enfurruñarse (POR algo)

hug¹ /hʌg/ *vt* **-gg-** 1▸ (embrace) abrazar* 2▸ (keep close to) ir* pegado a

hug² *n* abrazo *m*; **to give sb a ~** abrazar* *or* darle* un abrazo a algn

huge /ˈhjuːdʒ/ *adj* ‹*building/person*› enorme, inmenso, gigantesco; ‹*sum*› astronómico, enorme; ‹*response*› tremendo; **it was a ~ success** fue un exitazo (fam)

hugely /ˈhjuːdʒli/ *adv* 1▸ (*as intensifier*) ‹*successful*› tremendamente, enormemente; **to enjoy oneself ~** divertirse* en grande 2▸ (by large amount) ‹*increased/expanded*› enormemente

huh *interj* /hʌ/ (expressing surprise) ¿qué?; (expressing disbelief, derision) ¡ja!, sí, sí ...; (in inquiry) ¿eh?

hulk /hʌlk/ *n* 1▸ (body of ship) casco *m*; (worn-out ship) (pej) carraca *f*, barco *m* viejo 2▸ (wreck) restos *mpl* (*de un buque siniestrado*) 3▸ (large man) mole *f*, gigantón *m*

hulking /ˈhʌlkɪŋ/ *adj* (*before n*) (colloq) grandote (fam), descomunal; (*as adv*) **a ~ great brute** una bestia de hombre (fam)

hull¹ /hʌl/ *n*
A (of ship, plane, tank) casco *m*
B (of peas, beans) vaina *f*; (of strawberries) cabito *m*, calículo *m*; (of cereals) cáscara *f*, cascarilla *f*

hull² *vt* ‹*peas/beans*› pelar, quitarles la vaina a; ‹*strawberries*› quitarles el cabito a

hullabaloo /ˈhʌləbəluː/ *n* [u] (colloq) (noise) barullo *m*; (fuss) jaleo *m* (fam), escándalo *m*

hullo /həˈləʊ || hʌˈləʊ/ (esp BrE) ▸**hello**

hum¹ /hʌm/ **-mm-** *vi*
A «*machinery/bee/wire*» zumbar; «*person*» tararear (*con la boca cerrada*); **the place is ~ming with activity** el sitio bulle de actividad; ***to ~ and ha(w)*** (BrE colloq) vacilar
B (stink) (BrE colloq) oler* mal, apestar (fam), cantar (Esp fam)
■ **hum** *vt* ‹*tune*› tararear (*con la boca cerrada*)

hum² *n* (*no pl*) (of bees, machinery) zumbido *m*; (of voices, traffic) murmullo *m*

human¹ /ˈhjuːmən/ *adj* humano; **I'm only ~** (todos) somos humanos

human² *n* ser* *m* humano

human being *n* ser *m* humano; **she's a wonderful ~ ~** es una persona estupenda *or* una gran persona

humane /hjuːˈmeɪn/ *adj* humanitario, humano

humanely /hjuːˈmeɪnli/ *adv* humanitariamente, de manera humanitaria

humanism /ˈhjuːmənɪzəm/ *n* [u] humanismo *m*

humanist /ˈhjuːmənəst || ˈhjuːmənɪst/ *n* humanista *mf*

humanitarian /hjuːˈmænəˈteriən/ *adj* humanitario

humanities /hjuːˈmænətiz/ *n* 1▸ (+ *pl vb*) **the ~** las humanidades, las artes y las letras 2▸ (discipline) (+ *sing vb*) humanidades *fpl*; (*before n*) ‹*student/course*› de humanidades

humanity /hjuːˈmænəti/ *n* humanidad *f*; **crimes against ~** crímenes *mpl* contra la humanidad

humanize /ˈhjuːmənaɪz/ *vt* humanizar*

humankind /ˈhjuːmənkaɪnd || ˌhjuːmənˈkaɪnd/ *n* [u] (liter) el género humano (frml *o* liter)

humanly /ˈhjuːmənli/ *adv* humanamente

human: **~ nature** *n* [u] naturaleza *f* humana; **~ rights** *pl n* derechos *mpl* humanos

humble¹ /ˈhʌmbəl/ *adj* humilde, modesto; ‹*apology/request*› humilde; **in my ~ opinion** en mi modesta *or* humilde opinión; ▸**eat** *vt* **A**

humble² *vt* (make humble) darle* una lección de humildad a; (humiliate) humillar

humbly /ˈhʌmbli/ *adv* humildemente

humbug /ˈhʌmbʌg/ *n*
A [u] (nonsense) patrañas *fpl*
B [c] (sweet) (BrE) *caramelo de menta a rayas blancas y negras*

humdinger /ˈhʌmˈdɪŋər || ˌhʌmˈdɪŋə(r)/ *n* (colloq) maravilla *f*, portento *m*

humdrum /ˈhʌmdrʌm/ *adj* monótono, rutinario

humid /ˈhjuːməd || ˈhjuːmɪd/ *adj* húmedo

humidifier /hjuːˈmɪdəfaɪər || hjuːˈmɪdɪfaɪə(r)/ *n* humectador *m*, humidificador *m*

humidity /hjuːˈmɪdəti/ *n* [u] humedad *f*

humiliate /hjuːˈmɪlieɪt/ *vt* humillar

humiliating /hjuːˈmɪlieɪtɪŋ/ *adj* humillante

humiliation /hjuːˈmɪliˈeɪʃən/ *n* humillación *f*

humility /hjuːˈmɪləti/ *n* [u] humildad *f*

hummingbird /ˈhʌmɪŋbɜːrd/ *n* colibrí *m*, picaflor *m*

hummous, hummus /ˈhʊməs/ *n* [u] *puré de garbanzos al estilo griego*

humongous, humungous /hjuːˈmʌŋgəs/ *adj* (colloq) enorme, monumental (fam)

humor¹, (BrE) **humour** /ˈhjuːmər || ˈhjuːmə(r)/ *n*
A [u] (comic quality) humor *m*; **sense of ~** sentido *m* del humor
B (mood) (*no pl*) humor *m*, talante *m*
C [c] (Hist, Physiol) humor *m*

humor², (BrE) **humour** *vt* seguirle* la corriente a

humorist /ˈhjuːmərəst || ˈhjuːmərɪst/ *n* humorista *mf*

humorless, (BrE) **humourless** /ˈhjuːmərləs || ˈhjuːməlɪs/ *adj* ‹*person*› sin sentido del humor, sin gracia; ‹*smile*› forzado

humorous /ˈhjuːmərəs/ *adj* ‹*novel/play/speech*› humorístico; ‹*situation*› cómico, gracioso

humour *n/vt* (BrE) ▸**humor¹,²**

hump¹ /hʌmp/ *n* 1▸ (of camel) joroba *f*, giba *f*; (of person) joroba *f* 2▸ (in ground) montículo *m* 3▸ (bad mood) (BrE colloq): ***to get the ~*** enfurruñarse; ***to have the ~*** estar* de mal humor

hump² *vt*
A (hunch) ‹*back*› encorvar
B **~ (about)** (carry) (BrE colloq) cargar*, acarrear

humpback /ˈhʌmpbæk/, **humpbacked** /-bækt/ *adj* ‹*person*› jorobado; ‹*bridge*› (BrE) peraltado

humus /ˈhjuːməs/ *n* [u] humus *m*, mantillo *m*

hunch¹ /hʌntʃ/ *vt* ‹*back/shoulders*› encorvar
■ **hunch** *vi* encorvarse

hunch² *n* (intuitive feeling) (colloq) presentimiento *m*, pálpito *m*, corazonada *f*; **to have a ~ that ...** tener* el presentimiento de que ...

hunch: **~back** *n* (person) jorobado, -da *m,f*; (hump) joroba *f*; **~backed** /ˈhʌntʃbækt/ *adj* jorobado

hundred /ˈhʌndrəd/ *n* cien *m*; **a/one ~** cien; **a/one ~ and one** ciento uno; **two ~** doscientos; **five ~** quinientos; **five ~ pages** quinientas páginas; **twelve ~** mil doscientos; **fifteen ~** mil quinientos; **in (the year) fifteen ~**

en el (año) mil quinientos; **she lived in the seventeen ~s** vivió en el siglo XVIII; **ten ~s are a thousand** diez centenas son un millar; **they are sold by the ~** *o* **in ~s** se venden de a cien *or* (Esp) de cien en cien; **a/one ~ thousand/million** cien mil/millones; **~s of times** cientos de veces; **I've got a ~ and one things to do** tengo cientos *or* miles de cosas que hacer

hundred: **~fold** *adj/adv see* **-fold**; **~-percenter** /ˈhʌndrəd,pərˈsentər/ *n* (AmE) *nacionalista acérrimo*

hundredth[1] /ˈhʌndrədθ/ *adj* centésimo; *see also* **fifth**[1]

hundredth[2] *adv* en centésimo lugar; *see also* **fifth**[2]

hundredth[3] *n* 1 (Math) centésimo *m* 2 (part) centésima parte *f*

hundredweight /ˈhʌndrədweɪt/ *n* (*pl* ~) *unidad de peso equivalente a 45,36kg. en EEUU y a 50,80kg. en RU*

hung /hʌŋ/ *past & past p of* **hang**[1]

Hungarian[1] /hʌŋˈgeriən || hʌŋˈgeəriən/ *adj* húngaro

Hungarian[2] *n* 1 [u] (language) húngaro *m* 2 [c] (person) húngaro, -ra *m,f*

Hungary /ˈhʌŋgəri/ *n* Hungría *f*

hunger[1] /ˈhʌŋgər || ˈhʌŋgə(r)/ *n* 1 [u] (physical) hambre *f*‡ 2 (strong desire) (*no pl*): **a ~ for adventure/learning** un ansia *f*‡*or* (liter) hambre de aventura/de aprender

hunger[2] *vi* **to ~ FOR** *o* (liter) **AFTER sth** estar* sediento DE algo (liter)

hunger strike *n* huelga *f* de hambre

hung: **~ jury** *n*: *jurado que se disuelve al no ponerse de acuerdo sus miembros*; **~over** /ˈhʌŋˈəʊvər || ˌhʌŋˈəʊvə(r)/ *adj* con resaca, con guayabo (Col fam), con cruda (AmC, Méx fam), con ratón (Ven fam); **to be ~ over** tener* resaca (*or* guayabo *etc*); **~ parliament** *n*: *parlamento en el cual ningún partido tiene la mayoría absoluta*

hungrily /ˈhʌŋgrəli || ˈhʌŋgrɪli/ *adv* ávidamente

hungry /ˈhʌŋgri/ *adj* **-grier, -griest** hambriento; **to be ~** tener* hambre; **I'm getting ~** me está dando hambre; **to go ~** pasar hambre; **power-~** ansioso de poder; **to be ~ FOR sth** estar* ávido DE algo

hung up *adj* (sl)
A (Psych) (*pred*) **to be ~ ~ ABOUT sth/sb**: **she's really ~ ~ about men** tiene un trauma con los hombres; **he's very ~ ~ about his lack of education** tiene un gran complejo por no haber tenido estudios
B (AmE Auto) (*pred*) **to be ~ ~** estar* en un atasco

hunk /hʌŋk/ *n* 1 (chunk) trozo *m*, pedazo *m* 2 (man) (colloq): **he's quite a ~** está buenísimo (fam)

hunker down /ˈhʌŋkər/ [v ▸ adv] (AmE) agacharse

hunky-dory /ˈhʌŋkiˈdɔːri/ *adj* (colloq): **everything's ~** todo marcha sobre ruedas *or* a las mil maravillas

hunt[1] /hʌnt/ *vt*
A ‹*game/fox*› cazar*; **they were ~ed out of existence** fueron exterminados
B 1 (search for) buscar* 2 (drive away) **to ~ sb/sth FROM/OFF/OUT OF sth** echar *or* expulsar a algn/algo DE algo
■ **hunt** *vi* 1 (pursue game) **to ~ (FOR sth)** cazar* (algo); **to go ~ing** ir* de caza *or* de cacería 2 (search) buscar*; **to ~ (FOR sth)** buscar* (algo)

Phrasal verbs
- **hunt down** [v ▸ o ▸ adv, v ▸ adv ▸ o] darle* caza a
- **hunt out**, **hunt up** [v ▸ o ▸ adv, v ▸ adv ▸ o] buscar*

hunt[2] *n*
A 1 (chase) caza *f*, cacería *f* 2 (hunters) partida *f* de caza, cacería *f*
B (search) búsqueda *f*; **I'll have a ~ for the book at home** (colloq) voy a buscar en casa a ver si encuentro el libro; **to be on the ~ for sth** (colloq) andar* a la caza de algo

hunted /ˈhʌntəd || ˈhʌntɪd/ *adj* ‹*look*› atormentado; ‹*animal*› (at bay) acorralado; (pursued) perseguido

hunter /ˈhʌntər || ˈhʌntə(r)/ *n* (person) cazador, -dora *m,f*; (horse) caballo *m* de caza

hunting /ˈhʌntɪŋ/ *n* [u] (Sport) caza *f*, cacería *f*

hunting ground *n* tierras *fpl* de caza, cazadero *m*

huntsman /ˈhʌntsmən/ *n* (*pl* **-men** /-mən/) cazador *m*

hurdle /ˈhɜːrdl̩ || ˈhɜːdl/ *n* 1 (Sport) (obstacle) obstáculo *m*, valla *f*; *see also* **hurdles** 2 (Agr) valla *f* 3 (problem) obstáculo *m*

hurdler /ˈhɜːrdlər/ *n* corredor, -dora *m,f* de vallas

hurdles /ˈhɜːrdl̩z || ˈhɜːdl̩z/ *n* (+ *sing vb*) vallas *fpl*; **the 100 meters ~** los 100 metros vallas

hurl /hɜːrl || hɜːl/ *vt* tirar, arrojar, lanzar*; **to ~ abuse at sb** soltarle* una sarta de insultos a algn
■ *v refl* **to ~ oneself** tirarse, arrojarse, lanzarse*

hurly-burly /ˈhɜːrliˈbɜːrli/ *n* [u] bullicio *m*, alboroto *m*

hurrah /hʊˈrɑː/, **hurray** /hʊˈreɪ/ *interj* ▸**hooray**

hurricane /ˈhɜːrəkeɪn || ˈhʌrɪkən, -keɪn/ *n* huracán *m*

hurricane lamp *n* farol *m*

hurried /ˈhɜːrid || ˈhʌrid/ *adj* ‹*footsteps/movements*› rápido, apresurado; ‹*decision*› precipitado; ‹*piece of work*› hecho deprisa; **we had a ~ meal** comimos rápidamente *or* (fam) a las carreras

hurriedly /ˈhɜːridli || ˈhʌridli/ *adv* apresuradamente; **she left ~** se fue muy deprisa *or* (AmL tb) muy apurada

hurry[1] /ˈhɜːri || ˈhʌri/ *n* (*no pl*) prisa *f*, apuro *m* (AmL); **in all the ~, I forgot my umbrella** con la prisa *or* (AmL) con el apuro, se me olvidó el paraguas; **in a ~**: **I'm in a ~** tengo prisa, estoy apurado (AmL); **he wrote it in a ~** lo escribió deprisa *or* (fam) a las carreras (fam); **he won't try that again in a ~** (esp BrE colloq) no le va a quedar ni pizca de ganas de volver a hacerlo (fam); **to be in a ~ to + INF** tener* prisa *or* (AmL tb) apuro POR+INF; **what's the ~?** ¿qué prisa *or* (AmL tb) qué apuro hay?

hurry[2] **-ries, -rying, -ried** *vi* 1 (make haste) darse* prisa, apurarse (AmL); **there's no need to ~** no hay prisa, no hay apuro (AmL) 2 (move hastily) (+ *adv compl*): **she hurried after him** corrió tras él; **he hurried in/out** entró/salió corriendo
■ **hurry** *vt* 1 ‹*person*› meterle prisa a, apurar (AmL); **he was hurried to a waiting car** se lo llevaron rápidamente *or* a toda prisa a un coche que estaba esperando 2 ‹*work*› hacer* apresuradamente, hacer* a las carreras (fam)

Phrasal verbs
- **hurry along**
A [v ▸ adv] ir* deprisa, apurarse (AmL)
B [v ▸ o ▸ adv, v ▸ adv ▸ o] ‹*person*› meterle prisa a, apurar (AmL)
- **hurry away**, **hurry off**
A [v ▸ adv] alejarse rápidamente *or* corriendo
B [v ▸ o ▸ adv, v ▸ adv ▸ o] alejar rápidamente
- **hurry on** ▸**hurry along**
- **hurry up**
A [v ▸ adv] darse* prisa, apresurarse, apurarse (AmL)
B [v ▸ o ▸ adv, v ▸ adv ▸ o] ‹*person*› meterle prisa a, apurar (AmL); ‹*work*› acelerar, apurar (AmL)

hurt[1] /hɜːrt || hɜːt/ (*past & past p* **hurt**) *vt*
A 1 (cause pain): **you're ~ing her/me!** ¡le/me estás haciendo daño!, ¡la/me estás lastimando! (esp AmL); **my foot is ~ing me** me duele el pie 2 (injure): **I ~ my ankle** me hice daño en el tobillo, me lastimé el tobillo (esp AmL); **to ~ oneself, to get ~** hacerse* daño, lastimarse (esp AmL); **nobody got** *o* **was ~** a nadie le pasó nada; **30 passengers were badly ~** 30 pasajeros resultaron gravemente heridos
B 1 (distress emotionally): **I've been ~ too often** me han hecho sufrir demasiadas veces; **their remarks ~ me deeply** lo que dijeron me dolió *or* me lastimó mucho; **to ~ sb's feelings** herir* los sentimientos de algn 2 (affect adversely) ‹*government/economy*› perjudicar*; **hard work never ~ anyone** trabajar duro nunca le hizo daño *or* mal a nadie
■ **hurt** *vi*
A (be source of pain) doler*; **my leg/head ~s** me duele la pierna/la cabeza; **where does it ~?** ¿dónde le duele?; **do your shoes ~?** ¿te hacen daño los zapatos?
B (have adverse effects): **it won't ~ to postpone it for a while** no pasa nada si lo dejamos por el momento
C (colloq) 1 (feel pain): **I was ~ing all over** me dolía todo; **he was still ~ing after the divorce** (AmE) todavía estaba resentido por lo del divorcio 2 (suffer adverse effects) (AmE): **to be ~ing** estar* pasándola *or* pasándolo mal (fam)

hurt[2] *n* [u] (emotional) dolor *m*, pena *f*

hurt[3] *adj* 1 (physically) ‹*finger/foot*› lastimado; **she was badly ~** estaba gravemente herida, estaba malherida 2 (emotionally) ‹*feelings/pride*› herido; ‹*tone/expression*› dolido; **to feel/be ~** sentirse*/estar* dolido

hurtful /ˈhɜːrtfəl || ˈhɜːtfəl/ *adj* hiriente

hurtle /ˈhɜːrtḷ || ˈhɜːtḷ/ *vi* (+ *adv compl*): **to ~ along/by** *o* **past** ir*/pasar volando *or* a toda velocidad

husband /ˈhʌzbənd/ *n* marido *m*, esposo *m*; **they are ~ and wife** son marido y mujer

husbandry /ˈhʌzbəndri/ *n* [u] (Agr) agricultura *f*; **animal ~** cría *f* de animales

hush¹ /hʌʃ/ *n* (*no pl*) silencio *m*

hush² *vt* (quieten) hacer* callar; (calm down) calmar

Phrasal verb

• **hush up**

A [v ▸ o ▸ adv, v ▸ adv ▸ o] ‹*scandal/story*› acallar, echar tierra sobre

B [v ▸ adv] (be quiet) (AmE colloq) callarse

hush³ *interj*: **~!** ¡shh!, ¡chitón!

hushed /hʌʃt/ *adj* (*before n*) silencioso; **in ~ tones** en voz muy baja, en murmullos

hush: **~-hush** *adj* (colloq) super secreto (fam); **~ money** *n* [u] (sl) unto *m* de rana (arg) (*dinero con que se compra el silencio de alguien*); **~puppy** *n* (AmE) *torta de maíz frita*

husk¹ /hʌsk/ *n* (of wheat, rice) cáscara *f*, cascarilla *f*; (of maize) chala *f or* (Esp) farfolla *f*

husk² *vt* ‹*wheat/rice*› descascarillar; ‹*maize*› quitarle la chala *or* (Esp) farfolla a

husky¹ /ˈhʌski/ *adj* **-kier, -kiest** ronco

husky² *n* (*pl* **-kies**) husky *mf*, perro, -rra *m,f* esquimal

hussy /ˈhʌsi/ *n* (*pl* **-sies**) (dated *or* hum) fresca *f* (fam); **you brazen ~!** ¡qué desfachatada!

hustings /ˈhʌstɪŋz/ *pl n* **the ~** la campaña electoral

hustle¹ /ˈhʌsəl/ *vt*

A 1 (move hurriedly) (+ *adv compl*): **she was ~d into the car** la metieron en el coche a empujones; **he was ~d away by his bodyguards** sus guardaespaldas se lo llevaron precipitadamente 2 (pressure) apremiar, meterle prisa a, apurar (AmL); **to ~ sb INTO sth/-ING** empujar a algn A algo/+ INF

B (AmE colloq) 1 (obtain aggressively) hacerse* con; **to ~ sth OUT OF sb** sacarle* algo A algn; **to ~ sb FOR sth**: **he ~d them for cigarettes** les dio la lata para que le dieran cigarrillos (fam) 2 (hawk, sell) vender

■ **hustle** *vi*

A 1 (move quickly) darse* prisa, apurarse (AmL) 2 (jostle) empujar

B (AmE) 1 (work energetically) (colloq) trabajar (muy) duro, reventarse* (fam), darle* al callo (Esp fam), sobarse el lomo (Méx fam) 2 (swindle) (sl) hacer* chanchullos (fam), chanchullear (fam) 3 (solicit) (sl) «*prostitute*» hacer* la calle, talonear (Méx fam), patinar (Chi fam), yirar (RPl arg)

hustle² *n*

A [u] 1 (hurry) ajetreo *m*; **the ~ and bustle of the big city** el ajetreo y bullicio de la gran ciudad 2 (energy, initiative) (AmE) empuje *m*, garra *f* (fam)

B [c] (trick, swindle) (AmE colloq) chanchullo *m* (fam)

hustler /ˈhʌslər || ˈhʌslə(r)/ *n* (AmE) 1 (hard worker) (colloq) persona *f* trabajadora 2 (swindler) (sl) estafador, -dora *m,f* 3 (prostitute) (sl) puto, -ta *m,f* (vulg)

hut /hʌt/ *n* 1 (cabin) cabaña *f*; (of mud, straw) choza *f* 2 (hovel) casucha *f*

hutch /ˈhʌtʃ/ *n* (*rabbit* ~) conejera *f*

hwy (AmE) = **highway**

hyacinth /ˈhaɪəsɪnθ/ *n* jacinto *m*

hyaena /haɪˈiːnə/ *n* ▸ **hyena**

hybrid /ˈhaɪbrəd || ˈhaɪbrɪd/ *n* híbrido *m*

hydrangea /haɪˈdreɪndʒə/ *n* hortensia *f*

hydrant /ˈhaɪdrənt/ *n* boca *f* de riego, toma *f* de agua, hidrante *m* (AmC, Col)

hydraulic /haɪˈdrɔːlɪk/ *adj* hidráulico

hydraulics /haɪˈdrɔːlɪks || haɪˈdrɔːlɪks, haɪˈdrɒlɪks/ *n* 1 (+ *sing vb*) hidráulica *f* 2 (hydraulic system) (colloq) (+ *pl vb*) sistema *m* hidráulico

hydro- /ˈhaɪdrəʊ/ *pref* hidro-

hydrochloric acid /ˈhaɪdrəˈklɔːrɪk || ˌhaɪdrəˈklɒrɪk/ *n* [u] ácido *m* clorhídrico

hydroelectric /ˈhaɪdrəʊɪˈlektrɪk/ *adj* hidroeléctrico

hydroelectricity /ˌhaɪdrəʊɪlekˈtrɪsəti/ *n* [u] hidroelectricidad *f*

hydrofoil /ˈhaɪdrəfɔɪl/ *n* (vessel) hidrodeslizador *m*, alíscafo *m*

hydrogen /ˈhaɪdrədʒən/ *n* [u] hidrógeno *m*; (*before n*) **~ peroxide** agua *f‡* oxigenada, peróxido *m* de hidrógeno

hydrometer /haɪˈdrɑːmətər/ *n* hidrómetro *m*

hydroplane /ˈhaɪdrəpleɪn/ *n* (boat) hidroplano *m*

hydroxide /haɪˈdrɑːksaɪd/ *n* [u c] hidróxido *m*

hyena /haɪˈiːnə/ *n* hiena *f*

hygiene /ˈhaɪdʒiːn/ *n* higiene *f*

hygienic /haɪˈdʒiːnɪk/ *adj* higiénico

hygienist /haɪˈdʒiːnəst || ˈhaɪdʒiːnɪst/ *n* higienista *mf*

hymen /ˈhaɪmən/ *n* himen *m*

hymn /hɪm/ *n* 1 (Relig) cántico *m*, himno *m* 2 (paean) himno *m*, canto *m*

hymnal /ˈhɪmnəl/ *n* cantoral *m*, himnario *m*

hymnbook /ˈhɪmbʊk/ *n* cantoral *m*, himnario *m*

hype¹ /haɪp/ *n* [u] (colloq) despliegue *m or* bombo *m* publicitario

hype² *vt* (colloq) promocionar con bombos y platillos *or* (Esp) a bombo y platillo

Phrasal verb

• **hype up** [v ▸ adv ▸ o, v ▸ o ▸ adv] (colloq) ‹*movie*› promocionar con bombos y platillos *or* (Esp) a bombo y platillo; ‹*person*› poner* nervioso

hyper- /ˈhaɪpər || ˈhaɪpə(r)/ *pref* hiper-

hyperactive /ˈhaɪpərˈæktɪv/ *adj* hiperactivo

hyperbole /haɪˈpɜːrbəli || haɪˈpɜːbəli/ *n* [u c] hipérbole *f*

hypermarket /ˈhaɪpərˌmɑːrkət/ *n* (BrE) hipermercado *m*

hypersensitive /ˈhaɪpərˈsensətɪv/ *adj* hipersensible

hypertension /ˈhaɪpərˈtentʃən/ *n* [u] hipertensión *f*

hyperventilate /ˈhaɪpərˈventḷeɪt/ *vi* hiperventilarse

hyphen /ˈhaɪfən/ *n* guión *m*

hyphenate /ˈhaɪfəneɪt/ *vt* 1 escribir* *or* unir con (un) guión 2 **hyphenated** *past p* ‹*word*› con guión

hypnosis /hɪpˈnəʊsəs || hɪpˈnəʊsɪs/ *n* [u] hipnosis *f*; **under ~** hipnotizado, en estado de hipnosis

hypnotic /hɪpˈnɑːtɪk || hɪpˈnɒtɪk/ *adj* ‹*suggestion/state*› hipnótico; ‹*voice/eyes/rhythm*› hipnotizador, hipnotizante

hypnotism /ˈhɪpnətɪzəm/ *n* [u] hipnotismo *m*

hypnotist /ˈhɪpnətəst/ *n* hipnotizador, -dora *m,f*

hypnotize /ˈhɪpnətaɪz/ *vt* hipnotizar*

hypoallergenic /ˈhaɪpəʊˌælerˈdʒenɪk/ *adj* hipoalérgeno

hypochondria /ˈhaɪpəˈkɑːndriə/ *n* [u] hipocondría *f*

hypochondriac /ˈhaɪpəˈkɑːndriæk || ˌhaɪpəˈkɒndriæk/ *n* hipocondríaco, -ca *m,f*

hypocrisy /hɪˈpɑːkrəsi/ *n* [u c] (*pl* **-sies**) hipocresía *f*

hypocrite /ˈhɪpəkrɪt/ *n* hipócrita *mf*

hypocritical /ˈhɪpəˈkrɪtɪkəl/ *adj* hipócrita

hypodermic¹ /ˈhaɪpəˈdɜːrmɪk/ *adj* hipodérmico

hypodermic² *n* (aguja *f*) hipodérmica *f*

hypotenuse /haɪˈpɑːtṇuːs/ *n* hipotenusa *f*

hypothermia /ˈhaɪpəˈθɜːrmiə/ *n* [u] hipotermia *f*

hypothesis /haɪˈpɑːθəsəs/ *n* (*pl* **-ses** /-siːz/) hipótesis *f*

hypothesize /haɪˈpɑːθəsaɪz/ *vi* hacer* hipótesis

■ **hypothesize** *vt* plantear como hipótesis

hypothetical /ˈhaɪpəˈθetɪkəl/ *adj* hipotético

hypothetically /ˈhaɪpəˈθetɪkli/ *adv* hipotéticamente

hysterectomy /ˈhɪstəˈrektəmi/ *n* (*pl* **-mies**) histerectomía *f*

hysteria /hɪˈstɪriə || hɪˈstɪəriə/ *n* [u] histerismo *m*, histeria *f*; **mass ~** histeria colectiva

hysterical /hɪˈsterɪkəl/ *adj* 1 (Psych) histérico 2 (very funny) (colloq) para morirse de (la) risa

hysterically /hɪˈsterɪkli/ *adv* histéricamente; **it was ~ funny** (colloq) era para morirse de (la) risa

hysterics /hɪˈsterɪks/ *pl n* 1 (nervous agitation) histeria *f*, histerismo *m*; **to go into ~** ponerse* histérico; **she was almost in ~** estaba como loca 2 (laughter) (colloq) ataque *m* de risa; **to be in ~** estar* como loco

Hz (= **hertz**) Hz.

i

I, i /aɪ/ *n* I, i *f*; ***to dot the i's and cross the t's*** dar* los últimos toques

I /aɪ/ *pron* yo; **it is I** (frml) soy yo; **I live in London** vivo en Londres

IA = Iowa

IAEA *n* (= **International Atomic Energy Agency**) OIEA *f*

IBAN *n* (= **International Bank Account Number**) IBAN *m*

Iberia /aɪ'bɪriə || aɪ'bɪəriə/ *n* Iberia *f*

Iberian /aɪ'bɪriən || aɪ'bɪəriən/ *adj* ibérico; **the ~ Peninsula** la Península ibérica

ibex /'aɪbeks/ *n* (*pl* ~ *or* ~**es**) cabra *f* montés, íbice *m*

ibid /'ɪbɪd/ *adv* ibíd.

ibidem /'ɪbɪdəm/ *adv* ibídem

ibuprofen /ˌaɪbju:'prəʊfən/ *n* [u] ibuprofeno *m*

ice¹ /aɪs/ *n*

A [u] (frozen water) hielo *m*; **your hands are like ~!** ¡tienes las manos heladas!; **it's as cold as ~ in here** aquí hace un frío que te congelas; ***on ~***: **to put sth on ~** dejar algo en suspenso, aparcar* algo (Esp); ***to skate*** *o* ***walk*** *o* ***tread on thin ~*** andar* por *or* pisar terreno peligroso *or* resbaladizo; ***to break the ~*** (overcome reserve) romper* el hielo; (make a start) (AmE) dar* los primeros pasos; ***to cut no ~***: **it cuts no ~ with me** me deja frío, me deja tal cual

B [c u] **1** (sherbet) (AmE) sorbete *m*, helado *m* de agua (CS), nieve *f* (Méx) **2** (ice cream) (BrE) helado *m*

ice² *vt*

A ‹*drink*› enfriar*; (by adding ice cubes) ponerle* hielo a

B ‹*cake*› bañar (*con fondant*)

Phrasal verb

• **ice over, ice up** [v ▸ adv] (esp BrE) «*river/lake*» helarse*, congelarse; «*window*» cubrirse* de escarcha

ice: **~ age** *n*: **the I~ Age** la edad de hielo, la época glaciar; **~ ax,** (BrE) **axe** *n* piolet *m*, piqueta *f*; **~ bag** *n* ▸ **~ pack**

iceberg /'aɪsbɜ:rg || 'aɪsbɜ:g/ *n* iceberg *m*

iceberg lettuce *n* [c u] lechuga *f* repollada

ice: **~box** *n* **1** (refrigerator) (AmE colloq & dated) refrigerador *m*, nevera *f*, heladera *f* (RPl) **2** (freezing compartment) (BrE) congelador *m*; **~ bucket** *n* hielera *f* (AmL), cubitera *f* (Esp); **~ cap** *n* casquete *m* glaciar *or* de hielo; **~-cold** *adj* helado; **~ cream** *n* [u c] helado *m*; (*before n*) **~-cream parlor** heladería *f*; **~-cream sundae** copa *f* de helado; **~ cube** *n* cubito *m* de hielo

iced /aɪst/ *adj*

A (chilled) helado

B (Culin) glaseado

ice: **~ floe** *n* témpano *m* de hielo; **~ fog** *n* [u c] (AmE) niebla *f* helada; **~ hockey** *n* [u] hockey *m* sobre hielo

Iceland /'aɪslənd/ *n* Islandia *f*

Icelander /'aɪsləndər || 'aɪsləndə(r)/ *n* islandés, -desa *m,f*

Icelandic¹ /aɪs'lændɪk/ *adj* islandés

Icelandic² *n* [u] islandés *m*

ice: **~ lolly** *n* (BrE) paleta *f* helada *or* (Esp) polo *m or* (RPl) palito *m* helado *or* (CS) chupete *m* helado; **~man** /'aɪsmæn/ *n* (*pl* **-men**) (AmE) vendedor *m* de hielo; **~ pack** *n* **1** (for body) bolsa *f* de hielo; **2** (Geog) banco *m* de hielo flotante; **~ pick** *n* punzón *m* (*para romper hielo*); **~ rink** *n* (BrE) pista *f* de (patinaje sobre) hielo; **~ skate** *n* patín *m* de cuchilla; **~-skate** *vi* patinar sobre hielo; **~ skating** *n* [u] patinaje *m* sobre hielo

icicle /'aɪsɪkəl/ *n* carámbano *m* (de hielo)

icily /'aɪsəli || 'aɪsɪli/ *adv* glacialmente, con mucha frialdad

icing /'aɪsɪŋ/ *n* (Culin) glaseado *m*

icing sugar *n* [u] (BrE) azúcar *m or f* glas(é) *or* (RPl) impalpable *or* (Chi) flor *or* (Col) en polvo

icon /'aɪkɑ:n || 'aɪkɒn/ *n* icono *m*, ícono *m*

iconic /aɪ'kɑ:nɪk || aɪ'kɒnɪk/ *adj* icónico

iconoclast /aɪ'kɑ:nə'klæst || aɪ'kɒnəklæst/ *n* iconoclasta *mf*

iconography /'aɪkə'nɑ:grəfi || ˌaɪkə'nɒgrəfi/ *n* [u] iconografía *f*

icy /'aɪsi/ *adj* **icier, iciest** **1** ‹*wind/rain*› helado, glacial, gélido (liter); ‹*feet/hands*› helado; (*as adv*) **~ cold** helado **2** ‹*stare/reception*› glacial **3** ‹*roads/ground*› cubierto de hielo

ID **1** = **identification** **2** = **Idaho**

ID card *n* carné *or* carnet *m* de identidad, cédula *f* de identidad (AmL), identificación *f* (Méx)

idea /aɪ'di:ə || aɪ'dɪə/ *n*

A **1** (plan, suggestion) idea *f*; **then I had an ~** entonces se me ocurrió una idea; **it's a good ~ to check it regularly** conviene revisarlo con regularidad; **that's not a bad ~** no es mala idea; **it wasn't my ~** no fue idea mía **2** (purpose, principle) idea *f*; **the whole ~ of the operation was to attract publicity** habían hecho la operación con la idea de atraer publicidad; **that's the general ~** de eso se trata; **you get the ~ don't you?** entiendes ¿no?

B (notion, impression) idea *f*; **my ~ of Ireland** la idea que yo tengo *or* me hago de Irlanda; **that's not my ~ of fun** eso no es lo que yo entiendo por diversión; **the very ~!** ¡a quién se le ocurre!; **can you give me some ~ of what happened?** ¿me puedes dar una idea de lo que pasó?; **I've got a rough ~ of what you mean** ya me hago una idea aproximada de lo que quieres decir; **you have no ~ what I went through** no te puedes imaginar lo que pasé; **where is he? — (I've) no ~!** ¿dónde está? — (no tengo) ni idea; **she has no ~ how to handle people** no tiene idea de cómo tratar a la gente; **whatever gave you that ~?** ¿de dónde sacaste esa idea?; **you've got the wrong ~** has entendido mal; **to put ~s in** *o* **into sb's head, to give sb ~s** meterle ideas en la cabeza a algn

C (view) idea *f*, opinión *f*

ideal¹ /aɪ'di:əl/ *adj* ideal

ideal² *n* [u c] ideal *m*

idealism /aɪ'di:əlɪzəm/ *n* [u] idealismo *m*

idealistic /aɪ'di:ə'lɪstɪk || ˌaɪdɪə'lɪstɪk/ *adj* idealista

idealize /aɪ'di:əlaɪz || aɪ'dɪəlaɪz/ *vt* idealizar*

ideally /aɪ'di:əli || aɪ'dɪəli/ *adv* **1** ‹*located/placed/equipped*› inmejorablemente; **they are ~ suited** están hechos el uno para el otro, forman una pareja ideal **2** (*indep*): **~, no one would have to do it** lo ideal sería que nadie tuviera que hacerlo

identical /aɪ'dentɪkəl/ *adj* idéntico; **~ twins** gemelos *mpl* univitelinos (téc), gemelos *mpl* (AmL), gemelos *mpl* idénticos (Esp); **to be ~ TO** *o* **WITH sth** ser* idéntico A algo

identically /aɪ'dentɪkli/ *adv* ‹*dressed*› de idéntico modo, idénticamente; **they're ~ priced** tienen exactamente el mismo precio

identifiable /aɪ'dentəfaɪəbəl || aɪ'dentɪ,faɪəbəl/ *adj* identificable

identification /aɪ'dentəfə'keɪʃən || aɪ,dentɪfɪ'keɪʃən/ *n* [u] 1 (act of identifying) identificación *f* 2 (evidence of identity): **have you got any ~?** ¿tiene algún documento que acredite su identidad?; (*before n*) **~ papers** documentos *mpl*, papeles *mpl*, documentación *f*

identification parade *n* (BrE) rueda *f* de presos *or* de sospechosos *or* de reconocimiento *or* de identificación

identify /aɪ'dentəfaɪ || aɪ'dentɪfaɪ/ **-fies, -fying, -fied** *vt*
A 1 ‹*person/species*› identificar*; ‹*body*› identificar*, reconocer* 2 ‹*problem*› identificar*
B (associate, equate) identificar*
■ *v refl* 1 (reveal identity) **to ~ oneself** identificarse* 2 (link) **to ~ oneself WITH sth/sb** asociarse CON algo/algn
■ **identify** *vi* **to ~ WITH sb/sth** identificarse* CON algn/algo

Identikit® /aɪ'dentəkɪt || aɪ'dentɪkɪt/ *n* [u]: **~ picture** Identikit® *m*, retrato *m* hablado (AmL), retrato *m* robot (Esp)

identity /aɪ'dentəti/ *n* (*pl* **-ties**) identidad *f*; **you'll need some proof of ~** necesitará algún documento que acredite su identidad; (*before n*) **~ bracelet** esclava *f*; **~ card** carné *m or* (AmL tb) cédula *f* de identidad; **~ theft** robo *m* de identidad

ideological /'aɪdiə'lɑːdʒɪkəl || ,aɪdiə'lɒdʒɪkəl/ *adj* ideológico

ideology /'aɪdi'ɑːlədʒi/ *n* [u c] (*pl* **-gies**) ideología *f*

idiocy /'ɪdiəsi/ *n* [u c] (*pl* **-cies**) idiotez *f*, imbecilidad *f*

idiom /'ɪdiəm/ *n*
A [c] (expression) modismo *m*, giro *m* (idiomático)
B [u c] (language) lenguaje *m*

idiomatic /'ɪdiə'mætɪk/ *adj* idiomático; **~ expression** ▸**idiom A**

idiosyncrasy /'ɪdiə'sɪŋkrəsi/ *n* [c u] (*pl* **-sies**) idiosincrasia *f*; **he has his little idiosyncrasies** tiene sus pequeñas manías *or* rarezas

idiosyncratic /'ɪdiəsɪn'krætɪk || ,ɪdiəsɪŋ'krætɪk/ *adj* idiosincrásico

idiot /'ɪdiət/ *n* (foolish person) idiota *mf*, imbécil *mf*; **you stupid ~!** ¡idiota *or* imbécil!

idiotic /'ɪdi'ɑːtɪk || ,ɪdi'ɒtɪk/ *adj* idiota; **it was an ~ thing to say** fue una idiotez decir eso

idle[1] /'aɪdl/ *adj* **idler** /'aɪdlər || 'aɪdlə(r)/, **idlest** /'aɪdləst || 'aɪdlɪst/
A 1 (not in use or employment): **to be ~** «*worker*» no tener* trabajo, estar* sin hacer nada; «*machine/factory*» estar* parado; **don't let your money lie ~** no deje ocioso su dinero, no deje dormir su dinero 2 (unoccupied) ‹*hours/moment*› de ocio
B (lazy) holgazán, haragán, flojo (fam)
C 1 (frivolous): **it's just ~ chatter** no es más que cháchara (fam); **it was ~ curiosity** era pura curiosidad; **~ speculation** conjeturas *fpl* inútiles 2 ‹*promise*› vano

idle[2] *vi* 1 (be lazy) holgazanear, haraganear, flojear (fam) 2 (Auto) «*engine*» andar* *or* marchar al ralentí

Phrasal verb

• **idle away** [v ▸ adv ▸ o]: **they ~d away the hours chatting** pasaban las horas muertas charlando

idleness /'aɪdl̩nəs || 'aɪdl̩nɪs/ *n* 1 (inactivity — involuntary) inactividad *f*, desocupación *f*; (— reprehensible) ociosidad *f*, ocio *m*; (— pleasant) ocio *m*, descanso *m* 2 (laziness) holgazanería *f*, haraganería *f*, flojera *f* (fam)

idler /'aɪdlər || 'aɪdlə(r)/ *n* haragán, -gana *m,f*, vago, -ga *m,f* (fam), flojo, -ja *m,f* (fam)

idling speed *n* velocidad *f* de ralentí

idol /'aɪdl̩/ *n* ídolo *m*

idolatry /aɪ'dɑːlətri || aɪ'dɒlətri/ *n* [u] idolatría *f*

idolize /'aɪdl̩aɪz/ *vt* idolatrar

I'd've /'aɪdəv/ = **I would have**

idyll /'aɪdl̩ || 'ɪdɪl/ *n* idilio *m*

idyllic /aɪ'dɪlɪk || ɪ'dɪlɪk/ *adj* idílico

i.e. /'aɪ'iː/ (that is) (in writing) i.e.; (in speech) esto es, a saber

if[1] /ɪf/ *conj*
A 1 (on condition that) si; **~ you're good, I'll read you a story** si te portas bien, te leeré un cuento; **I'd help you ~ I could** te ayudaría si pudiera; **~ I were you, I wouldn't do it** yo en tu lugar *or* yo que tú, no lo haría 2 **if not**: **they were undernourished, ~ not (yet) actually starving** estaban desnutridos, si bien no se estaban muriendo de inanición; **she was very offhand, ~ not downright rude** estuvo muy brusca, por no decir verdaderamente grosera 3 **if nothing else** aunque no sea más que eso 4 **if only**: **~ only she could have seen him!** ¡si lo pudiera haber visto! 5 **if so** (*as linker*) si es así, de ser así
B (whether) si; **they asked ~ she had left** preguntaron si se había ido; **she doesn't care ~ you win or lose** no le importa que pierdas o ganes
C (though) aunque, si bien; **it's a good plot, ~ a complicated one** es un buen argumento, aunque complicado *or* si bien es complicado
D 1 (in requests): **~ you'll all follow me, please** síganme, por favor, ¿quieren seguirme, por favor? 2 (indicating surprise) (*with neg*): **well, ~ it isn't Mike Britton!** ¡pero si es Mike Britton!

if[2] *n*: **a lot of ~s and buts** muchas condiciones y salvedades

iffy /'ɪfi/ *adj* **iffier, iffiest** (colloq) 1 (uncertain) ‹*situation*› dudoso, incierto 2 ‹*person*› sospechoso, que da mala espina (fam)

igloo /'ɪgluː/ *n* iglú *m*

ignite /ɪg'naɪt/ *vt* prenderle fuego a, inflamar (frml)
■ **ignite** *vi* «*fuel/paper*» prenderse fuego, inflamarse (frml)

ignition /ɪg'nɪʃən/ *n* 1 [u] (act) encendido *m*, ignición *f* (frml); (*before n*) **~ key** llave *f* de contacto *or* (AmL tb) del arranque 2 (mechanism) (Auto) encendido *m*; **to turn on** *o* (BrE also) **switch on the ~** darle* al contacto *or* (AmL tb) al arranque

ignominious /'ɪgnə'mɪniəs/ *adj* (frml) ignominioso (frml)

ignominy /'ɪgnəmɪni/ *n* [u c] (*pl* **-nies**) (frml) ignominia *f* (frml), oprobio *m* (frml)

ignoramus /'ɪgnə'reɪməs/ *n* (hum) inculto, -ta *m,f*, analfabeto, -ta *m,f* (fam)

ignorance /'ɪgnərəns/ *n* [u] ignorancia *f*; **I was kept in ~ of the contents of the will** me ocultaron el contenido del testamento; **he acted in ~ of the enemy's intentions** actuó desconociendo *or* ignorando las intenciones del enemigo; **~ *is bliss*** ojos que no ven (corazón que no siente)

ignorant /'ɪgnərənt/ *adj* 1 (lacking knowledge) ignorante; **I'm totally ~ about politics** no tengo ni idea *or* no sé nada de política; **to be ~ OF sth** ignorar *or* desconocer* algo 2 (rude) (BrE colloq) maleducado

ignore /ɪg'nɔːr || ɪg'nɔː(r)/ *vt* ‹*warning*› hacer* caso omiso de; **he chose to ~ the remark** prefirió ignorar *or* pasar por alto el comentario; **we can't ~ the fact that ...** no podemos dejar de tener en cuenta el hecho de que ...; ‹*person*› ignorar; **just ~ him** no le hagas caso, haz como si no lo oyeras

iguana /ɪ'gwɑːnə/ *n* iguana *f*, garrobo *m* (AmC)

IL = **Illinois**

ilk /ɪlk/ *n* tipo *m*, clase *f*; **people of that ~** la gente de ese tipo *or* esa clase *or* (pey) esa calaña *or* ralea

ill[1] /ɪl/ *adj*
A **-er, -est** (unwell) enfermo, malo (Esp, Méx fam); **she's ~** está enferma; **he looked ~** tenía mala cara; **to feel ~** sentirse* mal; **to be taken ~** ponerse* enfermo, enfermarse (AmL); **to fall ~** enfermar, caer* enfermo
B (bad) (*before n*): **~ effects** efectos *mpl* negativos *or* adversos; **his ~ health** su mala salud

ill[2] *adv* (*no comp*) 1 (hardly): **I can ~ afford to buy a new car** mal puedo yo permitirme comprar un coche nuevo 2 (badly) (frml) mal; **to speak/think ~ of sb** hablar/pensar* mal de algn

ill[3] *n* mal *m*

ill. = **illustrated/illustration(s)**

Ill = **Illinois**

I'll /aɪl/ = **I will, I shall**

ill: **~-advised** /'ɪləd'vaɪzd/ *adj* ‹*action*› desacertado; **you would be ~-advised to go** no sería aconsejable que

i

fueras; ~ **at ease** *adj* (*pred*) [1] (uncomfortable) incómodo [2] (anxious) inquieto; ~**-bred** /ˈɪlˈbred/ *adj* sin educación, maleducado; ~**-considered** /ˈɪlkənˈsɪdərd || ˌɪlkənˈsɪdəd/ *adj* poco meditado; ~**-disposed** /ˈɪldɪsˈpəʊzd/ *adj* **to be ~-disposed TOWARD sb** estar* predispuesto EN CONTRA DE algn

illegal /ɪˈliːgəl/ *adj* [1] (unlawful) ilegal; ~ **immigrant** *o* (AmE also) **alien** inmigrante *mf* ilegal; **to make sth ~** prohibir* algo [2] (AmE Sport) antirreglamentario

illegible /ɪˈledʒəbəl/ *adj* ilegible

illegitimate /ˈɪlrˈdʒɪtəmət || ˌɪlrˈdʒɪtɪmət/ *adj* ilegítimo

ill: ~**-equipped** /ˈɪlrˈkwɪpt/ *adj* ‹*classroom/troops*› mal equipado; **I was ~-equipped for such a task** no estaba preparado para una tarea así; ~**-fated** /ˈɪlˈfeɪtəd || ˌɪlˈfeɪtɪd/ *adj* infortunado, desventurado, malhadado (liter); ~**-favored**, (BrE) ~**-favoured** /ˈɪlˈfeɪvərd || ˌɪlˈfeɪvəd/ *adj* (arch *or* liter) poco agraciado, mal parecido; ~ **feeling** *n* resentimiento *m*, rencor *m*; ~**-founded** /ˈɪlˈfaʊndəd || ˌɪlˈfaʊndɪd/ *adj* ‹*belief/suspicion*› infundado; ‹*rumor*› sin base, infundado; ~**-gotten** /ˈɪlˈgɑːtn̩ || ˌɪlˈgɒtn̩/*adj*: ~**-gotten gains** dinero *m* mal habido; ~**-humored**, (BrE) ~**-humoured** /ˈɪlˈhjuːmərd || ˌɪlˈhjuːməd/*adj* (frml) malhumorado

illicit /ɪˈlɪsət || ɪˈlɪsɪt/ *adj* ilícito

ill-informed /ˈɪlɪnˈfɔːrmd || ˌɪlɪnˈfɔːmd/ *adj* mal informado

i

illiteracy /ɪˈlɪtərəsi/ *n* [u] analfabetismo *m*

illiterate¹ /ɪˈlɪtərət/ *adj* [1] (unable to read or write) analfabeto [2] (linguistically incompetent) ‹*person*› ignorante, analfabeto; ‹*letter*› lleno de faltas

illiterate² *n* analfabeto, -ta *m,f*

ill-mannered /ˈɪlˈmænərd || ˌɪlˈmænəd/ *adj* maleducado, descortés

illness /ˈɪlnəs || ˈɪlnɪs/ *n* [u c] enfermedad *f*, dolencia *f* (frml)

illogical /ɪˈlɑːdʒɪkəl || ɪˈlɒdʒɪkəl/ *adj* ilógico

ill: ~**-suited** /ˌɪlˈsuːtəd || ˌɪlˈsuːtɪd/ *adj* poco indicado; **he's clearly ~-suited to** *o* **for the job** es claramente una persona poco indicada para el puesto; **they were ~-suited to** *o* **for each other** no estaban hechos el uno para el otro; ~**-treat** /ˈɪlˈtriːt/ *vt* maltratar; ~**-treatment** /ˈɪlˈtriːtmənt/ *n* [u] malos tratos *mpl*, maltrato *m*

illuminate /ɪˈluːməneɪt || ɪˈluːmɪneɪt/ *vt*
A ‹*room/street*› iluminar
B (Art) ‹*manuscript*› iluminar, miniar
C ‹*problem*› esclarecer*, dilucidar

illumination /ɪˈluːməˈneɪʃən || ɪˌluːmɪˈneɪʃən/ *n*
A [1] [u] (lighting) iluminación *f* [2] **illuminations** *pl* (decorative lighting) (BrE) luces *fpl*
B [c u] (Art) iluminación *f*, miniado *m*

illusion /ɪˈluːʒən/ *n* [1] [c u] (false appearance): **to give** *o* **create an ~ of sth** dar* la impresión de algo; (Art) crear la ilusión de algo; **an optical ~** una ilusión óptica [2] [c] (false idea) ilusión *f*; **she's under the ~ that they'll pay for it** se cree que *or* se hace ilusiones de que ellos lo van a pagar

illusory /ɪˈluːsəri/ *adj* (frml) ilusorio

illustrate /ˈɪləstreɪt/ *vt*
A ‹*book/magazine*› ilustrar
B [1] (explain by examples) ilustrar [2] (show) poner* de manifiesto, demostrar*

illustration /ˈɪləˈstreɪʃən/ *n*
A [c u] (picture, technique) ilustración *f*
B (example) ejemplo *m*

illustrator /ˈɪləstreɪtər || ˈɪləstreɪtə(r)/ *n* ilustrador, -dora *m,f*

illustrious /ɪˈlʌstriəs/ *adj* (liter) ‹*person/family*› ilustre, insigne (frml)

ill will *n* [u] [1] (hostility) inquina *f*, animadversión *f* [2] (spite) rencor *m*

ILO *n* (= **International Labor Organization**) OIT *f*

I'm /aɪm/ = **I am**

image /ˈɪmɪdʒ/ *n*
A (picture, statue) imagen *f*
B (public persona) imagen *f*; **to change one's ~** cambiar de imagen; **corporate ~** imagen de empresa
C [1] (likeness) imagen *f*; ***to be the (spitting) ~*** *o* ***spit and ~ of sb*** ser* la viva imagen *or* el vivo retrato de algn [2] (embodiment) viva imagen *f*, personificación *f*

imagery /ˈɪmɪdʒəri/ *n* [u] imaginería *f*, imágenes *fpl*

imaginable /ɪˈmædʒənəbəl || ɪˈmædʒɪnəbəl/ *adj* imaginable; **he's the laziest person ~** es la persona más perezosa que se pueda imaginar

imaginary /ɪˈmædʒəneri || ɪˈmædʒɪnəri/ *adj* imaginario

imagination /ɪˈmædʒəˈneɪʃən || ɪˌmædʒɪˈneɪʃən/ *n* [1] [u c] (faculty) imaginación *f*; **it's only your ~** son imaginaciones *or* figuraciones tuyas; **to capture the public ~** despertar* *or* atraer* el interés del público; **by no stretch of the ~** ni remotamente; **what were they doing? — use your ~!** ¿qué estaban haciendo? — pues, imagínatelo [2] [u] (inventiveness) inventiva *f*, imaginación *f*, idea *f*

imaginative /ɪˈmædʒənətɪv || ɪˈmædʒɪnətɪv/ *adj* imaginativo; **she's very ~** tiene mucha imaginación, es muy imaginativa

imagine /ɪˈmædʒən || ɪˈmædʒɪn/ *vt* [1] (picture to oneself) imaginarse; **I can just ~ her saying that** ya me la imagino diciendo eso; **(just) ~, leaving the poor child alone!** ¡figúrate *or* imagínate! ¡dejar al pobre niño solo!; **you can ~ how I felt!** ¡te imaginarás cómo me sentí!; **we can't begin to ~** no nos hacemos ni la más remota idea [2] (fancy, mistakenly suppose): **you're imagining things** son imaginaciones *or* figuraciones tuyas; **he ~d he was Napoleon** se creía que era Napoleón [3] (assume, believe) imaginarse, figurarse; **I ~ she's very tired** me imagino *or* me figuro que estará muy cansada

imbalance /ɪmˈbæləns/ *n* [c u] desequilibrio *m*

imbecile /ˈɪmbəsəl || ˈɪmbəsiːl/ *n* imbécil *mf*; **you ~!** ¡imbécil!

imbed /ɪmˈbed/ *vt/v refl* **-dd-** (AmE) ▸ **embed**

imbibe /ɪmˈbaɪb/ *vt* (frml) [1] (drink) beber, ingerir* (frml) [2] ‹*knowledge*› imbuirse* de (frml), empaparse de

imbue /ɪmˈbjuː/ *vt* (frml) **to ~ sb WITH sth** imbuir* a algn DE algo (frml)

IMF *n* (= **International Monetary Fund**) FMI *m*

imitate /ˈɪməteɪt || ˈɪmɪteɪt/ *vt* [1] (copy) ‹*person/mannerism*› imitar; (trying to be funny) imitar, remedar [2] (resemble) imitar

imitation¹ /ˈɪməˈteɪʃən || ˌɪmɪˈteɪʃən/ *n* [1] [u] (copying) imitación *f*; **to learn by ~** aprender imitando *or* por imitación [2] [c] (impersonation) imitación *f* [3] [c] (copy) imitación *f*; **beware of ~s** tenga cuidado con las imitaciones

imitation² *adj* ‹*gold/pearls*› de imitación

immaculate /ɪˈmækjələt || ɪˈmækjʊlət/ *adj* [1] ‹*clothes/room*› impecable, inmaculado; **she looked ~** estaba impecable [2] ‹*performance/taste*› impecable

Immaculate Conception *n* **the ~ ~** la Inmaculada Concepción

immaterial /ˈɪməˈtɪriəl || ˌɪməˈtɪəriəl/ *adj* (unimportant) irrelevante

immature /ˈɪməˈtʊr || ˌɪməˈtjʊə(r)/ *adj* [1] ‹*tree/animal*› joven; ‹*fruit*› verde, inmaduro [2] (childish) ‹*person/attitude*› inmaduro

immaturity /ˈɪməˈtʊrəti || ˌɪməˈtjʊərəti/ *n* [u] inmadurez *f*

immeasurable /ɪˈmeʒərəbəl/ *adj* [1] ‹*distance/amount*› inconmensurable, inmenso [2] ‹*harm*› incalculable

immediate /ɪˈmiːdiət/ *adj*
A [1] (instant, prompt) inmediato; **to take ~ action** actuar* inmediatamente; **the law will take ~ effect** la ley entrará en vigor inmediatamente [2] ‹*problem/need*› urgente, apremiante, perentorio; **my own ~ future is of more concern to me** a mí me preocupa más mi propio futuro
B (*before n*) (close): **in the ~ future** en el futuro inmediato; **in the ~ vicinity** en las inmediaciones, en los alrededores; **my ~ superior** mi superior inmediato *or* directo; **my ~ family** mis familiares más cercanos

immediately /ɪˈmiːdiətli/ *adv*
A [1] (at once) inmediatamente, de inmediato; **it's not ~ obvious** no resulta obvio a primera vista [2] (*as conj*) (BrE) en cuanto; **I'll send you a cheque ~ the goods arrive** le mandaré un cheque en cuanto llegue la mercancía
B [1] ‹*before/after*› inmediatamente; **my room is ~ above**

yours mi habitación está justo encima de la tuya 2 (directly) (BrE) directamente

immemorial /ˈɪməˈmɔːriəl/ *adj* (liter) inmemorial (liter); **from** *o* **since time ~** desde tiempos inmemoriales

immense /ɪˈmens/ *adj* ‹*problem/difference*› inmenso, enorme; ‹*person*› enorme

immensely /ɪˈmensli/ *adv* 1 ‹*enjoy/like*› enormemente 2 ‹*popular/powerful*› inmensamente, enormemente

immensity /ɪˈmensəti/ *n* [u] inmensidad *f*

immerse /ɪˈmɜːrs || ɪˈmɜːs/ *vt* 1 (submerge) **to ~ sth/sb (IN sth)** sumergir* algo/a algn (EN algo) 2 (absorb, involve) **to be ~d IN sth** estar* absorto *or* enfrascado EN algo

■ *v refl* **to ~ oneself IN sth**: **he ~d himself in his work** se metió de lleno *or* se sumergió en su trabajo

immersion /ɪˈmɜːrʒən || ɪˈmɜːʃən/ *n* [u] 1 (in liquid) (frml) inmersión *f* 2 (in work, activity) absorción *f*, enfrascamiento *m*

immersion heater *n* calentador *m* eléctrico (*de agua*), termo *m* (Chi), termofón *m* (RPl)

immigrant /ˈɪməgrənt || ˈɪmɪgrənt/ *n* inmigrante *mf*; (*before n*) ‹*worker/population*› inmigrante

immigration /ˈɪməˈgreɪʃən || ˌɪmɪˈgreɪʃən/ *n* 1 [u] inmigración *f* 2 **~ (control)** (at border, airport) (*no art*) (control *m* de) inmigración *f or* migración *f*

imminent /ˈɪmənənt || ˈɪmɪnənt/ *adj* inminente

immobile /ɪˈməʊbəl || ɪˈməʊbaɪl/ *adj* (motionless) inmóvil; (unable to walk) inmovilizado

immobilize /ɪˈməʊbəlaɪz || ɪˈməʊbɪlaɪz/ *vt* ‹*vehicle/limb*› inmovilizar*

immobilizer /ɪˈməʊbəlaɪz || ɪˈməʊbɪlaɪz/ *n* inmobilizador *m*

immoderate /ɪˈmɑːdərət || ɪˈmɒdərət/ *adj* 1 ‹*demands/appetite*› desmedido, desmesurado 2 ‹*views*› radical, extremista

immodest /ɪˈmɑːdəst || ɪˈmɒdɪst/ *adj* 1 (conceited) presuntuoso, inmodesto 2 (indecent) ‹*behavior/suggestion*› impúdico, inmodesto; ‹*dress*› poco recatado

immodesty /ɪˈmɑːdəsti || ɪˈmɒdɪsti/ *n* [u] 1 (conceit) falta *f* de modestia, inmodestia *f*, presunción *f* 2 (indecency) impudicia *f*, falta *f* de pudor, inmodestia *f*

immoral /ɪˈmɔːrəl || ɪˈmɒrəl/ *adj* inmoral; **to live off ~ earnings** (frml) vivir del proxenetismo *or* lenocinio

immorality /ˈɪmɔːˈræləti || ˌɪməˈræləti/ *n* [u] inmoralidad *f*

immortal¹ /ɪˈmɔːrtl̩ || ɪˈmɔːtl̩/ *adj* ‹*being/soul/words*› inmortal

immortal² *n* inmortal *mf*

immortality /ˈɪmɔːrˈtæləti || ˌɪmɔːˈtæləti/ *n* [u] inmortalidad *f*

immortalize /ɪˈmɔːrtl̩aɪz || ɪˈmɔːtl̩aɪz/ *vt* inmortalizar*

immovable /ɪˈmuːvəbəl/ *adj* 1 ‹*obstacle/object*› inamovible 2 (Law) ‹*property/asset*› inmueble

immune /ɪˈmjuːn/ *adj*

A 1 (not susceptible) **to be ~ TO sth** ser* inmune A algo; **I've had measles, so I'm ~** ya he tenido el sarampión, así que estoy inmunizado; **she was ~ to persuasion** nada logró persuadirla 2 (*before n*) ‹*system/response*› inmunológico; **~ deficiency** inmunodeficiencia *f*

B (exempt) **~ FROM sth**: **to be ~ from taxation** tener* inmunidad fiscal; **none of us is ~ from the effects of the recession** a todos nos afecta la recesión

immunity /ɪˈmjuːnəti/ *n* [u] 1 (Med) inmunidad *f* 2 (exemption): **parliamentary ~** inmunidad *f* parlamentaria

immunization /ˈɪmjənəˈzeɪʃən || ˌɪmjʊnaɪˈzeɪʃən/ *n* [u c] inmunización *f*

immunize /ˈɪmjənaɪz || ˈɪmjʊnaɪz/ *vt* inmunizar*; **to ~ sb AGAINST sth** inmunizar* a algn CONTRA algo

immunodeficient /ˌɪmjənəʊdɪˈfɪʃənt || ˌɪmjʊnəʊdɪˈfɪʃənt/ *adj* inmunodeficiente

immunologist /ˌɪmjəˈnɑːlədʒəst || ˌɪmjʊˈnɒlədʒɪst/ *n* inmunólogo, -ga *m,f*

immutable /ɪˈmjuːtəbəl/ *adj* (frml) inmutable

imp /ɪmp/ *n* diablillo *m* (fam)

impact /ˈɪmpækt/ *n* [u c] 1 (in collision) impacto *m*; **it exploded on ~** estalló al hacer impacto 2 (effect) impacto *m*; **this will have little ~ on the budget deficit** esto hará muy poca mella en el déficit presupuestario

impacted /ɪmˈpæktəd || ɪmˈpæktɪd/ *adj* ‹*tooth*› impactado

impair /ɪmˈper || ɪmˈpeə(r)/ *vt* ‹*hearing*› afectar, dañar; ‹*health*› afectar, perjudicar*; ‹*efficiency*› afectar, reducir*; **~ed vision/hearing** problemas *mpl* de vista/audición

impairment /ɪmˈpermənt || ɪmˈpeəmənt/ *n* [u c] (physical, mental) discapacidad *f*; **visual ~** problemas *fpl* de vista; **speech ~** impedimento *m* del habla; **I foresee no further ~s to her progress** no veo más impedimentos para su progreso

impale /ɪmˈpeɪl/ *vt* **to ~ sth/sb ON sth** ‹*on a sword/spear*› atravesar* algo/a algn CON algo; **she fell and was ~d on the railings** cayó y la reja le atravesó el cuerpo

impalpable /ɪmˈpælpəbəl/ *adj* 1 (intangible) impalpable 2 (hard to understand) sumamente sutil

impart /ɪmˈpɑːrt || ɪmˈpɑːt/ *vt* (frml) 1 ‹*news*› comunicar*; ‹*knowledge*› impartir, transmitir; ‹*secret*› divulgar* 2 ‹*feeling/quality*› conferir* (frml), dar*

impartial /ɪmˈpɑːrʃəl || ɪmˈpɑːʃəl/ *adj* imparcial

impartiality /ɪmˈpɑːrʃiˈæləti || ɪmˌpɑːʃiˈæləti/ *n* [u] imparcialidad *f*

impassable /ɪmˈpæsəbəl || ɪmˈpɑːsəbəl/ *adj* ‹*river/barrier*› infranqueable; ‹*road*› intransitable

impasse /ˈɪmpæs || ˈæmpæs/ *n* impasse *m*, punto *m* muerto; **to be at** *o* **in an ~** estar* en un impasse *or* en punto muerto

impassioned /ɪmˈpæʃənd/ *adj* apasionado, vehemente

impassive /ɪmˈpæsɪv/ *adj* impasible, imperturbable

impassively /ɪmˈpæsɪvli/ *adv* sin inmutarse

impatience /ɪmˈpeɪʃəns/ *n* [u] impaciencia *f*

impatient /ɪmˈpeɪʃənt/ *adj* 1 (unwilling to wait) (*usu pred*) impaciente 2 (irritable) ‹*person*› impaciente; ‹*gesture/voice*› de impaciencia; **to get ~ WITH sb** impacientarse CON algn

impatiently /ɪmˈpeɪʃəntli/ *adv* con impaciencia

impeach /ɪmˈpiːtʃ/ *vt*

A (Law) *acusar a un alto cargo de delitos cometidos en el desempeño de sus funciones*

B (discredit) ‹*testimony/motives*› impugnar, poner* en tela de juicio; ‹*witness*› tachar

impeachment /ɪmˈpiːtʃmənt/ *n*: *acusación formulada contra un alto cargo por delitos cometidos en el desempeño de sus funciones*

impeccable /ɪmˈpekəbəl/ *adj* impecable; **his French was ~** hablaba un francés impecable

impeccably /ɪmˈpekəbli/ *adv* impecablemente

impecunious /ˈɪmpɪˈkjuːniəs/ *adj* (liter *o* hum) sin peculio (liter *o* hum), pobretón (fam & hum)

impede /ɪmˈpiːd/ *vt* ‹*progress/communications*› dificultar, obstaculizar*; ‹*movement*› dificultar, impedir*; **to ~ the flow of traffic** obstruir* el tráfico

impediment /ɪmˈpedəmənt || ɪmˈpedɪmənt/ *n* 1 (hindrance) impedimento *m*; **~ TO sth** impedimento PARA algo; **lawful ~** impedimento *m* 2 (physical defect) defecto *m*; **a speech ~** un defecto del habla

impel /ɪmˈpel/ *vt* **-ll-** 1 (oblige) (frml) impeler (frml) 2 (push, move) impeler

impending /ɪmˈpendɪŋ/ *adj* (*before n*) inminente

impenetrable /ɪmˈpenətrəbəl/ *adj* 1 ‹*jungle/darkness*› impenetrable 2 ‹*subject*› impenetrable, abstruso (frml)

impenitent /ɪmˈpenətənt || ɪmˈpenɪtənt/ *adj* impenitente

imperative¹ /ɪmˈperətɪv/ *adj*

A 1 (essential) imprescindible, fundamental; **it is ~ that you be there** es fundamental que estés ahí 2 ‹*need*› imperioso, imperativo 3 (authoritative) (frml) imperioso, imperativo

B (Ling) ‹*mood*› imperativo; ‹*sentence*› en imperativo

imperative² *n*

A (Ling) imperativo *m*

B (compelling need) imperativo *m*

imperceptible /ˈɪmpərˈseptəbəl || ˌɪmpəˈseptəbəl/ *adj* imperceptible

imperfect¹ /ɪmˈpɜːrfɪkt || ɪmˈpɜːfɪkt/ *adj*

A (flawed) imperfecto; **these goods are slightly ~** estos artículos tienen algún pequeño defecto

B (Ling) imperfecto

imperfect² *n* imperfecto *m*

imperfection /ˈɪmpərˈfekʃən || ˌɪmpəˈfekʃən/ *n* [c u] imperfección *f*

imperial /ɪmˈpɪriəl || ɪmˈpɪəriəl/ *adj*

A *also* **Imperial** (of empire) (*before n*) imperial, del imperio

B (liter) ‹*pomp/bearing*› majestuoso, señorial

C *also* **Imperial** ‹*measures/weights*› *del antiguo sistema británico*

imperialism /ɪmˈpɪriəlɪzəm || ɪmˈpɪəriəlɪzəm/ *n* [u] imperialismo *m*

imperialist¹ /ɪmˈpɪriələst || ɪmˈpɪəriəlɪst/ *adj* imperialista

imperialist² *n* imperialista *mf*

imperil /ɪmˈperəl || ɪmˈperɪl, ɪmˈperəl/ *vt*, (BrE) **-ll-** poner* en peligro, hacer* peligrar

imperious /ɪmˈpɪriəs || ɪmˈpɪəriəs/ *adj* imperioso

impermeable /ɪmˈpɜːrmiəbəl || ɪmˈpɜːmiəbəl/ *adj* impermeable

impersonal /ɪmˈpɜːrsn̩əl || ɪmˈpɜːsənl̩/ *adj* impersonal

impersonate /ɪmˈpɜːrsəneɪt || ɪmˈpɜːsəneɪt/ *vt* **1** (pretend to be) hacerse* pasar por **2** (mimic) imitar, remedar, impersonar (Méx)

impersonation /ɪmˈpɜːrsəˈneɪʃən || ɪmˌpɜːsəˈneɪʃən/ *n* **1** (with intent to deceive) suplantación *f* **2** [u c] (mimicry) imitación *f*

impersonator /ɪmˈpɜːrsəneɪtər || ɪmˈpɜːsəneɪtə(r)/ *n* imitador, -dora *m,f*, impersonador, -dora *m,f* (Méx)

impertinence /ɪmˈpɜːrtn̩əns || ɪmˈpɜːtɪnəns/ *n* [u c] impertinencia *f*

impertinent /ɪmˈpɜːrtn̩ənt || ɪmˈpɜːtɪnənt/ *adj* impertinente

imperturbable /ˈɪmpərˈtɜːrbəbəl || ˌɪmpəˈtɜːbəbəl/ *adj* imperturbable

impervious /ɪmˈpɜːrviəs || ɪmˈpɜːviəs/ *adj* **1** ‹*rock/material*› impermeable, no poroso **2** (unaffected) **to be ~ TO sth** ‹*to criticism/doubt*› ser* impermeable *or* inmune A algo

impetuosity /ɪmˈpetʃuˈɑːsəti || ɪmˌpetʃʊˈɒsɪti/ *n* [u] impetuosidad *f*

impetuous /ɪmˈpetʃuəs/ *adj* ‹*person*› impetuoso, impulsivo; ‹*action/decision*› impulsivo, precipitado

impetuously /ɪmˈpetʃuəsli/ *adv* de manera impetuosa *or* impulsiva

impetus /ˈɪmpətəs || ˈɪmpɪtəs/ *n* [u] **1** (stimulus, boost) ímpetu *m*, impulso *m* **2** (momentum) ímpetu *m*

impinge /ɪmˈpɪndʒ/ *vi* **to ~ ON** *o* **UPON sth** (encroach on) ‹*privacy/freedom*› vulnerar algo

impious /ˈɪmpiəs/ *adj* impío

impish /ˈɪmpɪʃ/ *adj* pícaro, picaruelo (fam)

implacable /ɪmˈplækəbəl/ *adj* implacable

implant¹ /ɪmˈplænt || ɪmˈplɑːnt/ *vt* **1** ‹*idea/ideal*› inculcar* **2** ‹*embryo/hair*› implantar

implant² /ˈɪmplænt || ˈɪmplɑːnt/ *n* (of hair) implante *m*

implausible /ɪmˈplɔːzəbəl/ *adj* inverosímil, poco convincente

implement¹ /ˈɪmpləment || ˈɪmplɪment/ *vt* implementar, poner* en práctica, ejecutar

implement² /ˈɪmpləmənt || ˈɪmplɪmənt/ *n* instrumento *m*, implemento *m* (AmL)

implementation /ˈɪmpləmenˈteɪʃən || ˌɪmplɪmenˈteɪʃən/ *n* [u] implementación *f*, puesta *f* en práctica

implicate /ˈɪmpləkeɪt || ˈɪmplɪkeɪt/ *vt* implicar*, involucrar; **they are ~d in the murder** están implicados *or* involucrados en el asesinato

implication /ˈɪmpləˈkeɪʃən || ˌɪmplɪˈkeɪʃən/ *n*

A [c u] **1** (consequence, significance) repercusión *f*, implicación *f*, implicancia *f* (AmL); **to have/carry ~s for sth/sb** tener*/traer* consecuencias para algo/algn **2** (meaning) insinuación *f*; **by ~, he's blaming us** indirectamente *or* implícitamente nos está acusando

B [u] (involvement) implicación *f*

implicit /ɪmˈplɪsət || ɪmˈplɪsɪt/ *adj* **1** ‹*threat*› implícito, tácito **2** ‹*confidence/trust*› incondicional, total, absoluto

implicitly /ɪmˈplɪsətli || ɪmˈplɪsɪtli/ *adv* **1** (by implication) ‹*suggest*› implícitamente, tácitamente **2** ‹*trust/believe*› incondicionalmente, sin reservas

implode /ɪmˈpləʊd/ *vi* implosionar

implore /ɪmˈplɔːr || ɪmˈplɔː(r)/ *vt* ‹*help/mercy*› implorar; **don't go, I ~ you** no te vayas, te lo suplico; **to ~ sb to + INF** suplicarle* a algn QUE (+ *subj*)

imply /ɪmˈplaɪ/ *vt* **implies, implying, implied**

A (suggest, hint) dar* a entender, insinuar*; **what are you ~ing?** ¿qué insinúas?, ¿qué quieres decir?; **implied warranty** (AmE) garantía *f* implícita

B (involve) implicar*, suponer*

impolite /ˈɪmpəˈlaɪt/ *adj* ‹*person/remark*› maleducado, descortés; ‹*behavior*› descortés

imponderable¹ /ɪmˈpɑːndərəbəl || ɪmˈpɒndərəbəl/ *n* (frml) imponderable *m*

imponderable² *adj* (frml) imponderable

import¹ /ˈɪmpɔːrt || ˈɪmpɔːt/ *n*

A (Busn) **1** [u] (act) importación *f*; (*before n*) **~ duties** derechos *mpl* de importación **2** [c] (article): **a foreign ~** un artículo de importación

B [u] (significance) (frml) importancia *f*, trascendencia *f*

import² /ɪmˈpɔːrt || ɪmˈpɔːt/ *vt* **1** ‹*goods/idea*› importar **2** **imported** *past p* ‹*goods*› importado, de importación

importance /ɪmˈpɔːrtn̩s || ɪmˈpɔːtn̩s/ *n* [u] importancia *f*; **to be of the utmost ~** ser* de la mayor importancia; **it's of no ~** no tiene (ninguna) importancia, carece de importancia (frml); **she's so full of her own ~** se da una importancia *or* unos aires …, tiene unas ínfulas …

important /ɪmˈpɔːrtn̩t || ɪmˈpɔːtn̩t/ *adj* importante; **these services are ~ to the community** estos servicios tienen gran importancia para la comunidad; **the most ~ thing is that you eat well** lo más importante es que comas bien; **he's just trying to look ~** está tratando de darse importancia

importantly /ɪmˈpɔːrtn̩tli || ɪmˈpɔːtn̩tli/ *adv* (*indep*): **and, more ~, it costs half as much** y, lo que es más importante, cuesta la mitad

importation /ˈɪmpɔːrˈteɪʃən || ˌɪmpɔːˈteɪʃən/ *n* importación *f*

importer /ɪmˈpɔːrtər || ɪmˈpɔːtə(r)/ *n* importador, -dora *m,f*

importune /ˈɪmpərˈtuːn || ˌɪmpɔːˈtjuːn/ *vt* **1** (harass) (frml) importunar, asediar **2** (BrE Law) abordar con fines deshonestos

impose /ɪmˈpəʊz/ *vt* ‹*restriction/condition*› imponer*; **it's been ~d on us by management** la dirección nos lo ha impuesto; **the judge ~d the maximum sentence** el juez aplicó la pena máxima

■ *v refl* **to ~ oneself on sb**: **if I may ~ myself on you for a few more days** si puedo abusar de su amabilidad quedándome unos días más

■ **impose** *vi* molestar; **to ~ ON** *o* **UPON sb**: **I think I've ~d on him enough already** me parece que ya lo he molestado *or* importunado bastante; **to ~ on sb's goodwill** abusar de la buena voluntad de algn

imposing /ɪmˈpəʊzɪŋ/ *adj* imponente, impresionante

imposition /ˈɪmpəˈzɪʃən/ *n* **1** [u] (enforcement) imposición *f* **2** [c] (taking unfair advantage) abuso *m*

impossibility /ɪmˈpɑːsəˈbɪləti || ɪmˌpɒsəˈbɪləti/ *n* [u] imposibilidad *f*; **it's a physical ~** es físicamente imposible

impossible¹ /ɪmˈpɑːsəbəl || ɪmˈpɒsəbəl/ *adj* **1** ‹*job/request*› imposible; **she's making ~ demands on you** te está exigiendo lo imposible; **it's ~ for me to arrive by twelve** me es imposible llegar para las doce **2** (intolerable) intolerable; **to make life ~ for sb** hacerle* la vida imposible a algn

impossible² *n* **to ask/attempt the ~** pedir*/intentar lo imposible

impostor, imposter /ɪmˈpɑːstər || ɪmˈpɒstə(r)/ *n* impostor, -tora *m,f*

impotence /ˈɪmpətəns/ *n* [u] impotencia *f*

impotent /ˈɪmpətənt/ *adj* impotente

impound /ɪmˈpaʊnd/ *vt* **1** ‹*possessions/assets*› incautar, incautarse de **2** ‹*vehicle*› llevar al depósito municipal; ‹*stray dogs*› llevar a la perrera municipal

impoverished /ɪmˈpɑːvərɪʃt || ɪmˈpɒvərɪʃt/ *adj* (financially) empobrecido; (spiritually, intellectually) empobrecido; ‹*soil/diet*› pobre

impracticable /ɪm'præktɪkəbəl/ *adj* impracticable, imposible de llevar a cabo

impractical /ɪm'præktɪkəl/ *adj* 1 ‹*idea/suggestion*› poco práctico; **to be ~** no ser* práctico 2 ‹*person*› poco práctico

imprecise /'ɪmprɪ'saɪs/ *adj* impreciso

imprecision /'ɪmprɪ'sɪʒən/, **impreciseness** /'ɪmprɪ 'saɪsnɪs/ *n* imprecisión *f*, falta *f* de precisión

impregnable /ɪm'pregnəbəl/ *adj* 1 ‹*fortress*› inexpugnable, impenetrable; ‹*organization*› impenetrable 2 ‹*argument*› irrebatible, irrefutable; **the champion is in an ~ position** el campeón está en una posición invulnerable

impregnate /ɪm'pregneɪt || 'ɪmpregneɪt/ *vt*
A (saturate) **to ~ sth WITH sth** impregnar algo CON *or* DE algo
B (make pregnant) (frml) fecundar

impresario /'ɪmprə'sɑːriəʊ || ˌɪmprɪ'sɑːriəʊ/ (*pl* **-os**) *n* 1 (producer) empresario, -ria *m,f* teatral 2 (manager) director, -tora *m,f*

impress /ɪm'pres/ *vt*
A (make impression on): **we were ~ed by your work** tu trabajo nos causó muy buena impresión; **he only did it to ~ her** lo hizo sólo para impactarla *or* para dejarla admirada; **my excuse did not ~ them** mi excusa no los convenció
B (emphasize) **to ~ sth ON** *o* **UPON sb** recalcarle* algo a algn; **my father ~ed upon me the importance of work** mi padre me inculcó la importancia del trabajo
C (on paper, in wax) imprimir*, estampar
■ **impress** *vi* impresionar, impactar; **he does it to ~** lo hace para impresionar *or* impactar

impression /ɪm'preʃən/ *n*
A 1 (idea, image) impresión *f*; **it's my ~ that she doesn't want to go** tengo *or* me da la impresión de que no quiere ir; **I get the ~ that he wants me to leave** tengo *or* me da la impresión de que quiere que me vaya; **to give sb the ~ that ...** darle* a algn la impresión de que ...; **to be under the ~ (that) ...** creer* *or* pensar* que ..., tener* la impresión de que ... 2 (effect) impresión *f*; **to make** *o* **create a good/bad ~ on sb** causarle *or* producirle* a algn una buena/mala impresión; **it made no ~ at all on the stain** no surtió ningún efecto en la mancha; **she certainly made an ~!** ¡no hay duda de que causó impacto!
B 1 (imprint) impresión *f*, huella *f* 2 (Publ) impresión *f*
C (impersonation) imitación *f*

impressionable /ɪm'preʃṇəbəl/ *adj* 1 (easily influenced) influenciable 2 (easily frightened, upset) impresionable

impressionism /ɪm'preʃənɪzəm/ *n* [u] impresionismo *m*

impressionist¹ /ɪm'preʃənəst || ɪm'preʃənɪst/ *n* 1 (Art) impresionista *mf* 2 (impersonator) imitador, -dora *m,f*

impressionist² *adj* impresionista

impressive /ɪm'presɪv/ *adj* 1 ‹*record/work*› admirable, digno de admiración; **she's a very ~ speaker** es una excelente oradora 2 ‹*building/ceremony*› imponente, impresionante

imprint¹ /'ɪmprɪnt/ *n*
A (physical) marca *f*, huella *f*; **to leave an ~ on/in sth** dejar una marca *or* huella en algo
B (Publ): **a children's ~** (company) una editorial infantil; (series of books) una colección infantil; **it is published under the Axis ~** se publica bajo el sello (editorial) de Axis

imprint² /ɪm'prɪnt/ *vt* 1 (physically) imprimir* 2 (on mind) grabar; **her last words were ~ed on my memory** sus últimas palabras (se) me quedaron grabadas en la memoria

imprison /ɪm'prɪzən/ *vt* 1 (Law) encarcelar, meter en la cárcel 2 (lock up) ‹*dog/child*› encerrar*

imprisonment /ɪm'prɪzənmənt/ *n* [u] (act) encarcelamiento *m*; (state) prisión *f*; **ten years' ~** diez años de prisión; **he was sentenced to life ~** fue condenado a cadena perpetua

improbability /ɪm'prɑːbə'bɪləti || ɪmˌprɒbə'bɪləti/ *n* (*pl* **-ties**) 1 [u] (unlikeliness) improbabilidad *f*, lo poco probable 2 [u c] (implausibility) inverosimilitud *f*

improbable /ɪm'prɑːbəbəl || ɪm'prɒbəbəl/ *adj* 1 (unlikely) improbable, poco probable 2 (implausible) inverosímil

impromptu¹ /ɪm'prɑːmptu || ɪm'prɒmptjuː/ *adj* ‹*performance/speech*› improvisado; ‹*comment*› espontáneo

impromptu² *adv* ‹*perform*› de improviso, sin preparación; ‹*say*› espontáneamente

improper /ɪm'prɑːpər || ɪm'prɒpə(r)/ *adj*
A 1 (unseemly) ‹*behavior*› indecoroso, incorrecto; **it was considered ~ for a woman to dress this way** no estaba bien visto que una mujer vistiera así 2 (indecent) ‹*language*› indecoroso; ‹*suggestion*› deshonesto
B (incorrect) (frml) ‹*use*› indebido; ‹*term*› incorrecto, erróneo

improperly /ɪm'prɑːpərli || ɪm'prɒpəli/ *adv* ‹*used/applied*› indebidamente, incorrectamente; ‹*dressed*› incorrectamente

impropriety /'ɪmprə'praɪəti/ *n* (*pl* **-ties**) 1 [c] (breach of decorum) incorrección *f*; **a gross ~** una grave falta 2 [u] (quality) falta *f* de decoro, incorrección *f* 3 [u] (incorrectness) (frml) impropiedad *f*

improve /ɪm'pruːv/ *vt* 1 ‹*design/results*› mejorar; ‹*chances*› aumentar; **that new hairstyle has ~d her looks** ese nuevo peinado la favorece mucho; **to ~ one's mind** cultivarse, culturizarse* (hum) 2 ‹*property/premises*› hacer* mejoras en
■ **improve** *vi* «*situation/weather/health*» mejorar; «*chances*» aumentar; **to ~ with age/use** mejorar con el tiempo/uso
■ *v refl* **to ~ oneself** superarse

Phrasal verb
• **improve on**, **improve upon** [v ▸ prep ▸ o] ‹*result/record*› mejorar, superar; ‹*work*› mejorar; **if you can ~ on his offer** si puede ofrecer más que él

improvement /ɪm'pruːvmənt/ *n* [u c] (in design, situation) mejora *f*; (in health) mejoría *f*; **you're getting better, but there's still plenty of room for ~** has mejorado pero todavía puedes mejorar mucho más; **to be an ~ ON sth** ser* mejor QUE *or* superior A algo; **to make ~s** hacer* mejoras

improvisation /'ɪmprəvə'zeɪʃən || ˌɪmprəvaɪ'zeɪʃən/ *n* [u c] improvisación *f*

improvise /'ɪmprəvaɪz/ *vi/t* improvisar

imprudent /ɪm'pruːdṇt/ *adj* (frml) imprudente

impudence /'ɪmpjədəns || 'ɪmpjʊdəns/ *n* [u] insolencia *f*, descaro *m*, impudencia *f* (frml)

impudent /'ɪmpjədənt || 'ɪmpjʊdənt/ *adj* insolente, descarado; **an ~ remark** una insolencia *f*

impugn /ɪm'pjuːn/ *vt* (frml) ‹*reputation/integrity*› poner* en duda *or* en entredicho; ‹*evidence*› impugnar (frml)

impulse /'ɪmpʌls/ *n* 1 (urge) impulso *m*; **acting on (an) ~** llevado por un impulso; **I did it on ~** lo hice sin pensarlo; (*before n*) **~ buying** compras *fpl* impulsivas 2 (impetus, force) impulso *m*

impulsive /ɪm'pʌlsɪv/ *adj* impulsivo

impunity /ɪm'pjuːnəti/ (frml) *n* [u] impunidad *f*; **with ~** con impunidad, impunemente

impure /'ɪm'pjʊr || ɪm'pjʊə(r)/ *adj* 1 ‹*water/air/drug*› impuro 2 ‹*thought/act*› impuro

impurity /ɪm'pjʊrəti || ɪm'pjʊərəti/ *n* [u c] (*pl* **-ties**) impureza *f*

impute /ɪm'pjuːt/ *vt* (frml) **to ~ sth TO sth/sb** imputarle algo A algo/algn (frml)

in¹ /ɪn/ *prep*
A 1 (indicating place, location) en; **~ Detroit/Japan** en Detroit/en (el) Japón; **our friends ~ Detroit** nuestros amigos de Detroit; **he's ~ a meeting** está en una reunión, está reunido; **who's that ~ the photo?** ¿quién es ése de la foto?; **~ here/there** aquí/allí dentro *or* (esp AmL) adentro; **to lie ~ the sun** tumbarse al sol; **~ the rain** bajo la lluvia 2 (*with superl*) de; **the highest mountain ~ Italy** la montaña más alta de Italia; **the worst storm ~ living memory** la peor tormenta que se recuerda
B (indicating movement): **he went ~ the shop** entró en la tienda; **come ~ here** ven aquí dentro *or* (esp AmL) adentro
C 1 (during): **come ~ the afternoon** ven por la tarde, ven en la tarde (AmL), ven a la tarde *or* de tarde (RPl); **at four o'clock ~ the morning/afternoon** a las cuatro de la mañana/tarde; **~ spring/January/1924** en primavera/enero/1924; **I haven't seen her ~ years** hace años que no la veo; **he's ~ his forties** tiene cuarenta y tantos 2 (at the end of) dentro de; **~ two months** *o* **two months'**

time dentro de dos meses 3 (in the space of) en; **she did it ~ three hours** lo hizo en tres horas

D 1 (indicating manner) en; **~ a low voice** en voz baja; **~ dollars** en dólares; **~ French** en francés; **they sat ~ a circle** se sentaron en un círculo; **~ twos** de dos en dos, de a dos (AmL); **to break sth ~ two** partir algo en dos; **cut it ~ half** córtalo por la mitad; **they came ~ their thousands** vinieron miles y miles; **to paint ~ oils** pintar al óleo; **write ~ ink/pencil** escriba con tinta/lápiz 2 (wearing): **he turned up ~ a suit** apareció de traje; **I look terrible ~ this** esto me queda horrible; **are you going ~ that dress?** ¿vas a ir con ese vestido?

E (indicating circumstances, state): **the company is ~ difficulties** la empresa está pasando dificultades; **to be ~ a good mood** estar* de buen humor; **they gazed ~ admiration** miraban admirados; **he's ~ pain** está dolorido

F (indicating occupation, activity) en; **he's ~ insurance** trabaja en seguros; **we're all ~ this together** estamos todos metidos en esto

G (indicating personal characteristics): **I never thought she had it ~ her to get that far** nunca creí que iba a ser capaz de llegar tan lejos

H (in respect of, as regards): **low ~ calories** bajo en calorías; **she's deaf ~ one ear** es sorda de un oído; **~ itself** de por sí; **which is cheaper? — there's not much ~ it** ¿cuál es más barato? — no hay mucha diferencia; **what's ~ it for me?** ¿y yo qué gano *or* saco?

I (indicating ratio): **one ~ four** uno de cada cuatro; **she's one ~ a million** es única, como ella no hay otra

i

A 1 (+ *gerund*): **~ so doing, they set a precedent** al hacerlo, sentaron precedente 2 **in that** (*as conj*): **the case is unusual ~ that ...** el caso es poco común en el sentido de que *or* por el hecho de que ...

in[2] *adv*

A 1 (inside): **is the cat ~?** ¿el gato está dentro *or* (esp AmL) adentro?; **~ you go!** ¡entra!; **she's ~ for theft** está en la cárcel por robo 2 (at home, work): **is Lisa ~?** ¿está Lisa?; **there was nobody ~** no había nadie; **Jane's never ~ before one** Jane nunca llega antes de la una

B 1 (in position): **she had her curlers ~** llevaba *or* tenía los rulos puestos 2 (at destination): **the train isn't ~ yet** el tren no ha llegado todavía; **application forms must be ~ by October 5** las solicitudes deben entregarse antes del 5 de octubre 3 (available, in stock): **is the book I ordered ~ yet?** ¿ha llegado ya el libro que encargué? 4 (in power) en el poder

C (involved): **we were ~ on the planning stage** participamos en la planificación; ***to be ~ for sth***: **you're ~ for it now!** ¡ahora sí que te va a caer una buena!; **it looks like we're ~ for some rain** parece que va a llover; **you're ~ for a big surprise** te vas a llevar una buena sorpresa; ***to be ~ on sth***: **I wanted to be ~ on the deal** quería tener parte en el trato; ***to be ~ with sb***: **he's (well) ~ with the boss** es muy amigo del jefe; *see also* **get in with**

in[3] *adj*

A 1 (fashionable) (colloq) (*no comp*): **black is ~ this season** el negro está de moda *or* es lo que se lleva esta temporada; **the ~ place** el lugar de moda, el lugar in (fam) 2 (exclusive, private) (*before n*): **an ~ joke** un chiste para iniciados; **the ~ crowd** el grupito

B (*pred*) (in tennis, badminton, etc): **the ball was ~** la pelota fue buena *or* cayó dentro *or* (esp AmL) adentro

in[4] *n*

A (access to) (AmE colloq) (*no pl*): **to have an ~ with sb** tener* palanca *or* (Esp) enchufe con algn (fam)

B **ins** *pl*: **the ~s and outs (of sth)** los pormenores (de algo)

in[5] (*pl* **in** *or* **ins**) = **inch(es)**

IN = **Indiana**

inability /ˌɪnəˈbɪləti/ *n* [u] incapacidad *f*; **~ to + INF** incapacidad PARA + INF

inaccessibility /ˈɪnəkˌsesəˈbɪləti || ˌɪnæksesəˈbɪləti/ *n* [u] inaccesibilidad *f*

inaccessible /ˈɪnəkˈsesəbəl || ˌɪnækˈsesəbəl/ *adj* inaccesible

inaccuracy /ɪnˈækjərəsi/ *n* (*pl* **-cies**) 1 [u] (of information, instrument) inexactitud *f* 2 [c] (error) error *m* 3 [u] (of shot, aim) imprecisión *f*

inaccurate /ɪnˈækjərət/ *adj* 1 ‹*translation/estimate*› inexacto, erróneo; **these scales are very ~** esta balanza no es nada precisa 2 ‹*aim/shot*› impreciso

inaction /ɪnˈækʃən/ *n* [u] inactividad *f*, inacción *f*

inactive /ɪnˈæktɪv/ *adj* inactivo

inactivity /ˈɪnækˈtɪvəti/ *n* [u] inactividad *f*

inadequacy /ɪnˈædɪkwəsi/ *n* (*pl* **-cies**) 1 [u] (of resources) lo inadecuado 2 [u] (of person) ineptitud *f*, incompetencia *f* 3 [c] (weakness) deficiencia *f*

inadequate /ɪnˈædɪkwət/ *adj* 1 ‹*resources/measures*› insuficiente, inadecuado 2 ‹*person*› inepto, incompetente; **she felt ~** (for a particular task) se sentía inepta *or* incompetente; (in general) sentía que no estaba a la altura de las circunstancias

inadmissible /ˈɪnədˈmɪsəbəl/ *adj* inadmisible

inadvertently /ˈɪnədˈvɜːrtn̩tli || ˌɪnədˈvɜːtn̩tli/ *adv* sin querer, sin darse (*or* darme *etc*) cuenta

inadvisable /ˈɪnədˈvaɪzəbəl/ *adj* desaconsejable, poco aconsejable *or* recomendable

inalienable /ɪnˈeɪliənəbəl/ *adj* inalienable

inane /ɪˈneɪn/ *adj* estúpido, idiota, inane (frml)

inanimate /ɪnˈænəmət || ɪnˈænɪmət/ *adj* inanimado

inanity /ɪˈnænəti/ *n* (*pl* **-ties**) 1 [u] (stupidity) estupidez *f*, inanidad *f* (frml) 2 [c] (stupid remark) sandez *f*, estupidez *f*

inapplicable /ɪnˈæplɪkəbəl, ˌɪnəˈplɪkəbəl/ *adj* inaplicable, no aplicable

inappropriate /ˈɪnəˈprəʊpriət/ *adj* ‹*measure/dress*› inadecuado, poco apropiado; ‹*moment*› inoportuno; **a totally ~ comment** un comentario totalmente fuera de lugar; **it would be ~ for you to suggest it** no te corresponde a ti sugerirlo, no estaría bien que tú lo sugirieras

inappropriately /ˈɪnəˈprəʊpriətli/ *adv* de manera poco adecuada *or* apropiada; **they were ~ dressed** no iban adecuadamente vestidos

inarticulate /ˈɪnɑːrˈtɪkjələt || ˌɪnɑːˈtɪkjʊlət/ *adj* (in speech) ‹*babbling/grunt*› inarticulado; ‹*person*› con dificultad para expresarse

inasmuch as /ˈɪnəzˈmʌtʃ/ *conj* (frml) 1 (since, seeing that) ya que, puesto que, dado que 2 ▸ **insofar as**

inattention /ˈɪnəˈtentʃən || ˌɪnəˈtenʃən/ *n* [u] 1 (lack of attention) falta *f* de atención, distracción *f* 2 (neglect) desinterés *m*

inattentive /ˈɪnəˈtentɪv/ *adj* ‹*pupil/listener*› distraído, poco atento, desatento

inaudible /ɪnˈɔːdəbəl/ *adj* inaudible

inaugural[1] /ɪnˈɔːgjərəl || ɪˈnɔːgjʊrəl/ *adj* 1 ‹*speech/lecture*› inaugural, de apertura; ‹*flight/meeting*› inaugural 2 (of official) ‹*speech*› de toma de posesión; ‹*ceremony*› de investidura

inaugural[2] *n* (ceremony) (AmE) toma *f* de posesión, investidura *f*

inaugurate /ɪnˈɔːgjəreɪt || ɪˈnɔːgjʊreɪt/ *vt* 1 (begin) inaugurar 2 (open) inaugurar 3 (frml) ‹*president*› investir*; **to be ~d president** ser* investido como presidente

inauguration /ɪnˌɔːgjəˈreɪʃən || ɪˌnɔːgjʊˈreɪʃən/ *n* 1 (investiture) investidura *f*, toma *f* de posesión; (*before n*) **I~ Day** (in US) *día de la toma de posesión del presidente de los EEUU* 2 (opening) inauguración *f*

> **Inauguration Day**
>
> En EEUU, el día en que el nuevo Presidente asume oficialmente el poder. La ceremonia de investidura siempre tiene lugar el 20 de enero, en Washington DC

inauspicious /ˈɪnɔːˈspɪʃəs/ *adj* ‹*circumstances*› desfavorable, adverso; ‹*moment/start*› poco propicio

inbetween /ˈɪnbɪˈtwiːn/ *adj* (*before n*) intermedio

inborn /ˈɪnˈbɔːrn || ˈɪnbɔːn/ *adj* innato, connatural

inbox /ˈɪnbɑːks || ˈɪnbɒks/ *n*

A (AmE) ▸ **in-tray**

B (Comput) bandeja *f* de entrada

inbred /ˈɪnˈbred/ *adj*

A ‹*social group*› endogámico

B (innate) innato

inbreeding /ˈɪnˌbriːdɪŋ/ *n* [u] endogamia *f*

inbuilt /ˈɪnˈbɪlt/ *adj* ‹*system/program*› incorporado; ‹*inequalities*› consustancial, inherente; ‹*feeling*› innato

Inc /ɪnk/ (AmE) = **Incorporated**

Inca[1] /ˈɪŋkə/ *adj* incaico, inca

Inca[2] *n* inca *mf*

incalculable /ɪn'kælkjələbəl || ɪn'kælkjʊləbəl/ *adj* incalculable

incandescent /'ɪnkən'desn̩t || ˌɪnkæn'desn̩t/ *adj* incandescente

incantation /'ɪnkæn'teɪʃən/ *n* ensalmo *m*, conjuro *m*

incapable /ɪn'keɪpəbəl/ *adj (pred)* 1 (not able) **to be ~ OF -ING** ser* incapaz DE + INF; **she is ~ of jealousy** es incapaz de sentir celos 2 (helpless) inútil, incapaz

incapacitate /'ɪnkə'pæsəteɪt || ˌɪnkə'pæsɪteɪt/ *vt* 1 (disable) incapacitar; **to be ~d** estar* incapacitado *or* impedido 2 (Law) inhabilitar, incapacitar

incapacity /'ɪnkə'pæsəti/ *n* [u] incapacidad *f*; *(before n)* **I~ Benefit** (BrE) prestaciones *fpl* por invalidez

incarcerate /ɪn'kɑːrsəreɪt || ɪn'kɑːsəreɪt/ *vt* encarcelar

incarceration /ɪn'kɑːrsə'reɪʃən || ɪnˌkɑːsə'reɪʃən/ *n* encarcelación *f*

incarnate /ɪn'kɑːrnət || ɪn'kɑːnət/ *adj* (liter) *(usu pred)* encarnado; **the devil ~** el demonio encarnado *or* personificado

incarnation /'ɪnkɑːr'neɪʃən || ˌɪnkɑː'neɪʃən/ *n* encarnación *f*

incendiary /ɪn'sendieri || ɪn'sendiəri/ *adj* incendiario

incense[1] /'ɪnsens/ *n* [u] incienso *m*; *(before n)* **~ burner** incensario *m*

incense[2] /ɪn'sens/ *vt* indignar, darle* rabia a

incentive /ɪn'sentɪv/ *n* [c u] incentivo *m*, aliciente *m*, estímulo *m*; **a cash ~** una bonificación, un incentivo en efectivo *or* en metálico; **he had no ~ to diet** no tenía ningún aliciente *or* incentivo para hacer régimen; *(before n)* **~ scheme** plan *m* de incentivos

inception /ɪn'sepʃən/ *n* (frml) inicio *m*, comienzo *m*

incessant /ɪn'sesn̩t/ *adj* ‹*noise/rain*› incesante; ‹*effort*› ininterrumpido, constante

incessantly /ɪn'sesn̩tli/ *adv* sin cesar, incesantemente

incest /'ɪnsest/ *n* [u] incesto *m*

incestuous /ɪn'sestʃuəs || ɪn'sestjʊəs/ *adj* incestuoso

inch[1] /ɪntʃ/ *n* pulgada *f (2,54 centímetros)*; **two ~es of rain** dos pulgadas *or* (fam) cuatro dedos de lluvia; **I was within an ~ of getting that job** estuve a un paso *or* en un tris de que me dieran el trabajo; **I've searched every ~ of the house** he buscado hasta en el último rincón de la casa; **he looked every ~ the English aristocrat** de pies a cabeza parecía el típico aristócrata inglés; **she wouldn't budge** *o* **give an ~** no cedió ni un ápice; ***give them an ~ and they'll take a mile*** les das la mano y te toman *or* (esp Esp) te cogen el brazo

inch[2] *vi* moverse* lentamente *or* paso a paso; **to ~ forward** avanzar* lentamente *or* paso a paso

■ **inch** *vt*: ***to ~ one's way*** avanzar* lentamente

incidence /'ɪnsədəns || 'ɪnsɪdəns/ *n* [u]

A (frequency) índice *m*; **the high/low ~ of deaths among ...** el alto/bajo índice de muertes entre ...

B (Opt, Phys) incidencia *f*; **the angle of ~** al ángulo de incidencia

incident /'ɪnsədənt || 'ɪnsɪdənt/ *n* 1 (event) incidente *m*, episodio *m*; **the day passed without ~** el día transcurrió sin incidentes 2 (disturbance) (journ) incidente *m*; *(before n)* **~ room** (BrE) centro *m* de investigaciones

incidental /'ɪnsə'dentl̩ || ˌɪnsɪ'dentl̩/ *adj* 1 (accompanying) ‹*effect*› secundario; ‹*advantage/benefit*› adicional; ‹*expenses*› imprevisto; **~ music** música *f* incidental *or* de acompañamiento; **~ TO sth**: **these duties are ~ to the job** son responsabilidades que conlleva el trabajo 2 (minor) incidental, de menor importancia 3 (accidental) casual, fortuito

incidentally /'ɪnsə'dentl̩i || ˌɪnsɪ'dentl̩i/ *adv*

A *(indep)* a propósito, por cierto

B (casually) por casualidad, casualmente

incinerate /ɪn'sɪnəreɪt/ *vt* incinerar

incinerator /ɪn'sɪnəreɪtər || ɪn'sɪnəreɪtə(r)/ *n* incinerador *m*

incipient /ɪn'sɪpiənt/ *adj* incipiente

incision /ɪn'sɪʒən/ *n* [c u] incisión *f*

incisive /ɪn'saɪsɪv/ *adj* ‹*person/mind*› incisivo, penetrante; ‹*remark*› incisivo, mordaz

incisor /ɪn'saɪzər || ɪn'saɪzə(r)/ *n* incisivo *m*

incite /ɪn'saɪt/ *vt* ‹*hatred/violence*› instigar* a, incitar a; ‹*person*› **to ~ sb TO sth/+INF** instigar* *or* incitar a algn A algo/+ INF

incl *prep* (= **including** *o* **inclusive of**): **~ postage** franqueo incluido

inclement /ɪn'klemənt/ *adj* (frml) inclemente

inclination /'ɪnklə'neɪʃən || ˌɪnklɪ'neɪʃən/ *n* [u c]

A 1 (leaning) tendencia *f*, inclinación *f*; **~ TO sth** tendencia A algo 2 (desire): **my own ~ is to ignore them** yo me inclino por no hacerles caso; **to have an/no ~ to + INF** tener*/no tener* deseos *or* ganas de + INF; **she shows no ~ to relinquish her post** no da muestras de querer dejar su puesto; **to follow one's own ~(s)** dejarse llevar por su (*or* mi *etc*) instinto

B (tilt) inclinación *f*

incline[1] /ɪn'klaɪn/ *vt* (frml) 1 (dispose) **to ~ sb to + INF** predisponer* a algn A + INF 2 (bend, lower) ‹*head*› inclinar, bajar

■ **incline** *vi* (frml) **to ~ TO** *o* **TOWARD sth**: **she ~s to** *o* **toward the opposite view** se inclina a pensar lo contrario

incline[2] /'ɪnklaɪn/ *n* (frml) pendiente *f*

inclined /ɪn'klaɪnd/ *adj* (disposed) **~ to + INF**: **I'm ~ to agree** yo me inclino a pensar lo mismo; **she's ~ to be irritable in the morning** tiende a estar de mal humor por la mañana; **to be artistically ~** tener* inclinaciones artísticas; **anyone who feels so ~ can ...** cualquier persona que así lo desee, puede ...

include /ɪn'kluːd/ *vt* 1 (contain as part) incluir*; **does the rent ~ heating costs?** ¿el alquiler incluye *or* en el alquiler están incluidos los gastos de calefacción? 2 (put in) incluir*; (with letter) adjuntar, incluir*; **we're all ~d in the invitation** estamos todos invitados 3 (count in) incluir*; **service isn't ~d** el servicio no está incluido

including /ɪn'kluːdɪŋ/ *prep*: **~ the introduction, the book runs to 300 pages** incluyendo *or* contando la introducción, el libro tiene 300 páginas; **up to and ~ page 25** hasta la página 25 inclusive; **they all liked it, ~ Paul** a todos les gustó, incluso *or* hasta a Paul; **not ~ insurance** sin incluir el seguro

inclusion /ɪn'kluːʒən/ *n* [u] inclusión *f*

inclusive /ɪn'kluːsɪv/ *adj* 1 ‹*price/charge*› global, todo incluido; **to be ~ OF sth** incluir* algo 2 (including dates, figures mentioned) (BrE) *(after n)* inclusive; **from the 23rd to the 27th ~** del 23 al 27, ambos inclusive

incognito /ˌɪnkɑːg'niːtəʊ || ˌɪnkɒg'niːtəʊ/ *adv* de incógnito

incoherent /'ɪnkəʊ'hɪrənt || ˌɪnkəʊ'hɪərənt/ *adj* ‹*statement*› incoherente; ‹*argument/style*› falto de coherencia *or* ilación, incoherente

incoherently /'ɪnkəʊ'hɪrəntli || ˌɪnkəʊ'hɪərəntli/ *adv* ‹*speak*› incoherentemente, con incoherencia

income /'ɪnkʌm/ *n* [u c] ingresos *mpl*; (unearned) rentas *fpl*, ingresos *mpl*; **I live within my ~** vivo de acuerdo con mis ingresos

income: **~ support** *n* [u] (in UK) *subsidio otorgado a personas de bajos ingresos*; **~ tax** *n* [u] impuesto *m* sobre *or* a la renta, impuesto *m* a los réditos (Arg)

incoming /'ɪn'kʌmɪŋ/ *adj (before n)* 1 (inbound): **the area has been closed to ~ traffic** no se permite la entrada de vehículos a la zona; **the ~ tide** la marea *(que sube)*; **~ mail is sorted downstairs** la correspondencia que se recibe se clasifica abajo; **the secretary takes all ~ calls** la secretaria atiende todas las llamadas; Ⓢ **incoming calls only** sólo recibe llamadas 2 (about to take office) ‹*president*› entrante

incommunicado /'ɪnkə'mjuːnə'kɑːdəʊ || ˌɪnkəˌmjuːnɪ'kɑːdəʊ/ *adj (pred)* **to be ~** estar* incomunicado

incomparable /ɪn'kɑːmpərəbəl || ɪn'kɒmpərəbəl/ *adj* 1 (matchless) (liter) incomparable, sin par, sin igual 2 (totally different) (frml) *(pred)* **to be ~ WITH sth/sb** no poderse* comparar *or* no tener* comparación CON algo/algn

incompatible /'ɪnkəm'pætəbəl/ *adj* incompatible

incompetence /ɪn'kɑːmpətəns || ɪn'kɒmpɪtəns/ *n* [u] 1 (ineptitude) incompetencia *f*, ineptitud *f* 2 (Law) **~ (to + INF)** incapacidad *f* (PARA + INF)

incompetent /ɪn'kɑːmpətənt || ɪn'kɒmpɪtənt/ *adj* 1 (inept) ‹*person*› incompetente, inepto; ‹*work*› deficiente

[2] (disqualified) (Law) incapaz; **to be ~ to + INF** ser* incapaz PARA + INF

incomplete /ˈɪnkəmˈpliːt/ *adj* [1] (with sth or sb missing) incompleto; **the meal would be ~ without dessert** no sería una comida completa sin un postre [2] (unfinished) inacabado, inconcluso, sin terminar

incomprehensible /ɪnˈkɑːmprəˈhensəbəl || ɪnˌkɒmprɪˈhensəbəl/ *adj* incomprensible; **to be ~ TO sb** ser* incomprensible PARA algn

incomprehension /ɪnˈkɑːmprɪˈhentʃən || ɪnˌkɒmprɪˈhenʃən/ *n* [u] incomprensión *f*, falta *f* de comprensión

inconceivable /ˈɪnkənˈsiːvəbəl/ *adj* inconcebible

inconclusive /ˈɪnkənˈkluːsɪv/ *adj* ‹*evidence/findings*› no concluyente, inconcluyente; **the discussion was ~** la discusión no fue fructífera

incongruous /ɪnˈkɑːŋgruəs || ɪnˈkɒŋgruəs/ *adj* ‹*behavior/remark*› fuera de lugar, inapropiado; ‹*appearance*› extraño, raro

inconsequential /ɪnˈkɑːnsəˈkwentʃəl || ɪnˌkɒnsɪˈkwenʃəl/ *adj* [1] (unimportant) intrascendente, sin importancia [2] (illogical) (frml) ilógico, incoherente

inconsiderable /ˈɪnkənˈsɪdərəbəl/ *adj* (frml) (*usu neg*): **he inherited a not ~ sum** heredó una suma nada despreciable *or* desdeñable

inconsiderate /ˈɪnkənˈsɪdərət/ *adj* ‹*person/attitude*› desconsiderado; **it was very ~ of her** fue una gran falta de consideración de su parte

inconsistency /ˈɪnkənˈsɪstənsi/ *n* [u c] (*pl* **-cies**) falta *f* de coherencia, contradicción *f*

inconsistent /ˈɪnkənˈsɪstənt/ *adj* [1] (contradictory) ‹*statement/account*› contradictorio, incoherente; ‹*action*› contradictorio, inconsecuente; **to be ~ WITH sth** no concordar* CON algo; ‹*with principles/ideas*› no compadecerse* CON algo [2] (irregular, changeable) ‹*person/attitude*› inconsecuente, inconstante; ‹*performance*› desigual

inconsolable /ˈɪnkənˈsəʊləbəl/ *adj* inconsolable

inconspicuous /ˈɪnkənˈspɪkjuəs/ *adj* ‹*person/object*› que no llama la atención, que pasa desapercibido *or* inadvertido; ‹*gesture*› discreto, que no llama la atención; **he tried to make himself ~** trató de pasar desapercibido *or* inadvertido

incontinence /ɪnˈkɑːntṇəns || ɪnˈkɒntɪnəns/ *n* (Med) incontinencia *f*

incontinent /ɪnˈkɑːntṇənt || ɪnˈkɒntɪnənt/ *adj* (Med) incontinente

incontrovertible /ɪnˈkɑːntrəˈvɜːrtəbəl || ˌɪnkɒntrəˈvɜːtəbəl/ *adj* (frml) incontrovertible, indisputable

inconvenience[1] /ˈɪnkənˈviːniəns/ *n* [1] [u] (unsuitability, troublesomeness) inconveniencia *f*, incomodidad *f* [2] [u] (trouble) molestias *fpl*, inconvenientes *mpl* [3] [c] (drawback, nuisance) inconveniente *m*, desventaja *f*

inconvenience[2] *vt* causarle molestias a; **I don't want them to ~ themselves on my account** no quiero que se molesten por mí

inconvenient /ˈɪnkənˈviːniənt/ *adj* ‹*moment*› poco conveniente, inconveniente, inoportuno; ‹*position*› poco práctico; **I hope it's not too ~ for you** espero que no le cause muchos inconvenientes *or* muchas molestias

incorporate /ɪnˈkɔːrpəreɪt || ɪnˈkɔːpəreɪt/ *vt*
A [1] (take in) ‹*idea/plan*› incorporar; **to ~ sth INTO sth** incorporar algo A algo [2] (include, contain) incluir*, comprender
B (Busn, Law) ‹*business/enterprise*› constituir* (en sociedad); **a company ~d in the State of New Jersey** una compañía constituida en el estado de Nueva Jersey

incorporation /ɪnˈkɔːrpəˈreɪʃən || ɪnˌkɔːpəˈreɪʃən/ *n*
A (integration) incorporación *f*
B (Busn, Law) constitución *f* en sociedad

incorrect /ˈɪnkəˈrekt/ *adj* ‹*answer/translation/spelling*› incorrecto; ‹*statement/belief*› equivocado, erróneo; **that is ~** eso no es cierto

incorrectly /ˈɪnkəˈrektli/ *adv* incorrectamente; **the letter had been ~ addressed** la carta tenía la dirección equivocada

incorrigible /ɪnˈkɔːrədʒəbəl || ɪnˈkɒrɪdʒəbəl/ *adj* incorregible

incorruptible /ˈɪnkəˈrʌptəbəl/ *adj* incorruptible

increase[1] /ɪnˈkriːs/ *vi* «*number/size*» aumentar; «*prices*» aumentar, subir; «*influence/popularity*» crecer*, aumentar; «*trade/output*» aumentar, incrementarse (frml); **to ~ IN sth**: **to ~ in size/weight** aumentar de tamaño/peso; **to ~ in number/importance** crecer* en número/importancia; **to ~ in value** aumentar de valor, revalorizarse*

■ **increase** *vt* ‹*number/size*› aumentar; ‹*prices*› aumentar, subir; ‹*trade/output*› aumentar, incrementar (frml); ‹*wealth/knowledge*› aumentar, acrecentar*; **it will ~ your chances** te dará más posibilidades

increase[2] /ˈɪnkriːs/ *n* aumento *m*, incremento *m* (frml); **to be on the ~** estar* en aumento, ir* en aumento

increasing /ɪnˈkriːsɪŋ/ *adj* (*before n*) ‹*amount/number*› creciente, cada vez mayor; ‹*interest/pressure*› creciente

increasingly /ɪnˈkriːsɪŋli/ *adv*: **~ difficult/dangerous** cada vez más difícil/peligroso; **it is becoming ~ clear that ...** resulta cada vez más claro que ...

incredible /ɪnˈkredəbəl/ *adj* increíble; **~ though it may seem** aunque parezca increíble, aunque parezca mentira

incredibly /ɪnˈkredəbli/ *adv* [1] (colloq) (*as intensifier*) ‹*rich/weird/brave*› increíblemente [2] (*indep*) aunque parezca increíble, aunque parezca mentira

incredulous /ɪnˈkredʒələs || ɪnˈkredjʊləs/ *adj* ‹*expression/stare*› de incredulidad

increment /ˈɪŋkrəmənt/ *n* (in salary) incremento *m* (salarial) (frml), aumento *m* (de sueldo)

incriminate /ɪnˈkrɪməneɪt || ɪnˈkrɪmɪneɪt/ *vt* incriminar (frml)

incriminating /ɪnˈkrɪməneɪtɪŋ || ɪnˈkrɪmɪneɪtɪŋ/ *adj* ‹*evidence/document*› comprometedor; (Law) incriminatorio (frml)

incrust /ɪnˈkrʌst/ *vt* ▸ **encrust**

incubate /ˈɪŋkjəbeɪt || ˈɪŋkjʊbeɪt/ *vt* incubar
■ **incubate** *vi* «*bird*» empollar; «*egg/embryo/bacteria*» incubarse

incubation /ˈɪŋkjəˈbeɪʃən || ˌɪŋkjʊˈbeɪʃən/ *n* [u] incubación *f*; (*before n*) **~ period** período *m* de incubación

incubator /ˈɪŋkjəbeɪtər || ˈɪŋkjʊbeɪtə(r)/ *n* incubadora *f*

inculcate /ˈɪnkʌlkeɪt/ *vt* (frml) **to ~ sth IN(TO) sb, to ~ sb WITH sth** inculcarle* algo A algn, inculcar* algo EN algn

incumbent[1] /ɪnˈkʌmbənt/ *adj* (frml) **to be ~ ON** *o* **UPON sb** incumbirle A algn

incumbent[2] *n* (officeholder) titular *mf* del cargo; (Relig) titular *mf* del beneficio (eclesiástico)

incur /ɪnˈkɜːr || ɪnˈkɜː(r)/ *vt* **-rr-** (frml) ‹*anger/censure*› provocar*, incurrir en (frml); ‹*risk*› correr; ‹*penalty*› acarrear; ‹*damage/loss/injury*› sufrir; ‹*debt/liability*› contraer*; ‹*expense*› incurrir en (frml)

incurable /ɪnˈkjʊrəbəl || ɪnˈkjʊərəbəl/ *adj* [1] ‹*illness*› incurable [2] ‹*habit*› incorregible; ‹*optimist/romantic*› incorregible, recalcitrante, sin remedio

incursion /ɪnˈkɜːrʒən || ɪnˈkɜːʃən/ *n* [c u] incursión *f*

Ind = **Indiana**

indebted /ɪnˈdetəd || ɪnˈdetɪd/ *adj* [1] (owing gratitude) **to be ~ TO sb (FOR sth)** estar* en deuda CON algn (POR algo) [2] (owing money) endeudado, empeñado

indecency /ɪnˈdiːsṇsi/ *n* [u] indecencia *f*

indecent /ɪnˈdiːsṇt/ *adj* [1] (obscene) ‹*language/gesture*› indecente [2] (unseemly) indecoroso

indecent assault *n* [c u] abusos *mpl* deshonestos

indecipherable /ˈɪndɪˈsaɪfərəbəl/ *adj* indescifrable

indecision /ˈɪndɪˈsɪʒən/ *n* [u] indecisión *f*, irresolución *f* (frml)

indecisive /ˈɪndɪˈsaɪsɪv/ *adj* [1] (hesitant) indeciso, irresoluto (frml) [2] (inconclusive) ‹*result/outcome*› no decisivo, no concluyente

indeed[1] /ɪnˈdiːd/ *adv*
A [1] (*as intensifier*): **thank you very much ~** muchísimas gracias; **he's painted it very well ~** lo ha pintado realmente *or* verdaderamente bien [2] (emphatic): **this is ~ a great privilege** éste es un auténtico *or* verdadero privilegio; **what a lovely evening! — yes ~!** ¡que noche más agradable! — ¡ya lo creo! *or* ¡sí, por cierto! [3] (in response to question): **do you like champagne? — ~ I do** *o* **I do ~** ¿te gusta el champán? — sí, mucho; **I believe we've**

met before — ~ we have, a couple of years ago creo que nos conocemos — en efecto *or* así es, nos conocimos hace un par de años

B 1 (in fact): **the wheel was ~ loose** en efecto, la rueda estaba suelta 2 (indicating possibility): **if ~ he is right** si es que tiene razón; **this may ~ be the case, but ...** quizás sea así *or* no digo que no sea así, pero ... 3 (what is more) (*as linker*): **the situation hasn't improved; ~ it has worsened** la situación no ha mejorado; es más: ha empeorado; **a rare, ~ unique, example** un ejemplo, ya no poco común, sino único

C (in response to statement): **she says she's fat — fat ~!** dice que está gorda — sí, ya, gordísima; **he says he can do it better — does he ~?** (iro) dice que él lo puede hacer mejor — ¡no me digas!

indeed² *interj* ¡ya lo creo!

indefatigable /'ɪndɪ'fætɪgəbəl/ *adj* (frml) infatigable, incansable

indefensible /'ɪndɪ'fensəbəl/ *adj* ‹*rudeness/remark*› inexcusable, indefendible; ‹*view*› insostenible, indefendible

indefinable /'ɪndɪ'faɪnəbəl/ *adj* indefinible

indefinite /ɪn'defənət || ɪn'defɪnət/ *adj*

A 1 (*usu before n*) ‹*number/period*› indefinido, indeterminado 2 (vague) ‹*outline*› indefinido

B (Ling): **~ article** artículo *m* determinado *or* definido

indefinitely /ɪn'defənətli || ɪn'defɪnətli/ *adv* indefinidamente

indelible /ɪn'deləbəl/ *adj* ‹*stain/marker*› indeleble, imborrable; ‹*ink*› indeleble

indelicate /ɪn'delәkәt || ɪn'delɪkət/ *adj* 1 (vulgar) ‹*behavior/remark*› indelicado, descortés 2 (tactless) ‹*action/remark*› indiscreto, falto de tacto

indemnify /ɪn'demnəfaɪ || ɪn'demnɪfaɪ/ *vt* **-fies, -fying, -fied** 1 (insure) **to ~ sb (AGAINST sth)** asegurar a algn (CONTRA algo) 2 (compensate) **to ~ sb (FOR sth)** indemnizar* a algn (POR *or* DE algo)

indemnity /ɪn'demnəti/ *n* (*pl* **-ties**) 1 [u] (insurance) **~ (AGAINST sth)** indemnidad *f* (CONTRA algo) 2 [c] (compensation) **~ (FOR sth)** indemnización *f* (POR algo)

indent /ɪn'dent/ *vt* 1 ‹*line/paragraph*› sangrar 2 ‹*surface/edge*› marcar*, dejar marcas en

indentation /'ɪnden'teɪʃən/ *n*

A [c] 1 (along edge, border) mella *f* 2 (dent) hendidura *f*

B (Print) 1 [u] (act of indenting) sangría *f* 2 [c] (blank space) espacio *m*

independence /'ɪndɪ'pendəns/ *n* [u] independencia *f*

Independence Day *n* día *m* de la Independencia

> **Independence Day**
>
> En EEUU es el 4 de julio, día festivo oficial en que se celebra la independencia de la nación. En ese día, en 1776, el *Continental Congress* (el primer cuerpo de gobierno del naciente EEUU) sancionó la Declaración de Independencia (*Declaration of Independence*)

independent /'ɪndɪ'pendənt/ *adj*

A ‹*person/country/survey*› independiente; ‹*income*› independiente, propio, personal; **a person of ~ means** una persona que dispone de rentas; **Senegal became ~ in 1960** Senegal obtuvo la independencia *or* se independizó en 1960

B 1 ‹*company/newspaper/candidate*› independiente 2 (BrE) ‹*school*› particular, privado; ‹*sector*› privado; ‹*television/radio*› privado

independently /'ɪndɪ'pendəntli/ *adv*

A (without outside help): **is she capable of working the problem out ~?** ¿puede resolver el problema sola *or* por sí misma?; **~ OF sb**: **try to make up your mind ~ of anyone else** trata de decidir por ti misma *or* independientemente de lo que digan los demás

B 1 (separately) por separado 2 (by disinterested party) ‹*assessed/investigated*› independientemente

in-depth /'ɪn'depθ/ *adj* (*before n*) a fondo, en profundidad, exhaustivo

indescribable /'ɪndɪ'skraɪbəbəl/ *adj* indescriptible, inenarrable (liter); (*as intensifier*) ‹*mess/beauty/sadness*› indescriptible, increíble

indestructible /'ɪndɪ'strʌktəbəl/ *adj* indestructible

indeterminate /'ɪndɪ'tɜːrmənət || ˌɪndɪ'tɜːmɪnət/ *adj* indeterminado

index¹ /'ɪndeks/ *n*

A (*pl* **indexes**) 1 (in book, journal) índice *m* 2 (list) lista *f*; (*before n*) **~ card** ficha *f*

B (*pl* **indexes** *o* **indices**) (Econ, Fin) índice *m*; **the retail price ~** el índice de precios al consumo; (*before n*) **~ number** índice *m*

C (*pl* **indices**) (Math) índice *m*

index² *vt*

A (Publ) 1 (provide with index) ‹*book/journal*› ponerle* un índice a 2 (enter in index) ‹*name*› incluir* en un índice

B (Econ, Fin) ‹*prices/wages*› indexar, indiciar

index: **~ finger** *n* (dedo *m*) índice *m*; **~ fund** *n* fondo *m* indexado; **~-linked** /'ɪndeks'lɪŋkt/ *adj* (esp BrE) indexado, indiciado

India /'ɪndiə/ *n* la India

India ink, india ink *n* [u] tinta *f* china

Indian¹ /'ɪndiən/ *adj*

A (of India) indio

B (of America) indígena, indio

Indian² *n*

A 1 [c] (person from India) indio, -dia *m,f* 2 [c u] (food, meal) (BrE colloq) comida *f* india

B [c] (*American* ~) indígena *mf*, indio, -dia *m,f*

Indian: **~ file** *n* (BrE) **in ~ file** en fila india; **~ giver** *n* (AmE) *niño que regala algo y luego quiere que se lo devuelvan*; **~ ink, i~ ink** *n* [u] (esp BrE) ▸ **India ink**; **~ Ocean** *n* **the ~ Ocean** el (Océano) Índico; **~ summer** *n* (in northern hemisphere) ≈ veranillo *m* de San Martín *or* de San Miguel; (in southern hemisphere) ≈ veranillo *m* de San Juan

India rubber *n* caucho *m*, hule *m* (Méx)

indicate /'ɪndəkeɪt || 'ɪndɪkeɪt/ *vt*

A 1 (point out) ‹*object/direction*› señalar, indicar*; **to ~ sth TO sb** señalarle algo A algn 2 (Auto) indicar*, señalizar* 3 (mark) (*often pass*) señalar; **is it ~d on the map?** ¿está señalado en el mapa? 4 (register) ‹‹*instrument/scale*›› indicar*

B 1 (show) ‹*change/condition*› ser* indicio *or* señal de 2 (state) señalar

C (require) (*usu pass*): **a change in tactics is ~d, I feel** creo que se impone un cambio de táctica

■ **indicate** *vi* (BrE Auto) indicar*, señalizar*, poner* el intermitente *or* (Col, Méx) las direccionales *or* (Chi) el señalizador

indication /'ɪndə'keɪʃən || ˌɪndɪ'keɪʃən/ *n* 1 [c u] (sign, hint) indicio *m*; **there is every ~ that ...** todo parece indicar que ..., todo parece apuntar a que ... 2 [c] (Med) indicación *f*

indicative¹ /ɪn'dɪkətɪv/ *adj*

A (revealing) (frml) **to be ~ OF sth** ser* indicio DE algo, revelar algo

B (Ling) ‹*mood/form*› indicativo

indicative² *n* (Ling) **the ~** el indicativo

indicator /'ɪndəkeɪtər || 'ɪndɪkeɪtə(r)/ *n*

A 1 (pointer) indicador *m* 2 (instrument) indicador *m*

B (Auto) intermitente *m*, direccional *f* (Col, Méx), señalizador *m* (*de viraje*) (Chi)

C (sign) indicador *m*

indices /'ɪndəsiːz || 'ɪndɪsiːz/ *pl of* **index¹ B,C**

indict /ɪn'daɪt/ *vt* (Law) acusar; **to ~ sb FOR sth** acusar a algn DE algo

indictment /ɪn'daɪtmənt/ *n*

A [c u] (Law) acusación *f*; **to bring an ~ against sb** formular cargos contra algn

B [c] (criticism): **the report was an ~ of his management** el informe censuraba *or* criticaba su gestión

indie *n* 1 (Mus) indie *m* 2 (Cin) productora *f* independiente

indifference /ɪn'dɪfrəns/ *n* [u] **~ (TO/TOWARD sb/sth)** indiferencia *f* (ANTE/HACIA algn/algo)

indifferent /ɪn'dɪfrənt/ *adj*

A (uninterested) indiferente; **~ TO sth/sb**: **he is quite ~ to that sort of thing** ese tipo de cosa le es *or* le resulta totalmente indiferente

B (mediocre) ‹*performer*› mediocre, del montón (fam); **good, bad or ~?** ¿bueno, malo o regular?

indigenous /ɪn'dɪdʒənəs/ *adj* ‹*population/language*› indígena, autóctono; ‹*species*› autóctono; **~ TO sth**: **this tree/**

animal isn't ~ to Australia este árbol/animal no pertenece a la flora/fauna autóctona de Australia

indigent /'ɪndɪdʒənt/ *adj* (liter) indigente; **~ patient** (AmE) *paciente con derecho a recibir atención médica gratuita*

indigestible /'ɪndaɪ'dʒestəbəl, -də- || ˌɪndɪ'dʒestəbəl/ *adj* 1 (Physiol) (impossible to digest) no digerible; (hard to digest) indigesto, difícil de digerir 2 ‹*book/style*› pesado, difícil de digerir

indigestion /'ɪndaɪ'dʒestʃən, -də- || ˌɪndɪ'dʒestʃən/ *n* [u] indigestión *f*; **onions give me ~** las cebollas me resultan indigestas *or* me producen indigestión

indignant /ɪn'dɪgnənt/ *adj* indignado; **to be ~** estar* indignado; **~ AT sth/-ING: he was ~ at the suggestion** la sugerencia lo indignó; **they felt ~ at receiving such a small reward** se indignaron al recibir tan mezquina recompensa

indignantly /ɪn'dɪgnəntli/ *adv* con indignación

indignation /'ɪndɪg'neɪʃən/ *n* [u] indignación *f*; **~ AT sth** indignación ANTE algo

indignity /ɪn'dɪgnəti/ *n* [u c] (*pl* **-ties**) humillación *f*, indignidad *f*; (inflicted by others) humillación *f*, vejación *f*

indigo /'ɪndɪgəʊ/ *n* [u] índigo *m*, añil *m*; (*before n*) ‹*ink/sea*› color añil *adj inv*, azul añil *adj inv*; **~ blue** (azul *m*) índigo *m or* añil *m*

indirect /'ɪndə'rekt, -daɪ- || ˌɪndɪ'rekt, -daɪ-/ *adj*
A 1 ‹*route/method*› indirecto 2 (veiled) ‹*threat/criticism*› indirecto, velado 3 ‹*result/benefit*› indirecto 4 (Ling) ‹*statement/question*› indirecto; **~ discourse** *o* (BrE) **speech** estilo *m* indirecto
B (Fin) ‹*costs/taxes*› indirecto

indirectly /'ɪndə'rektli, -daɪ- || ˌɪndɪ'rektli, -daɪ-/ *adv* indirectamente

indiscernible /'ɪndɪ'sɜːrnəbəl || ˌɪndɪ'sɜːnəbəl/ *adj* imperceptible

indiscreet /'ɪndɪs'kriːt/ *adj* indiscreto; **it was ~ of you to tell him** cometiste una indiscreción al decírselo

indiscretion /'ɪndɪs'kreʃən/ *n* [c u] indiscreción *f*

indiscriminate /'ɪndɪs'krɪmənət || ˌɪndɪ'skrɪmɪnət/ *adj* 1 ‹*attacks/killings*› indiscriminado 2 ‹*viewing/reading*› hecho sin criterio *or* discernimiento

indispensable /'ɪndɪs'pensəbəl/ *adj* indispensable, imprescindible; **to be ~ TO sb/sth** ser* indispensable *or* imprescindible PARA algn/algo

indisposed /'ɪndɪ'spəʊzd/ *adj* (frml) (*pred*) 1 (ill) **to be ~** estar* *or* encontrarse* indispuesto (frml) 2 (disinclined) **~ to + INF: I feel very ~ to help them** no me siento nada dispuesto a ayudarlos

indisposition /'ɪndɪspə'zɪʃən/ *n* [u c] (frml) indisposición *f* (frml)

indisputable /'ɪndɪ'spjuːtəbəl/ *adj* ‹*evidence/proof*› irrefutable; ‹*leader/winner*› indiscutible, indiscutido

indissoluble /'ɪndɪ'sɑːljəbəl || ˌɪndɪ'sɒljʊbəl/ *adj* (frml) indisoluble

indistinct /'ɪndɪ'stɪŋkt/ *adj* ‹*sound/shape*› poco definido, indistinto; ‹*speech*› poco claro

indistinguishable /'ɪndɪ'stɪŋgwɪʃəbəl/ *adj* **~ (FROM sth)** indistinguible (DE algo); **the two products are quite ~** es imposible distinguir un producto del otro

individual¹ /'ɪndə'vɪdʒuəl || ˌɪndɪ'vɪdjʊəl/ *adj*
A (*before n*) (*no comp*) 1 (for one person) ‹*portion*› individual; ‹*tuition*› personal 2 (single, separate): **you can purchase the whole set or ~ items** se puede comprar el juego o cada pieza por separado 3 (particular, personal) ‹*style*› personal, propio
B (original, distinctive) personal, original

individual² *n* 1 (single person, animal) individuo *m* 2 (person) (colloq) individuo, -dua *m,f*, tipo, -pa *m,f* (fam)

individualism /'ɪndə'vɪdʒuəlɪzəm || ˌɪndɪ'vɪdjʊəlɪzəm/ *n* [u] individualismo *m*

individualist /'ɪndə'vɪdʒuələst || ˌɪndɪ'vɪdjʊəlɪst/ *n* individualista *mf*

individuality /'ɪndə'vɪdʒu'æləti || ˌɪndɪˌvɪdjʊ'æləti/ *n* [u] individualidad *f*

individually /'ɪndə'vɪdʒuəli || ˌɪndɪ'vɪdjʊəli/ *adv* (separately) por separado, individualmente

indivisible /'ɪndə'vɪzəbəl || ˌɪndɪ'vɪzəbəl/ *adj* indivisible

indoctrinate /ɪn'dɑːktrəneɪt || ɪn'dɒktrɪneɪt/ *vt* adoctrinar; **to ~ sb WITH** *o* **IN sth** adoctrinar a algn EN algo

indoctrination /ɪn'dɑːktrə'neɪʃən || ɪnˌdɒktrɪ'neɪʃən/ *n* [u] adoctrinamiento *m*

Indo-European /'ɪndəʊ'jʊrə'piːən || ˌɪndəʊjʊərə'piːən/ *adj* indoeuropeo

indolent /'ɪndələnt/ *adj* (frml) indolente

indomitable /ɪn'dɑːmətəbəl || ɪn'dɒmɪtəbəl/ *adj* (frml) indómito (liter), indomable

Indonesia /'ɪndə'niːʒə || ˌɪndə'niːziə/ *n* Indonesia *f*

Indonesian¹ /'ɪndə'niːʒən || ˌɪndə'niːziən/ *adj* indonesio

Indonesian² *n* 1 [c] (person) indonesio, -sia *m,f* 2 [u] (language) indonesio *m*

indoor /'ɪndɔːr || 'ɪndɔː(r)/ *adj* (*before n*) ‹*clothes/shoes*› para estar en casa; ‹*plants*› de interior(es); ‹*swimming pool*› cubierto, techado; **~ games** deportes *mpl* bajo techo

indoors /'ɪn'dɔːrz || ˌɪn'dɔːz/ *adv* dentro, adentro (esp AmL); **to stay ~** quedarse (a)dentro; **let's go ~** entremos

induce /ɪn'duːs || ɪn'djuːs/ *vt*
A (persuade, cause) **to ~ sb to + INF** inducir* a algn A + INF
B (Med) ‹*hypnosis/sleep/labor*› inducir*, provocar*

inducement /ɪn'duːsmənt || ɪn'djuːsmənt/ *n* (incentive) incentivo *m*, aliciente *m*

induction /ɪn'dʌkʃən/ *n* [u]
A 1 (introduction) **~ (INTO sth)** iniciación *f* (EN algo); (*before n*) ‹*course/period*› introductorio 2 (Relig) instalación *f* como párroco 3 (AmE Mil) reclutamiento *m*, conscripción *f* (AmL)
B (Med) (of labor) inducción *f*

indulge /ɪn'dʌldʒ/ *vt* ‹*child*› consentir*, mimar; ‹*desire/appetite*› satisfacer*; **it doesn't hurt to ~ oneself every now and again** es bueno darse algún gusto de vez en cuando
■ **indulge** *vi* **to ~ IN sth** permitirse algo

indulgence /ɪn'dʌldʒəns/ *n*
A 1 [c] (extravagance, luxury): **an occasional cigar is my only ~** un puro de vez en cuando es el único lujo que me permito 2 [u] (partaking): **too much ~ in anything is bad** es malo abusar de cualquier placer
B [u] 1 (satisfaction) complacencia *f* 2 (tolerance) indulgencia *f*
C [c u] (Relig) indulgencia *f*

indulgent /ɪn'dʌldʒənt/ *adj* indulgente; **to be ~ TOWARD** *o* **WITH sb** ser* indulgente CON algn

industrial /ɪn'dʌstriəl/ *adj* 1 ‹*town/production/engineering*› industrial 2 (Lab Rel): **~ accident** accidente *m* laboral *or* de trabajo; **~ dispute** conflicto *m* laboral

industrial: ~ action *n* [u] (BrE Lab Rel frml) *huelga o cualquier otra medida de presión ejercida en un conflicto laboral*; **~ estate** *n* (BrE) zona *f* industrial, polígono *m* industrial (Esp)

industrialist /ɪn'dʌstriələst || ɪn'dʌstriəlɪst/ *n* industrial *mf*

industrialize /ɪn'dʌstriəlaɪz/ *vi* industrializarse*
■ **industrialize** *vt* industrializar*

industrial: ~ park *n* (AmE) zona *f* industrial, polígono *m* industrial (Esp); **~ relations** *pl n* relaciones *fpl* laborales; **~ Revolution** *n* **the I~ Revolution** la Revolución Industrial; **~ tribunal** *n* (in UK) tribunal *m* laboral, magistratura *f* del trabajo

industrious /ɪn'dʌstriəs/ *adj* ‹*worker*› trabajador, laborioso, diligente; ‹*student*› aplicado, diligente

industry /'ɪndəstri/ *n* (*pl* **-tries**)
A 1 [u] (in general) industria *f*; **she works in ~** trabaja en el sector empresarial 2 [c] (particular branch) industria *f*; **the steel/textile ~** la industria siderúrgica/textil; **the tourist ~** el turismo
B [u] (hard work) (frml) laboriosidad *f*, diligencia *f*, aplicación *f*

inebriated /ɪn'iːbrieɪtəd || ɪn'iːbrieɪtɪd/ *adj* (frml) ‹*person*› beodo (frml), ebrio (frml); ‹*state*› de embriaguez (frml)

inebriation /ɪn'iːbri'eɪʃən/ *n* [u] (frml) embriaguez *f* (frml)

inedible /ɪn'edəbəl/ *adj* 1 (impossible to eat) no comestible 2 (unpalatable) incomible

ineffable /ɪn'efəbəl/ *adj* (liter) inenarrable (liter), inefable (liter), indescriptible

ineffective /'ɪnə'fektɪv || ˌɪnɪ'fektɪv/ *adj* ‹*measure/response*› ineficaz; ‹*attempt*› infructuoso, que no da resultado *or* no surte efecto; ‹*person*› incompetente, ineficiente

ineffectual /'ɪnə'fektʃuəl || ˌɪnɪ'fektʃʊəl/ *adj* ‹*person*› inútil, incapaz; ‹*action/response*› inútil

inefficiency /'ɪnə'fɪʃənsi || ˌɪnɪ'fɪʃənsi/ *n* [u] 1 (of machinery) falta *f* de eficiencia 2 (of persons, method) ineficiencia *f*

inefficient /'ɪnə'fɪʃənt || ˌɪnɪ'fɪʃənt/ *adj* 1 ‹*machine/method*› ineficiente, poco eficiente 2 ‹*person/worker*› ineficiente, incompetente

inefficiently /'ɪnə'fɪʃəntli || ˌɪnɪ'fɪʃəntli/ *adv* de manera ineficiente

inelegant /ɪn'elɪgənt/ *adj* poco elegante, inelegante

ineligible /ɪn'eləd͡ʒəbəl || ɪn'elɪd͡ʒəbəl/ *adj* (*usu pred*) ‹*candidate*› inelegible; **she was ~ to vote** no tenía derecho a votar

inept /ɪ'nept/ *adj* ‹*person*› inepto, incapaz, inútil; ‹*conduct/remark*› torpe

ineptitude /ɪ'neptətuːd || ɪ'neptɪtjuːd/ *n* [u] ineptitud *f*, inepcia *f* (frml)

inequality /'ɪnɪ'kwɑːləti || ˌɪnɪ'kwɒləti/ *n* (*pl* **-ties**) desigualdad *f*

inequitable /ɪn'ekwətəbəl || ɪ'nekwɪtəbəl/ *adj* (frml) injusto, no equitativo

inert /ɪ'nɜːrt || ɪ'nɜːt/ *adj* 1 (immobile) (frml) (*usu pred*) inerte (frml) 2 (Chem) ‹*gas*› inerte

inertia /ɪ'nɜːrʃə || ɪ'nɜːʃə/ *n* [u] 1 (inactivity) apatía *f*, inercia *f* 2 (Phys) inercia *f*

inescapable /'ɪnə'skeɪpəbəl/ *adj* ‹*necessity/responsibility*› ineludible; ‹*fate*› inexorable; ‹*outcome*› inevitable

inessential /'ɪnə'sentʃəl || ˌɪnɪ'senʃəl/ *adj* no esencial, innecesario, superfluo

inestimable /ɪn'estəməbəl || ˌɪn'estɪməbəl/ *adj* (frml) ‹*value/worth/service*› inestimable, inapreciable; ‹*damage*› incalculable

inevitable[1] /ɪn'evətəbəl || ɪn'evɪtəbəl/ *adj* 1 (certain, unavoidable) inevitable 2 (predictable) consabido, indefectible

inevitable[2] *n* **the ~** lo inevitable

inevitably /ɪn'evətəbli/ *adv* 1 (unavoidably) inevitablemente, forzosamente 2 (invariably) indefectiblemente

inexact /'ɪnɪg'zækt/ *adj* inexacto

inexcusable /'ɪnɪk'skjuːzəbəl/ *adj* imperdonable, inexcusable

inexhaustible /'ɪnɪg'zɔːstəbəl/ *adj* 1 ‹*funds/supply*› inagotable 2 ‹*athlete/hiker*› incansable, infatigable

inexorable /ɪn'eksərəbəl/ *adj* inexorable

inexpensive /'ɪnɪk'spensɪv/ *adj* económico, barato

inexperience /'ɪnɪk'spɪriəns || ˌɪnɪk'spɪəriəns/ *n* [u] inexperiencia *f*, falta *f* de experiencia

inexperienced /'ɪnɪk'spɪriənst || ˌɪnɪk'spɪəriənst/ *adj* ‹*nurse/pilot*› sin experiencia; ‹*swimmer/driver*› inexperto, novato; **to be ~ AT** *o* **IN sth** no tener* experiencia EN algo

inexpert /ɪn'ekspɜːrt || ɪn'ekspɜːt/ *adj* inexperto, poco hábil; **his ~ attempt at …** su torpe intento de …

inexpertly /ɪn'ekspɜːrtli || ɪn'ekspɜːtli/ *adv* con poca pericia *or* habilidad

inexplicable /'ɪnɪk'splɪkəbəl/ *adj* inexplicable

inexplicably /'ɪnɪk'splɪkəbli/ *adv* de forma inexplicable, inexplicablemente; **he felt ~ sad/happy** sentía una tristeza/alegría inexplicable

inexpressible /'ɪnɪk'spresəbəl/ *adj* ‹*joy/sorrow*› inexpresable, inefable (liter)

inextricably /'ɪnɪk'strɪkəbli/ *adv* inextricablemente

infallibility /ɪn'fælə'bɪləti/ *n* [u] infalibilidad *f*

infallible /ɪn'fæləbəl/ *adj* ‹*person/method*› infalible

infamous /'ɪnfəməs/ *adj* 1 (notorious) de triste fama, de infausta memoria (liter) 2 (shameful) infame

infamy /'ɪnfəmi/ *n* [c u] (*pl* **-mies**) (frml) infamia *f*

infancy /'ɪnfənsi/ *n* [u]

A (babyhood) primera infancia *f*; **this branch of science is still in its ~** esta rama de la ciencia está aún en pañales *or* en mantillas

B (Law) minoría *f* de edad

infant /'ɪnfənt/ *n*

A 1 (baby) bebé *m*, niño, -ña *m,f*; (*before n*) **~ mortality** mortalidad *f* infantil 2 (BrE Educ) niño, -ña *m,f* (*entre cinco y siete años de edad*); (*before n*) **~ school** (in UK) *escuela para niños de entre cinco y siete años de edad*

B (Law) menor *mf* (de edad)

infanticide /ɪn'fæntəsaɪd || ɪn'fæntɪsaɪd/ *n* [u c] (crime) infanticidio *m*

infantile /'ɪnfəntaɪl/ *adj* ‹*behavior/humor*› pueril, infantil

infantry /'ɪnfəntri/ *n* [u] (+ *sing or pl vb*) infantería *f*

infantryman /'ɪnfəntrimən/ *n* (*pl* **-men** /-mən/) soldado *m* de infantería, infante *m*

infatuated /ɪn'fætʃueɪtəd || ɪn'fætjʊeɪtɪd/ *adj* **to be ~ WITH sb** estar* encaprichado CON *or* (Esp tb) DE algn

infatuation /ɪn'fætʃu'eɪʃən || ɪnˌfætjʊ'eɪʃən/ *n* [u c] encaprichamiento *m*

infect /ɪn'fekt/ *vt*

A (Med) 1 ‹*wound/cut*› infectar; ‹*person/animal*› contagiar; **the wound became ~ed** la herida se infectó; **to ~ sb WITH sth** contagiarle algo A algn 2 (contaminate) contaminar

B (spread emotion): **his cheerfulness ~ed everyone around him** les contagiaba su alegría a todos los que lo rodeaban

infection /ɪn'fekʃən/ *n* 1 [c] (disease) infección *f* 2 [u] (of wound) infección *f*; (of person) contagio *m*

infectious /ɪn'fekʃəs/ *adj* 1 (Med) ‹*disease*› infeccioso, contagioso; **is she still ~?** ¿aún es contagioso lo que tiene? 2 ‹*laughter/enthusiasm*› contagioso; ‹*rhythm*› pegadizo, pegajoso (AmL exc RPl)

infer /ɪn'fɜːr || ɪn'fɜː(r)/ *vt* **-rr-** (deduce) **to ~ sth (FROM sth)** inferir* *or* deducir* *or* colegir* algo (DE algo)

inference /'ɪnfərəns/ *n* [c u] deducción *f*, conclusión *f*, inferencia *f* (frml); **to draw an ~** hacer* una deducción; **to draw an ~ from sth** sacar* una conclusión de algo

inferior[1] /ɪn'fɪriər || ɪn'fɪəriə(r)/ *adj* (*no comp*) ‹*product*› (de calidad) inferior; ‹*workmanship/rank*› inferior; **~ TO sth/sb** inferior A algo/algn

inferior[2] *n* [c] inferior *mf*

inferiority /ɪn'fɪri'ɔːrəti || ɪnˌfɪərɪ'ɒrəti/ *n* [u] inferioridad *f*; **~ TO sth/sb** inferioridad FRENTE A *or* CON RESPECTO A algo/algn; (*before n*) **~ complex** complejo *m* de inferioridad

infernal /ɪn'fɜːrnl̩ || ɪn'fɜːnl̩/ *adj*

A (colloq & dated) ‹*din/row*› infernal, de (los) mil demonios (fam)

B (liter) (of hell) infernal, de los infiernos

inferno /ɪn'fɜːrnəʊ || ɪn'fɜːnəʊ/ *n* (*pl* **-noes**) 1 (fire) (journ): **the building was a blazing ~** el edificio estaba totalmente envuelto en llamas *or* ardía como una hoguera 2 (hell) (liter) averno *m* (liter), infierno *m*

infertile /ɪn'fɜːrtl̩ || ɪn'fɜːtaɪl/ *adj* ‹*land/soil*› estéril, infecundo, yermo (liter); ‹*woman/man/animal*› estéril

infertility /'ɪnfər'tɪləti || ˌɪnfə'tɪləti/ *n* [u] (Agr) infecundidad *f*; (Biol) esterilidad *f*

infest /ɪn'fest/ *vt* infestar; **to be ~ed WITH sth** estar* infestado *or* plagado DE algo

infestation /'ɪnfes'teɪʃən/ *n* [u c] plaga *f*, infestación *f*

infidel /'ɪnfədl̩ || 'ɪnfɪdəl/ *n* (Hist, Relig) infiel *mf*

infidelity /'ɪnfə'deləti || ˌɪnfɪ'deləti/ *n* [u c] (*pl* **-ties**) infidelidad *f*

infield /'ɪnfiːld/ *n* [u] (in baseball) cuadro *m*

infighting /'ɪnˌfaɪtɪŋ/ *n* [u] luchas *fpl* internas *or* (frml) intestinas

infiltrate /ɪn'fɪltreɪt || 'ɪnfɪltreɪt/ *vt* infiltrarse en

infiltration /'ɪnfɪl'treɪʃən/ *n* [u] infiltración *f*

infiltrator /ɪn'fɪltreɪtər || 'ɪnfɪltreɪtə(r)/ *n* infiltrado, -da *m,f*

infinite /'ɪnfənət || 'ɪnfɪnət/ *adj* 1 (limitless) infinito 2 (great, extreme) infinito

infinitely /'ɪnfənətli || 'ɪnfɪnətli/ *adv* infinitamente

infinitesimal /'ɪnfɪnə'tesɪml̩/ *adj* infinitesimal

infinitive /ɪn'fɪnətɪv/ *n* infinitivo *m*

infinity /ɪn'fɪnəti/ *n* 1 [u] (Math) infinito *m* 2 [u] (endless space) infinito *m* 3 (vast number, quantity) (liter) (*no pl*) infinidad *f*

infirm /ɪn'fɜːrm || ɪn'fɜːm/ *adj* (weak) endeble, enfermizo; (ill) enfermo

infirmary /ɪn'fɜːrməri || ɪn'fɜːməri/ *n* (*pl* **-ries**) [1] (hospital) (used in titles) hospital *m* [2] (medical room) enfermería *f*

infirmity /ɪn'fɜːrməti || ɪn'fɜːməti/ *n* [c u] (*pl* **-ties**) dolencia *f* (frml), padecimiento *m*

inflame /ɪn'fleɪm/ *vt* [1] ‹*person/passion*› encender*, inflamar (liter); ‹*situation*› exacerbar; **the crowd was ~d by his speech** su discurso enardeció a la multitud [2] (Med) inflamar

inflamed /ɪn'fleɪmd/ *adj* inflamado; **to become ~** inflamarse

inflammable /ɪn'flæməbəl/ *adj* ‹*substance/material*› inflamable; ‹*situation*› explosivo

inflammation /'ɪnflə'meɪʃən/ *n* [u c] inflamación *f*

inflammatory /ɪn'flæmətɔːri || ɪn'flæmətri/ *adj* ‹*speech/writing*› incendiario, que exalta *or* (liter) inflama los ánimos

inflatable /ɪn'fleɪtəbəl/ *adj* inflable, hinchable (Esp)

inflate /ɪn'fleɪt/ *vt* [1] (with air, gas) inflar, hinchar (Esp) [2] ‹*prices/economy*› inflar

■ **inflate** *vi* «*balloon/dinghy*» inflarse, hincharse (Esp)

inflated /ɪn'fleɪtəd || ɪn'fleɪtɪd/ *adj* [1] (with air, gas) inflado, hinchado (Esp) [2] (exaggerated) ‹*prices*› inflado; **she has an ~ sense of her own importance** se cree muy importante

inflation /ɪn'fleɪʃən/ *n* [u] inflación *f*

inflationary /ɪn'fleɪʃəneri || ɪn'fleɪʃənri/ *adj* inflacionario, inflacionista

inflect /ɪn'flekt/ *vt* [1] (Ling) ‹*verb*› conjugar*; ‹*noun*› declinar [2] (vary pitch of) modular

■ **inflect** *vi* (Ling) tomar desinencias

inflection /ɪn'flekʃən/ *n* [u c] [1] (Ling) flexión *f*, inflexión *f*; (ending) desinencia *f*, inflexión *f* [2] (intonation) entonación *f*, inflexión *f*

inflexibility /ɪn'fleksə'bɪləti/ *n* [u] [1] (of person, system) inflexibilidad *f* [2] (of material) rigidez *f*

inflexible /ɪn'fleksəbəl/ *adj* [1] ‹*personality/regulations*› inflexible [2] ‹*material*› rígido

inflict /ɪn'flɪkt/ *vt* ‹*pain/damage*› causar, ocasionar, inferir* (frml); ‹*punishment*› imponer*, aplicar*, infligir*; **to ~ sth ON sb**: **the suffering which he ~ed on his family** el sufrimiento que le causó *or* ocasionó *or* (frml) infirió a su familia

in-flight /'ɪnflaɪt/ *adj* ‹*services*› de a bordo

influence[1] /'ɪnfluəns/ *n* [1] [c u] (effect) **~ (ON sb/sth)** influencia *f* (SOBRE algn/algo); **to be under the ~ of sb/sth** estar* bajo la influencia de algn/algo; **he was already under the ~** (colloq) ya estaba borracho [2] [c] (power) **~ (OVER/ON sb/sth)** influencia *f* (SOBRE algn/algo); **to have ~ over sb/sth** tener* influencia *or* (frml) ascendiente sobre algn/algo [3] [c] (source of effect): **she's a good/bad ~ on him** ejerce buena/mala influencia sobre él

influence[2] *vt* ‹*person/decision*› influir* en, influenciar

influential /'ɪnflu'entʃəl || ˌɪnflʊ'enʃəl/ *adj* influyente

influenza /'ɪnflu'enzə/ *n* [u] (Med) gripe *f or* (Chi tb) influenza *f or* (Col, Méx) gripa *f*

influx /'ɪnflʌks/ *n* [u c] (of people) afluencia *f*; (of goods) entrada *f*; (of ideas) llegada *f*

info /'ɪnfəʊ/ *n* [u] (colloq) información *f*

inform /ɪn'fɔːrm || ɪn'fɔːm/ *vt* (advise) informar; (by letter) informar, notificar*; **to keep sb ~ed** mantener* a algn informado *or* al corriente; **to ~ sb OF/ABOUT sth**: **we've not yet been ~ed of any change of plan** todavía no se nos ha informado de ningún cambio de plan; **its aim is to ~ people about the dangers of pollution** tiene por objeto informar al público sobre los peligros de la contaminación; **to ~ sb THAT** informarle a algn QUE; **I'm reliably ~ed that ...** me informan de buena fuente que ...

■ **inform** *vi* **to ~ ON** *o* **AGAINST sb** delatar *or* denunciar a algn

informal /ɪn'fɔːrməl || ɪn'fɔːməl/ *adj* [1] (casual) ‹*party/atmosphere*› informal; **we're very ~ in this office** en esta oficina el ambiente es muy informal [2] (not official) ‹*meeting/agreement*› informal

informality /'ɪnfɔːr'mæləti || ˌɪnfɔː'mæləti/ *n* [u] falta *f* de ceremonia, informalidad *f*

informally /ɪn'fɔːrməli || ɪn'fɔːməli/ *adv* [1] (casually) ‹*talk*› de manera informal, sin ceremonias; ‹*dress*› de manera informal [2] (unofficially) ‹*meet/discuss*› informalmente

informant /ɪn'fɔːrmənt || ɪn'fɔːmənt/ *n* informante *mf*, informador, -dora *m,f*

information /'ɪnfər'meɪʃən || ˌɪnfə'meɪʃən/ *n* [u] [1] (facts, news) información *f*; **a piece of ~** un dato; **for more/further ~ write to ...** para más/mayor información diríjase a ...; **~ ABOUT** *o* **ON sth/sb** información *f* ACERCA DE *or* SOBRE algo/algn; **we have no ~ as to his whereabouts** desconocemos su paradero; **for your ~** para su información, a título informativo (frml); **for your ~ I do *not* read other people's letters** para que te enteres, yo no tengo por costumbre leer la correspondencia ajena; (*before n*) **~ desk** información *f*; **~ network** red *f* informativa; **~ science** informática *f* [2] (AmE Telec) información *f*, servicio *m* de información telefónica

information technology *n* informática *f*

informative /ɪn'fɔːrmətɪv || ɪn'fɔːmətɪv/ *adj* ‹*article/lecture*› instructivo, informativo; ‹*guidebook*› lleno de información, informativo

informed /ɪn'fɔːrmd || ɪn'fɔːmd/ *adj* ‹*source/critic*› bien informado; ‹*criticism/approach*› bien fundado; **it's an ~ guess** se trata de una conjetura hecha sobre cierta base *or* con cierto fundamento

informer /ɪn'fɔːrmər || ɪn'fɔːmə(r)/ *n* informante *mf*

infrared /'ɪnfrə'red/ *adj* infrarrojo

infrastructure /'ɪnfrə'strʌktʃər || 'ɪnfrəˌstrʌktʃə(r)/ *n* infraestructura *f*

infrequent /ɪn'friːkwənt/ *adj* poco frecuente

infringe /ɪn'frɪndʒ/ *vt* ‹*contract*› no cumplir (con), incumplir; ‹*treaty/rule*› infringir*, transgredir, violar

■ **infringe** *vi* **to ~ ON** *o* **UPON sth** violar algo

infringement /ɪn'frɪndʒmənt/ *n* [c u] [1] (of law) contravención *f*, violación *f*; (of contract) incumplimiento *m*; (Sport) falta *f*; **they admitted ~ of copyright** reconocieron no haber respetado los derechos de autor [2] (of rights) violación *f*

infuriate /ɪn'fjʊrieɪt || ɪn'fjʊərieɪt/ *vt* enfurecer*, poner* furioso

infuriating /ɪn'fjʊrieɪtɪŋ || ɪn'fjʊərieɪtɪŋ/ *adj* exasperante, irritante

infuse /ɪn'fjuːz/ *vt* [1] (Culin) ‹*tea/herb*› hacer* una infusión de [2] (instill) (liter) **to ~ sb WITH sth, to ~ sth INTO sb** infundirle algo A algn

■ **infuse** *vi* (Culin): **let the tea bag ~ for three minutes** deje la bolsita de té en infusión durante tres minutos

infusion /ɪn'fjuːʒən/ *n* [c u]

A (extract) infusión *f*; (drink) infusión *f*, tisana *f*, agua *f*‡ (AmC, Andes)

B (of money, new life) inyección *f*

ingenious /ɪn'dʒiːnjəs || ɪn'dʒiːniəs/ *adj* ingenioso

ingenuity /ˌɪndʒə'nuːəti || ˌɪndʒə'njuːəti/ *n* [u] (of person) ingenio *m*, inventiva *f*, ingeniosidad *f*; (of gadget, idea) lo ingenioso

ingenuous /ɪn'dʒenjuəs/ *adj* [1] (naive) ingenuo [2] (frank, open) cándido, franco

ingest /ɪn'dʒest/ *vt* (frml) ingerir* (frml)

ingot /'ɪŋgət/ *n* lingote *m*

ingrained /'ɪn'greɪnd/ *adj* [1] ‹*belief/habit*› arraigado [2] ‹*dirt*› incrustado

ingratiate /ɪn'greɪʃieɪt/ *v refl* **to ~ oneself (WITH sb)** congraciarse (CON algn)

ingratiating /ɪn'greɪʃieɪtɪŋ/ *adj* halagador, obsequioso

ingratitude /ɪn'grætətuːd/ *n* [u] ingratitud *f*

ingredient /ɪn'griːdiənt/ *n* [1] (Culin) ingrediente *m* [2] (Pharm) componente *m* [3] (element) elemento *m*

ingrowing /'ɪn'grəʊɪŋ/ *adj* (BrE) ‹*toenail*› que crece hacia adentro, encarnado

ingrown /'ɪngrəʊn/ *adj* (Med): **~ toenail** uñero *m*, uña *f* encarnada, uña *f* enterrada (Méx)

inhabit /ɪn'hæbət || ɪn'hæbɪt/ *vt* ‹*region/building*› habitar (frml), vivir en

inhabitable /ɪn'hæbətəbəl || ɪn'hæbɪtəbəl/ *adj* habitable

inhabitant /ɪn'hæbətənt || ɪn'hæbɪtənt/ *n* habitante *mf*

inhabited /ɪn'hæbətəd || ɪn'hæbɪtɪd/ *adj* habitado

inhalation /ˈɪnhəˈleɪʃən/ *n* [u c] inhalación *f*

inhale /ɪnˈheɪl/ *vt* inhalar, aspirar

■ **inhale** *vi* aspirar; (when smoking) tragarse* el humo

inhaler /ɪnˈheɪlər || ɪnˈheɪlə(r)/ *n* inhalador *m*

inherent /ɪnˈhɪrənt, -ˈher- || ɪnˈhɪərənt, -ˈher-/ *adj* ‹*feature/quality*› inherente; **to be ~ IN sth** ser* inherente A algo; **with all its ~ difficulties** con todas las dificultades que conlleva

inherently /ɪnˈherəntli || ɪnˈhɪərəntli/ *adv* intrínsecamente

inherit /ɪnˈherət || ɪnˈherɪt/ *vt* **to ~ sth (FROM sb/sth)** heredar algo (DE algn/algo)

inheritance /ɪnˈherətəns || ɪnˈherɪtəns/ *n* 1 [c] (sth inherited) herencia *f*; **to come into an ~** heredar 2 [u] (act) sucesión *f*; (*before n*) **~ tax** impuesto *m* sucesorio *or* sobre sucesiones, impuesto *m* a la herencia

inhibit /ɪnˈhɪbət || ɪnˈhɪbɪt/ *vt* (frml) 1 ‹*person*› inhibir, cohibir*; **to ~ sb FROM -ING** impedirle* a algn + INF 2 ‹*growth/reaction*› inhibir

inhibited /ɪnˈhɪbətəd || ɪnˈhɪbɪtɪd/ *adj* inhibido, cohibido

inhibition /ˈɪnəˈbɪʃən || ˌɪnhɪˈbɪʃən/ *n* inhibición *f*

inhospitable /ˌɪnhɑːˈspɪtəbəl || ˌɪnhɒˈspɪtəbəl/ *adj* ‹*person*› poco hospitalario; ‹*climate/region*› inhóspito

in-house[1] /ˈɪnhaʊs/ *adj* ‹*training*› en la empresa (*or* organización *etc*); ‹*staff*› interno

in-house[2] /ɪnˈhaʊs/ *adv* en la empresa (*or* organización *etc*)

inhuman /ɪnˈhjuːmən/ *adj* inhumano

inhumane /ˈɪnhjuːˈmeɪn/ *adj* ‹*treatment*› inhumano; ‹*person*› cruel

inhumanity /ˈɪnhjuːˈmænəti/ *n* (*pl* **-ties**) 1 [u] (cruelty) crueldad *f*, inhumanidad *f* 2 [c] (cruel act) atrocidad *f*

inimitable /ɪnˈɪmətəbəl || ɪˈnɪmɪtəbəl/ *adj* inimitable; **in her own ~ way** en su característico e inimitable estilo

iniquitous /ɪˈnɪkwətəs/ *adj* inicuo (frml), injusto

iniquity /ɪˈnɪkwəti/ *n* (*pl* **-ties**) (frml) iniquidad *f* (frml)

initial[1] /ɪˈnɪʃəl/ *adj* inicial; **in the ~ stages** en la etapa inicial, al principio; **my ~ reaction** mi primera reacción

initial[2] *n* inicial *f*

initial[3] *vt*, (BrE) **-ll-** inicialar, ponerle* las iniciales a

initialize /ɪˈnɪʃəlaɪz/ *vt* (Comput) inicializar*

initially /ɪˈnɪʃəli/ *adv* inicialmente, al principio

initiate /ɪˈnɪʃieɪt/ *vt*

A (start) (frml) ‹*talks*› iniciar (frml), dar* comienzo a (frml), entablar; ‹*reform/plan*› poner* en marcha; ‹*fashion*› introducir*; **to ~ proceedings against sb** entablarle juicio a algn

B (admit, introduce) **to ~ sb (INTO sth)** iniciar a algn (EN algo)

initiation /ɪˈnɪʃiˈeɪʃən/ *n*

A [c u] (admission) **~ (INTO sth)** iniciación *f* (EN algo); (*before n*) **~ ceremony** ceremonia *f* iniciática *or* de iniciación

B [u] (of plan, talks) inicio *m* (frml), comienzo *m*

initiative /ɪˈnɪʃətɪv/ *n* [c u] iniciativa *f*; **on one's own ~** por iniciativa propia, (de) motu proprio; **to take the ~** tomar la iniciativa

inject /ɪnˈdʒekt/ *vt* 1 (Med) ‹*drug*› inyectar; **to ~ sth INTO sth** inyectar algo EN algo; **to ~ sb WITH sth** inyectar(le) algo A algn 2 **to ~ sth (INTO sth)** ‹*capital/resources*› inyectarle algo (A algo)

injection /ɪnˈdʒekʃən/ *n* 1 [c u] (Med) inyección *f*; **to give sb an ~** ponerle* *or* darle* una inyección a algn 2 [u] (*fuel ~*) inyección *f* de combustible 3 [c] (of capital, energy) inyección *f*

injudicious /ˈɪndʒʊˈdɪʃəs/ *adj* (frml) imprudente

injunction /ɪnˈdʒʌŋkʃən/ *n* 1 (Law) mandamiento *m* judicial 2 (order) (frml) orden *f*

injure /ˈɪndʒər || ˈɪndʒə(r)/ *vt* 1 ‹*person*› herir*, lesionar (frml); ‹*pride/feelings*› herir*, lastimar; ‹*reputation*› (frml) dañar; **she ~d her knee** se lesionó la rodilla (frml); **he was seriously ~d in the accident** resultó gravemente herido en el accidente 2 **injured** *past p*: **she gave me an ~d look** me miró con expresión ofendida; **I am the ~d party** soy yo quien sufrió el agravio

injured /ˈɪndʒərd || ˈɪndʒəd/ *pl n* **the ~** los heridos

injurious /ɪnˈdʒʊriəs || ɪnˈdʒʊəriəs/ *adj* (frml) perjudicial; **to be ~ TO sth** ser* perjudicial PARA algo

injury /ˈɪndʒəri/ *n* [c u] (*pl* **-ries**) herida *f*; **to do oneself an ~** hacerse* daño, lastimarse; (*before n*) **~ time** (BrE Sport) tiempo *m* de descuento

injustice /ɪnˈdʒʌstəs || ɪnˈdʒʌstɪs/ *n* [u c] injusticia *f*; **to do sb an ~** cometer una injusticia con algn, ser* injusto con algn

ink /ɪŋk/ *n* [u c] tinta *f*; **please write in ~** se ruega escribir con tinta

Phrasal verb

• **ink in** [v ▸ o ▸ adv, v ▸ adv ▸ o] repasar con tinta

ink: **~blot** *n* mancha *f* de tinta; **~-jet printer** *n* impresora *f* de chorro de tinta

inkling /ˈɪŋklɪŋ/ *n* [u]: **I had an ~ something had gone wrong** tuve el presentimiento *or* (CS, Per tb) el pálpito de que algo había salido mal

ink: **~pad** *n* tampón *m*, almohadilla *f*; **~well** *n* tintero *m* (*empotrado en un escritorio*)

inky /ˈɪŋki/ *adj* **inkier, inkiest** ‹*fingers/pen*› manchado de tinta

inlaid[1] /ˈɪnˈleɪd/ *past & past p of* **inlay**[2]

inlaid[2] *adj* ‹*design*› de marquetería *or* taracea; ‹*box/lid*› con incrustaciones

inland[1] /ˈɪnlənd/ *adj* (*before n*) 1 ‹*town*› del interior; ‹*sea*› interior; **~ waterways** canales *mpl* y ríos *mpl* 2 (domestic) (esp BrE) ‹*postal rates*› nacional; ‹*trade*› interior

inland[2] /ˈɪnˈlænd/ *adv* tierra adentro

Inland Revenue /ˈɪnlənd/ *n* (in UK) **the ~ ~** ≈ Hacienda, ≈ la Dirección General Impositiva (*en RPl*), ≈ Impuestos Internos (*en Chi*); ▸**HMRC** ▸**majesty**

in-laws /ˈɪnlɔːz/ *pl n* (colloq) (spouse's parents) suegros *mpl*; (spouse's family) parientes *mpl* políticos

inlay[1] /ˈɪnleɪ/ *n* [u c] (of wood, metal, ivory) incrustación *f*

inlay[2] /ɪnˈleɪ/ *vt* (*past & past p* **inlaid**) **to ~ sth WITH sth** hacer* incrustaciones de algo EN algo

inlet /ˈɪnlet/ *n*

A (in coastline) ensenada *f*, entrada *f*; (of river, sea) brazo *m*

B (Mech Eng) entrada *f*; (*before n*) ‹*valve/pipe*› de admisión

inmate /ˈɪnmeɪt/ *n* (of asylum) interno, -na *m,f*; (of prison) preso, -sa *m,f*; (of hospital) paciente hospitalizado, -da *m,f*

inmost /ˈɪnməʊst/ *adj* ▸**innermost**

inn /ɪn/ *n* (tavern) taberna *f*; (hotel) hostal *m*, hostería *f*; (Hist) posada *f*

innards /ˈɪnərdz || ˈɪnədz/ *pl n* tripas *fpl* (fam)

innate /ɪˈneɪt/ *adj* innato

innately /ɪˈneɪtli/ *adv* ‹*superior/inferior*› de manera innata; **to be ~ attracted to sth** sentirse* atraído de manera innata *or* por naturaleza hacia algo

inner /ˈɪnər || ˈɪnə(r)/ *adj* (*before n, no comp*) 1 ‹*room/part*› interior; **the ~ city** *la zona del centro urbano habitada por familias de escasos ingresos, caracterizada por problemas sociales etc*; **the ~ ear** el oído interno 2 (of person) ‹*life*› interior; ‹*thoughts*› íntimo; **~ self** fuero *m* interno

inner-city /ˈɪnərˈsɪti || ˌɪnəˈsɪti/ *adj* ‹*schools/problems*› de las zonas urbanas deprimidas

innermost /ˈɪnərməʊst || ˈɪnəməʊst/ *adj* 1 ‹*part/chamber*› más recóndito 2 ‹*thoughts/feelings*› más íntimo

inner tube *n* cámara *f*

inning /ˈɪnɪŋ/ *n* (in baseball) entrada *f*, manga *f*

innings /ˈɪnɪŋz/ *n* (*pl* **~**) (in cricket) entrada *f*, turno *m* de lanzamiento; **she had a good ~** (colloq) vivió sus buenos años

innkeeper /ˈɪnˌkiːpər || ˈɪnˌkiːpə(r)/ *n* posadero, -ra *m,f*, ventero, -ra *m,f*

innocence /ˈɪnəsəns/ *n* [u] inocencia *f*

innocent[1] /ˈɪnəsənt/ *adj* 1 (blameless, not guilty) inocente 2 (naive) inocente, ingenuo 3 (not malicious) ‹*game/mistake*› inocente

innocent[2] *n* (liter) inocente *mf*

innocuous /ɪˈnɑːkjuəs || ɪˈnɒkjuəs/ *adj* ‹*drug*› inocuo; ‹*person/comment*› inofensivo

innovation /ˈɪnəˈveɪʃən/ *n* [c u] innovación *f*, novedad *f*

innovative /ˈɪnəveɪtɪv || ˈɪnəvətɪv/ *adj* innovador

innuendo /ˈɪnjuˈendəʊ/ *n* [c u] (*pl* **-dos** *or* **-does**) indirecta *f*, insinuación *f*; **the article is full of ~s** el artículo hace muchas insinuaciones; **I am tired of all this ~** estoy harta de todas estas indirectas *or* insinuaciones

innumerable /ɪ'nu:mərəbəl || ɪ'nju:mərəbəl/ *adj* innumerable; **on ~ occasions** en innumerables ocasiones, en infinidad de ocasiones

innumerate /ɪ'nu:mərət || ɪ'nju:mərət/ *adj* (BrE) *incapaz de realizar cálculos aritméticos elementales*

inoculate /ɪ'nɑ:kjəleɪt || ɪ'nɒkjʊleɪt/ *vt* **to ~ sb (AGAINST sth)** inocular a algn (CONTRA algo)

inoculation /ɪ'nɑ:kjə'leɪʃən/ *n* [c u] inoculación *f*

inoffensive /'ɪnə'fensɪv/ *adj* inofensivo

inoperable /ɪn'ɑ:prəbəl / *adj* (Med) inoperable

inoperative /ɪn'ɑ:prətɪv || ɪn'ɒpərətɪv/ *adj* inoperante

inopportune /ɪn'ɑ:pər'tu:n || ɪn'ɒpətju:n/ *adj* inoportuno

inordinate /ɪ'nɔ:rdṇət || ɪn'ɔ:dɪnət/ *adj*: **an ~ amount of money** una cantidad exorbitante de dinero; **they are making ~ demands** lo que piden es excesivo

inorganic /'ɪnɔ:r'gænɪk || ˌɪnɔ:'gænɪk/ *adj* inorgánico

inpatient /'ɪnˌpeɪʃənt/ *n* paciente hospitalizado, -da *m,f*

input[1] /'ɪnpʊt/ *n*

A [u c] 1 (of resources) aportación *f*, aporte *m* (esp AmL) 2 (contribution) aportación *f*, aporte *m* (esp AmL)

B [u c] (Comput, Elec) entrada *f*

input[2] *vt* (*pres p* **inputting**; *past & past p* **input** *or* **inputted**) ‹*data/signal*› entrar

inquest /'ɪnkwest/ *n* investigación *f*, pesquisa *f* judicial; **coroner's ~** *investigación llevada a cabo por un* **coroner**

inquire, (BrE) **enquire** /ɪn'kwaɪr || ɪn'kwaɪə(r)/ *vt* preguntar, inquirir* (frml); **to ~ sth FROM** *o* (BrE) **OF sb** (frml) preguntarle algo A algn

■ **inquire** *vi* preguntar, informarse; **Ⓢ inquire within** infórmese aquí; **to ~ ABOUT sth** informarse *or* preguntar ACERCA DE *or* SOBRE algo; **to ~ AFTER sb/sth** (frml) preguntar POR algn/algo; **to ~ INTO sth** investigar* algo

inquiring, (BrE) **enquiring** /ɪn'kwaɪrɪŋ || ɪn'kwaɪərɪŋ/ *adj* (*before n*) ‹*nature/mind*› curioso, inquieto; ‹*look/expression*› inquisitivo, interrogante

inquiry, (BrE) **enquiry** /ɪn'kwaɪri, 'ɪnkwəri || ɪn'kwaɪəri/ *n* (*pl* **-ries**) 1 (question): **we made inquiries about** *o* **into his past** hicimos averiguaciones *or* indagaciones sobre su pasado; **they made inquiries about prices** pidieron *or* solicitaron información sobre precios; **all inquiries to ...** para cualquier información dirigirse a ...; **a man is assisting** *o* **helping police with their inquiries** (BrE) la policía está interrogando a un sospechoso; (*before n*) **~ desk** información *f* 2 (investigation) investigación *f*

inquisition /'ɪnkwə'zɪʃən || ˌɪnkwɪ'zɪʃən/ *n* 1 (severe questioning) interrogatorio *m*, inquisición *f* 2 **the Spanish I~** la (Santa) Inquisición, el Santo Oficio

inquisitive /ɪn'kwɪzətɪv/ *adj* ‹*mind/look*› inquisitivo, inquisidor; ‹*person/animal*› muy curioso

inquisitively /ɪn'kwɪzətɪvli/ *adv* con mucha curiosidad

inroads /'ɪnrəʊdz/ *pl n*: **to make ~ into sth**: **we are making ~ into the Japanese market** estamos haciendo avances en el mercado japonés; **this made substantial ~ into her savings** esto le comió buena parte de los ahorros

INS *n* (in US) = **Immigration and Naturalization Service**

insane[1] /ɪn'seɪn/ *adj* 1 (mad) demente, loco; **they drive you ~** te enloquecen, te sacan de quicio 2 (foolish) insensato; **it's an ~ idea** es una locura, es una idea descabellada

insane[2] *pl n* **the ~** los enfermos mentales

insanely /ɪn'seɪnli/ *adv* ‹*act/laugh*› como un loco; **he's/she's ~ jealous** está loco/loca de celos

insanitary /ɪn'sænəteri/ *adj* malsano, insalubre

insanity /ɪn'sænəti/ *n* [u] 1 (madness) demencia *f* 2 (foolishness) locura *f*, insensatez *f*

insatiable /ɪn'seɪʃəbəl/ *adj* insaciable

inscribe /ɪn'skraɪb/ *vt* 1 (engrave) **to ~ sth (ON sth)** ‹*words/letters*› inscribir* algo (EN algo); ‹*design*› grabar algo (EN algo); **to ~ sth (WITH sth)** ‹*locket/headstone*› grabar algo (CON algo) 2 (fix, impress) (*usu pass*) grabar 3 ‹*book*› dedicar*

inscription /ɪn'skrɪpʃən/ *n* 1 (on monument, coin) inscripción *f* 2 (in book) dedicatoria *f*

inscrutable /ɪn'skru:təbəl/ *adj* inescrutable

inseam /'ɪnsi:m/, **inseam measurement** *n* (AmE) entrepierna *f*

insect /'ɪnsekt/ *n* insecto *m*; (*before n*) **~ repellent** repelente *m* (para insectos)

insecticide /ɪn'sektəsaɪd || ɪn'sektɪsaɪd/ *n* [c u] insecticida *m*

insecure /'ɪnsɪ'kjʊr || ˌɪnsɪ'kjʊə(r)/ *adj* 1 (unsafe, exposed) inseguro 2 (not firmly fixed) ‹*lock/hinge*› poco seguro 3 (not confident) inseguro

insecurity /'ɪnsɪ'kjʊrəti || ˌɪnsɪ'kjʊərəti/ *n* [u c] (*pl* **-ties**) inseguridad *f*

insemination /ɪn'semə'neɪʃən || ɪnˌsemɪ'neɪʃən/ *n* [u c] inseminación *f*

insensible /ɪn'sensəbəl/ *adj* (frml)

A 1 (unconscious) inconsciente, sin conocimiento 2 (without sensation) insensible

B (*pred*) 1 (unaffected) **to be ~ TO sth** ser* insensible A algo 2 (unaware) **to be ~ OF sth**: **I am not ~ of the risks involved** soy consciente de *or* no ignoro los riesgos que acarrea

insensitive /ɪn'sensətɪv/ *adj* 1 (emotionally) ‹*person*› insensible; ‹*behavior*› falto de sensibilidad; **to be ~ TO sth** ser* insensible A algo 2 (physically) **to be ~ TO sth** ser* insensible A algo

insensitivity /ɪn'sensə'tɪvəti/ *n* [u] 1 (emotional) falta *f* de sensibilidad; **~ TO sth** ‹*to suffering/problems*› falta *f* de sensibilidad ANTE algo 2 (physical) **~ TO sth** insensibilidad *f* A algo

inseparable /ɪn'seprəbəl/ *adj* inseparable

insert[1] /ɪn'sɜ:rt || ɪn'sɜ:t/ *vt* ‹*coin/token*› introducir*, meter; ‹*zipper*› poner*; ‹*word/paragraph*› insertar; ‹*advertisement*› insertar, poner*

insert[2] /'ɪnsɜ:rt || 'ɪnsɜ:t/ *n* 1 (printed material) encarte *m*, encaje *m* 2 (Clothing) añadido *m*

insertion /ɪn'sɜ:rʃən/ *n* introducción *f*, inserción *f*

inshore[1] /'ɪn'ʃɔ:r || ˌɪn'ʃɔ:(r)/ *adj* costero

inshore[2] *adv* hacia la costa

inside[1] /'ɪn'saɪd/ *n*

A 1 (interior part) interior *m*; **the door had been locked from the ~** habían cerrado la puerta con llave por dentro 2 (inner side, surface) parte *f* de dentro *or* (esp AmL) de adentro; **the jacket's padded on the ~** la chaqueta es acolchada por dentro 3 (of racetrack) *parte más cercana al centro*; (of road): **he tried to pass me on the ~** me quiso adelantar por la derecha; (in UK etc) me quiso adelantar por la izquierda 4 (of organization): **we've got a man on the ~** tenemos a alguien infiltrado

B **insides** *pl* (internal organs) (colloq) tripas *fpl* (fam)

C **inside out** *adv*: **turn it ~ out** ponlo de adentro para fuera; **you've got your socks on ~ out** llevas los calcetines del *or* al revés; ***to know sth ~ and out*** *o* (BrE) ***~ out*** (colloq) saberse* algo al dedillo *or* al revés y al derecho; ***to turn sth ~ out***: **I turned the house ~ out looking for it** revolví toda la casa buscándolo; **he turned the bag ~ out** volvió la bolsa del revés, dio vuelta la bolsa (CS)

inside[2] *prep*

A 1 (within) dentro de 2 (into): **he followed her ~ the bar** la siguió al interior *or* hasta dentro del bar

B (colloq) (in expressions of time): **we did the journey ~ 3 hours** hicimos el viaje en menos de 3 horas; **she finished 2 seconds ~ (of) the previous record** batió el récord anterior por 2 segundos

inside[3] *adv* 1 (within) dentro, adentro (esp AmL); **~ and out** por dentro y por fuera, por adentro y por afuera (esp AmL); **deep down ~ I know that ...** en el fondo yo sé que ..., en mi fuero interno yo sé que ... 2 (indoors) dentro, adentro (esp AmL); **come ~** entra, pasa 3 (in prison) (colloq) entre rejas (fam), a la sombra (fam)

inside[4] *adj* (*before n*) 1 ‹*pages*› interior; ‹*pocket*› interior, de dentro, de adentro (esp AmL); **what's your ~ leg measurement?** ¿cuánto tiene *or* mide de entrepierna? 2 **the ~ lane** (Auto) el carril de la derecha; (in UK etc) el carril de la izquierda; (Sport) la calle número uno 3 (from within group) ‹*information*› de dentro, de adentro (esp AmL); **police think the robbery was an ~ job** la policía cree que alguien de la empresa (*or* casa *etc*) está implicado en el robo

insider /ɪn'saɪdər || ɪn'saɪdə(r)/ *n*: *persona que pertenece a una organización determinada o que tiene acceso a información confidencial*; (*before n*) ~ **dealing** *o* **trading** (Fin) abuso *m* de información privilegiada

insidious /ɪn'sɪdiəs/ *adj* insidioso

insight /'ɪnsaɪt/ *n* 1 [u] (perceptiveness) perspicacia *f*; **she has great** ~ es muy perspicaz 2 [c] (comprehension) ~ **INTO sth**: **to gain an** ~ **into sth** llegar* a comprender bien algo; **this gave me an** ~ **into the workings of the system** esto me permitió comprender mejor cómo funcionaba el sistema

insignia /ɪn'sɪgniə/ *n* (*pl* ~ *or* ~**s**) insignia *f*

insignificance /'ɪnsɪg'nɪfɪkəns/ *n* [u] insignificancia *f*; **to pale into** ~ **beside sth** ser* nimio *or* insignificante en comparación con algo

insignificant /'ɪnsɪg'nɪfɪkənt/ *adj* ‹*person/amount*› insignificante; ‹*detail*› nimio, insignificante, sin importancia

insincere /'ɪnsɪn'sɪr || ˌɪnsɪn'sɪə(r)/ *adj* ‹*offer*› poco sincero; ‹*person/smile*› falso, poco sincero

insincerity /'ɪnsɪn'serəti/ *n* [u] falta *f* de sinceridad

insinuate /ɪn'sɪnjueɪt/ *vt* insinuar*

■ *v refl* **to** ~ **oneself INTO sth** introducirse* EN algo

insinuation /ɪn'sɪnju'eɪʃən/ *n* [c u] insinuación *f*

insipid /ɪn'sɪpəd || ɪn'sɪpɪd/ *adj* ‹*food/drink*› insípido, soso (fam); ‹*person/novel*› insulso, soso (fam)

insist /ɪn'sɪst/ *vt* 1 (demand, require) **to** ~ **(THAT)** insistir EN QUE (+ *subj*) 2 (assert, maintain) **to** ~ **(THAT)** insistir EN QUE

■ **insist** *vi* insistir; **after you — no, after you, I** ~ usted primero — no, primero usted, no faltaba más

Phrasal verb

• **insist on, insist upon** [v ▸ prep ▸ o] **to** ~ **on -ING** insistir EN + INF/EN QUE (+ *subj*); **I** ~ **on seeing the manager** exijo ver al director, insisto en que quiero ver al director; **if you** ~ **on playing that music, I'm leaving** si te empeñas en seguir tocando esa música, yo me voy; **I** ~**ed on this point in my speech** insistí sobre *or* hice hincapié en este punto en mi charla

insistence /ɪn'sɪstəns/ *n* [u] insistencia *f*; ~ **ON sth/THAT ...** insistencia EN algo/EN QUE ...; **she took time off only at her doctor's** ~ se tomó tiempo libre sólo porque el médico le insistió

insistent /ɪn'sɪstənt/ *adj* 1 (persistent) insistente; **the salesman was very** ~ el vendedor insistió mucho; **to be** ~ **THAT** insistir EN QUE 2 (urgent, pressing) ‹*need*› apremiante

insistently /ɪn'sɪstəntli/ *adv* insistentemente, con insistencia

in situ /ɪn'sɪtju:/ *adv* (frml) in situ (frml)

insofar as /'ɪnsə'fɑ:r || ˌɪnsə'fɑ:(r)/ *conj* (frml) en la medida en que

insole /'ɪnsəʊl/ *n* plantilla *f*

insolence /'ɪnsələns/ *n* [u] insolencia *f*

insolent /'ɪnsələnt/ *adj* insolente

insoluble /ɪn'sɑ:ljəbəl || ɪn'sɒljʊbəl/ *adj* 1 (Chem) insoluble 2 ‹*equation/mystery*› insoluble, sin solución

insolvency /ɪn'sɑ:lvənsi || ɪn'sɒlvənsi/ *n* [u c] (*pl* **-cies**) insolvencia *f*

insolvent /ɪn'sɑ:lvənt || ɪn'sɒlvənt/ *adj* insolvente

insomnia /ɪn'sɑ:mniə || ɪn'sɒmniə/ *n* [u] insomnio *m*

insomniac /ɪn'sɑ:mniæk || ɪn'sɒmniæk/ *n* insomne *mf*

inspect /ɪn'spekt/ *vt* 1 (look closely at) ‹*car/camera*› revisar, examinar; (examine officially) ‹*school/restaurant*› inspeccionar; ‹*equipment*› inspeccionar, revisar; **to** ~ **sth FOR sth**: **we** ~**ed their hair for lice** les revisamos el pelo para ver si tenían piojos 2 ‹*troops*› pasar revista a

inspection /ɪn'spekʃən/ *n* [c u] 1 (official examination) inspección *f* 2 (of troops) revista *f* 3 (scrutiny) examen *m*, revisión *f*

inspector /ɪn'spektər || ɪn'spektə(r)/ *n* 1 (official) inspector, -tora *m,f*; (*ticket* ~) (BrE) inspector, -tora *m,f*, revisor, -sora *m,f* (Esp); **I**~ **of Taxes** (in UK) inspector, -tora *m,f* de Hacienda (*or* de la Dirección General Impositiva *etc*) 2 (police officer) inspector, -tora *m,f* (de policía)

inspectorate /ɪn'spektərət/ *n* cuerpo *m* de inspectores, inspección *f*

inspiration /'ɪnspə'reɪʃən/ *n* 1 [u] (for artistic creation) inspiración *f* 2 (encouragement, example) (*no pl*): **her bravery was a constant** ~ **to them** su valor fue una constante fuente de inspiración para ellos; **his hard work is an** ~ **to us** su tesón nos sirve de estímulo

inspire /ɪn'spaɪr || ɪn'spaɪə(r)/ *vt* 1 (arouse) ‹*love/confidence*› inspirar; ‹*fear/respect*› inspirar, infundir; ‹*hope/courage*› infundir; **to** ~ **sb WITH sth**: **she doesn't** ~ **me with confidence** no me inspira confianza 2 (influence, encourage) estimular; **to** ~ **sb TO sth**: **it** ~**d us to renewed efforts** nos sirvió de estímulo *or* de acicate para redoblar nuestros esfuerzos; **what** ~**d you to do that?** ¿qué te movió *or* te llevó a hacer eso? 3 (give inspiration for) ‹*music/painting*› inspirar

inspired /ɪn'spaɪrd || ɪn'spaɪəd/ *adj* inspirado; **I don't feel very** ~ **today** hoy no estoy muy inspirada; **the orchids were an** ~ **choice** las orquídeas fueron todo un acierto; **it was just an** ~ **guess** *o* **idea** fue sólo una inspiración

inspiring /ɪn'spaɪrɪŋ || ɪn'spaɪərɪŋ/ *adj* ‹*story/leader*› inspirador, que sirve de inspiración

instability /'ɪnstə'bɪləti/ *n* [u] inestabilidad *f*

install, instal /ɪn'stɔ:l/ *vt* **-ll-** 1 (fit) ‹*equipment/telephone*› instalar 2 (put in office): **once the new manager is** ~**ed** una vez que asuma el nuevo gerente 3 (settle) instalar; **he** ~**ed himself in front of the television** se instaló *or* (fam) se plantó delante del televisor 4 (Comput) ‹*program*› instalar

installation /'ɪnstə'leɪʃən/ *n*

A [u c] 1 (of equipment, machinery) instalación *f* 2 (of official) investidura *f*

B [c] (equipment) instalación *f*

installer /ɪn'stɔ:lər || ɪn'stɔ:lə(r)/ *n*

A (Comput) instalador *m*

B (person) instalador, -dora *m,f*

installment, (BrE) **instalment** /ɪn'stɔ:lmənt/ *n*

A (payment) plazo *m*, cuota *f* (esp AmL); **monthly** ~**s** mensualidades *fpl*, plazos *mpl* mensuales, cuotas *fpl* mensuales (esp AmL); **to pay in** *o* **by** ~**s** pagar* a plazos, pagar* en cuotas (esp AmL)

B (part — of publication) entrega *f*, fascículo *m*; (— of TV, radio serial) episodio *m*, capítulo *m*

installment plan *n* (AmE) plan *m* de financiación; **to buy sth on an** ~ ~ comprar algo a plazos, comprar algo en cuotas (esp AmL)

instance /'ɪnstəns/ *n* 1 (example) ejemplo *m*; **for** ~ por ejemplo 2 (case) caso *m*; **in this** ~ en este caso, en esta ocasión; **in the first** ~ en primer lugar

instant[1] /'ɪnstənt/ *adj*

A 1 (immediate) instantáneo, inmediato; **she took an** ~ **dislike to him** le cayó mal desde el primer momento 2 (Culin) ‹*coffee/mashed potatoes*› instantáneo

B (BrE Corresp frml) (*after n*): **in your letter of the 5th** ~ en su carta del 5 del corriente *or* (Esp tb) de los corrientes (frml), en su carta del 5 presente (Chi, Méx frml)

instant[2] *n* 1 (precise moment) instante *m*; **come here this** ~**!** ¡ven aquí en este mismo instante *or* ahora mismo!; **at that (very)** ~ en ese (mismo) instante *or* momento; (*as conj*) **let me know the** ~ **he arrives** avíseme en cuanto llegue *or* no bien llegue 2 (short time) momento *m*, instante *m*; **in an** ~ en un momento *or* instante

instantaneous /'ɪnstən'teɪniəs/ *adj* instantáneo

instantly /'ɪnstəntli/ *adv* al instante, en el acto

instant replay *n* [c u] repetición *f* (de la jugada)

instead /ɪn'sted/ *adv* 1 : **I couldn't go, so she went** ~ no pude ir, así que fue ella (en vez de mí *or* en mi lugar); **don't worry, I'll have tea** ~ no se preocupe, deme té entonces; **I thought I was going to be early:** ~**, I was half an hour late** creí que llegaría temprano; en cambio, llegué media hora tarde 2 **instead of** (*as prep*) en vez de, en lugar de; ~ **of going by train** en vez de ir en tren; **she volunteered to go** ~ **of me** se ofreció para ir en mi lugar

instep /'ɪnstep/ *n* 1 (of foot — arch) arco *m* (del pie); (— upper surface) empeine *m* 2 (of shoe) empeine *m*

instigate /'ɪnstəgeɪt || 'ɪnstɪgeɪt/ *vt* 1 (provoke) ‹*rebellion/mutiny*› instigar* a, incitar a 2 (initiate) ‹*scheme*› promover*

i

instigation /ˈɪnstəˈgeɪʃən || ˌɪnstɪˈgeɪʃən/ *n* [u] instigación *f*, incitación *f*; **it was carried out at the director's ~** se llevó a cabo a instancias del director

instigator /ˈɪnstəgeɪtər || ˈɪnstɪgeɪtə(r)/ *n* instigador, -dora *m,f*, incitador, -dora *m,f*

instill, instil /ɪnˈstɪl/ *vt* **-ll-**: **to ~ sth IN/INTO sb** ‹*habit/attitude*› inculcarle* algo A algn; ‹*courage/fear*› infundirle algo A algn

instinct /ˈɪnstɪŋkt/ *n* [c u] instinto *m*; **maternal/business ~** instinto maternal/para los negocios; **by ~** por instinto, instintivamente; **my first ~ was to escape** mi primera reacción fue escapar; **all his ~s told him to remain silent** su intuición le decía que era mejor callarse

instinctive /ɪnˈstɪŋktɪv/ *adj* instintivo

instinctively /ɪnˈstɪŋktɪvli/ *adv* instintivamente, por instinto

institute[1] /ˈɪnstətuːt || ˈɪnstɪtjuːt/ *vt* (frml) 1 ‹*search/inquiry*› iniciar; ‹*proceedings/action*› entablar, iniciar 2 (establish) ‹*rule*› instituir*; ‹*service/system*› establecer*

institute[2] *n* instituto *m*

institution /ˈɪnstəˈtuːʃən || ˌɪnstɪˈtjuːʃən/ *n*
A [c] (established practice, procedure) institución *f*
B [c] 1 (organization) organismo *m*, institución *f*; (building) institución *f*, establecimiento *m* 2 (hospital, asylum, home) *establecimiento sanitario, penitenciario o de asistencia social*; **she was frightened of ending up in an ~** temía terminar en un manicomio (*or* asilo *etc*)
C [u] (frml) 1 (initiation) iniciación *f* 2 (establishment) institución *f*, establecimiento *m*

institutional /ˈɪnstəˈtuːʃn̩əl || ˌɪnstɪˈtjuːʃən̩l/ *adj* institucional, de las instituciones

institutionalize /ˈɪnstəˈtuːʃn̩əlaɪz || ˌɪnstɪˈtjuːʃənəlaɪz/ *vt*
A (make an institution) institucionalizar*
B (put in an institution) internar (*en un establecimiento sanitario, penitenciario o de asistencia social*)

in-store /ˈɪnˈstɔːr || ˈɪnstɔː(r)/ *adj* (*before n*) dentro de una tienda

instruct /ɪnˈstrʌkt/ *vt*
A (command) **to ~ sb to + INF** ordenar a algn QUE (+ *subj*); **I've been ~ed to take you there** tengo instrucciones de llevarla allí
B (frml) 1 (teach) **to ~ sb IN sth** enseñarle algo a algn, instruir* a algn EN algo 2 (inform) informar

instruction /ɪnˈstrʌkʃən/ *n*
A [c] 1 (direction) instrucción *f*; ⓢ **instructions (for use)** instrucciones, modo de empleo 2 (order) instrucción *f*, orden *f*; **they were acting on the ~s of the chief of police** cumplían órdenes del jefe de policía
B [u] (teaching, training) (frml) **~ (IN sth)** instrucción *f* (EN algo)

instructive /ɪnˈstrʌktɪv/ *adj* instructivo

instructor /ɪnˈstrʌktər || ɪnˈstrʌktə(r)/ *n* 1 (teacher) (Mil) instructor, -tora *m,f*; **ski(ing) ~** instructor, -tora *m,f or* monitor, -tora *m,f* de esquí 2 (in US colleges) profesor, -sora *m,f* auxiliar

instrument /ˈɪnstrəmənt || ˈɪnstrʊmənt/ *n*
A (*musical* ~) instrumento *m* (musical)
B 1 (piece of equipment) instrumento *m*; **surgical ~s** instrumental *m* quirúrgico 2 **instruments** *pl n* (Aviat) instrumentos *mpl*, mandos *mpl*; (Auto) instrumentación *f*, instrumentos *mpl*

instrumental[1] /ˈɪnstrəˈmentl̩ || ˌɪnstrʊˈmentl̩/ *adj*
A (serving as a means) **to be ~ IN sth** jugar* un papel decisivo EN algo
B (Mus) instrumental

instrumental[2] *n* pieza *f* instrumental

instrumentalist /ˈɪnstrəˈmentl̩əst/ *n* instrumentista *mf*

instrumentation /ˈɪnstrəmənˈteɪʃən || ˌɪnstrʊmenˈteɪʃən/ *n* [u]
A (Mus) instrumentación *f*
B (Aviat, Naut) instrumentos *mpl*

instrument panel *n* (Auto) tablero *m* de mandos, salpicadero *m* (Esp); (Aviat) tablero *m* de mandos *or* de instrumentos

insubordinate /ˈɪnsəˈbɔːrdn̩ət || ˌɪnsəˈbɔːdɪnət/ *adj* (frml) insubordinado

insubordination /ˈɪnsəˈbɔːrdn̩ˈeɪʃən/ *n* [u] insubordinación *f*

insubstantial /ˈɪnsəbˈstæntʃəl || ˌɪnsəbˈstænʃəl/ *adj* 1 ‹*structure/object*› frágil, poco sólido; ‹*essay*› insustancial; **an ~ meal** una comida con poca sustancia 2 ‹*evidence/argument*› inconsistente, poco sólido

insufferable /ɪnˈsʌfrəbəl/ *adj* (frml) ‹*arrogance/rudeness*› insufrible, intolerable; ‹*heat/noise*› insoportable; ‹*person*› insufrible, insoportable, inaguantable

insufficient /ˈɪnsəˈfɪʃənt/ *adj* insuficiente

insufficiently /ˈɪnsəˈfɪʃəntli/ *adv* insuficientemente; **she was ~ prepared** no estaba lo suficientemente bien preparada

insular /ˈɪnsələr || ˈɪnsjʊlə(r)/ *adj* 1 ‹*mentality*› cerrado; ‹*person*› estrecho de miras, cerrado 2 (Geog) ‹*climate*› insular; ‹*people*› isleño, de las islas

insulate /ˈɪnsəleɪt || ˈɪnsjʊleɪt/ *vt*
A 1 ‹*building/wires*› aislar* 2 **insulating** *pres p* ‹*foam/felt*› aislante
B (protect) **to ~ sth/sb FROM sb/sth** proteger* algo/a algn DE algn/algo

insulating tape /ˈɪnsəleɪtɪŋ || ˈɪnsjʊleɪtɪŋ/ *n* [u] (BrE) cinta *f* aislante *or* aisladora

insulation /ˈɪnsəˈleɪʃən || ˌɪnsjʊˈleɪʃən/ *n* [u] 1 (against heat loss) aislamiento *m* (térmico); (Elec) aislamiento *m* 2 (material) (material *m*) aislante *m*

insulin /ˈɪnsələn || ˈɪnsjʊlɪn/ *n* [u] insulina *f*

insult[1] /ɪnˈsʌlt/ *vt* insultar, injuriar (frml); **I felt ~ed by his attitude** su actitud me ofendió

insult[2] /ˈɪnsʌlt/ *n* insulto *m*, injuria *f* (frml); **an ~ TO sb/sth** un insulto A algn/algo; ***to add ~ to injury*** por si fuera poco, para coronarla (fam)

insulting /ɪnˈsʌltɪŋ/ *adj* ‹*remarks/offer*› insultante, ofensivo; **he was extremely ~** lo que dijo fue muy insultante

insuperable /ɪnˈsuːpərəbəl/ *adj* (frml) insuperable

insurance /ɪnˈʃʊrəns || ɪnˈʃʊərəns, ɪnˈʃɔːrəns/ *n* seguro *m*; **he works in ~** trabaja en el ramo de los seguros; **medical/fire ~** seguro médico/de *or* contra incendios; **to take out ~** hacerse* *or* contratar un seguro; (*before n*) **~ broker** agente *mf* de seguros; **~ company** compañía *f* de seguros, (compañía *f*) aseguradora *f*; **~ premium** prima *f or* cuota *f* del seguro

insurance policy *n* póliza *f* de seguros

insure /ɪnˈʃʊr || ɪnˈʃʊə(r), ɪnˈʃɔː(r)/ *vt*
A (Fin) asegurar; **he ~d his life for $500,000** se hizo un seguro de vida de 500.000 dólares; **I'm ~d to drive any car** con mi seguro puedo manejar *or* (Esp) conducir cualquier coche; **to ~ sth/sb AGAINST sth** asegurar algo/a algn CONTRA algo
B (AmE) ▸**ensure**

insured /ɪnˈʃʊrd || ɪnˈʃʊəd, ɪnˈʃɔːd/ *n* (*pl* ~) (Fin) **the ~** el asegurado, la asegurada; (*pl*) los asegurados

insurer /ɪnˈʃʊrər || ɪnˈʃʊərə(r), ɪnˈʃɔːrə(r)/ *n* (company) compañía *f* de seguros, (compañía *f*) aseguradora *f*; (person) asegurador, -dora *m,f*

insurgency /ɪnˈsɜːdʒənsi/ *n* (*pl* **-cies**) (frml) insurgencia *f*

insurgent[1] /ɪnˈsɜːrdʒənt || ɪnˈsɜːdʒənt/ *adj* (frml) insurgente (frml), sublevado

insurgent[2] *n* (frml) insurgente *mf* (frml), insurrecto, -ta *m,f* (frml), sublevado, -da *m,f*

insurmountable /ˈɪnsərˈmaʊntəbəl || ˌɪnsəˈmaʊntəbəl/ *adj* (frml) ‹*difficulty/problem*› insalvable, insuperable; ‹*barrier*› infranqueable

insurrection /ˈɪnsəˈrekʃən/ *n* [c u] insurrección *f*

intact /ɪnˈtækt/ *adj* (*usu pred*) intacto; **he's kept his dignity ~** ha mantenido intacta su dignidad

intake /ˈɪnteɪk/ *n*
A (of water, air) entrada *f*; (of calories, protein) consumo *m*; **a sharp ~ of breath** una inhalación brusca
B (Tech) (pipe, vent) toma *f* (de aire, agua *etc*)
C (of trainees, students) (BrE) (+ *sing o pl vb*): **an ~ of 600** una matrícula de 600

intangible /ɪnˈtændʒəbəl/ *adj* intangible

integer /ˈɪntɪdʒər || ˈɪntɪdʒə(r)/ *n* (número *m*) entero *m*

integral /ˈɪntɪgrəl/ *adj*
A 1 ‹*part/feature*› integral, esencial; **to be ~ TO sth** ser* esencial A algo 2 (built-in) ‹*memory/microphone*› incorporado

B (Math) **1** ‹*number*› entero **2** ‹*equation/calculus*› integral

integrate /ˈɪntəgreɪt || ˈɪntɪgreɪt/ *vt* (combine) integrar; **to ~ sb/sth INTO sth**: **the new buildings have been successfully ~d with the old** se ha logrado integrar con éxito los nuevos edificios con los antiguos; **to ~ the handicapped into the community** hacer* que los minusválidos se integren en la sociedad

■ **integrate** *vi* «*parts/unit*» integrarse, combinarse (para formar un todo); «*immigrants/minorities*» integrarse; **to ~ INTO/WITH sth** integrarse EN/CON algo

integrated /ˈɪntəgreɪtəd || ˈɪntɪgreɪtɪd/ *adj* **1** (forming a whole) ‹*system/network*› integrado **2** (not separate) ‹*component/feature*› incorporado, integrado **3** (nonsegregated) no segregacionista, integrado

integrated circuit *n* circuito *m* integrado

integration /ˌɪntəˈgreɪʃən || ˌɪntɪˈgreɪʃən/ *n* [u] **1** (incorporation) **~ IN** *o* **INTO sth** integración *f* EN algo **2** (unification) unificación *f* **3** (desegregation) integración *f*

integrity /ɪnˈtegrəti/ *n* [u] integridad *f*

intellect /ˈɪntl̩ekt || ˈɪntəlekt/ *n* intelecto *m*, inteligencia *f*

intellectual¹ /ˈɪntəˈlektʃuəl/ *adj* intelectual

intellectual² *n* intelectual *mf*

intellectualize, intellectualise /ˈɪnteˈlektʃʊəlaɪz/ *vt* intelectualizar*

intellectual property *n* [u] (Law) propiedad *f* intelectual

intelligence /ɪnˈteləd͡ʒəns || ɪnˈtelɪd͡ʒəns/ *n*

A (mental capacity) inteligencia *f*; (*before n*) **~ test** prueba *f* *or* test *m* de inteligencia

B [u] (Govt, Mil) **1** (information) inteligencia *f*, información *f*; (*before n*) **~ agent** agente *mf* de inteligencia, agente secreto, -ta *m,f* **2** (department) servicio *m* de información *or* de inteligencia

intelligence quotient *n* coeficiente *m* *or* cociente *m* intelectual *or* de inteligencia

intelligent /ɪnˈteləd͡ʒənt || ɪnˈtelɪd͡ʒənt/ *adj* inteligente; **make an ~ guess** piensa un poco y trata de adivinar

intelligentsia /ɪnˈteləˈd͡ʒentsiə || ɪnˌtelɪˈd͡ʒentsiə/ *n* (+ *sing or pl vb*) **the ~** la intelectualidad, la inteligencia

intelligible /ɪnˈteləd͡ʒəbəl || ɪnˈtelɪd͡ʒəbəl/ *adj* inteligible, comprensible

intemperate /ɪnˈtempərət/ *adj* ‹*climate*› inclemente, riguroso

intend /ɪnˈtend/ *vt*: **no insult was ~ed** no fue mi intención ofender; **to ~ -ING** *o* **to ~ to + INF** pensar* + INF; **what do you ~ doing about it?** ¿qué piensas hacer al respecto?; **do it then! — I fully ~ to!** ¡pues hazlo! — ¡vaya que si lo haré!; **to ~ sb/sth to + INF** querer* QUE algn/algo (+ *subj*); **to ~ sth FOR sb**: **the present was ~ed for you** el regalo era para ti

intended¹ /ɪnˈtendəd || ɪnˈtendɪd/ *adj* **1** ‹*irony/slight*› intencionado, deliberado **2** ‹*response/effect*› deseado, buscado

intended² *n* (colloq & dated): **my/your ~** (fiancé) mi/tu futuro (fam); (fiancée) mi/tu futura (fam)

intense /ɪnˈtens/ *adj*

A (great) ‹*pain/activity*› intenso; **an ~ blue/green** un azul/verde intenso *or* vivo; **to my ~ relief** para mi gran alivio

B **1** (earnest) vehemente, apasionado; **she's terribly ~** se lo toma todo tan en serio **2** (emotionally taxing) duro

intensely /ɪnˈtensli/ *adv* **1** (*as intensifier*) ‹*moving*› profundamente, sumamente; **I dislike him ~** siento una profunda antipatía hacia él **2** (earnestly) apasionadamente

intensification /ɪnˈtensəfəˈkeɪʃən || ɪnˌtensɪfɪˈkeɪʃən/ *n* (of search, activity) intensificación *f*; (of fighting, problems) recrudecimiento *m*

intensify /ɪnˈtensəfaɪ || ɪnˈtensɪfaɪ/ **-fies, -fying, -fied** *vt* (increase) ‹*search*› intensificar*; ‹*efforts*› redoblar, intensificar*; ‹*pain/anxiety*› agudizar*, intensificar*

■ **intensify** *vi* «*pain*» agudizarse*, hacerse* más intenso; «*search*» intensificarse*; «*fighting*» recrudecer*

intensity /ɪnˈtensəti/ *n* intensidad *f*

intensive /ɪnˈtensɪv/ *adj* ‹*course/training*› intensivo; ‹*farming*› intensivo; ‹*fire/shelling*› intensivo; **they made an ~ search of the building** registraron el edificio detenidamente

intensive care *n* [u] cuidados *mpl* intensivos, terapia *f* intensiva (Méx, RPl); (*before n*) **~ ~ unit** unidad *f* de cuidados intensivos *or* (Esp tb) de vigilancia intensiva *or* (Arg, Méx) de terapia intensiva *or* (Chi) de tratamiento intensivo, centro *m* de tratamiento intensivo (Ur)

intent¹ /ɪnˈtent/ *adj* **1** (determined) (*pred*) **to be ~ ON sth/-ING** estar* decidido *or* resuelto A + INF **2** (attentive, concentrated) ‹*expression*› de viva atención, concentrado; ‹*look/stare*› penetrante, fijo; **to be ~ ON sth** estar* abstraído *or* concentrado EN algo

intent² *n* [u c] propósito *m*, intención *f*; **with evil/good ~** (frml) con malos/buenos propósitos, con malas/buenas intenciones; **with ~ to + INF** (frml) con el objeto *or* el propósito de + INF (frml); ***to all ~s and purposes*** a efectos prácticos

intention /ɪnˈtentʃən || ɪnˈtenʃən/ *n* **1** [u c] (aim, purpose) intención *f*, propósito *m*; **I have every ~ of going** tengo la firme intención de ir; **I have no ~ of writing to them** no tengo intenciones de escribirles, no pienso escribirles **2** [u] (Law) intencionalidad *f*

intentional /ɪnˈtentʃnəl || ɪnˈtenʃənl̩/ *adj* ‹*destruction*› intencional, deliberado; ‹*insult/cruelty*› deliberado

intentionally /ɪnˈtentʃn̩əli || ɪnˈtenʃn̩əli/ *adv* ‹*do/change/say*› adrede, a propósito; ‹*cruel/funny*› intencionadamente

intently /ɪnˈtentli/ *adv* ‹*listen*› atentamente; **he was staring ~ at them** tenía la mirada fija en ellos, los miraba de hito en hito (liter)

inter /ɪnˈtɜːr || ɪnˈtɜː(r)/ *vt* **-rr-** (frml *or* liter) inhumar (frml), sepultar (frml), enterrar*

interact /ˈɪntərˈækt/ *vi* «*people/organizations*» relacionarse, interactuar*; «*forces/particles/fields*» interactuar*; **to ~ WITH sth/sb** relacionarse CON algo/algn

interaction /ˈɪntərˈækʃən/ *n* [u c] interacción *f*, interrelación *f*

interactive /ˈɪntərˈæktɪv/ *adj* **1** ‹*forces/effects*› interactivo **2** (Comput, TV, Video) interactivo

interbreed /ˈɪntərˈbriːd || ˌɪntəˈbriːd/ (*past & past p* **-bred** /-ˈbred/) *vi* **1** (between groups, individuals) cruzarse* **2** (within group) reproducirse* entre sí (*dentro de un grupo cerrado*)

intercede /ˈɪntərˈsiːd || ˌɪntəˈsiːd/ *vi* interceder; **to ~ WITH sb FOR** *o* **ON BEHALF OF sb** interceder ANTE algn POR *or* EN FAVOR DE algn

intercept /ˈɪntərˈsept || ˌɪntəˈsept/ *vt* ‹*message/missile*› interceptar; **they were ~ed before they reached the building** les cerraron el paso antes de llegar al edificio

interception /ˈɪntərˈsepʃən || ˌɪntəˈsepʃən/ *n* **1** [u c] (catching in transit) interceptación *f*, intercepción *f* **2** [c] (Sport) corte *m*, intercepción *f*

interchange¹ /ˈɪntərˈtʃeɪnd͡ʒ/ *vt* intercambiar

interchange² /ˈɪntərtʃeɪnd͡ʒ || ˈɪntətʃeɪnd͡ʒ/ *n*

A [u c] (exchange) intercambio *m*, cambio *m*

B [c] (on road system) enlace *m*, intercambiador *m* (Esp)

interchangeable /ˈɪntərˈtʃeɪnd͡ʒəbəl || ˌɪntəˈtʃeɪnd͡ʒəbəl/ *adj* intercambiable

intercity /ˈɪntərˈsɪti || ˌɪntəˈsɪti/ *adj* rápido interurbano

intercom /ˈɪntərkɑːm || ˈɪntəkɒm/ *n* **1** (on plane, ship, in office) interfono *m*, intercomunicador *m* **2** (at building entrance) (AmE) portero *m* eléctrico *or* (Esp) automático, interfón *m* (Méx), intercomunicador *m* (Ven)

interconnect /ˈɪntərkəˈnekt || ˌɪntəkəˈnekt/ *vt* **1** (link) (*usu pass*): **to be ~ed** estar* conectados entre sí *or* interrelacionados **2** (Comput, Elec, Telec) ‹*circuits/speakers*› interconectar

■ **interconnect** *vi* **1** (link up) **to ~ (WITH sth)** interrelacionarse (CON algo) **2** (AmE Transp) **to ~ (WITH sth)** conectar *or* enlazar* (CON algo)

interconnecting /ˈɪntərkənektɪŋ || ˈɪntəkənektɪŋ/ *adj* ‹*cable/circuits*› interconectado; ‹*rooms/tunnels*› que se comunican entre sí

interconnection /ˈɪntərkəˈnekʃən || ˌɪntəkəˈnekʃən/ *n* **1** [u c] interconexión *f*, conexión *f* **2** [c] (AmE Transp) conexión *f*, enlace *m*

intercontinental /ˈɪntərˈkɑːntn̩ˈentl̩ || ˌɪntəˌkɒntɪˈnentl̩/ *adj* intercontinental

i

intercourse /ˈɪntərkɔːrs || ˈɪntəkɔːs/ *n* [u] **1** (sexual) coito *m* (frml), acto *m* sexual; **to have ~ with sb** tener* relaciones sexuales con algn **2** (liter & dated) (social) trato *m* social

interdependence /ˈɪntərdɪˈpendəns || ˌɪntədɪˈpendəns/ *n* [u] interdependencia *f*

interdisciplinary /ˈɪntərˈdɪsəpləneri || ˌɪntəˌdɪsɪˈplɪnəri/ *adj* interdisciplinario

interest¹ /ˈɪntrəst/ *n*

A **1** [u] (felt by person) interés *m*; **~ IN sb/sth/-ING** interés EN algn/algo/+ INF; **I have no ~ in getting to know them** no tengo ningún interés en conocerlos, no me interesa conocerlos; **to show (an) ~** demostrar* interés, mostrarse* interesado; **to take (an) ~ IN sth/sb** interesarse POR algo/algn **2** [c] (hobby) interés *m*

B [u] (possessed by object) interés *m*; **is this of any ~ to you?** ¿esto te interesa?; **it's a matter of public ~** es un asunto de interés público

C [c] **1** (stake) participación *f*, intereses *mpl*; **he has a number of business ~s abroad** tiene varios negocios en el extranjero; **I have to declare an ~** tengo que declarar que soy parte interesada **2** (advantage) (*often pl*) interés *m*; **you've got to look after your own ~(s)** tienes que velar por tus propios intereses; **to act in sb's ~(s)** actuar* en beneficio de algn; **it was not in our ~(s) to intervene** no nos convenía intervenir; **in the ~s of easing international tension** con el fin de relajar la tensión internacional

D [u] (Fin) interés *m*; **to earn/charge ~ of** *o* **at five per cent (per annum)** percibir/cobrar un interés del cinco por ciento (al año); ***to pay sth/sb back with ~***: **he repaid my affection with ~** me devolvió con creces el cariño que le había dado; **they'll pay me back with ~!** ¡me las van a pagar con creces!; (*before n*) **~ rate** tasa *f or* (esp Esp) tipo *m* de interés

interest² *vt* interesar; **can I ~ you in a raffle ticket?** ¿le puedo ofrecer un número de rifa?

interested /ˈɪntrəstəd || ˈɪntrəstɪd/ *adj*

A interesado; **would you be ~?** ¿le interesaría?; **sorry, I'm not ~** lo siento, no me interesa *or* no tengo interés; **anyone ~ should see Miss Bush** los interesados deben hablar con la señorita Bush; **to be ~ IN sb/sth/-ING**: **I am ~ in astronomy** me interesa la astronomía; **the company is ~ in acquiring new premises** la compañía está interesada en adquirir nuevos locales; **to be ~ to + INF**: **I'd be ~ to hear what they did** me interesaría saber qué hicieron

B (concerned): **~ party** parte *f* interesada

interesting /ˈɪntrəstɪŋ/ *adj* interesante

interestingly /ˈɪntrəstɪŋli/ *adv* **1** ‹*talk/write*› de manera interesante **2** (*indep*): **~ enough, he laughed** curiosamente, se rió

interface¹ /ˈɪntərfeɪs || ˈɪntəfeɪs/ *n*

A **1** (Comput) interface *f or m*, interfaz *f or m*, interfase *f or m* **2** (interaction) interrelación *f*

B **1** (Phys) punto *m or* superficie *f* de contacto **2** (point of contact) punto *m* de contacto

interface² *vi* (Comput) **to ~ WITH sth** funcionar en conjunto CON algo

interfere /ˈɪntərˈfɪr || ˌɪntəˈfɪə(r)/ *vi*

A (get involved) **to ~ (IN sth)** entrometerse *or* inmiscuirse* *or* interferir* (EN algo)

B **1** (disrupt) **to ~ WITH sth** afectar (A) algo **2** (tamper) **to ~ WITH sth** tocar* algo **3** (Rad, Telec) **to ~ WITH sth** interferir* algo

C (Sport) **1** (in US football) **to ~ WITH sb** hacerle* interferencia A algn **2** (in races) **to ~ WITH sb** obstaculizar* a algn

D (molest) (BrE euph) **to ~ WITH sb** abusar DE algn

interference /ˈɪntərˈfɪrəns || ˌɪntəˈfɪərəns/ *n* [u] **1** (interfering) intromisión *f*, injerencia *f* **2** (Phys, Rad, Telec) interferencia *f* **3** (Sport) interferencia *f*

interfering /ˈɪntərˈfɪrɪŋ/ *adj* entrometido, importuno

interim¹ /ˈɪntərəm || ˈɪntərɪm/ *adj* (*before n*) ‹*measure/solution*› provisional, provisorio (AmS); ‹*head/chairman*› interino; **an ~ payment** un pago a cuenta; **an ~ period** un período intermedio

interim² *n*: **in** *o* **during the ~** en el interín *or* ínterin, mientras tanto

interior¹ /ɪnˈtɪriər || ɪnˈtɪəriə(r)/ *n*

A **1** (of building) interior *m* **2** (Art) (escena *f or* cuadro *m* de) interior *m* **3** (Cin) interior *m*

B **1** (Geog) **the ~** el interior **2** (Govt) **the Ministry/Department of the I~** el Ministerio/Departamento del Interior

interior² *adj*

A **1** (inside) ‹*walls*› interior **2** (mental) interior

B (inland) del interior

interior: **~ decoration** *n* [u] (of house) decoración *f*; (profession) interiorismo *m*, decoración *f* (de interiores); **~ decorator** *n* (painter) pintor, -tora *m,f*; (designer) interiorista *mf*, decorador, -dora *m,f* (de interiores); **~ design** *n* [u] interiorismo *m*

interject /ˈɪntərˈdʒekt || ˌɪntəˈdʒekt/ *vt* ‹*cry*› lanzar*; ‹*remark*› agregar*, hacer*; **not necessarily, he ~ed** — no necesariamente — interpuso *or* terció

interjection /ˈɪntərˈdʒekʃən || ˌɪntəˈdʒekʃən/ *n* (Ling) interjección *f*; (exclamation) exclamación *f*

interlace /ˈɪntərˈleɪs || ˌɪntəˈleɪs/ *vt* **1** (interweave) entrelazar* **2** (intersperse) intercalar

interleave /ˈɪntərˈliːv || ˌɪntəˈliːv/ *vt* intercalar

interlink /ˈɪntərˈlɪŋk || ˌɪntəˈlɪŋk/ *vt* ‹*arms*› entrelazar*; ‹*factors/relationships*› interrelacionar

■ **interlink** *vi* entrelazarse*

interlock /ˈɪntərˈlɑːk || ˌɪntəˈlɒk/ *vi* **1** (join) entrelazarse*, trabarse **2** ‹‹*cogs*›› engranar

interlocutor /ˈɪntərˈlɑːkjətər || ˌɪntəˈlɒkjʊtə(r)/ *n* (frml *or* hum) interlocutor, -tora *m,f* (frml)

interloper /ˈɪntərləʊpər || ˈɪntələʊpə(r)/ *n* intruso, -sa *m,f*

interlude /ˈɪntərluːd || ˈɪntəluːd/ *n*

A (intervening period) intervalo *m*, paréntesis *m*

B **1** (Theat) (intermission) entreacto *m*, intermedio *m* **2** (Mus) interludio *m*

intermarriage /ˈɪntərˈmærɪdʒ || ˌɪntəˈmærɪdʒ/ *n* [u] **1** (between groups) matrimonio *m* mixto **2** (within group) matrimonio *m* endogámico

intermarry /ˈɪntərˈmæri || ˌɪntəˈmæri/ *vi* **-ries, -rying, -ried** **1** (between groups) casarse (*con gente de otros grupos raciales etc*) **2** (within group) casarse entre sí

intermediary /ˈɪntərˈmidieri || ˌɪntəˈmiːdiəri/ *n* (*pl* **-ries**) (frml) intermediario, -ria *m,f*

intermediate /ˈɪntərˈmiːdiət || ˌɪntəˈmiːdiət/ *adj* ‹*stage/step*› intermedio; ‹*size/weight/level*› medio, intermedio; ‹*course*› de nivel medio *or* intermedio

intermediate school *n* [c u] (in US) **1** (secondary) *escuela donde se cursa el primer ciclo de la enseñanza secundaria* **2** (primary) *escuela donde se cursa segundo ciclo de la enseñanza primaria*

interment /ɪnˈtɜːrmənt/ *n* [u c] (frml) sepelio *m* (frml)

interminable /ɪnˈtɜːrmənəbəl/ *adj* interminable

intermingle /ˈɪntərˈmɪŋgəl || ˌɪntəˈmɪŋgəl/ *vi* mezclarse, entremezclarse

intermission /ˈɪntərˈmɪʃən || ˌɪntəˈmɪʃən/ *n* intermedio *m*, intervalo *m*

intermittent /ˈɪntərˈmɪtn̩t/ *adj* intermitente

intern¹ /ɪnˈtɜːrn || ɪnˈtɜːn/ *vt* recluir*, confinar

■ **intern** *vi* /ˈɪntɜːrn || ˈɪntɜːn/ (AmE) **1** (Med) hacer* las prácticas, ser* interno **2** (Educ) hacer* las prácticas

intern² /ˈɪntɜːrn || ˈɪntɜːn/ *n* (AmE) **1** (Med) interno, -na *m,f* **2** (Educ) profesor, -sora *m,f* en prácticas

internal /ɪnˈtɜːrnl || ɪnˈtɜːnl/ *adj* interno; ❺ **not for internal use** para uso externo

internally /ɪnˈtɜːrnl̩i || ɪnˈtɜːnəli/ *adv* **1** (Med, Pharm, Physiol) ‹*digest/bleed*› internamente; ❺ **not to be taken internally** para uso externo **2** (Adm, Busn) ‹*distribute/review*› dentro de la organización

Internal Revenue Service *n* (in US) **the ~ ~ ~** ≈ Hacienda, ≈ la Dirección General Impositiva (*en RPl*), ≈ Impuestos Internos (*en Chi*)

international¹ /ˈɪntərˈnæʃn̩əl || ˌɪntəˈnæʃənl/ *adj* internacional

international² *n* (Sport) **1** (event) partido *m* internacional **2** (player) internacional *mf*

international: **~ Brigade** *n* **the I~ Brigade** las Brigadas Internacionales; **~ Court of Justice** *n* **the I~ Court of Justice** la Corte *or* el Tribunal Internacional de Justicia; **~ dateline** *n* **the ~ dateline** la línea (de cambio) de fecha

internationalism /ˈɪntərˈnæʃn̩əlɪzəm || ˌɪntəˈnæʃn̩əlɪzəm/ *n* [u] internacionalismo *m*

internationally /ˈɪntərˈnæʃn̩əli || ˌɪntəˈnæʃn̩əli/ *adv* 1 ‹*expand/trade*› internacionalmente 2 ‹*famous/known*› mundialmente

international: ~ **Monetary Fund** *n* **the I~ Monetary Fund** el Fondo Monetario Internacional; ~ **money order** *n* giro *m* postal internacional

internee /ɪnˌtɜːrˈniː || ˌɪntɜːˈniː/ *n* interno, -na *m,f*

Internet, internet /ˈɪntərnet || ˈɪntənet/ *n* [u] **the** ~ (el *or* la) Internet; **accessible via the** ~ accesible por *or* a través de Internet; **to be connected to** *o* **on the** ~ estar* conectado a Internet; (*before n*) ‹*access*› a Internet; ‹*auction/search*› en Internet; ‹*account/address/user*› de Internet; ~ **café** cibercafé *m*, café *m* Internet; ~ **shopping** compras *fpl* por Internet

Internet service provider /prəˈvaɪdər || prəˈvaɪdə(r)/ *n* proveedor *m* de servicios Internet

internist /ˈɪntɜːrnəst, ɪnˈtɜːrnəst || ɪnˈtɜːnɪst/ *n* (AmE) internista *mf*, especialista *mf* en medicina interna

internment /ɪnˈtɜːrnmənt/ *n* [u] internamiento *m*

internship /ˈɪntɜːrnʃɪp || ˈɪntɜːnʃɪp/ *n* [c u] (AmE) 1 (Med) internado *m* 2 (Educ) prácticas *fpl*

interpersonal /ˈɪntərˈpɜːrsn̩əl/ *adj* interpersonal

interplanetary /ˈɪntərˈplænəteri || ˌɪntəˈplænɪtri/ *adj* interplanetario

Interpol /ˈɪntərpəʊl || ˈɪntəpɒl/ *n* Interpol *f*

interpolation /ɪnˈtɜːrpəˈleɪʃən || ɪnˌtɜːpəˈleɪʃən/ *n* interpolación *f*

interpose /ˈɪntərˈpəʊz || ˌɪntəˈpəʊz/ *vt* 1 (in speech) ‹*question/objection*› interrumpir con; ‹*comment/remark*› interponer* (frml); **that's nonsense!, he ~d suddenly** —¡qué tontería! —exclamó interrumpiendo 2 (insert) (frml) interponer*

interpret /ɪnˈtɜːrprət || ɪnˈtɜːprɪt/ *vt* interpretar
■ **interpret** *vi* (Ling) (translate) traducir* (*oralmente*), interpretar; (work as interpreter) hacer* de *or* trabajar como intérprete

interpretation /ɪnˈtɜːrprəˈteɪʃən || ɪnˌtɜːprɪˈteɪʃən/ *n* [c u] interpretación *f*; **it's open to a number of different ~s** se puede interpretar de muchas maneras

interpreter /ɪnˈtɜːrprətər || ɪnˈtɜːprɪtə(r)/ *n* intérprete *mf*

interpreting /ɪnˈtɜːrprətɪŋ || ɪnˈtɜːprɪtɪŋ/ *n* [u] interpretación *f*

interracial /ˈɪntərˈreɪʃəl || ˌɪntəˈreɪʃəl/ *adj* ‹*discord/harmony*› interracial; ‹*marriage*› mixto

interrelate /ˈɪntərɪˈleɪt/ *vi* interrelacionarse

interrelated /ˈɪntərɪˈleɪtəd || ˌɪntərɪˈleɪtɪd/ *adj* 1 ‹*phenomena/events*› interrelacionado, relacionado entre sí 2 ‹*families/companies*› relacionado entre sí

interrogate /ɪnˈterəgeɪt/ *vt*
A ‹*criminal/suspect*› interrogar*, someter a un interrogatorio
B (Comput, Telec) ‹*computer/database*› interrogar* a

interrogation /ɪnˈterəˈgeɪʃən/ *n* [u c]
A (questioning) interrogatorio *m*
B (Comput, Telec) interrogación *f*

interrogation point *n* (AmE frml) signo *m* de interrogación

interrogative /ˈɪntəˈrɑːgətɪv || ˌɪntəˈrɒgətɪv/ *adj* interrogativo

interrogator /ɪnˈterəgeɪtər || ɪnˈterəgeɪtə(r)/ *n* interrogador, -dora *m,f*

interrupt /ˈɪntəˈrʌpt/ *vt/i* interrumpir; **if you'll excuse my ~ing** si me perdona la interrupción

interruption /ˈɪntəˈrʌpʃən/ *n* [c u] interrupción *f*; **without further ~** sin más interrupciones

intersect /ˈɪntərˈsekt || ˌɪntəˈsekt/ *vi*
A (cross) «*roads/paths*» cruzarse*
B (Math) 1 «*lines/curves*» cortarse, intersecarse* (frml) 2 «*sets*» formar intersección
■ **intersect** *vt* 1 ‹*road/path*› cruzar* 2 ‹*line/curve*› cortar

intersection /ˈɪntərˈsekʃən || ˌɪntəˈsekʃən/ *n* 1 (Transp) cruce *m*, intersección *f* (frml) 2 (Geog, Math) intersección *f*

intersperse /ˈɪntərˈspɜːrs || ˌɪntəˈspɜːs/ *vt* intercalar; **there were pictures ~d in the text** había fotografías intercaladas en el texto

interstate /ˈɪntərˈsteɪt || ˌɪntəˈsteɪt/ *adj* (*usu before n*) entre estados, interestatal

interstate (highway) /ˈɪntərsteɪt || ˈɪntəsteɪt/ *n* (AmE) carretera *f* interestatal, ≈ carretera *f* nacional

> **interstate (highway)**
>
> En Estados Unidos, una ruta nacional de larga distancia que cruza de un estado a otro. Están señalizadas con un símbolo rojo y azul que lleva la letra 'I' seguida del número de la ruta. Las que van de norte a sur tienen números impares y las que van de este a oeste tienen números pares. Cada calzada tiene cuatro carriles

intertwine /ˈɪntərˈtwaɪn || ˌɪntəˈtwaɪn/ *vi* «*fingers/plants*» entrelazarse*; «*paths/destinies*» entrecruzarse*
■ **intertwine** *vt* ‹*fingers*› entrelazar*

interval /ˈɪntərvəl || ˈɪntəvəl/ *n*
A 1 (time) intervalo *m*; **at ~s of 20 minutes, at 20-minute ~s** a intervalos de 20 minutos; **the ~(s) between their visits grew longer** cada vez espaciaban más sus visitas; **bright/sunny ~s** (Meteo) intervalos soleados/de sol 2 (distance) intervalo *m*, espacio *m*
B (pause) (BrE Cin, Mus) intermedio *m*; (BrE Theat) entreacto *m*, intermedio *m*; (Sport) descanso *m*, medio tiempo *m*, entretiempo *m* (Chi)
C (Mus) intervalo *m*

intervene /ˈɪntərˈviːn || ˌɪntəˈviːn/ *vi* 1 (interpose oneself) intervenir*; **he ~d with the authorities on our behalf** intervino *or* (frml) intercedió ante las autoridades en nuestro favor 2 (interrupt) «*fate*» interponerse*, intervenir*; «*event*» sobrevenir* 3 **intervening** *pres p*: **in the intervening period** en el interín *or* ínterin

intervention /ˈɪntərˈventʃən/ *n* intervención *f*

interventionism /ˈɪntərˈventʃənɪzəm || ˌɪntəˈvenʃənɪzəm/ *n* [u] intervencionismo *m*

interventionist /ˈɪntərˈventʃənəst || ˌɪntəˈvenʃənɪst/ *adj* intervencionista

interview¹ /ˈɪntərvjuː || ˈɪntəvjuː/ *n* 1 (for job, university place) entrevista *f*; **he was called for an ~** *o* (BrE also) **for ~** lo citaron para una entrevista 2 (with politician, entertainer) entrevista *f*, interviú *f* 3 (in market research) entrevista *f* 4 (BrE Law) interrogatorio *m*

interview² *vt* 1 ‹*candidate/celebrity*› entrevistar 2 (BrE Law) interrogar*
■ **interview** *vi* (conduct interview): **they're ~ing next Friday** las entrevistas tendrán lugar el próximo viernes

interviewee /ˈɪntərvjuːˈiː || ˌɪntəvjuːˈiː/ *n* entrevistado, -da *m,f*, candidato, -ta *m,f*

interviewer /ˈɪntərvjuːər || ˈɪntəvjuːə(r)/ *n* entrevistador, -dora *m,f*

interweave /ˈɪntərˈwiːv || ˌɪntəˈwiːv/ *vt* (*past* **-wove** *or* **-weaved**; *past p* **-woven** *or* **-weaved**) 1 ‹*threads/yarns*› entretejer 2 **interwoven** *past p* ‹*threads*› entretejido; **their lives were interwoven** sus vidas estaban inextricablemente unidas

intestate /ɪnˈtesteɪt/ *adj* intestado, abintestato (frml)

intestinal /ɪnˈtestənl̩ || ˌɪntesˈtaɪnl̩/ *adj* intestinal

intestine /ɪnˈtestən || ɪnˈtestɪn/ *n* (*often pl*) intestino *m*; **the small/large ~** el intestino delgado/grueso

intimacy /ˈɪntəməsi || ˈɪntɪməsi/ *n* (*pl* **-cies**)
A [u] 1 (close friendship) intimidad *f* 2 (sexual relations) (frml & euph) relaciones *fpl* íntimas (euf) 3 (of atmosphere) intimidad *f*
B **intimacies** *pl* intimidades *fpl*; (physical) arrumacos *mpl*

intimate¹ /ˈɪntəmət || ˈɪntɪmət/ *adj*
A 1 ‹*friendship/friend*› íntimo; ‹*talk/discussion*› de carácter íntimo *or* privado; **to be ~ WITH sb** tener* intimidad CON algn; **to be on ~ terms with sb** ser* íntimo de algn 2 (sexual) (frml) ‹*relationship*› íntimo; **to be ~ WITH sb** tener* relaciones íntimas con algn 3 ‹*atmosphere/restaurant*› íntimo
B (*usu before n*) (private) ‹*emotions/details*› íntimo
C 1 (close) ‹*link/association*› estrecho, íntimo 2 ‹*knowledge*› profundo

intimate² /ˈɪntəmeɪt || ˈɪntɪmeɪt/ *vt* **to ~ sth TO sb** insinuarle* algo A algn, darle* a entender algo A algn

intimately /ˈɪntəmətli || ˈɪntɪmətli/ *adv*
A **1** (familiarly) ‹*whisper/chat*› con familiaridad *or* intimidad **2** (sexually) (frml & euph) de modo íntimo
B **1** (closely) ‹*linked*› íntimamente, estrechamente **2** (in detail) ‹*know*› a fondo, en profundidad

intimation /ˈɪntəˈmeɪʃən || ˌɪntɪˈmeɪʃən/ *n* (sign) indicio *m*, indicación *f*; (inkling) presentimiento *m*; **we had no ~ of what was about to happen** nada nos hizo prever lo que ocurriría

intimidate /ɪnˈtɪmədeɪt || ɪnˈtɪmɪdeɪt/ *vt* intimidar; **don't be ~d by her manner** no te dejes intimidar por su actitud

intimidating /ɪnˈtɪmədeɪtɪŋ/ *adj* intimidante, amedrentador

intimidation /ɪnˈtɪməˈdeɪʃən/ *n* [u] intimidación *f*

into /ˈɪntu, *before consonant* ˈɪntə/ *prep*
A **1** (indicating motion, direction): **to walk ~ a building** entrar en *or* (esp AmL) a un edificio; **we drove ~ town** fuimos a la ciudad en coche; **they helped him ~ the chair** lo ayudaron a sentarse en el sillón; **she sat staring ~ space** estaba sentada mirando al vacío; **I dropped a coin ~ the water** dejé caer una moneda en el agua; **the cat shot up ~ the air** el gato salió volando por los aires; **a journey ~ the future** un viaje al futuro; **to translate sth ~ Spanish** traducir* algo al español **2** (against): **she walked ~ a tree** se dio contra un árbol; **he drove ~ the other car** chocó con el otro coche **3** (Math): **3 ~ 15 goes** *o* **is 5** 15 dividido (por) 3 *or* entre 3 es 5
B (in time, distance): **ten minutes ~ the game** a los diez minutos de empezar el partido; **they talked far ~ the night** hablaron hasta bien entrada la noche; **they penetrated deep ~ the jungle** entraron en el corazón de la selva; **the project is well ~ its third year** el proyecto ya está bien adentrado en su tercer año
C (indicating result of action): **we split ~ two groups** nos dividimos en dos grupos; **roll the dough ~ a ball** haga una bola con la masa; **the snowman had melted ~ a puddle** el muñeco de nieve había quedado convertido en un charco
D (involved in) (colloq) **to be ~ sth**: **she's really** *o* **heavily ~ jazz** le ha dado fuerte por el jazz (fam); **they're ~ drugs** se drogan; **at two, children are ~ everything** a los dos años, los niños son muy inquietos

intolerable /ɪnˈtɑːlərəbəl || ɪnˈtɒlərəbəl/ *adj* intolerable, insufrible

intolerance /ɪnˈtɑːlərəns || ɪnˈtɒlərəns/ *n* [u]
A (toward people, ideas) intolerancia *f*, intransigencia *f*
B (Biol, Med) intolerancia *f*

intolerant /ɪnˈtɑːlərənt || ɪnˈtɒlərənt/ *adj*
A ‹*person/attitude*› intolerante, intransigente; **to be ~ OF sb** ser* intolerante *or* intransigente CON algn; **to be ~ OF sth** no tolerar algo
B (Biol, Med): **the patient was ~ of** *o* **to penicillin** el paciente tenía intolerancia a la penicilina

intonation /ˈɪntəˈneɪʃən/ *n* [u c] entonación *f*

intone /ɪnˈtəʊn/ *vt* **1** ‹*psalm/Gloria*› entonar **2** ‹*list/names*› recitar

intoxicated /ɪnˈtɑːksəkeɪtəd || ɪnˈtɒksɪkeɪtɪd/ *adj* (frml) **1** (by alcohol) en estado de embriaguez (frml), en estado de intemperancia (Chi frml) **2** **~ WITH sth** ‹*with joy/success*› ebrio DE algo (liter)

intoxicating /ɪnˈtɑːksəkeɪtɪŋ || ɪnˈtɒksɪkeɪtɪŋ/ *adj* (frml) ‹*substance*› estupefaciente; **~ liquor** bebida *f* alcohólica

intoxication /ɪnˈtɑːksəˈkeɪʃən || ɪnˌtɒksɪˈkeɪʃən/ *n* [u] (frml)
A (by alcohol) embriaguez *f* (frml), intoxicación *f* etílica (frml), intemperancia *f* (Chi frml)
B (poisoning) (Med) intoxicación *f*

intractable /ɪnˈtræktəbəl/ *adj* (frml) **1** ‹*temperament*› obstinado; ‹*child*› incorregible **2** ‹*problem/dilemma*› inextricable (frml), insoluble

intramuscular /ˈɪntrəˈmʌskjələr || ˌɪntrəˈmʌskjʊlə(r)/ *adj* intramuscular

Intranet, intranet /ˈɪntrənet/ *n* Intranet *f*, intranet *f*

intransigence /ɪnˈtrænsədʒəns || ɪnˈtrænsɪdʒəns/ *n* [u] intransigencia *f*

intransigent /ɪnˈtrænsədʒənt || ɪnˈtrænsɪdʒənt/ *adj* intransigente

intransitive /ˈɪnˈtrænsətɪv/ *adj* intransitivo

intrauterine device /ˈɪntrəˈjuːtərən || ˌɪntrəˈjuːtəraɪn/ *n* dispositivo *m* intrauterino; (in the shape of a coil) espiral *f*

intravenous /ˈɪntrəˈviːnəs/ *adj* ‹*injection*› intravenoso, endovenoso

intravenously /ˈɪntrəˈviːnəsli/ *adv* por vía intravenosa *or* endovenosa

in-tray /ˈɪntreɪ/ *n* bandeja *f* de entrada *or* de asuntos pendientes

intrepid /ɪnˈtrepəd || ɪnˈtrepɪd/ *adj* intrépido

intricacy /ˈɪntrɪkəsi/ *n* **1** [u] (of pattern, embroidery) lo intrincado, complejidad *f* **2** **intricacies** *pl* (complexities) complejidades *fpl*

intricate /ˈɪntrɪkət/ *adj* complicado, intrincado

intrigue¹ /ˈɪntriːg/ *n* intriga *f*

intrigue² /ɪnˈtriːg/ *vt* intrigar*; **we were ~d to know how he had done it** nos tenía intrigados cómo lo había hecho, teníamos gran curiosidad por saber cómo lo había hecho

intriguing /ɪnˈtriːgɪŋ/ *adj* ‹*problem/text*› intrigante; ‹*possibility/suggestion*› fascinante; ‹*person*› interesante, enigmático

intrinsic /ɪnˈtrɪnzɪk/ *adj* intrínseco; **~ TO sth** (frml): **selfishness is ~ to his nature** el egoísmo le es connatural (frml); **it is ~ to the success of the plan that ...** para que el plan tenga éxito es esencial que ...

intrinsically /ɪnˈtrɪnzɪkli/ *adv* intrínsecamente

intro /ˈɪntrəʊ/ *n* (*pl* **intros**) **1** (to pop song) primeras notas *fpl* **2** (colloq) (to book, lecture) introducción *f*; (to performer) presentación *f*

introduce /ˈɪntrəˈduːs || ˌɪntrəˈdjuːs/ *vt*
A **1** (acquaint) presentar; **allow me to ~ myself** (frml) permítame que me presente; **to ~ sb TO sb** presentarle a algn A algn; **he ~d John to her** le presentó a John; **he ~d her to John** se la presentó a John **2** (initiate) **to ~ sb TO sth** introducir* a algn A algo, iniciar a algn EN algo **3** (present) ‹*speaker/program*› presentar; ‹*meeting/article*› iniciar
B **1** (bring in) ‹*subject/custom/practice*› introducir*; ‹*product*› lanzar*, sacar*; **introducing Juan Romero as Don Félix** presentando por primera vez (en pantalla) a Juan Romero en el papel de Don Félix **2** (Govt) ‹*legislation/tax*› introducir*; ‹*bill*› presentar
C (insert) (frml) **to ~ sth INTO sth** introducir* algo EN algo

introduction /ˈɪntrəˈdʌkʃən/ *n*
A [u c] **1** (to person) presentación *f*; **I was given an ~ to the manager** me dieron una carta de presentación para el director **2** (to activity, experience) **~ TO sth** introducción *f* A algo; **that was my ~ to France** ésa fue mi primera toma de contacto con Francia **3** (of speaker, performer) presentación *f*
B [u] **1** (bringing in): **the ~ of another color** el añadido de otro color **2** (of species, practice, legislation) introducción *f*; (of bill) presentación *f*
C [u] (insertion, entry) (frml) introducción *f*
D [c] **1** (to meeting, lecture) presentación *f* **2** (in book) introducción *f* **3** (Mus) introducción *f*
E [c] (elementary instruction) introducción *f*, iniciación *f*

introductory /ˈɪntrəˈdʌktəri/ *adj* **1** (prefatory, opening) ‹*notes/remarks*› preliminar; ‹*lecture/chapter*› de introducción; ‹*offer/discount*› (Busn) de lanzamiento **2** (elementary) ‹*course/lesson*› de introducción, de iniciación

introspection /ˈɪntrəˈspekʃən/ *n* [u] introspección *f*

introspective /ˈɪntrəˈspektɪv/ *adj* introspectivo

introvert /ˈɪntrəvɜːrt || ˈɪntrəvɜːt/ *n* introvertido, -da *m,f*

intrude /ɪnˈtruːd/ *vi* (disturb) importunar, molestar; (interfere) inmiscuirse*, meterse; **to ~ ON sb** importunar *or* molestar a algn; **to ~ ON sth**: **I didn't want to ~ on her grief** no quise importunarla en su dolor; **to ~ on sb's privacy** inmiscuirse* *or* meterse en la vida privada de algn

intruder /ɪnˈtruːdər || ɪnˈtruːdə(r)/ *n* intruso, -sa *m,f*

intrusion /ɪnˈtruːʒən/ *n* [u c] (unwelcome entry) intrusión *f*; (— in private life) intromisión *f*, intrusión *f*

intrusive /ɪnˈtruːsɪv/ *adj* **1** ‹*noise/smell*› molesto **2** ‹*questioning/reporter*› impertinente, indiscreto

intuit /ɪnˈtuːət || ɪnˈtjuːɪt/ *vt* intuir*

intuition /ˈɪntuːˈɪʃən || ˌɪntjuːˈɪʃən/ *n* [u c] intuición *f*; **I had an ~ about the outcome** intuí lo que iba a pasar; **female**

o **women's ~** intuición femenina

intuitive /ɪn'tu:ətɪv || ɪn'tju:ɪtɪv/ *adj* intuitivo; **an ~ feeling** una intuición; **she had an ~ dislike of him** le tenía una antipatía instintiva

Inuit /'ɪnuɪt || 'ɪnju:ɪt/ *n* (*pl* ~ *or* ~**s**) 1 [c] (person) esquimal *mf* 2 [u] (Ling) esquimal *m*

inundate /'ɪnʌndeɪt/ *vt* inundar; **to ~ sb WITH sth** inundar a algn DE algo; **we have been ~d with visitors** nos hemos visto inundados de visitantes, hemos recibido un aluvión de visitantes

inure /ɪ'nʊr || ɪ'njʊə(r)/ *vt* (frml) **to ~ sb TO sth** habituar* a algn A algo; **she had become ~d to their insults** se había hecho inmune *or* se había habituado a sus insultos

invade /ɪn'veɪd/ *vt* invadir; **to ~ sb's privacy** invadir la intimidad de algn
■ **invade** *vi* (Mil) invadir

invader /ɪn'veɪdər || ɪn'veɪdə(r)/ *n* invasor, -sora *m,f*

invalid¹ /ɪn'væləd || ɪn'vælɪd/ *adj* ‹*assumption/conclusion*› inválido; ‹*contract/will*› inválido, no válido; **~ in law** sin validez legal, sin valor ante la ley

invalid² /'ɪnvələd || 'ɪnvəli:d, 'ɪnvəlɪd/ *n* inválido, -da *m,f*; (*before n*) ‹*diet/food*› para enfermos; **~ car** coche *m* para minusválido

Phrasal verb
• **invalid out** [v ▸ o ▸ adv] (BrE) dar* de baja (*por invalidez*)

invalidate /ɪn'vælədeɪt || ɪn'vælɪdeɪt/ *vt* (frml) invalidar

invalidity /'ɪnvə'lɪdəti/ *n* [u] (frml)
A (of conclusion, will) invalidez *f*, falta *f* de validez
B (disablement, illness) invalidez *f*

invaluable /ɪn'væljuəbəl/ *adj* inapreciable, inestimable, invalorable (AmL)

invariable /ɪn'veriəbəl || ɪn'veəriəbəl/ *adj* 1 ‹*custom/practice*› invariable; ‹*pessimism*› eterno, constante 2 (Math) invariable

invariably /ɪn'veriəbli || ɪn'veəriəbli/ *adv* ‹*different/correct*› invariablemente, siempre; **he is ~ cheerful** siempre está alegre

invasion /ɪn'veɪʒən/ *n* (by army, of tourists) invasión *f*; **a gross ~ of my privacy/rights** una violación de mi intimidad/mis derechos

invective /ɪn'vektɪv/ *n* [u c] 1 (abuse) invectivas *fpl* (frml), improperios *mpl* 2 (condemnation) invectiva *f* (frml)

inveigh /ɪn'veɪ/ *vi* (frml *or* hum) **to ~ AGAINST sth/sb** arremeter CONTRA algo/algn

inveigle /ɪn'veɪgəl/ *vt* (frml) inducir* (*mediante engaño*); **she ~d him into compliance** *o* **into complying** lo persuadió con engaños *or* lo engatusó para que accediera

invent /ɪn'vent/ *vt* inventar; **she's ~ing the whole story** (se) lo está inventando todo

invention /ɪn'ventʃən || ɪn'venʃən/ *n*
A 1 [c] (device, machine) invento *m* 2 [u] (action, process) invención *f*
B 1 [u] (imagination): **(powers of) ~** inventiva *f* 2 [u c] (fabrication) (frml) invención *f*

inventive /ɪn'ventɪv/ *adj* ingenioso, lleno de inventiva; **you'll have to be ~** tendrás que usar tu inventiva *or* imaginación

inventiveness /ɪn'ventɪvnəs || ɪn'ventɪvnɪs/ *n* [u] inventiva *f*, ingenio *m*

inventor /ɪn'ventər || ɪn'ventə(r)/ *n* inventor, -tora *m,f*

inventory /'ɪnvəntɔ:ri || 'ɪnventri/ *n* (*pl* **-ries**) (Busn) inventario *m*; **to draw up an ~ of sth** hacer* (un) inventario de algo

inverse¹ /'ɪn'vɜ:rs, 'ɪnvɜ:rs || ˌɪn'vɜ:s, 'ɪnvɜ:s/ *adj* (*usu before n*) (opposite, reversed) inverso; **in ~ order** *o* **sequence** a la inversa, en orden inverso; **in ~ proportion/relation to sth** en proporción/relación inversa a algo

inverse² *n* (*no pl*) **the ~** (Math) el inverso; **the ~ is also true** lo inverso también es cierto

inversion /ɪn'vɜ:rʒən || ɪn'vɜ:ʃən/ *n* inversión *f*

invert /ɪn'vɜ:rt || ɪn'vɜ:t/ *vt* invertir*

invertebrate /ɪn'vɜ:rtəbrət || ɪn'vɜ:tɪbrət/ *n* invertebrado, -da *m,f*

inverted commas /ɪn'vɜ:rtəd || ɪn'vɜ:tɪd/ *pl n* (BrE) comillas *fpl*; **in ~ ~** entre comillas

invest /ɪn'vest/ *vt*
A **to ~ sth (IN sth)** ‹*money/time*› invertir* algo (EN algo)
B (endow) (frml) **to ~ sth WITH sth** conferirle* *or* otorgarle* algo A algo (frml)
C (frml) 1 (empower) **to ~ sb WITH sth** investir* a algn DE *or* CON algo (frml) 2 (put in office) investir* (frml); **they ~ed him as mayor** lo invistieron alcalde
■ **invest** *vi* **to ~ (IN sth)** invertir* (EN algo)

investigate /ɪn'vestəgeɪt || ɪn'vestɪgeɪt/ *vt* 1 ‹*crime/murder/cause*› investigar*; ‹*character/suspect*› hacer* indagaciones *or* averiguaciones sobre; ‹*complaint/possibility*› estudiar, examinar 2 (do research on) hacer* una investigación sobre, investigar*
■ **investigate** *vi* investigar*; **she went downstairs to ~** bajó a ver qué pasaba *or* a investigar

investigation /ɪn'vestə'geɪʃən || ɪnˌvestɪ'geɪʃən/ *n* [u c] 1 (detailed examination) estudio *m*; **upon closer ~** tras un examen más detenido 2 (official, scientific) investigación *f*; **she is under ~ by the police** la policía está haciendo averiguaciones sobre ella

investigator /ɪn'vestəgeɪtər || ɪn'vestɪgeɪtə(r)/ *n* 1 (*private ~*) investigador privado, investigadora privada *m,f*, detective *mf* 2 (official) inspector, -tora *m,f*

investiture /ɪn'vestətʃʊr || ɪn'vestɪtʃə(r)/ *n* [u c] (act, ceremony) investidura *f*

investment /ɪn'vestmənt/ *n* [u c] (of money, time) inversión *f*; **he had made a big emotional ~ in the relationship** había puesto mucho en la relación

investor /ɪn'vestər || ɪn'vestə(r)/ *n* inversor, -sora *m,f*, inversionista *mf*

inveterate /ɪn'vetərət/ *adj* (frml) (*usu before n*) 1 ‹*thief/liar*› empedernido 2 ‹*loathing/hostility*› inveterado

invidious /ɪn'vɪdiəs/ *adj* (frml) 1 ‹*task/role*› ingrato, odioso 2 ‹*comparison*› injusto

invigilate /ɪn'vɪdʒəleɪt || ɪn'vɪdʒɪleɪt/ (BrE) *vi* vigilar *or* supervisar un examen
■ **invigilate** *vt* ‹*examination*› vigilar, supervisar

invigilator /ɪn'vɪdʒəleɪtər || ɪn'vɪdʒɪleɪtə(r)/ *n* (BrE) *encargado de vigilar or supervisar un examen*

invigorate /ɪn'vɪgəreɪt/ *vt* «*breeze/shower*» vigorizar*, tonificar*; **I felt ~d after my swim** después de nadar me sentí lleno de energía

invigorating /ɪn'vɪgəreɪtɪŋ/ *adj* ‹*weather/walk*› vigorizante, tonificante; ‹*environment/change*› estimulante

invincible /ɪn'vɪnsəbəl/ *adj* ‹*army/foe*› invencible; ‹*lead*› insalvable, insuperable

inviolable /ɪn'vaɪələbəl/ *adj* inviolable

inviolate /ɪn'vaɪələt/ *adj* (frml) ‹*purity*› inmaculado; ‹*maiden*› sin mancillar (liter); ‹*integrity/reputation*› sin mácula (liter)

invisible /ɪn'vɪzəbəl/ *adj* 1 (unseen) invisible; **from the road the church is ~** desde la carretera no se ve la iglesia; **~ ink** tinta *f* invisible *or* simpática 2 (Econ, Fin) ‹*earnings/exports*› invisible

invitation /'ɪnvə'teɪʃən || ˌɪnvɪ'teɪʃən/ *n* 1 [c u] (act of inviting) invitación *f*; **to accept/decline an ~** aceptar/no aceptar una invitación; **at the ~ of** invitado por, por invitación de; **by ~ only** entrada por invitación 2 [c] (letter, card) invitación *f* 3 [c] (encouragement — to sth bad) incitación *f*; (— to sth good) invitación *f*

invite¹ /ɪn'vaɪt/ *vt*
A **to ~ sb (TO sth)** invitar a algn (A algo); **I've ~d her to** *o* **for dinner** la he invitado a cenar; **he was ~d for interview** lo citaron para una entrevista; **to ~ sb over for dinner** invitar a algn a cenar (en casa); **to ~ sb in/out** invitar a algn a pasar/a salir; **to ~ sb to + INF** invitar a algn A + INF *or* A QUE (+ *subj*)
B 1 (request politely) **to ~ sb to + INF** invitar a algn A + INF *or* A QUE (+ *subj*) 2 (call for) (frml): **he ~d questions from the audience** invitó al público a que formulara preguntas; **to ~ tenders for a new airport** llamar a un concurso *or* llamar a licitación para la construcción de un nuevo aeropuerto
C (encourage): **you're inviting trouble** te estás buscando problemas; **it ~s people to draw the wrong conclusions** se presta a que la gente saque conclusiones erróneas; **his work ~s comparison with the classics** su obra sugiere comparación con los clásicos

invite² /'ɪnvaɪt/ *n* (colloq) invitación *f*

i

inviting /ɪn'vaɪtɪŋ/ *adj* ‹*prospect/offer*› atractivo, atrayente; ‹*smile*› incitante

in vitro[1] /ɪn'vi:trəʊ/ *adj* in vitro *adj inv*; **~ ~ fertilization** fecundación *f* in vitro

in vitro[2] *adv* en vitro

invoice[1] /'ɪnvɔɪs/ *n* factura *f*

invoice[2] *vt* 1 (send invoice) **to ~ sb (FOR sth)** pasarle A algn factura (POR algo) 2 (list on invoice) ‹*goods/items*› facturar

■ **invoice** *vi* (Busn) facturar, hacer* facturas

invoke /ɪn'vəʊk/ *vt*

A 1 (use as authority) ‹*principle/precedent*› invocar* 2 (call into use) ‹*rule/law*› invocar*, acogerse* a

B ‹*devil/spirits*› invocar*, conjurar

involuntarily /ɪn'vɑ:lən'terəli || ɪn'vɒləntrəli/ *adv* involuntariamente, de manera involuntaria; **I let it slip out ~** se me escapó sin querer

involuntary /ɪn'vɑ:lənteri || ɪn'vɒləntri/ *adj* involuntario; **~ manslaughter** (in US) homicidio *m* involuntario

involve /ɪn'vɑ:lv || ɪn'vɒlv/ *vt*

A 1 (entail, comprise) suponer*; **what exactly does your work ~?** ¿en qué consiste exactamente tu trabajo?; **whenever there's money ~d** siempre que hay dinero de por medio 2 (affect, concern): **where national security is ~d ...** cuando se trata de la seguridad nacional ...; **it's my reputation that's ~d here** es mi reputación lo que está en juego

B **to ~ sb IN sth/-ING** (implicate) implicar* *or* involucrar a algn EN algo; (allow to participate) darle* participación a algn EN algo; **he doesn't ~ himself in the day-to-day running of the business** no toma parte en la gestión diaria del negocio; **don't try to ~ me in your problems** no intentes mezclarme en tus problemas

C **involved** *past p* 1 **to be/get ~d IN sth** (implicated, associated): **I was ~d in an accident last year** el año pasado me vi envuelto en un accidente; **whenever there's an argument, he has to get ~d** siempre que hay una pelea, él tiene que meterse; **several high-ranking officials were ~d in the affair** había varios oficiales de alto rango implicados en el asunto; **to be/get ~d WITH sb/sth**: **the people you're ~d with** la gente con la que andas metido *or* mezclado; **how did you get ~d with people like them?** ¿cómo te mezclaste con gente de esa calaña? 2 **to be ~d IN sth** (engrossed) estar* absorto *or* enfrascado EN algo; (busy) estar* ocupado CON algo; **to be/get ~d WITH sb/sth** estar* dedicado/dedicarse* A algn/algo 3 (emotionally) **to be/get ~d WITH sb**: **she doesn't want to get too ~d with him** no quiere llegar a una relación muy seria con él

involved /ɪn'vɑ:lvd || ɪn'vɒlvd/ *adj* enrevesado, complicado

involvement /ɪn'vɑ:lvmənt || ɪn'vɒlvmənt/ *n* [u c] 1 *n* (entanglement) participación *f*; **they deny any ~ in terrorist attacks** niegan estar implicados en ningún ataque terrorista 2 (relationship) relación *f* (sentimental), enredo *m* (fam)

involving /ɪn'vɑ:lvɪŋ || ɪn'vɒlvɪŋ/ *adj* apasionante

invulnerable /ɪn'vʌlnərəbəl/ *adj* invulnerable; ‹*fortifications*› inexpugnable

inward[1] /'ɪnwərd || 'ɪnwəd/ *adj* 1 (toward inside) ‹*curve*› hacia adentro 2 (private, mental) ‹*torment/serenity*› interior

inward[2], (BrE also) **inwards** *adv* 1 (toward inside) ‹*move/bend*› hacia adentro; ‹*travel*› hacia el interior 2 (toward mind, spirit): **meditation involves looking ~** la meditación exige introspección

inward-looking /'ɪnwərd'lʊkɪŋ || 'ɪnwəd,lʊkɪŋ/ *adj* encerrado en sí mismo, introvertido

inwardly /'ɪnwərdli || 'ɪnwədli/ *adv* ‹*agonize/gloat*› por dentro; **he smiled ~** sonrió para sus adentros *or* en su fuero interno

inwards /'ɪnwərdz || 'ɪnwədz/ *adv* (BrE) ▸ **inward**[2]

I/O /'aɪ'əʊ/ *adj* (= **input**/**output**) (*before n*) ‹*device/error*› de entrada-salida, de E/S

iodine /'aɪədaɪn || 'aɪədi:n/ *n* [u] yodo *m*, tintura *f* de yodo

ion /'aɪən, 'aɪɑ:n || 'aɪən/ *n* ión *m*

Ionian /aɪ'əʊniən/ *adj* jónico; **the ~ Sea** el mar Jónico

ionizer /'aɪənaɪzər || 'aɪənaɪzə(r)/ *n* ionizador *m*

iota /aɪ'əʊtə/ *n* (*usu with neg*) pizca *f*, ápice *m*; **there's not an ~ of truth in it** no hay ni un ápice de verdad en ello

IOU *n* (= **I owe you**) pagaré *m*

IPA *n* (= **International Phonetic Alphabet**) AFI *m*

iPod® /'aɪpɔ:d|| 'aɪpɒd/ *n* iPod® *m*

IQ *n* (= **intelligence quotient**) CI *m*

IRA *n* 1 /'aɪrə/ (in US) = **Individual Retirement Account** 2 (= **Irish Republican Army**) IRA *m*

IRA – Irish Republican Army

El IRA (Ejército Republicano Irlandés) es una organización paramilitar ilegal, fundada en 1919 para luchar por la independencia irlandesa del Reino Unido (**United Kingdom**). Después de la separación, en 1921, de los seis condados del noreste de la isla que siguieron bajo control británico como la provincia de Northern Ireland, su objetivo pasó a ser la unificación de la República de Irlanda e Irlanda del Norte. Posteriormente, como respuesta a lo que se percibía como represión contra la minoría católica en Irlanda del Norte, una facción del IRA (*Provisional IRA*) se reactivó en 1970, cometiendo actos de terrorismo en Irlanda del Norte e Inglaterra. El acuerdo de Viernes Santo (*Good Friday Agreement*), en 1998, ha llevado a la paz entre las comunidades enfrentadas en Irlanda del Norte y a la destrucción del arsenal de armas de la organización.

Iran /ɪ'rɑ:n, ɪ'ræn/ *n* Irán *m*

Iranian[1] /ɪ'reɪniən/ *adj* iraní

Iranian[2] *n* iraní *mf*

Iraq /ɪ'rɑ:k, ɪ'ræk/ *n* Irak *m*

Iraqi[1] /ɪ'rɑ:ki, ɪ'ræki/ *adj* iraquí

Iraqi[2] *n* iraquí *mf*

irascible /ɪ'ræsəbəl/ *adj* irascible

irate /aɪ'reɪt/ *adj* airado, furioso

ire /aɪr || 'aɪə(r)/ *n* [u] (liter) ira *f*, cólera *f*

Ireland /'aɪrlənd || 'aɪələnd/ *n* 1 (the island) Irlanda *f* 2 (the Republic) Irlanda *f*, (el) Eire

iridescent /'ɪrə'desn̩t || ,ɪrɪ'desn̩t/ *adj* (liter) irisado, iridiscente

iris /'aɪrəs || 'aɪərɪs/ *n*

A (Bot) lirio *m*

B (Anat) iris *m*

Irish[1] /'aɪrɪʃ || 'aɪərɪʃ/ *adj* 1 (of the island) irlandés; **the ~ Sea** el Mar de Irlanda 2 (of the Republic) irlandés

Irish[2] *n* 1 (people) (+ *pl vb*) **the ~** los irlandeses 2 [u] (language) irlandés *m*

Irish: **~ American** *n* norteamericano, -na *m,f* de origen irlandés; **~-American**/,aɪrɪʃə'merɪkən/ *adj* norteamericano de origen irlandés; **~ coffee** *n* [u c] café *m* irlandés; **~man** /'aɪrɪʃmən || 'aɪərɪʃmən/ *n* (*pl* **-men** /-mən/) irlandés *m*; **~ stew** *n* [u c] *guiso de carne y verduras*; **~ wolfhound** /'wʊlfhaʊnd/ *n* lebrel *m* irlandés; **~woman** *n* irlandesa *f*

irk /ɜ:rk || ɜ:k/ *vt* fastidiar, irritar

irksome /'ɜ:rksəm || 'ɜ:ksəm/ *adj* fastidioso, irritante

iron[1] /'aɪərn || 'aɪən/ *n*

A [u] 1 (metal) hierro *m*, fierro *m* (AmL); ***as hard as ~*** (duro) como el acero; **the ground will be as hard as ~ after all this frost** la tierra va a estar como piedra después de esta helada; ***to strike while the ~ is hot***: **there's nothing like striking while the ~'s hot** lo mejor es actuar de inmediato; (*before n*) **the I~ Age** la Edad de Hierro 2 (in food) hierro *m*

B (for clothes) plancha *f*

C 1 (*branding ~*) hierro *m* de marcar; ***to have several/too many ~s in the fire*** tener* varias/demasiadas cosas entre manos 2 (golf club) hierro *m*; **a seven ~** un hierro siete 3 (gun) (AmE sl) pistola *f*, pusca *f* (Esp arg)

D **irons** *pl* (fetters) grilletes *mpl*, grillos *mpl*

iron[2] *adj* 1 (made of iron) de hierro 2 (strong) (*before n*) ‹*constitution*› de hierro, fuerte como un roble; ‹*will/resolve*› férreo, de hierro

iron[3] *vt/i* planchar

Phrasal verb

• **iron out** [v ▸ o ▸ adv, v ▸ adv ▸ o] 1 ‹*problems*› resolver*; ‹*difficulties*› allanar, eliminar 2 ‹*crease*› planchar, quitar

iron: ~ **Curtain** *n* **the I~ Curtain** la cortina de hierro (AmL), el telón de acero (Esp); **~-gray**, (BrE) **~-grey** /ˈaɪərnˈgreɪ ‖ ˌaɪənˈgreɪ/ *adj* ‹*sky/sea*› gris acero *adj inv*; ‹*hair*› entrecano

ironic /aɪˈrɑːnɪk/, **ironical** /aɪˈrɒnɪkəl/ *adj* irónico; **it is ~ that ...** resulta irónico que ...

ironically /aɪˈrɑːnɪkli ‖ aɪˈrɒnɪkli/ *adv* irónicamente

ironing /ˈaɪərnɪŋ ‖ ˈaɪənɪŋ/ *n* [u] 1 (act): **to do the ~** planchar; **I'd better get on with the ~** más vale que siga planchando *or* con el planchado 2 (ironed clothes) ropa *f* planchada; (clothes to be ironed) ropa *f* para planchar

ironing board *n* tabla *f or* (Méx) burro *m* de planchar

iron: **~monger** /ˈaɪərnˌmɑːŋgər ‖ ˈaɪənˌmʌŋgə(r)/ *n* (BrE) ferretero, -ra *m,f*; **at the ~monger's** en la ferretería; **~ware** /ˈaɪərnwer ‖ ˈaɪənweə(r)/ *n* [u] 1 objetos *mpl* de hierro 2 (AmE Culin) utensilios *mpl* de cocina; **~-willed** /ˈaɪərnˈwɪld ‖ ˌaɪənˈwɪld/ *adj* con una voluntad férrea *or* de hierro; **~works** *n* (*pl* ~) (+ *sing or pl vb*) fundición *f*

irony /ˈaɪrəni/ *n* [c u] (*pl* **-nies**) ironía *f*; **the ~ of it is that ...** lo irónico del asunto es que ...; **he spoke with heavy ~** habló en un tono cargado de ironía

irradiate /ɪˈreɪdieɪt/ *vt* irradiar; ‹*tumor/cancer*› radiar, irradiar; ‹*food*› irradiar

irradiation /ɪˈreɪdiˈeɪʃən/ *n* [u] irradiación *f*, radiación *f*

irrational /ɪˈræʃnəl ‖ ɪˈræʃənl/ *adj* irracional

irreconcilable /ɪˈrekənˈsaɪləbəl/ *adj* ‹*principles/beliefs*› irreconciliable; **to be ~ WITH sth** ser* incompatible CON algo

irrecoverable /ˈɪrɪˈkʌvərəbəl/ *adj* (frml) irrecuperable

irredeemable /ˈɪrɪˈdiːməbəl/ *adj*
A 1 ‹*loss/error*› irremediable, irreparable 2 (Relig) ‹*sinner/soul*› irredimible
B (Fin) ‹*bond/debenture*› no amortizable

irrefutable /ɪˈrefjətəbəl, ˈɪrɪˈfjuː- ‖ ˌɪrɪˈfjuːtəbəl/ *adj* irrefutable

irregular /ɪˈregjələr ‖ ɪˈregjʊlə(r)/ *adj*
A (in shape, positioning, time) irregular; **to keep ~ hours** tener* un horario irregular
B (contrary to rules) inadmisible, contrario a las normas; **it would be most ~ for me to discuss a client with you** estaría totalmente fuera de lugar que yo hablara de un cliente con usted
C (Ling) irregular
D (Mil) ‹*troops*› irregular
E (substandard) (AmE) ‹*goods*› defectuoso

irregularity /ɪˈregjəˈlærəti ‖ ɪˌregjʊˈlærəti/ *n* [u c] (*pl* **-ties**)
A (in shape, positioning, time) irregularidad *f*
B (of action) lo inadmisible; **several irregularities** varias contravenciones de las normas

irrelevance /ɪˈreləvəns/ *n* [u c] irrelevancia *f*

irrelevant /ɪˈreləvənt/ *adj* ‹*fact/detail*› irrelevante, intrascendente; **the size of the building is quite ~** el tamaño del edificio no tiene ninguna importancia *or* no viene al caso; **to be ~ TO sth** no tener* relación *or* no tener* que ver CON algo; **to be ~ TO sb** serle* indiferente A algn

irreligious /ˈɪrɪˈlɪdʒəs/ *adj* (frml) irreligioso (frml)

irreparable /ɪˈreprəbəl/ *adj* irreparable

irreparably /ɪˈreprəbli/ *adv* irreparablemente

irreplaceable /ˈɪrɪˈpleɪsəbəl/ *adj* irreemplazable, insustituible

irrepressible /ˈɪrɪˈpresəbəl/ *adj* ‹*smile/laughter*› incontenible; ‹*urge/desire/anger*› irreprimible, incontenible; ‹*person*› indomable, irrefrenable

irreproachable /ˈɪrɪˈprəʊtʃəbəl/ *adj* irreprochable, intachable

irresistible /ˈɪrɪˈzɪstəbəl/ *adj* irresistible

irresolute /ɪˈrezəluːt/ *adj* (frml) ‹*person/conduct*› irresoluto (frml), indeciso

irrespective /ˈɪrɪˈspektɪv/ *adv* **~ OF sth**: **~ of what you say** independientemente de lo que usted diga, sin tener en cuenta lo que usted diga; **~ of age or sex** sin distinción de edad o sexo

irresponsible /ˈɪrɪˈspɑːnsəbəl ‖ ˌɪrɪˈspɒnsəbəl/ *adj* irresponsable

irresponsibly /ˈɪrɪˈspɑːnsəbli ‖ ˌɪrɪˈspɒnsəbli/ *adv* de modo irresponsable, irresponsablemente

irretrievable /ˈɪrɪˈtriːvəbəl/ *adj* (frml) irrecuperable; ‹*loss/damage*› irreparable

irreverent /ɪˈrevrənt, ɪˈrevərənt/ *adj* irreverente, irrespetuoso

irreverently /ɪˈrevrəntli/ *adv* irrespetuosamente, con irreverencia

irreversible /ˈɪrɪˈvɜːrsəbəl ‖ ˌɪrɪˈvɜːsəbəl/ *adj* ‹*decision/sentence*› irrevocable; ‹*process/decline/event*› irreversible

irrevocable /ɪˈrevəkəbəl/ *adj* irrevocable

irrevocably /ɪˈrevəkəbli/ *adv* irrevocablemente

irrigate /ˈɪrəgeɪt ‖ ˈɪrɪgeɪt/ *vt* 1 (Agr) irrigar*, regar* 2 (Med) irrigar*

irrigation /ˈɪrəˈgeɪʃən ‖ ˌɪrɪˈgeɪʃən/ *n* [u] 1 (Agr) irrigación *f*, riego *m* 2 (Med) irrigación *f*

irritable /ˈɪrətəbəl ‖ ˈɪrɪtəbəl/ *adj*
A (bad-tempered) ‹*person/mood*› irritable, quisquilloso; ‹*reply*› irritado
B (sensitive) ‹*skin/scalp*› sensible

irritant /ˈɪrətənt ‖ ˈɪrɪtənt/ *n* 1 (Med) agente *m* irritante 2 (person, thing) fastidio *m*, molestia *f*

irritate /ˈɪrəteɪt ‖ ˈɪrɪteɪt/ *vt*
A (annoy) irritar, molestar
B (make sore) ‹*skin/membrane*› irritar

irritated /ˈɪrəteɪtəd ‖ ˈɪrɪteɪtɪd/ *adj*
A ‹*look/frown*› de impaciencia, de irritación; **to be ~ WITH** *o* **AT sth/WITH sb** estar* irritado POR algo/CON algn
B ‹*skin/hands*› irritado

irritating /ˈɪrəteɪtɪŋ ‖ ˈɪrɪteɪtɪŋ/ *adj* irritante, molesto

irritatingly /ˈɪrəteɪtɪŋli ‖ ˈɪrɪteɪtɪŋli/ *adv* ‹*grumble/giggle*› de un modo irritante; ‹*smug/cheerful*› insufriblemente

irritation /ˈɪrəˈteɪʃən ‖ ˌɪrɪˈteɪʃən/ *n*
A [u c] (annoyance) irritación *f*; **one of life's minor ~s** uno de los pequeños inconvenientes de la vida
B [u] (soreness) irritación *f*

IRS *n* (in US) = **Internal Revenue Service**

is /ɪz/ *3rd pers sing pres of* **be**

Is = island(s) *o* **isle(s)**

ISBN *n* (= **International Standard Book Number**) ISBN *m*

ISDN *n* (= **Integrated Services Digital Network**) RDSI *f*

-ish /ɪʃ/ *suff*: **bigg~/long~** más bien grande/largo; **green~** verdoso; **eight~/tenn~** a eso de las ocho/diez; **she's thirty~** debe tener unos treinta años

Islam /ˈɪzlɑːm, ɪzˈlɑːm/ *n* [u] el Islam

Islamic /ɪzˈlæmɪk, ɪzˈlɑːmɪk/ *adj* islámico; **the ~ faith** la fe islámica *or* musulmana, el islamismo

Islamist¹ /ɪzˈlæməst ‖ ɪzˈlæmɪst/ *adj* islamista

Islamist² *n* islamista *mf*

island /ˈaɪlənd/ *n*
A (Geog) isla *f*; (*before n*) **he was welcomed by the ~ community** los isleños le dieron la bienvenida
B (in road) isla *f*

islander /ˈaɪləndər ‖ ˈaɪləndə(r)/ *n* isleño, -ña *m,f*

isle /aɪl/ *n* 1 (poet) isla *f*, ínsula *f* (liter) 2 (in place names): **the I~ of Wight** la Isla de Wight

Isles of Scilly /ˈaɪlzəvˈsɪli/ *pl n* **the ~ ~ ~** las islas Scilly *or* Sorlingas

isn't /ˈɪznt/ = **is not**

ISO *n* (= **International Standards Organization**) ISO *f*

isobar /ˈaɪsəbɑːr ‖ ˈaɪsəbɑː(r)/ *n* isobara *f*

isolate /ˈaɪsəleɪt/ *vt*
A (keep apart) **to ~ sth/sb (FROM sth/sb)** aislar* algo/a algn (DE algo/algn)
B (pick out, separate) ‹*cause/problem*› aislar*; **to ~ sth FROM sth** separar *or* desligar* algo DE algo

isolated /ˈaɪsəleɪtəd ‖ ˈaɪsəleɪtɪd/ *adj* ‹*place/incident*› aislado; **he leads a very ~ life** lleva una vida muy solitaria

isolation /ˈaɪsəˈleɪʃən/ *n* [u]
A 1 (state) aislamiento *m*; **in ~ (from sth)** aislado (de algo); **the events should not be studied in ~** los acontecimientos no se deberían estudiar aisladamente *or* fuera de su contexto 2 (Med) aislamiento *m*; **to keep sb in ~** mantener* a algn aislado; (*before n*) ‹*ward/hospital*› de infecciosos

[B] [1] (separation, identification) identificación *f* [2] (of virus, substance) aislamiento *m*

isolationism /'aɪsə'leɪʃənɪzəm/ *n* [u] aislacionismo *m*

isolationist /'aɪsə'leɪʃənəst/ *adj* aislacionista

isosceles /aɪ'sɑːsəliːz || aɪ'sɒsəliːz/ *adj* isósceles

isotope /'aɪsətəʊp/ *n* isótopo *m*

ISP *n* (= **Internet service provider**) ISP *m*

I-spy /'aɪ'spaɪ/ *n* [u] (BrE) veo-veo *m*

Israel /'ɪzreɪəl/ *n* Israel *m*

Israeli¹ /ɪz'reɪli/ *adj* israelí

Israeli² *n* israelí *mf*

issue¹ /'ɪʃuː || 'ɪʃjuː, ɪsjuː/ *n*

[A] [c] (subject discussed) tema *m*, cuestión *f*, asunto *m*; **to face the ∼** enfrentarse al *or* afrontar el problema; **let's not cloud** *o* **confuse** *o* **fog the ∼** no nos vayamos por la tangente, no desviemos la atención del verdadero problema; **we are campaigning on the ∼s** nuestra campaña se centra en los problemas que hay que resolver; ***at* ∼**: **the matter at ∼ is ...** de lo que se trata es de ...; ***to make an* ∼ *of sth***: **I don't want to make an ∼ of it but ...** no quiero insistir demasiado sobre el tema pero ..., no quiero exagerar la importancia del asunto pero ...; ***to take* ∼ *with sb/sth*** discrepar con algn/en algo

[B] [1] [u] (of documents) expedición *f*; (of library books) préstamo *m*; (of tickets) venta *f*, expedición *f*; (of supplies) reparto *m* [2] [u c] (of stamps, shares, bank notes) emisión *f* [3] [c] (of newspaper, magazine) número *m*

[C] [1] [u c] (emergence) (frml) flujo *m* [2] (outcome, result) (*no pl*) desenlace *m*; ***to force the* ∼** presionar (*para que se tome una decisión*)

[D] (progeny) (frml) (+ *sing or pl vb*) descendencia *f*

issue² *vt* [1] (give out) ‹*statement/report*› hacer* público; ‹*instructions*› dar*; ‹*tickets/visas*› expedir*; ‹*library books*› prestar; ‹*bank notes/stamps/shares*› emitir; ‹*writ/summons*› dictar, expedir*; **to ∼ sth TO sb, to ∼ sb WITH sth**: **the teacher ∼d library cards to the pupils** el profesor distribuyó tarjetas de lector entre los alumnos; **we can ∼ you with the necessary documents** le podemos proporcionar *or* suministrar los documentos necesarios [2] **issuing** *pres p* ‹*house/bank*› emisor

■ **issue** *vi* (frml)

[A] (result) **to ∼ FROM sth** derivar(se) *or* surgir* DE algo (frml)

[B] (emerge) salir*; «*liquid*» fluir*, manar

isthmus /'ɪsməs/ *n* (*pl* **-muses**) istmo *m*

it /ɪt/ *pron*

[A] (replacing noun — as direct object) lo, la (— as indirect object) le; (— as subject, after prep) *gen not translated*; **∼'s enormous** es enorme; **there's nothing behind/on top of ∼** no hay nada detrás/encima; **sign ∼** fírmalo/fírmala; **I gave ∼ another coat of paint** le di otra mano de pintura; **stop ∼!** ¡ya está bien!, ¡basta!; **I don't understand ∼** no lo entiendo; **∼'s all lies** son todas mentiras; **damn/blast ∼!** ¡maldita sea! (fam)

[B] (introducing person, thing, event): **who is ∼?** ¿quién es?; **∼'s me** soy yo; **∼'s Bill** es Bill; **∼ was you, wasn't ∼?** fuiste tú ¿no?; **what is ∼ you want me to do?** ¿qué es lo que quieres que haga?; **I'll see to ∼** yo me encargo (de ello); **∼'s his attitude that I don't like** su actitud es lo que no me gusta; **∼ was a dress, not a blouse she bought** fue un vestido, no una blusa lo que compró; **a little higher up ... that's ∼!** un poco más arriba ... ¡ahí está! *or* ¡eso es!; **one more and that's ∼** uno más y ya está *or* se acabó; **he's very ambitious — that's just ∼!** es muy ambicioso — ¡precisamente ahí está el problema!; **that's ∼, then** bueno, ya está

[C] (in impersonal constructions): **∼'s good to see you** da gusto verte; **∼'s raining** está lloviendo; **∼'s hot** hace calor; **∼'s two o'clock** son las dos; **how long is ∼ since we met?** ¿cuánto hace que nos conocimos?; **∼ would appear so** así *or* eso parece; **∼ says here that ...** aquí dice que ...; **∼ is known that ...** se sabe que ...

[D] (in children's games): **you're ∼** tú (la) paras

IT *n* [u] = **information technology**

Italian¹ /ɪ'tæljən/ *adj* italiano

Italian² *n* [1] [c] (person) italiano, -na *m,f* [2] [u] (language) italiano *m*

italics /ɪ'tælɪks/ *pl n* (letra *f*) cursiva *f or* bastardilla *f*

Italy /'ɪtḷi || 'ɪtəli/ *n* Italia *f*

itch¹ /ɪtʃ/ *vi*

[A] [1] «*scalp/toe*» picar* (+ *me/te/le etc*); **my nose ∼es** me pica la nariz; **I ∼ all over** me pica todo el cuerpo [2] (be impatient, eager) (colloq) **to be ∼ing to + INF**: **he was ∼ing to tell her** estaba que se moría por decírselo (fam)

[B] «*wool/underwear*» (cause irritation) picar*, hacer* picar

itch² *n* [1] (irritation) picor *m*, picazón *f*, comezón *f* [2] (desire) ansia *f*‡; **he felt the ∼ for travel** tenía el gusanillo de los viajes (fam)

itching /'ɪtʃɪŋ/ *n* [u c] ▸**itch²1**

itching powder *n* [u] polvos *mpl* pica-pica

itchy /'ɪtʃi/ *adj* **itchier, itchiest** [1] (feeling irritation): **I've got an ∼ nose/scalp** me pica la nariz/la cabeza [2] (causing irritation) ‹*garment/material*› que pica

it'd /'ɪtəd/ [1] **= it had** [2] **= it would**

item /'aɪtəm/ *n* [1] (article) (Busn) artículo *m*; (in collection) pieza *f*; (on agenda) punto *m*: **∼s of clothing** prendas *fpl* de vestir; **∼s of furniture** muebles *mpl* [2] (in newspaper) artículo *m*; (in show) número *m*; **news ∼** noticia *f*

itemize /'aɪtəmaɪz/ *vt* (break down) detallar, desglosar; (list) hacer* una lista de, enumerar

itinerant /aɪ'tɪnərənt/ *adj* (frml) ‹*worker/judge*› itinerante (frml); ‹*salesman/musician*› ambulante

itinerary /aɪ'tɪnəreri/ *n* (*pl* **-ries**) itinerario *m*

it'll /'ɪtḷ/ **= it will**

its /ɪts/ *adj* (*sing*) su; (*pl*) sus; **it has ∼ problems** tiene sus problemas; **it's lost ∼ handle** se le ha caído el asa

it's /ɪts/ [1] **= it is** [2] **= it has**

itself /ɪt'self/ *pron* [1] (reflexive): **it has earned ∼ a reputation** se ha hecho fama; **another problem presented ∼** se presentó otro problema [2] (emphatic use): **the town ∼ is small** la ciudad en sí *or* la ciudad propiamente dicha es pequeña; **he's kindness ∼** es la bondad personificada

itty-bitty /'ɪti'bɪti/, (BrE) **itsy-bitsy** /'ɪtsi'bɪtsi/ *adj* (colloq) chiquitito, chiquitín, pequeñito

ITV *n* (in UK) (*no art*) = **Independent Television**

IUD *n* (= **intrauterine device**) DIU *m*

IV *adj* (esp AmE) = **intravenous**

I've /aɪv/ **= I have**

Ivorian¹ /aɪ'ɔːrjæn/ *adj* marfilense, marfileño

Ivorian² *n* marfilense *mf*, marfileño -ña *m,f*

ivory¹ /'aɪvəri/ *n* (*pl* **-ries**) [1] (material) marfil *m* [2] (color) (color *m*) marfil *m*

ivory² *adj* ‹*paint/table*› de color marfil; ‹*skin*› marfil *adj inv*

ivory: **∼ Coast** *n* Costa *f* de Marfil; **∼ tower** *n* torre *f* de marfil

ivy /'aɪvi/ *n* [u] hiedra *f*

Ivy League *n* (AmE) **the ∼ ∼** *grupo de ocho universidades prestigiosas de EEUU*

Ivy League

El grupo de universidades más antiguas y más respetadas de EEUU, situadas en el noreste del país. Son: Harvard, Yale, Columbia University, Cornell University, Dartmouth College, Brown University, Princeton University y la University of Pennsylvania. El término proviene de la hiedra que crece en los antiguos edificios de las universidades

Jj

J, j /dʒeɪ/ *n* J, j *f*

jab¹ /dʒæb/ **-bb-** *vt*: **I ~bed myself with the needle** me pinché con la aguja, me piqué con la aguja (Méx); **she ~bed him in the ribs with her elbow** le dio un codazo en las costillas

■ **jab** *vi* **to ~ AT sth**: **he ~bed at my arm with his finger** me dio en el brazo con el dedo

jab² *n* 1 (prick) pinchazo *m*; (blow) golpe *m*; (with elbow) codazo *m* 2 (in boxing) jab *m*, corto *m* 3 (injection) (BrE colloq) inyección *f*

C (Scot colloq) ▸**jab² 1, 3**

jabber /ˈdʒæbər || ˈdʒæbə(r)/ *vi* farfullar; **to ~ away** parlotear

■ **jabber** *vt* farfullar

jack /dʒæk/ *n*

A (lifting device) gato *m*

B (socket) enchufe *m* hembra

C 1 (in French pack of cards) jota *f*, valet *m*; (in Spanish pack) sota *f* 2 (Games) ≈ taba *f* 3 (in bowls) boliche *m*

D **I'm all right, Jack!** (BrE set phrase: colloq) mientras yo esté bien ..., allá se pudran los demás (fam)

(Phrasal verbs)

- **jack in** [v ▸ o ▸ adv, v ▸ adv ▸ o] (BrE colloq) ‹*job/studies*› dejar, plantar (fam)
- **jack up** [v ▸ o ▸ adv, v ▸ adv ▸ o] 1 ‹*car*› levantar (*con el gato*) 2 (colloq) ‹*price*› subir, aumentar

jackal /ˈdʒækəl/ *n* chacal *m*

jack: **~ass** *n* asno *m*, burro *m*; **~boot** *n* bota *f* alta

jackdaw /ˈdʒækdɔː/ *n* grajilla *f*

jacket /ˈdʒækət || ˈdʒækɪt/ *n*

A (Clothing) chaqueta *f*; (*sports ~*) americana *f*, saco *m* (sport) (AmL)

B (of book) sobrecubierta *f*; (of record) (AmE) funda *f*

C (of potato) (BrE): **potatoes in their ~s, ~ potatoes** papas *fpl* asadas (*con la cáscara*) (AmL), patatas *fpl* asadas (*con la piel*) (Esp)

jack: **~hammer** *n* martillo *m* neumático; **~-in-the-box** /ˈdʒækənðəˈbɑːks || ˈdʒækɪnðəˌbɒks/ *n* caja *f* de sorpresas (*con muñeco a resorte*)

jackknife¹ /ˈdʒæknaɪf/ *n* (*pl* **-knives**) (knife) navaja *f*

jackknife² *vi* «*truck*» plegarse*

jack: **~ of all trades** /ˈdʒækəvˈɔːltreɪdz/ *n* (*pl* **~s of all trades**) hombre *m* *or* mujer *f* orquesta, manitas *mf* (Esp, Méx fam); **he's a ~ of all trades and master of none** (set phrase) sabe un poco de todo y mucho de nada; **~pot** *n* (in bingo, lottery) bote *m*, pozo *m*; ***to hit the ~pot*** (do very well) hacer* su (*or* mi *etc*) agosto, sacarse* la lotería; (win highest prize) sacarse* la lotería *or* (fam) el gordo; **~rabbit** *n*: *tipo de liebre de Norteamérica*

Jacobean /ˈdʒækəˈbiːən/ *adj* jacobeo

Jacuzzi®, jacuzzi /dʒəˈkuːzi/ *n* Jacuzzi® *m*

jade /dʒeɪd/ *n* [u] 1 (Min) jade *m* 2 (color) verde *m* jade; (*before n*) verde jade *adj inv*

jaded /ˈdʒeɪdəd || ˈdʒeɪdɪd/ *adj* ‹*person*› hastiado, harto; **to tempt even the most ~ palate** para tentar hasta los paladares más saturados

jade-green /ˈdʒeɪdˈgriːn/ *adj* (*pred* **jade green**) verde jade *adj inv*

jag /dʒæg/ *n* (AmE colloq)

A (binge) curda *f* (fam), mona *f* (fam), trompa *f* (Esp fam)

B (of emotion — crying) llorera *f* (fam), lloradera *f* (AmL fam); (— laughing) ataque *m* de risa

jagged /ˈdʒægəd || ˈdʒægɪd/ *adj* ‹*edge/cut*› irregular; ‹*rock/cliff*› recortado, con picos

jaguar /ˈdʒægwɑːr || ˈdʒægjʊə(r)/ *n* jaguar *m*

jail¹ /dʒeɪl/ *n* cárcel *f*, prisión *f*; **she's in ~** está presa *or* en la cárcel; **he went to ~** lo metieron preso; (*before n*) **~ sentence** pena *f* de prisión

jail² *vt* encarcelar; **he was ~ed for life** lo condenaron a cadena perpetua; **she was ~ed for theft** la metieron presa por robo

jail: **~bird** *n* (colloq) delincuente *mf* habitual; **~break** *n* (journ) fuga *f* (*de la cárcel*)

jailer, jailor /ˈdʒeɪlər || ˈdʒeɪlə(r)/ *n* carcelero, -ra *m,f*

jailhouse /ˈdʒeɪlhaʊs/ *n* (AmE) cárcel *f*

Jakarta /dʒəˈkɑːrtə || dʒəˈkɑːtə/ *n* Yakarta *f*

jalopy /dʒəˈlɑːpi || dʒəˈlɒpi/ *n* (*pl* **-pies**) (colloq) cacharro *m* (fam)

jam¹ /dʒæm/ *n*

A [u c] (Culin) mermelada *f*, dulce *m* (RPl)

B [c] (difficult situation) (colloq) aprieto *m*; **to be in a ~** estar* en un aprieto; **to get into a ~** meterse en un lío (fam)

C [c] (*traffic ~*) atasco *m*, embotellamiento *m*

jam² **-mm-** *vt*

A 1 (cram) **to ~ sth INTO sth** meter algo EN algo 2 (congest, block) ‹*road*› atestar; **the switchboard was ~med with calls** la centralita estaba saturada de llamadas

B (wedge firmly): **he ~med his foot in the door** metió el pie entre la puerta y el marco; **the car was ~med in between two trucks** el coche estaba atascado entre dos camiones

C (Rad) interferir*

■ **jam** *vi* «*brakes*» bloquearse; «*machine*» trancarse*; «*switch/lock*» trabarse; «*gun*» encasquillarse

(Phrasal verb)

- **jam on** [v ▸ o ▸ adv, v ▸ adv ▸ o]: **to ~ on the brakes** dar* un frenazo, frenar en seco; *see also* **jam²** *vt* **B**

Jamaica /dʒəˈmeɪkə/ *n* Jamaica *f*

Jamaican /dʒəˈmeɪkən/ *adj* jamaicano

jamb /dʒæm/ *n* jamba *f*

jamboree /ˈdʒæmbəˈriː/ *n* 1 (of Scouts) congreso *m* (*de exploradores*) 2 (party) juerga *f* (fam)

jam jar *n* (BrE) tarro *m* *or* bote *m* para mermelada

jammy /ˈdʒæmi/ *adj* (BrE colloq) (lucky) afortunado, suertudo (AmL fam); **you ~ so-and-so!** ¡qué suerte tienes!

jam: **~-packed** /ˈdʒæmˈpækt/ *adj* (colloq) repleto, atestado (de gente); **~ session** *n*: *sesión de un grupo de músicos de jazz o rock que se reúnen para improvisar*

Jan (= **January**) en.

Jane Doe *n* (AmE) persona *f* inidentificada, Juana Pérez

jangle¹ /ˈdʒæŋgəl/ *vt* hacer* sonar

■ **jangle** *vi* hacer* ruido (*metálico*), sonar*; **it sets my nerves jangling** me pone los nervios de punta; **her bracelets made a jangling noise** sus pulseras tintineaban al entrechocarse

jangle² *n* [c u] sonido *m* (*metálico*)

janitor /ˈdʒænətər || ˈdʒænɪtə(r)/ *n* conserje *m*, portero *m*

January /ˈdʒænjueri || ˈdʒænjʊəri/ *n* enero *m*; **~ 24** 24 de enero; **on the first of ~** el primero *or* (Esp tb) el uno de enero; **in ~** en enero; **early in ~, in early ~** a principios *or* a primeros de enero; **in the middle of ~** a mediados de enero; **at the end of ~** a fines *or* a finales de enero; **every ~** cada enero, todos los eneros; **there are 31 days in ~** enero tiene 31 días

Jap /dʒæp/ *n* (colloq & offensive) japonés, -nesa *m,f*, japo *mf* (fam & pey)

Japan /dʒə'pæn/ *n* (el) Japón *m*

Japanese[1] /ˌdʒæpə'ni:z/ *adj* japonés

Japanese[2] *n* (*pl* ~) [1] [u] (language) japonés *m* [2] [c] (person) japonés, -nesa *m,f*

jape /dʒeɪp/ *n* (dated) broma *f*

jar[1] /dʒɑ:r || dʒɑ:(r)/ *n*
A [1] (container) tarro *m*, bote *m* [2] (drink) (BrE colloq) cerveza *f*, caña *f* (Esp)
B (jolt) sacudida *f*

jar[2] **-rr-** *vi* [1] (clash) desentonar [2] (irritate) enervar; **her laugh ~s on my nerves** su risa me crispa los nervios
■ **jar** *vt* sacudir

jargon /'dʒɑ:rgən || 'dʒɑ:gən/ *n* [u] jerga *f*

jarring /'dʒɑ:rɪŋ/ *adj* ‹*sound*› discordante; **~ colors** colores que desentonan

jasmine /'dʒæzmən || 'dʒæsmɪn/ *n* [c u] jazmín *m*

jasper /'dʒæspər || 'dʒæspə(r)/ *n* [u] jaspe *m*

jaundice /'dʒɔ:ndəs || 'dʒɔ:ndɪs/ *n* [u] ictericia *f*

jaundiced /'dʒɔ:ndəst || 'dʒɔ:ndɪst/ *adj* [1] (Med) ‹*skin/baby*› ictérico [2] ‹*view/opinion*› negativo

jaunt /dʒɔ:nt/ *n* excursión *f*; **to go for** *o* **on a ~** salir* de excursión

jauntily /'dʒɔ:ntḷi || 'dʒɔ:ntɪli/ *adv* ‹*wave/whistle*› con desenfado *or* desenvoltura; ‹*walk*› con garbo

jaunty /'dʒɔ:nti/ *adj* **-tier, -tiest** (*usu before n*) ‹*air*› garboso, desenfadado; ‹*tune*› alegre

Java /'dʒɑ:və/ *n* Java *f*

javelin /'dʒævlən || 'dʒævlɪn/ *n* jabalina *f*

jaw /dʒɔ:/ *n* [1] (of person, animal) mandíbula *f*; (esp of animal) quijada *f*; **the lower/upper ~** el maxilar inferior/superior; **his ~ dropped** se quedó boquiabierto [2] **jaws** *pl* fauces *fpl*; **the ~s of death** las garras de la muerte [3] (of tool) mordaza *f*

jaw: **~bone** /'dʒɔ:bəʊn/ *n* mandíbula *f*, maxilar *m*; (of an animal) quijada *f*; **~-dropping** /'dʒɔ:ˌdrɑ:pɪŋ || 'dʒɔ:ˌdrɒpɪŋ/ *adj* (colloq) para quedarse con la boca abierta (fam), alucinante (Esp fam), abismante (Andes)

jay /dʒeɪ/ *n* arrendajo *m*

jay: **~bird** *n* (AmE) arrendajo *m*; ***as naked as a ~bird*** (colloq & dated) como Dios lo (*or* la *etc*) trajo al mundo; **~walk** *vi* cruzar* la calzada imprudentemente; **~walker** *n* peatón *m* imprudente

jazz /dʒæz/ *n* [u] (Mus) jazz *m*; ***... and all that*** ~ y todo eso, y toda esa historia (fam), y todo ese rollo (fam)

Phrasal verb
- **jazz up** [v ▸ o ▸ adv, v ▸ adv ▸ o] (colloq) [1] ‹*music*› tocar* con ritmo sincopado [2] ‹*room*› alegrar, darle* vida a

> **jazz**
>
> Un género musical, caracterizado por la síncopa y la improvisación, que tiene su origen en la música negra de Nueva Orleans de las postrimerías del siglo XIX. Desde entonces no ha dejado de evolucionar, desarrollando estilos sucesivos como son el *Chicago jazz* de los años 20 (Louis Armstrong), *swing* (Benny Goodman), el estilo orquestral de las *big bands* (Duke Ellington), el *bop* (Dizzy Gillespie, Charlie Parker, Lester Young), el *cool jazz* (Miles Davis, Stan Getz), el *free jazz* (John Coltrane), la *jazz rock fusion* (Weather Report) o la experimentación ecléctica con estilos del pasado practicado por Wynton Marsalis

jazzy /'dʒæzi/ *adj* **jazzier, jazziest**
A (flashy) (colloq) llamativo; **in ~ colors** de colores chillones
B (Mus) ‹*rhythm*› de jazz; ‹*version*› con ritmo de jazz

JCB® /ˌdʒeɪˌsi:'bi:/ *n* (BrE) excavadora *f* JCB

jealous /'dʒeləs/ *adj* [1] ‹*husband/wife*› celoso; **to be ~ OF sb** estar* celoso DE algn, tener* celos DE algn [2] (envious) envidioso; **don't you feel ~ when you see ...** ¿no te da envidia ver ...?; **to be ~ OF sth** envidiar algo; **to be ~ OF sb** tenerle* envidia A algn

jealously /'dʒeləsli/ *adv*
A [1] (enviously) con envidia [2] (possessively): **he ~ insisted she stop seeing her girlfriends** insistió, por celos, en que dejara de ver a sus amigas
B (protectively) celosamente; **a ~ guarded secret** un secreto celosamente guardado

jealousy /'dʒeləsi/ *n* (*pl* **-sies**) [1] [u] (fear of rivalry) celos *mpl* [2] [u c] (envy) envidia *f*

jeans /dʒi:nz/ *pl n* vaqueros *mpl*, jeans *mpl*, bluyines *mpl* (Andes); **a pair of ~** unos (pantalones) vaqueros, unos jeans, unos bluyines (Andes)

Jeep®, **jeep** /dʒi:p/ *n* Jeep® *m*

jeepers /'dʒi:pərz || 'dʒi:pəz/ *interj* (AmE colloq & dated) ¡cáspita! (fam), ¡Jesús! (fam)

jeer /dʒɪr || dʒɪə(r)/ *vi* (boo) abuchear; (mock) burlarse, mofarse; **to ~ AT sth/sb** burlarse *or* mofarse DE algo/algn; ‹‹*crowd*›› abuchear algo/a algn

jeez /dʒi:z/ *interj* (AmE colloq) ¡caray! (fam), ¡jo! (Esp fam)

Jehovah /dʒə'həʊvə/ *n* Jehová

Jehovah's Witness *n* testigo *mf* de Jehová

jell /dʒel/ *vi* ▸ **gel**[2]

Jell-O® /'dʒeləʊ/ *n* [u] (AmE) gelatina *f* (*con sabor a frutas*)

jelly /'dʒeli/ *n* [u c] (*pl* **-lies**)
A (Culin) [1] (clear jam) jalea *f* [2] (as dessert) (BrE) gelatina *f* (*con sabor a frutas*)
B (gelatinous substance) gelatina *f*; **my legs felt like ~** sentía que me temblaban las piernas

jelly: **~ baby** *n* (BrE) caramelo *m* de goma (*con forma de bebé*); **~ bean** *n* caramelo *m* de goma (*con forma de riñón*); **~fish** *n* (*pl* **-fish** *or* **-fishes**) medusa *f*, malagua *f* (Per), aguaviva *f* (RPl), aguamala *f* (Col, Méx); **~ roll** *n* (AmE) brazo *m* de gitano *or* (Andes) de reina, arrollado *m* (*dulce*) (RPl)

jemmy /'dʒemi/ *n* (BrE) ▸ **jimmy**

jeopardize /'dʒepərdaɪz || 'dʒepədaɪz/ *vt* poner* en peligro, hacer* peligrar

jeopardy /'dʒepərdi || 'dʒepədi/ *n* [u]: **in ~** en peligro; **to put** *o* **place sth in ~** poner* algo en peligro, hacer* peligrar algo

jerk[1] /dʒɜ:rk || dʒɜ:k/ *vi*: **his arms and legs ~ed nervously** sus brazos y piernas se agitaban nerviosamente; **the train ~ed to a stop** el tren se detuvo con una sacudida; **she ~ed away from him** se apartó de él con un movimiento brusco
■ **jerk** *vt*: **the impact ~ed him forward** el impacto lo propulsó hacia adelante

Phrasal verb
- **jerk off** [v ▸ adv] [v ▸ o ▸ adv] (vulg) **to ~ off** *o* **to ~ oneself off** hacerse* *or* (Chi, Per) correrse una *or* la paja (vulg), hacerse* una chaqueta (Méx vulg), hacerse* la manuela (Ven vulg)

jerk[2] *n*
A [1] (tug) tirón *m* [2] (sudden movement) sacudida *f*
B (contemptible person) (colloq) estúpido, -da *m,f*, pendejo, -ja *m,f* (AmL exc CS fam), gilipollas *mf* (Esp fam), huevón, -ona *m,f* (Andes, Ven fam)

jerkin /'dʒɜ:rkən || 'dʒɜ:kɪn/ *n* (sleeveless jacket) chaqueta *f* sin mangas; (Hist) jubón *m*

jerkwater /'dʒɜ:rkˌwɔ:tər || 'dʒɜ:kˌwɔ:tə(r)/ *adj* (AmE colloq) (*before n*) de mala muerte (fam)

jerky[1] /'dʒɜ:rki || 'dʒɜ:ki/ *adj* **-kier, -kiest** ‹*speech*› entrecortado; **he walked with short, ~ strides** andaba con pasos cortos y desacompasados, andaba a trompicones

jerky[2] *n* [u] (AmE) cecina *f*, tasajo *m*, charqui *m* (AmS)

jerry /'dʒeri/: **~-built** *adj* mal construido, construido por chapuceros; **~ can** *n* bidón *m*

jersey /'dʒɜrzi || 'dʒɜ:zi/ *n* (*pl* **-seys**)
A [1] [c] (sports shirt) camiseta *f* [2] [u] (Tex) jersey *m*, tejido *m* de punto [3] [c] (BrE) ▸ **sweater**
B [1] **Jersey** (la isla de) Jersey [2] *also* **Jersey** (cattle) *raza de ganado vacuno Jersey*

Jerusalem /dʒə'ru:sələm/ *n* Jerusalén *m*

Jerusalem artichoke *n* aguaturma *f*, pataca *f*

jest[1] /dʒest/ *n* (arch) broma *f*, chanza *f* (arc); **in ~** en broma; ▸ **word**[1] **B**

jest[2] *vi* bromear

jester /'dʒestər || 'dʒestə(r)/ *n* bufón *m*

Jesuit /'dʒeʒuət || 'dʒezjʊɪt/ *n* jesuita *m*

Jesus /'dʒi:zəs/ *n* [1] (Relig) Jesús; ~ **Christ** Jesucristo [2] (*as interj*) (colloq) ~ **(Christ)!** ¡por Dios!

jet¹ /dʒet/ *n*
A [c] (Aviat) [1] ~ **(engine)** motor *m* a reacción, reactor *m* [2] (plane) avión *m* (*con motor a reacción*)
B [c][1] (of water, air, gas) chorro *m* [2] (nozzle) surtidor *m*
C [u] (Min) azabache *m*

jet² *vi* **-tt-** (fly) (colloq) volar*; **where are you ~ting off to this time?** ¿a qué rincón del mundo te vas esta vez?

jet: **~-black** /'dʒet'blæk/ *adj* (*pred* ~ **black**) negro azabache *adj inv*; ~ **fighter** *n* caza *m* (*con motor a reacción*); ~ **lag** *n* [u] jet lag *m*, desfase *m* horario; **~-propelled** /'dʒetprə'peld/ *adj* a reacción de propulsión a chorro (ant); ~ **propulsion** *n* propulsión *f* a chorro

jetsam /'dʒetsəm/ *n* [u] echazón *f*; *see also* **flotsam**

jet: ~ **set** *n* **the ~ set** el jet set (AmL), la jet set (Esp); ~ **ski** *n* moto *f* acuática; **~-skiing** /'dʒet,ski:ɪŋ/ *n* [u] motociclismo *m* acuático

jettison /'dʒetəsən || 'dʒetɪsən/ *vt* (Naut) echar por la borda, echar al mar; (Aviat) deshacerse* de, arrojar; (get rid of) ‹*garbage*› deshacerse* de

jetty /'dʒeti/ *n* (*pl* **-ties**) (for landing) embarcadero *m*, malecón *m*; (breakwater) espigón *m*, malecón *m*

Jew /dʒu:/ *n* judío, -día *m,f*

jewel /'dʒu:əl/ *n* (gem) piedra *f* preciosa; (piece of jewelry) alhaja *f*, joya *f*; (in watch) rubí *m*; (sb, sth wonderful) joya *f*; (*before n*) ~ **box** *o* **case** joyero *m*

jeweler, (BrE) **jeweller** /'dʒu:ələr || 'dʒu:ələ(r)/ *n* joyero, -ra *m,f*; **a ~'s (shop)** una joyería

jewelry, (BrE) **jewellery** /'dʒu:əlri/ *n* [u] joyas *fpl*, alhajas *fpl*; **a piece of ~** una alhaja, una joya; (*before n*) ~ **box** joyero *m*; ~ **store** (AmE) joyería *f*

Jewish /'dʒu:ɪʃ/ *adj* judío

Jewry /'dʒu:ri/ *n* [u] (jews) judíos *mpl*; (religion) judaísmo *m*

jew's harp *n* birimbao *m*

jib /dʒɪb/ *n*
A (sail) foque *m*
B (of crane) brazo *m*

jibe¹ /dʒaɪb/ *n* pulla *f*, burla *f*

jibe² *vi*
A **to ~ AT sb/sth** burlarse *or* mofarse DE algn/algo
B (agree) (AmE colloq) **to ~ (WITH sth)** cuadrar (CON algo)

jiff /dʒɪf/, **jiffy** /'dʒɪfi/ *n* (colloq) (*no pl*) segundo *m*

Jiffy bag® /'dʒɪfi/ *n* sobre *m* acolchado

jig¹ /dʒɪg/ *n*
A (dance) giga *f*
B (Tech) plantilla *f* de guía

jig² *vi* **-gg-**: **they were ~ging around to the music** brincaban al son de la música

jigger /'dʒɪgər || 'dʒɪgə(r)/ *n* (tool, gadget) (AmE) cosa *f*, chisme *m* (Esp, Méx fam), coso *m* (AmS fam), vaina *f* (Col, Per, Ven fam)

jiggered /'dʒɪgərd || 'dʒɪgəd/ *adj* (colloq) (*pred*)
A (dated) (*in interj phrases*): **well, I'll be ~!** ¡caramba! (fam)
B (tired out) (BrE) **to be ~** estar* reventado *or* molido (fam)

jiggery-pokery /'dʒɪgəri'pəʊkəri/ *n* [u] (BrE colloq & dated) chanchullos *mpl* (fam), tejemanejes *mpl* (fam)

jiggle /'dʒɪgəl/ *vt* mover*, sacudir

jigsaw /'dʒɪgsɔ:/ *n*
A ~ **(puzzle)** rompecabezas *m*, puzzle *m*
B (saw) sierra *f* de vaivén, sierra *f* de puñal

jihad /dʒɪ'hæd/ *n* yihad *m or f*, jihad *m or f*, guerra *f* santa islámica

jihadi /dʒɪ'hædi/ **jihadist** /dʒɪ'hædɪst/ *n* yihadista *mf*

jilt /dʒɪlt/ *vt* dejar plantado, plantar (fam)

jim-crow /'dʒɪm'krəʊ/ *adj* (AmE) racista

jimmy /'dʒɪmi/, (BrE) **jemmy** /'dʒemi/ *n* (*pl* **-mies**) palanqueta *f*

jingle¹ /'dʒɪŋgəl/ *n*
A (sound) (*no pl*) tintineo *m*; (of harness bells) cascabeleo *m*, tintineo *m*
B [c] (Marketing) jingle *m* (publicitario)

jingle² *vi* tintinear

jingo /'dʒɪŋgəʊ/ *n*: **by ~!** (colloq & dated) ¡recórcholis! (fam), ¡pardiez! (arc)

jingoism /'dʒɪŋgəʊɪzəm/ *n* [u] patriotería *f*, jingoísmo *m*

jingoistic /'dʒɪŋgəʊ'ɪstɪk/ *adj* patriotero, jingoísta

jinks /dʒɪŋks/ *pl n* ▸ **high jinks**

jinx¹ /dʒɪŋks/ *n*: **there's a ~ on this project** a este proyecto le han echado una maldición

jinx² *vt* traer* mala suerte a

jitters /'dʒɪtərz || 'dʒɪtəz/ *pl n* (colloq) nervios *mpl*; **he got the ~** se puso nervioso, le dio el tembleque (fam)

jittery /'dʒɪtəri/ *adj* nervioso; **she got ~** se puso nerviosa, le dio el tembleque (fam)

jive¹ /dʒaɪv/ *n* [u] *baile de los años 40 y 50 con música de jazz o rock*

jive² *vi*: *bailar el* **jive¹**

Jnr (BrE) (= **Junior**) (h), Jr.

job /dʒɑ:b || dʒɒb/ *n*
A [1] (occupation, post) trabajo *m*, empleo *m*; **to have a teaching/publishing ~** *o* **a ~ in teaching/publishing** trabajar en la enseñanza/en una editorial; **my ~ involves a lot of traveling** en mi trabajo *or* puesto tengo que viajar mucho; **if you're late once more, you'll be out of a ~** como vuelvas a llegar tarde, te quedas sin trabajo; **is he the right person for the ~?** ¿es la persona idónea para el puesto?; ***~s for the boys*** (BrE colloq) amiguismo *m*; ***on the ~***: **I never drink on the ~** yo nunca bebo cuando estoy trabajando; **after three weeks on the ~ ...** tras tres semanas de trabajo ...; **on-the-~ training** cursos de capacitación en el trabajo; **if the nightwatchman hadn't been on the ~ ...** (AmE colloq) si el sereno no hubiera estado atento ...; (*before n*) ~ **creation** creación *f* de empleo *or* de puestos de trabajo; ~ **losses** pérdida *f* de puestos de trabajo; ~ **opportunity** oportunidad *f* laboral *or* de trabajo; **you get a lot of ~ satisfaction doing this** este trabajo es muy gratificante; ~ **security** seguridad *f* en el puesto [2] (duty, responsibility): **it's your ~ to make the tea** tú eres el encargado de hacer el té; **it's the leader's ~ to ensure party unity** al líder le corresponde velar por la unidad del partido; **I'm only doing my ~** sólo cumplo con mi deber
B [1] (task, piece of work) trabajo *m*; (Comput) trabajo *m*; **let's get on with the ~** vamos a ponernos a trabajar en serio; **concentrate on the ~ in hand** concéntrate en la tarea que tenemos entre manos; **she's had a nose ~** (colloq) se ha hecho la cirugía estética en la nariz; **a repair ~** (Auto) una reparación; **you're doing a fine ~** lo estás haciendo muy bien; **he did an excellent ~ on my car** me arregló el coche muy bien; **he's doing a good ~ of handling the crisis** está llevando bien la crisis; ***a good ~*** (BrE colloq) menos mal; **what a good ~ I brought my umbrella!** (BrE colloq) ¡menos mal que traje el paraguas!; ***to be just the ~!*** (BrE colloq) ser* lo ideal, ser* justo lo que hace falta; ***to give sth/sb up as a bad ~*** dejar algo/a algn por imposible; ***to make the best of a bad ~*** apechugar* y hacer* lo que se pueda; ***if a ~'s worth doing, it's worth doing well*** si vale la pena hacerlo, vale la pena hacerlo bien [2] (difficult task) (colloq): **I had a terrible ~ getting that nail out** me dio mucho trabajo sacar ese clavo; **we had a ~ to hear** nos las vimos negras para oír (fam)
C (crime) (sl) golpe *m*
D (thing) (sl) cosa *f*, chisme *m* (Esp, Méx fam), coso *m* (AmS fam), vaina *f* (Col, Per, Ven fam)

Job /dʒəʊb/ *n* Job; **~'s comforter** *persona que intentando consolar empeora la situación*

job action *n* [u] (AmE) movilización *f* (*de trabajadores*)

jobber /'dʒɑ:bər || 'dʒɒbə(r)/ *n* [1] (casual worker) trabajador, -dora *m,f* eventual [2] (wholesale dealer) intermediario, -ria *m,f*

jobbing /'dʒɑ:bɪŋ || 'dʒɒbɪŋ/ *adj* (*before n*) eventual, temporal

job: **~centre** *n* (in UK) oficina *f or* bolsa *f* de empleo; ~ **description** *n* descripción *f* del puesto; **~holder** *n* (AmE) trabajador, -dora *m,f*; **~-hunt** *vi* (*usu in -ing form*) buscar* trabajo; **to go ~hunting** salir* a buscar trabajo

jobless /'dʒɑ:bləs || 'dʒɒblɪs/ *adj* (journ) desempleado, sin trabajo, en paro (Esp), cesante (Chi)

job: ~ **lot** *n* lote *m*; ~ **security** *n* seguridad *f* en el puesto; ~ **sharing** /'ʃerɪŋ || 'ʃeərɪŋ/ *n* [u] *sistema en el cual dos personas comparten un puesto de trabajo*

jock /dʒɑ:k || dʒɒk/ *n*
A (colloq) (athlete, sportsman) (AmE) deportista *m*

B *also* **Jock** (Scotsman) (BrE sl & often pej) escocés *m*

jockey[1] /'dʒɑːki || 'dʒɒki/ *n* (*pl* ~**s**) jockey *mf*, jinete *mf*

jockey[2] *vi* **to ~ FOR sth: with her retirement coming up, many editors are ~ing for position** al acercarse su jubilación, muchos redactores están tratando de colocarse *or* (AmL tb) de ubicarse

Jockey shorts® /'dʒɑːki || 'dʒɒki/ *pl n* (AmE) calzoncillos *mpl*, calzones *mpl* (Méx), interiores *mpl* (Col, Ven)

jockstrap /'dʒɑːkstræp || 'dʒɒkstræp/ *n* suspensorio *m*, suspensor *m* (Per, RPl)

jocose /dʒəʊ'kəʊs, dʒə'kəʊs/ *adj* (liter) jocoso

jocular /'dʒɑːkjələr || 'dʒɒkjʊlə(r)/ *adj* jocoso

jocund /'dʒɑːkənd || 'dʒɒkənd/ *adj* (arch *or* poet) jocundo (liter)

jodhpurs /'dʒɑːdpərz || 'dʒɒdpəz/ *pl n* pantalones *mpl* de montar, breeches *mpl* (Col, RPl)

Joe /dʒəʊ/ *n* Pepe; **an average ~** (AmE colloq) un hombre cualquiera; **~ Public** (BrE colloq) el hombre de la calle, el ciudadano medio *or* de a pie

jog[1] /dʒɑːg || dʒɒg/ **-gg-** *vt*: **she ~ged his elbow just as ...** le dio en el codo justo cuando ...; **stop ~ging the table!** ¡deja de mover *or* sacudir la mesa!; **to ~ sb's memory** refrescarle* la memoria a algn

■ **jog** *vi* 1 (run) correr 2 (Leisure) hacer* footing *or* jogging; **to go ~ging** salir* a hacer footing *or* jogging

jog[2] *n*

A (*no pl*) (Leisure): **to go for a ~** hacer* footing *or* jogging

B (nudge): **she gave his arm a ~** le sacudió el brazo

C (in direction) (AmE): **the road makes a ~ to the left** el camino de pronto tuerce a la izquierda

jogger /'dʒɑːgər || 'dʒɒgə(r)/ *n*: *persona que hace footing*

jogging /'dʒɑːgɪŋ || 'dʒɒgɪŋ/ *n* [u] footing *m*, jogging *m*

joggle /'dʒɑːgəl || 'dʒɒgəl/ *vt* sacudir; **don't ~ me when I'm writing** no me muevas cuando estoy escribiendo

john /dʒɑːn || dʒɒn/ *n*

A (toilet) (AmE colloq) baño *m*, retrete *m*, váter *m* (Esp fam)

B **John**: **~ the Baptist/Evangelist** San Juan Bautista/Evangelista; **~ 6,31** (San) Juan 6,31; **~ Bull** (dated) *personificación de todo lo inglés*; **~ Doe** (AmE) (Law) persona *f* inidentificada; (colloq) el típico americano, el americano medio; **~ Q Public** (AmE) el hombre de la calle, el ciudadano medio *or* de a pie

joie de vivre /'ʒwɑːdə'viːv(r) || ˌʒwɑːdə'viːvrə/ *n* [u] alegría *f* de vivir, vitalidad *f*

join[1] /dʒɔɪn/ *vt*

A (fasten, link) ‹*ropes/wires*› unir; (put together) ‹*tables*› juntar; **to ~ two things together** unir dos cosas; **I ~ed an extra length onto the hosepipe** le añadí *or* le agregué un trozo a la manguera; **to ~ hands** tomarse *or* (esp Esp) cogerse* de la mano

B 1 (meet, keep company with): **we're going for a drink, won't** *o* **will you ~ us?** vamos a tomar algo ¿nos acompañas?; **you go ahead, I'll ~ you later** ustedes vayan que ya iré yo luego; **may I ~ you?** ¿le importa si me siento aquí?; **won't** *o* **will you ~ us for dinner?** ¿por qué no cenan con nosotros? 2 (associate oneself with): **I'd like you all to ~ me in a toast to ...** quiero proponer un brindis por ..., propongo que brindemos todos por ...; **my husband ~s me in wishing you a speedy recovery** (frml) tanto mi marido como yo le deseamos una pronta recuperación

C 1 (become part of) unirse a, sumarse a; **they have ~ed the ranks of the unemployed** se han sumado a las filas del desempleo; **I ~ed the line** me puse en la cola; **I ~ed the course in November** empecé el curso en noviembre, me uní al grupo en noviembre 2 (become member of) ‹*club*› hacerse* socio de; ‹*union*› afiliarse a; ‹*army*› alistarse en; ‹*firm*› entrar en *or* (AmL tb) entrar a, incorporarse a; **he ~ed our staff in July** pasó a formar parte de nuestro personal en julio

D 1 (merge with): **the path ~s the road a mile further on** el camino empalma con la carretera una milla más adelante; **this river eventually ~s the Thames** este río desemboca en *or* confluye con el Támesis; **where the wall ~s the roof** en la unión de la pared con el techo 2 (get onto): **we ~ the autobahn south of Frankfurt** entramos en la autopista al sur de Frankfurt; **he ~ed his ship at Boston** se unió a la tripulación en Boston

■ **join** *vi*

A **to ~ (together)** «*parts/components*» unirse; «*groups*» unirse; **to ~ WITH sb IN -ING: they ~ with me in congratulating you** se unen a mis felicitaciones, se hacen partícipes de mi enhorabuena (frml)

B (merge) «*streams*» confluir*; «*roads*» empalmar, unirse

C (become member) hacerse* socio

Phrasal verbs

• **join in**

A [v ▸ adv] participar, tomar parte; **when we get to the chorus I'd like you all to ~ in** cuando lleguemos al estribillo, quiero que todo el mundo cante

B [v ▸ adv ▸ o] ‹*celebrations*› participar *or* tomar parte en

• **join up**

A [v ▸ adv] 1 (enlist) alistarse, enrolarse 2 (fit together) «*pieces/parts*» encajar 3 (team up) «*people*» unirse

B [v ▸ o ▸ adv, v ▸ adv ▸ o] ‹*letters*› unir, juntar; **~ed-up writing** letra *f* cursiva *or* corrida (*manuscrita*)

join[2] *n* juntura *f*, unión *f*

joiner /'dʒɔɪnər || 'dʒɔɪnə(r)/ *n* carpintero, -ra *m,f* (de obra)

joinery /'dʒɔɪnəri/ *n* [u] (trade) carpintería *f* (de obra); (work) carpintería *f* (de obra)

joint[1] /dʒɔɪnt/ *n*

A (Anat) articulación *f*; **his shoulder was out of ~** tenía el hombro dislocado; ▸**nose**[1] **A**

B (Const) 1 (point of joining) unión *f*, junta *f*; (in woodwork) ensambladura *f* 2 (part that joins) empalme *m*, conexión *f*

C (Culin): **a ~ of lamb/pork** un trozo de cordero/cerdo (*para asar*)

D (place) (colloq): **this is a crummy ~** esto es un antro

E (of marijuana) porro *m* (arg), toque *m* (Méx arg), varillo *m* (Col arg), pito *m* (Chi fam)

joint[2] *adj* (*before n*) ‹*action*› conjunto; **~ ownership** copropiedad *f*; **~ owner** copropietario, -ria *m,f*; **~ committee** comisión *f* mixta; **they are ~ heirs** son coherederos; **~ first prize** primer premio compartido; **it was a ~ effort** fue un trabajo de equipo *or* realizado en conjunto; **they came ~ second** llegaron juntos en segundo lugar

joint account *n* cuenta *f* conjunta

jointly /'dʒɔɪntli/ *adv* ‹*decide/act*› conjuntamente

joint: **~ stock company** *n* sociedad *f* por acciones; **~ venture** *n* empresa *f* conjunta, joint venture *m*

joist /dʒɔɪst/ *n* viga *f*, vigueta *f*

joke[1] /dʒəʊk/ *n* 1 (verbal) chiste *m*; (directed at sb) broma *f*; **to tell** *o* **crack a ~** contar* un chiste; **they made endless ~s about my new hairstyle** no paraban de reírse de mi nuevo peinado; **I can't see the ~** no le veo la gracia; **he can't take a ~** no sabe aceptar una broma; **it's beyond a ~** se pasa de castaño oscuro; **it's no ~** maldita la gracia que tiene (fam); ***the ~'s on her/me/them*** le/me/les salió el tiro por la culata (fam) 2 (*practical ~*) broma *f*; **to play a ~ on sb** hacerle* *or* gastarle una broma a algn; **is that your idea of a ~?** ¿a ti te parece gracioso eso? 3 (contemptible person, thing): **as a teacher he's just a ~** como profesor es un desastre; **that interview was a ~** esa entrevista fue una farsa

joke[2] *vi* bromear, vacilar; **you must** *o* **have to be joking!** ¡tú debes estar loco! *or* ¡ni loco que estuviera!; **I was only joking** lo dije en broma; **he was always laughing and joking** siempre estaba de broma

joker /'dʒəʊkər || 'dʒəʊkə(r)/ *n*

A (cards) comodín *m*; ***the ~ in the deck*** *o* (BrE) ***pack*** la gran incógnita

B (prankster) bromista *mf*; (contemptible person) (colloq) tipo, -pa *m,f* (fam); **who was the ~ who put salt in my coffee?** ¿quién fue el gracioso que le puse sal a mi café? (iró)

jokey /'dʒəʊki/ *adj* ▸**joky**

joking[1] /'dʒəʊkɪŋ/ *adj* ‹*remark/reference*› jocoso

joking[2] *n* bromas *fpl*; **(all) ~ apart** *o* **aside** bromas aparte

jokingly /'dʒəʊkɪŋli/ *adv* en broma

joky /'dʒəʊki/ *adj* **jokier, jokiest** ‹*remark*› jocoso

jollity /'dʒɑːləti || 'dʒɒləti/ *n* [u] (attitude) jovialidad *f*; (merriment) regocijo *m*

jolly[1] /'dʒɑːli || 'dʒɒli/ *adj* **-lier, -liest** (merry) ‹*person*› jovial, alegre; ‹*laugh/tune*› alegre; **he was in a ~ mood** estaba muy contento *or* alegre

jolly² *adv* (BrE colloq) (*as intensifier*): **you were ~ lucky!** ¡qué suerte tuviste!; **you'll do as you're ~ well told!** ¡tú harás lo que se te diga y sanseacabó! (fam); **I've finished — ~ good!** ya he terminado — ¡muy bien! *or* ¡estupendo!

jolly³ *vt* **-lies, -lying, -lied** (colloq): **to ~ sb along** animar a algn

Jolly Roger /'dʒɑ:li'rɑ:dʒər || ˌdʒɒli'rɒdʒə(r)/ *n* bandera *f* pirata

jolt¹ /dʒəʊlt/ *vi*: **the cart ~ed along the path** el carro iba traqueteando *or* dando tumbos por el camino; **the train ~ed, and I spilled my coffee** el tren dio *or* pegó una sacudida y se me derramó el café

■ **jolt** *vt*: **the sudden stop ~ed me out of my seat** el frenazo repentino me hizo salir disparado del asiento; **she ~ed his arm** le movió el brazo; **this ~ed him out of his inertia** esto lo sacudió, sacándolo de su inercia

jolt² *n* sacudida *f*; **she awoke with a ~** se despertó sobresaltada

Joneses /'dʒəʊnzəz || 'dʒəʊnzɪz/ *pl n*: *see* **keep up** *Sense* **I B1**

Jordan /'dʒɔ:rdn̩ || 'dʒɔ:dn̩/ *n* 1▸ (country) Jordania *f* 2▸ **the ~, the ~ River** (AmE), **the River ~** (BrE) el Jordán

Jordanian /dʒɔ:r'deɪniən || dʒɔ:'deɪniən/ *adj* jordano

Joseph /'dʒəʊzəf || 'dʒəʊzɪf/ *n* José

josh /dʒɑ:ʃ || dʒɒʃ/ *vt* (esp AmE colloq) tomarle el pelo a

joss stick /dʒɑ:s || dʒɒs/ *n* varilla *f* de incienso, pebete *m*

jostle /'dʒɑ:səl || 'dʒɒsəl/ *vt* empujar; **he was ~d by protestors as he left** al salir fue zarandeado por unos manifestantes

■ **jostle** *vi*: **people were jostling trying to get out** la gente se empujaba tratando de salir; **to ~ FOR sth**: **hundreds of customers jostling for service** cientos de clientes peleando por ser atendidos

jot /dʒɑ:t || dʒɒt/ *n* (*no pl, usu with neg*): **he hasn't a ~ of sense** no tiene ni pizca *or* ni un ápice de sentido común; **it makes not a** *o* **one ~ of difference** da exactamente igual

(Phrasal verb)

• **jot down**: **-tt-** [v ▸ o ▸ adv, v ▸ adv ▸ o] apuntar *or* anotar (*rápidamente*)

jotter /'dʒɑ:tər || 'dʒɒtə(r)/ *n* (BrE) bloc *m*

jotting /'dʒɑ:tɪŋ || 'dʒɒtɪŋ/ *n* apunte *m*, nota *f*

joule /dʒu:l/ *n* julio *m*

journal /'dʒɜ:rnl̩ || 'dʒɜ:nl̩/ *n*

A (periodical) revista *f*, publicación *f*; (newspaper) periódico *m*

B (diary) (frml) diario *m*

journalese /'dʒɜ:rnl̩'i:z || ˌdʒɜ:nə'li:z/ *n* [u] (pej) jerga *f* periodística (pey)

journalism /'dʒɜ:rnl̩ɪzəm || 'dʒɜ:nəlɪzəm/ *n* [u] periodismo *m*

journalist /'dʒɜ:rnl̩əst || 'dʒɜ:n̩lɪst/ *n* periodista *mf*

journey¹ /'dʒɜ:rni || 'dʒɜ:ni/ *n* (*pl* **-neys**) viaje *m*; **an air/a rail ~** un viaje en avión/tren; **it's a three-hour ~ by car** en coche se tardan tres horas; **a 500-mile ~, a ~ of 500 miles** un viaje *or* trayecto de 500 millas; **the outward ~** el viaje de ida, la ida; **the return ~** el viaje de vuelta *or* de regreso, la vuelta, el regreso; **to go on** *o* **to make a ~** hacer* un viaje; **we usually break our ~ in York** normalmente paramos en York

journey² *vi* (liter) viajar

journeyman /'dʒɜ:rnimən || 'dʒɜ:nimən/ *n* (*pl* **-men** /-mən/) (worker) oficial *m*

joust /dʒaʊst/ *vi* justar

Jove /dʒəʊv/ *n* Júpiter; **by ~!** (BrE dated) ¡diantre! (ant)

jovial /'dʒəʊviəl/ *adj* jovial

jovially /'dʒəʊviəli/ *adv* jovialmente

jowls /dʒaʊlz/ *pl n* (*sometimes sing*) *parte inferior de los carrillos, que a veces cuelga de la mandíbula*

joy /dʒɔɪ/ *n*

A 1▸ [u] (emotion) alegría *f*, dicha *f*; **to my great ~** para mi gran alegría; **to jump for ~** saltar de alegría 2▸ [c u] (source of pleasure): **the children are a great ~ to them** los niños son una gran alegría para ellos; **she's a ~ to teach** es un verdadero placer *or* da gusto tenerla como alumna; **that's the ~ of it** eso es lo bueno que tiene; ***to be full of the ~s of Spring*** estar* como unas pascuas

B [u] (success) (BrE colloq): **any ~?** ¿hubo suerte?; **you'll get no ~ from** *o* **out of them** no vas a conseguir nada con ellos

joyful /'dʒɔɪfəl/ *adj* ‹*event*› feliz; ‹*dance/news*› alegre

joyfully /'dʒɔɪfəli/ *adv* alegremente, con regocijo

joyless /'dʒɔɪləs || 'dʒɔɪlɪs/ *adj* ‹*occasion*› falto de alegría; ‹*existence*› sombrío, triste

joyous /'dʒɔɪəs/ *adj* ‹*expression*› de dicha, de júbilo (liter); ‹*occasion*› feliz

joy: **~ride** *n* (in stolen car): **they took the car for a ~ride** robaron el coche para dar una vuelta; **~rider** *n*: *joven que roba un coche para dar una vuelta*; **~riding** *n* [u] *actividad delictiva del* **~rider**; **~stick** *n* (Aviat) palanca *f* de mando; (Electron, Comput) mando *m*, joystick *m*

JP *n* = **Justice of the Peace**

Jr (esp AmE) (= **Junior**) (h), Jr.

jubilant /'dʒu:bələnt || 'dʒu:bɪlənt/ *adj* ‹*expression*› de júbilo (liter), alborozado (liter); ‹*speech*› exultante (liter); **they were ~ at their win** estaban radiantes de alegría con la victoria

jubilation /'dʒu:bə'leɪʃən || ˌdʒu:bɪ'leɪʃən/ *n* [u] júbilo *m* (liter)

jubilee /'dʒu:bəli: || 'dʒu:bɪli:/ *n*: **the Queen's silver/golden ~** el vigésimo quinto *or* veinticinco/quincuagésimo *or* cincuenta aniversario de la reina

Judaism /'dʒu:dəɪzəm || 'dʒu:deɪɪzəm/ *n* [u] judaísmo *m*

Judas /'dʒu:dəs/ *n* 1▸ (Relig) Judas 2▸ (traitor) judas *m*

judder /'dʒʌdər || 'dʒʌdə(r)/ *vi* (BrE colloq) trepidar, retemblar*; **the car ~ed to a halt** el coche se paró con una sacudida

judge¹ /dʒʌdʒ/ *n*

A (Law) juez *mf*, juez, jueza *m,f*, magistrado, -da *m,f*; (of competition) juez *mf*, miembro *mf* del jurado; (Sport) juez *mf*; **the ~s' decision is final** la decisión del jurado es irrevocable

B (appraiser): **he's a good ~ of character** es muy buen psicólogo, tiene buen ojo para la gente; **she's an excellent ~ of wines** entiende mucho de vinos; **let me be the ~ of that** eso lo decidiré yo

judge² *vt*

A (Law) ‹*case/person*› juzgar*; ‹*contest*› ser* el juez de

B 1▸ (estimate) ‹*size/speed*› calcular; **I ~d her to be around 35** le calculaba unos 35 años 2▸ (assess) ‹*situation/position*› evaluar*; ‹*person*› juzgar*; ‹*advantages*› valorar 3▸ (deem) juzgar*, considerar

C (censure, condemn) juzgar*; **don't ~ her too harshly** no seas demasiado severo con ella

■ **judge** *vi* juzgar*; **you shouldn't ~ by appearances** no deberías juzgar *or* dejarte llevar por las apariencias; **judging by** a juzgar por

judgment, judgement /'dʒʌdʒmənt/ *n*

A [u c] 1▸ (Law) fallo *m*, sentencia *f*; (in arbitration) fallo *m*, laudo *m*; **to pass ~ on sth/sb** juzgar* algo/a algn; **to sit in ~ over sb** enjuiciar a algn 2▸ (Relig) castigo *m* de Dios; **the Last J~** el Juicio Final

B [u c] 1▸ (estimation) cálculo *m* 2▸ (view) opinión *f*; **I reserve ~ on that** sobre eso todavía no puedo dar una opinión; **in my ~** a mi juicio

C [u] (sense, discernment): **an error of ~** una equivocación, un desacierto; **I lent him the money against my better ~** le presté el dinero sabiendo que era un error

judgmental, judgemental /dʒʌdʒ'mentl̩/ *adj* ‹*attitude/assessment*› sentencioso

Judgment Day, Judgement Day *n* el día del Juicio Final

judicial /dʒu:'dɪʃəl/ *adj* judicial

judiciary /dʒu:'dɪʃieri || dʒu:'dɪʃəri/ *n* (judges) judicatura *f*; (arm of government) poder *m* judicial

judicious /dʒu:'dɪʃəs/ *adj* ‹*decision*› acertado, sensato; ‹*historian*› de criterio

judo /'dʒu:dəʊ/ *n* [u] judo *m*

jug /dʒʌg/ *n* (large) jarra *f*; (for milk, cream) jarrita *f*

juggernaut /'dʒʌgərnɔ:t || 'dʒʌgənɔ:t/ *n* (BrE) camión *m* grande

juggle /'dʒʌgəl/ *vi* hacer* malabarismos, hacer* juegos malabares *or* de manos

■ **juggle** *vt* ‹*balls/plates*› hacer* malabarismos *or* juegos malabares con; **to ~ the demands of work and family** hacer* malabarismos para compatibilizar las responsabilidades del trabajo con las del hogar; **I'm going to have to ~ my timetable** voy a tener que reorganizar mis actividades

juggler /'dʒʌglər || 'dʒʌglə(r)/ *n* malabarista *mf*

juggling /'dʒʌglɪŋ/ *n* [u] malabarismos *mpl*, juegos *mpl* malabares *or* de manos

Jugoslavia /'ju:gəʊ'slɑ:viə, 'ju:gə'slɑ:viə/ *etc* ▸**Yugoslavia** *etc*

jugular /'dʒʌgjələr || 'dʒʌgjʊlə(r)/ *n* (vena *f*) yugular *f*; ***to go for the ~*** tirar a matar

juice /dʒu:s/ *n*

A [u c] (from fruit, meat) jugo *m*; (fruit drink) jugo *m*, zumo *m*; (Physiol) jugo *m*; ▸**stew²** *vi*

B [u] (sl) 1 (liquid fuel) combustible *m* 2 (vitality) (AmE) vida *f*; **she's still full of ~** sigue tan llena de vida 3 (alcohol) (AmE) bebida *f*; **he's hitting the ~ again** le está dando a la bebida otra vez (fam)

juiced-up /'dʒu:st'ʌp/ *adj* (AmE colloq) borracho, cocido (fam)

juicer /'dʒu:sər || 'dʒu:sə(r)/ *n* exprimidor *m* (*gen eléctrico*), juguera *f* (CS)

juicy /'dʒu:si/ *adj* **-cier, -ciest** 1 (Culin) ‹*orange/steak*› jugoso 2 (colloq) ‹*part/role*› jugoso (fam); ‹*fee*› suculento (fam), jugoso (fam) 3 (racy) (colloq) ‹*gossip/details*› sabroso (fam), picante (fam)

jukebox /'dʒu:kbɑ:ks || 'dʒu:kbɒks/ *n* máquina *f* de discos, rocola *f* (AmL)

Jul (= **July**) jul.

July /dʒʊ'laɪ/ *n* julio *m*; *see also* **January**

jumble¹ /'dʒʌmbəl/ *vt* ~ **(up)** ‹*cards/pieces*› mezclar; **the clothes were all ~d up in the drawer** la ropa estaba toda revuelta en el cajón; **the instructions had got(ten) ~d (up) in her mind** se había hecho un embrollo *or* un lío con las instrucciones

jumble² *n* 1 (*no pl*) (of clothes, papers) revoltijo *m*; (of facts, data) embrollo *m*, confusión *f*, mezcolanza *f* 2 [u] (items for sale) (BrE) cosas *fpl* usadas

jumble sale *n* (BrE) *mercadillo de beneficencia donde se venden artículos de segunda mano*

jumbo /'dʒʌmbəʊ/ *adj* (*before n*) ‹*packet/size*› gigante

jumbo (jet) *n* jumbo *m*

jump¹ /dʒʌmp/ *vi*

A 1 (leap) saltar; **she ~ed across the ditch** cruzó la zanja de un salto; **the horse ~ed over the gate** el caballo saltó la verja 2 (move quickly): **he ~ed up from his seat** se levantó (del asiento) de un salto; **I ~ed out of bed** me levanté (de la cama) de un salto; **~ in, I'll give you a lift** súbete que te llevo; **to ~ AT sth: they'll ~ at the chance** no van a dejar pasar la oportunidad; **to ~ ON sb/sth** abalanzarse* SOBRE algn/algo; **to ~ to one's feet** ponerse* de pie *or* (AmL tb) pararse de un salto; **to ~ to attention** (Mil) cuadrarse, ponerse* firme; **~ to it!** ¡hazlo inmediatamente!

B 1 (change, skip) saltar, pasar 2 (increase, advance suddenly) subir de un golpe

C 1 (jerk) saltar 2 (in alarm) sobresaltarse; **you made me ~!** ¡qué susto me diste!

■ **jump** *vt*

A (leap over) ‹*hurdle*› saltar, brincar* (Méx); ‹*counter/piece*› (Games) comerse; **to ~ rope** (AmE) saltar a la cuerda *or* (Esp tb) a la comba *or* (Chi) al cordel, brincar* la reata (Méx)

B 1 (spring out of) ‹*rails/tracks*› salirse* de 2 (disregard) saltarse; **to ~ the lights** pasar el semáforo en rojo, pasarse el alto (Méx); **to ~ the line** *o* (BrE) **queue** colarse*

C (run away from) (colloq): **to ~ bail** huir* estando en libertad bajo fianza; **to ~ ship** desertar

D (ambush, attack) (colloq) asaltar, atacar*

E (catch) (AmE colloq) ‹*bus/plane*› agarrar (fam) *or* (esp Esp) coger*; (without paying fare): **he ~ed the train** se subió al tren sin pagar

jump² *n*

A 1 (leap) salto *m*; **I sat up with a ~** me incorporé sobresaltado; ***go (and) take a running ~!*** (colloq) ¡vete a freír espárragos! (fam); ***to be/stay one ~ ahead***: **this way, you'll be one ~ ahead of the competition** de esta manera le llevarás la delantera a la competencia; **she tried to stay one ~ ahead of her pupils** trataba de mantenerse un paso adelante de sus alumnos 2 (fence) valla *f*, obstáculo *m*

B 1 (sudden transition) salto *m* 2 (increase, advance) aumento *m*

jumped-up /'dʒʌmpt'ʌp/ *adj* (BrE) (*before n*): **he's nothing but a ~ clerk!** no es más que un empleadito con ínfulas

jumper /'dʒʌmpər || 'dʒʌmpə(r)/ *n* 1 (dress) (AmE) jumper *m or f* (AmL), pichi *m* (Esp) 2 (BrE) ▸**sweater**

jumper cables *pl n* (AmE) cables *mpl* de arranque

jump: **~ jet** *n* avión *m* de despegue vertical; **~ leads** *pl n* (BrE) ▸**jumper cables**; **~ rope** *n* (AmE) cuerda *f or* (Méx) reata *f or* (Chi) cordel *m* (de saltar), comba *f* (Esp); **~-start** *vt*: *hacer arrancar un coche ya sea empujándolo o haciendo un puente*; **~ suit** *n* mono *m*, enterito *m* (RPl)

jumpy /'dʒʌmpi/ *adj* **-pier, -piest** nervioso

Jun (= **June**) jun.

junction /'dʒʌŋkʃən/ *n* 1 (meeting point — of roads, rails) cruce *m*, empalme *m*; (— of rivers) confluencia *f*; **leave the motorway at ~ 13** (BrE) deje la autopista en la salida número 13 2 (Elec) empalme *m*

junction box *n* caja *f* de empalme

juncture /'dʒʌŋktʃər || 'dʒʌŋktʃə(r)/ *n* coyuntura *f*; **at this ~** en este momento, en esta coyuntura

June /dʒu:n/ *n* junio *m*; *see also* **January**

jungle /'dʒʌŋgəl/ *n* [c u] 1 (Geog) selva *f*, jungla *f*; **the law of the ~** la ley de la selva 2 (confusion, tangle) maraña *f*, laberinto *m* 3 (hostile place) jungla *f*; **concrete ~** la jungla de(l) asfalto

jungle warfare *n* [u] guerra *f* en la selva; (*before n*) **~ ~ operations** operaciones *fpl* de guerra en la selva; **~ ~ school** centro *m* de entrenamiento para operaciones de guerra en la selva

junior¹ /'dʒu:njər || 'dʒu:niə(r)/ *adj*

A 1 (lower in rank) ‹*official*› subalterno; ‹*position*› de subalterno; **~ minister** (in UK) ≈ subsecretario, -ria *m,f*; **~ partner** socio comanditario, socia comanditaria *m,f*; **~ senator** (in US) *senador de más reciente elección en un estado*; **to be ~ TO sb** ser* subalterno de algn, estar* por debajo de algn 2 (younger) más joven; **James D. Clark J~** (AmE) James D. Clark, hijo *or* junior

B (*before n*) 1 (for younger people) ‹*fashion/size*› para jóvenes; ‹*team*› juvenil, junior *adj inv* 2 (AmE Educ) de tercer año

junior² *n*

A 1 (younger person): **he is two years my ~, he is my ~ by two years** tiene dos años menos que yo, es dos años menor que yo 2 (person of lower rank) subalterno, -na *m,f*

B **Junior** (son) (AmE) *término usado para referirse o dirigirse a un hijo*

C 1 (Educ) (in US) *estudiante de tercer año de colegio secundario o universidad*; (in UK) *alumno de primaria o de los primeros años de secundaria* 2 (Sport) juvenil *mf*, junior *mf*

junior: **~ college** *n* (in US) *establecimiento universitario donde se estudian los dos primeros años de la carrera*; **~ high (school)** *n* (in US) *colegio en el que se imparten los dos o tres primeros años de la enseñanza secundaria*; **~ school** *n* (in UK) escuela *f* primaria (*para niños de 7 a 11 años*)

juniper /'dʒu:nəpər || 'dʒu:nɪpə(r)/ *n* (bush) enebro *m*; (*before n*) **~ berry** enebrina *f*

junk /dʒʌŋk/ *n*

A [u] 1 (discarded items) trastos *mpl* (viejos), cachivaches *mpl*; (*before n*) **~ shop** tienda *f* de viejo *or* de cosas usadas 2 (worthless stuff) (colloq) basura *f* (fam), porquería *f* (fam); (*before n*) **~ jewelry** bisutería *f*, quincalla *f* (pey); **~ mail** propaganda *f* que se recibe por correo

B [c] (boat) junco *m*

junket /'dʒʌŋkət || 'dʒʌŋkɪt/ *n*

A [u c] (Culin) (leche *f*) cuajada *f*

B [c] 1 (festivity) fiesta *f* 2 (trip) (AmE colloq) viajecito *m* pagado (fam)

junk: **~ food** *n* [u] comida *f* basura, porquerías *fpl* (fam), alimento *m* chatarra (Méx); **~ heap** *n* basurero *m*, vertedero *m*, deshuesadero *m* (Méx)

junkie /'dʒʌŋki/ *n* (colloq) yonqui *mf* (fam), drogadicto, -ta *m,f*, pichicatero, -ra (CS, Per fam)

junk: **~man** /'dʒʌŋkmæn/ *n* (*pl* **-men** /-men/) (AmE) ropavejero *m*, trapero *m*, botellero *m* (AmL); **~yard** *n* depósito *m* de chatarra, deshuesadero *m* (Méx)

junta /ˈhʊntə || ˈdʒʌntə/ *n* junta *f* militar

Jupiter /ˈdʒu:pətər || ˈdʒu:pɪtə(r)/ *n* Júpiter *m*

jurisdiction /ˈdʒʊrəsˈdɪkʃən || ˌdʒʊərɪsˈdɪkʃən/ *n* [u c] jurisdicción *f*, competencia *f*; **to have ~ (over sth)** tener* jurisdicción (sobre algo)

jurisprudence /ˈdʒʊrəsˈpru:dn̩s || ˌdʒʊərɪsˈpru:dn̩s/ *n* [u] jurisprudencia *f*

jurist /ˈdʒʊrəst || ˈdʒʊərɪst/ *n* [1] (expert) jurista *mf* [2] (judge) (AmE) magistrado, -da *m,f*

juror /ˈdʒʊrər || ˈdʒʊərə(r)/ *n* jurado *mf*, miembro *mf* de un jurado

jury /ˈdʒʊri || ˈdʒʊəri/ *n* (*pl* **-ries**) jurado *m*; **trial by ~** juicio *m* ante jurado; (*before n*) **to do ~ duty** *o* (BrE also) **service** ser* miembro de un jurado

juryman /ˈdʒʊrimæn || ˈdʒʊərimæn/ *n* (*pl* **-men** /-men/) jurado *m*, miembro *m* de un jurado

just¹ /dʒʌst/ *adj* ‹*decision/person*› justo

just² *adv*

A [1] (in recent past): **she's ~ left** se acaba de ir, recién se fue (AmL); **she'd only ~ finished** acababa de terminar, recién había terminado (AmL); Ⓢ **just married** recién casados; **~ recently I've begun to notice that ...** últimamente he empezado a darme cuenta de que ... [2] (now, at the moment): **she's ~ on her way** está en camino; **I was ~ about to leave when he called** estaba a punto de salir cuando llamó

B [1] (barely) justo; **I arrived ~ in time** llegué justo a tiempo; **it's only ~ over the recommended minimum** está apenas por encima del mínimo recomendado; **I ~ missed him** no lo vi por poco *or* por apenas unos minutos [2] (a little): **~ above the knee** justo *or* apenas encima de la rodilla; **I waited ~ outside the shop** esperé en la puerta de la tienda

C [1] (only) sólo; **I'll be with you in ~ a moment** enseguida *or* en un segundo estoy con usted; **there's ~ one left** queda sólo uno, queda uno nomás (AmL); **~ a moment, you're confusing two issues there** un momento: estás confundiendo dos problemas distintos; **I went there ~ once** fui sólo una vez; **she was ~ three when her father died** tenía apenas *or* sólo tres años cuando murió su padre; **would you like some more? — ~ a little, please** ¿quieres más? — bueno, un poquito; **~ occasionally** muy de vez en cuando [2] (simply): **I ~ stopped by to say hello** pasé para saludarte; **that's ~ gossip** no son más que chismes, son puros chismes (fam); **they're ~ friends** no son más que amigos, sólo son amigos; **it's ~ one of those things** son cosas que pasan; **~ because he's famous doesn't mean he can be rude** (colloq) el hecho de que sea famoso no le da derecho a ser grosero; **~ follow the instructions on the packet** simplemente siga las instrucciones impresas en el paquete; **I'll ~ have to pack up and go** no me queda otro remedio que hacer la maleta e irme; **he'll ~ make things worse** lo único que hará será empeorar las cosas

D [1] (exactly, precisely): **it's ~ what I wanted** es justo *or* precisamente *or* exactamente lo que quería; **the temperature was ~ right** la temperatura era la perfecta; **~ my luck!** ¡me tenía que pasar a mí! [2] (equally): **the desserts were ~ as good as the rest of the meal** los postres estuvieron tan buenos como el resto de la comida; **it's ~ as well you're leaving** menos mal que te vas

E (emphatic use): **I ~ can't understand it** simplemente no lo entiendo; **I ~ adore champagne** a mí me encanta el champán; **I'm feeling ~ fine now** ahora me siento muy bien; **~ leave it here** déjelo aquí, déjelo aquí nomás (AmL); **regret it? don't I ~!** ¿que si me arrepiento? ¡si me arrepentiré ... !; **~ you wait, you little rascal!** ¡ya vas a ver, bandido!; **~ go away, will you?** mira, vete, hazme el favor

F [1] (giving explanation): **it's ~ that ...** lo que pasa es que ... [2] (indicating possibility): **it may ~ happen** podría suceder

G **just about**: **I've ~ about finished now** casi he terminado, prácticamente he terminado; **did you get enough to eat? — ~ about** ¿te dieron bastante de comer? — más o menos

justice /ˈdʒʌstəs || ˈdʒʌstɪs/ *n*

A [u] (fairness) justicia *f*; **there's no ~!** ¡no es justo!, ¡es una injusticia!; **to do sb/sth ~**: **the portrait hardly does her ~** el retrato no le hace justicia *or* no la favorece; **he couldn't do ~ to the meal** no pudo hacerle honor a la comida; **she didn't do herself ~ in the exam** no rindió a la altura de su capacidad en el examen

B [u] (Law) justicia *f*; **court of ~** tribunal *m* de justicia; **~ was done** se hizo justicia; **in the end he was brought to ~** finalmente pagó sus culpas

C [c] (judge) juez *mf*, juez, jueza *m,f*, magistrado, -da *m,f*

Justice of the Peace *n* (*pl* **~s ~ ~ ~**) juez *mf* de paz, juez, jueza *m,f* de paz

justifiable /ˈdʒʌstəfaɪəbəl || ˈdʒʌstɪfaɪəbəl/ *adj* justificable; **~ homicide** (Law) homicidio *m* justificado

justifiably /ˈdʒʌstəfaɪəbli || ˈdʒʌstɪfaɪəbli/ *adv* justificadamente, con razón

justification /ˈdʒʌstəfəˈkeɪʃən || ˌdʒʌstɪfɪˈkeɪʃən/ *n* [u] justificación *f*

justified /ˈdʒʌstəfaɪd || ˈdʒʌstɪfaɪd/ *adj*

A (reasonable) justificado; **to be ~ IN sth/-ING**: **she is ~ in her concern** tiene motivos (justificados) para estar preocupada; **was he ~ in taking that step?** ¿tuvo motivos para dar ese paso?, ¿tuvo razón en dar ese paso?

B ‹*text/setting*› justificado

justify /ˈdʒʌstəfaɪ || ˈdʒʌstɪfaɪ/ *vt* **-fies, -fying, -fied**

A ‹*action/expense*› justificar*; **to ~ sth/oneself TO sb** justificar* algo/justificarse* ANTE *or* CON algn

B ‹*text/lines*› justificar*

just-in-time /ˌdʒʌstɪnˈtaɪm/ *adj* (*before n*) (Busn): justo a tiempo

justly /ˈdʒʌstli/ *adv* con razón, justamente

jut /dʒʌt/ **-tt-** *vi* [1] (stick out) sobresalir* [2] **jutting** *pres p* ‹*jaw/chin*› prominente, saliente; ‹*rock/cliff*› que sobresale, saliente

Phrasal verb

• **jut out** [v ▸ adv] sobresalir*

jute /dʒu:t/ *n* [u] yute *m*

juvenile¹ /ˈdʒu:vənaɪl, -vənl̩ || ˈdʒu:vənaɪl/ *adj* [1] (Law) (*before n*) ‹*court*› de menores; ‹*delinquent*› juvenil [2] (childish) (pej) infantil [3] ‹*literature*› (AmE) infantil y juvenil [4] (Theat) **~ lead** galán *m* joven

juvenile² *n* [1] (Law) menor *mf* [2] (Theat) *actor que hace papeles de joven*

juxtapose /ˈdʒʌkstəpəʊz || ˌdʒʌkstəˈpəʊz/ *vt* yuxtaponer*

juxtaposition /ˈdʒʌkstəpəˈzɪʃən/ *n* [u c] yuxtaposición *f*

j

Kk

K, k /keɪ/ *n* K, k *f*

K 1 (Comput) (= **kilobyte**) K 2 (a thousand pounds) mil libras *fpl* (esterlinas); **£30k** 30.000 libras (esterlinas)

kale /keɪl/ *n* [u] col *f* rizada

kaleidoscope /kə'laɪdəskəʊp/ *n* caleidoscopio *m*

Kampuchea /ˌkæmpu:'tʃiə/ *n* Kampuchea *f*

kangaroo /'kæŋgə'ru:/ *n* (*pl* **-roos**) canguro *m*

kangaroo court *n*: *tribunal irregular y arbitrario*

Kans = **Kansas**

kaolin /'keɪəlɪn/ *n* [u] caolín *m*

kapok /'keɪpɑ:k || 'keɪpɒk/ *n* [u] capoc *m*

kaput /kə'pʊt/ *adj* (colloq) (*pred*): **to be ~** estar* kaput (fam); **the business went ~** el negocio se fue al traste *or* al hoyo (fam)

k

karaoke /'kæri'əʊki/ *n* karaoke *m*

karat *n* (AmE) ▸**carat 1**

karate /kə'rɑ:ti/ *n* [u] kárate *m*, karate *m* (AmL)

kart¹ /kɑ:rt || kɑ:t/ *n* kart *m*

kart² *vi*: **to go ~ing** ir* a hacer karting

karting /'kɑ:rtɪŋ || 'kɑ:tɪŋ/ *n* [u] karting *m*

Kashmir /'kæʃmɪr || kæʃ'mɪə(r)/ *n* Cachemira *f*

kayak /'kaɪæk/ *n* kayak *m*

Kazakhstan /ˌkɑ:zɑ:k'stɑ:n/ *n* Kazajstán *m*

KBE *n* (in UK) = **Knight of the British Empire**

kebab /'kəbɑ:b || kɪ'bæb/ *n* pincho *m*, anticucho *m* (Bol, Chi, Per), brocheta *f* (Esp, Méx)

keel /ki:l/ *n* quilla *f*; ***on an even ~***: **to keep sth on an even ~** mantener* la estabilidad de algo; **to get sth back on an even ~** restablecer* el equilibrio de algo

Phrasal verb

• **keel over** [v ▸ adv] 1 (capsize) ⟨⟨*ship*⟩⟩ volcar(se)* 2 (collapse) (colloq) ⟨⟨*person*⟩⟩ caer* redondo (fam)

keen /ki:n/ *adj* **-er, -est**

A (enthusiastic) ⟨*photographer*⟩ entusiasta; ⟨*student*⟩ aplicado, que muestra mucho interés; **to be ~ to + INF**: **he was ~ to start work** tenía muchas ganas de empezar a trabajar; **to be ~ ON sth/-ING** (BrE): **I'm ~ on travel/golf** me encanta viajar/el golf; **he didn't seem too ~ on the idea** no parecía gustarle mucho la idea, no parecía estar muy entusiasmado con la idea; **they're ~ on joining the club** tienen muchas ganas de hacerse socios del club; **to be ~ ON sb** (BrE): **she's very ~ on him** le gusta muchísimo; **I'm not too ~ on their sister** su hermana no me cae muy bien

B 1 (sharp) ⟨*blade*⟩ afilado, filoso (AmL), filudo (Chi, Per); ⟨*breeze*⟩ cortante 2 (acute) ⟨*hearing*⟩ muy fino; ⟨*sight/sense of smell*⟩ agudo, muy bueno; ⟨*wit/intelligence*⟩ agudo; **she has a ~ eye for business** tiene mucha visión *or* (fam) mucho ojo para los negocios 3 (intense) ⟨*competition*⟩ muy reñido; ⟨*interest*⟩ vivo

keenly /'ki:nli/ *adv* 1 (intensely, acutely) profundamente; **a ~ contested match** un partido muy reñido 2 (enthusiastically) vivamente, con entusiasmo

keenness /'ki:nnəs || 'ki:nnɪs/ *n* [u] 1 (enthusiasm, eagerness) entusiasmo *m* 2 (of knife, blade) (liter) lo afilado; (of wind) lo cortante 3 (of sight, wit) agudeza *f* 4 (of pleasure, suffering) (frml) intensidad *f*

keep¹ /ki:p/ *n*

A (living) sustento *m*, manutención *f*; **he helped in the kitchen to earn his ~** ayudaba en la cocina a cambio de comida y techo; ***for ~s***: **if they win the cup again, it's theirs for ~s** si vuelven a ganar la copa, se la quedan para siempre

B (in castle, fortress) torre *f* del homenaje

keep² (*past & past p* **kept**) *vt*

A 1 (not throw away) ⟨*receipt/ticket*⟩ guardar, conservar; (not give back) quedarse con; (not lose) conservar; **~ the change** quédese (con) el cambio; **you can ~ your lousy job!** (colloq) ¡se puede guardar su porquería de trabajo! 2 (look after, reserve) **to ~ sth (FOR sb)** guardar(le) algo (A algn)

B (store) guardar; **where do you ~ the coffee?** ¿dónde guardas *or* tienes el café?; **S keep in a cool place** conservar en lugar fresco; **I like to ~ a first-aid kit in the car** me gusta tener un botiquín en el coche

C (reserve for future use) guardar, dejar

D 1 (raise) ⟨*pigs/bees*⟩ criar* 2 (manage, run) ⟨*stall/guesthouse*⟩ tener*

E 1 (support) mantener*; **it costs me a fortune to ~ them in clothes** me cuesta una fortuna vestirlos 2 (maintain): **she ~s a diary** escribe *or* lleva un diario; **I've kept a note** *o* **record of everything** he tomado nota de todo, lo tengo todo anotado

F 1 (cause to remain, continue) mantener*; **try and ~ it clean** trata de mantenerlo limpio; **~ her informed** manténla al tanto; **the noise kept me awake** el ruido no me dejó dormir; **to ~ sb/sth + -ING**: **to ~ sb guessing** tener* a algn en ascuas; **he kept the engine running** mantuvo el motor en marcha 2 (detain): **don't let me ~ you** no te quiero entretener; **what kept you?** ¿por qué tardaste?, ¿qué te retuvo?; **they kept her in hospital** la dejaron ingresada *or* (CS, Méx tb) internada

G (adhere to, fulfil) ⟨*promise/vow*⟩ cumplir; **she didn't ~ the appointment** faltó a la cita

H (observe, celebrate) celebrar; (Relig) guardar

■ **keep** *vi*

A (remain) mantenerse*: **to ~ fit** mantenerse* en forma; **to ~ awake** mantenerse* despierto, no dormirse*; **can't you ~ quiet?** ¿no te puedes estar callado?; **~ still!** ¡estáte quieto! *or* ¡quédate quieto!

B 1 (continue) seguir*; **~ left/right** siga por la izquierda/derecha; **to ~ -ING** seguir* + GER; **~ talking** sigue hablando 2 (repeatedly): **he ~s interfering** está continuamente entrometiéndose, no deja de entrometerse; **I ~ forgetting to bring it** nunca me acuerdo *or* siempre me olvido de traerlo

C 1 ⟨⟨*food*⟩⟩ conservarse (fresco); **this cake will ~ for several months** este pastel se conserva muchos meses 2 ⟨⟨*news/matter*⟩⟩ esperar; **I have something to tell you — will it ~ till later?** tengo algo que decirte — ¿puede esperar a más tarde? 3 (be in certain state of health) (colloq): **how are you ~ing?** ¿qué tal estás? (fam)

Phrasal verbs

• **keep ahead** [v ▸ adv] conservar la delantera; **to ~ ahead OF sb/sth** mantenerse* POR DELANTE DE algn/algo

• **keep at**

A [v ▸ prep ▸ o] (persevere with): **to ~ at it** seguir* dándole (fam); **you have to ~ at them to get them to do anything** hay que estarles encima para que hagan algo

B [v ▸ o ▸ prep ▸ o] (force to work): **I kept them (hard) at it all day** no los dejé levantar cabeza en todo el día

• **keep away**

A [v ▸ adv] **to ~ away (FROM sb/sth)**: **~ away from me!** ¡no te me acerques!; ~ **away from the fire!** ¡no se acerquen al fuego!; **I'll ~ away from them in future** evitaré tener nada que ver con ellos en (el) futuro

B [v ▸ o ▸ adv] **to ~ sb away FROM sb/sth**: **you'd better ~ her away from me** más vale que no dejes que se me acerque; **I kept him away from school** no lo mandé al colegio

• **keep back**

Sense I [v ▸ adv]: ~ **back!** ¡atrás!; **to ~ back FROM sth**: ~ **well back from the edge** mantente bien alejado del borde

Sense II [v ▸ o ▸ adv, v ▸ adv ▸ o]

A 1 (prevent from advancing) ‹*crowd/floodwaters*› contener*; **they tried to ~ demonstrators back from the gates** quisieron impedir que los manifestantes llegaran a las puertas 2 ‹*tears/sobs*› contener*

B 1 (not reveal) ‹*information/facts*› ocultar 2 (withhold) ‹*percentage*› retener*; ‹*profits*› guardarse, quedarse con

C [v ▸ o ▸ adv] (detain) (BrE) retener*; **he kept the whole class back after school** dejó a toda la clase castigada

• **keep down**

A [v ▸ adv] (not show oneself) no levantarse

B [v ▸ o ▸ adv] 1 (not raise): ~ **your head/voice down** no levantes la cabeza/la voz 2 (not vomit) retener*

C [v ▸ o ▸ adv, v ▸ adv ▸ o] 1 (not allow to increase): **they've kept prices ~** han mantenido los precios (al mismo nivel) 2 ‹*weeds*› contener*

• **keep from**

Sense I [v ▸ o ▸ prep ▸ o]

A (restrain, prevent) **to ~ sb from sth**: **I don't want to ~ you from your work** no quiero distraerte de *or* interrumpir tu trabajo; **to ~ sb from -ING**: **try to ~ him from working too hard** intenta que no trabaje demasiado; **I managed to ~ myself from laughing** pude aguantar la risa

B (not reveal to) ocultar; **he kept vital information from them/us** les/nos ocultó información vital

Sense II [v ▸ prep ▸ o] (refrain) **to ~ from + -ING**: **I could hardly ~ from crying/laughing** apenas si pude contener las lágrimas/aguantar la risa

• **keep in** [v ▸ o ▸ adv, v ▸ adv ▸ o] 1 (detain): **the teacher kept me in after school** el maestro me hizo quedar después de clase; **my mother kept me in** mi madre no me dejó salir; **he was kept in for observation** lo dejaron ingresado *or* (CS, Méx tb) internado en observación 2 ‹*anger/feelings*› contener*

• **keep in with** [v ▸ adv ▸ prep ▸ o] (colloq): **you have to ~ in with the teacher/boss** hay que estar en buenas relaciones con el profesor/el jefe

• **keep off**

A [v ▸ adv] (stay away): Ⓢ **keep off** prohibido el paso; **the rain kept off** no llovió

B [v ▸ prep ▸ o] 1 (stay away from): Ⓢ **keep off the grass** prohibido pisar el césped 2 (abstain from) ‹*cigarettes*› evitar, no tocar* (fam) 3 (avoid) ‹*subject*› evitar, no tocar*; **I should ~ off religion/politics while she's here** mientras esté ella, mejor no hables de religión/política

C [v ▸ o ▸ prep ▸ o] 1 (cause to stay away from): ~ **your hands off me!** ¡quítame las manos de encima! 2 (cause to avoid): ~ **her off the subject** no la dejes hablar del tema

D [v ▸ o ▸ adv, v ▸ adv ▸ o] (cause to stay away): **the smell ~s the mosquitoes off** el olor repele a los mosquitos

• **keep on**

A [v ▸ adv] 1 (continue) seguir*; ~ **straight on** siga (todo) recto *or* derecho; **to ~ on -ING** seguir* + GER 2 (repeatedly): **I ~ on forgetting to tell him** siempre me olvido *or* nunca me acuerdo de decírselo; **she kept on interrupting him** lo interrumpía constantemente 3 (talk incessantly) **to ~ on (ABOUT sth/sb)**: **she ~s on about her grandson** no hace más que hablar de su nieto; **she ~s on at me about my weight** me está siempre encima con que estoy muy gordo

B [v ▸ o ▸ adv, v ▸ adv ▸ o] (continue to employ) ‹*staff/cook*› no despedir*

C [v ▸ o ▸ adv] 1 (continue to wear): ~ **your coat on** no te quites el abrigo, déjate el abrigo puesto 2 (not get rid of) (BrE): **we decided to ~ the flat on** decidimos no deshacernos del apartamento

• **keep out**

A [v ▸ adv] (not enter) **to ~ out (OF sth)**: Ⓢ **keep out** prohibido el paso, prohibida la entrada; ~ **out of the kitchen** no entres en la cocina

B [v ▸ o ▸ adv, v ▸ adv ▸ o] (prevent from entering, exclude) **a roof to ~ the rain out** un techo para protegerse de la lluvia; **to ~ sb/sth out OF sth**: **the public must be kept out of the area** no debe permitirse la entrada del público a este sector; **they are fighting to ~ drugs out of schools** están luchando para impedir que las drogas entren en los colegios

• **keep out of**

A [v ▸ adv ▸ prep ▸ o] 1 (stay away from): **to ~ out of sb's way** (not bother) no molestar a algn; (avoid) rehuir* a algn, evitar encontrarse con algn 2 (avoid exposure to) ‹*danger*› no exponerse* a 3 (not get involved in) no meterse en; **you ~ out of this!** ¡no te metas (en esto)!

B [v ▸ o ▸ adv ▸ prep ▸ o] 1 (cause to stay away from): ~ **the children out of my way** quítame a los niños de en medio; **a hat will ~ the sun out of your eyes** un sombrero te protegerá los ojos del sol 2 (not involve in): **try to ~ your feelings out of the discussion** trata de mantener tus sentimientos al margen de la discusión

• **keep to**

A [v ▸ prep ▸ o] 1 (adhere to, fulfil) ‹*plan*› ceñirse* a; ‹*promise*› cumplir 2 (not deviate from) ‹*path*› seguir* por; ‹*script*› ceñirse* a; **please ~ to the point** por favor cíñase al tema 3 (stay on): ~ **to the right** (Auto) mantenga su derecha; ~ **to your side of the bed** quédate de tu lado de la cama

B [v ▸ o ▸ prep ▸ o] (not divulge): **to ~ sth to oneself** guardarse algo

C [v ▸ prep ▸ o] [v ▸ o ▸ prep ▸ o]: **to ~ (oneself) to oneself** no ser* muy sociable, no ir* mucho con gente

• **keep together**

A [v ▸ adv] no separarse

B [v ▸ o ▸ adv] ‹*papers*› mantener* juntos

• **keep up**

Sense I [v ▸ adv]

A (not stop) ‹‹*rain/noise*›› seguir*, continuar*; **to ~ up WITH sth** seguir* *or* continuar* CON algo

B 1 (maintain pace) **to ~ up (WITH sb/sth)**: **she walked so fast I couldn't ~ up** caminaba tan rápido que yo no podía seguirla *or* seguirle el ritmo; **he's finding it difficult to ~ up in class** le está resultando difícil mantenerse al nivel de la clase; **I couldn't ~ up with their discussion** no podía seguir su discusión; ***to ~ up with the Joneses*** no ser menos que los demás *or* que el vecino 2 (remain informed) **to ~ up WITH sth** mantenerse* al tanto *or* al corriente DE algo; **to ~ up with the times** mantenerse* al día

C (maintain contact) **to ~ up (WITH sb)** seguir* en contacto (CON algn)

Sense II [v ▸ o ▸ adv, v ▸ adv ▸ o]

A (maintain at present level) mantener*; **you've got to ~ your strength up** tienes que mantenerte fuerte

B (continue, not stop) ‹*payments*› mantenerse* al día con; ‹*friendship*› mantener*, seguir* con; ~ **up the good work** sigue así, muy bien

Sense III [v ▸ o ▸ adv]

A ‹*trousers/socks*› sujetar

B (prevent from sleeping): **I hope we're not ~ing you up** espero que no te estemos quitando el sueño; **my cough/the baby kept me up all night** la tos/el niño me tuvo toda la noche en vela

keeper /'ki:pər || 'ki:pə(r)/ *n* 1 (in zoo) guarda *mf*, cuidador, -dora *m,f*; (in museum) (BrE) conservador, -dora *m,f* 2 (Sport) ▸**goalkeeper**

keepfit /'ki:p'fɪt/ *n* [u] (BrE) gimnasia *f* (de mantenimiento)

keeping /'ki:pɪŋ/ *n* [u] 1 (conformity): **in ~ with** ‹*with law/tradition*› en conformidad con; **a building out of ~ with its surroundings** un edificio que desentona *or* no armoniza con su entorno 2 (trust, care): **to leave sth/sb in sb's ~** dejar algo/a algn al cuidado de algn

keepsake /'ki:pseɪk/ *n* recuerdo *m*

keester /'ki:stər || 'ki:stə(r)/ *n* (AmE colloq) ▸**keister**

keg /keg/ *n* barril *m*; (*before n*) ~ **beer** cerveza *f* de barril a presión

keister /'ki:stər, 'kaɪ- || 'ki:stə(r)/, **keester** *n* (AmE colloq) trasero *m* (fam); ***to be knocked on one's ~*** (colloq) quedarse boquiabierto *or* pasmado (fam)

kelp /kelp/ *n* [u] kelp *m* (*tipo de alga*)

ken /ken/ *n* [u]: **that is completely beyond my ~** eso me resulta totalmente incomprensible

k

kennel /'kenl̩/ *n* 1 (AmE) (for boarding) residencia *f* canina, hotel *m* de perros; (for breeding) criadero *m* de perros 2 (BrE) (hut) casa *f or* caseta *f or* casilla *f* del perro

kennels /'kenl̩z/ *n* (*pl* ~) (BrE) (+ *sing vb*) ►**kennel 1**

Kenya /'kenjə, 'ki:-/ *n* Kenia *f*

Kenyan /'kenjən, 'ki:-/ *adj* keniano

kept /kept/ *past & past p of* **keep²**

kerb /kɜ:rb || kɜ:b/ (BrE) ►**curb¹ B**

kerb-crawling /'kɜ:rb,krɔ:lɪŋ || 'kɜ:b,krɔ:lɪŋ/ *n* [u] (BrE) *solicitación de los servicios de una prostituta efectuada por quien conduce un coche*

kerfuffle /kər'fʌfəl || kə'fʌfəl/ *n* [u] (BrE colloq) escándalo *m*, jaleo *m* (fam), follón *m* (Esp fam)

kernel /'kɜ:rnl̩ || 'kɜ:nl̩/ *n* (of nut, fruit) almendra *f*; (of corn, wheat) grano *m*

kerosene, kerosine /'kerəsi:n/ *n* [u] queroseno *m*, kerosene *m*

kestrel /'kestrəl/ *n* cernícalo *m*

ketch /ketʃ/ *n* queche *m*

ketchup /'ketʃəp || 'ketʃʌp/ *n* [u] salsa *f* de tomate, ketchup *m*, catsup *m*

kettle /'ketl̩/ *n* pava *f*, tetera *f* (Andes, Méx), caldera *f* (Bol, Ur); **to put the ~ on** poner* agua a hervir; ***that's a different ~ of fish*** eso es harina de otro costal; ►**watch²** *vt* **B1**

kettledrum /'ketl̩drʌm/ *n* timbal *m*

key¹ /ki:/ *n* (*pl* ~**s**)

A (for lock) llave *f*; (on can) llave *f*, abridor *m*; **turn the ~ twice** dale dos vueltas a la llave; (*before n*) **~ ring** llavero *m*

B 1 (to puzzle, code etc) clave *f* 2 (to map) explicación *f* de los signos convencionales 3 (answers) soluciones *fpl*, respuestas *fpl*

C (crucial element) clave *f*; **patience is the ~** la paciencia es el factor clave *or* la clave

D (of typewriter, piano) tecla *f*; (of wind instrument) llave *f*

E (Mus) tono *m*, tonalidad *f*; **in the ~ of D minor** en (tono de) re menor; **to be in/off ~** estar*/no estar* en el tono; (*before n*) **~ signature** armadura *f*

key² *adj* ‹*man/question*› clave *adj inv*; **the ~ jobs** los puestos clave

(Phrasal verbs)

- **key in** [v ► o ► adv, v ► adv ► o] ‹*text/data*› teclear, grabar
- **key up** [v ► o ► adv, v ► adv ► o]: **he was all ~ed up about the interview** estaba nervioso por la entrevista

key: **~board** *n* teclado *m*; **~boarder** *n* operador, -dora *m,f*, teclista *mf*; **~board operator** *n* operador, -dora *m,f*, teclista *mf*; **~board player** *n* teclista *mf*, tecladista *mf* (Méx); **~hole** *n* ojo *m* de la cerradura; (*before n*) **~ surgery** *n* [u] cirugía *f* no invasiva; **~logging** *n* monitoreo *m* de teclado; **~note** *n* (Mus) tónica *f*; (central idea) tónica *f*; (*before n*) **~note speech** *discurso en que se intenta establecer la tónica de un congreso o asamblea*; **~pad** *n* (Comput, Telec, TV) teclado *m* numérico; **~stone** *n* (Archit) dovela *f*, sillar *m* de clave; (central principle) piedra *f* angular; **~stroke** *n* pulsación *f*; **~word** *n* palabra *f* clave; **~worker** *n* trabajador, -dora *m,f* clave

kg (= **kilo(s)** *o* **kilogram(s)**) Kg.

KGB (Hist) KGB *f*

khaki¹ /'kæki || 'kɑ:ki/ *n* [u] 1 /'kæki/ (color) caqui *m*, kaki *m* 2 (fabric) caqui *m*

khaki² *adj* caqui *or* kaki *adj inv*

Khartoum /kɑ:r'tu:m || kɑ:'tu:m/ *n* Jartum *m*

kHz (= **kilohertz**) KHz.

kibbutz /kɪ'bʊts/ *n* (*pl* **-butzim** /-bʊtsɪm/) kibbutz *m*

kibosh /kɪ'bɑ:ʃ || 'kaɪbɒʃ/ *n*: ***to put the ~ on sth*** (colloq) dar* al traste con algo (fam)

kick¹ /kɪk/ *n*

A [c] 1 (by person) patada *f*, puntapié *m*; (by horse) coz *f* 2 (in swimming) patada *f* 3 (of gun) culatazo *m*

B (colloq) 1 [c] (thrill, excitement) placer *m*; **he seems to get a ~ out of making her cry** parece que se deleitara haciéndola llorar; **just for ~s** nada más que por divertirse 2 (*no pl*) (stimulating effect): **this cocktail has a real ~ to it** este cóctel es explosivo 3 [c] (fad, phase): **I'm on a health food ~ now** ahora me ha dado por los alimentos dietéticos

kick² *vi* 1 ‹‹*person*›› dar* patadas, patalear; ‹‹*swimmer*›› patalear; ‹‹*horse*›› cocear, dar* coces; **they had to drag him there ~ing and screaming** tuvieron que llevarlo hasta allí a rastras 2 ‹‹*dancer*›› levantar una pierna 3 ‹‹*gun*›› dar* una coz *or* un culatazo *or* una patada

■ **kick** *vt*

A ‹*ball*› patear, darle* una patada *or* un puntapié a; **she ~ed him in the shins** le pegó una patada en la espinilla; **he ~ed the door open/shut** abrió/cerró la puerta de una patada; ***to ~ oneself*** darse* con la cabeza contra la pared; ***to ~ sb when he's/she's down*** pegarle* a algn en el suelo

B (stop) (colloq) ‹*habit*› dejar; ‹*heroin*› desengancharse de

(Phrasal verbs)

- **kick around**, (BrE also) **kick about** (colloq)

A [v ► o ► adv] 1 (treat badly) maltratar 2 ‹*idea*› estudiar 3 **to ~ a ball around** pelotear

B [v ► prep ► o] 1 (be present in) andar* por 2 (wander aimlessly around) deambular *or* andar* dando vueltas por

C [v ► adv] (be present): **this umbrella's been ~ing around for months** hace meses que este paraguas anda (dando vueltas) por aquí

- **kick down** [v ► o ► adv, v ► adv ► o] ‹*door*› echar abajo *or* derribar (*a patadas*)
- **kick in**

A [v ► o ► adv, v ► adv ► o] ‹*door*› echar abajo *or* derribar (*a patadas*)

B [v ► adv] (contribute money) (AmE colloq) contribuir*, poner*

- **kick off**

A [v ► adv] 1 (in football): **they ~ off at three** el partido empieza a las tres 2 (begin) (colloq) ‹‹*person/meeting*›› empezar*

B [v ► adv ► o] (begin) ‹*discussion*› iniciar, empezar*

- **kick out** [v ► o ► adv (► prep ► o)] echar; **he got ~ed out of the bar** lo echaron *or* lo sacaron del bar a patadas (fam)
- **kick up**

A [v ► o ► adv, v ► adv ► o] (raise) ‹*leaves/dust*› levantar

B [v ► adv ► o]: **to ~ up a fuss** *o* **stink** armar una bronca (fam); **to ~ up a din** *o* **row** armar un escándalo

kickback /'kɪkbæk/ *n* (colloq) soborno *m*, mordida *f* (Méx fam), coima *f* (CS, Per fam)

kickboxing /'kɪkbɑ:ksɪŋ || 'kɪkbɒksɪŋ/ *n* [u] kickboxing *m*

kicker /'kɪkər || 'kɪkə(r)/ *n*

A (Sport) pateador, -dora *m,f*

B (AmE colloq) 1 (surprise): **the news was a real ~** la noticia nos dejó helados (*or* me dejó helado *etc*) 2 (added inducement): **the ~ was the low price they were asking** lo que nos atraía era lo poco que pedían

kickoff /'kɪkɔ:f || 'kɪkɒf/ *n* (Sport) saque *m or* puntapié *m* inicial, patada *f* de inicio; **what time is the ~?** ¿a qué hora empieza el partido?; ***for a ~*** para empezar

kickstart¹ /'kɪkstɑ:rt || 'kɪkstɑ:t/ *vt* ‹*engine*› arrancar* (*con el pedal de arranque*); **to ~ the economy** darle* impulso a la reactivación de la economía

kickstart² *n* pedal *m or* palanca *f* de arranque

kid¹ /kɪd/ *n*

A [c] (colloq) 1 (child) niño, -ña *m,f*, chaval, -vala *m,f* (Esp fam), chavalo, -vala *m,f* (AmC, Méx fam), escuincle, -cla (Méx fam), pibe, -ba *m,f* (RPl fam), cabro, -bra *m,f* (Chi fam); **I loved swimming as a ~** de pequeño *or* (AmL tb) cuando era chico me encantaba nadar; ***to be ~ o ~'s stuff*** (easy) estar* tirado (fam), ser* un juego de niños; (lit: for children) ser* cosa de niños; (*before n*) **my ~ brother** mi hermano pequeño, mi hermanito 2 (young person) chico, -ca *m,f*

B 1 [c] (goat) cabrito, -ta *m,f*, choto, -ta *m,f* 2 [u] (leather) cabritilla *f*; ►**glove**

kid² **-dd-** *vi* (colloq) bromear; **I've won the lottery — no ~ding!** ¡me ha tocado la lotería! — ¡no me digas!

■ **kid** *vt* 1 (tease) **to ~ sb (ABOUT sth)** tomarle el pelo a algn (CON algo) 2 (deceive) engañar; **you can't ~ me you didn't know** no me vas a hacer creer que no lo sabías; **don't ~ yourself!** ¡no te hagas ilusiones!; **stop ~ding yourself!** ¡desengáñate!, ¡abre los ojos!

kiddie, kiddy /'kɪdi/ *n* (*pl* **-dies**) (colloq) ►**kid¹ A1**

kidnap¹ /'kɪdnæp/ *vt* **-pp-** *or* (AmE) **-p-** secuestrar, raptar

kidnap² *n* secuestro *m*, rapto *m*

kidnapper, (AmE also) **kidnaper** /'kɪdnæpər || 'kɪdnæpə(r)/ *n* secuestrador, -dora *m,f*, raptor, -tora *m,f*

kidnapping, (AmE also) **kidnaping** /'kɪdnæpɪŋ/ *n* secuestro *m*, rapto *m*

kidney /ˈkɪdni/ *n* (*pl* **-neys**) (Anat, Culin) riñón *m*; (*before n*) ‹*disease*› renal; **~ machine** riñón *m* artificial; **~ stone** cálculo *m* renal

kidney bean *n* frijol *m or* (Esp) judía *f or* (CS) poroto *m* (*con forma de riñón*)

kill¹ /kɪl/ *vt*

A (cause death of) ‹*person/animal*› matar, dar* muerte a (frml); **he ~ed himself** se suicidó; **she was ~ed in a car crash** se mató *or* murió en un accidente de coche; **the disease ~s thousands every year** la enfermedad se cobra miles de víctimas anualmente

B **1** (destroy) ‹*hopes*› acabar con; **her arrival ~ed the conversation stone dead** con su llegada se cortó la conversación en seco **2** (spoil) ‹*flavor/taste*› estropear **3** (deaden) ‹*pain*› calmar **4** (use up): **I went for a walk to ~ time** fui a dar un paseo para matar el tiempo; **I had an hour to ~** tenía una hora sin nada que hacer

C (colloq) **1** (cause discomfort) matar (fam); **my feet/shoes are ~ing me** los pies/zapatos me están matando (fam) **2** (tire out, exhaust) matar (fam); **don't ~ yourself!** (iro) ¡cuidado, no te vayas a herniar! (iró)

■ **kill** *vi* matar; **she was dressed to ~** se había vestido para dejar a todos boquiabiertos (fam)

Phrasal verb

• **kill off** [v ▸ o ▸ adv, v ▸ adv ▸ o] matar, acabar con

kill² *n* **1** [c] (act): **he went in for the ~** entró a matar; ***to be in at the ~*** estar* presente en el momento culminante **2** [u] (animal, animals killed) presa *f*

killer /ˈkɪlər ‖ ˈkɪlə(r)/ *n* (person) asesino, -na *m,f*; **the disease is a major ~** es una de las enfermedades que ocasionan más muertes; **the exam was a real ~** (colloq) el examen fue mortal *or* matador (fam); (*before n*) ‹*shark*› asesino; ‹*disease*› mortal; **the ~ instinct** el instinto asesino

killer whale *n* orca *f*

killing¹ /ˈkɪlɪŋ/ *n* [c u] (of person) asesinato *m*; (of animal) matanza *f*; ***to make a ~*** hacer* un gran negocio, forrarse (fam)

killing² *adj* (colloq) ‹*schedule*› matador (fam)

killjoy /ˈkɪldʒɔɪ/ *n* aguafiestas *mf*

kiln /kɪln/ *n* horno *m*

kilo /ˈkiːləʊ/ *n* (*pl* **-los**) kilo *m*

kilo- /ˈkɪləʊ/ *pref* kilo-

kilobyte /ˈkɪləbaɪt/ *n* kilobyte *m*, kiloocteto *m*

kilogram, (BrE also) **kilogramme** /ˈkɪləgræm/ *n* kilogramo *m*

kilohertz /ˈkɪləhɜːrts ‖ ˈkɪləhɜːts/ *n* (*pl* ~) kilohercio *m*

kilometer, (BrE) **kilometre** /ˈkɪləmiːtər ‖ kɪˈlɒmɪtə(r), ˈkɪləmiːtə(r)/ *n* kilómetro *m*

kilowatt /ˈkɪləwɑːt ‖ ˈkɪləwɒt/ *n* kilovatio *m*

kilowatt-hour /ˈkɪləwɑːtˈaʊr ‖ ˈkɪləwɒtˈaʊə(r)/ *n* kilovatio-hora *m*

kilt /kɪlt/ *n* falda *f or* (CS) pollera *f* escocesa

kilter /ˈkɪltər ‖ ˈkɪltə(r)/ *n*: **the strike has thrown our production out of ~** la huelga nos ha desbaratado la producción

kimono /kəˈməʊnəʊ ‖ kɪˈməʊnəʊ/ *n* (*pl* **-nos**) kimono *m*, quimono *m*

kin /kɪn/ *n* (+ *pl vb*) familiares *mpl*, parientes *mpl*

kind¹ /kaɪnd/ *n*

A (sort, type) **1** (of things) tipo *m*, clase *f*; **of all ~s** de todo tipo, de toda clase; **I like the ~ with walnuts in** me gustan las/los que tienen nueces; **the usual ~ of thing** lo de siempre; **and all that ~ of thing** y todo eso; **he has a business of some ~** tiene un negocio de algo; **I didn't say anything of the ~** yo no dije nada semejante **2** (of people) clase *f*, tipo *m*; **she's not that ~ of girl** no es de ésas; **what ~ of a fool do you take me for?** ¿tú te crees que soy tonta?; **they're not really our ~ of people** no son gente como uno

B (sth approximating to) especie *f*; **she was overcome by a ~ of yearning** la invadió una especie de añoranza

C (*in phrases*) **in kind**: **payment in ~** pago *m* en especie; **he repaid their insolence in ~** les pagó su insolencia con la misma moneda; **kind of** (colloq): **he seemed ~ of stupid** parecía como tonto (fam); **I ~ of thought he would** no sé por qué, pero pensé que lo haría; **of a kind**: **they served a meal, of a ~** sirvieron una especie de comida, si se le puede llamar así; **three of a ~** (Games) tres del mismo palo; **they're two of a ~** son tal para cual

kind² *adj* **-er, -est** ‹*offer*› amable; **he's very ~** es muy buena persona; **what a ~ thought!** ¡qué amabilidad!; **she has a ~ heart** tiene buen corazón; **to be ~ TO sb: she's always been ~ to me** siempre ha sido muy amable conmigo *or* se ha portado muy bien conmigo; **life has been ~ to him** la vida lo ha tratado bien; **it's very ~ to your skin** no daña la piel; **would you be ~ enough to** *o* (frml) **so ~ as to accompany me?** ¿tendría la amabilidad de acompañarme?

kindergarten /ˈkɪndərˌgɑːrtn ‖ ˈkɪndəgɑːtn/ *n* jardín *m* de infancia *or* de niños

kind-hearted /ˈkaɪndˈhɑːrtəd ‖ ˌkaɪndˈhɑːtɪd/ *adj* ‹*person*› de buen corazón, bondadoso

kindle /ˈkɪndl̩/ *vt* ‹*fire*› encender*, prender; ‹*interest*› despertar*; ‹*passion*› encender*

kindling /ˈkɪndlɪŋ/ *n* [u] (wood) astillas *fpl* para encender el fuego

kindly¹ /ˈkaɪndli/ *adv*

A **1** (generously) amablemente; **they ~ invited me to join them** tuvieron la gentileza de invitarme a ir con ellos **2** (adding polite emphasis) (frml): **passengers are ~ requested to ...** se ruega a los pasajeros tengan la amabilidad de ... **3** (expressing annoyance, impatience): **~ explain to me how ...** tenga la bondad de explicarme cómo ...

B (favorably): **they didn't take ~ to my suggestion** no recibieron demasiado bien mi sugerencia; **she doesn't take ~ to being contradicted** no le hace ninguna gracia que la contradigan

kindly² *adj* **-lier, -liest** bondadoso

kindness /ˈkaɪndnəs ‖ ˈkaɪndnɪs/ *n* **1** [u] (quality) **~ (TO** *o* **TOWARD sb)** amabilidad *f* PARA CON algn; **she did it out of the ~ of her heart** lo hizo de buena *or* generosa que es; ***to kill sb with ~*** abrumar a algn con atenciones **2** [c] (act) favor *m*, detalle *m*; **I thought I was doing him a ~** creí que le hacía un favor

kindred /ˈkɪndrəd ‖ ˈkɪndrɪd/ *adj* (*before n*) (similar) similar, análogo; **~ spirits** almas *fpl* gemelas

kinetic /kəˈnetɪk ‖ kɪˈnetɪk/ *adj* cinético

kinetics /kəˈnetɪks ‖ kɪˈnetɪks/ *n* (+ *sing vb*) cinética *f*

king /kɪŋ/ *n* **1** (ruler) rey *m*; **Christ the K~** Cristo Rey; **to live like a ~** vivir como un rey; ***a ~'s ransom*** un dineral; ***the ~ of the castle*** el amo y señor **2** (in cards, chess) rey *m*; (in checkers) dama *f*

kingdom /ˈkɪŋdəm/ *n* reino *m*; **the plant/animal ~** el reino vegetal/animal; ***to blow sth to ~ come*** hacer* saltar algo en pedacitos

king: **~fisher** *n* martín *m* pescador; **~pin** *n* **1** (in bowling) bolo *m or* (Méx) pino *m* central **2** (person) cerebro *m*; **~-size, ~-sized** *adj* ‹*cigarette*› extralargo; ‹*bed*› de matrimonio (*extragrande*)

kink /kɪŋk/ *n* (in rope, wire) vuelta *f*, curva *f*; (in hair) onda *f*

kinky /ˈkɪŋki/ *adj* **-kier, -kiest** (colloq) algo pervertidillo (fam)

kinship /ˈkɪnʃɪp/ *n* [u] (blood relationship) parentesco *m*

kinsman /ˈkɪnzmən/ *n* (*pl* **-men** /-mən/) familiar *m*, pariente *m*

kinswoman /ˈkɪnzˌwʊmən/ *n* (*pl* **-women**) familiar *f*

kiosk /ˈkiːɑːsk ‖ ˈkiːɒsk/ *n* **1** (stall) quiosco *m* **2** (*telephone* ~) (BrE) cabina *f* (telefónica)

kip¹ /kɪp/ *n* (BrE colloq) (sleep) (*no pl*): **to have a ~** echarse un sueño *or* una siestecita *or* siestita (fam), apolillar un rato (RPl fam); **let me get some ~** déjame dormir un rato

kip² *vi* **-pp-** (BrE colloq) dormir*

kipper /ˈkɪpər ‖ ˈkɪpə(r)/ *n* arenque *m* salado y ahumado

Kirghizia /kɪrˈgiːziə ‖ kɪəˈgɪziə/, **Kirghizstan** /ˌkɪrgiːˈstɑːn ‖ kɪəgɪˈstɑːn/ *n* Kirguizistán *m*

kirk /kɜːrk ‖ kɜːk/ *n* (Scot) iglesia *f*; **the K~** (colloq) la iglesia presbiteriana escocesa

kiss¹ /kɪs/ *vt* ‹*person*› besar; **they ~ed (each other)** se besaron, se dieron un beso; **to ~ sb goodbye/goodnight** darle* un beso de despedida/de buenas noches a algn

■ **kiss** *vi* besarse; **to ~ and make up** hacer* las paces

kiss² *n* beso *m*; **she blew ~es to the audience** tiró besos al público; **love and ~es** (Corresp) besos y abrazos; **she gave him the ~ of life** le hizo (la) respiración artificial *or* boca a boca; ~ ***of death*** golpe *m* de gracia

kiss-and-tell /ˌkɪsən(d)ˈtel/ *adj* (Journ) ‹*book/story*›: *en que el autor revela su vida íntima con una celebridad*

kiss curl *n* (BrE) caracol *m*, rizo *m*

kit /kɪt/ *n*

A [c] **1** (set of items): **first-aid ~** botiquín *m* de primeros auxilios; **sewing ~** costurero *m*; **tool ~** caja *f* de herramientas **2** (parts for assembly) kit *m*; **a model car ~** un coche para armar; (*before n*) **it comes in ~ form** venden el kit *or* las partes (y uno lo arma)

B [u] **1** (equipment) equipo *m* **2** (personal effects) cosas *fpl*; (Mil) petate *m* **3** (Clothing) (esp BrE) ropa *f*; **gym ~** (Sport) equipo *m* de gimnasia

Phrasal verb

• **kit out, kit up**: **-tt-** [v ▸ o ▸ adv, v ▸ adv ▸ o] (BrE) equipar; **she was ~ted out in tennis gear** llevaba puesto un equipo de tenis; **the room is ~ted out as a gymnasium** la habitación está habilitada como gimnasio

kitbag /ˈkɪtbæg/ *n* (BrE) bolsa *f*; (Mil) petate *m*

kitchen /ˈkɪtʃən || ˈkɪtʃɪn/ *n* cocina *f*; (*before n*) **~ unit** módulo *m* de cocina

kitchenette /ˈkɪtʃənˈet || ˌkɪtʃɪˈnet/ *n* kitchenette *f*, cocineta *f* (Méx)

kitchen: **~ garden** *n* huerto *m*; **~ sink** *n* fregadero *m or* (Andes) lavaplatos *m or* (RPl) pileta *f*; **he took everything but the ~ sink** (hum) se fue con la casa a cuestas; **~ware** /ˈkɪtʃənwer || ˈkɪtʃɪnweə(r)/ *n* [u] artículos *mpl* de cocina

kite /kaɪt/ *n*

A (toy) cometa *f or* (RPl tb) barrilete *m or* (AmC, Méx) papalote *m or* (Ven) papagayo *m or* (Chi) volantín *m*; ***to be as high as a ~*** (colloq) estar* totalmente colocado *or* volado (fam), estar* hasta atrás (Méx fam)

B (bird) milano *m*

kith /kɪθ/ *n*: **~ and kin** (frml) (+ *sing or pl vb*) familiares y amigos

kitsch /kɪtʃ/ *n* [u] kitsch *m*; (*before n*) ‹*ornaments/decor*› kitsch *adj inv*

kitten /ˈkɪtn̩/ *n* gatito, -ta *m,f*; ***to have ~s*** (colloq): **I nearly had ~s when I realized ...** casi me da un ataque cuando me di cuenta de que ...

kittiwake /ˈkɪtiweɪk/ *n* gaviota *f* tridáctida

kitty /ˈkɪti/ *n* (*pl* **-ties**)

A **1** (cards) banca *f*, bote *m* **2** (money) (colloq) bote *m*, fondo *m* común

B (cat) (colloq) minino *m* (fam)

kiwi /ˈkiːwiː/ *n* **1** (Zool) kiwi *m* **2** **K~** (New Zealander) (colloq) neozelandés, -desa *m,f* **3** **~ (fruit)** kiwi *m*

KKK *n* (in US) = **Ku Klux Klan**

klaxon /ˈklæksən/ *n* sirena *f*

Kleenex®, **kleenex** /ˈkliːneks/ *n* (*pl* ~) kleenex® *m*, pañuelo *m* de papel

kleptomania /ˈkleptəˈmeɪniə/ *n* [u] cleptomania *f*

kleptomaniac /ˈkleptəˈmeɪniæk/ *n* cleptómano, -na *m,f*

klutz /klʌts/ *n* (AmE colloq) torpe *mf*, ganso, -sa *m,f* (fam), patoso, -sa *m,f* (Esp fam)

klutzy /ˈklʌtsi/ *adj* **-zier, -ziest** (AmE colloq) torpe, ganso (fam), patoso (Esp fam)

km (= **kilometer(s)** *o* (BrE) **kilometre(s)**) Km.

knack /næk/ *n*: **there's a ~ to making omelettes** hacer tortillas tiene su truco *or* (Méx) su chiste; **I'll never get the ~ of this!** ¡nunca le voy a agarrar la onda (AmL fam) *or* (Esp) coger el tranquillo a esto!

knacker[1] /ˈnækər || ˈnækə(r)/ *n* (BrE) (of horses) matarife *m* de caballos; **it's for the ~'s yard** está para la basura

knacker[2] *vt* (BrE colloq) **1** (exhaust) dejar hecho polvo (fam) **2** (ruin) hacer* polvo (fam)

knackered /ˈnækərd || ˈnækəd/ *adj* (*pred*) (BrE colloq) hecho polvo (fam), reventado (fam)

knapsack /ˈnæpsæk/ *n* mochila *f*

knave /neɪv/ *n* **1** (rogue) (arch) truhán *m* (ant), bellaco *m* (arc) **2** (in French pack of cards) jota *f*; (in Spanish pack) sota *f*

knead /niːd/ *vt* (Culin) amasar, trabajar; ‹*muscles/shoulders*› masajear

knee[1] /niː/ *n* (Anat, Clothing) rodilla *f*; **I felt weak at the ~s** se me aflojaron las piernas; **to be on one's ~s** estar* arrodillado, estar* de rodillas *or* (liter) de hinojos; **to go** *o* **get down on one's ~s** ponerse* de rodillas, arrodillarse; **my/his ~s were knocking** (colloq) me/le temblaban las piernas; **my trousers have gone at the ~** se me han roto los pantalones en la rodilla; ***to bow*** *o* ***bend the ~ to sb*** doblar la cerviz ante algn; **on bended ~(s)** de rodillas, de hinojos (liter); ***to bring sth to its ~s***: **the strike brought the country to its ~s** la huelga llevó el país al borde del desastre

knee[2] *vt* darle* *or* pegarle* un rodillazo a

kneecap[1] /ˈniːkæp/ *n* rótula *f*

kneecap[2] *vt* **-pp-** (BrE) dispararle a las piernas a

knee: **~-deep** /ˈniːˈdiːp/ *adj* (*pred*): **the mud is ~-deep** el barro llega hasta la(s) rodilla(s); **to be ~-deep IN sth**: **they were ~-deep in mud** estaban con el barro hasta las rodillas; **~-high** /ˈniːˈhaɪ/ *adj* ‹*sock*› largo; **the weeds are ~-high** la maleza llega hasta las rodillas; **~ jerk** *n* reflejo *m* rotular; (*before n*) **~-jerk reaction** acto *m* reflejo, reacción *f* visceral *or* instintiva

kneel /niːl/ *vi* (*past & past p* **kneeled** *or* **knelt**) (get down on one's knees) arrodillarse; (be on one's knees) estar* arrodillado *or* de rodillas; **to ~ down** arrodillarse, ponerse* de rodillas

knee: **~-length** *adj* ‹*sock*› largo; ‹*skirt*› hasta la rodilla; **~-length boots** botas *fpl* altas *or* de caña alta; **~s-up** *n* (BrE colloq) fiesta *f*, fiestoca *f* (Chi fam), fiestichola *f* (RPl fam)

knell /nel/ *n* doble *m*, toque *m* de difuntos; **it was the death ~ of the party** fue la sentencia de muerte para el partido

knelt /nelt/ *past & past p of* **kneel**

knew /nuː || njuː/ *past of* **know**

knickerbockers /ˈnɪkərbɑːkərz || ˈnɪkəbɒkəz/ *pl n* pantalones *mpl* bombachos

knickers /ˈnɪkərz || ˈnɪkəz/ *pl n*

A (AmE) ▸**knickerbockers**

B (BrE) (undergarment) calzones *mpl* (AmS), bragas *fpl* (Esp), pantaletas *fpl* (AmC, Ven), bombacha *f* (RPl); ***to get one's ~ in a twist*** (colloq) ponerse* nervioso

knickknack /ˈnɪknæk/ *n* chuchería *f*, adornito *m*

knife[1] /naɪf/ *n* (*pl* **knives**) cuchillo *m*; (penknife) navaja *f*, cortaplumas *m or f*; (dagger) puñal *m*; ***the knives are out for him/her*** (BrE colloq) se la tienen jurada; ***to get one's ~ into sb*** (colloq) ensañarse con algn, atacar* a algn; ***to turn*** *o* ***twist the ~ (in the wound)*** hurgar* en la herida; ***under the ~*** (Med) en la mesa de operaciones; ***you could have cut the atmosphere with a ~*** se respiraba la tensión en el ambiente; (*before n*) **~ fight** pelea *f* con navajas (*or* cuchillos *etc*)

knife[2] *vt* acuchillar

knife: **~ edge** *n* filo *m* (*de cuchillo, navaja etc*); ***to be*** *o* ***rest*** *o* ***be balanced on a ~ edge*** pender de un hilo; **~-point** *n*: **he was robbed at ~-point** le robaron amenazándolo con un cuchillo

knifing /ˈnaɪfɪŋ/ *n* ataque *m* con cuchillo (*or* navaja *etc*)

knight[1] /naɪt/ *n* **1** (Hist) caballero *m*; **a ~ in shining armor** (dream man) un príncipe azul **2** (holder of title) sir *m* **3** (in chess) caballo *m*

knight[2] *vt* **1** (confer title upon) conceder el título de sir a **2** (Hist) armar caballero

knight errant *n* (*pl* **~s ~**) caballero *m* andante

knighthood /ˈnaɪthʊd/ *n* (title) título *m* de sir; **to receive a ~** recibir el título de sir

knit /nɪt/ (*pres p* **knitting**; *past & past p* **knitted** *or* **knit**) *vt*

A **1** ‹*sweater*› (by hand) hacer*, tejer; (with machine) tejer, tricotar (Esp); **~ one, purl one** uno (al) derecho, uno (al) revés **2** **knitted** *o* (AmE esp) **knit** *past p* de punto, tejido

B **1** **~ (together)** (join, unite) ‹*bones*› soldar*; **they are a tightly ~ family** son *or* es una familia muy unida **2** **to ~ one's brows** fruncir* el ceño

■ **knit** *vi* **1** (by hand) tejer, hacer* punto *or* calceta (Esp); (with machine) tejer, tricotar (Esp) **2** **~ (together)** «*bones*» soldarse*

knitting /ˈnɪtɪŋ/ *n* [u] **1** (piece of work) tejido *m*, punto *m* (Esp); **where did I put my ~?** ¿dónde habré dejado el tejido *or* (Esp) el punto? **2** (activity): **I really enjoy ~** me encanta tejer, me encanta hacer* punto *or* calceta (Esp);

(*before n*) ~ **pattern** patrón *m* (*de un suéter u otra prenda de punto*)

knitting: ~ **machine** *n* máquina *f* de tejer, tricotosa *f* (Esp); ~ **needle** *n* aguja *f* de tejer *or* (Esp) de hacer punto, palillo *m* (Chi)

knitwear /ˈnɪtwer || ˈnɪtweə(r)/ *n* [u] artículos *mpl or* géneros *mpl* de punto

knives /naɪvz/ *pl of* **knife**[1]

knob /nɑːb || nɒb/ *n* [1] (on door) pomo *m*, perilla *f* (AmL); (on drawer) tirador *m*, perilla *f* (AmL); (on walking stick) puño *m*; (on bedstead) perilla *f*; (on radio, TV) botón *m*; ***the same to you with (brass) ~s on!*** (BrE colloq) ¡y tú más! (fam) [2] (lump) bulto *m* [3] (small piece) (esp BrE): **a ~ of butter** un trocito *or* una nuez de mantequilla

knobbly /ˈnɑːbli || ˈnɒbli/ *adj* **-lier, -liest** ‹*tree/fingers*› nudoso; ‹*knees*› huesudo

knock[1] /nɑːk || nɒk/ *n*

A (sound) golpe *m*; (in engine) golpeteo *m*, cascabeleo *m* (AmL); **he gave a couple of ~s before entering** llamó *or* (AmL tb) tocó (a la puerta) un par de veces antes de entrar

B (blow) golpe *m*; **I got a ~ on the head** me di un golpe en la cabeza

C (colloq) [1] (setback) golpe *m*; **the company has taken some bad ~s recently** la compañía ha tenido serios reveses últimamente [2] (criticism) crítica *f*, palo *m* (fam)

knock[2] *vt*

A (strike, push): **to ~ one's head/knee on/against sth** darse* (un golpe) en la cabeza/rodilla con/contra algo; **to ~ a nail into the wall** clavar un clavo en la pared; **she ~ed the vase off the shelf** tiró el jarrón de la repisa; **he was ~ed to the ground by the blast/blow** la explosión/el golpe lo tiró al suelo *or* lo tumbó; **she ~ed the glass out of his hand** le hizo caer el vaso de la mano; **they ~ed a large hole in the wall** hicieron un gran boquete en la pared; **the blow ~ed her unconscious** el golpe la dejó inconsciente; ***to ~ sb sideways*** (colloq) dejar a algn de una pieza

B (criticize) (colloq) criticar*, hablar mal de

■ **knock** *vi* [1] (on door) llamar, golpear (AmL), tocar* (AmL) [2] (collide) **to ~ AGAINST/INTO sb/sth** darse* *or* chocar* CONTRA algn/algo [3] «*engine*» golpetear, cascabelear (AmL)

Phrasal verbs

• **knock about, knock around** (colloq)

A [v ▸ o ▸ adv] (beat) pegarle* a; **her husband used to ~ her about** su marido la maltrataba *or* le pegaba

B [1] [v ▸ adv] (be present): **I used to ~ around with him a lot** antes andaba *or* salía mucho con él [2] [v ▸ adv ▸ o] (travel) ‹*country/continent*› viajar por

• **knock back** (colloq)

A [v ▸ o ▸ adv, v ▸ adv ▸ o] (drink) beberse, tomarse

B [v ▸ o ▸ adv] (cost) costar*, salir*

• **knock down** [v ▸ o ▸ adv, v ▸ adv ▸ o]

A [1] (cause to fall) ‹*door/fence*› tirar abajo; ‹*obstacle*› derribar; **he ran into her and ~ed her down** chocó con ella y la hizo caer *or* la tiró al suelo [2] «*vehicle/driver*» atropellar [3] (demolish) echar abajo

B (colloq) (reduce) ‹*price/charge*› rebajar

• **knock off**

A [v ▸ adv] [v ▸ prep ▸ o] (stop work) (colloq): **when do you ~ off (work)?** ¿a qué hora sales del trabajo?, ¿hasta qué hora trabajas?; **let's ~ off for lunch** vamos a parar para comer

B [v ▸ o ▸ adv, v ▸ adv ▸ o] (stop) (colloq) dejar de; **~ it off, will you!** ¡déjala ya! (fam)

C [v ▸ o ▸ adv, v ▸ adv ▸ o] (deduct, eliminate) (colloq) rebajar; **I'll ~ off 25% for you** le hago un descuento del 25%

D [v ▸ o ▸ adv, v ▸ adv ▸ o] (do quickly, easily) (colloq): **he ~s off four novels a year** se escribe cuatro novelas por año (fam)

• **knock out**

A [v ▸ o ▸ adv, v ▸ adv ▸ o] [1] (make unconscious) dejar sin sentido, hacer* perder el conocimiento, noquear; **she hit her head and ~ed herself out** se dio un golpe en la cabeza y perdió el conocimiento; **he was ~ed out in the fourth round** lo dejó K.O. *or* lo noqueó en el cuarto asalto [2] (destroy, damage) (colloq) ‹*target*› destruir*

B [v ▸ o ▸ adv, v ▸ adv ▸ o] [1] (remove by hitting) ‹*contents*› vaciar*; **several teeth were ~ed out** perdió varios dientes [2] (of competition) eliminar

• **knock over** [v ▸ o ▸ adv, v ▸ adv ▸ o] [1] (cause to fall) tirar [2] «*vehicle*» atropellar

• **knock up**

A [v ▸ o ▸ adv, v ▸ adv ▸ o] (colloq) [1] (assemble hurriedly) improvisar, hacer*; **he ~ed up these shelves in a couple of hours** hizo esta estantería en un par de horas [2] (rouse, waken) (BrE) despertar*, llamar

B [v ▸ o ▸ adv] [1] (exhaust) (AmE colloq) dejar hecho polvo *or* para el arrastre *or* (AmL) de cama (fam) [2] (make pregnant) (sl) dejar embarazada

knock: **~about** *adj* (*before n*) bullicioso; **a ~about comedy** una astracanada; **~down** *adj* (*before n*) (reduced): **at a ~down price** a precio de ganga

knocker /ˈnɑːkər || ˈnɒkə(r)/ *n*

A (on door) aldaba *f*, llamador *m*

B **knockers** *pl* (sl) melones *mpl* (fam), tetas *fpl* (fam)

knocking /ˈnɑːkɪŋ || ˈnɒkɪŋ/ *n* [1] (noise) (*no pl*) golpes *mpl* [2] [u] (Auto) golpeteo *m*, cascabeleo *m* (AmL) [3] [u] (criticism) (colloq) palos *mpl* (fam)

knock: **~-kneed** /ˈnɑːkˈniːd || ˌnɒkˈniːd/ *adj* patizambo; **~-on** /ˈnɑːkˈɑːn || nɒkˈɒn/ *adj*: **~-on effect** repercusiones *fpl*

knockout[1] /ˈnɑːkaʊt || ˈnɒkaʊt/ *n* [1] (in boxing) nocaut *m*, K.O. *m* (*read as: nocaut or* (Esp) *cao*) [2] (person, thing) (colloq): **he/she's a ~** está super bien; **the show was a ~** el espectáculo fue un exitazo (fam)

knockout[2] *adj* [1] ‹*punch*› demoledor, fulminante [2] ‹*competition*› eliminatorio

knoll /nəʊl/ *n* loma *f*, montículo *m*

knot[1] /nɑːt || nɒt/ *n*

A [1] (in string, hair) nudo *m*; **to tie/untie a ~** hacer*/deshacer* un nudo; **I can't get the ~s out of my hair** no logro desenredarme el pelo; **I had a ~ in my stomach** tenía un nudo en el estómago; ***to tie sb up in ~s*** enredar *or* liar* a algn; ***to tie the ~*** (colloq) casarse [2] (in muscles) nódulo *m* [3] (in wood, tree) nudo *m* [4] (cluster) puñado *m*; **a ~ of people** un puñado de personas

B (measure of speed) nudo *m*; ***at a rate of ~s*** (BrE colloq) a toda mecha (fam)

knot[2] *vt* **-tt-** ‹*rope/thread*› hacer* un nudo en

knotted /ˈnɑːtəd || ˈnɒtɪd/ *adj* nudoso, lleno de nudos; ***get ~!*** (BrE colloq) ¡vete a que te zurzan! (fam)

knotty /ˈnɑːti || ˈnɒti/ *adj* **-tier, -tiest** [1] ‹*problem*› enredado, espinoso [2] ‹*wood*› nudoso

know[1] /nəʊ/ (*past* **knew**; *past p* **known**) *vt*

A [1] (have knowledge of, be aware of) saber*; **I don't ~ his name/how old he is** no sé cómo se llama/cuántos años tiene; **to ~ sth ABOUT sth** saber* algo DE algo; **not to ~ the first thing about sth** no saber* nada *or* no tener* ni idea de algo; **I knew it! you've changed your mind!** ¡ya sabía yo que ibas a cambiar de idea!; **how was I to ~ that ... ?** ¿cómo iba yo a saber que ... ?; **I should have ~n this would happen** tenía que haber(me) imaginado que iba a pasar esto; **I don't ~ that I agree/that I'll be able to come** no sé si estoy de acuerdo/si podré ir; **I'll have you ~ that ...** has de saber que ..., para que sepas, ...; **you ~ what he's like** ya sabes cómo es (él), ya lo conoces; **before I knew where I was, it was ten o'clock** cuando quise darme cuenta, eran las diez; **it is well ~n that ...** todo el mundo sabe que ...; **it soon became ~n that ...** pronto se supo que ...; **to be ~n to + INF**: **he's ~n to be dangerous** se sabe que es peligroso; **I ~ that for a fact** me consta que es así; **to let sb ~ sth** decirle* algo a algn, hacerle* saber *or* comunicarle* algo a algn (frml); (warn) avisarle algo a algn; **let me ~ how much it's going to cost** dime cuánto va a costar; **he let it be ~n that ...** dio a entender que ...; **to make sth ~n to sb** hacerle* saber algo a algn; **without our ~ing it** sin saberlo nosotros, sin que lo supiéramos; **there's no ~ing what he might do** quién sabe qué hará; **do you ~ what!** ¿sabes qué?; **I ~ what: let's go skating!** ¡tengo una idea: vayamos a patinar!; **wouldn't you ~ it: it's starting to rain!** ¡no te digo, se ha puesto a llover!; ***not to ~ which way o where to turn*** no saber* qué hacer; ***to ~ sth backwards***: **she ~s her part backwards** se sabe el papel al dedillo *or* al revés y al derecho [2] (have practical understanding of) ‹*French/shorthand*› saber* [3] (have skill, ability) **to ~ how to + INF** saber* + INF; **he doesn't ~ how to swim** no sabe nadar

B [1] (be acquainted with) ‹*person/place*› conocer*; **how well do you ~ her?** ¿la conoces mucho *or* bien?; **I only ~ her by**

name la conozco *or* (AmL tb) la ubico sólo de nombre; **you ~ me/him: ever the optimist** ya me/lo conoces: siempre tan optimista; **to get to ~ sb**: **how did they get to ~ each other?** ¿cómo se conocieron?; **I got to ~ him better/quite well** llegué a conocerlo mejor/bastante bien; **to get to ~ sth** ‹*subject/job*› familiarizarse* con algo; **we knew her as Mrs Balfour** para nosotros era la Sra Balfour 2 (have personal experience of): **he has ~n poverty/success** ha conocido la pobreza/el éxito; **he ~s no fear** no sabe lo que es *or* no conoce el miedo 3 (be restricted by) (liter) tener*; **her ambition ~s no limits** su ambición no tiene límites

C 1 (recognize, identify) reconocer*; **she ~s a good thing when she sees one** sabe lo que es bueno; **to ~ sth/sb BY sth** reconocer* algo/a algn POR algo 2 (distinguish) **to ~ sth/sb FROM sth/sb** distinguir* algo/a algn DE algo/algn; **I don't ~ one from the other** no los distingo, no distingo al uno del otro

D (see, experience) (*only in perfect tenses*): **I've never ~n her (to) lose her temper** nunca la he visto perder los estribos; **this has been ~n to happen before** esto ya ha ocurrido otras veces

■ **know** *vi* saber*; **what happened? — nobody ~s** ¿qué pasó? — no se sabe; **how do you ~?** ¿cómo lo sabes?; **I won't argue: you ~ best** no voy a discutir: tú sabrás; **I ~!** ¡ya sé!, ¡tengo una idea!; **I ought to ~!** ¡si lo sabré yo!; **you could have let me ~!** ¡me lo podrías haber dicho!; **you never ~** nunca se sabe; **the government didn't want to ~** el gobierno se desentendió completamente *or* no quiso saber nada; **I'm not stupid, you ~!** oye, que no soy tonto ¿eh? *or* ¿sabes?; **to ~ ABOUT sth/sb**: **he ~s about computers** sabe *or* entiende de computadoras; **did you ~ about John?** ¿sabías lo de John?, ¿estabas enterado de lo de John?; **can I invite him? — I don't ~ about that, we'll have to see** ¿lo puedo invitar? — no sé, veremos; **to get to ~ about sth** enterarse de algo; **to ~ OF sth/sb**: **she knew of their activities** tenía conocimiento *or* estaba enterada de sus actividades; **not that I ~ of** que yo sepa, no; **do you ~ of a good carpenter?** ¿conoces a *or* sabes de algún carpintero bueno?; **I don't actually ~ her, I ~ *of* her** no la conozco personalmente, sólo de oídas

know² *n*: ***to be in the ~*** estar* enterado

knowable /'nəʊəbəl/ *adj* conocible

know: **~-all** *n* (BrE) ▸**know-it-all**; **~how** *n* [u] know-how *m*, conocimientos *mpl* y experiencia

knowing /'nəʊɪŋ/ *adj* ‹*smile*› de complicidad; **she gave me a ~ look** me miró dándome a entender que ya lo sabía

knowingly /'nəʊɪŋli/ *adv* 1 ‹*smile/nod*› de manera cómplice 2 (deliberately) ‹*hurt/lie*› a sabiendas

know-it-all /'nəʊɪtɔːl/ *n* (colloq) sabelotodo *mf* (fam), sabihondo, -da *m,f* (fam)

knowledge /'nɑːlɪdʒ || 'nɒlɪdʒ/ *n* [u]

A (awareness) conocimiento *m*; **I had no ~ of their activities** no estaba enterado *or* (frml) no tenía conocimiento de sus actividades; **to the best of my ~** que yo sepa; **has he changed his mind? — not to my ~** ¿ha cambiado de opinión? — que yo sepa, no; **she did it in the ~ that ...** lo hizo sabiendo que *or* a sabiendas de que ...; **it is common ~ that ...** todo el mundo sabe que ...

B (facts known) saber *m*; (by particular person) conocimientos *mpl*; **the pursuit of ~** la búsqueda del saber; **my ~ of Spanish/the law is very limited** mis conocimientos de español/de la ley son muy limitados; **he has a thorough ~ of the subject** conoce el tema a fondo

knowledgeable /'nɑːlɪdʒəbəl || 'nɒlɪdʒəbəl/ *adj* ‹*person*› (about current affairs) informado; (about given subject) entendido; (in general) culto; **he's very ~ about wine/politics** sabe mucho de *or* está muy impuesto en tema de vinos/política

known¹ /nəʊn/ *past p of* **know**

known² *adj* ‹*fact*› conocido, sabido; **a little-~ artist** un artista poco conocido; **her last ~ address** la última dirección que se le conoce; **to be ~ AS sth** (have reputation) tener* fama DE algo; (be called): **he likes to be ~ as Alex** le gusta que lo llamen Alex; **you'll need what's ~ as an affidavit** vas a necesitar lo que se conoce como *or* lo que llaman un afidávit; **better ~ as ...** más conocido como ...; **before she became ~ as an author** antes de que se hiciera famosa como escritora; **to be ~ TO sb**: **she is ~ to the police** la policía la tiene fichada; **for reasons best ~ to herself** por motivos que ella conocerá; **to be ~ FOR sth**: **he's better ~ for his work in films** se le conoce mejor por su trabajo cinematográfico

know-nothing /'nəʊˌnʌθɪŋ/ *n* (colloq) ignorante *mf*, analfabeto, -ta *m,f* (fam)

knuckle /'nʌkəl/ *n* 1 (finger joint) nudillo *m*; ***to be near the ~*** (BrE colloq) pasarse de castaño oscuro (fam); ***to give sb a rap*** o ***to rap sb on*** o (esp BrE) ***over the ~s*** (rebuke) llamarle la atención a algn, echarle un rapapolvo a algn (Esp fam); (lit: hit) darle* en los nudillos a algn 2 (of pork) codillo *m*; (of veal) morcillo *m*, jarrete *m*

Phrasal verbs

- **knuckle down** [v ▸ adv] ponerse* a trabajar en serio; **to ~ down TO sth**: **you'd better ~ down to some hard work** va a ser mejor que te pongas a trabajar en serio
- **knuckle under** [v ▸ adv] ceder*, pasar por el aro

knuckleduster /'nʌkəlˌdʌstər || 'nʌkəlˌdʌstə(r)/ *n* (BrE) ▸**brass knuckles**

KO /'keɪ'əʊ/ *n* (in boxing) (colloq) K.O. *m*; (*read as: nocaut* o (Esp) *cao*)

koala /kəʊ'ɑːlə/ *n* **~ (bear)** koala *m*

kohlrabi /'kəʊl'rɑːbi/ *n* [u c] (*pl* **-bis**) colinabo *m*

kook /kuːk/ *n* (AmE colloq) chiflado, -da *m,f* (fam)

kooky /'kuːki/ *adj* **-kier, -kiest** (AmE colloq) ‹*person*› chiflado (fam)

kopeck, kopek /'kəʊpek/ *n* copec(k) *m*, kopek *m*

Koran /kə'rɑːn/ *n* **the ~** el Corán

Korea /kə'riːə/ *n* Corea *f*; **North/South ~** Corea del Norte/Sur

Korean¹ /kə'riːən/ *adj* coreano

Korean² *n* 1 [c] (person) coreano, -na *m,f*; **North ~** norcoreano, -na *m,f*; **South ~** surcoreano, -na *m,f* 2 [u] (language) coreano *m*

kosher /'kəʊʃər || 'kəʊʃə(r)/ *adj* ‹*food/butcher*› kosher *adj inv*; (genuine, legitimate) (colloq) legítimo, legal (fam)

Kotex® /'kəʊteks/ *n* (AmE) compresa *f*, toalla *f* higiénica

kowtow /'kaʊ'taʊ/ *vi* **to ~ TO sb** doblar la cerviz *or* doblegarse* ANTE algn

kph (= **kilometers** o (BrE) **kilometres per hour**) Km/h.

Kremlin /'kremlən || 'kremlɪn/ *n* **the ~** el Kremlin

KS = Kansas

kudos /'kuːdɑːs || 'kjuːdɒs/ *n* [u] prestigio *m*

Ku Klux Klan /'kuː'klʌks'klæn/ *n* (in US) **the ~ ~ ~** el Ku Klux Klan

Ku Klux Klan – KKK

Una organización secreta en EEUU que se opone a la igualdad de derechos para los afroamericanos (African-Americans). Se estableció en 1866, después de la abolición de la esclavitud. Declarada ilegal en 1871, resurgió en 1915, ampliando sus ataques para incluir también a los judíos, católicos y extranjeros. Durante los años 60 se opuso violentamente a la campaña por la igualdad de los derechos civiles de los afroamericanos. En la actualidad tiene poca influencia. Los miembros del KKK se visten con túnicas largas de color blanco y capuchones altos terminados en punta que les ocultan la cara

kumquat /'kʌmkwɑːt || 'kʌmkwɒt/ *n* naranjita *f* china, kumquat *m*, quinoto *m*

kung fu /'kʌŋ'fuː/ *n* [u] kung fu *m*

Kurd /kɜːrd || kɜːd/ *n* kurdo, -da *m,f*

Kurdish /'kɜːrdɪʃ || 'kɜːdɪʃ/ *adj* kurdo

Kuwait /kə'weɪt || kʊ'weɪt/ *n* Kuwait *m*

Kuwaiti¹ /kə'weɪti || kʊ'weɪti/ *adj* kuwaití

Kuwaiti² *n* kuwaití *mf*

KY, Ky = Kentucky

Ll

L, l /el/ *n* L, l *f*

l (= **liter(s)** *or* (BrE) **litre(s)**) l.

L [1] (BrE Auto) Ⓢ **L** (= **learner**) L (*conductor en aprendizaje*) [2] (Clothing) (= **large**) G (*talla grande*)

la /lɑː/ *n* (Mus) la *m*

La = Louisiana

LA [1] **= Los Angeles** [2] **= Louisiana**

lab /læb/ *n* (colloq) laboratorio *m*; (*before n*) ~ **coat** bata *f* blanca; ~ **technician** técnico *mf* de laboratorio

Lab= Labrador

label¹ /'leɪbəl/ *n*

A [1] (on bottle, file) etiqueta *f*, rótulo *m*; (on clothing, luggage) etiqueta *f*, marbete *m*; **address** ~ etiqueta con la dirección [2] (brand name) marca *f* [3] (record company) sello *m* discográfico [4] (Comput) etiqueta *f*

B (epithet) etiqueta *f*

label² *vt*, (BrE) **-ll-** [1] ‹*bottle/file*› etiquetar, ponerle* una etiqueta a; ‹*luggage*› ponerle* una etiqueta a; **to be ~ed** tener* *or* llevar una etiqueta [2] (categorize) **to ~ sth/sb (AS) sth** catalogar* *or* calificar* algo/a algn DE algo

labia /'leɪbiə/ *pl n* labios *mpl*

labor¹, (BrE) **labour** /'leɪbər || 'leɪbə(r)/ *n*

A [u] (Econ, Lab Rel) [1] (productive work) trabajo *m*; **Department of L~** (in US) Ministerio *m* de Trabajo, Secretaría *f* de Trabajo (Méx); (*before n*) ‹*dispute/laws*› laboral; ~ **costs** costo *m or* (Esp tb) coste *m* de la mano de obra; ~ **force** trabajadores *mpl*, mano *f* de obra; ~ **leader** (in US) líder *mf or* dirigente *mf* sindical; **the ~ movement** el movimiento obrero [2] (workers) mano *f* de obra

B **Labour** (in UK) (Pol) (*no art, + sing or pl vb*) los laboristas, el Partido Laborista; (*before n*) ‹*candidate/policy*› laborista

C [1] [u c] (effort) esfuerzos *mpl*, trabajo *m* [2] [c] (task) labor *f*, tarea *f*; **a ~ of love** una labor realizada con amor

D [u] (Med) parto *m*; **to be in ~** estar* de parto *or* en trabajo de parto; **to go into ~** entrar en trabajo de parto; (*before n*) ~ **pains** dolores *mpl or* contracciones *fpl* del parto

labor², (BrE) **labour** *vt*: **to ~ a point** insistir excesivamente sobre un punto

■ **labor** *vi*

A [1] (toil) trabajar; **to ~ AT sth** trabajar incansablemente EN algo [2] (work as laborer) (*only in -ing form*): **he got a job ~ing/a ~ing job** consiguió un trabajo de peón

B (struggle) ‹‹*engine*›› ahogarse*; **he ~ed up the hill** subió trabajosamente *or* penosamente la cuesta; **he was ~ing under the misapprehension** *o* **delusion that ...** se engañaba pensando que ...

laboratory /'læbərətɔːri || lə'bɒrətri/ *n* (*pl* **-ries**) laboratorio *m*

labor: ~ **camp** *n* campo *m* de trabajos forzados; ~ **Day** *n* Día *m* del Trabajo *or* de los trabajadores

labored, (BrE) **laboured** /'leɪbərd || 'leɪbəd/ *adj* ‹*breathing*› dificultoso, fatigoso; ‹*metaphor/joke*› forzado, torpe

laborer, (BrE) **labourer** /'leɪbərər || 'leɪbərə(r)/ *n* peón *m*; (in construction industry) peón *m* de albañil; **farm ~** peón *m*, trabajador *m* agrícola

labor-intensive, (BrE) **labour-intensive** /'leɪbərɪn'tensɪv/ *adj* que requiere mucha mano de obra

laborious /lə'bɔːriəs/ *adj* ‹*task/process*› laborioso; ‹*style*› farragoso, poco fluido; **in ~ detail** con excesivo detalle

labor: **~saving** *adj* (*before n*) que ahorra trabajo; ~ **union** *n* (AmE) sindicato *m*

labour *etc* (BrE) ▸**labor** *etc*

Labour Party *n* (in UK) Partido *m* Laborista

> **Labour Party**
>
> El Partido Laborista es uno de los tres principales partidos políticos de Gran Bretaña. Accedió por primera vez al poder en 1924 con el objetivo de representar los intereses de los trabajadores y sindicatos. En las últimas décadas, ha abandonado su postura de izquierda en puntos tales como la propiedad pública de la industria y los servicios, y hoy en día sus líderes prefieren denominarlo *New Labour*

labrador /'læbrədɔːr || 'læbrədɔː(r)/ *n* labrador *m*

labyrinth /'læbərɪnθ/ *n* laberinto *m*

lace¹ /leɪs/ *n*

A [u] (fabric) encaje *m*; (as border) puntilla *f*; (*before n*) ‹*handkerchief/curtains*› de encaje

B [c] (*shoe~*) cordón *m* (de zapato), agujeta *f* (Méx), pasador *m* (Per)

lace² *vt*

A ‹*shoes/boots*› ponerles* los cordones *or* (Méx) las agujetas *or* (Per) los pasadores a

B (fortify) **to ~ sth WITH sth**: **he ~d my drink with vodka** me echó un chorro de vodka en la bebida

lacerate /'læsəreɪt/ *vt* lacerar

laceration /'læsə'reɪʃən/ *n* laceración *f*, desgarro *m*

lace-up /'leɪsʌp/ *n* (BrE) (shoe) zapato *m* acordonado; (boot) bota *f* acordonada

lack¹ /læk/ *n* ~ **OF sth** falta *f or* (frml) carencia *f* DE algo; **there's no ~ of interest in the project** no hay falta de interés por el proyecto; **he was acquitted for ~ of evidence** lo absolvieron por falta de pruebas; **it won't be for ~ of trying** no será porque no lo haya intentado

lack² *vt* no tener*, carecer* de (frml); **it ~s originality** le falta *or* no tiene originalidad, carece de originalidad (frml)

■ **lack** *vi* (liter) **to ~ FOR sth**: **they ~ for nothing** no les falta nada, no carecen de nada (frml)

lackadaisical /'lækə'deɪzɪkəl/ *adj* (lacking vitality) apático, displicente; (lazy) indolente, perezoso

lackey /'læki/ *n* (*pl* **-eys**) (servile follower) lacayo, -ya *m,f*

lacking /'lækɪŋ/ *adj* (*pred*) [1] (absent): **the necessary resources are ~** faltan los recursos necesarios, se carece de los recursos necesarios (frml) [2] (deficient) **to be ~ IN sth** no tener* algo, carecer* DE algo (frml)

lackluster, (BrE) **lacklustre** /'læk,lʌstər || 'læk,lʌstə(r)/ *adj* [1] (dull) ‹*eyes*› apagado, sin brillo; ‹*hair*› opaco, sin brillo [2] (mediocre) ‹*performance/campaign*› deslucido; ‹*candidate*› mediocre

laconic /lə'kɑːnɪk || lə'kɒnɪk/ *adj* lacónico

laconically /lə'kɑːnɪkli || lə'kɒnɪkli/ *adv* lacónicamente

lacquer¹ /'lækər || 'lækə(r)/ *n* [u c] [1] (varnish) laca *f* [2] (*hair* ~) laca *f or* fijador *m* (para el pelo)

lacquer² *vt* laquear, lacar*

lacrosse /lə'krɔːs || lə'krɒs/ *n* [u] lacrosse *m*

lactate /'lækteɪt || læk'teɪt/ *vi* producir* leche

lactation /læk'teɪʃən/ *n* [u] lactancia *f*

lacy /'leɪsi/ *adj* (made of lace) de encaje; (like lace) como de encaje

lad /læd/ *n* [1] (boy) muchacho *m*, chaval *m* (Esp fam), pibe *m* (RPl fam), chavo *m* (Méx, Ven fam), chavalo *m* (AmC, Méx fam), cabro *m* (Chi fam); **when I was a ~** cuando yo era pequeño *or* (esp AmL) chico 2 (fellow) (BrE colloq) chico *m*, muchacho *m*, cuate *m* (Méx fam), gallo *m* (Chi fam); **he's one of the ~s** es uno del grupo (fam) *or* de la pandilla; **he's a bit of a ~** le gustan las faldas

ladder[1] /'lædər || 'lædə(r)/ *n*
A (Const) escalera *f* (de mano)
B (scale): **the social ~** la escala social; **you have to start at the bottom of the ~** hay que empezar desde abajo
C (in stocking, tights) (BrE) carrera *f*

ladder[2] (BrE) *vt*: **to ~ one's stockings** hacerse* una carrera en las medias
■ **ladder** *vi*: **my tights have ~ed** se me ha hecho una carrera en las medias

laddish /'lædɪʃ/ *adj* (BrE colloq) machista

laden /'leɪdn̩/ *adj* **~ WITH sth** cargado DE algo; **the table was ~ with food** la mesa estaba repleta de comida

la-di-da /'lɑ:di'dɑ:/ *adj* (colloq) afectado, repipi (Esp fam), pituco (CS, Per fam), popoff (Méx fam)

ladies[1] /'leɪdiz/ *pl of* **lady**

ladies[2] *n* (BrE) ▸ **ladies' room**

ladies' /'leɪdiz/: **~ fingers** *pl n* ▸ **okra**; **~ man** *n* donjuán *m*; **he's a bit of a ~ man** le gustan las faldas; **~ room** *n* (AmE) baño *m* *or* lavabo *m* *or* servicio *m* de señoras; Ⓢ **Ladies (Room)** Señoras, Damas

ladle[1] /'leɪdl/ *n* cucharón *m*, cazo *m*

ladle[2] *vt* servir* (*con cucharón*)

Phrasal verb
• **ladle out** [v ▸ o ▸ adv, v ▸ adv ▸ o] ‹*soup/stew*› servir* (*con cucharón*); ‹*advice/criticism*› prodigar*, repartir a diestra y siniestra *or* (Esp) a diestro y siniestro

lady /'leɪdi/ *n* (*pl* **ladies**)
A 1 (woman) señora *f*, dama *f* (frml); **ladies and gentlemen** señoras y señores, damas y caballeros; **ladies first!** ¡primero las damas *or* señoras!; **an old ~** una señora mayor; (*before n*) **a ~ doctor** una doctora; **he was with a ~ friend** estaba con una amiga; **~ mayoress** (BrE) alcaldesa *f* 2 (refined woman) señora *f*, dama *f* 3 (AmE colloq) (*as form of address*) señora 4 (appreciative use) mujer *f*
B (noblewoman or wife of a knight) lady *f*; **L~ Spencer** Lady Spencer
C (Relig) **Our L~** Nuestra Señora

lady: **~bug**, (AmE) **~bird** *n* (BrE) mariquita *f*, catarina *f* (Méx), petaca *f* (Col), chinita *f* (Chi), San Antonio *m* (Ur), vaca *f* de San Antón (Arg); **~-in-waiting** /'leɪdiɪn'weɪtɪŋ/ *n* (*pl* **ladies-in-waiting**) dama *f* de honor; **~-killer** *n* (colloq) donjuán *m* (fam), castigador *m* (Esp fam); **~like** *adj* fino, elegante, propio de una dama

ladyship /'leɪdiʃɪp/ *n*: **Her/Your L~** la señora

LAFTA /'læftə/ *n* (= **Latin American Free Trade Association**) ALALC *f*

lag[1] /læg/ *n*
A (interval) lapso *m*, intervalo *m*; (delay) retraso *m*, demora *f*
B (BrE colloq): **an old ~** un veterano de la cárcel

lag[2] **-gg-** *vi* **to ~ (behind)** quedarse atrás, rezagarse*; **to ~ behind sb/sth** ir* a la zaga de algn/algo
■ **lag** *vt* ‹*pipes/cylinder*› revestir* con aislantes

lager /'lɑ:gər || 'lɑ:gə(r)/ *n* [u c] cerveza *f* (rubia); (*before n*) **~ lout** (BrE) vándalo *m*, gamberro *m* (Esp)

lagging /'lægɪŋ/ *n* [u] aislamiento *m*, revestimiento *m*

lagoon /lə'gu:n/ *n* laguna *f*

lah /lɑ:/ *n* (BrE Mus) la *m*

lah-di-dah *adj* ▸ **la-di-da**

laid /leɪd/ *past & past p of* **lay**[2]

laid-back /'leɪd'bæk/ *adj* (colloq) ‹*person*› tranquilo y relajado, despreocupado; ‹*atmosphere*› relajado

lain /leɪn/ *past p of* **lie**[2] *Sense* II

lair /ler || leə(r)/ *n* guarida *f*

laird /lerd || leəd/ *n* (Scot) terrateniente *m*

laissez-faire, laisser-faire /'leɪseɪ'fer || ˌleɪseɪ'feə(r)/ *n* [u] laissez faire *m*, liberalismo *m* (económico); (*before n*) ‹*economics*› liberalista; ‹*attitude*› liberal

laity /'leɪəti/ *n* (+ *sing or pl vb*) **the ~** los laicos, el laicado

lake /leɪk/ *n* lago *m*; **milk/wine ~** (EC) excedentes *mpl* de leche/vino

lake: **~ District** *n* **the L~ District** el Lake District (*región de lagos al noroeste de Inglaterra*); **~side** *n*: **by the ~side** a orillas del lago

la-la-land /'lɑ:lɑ:lænd/ *n* [u] (AmE colloq) (*no art*)
A (Los Angeles) Los Angeles; (Hollywood) Hollywood *m*;
B (dream world) mundo *m* de ensueño, mundo *m* ideal; **he lives in ~** vive en las nubes

lam /læm/ *n* (AmE): ***to go on the ~*** (journ) darse* a la fuga, escaparse; **he's still on the ~** sigue fugitivo

lamb /læm/ *n* 1 [c] (young sheep) cordero *m*; (over one year old) borrego *m*; **she took it like a ~** se lo tomó muy mansamente; ***like a ~ to the slaughter*** como cordero que llevan al matadero 2 [u] (Culin) cordero *m*; (*before n*) **~ chop** chuleta *f* de cordero 3 [c] (*as term of endearment*): **the poor ~** el pobrecito

lambast /læm'bæst/, **lambaste** /-'beɪst/ *vt* arremeter contra

lambing /'læmɪŋ/ *n* [u] parición *f* (*de las ovejas*), (época *m* del) nacimiento *m* de los corderos

lambswool /'læmzwʊl/ *n* [u] lana *f* de cordero, lambswool *m*

lame[1] /leɪm/ *adj*
A (in foot, leg) cojo, renco, rengo (AmL); **to be ~ in one leg** cojear *or* renquear *or* (AmL tb) renguear de una pierna; **to go ~** quedarse cojo (*or* renco *etc*)
B (weak) ‹*excuse*› pobre, malo

lame[2] *vt* lisiar, dejar lisiado

lamé /lɑ:'meɪ || 'lɑ:meɪ/ *n* [u] lamé *m*

lame duck *n* fracaso *m*, caso *m* perdido; (*before n*) **a lame-duck president** *un presidente que no ha sido reelegido, en los últimos meses de su mandato*

lamely /'leɪmli/ *adv* ‹*argue/say*› (unconvincingly) de manera poco convincente; (without conviction) sin convicción

lameness /'leɪmnəs || 'leɪmnɪs/ *n* [u] cojera *f*, renquera *f*, renguera *f* (AmL)

lament[1] /lə'ment/ *n* 1 (expression of sorrow) lamento *m* 2 (Lit) elegía *f*

lament[2] *vt* 1 (deplore) ‹*misfortune/failure/absence*› lamentar 2 (mourn) (liter) ‹*death/loss*› llorar
■ **lament** *vi* (liter) llorar; **to ~ OVER sth** llorar algo

lamentable /'læməntəbəl/ *adj* lamentable, deplorable

lamentation /'læmən'teɪʃən/ *n* [u] lamentación *f*, lamento *m*

laminated /'læməneɪtəd || 'læmɪneɪtɪd/ *adj* ‹*plastic*› laminado; ‹*glass*› inastillable; **~ wood** madera *f* contrachapada; ‹*document/page*› plastificado

lamp /læmp/ *n* 1 (table, standard etc) lámpara *f*; **miner's ~** linterna *f* de minero 2 (Auto) luz *f*; *see also* **fog lamp, street lamp** *etc*

lamplight /'læmplaɪt/ *n* [u] (of table lamp) luz *f* de (la) lámpara; (of streetlamp) luz *f* de(l) farol *or* de (la) farola

lampoon[1] /læm'pu:n/ *n* sátira *f*

lampoon[2] *vt* satirizar*

lamp: **~post** *n* farol *m*, farola *f*; **~shade** *n* pantalla *f* (*de lámpara*)

lance[1] /læns || lɑ:ns/ *n* lanza *f*

lance[2] *vt* (Med) sajar, abrir* con lanceta

lance corporal *n* soldado *m* de primera clase

lancet /'lænsət || 'lɑ:nsɪt/ *n* (Med) lanceta *f*

land[1] /lænd/ *n*
A [u] 1 (Geog) tierra *f*; **over ~ and sea** por tierra y por mar; **on dry ~** en tierra firme; ***to know the lie*** *o* ***lay of the ~*** saber* qué terreno se pisa; ***to see how the ~ lies*** tantear el terreno; ***to spy out the ~*** reconocer* el terreno; (*before n*) ‹*animal/defenses*› de tierra, terrestre; **~ forces** fuerzas *fpl* terrestres *or* de tierra 2 (ground, property) tierra *f*; **a plot of ~** un terreno, una parcela; (*before n*) **~ registry** registro *m* catastral, catastro *m*; **~ reform** reforma *f* agraria 3 (Agr) **the ~** la tierra; **to live off the ~** vivir de la tierra
B [c] (country, realm) (liter) país *m*, nación *f*; (kingdom) reino *m*; ***the ~ of milk and honey*** el paraíso terrenal; ***to be in the ~ of Nod*** estar* dormido; ***to be in the ~ of the living*** (hum) estar* vivito y coleando (hum)

land[2] *vi*
A 1 (Aerosp, Aviat) ‹‹*aircraft/spaceship/pilot*›› aterrizar*; (on the moon) alunizar*; (on water) acuatizar*; (on sea) amarizar*,

amerizar*, amarar 2 (fall) caer*; **it ~ed on its side** cayó de lado

B (arrive, end up) (colloq) ir* a parar (fam)

C (Naut) «*ship*» atracar*; «*traveler/troops*» desembarcar*

■ **land** *vt*

A 1 (from sea) ‹*passengers/troops*› desembarcar*; ‹*cargo*› descargar* 2 (from air) ‹*plane*› hacer* aterrizar; ‹*troops*› desembarcar*; ‹*supplies*› descargar*

B 1 (in fishing) ‹*fish*› sacar* del agua 2 (win, obtain) ‹*contract*› conseguir*; ‹*job/husband*› conseguir*, pescar* (fam) 3 (strike home) (colloq) ‹*punch*› asestar (fam)

C (burden) (colloq) **to ~ sb WITH sth/sb, to ~ sth/sb ON sb** endilgarle* *or* encajarle algo/a algn A algn (fam); **I've ~ed myself with a lot of problems** me he metido en un montón de problemas

D (cause to end up) (colloq) **to ~ sb IN sth**: **that venture ~ed her in prison** con aquel negocio fue a parar a la cárcel (fam); **to ~ sb/oneself in trouble** meter a algn/meterse en problemas (fam)

Phrasal verb

- **land up** [v ▸ adv] (colloq): **to ~ up in jail** ir* a parar a la cárcel (fam); **to ~ up in trouble** terminar mal

landed /ˈlændəd || ˈlændɪd/ *adj* (*before n*): **the ~ gentry** la aristocracia terrateniente

landing /ˈlændɪŋ/ *n*

A 1 [u c] (Aerosp, Aviat) aterrizaje *m*; (on sea) amarizaje *m*, amerizaje *m*; (on water) acuatizaje *m*; (on moon) alunizaje *m*; (*before n*) **~ gear** tren *m* de aterrizaje; **~ strip** pista *f* de aterrizaje 2 [c] (Mil, Naut) desembarco *m*, desembarque *m*; (*before n*) **~ craft** lancha *f* de desembarco 3 [u] (of cargo) descarga *f*; (of troops) desembarco *m*

B [c] (on staircase) rellano *m*, descansillo *m*, descanso *m* (Col, CS)

landing: **~ card** *n* tarjeta *f* de desembarque; **~ party** *n* equipo *m* de reconocimiento; **~ stage** *n* embarcadero *m*, desembarcadero *m*

landlady /ˈlænd,leɪdi/ *n* (*pl* **-dies**) 1 (of rented dwelling) casera *f*, dueña *f* 2 (of small hotel) dueña *f*, patrona *f* 3 (BrE) (of pub — owner) dueña *f*, patrona *f*; (— manager) encargada *f*

landless /ˈlændləs || ˈlændlɪs/ *adj* sin tierra

land: **~locked** /ˈlændlɑːkt || ˈlændlɒkt/ *adj* sin salida al mar, sin litoral; **~lord** *n* 1 (of landed estate) terrateniente *m*, hacendado *m* 2 (of rented dwelling) casero *m*, dueño *m* 3 (BrE) (of pub — owner) dueño *m*, patrón *m*; (— manager) encargado *m*; **~lubber** /ˈlænd,lʌbər || ˈlænd,lʌbə(r)/ *n* marinero *m* de agua dulce; **~mark** *n* monumento *m* (*or* edificio *m etc*) famoso; **use the tower as a ~mark** utilice la torre como punto de referencia; **the promotion was a ~mark in his career** el ascenso marcó un hito en su carrera; **~mass** *n* masa *f* continental; **~ mine** *n* mina *f* (de tierra); **~owner** *n* terrateniente *mf*, hacendado, -da *m,f*

landscape¹ /ˈlændskeɪp/ *n* [u c] paisaje *m*; **the political ~** el panorama político; (*before n*) **~ gardener** jardinero, -ra *m,f* paisajista; **~ gardening** paisajismo *m*; **~ painter** paisajista *mf*

landscape² *vt* ‹*garden*› diseñar; ‹*public space*› ajardinar

landscape format *n* [u] 1 (Art, Phot) formato *m* apaisado 2 (in word processing) formato *m* horizontal *or* apaisado

landslide /ˈlændslaɪd/ *n* 1 (Geog) derrumbamiento *m or* desprendimiento *m* de tierras 2 (Pol) victoria *f* aplastante *or* arrolladora; (*before n*) ‹*victory*› aplastante, arrollador

lane /leɪn/ *n*

A (in countryside) camino *m*, sendero *m*; (alleyway) callejón *m*

B (Transp) 1 (for road traffic) carril *m or* (Chi) pista *f or* (RPl) senda *f*; **bus/bicycle ~** carril *m* de autobuses/bicicletas; ***to live in the fast ~*** (colloq) vivir a toda máquina, vivir a tope (Esp fam) 2 (for ships) ruta *f*; **sea/shipping ~** ruta marítima/de navegación

C (Sport) (in athletics) carril *m* (Andes, Ven), calle *f* (Esp); (in bowling) pista *f*

language /ˈlæŋgwɪdʒ/ *n*

A [c u] (means of communication, style of speech) lenguaje *m*; **bad ~** palabrotas *fpl*, malas palabras *fpl* (esp AmL)

B [c] 1 (particular tongue) idioma *m*, lengua *f*; **the English ~** la lengua inglesa, el idioma inglés; **first ~** (native tongue) lengua materna; (Educ) primera lengua extranjera; (*before n*) **~ barrier** barrera *f* idiomática *or* del idioma; **~ laboratory** laboratorio *m* de idiomas 2 (Comput) lenguaje *m*

languid /ˈlæŋgwəd || ˈlæŋgwɪd/ *adj* lánguido

languish /ˈlæŋgwɪʃ/ *vi* (liter) languidecer*, consumirse; (in prison) pudrirse*

languor /ˈlæŋgər || ˈlæŋgə(r)/ *n* [u] languidez *f*

languorous /ˈlæŋgərəs/ *adj* ‹*movement*› lánguido; ‹*heat*› aletargante, bochornoso

lank /læŋk/ *adj* ‹*hair*› lacio

lanky /ˈlæŋki/ *adj* **-kier, -kiest** desgarbado, larguirucho (fam)

lanolin, lanoline /ˈlænḷən || ˈlænəlɪn/ *n* [u] lanolina *f*

lantern /ˈlæntərn || ˈlæntən/ *n* (lamp) farol *m*

lantern-jawed /ˈlæntərnˈdʒɔːd || ,læntənˈdʒɔːd/ *adj* de cara larga

Laos /laʊs || ˈlɑːɒs, laʊs/ *n* Laos *m*

lap¹ /læp/ *n*

A (of body) rodillas *fpl*, regazo *m* (liter); **to sit on sb's ~** sentarse* en las rodillas *or* (liter) en el regazo de algn; **he dropped the problem in my ~** me pasó el problema, me endilgó el problema (fam); ***in the ~ of luxury*** en un lujo asiático; ***to be in the ~ of the gods***: **their fate is in the ~ of the gods** su destino queda librado al azar; ***to fall*** *o* ***drop into sb's ~*** caerle* como llovido del cielo a algn

B 1 (Sport) vuelta *f* 2 (stage) etapa *f*

lap² **-pp-** *vt*

A (Sport) ‹*opponent*› sacarle* una vuelta de ventaja a

B ‹*water/milk*› beber a lengüetazos

C (splash against) ‹*shore/bank*› lamer (liter), besar (liter)

■ **lap** *vi* chapalear; **to ~ AGAINST sth** lamer *or* besar algo (liter)

Phrasal verb

- **lap up** [v ▸ o ▸ adv, v ▸ adv ▸ o] 1 (drink) ‹*milk/water*› beber a lengüetazos 2 (relish) ‹*praise/news*› deleitarse *or* regodearse con

lapdog /ˈlæpdɔːg || ˈlæpdɒg/ *n* perrito *m* faldero

lapel /ləˈpel/ *n* solapa *f*

lapis lazuli /ˈlæpəsˈlæzəli || ,læpɪsˈlæzjʊli/ *n* [u] 1 (Min) lapislázuli *m* 2 (color) azul *m* ultramarino *or* (de) ultramar

Lapland /ˈlæplænd/ *n* Laponia *f*

Lapp¹ /læp/ *adj* lapón

Lapp² *n* 1 [c] (person) lapón, -pona *m,f* 2 [u] (language) lapón *m*

lapse¹ /læps/ *n*

A (fault, error) lapsus *m*, falla *f*, fallo *m* (Esp); **a security ~** una falla *or* (Esp) un fallo *or* descuido en el sistema de seguridad; **a ~ of memory** una falla (AmL) *or* (Esp) un fallo de memoria, un lapsus de memoria; **a ~ of concentration** una falta de concentración, un descuido

B (interval) lapso *m*, período *m*; **there was a ~ in the conversation** se hizo un silencio en la conversación

lapse² *vi*

A (fall, slip): **standards have ~d** el nivel ha decaído; **to ~ INTO sth**: **he ~d into silence** se calló, se quedó callado; **to ~ into bad habits** adquirir* malos hábitos; **she ~d into French** empezó a hablar en francés; **a ~d Catholic** un católico que ha dejado de practicar

B 1 (cease) «*project/plan*» cancelarse; «*custom/practice*» perderse*, caer* en desuso; **his concentration ~d** se desconcentró, perdió la concentración 2 (expire) «*policy/membership/contract*» caducar*, vencer*

C (pass) «*time/hours*» transcurrir

laptop¹ /ˈlæptɑːp || ˈlæptɒp/ *adj* (*before n*) portátil, laptop

laptop² *n* (**~** *computer*) laptop *f or* (Esp) *m*

lapwing /ˈlæpwɪŋ/ *n* avefría *f*‡

larceny /ˈlɑːrsəni || ˈlɑːsəni/ *n* [u] (in US) robo *m*; **petty ~** hurto *m*

larch /lɑːrtʃ || lɑːtʃ/ *n* alerce *m*

lard /lɑːrd || lɑːd/ *n* [u] manteca *f or* (RPl) grasa *f* de cerdo

larder /ˈlɑːrdər || ˈlɑːdə(r)/ *n* despensa *f*, alacena *f*

large¹ /lɑːrdʒ || lɑːdʒ/ *adj* **larger, largest** [*The usual translation,* **grande**, *becomes* **gran** *when it is used before a singular noun*] 1 (in size) ‹*area/room*› grande; **he's a ~ man** es un hombre corpulento *or* (fam) grandote 2 (in number, amount) ‹*family/crowd*› grande, numeroso; **a ~ proportion of my income** gran parte *or* una buena parte de mis ingresos;

the ~st collection of stamps in the world la mayor colección de sellos del mundo

large[2] *n*

A **at large** 1 (at liberty): **to be at ~** «*murderer/tiger*» andar* suelto 2 (as a whole) en general; **society/the public at ~** la sociedad/el público en general 3 (in US): **representative at ~** *representante de todo un estado o distrito en el Congreso o Senado de los EEUU*

B (size) (Clothing) talla *f or* (RPl) talle *m* grande

largely /ˈlɑːrdʒli || ˈlɑːdʒli/ *adv* en gran *or* en buena parte

large-scale /ˈlɑːrdʒˈskeɪl || ˈlɑːdʒˌskeɪl/ *adj* (*before n*) ‹*map/model*› a escala grande; ‹*search/inquiry*› en *or* a gran escala

largesse, (AmE also) **largess** /lɑːrˈdʒes || lɑːˈʒes/ *n* [u] (generosity) largueza *f*, esplendidez *f*

lariat /ˈlæriət/ *n* (lasso) lazo *m*

lark /lɑːrk || lɑːk/ *n*

A (Zool) alondra *f*; ***to be up o rise with the ~*** levantarse al cantar el gallo; ▸**happy A1**

B (BrE colloq) 1 (*no pl*) (bit of fun): **to do sth for a ~** hacer* algo por divertirse *or* de broma 2 (activity): **I'm too old for this ~** yo ya no estoy para estos trotes (fam); **this camping ~** esta historia del camping (fam)

Phrasal verb

- **lark about, lark around** [v ▸ adv] hacer* el tonto, (colloq) payasear (AmL fam)

larva /ˈlɑːrvə || ˈlɑːvə/ *n* (*pl* **-vae** /-viː/) larva *f*

laryngitis /ˈlærənˈdʒaɪtəs || ˌlærɪnˈdʒaɪtɪs/ *n* [u] laringitis *f*

larynx /ˈlærɪŋks/ *n* (*pl* **larynxes** *or* **larynges** /ləˈrɪndʒiːs/) laringe *f*

lasagna, lasagne /ləˈzɑːnjə || ləˈsænjə, leˈzænjə, -ɑːnjə/ *n* [u c] lasaña *f*

lascivious /ləˈsɪviəs/ *adj* lascivo

laser /ˈleɪzər || ˈleɪzə(r)/ *n* láser *m*; (*before n*) **~ beam** rayo *m* láser; **~ printer** impresora *f* láser; **~ surgery** cirujía *f* con láser

lash[1] /læʃ/ *n*

A (*eye~*) pestaña *f*

B 1 (whip) látigo *m* 2 (stroke — of whip) latigazo *m*, azote *m*; (— of tail) coletazo *m*

lash[2] *vt*

A 1 (whip) ‹*person*› azotar, darle* latigazos a; ‹*horse*› fustigar* 2 (beat against) azotar 3 (thrash): **the whale ~ed its tail** la ballena daba coletazos

B (bind) **to ~ sth/sb TO sth** amarrar *or* atar algo/a algn A algo; **to ~ sth down** amarrar *or* atar algo; (Naut) amarrar *or* trincar* algo

Phrasal verb

- **lash out** [v ▸ adv (▸ prep ▸ o)]

A (physically, verbally) atacar*; **to ~ out AT/AGAINST sb** (physically) emprenderla a golpes (*or* patadas *etc*) CON algn, arremeter CONTRA algn; (verbally) arremeter CONTRA algn

B (spend freely) (BrE colloq) **to ~ out (ON sth)**: **we decided to ~ out and buy a decent camera** decidimos tirar la casa por la ventana y comprarnos una cámara decente (fam); **I had ~ed out on a new dress** había gastado un montón en comprarme un vestido nuevo (fam)

lashing /ˈlæʃɪŋ/ *n*

A [c u] (whipping) azotaina *f*, latigazos *mpl*

B **lashings** *pl* (plenty) (BrE colloq) montones *mpl* (fam)

lass /læs/, **lassie** /ˈlæsi/ *n* (liter *or* dial) muchacha *f*, zagala *f* (liter & arc); (*as form of address*) nena

lassitude /ˈlæsətuːd || ˈlæsɪtjuːd/ *n* [u] (liter) lasitud *f* (liter)

lasso[1] /ˈlæsəʊ, læˈsuː || læˈsuː/ *n* (*pl* **-sos** *or* **-soes**) lazo *m*

lasso[2] *vt* **lassoes, lassoing, lassoed** echarle el lazo a, enlazar* (Col, RPl), lazar* (Méx), lacear (Chi)

last[1] /læst || lɑːst/ *adj*

A 1 (in series) ‹*chapter/lap*› último; **the second to ~ door, the ~ door but one** la penúltima puerta; **I do it ~ thing at night** es lo último que hago antes de acostarme; **to be ~** (in race, on arrival) ser* el último (en llegar), llegar* el último *or* (CS) llegar* último; **to be ~ to + INF** ser* el último EN + INF 2 (final, ultimate) ‹*chance/day*› último; **at the very ~ minute** *o* **moment** en el último momento, a última hora; **the ~ rites** *o* **sacraments** la extremaunción 3 (only remaining) último; **I'm down to my ~ few dollars** sólo me quedan unos pocos dólares

B (previous, most recent) (*before n*): **~ Tuesday** el martes pasado; **this time ~ week** la semana pasada a estas horas; **in my ~ letter** en mi última carta; **the ~ time I went** la última vez que fui

C (least likely or suitable): **that was the ~ thing I expected to hear from you** es lo que menos me esperaba que me dijeras; **that's the ~ thing I'd do!** ¡no se me ocurriría hacer eso!; ▸**laugh**[2] *vi*, **leg**[1] **A, straw 1** *etc*

last[2] *pron*

A 1 (in series, sequence) último, -ma *m,f*; **the ~ to + INF** el último/la última/los últimos/las últimas EN + INF; **the ~ I remember** lo último que recuerdo; **we haven't heard the ~ of him/it** nos va a seguir dando guerra, ya verás; **to breathe one's ~** (liter) exhalar el último suspiro 2 (only remaining) **the ~ OF sth**: **the ~ of its kind** el último de su clase; **that's the ~ of the jam** esa es toda la mermelada que queda 3 (*in phrases*) (liter) **at the last** al final; **to** *o* **until the ~** hasta el último momento, hasta el final

B (preceding one): **the night before ~** anteanoche, antenoche (AmL); **at the meeting before ~** en la penúltima reunión; **each hill seemed steeper than the ~** cada colina parecía más empinada que la anterior

last[3] *adv*

A 1 (at the end): **I went in ~** fui el último en entrar, entré el último, entré último (CS); **our team came** *o* **finished ~** nuestro equipo quedó en último lugar *or* (CS tb) terminó último 2 (finally, in conclusion): **~ of all** por último, lo último (de todo); **and ~ but not least** y por último, pero no por eso menos importante 3 (*in phrases*) **at last** por fin, al fin; **at long last** por fin, finalmente

B (most recently): **she was ~ seen a year ago** la última vez que se la vio fue hace un año; **when did you ~ see him** *o* **see him ~?** ¿cuándo fue la última vez que lo viste?

last[4] *n* (for shoemaking) horma *f*

last[5] *vi*

A 1 (continue) durar; **it ~ed (for) three hours** duró tres horas 2 (endure, survive) durar; **he wouldn't ~ five minutes in the army** no aguantaría *or* no duraría ni cinco minutos en el ejército

B (be sufficient) durar; **to make sth ~** hacer* durar algo

C (remain usable) durar; **it will ~ (for) a lifetime** durará toda la vida

■ **last** *vt* durar; **we have enough fuel to ~ us** el combustible que tenemos nos durará

Phrasal verb

- **last out** [v ▸ adv]

A (survive, endure) «*person*» aguantar, resistir

B (be sufficient) «*supplies/food*» alcanzar*

last: **~-ditch** /ˈlæstˈdɪtʃ || ˈlɑːstˈdɪtʃ/ *adj* (*before n*) desesperado; **~-gasp** /ˈlæstˈgɑsp || ˌlɑːstˈgɑːsp/ *adj* (*before n*) (colloq) ‹*penalty/goal*› de último momento; ‹*effort*› de última hora

lasting /ˈlæstɪŋ || ˈlɑːstɪŋ/ *adj* ‹*solution/peace*› duradero, perdurable; **to my ~ shame** para mi eterna vergüenza

lastly /ˈlæstli || ˈlɑːstli/ *adv* (*as linker*) por último, finalmente

last: **~-minute** /ˈlæstˈmɪnət || ˌlɑːstˈmɪnɪt/ *adj* (*before n*) de última hora; **~ post** *n* (BrE Mil) **the ~ post** el toque de silencio

lat (= **latitude**) lat.

latch /lætʃ/ *n* pasador *m*, pestillo *m*; (on lock) seguro *m*; **I've left the door on the ~** le he puesto el seguro al pestillo para que no se cierre la puerta

Phrasal verbs

- **latch on** [v ▸ adv (▸ prep ▸ o)] (understand) (colloq) agarrar *or* (Esp) coger* la onda; **to ~ on TO sth** entender* *or* captar algo; (realize) darse* cuenta DE algo
- **latch onto** [v ▸ prep ▸ o] (colloq) 1 (get hold of, catch) agarrarse de 2 (obtain) (AmE) hacerse* con, conseguir* 3 (attach oneself to) pegarse* a (fam)

latchkey /ˈlætʃkiː/ *n* llave *f* de (la) casa; (*before n*) **~ child** *niño cuyos padres trabajan y está solo en casa al regresar del colegio*

late[1] /leɪt/ *adj* **later, latest**

A (after correct, scheduled time): **the ~ arrival/departure of the train** el retraso en la llegada/salida del tren; **~ applications will not be accepted** no se aceptarán las solicitudes que lleguen fuera de plazo *or* con retraso; **to be ~** «*person*» llegar* tarde; **I'm sorry I'm ~** perdón por llegar tarde; **the train was an hour ~** el tren llegó con una hora de retraso; **to make sth/sb ~: she made me ~ for my class** me hizo llegar tarde a clase; **the accident made the train ~** el accidente hizo que el tren se retrasara; **to be ~ FOR/WITH sth: you'll be ~ for work/the train** vas a llegar tarde al trabajo/perder el tren; **I'm ~ with the rent** estoy atrasado con el alquiler

B [1] (after usual time): **to have a ~ night/breakfast** acostarse*/desayunar tarde; **Spring is ~ this year** la primavera se ha atrasado este año; **Ⓢ late opening Thursdays till 8 pm** jueves abierto hasta las 8 de la noche [2] ‹*chrysanthemum/potatoes*› tardío; **he was a ~ developer** (physically) se desarrolló tarde; (intellectually) maduró tarde

C [1] (far on in time): **it's ~** es tarde; **it's getting ~** se está haciendo tarde [2] (*before n*) ‹*shift/bus*› último; **the ~ film** la película de la noche *or* (CS) de trasnoche; **at this ~ hour** a estas horas; **to keep ~ hours** trasnochar; **at this ~ stage** a estas alturas; **they scored a ~ equalizer** marcaron el tanto del empate en los últimos minutos del partido; **in ~ April/summer** a finales *or* fines de abril/del verano; **the ~ 1950s** el final de la década del cincuenta; **she's in her ~ forties** tiene cerca de cincuenta años; **we caught a ~r train** tomamos un tren que salía más tarde

D (*before n*) [1] (deceased) difunto (frml); **the ~ John Doe** el difunto John Doe [2] (former) antiguo

late² *adv* **later, latest**

A (after correct, scheduled time) ‹*arrive/leave*› tarde; **the trains are running 20 minutes ~** los trenes llevan 20 minutos de retraso; ***better ~ than never*** más vale tarde que nunca

B (after usual time) ‹*work/sleep*› hasta tarde; ‹*mature/bloom*› tarde, más tarde de lo normal; **I'll be home ~ today** hoy llegaré tarde (a casa)

C [1] (recently): **as ~ as the thirteenth century** aún en el siglo trece [2] **of late** últimamente, en los últimos tiempos

D (toward end of period): **~ in the morning/afternoon** a última hora de la mañana/tarde; **~ in the week/year** a finales de la semana/del año; **he married ~ (in life)** se casó mayor *or* tarde; **~ in her career** hacia el final de su carrera

E (far on in time) tarde; **don't leave it too ~** no lo dejes para muy tarde; **we stayed up ~** nos quedamos levantados hasta tarde; **~ at night** tarde por la noche, bien entrada la noche; **~ into the night** hasta muy entrada la noche

latecomer /ˈleɪtˌkʌmər || ˈleɪtˌkʌmə(r)/ *n*: **~s will have to sit at the back** los que lleguen tarde tendrán que sentarse atrás

lately /ˈleɪtli/ *adv* últimamente, recientemente; **(up) until** *o* **till ~** hasta hace poco

lateness /ˈleɪtnəs || ˈleɪtnɪs/ *n* [u] [1] (of arrival) retraso *m*, tardanza *f*; **his continual ~** sus continuas llegadas tarde [2] (being late at night): **the ~ of the hour** lo tarde que era, lo avanzado de la hora

late-night /ˈleɪtˈnaɪt/ *adj* ‹*pharmacy*› que está abierta por la noche; ‹*show*› de noche; ‹*program*› de trasnoche

latent /ˈleɪtn̩t/ *adj* latente

later¹ /ˈleɪtər || ˈleɪtə(r)/ *adj* (*comp of* **late¹**) ‹*meeting/edition*› posterior, ulterior (frml); **we'll discuss it at a ~ date** lo discutiremos más adelante

later² *adv* (*comp of* **late²**) después, más tarde; **several glasses of brandy ~, ...** después de varias copas de coñac ...; **~ that day/night** más tarde *or* posteriormente ese día/esa noche; **not** *o* **no ~ than May 14** a más tardar el 14 de mayo; **~ I realized that ...** después *or* posteriormente me di cuenta de que ...; **~ on** más tarde, después; **see you ~!** ¡hasta luego!, ¡hasta ahora!

lateral /ˈlætərəl/ *adj* lateral; **~ thinking** pensamiento *m* lateral

latest¹ /ˈleɪtəst || ˈleɪtɪst/ *adj* [1] (*superl of* **late¹**) último [2] (most up to date) (*before n*) último; **the ~ fashion** la última moda; **this is the ~ in a series of similar incidents** éste es el más reciente en una serie de incidentes similares

latest² *n*

A [1] (most recent news, development): **have you heard the ~ on ... ?** ¿has oído lo último que se cuenta de ... ? [2] (most up to date) **the ~ IN sth** lo último *or* lo más actual EN algo

B (furthest on in time) (*as pron*): **when is the ~ I can let you know?** ¿para cuándo tengo que darte una respuesta?; **by the fifteenth at the (very) ~** a más tardar (para) el quince

latex /ˈleɪteks/ *n* [u] látex *m*

lathe /leɪð/ *n* torno *m*

lather¹ /ˈlæðər || ˈlɑːðə(r), læðə(r)/ *n* (*no pl*) [1] (from soap) espuma *f* [2] (sweat) sudor *m*; ***to be in/get into a ~ (about sth)*** (colloq) (nervous) estar*/ponerse* nervioso *or* histérico (por algo) (fam); (angry) estar*/ponerse* hecho una furia (por algo) (fam)

lather² *vt* ‹*face/hair*› enjabonar

■ **lather** *vi* «*soap/detergent*» hacer* espuma

Latin¹ /ˈlætn̩ || ˈlætɪn/ *adj* latino

Latin² *n* [1] [u] (language) latín *m* [2] [c] (person) latino, -na *m,f*

Latin America *n* América *f* Latina, Latinoamérica *f*

Latin American¹ *adj* latinoamericano

Latin American² *n* latinoamericano, -na *m,f*

Latino¹ /læˈtiːnəʊ/ *adj* (AmE) latinoamericano (*residente en EEUU*)

Latino² *n* (*pl* **-nos**) (AmE) latinoamericano, -na *m,f* (*residente en EEUU*)

latitude /ˈlætətuːd || ˈlætɪtjuːd/ *n* [1] [c u] (Geog) latitud *f* [2] [u] (freedom to choose) libertad *f*, flexibilidad *f*

latrine /ləˈtriːn/ *n* letrina *f*

latte /ˈlɑːteɪ, ˈlæteɪ/ *n* café *m* con leche

latter¹ /ˈlætər || ˈlætə(r)/ *n* (*pl* ~) **the ~** éste, -ta; (*pl*) éstos, -tas

latter² *adj* (*before n*) [1] (second of two) segundo, último [2] (later, last): **in the ~ part of the season** hacia el final de la temporada; **in his ~ years** (frml) en sus últimos años

Latter-day Saint /ˈlætərˈdeɪ || ˌlætəˈdeɪ/ *n* mormón, -mona *m,f*; **the Church of Jesus Christ of the ~ ~s** la Iglesia de Jesucristo de los Santos de los Últimos Días

latterly /ˈlætərli || ˈlætəli/ *adv* últimamente, en los últimos tiempos; **~ he was very ill** en los días que precedieron a su muerte estuvo muy enfermo

lattice /ˈlætəs || ˈlætɪs/ *n* (Archit, Const) entramado *m*, enrejado *m*; (*before n*) **~ window** celosía *f*

latticework /ˈlætəswɜːrk || ˈlætɪswɜːk/ *n* [u] celosía *f*

Latvia /ˈlætviə/ *n* Letonia *f*

Latvian¹ /ˈlætviən/ *adj* letón

Latvian² *n* [1] [c] (person) letón, -tona *m,f* [2] [u] (language) letón *m*

laudable /ˈlɔːdəbəl/ *adj* (frml) loable, laudable (frml)

laugh¹ /læf || lɑːf/ *n* [1] (act, sound) risa *f*; (loud) carcajada *f*, risotada *f*; **she gave a nervous ~** se rió nerviosamente, soltó una risa nerviosa; **to have a ~ (about/at sth)** reírse* (de algo); **to raise a ~** hacer* reír; ***the ~ is on me/you/him*** me/te/le salió el tiro por la culata; ***to have the last ~***: **I'll have the last ~** quien ríe (el) último ríe mejor (, y ésa voy a ser yo) [2] (joke, fun) (colloq): **it will be a ~** será divertido, va a ser un plato (AmL fam), va a ser un relajo (Méx); **she's a good ~** es muy divertida; **to do/say sth for a ~** hacer*/decir* algo por divertirse, hacer*/decir* algo de cachondeo (Esp) *or* (Méx) de puro relajo (fam)

laugh² *vi* reír(se)*; **she ~ed out loud/to herself** se rió a carcajadas/para sus adentros; **to burst out ~ing** soltar* una carcajada, echarse a reír; **I nearly died ~ing** casi me muero de (la) risa; **to make sb ~** hacer* reír a algn; **to ~ ABOUT sth** reírse* DE algo; **to ~ AT sb/sth** reírse* DE algn/algo; ***to ~ on the other side of one's face*** (colloq): **she'll be ~ing on the other side of her face when he finds out** se le van a quitar las ganas de reírse cuando él se entere; ***he who ~s last ~s best*** *o* (BrE) ***longest*** quien ríe *or* el que ríe (el) último, ríe mejor

■ **laugh** *vt*: **they were ~ed off the stage** se rieron tanto de ellos, que tuvieron que salir del escenario; **you don't say!, he ~ed** —¡no me digas! —dijo riendo

Phrasal verb

• **laugh off** [v ▸ o ▸ adv, v ▸ adv ▸ o] tomar a broma, reírse* de

laughable /ˈlæfəbəl || ˈlɑːfəbəl/ *adj* de risa, risible

laughing[1] /'læfɪŋ || 'lɑːfɪŋ/ *adj* ‹*eyes*› risueño, alegre; **this is no ~ matter** no es motivo de risa, no es para tomarlo a risa

laughing[2] *n* risas *fpl*; (loud) carcajadas *fpl*, risotadas *fpl*

laughing gas *n* [u] gas *m* hilarante

laughingly /'læfɪŋli || 'lɑːfɪŋli/ *adv*: **this is what he ~ calls leadership** ¡y a esto él lo llama liderazgo!

laughingstock /'læfɪŋstɑːk || 'lɑːfɪŋstɒk/ *n* hazmerreír *m*; **he made a ~ of his opponent** dejó *or* puso a su contrincante en ridículo

laughter /'læftər || 'lɑːftə(r)/ *n* [u] risas *fpl*; (loud) carcajadas *fpl*, risotadas *fpl*; **he roared with ~** se rió a carcajadas; (*before n*) **~ lines** arrugas *fpl* de gesto

launch[1] /lɔːntʃ/ *vt*

A 1 (Naut) ‹*new vessel*› botar; ‹*lifeboat*› echar al agua 2 (Aerosp, Mil) ‹*satellite/missile*› lanzar*; ‹*attack*› emprender, lanzar*

B 1 (Busn) ‹*product/campaign*› lanzar*; ‹*company*› fundar* 2 (Lit, Theat, Cin) ‹*book/play/actor*› lanzar*

Phrasal verbs

- **launch into** [v ▸ prep ▸ o]: **she ~ed into a lengthy account of her adventures** se puso a contar sus aventuras con lujo de detalles
- **launch out** [v ▸ adv] lanzarse*; **she decided to ~ out on her own** decidió lanzarse por su cuenta

launch[2] *n*

A (Naut) (motorboat) lancha *f* (a motor), motora *f*

B 1 (of new vessel) botadura *f*; (of lifeboat) lanzamiento *m* (*al agua*) 2 (of rocket, missile) lanzamiento *m*

C (of product, project, campaign) lanzamiento *m*; (of company) fundación *f*; (*before n*) ‹*date/party*› de lanzamiento

launcher /'lɔːntʃər || 'lɔːntʃə(r)/ *n* lanzador *m*; (*rocket* ~) lanzacohetes *m*; (*missile* ~) lanzamisiles *m*

launching /'lɔːntʃɪŋ/ *n* 1 ▸**launch**[2] B 2 ▸**launch**[2] C

launching pad, launchpad /'lɔːntʃpæd/ *n* 1 (Aerosp) rampa *f* or plataforma *f* de lanzamiento 2 (for ideas, career) trampolín *m*, plataforma *f*

launder /'lɔːndər || 'lɔːndə(r)/ *vt* 1 (wash and iron) (frml) lavar y planchar 2 ‹*money*› blanquear, lavar (AmL)

Launderette®, launderette /'lɔːndə'ret || lɔːn'dret/ *n* lavandería *f* automática

Laundromat®, laundromat /'lɔːndrəmæt/ *n* (AmE) lavandería *f* automática

laundry /'lɔːndri/ *n* (*pl* **-dries**) 1 [c] (commercial) lavandería *f*, lavadero *m* (RPl); (in home) lavadero *m* 2 [u] (dirty clothes) ropa *f* sucia *or* para lavar; (washed clothes) ropa *f* limpia *or* lavada; (*before n*) **~ basket** canasto *m* or cesto *m* de la ropa sucia

laureate /'lɔːriət || 'lɒriət/ *n* ▸**poet laureate**

laurel /'lɔːrəl || 'lɒrəl/ *n* 1 (Bot) laurel *m*; (*before n*) **~ wreath** corona *f* de laureles 2 **laurels** *pl* (glory) laureles *mpl*; ***to rest on one's ~s*** dormirse* sobre sus (*or* mis *etc*) laureles

lava /'lɑːvə/ *n* [u] lava *f*

lavatory /'lævətɔːri || 'lævətri/ *n* (*pl* **-ries**) 1 (room in house) (cuarto *m* de) baño *m*, váter *m* (Esp fam) 2 (public) (*often pl*) baños *mpl*, servicios *mpl* (Esp) 3 (receptacle) taza *f*, inodoro *m*, wáter *m*

lavender /'lævəndər || 'lævəndə(r)/ *n* [u] 1 (Bot) lavanda *f*, espliego *m*; (*before n*) **~ water** (agua *f*‡ de) lavanda *f* 2 (color) azul *m* lavanda; (*before n*) azul lavanda *adj inv*

lavish[1] /'lævɪʃ/ *adj* 1 (extravagant) ‹*lifestyle*› de derroche *or* despilfarro; **she was ~ in** *o* **with her praise** fue pródiga en elogios, no escatimó elogios 2 (large, sumptuous) ‹*gift*› espléndido, generoso; ‹*party/meal*› magnífico, espléndido; ‹*costumes/production*› fastuoso

lavish[2] *vt* **to ~ sth ON** *o* **UPON sb** prodigar(le)* algo A algn, no escatimar(le) algo A algn; **she ~es attention upon the children** se desvive por los niños

lavishly /'lævɪʃli/ *adv* 1 (in large measure) ‹*give*› con esplendidez *or* generosidad 2 (sumptuously) ‹*decorated/illustrated/produced*› magníficamente

law /lɔː/ *n*

A 1 [c] (rule, regulation) ley *f*; ***he's/she's a ~ unto himself/herself*** hace lo que le da la gana 2 [u] (collectively): **the ~** la ley; **to break the ~** violar *or* contravenir* *or* infringir* la ley; **it is against the ~** es ilegal *or* está prohibido por (la) ley; **to stay within the ~** actuar* dentro de la ley; **under French ~** según la ley *or* la legislación francesa; **these proposals became ~ in 1987** estas propuestas se hicieron ley en 1987; **his word is ~ in this house** en esta casa su palabra es ley; ***to lay down the ~*** dar* órdenes; ***to take the ~ into one's own hands*** tomarse la justicia por su (*or* mi *etc*) propia mano 3 [u] (as field, discipline) derecho *m*; (profession) abogacía *f*; **to enter the ~** (BrE) hacerse* abogado; (*before n*) **~ school** facultad *f* de Derecho

B [u] 1 (litigation): **to go to ~** (BrE) recurrir a los tribunales *or* a la justicia; **a court of ~** un tribunal de justicia 2 **the ~** (police) (colloq) la policía

C [c u] (code of conduct): **Islamic ~** (Relig) la ley del Corán

D [c] (scientific principle) ley *f*; **the ~s of nature** las leyes de la naturaleza

law: **~-abiding** *adj* respetuoso de la ley; **~ and order** *n* [u] (+ *sing o pl vb*) el orden público; **~breaker** *n* infractor, -tora *m,f* or transgresor, -sora *m,f* de la ley; **~ court** *n* (esp BrE) tribunal *m* (de justicia); **~ enforcement** *n* [u] *la imposición del cumplimiento de la ley*; **~-enforcement officer** agente *mf* de policía

lawful /'lɔːfəl/ *adj* ‹*ruler/heir*› legítimo; ‹*contract*› válido, legal; ‹*conduct/action*› lícito

lawfully /'lɔːfəli/ *adv* legalmente

lawless /'lɔːləs || 'lɔːlɪs/ *adj* ‹*mob/crowd*› desmandado, descontrolado; ‹*region*› anárquico, donde no rige la ley

lawlessness /'lɔːləsnəs || 'lɔːlɪsnɪs/ *n* [u] desorden *m*, anarquía *f*

law: **~maker** *n* legislador, -dora *m,f*; **~man** /'lɔːmən/ *n* (*pl* **-men** /-mən/) (AmE colloq) agente *m* del orden

lawn /lɔːn/ *n* césped *m*, pasto *m* (AmL), grama *f* (AmC, Ven)

lawn: **~mower** *n* máquina *f* de cortar el césped *or* (AmL tb) el pasto, cortadora *f* de césped *or* (AmL tb) de pasto, cortacésped *m* (Esp), cortagrama *m* (AmC, Ven); **~ tennis** *n* tenis *m* (*sobre hierba*)

lawsuit /'lɔːsuːt/ *n* juicio *m*, pleito *m*; **to bring a ~ against sb** llevar a algn a juicio, entablar una demanda contra algn

lawyer /'lɔːjər || 'lɔːjə(r)/ *n* abogado, -da *m,f*

lax /læks/ *adj* ‹*discipline/supervision*› poco estricto; ‹*morals/standards*› laxo, relajado

laxative /'læksətɪv/ *n* [c u] laxante *m*

laxity /'læksəti/, **laxness** /'læksnəs/ *n* [u] (of morals) relajación *f*, relajamiento *m*; (of rules) falta *f* de rigor, lo poco estricto

lay[1] /leɪ/ *past of* **lie**[2] *Sense* II

lay[2] (*past & past p* **laid**) *vt*

A (put, place) poner*; **~ the cloth flat on the table** extiende la tela sobre la mesa; **he laid a blanket over the sleeping child** cubrió al niño dormido con una manta

B (arrange, put down in position) ‹*bricks/carpet*› poner*, colocar*; ‹*cable/pipes*› tender*, instalar; ‹*mines*› sembrar*

C (prepare) ‹*trap/ambush*› tender*; ‹*plans*› hacer*; **to ~ the table** poner* la mesa

D (present, put forward): **to ~ a complaint against sb** formular *or* presentar una queja contra algn; ▸**claim**[1] B

E (impose): **to ~ a burden/fine on sb** imponer* una carga sobre/una multa a algn; *see also* **blame**[2] **1**, **stress**[1] **B1**, **emphasis**

F (cause to be): **one blow laid him flat on his back** de un golpe quedó tendido de espaldas en el suelo; **her statements laid her open to criticism** sus declaraciones la dejaron expuesta a críticas; ***to ~ sb low***: **he was laid low by malaria** estuvo postrado con malaria

G (Zool): **to ~ eggs** «*bird/reptile*» poner* huevos; «*fish/insects*» desovar*

H ‹*bet*› hacer*; ‹*money*› apostar*; ▸**odds A**

I (to have sex with) (sl): **to get laid** echar(se) un polvo (fam)

■ **lay** *vi*

A «*hen*» poner* huevos

B (crit) ▸**lie**[2] *Sense* II

Phrasal verbs

- **lay about** [v ▸ prep ▸ o]: **to ~ about sb** emprenderla a golpes con algn
- **lay aside** [v ▸ o ▸ adv, v ▸ adv ▸ o] 1 (put down) ‹*book/knitting*› dejar a un lado, apartar 2 (give up) ‹*pretense/differences*› olvidar, dejar de lado
- **lay down** [v ▸ o ▸ adv, v ▸ adv ▸ o] 1 (put down) ‹*tools/*

weapons› dejar (a un lado); ▸**arm¹ D** [2] (prescribe, fix) ‹*guidelines/procedure*› establecer*, determinar; ▸**law A2**

- **lay in** [v ▸ o ▸ adv, v ▸ adv ▸ o] ‹*food/water*› aprovisionarse de, proveerse* de
- **lay into** [v ▸ prep ▸ o] (colloq) (attack) emprenderla a golpes con, arremeter contra; (verbally) arremeter contra; **she really laid into me** se ensañó conmigo
- **lay off**

A [v ▸ adv ▸ o, v ▸ o ▸ adv] (AmE) despedir*; (BrE) *suspender temporalmente por falta de trabajo*

B [v ▸ adv] [v ▸ prep ▸ o] (colloq) [1] (stop pestering): **just ~ off, will you?** ¡basta ya!; **~ off me/her!** ¡déjame/déjala en paz! [2] (give up) dejar; **you should ~ off the drink** deberías dejar la bebida

- **lay on** [v ▸ adv ▸ o, v ▸ o ▸ adv]

A [1] (arrange, provide) ‹*transport/food*› hacerse* cargo de, proporcionar; ‹*entertainment*› ofrecer*, brindar [2] ‹*water/gas/electricity*› (BrE) conectar

B ***to ~ it on thick*** cargar* las tintas, exagerar

- **lay out** [v ▸ o ▸ adv, v ▸ adv ▸ o]

A [1] ‹*park/garden*› diseñar; ‹*town*› hacer* el trazado de; ‹*objects*› disponer*, arreglar [2] (Print) ‹*page*› diseñar, componer*

B (spend) gastar; (invest) invertir*

C (knock unconscious) dejar sin sentido; (in boxing) dejar KO *or* fuera de combate, noquear

D [1] ‹*dead body*› amortajar [2] ‹*clothes*› preparar, disponer*

- **lay up**

A [v ▸ o ▸ adv, v ▸ adv ▸ o] (render inactive) (*often passive*) ‹*boat/car*› guardar (*por una temporada*); **I was laid up with flu for two weeks** la gripe *or* (Col, Méx) la gripa me tuvo dos semanas en cama

B [v ▸ adv ▸ o] (store up) ‹*supplies*› almacenar, guardar; **to ~ up trouble for oneself** buscarse* *or* crearse problemas

lay³ *adj* (*before n*) [1] (secular) (Relig) ‹*organization/education*› laico; **~ preacher** predicador, -dora *m,f* seglar [2] (not expert): **the ~ reader** el lector profano en la materia, el lector no especializado

lay⁴ *n* (sl): **he's/she's a good ~** es muy bueno/buena en la cama (fam)

lay: **~about** *n* (BrE colloq) haragán, -gana *m,f*, vago, -ga *m,f* (fam); **~away** *n* [u] (AmE): **to have sth put on ~away** dejar algo reservado mediante el pago de un depósito; **~-by** *n* (BrE) área *f‡* de reposo

layer¹ /'leɪər || 'leɪə(r)/ *n* (of dust, paint, snow) capa *f*; (of rock, sediment) capa *f*, estrato *m*; **the novel has several ~s of meaning** la novela tiene varias lecturas *or* interpretaciones; (*before n*) **~ cake** pastel *m* relleno

layer² *vt*: **I had my hair ~ed** me corté el pelo en *or* (Esp) a capas, me rebajé el pelo (RPl)

layette /leɪ'et/ *n* ajuar *m* de bebé

lay: **~man** /'leɪmən/ *n* (*pl* **-men** /-mən/) [1] (non-expert): **a book written for the ~man** un libro dirigido al gran público; **in ~man's terms** en lenguaje accesible [2] (Relig) seglar *mf*, laico, -ca *m,f*; **~off** *n* (AmE) despido *m*; (BrE) *suspensión temporal por falta de trabajo*; **~out** *n* [1] (of house) distribución *f*; (of town, garden) trazado *m*, plan *m*; **the ~out of the room** la forma en que están dispuestos los muebles en la habitación [2] (in magazine, newspaper) diseño *m*, maquetación *f*; **~over** *n* (AmE) parada *f*, alto *m*; (Aviat) escala *f*

laze /leɪz/ *vi* haraganear, holgazanear; **the cat was lazing in the sun** el gato estaba tumbado al sol

lazily /'leɪzəli || 'leɪzɪli/ *adv* perezosamente

laziness /'leɪzinəs || 'leɪzɪnɪs/ *n* [u] pereza *f*, flojera *f* (fam)

lazy /'leɪzi/ *adj* **lazier, laziest** ‹*person*› perezoso, holgazán, flojo (fam); **we spent a ~ weekend on the beach** pasamos un fin de semana en la playa sin hacer nada; **to have a ~ eye** (Med) tener* un ojo perezoso

lazy: **~bones** *n* (*pl* **~bones**) (colloq) haragán, -gana *m,f*, vago, -ga *m,f* (fam), flojonazo, -za *m,f* (Chi, Méx fam), fiacún, -cuna *m,f* (RPl fam); **~ Susan** /'suːzən/ *n* (esp AmE) bandeja *f* giratoria

lb = **pound(s)**

LCD *n* = **liquid crystal display**

lead¹ *n*

Sense I /led/

A [u] (metal) plomo *m*; ***as heavy as ~***: **my feet felt as heavy as ~** los pies me pesaban como (un) plomo; (*before n*) **~ crystal** cristal *m* (*que contiene óxido de plomo y es muy preciado*); **~ poisoning** intoxicación *f* por plomo; (chronic disease) saturnismo *m*

B [c u] (in pencil) mina *f*; (*before n*) **~ pencil** lápiz *m* (de mina)

Sense II /liːd/

A (in competition) (*no pl*): **to be in/hold the ~** llevar/conservar la delantera; **to move into the ~, to take the ~** tomar la delantera; **she has a ~ of 20 meters/points over her nearest rival** le lleva 20 metros/puntos de ventaja a su rival más cercano

B (example, leadership) (*no pl*) ejemplo *m*; **to give a ~** dar* (el) ejemplo; **to follow** *o* **take sb's ~** seguir* el ejemplo de algn; **to take the ~ in doing sth** tomar la iniciativa en hacer algo

C [c] (clue) pista *f*

D [c] [1] (for dog) (BrE) correa *f*, traílla *f*; Ⓢ **dogs must be kept on a lead at all times** prohibido dejar a los perros sueltos [2] (Elec) cable *m*

E [c] [1] (main role) papel *m* principal; **the male/female ~** (role) el papel principal masculino/femenino; (person) el primer actor/la primera actriz [2] (Mus) solista *mf*; **to sing/play (the) ~** ser* la voz/el músico solista; (*before n*) ‹*guitar/singer*› principal

F [c] (cards) (*no pl*): **it was her ~** salía ella, ella era mano

lead² /liːd/ (*past & past p* **led**) *vt*

A [1] (guide, conduct) ‹*person/animal*› llevar, guiar*; **to ~ sb TO sth/sb** conducir* *or* llevar a algn A algo/ANTE algn; **they were led to safety by firemen** los bomberos los pusieron a salvo; **to ~ sb away/off** llevarse a algn; **~ the way!** ¡ve tú delante *or* (esp AmL) adelante! [2] (to a particular state, course of action): **to ~ sb into temptation** hacer* caer a algn en la tentación; **to ~ sb TO sth/+ INF: this led me to the conclusion that ...** esto me hizo llegar a la conclusión de que ...; **what led you to resign?** ¿qué te llevó a dimitir?; **I was led to believe that ...** me dieron a entender que ... [3] (influence): **he's easily led** se deja llevar fácilmente

B (head, have charge of) ‹*discussion*› conducir*; ‹*orchestra*› (conduct) (AmE) dirigir*; (play first violin in) (BrE) ser* el primer violín de; **the expedition was led by Smith** la expedición iba al mando de Smith

C [1] (be at front of) ‹*parade/attack*› encabezar*, ir* al frente de [2] (in race, competition) ‹*opponent*› aventajar; **they led the opposing team by ten points** aventajaban al equipo contrario por diez puntos, le llevaban diez puntos de ventaja al equipo contrario; **to ~ the field** (Sport) ir* en cabeza *or* a la cabeza, llevar la delantera; **they ~ the world in this kind of technology** son los líderes mundiales en este tipo de tecnología

D ‹*life*› llevar

E (play) ‹*trumps/hearts*› salir* con

■ **lead** *vi*

A **to ~ TO sth** ‹‹*road/path/steps*›› llevar *or* conducir* *or* dar* A algo; ‹‹*door*›› dar* A algo; **this discussion isn't ~ing anywhere** esta discusión no conduce a nada; **six streets ~ off the square** de la plaza salen seis calles

B [1] (be, act as leader): **you ~, we'll follow** ve delante *or* (esp AmL) adelante, que te seguimos [2] (in race, competition) ‹‹*competitor*›› ir* a la cabeza, puntear (AmL); **they are ~ing by three goals** van ganando por tres goles

C [1] (Journ): **'The Times' ~s with the budget deficit** 'The Times' dedica su artículo de fondo al déficit presupuestario [2] (in cards) salir*, ser* mano

Phrasal verbs

- **lead on**

A [v ▸ adv]: **~ on!** ¡adelante! (¡te seguimos!)

B [v ▸ o ▸ adv] (raise false hopes) engañar; **she's been ~ing him on for years** hace años que lo tiene agarrado de las narices dándole esperanzas (fam)

- **lead to** [v ▸ prep ▸ o] (result in) llevar *or* conducir* a; **one thing led to another and ...** una cosa llevó a la otra y ...
- **lead up to** [v ▸ adv ▸ prep ▸ o] [1] (precede) preceder a [2] (prepare for): **he was obviously ~ing up to something** era obvio que algo se proponía

leaded /'ledəd || 'ledɪd/ *adj* ‹*fuel*› con plomo

leaden /ˈledn̩/ *adj* (liter) 1 ‹*sky/sea*› plomizo 2 ‹*limbs*› pesado; ‹*spirit/heart*› triste, sombrío

leader /ˈliːdər || ˈliːdə(r)/ *n*
A 1 (of group, movement, political party) líder *mf*, dirigente *mf*; (of expedition) jefe, -fa *m,f*; (of gang) cabecilla *mf*, jefe, -fa *m,f*; **the L~ of the Opposition** (in UK) el líder de la oposición; **~ of the orchestra** (conductor) (AmE) director, -tora *m,f* (de orquesta); (first violin) (BrE) primer violín *mf* 2 (in race, competition) primero, -ra *m,f*; (in league) líder *m*, puntero *m*
B (BrE Journ) editorial *m*; (*before n*) **~ writer** editorialista *mf*

leadership /ˈliːdərʃɪp || ˈliːdəʃɪp/ *n* 1 [u] (direction, control — of party) liderazgo *m*, dirección *f*, jefatura *f*; (— of country) conducción *f* 2 [u] (quality) autoridad *f*, dotes *fpl* de mando; **this country needs strong ~** este país necesita una mano fuerte; (*before n*) **~ qualities** dotes *fpl* de mando 3 (leaders) (+ *sing o pl vb*) dirigentes *mpl*, directiva *f*

lead-free /ˈledˈfriː/ *adj* sin plomo

lead-in /ˈliːdɪn/ *n* [u c] **~ (TO sth)** introducción *f* (A algo)

leading /ˈliːdɪŋ/ *adj* (*before n*) 1 (principal) ‹*scientist/playwright*› destacado, importante; ‹*brand/company*› líder *adj inv*, puntero; **she played a ~ role in ...** tuvo un papel destacado en ...; **she was a ~ figure in the movement** fue una de las figuras principales del movimiento 2 (in front) ‹*runner/horse/driver*› que va a la cabeza *or* en cabeza, puntero

leading: **~ article** *n* 1 (main story) (AmE) artículo *m* de fondo (*gen en primera plana*) 2 (editorial) (BrE) editorial *m*; **~ edge** *n* 1 (Aviat) borde *m* anterior (*del ala*) 2 (forefront): (*before n*) **~-edge technology** tecnología *f* de avanzada *or* de vanguardia; **~ lady** *n* (Cin) protagonista *f*; (Theat) primera actriz *f*; **~ light** *n* estrella *f*; **~ question** *n*: *pregunta que sugiere la respuesta que se quiere obtener*

lead /liːd/: **~-off** *adj* (AmE) (in baseball) primero en turno, primero al bate; **~-off runner** primer, -mera *m,f* relevo; **~ time** *n* (before delivery) plazo *m* de entrega; **~-up** *n* **~-up (TO sth)**: **campaigning is intensifying in the ~-up to the election** la campaña se está intensificando a medida que se aproximan las elecciones

leaf¹ /liːf/ *n* (*pl* **leaves**)
A (of plant, tree) hoja *f*; **to come into ~** echar hojas; **to be in ~** tener* hojas; ***to shake o tremble like a ~*** temblar* como una hoja
B (page, sheet) hoja *f*; ***to take a ~ out of sb's book*** seguir* el ejemplo de algn; ***to turn (over) a new ~*** reformarse, hacer* borrón y cuenta nueva
C (of table) ala *f*‡; (of door, shutter) hoja *f*

leaf² *vi* (AmE) echar hojas

Phrasal verb
- **leaf through** [v ▸ prep ▸ o] hojear

leaflet¹ /ˈliːflət || ˈliːflɪt/ *n* (Print) folleto *m*; (Pol) panfleto *m*

leaflet² **-t-** *or* **-tt-** *vi* repartir folletos/panfletos
■ **leaflet** *vt* ‹*area*› repartir folletos/panfletos en

leafy /ˈliːfi/ *adj* **-fier, -fiest** ‹*boughs*› frondoso; ‹*lane*› arbolado

league /liːg/ *n*
A (alliance, association) liga *f*, asociación *f*, federación *f*; **the L~ of Nations** (Hist) la Sociedad de Naciones; ***to be in ~ (with sb)*** estar* aliado *or* confabulado (con algn)
B 1 (Sport) liga *f*; (*before n*) ‹*champion/game*› de liga; **~ standing** (AmE) posición *f* en la liga 2 (level, category): **not to be in the same ~ as sb/sth** no estar* a la misma altura *or* al mismo nivel que algn/algo; **they're in a different ~** no tienen ni punto de comparación
C (measure of distance) legua *f*

league table *n* (BrE) tabla *f* de clasificación *or* de posiciones, clasificación *f*

leak¹ /liːk/ *vi* 1 ‹‹*bucket/tank*›› gotear, perder* (RPl), salirse* (Chi, Méx); ‹‹*shoes/tent*›› dejar pasar el agua; ‹‹*faucet*›› gotear; ‹‹*pen*›› perder* tinta; **the roof is ~ing** hay una gotera/hay goteras en el techo, entra agua por el tejado 2 (escape) ‹‹*liquid*›› escaparse, salirse*; **water had ~ed through the ceiling** había entrado agua por el techo
■ **leak** *vt* 1 ‹*liquid/gas*› perder*, botar (AmL exc RPl) 2 ‹*information*› filtrar; **the report was ~ed to the press** filtraron el informe a la prensa

Phrasal verb
- **leak out** [v ▸ adv] ‹‹*news*›› filtrarse

leak² *n*
A 1 (in bucket, boat, pipe) agujero *m*; (in roof) gotera *f*; **the boat sprang a ~** el bote empezó a hacer agua 2 (escaping liquid, gas) escape *m*, fuga *f* 3 (of information) filtración *f*
B (act of urinating) (sl) (*no pl*): **to take** *o* (BrE also) **have a ~** hacer* pis (fam), mear (vulg)

leakage /ˈliːkɪdʒ/ *n* [c u] escape *m*, fuga *f*

leaky /ˈliːki/ *adj* **-kier, -kiest** agujereado; **we've got a ~ roof** tenemos goteras (en el techo)

lean¹ /liːn/ (*past & past p* **leaned** *or* (BrE also) **leant** /lent/) *vi*
1 (bend, incline): **the tower ~s to the left** la torre está inclinada hacia la izquierda; **she ~ed back in her chair** se echó hacia atrás *or* se reclinó en la silla; **don't ~ out of the window** no te asomes por la ventana; ▸**backward²** 1 2 (support oneself) apoyarse; **to ~ AGAINST sth** apoyarse CONTRA algo; **to ~ ON sth/sb** apoyarse EN algo/algn 3 (tend, incline) **to ~ TO/TOWARD sth**: **the party ~s to the left** el partido es de tendencia izquierdista; **they are ~ing toward a more conciliatory approach** se inclinan por un enfoque más conciliador
■ **lean** *vt* apoyar

Phrasal verb
- **lean on** [v ▸ prep ▸ o] (colloq) 1 (put pressure on) presionar, ejercer* presión sobre; **to ~ on sb to + INF** presionar a algn PARA QUE (+ *subj*) 2 (depend on) apoyarse en

lean² *adj* 1 ‹*person/build*› delgado, enjuto; ‹*animal*› flaco; **the company is now ~er and more efficient** la compañía ahora tiene menos personal y es más eficiente 2 ‹*meat*› magro, sin grasa 3 (poor) ‹*winter*› malo; **the ~ years** los años de escasez *or* de vacas flacas

leaning¹ /ˈliːnɪŋ/ *n* (*usu pl*) inclinación *f*, tendencia *f*

leaning² *adj* inclinado

leant /lent/ (BrE) *past & past p of* **lean¹**

lean-to /ˈliːntuː/ *n* (*pl* **-tos**) cobertizo *m* (*adosado a la casa*)

leap¹ /liːp/ (*past & past p* **leaped** *or* (BrE also) **leapt** /lept/) *vi* saltar; **to ~ over sth** saltar por encima de algo; **the dog ~ed at his throat** el perro le saltó *or* (esp Méx) le brincó al cuello; **he ~ed out of bed** se levantó (de la cama) de un salto *or* (esp Méx) de un brinco; **my heart ~ed at the news** (liter) el corazón me dio un brinco al recibir la noticia; **to ~ to sb's assistance** correr a ayudar a algn; **to ~ AT sth** ‹*at an opportunity/an offer/a chance*› no dejar pasar algo; **to ~ ON sb/sth**: **they ~ed on him** se le echaron encima, se abalanzaron sobre él; **his critics ~ed on this mistake** sus detractores se lanzaron sobre este error con ensañamiento
■ **leap** *vt* ‹*fence/stream*› saltar

leap² *n* 1 (jump) salto *m*, brinco *m*; ***by ~s and bounds*** a pasos agigantados 2 (in prices etc) subida *f* brusca

leapfrog¹ /ˈliːpfrɔːg || ˈliːpfrɒg/ *n* [u]: **to play ~** jugar* a la pídola, brincar* al burro (Méx), jugar* al rango (RPl)

leapfrog² *vi* **-gg-** saltar; **John ~ged over his brother** John saltó por encima de su hermano

leapt /lept/ (BrE) *past & past p of* **leap¹**

leap year *n* año *m* bisiesto

learn /lɜːrn || lɜːn/ (*past & past p* **learned** *or* (BrE also) **learnt**) *vt*
A 1 (gain knowledge of) aprender; **to ~ to + INF** aprender A + INF; **I've ~ed that from experience** eso lo he aprendido por propia experiencia; **you'll have to ~ to live with it** vas a tener que acostumbrarte 2 (memorize) aprender de memoria
B (become informed about) ‹*details*› enterarse de
■ **learn** *vi*
A (gain knowledge) aprender; **will he ever ~?** ¡cuándo aprenderá!
B (become informed) **to ~ ABOUT** *o* **OF sth** enterarse *or* saber* DE algo

learned /ˈlɜːrnəd || ˈlɜːnɪd/ *adj* ‹*scholar*› docto, sabio; **my ~ colleague** (BrE frml) mi distinguido colega

learner /ˈlɜːrnər || ˈlɜːnə(r)/ *n*: **he's a quick** *o* **fast ~** aprende con mucha rapidez; **he's a slow ~** tiene dificultades de aprendizaje; (*before n*) **~ (driver)** (esp BrE) *persona que está aprendiendo a conducir*

learning /ˈlɜːrnɪŋ || ˈlɜːnɪŋ/ *n* [u] 1 (knowledge) saber *m*, conocimientos *mpl*; (education) educación *f*; **book ~** aprendizaje *m* a través de los libros; **a man of ~** un erudito 2 (act) aprendizaje *m*; (*before n*) **~ difficulties** dificultades *fpl or* problemas *mpl* de aprendizaje

learnt /lɜːrnt || lɜːnt/ (BrE) *past & past p of* **learn**

lease¹ /liːs/ *n* ≈ contrato *m* de arrendamiento; (of real estate) ≈ usufructo *m*; ***to give sb/sth a new o fresh ~ on life*** *o* (BrE) **~ *of life***: **the operation has given him a new ~ on life** ha revivido con la operación; **the renovations have given the hotel a new ~ of life** el hotel ha quedado como nuevo con los arreglos

lease² *vt* 1 **~ (out)** (grant use of) arrendar*, dar* en arriendo; ‹*real estate*› dar* en usufructo 2 (hold under lease) arrendar*, tomar en arriendo; ‹*real estate*› tener* el usufructo de

lease: **~back** *n* cesión-arrendamiento *f*, retroarriendo *m*; **~hold** *n* [u c] arrendamiento *m*; **~holder** *n* arrendatario, -ria *m,f*

leash /liːʃ/ *n* correa *f*, traílla *f*; ***to keep sb on a ~*** mantener* *or* tener* a algn a raya; ***to strain at the ~*** (be impatient) morirse* de impaciencia; (lit) «*dog*» tirar de la correa, jalar la traílla *or* correa (AmL exc CS)

least¹ /liːst/ *adj*

A (*superl of* **little¹** *Sense* **II**): **she has the ~ money** es quien menos dinero tiene

B 1 (smallest, slightest) más mínimo; **I'm not the ~ bit interested** no me interesa en lo más mínimo; **that's the ~ of my worries** eso es lo que menos me preocupa 2 (lowest, humblest) (liter) más humilde

least² *pron*

A (*superl of* **little²**): **to say the ~** por no decir más; **it's the ~ I can do** es lo menos que puedo hacer

B (in adv phrases) **at least** por lo menos, como mínimo; **he can't afford it; at ~ that's what he says** no puede permitírselo; al menos eso es lo que dice; **in the least** en lo más mínimo; **am I disturbing you? — not in the ~** ¿te molesto? — en lo más mínimo *or* en absoluto

least³ *adv*

A (*superl of* **little³**): **~ of all you** tú menos que nadie; **when you ~ expect it** cuando menos te lo esperas

B (*before adj, adv*) menos; **John is the ~ intelligent** John es el menos inteligente

leastways /ˈliːstweɪz/, **leastwise** /-waɪz/ *adv* (colloq) por lo menos, al menos

leather /ˈleðər || ˈleðə(r)/ *n* 1 [u] (material) cuero *m*, piel *f* (Esp, Méx); (*before n*) **~ goods** artículos *mpl* de cuero *or* (Esp, Méx tb) de piel 2 [c] (chamois) (BrE) gamuza *f*

leathery /ˈleðəri/ *adj* ‹*skin*› curtido, áspero; ‹*steak*› correoso, duro como suela de zapatos (fam)

leave¹ /liːv/ *n*

A [u c] (authorized absence) permiso *m*, licencia *f* (esp AmL); (Mil) licencia *f*, permiso *m*; **one year's ~ of absence** un año de permiso *or* (esp AmL) de licencia *or* (Esp) de excedencia; **to be/go on ~** estar*/salir* de permiso *or* (esp AmL) de licencia

B [u] (permission) (frml) permiso *m*; **without so much as a by your ~** (colloq) sin ni siquiera pedir permiso

C [u] (departure) (frml): **to take ~ of sb** despedirse* de algn; **have you taken ~ of your senses?** ¿te has vuelto loco?

leave² (*past & past p* **left**) *vt*

A 1 (go away from): **she ~s home/the office at 6** sale de casa/de la oficina a las 6; **I left her reading a book** la dejé leyendo un libro; **may I ~ the table?** ¿puedo levantarme de la mesa?; **what are you going to do when you ~ school?** ¿qué vas a hacer cuando termines el colegio?; **he left school at 16** dejó *or* abandonó los estudios a los 16 años; **she left home at the age of 17** se fue de casa a los 17 años 2 (withdraw from) ‹*profession/organization/politics*› dejar; **to ~ sth FOR sth** dejar algo POR algo

B (abandon) dejar; **she left her husband for another man** dejó a su marido por otro (hombre); **he was left for dead** lo dieron por muerto; **they left him to die in the desert** lo abandonaron a su suerte en el desierto

C 1 (deposit in specified place) dejar; **~ your key at the desk** deje la llave en recepción; **to ~ sth FOR sb** dejarle algo A algn 2 (not take — deliberately) dejar; (— inadvertently) olvidarse de, dejarse 3 (not eat) ‹*food*› dejar

D (allow, cause to remain) dejar; **please ~ the window open** por favor dejen la ventana abierta; **she left her meal untouched** no probó la comida; **some things are better left unsaid** es mejor callar *or* no decir ciertas cosas; **let's ~ it at that** dejémoslo así

E (have as aftereffect) ‹*stain/scar*› dejar; **the hurricane left a trail of devastation** el huracán dejó la mayor desolación a su paso

F 1 (not attend to, postpone) dejar; **~ the dishes for later** deja los platos para más tarde 2 (not disturb or interfere) dejar; **~ me alone/in peace!** ¡déjame tranquilo/en paz!; **I was about to start cooking — I'll ~ you to it, then** iba a ponerme a cocinar — bueno, pues te dejo; **to ~ sth/sb to + INF** dejar algo/a algn + INF *or* QUE (+ *subj*); **~ her to finish on her own** déjala terminar *or* que termine sola; ▸**alone¹ 2**

G 1 (entrust) **to ~ sth TO sb/sth**: **~ it to me!** ¡déjalo por mi cuenta!; **we must ~ nothing to chance** no debemos dejar nada (librado) al azar 2 (allow, cause sb to do) dejar; **the teacher left us with a lot to do** el profesor nos dejó mucho trabajo; **to ~ sb to + INF** dejar QUE algn (+ *subj*); **he left his secretary to make the arrangements** dejó que su secretaria hiciera los preparativos

H 1 (Math): **6 from 10 ~s 4** si a 10 le quitamos 6, quedan 4 2 (after deduction, elimination): **that only ~s you and me** con eso sólo quedamos tú y yo; **there isn't much time left** no queda mucho tiempo 3 (make available) dejar; **~ a space** deja un espacio; **there's nothing left for it but to give in** no queda más remedio que ceder

I 1 (bequeath) **to ~ sth TO sb/sth** ‹*money/property*› dejar(le) algo A algn/algo 2 (after bereavement) dejar; **he ~s a wife and two sons** deja esposa y dos hijos

■ **leave** *vi* irse*, marcharse (esp Esp); **the train ~s at 5 o'clock** el tren sale a las 5 en punto; **he's already left for the airport** ya ha salido para el aeropuerto

Phrasal verbs

- **leave aside** [v ▸ o ▸ adv, v ▸ adv ▸ o] dejar de lado
- **leave behind** [v ▸ o ▸ adv, v ▸ adv ▸ o] 1 (not take or bring — deliberately) dejar; (— inadvertently) olvidarse de, dejarse 2 (abandon) ‹*worries/cares*› dejar atrás 3 (in race, at school) ‹*opponent/classmate*› dejar atrás; **slow learners get left behind** los niños con problemas de aprendizaje se quedan atrás *or* rezagados
- **leave in** [v ▸ o ▸ adv, v ▸ adv ▸ o] no omitir
- **leave off**

A [v ▸ adv] [v ▸ prep ▸ o] (discontinue) dejar; **I just carried on where she had left off** lo que hice fue continuar con su trabajo; **this book continues where the last one left off** este libro retoma el hilo del anterior; **where did we ~ off last time?** ¿dónde quedamos la última vez?; **~ off!** (colloq) ¡basta ya!; **to ~ off -ING** dejar *or* parar DE + INF

B [v ▸ o ▸ prep ▸ o] (not include) no incluir*

- **leave on** [v ▸ o ▸ adv, v ▸ adv ▸ o] 1 ‹*light/machine/television*› dejar encendido *or* (AmL tb) prendido 2 (keep wearing) no quitarse
- **leave out**

A [v ▸ o ▸ adv, v ▸ adv ▸ o] [v ▸ o ▸ adv (▸ prep ▸ o)] 1 (omit) omitir; **it won't taste right if you ~ out the garlic** no va a quedar bien si no le pones ajo 2 (exclude) excluir*, no incluir* 3 (not involve) **to ~ sb out OF sth** no meter a algn EN algo

B [v ▸ o ▸ adv] 1 (leave outside) dejar fuera *or* (esp AmL) afuera 2 (not put away) ‹*clothes/toys*› no guardar 3 (leave available) dejar preparado

- **leave over** [v ▸ o ▸ adv, v ▸ adv ▸ o] (*usu pass*): **tomorrow we can eat what's left over** mañana podemos comer lo que sobre *or* quede

leaves /liːvz/ *pl of* **leaf¹**

leave-taking /ˈliːvˌteɪkɪŋ/ *n* despedida *f*

leaving /ˈliːvɪŋ/ *adj* (*before n*) ‹*present*› de despedida; **~ party** despedida *f*

Lebanese /ˈlebəˈniːz/ *adj* libanés

Lebanon /ˈlebənɑːn || ˈlebənən/ *n* (el) Líbano

lecherous /ˈletʃərəs/ *adj* libidinoso, lascivo

lectern /ˈlektərn || ˈlektɜːn/ *n* atril *m*; (in church) facistol *m*

lecture¹ /ˈlektʃər || ˈlektʃə(r)/ *n* 1 (public address) conferencia *f*, (more informal) charla *f*, (Educ) clase *f*; (*before n*) **~ hall** sala *f* de conferencias; **~ notes** (Educ) apuntes *mpl* (de clase); (for public address) notas *fpl*; **~ theater** auditorio *m*, aula *f* magna 2 (talking-to) sermón *m*

lecture² *vi* (Educ) dar* clase, dictar clase (AmL frml), hacer* clase (Chi); **to ~ ON sth/TO sb** dar* una conferencia/clase SOBRE algo/A algn; **to ~ IN sth** dar* *or* (Chi) hacer* clase DE algo, dictar clase DE algo (AmL frml) (*en la universidad*)

■ **lecture** *vt* (scold, reprove) sermonear, darle* un sermón a

l

lecturer /ˈlektʃərər || ˈlektʃərə(r)/ *n* [1] (speaker) conferenciante *mf*, conferencista *mf* (AmL) [2] (esp BrE Educ) profesor universitario, profesora universitaria *m,f*

led /led/ *past & past p of* **lead**[2]

ledge /ledʒ/ *n* [1] (on wall) cornisa *f*; (*window* ~) (exterior) alféizar *m or* antepecho *m* (de la ventana); (interior) repisa *f* (de la ventana) [2] (on cliff) saliente *m or f*

ledger /ˈledʒər || ˈledʒə(r)/ *n* libro *m* de contabilidad

lee /liː/ *n*

A [u] (Naut) sotavento *m*

B **lees** *pl* (sediment) posos *mpl*

leech /liːtʃ/ *n* sanguijuela *f*

leek /liːk/ *n* puerro *m*

leer[1] /lɪr || lɪə(r)/ *vi* **to ~ AT sb** lanzarle* una mirada lasciva a algn

leer[2] *n* mirada *f* lasciva

leery /ˈlɪri || ˈlɪəri/ *adj* **-rier, -riest** receloso; **to be ~ OF sb/sth**: **I'm very ~ of them/their intentions** desconfío *or* recelo de ellos/de sus intenciones

leeward /ˈliːwərd || ˈliːwəd/ *n* [u] sotavento *m*; **to ~** a sotavento

leeway /ˈliːweɪ/ *n* [u] (margin of freedom): **I am given a lot of ~** me dan mucha libertad de acción; **there isn't much ~ in the budget** el presupuesto tiene poco margen de flexibilidad

left[1] /left/ *past & past p of* **leave**[2]

left[2] *n*

A [1] (left side) izquierda *f*; **on the ~** a la izquierda; **the one on the ~** el/la de la izquierda; **to drive on the ~** manejar *or* (esp Esp) conducir* por la izquierda; **keep (to the) ~** mantenga su izquierda; **to be on** *o* **to the ~ of sb** *o* **on sb's ~** estar* a la izquierda de algn [2] (left turn): **take the next ~** tome *or* (esp Esp) coja la próxima a la izquierda; **to make** *o* (BrE) **take a ~** girar *or* torcer* *or* doblar a la izquierda [3] (Sport) (hand) izquierda *f*; (blow) golpe *m* de izquierda, izquierdazo *m*

B (Pol) **the ~** la izquierda

left[3] *adj* (*before n*) ‹*side/ear/shoe*› izquierdo

left[4] *adv* ‹*turn/look*› a *or* hacia la izquierda; ***~ and right*** *o* (BrE) ***~, right and centre*** (colloq): **he was hitting out ~ and right** repartía golpes a diestra y siniestra *or* (Esp) a diestro y siniestro (fam); **complaints are coming in ~ and right** nos llegan quejas de todos lados

left-click /ˈleftˈklɪk/ *vi* hacer* clic *or* (fam) cliquear con el botón izquierdo *or* primario del ratón,

left: **~ field** *n* (in baseball) [1] (area) jardín *m* izquierdo; ***to be (out) in ~ field*** (AmE) «*person*» estar* *or* vivir en las nubes; ***to come from*** *o* ***out of ~ field*** no venir* a cuento [2] (position): **to play ~ field** jugar* de jardinero izquierdo; **~-hand** *adj* (*before n*) de la izquierda; **on the ~-hand side** a mano izquierda; **the car has ~-hand drive** el coche tiene el volante a la izquierda; **~-handed** /ˈleftˈhændəd || ˌleftˈhændɪd/ *adj* ‹*person*› zurdo; ‹*scissors/tool*› para zurdos; **~-luggage (office)** /ˈleftˈlʌgɪdʒ/ *n* (BrE) consigna *f* de equipajes; **~over** *adj* (*before n*) sobrante; **~overs** /ˈleftˌəʊvərz || ˈleftˌəʊvəz/ *pl n* sobras *fpl*, restos *mpl*; **~ wing** *n* [1] (Pol) (+ *sing or pl vb*) **the ~ wing** la izquierda, el ala izquierda [2] (Sport) banda *f or* ala *f*‡ izquierda; **~-wing** /ˈleftˈwɪŋ/ *adj* (Pol) de izquierda *or* (Esp) izquierdas, izquierdista; **~-winger** /ˈleftˈwɪŋər || ˌleftˈwɪŋə(r)/ *n* [1] (Pol) izquierdista *mf* [2] (Sport) extremo *mf or* alero *mf* izquierdo

lefty /ˈlefti/ *n* (*pl* **-ties**) (colloq) (Pol) rojillo, -lla *m,f*

leg[1] /leg/ *n*

A (Anat) (of person) pierna *f*; (of animal, bird) pata *f*; ***he/she can talk the hind ~s off a donkey!*** (colloq) habla como una cotorra *or* (hasta) por los codos (fam); ***not to have a ~ to stand on*** (colloq) llevar todas las de perder; ***to be on one's/its last ~s*** (colloq) estar* en las últimas (fam); ***to pull sb's ~*** (colloq) tomarle el pelo a algn (fam); ***to stretch one's ~s*** estirar las piernas; (*before n*) ‹*muscle*› de la pierna; ‹*injury*› en la pierna

B [1] (Culin) (of lamb, pork) pierna *f*, pernil *m*; (of chicken) pata *f*, muslo *m* [2] (Clothing) pierna *f*; (measurement) entrepierna *f* [3] (of chair, table) pata *f*

C (stage — of competition, race) manga *f*, vuelta *f*; (— of journey) etapa *f*

leg[2] *vt* **-gg-**: ***to ~ it*** (colloq) (go on foot) ir* a pata (fam); (run) ir* corriendo

legacy /ˈlegəsi/ *n* (*pl* **-cies**) legado *m*; **the hole in the wall is a ~ from the previous tenant** (hum) el agujero en la pared lo heredamos del inquilino anterior (hum)

legal /ˈliːgəl/ *adj*

A [1] (allowed) legal; ‹*tackle/move*› reglamentario [2] (founded upon law) ‹*contract/requirement/constraint/rights*› legal; **he is the ~ owner** es el legítimo propietario; **the contract is ~ and binding** el contrato tiene validez legal y es obligatorio para las partes

B (relating to legal system, profession) (*before n*) ‹*system/adviser/problem*› jurídico, legal; ‹*department*› jurídico; **~ costs** costas *fpl*; **the ~ profession** (lawyers) los abogados; (professional activity) la abogacía; **to seek ~ advice** consultar a un abogado; **we will be forced to take ~ action** nos veremos obligados a poner el asunto en manos de nuestro(s) abogado(s)

legal aid *n* [u] (in UK) asistencia *f* jurídica *or* legal, ≈ privilegio *m* de pobreza (*en Chi*)

legalese /ˈliːgəˈliːz/ *n* [u] (colloq & pej) jerigonza *f or* jerga *f* legal *or* de los abogados

legal holiday *n* (AmE) día *m* festivo oficial, feriado *m* oficial (esp AmL)

legality /liːˈgæləti/ *n* [u] legalidad *f*

legalization /ˈliːgələˈzeɪʃən || ˌliːgəlaɪˈzeɪʃən/ *n* [u] legalización *f*

legalize /ˈliːgəlaɪz/ *vt* legalizar*; ‹*cannabis*› despenalizar* el uso de

legally /ˈliːgəli/ *adv* legalmente; (*indep*) desde un punto de vista legal

legal tender *n* [u] moneda *f* de curso legal

legation /lɪˈgeɪʃən/ *n* legación *f*

legend /ˈledʒənd/ *n*

A [1] [c u] (story) leyenda *f* [2] [c] (person) mito *m*, leyenda *f*; **she was a ~ in her own lifetime** (set phrase) ya en vida era un mito *or* una leyenda

B [c] [1] (inscription) leyenda *f* [2] (on map) signos *mpl* convencionales; (on chart) clave *f*

legendary /ˈledʒənderi || ˈledʒəndri/ *adj* legendario

-legged /ˈlegəd || ˈlegɪd, legd/ *suff*: **long~** ‹*person*› de piernas largas; ‹*animal*› de patas largas; *see also* **bandy-legged, cross-legged** *etc*

leggings /ˈlegɪŋz/ *pl n* [1] (pants, trousers) leggings *mpl*, mallas *fpl*, calzas *fpl* (RPl) [2] (for lower leg) polainas *fpl*

leggy /ˈlegi/ *adj* **-gier, -giest** ‹*boy/girl*› de piernas largas, zanquilargo (fam)

legibility /ˈledʒəˈbɪləti/ *n* [u] legibilidad *f*

legible /ˈledʒəbəl/ *adj* legible

legibly /ˈledʒəbli/ *adv* de manera legible

legion[1] /ˈliːdʒən/ *n* legión *f*

legion[2] *adj* (frml) (*pred*): **the problems are ~** los problemas son innumerables

legionnaire /ˈliːdʒəˈner || ˌliːdʒəˈneə(r)/ *n* legionario *m*

Legionnaires' disease *n* [u] enfermedad *f* del legionario, legionella *f*

legislate /ˈledʒəsleɪt || ˈledʒɪsleɪt/ *vi* legislar

legislation /ˈledʒəsˈleɪʃən || ˌledʒɪsˈleɪʃən/ *n* [u] legislación *f*; **under existing ~** de acuerdo a *or* conforme a la legislación vigente; **a new piece of ~** una nueva ley (*or* un nuevo proyecto de ley *etc*)

legislative /ˈledʒəsleɪtɪv || ˈledʒɪslətɪv/ *adj* (*before n*) legislativo

legislator /ˈledʒəsleɪtər || ˈledʒɪsleɪtə(r)/ *n* legislador, -dora *m,f*

legislature /ˈledʒɪsleɪtʃər || ˈledʒɪsleɪtʃə(r)/ *n* asamblea *f* legislativa

legit /lɪˈdʒɪt/ *adj* (colloq) legal

legitimate /lɪˈdʒɪtəmət || lɪˈdʒɪtɪmət/ *adj* [1] (lawful) ‹*government/authority/claim*› legítimo; ‹*business*› legal; ‹*tackle/move*› reglamentario [2] (reasonable) ‹*excuse/complaint/interest*› legítimo, justificado

legitimately /lɪˈdʒɪtəmətli || lɪˈdʒɪtɪmətli/ *adv* [1] (lawfully) legítimamente [2] (reasonably): **he says, ~ in my opinion, that ...** dice, y en mi opinión con razón, que ...

legitimize /lɪˈdʒɪtəmaɪz || lɪˈdʒɪtɪmaɪz/ *vt* legitimar

legroom /ˈlegruːm, -rʊm/ *n* [u] espacio *m* para las piernas

legume /ˈleɡjuːm/ *n* legumbre *f*

leg: **~ up** *n* (colloq) (*no pl*): **to give sb a ~ up** ayudar a algn a subirse; **~work** *n* [u] (colloq): **to do the ~work** hacer* el trabajo preliminar *or* de campo

leisure /ˈliːʒər || ˈleʒə(r)/ *n* [u] tiempo *m* libre; **to live** *o* **lead a life of ~** llevar una vida de ocio; **now I'm a lady of ~** (hum) ahora me doy la gran vida; **read it at your ~** léalo cuando le venga bien; (*before n*) ‹*activity*› de tiempo libre; **~ center** (AmE) centro *m* recreativo; **~ centre** (BrE) centro *m* deportivo, polideportivo *m*; **~ time** tiempo *m* libre, ratos *mpl* libres; **~ wear** ropa *f* deportiva

leisurely /ˈliːʒərli || ˈleʒəli/ *adj* lento, pausado; **at a ~ pace** sin prisas

leitmotif, leitmotiv /ˈlaɪtməʊtiːf/ *n* leitmotiv *m*, tema *m* principal

lemming /ˈlemɪŋ/ *n* lemming *m* (*roedor del norte de Europa*)

lemon /ˈlemən/ *n*

A 1 [c u] (fruit) limón *m*, limón *m* francés (Méx, Ven); (*before n*) ‹*peel/juice/soufflé*› de limón; **~ squeezer** (BrE) exprimidor *m* (de limones), exprimelimones *m*; **~ tea** té *m* con limón 2 [c] **~ (tree)** limonero *m* 3 [u] (color) amarillo *m* limón; (*before n*) amarillo limón *adj inv*

B [c] (colloq) 1 (dud, failure) porquería *f* (fam) 2 (fool) (BrE) idiota *mf*

lemonade /ˈleməˈneɪd/ *n* [c u] 1 (with fresh lemons) limonada *f* 2 (fizzy drink) (BrE) (bebida *f*) gaseosa *f*

lemon: **~ cheese**, **~ curd** *n* [u] crema *f* de limón (*en conserva*); **~ sole** *n* [u] *tipo de platija similar al lenguado*; **~-yellow** /ˈlemənˈjeləʊ/ *adj* (*pred* **~ yellow**) amarillo limón *adj inv*

lend /lend/ (*past & past p* **lent**) *vt* 1 (loan) prestar, dejar (Esp fam); **to ~ sth TO sb** prestarle algo A algn 2 (give) **to ~ sth TO sth** darle* algo A algo; **this ~s an air of mystery to the scene** esto le da un aire de misterio a la escena

■ *v refl* **to ~ itself TO sth** prestarse A algo

Phrasal verb

• **lend out** [v ▸ o ▸ adv, v ▸ adv ▸ o] prestar, dejar (Esp fam); **to ~ sth out TO sb** prestarle *or* (Esp tb) dejarle algo A algn

lender /ˈlendər || ˈlendə(r)/ *n* (institution) entidad *f* crediticia; (person) prestamista *mf*

lending library /ˈlendɪŋ/ *n* biblioteca *f* pública (*en la que se permite sacar libros en préstamo*)

length /leŋθ/ *n*

A [u] 1 (of line, surface) longitud *f*, largo *m*; (of sleeve, coat) largo *m*; **it's the wrong ~** es demasiado largo/corto; **it's 5m in ~** mide *or* tiene 5 metros de largo; **he traveled the ~ and breadth of the country** viajó a lo largo y (a lo) ancho del país; **the beach is polluted along its entire ~** la playa está contaminada en toda su extensión; ***to go to great/any ~s***: **he went to great ~s to send me the money** hizo todo lo posible para enviarme el dinero; **he'd go to any ~s to get what he wants** es capaz de hacer cualquier cosa con tal de obtener lo que se propone 2 (of book, list) extensión *f*

B [u] 1 (duration) (of movie, play) duración *f*; **after a considerable ~ of time** después de mucho tiempo; **the ~ of his absence** lo prolongado de su ausencia; **~ of service** antigüedad *f* (*en el trabajo*) 2 **at length** (finally) finalmente, por fin; (for a long time) extensamente, por extenso; (in detail) detenidamente, con detenimiento; **to talk at ~** hablar largo y tendido

C [c] (section — of wood, pipe) trozo *m*; (— of river, road) tramo *m*, parte *f*; **a ~ of cloth** un corte de tela, una tela

D [c] (Sport) 1 (in swimming) largo *m* 2 (in horse, dog racing) cuerpo *m*; (in rowing) largo *m*

lengthen /ˈleŋθən/ *vt* ‹*skirt/novel*› alargar*; ‹*line/speech/visit*› alargar*, prolongar*

■ **lengthen** *vi* «*day/shadow*» alargarse*; **the odds have ~ed** las probabilidades han disminuido

lengthwise /ˈleŋθwaɪz/, (esp BrE) **lengthways** /-weɪz/ *adv* a lo largo, longitudinalmente

lengthy /ˈleŋθi/ *adj* **-thier -thiest** (long) largo, prolongado; (tedious) largo y pesado

leniency /ˈliːniənsi/, **lenience** /-əns/ *n* [u] **~ (TO** *o* **TOWARD sb)** indulgencia *f or* (frml) lenidad *f* (CON *or* HACIA algn)

lenient /ˈliːniənt/ *adj* ‹*attitude/view*› indulgente; ‹*sentence*› poco severo; **to be ~ TO** *o* **TOWARD** *o* **WITH sb** ser* indulgente *or* benévolo CON algn

lens /lenz/ *n* (*pl* **lenses**) 1 (Opt) lente *f* 2 (for magnifying) lupa *f* 3 (in spectacles) cristal *m* 4 ▸**contact lens** 5 (Phot) lente *f*; (compound) objetivo *m*

lent /lent/ *past & past p of* **lend**

Lent /lent/ *n* Cuaresma *f*

lentil /ˈlentl̩/ *n* lenteja *f*

Leo /ˈliːəʊ/ *n* (*pl* **-os**) 1 (sign) (*no art*) Leo 2 [c] (person) Leo *or* leo *mf*; *see also* **Aquarius**

leopard /ˈlepərd || ˈlepəd/ *n* leopardo *m*

leotard /ˈliːətɑːrd || ˈliːətɑːd/ *n* malla *f*

leper /ˈlepər || ˈlepə(r)/ *n* (Med) leproso, -sa *m,f*; **he's a social ~** lo tratan como a un paria; (*before n*) **~ colony** leprosería *f or* (CS) leprosario *m*

leprechaun /ˈleprəkɔːn/ *n* duende *m* (*en la leyenda irlandesa*)

leprosy /ˈleprəsi/ *n* [u] lepra *f*

lesbian¹ /ˈlezbiən/ *n* lesbiana *f*

lesbian² *adj* lesbiano, lésbico

lesbianism /ˈlezbiənɪzəm/ *n* [u] lesbianismo *m*

lesion /ˈliːʒən/ *n* lesión *f*

less¹ /les/ *adj* (*comp of* **little¹** *Sense* **II**) menos; **~ and ~ money** cada vez menos dinero; **of ~ importance** de menor importancia; **no ~ a person than the Queen** nada menos que la Reina, ni más ni menos que la Reina

less² *pron* (*comp of* **little²**) menos; **a sum of ~ than $1,000** una suma inferior a los 1.000 dólares

less³ *adv* (*comp of* **little³**) menos; **I see them ~ often than I'd like** los veo menos de lo que me gustaría; **the situation is no ~ serious than it was** la situación sigue siendo tan grave como antes; **I was none the ~ grateful for it** no por ello te (*or* se *etc*) lo agradecí menos

less⁴ *prep* menos

-less /ləs || lɪs/ *suff* sin; **hat~** sin sombrero

lessee /leˈsiː/ *n* arrendatario, -taria *m,f*

lessen /ˈlesn̩/ *vt* ‹*pain*› aliviar, atenuar*; ‹*cost/risk*› reducir*, disminuir*

■ **lessen** *vi* «*noise*» disminuir*; «*pain*» aliviarse; «*interest*» decrecer*, menguar*

lessening /ˈlesn̩ɪŋ/ *n* (*no pl*) disminución *f*, reducción *f*

lesser /ˈlesər || ˈlesə(r)/ *adj* (*before n*) menor; **to a ~ extent** *o* **degree** en menor grado; **a ~ man than him would have given up the struggle** un hombre de menos valía hubiera abandonado la lucha; ▸**evil²**

lesson /ˈlesn̩/ *n*

A (Educ) 1 (class, period) clase *f*; **to give ~s in sth** dar* *or* (Chi) hacer* clases de algo; **to take ~s in sth** tomar clases de algo, dar* clases de algo (Esp) 2 (in textbook) lección *f*

B (from experience) lección *f*; **to learn one's ~** aprender la lección, escarmentar*; **she needs to be taught a ~** hay que darle una lección; **that'll teach you a ~!** ¡que te sirva de lección *or* de escarmiento!

C (Relig) lectura *f*

lessor /leˈsɔːr || leˈsɔː(r)/ *n* arrendador, -dora *m,f*

lest /lest/ *conj* (liter) 1 (to prevent) no sea que (+ *subj*); **hide, ~ they discover you** escóndete, no sea que *or* no vaya a ser que te descubran; **~ we forget** para que no olvidemos 2 (in case): **~ he be a spy** por si acaso fuera un espía

let¹ /let/ *n* (BrE) contrato *m* de arrendamiento *m*; **they specialize in holiday ~s** se especializan en el alquiler *or* el arrendamiento de residencias de vacaciones

let² (*pres p* **letting**; *past & past p* **let**) *vt*

A (*no pass*) 1 (allow to) dejar; **to ~ sb/sth + INF**: **~ her speak** déjala hablar; **he ~ his hair grow** se dejó crecer el pelo; **~ me help you** deja que te ayude; **don't ~ me keep you** no te quiero entretener; **~ me see** ¿a ver?, deja *or* déjame ver; **you shouldn't ~ her talk to you like that** no deberías permitir que te hable así; **don't ~ me catch you here again!** ¡que no te vuelva a pescar por aquí!; ▸**be** *Sense* **II A1, drop²** *vt* **E, rip¹** *vi* **B** 2 (cause to, make) **to ~ sb/sth + INF**: **~ me have your answer tomorrow!** dame la respuesta mañana; **~ me know if there are any problems** avísame si hay algún problema; **he ~ it be known that ...** hizo saber que ... 3 **to ~ go** soltar*;

l

~ **go! you're hurting me!** ¡suelta *or* suéltame, que me haces daño!; ~ **go of my hand!** ¡suéltame la mano!; ***to ~ sb go*** (release sb) soltar* a algn; (give sb permission to go) dejar ir a algn; (fire sb) (euph) despedir* a algn; ***to ~ oneself go*** (enjoy oneself) soltarse*, soltarse* la melena (fam); (neglect oneself) abandonarse; ***to ~ sth go*** ‹*garden*› descuidar algo; (let sth pass) **we'll ~ it go this time** por esta vez (que) pase, por esta vez lo pasaremos por alto

B (+ *adv compl*): **to ~ sth/sb by** *o* **past** dejar pasar algo/a algn; **she ~ herself into the house** abrió la puerta y entró en la casa; *see also* **let in, off, out**

C [*Used to form 1st pers pl imperative*] **1** (in suggestions): **~'s go** vamos, vámonos; **~'s dance!** ¡vamos a bailar!; **don't ~'s** *o* **~'s not argue** no discutamos **2** (in requests, proposals, commands): **if we were to sell it for, ~'s say, $500** si lo vendiéramos por, digamos, $500; **~'s be honest!** ¡seamos honestos!; **~'s be quite clear about this** que esto quede bien claro; **~ us pray** (frml) oremos

D [*Used to form 3rd pers imperative, gen translated by* QUE + SUBJ *in Spanish*] **1** (in commands): **~ that be a lesson to you** que te sirva de lección; **never ~ it be said that ...** que no se diga que ... **2** (expressing defiance, warning, threat): **just ~ them try!** ¡que se atrevan! **3** (in suppositions): **~ x equal 4** supongamos que x es igual a 4

E (rent) (esp BrE) alquilar; **to ~ sth TO sb** alquilarle algo A algn; **⊜ to let** se alquila

(Phrasal verbs)

• **let down**

(Sense I) [v ▸ o ▸ adv, v ▸ adv ▸ o]

A **1** (lower) ‹*rope/bucket*› bajar; ***to ~ sb down gently*** suavizarle* el golpe a algn; ▸ **hair A** **2** (lengthen) ‹*skirt*› alargar*; (lower) ‹*hem*› bajar, sacar **3** (deflate) ‹*tire/balloon*› desinflar

B (disappoint) fallar, defraudar; **you're ~ting your parents down by giving up your studies** al dejar los estudios estás decepcionando *or* defraudando a tus padres; **he always ~s the side down** siempre nos (*or* los *etc*) hace quedar mal; **her spelling ~s her down** su ortografía no le hace justicia a su trabajo

(Sense II) [v ▸ adv] (slow up) (AmE colloq) aflojar (fam), aminorar la marcha

• **let in** [v ▸ o ▸ adv, v ▸ adv ▸ o]

A **1** (allow to enter) dejar entrar; (open the door for) abrirle* la puerta a, hacer* pasar; **here's the key, ~ yourself in** aquí tienes la llave, abre y entra; ***to ~ oneself in for sth***: **she doesn't know what she's ~ting herself in for** ¡no sabe en lo que se está metiendo!; ***to ~ sb in on sth***: **I'll ~ you in on a secret** te voy a contar *or* confiar un secreto **2** (allow to penetrate) ‹*light/air*› dejar entrar

B (release) ‹*clutch*› soltar*

• **let off**

(Sense I)

A **1** [v ▸ o ▸ adv] (not punish, forgive) perdonar; **to ~ sb off WITH sth**: **she was ~ off with a reprimand** sólo le hicieron una amonestación **2** [v ▸ o ▸ adv] [v ▸ o ▸ prep ▸ o] (exempt, excuse from) perdonar; **I'll ~ you off the 80 cents** te perdono los 80 centavos

B [v ▸ o ▸ adv] (allow to go) dejar salir

(Sense II) [v ▸ o ▸ adv, v ▸ adv ▸ o]

A (allow to get off) ‹*passenger*› dejar bajar

B (fire, explode) ‹*fireworks*› hacer* estallar; ‹*rocket/cracker*› tirar

• **let on**

A [v ▸ adv] [v ▸ adv ▸ o] (reveal): **don't ~ on!** no digas nada, no levantes la liebre *or* (RPl) la perdiz; **to ~ on ABOUT sth (TO sb)**: **you mustn't ~ on about this to Jim** no le vayas a decir nada de esto a Jim; **to ~ on (THAT)**: **don't ~ on (that) you know me!** no digas que me conoces

B [v ▸ o ▸ adv, v ▸ adv ▸ o] ‹*passenger*› dejar subir

• **let out**

(Sense I) [v ▸ o ▸ adv, v ▸ adv ▸ o]

A (disclose) ‹*secret*› revelar; **she inadvertently ~ out the fact that ...** se le escapó sin darse cuenta que ...

B (rent out) (esp BrE) alquilar

C (make wider) ‹*skirt/dress*› ensanchar, agrandar

(Sense II) [v ▸ o ▸ adv, v ▸ adv ▸ o] [v ▸ o ▸ adv (▸ prep ▸ o)] **1** (allow to leave) dejar salir; **~ me out of here!** ¡ábreme!, ¡déjame salir de aquí!; **who ~ the canary out?** ¿quién soltó al canario?; **I'll ~ myself out** no me acompañes, salgo solo **2** (allow to get out — from bus) dejar bajar; (— from taxi) dejar **3** (allow to escape) ‹*water/smoke*› dejar salir; **you're ~ting the heat out** estás dejando salir *or* escapar el calor; **someone ~ the air out of my tires** alguien me desinfló los neumáticos

(Sense III)

A [v ▸ adv ▸ o] (utter) ‹*scream/yell*› soltar*, pegar*; ‹*guffaw*› soltar*

B [v ▸ adv] (be dismissed) (AmE colloq) ‹‹*school*›› terminar

• **let up** [v ▸ adv] **1** (diminish, slacken) ‹‹*wind/storm*›› amainar; ‹‹*pressure/work*›› disminuir*, aflojar (fam); **the rain is beginning to ~ up** está lloviendo menos **2** (relax efforts): **you can't afford to ~ up now!** no puedes aflojar el ritmo *or* dejarte estar justo ahora; **to ~ up (ON sb)**: **she won't ~ up until she gets what she wants** no va a aflojar hasta conseguir lo que quiere; **he'd do better if the teacher ~ up on him a bit** trabajaría mejor si el maestro no estuviera constantemente encima de él **3** (stop) (colloq) (*usu with neg*) parar

letdown /'letdaʊn/ *n* decepción *f*, chasco *m*

lethal /'li:θəl/ *adj* ‹*blow/substance/dose*› mortal, letal; ‹*weapon*› mortífero; ‹*alcoholic drink*› (hum) explosivo (hum)

lethargic /lə'θɑ:rdʒɪk || lɪ'θɑ:dʒɪk/ *adj* ‹*mood/movement*› aletargado; ‹*response*› sin energía, apático

lethargy /'leθərdʒi || 'leθədʒi/ *n* [u] aletargamiento *m*

let's /lets/ (= **let us**) *see* **let² C**

letter /'letər || 'letə(r)/ *n*

A (written message) carta *f*; **~ of introduction** carta *f* de recomendación; (*before n*) **I'm not much of a ~ writer** no soy muy buen corresponsal

B **1** (of alphabet) letra *f*; **a two-letter word** una palabra de dos letras; **the ~ of the law** la letra de la ley; ***to the ~*** al pie de la letra **2** **letters** *pl* (literature) (frml): **a man/woman of ~s** un hombre/una mujer de letras, un literato/una literata

letter: **~ bomb** *n* carta *f* bomba; **~ box** *n* buzón *m*; **~ carrier** *n* (AmE) cartero, -ra *m,f*; **~head** /'letərhed || 'letəhed/ *n* membrete *m*

lettering /'letərɪŋ/ *n* [u] (words) caracteres *mpl*

letter: **~-perfect** /'letər'pɜ:rfɪkt || ˌletə'pɜ:fɪkt/ *adj* (AmE) ‹*document/speech*› impecable, perfecto; **~press** *n* [u] tipografía *f*, impresión *f* tipográfica

lettuce /'letəs || 'letɪs/ *n* [u c] lechuga *f*

let-up /'letʌp/ *n* interrupción *f*, pausa *f*; **there's no sign of any ~ in demand** no parece que vaya a disminuir la demanda

leukemia, (esp BrE) **leukaemia** /lu:'ki:miə/ *n* [u] leucemia *f*

levee /'levi/ *n* **1** (Agr) (embankment) dique *m* **2** (landing stage) (AmE) atracadero *m*

level¹ /'levəl/ *n*

A (height) nivel *m*; **at eye/shoulder ~** a la altura de los ojos/hombros; ***on the ~*** (honest) (colloq): **is it all on the ~ ?** ¿es un asunto limpio?; **he's on the ~** es un tipo derecho (fam) *or* (Esp arg) legal *or* (RPl fam) bien

B (rank) nivel *m*; **at ministerial ~** a nivel ministerial; **a top-~ meeting** una reunión de *or* a alto nivel; **to be on a ~ with sb/sth** estar* a la par de *or* a la altura de algn/algo; **this latest scandal is on a ~ with ...** este último escándalo es equiparable a *or* comparable con ...

level² *adj*

A ‹*ground/surface*› plano, llano; **that picture's not ~** ese cuadro no está derecho; **a ~ spoonful** una cucharada rasa; **to do** *o* **try one's ~ best** hacer* todo lo posible

B **1** (at same height) **to be ~ (WITH sth)** estar* al nivel *or* a ras (DE algo) **2** (abreast, equal): **the two teams were ~ at half-time** al medio tiempo los dos equipos iban *or* estaban empatados; **to draw ~ with sb** (in a race) alcanzar* a algn

C (unemotional, calm) ‹*voice/tone*› desapasionado; **to keep a ~ head** no perder* la cabeza

level³, (BrE) **-ll-** *vt*

A **1** (make flat) ‹*ground/surface*› nivelar, aplanar **2** (raze, flatten) ‹*building/town*› arrasar

B (make equal) igualar

C (direct) **to ~ sth AT sb/sth** ‹*weapon*› apuntarle A algn/A algo CON algo; **to ~ an accusation at sb** acusar a algn

■ **level** *vi* (be honest) (colloq) **to ~ WITH sb** ser* franco *or* sincero CON algn

Phrasal verbs
- **level off**

A [v ▸ adv] **1** «*aircraft*» nivelarse, enderezarse* **2** «*prices/growth/inflation*» estabilizarse*
B [v ▸ o ▸ adv, v ▸ adv ▸ o] ‹*surface/board*› nivelar, emparejar
- **level out** [v ▸ adv] ▸**level off A**

level: ~ **crossing** *n* (BrE) paso *m* a nivel, crucero *m* (Méx); ~**-headed** /'levəl'hedəd || ˌlevəl'hedɪd/ *adj* sensato; ~**-peg** /'levəl'peg/ *vi* **-gg-** (BrE) (*usu in -ing form*): **at half time it was ~-pegging** al final del primer tiempo los dos equipos estaban *or* iban empatados

lever[1] /'levər || 'li:və(r)/ *n* palanca *f*

lever[2] *vt* (+ *adv compl*): **to ~ sth open** abrir* algo haciendo palanca

leverage[1] /'levərɪdʒ || 'li:vərɪdʒ/ *n* [u] **1** (Phys, Fin) apalancamiento *m* **2** (influence) influencia *f*, palanca *f* (fam)

leverage[2] *vt* (esp US) **1** (bring about) provocar* **2** ‹*assets/investments*› apalancar*

leveraged buyout /'levərɪdʒd || 'li:vərɪdʒd/ *n* compra *f* apalancada *or* con financiación ajena

leveret /'levərət || 'levərɪt/ *n* lebrato *m*

leviathan /lɪ'vaɪəθən/ *n* (giant) (liter) gigante *m*

levitate /'levəteɪt || 'levɪteɪt/ *vi* levitar

levitation /'levə'teɪʃən || ˌlevɪ'teɪʃən/ *n* [u] levitación *f*

levity /'levəti/ *n* [u] (frml) ligereza *f*, frivolidad *f*

levy[1] /'levi/ *vt* **levies, levying, levied** **1** ‹*tax/duty*› (impose) imponer*; (collect) recaudar; **to ~ sth ON sth**: **the government intends to ~ a new tax on imports** el gobierno tiene la intención de gravar las importaciones con un nuevo impuesto **2** ‹*fee/charge*› cobrar **3** ‹*fine*› imponer*

levy[2] *n* (*pl* **levies**) **1** [u] (raising of tax, contributions): **the strike was funded by a ~ on all members** la huelga se financió mediante el cobro de una cuota a todos los miembros **2** [c] (tax) impuesto *m*, gravamen *m*

lewd /lu:d || lju:d/ *adj* **-er, -est** lascivo; ‹*joke/song*› verde (fam), colorado (Méx fam)

lexica /'leksəkə || 'leksɪkə/ *pl n* ▸**lexicon**

lexicographer /'leksə'kɑ:grəfər || ˌleksɪ'kɒgrəfə(r)/ *n* lexicógrafo, -fa *m,f*

lexicography /'leksə'kɑ:grəfi/ *n* [u] lexicografía *f*

lexicon /'leksəkɑ:n/ *n* (*pl* **-cons** *or* **-ca**) léxico *m*

liability /'laɪə'bɪləti/ *n* (*pl* **-ties**)
A [u] **1** (responsibility) responsabilidad *f*; **to deny/admit ~ for sth** negar*/admitir ser responsable de algo **2** [u] (eligibility): **tax ~** pasivo *m* exigible en concepto de impuestos; **~ FOR sth**: **his ~ for military service** su obligación de prestar servicio militar **3** (proneness) **~ TO sth/to + INF** propensión *f* A algo/+ INF
B **liabilities** *pl* (debt) (Fin) pasivo *m*
C (drawback, disadvantage) (*no pl*): **she's a positive ~** es un verdadero lastre; **the car turned out to be a ~** el coche terminó dándonos más problemas que otra cosa

liable /'laɪəbəl/ *adj* (*pred*)
A **1** (responsible) reponsable; **to be ~ FOR sth** ser* responsable DE algo, responder DE algo; **to hold sb ~** responsabilizar* a algn, considerar a algn responsable **2** (subject) **to be ~ FOR/TO sth**: **any income is ~ for tax** cualquier ingreso es gravable *or* está sujeto a impuestos; **you will be ~ to a 15% surcharge** le pueden hacer un recargo del 15%
B **1** **to be ~ to + INF**: **I'm ~ to forget** es probable que me olvide; **the earlier model was ~ to overheat** el modelo anterior tenía tendencia a recalentarse **2** (susceptible) **to be ~ TO sth** ser* propenso A algo, tener* propensión A algo

liaise /li'eɪz/ *vi* (esp BrE) **to ~ (WITH sb)** actuar* de enlace (CON algn); **the departments will ~ closely** los departamentos mantendrán un estrecho contacto

liaison /li'eɪzɑ:n || li'eɪzn̩/ *n*
A [u] (coordination) enlace *m*, coordinación *f*; (*before n*) **~ officer** oficial *m* de enlace
B [c] (affair) (liter) affaire *m*, relación *f*

liar /'laɪər || 'laɪə(r)/ *n* mentiroso, -sa *m,f*, embustero, -ra *m,f*

libel[1] /'laɪbəl/ *n* [u c] (defamation) difamación *f*; (where a crime is implied) calumnia *f*; **to sue (sb) for ~** demandar (a algn) por difamación/calumnia; (*before n*) ‹*suit/action*› por difamación/calumnia

libel[2] *vt*, (BrE) **-ll-** (defame) difamar; (where a crime is implied) calumniar

libelous, (BrE) **libellous** /'laɪbələs/ *adj* ‹*article/remark*› difamatorio; ‹*accusation/charge*› calumnioso

liberal[1] /'lɪbərəl/ *adj*
A **1** (tolerant) ‹*ideas/attitude*› liberal; ‹*interpretation*› libre **2** **Liberal** (Pol) del Partido Liberal; **the L~ Party** el Partido Liberal; **the L~ Democratic Party** (in UK) el Partido Democrático Liberal
B (generous) ‹*sponsor/backer*› generoso

liberal[2] *n* **1** (progressive thinker) liberal *mf* **2** **Liberal** (party member) liberal *mf*; **L~ Democrat** (in UK) demócrata *mf* liberal

liberal arts *pl n* **the ~ ~** las humanidades, las artes liberales

liberalism /'lɪbərəlɪzəm/ *n* [u] liberalismo *m*

liberalize /'lɪbərəlaɪz/ *vt* liberalizar*

liberally /'lɪbərəli/ *adv* **1** (generously) ‹*give/compliment*› generosamente; ‹*apply/spread*› abundantemente, generosamente **2** (not strictly) ‹*translate/interpret*› libremente

liberate /'lɪbəreɪt/ *vt* **1** ‹*people/nation*› liberar, libertar; ‹*woman*› liberar **2** (set free) (frml) ‹*prisoner/hostage*› poner* *or* dejar en libertad, liberar

liberation /'lɪbə'reɪʃən/ *n* [u] liberación *f*

liberator /'lɪbəreɪtər || 'lɪbəreɪtə(r)/ *n* libertador, -dora *m,f*

Liberia /laɪ'bɪriə || laɪ'bɪəriə/ *n* Liberia *f*

Liberian /laɪ'bɪriən || laɪ'bɪəriən/ *adj* liberiano

libertarian[1] /'lɪbər'teriən || ˌlɪbə'teəriən/ *n* (Pol) libertario, -ria *m,f*

libertarian[2] *adj* (Pol) libertario

liberty /'lɪbərti || 'lɪbəti/ *n* (*pl* **-ties**)
A [u] (freedom) libertad *f*; **to be at ~** estar* libre *or* en libertad; **to be at ~ to + INF** (frml): **I'm not at ~ to tell you** no se lo puedo decir; **you're not at ~ to alter the text** no tienes autorización para cambiar el texto
B [c] (presumptuous action) (esp BrE): **what a ~!** ¡qué descaro *or* atrevimiento!; **to take the ~ of -ING** tomarse la libertad DE + INF, permitirse + INF (frml); **to take liberties with sb** tomarse libertades *or* confianzas con algn
C [c] (leave) (AmE Naut) licencia *f*, permiso *m*

libido /lə'bi:dəʊ || lɪ'bi:dəʊ/ *n* libido *f*, líbido *f*

Libra /'li:brə, 'laɪbrə || 'li:brə/ *n* **1** (sign) (*no art*) Libra **2** [c] (person) Libra *or* libra *mf*; *see also* **Aquarius**

librarian /laɪ'breriən || laɪ'breəriən/ *n* bibliotecario, -ria *m,f*

librarianship /laɪ'breriənʃɪp || laɪ'breəriənʃɪp/ *n* [u] biblioteconomía *f*

library /'laɪbreri || 'laɪbrəri/ *n* (*pl* **-ries**) biblioteca *f*; **public ~** biblioteca pública; (*before n*) **~ card** *o* **ticket** (BrE) tarjeta *f* *or* (Méx) credencial *f* de lector

> **Library of Congress**
>
> La biblioteca nacional de EEUU, situada en Washington DC. Fundada por el Congreso (**Congress**), alberga más de 80 millones de libros, en 470 idiomas, y otros objetos

libretto /lə'bretəʊ || lɪ'bretəʊ/ *n* (*pl* **-tos** *or* **-ti** /-ti:/) libreto *m*

Libya /'lɪbiə/ *n* Libia *f*

Libyan /'lɪbiən/ *adj* libio

lice /laɪs/ *pl of* **louse 1**

license[1], (BrE) **licence** /'laɪsn̩s/ *n*
A [c] **1** (permit) permiso *m*, licencia *f*; **import/export ~** permiso de importación/exportación; **to manufacture sth under ~** fabricar* algo bajo licencia; (*before n*) **~ number** (AmE Auto) número *m* de matrícula *or* (CS) de patente; **~ plate** matrícula *f*, placa *f* (AmL), patente *f* (CS), chapa *f* (RPl) **2** ▸**driver's license**
B [u] **1** (freedom): **poetic ~** licencia *f* poética **2** (excessive freedom) (frml) libertinaje *m*

license[2] /'laɪsn̩s/ *vt* otorgarle* un permiso *or* una licencia a

licensed /'laɪsn̩st/ *adj* ‹*practitioner*› autorizado para ejercer; ‹*premises/restaurant*› (BrE) autorizado para vender bebidas alcohólicas

licensee /ˈlaɪsn̩ˈsiː/ *n* 1▸ (holder of licence) *titular de un permiso o licencia* 2▸ (publican) (BrE) *persona al frente de un* **pub**

licensing /ˈlaɪsn̩sɪŋ/ *adj (before n)*: **~ laws** (BrE) *legislación que regula la venta de bebidas alcohólicas*

licentious /laɪˈsentʃəs || laɪˈsenʃəs/ *adj* licencioso

lichee /ˈlaɪtʃi/ *n* lichi *m*

lichen /ˈlaɪkən, ˈlɪtʃən/ *n* [u c] liquen *m*

lick¹ /lɪk/ *vt*

A ‹*spoon/ice-cream*› lamer; ‹*stamp*› pasarle la lengua a; **the cat ~ed the cream off the cake** el gato le quitó la crema al pastel a lengüetazos; **I ~ed my finger** me humedecí el dedo con saliva

B (colloq) (defeat) barrer con, darle* una paliza a (fam)

■ **lick** *vi* **to ~ AT sth** lamer algo

lick² *n* 1▸ [c] (act) lamida *f*, lengüetazo *m* 2▸ (application, coat) (colloq) (*no pl*): **a ~ of paint** una mano de pintura

lickety-split /ˌlɪkətiˈsplɪt/ *adv* (AmE colloq) 1▸ (full speed) a todo lo que da (fam), a todo gas (fam) 2▸ (right away) en menos de lo que canta un gallo

licking /ˈlɪkɪŋ/ *n* (colloq) paliza *f* (fam)

licorice, (BrE) **liquorice** /ˈlɪkərɪʃ, -ɪs/ *n* [u] regaliz *f*, orozuz *m*

lid /lɪd/ *n*

A (of container) tapa *f*; ***to flip one's ~*** (colloq) (go mad) perder* la chaveta (fam); (become angry) poner* el grito en el cielo (fam); ***to keep the ~ on sth*** mantener* algo tapado; ***to take*** *o* ***lift*** *o* ***blow the ~ off sth*** destapar algo

B (*eye ~*) párpado *m*

lido /ˈliːdəʊ/ *n* (*pl* **-dos**) 1▸ (pool) (BrE) piscina *f or* (RPl tb) pileta *f or* (Méx) alberca *f* (*al aire libre*) 2▸ (beach resort) centro *m* turístico costero, balneario *m* (AmS)

lie¹ /laɪ/ *n* (untruth) mentira *f*; **that's a ~!** ¡(eso es) mentira!; **to tell ~s** decir* mentiras, mentir*; ***to give the ~ to sth*** desmentir* algo

lie² *vi*

(Sense I) (*3rd pers sing pres* **lies**; *pres p* **lying**; *past & past p* **lied**) (tell untruths) mentir*; ***to ~ one's way out of/into sth*** salir* de un problema/conseguir* algo a base de mentiras

(Sense II) (*3rd pers sing pres* **lies**; *pres p* **lying**; *past* **lay**; *past p* **lain**)

A 1▸ (lie down) echarse, acostarse*, tenderse* 2▸ (be in lying position) estar* tendido, yacer* (liter); **he often ~s in bed until noon** con frecuencia se queda en la cama hasta el mediodía; **~ still!** ¡quédate quieto!; **I lay awake for hours** estuve horas sin poder dormir; ***to ~ low*** tratar de pasar inadvertido 3▸ (be buried) yacer* (liter), estar* sepultado (frml); Ⓢ **here lies John Brown** aquí yacen los restos de John Brown

B (be) «*object*» estar*; **the snow lay two feet deep** la nieve tenía dos pies de espesor; **the book lay open at page 304** el libro estaba abierto en la página 304; **the factory still lay idle** la fábrica seguía parada; **the ship lay at anchor** el barco estaba fondeado *or* anclado

C 1▸ (be located) «*building/city*» encontrarse*, estar* (situado *or* ubicado); **a group of islands lying off the west coast** un conjunto de islas situadas cerca de la costa occidental 2▸ (stretch) extenderse*

D «*problem/difference*» radicar*, estribar, estar*; «*answer*» estar*; **where do your sympathies ~?** ¿con quién simpatizas?; **it's hard to see where the problem ~s** es difícil ver en qué estriba *or* radica el problema; **victory lay within his grasp** tenía la victoria al alcance de la mano

(Phrasal verbs)

- **lie about** (BrE) ▸**lie around**
- **lie ahead** [v ▸ adv] **to ~ ahead (OF sb/sth)**: **miles of desert lay ahead of us** teníamos por delante millas de desierto; **who knows what may ~ ahead?** ¡quién sabe qué nos depara el futuro!
- **lie around** [v ▸ adv] 1▸ (be scattered) (*usu in -ing form*) estar* tirado, estar* botado (AmL exc RPl) 2▸ (be idle) estar* tumbado *or* echado sin hacer nada
- **lie back** [v ▸ adv] recostarse*
- **lie down** [v ▸ adv] 1▸ (adopt lying position) echarse, acostarse*, tenderse* 2▸ (be lying) estar* echado *or* acostado *or* tendido; ***to take sth lying down***: **I won't take this lying down** no voy a permitir que me traten (*or* me hablen, *etc*) así sin protestar *or* pelear
- **lie in** [v ▸ adv] (BrE) dormir* hasta tarde, levantarse tarde

lie: **~ detector** *n* detector *m* de mentiras; **~-down** /ˈlaɪˈdaʊn/ *n* (BrE colloq) (*no pl*): **to have a ~-down** echarse *or* recostarse* un rato (a descansar); **~-in** /ˈlaɪˈɪn/ *n* (BrE colloq): **to have a ~-in** quedarse en la cama, no levantarse hasta tarde

lieu /luː || ljuː/ *n* (frml): **in ~ of** en lugar de, en vez de; **time off in ~** horas *fpl*/días *mpl* libres a cambio

lieutenant /luːˈtenənt || lefˈtenənt/ *n* 1▸ (in navy) teniente *mf* de navío, teniente *mf* primero (*en Chi*) 2▸ (in other services) teniente *mf* 3▸ (deputy, assistant) lugarteniente *mf*

lieutenant governor *n* 1▸ (in Canada) vicegobernador, -dora *m,f* 2▸ (in US) lugarteniente *mf* del gobernador

life /laɪf/ *n* (*pl* **lives**)

A [c u] (existence) vida *f*; **it will last you for ~** te durará toda la vida; **maimed for ~** lisiado de por vida; **for the rest of my ~** por el resto de mis días; **early in ~** en su (*or* mi, *etc*) juventud; **in later ~** más tarde *or* más adelante; **at my time of ~** a mi edad, con la edad que tengo; **he began ~ as a car salesman** empezó vendiendo coches; **the man/woman in your ~** el hombre/la mujer de tu vida; **to have the time of one's ~** divertirse* como nunca *or* (fam) de lo lindo; **to live ~ to the full** vivir la vida al máximo; **to see ~** ver* mundo; **you can bet your ~ we'll be late!** (colloq) ¡te apuesto lo que quieras a que llegamos tarde!; **to lose one's ~** perder* la vida; **no lives were lost** no hubo muertos; **to risk one's ~** arriesgar* la vida; **to save sb's ~** salvarle la vida a algn; **to take sb's ~** (frml) darle* muerte a algn (frml); **to take one's (own) ~** (frml) quitarse la vida (frml); ***a matter of ~ and death*** una cuestión de vida o muerte; ***as large as ~*** en carne y hueso; ***he couldn't darn a sock to save his ~*** no sería capaz de zurcir un calcetín ni aun si le fuera la vida en ello; ***larger than ~***: **the characters are all larger than ~** todos los personajes son creaciones que desbordan la realidad; **he was a larger-than-~ character** era un personaje exuberante; ***not for the ~ of one***: **I can't remember for the ~ of me** no me puedo acordar por nada del mundo; ***not on your ~!*** ¡ni muerto!; ***to cling/hold on for dear ~*** aferrarse/agarrarse desesperadamente; ***to fight/run for one's ~***: **they had to run for their lives** tuvieron que correr como alma que lleva el diablo; **run for your lives!** ¡sálvese quien pueda!; **he was fighting for (his) ~** se debatía entre la vida y la muerte; ***to frighten*** *o* ***scare the ~ out of sb*** darle* *or* pegarle* un susto mortal a algn; ***(to have) the shock of one's ~*** llevarse el susto de su (*or* mi *etc*) vida; **she gave the performance of her ~** actuó como nunca; ***to risk ~ and limb*** arriesgar* la vida; ***to take one's ~ in one's hands*** jugarse* la vida; (*before n*) ‹*member/pension/president*› vitalicio; **~ force** fuerza *f* vital; **~ imprisonment** cadena *f* perpetua; **~ sentence** condena *f* a perpetuidad *or* a cadena perpetua; **his ~ story** la historia de su vida

B [u] 1▸ (vital force) vida *f*; **it brings the history of this period to ~** hace cobrar vida a este período de la historia; **to bring sb back to ~** resucitar a algn; **to come to ~** «*party*» animarse; «*puppet/doll*» cobrar vida 2▸ (vitality) vida *f*, vitalidad *f*; **to inject new ~ into sth** revitalizar* algo; ***to be the ~*** *o* (esp BrE) ***the ~ and soul of the party*** ser* el alma de la fiesta

C [u] (lifestyle) vida *f*; **married ~** la vida de casado; **this is the ~ (for me)!** ¡esto sí que es vida!; ***to live the ~ of Riley*** darse* la gran vida, vivir a cuerpo de rey

D [u] (living things) vida *f*; **animal/plant ~** vida animal/vegetal

E [u] (duration — of battery) duración *f*, vida *f*; (— of agreement) vigencia *f*

F [u] (imprisonment) (colloq) cadena *f* perpetua; **he got ~** lo condenaron a cadena perpetua

G [u] (Art): **to paint/draw from ~** pintar/dibujar del natural

H [c] (biography) vida *f*

life: **~-and-death** /ˌlaɪfən(d)ˈdeθ/ *adj* de vida o muerte; **a ~-and-death struggle** una lucha a vida o muerte; **~ assurance** *n* [u] (BrE) ▸**~ insurance**; **~ belt** *n* (BrE) salvavidas *m*; **~blood** *n* [u] 1▸ (mainstay) parte *f* vital, alma *f* 2▸ (life) (liter): **his ~blood was draining away** su vida se apagaba (liter); **~boat** *n* (on ship) bote *m* salvavidas; (shore-based) lancha *f* de salvamento; **~ buoy** *n* salvavidas *m*; **~ cycle** *n* ciclo *m* vital; **~ expectancy** *n* esperanza *f or* expectativas *fpl* de vida; **~-form** *n* ser *m* vivo, criatura *f*; (in science fiction) ser *m*; **~guard** *n* salvavidas *mf*, socorrista *mf*; **~ insurance** *n* seguro *m* de vida; (*before n*) ‹*company*› de seguros de vida; ‹*policy*› de seguro de vida; **~ jacket** *n* chaleco *m* salvavidas

lifeless /ˈlaɪfləs || ˈlaɪflɪs/ *adj* **1** ‹*body*› (dead) sin vida, inánime (frml), exánime (liter); (unconscious) inerte **2** (listless) ‹*appearance/prose*› anodino, sin vida; ‹*hair/painting*› sin vida; ‹*eyes*› apagado, sin vida; ‹*party*› poco animado

life: **~like** *adj* ‹*character*› muy real, verosímil; ‹*waxwork*› que parece vivo, verosímil; ‹*situation*› verosímil; **~line** *n* (rope) cuerda *f* de salvamento; **his letters were my ~line** sus cartas eran lo único que me mantenía viva; **the bank threw them a ~line** el banco les tendió una mano; **~long** *adj* (*before n*): **a ~long friend** un amigo de toda la vida; **~ preserver** /prɪˈzɜːrvər || prɪˈzɜːvə(r)/ *n* (AmE) **1** ▸**life buoy** **2** ▸**life jacket**; **~ raft** *n* balsa *f* salvavidas; **~ ring** *n* (AmE) salvavidas *m*; **~saver** *n* **1** ▸**lifeguard** **2** (from bad situation) salvación *f*; **~-saving** *adj* (*before n*) ‹*drug/operation/device*› que salva vidas; ‹*mission*› de socorro; **~ sciences** *pl n* ciencias *fpl* biológicas; **~-size** /ˈlaɪfˈsaɪz/, **~-sized** /-d/ *adj* (de) tamaño natural; **~ span** *n* (of living creature) vida *f*; (of project) duración *f*; (of equipment) vida *f* útil; **~style** *n* estilo *m* de vida; **~-support system** /ˈlaɪfsəˈpɔːrt || ˈlaɪfsə,pɔːt/ *n*: **the patient is on a ~-support system** el paciente está conectado a una máquina que mantiene sus constantes vitales; **~time** *n* vida *f*; **once in a ~time** una vez en la vida; **the opportunity of a ~time** la oportunidad de su (*or* mi *etc*) vida; **it won't happen in my ~time** no lo verán mis ojos, no sucederá mientras yo viva; (*before n*) ‹*appointment/post*› vitalicio; **a once-in-a-~time chance** una oportunidad única (en la vida) *or* irrepetible; **~time guarantee** garantía *f* para toda la vida; **~ vest** *n* (AmE) chaleco *m* salvavidas; **~work**, **~'s work** *n* trabajo *m* de toda una vida

lift¹ /lɪft/ *n*

A **1** [u c] (boost) impulso *m*; **the news gave her a big ~** la noticia le levantó mucho la moral *or* el ánimo **2** [u] (Aviat) fuerza *f* propulsora, propulsión *f*

B [c] (ride): **can I give you a ~?** ¿quieres que te lleve *or* (Per fam) te jale?, ¿quieres que te dé un aventón (Méx) *or* (Col fam) una palomita?

C [c] (elevator) (BrE) ascensor *m*; (*before n*) **~ attendant** ascensorista *mf*; **~ shaft** hueco *m* del ascensor

lift² *vt*

A (raise) ‹*weight/box/eyes/head*› levantar; **shall I ~ your suitcase down for you?** ¿quieres que te baje la maleta?; **I ~ed the child into his chair** subí al niño a la silla

B (end) ‹*ban/blockade/siege*› levantar

C **1** (take, remove) (*usu pass*) sacar* **2** (plagiarize) (colloq) **to ~ sth (FROM sth)** ‹*idea/sentence*› copiar *or* plagiar algo (DE algo) **3** (steal) (colloq) birlar (fam)

■ **lift** *vi* **1** (rise) «*curtain*» levantarse; **to ~ into the air** «*aircraft/balloon/kite*» elevarse en el aire **2** (clear) «*mist*» disiparse

Phrasal verbs

• **lift off** [v ▸ adv] «*rocket*» despegar*

• **lift up** [v ▸ o ▸ adv, v ▸ adv ▸ o] levantar

lift-off /ˈlɪftɔːf || ˈlɪftɒf/ *n* (Aerosp) despegue *m*; **we have ~** hemos completado el despegue

ligament /ˈlɪgəmənt/ *n* ligamento *m*

ligature /ˈlɪgətʃʊr || ˈlɪgətʃə(r)/ *n* (Med, Mus) ligadura *f*

light¹ /laɪt/ *n*

A [u] luz *f*; **~ and shade** luz y sombra; (Art) claroscuro *m*; **by the ~ of the moon** a la luz de la luna; **hold it up to the ~** ponlo al trasluz *or* a contraluz; **in** *o* **by the cold ~ of day it didn't seem such a good idea** al pensarlo mejor *or* en frío, no parecía tan buena idea; **at first ~** al clarear (el día), con las primeras luces; ***to bring sth to ~*** sacar* algo a la luz; ***to come to ~*** salir* a la luz; ***to hide one's ~ under a bushel*** ser* modesto; ***to see the ~*** abrir* los ojos, comprender las cosas; ***to see (the) ~ at the end of the tunnel*** vislumbrar el fin de sus (*or* mis *etc*) problemas; ***to see the ~ (of day)*** ver* la luz (del día); ***to throw*** *o* ***cast*** *o* ***shed ~ on sth*** arrojar luz sobre algo; (*before n*) **~ meter** fotómetro *m*

B [c] **1** (source of light) luz *f*; (lamp) lámpara *f*; **to turn the ~ off** apagar* la luz; **to turn the ~ on** encender* *or* (AmL tb) prender *or* (Esp tb) dar* la luz; **warning ~** señal *f* luminosa; ***to go out like a ~*** (colloq) (become unconscious) caer(se)* redondo; (fall asleep) dormirse* como un tronco, caer* como piedra (AmL fam); (*before n*) **~ switch** interruptor *m* **2** (of car, bicycle) luz *f*; **brake ~s** luces de frenado **3** (*traffic ~*) semáforo *m*; **the ~s were against us** nos tocaron los semáforos en contra *or* en rojo

C **1** (aspect) (*no pl*): **to see sth/sb in a good/bad/new** *o* **different ~** ver* algo/a algn con buenos/malos/otros ojos; **it didn't show him in a very good ~** no daba una imagen demasiado buena de él **2** **in the ~ of** *o* (AmE also) **in ~ of** (*as prep*) a la luz de, en vista de

D [c] (for igniting): **have you got a ~?** ¿tienes fuego?; **to put a** *o* **set ~ to sth** prender fuego a algo

E **lights** *pl* (Culin) pulmón *m*

light² *adj* **-er, -est**

Sense I

A (not heavy) ligero, liviano (esp AmL); ‹*voice*› suave; **it's ~er than the other one** pesa menos que el otro, es más ligero *or* (esp AmL) liviano que el otro; **with a ~ heart** tranquilo; **she's a very ~ sleeper** tiene el sueño muy ligero

B **1** (Meteo) ‹*breeze/wind*› suave; **~ rain** llovizna *f* **2** (sparse): **the losses were fairly ~** las pérdidas fueron de poca consideración *or* de poca monta **3** (not strenuous) ‹*work/duties*› ligero, liviano (esp AmL) **4** (not severe) ‹*sentence*› leve

C (not serious) ‹*music/comedy/reading*› ligero; **a program of ~ entertainment** un programa de variedades; ***to make ~ of sth*** quitarle *or* restarle importancia a algo

Sense II **1** (pale) ‹*green/brown*› claro **2** (bright): **it gets ~ very early these days** ahora amanece *or* aclara muy temprano; **it's already ~** ya es de día, ya está claro

light³ *adv*: **to travel ~** viajar con el mínimo de equipaje

light⁴ *vt*

A (*past & past p* **lighted** *or* **lit**) (set alight) encender*, prender

B (*past & past p* **lit**) (illuminate) ‹*room/scene*› iluminar; **dimly/brightly lit** poco/muy iluminado

■ **light** *vi* (*past & past p* **lighted** *or* **lit**) encenderse*

Phrasal verb

• **light up** (*past & past p* **lit**)

A [v ▸ adv] **1** «*eyes/face*» iluminarse **2** «*smoker*» encender* *or* prender un cigarrillo (*or* un puro *etc*)

B [v ▸ o ▸ adv, v ▸ adv ▸ o] **1** ‹*street/square*› iluminar **2** ‹*cigar/pipe*› encender*, prender

light: **~ bulb** *n* ▸**bulb B**; **~-colored**, (BrE) **~-coloured** /ˈlaɪtˈkʌlərd || ˌlaɪtˈkʌləd/ *adj* (de color) claro; **~ cream** *n* (AmE) crema *f* líquida, nata *f* líquida (Esp)

lighten /ˈlaɪtn̩/ *vt*

A (make less heavy) ‹*load/workload*› aligerar; ‹*responsibility/conscience*› descargar*; **to ~ the tone of a speech** darle* un tono menos grave a un discurso

B **1** (make brighter) ‹*room*› dar* más luz a; ‹*sky*› iluminar **2** (make paler) ‹*color/hair*› aclarar

C (liter) ‹*cares*› aliviar; ‹*heart*› alegrar

■ **lighten** *vi*

A (become less heavy) «*load/weight*» hacerse* más ligero *or* (esp AmL) liviano, aligerarse

B (become brighter) «*sky*» despejarse; «*face*» iluminarse; «*atmosphere*» relajarse

Phrasal verb

• **lighten up** (colloq) [v ▸ adv] relajarse

lighter /ˈlaɪtər || ˈlaɪtə(r)/ *n* (*cigarette ~*) encendedor *m*, mechero *m* (Esp)

light: **~-fingered** /ˈlaɪtˈfɪŋgərd || ˌlaɪtˈfɪŋgəd/ *adj* (colloq): **to be ~-fingered** tener* (la) mano larga *or* las manos largas (fam); **~-headed** /ˈlaɪtˈhedəd || ˌlaɪtˈhedɪd/ *adj* (dizzy) mareado; (excited) exaltado; **~-hearted** /ˈlaɪtˈhɑːrtəd || ˌlaɪtˈhɑːtɪd/ *adj* ‹*book/account*› alegre, desenfadado; **she was in a ~-hearted mood** estaba de buen humor; **~house** *n* faro *m*; (*before n*) **~house keeper** farero, -ra *m,f*, guardafaro *mf* (CS)

lighting /ˈlaɪtɪŋ/ *n* [u] (illumination) iluminación *f*; (on streets) alumbrado *m*; (Theat) iluminación *f*

lightly /ˈlaɪtli/ *adv*

A **1** ‹*touch*› suavemente; ‹*snow*› ligeramente; **she brushed ~ against me as she passed** me rozó al pasar **2** (Culin) ‹*grill/beat*› ligeramente

B **1** (frivolously) ‹*dismiss/undertake*› a la ligera **2** (not severely): **they were let off ~** los trataron con indulgencia; **they got off very ~ with a small fine** se libraron con sólo una pequeña multa

lightness /ˈlaɪtnəs || ˈlaɪtnɪs/ *n* [u]
A (of fabric) ligereza *f*, lo liviano (esp AmL); (of cake) lo ligero *or* (esp AmL) liviano; **~ of touch** delicadeza *f*
B 1 (brightness) claridad *f*, luminosidad *f* 2 (of color) lo claro

lightning¹ /ˈlaɪtnɪŋ/ *n* [u]: **a bolt** *o* **flash of ~** un relámpago; **a streak of ~** un rayo; **he was struck by ~** le cayó *or* lo alcanzó un rayo; ***as quick as ~*** como un rayo; ***like greased ~*** como un relámpago; ***~ never strikes twice (in the same place)*** tales cosas sólo pasan una vez; (*before n*) **~ conductor** *o* **rod** pararrayos *m*

lightning² *adj* ‹*attack/raid/strike*› relámpago *adj inv*; **with ~ speed** como un rayo

lightning bug *n* (AmE) luciérnaga *f*

light: **~ pen** *n* lápiz *m* óptico *or* fotosensible; **~-skinned** /ˈlaɪtˈskɪnd/ *adj* de piel clara

lightweight¹ /ˈlaɪtweɪt/ *adj* ‹*coat/tent/metal*› ligero, liviano (esp AmL); ‹*book/writer/performance*› de poco peso, superficial

lightweight² *n* (in boxing, wrestling) peso *m* ligero; (minor figure) persona *f* de poco peso

light year *n* (Astron) año *m* luz

likable /ˈlaɪkəbəl/ *adj* agradable, simpático

like¹ /laɪk/ *vt*
A (enjoy, be fond of): **I/we ~ tennis** me/nos gusta el tenis; **she ~s him, but she doesn't love him** le resulta simpático pero no lo quiere; **I ~ that one best** el que más me gusta es ése; **how do you ~ my dress?** ¿qué te parece mi vestido?; **how would you ~ an ice-cream?** ¿quieres *or* (Esp tb) te apetece un helado?; **orchids ~ a damp climate** las orquídeas prefieren un clima húmedo; **I ~ it!** (joke) ¡muy bueno!; (suggestion) ¡buena idea!; **I ~ that!** (iro) ¡muy bonito! (iró), ¡habráse visto!; **as much as you ~** todo lo que quieras; **do as** *o* **what you ~** haz lo que quieras *or* lo que te parezca; **to ~ -ING/to + INF**: **I ~ dancing** me gusta bailar; **she ~s to have breakfast before eight** le gusta desayunar antes de las ocho; **I don't ~ to mention it, but ...** no me gusta (tener que) decírtelo pero ...; **to ~ sb to + INF**: **we ~ him to write to us every so often** nos gusta que nos escriba de vez en cuando
B (in requests, wishes) querer*; **we would just ~ to say how grateful we are** queríamos decirle lo agradecidos que estamos; **would you ~ a cup of tea/me to help you?** ¿quieres una taza de té/que te ayude?; **I'd ~ two melons, please** (me da) dos melones, por favor
■ **like** *vi* querer*; **if you ~** si quieres, si te parece

like² *n*
A (sth liked): **her/his ~s and dislikes** sus preferencias *or* gustos, lo que le gusta y no le gusta
B (similar thing, person) **the ~**: **judges, lawyers and the ~** jueces, abogados y (otra) gente *or* (otras) personas por el estilo; **I've never seen/heard the ~ (of this)** nunca he visto/oído cosa igual; **he doesn't mix with the ~s of me/us** (colloq) no se codea con gente como yo/nosotros

like³ *adj* (dated *or* frml) parecido, similar; **people of ~ minds** gente *f* con ideas afines; ▸**pea**

like⁴ *prep*
A 1 (similar to) como; **I want a hat ~ this one** quiero un sombrero como éste; **I heard a noise ~ (that of) a woman crying** me pareció oír a una mujer llorando; **she's very ~ her mother** se parece mucho *or* es muy parecida a su madre; **that photo isn't ~ you at all!** estás completamente distinta en esa foto; **try this one — now, that's more ~ it!** prueba éste — ah, esto ya es otra cosa; **come on, stop crying! ... that's more ~ it!** vamos, para de llorar ... ¡ahí está! *or* ¡así me gusta!; **what's the food ~?** ¿cómo *or* (fam) qué tal es la comida?; **she's always ~ that** siempre es así; **it cost £20, or something ~ that** costó 20 libras o algo así *or* o algo por el estilo; **I've never known anything ~ it!** ¡nunca he visto cosa igual! 2 (typical of): **that's not ~ her** es muy raro en ella; **it's not ~ him to forget** ¡qué raro que se le haya olvidado!; **it's just ~ you to think of food** ¡típico! *or* ¡cuándo no! ¡tú pensando en comida!
B (indicating manner): **~ this/that** así; **to run ~ mad** correr como un loco
C (such as, for example) como; **don't do anything silly, ~ running away** no vayas a hacer una tontería, como escaparte por ejemplo

like⁵ *conj* (crit) 1 (as if): **she looks ~ she knows what she's doing** parece que *or* da la impresión de que sabe lo que hace; **they stared at him ~ he was crazy** se quedaron mirándolo como si estuviera loco 2 (as, in same way) como; **you don't know him ~ I do** tú no lo conoces como yo

like⁶ *adv* 1 (likely): **as ~ as not, she won't come** lo más probable es que no venga 2 (nearly): **this film is nothing ~ as good as the first** esta película no es tan buena como la primera ni mucho menos

-like /laɪk/ *suff*: **prison~** parecido a *or* como una prisión; **snake~** ‹*appearance*› (como) de serpiente; ‹*movement*› serpenteante

likeable *adj* ▸**likable**

likelihood /ˈlaɪklihʊd/ *n* [u] probabilidad *f*, posibilidad *f*; **there is little/every ~ that she'll agree** es poco/muy probable que acepte; **in all ~ it will be finished by then** lo más probable es que esté terminado para entonces; **what is the ~ of a spring election?** ¿qué posibilidades hay de que haya elecciones en primavera?

likely¹ /ˈlaɪkli/ *adj* **-lier, -liest** 1 (probable) ‹*outcome/winner*› probable; **rain is ~** es posible *or* probable que llueva; **it's more than ~ that she's out** lo más seguro es que no esté; **a ~ story!** (iro) ¡cuéntame otra! (iró), ¡no me digas! (iró); **to be ~ to + INF**: **it is ~ to be a tough match** lo más probable es que sea un partido difícil; **are you ~ to be in tomorrow?** ¿estarás en casa mañana? 2 (promising): **she's the most ~ applicant** es la candidata con más posibilidades; **this is a ~ place to find a telephone** aquí tiene que haber un teléfono

likely² *adv*: **most ~ she'll forget** lo más probable es que se olvide; **as ~ as not it'll be closed** lo más probable es que esté cerrado

like-minded /ˈlaɪkˈmaɪndəd || ˌlaɪkˈmaɪndɪd/ *adj* de ideas afines

liken /ˈlaɪkən/ *vt* **to ~ sth/sb TO sth/sb** comparar algo/a algn CON *or* A algo/algn

likeness /ˈlaɪknəs || ˈlaɪknɪs/ *n* 1 [u c] (resemblance) parecido *m*, semejanza *f*; **there is a certain ~ between them** tienen un cierto parecido *or* una cierta semejanza; **a family ~** un aire de familia 2 [c] (referring to a portrait): **it's a good ~** es un buen retrato

likewise /ˈlaɪkwaɪz/ *adv* 1 (in the same way) asimismo, de la misma manera 2 (the same): **to do ~** hacer* lo mismo, hacer* otro tanto

liking /ˈlaɪkɪŋ/ *n* 1 (fondness) **~ (FOR sth)** afición *f* (A algo); **she has a ~ for reading/cats** es aficionada a la lectura/le gustan los gatos; **to take a ~ to sb/sth** tomarle *or* (esp Esp) cogerle* simpatía a algn/gusto a algo 2 (satisfaction) gusto *m*; **to be to sb's ~** ser* del gusto *or* del agrado de algn; **it's too sweet for my ~** es demasiado dulce para mi gusto

lilac /ˈlaɪlək/ *n* 1 **~ (bush)** lila *f*, lilo *m*; (*before n*) **~ flower** lila *f* 2 (color) lila *m*; (*before n*) lila *adj inv*

Lilo®, lilo /ˈlaɪləʊ/ *n* (*pl* **lilos**) (BrE) colchoneta *f* inflable *or* (Esp) hinchable

lilt /lɪlt/ *n* (of song, tune) cadencia *f*; **to speak with a ~** hablar con un tono cantarín

lilting /ˈlɪltɪŋ/ *adj* ‹*voice*› cantarín, musical; ‹*melody*› cadencioso

lily /ˈlɪli/ *n* (*pl* **lilies**) (Bot) liliácea *f*; (*white ~*) azucena *f*, lirio *m* blanco; ***to paint*** *o* ***gild the ~*** rizar* el rizo

lily: **~-of-the-valley** /ˈlɪliəvðəˈvæli/ *n* (*pl* **lilies-of-the-valley**) lirio *m* de los valles, muguete *m*; **~-white** *adj* (*pred* **~ white**) 1 (in color) blanco como la nieve *or* como una azucena 2 (pure) (pej) ‹*ideals*› puro

lima bean /ˈlaɪmə || ˈliːmə/ *n* frijol *m* *or* (CS) poroto *m* blanco *or* (Esp) judía *f* blanca

limb /lɪm/ *n* 1 (Anat) miembro *m*; **to tear sb ~ from ~** despedazar* a algn 2 (of tree) rama *f* (*principal*), brazo *m*; ***to be (left) out on a ~*** quedarse en la estacada; ***to go out on a ~*** aventurarse

limber up /ˈlɪmbər || ˈlɪmbə(r)/ [v ▸ adv] «*sportsman*» hacer* ejercicios de calentamiento

limbo /ˈlɪmbəʊ/ *n*
A **Limbo** (Relig) limbo *m*; ***to be in ~*** estar* a la expectativa
B (dance) limbo *m*

lime /laɪm/ *n*

A [u] (calcium oxide) cal *f*

B 1 [c] (fruit) lima *f* 2 [c] (tree) limero *m*, lima *f* 3 [u] (color) verde *m* lima; (*before n*) verde lima *adj inv*

C [c] (linden) (BrE) tilo *m*

lime: **~-green** /'laɪm'gri:n/ *adj* (*pred* **~ green**) verde lima *adj inv*; **~light** *n*: **to be in the ~light** estar* en primer plano, ser* el centro de atención; **to steal the ~light** acaparar la atención del público

limerick /'lɪmərɪk/ *n*: *poema humorístico de cinco versos*

limescale /'laɪmskeɪl/ *n* [u] sarro *m*

limestone /'laɪmstəʊn/ *n* [u] (piedra *f*) caliza *f*

limey /'laɪmi/ *n* (*pl* **limeys** *or* **limies**) (AmE sl & often offensive) inglés, -glesa *m,f*

limit¹ /'lɪmət || 'lɪmɪt/ *n*

A 1 [c u] (boundary) límite *m*; ***to be off ~s*** (esp AmE) estar* en zona prohibida 2 [c u] (furthest extent): **she pushes herself to the ~** se esfuerza al máximo; **they stretched my patience to the ~** realmente pusieron a prueba mi paciencia 3 (*no pl*) (colloq) (*in interj phrases*): **you're/that's the ~!** ¡eres/es el colmo! (fam)

B [c u] (restriction, maximum) límite *m*; **what's the (speed) ~?** ¿cuál es la velocidad máxima *or* el límite de velocidad?; **within ~s** dentro de ciertos límites; **to put a ~ on sth** poner* un límite a algo

limit² *vt* ‹*possibility/extent/number*› limitar; ‹*imports*› restringir*; **they ~ed me to one drink a week** me pusieron como límite una copa por semana; **to ~ oneself TO sth/-ING** limitarse A algo/+ INF

limitation /'lɪmə'teɪʃən || ,lɪmɪ'teɪʃən/ *n*

A [u c] (restriction) limitación *f*, restricción *f*

B **limitations** *pl* (weaknesses) (*sometimes sing*) limitaciones *fpl*

limited /'lɪmətəd || 'lɪmɪtɪd/ *adj* 1 ‹*number/space*› limitado, restringido; ‹*knowledge/experience/scope*› limitado; **to a ~ extent/degree** hasta cierto punto/en cierta medida; **~ edition** edición *f* limitada *or* numerada; **my time is ~** no dispongo de mucho tiempo 2 (AmE Transp) ‹*express/train/bus*› semi-directo 3 (Busn) ‹*liability*› limitado; **~ (liability) company** sociedad *f* de responsabilidad limitada; **public ~ company** (BrE) sociedad *f* anónima

limiting /'lɪmətɪŋ || 'lɪmɪtɪŋ/ *adj* restrictivo

limitless /'lɪmətləs || 'lɪmɪtlɪs/ *adj* ilimitado, sin límites

limo /'lɪməʊ/ *n* (colloq) limusina *f*

limousine /'lɪməzi:n, lɪmə'zi:n/ *n* limusina *f*

limp¹ /lɪmp/ *vi* cojear, renquear, renguear (AmL)

limp² *n* cojera *f*, renquera *f*, renguera *f* (AmL); **she walks with a ~** cojea *or* renquea *or* (AmL tb) renguea

limp³ *adj* ‹*handshake*› flojo; ‹*lettuce*› mustio; ‹*hair*› lacio y sin vida; **let yourself go ~** relaja los músculos

limpet /'lɪmpət || 'lɪmpɪt/ *n* lapa *f*

limpid /'lɪmpəd || 'lɪmpɪd/ *adj* (liter) límpido

linchpin /'lɪntʃpɪn/ *n* 1 (vital factor) eje *m* 2 (on tractor) pezonera *f*

linden /'lɪndən/ *n* (AmE) tilo *m*

line¹ /laɪn/ *n*

A [c] 1 (mark, trace) línea *f*, raya *f*; (Math) recta *f*; **to draw a ~** trazar* una línea; **to put** *o* **draw a ~ through sth** tachar algo; ***to be on the ~*** (colloq) estar* en peligro, peligrar; ***to lay it on the ~*** (colloq) no andarse* con rodeos; ***to lay*** *o* ***put sth on the ~*** (colloq) jugarse* algo; (*before n*) **~ drawing** dibujo *m* lineal 2 (on face, palm) línea *f*; (wrinkle) arruga *f*

B 1 [c] (boundary, border) línea *f*; **the county/state ~** (AmE) (la línea de) la frontera del condado/estado; ***to draw the ~ (at sth)***: **I don't mind untidiness, but I draw the ~ at this** no me importa el desorden, pero esto es intolerable *or* esto ya es demasiado; **one has to draw the ~ somewhere** en algún momento hay que decir basta 2 [c] (Sport) línea *f*; (*before n*) **~ judge** juez *mf* de línea 3 [c u] (contour) línea *f*

C 1 [c u] (cable, rope) cuerda *f*; (*clothes o washing* **~**) cuerda (de tender la ropa); (*fishing* **~**) sedal *m*; **power ~** cable *m* eléctrico 2 [c] (Telec) línea *f*; **the ~s are down** no hay línea; **hold the ~, please** no cuelgue *or* (CS tb) no corte, por favor; **it's a very bad ~** se oye muy mal

D [c] (Transp) 1 (company, service) línea *f*; **shipping ~** línea de transportes marítimos, (compañía *f*) naviera *f* 2 (Rail) línea *f*; (track) (BrE) vía *f*

E [u c] 1 (path, direction) línea *f*; **~ of fire** línea de fuego; **it was right in my ~ of vision** me obstruía la visual; ▸**resistance** 2 (attitude, policy) postura *f*, línea *f*; **to take a firm/hard ~ (with sb/on sth)** adoptar una postura *or* línea firme/dura (con algn/con respecto a algo); **she takes the ~ that ...** su actitud es que ...; ***to toe*** *o* (AmE also) ***hew the ~*** acatar la disciplina 3 (method, style): **~ of inquiry** línea *f* de investigación; **~ of argument** argumento *m*; **I was thinking of something along the ~s of ...** pensaba en algo del tipo de *or* por el estilo de ...; **we're thinking along similar ~s** pensamos de la misma manera

F [c] 1 (row) fila *f*, hilera *f*; (queue) (AmE) cola *f*; **they formed a** *o* **fell into ~ behind their teacher** se pusieron en fila detrás del profesor; **the soldiers fell into ~** los soldados se alinearon; **to wait in ~** (AmE) hacer* cola; **to get in ~** (AmE) ponerse* en la cola; **to cut in ~** (AmE) colarse* (fam), brincarse* *or* saltarse la cola (Méx fam); ***all/somewhere along the ~***: **she's had bad luck all along the ~** ha tenido mala suerte desde el principio; **we must have made a mistake somewhere along the ~** debemos de haber cometido un error en algún momento; ***in ~ with sth***: **wages haven't risen in ~ with inflation** los sueldos no han aumentado a la par de la inflación; **the new measures are in ~ with government policy** las nuevas medidas siguen la línea de la política del gobierno; ***out of ~***: **that remark was out of ~** ese comentario estuvo fuera de lugar; **their ideas were out of ~ with mine** sus ideas no coincidían con las mías; **to step out of ~** mostrar* disconformidad, desobedecer*; ***to bring sb/sth into ~***: **he needs to be brought into ~** hay que llamarlo al orden *or* (fam) meterlo en vereda; **the province was brought into ~ with the rest of the country** la situación de la provincia se equiparó a la del resto del país; ***to fall in/into ~***: **they had to fall in ~ with company policy** tuvieron que aceptar *or* acatar la política de la compañía; ***to keep sb in ~*** tener* a algn a raya; *see also* **on line** 2 (series) serie *f*; **he's the latest in a long ~ of radical leaders** es el último de una larga serie de dirigentes radicales 3 (succession) línea *f*; **the title passes through the female ~** el título se transmite por línea materna; **he's next in ~ to the throne** es el siguiente en la línea de sucesión al trono

G [c] (Mil) línea *f*; **behind enemy ~s** tras las líneas enemigas

H 1 [c] (of text) línea *f*, renglón *m*; (of poem) verso *m*; **the best ~ in the movie** la mejor frase de la película; **new ~** (when dictating) punto y aparte; ***to read between the ~s*** leer* entre líneas 2 **lines** *pl* (Theat): **to learn one's ~s** aprenderse el papel; **he forgot his ~s** se olvidó de lo que le tocaba decir 3 (note): **to drop sb a ~** escribirle* a algn unas líneas

I [c] 1 (area of activity): **what ~ are you in?** ¿a qué te dedicas?; **in my ~ of business** en mi trabajo *or* profesión 2 (of merchandise) línea *f*

line² *vt*

A 1 ‹*skirt/box*› forrar 2 (form lining along) cubrir*; **books ~d the walls, the walls were ~d with books** las paredes estaban cubiertas de libros

B (mark with lines) ‹*paper*› rayar

C (border): **the avenue is ~d with trees** la avenida está bordeada de árboles; **crowds ~d the route** cientos de personas estaban alineadas a ambos lados del camino

Phrasal verbs

- **line up**

A [v ▸ adv] (form line, row) ponerse* en fila, formar fila; (queue up) (AmE) hacer* cola

B [v ▸ o ▸ adv, v ▸ adv ▸ o] 1 (form into line) ‹*soldiers/prisoners*› poner* en fila 2 (arrange): **we've a busy program ~d up for you** le tenemos preparada una apretada agenda; **have you got anything ~d up for the weekend?** ¿tienes algo planeado para el fin de semana? 3 (align) alinear

- **line up with** [v ▸ adv ▸ prep ▸ o] alinearse con

lineage /'lɪniɪdʒ/ *n* [u] (descent) linaje *m*

linear /'lɪniər || 'lɪniə(r)/ *adj* ‹*path/motion*› lineal; ‹*approach*› directo; **~ measure** medida *f* de longitud; **~ programming** (Comput) programación *f* lineal

lined /laɪnd/ *adj* 1 ‹*paper*› con renglones *or* (Chi) reglones 2 ‹*jacket/boots/curtains*› forrado; **to be ~ (WITH sth)** estar* forrado (DE algo) 3 (Tech) revestido 4 ‹*face/skin*› arrugado; **his face was deeply ~** tenía la cara surcada de arrugas (liter)

-lined /laɪnd/ *suff*: **fur~/silk~** forrado de piel/seda; **copper~/steel~** revestido de cobre/acero

line: **~man** /ˈlaɪnmən/ *n* (*pl* **-men** /-mən/) (in US football): **defensive/offensive ~man** *cualquier jugador de la línea defensiva/ofensiva*; **~ management** *n* [u] dirección *f* de línea, gerencia *f* de línea; (*before n*) **~ management position** cargo *m* de gerente de línea; **~ manager** *n* gerente *mf* de línea, jefe, -fa *m,f* de línea

linen /ˈlɪnən/ *n* [u]
A (cloth) hilo *m*, lino *m*
B (*bed* ~) ropa *f* blanca *or* de cama; (*table* ~) mantelerías *fpl*; ***to wash one's dirty ~ in public*** sacar* los trapos (sucios) a relucir, sacar* los trapitos al sol (AmL); (*before n*) **~ basket** canasto *m or* cesto *m* de la ropa sucia

lineout /ˈlaɪnaʊt/ *n* (in rugby) saque *m* de banda

liner /ˈlaɪnər || ˈlaɪnə(r)/ *n*
A [c] (ship) buque *m* (de pasaje *or* pasajeros); (*ocean* ~) transatlántico *m*
B [c] **1** (lining) forro *m*; **(dust)bin ~** (BrE) bolsa *f* para la basura **2** (record sleeve) (AmE) funda *f*

line: **~sman** /ˈlaɪnzmən/ *n* (*pl* **-men** /-mən/) (Sport) juez *m* de línea; **~up** *n* **1** (Sport) alineación *f*; **the band's original ~up** la integración original del grupo **2** (of suspects) (AmE) rueda *f* de identificación *or* de sospechosos

linger /ˈlɪŋgər || ˈlɪŋgə(r)/ *vi* **1** (delay leaving) quedarse *or* entretenerse* (un rato) **2** **~ (on)** (remain) ‹‹*aftertaste/smell*›› persistir; ‹‹*tradition*›› perdurar, sobrevivir; **his memory ~s on** aún se lo recuerda, su recuerdo sigue vivo **3** **lingering** *pres p* ‹*doubts/memory*› persistente, que no desaparece; ‹*embrace/look/illness*› prolongado **4** (take one's time) **to ~ ON/OVER sth**: **to ~ on a subject** extenderse* largamente sobre un tema; **her eyes ~ed on the child** se quedó largo rato mirando al niño; **they ~ed over their coffee** se entretuvieron tomando el café; (after meal) alargaron la sobremesa

lingerie /ˈlɑːnʒəˈreɪ || ˈlænʒəri/ *n* [u] lencería *f*, ropa *f* interior femenina

lingo /ˈlɪŋgəʊ/ *n* (*pl* **-goes**) (colloq) (language) idioma *m*; (jargon) jerga *f*

linguist /ˈlɪŋgwəst || ˈlɪŋgwɪst/ *n* **1** (language speaker): **she's quite a ~** (learns languages easily) tiene facilidad para los idiomas; (knows several languages) habla varios idiomas **2** (expert in linguistics) lingüista *mf*

linguistic /lɪŋˈgwɪstɪk/ *adj* lingüístico

linguistics /lɪŋˈgwɪstɪks/ *n* [u] (+ *sing vb*) lingüística *f*

liniment /ˈlɪnəmənt || ˈlɪnɪmənt/ *n* [u c] linimento *m*

lining /ˈlaɪnɪŋ/ *n* (of clothes, suitcase) forro *m*; (of brakes) forro *m*, guarnición *f*; (Tech) revestimiento *m*

link¹ /lɪŋk/ *n*
A **1** (in chain) eslabón *m*; **the missing ~** (Anthrop) el eslabón perdido; **the weak ~** el punto débil **2** ► **cuff link**
B **1** (connection) conexión *f* **2** (tie, bond) vínculo *m*, lazo *m* **3** (Telec, Transp) conexión *f*, enlace *m*; **rail/air ~** conexión ferroviaria/aérea **4** (Comput) (between programs, terminals) enlace *m*; (in compilation) montaje *m*

link² *vt* **1** ‹*components*› unir, enlazar*; ‹*terminals*› conectar; **to ~ arms** tomarse *or* (esp Esp) cogerse* del brazo **2** ‹*buildings/towns*› unir, conectar; **the two groups are closely ~ed** los dos grupos están estrechamente vinculados **3** ‹*facts/events*› relacionar; **to ~ sth TO/WITH sth** relacionar algo CON algo
■ **link** *vi* **1** ► **link up A** **2** (Comput, Telec) **to ~ INTO sth** conectar *or* enlazar* CON algo

Phrasal verb
• **link up**
A [v ► adv] conectar; ‹‹*spacecraft*›› acoplarse
B [v ► o ► adv, v ► adv ► o] conectar

links /lɪŋks/ *n* (*pl* ~) (+ *sing o pl vb*) campo *m* de golf (*esp a orillas del mar*), link *m*

linkup /ˈlɪŋkʌp/ *n* **1** [c u] (connection) conexión *f*; (of spacecraft) acoplamiento *m* **2** [c] (Rad, TV) conexión *f*, enlace *m* **3** [c] (meeting) encuentro *m*

lino /ˈlaɪnəʊ/ *n* [u] (BrE colloq) linóleo *m*

linoleum /lɪˈnəʊliəm/ *n* [u] linóleo *m*

linseed /ˈlɪnsiːd/ *n* [u] linaza *f*; (*before n*) **~ oil** aceite *m* de linaza

lint /lɪnt/ *n* [u] hilas *fpl*

lintel /ˈlɪntl/ *n* dintel *m*

lion /ˈlaɪən/ *n* león *m*; ***the ~'s share*** la mejor parte; (*before n*) **~ cub** cachorro *m* de león; ► **throw¹** *vt* **B**

lioness /ˈlaɪənəs || ˈlaɪənes/ *n* leona *f*

lion tamer /ˈlaɪənˈteɪmər || ˈlaɪən,teɪmə(r)/ *n* domador, -dora *m,f* de leones

lip /lɪp/ *n*
A [c] **1** (Anat) labio *m*; **to read sb's ~s** leerle* los labios a algn; **to bite one's ~** morderse* la lengua; **her name was on everyone's ~s** su nombre estaba en boca de todo el mundo; **to lick/smack one's ~s** relamerse; ***my ~s are sealed***: **I can't tell you, my ~s are sealed** no puedo decírtelo, he prometido no decir nada; **don't worry, my ~s are sealed** no te preocupes, no diré una palabra *or* de mi boca no saldrá; ***to button one's ~*** (colloq) callarse la boca (fam); ***to keep a stiff upper ~*** guardar la compostura, no inmutarse **2** (of cup, tray) borde *m*
B [u] (insolence) (colloq): **that's enough of your ~!** ¡ya basta de insolencias!

lip gloss *n* [u] brillo *m* de labias

liposuction /ˈlaɪpəʊ,sʌkʃən/ *n* liposucción *f*

lip: **~read** (*past & past p* **-read** /-red/) *vi* leer* los labios
■ **lip** *vt*: **she ~read what I was saying** me leyó los labios; **~ salve** *n* bálsamo *m* labial; **~ service** *n*: **he just pays ~ service to feminism** es feminista de los dientes para afuera *or* de boquilla; **~stick** *n* **1** [c] (stick) lápiz *m or* barra *f* de labios, lápiz *m* labial (AmL), pintalabios *m* (Esp fam) **2** [u] (substance) rouge *m*, carmín *m*

liquefy /ˈlɪkwəfaɪ || ˈlɪkwɪfaɪ/ **-fies, -fying, -fied** *vi* licuarse*
■ **liquefy** *vt* licuar*

liqueur /lɪˈkɜːr || lɪˈkjʊə(r)/ *n* [u c] licor *m*

liquid¹ /ˈlɪkwəd || ˈlɪkwɪd/ *n* [u c] líquido *m*; (*before n*) **~ measure** medida *f* de capacidad para líquidos

liquid² *adj* **1** líquido **2** (Fin) líquido; **~ assets** activo *m* líquido **3** (limpid) (liter) límpido, transparente

liquidate /ˈlɪkwədeɪt || ˈlɪkwɪdeɪt/ *vt* (Fin, Law) liquidar

liquidation /ˈlɪkwəˈdeɪʃən || ˌlɪkwɪˈdeɪʃən/ *n* [u c] (Fin, Law) liquidación *f*; **to go into ~** entrar en liquidación; **voluntary ~** disolución *f*

liquid crystal display *n* pantalla *f* de cristal líquido

liquidity /lɪˈkwɪdəti/ *n* [u] (Fin, Law) liquidez *f*

liquidize /ˈlɪkwədaɪz || ˈlɪkwɪdaɪz/ *vt* licuar*

liquidizer /ˈlɪkwədaɪzər || ˈlɪkwɪdaɪzə(r)/ *n* (BrE) licuadora *f*

liquid paraffin *n* (BrE) parafina *f* liquida, aceite *m* de parafina

liquor /ˈlɪkər || ˈlɪkə(r)/ *n* [u] (alcohol) alcohol *m*, bebidas *fpl* alcohólicas; **hard ~** bebidas *fpl* (alcohólicas) fuertes; (*before n*) **~ cabinet** (AmE) mueble-bar *m*

liquorice (BrE) ► **licorice**

liquor store *n* (AmE) ≈ tienda *f* de vinos y licores, botillería *f* (Chi)

lira /ˈlɪrə || ˈlɪərə/ *n* (*pl* **lire** /ˈlɪrə || ˈlɪəre, ˈlɪəri/) lira *f*

Lisbon /ˈlɪzbən/ *n* Lisboa *f*

lisp¹ /lɪsp/ *n* ceceo *m*; **to speak with a ~** cecear

lisp² *vi* cecear

lissom, lissome /ˈlɪsəm/ *adj* (liter) grácil (liter)

list¹ /lɪst/ *n*
A (of items) lista *f*, relación *f* (frml); **shopping ~** lista de la compra; **to be high/low on the ~** ‹‹*matter/problem*›› tener*/no tener* prioridad; (*before n*) **~ price** precio *m* de catálogo *or* de lista
B (Naut) escora *f*

list² *vt* **1** (enumerate) hacer* una lista de; (verbally) enumerar **2** (include) incluir*; **he's/it's not ~ed** no aparece *or* figura en la lista; **~ed building** (in UK) edificio *m* protegido (*por su interés histórico o arquitectónico*) **3** (Fin) ‹*securities/stocks*› cotizar*; **~ed company** compañía *f* que cotiza en Bolsa
■ **list** *vi* (Naut) escorar

listen /ˈlɪsn̩/ *vi* **1** (focus hearing) escuchar; **to ~ TO sth/sb** escuchar algo/a algn; **as she lay in bed she ~ed to them arguing** acostada en su cama, los oía discutir; **to ~ FOR sth**: **they ~ed for her footsteps** estaban atentos a ver si la oían venir **2** (pay attention, heed) **to ~ (TO sth/sb)** escuchar (algo/a algn); **I never used to ~ in class** nunca atendía *or* prestaba atención en clase; **he doesn't ~ to a word I say!** no me hace ningún caso

(Phrasal verb)

- **listen in** [v ▸ adv] escuchar; **to ~ in TO/ON sth** escuchar algo

listener /'lɪsn̩ər || 'lɪsnə(r)/ *n* 1 (Rad) oyente *mf*, radioyente *mf* 2 (in conversation): **he's a good ~** es una persona que sabe escuchar

listening device /'lɪsnɪŋ/ *n* aparato *m* de escucha

listeria /lɪs'tɪriə || lɪ'stɪəriə/ *n* [u] listeria *f*

listing /'lɪstɪŋ/ *n* 1 (list) lista *f*, listado *m*; **TV ~s** programación *f* televisiva *or* de televisión; **~s magazine** guía *f* de espectáculos, ≈ guía *f* del ocio (*en Esp*) 2 (entry) entrada *f*; (Fin) cotización *f* bursátil

listless /'lɪstləs || 'lɪstlɪs/ *adj* (lacking enthusiasm) apático, indiferente; (lacking energy) lánguido

list processing *n* [u] procesamiento *m* de listas

lit /lɪt/ *past & past p of* **light**[4]

litany /'lɪtəni/ *n* (*pl* **-nies**) (Relig) letanía *f*; **the L~** *oración de la liturgia anglicana en forma de letanías*

litchi /'laɪtʃi:/ *n* (*pl* **~s**) (AmE) lichi *m*

lite /laɪt/ *adj*

A (low-fat/low-sugar) light *adj inv*, bajo en calorías, dietético (AmL)

B (facile) (colloq) light *adj inv*, de poco peso; **the performance was Shakespeare ~** la interpretación fue sakespeariana light *or* de poco peso

liter, (BrE) **litre** /'li:tər || 'li:tə(r)/ *n* litro *m*

literacy /'lɪtərəsi/ *n* [u] alfabetismo *m*; **adult ~ is below 50%** más del 50% de los adultos son analfabetos; (*before n*) **~ program** programa *f* de alfabetización; **~ teaching** alfabetización *f*

literal /'lɪtərəl/ *adj* literal; **~-minded** sin imaginación

literally /'lɪtərəli/ *adv* ‹*translate*› literalmente, palabra por palabra; **I didn't mean it ~** no lo decía en sentido literal; **he was ~ starving** se estaba muriendo de hambre, en el verdadero sentido de la palabra

literary /'lɪtəreri || 'lɪtərəri/ *adj* literario; **~ agent** agente literario, -ria *m,f*

literate /'lɪtərət/ *adj* 1 (able to read) alfabetizado; **barely ~** casi analfabeto 2 (well-educated) instruido; (cultured) cultivado, culto

literature /'lɪtərətʃʊr || 'lɪtrətʃə(r)/ *n* 1 [u] (art) literatura *f* 2 [u c] (published works) bibliografía *f*, material *m* publicado 3 [u] (promotional material) folletos *mpl*, información *f*

lithe /laɪð/ *adj* **lither, lithest** ágil

lithium /'lɪθiəm/ *n* [u] litio *m*

lithograph /'lɪθəgræf || 'lɪθəgrɑ:f/ *n* litografía *f*

lithography /lɪ'θɑ:grəfi || lɪ'θɒgrəfi/ *n* [u] litografía *f*

Lithuania /'lɪθju'eɪniə/ *n* Lituania *f*

Lithuanian[1] /'lɪθju'eɪniən/ *adj* lituano

Lithuanian[2] *n* 1 [c] (person) lituano, -na *m,f* 2 [u] (language) lituano *m*

litigation /'lɪtə'geɪʃən || ˌlɪtɪ'geɪʃən/ *n* [u] litigio *m*

litigious /lɪ'tɪdʒəs/ *adj* pleiteador

litmus /'lɪtməs/: **~ paper** *n* papel *m* (de) tornasol; **~ test** *n* (Chem) prueba *f* de acidez *or* de tornasol

litre /'li:tər || 'li:tə(r)/ *n* (BrE) ▸ **liter**

litter[1] /'lɪtər || 'lɪtə(r)/ *n*

A [u] (refuse) basura *f*, desperdicios *mpl*; **don't drop ~** no tire basura

B [c] (offspring) (Zool) camada *f*, cría *f*

C [u] (for horses, cows) lecho *m* de paja; (for cats) arena *f* higiénica

D [c] 1 (stretcher) camilla *f* 2 (couch) (Hist) litera *f*

litter[2] *vt*: **newspapers ~ed the floor** el suelo estaba cubierto de papeles, había papeles tirados por (todo) el suelo; **to be ~ed WITH sth** estar* lleno DE algo

litter: **~ bin** *n* (BrE) papelera *f or* (AmL tb) papelero *m or* (Col) caneca *f*; **~bug** *n*: *persona que tira basura en lugares públicos*; **~ pick** *n* (BrE) *recogida de basura en las calles por parte de los vecinos*

little[1] /'lɪtl̩/ *adj*

(Sense I) (*comp* **littler** /'lɪtl̩ər || 'lɪtl̩ə(r)/; *superl* **littlest** /'lɪtl̩əst || 'lɪtl̩ɪst/)

A 1 (small) pequeño, chico (esp AmL); **a lovely ~ dog** un perrito precioso; **a ~ old lady** una viejecita; **a ~ while** un ratito; **she is a ~ bit better** está un poquito mejor *or* algo mejor 2 (young) pequeño, chico (esp AmL); **when I was ~** cuando era pequeña *or* pequeñita *or* (esp AmL) chica *or* chiquita; **my ~ sister/brother** mi hermanita/hermanito 3 (insignificant) pequeño; **then there's the ~ matter of ...** (iro) está también el pequeño detalle de ... (iró)

B (expressing speaker's attitude) (colloq) (*before n*): **I know your ~ game!** ¡ya te conozco el jueguito! (fam); **you poor ~ thing!** ¡pobrecito!

(Sense II) (*comp* **less**; *superl* **least**) 1 (not much) poco; **there is very ~ bread left** queda muy poco pan; **from what ~ information we have** por lo poco que sabemos; **it uses less electricity than a toaster** gasta menos electricidad que una tostadora; **he had ~ talent and even less charm** tenía poco talento y aún menos encanto; **he has (the) least talent of all** es el que menos talento tiene 2 **a little** (some) un poco de; **with not a ~ sadness** (frml) con no poca tristeza

little[2] *pron* (*comp* **less**; *superl* **least**) 1 (not much) poco, -ca; **there was ~ to do** había poco que hacer; **we see very ~ of him nowadays** lo vemos muy poco últimamente; **the ~ that she earns** lo poco que gana; **from as ~ as $2,000** a partir de tan sólo 2.000 dólares; **~ by ~** poco a poco; **I get paid less than you** me pagan menos que a ti; **Jean earns (the) least of all** Jean es la que menos gana de todos; **the (very) least you can do is apologize** lo menos que puedes hacer es pedir perdón; **he was rather abrupt, to say the least** estuvo un poco brusco, por no decir otra cosa; **that's the least of it** eso es lo de menos 2 **a little** (some) un poco, algo; **she ate a ~** comió algo *or* un poco

little[3] *adv* (*comp* **less**; *superl* **least**) 1 (not much) poco; **he goes out very ~** sale muy poco; **it is a ~ known fact that ...** es un hecho poco conocido que ...; **the campaign has been somewhat less than a success** la campaña no ha tenido mucho éxito que digamos; **just when we were least expecting it** cuando menos lo esperábamos 2 (hardly, not): **~ did he know that ...** lo que menos se imaginaba era que ...; **he's ~ better than a thief** es poco menos que un ladrón; **no one likes him, least of all his brother** nadie lo quiere, y su hermano menos que nadie 3 **a little** (somewhat) un poco; **do you speak French? — a ~** ¿hablas francés? — algo *or* un poco; **a ~ less noise, please** hagan menos ruido, por favor

little: **~ finger** *n* (dedo *m*) meñique *m*; ***to twist sb around one's ~ finger*** meterse a algn en el bolsillo; **~ Red Riding Hood** *n* Caperucita Roja

littoral /'lɪtərəl/ *n* litoral *m*

liturgy /'lɪtərdʒi || 'lɪtədʒi/ *n* (*pl* **-gies**) liturgia *f*

livable /'lɪvəbəl/ *adj* 1 (habitable) (AmE) habitable, en el que se puede vivir; **to be ~** o (BrE) **to be ~ in** ser* habitable 2 (endurable) ‹*life*› llevadero

live[1] /lɪv/ *vi*

A 1 (be, remain alive) vivir; **(for) as long as I ~** mientras viva, toda la vida; **she ~d to be 100** llegó a cumplir 100 años; **you'll ~ to regret it** algún día te arrepentirás; **she had three months to ~** le quedaban tres meses de vida; **you'll ~** (colloq) no te vas a morir (fam); **long ~ the king!** ¡viva el rey!; **you ~ and learn** (set phrase) todos los días se aprende algo nuevo; **~ and let ~** (set phrase) vive y deja vivir a los demás 2 (experience life) vivir; **never eaten paella? you haven't ~d!** ¿no has comido nunca una paella? ¡pues no sabes lo que te pierdes *or* lo que es bueno!

B 1 (conduct one's life) vivir; **we ~ very quietly** llevamos una vida tranquila; ***to ~ like a king*** o ***lord*** vivir a cuerpo de rey 2 (support oneself) vivir

C 1 (reside) vivir; **where do you ~?** ¿donde vives?; **this house is not fit to ~ in** esta casa no está en condiciones 2 (belong) (esp BrE colloq) ir*; **where do these dishes ~?** ¿dónde van estos platos?

■ **live** *vt* 1 (exist in specified way) vivir; **she ~s a happy life** lleva una vida feliz, vive feliz; **to ~ life to the full** vivir la vida al máximo 2 (throw oneself into): **she really ~d the part** realmente se identificó con el personaje

(Phrasal verbs)

- **live down** [v ▸ o ▸ adv, v ▸ adv ▸ o]: **if they see you wearing that, you'll never ~ it down** si te ven con eso no lo van a olvidar nunca *or* (fam) te van a tomar el pelo toda la vida
- **live for** [v ▸ prep ▸ o]: **she ~s for her work** vive para su trabajo; **I've nothing left to ~ for** ya no tengo nada por

l

lo que vivir; **he's living for the day of her return** vive esperando su retorno

- **live in** [v ▸ adv] *vivir en el lugar de trabajo*
- **live off** [v ▸ prep ▸ o] 1 (be supported by) ‹*family/friends*› vivir a costa *or* a costillas de; ‹*crime/social security/the land*› vivir de; **you could ~ off the interest** podrías vivir de los intereses 2 (feed on) ‹*fruits/seeds*› alimentarse de
- **live on**

A [v ▸ adv] (continue in existence) ‹‹*memory*›› seguir* presente; ‹‹*tradition*›› seguir* existiendo

B [v ▸ prep ▸ o] 1 (feed on) alimentarse de; **we ~d on pizza for a week** no comimos más que pizzas toda la semana 2 (support oneself with): **she ~s on $75 a week** vive *or* se las arregla con 75 dólares a la semana; **the pension is barely enough to ~ on** la pensión apenas alcanza para vivir

- **live out**

A [v ▸ adv] (off premises) vivir fuera (*del lugar de trabajo o estudio*)

B [v ▸ adv ▸ o] 1 ‹*one's life/days*›: **he wanted to ~ out his days in that house** quería vivir *or* pasar el resto de sus días en aquella casa 2 (enact) ‹*fantasy/dream*› vivir

- **live through** [v ▸ prep ▸ o] ‹*war/experience*› vivir, pasar por; **I don't think she'll ~ through the night** no creo que pase de esta noche
- **live together** [v ▸ adv] 1 (cohabit) vivir juntos 2 (coexist) convivir
- **live up** [v ▸ o ▸ adv]: ***to ~ it up*** (colloq) darse* la gran vida (fam)
- **live up to** [v ▸ adv ▸ prep ▸ o]: **it didn't ~ up to its reputation** no estuvo a la altura de su reputación; **she didn't ~ up to her father's expectations** defraudó las esperanzas *or* expectativas de su padre; **they ~ up to their name** hacen honor a su nombre
- **live with** [v ▸ prep ▸ o] 1 (share house with) vivir con 2 (accept, tolerate) ‹*fact/situation*› aceptar

live² /laɪv/ *adj*

A (alive) vivo; **wow, a real ~ princess!** ¡uy, una princesa de verdad *or* de carne y hueso!

B (of current interest) ‹*issue*› candente, de actualidad

C (Rad, TV): **the show was ~** el programa era en directo *or* en vivo; **the program is recorded before a ~ audience** el programa se graba con público en la sala *or* en presencia de público

D 1 (Mil): **~ ammunition** fuego *m* real; **~ bomb** bomba *f* que no ha estallado 2 (Elec) ‹*circuit/terminal*› con corriente, cargado 3 (on fire) encendido; **~ coal** brasa *f*

live³ /laɪv/ *adv* (Rad, TV) ‹*broadcast*› en directo, en vivo

liveable /ˈlɪvəbəl/ *adj* ▸**livable**

lived-in /ˈlɪvdɪn/ *adj* (*pred* **lived in**): **the pictures made the room feel ~ ~** los cuadros le daban un ambiente acogedor *or* cálido a la habitación

live-in /ˈlɪvˈɪn/ *adj* (*before n*) ‹*staff*› residente; ‹*nanny/maid*› con cama, de planta (Méx), puertas adentro (Chi); **she has a ~ lover** su amante vive con ella

livelihood /ˈlaɪvlihʊd/ *n* (*no pl*): **farming is their ~** viven de la agricultura; **to earn one's/a ~** ganarse la vida *or* el sustento

liveliness /ˈlaɪvlinəs || ˈlaɪvlinɪs/ *n* [u] (of person) vivacidad *f*; (of atmosphere) animación *f*; (of debate) lo animado

lively /ˈlaɪvli/ *adj* **-lier, -liest** ‹*place/atmosphere/debate*› animado; ‹*music*› alegre; ‹*description/account*› vívido; **he's a ~ character** es un tipo de lo más animado y alegre; **they take a ~ interest in developments** toman un vivo interés en el desarrollo de los acontecimientos

liven up /ˈlaɪvən/

A [v ▸ adv] animarse

B [v ▸ o ▸ adv, v ▸ adv ▸ o] animar

liver /ˈlɪvər || ˈlɪvə(r)/ *n* (Anat, Culin) hígado *m*; (*before n*) **~ disease** enfermedad *f* del hígado, afección *f* hepática (frml); **~ sausage** (BrE) embutido *m* de paté de hígado

Liverpudlian¹ /ˈlɪvərˈpʌdliən || ˌlɪvəˈpʌdliən/ *adj* de Liverpool

Liverpudlian² *n*: *habitante o persona oriunda de Liverpool*

liver spot *n* mancha *f* (de la vejez)

liverwurst /ˈlɪvərwɜːrst || ˈlɪvəwɜːst/ *n* [u] (AmE) embutido *m* de paté de hígado

livery /ˈlɪvəri/ *n* (*pl* **-ries**) 1 (uniform) librea *f* 2 (of aircraft, vehicle) colores *mpl* distintivos

lives /laɪvz/ *pl of* **life**

live /laɪv/: **~stock** *n* [u] (+ *sing or pl vb*) animales *mpl* (de cría); (cattle) ganado *m*; **~ wire** *n* (colloq): **he's a real ~ wire** es una persona llena de vida

livid /ˈlɪvəd || ˈlɪvɪd/ *adj*

A (furious) (colloq) furioso, furibundo (fam)

B 1 (blueish) ‹*bruise*› amoratado 2 (white) ‹*face*› lívido

living¹ /ˈlɪvɪŋ/ *n*

A (livelihood) (*no pl*): **to earn** *o* **make one's/a ~** ganarse la vida; **they scrape** *o* **scratch a ~ selling trinkets** sobreviven *or* malviven vendiendo chucherías; **what do you do for a ~?** ¿en qué trabajas?, ¿a qué te dedicas?; **to work for a ~** trabajar para vivir; **the world doesn't owe you a ~** no tienes derecho a vivir sin trabajar

B [u] (style of life) vida *f*; **clean/loose ~** vida ordenada/disoluta; ‹*space/area*› destinado a vivienda; ‹*conditions*› de vida; **~ standards** nivel *m* de vida

C (people) (+ *pl vb*) **the ~** los vivos

living² *adj* (*before n*) ‹*person/creature*› vivo; **Spain's greatest ~ painter** el pintor vivo más importante de España; **he was ~ proof of the power of the media** era prueba evidente *or* palpable del poder de los medios de comunicación

living: **~ room** *n* sala *f* (de estar) , living *m* (esp AmS), salón *m* (esp Esp); **~ wage** *n* salario *m* digno; **~ will** *n* testamento *m* vital

lizard /ˈlɪzərd || ˈlɪzəd/ *n* lagarto *m*; (*wall* ~) lagartija *f*

'll /l̩/ 1 **= will** 2 **= shall**

llama /ˈlɑːmə/ *n* llama *f*

LLB *n* **= Bachelor of Laws**

'll've /l̩əv/ 1 **= will have** 2 **= shall have**

lo /ləʊ/ *interj* (arch *or* hum): **~ and behold** ¡y quién lo iba a decir!

load¹ /ləʊd/ *n*

A [c] (cargo) carga *f*; (burden) carga *f*, peso *m*; **four ~s of washing** cuatro lavados *or* (Esp) coladas; **the project will create a heavy administrative ~** el proyecto generará mucho trabajo administrativo; ***to have a ~ on*** (AmE colloq) estar* como una cuba (fam), estar* tomado (AmL fam)

B (*often pl*) (colloq) 1 (much, many) cantidad *f*, montón *m* (fam), pila *f* (AmS fam); **I've done this ~s of times** esto lo he hecho cantidad *or* montones *or* (AmS tb) pilas de veces (fam); **what a ~ of nonsense!** ¡qué sarta de estupideces!; **the play is a ~ of rubbish** la obra no vale nada *or* (fam) es una porquería 2 (*as intensifier*) (colloq): **my room's ~s bigger than hers** mi cuarto es muchísimo más grande que el suyo

C (Civil Eng) carga *f*; ⊜ **maximum load 15 tons** peso máximo: 15 toneladas

load² *vt* 1 (Transp) ‹*truck/plane*› cargar* 2 (charge) ‹*gun*› cargar*; **to ~ a program (into a computer)** cargar* un programa (en una computadora)

■ **load** *vi* cargar*; ⊜ **loading prohibited** carga y descarga prohibidas

Phrasal verbs

- **load down** [v ▸ o ▸ adv, v ▸ adv ▸ o] (*usu pass*) **to be ~ed down WITH sth** (with parcels) ir* cargado DE algo; (with problems) estar* abrumado *or* agobiado POR algo
- **load up**

A [v ▸ o ▸ adv, v ▸ adv ▸ o] ‹*truck/ship/person*› cargar*; **to ~ sth up WITH sth** cargar* algo DE algo

B [v ▸ adv] cargar*

loaded /ˈləʊdəd || ˈləʊdɪd/ *adj*

A 1 ‹*vehicle/gun/camera*› cargado 2 (richly provided) (*pred*) **to be ~ WITH sth** estar* repleto *or* plagado DE algo 3 (weighted) ‹*dice*› cargado; ‹*question/remark*› tendencioso

B (colloq) (*pred*) 1 (rich) forrado (fam) 2 (drunk) (AmE) como una cuba (fam), tomado (AmL fam)

loading dock, (BrE) **loading bay** /ˈləʊdɪŋ/ zona *f or* área *f*‡ de carga

loaf¹ /ləʊf/ *n* (*pl* **loaves**): **a ~ (of bread)** un pan; (of French bread) una barra de pan, una flauta (CS); (baked in tin) un pan de molde; ***use your ~!*** (BrE colloq) ¡usa el coco *or* (Esp tb) la cocorota *or* (Col tb) la tusta! (fam)

loaf² *vi* (colloq): **to ~ (around** *o* **about)** holgazanear, haraganear, flojear (fam)

loafer /ˈləʊfər || ˈləʊfə(r)/ *n* holgazán, -zana *m,f*, vago, -ga *m,f*

Loafer®, **loafer** /ˈləʊfər || ˈləʊfə(r)/ *n* mocasín *m*

l

loan¹ /ləʊn/ *n* **1** (of money) préstamo *m*; (Fin) préstamo *m*, crédito *m*, empréstito *m* (frml); **bank ~** préstamo *or* crédito bancario; (*before n*) **~ account** (BrE) cuenta *f* crediticia **2** (temporary use): **may I have the ~ of your umbrella?** ¿me prestas el paraguas?; **the book you want is out on ~** el libro que quieres está prestado

loan² *vt* prestar; **many sports clubs will ~ out equipment** muchos clubs deportivos prestan el equipo; **to ~ sb sth, to ~ sth TO sb** prestarle algo A algn

loan: **~ shark** *n* usurero, -ra *m,f*, agiotista *mf* (AmL); **~word** *n* préstamo *m* (lingüístico)

loath /ləʊθ/ *adj* (*pred*) **to be ~ to + INF** resistirse A + INF

loathe /ləʊð/ *vt* odiar, detestar; **to ~ -ING** odiar + INF

loathing /'ləʊðɪŋ/ *n* [u] aversión *f*, odio *m*

loathsome /'ləʊðsəm/ *adj* repugnante, odioso

loaves /ləʊvz/ *pl of* **loaf¹**

lob¹ /lɑːb || lɒb/ *vt* **-bb-** ‹*ball*› lanzar* por lo alto; ‹*stone/grenade*› tirar *or* lanzar* por lo alto

lob² *n* (Sport) globo *m*, lob *m*

lobby¹ /'lɑːbi || 'lɒbi/ *n* (*pl* **-bies**)
A (entrance hall) vestíbulo *m*, hall *m*; (in theater) foyer *m*
B (pressure group) grupo *m* de presión, lobby *m*

lobby², **-bies, -bying, -bied** *vt* ejercer* presión sobre
■ **lobby** *vi* **to ~ FOR sth** ejercer* presión *or* cabildear para obtener algo

lobbying /'lɑːbiɪŋ || 'lɒbiɪŋ/ *n* [u] cabildeo *m*

lobbyist /'lɑːbiəst || 'lɒbiɪst/ *n* miembro *mf* de un grupo de presión

lobe /ləʊb/ *n* lóbulo *m* (de la oreja)

lobotomy /ləʊ'bɑːtəmi || lə'bɒtəmi/ *n* (*pl* **-mies**) lobotomía *f*

lobster /'lɑːbstər || 'lɒbstə(r)/ *n* langosta *f*, bogavante *m* (Esp); (*before n*) **~ pot** nasa *f*, langostera *f*

local¹ /'ləʊkəl/ *adj*
A ‹*dialect/custom/newspaper*› local; ‹*council/election*› ~ municipal; **he's a ~ man** es de aquí (*or* de allí); **the ~ community** los vecinos *or* habitantes de la zona; **a ~ specialty** una especialidad de la localidad (*or* de la región *etc*)
B (Med) ‹*anesthetic*› local; ‹*infection*› localizado

local² *n* **1** (inhabitant): **he's not a ~** no es de aquí (*or* de allí); **the ~s say it's true** los (vecinos) del lugar dicen que es verdad **2** (pub) (BrE colloq): **our ~** el bar de nuestro barrio (*or* de nuestra zona *etc*)

local: **~ authority** *n* (BrE) ≈ ayuntamiento *m*, ≈ alcaldía *f*, ≈ municipio *m*; **~ area network** *n* red *f* de área local

locale /ləʊ'kæl || ləʊ'kɑːl/ *n* escenario *m*

local government *n* [u] ≈ administración *f* municipal; (*before n*) ‹*elections*› ≈ municipal

locality /ləʊ'kæləti/ *n* (*pl* **-ties**) (frml) localidad *f*

localize /'ləʊkəlaɪz/ *vt* localizar*

locally /'ləʊkəli/ *adv* ‹*live/work*› en la zona; **do you shop ~?** ¿compras en las tiendas del barrio (*or* de la zona *etc*)?; **these issues should be decided ~** estas decisiones deben tomarse a nivel local; **were you born ~?** ¿naciste aquí?, ¿eres de (por) aquí?

locate /'ləʊkeɪt || ləʊ'keɪt/ *vt*
A (find) ‹*fault/leak*› localizar*, ubicar* (esp AmL)
B (position) ‹*building/business*› situar*, ubicar* (esp AmL); **the switch is ~d under the seat** el interruptor está *or* se encuentra debajo del asiento
■ **locate** *vi* (settle) (AmE) establecerse*

location /ləʊ'keɪʃən/ *n*
A [c] (position) posición *f*, ubicación *f* (esp AmL)
B [c u] (Cin) lugar *m* de filmación; **we were filming on ~ in Italy** estábamos rodando los exteriores en Italia
C [u] **1** (siting) emplazamiento *m*, ubicación *f* (esp AmL) **2** (discovery of position) localización *f*

locative /'lɑːkətɪv || 'lɒkətɪv/ *n* locativo *m*

loch /lɑːk, lɑːx || lɒk, lɒx/ *n* **1** (lake) lago *m* **2** (*sea ~*) fiordo *m*, ría *f*

lock¹ /lɑːk || lɒk/ *n*
A [c] (device) cerradura *f*, cerrojo *m*, chapa *f* (AmL); **under ~ and key** bajo llave; ***~, stock and barrel***: **he sold up ~, stock and barrel** vendió absolutamente todo
B [c] (on canal) esclusa *f*
C [c] (of hair) mechón *m*
D [c] (in wrestling) llave *f*; ***to have a ~ on sth*** (AmE) tener* el control de algo
E [u] (BrE Auto) tope *m*, retén *m*; **keep it on full ~** dale al volante hasta el tope
F [c] **~ (forward)** (in rugby) delantero, -ra *m,f* de segunda línea *m*

lock² *vt* **1** (fasten) ‹*door/room/car*› cerrar* (con llave); **to ~ sb in a room** encerrar* a algn en una habitación **2** (immobilize) ‹*steering wheel*› bloquear; **to be ~ed IN sth**: **~ed in a passionate embrace** fundidos en un apasionado abrazo; **they are ~ed in a battle of wills** están enzarzados en una lucha de resistencia
■ **lock** *vi* **1** (fasten, secure) «*door/case*» cerrarse* con llave **2** (become immobile) «*catch*» trabarse; «*wheel*» bloquearse

Phrasal verbs

• **lock away** [v ▸ o ▸ adv, v ▸ adv ▸ o] ‹*valuables*› guardar bajo llave; ‹*person*› encerrar*
• **lock in** [v ▸ o ▸ adv, v ▸ adv ▸ o] encerrar*
• **lock out** [v ▸ o ▸ adv, v ▸ adv ▸ o]: **I ~ed myself out (of the house)** me quedé afuera sin llaves
• **lock up**
A [v ▸ o ▸ adv, v ▸ adv ▸ o] **1** ‹*valuables*› guardar bajo llave; ‹*person*› encerrar* **2** ‹*house/shop*› cerrar* con llave **3** (make sure of) (AmE colloq) asegurar
B [v ▸ adv] cerrar* (con llave)

locker /'lɑːkər || 'lɒkə(r)/ *n* armario *m*, locker *m* (AmL); (at bus, railway station) (casilla *f* de la) consigna *f* automática

locker room *n* (esp AmE) vestuario *m*; (*before n*) ‹*humor/joke*› de machos (fam)

locket /'lɑːkət || 'lɒkɪt/ *n* relicario *m*, guardapelo *m*

lock: **~jaw** *n* [u] tétano(s) *m*; **~out** *n* cierre *m* patronal, paro *m* patronal (AmL); **~smith** *n* cerrajero, -ra *m,f*; **~-up** *n* **1** (cell) (esp AmE) calabozo *m* **2** **~-up (garage)** (BrE) garaje *m* (*separado de la vivienda*) **3** **~-up (shop)** (BrE) local *m* (comercial) (*pequeño y sin vivienda*)

locomotion /'ləʊkə'məʊʃən/ *n* [u] (frml) locomoción *f*

locomotive /'ləʊkə'məʊtɪv/ *n* locomotora *f*

locum /'ləʊkəm/ *n* (esp BrE) suplente *mf* (*de un médico*)

locust /'ləʊkəst/ *n* (Zool) langosta *f*

lode /ləʊd/ *n* veta *f*, filón *m*

lodestone /'ləʊdstəʊn/ *n* piedra *f* imán

lodge¹ /lɑːdʒ || lɒdʒ/ *n*
A **1** (for gatekeeper) (BrE) casa *f* del guarda **2** (for porter) portería *f* **3** (on private estate) pabellón *m* **4** (at resort) (AmE) hotel *m*
B (branch, meeting place of society) logia *f*
C (of beaver) madriguera *f*

lodge² *vt*
A ‹*appeal*› interponer*; ‹*complaint/objection*› presentar
B (place, deposit) depositar
C (fix): **the bullet had ~d itself in his thigh** la bala se le había alojado en el muslo; **I have something ~d between my teeth** tengo algo metido entre los dientes
■ **lodge** *vi*
A (become stuck, implanted): **the bullet had ~d in his spine** la bala se le había alojado en la columna
B (live as lodger) alojarse, hospedarse

lodger /'lɑːdʒər || 'lɒdʒə(r)/ *n* inquilino, -na *m,f* (*de una habitación en una casa particular*); **they take (in) ~s** alquilan habitaciones

lodging /'lɑːdʒɪŋ || 'lɒdʒɪŋ/ *n* **1** [u] (accommodations) alojamiento *m* **2** **lodgings** *pl* (rented): **to live in ~s** vivir en una habitación alquilada (*or* en una pensión *etc*); **I'm looking for ~s** estoy buscando alojamiento

lodging house *n* (BrE) casa *f* de inquilinato

loft /lɔːft || lɒft/ *n* **1** (attic) (BrE) desván *m*, buhardilla *f*, altillo *m*, zarzo *m* (Col) **2** (*hay ~*) pajar *m* **3** (in warehouse) (AmE) loft *m* (*espacio comercial convertido en residencia*)

loftily /'lɔːftəli || 'lɒftɪli/ *adv* con altivez, altaneramente

lofty /'lɔːfti || 'lɒfti/ *adj* **-tier, -tiest** **1** (elevated, grand) ‹*aims/ideals/sentiments*› noble, elevado **2** (haughty) altivo, altanero **3** (high) (liter) alto, majestuoso (liter)

log¹ /lɔːg || lɒg/ *n*
A (wood) tronco *m*; (as fuel) leño *m*; ***to be as easy as falling off a ~*** ser* pan comido (fam), ser* coser y cantar (fam); ***to sleep like a ~*** dormir* como un tronco (fam); (*before n*) **~ cabin** cabaña *f* de troncos; **~ fire** fuego *m* de leña

L

B 1 (record) diario *m* 2 (device for measuring speed) corredera *f*
C (Math) logaritmo *m*; (*before n*) ~ **tables** tabla *f* de logaritmos

log² **-gg-** *vt* 1 (record) ‹*speed/position/time*› registrar, anotar; ‹*call*› registrar 2 ~ **(up)** (accomplish) anotarse; **he has ~ged (up) 100 hours in the air** tiene *or* ha hecho 100 horas de vuelo

Phrasal verbs
- **log in, log on** [v ▸ adv] (Comput) entrar (al sistema)
- **log off, log out** [v ▸ adv] (Comput) salir* (del sistema)

loganberry /'ləʊgən,beri || 'ləʊgənbəri/ *n* (*pl* **-ries**) frambuesa *f* de Logan

logarithm /'lɔːgərɪðəm || 'lɒgərɪðəm/ *n* logaritmo *m*

logbook /'lɔːgbʊk || 'lɒgbʊk/ *n* 1 (register) diario *m*; (Naut) diario *m* de navegación *or* de a bordo; (Aviat) diario *m* de vuelo 2 (of car) (BrE) documentación *f* del automóvil

logger /'lɔːgər || 'lɒgə(r)/ *n* leñador, -dora *m,f*

loggerheads /'lɔːgərhedz || 'lɒgəhedz/ *pl n*: ***to be at ~***: **they were constantly at ~** siempre estaban en desacuerdo

logging /'lɔːgɪŋ || 'lɒgɪŋ/ *n* [u] tala *f* (de árboles); (*before n*) ‹*industry/town*› maderero

logic /'lɑːdʒɪk || 'lɒdʒɪk/ *n* [u] lógica *f*; (*before n*) (Comput) ‹*circuit/diagram*› lógico

logical /'lɑːdʒɪkəl || 'lɒdʒɪkəl/ *adj* lógico

logically /'lɑːdʒɪkli || 'lɒdʒɪkli/ *adv* 1 ‹*reason/argue*› lógicamente, de manera lógica 2 (*indep*) lógicamente

logistics /lə'dʒɪstɪks/ *n* 1 (Mil) (+ *sing vb*) logística *f* 2 (practicalities) (+ *pl vb*) problemas *mpl* logísticos

logo /'ləʊgəʊ, 'lɑː- || 'ləʊgəʊ/ *n* (*pl* **logos**) logo *m*, logotipo *m*

logrolling /'lɔːg,rəʊlɪŋ || 'lɒg,rəʊlɪŋ/ *n* [u] (AmE) amiguismo *m*, camarillismo *m*

loin /lɔɪn/ *n* 1 (meat) lomo *m*; (*before n*) ~ **chop** chuleta *f* de lomo *or* de vacío 2 **loins** *pl* (Anat) (liter) entrañas *fpl*; ***to gird (up) one's ~s*** (liter) prepararse para la lucha, ponerse* lanza en ristre

loincloth /'lɔɪnklɔːθ || 'lɔɪnklɒθ/ *n* taparrabos *m*

loiter /'lɔɪtər || 'lɔɪtə(r)/ *vi* perder* el tiempo, holgazanear; **he was ~ing outside the building** andaba merodeando alrededor del edificio

loll /lɑːl || lɒl/ *vi*: **I found him ~ing in an armchair** me lo encontré apoltronado en un sillón; **the dog's tongue ~ed out** al perro le colgaba la lengua

lollipop /'lɑːlipɑːp || 'lɒlipɒp/ *n* piruleta *f or* (Esp) chupachup(s)® *m or* (Andes, Méx) paleta *f or* (RPl) chupetín *m or* (Col) colombina *f or* (Chi, Per) chupete *m*; (*before n*) ~ **lady/man** (BrE) *persona que detiene el tráfico para permitir que los escolares atraviesen la calzada*

lolly /'lɑːli || 'lɒli/ *n* (*pl* **-lies**) (BrE)
A [c] (*ice* ~) paleta *f* (helada) *or* (Esp) polo *m or* (RPl) palito *m or* (CS) chupete *m* helado
B [u] (money) (sl) guita *f* (arg), lana *f* (AmL fam), plata *f* (AmL fam)

London /'lʌndən/ *n* Londres; (*before n*) londinense

Londoner /'lʌndənər || 'lʌndənə(r)/ *n* londinense *mf*

lone /ləʊn/ *adj* ‹*existence*› solitario; ‹*explorer/sailor*› en solitario

loneliness /'ləʊnlinəs || 'ləʊnlinɪs/ *n* [u] soledad *f*

lonely /'ləʊnli/ *adj* **-lier, -liest** 1 (feeling alone): **to feel ~** sentirse* solo; ~ **evenings** noches de soledad; **a ~ life** una vida solitaria 2 (isolated) ‹*spot/farm*› solitario, aislado

loner /'ləʊnər || 'ləʊnə(r)/ *n*: **she's a bit of a ~** le gusta estar sola

lonesome /'ləʊnsəm/ *adj* (esp AmE) 1 ▸**lonely** 2 ***all on o by one's ~*** (AmE colloq) solito y desamparado (fam)

lone wolf *n* lobo *m* solitario

long¹ /lɔːŋ || lɒŋ/ *adj* **longer** /'lɔːŋgər || 'lɒŋgə(r)/, **longest** /'lɔːŋgəst || 'lɒŋgɪst/
A 1 (in space) ‹*distance/hair/legs*› largo; **how ~ do you want the skirt?** ¿cómo quieres la falda de larga?; **the wall is 200 m ~** el muro mide 200 m de largo; **it's a ~ way to Tulsa from here** Tulsa queda bastante lejos de aquí; **a ~ drink** un trago largo; ***the ~ and the short of it***: **the ~ and the short of it is that we have no money** en resumidas cuentas *or* en una palabra: no tenemos dinero 2 (extensive) ‹*book/letter/list*› largo; **the book is over 300 pages ~** el libro tiene más de 300 páginas
B (in time) ‹*struggle/investigation*› largo; ‹*period/illness*› prolongado, largo; **how ~ was your flight?** ¿cuánto duró el vuelo?; **two months isn't ~ enough** dos meses no son suficientes *or* no es tiempo suficiente; **she's been gone a ~ time/while** hace tiempo/rato que se fue; **he works ~ hours** trabaja muchas horas

long² *adv* **-er, -est**
A (in time): **are you going to stay ~** ¿te vas a quedar mucho tiempo?; **how much ~er must we wait?** ¿hasta cuándo vamos a tener que esperar?; **how ~ did it take you to get there?** ¿cuánto tardaste en llegar?, ¿cuánto tiempo te llevó el viaje?; **how ~ have you been living here?** ¿cuánto hace que vives aquí?; **I didn't have ~ enough to answer all the questions** no me alcanzó el tiempo para contestar todas las preguntas; **people live ~er now** ahora la gente vive más (años); **it won't be ~ before they get here** no tardarán en llegar; **sit down, I won't be ~** siéntate, enseguida vuelvo (*or* termino *etc*); **all day ~** todo el día; **not ~ afterwards** poco después; **~ ago** hace (ya) mucho tiempo; **it has ~ since been lost** lleva perdido desde hace tiempo; **not ~ ago** *o* **since** no hace mucho; **a ~ forgotten hero** un héroe olvidado desde hace tiempo
B 1 (*in phrases*) **before long**: **you'll be an aunt before ~** dentro de poco serás tía; **before ~ they had bought more offices** poco después ya habían comprado más oficinas; **for long**: **she wasn't gone for ~** no estuvo fuera mucho tiempo; **no longer, not any longer**: **I can't stand it any ~er** ya no aguanto más; **they no ~er live here** ya no viven aquí 2 **as long as, so long as** (*as conj*) (for the period) mientras; (providing that) con tal de que (+ *subj*), siempre que (+ *subj*); **I'll remember it as** *o* **so ~ as I live** lo recordaré mientras viva; **for as ~ as I can remember** desde que tengo memoria; **you can go so** *o* **as ~ as you're back by 12** puedes ir con tal de que *or* siempre que vuelvas antes de las 12

long³ *vi* **to ~ to + INF** estar* deseando + INF, anhelar + INF (liter)

Phrasal verb
- **long for** [v ▸ prep ▸ o] ‹*mother/friend*› echar de menos, extrañar (esp AmL); **he was ~ing for her return** anhelaba su regreso (liter); **she ~ed for Friday to arrive** estaba deseando que llegara el viernes; **the ~ed-for moment had arrived** había llegado el tan anhelado *or* esperado momento

long⁴ (= **longitude**) Long.

-long /lɔːŋ || lɒŋ/ *suff*: **an hour~ wait** una espera de una hora; **inch~ nails** clavos de una pulgada (de largo)

longbow /'lɔːŋbəʊ || 'lɒŋbəʊ/ *n* arco *m*

long-distance¹ /'lɔːŋ'dɪstəns || ,lɒŋ'dɪstəns/ *adj* (*before n*) ‹*truck driver*› que hace largos recorridos; ‹*train*› de largo recorrido; ‹*race/runner*› de fondo; **a ~ telephone call** una llamada de larga distancia, una conferencia (interurbana) (Esp)

long-distance² *adv* (esp AmE): **to call ~** hacer* una llamada de larga distancia, poner* una conferencia (Esp)

long drawn-out /'drɔːn'aʊt/ *adj* interminable, larguísimo

longevity /lɑːn'dʒevəti || lɒn'dʒevəti/ *n* [u] (frml) longevidad *f*; (of material) larga duración *f*

long: **~-grain** *adj* ‹*rice*› de grano largo; **~-haired** /'lɔːŋ'herd || ,lɒŋ'heəd/ *adj* ‹*person*› de pelo largo, melenudo (fam & pey); ‹*animal*› de pelo largo; **~hand** *n* [u]: **written in ~hand** en escritura normal (*no en taquigrafía*); **~-haul** /'lɔːŋ'hɔːl || ,lɒŋ'hɔːl/ *adj* (*before n*) de larga distancia

longing /'lɔːŋɪŋ || 'lɒŋɪŋ/ *n* [u c] (nostalgia) añoranza *f*, nostalgia *f*; (desire) vivo *or* vehemente deseo *m*

longingly /'lɔːŋɪŋli || 'lɒŋɪŋli/ *adv* 1 (nostalgically) con nostalgia 2 (desirously) con ansia

longitude /'lɑːndʒətuːd || 'lɒŋgɪtjuːd, 'lɒndʒɪtjuːd/ *n* [u] longitud *f*

long: **~ johns** /dʒɑːnz || dʒɒnz/ *pl n* calzoncillos *mpl* largos; **~ jump** *n* [u c] salto *m* de longitud, salto *m* (en) largo (AmL); **~-lasting** /'lɔːŋ'læstɪŋ || ,lɒŋ'lɑːstɪŋ/ *adj* duradero; **~-life** /'lɔːŋ'laɪf || 'lɒŋlaɪf/ *adj* ‹*milk/orange juice*› (BrE) uperizado, sometido al proceso UHT; ‹*battery/*

bulb› de larga duración; **~-lived** /ˈlɔːŋˈlɪvd ‖ ˌlɒŋˈlɪvd/ *adj* longevo, de larga vida; **~-lost** /ˈlɔːŋˈlɔːst ‖ ˈlɒŋlɒst/ *adj* (*before n*): **she had a ~-lost uncle in Australia** tenía un tío en Australia a quien había perdido de vista hacía mucho tiempo; **~-playing record** /ˈlɔːŋˈpleɪɪŋ ‖ ˈlɒŋ ˌpleɪɪŋ/ *n* disco *m* de larga duración, elepé *m*; **~-range** /ˈlɔːŋˈreɪndʒ ‖ ˈlɒŋreɪndʒ/ *adj* (*before n*) ‹*missile*› de largo alcance; ‹*aircraft*› para vuelos largos; **~-running** /ˈlɔːŋ ˈrʌnɪŋ ‖ ˈlɒŋˌrʌnɪŋ/ *adj* ‹*musical/farce*› que lleva tiempo en cartelera; ‹*feud/controversy*› que viene (*or* venía *etc*) de largo; **~shoreman** /ˈlɔːŋˈʃɔːrmən ‖ ˈlɒŋˌʃɔːmən/ *n* (*pl* **-men** /-mən/) (AmE) estibador *m*, changador *m* (RPl); **~sighted** /ˈlɔːŋˈsaɪtəd ‖ ˌlɒŋˈsaɪtɪd/ *adj* hipermétrope; **~-sleeved** /ˈlɔːŋˈsliːvd ‖ ˈlɒŋsliːvd/ *adj* de manga larga; **~standing** /ˈlɔːŋˈstændɪŋ ‖ ˌlɒŋˈstændɪŋ/ *adj* ‹*grievance/relationship*› antiguo, que viene (*or* venía *etc*) de largo; **~-stay** /ˈlɔːŋˈsteɪ ‖ ˈlɒŋsteɪ/ *adj* ‹*patient*› de estancia *or* (AmL) estadía prolongada; ‹*car park*› (BrE) para estacionamiento *or* (Esp) aparcamiento prolongado; **~-suffering** /ˈlɔːŋˈsʌfərɪŋ ‖ ˌlɒŋˈsʌfərɪŋ/ *adj* ‹*person*› sufrido; ‹*expression*› de resignación; **~-term** /ˈlɔːŋˈtɜːrm ‖ ˈlɒŋtɜːm/ *adj* (*usu before n*) [1] (in the future) ‹*effects/benefits*› a largo plazo [2] (for a long period) ‹*solution*› duradero; ‹*effects*› prolongado; ‹*unemployment*› de larga duración; ‹*parking lot*› (AmE) para estacionamiento *or* (Esp) aparcamiento prolongado; **~time** *adj* (*before n*) ‹*friend*› viejo; **his ~time enemy** su enemigo de toda la vida; **his ~time companion** su compañero de tantos años; **~ wave** *n* onda *f* larga; **~-winded** /ˈlɔːŋˈwɪndəd ‖ ˌlɒŋˈwɪndɪd/ *adj* ‹*speech/article*› denso, prolijo; ‹*procedure*› interminable, larguísimo

loo /luː/ *n* (BrE colloq) baño *m* (esp AmL), váter *m* (Esp fam); (*before n*) **~ paper** papel *m* higiénico

loofah, loofa /ˈluːfə/ *n*: *esponja para el baño que se obtiene del fruto del paste*

look¹ /lʊk/ *n*

A (glance) mirada *f*; **if ~s could kill …** si las miradas mataran …; **she got some odd ~s** la miraron como a un bicho raro (fam); **to have** *o* **take a ~ at sth/sb** echarle un vistazo a algo/algn; **I bought this — let's have a ~** compré esto — ¿a ver?; **let's have a ~ at you** déjame que te vea (bien); **have** *o* **take a good ~ at the picture** fíjate bien en el cuadro, mira bien el cuadro; **I had a quick ~ at the newspaper** le eché una ojeada al periódico; **I'll have to take a long, hard ~ at the figures** tendré que estudiar detenidamente las cifras; **a ~ back over the week's events** un vistazo a los acontecimientos de la semana

B (search, examination): **have a ~ for my pipe, will you?** mira a ver si me encuentras la pipa, por favor; **do you mind if I take a ~ around?** ¿le importa si echo un vistazo?

C [1] (expression) cara *f*; **with a ~ of despair** con cara de desesperación [2] (appearance) aire *m*; **the house had a familiar ~ about it** la casa tenía un aire familiar; **I don't like the ~ of his friend** no me gusta el aspecto *or* (fam) la pinta de su amigo; **by the ~(s) of things** según parece; **he's down on his luck by the ~(s) of him** a juzgar por su aspecto, está pasando una mala racha [3] (Clothing) moda *f*, look *m*; **I need a new ~** tengo que cambiar de imagen [4] **looks** *pl* (beauty) belleza *f*; **she was attracted by his good ~s** la atrajo lo guapo *or* (AmL tb) lo buen mozo que era; **she hasn't lost her ~s** sigue tan guapa como siempre

look² *vi*

Sense I

A [1] (see, glance) mirar; **I ~ed around** (behind) me volví a mirar *or* miré hacia atrás; (all around) miré a mi alrededor; **to ~ away** apartar la vista; **to ~ down** (lower eyes) bajar la vista; (from tower, clifftop) mirar hacia abajo; **we ~ed down over the city** contemplamos la ciudad que se extendía a nuestros pies; **~ into my eyes** mírame a los ojos; **~ out (of) the window** mira por la ventana; **he ~ed straight** *o* **right through me** me miró sin verme; **to ~ up** (raise eyes) levantar la vista; (toward ceiling, sky) mirar hacia arriba; **he ~ed up at the moon** miró a la luna; **she ~ed up from her book** levantó la vista del libro; ***to ~ on the bright side of sth*** ver* el lado bueno *or* positivo de algo; ***to ~ the other way*** (ignore) hacer* la vista gorda; (lit) mirar para otro lado, apartar la vista [2] (*as interj*): **~! a squirrel!** ¡mira! ¡una ardilla!; **(now) ~ here** ¡oye tú!, ¡escucha un momento! [3] (face): **our window ~s north** nuestra ventana da al norte *or* está orientada al norte; **to ~ ONTO sth** dar* A algo

B (search, investigate) mirar, buscar*; **~ and see if there's any mail** fíjate a ver si hay correo; **you need ~ no further** no necesita buscar más; **~ *before you leap*** mira lo que haces, mira dónde te metes

Sense II (seem, appear): **he ~s well/ill** tiene buena/mala cara; **she ~s unhappy** parece (que está) triste, se la ve triste (AmL); **don't ~ so shocked** no pongas esa cara de asombro; **he ~s like his father** se parece a su padre; **it ~s like a camel** parece un camello; **he's 60, but ~s 20 years younger** tiene 60 años, pero aparenta 20 menos; **you made me ~ a fool** me hiciste quedar en ridículo; **I wanted to ~ my best** quería estar lo mejor posible; **how does it ~ to you?** ¿a ti qué te parece?; **it ~s like rain** parece que va a llover; **will they stay? — it ~s like it** ¿se quedarán? — parece que sí *or* eso parece; **to ~ as if** *o* **as though**: **it ~s as though it's healing nicely** parece que está cicatrizando bien; **you ~ as though you could use a drink** me da la impresión de que no te vendría mal un trago; ***to ~ alive*** *o* ***lively*** *o* (BrE also) ***sharp*** (colloq) espabilar (fam)

■ **look** *vt* mirar; **he ~ed me straight in the eye** me miró a los ojos; **to ~ sb up and down** mirar a algn de arriba (a) abajo; **~ where you're going!** ¡mira por dónde vas!; **~ who's here!** ¡mira quién está aquí!

Phrasal verbs

- **look after** [v ▸ prep ▸ o] [1] (care for, protect) ‹*invalid/child/animal*› cuidar, cuidar de; ‹*guest/tourist*› atender*; **he's old enough to ~ after himself** ya es grandecito y puede arreglárselas solo; **~ after yourself!** ¡cuídate! [2] (keep watch on) cuidar, vigilar; **will you ~ after Tommy for a minute?** ¿me cuidas a Tommy un momento? [3] (be responsible for) encargarse* *or* ocuparse de
- **look ahead** [v ▸ adv] [1] (in space) mirar hacia adelante [2] (into the future) mirar hacia el futuro
- **look around**

A [v ▸ adv] [v ▸ prep ▸ o] (survey, investigate) mirar; **could we ~ around the house?** ¿podríamos ver la casa?

B [v ▸ adv] (seek) **to ~ around FOR sth** buscar* algo; *see also* **look² A1**

- **look at** [v ▸ prep ▸ o]

A ‹*person/picture/diagram*› mirar; **he's not much to ~ at** muy atractivo no es; **to ~ at her, you'd think she was really weak** tiene todo el aspecto de una persona débil; **~ at the time!** ¡mira qué hora es!; **~ at me for instance** mírame a mí, por ejemplo; **he said he'd never marry, and ~ at him now!** ¡decía que no se casaría nunca y ahí lo tienes!

B (consider) ‹*possibilities*› considerar, estudiar; **~ at it from my point of view** míralo *or* considéralo desde mi punto de vista; **the program ~s at university life** el programa enfoca la vida universitaria

C (examine, check) ‹*patient/arm/graze*› examinar; ‹*car/valve/pump*› revisar, chequear

- **look back** [v ▸ adv] [1] (in space) mirar (hacia) atrás [2] (into the past): **~ing back, it seems foolish** mirándolo ahora, parece una locura; **the program ~s back over the last 20 years** el programa es una retrospectiva de los últimos veinte años; **they married five weeks later and they've never ~ed back** se casaron cinco semanas después y desde entonces todo ha marchado sobre ruedas
- **look down on** [v ▸ adv ▸ prep ▸ o] (regard with contempt) mirar por encima del hombro a, menospreciar
- **look for** [v ▸ prep ▸ o] (seek, search for) buscar*; **what do you ~ for in a secretary/friend?** ¿qué esperas de una secretaria/un amigo?
- **look forward to** [v ▸ adv ▸ prep ▸ o]: **I'm ~ing forward to tomorrow/my birthday** estoy deseando que llegue mañana/mi cumpleaños; **I'm really ~ing forward to the trip** tengo muchas ganas de hacer el viaje, el viaje me hace mucha ilusión (Esp); **see you on Friday, then — I'll ~ forward to that** lo vemos el viernes, entonces — sí, por supuesto, con mucho gusto; **to ~ forward to -ING**: **I ~ forward to hearing from you soon** (Corresp) esperando tener pronto noticias suyas; **I'm ~ing forward to meeting him** tengo ganas de conocerlo; **I'm not ~ing forward to having to work with her** la idea de tener que trabajar con ella no me hace ninguna gracia
- **look in** [v ▸ adv] (pay visit): **I just ~ed in to say hello** sólo

l

pasé a saludar; **I ~ed in at the library** pasé por la biblioteca; **to ~ in ON sb** ir* a ver a algn

- **look into** [v ▸ prep ▸ o] ‹*matter/problem/case*› investigar*; ‹*possibility*› estudiar, considerar
- **look on**

A [v ▸ adv] (watch passively) mirar

B [v ▸ prep ▸ o] (regard) considerar; **they ~ on us as cheap labor** nos consideran mano de obra barata

- **look out**

A [v ▸ adv] **1** (be careful) tener* cuidado; **~ out!** ¡cuidado! **2** (overlook) **to ~ out ON** *o* **OVER sth** ‹‹*window/room*›› dar* A algo

B [v ▸ o ▸ adv, v ▸ adv ▸ o] (search for) (BrE) buscar*

- **look out for** [v ▸ adv ▸ prep ▸ o] **1** (be on the watch for): **~ out for her at the station** fíjate a ver si la ves en la estación; **we were warned to ~ out for thieves** nos advirtieron que tuviéramos cuidado con los ladrones; **common pitfalls to ~ out for** errores comunes de los que hay que cuidarse **2** (protest on behalf of) (AmE) salir* en defensa de
- **look over**

A [v ▸ o ▸ adv, v ▸ adv ▸ o] (examine, check) ‹*work/contract*› revisar, chequear; ‹*house/building*› inspeccionar

B [v ▸ prep ▸ o] (make tour of) ‹*house/factory*› visitar

- **look round** (esp BrE) ▸ **look around**
- **look through** **1** [v + o + adv, v + adv + o] (check) ‹*work/sums*› revisar, chequear **2** [v+ prep + o] (peruse) ‹*magazine/book*› echarle* un vistazo a, hojear
- **look to** [v ▸ prep ▸ o] (rely on): **they are ~ing to you for guidance** esperan que tú los guíes
- **look up**

A [v ▸ o ▸ adv, v ▸ adv ▸ o] **1** (try to find) ‹*word*› buscar* (*en el diccionario*) **2** (visit) ‹*person*› ir* a ver

B [v ▸ adv] (improve) mejorar; **things are/business is ~ing up** las cosas/los negocios van mejorando

- **look upon** ▸ **look on B**
- **look up to** [v ▸ adv ▸ prep ▸ o] admirar, respetar

look: **~-alike** *n* (colloq) (person) doble *mf*, sosia *mf*; **~-in** *n* (colloq): **if they're taking part, we won't get a ~-in** si ellos toman parte, nosotros no tenemos ni la más remota posibilidad; **she dominated the discussion and no one else got a ~-in** acaparó la palabra y nadie más pudo meter baza *or* abrir la boca (fam)

-looking /ˌlʊkɪŋ/ *suff* (indicating appearance): **a funny~ character** un individuo de aspecto extraño

looking glass *n* (dated) espejo *m*

look: **~out** *n* **1** (watch) (*no pl*): **to be on the ~out for sth/sb** andar* a la caza de algo/algn; (*before n*) **~out post** puesto *m* de observación **2** (person) (Mil) vigía *mf*; **3** (concern) (colloq) problema *m*; **that's your ~out** ése es tu problema; **~-see** /ˈlʊksiː/ *n* (colloq) (*no pl*) vistazo *m*

loom¹ /luːm/ *n* telar *m*

loom² *vi* **1** (be imminent) avecinarse **2** (look threatening): **the mountain ~ed high above them** la montaña surgió imponente ante ellos **3** (figure) **to ~ large**: **the problem ~ed large in his mind** el problema dominaba sus pensamientos

Phrasal verb

- **loom up** [v ▸ adv]: **a figure ~ed up in the mist** una figura surgió de entre las tinieblas

loony¹, **looney** /ˈluːni/ *adj* **-nier, -niest** (colloq) ‹*person*› chiflado (fam); ‹*idea*› disparatado; **the ~ left** los fanáticos de la izquierda

loony², **looney** *n* (*pl* **-nies**) (colloq) loco, -ca *m,f*, chiflado, -da *m,f* (fam)

loony bin *n* (colloq) loquero *m* (fam), manicomio *m*

loop¹ /luːp/ *n*

A **1** (shape) curva *f*; (in river) meandro *m* **2** (in string, cable) lazada *f* **3** (in sewing) presilla *f* **4** (Aviat): **to loop the ~** rizar* el rizo

B **1** (circuit) circuito *m* cerrado, lazo *m*; ***to be in/out of the ~*** (colloq) estar* dentro/fuera del círculo de información **2** (Comput) bucle *m*

loop² *vt*: **~ the wool** haz una lazada con la lana; **I ~ed the dog's lead over the post** enganché la correa del perro en el poste

■ **loop** *vi* ‹‹*road*›› serpentear

loophole /ˈluːphəʊl/ *n*: **a legal ~, a ~ in the law** una fisura legal, una laguna jurídica *or* legal

loopy /ˈluːpi/ *adj* **-pier, -piest** (colloq) ‹*idea*› descabellado; ‹*person*› chiflado (fam)

loose¹ /luːs/ *adj* **looser, loosest**

A **1** (not tight) ‹*jacket/blouse*› suelto, holgado, amplio; **these jeans are ~ around the waist** estos vaqueros me quedan flojos de cintura **2** (not secure) ‹*screw/knot*› flojo, suelto; ‹*thread/end*› suelto; **a ~ connection** un mal contacto; **the knot had come ~** el nudo se había aflojado; **the piece had worked (itself) ~** la pieza se había soltado *or* desprendido; **to wear one's hair ~** llevar el pelo suelto; ***to be at a ~ end*** no tener* nada que hacer; ***to tie up the ~ ends*** atar (los) cabos sueltos **3** (separate, not packaged) ‹*cigarettes*› suelto; ‹*tea/lentils*› a granel, suelto; **~ change** calderilla *f*, dinero *m* suelto, sencillo *m* (AmL) **4** (not compact) ‹*earth*› suelto; ‹*weave*› abierto, flojo

B (free) (*pred*) suelto; **a tiger is ~ in the town** un tigre anda suelto por la ciudad; **to break ~** soltarse*; **to let** *o* **set** *o* **turn sb ~** soltar* a algn; **don't go and let him ~ on the new computer** no lo vayas a dejar usar la computadora nueva; ***to be on the ~*** andar* suelto

C **1** (not precise) ‹*definition*› poco preciso; ‹*translation*› libre, aproximado **2** (flexible) ‹*structure*› flexible; ‹*organization*› poco rígido

D **1** (immoral) ‹*morals*› relajado; ‹*life*› disoluto; **a ~ woman** una mujer fácil **2** (indiscreet) ‹*tongue*› suelto; **~ talk is dangerous** la indiscreción es peligrosa

loose² *vt* (liter) **1** ‹*prisoner*› poner* en libertad, soltar*; ‹*horse*› soltar* **2** ‹*arrow*› lanzar*; ‹*violence/wrath*› desatar

Phrasal verb

- **loose off** [v ▸ adv ▸ o] (fire) ‹*gun/bullet*› disparar; ‹*arrow*› lanzar*

loose cannon *n* (colloq) elemento *m* peligroso

loose: **~-fitting** /ˈluːsˈfɪtɪŋ/ *adj* suelto; ‹*clothes*› holgado, amplio; **~-leaf** /ˈluːsˈliːf/ *adj* ‹*binder*› de anillas; **~-limbed** /ˈluːsˈlɪmd/ *adj* ágil

loosely /ˈluːsli/ *adv*

A (not tightly) ‹*tie/bandage*› sin apretar; **the dress fits ~** el vestido no es entallado

B **1** (not precisely) ‹*define*› sin excesivo rigor; ‹*translate*› libremente; **they're ~ connected** tienen una cierta relación **2** (*indep*): **~ speaking** (hablando) en términos generales **3** (flexibly) ‹*structured/organized*› de forma flexible *or* poco rígida

loosen /ˈluːsn̩/ *vt* **1** (partially dislodge) ‹*tooth*› aflojar **2** (make less tight) ‹*collar/knot/bolt*› aflojar, soltar*; **she ~ed her grip on the steering wheel** dejó de apretar con tanta fuerza el volante

■ **loosen** *vi* ‹‹*knot/bolt*›› aflojarse, soltarse*

Phrasal verb

- **loosen up** [v ▸ adv] **1** (physically) entrar en calor **2** (emotionally) relajarse

loot¹ /luːt/ *n* [u] **1** (plunder) botín *m* **2** (money) (sl) guita *f* (arg), lana *f* (AmL fam), pasta *f* (Esp fam)

loot² *vt* ‹*warehouse/store*› saquear; ‹*goods*› robar

■ **loot** *vi* saquear

looter /ˈluːtər || ˈluːtə(r)/ *n* saqueador, -dora *m,f*

looting /ˈluːtɪŋ/ *n* [u] saqueo *m*, pillaje *m*

lop /lɑːp || lɒp/ *vt* **-pp-** **1** ‹*tree*› podar **2** **~ (off)** ‹*branch*› cortar, podar

lope /ləʊp/ *vi* ‹‹*wolf/dog*›› trotar; **he ~d along behind her** la seguía corriendo a paso largo

loppers /ˈlɔːpərz/ *pl n* podadera *f*

lopsided /ˈlɑːpˈsaɪdəd || ˌlɒpˈsaɪdɪd/ *adj* **1** (not straight) torcido, chueco (AmL) **2** (asymmetric) ‹*face/smile*› torcido; ‹*shape*› asimétrico **3** (unbalanced) ‹*distribution*› desigual

loquacious /ləʊˈkweɪʃəs/ *adj* (frml) locuaz

lord¹ /lɔːrd || lɔːd/ *n*

A **1** (nobleman) señor *m*, noble *m*; **an English ~** un lord inglés; ▸ **live¹** *vi* **B1** **2** **Lord** (in UK) lord *m*; **the (House of) L~s** la cámara de los lores **3** **my L~** (addressing judge) (BrE) (su) señoría; (addressing bishop) Ilustrísima; (to nobleman) milord, señor **4** (in UK titles) **L~ Mayor** *alcalde de ciertos municipios*

B **Lord** **1** (God): **the/our L~** el/nuestro Señor; **the L~'s Prayer** el Padrenuestro **2** (*in interj phrases*): **good L~** ¡Dios bendito!; **oh L~** (colloq) ¡ay, no! (fam)

lord² *vt* ***to ~ it over sb*** tratar a algn con prepotencia

lordly /'lɔːrdli || 'lɔːdli/ *adj* **-lier, -liest** [1] (superior, arrogant) ‹*manner/bearing*› altanero, arrogante [2] (magnificent) ‹*mansion/estate*› señorial

lordship /'lɔːrdʃɪp || 'lɔːdʃɪp/ *n*: **His/Your L~** (of or to peers, judges) (su) señoría; (of or to bishops) (su) Ilustrísima

lore /lɔːr || lɔː(r)/ *n* [u]: **French peasant ~** las tradiciones rurales francesas

lorry /'lɔːri || 'lɒri/ *n* (*pl* **-ries**) (BrE) camión *m*; (*before n*) **~ driver** camionero, -ra *m,f*

lose /luːz/ *vt* (*past & past p* **lost**)

(Sense I)

A (mislay) perder*; **I've lost my key** he perdido *or* se me ha perdido la llave; **to ~ one's way** perderse*

B (be deprived of) ‹*sight/territory/right*› perder*; **to ~ one's voice** quedarse afónico; **she lost the use of her legs** quedó paralítica

C [1] (fail to keep) ‹*customers/popularity/speed*› perder*; **we are losing our best teachers to industry** los mejores profesores se nos están yendo a trabajar a la industria [2] (rid oneself of) ‹*inhibitions*› perder*; **to ~ weight** adelgazar*, perder* peso

D [1] (shake off) ‹*pursuer*› deshacerse* de [2] (lose sight of) perder* de vista

E (confuse) confundir; **you've lost me there!** no entiendo, no te sigo

F (cause to lose) costar*, hacer* perder; **their hesitation lost them the contract** la falta de decisión les costó *or* les hizo perder el contrato

G [1] (miss) ‹*train/flight/connection*› perder* [2] (let pass) ‹*time/opportunity*› perder*; **my watch ~s three minutes every day** mi reloj (se) atrasa tres minutos por día

(Sense II) (fail to win) ‹*game/battle/election*› perder*

■ **lose** *vi*

A [1] (be beaten) «*team/contestant/party*» perder*; **they're losing 3-1** van perdiendo 3 a 1; **to ~ TO sb** perder* FRENTE A algn [2] **losing** *pres p* ‹*team/party*› perdedor; **to be on the losing side** ser* de los perdedores

B [1] (suffer losses) perder*; **to ~ on a deal** salir* perdiendo en un negocio [2] (be less effective) perder*; **the poem ~s in translation** el poema pierde con la traducción *or* al ser traducido

C «*watch/clock*» atrasar, atrasarse

■ *v refl* **to ~ oneself (in sth)** ensimismarse (en algo)

(Phrasal verb)

• **lose out** [v ▸ adv] salir* perdiendo

loser /'luːzər || 'luːzə(r)/ *n* [1] (in game, contest) perdedor, -dora *m,f*; **he's a good/bad** *o* (AmE also) **sore ~** es buen/mal perdedor; **the biggest ~s will be the farmers** los granjeros serán quienes se verán más perjudicados [2] (habitually) (colloq) fracasado, -da *m,f*, perdedor, -dora *m,f* [3] (sth unsuccessful) (colloq): **to be on a ~** llevar todas las de perder

loss /lɔːs || lɒs/ *n*

A (of possessions, jobs, faculties) pérdida *f*; **the ship sank with the ~ of 21 lives** el naufragio se cobró 21 vidas; **without ~ of life** sin que hubiera que lamentar víctimas *or* sin derramamiento de sangre; **it's their ~** son ellos los que salen perdiendo *or* los que se lo pierden; **they were filled with a keen sense of ~** sintieron un gran vacío; ***to be at a ~***: **I'm at a ~ to know what to do next** no sé qué hacer ahora; **I was at a ~ for words** no supe qué decir

B (Busn, Fin) pérdida *f*; **the company made a huge ~** la compañía sufrió grandes pérdidas; **I made a ~ of $100 on the deal** perdí 100 dólares en el negocio; **to sell sth at a ~** vender algo con pérdida; **we cannot continue trading at a ~** no podemos seguir operando con déficit; ***to be a dead ~*** (colloq): **this typewriter is a dead ~** esta máquina de escribir no sirve para nada *or* (fam) es una porquería; **he's a dead ~ as an organizer** como organizador es un desastre *or* una calamidad; ***to cut one's ~es*** cortar por lo sano; (Fin) reducir* las pérdidas

C [1] (bereavement) (euph) pérdida *f* (euf) [2] **losses** *pl* (deaths) (Mil) bajas *fpl*

loss: **~-adjustor** /ə'dʒʌstər || ə'dʒʌstə(r)/ *n* tasador, -dora *m,f* de pérdidas; **~-making** /'lɔːsˌmeɪkɪŋ || 'lɒsˌmeɪkɪŋ/ *adj* (BrE) deficitario

lost¹ /lɔːst || lɒst/ *past & past p of* **lose**

lost² *adj*

(Sense I)

A (mislaid, missing) perdido; **to get ~** perderse*, extraviarse* (frml); **get ~!** (sl) ¡vete al diablo! (fam), ¡andá a pasear! (RPl fam)

B (dead, destroyed) (euph): **to give sb up for** *o* **as ~** dar* a algn por desaparecido; **to give sth up for** *o* **as ~** dar* algo por perdido

C (wasted) ‹*time*› perdido; ‹*opportunity*› desperdiciado, perdido; **to make up for ~ time** recuperar el tiempo perdido; ***to be ~ on sb***: **these subtleties are ~ on him** se le escapan *or* no sabe apreciar estas sutilezas; **the joke was completely ~ on her** no entendió el chiste

D (*pred*) [1] (confused) perdido; **you're going too fast: I'm ~** vas demasiado rápido y me confundo *or* no te sigo [2] (at a loss) **to be ~ WITHOUT sth/sb** estar* perdido SIN algo/algn; **I was ~ for words** no supe qué decir [3] (absorbed) **to be ~ IN sth** estar* ensimismado EN algo; **~ in thought/meditation** sumido en la reflexión, absorto, ensimismado

(Sense II) (not won) ‹*battle/election*› perdido; **a ~ cause** una causa perdida

lost and found /'lɔːstən'faʊnd || ˌlɒstən'faʊnd/ *n* [u] (AmE) objetos *mpl* perdidos

lost property *n* [u] (esp BrE) objetos *mpl* perdidos

lot /lɑːt || lɒt/ *n*

A (large number, quantity) [1] (*no pl*): **a ~ of wine** mucho vino; **a ~ of people** mucha gente; **a ~ of the play is boring** gran parte de la obra es aburrida; **I've seen a ~ of her recently** la he visto mucho últimamente; **quite a ~ of money** bastante dinero; **what a ~ of books you've got!** ¡cuántos libros tienes!; **what a ~ of fuss over nothing!** ¡tanto lío por una tontería!; ▸**fat¹ C** [2] **a ~** (*as adv*) mucho; **I like her a ~** me gusta mucho, me cae muy bien; **a ~ better** mucho mejor; **thanks a ~!** ¡muchas gracias! [3] **lots** *pl* (colloq): **how many seats are there left? — lots** ¿cuántos asientos quedan? — muchos *or* (fam) montones; **~s of people liked it** a mucha gente le gustó

B [1] (group, mass of things) montón *m*, pila *f* [2] (group of people) (colloq): **they're a funny ~** son raros, son gente rara; **come on, you ~!** ¡vamos, ustedes *or* (Esp) vosotros! [3] **the ~** (esp BrE): **they ate the ~** se lo comieron todo (*or* se las comieron todas *etc*); **one more story, then that's your ~!** ¡un cuento más y se acabó!

C (at auction) lote *m*

D [1] (parcel of land) terreno *m*, solar *m*; **film ~** (Cin) plató *m* [2] (AmE) ▸**parking lot**

E [1] (for random choice): **to draw** *o* **cast ~s for sth** echar algo a suertes [2] (fate) suerte *f*; ***to throw in one's ~ with sb*** unirse a algn

loth /ləʊθ/ *adj* ▸**loath**

lotion /'ləʊʃən/ *n* [c u] loción *f*

lottery /'lɑːtəri || 'lɒtəri/ *n* (*pl* **-ries**) lotería *f*

lotus /'ləʊtəs/ *n* (*pl* **~es**) loto *m*

loud¹ /laʊd/ *adj* **-er, -est** [1] ‹*noise/scream/applause*› fuerte; **he said it in a ~ voice** lo dijo en voz alta [2] (vigorous) ‹*protests/complaints*› enérgico [3] (ostentatious) ‹*color*› llamativo, chillón [4] ▸**loudmouthed**

loud² *adv* **-er, -est** ‹*speak*› alto; **she laughed (the) ~est of all** fue la que se rió más fuerte; **he always turns the TV up too ~** siempre pone la televisión demasiado alta *or* fuerte; **out ~** en voz alta; **I'm receiving you ~ and clear** (Telec) te recibo perfectamente

loudhailer /'laʊd'heɪlər || ˌlaʊd'heɪlə(r)/ *n* (BrE) megáfono *m*

loudly /'laʊdli/ *adv* [1] ‹*shout*› fuerte; ‹*speak*› alto, en voz alta [2] ‹*complain/proclaim*› a voz en grito *or* en cuello

loud: **~mouth** *n* (colloq) gritón, -tona *m,f*, escandaloso, -sa *m,f*; **~mouthed** /'laʊd'maʊðd || 'laʊdmaʊðd/ *adj* (colloq) gritón

loudness /'laʊdnəs || 'laʊdnɪs/ *n* [u] (volume) volumen *m*; (of explosion) estruendo *m*, estrépito *m*

loudspeaker /'laʊd'spiːkər || ˌlaʊd'spiːkə(r)/ *n* altavoz *m*, altoparlante *m* (AmL)

Louisiana /lu'iːzi'ænə/ *n* Luisiana *f*

lounge¹ /laʊndʒ/ *n* (on ship, in hotel) salón *m*; (in house) (BrE) sala *f* (de estar), living *m* (esp AmS), salón *m* (esp Esp)

lounge² *vi* [1] (laze) **to ~ around** *o* **about** no hacer* nada, holgazanear [2] (loll): **he ~d in his chair** estaba repanti (n)gado *or* (AmL tb) repatingado en su sillón

lounge: ~ **bar** *n* salón-bar *m*; ~ **suit** *n* (BrE) traje *m* (de calle)

louse /laʊs/ *n* 1 (*pl* **lice**) (Zool) piojo *m* 2 (*pl* ~**s**) (person) (colloq) canalla *mf*

Phrasal verb

- **louse up** /laʊs, laʊz/ [v ▸ o ▸ adv, v ▸ adv ▸ o] (AmE colloq) estropear, fastidiar (fam)

lousy /ˈlaʊzi/ *adj* **-sier, -siest**
A (bad) (colloq) ‹*food/weather*› asqueroso (fam); **a ~ movie/party** una película/fiesta malísima; **we had a ~ time** lo pasamos pésimo *or* (Esp tb) fatal (fam); **I'm feeling ~ today** hoy me siento pésimo, hoy estoy fatal (Esp fam); **I got a ~ $50** me saqué 50 cochinos dólares (fam)
B (infested with lice) lleno *or* plagado de piojos

lout /laʊt/ *n* patán *m* (fam), gandalla *m* (Méx fam), jallán *m* (AmC)

louver, (BrE) **louvre** /ˈluːvər || ˈluːvə(r)/ *n* lama *f*, listón *m* (*de persiana*); (*before n*) ‹*door/window*› de lamas, tipo persiana

lovable /ˈlʌvəbəl/ *adj* adorable, amoroso (AmL)

love[1] /lʌv/ *n*
A 1 (affection, emotional attachment) amor *m*; **their ~ for each other** el amor *or* el cariño que se tenían; **to feel ~ for sb** sentir* cariño *or* amor por algn; **to fall/be in ~ with sb/sth** enamorarse/estar* enamorado de algn/algo; **to make ~ to sb** (sexually) hacer* el amor con algn; (flirt) (dated) hacer(le)* el amor *or* la corte (a algn) (ant); **a ~-hate relationship** una relación de amor y odio; ***not for ~ or*** *o* (esp BrE) ***nor money*** por nada del mundo; ***there's no ~ lost between them*** no se pueden ver; **~ bite** mordisco *m or* (CS fam) chupón *m or* (Méx fam) chupete *m*; 2 (enthusiasm, interest) ~ **OF sth** amor *m* A *or* POR algo; **her ~ of reading** su amor a *or* por la lectura, su afición por la lectura
B 1 (greetings, regards): **give my ~ to your parents** (dale) recuerdos a tus padres (de mi parte), cariños a tus padres (AmL) 2 (in letters) ~ **from John** *o* ~, **John** un abrazo, John *or* (AmL tb) cariños, John; **lots of ~, John** un apretado abrazo, John; **all my ~, John** con todo mi cariño, John
C 1 (person loved) amor *m* 2 (thing loved) pasión *f*; **the theater remained her first ~** el teatro siguió siendo su gran pasión
D (colloq) (*as form of address*) 1 (to loved one) cariño, cielo; **don't cry, my ~** no llores, mi vida *or* mi amor 2 (BrE) (to older woman) señora; (to younger woman) señorita, guapa (Esp); (to older man) señor; (to younger man) joven, guapo (Esp)
E (in tennis) cero *m*

love[2] *vt* 1 (care for) querer*, amar (liter); **children need to be ~d** los niños necesitan cariño 2 (like) **to ~ sth/-ING/to + INF**: **I ~ music/reading/to get presents** me encanta la música/leer/recibir regalos; **I'd ~ a cup of tea** una taza de té me vendría de maravilla; **I'd ~ to come** me encantaría ir, me gustaría muchísimo ir

loveable *adj* ▸ **lovable**

love: ~ **affair** *n* aventura *f*, amoríos *mpl* (pey); ~**birds** *pl n* (lovers) (colloq) tórtolos *mpl* (fam), tortolitos *mpl* (fam); ~ **child** *n* hijo, -ja *m,f* natural

loved one /lʌvd/ *n* ser *m* querido

loveless /ˈlʌvləs || ˈlʌvlɪs/ *adj* sin amor

love life *n* [u] vida *f* amorosa *or* sentimental

lovelorn /ˈlʌvlɔːrn || ˈlʌvlɔːn/ *adj* (liter *or* hum) perdidamente enamorado

lovely /ˈlʌvli/ *adj* **-lier, liest** 1 (very nice) ‹*face/hair/voice/figure*› precioso, bonito, lindo (esp AmL); ‹*person/nature*› encantador, amoroso (AmL); ‹*soup/ice cream/meal/taste*› (BrE) riquísimo, buenísimo; **the weather was ~** hacía un tiempo buenísimo *or* precioso; **we had a ~ time** lo pasamos estupendo *or* muy bien; **it was ~ to see them again** fue un gran placer volver a verlos; **what's a ~ surprise!** ¡que sorpresa más grande! 2 (*as intensifier*) (esp BrE): **it was ~ and warm by the fire** se estaba muy calentito *or* a gusto junto al fuego

love: ~**making** *n* [u] relaciones *fpl* sexuales; ~ **match** *n* matrimonio *m* por amor; ~ **nest** *n* (esp BrE journ) nidito *m* de amor

lover /ˈlʌvər || ˈlʌvə(r)/ *n*
A (partner in love) amante *mf*
B (fan) ~ **OF sth** amante *mf* DE algo; **music-~s** los aficionados a *or* los amantes de la música

lovesick /ˈlʌvsɪk/ *adj* enfermo de amor

lovey-dovey /ˈlʌviˈdʌvi/ *adj* (colloq & pej) acaramelado (fam & pey)

loving /ˈlʌvɪŋ/ *adj* ‹*person/disposition*› cariñoso, afectuoso; **with ~ care** con tierno cuidado; **from your ~ son, Henry** (in letters) de tu hijo que te quiere, Henry

lovingly /ˈlʌvɪŋli/ *adv* ‹*gaze/whisper*› tiernamente, cariñosamente; ‹*handwritten/prepared*› con amor *or* cariño; ‹*restored*› con el mayor cuidado

low[1] /ləʊ/ *adj* **-er, -est**
A (in height) bajo; **to fly at ~ altitude** volar* bajo *or* a poca altura; **the dress had a very ~ back** el vestido era muy escotado por la espalda; **he gave a ~ bow** hizo una profunda reverencia; **a ~ point in his career** un momento bajo en su carrera
B 1 (in volume) ‹*voice*› bajo, quedo; ‹*sound/whisper*› débil, quedo; **turn the radio down ~** bájale al radio (AmL exc CS), baja la radio (CS, Esp) 2 (in pitch) ‹*key/note/pitch*› grave, bajo
C (in intensity, amount, quality) ‹*pressure/temperature*› bajo; ‹*wages/prices*› bajo; ‹*proportion*› pequeño; ‹*standard/quality*› bajo, malo; ‹*number/card*› bajo; **cook on a ~ flame** *o* **heat** cocinar a fuego lento; **student numbers fell as ~ as five** el número de estudiantes bajó a tan sólo cinco; **attendance has been ~ lately** últimamente no ha habido muchos asistentes; **the temperature was in the ~ sixties** la temperatura apenas pasaba de 60° Fahrenheit; **he has a ~ opinion of doctors** no tiene muy buena opinión de los médicos
D (in short supply): **supplies are ~** los suministros escasean *or* están empezando a faltar; **stocks are running ~** se están agotando las existencias; **to be ~ ON sth**: **we're rather ~ on milk** tenemos *or* nos queda poca leche
E (in health, spirits): **to feel ~** (physically) sentirse* débil; (emotionally) estar* deprimido; **to be in ~ spirits** estar* bajo de moral *or* con la moral baja
F 1 (humble) (liter) bajo, humilde; **of ~ birth** de humilde cuna (liter); **the ~est of the ~** lo más bajo 2 (despicable) bajo, mezquino; **a ~ trick** una mala jugada, una mala pasada

low[2] *adv* **-er, -est**
A bajo; **to fly ~** volar* bajo *or* a poca altura; **to bow ~** hacer* una profunda reverencia; **get down ~er if you don't want them to see you** agáchate más si no quieres que te vean; **put the shelf ~er down** coloca el estante más abajo; **he rates ~ in my estimation** no lo tengo en gran estima; **I wouldn't sink** *o* **stoop so ~ as to do that** no me rebajaría a hacer una cosa así, nunca caería tan bajo
B 1 (softly, quietly) bajo 2 (in pitch) bajo

low[3] *n* 1 (low point) punto *m* más bajo; **the peso has dropped to a new (record) ~ against the dollar** la cotización del peso ha alcanzado un nuevo mínimo (histórico) con respecto al dólar; **relations between the two countries are at an all-time ~** las relaciones entre los dos países nunca han sido peores 2 (Meteo) zona *f* de bajas presiones

low[4] *vi* mugir*

low- /ləʊ/ *pref*: ~**priced** de bajo precio; ~**income** de bajos ingresos; ~**tension** de baja tensión

low: ~ **beam** *n* luces *fpl* de cruce, luces *fpl* cortas *or* (Chi) bajas; **keep the headlights on ~ beam** deja puestas las luces de cruce (*or* cortas *etc*); ~**brow** *adj* ‹*tastes/person*› poco intelectual; ‹*culture/writer*› popular; ~**-budget** /ˈləʊˈbʌdʒət || ˌləʊˈbʌdʒɪt/ *adj* ‹*production*› barato; ‹*traveler/tourist*› con un presupuesto limitado; ~**-calorie** /ˈləʊˈkæləri/ *adj* bajo en calorías; ~**-class** /ˈləʊˈklæs || ˌləʊˈklɑːs/ *adj* ‹*place*› de mala muerte (fam); ‹*clientele*› de poca categoría; ~ **Countries** *pl n* **the L~ Countries** los Países Bajos; ~**-cut** /ˈləʊˈkʌt/ *adj* escotado; ~**down** *n* [u] (colloq): **to give sb the ~down (on sth)** poner* a algn al tanto (de algo); ~**-down** /ˈləʊˈdaʊn/ *adj* (colloq & pej) (*before n*): **that was a ~-down thing to do** ¡qué cochinada *or* marranada! (fam)

lower[1] /ˈləʊər || ˈləʊə(r)/ *adj*
A *comp of* **low**[1,2]
B (*before n*) 1 (spatially, numerically) ‹*jaw/lip*› inferior; **~ age limit** edad *f* mínima 2 (in rank, importance) ‹*rank/echelons*› inferior, más bajo; **the ~ chamber/L~ House** la cámara

baja 3 ‹*mammals/apes/life-forms*› inferior
C (Geog) bajo; **the ~ reaches of the Nile** el curso bajo del Nilo; **~ Manhattan** el sur de Manhattan

lower² /ˈləʊər || ˈləʊə(r)/ *vt*
A (let down) ‹*blind/ceiling*› bajar; ‹*flag/sail*› bajar, arriar*; **to ~ the lifeboats** echar al agua los botes salvavidas; **he ~ed himself into his chair** se sentó en el sillón; **to ~ one's eyes** bajar la vista *or* los ojos
B (reduce, diminish) ‹*temperature/volume/price*› bajar; **~ your voice** baja la voz; **to ~ sb's morale** bajarle la moral a algn, desmoralizar* a algn; **it ~ed his resistance to disease** le minó *or* le disminuyó las defensas
■ *v refl* **to ~ oneself** rebajarse
■ **lower** *vi* «*prices/standards/temperature*» bajar

lower³ /ˈlaʊr || ˈlaʊə(r)/ *vi* (liter) 1 (darken) «*sky*» encapotarse 2 (frown) fruncir* el ceño 3 **lowering** *pres p* ‹*sky*› encapotado; ‹*expression/look*› ceñudo

lower: **~-case** /ˈləʊerˈkeɪs || ˌləʊəˈkeɪs/ *adj* ‹*word*› en minúsculas; **~-case letter** (letra *f*) minúscula *f*; **~-class** /ˈləʊərˈklæs || ˌləʊəˈklɑːs/ *adj* de clase baja

lowest common denominator *n* (Math) mínimo común denominador *m*; **a series aimed at the ~ ~ ~** una serie dirigida al público de nivel más bajo

low: **~-fat** /ˈləʊˈfæt/ *adj* bajo en grasas; **~-flying** /ˈləʊˈflaɪɪŋ/ *adj* ‹*aircraft*› que vuela bajo *or* a poca altura; **~-grade** /ˈləʊˈgreɪd/ *adj* ‹*oil*› de baja calidad; ‹*ore*› pobre; **~-key** /ˈləʊˈkiː/, **~-keyed** /-d/ *adj* ‹*speech/tone*› mesurado, medido; ‹*ceremony*› sencillo, discreto; **~land** /ˈləʊlənd/ *adj* (*before n*) de las tierras bajas; (in tropical countries) de tierra caliente; **~lands** /ˈləʊləndz/ *pl n* tierras *fpl* bajas; (in tropical countries) tierras *fpl* calientes; **~-level** /ˈləʊˈlevəl/ *adj* 1 ‹*talks*› a bajo nivel 2 ‹*radiation*› de baja intensidad 3 (Comput): **~-level language** lenguaje *m* de bajo nivel; **~life** *n* (colloq) 1 [u] (people, environment) bajos fondos *mpl* 2 [c] (*pl* **~s**) (person) (AmE) delincuente *mf*; **~lights** /ˈləʊlaɪts/ *pl n* (in hair) reflejos *mpl* oscuros, mechas *fpl or* (RPl) mechitas *fpl* oscuras, rayitos *mpl* oscuros (Chi); (colloq) (disappointing aspect) lo menos destacado

lowly /ˈləʊli/ *adj* **-lier, -liest** humilde

low: **~-lying** /ˈləʊˈlaɪɪŋ/ *adj* bajo; **~-necked** /ˈləʊˈnekt/ *adj* escotado; **~-paid** /ˈləʊˈpeɪd/ *adj* mal remunerado, mal pagado; **~-pitched** /ˈləʊˈpɪtʃt/ *adj* ‹*note/voice*› grave; **~-pressure** /ˈləʊˈpreʃər || ˌləʊˈpreʃə(r)/ *adj* (*before n*) 1 (Tech) de baja presión 2 (Meteo) ‹*area*› de bajas presiones; **~-profile** /ˈləʊˈprəʊfaɪl/ *adj* poco prominente; **they kept the meeting ~-profile** le dieron poca publicidad a la reunión; **~-ranking** /ˈləʊˈræŋkɪŋ/ *adj* ‹*officer*› de baja graduación; ‹*official*› subalterno; **~-rise** /ˈləʊˈraɪz/ *adj* de poca altura; **~-risk** /ˈləʊˈrɪsk/ *adj* ‹*business/occupation*› poco arriesgado; ‹*operation/investment*› de poco *or* bajo riesgo; **~ season** *n* [u] (BrE) temporada *f* baja; **~-tech** /ˈləʊˈtek/ *adj* (*before n*) de baja tecnología; **~-water mark** *n* línea *f* de bajamar

lox /lɑːks || lɒks/ *n* [u] (AmE) salmón *m* ahumado

loyal /ˈlɔɪəl/ *adj* ‹*follower/friend*› fiel, leal; ‹*customer*› fiel; **to be ~ TO sth** ‹*to the state/party*› ser* leal A algo; ‹*to one's ideals/principles*› ser* fiel A algo; **he is ~ to his friends** es un amigo leal *or* fiel

loyalist /ˈlɔɪələst || ˈlɔɪəlɪst/ *n* partidario, -ria *m,f* del régimen; **L~** (in US history) *colono leal a la corona británica durante la guerra de independencia*; (in N Ireland) unionista *mf*; (in Spain) republicano, -na *m,f*

loyalty /ˈlɔɪəlti/ *n* (*pl* **-ties**) 1 [u] (quality, state) lealtad *f* 2 (allegiance) (*often pl*) **~ TO sb/sth** lealtad *f* A algn/algo; **divided loyalties** conflicto de lealtades

loyalty card *n* (BrE) tarjeta *f* de fidelidad

lozenge /ˈlɑːzṇdʒ || ˈlɒzɪndʒ/ *n* (Med) pastilla *f*

LP *n* (= **long-playing record**) LP *m*, elepé *m*

L-plate /ˈelpleɪt/ *n* (in UK) placa *f* de la L *or* de prácticas (*placa que se debe exhibir en el coche cuando se aprende a conducir*)

LSD *n* (= **lysergic acid diethylamide**) LSD *m*

L-shaped /ˈelʃeɪpt/ *adj* en forma de L

LST (in US) = **Local Standard Time**

Lt = **Lieutenant**

Ltd (= **Limited**) Ltda., S.A.

lubricant /ˈluːbrɪkənt/ *n* [u c] lubricante *m*

lubricate /ˈluːbrɪkeɪt/ *vt* lubricar*

lubrication /ˈluːbrɪˈkeɪʃən/ *n* [u] lubricación *f*

lucid /ˈluːsəd || ˈluːsɪd/ *adj* lúcido

lucidity /luːˈsɪdəti/ *n* [u] lucidez *f*

Lucifer /ˈluːsəfər || ˈluːsɪfə(r)/ *n* Lucifer

luck /lʌk/ *n* [u] suerte *f*; **you never know your ~** a lo mejor tienes suerte; **knowing my ~ ...** con la (mala) suerte que tengo ...; **good/bad ~** buena/mala suerte; **to wish sb (good) ~** desearle (buena) suerte a algn; **good ~!** ¡(buena) suerte!; **best of ~!** ¡mucha suerte!, te deseo la mejor de las suertes; **bad** *o* **hard ~!** ¡mala suerte!; **better ~ next time** otra vez será; **it's bad ~ to break a mirror** romper un espejo trae mala suerte; **to have the good/bad ~ to + INF** tener* la (buena)/mala suerte DE + INF; **a piece** *o* **stroke of ~** un golpe de suerte; **if our ~ holds** si seguimos con suerte; **with any/a bit of ~** con un poco de suerte; **to be in/out of ~** estar*/no estar* de suerte; **still working there? — yes, worse ~** (colloq) ¿todavía trabajas ahí? — sí, ¡qué le vamos a hacer!; **did you get a taxi? — no such ~** ¿conseguiste un taxi? — ¡qué va!; ***as ~ would have it ...*** quiso la suerte que (+ *subj*); ***it's the ~ of the draw*** es cuestión de suerte; ***to be down on one's ~*** estar* de mala racha; ***to have the ~ of the devil*** *o* ***the devil's own ~*** tener* mucha suerte, ser* muy suertudo (AmL fam); ***to push one's ~*** desafiar* a la suerte; ***to try one's ~*** probar* suerte

luckily /ˈlʌkəli || ˈlʌkɪli/ *adv* (*indep*) por suerte, afortunadamente

luckless /ˈlʌkləs || ˈlʌklɪs/ *adj* desafortunado

lucky /ˈlʌki/ *adj* **luckier, luckiest** 1 ‹*person*› con suerte, afortunado, suertudo (AmL fam); **he was born ~** nació con suerte; **if we're ~ ...** si tenemos suerte ..., con un poco de suerte ...; **you can think yourself ~ I didn't tell her** puedes darte por contento de que no se lo dijera; **to be ~ to + INF**: **he's ~ to be alive** tuvo suerte de no matarse; **you'll be ~ to find him there** me extrañaría que lo encontraras allí; **~ you/him!** (colloq) ¡qué suerte (tienes/tiene)!; **borrow my car? you should be so ~** *o* (BrE) **you'll be ~** (colloq) ¿que te preste el coche? ¡ni soñarlo! *or* ¡ni lo sueñes! (fam); **a pay increase? I should be so ~** (colloq) ¿un aumento de sueldo? ¡qué más quisiera (yo)! (fam); **third time ~** la tercera es la vencida 2 (fortuitous): **it was just a ~ guess** acertó (*or* acerté *etc*) por pura casualidad; **he had a ~ escape** se salvó de milagro; **a ~ break** un golpe de suerte; **it was ~ (that) you were there** fue una suerte que estuvieras ahí 3 (bringing luck): **~ charm** amuleto *m* (de la suerte); **seven is my ~ number** el siete es mi número de la suerte; **it's my ~ day** hoy estoy de suerte

lucky dip *n* (BrE) ≈ pesca *f* milagrosa

lucrative /ˈluːkrətɪv/ *adj* lucrativo

lucre /ˈluːkər || ˈluːkə(r)/ *n* [u] (profit) lucro *m*; ***filthy ~*** (hum) dinero cochino

Luddite /ˈlʌdaɪt/ *n* 1 (Hist) ludita *m* 2 (opponent of new technology) ludita *mf*

ludicrous /ˈluːdɪkrəs/ *adj* ridículo, absurdo

ludo /ˈluːdəʊ/ *n* [u] (in UK) ludo *m or* (Esp, Méx) parchís *m*

lug /lʌg/ *vt* **-gg-** (colloq) arrastrar; **I've been ~ging this box around all day** llevo todo el día con esta caja a cuestas

luggage /ˈlʌgɪdʒ/ *n* [u] equipaje *m*

luggage: **~ checkroom** /ˈtʃekruːm, -rʊm/ *n* (AmE) consigna *f* (de equipajes); **~ rack** *n* 1 (Rail) rejilla *f* (portaequipajes) 2 (Auto) baca *f*, portaequipajes *m*, parrilla *f* (Andes)

lugubrious /lʊˈguːbriəs/ *adj* lúgubre

Luke /luːk/ *n* (Bib) (San) Lucas

lukewarm /ˈluːkˈwɔːrm || ˌluːkˈwɔːm/ *adj* 1 ‹*water/milk*› tibio 2 ‹*support/reaction*› poco entusiasta

lull¹ /lʌl/ *vt* 1 ‹*baby*›: **to ~ a baby to sleep** arrullar *or* mecer* a un niño hasta dormirlo; **the gentle rocking of the boat ~ed me to sleep** me dormí arrullado por el suave balanceo de la barca 2 ‹*fears*› calmar; ‹*suspicions*› desvanecer, ahuyentar 3 (deceive): **we were ~ed into a false sense of security** nos confiamos demasiado

lull² *n* (in activity) período *m* de calma; (in fighting) tregua *f*; (in conversation) pausa *f*, paréntesis *m*; ***the ~ before the storm*** la calma que precede a la tormenta

lullaby /ˈlʌləbaɪ/ *n* (*pl* **-bies**) canción *f* de cuna, nana *f*

lumbago /lʌmˈbeɪgəʊ/ *n* [u] lumbago *m*

lumbar /ˈlʌmbər || ˈlʌmbə(r)/ *adj* lumbar

lumber[1] /ˈlʌmbər || ˈlʌmbə(r)/ *n* [u] 1 (timber) (AmE) madera *f*; (*before n*) ‹*trade/company*› maderero; ~ **mill** aserradero *m* *or* (Col, Ec) aserrío *m* 2 (junk) cachivaches *mpl*, trastos *mpl* viejos

lumber[2] *vt*
A (burden) (colloq) **to ~ sb WITH sth** enjaretarle *or* endilgarle* algo A algn (fam); **I got ~ed with the job** me enjaretaron *or* me endilgaron el trabajo a mí (fam)
B (chop down) (AmE) talar
■ **lumber** *vi*
A 1 (move awkwardly) avanzar* pesadamente 2 **lumbering** *pres p* ‹*gait/step/footsteps*› torpe, pesado
B (cut timber) (AmE) aserrar*

lumber: **~jack** *n* leñador *m*; **~jacket** *n* chaquetón *m* *or* chamarra *f* de leñador (*a cuadros*); **~yard** *n* (AmE) almacén *m* de maderas, barraca *f* (CS)

luminous /ˈlu:mənəs || ˈlu:mɪnəs/ *adj* luminoso

lump[1] /lʌmp/ *n*
A (swelling, protuberance) bulto *m*; (as result of knock, blow to head) chichón *m*; ***a ~ in one's throat*** un nudo en la garganta
B 1 (piece — of coal, iron, clay, cheese) trozo *m*, pedazo *m*; (— of sugar) terrón *m*; **there were ~s in the sauce** había grumos en la salsa 2 (whole, total): **in one ~** de una vez, de golpe (fam)

lump[2] *vt* 1 (put up with) (colloq): ***to ~ it*** aguantarse (fam); **if you don't like it, (you can) ~ it** si no te gusta, te aguantas 2 (place together): **to ~ sth together**: **you can ~ all those items together under one heading** todo eso puede ir junto *or* agruparse bajo el mismo epígrafe; **they can't all be ~ed together as reactionaries** no se puede tachar a todos indiscriminadamente de reaccionarios

lump sum *n* cantidad *f* *or* suma *f* global (*que se paga o recibe para saldar totalmente una obligación*)

l

lumpy /ˈlʌmpi/ *adj* **-pier, -piest** 1 ‹*sauce*› lleno de grumos 2 ‹*mattress/cushion*› lleno de bultos

lunacy /ˈlu:nəsi/ *n* (*pl* **-cies**) locura *f*; **an act of ~** una locura

lunar /ˈlu:nər || ˈlu:nə(r)/ *adj* (Aerosp, Astron) lunar; **~ landing** alunizaje *m*

lunatic[1] /ˈlu:nətɪk/ *n* loco, -ca *m,f*

lunatic[2] *adj* ‹*idea/scheme*› alocado, disparatado; **the ~ fringe** el sector más fanático

lunatic asylum *n* manicomio *m*

lunch[1] /lʌntʃ/ *n* [u c] almuerzo *m*, comida *f* (esp Esp, Méx); **to have ~** almorzar*, comer (esp Esp, Méx)

lunch[2] *vi* (frml) almorzar*, comer (esp Esp, Méx)

lunchbox /ˈlʌntʃbɑ:ks || ˈlʌntʃbɒks/ *n* lonchera *f* (AmL), fiambrera *f* (Esp)

luncheon /ˈlʌntʃən/ *n* (frml) almuerzo *m*; (*before n*) **~ party** lunch *m*

luncheon: **~ meat** *n* [u] *tipo de fiambre de cerdo*; **~ voucher**, **~ Voucher**® *n* (BrE) cheque-comida *m*, ticket *m* restaurant

lunch: **~room** *n* (AmE) comedor *m*, refectorio *m*; **~time** *n* hora *f* de almorzar *or* del almuerzo, hora *f* de comer *or* de la comida (esp Esp, Méx); (*before n*) ‹*concert/program*› de mediodía

lung /lʌŋ/ *n* (*often pl*) pulmón *m*; (*before n*) ‹*disease*› pulmonar; **~ cancer** cáncer *m* de pulmón

lunge[1] /lʌndʒ/ *vi* embestir*; (in fencing) atacar*, entrar a fondo; **to ~ AT sb/sth** arremeter CONTRA algn/algo

lunge[2] *n* arremetida *f*; (in fencing) estocada *f*, entrada *f* a fondo; **he made a ~ toward the door** se lanzó hacia la puerta

lupine, (BrE) **lupin** /ˈlu:pən || ˈlu:pɪn/ *n* altramuz *m*, lupino *m*

lurch[1] /lɜ:rtʃ || lɜ:tʃ/ *vi* ‹‹*vehicle*›› dar* bandazos *or* sacudidas; ‹‹*person*›› tambalearse; **the train ~ed to a halt** el tren dio una sacudida y se paró

lurch[2] *n* bandazo *m*, sacudida *f*; **to give a ~** dar* un bandazo *or* una sacudida; ***to leave sb in the ~*** (colloq) dejar a algn plantado

lure[1] /lʊr || ljʊə(r), lʊə(r)/ *vt* atraer*; **he was ~d by the offer of a higher salary** lo atrajeron ofreciéndole un sueldo más alto; **it was easily ~d into the trap** fue fácil hacer que cayera en la trampa

lure[2] *n* 1 [c u] (attraction) atractivo *m* 2 [c] (enticement, bait) señuelo *m*, aliciente *m*

lurid /ˈlʊrəd || ˈlʊərɪd/ *adj* 1 (sensational) ‹*details/tale*› escabroso, morboso; ‹*imagination*› morboso 2 (garish) ‹*color/garment*› chillón, charro (AmL fam)

lurk /lɜ:rk || lɜ:k/ *vi* 1 ‹‹*thief*›› merodear, acechar; **to ~ around** *o* **about** merodear 2 (be hidden): **any ~ing doubts were soon allayed** pronto se disiparon las dudas que aún quedaban

lurker /ˈlɜ:kər/ *n* fisgón, -gona *m,f*, lurker *mf*

luscious /ˈlʌʃəs/ *adj* 1 ‹*girl*› seductor 2 ‹*scent/sweetness*› exquisito, delicioso; **ripe, ~ grapes** maduras y suculentas uvas

lush[1] /lʌʃ/ *adj* **-er, -est** 1 ‹*vegetation*› exuberante, lozano 2 ‹*surroundings/upholstery*› suntuoso

lush[2] *n* (sl) borrachín, -china *m,f* (fam)

lust[1] /lʌst/ *n* 1 [u] (sexual) lujuria *f*, concupiscencia *f* 2 [c] (craving) deseo *m*; **~ FOR sth** ‹*for power/vengeance/adventure*› ansia *f*‡ *or* (liter) sed *f* DE algo

lust[2] *vi* **to ~ AFTER sb** desear a algn; **to ~ AFTER sth** codiciar algo; **to ~ FOR sth** ambicionar algo

luster, (BrE) **lustre** /ˈlʌstər || ˈlʌstə(r)/ *n* [u] (gloss, sheen) (liter) lustre *m*, brillo *m*

lustful /ˈlʌstfəl/ *adj* lujurioso, concupiscente

lustily /ˈlʌstəli || ˈlʌstɪli/ *adv* ‹*cheer*› animadamente; ‹*cry*› con mucha energía

lustre /ˈlʌstər || ˈlʌstə(r)/ *n* (BrE) ▸ **luster**

lustrous /ˈlʌstrəs/ *adj* (liter) ‹*hair*› brillante, brilloso (AmL); ‹*eyes*› luminoso, brillante

lusty /ˈlʌsti/ *adj* **-tier, tiest** ‹*person*› sano, lozano; **he has a ~ appetite** tiene muy buen apetito

lute /lu:t/ *n* laúd *m*

Lutheran /ˈlu:θərən/ *adj* luterano

Luxembourg, Luxemburg /ˈlʌksəmbɜ:rg || ˈlʌksəm bɜ:g/ *n* Luxemburgo *m*

luxuriant /lʌgˈʒʊriənt || lʌgˈzjʊəriənt/ *adj* ‹*vegetation/growth*› exuberante; ‹*hair*› hermoso y abundante

luxuriate /lʌgˈʒʊrieɪt || lʌgˈzjʊərieɪt/ *vi* (revel) **to ~ IN sth** deleitarse CON algo

luxurious /lʌgˈʒʊriəs || lʌgˈzjʊəriəs/ *adj* ‹*home/surroundings*› lujoso

luxuriously /lʌgˈʒʊriəsli/ *adv* lujosamente

luxury /ˈlʌkʃəri/ *n* (*pl* **-ries**) 1 [u] (indulgence) lujo *m*; **a life of ~** una vida de lujos; **to live in ~** vivir rodeado de lujos; (*before n*) ‹*car/hotel*› de lujo; **~ goods** (Busn) artículos *mpl* suntuarios *or* de lujo 2 [c] (item) lujo *m*

lychee /ˈlaɪtʃi || ˈlaɪtʃi:, ˌlaɪˈtʃi:/ *n* lichi *m*

lying[1] /ˈlaɪɪŋ/ *n* [u] mentiras *fpl*

lying[2] *adj* (*before n*) mentiroso

lymph /lɪmf/ *n* [u] linfa *f*; (*before n*) **~ gland** glándula *f* linfática

lymphoma /lɪmˈfəʊmə/ *n* (*pl* **-mas** *or* **-mata** /-mətə/) linfoma *f*

lynch /lɪntʃ/ *vt* linchar

lynching /ˈlɪntʃɪŋ/ *n* linchamiento *m*

lynx /lɪŋks/ *n* (*pl* **~es** *or* **~**) lince *m*

lyre /ˈlaɪr || ˈlaɪə(r)/ *n* lira *f*

lyric[1] /ˈlɪrɪk/ *n* 1 (poem) poema *m* lírico 2 **lyrics** *pl n* (Mus) letra *f*

lyric[2] *adj* lírico

lyrical /ˈlɪrɪkəl/ *adj* (Lit) lleno de lirismo; ***to wax ~ about sth/sb*** (hum) poner* algo/a algn por las nubes

lyricist /ˈlɪrəsəst || ˈlɪrɪsɪst/ *n* (Mus) letrista *mf*

M, m /em/ *n* M, m *f*

m 1 (= **million(s)**) m 2 (= **meter(s)** *o* (BrE) **metre(s)**) m 3 (= **male**) de sexo masculino 4 (Ling) (= **masculine**) m 5 (= **married**) casóse con

M 1 (Clothing) (= **medium**) M, talla *f* mediana *or* (RPl) talle *m* mediano 2 (in UK) (Transp) (= **motorway**) *indicador de autopista*

ma /mɑː/ *n* (colloq) mamá *f*

MA /ˈemˈeɪ/ *n* 1 = **Master of Arts** 2 = **Massachusetts**

ma'am /mæm/ *n* (*as form of address*) señora; (to a younger woman) señorita; (to royalty) Majestad

mac /mæk/ *n* (colloq)
A *also* **Mac** (AmE colloq) (*as form of address*) amigo (fam)
B (raincoat) (BrE) impermeable *m*

Mac® /mæk/ *n* (Comput) Mac® *m or* (Esp) *f* (fam)

macabre /məˈkɑːbrə/ *adj* macabro

macadamia (nut) /ˈmækəˈdeɪmiə/ *n* macadamia *f*

macaroni /ˈmækəˈrəʊnɪ/ *n* [u] macarrones *mpl*; ~ **and cheese** (AmE), ~ **cheese** (BrE) macarrones *mpl* gratinados *or* al gratín

macaroon /ˈmækəˈruːn/ *n* macarrón *m*

macaw /məˈkɔː/ *n* guacamayo *m*, ara *m*

mace /meɪs/ *n*
A (Art, Hist, Mil) maza *f*
B (Culin) macis *f*, macia *f*
C **Mace**® (tear gas) (AmE) *gas para defensa personal*

Macedonia /ˈmæsəˈdəʊniə || ˌmæsɪˈdəʊniə/ *n* Macedonia *f*

Mach /mɑːk, mæk/ *adj*: ~ **3** 3 Mach; ~ **number** Mach *m*

machete /məˈʃeti, məˈtʃeti/ *n* machete *m*

Machiavellian, (BrE also) **Machiavelian** /ˈmækiəˈveliən/ *adj* maquiavélico

machinations /ˈmækəˈneɪʃənz, ˈmæʃ- || ˌmækɪˈneɪʃənz, ˈmæʃ-/ *pl n* (liter) maquinaciones *fpl*, intrigas *fpl*

machine[1] /məˈʃiːn/ *n* máquina *f*; ~ **made** hecho a máquina; (*washing* ~) lavadora *f*, máquina *f* (de lavar), lavarropas *m* (RPl); **I got $20 out of the** ~ saqué 20 dólares del cajero (automático); **the party** ~ (Pol) el aparato del partido; (*before n*) ~ **operator** operario, -ria *m,f*

machine[2] *vt* 1 (Tech) ‹*metal/edge*› trabajar a máquina; (on lathe) tornear 2 (sewing) coser a máquina

machine: ~ **code** *n* [u] (Comput) código *m* máquina; ~ **gun** *n* ametralladora *f*; **~-readable** /məˈʃiːnˈriːdəbəl/ *adj* legible por máquina

machinery /məˈʃiːnəri/ *n* [u] (machines) maquinaria *f*; (working parts) mecanismo *m*; **the** ~ **of government** la maquinaria de gobierno

machine: ~ **tool** *n* máquina *f* herramienta; ~ **translation** *n* [u] traducción *f* automática; **~-washable** /məˈʃiːnˈwɔːʃəbəl/ *adj* lavable a máquina

machinist /məˈʃiːnəst || məˈʃiːnɪst/ *n* maquinista *mf*, operario, -ria *m,f*

machismo /mɑːˈtʃɪzməʊ/ *n* [u] machismo *m*

macho /ˈmɑːtʃəʊ || ˈmætʃəʊ/ *adj* 1 (male chauvinist) ‹*behavior/attitude*› machista 2 (virile) ‹*image*› de macho; **she likes** ~ **men** le gustan los hombres muy machos *or* (fam) machotes

macintosh *n* ▸ **mackintosh**

mackerel /ˈmækrəl/ *n* [c u] (*pl* ~ *or* ~**s**) caballa *f*

mackinaw /ˈmækənɔː || ˈmækɪnɔː/ *n* (AmE) chaquetón *m*

mackintosh /ˈmækəntɑːʃ/ *n* impermeable *m*

macro /ˈmækrəʊ/ *n* (*pl* **-ros**) (Comput) macro *m*, macroinstrucción *f*

macrobiotic /ˈmækrəʊbaɪˈɑːtɪk || ˌmækrəʊbaɪˈɒtɪk/ *adj* macrobiótico

macrocosm /ˈmækrəʊkɑːzəm || ˈmækrəʊkɒzəm/ *n* macrocosmo(s) *m*

macroeconomics /ˈmækrəʊˌekəˈnɑːmɪks || ˌmækrəʊiːkəˈnɒmɪks/ *n* (+ *sing vb*) macroeconomía *f*

mad /mæd/ *adj* **-dd-**
A 1 (insane) loco, demente; ~ **dog** (rabid) perro *m* rabioso; **to go** ~ (become insane) volverse* loco, enloquecer(se)*; (become angry) ponerse* como loco *or* como una fiera; **don't go** ~ **with the salt** no te pases con la sal (fam); **to drive sb** ~ volver* *or* traer* loco a algn; **to work/run/fight like** ~ trabajar/correr/pelear como un loco; ***to be as*** ~ ***as a hatter*** *o* ***as a March hare*** estar* loco de atar *or* más loco que una cabra (fam) 2 ‹*rush*› loco, demencial; **we made a** ~ **dash for the airport** salimos como locos para el aeropuerto 3 ‹*scheme/idea*› disparatado, descabellado
B (angry) (esp AmE) (*pred*) **to be** ~ **(WITH/AT sb)** estar* furioso *or* (esp AmL) enojadísimo *or* (esp Esp) enfadadísimo (CON algn); **to get** ~ ponerse* furioso; **to make sb** ~ poner* furioso a algn
C (very enthusiastic) (colloq) (*pred*) **to be** ~ **ABOUT sb** estar* loco POR algn; **to be** ~ **ABOUT/ON sth**: **she's** ~ **about** *o* **on African music** la música africana la vuelve loca, le encanta *or* le chifla la música africana

-mad /ˈmæd/ *suff*: **to be car~/baseball~** ser* un fanático de los coches/del béisbol

Madagascan /ˈmædəˈgæskən/ *adj* malgache

Madagascar /ˈmædəˈgæskər/ *n* Madagascar *m*

madam /ˈmædəm/ *n* 1 (as title) señora *f*; **Dear M~** (Corresp) Estimada Señora; **M~ President/Chairman** señora presidenta/directora 2 (of brothel) madam(e) *f*, madama *f*, regenta *f* (Chi) 3 (bossy girl) (BrE pej): **she's a proper little** ~**!** mira que aires *or* importancia se da la mocosa esta (fam)

mad: ~**cap** *adj* ‹*plan*› descabellado, disparatado; ~ **cow disease** *n* encefalopatía *f* espongiforme bovina

madden /ˈmædn̩/ *vt* (make angry) enfurecer*; (drive mad) enloquecer*

maddening /ˈmædn̩ɪŋ/ *adj* ‹*indecision/habit*› exasperante; ‹*delay*› desesperante

made[1] /meɪd/ *past & past p of* **make**[1]

made[2] *adj* (*pred*) 1 (assured of success) ***to have it*** ~ tener* el éxito asegurado 2 (ideally suited): **they were** ~ **for each other** estaban hechos el uno para el otro

-made /ˈmeɪd/ *suff*: **Italian~ products** productos de fabricación italiana

Madeira /məˈdɪrə || məˈdɪərə/ *n* Madeira *f*, Madera *f*; (wine) madeira *m*, vino *m* de Madeira *or* Madera; (*before n*) ~ **cake** (BrE) bizcocho *m* de mantequilla

made-to-measure /ˈmeɪdtəˈmeʒər || ˌmeɪdtəˈmeʒə(r)/ *adj* (*pred* **made to measure**) hecho a (la) medida

madhouse /ˈmædhaʊs/ *n* (colloq) manicomio *m*

madly /ˈmædli/ *adv* 1 (frantically) ‹*rush/work*› como un loco; ‹*love*› locamente 2 (very) (*as intensifier*): ~ **in love**

locamente *or* perdidamente enamorado

madman /ˈmædmən/ *n* (*pl* **-men** /-mən/) loco *m*

madness /ˈmædnəs || ˈmædnɪs/ *n* [u] locura *f*, demencia *f*

madonna /məˈdɑːnə || məˈdɒnə/ *n* 1 (Relig) **Madonna**: **the M~** la Virgen 2 (Art) virgen *f*, madona *f*

Madrid /məˈdrɪd/ *n* Madrid *m*; (*before n*) madrileño

madwoman /ˈmædˌwʊmən/ *n* (*pl* **-women**) loca *f*

maelstrom /ˈmeɪlstrəm/ *n* (liter) vorágine *f* (liter)

maestro /ˈmaɪstrəʊ/ *n* (*pl* **-tros**) maestro *m*

Mafia /ˈmɑːfiə, ˈmæ- || ˈmæfiə/ *n* Mafia *f*

mag /mæg/ *n* (colloq) revista *f*

magazine /ˈmægəˈziːn/ *n*

A 1 (Publ) revista *f*; (*before n*) **~ rack** revistero *m* 2 **~ (program)** (Rad, TV) programa *m* de entrevistas y variedades

B (on gun — compartment) recámara *f*; (— bullet case) cargador *m*

magenta /məˈdʒentə/ *adj* (color) magenta *adj inv*, morado

maggot /ˈmægət/ *n* gusano *m*

Maghreb /ˈmɑːgreb || ˈmʌgrəb/ *n* **the ~** el Magreb

Magi /ˈmeɪdʒaɪ/ *pl n* **the ~** los Reyes Magos

magic[1] /ˈmædʒɪk/ *n* [u] magia *f*; **as if by ~** como por encanto, como por arte de magia; **the place has lost its ~ for me** el lugar ha perdido el encanto para mí

magic[2] *adj* 1 ‹*power/potion*› mágico; ‹*trick*› de magia; **~ spell** hechizo *m*, encanto *m*; **say the ~ word!** di la palabra mágica 2 (enchanting) ‹*moment/beauty*› mágico; (marvellous) (colloq) sensacional, fabuloso

magic bullet *n* (colloq) bala *f* mágica

magical /ˈmædʒɪkəl/ *adj* ‹*powers*› mágico; ‹*improvement*› milagroso

magically /ˈmædʒɪkli/ *adv* ‹*transformed/cured/transported*› como por encanto, como por arte de magia

magician /məˈdʒɪʃən/ *n* (sorcerer) mago *m*; (conjurer) mago, -ga *m,f*, prestidigitador, -dora *m,f*

magic realism *n* [u] realismo *m* mágico

magisterial /ˈmædʒəˈstɪriəl || ˌmædʒɪˈstɪəriəl/ *adj* ‹*treatise/performance*› magistral; ‹*wave/command*› autoritario

magistrate /ˈmædʒəstreɪt || ˈmædʒɪstreɪt/ *n* (in UK) *juez que conoce de faltas y asuntos civiles de menor importancia*

magna cum laude /ˈmægnəkʌmˈlaʊdeɪ/ *adv* (AmE) ‹*graduate*› con promedio (de) sobresaliente

magnanimity /ˈmægnəˈnɪməti/ *n* [u] magnanimidad *f*

magnanimous /mægˈnænəməs/ *adj* magnánimo

magnate /ˈmægneɪt/ *n* magnate *mf*, potentado, -da *m,f*

magnesia /məgˈniːʃə, -ʒə/ *n* [u] magnesia *f*

magnesium /mægˈniːziəm/ *n* [u] magnesio *m*

magnet /ˈmægnət || ˈmægnɪt/ *n* (Phys) imán *m*; **to be a ~ FOR sth/sb** atraer* como un imán a algo/algn

magnetic /mægˈnetɪk/ *adj* 1 ‹*field/north/tape*› magnético; **~ compass** brújula *f* 2 ‹*charm*› magnético; ‹*personality*› lleno de magnetismo

magnetic resonance imaging *n* representación *f* óptica por resonancia

magnetism /ˈmægnətɪzəm/ *n* [u] magnetismo *m*

magnetize /ˈmægnətaɪz/ *vt* imantar, magnetizar*

magnification /ˈmægnəfəˈkeɪʃən || ˌmægnɪfɪˈkeɪʃən/ *n* 1 [u] (Opt) aumento *m* 2 [c] (copy, print) ampliación *f*

magnificence /mægˈnɪfəsəns || mægˈnɪfɪsəns/ *n* [u] magnificencia *f*, esplendor *m*

magnificent /mægˈnɪfəsənt || mægˈnɪfɪsənt/ *adj* magnífico, espléndido

magnify /ˈmægnəfaɪ || ˈmægnɪfaɪ/ *vt* **-fies, -fying, -fied**

A 1 ‹*image*› ampliar*, aumentar de tamaño 2 ‹*problem/difficulty*› exagerar

B (exalt) (Relig) magnificar*

magnifying glass /ˈmægnəfaɪɪŋ/ *n* lupa *f*

magnitude /ˈmægnətuːd || ˈmægnɪtjuːd/ *n* (size) magnitud *f*; (importance) envergadura *f*

magnolia /mægˈnəʊljə || mægˈnəʊliə/ *n* 1 (flower) magnolia *f*; (tree) magnolio *m*, magnolia *f* 2 (color) (BrE) color *m* magnolia (*color crema con un ligero matiz rosado*)

magnum /ˈmægnəm/ *n* (*pl* **-nums**) 1 (bottle) mágnum *m* (*botella de litro y medio*) 2 **~ (revolver)** mágnum *f or m*

magpie /ˈmægpaɪ/ *n* 1 (Zool) urraca *f*, picaza *f* 2 (hoarder) urraca *mf* 3 (chatterbox) (AmE) cotorra *f* (fam)

maharajah /ˈmɑːhəˈrɑːdʒə/ *n* maharajá *m*, marajá *m*

mahogany /məˈhɑːgəni || məˈhɒgəni/ *n* (*pl* **-nies**) 1 [u] (wood) caoba *f* 2 [c] **~ (tree)** caoba *f*

maid /meɪd/ *n*

A 1 (servant) sirvienta *f*, criada *f*, mucama *f* (AmL), empleada *f* doméstica (frml); (*parlor/lady's* **~**) (primera) doncella *f*; **kitchen ~** pinche *f*, ayudanta *f* de cocina 2 (in hotel) camarera *f*, mucama *f* (AmL) 3 (occasional housekeeper) (AmE) señora *f* de la limpieza, limpiadora *f*

B (young woman) (arch) doncella *f* (arc); *see also* **old maid**

maiden[1] /ˈmeɪdn̩/ *n* (arch *or* liter) doncella *f* (arc *o* liter)

maiden[2] *adj* (*before n*) 1 (unmarried) soltera; **~ aunt** tía *f* soltera 2 ‹*flight/speech*› inaugural

maiden name *n* apellido *m* de soltera

maid: **~ of honor**, (BrE) **~ of honour** *n* (*pl* **~s of honor**) dama *f* de honor; **~servant** *n* sirvienta *f*

mail[1] /meɪl/ *n* [u]

A 1 (system) correo *m*; **by ~** por correo; (*before n*) **~ train** tren *m* correo 2 (letters, parcels) correspondencia *f*, correo *m*

B (armor) malla *f*

mail[2] *vt* (esp AmE): **to ~ a letter** echar una carta al correo *or* al buzón; **to ~ sth TO sb** mandarle *or* enviarle* algo por correo A algn

mail: **~bag** *n* bolsa *f* del correo (AmL), saca *f* del correo (Esp); **~ bomb** *n* 1 (letter bomb) (AmE) carta *f* bomba; (parcel) paquete *m* bomba; 2 (e-mails) bombardeo *m* de emails; **~box** *n* 1 (for receiving mail) (AmE) buzón *m*, casillero *m* (Ven) 2 (for sending mail) (AmE) buzón *m* (de correos) 3 (electronic) buzón *m*; **~ carrier** *n* (AmE) cartero, -ra *m,f*; **~ drop** *n* (AmE) dirección *f* postal

mailing list *n* (Marketing) banco *m or* lista *f* de direcciones

mail: **~man** /ˈmeɪlmæn/ *n* (*pl* **-men** /-men/) (AmE) cartero *m*; **~ merge** *n* [u] fusión *f* de correo; (*before n*) **~ merge facility** función *f* de fusión de correo; **~ order** *n* [u] venta *f* por correo; **to buy sth by** *o* **on ~ order** comprar algo por correo; (*before n*) **~-order catalog/firm** catálogo *m*/compañía *f* de venta por correo; **~-out** /ˈmeɪlaʊt/ *n* 1 [u] (practice) buzoneo *m*, mailing *m* 2 [c] (item) mailing *m*; **~ shot** *n* (BrE) mailing *m*

maim /meɪm/ *vt* (cripple) lisiar; (mutilate) mutilar

main[1] /meɪn/ *adj* 1 (*before n, no comp*) ‹*purpose/idea*› principal, fundamental, más importante; ‹*door/bedroom*› principal; ‹*office*› central; **the ~ thing** lo principal, lo fundamental, lo más importante; **~ course** plato *m* principal *or* fuerte, segundo plato *m*; **~ street** calle *f* principal; ***M~ Street*** (AmE) ≈ la Calle Mayor 2 **in the main** en general, por lo general, por regla general

main[2] *n*

A (Civil Eng, Const) 1 [c] (pipe) cañería *f or* tubería *f* principal *or* de distribución; (cable) cable *m* principal 2 (supply) **the ~** *o* (BrE) **the ~s** la red de suministro; **to turn the water/gas off at the ~** *o* (BrE) **the ~s** cerrar la llave (principal) del agua/del gas

B [u] (open sea) (liter) **the ~** la mar océana (liter)

main: **~ drag** *n* (AmE sl) **the ~ drag** la calle principal; **~frame** *n* unidad *f* central *or* principal, computadora *f or* (Esp tb) ordenador *m* central; **~land** /ˈmeɪnlənd, -lænd/ *n*: **the ~land** *la masa territorial de un país o continente excluyendo sus islas*; (*before n*) **~land China** (la) China continental; **~ line** *n* (Rail) línea *f* principal; (*before n*) **~-line station** estación *f* interurbana

mainly /ˈmeɪnli/ *adv* 1 (chiefly) principalmente, fundamentalmente 2 (for the most part): **the people in the streets were ~ tourists** la mayoría de la gente que había en la calle eran turistas

main: **~ man** *n* (AmE colloq) 1 (close friend) mejor amigo *m* 2 (principal figure) gran figura *f*; **~ road** *n* (BrE) carretera *f* principal; **~sail** /ˈmeɪnseɪl, -səl/ *n* vela *f* mayor; **~spring** *n* muelle *m* real; **~stay** *n* (Naut) estay *m* mayor; (chief support) pilar *m*, puntal *m*

mainstream[1] /ˈmeɪnstriːm/ *n* corriente *f* dominante, línea *f* central

mainstream[2] *adj* ‹*culture*› establecido; ‹*ideology*› dominante; **~ politics** la política a nivel de los partidos mayoritarios

maintain /meɪn'teɪn/ *vt*
A 1 ‹*speed/lead*› mantener*; ‹*silence*› guardar 2 ‹*house/machine*› ocuparse del mantenimiento de; ‹*aircraft*› mantener* 3 ‹*family/dependents/army*› mantener*
B (claim) mantener*, sostener*

maintenance /'meɪntṇəns || 'meɪntənəns/ *n* [u]
A (repairs) mantenimiento *m*; **I do all my own ~ on the car/house** hago todo el mantenimiento del coche/todos los arreglos de la casa yo mismo
B (money) (BrE Law) pensión *f* alimenticia, alimentos *mpl*

maisonette /'meɪzṇ'et || ˌmeɪzə'net/ *n* (BrE) (apartment) dúplex *m*; (house) *vivienda independiente de dos pisos que forma parte de una casa*

maitre d' /'meɪtrə'diː/ *n* (AmE) maître *mf*

maize /meɪz/ *n* [u] 1 (plant) maíz *m*; (*before n*) **~ field** maizal *m* 2 (grains) maíz *m*, choclo *m* (CS, Per), elote *m* (Méx)

Maj (title) = **Major**

majestic /mə'dʒestɪk/ *adj* majestuoso

majesty /'mædʒəsti/ *n* (*pl* **-ties**) 1 [u] (of appearance, landscape) majestuosidad *f* 2 [c] **Majesty** (as title) Majestad; **Her/Your M~** su Majestad; **Her M~'s Revenue and Customs** (in UK) ≈ Hacienda, ≈ la Dirección General Impositiva (en RPl), ≈ Impuestos Internos (en Chi)

major¹ /'meɪdʒər || 'meɪdʒə(r)/ *adj*
A ‹*change/client*› muy importante; ‹*setback*› serio; ‹*revision*› a fondo; ‹*illness*› grave; **she is at a ~ disadvantage** está en franca desventaja; **all ~ credit cards accepted** se aceptan las principales tarjetas de crédito
B (Mus) mayor; **B/C ~** si/do mayor

major² *n*
A (Mil) mayor *mf* (*en AmL*), comandante *mf* (*en Esp*)
B (AmE Educ) (subject) asignatura *f* principal; (student): **she's a geography ~** estudia geografía (*asignatura principal*)
C **majors** *pl* (AmE) 1 (companies) grandes *or* importantes empresas *fpl* 2 (Sport) **the ~s** las grandes ligas (*esp de béisbol*)

major³ *vi* (AmE Educ) **to ~ IN sth** especializarse* EN algo

Majorca /mə'jɔːrkə || mə'jɔːkə, mə'dʒɔːkə/ *n* Mallorca *f*

majorette /'meɪdʒə'ret/ *n* batonista *f*

major general *n* (in army) general *mf* de división (*este grado tiene diversos equivalentes en Latinoamérica, entre ellos* **brigadier mayor, mayor general** *y* **teniente general**)

majority /mə'dʒɔːrəti || mə'dʒɒrəti/ *n* (*pl* **-ties**)
A 1 (greater number) (+ *sing o pl vb*) mayoría *f*; **to be in the ~** ser* mayoría; **the silent ~** la mayoría silenciosa; (*before n*) ‹*decision/party*› mayoritario; **~ holding** *o* **interest** participación *f* mayoritaria; **~ rule** gobierno *m* de la mayoría 2 (margin) mayoría *f*, margen *m*; **absolute ~** mayoría absoluta
B (adulthood) mayoría *f* de edad

major league *n* (Sport) liga *f* nacional; (*before n*) **major-league companies** compañías *fpl* de primera línea

make¹ /meɪk/ (*past & past p* **made**) *vt*

Sense I

A (create, produce) ‹*paint/cars*› hacer*, fabricar*; ‹*dress*› hacer*, confeccionar (frml); ‹*meal/cake/sandwich/coffee*› hacer*, preparar; ‹*film*› hacer*, rodar; ‹*record*› grabar; ‹*fire/nest/hole*› hacer*; ‹*list/will*› hacer*; **to ~ a noise** hacer* ruido; **to ~ a note of sth** anotar algo; Ⓢ **made in Spain/Mexico** hecho *or* fabricado en España/México; Ⓢ **made in Argentina/Peru** industria *or* fabricación argentina/peruana; **to ~ sth INTO sth: I'll ~ this material into a skirt** con esta tela me haré una falda; **to ~ sth OUT OF/FROM/OF sth: she made the dress out of an old sheet** se hizo el vestido con/de una sábana vieja; **we made another meal from the leftovers** hicimos otra comida con las sobras; **it's made of wood/plastic** es de madera/plástico; **don't ~ an enemy of her** no te la eches encima como enemiga; *see also* **difference A2, fuss¹, mess¹ A, B** *etc*
B 1 (carry out) ‹*repairs/changes/payment*› hacer*, efectuar* (frml); ‹*preparations/arrangements*› hacer*; ‹*journey*› hacer*; **~ a left (turn) here** (AmE) dobla *or* gira a la izquierda aquí 2 ‹*remark/announcement*› hacer*

Sense II

A (cause to be): **I'll ~ you happy/rich** te haré feliz/rica; **don't ~ life difficult for yourself** no te compliques la vida; **that made me sad** eso me entristeció *or* me apenó; **the work made me thirsty/sleepy** el trabajo me dio sed/sueño; **what ~s me angry is ...** lo que me da rabia es ...; **I couldn't ~ myself heard above the noise** no podía conseguir que me oyeran con el ruido; **they've made him supervisor** lo han nombrado supervisor, lo han ascendido a supervisor; **we'll ~ a man of you** haremos de ti un hombre; **if nine o'clock is too early, ~ it later** si las nueve es muy temprano, podemos reunirnos (*or* encontrarnos *etc*) más tarde; **two large pizzas ... , no, ~ that three** dos pizzas grandes ... , no, mire, mejor déme tres
B 1 (cause to) hacer*; **whatever made you do it?** ¿por qué lo hiciste?, ¿qué te llevó a hacer eso? 2 (compel) obligar* a, hacer*; **she was made to apologize** la obligaron a *or* la hicieron pedir perdón 3 (*in phrases*) **to make believe**: **you can't just ~ believe it never happened** no puedes pretender que no sucedió, no puedes hacer como si no hubiera sucedido; **to make do (with sth), to make sth do** arreglárselas con algo

Sense III

A 1 (constitute, be) ser*; **perfume ~s the ideal gift** el perfume es el regalo ideal; **it would ~ a nice change** sería un cambio agradable; **you'd ~ a useless nurse** como enfermera serías un desastre; **they ~ a nice couple** hacen buena pareja 2 (equal, amount to) ser*; **five plus five ~s ten** cinco y *or* más cinco son diez; **that ~s two of us** ya somos dos
B (calculate): **what do you ~ the total?** ¿(a ti) cuánto te da?; **I ~ it 253** (a mí) me da 253; **what time do you ~ it, what do you ~ the time?** ¿qué hora tienes?
C (make fuss): **I think you're making too much of what she said** creo que le estás dando demasiada importancia a lo que dijo
D 1 (understand) **to ~ sth OF sth**: **I could ~ nothing of the message** no entendí el mensaje; **~ of that what you will** tú saca tus propias conclusiones 2 (think) **to ~ sth OF sb/sth**: **what did you ~ of him?** ¿qué te pareció?; **I don't know what to ~ of it** no sé qué pensar

Sense IV

A 1 (gain, earn) ‹*money*› hacer*; **they made a loss/profit** perdieron/ganaron dinero; **they made a profit of $20,000** ganaron *or* sacaron 20.000 dólares; **how much did you ~ on the deal?** ¿cuánto sacaste *or* ganaste con el trato? 2 (acquire) ‹*friends*› hacer*; **I made a few acquaintances there** conocí a *or* (frml) trabé conocimiento con algunas personas allí; **to ~ a name for oneself** hacerse* un nombre
B (colloq) (manage to attend, reach): **I'm afraid I can't ~ Saturday** me temo que el sábado no puedo; **we just made the 3 o'clock train** llegamos justo a tiempo para el tren de las tres; ***to ~ it***: **he'll never ~ it as a doctor** nunca será un buen médico; **they made it through to the finals** llegaron a la final
C (assure success of): **if you go to Harvard, you're made for life** si vas a Harvard, tienes el futuro asegurado; ***to ~ or break sth/sb*** ser* el éxito o la ruina de algo/algn

■ **make** *vi*
A (make preliminary move): **to ~ as if** *o* **as though to + INF** hacer* ademán de + INF
B (move, proceed): **they made toward the door** se dirigieron hacia la puerta; *see also* **make for**

Phrasal verbs

• **make for** [v ▸ prep ▸ o]
A (head toward) dirigirse* hacia/a; **she made straight for the bar** se fue derecho al bar
B (encourage, promote) contribuir* a; **mutual distrust doesn't ~ for a good relationship** la desconfianza mutua no contribuye a una buena relación

• **make off** [v ▸ adv] salir* corriendo, largarse* (fam); **to ~ off with sth** llevarse algo, escaparse *or* (fam) largarse* con algo

• **make out**

Sense I [v ▸ o ▸ adv, v ▸ adv ▸ o]

A 1 (discern) ‹*object/outline*› distinguir*; (from a distance) divisar; ‹*sound*› distinguir*; **I can't ~ out what she's saying** no entiendo lo que dice; **I can't ~ out the address** no logro descifrar la dirección 2 (figure out) (colloq) entender*, comprender
B 1 (write) ‹*list/invoice*› hacer*; ‹*receipt*› hacer*, extender* (frml); **~ the check out to P. Jones** haga el cheque pagadero a *or* a favor de P. Jones 2 (put forward): **to ~ out a**

m

case for/against sth/sb presentar argumentos a favor/en contra de algo/algn

(Sense II) [v ▸ adv] [1] (do, fare) (colloq): **how did you ~ out in the exam?** ¿qué tal te fue en el examen? (fam) [2] (sexually) (AmE sl) ▸**neck²**

(Sense III) (claim, pretend) [1] [v ▸ adv ▸ o]: **she made out it was her own work** dio a entender que lo había hecho ella misma; **you're not as ill as you ~ out** no estás tan enfermo como pretendes *or* como quieres hacer creer [2] [v ▸ o ▸ adv]: **he's not as rich as he ~s himself out to be** no es tan rico como pretende

• **make over**

A [v ▸ o ▸ adv, v ▸ adv ▸ o] ‹*property/money*›, ceder

B [v ▸ o ▸ adv, v ▸ adv ▸ o] (reuse) ‹*clothes*› (AmE) arreglar

C [v ▸ o ▸ adv] (AmE) [1] (with cosmetics) maquillar [2] (change image of) transformar la imagen de; **the candidate had been made over in an effort to win votes** habían transformado la imagen del candidato en un intento de ganar votos

• **make up**

(Sense I) [v ▸ o ▸ adv, v ▸ adv ▸ o]

A ‹*story/excuse*› inventar

B [1] (assemble, prepare) ‹*prescription/food parcel*› preparar; **to ~ up a sweater** coser *or* armar un suéter; **to ~ up a foursome** formar un grupo de cuatro personas; **we can ~ up a bed for you on the sofa** podemos prepararte una cama en el sofá [2] (draw up) ‹*agenda/list*› hacer*

C [1] (complete, add) completar; **she came along to ~ up the numbers** vino para completar el grupo [2] (compensate for): **I'll take the afternoon off, and ~ up the time later** me tomaré la tarde libre y ya recuperaré el tiempo más tarde; *see also* **make up for**

(Sense II) [v ▸ adv ▸ o] (constitute) formar; **it is made up of three parts** está compuesto de tres partes

(Sense III) [v ▸ adv, v ▸ o ▸ adv] (achieve reconciliation) **to ~ (it) up (WITH sb)** hacer* las paces (CON algn), reconciliarse (CON algn)

(Sense IV) [1] [v ▸ adv] (with cosmetics) maquillarse, pintarse [2] [v ▸ adv ▸ o, v ▸ o ▸ adv] ‹*person/eyes*› maquillar, pintar; ‹*actor*› maquillar, caracterizar*; **to ~ oneself up** maquillarse, pintarse

• **make up for** [v ▸ adv ▸ prep ▸ o] compensar; **to ~ up for lost time** recuperar el tiempo perdido; **what she lacks in technique she ~s up for in style** lo que le falta de técnica lo compensa con estilo

• **make up to**

A [v ▸ adv ▸ prep ▸ o] (make advances to) tratar de ganarse el favor de

B [v ▸ o ▸ adv ▸ prep] [1] (bring, raise): **I'll ~ the total up to $200** yo pondré lo que falte para llegar a 200 dólares; **add water to ~ the juice up to a pint** añadir agua al jugo hasta obtener una pinta [2] (compensate) ***to ~ it up to sb***: **just give me one more chance: I'll ~ it all up to you** dame otra oportunidad y te resarciré de todo; **thank you for your help: I don't know how to ~ it up to you** gracias por tu ayuda, no sé cómo podré pagarte lo que has hecho

make² *n*

A (brand) marca *f*; **what ~ is it?** ¿de qué marca es?

B ***to be on the ~*** (colloq) (out for gain) estar* intentando sacar tajada (fam); (looking for a date) estar* de ligue *or* (AmS) de levante *or* (Chi) de pinche (fam)

make: **~-believe** *n* [u] [1] (fantasy) fantasía *f*; **the land of ~-believe** el mundo de la fantasía [2] (pretense): **don't be frightened, it's only ~-believe** no te asustes, es de mentira **~over** *n* [1] (of organization) gran reorganización *f or* restructuración *f* [2] (of person) transformación *f* completa (*del aspecto exterior*) [3] (of image) cambio *m* de imagen [4] (repairs) reformas *fpl*

maker /'meɪkər || 'meɪkə(r)/ *n*

A (manufacturer) fabricante *mf*

B **Maker** (God) Creador *m*, Hacedor *m*; **she has gone to meet her M~** (euph) Dios la ha llamado a su seno *or* a su lado (euf)

make: **~shift** *adj* ‹*repair*› provisional, provisorio (AmS); ‹*bed*› improvisado; **~up** *n* [1] [u] (cosmetics) maquillaje *m*; **to put on one's ~up** maquillarse, pintarse; **she doesn't wear ~up** no se maquilla, no se pinta; (*before n*) **~up artist** maquillador, -dora *m,f*; **~up remover** desmaquillador *m*; [2] (*no pl*) (of person) carácter *m*, modo *m* de ser; **its genetic ~up** su estructura genética; [3] [c] (AmE Educ) examen *m* de recuperación; (*before n*) **~up course** curso *m* de recuperación

making /'meɪkɪŋ/ *n* [u] [1] (production, creation): **a book about the ~ of the TV series** un libro que trata de cómo se hizo la serie de televisión; **the encyclopedia has been nine years in the ~** ha llevado nueve años compilar la enciclopedia; **this is history in the ~** esto va a pasar a la historia; **her problems are of her own ~** ella se crea sus propios problemas; ***to be the ~ of sb/sth***: **her years in New York were the ~ of her** los años que pasó en Nueva York fueron decisivos (en su vida); **the merger proved to be the ~ of Acmeco** el éxito de Acmeco se debió a la fusión [2] **makings** *pl* **the ~s OF sth**: **you have the ~s of a good story there** allí tienes material *or* tienes todos los ingredientes para una buena historia; **she has the ~s of a great actress** es una gran actriz en ciernes

maladjusted /'mælə'dʒʌstəd || ˌmælə'dʒʌstɪd/ *adj* (Psych) inadaptado, desadaptado

maladroit /'mælə'drɔɪt/ *adj* torpe

malady /'mælədi/ *n* (*pl* **-dies**) (liter) mal *m* (liter)

malaise /mæ'leɪz/ *n* [c u] malestar *m*

malapropism /'mæləprɑːpɪzəm || 'mæləprɒpɪzəm/ *n* [c u] *error cometido al confundir un vocablo con otro similar, esp cuando causa un efecto ridículo*

malaria /mə'leriə/ *n* [u] malaria *f*, paludismo *m*

Malawi /mə'lɑːwi/ *n* Malaui *m*, Malawi *m*

Malawian /mə'lɑːwiən/ *adj* malauiano

Malay¹ /mə'leɪ/ *adj* malayo

Malay² *n* [1] [c] (person) malayo, -ya *m,f* [2] [u] (language) malayo *m*

Malaysia /mə'leɪʒə || mə'leɪziə/ *n* Malaisia *f*; (continental part) Malasia *f*

Malaysian¹ /mə'leɪʒən || mə'leɪziən/ *adj* malaisio; (from continental part) malasio

Malaysian² *n* malaisio, -sia *m,f*; (from continental part) malasio, -sia *m,f*

Maldive Islands /'mɔːldiːv, -daɪv/, **Maldives** /-z/ *pl n* **the ~ ~** las (islas) Maldivas

male¹ /meɪl/ *adj*

A [1] ‹*animal/plant*› macho; ‹*hormone/sex*› masculino [2] ‹*attitude*› masculino; ‹*workforce*› de hombres; **~ doctor** médico *m*, doctor *m*; **~ chauvinism** machismo *m*; **~ model** modelo *m* (masculino); **~ nurse** enfermero *m*; **there were several ~ applicants** se presentaron varios candidatos varones

B (Mech Eng) ‹*plug/thread*› macho

male² *n* (animal) macho *m*; (person) varón *m*

male-voice choir /'meɪl'vɔɪs/ *n* (BrE) coro *m* de voces masculinas

malevolence /mə'levələns/ *n* [u] malevolencia *f*

malevolent /mə'levələnt/ *adj* ‹*grin*› malévolo; ‹*deity*› maligno

malformation /'mælfɔːr'meɪʃən || ˌmælfɔː'meɪʃən/ *n* [u c] deformación *f* (*esp congénita*), malformación *f*

malformed /'mæl'fɔːrmd/ *adj* deforme, mal formado

malfunction¹ /'mæl'fʌŋkʃən/ *n* [1] [u] (defective functioning) mal funcionamiento *m*; **heart/liver ~** (Med) disfunción *f* cardíaca/hepática [2] [c] (failure) falla *f or* (Esp) fallo *m*

malfunction² *vi* (Med, Tech) fallar, funcionar mal

malice /'mæləs || 'mælɪs/ *n* [u] [1] (ill will) mala intención *f*, maldad *f*; **to bear sb ~** guardarle rencor a algn [2] (Law) dolo *m* (penal), intención *f* delictuosa; **with ~ aforethought** con premeditación

malicious /mə'lɪʃəs/ *adj* ‹*person/gossip*› malicioso, malintencionado; ‹*damage*› doloso, intencional

malign¹ /mə'laɪn/ *vt* ‹*person*› calumniar, difamar; **the much ~ed director** el vilipendiado director

malign² *adj* maligno

malignant /mə'lɪgnənt/ *adj* maligno

malinger /mə'lɪŋgər/ *vi* hacerse* el enfermo

malingerer /mə'lɪŋgərər/ *n*: *persona que se finge enferma*

mall /mɔːl || mæl, mɔːl/ *n* [1] (for shopping) centro *m* comercial [2] (avenue) paseo *m*, bulevar *m*

mallard /'mælərd || 'mælɑːd/ *n* pato *m or* ánade *m* real

malleable /'mæliəbəl/ *adj* ‹*material*› maleable; ‹*person*› dócil

mallet /'mælət || 'mælɪt/ *n* 1 (tool) mazo *m* 2 (Sport) (in polo) maza *f*; (in croquet) mazo *m*

malnourished /'mæl'nɜːrɪʃt/ *adj* desnutrido

malnutrition /'mælnuː'trɪʃən/ *n* [u] desnutrición *f*

malodorous /mæl'əʊdərəs/ *adj* (frml *or* hum) maloliente, hediondo

malpractice /'mæl'præktəs/ *n* [u] mala práctica *f*, conducta *f* incorrecta (*en el ejercicio de la profesión*)

malt /mɔːlt/ *n* 1 [u] (grain) malta *f*; (*before n*) ~ **extract/vinegar** extracto *m*/vinagre *m* de malta 2 [u c] ~ **(whisky)** whisky *m* de malta

Malta /'mɔːltə/ *n* Malta *f*

malted milk /'mɔːltəd || 'mɔːltɪd/ *n* (AmE) batido *m* de leche malteada; (BrE) leche *f* malteada

Maltese[1] /'mɔːl'tiːz/ *adj* maltés

Maltese[2] *n* (*pl* ~) 1 [c] (person) maltés, -tesa *m,f* 2 [u] (language) maltés *m*

maltreat /'mæl'triːt/ *vt* maltratar, tratar mal

maltreatment /'mæl'triːtmənt/ *n* [u] malos tratos *mpl*

mamma *n* ▸ **momma**

mammal /'mæməl/ *n* mamífero *m*

mammary gland /'mæməri/ *n* glándula *f* mamaria

mammogram /'mæməgræm/, **mammograph** /'mæməgræf || -grɑːf/ *n* mamografía *f*

mammoth[1] /'mæməθ/ *n* mamut *m*

mammoth[2] *adj* ‹*building/cost*› gigantesco, enorme, colosal; ‹*task*› de titanes

mammy /'mæmi/ *n* (*pl* **-mies**) (black nurse) (Hist) ama *f*‡ negra; (black woman) (pej & dated) negra *f*

man[1] /mæn/ *n* (*pl* **men** /men/)

A 1 (adult male) hombre *m*; **a young ~** un joven; **I'm not half the ~ I used to be** ya no soy lo que era; **he was ~ enough to admit his error** fue lo bastante hombre como para admitir su error; **he's a sick ~** está muy enfermo; **I feel a new ~** me siento como nuevo; **the ~'s a fool** es un estúpido; **he's the ~ to ask** es a él a quien hay que preguntar(le); **the police think he's their ~** la policía cree que es la persona que andan buscando; **a ~'s gotta do what a ~'s gotta do** (set phrase) un hombre tiene que cumplir con su deber; **are you a ~ or a mouse?** (set phrase) ¿eres hombre o gallina?; ***to be low ~ on the totem pole*** (AmE) ser* el último mono (fam); ***to be one's own ~*** ser* independiente, ir* por libre (Esp fam); ***to separate*** *o* (BrE also) ***sort out the men from the boys*** ser* una verdadera prueba de fuego 2 (husband/boyfriend): **her new ~** su nueva pareja (*or* su nuevo compañero *etc*); **to live together as ~ and wife** vivir como marido y mujer; **her young ~** (dated) su novio, su galán (ant) 3 (type): **he's a Harvard ~** estudió en Harvard; **he's a local/Boston ~** es del lugar/de Boston; **he's a family ~** es un padre de familia; **the ~ in the street** el hombre de la calle, el ciudadano medio *or* de a pie; **the ~ of the match** (BrE) el mejor jugador

B 1 (person) persona *f*; **no ~ has the right to take life** (frml) nadie *or* ningún ser humano tiene derecho a matar; **every ~ for himself** (set phrase) sálvese quien pueda (fr hecha); ***as one ~*** como un solo hombre; ***to a ~***: **they're loyal citizens to a ~** todos ellos (sin excepción) son ciudadanos leales; ▸ **meat 1** 2 *also* **Man** (mankind) (*no art*) el hombre; **~ shall not live by bread alone** no sólo de pan vive el hombre

C 1 (representative, employee): **our ~ in Cairo** nuestro representante (*or* corresponsal *or* agente *etc*) en el Cairo; **he's the PR ~ for Acme UK** es el encargado de relaciones públicas en Acme UK 2 (manservant) (dated) criado *m*

D **men** *pl*: **the men** (troops) los soldados, la tropa; (employees) los trabajadores; **officers and men** los oficiales y los soldados *or* la tropa

E (in chess) pieza *f*; (in draughts) ficha *f*

F (*as form of address*) (colloq): **hey, ~!** ¡oiga, amigo!, ¡oye, tío (Esp) *or* (AmL exc CS) mano *or* (Chi) gallo! (fam), ¡oíme, che! (RPl fam)

G (*as interj*) (esp AmE): **~, it was hot!** ¡hacía un calor ...!

man[2] *vt* **-nn-** ‹*switchboard*› encargarse* *or* ocuparse de; ‹*ship*› tripular; **the inquiry desk is ~ned at all times** el mostrador de informaciones está atendido a toda hora; **soldiers ~ned the barricades/guns** había soldados apostados en las barricadas/a las armas

Man = **Manitoba**

man-about-town /'mænəbaʊt'taʊn/ *n* (*pl* **men-about-town** /men-/) hombre *m* de mundo

manacle /'mænəkəl/ *vt* esposar

manacles /'mænəkəlz/ *pl n* (for wrists) esposas *fpl*; (for legs) grillos *mpl*

manage /'mænɪdʒ/ *vt*

A (Busn) ‹*company/bank*› dirigir*, administrar, gerenciar (AmL); ‹*staff/team*› dirigir*; ‹*land/finances*› administrar

B (handle, cope with) ‹*children*› manejar, controlar; ‹*household*› llevar, administrar; **he seems unable to ~ his life** parece incapaz de organizar su vida; **can you ~ those suitcases on your own?** ¿puedes con esas maletas tú sola?; **she can't ~ the stairs** no puede subir la escalera

C (achieve): **I can ~ 60 words per minute** puedo hacer 60 palabras por minuto; **he ~d a smile** esbozó una sonrisa forzada; **I can't ~ the meeting** no puedo *or* no me es posible ir a la reunión; **to ~ to + INF** lograr *or* poder* + INF; **I ~d to get four tickets** conseguí *or* pude conseguir cuatro entradas; **how did they ~ to get away with it?** ¿cómo se las arreglaron para salirse con la suya?

■ **manage** *vi*

A (Busn) dirigir*, administrar

B (cope): **can I help you? — thank you, I can ~** ¿me permite que la ayude? — gracias, yo puedo sola; **they have to ~ on $300 a week** tienen que arreglarse *or* arreglárselas con 300 dólares a la semana

manageable /'mænɪdʒəbəl/ *adj* ‹*child/animal*› dócil; ‹*hair*› dócil, manejable; ‹*task/goal*› posible de alcanzar; ‹*size/amount/portion*› razonable

management /'mænɪdʒmənt/ *n*

A [u] (act) 1 (Busn) dirección *f*, administración *f*, gestión *f*; ⓢ **under new management** bajo nueva dirección, cambio de firma; **she's studying ~** está estudiando administración de empresas 2 (handling, control) manejo *m*; **personnel ~** gestión *f or* gerencia *f* de personal

B (managers) 1 (as group) (*no art*, + *sing o pl vb*) directivos *mpl*; **~ and workers** los directivos *or* la patronal y los trabajadores; **senior ~** altos cargos *mpl* 2 [c] (of particular company) dirección *f*, gerencia *f*

manager /'mænɪdʒər || 'mænɪdʒə(r)/ *n* (Busn) (of company, department) director, -tora *m,f*, gerente *mf*; (of store, restaurant) gerente *mf*, encargado, -da *m,f*; (of estate, fund) administrador, -dora *m,f*; (of pop group, boxer) manager *mf*; (Sport) agente *mf*; (in soccer) entrenador, -dora *m,f*, director técnico, directora técnica *m,f* (AmL); **she's a good ~** es buena administradora

manageress /'mænɪdʒərəs/ *n* (esp BrE) encargada *f*

managerial /'mænə'dʒɪriəl || ˌmænɪ'dʒɪəriəl/ *adj* directivo, de dirección, gerencial (AmL)

managing director /'mænɪdʒɪŋ/ *n* (esp BrE) /'mænədʒɪŋ/ director ejecutivo, directora ejecutiva *m,f*

manatee /'mænətiː || ˌmænə'tiː/ *n* manatí *m*

> **Man Booker Prize**
>
> En el Reino Unido, un premio que se otorga cada octubre al autor de la mejor novela de ficción que se haya publicado el año anterior. Antes de 2002 su nombre era el *Booker Prize*

Mancunian[1] /mæn'kjuːniən/ *adj* de Manchester, Inglaterra

Mancunian[2] *n*: *habitante o persona oriunda de Manchester, Inglaterra*

mandarin /'mændərən || 'mændərɪn/ *n*

A [c] 1 (Chinese official) (Hist) mandarín *m* 2 (top establishment figure) (journ) jerarca *mf*, mandarín *m*

B [c] ~ **(orange)** mandarina *f*

C [u] **Mandarin (Chinese)** (language) mandarín *m*, lengua *f* mandarina

mandate /'mændeɪt/ *n* mandato *m*

mandatory /'mændətɔːri || 'mændətəri/ *adj* (frml) obligatorio

mandible /'mændəbəl || 'mændɪbəl/ *n* 1 (lower jaw) mandíbula *f* inferior 2 (of bird) mandíbula *f*

mandolin, mandoline /ˌmændə'lɪn/ *n* mandolina *f*

m

mandrake /'mændreɪk/ *n* mandrágora *f*
mane /meɪn/ *n* (of horse) crin(es) *f(pl)*; (of lion) melena *f*
man-eating /'mæn,i:tɪŋ/ *adj* (*before n*) que come carne humana
maneuver¹, (BrE) **manoeuvre** /mə'nu:vər || mə'nu:və(r)/ *n* [1] (movement) maniobra *f* [2] (tactical move) maniobra *f*, estratagema *f* [3] **maneuvers** *pl* (Mil) maniobras *fpl*
maneuver², (BrE) **manoeuvre** *vt* [1] (move): **they ~ed the piano up the stairs** subieron trabajosamente el piano por la escalera; **she ~ed the car out of the garage** sacó el coche del garaje maniobrando [2] (lead, trick) **to ~ sb INTO sth**: **he has ~ed them into an impossible negotiating position** ha logrado ponerlos en una posición muy difícil para negociar
■ **maneuver** *vi* [1] ‹‹*vehicle/driver*›› maniobrar, hacer* una maniobra; **to have room to ~** ‹‹*driver*›› tener* espacio para maniobrar; ‹‹*diplomat*›› tener* libertad de acción [2] ‹‹*army/troops*›› hacer* maniobras, maniobrar
manfully /'mænfəli/ *adv* valientemente
manganese /'mæŋgəni:z/ *n* [u] manganeso *m*
mange /meɪndʒ/ *n* [u] sarna *f*
manger /'meɪndʒər || 'meɪndʒə(r)/ *n* pesebre *m*, comedero *m*
mangetout /mɑ:nʒ'tu:/ *n* (BrE) tirabeque *m*, arveja *f* *or* (Esp) guisante *m* *or* (esp Méx) chícharo *m* mollar
mangle¹ /'mæŋgəl/ *vt* destrozar*
mangle² *n* rodillo *m* (escurridor)
mango /'mæŋgəʊ/ *n* (*pl* **-goes** *or* **-gos**) [1] (fruit) mango *m* [2] **~ (tree)** mango *m*
mangrove /'mæŋgrəʊv/ *n* mangle *m*; (*before n*) **~ swamp** manglar *m*
mangy /'meɪndʒi/ *adj* **-gier, -giest** ‹*cat*› sarnoso; ‹*sofa/blanket*› (colloq) raído, gastado
man: **~handle** *vt* [1] (move by hand) mover* a pulso [2] (treat roughly) maltratar; **~hole** *n* registro *m*, pozo *m* de inspección; (into sewer) boca *f* de registro *m*
manhood /'mænhʊd/ *n* [u] [1] (adulthood) madurez *f*, edad *f* adulta (*en un hombre*) [2] (adult males) (+ *sing o pl vb*) hombres *mpl* [3] (virility) hombría *f*, virilidad *f*
man: **~-hour** *n* hora *f* hombre; **500 ~-hours** 500 horas hombre; **~hunt** *n* persecución *f*, búsqueda *f*
mania /'meɪniə/ *n* (*pl* **-nias**) [1] [u c] (Psych) manía *f* [2] [c] (obsession) manía *f*, obsesión *f*
maniac /'meɪniæk/ *n* maniaco, -ca *m,f*, maníaco, -ca *m,f*; **homicidal ~** maniaco homicida; **a religious ~** un fanático (religioso)
manic /'mænɪk/ *adj* ‹*behavior*› maniaco, maníaco; ‹*activity*› frenético
manic: **~ depression** *n* [u] maniacodepresión *f*, depresión *f* maniaca, trastorno *m* bipolar (téc); **~-depressive** /'mænɪkdɪ'presɪv/ *n* maniacodepresivo, -va *m,f*
manicure¹ /'mænəkjʊr || 'mænɪkjʊə(r)/ *n* [u c] manicura *f*, manicure *f* (AmL exc RPl); **to have a ~** arreglarse las manos *or* las uñas, hacerse* la manicura
manicure² *vt* arreglarle las manos *or* las uñas a
manifest¹ /'mænəfest || 'mænɪfest/ *v refl* (frml) **to ~ itself** ‹‹*ghost*›› aparecerse*; ‹‹*disease/fear*›› manifestarse*
■ **manifest** *vt* (express) manifestar*, expresar
manifest² *adj* manifiesto, evidente; **to make sth ~** poner* algo de manifiesto
manifestation /'mænəfə'steɪʃən || ,mænɪfə'steɪʃən/ *n* [1] (embodiment) manifestación *f* [2] (sign, symptom) manifestación *f*, indicio *m* [3] (of ghost) aparición *f*
manifesto /'mænə'festəʊ || ,mænɪ'festəʊ/ *n* (*pl* **-toes** *or* **-tos**) manifiesto *m*; (for a specific election) (esp BrE) plataforma *f* electoral
manifold¹ /'mænəfəʊld/ *adj* (frml) múltiples, diversos
manifold² *n* colector *m*
manikin /'mænɪkən || 'mænɪkɪn/ *n* ▸**mannequin**
manila, manilla /mə'nɪlə/ *n* [u] papel *m* Manila
Manila /mə'nɪlə/ *n* Manila *f*
manioc /'mæniɑ:k || 'mæniɒk/ *n* [u] mandioca *f*, yuca *f*
manipulate /mə'nɪpjəleɪt || mə'nɪpjʊleɪt/ *vt* [1] (handle) manejar, manipular [2] (Med) manipular [3] (influence, control) manipular
manipulation /mə'nɪpjə'leɪʃən || mə,nɪpjʊ'leɪʃən/ *n* [u] [1] (handling) manejo *m*, manipulación *f* [2] (Med) manipulación *f* [3] (influence) manipulación *f*
manipulative /mə'nɪpjələtɪv || mə'nɪpjʊlətɪv/ *adj* (interfering) manipulador
mankind /mæn'kaɪnd/ *n* [u] humanidad *f*, género *m* humano
manly /'mænli/ *adj* **-lier, -liest** [1] ‹*physique/pursuits*› varonil, masculino, viril [2] (courageous): **it's not very ~ to run away like that** no es de hombres *or* de valientes salir corriendo así
man-made /'mæn'meɪd/ *adj* ‹*lake*› artificial; ‹*material*› sintético
manna /'mænə/ *n* [u] maná *m*; **~ *from heaven*** maná del cielo
mannequin /'mænɪkən || 'mænɪkɪn/ *n* (dummy) maniquí *m*; (fashion model) maniquí *f*, modelo *f*
manner /'mænər || 'mænə(r)/ *n*
A (way, fashion) forma *f*, modo *m*, manera *f*; **he was behaving in a ridiculous ~** se estaba comportando de forma *or* manera ridícula *or* de modo ridículo; **in a ~ of speaking** en cierto modo *or* en cierta medida *or* hasta cierto punto; ***(as) to the ~ born*** como si hubiera nacido para ello
B [1] (bearing, demeanor) actitud *f*; **she has an abrupt ~** es brusca; **a good telephone ~ is essential** es imprescindible tener buen trato por teléfono [2] (style) (Art) estilo *m*
C (variety) tipo *m*, suerte *f*, clase *f*; **by no ~ of means** de ningún modo, de ninguna manera
D **manners** *pl* [1] (personal conduct) modales *mpl*, educación *f*; **it's (good) ~s to say 'please'** es de buena educación decir 'por favor'; **~s!** ¡qué modales son ésos! [2] (lifestyle) (frml) costumbres *fpl*; **a comedy of ~s** (Lit) una comedia costumbrista
mannered /'mænərd || 'mænəd/ *adj* afectado, amanerado
mannerism /'mænərɪzəm/ *n* (peculiarity, habit) peculiaridad *f*; (gesture) gesto *m*
mannish /'mænɪʃ/ *adj* ‹*woman/appearance*› masculino, hombruno; ‹*clothes/fashion*› masculino
manoeuvre *n/vt/vi* (BrE) ▸**maneuver¹,²**
man-of-war /'mænəv'wɔ:r || ,mænə'wɔ:(r)/ *n* (*pl* **men-of-war** /men-/) buque *m* de guerra
manor /'mænər || 'mænə(r)/ *n* [1] (estate) (Hist) feudo *m*, heredad *f* [2] **~ (house)** casa *f* solariega
manpower /'mænpaʊər/ *n* [u] (workers) personal *m*, recursos *mpl* humanos; (blue-collar) mano *f* de obra
manse /mæns/ *n*: *casa de un pastor protestante*
manservant /'mæn,sɜ:rvənt || 'mænsɜ:vənt/ *n* (*pl* **menservants** /'men-/ *or* **manservants**) criado *m*, sirviente *m*; (valet) valet *m*
mansion /'mænʃən/ *n* mansión *f*
man: **~-sized** /'mænsaɪzd/, (BrE also) **~-size** *adj* grande; **~slaughter** *n* [u] homicidio *m* sin premeditación
mantelpiece /'mæntḷpi:s/, **mantelshelf** /'mæntḷʃelf/ *n* repisa *f* de la chimenea
mantis /'mæntəs || 'mæntɪs/ *n* (*pl* **-tises**) ▸**praying mantis**
mantle /'mæntḷ/ *n*
A [1] (cloak) (arch) manto *m* [2] (covering) (liter) manto *m* (liter)
B (on gas lamp) camisa *f*, mantilla *f*
C (Geol) manto *m*, sima *f*
man: **~ to man** *adv* de hombre a hombre; **~trap** *n* trampa *f*, cepo *m*
manual¹ /'mænjuəl/ *adj* manual
manual² *n* manual *m*
manually /'mænjuəli/ *adv* manualmente, a mano
manufacture¹ /'mænjə'fæktʃər || ,mænjʊ'fæktʃə(r)/ *vt* ‹*cars/toys*› fabricar*, manufacturar; ‹*clothes*› confeccionar; ‹*foodstuffs*› elaborar, producir*; **~d goods** productos *mpl* manufacturados, manufacturas *fpl*
manufacture² *n* [u] (act) fabricación *f*, manufactura *f*; (of clothes) confección *f*; (of foodstuffs) elaboración *f*
manufacturer /'mænjə'fæktʃərər/ *n* fabricante *mf*
manufacturing /'mænjə'fæktʃərɪŋ || ,mænjʊ'fæktʃərɪŋ/ *adj* ‹*sector/town*› manufacturero, industrial; ‹*output/capacity*› industrial; **~ industry** industria *f* manufacturera

manure /mə'nʊr || mə'njʊə(r)/ *n* [u c] estiércol *m*

manuscript /'mænjəskrɪpt/ *n* manuscrito *m*

Manx[1] /mæŋks/ *adj* manés, de la isla de Man

Manx[2] *n* [u] (language) manés *m*

Manx cat *n: gato rabón de pelo corto*

many[1] /'meni/ *adj*

A muchos, -chas; **how ~ plates/cups?** ¿cuántos platos/cuántas tazas?; **a great/good ~ people** muchísima/mucha gente; **I've had as ~ jobs as you** he tenido tantos trabajos como tú; **use as ~ colors as you need** utiliza todos los colores que necesitas; **she read 15 books in as ~ days** se leyó 15 libros en el mismo número de días; **too ~ problems/people** demasiados problemas/demasiada gente; **one chair too ~, one too ~ chairs** una silla de más

B **many a** (liter) muchos, -chas; **~ a time** muchas veces

many[2] *pron* muchos, -chas; **how ~ of you smoke?** ¿cuántos/cuántas de ustedes fuman?; **~ of us** muchos de nosotros; **a good ~ of the houses** muchas de las casas; **~'s the time I've asked myself that** más de una vez me he preguntado eso; **answer as ~ of the questions as possible** conteste todas las preguntas que pueda; **I've got twice as ~ as you** tengo el doble que tú; **as ~ as 26 are missing** faltan nada menos que 26; **however ~ you eat** te comas las *or* los que te comas; **I don't want this ~** yo no quiero tantos/tantas; **would ten be too ~?** ¿diez serían demasiados?; **you've given me one/two too ~** me has dado uno/dos de más; **~ would disagree with that** muchos no estarían de acuerdo con eso

Maoist /'maʊəst || 'maʊɪst/ *adj* maoísta

Maori[1] /'maʊri/ *adj* maorí

Maori[2] *n* maorí *mf*

map[1] /mæp/ *n* (of country, region) mapa *m*; (of town, subway, building) plano *m*; **a ~ of the world** un planisferio, un mapamundi; ***to put sth on the ~*** dar* notoriedad a algo

map[2] **-pp-** *vt* trazar* el mapa de

Phrasal verb

• **map out** [v ▸ o ▸ adv, v ▸ adv ▸ o] ‹*itinerary/holiday*› planear, planificar*

maple /'meɪpəl/ *n* ~ **(tree)** arce *m*; (*before n*) **~ syrup** jarabe *m or* sirope *m* de arce

map-reading /'mæp,ri:dɪŋ/ *n* [u] interpretación *f* de mapas

mar /mɑ:r || mɑ:(r)/ *vt* **-rr-** estropear

Mar (= **March**) mar.

maraschino /'mærə'ski:nəʊ, -'ʃi:nəʊ/ *n* (*pl* **-nos**) **~ (cherry)** cereza *f* al marrasquino

marathon /'mærəθɑ:n || 'mærəθən/ *n* (race) maratón *m or f*; (endurance test) concurso *m* de resistencia; (*before n*) ‹*speech*› maratoniano; ‹*task*› monumental

marauder /mə'rɔ:dər || mə'rɔ:də(r)/ *n* (criminal) maleante *mf*; (prowler) merodeador, -dora *m,f*

marauding /mə'rɔ:dɪŋ/ *adj*: **they were attacked by ~ pirates** unos piratas que merodeaban en la zona los atacaron; **they are being terrorized by ~ bands of youths** las pandillas de jóvenes maleantes que merodean por el lugar los tienen aterrorizados

marble /'mɑ:rbəl || 'mɑ:bəl/ *n*

A 1 [u] (Min) mármol *m* 2 [c] (Art) escultura *f*/estatua *f* de mármol

B [c] (Games) canica *f or* (AmS) bolita *f*; **to play ~s** jugar* a las canicas *or* (AmS) bolitas; ***to lose one's ~s*** (colloq & hum) perder* la chaveta (fam)

march[1] /mɑ:rtʃ || mɑ:tʃ/ *n*

A 1 (Mil, Mus) marcha *f* 2 (demonstration) marcha *f* (de protesta)

B (of time) paso *m*; (of science, technology) avance *m*

march[2] *vi* 1 «*troops*» marchar; **when Saddam ~ed into** *o* **on Kuwait** cuando Saddam invadió Kuwait; **they ~ed past the visiting dignitaries** desfilaron ante los dignatarios visitantes; **time ~es on** el tiempo sigue su curso inexorablemente 2 (stride): **she ~ed into the office** entró con paso firme en *or* (esp AmL) a la oficina; **he ~ed up to the referee** se dirigió resueltamente hacia el árbitro

■ **march** *vt* hacer* marchar, obligar* a caminar; **the prisoner was ~ed in** hicieron entrar al prisionero

March /mɑ:rtʃ || mɑ:tʃ/ *n* marzo *m*; *see also* **January**

marchioness /'mɑ:rʃənəs || ,mɑ:ʃə'nes/ *n* marquesa *f*

march-past /'mɑ:rtʃpæst/ *n* desfile *m*, parada *f*

Mardi Gras /'mɑ:rdigrɑ: || ,mɑ:di'grɑ:/ *n* martes *m* de Carnaval

mare /mer || meə(r)/ *n* yegua *f*

margarine /'mɑ:rdʒərən || ,mɑ:dʒə'ri:n/ *n* [u] margarina *f*

margin /'mɑ:rdʒən || 'mɑ:dʒɪn/ *n*

A (on page, typewriter) margen *m*; **to set the ~s** fijar los márgenes, marginar

B 1 [c u] (leeway) margen *m*; **he won by a comfortable ~** ganó holgadamente; **~ of error/safety** margen de error/de seguridad 2 (Busn) (of profit) margen *m* (de ganancia *or* de beneficio)

C (fringe — of lake) (*often pl*) margen *f*; (— of society, debate) margen *m*; **they live on the ~(s) of society** viven marginados (de la sociedad)

marginal[1] /'mɑ:rdʒn̩əl || 'mɑ:dʒɪnl̩/ *adj*

A (minor) ‹*difference*› mínimo; ‹*role*› menor

B 1 (not very productive) ‹*land/well*› poco rentable 2 (Econ, Fin) ‹*cost*› marginal 3 (Pol BrE): **~ constituency** *distrito electoral cuyo representante obtuvo el escaño por escasa mayoría*

marginal[2] *n* (BrE) *escaño obtenido por escasa mayoría*

marginalize /'mɑ:rdʒn̩əlaɪz/ *vt* marginar

marginally /'mɑ:rdʒn̩əli || 'mɑ:dʒɪnəli/ *adv* ligeramente, un poquito

marigold /'mærəgəʊld/ *n* caléndula *f*, maravilla *f*

marijuana, /'mærə'wɑ:nə, -'hwɑ:- || ,mæri'wɑ:nə/ *n* [u] marihuana *f*

marina /mə'ri:nə/ *n* puerto *m* deportivo

marinade[1] /'mærə'neɪd || ,mærɪ'neɪd/ *n* [c u] adobo *m*

marinade[2], **marinate** /'mærəneɪd, -eɪt || 'mærɪneɪd, -eɪt/ *vt* dejar en adobo, marinar

marine[1] /mə'ri:n/ *n also* **Marine** (Mil) ≈ infante *m* de marina, **the M~s** (in US) los marines; (in UK) infantería *f* de marina; ***you can tell that to the ~s!*** (colloq) ¡a otro perro con ese hueso! (fam)

marine[2] *adj* (*before n*) ‹*biology*› marino; ‹*engineering*› naval; ‹*insurance*› marítimo

mariner /'mærənər/ *n* (arch & poet) navegante *m* (liter)

marionette /'mæriə'net/ *n* marioneta *f*, títere *m*

marital /'mærətl̩ || 'mærɪtl̩/ *adj* ‹*problems*› matrimonial; ‹*bliss*› conyugal; **~ status** estado *m* civil

maritime /'mærətaɪm || 'mærɪtaɪm/ *adj* marítimo

marjoram /'mɑ:rdʒərəm || 'mɑ:dʒərəm/ *n* [u] mejorana *f*

mark[1] /mɑ:rk || mɑ:k/ *n*

A (sign, symbol) marca *f*; (stain) mancha *f*; (imprint) huella *f*; (on body) marca *f*; **a ~ of quality** un signo de calidad; **as a ~ of respect** en señal de respeto; **it's the ~ of a gentleman** es lo que distingue a un caballero; ***to leave*** *o* ***stamp one's ~ on sb/sth*** dejar su impronta en algn/algo; **five years in prison have left their ~** cinco años en la cárcel le han dejado huella; ***to make one's ~*** dejar su impronta

B (Educ) nota *f*; (Sport) punto *m*; **to give sb/get a good ~** ponerle* a algn/sacar* una buena nota; (Sport) darle* a algn/obtener* un buen puntaje *or* (esp Esp) una buena puntuación; **I give her full ~s for trying** se merece un premio por intentarlo

C 1 (indicator): **the cost has reached the $100,000 ~** el costo ha llegado a los 100.000 dólares; **(gas) ~ 6** (BrE) el número 6 (*de un horno de gas*); ***to overstep the ~*** pasarse de la raya 2 (for race) línea *f* de salida; **on your ~s!** *o* **take your ~s!** ¡a sus marcas!; ***to be quick/slow off the ~*** ser* rápido/lento

D (target) blanco *m*; **$300? $3,000 would be nearer the ~!** ¿300 dólares? ¡yo diría más bien 3.000!; ***to be*** *o* ***fall wide of the ~***: **his estimate was wide of the ~** erró por mucho en su cálculo; ***to hit/miss the ~*** «*warning*» hacer*/no hacer* mella

E *also* **Mark** (type, version) modelo *m*

F (Fin) marco *m*

mark[2] *vt*

A 1 (stain, scar) manchar, dejar (una) marca en 2 (pattern) (*usu pass*): **the male's throat is ~ed with two white bars** el macho tiene dos franjas blancas en el cuello

B (indicate) señalar, marcar*; **the letter was ~ed 'Urgent'** en el sobre decía *or* (esp Esp) ponía 'urgente'

C 1 ‹*anniversary*› celebrar; ‹*beginning*› marcar*, señalar; **1997 ~s the centenary** en 1997 se cumple el centenario 2 (characterize) caracterizar*

D ‹*exam*› (make corrections in) corregir*; (grade) poner(le)* nota a, calificar*; **he ~ed it wrong** lo marcó como erróneo

E (heed): **(you) ~ my words!** ¡ya verás!, ¡vas a ver!

F (BrE Sport) ‹*opponent*› marcar*

(Phrasal verbs)

- **mark down** [v ▸ o ▸ adv, v ▸ adv ▸ o] 1 (Busn) ‹*goods*› rebajar 2 (BrE Educ) ‹*person/work*› bajarle la nota a
- **mark off** [v ▸ o ▸ adv, v ▸ adv ▸ o] 1 (divide off) ‹*area*› delimitar; ‹*boundary*› demarcar*; **to ~ sth off** FROM **sth** separar *or* deslindar algo DE algo 2 (check off) marcar*; (cross out) tachar
- **mark out** [v ▸ o ▸ adv, v ▸ adv ▸ o] 1 ‹*sports ground*› marcar* 2 (select) señalar 3 (distinguish) distinguir*
- **mark up** [v ▸ o ▸ adv, v ▸ adv ▸ o] 1 (note) anotar, apuntar 2 (Busn) ‹*goods*› aumentar el precio de 3 (BrE Educ) ‹*person/work*› subirle la nota a

Mark /mɑːrk || mɑːk/ *n* (Bib) (San) Marcos

marked /mɑːrkt || mɑːkt/ *adj* 1 (pronounced) ‹*improvement*› marcado, notable, notorio; ‹*accent*› marcado, fuerte; ‹*contrast*› acusado 2 **a ~ man** un hombre fichado

markedly /ˈmɑːrkədli/ *adv*: **~ different** muy diferente; **~ inferior** marcadamente *or* notablemente inferior

marker /ˈmɑːrkər || ˈmɑːkə(r)/ *n* 1 (to show position) indicador *m* 2 **~ (pen)** rotulador *m* 3 (Educ) *persona que corrige exámenes etc*

market[1] /ˈmɑːrkət || ˈmɑːkɪt/ *n*

A (Busn) mercado *m*; (exchange) lonja *f*; (*street ~*) mercado *m or* mercadillo *m or* (CS, Per) feria *f*

B 1 (trading activity) mercado *m*; **to be on/come on (to) the ~** estar*/salir* a la venta; **to put a product on the ~** lanzar* un producto al mercado; **we put the house on the ~ at $320,000** pusimos la casa en venta en $320.000; **they're in the ~ for semiconductors** están buscando semiconductores; **a buyer's/seller's ~** un mercado favorable al comprador/al vendedor; (*before n*) **~ forces** fuerzas *fpl* del mercado 2 (area of business) mercado *m*; (*before n*) **a ~ leader** un líder del mercado *or* de su sector en el mercado 3 (demand): **they have created a ~ for their products** han creado un mercado para sus productos; **the ~ for steel** la demanda de acero

C (*stock ~*) bolsa *f* (de valores); ***to corner the ~ (in sth)*** hacerse* con el mercado (de algo)

market[2] *vt* comercializar*

▪ **market** *vi* (AmE): **to go ~ing** ir* a hacer la compra *or* (AmS) las compras, ir* a hacer el mercado (Col, Ven)

marketable /ˈmɑːrkətəbəl || ˈmɑːkɪtəbəl/ *adj* ‹*goods/product*› comercializable, mercadeable; ‹*image*› comercial; ‹*skill*› que se cotiza muy bien en el mundo laboral

market: **~-driven** /ˈmɑːrkətˌdrɪvən || ˈmɑːkɪtˌdrɪvən/ *adj* dirigido por el mercado, manejado por el mercado; **~ garden** *n* (BrE) huerta *f*

marketing /ˈmɑːrkətɪŋ || ˈmɑːkɪtɪŋ/ *n* [u] (Busn) marketing *m*, mercadotecnia *f*

market: **~place** *n* (in town) mercado *m*, plaza *f* del mercado; (Busn) mercado *m*; **~ research** *n* [u] estudio *m or* investigación *f* de mercado; **~ town** *n* (in UK) *población con mercado*

marking /ˈmɑːrkɪŋ || ˈmɑːkɪŋ/ *n*

A [c] 1 (on animal, plant) mancha *f* 2 (manmade) marca *f*; **road ~s** líneas *fpl* de señalización vial

B [u] (Educ): **I've got a lot of ~ to do** tengo muchos ejercicios (*or* cuadernos *etc*) que corregir

marksman /ˈmɑːrksmən || ˈmɑːksmən/ *n* (*pl* **-men** /-mən/) tirador *m*; **he's a good ~** tiene buena puntería

marksmanship /ˈmɑːrksmənʃɪp || ˈmɑːksmənʃɪp/ *n* [u] puntería *f*

markup /ˈmɑːrkʌp/ *n* margen *m* de ganancia *or* beneficio

marmalade /ˈmɑːrməleɪd || ˈmɑːməleɪd/ *n* [u c] mermelada *f* (*de cítricos*)

maroon[1] /məˈruːn/ *adj* granate *adj inv*

maroon[2] *n* [u] granate *m*

maroon[3] *vt* (*usu pass*) ‹*castaway*› abandonar (*en una isla desierta*)

marquee /mɑːrˈkiː || mɑːˈkiː/ *n* 1 (canopy) (AmE) marquesina *f* 2 (tent) (BrE) entoldado *m*, toldo *m*

marquess, marquis /ˈmɑːrkwəs || ˈmɑːkwɪs/ *n* marqués *m*

marriage /ˈmærɪdʒ/ *n*

A 1 [u] (act) casamiento *m*, matrimonio *m*, enlace *m* (frml); (*before n*) **~ certificate** certificado *m* de matrimonio 2 [u c] (relationship) matrimonio *m*; **~** TO **sb**: **her ~ to the poet lasted two years** estuvo dos años casada con el poeta; **a ~ of convenience** un matrimonio de conveniencias; (*before n*) **~ counseling** *o* (BrE) **guidance** terapia *f* de pareja; **~ counselor** *o* (BrE) **~ guidance counsellor** consejero, -ra *m,f* matrimonial

B (union) (liter) (*no pl*) maridaje *m*, unión *f*

marriageable /ˈmærɪdʒəbəl/ *adj* (*usu before n*): **of ~ age** casadero, en edad de casarse

married /ˈmærid/ *adj* ‹*man/woman*› casado; **a ~ couple** un matrimonio; **~ life** la vida matrimonial *or* conyugal *or* de casado; **they have been ~ for two years** llevan dos años casados, hace dos años que se casaron; **he's ~** está *or* (esp AmS tb) es casado; **he's ~ to Mary** está casado con Mary; **to get ~ (to sb)** casarse (con algn)

marrow /ˈmærəʊ/ *n*

A [u] (*bone ~*) médula *f*, tuétano *m*; **frozen** *o* **chilled to the ~** helado hasta la médula

B [c] **~ squash** *o* (BrE) **~** (Culin) *tipo de calabaza alargada y de cáscara verde*

marrowbone /ˈmærəʊbəʊn/ *n* hueso *m* con tuétano *or* (RPl tb) caracú

marry /ˈmæri/ **-ries, -rying, -ried** *vt* 1 (get married to) casarse con, contraer* matrimonio con (frml) 2 (perform ceremony) casar 3 ▸**marry off** 4 (unite, combine) unir

▪ **marry** *vi* casarse, contraer* matrimonio (frml); **he's not the ~ing kind** él no es de los que se casan

(Phrasal verb)

- **marry off** [v ▸ o ▸ adv, v ▸ adv ▸ o] casar

Mars /mɑːrz || mɑːz/ *n* Marte *m*

marsh /mɑːrʃ || mɑːʃ/ *n* [c u] (*often pl*) pantano *m*; (on coast) marisma *f*

marshal[1] /ˈmɑːrʃəl || ˈmɑːʃəl/ *n*

A *also* **Marshal** (as title) (Mil) mariscal *m*

B (as title) (AmE) 1 (police chief) jefe, -fa *m,f* de policía; (fire chief) jefe, -fa *m,f* de bomberos 2 (Law) *supervisor de los tribunales de un distrito judicial*

C (at public gathering) miembro *m* del servicio de vigilancia

marshal[2] *vt*, (BrE) **-ll-** ‹*troops/crowd*› reunir*; ‹*support*› conseguir*; ‹*courage*› armarse de; ‹*thoughts*› poner* en orden; ‹*evidence*› reunir*

marsh: **~land** *n* [u] (*sometimes pl*) pantanal *f*, pantanos *mpl*; (on coast) marismas *fpl*; **~mallow** *n* [c u] (Culin) malvavisco *m*, gomita *f* (Ven), bombón *m* (Méx)

marsupial /mɑːrˈsuːpiəl || mɑːˈsuːpiəl/ *n* marsupial *m*

martial /ˈmɑːrʃəl || ˈmɑːʃəl/ *adj* marcial, castrense

martial: **~ arts** *pl n* artes *fpl* marciales; **~ law** *n* [u] ley *f* marcial

Martian[1] /ˈmɑːrʃən || ˈmɑːʃən/ *n* marciano, -na *m,f*

Martian[2] *adj* marciano

martin /ˈmɑːrtn̩ || ˈmɑːtɪn/ *n*: *cualquier pájaro de la familia del avión y el vencejo*

martini /mɑːrˈtiːni || mɑːˈtiːni/ *n* 1 (cocktail) *cóctel de vodka o ginebra y vermú* 2 **Martini®** Martini® *m*, vermú *m*, vermut *m*

martyr[1] /ˈmɑːrtər || ˈmɑːtə(r)/ *n* mártir *mf*; **he's a ~ to arthritis** la artritis lo tiene martirizado

martyr[2] *vt* (*usu pass*): **to be ~ed** sufrir el martirio

martyrdom /ˈmɑːrtərdəm || ˈmɑːtədəm/ *n* martirio *m*

marvel[1] /ˈmɑːrvəl || ˈmɑːvəl/ *n* maravilla *f*; **it's a ~ (to me) there wasn't an accident!** fue un milagro que no ocurriera un accidente

marvel[2], (BrE) **-ll-** *vi* **to ~** (AT **sth**) maravillarse (DE algo)

marvelous, (BrE) **marvellous** /ˈmɑːrvl̩əs || ˈmɑːvələs/ *adj* maravilloso

Marxism /ˈmɑːrksɪzəm || ˈmɑːksɪzəm/ *n* [u] marxismo *m*

Marxist[1] /ˈmɑːrksəst || ˈmɑːksɪst/ *n* marxista *mf*

Marxist[2] *adj* marxista

Mary /ˈmeri || ˈmeəri/ *n*: **the Virgin ~** la Virgen María; **~ Magdalene** María Magdalena, la Magdalena

marzipan /ˈmɑːrzəpɑːn/ *n* [u] mazapán *m*

mascara /mæ'skærə || mæ'skɑːrə/ *n* [u c] rímel® *m*

mascot /'mæskɑːt || 'mæskət, -skɒt/ *n* mascota *f*

masculine¹ /'mæskjələn || 'mæskjʊlɪn/ *adj*
A (manly) masculino, varonil
B (Ling, Lit) ‹*noun*› masculino

masculine² *n* [u] (Ling): **in the ~** en masculino

masculinity /'mæskjə'lɪnəti || ˌmæskjʊ'lɪnəti/ *n* [u] masculinidad *f*

mash¹ /mæʃ/ *n* **1** [u] (mashed potato) (BrE colloq) puré *m* de papas *or* (Esp) de patatas **2** [u c] (animal feed) afrecho *m*

mash² *vt* (Culin) ‹*potatoes/bananas*› hacer* puré de, moler* (Chi, Méx), pisar (RPl, Ven), espichar (Col); **~ed potato(es)** puré *m* de papas *or* (Esp) de patatas

mask¹ /mæsk || mɑːsk/ *n* **1** (for disguise, ritual) máscara *f*, careta *f* **2** (in fencing, ice-hockey) careta *f*; (used by doctors) mascarilla *f*, barbijo *m*; (for diving) gafas *fpl or* anteojos *mpl* de bucear *or* de buceo; (against dust, fumes) mascarilla *f*

mask² *vt* **1** (conceal) ocultar **2** (cover) cubrir*, tapar

masked /mæskt || mɑːskt/ *adj* ‹*gunman*› enmascarado; **~ ball** baile *m* de disfraces *or* de máscaras

masking tape /'mæskɪŋ || 'mɑːskɪŋ/ *n* cinta *f* adhesiva protectora, cinta *f* de enmascarar (Col), tirro *m* (Ven)

masochism /'mæsəkɪzəm/ *n* masoquismo *m*

masochist /'mæsəkəst || 'mæsəkɪst/ *n* masoquista *mf*

masochistic /'mæsə'kɪstɪk/ *adj* masoquista

mason /'meɪsn̩/ *n* **1** (Const) albañil *mf*; (*stone* **~**) mampostero *m* **2** *also* **Mason** (*Free~*) masón *m*, francmasón *m*

Mason-Dixon line /ˌmeɪsn̩'dɪksn̩/ *n* (in US) línea *f* Mason-Dixon (*que divide el sur del norte de EE UU*)

> **Mason–Dixon Line**
>
> Una línea divisoria medida y trazada en el siglo XVIII, entre los estados de Pensilvania y Maryland en EEUU, a fin de resolver un litigio entre los dos estados. En su época llegó a considerarse un símbolo de la división entre los estados del norte de EEUU, que no tenían esclavos y los estados del sur que sí los tenían

Masonic, masonic /mə'sɑːnɪk/ *adj* masónico

Masonite® /'meɪsənaɪt/ *n* [u] (AmE) conglomerado *m*

Mason jar /'meɪsn̩/ *n* (AmE) frasco *m* de conservas

masonry /'meɪsn̩ri || 'meɪsənri/ *n* [u] (Const) (craft of mason) albañilería *f*; (*stone* **~**) mampostería *f*

masquerade¹ /'mæskə'reɪd || ˌmɑːskə'reɪd, ˌmæ-/ *n* **1** (pretense) mascarada *f*, farsa *f* **2** (masked ball) mascarada *f*, baile *m* de disfraces *or* de máscaras

masquerade² *vi* **to ~ AS sb** hacerse* pasar POR algn

mass¹ /mæs/ *n*
A (bulk, body) masa *f*; **her hair was a ~ of curls** tenía la cabeza cubierta de rizos
B masses *pl* **1** (great quantity) (BrE colloq): **we received ~es of complaints** recibimos cantidades *or* (fam) montones de quejas **2** **the ~es** las masas
C [u] (Phys) masa *f*
D [c] *also* **Mass** (Mus, Relig) misa *f*; **to go to ~** ir* a misa

mass² *vi* «*crowd/clouds*» concentrarse

mass³ *adj* (*before n*) ‹*culture/market*› de masas; ‹*hysteria/suicide*› colectivo; ‹*protest*› masivo, en masa; ‹*unemployment*› generalizado, masivo; **~ grave** fosa *f* común; **a ~ meeting** una reunión de todo el personal (*or* el estudiantado *etc*); **~ murder** matanza *f*; **~ transit** (AmE) transporte *m* público

Mass = **Massachusetts**

massacre¹ /'mæsəkər || 'mæsəkə(r)/ *vt* **1** (slaughter) masacrar, matar **2** (defeat heavily) (colloq) aniquilar (fam)

massacre² *n* [c u] matanza *f*, masacre *f*, carnicería *f*

massage¹ /mə'sɑːʒ || 'mæsɑːʒ/ *vt* masajear

massage² *n* [c u] masaje *m*; **to give sb a ~** darle* un masaje a algn; **heart ~** masaje cardíaco

masseur /mæ'sɜːr || mæ'sɜː(r)/ *n* masajista *m*

masseuse /mæ'sɜːz/ *n* masajista *f*

massive /'mæsɪv/ *adj* ‹*wall/façade*› sólido, macizo; ‹*support/task*› enorme, grande; ‹*heart attack/overdose*› masivo

mass: ~ media *pl n* **the ~ media** los medios de comunicación (de masas); **~-produce** /'mæsprə'duːs || ˌmæsprə'djuːs/ *vt* fabricar* en serie

mast /mæst || mɑːst/ *n* **1** (Naut) mástil *m* **2** (flagpole) mástil *m* **3** (*relay* **~**) antena *f* repetidora, repetidor *m*

mastectomy /mæ'stektəmi/ *n* [u c] (*pl* **-mies**) mastectomía *f*

master¹ /'mæstər || 'mɑːstə(r)/ *n*
A (of household) señor *m*, amo *m*; (of animal) amo *m*, dueño *m*; (of servant) amo *m*, patrón *m*; **to be one's own ~** no tener* que darle cuentas a nadie
B (expert) **~ OF sth** maestro, -tra *m,f* DE algo, experto, -ta *m,f* EN algo; ***to be a past ~ of sth*** ser* un maestro consumado en algo
C (Educ) **1** (degree) **~'s (degree)** master *m*, maestría *f*; **M~ of Arts/Science** *poseedor de una maestría en Humanidades/Ciencias* **2** (BrE) (in secondary school) profesor *m*
D (Naut) capitán *m*
E Master **1** (Hist) (as form of address used by servants) el señor; (to younger man) señorito **2** (on letters to young boys) Sr.
F (for copies) (Audio, Comput, Print) original *m*

master² *vt* ‹*technique/subject*› llegar* a dominar

master³ *adj* (*before n, no comp*) **1** (expert): **~ baker/builder** maestro *m* panadero/de obras **2** (main) ‹*switch/key*› maestro; **~ bedroom** dormitorio *m* principal **3** (original) ‹*tape*› original, matriz; **~ copy** original *m*; **~ plan** plan *m* general

masterful /'mæstərfəl || 'mɑːstəfəl/ *adj* ‹*manner/gesture*› autoritario, imperioso; ‹*voice*› potente; ‹*person*› de porte autoritario

masterly /'mæstərli || 'mɑːstəli/ *adj* magistral

mastermind¹ /'mæstərmaɪnd/ *n* cerebro *m*

mastermind² *vt* planear y organizar*

master: ~ of ceremonies *n* maestro, -tra *m,f* de ceremonias; **~piece** *n* obra *f* maestra; **~ sergeant** *n* (in US) sargento *m* mayor; **~stroke** *n* golpe *m* maestro

mastery /'mæstəri || 'mɑːstəri/ *n* [u] **1** (expertise, skill) maestría *f*; (of language, technique) dominio *m* **2** (control) dominio *m*

masticate /'mæstəkeɪt || 'mæstɪkeɪt/ *vt/i* masticar*

mastiff /'mæstəf || 'mæstɪf/ *n* mastín *m*, alano *m*

mastitis /mæ'staɪtəs || mæ'staɪtɪs/ *n* [u] mastitis *f*

masturbate /'mæstərbeɪt || 'mæstəbeɪt/ *vi* masturbarse

masturbation /'mæstər'beɪʃən || ˌmæstə'beɪʃən/ *n* [u] masturbación *f*

mat¹ /mæt/ *n* (of rushes, straw) estera *f*, esterilla *f*; (*door* **~**) felpudo *m*, tapete *m* (Col, Méx); (*bath* **~**) alfombrilla *f or* alfombrita *f or* (Col, Méx) tapete *m* del baño; (*table~*) (individual) (mantel *m*) individual *m*; (in center of table) salvamanteles *m*, posafuentes *m* (CS)

mat² *adj* (AmE) ▸ **matt**

match¹ /mætʃ/ *n*
A (for fire) fósforo *m*, cerilla *f* (Esp), cerillo *m* (esp AmC, Méx)
B (Sport): **boxing/wrestling ~** combate *m or* match *m* de boxeo/de lucha libre; **tennis ~** partido *m* de tenis; **football/hockey ~** (BrE) partido *m* de fútbol/de hockey
C (equal) (*no pl*): **to be a/no ~ for sb** estar*/no estar* a la altura de algn, poder*/no poder* competir con algn; **to meet one's ~** encontrar* la horma de su zapato
D (*no pl*) (sth similar): **they are a good ~** «*couple*» hacen buena pareja; **that shirt is a perfect ~ for my suit** esa camisa va *or* queda perfecta con mi traje

match² *vt*
A (equal) igualar; **we have nothing to ~ their new line** no tenemos nada equiparable a su nueva línea; **I'll ~ any offer he makes** estoy dispuesto a igualar cualquier oferta que él haga
B **1** (correspond to) ajustarse a, corresponder a; **does it ~ the description?** ¿se ajusta *or* corresponde a la descripción? **2** (harmonize with) hacer* juego con; **it ~es my shoes** hace juego con mis zapatos, queda bien con mis zapatos **3** (make correspond, find equivalent for): **~ the words with the pictures** encuentra la palabra que corresponda a cada dibujo; **to be well ~ed** «*competitors*» ser* del mismo nivel, ser* muy parejos (esp AmL); «*couple*» hacer* buena pareja **4** **matching** *pres p* haciendo juego, a juego (Esp)

■ **match** *vi* **1** (go together) «*clothes/colors*» hacer* juego, combinar, pegar* (fam); **a coat and a scarf to ~** un abrigo y una bufanda haciendo juego *or* (Esp) a juego; **a demanding job with a salary to ~** un trabajo que exige mucho

m

con un salario acorde 2 (tally) coincidir, concordar*

Phrasal verb

- **match up**

A [v ▸ o ▸ adv, v ▸ adv ▸ o] 1 ‹*pattern/design*› hacer* coincidir 2 (compare, find equivalent for) **to ~ sth up (WITH sth)** comparar *or* cotejar algo (CON algo)

B [v ▸ adv] (tally) coincidir, concordar*

match: **~book** *n* (AmE) librito *m* de fósforos *or* (Esp) de cerillas *or* (AmC, Méx tb) de cerillos; **~box** *n* caja *f* de fósforos *or* (Esp) de cerillas *or* (esp AmC, Méx) de cerillos

matchless /ˈmætʃləs || ˈmætʃlɪs/ *adj* (liter) incomparable, inigualable, sin igual (liter)

match: **~maker** *n* (marriage arranger — woman) celestina *f*, casamentera *f*; (— man) casamentero *m*; **~making** *n* [u]: **you'll be accused of ~making** te van a acusar de andar haciendo de casamentero; **~ point** *n* punto *m* de partido; **~stick** *n* 1 ▸**match¹** A 2 (stick) palillo *m*; **her legs are like ~sticks** tiene unas piernas como palillos; (*before n*) ‹*drawing*› de palotes; **~stick man** monigote *m*

mate¹ /meɪt/ *n*

A 1 (assistant) ayudante *mf* 2 (Naut) oficial *mf* de cubierta; **first ~** primer oficial *m*

B 1 (Zool) (male) macho *m*; (female) hembra *f* 2 (of person) pareja *f*, compañero, -ra *m,f* 3 (of shoe, sock etc) (esp AmE) compañero, -ra *m,f*

C (BrE colloq) 1 (friend) amigo, -ga *m,f*, cuate, -ta *m,f* (Méx fam) 2 (as form of address — to a friend) hermano (fam), tío *or* macho (Esp fam), mano (AmL exc CS fam), che (RPl fam), gallo (Chi fam); (— to a stranger) amigo, jefe, maestro (AmL)

D (*check~*) (jaque *m*) mate *m*

mate² *vi* (copulate) aparearse, copular

material¹ /məˈtɪriəl || məˈtɪəriəl/ *n*

A 1 [c u] (used in manufacturing etc) material *m* 2 **materials** *pl* (equipment) material *m*; **teaching ~s** material *m* didáctico; **writing ~s** artículos *mpl* de escritorio

B [u c] (cloth) tela *f*, género *m*, tejido *m*

C [u] 1 (for book, show etc) material *m* 2 (potential, quality): **this is bestseller ~** éste es un bestseller en potencia; **she's champion ~** tiene madera de campeona

material² *adj*

A (worldly, physical) ‹*gain/needs*› material

B (Law) ‹*evidence*› sustancial

materialism /məˈtɪriəlɪzəm/ *n* [u] materialismo *m*

materialistic /məˈtɪriəˈlɪstɪk/ *adj* materialista

materialize /məˈtɪriəlaɪz || məˈtɪəriəlaɪz/ *vi* «*object/ghost*» aparecer*; «*hope/idea*» hacerse* realidad, concretarse, materializarse*

maternal /məˈtɜːrnl̩ || məˈtɜːnl̩/ *adj* 1 (motherly) maternal 2 (on mother's side) (*before n*) ‹*grandfather*› materno

maternity /məˈtɜːrnəti || məˈtɜːnəti/ *n* [u] maternidad *f*; (*before n*) ‹*clinic/ward*› de obstetricia; ‹*dress/clothes*› de embarazada, de futura mamá, premamá *adj inv* (Esp); ‹*pay/leave*› por maternidad; **~ hospital** maternidad *f*

math /mæθ/ *n* [u] (AmE) matemática(s) *f(pl)*, mates *fpl* (fam)

mathematical /ˈmæθəˈmætɪkəl/ *adj* matemático; **she's a ~ genius** es un genio para las matemáticas

mathematician /ˈmæθəməˈtɪʃən/ *n* matemático, -ca *m,f*

mathematics /ˈmæθəˈmætɪks/ *n* (+ *sing vb*) matemática(s) *f(pl)*

maths /mæθs/ *n* [u] (BrE) (+ *sing vb*) matemática(s) *f(pl)*, mates *fpl* (fam)

matinee, matinée /ˈmætn̩ˈeɪ || ˈmætɪneɪ/ *n* (Cin) primera sesión *f* (*de la tarde*), matiné(e) *f* (AmS); (Theat) función *f* de tarde, matiné(e) *f* (AmS)

mating /ˈmeɪtɪŋ/ *n* [u] apareamiento *m*; (*before n*) **~ season** época *f* de celo

matriarch /ˈmeɪtriɑːrk || ˈmeɪtriɑːk/ *n* matriarca *f*

matriarchy /ˈmeɪtriɑːrki || ˈmeɪtriɑːki/ *n* [c u] (*pl* **-chies**) matriarcado *m*

matrices /ˈmeɪtrəsiːz, ˈmæt- || ˈmeɪtrɪsiːz/ *pl of* **matrix**

matricide /ˈmætrəsaɪd || ˈmeɪtrɪsaɪd/ *n* [u c] (frml) (crime) matricidio *m*

matriculate /məˈtrɪkjəleɪt/ *vi* (frml) matricularse

matriculation /məˈtrɪkjəˈleɪʃən/ *n* [u] matrícula *f*

matrimonial /ˈmætrəˈməʊniəl || ˌmætrɪˈməʊniəl/ *adj* (*before n*) matrimonial

matrimony /ˈmætrəməʊni || ˈmætrɪməni/ *n* [u] (frml) matrimonio *m*; **holy ~** el sacramento del matrimonio

matrix /ˈmeɪtrɪks/ *n* (*pl* **matrices** *or* **~es**) matriz *f*

matron /ˈmeɪtrən/ *n* 1 (dignified woman) matrona *f* 2 (in prison) (AmE) matrona *f* 3 (in hospital) (BrE dated) enfermera *f* jefe *or* jefa 4 (in school) ≈ enfermera *f*

matronly /ˈmeɪtrənli/ *adj* matronil

matt, (AmE also) **matte**, **mat** /mæt/ *adj* mate

matted /ˈmætəd/ *adj* enmarañado y apelmazado

matter¹ /ˈmætər || ˈmætə(r)/ *n*

A [u] 1 (substance) (Phil, Phys) materia *f*, sustancia *f* 2 (discharge) (Med) pus *m*, materia *f* 3 (*subject ~*) temática *f*, tema *m*; **form and ~** forma y contenido 4 (written, printed material): **printed ~** impresos *mpl*; **reading ~** material *m* de lectura

B 1 (question, affair) asunto *m*, cuestión *f*; **that's another** *o* **a different ~** eso es otra cosa, eso es diferente; **this is a ~ for the police** esto requiere la intervención de la policía; **it's only a ~ of time** sólo es cuestión de tiempo; **that's a ~ of opinion** eso es discutible; **as a ~ of interest, what does he do for a living?** por pura curiosidad ¿en qué trabaja?; **it's no laughing ~** no es motivo de risa, no es (como) para reírse 2 **matters** *pl*: **as ~s stand** tal y como están las cosas; **to make ~s worse** para colmo (de males); **that didn't help ~s** aquello no ayudó a mejorar la situación; **~s arising** asuntos *mpl* varios 3 (approximate amount) **a ~ OF sth** cuestión *f or* cosa *f* DE algo; **it was all over in a ~ of seconds** todo acabó en cuestión *or* cosa de segundos 4 (*in phrases*) **as a matter of fact**: **as a ~ of fact, I've never been to Spain** la verdad es que *or* en realidad nunca he estado en España; **for that matter** en realidad; **no matter** (*as interj*) no importa; (*as conj*): **no ~ how hard I try** por mucho que me esfuerce; **I want you back by 9 o'clock, no ~ what** quiero que estés de vuelta a las nueve, pase lo que pase

C (problem, trouble): **what's the ~?** ¿qué pasa?; **what's the ~ with Jane/the typewriter?** ¿qué le pasa a Jane/a la máquina de escribir?; **is anything the ~ with Alice?** ¿le pasa algo a Alice?

matter² *vi* importar; **it doesn't ~** no importa, da igual; **to ~ TO sb**: **money is the only thing that ~s to her/them** el dinero es lo único que le/les importa

matter-of-fact /ˈmætərəvˈfækt/ *adj* ‹*person*› práctico, realista; **he explained it in a very ~ way** lo explicó con total naturalidad

matter-of-factly /ˈmætərəvˈfæktli/ *adv* con total naturalidad

Matthew /ˈmæθjuː/ *n* (Bib) (San) Mateo

matting /ˈmætɪŋ/ *n* [u] esteras *fpl*

mattress /ˈmætrəs || ˈmætrɪs/ *n* colchón *m*

mature¹ /məˈtʊr || məˈtjʊə(r)/ *adj* 1 (developed) ‹*animal/tree*› adulto; ‹*fruit*› maduro; ‹*artist/ideas*› maduro; **a ~ student** (BrE) un estudiante mayor 2 (sensible) maduro 3 (Culin) ‹*whiskey*› añejo; ‹*cheese*› curado; ‹*wine*› añejo, de crianza 4 (Fin) ‹*policy/bond*› vencido

mature² *vi* 1 (develop) «*plant/animal/person*» desarrollarse; «*artist/work*» madurar; «*wine*» añejarse; **to ~ with age** «*person*» madurar con la edad; «*cheese/wine*» madurar con los años *or* el tiempo 2 (become sensible) madurar 3 (Fin) «*bond/policy*» vencer*

maturity /məˈtʊrəti/ *n* [u] 1 (physical) madurez *f*, edad *f* adulta; (of temperament) madurez *f* 2 (of bond, security) vencimiento *m*

maudlin /ˈmɔːdlən || ˈmɔːdlɪn/ *adj* llorón, sensiblero

maul /mɔːl/ *vt* atacar* (y herir*)

Maundy Thursday /ˈmɔːndi/ *n* Jueves *m* Santo

Mauritius /mɔːˈrɪʃəs || məˈrɪʃəs/ *n* Mauricio *m*

mausoleum /ˈmɔːsəˈliːəm/ *n* (*pl* **-ums**) mausoleo *m*

mauve¹ /məʊv/ *adj* malva *adj inv*

mauve² *n* [u] malva *m*

maven /ˈmeɪvən/ *n* (AmE colloq) experto, -ta *m,f*

maverick /ˈmævərɪk/ *n* 1 (person) inconformista *mf* 2 (unbranded calf) (AmE) ternero *m* no marcado

maw /mɔː/ *n* (liter) fauces *fpl* (liter)

mawkish /ˈmɔːkɪʃ/ *adj* sensiblero, empalagoso

max /mæks/ (= **maximum**) máx.; **to the ~** (AmE colloq) al máximo, a tope (Esp fam)

maxillofacial /ˈmæksɪləʊˈfeɪsjəl/ *adj* maxilofacial

maxim /ˈmæksəm || ˈmæksɪm/ *n* máxima *f*

maximize /ˈmæksəmaɪz || ˈmæksɪmaɪz/ *vt* maximizar*, potenciar al máximo

maximum[1] /ˈmæksəməm || ˈmæksɪməm/ *n* máximo *m*; **I sleep a ~ of five hours** duermo cinco horas como máximo; **to the ~** al máximo

maximum[2] *adj* (*before n*) ‹*speed/amount/temperature*› máximo; **it was planned to cause ~ disruption** estaba planeado para causar el mayor trastorno posible

maximum[3] *adv* como máximo

maximum security *adj* (*before n*) de alta seguridad

may[1] /meɪ/ *v mod* (*past* **might**)

A (asking, granting permission) poder*; **~ I smoke?** ¿puedo fumar?, ¿me permite fumar?; **and who, ~ I ask, are you?** ¿y quién es usted, si se puede saber?; **~ we see the menu, please?** ¿podríamos ver *or* nos podría traer el menú, por favor?; **~ I have your name and address, please?** ¿quiere darme su nombre y dirección, por favor?

B 1 (indicating probability) [*El grado de probabilidad que indica* **may** *es mayor que el que expresan* **might** *o* **could**]: **we ~ increase the price** quizás *or* tal vez aumentemos el precio; **it ~ or ~ not be true** puede o no ser cierto; **I was worried he might do something foolish** tenía miedo de que hiciera un disparate 2 (in generalizations): **no matter what they ~ say** digan lo que digan; **come what ~** pase lo que pase

C (indicating sth is natural): **you ~ well ask!** ¡buena pregunta!, ¡eso (mismo) digo yo!; **you ~ well feel embarrassed** no me extraña que te sientas avergonzado

D (conceding): **he ~ not be clever, but he's very hard-working** no será inteligente, pero es muy trabajador; **be that as it ~** sea como sea; **that's as ~ be** puede ser

E (in wishes) (liter): **~ that day never come** que ese día no llegue nunca; **long ~ she reign!** ¡que reine por muchos años!; *see also* **might**[1]

may[2] *n* [u] espino *m*

May /meɪ/ *n* mayo *m*; *see also* **January**

Maya /ˈmaɪə/ *n* (*pl* **Mayas** *or* **Maya**) maya *mf*

Mayan[1] /ˈmaɪən/ *adj* maya

Mayan[2] *n* ▸**Maya**

maybe /ˈmeɪbi:/ *adv* quizá(s), tal vez, a lo mejor; **~ I'll come later** quizá(s) *or* tal vez venga luego

Mayday, mayday /ˈmeɪdeɪ/ *n* señal *f* de socorro *or* auxilio; (*as interj*) ¡socorro!, ¡auxilio!

May: ~ Day *n* el primero de mayo; (in some countries) el día del trabajo *or* de los trabajadores; **~fly** *n* efímera *f*

mayhem /ˈmeɪhem/ *n* [u] caos *m*, tumulto *m*; (in US) (Law) delito *m* de mutilación

mayo /ˈmeɪəʊ/ *n* [u] (AmE colloq) ▸**mayonnaise**

mayonnaise /ˈmeɪəˈneɪz/ *n* [u] mayonesa *f*, mahonesa *f*

mayor /ˈmeɪər || meə(r)/ *n* alcalde, -desa *m,f*, intendente *mf* (municipal) (RPl)

mayoress /ˈmeɪərəs || ˈmeəres/ *n* (BrE) (mayor) alcaldesa *f*, intendente *f* (RPl); (mayor's wife) alcaldesa *f*

maypole /ˈmeɪpəʊl/ *n* mayo *m*

maze /meɪz/ *n* laberinto *m*

MB (= **megabyte(s)**) Mb.

MBA *n* = **Master of Business Administration**

MBE *n* (in UK) = **Member of the British Empire**

MC *n* = **master of ceremonies**

McCoy /məˈkɔɪ/ *n* ***the real ~***: **it isn't sparkling wine, it's the real ~** no es vino espumoso, es champán de verdad

Md = **Maryland**

MD 1 (Med): **John Jones, ~** (el) Dr. John Jones 2 (BrE Busn colloq) = **managing director**

me[1] /mi:, *weak form* mi/ *pron*

A 1 (as direct object) me; **she helped ~** me ayudó; **help ~** ayúdame 2 (as indirect object) me; **he bought ~ flowers** me compró flores; **tell ~ something** dime una cosa; **give it to ~** dámelo 3 (after prep) mí; **for/behind/without ~** para mí/detrás de mí/sin mí; **come with ~** ven conmigo; **she's older than ~** es mayor que yo

B (emphatic use) yo; **it's ~** soy yo; **it was ~ who did it** fui yo que lo hice *or* quien lo hizo; **silly ~!** ¡qué tonto soy!; **~ join the army? never!** ¿meterme yo en el ejército? ¡ni soñar!

C (for myself) (AmE colloq *or* dial) me; **I'm going to get ~ a wife** voy a encontrar una mujer para casarme con ella

me[2] /mi:/ *n* (Mus) mi *m*

ME

A (Geog) = **Maine**

B = **myalgic encephalomyelitis**

mead /mi:d/ *n* [u] hidromiel *m*, aguamiel *f*‡

meadow /ˈmedəʊ/ *n* [c u] prado *m*, pradera *f*

meager, (BrE) **meagre** /ˈmi:gər || ˈmi:gə(r)/ *adj* ‹*portion/salary*› escaso, exiguo; ‹*existence*› precario

meal /mi:l/ *n*

A [c] (Culin) comida *f*; **she has four ~s a day** hace cuatro comidas al día, come cuatro veces al día; ***to make a ~ of sth*** (esp BrE): **a short letter will do: there's no need to make a ~ of it** con una carta corta alcanza: no hay por qué exagerar

B [u] (Agr, Culin) harina *f* (*de avena, maíz etc*)

meal: ~ ticket *n* 1 (source of income) (colloq): **his rich wife is his ~ ticket** como su mujer es millonaria tiene el futuro asegurado 2 (AmE) (voucher) cheque-comida *m*; **~time** *n* hora *f* de comer; **at ~times** a la hora de comer

mealy-mouthed /ˈmi:liˈmaʊðd/ *adj* (pej) que no habla claro; **don't be so ~** habla claro, déjate de rodeos

mean[1] /mi:n/ *vt* (*past & past p* **meant**)

A (represent, signify) ‹‹*word/symbol*›› significar*, querer* decir; **dark clouds ~ rain** los nubarrones son señal de lluvia; **that ~s trouble** eso quiere decir que va a haber problemas; **to ~ sth TO sb: does the number 0296 ~ anything to you?** ¿el número 0296 te dice algo?; **fame ~s nothing/a lot to her** la fama la tiene sin cuidado/es muy importante para ella

B 1 (refer to, intend to say) ‹‹*person*›› querer* decir; **what do you ~?** ¿qué quieres decir (con eso)?; **do you know what I ~?** ¿me entiendes?, ¿me comprendes?; **that's not what I ~t** no es eso lo que quise decir; **he's Swedish, I ~, Swiss** es sueco, (qué) digo, suizo; **I know who you ~** ya sé de quién hablas *or* a quién te refieres; **what's that supposed to ~?** ¿a qué viene eso? 2 (be serious about) decir* en serio; **I ~ it!** ¡va *or* lo digo en serio!

C (equal, entail) significar*; **being 40 doesn't ~ I can't wear fashionable clothes** (el) que tenga 40 años no quiere decir que no me pueda vestir a la moda; **to ~ -ING: that would ~ repainting the kitchen** eso supondría *or* implicaría volver a pintar la cocina

D 1 (intend): **he didn't ~ (you) any harm** no quiso hacerte daño, no lo hizo por mal; **to ~ to + INF: I ~ to succeed** mi intención es triunfar, me propongo triunfar; **I'm sorry, I didn't ~ to do it** perdón, lo hice sin querer; **I ~t to do it but I forgot** tenía toda la intención de hacerlo pero me olvidé; **I've been ~ing to talk to you** hace tiempo que quiero hablar contigo; **I ~t it to be a surprise** yo quería que fuera una sorpresa; **the bullet was ~t for me** la bala iba dirigida a mí; **we were ~t for each other** estamos hechos el uno para el otro 2 **to be ~t to + INF** (supposed, intended): **you weren't ~t to get the job** el trabajo no era para ti; **you weren't ~t to hear that** no pensaron (*or* pensé *etc*) que tú estarías escuchando; **I was never ~t to be a teacher** yo no estoy hecho para enseñar; **the money was ~t to last** se suponía que el dinero iba a durar

mean[2] *adj*

A (miserly) ‹*person*› tacaño, mezquino; ‹*portion*› mezquino, miserable

B 1 (unkind, nasty) malo; **it was really ~ of you** fue una maldad (de tu parte); **you were really ~ to me** me trataste muy mal 2 (excellent) (esp AmE sl) genial, fantástico

C (inferior, humble) (liter) humilde; **that's no ~ feat/achievement** no es poca cosa, no es moco de pavo (fam)

D (Math) (*before n*) medio

mean[3] *n* media *f*, promedio *m*; *see also* **means**

mean[4] *adv* (AmE colloq & dial): **they treated us real ~** nos trataron muy mal

meander /miˈændər || miˈændə(r)/ *vi* ‹‹*river*›› serpentear; ‹‹*person*›› deambular, vagar*, andar* sin rumbo fijo

meandering /miˈændərɪŋ/ *adj* ‹*river/course*› serpenteante; **a ~ speech** un discurso lleno de divagaciones

meaning /'mi:nɪŋ/ *n* [c u] (of word) significado *m*, acepción *f*; (of symbol, act) significado *m*; **literal/figurative ~** sentido *m* literal/figurado; **work? you don't know the ~ of the word** ¿trabajar? ¡tú no sabes qué significa trabajar!; **if you take** *o* **get my ~** si me entiendes

meaningful /'mi:nɪŋfəl/ *adj* ‹*look*› significativo, elocuente; ‹*explanation*› con sentido, coherente; ‹*results*› significativo; ‹*experience/relationship*› significativo, valioso; ‹*discussions*› positivo

meaningless /'mi:nɪŋləs || 'mi:nɪŋlɪs/ *adj* ‹*word*› sin sentido; **the term is ~ to most people** para la mayoría de la gente el término no significa nada

meanness /'mi:nnəs || 'mi:nnɪs/ *n* [u] 1 (stinginess) tacañería *f*, mezquindad *f* 2 (nastiness) maldad *f*

means /mi:nz/ *n* (*pl* ~)
A (+ *sing vb*) 1 (method) medio *m*; **a ~ to an end** un medio para lograr un fin; **does the end justify the ~?** ¿el fin justifica los medios?; **~ of transport** medio de transporte; **there's no ~ of finding out** no hay manera *or* forma de saberlo; *see also* **ways and means** 2 (*in phrases*) **by all means** por supuesto, ¡cómo no! (esp AmL); **by no means, not by any means**: **we are by no ~ rich** no somos ricos ni mucho menos: **it's not a perfect film by any ~** de ninguna manera *or* de ningún modo es una película perfecta; **by means of** (*as prep*) por medio de, mediante
B (frml) (+ *pl vb*) (wealth) medios *mpl* (económicos), recursos *mpl*; (income) ingresos *mpl*; **a woman of ~** una mujer de buena posición económica; **they live beyond their ~** llevan un tren de vida que no se pueden costear *or* que sus ingresos no les permiten

means test *n*: *investigación de los ingresos de una persona para determinar si tiene derecho o no a ciertas prestaciones*

meant /ment/ *past & past p of* **mean**[1]

meantime[1] /'mi:ntaɪm/ *n*: **in the ~** (while sth else happens) mientras tanto, entretanto; (in the intervening period) en el ínterin *or* interín; **for the ~** por ahora, por el momento

meantime[2] *adv* ▸**meanwhile**[1]

meanwhile[1] /'mi:nhwaɪl/ *adv* mientras tanto

meanwhile[2] *n* ▸**meantime**[1]

measles /'mi:zəlz/ *n* (+ *sing or pl vb*) (Med) sarampión *m*

measly /'mi:zli/ *adj* **-lier, -liest** (colloq) mísero

measurable /'meʒərəbəl/ *adj* 1 (quantifiable) mensurable, medible, susceptible de ser medido 2 (perceptible) apreciable, perceptible

measure[1] /'meʒər || 'meʒə(r)/ *n*
A 1 [u] (system) medida *f* 2 [c] (unit) medida *f*, unidad *f* 3 [c u] (amount) cantidad *f*; **with a (certain) ~ of success** con cierto éxito; **in large** *o* **great** *o* **no small ~** (frml) en gran medida, en gran parte; ***for good ~***: **take two for good ~** lleva dos por si acaso *or* para que no vaya a faltar 4 [c u] (size) (BrE) medida *f*; **he had it made to ~** se lo mandó hacer a (la) medida; **the true ~ of the problem** la verdadera magnitud *or* envergadura del problema; ***to have the ~ of sb***: **fortunately I had his ~** *o* **the ~ of him** por suerte yo ya lo tenía calado (fam)
B [c] (device) medida *f*
C [c] (step) medida *f*; **to take ~s to + INF** tomar medidas para + INF
D (AmE Mus) compás *m*

measure[2] *vt*
A ‹*length/speed/waist*› medir*; ‹*weight*› pesar; **to ~ sb for a suit** tomarle las medidas a algn para un traje
B (assess) calcular, evaluar*; **to ~ sth AGAINST sth** comparar algo CON algo
■ **measure** *vi* medir*; **what does it ~?** ¿cuánto mide?

Phrasal verbs
- **measure off** [v ▸ o ▸ adv, v ▸ adv ▸ o] ‹*length/area*› medir*
- **measure out** [v ▸ o ▸ adv, v ▸ adv ▸ o] ‹*length*› medir*; ‹*weight*› pesar
- **measure up** [v ▸ adv] estar* a la altura de las circunstancias; **to ~ up TO sth** estar* a la altura DE algo

measured /'meʒərd || 'meʒəd/ *adj* ‹*stride/step*› acompasado; ‹*words/language*› moderado, comedido, mesurado

measurement /'meʒərmənt || 'meʒəmənt/ *n* 1 [u c] (act) medición *f* 2 [c] (dimension) medida *f*; **to take sb's ~s** tomarle las medidas a algn

measuring /'meʒərɪŋ/: **~ cup**, (BrE) **~ jug** *n* jarra *f* graduada; **~ spoon** *n* cuchara *f* de medir

meat /mi:t/ *n* 1 [u c] carne *f*; **cold** *o* **cooked ~s** fiambres *mpl*, carnes *fpl* frías (Méx); ***the ~ and potatoes*** (AmE) lo básico; ***one man's ~ is another man's poison*** lo que a uno cura a otro mata; (*before n*) ‹*product*› cárnico 2 [u] (substance) sustancia *f*, enjundia *f*

meat: **~ball** *n* (Culin) albóndiga *f*; (stupid person) (AmE sl) pánfilo, -la *m,f* (fam); **~-eater** *n* (animal) carnívoro, -ra *m,f*; (person) *persona que come carne*; **~loaf** *n* [u c] pan *m* de carne

meaty /'mi:ti/ *adj* **-tier, -tiest** 1 ‹*taste/smell*› a carne; ‹*soup/stew*› con mucha carne; ‹*rabbit/bone*› carnoso, con mucha carne 2 ‹*article/book*› sustancioso, enjundioso

Mecca /'mekə/ *n* 1 La Meca 2 *also* **mecca** (center of attraction) meca *f*; **Monte Carlo is a ~ for gamblers** Montecarlo es la meca de los jugadores

mechanic /mə'kænɪk || mɪ'kænɪk/ *n* mecánico, -ca *m,f*; *see also* **mechanics**

mechanical /mə'kænɪkəl || mɪ'kænɪkəl/ *adj* ‹*problem/toy*› mecánico, maquinal; ‹*action/reply*› mecánico

mechanical: **~ engineer** *n* ingeniero mecánico, ingeniera mecánica *m,f*; **~ engineering** *n* [u] ingeniería *f* mecánica

mechanically /mə'kænɪkli || mɪ'kænɪkli/ *adv* ‹*driven/operated*› mecánicamente, maquinalmente; ‹*answer/repeat*› mecánicamente

mechanics /mə'kænɪks || mɪ'kænɪks/ *n*
A (+ *sing vb*) (Phys, Mech Eng) mecánica *f*
B (+ *pl vb*) **the ~** (practical details) los aspectos prácticos; (mechanical parts) el mecanismo

mechanism /'mekənɪzəm/ *n* mecanicismo *m*

mechanize /'mekənaɪz/ *vt* ‹*process/agriculture*› mecanizar*; ‹*unit/regiment*› motorizar*

Med /med/ *n* (colloq) **the ~** el Mediterráneo

M Ed *n* = **Master of Education**

medal /'medḷ/ *n* medalla *f*; (*before n*) **~ winner** ▸**medalist**

medalist, (BrE) **medallist** /'medḷəst || 'medəlɪst/ *n* medallista *mf*; **gold/silver ~** medalla *mf* de oro/plata

medallion /mə'dæljən/ *n* medallón *m*

medallion man *n* (colloq) macho *m* prototípico (*que lleva ropa llamativa y medallón*), macho *m* ibérico (Esp)

medallist (BrE) ▸**medalist**

meddle /'medḷ/ *vi* 1 (interfere) **to ~ (IN/WITH sth)** meterse *or* entrometerse *or* inmiscuirse* (EN algo) 2 (tamper) **to ~ WITH sth** toquetear algo

meddlesome /'medḷsəm/ entrometido

media[1] /'mi:diə/ *n*: **the ~** (+ *pl or* (crit) *sing vb*) los medios de comunicación *or* difusión; (*before n*) **~ coverage** cobertura *f* periodística; **~ studies** periodismo *m*

media[2] *pl of* **medium**[2] **A,2**

mediaeval /'mi:di'i:vəl, 'me- || ˌmedi'i:vəl/ ▸**medieval**

median[1] /'mi:diən/ *adj* (Math) medio

median[2] *n*
A (Math) mediana *f*
B **~ (strip)** (AmE) mediana *f*, bandejón *m* (central) (Chi), camellón *m* (Méx)

mediate /'mi:dieɪt/ *vi* mediar, actuar* de mediador

mediator /'mi:dieɪtər/ *n* mediador, -dora *m,f*

medic /'medɪk/ *n* (colloq) 1 (physician) médico, -ca *m,f* 2 (student) estudiante *mf* de medicina 3 ▸**paramedic**

Medicaid /'medɪkeɪd/ *n* (in US) *organismo y programa estatal de asistencia sanitaria a personas de bajos ingresos*

medical[1] /'medɪkəl/ *adj* ‹*care/examination/insurance*› médico; ‹*student*› de medicina; ‹*case*› clínico; **~ certificate** certificado *m* médico; **~ history** (of patient) historial *m* médico *or* clínico, historia *f* clínica (AmL); **the ~ profession** los médicos, la profesión médica, el cuerpo médico; **on ~ grounds** por razones de salud; **~ school** facultad *f* de medicina

medical[2] *n* revisión *f* médica, examen *m* médico

medical examiner *n* (AmE Law) médico, -ca *m,f* forense

medically /'medɪkli/ *adv* 1 **~ qualified** titulado en medicina; **to be ~ examined** ser* reconocido por un médico 2 (*indep*) desde el punto de vista médico *or* clínico

medical officer, **Medical Officer** *n* (in company) médico, -ca *m,f* (*de una empresa*); (Mil) médico, -ca *m,f* militar

Medicare /'medɪker || 'medɪkeə(r)/ *n* (in US) *programa estatal de asistencia sanitaria a personas mayores de 65 años*

medicated /'medəkeɪtəd || 'medɪkeɪtɪd/ *adj* medicinal

medication /'medə'keɪʃən || ˌmedɪ'keɪʃən/ *n* [1] [u c] (substance) medicamento *m* [2] [u] (drugs) medicación *f*

medicinal /mə'dɪsṇəl || mɪ'dɪsɪnl/ *adj* medicinal

medicine /'medəsən || 'medsən, 'medəsən/ *n*

A [c u] (substance) medicamento *m*, medicina *f*, remedio *m* (esp AmL); ***to give sb a taste*** *o* ***dose of her/his own ~*** pagarle* a algn con la misma moneda

B [u] (science) medicina *f*

medicine man *n* curandero *m*, hechicero *m*

medieval /'mi:di'i:vəl, 'me- || ˌmedi'i:vəl/ *adj* medieval, medioeval

mediocre /'mi:di'əʊkər || ˌmi:dɪ'əʊkə(r)/ *adj* mediocre

mediocrity /'mi:di'ɑ:krəti/ *n* (*pl* **-ties**) [1] [u] (quality) mediocridad *f*, medianía *f* [2] [c] (person) mediocre *mf*

meditate /'medəteɪt || 'medɪteɪt/ *vi* **to ~ (ON** *o* **UPON sth)** meditar (SOBRE algo)

meditation /'medə'teɪʃən/ *n* [1] [u] (Psych, Relig) meditación *f* [2] [u c] (reflection) meditación *f*, reflexión *f*

Mediterranean¹ /'medətə'reɪmiən || ˌmedɪtə'reɪmiən/ *adj* mediterráneo

Mediterranean² *n* [1] **the ~ (Sea)** el (mar) Mediterráneo [2] (region) **the ~** el Mediterráneo

medium¹ /'mi:diəm/ *adj*

A (intermediate) ‹*size*› mediano; **of ~ height/build** de estatura *or* talla media *or* mediana/de complexión normal

B (Culin) [1] ‹*steak*› a punto, término medio (Méx) [2] (*as adv*): **~ rare** ‹*steak*› poco hecho, a la inglesa (Méx); **~ dry** ‹*wine*› semi-seco

medium² *n*

A [c] (*pl* **media**) (means, vehicle) medio *m*: **through the ~ of** a través de *or* por medio de

B (*pl* **media**) [1] [c] (environment) medio *m* (ambiente) [2] [c] (for growing cultures) caldo *m* de cultivo

C (middle position) (*no pl*) punto *m* medio; **to strike a happy ~** lograr un término medio

D [c] (*pl* **mediums**) (Occult) médium *mf*, medio *mf*

medium: **~-range** /'mi:diəm'reɪndʒ/ *adj* (*before n*) ‹*missile/aircraft*› de alcance medio *or* intermedio; ‹*plans/forecast*› a medio *or* mediano plazo; **~-size** /'mi:diəm'saɪz/, (BrE also) **~-sized** /-d/ *adj* ‹*book/house*› de tamaño mediano; ‹*person*› de talla *or* estatura media *or* mediana; **~-term** /'mi:diəm'tɜ:rm/ *adj* (*before n*) a medio *or* mediano plazo; **~ wave** *n* (BrE) (*no pl*) onda *f* media

medlar /'medlər || 'medlə(r)/ *n* níspero *m*

medley /'medli/ *n* [1] (mixture) mezcla *f*, combinación *f* [2] (Mus) popurrí *m*

meek /mi:k/ *adj* **-er, -est** dócil, sumiso, manso (liter); ***~ and mild*** como una malva

meet¹ /mi:t/ (*past & past p* **met**) *vt*

A [1] (encounter) encontrarse* con; **~ me on the corner at 6 o'clock** encontrémonos en la esquina a las 6; ***to ~ sb halfway*** *o* ***in the middle*** llegar* a un arreglo con algn [2] (welcome) recibir; (collect on arrival) ir* a buscar; **she ran to ~ me** corrió a mi encuentro; **he met me off the train** me fue a buscar *or* a esperar a la estación [3] (oppose) ‹*opponent/enemy*› enfrentarse a

B (make acquaintance of) conocer*; **John, ~ Mr Clark** (frml) John, le presento al señor Clark; **pleased to ~ you** encantado de conocerlo, mucho gusto

C [1] (come up against, experience) encontrar*, toparse con; **he met his death there** allí encontró su muerte; **to be met BY/WITH sth** encontrarse* CON algo; **there's more to this than ~s the eye** esto es más complicado de lo que parece [2] (counter, respond to): **she met their threats with defiance** hizo frente desafiante a sus amenazas; **she was met with applause** fue recibida con aplausos

D ‹*demands/wishes*› satisfacer*; ‹*deadline/quota*› cumplir con; ‹*debt*› satisfacer*, pagar*; ‹*obligation*› cumplir con; ‹*requirements*› reunir*, cumplir; ‹*cost*› hacerse* cargo de; **his income is inadequate to ~ his needs** su salario le es insuficiente para hacer frente a sus necesidades

E [1] (come together with, join): **East ~s West in this beautiful city** Oriente y Occidente se dan la mano en esta bella ciudad; **her gaze met his** sus miradas se cruzaron; **she could not ~ his eye** *o* **gaze** no se atrevía a mirarlo a la cara [2] (strike) dar* contra

■ **meet** *vi*

A [1] (encounter each other) encontrarse*; **where shall we ~?** ¿dónde nos encontramos?, ¿dónde quedamos? (esp Esp); **until we ~ again!** ¡hasta la vista! [2] (hold meeting) «*club*» reunirse*; «*heads of state/ministers*» entrevistarse [3] (make acquaintance) conocerse*; **have you two already met?** ¿ya se conocen?, ¿ya los han presentado? [4] (as opponents) enfrentarse

B (come into contact): **the vehicles met head on** los vehículos chocaron *or* se dieron de frente; **where the three roads ~** en el empalme *or* en la confluencia de las tres carreteras; **their eyes met** sus miradas se cruzaron

Phrasal verbs

- **meet up** [v ▸ adv] [1] (get together) **to ~ up (WITH sb)** encontrarse* (CON algn) [2] (join) «*roads*» **to ~ up WITH sth** empalmar CON algo
- **meet with** [v ▸ prep ▸ o] [1] ‹*opposition/hostility*› ser* recibido con; **to ~ with failure** fracasar; **to ~ with success** tener* éxito; **the proposal met with general approval** la propuesta recibió la aprobación general; **she met with an unfortunate accident** le ocurrió un lamentable accidente [2] (meet) (AmE) encontrarse* con

meet² *n* [1] (AmE Sport) encuentro *m* [2] (in hunting) partida *f* (de caza)

meeting /'mi:tɪŋ/ *n*

A (assembly) reunión *f*; **to call/hold a ~** convocar*/celebrar una reunión; **political ~** mitin *m*, mítin *m*; **to have a ~** reunirse*, tener* una reunión; **the ~ decided to accept the proposals** la asamblea decidió *or* los presentes decidieron aceptar las propuestas; **to be in a ~** estar* en una reunión *or* (Esp tb) estar* reunido; **the ~ is adjourned** se levanta la sesión

B (encounter) encuentro *m*; (between presidents) entrevista *f*: **I remember our last ~** recuerdo la última vez que nos vimos

C (BrE Sport) encuentro *m*; **athletics ~** competencia *f* *or* (Esp) competición *f* de atletismo; **race ~** (Equ) jornada *f* de carreras

mega- /'megə/ *pref* mega-

megabuck /'megəbʌk/ *adj* (AmE colloq) (*before n*) multimillonario

megabucks /'megəbʌks/ *pl n* (colloq) un dineral, un platal (AmS fam), un pastón (Esp fam), un lanón (Méx fam)

megabyte /'megəbaɪt/ *n* megabyte *m*, megaocteto *m*

megalomaniac /'megələʊ'meɪniæk/ *n* megalómano, -na *m,f*

megaphone /'megəfəʊn/ *n* megáfono *m*

megaton /'megətʌn/ *n* megatón *m*

megawatt /'megəwɑ:t || 'megəwɒt/ *n* megavatio *m*

melancholy /'melənkɑ:li || 'melənkəli/ *adj* ‹*person/mood*› melancólico; ‹*sound*› triste

mélange, melange /meɪ'lɑ:nʒ/ *n* (liter) mezcla *f*

melanoma /'melə'nəʊmə/ *n* [u c] melanoma *m*

melee, mêlée /'meɪleɪ || 'meleɪ/ *n* (confusion) tumulto *m*; (fight) riña *f*, refriega *f*

mellow¹ /'meləʊ/ *adj* **-er, -est** [1] ‹*fruit*› maduro; ‹*wine*› añejo; ‹*sound/voice*› dulce, melodioso; ‹*light/color*› tenue, suave [2] ‹*person/mood*› apacible, sosegado; **the wine had made him ~** el vino lo había hecho más afable

mellow² *vt* suavizar*

■ **mellow** *vi* «*color/voice*» suavizarse*; «*views*» moderarse; «*wine*» añejarse; **he has ~ed with age** se le ha suavizado el carácter con los años

melodic /mə'lɑ:dɪk || mə'lɒdɪk/ *adj* ▸**melodious**

melodious /mə'ləʊdiəs || mə'ləʊdiəs/ *adj* melodioso

melodrama /'melədrɑ:mə/ *n* [c u] melodrama *m*

melodramatic /'melədrə'mætɪk/ *adj* melodramático

melody /'melədi/ *n* (*pl* **-dies**) melodía *f*

melon /'melən/ *n* [c u] melón *m*

melt /melt/ *vi* [1] «*ice/butter*» derretirse*; «*metal/wax*» fundirse; **the candy ~ed in his mouth** el caramelo se le deshizo *or* se le disolvió en la boca [2] (become mild, gentle) «*person*» ablandarse; «*anger*» desaparecer*; **he ~ed in her arms** se derritió en sus brazos [3] **to ~ INTO sth**: **they ~ed into the crowd** se perdieron en la muchedumbre;

m

the scenes ~ into one another las escenas se funden unas con otras

■ **melt** *vt* 1 (liquefy) ‹*snow/butter*› derretir* 2 (make gentle, compassionate): **their cries ~ed her heart** su llanto la conmovió

Phrasal verbs

• **melt away** [v ▸ adv] 1 «*ice/snow*» derretirse* 2 (disappear) «*mist/fog*» levantarse, disiparse; «*fear/suspicion*» disiparse, desvanecerse*; «*confidence*» desvanecerse*, esfumarse; «*resistance/opposition*» desaparecer*, esfumarse; **they ~ed away into the woods** desaparecieron ocultándose en el bosque

• **melt down** [v ▸ o ▸ adv, v ▸ adv ▸ o] ‹*gold/coins*› fundir

meltdown /'meltdaʊn/ *n*: *fusión accidental del núcleo de un reactor*

melting /'meltɪŋ/: **~ point** *n* punto *m* de fusión; **~ pot** *n* crisol *m*; ***to be in the ~ pot*** estar* sobre el tapete

member /'membər || 'membə(r)/ *n*

A (of committee, board) miembro *mf*; (of club) socio, -cia *m,f*; (of church) feligrés, -gresa *m,f*; **~ of staff** empleado, -da *m,f*; **he's a ~ of the union** está afiliado al sindicato; **a ~ of the House of Representatives** un diputado, un miembro de la Cámara de Representantes *or* Diputados; **the ~ for Rye** (in UK) el diputado por Rye; **a ~ of the audience** un espectador, un asistente; **the offer is open to any ~ of the public** la oferta está abierta al público en general; **Spain is a ~ of the EC** España es miembro de la CE; (*before n*) **~ states** países *mpl* miembros

B (limb) (arch) miembro *m*

member: **~ of Congress** *n* (in US) miembro *mf* del Congreso; **~ of Parliament** *n* (in UK etc) diputado, -da *m,f*, parlamentario, -ria *m,f*

membership /'membərʃɪp || 'membəʃɪp/ *n* 1 [u] (being a member): **~ of the club is restricted to residents** sólo los residentes pueden hacerse socios del club; **to apply for ~** solicitar el ingreso *or* la admisión en un club (*or* partido *etc*); **she gave up her party ~** dejó de pertenecer al partido; (*before n*) **~ card** carné *m* de socio; **~ fee(s)** cuota *f* (de socio) 2 [c] (members) (+ *sing or pl vb*) socios *mpl* (*or* afiliados *mpl etc*); (number of members) número *m* de socios (*or* afiliados *etc*)

membrane /'membreɪn/ *n* membrana *f*

memento /mə'mentəʊ/ *n* (*pl* **-tos** *or* **-toes**) recuerdo *m*

memo /'meməʊ/ *n* (*pl* **-os**) memorándum *m*, nota *f*

memoirs /'memwɑːrz || 'memwɑːz/ *pl n* memorias *fpl*

memorabilia /'memərə'bɪliə/ *pl n* objetos *mpl* de interés

memorable /'memərəbəl/ *adj* memorable

memorandum /'memə'rændəm/ *n* (*pl* **-dums** *or* **-da** /-də/) memorándum *m*

memorial[1] /mə'mɔːriəl/ *n* monumento *m*

memorial[2] *adj* conmemorativo

Memorial Day *n* (in US) *día en que se recuerda a los caídos*

Memorial Day

Un día festivo en EEUU en honor a los americanos caídos en la guerra. Tiene lugar, por lo general, el último lunes de mayo

memorize /'meməraɪz/ *vt* memorizar*, aprender de memoria

memory /'meməri/ *n* (*pl* **-ries**)

A 1 [u c] (faculty) memoria *f*; **if (my) ~ serves me right** si mal no recuerdo, si la memoria no me falla; **to play sth from ~** tocar* algo de memoria; ***to have a ~ like a sieve*** tener* la cabeza como un colador, tener* muy mala memoria; **~ *lane*: to take a trip** *o* **stroll down ~ lane** rememorar el pasado 2 [u] (period): **the worst storm in living ~** la peor tormenta que se recuerde *or* de que se tenga memoria

B 1 [c] (recollection) recuerdo *m*; **I have no ~ of it** no lo recuerdo; **his ~ will live on** su recuerdo permanecerá vivo 2 [u] (remembrance) memoria *f*; **in ~ of sb** a la memoria *or* en memoria de algn; **in ~ of sth** en conmemoración de algo

C [c u] (Comput) memoria *f*

memory stick *n* lápiz *m* de memoria, tarjeta *f* de memoria flash

men /men/ *pl of* **man**[1]

menace /'menəs || 'menɪs/ *n*

A 1 [u] (threatening quality): **the ~ in his voice** el tono amenazador de su voz; **an air of ~** un aire amenazador 2 [c] (threat) amenaza *f*; **to demand money with ~s** (BrE Law) exigir* dinero con intimidación

B [c] 1 (danger) amenaza *f*; **a ~ TO sb/sth** una amenaza PARA algn/algo 2 (nuisance) (colloq) peligro *m* público

menacing /'menəsɪŋ || 'menɪsɪŋ/ *adj* ‹*look/voice*› amenazador, amenazante; ‹*sky/clouds*› que amenaza tormenta/lluvia, amenazador (liter)

menagerie /mə'nædʒəri/ *n* colección *f* de animales salvajes

mend[1] /mend/ *vt* 1 (repair) ‹*garment*› coser, arreglar; ‹*shoe*› arreglar; ‹*clock/roof*› arreglar, reparar 2 (set to rights): **she tried to ~ matters** trató de arreglar las cosas; **to ~ one's ways** enmendarse*

■ **mend** *vi* (heal) «*injury*» curarse; «*fracture/bone*» soldarse*

mend[2] *n* remiendo *m*; (darn) zurcido *m*; ***to be on the ~*** (colloq) ir* mejorando, estar* reponiéndose

mendacious /men'deɪʃəs/ *adj* (frml) ‹*person*› mendaz (liter), mentiroso; ‹*report/statement*› falaz (liter), falso

mender /'mendər / *n* (BrE): **to collect one's shoes from the ~('s)** ir* a buscar los zapatos al zapatero

menfolk /'menfəʊk/, (AmE also) **menfolks** /-s/ *pl n*: **the ~** los hombres; **their ~** sus maridos (*or* compañeros *etc*)

menial /'miːniəl/ *adj* de ínfima importancia, de baja categoría

meningitis /'menən'dʒaɪtəs/ *n* [u] meningitis *f*

menopausal /'menə'pɔːzəl/ *adj* menopáusico

menopause /'menəpɔːz/ *n* **the ~** la menopausia; **the male ~** la andropausia

men's room *n* (AmE) baño *m mpl* de caballeros

menstrual /'menstruəl/ *adj* (*before n*) menstrual

menstruate /'menstrueɪt/ *vi* menstruar*

menstruation /'menstru'eɪʃən/ *n* [u] menstruación *f*

menswear /'menzwer || 'menzweə(r)/ *n* [u] ropa *f* de caballero

mental /'mentl̩/ *adj*

A (*before n*) ‹*powers/illness*› mental; ‹*hospital/patient*› psiquiátrico; **~ age** edad *f* mental; **to make a ~ note of sth** tomar nota de algo mentalmente

B (mad) (BrE colloq) (*pred*) **to be ~** estar* chiflado (fam)

mental arithmetic *n* [u] cálculos *mpl* mentales

mentality /men'tæləti/ *n* (*pl* **-ties**) mentalidad *f*

mentally /'mentəli/ *adv* mentalmente; **he's ~ ill/handicapped** es un enfermo mental/un disminuido psíquico

menthol /'menθɔːl || 'menθɒl/ *n* [u] mentol *m*; (*before n*) ‹*cigarettes*› mentolado

mentholated /'menθəleɪtəd/ *adj* mentolado

mention[1] /'mentʃən || 'menʃən/ *vt* mencionar; **your name was ~ed** se mencionó tu nombre; **I won't ~ any names** no daré nombres; **the village is ~ed in the book** el pueblo aparece mencionado en el libro; **have I ~ed John already?** ¿ya te he hablado de John?; **did I hear somebody ~ coffee?** ¿ha dicho alguien algo acerca de un cafe?; **to ~ only a few** por nombrar sólo a unos pocos; **there's the problem of time, not to ~ the cost** está el problema del tiempo y no digamos ya el costo; **don't ~ it** (on being thanked) no hay de qué, de nada

mention[2] *n* mención *f*; **it didn't even get a ~ in the press** la prensa ni siquiera lo mencionó; **at the ~ of her name** al oír (mencionar) su nombre

mentor /'mentɔːr/ *n* (liter) mentor, -tora *m,f* (liter)

menu /'menjuː/ *n* 1 (in restaurant) carta *f*, menú *m* (esp AmL); **Ⓢ set menu** menú de la casa 2 (Comput) menú *m*

meow[1] /mi'aʊ/ *n* maullido *m*, miau *m*

meow[2] *vi* maullar*

MEP *n* (= **Member of the European Parliament**) eurodiputado, -da *m,f*

mercantile /'mɜːrkəntiːl || 'mɜːkəntaɪl/ *adj* mercantil

mercantile marine *n* marina *f* mercante

mercenary[1] /'mɜːrsn̩eri || 'mɜːsɪnəri/ *n* (*pl* **-ries**) mercenario, -ria *m,f*

mercenary[2] *adj* materialista, interesado

merchandise /'mɜːrtʃəndaɪz || 'mɜːtʃəndaɪz/ *n* [u] mercancía *f*, mercadería *f* (AmS)

merchandising /ˈmɜːrtʃəndaɪzɪŋ || ˈmɜːtʃəndaɪzɪŋ/ *n* [u] comercialización *f* (*esp de subproductos*)

merchant /ˈmɜːrtʃənt || ˈmɜːtʃənt/ *n*
A 1 (retailer) comerciante *mf*; **coal ~** comerciante en carbón 2 (Hist) mercader *m*
B (BrE colloq): **~ of doom** agorero, -ra *m,f*; **they're rip-off ~s** son unos ladrones

merchant: **~ bank** *n* (BrE) banco *m* mercantil; **~ banker** *n* (BrE) *ejecutivo de un banco mercantil*; **~ marine**, (BrE also) **~ navy** *n* marina *f* mercante; **~ shipping** *n* [u] 1 (industry) industria *f* de la marina mercante 2 (ships) barcos *mpl* mercantes

merciful /ˈmɜːrsɪfəl || ˈmɜːsɪfəl/ *adj* misericordioso, compasivo, clemente; **her death was a ~ release** en las circunstancias, su muerte fue una bendición

mercifully /ˈmɜːrsɪfəli/ *adv* 1 (leniently) con clemencia 2 (fortunately) (*indep*) gracias a Dios

merciless /ˈmɜːrsɪləs || ˈmɜːsɪlɪs/ *adj* despiadado

mercilessly /ˈmɜːrsɪləsli || ˈmɜːsɪlɪsli/ *adv* despiadadamente, sin piedad *or* clemencia

mercurial /mɜːrˈkjʊriəl || mɜːˈkjʊəriəl/ *adj* ‹*person/temperament*› voluble, volátil; ‹*wit*› vivo

mercury /ˈmɜːrkjəri || ˈmɜːkjʊri/ *n* [u] mercurio *m*

Mercury /ˈmɜːrkjəri || ˈmɜːkjʊri/ *n* Mercurio *m*

mercy /ˈmɜːrsi || ˈmɜːsi/ *n* (*pl* **-cies**) 1 [u] (clemency) misericordia *f*, clemencia *f*; **to have ~ (on sb)** tener* misericordia *or* piedad (de algn), apiadarse (de algn); **he begged for ~** pidió clemencia; **they showed the traitor no ~** no fueron clementes con el traidor; **to throw oneself on sb's ~** abandonarse a la merced de algn; **at the ~ of the elements** a merced de los elementos; (*before n*) ‹*mission/flight*› (journ) de ayuda *or* socorro 2 [c] (blessing) bendición *f*; **it's a ~ that ...** (colloq) es una suerte que ..., gracias a Dios, ...; **let's be grateful** *o* **thankful for small mercies** (set phrase) seamos positivos, podría haber sido peor

mercy killing *n* 1 [u] (practice) eutanasia *f* 2 [c] (instance) acto *m* de eutanasia

mere /mɪr || mɪə(r)/ *adj* (*superl* **merest**) (*before n*) simple, mero; **the ~ mention of his name** la mera *or* sola mención de su nombre; **a ~ six months ago** hace apenas seis meses; ▸**merest**

merely /ˈmɪrli || ˈmɪəli/ *adv* simplemente, solamente, sólo; **she ~ has to raise her voice and he ...** no tiene más que levantar la voz y él ...

merest /ˈmɪrəst || ˈmɪərɪst/ *adj* (*superl of* **mere**): **the ~ noise makes her jump** el menor ruido *or* el más leve ruido la hace saltar

meretricious /ˈmerəˈtrɪʃəs / *adj* ‹*style*› ampuloso, rimbombante; ‹*argument*› engañoso, especioso (frml)

merge /mɜːrdʒ/ *vi* «*roads/rivers*» confluir*; «*colors*» fundirse; «*companies*» fusionarse, unirse; **to ~ INTO sth**: **he ~d into the crowd** se perdió entre el gentío; **the red ~s into the blue** el rojo se funde con el azul

■ **merge** *vt* ‹*companies/organizations*› fusionar, unir; ‹*colors*› combinar, fundir; ‹*programs/data*› fusionar

merger /ˈmɜːrdʒər || ˈmɜːdʒə(r)/ *n* 1 (Busn) fusión *f* 2 (of organizations etc) fusión *f*, unión *f*

meridian /məˈrɪdiən/ *n* (Geog, Astron) meridiano *m*

meringue /məˈræŋ/ *n* [c u] merengue *m*

merit[1] /ˈmerət || ˈmerɪt/ *n*
A 1 [u] (excellence) mérito *m*; **he was chosen on ~** lo eligieron por sus méritos 2 [c] (praiseworthy quality): **each case is judged on its (own) ~s** se juzga cada caso individualmente *or* por separado; **there is no** *o* **isn't any ~ in prolonging the dispute** no tiene ningún sentido prolongar el conflicto
B [c] (BrE Educ) ≈ mención *f* especial

merit[2] *vt* merecer*, ser* digno de

meritocracy /ˈmerəˈtɑːkrəsi || ˌmerɪˈtɒkrəsi/ *n* [u c] (*pl* **-cies**) meritocracia *f*

mermaid /ˈmɜːrmeɪd || ˈmɜːmeɪd/ *n* sirena *f*

merrily /ˈmerəli || ˈmerɪli/ *adv* 1 (joyfully) alegremente 2 (unconcernedly) tranquilamente

merriment /ˈmerɪmənt/ *n* [u] (joy) alegría *f*, júbilo *m*; (laughter) risas *fpl*

merry /ˈmeri/ *adj* **-rier, -riest** 1 (joyful) alegre; **the more the merrier** (set phrase) cuantos más, mejor; **~ Christmas!** ¡feliz Navidad!, ¡felices Pascuas!; ***to make ~*** (liter) divertirse* 2 (unconcerned): **to go one's ~ way** (iro): **he went his own ~ way** se fue tan campante 3 (drunk) (colloq) alegre, achispado

merry: **~-go-round** *n* carrusel *m*, tiovivo *m* (Esp), calesita *f* (Per, RPl); **~making** *n* [u] juerga *f*; (celebrations) festejos *mpl*

mesh /meʃ/ *n* 1 [c] (opening) malla *f*; **a broad/fine ~** malla abierta/fina 2 [u] (material) malla *f*; **wire ~** tela *f or* malla *f* metálica

mesmerize /ˈmezməraɪz/ *vt* 1 (fascinate) cautivar, fascinar 2 (hypnotize) (dated) hipnotizar*; **I was ~d** me quedé pasmada *or* boquiabierta

mess /mes/ *n*
A 1 (*no pl*) (untidiness) desorden *m*, revoltijo *m*; **what a ~!** ¡qué desorden!; **the bedroom was (in) a ~** el dormitorio estaba todo desordenado *or* (fam) patas para arriba; **my hair is a ~** (colloq) tengo el pelo hecho un desastre; **he made a ~ in the kitchen** dejó la cocina hecha un desastre (fam); **don't make a ~** no desordenes nada 2 (dirt): **what a ~!** ¡qué desastre *or* (RPl tb) enchastre! (fam); **they made a ~ on the carpet/in the kitchen** dejaron la alfombra/cocina hecha un asco (fam); **don't make a ~** no ensucies nada 3 [u] (excrement) (BrE colloq & euph) caca *f* (fam)
B (*no pl*) (confused, troubled state): **their marriage was (in) a ~** su matrimonio andaba muy mal; **the country is (in) a complete ~** la situación del país es caótica; **my life's a ~** mi vida es un desastre; **to get into a ~** meterse en un lío; **to make a ~ of sth**: **you made a real ~ of this job** hiciste muy mal este trabajo; **she made a real ~ of her life** se arruinó la vida
C [c] (Mil): **officers' ~** casino *m or* comedor *m* de oficiales
D (*no pl*) (large quantity) (AmE colloq) montón *m*

Phrasal verbs

• **mess around**, (BrE also) **mess about** (colloq)
A [v ▸ adv] 1 (misbehave) «*children*» hacer* travesuras, tontear; **she found out he'd been ~ing around** descubrió que había tenido líos *or* enredos con otras; **he started ~ing around with drugs** empezó a meterse con drogas 2 (fiddle, waste time): **he enjoys ~ing around in boats** le gusta entretenerse *or* pasar el tiempo navegando; **she didn't ~ around: she told him straight out** no se anduvo con vueltas; se lo dijo sin más (fam) 3 (interfere) **to ~ around (WITH sth/sb)**: **stop ~ing around with my things!** ¡deja mis cosas tranquilas!; **don't ~ around with me** no juegues conmigo, no me tomes el pelo (fam)
B [v ▸ o ▸ adv] (BrE) 1 (treat inconsiderately): **don't ~ me around: are you going to come or not?** no me fastidies *or* decídete de una vez ¿vienes o no? (fam) 2 (muddle) armar un lío con (fam)

• **mess up**
A [v ▸ o ▸ adv, v ▸ adv ▸ o] 1 (make untidy) desordenar, desarreglar 2 (make dirty) ensuciar 3 (spoil) ‹*plans*› estropear
B [v ▸ adv] (AmE colloq) echarlo todo a perder, embarrarla (fam)

• **mess with** [v ▸ prep ▸ o] (colloq) (provoke) meterse con (fam)

message[1] /ˈmesɪdʒ/ *n* mensaje *m*; **would you like to leave a ~, can I take a ~?** ¿quiere dejar algún recado *or* (esp AmL) mensaje?, ¿quiere dejar algo dicho? (CS); **error ~** (Comput) mensaje de error; ***to get the ~*** (colloq) entender*, darse* cuenta

message[2] *vt* enviar un mensaje de texto

messenger /ˈmesn̩dʒər || ˈmesɪndʒə(r)/ *n* mensajero, -ra *m,f*; (*before n*) **~ boy** recadero *m*, mandadero *m* (AmL)

mess hall *n* (AmE) comedor *m*

Messiah /məˈsaɪə/ *n* Mesías *m*

Messrs /ˈmesərz || ˈmesəz/ *pl of* **Mr** Sres.

messy /ˈmesi/ *adj* **-sier, -siest** 1 (untidy) ‹*room*› desordenado; ‹*writing*› sucio y descuidado, desprolijo (CS) 2 (dirty) sucio; **he's a ~ eater** no sabe comer, come sin modales 3 (unpleasant, confused) ‹*affair/business*› turbio

met /met/ *past & past p of* **meet**[1]

metabolic /ˈmetəˈbɑːlɪk || ˌmetəˈbɒlɪk/ *adj* metabólico

metabolism /məˈtæbəlɪzəm/ *n* metabolismo *m*

metal /ˈmetl̩/ *n* [u c] (Chem, Metall) metal *m*; (*before n*) ‹*box*› metálico, de metal; **~ detector** detector *m* de metales; **~ fatigue** fatiga *f* del metal

metallic /məˈtælɪk/ *adj* metálico

metallurgy /ˈmetḷɜːrdʒi || məˈtælədʒi/ *n* [u] metalurgia *f*
metalwork /ˈmetḷwɜːrk || ˈmetḷwɜːk/ *n* [u] trabajo *m* en metales, metalistería *f*
metamorphose /ˈmetəˈmɔːrfəʊz || ˌmetəˈmɔːfəʊz/ *vi* **to ~ INTO sth** convertirse* *or* transformarse *or* (frml) metamorfosearse EN algo
metamorphosis /ˈmetəˈmɔːrfəsəs || ˌmetəˈmɔːfəsɪs/ *n* [c u] (*pl* **-phoses** /-fəsiːz/) metamorfosis *f*
metaphor /ˈmetəfɔːr || ˈmetəfɔː(r)/ *n* [c u] metáfora *f*
metaphorical /ˈmetəˈfɔːrɪkəl/ *adj* metafórico
metaphysical /ˈmetəˈfɪzɪkəl/ *adj* metafísico
metaphysics /ˈmetəˈfɪzɪks/ *n* [u] (+ *sing vb*) metafísica *f*
mete /miːt/ *see* **mete out**
meteor /ˈmiːtiər, -ɔːr || ˈmiːtiə(r), -ɔː(r)/ *n* meteorito *m*
meteoric /ˈmiːtiˈɔːrɪk || ˌmiːtɪˈɒrɪk/ *adj* ‹*rise/progress*› meteórico; **~ rock** piedra *f* meteórica
meteorite /ˈmiːtiəraɪt/ *n* meteorito *m*
meteorologist /ˈmiːtiəˈrɑːlədʒəst || ˌmiːtiəˈrɒlədʒɪst/ *n* meteorólogo, -ga *m,f*
meteorology /ˈmiːtiəˈrɑːlədʒi || ˌmiːtiəˈrɒlədʒi/ *n* [u] meteorología *f*
mete out [v ▸ o ▸ adv, v ▸ adv ▸ o] ‹*fine/punishment*› imponer*
meter[1] /ˈmiːtər || ˈmiːtə(r)/ *n*
A [c] **1** (measuring device): **gas/electricity/water ~** contador *m or* (AmL tb) medidor *m* de gas/electricidad/agua; **volt ~** voltímetro *m*; **light ~** fotómetro *m* **2** (*parking ~*) parquímetro *m*
B [u c] (AmE Mus) compás *m*
C [c] (BrE) **metre** (measure) metro *m*
D [c u] (BrE) **metre** (Lit) metro *m*
meter[2] *vt* medir* (*con contador*)
meth /meθ/ *n* [u] (AmE colloq) (+ *sing vb*) alcohol *m* azul *or* de quemar
methadone /ˈmeθədəʊn/ *n* [u] metadona *f*
methane /ˈmeθeɪn || ˈmiːθeɪn/ *n* [u] metano *m*
methinks /miˈθɪŋks/ *adv* (arch) a mi parecer
method /ˈmeθəd/ *n*
A [c u] método *m*; **~ of payment** forma *f* de pago; ***there's ~ in his/her madness*** no es tan loco/loca como parece
B (Theat) (*before n*) **a M~ actor** un actor del método (Stanislavsky-Strasberg)
methodical /məˈθɑːdɪkəl || mɪˈθɒdɪkəl/ *adj* metódico
methodically /məˈθɑːdɪkli/ *adv* métodicamente
Methodism /ˈmeθədɪzəm/ *n* [u] metodismo *m*
Methodist[1] /ˈmeθədəst || ˈmeθədɪst/ *n* metodista *mf*
Methodist[2] *adj* metodista
methodology /ˈmeθəˈdɑːlədʒi || ˌmeθəˈdɒlədʒi/ *n* (*pl* **-gies**) metodología *f*
meths /meθs/ *n* [u] (BrE colloq) ▸**meth**
methylated spirit(s) /ˈmeθəleɪtəd/ *n* [u] (+ *sing vb*) alcohol *m* desnaturalizado *or* azul *or* de quemar
meticulous /məˈtɪkjələs || məˈtɪkjʊləs/ *adj* meticuloso
meticulously /məˈtɪkjələsli || məˈtɪkjʊləsli/ *adv* meticulosamente, minuciosamente
metier /meɪˈtjeɪ || ˈmetjeɪ/ *n* (profession) profesión *f*, oficio *m*; (strong point) fuerte *m*, especialidad *f*
metre (BrE) ▸**meter**[1] **C,4**
metric /ˈmetrɪk/ *adj* métrico; **the ~ system** el sistema métrico (decimal)
metrication /ˈmetrɪˈkeɪʃən/ *n* [u] conversión *f* al sistema métrico (decimal)
metric ton *n* tonelada *f* (métrica)
metro[1] /ˈmetrəʊ/ *n* (*pl* **-ros**) (Rail, Transp) metro *m*, subterráneo *m* (RPl)
metro[2] *adj* (AmE journ) (*before n*) metropolitano
metronome /ˈmetrənəʊm/ *n* metrónomo *m*
metropolis /məˈtrɑːpələs || məˈtrɒpəlɪs/ *n* (*pl* **-polises**) metrópoli(s) *f*
metropolitan /ˈmetrəˈpɑːlətn̩ || ˌmetrəˈpɒlɪtən/ *adj* (frml) metropolitano; **the M~ Police** (in UK) la policía londinense
mettle /ˈmetḷ/ *n* [u] temple *m*, entereza *f*; **to show one's ~** demostrar* lo que se vale; ***to be on one's ~*** estar* dispuesto a dar lo mejor de sí

mew /mjuː/ *vi* maullar*
mewl /mjuːl/ *vi* «*tomcat*» maullar*; «*baby*» lloriquear
mews /mjuːz/ *n* (*pl* ~) (esp BrE) *calle flanqueada de antiguas caballerizas convertidas en viviendas, talleres etc*
Mexican[1] /ˈmeksɪkən/ *adj* mexicano, mejicano
Mexican[2] *n* mexicano, -na *m,f*, mejicano, -na *m,f*
Mexico /ˈmeksɪkəʊ/ *n* México *m*, Méjico *m*
Mexico City *n* (ciudad *f* de) México *m or* Méjico *m*; (within Mexico) el Distrito Federal *or* DF
mezzanine /ˈmezəniːn/ *n* **1** **~ (floor)** entresuelo *m*, *m*, mezzanine *f or m* (AmL) **2** (AmE Theat) platea *f* alta
mezzo-soprano /ˈmetsəʊsəˈprɑːnəʊ/ *n* mezzosoprano *f*
mg (= **milligrams(s)**) mg.
mi /miː/ *n* (Mus) mi *m*
MI = Michigan
MI5 *n* (in UK) *departamento de contraespionaje británico*
MI6 *n* (in UK) *departamento de inteligencia británico*
miaow /miˈaʊ/ *n/vi* ▸**meow**[1,2]
mice /maɪs/ *pl of* **mouse**
Mich = Michigan
Michelangelo /ˈmaɪkəlˈændʒələʊ/ *n* Miguel Ángel
mickey /ˈmɪki/ *n* ***to take the ~ (out of sb)*** (BrE colloq) reírse* de algn; (face to face) tomarle el pelo a algn
Mickey Mouse® *adj* (colloq & pej) (*before n*) ‹*approach*› muy poco serio (fam)
micro /ˈmaɪkrəʊ/ *n* (*pl* **-cros**) ▸**microcomputer**
microbe /ˈmaɪkrəʊb/ *n* microbio *m*
microbiology /ˈmaɪkrəʊbaɪˈɑːlədʒi || ˌmaɪkrəʊbaɪˈɒlədʒi/ *n* [u] microbiología *f*
microbrewery /ˈmaɪkrəʊbruːəri/ *n* (*pl* **-ries**) (AmE) destilería *f* de cerveza artesanal
microchip /ˈmaɪkrəʊtʃɪp/ *n* (micro)chip *m*
microclimate /ˈmaɪkrəʊklaɪmət/ *n* microclima *m*
microcomputer /ˈmaɪkrəʊkəmˌpjuːtər/ *n* microcomputadora *f* (esp AmL), microordenador *m* (Esp)
microcosm /ˈmaɪkrəkɑːzəm/ *n* microcosmo(s) *m*
microeconomics /ˈmaɪkrəʊˌekəˈnɑːmɪks || -ˌiːk-/ *n* (+ *sing vb*) microeconomía *f*
microelectronics /ˈmaɪkrəʊelekˈtrɑːnɪks || ˌmaɪkrəʊɪlekˈtrɒnɪks/ *n* (+ *sing vb*) microelectrónica *f*
microfiche /ˈmaɪkrəʊfiːʃ/ *n* [c u] microficha *f*
microfilm /ˈmaɪkrəʊfɪlm/ *n* [c u] microfilm *m*, microfilme *m*
microlight /ˈmaɪkrəʊlaɪt/ *n* aeroligero *m*
micrometer /maɪˈkrɑːmətər/ *n* micrómetro *m*
micron /ˈmaɪkrɑːn || ˈmaɪkrɒn/ *n* micrón *m*
microorganism /ˈmaɪkrəʊˈɔːrgənɪzəm || ˌmaɪkrəʊˈɔːgənɪzəm/ *n* microorganismo *m*
microphone /ˈmaɪkrəfəʊn/ *n* micrófono *m*
microprocessor /ˈmaɪkrəʊˈprɑːsesər || ˈmaɪkrəʊˌprəʊsesə(r)/ *n* microprocesador *m*
microscope /ˈmaɪkrəskəʊp/ *n* microscopio *m*; ***to put sth under the ~*** examinar algo detenidamente
microscopic /ˈmaɪkrəˈskɑːpɪk || ˌmaɪkrəˈskɒpɪk/ *adj* microscópico, al microscopio
microsurgery /ˈmaɪkrəʊˈsɜːrdʒəri/ *n* microcirugía *f*
microwave /ˈmaɪkrəʊweɪv/ *n*
A (Phys, Telec) microonda *f*
B **~ (oven)** (horno *m* de) microondas *m*
mid- /mɪd/ *pref*: **in ~January/the ~1980s** a mediados de enero/de la década de los 80; **~morning/~afternoon** a media mañana/tarde; **she was in her ~forties** tenía alrededor de 45 años
midair /ˈmɪdˈer || ˌmɪdˈeə(r)/ *n*: **in ~** en el aire
Midas /ˈmaɪdəs/ *n* Midas; ***to have the ~ touch***: **she has the ~ touch** es como el rey Midas, todo lo que toca se convierte en oro
midday /ˈmɪdˈdeɪ/ *n* mediodía *m*; **at/before ~** al/antes del mediodía
middle[1] /ˈmɪdḷ/ *n*
A (of object, place — center) centro *m*, medio *m*; (— half-way line) mitad *f*; **in the ~ of nowhere** quién sabe dónde, en el quinto pino (Esp fam), donde el diablo perdió el poncho

(AmS fam); ***to split sth down the* ~** dividir algo por la mitad

B (of period, activity): **in the ~ of the week/month** a mediados de semana/mes; **it's the ~ of winter** estamos en pleno invierno; **in the ~ of the day** alrededor del medio día; **in the ~ of the night** en la mitad de la noche; **to be in the ~ of sth/-ING**: **I'm in the ~ of a really exciting novel at the moment** en este momento estoy leyendo una novela muy interesante; **I'm in the ~ of cooking dinner** estoy preparando la cena

C (waist) cintura *f*

middle[2] *adj* (*before n*): **the ~ house of the three** de las tres, la casa de en medio *or* del medio; **~ finger** dedo *m* medio *or* del corazón

middle: **~ age** *n* [u] madurez *f*; (*before n*) **~-age spread** ≈ la curva de la felicidad (euf); **~-aged** /ˈmɪdl̩ˈeɪdʒd/ *adj* de mediana edad, de edad madura; **~ Ages** *pl n* **the M~ Ages** la Edad Media; **~ America** *n* [1] (Geog) Mesoamérica, México y América Central; (in US) *la zona central de los EEUU* [2] (Sociol) la clase media norteamericana; **~brow** *adj* ‹*public/tastes*› medianamente cultivado; ‹*reading*› de nivel intelectual medio; **~ class** *n* [c u] (*often pl*) clase *f* media; **~-class** /ˈmɪdl̩ˈklæs ‖ ˌmɪdl̩ˈklɑːs/ *adj* ‹*family/district*› de clase media; ‹*attitudes*› burgués, convencional; **~ distance** *n* (in picture) segundo plano *m*; **~-distance** /ˈmɪdl̩ˈdɪstəns/ *adj* (*before n*) ‹*running/race*› de medio fondo; **~-distance runner** mediofondista *mf*; **~ East** *n* **the M~ East** el Oriente Medio, el Medio Oriente; **~ Eastern** *adj* medio-oriental, del Oriente Medio *or* Medio Oriente; **~ ground** *n* **the ~ ground** el terreno propicio para un avenimiento; **~man** /ˈmɪdl̩mæn/ *n* (*pl* **-men** /-men/) intermediario *m*; **to cut out the ~man** eliminar al intermediario; **~ management** *n* mandos *mpl or* cuadros *mpl* (inter)medios, gerencia *f* media; **~ name** *n* segundo nombre *m*; **thrift is her ~ name** (colloq & hum) es la tacañería personificada; **~-of-the-road** /ˈmɪdl̩əvðəˈrəʊd/ *adj* ‹*politician/views*› moderado; ‹*artist*› del montón; **~-ranking** /ˈmɪdl̩ˈræŋkɪŋ/ *adj* (*before n*) [1] (of intermediate rank) ‹*officer*› de medio rango [2] (average) ‹*book/film/author*› de mediana categoría; **~ school** *n* (in US) *colegio para niños de 12 a 14 años*; (in UK) *colegio para niños de 9 a 13 años*; **~weight** *n* (Sport) peso *m* mediano *or* medio; **~ West** *n* ▸**Midwest**

middling /ˈmɪdlɪŋ/ *adj* (in size) mediano; (in quality) regular; ▸**fair**[1] **D1**

Mideast /mɪdˈiːst/ *n* (AmE) ▸**Middle East**

midfield /ˈmɪdfiːld ‖ ˌmɪdˈfiːld/ *n* (area, players) centro *m* del campo, mediocampo *m*; (*before n*) **~ player** centrocampista *mf*, mediocampista *mf*

midge /mɪdʒ/ *n*: *especie de mosquito pequeño*

midget /ˈmɪdʒət ‖ ˈmɪdʒɪt/ *n* enano, -na *m,f* (*de proporciones normales*)

midi /ˈmɪdɪ/ *adj* (Audio): **~ system** cadena *f* musical compacta

Midi /mɪˈdi/ *n* **the ~** el sur de Francia

Midlands /ˈmɪdləndz/ *pl n* (in UK) **the ~** *la región central de Inglaterra*

midlife /ˈmɪdˈlaɪf/ *n*: (*before n*) **~ crisis** crisis *f* de los 40

midnight /ˈmɪdnaɪt/ *n* medianoche *f*; **at ~** a medianoche; (*before n*) **M~ Mass** misa *f* de *or* del gallo; ▸**oil**[1] **A4**

midpoint /ˈmɪdpɔɪnt/ *n* punto *m* medio

midriff /ˈmɪdrɪf/ *n* estómago *m*; (Anat) diafragma *m*

midshipman /ˈmɪdʃɪpmən/ *n* (*pl* **-men** /-mən/) guardiamarina *m*

midst /mɪdst/ *n*: **in the ~ of sth** en medio de algo; **in our/their ~** entre nosotros/ellos

midstream /ˈmɪdˈstriːm/ *n*: **it was floating in ~** estaba flotando en el medio de la corriente; **I interrupted him in ~** lo interrumpí (en plena parrafada); ▸**horse A**

midsummer /ˈmɪdˈsʌmər ‖ ˌmɪdˈsʌmə(r)/ *n* [u] pleno verano *m*; **M~'s Day** el solsticio estival *or* vernal; (in the Northern hemisphere) el día de San Juan; (*before n*) **~ madness** locura *f* de verano

midterm /ˈmɪdtɜːrm ‖ ˌmɪdˈtɜːm/ *n*

A (Govt) mitad *f* del período de gobierno

B **midterms** *pl* (AmE Educ) exámenes *mpl* parciales

midtown /ˈmɪdˈtaʊn/ *n* casco *m*, centro *m*; (*before n*) ‹*apartment/hotel*› de la periferia del centro

midway /ˈmɪdˈweɪ/ *adv* ‹*stop*› a mitad de camino, a medio camino; **~ through the morning** a media mañana

midweek[1] /ˈmɪdˈwiːk/ *n*: **around ~** a mediados de semana; (*before n*) ‹*concert/flight*› de entre semana

midweek[2] *adv* entre semana, los días de semana

Midwest /ˈmɪdˈwest/ *n* **the ~** *la región central de los EEUU*

midwife /ˈmɪdwaɪf/ *n* (*pl* **-wives**) partera *f*, comadrona *f*, matrona *f*; **male ~** partero *m*

midwinter /ˈmɪdˈwɪntər/ *n* [u] pleno invierno *m*

miffed /mɪft/ *adj* (colloq) (*pred*) picado (fam), ofendido

might[1] /maɪt/ *v mod*

A *past of* **may**[1]

B [1] (asking permission) (esp BrE) podría (*or* podríamos *etc*); **~ I make a suggestion?** si se me permite (hacer) una sugerencia …, ¿podría hacer una sugerencia? [2] (in suggestions, expressing annoyance, regret) poder*; **you ~ at least listen** al menos podrías *or* podías escuchar

C (indicating possibility) [*La posibilidad que indica* **might** *es más remota que la que expresan* **may** *o* **could**]: **somebody ~ have found it** pudiera ser que alguien lo hubiera encontrado, a lo mejor alguien lo encontró; **it ~ (well) have been disastrous if the police hadn't arrived** podría haber sido catastrófico si no hubiera llegado la policía; **as you ~ imagine** como te podrás imaginar

D (indicating sth is natural): **he rang to apologize — and** *o* **as well he ~!** llamó para pedir perdón — ¡era lo menos que podía hacer!

E [1] (conceding): **the house ~ not be big, but …** la casa no será grande pero …, puede ser que la casa no sea grande, pero … [2] (asking for information) (frml): **who ~ that gentleman be?** ¿quién es ese caballero?

F (indicating purpose): **he died that others ~ live** (liter) murió para que otros vivieran

might[2] *n* [u] poder *m*, poderío *m*; **with all one's ~** con todas sus (*or* mis *etc*) fuerzas; ***to struggle with* ~ *and main*** luchar con todas sus (*or* mis *etc*) fuerzas

mighty[1] /ˈmaɪti/ *adj* **-tier, -tiest** [1] (powerful) ‹*empire/ruler*› poderoso; ‹*kick/blow*› fortísimo, tremendo (fam) [2] (imposing) ‹*ocean/river*› imponente, inmenso

mighty[2] *pl n* (liter) **the ~** los poderosos; **how are the ~ fallen!** (set phrase, hum) ¡cómo caen los poderosos!

mighty[3] *adv* (colloq) (*as intensifier*) muy; **a ~ fine pair of boots** unas botas sensacionales *or* estupendas

migraine /ˈmaɪgreɪn/ *n* [c u] jaqueca *f*, migraña *f*

migrant[1] /ˈmaɪgrənt/ *n* [1] (Zool) (species) especie *f* migratoria; (bird) ave *f*‡ migratoria [2] (person) trabajador, -dora *m,f* itinerante; (foreign) trabajador extranjero, trabajadora extranjera *m,f*

migrant[2] *adj* [1] (Zool) migratorio [2] (*before n*) ‹*worker/labor*› itinerante; (foreign) extranjero

migrate /ˈmaɪgreɪt ‖ maɪˈgreɪt/ *vi* emigrar

migration /maɪˈgreɪʃən/ *n* [u c] migración *f*, emigración *f*

mike /maɪk/ *n* (colloq) micro *m* (fam)

milage *n* ▸**mileage**

Milan /mɪˈlæn/ *n* Milán *m*

mild /maɪld/ *adj* **-er, -est**

A [1] (gentle) ‹*person*› afable, dulce; ‹*manner*› suave; ‹*criticism*› suave, leve [2] (not serious or potent) ‹*attack/form*› ligero, leve; ‹*discomfort*› ligero, leve; **a ~ bout of flu** una gripe no muy fuerte

B ‹*climate*› templado, benigno; ‹*winter*› no muy frío

C ‹*cheese/tobacco/detergent/sedative*› suave

mildew /ˈmɪlduː ‖ ˈmɪldjuː/ *n* [u] (on plants) mildeu *m*, mildiu *m*; (on wall, fabric) moho *m*

mildly /maɪldli/ *adv* [1] (gently) ‹*rebuke*› suavemente, gentilmente; **to put it ~** por no decir algo peor [2] (slightly) ligeramente

mild-mannered /ˈmaɪldˈmænərd ‖ ˌmaɪldˈmænəd/ *adj* afable, de modales suaves

mile /maɪl/ *n* milla *f* (*1.609 metros*); **how many ~s to the gallon?** ¿cuántas millas por galón?; **that's ~s away from here** (colloq) eso está lejísimos de aquí; **I'd recognize that voice a ~ off** reconocería esa voz en cualquier sitio; **sorry, I was ~s away** perdona, estaba pensando en otra cosa *or* no estaba prestando atención; ***it sticks*** *o* ***stands out a* ~** se ve *or* se nota a la legua; ▸**inch**[1]

m

mileage /'maɪlɪdʒ/ *n*
A (Auto) **1** [c u] (distance traveled) distancia *f* recorrida (*en millas*), ≈ kilometraje *m*; (in aviation, etc) millaje *m*; **this car has (a) high ~** este coche ha hecho muchas millas **2** [u] (charge) tarifa *f* por milla **3** [u] (allowance) pago *m* por milla recorrida
B [u] (advantage, profit): **they want to extract maximum ~ from the Pope's visit** quieren explotar al máximo la visita del Papa
mileometer /maɪ'lɑːmətər || maɪ'lɒmɪtə(r)/ *n* (BrE) ≈ cuentakilómetros *m*
milestone /'maɪlstəʊn/ *n* (on road) mojón *m*; (significant event) hito *m*, jalón *m*
milieu /miːl'jɜː/ *n* (frml) entorno *m*, medio *m*
militant¹ /'mɪlɪtənt/ *adj* militante, combativo
militant² *n* militante *mf*
militarism /'mɪlətərɪzəm/ *n* [u] militarismo *m*
militaristic /,mɪlətə'rɪstɪk || ,mɪlɪtə'rɪstɪk/ *adj* militarista
militarize /'mɪlətəraɪz || 'mɪlɪtəraɪz/ *vt* militarizar*
military¹ /'mɪləteri || 'mɪlɪtri/ *adj* militar; **~ academy** (in US) escuela *f* militar; **~ coup** golpe *m* militar; **to do ~ service** hacer* *or* prestar el servicio militar
military² *n* **the ~** los militares, el ejército
military police *n* [u] policía *f* militar
militate /'mɪləteɪt || 'mɪlɪteɪt/ *vi* (frml): **this problem ~s against his chances of success** este problema incide negativamente en sus posibilidades de éxito
militia /mə'lɪʃə || mɪ'lɪʃə/ *n* (+ *sing or pl vb*) milicia *f*
militiaman /mə'lɪʃəmən/ *n* (*pl* **-men** /-mən/) miliciano *m*
milk¹ /mɪlk/ *n* [u] **1** leche *f*; ***it's no use crying over spilt ~*** a lo hecho pecho; (*before n*) ‹*production/bottle*› de leche; ‹*product*› lácteo; **~ chocolate** chocolate *m* con leche **2** (lotion) (BrE) leche *f*, crema *f*
milk² *vt* **1** ‹*cow/herd*› ordeñar **2** (exploit) explotar; **they ~ the benefit system for all it's worth** sacan todo lo que pueden del sistema de seguridad social
milking /'mɪlkɪŋ/ *n* [u] ordeña *f* (AmL), ordeño *m* (esp Esp); **to do the ~** ordeñar
milk: **~maid** *n* lechera *f*, ordeñadora *f*; **~man** /'mɪlkmən/ *n* (*pl* **-men** /-mən/) lechero *m*; **~ round** *n* (BrE) (delivery) reparto *m* de leche; (Busn, Educ) *visitas que hacen las industrias a las universidades en busca de personal*; **~ run** *n*: *viaje rutinario y sin complicaciones*; **~ shake** *n* batido *m*, (leche *f*) malteada *f* (AmL), merengada *f* (Ven); **~ tooth** *n* diente *m* de leche
milky /'mɪlki/ *adj* **-kier, -kiest** lechoso; ‹*coffee/tea*› con mucha leche; **a ~ drink** una bebida con leche
Milky Way *n* **the ~** la Vía Láctea
mill¹ /mɪl/ *n*
A **1** (building, machine) molino *m*; ***to go through the ~*** «*person*» vérselas* negras (fam), pasarlas duras **2** (for pepper etc) molinillo *m*
B (*cotton ~*) fábrica *f* de tejidos de algodón; (*paper ~*) fábrica *f* de papel, papelera *f*; (*saw ~*) aserradero *m*, aserrío *m* (Col, Ec)
C (in US) (Fin) milésima *f* de dólar (*unidad usada en el cálculo de impuestos*)
mill² *vt*
A ‹*flour*› moler*
B ‹*lumber*› aserrar*, serrar*; ‹*cloth*› abatanar, batanar
▪ **mill** *vi* (circulate) «*crowd*» dar* vueltas, pulular, arremolinarse; **a ~ing crowd** un remolino de gente
Phrasal verb
• **mill about, mill around** [v ▸ adv] «*crowd*» dar* vueltas, pulular, arremolinarse
millage /'mɪlɪdʒ/ *n* [u] (in US) *tasa impositiva expresada en milésimas de dólar por dólar*
millennium /mɪ'leniəm/ *n* (*pl* **-niums** *or* **-nia** /-niə/) milenio *m*
miller /'mɪlər || 'mɪlə(r)/ *n* molinero, -ra *m,f*
millet /'mɪlət || 'mɪlɪt/ *n* [u] mijo *m*
milli- /'mɪli/ *pref* mili-
milligram /'mɪləgræm || 'mɪlɪgræm/ *n* miligramo *m*
milliliter, (BrE) **millilitre** /'mɪlə,liːtər/ *n* mililitro *m*
millimeter, (BrE) **millimetre** /'mɪlə,miːtər || 'mɪlɪmiːtə(r)/ *n* milímetro *m*
milliner /'mɪlənər/ *n* sombrerero, -ra *m,f* de señoras
million /'mɪljən/ *n* millón *m*; **thanks a ~!** (colloq) un millón de gracias; **a ~/two ~ people** un millón/dos millones de personas; **she really is one in a ~** es única, como ella no hay dos; *see also* **hundred**
millionaire /'mɪljə'ner || ,mɪljə'neə(r)/ *n* millonario, -ria *m,f*; (*before n*) **M~'s Row** calle *f* de los millonarios
millionairess /'mɪljə'nerəs/ *n* millonaria *f*
millionth¹ /'mɪljənθ/ *adj* millonésimo; *see also* **fifth¹**
millionth² *n* **1** (Math) millonésimo *m* **2** (part) millonésima parte *f*
millipede /'mɪləpiːd || 'mɪlɪpiːd/ *n* milpiés *m*
millisecond /'mɪlə,sekənd || 'mɪlɪ,sekənd/ *n* milésima *f* de segundo, milisegundo *m*
mill: **~pond** *n* represa *f* de molino; ***as calm*** *o* ***smooth as a ~pond*** como una balsa de aceite; **~stone** *n* muela *f*, rueda *f* de molino; ***to be (like) a ~stone around sb's neck*** ser* una cruz *or* una carga para algn
milometer /maɪ'lɑːmətər/ *n* ▸**mileometer**
mime¹ /maɪm/ *n* **1** [u] (technique) mímica *f* **2** [c] **~ (artist)** mimo *mf* **3** [c] (performance) pantomima *f*
mime² *vt* imitar, hacer* la mímica de
▪ **mime** *vi* hacer* la mímica
mimic¹ /'mɪmɪk/ *vt* **-ck-** ‹*voice/accent*› imitar, remedar
mimic² *n* imitador, -dora *m,f*
mimicry /'mɪmɪkri/ *n* [u] (imitation) imitación *f*; (Biol) mimetismo *m*
min /mɪn/
A (= **minimum**) mín.
B (*pl* **mins**) (= **minutes**) min.
minaret /'mɪnə'ret/ *n* minarete *m*, alminar *m*
mince¹ /mɪns/ *vt* ‹*onions*› picar* (*en trozos menudos*); ‹*meat*› moler* *or* (Esp, RPl) picar*; ***not to ~ (one's) words*** no andar(se)* con rodeos, no tener* pelos en la lengua (fam)
▪ **mince** *vi* caminar con afectación *or* amaneramiento
mince² *n* [u] (BrE) carne *f* molida *or* (Esp, RPl) picada
mince: **~meat** *n* [u] *picadillo de frutos secos, grasa y especias usado en pastelería*; ***to make ~meat of sb*** (colloq) hacer* picadillo *or* puré a algn (fam); **~ pie** *n* (BrE) *pastelillo hecho con* **~meat**
mincer /'mɪnsər || 'mɪnsə(r)/ *n* (BrE) máquina *f* de moler *or* (Esp, RPl) de picar carne
mind¹ /maɪnd/ *n*
A **1** (Psych) mente *f*; **the unconscious ~** el inconsciente; **with an open/a closed ~** sin/con ideas preconcebidas; **to keep an open ~ on sth** mantener* una mentalidad abierta *or* no cerrarse* frente a algo; **I'm convinced in my own ~ that ...** yo estoy plenamente convencido de que ...; **I tried to push it to the back of my ~** traté de no pensar en ello; **to bear** *o* **keep sth/sb in ~** tener* algo/a algn en cuenta, tener* presente algo/a algn; **to bring** *o* **call sth to ~**: **this case brings to ~ another incident** este caso (nos) recuerda otro incidente; **to come to ~**: **nothing in particular comes to ~** no se me ocurre nada en particular; **to have sth/sb in ~** tener* algo/a algn en mente; **with that in ~** pensando en eso; **to have sth on one's ~**: **what's on your ~?** ¿qué es lo que te preocupa?; **to prey** *o* **weigh on sb's ~**: **it's been preying** *o* **weighing on my ~** me ha estado preocupando; **that put my ~ at rest** con eso me tranquilicé *or* me quedé tranquilo; **put it out of your ~!** ¡no pienses más en eso!; **I can see her now in my ~'s eye** es como si la estuviera viendo; **you're not ill: it's all in the ~** no estás enfermo, es pura sugestión; **I can't get him/the thought out of my ~** no puedo quitármelo de la cabeza, no hago más que pensar en él/en eso; **it never crossed my ~ that ...** ni se me ocurrió pensar que ..., nunca me habría imaginado que ..., ni se me pasó por la cabeza que ...; ***to take a load*** *o* ***weight off sb's ~*** quitarle a algn un peso de encima; ***great ~s think alike*** (hum) los genios pensamos igual **2** (mentality) mentalidad *f* **3** (Phil) (*no art*) espíritu *m*; **it's a question of ~ over matter** es cuestión de voluntad
B (attention): **her ~ wandered** divagaba; **my ~ was on other things** tenía la cabeza en otras cosas; **to put one's ~ to sth**: **he can be quite charming if he puts his ~ to it** cuando quiere *or* cuando se lo propone, es un verdadero encanto; **you could finish it today if you put your ~ to it** si te lo propones puedes terminarlo hoy; **he needs**

m

something to take his ~ off it necesita algo que lo distraiga; **it slipped my ~** se me olvidó
C **1** (opinion): **to change one's ~** cambiar de opinión *or* de parecer *or* de idea; **to make up one's ~** decidirse; **my ~'s made up** lo he decidido, estoy decidido; **he spoke his ~** dijo lo que pensaba, habló sin tapujos; **to my ~** a mi parecer, en mi opinión; ***to be in** o **of two ~s about sth*** estar* indeciso respecto a algo **2** (will, intention): **he has a ~ of his own** (he is obstinate) es muy empecinado *or* porfiado *or* testarudo; (he knows his own mind) sabe muy bien lo que quiere; **this machine seems to have a ~ of its own!** ¡parece que esta máquina estuviera embrujada!; **to have a ~ to + INF**: **when he has a ~ to** cuando quiere, cuando se lo propone; **I've a good ~ to complain to the manager** tengo ganas de ir a quejarme al gerente; **I've half a ~ to tell her myself** casi estoy por decírselo *or* casi se lo diría yo mismo; **she certainly knows her own ~** ciertamente sabe lo que quiere
D (mental faculties) juicio *m*, razón *f*; **to be of sound ~** (frml) estar* en pleno uso de sus (*or* mis *etc*) facultades (mentales) (frml); **to be/go out of one's ~** estar*/volverse* loco; **no one in her/his right ~ ...** nadie en su sano juicio *or* en sus cabales ...; ***to blow sb's ~*** (colloq) alucinar a algn (fam)
E (person) mente *f*, cabeza *f*, cerebro *m*

mind² *vt*
A (look after) ‹*children*› cuidar, cuidar de; ‹*seat/place*› guardar, cuidar; ‹*shop/office*› atender*
B (*usu in imperative*) **1** (be careful about): **you'd better ~ your temper!** ¡más vale que controles ese genio!; **~ your head!** ¡ojo *or* cuidado con la cabeza!; **~ how you go!** (colloq) cuídate, vete con cuidado; **~ (that) you don't forget!** procura no olvidarte **2** (concern oneself about) preocuparse por; **never ~ him!** ¡no le hagas caso!; **don't ~ me** no se preocupen por mí, hagan como si yo no estuviera **3** **never mind** (let alone): **we didn't break even, never ~ make a profit** ni siquiera cubrimos los gastos, ni hablar pues de ganancias
C (object to) (*usu neg or interrog*): **I don't ~ the noise/cold** no me molesta *or* no me importa el ruido/frío; **I don't ~ him, but I can't stand her** él no me disgusta, pero a ella no la soporto; **I wouldn't ~ a drink** (colloq) no me vendría mal un trago; **I don't ~ what you do** me da igual *or* me da lo mismo lo que hagas; **to ~ -ING**: **would you ~ waiting?** ¿le importaría esperar?, espere, por favor; **if you don't ~ me saying so** si me permites

■ **mind** *vi*
A (*in imperative*) **1** (take care): **~!** ¡ojo!, ¡cuidado! **2** (concern oneself) **never ~** no importa, no te preocupes (*or* no se preocupen *etc*); **never you ~!** ¡(a ti) qué te importa!
B (object) (*usu neg or interrog*): **I don't ~** me da igual *or* lo mismo; **have another one — I don't ~ if I do!** (BrE hum) tómate otro — hombre, no te diría que no; (expressing indignation) **do you ~ if I smoke? — yes, I do ~!** ¿te importa si fumo? — ¡sí que me importa!; **do you ~!** (expressing indignation) ¡hágame el favor!
C (take note) (*only in imperative*): **I'm not promising, ~!** mira que no te lo prometo ¿eh?; **he's very generous; ~ you, he can afford to be!** es muy generoso; pero claro, puede permitírselo

Phrasal verb
• **mind out** [v ▸ adv] tener* cuidado; **~ out!** ¡cuidado!

mind: **~-blowing** /ˈmaɪndˌbləʊɪŋ/ *adj* (colloq) alucinante, de alucine (Esp arg); **~-boggling** /ˈmaɪndˌbɑːglɪŋ || ˈmaɪndˌbɒglɪŋ/ *adj* (colloq) que no le cabe a uno en la cabeza, inconcebible, alucinante

-minded /ˈmaɪndəd || ˈmaɪndɪd/ *suff*: **business~** con mentalidad para los negocios; **reform~** reformista

minder /ˈmaɪndər || ˈmaɪndə(r)/ *n* (BrE colloq) guardaespaldas *m*, gorila *m* (arg), guarura *m* (Méx)

mindful /ˈmaɪndfəl/ *adj* (*pred*) **~ OF sth** consciente DE algo

mind game *n* estratagema *f*, juego *m* psicológico

mindless /ˈmaɪndləs || ˈmaɪndlɪs/ *adj* ‹*activity*› mecánico, tonto; ‹*violence/obedience*› ciego, sin sentido

mind: **~-reader** *n* adivino, -na *m,f*; **~-set** *n* modo *m* de pensar; **~share** /ˈmaɪndʃer || ˈmaɪndʃeə(r)/ *n* [u] conciencia *f* de marca

mine¹ /maɪn/ *n*
A (Min) mina *f*; **to go down the ~(s)** trabajar en las minas; ***to be a ~ of information*** ser* una mina de información
B (Mil) mina *f*

mine² *pron* (*sing*) mío, mía; (*pl*) míos, mías; **~ is here** el mío/la mía está aquí; **a friend of ~** un amigo mío; **it's a hobby of ~** es uno de mis hobbies, es un hobby que tengo

mine³ *vt*
A (Min) ‹*gold/coal*› extraer*; ‹*area/seam*› explotar
B (Mil) minar

minefield /ˈmaɪnfiːld/ *n* (Mil) campo *m* minado, campo *m* de minas; **a political ~** un polvorín político

miner /ˈmaɪnər || ˈmaɪnə(r)/ *n* minero, -ra *m,f*; **coal ~** minero del carbón

mineral /ˈmɪnərəl/ *n* **1** mineral *m* **2** **minerals** *pl* (BrE Culin) refrescos *mpl*, (bebidas *fpl*) gaseosas *fpl* (CS)

mineralogy /ˈmɪnəˈrælədʒi/ *n* [u] mineralogía *f*

mineral: **~ oil** *n* [u] (AmE Pharm) aceite *m* de parafina, parafina *f* líquida; **~ water** *n* [u] agua *f*‡ mineral

mineshaft /ˈmaɪnʃæft/ *n* pozo *m* (*de una mina*)

minestrone (soup) /ˈmɪnəˈstrəʊni || ˌmɪnɪˈstrəʊni/ *n* [u] minestrón *m* *or* (Esp) minestrone *f* *or* *m*

minesweeper /ˈmaɪnˌswiːpər || ˈmaɪnˌswiːpə(r)/ *n* dragaminas *m*

mingle /ˈmɪŋgəl/ *vi* **1** «*people*» mezclarse; (at a party etc) circular **2** «*liquids*» mezclarse; «*sounds*» fundirse
■ **mingle** *vt* **to ~ sth WITH sth** mezclar algo CON algo

mingy /ˈmɪndʒi/ *adj* **-gier, -giest** (colloq) ‹*person*› agarrado (fam), amarrete (AmS fam), pinche (AmC fam); ‹*portion*› miserable

mini /ˈmɪni/ *n* **1** (Comput) mini *m*, minicomputadora *f* (esp AmL), miniordenador *m* (Esp) **2** (miniskirt) mini *f* (fam), minifalda *f*

mini- /ˈmɪni/ *pref* mini-

miniature¹ /ˈmɪnɪtʃʊr || ˈmɪnɪtʃə(r)/ *n* **1** (small copy, version) miniatura *f* **2** (Art) miniatura *f* **3** (bottle) *botellita en miniatura de una bebida alcohólica*

miniature² *adj* (*before n*) ‹*portrait*› en miniatura; ‹*poodle*› enano; **~ golf** minigolf *m*, golfito *m* (AmL)

minibus /ˈmɪnibʌs/ *n* microbús *m*, micro *m*

minicab /ˈmɪnikæb/ *n* (BrE) taxi *m* (*que se pide por teléfono*)

minicomputer /ˈmɪnikəmˌpjuːtər || ˌmɪnikəmˈpjuːtə(r)/ *n* minicomputadora *f*, miniordenador *m* (Esp)

minim /ˈmɪnəm || ˈmɪnɪm/ *n* (BrE) blanca *f*

minimal /ˈmɪnəməl || ˈmɪnɪməl/ *adj* mínimo

minimalize /ˈmɪnəməlaɪz || ˈmɪnɪməlaɪz/ *vt* minimizar*

minimize /ˈmɪnəmaɪz/ *vt* ‹*risk/cost*› minimizar*

minimoto /ˌmɪnɪˈməʊtəʊ/ *n* (BrE) minimoto *f*

minimum¹ /ˈmɪnəməm || ˈmɪnɪməm/ *n* mínimo *m*; **he always does the absolute ~** siempre sigue la ley del menor *or* mínimo esfuerzo; **to reduce sth to a ~** reducir* algo al mínimo

minimum² *adj* (*before n*) mínimo

mining /ˈmaɪnɪŋ/ *n* [u] minería *f*; **coal/gold ~** extracción *f* de carbón/oro; (*before n*) ‹*company/town*› minero

minion /ˈmɪnjən/ *n* (underling) (liter) subalterno, -na *m,f*, adlátere *mf*

miniskirt /ˈmɪniskɜːrt || ˈmɪniskɜːt/ *n* minifalda *f*

minister¹ /ˈmɪnəstər || ˈmɪnɪstə(r)/ *n*
A (Relig) pastor, -tora *m,f*
B (Pol) ministro, -tra *m,f*, secretario, -ria *m,f* (Méx)

minister² *vi* **to ~ TO sb** cuidar DE algn, atender* a algn

ministerial /ˈmɪnəˈstɪriəl || ˌmɪnɪˈstɪəriəl/ *adj* (*before n*) ‹*duties/rank*› ministerial

minister of state *n* (in UK) viceministro, -tra *m,f*

ministry /ˈmɪnəstri || ˈmɪnɪstri/ *n* (*pl* **-tries**)
A (Relig): **the ~** la clerecía; (esp in the Catholic church) el ministerio sacerdotal, el sacerdocio; **to go into** *o* **enter the ~** hacerse* clérigo; (esp in the Catholic church) hacerse* sacerdote
B (Pol) **1** **Ministry** (department) ministerio *m*, secretaría *f* (Méx) **2** (period of office) gestión *f* ministerial

mink /mɪŋk/ *n* (*pl* **~s** *or* **~**) **1** [c] (animal) visón *m* **2** [u] (fur) visón *m*, piel *f* de visón; (*before n*) **a ~ coat** un abrigo de visón

Minn = **Minnesota**

minnow /ˈmɪnəʊ/ *n*: *pez pequeño de agua dulce*

m

minor¹ /'maɪnər || 'maɪnə(r)/ *adj*
A (unimportant) ‹*poet/work*› menor; ‹*role*› secundario, menor; ‹*road*› (in UK) secundario; ‹*operation*› de poca importancia *or* gravedad
B (Mus) menor; **B flat ~/C ~** si bemol menor/do menor

minor² *n*
A (Law) menor *mf* (de edad)
B (Educ) asignatura *f* secundaria
C **minors** *pl* (in US) (Sport colloq) **the ~s** las ligas menores

minor³ *vi* (in US) (Educ) **to ~ IN sth** estudiar algo como asignatura secundaria

Minorca /mə'nɔːrkə || mɪ'nɔːkə/ *n* Menorca *f*

minority /mə'nɔːrəti || maɪ'nɒrɪti/ *n* (*pl* **-ties**)
A 1 (smaller number) (+ *sing o pl vb*) minoría *f*; **to be in a/the ~** estar* en minoría; **a ~ of students share that view** los estudiantes que comparten ese punto de vista son una minoría; (*before n*) ‹*group/vote*› minoritario 2 (in US) (Govt) oposición *f*
B (Law) minoría *f* de edad

minor league *n* (in US) (Sport) liga *f* menor; (*before n*) ‹*baseball/player*› de la liga menor; ‹*politician*› de segundo orden, de segunda fila

minstrel /'mɪnstrəl/ *n* trovador *m*, juglar *m*

mint¹ /mɪnt/ *n*
A (Bot, Culin) 1 [u] (*spear~*) menta *f* (verde) 2 [u] (*pepper~*) menta *f*, hierbabuena *f* 3 [c] (confection) pastilla *f* de menta
B [c] (Fin) casa *f* de la moneda; **to make/cost/be worth a ~** hacer*/costar*/valer* un dineral *or* una fortuna

mint² *vt* ‹*coin*› acuñar

mint³ *adj* (*before n*) ‹*coin/stamp*› sin usar; **in ~ condition** en perfecto estado, como nuevo

minuet /'mɪnju'et/ *n* minué *m*

minus¹ /'maɪnəs/ *n* (*pl* **-nuses** *or* **-nusses**) 1 **~ (sign)** signo *m* de menos, menos *m* 2 (disadvantage) (colloq) desventaja *f*, contra *m*

minus² *adj* 1 (disadvantageous) (colloq) (*before n*) **on the ~ side, ...** un factor negativo *or* en contra es que ... 2 (negative) (*before n*) ‹*number/ion*› negativo; **-3** *(léase: minus three)* -3 *(read as: menos tres)* 3 (Educ): **A-** *(léase: A minus) calificación entre A y B, más alta que B+*

minus³ *prep* 1 menos; **3 - 1 = 2** *(léase: three minus one equals two)* 3 - 1 = 2 *(read as: tres menos uno es igual a dos)* 2 (without, missing) (colloq) sin

minuscule /'mɪnəskjuːl/ *adj* minúsculo

minute¹ /'mɪnət || 'mɪnɪt/ *n*
A 1 (unit of time) minuto *m*; **seven ~s to eight** las ocho menos siete minutos, siete minutos para las ocho (AmL exc RPl); **he lives about five ~s from here** vive a unos cinco minutos de aquí; **there's one born every ~** (set phrase) ¡hay cada idiota ...! (fam); (*before n*) **~ hand** minutero *m*; **~ steak** filete *m* (*delgado*) 2 (short period) minuto *m*, momento *m*; **I won't be a ~** no tardo ni un minuto; **could I see you for a ~?** ¿puedo hablar contigo un momento?; **without a ~ to spare** en el último minuto; **not a ~ too soon!** ¡en buena hora! 3 (instant) minuto *m*; **I enjoyed every ~ of the vacation** disfruté de las vacaciones al máximo; **any ~ (now)** de un momento a otro; **at this very ~** en este preciso instante; **at the last ~** a última hora; **the ~ (that) I saw the house** en cuanto vi la casa
B 1 (memorandum) acta *f* 2 (of meeting): **the ~s** el acta

minute² /maɪ'nuːt || maɪ'njuːt/ *adj* 1 (very small) ‹*amount*› mínimo; ‹*object*› diminuto 2 (detailed) (*before n*) ‹*scrutiny/care*› minucioso

minutely /maɪ'nuːtli || maɪ'njuːtli/ *adv* ‹*examine*› minuciosamente, con minuciosidad; ‹*compare*› detalladamente

minutiae /mə'nuːʃiiː || maɪ'njuːʃiː, mɪ-/ *pl n* (frml) minucias *fpl*, nimiedades *fpl*

miracle /'mɪrɪkəl || 'mɪrəkəl/ *n* milagro *m*; **to work ~s** hacer* milagros; (*before n*) ‹*drug/cure*› milagroso

miraculous /mə'rækjələs || mɪ'rækjʊləs/ *adj* milagroso

miraculously /mə'rækjələsli/ *adv* milagrosamente

mirage /mə'rɑːʒ || 'mɪrɑːʒ, mɪ'rɑːʒ/ *n* espejismo *m*

mire /maɪr || 'maɪə(r)/ *n* [c u] (liter) lodo *m* (liter), fango *m*

mirror¹ /'mɪrər || 'mɪrə(r)/ *n* espejo *m*; (*driving ~*) (espejo *m*) retrovisor *m*; **a true ~ of public opinion** un verdadero reflejo de la opinión pública

mirror² *vt* reflejar

mirror image *n* 1 (Math, Opt) imagen *f* especular 2 (direct opposite) reflejo *m*

mirth /mɜːrθ/ *n* [u] (liter) regocijo *m* (liter), alborozo *m* (liter)

mirthless /'mɜːrθləs || 'mɜːθlɪs/ *adj* triste, amargo

MIS *n* = **management information system**

misadventure /'mɪsəd'ventʃər || ˌmɪsəd'ventʃə(r)/ *n* desventura *f*; **death by ~** (BrE Law) muerte *f* accidental

misanthropist /mɪ'sænθrəpəst/ misántropo, -pa *m,f*

misapply /'mɪsə'plaɪ/ *vt* **-plies, -plying, -plied** ‹*word/expression*› usar indebidamente, emplear mal; ‹*law/regulation*› aplicar* mal; ‹*funds/contribution*› malversar

misapprehension /mɪs'æprɪ'hentʃən || ˌmɪsæprɪ'henʃən/ *n* [c u] (frml) malentendido *m*; **to be under a ~** estar* en un error; **they are laboring under the ~ that ...** siguen convencidos de que ...

misappropriate /'mɪsə'prəʊprieɪt/ *vt* malversar

misappropriation /'mɪsə'prəʊpri'eɪʃən/ *n* [u c] malversación *f*

misbehave /'mɪsbɪ'heɪv/ *vi* portarse mal

misbehavior, (BrE) **misbehaviour** /'mɪsbɪ'heɪvjər || ˌmɪsbɪ'heɪvɪə(r)/ *n* [u] mala conducta *f*

misc /mɪsk/ = **miscellaneous**

miscalculate /'mɪs'kælkjəleɪt/ *vt/i* calcular mal

miscalculation /'mɪskælkjə'leɪʃən || ˌmɪskælkjʊ'leɪʃən/ *n* [c u] error *m* de cálculo

miscarriage /'mɪs'kærɪdʒ/ *n*
A (Med) aborto *m* espontáneo *or* no provocado; **to have/suffer a ~** tener*/sufrir un aborto, perder* un niño
B **a ~ of justice** una injusticia, un fallo injusto

miscarry /'mɪs'kæri/ *vi* **-ries, -rying, -ried** 1 (Med) abortar (*espontáneamente*), tener* un aborto, perder* el niño *or* el bebé (fam) 2 (liter) ‹‹*plan*›› malograrse (liter)

miscast /'mɪs'kæst || ˌmɪs'kɑːst/ *vt* (*past & past p* **-cast**) ‹*actor*› darle* un papel inapropiado a

miscellaneous /'mɪsə'leɪniəs/ *adj* ‹*collection/crowd*› heterogéneo; ‹*assortment*› variado; **~ objects** objetos *mpl* de todo tipo; **file it under ~** archívalo en 'varios'

miscellany /'mɪsəleɪni || mɪ'seləni/ *n* (*pl* **-nies**) (of objects) miscelánea *f*; (Lit) antología *f*

mischance /'mɪs'tʃæns || ˌmɪs'tʃɑːns/ *n* [u c] infortunio *m*, desgracia *f*; **by (some) ~** desafortunadamente

mischief /'mɪstʃəf || 'mɪstʃɪf/ *n* 1 [u] (naughtiness): **to be up to ~** estar* haciendo travesuras *or* diabluras; **don't get into any ~** no hagas diabluras *or* travesuras 2 [u c] (trouble, harm) daño *m*; **to make ~** causar daños; **to do oneself a ~** (BrE colloq) hacerse* daño, lastimarse (AmL)

mischief-maker /'mɪstʃəfˌmeɪkər || 'mɪstʃɪfˌmeɪkə(r)/ *n* alborotador, -dora *m,f*

mischievous /'mɪstʃəvəs || 'mɪstʃɪvəs/ *adj* ‹*child*› travieso; ‹*grin*› pícaro

mischievously /'mɪstʃəvəsli || 'mɪstʃɪvəsli/ *adv* ‹*grin*› pícaramente; ‹*tease*› con picardía, juguetonamente

misconceived /'mɪskən'siːvd/ *adj* desacertado, equivocado; ‹*plan*› descabellado

misconception /'mɪskən'sepʃən/ *n* error *m*, idea *f* falsa

misconduct /'mɪs'kɑːndʌkt || ˌmɪs'kɒndʌkt/ *n* [u] (frml) mala conducta *f*; **professional ~** mala conducta en el ejercicio de la profesión, falta *f* de ética profesional

misconstrue /'mɪskən'struː/ *vt* (frml) malinterpretar

misdeed /'mɪs'diːd/ *n* fechoría *f*, delito *m*

misdemeanor, (BrE) **misdemeanour** /'mɪsdɪ'miːnər || ˌmɪsdɪ'miːnə(r)/ *n* 1 (Law) delito *m* menor, falta *f* 2 (minor misdeed) fechoría *f*, jugarreta *f* (fam)

misdirect /'mɪsdə'rekt, -daɪ- || ˌmɪsdaɪ'rekt, -dɪ-/ *vt* 1 ‹*money*› emplear mal; ‹*effort*› encauzar* mal; ‹*funds*› malversar 2 (misadvise) ‹*person*› malaconsejar; **he got lost because someone ~ed him** se perdió porque le indicaron mal el camino

miser /'maɪzər/ *n* avaro, -ra *m,f*, tacaño, -ña *m,f*

miserable /'mɪzərəbəl/ *adj*
A 1 (in low spirits) abatido; **we were tired and ~** estábamos cansados y con el ánimo por los suelos; **don't look so ~** ¡alegra esa cara! 2 (depressing) ‹*weather*› deprimente; ‹*prospect*› triste; **to make sb's life ~** amargarle* la vida a algn

m

B 1 (mean-spirited) miserable; **a ~ $2** dos míseros dólares 2 (wretched, poor) mísero 3 ‹*episode/failure*› lamentable

miserably /ˈmɪzərəbli/ *adv* 1 (unhappily) con abatimiento 2 ‹*dressed/housed*› miserablemente, míseramente 3 ‹*fail*› de manera lamentable

miserly /ˈmaɪzərli ‖ ˈmaɪzəli/ *adj* mezquino, ruin

misery /ˈmɪzəri/ *n* (*pl* **-ries**) 1 [u] (unhappiness) sufrimiento *m*; **the ~ of toothache** el suplicio de un dolor de muelas; **they put the dog out of its ~** sacrificaron al perro para que no sufriera más; **to put them out of their ~ he told them the final score** para que no siguieran torturándose, les dijo el resultado final; **to make sb's life a ~** amargarle* la vida a algn 2 [c] (miserable person) (BrE colloq) amargado, -da *m,f*

misfire /ˌmɪsˈfaɪr ‖ ˌmɪsˈfaɪə(r)/ *vi* «*gun/engine/plan*» fallar; **the joke ~d** a nadie le hizo gracia el chiste

misfit /ˈmɪsfɪt/ *n*: **a social ~** un inadaptado social

misfortune /mɪsˈfɔːrtʃən ‖ ˌmɪsˈfɔːtʃən, ˌmɪsˈfɔːtʃuːn/ *n* [c u] (frml) desgracia *f*; **to have the ~ to + INF** tener* la desgracia *or* la mala fortuna DE + INF

misgiving /mɪsˈgɪvɪŋ/ *n* [c u] recelo *m*, duda *f*

misgovernment /ˈmɪsˈgʌvərnmənt ‖ ˌmɪsˈgʌvənmənt/ *n* [u] mal gobierno *m*, desgobierno *m*

misguided /ˈmɪsˈgaɪdəd ‖ ˌmɪsˈgaɪdɪd/ *adj* equivocado; **a ~ attempt to help** un torpe intento de ayuda

mishandle /ˈmɪsˈhændl̩/ *vt* (deal with ineptly) llevar mal

mishap /ˈmɪshæp/ *n* percance *m*, contratiempo *m*

mishear /ˈmɪsˈhɪr ‖ ˌmɪsˈhɪə(r)/ (*past & past p* **-heard**) *vt* entender* mal

■ **mishear** *vi* entender* *or* oír* mal

mishit[1] /ˈmɪsˈhɪt/ *vt* (*pres p* **-hitting**; *past & past p* **-hit**) ‹*ball*› golpear mal, darle* mal a

mishit[2] /ˈmɪshɪt/ *n* golpe *m* defectuoso

mishmash /ˈmɪʃmæʃ/ *n* mezcolanza *f* (fam), batiburrillo *m* (fam)

misinform /ˈmɪsn̩ˈfɔːrm/ *vt* (frml) informar mal

misinformation /ˈmɪsn̩fərˈmeɪʃən ‖ ˌmɪsɪnfəˈmeɪʃən/ *n* [u] (frml) información *f* errónea

misinterpret /ˈmɪsn̩ˈtɜːrprət ‖ ˌmɪsɪnˈtɜːprɪt/ *vt* ‹*statement/action*› interpretar mal, malinterpretar; (deliberately) tergiversar; **he ~ed her nosiness as concern** tomó por interés lo que sólo era curiosidad

misinterpretation /ˈmɪsn̩ˈtɜːrprəˈteɪʃən ‖ ˌmɪsɪntɜːprɪˈteɪʃən/ *n* [c u] mala interpretación *f*

misjudge /ˈmɪsˈdʒʌdʒ/ *vt* 1 (judge unfairly) juzgar* mal 2 (miscalculate) calcular mal

mislay /ˈmɪsˈleɪ/ *vt* (*past & past p* **-laid**) perder* (*momentáneamente*)

mislead /ˈmɪsˈliːd/ *vt* (*past & past p* **-led**) engañar; ‹*court/parliament*› inducir* a error

misleading /ˈmɪsˈliːdɪŋ/ *adj* ‹*statement*› engañoso

misled /mɪsˈled/ *past & past p of* **mislead**

mismanage /ˈmɪsˈmænɪdʒ/ *vt* ‹*affair*› llevar *or* dirigir* mal; ‹*company*› administrar mal

mismanagement /ˈmɪsˈmænɪdʒmənt/ *n* [u] mala administración *f*

mismatch /ˈmɪsˈmætʃ/ *n* [u c] (of combination): **the armchairs and sofa were a ~** los sillones y el sofá no hacían juego

mismatched /ˈmɪsˈmætʃt/ *adj* ‹*teams/opponents*› desigual; **a ~ couple** una pareja dispareja

misnomer /ˈmɪsˈnəʊmər ‖ ˌmɪsˈnəʊmə(r)/ *n* (frml) nombre *m* poco apropiado

misogynist /mɪˈsɑːdʒənəst ‖ mɪˈsɒdʒɪnɪst/ *n* misógino *m*

misplace /ˈmɪsˈpleɪs/ *vt* perder* (*momentáneamente*)

misplaced /ˈmɪsˈpleɪst/ *adj* ‹*confidence*› depositado en quien no lo merece; ‹*enthusiasm*› que no viene al caso

misprint /ˈmɪsprɪnt/ *n* errata *f*, error *m* de imprenta

mispronounce /ˈmɪsprəˈnaʊns/ *vt* pronunciar mal

misquote /ˈmɪsˈkwəʊt/ *vt* citar incorrectamente

misread /ˈmɪsˈriːd/ *vt* (*past & past p* **-read** /-ˈred/) ‹*word*› leer* mal; ‹*intention*› interpretar mal, malinterpretar

misrepresent /ˈmɪsreprɪˈzent/ *vt* ‹*event*› deformar, falsear; ‹*remarks/views*› tergiversar; **she's been ~ed** han tergiversado sus palabras (*or* su declaración *etc*)

miss[1] /mɪs/ *n*

A 1 **Miss** (as title) señorita *f*; **M~ Jane Smith** la señorita Jane Smith; (in correspondence) Sra Jane Smith; **M~ World** Miss Mundo; **M~ Elizabeth** (dated) (in US: matron) doña Elizabeth; (in UK: younger sister) la señorita Elizabeth, la niña Elizabeth (AmL) 2 (*as form of address*) señorita

B (failure to hit) fallo *m*; **she had two unlucky ~es** erró el tiro dos veces por mala suerte; ***to give sth a ~*** (colloq): **I think I'll give swimming a ~ this afternoon** creo que esta tarde no voy a ir a nadar

miss[2] *vt*

(Sense I)

A 1 (fail to hit): **the bomb ~ed its target** la bomba no cayó en el blanco *or* objetivo; **he ~ed the target completely** no dio en el blanco; **the bullet just ~ed him** la bala le pasó rozando; **the car only just ~ed him** el coche por poco lo atropella 2 (overlook, fail to notice): **you ~ed three mistakes** se te pasaron (por alto) tres errores; **we ~ed the turning** nos pasamos (de donde deberíamos haber doblado); **you can't ~ it** lo va a ver enseguida, no tiene pérdida (Esp); **you've ~ed a bit** te quedó un pedacito sin pintar (*or* limpiar *etc*); **he never ~es my birthday** nunca se olvida de mi cumpleaños 3 (fail to hear, understand) no oír*; **sorry, I ~ed that** perdona, no te oí; **she doesn't ~ a thing** no se le escapa una (fam); **he's ~ed the point** no ha entendido; ▸**trick**[1] D 4 ‹*chance*› perder*, dejar pasar

B (fail to catch) ‹*bus/flight*› perder*; **sorry, you've just ~ed him** lo siento, acaba de irse; **I ~ed her in the crowd** había tanta gente que no la vi; ***to ~ the boat*** *o* ***bus*** perder* el tren

C 1 (fail to experience) perderse*; **I wouldn't have ~ed it for anything** no me lo hubiera perdido por nada (en el mundo); **you didn't ~ much** no te perdiste nada 2 (fail to attend) ‹*meeting*› faltar a; ‹*party/show*› perderse*

D (avoid) ‹*town/crowds*› evitar; **to ~ -ING**: **he just ~ed getting soaked** por poco se empapa

(Sense II) 1 (regret absence of) ‹*friend/country*› echar de menos, extrañar (esp AmL); **I ~ you (terribly)** te echo (muchísimo) de menos, te extraño (muchísimo) (esp AmL); **to ~ -ING**: **I ~ going for walks in the country** echo de menos *or* (esp AmL) extraño mis paseos por el campo 2 (notice absence of) echar en falta *or* de menos; **when did you first ~ the necklace?** ¿cuándo te diste cuenta de que te faltaba el collar?

■ **miss** *vi* 1 «*marksman*» errar* el tiro, fallar; «*bullet*» no dar* en el blanco 2 (fail) (colloq) fallar; **she goes every year, she never ~es** va todos los años sin falta, va todos los años, nunca falla

(Phrasal verb)

• **miss out**

A [v ▸ o ▸ adv, v ▸ adv ▸ o] ‹*line/paragraph*› saltarse, comerse (fam); **I felt I'd been ~ed out deliberately** (BrE) sentí que me habían excluido deliberadamente

B [v ▸ adv] (fail to profit): **don't ~ out; reserve your free tickets** no se lo pierda, reserve sus entradas gratuitas; **to ~ out ON sth** perderse* algo; **I feel I'm ~ing out on life** siento que estoy desaprovechando *or* desperdiciando mi vida

Miss = Mississippi

missal /ˈmɪsəl/ *n* misal *m*

misshapen /ˈmɪsˈʃeɪpən/ *adj* deforme

missile /ˈmɪsəl ‖ ˈmɪsaɪl/ *n* (Mil) misil *m*, vector *m*; (sth thrown) proyectil *m*

missing /ˈmɪsɪŋ/ *adj* 1 (lost): **the ~ papers** los papeles que faltan; **~ person** desaparecido, -da *m,f*; **~, presumed dead** desaparecido, dado por muerto; **to be ~** faltar; **one of the coins is ~** falta una de las monedas; **to go ~** (BrE) «*person/object*» desaparecer* 2 (lacking): **it has two strings ~** le faltan dos cuerdas

mission /ˈmɪʃən/ *n*

A 1 (task) misión *f* 2 (vocation, aim) misión *f*; **her ~ in life is to help the poor** su misión en la vida es ayudar a los pobres

B (group of delegates) misión *f*, delegación *f*

C (Relig) misión *f*

missionary /ˈmɪʃəneri ‖ ˈmɪʃənəri/ *n* misionero, -ra *m,f*

mission: **~ control** *n* (*no art*) centro *m* de control; **~ statement** *n* declaración *f* de propósitos *or* objetivos

m

Mississippi /ˈmɪsəˈsɪpi || ˌmɪsɪˈsɪpi/ *n* (state) Misisipí *m*; **the ~ (River)** el Misisipí

missive /ˈmɪsɪv/ *n* (hum) misiva *f* (frml *o* hum)

Missouri /məˈzʊri || mɪˈzʊəri/ *n* (state) Misuri *m*; **the ~ (River)** el Misuri

misspell /ˈmɪsˈspel/ *vt* (*past & past p* **-spelled** *or* (BrE) **-spelt**) escribir* mal; (orally) deletrear mal

misspent /ˈmɪsˈspent/ *adj* (*before n*) ‹*money*› malgastado; ‹*hours*› perdido; **a ~ youth** (set phrase) una juventud disipada

misstate /ˈmɪsˈsteɪt/ *vt* (frml) exponer* mal

mist /mɪst/ *n* 1 [u c] (Meteo) neblina *f*; **sea ~** bruma *f*; **it is lost in the ~s of time** se pierde en la noche de los tiempos 2 [u] (condensation) vaho *m* 3 [u] (spray) vaporización *f*

Phrasal verbs

- **mist over** [v ▸ adv] «*landscape*» cubrirse* de neblina; «*eyes*» empañarse; «*glass/mirror*» empañarse
- **mist up** [v ▸ adv] «*glass/mirror*» empañarse

mistake¹ /məˈsteɪk/ *n* error *m*; **a spelling ~** una falta de ortografía; **sorry, my ~** lo siento, es culpa mía; **to make a ~** cometer un error, equivocarse*; **make no ~ (about it)** no te quepa la menor duda (de ello); **it's hot today and no ~** hoy sí que hace calor; **by ~** por error

mistake² *vt* (*past* **-took**; *past p* **-taken**) confundir; **to ~ sth/sb FOR sth/sb** confundir algo/a algn CON algo/algn; **her shyness can be ~n for rudeness** su timidez a veces parece grosería; **there's no mistaking that voice!** ¡esa voz es inconfundible!

mistaken¹ /məˈsteɪkən || mɪˈsteɪkən/ *past p of* **mistake²**

mistaken² *adj* ‹*impression/idea*› equivocado, falso; **in the ~ belief that ...** creyendo equivocadamente que ...; **unless I'm (very) much ~** si no me equivoco, a menos que esté muy equivocado

mistakenly /məˈsteɪkənli/ *adv* equivocadamente

mister /ˈmɪstər || ˈmɪstə(r)/ *n* 1 (as title) señor *m* 2 (colloq) (*as form of address*) ¡oiga!

mistime /ˈmɪsˈtaɪm/ *vt* ‹*speech/shot*› calcular mal el momento de; **they ~d their arrival/attack** llegaron/atacaron a destiempo

mistletoe /ˈmɪsəltəʊ/ *n* [u] muérdago *m*

mistook /mɪˈstʊk/ *past of* **mistake²**

mistranslation /ˈmɪstrænsˈleɪʃən/ *n* [u c] traducción *f* errónea

mistreat /ˈmɪsˈtriːt/ *vt* maltratar, tratar mal

mistress /ˈmɪstrəs || ˈmɪstrɪs/ *n* 1 (of dog) dueña *f*, ama *f*‡; (of servant) señora *f*; **the ~ of the house** la señora de la casa, la dueña de casa (AmL) 2 (teacher) (BrE) (in secondary school) profesora *f*; (in primary school) maestra *f* 3 (lover) amante *f*, querida *f*

mistrial /ˈmɪsˈtraɪəl/ *n* 1 (in US and UK) *proceso declarado nulo por contener vicios de procedimiento* 2 (in US) *proceso en el cual el jurado no llega a un acuerdo*

mistrust¹ /ˈmɪsˈtrʌst/ *vt* desconfiar* de, recelar de

mistrust² *n* [u] desconfianza *f*, recelo *m*

mistrustful /ˈmɪsˈtrʌstfəl/ *adj* desconfiado, receloso; **to be ~ OF sb/sth** desconfiar* *or* recelar DE algn/algo

misty /ˈmɪsti/ *adj* **-tier, -tiest** 1 ‹*day/morning*› neblinoso; **it's ~** hay neblina; (it's drizzling) (AmE) está lloviznando 2 ‹*mirror/glasses*› empañado 3 ‹*eyes*› empañado, lloroso 4 ‹*recollection*› borroso, vago; ‹*outline*› borroso

misty-eyed /ˈmɪstiˈaɪd/ *adj* con los ojos empañados *or* llorosos; **he went all ~** se le empañó la mirada

misunderstand /ˈmɪsʌndərˈstænd || ˌmɪsˌʌndəˈstænd/ (*past & past p* **-stood**) *vt* ‹*idea/instructions*› entender* *or* comprender mal; ‹*remark/motives*› malinterpretar; ‹*artist/work*› interpretar mal, no entender* *or* comprender

■ **misunderstand** *vi* entender* *or* comprender mal

misunderstanding /ˈmɪsʌndərˈstændɪŋ || ˌmɪsˌʌndəˈstændɪŋ/ *n* [u c] malentendido *m*; **they had a ~** (euph) tuvieron una diferencia (euf)

misunderstood¹ /ˈmɪsʌndərˈstʊd || ˌmɪsˌʌndəˈstʊd/ *past & past p of* **misunderstand**

misunderstood² *adj* incomprendido

misuse¹ /ˈmɪsˈjuːs/ *n* [u] (of word) mal uso *m*, uso *m* incorrecto; (of power) abuso *m*; (of funds) malversación *f*; (of resources) despilfarro *m*

misuse² /ˈmɪsˈjuːz/ *vt* ‹*language/tool*› utilizar* *or* emplear mal; ‹*resources*› despilfarrar; ‹*funds*› malversar

mite /maɪt/ *n* 1 (Zool) ácaro *m* 2 (small child, animal): **the poor little ~!** ¡pobrecito! 3 **a mite** (*as adv*) un tanto

miter, (BrE) **mitre** /ˈmaɪtər || ˈmaɪtə(r)/ *n*

A (Relig) mitra *f*

B (Const) **~ (joint)** unión *f* a inglete, inglete *m*

mitigate /ˈmɪtəgeɪt || ˈmɪtɪgeɪt/ *vt* (frml) 1 (soften, lessen) mitigar* (frml); **to ~ the harmful effects of the drug** para paliar *or* atenuar los efectos nocivos del fármaco 2 **mitigating** *pres p* ‹*factor*› atenuante; **mitigating circumstances** (circunstancias *fpl*) atenuantes *fpl or mpl*

mitigation /ˈmɪtəˈgeɪʃən || ˌmɪtɪˈgeɪʃən/ *n* [u] (frml) 1 (extenuation) atenuante *f or m*; **in ~** como (circunstancia) atenuante 2 (alleviation) alivio *m*

mitre /ˈmaɪtər || ˈmaɪtə(r)/ *n* (BrE) ▸ **miter**

mitt /mɪt/ *n* 1 (mitten) mitón *m* 2 (in baseball) manopla *f*, guante *m* (de béisbol) 3 (hand) (colloq) manaza *f* (fam), manota *f* (fam)

mitten /ˈmɪtn̩/ *n* mitón *m*

mix¹ /mɪks/ *n* 1 (mixture, ingredients) mezcla *f*; **cake ~** *preparado comercial para hacer pasteles* 2 (Audio) mezcla *f*

mix² *vt* 1 ‹*ingredients/paint*› mezclar; ‹*cocktail*› preparar; **to ~ one's drinks** mezclar las bebidas; **to ~ sth INTO sth** mezclar algo CON algo, incorporar algo A algo; **~ together the flour and the eggs** mezclar la harina con los huevos 2 (Audio) mezclar

■ **mix** *vi* 1 (combine) «*substances*» mezclarse 2 (go together) «*foods/colors*» combinar (bien) 3 (socially): **she doesn't ~ well at parties** le cuesta entablar conversación con la gente en una reunión; **to ~ WITH sb** tratarse CON algn

Phrasal verb

- **mix up**

Sense I [v ▸ o ▸ adv, v ▸ adv ▸ o]

A (throw into confusion) desordenar, revolver*; **don't get your books ~ed up with mine** no mezcles tus libros con los míos

B 1 (confuse) ‹*names/dates*› confundir; ***to ~ it up*** (AmE colloq) pelearse, sacarse* la mugre (CS fam) 2 (bewilder) ‹*person*› confundir

Sense II (*usu pass*) 1 (involve) **to be/get ~ed up IN sth** estar* metido *or* enredado/meterse EN algo; **to be/get ~ed up WITH sb** andar* liado/liarse* CON algn 2 (confuse): **to get ~ed up** confundirse, hacerse* un lío (fam)

mixed /mɪkst/ *adj* 1 (various) mezclado, variado; **~ fruit** frutas *fpl* surtidas; **~ grill** parrillada *f* mixta; **~ spice** mezcla *f* de especias; **person of ~ race** mestizo, -za *m,f*; (of black and white descent) mulato, -ta *m,f*; **she invited quite a ~ crowd** invitó a gente de todo tipo *or* a un grupo muy variopinto 2 (male and female) ‹*sauna/bathing*› mixto 3 (ambivalent) ‹*fortunes*› desigual; ‹*reception*› tibio, poco entusiasta; **I have ~ feelings about it** no sé muy bien qué pensar sobre el asunto

mixed: **~ doubles** *n* (+ *sing vb*) dobles *mpl* mixtos; **~ economy** *n* economía *f* mixta; **~-up** /ˈmɪkstˈʌp/ *adj* confuso, desorientado; **a crazy, ~-up kid** un chico con problemas

mixer /ˈmɪksər || ˈmɪksə(r)/ *n* 1 [c] (Culin) batidora *f* 2 [c] (Audio, Cin, TV) (person) operador, -dora *m,f* de sonido; (machine) mezcladora *f* 3 [c] (sociable person) persona *f* sociable; **to be a good/bad ~** ser* muy/poco sociable 4 [c] (dance) (AmE) baile *m*, fiesta *f* 5 [u c] (drink) refresco *m* (*para mezclar con alcohol*)

mixing bowl /ˈmɪksɪŋ/ *n* bol *m* (*grande, para mezclar ingredientes*)

mixture /ˈmɪkstʃər || ˈmɪkstʃə(r)/ *n* 1 [c] (of diverse things) mezcla *f* 2 [c u] (Culin) mezcla *f* 3 [c u] (Pharm) preparado *m*, mixtura *f* (ant)

mix-up /ˈmɪksʌp/ *n* (colloq) lío *m* (fam), confusión *f*

ml (= **milliliter(s)** *o* (BrE) **millilitre(s)**) ml.

mm (= **millimeter(s)** *o* (BrE) **millimetre(s)**) mm.

MN = **Minnesota**

mnemonic /nɪˈmɑːnɪk/ *n* ayuda *f* nemotécnica

MO 1 = **Missouri** 2 = **Medical Officer**

moan¹ /məʊn/ *vi* 1 (make sound) «*person/wind*» gemir* 2 (complain) (pej) **to ~ (ABOUT sth)** quejarse (DE algo), protestar (POR algo)

moan² *n* [1] (sound) gemido *m* [2] (complaint) (colloq) (*no pl*) queja *f*; **to have a ~ about sth** quejarse de algo

moaner /'məʊnər || 'məʊnə(r)/ *n* (colloq) llorón, -rona *m,f*, protestón, -tona *m,f* (fam)

moat /məʊt/ *n* foso *m*

mob¹ /mɑ:b || mɒb/ *n* [1] (crowd) turba *f*, muchedumbre *f*; (populace) populacho *m*; (*before n*) **~ rule** la ley de la calle [2] (gang) (sl) banda *f*; **the M~** (AmE) la mafia

mob² *vt* **-bb-** [1] (attack) atacar* en grupo [2] (swarm up to) acosar, asediar

mobile¹ /'məʊbəl || 'məʊbaɪl/ *adj* [1] ‹*library/shop*› ambulante, móvil [2] (able to move): **we try and get the patient ~ as soon as possible** tratamos de que el paciente recupere su movilidad lo más pronto posible; **are you ~?** (colloq) ¿estás motorizado? (fam) [3] (Sociol) con movilidad

mobile² *n* [1] (hanging) móvil *m* [2] (*~ phone*) teléfono *m* celular *m or* (Esp) móvil *m*

mobile: **~ home** *n* trailer *m* (AmL), caravana *f* fija (Esp); **~ phone** *n* (teléfono *m*) celular *m* (AmL), (teléfono *m*) móvil *m* (Esp)

mobility /məʊ'bɪləti/ *n* [u] movilidad *f*

mobilize /'məʊbəlaɪz || 'məʊbɪlaɪz/ *vt* movilizar*

■ **mobilize** *vi* (Mil) movilizarse*

mobster /'mɑ:bstər || 'mɒbstə(r)/ *n* (AmE) gángster *mf*

moccasin /'mɑ:kəsən || 'mɒkəsɪn/ *n* mocasín *m*

mocha /'məʊkə || 'mɒkə/ *n* [u] (coffee) moca *m*, café *m* moca; (coffee and chocolate) *mezcla de café y chocolate*

mock¹ /mɑ:k || mɒk/ *vt* burlarse *or* mofarse de; **he ~ed her accent** imitó *or* remedó su acento burlonamente

mock² *adj* (*before n*) ‹*examination/interview*› de práctica, de prueba; ‹*anger/outrage*› fingido, simulado; **a ~ battle** un simulacro de batalla

mockery /'mɑ:kəri || 'mɒkəri/ *n* [1] [u] (ridicule) burla *f*, mofa *f* (liter) [2] (travesty) (*no pl*) farsa *f*, pantomima *f*; **a ~ of justice** una parodia de justicia; **to make a ~ of sth** ridiculizar* algo

mocking /'mɑ:kɪŋ || 'mɒkɪŋ/ *adj* burlón, socarrón

mockingbird /'mɑ:kɪŋbɜ:rd || 'mɒkɪŋbɜ:d/ *n* sinsonte *m*

mockup /'mɑ:kʌp || 'mɒkʌp/ *n* maqueta *f*

MOD *n* (in UK) = **Ministry of Defence**

modal /'məʊdl/ *adj* modal

mod cons /'mɑ:d'kɑ:nz || ,mɒd'kɒnz/ *pl n* (= **modern conveniences**) (BrE colloq & journ) comodidades *fpl*

mode /məʊd/ *n*

A [1] (means) medio *m*; (kind) modo *m*; **~ of transport** medio de transporte [2] (operating method) (Comput, Tech) modalidad *f*, modo *m*

B (Math) modo *m*

C (Clothing) moda *f*

model¹ /'mɑ:dl || 'mɒdl/ *n*

A (reproduction) maqueta *f*, modelo *m*; **a scale ~** un modelo a escala

B (paragon, example) modelo *m*; **a ~ of efficiency** un modelo de eficiencia

C (design) modelo *m*; **the most popular ~ in our range** el modelo más popular de nuestra serie

D (person) modelo *mf*; **a male ~** un modelo

model², (BrE) **-ll-** *vt*

A ‹*clay/shape*› modelar

B (base): **their education system was ~ed on that of France** su sistema educativo se inspiró en el francés; **to ~ oneself on sb** tomar a algn como modelo

C ‹*garment*›: **she ~s sportswear** es modelo de ropa sport

■ **model** *vi*

A (make shapes) modelar

B (pose) (Clothing) trabajar de modelo; (Art) posar; (Phot) ser* modelo

model³ *adj* (*before n, no comp*)

A (miniature) ‹*railway/village*› en miniatura, a escala; **~ aeroplane** aeromodelo *m*

B (ideal) ‹*citizen/husband/pupil*› modelo *adj inv*, ejemplar; ‹*answer*› tipo *adj inv*; **a ~ prison** una cárcel modelo

model home *n* (AmE) casa *m* piloto

modeling, (BrE) **modelling** /'mɑ:dlɪŋ || 'mɒdəlɪŋ/ *n* [u]

A (making models) modelismo *m*

B (Clothing, Phot) profesión *f* de modelo; **she did some ~** trabajó de *or* como modelo

modem /'məʊdem/ *n* módem *m*

moderate¹ /'mɑ:dərət || 'mɒdərət/ *adj* ‹*price*› moderado, módico; ‹*heat/wind*› moderado; ‹*views*› moderado; ‹*ability*› regular, pasable; **he's a ~ drinker** bebe con moderación

moderate² /'mɑ:dəreɪt || 'mɒdəreɪt/ *vt* [1] moderar; **kindly ~ your language** ten la bondad de cuidar el vocabulario que empleas [2] **moderating** *pres p* ‹*influence/effect*› moderador

moderate³ /'mɑ:dərət || 'mɒdərət/ *n* moderado, -da *m,f*

moderately /'mɑ:dərətli || 'mɒdərətli/ *adv* ‹*good*› medianamente; **~ priced** de precio módico *or* razonable; **they played ~ well** jugaron a un nivel aceptable

moderation /'mɑ:də'reɪʃən || ,mɒdə'reɪʃən/ *n* [u] moderación *f*; **drinking is not harmful, in ~** beber no es nocivo, si se hace con moderación

moderator /'mɑ:dəreɪtər || 'mɒdəreɪtə(r)/ *n* (in debates) moderador, -dora *m,f*

modern /'mɑ:dərn || 'mɒdn/ *adj* moderno

modern-day /'mɑ:dərn'deɪ || ,mɒdn'deɪ/ *adj* de hoy (en) día, de nuestro tiempo

modernism, Modernism /'mɑ:dərnɪzəm || 'mɒdənɪzəm/ *n* [u] (Art, Lit) modernismo *m*

modernization /'mɑ:dərnə'zeɪʃən || ,mɒdənaɪ'zeɪʃən/ *n* [u c] modernización *f*, actualización *f*

modernize /'mɑ:dərnaɪz || 'mɒdənaɪz/ *vt* ‹*system/service*› modernizar*, actualizar*; ‹*building*› modernizar*

modest /'mɑ:dəst || 'mɒdɪst/ *adj* [1] (not boastful) ‹*person/remark*› modesto [2] ‹*income/gift*› modesto; ‹*improvement*› moderado, pequeño; ‹*success*› moderado [3] (chaste) pudoroso, púdico

modestly /'mɑ:dəstli || 'mɒdɪstli/ *adv* [1] (not boastfully) modestamente [2] (moderately) ‹*rise/improve*› moderadamente; **it was ~ priced** tenía un precio módico [3] (with propriety) ‹*behave/dress*› recatadamente, pudorosamente, con pudor

modesty /'mɑ:dəsti || 'mɒdɪsti/ *n* [u] [1] (absence of conceit) modestia *f* [2] (propriety) recato *m*, pudor *m*

modicum /'mɑ:dɪkəm || 'mɒdɪkəm/ *n* (*no pl*) (frml) **a ~ OF sth** un atisbo DE algo (frml), un mínimo DE algo

modification /'mɑ:dəfə'keɪʃən || ,mɒdɪfɪ'keɪʃən/ *n* [c u] modificación *f*

modify /'mɑ:dəfaɪ || 'mɒdɪfaɪ/ *vt* **-fies, -fying, -fied** [1] (alter) modificar* [2] (moderate) ‹*demands*› moderar

modish /'məʊdɪʃ/ *adj* ‹*outfit/design*› de moda, a la moda; ‹*idea/expression*› de moda, in *adj inv* (fam)

modular /'mɑ:dʒələr || 'mɒdjʊlə(r)/ *adj* ‹*furniture*› modular, a base de módulos; ‹*degree/course*› dividido en módulos; ‹*program*› (Comput) modular

modulate /'mɑ:dʒəleɪt || 'mɒdjʊleɪt/ *vt* modular

modulation /'mɑ:dʒə'leɪʃən || ,mɒdjʊ'leɪʃən/ *n* modulación *f*; **frequency ~** frecuencia *f* modulada

module /'mɑ:dʒu:l || 'mɒdju:l/ *n* módulo *m*

moggy /'mɑ:gi/ *n* (*pl* **-gies**) (BrE colloq & hum) gato, -ta *m,f*

Mogul /'məʊgəl/ *n* [1] (in India) mogol *m* [2] **mogul** (powerful person) magnate *mf*

mohair /'məʊher || 'məʊheə(r)/ *n* [u] mohair *m*

Mohammed /məʊ'hæməd || məʊ'hæmɪd/ *n* Mahoma

Mohican /məʊ'hi:kən/ *n* (American Indian) mohicano, -na *m,f*

moist /mɔɪst/ *adj* ‹*climate/soil*› húmedo; ‹*cake*› no seco

moisten /'mɔɪsn/ *vt* humedecer*

moisture /'mɔɪstʃər || 'mɔɪstʃə(r)/ *n* [u] humedad *f*; (condensation) vaho *m*

moisturize /'mɔɪstʃəraɪz/ *vt* hidratar, humectar

moisturizer /'mɔɪstʃəraɪzər || 'mɔɪstʃəraɪzə(r)/, **moisturizing cream** /'mɔɪstʃəraɪzɪŋ/ *n* [u c] crema *f* hidratante *or* humectante

molar /'məʊlər || 'məʊlə(r)/ *n* muela *f*, molar *m* (frml)

molasses /mə'læsəz || mə'læsɪz/ *n* [u] (+ *sing vb*) melaza *f*

mold¹, (BrE) **mould** /məʊld/ *n*

A [1] [c] (hollow vessel) molde *m*; ***to break the ~*** romper* moldes [2] (type) (*no pl*): **to be cast** *o* **set in the same ~** estar* cortado por el mismo patrón [3] [c u] (dish) timbal *m*

B [u c] (fungus) moho *m*

m

mold[2], (BrE) **mould** *vt* ‹*steel/plastic*› moldear; ‹*character/attitudes*› formar, moldear; **the leather should ~ itself to the foot** el cuero debe amoldarse al pie

Moldavia /mɑːl'deɪvjə || mɒl'deɪviə/ *n* Moldavia *f*

molder, (BrE) **moulder** /'məʊldər || 'məʊldə(r)/ *vi* 1 «*buildings*» desmoronarse; «*corpse/leaves*» descomponerse* 2 **moldering** *pres p* ‹*leaves/corpse*› en estado de descomposición

molding, (BrE) **moulding** /'məʊldɪŋ/ *n* 1 [c u] (Archit) moldura *f* 2 [c] (thing cast) molde *m* 3 [u] (shaping) modelado *m*

Moldova /mɑːl'dəʊvə || mɒl'dəʊvə/ *n* Moldova *f*

moldy, (BrE) **mouldy** /'məʊldi/ *adj* 1 (covered in mold) mohoso; **to become** *o* (BrE) **go ~** enmohecerse* 2 (stale) ‹*smell*› a humedad, a moho

mole /məʊl/ *n*
A 1 (Zool) topo *m* 2 (spy, informant) topo *mf*, espía *mf*
B (on skin) lunar *m*

molecular /mə'lekjələr || mə'lekjʊlə(r)/ *adj* molecular

molecule /'mɑːlɪkjuːl || 'mɒlɪkjuːl/ *n* molécula *f*

molehill /'məʊlhɪl/ *n* topera *f*

molest /mə'lest/ *vt* 1 (sexually) abusar (sexualmente) de 2 (harass) importunar, molestar

moll /mɑːl || mɒl/ *n* chica *f* (*de un gángster*)

mollify /'mɑːləfaɪ || 'mɒlɪfaɪ/ *vt* **-fies, -fying, -fied** aplacar*, calmar

mollusk, mollusc /'mɑːləsk || 'mɒləsk/ *n* molusco *m*

mollycoddle /'mɑːlikɑːdl || 'mɒlɪkɒdl/ *vt* (colloq & pej) mimar, consentir*

molt, (BrE) **moult** /məʊlt/ *vi* «*snake*» mudar *or* cambiar de piel; «*bird*» mudar *or* cambiar de plumas; «*dog/cat*» pelechar, mudar *or* cambiar de pelo

molten /'məʊltən/ *adj* ‹*rock/metal*› fundido; ‹*lava*› líquido

mom /mɑːm || mɒm/ *n* (AmE colloq) mamá *f* (fam)

mom-and-pop /'mɑːmən'pɑːp || ˌmɒmən'pɒp/ *adj* (AmE colloq) familiar

moment /'məʊmənt/ *n*
A [c] 1 (short period) momento *m*; **just a ~** un momento, un momentito; **could I speak to you for a ~?** ¿podría hablar con usted un momento?; **doctor Davies will see you in a ~** enseguida la atiende el doctor Davies; **not for a ~** ni por un instante *or* momento; **I'm going out to get some milk: I won't be a ~** salgo a comprar leche, enseguida vuelvo; **a ~ later** poco después; **at the ~** en este momento; **at that ~** en ese momento; **for the ~** de momento, por el momento; **the man/woman of the ~** el hombre/la mujer del momento; **they'll be here any ~** estarán aquí en cualquier momento *or* de un momento a otro; **at that very ~** en ese preciso instante; **it was the wrong ~ to tell her** no era el momento de decírselo; **the ~ of truth** la hora de la verdad; ***to have one's ~s*** tener* sus (*or* mis *etc*) buenos momentos 2 **the moment (that)** (*as conj*) en cuanto; **the ~ they arrive** en cuanto lleguen
B [u] (Phys) momento *m*
C [u] (importance) (frml) trascendencia *f*, importancia *f*

momentarily /'məʊmən'terəli || 'məʊməntrəli/ *adv* 1 (briefly) momentáneamente, por un momento 2 (shortly) (AmE crit) de un momento a otro

momentary /'məʊmənteri || 'məʊməntri/ *adj* ‹*feeling/glimpse*› momentáneo, pasajero

momentous /məʊ'mentəs/ *adj* ‹*occasion/decision*› trascendental, de capital importancia; ‹*day*› memorable

momentum /məʊ'mentəm/ *n* [u c] (*pl* **-ta** /-tə/ *or* **-tums**) 1 (Phys) momento *m* 2 (speed) velocidad *f*; **to gather/gain/lose ~** ir* adquiriendo/cobrar/perder* velocidad 3 (of movement, project) impulso *m*, empuje *m*, ímpetu *m*

momma /'mɑːmə || 'mɒmə/ *n* (AmE) 1 (mother) (colloq) mamá *f* (fam) 2 (woman) (sl) mamita *f* (fam), tía *f* (Esp fam), mamacita *f* (Méx fam)

mommy /'mɑːmi || 'mɒmi/ *n* (*pl* **-mies**) (AmE colloq) mami *f* (fam), mamita *f* (fam)

Mon (= **Monday**) lun.

Monaco /'mɑːnəkəʊ, mə'nɑː- || 'mɒnəkəʊ/ *n* Mónaco *m*

monarch /'mɑːnərk || 'mɒnək/ *n* monarca *mf*

monarchist /'mɑːnərkəst/ *n* monárquico, -ca *m,f*

monarchy /'mɑːnərki || 'mɒnəki/ *n* [c u] monarquía *f*

monastery /'mɑːnəsteri/ *n* (*pl* **-ries**) monasterio *m*

monastic /mə'næstɪk/ *adj* monástico

Monday /'mʌndeɪ, -di/ *n*
A (day) lunes *m*; **it's ~ today, today's ~** (hoy) es lunes; **on ~** el lunes; **last ~** el lunes pasado; **next ~** el próximo lunes *or* el lunes que viene; **(on) ~s** *o* (BrE) **on a ~** los lunes; **I got the reply on a/the ~** la respuesta me llegó un/el lunes; **every ~** todos los lunes; **every second ~** cada dos lunes, un lunes sí y otro no, lunes por medio (CS, Per); **the ~ after next** el lunes que viene no, el siguiente *or* el otro; (*before n*) **~ afternoon/morning** el lunes por la tarde/mañana, la tarde/mañana del lunes
B **Mondays** (*as adv*) los lunes

monetarism /'mɑːnətərɪzəm/ *n* [u] monetarismo *m*

monetarist /'mɑːnətərəst || 'mʌnɪtərɪst/ *adj* monetarista

monetary /'mɑːnəteri || 'mʌnɪtəri/ *adj* monetario

money /'mʌni/ *n* [u] (*pl* **-nies** *or* **-neys**)
A dinero *m*, plata *f* (AmL fam), lana *f* (AmL fam), pasta *f* (Esp fam); (currency) moneda *f*, dinero *m*; **paper ~** papel *m* moneda, billetes *mpl*; **it cost $300, but it was worth the ~** costó 300 dólares, pero valió la pena; **I've had my ~'s worth out of this car** le he sacado mucho jugo a este coche (fam); **what's the ~ like where you work?** (colloq) ¿qué tal pagan donde trabajas? (fam); **he's earning good ~** está ganando un buen sueldo, está ganando bien; **there's ~ in secondhand books** los libros de segunda mano son un buen negocio; **she married ~** se casó con un hombre de dinero; **to come into ~** heredar dinero; **their European operation is making a lot of ~** su operación europea está dando mucho *or* produciendo grandes beneficios; **to put ~ into sth** invertir* *or* poner* dinero en algo; **you pay(s) your ~ and you take(s) your choice** (set phrase) es a gusto del consumidor; ***for my ~*** (colloq) para mí; ***it's ~ for jam*** *o* ***for old rope*** (BrE) es dinero regalado; ***to be in the ~*** estar* forrado (fam); ***to be made of ~*** nadar en la abundancia, tener* mucho dinero; ***to have ~ to burn*** tener* dinero de sobra; ***to put one's ~ where one's mouth is*** (colloq) obrar de acuerdo a sus (*or* mis *etc*) opiniones; ***to spend ~ like water*** gastar dinero como si fuera agua; ***to throw good ~ after bad*** seguir* tirando dinero (a la basura); **~ *talks*** poderoso caballero es don Dinero
B **monies** *o* **moneys** *pl* (Fin, Law) sumas *fpl* de dinero

money: **~bags** *n* (*pl* **~bags**) (colloq) ricachón, -chona *m,f* (fam); **~ belt** *n* faltriquera *f*; **~box** *n* alcancía *f* (AmL), hucha *f* (Esp); **~changer** /'mʌni'tʃeɪndʒər || 'mʌniˌtʃeɪndʒə(r)/ *n* (person) cambista *mf*; (dispenser) (AmE) *aparato que contiene monedas para dar el cambio*

moneyed /'mʌnid/ *adj* adinerado

money: **~-grubbing** /'mʌniˌgrʌbɪŋ/ *adj* ‹*scheme*› para enriquecerse; ‹*person*› avaro, avariento; **~ laundering** *n* blanqueo *m* de dinero, lavado *m* de dinero (AmL); **~lender** *n* prestamista *mf*; **~-making** *adj* lucrativo, rentable; **~ market** *n* mercado *m* monetario; **~ order** *n* ≈ giro *m* postal; **~-spinner** *n* (BrE colloq) mina *f* de oro (fam), filón *m* (fam); **~ supply** *n* **the ~ supply** la masa monetaria

Mongol /'mɑːŋgəl || 'mɒŋgəl/ *n* (Geog) mongol *mf*

Mongolia /mɑːn'gəʊliə || mɒŋ'gəʊliə/ *n* Mongolia *f*

Mongolian[1] /mɑːn'gəʊliən || mɒŋ'gəʊliən/ *adj* mongol

Mongolian[2] *n* mongol *mf*

mongoose /'mɑːnguːs/ *n* (*pl* **-gooses**) mangosta *f*

mongrel /'mɑːŋgrəl || 'mʌŋgrəl/ *n*: *perro mestizo*, chucho, -cha *m,f* (fam), gozque *mf* (Col), quiltro, -tra *m,f* (Chi fam)

monicker /'mɑːnəkər || 'mɒnɪkə(r)/ *n* (colloq) apodo *m*

monied /mʌnid/ *adj* ▸**moneyed**

monitor[1] /'mɑːnətər || 'mɒnɪtə(r)/ *n*
A 1 (screen) monitor *m* 2 (for measuring) monitor *m*
B (listener) escucha *mf*
C (Educ) encargado, -da *m,f*, monitor, -tora *m,f* (CS)

monitor[2] *vt* 1 ‹*elections*› observar; ‹*process/progress*› seguir*, controlar; (esp electronically) monitorizar*; **the project will be closely ~ed** se seguirá muy de cerca el desarrollo del proyecto 2 ‹*radio station*› escuchar

monk /mʌŋk/ *n* monje *m*

monkey /'mʌŋki/ *n* 1 mono, -na *m,f*, mico, -ca *m,f*; ***not to give a ~'s***: **he doesn't give a ~'s** (BrE sl) le importa un rábano *or* un pepino *or* un pito (fam) 2 (mischievous child) diablillo, -lla *m,f*

m

Phrasal verbs

- **monkey around**, (BrE) **monkey about** [v ▸ adv] tontear
- **monkey with** [v ▸ prep ▸ o] 1 (tamper with) andar* tocando 2 (cross): **don't ~ with me!** ¡no me tomes el pelo!

monkey: **~ business** *n* [u] (colloq) (trickery) trapicheo *m* (fam), chanchullos *mpl* (fam); (of children) diabluras *fpl*, travesuras *fpl*; **~ nut** *n* (BrE) maní *m or* (Esp) cacahuete *m or* (Méx) cacahuate *m*; **~ puzzle (tree)** *n* araucaria *f*; **~ shines** *pl n* (AmE colloq), **~ tricks** *pl n* (BrE colloq) diabluras *fpl*, travesuras *fpl*; **~ wrench** *n* llave *f* inglesa; ***to throw a ~ wrench in the works*** *o* ***the machinery*** (AmE) fastidiarlo todo

monkfish /ˈmʌŋkfɪʃ/ *n* (*pl* **-fish**) rape *m*

mono /ˈmɑːnəʊ || ˈmɒnəʊ/ *n* [u] (Audio) monofonía *f*

monochrome /ˈmɑːnəkrəʊm || ˈmɒnəkrəʊm/ *adj* ‹*picture*› monocromático, monocromo

monocle /ˈmɑːnɪkəl || ˈmɒnəkəl/ *n* monóculo *m*

monogamous /məˈnɑːgəməs/ *adj* monógamo

monogamy /məˈnɑːgəmi/ *n* [u] monogamia *f*

monogram /ˈmɑːnəgræm/ *n* monograma *m*

monolingual /ˈmɑːnəˈlɪŋgwəl/ *adj* monolingüe

monolith /ˈmɑːnl̩ɪθ || ˈmɒnəlɪθ/ *n* monolito *m*

monolithic /ˈmɑːnl̩ˈɪθɪk || ˌmɒnəˈlɪθɪk/ *adj* monolítico

monologue /ˈmɑːnəlɔːg/ *n* monólogo *m*

monoplane /ˈmɑːnəpleɪn || ˈmɒnəpleɪn/ *n* monoplano *m*

monopolize /məˈnɑːpəlaɪz/ *vt* ‹*market/industry*› monopolizar*; ‹*conversation/television*› acaparar, monopolizar*

monopoly /məˈnɑːpəli || məˈnɒpəli/ *n* [c u] (*pl* **-lies**) monopolio *m*; **they have a ~ of the market** monopolizan el mercado; **she doesn't have a ~ on my affections** no tiene el monopolio de mis sentimientos

Monopoly® *n* [u] Monopoly® *m*

monorail /ˈmɑːnəreɪl || ˈmɒnəʊreɪl/ *n* monocarril *m*, monorriel *m* (AmL), monorraíl *m* (Esp)

monoskiing /ˈmɑːnəskiːɪŋ/ *n* [u] monoesquí *m*

monosyllabic /ˈmɑːnəsəˈlæbɪk || ˌmɒnəsɪˈlæbɪk/ *adj* ‹*word*› monosilábico; ‹*reply*› lacónico, monosilábico

monosyllable /ˈmɑːnəˌsɪləbəl || ˈmɒnəsɪləbəl/ *n* monosílabo *m*; **he answered in ~s** contestó con monosílabos

monotone /ˈmɑːnətəʊn || ˈmɒnətəʊn/ *n* tono *m* monocorde; **in a dull ~** con voz monótona

monotonous /məˈnɑːtn̩əs || məˈnɒtənəs/ *adj* monótono; **with ~ regularity** con exasperante regularidad

monotony /məˈnɑːtn̩i || məˈnɒtəni/ *n* [u] monotonía *f*

monsoon /mɑːnˈsuːn || mɒnˈsuːn/ *n* monzón *m*

monster /ˈmɑːnstər || ˈmɒnstə(r)/ *n* monstruo *m*; **a ~ of a dog** un perro enorme, un perrazo (fam)

monstrance /ˈmɑːnstrəns || ˈmɒnstrəns/ *n* custodia *f*

monstrosity /mɑːnˈstrɑːsəti || mɒnˈstrɒsɪti/ *n* [u c] (*pl* **-ties**) monstruosidad *f*

monstrous /ˈmɑːnstrəs || ˈmɒnstrəs/ *adj* 1 (huge) gigantesco 2 (shocking) monstruoso, escandaloso

Mont = **Montana**

montage /mɑːnˈtɑːʒ || mɒnˈtɑːʒ/ *n* [u c] montaje *m*

Montenegro /mɑːntəˈniːgrəʊ/ *n* Montenegro *m*

month /mʌnθ/ *n* mes *m*; **lunar ~** mes lunar; **calendar ~** mes civil *or* del calendario; **$900 a ~** 900 dólares mensuales *or* por mes *or* al mes; **in a ~'s time** *o* **in a ~** dentro de un mes; **I haven't seen him for** *o* **in ~s** hace meses que no lo veo; ***never in a ~ of Sundays*** ni por casualidad

monthly¹ /ˈmʌnθli/ *adj* ‹*journal/event*› mensual; **~ payment** mensualidad *f*, cuota *f* mensual (esp AmL)

monthly² *adv* mensualmente, una vez al *or* por mes

monthly³ *n* (*pl* **-lies**) publicación *f* mensual

monument /ˈmɑːnjəmənt/ *n* monumento *m*

monumental /ˈmɑːnjəˈmentl̩ || ˌmɒnjʊˈmentl̩/ *adj* 1 (enormous) ‹*building/task*› monumental; ‹*error*› garrafal 2 ‹*arch/sculpture*› monumental; **~ mason** marmolista *mf* (*especializado en monumentos funerarios*)

moo¹ /muː/ *n* mugido *m*

moo² *vi* **moos, mooing, mooed** mugir*

mooch /muːtʃ/ *vt* (AmE colloq) gorronear (fam), gorrear (fam), garronear (RPl fam), bolsear (Chi fam)

■ **mooch** *vi* (BrE) (+ *adv compl*): **to ~ around** *o* **about the house/town** dar* vueltas por la casa/deambular por la ciudad

mood /muːd/ *n*

A 1 (state of mind) humor *m*; **to be in a good/bad ~** estar* de buen humor/de mal humor *or* de mal genio; **as the ~ takes him** según de qué humor esté, según le dé (la vena) (fam); **I'm not in the ~** no tengo ganas; **I'm not in the ~ for jokes/dancing** no estoy (de humor) para chistes/no tengo ganas de bailar; **she's in a ~** *o* **in one of her ~s** está *or* anda de mal humor 2 (atmosphere) atmósfera *f*, clima *m*

B (Ling) modo *m*

moodily /ˈmuːdl̩i || ˈmuːdɪli/ *adv* 1 (irritably) malhumoradamente 2 (gloomily) con aire taciturno

moodiness /ˈmuːdinəs || ˈmuːdɪnɪs/ *n* [u] 1 (irritability) mal humor *m*; (gloom) depresión *f* 2 (changeable moods) carácter *m* temperamental

moody /ˈmuːdi/ *adj* **-dier, -diest** 1 (irritable, sulky) de mal humor, malhumorado; (gloomy) deprimido, taciturno 2 (changeable) ‹*person*› temperamental

moola, moolah /ˈmuːlə/ *n* [u] (AmE sl) guita *f* (arg), plata *f* (AmL fam), lana *f* (AmL fam)

moon¹ /muːn/ *n* luna *f*; **to land on the ~** alunizar*; **many ~s ago** hace muchas lunas, hace mucho tiempo; ***once in a blue ~*** muy de vez en cuando; ***to be over the ~*** (esp BrE) estar* como unas Pascuas *or* loco de contento; ***to promise the ~*** prometer el oro y el moro; (*before n*) **~ buggy** vehículo *m* lunar; **~ landing** alunizaje *m*

moon² *vi*: **she spent the whole day ~ing in her room** se pasó el día en su habitación pensando en las musarañas; **to ~ OVER sb** soñar* CON algn

moonbeam /ˈmuːnbiːm/ *n* rayo *m* de luna

Moonie /ˈmuːni/ *n* moonie *mf*

moonlight¹ /ˈmuːnlaɪt/ *n* [u] luz *f* de la luna; **by ~** a la luz de la luna

moonlight² *vi* tener* un segundo empleo, estar* pluriempleado; **he ~s as a cab driver** trabaja además como taxista

moon: **~light flit** *n*: **to do a ~light flit** (BrE) largarse* (fam) (*para no pagar*); **~lighting** *n* [u] pluriempleo *m*; **~lit** *adj* iluminado por la luna; **a ~lit night** una noche de luna; **~shine** *n* [u] 1 (nonsense) tonterías *fpl*, pamplinas *fpl* 2 (liquor) (AmE) *bebida alcohólica destilada ilegalmente*; **~stone** *n*: *tipo de ópalo o feldespato*; **~struck** *adj* lunático, trastornado

moor¹ /mʊr || mʊə(r), mɔː(r)/ *n* 1 (boggy area) llanura *f* anegadiza 2 (high exposed area) (esp BrE) páramo *m*; (covered with heather) brezal *m*

moor² *vt* amarrar

■ **moor** *vi* echar amarras

Moor /mʊr || mʊə(r), mɔː(r)/ *n* moro, -ra *m,f*

moorhen /ˈmʊrhen || ˈmʊəhen, ˈmɔːhen/ *n* polla *f* de agua

mooring /ˈmʊrɪŋ || ˈmʊərɪŋ, ˈmɔːrɪŋ/ *n* 1 (place) amarradero *m*, atracadero *m* 2 **moorings** *pl* (ropes) amarras *fpl*

Moorish /ˈmʊrɪʃ || ˈmʊərɪʃ, ˈmɔːrɪʃ/ *adj* 1 ‹*conquest*› árabe 2 ‹*art/style*› morisco; (in post-Reconquest Spain) mudéjar

moorland /ˈmʊrlənd || ˈmʊələnd, ˈmɔːlənd/ *n* [u] 1 (boggy area) llanura *f* anegadiza 2 (high exposed area) (esp BrE) páramo *m*

moose /muːs/ *n* (*pl* **moose**) alce *m* americano

moot¹ /muːt/ *adj* (*before n*) discutible; **that remains a ~ point** eso sigue siendo discutible

moot² *vt* (*usu pass*) someter a discusión, plantear

mop¹ /mɑːp || mɒp/ *n* 1 (for floor) trapeador *m* (AmL), fregona *f* (Esp) 2 **~ of hair** mata *f* de pelo, pelambre *f*

mop² **-pp-** *vt* ‹*floor/room*› limpiar, trapear (AmL), pasarle la fregona a (Esp); **to ~ one's brow** secarse* la frente

Phrasal verb

- **mop up**

A [v ▸ o ▸ adv, v ▸ adv ▸ o] 1 ‹*water*› secar*; ‹*mess*› limpiar 2 ‹*resistance*› sofocar*

B [v ▸ adv] limpiar

mope /məʊp/ *vi* (colloq) estar* deprimido *or* alicaído

m

moped /ˈməʊped/ *n* ciclomotor *m*, bicimoto *m*

mopping-up operation /ˈmɑːpɪŋˈʌp || ˌmɒpɪŋˈʌp/ *n* operación *f* de limpieza

moral¹ /ˈmɔːrəl/ *adj* moral; **the decline in ~ standards** la decadencia moral; **~ support** apoyo *m* moral

moral² *n*

A (message) moraleja *f*

B **morals** *pl* (principles) moralidad *f*; **have you no ~s?** ¿no tienes ningún sentido moral?

moral hazard *n* riesgo *m* moral

morale /məˈræl || məˈrɑːl/ *n* [u] moral *f*; **~ is high/low** tienen (*or* tenemos *etc*) la moral alta/baja; **to boost sb's ~** levantarle la moral a algn

morale-booster /məˈræl,buːstər || məˈrɑːl,buːstə(r)/ *n*: **it was intended as a ~** tenía por objeto levantarles (*or* levantarnos *etc*) la moral

moralistic /ˈmɔːrəˈlɪstɪk || ˌmɒrəˈlɪstɪk/ *adj* moralizador

morality /məˈræləti/ *n* [u c] (*pl* **-ties**) (ethics) moralidad *f*, moral *f*

moralize /ˈmɔːrəlaɪz || ˈmɒrəlaɪz/ *vi* 1 (make moral pronouncement) moralizar* 2 **moralizing** *pres p* ‹*tone/speech*› moralizador

morally /ˈmɔːrəli || ˈmɒrəli/ *adv* 1 (from moral standpoint) moralmente; **a ~ bankrupt society** una sociedad en la bancarrota moral 2 ‹*behave*› moralmente, éticamente

morass /məˈræs/ *n* ciénaga *f*; **a ~ of paperwork** un lío de papeles; **a ~ of regulations** un laberinto de reglamentos

moratorium /ˈmɔːrəˈtɔːriəm || ˌmɒrəˈtɔːriəm/ *n* (*pl* **-riums** *or* **-ria** /-riə/) **~ (ON sth)** moratoria *f* (EN algo)

morbid /ˈmɔːrbəd || ˈmɔːbɪd/ *adj* 1 ‹*curiosity*› morboso, malsano; ‹*fear/mind*› morboso 2 (Med) mórbido

mordant /ˈmɔːrdn̩t || ˈmɔːdn̩t/ *adj* (liter) mordaz

more¹ /mɔːr || mɔː(r)/ *adj* 1 (additional number, amount) más; **would you like some ~?** ¿quieres más?; **there'll be no ~ talking** se acabó la charla; **how much ~ flour?** ¿cuánta harina más?; **for ~ information call 387351** para mayor información llamar al 38-73-51; **one ~ question** una pregunta más; **~ and ~ people** cada vez más gente; **the ~ money you earn, the ~ tax you have to pay** cuanto más dinero se gana, (tantos) más impuestos hay que pagar 2 (in comparisons) más; **I eat ~ meat than you** yo como más carne que tú

more² *pron* 1 (additional number, amount) más; **let's say no ~ about it** no hablemos más del asunto; **and, what is ~, ...** y lo que es más, ...; **the ~ she eats, the thinner she gets** cuanto más come, más adelgaza; **have you anything ~ to say?** ¿tiene algo más que decir? 2 (in comparisons) más; **you eat ~ than me** tú comes más que yo; **we had four ~ than we needed** nos sobraron cuatro, había cuatro de más; **there's ~ to life than politics** hay cosas más importantes en la vida que la política; **my brother is ~ of a businessman than I am** mi hermano tiene mucha más idea para los negocios que yo

more³ *adv*

A 1 (to greater extent) más; **you watch television ~ than I do** tú ves más televisión que yo; **I couldn't agree ~** estoy totalmente de acuerdo; **I don't go there any ~ than I have to** no voy ahí más de lo necesario; **I love you ~ and ~ each day** te quiero cada día más; **~ or less** más o menos; **I was ~ than a little surprised by your attitude** tu actitud me sorprendió bastante 2 (*before adj, adv*) más; **could you please speak ~ clearly?** ¿podría hacer el favor de hablar más claro?; **~ often** con más frecuencia, más a menudo; **this made her all the ~ determined** esto la afirmó aún más en su resolución

B (again, longer) más; **once/twice ~** una vez/dos veces más; **I don't eat meat any ~** ya no como carne

C (rather): **it's ~ an encyclopedia than a dictionary** es más una enciclopedia que un diccionario; **I was ~ surprised than anything** me causó más que nada sorpresa

moreish /ˈmɔːrɪʃ/ *adj* (BrE colloq): **these biscuits are very ~** uno no puede parar de comer estas galletas

morello (cherry) /məˈreləʊ/ *n* guinda *f*

moreover /mɔːrˈəʊvər || mɔːˈrəʊvə(r)/ *adv* (frml) (*as linker*) además, por otra parte; **it appears, ~, that ...** es más, parece ser que ...

mores /ˈmɔːreɪz/ *pl n* costumbres *fpl* y convenciones *fpl*

morgue /mɔːrg || mɔːg/ *n* depósito *m* de cadáveres, morgue *f* (AmL)

moribund /ˈmɔːrəbʌnd || ˈmɒrɪbʌnd/ *adj* moribundo

Mormon¹ /ˈmɔːrmən || ˈmɔːmən/ *n* mormón, -mona *m,f*

Mormon² *adj* mormón

> **Mormon**
>
> La *Church of Jesus Christ of Latter-Day Saints* cuenta hoy con unos 10 millones de miembros, denominados *Mormons*. Fue fundada en 1830 por Joseph Smith. Posteriormente, guiados por Brigham Young, sus miembros se trasladaron hacia el oeste para fundar Salt Lake City en el estado de Utah, la mayoría de cuyos habitantes son hoy mormones. Tienen reglas morales muy estrictas y no beben alcohol ni café

morn /mɔːrn || mɔːn/ *n* (poet) mañana *f*

morning /ˈmɔːrnɪŋ || ˈmɔːnɪŋ/ *n*

A (time of day) mañana *f*; **he hasn't been in all ~** no ha venido en toda la mañana; **yesterday/tomorrow ~** ayer/mañana por la mañana *or* (AmL tb) en la mañana *or* (RPl tb) a la mañana *or* de mañana; **every Saturday ~** todos los sábados por la mañana (*or* en la mañana *etc*); **at eight o'clock in the ~** a las ocho de la mañana; **until three in the ~** hasta las tres de la mañana *or* madrugada; **we'll do it first thing in the ~** lo haremos por la mañana a primera hora; **on the ~ of August 16** la mañana del 16 de agosto; **(good) ~!** ¡buenos días!, ¡buen día! (RPl); (*before n*) **~ paper** diario *m or* periódico *m* de la mañana, matutino *m*

B **mornings** (*as adv*) por las mañanas, en las mañanas (AmL), a la *or* de mañana (RPl)

morning: ~-after pill /ˈmɔːrnɪŋˈæftər/ *n* píldora *f* del día siguiente; **~ coat** *n* chaqué *m*, frac *m*; **~ sickness** *n* [u] náuseas *fpl* (matinales) (*del embarazo*)

Moroccan¹ /məˈrɑːkən || məˈrɒkən/ *adj* marroquí

Moroccan² *n* marroquí *mf*

Morocco /məˈrɑːkəʊ || məˈrɒkəʊ/ *n* Marruecos *m*

moron /ˈmɔːrɑːn || ˈmɔːrɒn/ *n* (colloq & pej) imbécil *mf*, tarado, -da *m,f* (fam)

moronic /mɔːˈrɑːnɪk || məˈrɒnɪk/ *adj* imbécil

morose /məˈrəʊs/ *adj* taciturno

morphine /ˈmɔːrfiːn || ˈmɔːfiːn/ *n* [u] morfina *f*

morris dancing /ˈmɑːrɪs || ˈmɒrɪs/ *n*: *bailes folklóricos ingleses*

Morse /mɔːrs || mɔːs/ *n* [u] morse *m*; **in ~ (code)** en (código) morse

morsel /ˈmɔːrsəl || ˈmɔːsəl/ *n* (of food) bocado *m*; **this ~ of information** este dato

mortal¹ /ˈmɔːrtl̩ || ˈmɔːtl̩/ *adj* 1 (subject to death) mortal 2 (liter) ‹*blow/injury*› mortal; **~ sin** pecado *m* mortal 3 (until death) (liter): **~ enemy** enemigo, -ga *m,f* mortal; **~ combat** combate *m* a muerte

mortal² *n* mortal *mf*

mortality /mɔːrˈtæləti/ *n* [u] 1 (death rate) mortalidad *f* 2 (loss of life) mortandad *f* 3 (condition) mortalidad *f*

mortally /ˈmɔːrtl̩i || ˈmɔːtəli/ *adv* ‹*wounded*› de muerte, mortalmente; ‹*offended/afraid*› terriblemente

mortar /ˈmɔːrtər || ˈmɔːtə(r)/ *n*

A [u] (cement) argamasa *f*, mortero *m*

B [c] (weapon) mortero *m*

C [c] (bowl) mortero *m*, almirez *m*, molcajete *m* (Méx)

mortarboard /ˈmɔːrtərbɔːrd || ˈmɔːtəbɔːd/ *n* (academic cap) birrete *m*

mortgage¹ /ˈmɔːrgɪdʒ || ˈmɔːgɪdʒ/ *n* (charge) hipoteca *f*; (loan) préstamo *m or* crédito *m* hipotecario, hipoteca *f*; **to pay off a ~** terminar de pagar una hipoteca, redimir una hipoteca (frml); **to take out a ~ on a property** hipotecar* una propiedad

mortgage² *vt* hipotecar*

mortice /ˈmɔːrtəs || ˈmɔːtɪs/ *n* ▸ **mortise**

mortician /mɔːrˈtɪʃən || mɔːˈtɪʃən/ *n* (AmE) (employee) *persona que trabaja en una funeraria*; (funeral director) director, -tora *m,f* de pompas fúnebres

mortify /ˈmɔːrtəfaɪ || ˈmɔːtɪfaɪ/ *vt* **-fies, -fying, -fied**

A (Relig) mortificar*

B **mortified** *past p*: **I was mortified** me dio mucha vergüenza, me sentí muy avergonzado

mortise /ˈmɔːrtəs || ˈmɔːtɪs/ *n* mortaja *f*, entalladura *f*; (*before n*) **~ lock** cerradura *f* embutida

mortuary /'mɔːrtʃueri || 'mɔːtjʊəri/ *n* (*pl* **-ries**) depósito *m* de cadáveres, morgue *f* (AmL)

mosaic /məʊ'zeɪɪk/ *n* mosaico *m*

Moscow /'mɑːskaʊ || 'mɒskəʊ/ *n* Moscú *m*

Moses /'məʊzəz || 'məʊzɪz/ *n* Moisés

mosey /'məʊzi/ *vi* **moseys, moseying, moseyed** (colloq): **well, guess I'll just ~ along** bueno, pues me voy yendo

Moslem /'mɑːzləm || 'mɒzləm/ *n/adj* ▸**Muslim**[1,2]

mosque /mɑːsk || mɒsk/ *n* mezquita *f*

mosquito /mə'skiːtəʊ || mɒs'kiːtəʊ/ *n* (*pl* **-toes** *or* **-tos**) mosquito *m*, zancudo *m* (AmL); (*before n*) **~ net** mosquitero *m*, mosquitera *f*

moss /mɔːs || mɒs/ *n* [u c] musgo *m*

most[1] /məʊst/ *adj* 1 (nearly all) la mayoría de, la mayor parte de; **~ people** casi todo el mundo *or* la mayoría de la gente; **~ days** casi todos los días 2 (*as superl*) más; **who eats (the) ~ meat in your family?** ¿quién es el que come más carne de tu familia?

most[2] *pron* 1 (nearly all) la mayoría, la mayor parte; **~ of us/them** la mayoría de nosotros/ellos; **~ of the wine** casi todo el vino; **I read ~ of it** lo leí casi todo 2 (*as superl*): **she ate the ~** fue la que más comió, comió más que nadie; **it is the ~ we can offer you** es todo lo que podemos ofrecerle; **at (the) ~** como máximo, a lo sumo; ***to make the ~ of sth*** sacar* el mejor provecho posible de algo; **make the ~ of it** aprovéchalo al máximo 3 (people) la mayoría

most[3] *adv*

A 1 (to greatest extent) más; **what I like/dislike (the) ~ about him is ...** lo que más/menos me gusta de él es ...; **I enjoyed the last act ~ of all** el último acto fue el que más me gustó 2 (*before adj, adv*) más; **which is the ~ expensive?** ¿cuál es el más caro?; **it's Joe who visits us (the) ~ often** es Joe el que nos visita más a menudo

B (*as intensifier*): **what happened was ~ interesting** lo que sucedió fue de lo más interesante; **it was ~ kind of you** fue muy amable de su parte; **~ probably** *o* **likely** muy probablemente

C (almost) (AmE colloq) casi; **she ate ~ all the food** se comió casi toda la comida

mostly /'məʊstli/ *adv*: **her friends are ~ students** la mayoría de sus amigos son estudiantes; **the land is ~ flat** el terreno es en su mayor parte llano; **she works ~ in the evenings** trabaja sobre todo por las noches

most valuable player *n* (AmE) jugador más destacado, jugadora más destacada *m,f*

MOT *n* (in UK) ~ **(test)** *inspección técnica a la que deben someterse anualmente todos los vehículos de más de tres años*, ITV *f* (en Esp)

motel /məʊ'tel/ *n* motel *m*

moth /mɔːθ || mɒθ/ *n* mariposa *f* de la luz, palomilla *f*; (*clothes* ~) polilla *f*

moth: **~ball** *n* bola *f* de naftalina; **~-eaten** *adj* apolillado

mother[1] /'mʌðər || 'mʌðə(r)/ *n* madre *f*; (*before n*) **~ country** madre patria *f*

mother[2] *vt* mimar

mother[3] *adv*: **~ naked** (AmE colloq) como Dios lo (*or* me *etc*) trajo al mundo (fam)

mother: **~board** *n* placa *f* madre; **~ earth** *n* la madre tierra, la Pachamama (AmS); **~fucker** *n* (AmE vulg) (person) hijo *m* de puta *or* (Méx) de la chingada (vulg); (thing) mierda *f* (vulg), madre *f* (Méx vulg)

motherhood /'mʌðərhʊd/ *n* [u] maternidad *f*

Mothering Sunday *n* (BrE) ▸**Mother's Day**

mother: **~-in-law** *n* (*pl* **~s-in-law**) suegra *f*, madre *f* política (frml); **~land** *n* patria *f*

motherless /'mʌðərləs/ *adj* huérfano de madre

motherly /'mʌðərli || 'mʌðəli/ *adj* maternal

mother: **~ Nature** *n* la (Madre) Naturaleza; **~-of-pearl** /'mʌðərəv'pɜːrl || ,mʌðərəv'pɜːl/ *n* [u] nácar *m*, madreperla *f*, concha *f* nácar (Méx), concha *f* de perla (Chi); **~'s Day** *n* el día de la Madre (*el segundo domingo de mayo en EEUU y el cuarto domingo de Cuaresma en GB*); **~ Superior** *n* Madre *f* Superiora; **~-to-be** /'mʌðərtə'biː || ,mʌðətə'biː/ *n* (*pl* **~s-to-be**) futura madre *f*, futura mamá *f*; **~ tongue** *n* lengua *f* materna

> **Mother's Day/Mothering Sunday**
>
> En EEUU, el Día de la Madre cae el segundo domingo de mayo y es la ocasión en que, por tradición, todas las madres reciben regalos y tarjetas por parte de sus hijos y se las invita a cenar fuera de casa. En el Reino Unido se emplea también el término más tradicional *Mothering Sunday*. Aquí cae el cuarto domingo de Cuaresma y también es una ocasión en que las madres reciben pequeños regalos y tarjetas

motif /məʊ'tiːf/ *n* 1 (theme) tema *m*, motivo *m* 2 (design) motivo *m*

motion[1] /'məʊʃən/ *n*

A 1 [u] (movement) movimiento *m*; **to be in ~** estar* en movimiento, moverse*; **to set** *o* **put sth in ~** ‹*wheel*› poner* algo en movimiento; ‹*project/plan*› poner* algo en marcha; **it set in ~ a whole chain of consequences** desencadenó toda una serie de consecuencias; (*before n*) **~ sickness** mareo *m*; *see also* **slow motion** 2 [c] (action, gesture) gesto *m*, movimiento *m*; **he made a cutting ~ with his hand** hizo ademán de cortar algo con la mano; ***to go through the ~s***: **he went through the ~s of interviewing them** los entrevistó por pura fórmula

B 1 (for vote) moción *f*; **to carry** *o* **pass a ~** aprobar* una moción; **the ~ was rejected/defeated** se rechazó/no se aprobó la moción 2 (Law) petición *f*

motion[2] *vi*: **she ~ed to her assistant** le hizo una señal a su ayudante; **they ~ed to us to sit down** nos hicieron señas para que nos sentáramos

motionless /'məʊʃənləs/ *adj* inmóvil, sin moverse

motion picture *n* película *f*

motivate /'məʊtəveɪt || 'məʊtɪveɪt/ *vt* motivar; **a politically ~d strike** una huelga con motivaciones políticas *or* por motivos políticos

motivated /'məʊtəveɪtəd || 'məʊtɪveɪtɪd/ *adj* motivado; **to be highly ~** estar* muy motivado

motivation /'məʊtə'veɪʃən || ,məʊtɪ'veɪʃən/ *n* 1 [u] (drive) motivación *f* 2 [c] (motive) motivo *m*, móvil *m* (frml)

motive[1] /'məʊtɪv/ *n* motivo *m*, móvil *m* (frml); **she acted out of the best of ~s** lo hizo con la mejor intención; **his ~ was greed** actuó movido por la avaricia

motive[2] *adj* (*before n*) motor [*The feminine of* **motor** *is* **motriz** *or* **motora**]; **~ power** fuerza *f* motriz

motley /'mɑːtli || 'mɒtli/ *adj* variopinto, heterogéneo; **they're a ~ crew** forman una pandilla de lo más variopinto

motor[1] /'məʊtər || 'məʊtə(r)/ *n* 1 (engine) motor *m* 2 (car) (BrE colloq) coche *m*, carro *m* (AmL exc CS), auto *m* (esp CS)

motor[2] *adj* (*before n*)

A (Auto, Mech Eng) ‹*parts/spares*› de automóvil; ‹*mechanic*› de automóviles; **~ racing** carreras *fpl* automovilísticas; **~ show** salón *m* del automóvil; **~ sport** automovilismo *m*; **~ vehicle** (vehículo *m*) automóvil *m* (frml)

B (Physiol) ‹*neuron/nerve*› motor [*The feminine of* **motor** *is* **motriz** *or* **motora**]

motor: **~bike** *n* moto *f*; **~boat** *n* lancha *f* a motor

motorcade /'məʊtərkeɪd || 'məʊtəkeɪd/ *n* desfile *m* de vehículos, caravana *f*

motor: **~car** *n* (Auto frml) automóvil *m* (frml); **~cycle** *n* motocicleta *f*; **~cyclist** *n* motorista *mf*

motoring /'məʊtərɪŋ/ *n* [u] automovilismo *m*; **school of ~** (in UK) autoescuela *f*, escuela *f* de conductores *or* de choferes (AmL), escuela *f* de manejo (Méx); (*before n*) **~ offence** (BrE) infracción *f* de tráfico

motorist /'məʊtərəst || 'məʊtərɪst/ *n* automovilista *mf*, conductor, -tora *m,f*

motor: **~man** /'məʊtərmən || 'məʊtəmən/ *n* (*pl* **-men** /-mən/) (AmE) maquinista *m*, conductor *m*; **~way** *n* (BrE) autopista *f*

mottled /'mɑːtḷd || 'mɒtḷd/ *adj* ‹*skin*› manchado, moteado; ‹*marble*› veteado, jaspeado; **~ with black** a *or* con manchas negras

motto /'mɑːtəʊ || 'mɒtəʊ/ *n* (*pl* **-toes**) (of family, school) lema *m*, divisa *f*

mould *etc* (BrE) ▸**mold** *etc*

moult *vi* (BrE) ▸**molt**

m

mound /maʊnd/ *n* [1] (hillock) montículo *m* [2] (man-made) túmulo *m*; **burial ~** túmulo funerario [3] (in baseball) (*pitcher's* ~) montículo *m* (del lanzador *or* pítcher) [4] (heap) montón *m*

mount¹ /maʊnt/ *n*
A (mountain) (liter) monte *m*; **M~ Everest** el Everest
B (Equ) montura *f*
C [1] (for machine, gun) soporte *m* [2] (for picture — surround) paspartú *m*, marialuisa *f* (Méx); (— backing) fondo *m*; (for slide) marco *m* [3] (for stamp) fijasellos *m* [4] (for jewel) montura *f*, engaste *m*

mount² *vt*
A [1] ‹*horse*› montar, montarse en; **I ~ed my bicycle** (me) monté en *or* me subí a la bicicleta [2] ‹*platform/throne*› subir a; **the car ~ed the pavement** el coche se subió a la acera
B ‹*gun/picture*› montar; ‹*stamp/butterfly*› fijar; ‹*gem*› engarzar*, engastar, montar
C (copulate with) (Zool) montar
D ‹*attack/offensive*› preparar, montar; ‹*campaign/event*› organizar*, montar
■ **mount** *vi*
A [1] «*cost/temperature*» subir, elevarse (frml); «*excitement/alarm*» crecer*, aumentar [2] **mounting** *pres p* ‹*cost/fears/tension*› cada vez mayor, creciente
B (climb onto horse) montar

Phrasal verb
• **mount up** [v ▸ adv] «*bills*» irse* acumulando

mountain /ˈmaʊntn̩ || ˈmaʊntɪn/ *n* (Geog) montaña *f*; **the butter ~** (BrE EC) los excedentes de mantequilla; ***to make a ~ out of a molehill*** hacer* una montaña de un grano de arena; (*before n*) ‹*stream/path*› de montaña; ‹*scenery*› montañoso; **~ range** cordillera *f*; (shorter) sierra *f*; **~ sickness** *see* **altitude sickness, altitude**

mountain bike *n* bicicleta *f* de montaña

mountaineer /ˈmaʊntn̩ˈɪr || ˌmaʊntɪˈnɪə(r)/ *n* alpinista *mf*, andinista *mf* (AmL)

mountaineering /ˈmaʊntn̩ˈɪrɪŋ || ˌmaʊntɪˈnɪərɪŋ/ *n* [u] alpinismo *m*, andinismo *m* (AmL)

mountain: **~ goat** *n* cabra *f* montés; **~ lion** *n* puma *m*, león, leona *m,f* (AmC, Méx)

mountainous /ˈmaʊntn̩əs || ˈmaʊntɪnəs/ *adj* [1] montañoso [2] (large) descomunal, gigantesco

mountain: **~side** *n* ladera *f* de la montaña; **~top** *n* cima *f or* cumbre *f* (de la montaña)

mounted /ˈmaʊntəd || ˈmaʊntɪd/ *adj* montado: **~ police** policía *f* montada *or* a caballo

mounting /ˈmaʊntɪŋ/ *n* ▸**mount¹ C**

mourn /mɔːrn || mɔːn/ *vt* ‹*loss/tragedy*› llorar, lamentar; **she is still ~ing him** todavía lo llora
■ **mourn** *vi* **to ~ FOR sb** llorar a algn, llorar la pérdida *or* la muerte de algn

mourner /ˈmɔːrnər || ˈmɔːnə(r)/ *n* doliente *mf*; **to be the chief ~** presidir el duelo

mournful /ˈmɔːrnfəl || ˈmɔːnfəl/ *adj* ‹*expression/glance*› de profunda tristeza, acongojado (liter); ‹*sigh/cry*› lastimero

mourning /ˈmɔːrnɪŋ || ˈmɔːnɪŋ/ *n* [u] (action, period) duelo *m*, luto *m*; **to be in ~ for sb** estar* de luto por algn, guardar luto por algn; **to go into/come out of ~** ponerse* de/quitarse el luto

mouse /maʊs/ *n* (*pl* **mice**)
A [1] (animal) ratón *m*, laucha *f* (CS); ***as poor as a church ~*** más pobre que las ratas [2] (timid person) timorato, -ta *m,f*
B (Comput) ratón *m*

Phrasal verb
• **mouse over** [v ▸ prep ▸ o]: **to ~ over a link** pasar el ratón sobre/por encima de un enlace

mouse: **~hole** *n* ratonera *f*; **~mat** (Comput) /ˈmaʊsmæt/ *n* alfombrilla *f* de *or* para ratón; **~trap** *n* ratonera *f*

mousey *adj* ▸**mousy**

mousse /muːs/ *n* [u c] [1] (Culin) mousse *f or m*, espuma *f* [2] (for hair) mousse *f*, espuma *f*

moustache *n* (BrE) ▸**mustache**

mousy /ˈmaʊsi/ *adj* **-sier, -siest** ‹*hair*› castaño desvaído *adj inv*

mouth¹ /maʊθ/ *n* (*pl* **mouths** /maʊðz/)
A (of person, animal) boca *f*; **shut your ~!** (colloq) ¡cállate la boca! (fam), ¡cierra el pico! (fam); **keep your ~ shut about this** no digas ni media palabra de esto a nadie; **watch your ~!** (be careful) ¡ojo con lo que dices!; (response to obscenity) ¡qué boca!, ¡no digas palabrotas!; ***down in the ~*** alicaído, bajo de moral; ***to be all ~*** (sl) ser* un fanfarrón (fam); ***to have a big ~*** ser* un bocazas *or* (Andes, Méx) un bocón *or* (RPl) (un) estómago resfriado (fam); **me and my big ~!** ¡quién me mandaría abrir la boca!; ***to make sb's ~ water***: **it made my ~ water** se me hizo agua la boca *or* (Esp) se me hizo la boca agua; ***to shoot one's ~ off*** (colloq) (boast) fanfarronear (fam)
B (of bottle) boca *f*; (of tunnel, cave) entrada *f*; (of river) desembocadura *f*

mouth² /maʊð/ *vt* [1] (silently): **it's him, she ~ed** —es él —me/le dijo articulando para que le leyera los labios [2] (say) (pej) decir*; **to ~ platitudes** decir* lugares comunes

Phrasal verb
• **mouth off** [v ▸ adv (▸ prep ▸ o)] (colloq) (brag) fanfarronear (fam); **to ~ off ABOUT sth** jactarse DE algo

mouthful /ˈmaʊθfʊl/ *n* (of food) bocado *m*; (of drink) trago *m*; (of air) bocanada *f*; **it's a bit of a ~ (to say)** (difficult to pronounce) es un trabalenguas; (long) es larguísimo; ***to give sb a ~*** soltarle* una sarta de insultos a algn

mouth: **~ organ** *n* armónica *f*; **~piece** *n* [1] (of telephone) micrófono *m*; (Mus) boquilla *f*; (AmE Sport) protector *m* (de dentadura); [2] (spokesperson) portavoz *mf*; **~-to-mouth** /ˈmaʊθtəˈmaʊθ/ *adj* (*before n*) boca a boca; **~wash** *n* [u c] enjuague *m* (bucal), elixir *m* (bucal); **~-watering** /ˈmaʊθˌwɔːtərɪŋ/ *adj* delicioso

movable /ˈmuːvəbəl/ *adj* ‹*part*› movible, móvil; ‹*apparatus*› portátil; **~ property** (Law) bienes *mpl* muebles

move¹ /muːv/ *n*
A (movement) movimiento *m*; **she watched their every ~** vigilaba todos sus movimientos; **she made a ~ to get up/for the door** hizo ademán de levantarse/ir hacia la puerta; **it's time we made a ~** ya es hora de que nos vayamos; ***on the ~***: **she's always on the ~** siempre está de un lado para otro; ***to get a ~ on*** (colloq) darse* prisa, apurarse (AmL)
B (change — of residence) mudanza *f*, trasteo *m* (Col); (— of premises) traslado *m*, mudanza *f*
C [1] (action, step) paso *m*; (measure) medida *f*; **what's the next ~?** ¿cuál es el siguiente paso?, ¿ahora qué hay que hacer?; **to make the first ~** dar* el primer paso [2] (in profession, occupation): **it would be a good career ~** sería un cambio muy provechoso para mi (*or* su *etc*) carrera profesional
D (Games) movimiento *m*, jugada *f*; **whose ~ is it?** ¿a quién le toca mover *or* jugar?

move² *vi*
A [1] (change place): **he ~d nearer the fire** se acercó *or* se arrimó al fuego; **we could ~ to another table** podríamos cambiarnos de mesa; **government troops have ~d into the area** tropas del gobierno se han desplazado *or* se han trasladado a la zona; **to ~ to a new job/school** cambiar de trabajo/colegio [2] (change location, residence) mudarse, cambiarse; *see also* **move in, move out**
B (change position) moverse*; **don't you ~, I'll answer the door** tú tranquilo, que voy yo a abrir la puerta
C (proceed, go): **the procession/vehicle began to ~** la procesión/el vehículo se puso en marcha; **get moving!** ¡muévete! (fam); **the police kept the crowds moving** la policía hacía circular a la multitud; **it's time we were moving** ya es hora de que nos vayamos; **the earth ~s around the sun** la Tierra gira alrededor del sol; **we ~d aside** *o* **to one side** nos apartamos, nos hicimos a un lado
D (advance, develop): **things seem to be moving** parece que las cosas marchan; **events ~d rapidly** los acontecimientos se desarrollaron rápidamente; **to ~ with the times** mantenerse* al día; **the conflict has ~d into a new phase** el conflicto ha entrado en una nueva fase; **to ~ into the lead** pasar a ocupar el primer lugar; **the company plans to ~ into the hotel business** la compañía tiene planes de introducirse en el ramo hotelero
E (carry oneself) moverse*
F (go fast) (colloq) correr
G (take steps, act): **we must ~ now** tenemos que actuar ahora; **she ~d quickly to scotch rumors** inmediatamente tomó medidas para acallar los rumores
H (Games) mover*, jugar*

I (circulate socially) moverse*; **he ~s in fashionable circles** se mueve en círculos que están de moda

■ **move** *vt*

A (transfer, shift position of): **let's ~ the sofa over there** pongamos el sofá allí; **why have you ~d the television?** ¿por qué has cambiado la televisión de sitio *or* de lugar?; **~ your chair a little** corre un poco la silla; **ask him to ~ the boxes out of the way** dile que quite las cajas de en medio; **we shall not be ~d!** ¡no nos moverán!; **I can't ~ my leg/neck** no puedo mover la pierna/el cuello

B 1 (transport) transportar, trasladar 2 (relocate, transfer) trasladar; **she was ~d to head office** la trasladaron a la oficina central; **I'll ~ this paragraph further down** pondré este párrafo más abajo 3 (change residence, location): **the firm that ~d us** la compañía que nos hizo la mudanza; **to ~ house** (BrE) mudarse de casa

C 1 (arouse emotionally) conmover*, emocionar; **he's easily ~d** es muy sensible; **to ~ sb to tears** hacer* llorar a algn de la emoción 2 (prompt) **to ~ sb to + INF**: **this ~d her to remonstrate** esto la indujo a protestar

D (propose) (Adm, Govt) proponer*

E (Games) mover*

Phrasal verbs

- **move about** (BrE) ▸**move around**
- **move along**

A [v ▸ adv] 1 (go further along) correrse; **~ along, so I can sit down too** córrete *or* arrímate para que pueda sentarme yo también 2 (disperse) circular

B [v ▸ o ▸ adv] (cause to disperse) hacer* circular; **the police ~d us along** la policía nos hizo circular

- **move around,** (BrE also) **move about**

A [v ▸ adv] 1 (walk) andar* 2 (change residence) mudarse, cambiarse (*a menudo*); (change job) cambiar de trabajo (*a menudo*)

B [v ▸ o ▸ adv] ‹*furniture*› cambiar de sitio *or* de lugar; ‹*employee/troops*› trasladar

- **move away** [v ▸ adv] 1 (move house) mudarse (*de la ciudad, el barrio etc*) 2 ▸**move off**
- **move back**

A [v ▸ adv]: **they ~d back here in 1979** volvieron a vivir aquí en 1979; **they ~d back to let him pass** retrocedieron para dejarlo pasar

B [v ▸ o ▸ adv]: **~ the microphone back a bit** coloca el micrófono un poco más atrás; **she's ~d the date of the meeting back again** ha vuelto a aplazar la fecha de la reunión

- **move down**

A [v ▸ adv] bajar

B [v ▸ o ▸ adv] bajar

- **move forward**

A [v ▸ adv] «*car/troops*» avanzar*; **I ~d forward to get a better view** me puse más adelante para ver mejor

B [v ▸ o ▸ adv] ‹*troops*› hacer* avanzar; ‹*date/event*› adelantar

- **move in** [v ▸ adv] 1 (set up home) mudarse, cambiarse (*a una casa etc*); **to ~ in WITH sb** irse* a vivir CON algn 2 (draw closer) acercarse* 3 (go into action) «*police*» intervenir*; **they ~d in at dawn** (Mil) atacaron al amanecer
- **move in on** [v ▸ adv ▸ prep ▸ o] 1 (advance upon) ‹*enemy*› avanzar* sobre 2 (encroach upon) ‹*territory/business*› invadir
- **move off** [v ▸ adv] «*procession*» ponerse* en marcha; «*car*» arrancar*, ponerse* en marcha
- **move on**

Sense I [v ▸ adv]

A (walk further) seguir* adelante; (continue journey) continuar* el viaje

B 1 (proceed) pasar; **shall we ~ on?** ¿pasamos al punto siguiente? 2 (progress) progresar, avanzar*

Sense II [v ▸ o ▸ adv] (cause to disperse) hacer* circular

- **move out** [v ▸ adv] irse*, mudarse, cambiarse (*de una casa etc*)
- **move over** [v ▸ adv] (make room) correrse
- **move up**

A [v ▸ adv] 1 (rise) subir; **they've ~d up in the world** han prosperado mucho 2 (make room) correrse

B [v ▸ o ▸ adv] ‹*picture/shelf*› subir; **they ~d him up a class** lo pusieron en la clase inmediatamente superior

moveable *adj* ▸**movable**

movement /'mu:vmənt/ *n*

A 1 [u] (motion) movimiento *m* 2 [c] (action, gesture) movimiento *m*; (with the hand) ademán *m*; **there was a sudden ~ in the bushes** de repente algo se movió entre los arbustos 3 [c u] (change — of position) movimiento *m*; (— in opinion) giro *m* 4 **movements** *pl* (activities, whereabouts) desplazamientos *mpl*, movimientos *mpl*

B [u] 1 (transportation) movimiento *m* 2 (travel) desplazamiento *m*

C [c] (Art, Pol, Relig) movimiento *m*

D [c] (Mus) movimiento *m*

mover /'mu:vər || 'mu:və(r)/ *n* 1 (in debate) ponente *mf* 2 (in dancing) (colloq): **he's/she's a clumsy ~** tiene muy poco garbo 3 (of furniture, belongings): **a firm of ~s** una compañía de mudanzas

movie /'mu:vi/ *n* (esp AmE)

A (film) película *f*, film(e) *m* (period); (*before n*) ‹*actor/director*› de cine; **~ theater** (AmE) cine *m*

B **movies** *pl* (esp AmE) 1 (building) **the ~s** el cine; **to go to the ~s** ir* al cine *or* a ver una película, ir* a cine (Col) 2 (industry) cine *m*

movie: **~ camera** *n* (esp AmE) filmadora *f or* (Esp) tomavistas *m*; (large, professional) cámara *f* cinematográfica; **~goer** *n* (esp AmE): **he's a keen ~goer** va mucho al cine, es muy aficionado al cine

moving /'mu:vɪŋ/ *adj*

A (emotionally) emotivo, conmovedor

B (in motion) (*before n*) **~ part** pieza *f* movible *or* móvil; **~ target** blanco *m* móvil *or* en movimiento

C (AmE) (*before n*) ‹*van/company*› de mudanzas

D ‹*force/spirit*› impulsor

mow /məʊ/ *vt* (*past* **mowed**; *past p* **mown** *or* **mowed**) ‹*hay*› segar*; ‹*lawn*› cortar

Phrasal verb

- **mow down** [v ▸ o ▸ adv, v ▸ adv ▸ o] acribillar, segar* (liter)

mower /'məʊər || 'məʊə(r)/ *n* 1 (Hort) ▸**lawnmower** 2 (on farm) segadora *f*

mown /məʊn/ *past p of* **mow**

Mozambique /'məʊzəm'bi:k || ˌməʊzæm'bi:k/ *n* Mozambique *m*

MP *n* 1 (in UK) (Govt) = **Member of Parliament** 2 (= **military police**) PM *f*

MP3 player *n* equipo *m* MP3, equipo *m* emepetres

mpg = **miles per gallon**

mph = **miles per hour**

Mr /'mɪstər || 'mɪstə(r)/ (= **Mister**) Sr.; **~ J.B. Jones** Sr. (D.) J.B.Jones *or* Sr.Dn. J.B.Jones; **she's waiting for ~ Right** está esperando al príncipe azul

Mrs /'mɪsəs || 'mɪsɪz/ Sra.; **~ A.J. Rees** Sra. (Dña.) A.J. Rees

Ms /mɪz || məz/ ≈ Sra. (*tratamiento que no indica su estado civil*); **~ Jane Brown** Sra. Jane Brown

MS *n* 1 [c] **ms** (*pl* **MSS** *or* **mss**) (= **manuscript**) ms. 2 [u] (= **multiple sclerosis**) E.M. *f* 3 [c] (AmE) = **Master of Science** 4 = **Mississippi**

MSc *n* (BrE) = **Master of Science**

MS-DOS® /'emes'dɑ:s || ˌemes'dɒs/ *n* (= **Microsoft disk operating system**) MS-DOS® *m*

MSF *n* (in UK) (= **Manufacturing Science Finance**) *sindicato general de trabajadores*

MST (in US) = **Mountain Standard Time**

mt, mtn = **mountain**

Mt (= **Mount**) **~ Rushmore** el monte Rushmore

MT = **Montana**

much¹ /mʌtʃ/ *adj* mucho, -cha; **I don't earn very ~ money** no gano mucho dinero; **$2 too ~** 2 dólares de más; **without ~ effort** sin mucho *or* sin demasiado esfuerzo; **I do as ~ work as anybody** trabajo tanto como cualquiera; **use as ~ paper as you need** utiliza todo el papel que necesites; **too ~ coffee/water** demasiado café/demasiada agua; **how ~ coffee/milk?** ¿cuánto café/cuánta leche?

much² *pron* mucho, -cha; **an ice cream isn't ~ of a meal** un helado no es comida; **he's not ~ of a swimmer** no nada muy bien; **what do you think of the new boss? — not ~** (colloq) ¿qué te parece el nuevo jefe? — no gran cosa (fam); **do you see ~ of the Smiths?** ¿ves mucho a los Smith?, ¿ves a menudo a los Smith?; **she won, though not by ~** *o* (BrE also) **though there wasn't ~ in it** ganó, pero por poco; **how ~ does it cost?** ¿cuánto cuesta?;

m

~ **of the day** gran parte *or* la mayor parte del día; **the cat eats as ~ as the dog** el gato come tanto como el perro; **I've done as ~ as I can** he hecho todo lo que he podido; **three times as ~ as yesterday** tres veces más que ayer; **you can lose as ~ as 2 kilos in one week** puedes adelgazar hasta dos kilos en una semana; **I thought/suspected as ~** (ya) me lo figuraba; **you need twice as ~** necesitas el doble; **and as ~ again** y otro tanto; **without so ~ as a goodbye** sin decir ni adiós; **if you so ~ as touch him, I'll kill you!** como le llegues a poner la mano encima, te mato; **so ~ for true love!** ¡pues si eso es amor ...! (iró); **however ~ she eats** coma lo que coma; **you've drunk too ~** has bebido demasiado; **it's a bit ~!** ¡ya es demasiado!, ¡es pasarse un poco! (fam); **it's not up to ~** no vale gran cosa

much[3] *adv*

A 1 (to large extent) mucho; **I like it very ~** me gusta mucho; **it is snowing, but not ~** está nevando, pero poco *or* no mucho; **I ~ prefer dogs to cats** me gustan mucho más los perros que los gatos; **I'd very ~ like to meet her** me gustaría mucho conocerla; **you deserve the prize just as ~ as I do** te mereces el premio tanto como yo; **the house is as ~ mine as yours** la casa es tan mía como tuya; **so ~ the better** tanto mejor; **you talk too ~** hablas demasiado; **~ to my surprise** para mi gran sorpresa 2 (often) mucho; **she doesn't get out as ~ as she used to** no sale tanto como antes *or* como solía

B (*before adj, adv*) mucho; **your house is ~ older than mine** tu casa es mucho más vieja que la mía; **this church is ~ the larger of the two** de las dos iglesias ésta es, con mucho, la más grande; **I'm ~ too busy to do it** estoy demasiado ocupada para hacerlo; **I'd ~ rather be at home** preferiría mil veces estar en mi casa; **it won't be ~ different from mine** no será muy distinto del mío

C (more or less, approximately): **he was of ~ the same opinion** en gran medida opinaba igual; **one bed is ~ like another** todas las camas son parecidas

muchness /ˈmʌtʃnəs || ˈmʌtʃnɪs/ *n*: ***to be much of a ~*** (BrE) ser* tres cuartos de lo mismo (fam)

muck /mʌk/ *n* [u] 1 (dung) (Agr) estiércol *m*; ***Lady/Lord M~*** (BrE colloq) la marquesa/el marqués de Carabás (iró); ***to be as common as ~*** (colloq) ser* muy ordinario, ser* más basto que el papel de lija (fam) 2 (dirt, filth) mugre *f*

Phrasal verbs

• **muck about, muck around** (BrE colloq)

A [v ▸ adv] 1 (play the fool) tontear, mamar gallo (Col, Ven fam) 2 (tinker) **to ~ about** *o* **around WITH sth** andar* tocando algo

B [v ▸ o ▸ adv] (treat badly): **to ~ sb about** *o* **around** jugar* con algn, tomarle el pelo a algn (fam)

• **muck in** [v ▸ adv] (BrE colloq) poner* *or* arrimar el hombro

• **muck out** [v ▸ o ▸ adv, v ▸ adv ▸ o] limpiar

• **muck up** (BrE colloq) [v ▸ o ▸ adv, v ▸ adv ▸ o] (make a hash of): **I ~ed up the first question** metí la pata en la primera pregunta (fam)

muckraking /ˈmʌkˌreɪkɪŋ/ *n* [u] (pej): **this newspaper specializes in ~** este periódico se especializa en escándalos *or* (fam) en sacar trapos sucios al sol

mucky /ˈmʌki/ *adj* **muckier, muckiest** (colloq): **I got all ~ changing the oil** quedé hecho un asco cambiando el aceite (fam); **you ~ pup!** (BrE) ¡mira que eres cochino!

mucus /ˈmjuːkəs/ *n* [u] mucosidad *f*

mud /mʌd/ *n* [u] barro *m*, fango *m*, lodo *m*; ***to be as clear as ~*** (iro) ser* un galimatías; ***to throw*** *o* ***sling ~ (at sb)*** insultar (a algn); (*before n*) ‹*brick/hut*› de barro, de adobe

mudbath /ˈmʌdbæθ || ˈmʌdbɑːθ/ *n* baño *m* de lodo

muddle[1] /ˈmʌdl̩/ *n* lío *m*, follón *m* (Esp fam); **to be in a ~** ‹‹*papers*›› estar* (todo) revuelto *or* desordenado; ‹‹*person*›› estar* liado *or* hecho un lío (fam); **to get into a ~** ‹‹*person*›› armarse *or* hacerse* un lío (fam)

muddle[2] *vt* ▸ **muddle up**

Phrasal verbs

• **muddle along** [v ▸ adv] ir* tirando (fam)

• **muddle through** [v ▸ adv] arreglárselas

• **muddle up** [v ▸ o ▸ adv, v ▸ adv ▸ o] 1 ‹*papers*› entreverar, desordenar; **to get ~d up** entreverarse, desordenarse 2 (mix up) confundir 3 (bewilder) confundir; **to get ~d up** confundirse

muddled /ˈmʌdl̩d/ *adj* confuso; **to get ~** hacerse* un lío (fam)

muddy /ˈmʌdi/ *adj* **-dier, -diest** ‹*boots/hands/road*› lleno *or* cubierto de barro *or* de lodo, enlodado, embarrado; ‹*water*› turbio; ‹*green/brown*› sucio; ▸ **water**[1] **C1**

mud: **~flat** *n* (*often pl*) marisma *f*; **~guard** *n* guardabarros *m*, salpicadera *f* (Méx), tapabarros *m* (Chi, Per); **~pack** *n* mascarilla *f* facial; **~slinging** /ˈmʌdˌslɪŋɪŋ/ *n* [u] (journ) vilipendio *m*, insultos *mpl*

muesli /ˈmjuːzli/ *n* [u] (esp BrE) musli *m*, muesli *m*

muff[1] /mʌf/ *vt* (colloq) ‹*shot*› errar*; ‹*chance*› desperdiciar; **he ~ed his lines** le salió mal lo que tenía que decir

muff[2] *n* (Clothing) manguito *m*

muffin /ˈmʌfən || ˈmʌfɪn/ *n* (AmE) mollete *m* (*bollo dulce hecho con huevos*); (BrE) *bollo de pan que suele servirse tostado*

muffle /ˈmʌfl̩/ *vt*

A 1 ‹*sound*› amortiguar* 2 ‹*oars/hooves*› enfundar, envolver* (*en una tela para amortiguar el ruido*)

B **~ (up)**: **her face was ~d (up) in a scarf** una bufanda casi le tapaba *or* le cubría la cara

muffled /ˈmʌfl̩d/ *adj* ‹*sound/shot*› sordo, apagado

muffler /ˈmʌflər || ˈmʌflə(r)/ *n*

A (scarf) bufanda *f*

B 1 (Mus) sordina *f* 2 (AmE Auto) silenciador *m*, mofle *m* (AmC, Méx)

mufti /ˈmʌfti/ *n* [u] (colloq): **in ~** sin uniforme; (Mil) (vestido) de paisano *or* de civil

mug[1] /mʌg/ *n*

A (cup) taza *f* (*alta y sin platillo*), tarro *m* (Méx, Ven); **beer ~** jarra *f or* (Méx, Ven) tarro *m* de cerveza

B (gullible person) (BrE colloq) idiota *mf*, ingenuo, -nua *mf*; **that's a ~'s game** es cosa de idiotas

C (face) (sl) cara *f*, jeta *f* (arg), careto *m* (Esp arg)

mug[2] **-gg-** *vt* atracar*, asaltar

■ **mug** *vi* (make faces) (AmE) hacer morisquetas

Phrasal verb

• **mug up** (BrE colloq) [v ▸ adv] **to ~ up ON sth** darle* duro a *or* (Esp tb) empollar *or* (RPl tb) tragar* *or* (Méx tb) matarse EN *or* (Ven tb) puñalearse algo (fam)

mugger /ˈmʌgər || ˈmʌgə(r)/ *n* atracador, -dora *m,f*

mugging /ˈmʌgɪŋ/ *n* (Law) 1 [u] (crime) atracos *mpl* 2 [c] (instance) atraco *m*

muggins /ˈmʌgɪnz/ *n* (*pl* ~) (BrE colloq): **and ~ had to pay!** y yo, el idiota de siempre tuve que pagar

muggle /mʌgl/ *n* (colloq) pesado, -da *m,f* (fam), aburrido, -da *m,f*

muggy /ˈmʌgi/ *adj* **-gier, -giest** ‹*weather/day*› pesado

mug shot *n* (colloq) foto *f* (*de archivo policial*)

mugwump /ˈmʌgwʌmp/ *n* (AmE) independiente *mf*

Muhammad /məˈhæməd || məˈhæmɪd/ *n* Mahoma

mulatto /mjʊˈlætəʊ/ *n* (*pl* **-toes** *or* **-tos**) mulato, -ta *m,f*

mulberry /ˈmʌlˌberi || ˈmʌlbəri/ *n* (*pl* **-ries**) (tree) morera *f*; (fruit) mora *f* (de morera)

mulch /mʌltʃ/ *vt* cubrir* con mantillo

mule /mjuːl/ *n*

A (Zool) mula *f* (*cruce de burro y yegua*); ***as stubborn as a ~*** más terco que una mula

B (Clothing) chinela *f*, pantufla *f* (*sin talón*)

mull /mʌl/ *vt* 1 (Culin): **~ed wine** *ponche caliente de vino y especias* 2 (AmE) ▸ **mull over**

Phrasal verb

• **mull over** [v ▸ o ▸ adv, v ▸ adv ▸ o] reflexionar *or* meditar sobre

mullet /ˈmʌlət || ˈmʌlɪt/ *n* [c u] (*pl* ~) (*gray* ~) mújol *m*, múgil *m*; (*red* ~) (esp BrE) salmonete *m*

multiaccess /ˈmʌltiˈækses || ˌmʌltɪˈækses/ *adj* de acceso múltiple, multiacceso *adj inv*

multicolored, (BrE) **multi-coloured** /ˈmʌltiˌkʌlərd || ˌmʌltɪˈkʌləd/ *adj* multicolor

multicultural /ˈmʌltiˈkʌltʃərəl/ *adj* multicultural

multifaceted /ˈmʌltiˈfæsətəd/ *adj* multifacético

multifarious /ˈmʌltiˈferiəs/ *adj* variopinto, muy diverso

multifunctional /ˌmʌltiˈfʌŋkʃnəl/ *adj* multifuncional

multilateral /ˈmʌltiˈlætərəl/ *adj* multilateral

multilevel /ˈmʌltiˈlevl̩/ *adj* (AmE) de varias plantas

multilingual /mʌltiˈlɪŋgwəl/ *adj* plurilingüe, multilingüe

multimedia /ˈmʌltiˈmiːdiə/ *adj* (*before n*) multimedia *adj inv*

multimillion /ˈmʌltiˈmɪljən/ *adj* (journ) multimillonario

multimillionaire /ˈmʌltiˈmɪljəˈner || ˌmʌltiˌmɪljəˈneə(r)/ *n* multimillonario, -ria *m,f*

multinational¹ /ˈmʌltiˈnæʃn̩əl/ *adj* multinacional

multinational² *n* multinacional *f*

multiparty /ˈmʌltipɑːrti/ *adj* multipartidista

multiple¹ /ˈmʌltəpəl || ˈmʌltɪpəl/ *adj* **1** (involving many elements) múltiple; ~ **birth** parto *m* múltiple **2** (many) múltiples; ~ **errors** múltiples errores

multiple² *n* múltiplo *m*

multiple: **~-choice** /ˈmʌltəpəlˈtʃɔɪs || ˌmʌltɪpəlˈtʃɔɪs/ *adj* de opción múltiple, tipo test; ~ **sclerosis** /skləˈrəʊsəs/ *n* [u] esclerosis *f* múltiple

multiplex /ˈmʌltɪpleks/ *n* multicine *m*

multiplication /ˈmʌltəpləˈkeɪʃən || ˌmʌltɪplɪˈkeɪʃən/ *n* [u] multiplicación *f*; (*before n*) ~ **table** tabla *f* de multiplicar

multiply /ˈmʌltəplaɪ || ˈmʌltɪplaɪ/ **-plies, -plying, -plied** *vt* **1** (Math) **to ~ sth (BY sth)** multiplicar* algo (POR algo) **2** (increase) multiplicar*

■ **multiply** *vi* **1** (Math) multiplicar* **2** (increase, reproduce) multiplicarse*

multipurpose /ˈmʌltiˈpɜːrpəs || ˌmʌltiˈpɜːpəs/ *adj* ‹*tool/appliance*› multiuso *adj inv*; ‹*building*› para usos diversos

multiracial /ˈmʌltiˈreɪʃəl/ *adj* multirracial

multistory, (BrE) **multistorey** /ˈmʌltiˈstɔːri/ *adj* de varias plantas, de varios pisos

multitasking /ˈmʌltiˈtæskɪŋ || ˌmʌltiˈtɑːskɪŋ/ *n* [u] (función *f*) multitarea *f*

multitude /ˈmʌltətuːd || ˈmʌltɪtjuːd/ *n* **1** (large number) (frml) (*no pl*) **a ~ OF sth**: **a ~ of problems** innumerables *or* múltiples problemas; **this covers a ~ of sins** (hum) con esto se disimulan muchas cosas **2** [c] (crowd) (arch *or* liter) multitud *f*, muchedumbre *f*

multiuser /ˈmʌltiˈjuːzər/ *adj* multiusuario *adj inv*

mum /mʌm/ *n*

A (mother) (BrE colloq) mamá *f* (fam)

B (silence) (colloq): **~'s *the word*** ¡punto en boca! (fam), ¡chitón! (fam); ***to keep*** ~ no decir* ni pío (fam)

mumble /ˈmʌmbəl/ *vi* hablar entre dientes, farfullar

■ **mumble** *vt* mascullar, farfullar

mumbo jumbo /ˈmʌmbəʊˈdʒʌmbəʊ/ *n* [u] (pej): **religion, he said, was a lot of ~ ~** dijo que la religión no era más que supercherías *or* (fam) paparruchas

mummify /ˈmʌmɪfaɪ/ *vt* **-fies, -fying, -fied** momificar*

mummy /ˈmʌmi/ *n* (*pl* **-mies**)

A (mother) (BrE colloq: esp used by children) mami *f*, mamita *f* (fam)

B (Archeol) momia *f*

mumps /mʌmps/ *n* [u] paperas *fpl*

munch /mʌntʃ/ *vt/i* mascar*, masticar*

mundane /mʌnˈdeɪn/ *adj* **1** ‹*existence*› prosaico; ‹*activity*› rutinario **2** ‹*comments*› trivial

mung bean /mʌŋ/ *n*: *semilla cuyo brote se utiliza en la cocina oriental*

municipal /mjʊˈnɪsəpəl/ *adj* (*usu before n*) municipal

municipality /mjʊˈnɪsəˈpæləti/ *n* (*pl* **-ties**) municipio *m*, municipalidad *f*

munitions /mjʊˈnɪʃənz || mjuːˈnɪʃənz/ *pl n* municiones *fpl*

mural /ˈmjʊrəl || ˈmjʊərəl/ *n* mural *m*

murder¹ /ˈmɜːrdər || ˈmɜːdə(r)/ *n*

A [u c] (killing) asesinato *m*; (Law) homicidio *m*; **to commit ~** cometer un asesinato *or* un crimen; ***to get away with ~***: **she lets them get away with ~** les permite cualquier cosa, los deja hacer lo que les da la gana (fam); ***to scream bloody*** *o* (esp BrE) ***blue ~*** poner* el grito en el cielo

B [u] (sth unpleasant): **to be ~** (colloq) ser* la muerte (fam)

murder² *vt* **1** (kill) asesinar, matar **2** (ruin) ‹*music/play*› destrozar*, masacrar (hum) **3** (devour) (colloq): **I could ~ a beer** ¡con qué gusto me tomaría una cerveza!

■ **murder** *vi* matar

murderer /ˈmɜːrdərər || ˈmɜːdərə(r)/ *n* asesino, -na *m,f*, criminal *mf*, homicida *mf* (frml)

murderous /ˈmɜːrdərəs/ *adj* ‹*instinct/look*› asesino; ‹*individual*› de instintos asesinos; ‹*plan*› criminal

murky /ˈmɜːrki || ˈmɜːki/ *adj* **-kier, -kiest** ‹*water*› turbio, opaco; ‹*green/brown*› sucio; ‹*past*› turbio; **the ~ depths of the lake** las tenebrosas profundidades del lago (liter)

murmur¹ /ˈmɜːrmər || ˈmɜːmə(r)/ *n*

A **1** (speech) murmullo *m*, susurro *m*; **to speak in a ~** hablar en voz baja *or* susurrando; **without a ~** sin chistar **2** (of stream, wind) murmullo *m* (liter); (of traffic) rumor *m*

B (*heart ~*) soplo *m* en el corazón

murmur² *vt* ‹*remark/name*› murmurar

■ **murmur** *vi* «*wind/stream*» murmurar, susurrar (liter)

muscatel /ˈmʌskəˈtel/ *n* [u] (wine) moscatel *m*; (fortified wine) (AmE) *vino dulce de mala calidad*

muscle /ˈmʌsəl/ *n* **1** [c u] (Anat) músculo *m*; **don't move a ~!** ¡no te muevas!, ¡no muevas ni un pelo! (fam) **2** [u] (power) fuerza *f*, poder *m* efectivo; **they have no political ~** políticamente, no tienen influencia

Phrasal verb

• **muscle in** [v ▸ adv] (colloq) meterse por medio (*con prepotencia*) **to ~ in ON sth**: **a rival company ~d in on their market** una compañía de la competencia se introdujo en su sector del mercado

muscle-bound /ˈmʌsəlbaʊnd/ *adj* demasiado musculoso

Muscovite *n* moscovita *mf*

muscular /ˈmʌskjələr || ˈmʌskjʊlə(r)/ *adj* **1** ‹*arms/build*› musculoso **2** ‹*strain/contraction*› muscular

muscular dystrophy /ˈdɪstrəfi/ *n* [u] distrofia *f* muscular

muse¹ /mjuːz/ *vi* **to ~ (ON *o* UPON sth)** cavilar *or* reflexionar (SOBRE algo)

muse², **Muse** *n* musa *f*

museum /mjʊˈziːəm/ *n* museo *m*

museum piece *n* pieza *f* de museo

mush /mʌʃ/ *n* [u] (soft mass) papilla *f*, pasta *f*, pasteta *f* (fam); (**corn meal**) ▸ (AmE) *harina de maíz cocida en leche*

mushroom¹ /ˈmʌʃrʊm, -ruːm/ *n* hongo *m* (esp AmL), seta *f* (esp Esp), callampa *f* (Chi); (rounded, white) champiñón *m*; (*before n*) ~ **soup** (sopa *f*) crema *f* de champiñones; ~ **cloud** hongo *m* atómico *or* nuclear

mushroom² *vi* «*town/population*» crecer* rápidamente; «*companies/buildings*» aparecer* *or* brotar como hongos *or* (Chi) como callampas, multiplicarse*

mushy /ˈmʌʃi/ *adj* **mushier, mushiest** **1** ‹*vegetables/fruit*› blando **2** ‹*play/scene*› sentimentaloide (fam)

music /ˈmjuːzɪk/ *n* [u] **1** (art form) música *f*; **the news was ~ to her ears** la noticia le sonó a música celestial; ***to face the ~*** afrontar las consecuencias **2** (written notes) partitura *f*, música *f*; **can you read ~?** ¿sabes solfeo?, ¿sabes leer música?; (*before n*) ~ **stand** atril *m*

musical¹ /ˈmjuːzɪkəl/ *adj* **1** (Mus) (*before n*) ‹*ability/tradition*› musical **2** (musically gifted) con aptitudes para la música, con dotes musicales **3** ‹*voice/laugh*› musical

musical² *n* musical *m*

musical: ~ **box** *n* (BrE) caja *f* de música; ~ **chairs** *n* (+ *sing vb*): **to play ~ chairs** jugar* a las sillitas *or* al stop

music: ~ **box** *n* caja *f* de música; ~ **centre** *n* (BrE) equipo *m* de música; ~ **hall** *n* **1** [u] (entertainment) music hall *m*, ≈ revista *f* de variedades **2** [c] (building) teatro *m* de variedades

musician /mjʊˈzɪʃən/ *n* músico, -ca *m,f*

musicology /ˈmjuːzɪˈkɑːlədʒi/ *n* [u] musicología *f*

musings /ˈmjuːzɪŋz/ *pl n* reflexiones *fpl*, cavilaciones *fpl*

musk /mʌsk/ *n* [u] almizcle *m*

musket /ˈmʌskət || ˈmʌskɪt/ *n* mosquete *m*

muskrat /ˈmʌskræt/ *n* (*pl* **~s** *or* ~) **1** [c] (animal) almizclera *f*, rata *f* almizclada **2** [u] (AmE) ▸ **musquash 1**

Muslim¹ /ˈmʊzləm || ˈmʊzlɪm/ *n* musulmán, -mana *m,f*

Muslim² *adj* musulmán

muslin /ˈmʌzlən || ˈmʌzlɪn/ *n* [u] muselina *f* (*de algodón*); **a piece of ~** una gasa

musquash /ˈmʌskwɑːʃ/ *n* **1** [u] (Clothing) piel *f* de almizclera *or* de rata almizclada **2** [c] ▸ **muskrat 1**

muss /mʌs/ *vt* ~ **(up)** (AmE colloq) ‹*room*› desordenar; **she ~ed her hair** se despeinó

mussel /ˈmʌsəl/ *n* mejillón *m*

must¹ /mʌst, *weak form* məst/ *v mod*

A **1** (expressing obligation) tener* que *or* deber; **it ~ be remembered that ...** hay que recordar que ..., tenemos que *or* debemos recordar que ...; **she ~ not know that I am here** no debe enterarse de que estoy aquí, que no se entere de que estoy aquí; ***must* you make so much noise?** ¿hace falta *or* es necesario hacer tanto ruido?; **I'll read you my poem — oh well, if you ~(, you ~)** te voy a leer mi poema — bueno, si te empeñas; **I ~ say, everywhere looks very tidy** tengo que reconocer que está todo muy ordenado **2** (in invitations, suggestions): **you ~ come and see us more often** a ver si nos vienes a ver más a menudo

B (expressing certainty, supposition) deber (de) *or* (esp AmL) haber* de; **it ~ be six o'clock** deben (de) ser *or* (esp AmL) han de ser las seis, serán las seis; **there ~ be another way!** ¡debe (de) *or* tiene que haber otra manera!

must² /mʌst/ *n*

A [c] (essential thing, activity): **a car is a ~ here** aquí es indispensable *or* imprescindible tener coche; **this book is a ~** éste es un libro que hay que leer

B [u] (Culin) mosto *m*

mustache /'mʌstæʃ/, (BrE) **moustache** /mə'stɑːʃ/ *n* bigote(s) *m(pl)*; **to grow a ~** dejarse bigote(s) *or* el bigote

mustard /'mʌstərd/ *n* [u] **1** (Culin, Bot) mostaza *f* **2** (color) color *m* mostaza; (*before n*) (color) mostaza *adj inv*

mustard gas *n* [u] gas *m* mostaza

muster¹ /'mʌstər || 'mʌstə(r)/ *vt* **1** (Mil) ‹*soldiers*› reunir*, llamar a asamblea **2** (succeed in raising) **to ~ (up)** ‹*team/army*› lograr formar; **if they can ~ enough support** si logran el apoyo que necesitan

muster² *n* asamblea *f*; ***to pass ~***: **that kind of excuse will not pass ~** ese tipo de excusa no va a colar (fam); **the car didn't pass ~** el coche no pasó la inspección

mustn't /'mʌsn̩t/ = **must not**

musty /'mʌsti/ *adj* **-tier, tiest** que huele a humedad *or* a moho; ‹*ideas/methods*› anticuado, desfasado

mutant¹ /'mjuːtn̩t || 'mjuːtənt/ *adj* mutante

mutant² *n* (Biol) mutante *m*; (in science fiction) mutante *mf*

mutate /'mjuːteɪt || mjuː'teɪt/ *vi* **1** (Biol) mutar **2** (change) (frml) sufrir una transformación/transformaciones **3** (Ling) mutar, transformarse

mutation /mjuː'teɪʃən/ *n* [u c] **1** (Biol, Ling) mutación *f* **2** (change) (frml) transformación *f*

mute¹ /mjuːt/ *adj* mudo

mute² *n*

A (dumb person) mudo, -da *m,f*

B **1** (Mus) sordina *f* **2** (Audio) mute *m*

mute³ *vt* (Mus) ponerle* sordina a

muted /'mjuːtəd || 'mjuːtɪd/ *adj* ‹*sound*› sordo; ‹*voice*› apagado; ‹*trumpet*› con sordina; ‹*shade/red*› apagado; ‹*protest/reaction*› débil

mutilate /'mjuːtl̩eɪt || 'mjuːtɪleɪt/ *vt* mutilar

mutilation /'mjuːtl̩'eɪʃən/ *n* [u c] mutilación *f*

mutineer /'mjuːtn̩'ɪr/ *n* amotinado, -da *m,f*

mutinous /'mjuːtn̩əs || 'mjuːtɪnəs/ *adj* ‹*crew/troops*› amotinado; ‹*atmosphere*› de rebelión

mutiny¹ /'mjuːtn̩i || 'mjuːtɪni/ *n* (*pl* **-nies**) **1** [c] (instance) motín *m*, amotinamiento *m* **2** [u] (offense) amotinamiento *m*

mutiny² *vi* **-nies, -nying, -nied** amotinarse

mutt /mʌt/ *n* (AmE colloq) (dog) chucho *m* (fam), gozque *m* (Col fam), quiltro *m* (Chi fam), pichicho *m* (RPl fam)

mutter /'mʌtər || 'mʌtə(r)/ *vi* hablar entre dientes; (grumble) refunfuñar, rezongar*

■ **mutter** *vt* mascullar, farfullar

mutton /'mʌtn̩/ *n* [u] carne *f* de ovino (*de más de un año*), añojo *m* (Esp), capón *m* (RPl); **~ *dressed as lamb*** (BrE) una vieja vestida de jovencita

mutual /'mjuːtʃuəl/ *adj* **1** (reciprocal) mutuo; **the feeling is ~** el sentimiento es mutuo *or* correspondido **2** (shared, common) (*before n*) ‹*friend/enemy*› común; **it will be to our ~ benefit** será beneficioso para ambos/para todos

mutual fund *n* (AmE) fondo *m* de inversión mobiliaria

mutually /'mjuːtʃuəli/ *adv* **1** (reciprocally): **they are ~ exclusive options** son opciones que se excluyen mutuamente *or* entre sí **2** (by, to, for all parties): **it was ~ acceptable/beneficial** era aceptable/beneficioso para ambos/para todos

Muzak® /'mjuːzæk/ *n* [u] música *f* ambiental, música *f* funcional (RPl)

muzzle¹ /'mʌzəl/ *n* **1** (snout) hocico *m* **2** (for dog) bozal *m* **3** (of gun) boca *f*

muzzle² *vt* ‹*dog*› ponerle* un bozal a; ‹*press/critics*› amordazar*

my¹ /maɪ/ *adj* (*sing*) mi; (*pl*) mis; **I put ~ hat on** me puse el sombrero; **I broke ~ arm** me rompí el brazo

my² *interj* ¡caramba!

myalgic encephalomyelitis /maɪ'ældʒɪken ˌsefələʊmaɪə'laɪtəs || maɪˌældʒɪkenˌsefələʊˌmaɪə'laɪtɪs/ *n* encefalomielitis *f* miálgica, síndrome *m* de fatiga crónica

myna (bird), mynah (bird) /'maɪnə/ *n* mina *f*, mainato *m* (*pájaro tropical capaz de imitar sonidos humanos*)

myopia /maɪ'əʊpiə/ *n* [u] (frml) miopía *f*

myopic /maɪ'əʊpɪk, -'ɑːpɪk || maɪ'ɒpɪk/ *adj* (frml) ‹*person*› miope; ‹*attitude*› corto de miras

myriad¹ /'mɪriəd/ *adj* (liter): **the ~ varieties of butterfly** los miles *or* millares de tipos de mariposas

myriad² *n* (liter) miríada *f* (liter)

myrrh /mɜːr || mɜː(r)/ *n* [u] mirra *f*

myself /maɪ'self/ *pron* **1** (reflexive): **I cut/hurt ~** me corté/lastimé; **I fixed ~ a drink** me serví una copa; **I was talking to ~** estaba hablando solo/sola; **that's wrong, I thought to ~** eso está mal —pensé para mí *or* para mis adentros; **I was by ~** estaba solo/sola; **I behaved ~** me porté bien **2** (*emphatic use*) yo mismo, yo misma; **I made it ~** lo hice yo mismo/misma; **(even) though I say so ~** modestia aparte **3** (normal self): **I haven't been feeling ~ lately** no me encuentro muy bien últimamente

mysterious /mɪ'stɪriəs || mɪ'stɪəriəs/ *adj* **1** (unexplained, strange) misterioso **2** (suggesting) ‹*look/smile*› misterioso, lleno de misterio

mysteriously /mɪ'stɪriəsli || mɪ'stɪəriəsli/ *adv* **1** ‹*disappear/vanish*› misteriosamente **2** ‹*say/smile*› con cierto misterio

mystery /'mɪstəri/ *n* (*pl* **-ries**)

A **1** [c] (puzzle) misterio *m*; **it's a ~ to me how she puts up with him** para mí es un misterio cómo logra aguantarlo **2** [u] (quality) misterio *m*; (*before n*) ‹*guest/tour*› sorpresa *adj inv*

B [c] (Cin, Lit, Theat) película *f* (*or* novela *f etc*) de misterio *or* de suspenso *or* (Esp) de suspense

mystical /'mɪstɪkəl/ *adj* místico

mysticism /'mɪstəsɪzəm || 'mɪstɪsɪzəm/ *n* [u] misticismo *m*

mystify /'mɪstəfaɪ || 'mɪstɪfaɪ/ *vt* **-fies, -fying, -fied** desconcertar*, dejar perplejo; **I'm totally mystified** estoy perplejo

mystique /mɪ'stiːk/ *n* [u] aura *f‡ or* halo *m* de misterio

myth /mɪθ/ *n* mito *m*

mythical /'mɪθɪkəl/ *adj* **1** (Lit) ‹*country/hero*› mítico **2** (not real): **the ~ wisdom of old age** la supuesta sabiduría que da la vejez

mythological /'mɪθə'lɑːdʒɪkəl/ *adj* mitológico

mythology /mɪ'θɑːlədʒi/ *n* (*pl* **-gies**) mitología *f*

myxomatosis /mɪkˌsəʊmə'təʊsəs/ *n* [u] mixomatosis *f*

Nn

N, n /en/ *n* [1] (letter) N, n *f* [2] (indeterminate number) (Math) (número *m*) n; **there are n different ways of doing it** (colloq) hay ene *or* equis maneras de hacerlo

'n' /ən/ **= and**

N (**= north**) N

NA [1] (**= not applicable**) no corresponde [2] (AmE) **= North America**

NAACP /ˈendʌbəlˈeɪsiːˈpiː/ *n* (in US) **= National Association for the Advancement of Colored People**

nab /næb/ *vt* **-bb-** (colloq) [1] (catch) ‹*person*› pescar* (fam), pillar (fam) [2] (snatch) agarrar *or* (Esp) coger*

nadir /ˈneɪdɪr || ˈneɪdiə(r)/ *n* (Astron) nadir *m*; (lowest point) punto *m* más bajo

naff /næf/ *adj* (BrE colloq) [1] (in poor taste) de mal gusto, hortera (Esp fam), naco (Méx fam), meosa (RPl fam), lobo (Col fam), huachaca (Chi fam), huachafo (Per fam) [2] (inferior) malo, rasca (CS fam)

NAFTA /ˈnæftə/ *n* (**= North American Free Trade Agreement**) NAFTA *m*

NAFTA – the North American Free Trade Agreement

Un acuerdo entre EEUU, Canadá y México firmado en 1989 y vigente desde 1994. Tiene por objeto permitir un más fácil transporte y venta de mercancías a través de sus fronteras

nag¹ /næg/ **-gg-** *vt* [1] (pester) fastidiar; **don't ~ me** deja de fastidiarme *or* (fam) darme la lata; **to ~ sb to + INF** darle* la lata a algn para que (+ *subj*) [2] (criticize): **he's always ~ging her for being untidy** siempre le está encima con que es desordenada

■ **nag** *vi*

A [1] (pester) fastidiar; **to ~ AT sb** fastidiar *or* (fam) darle* la lata a algn [2] (criticize, scold) rezongar*; **to ~ AT sb** estarle* encima A algn

B **nagging** *pres p* ‹*doubt/worry*› persistente, acuciante; ‹*husband/wife*› rezongón (fam)

nag² *n*

A (scolder) rezongón, -gona *m,f* (fam), gruñón, -ñona *m,f*

B (horse) (colloq & pej) jamelgo *m* (fam & pey), cuaco *m* (Méx fam & pey)

nail¹ /neɪl/ *n*

A (Const) clavo *m*; (smaller) puntilla *f*; ***a ~ in sb's coffin***: **this failure is another ~ in his coffin** este fracaso es otro paso camino a su derrota; ***to be as hard as ~s*** ser* muy duro (de corazón); ***to hit the ~ on the head*** dar* en el clavo; ***to pay on the ~*** (colloq) pagar* en el acto; **they paid cash on the ~** pagaron a tocateja (Esp) *or* (RPl) pagaron taca taca *or* (Chi, Ven) chin-chin *or* (Méx) en caliente (y de repente) (fam)

B (Anat) uña *f*; **to cut one's ~s** cortarse las uñas; (*before n*) **~ polish** *o* (BrE also) **varnish** esmalte *m* de uñas; **~ polish** *o* (BrE also) **varnish remover** quitaesmalte *m*

nail² *vt*

A (fix) clavar; **he was ~ed to the spot in fear** se quedó clavado en el sitio de puro miedo

B (colloq) (apprehend) agarrar *or* (esp Esp) coger

Phrasal verbs

• **nail down** [v ▸ o ▸ adv, v ▸ adv ▸ o] [1] ‹*lid/floorboard*› clavar, asegurar con clavos [2] ‹*cause*› establecer* con certeza [3] ‹*person*›: **see if you can ~ him down on this issue** a ver si logras que te dé una respuesta concreta sobre este asunto; **to ~ sb down TO sth**: **we must ~ them down to a precise date** tenemos que hacer que se comprometan a una fecha concreta

• **nail up** [v ▸ o ▸ adv, v ▸ adv ▸ o] [1] ‹*crate*› cerrar* con clavos; ‹*door/window*› tapar (*con tablas*) [2] ‹*sign*› clavar

nail: **~-biting** *adj* ‹*suspense/tension*› angustioso; ‹*finish/contest*› lleno de tensión; **~brush** *n* cepillo *m* de uñas; **~ clippers** *pl n* cortaúñas *m*; **a pair of ~ clippers** un cortaúñas; **~ file** *n* lima *f* (de uñas)

naive, naïve /nɑːˈiːv, naɪˈiːv/ *adj* [1] ‹*person/belief/view*› ingenuo, cándido, inocentón (fam); ‹*book/article*› simplista; **don't be so ~!** ¡no seas tan ingenuo! [2] ‹*art/artist*› naif *adj inv*

naively, naïvely /nɑːˈiːvli, naɪ-/ *adv* ingenuamente

naivety /nɑːˈiːvti, naɪ-/, (AmE esp) **naïveté** /-teɪ/ *n* [u] ingenuidad *f*, candor *m*

naked /ˈneɪkəd || ˈneɪkɪd/ *adj* [1] (unclothed) desnudo; **~ to the waist** desnudo hasta la cintura [2] ‹*sword/blade*› desenvainado, **❶ do not use near a naked flame** no acercar a la llama; **visible/invisible to the ~ eye** que se puede ver/invisible a simple vista; **do not look at the sun with the ~ eye** no mire el sol sin protección [3] (stark, plain) ‹*aggression*› manifiesto; ‹*ambition*› puro; **the ~ truth** la verdad desnuda

nakedness /ˈneɪkɪdnəs || ˈneɪkɪdnɪs/ *n* [u] desnudez *f*

namby-pamby /ˈnæmbiˈpæmbi/ *n* (*pl* **-bies**) (colloq) ñoño, -ña *m,f* (fam), remilgado, -da *m,f*

name¹ /neɪm/ *n*

A (of person, thing) nombre *m*; (surname) apellido *m*; **what's your ~?** ¿cómo te llamas?, ¿cómo se llama (Ud)?, ¿cuál es su nombre? (frml); **my ~ is John Baker** me llamo John Baker; **the ~'s Smith** me llamo Smith; **a woman by the ~ of Green** una mujer llamada Green; **he knows them all by ~** los conoce a todos por su nombre; **I only know her by ~** sólo la conozco de oídas *or* de nombre; **she goes by** *o* **under the ~ of Shirley Lane** se hace llamar Shirley Lane; **he writes under the ~ (of) ...** escribe bajo el seudónimo de ...; **in ~ only** sólo de nombre; **she's manager in all but ~** a todos los efectos *or* en la práctica, la directora es ella; **the house is in her husband's ~** la casa está a nombre de su marido; **what in God's** *o* **heaven's ~ is this?** ¿qué diablos es esto?; **he doesn't have a penny to his ~** no tiene dónde caerse muerto; **mentioning no ~s, without mentioning any ~s** sin mencionar a nadie; **to take sb's ~** ‹‹*referee*›› (BrE) sacarle* la tarjeta a algn; **the policeman took my ~** el policía me tomó los datos; **he's put his ~ down for a transfer** ha solicitado un traslado; ***to call sb ~s*** insultar a algn; (*before n*) **~ tag** etiqueta *f* de identificación, chapa *f*; ***to name ~s*** dar* nombres

B [1] (reputation) fama *f*; **to give sb/sth a bad ~** darle* mala fama a algn/algo; **he has made quite a ~ for himself as a designer** se ha hecho bastante fama como diseñador [2] (person) figura *f*; (company) nombre *m*; **all the big ~s** todas las grandes figuras; ***to drop ~s*** mencionar a gente importante (*para darse tono*)

name² *vt*

A (give name to) ‹*company/town*› ponerle* nombre a; ‹*boat*› bautizar*, ponerle* nombre a; **they ~d the baby George** le pusieron George al niño, al niño le pusieron por nombre George (liter); **a man ~d Smith** un hombre llamado Smith; **to ~ sb/sth AFTER** *o* (AmE also) **FOR sb**: **they ~d**

n

her after Ann's mother le pusieron el nombre de la madre de Ann; **the city is ∼d after the national hero** la ciudad lleva el nombre del héroe nacional
B (identify, mention): **police have ∼d the suspect** la policía ha dado el nombre del sospechoso; **to ∼ but a few** por mencionar a unos pocos; **to ∼ the day** fijar la fecha de la boda; ***you ∼ it*** (colloq): **you ∼ it, she's done it** ha hecho de todo lo habido y por haber
C (appoint) nombrar

name: **∼ day** *n* (Relig) día *m* del santo, día *m* del onomástico (AmL), día *m* de la onomástica (Esp); **∼-dropper** /ˈneɪm,drɑːpər || ˈneɪmdrɒpə(r)/ *n* (colloq): **she's a terrible ∼-dopper** le encanta darse tono mencionando a gente importante

nameless /ˈneɪmləs || ˈneɪmlɪs/ *adj*
A (not specified) anónimo
B 1 ‹*fear/yearning*› indescriptible 2 ‹*atrocities*› nefando (liter), indescriptible

namely /ˈneɪmli/ *adv* (frml) a saber (frml), concretamente

name: **∼plate** *n* (on door) placa *f* (*con el nombre*); **∼sake** *n* tocayo, -ya *m,f*, homónimo, -ma *m,f*

nanny /ˈnæni/ *n* (*pl* **-nies**)
A (nursemaid) (esp BrE) niñera *f*; **the ∼ state** el estado protector
B (granny) (used to or by children) abuelita *f* (fam)

nanosecond /ˈnænəʊsekənd/ *n* nanosegundo *m*

nap[1] /næp/ *n*
A (sleep) sueñecito *m* (fam), sueñito *m* (esp AmL fam); (esp in the afternoon) siesta *f*; **to have** *o* **take a ∼** echarse un sueñecito (*or* una siesta *etc*)
B (Tex) pelo *m*

nap[2] *vi* **-pp-** dar* cabezadas; ***to catch sb ∼ping*** agarrar *or* (Esp) coger* a algn desprevenido

napalm /ˈneɪpɑːm/ *n* [u] napalm *m*

nape /neɪp/ *n* nuca *f*, cogote *m* (fam)

napkin /ˈnæpkɪn/ *n* servilleta *f*; (*before n*) **∼ ring** servilletero *m*

Naples /ˈneɪpəlz/ *n* Nápoles *m*

nappy /ˈnæpi/ *n* (*pl* **-pies**) (BrE) pañal *m*; **∼ rash** ▸ **diaper rash**

narcissus /nɑːrˈsɪsəs || nɑːˈsɪsəs/ *n* [c u] (*pl* **-cissuses** *or* **-cissi**) narciso *m*

narcoterrorism /ˌnɑːrkəʊˈterərɪzəm || ˌnɑːkəʊˈterərɪzəm/ *n* [u] narcoterrorismo *m*

narcotic /nɑːrˈkɑːtɪk || nɑːˈkɒtɪk/ *n* estupefaciente *m*, narcótico *m*

narrate /ˈnæreɪt || nəˈreɪt/ *vt* 1 (Lit frml) ‹*story/events*› narrar, relatar 2 ‹*film/documentary*› hacer* el comentario de

narration /næˈreɪʃən || nəˈreɪʃən/ *n* [u c] 1 (Lit frml) narración *f* 2 (Cin, Theat, TV) comentario *m*

narrative[1] /ˈnærətɪv/ *adj* narrativo

narrative[2] *n* 1 [c] (story) (frml) narración *f*, relato *m* 2 [u] (Lit) (narrated part) narración *f*

narrator /ˈnæreɪtər || nəˈreɪtə(r)/ *n* 1 (Lit) narrador, -dora *m,f* 2 (Cin, Theat, TV) comentarista *mf*

narrow[1] /ˈnærəʊ/ *adj*
A 1 (not wide) ‹*path/opening/hips*› estrecho, angosto (esp AmL); **to get** *o* **become ∼er** estrecharse, angostarse (esp AmL) 2 (slender) ‹*margin*› escaso; ‹*win/victory*› conseguido por un escaso margen; **to have a ∼ escape** salvarse de milagro
B (restricted) ‹*range/view*› limitado; ‹*attitude/ideas*› cerrado

narrow[2] *vt* 1 (reduce width of) estrechar, angostar (esp AmL); **to ∼ the gap** reducir* la distancia 2 (restrict) ‹*range/field*› restringir*, limitar
■ **narrow** *vi* 1 ‹‹*road/river/valley*›› estrecharse, angostarse (esp AmL) 2 ‹‹*options/odds*›› reducirse*

Phrasal verb
• **narrow down**
A [v ▸ o ▸ adv, v ▸ adv ▸ o]: **they've ∼ed their investigation down to this area** han restringido su investigación a esta área; **we ∼ed it down to only three candidates** fuimos descartando candidatos hasta quedar con sólo tres
B [v ▸ adv] **to ∼ down (TO sth)** reducirse* (A algo)

narrowly /ˈnærəʊli/ *adv* por poco, por un escaso margen

narrow-minded /ˈnærəʊˈmaɪndəd || ˌnærəʊˈmaɪndɪd/ *adj* ‹*person*› de mentalidad cerrada, intolerante; ‹*attitude*› cerrado, intolerante

narrow-mindedness /ˈnærəʊˈmaɪndədnəs || ˌnærəʊˈmaɪndɪdnɪs/ *n* [u] intolerancia *f*

narrowness /ˈnærəʊnəs || ˈnærəʊnɪs/ *n* [u] estrechez *f*

NASA /ˈnæsə/ *n* (in US) (*no art*) (= **National Aeronautics and Space Administration**) la NASA

nasal /ˈneɪzəl/ *adj* (Anat, Ling) nasal; ‹*voice/accent*› gangoso, (de timbre) nasal

NASDAQ /ˈnæzdæk/ *n* (= **National Association of Securities Dealers Automated Quotations**) NASDAQ *m*

nastily /ˈnæstəli || ˈnɑːstɪli/ *adv* ‹*say/behave*› con maldad

nastiness /ˈnæstinəs || ˈnɑːstɪnɪs/ *n* [u] maldad *f*

nasturtium /nəˈstɜːrʃəm || nəˈstɜːʃəm/ *n* capuchina *f*

nasty /ˈnæsti || ˈnɑːsti/ *adj* **-tier, -tiest**
A 1 ‹*taste/smell/medicine*› asqueroso, repugnante; ‹*habit*› feo, desagradable 2 ‹*film/book*› asqueroso, inmundo
B (spiteful) ‹*person*› malo, asqueroso; **that was a ∼ thing to say!** fue una maldad decirle eso; **they are really ∼ to him** son realmente malos *or* crueles con él; **to have a ∼ temper** tener* muy mal carácter; **what a ∼ trick!** ¡qué canallada!; ▸ **piece B**
C 1 (severe) ‹*cut/injury/cough*› feo; ‹*accident*› serio; (stronger) horrible; **I had a ∼ shock** me llevé una sorpresa de lo más desagradable 2 (difficult, dangerous) ‹*question/exam*› peliagudo, muy difícil; ‹*corner/intersection*› muy peligroso 3 (unpleasant) ‹*situation/experience*› desagradable

nation /ˈneɪʃn̩/ *n* nación *f*; **the British ∼** los británicos, la nación británica

national[1] /ˈnæʃn̩əl || ˈnæʃənl̩/ *adj* nacional; **our ∼ anthem** nuestro himno nacional; **they were wearing their ∼ costume** llevaban sus trajes típicos; **the ∼ debt** la deuda nacional; **∼ holiday** fiesta *f* nacional, fiesta *f* patria (AmL)

national[2] *n* ciudadano, -na *m,f*; **foreign ∼s** los ciudadanos extranjeros

> **National Guard**
> Una milicia voluntaria, reclutada por cada uno de los estados norteamericanos, cuya historia remonta a la época colonial. En tiempos de desastre natural o emergencia civil puede ser declarada bajo mando federal. Hoy día se la considera parte del ejército nacional

> **National Rifle Association – NRA**
> Una organización en EEUU que apoya el uso de armas de fuego para la caza, el deporte y la legítima defensa. Sus 3,4 millones de miembros sostienen que la Constitución otorga a los ciudadanos el derecho a poseerlas

> **National Trust – The National Trust**
> Una fundación británica que tiene como objetivo la conservación de lugares de interés histórico o de belleza natural. Se financia mediante legados y subvenciones privadas y es la mayor propietaria de tierras en Gran Bretaña. A lo largo del tiempo ha obtenido, mediante compra o cesión, enormes extensiones de tierra y de litoral, así como pueblos y casas, muchas de las cuales están abiertas al público en determinadas épocas del año. En Escocia la organización recibe el nombre de *National Trust for Scotland* y es independiente

national: **∼ bank** *n* (Fin) (state-owned) banco *m* estatal *or* nacional; (in US) *banco que opera según las normas del Federal Reserve System*; **∼ Guard** *n* (in US) **the N∼ Guard** la Guardia Nacional; **∼ Health (Service)** *n* [u] (in UK) **the N∼ Health (Service)** *servicio de asistencia sanitaria de la Seguridad Social*; (*before n*) ‹*hospital/doctor*› de la Seguridad Social, del Seguro; **∼ Insurance** *n* [u] (in UK) Seguridad *f* Social; (*before n*) **N∼ Insurance contributions** aportaciones *fpl or* (Esp) cotizaciones *fpl or* (RPl) aportes *mpl or* (Chi) imposiciones *fpl* a la Seguridad Social

nationalism /ˈnæʃn̩əlɪzəm/ *n* [u] nacionalismo *m*

nationalist[1] /ˈnæʃn̩ələst || ˈnæʃn̩əlɪst/ *adj* nacionalista

nationalist[2] *n* nacionalista *mf*

nationalistic /ˌnæʃn̩əˈlɪstɪk/ *adj* nacionalista

nationality /ˌnæʃəˈnæləti/ *n* (*pl* **-ties**) 1 [u] (citizenship) nacionalidad *f*, ciudadanía *f*; **what's your ∼?, what ∼ are**

you? ¿de qué nacionalidad eres? 2 (c) (national group) nacionalidad *f*

nationalization /ˈnæʃn̩əlaˈzeɪʃən || ˌnæʃnəlaɪˈzeɪʃən/ *n* [u] nacionalización *f*

nationalize /ˈnæʃn̩əlaɪz || ˈnæʃnəlaɪz/ *vt* nacionalizar*

nationally /ˈnæʃn̩əli || ˈnæʃn̩əli/ *adv* a escala nacional

national: ~ **park** *n* parque *m* nacional; ~ **Security Council** *n* (in US) **the N~ Security Council** el Consejo Nacional de Seguridad de los EEUU; ~ **service** *n* [u] (BrE) servicio *m* militar; ~ **Socialism** *n* [u] nacionalsocialismo *m*

nationwide¹ /ˈneɪʃənwaɪd/ *adj* ‹*campaign*› a escala nacional; ‹*appeal*› a toda la nación; **a ~ survey** un estudio realizado a nivel nacional

nationwide² *adv* ‹*distribute/operate*› a escala nacional

native¹ /ˈneɪtɪv/ *adj*

A 1 (of or by birth) ‹*country/town*› natal, nativo; ‹*customs*› nativo; ‹*language*› materno; **his ~ land** su patria, su tierra natal; **a ~ speaker of ...** un hablante nativo de ... 2 (innate) ‹*ability/wit/charm*› innato

B (indigenous) ‹*plant/animal*› autóctono; **to be ~ TO sth** ser* originario DE algo

native² *n* 1 (referring to place of birth): **he is a ~ of Texas** es natural *or* oriundo de Tejas; **she speaks French like a ~** habla (el) francés como si fuera su lengua materna 2 (Anthrop) nativo, -va *m,f*, indígena *mf* 3 (plant, animal): **the dingo is a ~ of Australia** el dingo es originario de Australia

Native American *n* indio americano, india americana *m,f*

> **Native American**
>
> El término de más amplia aceptación para referirse a los pueblos indígenas de América y el Caribe. De acuerdo al *Bureau of Indian Affairs*, organización del gobierno de EEUU que trata todo los asuntos relacionados con los indios, existen en ese país cerca de 550 tribus que totalizan alrededor de 1,2 millones de personas. De éstas, cerca de un millón vive en reservaciones y alrededor del 37% están desempleadas. Muchas reservaciones abren casinos basándose en el hecho de que pueden establecer sus propias normas

nativity /nəˈtɪvəti/ *n*: **The N~** (Relig) la Natividad; (*before n*) **~ play** función *f* or obra *f* de Navidad, pastorela *f* (Méx)

NATO /ˈneɪtəʊ/ *n* (*no art*) (= **North Atlantic Treaty Organization**) la OTAN

natter¹ /ˈnætər || ˈnætə(r)/ *vi* (BrE colloq) charlar (fam), cotorrear (fam)

natter² *n* (BrE colloq) (*no pl*) charla *f* (fam); **to have a ~** charlar

natural¹ /ˈnætʃrəl/ *adj*

A (as in nature) natural; **these animals are ~ enemies** estos animales son enemigos por naturaleza; **I'm a ~ blonde** soy rubia natural; **death from ~ causes** muerte *f* natural *or* por causas naturales

B 1 ‹*talent/propensity*› innato 2 (*before n*) ‹*leader/troublemaker*› nato, por naturaleza 3 ‹*reaction/response*› natural, normal; ‹*successor*› lógico; **she's the ~ choice for the job** lo natural es que le ofrezcan el puesto a ella; **it is ~ THAT** es natural QUE (+ *subj*)

C (not forced) ‹*warmth/enthusiasm/style*› natural

D (related by blood) ‹*child/parent*› biológico

natural² *n* (person): **to be a ~** tener* un talento innato

natural³ *adv*: **act ~** (colloq) disimula

natural history *n* [u] historia *f* natural

naturalist /ˈnætʃrələst || ˈnætʃrəlɪst/ *n* naturalista *mf*

naturalization /ˈnætʃrələˈzeɪʃən || ˌnætʃrəlaɪˈzeɪʃən/ *n* [u] naturalización *f*, nacionalización *f*

naturalize /ˈnætʃrəlaɪz/ *vt* naturalizar*, nacionalizar*

naturalized /ˈnætʃrəlaɪzd/ *adj* 1 ‹*citizen/American*› naturalizado, nacionalizado 2 (Bot, Zool) aclimatado

naturally /ˈnætʃrəli/ *adv*

A 1 (inherently) ‹*shy/tidy*› por naturaleza; ***to come ~***: **lying comes ~ to him** miente con toda naturalidad 2 (unaffectedly) ‹*smile/behave/speak*› con naturalidad

B (without artifice) ‹*form/heal*› de manera natural

C 1 (logically) lógicamente 2 (*indep*) (of course) naturalmente, por supuesto, claro

natural science *n* [u c] ciencias *fpl* naturales

nature /ˈneɪtʃər || ˈneɪtʃə(r)/ *n*

A [u] (universe, way of things) naturaleza *f*; **against ~** contranatural

B 1 [u c] (of people) carácter *m*, natural *m*; **he has a kind ~** es de natural bondadoso; **it's not (in) his ~ to complain** no es de los que se quejan; **by ~** por naturaleza; ***to be second ~ (to sb)***: **it's second ~ to me to put my seat belt on** ponerme el cinturón de seguridad es un acto reflejo *or* es algo que hago automáticamente 2 [u] (of things, concepts) naturaleza *f*; **the ~ of the material/problem** la naturaleza del material/problema; **it's in the ~ of things that ...** es algo natural que ...; **something of that ~** algo de esa índole

-natured /ˈneɪtʃərd || ˈneɪtʃəd/ *suff*: **evil~** de carácter *or* de natural perverso; **sweet~** dulce

nature: ~ **reserve** *n* reserva *f* natural; ~ **study** *n* historia *f* natural; ~ **trail** *n* ruta *f* ecológica (*circuito educativo en un bosque etc*)

naturism /ˈneɪtʃərɪzəm/ *n* [u] (esp BrE) naturismo *m*

naturist /ˈneɪtʃərəst || ˈneɪtʃərɪst/ *n* (esp BrE) naturista *mf*; (*before n*) **~ beach** playa *f* naturista *or* nudista

naught /nɔːt/ *n* 1 [u] (nothing) (arch *or* liter) **to come to ~** malograrse 2 (esp AmE) (zero) cero *m*

naughty /ˈnɔːti/ *adj* **-tier, -tiest** 1 (mischievous) ‹*child/dog*› malo, travieso, pícaro; **(you) ~ girl!** ¡mala!; (more affectionate) ¡pícara!, ¡pillina! (fam); **don't do that, it's ~** eso no se hace 2 ‹*word*› feo 3 (in adult context): **he was a bit ~ not to consult them** estuvo mal en no consultarlos 4 (risqué) ‹*joke*› atrevido, picante

nausea /ˈnɔːsiə, -ziə/ *n* [u] náusea *f*; **it fills me with ~** me da náuseas

nauseate /ˈnɔːsieɪt, ˈnɔːz-/ *vt* 1 (disgust) (colloq) asquear, repugnar; **I was ~d by it** me asqueó, me repugnó, me dio asco 2 (Med): **the sight of the food ~d me** me dieron náuseas de sólo ver la comida

nauseating /ˈnɔːsieɪtɪŋ, ˈnɔːz-/ *adj* ‹*violence/brutality*› repugnante; ‹*smell*› nauseabundo

nauseous /ˈnɔːʃəs, ˈnɔːziəs || ˈnɔːsiəs, nɔːz-/ *adj* 1 (bilious): **to feel ~** sentir* náuseas 2 (sickening) ‹*smell/taste/color*› nauseabundo

nautical /ˈnɔːtɪkl̩ || ˈnɔːtɪkəl/ *adj* náutico, marítimo; **~ mile** milla *f* marina

naval /ˈneɪvəl/ *adj* ‹*warfare/base/forces*› naval; ‹*supremacy/history/power*› naval, marítimo; ‹*officer/recruit*› de marina; **~ attaché** agregado *m* naval; **~ officer** oficial *mf* de marina

nave /neɪv/ *n* nave *f*

navel /ˈneɪvəl/ *n* ombligo *m*

navigable /ˈnævɪgəbəl/ *adj* ‹*river/channel*› navegable

navigate /ˈnævəgeɪt || ˈnævɪgeɪt/ *vi* 1 (Aviat, Naut) navegar* 2 (in car) hacer* de copiloto

■ **navigate** *vt* 1 (steer) ‹*ship/plane*› conducir*, llevar 2 (travel across, along) ‹*sea/river*› navegar* por

navigation /ˈnævəˈgeɪʃən || ˌnævɪˈgeɪʃən/ *n* [u] navegación *f*; (— in car) dirección *f*; (*before n*) **~ lights** luces *fpl* de navegación

navigator /ˈnævəgeɪtər || ˈnævɪgeɪtə(r)/ *n* (crew member) (Naut) oficial *mf* de derrota; (Aviat) navegante *mf*

navvy /ˈnævi/ *n* (*pl* **navvies**) (BrE) peón *m*

navy¹ /ˈneɪvi/ *n* (*pl* **navies**)

A [c] (Mil, Naut) marina *f* de guerra, armada *f*; **the US N~** la armada *or* marina de los EEUU; **the Royal N~** la armada *or* marina británica; (*before n*) **N~ Department** (in US) Ministerio *m* de Marina de los EEUU

B [u] **~ (blue)** azul *m* marino

navy², navy-blue /ˈneɪviˈbluː/ (*pred* **navy blue**) *adj* azul marino *adj inv*

naysayer /ˈneɪˌseɪər || ˈneɪˌseɪə(r)/ *n* (AmE journ) negativista *mf*

Nazi¹ /ˈnɑːtsi/ *n* nazi *mf*, nazista *mf*

Nazi² *adj* nazi, nazista

Nazism /ˈnɑːtsɪzəm/ *n* [u] nazismo *m*

NB (= **nota bene**) NB

NBC *n* (in US) (*no art*) (= **National Broadcasting Company**) la NBC

NC 1 = **no charge** 2 = **North Carolina**

n

NCO *n* = **noncommissioned officer**

ND, N Dak = **North Dakota**

NE 1 (= **northeast**) NE 2 = **Nebraska**

near¹ /nɪr || nɪə(r)/ *adj* **-er, -est**

A 1 (in position) cercano, próximo; **the ~est store** la tienda más cercana 2 (in time) cercano, próximo 3 (in approximation) parecido; **that's the ~est thing to an apology you can expect from him** eso es lo más parecido a una disculpa que se puede esperar de él 4 ‹*relative*› cercano

B (virtual) (*before n*): **there was ~ panic when the alarms sounded** casi se produjo el pánico cuando sonaron las alarmas; **in a state of ~ exhaustion** prácticamente en estado de agotamiento

C (BrE Auto, Equ) izquierdo

near² *adv* **-er, -est**

A 1 (in position) cerca; **don't go any ~er to the edge** no te acerques más al borde; **from ~ and far** de todas partes 2 (in time): **we're getting ~ to Christmas** ya falta poco para Navidad 3 (in approximation): **the total will be ~er to $1,000 than $500** el total va a estar más cerca de 1.000 que de 500 dólares 4 (on the verge of) **~ TO sth/-ING**: **she was ~ to tears** estaba al borde de las lágrimas *or* a punto de echarse a llorar; **I came very ~ to hitting him** estuve a punto de pegarle, por poco le pego

B (nearly) casi; **I'm nowhere ~ finished** me falta mucho *or* (colloq) un montón para terminar; **that's nowhere ~ enough** (colloq) con eso no alcanza, ni mucho menos; **it'll cost $1,000, ~ enough** (colloq) costará 1.000 dólares, o por ahí (fam)

near³ *prep* **-er, -est** 1 (in position) cerca de; **the room ~est the entrance** la habitación que está más cerca de la entrada; **don't go too ~ the fire** no te acerques demasiado al fuego 2 (in time): **we're getting very ~ Christmas** falta muy poco para Navidad 3 (in approximation): **damage was estimated at somewhere ~ $2,000** los daños se calcularon en cerca de 2.000 dólares; **I'd say he's ~er 70 than 60** yo diría que está más cerca de los 70 que de los 60; **no one comes ~ her in stamina** los deja a todos muy atrás en resistencia 4 (on the verge of): **the project is now ~ completion** el proyecto está a punto de acabarse

near⁴ *vt* acercarse* a; **we are ~ing our destination** nos estamos acercando a nuestro destino; **he must be ~ing his 80th birthday** debe faltarle poco para cumplir los 80; **the project is ~ing completion** el proyecto se está por acabar

near- /nɪr || 'nɪə(r)/ *pref* casi; **~perfect** casi perfecto

nearby¹ /'nɪrbaɪ || nɪə'baɪ/ *adj* cercano

nearby² *adv* cerca

near-death experience /'nɪr'deθ || 'nɪə'deθ/ *n* experiencia *f* cercana a la muerte

nearly /'nɪrli || 'nɪəli/ *adv*

A (almost) casi; **I'm ~ ready** estoy casi listo; **I ~ said something rude** casi digo *or* por poco digo una grosería, estuve a punto de decir una grosería; **she very ~ died** por poco *or* casi se muere; **we're very ~ there** ya falta poco para llegar; **not ~** ni con mucho; **I didn't prepare ~ enough food** no preparé ni con mucho suficiente comida, me quedé cortísima con la comida

B (closely) (frml): **what language does Hungarian most ~ resemble?** ¿a qué idioma se parece más el húngaro?

near miss *n* 1 (in dropping bomb, etc): **it was a ~ ~** la bala/bomba por poco falló el blanco 2 (near collision): **we had a ~ ~** (Auto) casi chocamos; (Aviat) casi nos estrellamos

nearness /'nɪrnəs || 'nɪənɪs/ *n* [u] cercanía *f*, proximidad *f*

near: **~side** *n* (in most countries) lado *m* derecho; (in UK) lado *m* izquierdo; **~sighted** /'nɪr'saɪtəd || ˌnɪə'saɪtɪd/ *adj* miope, corto de vista

neat /ni:t/ *adj* **-er, -est**

A 1 (tidy, orderly) ‹*appearance*› arreglado, cuidado, prolijo (RPl); ‹*person*› pulcro, prolijo (RPl); ‹*room*› ordenado; ‹*garden*› muy cuidado; **her hair is always very ~** va siempre muy bien peinada *or* con el pelo muy arreglado; **his handwriting is very ~** tiene muy buena letra 2 (trim, compact): **a ~ little car** un cochecito compacto; **she has a ~ figure** tiene muy buena figura *or* (Esp) muy buen tipo 3 (deft) ‹*catch*› bueno, hábil 4 (ingenious) ‹*gadget/solution*› ingenioso, bueno

B (good, nice) (AmE colloq) fantástico (fam), padre (Méx fam), chévere (AmL exc CS fam), chulo (Esp fam), encachado (Chi fam); **he's a ~ ballplayer** es un jugador buenísimo

C (BrE) ‹*brandy/alcohol*› solo; **she drank half a bottle of ~ vodka** se bebió media botella de vodka puro

neatly /'ni:tli/ *adv* 1 (tidily): **the papers were ~ organized into piles** los papeles estaban cuidadosamente apilados; **the garden is very ~ kept** el jardín está muy bien cuidado; **she was ~ dressed** iba bien arreglada 2 (snugly): **the table fits ~ into the alcove** la mesa cabe perfectamente en el hueco 3 ‹*explain/evade*› hábilmente

neatness /'ni:tnəs || 'ni:tnɪs/ *n* [u] 1 (of appearance) pulcritud *f*, prolijidad *f* (RPl); **the ~ of the room surprised me** me sorprendió lo limpia y ordenada *or* (RPl tb) lo prolija que estaba la habitación 2 (cleverness) ingenio *m*

Neb, Nebr = **Nebraska**

nebulous /'nebjələs || 'nebjʊləs/ *adj* ‹*idea*› nebuloso, vago; ‹*argument/concept*› vago, impreciso

necessarily /'nesə'serəli || ˌnesə'serɪli/ *adv* forzosamente, necesariamente

necessary¹ /'nesəseri || 'nesəsəri / *adj*

A (required) necesario; **it is absolutely ~** es imprescindible *or* preciso; **we can always give it another coat of paint, if ~** siempre le podemos dar otra mano de pintura, si fuera necesario; **to be ~ (FOR sb) to + INF**: **it's ~ for you all to be there** es necesario que estén todos allí; **was it really ~ to be so rude?** ¿había necesidad de ser tan grosero?

B (inevitable) ‹*conclusion/result*› inevitable, lógico; **a ~ evil** un mal necesario

necessary² *n* (what is required) (colloq): **the ~** lo que hace falta, lo necesario

necessitate /nə'sesɪteɪt || nɪ'sesɪteɪt/ *vt* (frml) exigir*, hacer* necesario

necessity /nə'sesəti || nɪ'sesəti/ *n* (*pl* **-ties**)

A 1 (imperative need) (*no pl*) necesidad *f*; **~ FOR sth** necesidad DE algo; **there was no ~ for you to call the police** no había necesidad de que llamaras a la policía; **out of ~** por necesidad 2 [u] (inevitability) inevitabilidad *f*; **of ~** (frml) forzosamente, necesariamente

B [c] (necessary item): **the bare necessities** lo indispensable, lo imprescindible; **a car is a ~ for me** para mí tener coche es una necesidad

neck¹ /nek/ *n*

A (Anat) (of person) cuello *m*; (of animal) cuello *m*, pescuezo *m*; **the back of the ~** la nuca; **I've got a stiff ~** tengo tortícolis; **if you say that again, I'll break your ~** (colloq) si vuelves a decir eso te rompo la crisma (fam); ***to be up to one's ~ in sth*** (colloq): **she's up to her ~ in work/trouble** está hasta aquí de trabajo/problemas (fam); **they're up to their ~s in debt** deben hasta la camisa (fam); ***to break one's ~*** (work hard) (colloq) matarse (trabajando), deslomarse (fam); (lit: in accident) desnucarse*, romperse* el cuello; ***to breathe down sb's ~*** (colloq) estarle* encima a algn; ***to get it*** *o* ***catch it in the ~*** (colloq) llevarse una buena (fam); ***to risk one's ~*** (colloq) jugarse* *or* arriesgar* el pellejo (fam); ***to stick one's ~ out*** (colloq) aventurarse, arriesgarse*; (*before n*) ‹*muscle/injury*› del cuello; ▸ **save¹** *vt* **A1**

B (Clothing) cuello *m*, escote *m*; (measurement) cuello *m*; **a high ~** un cuello cerrado; **the dress has a low ~** el vestido es muy escotado

C 1 (of pork, beef, lamb) (esp BrE) cuello *m* 2 (in horse-racing) cabeza *f*: **to win/lose by a (short) ~** ganar/perder* por una cabeza

D (of bottle, vase) cuello *m*; (of guitar, violin) mástil *m*; **a ~ of land** un istmo; ***my/this ~ of the woods*** (colloq) mis/estos pagos (fam)

neck² *vi* (colloq) besuquearse (fam), darse* *or* pegarse* el lote (Esp fam), fajar (Méx fam), chapar (RPl fam), amacizarse* (Col fam), atracar* (Chi fam), jamonearse (Ven fam)

neck-and-neck /'nekən'nek/ *adj* (*pred* **neck and neck**): **a ~ finish** un final muy reñido; **they were ~ ~ ~** iban a la par, iban parejos (esp AmL)

-necked /'nekt/ *suff*: **long~** de cuello largo; **round~** (Clothing) de cuello *or* escote redondo

neckerchief /'nekərtʃɪf || 'nekətʃɪf/ *n* pañuelo *m* (*que se lleva atado al cuello*)

necklace /'nekləs || 'neklɪs/ *n* collar *m*

neck: **~line** *n* escote *m*; **~tie** *n* (AmE) corbata *f*

nectar /'nektər || 'nektə(r)/ *n* [u] néctar *m*

nectarine /'nektəri:n || 'nektərɪn, -ri:n/ *n* nectarina *f*, pelón *m* (RPl), durazno *m* pelado (Chi)

née /neɪ/ *adj* de soltera

need¹ /ni:d/ *n*

A [c u] (requirement, necessity) necesidad *f*; **an urgent** *o* **a pressing ~** una imperiosa necesidad, una necesidad acuciante; **your daily vitamin ~s** las vitaminas que necesita diariamente; **~ FOR sth/to + INF** necesidad DE algo/DE + INF; **I see no ~ for that** no creo que eso haga falta *or* sea necesario; **there's no ~ to tell her** no hay ninguna necesidad de decírselo; **if ~ be** si hace falta, si es necesario; **the house is badly in ~ of renovation** a la casa le hacen muchísima falta unos arreglos; **your ~ is greater than mine** a ti te hace más falta (que a mí), tú lo necesitas más (que yo)

B [u] **1** (emergency): **he abandoned them in their hour of ~** los abandonó cuando más falta les hacía; ▸**friend A** **2** (poverty) necesidad *f*; **those in ~** los necesitados

need² *vt* necesitar; **just what I ~ed!** ¡justo lo que necesitaba *or* lo que me hacía falta!; **you really ~ a shower!** ¡qué falta te hace una ducha!; **all it ~ed was a bit of salt** sólo le faltaba un poco de sal; **that's all we ~!** (iro) ¡lo que nos faltaba! (iró); **I ~ someone to look after the children** necesito a alguien que me cuide a los niños; **the soup ~s another twenty minutes** a la sopa le faltan 20 minutos; **I took a badly ~ed break** me tomé un descanso, que buena falta me hacía; **it ~s great concentration** requiere gran concentración; **to ~ -ING, to ~ to be + PP**: **the plants ~ watering** *o* **to be watered** hay que regar las plantas; **the car ~s looking at** *o* **to be looked at** el coche necesita una revisión; **she didn't ~ telling** *o* **to be told twice** no hubo que decírselo dos veces; **to ~ to + INF** tener* QUE + INF; **I ~ to wash my hair** tengo que lavarme la cabeza; **you don't ~ to be a genius to see that it's wrong** no hay que ser un genio para darse cuenta de que está mal; **you only ~ed to ask me** no tenías más que pedírmelo

■ **need** *v mod* (*usu with neg or interrog*) **1** (be obliged to): **you ~n't come if you don't want to** no hay necesidad de que vengas *or* no hace falta que vengas *or* no tienes por qué venir si no tienes ganas; **she ~ never know** no tiene por qué enterarse, no hay necesidad de que se entere; **I ~ hardly say that ...** de más está decir que ..., ni falta hace que diga que ... **2** (be necessarily): **that ~n't always be the case** no tiene por qué ser así, no necesariamente tiene que ser así; **that ~n't mean that ...** eso no significa necesariamente que ...

needle¹ /'ni:dl/ *n*[c] **1** (for sewing, on syringe, for etching) aguja *f*; (on record player) aguja *f*, púa *f* (RPl); (*knitting* ~) aguja *f* de tejer *or* (Esp) de hacer punto, palillo *m* (Chi); ***to give sb the ~*** (colloq) (taunt) (AmE) pinchar a algn (fam); (irritate) (BrE) sacar* de quicio a algn; ***to look for a ~ in a haystack*** buscar* una aguja en un pajar **2** (on gauge) aguja *f* **3** (Bot) aguja *f*

needle² *vt* pinchar (fam); **what really ~s me is that ...** lo que de verdad me saca de quicio *or* me fastidia es que ...

needless /'ni:dləs || 'ni:dlɪs/ *adj* innecesario, superfluo; **~ to say, no one asked me** de más está decir *or* huelga decir que nadie me preguntó

needlessly /'ni:dləsli || 'ni:dlɪsli/ *adv* innecesariamente, sin ninguna necesidad

needlework /'ni:dlwɜ:rk || 'ni:dlwɜ:k/ *n* [u] **1** (activity, skill) labores *fpl* de aguja **2** (stitching) bordado *m*

needn't /'ni:dnt/ = **need not**

need-to-know /,ni:dtə'nəʊ/ *adj* ⟨*policy/principle*⟩ de informar sólo lo estrictamente necesario; **employees will be kept informed on a ~ basis** se mantendrá informados a los empleados sólo sobre lo que es estrictamente necesario saber

needy¹ /'ni:di/ *adj* **-dier, -diest** necesitado

needy² *pl n* **the ~** los necesitados

negate /nɪ'geɪt/ *vt* (frml) invalidar

negation /nɪ'geɪʃən/ *n* [u c] negación *f*

negative¹ /'negətɪv/ *adj* negativo; **you're too ~** eres demasiado negativo; **~ image** imagen *f* en negativo

negative² *n*

A **1** (word, particle) negación *f*; **put this sentence into the ~** pon esta frase en negativo **2** (no) negativa *f*; **he answered in the ~** contestó negativamente *or* con una negativa

B (Phot) negativo *m*

C (Elec) polo *m* negativo

neglect¹ /nɪ'glekt/ *vt* **1** (leave uncared-for) ⟨*family/child*⟩ desatender*; ⟨*house/health*⟩ descuidar; **he ~ed his appearance** dejó de arreglarse, se abandonó **2** (not carry out) ⟨*duty/obligations*⟩ desatender*, no cumplir con; ⟨*studies/business*⟩ descuidar; **he ~ed to inform the authorities** (frml) faltó a su deber de informar a las autoridades

neglect² *n* [u] (lack of care) abandono *m*; (negligence) negligencia *f*; **the garden has fallen into ~** el jardín está muy abandonado *or* descuidado

neglected /nɪ'glektəd || nɪ'glektɪd/ *adj* **1** (uncared-for) ⟨*building/garden*⟩ abandonado, descuidado; ⟨*appearance*⟩ dejado, abandonado **2** (forgotten): **I'm feeling ~** me tienen abandonado

neglectful /nɪ'glektfəl/ *adj* ⟨*owner/parents*⟩ negligente

negligee, negligé /'neglə'ʒeɪ || 'neglɪʒeɪ/ *n* negligé *m*

negligence /'neglɪdʒəns/ *n* [u] negligencia *f*

negligent /'neglɪdʒənt/ *adj* negligente

negligible /'neglɪdʒəbəl/ *adj* insignificante, desdeñable

negotiable /nɪ'gəʊʃəbəl/ *adj* **1** (subject to negotiation) ⟨*contract/claim*⟩ negociable; **salary ~** sueldo negociable *or* a negociar **2** (Fin) negociable; **not ~** no negociable **3** (passable) ⟨*road*⟩ transitable; ⟨*obstacle*⟩ superable

negotiate /nɪ'gəʊʃieɪt/ *vi* (confer, talk) negociar; **after months of negotiating** tras meses de negociaciones

■ **negotiate** *vt*

A (obtain by discussion) ⟨*contract/treaty*⟩ negociar; ⟨*loan*⟩ gestionar, tramitar

B (pass, deal with) ⟨*obstacle*⟩ sortear, salvar; ⟨*difficulty*⟩ superar; **they ~d the rocky path** salvaron *or* pasaron el camino rocoso

C (Fin) ⟨*bill/draft*⟩ negociar

negotiation /nɪ'gəʊʃi'eɪʃən/ *n* [u] (discussion) (*sometimes pl*) negociación *f*; **by ~** mediante negociaciones *or* negociación; **to enter into ~s/be in ~ with sb** entrar/estar* en negociaciones *or* (CS tb) en tratativas con algn

negotiator /nɪ'gəʊʃɪeɪtər || nɪ'gəʊʃɪeɪtə(r)/ *n* negociador, -dora *m,f*

Negro /'ni:grəʊ/ *n* (*pl* **Negroes**) (often offensive) negro, -gra *m,f*

neigh /neɪ/ *vi* relinchar

neighbor¹, (BrE) **neighbour** /'neɪbər || 'neɪbə(r)/ *n* (in street, district) vecino, -na *m,f*; **she turned to her ~ on the right** se volvió hacia la persona que estaba a su derecha; **love thy ~** (Bib) ama a tu prójimo

neighbor², (BrE) **neighbour** *vi* **to ~ ON sth** lindar *or* colindar CON algo

neighborhood, (BrE) **neighbourhood** /'neɪbərhʊd || 'neɪbəhʊd/ *n* **1** (residential area) barrio *m*; (*before n*) ⟨*school/policeman*⟩ del barrio, del vecindario; **~ watch** *o* (AmE also) **patrol** *vigilancia de una calle, barrio etc a cargo de sus propios habitantes* **2** (inhabitants) vecindario *m* **3** (vicinity) zona *f*; **in the ~** en los alrededores, en *or* por la zona

neighboring, (BrE) **neighbouring** /'neɪbərɪŋ/ *adj* ⟨*country*⟩ vecino; **the town and the ~ villages** la ciudad y los pueblos de los alrededores

neighborly, (BrE) **neighbourly** /'neɪbərli || 'neɪbəli/ *adj* amable

neither¹ /'ni:ðər, 'naɪ- || 'naɪðə(r), 'ni:ð-/ *conj*

A **neither ... nor ...** ni ... ni ...; **she ~ knows nor cares!** ¡ni sabe ni le importa!

B (nor) tampoco; **I don't want to go — ~ do I** *o* (colloq) **me ~** no quiero ir — yo tampoco *or* ni yo

neither² *adj*: **~ proposal was accepted** no se aceptó ninguna de las (dos) propuestas

neither³ *pron* ninguno, -na

neo- /'ni:əʊ/ *pref* neo-

neoclassical /'niəʊ'klæsɪkəl/ *adj* neoclásico

neolithic, Neolithic /'ni:ə'lɪθɪk/ *adj* neolítico; **the ~ (period)** el Neolítico

neologism /ni:'ɑ:lədʒɪzəm || ni:'ɒlədʒɪzəm/ *n* neologismo *m*

neon /'ni:ɑ:n || 'ni:ɒn/ *n* [u] neón *m*; (*before n*) ⟨*glow/lighting*⟩ de neón; **~ sign** letrero *m* de neón

n

Nepal /nəˈpɔːl || nɪˈpɔːl/ *n* Nepal *m*

Nepalese /ˌnepəˈliːz/ *adj* nepalés

nephew /ˈnefjuː || ˈnevjuː, ˈnef-/ *n* sobrino *m*

nepotism /ˈnepətɪzəm/ *n* [u] nepotismo *m*

Neptune /ˈneptuːn || ˈneptjuːn/ *n* Neptuno *m*

nerd /nɜːrd || nɜːd/ *n* (colloq) ganso, -sa *m,f* (fam), pendejo, -ja *m,f* (AmL exc CS fam)

nerve[1] /nɜːrv || nɜːv/ *n*

A [c] (Anat, Bot) nervio *m*; ***to touch a (raw) ~*** meter *or* poner* el dedo en la llaga; (*before n*) ‹*fiber/ending*› nervioso; **~ gas** (Mil) gas *m* nervioso

B **nerves** *pl* 1▸ (emotional constitution) nervios *mpl*; **their ~s were on edge** tenían los nervios de punta; **to have ~s of steel** tener* nervios de acero; **a war of ~s** una guerra de nervios; ***to get on sb's ~s*** (colloq) ponerle* los nervios de punta a algn; ***to live on one's ~s*** estar* en permanente estado de tensión 2▸ (anxiety) nervios *mpl*, nerviosismo *m*; **I had terrible ~s** pasé unos nervios tremendos; ***to be a bag*** *o* ***bundle of ~s*** ser* un manojo de nervios, ser* puro nervio

C 1▸ [u] (resolve) valor *m*, coraje *m*; **to lose/keep one's ~** perder*/mantener* el valor; **it takes some ~ to do it** hay que tener valor *or* coraje *or* (fam) agallas para hacerlo 2▸ (effrontery) (colloq) (*no pl*) frescura *f* (fam), cara *f* (fam); **you've/he's got a ~!** ¡qué frescura *or* cara tienes/tiene!; **to have the ~ to + INF** tener* la frescura *or* la cara de + INF (fam); **what a ~!** ¡qué frescura *or* cara! (fam)

nerve[2] *v refl* **to ~ oneself FOR sth** armarse de valor PARA algo

nerve: **~-center**, (BrE) **~-centre** *n* (of organization) centro *m* neurálgico; **~-racking** /ˈnɜːrvˈrækɪŋ || ˈnɜːv ˌrækɪŋ/ *adj* que destroza los nervios

nervous /ˈnɜːrvəs || ˈnɜːvəs/ *adj*

A (apprehensive, tense) nervioso; **to feel/get ~** estar*/ponerse* nervioso; **to be ~ ABOUT sth/-ING**: **there's nothing to be ~ about** no tienes por qué ponerte nervioso; **I was ~ about making a mistake** tenía miedo de equivocarme; **she's been ~ of traffic since the accident** desde el accidente le tiene miedo al tráfico; **to make sb ~** poner* nervioso a algn

B ‹*system/tissue/tension*› nervioso; **a ~ complaint** un problema nervioso; **she's a ~ wreck** (colloq) es un manojo de nervios

nervously /ˈnɜːrvəsli || ˈnɜːvəsli/ *adv* nerviosamente

nervousness /ˈnɜːrvəsnəs || ˈnɜːvəsnɪs/ *n* [u] nerviosismo *m*

nervy /ˈnɜːrvi || ˈnɜːvi/ *adj* **-vier, -viest** 1▸ (bold, brash) (AmE colloq) fresco (fam), caradura (fam) 2▸ (courageous) (AmE colloq) valiente, agalludo (AmL fam) 3▸ (tense, edgy) (BrE) nervioso

nest[1] /nest/ *n*

A (of birds, reptiles) nido *m*; (of mice) ratonera *f*, nido *m*; **ants' ~** hormiguero *m*; **to fly** *o* **leave the ~** ‹‹*bird/child*›› volar* del *or* dejar el nido; ***to feather one's (own) ~*** barrer hacia adentro

B (set) juego *m*; **~ of tables** mesa *f* nido

nest[2] *vi* ‹‹*birds*›› anidar

nest egg *n* (colloq) ahorros *mpl*

nestle /ˈnesəl/ *vi* (snuggle) acurrucarse*; **he ~d up to her** se acurrucó contra ella; **the village ~s at the foot of the hill** el pueblo está enclavado al pie de la montaña

■ **nestle** *vt* (lay) (*often pass*): **her head was ~d against his shoulder** tenía la cabeza recostada en su hombro

net[1] /net/ *n*

A [c] red *f*; ***to cast one's ~ wide*** buscar* en un radio muy amplio; ***to slip through the ~***: **she/it slipped through the ~** se les (*or* nos *etc*) escapó; ***to spread one's ~*** tender* su (*or* mi *etc*) red

B [c] (Sport) red *f*

C [u] (fabric) tela *f* de visillos; (*before n*) **~ curtains** visillos *mpl*

net[2] *vt* **-tt-**

A (catch) ‹*butterfly*› cazar* (*con red*); ‹*fish*› pescar* (*con red*)

B (earn) ‹‹*company/sale*›› producir*; **he ~ted $50,000** se embolsó 50.000 dólares limpios (fam)

net[3] *adj* 1▸ (Busn, Fin) ‹*income/profit/cost/weight*› neto 2▸ (overall, final) ‹*effect/result*› global

NET *n* (in US) (*no art*) = **National Educational Television**

netball /ˈnetbɔːl/ *n* [u] (in UK) *deporte similar al baloncesto jugado esp por mujeres*

nethead /ˈnethed/ *n* (colloq) cerebrito *mf* de Internet (fam)

Netherlands /ˈneðərləndz || ˈneðələndz/ *n* (+ *sing or pl vb*) **the ~** los Países Bajos

netiquette *n* /ˈnetɪket/ netiqueta *f* (fam)

nett *adj* (BrE) ▸**net**[3] **1**

netting /ˈnetɪŋ/ *n* [u] (mesh) redes *fpl*, mallas *fpl*; **wire ~** tela *f* metálica *or* de alambre, tejido *m* metálico (RPl), anjeo *m* (Col)

nettle[1] /ˈnetl̩/ *n* ortiga *f*; (*stinging ~*) ortiga *f* (romana); ***to grasp the ~*** agarrar al toro por las astas *or* (esp Esp) coger* el toro por los cuernos

nettle[2] *vt* molestar, irritar

network[1] /ˈnetwɜːrk || ˈnetwɜːk/ *n* 1▸ (system) red *f* 2▸ (Elec) red *f* 3▸ (Rad, TV) cadena *f*; (*before*) **~ television** (in US) emisiones *fpl* televisivas en cadena

network[2] *vt*

A (BrE Rad, TV) transmitir en cadena

B (link together) (Comput) interconectar

networking /ˈnetˌwɜːrkɪŋ || ˈnetˌwɜːkɪŋ/ *n* [u] 1▸ (Comput) interconexión *f* 2▸ (Rad, TV) transmisión *f* en cadena 3▸ (using contacts) creación *f or* establecimiento *m* de una red de contactos *or* (AmL tb) conexiones

neuralgia /nʊˈrældʒə || njʊəˈrældʒə/ *n* [u] neuralgia *f*

neurological /ˈnʊrəˈlɑːdʒɪkəl || ˌnjʊərəˈlɒdʒɪkəl/ *adj* neurológico

neurologist /nʊˈrɑːlədʒəst || ˌnjʊəˈrɒlədʒɪst/ *n* neurólogo, -ga *m,f*

neurology /nʊˈrɑːlədʒi || ˌnjʊəˈrɒlədʒi/ *n* [u] neurología *f*

neuron /ˈnuːrɑːn || ˈnjʊərɒn/, **neurone** /-rəʊn/ *n* neurona *f*

neurosis /nʊˈrəʊsəs || njʊəˈrəʊsɪs/ *n* [c u] (*pl* **-roses** /-ˈrəʊsiːz/) neurosis *f*

neurotic /nʊˈrɑːtɪk || njʊəˈrɒtɪk/ *adj* neurótico; **he's ~ about his weight** está obsesionado con su peso

neuter[1] /ˈnuːtər || ˈnjuːtə(r)/ *adj*

A (Ling) neutro

B (sexless) (Bot, Zool) neutro, asexuado

neuter[2] *n* (Ling) neutro *m*; **in the ~** en género neutro

neuter[3] *vt* castrar, capar

neutral[1] /ˈnuːtrəl || ˈnjuːtrəl/ *adj* 1▸ (impartial) neutral; **to remain ~** permanecer* neutral 2▸ (not bright) ‹*shade/tone*› neutro 3▸ (Chem, Elec, Ling) neutro

neutral[2] *n* (Auto): **to be in ~** ‹‹*car/gear*›› estar* en punto muerto

neutrality /nuːˈtræləti || njuːˈtræləti/ *n* [u] neutralidad *f*

neutralize /ˈnuːtrəlaɪz || ˈnjuːtrəlaɪz/ *vt* neutralizar*

neutron /ˈnuːtrɑːn || ˈnjuːtrɒn/ *n* neutrón *m*

Nev = **Nevada**

never /ˈnevər || ˈnevə(r)/ *adv*

A (at no time) nunca; (more emphatic) jamás; **he ~ helps** nunca ayuda, no ayuda nunca; **~ in all my life have I been so insulted** en mi vida me habían insultado de ese modo; **~ again** nunca más; **~ before had she experienced such pain** nunca había sentido tanto dolor; **as ~ before** como nunca, más que nunca

B 1▸ (*used for emphasis*): **she said she'd call but she ~ did** dijo que llamaría pero no llamó; **really? I ~ knew that** ¿ah sí? no sabía; **they ~ once thanked me** no me dieron las gracias ni una vez; **this will ~ do!** ¡esto no puede ser! 2▸ (expressing incredulity) (colloq) (*in interj phrases*): **I walked all the way — never!** hice todo el camino a pie — ¡no me digas!; **well, I ~!** ¡pues, vaya!

never: **~-ending** /ˈneverˈendɪŋ/ *adj* (*pred* **~ ending**) ‹*dispute/saga*› interminable; ‹*devotion/supply*› inagotable; **~-never** /ˈnevərˈnevər || ˈnevəˈnevə(r)/ *n* (BrE colloq & hum): **to pay for/buy sth on the ~-~** pagar*/comprar algo a plazos *or* (fam & hum) a plazoletas; **~theless** /ˌnevərðəˈles || ˌnevəðəˈles/ *adv* sin embargo, no obstante (frml); **I'm going to try ~theless** de todas maneras lo voy a intentar, no obstante lo voy a intentar (frml)

new[1] /nuː || njuː/ *adj* **-er, -est**

A 1▸ (unused) nuevo; **brand ~** flamante; **is that a ~ suit you're wearing?** ¿estás estrenando traje?, ¿es nuevo ese traje?; **as ~** como nuevo; **to be/look like ~** ser*/parecer* nuevo 2▸ (recent, novel) nuevo; **hi, what's ~?** (colloq) ¿que tal? ¿qué hay (de nuevo)? (fam); **that's nothing ~** eso no es nada nuevo [3] (recently arrived) ‹*member/recruit*› nuevo; **I'm ~ here** soy nueva aquí; **to be ~ TO sth**: **she's ~ to this company** es nueva en la empresa

B (different, other) ‹*address/job/era*› nuevo; **after the shower I felt like a ~ man** la ducha me dejó como nuevo

C [1] (freshly made) ‹*wine*› joven; ‹*bread*› fresco, recién hecho [2] (tender, young) ‹*buds/leaves*› nuevo [3] (early) ‹*crop/potatoes*› nuevo

new² *adv* recién

> **New Age**
>
> El movimiento de la New Age cree que se debe tener un enfoque más holístico de la vida. Se originó en California en los años 70 y se extendió rápidamente a través de EEUU. Sus adherentes rechazan el materialismo y respetan los ciclos de la naturaleza ya que pueden ayudar a restablecer el balance espiritual y restablecer la armonía dentro del entorno

new: **~born** /'nu:bɔ:n || 'nju:bɔ:n/ *adj* recién nacido; **~comer** /'nu:kʌmər || 'nju:kʌmə(r)/ *n* (person) recién llegado, -da *m,f*; **he's a relative ~comer to politics** no lleva mucho tiempo en la política; **~ England** *n* Nueva Inglaterra *f*; **~fangled** /'nu:'fæŋgəld || 'nju:'fæŋgəld/ *adj* (*before n*) (pej) moderno; **~found** /'nju:ˌfaʊnd/ *adj* nuevo, recién descubierto; **~foundland** /'nu:fəndlənd || nju:'fəndlənd/ *n* (Geog) Terranova *f*; **~ Hampshire** /'hæmpʃər || 'hæmpʃi:ə(r)/ *n* Nueva Hampshire *f*, Nuevo Hampshire *m*; **~ Jersey** /'jɜrzi || 'jɜ:zi/ *n* Nueva Jersey *f*; **~-laid** /'nu:'leɪd || 'nju:'leɪd/ *adj* recién puesto, fresco

newly /'nu:li || 'nju:li/ *adv* recién; **~ baked/arrived** recién horneado/llegado

newlyweds /'nu:liwedz || 'nju:liwedz/ *pl n* recién casados *mpl*

New Mexico *n* Nuevo México *m*

newness /'nu:nəs || 'nju:nɪs/ *n* [u] [1] (novelty, unfamiliarity) novedad *f* [2] (of purchase, object, clothes etc) lo nuevo

New Orleans /'nu:'ɔ:rliənz, ɔ:r'li:nz || 'nju:'ɔ:liənz, -ɔ:'li:nz/ *n* Nueva Orleáns *f*

news /nu:z || nju:z/ *n* [u]

A (fresh information): **a piece** *o* **an item of ~** una noticia; **I have (some) good/bad ~** tengo buenas/malas noticias; **we've had some sad ~** hemos recibido una triste noticia *or* noticias muy tristes; **I had to break the ~ to him** me tocó a mí darle la (mala) noticia; **tell me all your ~!** ¡cuéntame qué novedades tienes!; **we've had no ~ of him** no hemos tenido noticias de él, no hemos sabido nada de él; **the fall in the dollar is good ~ for some** la caída del dolar les viene muy bien a algunos; **he's bad ~!** (colloq) no trae más que problemas; **it was ~ to me that ...** para mí era una novedad que ..., recién me enteraba de que ... (AmL); **~ travels fast** ¡cómo corren las noticias!; **no ~ is good ~** (set phrase) que no haya noticias es buena señal

B (Journ, Rad, TV) noticias *fpl*; **the international/sports ~** la información internacional/deportiva; **the six o'clock ~** las noticias *or* el informativo *or* el noticiario *or* (AmL tb) el noticiero de las seis; (*before n*) **~ agency** agencia *f* de noticias; **~ bulletin** boletín *m* informativo; **the ~ headlines** el resumen informativo *or* de noticias

news: **~agent** *n* (BrE) *dueño o empleado de una tienda que vende prensa, caramelos etc*; **~boy** *n* (AmE) repartidor *m* de periódicos, periodiquero *m* (Méx), diariero *m or* diarero *m* (CS); **~cast** *n* (esp AmE) informativo *m*, noticiario *m*, noticiero *m* (AmL); **~caster** *n* locutor, -tora *m,f*, presentador, -dora *m,f* (*de un informativo*); **~dealer** *n* (AmE) vendedor, -dora *m,f* de periódicos *or* de prensa; **~ flash** *n* (BrE) información *f* de última hora, flash *m* informativo; **~girl** *n* (AmE) repartidora *f* de periódicos, periodiquera *f* (Méx), diariera *f or* diarera *f* (CS); **~group** /'nu:zgru:p || 'nju:zgru:p/ *n* grupo *m* de noticias; **~letter** *n* boletín *m* informativo; **church ~letter** ≈ hoja *f* parroquial; **~man** /'nu:zmæn || 'nju:zmæn/ *n* (*pl* **-men** /-men/) (reporter) periodista *m*, reportero *m*; (newscaster) (AmE) locutor *m*, presentador *m*

newspaper /'nu:zˌpeɪpər || 'nju:sˌpeɪpə(r)/ *n* (Journ) periódico *m*, diario *m*; (*before n*) **~ article** artículo *m* periodístico; **~ cutting** recorte *m* de periódico *or* de prensa

news: **~print** *n* [u] (paper) papel *m* de prensa; (ink) tinta *f* de periódico; **~reel** *n* [c u] noticiario *m or* (AmL tb) noticiero *m* (cinematográfico), documental *m* de actualidades, nodo *m* (Esp); **~stand** *n* kiosco *m or* puesto *m* de periódicos; **~woman** *n* periodista *f*, reportera *f*; **~worthy** *adj* de interés periodístico

newsy /'nu:zi || 'nju:zi/ *adj* **-sier, -siest** (colloq): **a ~ letter** una carta llena de novedades

newt /nu:t || nju:t/ *n* tritón *m*

New Testament *n* **the ~ ~** el Nuevo Testamento

newton /'nu:tn̩ || 'nju:tn̩/ *n* newton *m*

new: **~ World** *n* **the N~ World** el Nuevo Mundo; **~ Year** *n* Año *m* Nuevo; **happy N~ Year!** ¡Feliz Año (Nuevo)!; **~ Year's Day** *n* día *m* de Año Nuevo; **~ Year's Eve** *n* la noche de Fin de Año, la Nochevieja (Esp); **~ York** *n* Nueva York *f*; (*before n*) neoyorquino; **~ Yorker** /'jɔ:rkər || 'jɔ:kə(r)/ *n* neoyorquino, -na *m,f*; **~ Zealand** /'zi:lənd/ *n* Nueva Zelanda; (*before n*) neocelandés; **~ Zealander** /'zi:ləndər || 'zi:ləndə(r)/ *n* neocelandés, -desa *m,f*

next¹ /nekst/ *adj* [1] (in time — talking about the future) próximo; (— talking about the past) siguiente; **I'll see you ~ month/Thursday** nos vemos el mes/el jueves que viene *or* el mes/el jueves próximo; **the matter will be/was discussed at the ~ meeting** el asunto se tratará en la próxima reunión/se trató en la reunión siguiente; **the week after ~** la semana que viene no, la otra *or* la siguiente; **I'll have been here two months ~ Tuesday** el martes que viene hará dos meses que estoy aquí; **from one day to the ~** de un día para otro [2] (in position) siguiente; **I'm getting off at the ~ stop** me bajo en la próxima *or* la siguiente parada; **the nearest station is in the ~ village** la estación más cercana queda en el pueblo de al lado; **take the ~ turning on the right** tome la próxima *or* la siguiente a la derecha [3] (in sequence): **who's ~?** ¿quién sigue?, ¿a quién le toca?; **~(, please)!** (at doctor's) el siguiente, por favor; **excuse me, I was** *o* **I'm ~** perdone, me toca a mí; **have you got the ~ size up/down?** ¿tiene una talla más grande/más pequeña?; **to be (the) ~ to + INF**: **you're the ~ to speak** luego te toca a ti hablar, tú eres el próximo orador

next² *adv*

A [1] (then) luego, después; **what did you do/say ~?** ¿y luego *or* después qué hiciste/dijiste? [2] (now): **what shall we do ~?** ¿y ahora qué hacemos?; **what comes ~?** ¿qué sigue (ahora)?; **whatever ~!** ¡adónde vamos (a ir) a parar! [3] (the first time after now): **when you see me ~** *o* **when you ~ see me** la próxima vez que me veas

B (second): **Tom is the tallest in the class, Bob the ~ tallest** Tom es el más alto de la clase y (a Tom) le sigue Bob; **it's the ~ best thing to champagne** después del champán, es lo mejor que hay

C **next to** [1] (beside) al lado de; **we live ~ to the hospital** vivimos al lado del hospital; **come and sit ~ to me** ven y siéntate a mi lado *or* junto a mí [2] (compared with) al lado de [3] (second): **the ~ to last page** la penúltima página [4] (almost, virtually); **I bought it for ~ to nothing** lo compré por poquísimo dinero; **I'll have it ready in ~ to no time** lo termino en un segundo

next: **~ door** *adv* al lado; **who lives ~ door?** ¿quién vive al lado *or* en la casa de al lado?; **~ door TO sb/sth** al lado DE algn/algo; **~-door** /'neks'dɔ:r || 'neks'dɔ:(r)/ *adj* (*before n*) de al lado; **~ of kin** *n* (*pl* **~ of kin**) familiar(es) *m(pl) or* pariente(s) *m(pl)* más cercano(s)

NF [1] (Geog) = **Newfoundland** [2] (in UK) = **National Front**

NFL *n* (in US) = **National Football League**

Nfld = **Newfoundland**

NGO *n* (= **Non-Governmental Organization**) ONG *f*

NH = **New Hampshire**

NHL *n* (in US) = **National Hockey League**

NHS *n* (in UK) = **National Health Service**

nib /nɪb/ *n* plumín *m*, pluma *f*

nibble /'nɪbəl/ *vt* [1] (bite) mordisquear [2] (eat, pick at) picar*

■ **nibble** *vi* [1] (bite, gnaw) **to ~ AT/ON sth** mordisquear algo [2] (eat) picar*

NICAM /'naɪkæm/ *n* (= **near-instantaneous companded system**) NICAM *m*

Nicaragua /ˈnɪkəˈrɑːgwə || ˌnɪkəˈrægjʊə/ *n* Nicaragua *f*

Nicaraguan[1] /ˈnɪkəˈrɑːgwən/ *adj* nicaragüense

Nicaraguan[2] *n* nicaragüense *mf*

nice /naɪs/ *adj* **nicer, nicest**

A 1 (kind, amiable) amable; (kind-hearted) bueno; (friendly) simpático; **he's a very ~ person** es muy buena persona, es muy majo (Esp fam); **to be ~ ABOUT sth: it was entirely our fault, but he was very ~ about it** fue todo por culpa nuestra, pero él estuvo muy comprensivo; **to be ~ TO sb** ser* amable CON algn, tratar bien a algn; **how ~ of you to ask us** muchas gracias por invitarnos 2 (attractive, appealing) ‹*place/dress/face*› bonito, lindo (esp AmL); ‹*food*› bueno, rico; **you look very ~ today!** (to a woman) ¡estás muy guapa *or* bonita hoy!, ¡estás *or* te ves muy linda hoy! (AmL); (to a man) ¡estás muy guapo hoy!, ¡estás *or* te ves muy buen mozo hoy! (AmL); **the soup smells ~** la sopa huele bien 3 (enjoyable) ‹*walk/surprise*› agradable, lindo (esp AmL); **(it was) ~ meeting you** me alegro de haberlo conocido, encantado

B (*as intensifier*): **I had a ~ hot shower** me di una buena ducha caliente; **her apartment is ~ and sunny** tiene un apartamento muy *or* de lo más soleado

C (respectable, decent): **he seemed such a ~ boy** parecía tan buen chico; **it isn't a very ~ area** es un barrio bastante feo

D (skilful) ‹*move/shot/job*› bueno; **~ work!** ¡así me gusta!, ¡bien hecho!

E (fine, subtle) ‹*distinction/point/detail*› sutil, fino

NICE *n* (in UK) = **National Institute for Health and Clinical Excellence**

nice-looking /ˈnaɪsˈlʊkɪŋ/ *adj* atractivo, guapo

nicely /ˈnaɪsli/ *adv*

A 1 (amiably) ‹*treat/smile*› amablemente 2 (politely, respectably) con buenos modales

B 1 (attractively) ‹*presented/dressed*› bien 2 (well, satisfactorily) ‹*get on/work*› bien

C (finely, precisely) ‹*judged/timed*› (muy) bien, con precisión

niceties /ˈnaɪsətiz/ *pl n* sutilezas *fpl*, detalles *mpl*

niche /nɪtʃ, niːʃ/ *n* 1 (Archit) nicho *m*, hornacina *f* 2 (suitable place): **she's found a little ~ for herself in the business** se ha hecho su huequito en la empresa (fam) 3 (Busn, Marketing) nicho *m* 4 (Ecol) nicho *m*

nick[1] /nɪk/ *n*

A (notch — in wood) muesca *f*; (— in blade) mella *f*; **did you cut yourself? — it's just a little ~** ¿te cortaste? — es sólo un rasguño; ***in the ~ of time*** justo a tiempo

B (condition) (BrE colloq): **to be in good/bad ~** estar* en buen/mal estado

C (BrE sl) (prison) cárcel *f*, chirona *f* (fam), cana *f* (AmS arg), trullo *m* (Esp arg), bote *m* (Méx, Ven arg)

nick[2] *vt*

A (notch) hacer* una muesca en; **I ~ed myself shaving** me corté al afeitarme

B (steal) (BrE colloq) afanar (arg), volar* (Méx, Ven fam), robar; **to ~ sth FROM sb** afanarle (arg) *or* (Méx, Ven fam) volarle* algo A algn

C (catch, arrest) (BrE sl): **he got ~ed** lo agarraron (fam) *or* (Esp arg) lo trincaron *or* (Méx arg) lo apañaron

nickel /ˈnɪkəl/

A *n* [u] (Chem, Metall) níquel *m*

B [c] (US coin) *moneda de cinco centavos*

nickel-and-dime /ˈnɪkələnˈdaɪm/ *adj* (AmE colloq) de poca monta (fam)

nickelodeon /ˈnɪkəˈləʊdiən/ *n* (AmE Hist) 1 (jukebox) máquina *f* de discos, juke-box *m*, rocola *f* (AmC, Col, Méx) 2 (Cin) *sala de proyección en la primera época del cine*

nickname[1] /ˈnɪkneɪm/ *n* apodo *m*, sobrenombre *m*; (relating to personal characteristics) mote *m*

nickname[2] *vt* apodar

nicotine /ˈnɪkətiːn/ *n* [u] nicotina *f*

niece /niːs/ *n* sobrina *f*

nifty /ˈnɪfti/ *adj* **-tier, -tiest** (colloq) 1 (adroit) hábil, diestro 2 (ingenious) ingenioso 3 (neat) (AmE) ‹*clothes*› bonito, chulo (Esp, Méx fam) 4 (speedy) (BrE) rápido

Nigeria /naɪˈdʒɪriə || naɪˈdʒɪəriə/ *n* Nigeria *f*

Nigerian[1] /naɪˈdʒɪriən || naɪˈdʒɪəriən/ *adj* nigeriano

Nigerian[2] *n* nigeriano, -na *m,f*

niggardly /ˈnɪgərdli || ˈnɪgədli/ *adj* ‹*person/gift*› mezquino; ‹*sum*› mísero

nigger /ˈnɪgər || ˈnɪgə(r)/ *n* (offensive) negro, -gra *m,f*

niggle /ˈnɪgəl/ *vi* 1 (complain) quejarse, rezongar* 2 **niggling** *pres p* ‹*doubt/worry*› constante; ‹*detail/job*› engorroso

■ **niggle** *vt*: **something's niggling him** algo le preocupa, algo lo tiene inquieto

night /naɪt/ *n*

A [c u] (period of darkness) noche *f*; **~ fell** cayó la noche (liter); **at this time of ~** a estas horas de la noche; **all ~ (long)** toda la noche; **at ~** por la noche, de noche; **it was eleven o'clock at ~** eran las once de la noche; **she woke up in the middle of the ~** se despertó por la noche *or* durante la noche; **~ and day** día y noche; **last ~** anoche; **the ~ before last** anteanoche, antenoche (AmL); **we stayed (for) the ~** nos quedamos a dormir; **to spend a sleepless ~** pasar una noche en vela *or* en blanco; **to have a good/bad ~** pasar (una) buena/mala noche; **to have a late/an early ~** acostarse* tarde/temprano; (*before n*) ‹*flight/patrol*› nocturno; **~ shift** turno *m* nocturno *or* de la noche

B [c] (evening) noche *f*; **last ~** anoche, ayer por la noche; **on the ~ of the party** la noche de la fiesta; **a ~ on the town** una noche de juerga; **we haven't had a ~ out for ages** hace muchísimo que no salimos por la noche; **first ~** (Theat) noche *f* del estreno

C **nights** (*as adv*) por las noches

night: **~cap** *n* 1 (Clothing) gorro *m* de dormir 2 (drink) *bebida alcohólica o caliente tomada antes de acostarse*; **~clothes** *pl n* ropa *f* de dormir; **~club** *n* club *m* nocturno; **~dress** *n* camisón *m*; **~fall** *n* [u] anochecer *m*; **at ~fall** al anochecer; **~gown** *n* camisón *m*

nightie /ˈnaɪti/ *n* (colloq) camisón *m*

nightingale /ˈnaɪtn̩geɪl || ˈnaɪtɪŋgeɪl/ *n* ruiseñor *m*

nightlife /ˈnaɪtlaɪf/ *n* [u] vida *f* nocturna

nightly[1] /ˈnaɪtli/ *adj* diario, de todas las noches

nightly[2] *adv* todas las noches; **twice ~** dos veces cada noche

nightmare /ˈnaɪtmer || ˈnaɪtmeə(r)/ *n* pesadilla *f*; (*before n*) ‹*journey/situation*› de pesadilla

night: **~ owl** *n* (colloq) ave *f*‡ nocturna (fam), noctámbulo, -la *m,f*; **~ school** *n* clases *fpl* nocturnas; **~stick** *n* (esp AmE) porra; **~time** *n* noche *f*; **at ~time** de noche; **in the ~time** por la noche, durante la noche; **~ watchman** /ˈwɑːtʃmən || ˈwɒtʃmən/ *n* sereno *m*, vigilante *m* nocturno

nihilism /ˈnaɪəlɪzəm || ˈnaɪlɪzəm, ˈnɪhɪl-/ *n* [u] nihilismo *m*

nil /nɪl/ *n* 1 (nothing): **its food value is virtually ~** su valor nutritivo es casi nulo 2 (BrE Sport) cero *m*; **we lost two ~** perdimos por dos a cero

Nile /naɪl/ *n* **the ~** el Nilo

nimble /ˈnɪmbəl/ *adj* **-bler** /-blər/, **-blest** /-bləst/ ‹*person/step/mind*› ágil; ‹*fingers*› diestro, hábil

nimbly /ˈnɪmbli/ *adv* ‹*leap/climb*› ágilmente, con agilidad; ‹*work*› con destreza *or* habilidad

NIMBY /ˈnɪmbi/ *n* (hum & pej) = **not in my back yard**

nincompoop /ˈnɪŋkəmpuːp/ *n* (colloq) papanatas *mf* (fam)

nine[1] /naɪn/ *n* nueve *m*; (in baseball) equipo *m*; ***to be dressed up*** *o* ***done up to the ~s*** (colloq) estar* *or* ir* de punta en blanco, ir* de tiros largos (fam); *see also* **four**[1]

nine[2] *adj* nueve *adj inv*; **~ times out of ten he's late/right** casi siempre llega tarde/tiene razón; *see also* **four**[2]

ninefold /ˈnaɪnfəʊld/ *adj/adv see* **-fold**

nineteen /ˈnaɪnˈtiːn/ *adj/n* diecinueve *adj inv/m*; ***to talk ~ to the dozen*** hablar (hasta) por los codos *or* como una cotorra (fam)

nineteenth[1] /ˈnaɪnˈtiːnθ/ *adj* decimonoveno; *see also* **fifth**[1]

nineteenth[2] *adv* en decimonoveno lugar; *see also* **fifth**[2]

nineteenth[3] *n* 1 (Math) diecinueveavo *m* 2 (part) diecinueveava parte *f*

ninetieth[1] /ˈnaɪntiəθ/ *adj* nonagésimo; *see also* **fifth**[1]

ninetieth[2] *adv* en nonagésimo lugar; *see also* **fifth**[2]

ninetieth[3] *n* 1 (Math) noventavo *m* 2 (part) noventava *or* nonagésima parte *f*

nine-to-five /ˈnaɪntəˈfaɪv/ *adj* ‹*job/worker*› de oficina (*con horario de nueve a cinco*)

ninety /ˈnaɪnti/ *adj/n* noventa *adj inv/m*; **temperatures in the nineties** temperaturas superiores a los noventa grados Fahrenheit; *see also* **seventy**

ninth[1] /naɪnθ/ *adj* noveno; *see also* **fifth**[1]

ninth[2] *adv* en noveno lugar; *see also* **fifth**[2]

ninth[3] *n* 1 (Math) noveno *m* 2 (part) novena parte *f*

nip[1] /nɪp/ *n*
A 1 (pinch) pellizco *m*; (bite) mordisco *m* 2 (chill): **there's a ~ in the air** hace bastante fresco 3 (tang) (AmE) sabor *m* fuerte
B (drink) traguito *m* (fam), dedal *m* (fam)

nip[2] **-pp-** *vt* 1 (pinch) pellizcar*; (bite) mordisquear 2 (damage) «*frost*» ‹*plants*› quemar
■ **nip** *vi*
A (bite, snap) **to ~ AT sth** «*dog*» mordisquear algo
B (go quickly) (BrE colloq): **~ upstairs and fetch my pipe** sube un momento a buscarme la pipa; **to ~ out** salir* un momento

nipple /ˈnɪpəl/ *n* 1 (on breast — of woman) pezón *m*; (— of man) tetilla *f* 2 (on bottle) (AmE) tetina *f*, chupón *m* (Méx)

nippy /ˈnɪpi/ *adj* **-pier, -piest**
A (chilly) (colloq) frío; **it's ~** hace frío
B (of flavor) (AmE) ‹*cheese/taste*› fuerte
C (BrE colloq) ‹*car/person*› rápido

nit /nɪt/ *n* 1 (Zool) liendre *f* 2 (silly person) (BrE colloq) bobo, -ba *m,f* (fam), zonzo, -za *m,f* (AmL fam)

nit: **~pick** *vi* encontrarle* defectos a todo, buscarle* tres *or* cinco pies al gato (fam); **~picking** *adj* quisquilloso, chinche (fam)

nitrate /ˈnaɪtreɪt/ *n* [c u] nitrato *m*

nitric acid /ˈnaɪtrɪk/ *n* [u] ácido *m* nítrico

nitrogen /ˈnaɪtrədʒən/ *n* [u] nitrógeno *m*

nitroglycerin, nitroglycerine /ˈnaɪtrəʊˈglɪsərən || ˌnaɪtrəʊˈglɪsəriːn/ *n* [u] nitroglicerina *f*

nitty-gritty /ˈnɪtiˈgrɪti/ *n* (colloq): **to get down to the ~** ir* al meollo de la cuestión, ir* al grano

nix[1] /nɪks/ *interj* (AmE sl): **~ on that!** ¡ni hablar! (fam)

nix[2] *vt* (AmE colloq) rechazar*

NJ = **New Jersey**

NL *n* (in US) = **National League**

NLRB *n* (in US) = **National Labor Relations Board**

NM, N Mex = **New Mexico**

NNE (= **north-northeast**) NNE

NNW (= **north-northwest**) NNO

no[1] /nəʊ/ *adj*
A 1 (+ *pl n*): **they have ~ children** no tienen hijos; **the room has ~ windows** la habitación no tiene ninguna ventana *or* no tiene ventanas; **I am under ~ illusions** no me hago ilusiones 2 (+ *uncount n*): **there's ~ food left** no queda nada de comida; **there's ~ time for that now** no tenemos tiempo para eso ahora; **how can we cook with ~ electricity?** ¿cómo vamos a cocinar sin electricidad? 3 (+ *sing count n*): **this cup has ~ handle** esta taza no tiene asa; **~ intelligent person would do that** ninguna persona inteligente haría eso
B (in understatements): **I'm ~ expert, but ...** no soy ningún experto, pero ...; **she told him what she thought in ~ uncertain terms** le dijo lo que pensaba muy claramente
C 1 (prohibiting, demanding): Ⓢ **no smoking** prohibido fumar; Ⓢ **no dogs allowed** no se admiten perros 2 (*with -ing form*): **there's ~ pleasing some people** no hay manera de complacer a cierta gente; **there'll be ~ stopping them now** ahora no hay quien los pare
D (very little): **it's ~ distance** no queda muy lejos; **I'll be finished in ~ time (at all)** termino enseguida

no[2] *adv* (*before adj or adv*): **my house is ~ larger than yours** mi casa no es más grande que la tuya; **I ~ longer work for them** ya no trabajo para ellos, no trabajo más para ellos; **~ fewer than 200 guests are expected** se espera nada menos que a unos 200 invitados

no[3] *interj* no; **to say ~** decir* que no; **don't take ~ for an answer** no te conformes con un no; **no, thank you** no, gracias; **have you seen John? — ~, I haven't** ¿has visto a John? — no; **oh ~, you don't!** ¡eso sí que no!; **oh ~, not again!** ¡ay no, otra vez!

no[4] *n* (*pl* **noes**) 1 (negative answer) no *m* 2 (vote) voto *m* en contra

no[5] (*pl* **nos**) (= **number**) nº, Nº; **phone ~ 34682** (nº de) Tel.: 34682

no-account /ˈnəʊəkaʊnt/ *adj* (AmE colloq) (*before n*) que no vale nada, despreciable

Noah /ˈnəʊə/ *n* Noé

nobble /ˈnɑːbəl || ˈnɒbəl/ *vt* (BrE) 1 (sl) ‹*witness/jury*› (bribe) comprar, coimear (CS fam), darle* una mordida a (Méx fam); (threaten) amenazar* 2 ‹*horse/dog*› drogar* (*para evitar que gane*) 3 (catch) (colloq) ‹*intruder/thief*› pescar* (fam), agarrar (esp AmL)

Nobel Prize *n* **the ~ ~** el Premio Nobel

nobility /nəʊˈbɪləti/ *n* [u] nobleza *f*; **the ~** la nobleza

noble[1] /ˈnəʊbəl/ *adj* **nobler** /-blər/, **noblest** /-bləst/
A (aristocratic) ‹*family/birth*› noble
B (virtuous) ‹*sentiments/deed/sacrifice*› noble

noble[2] *n* noble *mf*, aristócrata *mf*

noble: **~man** /ˈnəʊbəlmən/ *n* (*pl* **-men** /-mən/) noble *m*, aristócrata *m*; **~woman** *n* noble *f*, aristócrata *f*

nobly /ˈnəʊbli/ *adv* ‹*act*› noblemente

nobody[1] /ˈnəʊˌbɑːdi || ˈnəʊbədi/ *pron* nadie; **~ must hear about this** que no se entere nadie de esto; **there was ~ there** no había nadie; **~ else** nadie más

nobody[2] *n* (*pl* **-dies**): **to be (a) ~** ser* un don nadie

no-brainer /nəʊˈbreɪnə(r)/ *n* (colloq) 1 (movie) película *f* tonta (fam); (TV show) programa *m* tonto (fam) 2 (task) tarea *f* para tontos (fam); **the problem is a ~** no se necesita mucho seso para solucionar el problema 3 (stupid person) tonto, -ta *m,f*

no-claim bonus /ˈnəʊˈkleɪm/, **no-claims bonus** /ˈnəʊˈkleɪmz/ *n* (BrE) bonificación *f* por ausencia de siniestros

nocturnal /nɑːkˈtɜːrnl || nɒkˈtɜːnl/ *adj* nocturno

nocturne /ˈnɑːktɜːrn || ˈnɒktɜːn/ *n* nocturno *m*

nod[1] /nɑːd || nɒd/ *n*: **he greeted her with a ~** la saludó con un movimiento de cabeza; **she gave a ~ of agreement** asintió con un movimiento de cabeza; ***to give sb/sth the ~*** darle* luz verde a algn/algo

nod[2] **-dd-** *vt* 1 : **he ~ded his head (in agreement)** asintió con la cabeza; **he ~ded his approval** hizo un gesto de aprobación con la cabeza 2 (Sport) ‹*ball*› cabecear
■ **nod** *vi* (dip head): **she smiled at me and I ~ed to her** me sonrió y la saludé con la cabeza; **they ~ded in assent** asintieron con la cabeza

Phrasal verb
• **nod off** [v ▸ adv] (colloq) dormirse*, quedarse dormido

node /nəʊd/ *n*
A 1 (Anat) nódulo *m*, ganglio *m* 2 (Bot) nódulo *m*
B (Math) nodo *m*

nodule /ˈnɑːdʒuːl || ˈnɒdjuːl/ *n* nódulo *m*

noes /nəʊz/ *pl of* **no**[4]

no-go /ˈnəʊˈgəʊ/ *adj* (*before n*): **~ area** (Law, Mil) zona *f* prohibida; **that neighborhood is a ~ area** no se puede poner pie en ese barrio

no-good /ˈnəʊˈgʊd/ *adj* (AmE colloq) maldito (fam)

no-hoper /ˈnəʊˈhəʊpər || ˌnəʊˈhəʊpə(r)/ *n* (BrE colloq): **he's a complete ~** es un caso perdido

nohow /ˈnəʊhaʊ/ *adv* (AmE dial) de ninguna manera, de ningún modo

noise /nɔɪz/ *n* 1 [c u] (sound) ruido *m*; **to make a ~** hacer* ruido; ***to make a ~ about sth*** quejarse de algo; (*before n*) **~ level** nivel *m* sonoro *or* de ruido 2 **noises** *pl* (remarks, comments) (colloq): **all I could do was to make sympathetic ~s** lo único que pude hacer fue mostrarme comprensivo; **I don't know if she liked it, but she made all the right ~s** no sé si le gustó, pero fue muy cortés *or* dio la impresión de que sí

noiseless /ˈnɔɪzləs || ˈnɔɪzlɪs/ *adj* silencioso, quedo (liter)

noisily /ˈnɔɪzəli || ˈnɔɪzɪli/ *adv* ‹*laugh/cough/clatter*› ruidosamente, haciendo mucho ruido; ‹*protest/argue*› a gritos, ruidosamente

noisy /ˈnɔɪzi/ *adj* **-sier, -siest** ‹*machine/train*› ruidoso, que hace mucho ruido; ‹*office/street*› ruidoso; ‹*person/child/party*› bullicioso; ‹*meeting*› acalorado; **it's so ~ in here** aquí hay tanto ruido

nomad /ˈnəʊmæd/ *n* nómada *mf*, nómade *mf* (CS)

nomadic /nəʊˈmædɪk/ *adj* nómada, nómade (CS)

no-man's land /ˈnəʊmænzlænd/ *n* [u c] tierra *f* de nadie

n

nominal /'nɑːmənḷ || 'nɒmɪnḷ/ *adj* [1] (in name) nominal [2] (stated) nominal; ~ **value** valor *m* nominal [3] (token) ‹*fee/rent*› simbólico

nominally /'nɑːmənḷi || 'nɒmɪnəli/ *adv* (in theory) ‹*lead/head*› nominalmente; ‹*free/democratic*› sólo de nombre

nominate /'nɑːməneɪt || 'nɒmɪneɪt/ *vt* [1] (propose) **to ~ sb (FOR sth)** ‹*for a post*› proponer* *or* (AmL tb) postular a algn (PARA algo) [2] (appoint, choose) nombrar, designar; ‹*candidate*› (Pol AmE) proclamar, nominar

nomination /'nɑːmə'neɪʃən || ˌnɒmɪ'neɪʃən/ *n* [c u] [1] (choice, appointment) nombramiento *m*, designación *f*; (of candidate) (Pol AmE) proclamación *f*, nominación *f* [2] (proposal) propuesta *f*, postulación *f* (AmL)

nominative /'nɑːmṇətɪv || 'nɒmɪnətɪv/ *n* nominativo *m*

nominee /'nɑːmə'niː || ˌnɒmɪ'niː/ *n* [1] (person proposed) candidato, -ta *m,f* [2] (person appointed) persona *f* nombrada; (candidate) (AmE Pol) candidato, -ta *m,f*

non- /nɑːn || nɒn/ *pref* no; **~swimmers must ...** las personas que no saben nadar deben ...

nonaggression /ˌnɑːnə'greʃən || ˌnɒnə'greʃən/ *adj* (*before n*) ‹*pact/treaty*› de no agresión

nonalcoholic /ˌnɑːnælkə'hɑːlɪk || ˌnɒnælkə'hɒlɪk/ *adj* no alcohólico, sin alcohol

nonaligned /ˌnɑːnə'laɪnd || ˌnɒnə'laɪnd/ *adj* no alineado

nonbeliever /ˌnɑːnbə'liːvər || ˌnɒnbɪ'liːvə(r)/ *n* no creyente *mf*

nonchalance /'nɑːnʃə'lɑːns || 'nɒnʃələns/ *n* [u] despreocupación *f*

nonchalant /'nɑːnʃə'lɑːnt || 'nɒnʃələnt/ *adj* ‹*person*› (casual, relaxed) despreocupado; (indifferent) indiferente; ‹*gesture*› desenfadado

nonchalantly /'nɑːnʃə'lɑːntli || 'nɒnʃələntli/ *adv* ‹*behave/react*› con toda tranquilidad

noncombatant /ˌnɑːnkəm'bætṇt || nɒn'kɒmbətənt/ *n* no combatiente *mf*

noncommissioned officer /ˌnɑːnkə'mɪʃənd || ˌnɒnkə'mɪʃənd/ *n* ≈ suboficial *mf*

noncommittal /ˌnɑːnkə'mɪtḷ || ˌnɒnkə'mɪtḷ/ *adj* ‹*reply*› evasivo, que no compromete a nada; **he was very ~ about it** no se definió al respecto

nonconformist[1] /ˌnɑːnkən'fɔːrməst || ˌnɒnkən'fɔːmɪst/ *n* [1] (rebel, eccentric) inconformista *mf* [2] **Nonconformist** (in UK) *protestante que no pertenece a la Iglesia Anglicana*

nonconformist[2] *adj* inconformista

noncontributory /ˌnɑːnkən'trɪbjətɔːri || ˌnɒnkən'trɪbjʊtəri/ *adj* ‹*pension plan*› sin aportaciones por parte del empleado

noncooperation /ˌnɑːnkəʊɑːpə'reɪʃən || ˌnɒnkəʊˌɒpə'reɪʃən/ *n* no cooperación *f*

nondenominational /ˌnɑːndɪnɑːmɪ'neɪʃṇəl || ˌnɒndɪˌnɒmɪ'neɪʃənḷ/ *adj* no confesional

nondescript /'nɑːndɪ'skrɪpt || 'nɒndɪskrɪpt/ *adj* ‹*person/appearance*› (not unusual or outstanding) anodino; (dull) insulso, soso (fam)

none[1] /nʌn/ *pron*

[A] (not any, not one) (*referring to count n*) ninguno, ninguna; **I tried to get tickets, but there were ~ left** traté de comprar entradas pero no quedaba ninguna *or* ni una; **any objections? — ~ at all** ¿tienes alguna objeción? — no, ninguna; **~ of us know** *o* **knows her** ninguno de nosotros la conoce; **we want ~ of your comments** guárdate tus comentarios

[B] (no amount or part) (*referring to uncount n*): **did you buy any milk? there's ~ left** ¿compraste leche? no hay más *or* se ha acabado; **does she have any experience? — ~ that I know of** ¿tiene experiencia? — que yo sepa no

none[2] *adv*

[A] [1] **none the** (not, in no way) (*with comp*): **I was ~ the wiser after his explanation** su explicación no me aclaró nada [2] **none too** (not very) (*with adj or adv*): **she was ~ too pleased to see me** no le hizo demasiada gracia verme

[B] (AmE crit) (*with neg*): **it didn't hurt ~** no me dolía nada

nonentity /nɑː'nentəti || nɒ'nentəti/ *n* (*pl* **-ties**) persona *f* insignificante

nonetheless /'nʌnðə'les/ *adv* ▸**nevertheless**

nonevent /'nɑːnɪvent || ˌnɒnɪ'vent/ *n* fiasco *m*

non-existent /ˌnɑːnɪg'zɪstənt || ˌnɒnɪg'zɪstənt/ *adj* ‹*person/country*› inexistente; **her chances are practically ~** prácticamente no tiene ninguna posibilidad

nonfiction /'nɑːn'fɪkʃən || ˌnɒn'fɪkʃən/ *n* [u] no ficción *f* (*ensayos, biografías, obras de divulgación etc*)

nonintervention /ˌnɑːnɪntər'ventʃən || ˌnɒnɪntə'venʃən/ *n* no intervención *f*

nonissue /nɑː'nɪʃuː || nɒn'ɪʃuː/ *n*: **right now inflation is a ~** en estos momentos la inflación no es un asunto de importancia

nonmember /'nɑːn'membər || nɒn'membə(r)/ *n* no socio, -cia *m,f*

nonnuclear /'nɑːn'nuːkliər || nɒn'njuːkliə(r)/ *adj* no nuclear

no-nonsense /'nəʊ'nɑːnsens || ˌnəʊ'nɒnsəns/ *adj* (*before n*) ‹*approach/attitude*› sensato, serio; ‹*management*› firme y eficiente

nonpayment /'nɑːn'peɪmənt || ˌnɒn'peɪmənt/ *n* impago *m*

nonplus /nɑːn'plʌs || nɒn'plʌs/ *vt* **-ss-** desconcertar*, confundir

nonplused, nonplussed /nɑːn'plʌst || ˌnɒn'plʌst/ *adj* desconcertado, perplejo

nonprofit /'nɑːn'prɑːfət || ˌnɒn'prɒfɪt/, (BrE) **non-profit-making** /'nɑːn'prɑːfətˌmeɪkɪŋ || ˌnɒn'prɒfɪtmeɪkɪŋ/ *adj* sin fines lucrativos *or* de lucro

nonproliferation /ˌnɑːnprə'lɪfə'reɪʃən || ˌnɒnprəlɪfə'reɪʃən/ *n* [u] no proliferación *f*; (*before n*) **~ treaty** tratado *m* de no proliferación

nonresident /'nɑːn'rezədənt || ˌnɒn'rezɪdənt/ *n* [1] (of country) (Govt, Soc Adm) no residente *mf*, transeúnte *mf* [2] (of hotel): **the restaurant is open to ~s** el restaurante está abierto al público en general

nonreturnable /ˌnɑːnrɪ'tɜːrnəbəl || ˌnɒnrɪ'tɜːnəbəl/ *adj* ‹*deposit*› no reembolsable, a fondo perdido; ‹*bottle*› no retornable

nonsense /'nɑːnsens || 'nɒnsəns/ *n* [u]

[A] (rubbish) tonterías *fpl*, estupideces *fpl*; **to talk ~** decir* tonterías *or* estupideces *or* disparates; **that's absolute ~** eso es una tontería *or* una estupidez; **what's all this ~ about you not coming to the party?** ¿qué tonterías son ésas de que no vienes a la fiesta?; **to make (a) ~ of sth** hacer* que algo resulte absurdo; (*as interj*) **~!** ¡tonterías! *or* ¡qué ridículo!

[B] (bad behavior) tonterías *fpl*

nonsensical /nɑːn'sensɪkəl || nɒn'sensɪkəl/ *adj* disparatado, absurdo

nonshrink /'nɑːn'ʃrɪŋk || ˌnɒn'ʃrɪŋk/ *adj* que no encoge

nonsmoker /'nɑːn'sməʊkər || ˌnɒn'sməʊkə(r)/ *n* no fumador, -dora *m,f*, persona *f* que no fuma

nonsmoking /ˌnɑːn'sməʊkɪŋ || ˌnɒn'sməʊkɪŋ/ *adj* para no fumadores

nonstarter /'nɑːn'stɑːrtər || ˌnɒn'stɑːtə(r)/ *n* (colloq): **her proposal is a complete ~** su propuesta no tiene la más mínima posibilidad *or* (AmL tb) la más mínima chance

nonstick /'nɑːn'stɪk || ˌnɒn'stɪk/ *adj* antiadherente, de teflón®, de tefal®

nonstop[1] /'nɑːn'stɑːp || ˌnɒn'stɒp/ *adj* ‹*journey*› directo, sin paradas; ‹*flight*› sin escalas, directo

nonstop[2] *adv* [1] ‹*work/talk*› sin parar [2] ‹*sail/fly*› sin hacer escalas

nontoxic /'nɑːn'tɑːksɪk || ˌnɒn'tɒksɪk/ *adj* no tóxico

nonviolent /'nɑːn'vaɪələnt || ˌnɒn'vaɪələnt/ *adj* no violento, pacífico

noodle /'nuːdḷ/ *n* [1] (Culin) fideo *m*; (*before n*) **~ soup** sopa *f* de fideos [2] (head) (AmE colloq) coco *m* (fam)

nook /nʊk/ *n* rincón *m*; ***to search every ~ and cranny*** mirar/buscar* hasta en el último rincón *or* recoveco

noon /nuːn/ *n* mediodía *m*; **at ~** a mediodía; **until ~** hasta (el) mediodía

no one *pron* ▸**nobody**[1]

noose /nuːs/ *n* (for hanging) soga *f*, dogal *m*; (for trapping) lazo *m*; ***to put one's head in a ~*** firmar su (*or* mi *etc*) sentencia de muerte

nope /nəʊp/ *interj* (sl) no

noplace /'nəʊpleɪs/ *adv* (AmE) ▸**nowhere**[1] **A**

nor /nər, nɔːr || nɔː(r)/ *conj* [1] **neither ... nor ...** *see* **neither**[1] **A** [2] (*usu with neg*) tampoco; **I mustn't be late —**

~ **(must) I** no debo llegar tarde — yo tampoco *or* ni yo; ~ **does my client deny the fact that ...** tampoco niega mi cliente el hecho de que ...

norm /nɔːrm || nɔːm/ *n* 1 (standard, rule) norma *f*; **social ~s** normas sociales 2 (average): **that's not the ~** eso no es lo normal

normal /'nɔːrməl || 'nɔːməl/ *adj* normal; **above/below ~** por encima/por debajo de lo normal; **when things get back to ~** cuando todo vuelva a la normalidad, cuando la situación se normalice; **it's ~ to tip the driver** se acostumbra *or* se suele dar una propina al conductor; **it's ~ for them to react like that** es normal que reaccionen así

normalcy /'nɔːrməlsi || 'nɔːməlsi/ *n* [u] (AmE) ▸**normality**

normality /nɔːr'mæləti || nɔːmæləti/ *n* [u] normalidad *f*

normalize /'nɔːrməlaɪz || 'nɔːməlaɪz/ *vt* normalizar*

normally /'nɔːrməli || 'nɔːməli/ *adv* normalmente

north¹ /nɔːrθ || nɔːθ/ *n* [u]

A 1 (point of the compass, direction) norte *m*; **it lies to the ~ of the city** está al norte de la ciudad; **the wind is blowing from** *o* **is in the ~** el viento sopla *or* viene del norte *or* Norte; **~ by west** norte cuarta al noroeste; **~-~west** nornoroeste 2 (region) **the ~, the N~** el norte; **a town in the ~ of Spain** una ciudad del norte *or* en el norte de España; **the Far N~** el Polo Norte

B **the North** (in US history) el Norte, los estados nordistas

C **North** (in bridge) Norte *m*

north² *adj* (*before n*) ‹*wall/face*› norte *adj inv*, septentrional; **a strong ~ wind** un fuerte viento norte *or* del norte

north³ *adv* al norte; **the house faces ~** la casa está orientada *or* da al norte; **we sailed ~ for three hours** navegamos tres horas en dirección norte; **~ OF sth** al norte DE algo; **it is ~ of Rome** está al norte de Roma; **they live up ~** viven en el norte

north: **~ America** *n* Norteamérica *f*, América *f* del Norte; **~ American** *adj* de América del Norte, norteamericano; **~bound** *adj* ‹*traffic/train*› que va (*or* iba *etc*) en dirección norte

northeast¹, **Northeast** /'nɔːrθ'iːst || ,nɔːθ'iːst/ *n* [u] **the ~** 1 (direction) nor(d)este, Nor(d)este 2 (region) **the ~** el nor(d)este

northeast² *adj* nor(d)este *adj inv*, del nor(d)este, nororiental

northeast³ *adv* hacia el nor(d)este, en dirección nor(d)este

northeasterly¹ /'nɔːrθ'iːstərli || ,nɔːθ'iːstəli/ *adj* ‹*wind*› del nor(d)este; **in a ~ direction** hacia el nor(d)este, en dirección nor(d)este

northeasterly² *n* (*pl* **-lies**) viento *m* del nor(d)este

northeastern /'nɔːrθ'iːstərn || ,nɔːθ'iːstən/ *adj* nor(d)este *adj inv*, del nor(d)este, nororiental

northerly¹ /'nɔːrðərli || 'nɔːðəli/ *adj* ‹*wind*› del norte; ‹*latitude*› norte *adj inv*; **in a ~ direction** hacia el *or* en dirección norte

northerly² *n* (*pl* **-lies**) viento *m* del norte

northern /'nɔːrðərn || 'nɔːðən/ *adj* ‹*region/country*› del norte, septentrional, norteño, nortino (Chi, Per); **~ England** el norte de Inglaterra; **the ~ states** (in US) los estados del norte; **N~ Europe** Europa septentrional, el Norte de Europa; **the N~ Hemisphere** el hemisferio norte *or* septentrional; **the ~ lights** la aurora boreal

Northerner, northerner /'nɔːrðərnər || 'nɔːðənə(r)/ *n*: *habitante o persona oriunda del norte de un país o de una región*

Northern Ireland *n* Irlanda *f* del Norte

northernmost /'nɔːrðərnməʊst || 'nɔːðənməʊst/ *adj* (*before n*) ‹*point/town/island*› más septentrional; **the ~ tip of the island** el extremo norte *or* septentrional de la isla

north: **~ Sea** *n* Mar *m* del Norte; **~ Star** *n* estrella *f* polar

northward¹ /'nɔːrθwərd 'nɔːθwəd/, **northwardly** /-li/ *adj* (*before n*): **in a ~ direction** en dirección norte, hacia el norte

northward², (BrE) **northwards** /-z/ *adv* ‹*drive/travel/turn*› hacia el norte

northwest¹, **Northwest** /'nɔːrθ'west || ,nɔːθ'west/ *n* [u] **the ~** 1 (direction) el noroeste *or* Noroeste 2 (region) el noroeste *or* Noroeste

northwest² *adj* noroeste *adj inv*, del noroeste

northwest³ *adv* hacia el noroeste, en dirección noroeste

northwesterly¹ /'nɔːrθ'westərli || ,nɔːθ'westəli/ *adj* ‹*wind*› del noroeste

northwesterly² *n* (*pl* **-lies**) viento *m* del noroeste

northwestern /'nɔːrθ'westərn || ,nɔːθ'westən/ *adj* noroccidental, noroeste *adj inv*, del noroeste

Norway /'nɔːrweɪ || 'nɔːweɪ/ *n* Noruega *f*

Norwegian¹ /nɔːr'wiːdʒən || nɔː'wiːdʒən/ *adj* noruego

Norwegian² *n* 1 [c] (person) noruego, -ga *m,f* 2 [u] (language) noruego *m*

nose¹ /nəʊz/ *n*

A (of person, animal) nariz *f*; **to blow one's ~** sonarse* (la nariz); **her ~ was bleeding** le salía sangre de la nariz, le sangraba la nariz; ***not to look/see beyond the end of one's ~*** no ver* más allá de sus (*or* mis *etc*) narices; ***(right) under sb's ~*** (colloq): **it was right under my ~ all the time** lo tenía delante de las narices (fam); **he stole it from under our very ~s** se lo robó en nuestras propias narices (fam); ***to cut off one's ~ to spite one's face*** tirar piedras al *or* contra el propio tejado; ***to follow one's ~*** (go straight on) seguir* derecho *or* todo recto; (act intuitively) dejarse guiar por la intuición; ***to get up sb's ~*** (BrE colloq): **that's the sort of thing that gets right up my ~** ése es el tipo de cosa que me enferma *or* me revienta (fam); ***to keep one's ~ clean*** (colloq) no meterse en líos (fam); ***to keep one's ~ out of sth*** no meter las narices en algo (fam), no meterse en algo; ***to keep one's ~ to the grindstone*** trabajar duro, darle* al callo (Esp fam); ***to lead sb by the ~*** tener* a algn agarrado por las narices, manejar a algn a su (*or* mi *etc*) antojo; ***to look down one's ~ at sb*** mirar a algn por encima del hombro; **he looked down his ~ at the idea** la idea le pareció tonta (*or* ridícula *etc*); ***to pay through the ~*** (colloq) pagar* un ojo de la cara *or* un riñón (fam); ***to poke*** *o* ***stick one's ~ in*** (colloq) meter las narices en algo (fam); ***to put sb's ~ out of joint*** (colloq) hacer* que algn se moleste *or* se ofenda; ***to rub sb's ~ in sth*** (colloq) restregarle* *or* refregarle* algo a algn por las narices (fam); ***to turn one's ~ up at sth/sb*** (colloq) despreciar algo/a algn; (*before n*) **~ drops** gotas *fpl* nasales

B (of plane, car) parte *f* delantera, morro *m*, trompa *f* (RPl); (of boat) proa *f*

nose² *vi* 1 (rummage, pry) entrometerse; **to ~ around** *o* **about in sth** husmear *or* fisgonear en algo 2 (move slowly) (+ *adv compl*): **to ~ past/out/in** pasar/salir*/entrar lentamente

■ **nose** *vt*: ***to ~ one's way*** avanzar* con precaución

Phrasal verb

• **nose out** [v ▸ o ▸ adv, v ▸ adv ▸ o] 1 (narrowly defeat) (esp AmE) escamotearle la victoria a 2 (discover) ‹*truth/secret*› enterarse de, descubrir*

nose: **~bag** *n* (Equ) morral *m*; **~bleed** *n* hemorragia *f* nasal (frml); **I've got a ~bleed** me sangra la nariz

nosedive¹ /'nəʊzdaɪv/ *n* **to take a ~** «*plane/pilot*» descender* *or* bajar en picada *or* (Esp) en picado; «*prices*» caer* en picada *or* (Esp) en picado

nosedive² *vi* 1 (Aviat) «*plane/pilot*» descender* *or* bajar en picada *or* (Esp) en picado 2 (drop sharply) «*prices*» caer* en picada *or* (Esp) en picado

nosepiece /'nəʊzpiːs/ *n* (AmE) 1 (Equ) muserola *f* 2 (on glasses) puente *m*

nosey /'nəʊzi/ *adj* (BrE) ▸**nosy**

nosh /nɑːʃ || nɒʃ/ *n* (BrE colloq) 1 [u] (food) comida *f*, manye *m* (CS arg) 2 (meal) (*no pl*): **we had a good ~** nos dimos una comilona (fam)

nosh-up /'nɑːʃʌp || 'nɒʃʌp/ *n* (BrE colloq) comilona *f* (fam)

no-smoking /'nəʊ'sməʊkɪŋ/ *adj* ‹*compartment/section*› para no fumadores

nostalgia /nɑː'stældʒə || nɒ'stældʒə/ *n* [u] nostalgia *f*

nostalgic /nɑː'stældʒɪk || nɒ'stældʒɪk/ *adj* nostálgico

nostril /'nɑːstrəl || 'nɒstrɪl/ *n* ventana *f* de la nariz, orificio *m* nasal (frml)

nosy, (BrE also) **nosey** /'nəʊzi/ *adj* **nosier, nosiest** (colloq) ‹*person*› entrometido, metiche (AmL fam), metido

n

(AmL fam); ‹*question*› impertinente

not /nɑːt || nɒt/ *adv* 1 no; **I asked them ~ to tell anyone** les pedí que no se lo dijeran a nadie; **~ to go would have been rude** no ir hubiera sido una grosería; **~ to worry** (BrE) no importa; **a ~ inconsiderable sum of money** (frml) una suma de dinero bastante considerable; **oh, no, ~ you again!** ¡Dios mío! ¿tú otra vez?; **that's mine — it is *not*!** eso es mío — ¡no, señor! 2 **not that** (*as conj*): **I'm going to London, ~ that it's any business of yours** voy a Londres, no es que a ti te importe, pero … 3 (emphatic) ni; **~ a penny more** ni un penique más 4 (replacing clause): **I hope ~** — espero que no; **I should think ~!** ¡claro que no!; ¡faltaría más!; **certainly ~!** ¡de ninguna manera!; **of course ~!** ¡por supuesto *or* claro que no!; **are you going to help me or ~?** ¿me vas a ayudar o no?

notable /ˈnəʊtəbəl/ *adj* ‹*author/actor*› distinguido; ‹*success*› señalado; ‹*improvement/difference*› notable, considerable, marcado; **it is ~ that …** es de notar que …

notably /ˈnəʊtəbli/ *adv* 1 (noticeably) notablemente 2 (in particular) particularmente, en particular

notary (public) /ˈnəʊtəri/ *n* (*pl* **notaries (public)**) notario, -ria *m,f*, escribano (público), escribana (pública) *m,f* (RPl)

notation /nəʊˈteɪʃən/ *n* 1 [u] (system) notación *f* 2 [c] (jotting) (AmE) anotación *f*, nota *f*

notch¹ /nɑːtʃ || nɒtʃ/ *n* (in wood, metal) muesca *f*, corte *m*; (on belt) agujero *m*

notch² *vt* hacer* una muesca *or* un corte en, marcar*

Phrasal verb

- **notch up** [v ▸ adv ▸ o] (colloq) apuntarse

note¹ /nəʊt/ *n*

A [c] 1 (record, reminder) nota *f*; **to make a ~ of sth** anotar *or* apuntar algo; **to make ~s** hacer* anotaciones; **to take ~s** tomar apuntes *or* notas; **to compare ~s** cambiar impresiones 2 (comment) nota *f*, comentario *m*

B [c] (message) nota *f*

C [c] 1 (Mus) nota *f* 2 (tone): **it strikes a familiar ~** suena conocido; **I detected a ~ of sarcasm in his voice** percibí un tono de sarcasmo en su voz; **if I may sound a ~ of caution …** si se me permite llamar a la precaución …; **the evening ended on a sad ~** la velada terminó con una nota triste 3 (element, hint) toque *m*

D [c] (esp BrE) (*bank~*) billete *m*

E [u] 1 (importance, interest): **a surgeon of ~** un cirujano de renombre, un eminente cirujano; **nothing worthy of ~** nada digno de mención 2 (attention): **take ~ of what he says** toma nota de *or* presta atención a lo que dice

note² *vt* 1 (observe, notice) observar, fijarse en; ‹*objections*› tomar (debida) nota de; **to ~ THAT** observar *or* notar QUE 2 (record) ‹*information/details*› apuntar, anotar

Phrasal verb

- **note down** [v ▸ adv ▸ o, v ▸ o ▸ adv] apuntar, anotar

notebook /ˈnəʊtbʊk/ *n* 1 (exercise book) cuaderno *m* 2 (ring binder) (AmE) carpeta *f* de anillos *or* (Esp) anillas

noted /ˈnəʊtəd || ˈnəʊtɪd/ *adj* ‹*historian/surgeon*› renombrado, de nota; **to be ~ FOR sth/-ING** ser* conocido POR algo/+ INF

note: **~pad** *n* bloc *m*; **~paper** *n* [u] papel *m* de carta(s); **~worthy** *adj* ‹*event/building*› notable, de interés; **it is ~worthy that …** es de notar que …

nothing¹ /ˈnʌθɪŋ/ *pron*

A nada; **~ has changed** nada ha cambiado; **he gave us ~** no nos dio nada; **she said ~ else** no dijo nada más; **it's better than ~, I suppose** hombre, peor es nada; **there's ~ to eat** no hay nada de comer; **I have ~ more to say** no tengo nada más que decir; **there's ~ we can do** no podemos hacer nada; ***~ doing!*** ¡de eso nada!; ***there's ~ for it*** no hay más remedio; ***there's ~ in it***: **this one may cost a bit more but there's ~ in it really** puede que éste cueste algo más pero la diferencia es mínima; ***there's ~ to it*** (it's easy) es muy fácil; (it's groundless) no es cierto

B (*in phrases*) **for nothing**: **she gave it to me for ~** me lo dio gratis; **it was all for ~** todo fue en vano; **not for ~ was he called Ivan the Terrible** no en vano *or* no por nada se le llamaba Iván el Terrible; **if nothing else** al menos, por lo menos; **nothing but**: **she's caused ~ but trouble** no ha causado (nada) más que problemas; **nothing if not**: **he's ~ if not reliable** es totalmente de fiar; **nothing less than**: **it's ~ less than scandalous** es verdaderamente escandaloso; **nothing like**: **there's ~ like a shower to freshen you up** no hay (nada) como una ducha para refrescarse; **there's ~ like it** es lo mejor que hay; **she's ~ like her mother** no se parece en nada a su madre; **nothing more than**: **it's ~ more than a scratch** no es más que un rasguño; **nothing much**: **~ much happened** no pasó gran cosa; **nothing short of**: **the consequences would be ~ short of disastrous** las consecuencias no serían ni más ni menos que desastrosas

nothing² *n*

A (Math) cero *m*

B (worthless thing): **this is a mere ~ to what they spend on food and drink** esto no es nada comparado con lo que gastan en comida y bebida; ***to whisper sweet ~s*** susurrar palabras de amor; **he whispered sweet ~s in her ear** le susurraba palabras de amor al oído

notice¹ /ˈnəʊtəs || ˈnəʊtɪs/ *n*

A [c] 1 (written sign) letrero *m*, aviso *m*; **to put up a ~** poner* un letrero *or* aviso 2 (item of information) anuncio *m*; **the birth/marriage ~s** (in newspaper) los anuncios *or* (AmL tb) avisos de nacimientos/matrimonios 3 (review) reseña *f*, crítica *f*

B [u] (attention): **it has come/been brought to my ~ that …** (frml) ha llegado a mi conocimiento que …/se me ha señalado que … (frml); **it was never brought to his ~** no se le dijo nada al respecto; **to take ~ (of sth/sb)**: **she took no ~** no hizo caso; **don't take any ~ of him** no le hagas caso; **take special ~ of these instructions** preste especial atención a estas instrucciones; **this will make them sit up and take ~** esto hará que presten atención

C [u] 1 (notification) aviso *m*; **without prior ~** sin previo aviso; **until further ~** hasta nuevo aviso; **I can't drop everything at a moment's ~** no puedo abandonarlo todo así, de un momento a otro; **I'll try and get there, but it's rather short ~** (colloq) procuraré ir, pero me avisas con muy poca antelación *or* anticipación; **it's impossible to do it at such short ~** es imposible hacerlo a tan corto plazo; **~ OF sth**: **we require at least two days' ~ of any changes** cualquier cambio nos debe ser comunicado con por lo menos dos días de antelación *or* anticipación 2 (of termination of employment) preaviso *m*; **I have to give (the company) a month's ~** tengo que dar un mes de preaviso; **she was given (her) ~** la despidieron; **to give** *o* **hand in one's ~** presentar su (*or* mi *etc*) renuncia *or* dimisión

notice² *vt* notar; **he pretended not to ~ me** hizo como si no me hubiera visto; **I managed to sneak out without being ~d** logré escabullirme sin que nadie se diera cuenta; **to get oneself ~d** hacerse* notar; **I couldn't help noticing that …** no pude menos que notar que…; **to ~ sb/sth + INF/-ING**: **nobody ~d him put it in his pocket** nadie lo vio ponérselo en el bolsillo; **I ~d water dripping from the ceiling** noté que caían gotas de agua del techo

■ **notice** *vi* 1 (realize, observe) darse* cuenta; **he did it without my noticing** lo hizo sin que me diera cuenta 2 (BrE) (show) (colloq) notarse; **it hardly ~s** apenas se nota

noticeable /ˈnəʊtəsəbəl || ˈnəʊtɪsəbəl/ *adj* ‹*change/difference*› perceptible, evidente; **it's hardly ~** apenas se nota; **there's been a ~ improvement in his condition** ha experimentado una sensible mejoría

noticeably /ˈnəʊtəsəbli || ˈnəʊtɪsəbli/ *adv* ‹*different*› perceptiblemente; ‹*better*› sensiblemente; **it's ~ colder there** ahí se nota que hace más frío

noticeboard /ˈnəʊtəsbɔːrd || ˈnəʊtɪsbɔːd/ *n* (esp BrE) tablero *m or* (Esp) tablón *m* de anuncios, cartelera *f* (AmL), diario *m* mural (Chi)

notifiable /ˈnəʊtəˈfaɪəbəl || ˈnəʊtɪfaɪəbəl/ *adj* (esp BrE) ‹*disease*› de la que hay que dar parte

notification /ˈnəʊtəfəˈkeɪʃən || ˌnəʊtɪfɪˈkeɪʃən/ *n* [u] notificación *f*

notify /ˈnəʊtəfaɪ || ˈnəʊtɪfaɪ/ *vt* **-fies, -fying, -fied** 1 (inform) informar; (in writing) notificar*; **the authorities must be notified** se debe dar parte *or* informar a las autoridades; **to ~ sb OF sth** comunicarle* algo A algn 2 (instruct) (frml) ‹*agent/lawyer/accountant*› darle* instrucciones a

notion /ˈnəʊʃən/ *n*

A [c] 1 (idea) idea *f*; **she hadn't the slightest ~ of how to behave in public** no tenía ni la menor idea de cómo comportarse en público; **I had a ~ that …** me dio la impresión de que …, me pareció que … 2 (inclination) (colloq):

I've a ~ to tell him just what I think tengo ganas de decirle exactamente lo que pienso
B [c] (concept) concepto *m*
C **notions** *pl* 1 (in sewing) artículos *mpl* de mercería 2 (AmE): **household/gift ~s** artículos *mpl* para el hogar/de regalo

notoriety /ˈnəʊtəˈraɪəti/ *n* [u] mala reputación *f*, mala fama *f*

notorious /nəʊˈtɔːriəs/ *adj* ‹*thief/womanizer/gossip*› (bien) conocido; ‹*place*› de mala fama *or* mala reputación; **to be ~ FOR sth/-ING** ser* (bien) conocido POR algo/+ INF, tener* fama DE algo/+ INF

notoriously /nəʊˈtɔːriəsli/ *adv*: **he's ~ lazy** tiene fama de holgazán; **it's ~ difficult** es de notoria dificultad, se sabe que es muy difícil

notwithstanding¹ /ˈnɑːtwɪðˈstændɪŋ || ˌnɒtwɪθˈstændɪŋ/ *prep* (frml) a pesar de, pese a, no obstante (frml)

notwithstanding² *adv* (frml) no obstante (frml)

notwithstanding³ *conj* (frml) a pesar de que

nougat /ˈnuːgət || ˈnuːgɑː/ *n* [u] ≈ turrón *m*

nought /nɔːt/ *n* (esp BrE) 1 (zero) cero *m* 2 ▸ **naught¹ 1**

noughts and crosses *n* [u] (BrE) (+ *sing vb*) tres en raya *m*, tres en línea *m* (Col), gato *m* (Chi, Méx), ta-te-ti *m* (RPl)

noun /naʊn/ *n* sustantivo *m*, nombre *m*

nourish /ˈnɜːrɪʃ || ˈnʌrɪʃ/ *vt* 1 (feed) ‹*person/animal/plant*› nutrir, alimentar 2 (foster, cherish) ‹*hope*› abrigar*, alentar*; ‹*ambition*› alentar*

nourishing /ˈnɜːrɪʃɪŋ || ˈnʌrɪʃɪŋ/ *adj* nutritivo, alimenticio

nourishment /ˈnɜːrɪʃmənt || ˈnʌrɪʃmənt/ *n* [u] alimento *m*; **it provides the ~ the plant requires** aporta los nutrientes que la planta necesita

nouveau riche /ˈnuːvəʊˈriːʃ/ *n* (*pl* **~x ~s** /ˈnuːvəʊˈriːʃ/) (pej) nuevo rico, nueva rica *m,f* (pey)

Nov (= **November**) nov.

Nova Scotia /ˈnəʊvəˈskəʊʃə/ *n* Nueva Escocia *f*

novel¹ /ˈnɑːvəl || ˈnɒvəl/ *n* novela *f*

novel² *adj* original, novedoso (esp AmL)

novelist /ˈnɑːvələst || ˈnɒvəlɪst/ *n* novelista *mf*

novelty /ˈnɑːvəlti || ˈnɒvəlti/ *n* (*pl* **-ties**) 1 [u] (newness): **the ~ will soon wear off** pronto dejará de ser novedad *or* (esp AmL) novedoso 2 [c] (new thing, situation) novedad *f*; **to be a ~** ser* una novedad 3 [c] (small toy, trinket) (esp BrE) chuchería *f*

November /nəʊˈvembər || nəʊˈvembə(r)/ *n* noviembre *m*; *see also* **January**

novice /ˈnɑːvəs || ˈnɒvɪs/ *n* 1 (beginner) principiante *mf*, novato, -ta *m,f*; (*before n*) ‹*skier/programmer*› principiante, novato 2 (Relig) novicio, -cia *m,f*

now¹ /naʊ/ *adv*
A 1 (at this time) ahora; **I feel better ~** ahora me siento mejor; **they've all gone home ~** ya se han ido todos a casa; **you can come in ~** ya puedes entrar; **any minute ~** en cualquier momento, están al caer (fam); **~'s your chance** ésta es tu oportunidad 2 (at that time): **it was ~ time to say goodbye** había llegado el momento de decir adiós; **it was ~ too late to change** ya era demasiado tarde para cambiar 3 (nowadays) hoy en día, actualmente 4 (*in phrases*) **(every) now and then** *o* **again** de vez en cuando; **for now** por ahora, por el momento; **now ..., now ...** (showing alternation) de repente ..., de repente ..., ora ..., ora ... (liter)
B 1 (at once, immediately) ahora (mismo); **ready? ~!** ¿listos? ¡ya!; **it's ~ or never!** ¡ahora o nunca! 2 (*in phrases*) **just now**: **he left just ~** acaba de irse; **he's talking to a client just ~** en este momento está hablando con un cliente; **right now** (immediately) ahora mismo, inmediatamente; (at present) ahora mismo, en este momento
C (to follow that) ahora; **what shall I do ~?** ¿ahora qué hago?
D 1 (showing length of time) ya; **we've been living here for 40 years ~** ya hace 40 años que vivimos aquí, llevamos 40 años viviendo aquí 2 (*after prep*): **he'd have called before ~** ya habría llamado; **between ~ and Friday** de aquí al viernes; **she should be here by ~** ya debería estar aquí; **the by ~ furious customer said that ...** el cliente, que a estas alturas ya estaba furioso, dijo que ...; **100 years from ~** dentro de 100 años; **from ~ on(ward)** a partir de ahora, de ahora en adelante; **(up) until** *o* **till ~, up to ~** hasta ahora
E 1 (indicating pause, transition): **~, who's next?** bueno ¿(ahora) a quién le toca? 2 (introducing statement or question): **~ that's what I call real food!** ¡eso sí que es comida como Dios manda!; **~ where did I put my book?** ¿dónde habré puesto el libro? 3 (emphasizing command, request, warning, advice): **~ look here!** ¡espera un momento!; **don't get me wrong, ~!** no me vayas a malinterpretar 4 (*in phrases*) **now, now** ¡vamos, vamos!; **now then ...** a ver ...

now² *conj* **~ (that)** ahora que

NOW *n* (in US) = **National Organization for Women**

nowadays /ˈnaʊədeɪz/ *adv* hoy (en) día, actualmente, en la actualidad

nowhere¹ /ˈnəʊhwer || ˈnəʊweə(r)/ *adv*
A : **where did you go last night? — nowhere** ¿adónde fuiste anoche? — a ningún lado *or* a ninguna parte; **~ else will you find such beautiful scenery** en ninguna otra parte encontrarás un paisaje tan hermoso; **she was ~ to be found/seen** no se la encontraba/se la veía por ningún lado *or* por ninguna parte; ***to get* ~** no conseguir* *or* no lograr nada; **we're getting ~ fast** (colloq) no estamos avanzando nada de nada (fam); ***to go* *o* *lead* ~** no conducir* a nada
B **nowhere near**: **Warsaw is ~ near Moscow** Varsovia está lejísimos de Moscú; **my house is ~ near as big as theirs** mi casa no es tan grande como la suya ni mucho menos

nowhere² *pron*: **~ was open yet** todavía no había nada (*or* ningún lugar *etc*) abierto; **Paris is like ~ else** París es único; **he had ~ to go/hide** no tenía dónde ir/dónde esconderse; **the car just appeared from** *o* **out of ~** el coche apareció de la nada

no-win /ˈnəʊˈwɪn/ *adj* (*before n*): **to be in a ~ situation** estar* en una situación sin salida

noxious /ˈnɑːkʃəs || ˈnɒkʃəs/ *adj* (frml) ‹*substance/fumes*› nocivo, tóxico

nozzle /ˈnɑːzəl || ˈnɒzəl/ *n* (on hose) boca *f*; (on fire extinguisher) boquilla *f*, boca *f*; (on oil can) pico *m*, pitorro *m* (Esp)

NRC *n* (in US) = **Nuclear Regulatory Commission**

NSA *n* (in US) = **National Security Agency**

NSC *n* (in US) = **National Security Council**

NSPCC *n* (in UK) = **National Society for the Prevention of Cruelty to Children**

nth /enθ/ *adj* (*before n*) 1 (Math): **to the ~ degree** a la enésima potencia 2 (colloq): **for the ~ time** por enésima vez; **unreliable to the ~ degree** informal hasta decir basta

nuance /ˈnuːɑːns || ˈnjuːɑːns/ *n* matiz *m*

nubile /ˈnuːbəl, -aɪl || ˈnjuːbaɪl/ *adj* núbil (liter)

nuclear /ˈnuːkliər || ˈnjuːkliə(r)/ *adj* nuclear; **the ~ debate** el debate sobre la cuestión nuclear; **~ power** energía *f* nuclear; **~ power station** central *f* nuclear

nuclear: **~ family** *n* familia *f* nuclear; **~ physics** *n* [u] (+ *sing vb*) física *f* nuclear; **~-powered** /ˈnuːkliərˈpaʊərd || ˈnjuːklɪəˈpaʊəd/ *adj* nuclear; **~ reactor** *n* reactor *m* nuclear

nucleus /ˈnuːkliəs || ˈnjuːkliəs/ *n* (*pl* **-clei** /-kliaɪ/) núcleo *m*

nude¹ /nuːd || njuːd/ *n* (Art) desnudo *m*; **in the ~** desnudo

nude² *adj* desnudo; **a ~ portrait** un desnudo

nudge¹ /nʌdʒ/ *vt* codear (ligeramente)

nudge² *n* golpe *m* (suave) con el codo

nudism /ˈnuːdɪzəm || ˈnjuːdɪzəm/ *n* [u] nudismo *m*

nudist /ˈnuːdəst || ˈnjuːdɪst/ *n* nudista *mf*; (*before n*) ‹*beach/camp/club*› nudista

nudity /ˈnuːdəti || ˈnjuːdəti/ *n* [u] desnudez *f*

nugget /ˈnʌgət || ˈnʌgɪt/ *n* (Min) pepita *f*; **a gold ~** una pepita de oro

nuisance /ˈnuːsn̩s || ˈnjuːsn̩s/ *n* 1 (occurrence, thing): **to be a ~** ser* una molestia *or* (fam) una lata *or* una pesadez, ser* un incordio (Esp); **what a ~!** ¡qué molestia!, ¡qué lata! (fam) 2 (person) pesado, -da *m,f*, incordio *m* (Esp fam); **he's always making a ~ of himself** siempre está dando la lata (fam) 3 (Law): **a public ~** una alteración del orden público

nuisance tax *n* (AmE) *impuesto cobrado directamente al consumidor*

NUJ *n* (in UK) = **National Union of Journalists**

null /nʌl/ *adj* (Law): **to declare sth ~ and void** declarar nulo algo

nullify /ˈnʌləfaɪ || ˌnʌlɪfaɪ/ *vt* **-fies, -fying, -fied** ‹*decree/claim*› anular, invalidar; ‹*effect/efforts*› anular

NUM *n* (in UK) = **National Union of Mineworkers**

numb[1] /nʌm/ *adj* **-er, -est** (with cold) entumecido; **the injection made my gums go ~** la inyección me durmió las encías; **I just felt ~ after the funeral** me quedé como insensible después del funeral; **my fingers were ~ with cold** tenía los dedos entumecidos de frío

numb[2] *vt* «*cold*» entumecer*; «*drug*» adormecer*

number[1] /ˈnʌmbər || ˈnʌmbə(r)/ *n*

A (digit) número *m*; **in round ~s** en números redondos

B (for identification) número *m*; (*telephone ~*) número de teléfono; **wrong ~** número equivocado; **page/room ~** número de página/de habitación; **I'm in ~ 17** estoy en la (habitación) 17; **she lives at ~ 48** vive en el número 48; ***her/my ~ is up*** le/me ha llegado la hora; ***to do a ~ on sb*** (AmE sl) hacérsela* buena a algn (fam); ***to do sth by the ~s*** (AmE) hacer* algo como Dios manda; ***to have sb's ~*** (esp AmE colloq) tener* calado a algn (fam); ***to look out for*** *o* ***after ~ one*** pensar* ante todo en el propio interés; (*before n*) **he's hardly your ~ one fan** no eres precisamente santo de su devoción

C 1 (amount, quantity) número *m*; **student ~s** el número de estudiantes; **in a large ~ of cases** en un gran número de casos; **in a small ~ of cases** en unos pocos casos, en contados casos; **on a ~ of occasions** en varias ocasiones, varias veces; **any ~ of things could go wrong** hay (una) cantidad de cosas que podrían fallar 2 (group): **among** *o* **in their ~** entre ellos, en su grupo

D 1 (song, tune) número *m* 2 (issue of magazine, journal) número *m* 3 (garment) (colloq) modelo *m*; **she wore a smart little red ~** llevaba un elegante modelito rojo

E numbers *pl* (AmE colloq) 1 (lottery) lotería *f* clandestina, ≈ chance *m* (*en Col*) 2 (results): **I can't say anything till I see the ~s** no puedo decir nada hasta ver las cifras

number[2] *vt* 1 (assign number to) ‹*houses/pages/items*› numerar; **a ~ed (bank) account** una cuenta (bancaria) numerada 2 (amount to): **the spectators ~ed 50,000** había (un total de) 50.000 espectadores, el número de espectadores ascendía a 50.000; **they ~ thousands** son miles, hay miles de ellos 3 (count) contar*; **they are worthy to be ~ed among the saints** merecen que se los cuente entre los santos; **his days are ~ed** tiene los días contados

■ **number** *vi* (figure) figurar

number: **~plate** *n* (BrE) matrícula *f*, placa *f* (AmL), patente *f* (CS), chapa *f* (RPl); **~ sign** *n* (AmE) tecla *f* (del signo) de número, tecla *f* numeral, tecla *f* de almohadilla (Esp); **~s game** *n* (AmE) ▸**number**[1] **E1**

numbing /ˈnʌmɪŋ/ *adj* ‹*cold*› entumecedor; ‹*banality/monotony*› soporífero

numbness /ˈnʌmnəs || ˈnʌmnɪs/ *n* [u]: **I still experience some ~ in my fingers** todavía siento los dedos medio dormidos; **I was left with a feeling of ~ after she died** su muerte me dejó como insensible

numbskull /ˈnʌmskʌl/ *n* ▸**numskull**

numeracy /ˈnuːmərəsi || ˈnjuːmərəsi/ *n* [u] (esp BrE) nociones *fpl* elementales de cálculo aritmético

numeral /ˈnuːmərəl || ˈnjuːmərəl/ *n* número *m*

numerate /ˈnuːmərət || ˈnjuːmərət/ *adj* (esp BrE) *capaz de realizar cálculos aritméticos elementales*

numerical /nʊˈmerɪkəl || njuːˈmerɪkəl/ *adj* numérico; **in ~ order** *o* **sequence** por *or* en orden numérico

numerous /ˈnuːmərəs || ˈnjuːmərəs/ *adj* numeroso

numskull /ˈnʌmskʌl/ *n* (esp AmE colloq) zoquete *m* (fam), tarugo, -ga *m,f* (fam)

nun /nʌn/ *n* monja *f*, religiosa *f* (frml)

nunnery /ˈnʌnəri/ *n* (*pl* **-ries**) convento *m*

nuptial /ˈnʌpʃəl/ *adj* (frml *or* hum) ‹*ceremony*› nupcial (frml); ‹*mass*› de esponsales (frml)

nuptials /ˈnʌpʃəlz/ *pl n* (frml *or* hum) nupcias *fpl* (frml)

nurse[1] /nɜːrs || nɜːs/ *n* 1 (Med) enfermero, -ra *m,f* 2 (nanny) niñera *f*

nurse[2] *vt*

A 1 (Med) ‹*patient*› atender*, cuidar (de); **he ~d her back to health** la atendió *or* cuidó hasta que se repuso, cuidó de ella hasta que se repuso 2 ‹*wound/injury*› cuidar; **I'm staying in to ~ my cold** me voy a quedar en casa a ver si me mejoro de este resfriado

B 1 (cradle) ‹*baby*› arrullar, tener* en brazos 2 ‹*drink*› tener* en la mano

C (suckle) ‹*baby*› amamantar

D (harbor) ‹*hope/ambition*› abrigar*

nursemaid /ˈnɜːrsmeɪd || ˈnɜːsmeɪd/ *n* (dated) niñera *f*

nursery /ˈnɜːrsri || ˈnɜːsəri/ *n* (*pl* **-ries**) 1 (*day ~*) guardería *f* 2 (room in house) cuarto *m or* habitación *f* de los niños 3 (Agr, Hort) vivero *m*

nursery: **~ rhyme** *n* canción *f* infantil; **~ school** *n* jardín *m* de infancia, jardín *m* infantil (AmL), kindergarten *m* (AmL); (preschool) pre-escolar *m*

nursing /ˈnɜːrsɪŋ || ˈnɜːsɪŋ/ *n* [u] 1 (profession) enfermería *f*; (*before n*) ‹*staff/studies*› de enfermería 2 (care) atención *f*, cuidado *m*

nursing home *n* (for the aged) residencia *f* de ancianos *con mayor nivel de asistencia médica*; (for convalescence) clínica *f*, casa *f* de reposo *or* (Ur) de salud

nurture /ˈnɜːrtʃər || ˈnɜːtʃə(r)/ *vt* ‹*child/person*› criar*, educar*; ‹*plant/crop*› cuidar; ‹*friendship*› cultivar; ‹*emotion/feeling*› nutrir, alimentar

nut /nʌt/ *n*

A (Agr, Bot, Culin) fruto *m* seco (*nuez, almendra, avellana etc*); ***a hard*** *o* ***tough ~*** (BrE colloq) un tipo duro (fam); ***a hard*** *o* ***tough ~ to crack*** un hueso duro de roer, un problema difícil de resolver; (*before n*) ‹*cutlet/loaf*› (Culin) de frutos secos

B (Tech) tuerca *f*; **~s and bolts** tuercas y tornillos; ***the ~s and bolts (of sth)***: **the ~s and bolts of accounting** las bases *or* los elementos básicos de contabilidad

C (colloq) 1 (crazy person) chiflado, -da *m,f* (fam) 2 (fanatic): **a baseball/an opera ~** un fanático *or* (Esp fam) un forofo del béisbol/de la ópera

D (head) (BrE colloq): ***to be off one's ~*** (crazy, reckless) estar* mal del coco (fam), estar* chiflado (fam); (angry): ***to do one's ~*** (BrE) salirse* de sus (*or* mis *etc*) casillas

E nuts *pl* (testicles) (vulg) huevos *mpl* (vulg), cojones *mpl* (vulg), pelotas *fpl* (CS, Esp vulg), tanates *mpl* (Méx vulg)

nut: **~case** *n* (colloq) chiflado, -da *m,f* (fam), loco, -ca *m,f*; **~crackers** *pl n* (BrE) cascanueces *m*; **a pair of ~crackers** un cascanueces

nutmeg /ˈnʌtmeg/ *n* [u c] (spice) nuez *f* moscada; (tree) mirística *f*

nutrient /ˈnuːtriənt || ˈnjuːtriənt/ *n* nutriente *m*, sustancia *f* nutritiva

nutrition /nʊˈtrɪʃən || njuːˈtrɪʃən/ *n* [u] nutrición *f*

nutritious /nʊˈtrɪʃəs || njuːˈtrɪʃəs/ *adj* nutritivo

nuts /nʌts/ *adj* (colloq) (*pred*) chiflado (fam), chalado (fam); **to go ~ (over sth/sb)** chalarse *or* chiflarse (por algo/algn) (fam); **this job is enough to drive you ~** este trabajo es capaz de enloquecer a cualquiera; **she's absolutely ~ about him** está loca por él (fam), se derrite por él (fam)

nutshell /ˈnʌtʃel/ *n* cáscara *f* de nuez; ***in a ~*** en dos *or* en pocas palabras

nutter /ˈnʌtər || ˈnʌtə(r)/ *n* (BrE sl) chiflado, -da *m,f* (fam), chalado, -da *m,f* (fam), loco, -ca *m,f* (de remate)

nutty /ˈnʌti/ *adj* **-tier, -tiest**

A ‹*taste*› a nueces (*or* almendras *etc*)

B (colloq) (eccentric) ‹*professor*› chiflado (fam), chalado (fam); ‹*idea*› de loco

nuzzle /ˈnʌzəl/ *vi* (rub against) **to ~ AGAINST sth/sb**: **the dog ~d against my leg** el perro me acarició la pierna con el hocico

NW (= **northwest**) NO

NWT = **North West Territories**

NY = **New York**

NYC = **New York City**

nylon /ˈnaɪlɑːn || ˈnaɪlɒn/ *n* 1 [u] (Tex) nylon *m* 2 **nylons** *pl* (dated) medias *fpl* de nylon

nymph /nɪmf/ *n* (Myth, Zool) ninfa *f*

nymphomaniac /ˌnɪmfəˈmeɪniæk/ *n* ninfómana *f*

NYSE *n* (in US) (= **New York Stock Exchange**) la Bolsa de Nueva York

NZ = **New Zealand**

Oo

O, o /əʊ/ *n* O, o *f*
O /əʊ/ *interj* oh
oaf /əʊf/ *n* zoquete *mf* (fam), zopenco, -ca *m,f* (fam)
oafish /ˈəʊfɪʃ/ *adj* zafio y torpe
oak /əʊk/ *n* 1 [c] ~ **(tree)** roble *m*; ***great*** *o* ***mighty ~s from little acorns grow*** *las cosas importantes tienen orígenes humildes* 2 [u] (wood) roble *m*
OAP *n* (BrE) = **old age pensioner**
oar /ɔːr || ɔː(r)/ *n* remo *m*; ***to put*** *o* ***shove*** *o* ***stick one's ~ in*** (colloq) meter las narices (fam), entrometerse
oar: **~sman** /ˈɔːrzmən || ˈɔːzmən/ *n* (*pl* **-men** /-mən/) remero *m*; **~swoman** *n* remera *f*
OAS *n* (= **Organization of American States**) OEA *f*
oasis /əʊˈeɪsɪs/ *n* (*pl* **oases** /əʊˈeɪsiːz/) oasis *m*
oat /əʊt/ *n* 1 (plant) avena *f*; **wild ~** avena loca, ballueca *f* 2 **oats** *pl* (cereal) avena *f*, copos *mpl* de avena, Quáker® *m* (CS); ***to know one's ~s*** (AmE) ser* un experto en la materia; ***to sow one's wild ~s*** correrla (mientras se es joven) (fam)
oath /əʊθ/ *n* (*pl* **~s** /əʊðz/) 1 (promise) juramento *m*; **to break one's ~** romper* su (*or* mi *etc*) juramento; **to make** *o* **swear** *o* **take an ~** jurar, hacer* (un) juramento; **to take the ~** (Law) jurar; **under** *o* (BrE also) **on ~** (Law) bajo juramento 2 (curse) (liter) juramento *m* (liter)
oatmeal /ˈəʊtmiːl/ *n* [u] (Culin) (flour) harina *f* de avena; (flakes) (AmE) avena *f* (*en copos*)
OAU *n* (= **Organization of African Unity**) OUA *f*
obdurate /ˈɑːbdərət || ˈɒbdjʊrət/ *adj* (frml) ‹*refusal/stand*› obstinado; ‹*pride*› irreductible, contumaz (frml)
OBE *n* (in UK) = **Order of the British Empire**
obedience /əˈbiːdiəns, əʊ-/ *n* [u] obediencia *f*; **to show ~ to sb/sth** obedecer* a algn/algo
obedient /əˈbiːdiənt, əʊ-/ *adj* obediente
obediently /əˈbiːdiəntli, əʊ-/ *adv* obedientemente
obelisk /ˈɑːbəlɪsk || ˈɒbəlɪsk/ *n* obelisco *m*
obese /əʊˈbiːs/ *adj* obeso
obesity /əʊˈbiːsəti/ *n* [u] obesidad *f*
obey /əˈbeɪ, əʊ-/ *vt* obedecer*; ‹*instincts*› seguir*
■ **obey** *vi* obedecer*
obit /ˈəʊbɪt/ *n* (colloq) obituario *m*, necrológicas *fpl*
obituary /əˈbɪtʃueri || əˈbɪtʃʊəri/ *n* (*pl* **-ries**) obituario *m*, nota *f* necrológica; (*before n*) ‹*column/notice*› necrológico
object¹ /ˈɑːbdʒɪkt || ˈɒbdʒɪkt/ *n*
A 1 (thing) objeto *m* 2 ***no ~***: **distance is no ~** la distancia no importa *or* no es inconveniente; **money's no ~ for them** el dinero no les preocupa 3 (of actions, feelings) objeto *m*; **he was the ~ of a smear campaign** fue objeto de una campaña de difamación
B (aim, purpose) objetivo *m*, propósito *m*, fin *m*; **with this ~ in mind** teniendo en mente este objetivo *or* propósito
C (Ling) complemento *m*; **direct/indirect ~** complemento (de objeto) directo/indirecto
object² /əbˈdʒekt/ *vi* 1 (express objection, oppose) **to ~ (TO sth)** oponerse* *or* poner* objeciones (A algo); **I ~!** ¡protesto!; **to ~ to a question** (Law) oponerse* a *or* objetar una pregunta 2 (disapprove, mind): **if you don't ~** si no le molesta *or* (frml) importuna; **to ~ TO -ING**: **do you ~ to my smoking?** ¿le molesta que fume?; **I ~ to your using this house as a hotel** no estoy dispuesta a aceptar que uses esta casa como un hotel
■ **object** *vt* objetar; **she ~ed that he was too young** objetó que era demasiado joven
objection /əbˈdʒekʃən/ *n* 1 [c] (argument against) objeción *f*; **to make/raise/voice an ~** hacer*/poner*/expresar una objeción; **I'm going out: any ~s?** voy a salir ¿alguna objeción *or* algún inconveniente?; **~ TO sth** objeción A algo; **is there any ~ to my being present?** ¿existe alguna objeción a que *or* algún inconveniente en que yo asista? 2 [c] (Law): **~!** ¡protesto!; **~ overruled** no ha lugar a la protesta; **~ sustained** *o* **upheld** ha lugar a la protesta 3 [u] (disapproval, dislike): **I have no ~ to her** no tengo nada en contra de ella; **I have no ~ to his coming too** no tengo ningún inconveniente en que venga él también
objectionable /əbˈdʒekʃn̩əbəl || əbˈdʒekʃn̩əbəl/ *adj* ‹*attitude/remark*› censurable, inaceptable; ‹*person/tone*› desagradable; ‹*language*› soez; **a most ~ smell** un olor desagradabilísimo
objective¹ /ɑːbˈdʒektɪv || əbˈdʒektɪv/ *adj* objetivo
objective² *n* objetivo *m*
objectively /ɑːbˈdʒektɪvli || əbˈdʒektɪvli/ *adv* objetivamente; **~ speaking** si se es objetivo, desde un punto de vista objetivo
objectivity /ˈɑːbdʒekˈtɪvəti || ˌɒbdʒekˈtɪvəti/ *n* [u] objetividad *f*
object lesson *n*: **it was an ~ ~ in how not to do it** fue la perfecta demostración de cómo no se debe hacer; **his success is an ~ ~ in willpower** su éxito es una verdadera lección de fuerza de voluntad
objector /əbˈdʒektər || əbˈdʒektə(r)/ *n*: **there were many ~s to the new plan** mucha gente se opuso *or* puso objeciones al nuevo plan
obligate /ˈɑːbləgeɪt || ˈɒblɪgeɪt/ *vt* (esp AmE frml) **to ~ sb to + INF** obligar* a algn A + INF; **to be/feel ~d (to + INF)** estar*/sentirse* obligado (A + INF); **to be/feel ~d to sb** estar*/quedar en deuda con algn
obligation /ˈɑːbləˈgeɪʃən || ˌɒblɪˈgeɪʃən/ *n* 1 [c u] (duty, requirement) obligación *f*; **family/professional ~s** compromisos *mpl* familiares/profesionales; **I feel/have an ~ to my parents** me siento obligado/tengo una obligación para con mis padres; **~ to + INF** obligación DE + INF; **I understand that I am under no ~** entiendo que no contraigo ninguna obligación 2 [c] (financial commitment) (Busn) compromiso *m*
obligatory /əˈblɪgətɔːri || əˈblɪgətri/ *adj* obligatorio
oblige /əˈblaɪdʒ/ *vt*
A (require, compel) **to ~ sb to + INF** obligar* a algn A + INF; **to be ~d to + INF**: **you're not ~d to attend** no estás obligado a asistir, no tienes obligación de asistir
B (do favor for): **he was always ready to ~ a friend** estaba siempre dispuesto a hacerle un favor a un amigo; **much ~d!** muchas gracias, le agradezco mucho; **I'd be much ~d if you could help me** le quedaría muy agradecido si pudiera ayudarme
■ **oblige** *vi*: **he's always willing to ~** siempre está dispuesto a hacer un favor; **anything to ~** (colloq) con mucho gusto
obliging /əˈblaɪdʒɪŋ/ *adj* atento, servicial
oblique¹ /əˈbliːk, əʊ- || əˈbliːk/ *adj* ‹*line/plane/angle*› oblicuo; ‹*reply/reference/style*› indirecto
oblique² *n* barra *f* (*inclinada*)

obliquely /əˈbliːkli, əʊ- || əˈbliːkli/ *adv* (at an angle) oblicuamente; (indirectly) ‹*reply*› indirectamente

obliterate /əˈblɪtəreɪt/ *vt* 1 (destroy) arrasar, destruir* totalmente 2 (obscure, erase) borrar, obliterar (frml)

oblivion /əˈblɪviən/ *n* [u] 1 (obscurity) olvido *m*; **to fall** *o* **sink into ~** caer* en el olvido 2 (unconsciousness) inconsciencia *f*

oblivious /əˈblɪviəs/ *adj* (*pred*) **to be ~ OF** *o* **TO sth**: **she was quite ~ of** *o* **to her surroundings** estaba totalmente ajena a *or* no parecía darse cuenta de lo que la rodeaba; **~ of** *o* **to the danger** (unaware of) ignorante del peligro; (not mindful of) haciendo caso omiso del peligro

oblong[1] /ˈɑːblɔːŋ || ˈɒblɒŋ/ *adj* alargado, oblongo

oblong[2] *n* rectángulo *m*

obnoxious /ɑːbˈnɑːkʃəs || əbˈnɒkʃəs/ *adj* ‹*smell/person*› detestable; **he was really ~ last night** anoche estuvo de lo más insoportable

oboe /ˈəʊbəʊ/ *n* oboe *m*

oboist /ˈəʊbəʊəst || ˈəʊbəʊɪst/ *n* oboe *mf*

obscene /ɑːbˈsiːn || əbˈsiːn/ *adj* 1 (indecent) obsceno 2 (abhorrent) espantoso; **he earns an ~ amount of money** (colloq) es escandaloso *or* es un escándalo lo que gana

obscenely /ɑːbˈsiːnli || əbˈsiːnli/ *adv* 1 (indecently) ‹*pose/gesture*› obscenamente 2 (abhorrently) ‹*rich*› indecentemente, escandalosamente

obscenity /ɑːbˈsenəti || əbˈsenəti/ *n* (*pl* **-ties**) 1 [u] (indecency) obscenidad *f* 2 [c] (repulsive thing or action) aberración *f*, espanto *m* 3 [c] (obscene word) obscenidad *f*

obscure[1] /əbˈskjʊr || əbˈskjʊə(r)/ *adj* **obscurer, obscurest** 1 (not easily understood) ‹*meaning*› oscuro, poco claro; ‹*message/reference*› críptico; **for some ~ reason** por alguna extraña razón 2 (vague) ‹*impression/feeling*› confuso, vago 3 (little known) ‹*writer/journal*› oscuro, poco conocido; ‹*island/town*› recóndito, perdido

obscure[2] *vt* 1 (conceal) ‹*object/beauty/sun*› ocultar; ‹*sky*› oscurecer*; **her view of the stage was ~d by the man in front** el hombre que tenía delante le impedía ver todo el escenario 2 (make unclear, cover up): **these irrelevant details ~ the central problem** estos detalles superfluos impiden ver claramente el problema central

obscurely /əbˈskjʊrli || əbˈskjʊəli/ *adv* 1 (unclearly) ‹*talk/write/argue*› de manera confusa 2 (vaguely) ‹*remember/sense*› confusamente, vagamente

obscurity /əbˈskjʊrəti || əbˈskjʊərəti/ *n* [u c] (*pl* **-ties**) oscuridad *f*

obsequious /əbˈsiːkwiəs/ *adj* servil, excesivamente obsequioso

observance /əbˈzɜːrvəns || əbˈzɜːvəns/ *n* 1 [u] (of law, custom, agreement, religious festival) observancia *f*, cumplimiento *m* 2 [c] (rite, practice) práctica *f*; **religious ~s** prácticas religiosas

observant /əbˈzɜːrvənt || əbˈzɜːvənt/ *adj* observador, perspicaz

observation /ˈɑːbzərˈveɪʃən || ˌɒbzəˈveɪʃən/ *n*
A 1 [u c] (examination, study) observación *f*; **to keep sb under ~** mantener* a algn bajo vigilancia; (Med) tener* algo/a algn en observación; (*before n*) ‹*post/tower/ward*› de observación 2 [c] (recording, measurement) observación *m*; **to take an ~** observar
B [c] (comment) observación *f*, comentario *m*

observatory /əbˈzɜːrvətɔːri || əbˈzɜːvətri/ *n* (*pl* **-ries**) observatorio *m*

observe /əbˈzɜːrv || əbˈzɜːv/ *vt*
A (watch, notice) observar; ‹*patient*› observar; **he was ~d leaving the building** se lo vio salir del edificio
B (comment) (liter) observar
C ‹*custom*› observar; ‹*law*› respetar, cumplir, obedecer*; ‹*religious festival*› guardar, celebrar
■ **observe** *vi* (watch) observar, mirar

observer /əbˈzɜːrvər || əbˈzɜːvə(r)/ *n* observador, -dora *m,f*

obsess /əbˈses/ *vt* obsesionar

obsessed /əbˈsest/ *adj* (*pred*) obsesionado; **to be ~ (WITH sb/sth)** estar* obsesionado (CON algn/algo)

obsession /əbˈseʃən/ *n* obsesión *f*; **my boss has an ~ with punctuality** mi jefe tiene la manía de la puntualidad

obsessional /əbˈseʃnəl || əbˈseʃənl̩/ *adj* obsesivo

obsessive /əbˈsesɪv/ *adj* obsesivo; **she's an ~ reader** leer es como una obsesión para ella

obsessively /əbˈsesɪvli/ *adv* obsesivamente

obsolescence /ˈɑːbsəˈlesn̩s || ˌɒbsəˈlesn̩s/ *n* [u] caída *f* en desuso, obsolescencia *f* (téc *o* frml); **to fall into ~** volverse* obsoleto; **built-in ~** obsolescencia planificada

obsolete /ˈɑːbsəliːt || ˈɒbsəliːt/ *adj* ‹*machinery/word/vehicle*› obsoleto; ‹*ideas/approach*› anticuado, obsoleto; ‹*spelling*› caído en desuso

obstacle /ˈɑːbstɪkəl || ˈɒbstəkəl/ *n* obstáculo *m*; **~ TO sth/sb** obstáculo PARA algo/algn; (*before n*) **~ course/race** pista *f*/carrera *f* de obstáculos

obstetric /əbˈstetrɪk/ *adj* ‹*ward*› de obstetricia *or* tocología; ‹*care*› obstétrico

obstetrician /ˈɑːbstəˈtrɪʃən || ˌɒbstəˈtrɪʃən/ *n* obstetra *mf*, tocólogo, -ga *m,f*

obstetrics /əbˈstetrɪks/ *n* (+ *sing vb*) obstetricia *f*, tocología *f*

obstinacy /ˈɑːbstənəsi || ˈɒbstɪnəsi/ *n* [u] 1 (stubbornness) obstinación *f*, terquedad *f* 2 (of efforts, resistance) tenacidad *f*, determinación *f*

obstinate /ˈɑːbstənət || ˈɒbstɪnət/ *adj* ‹*person*› obstinado, terco; ‹*refusal/attitude*› obstinado; ‹*efforts*› tenaz

obstinately /ˈɑːbstənətli || ˈɒbstɪnətli/ *adv* (stubbornly) obstinadamente, porfiadamente; (determinedly) tenazmente

obstreperous /əbˈstrepərəs/ *adj* escandaloso

obstruct /əbˈstrʌkt/ *vt* 1 (block) obstruir* 2 (impede, hinder) ‹*traffic*› bloquear, obstruir*; ‹*plan/progress*› obstaculizar*, dificultar 3 (Sport) obstruir*, bloquear

obstruction /əbˈstrʌkʃən/ *n* [u c] (in traffic, pipeline) obstrucción *f*; (Med) obstrucción *f*, oclusión *f*; (to plans) obstáculo *m*, impedimento *m*; **move on please: you're causing an ~** circule: está obstruyendo el paso; **an ~ to traffic** una obstrucción del tráfico

obstructive /əbˈstrʌktɪv/ *adj* ‹*policy/measure*› obstruccionista; ‹*person*› que pone obstáculos *or* dificultades

obtain /əbˈteɪn/ *vt* conseguir*, obtener* (frml); **to ~ sth FOR sb** conseguirle* algo A algn

obtainable /əbˈteɪnəbəl/ *adj*: **it's not ~ in this country** no se puede conseguir en este país; **passes are easily ~** los pases son fáciles de conseguir *or* se pueden conseguir fácilmente

obtrusive /əbˈtruːsɪv/ *adj* ‹*presence/building*› demasiado prominente; ‹*noise*› molesto; ‹*smell*› penetrante

obtuse /ɑːbˈtuːs || ɒbˈtjuːs/ *adj*
A (Math) ‹*angle*› obtuso
B (frml) (stupid) obtuso

obverse[1] /ˈɑːbvɜːrs || ˈɒbvɜːs/ *n* (frml) **the ~** (of coin, medal) el anverso

obverse[2] *adj* (frml) (*before n*) ‹*face/surface*› del anverso

obviate /ˈɑːbvieɪt || ˈɒbvieɪt/ *vt* (frml) ‹*difficulty/danger*› eludir; **to ~ the need for reform** hacer* innecesaria cualquier reforma

obvious[1] /ˈɑːbviəs || ˈɒbviəs/ *adj* 1 (evident, clear) ‹*answer/solution*› obvio, lógico; ‹*advantage/implication/difference*› obvio, claro; **the ~ thing to do is ...** no cabe duda de que lo que hay que hacer es ...; **it was ~ to anyone that it was too heavy** cualquiera se hubiera dado cuenta de que pesaba demasiado; **they made it very ~ (that) they hadn't enjoyed the party** hicieron muy patente el hecho que no les había gustado la fiesta 2 (unmistakable) (*before n*): **it's an ~ lie** es claramente mentira, es una burda mentira; **she's the ~ candidate for the job** es la candidata indiscutible *or* obvia para el puesto 3 (unsubtle): **it was such an ~ ploy** el ardid era tan evidente *or* obvio

obvious[2] *n*: **to say we're alarmed would be stating the ~** de más está decir *or* huelga decir que estamos alarmados

obviously /ˈɑːbviəsli || ˈɒbviəsli/ *adv* 1 obviamente; **they're ~ not coming** está visto *or* claro que no van a venir; **the child is ~ tired** se nota *or* se ve claramente que el niño está cansado; **the two ideas are ~ not related** es evidente *or* obvio que las dos ideas no tienen relación; **the two ideas are not ~ related** a primera vista las dos ideas no tienen relación 2 (*indep*): **~, I'm sad, but what can I do?** como es lógico *or* lógicamente estoy triste pero ¿qué puedo hacer?

O

OCAS (= **Organization of Central American States**) *n* ODECA *f*

occasion¹ /ə'keɪʒən/ *n*

A [c] **1** (particular time, instance) ocasión *f*; **on that (particular) ~** en aquella ocasión **2** (special event): **I only wear it on special ~s** sólo me lo pongo en *or* para las grandes ocasiones; **what's the ~?** ¿qué se celebra?; **he has no sense of ~** no sabe vestirse (*or* comportarse *etc*) en las grandes ocasiones; **on the ~ of her retirement** con ocasión *or* motivo de su jubilación; ***to rise*** *o* ***be equal to the ~*** estar* a la altura de las circunstancias, dar* la talla

B [u] (frml) **1** (opportunity) ocasión *f*, oportunidad *f*; **may I take this ~ to remind you that ...** permítame que aproveche la ocasión *or* la oportunidad para recordarle que ... **2** (cause) ocasión *f*, motivo *m*

occasion² *vt* (frml) ocasionar, dar* lugar a

occasional /ə'keɪʒnəl || ə'keɪʒənl/ *adj* ‹*showers/sunny spells*› aislado, esporádico; **I like an** *o* **the ~ glass of wine** de tanto en tanto *or* de vez en cuando me gusta tomarme un vaso de vino; **we get the ~ complaint/visitor** recibimos alguna que otra queja/algún que otro visitante; **~ table** mesa *f* auxiliar

occasionally /ə'keɪʒnəli/ *adv* de vez en cuando, alguna que otra vez, ocasionalmente (frml)

occidental /ˌɑːksə'dentl || ˌɒksɪ'dentl/ *adj* (liter) occidental

occult¹ /ə'kʌlt || ɒ'kʌlt/ *n* **the ~** las ciencias ocultas, el ocultismo

occult² *adj* ‹*arts/powers*› oculto; ‹*ritual*› ocultista

occupancy /'ɑːkjəpənsi || 'ɒkjʊpənsi/ *n* [u] (of building) ocupación *f*; **during his ~ of the post** mientras ocupó el cargo, mientras estuvo en posesión del cargo

occupant /'ɑːkjəpənt || 'ɒkjʊpənt/ *n* (of house, building) ocupante *mf*; (tenant) inquilino, -na *m,f*; (of room, vehicle) ocupante *mf*; (of office, post) titular *mf*; **O~** (on letter) (AmE) al ocupante de la vivienda

occupation /ˌɑːkjə'peɪʃən || ˌɒkjʊ'peɪʃən/ *n*

A [c] (profession, activity) ocupación *f*

B [u c] (Mil) ocupación *f*; **to be under ~** estar* ocupado

C [u] (of accommodations) ocupación *f*

occupational /ˌɑːkjə'peɪʃnəl || ˌɒkjʊ'peɪʃənl/ *adj* ‹*training*› ocupacional, profesional; ‹*disease*› profesional; **it's an ~ hazard** son riesgos de la profesión/del oficio; (hum) son gajes del oficio (hum)

occupational: **~ therapist** *n* terapeuta *mf* ocupacional; **~ therapy** *n* terapia *f* ocupacional

occupier /'ɑːkjəpaɪər || 'ɒkjʊpaɪə(r)/ *n* (BrE) ocupante *mf*; **to the ~** al ocupante de la vivienda

occupy /'ɑːkjəpaɪ || 'ɒkjʊpaɪ/ *vt* **-pies, -pying, -pied**

A ‹*offices/site/seat/position*› ocupar

B ‹*country/town/factory/premises*› ocupar; **~ing forces** fuerzas *fpl* de ocupación

C ‹*space/attention*› ocupar; ‹*time*› llevar, ocupar; **to keep sb occupied** mantener* a algn ocupado; **to ~ oneself** ocupar el tiempo, entretenerse*

occur /ə'kɜːr || ə'kɜː(r)/ *vi* **-rr-**

A **1** (take place) (frml) «*event/incident*» tener* lugar (frml), ocurrir, suceder; «*change*» producirse* (frml), tener* lugar (frml) **2** (appear, be found) «*disease/species*» darse*, encontrarse*

B (come to mind) **to ~ TO sb (to + INF)** ocurrírsele A algn (+ INF); **it didn't ~ to me to ask** ni se me ocurrió preguntar

occurrence /ə'kɜːrəns || ə'kʌrəns/ *n* **1** [c] (event, instance): **it is a frequent/rare ~** es/no es algo frecuente, ocurre/no ocurre con frecuencia; **the unusual ~s of the previous evening** los extraños acontecimientos de la noche anterior; **there were two separate ~s** hubo dos casos independientes **2** [u] (incidence) incidencia *f*

ocean /'əʊʃən/ *n* **1** (sea) océano *m*; (*before n*) **~ cruise** crucero *m* (*por el Atlántico, Índico, etc*); **~ liner** transatlántico *m* **2** **oceans** *pl* (large quantity) (colloq) un montón (fam), la mar (fam)

ocean-going /'əʊʃən,gəʊɪŋ/ *adj* ‹*vessel*› transatlántico

Oceania /ˌəʊʃi'æniə || ˌəʊʃi'ɑːniə/ *n* Oceanía *f*

oceanographer /'əʊʃə'nɑːgrəfər || ˌəʊʃə'nɒgrəfə(r)/ *n* oceanógrafo, -fa *m,f*

oceanography /'əʊʃə'nɑːgrəfi || ˌəʊʃə'nɒgrəfi/ *n* [u] oceanografía *f*

ocher, (BrE) **ochre** /'əʊkər || 'əʊkə(r)/ *n* [u] **1** (Min) ocre *m* **2** (color) ocre *m*; (*before n*) color ocre *adj inv*

ocker /'ɔːkər || 'ɒkə/ *n* (Austral colloq) australiano *m* basto; (*before n*) **~ sports/writer/politician** australiano

o'clock /ə'klɑːk || ə'klɒk/ *adv*: **it's four ~** son las cuatro; **it's one ~** es la una; **at two ~ in the afternoon/morning** a las dos de la tarde/mañana *or* madrugada; **it's twelve ~ exactly** son las doce en punto; **it's just after one ~** acaba de dar la una; **the five ~ train** el tren de las cinco

OCR *n* (Comput) **1** [c] (= **optical character reader**) LOC *m* **2** [u] (= **optical character recognition**) ROC *m*

Oct (= **October**) oct.

octagon /'ɑːktəgɑːn/ *n* octágono *m*, octógono *m*

octagonal /ɑːk'tægənl || ɒk'tægənl/ *adj* octagonal, octogonal

octane /'ɑːkteɪn || 'ɒkteɪn/ *n* octano *m*

octave /'ɑːktɪv || 'ɒktɪv/ *n* (Lit, Mus) octava *f*

October /ɑːk'təʊbər/ *n* octubre *m*; *see also* **January**

octogenarian /'ɑːktədʒə'neriən || ˌɒktədʒɪ'neəriən/ *n* octogenario, -ria *m,f*

octopus /'ɑːktəpəs || 'ɒktəpəs/ *n* (*pl* **-puses**) pulpo *m*

OD *vi* (colloq) = **overdose²**

odd /ɑːd || ɒd/ *adj* **-er, -est**

A (strange) raro, extraño; **the ~ thing is that ...** lo raro *or* lo curioso es que ...

B (occasional, random) (*no comp*): **she smokes the ~ cigarette** se fuma algún *or* alguno que otro cigarrillo; **except for the ~ fisherman ...** a excepción de algún *or* alguno que otro pescador ...; **he's done ~ jobs for us** nos ha hecho algunos trabajitos

C (*no comp*) **1** (unmatched, single) desparejado, sin pareja; **the ~ one** *o* **the ~ man out** la excepción **2** (Math) ‹*number*› impar

D (*no comp*) **1** (being left over, spare): **if you've got the ~ moment to spare** si tienes algún momento libre; **I have a few ~ bits of fabric left over** me han sobrado unos retazos *or* (Esp) retales **2** (approximately) (colloq): **it cost me 30 pounds ~** *o* **30-~ pounds** me costó 30 y tantas libras *or* 30 y pico libras (fam); **she must be 80 ~ by now** debe tener 80 y tantos años *or* 80 y pico (de) años (fam)

oddball /'ɑːdbɔːl || 'ɒdbɔːl/ *n* (colloq) **1** (person) bicho *m* raro (fam), excéntrico, -ca *m,f* **2** (object) (AmE) cosa *f* rara, rareza *f*

oddity /'ɑːdəti || 'ɒdɪti/ *n* (*pl* **-ties**)

A [c] **1** (person): **(s)he's a bit of an ~** es un bicho raro **2** (thing) rareza *f*, cosa *f* rara

B [u c] (strangeness) lo raro, rareza *f*

odd-job man /'ɑːd'dʒɑːbmæn || ˌɒd'dʒɒbmæn/ *n* (*pl* **-men** /-men/) *hombre que hace pequeños trabajos o arreglos*

oddly /'ɑːdli || 'ɒdli/ *adv* **1** ‹*dress/behave*› de una manera rara *or* extraña **2** (*indep*): **~ enough, she forgot to mention that** curiosamente *or* por extraño que parezca, se olvidó de mencionarlo

oddment /'ɑːdmənt || 'ɒdmənt/ *n*: **an ~s sale** una venta de restos de serie; **~s of fabric** *o* **material** retazos *mpl or* (Esp) retales *mpl*

oddness /'ɑːdnəs || 'ɒdnɪs/ *n* [u] lo raro, rareza *f*

odds /ɑːdz || ɒdz/ *pl n*

A (in betting) *proporción en que se ofrece pagar una apuesta, que refleja las posibilidades de acierto de la misma*; **bookmakers are giving** *o* **laying ~ of ten to one** los corredores de apuestas están dando *or* ofreciendo diez contra uno; ***by all ~*** (AmE) sin lugar a dudas, indiscutiblemente; ***to pay over the ~*** (BrE) pagar* más de la cuenta

B (likelihood, chances) probabilidades *fpl*, posibilidades *fpl*; **all the ~ are in your favor** tienes todas las de ganar, lo tienes todo a tu favor; **the ~ on him recovering were never good** nunca hubo muchas probabilidades de que se recuperase; **the pilot survived against (all) the ~** aunque parezca increíble, el piloto sobrevivió; **despite overwhelming ~** a pesar de tenerlo todo en contra

C (difference) (BrE colloq): **it makes no ~ (to me)** (me) da igual *or* da lo mismo, no (me) importa

D (variance) **to be at ~ with sb/sth: those two are always at ~ with each other** esos dos siempre están en desacuerdo; **that's at ~ with the official version** eso no concuerda con la versión oficial

O

odds: **~ and ends** /'ɑdzən'endz || ˌɒdzən'endz/ *pl n* (colloq) cosas *fpl* sueltas; (trinkets) chucherías *fpl*; (junk) cachivaches *mpl*, trastos *mpl* viejos; **~ and sods** /'ɑːdzən'sɑːdz || ˌɒdzən'sɒdz/ *pl n* (BrE sl) ▸**bits and pieces** *see* **bit**² **A 1**; **~-on** /'ɑːdz'ɑːn || 'ɒdz'ɒn/ *adj*: **he's the ~-on favorite** es el favorito, es el que tiene todas las de ganar; **they're ~-on to win this year's elections** es casi seguro que ganarán las elecciones de este año

ode /əʊd/ *n* oda *f*

odious /'əʊdiəs/ *adj* (frml) detestable, odioso

odium /'əʊdiəm/ *n* [u] (liter) odio *m*

odometer /əʊ'dɑːmətər || ɒ'dɒmɪtə(r), əʊ-/ *n* (AmE) cuentarrevoluciones *m*

odor, (BrE) **odour** /'əʊdər || 'əʊdə(r)/ *n* olor *m*; (pleasant) aroma *m*, perfume *m*

odorless, (BrE) **odourless** /'əʊdərləs || 'əʊdəlɪs/ *adj* inodoro

odour *n* (BrE) ▸**odor**

odyssey /'ɑːdəsi || 'ɒdɪsɪ/ *n* (*pl* **-seys**) (liter) odisea *f*

OECD *n* (= **Organization for Economic Cooperation and Development**) OCDE *f*

oedema /ɪ'diːmə/ *n* (BrE) ▸**edema**

Oedipus /'edəpəs || 'iːdɪpəs/ *n* Edipo; (*before n*) **~ complex** complejo *m* de Edipo

o'er /'əʊər || ɔː(r)/ *adv* (poet) (= **over**): **~ land and sea** por tierras y mares (liter)

oesophagus /ɪ'sɑːfəgəs || iː'sɒfəgəs/ *n* (BrE) esófago *m*

oestrogen /'estrədʒen || 'iːstrədʒən/ *n* [u] (BrE) estrógeno *m*

oeuvre /'ərvrə || 'ɜːvrə/ *n* (liter) obra *f*

of /ɑːv || ɒv, *weak form* əv/ *prep*

A (indicating relationship, material, content) de; **the son ~ Mr and Mrs T Phipps** el hijo de los señores Phipps; **it's made ~ wood** es de madera, está hecho de madera; **a kilo ~ grapes** un kilo de uvas; **a colleague ~ mine/his** un colega mío/suyo

B (descriptive use): **the city ~ Athens** la ciudad de Atenas; **a boy ~ ten** un niño de diez años; **a woman ~ courage** una mujer valiente; **he's a giant ~ a man** es un gigante

C **1** (partitive use): **there were eight ~ us** éramos ocho; **he invited the eight ~ us** nos invitó a los ocho; **six ~ them survived** seis de ellos sobrevivieron; **~ all the stupid things to say!** ¡mira qué cosa de ir a decir!; **you ~ all people should have known better** tú deberías haberlo sabido mejor que nadie **2** (with superl) de; **the wisest ~ men** el más sabio de los hombres; **most ~ all** más que nada

D **1** (indicating date) de; **the sixth ~ October** el seis de octubre **2** (indicating time): **it's ten (minutes) ~ five** (AmE) son las cinco menos diez, son diez para las cinco (AmL exc RPl); **it's a quarter ~ five** (AmE) son las cinco menos cuarto, son un cuarto para las cinco (AmL exc RPl); **Jane, his wife ~ six months ...** Jane, con la que lleva/llevaba casado seis meses ...

E (on the part of): **it was very kind ~ you** fue muy amable de su parte

F (inherent in): **the senselessness ~ it all, that's what depresses me** es lo absurdo de todo el asunto lo que me deprime

G (indicating cause): **it's a problem ~ their own making** es un problema que ellos mismos se han creado; **what did he die ~?** ¿de qué murió?; **~ itself** de por sí

off¹ /ɔːf || ɒf/ *prep*

A **1** (from the surface) de; **she picked it up ~ *o* (crit) ~ of the floor** lo recogió del suelo; **to eat ~ paper plates** comer en platos de papel **2** (indicating removal, absence): **there's a button ~ this shirt** a esta camisa le falta un botón; **the lid was ~ the pan** la cacerola estaba destapada **3** (from) (colloq): **he bought it ~ a friend** se lo compró a un amigo; **I caught the cold ~ her** (BrE) ella me pegó el resfriado (fam)

B **1** (distant from): **3 ft ~ the ground** a 3 pies del suelo; **five miles ~ Dover** a cinco millas de Dover; **just ~ the coast of Florida** a poca distancia de la costa de Florida **2** (leading from): **a street ~ the square** una calle que sale de *or* desemboca en la plaza; **it's just ~ Oxford Street** está en una bocacalle de Oxford Street; **the bathroom's ~ the bedroom** el baño da al dormitorio

C **1** (absent from): **I've been ~ work for a week** hace una semana que no voy a trabajar *or* que falto al trabajo **2** (indicating repugnance, abstinence) (BrE): **he's ~ his food** anda sin apetito; **is he ~ drugs now?** ¿ha dejado las drogas?

off² *adv*

A **1** (removed): **the lid was ~** la tapa no estaba puesta; **once the old wallpaper is ~ ...** en cuanto se quite el papel viejo ...; **he sat there with his shirt ~** estaba ahí sentado sin camisa; **~!** (BrE Sport) ¡fuera!; **hands ~!** ¡no (me *or* lo *etc*) toques!; **20% ~** 20% de descuento **2** **off and on** ▸**on**² **C3**

B (indicating departure): **I must be ~** me tengo que ir; **~ we go!** ¡vámonos!; **oh, no, he's ~ again** ¡ya empieza *or* ya está otra vez!

C (distant): **the nearest village is five miles ~** el pueblo más cercano queda a cinco millas; **some way ~** a cierta distancia; **my birthday is a long way ~** falta mucho para mi cumpleaños

off³ *adj*

A (*pred*) **1** (not turned on): **the TV/light is ~** la televisión/luz está apagada; **the handbrake is ~** el freno de mano no está puesto; **make sure the electricity is ~** asegúrate de que la electricidad esté desconectada **2** (canceled): **the game/wedding is ~** el partido/la boda se ha suspendido; **the deal is ~** ya no hay trato

B (absent, not on duty) libre; **a day ~ *o* (AmE also) an ~ day** un día libre; **I'm ~ at five** salgo de trabajar *or* acabo a las cinco

C **1** (poor, unsatisfactory) (*before n*) malo; **to have an ~ day** tener* un mal día **2** (unwell) (*pred*): **to feel ~** sentirse* mal **3** (rude, unfair) (BrE colloq) (*pred*): **they didn't ask her in — that's a bit ~** no la hicieron pasar — ¡qué mal estuvieron! *or* ¡qué poco amables!

D (Culin) (*pred*) **to be ~** ‹‹*meat/fish*›› estar* malo *or* pasado; ‹‹*milk*›› estar* cortado; ‹‹*butter/cheese*›› estar* rancio; *see also* **go off** *Sense* **I B**

E (talking about personal situation): **they are comfortably ~** están bien económicamente, están bien de dinero; **how are you ~ for cash?** (BrE) ¿qué tal andas de dinero?; *see also* **well-off, better-off, badly off** *etc*

F ▸**offside**² **B**

offal /'ɔːfəl || 'ɒfəl/ *n* [u] **1** (Culin) despojos *mpl*, asaduras *fpl*, achuras *fpl* (RPl), interiores *mpl* (Chi) **2** (garbage) (AmE) basura *f*

off: **~beat** *adj* poco convencional; **~-center**, (BrE) **~-centre** /'ɔːf'sentər || ˌɒf'sentə(r)/ *adj* (*pred*) **1** (unconventional) poco convencional **2** (not in middle) descentrado; **~-chance** *n*: **on the ~-chance** por si acaso; **I just asked on the ~-chance (that) you might know** pregunté por si acaso *or* para ver si por casualidad tú lo sabías; **~-color**, (BrE) **~-colour** /'ɔːf'kʌlər || ˌɒf'kʌlə(r)/ *adj* (*pred* **~ color**) **1** (unwell) (*pred*): **to feel ~ color** no encontrarse* muy bien, sentirse* indispuesto **2** (risqué) (esp AmE) ‹*joke*› subido de tono; **~cut** *n* (of leather fabric, paper, wood) recorte *m*, trozo *m*; (of meat) resto *m*

offence /ə'fens/ *n* (BrE) ▸**offense**

offend /ə'fend/ *vt* **1** (hurt feelings of) ofender; **many people were deeply ~ed by this remark** mucha gente se sintió muy ofendida por este comentario; **don't be ~ed, but ...** no te vayas a ofender, pero ...; **he's easily ~ed** es muy susceptible **2** (cause displeasure to): **their behavior ~s one's sense of decency/justice** su conducta atenta contra el sentido de la moral/justicia

■ **offend** *vi* **1** (cause displeasure) ‹‹*person/action/remark*›› ofender **2** **offending** *pres p*: **he rewrote it omitting the ~ing paragraph** volvió a escribirlo omitiendo el párrafo que había causado controversia; **the ~ing smell** el desagradable olor **3** (violate) **to ~ AGAINST sth** atentar CONTRA algo **4** (Law frml) infringir* la ley (*or* el reglamento *etc*); (criminally) cometer un delito, delinquir* (frml)

offender /ə'fendər || ə'fendə(r)/ *n* infractor, -tora *m,f*; (criminal) delincuente *mf*; **young ~** menor *mf* (*que ha cometido un delito*); **as he was a first ~** como era su primera infracción/su primer delito, como no tenía antecedentes penales; **previous ~** reincidente *mf*; **as far as wasting paper's concerned, he's the worst ~** en cuanto a desperdiciar papel, él es más culpable que nadie

offense, (BrE) **offence** /ə'fens/ *n*

A [c] (breach of law, regulations) infracción *f*; (*criminal* ~) delito *m*

B **1** (cause of outrage) (*no pl*) atentado *m* **2** (resentment, displeasure): **to cause/give ~ to sb** ofender a algn; **to take ~ at sth** ofenderse *or* sentirse* ofendido por algo

C (AmE) *also* /'ɑːfens/ **1** [u] (attack) ataque *m*, ofensiva *f*; **weapons of ~** armas *fpl* ofensivas **2** [u c] (Sport) (línea *f* de) ataque *m*, (línea *f*) ofensiva *f*

offensive¹ /ə'fensɪv/ *adj*

A **1** ‹*remark/language/gesture*› ofensivo, insultante; **to be ~ TO sb** ofender *or* insultar a algn **2** ‹*sight/smell*› desagradable

B **1** ‹*strategy*› ofensivo; **~ weapon** arma *f*‡ ofensiva **2** (AmE Sport) ‹*play/tactics*› de ataque

offensive² *n* ofensiva *f*

offensively /ə'fensɪvli/ *adv*

A (insultingly) ‹*behave*› de (una) manera ofensiva *or* insultante

B (in attack) de manera ofensiva

offer¹ /'ɔːfər || 'ɒfə(r)/ *vt*

A **1** (proffer) ofrecer*; **may I ~ you a drink?** ¿quisiera beber algo?; **I ~ed him my hand, but he refused it** le tendí la mano, pero la rechazó; **she ~ed her resignation** puso su cargo a disposición del presidente (*or* de su jefe *etc*) **2** (show willingness) **to ~ to + INF** ofrecerse* A + INF

B (put forward) ‹*idea/solution*› proponer*, sugerir*; ‹*excuse/alibi*› presentar; **he never even ~ed any suggestions** ni siquiera hizo ninguna sugerencia

C (provide) ‹*reward*› ofrecer*; ‹*opportunity*› brindar, ofrecer*; **to have sth to ~** tener* algo que ofrecer

D (give, show) ‹*resistance*› ofrecer*, oponer*

E **~ (up)** ‹*prayers/sacrifice*› ofrecer*

■ *v refl* **to ~ itself** «*opportunity*» presentarse

■ **offer** *vi* (show willingness) ofrecerse*

offer² *n*

A **1** (proposal— of job, money) oferta *f*; (— of help, mediation) ofrecimiento *m*; **the ~ still stands** la oferta sigue en pie; **they refused my ~ of the car** no quisieron que les prestara el coche; **an ~ of marriage** una proposición matrimonial *or* de matrimonio; **I've had the ~ of a job in Rome** me han ofrecido un trabajo en Roma; **the windows need cleaning: any ~s?** hay que limpiar las ventanas: ¿quién se ofrece? **2** (bid) oferta *f*; **$650 or nearest ~** 650 dólares negociables *or* a convenir

B (bargain, reduced price) oferta *f*; **introductory ~** oferta de lanzamiento

C **on offer** (BrE) **1** (available): **there's not much on ~ at this year's fair** no hay mucho para comprar en la feria de este año **2** (at reduced price) de oferta

offering /'ɔːfərɪŋ || 'ɒfərɪŋ/ *n* **1** (sacrifice) ofrenda *f* **2** (donation) ofrenda *f*, donativo *m* **3** (creation) creación *f*

offertory /'ɔːfərtɔːri || 'ɒfətəri/ *n* (*pl* **-ries**) (part of service) ofertorio *m*; (collection) colecta *f* (*que se hace durante el ofertorio*); (*before n*) **~ box** cepillo *m*

offhand¹ /'ɔːf'hænd || ˌɒf'hænd/ *adj*: **he dismissed the whole scheme in a very ~ way** *o* **manner** descartó todo el proyecto muy a la ligera; **she was very ~ with me** estuvo muy brusca conmigo

offhand² *adv* así de pronto *or* de improviso, en este momento

off-hours¹ /'ɔːf'aʊrz || 'ɒfˌaʊəz/ *pl n* (AmE): **during ~** fuera de las horas pico *or* (Esp) punta

off-hours² *adj* (AmE) fuera de las horas pico *or* (Esp) punta

office /'ɑːfəs || 'ɒfɪs/ *n*

A [c] (room) oficina *f*, despacho *m*; (building, set of rooms) oficina *f*, oficinas *fpl*; (staff) oficina *f*; (*lawyer's* **~**) bufete *m* *or* despacho *m* (de abogado); (*doctor's* **~**) (AmE) consultorio *m*, consulta *f*; **the company's New York ~** las oficinas de la compañía en Nueva York; (*before n*) ‹*work/furniture*› de oficina; ‹*block/building*› de oficinas; **during ~ hours** en horas de oficina; **~ worker** oficinista *mf*, empleado, -da *m,f* de oficina, administrativo, -va *m,f*

B [u] (post, position) cargo *m*; **to take ~** tomar posesión del cargo; **he was in ~ for three years** ocupó el cargo durante tres años; **the party was in/out of ~** el partido estaba/ya no estaba en el poder; **term of** *o* (AmE also) **in ~** mandato *m*

C [c] (Relig) oficio *m*

officer /'ɑːfəsər || 'ɒfɪsə(r)/ *n* **1** (Mil, Naut) oficial *mf* **2** (*police* **~**) policía *mf*, agente *mf* de policía; (*as form of address*) agente **3** (official — in government service) funcionario, -ria *m,f*; (— of union, party) dirigente *mf*; (—of club) directivo, -va *m,f*

official¹ /ə'fɪʃəl/ *adj* oficial; **the election will be in March and that's ~** las elecciones serán en marzo: está confirmado

official² *n* (*government* **~**) funcionario, -ria *m,f* del Estado *or* gobierno; (*party/union* **~**) dirigente *mf* (del partido/sindicato)

officialdom /ə'fɪʃəldəm/ *n* [u] los círculos oficiales; (pej) la burocracia

officialese /ə'fɪʃə'liːz/ *n* (pej) jerga *f* burocrática (pey)

officially /ə'fɪʃəli/ *adv* oficialmente

officiate /ə'fɪʃieɪt/ *vi* **to ~ AT sth** ‹*at mass/at a wedding*› oficiar (EN) *or* celebrar algo

officious /ə'fɪʃəs/ *adj* oficioso

offing /'ɔːfɪŋ || 'ɒfɪŋ/ *n*: **in the ~** en perspectiva

off: **~ key** *adv*: **to play/sing ~ key** desafinar; **~-licence** *n* (in UK) ≈ tienda *f* de vinos y licores, botillería *f* (Chi); **~ limits** /'lɪməts || 'lɪmɪts/ *adv*: **to go/be ~ limits** entrar/estar* en zona prohibida; **~-line** /'ɔːf'laɪn || ˌɒf'laɪn/ *adj* (*pred* **~ line**) ‹*storage/printer*› autónomo; **~load** /'ɔːf'ləʊd || ˌɒf'ləʊd/ *vt* **1** (unload) ‹*cargo*› desembarcar*, descargar*; ‹*ship/truck*› descargar*; ‹*passengers*› hacer* bajar **2** (discard) (colloq) **to ~load sth ONTO sb** endilgarle* *or* endosarle *or* (AmL tb) encajarle algo A algn (fam); **~-message** /'ɔːfmesɪdʒ || 'ɒfmesɪdʒ/ *adj* (Pol) que se sale de la línea del partido; **~-peak** /'ɔːf'piːk || ˌɒf'piːk/ *adj* (*before n*) ‹*travel/fare*› fuera de las horas pico *or* (Esp) punta; (Elec) fuera de (las) horas pico *or* (Esp) punta, en horas de menor consumo; **~-putting** /'ɔːf'pʊtɪŋ || ˌɒf'pʊtɪŋ/ *adj* (BrE) **1** (disagreeable) desagradable; **I found the thought of it rather ~-putting** sólo de pensar en ello se me quitaban las ganas **2** (discouraging) desmoralizador, desalentador **3** (distracting) molesto; **~-roading** /ˌɔːf'rəʊdɪŋ || ˌɒf'rəʊdɪŋ/ *n* [u] conducción *f* (de un) todoterreno; **~ season** *n* temporada *f* baja

off-ramp /'ɔːfræmp || 'ɒfræmp/ *n* (AmE) vía de salida (*de una autopista*)

offset¹ /'ɔːf'set || 'ɒfset/ *vt* (*pres* **-sets**; *pres p* **-setting**; *past & past p* **-set**) compensar; **to ~ sth AGAINST sth** deducir* algo DE algo

offset² /'ɔːfset || 'ɒfset/ *n* (Print) offset *m*; (*before n*) ‹*printing/reproduction*› en offset

offshoot /'ɔːfʃuːt || 'ɒfʃuːt/ *n* **1** (of plant, tree) retoño *m*, vástago *m*, renuevo *m* **2** (of family) rama *f*; (of company, organization) filial *f*

offshore¹ /'ɔːf'ʃɔːr || ˌɒf'ʃɔː(r)/ *adj* **1** ‹*oilfield/pipeline*› submarino; ‹*exploration/drilling*› off-shore *adj inv*, costa afuera **2** ‹*funds/account*› en el exterior, offshore *adj inv*; (with tax advantages) en un paraíso fiscal

offshore² *adv* ‹*anchor*› a cierta distancia de la costa

offside¹ /'ɔːf'saɪd || ˌɒf'saɪd/ *n*

A (Sport) fuera de juego *or* (AmL tb) de lugar *m*, off side *m*, orsay *m*

B (BrE Auto): **the ~** el lado del conductor

offside² *adj*

A (Sport) ‹*player*› en fuera de juego *or* (AmL tb) de lugar, en off side, en orsay

B (BrE Auto) (*before n*) del lado del conductor

offside³ *adv* (Sport) fuera de juego *or* (AmL tb) de lugar, en off side, en orsay

offspring /'ɔːfsprɪŋ || 'ɒfsprɪŋ/ *n* (*pl* **~**) **1** (animal) cría *f* **2** (hum) (child) hijo, -ja *m,f*, crío, cría *m,f* (fam), vástago *m* (liter *o* hum); (children) prole *f* (fam & hum), críos *mpl* (fam)

offstage¹ /'ɔːf'steɪdʒ || ˌɒf'steɪdʒ/ *adj* (*before n*) de entre bastidores, de fuera del escenario

offstage² *adv* fuera del escenario

off: **~-the-wall** /'ɔːfðə'wɔːl || ˌɒfðə'wɔːl/ *adj* (*pred* **~ the wall**) (colloq) estrambótico (fam), estrafalario; **~-white** /'ɔːf'hwaɪt || ˌɒf'waɪt/ *adj* color hueso *adj inv*; **~ year** *n* (AmE) *año durante el cual no se celebran elecciones importantes*

oft- /'ɔːft || 'ɒft/ *pref*: **~quoted/~repeated** muy citado/repetido

often /'ɔːfən, 'ɔːftən || 'ɒfən, 'ɒftən/ *adv* a menudo; **I see her quite ~** la veo bastante a menudo *or* (AmL tb) seguido; **how ~ do you see her?** ¿con qué frecuencia la ves?, ¿cada cuánto la ves?; **as ~ as I can** siempre que puedo;

every so ~ de vez en cuando; **we've ~ thought of emigrating** hemos pensado muchas veces en emigrar; **he's right more ~ than not** la mayoría *or* las más de las veces tiene razón; **you'll do that once too ~ and you'll hurt yourself** si sigues haciendo eso, vas a acabar haciéndote daño

ogle /'əʊgəl/ *vt* comerse con los ojos

ogre /'əʊgər || 'əʊgə(r)/ *n* ogro *m*

oh /əʊ/ *interj*: **~, what a surprise!** ¡anda *or* vaya, qué sorpresa!; **~, it's you** ah, eres tú; **~ no, not him again!** ¡ay no, es él otra vez!; **~, really?** ¿de veras?, ¡no me digas!; **~ well, never mind** bueno, no importa

OH = **Ohio**

ohm /əʊm/ *n* ohmio *m*, ohm *m*

OHMS (in UK) = **on Her/His Majesty's Service**

oil¹ /ɔɪl/ *n*

A [u] **1** (petroleum) petróleo *m*; ***to strike ~*** (colloq) dar* con una mina de oro *or* con la gallina de los huevos de oro (fam); (lit: reach oil) encontrar* petróleo; (*before n*) **the ~ industry** la industria petrolera; **~ pipeline** oleoducto *m*; **~ refinery** refinería *f* de petróleo; **~ tanker** (ship) petrolero *m*; (truck) camión *m* cisterna (*para petróleo*) **2** (lubricant) aceite *m*; ***to pour ~ on troubled waters*** tratar de apaciguar los ánimos **3** (*fuel ~*) fuel-oil *m*, gasoil *m* **4** (for domestic lamps, stoves) queroseno *m*, kerosene *m*, parafina *f* (AmL); ***to burn the midnight ~*** quemarse las cejas

B [u c] (Culin) aceite *m*

C **1** [c] (painting) óleo *m* **2** **oils** *pl* (paints): **he paints in ~s** pinta al óleo

oil² *vt* ‹*machine/hinge*› lubricar*, aceitar, engrasar; ‹*wood/bat*› darle* aceite a

oil: **~can** *n* aceitera *f*; **~cloth** *n* [u] hule *m*; **~ color**, (BrE) **~ colour** *n* ▸ **~ paint**; **~ drum** *n* bidón *m* de aceite; **~field** *n* yacimiento *m* petrolífero *or* de petróleo; **~ paint** *n* [u c] óleo *m*; **~ painting** *n* **1** [c] (picture) óleo *m*; ***he's no ~ painting*** no es ninguna belleza *or* ningún Adonis **2** [u] (medium) pintura *f* al óleo; **~ patch** *n* **1** (patch of oil) mancha *f* de petróleo **2** (oilfield) (AmE sl) yacimiento *m* de petróleo **3** (the oil industry) (AmE) industria *f* petrolífera; **~ rig** *n* plataforma *f* petrolífera *or* petrolera; (derrick) torre *f* de perforación; **~skin** *n* **1** [u] (Tex) hule *m* **2** **~skins** *pl* chubasquero *m*, impermeable *m*; **~ slick** *n* marea *f* negra, mancha *f* de petróleo; **~ well** *n* pozo *m* petrolero *or* de petróleo

oily /'ɔɪli/ *adj* **oilier, oiliest** **1** ‹*substance*› oleaginoso; ‹*rag*› manchado de aceite; ‹*fingers*› grasiento; ‹*food*› aceitoso, grasiento; ‹*skin/hair*› graso, grasoso (AmL) **2** (unctuous) empalagoso

ointment /'ɔɪntmənt/ *n* [u c] pomada *f*, ungüento *m*

OK¹, **okay** /'əʊ'keɪ/ *interj* (colloq) ¡bueno!, ¡okey! (esp AmL fam), ¡vale! (Esp fam), ¡vaya (pues) *or* va pues! (AmC)

OK², **okay** *adj* **1** (all right) (colloq) (*pred*): **how are you? — ~, thanks** ¿qué tal estás? — bien, gracias; **the job's ~, but ...** el trabajo no está mal, pero ...; **will it be ~ if I bring a friend?** ¿te importa si traigo a un amigo?; **it's ~ with me** yo no tengo ningún inconveniente **2** (acceptable) (sl) (*before n*): **he's really an ~ guy** es un tipo muy bien (fam), es un tío legal (Esp arg)

OK³, **okay** *adv* (colloq) bastante bien

OK⁴, **okay** *vt* (*pres* **OK's**; *pres p* **OK'ing**; *past & past p* **OK'ed**) (colloq) darle* el visto bueno a

OK⁵, **okay** *n* (*pl* **OK's**) (colloq) visto bueno *m*

OK⁶, **Okla** = **Oklahoma**

okra /'əʊkrə/ *n* [u] quingombó *m*, calalú *m* (*verdura muy usada en la cocina africana e india*)

old¹ /əʊld/ *adj*

A (of certain age): **he's 10 years ~** tiene 10 años; **how ~ are you?** ¿cuántos años tienes?, ¿qué edad tienes?; **she's two years ~er than me** me lleva dos años, es dos años mayor que yo; **a month-~ puppy** un cachorro de un mes; **a group of six-year-/fifteen-year-~s** un grupo de niños de seis años/de quinceañeros; **she's not ~ enough to go to school** no tiene edad de ir a la escuela; **you're ~ enough to know better!** ¡a tu edad ...!

B (not young) mayor; (less polite) viejo; **~ people feel the cold more** los ancianos *or* las personas mayores *or* de edad sienten más el frío; **to get** *o* **grow ~/~er** envejecer*; **doesn't she look ~!** ¡qué vieja *or* avejentada está!

C **1** (not new) ‹*clothes/car/remedy*› viejo; ‹*city/civilization*› antiguo; ‹*custom/tradition*› viejo, antiguo; **it's a very ~ family** es una familia de abolengo **2** (longstanding, familiar) (*before n*) ‹*friend/enemy/rivalry*› viejo; ‹*injury/problem*› antiguo; **it's the same ~ story** es la misma historia de siempre

D (former, previous) (*before n*) antiguo

E **Old** (Ling) (*before n*) antiguo

F (colloq) (*before n*) **1** (*as intensifier*): **just wear any ~ thing** ponte cualquier cosa; **this book is a load of ~ rubbish** este libro es una porquería (fam) **2** (in familiar references): **good ~ John!** ¡el bueno de John! (Esp); **lucky ~ you!** ¡qué suerte tienes!

old² *n*

A (old people) (+ *pl vb*) **the ~** los ancianos, las personas mayores *or* de edad; (less polite) los viejos

B (former times) (liter): **in days of ~** antaño (liter), antiguamente

old: **~ age** *n* [u] vejez *f*; **to die of ~ age** morir(se)* de viejo; **it's just ~ age** son los años; **~ age pensioner** *n* (BrE) pensionista *mf* (de la tercera edad); **~ boy** *n* (ex-pupil) (BrE) ex-alumno *m*; (*before n*) **the ~-boy network** el amiguismo (*esp entre ex-alumnos de colegios de elite*)

olden /'əʊldən/ *adj* (liter): **in ~ days** *o* **times** antaño (liter)

olde-worlde /'əʊldi'wɜːrldi || 'əʊldi'wɜːldi/ *adj* (BrE hum) pintoresco

old: **~-fashioned** /'əʊld'fæʃənd/ *adj* **1** (outdated) anticuado, pasado de moda; **he's a bit ~-fashioned** es un poco chapado a la antigua **2** (traditional) tradicional; **~ folks' home** *n* residencia *f* de ancianos; **~ girl** *n* (ex-pupil) (BrE) ex-alumna *f*; **~ Glory** *n* (AmE) la bandera de los EEUU; **~ lady** *n* (colloq): **my/his ~ lady** (mother) mi/su vieja (fam); (wife) mi/su señora, mi/su vieja (Méx fam), la parienta (Esp fam), la patrona (CS fam & hum); **~-line** /'əʊld'laɪn/ *adj* (AmE) (*before n*) ‹*views*› tradicional; ‹*supporter*› tradicionalista, de la vieja guardia; **~ maid** *n* (colloq) solterona *f* (fam); **~ man** *n* (colloq) **1** : **my/her ~ man** (father) mi/su viejo (fam); (husband) mi/su marido, mi/su viejo (Méx fam) **2** (boss): **the ~ man** el jefe *or* patrón; **~ master** *n* (painter) gran maestro *m* de la pintura; (painting) obra *f* maestra de la pintura clásica; **~ people's home** *n* residencia *f* de ancianos; **~ school** *n*: **a politician in** *o* **of the ~ school** un político de la vieja escuela; **~ school tie** (Clothing) *corbata con los colores de la escuela*; (attitude, system) **the ~ school tie** el amiguismo (*esp entre ex-alumnos de colegios de elite*); **~-style** /'əʊld'staɪl/ *adj* (*before n*) de la vieja guardia, a la antigua; **~ Testament** *n* Antiguo Testamento *m*; **~-time** /'əʊld'taɪm/ *adj* (*before n*) antiguo; **~-timer** /'əʊld'taɪmər || ˌəʊld'taɪmə(r)/ *n* (colloq) (veteran) veterano, -na *m,f*; (old man) (AmE) viejo *m* (fam); **~ wives' tale** *n* cuento *m* de viejas; **~ woman** *n* ▸ **~ lady**; **~-world** /'əʊld'wɜːrld || 'əʊld,wɜːld/ *adj* ‹*atmosphere*› con sabor antiguo; ‹*courtesy*› a la antigua (usanza)

> **Old Glory**
>
> ▸ Stars and Stripes

oleaginous /'əʊli'ædʒənəs/ *adj* ‹*substance/film*› oleaginoso; (unctuous) empalagoso

O level *n* (formerly in UK) *estudios de una asignatura en preparación del examen al cual solía presentarse alrededor de los 16 años y certificado otorgado*

oligarchy /'ɑːləgɑːrki || 'ɒlɪgɑːki/ *n* [c u] (*pl* **-chies**) oligarquía *f*

olive¹ /'ɑːlɪv || 'ɒlɪv/ *n*

A [c] **1** (Culin) aceituna *f*, oliva *f*; (*before n*) **~ oil** aceite *m* de oliva **2** **~ (tree)** olivo *m*; (*before n*) **~ grove** olivar *m*

B [u] (color) (color) aceituna *m*

olive² *adj* ‹*coat/paint*› color aceituna *adj inv*; ‹*skin*› aceitunado

olive: **~ branch** *n* rama *f* de olivo; **to extend** *o* **hold out** *o* **proffer the ~ branch to sb** tenderle* la mano a algn en son de paz; **~ drab** *n* (AmE) **1** [u] (color, cloth) caqui *m* **2** **~ drabs** *pl* (uniform) *uniforme de la infantería estadounidense*; **~-green** /'ɑːlɪv'griːn || ˌɒlɪv'griːn/ *adj* (*pred* **~ green**) verde aceituna *or* oliva *adj inv*

Olympiad /ə'lɪmpiæd/ *n* olimpiada *f*, olimpíada *f*

Olympic /ə'lɪmpɪk/ *adj* olímpico

Olympic Games *pl n* **the ~ ~** los juegos Olímpicos

O

Olympics /ə'lɪmpɪks/ *pl n* **the ~** las Olimpíadas *or* Olimpiadas

Oman /əʊ'mɑːn/ *n* Omán *m*

ombudsman /'ɑːmbʊdzmən || 'ɒmbʊdzmən/ *n* (*pl* **-men** /-mən/) ombudsman *mf or* (Esp, Per) defensor, -sora *m,f* del pueblo

omega /əʊ'meɪgə || 'əʊmɪgə/ *n* omega *f*

omelet, (BrE) **omelette** /'ɑːmlət || 'ɒmlɪt/ *n* omelette *f or* (Esp) tortilla *f* francesa; **Spanish ~** tortilla *f* de papas *or* (Esp) patatas, tortilla *f* española; ***you can't make an ~ without breaking eggs*** nada que valga la pena se logra sin crear conflictos

omen /'əʊmən/ *n*: **it's a good/bad ~** es un buen/mal augurio, es de buen/mal agüero; **they saw this as an ~ of victory** lo tomaron como un presagio de victoria; **bird of ill ~** pájaro *m* de mal agüero

ominous /'ɑːmənəs || 'ɒmɪnəs/ *adj*: **there was an ~ silence** se hizo un silencio que no presagiaba *or* no auguraba nada bueno; **that's ~** eso es de mal agüero *or* es un mal augurio

ominously /'ɑːmənəsli || 'ɒmɪnəsli/ *adv*: **he was ~ silent** su silencio no presagiaba nada bueno; **there is worse to come, he said ~** —todavía queda lo peor —dijo en tono alarmante *or* inquietante

omission /əʊ'mɪʃən || ə'mɪʃən/ *n* [u c] omisión *f*, supresión *f*

omit /əʊ'mɪt || ə'mɪt/ *vt* **-tt-** 1 (leave out) omitir, suprimir; (accidentally) olvidar incluir 2 (fail) (frml) **to ~ to + INF** omitir + INF (frml)

omnibus /'ɑːmnɪbəs || 'ɒmnɪbəs/ *n* (*pl* **-buses**)

A (Publ) antología *f*

B (Transp dated) ómnibus *m* (ant exc en Per y RPl)

omnipotent /ɑːm'nɪpətənt || ɒm'nɪpətənt/ *adj* (frml) omnipotente

omnipresent /'ɑːmnɪ'prezn̩t || ˌɒmnɪ'prezn̩t/ *adj* (frml) omnipresente

omniscient /ɑːm'nɪʃənt || ɒm'nɪsɪənt/ *adj* omnisciente

omnivore /'ɑːmnɪvɔːr || 'ɒmnɪvɔː(r)/ *n* omnívoro, -ra *m,f*

omnivorous /ɑːm'nɪvərəs || ɒm'nɪvərəs/ *adj* ‹*animal*› omnívoro; ‹*reader/viewer*› voraz

on[1] /ɑːn || ɒn/ *prep*

A 1 (indicating position) en; **put it ~ the table** ponlo en *or* sobre la mesa; **~ the ground** en el suelo; **he hung it ~ a hook** lo colgó de un gancho; **yellow ~ a black background** amarillo sobre un fondo negro; **I live ~ Acacia Avenue** (esp AmE) vivo en Acacia Avenue; **~ the right/left** a la derecha/izquierda 2 (belonging to) de; **the handle ~ the cup** el asa de la taza 3 (against): **I hit my head ~ the shelf** me di con la cabeza contra el estante; **he cut his hand ~ the glass** se cortó la mano con el vidrio

B 1 (of clothing): **it looks better ~ you than me** te queda mejor a ti que a mí 2 (about one's person): **I didn't have any cash ~ me** no llevaba dinero encima; **they found heroin ~ him** le encontraron heroína (encima)

C (indicating means of transport): **I went ~ the bus** fui en autobús; **we had lunch ~ the train** comimos en el tren; **~ a bicycle/horse** en bicicleta/a caballo; **~ foot** a pie

D 1 (playing instrument) a; **George Smith ~ drums** George Smith a la *or* en la batería 2 (Rad, TV): **I heard it ~ the radio** lo oí por la radio; **I was ~ TV last night** anoche salí por televisión; **the play's ~ channel 4** la obra la dan en el canal 4 3 (recorded on) en; **~ tape** en cinta

E 1 (using equipment): **who's ~ the computer?** ¿quién está usando la computadora?; **you've been ~ the phone an hour!** ¡hace una hora que estás hablando por teléfono!, ¡hace una hora que estás colgado del teléfono! (fam) 2 (on duty at) en; **to be ~ the door** estar* en la puerta 3 (contactable via): **call us ~ 800 7777** llámenos al 800 7777

F (a member of): **she's ~ the committee** está en la comisión, es miembro de la comisión; **~ a team** (AmE) en un equipo

G (indicating time): **I went ~ Monday** fui el lunes; **~ Wednesdays she goes swimming** los miércoles va a nadar; **~ the anniversary of her death** en el aniversario de su muerte; **~ -ING** al + INF; **~ hearing the news** al enterarse de la noticia

H (about, concerning) sobre; **while we're ~ the subject** a propósito, ya que estamos hablando de esto

I 1 (indicating activity, undertaking): **~ vacation/safari** de vacaciones/safari; **we went ~ a trip to London** hicimos un viaje a Londres, nos fuimos de viaje a Londres; **I went there ~ business** fui allí en viaje de negocios; **he's ~ a diet** está a dieta, está a *or* de régimen 2 (working on, studying): **we're ~ page 45 already** ya vamos por la página 45; **I'm still ~ question 1** todavía estoy con la pregunta número 1

J (taking, consuming): **she's ~ antibiotics** está tomando antibióticos; **he's ~ heroin** es heroinómano

K (talking about income, available funds): **I manage ~ less than that** yo me las arreglo con menos de eso; **she's ~ £30,000** (BrE) gana 30.000 libras al año

L (according to): **she wants to stay ~ her terms** quiere quedarse pero imponiendo sus condiciones; **acting ~ his advice** siguiendo sus consejos

M (at the expense of): **this round's ~ me** a esta ronda invito yo, esta ronda la pago yo; **it's ~ the house** invita la casa, atención de la casa

N 1 (in comparison with): **profits are up ~ last year** los beneficios han aumentado respecto al año pasado 2 (in) (AmE): **20 cents ~ the dollar** el 20 por ciento

on[2] *adv*

A 1 (worn): **she had a blue dress ~** llevaba (puesto) *or* tenía puesto un vestido azul; **with no clothes ~** sin ropa, desnudo; **let's see what it looks like ~** a ver cómo queda puesto; *see also* **have on, put on** 2 (in place): **the lid's not ~ properly** la tapa no está bien puesta; **to sew a button ~** coser *or* pegar* un botón

B (indicating relative position): **head ~** de frente; **sideways ~** de lado

C (indicating progression) 1 (in space): **drive ~** sigue adelante; **further ~** un poco más allá *or* más adelante; **go ~ up; I'll follow in a minute** tú ve subiendo que yo ya voy 2 (in time, activity): **from then ~** a partir de ese momento; **from now ~** de ahora en adelante; **I have nothing ~ that day** ese día no tengo ningún compromiso 3 **on and off, off and on**: **we still see each other ~ and off** todavía nos vemos de vez en cuando; **it rained ~ and off** *o* **off and ~ all week** estuvo lloviendo y parando toda la semana 4 **on and on**: **the film went ~ and ~** la película se hizo interminable *or* (fam) pesadísima; **you don't have to go ~ and ~ about it!** no hace falta que sigas dale y dale con lo mismo (fam)

D (in phrases) 1 **on about** (BrE colloq): **what's she ~ about?** ¿de qué está hablando?, pero ¿qué dice? 2 **on at** (BrE colloq): **he's always ~ at her about the same thing** siempre le está encima con lo mismo

on[3] *adj*

A (*pred*) 1 (functioning): **to be ~** «*light/TV/radio*» estar* encendido, estar* prendido (AmL); «*faucet*» estar* abierto; **the electricity/water isn't ~ yet** la electricidad/el agua todavía no está conectada; **the handbrake is ~** el freno de mano está puesto 2 (on duty): **we work four hours ~, four hours off** trabajamos cuatro horas y tenemos otras cuatro de descanso; **which of the doctors is ~ today?** ¿qué médico está de guardia hoy?

B (*pred*) 1 (taking place): **there's a lecture ~ in there** hay *or* están dando una conferencia allí; **while the conference is ~** mientras dure el congreso, hasta que termine el congreso 2 (due to take place): **the party's definitely ~ for Friday** la fiesta es *or* se hace el viernes seguro; **is the wedding still ~?** ¿no se ha suspendido la boda? 3 (being presented): **what's ~ at the Renoir?** (Cin, Rad, Theat, TV) ¿qué dan *or* (Esp tb) ponen *or* echan en el Renoir?; **is that play still ~?** ¿sigue en cartelera la obra?; **the exhibition is still ~** la exposición sigue abierta 4 (performing, playing): **you're ~!** (Theat) ¡a escena!; **I'm only ~ for about five minutes in Act 3** sólo salgo cinco minutos en el tercer acto; **he has been ~ for most of the game** ha estado jugando casi todo el partido; *see also* **bring, come, go** *etc* **on**

C 1 (indicating agreement, acceptance) (colloq): **you teach me Spanish and I'll teach you French — you're ~!** tú me enseñas español y yo te enseño francés — ¡trato hecho! *or* ¡te tomo la palabra! 2 **not on** (esp BrE colloq): **that sort of thing just isn't ~** ese tipo de cosa no se puede tolerar; **the idea of finishing by April was never really ~** la idea de terminar para abril nunca fue viable

once[1] /wʌns/ *adv*

A 1 (one time, on one occasion) una vez; **~ a week** una vez por semana, una vez a la semana; **~ was enough** con una vez me (*or* le *etc*) alcanzó; **not ~ did I ask them for help** ni una sola vez les pedí ayuda; ▸**bite** 2▸ (formerly): **a health care system which was ~ the pride of the nation** un sistema de asistencia sanitaria que antes era *or* que en su día fue el orgullo de la nación; **~ upon a time there was ...** érase una vez ..., había una vez ...

B (*in phrases*) **all at once** (suddenly) de repente; **at once**: **come here at ~!** ¡ven aquí inmediatamente *or* ahora mismo!; **don't all shout at ~** no griten todos al mismo tiempo *or* a la vez; **for once** por una vez; **once again** *o* **once more** otra vez, una vez más; **do that ~ more and I'll tell your father!** como vuelvas a hacer eso, se lo digo a tu padre; **once (and) for all** de una vez por todas; **(every) once in a while** de vez en cuando; **once or twice** una o dos veces, un par de veces

once[2] *conj* una vez que; (with verb omitted) una vez; **~ you get started, it's hard to stop** una vez que empiezas, es difícil parar; **~ inside the house, she felt safer** una vez dentro de la casa, se sintió más segura

once[3] *n*: **the/this ~** una/esta vez; **I'll let you off this ~** por esta vez que pase

once- /ˈwʌns/ *pref* otrora (liter)

once: **~-over** *n*: ***to give sth/sb a*** *o* ***the ~-over*** (colloq): **we gave the house a quick ~-over** le dimos una pasada por encima a la casa (fam); **he gave her a quick ~-over out of the corner of his eye** le echó un vistazo de reojo; **~-over-lightly** /ˈwʌnsəʊvərˈlaɪtli || ˌwʌnsəʊvəˈlaɪtli/ *n* (AmE) (*no pl*): **the ~-over-lightly** un repaso rápido, una pasada por encima (fam)

oncology /ɑːŋˈkɑːlədʒi || ɒŋˈkɒlədʒi/ *n* [u] oncología *f*

oncoming /ˈɑːnˌkʌmɪŋ || ˈɒnkʌmɪŋ/ *adj* (*before n*) ‹*vehicle*› que viene (*or* venía) en dirección contraria

one[1] /wʌn/ *n*

A 1▸ (number) uno *m*; **has anybody got five ~s?** ¿alguien tiene cinco billetes de un dólar (*or* un peso *etc*)?; ***to be at ~ with sb/sth*** estar* en paz *or* en armonía con algn/algo; *see also* **four**[1] 2▸ (elliptical use): **he's nearly ~** tiene casi un año; **it's nearly ~** es casi la una; **it was interesting in more ways than ~** fue interesante en más de un sentido/en muchos sentidos; **the chances are ~ in a million** la probabilidad es de uno en un millón; **I only want the ~** sólo quiero uno/una; **did you see many cows? — ~ or two** ¿viste muchas vacas? — alguna que otra

B (*in phrases*) **as one**: **they rose as ~** se pusieron de pie todos a la vez *or* como un solo hombre; **for one** por lo pronto; **who's going? — well, I am for ~** ¿quién va? — yo, por lo pronto; **in one**: **it's a TV and a video in ~** es televisión y vídeo a la vez *or* todo en uno; **one by one** uno a uno, uno por uno

one[2] *adj*

A 1▸ (stating number) un, una; **~ button/pear** un botón/una pera; **~ hundred** cien; **~ thousand, three hundred** mil trescientos; **~ fifth of the population** la quinta parte de la población 2▸ (certain, particular): **~ boy was tall, the other short** uno de los niños era alto, el otro era bajo; **~ window looks out over the park** una de las ventanas da al parque

B 1▸ (single): **she was the ~ person I trusted** era la única persona en quien confiaba; **it is too much for any ~ person** es demasiado para una sola persona; **there is not ~ shred of evidence** no existe ni la más mínima prueba; **the ~ and only Frank Sinatra** el incomparable *or* inimitable Frank Sinatra; **my ~ and only coat is at the cleaners** el único abrigo que tengo *or* mi único abrigo está en la tintorería 2▸ (same) mismo, misma; **we drank out of the ~ glass cup** bebimos del mismo vaso/de la misma taza; **Clark Kent and Superman are ~ and the same** Clark Kent y Superman son la misma persona

C (unspecified) un, una; **you must come over ~ evening** tienes que venir una noche; **I'll get even with you ~ day** algún día me las pagarás

D (with names): **in the name of ~ John Smith/Sarah Brown** a nombre de un tal John Smith/una tal Sarah Brown

one[3] *pron*

A (thing): **this ~** éste/ésta; **that ~** ése/ésa; **which ~?** ¿cuál?; **the ~ on the right/left** el/la de la derecha/izquierda; **the ~s on the table** los/las que están en la mesa; **the blue ~s** los/las azules; **I want the big ~** quiero el/la grande; **it's my last ~** es el último/la última que me queda; **~ of the oldest cities in Europe** una de las ciudades más antiguas de Europa; **every ~ of them was broken** todos estaban rotos; **he's had ~ too many** ha bebido de más, ha bebido más de la cuenta; **have you heard the ~ about ...?** ¿has oído el chiste de ...?; **he ate all the apples ~ after another** *o* **the other** se comió todas las manzanas, una detrás de otra

B (person): **the ~ on the right's my cousin** el/la de la derecha es mi primo/prima; **it could be any ~ of us** podría ser cualquiera de nosotros; **our loved ~s** nuestros seres queridos; **he's a sly ~, that Jack Tibbs** es un zorro ese Jack Tibbs; **I'm not ~ to gossip, but ...** no me gustan los chismes pero ...; **~ after another** *o* **the other** uno tras otro *or* detrás de otro

one[4] *pron* uno, una; **~ simply never knows** realmente nunca se sabe *or* uno nunca sabe; **it certainly makes ~ think** le da que pensar a uno; **~ another** ▸**each other, each**[2] **B**

one: **~-arm bandit** *n* (colloq) máquina *f* tragamonedas *or* (Esp) tragaperras; **~-armed** /ˈwʌnˈɑːrmd || ˈwʌnˌɑːmd/ *adj* manco; **~-armed bandit** *n* ▸**~-arm bandit**; **~-dimensional** /ˈwʌndəˈmentʃṇəl, -ˈdaɪ- || ˌwʌndɪˈmenʃənḷ/ *adj* (Math) unidimensional; (pej) ‹*characters/description*› superficial, sin fondo *or* sin profundidad; **~-eyed** /ˈwʌnˈaɪd/ *adj* tuerto; **~-handed** /ˈwʌn ˈhændəd || ˌwʌnˈhændɪd/ *adv/adj* con una sola mano; **~-horse** /ˈwʌnˈhɔːrs || ˌwʌnˈhɔːs/ *adj* (*before n*) 1▸ (small) (pej): **a ~-horse town** un pueblucho (pey), un pueblo de mala muerte (fam & pey) 2▸ (one-sided) (colloq): **it was a ~-horse race** el resultado estaba cantado (fam); **~-legged** /ˈwʌnˈlegəd || ˌwʌnˈlegɪd/ *adj* con una sola pierna; **~-liner** /ˈwʌnˈlaɪnər || ˌwʌnˈlaɪnə(r)/ *n* dicho *m* ingenioso; **~-man** /ˈwʌnˈmæn/ *adj* (*before n*) ‹*business*› unipersonal; ‹*operation*› dirigido por una sola persona; **she's a ~-man woman** es mujer de un solo hombre; **~-man band** *n* hombre-orquesta *m*

oneness /ˈwʌnnəs || ˈwʌnnɪs/ *n* [u] (frml) 1▸ (homogeneity) unidad *f* 2▸ (unity): **he felt a sense of ~ with the universe** se sentía uno con el universo

one-night stand /ˈwʌnnaɪt/ *n* 1▸ (sexual encounter) (colloq) ligue *m* *or* (CS) programa *m* de una noche (fam) 2▸ (Mus, Theat) función *f* única

one-off[1] /ˈwʌnˈɔːf || ˌwʌnˈɒf/ *n* (BrE colloq): **this payment is strictly a ~** este pago es una excepción

one-off[2] *adj* (BrE) excepcional

one on one *adv* (AmE) uno a uno

one-on-one[1] /ˈwʌnɑːnˈwʌn || ˈwʌnɒnˈwʌn/ *adj* (AmE) ‹*defense*› individual, uno a uno; ‹*confrontation*› uno a uno

one-on-one[2] *n* (AmE) tête *m* à tête, mano *m* a mano

one-piece /ˈwʌnpiːs/ *adj* ‹*swimsuit*› entero

onerous /ˈəʊnərəs/ *adj* ‹*task*› pesado; ‹*debt*› oneroso

one: **~self** /wʌnˈself/ *pron* (frml) (reflexive) se; (after prep) sí mismo; (emphatic use) uno mismo; **to cut ~self** cortarse; **to talk about ~self** hablar de sí mismo; **to experience sth for ~self** experimentar algo uno mismo; **~-shot** *adj* (AmE) 1▸ (effective) (*before n*) ‹*remedy*› de efecto inmediato 2▸ (exceptional) excepcional; **~-sided** /ˈwʌnˈsaɪdəd || ˌwʌnˈsaɪdɪd/ *adj* ‹*account/version*› parcial, tendencioso; ‹*game/contest*› desigual; **~-stop** /ˈwʌnˈstɑːp || ˈwʌnˈstɒp/ *adj* (*before n*): **~-stop banking** servicios *mpl* bancarios integrados; **~-time** *adj* antiguo; **~-to-one** /ˈwʌntə ˈwʌn/ *adj* 1▸ (individual) ‹*teaching/attention*› individualizado; ‹*discussion*› mano a mano; **on a ~-to-~ basis** de uno a uno 2▸ (exact) ‹*correlation*› de uno a uno; **~-track mind** /ˈwʌnˈtræk/ *n*: **to have a ~-track mind** ser* un obseso, no tener* más que una idea en la cabeza

one-size-fits-all /ˌwʌnˌsaɪzˌfɪtsˈɔːl/ *adj* (*before n*) 1▸ (Clothing) de talla única 2▸ (universal) ‹*solution/judgment*› para dejar contentos a todos

one-upmanship /ˈwʌnˈʌpmənʃɪp/ *n* [u] (colloq) *arte de colocarse siempre en una situación de superioridad con respecto a los demás*

one-way /ˈwʌnˈweɪ/ *adj* 1▸ ‹*street*› de sentido único 2▸ (for one journey): **~ or round trip?** ¿ida sólo o ida y vuelta?, ¿sencillo o redondo? (Méx)

ongoing /ˈɑːnˌgəʊɪŋ || ˈɒngəʊɪŋ/ *adj*: **the ~ talks** las conversaciones en curso; **the investigations have been ~ for several months** se están llevando a cabo investigaciones desde hace meses

onion /ˈʌnjən/ *n* [c u] cebolla *f*

on: ~ **line** *adv*: **to edit/work ~ line** (Comput) editar/trabajar en línea; **~-line** /ˈɑːnˈlaɪn || ˌɒnˈlaɪn/ *adj* (*pred* ~ **line**) (Comput) conectado, en línea; **~-line banking** banca *f* en línea; **~looker** *n* espectador, -dora *m,f*

only[1] /ˈəʊnli/ *adv* 1 (merely, no more than) sólo, solamente; **you'll ~ make matters worse** lo único que vas a lograr es empeorar las cosas; **you ~ have** *o* **have ~ to ask** no tienes más que pedir; **I was ~ joking!** ¡te lo decía en broma! 2 (exclusively) sólo, solamente, únicamente; Ⓢ **staff only** sólo personal autorizado 3 (no earlier than) sólo, recién (AmL); **~ then did I learn the truth** sólo *or* (AmL tb) recién entonces me enteré de la verdad 4 (no longer ago than): **~ last week the very same problem came up** la semana pasada, sin ir más lejos, surgió el mismo problema 5 (*in phrases*) **if only**: **if ~ I were rich!** ¡ojalá fuera rico!; **if ~ I'd known** si lo hubiera sabido; **only just**: **they've ~ just arrived** ahora mismo acaban de llegar; **he ~ just escaped being arrested** se libró por poco de que lo detuvieran, se libró por un pelo *or* por los pelos de que lo detuvieran (fam); **will it fit in? — ~ just** ¿cabrá? — apenas *or* (fam) justito; **not only ... , but also ...** no sólo ... , sino también ...

only[2] *adj* (*before n*) único; **she's an ~ child** es hija única; **my ~ regret is that ...** lo único que siento es que ...

only[3] *conj* (colloq) pero; **I'd like to, ~ I'm very busy** me gustaría, pero *or* lo que pasa es que estoy muy ocupado

-only /ˈəʊnli/ *suff*: **a men~/women~ session** una sesión sólo *or* exclusivamente para hombres/mujeres

on-message /ˈɑːnˌmesɪdʒ || ˈɒnˌmesɪdʒ/ *adj* que sigue la línea del partido

o.n.o. (esp BrE) (= **or near(est) offer**): **£500 ~** 500 libras, negociable

onomatopoeia /ˈɑːnəˈmætəˈpiːə || ˌɒnəˌmætəˈpiə/ *n* [u] onomatopeya *f*

on: **~-ramp** *n* (AmE) vía *f* de acceso (*a una autopista*); **~rush** *n* (of waves) embate *m*; (of people) avalancha *f*; **~set** *n* (of winter, rains) llegada *f*, comienzo *m*; (of disease) aparición *f*

onshore[1] /ˈɑːnˈʃɔːr || ˈɒnʃɔː(r)/ *adj* 1 ‹*wind*› que sopla desde el mar 2 (on land) ‹*oil terminal/location*› en tierra

onshore[2] *adv* tierra adentro

onside /ˈɑːnˈsaɪd || ˌɒnˈsaɪd/ *adj* en posición reglamentaria

onslaught /ˈɑːnslɔːt || ˈɒnslɔːt/ *n* ataque *m*, arremetida *f*; **the ~ of summer visitors** la invasión *or* avalancha de visitantes veraniegos

on: **~stage** /ˈɑːnˈsteɪdʒ || ˌɒnˈsteɪdʒ/ *adv*: **to come ~stage** salir* a escena; **to appear ~stage** aparecer* en escena; **~-street** /ˈɑːnˈstriːt || ˈɒnˌstriːt/ *adj* (*before n*): **~-street parking** estacionamiento *m* *or* (Esp) aparcamiento *m* en la vía pública

Ont = **Ontario**

onto /ˈɑːntuː || ˈɒntuː, *before consonant* ˈɑːntə || ˈɒntə/ *prep*
A (on): **it fell ~ the table** cayó sobre la mesa; **he climbed ~ the cart** se subió al carro
B (aware of) (colloq) **to be ~ sb/sth**: **the police are ~ her** la policía anda tras ella *or* le está siguiendo la pista; **I think we're ~ something big** creo que hemos dado con algo importante *or* (fam) algo gordo
C **to be ~ sb** (BrE colloq) 1 (in contact with): **I've just been ~ them** acabo de hablar con ellos 2 (nagging): **I've been ~ them all week to send it to us** llevo toda la semana dándoles la lata para que nos lo manden (fam)

onus /ˈəʊnəs/ *n* (frml) responsabilidad *f*; **the ~ is on him to prove his theory** le corresponde *or* le incumbe a él probar su teoría

onward[1] /ˈɑːnwərd || ˈɒnwəd/ *adj* (*before n*) hacia adelante

onward[2], (BrE also) **onwards** /-z/ *adv* (hacia) adelante; **from now ~** de ahora en adelante, a partir de ahora

onyx /ˈɑːnɪks || ˈɒnɪks/ *n* [u] ónix *m*

oodles /ˈuːdlz/ *pl n* (colloq) cantidad *f* (fam), montones *mpl* (fam)

ooh[1] /uː/ *interj*: **~, what a beautiful sunset!** ¡ah, qué puesta de sol tan bonita!; **~, that hurt** ¡ay, eso me dolió!

ooh[2] *vi*: **to ~ and aah** (colloq) exclamar extasiado

oops /ʊps || uːps/ *interj* (colloq) ¡uy! (fam)

ooze /uːz/ *vi*: **blood ~d from his wound** le salía sangre de la herida; **to ~ WITH sth**: **the walls were oozing with damp** las paredes rezumaban humedad

■ **ooze** *vt*: **the wound ~d pus** la herida (le) supuraba; **the walls ~d damp** las paredes rezumaban humedad; **he ~s charm** irradia simpatía

opal /ˈəʊpəl/ *n* [u c] ópalo *m*

opaque /əʊˈpeɪk/ *adj* opaco

OPEC /ˈəʊpek/ *n* (*no art*) (= **Organization of Petroleum Exporting Countries**) la OPEC *or* la OPEP

open[1] /ˈəʊpən/ *adj*
A 1 (not shut or sealed) abierto; **with ~ arms** con los brazos abiertos; **to cut sth ~** abrir* algo cortándolo; **he pushed the door ~** abrió la puerta de un empujón 2 (not fastened) ‹*shirt/jacket*› abierto, desabrochado 3 (not folded) ‹*flower/newspaper/book*› abierto
B 1 (not enclosed) abierto; **it's ~ country all around here** aquí estamos en campo abierto; **~ prison** cárcel *f* en régimen abierto; **on the ~ seas** en alta mar, en mar abierto 2 (not blocked) abierto; **the road is now ~ to traffic once more** la carretera vuelve a estar abierta al tráfico 3 ‹*cheque*› (in UK) no cruzado, al portador, a la orden
C 1 (not covered) ‹*carriage*› abierto, descubierto; ‹*sewer*› a cielo abierto, descubierto; **an ~ fire** una chimenea, un hogar 2 (exposed, vulnerable) **~ TO sth** ‹*to elements/enemy attack*› expuesto A algo; **to lay** *o* **leave oneself ~ to sth** exponerse* a algo; **this is ~ to misunderstanding/abuse** esto se presta a malentendidos/a que se cometan abusos
D (*pred*) (ready for business) **to be ~** ‹‹*shop/museum*›› estar* abierto; **the new section is ~ for traffic** el nuevo tramo está abierto al tráfico
E (unrestricted) ‹*membership*› abierto al público en general; ‹*meeting*› a puertas abiertas, abierto al público; ‹*ticket/reservation*› abierto; ‹*government/marriage*› abierto; **~ letter** carta *f* abierta; **in the ~ market** en el mercado libre *or* abierto; **to sell sth ~ stock** (AmE) vender algo por piezas *or* por unidad; **let's throw the topic ~ for debate** abramos el debate sobre el tema; **to be ~ TO sb/sth**: **the competition is ~ to everybody** cualquiera puede presentarse al certamen; **the palace gardens are ~ to the public** los jardines del palacio están abiertos al público
F 1 (available) (*pred*): **several options are ~ to us** tenemos *or* se nos presentan varias opciones *or* alternativas 2 (not decided): **that's still an ~ question** eso aún está por decidirse; **let's leave things ~ for the time being** no descartemos ninguna posibilidad de momento; **let's leave the date ~** no concretemos la fecha todavía; **~ verdict** *veredicto que se emite cuando no se puede establecer la causa de la muerte de una persona*
G 1 (receptive) abierto; **I'm always ~ to suggestions** siempre estoy abierto a todo tipo de sugerencias, siempre estoy dispuesto a recibir sugerencias; **to have an ~ mind** tener* una actitud abierta 2 (frank, candid): **to be ~ WITH sb** ser* sincero *or* franco CON algn
H (not concealed) ‹*resentment/hostility*› abierto, manifiesto

open[2] *vt*
A 1 ‹*door/box/parcel*› abrir*; ‹*bottle*› abrir*, destapar; **to ~ one's mouth/eyes** abrir* la boca/los ojos 2 (unfold) ‹*newspaper/book*› abrir*
B 1 (clear, remove obstructions from) ‹*road/channel*› abrir* 2 (make accessible, available) abrir*; **they have ~ed the house to the public** han abierto la casa al público
C 1 (set up, start) ‹*branch/department*› abrir*; ‹*shop/business*› abrir*, poner* 2 (declare open) abrir*, inaugurar
D (begin) ‹*debate*› abrir*, iniciar; ‹*meeting*› abrir*, dar* comienzo a; ‹*bidding*› iniciar; ‹*talks*› entablar; **to ~ fire on sb/sth** abrir* fuego contra algn/algo
E (make receptive) **to ~ sth TO sth** abrir* algo A algo; **you must ~ your mind to new ideas** debes abrirte a nuevas ideas

■ **open** *vi*
A 1 ‹‹*door/window/wound*›› abrirse*; **~ wide!** abra bien la boca, abra bien grande; **the heavens** *o* **skies ~ed** empezó a diluviar 2 (unfold) abrirse*
B (give access) **to ~ ONTO/INTO sth** dar* A algo
C (for business) ‹‹*shop/museum*›› abrir*
D (begin) ‹‹*play/book*›› comenzar*, empezar*; (in card games) abrir* (el juego); **her new movie ~s next week** su nueva película se estrena la semana próxima

Phrasal verbs

• **open out**
A [v ▸ adv] 1 (become wider) ‹‹*river/valley/road*›› ensancharse

O

2 (unfold) abrirse*; **the center pages ~ out into a poster** las páginas centrales forman un póster al abrirse
B [v ▸ o ▸ adv , v ▸ adv ▸ o] ‹*map/newspaper*› abrir*, desplegar*
• **open up**
Sense I [v ▸ o ▸ adv, v ▸ adv ▸ o]
A 1 (undo, unlock) abrir* 2 (cut, create) ‹*channel/breach*› abrir*
B 1 (make accessible, available) abrir* 2 (reveal) ‹*new horizons*› abrir*
C (set up) ‹*shop/store*› abrir*, poner*
Sense II [v ▸ adv]
A 1 (open building) abrir*; **~ up! police!** ¡abran! ¡policía! 2 (become open) abrirse*
B (become accessible, available) «*country/market*» abrirse*; **to ~ up (TO sb/sth)** abrirse* (A algn/algo); **to ~ up to new ideas** abrirse* a nuevas ideas
C (talk freely) (colloq): **he found it difficult to ~ up to his father** le costaba ser abierto *or* franco con su padre
D (start up) «*business/factory/store*» abrir*

open³ *n*
A : **in the ~** (in open space or country) al aire libre; (Mil) al descubierto; **I feel better now it's all out in the ~** me siento mejor ahora que todo el mundo lo sabe; **to bring sth (out) into the ~** hacer* público algo, sacar* algo a la luz
B **Open** (Sport) (campeonato *m*) abierto *m*, Open *m*

open: **~ air** *n*: **in the ~ air** al aire libre; **~-and-shut** /ˈəʊpənənˈʃʌt/ *adj*: **an ~-and-shut case** un caso clarísimo; **~ day** *n* (BrE) *día en que un establecimiento educativo, científico etc puede ser visitado por el público*; **~-ended** /ˈəʊpənˈendəd || ˌəʊpənˈendɪd/ *adj* 1 ‹*contract/lease*› de duración indefinida, sin plazo definido 2 ‹*discussion*› abierto

opener /ˈəʊpn̩ər || ˌəʊpn̩ə(r)/ *n*
A (for bottle) abridor *m*, abrebotellas *m*, destapador *m* (AmL); (for can) abrelatas *m*
B (of show) primer número *m*; ***for ~s*** para empezar

open: **~-eyed** /ˈəʊpənˈaɪd/ *adj* con los ojos abiertos; **~handed** /ˈəʊpənˈhændəd || ˌəʊpənˈhændɪd/ *adj* ‹*generosity*› a manos llenas; ‹*gesture*› generoso; **~-heart** /ˈəʊpənˈhɑːrt || ˌəʊpənˈhɑːt/ *adj* (*before n*) de corazón abierto; **~-hearted** /ˈəʊpənˈhɑːrtəd || ˌəʊpənˈhɑːtɪd/ *adj* ‹*person*› de gran corazón; ‹*welcome*› cálido; **~ house** *n* 1 [u] (*no art*): **to keep ~ house** tener* las puertas siempre abiertas a todos; 2 (informal reception) *fiesta que dura varias horas y a la que se puede llegar en cualquier momento* 3 (AmE) *día en que un establecimiento educativo, científico etc puede ser visitado por el público*

opening¹ /ˈəʊpnɪŋ/ *n*
A [c] (in hedge, fence) abertura *f*
B 1 [u c] (beginning, initial stage) apertura *f*, comienzo *m* 2 [c] (Games) apertura *f*
C [c u] (of exhibition, building) inauguración *f*; (Cin, Theat) estreno *m*; **the ~ of Parliament** la apertura del Parlamento; (*before n*) ‹*ceremony*› inaugural, de inauguración; ‹*speech*› inaugural; **~ night** noche *f* del estreno
D [u] (period when open): **hours of ~** (of shop) horario *m* comercial; (of bank, office) horario *m* de atención al público; Ⓢ **late opening till 8pm on Thursdays** los jueves abierto hasta las 8; (*before n*) **~ time** (BrE) *hora en que se abren los pubs*
E [c] 1 (favorable opportunity) oportunidad *f* 2 (job vacancy) oportunidad *f*, vacante *f*

opening² *adj* ‹*remarks*› inicial; ‹*move/gambit*› de apertura *or* salida; **the ~ scene** la primera escena

openly /ˈəʊpənli/ *adv* 1 ‹*acknowledge/admit*› abiertamente 2 ‹*boast/ridicule*› descaradamente

open: **~-minded** /ˈəʊpənˈmaɪndəd || ˌəʊpənˈmaɪndɪd/ *adj* ‹*person*› de actitud abierta, sin prejuicios; ‹*approach*› imparcial, que no parte de ideas preconcebidas; **~-mouthed** /ˈəʊpənˈmaʊðd/ *adj* boquiabierto; **~-necked** /ˈəʊpənˈnekt/ *adj*: **he was wearing an ~-necked shirt** llevaba una camisa desabotonada *or* desabrochada en el cuello; (informally dressed) no llevaba corbata

openness /ˈəʊpənnəs || ˈəʊpənnɪs/ *n* [u] 1 (frankness) franqueza *f* 2 (lack of concealment) transparencia *f*

open: **~-plan** /ˈəʊpənˈplæn/ *adj* abierto, de planta abierta, open-plan *adj inv*; **~ season** *n* (Sport) temporada *f* de caza; ***to declare ~ season on sth/sb*** declararle la guerra a muerte a algo/algn; **~ secret** *n* secreto *m* a voces; **~-source** /ˈəʊpənˈsɔːrs/ *adj* ‹*software*› de código abierto; **~-toed** /ˈəʊpənˈtəʊd/ *adj* sin punta; **~-top** /ˈəʊpənˈtɑːp || ˌəʊpənˈtɒp/ *adj* descubierto; **~ University** *n* (in UK) *la universidad a distancia del Reino Unido*

> **Open University – OU**
>
> Universidad a distancia británica, fundada en 1969. La enseñanza se lleva a cabo mediante una mezcla de materiales impresos, programas de televisión y radio emitidos por la BBC y en algunos casos mediante material enviado por internet. Los estudiantes deben estudiarlo y enviar sus trabajos por correo a un tutor. La mayoría de los estudiantes toma cursos a tiempo parcial durante cuatro o cinco años, aunque no hay un límite de tiempo

opera /ˈɑːprə || ˈɒprə/ *n* [c u] (*pl* **-ras**) ópera *f*; (*before n*) ‹*singer/company*› de ópera; **~ house** ópera *f*, teatro *m* de ópera

operable /ˈɑːpərəbəl || ˈɒpərəbəl/ *adj* (Med) operable

operate /ˈɑːpəreɪt || ˈɒpəreɪt/ *vi*
A «*machine/mechanism*» funcionar
B 1 (act): **the law ~s to our advantage** la ley nos favorece 2 (be applicable) «*rules/laws*» regir*; **a Sunday service will ~ on New Year's Day** (Transp) el día de Año Nuevo habrá un servicio dominical
C (pursue one's business) «*company/airline/gang*» operar; **he ~s from a base in Montevideo** tiene su base de operaciones en Montevideo
D (Med) operar, intervenir* (frml); **to ~ ON sb (FOR sth)** operar A algn (DE algo)
■ **operate** *vt*
A ‹*machine*› manejar, operar; ‹*controls*› manejar, accionar
B ‹*policy/system*› aplicar*, tener*
C (manage, run): **she ~s a small business from home** lleva un pequeño negocio desde su casa; **we ~ a bus service between here and the capital** tenemos un servicio de autobuses que van de aquí a la capital

operatic /ˈɑːpəˈrætɪk || ˌɒpəˈrætɪk/ *adj* operístico

operating /ˈɑːpəreɪtɪŋ || ˈɒpəreɪtɪŋ/ *adj* (*before n*)
A 1 (Busn) ‹*profit/loss/costs*› de explotación 2 (Tech) ‹*conditions/speed*› de funcionamiento
B (Med): **~ room** *o* (BrE) **theatre** quirófano *m*, sala *f* de operaciones; **~ table** mesa *f* de operaciones

operating system *n* sistema *m* operativo

operation /ˈɑːpəˈreɪʃən || ˌɒpəˈreɪʃən/ *n*
A [u] (functioning) funcionamiento *m*; **to be in ~** «*machine*» estar* en funcionamiento; «*system*» regir*; **a bus service will be in ~** habrá un servicio de autobuses; **to put a plan into ~** poner* en marcha un plan, implementar un plan (AmL)
B [u] (running — of machine) manejo *m*; (— of system) uso *m*
C [c] 1 (activity, series of activities) operación *f*; **to mount a rescue ~** montar una operación de rescate 2 (enterprise) operación *f*; (Busn) operación comercial
D [c] (Mil) operación *f*
E [c] (Med) operación *f*, intervención *f* quirúrgica (frml); **who performed the ~?** ¿quién la (*or* lo) operó?; **he has to have an ~** se tiene que operar, lo tienen que operar; **he had an ~ on his knee** le operaron la rodilla, lo operaron de la rodilla
F [c] (Math, Comput) operación *f*

operational /ˈɑːpəˈreɪʃn̩əl || ˌɒpəˈreɪʃənl̩/ *adj* 1 (functioning) (*pred*) **to be ~** estar* en funcionamiento 2 (*before n*) ‹*capacity*› de operación *or* funcionamiento

operative¹ /ˈɑːpərətɪv || ˈɒpərətɪv/ *adj*
A (having effect): **to be ~** «*rules/measures*» estar* en vigor *or* en vigencia; **the ~ word** la palabra clave
B (Med) (*before n*) quirúrgico

operative² *n* (frml) operario, -ria *m,f*

operator /ˈɑːpəreɪtər || ˈɒpəreɪtə(r)/ *n*
A 1 (Telec) operador, -dora *m,f*; **telephone/switchboard ~** telefonista *mf*, operador, -dora *m,f* 2 (of equipment) operario, -ria *m,f*; (Comput) operador, -dora *m,f*
B 1 (company): **tour ~** tour operador *m*, operador *m* turístico 2 (person) (colloq): **he's a smooth** *o* **slick ~** es de los que saben conseguir lo que quieren

operetta /ˈɑːpəˈretə || ˌɒpəˈretə/ *n* [c u] opereta *f*

ophthalmic /ɑːp'θælmɪk, ɑːf- || ɒf'θælmɪk/ *adj* oftalmológico; ~ **optician** ≈ oculista *mf*

ophthalmologist /'ɑːpθəl'mɑːlədʒəst, 'ɑːf- || ˌɒfθæl'mɒlədʒɪst/ *n* oftalmólogo, -ga *m,f*, oculista *mf*

ophthalmology /'ɑːpθəl'mɑːlədʒi, 'ɑːf- || ˌɒfθæl'mɒlədʒi/ *n* [u] oftalmología *f*

opinion /ə'pɪnjən/ *n*

A [c] (belief) opinión *f*; **what's your ~?** ¿qué opinas?, ¿qué te parece?, ¿cuál es tu opinión *or* parecer?; **to be of the ~ that** ser* de la opinión *or* del parecer de que; **in my ~** en mi opinión, a mi parecer, a mi juicio; **that's a matter of ~** eso es discutible; **~ ON** *o* **ABOUT sth** opinión SOBRE *or* ACERCA DE algo; **~ OF sth/sb**: **what's your ~ of the plan/of Robinson?** ¿qué opina del plan/de Robinson?, ¿qué opinión le merece el plan/Robinson?; **to have a good** *o* **high/poor** *o* **low ~ of sth/sb** tener* buena/mala opinión de algo/algn

B [c] (evaluation, judgment) opinión *f*; **I'd like a second ~** me gustaría consultarlo con otro especialista

C [u] (of body of people) opinión *f*; **~ is moving away from the nuclear option** el consenso de opinión está dejando de lado la opción nuclear; **literary ~ is divided** la opinión del mundo literario está dividida

opinionated /ə'pɪnjəneɪtəd || ə'pɪnjəˌneɪtɪd/ *adj* dogmático, aferrado a sus (*or* tus *etc*) opiniones *or* ideas

opinion poll *n* sondeo *m or* encuesta *f* de opinión

opium /'əʊpiəm/ *n* [u] opio *m*; (*before n*) **~ addict** opiómano, -na *m,f*; **~ poppy** adormidera *f*

opossum /ə'pɑːsəm || ə'pɒsəm/ *n* zarigüeya *f*, oposum *m*, comadreja *f* (CS), zorro *m* (AmC, Méx)

opp = opposite

opponent /ə'pəʊnənt/ *n* **1** (of a regime, policy) opositor, -tora *m,f*; (in debate) adversario, -ria *m,f*, oponente *mf*; **~s of the government's defense policy** quienes se oponen a *or* los opositores de la política de defensa del gobierno **2** (Games, Sport) contrincante *mf*, rival *mf*, oponente *mf*

opportune /'ɑːpər'tuːn || 'ɒpətjuːn/ *adj* (frml) oportuno

opportunely /'ɑːpər'tuːnli || 'ɒpətjuːnli/ *adv* (frml) ‹*arrive/intervene*› oportunamente

opportunism /'ɑːpər'tuːnɪzəm || ˌɒpə'tjuːnɪzəm/ *n* [u] oportunismo *m*

opportunist[1] /'ɑːpər'tuːnəst || ˌɒpə'tjuːnɪst/ *n* oportunista *mf*

opportunist[2], **opportunistic** /-tuː'nɪstɪk || -tjuː-/ *adj* oportunista

opportunity /'ɑːpər'tuːnəti || ˌɒpə'tjuːnəti/ *n* [c u] (*pl* **-ties**) oportunidad *f*, ocasión *f*; **she never misses an ~** nunca deja pasar una oportunidad *or* ocasión; **at the earliest** *o* **first ~** cuanto antes, en la primera oportunidad que se presente; **~ to + INF/OF -ING** oportunidad DE + INF; **we took the ~ of looking around the city** aprovechamos (la oportunidad) para recorrer la ciudad; **~ FOR sth/-ING**: **the job offers excellent opportunities for promotion** el trabajo ofrece excelentes posibilidades de ascenso; **this left us little ~ for sightseeing** esto nos dejó poco tiempo para hacer turismo

oppose /ə'pəʊz/ *vt*

A **1** (be against) ‹*measure/policy/actions*› oponerse* a, estar* en contra de **2** (resist) ‹*decision/plan*› combatir, luchar contra

B (contrast) contraponer*

opposed /ə'pəʊzd/ *adj*

A (against, in disagreement with) (*pred*) **to be ~ TO sth** oponerse* A algo, estar* en contra DE algo

B **as opposed to** a diferencia de, en contraposición a

opposing /ə'pəʊzɪŋ/ *adj* (*before n*) ‹*viewpoint/faction*› contrario, opuesto; ‹*team*› contrario; ‹*army*› enemigo

opposite[1] /'ɑːpəzət || 'ɒpəzɪt/ *adj*

A (facing) ‹*side/wall/seat*› de enfrente; ‹*page*› de enfrente, contiguo; **they sat at ~ ends of the table** estaban sentados en extremos opuestos de la mesa

B (contrary) ‹*opinions/news*› opuesto; **we set off in ~ directions** partimos en direcciones opuestas; **it was coming in the ~ direction** venía en dirección contraria; **the ~ sex** el sexo opuesto

opposite[2] *adv* enfrente; **the people ~ have bought a new car** los de enfrente se han comprado un coche nuevo

opposite[3] *prep* enfrente de, frente a

opposite[4] *n* lo contrario; **quite the ~** todo lo contrario, al contrario; **she's the exact ~ of her mother** es la antítesis de su madre

opposite number *n* homólogo, -ga *m,f*

opposition /'ɑːpə'zɪʃən || ˌɒpə'zɪʃən/ *n*

A [u] (antagonism, resistance) oposición *f*; **~ TO sth/sb** oposición A algo/algn

B (+ *sing or pl vb*) **1** (rivals, competitors) (Busn) competencia *f*; (Sport) adversarios *mpl* **2** (Pol): **the ~ is** *o* **are divided on this issue** la oposición está dividida al respecto; **to be in ~** estar* en la oposición; (*before n*) ‹*spokesperson/benches*› de la oposición

oppress /ə'pres/ *vt* ‹*nation/minority*› oprimir; «*heat/humidity*» agobiar; «*anxiety/foreboding*» oprimir, agobiar

oppression /ə'preʃən/ *n* [u] (Pol) opresión *f*; (feeling) agobio *m*

oppressive /ə'presɪv/ *adj* (Pol) opresivo; ‹*heat/humidity*› agobiante; ‹*fears/guilt*› agobiante, opresivo

oppressor /ə'presər || ə'presə(r)/ *n* opresor, -sora *m,f*

opprobrium /ə'prəʊbriəm/ *n* [u] (frml) oprobio *m* (frml)

opt /ɑːpt || ɒpt/ *vi* optar; **to ~ FOR sth** optar POR algo; **to ~ to + INF** optar POR + INF

Phrasal verb

- **opt out** [v ▸ adv] **1** «*person*» **to ~ out (OF sth)** decidir no tomar parte *or* no participar (EN algo); (when already involved) dejar de tomar parte (EN algo); **I've ~ed out of the scheme** me he borrado del plan **2** «*school/hospital*» (in UK) *pasar a depender directamente del gobierno central*

optic /'ɑːptɪk/ *adj* (*before n*) óptico

optical /'ɑːptɪkəl || 'ɒptɪkəl/ *adj* óptico; **~ character reader** lectora *f* óptica *or* lector *m* óptico de caracteres; **~ character recognition** reconocimiento *m* óptico de caracteres; **~ illusion** ilusión *f* óptica

optical fiber, (BrE) **fibre** *n* fibra *f* óptica

optician /ɑːp'tɪʃən || ɒp'tɪʃən/ *n* óptico, -ca *m,f*; (esp in UK) ≈ oculista *mf*

optics /'ɑːptɪks || 'ɒptɪks/ *n* (+ *sing vb*) óptica *f*

optimism /'ɑːptəmɪzəm || 'ɒptɪmɪzəm/ *n* [u] optimismo *m*

optimist /'ɑːptəməst || 'ɒptɪmɪst/ *n* optimista *mf*

optimistic /'ɑːptə'mɪstɪk || ˌɒptɪ'mɪstɪk/ *adj* optimista

optimistically /'ɑːptə'mɪstɪkli || ˌɒptɪ'mɪstɪkli/ *adv* con optimismo

optimize /'ɑːptəmaɪz || 'ɒptɪmaɪz/ *vt* optimar, optimizar* (frml)

optimum /'ɑːptəməm || 'ɒptɪməm/ *adj* (*before n*) óptimo

option /'ɑːpʃən || 'ɒpʃən/ *n*

A (choice) opción *f*, posibilidad *f*; **I had no ~ but to resign** no me quedó más remedio que renunciar, no tuve otra alternativa que renunciar; **to keep** *o* **leave one's ~s open** dejar todas las puertas abiertas, no descartar ninguna posibilidad *or* opción

B **1** (optional feature) (Audio, Auto) extra *m* **2** (Educ) (asignatura *f*) optativa *f*

C (Busn, Fin) opción *f*; **we want first ~ (to buy)** queremos la primera opción de compra

optional /'ɑːpʃənḷ || 'ɒpʃənḷ/ *adj* ‹*accessories/features*› opcional; ‹*course/subject*› optativo; **~ extra** accesorio *m* opcional, extra *m*; **evening dress is ~** el traje de etiqueta no es de rigor

optometrist /ɑːp'tɑːmətrəst || ɒp'tɒmɪtrɪst/ *n* (AmE) optometrista *mf*

optometry /ɑːp'tɑːmətri || ɒp'tɒmɪtri/ *n* [u] optometría *f*

opulence /'ɑːpjələns || 'ɒpjʊləns/ *n* [u] opulencia *f*

opulent /'ɑːpjələnt || 'ɒpjʊlənt/ *adj* opulento, de gran opulencia

opus /'əʊpəs/ *n* obra *f*, (Mus) opus *m*

or /ər, ɔːr || ɔː(r)/ *conj* [*The usual translation* **o** *becomes* **u** *when it precedes a word beginning with* **o** *or* **ho-**]

A **1** (indicating alternative) o; (with negative) ni; **one ~ the other** uno u otro; **that's not clever ~ funny** eso no tiene ni ingenio ni gracia **2** **either ... or ...** *see* **either**[1] **3** (in approximations) o; **five minutes ~ so** unos cinco minutos **4** (showing alternative designation) o; **an environmentalist, ~ green, policy** una política ecologista o verde

B (otherwise) o; **do as I say, ~ else!** ¡haz lo que digo o vas a ver!

O

OR = Oregon

oracle /'ɔːrəkəl || 'ɒrəkəl/ *n* oráculo *m*

oral¹ /'ɔːrəl/ *adj* (*usu before n*) oral; ‹*tradition*› transmitido oralmente *or* verbalmente; ~ **sex** sexo *m* oral

oral² *n* (examen *m*) oral *m*

orally /'ɔːrəli/ *adv* [1] (in speech) oralmente, verbalmente [2] (with, through the mouth) ‹*take/administer*› por vía oral, por boca

orange¹ /'ɑːrɪndʒ || 'ɒrɪndʒ/ *n*
A [1] (fruit) naranja *f*; (*before n*) ~ **blossom** azahar *m*, flor *f* del naranjo; ~ **drink** naranjada *f*; ~ **juice** jugo *m or* (Esp) zumo *m* de naranja [2] ~ **(tree)** naranjo *m*
B (color) naranja *m*

orange² *adj* naranja *adj inv*, de color naranja

orangeade /'ɑːrɪndʒ'eɪd || ˌɒrɪndʒ'eɪd/ *n* [u] naranjada *f*

orangutan /ə'ræŋəˌtæn || ɔːˌræŋuː'tæn/, **orang-outang** /ə'ræŋə'tæŋ || ɔːˌræŋuː'tæŋ/ *n* orangután *m*

oration /ɔː'reɪʃən, ə-/ *n* discurso *m*, alocución *f* (frml)

orator /'ɔːrətər || 'ɒrətə(r)/ *n* orador, -dora *m,f*

oratorio /'ɔːrə'tɔːriəʊ || ˌɒrə'tɔːriəʊ/ *n* (*pl* **-rios**) oratorio *m*

oratory /'ɔːrətɔːri || 'ɒrətəri/ *n* (*pl* **-ries**)
A [u] (rhetoric, formal speech) oratoria *f*
B [c] (building) oratorio *m*

orbit¹ /'ɔːrbət || 'ɔːbɪt/ *n* órbita *f*; **to put a satellite into** ~ poner* un satélite en órbita

orbit² *vt* girar *or* orbitar alrededor de, describir* una órbita alrededor de
■ **orbit** *vi* orbitar

orbiter /'ɔːrbətər || 'ɔːbɪtə(r)/ *n* módulo *m* orbital, orbitador *m*

orchard /'ɔːrtʃərd || 'ɔːtʃəd/ *n* huerto *m* (*de árboles frutales*)

orchestra /'ɔːrkəstrə || 'ɔːkɪstrə/ *n*
A (Mus) orquesta *f*; (*before n*) ~ **pit** foso *m* orquestal *or* de la orquesta
B (AmE Theat) platea *f*, patio *m* de butacas

orchestral /ɔːr'kestrəl || ɔː'kestrəl/ *adj* ‹*music*› orquestal; ‹*piece*› para orquesta, orquestal

orchestrate /'ɔːrkəstreɪt || 'ɔːkɪstreɪt/ *vt* [1] (Mus) orquestar [2] ‹*revolt/violence*› orquestar; ‹*campaign*› organizar*, montar, orquestar

orchestration /'ɔːrkə'streɪʃən || ˌɔːkɪ'streɪʃən/ *n* [1] [u c] (Mus) orquestación *f* [2] [u] (of revolt) orquestación *f*; (of campaign) organización *f*, orquestación *f*

orchid /'ɔːrkəd || 'ɔːkɪd/ *n* orquídea *f*

ordain /ɔːr'deɪn || ɔː'deɪn/ *vt*
A (Relig) ordenar
B [1] (decree) (frml) **to** ~ THAT decretar QUE (+ *subj*) [2] (predestine) predestinar

ordeal /ɔːr'diːl || ɔː'diːl/ *n* (painful experience) terrible experiencia *f*, dura prueba *f*; **I hate shopping on a Saturday, it's such an** ~ detesto ir de compras los sábados, es un verdadero suplicio

order¹ /'ɔːrdər || 'ɔːdə(r)/ *n*

(*Sense I*)
A [c] [1] (command) orden *f*; **to await** ~**s** esperar órdenes; **I don't take** ~**s from anyone** a mí nadie me da órdenes; ~**s are** ~**s** órdenes son órdenes; ~ **to** + INF orden DE + inf; **he gave the** ~ **to fire** dio orden de disparar; ~ THAT orden DE QUE (+ *subj*); **I left** ~**s that she was not to be disturbed** dejé órdenes de que no se la molestara; **on whose** ~**s are you doing this?** ¿quién le ordenó hacer esto?; **by** ~ **of ...** por orden de ...; ***to get one's marching*** ~***s*** (colloq) ser* despedido [2] (court decree) (Law) orden *f*; *see also* **order of the day**
B [c] (request, goods requested) pedido *m*; **to place an** ~ **for sth** hacer* un pedido de algo, encargar* algo; **the books are on** ~ los libros están pedidos; **we make them to** ~ los hacemos por encargo; **the waiter took my** ~ el camarero tomó nota de lo que quería; ***a tall*** ~: **it's a bit of a tall** ~, **but I'll see what I can do** es algo difícil, pero veré qué puedo hacer
C [u] (instructions to pay) (Fin) orden *f*; *see also* **postal order, standing order** *etc*

(*Sense II*) [u]
A (sequence) orden *m*; **in alphabetical/numerical** ~ en *or* por orden alfabético/numérico; **the photos were all in the wrong** ~ las fotos estaban todas desordenadas; **to put sth in(to)** ~ poner* algo en orden, ordenar algo
B (satisfactory condition) orden *m*; **let's get this room into some sort of** ~ tratemos de ordenar un poco esta habitación; **I'm trying to put my affairs in** ~ estoy tratando de poner mis asuntos en orden *or* de arreglar mis asuntos; **the car was in perfect working** ~ el coche funcionaba perfectamente bien
C (harmony, discipline) orden *m*; **to keep** ~ mantener* el orden; ~ **in (the) court!** ¡silencio en la sala!; **to call sb to** ~ llamar a algn al orden
D (rules, procedure) orden *m*; **point of** ~ cuestión *f* de orden *or* de procedimiento; **to call a meeting to** ~ (start) empezar* una reunión; (resume) reanudar una reunión
E (in phrases) [1] **in order**: **is your bedroom in** ~**?** ¿tu cuarto está ordenado *or* en orden?; **are her papers in** ~**?** ¿tiene los papeles en regla?; **is everything in** ~ **for tomorrow's performance?** ¿está todo dispuesto para la función de mañana?; **an apology would seem to be in** ~ parecería que lo indicado sería disculparse [2] **in order to** para [3] **in order that** para que (+ *subj*) [4] **out of order** (not in sequence) desordenado; (not working) averiado, descompuesto (AmL); Ⓢ **out of order** no funciona; (uncalled-for, not following procedure): **that remark was out of** ~ ese comentario estuvo fuera de lugar

(*Sense III*)
A [c] [1] (kind, class): **the lower** ~**s** las clases bajas; **a performance of the first** ~ una interpretación de primera clase; **a fool of the first** ~ un tonto de marca mayor [2] (Biol) orden *m* [3] (*in phrases*) **on** *o* (BrE) **in the order of**: **it cost something on the** ~ **of $100** costó alrededor de 100 dólares, el costo fue del orden de 100 dólares
B [c] [1] (of monks, nuns) orden *f* [2] (insignia) condecoración *f*
C **orders** *pl* (Relig) órdenes *fpl* sagradas; **to take (holy)** ~**s** recibir las órdenes (sagradas), ordenarse sacerdote

order² *vt*
A [1] (command) ordenar; **to** ~ **sb to** + INF ordenarle a algn QUE (+ *subj*); **to** ~ **sth (to be) done** ordenar que se haga algo; **to** ~ THAT ordenar QUE (+ *subj*); **he** ~**ed me out of the room** me ordenó *or* me mandó salir de la habitación [2] (Med) mandar; **he** ~**ed complete rest** le mandó hacer reposo absoluto
B (request) pedir*; ‹*goods*› encargar*, pedir*; **I** ~**ed three boxes of pencils** hice un pedido de *or* encargué tres cajas de lápices; **to** ~ **a taxi** llamar un taxi
C (put in order) ‹*work/life/affairs*› ordenar, poner* en orden
■ **order** *vi* (in restaurant): **are you ready to** ~**?** ¿ya han decidido qué van a tomar *or* pedir?

(Phrasal verb)
• **order around**, (BrE also) **order about** [v ▸ o ▸ adv] mandonear (fam)

order book *n* libro *m* de pedidos

ordered /'ɔːrdərd || 'ɔːdəd/ *adj* ordenado

orderly¹ /'ɔːrdərli || 'ɔːdəli/ *adj* [1] ‹*life/mind*› ordenado, metódico [2] ‹*crowd*› disciplinado; **the demonstration passed off in an** ~ **fashion** la manifestación transcurrió de forma pacífica

orderly² *n* (*pl* **-lies**) [1] (in hospital) camillero *m* [2] (Mil) ordenanza *m*

order of the day *n* [1] (agenda) orden *m* del día [2] (Mil) orden *f* del día [3] (rule, custom) **to be the** ~ ~ ~ ~ estar* a la orden del día

ordinal (number) /'ɔːrdn̩əl || 'ɔːdɪnəl/ *n* (número *m*) ordinal *m*

ordinance /'ɔːrdn̩əns || 'ɔːdnəns/ *n* (frml) ordenanza *f*

ordinarily /'ɔːrdn̩'erəli || 'ɔːdənrəli/ *adv* [1] (usually) normalmente [2] (averagely) medianamente

ordinary¹ /'ɔːrdn̩eri || 'ɔːdənri/ *adj* [1] (average, normal) ‹*person/object*› normal, corriente, común [2] (usual) normal, habitual; **I'll just wear my** ~ **clothes** me pondré la ropa de todos los días, nada especial

ordinary² *n* [1] (average): **out of the** ~ fuera de lo común, excepcional [2] ~ **(degree)** (Educ) *título universitario que no alcanza la categoría de* **honors degree**

ordinary level *n* (formerly in UK) (frml) ▸ **O level**

ordination /'ɔːrdn̩'eɪʃən || ˌɔːdɪ'neɪʃən/ *n* [u] ordenación *f*

ordnance /ˈɔːrdnəns || ˈɔːdnəns/ *n* [u] 1 (artillery) artillería *f*; (*before n*) **O~ Survey** (in UK) *servicio oficial de cartografía* 2 (supplies) pertrechos *mpl*

ore /ɔːr || ɔː(r)/ *n* mena *f*, mineral *m* metalífero; **gold/iron ~** mineral *m* de oro/hierro

Ore, Oreg = Oregon

oregano /əˈregənəʊ || ˌɒrɪˈɡɑːnəʊ/ *n* [u] orégano *m*

organ /ˈɔːrgən || ˈɔːgən/ *n*
A (Anat) órgano *m*
B 1 (agency) organismo *m* 2 (mouthpiece) órgano *m*
C (Mus) órgano *m*

organ grinder *n* organillero, -ra *m,f*

organic /ɔːrˈgænɪk || ɔːˈgænɪk/ *adj* orgánico; ‹*farming*› ecológico; ‹*vegetable*› biológico, cultivado sin pesticidas ni fertilizantes artificiales

organically /ɔːrˈgænɪkli || ɔːˈgænɪkli/ *adv* (Agr, Hort) biológicamente

organism /ˈɔːrgənɪzəm || ˈɔːgənɪzəm/ *n* organismo *m*

organist /ˈɔːrgənəst || ˈɔːgənɪst/ *n* organista *mf*

organization /ˌɔːrgənəˈzeɪʃən || ˌɔːgənaɪˈzeɪʃən/ *n* 1 [c] (group) organización *f*; (*before n*) **~ chart** organigrama *m* 2 [u] (organizing) organización *f* 3 [u] (order, system) método *m*, sistema *m*

organizational /ˌɔːrgənəˈzeɪʃn̩əl || ˌɔːgənaɪˈzeɪʃənl̩/ *adj* organizativo, de organización

organize /ˈɔːrgənaɪz || ˈɔːgənaɪz/ *vt*
A 1 (arrange, set up) organizar*; **have you got anything ~d for this evening?** ¿tienes algún plan para esta noche? 2 **organizing** *pres p* (*before n*) ‹*body/committee*› organizador
B (systematize) ‹*ideas/life*› ordenar; **you've got to ~ your time better** tienes que organizarte mejor para aprovechar bien el tiempo; **I haven't had time to get myself ~d** no he tenido tiempo de organizarme
C (Lab Rels) sindicalizar* (esp AmL), sindicar* (esp Esp)
■ **organize** *vi*
A (arrange things) organizar*
B (Lab Rels) sindicalizarse* (esp AmL), sindicarse* (esp Esp)

organized /ˈɔːrgənaɪzd || ˈɔːgənaɪzd/ *adj*
A (methodical, systematic) organizado: **his work is badly ~** su trabajo está mal organizado
B (Lab Rels) sindicalizado (esp AmL), sindicado (esp Esp)
C ‹*crime*› organizado

organizer /ˈɔːrgənaɪzər || ˈɔːgənaɪzə(r)/ *n* organizador, -dora *m,f*

orgasm /ˈɔːrgæzəm || ˈɔːgæzəm/ *n* orgasmo *m*

orgy /ˈɔːrdʒi || ˈɔːdʒi/ *n* (*pl* **orgies**) orgía *f*

orient[1], **Orient** /ˈɔːriənt/ *n* **the ~** (el) Oriente

orient[2] *vt* (esp AmE) orientar; **to ~ oneself** orientarse

oriental /ˌɔːriˈentl̩/ *adj* oriental

Oriental *n* (dated) oriental *mf*

orientate /ˈɔːrienteɪt/ *vt* (esp BrE) ▸**orient**[2]

orientated /ˈɔːrienteɪtəd || ˈɔːriənteɪtɪd/ *adj* (esp BrE) ▸**oriented**

orientation /ˌɔːrienˈteɪʃən/ *n* [u] 1 (leanings, preference) tendencia *f* 2 (guidance) orientación *f*

oriented /ˈɔːrientəd || ˈɔːrientɪd/ *adj* **to be ~ TOWARD sth** orientarse HACIA algo

orienteering /ˌɔːrienˈtɪrɪŋ || ˌɔːriənˈtɪərɪŋ/ *n* [u] orientación *f*

orifice /ˈɔːrəfəs || ˈɒrɪfɪs/ *n* orificio *m*

origami /ˌɔːrəˈgɑːmi || ˌɒrɪˈgɑːmi/ *n* [u] origami *m*, papiroflexia *f*

origin /ˈɔːrədʒən || ˈɒrɪdʒɪn/ *n* origen *m*; **of humble ~s** de origen *or* de cuna humilde

original[1] /əˈrɪdʒənl̩/ *adj*
A (first) original, originario; **the ~ inhabitants** los primeros habitantes, los habitantes originarios; **~ sin** pecado *m* original
B 1 (not copied) original 2 (unusual) original

original[2] *n* 1 (document, painting, sculpture) original *m*; **in the ~** en versión original; **the songs on the album are all ~s** los temas del álbum son todos nuevos 2 (unusual person): **she's a complete ~!** ¡es de lo más original!

originality /əˌrɪdʒəˈnæləti/ *n* [u] originalidad *f*

originally /əˈrɪdʒənl̩i/ *adv* 1 (in the beginning) originariamente, al principio; **she's from Russia ~** es de origen ruso 2 (unusually) con originalidad, de manera original

originate /əˈrɪdʒəneɪt || əˈrɪdʒɪneɪt/ *vi* 1 (begin) «*custom*» originarse; «*fire*» empezar*, iniciarse 2 **to ~ from sth** (develop from) tener* su origen en algo; **the film ~d from a short story** la película tuvo su origen en un cuento corto; **the noise seemed to ~ from the first floor** el ruido parecía venir de la planta baja 3 (AmE Transp) salir* de; **the flight, which ~d in New York, stopped over in Chicago** el vuelo, procedente de *or* que venía de Nueva York, hizo escala en Chicago
■ **originate** *vt* ‹*idea/style*› crear

originator /əˈrɪdʒəneɪtər || əˈrɪdʒɪneɪtə(r)/ *n* (of an idea, style) creador, -dora *m,f*

Orkney Islands /ˈɔːrkni || ˈɔːkni/, **Orkneys** /-z/ *pl n* (Islas *fpl*) Órcadas *fpl*

ornament[1] /ˈɔːrnəmənt || ˈɔːnəmənt/ *n* 1 [c] (object) adorno *m* 2 [c u] (decoration) (frml) adorno *m*, ornamento *m* (frml)

ornament[2] /ˈɔːrnəment/ *vt* adornar, decorar

ornamental /ˌɔːrnəˈmentl̩ || ˌɔːnəˈmentl̩/ *adj* ornamental, decorativo

ornamentation /ˌɔːrnəmenˈteɪʃən || ˌɔːnəmənˈteɪʃən/ *n* [u c] decoración *f*, ornamentación *f*

ornate /ɔːrˈneɪt || ɔːˈneɪt/ *adj* ‹*decoration/vase*› ornamentado, elaborado; (pej) recargado; ‹*language/style*› florido; (pej) ampuloso

ornately /ɔːrˈneɪtli || ɔːˈneɪtli/ *adv* ‹*decorate*› de manera ornamentada *or* elaborada; (pej) recargadamente; ‹*write*› en estilo florido; (pej) ampulosamente

ornery /ˈɔːrnəri || ˈɔːnəri/ *adj* (AmE colloq) de mal genio, de malas pulgas (fam); **to be ~** tener* mal genio *or* (fam) malas pulgas

ornithologist /ˌɔːrnəˈθɑːlədʒəst || ˌɔːnɪˈθɒlədʒɪst/ *n* ornitólogo, -ga *m,f*

ornithology /ˌɔːrnəˈθɑːlədʒi || ˌɔːnɪˈθɒlədʒi/ *n* [u] ornitología *f*

orphan[1] /ˈɔːrfən || ˈɔːfən/ *n* huérfano, -na *m,f*; **he was left an ~** quedó huérfano

orphan[2] *vt* (*usu pass*): **she was ~ed at the age of two** quedó huérfana a los dos años

orphanage /ˈɔːrfənɪdʒ || ˈɔːfənɪdʒ/ *n* orfanato *m*, orfelinato *m*

orthodox /ˈɔːrθədɑːks || ˈɔːθədɒks/ *adj* ortodoxo; **the O~ Church** la Iglesia Ortodoxa

orthodoxy /ˈɔːrθədɑːksi || ˈɔːθədɒksi/ *n* [c u] (*pl* **-xies**) ortodoxia *f*

orthographic /ˌɔːrθəˈgræfɪk || ˌɔːθəˈgræfɪk/, **-ical** /-ɪkəl/ *adj* ortográfico

orthography /ɔːrˈθɑːgrəfi || ɔːˈθɒgrəfi/ *n* [u] ortografía *f*

orthopedic, orthopaedic /ˌɔːrθəˈpiːdɪk || ˌɔːθəˈpiːdɪk/ *adj* ‹*device*› ortopédico; ‹*ward*› de ortopedia, de traumatología; **~ surgeon** ortopedista *mf*

orthopedics, orthopaedics /ˌɔːrθəˈpiːdɪks || ˌɔːθəˈpiːdɪks/ *n* [u] (+ *sing vb*) ortopedia *f*

Oscar /ˈɑːskər || ˈɒskə(r)/ *n* oscar *m*

> **Oscar awards**
>
> En la *Oscar Ceremony*, celebrada en Los Ángeles cada año desde 1929 por la *Academy of Motion Picture Arts and Sciences*, se otorgan los *Academy Awards*, apodados los *Oscars*, a aquellos artistas, directores, productores y guionistas de cine considerados los mejores del año según la votación de sus colegas

oscillate /ˈɑːsəleɪt || ˈɒsɪleɪt/ *vi* 1 (Elec, Phys) oscilar 2 (fluctuate) (frml) «*prices/values*» oscilar, fluctuar*; «*person*» oscilar

oscillation /ˌɑːsəˈleɪʃən || ˌɒsɪˈleɪʃən/ *n* [u c] 1 (Elec, Phys) oscilación *f* 2 (wavering) oscilación *f*, fluctuación *f*

osmosis /ɑːzˈməʊsəs || ɒzˈməʊsɪs/ *n* [u] ósmosis *f*, osmosis *f*

ossify /ˈɑːsəfaɪ || ˈɒsɪfaɪ/ *vi* **-fies, -fying, -fied** 1 (Physiol) osificarse* 2 (frml) «*institution/attitude*» anquilosarse

ostensible /ɑːˈstensəbəl || ɒˈstensəbəl/ *adj* aparente, pretendido

ostensibly /ɑːˈstensəbli || ɒˈstensəbli/ *adv* aparentemente, en apariencia; **she came ~ to help** vino con el pretexto de ayudar

O

ostentation /ˈɑːstənˈteɪʃən || ˌɒstenˈteɪʃən/ *n* [u] ostentación *f*

ostentatious /ˈɑːstənˈteɪʃəs || ˌɒstenˈteɪʃəs/ *adj* ostentoso

ostentatiously /ˈɑːstənˈteɪʃəsli || ˌɒstenˈteɪʃəsli/ *adv* ostentosamente, con ostentación

osteoarthritis /ˈɑːstiəʊɑːrˈθraɪtəs || ˌɒstiəʊɑːˈθraɪtɪs/ *n* [u] osteoartritis *f*

osteopath /ˈɑːstiəpæθ || ˈɒstiəpæθ/ *n* osteópata *mf*

osteoporosis /ˈɑːsteəʊpəˈrəʊsɪs || ˌɒstiəʊpəˈrəʊsɪs/ *n* [u] osteoporosis *f*

ostracism /ˈɑːstrəsɪzəm/ *n* [u] ostracismo *m*

ostracize /ˈɑːstrəsaɪz || ˈɒstrəsaɪz/ *vt* hacerle* el vacío a, aislar*

ostrich /ˈɑːstrɪtʃ || ˈɒstrɪtʃ/ *n* avestruz *m*

OT (= **Old Testament**) A.T.

other[1] /ˈʌðər || ˈʌðə(r)/ *adj* 1 (different, alternative) otro, otra; (*pl*) otros, otras; **are there any ~ possibilities?** ¿hay alguna otra posibilidad?; **he doesn't relate easily to ~ people** no se relaciona fácilmente con los demás; **some ~ time** en otro momento 2 (the remaining one or ones) otro, otra; (*pl*) otros, otras; **the ~ children are all older than me** los otros *or* los demás niños son todos mayores que yo 3 (in addition) otro, otra; (*pl*) otros, otras; **answer Section A and two ~ questions** conteste la sección A y dos preguntas más *or* y otras dos preguntas 4 (recent): **the ~ day** el otro día

other[2] *pron* (*pl* **others**)

A 1 (different, alternative one or ones) otro, otra; **~s** otros, otras; **somebody or ~ must be responsible** alguien tiene que ser el responsable; **something or ~ is bound to happen** tiene que pasar algo; **he was called Richard something or ~** se llamaba Richard no sé cuánto *or* no sé qué (fam) 2 (the remaining one or ones) otro, otra; **~s** otros, otras; **what do the ~s think?** ¿qué piensan los demás *or* los otros? 3 (additional one or ones) otro, otra; **~s** otros, otras; **answer the first three questions and one ~** conteste las tres primeras preguntas y otra *or* y una más

B **other than** (apart from) aparte de; (different from) distinto (*or* distinta *etc*) de *or* a; **~ than John, who's going to go with you?** ¿quién va a ir contigo aparte de John *or* además de John?; **it was none ~ than Uncle Bob** no era ni más ni menos que el tío Bob

other[3] *adv*: **somehow or ~** de alguna manera, de algún modo; **somewhere/sometime or ~** en algún sitio *or* lugar/momento; **I could not have intervened ~ than when I did** no podría haber intervenido más que cuando lo hice; **where would you like to live? — anywhere ~ than London** ¿dónde te gustaría vivir? — en cualquier (otro) sitio *or* lugar menos en Londres, en cualquier sitio *or* lugar que no sea Londres

otherwise /ˈʌðərwaɪz || ˈʌðəwaɪz/ *adv*

A (if not) (*as linker*) si no

B (in other respects) por lo demás, aparte de eso

C 1 (in a different way): **he could not have done ~** no podía haber hecho otra cosa *or* (frml) obrado de otro modo: **we all thought it was too dangerous, but she thought ~** todos pensamos que era demasiado peligroso, pero no así ella; **they believe they are right and nothing will convince them ~** creen que están en lo cierto y nada los convencerá de lo contrario *or* de que no es así; **unless ~ agreed, payments ...** a menos que se convenga otra cosa, los pagos ... 2 (other, different): **there are many problems, legal and ~** hay muchos problemas, legales y de otro tipo; **how can it be ~?** ¿cómo no va a ser así?

otherworldly /ˈʌðərˈwɜːrdli || ˌʌðəˈwɜːldli/ *adj* 1 (dreamlike) de otro mundo, de ensueño 2 (mystical) místico, espiritual

otter /ˈɑːtər || ˈɒtə(r)/ *n* nutria *f*

ottoman /ˈɑːtəmən || ˈɒtəmən/ *n* (*pl* **-mans**) otomana *f*

ouch /aʊtʃ/ *interj* (colloq) ¡ay!

ought /ɔːt/ *v mod* **~ to + INF**

A (indicating obligation, desirability) debería (*or* deberías *etc*) + INF, debiera (*or* debieras *etc*) + INF; **you ~ to be grateful** deberías *or* debieras estar agradecido, tendrías que estar agradecido; **she ~ not to have said that** no debería haber dicho eso, no tendría *or* no tenía que haber dicho eso; **you ~ to have seen her face!** ¡tenías *or* tendrías que haber visto la cara que puso!

B (expressing logical expectation) debería (*or* deberías *etc*) + INF, debiera (*or* debieras *etc*) + INF; **she ~ to be here by now** ya debería *or* debiera estar aquí

Ouija board® /ˈwiːdʒə/ *n* (tablero *m* de) ouija *f*

ounce /aʊns/ *n* 1 (unit) onza *f* (*28,35 gramos*) 2 (AmE) ▸**fluid ounce** 3 (small quantity) (*no pl*): **if you had an ~ of decency/sense ...** si tuvieras una pizca de vergüenza/sentido común ...

our /ˈaʊə(r)/ *adj* (*sing*) nuestro, -tra; (*pl*) nuestros, -tras

ours /aʊrz || ˈaʊəz/ *pron* (*sing*) nuestro, -tra; (*pl*) nuestros, -tras; **~ is blue** el nuestro/la nuestra es azul; **a friend of ~** un amigo nuestro

ourselves /aʊrˈselvz || aʊəˈselvz, ɑː-/ *pron* 1 (reflexive): **we behaved ~** nos portamos bien; **we thought only of ~** sólo pensamos en nosotros mismos/nosotras mismas; **we were by ~** estábamos solos/solas 2 (emphatic use): **we did it ~** lo hicimos nosotros mismos/nosotras mismas

oust /aʊst/ *vt* ‹*rival/leader*› desbancar*; ‹*government*› derrocar*, hacer* caer; **she was ~ed from office** la destituyeron, la alejaron *or* la separaron del cargo (euf)

ouster /ˈaʊstər/ *n* (AmE) expulsión *f*, destitución *f*

out[1] /aʊt/ *adv*

Sense **I**

A 1 (outside) fuera, afuera (esp AmL); **is the cat in or ~?** ¿el gato está (a)dentro *or* (a)fuera?; **all the books on Dickens are ~** todos los libros sobre Dickens están prestados; **the jury is still ~** el jurado todavía está deliberando; **the jury's ~ on which will prove to be the right formula** está por ver(se) cuál será la fórmula correcta; *see also* **out of** 2 (not at home, work): **tell him I'm ~** dile que no estoy; **he's ~ to** *o* **at lunch** ha salido a comer; **I was ~ most of the day** estuve (a)fuera casi todo el día; **we haven't had a night ~ for months** hace meses que no salimos de noche; **they had a day ~ in York** pasaron un día en York; **to eat** *o* (frml) **dine ~** cenar/comer fuera *or* (esp AmL) afuera; **~ and about**: **you must get ~ and about more** tienes que salir más; *see also* **go out**

B (removed): **I'm having my stitches ~ next week** la semana que viene me sacan los puntos

C 1 (indicating movement, direction): **~!** ¡fuera!; Ⓢ **out** salida; **she went over to the window and looked ~** se acercó a la ventana y miró para afuera 2 (outstretched, projecting): **the dog had its tongue ~** el perro tenía la lengua fuera *or* (esp AmL) afuera; **arms ~, legs together** brazos extendidos, piernas juntas

D (indicating distance): **~ here in Japan** aquí en Japón; **they worked ~ in Brunei for a while** estuvieron un tiempo trabajando en Brunei; **we live ~ Brampton way** vivimos en la dirección de Brampton; **ten miles ~** (Naut) a diez millas de la costa

E 1 (ejected, dismissed): **any more foul language and she's ~!** ¡otra palabrota más y se va *or* la echo!; **he couldn't get the tenants ~** no pudo echar a los inquilinos 2 (from hospital, jail): **he's been ~ for a month now** ya hace un mes que salió 3 (out of office): **the socialists will be ~ next time** los socialistas van a perder las próximas elecciones; **Jones ~!** ¡fuera Jones!

F (in phrases) **out for**: **Lewis was ~ for revenge** Lewis quería vengarse; **out to + INF**: **she's ~ to beat the record** está decidida a batir el récord; **they're only ~ to make money** su único objetivo es hacer dinero; **they're ~ to get you!** ¡andan tras de ti!, ¡van a por ti! (Esp); *see also* **out of**

Sense **II**

A 1 (displayed, not put away): **are the plates ~ yet?** ¿están puestos ya los platos? 2 (in blossom) en flor 3 (shining): **when the sun's ~** cuando hay *or* hace sol; **the stars are ~** hay estrellas

B 1 (revealed, in the open): **once the news was ~, she left the country** en cuanto se supo la noticia, se fue del país; **~ with it! who stole the documents?** ¡dilo ya! ¿quién robó los documentos? 2 (published, produced): **a report ~ today points out that ...** un informe publicado hoy señala que ...; **their new album will be ~ by April** sacarán el nuevo disco para abril; **the results are due ~ next week** los resultados salen la semana que viene 3 (in existence) (colloq): **it's the fastest car ~** es el coche más rápido que hay (en el mercado)

C (clearly, loudly): **he read ~ the names of the winners** leyó (en voz alta) los nombres de los ganadores; **he said it ~ loud** lo dijo en voz alta; *see also* **call, cry, speak** *etc* **out**

out[2] *adj*

A (*pred*) **1** (extinguished) **to be ~** «*fire/light/pipe*» estar* apagado **2** (unconscious) inconsciente, sin conocimiento; **after five vodkas she was ~ cold** con cinco vodkas, quedó fuera de combate (fam)

B (*pred*) **1** (at an end): **before the month/year is ~** antes de que acabe el mes/año **2** (out of fashion) pasado de moda; *see also* **go out G1** **3** (out of the question) (colloq): **smoking in the bedrooms is absolutely ~** ni hablar de fumar en los dormitorios (fam), está terminantemente prohibido fumar en los dormitorios

C (Sport) **1** (eliminated) **to be ~** ‹*batter/batsman*› quedar out *or* fuera; ‹*team*› quedar eliminado; *see also* **out of C** **2** (outside limit) (*pred*) fuera; **it was ~** cayó *or* fue fuera; **~!** (call by line-judge or umpire) ¡out!

D (inaccurate) (*pred*): **they were ~ in their calculations** se equivocaron en los cálculos; **you're not far ~** no andas muy descaminado; **you're way** *o* **a long way** *o* **miles ~** andas muy lejos *or* muy errado

E (without, out of) (colloq) (*pred*): **coffee? sorry, I'm completely ~** ¿café? lo siento, no me queda ni gota (fam); *see also* **out of 6**

F ‹*homosexual*› declarado

out[3] *prep*: **he looked ~ the window** miró (hacia afuera) por la ventana; *see also* **out of A**

out[4] *n*

A **1** (in baseball) out *m*, hombre *m* fuera **2** (escape) (AmE colloq) escapatoria *f*

B **outs** *pl* (AmE) **1** : ***to be on the ~s with sb*** estar* enemistado con algn **2** (those not in power): **the ~s** los partidos de la oposición

out[5] *vt* revelar la homosexualidad de

out- /'aʊt/ *pref*: **he can ~argue me any day** me puede ganar cualquier discusión sin problemas; *see also* **outgrow, outstay** *etc*

out: **~-and-out** /'aʊtn̩'aʊt/ *adj* (*as intensifier*) ‹*villain/liar*› consumado, redomado; ‹*radical/feminist*› acérrimo; ‹*defeat/disgrace*› total, absoluto; **~back** *n* **the ~back** el interior (*zona despoblada de Australia*); **~bid** /'aʊt'bɪd/ *vt* (*pres p* **-bidding**; *past* **-bid**; *past p* **-bid** *or* (AmE also) **-bidden**) **to ~bid sb (FOR sth)** pujar *or* ofrecer* más que algn (POR algo); **~board** *n* **1** **~board (motor)** motor *m* fuera de borda, fueraborda *m* **2** (boat) lancha *f* con motor fuera de borda, fueraborda *m*; **~bound** *adj*: **~bound flights from Dallas were delayed** los vuelos que partían de Dallas estaban saliendo con retraso; **~break** *n* (of war) estallido *m*; (of hostilities) comienzo *m*; (of cholera, influenza) brote *m*; **there were ~breaks of violence/protest** hubo brotes de violencia/protesta; **~building** *n* edificación *f* anexa; **~burst** *n* (of emotion) arrebato *m*, arranque *m*; **I apologize for my ~burst** perdonen que perdiera los estribos; **there was a sudden ~burst of shouting/applause** de repente se oyeron unos gritos/el público prorrumpió en aplausos; **~cast** *n* paria *mf*; **a social ~cast** un marginado de la sociedad; **~class** /'aʊt'klæs || ˌaʊt'klɑːs/ *vt* superar, aventajar; **~come** *n* (result) resultado *m*; (consequences) consecuencias *fpl*; **~crop** *n* afloramiento *m*; **~cry** *n* [u c] protesta *f* (*enérgica*); **there was a public ~cry** hubo protestas generalizadas; **~dated** /'aʊt'deɪtəd || ˌaʊt'deɪtɪd/ *adj* ‹*style/custom*› pasado de moda, anticuado; ‹*idea/theory*› anticuado, trasnochado; **~did** /'aʊt'dɪd/ *past of* **~do**; **~distance** /'aʊt'dɪstəns/ *vt* dejar atrás, aventajar; **~do** /'aʊt'duː/ *vt* (*3rd pers sing pres* **-does**; *past* **-did**; *past p* **-done**) ‹*person/team*› superar, ganarle a; ‹*result/achievement*› mejorar, superar; **not to be ~done, she bought an even bigger one** para no ser menos, se compró uno aún más grande; **~door** /'aʊtdɔːr || 'aʊtdɔː(r)/ *adj* (*before n*) ‹*clothes*› de calle; ‹*plants*› de exterior; ‹*swimming pool*› descubierto, al aire libre; **he's very much the ~door type** es el tipo de persona a la que le gusta la vida al aire libre; **~door games** juegos *mpl* al aire libre

outdoors[1] /'aʊt'dɔːrz || ˌaʊt'dɔːz/ *adv* al aire libre

outdoors[2] *n*: **the great ~** el aire libre, la naturaleza

outer /'aʊtər || 'aʊtə(r)/ *adj* (*before n*) exterior; **~ space** el espacio sideral

outermost /'aʊtərməʊst || 'aʊtəməʊst/ *adj* exterior; **the ~ island in the archipelago** la isla más remota del archipiélago

out: **~fall** *n* desagüe *m*; **~field** *n* **the ~field** (area) los jardines, las praderas (*el perímetro del campo de juego*); (players) (+ *sing or pl vb*) los jardineros; **~fielder** *n* jardinero, -ra *m,f* (*jugador en el perímetro del campo de juego*); **~fit** *n* **1** (clothes) conjunto *m*, tenida *f* (Chi) **2** (equipment) equipo *m* **3** (organization, unit) (colloq): **they've set up a small electronics ~fit** han montado un pequeño negocio de electrónica; **~fitter** *n*: Ⓢ **gentlemen's outfitters** confecciones *fpl* para caballeros; Ⓢ **sports outfitters** artículos *mpl* para el deportista; **~flow** *n* (of water) desagüe *m*, flujo *m*; **cash ~flows** salidas *fpl* de efectivo; **~go** *n* [u c] (AmE) salida *f*; **~going** *adj* **1** (sociable) sociable, extrovertido; **2** (*before n*) (outbound): **delays are reported on all ~going flights** todos los vuelos están saliendo con retraso **3** ‹*president/administration*› saliente; **~goings** *pl n* (esp BrE) gastos *mpl*, salidas *fpl*; **~grow** /'aʊt'grəʊ/ *vt* (*past* **-grew**; *past p* **-grown**) **1** (grow taller than): **you have ~grown your father** estás más alto que tu padre **2** (grow too big for): **he's already ~grown his new shoes** los zapatos nuevos ya le han quedado chicos *or* (Esp) ya se le han quedado pequeños; **he's ~grown the disco phase** ya ha dejado atrás la etapa de las discotecas; **~house** *n* **1** (building) (BrE) edificación *f* anexa **2** (outdoor privy) (AmE) excusado *m* exterior

outing /'aʊtɪŋ/ *n* excursión *f*, salida *f*; **to go on an ~** salir* de excursión

outlandish /aʊt'lændɪʃ/ *adj* ‹*clothes/expression*› extravagante, estrafalario; ‹*idea/suggestion*› descabellado

outlast /'aʊt'læst || ˌaʊt'lɑːst/ *vt* **1** (last longer than) durar más que **2** (survive) sobrevivir a

outlaw[1] /'aʊtlɔː/ *n* forajido, -da *m,f*, bandido, -da *m,f*, bandolero, -ra *m,f*

outlaw[2] *vt* ‹*activity/product*› prohibir*, declarar ilegal; ‹*organization*› proscribir*; ‹*person*› declarar fuera de la ley

out: **~lay** *n* desembolso *m*; **~lay ON sth** gasto *m* *or* inversión *m* EN algo; **~let** *n* **1** (for liquid, gas) salida *f*; (*before n*) ‹*valve*› de escape, de vaciado **2** (AmE Elec) toma *f* de corriente, tomacorriente *m* (AmL); **3** (means of expression): **she found an ~let for her feelings** encontró cómo canalizar sus sentimientos; **4** (Busn, Marketing) punto *m* de venta; **retail ~let** tienda *f* al por menor

outline[1] /'aʊtlaɪn/ *n*

A **1** (contour) contorno *m* **2** (shape) perfil *m*

B (summary): **a brief ~ of events so far** un breve resumen de lo sucedido hasta ahora

outline[2] *vt* **1** (sketch) ‹*shape*› bosquejar; ‹*map*› trazar*; **the trees stood ~d against the sky** el perfil de los árboles se recortaba contra el cielo **2** (summarize) esbozar*, explicar* resumidamente, dar* una idea general de

out: **~live** /'aʊt'lɪv/ *vt* sobrevivir a; **~look** *n* **1** (attitude) punto *m* de vista; **~look ON sth** actitud *f* ANTE algo **2** (prospects) perspectivas *fpl*; **the ~look for tomorrow** (Meteo) la previsión del tiempo para mañana, las perspectivas para mañana **3** (view) (esp BrE) vista *f*, panorama *m*; **~lying** *adj* (*before n*) ‹*villages/islands*› alejado, distante; ‹*area/hills/suburbs*› de la periferia; **~maneuver**, (BrE) **~manoeuvre** /'aʊtmə'nuːvər || ˌaʊtmə'nuːvə(r)/ *vt* ‹*opponent*› mostrarse* más hábil que; ‹*vehicle/plane*› ser* más maniobrable que; **~moded** /'aʊt'məʊdəd || ˌaʊt'məʊdɪd/ *adj* anticuado, pasado de moda; **~number** /'aʊt'nʌmbər || ˌaʊt'nʌmbə(r)/ *vt* superar en número a; **they were ~numbered (by) two to one** los doblaban en número

out of *prep*

A (from inside): **it fell ~ ~ her hand** se le cayó de la mano; **(come) ~ ~ there!** ¡salgan de ahí!; **to look ~ ~ the window** mirar (hacia afuera) por la ventana

B **1** (outside): **I was ~ ~ the room for two minutes** estuve dos minutos fuera *or* (AmL tb) afuera de la habitación; **I want you ~ ~ those wet clothes/this office immediately** haz el favor de quitarte esa ropa mojada/salir de esta oficina inmediatamente **2** (distant from): **100 miles ~ ~ Murmansk** (Naut) a 100 millas de Murmansk

C (eliminated, excluded): **Korea is ~ ~ the tournament** Corea ha quedado eliminada; **he was left ~ ~ the team** no lo incluyeron en el equipo; ***to be/feel* ~ ~ *it*** (colloq) sentirse* excluido

D 1 (indicating source, origin) de; **you look like something ~ ~ a horror movie** pareces salido de una película de terror 2 (indicating substance, makeup) de; **made ~ ~ steel** hecho de acero 3 (indicating motive) por; **~ ~ charity** por caridad

E (from among) de; **eight ~ ~ ten people** ocho de cada diez personas

F (indicating lack): **we're ~ ~ bread** nos hemos quedado sin pan, no nos queda pan

out: **~-of-date** /ˈaʊtəvˈdeɪt/ *adj* (*pred* **~ of date**) ‹*ideas/technology*› desfasado, obsoleto, perimido (RPl); ‹*ticket/check*› caducado, vencido (AmL); ‹*clothes*› pasado de moda; **~ of doors** *adv* ▸ **outdoors**[1]; **~-of-doors** *n* (AmE) (+ *sing vb*) **the ~-of-doors** el aire libre, la naturaleza; **~-of-pocket** /ˈaʊtəvˈpɑːkət || ˌaʊtəvˈpɒkɪt/ *adj* (*pred* **~ of pocket**) 1 (Busn) (*before n*) **~-of-pocket expenses** desembolsos *mpl* varios 2 (*pred*): **the deal left them ~ of pocket** perdieron dinero en el trato; **~-of-the-way** /ˈaʊtəvðəˈweɪ/ *adj* ‹*place*› apartado, poco conocido; **~patient** *n* paciente ambulatorio, -ria *m,f*, paciente externo, -na *m,f*; **~patients** *n* (+ *sing vb*) consultas *fpl* (*para pacientes externos*); **~perform** /ˌaʊtpərˈfɔːrm || ˌaʊtpəˈfɔːm/ *vt* 1 (perform better than) ‹*employee/car*› superar 2 (be more profitable than) ‹*index/benchmark*› sobrepasar; **~placement** /ˈaʊtpleɪsmənt/ *n* [u] outplacement *m* (*asesoría, apoyo y capacitación a los trabajadores que son despedidos a fin de que se reintegren al mercado laboral en el menor tiempo posible*); **~play** /ˈaʊtˈpleɪ/ *vt* jugar* mejor que; **~post** *n* 1 (Mil) avanzada *f* 2 (settlement) puesto *m* de avanzada; **~pouring** *n*: **the ~pourings of a tormented soul** el desahogo de un alma atormentada

output[1] /ˈaʊtpʊt/ *n* [u c]

A 1 (of factory) producción *f*; (of worker, machine) rendimiento *m* 2 (literary, artistic) producción *f* 3 (Comput) salida *f*

B (Elec) salida *f*

output[2] *vt* (*pres p* **-putting**; *past & past p* **-put** *or* **-putted**) imprimir*

outrage[1] /ˈaʊtreɪdʒ/ *n* 1 [c] (cruel act) atrocidad *f*; (terrorist act) atentado *m* 2 [c] (scandal) escándalo *m*; **~ AGAINST sth/sb** atropello *m* CONTRA *or* A algo/algn 3 [u] (feeling) **~ (AT sth)** indignación *f* (ANTE algo)

outrage[2] *vt* 1 (offend) indignar, ultrajar (frml); **to be ~d AT sth** indignarse ANTE algo 2 (scandalize) escandalizar*

outrageous /aʊtˈreɪdʒəs/ *adj* 1 (scandalous) ‹*behavior/state of affairs*› vergonzoso, escandaloso, atroz; ‹*injustice*› indignante, atroz; ‹*manners/language*› injurioso; ‹*demands/price*› escandaloso, exorbitante, abusivo; **how dare you! this is ~!** ¡cómo te atreves! ¡esto es intolerable! 2 (unconventional) ‹*clothes*› extravagante, estrafalario; **he tries hard to be ~** se esfuerza por resultar atrevido *or* por escandalizar

outrageously /aʊtˈreɪdʒəsli/ *adv* 1 (scandalously): **they treated her ~** fue indignante *or* escandaloso cómo la trataron 2 (unconventionally) ‹*dress*› de modo extravagante *or* estrafalario; **an ~ funny play** una obra desternillante

out: **~ran** /ˈaʊtˈræn/ *past of* **outrun**; **~rank** /ˈaʊtˈræŋk/ *vt* estar* jerárquicamente por encima de; **~reach** /ˈaʊtriːtʃ/ *n* [u] (extent of influence) alcance *m*; (*before n*) **~reach worker** (in UK) *funcionario de los Servicios Sociales cuyo cometido es promover la solicitud de ciertas prestaciones o ayudas sociales por parte de los individuos o grupos que tienen derecho a ellas*

outright[1] /ˈaʊtraɪt/ *adj* (*before n*) ‹*refusal/opposition*› rotundo, total, categórico; ‹*hostility*› declarado, abierto; ‹*majority*› claro; ‹*winner*› indiscutido; ‹*lie*› descarado

outright[2] *adv* 1 (completely) ‹*refuse/reject*› rotundamente, categóricamente, terminantemente; ‹*ban*› totalmente; ‹*win*› indiscutiblemente 2 (directly, frankly) ‹*ask/say*› abiertamente, directamente 3 (instantly) ‹*kill*› en el acto

out: **~run** /ˈaʊtˈrʌn/ *vt* (*pres p* **-running**; *past* **-ran**; *past p* **-run**) ‹*competitor/pursuer*› dejar atrás; **~sell** /ˈaʊtˈsel/ *vt* (*past and past p* **-sold**) ‹*product*› venderse más que; **~set** *n*: **from the ~set** desde el principio *or* comienzo, de entrada; **~shine** /ˈaʊtˈʃaɪn/ *vt* (*past & past p* **-shone**) eclipsar

outside[1] /ˈaʊtˈsaɪd/ *n*

A 1 (exterior part) exterior *m*; (surface) parte *f* de fuera *or* (esp AmL) de afuera; **the house looks really nice from the ~** la casa parece muy bonita vista desde (a)fuera; **on the ~ she appeared very calm** aparentemente estaba muy tranquila, por fuera parecía muy tranquila 2 (of road): **he overtook me on the ~** me adelantó por la izquierda; (in UK etc) me adelantó por la derecha

B **the ~** 1 (of group, organization): **to be on the ~ looking in** ser* un mero espectador; **seen from the ~** visto desde fuera *or* (esp AmL) desde afuera 2 (of prison) (colloq) fuera, afuera (esp AmL); **he's got a friend on the ~** tiene un amigo (a)fuera

C **at the (very) outside** como máximo, a lo sumo

outside[2] *adv* 1 (place) fuera, afuera (esp AmL) 2 (outdoors) fuera, afuera (esp AmL); **what's it like ~?** ¿qué tiempo hace (a)fuera? 3 (indicating movement): **to run ~** salir* corriendo

outside[3] *prep* 1 (of a place) fuera de; **you wear the blouse ~ the skirt** la blusa se lleva por fuera (de la falda); **it's just ~ London** está en las afueras de Londres; **it's five miles ~ Oxford** está a cinco millas de Oxford; **I'll see you ~ the theater** te veo en la puerta del teatro 2 (beyond) fuera de; **it's ~ my responsibilities** no está dentro de mis responsabilidades 3 (in time): **~ office hours** fuera del horario de oficina; **only 2 seconds ~ the world record** sólo a 2 segundos del récord mundial

outside[4] *adj* (*before n*)

A 1 (exterior, outward) exterior 2 (outdoor) ‹*toilet*› fuera de la vivienda, exterior; ‹*swimming pool*› descubierto, al aire libre 3 (outer) exterior; **the ~ lane** (Auto) el carril *or* (Chi) la pista *or* (Ur) la senda de la izquierda; (in UK etc) el carril *or* la pista *etc* de la derecha; (Sport) el carril (AmL) *or* (Esp) la calle número ocho (*or* seis *etc*) 4 (external) ‹*interference/pressure*› externo; **the ~ world** el mundo exterior

B (remote) ‹*chance*› remoto

outside of *prep* (AmE colloq) fuera de

outsider /ˈaʊtˈsaɪdər || ˌaʊtˈsaɪdə(r)/ *n* 1 (person not belonging) persona *f* de fuera, afuerano, -na *m,f* 2 (in competition): **he was beaten by an ~** fue derrotado por un desconocido (*un competidor que se consideraba tenía pocas probabilidades de ganar*); **a rank ~** un segundón

out: **~size** /ˈaʊtˈsaɪz/, (esp AmE) **~-sized** /-d/ *adj* (Clothing) de talla *or* (RPl) talle gigante; (very large) gigantesco, enorme; **~skirts** *pl n* afueras *fpl*, alrededores *mpl*, extrarradio *m*; **~smart** /ˈaʊtˈsmɑːrt || ˌaʊtˈsmɑːt/ *vt* (esp AmE colloq) burlar; **~sold** /ˈaʊtˈsəʊld/ *past & past p of* **outsell**; **~source** /aʊtˈsɔːrs || aʊtˈsɔːs/ *vt* ‹*work/service*› externalizar*; ‹*goods/components*› externalizar*, adquirir ... de fuentes externas; **~sourcing** /aʊtˈsɔːrsɪŋ || aʊtˈsɔːsɪŋ/ *n* [u] externalización *f*; **~spoken** /ˈaʊtˈspəʊkən/ *adj* ‹*criticism/person*› directo, franco; **she was ~spoken in her condemnation** fue categórica al expresar su condena; **~spread** /ˈaʊtˈspred/ *adj* ‹*wings*› extendido, desplegado; **~standing** /aʊtˈstændɪŋ/ *adj* 1 (excellent) ‹*ability/beauty*› extraordinario, excepcional; ‹*achievement/performer*› destacado 2 (prominent) (*before n*) ‹*feature*› destacado; 3 (unpaid) ‹*debt/account*› pendiente (de pago) 4 (remaining) ‹*request/problem*› pendiente, por resolver 5 (AmE) **~standing stock** *o* **shares** acciones *fpl* en circulación

outstandingly /aʊtˈstændɪŋli/ *adv* excepcionalmente, extraordinariamente

out: **~stay** /ˈaʊtˈsteɪ/ *vt* **to ~stay one's welcome**: **I don't want to ~stay my welcome** no quiero abusar de la hospitalidad; **I think we've ~stayed our welcome** creo que nos hemos quedado más de la cuenta; **~stretched** /ˈaʊtˈstretʃt/ *adj* extendido; **~strip** /ˈaʊtˈstrɪp/ *vt* **-pp-** 1 (run faster than): **to ~strip a runner** tomarle la delantera a *or* aventajar a un corredor 2 (exceed) sobrepasar; **~vote** /ˈaʊtˈvəʊt/ *vt*: **to be ~voted** perder* la votación

outward[1] /ˈaʊtwərd || ˈaʊtwəd/ *adj* (*before n*) 1 ‹*appearance*› exterior; ‹*sign*› externo; **his ~ cheerfulness** su aparente buen humor 2 ‹*journey/flight*› de ida

outward[2], (BrE also) **outwards** /-z/ *adv* hacia afuera, hacia el exterior

outward bound *adj*: **the ship was ~ ~** el barco hacía su viaje de ida

O

outwardly /'aʊtwərdli || 'aʊtwədli/ *adv* en apariencia, aparentemente

out: ~weigh /'aʊt'weɪ/ *vt* ser* mayor que; **the rewards far ~weigh the difficulties** la recompensa compensa con creces las dificultades; **~wit** /'aʊt'wɪt/ *vt* **-tt-** burlar; **~worker** *n* (Busn) *persona que realiza trabajo en su domicilio*; **~worn** /'aʊt'wɔːrn || ,aʊt'wɔːn/ *adj* ‹*joke/slogan/metaphor*› trillado, manido; ‹*belief/custom*› desfasado, perimido (RPl)

oval¹ /'əʊvəl/ *n* óvalo *m*

oval² *adj* ovalado, oval; **the O~ Office** (in US) el despacho oval, el despacho del presidente

ovarian /əʊ'veriən || əʊ'veəriən/ *adj* ovárico

ovary /'əʊvəri/ *n* (*pl* **-ries**) ovario *m*

ovation /əʊ'veɪʃən/ *n* (frml) ovación *f* (frml); **he got a standing ~ from the delegates** los delegados se pusieron de pie para aplaudirlo *or* (frml) para ovacionarlo

oven /'ʌvən/ *n* horno *m*; **~ baked** hecho al horno, horneado; **it's like an ~ in here!** (colloq) ¡esto es un horno! (fam); (*before n*) **~ glove** *o* **mitt** guante *m or* manopla *f* para el horno

oven: ~proof *adj* refractario, de horno; **~-ready** /'ʌvən'redi/ *adj* listo para el horno; **~ware** /'ʌvənwer || 'ʌvənweə(r)/ *n* [u] vajilla *f* refractaria

over¹ /'əʊvər || 'əʊvə(r)/ *adv*

(Sense I)

A 1 (across): **come ~ here!** ¡ven aquí!; **look ~ there!** ¡mira allí!; **he came ~ to say hello** vino *or* se acercó a saludar; **she called me ~** me llamó (desde el otro lado); **you must come ~ sometime!** ¡tienes que venir un día!; **I'll be right ~** enseguida estoy allí; **he reached ~ and took the money** se estiró y tomó el dinero; **we can jump ~** podemos saltar por encima; **the journey ~ to/from France** el viaje hasta/desde Francia; **how did you come? — I drove/flew ~** ¿cómo viniste? — en coche/avión 2 (overhead) por encima; **a plane flies ~ every five minutes** pasa un avión cada cinco minutos

B 1 (in another place): **she was sitting ~ there/here** estaba sentada allí/aquí; **~ on the far bank** en la otra orilla; **he's ~ in England** está en Inglaterra; **she's ~ from London** ha venido de Londres; **how long are you ~ (here) for?** ¿cuánto tiempo te vas a quedar (aquí)?; ▸**come over, go over** 2 (on other page, TV station etc): **see ~** véase al dorso; **for the latest news, ~ to New York** para las últimas noticias, conectamos ahora con Nueva York 3 (Rad, Telec) corto; **~ and out!** corto y fuera

C 1 (out of upright position): **to knock sth ~** tirar *or* (AmL exc RPl) botar algo (de un golpe); **to tip sth ~** volcar* algo 2 (onto other side): **let's get her ~ onto her back** pongámosla boca arriba; *see also* **turn over D**

(Sense II)

A (finished): **the film was ~ by 11 o'clock** la película terminó *or* acabó antes de las 11; **it's all ~ between us** lo nuestro se ha acabado, ya no hay nada entre nosotros; **the worst is ~** ya ha pasado lo peor; ***to be ~ (and done) with*** haber* terminado *or* acabado

B (remaining): **if you have any material ~** si te sobra *or* te queda tela; **3 into 10 goes 3 and 1 ~** 10 dividido (por) 3 cabe a 3 y sobra 1

C 1 (*as intensifier*): **twice/ten times ~** dos/diez veces 2 (again) (AmE) otra vez; **we had to start ~** tuvimos que volver a empezar

D (more) más; **all words of six letters and ~** todas las palabras de seis letras o más

E (excessively) ‹*careful/aggressive*› demasiado

(Sense III) (*in phrases*)

A **all over** 1 (everywhere) por todas partes; **I've been looking all ~ for you** te he estado buscando por todas partes 2 (over entire surface): **the tabletop is scratched all ~** el tablero de la mesa está todo rayado; **I'm aching/itching all ~** me duele/pica todo (el cuerpo) 3 (through and through) (colloq): **that's her/Dee all ~** eso es típico de ella/de Dee 4 (finished) **to be all ~** *see Sense* **II A**

B **(all) over again**: **to start (all) ~ again** volver* a empezar (desde cero), empezar* de nuevo

C **over and over** (repeatedly) una y otra vez; (rolling): **turning ~ and ~ as it fell** rodando al caer

over² *prep*

(Sense I)

A (across): **he jumped ~ the fence** saltó (por encima de) la valla; **they built a bridge ~ the river** construyeron un puente sobre el río; **she peered ~ his shoulder** atisbó por encima de su hombro; **to sling sth ~ one's shoulder** colgarse* algo del hombro; **they live ~ the road** (BrE) viven en frente

B 1 (above) encima de; **the portrait hangs ~ the fireplace** el retrato está colgado encima de *or* (AmL tb) arriba de la chimenea; **a cold front ~ the Atlantic** un frente frío sobre el Atlántico 2 (Math) sobre

C (covering, on): **there are grilles ~ the windows** hay rejas en las ventanas; **snow was falling ~ the countryside** nevaba sobre la campiña; **my room looks out ~ the square** mi habitación da a la plaza; **he pulled his hat down ~ his eyes** se encasquetó el sombrero tapándose los ojos; **he put a coat on ~ his pajamas** se puso un abrigo encima del pijama; **she hit me ~ the head with her stick** me dio con el bastón en la cabeza

D 1 (through, all around): **to show sb ~ a building/an estate** mostrarle* *or* (esp Esp) enseñarle un edificio/una finca a algn; **~ an area of 50km²** en un área de 50km²; **I've been ~ the details with her** he repasado los detalles con ella; **we've been ~ and ~ what happened** hemos vuelto una y otra vez sobre lo que sucedió 2 (referring to experiences, illnesses): **is she ~ her measles yet?** ¿ya se ha repuesto del sarampión?; **we're ~ the worst now** ya hemos pasado lo peor; **he isn't ~ her yet** todavía la quiere

E (during, in the course of): **~ the past/next few years** en *or* durante los últimos/próximos años; **we can discuss it ~ lunch** podemos hablarlo mientras comemos; **we'll be in Italy ~ the summer** pasaremos el verano en Italia; **spread (out) ~ a six-week period** a lo largo de seis semanas, en un plazo de seis semanas

F (by the medium of) por; **~ the loudspeaker** por el altavoz

G (about, on account of): **to cry ~ sth** llorar por algo; **they argued ~ money** discutieron por asuntos de dinero

H **all over** 1 (over entire surface of): **there are black marks all ~ the floor** hay marcas negras por todo el suelo; ***to be all ~ sb*** (colloq) (defeat heavily) darle* una paliza a algn (fam); (be demonstrative toward): **they were all ~ each other** estaban de lo más acaramelados (fam) 2 (throughout): **all ~ town** por toda la ciudad; **I've been all ~ the place looking for you** te he estado buscando por todas partes

(Sense II)

A 1 (more than) más de; **think of a number ~ 10** piensa en un número mayor de *or* que 10 2 **over and above** (in addition to) además de

B 1 (senior to) por encima de 2 (indicating superiority) sobre; **to have control ~ sb/sth** tener* control sobre algn/algo

C (in comparison to): **sales are up 20% ~ last year** las ventas han aumentado un 20% con respecto al año pasado; **she has one great advantage ~ her rivals** tiene una gran ventaja sobre sus rivales

over³ *n* (in cricket) over *m* (*serie de seis lanzamientos*)

over- /'əʊvər || 'əʊvə(r)/ *pref* 1 (excessively) demasiado, excesivamente; *see also* **overeat, oversleep** *etc* 2 (in deliberate understatement): **she wasn't ~enthusiastic** no demostró mucho entusiasmo que digamos

over: ~abundance /'əʊvərə'bʌndəns/ *n* (*no pl*) superabundancia *f*; **~abundant** /'əʊvərə'bʌndənt/ *adj* superabundante; **~achieve** /'əʊvərə'tʃiːv/ *vi* rendir* más de lo esperado; **~act** /'əʊvər'ækt/ *vi* sobreactuar*; **~active** /'əʊvər'æktɪv/ *adj* ‹*imagination/mind*› febril; ‹*thyroid/gland*› hiperactivo

overall¹ /'əʊvərɔːl/ *adj* (*before n*) ‹*length*› total; ‹*result/reduction/cost*› global; **the ~ impression** la impresión general *or* de conjunto; **he was the ~ winner** fue (el) campeón absoluto

overall² *adv*: **she was third ~** quedó tercera en la clasificación general; **~, one could say that ...** (*indep*) en términos generales podría decirse que ...

overall³ *n*

A (protective garment) (esp BrE) bata *f*, túnica *f*

B **overalls** *pl* 1 (dungarees) (AmE) overol *m* (AmL), (pantalones *mpl* de) peto *m* (Esp), mameluco *m* (CS) 2 (boiler suit)

(BrE) overol *m* (AmL), mono *m* (Esp)

over: **~anxious** /'əʊvər'æŋkʃəs/ *adj* aprensivo; ‹*parent*› sobreprotector; **~arm** *adv* (esp BrE) por encima de la cabeza; **~ate** /'əʊvər'et/ *past of* **overeat**; **~awe** /'əʊvər'ɔː/ *vt* intimidar; **we were ~awed** nos sentimos sobrecogidos; **~balance** /'əʊvər'bæləns || ˌəʊvə 'bæləns/ *vi* perder* el equilibrio; **~bearing** /'əʊvər 'berɪŋ || ˌɛʊvə'beərɪŋ/ *adj* autoritario, dominante; **~blown** /'əʊvər'bləʊn || ˌəʊvə'bləʊn/ *adj* ‹*rhetoric/prose*› ampuloso, rimbombante; **~board** *adv*: **man ~board!** ¡hombre al agua!; **they threw him ~board** lo echaron por la borda; ***to go ~board*** (colloq): **there's no need to go ~board** no hay por qué exagerar, tampoco hay que pasarse (fam); **~book** /'əʊvər'bʊk || ˌəʊvə'bʊk/ *vt*: **the flight was ~booked** habían aceptado demasiadas reservas *or* (AmL tb) reservaciones para el vuelo; *vi* sobrecontratar (*aceptar reservas por encima del número de plazas disponibles*); **~burden** /'əʊvər'bɜːrdn || ˌəʊvə'bɜːdn/ *vt* **to ~burden sb (WITH sth)**: **they ~burdened her with work** la sobrecargaron de trabajo; **~came** /'əʊvər'keɪm || ˌəʊvə'keɪm/ *past of* **~come**; **~cast** *adj* ‹*sky*› cubierto; ‹*day*› nublado; **~charge** /'əʊvər'tʃɑːrdʒ || ˌəʊvə'tʃɑːdʒ/ *vt* **to ~charge sb (FOR sth)** cobrarle de más A algn (POR algo); *vi* **to ~charge (FOR sth)** cobrar de más (POR algo); **~coat** *n* abrigo *m*, sobretodo *m* (esp RPl); **~come** /'əʊvər'kʌm || ˌəʊvə'kʌm/ (*past* **-came**; *past p* **-come**) *vt* 1 ‹*opponent*› reducir*, vencer* 2 (overwhelm) invadir, apoderarse de; **to be ~come BY sth**: **he was ~come by sleep/fatigue** lo venció el sueño/la fatiga; **they were ~come by emotion** los embargó la emoción; **to be ~come WITH sth** ‹*with guilt/remorse*› sentirse* abrumado POR algo 3 (prevail over) ‹*fear*› superar, dominar, vencer*; ‹*inhibitions*› vencer*; *vi*: **we shall ~come** venceremos; **~compensate** /'əʊvər'kɑːmpənseɪt || ˌəʊvə 'kɒmpenseɪt/ *vi* sobrecompensar; **to ~compensate FOR sth** sobrecompensar algo; **~confident** /'əʊvər'kɑːnfədənt || ˌəʊvə'kɒnfɪdənt/ *adj* ‹*person*› demasiado seguro de sí mismo, suficiente; ‹*prediction*› demasiado confiado; **~cook** /'əʊvər'kʊk || ˌəʊvə'kʊk/ *vt* cocinar demasiado, recocer*, dejar pasar; **~crowded** /'əʊvər'kraʊdəd || ˌəʊvə'kraʊdɪd/ *adj* abarrotado *or* atestado (de gente); ‹*country*› superpoblado; **our universities are ~crowded** nuestras universidades están masificadas; **~crowding** /'əʊvər'kraʊdɪŋ || ˌəʊvə'kraʊdɪŋ/ *n* [u]: **they complained about the ~crowding on the trains** se quejaron de lo abarrotados que iban los trenes; **the severe ~crowding in our prisons** el hacinamiento en nuestras cárceles; **~developed** /'əʊvərdɪ'veləpt || ˌəʊvədɪ'veləpt/ *adj* ‹*muscles/imagination*› excesivamente desarrollado; **~do** /'əʊvər'duː || ˌəʊvə'duː/ *vt* (*3rd pers sing pres* **-does**; *past* **-did**; *past p* **-done**) 1 (exaggerate) exagerar, pasarse con (fam); ***to ~do it, to ~do things*** (go too far) írsele la mano a algn; (overexert oneself) exigir* demasiado; 2 (Culin) cocinar demasiado, recocer*, dejar pasar; **~done** /'əʊvər'dʌn || ˌəʊvə'dʌn/ *adj* 1 (exaggerated) exagerado; 2 (Culin) recocido

overdose¹ /'əʊvərdəʊs || 'əʊvədəʊs/ *n* sobredosis *f*; **to take an ~** tomar una sobredosis

overdose² *vi* **to ~ ON sth** tomar una sobredosis de algo

over: **~draft** *n* descubierto *m*, sobregiro *m*; (*before n*) **~draft facility** crédito *m* al descubierto; **~draw** /'əʊvər'drɔː || ˌəʊvə'drɔː/ (*past* **-drew**; *past p* **-drawn**) *vt* (Fin): **I'm ~drawn** tengo un descubierto, estoy sobregirado; *vi* (BrE Fin) girar al descubierto, sobregirarse; **~drive** /'əʊvərdraɪv || 'əʊvədraɪv/ *n* superdirecta *f*; **~due** /'əʊvər'duː || ˌəʊvə'djuː/ *adj*: **the book is a month ~due** el plazo de devolución del libro venció hace un mes; **payment is now ~due** el plazo ha vencido y se requiere pago inmediato; **such measures are long ~due** tales medidas deberían haberse adoptado mucho antes; **she's a week ~due** debería haber dado a luz hace una semana, salió de cuentas hace una semana (Esp); **to be ~due FOR sth**: **you're ~due for promotion** hace tiempo que te deberían haber ascendido; **~eat** /'əʊvər'iːt/ *vi* (*past* **-ate**; *past p* **-eaten**) comer demasiado, sobrealimentarse; **~estimate** /'əʊvər'estəmeɪt || ˌəʊvər'estɪmeɪt/ *vt* ‹*cost/strength*› sobreestimar; ‹*importance*› exagerar; **~excited** /'əʊvərɪk'saɪtəd || ˌəʊvərɪk'saɪtɪd/ *adj* sobreexcitado; **~exert** /'əʊvərɪg'zɜːrt || ˌəʊvərɪg'zɜːt/ *v refl* **to ~exert oneself** hacer* un esfuerzo excesivo; **~expose** /'əʊvərɪk'spəʊz/ *vt* (Phot) sobreexponer*; **~feed** /'əʊvər'fiːd || ˌəʊvə'fiːd/ *vt* (*past & past p* **-fed**) sobrealimentar

overflow¹ /'əʊvər'fləʊ || ˌəʊvə'fləʊ/ *vi* 1 «*liquid*» derramarse, desbordarse; «*bucket/bath/river*» desbordarse; **the party had ~ed into the garden** la fiesta se había extendido al jardín; **to fill sth to ~ing** llenar algo hasta el borde 2 (be more than full of) **to ~ WITH sth**: **the house is ~ing with junk** la casa está hasta el techo de cachivaches

■ **overflow** *vt* (flow over) desbordar

overflow² /'əʊverfləʊ || 'əʊvəfləʊ/ *n* 1 [u c] (excess): **we put a bowl there to catch the ~** pusimos un bol para recoger el líquido que se derramaba *or* que salía; **the ~ from the church stood outside** los que no cabían en la iglesia se quedaron fuera 2 [c] (outlet) rebosadero *m*

over: **~grown** /'əʊvər'grəʊn || ˌəʊvə'grəʊn/ *adj* 1 ‹*garden*› lleno de maleza, abandonado; **to be ~grown WITH sth** estar* cubierto DE algo 2 (too big) demasiado grande; **~hand** *adv* (AmE) por encima de la cabeza

overhang¹ /'əʊvər'hæŋ || ˌəʊvə'hæŋ/ (*past & past p* **-hung**) *vt* sobresalir* por encima de

■ **overhang** *vi* sobresalir*; **he tried to grab an ~ing branch** trató de agarrarse de una rama que colgaba por encima

overhang² /'əʊvərhæŋ || 'əʊvəhæŋ/ *n* saliente *f or* (Esp) *m*

overhaul¹ /'əʊvər'hɔːl || ˌəʊvə'hɔːl/ *vt* (examine and repair) ‹*machinery/car/system*› revisar, poner* a punto

overhaul² /'əʊvərhɔːl || 'əʊvəhɔːl/ *n* (of machinery, system) revisión *f* (general), puesta *f* a punto, overjol *m* (AmC)

overhead¹ /'əʊvər'hed || ˌəʊvə'hed/ *adv*: **the lights shone ~** las luces brillaban en lo alto; **the sun was directly ~** el sol caía de pleno; **a plane flew ~** pasó un avión

overhead² /'əʊvərhed || 'əʊvəhed/ *adj*

A 1 (high up) ‹*cable*› aéreo; ‹*railway*› elevado 2 (Sport) por encima de la cabeza

B (Busn, Fin) (*before n*) ‹*costs/charges*› indirecto, general, de estructura

overhead projector *n* retroproyector *m*

overheads /'əʊvərhedz || 'əʊvəhedz/ *pl n*[c u] (BrE) gastos *mpl* indirectos *or* generales *or* de estructura

over: **~hear** /'əʊvər'hɪr || ˌəʊvə'hiə(r)/ *vt* (*past & past p* **-heard**) oír* (*por casualidad*); **I ~heard her talking about me** la oí hablar de mí

■ **over** *vi*: **excuse me, but I couldn't help ~hearing** perdone, pero no pude evitar escuchar lo que decía (*or* dijo *etc*); **~heat** /'əʊvər'hiːt || ˌəʊvə'hiːt/ *vi* recalentarse*; **~heated** /əʊvər'hiːtəd || ˌəʊvə'hiːtɪd/ *adj* recalentado; ‹*person/argument*› acalorado; **~hung** *past & past p of* **overhang¹**; **~indulge** /'əʊvərɪn'dʌldʒ/ *vi* excederse; **to ~indulge IN sth** abusar DE algo

■ **over** *vt* ‹*child*› consentir* demasiado; **I ~indulged my fondness for chocolate** comí todo el chocolate que se me antojó, me dejé llevar por mi pasión por el chocolate; **~indulgence** /'əʊvərɪn'dʌldʒəns/ *n* [u] 1 (lenience) consentimiento *m* (excesivo) 2 (having too much) **~indulgence (IN sth)** ‹*in food/drink*› abuso *m* (DE algo); **~indulgent** /'əʊvərɪn'dʌldʒənt/ *adj* demasiado blando, que lo consiente todo; **~joyed** /'əʊvər'dʒɔɪd || ˌəʊvə'dʒɔɪd/ *adj* encantado, rebosante de alegría; **to be ~joyed AT/ABOUT sth**: **I was ~joyed at the news** la noticia me causó gran alegría; **they are ~joyed about the baby** están que no caben en sí de alegría con el niño; **~kill** *n* [u] exageración *f*; **~laid** /'əʊvər'leɪd || ˌəʊvə'leɪd/ *past & past p of* **overlay¹**; **~land** *adj/adv* por tierra

overlap¹ /'əʊvər'læp || ˌəʊvə'læp/ **-pp-** *vi* 1 «*tiles/planks*» estar* montados unos sobre otros, traslaparse 2 «*responsibilities*» coincidir en parte; **our vacations ~ by one week** durante una semana estamos los dos de vacaciones

■ **overlap** *vt* ‹*boards/planks*› colocar* montados unos sobre otros, traslapar

overlap² /'əʊvərlæp || 'əʊvəlæp/ *n* [u c]: **there will be an inch ~ on either side** se traslaparán una pulgada por cada lado; **there will be a period of ~ between the two**

secretaries las dos secretarias coincidirán durante un tiempo

overlay[1] /'əʊvər'leɪ || ˌəʊvə'leɪ/ *vt* (*past & past p* **-laid**) **to ~ sth WITH sth** recubrir* algo DE algo

overlay[2] /'əʊvərleɪ || 'əʊvəleɪ/ *n* revestimiento *m*

overleaf /'əʊvər'li:f || ˌəʊvə'li:f/ *adv* al dorso; **see ~** véase al dorso

overload[1] /'əʊvər'ləʊd || ˌəʊvə'ləʊd/ *vt* sobrecargar*; **we are ~ed with work** estamos agobiados de trabajo

■ **overload** *vi* sobrecargarse*

overload[2] /'əʊvərləʊd || 'əʊvələʊd/ *n* [u] (Elec) sobrecarga *f*

overlook /'əʊvər'lʊk || ˌəʊvə'lʊk/ *vt*

A 1 (not notice) pasar por alto 2 (disregard) disculpar, dejar pasar 3 (pass over): **he was ~ed for promotion** no lo tuvieron en cuenta para el ascenso

B (have view over): **a room ~ing the sea** una habitación con vista al mar *or* que da al mar

overly /'əʊvərli || 'əʊvəli/ *adv* demasiado

over: **~manned** /'əʊvər'mænd || ˌəʊvə'mænd/ *adj* ‹*factory/office*› con demasiado personal; ‹*ship*› con excesiva tripulación; **~manning** /'əʊvər'mænɪŋ || ˌəʊvə'mænɪŋ/ *n* [u] exceso *m* de personal/tripulación; **~much** /'əʊvər'mʌtʃ || ˌəʊvə'mʌtʃ/ *adv* en exceso, en demasía (frml)

overnight[1] /'əʊvər'naɪt || ˌəʊvə'naɪt/ *adv* 1 (through the night): **to stay ~** quedarse a pasar la noche, hacer* noche; **there had been a heavy fall of snow ~** durante la noche había nevado mucho; **soak the chickpeas ~** ponga los garbanzos en remojo la noche anterior 2 (suddenly) ‹*change/disappear*› de la noche a la mañana

overnight[2] /'əʊvərnaɪt || 'əʊvənaɪt/*adj* 1 (through the night) ‹*journey*› de noche; ‹*stay*› de una noche 2 (sudden) ‹*change/success*› repentino; **she became an ~ sensation** de la noche a la mañana, empezó a causar sensación

overnight[3] /ˌəʊvər'naɪt || ˌəʊvə'naɪt/ *vt* (convey at night) (AmC) transportar durante la noche

■ **overnight** *vi* (stay for the night) pasar la noche, hacer* noche, pernoctar (frml)

overnight bag *n* bolso *m* de viaje *or* de fin de semana, fin *m* de semana (Esp)

overpaid[1] /'əʊvər'peɪd || ˌəʊvə'peɪd/ *past & past p of* **overpay**

overpaid[2] *adj*: **she's ~** le pagan demasiado; **he's vastly ~, considering what he does** le pagan un dineral para lo que hace

over: **~pass** *n* paso *m* elevado, paso *m* a desnivel (Méx); **~pay** /'əʊvər'peɪ || ˌəʊvə'peɪ/ *vt* (*past & past p* **-paid**) (deliberately) pagarle* demasiado *or* en exceso a; (in error) pagarle* de más a; **~play** /'əʊvər'pleɪ || ˌəʊvə'pleɪ/ *vt* ‹*problem*› exagerar; **to ~play the importance of sth** darle* demasiada importancia a algo; **~populated** /'əʊvər'pɑ:pjəleɪtəd || ˌəʊvə'pɒpjʊleɪtɪd/ *adj* superpoblado, sobrepoblado (AmL); **~power** /'əʊvər'paʊər || ˌəʊvə'paʊə(r)/ *vt* 1 (render helpless) dominar 2 (affect greatly) «*smell*» marear; «*heat*» sofocar*, agobiar; «*emotion*» abrumar; **~powering** /'əʊvər'paʊrɪŋ || ˌəʊvə'paʊərɪŋ/ *adj* 1 ‹*smell*› muy fuerte, embriagador (liter); ‹*heat*› aplastante, agobiante; ‹*desire*› irresistible, inaguantable 2 ‹*personality*› apabullante, abrumador; **~price** /'əʊvər'praɪs || ˌəʊvə'praɪs/ *vt* ‹*product*› fijar un precio excesivo a; **the food is reasonable, but a little ~priced** la comida no es mala, pero un poco cara para lo que es; **~production** /'əʊvərprə'dʌkʃən || ˌəʊvəprə'dʌkʃən/ *n* [u] sobreproducción *f*, superproducción *f*; **~protect** /'əʊvərprə'tekt || ˌəʊvəprə'tekt/ *vt* sobreproteger*, proteger* demasiado; **~protective** /'əʊvərprə'tektɪv || ˌəʊvəprə'tektɪv/ *adj* sobreprotector; **he is ~protective toward** *o* **to his little brother** sobreprotege a su hermano pequeño; **~qualified** /'əʊvər'kwɑ:ləfaɪd || ˌəʊvə'kwɒlɪfaɪd/ *adj* con más titulación de la requerida; **~ran** /'əʊvər'ræn || ˌəʊvə'ræn/ *past of* **~run**; **~rated** /'əʊvər'reɪtəd || ˌəʊvə'reɪtɪd/ *adj* sobrevalorado, sobreestimado; **~reach** /'əʊvər'ri:tʃ || ˌəʊvə'ri:tʃ/ *v refl*: **to ~reach oneself** intentar hacer demasiado; **~react** /'əʊvərri'ækt || ˌəʊvəri'ækt/ *vi* reaccionar en forma exagerada; **to ~react TO sth** tener* una reacción exagerada FRENTE A algo; **~ride** /'əʊvər'raɪd || ˌəʊvə'raɪd/ *vt* (*past* **-rode**; *past p* **-ridden**) ‹*decision/recommendation*› invalidar, anular; ‹*wishes/advice*› hacer* caso omiso de; **~riding** /'əʊvər'raɪdɪŋ || ˌəʊvə'raɪdɪŋ/ *adj* ‹*importance/need/consideration*› primordial; ‹*priority*› absoluto; **~ripe** /'əʊvər'raɪp || ˌəʊvə'raɪp/ *adj* demasiado maduro, pasado; **~rode** /'əʊvər'rəʊd || ˌəʊvə'rəʊd/ *past of* **~ride**; **~rule** /'əʊvər'ru:l || ˌəʊvə'ru:l/ *vt* ‹*decision/verdict*› anular, invalidar; ‹*objection*› rechazar*, no admitir; **~run** /'əʊvər'rʌn || ˌəʊvə'rʌn/ (*past* **-ran**; *past p* **-run**) *vt* 1 (invade, swarm over) invadir; **to be ~run WITH sth** estar* plagado DE algo 2 (exceed) exceder

■ **over** *vi*: **the meeting ~ran by half an hour** la reunión se prolongó media hora más de lo previsto; **~saw** /'əʊvər'sɔ: || ˌəʊvə'sɔ:/ *past of* **oversee**

overseas[1] /'əʊvər'si:z || 'əʊvəˌsi:z/ *adj* (*before n*) ‹*trade*› exterior; ‹*investments/branches*› en el exterior *or* extranjero; ‹*student/visitor*› extranjero; ‹*news*› del exterior; **~ aid** (BrE) ayuda *f* a los países en vías de desarrollo

overseas[2] /'əʊvər'si:z || ˌəʊvə'si:z/ *adv* ‹*live*› en el extranjero; ‹*travel/send*› al extranjero

over: **~see** /'əʊvər'si: || ˌəʊvə'si:/ *vt* (*past* **-saw**; *past p* **-seen**) supervisar; **~seer** /'əʊvər'sɪr, -'si:ər || 'əʊvəsi:ə(r)/ *n* capataz *mf*, supervisor, -sora *m,f*; **~sensitive** /'əʊvər'sensətɪv || ˌəʊvə'sensɪtɪv/ *adj* demasiado susceptible; **~shadow** /'əʊvər'ʃædəʊ || ˌəʊvə'ʃædəʊ/ *vt* (diminish) eclipsar; **~shoe** /'əʊvərʃu: || 'əʊvəʃu:/ *n* chanclo *m or* (CS) galocha *f*; **~shoot** /'əʊvər'ʃu:t || ˌəʊvə'ʃu:t/ *vt* (*past & past p* **-shot**) ‹*runway*› salirse* de; ‹*turning*› pasarse de; ‹*target/budget*› exceder, rebasar; **~sight** /'əʊvərsaɪt || 'əʊvəsaɪt/ *n* [u c] (carelessness) descuido *m*; **~simplify** /'əʊvər'sɪmpləfaɪ || ˌəʊvə'sɪmplɪfaɪ/ *vt/i* **-fies, -fying, -fied** simplificar* excesivamente; **~size** /'əʊvər'saɪz || 'əʊvəsaɪz/, **~sized** *adj* (larger than normal) mayor de lo normal, extra grande; (too large) tremendo, descomunal; **~sleep** /'əʊvər'sli:p || ˌəʊvə'sli:p/ *vi* (*past & past p* **-slept**) quedarse dormido; **~spend** /'əʊvər'spend || ˌəʊvə'spend/ *vi* (*past & past p* **-spent**) gastar más de la cuenta; **I've overspent by £5** he gastado 5 libras de más; **~spill** *n* [u] excedente *m* de población; **~staffed** /'əʊvər'stæft || ˌəʊvə'stɑ:ft/ *adj* con exceso de personal *or* (Esp tb) de plantilla; **~staffing** /'əʊvər'stæfɪŋ || ˌəʊvə'stɑ:fɪŋ/ *n* [u] exceso *f* de personal *or* (Esp tb) de plantilla; **~state** /'əʊvər'steɪt || ˌəʊvə'steɪt/ *vt* exagerar; **~stay** /'əʊvər'steɪ || ˌəʊvə'steɪ/ *vt* ▸**outstay**; **~step** /'əʊvər'step || ˌəʊvə'step/ *vt* **-pp-** sobrepasar, rebasar, pasarse de; ▸**mark**[1] **C1**

overstock[1] /'əʊvər'stɑ:k || ˌəʊvə'stɒk/ *vt* abarrotar

■ **overstock** *vi* comprar de más

overstock[2] *n* excedentes *mpl* de stock, excedentes *mpl* de existencias; (*before n*) **~ sale** liquidación *f* de excedentes de stock *or* de existencias

over: **~stretch** /'əʊvər'stretʃ || ˌəʊvə'stretʃ/ *vt*: **the sales staff are ~stretched** los vendedores están trabajando al máximo; **the already ~stretched education system ...** el sistema educativo, cuyos recursos ya no dan más de sí ...; **~subscribed** /'əʊvərsəb'skraɪbd || ˌəʊvəsəb'skraɪbd/ *adj*: **the trip to London is already ~subscribed** el viaje a Londres ya está sobrevendido, ya hay demasiada gente anotada para el viaje a Londres; **the issue was ~subscribed** la demanda de acciones superó a la oferta

overt /əʊ'vɜ:rt || 'əʊvɜ:t/ *adj* ‹*hostility*› declarado, manifiesto; ‹*criticism*› abierto

over: **~take** /'əʊvər'teɪk || ˌəʊvə'teɪk/ (*past* **-took**; *past p* **-taken**) *vt* 1 (go past) ‹*horse/runner*› adelantar, pasar, rebasar (Méx) 2 (surpass) superar, tomarle la delantera a

■ **over** *vi* (BrE Auto) adelantar, rebasar (Méx); **~taking** /'əʊvər'teɪkɪŋ || ˌəʊvə'teɪkɪŋ/ *n* [u] (BrE) adelantamiento *m*, rebase *m* (Méx); **~tax** /'əʊvər'tæks || ˌəʊvə'tæks/ *vt* 1 (strain) poner* a prueba 2 (Tax) gravar en exceso ‹*con impuestos*›; **~-the-counter** /'əʊvərðə'kaʊntər || ˌəʊvəðə'kaʊntə(r)/ *adj*: **~-the-counter medicine** medicamento *m* que se puede comprar sin receta

overthrow[1] /'əʊvər'θrəʊ || ˌəʊvə'θrəʊ/ *vt* (*past* **-threw**; *past p* **-thrown**) ‹*government*› derrocar*

overthrow[2] /'əʊvərθrəʊ || 'əʊvəθrəʊ/ *n* (of ruler, government) derrocamiento *m*

overtime /'əʊvərtaɪm || 'əʊvətaɪm/ *n* [u]

A 1 (extra work hours) horas *fpl* extra(s), sobretiempo *m* (Chi, Per); **to work ~** hacer* horas extra(s), trabajar sobretiempo (Chi, Per); **my brain was working ~** mi cerebro estaba

trabajando a toda máquina 2 (pay) horas *fpl* extra(s), sobretiempo *m* (Chi, Per)
B (AmE Sport) prórroga *f*, tiempo *m* suplementario

overtly /əʊ'vɜːrtli || 'əʊvɜːtli/ *adv* abiertamente

over: **~tone** *n* (suggestion, hint) (*usu pl*) dejo *m*, deje *m* (Esp); **the film had clear political ~tones** la película tenía un claro trasfondo político; **~took** /'əʊvər'tʊk || ˌəʊvə'tʊk/ *past of* **overtake**

overture /'əʊvərtʃʊr || 'əʊvətjʊə(r)/ *n*
A (Mus) obertura *f*
B **overtures** *pl* (approaches) (frml) intento *m or* tentativa *f* de acercamiento; (sexual) insinuación *f*; **to make ~s to sb**: **he made ~s to several European leaders** intentó acercamientos con varios líderes europeos

overturn /'əʊvər'tɜːrn || ˌəʊvə'tɜːn/ *vt* 1 (tip over) ‹*table/boat*› darle* la vuelta a, dar* vuelta (CS) 2 (depose) ‹*government*› derrocar*, derribar 3 (nullify) ‹*decision/ruling*› anular
■ **overturn** *vi* «*vehicle*» volcar*, dar* una vuelta de campana, capotar

overuse[1] /'əʊvər'juːz || ˌəʊvə'juːz/ *vt* abusar de, usar demasiado

overuse[2] /'əʊvər'juːs || ˌəʊvə'juːs/ *n* [u] uso *m* excesivo

overview /'əʊvərvjuː || 'əʊvəvjuː/ *n* perspectiva *f* general

overweight /'əʊvər'weɪt || ˌəʊvə'weɪt/ *adj* ‹*person*› demasiado gordo; **I am 10lb ~** peso 10 libras de más, tengo un sobrepeso de 10 libras (Chi, Méx); **the parcel is ~** el paquete pesa más de la cuenta

overwhelm /'əʊvər'hwelm || ˌəʊvə'welm/ *vt* 1 (emotionally) abrumar; **I was ~ed with rage** sentí una rabia incontenible 2 (defeat) ‹*army/post*› aplastar, arrollar 3 (swamp) inundar, anegar*; **to be ~ed WITH sth**: **they've been ~ed with applications/complaints** han recibido infinidad de solicitudes/quejas

overwhelming /'əʊvər'hwelmɪŋ || ˌəʊvə'welmɪŋ/ *adj* ‹*grief*› inconsolable; ‹*urge*› irresistible; ‹*anger*› incontenible; ‹*boredom*› insoportable; ‹*defeat*› aplastante; ‹*majority*› abrumador

overwhelmingly /'əʊvər'hwelmɪŋli || ˌəʊvə'welmɪŋli/ *adv*: **they voted ~ against it** una abrumadora mayoría votó en contra

overwind /'əʊvər'waɪnd || ˌəʊvə'waɪnd/ *vt* (*past & past p* **-wound** /-waʊnd/) dar* demasiada cuerda a

O

overwork[1] /'əʊvər'wɜːrk || ˌəʊvə'wɜːk/ *vt* hacer* trabajar demasiado

overwork[2] *n* [u] agotamiento *m*

over: **~write** /'əʊvər'raɪt || ˌəʊvə'raɪt/ *vt* (*past* **-wrote**; *past p* **-written**) (Comput) 1 (write) **to ~write sth ON sth** superponer* algo A algo 2 (delete) machacar*, borrar; **~wrought** /'əʊvər'rɔːt || ˌəʊvə'rɔːt/ *adj* 1 (agitated) alterado, exaltado 2 (elaborate) (pej) ‹*prose/style*› recargado

ovulate /'ɑːvjəleɪt || 'ɒvjʊleɪt/ *vi* ovular

ovulation /'ɑːvjə'leɪʃən || ˌɒvjʊ'leɪʃən/ *n* [u] ovulación *f*

owe /əʊ/ *vt*
A 1 (financially) deber, adeudar (frml); **to ~ sb sth, ~ sth TO sb** deberle algo A algn; **I'll ~ it to you** te lo quedo debiendo; **to ~ sb FOR sth** deberle algo A algn; **how much do I ~ you for the tickets?** ¿cuánto te debo por las entradas? 2 (be obliged to give, do) ‹*explanation/apology/favor*› deber; **take a break; you ~ it to yourself** tómate un descanso, te lo has ganado
B 1 (be indebted for) deber; **to what do we ~ the pleasure of your company?** (hum) ¿a qué debemos el placer de tu compañía? (hum) 2 (be influenced by) deber
■ **owe** *vi* **to ~ FOR sth** deber algo

owing /'əʊɪŋ/ *adj*
A (*pred*): **the money still ~** el dinero que aún se debe *or* (frml) adeuda
B **owing to** (*as prep*) debido a

owl /aʊl/ *n* búho *m*, tecolote *m* (Méx); (*barn* ~) lechuza *f*

own[1] /əʊn/ *vt*
A (possess) ‹*property*› tener*, ser* dueño de, poseer* (frml); **do you ~ the house?** ¿la casa es tuya?; **she acts as if she ~s the place** se comporta como si fuera la dueña y señora del lugar
B (admit) (frml) reconocer*, admitir

Phrasal verb

- **own up** [v ▸ adv]: **no one ~ed up** nadie reconoció *or* admitió tener la culpa; **come on, ~ up** anda, reconócelo *or* confiésalo; **to ~ up TO sth/-ING**: **no one would ~ up to having left the window open** nadie quiso reconocer *or* admitir que había sido quien dejó la ventana abierta

own[2] *adj* **my/her/your** *etc* **~**: **in our ~ house** en nuestra propia casa; **I saw it with my (very) ~ eyes** lo vi con mis propios ojos; **she makes her ~ clothes** se hace la ropa ella misma; **it's all my ~ work** lo hice todo yo; **I'll find my ~ way out** no hace falta que me acompañe hasta la salida

own[3] *pron* **my/her/your** *etc* **~**: **it isn't a company car: it's her ~** no es un coche de la empresa, es suyo (propio); **she wanted a room of her ~** quería una habitación para ella sola; **she has enough work of her ~ without helping you too** tiene bastante trabajo propio como para estar ayudándote a ti; **Florence has a charm all (of) its ~** Florencia tiene un encanto muy particular; **on one's ~** solo; **you're on your ~ from now on** de ahora en adelante te las arreglarás por tu cuenta; **to call sth one's ~**: **I don't have a moment to call my ~** no tengo ni un minuto para mí; ***to come into one's ~***: **she really comes into her ~ in the final act** en el último acto es cuando verdaderamente se luce; ***to get one's ~ back*** (BrE colloq) desquitarse; **I can't wait to get my ~ back on him** no veo el momento de desquitarme *or* de hacérselas pagar; ***to hold one's ~*** saber* defenderse

own-brand /'əʊn'brænd/ *adj* (BrE) ‹*product*› *de marca propia del supermercado o la tienda que lo vende*

-owned /əʊnd/ *suff*: **company/state~** de propiedad de la compañía/del estado

owner /'əʊnər || 'əʊnə(r)/ *n* dueño, -ña *m,f*; **who is the ~ of this shop/dog?** ¿quién es el propietario *or* dueño de esta tienda/el dueño de este perro?; **if you are a car-/dog-~** si usted tiene coche/un perro

ownership /'əʊnərʃɪp || 'əʊnəʃɪp/ *n* [u] propiedad *f*; **the company is in private/state ~** la compañía es de propiedad privada/estatal

own goal *n* autogol *m*, gol *m* en contra (CS)

ox /ɑːks || ɒks/ *n* (*pl* **oxen**) buey *m*; ***as strong as an ~*** fuerte como un toro *or* un roble

Oxbridge /'ɑːksbrɪdʒ || 'ɒksbrɪdʒ/ *n* (in UK) *las universidades británicas de Oxford y Cambridge*

oxen /'ɑːksən || 'ɒksən/ *pl of* **ox**

oxford, Oxford /'ɑːksfərd || 'ɒksfəd/ *n* (AmE) zapato *m* acordonado (*de hombre*)

oxide /'ɑːksaɪd || 'ɒksaɪd/ *n* [u c] óxido *m*

oxidize /'ɑːksədaɪz || 'ɒksɪdaɪz/ *vt* oxidar
■ **oxidize** *vi* oxidarse

oxtail /'ɑːksteɪl || 'ɒksteɪl/ *n* [u c] rabo *m* de buey

oxygen /'ɑːksədʒən || 'ɒksɪdʒən/ *n* [u] oxígeno *m*; (*before n*) **~ mask** (Aviat, Med) mascarilla *f or* máscara *f* de oxígeno

oyster /'ɔɪstər || 'ɔɪstə(r)/ *n* (Culin, Zool) ostra *f*, ostión *m* (Méx)

oz = ounce(s)

ozone /'əʊzəʊn/ *n* [u] (Chem) ozono *m*; (*before n*) **the ~ layer** la capa de ozono

ozone: **~-friendly** /'əʊzəʊn'frendli/ *adj* que no daña la capa de ozono; **~ hole** *n* agujero *m* (en la capa) de ozono

P, p /piː/ *n* P, p *f*; ***to mind one's Ps and Qs*** tener* mucho cuidado

p (in UK) (= **penny/pence**) penique(s) *m(pl)*

p. (*pl* **pp.**) (= **page**) pág., p.; **pp. 12-48** págs. 12 a 48

P (= **parking**) Ⓢ **P** P, E

pa¹ /pɑː/ *n* (dial & dated) papá *m*

pa², p.a. /ˈpiːˈeɪ/ = **per annum**

PA *n* [1] /ˈpiːˈeɪ/ ~ **(system)** = **public-address system** [2] /piːˈeɪ/ (BrE) = **personal assistant** [3] *also* **Pa** = **Pennsylvania**

pace¹ /peɪs/ *n*

A (stride) paso *m*; ***to put sb through her/his ~s*** poner* a algn a prueba, hacerle* demostrar a algn de lo que es capaz

B (speed) (*no pl*) ritmo *m*; **at a slow ~** a ritmo lento, lentamente; **at my own ~** a mi ritmo; **I can't keep ~ with her** no le puedo seguir el ritmo *or* (CS tb) el tren; **salaries have not kept ~ with inflation** los sueldos no han aumentado en la misma proporción que la inflación; **to set the ~** marcar* la pauta; **he gave up the job because he couldn't take** *o* **stand the ~** dejó el trabajo porque no podía aguantar el ritmo

pace² *vi*: **to ~ up and down** caminar *or* (esp Esp) andar de un lado para otro *or* de para arriba para abajo

■ **pace** *vt*

A (walk across): **he ~d the room anxiously** caminaba preocupado de un lado a otro de la habitación

B (regulate speed of): **to ~ a runner** marcarle* el ritmo a un corredor; **to ~ oneself** controlarse el tiempo

(Phrasal verb)

• **pace out** [v ▸ o ▸ adv, v ▸ adv ▸ o] ‹*distance*› medir* a pasos

pace: **~maker** *n* (Sport) liebre *f*; (Med) marcapasos *m*; **~setter** *n* (Sport) liebre *f*; (pioneer) líder *mf*

pacific /pəˈsɪfɪk/ *adj* (liter) pacífico

Pacific /pəˈsɪfɪk/ *n* **the ~ (Ocean)** el (Océano) Pacífico

pacifier /ˈpæsəfaɪər || ˈpæsɪfaɪə(r)/ *n* (AmE) chupete *m*, chupón *m* (AmL exc CS), chupo *m* (Col), chupa *f* (Ven)

pacifism /ˈpæsəfɪzəm || ˈpæsɪfɪzəm/ *n* [u] pacifismo *m*

pacifist /ˈpæsəfəst || ˈpæsɪfɪst/ *n* pacifista *mf*

pacify /ˈpæsəfaɪ || ˈpæsɪfaɪ/ *vt* **-fies, -fying, -fied** [1] (calm, satisfy) apaciguar*, calmar [2] (restore to peace) ‹*country/area*› pacificar*

pack¹ /pæk/ *n*

A (bundle, load) fardo *m*; (rucksack) mochila *f*; (*before n*) **~ animal** bestia *f* de carga

B [1] (packet, package) paquete *m*; **a ~ of cigarettes** (esp AmE) un paquete *or* una cajetilla *or* (RPl) una cajilla de cigarrillos [2] (of cards) (BrE) baraja *f*, mazo *m* (esp AmL)

C [1] (of animals): **a ~ of wolves** una manada de lobos; **a ~ of hounds** (Sport) una jauría; ***to run with the ~*** seguir* la corriente [2] (in race) pelotón *m* [3] (in rugby) delanteros *mpl*

D (of thieves, fools) (pej) partida *f* (pey), pandilla *f* (pey); **a ~ of lies** una sarta de mentiras

E [1] (compress) compresa *f* [2] (cosmetic) mascarilla *f*

pack² *vt*

A [1] (Busn) ‹*goods/products*› (put into container) envasar; (make packets with) empaquetar; (for transport) embalar [2] (put into suitcase, bag): **have you ~ed your toothbrush?** ¿llevas el cepillo de dientes?; **I ~ed my winter clothes away in a trunk** guardé la ropa de invierno en un baúl; **she takes a ~ed lunch to work** se lleva el almuerzo *or* (esp Esp, Méx) la comida al trabajo [3] (fill): **to ~ one's suitcase** hacer* la maleta *or* (RPl) la valija, empacar (AmL); **he was told to ~ his bags** le dijeron que (hiciera las maletas y) se fuera

B [1] (press tightly together): **~ the soil (down) firmly** apisone bien la tierra [2] (cram full): **~ the gaps tightly** rellena bien los huecos; **the book is ~ed with useful information** el libro está lleno de información útil

C (fill with sympathizers) **to ~ a jury** formar un jurado tendencioso

■ **pack** *vi*

A (fill suitcase) hacer* la(s) maleta(s) *or* (RPl) la(s) valija(s), empacar* (AmL); ▸**send** *vt* **B**

B (squeeze) **to ~ INTO sth**: **the crowd ~ed into the station** el gentío se apiñó en la estación

(Phrasal verbs)

• **pack in** [v ▸ o ▸ adv, v ▸ adv ▸ o]

A (quit) (colloq) ‹*job/course*› dejar; **~ it in!** ¡para ya! (fam), ¡ya párale! (Méx fam), ¡terminala! (RPl fam), ¡ya córtala! (Chi fam)

B (cram in): **we managed to ~ in 50 people** pudimos meter a 50 personas; **we were only there for a weekend, but we ~ed a lot in** sólo estuvimos un fin de semana pero hicimos un montón de cosas (fam)

• **pack off** [v ▸ o ▸ adv, v ▸ adv ▸ o] despachar, mandar; **she ~ed the children off to school** mandó a los niños al colegio

• **pack up**

A [v ▸ adv] [1] (assemble belongings) liar* el petate, hacer* su itacate (Méx) [2] (stop) (colloq): **let's ~ up for the day** dejémoslo por hoy [3] (break down) (colloq) «*motor/radio*» dejar de funcionar, descomponerse* (esp AmL), tronarse* (Méx fam)

B [v ▸ o ▸ adv, v ▸ adv ▸ o] [1] ‹*tools/belongings*› recoger*, guardar [2] ▸**pack in A**

package¹ /ˈpækɪdʒ/ *n*

A [1] (parcel) paquete *m* [2] (packet, carton) (esp AmE) paquete *m*

B (collection, set) paquete *m*; **a ~ of reforms** un paquete de reformas; **a software ~** un paquete de software

C (colloq) ▸**package vacation**

package² *vt* [1] (pack) embalar, empaquetar [2] (Marketing): **the product is attractively ~d** la presentación del producto es atractiva

package: **~ holiday** (BrE) ▸**~ vacation**; **~ store** *n* (AmE) tienda *f* de bebidas alcohólicas; **~ tour** *n* viaje *m* organizado (*en el que se recorren diferentes localidades*); **~ vacation** *n* (AmE) vacaciones *fpl* organizadas, viaje *m* organizado

packaging /ˈpækɪdʒɪŋ/ *n* [u] [1] (packing) embalaje *m* [2] (wrapping) envoltorio *m* [3] (Marketing) presentación *f*

packed /pækt/ *adj* ‹*hall/restaurant*› lleno *or* atestado de gente, de bote en bote, repleto; **the group played to ~ houses** el grupo tocó con llenos completos; **the theater was ~ed out** (BrE) el teatro estaba de bote en bote *or* estaba repleto

packer /ˈpækər || ˈpækə(r)/ *n* embalador, -dora *m,f*, empacador, -dora *m,f*

packet /ˈpækət || ˈpækɪt/ *n*

A (container) (esp BrE) paquete *m*; **a ~ of cigarettes** (BrE) un

paquete *or* una cajetilla de cigarrillos; (*before n*) ‹*soup/cake mix*› de sobre
B (large sum) (BrE colloq) (*no pl*) dineral *m*, fortunón *m* (fam)

pack: **~horse** *n* caballo *m* de carga; **~ ice** *n* [u] banco *m* de témpanos

packing /'pækɪŋ/ *n* [u] **1** (of suitcase): **to do one's ~** hacer* la(s) maleta(s) *or* (RPl) la(s) valija(s), empacar* (AmL) **2** (in factory) embalaje *m* **3** (material for packing) embalaje *m*

packing case *n* caja *f* de embalaje

packsack /'pæksæk/ *n* (AmE) mochila *f*

pact /pækt/ *n* pacto *m*; (Pol, Lab Rel) pacto *m*, convenio *m*; **suicide ~** pacto suicida; **to make a ~ with sb** pactar con algn, hacer* un pacto con algn

pad¹ /pæd/ *n*
A (cushioning) almohadilla *f*; **shoulder ~s** hombreras *fpl*; **knee ~s** rodilleras *fpl*
B (of paper) bloc *m*; **desk ~** bloc de notas
C (*launch ~*) plataforma *f* de lanzamiento

pad² **-dd-** *vt*
A **1** (line) ‹*seat/panel*› acolchar, enguatar (Esp) **2** **padded** *past p* ‹*jacket*› acolchado, enguatado (Esp); ‹*bra*› con relleno; ‹*envelope*› acolchado; **~ded cell** celda *f* de aislamiento
B **~ (out)** (expand) ‹*essay*› rellenar, meter* paja en (fam)
■ **pad** *vi* andar*, caminar (*con paso suave*)

padding /'pædɪŋ/ *n* [u] **1** (material) relleno *m*, guata *f* (Esp); (for protection) almohadillas *fpl* **2** (in essay, speech) paja *f* (fam), hojarasca *f*

paddle¹ /'pædḷ/ *n*
A [c] **1** (oar) zagual *m*, pala *f*, remo *m* pequeño **2** **~ (wheel)** rueda *f* hidráulica de paletas **3** (on paddle wheel) paleta *f*
B (*no pl*): **to go for a ~** ir* a mojarse los pies

paddle² *vi*
A (wet feet) mojarse los pies (*en la orilla*)
B **1** (in canoe) remar **2** (swim) ‹‹*duck/dog*›› chapotear
■ **paddle** *vt* ‹*boat/canoe*› llevar (*remando con pala or zagual*)

paddle: **~ boat** *n* **1** ▸ **~ steamer** **2** (pedalo) bote *m* de pedales, patín *m* (Esp); **~ steamer** *n* barco *m* de vapor con paletas

paddling pool /'pædlɪŋ/ *n* (BrE) (in park) estanque *m*; (inflatable) piscina *f* or (Méx) alberca *f* inflable (*para niños*)

paddock /'pædək/ *n* prado *m*, cercado *m*, potrero *m*

paddy /'pædi/ *n* (*pl* **-dies**) **~ (field)** arrozal *m*

padlock¹ /'pædlɑːk || 'pædlɒk/ *n* candado *m*

padlock² *vt* cerrar* con candado

padre /'pɑːdreɪ/ *n* capellán *m*

paediatric *etc* (BrE) ▸ **pediatric** *etc*

paedophile *etc* (BrE) ▸ **pedophile** *etc*

pagan¹ /'peɪgən/ *n* pagano, -na *m,f*

pagan² *adj* pagano

page¹ /peɪdʒ/ *n*
A (of book, newspaper) página *f*
B **1** (attendant) paje *m*; (in hotel) botones *m* **2** (in legislature) (in US) mensajero *m*

page² *vt* (over loudspeaker) llamar por megafonía

pageant /'pædʒənt/ *n* **1** (show, ceremony) festividades *fpl* **2** (historical show) *espectáculo histórico al aire libre*

pageantry /'pædʒəntri/ *n* [u] fausto *m*, pompa *f*, esplendor *m*

page: **~boy** /'peɪdʒbɔɪ/ *n* **1** ▸ **page¹ B1**; **2** (hairstyle) peinado *m* or corte *m* a lo paje; **~ break** *n* salto *m* de página

pager /'peɪdʒər || 'peɪdʒə(r)/ *n* (Telec) buscapersonas *m*, localizador *m* (de personas), bip *m* (Méx fam), busca *m* (Esp fam), bíper *m* (Chi)

pagination /'pædʒə'neɪʃən || ˌpædʒɪ'neɪʃən/ *n* [u] paginación *f*

pagoda /pə'gəʊdə/ *n* pagoda *f*

paid¹ /peɪd/ *past & past p of* **pay¹**

paid² *adj* **1** ‹*employment*› remunerado; ‹*worker*› asalariado; ‹*vacation*› pagado; ‹*leave*› con goce de sueldo; ***to put ~ to sth*** (BrE) echar por tierra algo, acabar con algo **2** (AmE) ‹*member/supporter*› que ha pagado su cuota de afiliación

paid-up /'peɪdʌp/ *adj* (*pred* **paid up**) (BrE) ▸ **paid² 2**

pail /peɪl/ *n* balde *m*, cubo *m* (Esp), cubeta *f* (Méx)

pain¹ /peɪn/ *n*
A **1** [u c] (physical) dolor *m*; **I'm in constant ~** siento dolor constantemente; **she was in great ~** estaba muy dolorida *or* (AmL tb) adolorida, sentía mucho dolor; **to cry out in** *o* **with ~** gritar de dolor; **I've got a ~ in my leg** me duele la pierna; ***to be a ~ in the neck*** *o* (AmE vulg) ***ass*** *o* (BrE vulg) ***arse*** ser* un pesado, ser* insoportable, ser* un coñazo (Esp vulg) **2** [u] (mental) dolor *m*, pena *f*; **it takes the ~ out of accounting** hace más fácil la contabilidad **3** **on ~ of sth/-ING** (*as prep*) bajo *or* so pena de algo/+ INF **4** [u] (annoying person or thing) (colloq) lata *f* (fam)
B **pains** *pl* (effort): **that's all you get for your ~s** así te pagan la molestia; **she was at great ~s to deny the rumor** trató por todos los medios de desmentir el rumor; **I took considerable ~s** *o* **went to great ~s to explain it to them carefully** puse mucho esmero *or* me esforcé mucho en explicárselo

pain² *vt*: **it ~s me to see that ...** me duele *or* me apena *or* me da pena ver que ...

pained /peɪnd/ *adj* afligido, apenado; ‹*expression*› de pena

painful /'peɪnfəl/ *adj* **1** (physically) doloroso; **is it very ~?** ¿duele mucho? **2** (mentally) ‹*task*› desagradable; ‹*reminder*› doloroso; **it was ~ to watch her wasting away** daba pena *or* lástima *or* era doloroso ver como se consumía **3** (bad) (colloq) de pena (fam), pésimo

painfully /'peɪnfəli/ *adv*: **she dragged herself ~ along** se iba arrastrando con mucho dolor; **he's ~ slow** es tan lento que te exaspera; **she's ~ shy** es tan tímida que da pena; **I'm ~ aware of it** tengo plena conciencia de ello

painkiller /'peɪnˌkɪlər || 'peɪnˌkɪlə(r)/ *n* [u c] analgésico *m*, calmante *m* (*para el dolor*)

painless /'peɪnləs || 'peɪnlɪs/ *adj* **1** (causing no pain) indoloro; **~ childbirth** parto *m* sin dolor **2** (easy, pleasant) (colloq) ‹*method*› sencillo; **the experience was fairly ~** la experiencia fue bastante llevadera

painstaking /'peɪnzˌteɪkɪŋ/ *adj* ‹*research/efforts*› concienzudo; ‹*person/personality*› meticuloso, minucioso

paint¹ /peɪnt/ *n* [u c] pintura *f*

paint² *vt* **1** (Art) ‹*portrait/landscape*› pintar **2** (apply paint to) ‹*wall/door/house*› pintar; **I ~ed the kitchen pink** pinté la cocina de rosa; **to ~ sth out**, **to ~ over sth** pintar encima de algo, tapar algo con pintura **3** (describe) pintar; **to ~ a glowing/gloomy picture of sth** pintar algo favorablemente/muy negro; ***as black as it's been ~ed***: **the situation isn't as black as it's been ~ed** la situación no es tan negra como la pintan **4** (make up): **to ~ one's face** pintarse, maquillarse
■ **paint** *vi* pintar

paint: **~box** *n* caja *f* de acuarelas; **~brush** *n* pincel *m*; (large, for walls) brocha *f*

painter /'peɪntər || 'peɪntə(r)/ *n* (Art, Const) pintor, -tora *m,f*

painting /'peɪntɪŋ/ *n* **1** [c] (picture) cuadro *m*, pintura *f* **2** [u] (Art) pintura *f*

paintwork /'peɪntwɜːrk || 'peɪntwɜːk/ *n* [u] pintura *f*

pair¹ /per || peə(r)/ *n*
A **1** (of shoes, socks, gloves) par *m*; **a ~ of trousers** unos pantalones, un par de pantalones; **a ~ of scissors** unas tijeras; **a ~ of glasses** unas gafas, unos lentes *or* anteojos (AmL); **I've only got one ~ of hands** sólo tengo dos manos **2** (in cards) pareja *f*, par *m*
B (couple) pareja *f*; **the seats were arranged in ~s** los asientos estaban colocados de dos en dos *or* (AmL tb) de a dos

pair² *vt* ‹*objects*› emparejar, formar pares con; **she was ~ed with Paul** le pusieron a Paul de pareja
■ **pair** *vi* (Zool) aparearse

Phrasal verbs

• **pair off**
A [v ▸ o ▸ adv, v ▸ adv ▸ o] ‹*pupils/dancers*› poner* en parejas; ‹*objects/words*› emparejar, formar pares con; **my friends tried to ~ me off with John** mis amigos me quisieron hacer gancho con John (fam)
B [v ▸ adv] formar parejas

• **pair up** [v ▸ adv] formar parejas

paisley /'peɪzli/ *n* [u] estampado *m* de cachemir(a)

pajamas, (BrE) **pyjamas** /pəˈdʒɑːməz/ *pl n* pijama *m*, piyama *m or f* (AmL); **a pair of ~** un pijama, unos pijamas, un *or* una piyama (AmL); ▸**cat**

Pakeha /ˈpɑːkɪːhɑe:/ *n* (NZ colloq) *neozelandés de origen europeo*

Paki /ˈpæki/ *n* (BrE sl & offensive) pakistaní *mf*, paquistaní *mf*

Pakistan /ˈpækɪˈstæn/ *n* Pakistán *m*, Paquistán *m*

Pakistani¹ /ˈpækɪˈstæni/ *adj* pakistaní, paquistaní

Pakistani² *n* pakistaní *mf*, paquistaní *mf*

pal /pæl/ *n* **1** (friend) (colloq) amigo *m*, compinche *m* (fam), cuate *m* (Méx fam); **you're a ~!** ¡eso es un amigo! **2** (*as form of address*) compadre *or* (Esp) tío *or* (Méx) cuate

Phrasal verb

• **pal up**: **-ll-** [v ▸ adv] (colloq) hacerse* amigos; **to ~ up WITH sb** hacerse* amigo DE algn

palace /ˈpæləs || ˈpælɪs/ *n* palacio *m*; **the P~** la Casa Real

Palaeolithic *etc* (BrE) ▸**Paleolithic** *etc*

palatable /ˈpælətəbəl/ *adj* agradable; **a very ~ wine** un vino de muy buen paladar; **he tried to make the figures more ~** trató de que las cifras resultaran más aceptables

palate /ˈpælət/ *n* **1** (Anat) paladar *m* **2** (sense of taste) paladar *m*

palatial /pəˈleɪʃəl/ *adj* ‹*home*› palaciego; ‹*room*› grandioso

palaver /pəˈlævər || pəˈlɑːvə(r)/ *n* [u] (colloq) (bother) (esp BrE) jaleo *m* (fam), lío *m*, borlote *m* (Méx fam)

pale¹ /peɪl/ *adj* **1** ‹*skin/person*› (naturally) blanco; (pallid) pálido; **to turn ~** palidecer* **2** ‹*blue/pink*› pálido; **a ~ imitation** una burda imitación

pale² *vi* **1** «*person*» palidecer* **2** (seem minor) **to ~ BESIDE** *o* **BEFORE sb/sth** palidecer* JUNTO A algn/algo

pale³ *n*; ***beyond the ~*** intolerable, inaceptable

pale: **~ ale** *n* [u c] *cerveza rubia suave*; **~-faced** /ˈpeɪlfeɪst/ *adj* pálido (de cara)

paleness /ˈpeɪlnəs || ˈpeɪlnɪs/ *n* [u] palidez *f*

Paleolithic, (BrE also) **Palaeolithic** /ˈpeɪliəˈlɪθɪk || ˌpæliəʊˈlɪθɪk, ˌpeɪ-/ *adj* paleolítico

paleontology, (BrE also) **palaeontology** /ˈpeɪliɑːnˈtɑːlədʒi || ˌpælɪɒnˈtɒlədʒi, ˌpeɪ-/ *n* [u] paleontología *f*

Palestine /ˈpæləstaɪn/ *n* Palestina *f*

Palestinian¹ /ˈpæləˈstɪniən/ *adj* palestino

Palestinian² *n* palestino, -na *m,f*

palette /ˈpælət || ˈpælɪt/ *n* **1** (board) paleta *f* **2** (range of color) gama *f*

palette knife *n* **1** (Art) espátula *f* **2** (AmE also **pallet knife**) (Culin) espátula *f*, paleta *f*

paling /ˈpeɪlɪŋ/ *n* **1** [u c] (fence) (*often pl*) empalizada *f* **2** [c] (stake) estaca *f*

palisade /ˈpæləˈseɪd || ˌpælɪˈseɪd/ *n* **1** (fence) empalizada *f*, palizada *f* **2** (cliff) (AmE) (*usu pl*) acantilado *m*

pall¹ /pɔːl/ *n* **1** (cloth) paño *m* mortuorio; **a ~ of smoke** una cortina de humo; ***to cast a ~ on*** *o* ***over sth*** empañar algo **2** (bier) (AmE) andas *fpl*, parihuelas *fpl*

pall² *vi* hacerse* pesado; **his jokes began to ~ (on us)** sus chistes empezaron a aburrirnos

pallbearer /ˈpɔːlˌberər || ˈpɔːlˌbeərə(r)/ *n* portador, -dora *m,f* del féretro

pallet /ˈpælət || ˈpælɪt/ *n* **1** (for forklift) paleta *f* **2** (bed) camastro *m*

pallet knife *n* (AmE) ▸**palette knife 2**

palliative¹ /ˈpælieɪtɪv || ˈpæliətɪv/ *n* paliativo *m*

palliative² *adj* paliativo

pallid /ˈpæləd || ˈpælɪd/ *adj* pálido

pallor /ˈpælər || ˈpælə(r)/ *n* [u] palidez *f*

pally /ˈpæli/ *adj* **-lier, -liest** (colloq) (*pred*) **to be ~ WITH sb** ser* muy amigo DE algn; **he's very ~ with the boss** está íntimo con el jefe (fam), él y el jefe son muy cuates (Méx fam)

palm /pɑːm/ *n*

A **1** **~ (tree)** palmera *f*; (*before n*) **~ leaf** palma *f* **2** (leaf, branch) palma *f*

B (Anat) palma *f*; **to read sb's ~** leerle* la mano a algn; ***to grease*** *o* ***oil sb's ~*** untarle la mano a algn; ***to have sb in the ~ of one's hand***: **she's got him in the ~ of her hand** se lo ha metido en el bolsillo, hace lo que le da la gana con él

Phrasal verb

• **palm off** [v ▸ o ▸ adv] **to ~ sth off ON** *o* **ONTO sb** encajarle *or* endilgarle algo a algn (fam); **to ~ sb off WITH sth** quitarse a algn de encima CON algo

palm: **~corder** /ˈpɑːmkɔːrdər || ˈpɑːmkɔːdə(r)/ *n* videocámara *f* de bolsillo, palmcorder *f*; **~top** /ˈpɑːmtɑːp || ˈpɑːmtɒp/ *n* computadora *f or* (Esp) ordenador *m* de mano, palm *m or f*

palmist /ˈpɑːməst || ˈpɑːmɪst/ quiromántico, -ca *m,f*

palmistry /ˈpɑːməstri || ˈpɑːmɪstri/ *n* [u] quiromancia *f*

Palm Sunday *n* Domingo *m* de Ramos

palomino /ˈpæləˈmiːnəʊ/ *n* (*pl* **-nos**) *caballo claro con crin blanca*

palpable /ˈpælpəbəl/ *adj* (frml) ‹*pride/anxiety*› palmario, palpable

palpate /ˈpælpeɪt || pælˈpeɪt/ *vt* palpar

palpitate /ˈpælpəteɪt || ˈpælpɪteɪt/ *vi* palpitar

palpitation /ˈpælpəˈteɪʃən || ˌpælpɪˈteɪʃən/ *n* [u c] (Med) palpitación *f*

palsy /ˈpɔːlzi/ *n* [u] parálisis *f*

paltry /ˈpɔːltri/ *adj* **-trier -triest** ‹*sum/amount*› mísero, mezquino; ‹*excuse*› malo

pampas /ˈpæmpəs/ *n* (+ *sing or pl vb*) pampa *f*; **the ~** la pampa, las pampas; **the P~** la Pampa

pamper /ˈpæmpər || ˈpæmpə(r)/ *vt* mimar

pampered /ˈpæmpərd || ˈpæmpəd/ *adj* mimado, consentido

pamphlet /ˈpæmflət || ˈpæmflɪt/ *n* (informative) folleto *m*; (political) panfleto *m*, volante *m*

pan¹ /pæn/ *n*

A **1** (Culin) cacerola *f*; (large, with two handles) olla *f*; (small) cacerola *f*, cazo *m* (Esp); (*frying ~*) sartén *f*; **pots and ~s** cacharros *mpl* (fam), trastes *mpl* (Méx); **loaf ~** (AmE) molde *m* para pan **2** (for prospecting) batea *f* **3** (on scales) platillo *m*, bandeja *f*

B (of toilet) (BrE) taza *f*; ***to go down the ~*** (colloq) irse* al traste (fam)

pan² **-nn-** *vt* (Min) **1** ‹*gravel/soil*› cribar **2** ‹*gold*› separar cribando

■ **pan** *vi*

A (Min): **to ~ for gold** lavar oro

B (Cin): **the camera ~s across to the two figures** la cámara recorre hasta enfocar en las dos figuras

Phrasal verb

• **pan out** [v ▸ adv] (colloq) salir*, resultar

panacea /ˈpænəˈsiːə/ *n* (frml) panacea *f*

panache /pəˈnæʃ/ *n* [u] garbo *m*, salero *m*

Panama /ˈpænəmɑː/ *n* **1** (Geog) Panamá *m*; (*before n*) **~ Canal** el Canal de Panamá; **~ City** Ciudad *f* de Panamá **2** **~ (hat)** *or* **panama (hat)** panamá *m*, (sombrero *m* de) jipijapa *m*

Panamanian¹ /ˈpænəˈmeɪniən/ *adj* panameño

Panamanian² *n* panameño, -ña *m,f*

Pan-American /ˌpænəˈmerɪkən/ *adj* panamericano

pancake /ˈpænkeɪk/ *n* [c] (Culin) crep(e) *m*, panqueque *m* (AmL), crepa *f* (Méx), panqué *m* (AmC, Col), panqueca *f* (Ven); ***as flat as a ~*** liso como una tabla; (*before n*) **P~ Day** martes *m* de Carnaval

pancreas /ˈpæŋkriəs/ *n* páncreas *m*

panda /ˈpændə/ *n* (oso, osa *m,f*) panda *mf*; **giant ~** panda gigante

panda car *n* (BrE) coche *m* de policía

pandemonium /ˈpændəˈməʊniəm/ *n* [u] pandemonio *m*, pandemónium *m*

pander /ˈpændər || ˈpændə(r)/ *vi*: **to ~ to sb's whims** consentirle* los caprichos a algn

p & p /ˈpiːənˈpiː/ (BrE) = **postage and packing**

pane /peɪn/ *n* (hoja *f* de) vidrio *m*, cristal *m* (Esp)

P

panel¹ /ˈpænl̩/ *n*
A 1 (of door, car body, plane wing) panel *m*; (of garment) pieza *f* 2 (*instrument* ~) tablero *m or* panel *m* (de instrumentos); (*control* ~) tablero *m* (de control) 3 (Art) tabla *f*
B (in discussion, interview) panel *m or* (Col, Ven) pánel *m*; (in quiz, contest) equipo *m*; (in exam) mesa *f*, tribunal *m*, comisión *f* (Chi)

panel² *vt*, (BrE) **-ll-** 1 ‹*room/wall*› revestir* con paneles 2 **paneled**, (BrE) **panelled** *past p* ‹*door*› de paneles; **an oak-~ed room** una habitación con paneles de roble

panel: **~ beater** *n* (BrE) chapista *mf*, hojalatero *mf* (Méx); **~ beating** *n* (BrE) [u] 1 (work produced) chapistería *f*, hojalatería *f* (Méx), latonería *f* (Col) 2 (action) arreglo *m* de chapa

paneling, (BrE) **panelling** /ˈpænl̩ɪŋ || ˈpænəlɪŋ/ *n* [u] paneles *mpl*

panelist, (BrE) **panellist** /ˈpænl̩əst || ˈpænəlɪst/ *n* (in discussion, interview) miembro *mf* del panel *or* (Col, Ven) del pánel

pan-fry /ˈpænfraɪ/ *vt* freír en sartén (*con poco aceite*)

pang /pæŋ/ *n* punzada *f*; **~s of hunger** retorcijones *mpl or* (Esp) retortijones *mpl* de hambre; **to feel ~s of remorse** sentir* remordimiento (de conciencia)

panhandle¹ /ˈpænˌhændl̩/ *n* (AmE) *faja estrecha de territorio de un estado que penetra en otro*

panhandle² *vi* (AmE colloq) pordiosear, mendigar*

panhandler /ˈpænˌhændlər || ˈpænˌhændlə(r)/ *n* (AmE colloq) mendigo *m*

panic¹ /ˈpænɪk/ *n*
A [u c] (fear, anxiety) pánico *m*; **people fled in ~** la gente huyó, despavorida *or* presa del pánico; **don't get into a ~** no te dejes llevar por el pánico; (*before n*) **~ button** botón *m* de alarma; **the strike led to ~ food-buying** la gente se asustó con la huelga y se lanzó a comprar alimentos; **it was ~ stations** (colloq) reinaba el pánico
B [c] (funny person, thing) (AmE colloq): **he is a ~** es divertidísimo *or* comiquísimo, es un plato (AmL fam)

panic² **-ck-** *vi* dejarse llevar por el pánico; **he ~ked and pressed the alarm bell** le entró el pánico y apretó la alarma; **don't ~!** ¡tranquilo!, ¡cálmate!; **there's no need to ~** no hay por qué alarmarse
■ **panic** *vt* infundirle pánico a; **to ~ sb INTO sth**: **we were ~ked into a hasty decision** lo que nos dijeron (*or* lo que leímos, *etc*) nos infundió pánico y tomamos una decisión precipitada

panicky /ˈpænɪki/ *adj* ‹*person*› muy nervioso; ‹*behavior/decision*› precipitado; **to get/grow ~** dejarse llevar por el pánico

panic-stricken /ˈpænɪkˌstrɪkən/ *adj* aterrorizado

pannier /ˈpæniər || ˈpæniə(r)/ *n* alforja *f*; (on cycle) maletero *m*

panoply /ˈpænəpli/ *n* (*pl* **-plies**) 1 (array) (frml) colección *f* 2 (armor) (Hist) panoplia *f*

panorama /ˈpænəˈræmə || ˌpænəˈrɑːmə/ *n* panorama *m*

panoramic /ˈpænəˈræmɪk/ *adj* panorámico

panpipes /ˈpænpaɪps/ *pl n* zampoña *f*, guaira *f* (AmC)

pansy /ˈpænzi/ *n* (*pl* **-sies**) 1 (Bot) pensamiento *m* 2 (effeminate male) (colloq & pej) mariquita *m* (fam & pey)

pant¹ /pænt/ *vi* (breathe quickly) jadear, resollar
■ **pant** *vt* decir* jadeando

pant² *n* jadeo *m*; *see also* **pants**

pantheon /ˈpænθiːɑːn || ˈpænθiən/ *n* panteón *m*

panther /ˈpænθər || ˈpænθə(r)/ *n* pantera *f*

panties /ˈpæntiz/ *pl n* calzones *mpl* (AmL), bragas *fpl* (Esp), pantaletas *fpl* (Méx, Ven), bombacha *f* (RPl), calzoneta *f* (AmC)

pantihose /ˈpæntihəʊz/ *pl n* ▸**pantyhose**

panto /ˈpæntəʊ/ *n* [c u] (*pl* **-tos**) (BrE colloq) ▸**pantomime 2**

pantomime /ˈpæntəmaɪm/ *n* [c u] 1 (mime) pantomima *f* 2 (in UK) *comedia musical navideña, basada en cuentos de hadas*

> **pantomime**
> Un tipo de representación teatral, dirigida a los niños y comúnmente conocida como *panto*, que tradicionalmente presentan los teatros británicos durante la época navideña. El argumento suele ser una adaptación cómica de un cuento tradicional y cuenta con un número de personajes de características exageradas e increíbles. También requiere de un gran nivel de participación por parte del público

pantry /ˈpæntri/ *n* (*pl* **-tries**) despensa *f*

pants /pænts/ *pl n*
A (trousers) (AmE) pantalón *m*, pantalones *mpl*; **a pair of ~** un par de pantalones, unos pantalones, un pantalón; ***to bore the ~ off sb*** (also BrE colloq) matar a algn de aburrimiento; ***to scare the ~ off sb*** (also BrE colloq) darle* a algn un susto de muerte; ▸**wear²** *vt* **A2**
B (underwear) (BrE) 1 (men's) calzoncillos *mpl*, calzones *mpl* (Méx), interiores *mpl* (Col, Ven); ***to catch sb with his ~ down*** (colloq) agarrar *or* (esp Esp) coger* a algn desprevenido 2 (women's) ▸**panties**

pantsuit /ˈpæntsuːt/, **pants suit** *n* (AmE) traje *m* pantalón

pantyhose /ˈpæntihəʊz/ *pl n* (AmE) medias *fpl*, panti(e)s *mpl or fpl*, pantimedias *fpl* (Méx), medias *fpl* bombacha (RPl) *or* (Col) pantalón *or* (Ven) panty

pap /pæp/ *n* [u] 1 (soft food) papilla *f* 2 (drivel): **this book is mindless ~!** este libro es una estupidez *or* una tontería

papa *n* 1 /ˈpɑːpə/ (AmE) papá *m* 2 /pəˈpɑː/ (BrE dated) padre *m* (ant), papá *m*

papacy /ˈpeɪpəsi/ *n* (*pl* **-cies**) papado *m*, pontificado *m*

papal /ˈpeɪpəl/ *adj* (*before n*) papal, pontificio

papaw *n* (esp AmE)
A /pəˈpɔː/ (custard apple) asimina *f*
B /ˈpɔːpɔː/ ▸**papaya**

papaya /pəˈpaɪə/ *n* 1 [c u] (fruit) papaya *f* 2 [c] ~ **(tree)** papayo *m*

paper¹ /ˈpeɪpər || ˈpeɪpə(r)/ *n*
A 1 [u] (material) papel *m*; **don't throw ~ on the floor** no tiren papeles al suelo; **it's made of ~** es de papel; **a sheet of ~** una hoja de papel; **a piece of ~** un papel; **this agreement/contract is not worth the ~ it's printed on** este acuerdo/contrato es papel mojado *or* no tiene el menor valor; ***on ~*** en teoría; ***to get** o **put sth down on ~*** poner* algo por escrito; (*before n*) ‹*towel/handkerchief*› de papel; **~ knife** abrecartas *m*, cortapapeles *m*; **~ mill** fábrica *f* de papel, papelera *f*; **~ money** papel *m* moneda 2 [c] (wrapper) (esp BrE) envoltorio *m*, papel *m*
B [c] (newspaper) diario *m*, periódico *m*; (*before n*) **~ boy/girl** repartidor, -dora *m,f* de periódicos *or* diarios, diar(i)ero, -ra *m,f* (CS); **~ round** reparto *m* de diarios *or* periódicos; **~ shop** (BrE) tienda *f* de periódicos, ≈ quiosco *m* (*de periódicos*)
C [c] 1 (for journal) trabajo *m*, artículo *m*; (at conference) ponencia *f* 2 (Govt) *see* **white paper**
D [c] (*exam* ~) (BrE) examen *m*; (part) parte *f*
E **papers** *pl* (documents) documentos *mpl*, papeles *mpl*; **identity ~s** documentos de identidad, documentación *f* personal; **ship's ~s** documentación *f* del barco; ***to give sb her/his walking ~s*** (AmE colloq) poner* a algn de patitas en la calle (fam)

paper² *vt* ‹*wall/room*› empapelar *or* (Méx tb) tapizar*

Phrasal verb

• **paper over** [v ▸ o ▸ adv, v ▸ adv ▸ o] ‹*hole/crack*› tapar con papel; ‹*rift/quarrel*› tapar, disimular

paper: **~back** *n* libro *m* en rústica *or* (Méx) de pasta blanda; **available in ~back** a la venta en (edición) rústica; **~ bag** *n* bolsa *f* de papel; **~clip** *n* clip *m*, sujetapapeles *m*; **~ tiger** *n* tigre *m* de papel (*persona o institución que parece poderosa pero en realidad es débil o insignificante*); **~weight** *n* pisapapeles *m*; **~work** *n* [u] papeleo *m* (fam), trabajo *m* administrativo, tareas *fpl* administrativas

papier mâché /ˈpeɪpərməˈʃeɪ || ˌpæpjerˈmæʃeɪ/ *n* [u] papel *m* maché, cartón *m* piedra (Esp)

papist /ˈpeɪpəst || ˈpeɪpɪst/ *n* (pej) papista *mf*

papoose /pəˈpuːs/ *n*: *bebé o niño indio norteamericano*

pappy /ˈpæpi/ *n* (*pl* **-pies**) (AmE dial) papá *m*, papi *m* (fam)

paprika /pəˈpriːkə || ˈpæprɪkə/ *n* [u] pimentón *m* dulce, paprika *f*

Pap smear, Pap test (AmE) /pæp/ *n* citología *f*, frotis *m*, Papanicolau *m* (AmL)

Papua New Guinea /'pɑːpuə || 'pæpjʊə/ *n* Papua Nueva Guinea *f*

papyrus /pə'paɪrəs/ *n* (*pl* **-ruses** *or* **-ri** /-raɪ/) papiro *m*

par /pɑːr || pɑː(r)/ *n* [u]

A 1 (equal level) **on a ~ (with sb/sth): the two athletes are on a ~** los dos atletas son del mismo nivel; **the two systems are more or less on a ~** los dos sistemas son más o menos parecidos *or* equivalentes; **the new law puts us on a ~ with workers in other countries** la nueva ley nos pone en igualdad de condiciones *or* nos equipara con los trabajadores de otros países 2 (accepted standard): **your work is below** *o* **not up to ~** tu trabajo no está a la altura de lo que se esperaba; **not to be/feel up to ~, to be/feel below ~** (colloq) no estar*/sentirse* del todo bien

B (Fin): **at ~ (value)** a la par; **above/below ~ (value)** por encima/por debajo de la par

C (in golf) par *m*; **three under/over ~** tres bajo/sobre par; **~ *for the course*** (normal, standard) lo normal, lo habitual

parable /'pærəbəl/ *n* parábola *f*

parabola /pə'ræbələ/ *n* (Math) parábola *f*

paracetamol /'pærə'siːtəmɔːl || ˌpærə'setəmɒl/ *n* [u c] (esp BrE) paracetamol *m*

parachute¹ /'pærəʃuːt/ *n* paracaídas *m*; (*before n*) **~ jump** salto *m* en *or* con paracaídas

parachute² *vi* saltar *or* lanzarse* en *or* con paracaídas
■ **parachute** *vt* ‹*troops/supplies*› lanzar* en *or* con paracaídas

parachutist /'pærəʃuːtəst || 'pærəʃuːtɪst/ *n* paracaidista *mf*

parade¹ /pə'reɪd/ *n* 1 (procession) desfile *m*; (Mil) desfile *m*, parada *f* 2 (assembly) (Mil) formación *f*; **to be on ~** (Mil) estar* formado *or* en formación; (on display) estar* en exposición *or* a la vista de todos; (*before n*) **~ ground** plaza *f* de armas 3 (of shops) (BrE) hilera *f* de tiendas

parade² *vt* 1 (display) ‹*placards*› desfilar con; ‹*feelings/knowledge*› hacer* alarde *or* ostentación de, alardear de; ‹*wealth*› hacer* ostentación de, ostentar 2 (march, walk) ‹*streets*› desfilar por 3 (assemble) ‹*troops*› hacer* formar
■ **parade** *vi* 1 (march, walk) desfilar; **to ~ up and down** «*soldier/model/child*» desfilar; (swagger, strut) andar* de aquí para allá pavoneándose 2 (masquerade): **self-interest parading as humanitarianism** el propio interés haciéndose pasar por humanitarismo 3 (assemble) (Mil) formar

paradigm /'pærədaɪm/ *n* (frml) paradigma *m*, ejemplo *m*

paradise /'pærədaɪs/ *n* [u] 1 (heaven) paraíso *m* 2 **Paradise** (Garden of Eden) Paraíso *m* (Terrenal)

paradox /'pærədɑːks || 'pærədɒks/ *n* [c u] paradoja *f*

paradoxical /'pærə'dɑːksɪkəl || ˌpærə'dɒksɪkəl/ *adj* paradójico

paraffin /'pærəfən || 'pærəfɪn/ *n* [u] 1 **~ (wax)** parafina *f* 2 **~ (oil)** (BrE) queroseno *m*, kerosene *m*, parafina *f* (Chi)

paraglide /'pærəglaɪd/ *vi* hacer* *or* practicar* parapente

paraglider /'pærəglaɪdər || 'pærəglaɪdə(r)/ *n* 1 (device) parapente *m* 2 (person) parapentista *mf*

paragliding /'pærəglaɪdɪŋ/ *n* [u] parapente *m*

paragon /'pærəgɑːn || 'pærəgən/ *n*: **a ~ of virtue** (set phrase) un dechado de virtudes (fr hecha)

paragraph /'pærəgræf || 'pærəgrɑːf/ *n* 1 (subdivision) párrafo *m*; **period** (AmE) *o* (BrE) **full stop; new ~** punto y aparte 2 (in newspaper) artículo *m* corto

Paraguay /'pærəgwaɪ/ *n* Paraguay *m*

Paraguayan¹ /'pærə'gwaɪən/ *adj* paraguayo

Paraguayan² *n* paraguayo, -ya *m,f*

parakeet /'pærəkiːt/ *n* periquito *m*

parallel¹ /'pærəlel/ *adj*

A 1 ‹*streets/rows*› paralelo; **~ lines** rectas *fpl* paralelas; **~ TO sth** paralelo A algo 2 (similar) paralelo, análogo

B 1 (Comput) en paralelo 2 (Electron) ‹*circuit*› paralelo

parallel² *n*

A 1 (Math) (line) paralela *f* 2 (Geog) paralelo *m*

B 1 (similarity): **one is struck by the ~s with contemporary Africa** llama la atención el paralelismo que existe con el África contemporánea; **without ~** sin parangón, sin paralelo 2 (comparison): **to draw a ~** establecer* un paralelismo *or* un paralelo

C **in parallel** (together, simultaneously) paralelamente; (Elec) en paralelo

parallel³ *vt* **-l-** *or* (BrE also) **-ll-** (frml) ser* análogo *or* paralelo a

parallel bars *pl n* (barras *fpl*) paralelas *fpl*

parallelogram /'pærə'leləgræm/ *n* paralelogramo *m*

parallel port *n* puerto *m* paralelo

Paralympics /ˌpærə'lɪmpɪks/ *pl n* juegos *mpl* paralímpicos

paralysis /pə'ræləsəs || pə'ræləsɪs/ *n* (*pl* **-ses** /-siːz/) 1 [u c] (Med) parálisis *f*; **creeping ~** parálisis progresiva 2 [u] (inactivity, powerlessness) paralización *f*

paralytic¹ /'pærə'lɪtɪk/ *adj* 1 (Med) paralítico 2 (very drunk) (BrE colloq) como una cuba (fam)

paralytic² *n* paralítico, -ca *m,f*

paralyze /'pærəlaɪz/ *vt* paralizar*

paramedic /'pærə'medɪk/ *n*: *profesional conectado con la medicina, como enfermero, kinesiólogo etc*

parameter /pə'ræmətər || pə'ræmɪtə(r)/ *n* parámetro *m*

paramilitary /'pærə'mɪləteri || ˌpærə'mɪlɪtəri/ *adj* paramilitar

paramount /'pærəmaʊnt/ *adj* (frml) primordial; **of ~ importance** de primordial importancia

paranoia /'pærə'nɔɪə/ *n* [u] paranoia *f*

paranoiac /'pærənɔɪæk/ *adj* paranoico

paranoid /'pærənɔɪd/ *adj* paranoico; **~ schizophrenia** esquizofrenia *f* paranoide

paranormal¹ /'pærə'nɔːrməl || ˌpærə'nɔːməl/ *adj* paranormal

paranormal² *n* [u] **the ~** lo paranormal

parapet /'pærəpət || 'pærəpɪt/ *n* parapeto *m*, pretil *m*; (Mil) parapeto *m*

paraphernalia /'pærəfər'neɪljə || ˌpærəfə'neɪliə/ *n* [u] parafernalia *f*

paraphrase /'pærəfreɪz/ *vt* parafrasear

paraplegic¹ /'pærə'pliːdʒɪk/ *adj* parapléjico

paraplegic² *n* parapléjico, -ca *m,f*

parasail /'pærəseɪl/ *vi* hacer* parasail, hacer* paravela

parasailing /'pærəseɪlɪŋ/ *n* [u] parasail *m*, paravela *f*

parasite /'pærəsaɪt/ *n* parásito *m*

parasitic /'pærə'sɪtɪk/ *adj* 1 ‹*animal/plant*› parásito; ‹*disease*› parasitario 2 ‹*person*› parásito

parasol /'pærəsɔːl || 'pærəsɒl/ *n* sombrilla *f*, quitasol *m*

paratrooper /'pærəˌtruːpər || 'pærəˌtruːpə(r)/ *n* (Mil) paracaidista *mf* (*del ejército*)

paratroops /'pærətruːps/ *pl n* (Mil) paracaidistas *mpl* (*del ejército*)

parboil /'pɑːrbɔɪl || 'pɑːbɔɪl/ *vt* dar* un hervor a

parcel¹ /'pɑːrsəl || 'pɑːsəl/ *n*

A (package) (BrE) paquete *m*; (*before n*) **~ post** servicio *m* de paquetes postales *or* (AmL tb) de encomiendas

B (of land) parcela *f*; ▸ **part¹ A2**

parcel² *vt*, (BrE) **-ll-**: **~ (up)** empaquetar

Phrasal verb

• **parcel out** [v ▸ o ▸ adv, v ▸ adv ▸ o] dividir, repartir; ‹*land*› parcelar, dividir en parcelas

parched /pɑːrtʃt || pɑːtʃt/ *adj* 1 (very dry) reseco, agostado 2 (very thirsty) (colloq) (*pred*) **to be ~** estar* muerto de sed (fam)

parchment /'pɑːrtʃmənt || 'pɑːtʃmənt/ *n* pergamino *m*

pardon¹ /'pɑːrdn̩ || 'pɑːdn̩/ *n*

A 1 [u] (forgiveness) perdón *m*; **to ask sb's ~** pedirle* perdón a algn 2 (*as interj*): **~?** *o* (frml) **I beg your ~?** (requesting repetition) ¿cómo?, ¿cómo dice? (frml), ¿mande? (Méx); **I beg your ~** (apologizing) perdón, perdone (usted), disculpe; (expressing disagreement) perdone, con perdón; **that's a lie — I *beg* your ~?** (expressing annoyance, shock) eso es mentira — ¿qué has dicho?

B [c] (Law) indulto *m*; **to grant sb a ~** indultar a algn

pardon² *vt*

A (forgive) perdonar; **to ~ sb sth** perdonarle algo a algn; **~ me!** (apologizing) ¡perdón!, ¡ay, disculpe!; **~ me?** (requesting repetition) (esp AmE) ¿cómo?, ¿cómo dice? (frml)

B (Law) ‹*offender*› indultar

pardonable /'pɑːrdn̩əbəl || 'pɑːdn̩əbəl/ *adj* perdonable, comprensible

P

pare /per || peə(r)/ *vt* 1 (peel) pelar, mondar 2 (trim) ‹*nails*› cortar 3 ▸**pare down**

Phrasal verb

• **pare down** [v ▸ o ▸ adv, v ▸ adv ▸ o] reducir*, recortar

parent /ˈperənt || ˈpeərənt/ *n*: **my/his ~s** mis/sus padres; **it has to be signed by a ~** tiene que firmarlo uno de los padres; **the responsibility of being a ~** las responsabilidades que conlleva el ser padre/madre, las responsabilidades de la paternidad/maternidad; (*before n*) ‹*plant/birds*› progenitor; ‹*cell*› madre; **~ company** *o* **corporation** sociedad *f or* empresa *f* matriz

parentage /ˈperəntɪdʒ || ˈpeərəntɪdʒ/ *n* (frml): **of humble/noble ~** de origen humilde/noble

parental /pəˈrentl/ *adj* de los padres

parenthesis /pəˈrenθəsəs || pəˈrenθəsɪs/ *n* (*pl* **-theses** /-θəsi:z/) paréntesis *m*; **in parentheses** entre paréntesis

parenthood /ˈperənthʊd || ˈpeərənthʊd/ *n* [u] el ser padre/madre, la paternidad/maternidad

parenting /ˈperəntɪŋ || ˈpeərəntɪŋ/ *n* [u] crianza *f* de los hijos

parent-teacher association /ˈperəntˈti:tʃər || ˌpeərəntˈti:tʃə(r)/ *n* asociación *f* de padres y maestros

par excellence /ˈpɑ:rˈeksəˈlɑ:ns/ *adj* (frml) (*after n*) por excelencia

pariah /pəˈraɪə/ *n* paria *mf*

parings /ˈperɪŋz || ˈpeərɪŋz/ *pl n* 1 (of fruit, vegetables) cáscaras *fpl*, mondas *fpl* 2 (of nails) trozos *mpl* (de uña)

Paris /ˈpærəs || ˈpærɪs/ *n* París *m*; (*before n*) parisino, parisiense

parish /ˈpærɪʃ/ *n*
A (Relig) parroquia *f*; (*before n*) ‹*newsletter/community*› parroquial; **~ church** parroquia *f*, iglesia *f* parroquial; **~ council** (in England) consejo *m* del distrito; **~ priest** (cura *m*) párroco *m*
B (Govt) distrito *m*

parishioner /pəˈrɪʃənər || pəˈrɪʃənə(r)/ *n* feligrés, -gresa *m,f* (*de una parroquia*)

Parisian[1] /pəˈrɪʒən || pəˈrɪziən/ *adj* parisino, parisiense

Parisian[2] *n* parisino, -na *m,f*, parisiense *mf*

parity /ˈpærəti/ *n* (*pl* **-ties**) 1 [u] (equality) (frml) igualdad *f*, paridad *f* 2 [u c] (Fin) paridad *f* 3 [u] (Phys, Math, Comput) paridad *f*

park[1] /pɑ:rk || pɑ:k/ *n*
A 1 (in town) parque *m*; (*before n*) **~ bench** banco *m or* (Méx) banca *f* (de plaza) 2 (in a private estate) jardines *mpl*
B (stadium) (AmE) estadio *m*

park[2] *vt* 1 ‹*car*› estacionar (esp AmL), aparcar* (Esp), parquear (AmL) 2 (put) (colloq) ‹*bags/books*› dejar, poner*; **~ yourself there** ponte ahí
■ **park** *vi* (Auto) estacionar (esp AmL), aparcar* (Esp), parquear (AmL), estacionarse (Chi, Méx)

parka /ˈpɑ:rkə || ˈpɑ:kə/ *n* parka *f*

park-and-ride /ˈpɑ:rkn̩ˈraɪd || ˌpɑ:kənˈraɪd/ *n*: *sistema de estacionamiento en zonas adyacentes al centro, desde donde se puede utilizar el transporte colectivo*

parking /ˈpɑ:rkɪŋ || ˈpɑ:kɪŋ/ *n* [u] estacionamiento *m* (esp AmL), aparcamiento *m* (Esp); **no parking** prohibido estacionar (esp AmL) *or* (Esp) aparcar *or* (AmL) parquear; (*before n*) **~ attendant** guardacoches *mf*; **a ~ place** *o* **space** un lugar para estacionar (*or* aparcar *etc*); **~ ticket** multa *f* (por estacionamiento indebido)

parking: **~ garage** *n* (AmE) estacionamiento *m* (esp AmL), aparcamiento *m* (Esp), parking *m* (Esp); **~ lot** *n* (AmE) estacionamiento *m* (esp AmL), aparcamiento *m* (Esp), parking *m* (Esp), parqueadero *m* (Col); **~ meter** *n* parquímetro *m*

Parkinson's Disease /ˈpɑ:rkənsənz || ˈpɑ:kɪnsənz/ *n* [u] enfermedad *f or* mal *m* de Parkinson, Parkinson *m*

park: **~land** *n* [u] (surrounding mansion) jardines *mpl*; (public) parques *mpl*, zona *f* verde; **~ ranger** *n* guardaparques *mf*, guardaparque *mf* (AmL); **~way** *n* (AmE) carretera *f*/avenida *f* ajardinada, paseo *m*

parlance /ˈpɑ:rləns || ˈpɑ:ləns/ *n* [u] (frml) lenguaje *m*, habla *f*‡; **in common ~** de uso común

parley /ˈpɑ:rli || ˈpɑ:li/ *vi* **to ~ (WITH sb)** negociar *or* parlamentar (CON algn)

parliament /ˈpɑ:rləmənt || ˈpɑ:ləmənt/ *n* 1 (assembly) parlamento *m* 2 **Parliament** (in UK etc — body) Parlamento *m*; (period) legislatura *f*

parliamentarian /ˈpɑ:rləmenˈteriən || ˌpɑ:ləmenˈteəriən/ *n* parlamentario, -ria *m,f*

parliamentary /ˈpɑ:rləˈmentəri || ˌpɑ:ləˈmentri/ *adj* parlamentario; **~ democracy** democracia *f* parlamentaria

parlor, (BrE) **parlour** /ˈpɑ:rlər || ˈpɑ:lə(r)/ *n*
A (dated in BrE) (in house) salón *m* (esp Esp), sala *f* (de estar)
B (for business) (AmE) sala *f*; **billiard ~** (sala *f* de) billar *m*; **ice-cream ~** heladería *f*

parlor car *n* (AmE) ≈ vagón *m* de primera clase

parlour *n* (BrE) ▸**parlor**

parlous /ˈpɑ:rləs || ˈpɑ:ləs/ *adj* (frml *or* hum) lamentable, calamitoso

Parmesan (cheese) /ˈpɑ:rməzɑ:n || ˈpɑ:mɪzæn/ *n* [u c] (queso *m*) parmesano *m*

parochial /pəˈrəʊkiəl/ *adj* 1 (narrow) (pej) ‹*person/attitude/outlook*› provinciano, pueblerino 2 (Relig) parroquial; **~ school** (AmE) colegio *m* privado religioso

parody[1] /ˈpærədi/ *n* (*pl* **-dies**) parodia *f*

parody[2] *vt* **-dies, -dying, -died** parodiar

parole[1] /pəˈrəʊl/ *n* [u] libertad *f* condicional; **he was released on ~** fue dejado en libertad condicional

parole[2] *vt* ‹*prisoner*› dejar en libertad condicional

paroxysm /ˈpærəksɪzəm/ *n* (Med) paroxismo *m*, acceso *m* violento; (outburst): **the news sent them into ~s of laughter** la noticia los hizo desternillarse de risa

parquet /pɑ:rˈkeɪ || ˈpɑ:keɪ/ *n* [u]
A (Const) parqué *m*, parquet *m*
B (AmE Theat) platea *f*

parrot /ˈpærət/ *n* (Zool) loro *m*, papagayo *m*

parrot-fashion /ˈpærətˌfæʃən/ *adv* (BrE) como un loro *or* papagayo

parry[1] /ˈpæri/ *vt* **-ries, -rying, -ried** ‹*blow/thrust*› parar; ‹*attack*› rechazar*; ‹*question*› eludir

parry[2] *n* (*pl* **-ries**) (in fencing, boxing) parada *f*

parse /pɑ:rz || pɑ:z/ *vt* analizar* sintácticamente

parser /ˈpɑ:rzər || ˈpɑ:zə(r)/ *n* parser *m*, analizador *m* sintáctico *or* de sintaxis

parsimonious /ˈpɑ:rsəˈməʊniəs || ˌpɑ:sɪˈməʊniəs/ *adj* (frml) mezquino

parsley /ˈpɑ:rsli || ˈpɑ:sli/ *n* [u] perejil *m*

parsnip /ˈpɑ:rsnəp || ˈpɑ:snɪp/ *n* [c u] chirivía *f*, pastinaca *f*

parson /ˈpɑ:rsn̩ || ˈpɑ:sn̩/ *n* clérigo *m*; (vicar) ≈ (cura *m*) párroco *m*

parsonage /ˈpɑ:rsn̩ɪdʒ || ˈpɑ:sənɪdʒ/ *n* ≈ casa *f* del párroco

part[1] /pɑ:rt || pɑ:t/ *n*
A 1 [c] (section) parte *f*; **the book is funny in ~s** el libro tiene partes divertidas; **in my ~ of the world** en mi país (*or* región *etc*); **the worst ~ of it was that ...** lo peor de todo fue que ...; **for the best ~ of a week/month** durante casi una semana/un mes 2 [c] (integral constituent) (*no pl*) parte *f*; **it's all ~ of growing up** todos tenemos que pasar por eso; ***to be ~ and parcel of sth*** formar parte de algo 3 (*in phrases*) **in part** en parte; **for the most part** en su mayor parte; *see also* **part of speech**
B [c] (measure) parte *f*; **two ~s milk to one ~ water** dos partes de leche por cada parte de agua
C [c] (component) pieza *f*; (*spare* **~**) repuesto *m*, pieza *f* de recambio, refacción *f* (Méx)
D [c] 1 (in play) papel *m*; **a bit ~** un papel secundario, un papelito (fam); **he acted/played the ~ of Hamlet** representó/hizo el papel de Hamlet; **if you're a manager, you must act/look the ~** si eres director, tienes que actuar/vestir como tu rol lo exige 2 (role, share) papel *m*; **she had** *o* **played a major ~ in ...** tuvo *or* jugó *or* desempeñó un papel fundamental en ...; **I want no ~ in it** yo no quiero tener nada que ver con eso; **to take ~ in sth** tomar parte *or* participar en algo
E (side): **for my ~** por mi parte, por mi lado; ***to take sb's ~*** ponerse* de parte *or* de lado de algn, tomar partido por algn; ***to take sth in good ~*** tomarse algo bien, no tomarse algo a mal
F [c] (section of book, play) parte *f*; (episode of TV, radio serial) episodio *m*; (Publ) fascículo *m*

G [c] (Mus) (vocal, instrumental line) parte *f*
H [c] (in hair) (AmE) raya *f*, carrera *f* (Col, Ven), partidura *f* (Chi)
I **parts** *pl* 1 (area): **in/around these ~s** por aquí, por estos lares (arc), por estos pagos (fam); **in foreign ~s** en el extranjero 2 (capabilities): **a man of many ~s** un hombre de muchas facetas

part² *vt* 1 (separate) separar 2 (divide): **she ~s her hair down the middle** se peina con raya al *or* (Esp) en medio, se peina con la carrera por el medio (Col, Ven), se peina con partidura al medio (Chi)

■ **part** *vi* 1 (separate) «*lovers*» separarse; **they ~ed as friends** quedaron como amigos 2 «*curtains/lips*» (open up) abrirse* 3 (break) «*rope/cable*» romperse*

Phrasal verb

• **part with** [v ▸ prep ▸ o] ‹*possession*› desprenderse *or* deshacerse* de; **they don't want to ~ with their money** no quieren desembolsar *or* (fam) soltar dinero

part³ *adv* en parte; **I was ~ angry, ~ relieved** en parte *or* por un lado me dio rabia, pero al mismo tiempo fue un alivio; **he's ~ Chinese and ~ French** tiene sangre china y francesa; *see also* **part exchange**

part⁴ *adj* (*before n*) ‹*payment*› parcial; **~ owner** copropietario, -ria *m,f*

partake /pɑːr'teɪk || pɑː'teɪk/ *vi* (*past* **partook**; *past p* **partaken**)
A (consume) (frml *or* hum) **to ~ OF sth**: **he wouldn't ~ of the meal** no quiso aceptar la invitación a compartir la comida
B (take part) (liter) **to ~ IN sth** ser* partícipe DE algo (frml)

part exchange *n* [u] (esp BrE): **in ~ ~** a cuenta *or* como parte del pago

partial /'pɑːrʃəl || 'pɑːʃəl/ *adj*
A (not complete) ‹*paralysis/solution/payment*› parcial; **a ~ success** un éxito a medias; **she made a ~ recovery** se recuperó parcialmente
B 1 (fond) (*pred*) **to be ~ TO sth** tener* debilidad POR algo 2 (biased) (frml) ‹*judge/arbiter*› parcial

partiality /'pɑːrʃi'æləti || ˌpɑːʃi'æləti/ *n* [u] 1 (bias) parcialidad *f* 2 (fondness) **~ FOR sth** debilidad *f* POR algo

partially /'pɑːrʃəli || 'pɑːʃəli/ *adv* 1 (partly) parcialmente 2 (with bias) con parcialidad

participant /pər'tɪsəpənt, pɑːr- || pɑː'tɪsɪpənt/ *n* participante *mf*

participate /pər'tɪsəpeɪt, pɑːr- || pɑː'tɪsɪpeɪt/ *vi* **to ~ (IN sth)** participar *or* tomar parte (EN algo)

participation /pər'tɪsə'peɪʃən, pɑːr- || pɑːˌtɪsɪ'peɪʃən/ *n* [u] participación *f*

participatory /pər'tɪsəpətɔːri, pɑːr- || pɑː'tɪsəpətəri/ *adj* participativo

participle /'pɑːrtəsɪpəl || 'pɑːtɪsɪpəl/ *n* participio *m*; **past/present ~** participio pasado *or* pasivo/activo *or* de presente

particle /'pɑːrtɪkəl || 'pɑːtɪkəl/ *n* partícula *f*

particular¹ /pər'tɪkjələr || pə'tɪkjʊlə(r)/ *adj*
A (specific, precise): **in this ~ instance** en este caso concreto *or* particular; **this ~ specimen** este ejemplar en concreto *or* en particular; **is there any ~ style you'd prefer?** ¿tiene preferencia por algún estilo determinado *or* en particular?; **why did you do it? — no ~ reason** ¿por qué lo hiciste? — por nada en especial *or* en particular
B (special) ‹*interest/concern*› especial; **I want you to take ~ care with this** quiero que pongas especial cuidado en esto
C (fastidious) (*pred*) **to be ~ (ABOUT sth)**: **she's very ~ about what she eats** es muy especial *or* (pey) maniática con la comida, no se come cualquier cosa; **you can't afford to be too ~** no puedes ponerte a exigir demasiado

particular² *n*
A (detail) (frml) (*usu pl*) detalle *m*; **please send me full ~s** por favor envíeme información detallada; **in every ~** *o* **in all ~s** en todo sentido; **just fill in your ~s on this form** (BrE) rellene este formulario con sus datos
B 1 (specific points): **from the general to the ~** de lo general a lo particular 2 **in particular** en particular, en especial

particularly /pər'tɪkjələrli || pə'tɪkjʊləli/ *adv* 1 (specifically) específicamente, en particular, en especial 2 (especially) particularmente, especialmente; **I'm ~ fond of Sarah** le tengo especial cariño a Sarah; **are you cold? — not ~** ¿tienes frío? — no mucho

parting¹ /'pɑːrtɪŋ || 'pɑːtɪŋ/ *n*
A [u] (separation) despedida *f*; **so this is the ~ of the ways** así que ésta es la despedida definitiva
B [c] (in hair) (BrE) raya *f*, carrera *f* (Col, Ven), partidura *f* (Chi)

parting² *adj* (*before n*) ‹*kiss/words*› de despedida; **her ~ shot was …** lo último que dijo al despedirse fue …

partisan¹ /'pɑːrtəzən || 'pɑːtɪzæn/ *n* 1 (guerrilla) partisano, -na *m,f*, miembro *mf* de la resistencia 2 (supporter) partidario, -ria *m,f*

partisan² *adj* ‹*crowd/decision*› partidista; ‹*account*› parcial

partition¹ /pər'tɪʃən, pɑːr- || pɑː'tɪʃən/ *n*
A [c] 1 (screen) tabique *m*; **a glass ~** una mampara de vidrio *or* (Esp) de cristal 2 (divider) separador *m*
B [u c] (of country, territory) división *f*, partición *f*

partition² *vt* 1 ‹*country/territory*› dividir 2 ‹*room/corridor*› dividir con un tabique/con una mampara

Phrasal verb

• **partition off** [v ▸ o ▸ adv, v ▸ adv ▸ o] separar, dividir (*con un tabique, una mampara etc*)

partly /'pɑːrtli || 'pɑːtli/ *adv* en parte; **it's only ~ true** sólo es verdad en parte; **it was ~ destroyed** fue parcialmente destruido

partner¹ /'pɑːrtnər || 'pɑːtnə(r)/ *n* 1 (in an activity) compañero, -ra *m,f*; (in dancing, tennis) pareja *f* 2 (Busn) socio, -cia *m,f*; **~s in crime** cómplices *mpl or fpl*, compinches *mpl or fpl* (fam) 3 (in personal relationship) pareja *f*, compañero, -ra *m,f*

partner² *vt* 1 (act as partner to): **he ~ed Moira** jugó (*or* bailó *etc*) en pareja con Moira 2 (pair) **to ~ sb WITH sb** poner* a algn CON algn (como pareja)

partnership /'pɑːrtnərʃɪp || 'pɑːtnəʃɪp/ *n* 1 [u c] (relationship) asociación *f*; **the teachers work in ~ with the parents** los profesores trabajan conjuntamente con los padres 2 [u c] (Busn) sociedad *f* (colectiva); **he went into ~ with his brother-in-law** se asoció con su cuñado 3 [c] (position as partner): **he aspires to a ~ in the firm** aspira a ser socio de la empresa

part of speech *n* (*pl* **~s ~ ~**): **what ~ ~ ~ is it?** ¿qué función gramatical tiene?, ¿a qué categoría gramatical pertenece?; **the ~s ~ ~** las partes de la oración

partook /pɑːr'tʊk || pɑː'tʊk/ *past of* **partake**

partridge /'pɑːrtrɪdʒ || 'pɑːtrɪdʒ/ *n* (*pl* **~s** *or* **~**) perdiz *f*

part-time¹ /'pɑːrt'taɪm || ˌpɑːt'taɪm/ *adj* de medio tiempo (AmL), a tiempo parcial

part-time² *adv* de medio tiempo (AmL), a tiempo parcial (Esp); **to work ~** trabajar de medio tiempo (AmL) *or* (Esp) a tiempo parcial

part: **~-timer** /'pɑːrt'taɪmər || ˌpɑːt'taɪmə(r)/ *n* trabajador, -dora *m,f* de medio tiempo (AmL) *or* (Esp) a tiempo parcial; **~way** /'pɑːrt'weɪ || ˌpɑːt'weɪ/ *adv*: **the TV broke down ~way through the film** la televisión se estropeó al rato de empezar la película

party¹ /'pɑːrti || 'pɑːti/ *n*
A (event) fiesta *f*; **I was invited to a tea/dinner ~** me invitaron a un té/a una cena; **to have** *o* (colloq) **throw a ~** dar* *or* hacer* una fiesta; (*before n*) ‹*mood*› festivo; ‹*game*› de salón; ‹*dress*› de fiesta
B (Pol) partido *m*; (*before n*) ‹*member/leader*› del partido; **~ politics** política *f* de partido; (pej) partidismo *m*
C (group) grupo *m*; (in hunting) partida *f*
D (person or body involved) parte *f*; **a third ~** un tercero; **all parties concerned** todos los interesados; **the guilty/innocent ~** el culpable/inocente; **to be (a) ~ to a crime** ser* cómplice de un crimen

party² *vi* (esp AmE colloq) (go to parties) ir* a fiestas; (have fun) divertirse*; **let's ~!** ¡vámonos de juerga! (fam)

party-goer *n*: **the street was full of ~s** la calle estaba llena de gente que iba de fiesta; **I'm not a great ~** no soy muy dado a ir a fiestas

partying /'pɑːrtiɪŋ || 'pɑːtiɪŋ/ *n* [u]: **he loves ~** le gusta la parranda (fam), le va la marcha (Esp fam), le gusta el carrete (Chi fam)

party: **~ line** *n* 1 (Pol) **the ~ line** la línea del partido; 2 (Telec) línea *f* colectiva (*línea telefónica compartida por dos o más abonados*); **~ list** *n* lista *f* de partido; **~ piece** *n*

P

[u] (BrE) numerito *m* (fam); **~ political broadcast** *n* (BrE TV) *emisión de propaganda de un partido político*

pass¹ /pæs || pɑːs/ *n*
A (document, permit) pase *m*; (ticket) abono *m*; **bus/rail ~** abono de autobús/tren
B (Geog) paso *m*; (narrow) desfiladero *m*
C (in test, examination) (BrE) aprobado *m*; (*before n*) **the ~ mark** la nota mínima para aprobar
D (Sport) pase *m*
E (sexual advance): **to make a ~ at sb** intentar besar a algn
F (state of affairs) (*no pl*): **things have come to a pretty ~** hay que ver a dónde hemos llegado

pass² *vt*
(Sense I)
A 1 (go by, past) ‹*shop/house*› pasar por; **I ~ed him in the street** me crucé con él en la calle; **not a drop has ~ed my lips** no he bebido ni gota 2 (overtake) pasar, adelantar, rebasar (Méx)
B 1 (cross, go beyond) ‹*limit*› pasar; ‹*frontier*› pasar, cruzar* 2 (surpass) sobrepasar
C (spend) ‹*time*› pasar; **to ~ the time** pasar el rato
(Sense II)
A 1 (convey, hand over) **to ~ sb sth, to ~ sth TO sb** pasarle algo A algn; **~ (me) the sugar, please** ¿me pasas el azúcar, por favor? 2 (Sport) ‹*ball*› pasar
B (Med): **to ~ water** orinar
C (utter) ‹*comment/remark*› hacer*; **to ~ sentence** dictar sentencia, fallar
(Sense III) 1 (succeed in) ‹*exam/test*› aprobar*, salvar (Ur); **it ~es all the safety requirements** cumple con todos los requisitos de seguridad 2 (approve) ‹*candidate/work*› aprobar*; **he was ~ed fit for military service** fue declarado apto para el servicio militar 3 ‹*law/motion*› aprobar*
■ **pass** *vi*
(Sense I)
A (move, travel) pasar; **~ along the car, please** córranse *or* pasen adelante, por favor; **her name ~ed into history/oblivion** su nombre pasó a la historia/fue relegado al olvido; **we watched until he ~ed out of sight** nos quedamos mirando hasta que lo perdimos de vista; **we are now ~ing over Washington** estamos sobrevolando Washington; **the rope ~es through this ring** la cuerda pasa por esta anilla; **the thought ~ed through my mind** la idea (se) me pasó por la cabeza; **the road ~es under a bridge** la carretera pasa por debajo de un puente
B 1 (go, move past) pasar; **I was just ~ing** pasaba por aquí; **they ~ed on the stairs** se cruzaron en la escalera; **his mistake ~ed unnoticed** su error pasó desapercibido; **it was a stupid remark, but let it ~** fue un comentario estúpido pero dejémoslo correr *or* no hagamos caso 2 (overtake) adelantarse, rebasar (Méx); **S no passing** (AmE) prohibido adelantar *or* (Méx) rebasar
C 1 (elapse) «*time*» pasar, transcurrir (frml); **time ~ed** pasó el tiempo 2 (disappear) «*feeling/pain*» pasarse
D (be transferred) «*title/estate/crown*» pasar; **to ~ TO sb** pasar A algn
E (happen) (arch): **to come to ~** acaecer* (liter), acontecer* (liter), suceder
F (decline chance to play) pasar; (*as interj*) ¡paso!; **I'll ~ on the dessert, thanks** no voy a tomar postre *or* (fam) voy a pasar del postre, gracias
G (Sport) **to ~ (TO sb)** pasar(le) la pelota (*or* el balón *etc*) (A algn)
H (rule) (AmE) **to ~ ON sth** pronunciarse SOBRE algo
(Sense II) 1 (be acceptable) pasar; **it's not brilliant, but it'll ~** (colloq) una maravilla no es, pero pasa; **to ~ AS sth** pasar POR algo 2 (in an exam) aprobar*, pasar
(Phrasal verbs)
• **pass away** [v ▸ adv] (frml & euph) 1 (die) fallecer* (frml) 2 (cease to exist) desaparecer*
• **pass by**
A [v ▸ adv] (go past) pasar; **we were just ~ing by** pasábamos por aquí
B [v ▸ o ▸ adv] (not affect): **time had ~ed the village by** el tiempo no había pasado por el pueblo; **he felt life had ~ed him by** sentía que no había vivido
• **pass down** [v ▸ o ▸ adv, v ▸ adv ▸ o] (*often pass*) ‹*heirloom*› pasar; ‹*story/tradition*› transmitir
• **pass for** [v ▸ prep ▸ o] pasar por
• **pass off**
A [v ▸ adv] 1 (take place): **the march ~ed off without incident** la marcha transcurrió *or* se llevó a cabo *or* se desarrolló sin incidentes 2 (cease) «*pain/depression*» pasarse, quitarse, irse*
B [v ▸ o ▸ adv, v ▸ adv ▸ o] (represent falsely) hacer* pasar; **she ~ed herself off as a journalist** se hizo pasar por periodista
• **pass on**
A [v ▸ o ▸ adv, v ▸ adv ▸ o] ‹*information*› pasar, dar*; ‹*infection*› contagiar, pegar* (fam); **the costs are ~ed on to the customer** los costos los paga el cliente, los costos se repercuten en *or* sobre el cliente
B [v ▸ adv] 1 **to ~ on TO sth** pasar A algo 2 ▸ **pass away**
• **pass out**
A [v ▸ adv] 1 (become unconscious) desmayarse, perder* el conocimiento 2 (graduate) (BrE) «*cadet*» graduarse*
B [v ▸ o ▸ adv, v ▸ adv ▸ o] (distribute) repartir
• **pass over**
A [v ▸ adv ▸ o] 1 (omit) ‹*fact/detail*› pasar por alto 2 (overlook) ‹*remark/behavior*› pasar por alto, dejar pasar
B [v ▸ o ▸ adv] (disregard for promotion) (*usu pass*) pasarle por encima a
• **pass through**
A 1 [v ▸ adv] pasar; **we're just ~ing through** estamos sólo de paso 2 [v ▸ prep ▸ o] ‹*town/area*› pasar por
B [v ▸ prep ▸ o] (experience) ‹*period/phase*› pasar por
• **pass up** [v ▸ o ▸ adv, v ▸ adv ▸ o] (colloq) ‹*opportunity*› dejar pasar, desperdiciar

passable /ˈpæsəbəl || ˈpɑːsəbəl/ *adj* 1 (adequate) pasable, aceptable 2 ‹*road/route*› transitable

passage /ˈpæsɪdʒ/ *n*
A [c] 1 (alleyway) callejón *m*, pasaje *m*; (narrow) pasadizo *m* 2 (corridor) (esp BrE) pasillo *m*, corredor *m*; **secret ~** pasadizo *m* secreto 3 (Anat) conducto *m*; **back ~** (euph) recto *m*
B [u] 1 (right to pass) (frml) derecho *m* de tránsito; (movement) paso *m*; **the ~ of the bill through parliament** la discusión del proyecto en el parlamento 2 (transition) paso *m* 3 (lapse): **the ~ of time** el paso *or* el transcurso del tiempo
C [c] (voyage) viaje *m*, travesía *f*; (fare) pasaje *m*
D [c] (extract) pasaje *m*, trozo *m*

passageway /ˈpæsɪdʒweɪ/ *n* pasillo *m*, corredor *m*

passbook /ˈpæsbʊk || ˈpɑːsbʊk/ *n* libreta *f* de ahorros

passé /pæˈseɪ || ˈpæseɪ/ *adj* pasado de moda, demodé *adj inv* (fam)

passenger /ˈpæsndʒər || ˈpæsɪndʒə(r)/ *n* pasajero, -ra *m,f*; (*before n*) **~ list** lista *f* de pasajeros; **~ seat** asiento *m* del pasajero

passer-by /ˈpæsərˈbaɪ || ˌpɑːsəˈbaɪ/ *n* (*pl* **passers-by**) transeúnte *mf*

passing¹ /ˈpæsɪŋ || ˈpɑːsɪŋ/ *adj* (*before n*)
A (going past): **she hailed a ~ taxi** llamó a un taxi que pasaba
B 1 ‹*fad/fashion*› pasajero; ‹*glance*› rápido 2 (casual): **he made a ~ reference to ...** se refirió de pasada a ...; **it was only a ~ thought** simplemente fue algo que se me ocurrió

passing² *n* [u]
A (of person) (frml & euph) fallecimiento *m* (frml), defunción *f* (frml); (of custom) (frml) desaparición *f*
B **in passing** (incidentally) al pasar, de pasada

passing: **~ lane** *n* (AmE) carril *m* de adelantamiento; **~-out** /ˈpæsɪŋˈaʊt || ˌpɑːsɪŋˈaʊt/ *n* [u] (BrE) graduación *f*; **~ shot** *n* tiro *m* pasado

passion /ˈpæʃən/ *n*
A [c u] 1 (emotion) pasión *f*; **he played with ~** tocó apasionadamente *or* con pasión; **she spoke with ~** habló con vehemencia *or* ardor; **~s were aroused by the controversy** la polémica exaltó los ánimos 2 (love, enthusiasm) pasión *f*; **crime of ~** crimen *m* pasional; **he has a ~ for opera** le apasiona la ópera 3 (rage) ira *f*, cólera *f*; **to fly into a ~** montar en cólera
B (Relig) **the P~** la Pasión; (*before n*) **P~ play** misterio *m*

passionate /ˈpæʃənət/ *adj* ‹*love*› apasionado; ‹*hatred*› mortal; ‹*admirer*› ardiente, ferviente; ‹*speech*› vehemente, ardoroso

P

passionately /ˈpæʃənətli/ *adv* ‹*love*› apasionadamente; ‹*believe*› fervientemente; ‹*desire*› ardientemente, fervientemente; ~ **in love** perdidamente enamorado; **he was ~ committed to the cause** su entrega a la causa era total; **I hate you, he said ~** te odio —dijo con vehemencia

passion fruit *n* granadilla *f*, maracuyá *m*, parchita *f* (Ven)

passive¹ /ˈpæsɪv/ *adj* 1 ‹*person/attitude*› pasivo 2 (Ling) pasivo

passive² *n* voz *f* pasiva; **in the ~** en voz pasiva

passively /ˈpæsɪvli/ *adv* pasivamente

passive: **~ smoker** *n* fumador pasivo, fumadora pasiva *m,f*; **~ smoking** *n* [u] tabaquismo *m* pasivo

passivity /pæˈsɪvəti/ *n* [u] pasividad *f*

pass: **~key** *n* llave *f* maestra; **~over** *n* Pascua *f* (*judía*); **~port** *n* pasaporte *m*; (*before n*) **~port control** control *m* de pasaportes; **~port office** *organismo que expide pasaportes*; **~port picture** *o* (BrE also) **photograph** foto *f* de carné; **~word** *n* contraseña *f*, santo *m* y seña

past¹ /pæst || pɑːst/ *adj*

A 1 (former) anterior; ‹*life*› pasado; (old) antiguo; **she knew from ~ experience that ...** sabía por experiencia que ...; **in times ~** (liter) antaño (liter), años ha (liter), antiguamente 2 (most recent) ‹*week/month/year*› último; **in the ~ few days** en los últimos días; **for some time ~** desde hace tiempo 3 (finished, gone) (*pred*): **what's ~ is ~** lo pasado, pasado; **in days long ~** en tiempos remotos

B (Ling): **the ~ tense** el pasado, el pretérito

past² *n*

A 1 [u] (former times) pasado *m*; **steam trains are a thing of the ~** las locomotoras de vapor han pasado a la historia; **in the ~, women ...** antes *or* antiguamente *or* en otros tiempos las mujeres ...; **that's all in the ~** eso forma parte del pasado, eso ya es historia 2 [c] (of person) pasado *m*; (of place) historia *f*

B [u] (Ling) pasado *m*, pretérito *m*

past³ *prep*

A 1 (by the side of): **I go ~ their house every morning** paso por (delante de) su casa todas las mañanas; **she walked straight ~ him** pasó de largo por su lado 2 (beyond): **it's just ~ the school** queda un poco más allá de la escuela; **how did you get ~ the guard?** ¿cómo hiciste para que el guardia te dejara pasar?; **the second turning ~ the lights** la segunda calle después del semáforo

B 1 (after) (esp BrE): **it's ten ~ six/half ~ two** son las seis y diez/las dos y media; **it was ~ eleven** eran las once pasadas; **it's long ~ midnight** son mucho más de las doce; **till ~ midnight** hasta después de la medianoche; **it's ~ your bedtime** ya deberías estar acostado 2 (older than): **once you get ~ 40 ...** después de los 40 ..., una vez pasados los 40 ...; **I'm ~ the age/stage when ...** ya he pasado la edad/superado la etapa en que ...

C (outside, beyond): **to be ~ -ING**: **I'm ~ caring** ya no me importa; **I wouldn't put it ~ her** no me extrañaría que lo hiciera, la creo muy capaz de hacerlo; ***to be ~ it*** (colloq): **they think everyone over 40 is ~ it** piensan que cualquiera que tenga más de 40 ya está para el arrastre (fam) *or* para cuarteles de invierno

past⁴ *adv* 1 (with verbs of motion): **to fly/cycle/drive ~** pasar volando/en bicicleta/en coche; **he hurried ~** pasó a toda prisa; **we watched the troops march ~** vimos desfilar a las tropas 2 (giving time) (esp BrE): **it's twenty-five ~** son y veinticinco

pasta /ˈpɑːstə || ˈpæstə/ *n* [u] pasta(s) *f(pl)*

paste¹ /peɪst/ *n* 1 [u c] (thick mixture) pasta *f*; **meat/fish ~** (BrE) paté *m* de carne/pescado; **tomato ~** extracto *m or* concentrado *m* de tomate 2 [u] (glue) engrudo *m*; (*wallpaper* ~) pegamento *m*, cola *f* 3 [u] (imitation gem) estrás *m*; **all her jewels are ~** todas sus joyas son de fantasía *or* bisutería

paste² *vt* **to ~ sth INTO/ONTO sth** pegar* algo EN algo

Phrasal verb

- **paste up** [v ▸ o ▸ adv, v ▸ adv ▸ o] 1 ‹*poster/notice*› pegar* 2 (Publ) armar 3 (Comput) ‹*text/paragraph*› pegar*

pastel /pæsˈtel || ˈpæstl/ *n*

A (Art) 1 (crayon) pastel *m* 2 (drawing) dibujo *m* al pastel

B (pale shade) tono *m* pastel; (*before n*) ‹*shades/color*› pastel *adj inv*

pasteurize /ˈpæstʃəraɪz || ˈpɑːstʃəraɪz/ *vt* pasteurizar*, pasterizar*

pastiche /pæsˈtiːʃ/ *n* [c u] imitación *f*, pastiche *m*

pastille /pæsˈtiːl || ˈpæstɪl/ *n* pastilla *f*

pastime /ˈpæstaɪm || ˈpɑːstaɪm/ *n* pasatiempo *m*

pasting /ˈpeɪstɪŋ/ *n* (sl) paliza *f*; **the critics gave the play a sound ~** los críticos pusieron la obra por el suelo *or* por los suelos

pastor /ˈpæstər || ˈpɑːstə(r)/ *n* pastor, -tora *m,f*

pastoral /ˈpæstərəl || ˈpɑːstərəl/ *adj*

A ‹*painting/scene*› pastoril, bucólico

B (Relig) ‹*care/duties*› pastoral

pastrami /pəˈstrɑːmi || pæˈstrɑːmi/ *n* [u] pastrami *m* (*fiambre de carne vacuna y especias*)

pastry /ˈpeɪstri/ *n* (*pl* **-tries**) 1 [u] (substance) masa *f*; (*before n*) **~ cutter** cortapastas *m* 2 [c] (cake) pastelito *m or* (RPl) masa *f*

pastrycook /ˈpeɪstrikʊk/ *n* pastelero, -ra *m,f*, repostero, -ra *m,f*

pasture¹ /ˈpæstʃər || ˈpɑːstʃə(r)/ *n* 1 [u] (grazing land) pastos *mpl* 2 [c] (tract of grazing land) prado *m*, potrero *m* (AmL); ***to move on to ~s new*** cambiar de aires, buscar* nuevos horizontes; ***to put sb out to ~*** jubilar a algn (fam) 3 [u] (grass) pasto *m*, pastura *f*; (*before n*) **~ land** tierra *f* de pastoreo, pradera *f*

pasture² *vt* apacentar*, pastar

pasty¹ /ˈpeɪsti/ *adj* **-tier, -tiest** 1 (pale) ‹*complexion*› pálido 2 ‹*substance/consistency*› pastoso

pasty² /ˈpæsti/ *n* (*pl* **-ties**) (esp BrE) empanada *f* (AmL), empanadilla *f* (Esp); **Cornish ~** *empanada de papa, cebolla y carne*

pasty-faced /ˈpeɪstiˈfeɪst/ *adj* pálido

pat¹ /pæt/ *vt* **-tt-** darle* palmaditas a; ***to ~ sb on the back*** (congratulate) felicitar a algn; (lit) darle* una palmadita en la espalda a algn

pat² *n*

A (tap) palmadita *f*, golpecito *m*; (touch) toque *m*; ***to give sb a ~ on the back*** (congratulate) felicitar a algn; (lit) darle* una palmadita en la espalda a algn

B (Culin) (of butter) porción *f*

pat³ *adj* (pej) ‹*answer*› fácil

pat⁴ *adv* 1 (by heart): **to have** *o* **know sth down** *o* (BrE) **off ~** saberse* algo al dedillo *or* de memoria 2 (AmE): **to stand ~** mantenerse* en sus (*or* mis *etc*) trece

pat⁵ (= **patent**) Pat.; **~ pending** Pat. solicitada *or* en trámite

patch¹ /pætʃ/ *n*

A 1 (for mending clothes) remiendo *m*, parche *m*; (for reinforcing) refuerzo *m*; (on knee) rodillera *f*; (on elbow) codera *f*; (for a puncture, wound) parche *m*; ***not to be a ~ on sb/sth*** (BrE colloq) no tener* ni punto de comparación con algn/algo 2 (*eye* ~) parche *m* (*en el ojo*) 3 (AmE Mil) insignia *f*

B 1 (area): **test the product on a small ~ of material** pruebe el producto en un pequeño trozo de tela; **she slipped on a ~ of ice/oil** resbaló en el hielo/en una mancha de aceite; **a damp ~** una mancha de humedad; **fog ~es** zonas *fpl* de niebla; ***to go through a bad*** *o* ***rough*** *o* ***sticky ~*** (BrE) pasar por *or* atravesar* una mala racha 2 (small plot of land): **a vegetable ~** un huerto, una parcela para verduras 3 (territory) (BrE colloq): **my/his ~** mi/su territorio

C (Comput, Rad, Telec) ajuste *m*

patch² *vt* 1 (repair) remendar*, parchar (esp AmL) 2 (connect) (Comput, Rad, Telec) conectar

Phrasal verb

- **patch up** [v ▸ o ▸ adv, v ▸ adv ▸ o] 1 (mend) ‹*roof/furniture*› hacerle* un arreglo a (*provisionalmente*); ‹*clothes*› remendar*, parchar (esp AmL); ‹*hole*› ponerle* un parche a 2 (resolve, settle): **it will be difficult to ~ things up now** ahora va a ser difícil arreglar las cosas; **I tried to help ~ things up betweem them** quise ayudar para que hicieran las paces

patchwork /ˈpætʃwɜːrk || ˈpætʃwɜːk/ *n* 1 [u] (craft) patchwork *m*, labor *f* de retazos *or* (Esp) retales; (*before n*) ‹*quilt*› de patchwork, de retazos *or* (Esp) retales 2 [c] (medley): **a ~ of fields** un mosaico de campos

patchy /ˈpætʃi/ *adj* **-chier, -chiest** ‹*paintwork/color*› disparejo, poco uniforme; ‹*coverage*› incompleto; ‹*attendance*› irregular; ‹*description*› fragmentario; ‹*performance/work*› irregular

pâté /pɑːˈteɪ || ˈpæteɪ/ *n* [u c] paté *m*

patent¹ /ˈpætn̩t || ˈpeɪtn̩t, ˈpætn̩t/ *n* patente *f*; **to take out a ~ on sth** patentar algo; (*before n*) **~ agent** agente *mf* de patentes; **~ attorney** (in US) abogado, -da *m,f* especialista en patentes; **P~ Office** ≈ Registro *m* de la propiedad industrial

patent² /ˈpætn̩t || ˈpeɪtn̩t, ˈpætn̩t/ *vt* patentar

patent³ *adj*

A /ˈpeɪtn̩t, ˈpæt- || ˈpeɪtn̩t/ (obvious) (frml) patente, evidente

B /ˈpætn̩t || ˈpeɪtn̩t, ˈpætn̩t/ (patented) ‹*invention*› patentado; **~ medicine** especialidad *f* medicinal

patent leather /ˈpætn̩t || ˈpeɪtn̩t, ˈpæt-/ *n* [u] charol *m*

patently /ˈpeɪtn̩tli, ˈpæt- || ˈpeɪtn̩tli/ *adv*: **it's ~ clear** *o* **obvious that ...** salta a la vista *or* está clarísimo que ...

paternal /pəˈtɜːrnl̩ || pəˈtɜːnl̩/ *adj* **1** (fatherly) ‹*affection*› paternal; ‹*pride*› de padre; ‹*trait/inheritance*› paterno **2** (on father's side) (*before n*) por parte de padre; **~ grandmother** abuela *f* paterna, abuela *f* por parte de padre

paternalist /pəˈtɜːrnl̩əst || pəˈtɜːnl̩ɪst/, **-istic** /-ˈɪstɪk/ *adj* paternalista

paternity /pəˈtɜːrnəti || pəˈtɜːnəti/ *n* [u] (frml) paternidad *f*; (*before n*) **~ leave** permiso *m or* (esp AmL) licencia *f* por paternidad; **~ suit** litigio *m* por paternidad

path /pæθ || pɑːθ/ *n* **1** (track, walkway) sendero *m*, senda *f*, camino *m*; **the ~ to success** el camino al éxito **2** (of missile) trayectoria *f*; **the ~ of the sun** el recorrido *or* el trayecto del sol; **he stepped into the ~ of the oncoming vehicle** se cruzó en el camino del vehículo que se acercaba; ***to cross sb's ~*** cruzarse* *or* toparse con algn; **if you cross my ~ again ...** si te me vuelves a cruzar en el camino ... **3** (course of action): **if you take that ~ ...** si optas por hacer eso ...

pathetic /pəˈθetɪk/ *adj* **1** (pitiful) ‹*sight/moan/gesture*› patético **2** (feeble) (colloq): **what a ~ excuse!** ¡qué excusa más pobre!; **a ~ performance** una pésima actuación, una actuación que daba pena; **you're ~** ¡eres despreciable!

pathetically /pəˈθetɪkli/ *adv* **1** (pitiably) ‹*moan/weep*› lastimeramente; **he was ~ thin** era de una delgadez que daba pena **2** (lamentably) (colloq): **they played ~** jugaron que daba pena (fam)

path: ~finder /ˈpæθˌfaɪndər || ˈpɑːθˌfaɪndə(r)/ *n* explorador, -dora *m,f*; **~name** /ˈpæθneɪm || ˈpɑːθneɪm/ *n* (Comput) nombre *m* de ruta

pathological /ˈpæθəˈlɑːdʒɪkəl || ˌpæθəˈlɒdʒɪkəl/ *adj* patológico

pathologist /pəˈθɑːlədʒəst || pəˈθɒlədʒɪst/ *n* patólogo, -ga *m,f*

pathology /pəˈθɑːlədʒi || pəˈθɒlədʒi/ *n* [u] patología *f*

pathos /ˈpeɪθɑːs || ˈpeɪθɒs/ *n* [u] patetismo *m*

pathway /ˈpæθweɪ || ˈpɑːθweɪ/ *n* camino *m*, sendero *m*

patience /ˈpeɪʃəns/ *n* [u]

A (quality) paciencia *f*; **to try sb's ~** poner* a prueba la paciencia de algn; **~ is a virtue** (set phrase) la paciencia es la madre de la ciencia (fr hecha); ***to have the ~ of a saint*** tener* más paciencia que un santo

B (cards) (BrE) solitario *m*; **to play ~** hacer* solitarios

patient¹ /ˈpeɪʃənt/ *adj* paciente; ‹*research*› hecho con paciencia y detenimiento; **to be ~** ser* paciente, tener* paciencia; **to be ~ WITH sb** tener* paciencia CON algn

patient² *n* paciente *mf*

patiently /ˈpeɪʃəntli/ *adv* pacientemente

patina /pəˈtiːnə || ˈpætɪnə/ *n* pátina *f*

patio /ˈpætiəʊ/ *n* patio *m*

patois /ˈpætwɑː/ *n* (*pl* **~** /-wɑːz/) dialecto *m*

patriarch /ˈpeɪtriɑːrk || ˈpeɪtriɑːk/ *n* patriarca *m*

patriarchy /ˈpeɪtriɑːrki || ˈpeɪtriɑːki/ *n* [u c] (*pl* **-chies**) patriarcado *m*

patricide /ˈpætrəsaɪd || ˈpætrɪsaɪd/ *n* [u c] (crime) parricidio *m*

patrimony /ˈpætrəməʊni || ˈpætrɪməni/ *n* (*pl* **-nies**) (frml) patrimonio *m*

patriot /ˈpeɪtriət || ˈpætriət, ˈpeɪ-/ *n* patriota *mf*

patriotic /ˈpeɪtriˈɑːtɪk || ˌpætriˈɒtɪk, ˈpeɪ-/ *adj* patriótico

patriotism /ˈpeɪtriətɪzəm || ˈpætriətɪzəm, ˈpeɪ-/ *n* [u] patriotismo *m*

patrol¹ /pəˈtrəʊl/ *n* **1** [u c] (act) patrulla *f*, ronda *f*; **to be on ~** estar* patrullando, estar* de patrulla; (*before n*) **~ boat** (lancha *f*) patrullera *f*; **~ car** coche *m* patrulla, patrullero *m* (RPl), auto *m* patrulla (Chi); **~ wagon** (AmE) furgón *m* policial, (coche *m*) celular *m* (Esp), patrulla *f* (Col, Méx) **2** (group) patrulla *f*

patrol² *vt/i* **-ll-** patrullar

patrolman /pəˈtrəʊlmən/ *n* (*pl* **-men** /-mən/) **1** (police) (AmE) policía *m*, guardia *m* **2** (from motoring organization) (BrE) mecánico *m*

patron /ˈpeɪtrən/ *n* **1** (sponsor) patrocinador, -dora *m,f*; **a ~ of the arts** un mecenas **2** (customer) (frml) cliente, -ta *m,f* **3** (patron saint) patrono, -na *m,f*

patronage /ˈpætrənɪdʒ/ *n* [u]

A **1** (custom) clientela *f* **2** (sponsorship) patrocinio *m*, auspicio *m*; **under the ~ of** bajo *or* con el patrocinio de, con los auspicios de

B (Pol) influencia *f*

patronize /ˈpeɪtrənaɪz || ˈpætrənaɪz/ *vt*

A (condescend to) tratar con condescendencia

B **1** (frequent) (frml) ‹*shop/hotel*› ser* cliente de; ‹*theater/cinema*› frecuentar **2** (sponsor) patrocinar, auspiciar

patronizing /ˈpeɪtrənaɪzɪŋ || ˈpætrənaɪzɪŋ/ *adj* condescendiente

patsy /ˈpætsi/ *n* (*pl* **-sies**) (AmE sl) **1** (scapegoat) cabeza *mf* de turco, chivo *m* expiatorio **2** (easy victim) presa *f* fácil (fam), primo, -ma *m,f* (Esp fam)

patter¹ /ˈpætər || ˈpætə(r)/ *vi* ‹‹*rain*›› golpetear, tamborilear; ‹‹*feet/person*›› golpetear

patter² *n* [u]

A (of rain) golpeteo *m*, tamborileo *m*; **the ~ of tiny feet** (hum) pasitos *mpl* de niño

B (talk): **he has a good sales ~** tiene mucha labia para vender, sabe convencer al cliente; **the salesman gave me the usual ~** el vendedor me soltó el rollo de costumbre

pattern¹ /ˈpætərn || ˈpætən/ *n*

A **1** (decoration) diseño *m*, dibujo *m*; (on fabric) diseño *m*, estampado *m* **2** (order, arrangement): **it follows the normal ~** sigue las pautas normales; **the murders all seem to follow a ~** todos los asesinatos parecen responder al mismo patrón; **behavior ~** (Psych) patrón *m* conductual *or* de conducta; **the familiar ~ of events repeated itself** volvió a repetirse la historia de siempre

B **1** (model) modelo *m* **2** (in dressmaking) patrón *m*, molde *m* (CS) **3** (sample) muestra *f*

pattern² *vt* **to ~ sth ON sth** basar algo EN algo

pattern book *n* **1** (of wallpaper, fabrics) muestrario *m* **2** (of dress designs) revista *f* de patrones *or* (CS) de moldes, figurín *m*

patterned /ˈpætərnd || ˈpætənd/ *adj* con dibujos *or* motivos; ‹*fabric*› estampado

patty /ˈpæti/ *n* (*pl* **-ties**) **1** (meat cake) fritura *f* de carne (AmL) **2** (pie) empanada *f* (AmL), empanadilla *f* (Esp)

paunch /pɔːntʃ/ *n* panza *f* (fam), barriga *f* (fam)

pauper /ˈpɔːpər || ˈpɔːpə(r)/ *n* pobre *mf*, indigente *mf*

pause¹ /pɔːz/ *n* pausa *f*; **without ~** sin interrupción; **there was a ~ in the conversation** hubo una pausa *or* se hizo un silencio en la conversación; ***to give (sb) ~ for thought*** dar* que pensar (a algn)

pause² *vi* (in speech) hacer* una pausa; (in movement) detenerse*; **to ~ for breath** parar para recobrar el aliento

pave /peɪv/ *vt* (with concrete) pavimentar; (with flagstones) enlosar; (with stones) empedrar*, adoquinar; ***to ~ the way for sth*** preparar el terreno para algo

pavement /ˈpeɪvmənt/ *n* **1** [c u] (paved area) pavimento *m* **2** [u] ▸**paving 2** **3** [c] (beside road) (BrE) ▸**sidewalk**

pavement café *n* (BrE) café *m* con terraza

pavilion /pəˈvɪljən/ *n* **1** (tent, stand) pabellón *m* **2** (BrE Sport) caseta *f*

paving /ˈpeɪvɪŋ/ *n* [u] **1** (paved area) pavimento *m*; (of flagstones) enlosado *m*; (of tiles) embaldosado *m*; (of stones) empedrado *m*, adoquinado *m*; (*before n*) **~ slab** *o* **stone** losa *f* **2** (road surface) (AmE) calzada *f*

paw¹ /pɔː/ *n* **1** (Zool) pata *f* **2** (hand) (colloq & pej) manaza *f* (fam & pey), zarpa *f* (fam & pey)

paw² *vt* 1 «*animal*» tocar* con la pata; **to ~ the ground** «*horse*» piafar 2 «*person*» (pej) manosear (pey), toquetear (pey)

pawn¹ /pɔːn/ *n*
A [c] 1 (in chess) peón *m* 2 (manipulated person) títere *m*
B [c u] (pledge) prenda *f*; **to place sth in ~** empeñar algo, dejar algo en prenda

pawn² *vt* empeñar

pawn: **~broker** *n* prestamista *mf*; **~shop** *n* casa *f* de empeños, monte *m* de piedad

pawpaw /'pɔːpɔː/ *n* (esp BrE)
A [c u] (fruit) asimina *f*
B ▸**papaya**

pay¹ /peɪ/ (*past & past p* **paid**) *vt*
A 1 ‹*tax/rent*› pagar*; ‹*amount/fees*› pagar*, abonar (frml); ‹*bill*› pagar*, saldar; ‹*debt*› pagar*, saldar, cancelar; **this account ~s 8% interest** esta cuenta da *or* produce un interés del 8%; **to ~ sth FOR sth/to + INF**: **how much did you ~ for the painting?** ¿cuánto te costó el cuadro?, ¿cuánto pagaste por el cuadro?; **I paid a fortune to have it cleaned** me costó un dineral hacerlo limpiar, me cobraron un dineral por limpiarlo; **they ~ my salary directly into the bank** me depositan *or* (esp Esp) me ingresan el sueldo directamente en el banco 2 ‹*employee/creditor/tradesperson*› pagarle* a; **to ~ sb FOR sth** pagarle* algo A algn; **they haven't paid me for the tickets** no me han pagado las entradas; **I paid him £20 for the table** le di 20 libras por la mesa; ***to ~ one's way***: **I've always paid my own way** siempre he pagado lo que me correspondía
B ‹*respects*› presentar; ‹*attention*› prestar; **to ~ sb a visit** *o* **call** hacerle* una visita a algn; ▸**compliment¹ 1, heed¹, homage** *etc*

■ **pay** *vi*
A (with money) pagar*; **to ~ FOR sth** pagar* algo; **that won't even ~ for the food** eso no da ni para la comida; **to ~ FOR sb (to + INF)**: **I'll ~ for Matthew** yo pago lo de Matthew; **I'll ~ for you to go to Paris** yo te pago el viaje a París; **teaching doesn't ~ very well** la enseñanza no está muy bien pagada *or* remunerada
B (suffer) **to ~ FOR sth** pagar* algo; **he paid for his mistake with his life** el error le costó la vida; **I'll make you ~** me las pagarás; ***there'll be hell*** *o* ***the devil to ~*** se va a armar la de San Quintín
C **paying** *pres p*: **the ~ing public** el público; **~ing guest** huésped *mf* (*que paga el alojamiento*)

■ **pay** *v impers* convenir*; **it ~s to be polite to people** merece la pena ser amable con la gente

Phrasal verbs

• **pay back** [v ▸ o ▸ adv, v ▸ adv ▸ o]
A (repay) ‹*money*› devolver*, reintegrar (frml), regresar (AmL exc CS); ‹*loan/mortgage*› pagar*; **to ~ sb back FOR sth**: **I must ~ her back for the meal** tengo que devolverle *or* (AmL exc CS tb) regresarle el dinero de la comida; **how can I ~ you back for your kindness?** ¿cómo puedo retribuir tu amabilidad?
B (take revenge on): **I'll ~ you back (one day)!** ¡ya me las vas a pagar!, ¡ya me las cobraré *or* me vengaré!

• **pay in** [v ▸ o ▸ adv, v ▸ adv ▸ o] (BrE) ‹*money*› depositar *or* (Esp) ingresar *or* (Col) consignar

• **pay off**
A [v ▸ o ▸ adv, v ▸ adv ▸ o] 1 (settle, repay) ‹*debt*› cancelar, saldar, liquidar, pagar*; ‹*creditor*› pagarle* a 2 ‹*worker*› liquidarle el sueldo (*or* jornal *etc*) a (*al despedirlo*) 3 (bribe) (colloq) untarle la mano a (fam), coimear (CS, Per fam), darle* una mordida a (Méx fam)
B [v ▸ adv] (prove worthwhile) valer* *or* merecer* la pena, tener* su compensación; «*gamble*» resultar

• **pay out**
A [v ▸ o ▸ adv, v ▸ adv ▸ o] 1 (distribute) ‹*dividend/compensation/prize money*› pagar* 2 (spend) (colloq) desembolsar, aflojar (fam)
B [v ▸ o ▸ adv, v ▸ adv ▸ o] ‹*rope*› ir* soltando
C [v ▸ adv] «*insurance company*» pagar* (*una indemnización etc*)

• **pay up**
A [v ▸ adv] pagar*; **in the end the company paid up** al final la empresa le pagó lo que le debía (*or* la indemnizó *etc*)
B [v ▸ adv ▸ o] ‹*subscription*› abonar (frml), pagar*

pay² *n* [u] (of manual worker) paga *f*, salario *m* (frml); (of employee) sueldo *m*; **equal ~** igualdad *f* salarial; **to be in sb's ~** estar* a sueldo de algn; (*before n*) **~ envelope** *o* (BrE) **packet** sobre *m* de la paga; **~ increase** aumento *m or* (frml) incremento *m* salarial

payable /'peɪəbəl/ *adj* (frml) (*pred*) pagadero; **the rent becomes ~ on the first of the month** el alquiler vence el primero de mes; **make the check ~ to ...** extienda el cheque a nombre de *or* a favor de ...

pay: **~back** /'peɪbæk/ *n*
A [u] (on investment) recuperación *f*; (*before n*) **~back period** plazo *m* de recuperación (*de la inversión*);
B [c] (revenge) venganza *f*; **~check**, (BrE) **~ cheque** *n* cheque *m* del sueldo *or* de la paga; (salary) sueldo *m*; **~day** *n* día *m* de paga *or* de cobro; **Friday is ~day** cobramos (*or* cobran *etc*) el viernes

PAYE /'piːeɪwaɪ'iː/ *n* [u] (in UK) = **pay as you earn**; (*before n*) **the ~ system** *sistema de recaudación de impuestos por medio de retenciones sobre el salario*

payee /peɪ'iː/ *n* beneficiario, -ria *m,f*

payer /'peɪər || 'peɪə(r)/ *n* pagador, -dora *m,f*

pay: **~load** *n* 1 (load) (Aerosp, Transp) carga *f* útil 2 (explosive capacity) carga *f* explosiva; **~master** *n* pagador, -dora *m,f* (*encargado de la nómina*)

payment /'peɪmənt/ *n* 1 [u] (of debt, money, wage) pago *m*; **on ~ of the outstanding charges** previo pago de las cantidades pendientes; **~ FOR sth**: **he received no ~ for what he did** no recibió remuneración por lo que hizo (frml) 2 [c] (installment) plazo *m*, cuota *f* (AmL); **I've made the first ~ on the house** he pagado el primer plazo *or* (AmL) la primera cuota de la casa; **she made several ~s into her account** hizo varios depósitos *or* (esp Esp) ingresos *or* (Col) consignaciones en su cuenta 3 [u] (reward, thanks) pago *m*, recompensa *f*

pay-off /'peɪɔːf || 'peɪɒf/ *n*
A 1 (final payment) pago *m*, ajuste *m* de cuentas; (of debt) liquidación *f* 2 (bribe) (colloq) soborno *m*, coima *f* (CS, Per fam), mordida *f* (Méx fam) 3 (benefit) (colloq) compensación *f*, beneficios *mpl*
B (climax of story) (esp AmE colloq) desenlace *m*

payola /peɪ'əʊlə/ *n* [u] (esp AmE colloq) soborno *m*, coima *f* (CS, Per fam), mordidas *fpl* (Méx fam)

pay: **~out** *n* pago *m*; **~ phone** *n* teléfono *m* público, monedero *m* (público) (Ur); **~roll** *n* 1 (list) nómina *f*, planilla *f* (de sueldos) (AmL), plantilla *f* (Esp); **the company has 50 employees on its ~roll** la empresa tiene 50 empleados en planilla *or* (Esp) en plantilla 2 (wages) nómina *f*; **~ slip** *n* nómina *f*, recibo *m* del sueldo

PC¹ *n*
A = **personal computer**
B (in UK) = **police constable**

PC² *adj* = **politically correct**

PD *n* (in US) = **Police Department**

PE *n* [u] = **physical education**

pea /piː/ *n* arveja *f or* (Esp) guisante *m or* (AmC, Méx) chícharo *m*; ***as (a)like as two ~s in a pod*** como dos gotas de agua

peace /piːs/ *n*
A [u] paz *f*; **in** *o* **at ~** en paz; **to be at ~ with the world** estar* satisfecho de la vida; **to make ~ with sb** hacer* las paces con algn; (*before n*) para la paz; ‹*proposal/initiative/treaty*› de paz; ‹*talks/march/campaign*› por la paz; **the ~ movement** el movimiento pacifista; **as a ~ offering** en señal de reconciliación
B (Law): **to keep the ~** mantener* el orden; **to breach** *o* (BrE) **disturb the ~** alterar el orden público
C (tranquillity) paz *f*; **I went to the library for some ~ and quiet** me fui a la biblioteca para poder estar tranquilo; **the ~ of mind that comes with old age** la serenidad que da la edad; **I turned off the gas for my own ~ of mind** apagué el gas para quedarme tranquilo; **rest in ~** que en paz descanse; **speak now or forever hold your ~** que hable ahora o que calle para siempre

peaceable /'piːsəbəl/ *adj* 1 ‹*person/nation*› amante de la paz 2 ‹*agreement/settlement*› pacífico

peaceably /'piːsəbli/ *adv* pacíficamente

Peace Corps *n* (in US) **the ~ ~** el Cuerpo de Paz (de los EEUU)

peaceful /'piːsfəl/ *adj* 1 (calm, quiet) ‹*place*› tranquilo 2 (non-violent) ‹*protest*› pacífico, no violento; **they are a ~ people** son un pueblo amante de la paz

P

peacefully /ˈpiːsfəli/ *adv* 1 (serenely, quietly) ‹*sleep*› plácidamente; ‹*read/sit*› tranquilamente; **he died ~** murió sin sufrir 2 (without violence) ‹*protest*› pacíficamente, de forma no violenta

peace: **~keeping** *adj* (*before n*): **~keeping forces** fuerzas *fpl* de paz, fuerzas *fpl* encargadas del mantenimiento de la paz; **~maker** *n* conciliador, -dora *m,f*; **~time** *n* [u] época *f or* tiempos *mpl* de paz

peach /piːtʃ/ *n* 1 (fruit) durazno *m*, melocotón *m* (Esp) 2 **~ (tree)** duraznero *m or* (Esp) melocotonero *m* 3 (color) color *m* durazno *or* (Esp) melocotón

peacock /ˈpiːkɑːk || ˈpiːkɒk/ *n* pavo *m* real

peacock-blue /ˈpiːkɑːkˈbluː || ˌpiːkɒkˈbluː/ *adj* (*pred* **peacock blue**) azul eléctrico *adj inv*

pea-green /ˈpiːˈgriːn/ *adj* (*pred* **pea green**) verde manzana *adj inv*

peahen /ˈpiːhen/ *n* pava *f* real

peak¹ /piːk/ *n* 1 (of mountain) cima *f*, cumbre *f*, cúspide *f* (frml *or* liter); (mountain) pico *m*; (of cap) visera *f* 2 (highest point): **to reach a ~** alcanzar* su punto álgido; **at the ~ of her career** en el apogeo *or* la cúspide de su carrera

peak² *adj* (*before n*) 1 (maximum) ‹*level/power*› máximo; **to be in ~ condition** «*athlete/horse*» estar* en plena forma 2 (busiest): **during ~ hours** durante las horas de mayor demanda (*or* consumo *etc*); **~ viewing figures** cifras *fpl* de máxima audiencia; **~ rate** tarifa *f* máxima; **~ season** temporada *f* alta

peak³ *vi* alcanzar* su nivel más alto *or* su punto máximo/su mejor momento

peaked /piːkt/ *adj* 1 (with visor) (BrE) ‹*cap*› de *or* con visera 2 (pointy) (AmE) ‹*hat*› de pico

peaky /ˈpiːki/ *adj* **-kier, -kiest** (BrE) paliducho

peal¹ /piːl/ *n*: **~ of bells** (sound, musical pattern) repique *m* de campanas; (set) carillón *m*; **~s of laughter** carcajadas *fpl*; **a ~ of thunder** un trueno

peal² *vi* **~ (out)** (liter) «*bells*» repicar*, tocar* a vuelo

peanut /ˈpiːnʌt/ *n* 1 (Agr, Culin) maní *m or* (Esp) cacahuete *m or* (Méx) cacahuate *m* 2 **peanuts** *pl* (small sum) (colloq) una miseria (fam)

peanut butter *n* [u] mantequilla *f* de maní *or* (Esp) de cacahuete *or* (Méx) de cacahuate, manteca *f* de maní (RPl)

peapod /ˈpiːpɑːd || ˈpiːpɒd/ *n* vaina *f* (*de arveja, guisante o chícharo*)

pear /per || peə(r)/ *n* 1 (fruit) pera *f*; **~-shaped** con forma de pera 2 **~ (tree)** peral *m*

pearl /pɜːrl || pɜːl/ *n* 1 [c] perla *f*; **a string of ~s** un collar de perlas; **~s of wisdom** sabias palabras *fpl*; (iro) joyitas *fpl* (iró); ***to cast ~s before swine*** echarles margaritas a los cerdos; (*before n*) ‹*necklace/earrings*› de perlas; **~ diver** pescador *m* de perlas; **~ oyster** madreperla *f*, ostra *f* perlífera 2 [u] (*mother-of-~*) nácar *m*, madreperla *f*, concha *f* nácar (Méx), concha *f* de perla (Chi); (*before n*) ‹*brooch/buttons*› de nácar (*or* de madreperla *etc*)

pearl barley *n* [u] cebada *f* perlada

pearly /ˈpɜːrli || ˈpɜːli/ *adj* **-lier, -liest** ‹*finish/gloss*› nacarado, perlado; **the P~ Gates** (hum) las puertas del Paraíso

peasant /ˈpeznt/ *n* 1 (Agr) campesino, -na *m,f*; (*before n*) ‹*population*› campesino, rural; **a ~ farmer** un pequeño agricultor; **~ woman** campesina *f* 2 (uncultured person) (pej) ordinario, -ria *m,f*, palurdo, -da *m,f*

peasantry /ˈpezntri/ *n* (+ *sing or pl vb*) campesinado *m*

peashooter /ˈpiːˌʃuːtər || ˈpiːˌʃuːtə(r)/ *n* canuto *m*, cerbatana *f*

peat /piːt/ *n* [u] turba *f*; (*before n*) **~ bog** turbera *f*

peaty /ˈpiːti/ *adj* **-tier, -tiest** ‹*soil*› de turba

pebble /ˈpebəl/ *n* guijarro *m*, piedrecita *f or* (esp AmL) piedrita *f*; ***not to be the only ~ on the beach*** (BrE): **he's not the only ~ on the beach** no es el único hombre (*or* candidato *etc*), hay mucho más donde elegir; (*before n*) **~ beach** playa *f* de guijarros

pebbly /ˈpebḷi/ *adj* **-lier, -liest** de guijarros

pecan /pɪˈkæn || ˈpiːkən/ *n* pacana *f*, nuez *f* (Méx)

peccadillo /ˌpekəˈdɪləʊ/ *n* (*pl* **-loes** *or* **-los**) desliz *m*

peck¹ /pek/ *n* 1 (of bird) picotazo *m* 2 (kiss) beso *m*

peck² *vt* picotear, picar*

▪ **peck** *vi* **to ~ (AT sth)** «*bird*» picar* *or* picotear (algo); (nibble) picotear *or* picar* (algo)

pecker /ˈpekər || ˈpekə(r)/ *n*

A (AmE vulg) verga *f* (vulg), polla *f* (Esp vulg), pija *f* (RPl vulg), pico *m* (Chi vulg)

B (spirits, courage) **to keep one's ~ up** (BrE colloq & dated) no desanimarse

pecking order /ˈpekɪŋ/ *n* jerarquía *f*

peckish /ˈpekɪʃ/ *adj* (esp BrE colloq) (*pred*) **to be** *o* **feel ~** tener* un poco de hambre

pectorals /ˈpektərəlz/ *pl n* (músculos *mpl*) pectorales *mpl*

peculiar /pɪˈkjuːljər || pɪˈkjuːliə(r)/ *adj*

A (strange) raro, extraño; **to feel ~** tener* una sensación extraña

B (particular, exclusive) peculiar, característico; **~ TO sth**: **an animal ~ to that region** un animal que sólo existe en esa región; **the problem is not ~ to this country** el problema no es exclusivo *or* particular de este país

peculiarity /pɪˈkjuːlˈjærəti || pɪˌkjuːliˈærəti/ *n* (*pl* **-ties**) 1 [c] (sth unusual) rasgo *m* singular; (oddity) rareza *f* 2 [u] (strangeness) lo raro *or* extraño 3 [c] (particular, exclusive quality) peculiaridad *f*, singularidad *f*

peculiarly /pɪˈkjuːljərli || pɪˈkjuːliəli/ *adv* 1 (strangely) de forma rara *or* extraña 2 (more than usually) ‹*difficult*› especialmente, particularmente

pecuniary /pɪˈkjuːnieri || pɪˈkjuːniəri/ *adj* (frml) ‹*motives/gain*› pecuniario (frml); ‹*difficulties*› monetario, financiero

pedagogic /ˈpedəˈgɑːdʒɪk || ˌpedəˈgɒdʒɪk/, **-ical** /-ɪkəl/ *adj* (frml) pedagógico

pedagogue, (AmE also) **pedagog** /ˈpedəgɑːg || ˈpedəgɒg/ *n* (frml) pedagogo, -ga *m,f*

pedal¹ /ˈpedḷ/ *n* pedal *m*

pedal², (BrE) **-ll-** *vi* pedalear

▪ **pedal** *vt* darle* a los pedales de

pedal: **~ bin** *n* (BrE) cubo *m or* (Méx) bote *m or* (CS) tacho *m or* (Ven) tobo *m or* (Col) caneca *f* de la basura (*con pedal*); **~ car** *n* cochecito *m* de pedales

pedalo /ˈpedḷəʊ/ *n* (*pl* **-los** *or* **-loes**) (BrE) bote *m* de pedales, patín *m* (Esp)

pedant /ˈpednt/ *n* pedante *mf*

pedantic /pɪˈdæntɪk/ *adj* pedante

pedantry /ˈpedntri/ *n* [u c] (*pl* **-ries**) pedantería *f*

peddle /ˈpedḷ/ *vt* vender (*en las calles o de puerta en puerta*); **to ~ an ideology** hacer* proselitismo; **to ~ drugs** traficar* con drogas, pasar droga (arg)

peddler /ˈpedlər || ˈpedlə(r)/ *n* vendedor, -dora ambulante *m,f*, mercachifle *mf* (pey); (in former times) buhonero *m*; **a drug ~** un traficante de drogas

pederast /ˈpedəræst/ *n* pederasta *m*

pedestal /ˈpedəstḷ || ˈpedɪstḷ/ *n* pedestal *m*; ***to knock sb off her/his ~*** bajarle los humos a algn; ***to put*** *o* ***set sb on a ~*** poner* a algn en un pedestal

pedestrian¹ /pəˈdestriən || pɪˈdestriən/ *n* peatón, -tona *m,f*; (*before n*) **~ crossing** paso *m* de peatones; **~ mall** *o* (BrE) **precinct** zona *f* peatonal

pedestrian² *adj* pedestre

pedestrianize /pəˈdestriənaɪz || pɪˈdestriənaɪz/ *vt* (BrE) convertir* en zona (*or* calle *etc*) peatonal

pediatric, (BrE also) **paediatric** /ˈpiːdiˈætrɪk/ *adj* ‹*hospital*› pediátrico; ‹*specialist*› en pediatría

pediatrician, (BrE also) **paediatrician** /ˈpiːdiəˈtrɪʃən/ *n* pediatra *mf*

pediatrics, (BrE also) **paediatrics** /ˈpiːdiˈætrɪks/ *n* (+ *sing vb*) pediatría *f*

pedicure /ˈpedɪkjʊr || ˈpedɪkjʊə(r)/ *n* [u c]: **to have a ~** arreglarse/hacerse* arreglar los pies

pedigree /ˈpedəgriː || ˈpedɪgriː/ *n* 1 (ancestry — of animal) pedigrí *m*; (— of person) linaje *m*; (*before n*) ‹*bull/dog*› de raza 2 (certificate, document) pedigrí *m*

pedlar /ˈpedlər || ˈpedlə(r)/ *n* (BrE) ▸ **peddler**

pedophile, (BrE) **paedophile** /ˈpiːdəfaɪl/ *n* pedófilo, -la *m,f*

pedophilia, (BrE) **paedophilia** /ˈpiːdəˈfɪliə/ *n* [u] pedofilia *f*

pee¹ /piː/ *vi* (*past & past p* **peed**) (colloq) hacer* pis *or* pipí (fam), hacer* del uno (Méx, Per fam & euf)

P

pee² *n* (colloq (*no pl*) pis *m* (fam), pipí *m* (fam); **to go for/have a ~** ir* a hacer/hacer* pis *or* pipí (fam)

peek¹ /pi:k/ *vi* **~ (AT sth/sb)** mirar (algo/a algn) (*a hurtadillas*), vichar (algo/a algn) (RPl fam)

peek² *n* **~ (AT sth/sb): may I have** *o* **take a ~ (at it)?** ¿puedo echar(le) una miradita? (fam), ¿puedo vichar? (RPl fam)

peel¹ /pi:l/ *vt* 1 ‹*apple/potato*› pelar, mondar 2 (remove): **he ~ed back the plastic film** quitó *or* despegó la película de plástico

■ **peel** *vi* «*person*» pelarse, despellejarse; «*paint*» desconcharse, salirse*; «*wallpaper*» despegarse*; **to ~ away** «*paint/plaster*» desconcharse

Phrasal verb

• **peel off**

A [v ▸ adv] 1 «*wallpaper/label*» despegarse*; ‹*paint*› desconcharse, salirse* 2 (leave group) (colloq) «*person*» irse* por su lado, separarse del grupo

B [v ▸ o ▸ adv, v ▸ adv ▸ o] ‹*stamp/sticker*› despegar*, quitar; ‹*paint/bark*› quitar; **she ~ed off her clothes** se quitó la ropa

peel² *n* [u] (of potato, apple) piel *f*, cáscara *f* (esp AmL); (of orange, lemon) cáscara *f*

peeler /ˈpi:lər || ˈpi:lə(r)/ *n* ▸**potato peeler**

peelings /ˈpi:lɪŋz/ *pl n* cáscaras *fpl*, peladuras *fpl*, mondaduras *fpl*

peep¹ /pi:p/ *vi*

A 1 (watch) espiar*, vichar (RPl fam); (look quickly) mirar (*a hurtadillas*), echar un vistazo, vichar (RPl fam); **she ~ed out of the window** se acercó a la ventana y se asomó a mirar; **to ~ AT sb/sth** espiar* *or* atisbar a algn/algo 2 (show, stick out) **~ (out)** asomar

B (make high-pitched sound) «*bird*» piar*; «*horn/whistle*» sonar*; **he ~ed at them as he drove by** les tocó la bocina *or* les pitó al pasar

■ **peep** *vt* (colloq): **I ~ed the horn** toqué la bocina *or* el claxon

peep² *n*

A (quick or furtive look) vistazo *m*; **can I have a ~?** ¿puedo ver?, ¿a ver?, ¿puedo vichar? (RPl fam); **to have a ~ AT sth** echarle un vistazo A algo

B (sound): **the ~, ~ of the canary** el pío, pío del canario; **the ~ of a car horn** el pitido de un claxon; **we didn't hear another ~ from her all evening** no volvió a decir ni pío *or* ni mu en toda la noche (fam)

peephole /ˈpi:phəʊl/ *n* mirilla *f*

peeping Tom /ˈpi:pɪŋˈtɑ:m || ˌpi:pɪŋˈtɒm/ *n* mirón *m*

peepshow /ˈpi:pʃəʊ/ *n* 1 (live show) *espectáculo de striptease* 2 (machine) cosmorama *m*, mundonuevo *m*

peer¹ /pɪr || pɪə(r)/ *n*

A 1 (equal) par *mf*, igual *mf* 2 (contemporary) coetáneo, -nea *m,f*; **among her ~s** entre sus coetáneos *or* los de su edad

B (lord) (in UK) par *m*, lord *m*; **he's a life ~** tiene un título vitalicio

peer² *vi*: **to ~ AT sth/sb** (with difficulty) mirar algo/a algn con ojos de miope; (closely) mirar algo/a algn detenidamente; **he climbed the wall and ~ed over** se trepó al muro y atisbó por encima

peerage /ˈpɪrɪdʒ || ˈpɪərɪdʒ/ *n* 1 (title, honor) título *m or* dignidad *f* de lord 2 (nobility, aristocracy) **the ~** la nobleza; **to raise** *o* **elevate sb to the ~** concederle a algn el título de lord

peeress /ˈpɪrəs || ˈpɪəres/ *n* (in UK) paresa *f*

peer group *n* grupo *m* paritario (frml); (*before n*) **peer-group pressure** la presión que ejercen los compañeros *or* (frml) que ejerce el grupo paritario

peerless /ˈpɪrləs || ˈpɪəlɪs/ *adj* (liter) incomparable, sin igual, sin par (liter)

peeved /pi:vd/ *adj* ‹*expression/look*› de fastidio; **to be** *o* **feel ~** estar* molesto *or* (fam) picado

peevish /ˈpi:vɪʃ/ *adj* ‹*remark*› desagradable, malhumorado; **to be ~** estar* fastidioso

peevishly /ˈpi:vɪʃli/ *adv* de mala manera

peg¹ /peg/ *n*

A 1 (in ground) estaca *f*; (in furniture, barrel) estaquilla *f*; (in mountaineering) clavija *f*; (on violin, guitar) clavija *f*; (*tent* ~) estaquilla *f*; (on board game) *pieza o ficha que encaja en un tablero*; ***like a square ~ in a round hole*** totalmente fuera de lugar, como gallina en corral ajeno (fam) *or* (Ven fam) como cucaracha en fiesta de gallina *or* (RPl fam) como sapo de otro pozo; ***to take** o **bring sb down a ~ (or two)*** bajarle los humos a algn, poner* a algn en su sitio 2 (*clothes ~*) (BrE) *see* **clothes**

B (hook, hanger) colgador *m*, perchero *m*, gancho *m*; (*before n*) **an off-the-~ suit** (esp BrE) un traje de confección

peg² **-gg-** *vt*

A (attach, secure) sujetar, asegurar (*con estaquillas etc*); **to ~ the clothes (out)** (BrE) tender* la ropa

B (Econ, Fin) 1 (fix, limit) ‹*price/salary*› congelar 2 (link) **to ~ sth TO sth** vincular algo A algo

Phrasal verbs

• **peg down** [v ▸ o ▸ adv, v ▸ adv ▸ o] (BrE) ‹*tent*› sujetar (*con estaquillas*); ‹*prices/wages*› fijar

• **peg out** [v ▸ adv] (colloq) 1 (die) estirar la pata (fam), palmarla (Esp fam), petatearse (Méx fam) 2 (collapse from exhaustion) desplomarse, tronar* (Méx fam) 3 (break down) «*engine/car*» quedarse (fam), tronarse* (Méx fam)

pegboard /ˈpegbɔ:rd || ˈpegbɔ:d/ *n* tablero *m* (*con agujeros para insertar las fichas*)

PEI = Prince Edward Island

pejorative /pɪˈdʒɔ:rətɪv || pɪˈdʒɒrətɪv/ *adj* peyorativo, despectivo

Pekinese /ˈpi:kəˈni:z || ˌpi:kɪˈni:z/, (AmE) **Pekingese** /ˈpi:kɪŋˈi:z/ *n* pequinés, -nesa *m,f*

Peking /ˈpi:ˈkɪŋ/ *n* Pekín *m*

pelican /ˈpelɪkən/ *n* pelícano *m*

pellet /ˈpelət || ˈpelɪt/ *n* 1 (of bread, paper) bolita *f* 2 (Zool) (of regurgitated food) bola *f*; (feces) cagadita *f* (fam) 3 (ammunition) perdigón *m*

pell-mell /ˈpelˈmel/ *adv* desordenadamente, sin orden ni concierto; **they rushed ~ into the sea** corrieron en tropel hacia el mar

pelmet /ˈpelmət || ˈpelmɪt/ *n* (esp BrE) galería *f*, bastidor *m* (*que cubre la barra de donde cuelgan las cortinas*)

pelt¹ /pelt/ *vt*: **to ~ sb with tomatoes** lanzarle* *or* tirarle tomates a algn; **to ~ sb with stones** apedrear a algn

■ **pelt** *vi* (colloq)

A (rush): **they came ~ing down the hill** bajaron la cuesta (corriendo) a toda velocidad *or* prisa

B (fall heavily): **it was ~ing with rain** llovía a cántaros *or* a mares; **the hail was ~ing down** estaba granizando fuertísimo

pelt² *n*

A (animal skin) piel *f*; (stripped) cuero *m*

B (pace) (esp BrE colloq): **at full ~** a toda máquina, a todo lo que da (fam)

pelvic /ˈpelvɪk/ *adj* pélvico

pelvis /ˈpelvəs || ˈpelvɪs/ *n* (*pl* **-vises**) pelvis *f*

pen¹ /pen/ *n*

A (*fountain ~*) pluma *f* estilográfica, pluma *f* fuente (AmL); (*ballpoint ~*) bolígrafo *m*, boli *m* (Esp fam), birome *f* (RPl), pluma *f* atómica (Méx), lápiz *m* de pasta (Chi); (*felt ~*) rotulador *m*; **to put** *o* **set ~ to paper** ponerse* a escribir; ***the ~ is mightier than the sword*** más puede la pluma que la espada

B 1 (Agr) (*sheep ~*) redil *m*; (*cattle ~*) corral *m* 2 (prison) (AmE sl) cana *f* (AmS arg), talego *m* (Esp arg), tanque *m* (Méx arg); **in the ~** a la sombra (fam)

pen² **-nn-** *vt* ‹*letter/article*› redactar, escribir*; ‹*verse*› componer*

Phrasal verb

• **pen in** [v ▸ o ▸ adv, v ▸ adv ▸ o] encerrar*, cercar*

penal /ˈpi:nl/ *adj* penal; **~ code** código *m* penal; **~ colony** penal *m*, colonia *f* penal *or* penitenciaria; **~ offense** (AmE) delito *m* penal

penalize /ˈpi:nlaɪz || ˈpi:nəlaɪz/ *vt* 1 (punish) ‹*player*› sancionar, penalizar*; **candidates will be ~d for ...** (Educ) se quitarán puntos *or* se bajará la nota por ... 2 (make punishable, illegal) penalizar*, penar

penalty /ˈpenlti/ *n* (*pl* **-ties**)

A (punishment) pena *f*, castigo *m*; (fine) multa *f*; **the ~ for disobedience is death** la desobediencia está penada con la muerte; **on ~ of death** bajo *or* so pena de muerte; **to pay the ~** pagar* las consecuencias; (*before n*) **~ clause** cláusula *f* penal *or* punitiva

P

B (Sport) (in rugby) penalty *m*, golpe *m* de castigo; (in US football) castigo *m*; **~ (kick)** (in soccer) penalty *m*, penalti *m*, penal *m* (AmL), pénal *m* (Andes); (*before n*) **~ area** (in soccer) área *f*‡ de penalty *or* de castigo

penalty: **~ box** *n* **1** (in soccer) área *f*‡ de penalty *or* de castigo **2** (in ice hockey) banquillo *m* (*de castigo*); **~ shoot-out** *n* lanzamiento *m or* tanda *f* de penaltys (*or* penaltis *etc*); **~ spot** punto *m* de penalty (*or* penalti *etc*)

penance /'penəns/ *n* [u c] **1** (Relig) penitencia *f* **2** (punishment) (hum) castigo *m*

pence /pens/ *n pl of* **penny A1**

penchant /'pentʃənt || 'pɒŋʃɒŋ/ *n* (frml) **~ (FOR sth)** (liking) inclinación *f or* afición *f* (POR algo); (tendency) tendencia *f* (A algo)

pencil[1] /'pensəl/ *n* lápiz *m*; **colored ~s** lápices de colores; **in ~** con lápiz; (*before n*) **~ drawing** dibujo *m* a lápiz

pencil[2], (BrE) **-ll-** *vt* anotar (*con lápiz*); ‹*outline*› hacer* un esbozo de

Phrasal verb

- **pencil in** [v ▸ o ▸ adv, v ▸ adv ▸ o] apuntar, anotar (*provisionalmente*)

pencil: **~ case** *n* estuche *m* (para lápices), plumier *m* (Esp), chuspa *f* (Col), cartuchera *f* (RPl); **~ pusher** *n* (AmE) ▸**pen pusher**; **~ sharpener** *n* sacapuntas *m*, tajalápiz *m* (Col); (larger) afilalápices *m*, sacapuntas *m*

pendant /'pendənt/ *n* colgante *m*

pending /'pendɪŋ/ *adj* **1** (awaiting action) (*pred*): **to be ~** estar* pendiente; (*before n*) **~ tray** ≈ carpeta *f* de asuntos pendientes **2** (imminent) ‹*elections/retirement*› próximo

pendrive *n* lápiz *m* de memoria

pendulum /'pendʒələm || 'pendjʊləm/ *n* (*pl* **-lums**) péndulo *m*

penes /'pi:ni:z/ *pl of* **penis**

penetrate /'penətreɪt || 'penɪtreɪt/ *vt* **1** (enter into or through) ‹*membrane/defenses*› penetrar (en); ‹*clothing/armor*› atravesar*, traspasar; ‹*enemy lines*› adentrarse en; ‹*building/territory*› penetrar en; ‹*organization*› infiltrarse en; ‹*market*› introducirse* *or* entrar en **2** (in sex act) penetrar **3** (seep into) ‹‹*liquid*›› penetrar *or* calar (en)

■ **penetrate** *vi* **1** ‹‹*arrow/water/light*›› penetrar, entrar; **to ~ THROUGH sth** atravesar* algo **2** (sink in mentally): **it took a long time to ~** tardé (*or* tardó *etc*) en entenderlo

penetrating /'penətreɪtɪŋ || 'penɪtreɪtɪŋ/ *adj* ‹*voice/sound/gaze*› penetrante; ‹*insight/analysis*› penetrante, agudo, perspicaz

penetration /'penə'treɪʃən || ,penɪ'treɪʃən/ *n* [u] penetración *f*; (insight) penetración *f*, perspicacia *f*, agudeza *f*

pen friend *n* (esp BrE) ▸**pen pal**

penguin /'peŋgwən || 'peŋgwɪn/ *n* pingüino *m*

penicillin /'penə'sɪlən || ,penɪ'sɪlɪn/ *n* [u] penicilina *f*

peninsula /pə'nɪnsələ || pə'nɪnsjʊlə/ *n* península *f*

peninsular /pə'nɪnsələr || pə'nɪnsjʊlə(r)/ *adj* peninsular

penis /'pi:nəs || 'pi:nɪs/ *n* (*pl* **penises** *or* **penes**) pene *m*

penitence /'penətəns || 'penɪtəns/ *n* [u] arrepentimiento *m*, penitencia *f* (frml)

penitent[1] /'penətənt || 'penɪtənt/ *adj* arrepentido

penitent[2] *n* (Relig) penitente *mf*

penitential /'penə'tentʃəl || ,penɪ'tenʃəl/ *adj* penitencial

penitentiary /'penə'tentʃəri || ,penɪ'tenʃəri/ *n* (*pl* **-ries**) (AmE) prisión *f*, penitenciaría *f*

penknife /'pennaɪf/ *n* (*pl* **-knives**) navaja *f*, cortaplumas *m*

Penn, Penna = Pennsylvania

pen name *n* seudónimo *m*, nombre *m* de guerra *or* (AmL) de batalla

penniless /'penɪləs || 'penɪlɪs/ *adj* pobre, sin un céntimo; **to leave sb ~** dejar a algn en la miseria

Pennsylvania /'pensəl'veɪnjə || ,pensɪl'veɪniə/ *n* Pensilvania *f*

penny /'peni/ *n*

A (in UK) **1** (*pl* **pence**) penique *m*; **it only costs four pence** sólo cuesta cuatro peniques **2** (*pl* **pennies**) (coin) penique *m*

B (*pl* **pennies**) (cent coin) (in US, Canada) (colloq) (moneda *f* de un) centavo *m*

C (*pl* **pennies**) (small sum) céntimo *m*, centavo *m*; **she hasn't a ~ to her name** no tiene un céntimo, no tiene donde caerse muerta (fam); **it's worth every ~** vale lo que cuesta; **to count the pennies** mirar el dinero, mirar la plata (AmL fam); ***he/she keeps turning up like a bad ~*** te lo/la encuentras hasta en la sopa (fam); ***the ~ (finally) dropped*** (esp BrE colloq) al final se dio (*or* me di *etc*) cuenta; ***to cost/be worth a pretty ~*** costar*/valer* un dineral; ***to spend a ~*** (BrE colloq) hacer* pis (fam); ***in for a ~, in for a pound*** (BrE) de perdidos, al agua *or* ya que estamos en el baile, bailemos; ▸**rub**[1] *vt* **1**

penny arcade *n* salón *m* recreativo, sala *f* de juegos

penny-pinching[1] /'peni,pɪntʃɪŋ/ *adj* ‹*person*› cicatero, tacaño, agarrado (fam); ‹*policy*› cicatero

penny-pinching[2] *n* [u] cicatería *f*, tacañería *f*

penny: **~-whistle** /'peni'hwɪsəl || ,peni'wɪsəl/ *n* flautín *m*; **~worth** /'peniwɜ:rθ || 'peniwɜ:θ, 'penəθ/ *n*: **a ~worth of pins** un penique de alfileres; ***to put in one's (two) ~worth*** (BrE colloq) meter baza *or* cuchara (fam)

pen: **~ pal** *n* (esp AmE) amigo, -ga *m,f* por correspondencia; **~ pusher** *n* chupatintas *mf* (fam), tinterillo, -lla *m,f* (fam), suche *mf* (Chi fam)

pension /'pentʃən || 'penʃən/ *n* pensión *f*; **retirement ~** pensión de jubilación, jubilación *f*, pensión *f*; **to be on** *o* **draw a ~** cobrar una pensión/una jubilación; (*before n*) **~ fund** fondo *m* de pensiones; **~ plan** *o* **scheme** plan *m* de pensiones

Phrasal verb

- **pension off** [v ▸ o ▸ adv, v ▸ adv ▸ o] jubilar

pensionable /'pentʃənəbəl || 'penʃənəbəl/ *adj* (BrE) ‹*age*› jubilatorio, de jubilación *or* retiro; **this post is ~** este puesto da derecho a jubilación

pensioner /'pentʃənər || 'penʃənə(r)/ *n* pensionado, -da *m,f*, pensionista *mf*; (retired person) jubilado, -da *m,f*

pensive /'pensɪv/ *adj* pensativo, meditabundo; **to be in a ~ mood** estar* pensativo *or* meditabundo

pentagon /'pentəgɑ:n || 'pentəgən/ *n* **1** (Math) pentágono *m* **2** (in US) **the Pentagon** el Pentágono

> **Pentagon – the Pentagon**
>
> El edificio de forma pentagonal, situado en Washington, donde se encuentra la oficina central del Ministerio de Defensa y de las fuerzas armadas de EEUU. Fue blanco de uno de los atentados terroristas del 11 de septiembre de 2001. A menudo la prensa utiliza el término "The Pentagon" para referirse al Estado Mayor

pentameter /pen'tæmətər || pen'tæmɪtə(r)/ *n* pentámetro *m*

pentathlon /pen'tæθlən/ *n* pentatlón *m*

Pentecost /'pentəkɔ:st || 'pentɪkɒst/ *n* Pentecostés *m*

Pentecostal /'pentə'kɔ:stəl || ,pentɪ'kɒstəl/ *adj* ‹*church/minister*› pentecostal

penthouse /'penthaʊs/ *n* penthouse *m*, ático *m* (*gen de lujo*)

pent-up /'pent'ʌp/ *adj* (*pred* **pent up**) ‹*emotions/anger/frustration*› contenido, reprimido; ‹*energy*› acumulado

penultimate /pɪ'nʌltəmət || pen'ʌltɪmət/ *adj* (*before n*) penúltimo

penurious /pə'nʊriəs || pɪ'njʊəriəs/ *adj* (liter) mísero

penury /'penjəri || 'penjʊri/ *n* [u] (liter) penuria *f*, miseria *f*

peony /'pi:əni/ *n* (*pl* **-nies**) peonía *f*, peonia *f*

people[1] /'pi:pəl/ *n*

A (+ *pl vb, no art*) **1** (in general) gente *f*; **what will ~ say?** ¿qué dirá la gente?; **~ say that ...** dicen que ..., se dice que ...; **some ~ don't like it** a algunos no les gusta, a algunas personas no les gusta, hay gente a la que no le gusta **2** (individuals) personas *fpl*; **the hall seats 200 ~** la sala tiene un aforo de 200 personas; **well, really, some ~!** ¡hay cada uno!; **you ~ don't understand** ustedes no entienden; **you of all ~ ought to know** tú más que nadie deberías saberlo **3** (specific group): **tall/rich ~** la gente alta/rica, las personas altas/ricas, los altos/ricos; **young ~** los jóvenes, la juventud; **local ~** la gente del lugar, los lugareños; **my ~ are from Illinois** mi familia *or* (fam) mi gente es de Illinois; **he wasn't one of our ~** no era uno de los nuestros

B **1** (inhabitants) (+ *pl vb*): **the ~ of this country** la gente de este país, este pueblo; **she got to know the country and**

its ~ llegó a conocer bien el país y su(s) gente(s) **2** (citizens, nation) (+ *pl vb*) **the ~** el pueblo; **a ~'s republic** una república popular **3** (race) (+ *sing vb*) pueblo *m*

people² *vt* poblar*; **a land ~d by savage tribes** una tierra habitada por tribus salvajes

people: **~ carrier** *n* monovolumen *m*; **~ trafficker** *n* traficante *mf* de personas

pep /pep/ *n* [u] (colloq) energía *f*, vitalidad *f*

Phrasal verb

- **pep up**: **-pp-** [v ▸ o ▸ adv, v ▸ adv ▸ o] (colloq) ‹*person*› animar, levantarle el ánimo a; (physically) darle* energía a; ‹*food*› hacer* más sabroso

pepper¹ /ˈpepər || ˈpepə(r)/ *n*

A [u] (spice) pimienta *f*; **black/white ~** pimienta negra/blanca; (*before n*) **~ mill** molinillo *m* de pimienta; **~ shaker** (AmE) pimentero *m*

B [c u] (capsicum fruit, plant) (*sweet* **~**) pimiento *m*, pimentón *m* (AmS exc RPl), ají *m* (RPl), rocote *or* rocoto *m* (AmL exc CS); **green ~** pimiento (*or* pimentón *etc*) verde; **red ~** pimiento (*or* pimentón *etc*) rojo *or* colorado, ají *m* morrón (RPl)

pepper² *vt* **1** (Culin) ponerle* *or* echarle pimienta a **2** (intersperse) **to ~ sth WITH sth** salpicar* algo DE algo

pepper: **~box** *n* (AmE) pimentero *m*; **~corn** *n* grano *m* de pimienta; **~mint** *n* **1** [u] (plant) menta *f*; (*before n*) ‹*tea/oil*› de menta; ‹*flavor*› a menta **2** [c] (sweet) caramelo *m* de menta; (lozenge) pastilla *f* de menta

pepperoni /ˈpepəˈrəʊni/ *n* [u] salchichón *m*

pepperpot /ˈpepərpɑːt || ˈpepəpɒt/ *n* (BrE) pimentero *m*

peppery /ˈpepəri/ *adj* **-rier, -riest** **1** (Culin) ‹*taste*› a pimienta; (hot) picante **2** (irascible) cascarrabias *adj inv*

pep talk *n*: **he gave them a ~ ~** les habló para levantarles la moral/infundirles ánimo

per /pɜːr || pɜː(r)/ *prep* (for each) por; **£10 ~ head** 10 libras por cabeza; **at $25 ~ kilo** a 25 dólares el kilo; **£20 ~ person ~ night** 20 libras por persona y noche; **30 miles ~ hour** 30 millas por hora; *see also* **as per**

per: **~ annum** /pərˈænəm/ *adv* al año, por año; **$40,000 ~ annum** 40.000 dólares anuales; **~ capita** /pərˈkæpətə || pəˈkæpɪtə/ *adv* per cápita

perceive /pərˈsiːv || pəˈsiːv/ *vt* **1** (Psych) ‹*object/sound*› percibir **2** (realize) percatarse de, notar, darse* cuenta de **3** (regard) ver*; **he is ~d as ...** se lo ve *or* se lo considera como ...; **the ~d image of the organization** la imagen que se tiene de la organización

percent¹, **per cent** /pərˈsent || pəˈsent/ *n* (percentage) (*no pl*) porcentaje *m*; (*before n*) **a five ~ discount** un descuento del cinco por ciento, un cinco por ciento de descuento

percent², **per cent** *adv* por ciento; **I'm a hundred ~ certain** estoy cien por cien(to) seguro; **I don't feel a hundred ~** no estoy lo que se dice bien del todo

percentage /pərˈsentɪdʒ || pəˈsentɪdʒ/ *n* **1** [c] (Math) porcentaje *m*; (*before n*) **~ increase/point** aumento *m*/punto *m* porcentual; **~ sign** signo *m* del tanto por ciento **2** [c] (part) porcentaje *m*; **she gets a ~ of the profits** recibe un tanto por ciento *or* un porcentaje de los beneficios **3** [u] (advantage) (AmE colloq): **there must be some ~ in it for him** él debe de sacar tajada (fam) **4** [c] (average) (AmE) promedio *m*

perceptible /pərˈseptəbəl || pəˈseptəbəl/ *adj* ‹*difference/effect*› perceptible, apreciable; ‹*sound*› perceptible, audible

perceptibly /pərˈseptəbli || pəˈseptəbli/ *adv* ‹*improve/change/increase*› de manera perceptible *or* apreciable, perceptiblemente, apreciablemente

perception /pərˈsepʃən || pəˈsepʃən/ *n*

A [u] (faculty) percepción *f*; **sense ~** percepción sensorial

B [c] (idea) idea *f*; (image) imagen *f*

C [u] (insight) perspicacia *f*, agudeza *f*

perceptive /pərˈseptɪv || pəˈseptɪv/ *adj* ‹*person*› perspicaz, agudo; ‹*analysis*› perspicaz, penetrante

perch¹ /pɜːrtʃ || pɜːtʃ/ *n*

A **1** (in birdcage) percha *f* **2** (high position) posición *f* privilegiada; ***to knock sb off her/his ~*** bajarle los humos a algn

B (*pl* **~** *or* **~es**) (fish) perca *f*

perch² *vi* «*bird*» posarse; **he ~ed on the edge of the table** se sentó en el borde de la mesa

■ **perch** *vt*: **she ~ed herself on the arm of the chair** se sentó en el brazo del sillón; **the village is ~ed halfway up the mountainside** el pueblo está como colgado en mitad de la ladera

perchance /pərˈtʃæns || pəˈtʃɑːns/ *adv* (arch) (perhaps) tal vez; (by chance) por ventura (liter)

percolate /ˈpɜːrkəleɪt || ˈpɜːkəleɪt/ *vi* **1** (filter) **to ~ THROUGH sth** filtrarse A TRAVÉS DE algo; **to ~ through** filtrarse **2** (Culin) «*coffee*» hacerse*, filtrarse **3** (spread) «*news/idea*» difundirse, propagarse*

■ **percolate** *vt*: **to ~ coffee** hacer* café (*en una cafetera eléctrica*)

percolator /ˈpɜːrkəleɪtər/ *n* cafetera *f* eléctrica

percussion /pərˈkʌʃən || pəˈkʌʃən/ *n* [u] percusión *f*

percussionist /pərˈkʌʃənəst/ *n* percusionista *mf*

peregrine (falcon) /ˈperəgrən || ˈperɪgrɪn/ *n* halcón *m* peregrino

peremptory /pəˈremptəri/ *adj* ‹*person/manner*› autoritario, imperioso; ‹*order/tone*› perentorio, imperioso

perennial¹ /pəˈreniəl/ *adj* **1** (Bot) perenne, vivaz **2** (recurring) ‹*problem/shortage*› perenne, perpetuo, eterno

perennial² *n* planta *f* perenne *or* vivaz

perfect¹ /ˈpɜːrfɪkt || ˈpɜːfɪkt/ *adj*

A **1** (precise, exact) ‹*circle/copy*› perfecto **2** (faultless) perfecto; **he speaks ~ French** habla francés perfectamente *or* a la perfección; **I'm in ~ health** estoy perfectamente bien de salud **3** (ideal) ‹*weather/day*› ideal, perfecto; ‹*example/excuse*› perfecto; ‹*opportunity*› ideal

B (complete) (*before n*): **a ~ idiot** un perfecto idiota, un idiota redomado; **he's a ~ stranger to me** me es totalmente desconocido

C (Ling) ‹*tense*› perfecto

perfect² /pərˈfekt || pəˈfekt/ *vt* perfeccionar

perfect³ /ˈpɜːrfɪkt || ˈpɜːfɪkt/ *n*: **the future/present ~** el futuro/pretérito perfecto; **the past ~** el pluscuamperfecto

perfection /pərˈfekʃən || pəˈfekʃən/ *n* [u] **1** (state, quality) perfección *f*; **to do sth to ~** hacer* algo a la perfección **2** (act) perfeccionamiento *m*

perfectionist /pərˈfekʃənəst || pəˈfekʃənɪst/ *n* perfeccionista *mf*

perfectly /ˈpɜːrfɪktli || ˈpɜːfɪktli/ *adv*

A **1** (exactly) ‹*round/straight*› totalmente; ‹*fit/match*› perfectamente **2** (faultlessly, ideally) perfectamente; **your arrival was ~ timed** llegaste en el momento justo

B (completely, utterly) ‹*safe/ridiculous*› totalmente, absolutamente; **that's ~ obvious** eso está clarísimo, eso salta a la vista; **they are ~ suited** están hechos el uno para el otro; **that's ~ true** tienes (*or* tiene *etc*) toda la razón; **to be ~ honest, ...** si he de serte absolutamente franco ...; **he knows ~ well that ...** sabe perfectamente que ...; **it's ~ possible** es muy posible

perfidious /pərˈfɪdiəs || pəˈfɪdiəs/ *adj* (liter) pérfido (liter)

perfidy /ˈpɜːrfədi || ˈpɜːfɪdi/ *n* [u c] (*pl* **-dies**) (liter) perfidia *f* (liter)

perforate /ˈpɜːrfəreɪt || ˈpɜːfəreɪt/ *vt* perforar

perforated /ˈpɜːrfəreɪtəd || ˈpɜːfəreɪtɪd/ *adj* ‹*lung/ulcer*› perforado; ‹*edge*› con línea perforada de puntos

perforation /ˈpɜːrfəˈreɪʃən || ˌpɜːfəˈreɪʃən/ *n* [c u] perforación *f*; **~s** (on sheet of stamps etc) perforado *m*

perforce /pərˈfɔːrs || pəˈfɔːs/ *adv* (liter) ineludiblemente, forzosamente

perform /pərˈfɔːrm || pəˈfɔːm/ *vi*

A (Mus, Theat) «*actor/comedian*» actuar*, trabajar; «*singer*» cantar; «*musician*» tocar*; «*dancer*» bailar

B (work, produce results) «*student/worker*» rendir*, trabajar; «*team/athlete/vehicle*» responder; «*company/stocks*» rendir*; «*economy*» marchar

■ **perform** *vt*

A (Mus, Theat) ‹*play*› representar, dar*; ‹*role*› interpretar, representar; ‹*aria*› interpretar, cantar; ‹*symphony*› tocar*, interpretar, ejecutar

B (carry out, fulfill) ‹*function*› desempeñar, cumplir; ‹*role*› desempeñar; ‹*task*› ejecutar, llevar a cabo; ‹*experiment*› realizar*; ‹*ceremony*› celebrar; ‹*rites*› practicar*

performance /pərˈfɔːrməns || pəˈfɔːməns/ *n*

A [c] (Cin, Mus, Theat) **1** (session) (Theat) representación *f*, fun-

P

ción *f*; (Cin) función *f*; (by circus, cabaret artist) número *m*, espectáculo *m*; **in ~** (live) (actuando) en directo **2** (of symphony, song) interpretación *f*; (of play) representación *f*; **the first ~ of the play** el estreno de la obra **3** (of actor) interpretación *f*, actuación *f*; (of pianist, tenor) interpretación *f*; (of entertainer) actuación *f*

B [c u] (of employee) rendimiento *m*, desempeño *m* (AmL); (of student) rendimiento *m*; (of team, athlete) actuación *f*, desempeño *m*, performance *f* (AmL period); (of machine, vehicle) comportamiento *m*, performance *f* (AmL); (of company) resultados *mpl*; (of stocks) rendimiento *m*; **a high-~ engine** un motor de alto rendimiento; **~-related pay** remuneración *f* según rendimiento

C [c] (fuss, bother) (colloq): **what a ~!** ¡qué historia! (fam), ¡qué lata! (fam), ¡qué rollo! (Esp fam)

performer /pərˈfɔːrmər || pəˈfɔːmə(r)/ *n* (Theat) actor, -triz *m,f*; (Cin) actor, -triz *m,f*, artista *mf*; (entertainer, artiste) artista *mf*; (of role, piece of music) intérprete *mf*

performing /pərˈfɔːrmɪŋ || pəˈfɔːmɪŋ/ *adj* (*before n*) **1** (Mus, Theat): **the ~ arts** las artes interpretativas; **~ artists** artistas *mpl* del espectáculo **2** ‹*seal/dog*› amaestrado

perfume¹ /ˈpɜːrfjuːm || ˈpɜːfjuːm/ *n* perfume *m*

perfume² /pərˈfjuːm || ˈpɜːfjuːm/ *vt* perfumar; **~d soap** jabón *m* perfumado *or* de olor

perfumery /pərˈfjuːməri || pəˈfjuːməri/ *n* (*pl* **-ries**) perfumería *f*

perfunctorily /pərˈfʌŋktərəli || pəˈfʌŋktrəli/ *adv* ‹*inspect*› someramente, superficialmente; ‹*greet/smile*› como por obligación, mecánicamente

perfunctory /pərˈfʌŋktəri || pəˈfʌŋktəri/ *adj* ‹*inspection/description*› somero, superficial; ‹*greeting*› mecánico

perhaps /pərˈhæps || pəˈhæps/ *adv* quizá(s), tal vez; **~ they'll come later** tal vez *or* quizá(s) vengan más tarde, puede que vengan más tarde, a lo mejor vienen más tarde; **are you coming out tonight? — perhaps** ¿vas a salir esta noche? — quizá(s) *or* tal vez *or* a lo mejor

peril /ˈperəl || ˈperɪl, ˈperəl/ *n* [c u] peligro *m*; **do it at your ~** hazlo por tu cuenta y riesgo

perilous /ˈperələs || ˈperɪləs, ˈperələs/ *adj* peligroso, arriesgado

perilously /ˈperələsli || ˈperɪləsli, ˈperələsli/ *adv* peligrosamente; **they came ~ close to the edge of the cliff** se acercaron peligrosamente al borde del acantilado

perimeter /pəˈrɪmətər || pəˈrɪmɪtə(r)/ *n* perímetro *m*; (*before n*) **the ~ fence** la valla que cerca el recinto

perinatal /ˌperɪˈneɪtl/ *adj* perinatal

period¹ /ˈpɪriəd || ˈpɪəriəd/ *n* [*the forms* **período** *and* **periodo** *are equally acceptable in Spanish where this translation applies*]

A **1** (interval, length of time) período *m*; (when specifying a time limit) plazo *m*; **she is away for long ~s** pasa mucho tiempo fuera, pasa largas temporadas fuera; **a short ~ of time** un breve período de tiempo; **for a ~ of five hours/12 months** por un espacio de cinco horas/período de 12 meses; **during her ~ in office** durante el tiempo *or* período en que desempeñó el cargo **2** (epoch) época *f*; **the Tudor ~** la época de los Tudor; **the postwar ~** la posguerra

B (menstruation) periodo *m*, regla *f*; (*before n*) **~ pain** (BrE) dolor *m* menstrual

C **1** (in school) hora *f* (*de clase*) **2** (Sport) tiempo *m*

D (in punctuation) (AmE) punto *m*; (*as interj*) y punto, y sanseacabó (fam)

period² *adj* ‹*costume/furniture*› de época; **the house retains many ~ features** la casa conserva muchos detalles arquitectónicos de la época; *see also* **period piece**

periodic /ˈpɪriˈɑːdɪk || ˌpɪəriˈɒdɪk/ *adj* periódico

periodical¹ /ˈpɪriˈɑːdɪkəl || ˌpɪəriˈɒdɪkəl/ *n* publicación *f* periódica

periodical² *adj* ▸ **periodic**

periodically /ˈpɪriˈɑːdɪkli || ˌpɪəriˈɒdɪkli/ *adv* periódicamente

period piece *n*: **his paintings are charming ~ ~s** sus cuadros son deliciosas estampas de época

peripatetic /ˈperəpəˈtetɪk || ˌperɪpəˈtetɪk/ *adj* que trabaja en más de un centro

peripheral¹ /pəˈrɪfərəl/ *adj* **1** (minor, secondary) secundario **2** (Comput) ‹*device/unit*› periférico **3** (Anat, Med) periférico

peripheral² *n* periférico *m*

periphery /pəˈrɪfəri/ *n* (*pl* **-ries**) (frml) (of city) periferia *f*; (of society) margen *m*

periscope /ˈperəskəʊp || ˈperɪskəʊp/ *n* periscopio *m*

perish /ˈperɪʃ/ *vi* **1** (die) (liter) perecer* (liter), morir*; **~ the thought!** ¡Dios nos libre! **2** (decay) «*rubber/leather*» deteriorarse, picarse*; «*foodstuffs*» echarse a perder, estropearse

perishable /ˈperɪʃəbəl/ *adj* perecedero

perishables /ˈperɪʃəbəlz/ *pl n* (Busn) productos *mpl* perecederos

perisher /ˈperɪʃər || ˈperɪʃə(r)/ *n* (BrE) (naughty child) pillo, -lla *m,f*; **you little ~!** ¡pilluelo!

perishing /ˈperɪʃɪŋ/ *adj* (BrE colloq): **it's ~ (cold)!** ¡hace un frío que pela! (fam)

periwinkle /ˈperɪwɪŋkəl/ *n* **1** (Zool) bígaro *m* **2** (Bot) hierba *f* doncella, vincapervinca *f*

perjure /ˈpɜːrdʒər || ˈpɜːdʒə(r)/ *v refl* (Law) **to ~ oneself** perjurar(se), cometer perjurio, jurar en falso

perjury /ˈpɜːrdʒəri || ˈpɜːdʒəri/ *n* [u] perjurio *m*; **to commit ~** cometer perjurio, jurar en falso, perjurar(se)

perk /pɜːrk || pɜːk/ *n* (colloq) (perquisite of job) (beneficio *m*) extra *m*; (particular advantage) ventaja *f*; **one of the ~s of the job is that ...** una de las ventajas es que ...

Phrasal verb

• **perk up**

A [v ▸ adv] «*person*» animarse, reanimarse; «*business/weather*» mejorar

B [v ▸ o ▸ adv] (enliven) animar, reanimar

perky /ˈpɜːrki || ˈpɜːki/ *adj* **-kier, -kiest** (cheerful) alegre, animado, lleno de vida; (pert) desenfadado

perm¹ /pɜːrm || pɜːm/ *n* (hairdressing) permanente *f or* (Méx) *m*; **to have a ~** hacerse* la *or* (Méx) un permanente

perm² *vt*: **to have one's hair ~ed** hacerse* la *or* (Méx) un permanente

permanence /ˈpɜːrmənəns || ˈpɜːmənəns/ *n* [u] permanencia *f*, lo permanente

permanent¹ /ˈpɜːrmənənt || ˈpɜːmənənt/ *adj* permanente; ‹*address/job*› fijo, permanente; ‹*damage*› irreparable; ‹*relationship*› estable; ‹*dye/ink*› indeleble; **~ wave** permanente *f or* (Méx) *m*

permanent² *n* (AmE) ▸ **perm¹**

permanently /ˈpɜːrmənəntli || ˈpɜːmənəntli/ *adv* ‹*work/settle*› permanentemente, de forma permanente; ‹*damaged*› irreparablemente; ‹*stained/marked/disfigured*› para siempre; **they decided to split up ~** decidieron separarse definitivamente *or* para siempre

permeable /ˈpɜːrmiəbəl || ˈpɜːmiəbəl/ *adj* permeable

permeate /ˈpɜːrmieɪt || ˈpɜːmieɪt/ *vt* «*liquid*» calar, impregnar; «*smoke/smell*» impregnar; **this pessimism ~s his entire work** este pesimismo se evidencia *or* está presente en toda su obra

■ **permeate** *vi* **to ~ THROUGH/INTO sth** «*liquid/smell/smoke*» penetrar A TRAVÉS DE/EN algo

permissible /pərˈmɪsəbəl || pəˈmɪsəbəl/ *adj* (permitted) permisible, lícito; (acceptable) tolerable, aceptable

permission /pərˈmɪʃən || pəˈmɪʃən/ *n* [u] permiso *m*; **she gave me ~** me dio (su) permiso; **by ~ of the author** con permiso *or* autorización del autor

permissive /pərˈmɪsɪv || pəˈmɪsɪv/ *adj* permisivo

permissiveness /pərˈmɪsɪvnəs || pəˈmɪsɪvnɪs/ *n* [u] permisividad *f*

permit¹ /pərˈmɪt || pəˈmɪt/ **-tt-** *vt* permitir; **photography is not ~ted** no se permite tomar fotografías; **to ~ sb to + INF**: **I will not ~ you to insult my family like this** no te permito que insultes así a mi familia; **may I be ~ted to make a suggestion?** (frml) ¿me permiten que haga una sugerencia?

■ **permit** *vi*: **weather ~ting** si hace buen tiempo; **if time ~s** si hay tiempo

permit² /ˈpɜːrmɪt || ˈpɜːmɪt/ *n* permiso *m* (*por escrito*); **work/residence ~** permiso de trabajo/de residencia; **gun ~** (AmE) licencia *f* de armas

permutation /ˈpɜːrmjʊˈteɪʃən || ˌpɜːmjʊˈteɪʃən/ *n* 1 [c] (arrangement) variante *f* 2 [u c] (Math) permutación *f*

pernicious /pərˈnɪʃəs || pəˈnɪʃəs/ *adj* pernicioso

pernickety /pərˈnɪkəti || pəˈnɪkəti/ *adj* (BrE) ▸**persnickety 1**

peroxide /pərˈɑːksaɪd || pəˈrɒksaɪd/ *n* [u] peróxido *m*; (*before n*) **a ~ blonde** una rubia teñida *or* oxigenada *or* (Esp fam) de bote

perpendicular¹ /ˈpɜːrpənˈdɪkjələr || ˌpɜːpənˈdɪkjʊlə(r)/ *adj* 1 (vertical) ‹*wall/surface*› perpendicular al horizonte 2 (Math) **~ TO sth** perpendicular A algo

perpendicular² *n* perpendicular *f*

perpetrate /ˈpɜːrpətreɪt || ˈpɜːpɪtreɪt/ *vt* (frml) perpetrar, cometer

perpetrator /ˈpɜːrpətreɪtər || ˈpɜːpɪtreɪtə(r)/ *n* (frml *or* hum) autor, -tora *m,f* (*de un crimen etc*)

perpetual /pərˈpetʃuəl || pəˈpetjʊəl/ *adj* ‹*problem/nuisance*› eterno, perpetuo; **~ motion** movimiento *m* continuo

perpetually /pərˈpetʃuəli || pəˈpetjʊəli/ *adv* permanentemente

perpetuate /pərˈpetʃueɪt || pəˈpetjʊeɪt/ *vt* perpetuar*

perpetuity /ˈpɜːrpəˈtuːəti || ˌpɜːpɪˈtjuːəti/ *n* [u] (frml) perpetuidad *f*; **in ~** (Law) a perpetuidad

perplex /pərˈpleks || pəˈpleks/ *vt* dejar perplejo, desconcertar*

perplexed /pərˈplekst || pəˈplekst/ *adj* perplejo; ‹*frown*› de perplejidad

perquisite /ˈpɜːrkwəzət || ˈpɜːkwɪzɪt/ *n* (frml) (beneficio *m*) extra *m*, incentivo *m*

per se /ˈpɜːrˈseɪ || ˌpɜːˈseɪ/ *adv* en sí, per se

persecute /ˈpɜːrsɪkjuːt || ˈpɜːsɪkjuːt/ *vt* perseguir*

persecution /ˈpɜːrsɪˈkjuːʃən || ˌpɜːsɪˈkjuːʃən/ *n* [u c] persecución *f*

persecutor /ˈpɜːrsɪkjuːtər || ˈpɜːsɪkjuːtə(r)/ *n* perseguidor, -dora *m,f*

perseverance /ˈpɜːrsəˈvɪrəns || ˌpɜːsɪˈvɪərəns/ *n* [u] perseverancia *f*

persevere /ˈpɜːrsəˈvɪr || ˌpɜːsɪˈvɪə(r)/ *vi* perseverar; **I ~d, and it worked** seguí insistiendo y funcionó

persevering /ˈpɜːrsəˈvɪrɪŋ || ˌpɜːsɪˈvɪərɪŋ/ *adj* perseverante, tenaz

Persia /ˈpɜːrʒə || ˈpɜːʃə/ *n* Persia *f*

Persian¹ /ˈpɜːrʒən || ˈpɜːʃən/ *adj* persa; **the ~ Gulf** el Golfo Pérsico; **a ~ carpet** una alfombra persa

Persian² *n*

A 1 [u] (language) persa *m* 2 [c] (person) persa *mf*

B [c] **~ (cat)** gato *m* persa

persist /pərˈsɪst || pəˈsɪst/ *vi* 1 «*person*» (continue doggedly) **to ~ IN sth/-ING**: **they ~ed in the belief** *o* **in believing that ...** persistieron en la creencia de que ... 2 «*belief/doubts/pain*» persistir; **if the rain ~s ...** si continúa *or* sigue lloviendo ...

persistence /pərˈsɪstəns || pəˈsɪstəns/ *n* [u] 1 (tenacity) perseverancia *f*, tenacidad *f* 2 (continued existence) persistencia *f*

persistent /pərˈsɪstənt || pəˈsɪstənt/ *adj* 1 (unceasing) ‹*demands/warnings*› continuo, constante, repetido; ‹*cough/fog*› persistente; ‹*rain*› continua, persistente 2 (undaunted) ‹*salesman/suitor*› insistente, persistente; **he's very ~** es muy persistente

persistently /pərˈsɪstəntli || pəˈsɪstəntli/ *adv*: **he is ~ late** llega tarde continuamente; **he ~ denied it** persistió en su negativa, lo negó una y otra vez

persnickety /pərˈsnɪkəti || pəˈsnɪkəti/ *adj* (AmE) 1 (fussy) puntilloso, chinche (fam), mañoso (AmL fam) 2 (delicate, awkward) ‹*task*› que requiere minuciosidad

person /ˈpɜːrsn̩ || ˈpɜːsn̩/ *n*

A (*pl* **people**) persona *f*; **she's a charming ~** es (una persona) encantadora; **Sue's the ~ to ask** a quien hay que preguntarle es a Sue; **who is this Davies ~?** ¿quién es el tal Davies?; **help arrived in the ~ of his father** su padre llegó en el momento más oportuno; *see also* **people¹ A 2**

B (*pl* **persons**) 1 (individual) (frml) persona *f* 2 (body) persona *f*; **to have a weapon on** *o* **about one's ~** (BrE frml) ser* portador de arma; **in ~** en persona

C (Ling) (*pl* **persons**) persona *f*

persona /pərˈsəʊnə || pɜːˈsəʊnə/ *n* 1 (*pl* **personas**) (image) imagen *f* 2 (*pl* **personae** /-niː/) (character) personaje *m*

personable /ˈpɜːrsn̩əbəl || ˈpɜːsn̩əbəl/ *adj* agradable, afable

personal¹ /ˈpɜːrsn̩əl || ˈpɜːsənl̩/ *adj*

A 1 (own) ‹*experience/preference*› personal; ‹*property*› privado 2 (private) personal; **this is a ~ matter** éste es un asunto privado *or* personal; **no ~ calls are allowed** no se permite hacer llamadas particulares; **don't ask ~ questions** no hagas preguntas indiscretas 3 (individual) ‹*account/loan*› personal; **~ identification number** número *m* de identificación personal, PIN *m*

B 1 (in person) ‹*appearance*› en persona 2 (physical) ‹*hygiene*› íntimo; ‹*appearance*› personal 3 (directed against individual): **let's not get ~** no llevemos las cosas al plano personal; **it's nothing ~, but ...** no tengo nada contra ti (*or* ella *etc*), pero ...

personal² *n* (AmE) anuncio *m* personal

personal: **~ assistant** *n* (Busn) secretario, -ria *m,f* personal; **~ column** *n* sección *f* de anuncios personales; **~ computer** *n* computadora *f* *or* (Esp tb) ordenador *m* personal

personality /ˈpɜːrsn̩ˈæləti || ˌpɜːsəˈnæləti/ *n* (*pl* **-ties**)

A 1 [c] (nature, disposition) personalidad *f* 2 [u] (personal appeal) personalidad *f*

B [c] (public figure) personalidad *f*, figura *f*

personalize /ˈpɜːrsn̩əlaɪz || ˈpɜːsn̩əlaɪz/ *vt* personalizar*, individualizar*; **~d stationery** papel *m* de carta con membrete

personally /ˈpɜːrsn̩əli || ˈpɜːsn̩əli/ *adv*

A 1 ‹*responsible/liable*› personalmente; **she wrote to me ~** me escribió personalmente *or* ella misma; **to take sth ~** ofenderse 2 (in person) personalmente; **do you know him ~?** ¿lo conoces personalmente?

B (*indep*) (for my part) personalmente, **~, I can't stand him** yo, personalmente, no lo aguanto

personal organizer *n* agenda *f* de uso múltiple, Filofax® *m*

persona non grata /ˈnɑːnˈgrɑːtə || ˌnɒnˈgrɑːtə/ *n* (*pl* **personae non gratae** /pərˈsəʊniːˌnɑːnˈgrɑːtiː || pəˈsəʊniːˌnɒnˈgrɑːtiː/) persona *f* non grata

personification /pərˈsɑːnəfəˈkeɪʃən || pəˌsɒnɪfɪˈkeɪʃən/ *n* [u c] personificación *f*

personify /pərˈsɑːnəfaɪ || pəˈsɒnɪfaɪ/ *vt* **-fies, -fying, -fied** personificar*

personnel /ˈpɜːrsn̩ˈel || ˌpɜːsəˈnel/ *n* 1 (staff) (+ *pl vb*) personal *m*; (*before n*) **~ manager** jefe, -fa *m,f* de personal 2 **Personnel** (department) (+ *sing vb*) sección *f* de personal 3 (field) (+ *sing vb*) administración *f* *or* gestión *f* de personal

perspective /pərˈspektɪv || pəˈspektɪv/ *n* 1 [u] (Art) perspectiva *f* 2 [u c] (angle, view) perspectiva *f*; **from a historical ~** con una perspectiva histórica; **I'm trying to get things into ~** me gustaría poder ver las cosas objetivamente; **you have to keep things in ~** no tienes que perder de vista la verdadera dimensión de las cosas

Perspex® /ˈpɜːrspeks || ˈpɜːspeks/ *n* [u] (BrE) acrílico *m*, Plexiglas® *m* (Esp)

perspicacious /ˈpɜːrspəˈkeɪʃəs || ˌpɜːspɪˈkeɪʃəs/ *adj* (frml) perspicaz

perspiration /ˈpɜːrspəˈreɪʃən || ˌpɜːspɪˈreɪʃən/ *n* [u] transpiración *f*

perspire /pərˈspaɪr || pəˈspaɪə(r)/ *vi* transpirar

persuade /pərˈsweɪd || pəˈsweɪd/ *vt* ‹*person*› convencer*, persuadir; **she didn't need much persuading** no hubo que insistirle; **he's easily ~d** se deja convencer fácilmente; **to ~ sb to + INF** convencer* *or* persuadir a algn DE QUE *or* PARA QUE (+ *subj*); **they ~d him to give himself up** lo convencieron de que se entregara, lo persuadieron de *or* para que se entregara; **nothing would ~ her to change her mind** nada la haría cambiar de opinión; **to ~ sb THAT** convencer* a algn DE QUE

persuasion /pərˈsweɪʒən || pəˈsweɪʒən/ *n* 1 [u] (act) persuasión *f*; **we tried various means of ~** usamos varios medios de persuasión 2 [c] (belief) (frml): **people of all ~s** (Relig) gente de todas las creencias; **others of that/her ~** otros que opinan así/como ella

P

persuasive /pər'sweɪsɪv || pə'sweɪsɪv/ *adj* ‹*person*/*manner*› persuasivo; ‹*argument*› convincente

pert /pɜːrt || pɜːt/ *adj* [1] (saucy) ‹*reply*› descarado [2] (neat and stylish) ‹*hat*/*dress*› coqueto; **her ~ little nose** su naricilla respingona *or* (AmL tb) respingada

pertain /pɜːr'teɪn || pɜː'teɪn/ *vi* (frml) **to ~ TO sth** (have to do with) concernir A algo

pertinent /'pɜːrtṇənt || 'pɜːtɪnənt/ *adj* (frml) pertinente; **to be ~ TO sth** guardar relación CON algo

perturb /pər'tɜːrb || pə'tɜːb/ *vt* (*usu pass*) perturbar

Peru /pə'ruː/ *n* (el) Perú *m*

perusal /pə'ruːzəl/ *n* [u c] (frml): **I enclose the document for your ~** le adjunto el documento para que lo examine

peruse /pə'ruːz/ *vt* [1] (read through) (frml or hum) leer* detenidamente [2] (examine, study) (frml) examinar

Peruvian[1] /pə'ruːviən/ *adj* peruano

Peruvian[2] *n* peruano, -na *m,f*

pervade /pər'veɪd || pə'veɪd/ *vt* «*idea*/*mood*» dominar; «*smell*» llenar, haber* invadido; **images of death ~ his writing** las imágenes de la muerte son una constante en su obra

pervasive /pər'veɪsɪv || pə'veɪsɪv/ *adj* ‹*smell*› penetrante, que todo lo invade; ‹*idea*/*mood*› dominante; ‹*influence*› omnipresente

perverse /pər'vɜːrs || pə'vɜːs/ *adj* (stubborn) obstinado, terco; (wayward, contrary) retorcido, avieso (liter); **a ~ delight** un placer malsano

perversely /pər'vɜːrsli || pə'vɜːsli/ *adv* con obstinación, porfiadamente, contra toda lógica

perversion /pər'vɜːrʒən || pə'vɜːʃən/ *n* [c u] [1] (distortion) distorsión *f*, tergiversación *f*; **a ~ of justice** una deformación de la justicia [2] (Psych) perversión *f*

perversity /pər'vɜːrsəti || pə'vɜːsəti/ *n* [u c] (*pl* **-ties**) obstinación *f* malsana

pervert[1] /pər'vɜːrt || pə'vɜːt/ *vt* [1] (corrupt) pervertir* [2] (misdirect) distorsionar

pervert[2] /'pɜːrvɜːrt || 'pɜːvɜːt/ *n* pervertido, -da *m,f*

perverted /pər'vɜːrtəd || pə'vɜːtɪd/ *adj* pervertido

peseta /pə'seɪtə/ *n* peseta *f*

pesky /'peski/ *adj* **-kier, -kiest** (AmE colloq) latoso (fam), molesto

peso /'peɪsəʊ/ *n* (*pl* **~s**) peso *m*

pessimism /'pesəmɪzəm || 'pesɪmɪzəm/ *n* [u] pesimismo *m*

pessimist /'pesəməst || 'pesɪmɪst/ *n* pesimista *mf*

pessimistic /'pesə'mɪstɪk || ˌpesɪ'mɪstɪk/ *adj* pesimista

pessimistically /'pesə'mɪstɪkli || ˌpesɪ'mɪstɪkli/ *adv* de forma pesimista

pest /pest/ *n* [1] (Agr, Hort) plaga *f*; (*before n*) **~ control** (of insects) lucha *f* contra los insectos; (of rats) desratización *f* [2] (person, thing) (colloq) peste *f* (fam)

pester /'pestər || 'pestə(r)/ *vt* molestar; **he ~s me with questions** me acosa con preguntas; **to ~ sb FOR sth/to + INF**: **he keeps ~ing me for an ice-cream/to take him to the zoo** no hace más que darme la lata para que le compre un helado/para que lo lleve al zoo (fam)

pesticide /'pestəsaɪd || 'pestɪsaɪd/ *n* [u c] pesticida *m*

pestilence /'pestələns || 'pestɪləns/ *n* [c u] (liter) pestilencia *f*

pestilential /'pestə'lentʃəl || ˌpestɪ'lenʃəl/ *adj* (hum) pesado, cargante

pestle /'pesəl/ *n* mano *f* de mortero

pet[1] /pet/ *n* [1] (animal) animal *m* doméstico *or* de compañía, mascota *f*; (*before n*) **~ food** comida *f* para animales; **~ shop** ≈ pajarería *f* [2] (favorite): **he's teacher's ~** es el niño mimado de la maestra [3] (term of endearment) (colloq) cielo (fam)

pet[2] *adj* (*before n*) [1] (kept as pet): **his ~ budgie** su periquito [2] (favorite) ‹*subject*/*theory*› favorito, preferido; **my ~ hate** lo que más odio

pet[3] **-tt-** *vt* ‹*animal*› acariciar, mimar

■ **pet** *vi* acariciarse, tocarse*, manosearse (pey)

petal /'petḷ/ *n* pétalo *m*

petard /pə'tɑːrd || pɪ'tɑːd/ *n*: ***to be hoist with one's own ~***: **he was hoist with his own ~** le salió el tiro por la culata

peter out /'piːtər/ [v ▸ adv] «*enthusiasm*» decaer*, irse* apagando; «*supplies*» irse* agotando; «*engine*» parar, quedarse (AmL fam); «*conversation*» apagarse*; **the road narrows and finally ~s out altogether** la carretera se estrecha y finalmente desaparece

petit bourgeois /'peti/ *adj* pequeñoburgués

petite /pə'tiːt/ *adj* ‹*woman*› chiquita, menuda

petition[1] /pə'tɪʃən/ *n* [1] (written document) petición *f* [2] (Law) demanda *f*; **to file** *o* **lodge a ~** presentar una demanda

petition[2] *vt* (frml) elevar una petición a (frml), peticionar (AmL)

■ **petition** *vi* **to ~ FOR sth** elevar una petición solicitando algo (frml); **to ~ for divorce** (BrE Law) presentar una demanda de divorcio

petitioner /pə'tɪʃənər || pə'tɪʃənə(r)/ *n* [1] (frml) peticionario, -ria *m,f* (frml) [2] (Law) demandante *mf*

pet name *n* apodo *m*, sobrenombre *m*

petrified /'petrɪfaɪd/ *adj* [1] (terrified) muerto de miedo [2] (Geol) petrificado

petrify /'petrɪfaɪ/ **-fies, -fying, -fied** *vt* [1] (terrify) aterrorizar* [2] (Geol) petrificar*

petrochemical /'petrəʊ'kemɪkəl/ *n* producto *m* petroquímico; (*before n*) ‹*industry*/*plant*› petroquímico

petrol /'petrəl/ *n* [u] (BrE) gasolina *f*, bencina *f* (Andes) nafta *f* (RPl); (*before n*) **~ bomb** coctel *m or* (CS, Esp) cóctel *m* molotov; **~ pump** surtidor *m*; **~ station** estación *f* de servicio, gasolinera *f*, bomba *f* (Andes, Ven), estación *f* de nafta (RPl), bencinera *f* (Andes), grifo *m* (Per)

petroleum /pə'trəʊliəm/ *n* [u] petróleo *m*; (*before n*) ‹*derivatives*› del petróleo; **~ jelly** vaselina *f*

petticoat /'petikəʊt/ *n* [1] (underskirt) enagua *f or* (Méx) fondo *m* [2] (slip) (BrE) combinación *f*, viso *m*

pettifogging /'petifɔːgɪŋ || 'petifɒgɪŋ/ *adj* ‹*lawyer*› pedante, puntilloso; **~ details** detalles *mpl* insignificantes, nimiedades *fpl*

pettiness /'petinəs || 'petinɪs/ *n* [u] mezquindad *f*, pequeñez *f* de espíritu

petting /'petɪŋ/ *n* [u] caricias *fpl*, manoseo *m* (pey)

petty /'peti/ *adj* **-tier, -tiest** [1] (unimportant) ‹*details*› insignificante, nimio; **~ crime** delito *m* menor, falta *f*; **~ thief** ladronzuelo, -la *m,f* [2] (small-minded) mezquino

petty: **~ cash** *n* [u] caja *f* chica, dinero *m* para gastos menores; **~ officer** *n* suboficial *mf* de marina; **~ theft** *n* hurto *m* menor

petulance /'petʃələns || 'petjʊləns/ *n* [u] mal genio *m*

petulant /'petʃələnt || 'petjʊlənt/ *adj* de mal genio, irascible (frml)

pew /pjuː/ *n* banco *m* (*de iglesia*); **take a ~!** (BrE colloq & hum) ¡toma asiento!

pewter /'pjuːtər || 'pjuːtə(r)/ *n* [u] peltre *m*

PG (= **parental guidance**) menores acompañados

PG-13 (in US) mayores de 13 años o menores acompañados

PGCE *n* (in UK) = **Postgraduate Certificate of Education**

pH *n* pH *m*; **it has a ~ of 7** tiene el pH 7

phalanx /'feɪlæŋks || 'fælæŋks/ *n*
A (*pl* **-anxes**) (Hist, Mil) falange *f*
B (*pl* **-anges** /-ændʒiːz/) (Anat) falange *f*

phallic /'fælɪk/ *adj* fálico; **~ symbol** símbolo *m* fálico

phallus /'fæləs/ *n* (*pl* **-luses** *or* **-li** /-laɪ/) falo *m*

phantasmagoric /fænˌtæzmə'gɔːrɪk || ˌfæntæzmə'gɒrɪk/, **-ical** /-ɪkəl/ *adj* fantasmagórico

phantom[1] /'fæntəm/ *n* (liter) fantasma *m*

phantom[2] *adj* [1] (ghostly) (liter) (*before n*) ‹*shape*› fantasmal; ‹*horseman*› fantasma *adj inv* [2] (imaginary) ilusorio, imaginario; **~ pregnancy** embarazo *m* psicológico *or* fantasma

Pharaoh /'ferəʊ || 'feərəʊ/ *n* faraón *m*

pharmaceutical /'fɑːrmə'suːtɪkəl || ˌfɑːmə'sjuːtɪkəl/ *adj* farmacéutico

pharmacist /ˈfɑːrməsəst || ˈfɑːməsɪst/ *n* farmacéutico, -ca *m,f*, farmaceuta *mf* (Col, Ven)

pharmacologist /ˈfɑːrməˈkɑːlədʒəst || ˌfɑːməˈkɒlədʒɪst/ *n* farmacólogo, -ga *m,f*

pharmacology /ˈfɑːrməˈkɑːlədʒi || ˌfɑːməˈkɒlədʒi/ *n* [u] farmacología *f*

pharmacy /ˈfɑːrməsi / *n* (*pl* **-cies**) 1 [u] (discipline) química *f* farmacéutica 2 [c] (dispensary) farmacia *f*

pharyngitis /ˈfærənˈdʒaɪtəs/ *n* [u] faringitis *f*

pharynx /ˈfærɪŋks/ *n* (*pl* **-rynxes** *or* **-rynges**) faringe *f*

phase¹ /feɪz/ *n*
A (stage) fase *f*, etapa *f*; **it's just a ~ you're going through** ya se te pasará
B (synchronization): **to be out of/in ~** estar* desfasado/sincronizado

phase² *vt* 1 (do in stages) escalonar, realizar* por etapas 2 (coordinate) sincronizar* 3 **phased** *past p* ‹*withdrawal/increase*› progresivo, gradual; ‹*traffic signals*› sincronizado

Phrasal verbs

- **phase in** [v ▸ o ▸ adv, v ▸ adv ▸ o] introducir* paulatinamente
- **phase out** [v ▸ o ▸ adv, v ▸ adv ▸ o] ‹*service*› retirar paulatinamente; ‹*old model*› dejar de producir

PhD *n* (award) doctorado *m*; (person) Dr., Dra.; **John Smith, ~** Dr. John Smith

pheasant /ˈfeznt/ *n* (*pl* **~s** *or* **~**) faisán *m*

phenomena /fɪˈnɑːmənə/ *pl of* **phenomenon**

phenomenal /fɪˈnɑːmənl/ *adj* (colloq) ‹*success/achievement*› espectacular, extraordinario; ‹*strength*› increíble

phenomenally /fɪˈnɑːmənli || fəˈnɒmɪnəli/ *adv* (colloq) super (fam), increíblemente

phenomenon /fɪˈnɑːmənɑːn/ *n* (*pl* **-mena**) fenómeno *m*

pheromone /ˈferəməʊn/ *n* feromona *f*

phew /fjuː/ *interj* (colloq) ¡uf!

phial /ˈfaɪəl/ *n* ampolla *f*

Philadelphia /ˈfɪləˈdelfiə/ *n* Filadelfia *f*

philanderer /fəˈlændərər || fɪˈlændərə(r)/ *n* (pej) mujeriego *m* (pey), tenorio *m* (ant *o* hum)

philandering /fəˈlændərɪŋ || fɪˈlændərɪŋ/ *n* (pej) aventuras amorosas *fpl*

philanthropic /ˈfɪlənˈθrɑːpɪk/ *adj* filantrópico

philanthropist /fəˈlænθrəpəst || fɪˈlænθrəpɪst/ *n* filántropo, -pa *m,f*

philanthropy /fəˈlænθrəpi / *n* (*pl* **-pies**) 1 [u] (charitableness) filantropía *f* 2 [c] (cause) (AmE) obra *f* benéfica

philately /fəˈlætli || fɪˈlætəli/ *n* [u] (frml) filatelia *f*

-phile /faɪl/ *suff* -filo; **Russophile** rusófilo

philharmonic /ˈfɪlərˈmɑːnɪk || ˌfɪlhɑːˈmɒnɪk, ˌfɪlɑː-/ *adj* filarmónico

-philia /ˈfɪliə/ *suff* -filia

Philippine /ˈfɪləpiːn || ˈfɪlɪpiːn/ *adj* filipino

Philippines /ˈfɪləpiːnz / *pl n* **the ~** (las) Filipinas

philistine /ˈfɪləstiːn, -aɪn || ˈfɪlɪstaɪn/ *n* 1 (boor) ignorante *mf*, cernícalo, -la *m,f* 2 **Philistine** (Bib) filisteo, -tea *m,f*

philology /fəˈlɑːlədʒi || fɪˈlɒlədʒi/ *n* [u] filología *f*

philosopher /fəˈlɑːsəfər || fɪˈlɒsəfə(r)/ *n* filósofo, -fa *m,f*

philosophic /ˈfɪləˈsɑːfɪk || ˌfɪləˈsɒfɪk/, **-ical** /-ɪkəl/ *adj* filosófico; **to be ~ ABOUT sth** tomarse algo con filosofía

philosophically /ˈfɪləˈsɑːfɪkli || ˌfɪləˈsɒfɪkli/ *adv* filosóficamente

philosophize /fəˈlɑːsəfaɪz || fɪˈlɒsəfaɪz/ *vi* **to ~ (ABOUT sth)** filosofar (SOBRE algo)

philosophy /fəˈlɑːsəfi || fɪˈlɒsəfi/ *n* [u c] filosofía *f*

philter, (BrE) **philtre** /ˈfɪltər || ˈfɪltə(r)/ *n* (liter) filtro *m* (de amor) (liter)

phlegm /flem/ *n* [u] flema *f*

phlegmatic /flegˈmætɪk/ *adj* flemático

-phobe /fəʊb/ *suff* -fobo

phobia /ˈfəʊbiə/ *n* fobia *f*

-phobia /ˈfəʊbiə/ *suff* -fobia

-phobic /ˈfəʊbɪk/ *suff* -fóbico

phoenix /ˈfiːnɪks/ *n* Ave *f‡* Fénix, fénix *m or f*

phone¹ /fəʊn/ *n* teléfono *m*; **by ~/over the ~** por teléfono; **to be on the ~** (be speaking) estar* hablando por teléfono; (subscribe) (BrE) tener* teléfono; **you're wanted on the ~** te llaman por teléfono; (*before n*) ‹*message*› telefónico; **~ call** llamada *f* (telefónica); **~ number** (número *m* de) teléfono *m*

phone² *vt* ‹*person*› llamar (por teléfono), telefonear, hablarle a (Méx); ‹*place/number*› llamar (por teléfono) a; **she ~d the results to us** telefoneó para darnos los resultados

■ **phone** *vi* llamar (por teléfono), telefonear

Phrasal verbs

- **phone around** [v ▸ adv] llamar (*a varias personas*); **I ~ed around to find a cheaper flight** hice unas cuantas llamadas tratando de encontrar un pasaje más barato
- **phone in** 1 [v ▸ adv] llamar (por teléfono), telefonear, fono *m* (Chi); **she ~d in sick** llamó para dar parte de enferma, se reportó enferma (AmL) 2 [v ▸ adv ▸ o]: **I ~d in my order** llamé para hacer un pedido
- **phone round** [v ▸ adv] (BrE) ▸ **phone around**
- **phone up** 1 [v ▸ adv] llamar, telefonear 2 [v ▸ adv ▸ o, v ▸ o ▸ adv] llamar, telefonear

phone: **~ book** *n* (colloq) guía *f* (telefónica *or* de teléfonos) *or* (Col, Méx) directorio *m*; **~ booth**, (BrE) **~ box** *n* cabina *f* telefónica *or* de teléfonos; **~card** *n* tarjeta *f* telefónica; **~-in** *n*: *programa de radio o TV en el que el público participa por teléfono*

phonetic /fəˈnetɪk/ *adj* fonético

phonetics /fəˈnetɪks/ *n* (+ *sing vb*) fonética *f*

phoney¹, (AmE also) **phony** /ˈfəʊni/ *adj* **-nier, -niest** (colloq & pej) falso; **a ~ British accent** un acento británico fingido

phoney², (AmE also) **phony** *n* (*pl* **-neys** *or* **-nies**) (colloq & pej) 1 (person) farsante *mf* (fam) 2 (thing) falsificación *f*

phonograph /ˈfəʊnəgræf || ˈfəʊnəgrɑːf/ *n* 1 (for records) (AmE) tocadiscos *m* 2 (Hist) fonógrafo *m*

phonology /fəˈnɑːlədʒi/ *n* (*pl* **-gies**) [uc] fonología *f*

phony *n/adj* (AmE) ▸ **phoney¹,²**

phooey /ˈfuːi/ *interj* (colloq) ¡cuentos chinos! (fam)

phosphate /ˈfɑːsfeɪt || ˈfɒsfeɪt/ *n* 1 (Chem) fosfato *m* 2 **phosphates** *pl* (Agr) fertilizantes *mpl* a base de fosfatos 3 (drink) (AmE) gaseosa *f* (*con sabor a frutas*)

phosphorescent /ˈfɑːsfəˈresnt || ˌfɒsfəˈresnt/ *adj* fosforescente

phosphorus /ˈfɑːsfərəs || ˈfɒsfərəs/ *n* [u] fósforo *m*

photo /ˈfəʊtəʊ/ *n* (*pl* **-tos**) (colloq) foto *f*; **to take a ~ (of sb/sth)** sacar(le)* *or* tomar(le) *or* (Esp tb) hacer(le)* una foto (a algn/algo); (*before n*) **~ booth** *máquina automática para sacarse fotos de carné*, fotomatón *m* (Esp)

photo- /ˈfəʊtəʊ/ *pref* foto-; **~journalist** reportero gráfico, reportera gráfica *m,f*

photo: **~call** *n* sesión *f* fotográfica para la prensa, foto *f* protocolaria; **~composition** /ˌfəʊtəʊkɑːmpəˈzɪʃən/ *n* [u] fotocomposición *f*; **~copiable** /ˈfəʊtəʊkɑːpiəbəl/ *adj* fotocopiable, que se puede fotocopiar; **~copier** *n* fotocopiadora *f*

photocopy¹ /ˈfəʊtəʊˌkɑːpi/ *n* (*pl* **-copies**) fotocopia *f*

photocopy² *vt* **-copies, -copying, -copied** fotocopiar

photo: **~ finish** *n* foto(-)finish *f*; **~fit**® *n* (BrE): **P~fit (picture)** retrato *m* hablado (AmS) *or* (Esp) robot *or* (Méx) reconstruido

photogenic /ˈfəʊtəˈdʒenɪk/ *adj* fotogénico

photograph¹ /ˈfəʊtəgræf/ *n* fotografía *f*, foto *f*; **to take a ~ (of sb/sth)** sacar(le)* *or* tomar(le) *or* (Esp tb) hacer(le)* una foto *or* una fotografía (a algn/algo); (*before n*) **~ album** álbum *m* de fotos *or* de fotografías, álbum *m* fotográfico

photograph² *vt* fotografiar*, sacarle* *or* tomarle *or* (Esp tb) hacerle* una foto *or* una fotografía a

■ **photograph** *vi*: **to ~ well/badly** salir* bien/mal en las fotos *or* fotografías

photographer /fəˈtɑːgrəfər || fəˈtɒgrəfə(r)/ *n* fotógrafo, -fa *m,f*; **press ~** reportero gráfico, reportera gráfica *m,f*; **she's a keen ~** le gusta la fotografía *or* sacar fotos

photographic /ˈfəʊtəˈgræfɪk/ *adj* ‹*copy/evidence/memory*› fotográfico; ‹*shop/equipment*› de fotografía

photographically /ˈfəʊtəˈgræfɪkli/ *adv* fotográficamente

photography /fə'tɑːgrəfi || fə'tɒgrəfi/ *n* [u] fotografía *f*

photo: **~gravure** /ˌfəʊtəʊgrə'vjʊr/ *n* [u c] fotograbado *m*; **~journalism** /ˌfəʊtəʊ'dʒɜːrnlɪzəm/ *n* [u] periodismo *m* fotográfico, fotoperiodismo *m*; **~lithography** /ˌfəʊtəʊlɪ'θɑːgrəfi/ *n* [u] fotolitografía *f*; **~montage** /'fəʊtəmɑːn'tɑːʒ/ *n* [u c] fotomontaje *m*; **~opportunity** /'fəʊtəʊɑːpər'tuːnəti/ *n* ▸**photocall**; **~sensitive** /'fəʊtəʊ'sensətɪv/ *adj* fotosensible; **~ shoot** *n* sesión *f* de fotos; **~stat**®, **~stat** /'fəʊtəstæt/ *n* fotocopia *f*; **~synthesis** /'fəʊtəʊ'sɪnθəsəs/ *n* [u] fotosíntesis *f*

phrasal verb /'freɪzl/ *n* verbo *m* con partícula(s)

phrase[1] /freɪz/ *n* frase *f*, locución *f*; **to coin a ~** por así decirlo; (*before n*) **~ book** manual *m* de conversación, ≈ guía *f* de bolsillo para el viajero

phrase[2] *vt* expresar, formular; **a carefully ~d letter** una carta redactada con gran cuidado

phraseology /'freɪzi'ɑːlədʒi/ *n* [u] fraseología *f*

phrasing /'freɪzɪŋ/ *n* [u] 1 (Mus) fraseo *m* 2 (wording) expresión *f*; (in writing) redacción *f*

phrenology /frɪ'nɑːlədʒi || frə'nɒlədʒi/ *n* [u] frenología *f*

physiatrics /ˌfɪzɪ'ætrɪks/ *n* (+ *sing vb*) (AmE) ▸**physiotherapy**

physical[1] /'fɪzɪkəl/ *adj*

A 1 (bodily) físico; ‹*illness*› orgánico; **the ~ effects of alcohol consumption** los efectos del alcohol en el organismo; **~ examination** reconocimiento *m* médico, chequeo *m* (médico); **~ education** educación *f* física 2 (rough): **it was a very ~ game** jugaron muy duro

B (material) ‹*world*› material; **that's a ~ impossibility** eso es materialmente imposible

physical[2] *n* reconocimiento *m* médico, chequeo *m* (médico)

physically /'fɪzɪkli/ *adv* ‹*attractive*› físicamente; ‹*dangerous/demanding*› desde el punto de vista físico; **to be ~ fit** estar* en forma; **it's ~ impossible** es materialmente imposible; **he was ~ ejected from the club** lo sacaron a viva fuerza del club

physical: **~ therapist** *n* (AmE) ▸**physiotherapist**; **~ therapy** *n* [u] (AmE) ▸**physiotherapy**

physician /fə'zɪʃən || fɪ'zɪʃən/ *n* (frml) médico, -ca *m,f*

physicist /'fɪzəsəst || 'fɪzɪsɪst/ *n* físico, -ca *m,f*

physics /'fɪzɪks/ *n* (+ *sing vb*) física *f*

physio /'fɪziəʊ/ *n* (colloq) 1 [u] ▸**physiotherapy** 2 [c] ▸**physiotherapist**

P

physiognomy /'fɪzi'ɑːgnəmi/ *n* [u] (liter) fisonomía *f*

physiological /'fɪziə'lɑːdʒɪkəl/ *adj* fisiológico

physiologist /'fɪzi'ɑːlədʒəst/ *n* fisiólogo, -ga *m,f*

physiology /'fɪzi'ɑːlədʒi || ˌfɪzi'ɒlədʒi/ *n* [u] fisiología *f*

physiotherapist /'fɪziəʊ'θerəpəst || ˌfɪziəʊ'θerəpɪst/ *n* fisioterapeuta *mf*, kinesiólogo, -ga *m,f*

physiotherapy /'fɪziəʊ'θerəpi/ *n* [u] (discipline) kinesiología *f*; (treatment) fisioterapia *f*, kinesiterapia *f*

physique /fə'ziːk || fɪ'ziːk/ *n* físico *m*

pianist /pi'ænəst || 'piənɪst/ *n* pianista *mf*

piano /pi'ænəʊ/ *n* (*pl* **-os**) piano *m*; (*before n*) ‹*duet/concerto*› para piano; **~ player** pianista *mf*; **~ stool** banqueta *f* or taburete *m* (del piano); **~ tuner** afinador, -dora *m,f* de pianos

piazza /pi'ætsə/ *n* 1 (square) plaza *f* 2 (veranda) (AmE) galería *f*, veranda *f*

picaresque /'pɪkə'resk/ *adj* picaresco

piccolo /'pɪkələʊ/ *n* flautín *m*, piccolo *m*

pick[1] /pɪk/ *n*

A 1 ▸**pickax** 2 (*ice ~*) piolet *m* 3 (plectrum) púa *f*, plectro *m*, uñeta *f* (CS), uña *f* (Méx, Ven)

B 1 (choice) (*no pl*): **take your ~** elige *or* escoge el (*or* los *etc*) que quieras 2 (best): **the ~ of sth** lo mejor de algo; ***to be the ~ of the bunch*** ser* el mejor de todos 3 (tip) (AmE) pronóstico *m*, fija *f* (CS)

pick[2] *vt*

A 1 (choose, select) ‹*number/color*› elegir*, escoger*; ‹*team/crew*› seleccionar; **to ~ a winner** (in racing) pronosticar* el ganador; (choose well) elegir* *or* escoger* bien; ***to ~ one's way*** andar* con mucho cuidado 2 (provoke): **to ~ a fight** buscar* pelea; **to ~ a fight with sb** meterse con algn; **are you trying to ~ a quarrel with me?** ¿quieres que discutamos?

B (gather) ‹*flower*› cortar, coger* (esp Esp); ‹*fruit/cotton/tea*› recoger*, coger* (esp Esp), pizcar* (Méx)

C 1 (remove matter from): **to ~ one's nose** meterse el dedo en la nariz, hurgarse* la nariz; **to ~ one's teeth** escarbarse los dientes; **don't ~ your spots** no te toques los granitos; **the vultures ~ed the bones clean** los buitres dejaron los huesos limpios; **to ~ sb's pocket** robarle la billetera (*or* las llaves *etc*) a algn del bolsillo, bolsear a algn (Mex fam), carterear a algn (Chi fam) 2 (open) ‹*lock*› abrir* con una ganzúa (*or* una horquilla *etc*)

■ **pick** *vi* 1 : **you can't (afford to) ~ and choose** no puedes (permitirte el lujo de) ser exigente *or* andarte con remilgos 2 (take bits): **they were ~ing through the rubbish** estaban escarbando en la basura; **to ~ AT sth** ‹*at scab*› tocar* algo; **he was ~ing at his dinner** comía desganado

Phrasal verbs

• **pick off** [v ▸ o ▸ adv, v ▸ adv ▸ o] (shoot) eliminar, liquidar

• **pick on** [v ▸ prep ▸ o] 1 (victimize) (colloq) meterse con, agarrársela(s) con (AmL fam) 2 (choose) elegir*, escoger*

• **pick out** [v ▸ o ▸ adv, v ▸ adv ▸ o]

A (choose, select) elegir*, escoger*

B 1 (recognize, identify) reconocer* 2 (discern) distinguir*

C (highlight) destacar*, hacer* resaltar

• **pick up**

Sense I [v ▸ o ▸ adv, v ▸ adv ▸ o]

A (gather off floor, ground) recoger*; (take) tomar, agarrar (esp AmL), coger* (esp Esp); (lift up) levantar; ***to ~ oneself up*** reponerse*; (lit: after falling) levantarse; ***to ~ up the tab*** *o* (BrE also) ***bill*** cargar* con la cuenta, cargar* con el muerto (fam); **she ~ed up the check** (AmE) pagó ella

B 1 (learn) ‹*language*› aprender; ‹*habit*› adquirir, agarrar (esp AmL), coger* (esp Esp); **it's not hard, you'll soon ~ it up** no es difícil, ya verás cómo enseguida le agarras la onda *or* (Esp) le coges el tranquillo (fam) 2 (acquire) ‹*bargain*› conseguir*, encontrar*

C 1 (collect, fetch) recoger*, pasar a buscar; **could you ~ up some eggs for me?** ¿me traes unos huevos? 2 (take on board) ‹*passenger*› recoger* 3 (rescue) rescatar 4 (arrest) detener* 5 (colloq) ‹*man/woman*› ligarse* (fam), levantar (AmS fam)

D 1 (receive) ‹*signal*› captar, recibir 2 (detect) detectar

E (resume) ‹*conversation*› reanudar

Sense II [v ▸ adv ▸ o]

A 1 (earn) (colloq) hacer* (fam), sacar* (fam) 2 (gain) ‹*speed*› agarrar, coger* (esp Esp)

B (tidy) (AmE colloq) ‹*room/house*› ordenar

Sense III [v ▸ o ▸ adv] 1 (revive) reanimar 2 (correct) corregir*; **to ~ sb up ON sth**: **she ~ed him up on a few points of historical detail** le señaló algunos detalles históricos donde se había equivocado

Sense IV [v ▸ adv]

A 1 (improve) «*prices/sales*» subir, repuntar; «*economy/business*» repuntar; «*invalid*» mejorar, recuperarse; «*weather*» mejorar 2 (resume) seguir*, continuar*

B (notice) (colloq) **to ~ up ON sth** darse* cuenta DE algo

pick: **~aback** /'pɪkəbæk/ *n* ▸**piggyback**; **~ax**, (BrE) **~axe** *n* pico *m*, piqueta *f*

picker /'pɪkər || 'pɪkə(r)/ *n* 1 (person) recolector, -tora *m,f* 2 (machine) recolectora *f*

picket[1] /'pɪkət || 'pɪkɪt/ *n*

A 1 (group) piquete *m*; (*before n*) **~ line** piquete *m* 2 (individual) *miembro de un piquete*

B (stake) estaca *f*; (*before n*) **~ fence** cerca *f*, valla *f*

picket[2] *vt* ‹*factory/workplace*› formar un piquete frente a, piquetear (esp AmL)

■ **picket** *vi* tomar parte en un piquete, piquetear (esp AmL)

pickings /'pɪkɪŋz/ *pl n* 1 (profits) ganancias *fpl*; **rich ~** suculentas ganancias 2 (food) sobras *fpl*, restos *mpl* (esp AmL)

pickle[1] /'pɪkəl/ *n* 1 [c] (*dill ~*) (AmE) pepinillo *m* en vinagre al eneldo 2 [c]: **~s** (vegetables) encurtidos *mpl*, pickles *mpl* (CS) 3 [u] (relish) (BrE) *condimento a base de encurtidos en una salsa* 4 ***to be in a (pretty) ~*** estar* metido en un lío *or* en un berenjenal (fam)

pickle² *vt* conservar en vinagre *or* (Chi tb) en escabeche, encurtir

pickled /'pɪkəld/ *adj* ‹*onions*› en vinagre, escabechado (Chi); ‹*herring*› ≈ escabechado

pick: **~-me-up** *n* (colloq) estimulante *m*; **~pocket** *n* carterista *mf*, bolsista *mf* (Méx); **~up** *n* 1 **~ (truck)** camioneta *f or* furgoneta *f* (de reparto); 2 (by taxi, bus, truck): **I've got two ~ups to make** tengo que pasar a recoger dos paquetes (*or* a dos personas *etc*); (*before n*) **~up point** lugar *m* de recogida; 3 (Audio, Mus) **~up (arm)** (BrE) brazo *m* (del tocadiscos); 4 (sexual) (sl) ligue *m* (fam), levante *m* (AmS fam)

picky /'pɪki/ *adj* **pickier, pickiest** (colloq) quisquilloso

picnic¹ /'pɪknɪk/ *n* picnic *m*; **to go for** *o* **on a ~** ir* de picnic; ***it's no* ~** no es (ninguna) broma (fam); (*before n*) **~ lunch** almuerzo *m or* comida *f* campestre

picnic² *vi* **-ck-** (go on a picnic) ir* de picnic; (eat) comer

picnicker /'pɪknɪkər || 'pɪknɪkə(r)/ *n* excursionista *mf*

pictogram /'pɪktə(ʊ)græm/ *n* pictograma *m*

pictograph /'pɪktə(ʊ)græf/ *n* pictografía *f*

pictorial /pɪk'tɔːriəl/ *adj* ‹*representation*› pictórico; ‹*account/history*› en imágenes, gráfico; ‹*magazine*› ilustrado

picture¹ /'pɪktʃər || 'pɪktʃə(r)/ *n*

A 1 (illustration) ilustración *f*; (drawing) dibujo *m*; (painting) cuadro *m*, pintura *f*; (print) cuadro *m*, lámina *f*; (portrait) retrato *m*; **to draw a ~ of sth** hacer* un dibujo de algo, dibujar algo; **to paint a ~ of sth/sb** pintar algo/a algn; **the book paints a gloomy ~ of ...** el libro pinta un cuadro sombrío de ...; ***to be as pretty as a* ~** ser* precioso: (*before n*) **~ frame** marco *m*; **~ gallery** (museum) pinacoteca *f*, museo *m*; (shop) galería *f* de arte 2 (photo) foto *f*; **to take a ~ of sth/sb** sacarle* *or* tomarle *or* (Esp tb) hacerle* una foto a algo/algn

B (situation) panorama *m*; **that's not the whole ~** ésa es una visión parcial del asunto; ***to get the* ~** (colloq): **you're not welcome here, get the ~?** aquí no eres bienvenido ¿entiendes *or* te enteras?; ***to put sb in the* ~** poner* a algn al tanto (de la situación)

C (idea) idea *f*; **you get a very different ~ from these figures** estas cifras te dan una idea muy distinta

D (TV) imagen *f*

E (Cin) 1 (movie) película *f* 2 **pictures** *pl* (cinema) (BrE dated) **the ~s** el cine

F 1 (embodiment) imagen *f*; **he looks the very ~ of health** es la viva imagen de la salud 2 (beautiful sight) espectáculo *m*; **doesn't she look a ~?** ¿no está preciosa?

picture² *vt* 1 (imagine) imaginarse; **I can't ~ myself with a baby** no me veo con un niño 2 (depict) (*usu pass*): **the minister, ~d here next to ...** el ministro, que aparece en la foto junto a ...

picture: **~ book** *n* libro *m* ilustrado; **~ postcard** *n* (BrE) (tarjeta *f*) postal *f*

picturesque /'pɪktʃə'resk/ *adj* pintoresco

piddling /'pɪdlɪŋ/ *adj* (colloq & pej) ‹*amount*› insignificante

pidgin /'pɪdʒən || 'pɪdʒɪn/ *n* [c u] *versión simplificada y rudimentaria de una lengua, usada como lengua franca*

pie /paɪ/ *n* [u c] pastel *m*, pay *m* (AmC, Méx); (savory) empanada *f*, pastel *m*; **~ *in the sky*** castillos en el aire; ***to be as easy as* ~** ser* pan comido (fam); ***to eat humble* ~** morder* el polvo

piebald /'paɪbɔːld/ *adj* ‹*horse*› picazo

piece /piːs/ *n*

A 1 (part of sth broken, torn, cut, divided) pedazo *m*, trozo *m*; **she ripped the letter into ~s** rompió la carta en pedacitos, hizo trizas la carta; **a ~ of land** un terreno, una parcela; **to come** *o* **fall to ~s** hacerse* pedazos; **she smashed the vase to ~s** hizo añicos el jarrón; **her life was in ~s** su vida estaba arruinada; ***in one* ~**: **they got back in one ~** volvieron sanos y salvos; **I dropped it, but it's still in one ~** se me cayó, pero está intacto; ***to be a* ~ *of cake*** (colloq) ser* pan comido; ***to go to* ~s** (be very upset) quedar deshecho *or* destrozado; (break down) perder* el control; ***to pick up the* ~s**: **he gets himself into trouble and expects me to pick up the ~s** se mete en líos y después pretende que yo le saque las castañas del fuego; **he's trying to pick up the ~s of his life** está tratando de rehacer su vida; ***to pull sth/sb to* ~s** destrozar* algo/a algn; ***to say one's* ~** dar* su (*or* mi *etc*) opinión, opinar 2 (component) pieza *f*, parte *f*; **he's taken the clock to ~s** ha desarmado *or* desmontado el reloj; **it comes to ~s** es desmontable; **a three-~ suit** un traje de tres piezas, un terno

B (item): **a ~ of advice** un consejo; **a ~ of furniture** un mueble; **a ~ of paper** un papel; **an excellent ~ of work** un trabajo excelente; ***to be a nasty* ~ *of work*** (esp BrE colloq) ser* una basura *or* (fam) una porquería; ***to give sb a* ~ *of one's mind*** cantarle las cuarenta *or* decirle* cuatro verdades a algn

C 1 (Mus): **a ~ (of music)** una pieza (de música) 2 (Journ) artículo *m* 3 (Art) pieza *f*

D (coin) moneda *f*, pieza *f*

E (in board games) ficha *f*, pieza *f*; (in chess) figura *f*

Phrasal verb

- **piece together** [v ▸ o ▸ adv, v ▸ adv ▸ o] 1 ‹*fragments*› juntar*; ‹*events/facts*› reconstruir* 2 ‹*alibi*› idear; ‹*argument*› estructurar

pièce de résistance /pi'esdə'rezɪs'tɑːns || ˌpjesdərə'zɪstɑːns/ *n* plato *m* fuerte

piecemeal¹ /'piːsmiːl/ *adj* poco sistemático

piecemeal² *adv* (gradually) poco a poco; (unsystematically) de manera poco sistemática

piece: **~work** *n* [u] trabajo *m* a destajo; **to do ~work** trabajar a destajo; **~worker** *n* destajista *mf*, trabajador, -dora *m,f* a destajo

pie chart *n* gráfico *m or* gráfica *f* circular

pied /paɪd/ *adj* ‹*horse*› ruano

pied-a-terre /pi'eɪdɑː'ter || ˌpjeɪdɑː'teə(r)/ *n*: *apartamento o casa en la ciudad que se tiene como segunda residencia*

pier /pɪr || pɪə(r)/ *n* 1 (landing place) embarcadero *m* 2 (with amusements) *paseo con juegos y atracciones sobre un muelle*

pierce /pɪrs || pɪəs/ *vt* 1 (make a hole in) agujerear, perforar; (go through) atravesar*; **to ~ a hole in sth** hacer* un agujero en algo, agujerear algo; **she's had her ears ~d** se ha hecho hacer agujeros en las orejas 2 ‹‹*sound/light*›› (liter) rasgar* (liter)

piercing /'pɪrsɪŋ || 'pɪəsɪŋ/ *adj* ‹*eyes/look*› penetrante; ‹*scream*› desgarrador

piety /'paɪəti/ *n* [u] piedad *f*, devoción *f*

piffle /'pɪfəl/ *n* [u] (colloq) estupideces *fpl* (fam), paparruchas *f* (fam)

piffling /'pɪflɪŋ/ *adj* (colloq) ‹*affair/matter*› insignificante; ‹*sum/amount*› ridículo

pig¹ /pɪg/ *n*

A (Agr, Zool) cerdo *m*, chancho *m* (AmL); **a ~ *in a poke***: **you've bought yourself a ~ in a poke** te han dado gato por liebre; **~*s might fly*** *o* ***if* ~*s had wings*** cuando las ranas críen pelo (fam), la semana de tres jueves (fam); ***to make a* ~*'s ear of sth*** (BrE colloq) hacer* algo muy mal *or* (CS fam) como la mona

B 1 (obnoxious person) (colloq) cerdo, -da *m,f* (fam) 2 (glutton) (colloq) glotón, -tona *m,f*, angurriento, -ta *m,f* (CS fam); **to make a ~ of oneself** darse* un atracón (fam), ponerse* morado *or* ciego (Esp fam) 3 (policeman) (pej & sl) policía *m*, mono *m* (Esp arg & pey), tombo *m* (Col, Ven fam & pej), paco *m* (Chi fam & pey), cana *m* (RPl arg & pey), tira (Méx fam & pey)

pig² **-gg-** *vt*: ***to* ~ *it*** (colloq) (AmE) compartir la cama

Phrasal verb

- **pig out** [v ▸ adv] (eat to excess) (colloq) **to ~ out (ON sth)** darse* un atracón (DE algo) (fam)

pigeon /'pɪdʒən || 'pɪdʒɪn, 'pɪdʒən/ *n* [c u] (Zool) paloma *f*; (Culin) pichón *m*; (*before n*) **~ fancier** colombófilo, -la *m,f*

pigeon: **~hole** *n* 1 (on wall, desk) casillero *m* 2 (category) casilla *f*; **to put sb/sth in a ~hole** encasillar a algn/algo; **~-toed** /'pɪdʒən'təʊd || ˌpɪdʒɪn'təʊd, ˌpɪdʒən-/ *adj*: **he's ~-toed** tiene las puntas de los pies hacia dentro

piggy /'pɪgi/ *n* (*pl* **-gies**) (used to or by children) cerdito *m*, chanchito *m* (AmL)

piggy: **~back** *n*: **to give sb a ~back** llevar a algn a caballo; **~bank** *n* alcancía *f* (AmL), hucha *f* (Esp) (*en forma de cerdito*); **~ in the middle** *n* ▸**pig in the middle**

pig: **~headed** /'pɪg'hedəd || ˌpɪg'hedɪd/ *adj* ‹*person*› terco, testarudo, cabeza dura (fam); ‹*attitude/refusal*› obstinado, empecinado; **~ in the middle** *n* [u] ***to be (the)* ~ *in the middle*** ser* el tercero en discordia; **~ iron** *n* [u] hierro *m* en lingotes

piglet /'pɪglət/ *n* cochinillo *m*, chanchito *m* (AmL)

pigment /ˈpɪgmənt/ *n* [c u] pigmento *m*

pigmentation /ˈpɪgmənˈteɪʃən/ *n* [u] pigmentación *f*

pigmy /ˈpɪgmi/ *n* ▸ **pygmy**

pig: **~-out** *n* (AmE colloq) comilona *f* (fam), atracón *m* (fam); **~-pen** *n* (AmE) ▸ **~ sty**; **~skin** *n* [1] [u] (leather) cuero *m* de chancho *or* (Esp) piel *f* de cerdo [2] [c] (AmE Sport) pelota *f*, balón *m*; **~sty** *n* pocilga *f*, chiquero *m* (AmL); **~swill** *n* [u] (BrE) bazofia *f*; **~tail** *n* (bunch) coleta *f*, chape *m* (Chi); (plait) trenza *f*

pike /paɪk/ *n* [1] (*pl* ~) (Zool) lucio *m* [2] (weapon) (Hist) pica *f* [3] (*turn*~) (AmE) carretera *f*

piker /ˈpaɪkər || ˈpaɪkə(r)/ *n* (AmE sl) (stingy person) roñoso, -sa *m,f* (fam), agarrado, -da *m,f* (fam)

Pilates /pɪˈlɑːteɪz/ *n* [u] Pilates *m*; **to go to ~** hacer* Pilates

pilau /pɪˈlaʊ/, **pilaw** /pɪˈlɔː/ *n*: *plato de arroz*

pilchard /ˈpɪltʃərd || ˈpɪltʃəd/ *n* sardina *f* (*grande*)

pile¹ /paɪl/ *n*

A [c] [1] (stack, heap) montón *m*, pila *f* [2] (fortune) (colloq) fortuna *f*

B [c u] (Tex) pelo *m*; **with a thick ~** de pelo tupido

C **piles** *pl* (BrE Med) hemorroides *fpl*, almorranas *fpl*

D [c] (Const) pilote *m*

E [c] (large building) (hum) mole *f*

pile² *vt* amontonar, apilar, hacer* un montón *or* una pila con; **my desk was ~d high with boxes** había un montón de cajas sobre mi escritorio; **he ~d more rice onto his plate** se sirvió otro montón de arroz

Phrasal verbs

- **pile in** [v ▸ adv] (colloq) (squeeze in) meterse
- **pile into** [v ▸ prep ▸ o] (colloq) [1] (squeeze into) ‹*car*› meterse en [2] (attack) arremeter contra [3] (crash into) «*vehicle*» estrellarse contra
- **pile on** [v ▸ o ▸ adv, v ▸ adv ▸ o] [1] (add): **she ~d on the mayonnaise** le puso un montón de mayonesa (fam); **they keep piling on the work** nos dan cada vez más trabajo [2] (exaggerate) (colloq) exagerar; **to ~ it on** pasarse de dramático, exagerar mucho
- **pile up**

A [v ▸ adv] (accumulate) amontonarse, acumularse

B [v ▸ o ▸ adv, v ▸ adv ▸ o] [1] (form into pile) ‹*books/boxes*› apilar, amontonar [2] (collect) ‹*fortune*› amasar; ‹*sum*› juntar, reunir*; **they ~d up huge debts** se llenaron de deudas

pile: **~ driver** *n* (Const) martinete *m*; **~up** *n* choque *m* múltiple *or* en cadena, colisión *f* en cadena

pilfer /ˈpɪlfər || ˈpɪlfə(r)/ *vt/i* robar (*cosas de poco valor*), ratear, hurtar

pilfering /ˈpɪlfərɪŋ/ *n* [u] robos *mpl*, raterías *fpl*

pilgrim /ˈpɪlgrəm || ˈpɪlgrɪm/ *n* peregrino, -na *m,f*; (*before n*) **the P~ Fathers** *los primeros colonizadores de Nueva Inglaterra*

Pilgrim Fathers – the Pilgrim Fathers

Se denomina así a las 102 personas que zarparon rumbo a América, en 1620, a bordo del *Mayflower*. El grupo incluía 35 puritanos cuyo objetivo era fundar una comunidad religiosa segura en el Nuevo Mundo y lejos de la persecución de la que habían sido objeto en Inglaterra. Probablemente atracaron en Plymouth Rock, Massachusetts, donde fundaron la colonia de Plymouth

pilgrimage /ˈpɪlgrəmɪdʒ || ˈpɪlgrɪmɪdʒ/ *n* peregrinación *f*; **to go on a ~** ir* de peregrinación

pill /pɪl/ *n* [1] (tablet) pastilla *f*, píldora *f*; ***a bitter ~ to swallow*** un trago amargo; ***to sugar*** *o* ***sweeten the ~*** dorar la píldora [2] (contraceptive) **the P~** la píldora (anticonceptiva); **to be on the P~** tomar la píldora

pillage¹ /ˈpɪlɪdʒ/ *n* [u] pillaje *m*, saqueo *m*

pillage² *vt* saquear

■ **pillage** *vi* saquear, pillar

pillar /ˈpɪlər || ˈpɪlə(r)/ *n* [1] (column) pilar *m*, columna *f*; ***from ~ to post*** de la ceca a la Meca [2] (exemplary member) pilar *m*, baluarte *m*; **he is a ~ of the community** es uno de los pilares *or* baluartes de la comunidad

pillar box *n* (BrE) buzón *m*

pillbox /ˈpɪlbɑːks || ˈpɪlbɒks/ *n* [1] (for pills) pastillero *m* [2] **~ (hat)** (worn by women) casquete *m*; (worn by soldiers, bellboys) gorra *f*

pillion¹ /ˈpɪljən/ *n* (Auto) asiento *m* trasero (*de una moto*)

pillion² *adv* en el asiento trasero, de paquete (fam)

pillory¹ /ˈpɪləri/ *n* **-ries** picota *f*

pillory² *vt* **-ries, -rying, -ried** ridiculizar*, burlarse de

pillow¹ /ˈpɪləʊ/ *n* almohada *f*; (*before n*) **~ talk** conversaciones *fpl* íntimas (*en la cama*)

pillow² *vt* recostar*, apoyar

pillowcase /ˈpɪləʊkeɪs/, (BrE also) **pillow slip** *n* funda *f*

pill-popper /ˈpɪlpɑːpər || ˈpɪlpɒpə(r)/ *n* (colloq) [1] (pill-taker) adicto, -ta *m,f* a las pastillas [2] (barbiturate addict) adicto, -ta *m,f* a los barbitúricos

pilot¹ /ˈpaɪlət/ *n*

A (Aerosp, Aviat) piloto *mf*

B (Naut) práctico *mf* (de puerto)

C (Rad, TV) programa *m* piloto; (Busn) producto *m* piloto

pilot² *adj* (*before n*) piloto *adj inv*, experimental

pilot³ *vt*

A [1] (Aviat, Naut) pilotar, pilotear (AmL) [2] (guide, lead) dirigir*; **to ~ a bill through Congress** lograr la aprobación de un proyecto de ley

B (test) poner* a prueba

pilot: **~light** *n* piloto *m*; **~fish** /ˈpaɪlətfɪʃ/ *n* (*pl* **~fish** *or* **~fishes**) pez *m* piloto

pimento /pɪˈmentəʊ/, **pimiento** /pɪˈmjentəʊ/ *n* (*pl* **-tos**)

A (sweet pepper) pimiento *m or* (AmS exc RPl) pimentón *m* rojo *or* colorado, ají *m* morrón (RPl)

B (allspice) pimienta *f* de Jamaica

pimp /pɪmp/ *n* proxeneta *m*, chulo *m* (de putas) (Esp fam), padrote *m* (Méx fam), cafiche *m* (CS fam)

pimple /ˈpɪmpəl/ *n* grano *m*, espinilla *f* (AmL)

pimply /ˈpɪmpli/ *adj* **-plier, -pliest** lleno de granos

pin¹ /pɪn/ *n*

A (for cloth, paper) alfiler *m*; **it was so quiet you could have heard a ~ drop** había tanto silencio que se podía oír el vuelo de una mosca; ***as clean as a (new) ~*** limpio como un jaspe *or* como los chorros del oro

B (brooch, badge) (AmE) insignia *f*

C [1] (on grenade) anilla *f* [2] (on plug) (BrE Elec) clavija *f*, borne *m* [3] (peg) (Tech) perno *m* [4] (*clothes* ~) (AmE) *see* **clothes**

D **pins** *pl* (legs) (colloq) patas *fpl* (fam)

pin² **-nn-** *vt*

A (fasten, attach) ‹*dress/seam*› prender con alfileres; **I ~ned the papers together** sujeté los papeles con un alfiler; **she wore her hair ~ned up** llevaba el pelo recogido (con horquillas/pasadores); **~ the list (up) on the board** pon la lista en el tablero de anuncios; **I ~ned the clothes on the line** (AmE) tendí la ropa; **she had ~ned her hopes on getting a scholarship** había depositado sus esperanzas en conseguir la beca; **they tried to ~ the blame on him** trataron de hacerle cargar con la culpa

B (hold motionless): **they ~ned him against the wall** lo inmovilizaron contra la pared; **he ~ned my arms to my sides** me sujetó los brazos a ambos lados

Phrasal verbs

- **pin back** [v ▸ o ▸ adv, v ▸ adv ▸ o] sujetar, fijar
- **pin down** [v ▸ o ▸ adv, v ▸ adv ▸ o]

A (prevent from moving): **they ~ned him down** (se echaron sobre él y) lo inmovilizaron

B [1] (define) ‹*cause/identity*› definir, precisar; **something's wrong with me, but I can't ~ it down** algo tengo, pero no sabría decir exactamente qué [2] (force to state position): **it's useless trying to ~ politicians down** es inútil intentar que los políticos se definan; **I managed to ~ him down to a definite date** conseguí que se comprometiera para una fecha concreta

PIN /pɪn/ *n* (= **personal identification number**) PIN *m*

pinafore /ˈpɪnəfɔːr || ˈpɪnəfɔː(r)/ *n* [1] **~ (dress)** (sleeveless dress) jumper *m or* (Esp) pichi *m* [2] (apron) (BrE) delantal *m or* (esp Méx) mandil *m* (*con peto*) [3] (protective overdress) delantal *m*

pinball /ˈpɪnbɔːl/ *n* [u] (*before n*) **~ machine** flipper *m*

pince-nez /ˈpænsˈneɪ/ *n* (*pl* ~ /-z/) quevedos *mpl*

pincer /ˈpɪnsər || ˈpɪnsə(r)/ *n* [1] (Zool) pinza *f*; (*before n*) **~ movement** (Mil) movimiento *m* de tenazas [2] **pincers** *pl* (tool) tenazas *fpl*, tenaza *f*; **a pair of ~s** unas tenazas, una tenaza

pinch¹ /pɪntʃ/ *n* 1 (act) pellizco *m*; **to give sb a ~** pellizcar* *or* darle* un pellizco a algn; ***in*** *o* (BrE) ***at a ~*** (if necessary) si fuera necesario; (at the most) como máximo; ***to feel the ~*** estar* apretado (de dinero), pasar estrecheces 2 (small quantity) pizca *f*, pellizco *m*; ▸**salt¹ 1**

pinch² *vt*
A «*person*» pellizcar*; «*shoes*» apretar*
B (BrE colloq) (steal) ‹*wallet*› robar; ‹*boyfriend*› levantar (fam); ‹*idea*› robar, quitar
■ **pinch** *vi* 1 (be too tight) «*shoes*» apretar* 2 (be frugal): **to ~ and scrape** *o* **save** hacer* economías

pinched /pɪntʃt/ *adj*: **she had a ~ look** tenía mala cara; **faces ~ with grief** caras transidas de dolor

pinch-hit /ˈpɪntʃˈhɪt/ *vi* **-tt-** 1 (in baseball) batear de emergencia 2 (act as substitute) (AmE colloq) **to ~ FOR sb** sustituir* A algn

pincushion /ˈpɪnˌkʊʃən/ *n* alfiletero *m*, acerico *m*

pine¹ /paɪn/ *n* 1 [c] **~ (tree)** pino *m*; (*before n*) **~ cone** piña *f*; **~ needle** hoja *f* de pino; **~ nut** piñón *m* 2 [u] (wood) (madera *f* de) pino *m*

pine² *vi* estar* triste, sufrir; **to ~ FOR sth** suspirar POR algo; **the dog was pining for its master** el perro echaba muchísimo de menos a su amo

(Phrasal verb)
• **pine away** [v ▸ adv] languidecer* *or* consumirse de añoranza

pineapple /ˈpaɪnˌæpəl/ *n* piña *f* *or* (esp RPl) ananá *f*

pine: **~ marten** /ˈmɑːrtn̩ || ˈmɑːtɪn/ *n* marta *f*; **~wood** *n* 1 [c] (forest) (*often pl*) pinar *m*, bosque *m* de pinos 2 [u] ▸**pine¹ 2**

ping¹ /pɪŋ/ *n* sonido *m* metálico

ping² *vi* sonar*, hacer* tin (fam)

Ping-Pong®, **ping-pong** /ˈpɪŋpɑːŋ/ *n* [u] ping-pong *m*

pin: **~head** *n* cabeza *f* de alfiler; **~hole** *n* agujerito *m*

pinion¹ /ˈpɪnjən/ *vt* ‹*person*› inmovilizar* (*esp sujetándole los brazos*)

pinion² *n* (cogwheel) piñón *m*

pink¹ /pɪŋk/ *adj* **-er, -est** rosa *adj inv*, rosado (AmL); ‹*cheeks*› sonrosado; ▸**tickle¹ 2**

pink² *n*
A [u] (color) rosa *m*, rosado *m* (AmL); ***to be in the ~*** (in top form) estar* en plena forma
B [c] (Bot) clavelina *f*

pink³ *vt* cortar con tijera dentada

pinking shears /ˈpɪŋkɪŋ/ *pl n* tijeras *fpl* dentadas

pink slip *n* (AmE) notificación *f* de despido

pin money *n* [u] *dinero para gastos personales*

pinnacle /ˈpɪnɪkəl || ˈpɪnəkəl/ *n* 1 (Archit) pináculo *m*; **the ~ of fame** el pináculo de la fama 2 (mountain peak) cumbre *f*, cima *f*

pinny /ˈpɪni/ *n* (*pl* **-nies**) (BrE colloq) ▸**pinafore 2**

pinpoint¹ /ˈpɪnpɔɪnt/ *vt* 1 (determine) ‹*position/aircraft*› localizar* *or* (AmL tb) ubicar* con exactitud; **to ~ the causes of the problem** establecer* con exactitud cuáles son las causas del problema 2 (pick out) ‹*fact*› señalar

pinpoint² *n* puntito *m*

pin: **~prick** *n* (sensation) pinchazo *m*; (minor irritation) pequeño inconveniente *m*; **~s and needles** *pl n* hormigueo *m*; **~stripe**, **~striped** *adj*: **~stripe(d) suit** traje *m* oscuro de raya diplomática

pint /paɪnt/ *n* pinta *f* (*EEUU: 0,47 litros, RU: 0,57 litros*); **to go for a ~** (BrE colloq) salir* a tomar una cerveza

pinto /ˈpɪntəʊ/ *n* (*pl* **-tos**) (AmE) caballo *m* pinto

pint-size /ˈpaɪntsaɪz/, **pint-sized** /-d/ *adj* pequeñito (fam), chiquito (esp AmL fam)

pinup /ˈpɪnʌp/ *n* foto *f* (*de chica atractiva, actor famoso etc*); (*before n*) **~ girl** pin-up *f*

pioneer¹ /ˈpaɪəˈnɪr || ˌpaɪəˈnɪə(r)/ *n* 1 (settler) pionero, -ra *m,f*, colonizador, -dora *m,f* 2 (originator) pionero, -ra *m,f*, precursor, -sora *m,f*

pioneer² *vt* 1 ‹*policy*› promover*; ‹*technique*› ser* el primero (*or* la primera *etc*) en aplicar 2 **pioneering** *pres p* ‹*research*› pionero

pious /ˈpaɪəs/ *adj* 1 (devout) piadoso 2 (sanctimonious) beato, santurrón

pip¹ /pɪp/ *n*
A (seed) pepita *f*, semilla *f*
B (BrE Mil) (on uniform) estrella *f*
C (BrE Rad, Telec) pitido *m*; **wait for the ~s** espere a oír la señal
D : ***to give sb the ~*** (BrE colloq) sacar* de quicio a algn

pip² *vt* **-pp-** (BrE colloq): **he was ~ped at the post** perdió por un pelo (fam)

pipe¹ /paɪp/ *n*
A (for liquid, gas) caño *m*, tubería *f*, cañería *f*
B (for tobacco) pipa *f*; **to smoke a ~** fumar en pipa; ***put that in your ~ and smoke it!*** (colloq) ¡chúpate ésa! (fam); (*before n*) **~ cleaner** desatascador *m*
C (Mus) 1 (wind instrument) caramillo *m* 2 (of organ) tubo *m*, cañón *m* 3 **pipes** *pl* gaita *f*

pipe² *vt*
A (transport by pipe) (+ *adv compl*) llevar (*por tuberías, gasoducto, oleoducto*)
B 1 (Culin) ‹*icing*› poner* (*con manga de repostería*) 2 (Clothing) (*usu pass*) ribetear

(Phrasal verbs)
• **pipe down** [v ▸ adv] (colloq) (*usu in imperative*) callarse la boca (fam)
• **pipe up** [v ▸ adv] (colloq): **her friend ~d up and said she knew too** su amiga saltó con que ella también lo sabía (fam); **he always ~s up with some stupid comment** siempre sale con alguna tontería

piped music /paɪpt/ *n* [u] música *f* ambiental

pipe: **~ dream** *n* quimera *f*, sueño *m*, sueño *m* guajiro (Méx); **~line** *n* conducto *m*, ducto *m* (Méx); **a gas ~line** un gasoducto; **an oil ~line** un oleoducto; ***in the ~line***: **it's in the ~line** está proyectado, hay planes al respecto

piper /ˈpaɪpər || ˈpaɪpə(r)/ *n* gaitero, -ra *m,f*; ***he who pays the ~ calls the tune*** quien paga manda *or* elige

piping¹ /ˈpaɪpɪŋ/ *n* [u]
A (pipe) cañería *f*, tubería *f*; **a length of lead ~** un tubo *or* un caño *or* una cañería *or* una tubería de plomo
B (cord) ribete *m* (*con cordón*)
C (sound) trinar *m*

piping² *adv* (*as intensifier*): **~ hot** bien *or* muy caliente

pippin /ˈpɪpən || ˈpɪpɪn/ *n*
A (Bot) camuesa *f* (*tipo de manzana*)
B (AmE colloq) (excellent — person) cielo *m* (fam); (- thing) maravilla *f*

piquancy /ˈpiːkənsi/ *n* [u] 1 (of situation) gracia *f*, interés *m* 2 (of sauce) lo sabroso, lo bien sazonado

piquant /pɪˈkɑːnt || ˈpiːkənt/ *adj* 1 ‹*contrast/irony*› punzante, agudo 2 ‹*sauce*› sabroso, bien sazonado; ‹*taste*› pronunciado, fuerte

pique¹ /piːk/ *n* [u] despecho *m*, resentimiento *m*; **he did it in a fit of ~** lo hizo sólo por despecho

pique² *vt* 1 (irritate): **he was ~d by her lack of interest** se resintió *or* (fam) se picó por su falta de interés 2 (arouse) ‹*curiosity*› picar*

piracy /ˈpaɪrəsi/ *n* [u] piratería *f*

piranha /pəˈrɑːnə || pɪˈrɑːnə/ *n* piraña *f*

pirate¹ /ˈpaɪrət/ *n* 1 (at sea) pirata *mf* 2 (*before n*) ‹*tape/video/radio station*› pirata *adj inv*

pirate² *vt* piratear; **a ~d copy** una copia pirata

pirouette¹ /ˈpɪruˈet/ *n* giro *m*, vuelta *f*; (in ballet) pirueta *f*

pirouette² *vi* girar, dar* vueltas

Pisces /ˈpaɪsiːz/ *n* 1 (sign) (*no art*) Piscis 2 [c] (person) Piscis *or* piscis *mf*; *see also* **Aquarius**

piss¹ /pɪs/ *n* (sl) 1 (act) (*no pl*) meada *f* (vulg) 2 [u] (urine) meados *mpl* (vulg); ***to take the ~ out of sb*** (BrE) tomarle el pelo a algn (fam), cachondearse de algn (Esp fam)

piss² *vi* (sl) mear (vulg)
■ **piss** *v impers* (BrE sl): **it was ~ing down (with rain)** estaba lloviendo a cántaros *or* a chuzos

(Phrasal verb)
• **piss off** (sl)
A [v ▸ adv] (go away) (BrE): **~ off!** ¡vete a la mierda (vulg)
B [v ▸ o ▸ adv] (anger): **it ~es me off** me revienta (fam), me cabrea (fam), me encabrona (Esp, Méx vulg)

pissed /pɪst/ *adj* (sl) 1 (AmE) (fed up) cabreado (fam), encabronado (Esp, Méx vulg), choreado (Chi fam); **I'm really ~ at her** estoy cabreado con ella (fam), me tiene harto (fam), me

P

tiene podrido (RPI fam) 2 (drunk) (BrE) como una cuba (fam), tomado (AmL fam)

pissed-off /ˈpɪstˈɔːf || ˌpɪstˈɒf/ *adj* (*pred* **pissed off**) (BrE sl) cabreado (fam), encabronado (Esp, Méx vulg), choreado (Chi fam)

piss-up /ˈpɪsʌp/ *n* (BrE sl) juerga *f* (fam) (*donde se bebe mucho*)

pistachio /pɪˈstæʃiəʊ/ *n* ~ **(nut)** pistacho *m*, pistache *m* (Méx)

piste /piːst/ *n* pista *f*

pistol /ˈpɪstl̩/ *n* pistola *f*, revólver *m*; ***to hold a ~ to sb's head*** poner* a algn entre la espada y la pared

piston /ˈpɪstən/ *n* émbolo *m*, pistón *m*

pit¹ /pɪt/ *n*

A (hole — in ground) hoyo *m*, pozo *m*; (— for burying) fosa *f*; (— as trap) trampa *f*, fosa *f*; **(inspection)** ~ (Auto) foso *m* *or* (RPI) fosa *f*; **the ~ of the stomach** la boca del estomago; ***a bottomless ~*** (costly business, enterprise) un pozo sin fondo; (person who eats a lot): **he's a bottomless ~** tiene la solitaria (fam), es un barril sin fondo (AmL fam)

B 1 (coalmine) mina *f* (*de carbón*) 2 (quarry) cantera *f*

C (*orchestra* ~) foso *m* orquestal *or* de la orquesta

D (in Stock Exchange) (AmE) parqué *m*

E **pits** *pl* 1 (in motor racing) **the ~s** los boxes, los pits 2 (the very worst) (sl) **the ~s** lo peor que hay (fam)

F (in fruit) (AmE) hueso *m*, cuesco *m*, carozo *m* (CS), pepa *f* (Col)

pit² **-tt-** *vt*

A (mark) ‹*surface/metal*› picar*, marcar*

B (remove stone) (AmE) ‹*fruit/olive*› quitarle el hueso *or* el cuesco *or* (CS) el carozo *or* (Col) la pepa a, deshuesar, descarozar* (CS)

(Phrasal verb)

- **pit against** [v ▸ o ▸ prep ▸ o] enfrentar a; **to ~ oneself against sb** enfrentarse a algn, medir* fuerzas con algn; **you'll be ~ting your wits against the experts** vas a estar compitiendo con los expertos

pita (bread), /ˈpɪtə/ *n* [u] pan *m* árabe

pit-a-pat /ˈpɪtəˈpæt/ *n/adv/vi* ▸**pitter-patter¹,²,³**

pitbull terrier /ˈpɪtbʊl/ *n*: *perro de la familia del bulterrier*

pitch¹ /pɪtʃ/ *n*

A 1 (level, degree) (*no pl*) punto *m*, extremo *m*, grado *m*; **tension had risen to an unbearable ~** la tensión había aumentado hasta hacerse insoportable 2 [u c] (Mus) tono *m*; **to have perfect ~** tener* oído absoluto

B [c] (in baseball) lanzamiento *m*

C [c] (Sport) (playing area) (BrE) campo *m*, cancha *f* (AmL)

D [c] 1 (position, site) (BrE) lugar *m*, sitio *m*; (in market, fair) puesto *m* 2 (*sales ~*): **he had a very effective sales ~** tenía buena labia para vender

E [u] (substance) brea *f*

pitch² *vt*

A (set up) ‹*tent*› armar, montar; ‹*camp*› montar, hacer*

B (sport) ‹*ball*› lanzar*, pichear

C 1 (aim, set, address): **she doesn't know at what level to ~ her talk** no sabe qué nivel darle a la charla; **they ~ed their opening offer at 3%** situaron su oferta inicial en un 3% 2 (Mus): **her instrument was ~ed lower** su instrumento tenía un tono más bajo

■ **pitch** *vi*

A 1 (fall) (+ *adv compl*) caerse*; **he ~ed forward onto his face** se fue *or* cayó de bruces 2 (lurch) «*ship/plane*» cabecear

B (Sport) 1 (in baseball) lanzar*, pichear 2 (in golf, cricket) «*ball*» caer*, dar*

C (campaign, fight) (AmE) **to ~ FOR sth** pelear POR algo; ***to be in there ~ing*** (colloq) estar* en la brecha *or* al pie del cañón

(Phrasal verbs)

- **pitch in** [v ▸ adv] (colloq) 1 (join in) arrimar el hombro, dar* una mano 2 (start eating) atacar* (fam), entrarle (Méx fam)
- **pitch into** [v ▸ prep ▸ o] (colloq) 1 (set about) **to ~ into sth** ponerse* a hacer algo 2 (start eating) atacar* (fam), entrarle a (Méx fam) 3 (attack) arremeter contra

pitch: **~-and-putt** /ˈpɪtʃənˈpʌt/ *n* minigolf *m*, golfito *m* (AmL); **~-black** /ˈpɪtʃˈblæk/ *adj* ‹*night*› (oscuro) como boca de lobo (fam), muy oscuro; ‹*surface*› negro como el azabache; **~-dark** /ˈpɪtʃˈdɑːrk || ˌpɪtʃˈdɑːk/ *adj* ▸**~-black**

pitched battle /pɪtʃt/ *n* batalla *f* campal

pitcher /ˈpɪtʃər || ˈpɪtʃə(r)/ *n*

A (for pouring) jarra *f*, jarro *m*, pichel *m* (AmC); (of clay) (BrE) cántaro *m*

B (in baseball) lanzador, -dora *m,f*, pítcher *mf*

pitch: **~fork** /ˈpɪtʃfɔːrk || ˈpɪtʃfɔːk/ *n* horca *f*, horquilla *f*, horqueta *f* (Chi); **~man** /ˈpɪtʃmæn/ *n* (*pl* **-men** /-men/) (AmE colloq): *persona que usa su labia para convencer, vender una idea, producto etc*

piteous /ˈpɪtiəs/ *adj* ‹*sound/cry*› lastimero; **in a ~ condition** en un estado lastimoso

piteously /ˈpɪtiəsli/ *adv* lastimeramente

pitfall /ˈpɪtfɔːl/ *n* (difficulty) dificultad *f*, escollo *m*; (risk) riesgo *m*

pith /pɪθ/ *n* [u] 1 (Bot) (of citrus fruit) *tejido blanco fibroso que recubre el interior de la cáscara de los cítricos*; (of palms, rushes) médula *f* 2 (of argument, theory) meollo *m*

pithead /ˈpɪthed/ *n* bocamina *f* (*en una mina de carbón*)

pithy /ˈpɪθi/ *adj* **pithier, pithiest** 1 ‹*remark/reply*› sucinto *or* conciso y expresivo 2 (Bot) medular

pitiable /ˈpɪtiəbəl/ *adj* (frml) 1 (arousing pity) lastimoso 2 (arousing contempt) lamentable

pitiful /ˈpɪtɪfəl/ *adj* 1 (arousing pity) ‹*cry/moan*› lastimero; ‹*sight*› lastimoso 2 (wretched, inadequate) lamentable; **you're ~!** ¡das pena *or* lástima!

pitifully /ˈpɪtɪfli, ˈpɪtɪfəli/ *adv* (pathetically) lastimosamente; (deplorably) lamentablemente

pitiless /ˈpɪtɪləs || ˈpɪtɪlɪs/ *adj* despiadado

pit stop *n* 1 (in motor racing) entrada *f* a los botes *or* pits 2 (break) descanso *m* breve; **let's have a five minute ~ ~** paremos cinco minutos para descansar

pitta (bread) *n* [u] ▸**pita (bread)**

pittance /ˈpɪtn̩s/ *n* miseria *f*

pitter-pat /ˈpɪtərpæt || ˈpɪtəpæt/ *adv* ▸**pitter-patter²**

pitter-patter¹ /ˈpɪtərˌpætər/ *n* (of rain) golpeteo *m*

pitter-patter² *adv*: **the rain went ~ on the window** la lluvia repiqueteaba en la ventana

pitter-patter³ *vi* «*rain*» golpetear, repiquetear

pituitary (gland) /pəˈtuːəteri/ *n* glándula pituitaria *f*

pity¹ /ˈpɪti/ *n*

A (*no pl*) (cause of regret) lástima *f*, pena *f*; **it's a ~ (THAT)** es una lástima *or* una pena QUE (+ *subj*); **what a ~!** ¡qué lástima!, ¡que pena!; **more's the ~** es una lástima *or* una pena

B [u] (compassion) piedad *f*, compasión *f*; **he showed no ~** se mostró implacable; **to take ~ on sb/sth** apiadarse *or* compadecerse* de algn/algo; **to have ~ on sb** tener* piedad de algn; **for ~'s sake!** ¡por (el) amor de Dios!

pity² *vt* **pities, pitying, pitied** tenerle* lástima a, compadecer*; **I ~ you if he finds out** pobre de ti como se entere

pitying /ˈpɪtiɪŋ/ *adj* 1 (compassionate) de lástima 2 (contemptuous) de desdén

pivot¹ /ˈpɪvət/ *n* 1 (Tech) pivote *m* 2 (of play, plot) eje *m* central 3 (Sport) (AmE) (key player) jugador, -dora clave; (in basketball) pívot *mf*

pivot² *vi* (Mech Eng) pivotar; **to ~ ON sth/sb**: **he ~ed on his heel** giró sobre sus talones; **the whole organization ~s on one man** la organización entera gira alrededor de un solo hombre

pivotal /ˈpɪvətl̩/ *adj* capital, fundamental

pixie /ˈpɪksi/ *n* (elf) duendecillo *m*, elfo *m*; (fairy) hadita *f*

pizazz /pəˈzæz || pɪˈzæz/ *n* [u] (colloq) dinamismo *m*

pizza /ˈpiːtsə/ *n* pizza *f*

pizzeria /ˈpiːtsəˈriːə/ *n* pizzería *f*

pkt = packet

placard /ˈplækɑːrd || ˈplækɑːd/ *n* letrero *m*, cartel *m*; (at demonstration) pancarta *f*

placate /ˈpleɪkeɪt/ *vt* apaciguar*, aplacar* la cólera de

placatory /ˈpleɪkətɔːri/ *adj* conciliatorio, apaciguador

place¹ /pleɪs/ *n*

A 1 [c] (spot, position, area) lugar *m*, sitio *m*; **she was in the right ~ at the right time and got the job** tuvo la suerte de estar allí en el momento oportuno y le dieron el trabajo; **there's no ~ like home** no hay nada como estar en casa; **from ~ to ~** de un lugar *or* un sitio *or* un lado a otro; **this is no ~ for a dog** éste no es un lugar apropiado para

p

tener un perro; **there's a time and (a) ~ for everything** todo a su debido tiempo y en su debido lugar; **to have friends in high ~s** tener* amigos influyentes; ***all over the ~*** por todas partes, por todos lados; ***to fall into ~*** aclararse; ***to go ~s***: **this boy will go ~s** este chico va a llegar lejos **2** (specific location) lugar *m*; **~ of birth** lugar de nacimiento **3** (*in phrases*) **in place**: **when the new accounting system is in ~** cuando se haya implementado el nuevo sistema de contabilidad; **to hold sth in ~** sujetar algo; **out of place**: **modern furniture would look out of ~ in this room** quedaría mal *or* no resultaría apropiado poner muebles modernos en esta habitación; **I felt very out of ~ there** me sentí totalmente fuera de lugar allí **4** [u] (locality) lugar *m*

B [c] **1** (building, shop, restaurant etc) sitio *m*, lugar *m*; **the hotel was a depressing ~** el hotel era deprimente; **they've moved to a bigger ~** se han mudado a un local (*or* a una casa) más grande; **there's a good pizza ~ nearby** hay una buena pizzería cerca **2** (home) casa *f*; **my ~** mi casa; **we went back to Jim's ~** después fuimos a (la) casa de Jim *or* (AmL tb) fuimos donde Jim *or* (RPl tb) a lo de Jim

C [c] **1** (position, role) lugar *m*; **if I were in your ~** yo en tu lugar, yo que tú; **it's not my ~ to interfere** yo no soy quién para meterme; **I wouldn't change ~s with her for anything** no me cambiaría por ella por nada; **nobody can ever take your ~** nadie podrá jamás ocupar tu lugar *or* reemplazarte; ***to know one's ~*** (dated *or* hum) saber* el lugar que le corresponde a uno; ***to put sb in her/his ~*** poner* a algn en su lugar **2** **in place of** (*as prep*) en lugar de **3** **to take place** (occur) ‹‹*meeting/concert/wedding*›› tener* lugar; **we don't know what took ~ that night** no sabemos qué ocurrió *or* qué sucedió aquella noche

D [c] **1** (seat): **save me a ~** guárdame un asiento *or* un sitio; **the hall has ~s for 500 people** la sala tiene capacidad *or* cabida para 500 personas **2** (at table) cubierto *m*; **to lay/set a ~ for sb** poner* un cubierto para algn

E [c] (in contest, league) puesto *m*, lugar *m*; **he took first ~** obtuvo el primer puesto *or* lugar; **your social life will have to take second ~** tu vida social va a tener que pasar a un segundo plano

F [c] (in book, script, sequence): **you've made me lose my ~** me has hecho perder la página (*or* la línea *etc*) por donde iba; **the audience laughed in all the right ~s** el público se rió cuando había que reírse

G [c] **1** (job) puesto *m*; **to fill a ~** cubrir* una vacante **2** (BrE Educ) plaza *f* **3** (on team) puesto *m*

H (in argument) lugar *m*; **in the first/second ~** en primer/segundo lugar

place² *vt*

A (put, position) ‹*object*› poner*; (carefully, precisely) colocar*; ‹*guards/sentries*› poner*, apostar*, colocar*; **how are you ~d (for) next week?** ¿cómo estás de tiempo la semana que viene?; **to ~ one's confidence** *o* **trust in sb/sth** depositar su (*or* mi *etc*) confianza en algn/algo

B **1** (in hierarchy, league, race): **national security should be ~d above everything else** la seguridad nacional debería ponerse por encima de todo; **this victory ~s her among the top three** este triunfo la sitúa entre las tres primeras; **the team is currently ~d fourth** actualmente el equipo ocupa el cuarto puesto *or* lugar **2** (in horseracing): **to be ~d** llegar* placé *or* colocado (*en segundo o tercer lugar*)

C **1** (find a home, job for) colocar*; **they ~d her with a Boston firm** la colocaron *or* le encontraron trabajo en una empresa de Boston **2** ‹*advertisement*› poner*; ‹*phone call*› pedir*; ‹*goods/merchandise*› colocar*; **we ~d an order with Acme Corp** hicimos un pedido a Acme Corp

D (identify) ‹*tune*› identificar*, ubicar* (AmL); **her face is familiar, but I can't quite ~ her** su cara me resulta conocida pero no sé de dónde *or* (AmL tb) pero no la ubico

E (direct carefully) ‹*ball/shot*› colocar*

placebo /plə'si:bəʊ/ *n* (*pl* **~s** *or* **~es**) placebo *m*

place: **~ kick** *n* (in American football, rugby) patada *f* fija; (in soccer) tiro *m* libre; **~ mat** *n* (mantel *m*) individual *m*

placement /'pleɪsmənt/ *n* **1** [c] (in employment) colocación *f*; **the course included a year's ~ with a company** el curso incluía un año de prácticas en una empresa **2** [c u] (positioning) colocación *f*, ubicación *f* (esp AmL); (*before n*) **~ test** (AmE) test *m* de aptitud (*para determinar qué curso se ha de seguir*)

place name *n* topónimo *m*, nombre *m* geográfico

placenta /plə'sentə/ *n* (*pl* **~s** *or* **~e** /-ti:/) placenta *f*

placid /'plæsəd || 'plæsɪd/ *adj* plácido, tranquilo, apacible

plagiarism /'pleɪdʒərɪzəm/ *n* [uc] plagio *m*

plagiarize /'pleɪdʒəraɪz/ *vt* plagiar

plague¹ /pleɪg/ *n* **1** [u c] (disease) peste *f*; ***to avoid sb like the ~*** huirle* a algn como a la peste; **I avoid Saturday shopping like the ~** ni loco voy de compras un sábado (fam) **2** [c] (horde) plaga *f*; **a ~ of locusts/tourists** una plaga de langostas/turistas

plague² *vt* **1** (afflict): **a country ~d by strikes** un país asolado por constantes huelgas; **~d with problems** plagado de problemas **2** (pester) acosar, asediar

plaice /pleɪs/ *n* [c u] (*pl* **~**) platija *f*

plaid /plæd/ *n* [u] (pattern) cuadros *mpl* escoceses; (material) tela *f* escocesa; (*before n*) ‹*skirt/trousers/scarf*› escocés

plain¹ /pleɪn/ *adj* **-er, -est**

A **1** (unadorned) ‹*decor/cooking*› sencillo; ‹*language*› sencillo, llano; ‹*fabric*› liso; **tell me in ~ English** dímelo en términos sencillos *or* (fam & hum) en cristiano; **just ~ water, thank you** agua nada más, gracias **2** (Culin): **~ chocolate** (BrE) chocolate *m* sin leche; **~ flour** harina *f* común

B **1** (clear) claro; **to make sth ~** dejar algo (en) claro; **the reasons are ~ to see** las razones saltan a la vista *or* son obvias **2** (blunt, straightforward): **the ~ truth** la pura verdad, la verdad lisa y llana; **the time has come for some ~ speaking** ya es hora de que hablemos con franqueza *or* sin rodeos; **I'll be ~ with you, Mr Andrews** seré franco *or* sincero con usted, señor Andrews

C (not good-looking) feo, poco agraciado

plain² *adv* **1** (downright) (*as intensifier*) totalmente; **she's not incapable, she's just ~ lazy** no es que sea incapaz: lo que es es vaga; **that's just ~ stupid** eso es una completa estupidez **2** (bluntly) ‹*tell*› claramente, francamente

plain³ *n* llanura *f*; **the (Great) P~s** las grandes llanuras

plain clothes *pl n*: **in ~ ~** de civil *or* (Esp tb) de paisano; (*before n*) **a plain-clothes policeman** un policía de civil

plainly /'pleɪnli/ *adv* **1** (obviously, visibly) claramente; **~, this is not the solution** (*indep*) es obvio *or* está claro que ésta no es la solución, obviamente, ésta no es la solución **2** (clearly, distinctly) ‹*explain*› claramente; ‹*remember*› perfectamente **3** (bluntly) ‹*speak*› claramente, sin rodeos, claro **4** ‹*dress*› con sencillez

plainness /'pleɪnnəs || 'pleɪnnɪs/ *n* [u]

A (simplicity) sencillez *f*

B (bluntness) franqueza *f*

plainspoken /'pleɪn'spəʊkən/ *adj* franco, sincero

plaintiff /'pleɪntəf/ *n* demandante *mf*, actor, -tora *m,f*

plaintive /'pleɪntɪv/ *adj* lastimero, quejumbroso

plait¹ /plæt/ *n* trenza *f*; **she wore her hair in ~s** llevaba trenzas

plait² *vt* trenzar*

plan¹ /plæn/ *n*

A **1** (diagram, map) plano *m*; **seating ~** disposición *f* de los comensales; **to draw up a ~** hacer* un plano **2** (of book, essay) esquema *m*

B (arrangement, scheme) plan *m*; **to go according to ~** salir* conforme estaba planeado, salir* según el plan; **do you have any ~s for tonight?** ¿tienes algún plan *or* programa para esta noche?; **to make a ~** hacer* un plan; **we're making ~s for the wedding** estamos planeando la boda; **there's been a change of ~** ha habido un cambio de planes; **~ of action** plan de acción

plan² **-nn-** *vt* **1** ‹*journey/itinerary*› planear, programar; ‹*raid/assault*› planear; ‹*garden/house*› diseñar, proyectar; ‹*economy/strategies*› planificar*; ‹*essay*› hacer* un esquema de; **it's all ~ned out in advance** todo está planeado de antemano; **as ~ned** según lo planeado, tal y como estaba previsto *or* planeado **2** (intend): **they're ~ning a surprise for her birthday** le están preparando una sorpresa para el cumpleaños; **to ~ to + INF**: **where are you ~ning to spend Christmas?** ¿dónde tienes pensado *or* dónde piensas pasar las Navidades?

■ **plan** *vi*: **to ~ ahead** planear las cosas de antemano; **to ~ FOR sth**: **we need to ~ for the future** tenemos que pensar en el futuro; **we hadn't ~ned for this** esto no lo habíamos previsto

Phrasal verb

• **plan on** [v ▸ prep ▸ o]
A (intend) pensar*; **I'd ~ned on going out** había pensado salir
B (expect, count on) contar* con

plane¹ /pleɪn/ *n*
A (aircraft) avión *m*; **we went by ~** fuimos en avión
B ~ **(tree)** plátano *m*
C (tool) cepillo *m* de carpintero; (longer) garlopa *f*
D **1** (surface) plano *m* **2** (level) nivel *m*; **she is on a different ~** está a otro nivel, es de otra categoría

plane² *vt* ‹*wood/surface*› cepillar; **to ~ sth down** desbastar algo
■ **plane** *vi* (glide) planear

planeload /'pleɪnləʊd/ *n*: **~s of supplies** aviones *mpl* cargados de suministros; **tourists came by the ~** llegaba avión tras avión cargado de turistas

planet /'plænət || 'plænɪt/ *n* planeta *m*

planetary /'plænəteri/ *adj* (*before n*) planetario

plank /plæŋk/ *n* tabla *f*, tablón *m*; **to walk the ~** pasear la tabla

plankton /'plæŋktən/ *n* [u] plancton *m*

planned /plænd/ *adj* planeado; **~ economy** economía *f* dirigida; **~ parenthood** (AmE) planificación *f* familiar, paternidad *f* responsable

planner /'plænər || 'plænə(r)/ *n* **1** (of project, strategy) planificador, -dora *m,f* **2** (*town* ~) urbanista *mf*

planning /'plænɪŋ/ *n* [u] **1** (of project) planificación *f* **2** (*town* ~) urbanismo *m*; (*before n*) **~ permission** (BrE) permiso *m* de obras

plant¹ /plænt || plɑːnt/ *n*
A [c] (Bot) planta *f*; (*before n*) **~ life** vida *f* vegetal, flora *f*; **~ pot** maceta *f*, tiesto *m*, macetero *m* (AmS)
B **1** [c] (factory, installation) planta *f* **2** [u] (equipment) maquinaria *f*

plant² *vt*
A **1** ‹*flower/trees*› plantar; ‹*seeds*› sembrar* **2** ‹*garden/hillside*› **to ~ sth (WITH sth)** plantar algo (DE algo)
B (place) ‹*bomb*› colocar*, poner*; **she ~ed a kiss on his cheek** le dio *or* (fam) le plantó un beso en la mejilla; **she ~ed herself right next to me** se me plantó *or* se me plantificó justo al lado (fam)
C (Law) **1** ‹*drugs/evidence*› colocar*; **they had ~ed the gun on him** le habían colocado la pistola para inculparlo **2** ‹*agent/informer*› infiltrar, colocar*

Phrasal verb

• **plant out** [v ▸ o ▸ adv, v ▸ adv ▸ o] ‹*seedlings*› trasplantar (*a la intemperie*)

plantain /'plæntn̩ || 'plæntɪn/ *n* [c] plátano *m* grande (*para cocinar*), plátano *m* (Col, Ven), plátano *m* macho (Méx)

plantation /plæn'teɪʃən/ *n* plantación *f*

planter /'plæntər || 'plɑːntə(r)/ *n* **1** (owner of plantation) hacendado, -da *m,f* **2** (machine) (Agr) sembradora *f* **3** (container) tiesto *m*, maceta *f*

plaque /plæk/ *n*
A [c] (tablet) placa *f*
B [u] (Dent) sarro *m*, placa *f* (dental)

plasma /'plæzmə/ *n* [u] (Physiol, Phys) plasma *m*

plaster¹ /'plæstər || 'plɑːstə(r)/ *n*
A [u] **1** (Const) (powder, mixture) yeso *m*; (on walls) revoque *m*, enlucido *m* **2** **~ (of Paris)** (Art, Med) yeso *m*, escayola *f* (Esp); **to have one's leg in ~** tener* la pierna enyesada *or* (Esp) escayolada
B [c] (*sticking* ~) (BrE) ▸ **Band-Aid**

plaster² *vt*
A ‹*wall/room*› revocar*, enlucir*; ‹*cracks*› rellenar con yeso
B (cover): **they ~ed the wall with posters** cubrieron *or* empapelaron la pared de afiches; **she ~ed herself with make-up** se pintarrajeó toda
C (defeat) (AmE colloq) darle* una paliza a (fam)

plaster: **~board** *n* [u] (Const) placa *f* de yeso, pladur® *m* (Esp); **~ cast** *n* **1** (Med) yeso *m* *or* (Esp) escayola *f* **2** (Art) molde *m* *or* vaciado *m* de yeso, escayola *f*

plastered /'plæstərd || 'plɑːstəd/ *adj* (colloq): **to be/get ~** estar*/ponerse* como una cuba (fam)

plasterer /'plæstərər || 'plɑːstərə(r)/ *n* yesero, -ra *m,f*, enlucidor, -dora *m,f*

plastic¹ /'plæstɪk/ *n* **1** [u c] (substance) plástico *m*; (*before n*) de plástico **2** [u] (credit cards) (colloq) plástico *m* (fam), tarjetas *fpl* de crédito

plastic² *adj*
A (artificial) (pej) ‹*smile/people*› de plástico (pey)
B **1** (malleable) (Tech) plástico, moldeable **2** (Art) plástico; **the ~ arts** las artes plásticas

plastic: **~ bullet** *n* bala *f* de plástico; **~ explosive** *n* [cu] explosivo *m* plástico, goma (-) dos *f*

Plasticine® /'plæstəsiːn/ *n* [u] plastilina® *f*, plasticina® *f* (CS)

plastic: **~ money** *n* [u] (colloq) dinero *m* de plástico (fam); **~ surgeon** *n* cirujano plástico, cirujana plástica *m,f* (AmL), especialista *mf* en cirugía estética *or* plástica; **~ surgery** *n* [u] cirugía *f* estética *or* plástica; **~ wrap** *n* [u] (AmE) film *m* *or* película *f* adherente (*para envover alimentos*), Egapac® *m* (Méx)

plate¹ /pleɪt/ *n*
A **1** [c] (dish) plato *m*; ***to hand o give sth to sb on a ~*** servirle* algo a algn en bandeja; ***to have a lot/too much on one's ~*** tener* muchas/demasiadas cosas entre manos; (*before n*) **~ rack** escurreplatos *m* **2** [u] (dishes) vajilla *f* (*de plata u oro*)
B **1** [c] (of metal) chapa *f*, placa *f*; (thin) lámina *f*; (of glass) placa *f* **2** [u] (coating) enchapado *m*
C [c] **1** (Phot) placa *f* **2** (Art, Print) plancha *f* **3** (illustration) ilustración *f*, lámina *f*
D [c] **1** (Auto) **(license** *or* (BrE) **number) ~** matrícula *f*, placa *f* de matrícula, patente *f* (CS), chapa *f* (RPl) **2** (plaque) placa *f*
E [c] (Dent) (denture) dentadura *f* postiza
F (*home* ~) (in baseball) (AmE) home (plate) *m*, pentágono *m*

plate² *vt* **1** (coat) (Metall) **to ~ sth WITH sth** recubrir* algo DE algo; **gold-~d** enchapado en oro **2** (encase) ‹*machine/armored car*› blindar

plateau /plæ'təʊ || 'plætəʊ/ *n* (*pl* **-teaus** *or* **-teaux** /-z/) meseta *f*; **high ~** altiplanicie *f*, altiplano *m*; **she lost 8 lbs, then reached a ~** adelgazó 8 libras y se estancó

plateful /'pleɪtfʊl/ *n* plato *m*

plate glass *n* [u] vidrio *m* *or* (Esp tb) cristal *m* cilindrado

platform /'plætfɔːrm || 'plætfɔːm/ *n*
A **1** (raised structure) plataforma *f*; (for orator) estrado *m*, tribuna *f* **2** (Rail) andén *m*
B (Pol) **1** (opportunity to air views) plataforma *f*, tribuna *f* **2** (program) plataforma *f*, programa *m*
C **~ (shoe)** zapato *m* de plataforma

plating /'pleɪtɪŋ/ *n* (*no pl*) **1** (coating) baño *m*, (en)chapado *m* **2** (casing) coraza *f*

platinum /'plætn̩əm || 'plætɪnəm/ *n* [u] platino *m*

platinum blonde *n* rubia *f* platino *or* platinada

platitude /'plætətuːd/ *n* lugar *m* común, tópico *m*

platonic /plə'tɑːnɪk || plə'tɒnɪk/ *adj* platónico

platoon /plə'tuːn/ *n* (Mil) sección *f*

platter /'plætər || 'plætə(r)/ *n* (plate) fuente *f*

platypus /'plætɪpəs/ *n* (*pl* **~es**) (*duck-billed* ~) ornitorrinco *m*

plausible /'plɔːzəbəl/ *adj* ‹*argument/story/excuse*› verosímil; ‹*liar/salesman*› convincente

plausibly /'plɔːzəbli/ **1** ‹*explain*› de forma verosímil **2** ‹*act*› convincentemente

play¹ /pleɪ/ *n*
A **1** [u] (recreation) juego *m*; **she watched them at ~** los observaba mientras jugaban **2** [u] (Sport) juego *m*; **~ was interrupted** se interrumpió el juego *or* el partido; ***to bring sth/come into ~*** poner* algo/entrar en juego **3** [c] (AmE Sport) (maneuver) jugada *f*; ***to make a ~ for sb/sth*** (also BrE): **he made a ~ for her** trató de ganársela *or* de conquistársela; **the company made a ~ for ownership of ABC Industries** la compañía intentó hacerse con ABC Industries
B [u] (interplay) juego *m*; **the ~ of light and shadow** el juego de luces y sombras
C [u] (slack) (Tech) juego *m*
D [c] (Theat) obra *f* (de teatro), pieza *f* (teatral), comedia *f*; **radio ~** obra *f* radiofónica
E [c] (pun): **a ~ on words** un juego de palabras

play² *vt*

(Sense I)

A 1 ‹*cards/hopscotch*› jugar* a; **let's ~ a game** vamos a jugar; **to ~ a joke/trick on sb** hacerle* *or* gastarle una broma/una jugarreta a algn 2 ‹*football/chess*› jugar* (AmL exc RPl), jugar* a (Esp, RPl)

B 1 (compete against) ‹*opponent*› jugar* contra; **to ~ sb AT sth**: **I used to ~ her at chess** jugaba ajedrez *or* (Esp, RPl) al ajedrez con ella 2 ‹*ball*› pasar; ‹*card*› tirar, jugar*; ‹*piece*› mover* 3 (in particular position) jugar* de 4 (use in game) ‹*reserve*› alinear, sacar* a jugar

C (gamble on) jugar* a; **to ~ the market** (Fin) jugar* a la bolsa

(Sense II)

A (Theat) 1 ‹*villain/Hamlet*› representar el papel de, hacer* de, actuar* de; **to ~ the innocent** hacerse* el inocente 2 ‹*scene*› representar; ***to ~ it cool*** hacer* como si nada; ***to ~ (it) safe*** ir* a la segura, no arriesgarse*; ***to ~ (it) straight*** ser* sincero *or* honesto 3 ‹*theater/town*› actuar* en

B (Mus) ‹*instrument/note*› tocar*; ‹*piece*› tocar*, interpretar (frml)

C (Audio) ‹*tape/record*› poner*

(Sense III) (move) (+ *adv compl*): **they ~ed the hoses over the blaze** movían las mangueras sobre las llamas

■ **play** *vi*

(Sense I)

A (amuse oneself) «*children*» jugar*; **to ~ AT sth** jugar* A algo; **what are you ~ing at?** ¿a qué estás jugando?, ¿qué es lo que te propones?; **to ~ WITH sth/sb** jugar* CON algo/algn; **we don't have much time to ~ with** no disponemos de mucho tiempo; **to ~ with oneself** (euph) toquetearse (euf)

B (Games, Sport) jugar*; ***to ~ fair*** jugar* limpio; ***to ~ fair with sb*** ser* justo con algn

(Sense II)

A 1 (Theat) «*cast*» actuar*, trabajar; «*show*» ser* representado; **the musical has been ~ing to packed houses** el musical ha estado llenando las salas 2 (pretend): **to ~ dead** hacerse* el muerto; ***to ~ hard to get*** hacerse* el (*or* la *etc*) interesante

B (Mus) «*musician*» tocar*; **music was ~ing in the background** se escuchaba una música de fondo

(Sense III) (move): **lights ~ed across the sky** un juego de luces recorrió el cielo; **a smile ~ed about his lips** un atisbo de sonrisa rondaba sus labios

(Phrasal verbs)

- **play about** [v ▸ adv] (BrE) juguetear (fam & pey)
- **play along**

A [v ▸ adv] (cooperate): **I refuse to ~ along with him/his schemes** me niego a hacerle el juego/a tener nada que ver con sus enjuagues (fam)

B [v ▸ o ▸ adv] (deceive, manipulate) manipular, utilizar*

- **play around** [v ▸ adv] jugar*, juguetear (fam & pey); **I don't want them ~ing around with my tools** no quiero que anden (jugando) con mis herramientas (fam)
- **play back** [v ▸ o ▸ adv, v ▸ adv ▸ o] poner* (*una grabación*)
- **play down** [v ▸ o ▸ adv, v ▸ adv ▸ o] ‹*importance*› minimizar*; ‹*risk/achievement*› quitarle *or* restarle importancia a
- **play off** 1 [v ▸ o ▸ adv] oponer*; ***to ~ sb off against sb***: **she ~s her parents off against each other** hace pelear a sus padres para lograr sus propósitos 2 [v ▸ adv] jugar* el desempate
- **play on** [v ▸ adv ▸ o] ‹*fears/generosity*› aprovecharse de
- **play out** [v ▸ o ▸ adv, v ▸ adv ▸ o] 1 (enact) (*usu pass*) interpretar 2 (finish) ‹*game*› terminar, acabar; **to ~ out time** (Sport) hacer* tiempo
- **play up**

A [v ▸ adv] (BrE) 1 (cause trouble) (colloq) «*child*» dar* guerra (fam), portarse mal; **the car is ~ing up** el coche anda mal *or* (fam) está haciendo de las suyas; **my back has been ~ing up** la espalda me ha estado fastidiando *or* (fam) dando la lata 2 (flatter) **to ~ up TO sb** halagar* a algn, darle* coba A algn (Esp fam)

B [v ▸ o ▸ adv] (cause trouble) (BrE colloq) «*child*» darle* guerra a (fam); **my shoulder's ~ing me up** el hombro me está fastidiando *or* (fam) dando la lata

C [v ▸ o ▸ adv, v ▸ adv ▸ o] (exaggerate) exagerar

- **play upon** ▸**play on**

play: **~-act** *vi* hacer* teatro; **~back** *n* play-back *m*; **~boy** *n* playboy *m*; **~-by-play** /ˈpleɪbaɪˈpleɪ/ *adj* (AmE Sport) (*before n*) jugada a jugada

player /ˈpleɪər || ˈpleɪə(r)/ *n*

A (Games, Sport) jugador, -dora *m,f*; **he's a keen tennis ~** le gusta mucho jugar tenis *or* (Esp, RPl) al tenis

B 1 (Mus) músico *mf*, músico, -ca *m,f*, instrumentista *mf*; **guitar-~** guitarrista *mf* 2 (actor) (arch *or* frml) actor, -triz *m,f*

player: **~-coach** *n* ▸**player-manager**; **~-manager** *n* jugador-entrenador, jugadora-entrenadora *m,f*, director técnico y jugador, directora técnica y jugadora *m,f* (AmL)

playful /ˈpleɪfəl/ *adj* 1 (boisterous) juguetón 2 (not serious) pícaro, travieso; **a ~ remark** un comentario hecho en broma

playfully /ˈpleɪfəli/ *adv* 1 (boisterously) juguetonamente, alegremente 2 (humorously) ‹*remark/slap*› en broma

play: **~ground** *n* 1 (at school) (BrE) patio *m* (de recreo) 2 (resort): **Marbella, the ~ground of the jet set** Marbella, lugar de diversiones del jet-set *or* (Esp) de la jet-set; **~group** *n*: *grupo de actividades lúdico-educativas para niños de edad preescolar*; **~house** *n* 1 (Theat) teatro *m*; 2 (for children) casa *f* de juguete

playing /ˈpleɪɪŋ/: **~ card** *n* naipe *m*, carta *f*; **~ field** *n* (BrE) (*often pl*) campo *m* de juego, cancha *f* de deportes

play: **~list** *n* lista *f* de reproducción; **~mate** *n* compañero, -ra *m,f* de juegos, amiguito, -ta *m,f* (fam); **~off** *n* 1 (after a tie) desempate *m* 2 **the ~offs** (in US football etc) las finales; (in soccer) la promoción; **~pen** *n* corral *m*, parque *m* (Esp); **~room** *n* cuarto *m* de los juguetes; **~thing** *n* juguete *m*; **~time** *n* [u] (*no art*) (BrE) hora *f* del recreo, recreo *m*; **~wright** /ˈpleɪraɪt/ *n* dramaturgo, -ga *m,f*, autor, -tora *m,f* teatral

plaza /ˈplæzə/ *n* 1 (square) plaza *f*; (in front of large building) explanada *f* 2 (complex) (AmE) centro *m* comercial

plc, Plc (in UK) (= **public limited company**) ≈ S.A.

plea /pliː/ *n*

A (appeal) (frml) petición *f*; (in supplication) ruego *m*, súplica *f*; **~ FOR sth**: **she made a ~ for mercy** rogó *or* suplicó *or* imploró clemencia

B (Law): **to enter a ~ of guilty/not guilty** declararse culpable/inocente

C (excuse) (frml) pretexto *m*, excusa *f*

plead /pliːd/ (*past & past p* **pleaded** *or* (AmE also) **pled**) *vt* 1 (give as excuse) alegar*; **he ~s ignorance of the whole affair** alega *or* aduce no saber nada del asunto; **she's not coming, she ~ed poverty** no viene, dijo que no tenía dinero 2 (argue) abogar* por, defender*; **he ~ed the cause of the poor** abogaba en favor de los pobres; **to ~ the case for sth** abogar* en favor de algo; **to ~ sb's case** (Law) llevar el caso de algn

■ **plead** *vi* 1 (implore, beg) suplicar*; **to ~ FOR sth** suplicar* algo; **to ~ WITH sb to + INF** suplicarle* a algn QUE (+ *subj*) 2 (Law): **to ~ guilty/not guilty** declararse culpable/inocente

pleading¹ /ˈpliːdɪŋ/ *n* (*often pl*) 1 (begging) súplica *f* 2 (Law) alegato *m*

pleading² *adj* suplicante

pleasant /ˈpleznt/ *adj* **-er, -est** agradable; ‹*person*› simpático, agradable; **what a ~ surprise!** ¡qué agradable *or* grata sorpresa!; **it makes a ~ change** es un cambio que resulta agradable; **~ dreams!** ¡felices sueños!

pleasantly /ˈplezntli/ *adv* ‹*say/speak*› en tono agradable; ‹*smile*› con simpatía; **I was ~ surprised by the changes** los cambios me causaron una grata sorpresa; **we passed the afternoon very ~** pasamos una tarde muy agradable, pasamos la tarde muy a gusto

pleasantry /ˈplezntri/ *n* [c] (*pl* **-ries**) 1 (polite remark) cortesía *f* 2 (joking remark) gracia *f*, comentario *m* gracioso

please¹ /pliːz/ *interj* por favor; **~ sit down** (por favor) siéntese; **pass the salt, ~** pásame la sal, por favor, ¿me pasas la sal?; **yes, ~** sí, gracias; **~ do!** ¡sí, cómo no!, ¡no faltaba más!; **say ~** las cosas se piden por favor

please² *vt* (make happy) complacer*; (satisfy) contentar, complacer*; **her progress ~d her parents** sus padres estaban contentos con los progresos que hacía; **she's easily ~d** se contenta con poco *or* con cualquier cosa

P

■ **please** *vi* 1 (satisfy): **we do our best to ~** hacemos todo lo posible por complacer al cliente (*or* a todo el mundo *etc*); **he's eager to ~** busca la aprobación de los demás 2 (choose) querer*; **do as you ~** haz lo que quieras *or* lo que te parezca *or* (fam) lo que te dé la gana; **just as you ~** como quieras; **I'll have no arguing, if you ~** haga el favor de no discutir

■ *v refl* **to ~ oneself**: **~ yourself** haz lo que quieras *or* lo que te parezca *or* (fam) lo que te dé la gana

please³ *n*: **without so much as a ~ or thank-you** sin pedir por favor ni dar las gracias

pleased /pli:zd/ *adj* (satisfied) satisfecho; (happy) contento; **she is very ~ with the results** está muy contenta/satisfecha con los resultados; **I'm very ~ for you!** me alegro mucho por ti; **she was very ~ with herself** estaba muy ufana, estaba muy satisfecha consigo misma; **I'm so ~ you could come!** ¡(cuánto) me alegro de que hayas podido venir!; **to be ~ AT/ABOUT sth**: **I was ~ at the news** me alegré con la noticia; **they were ~ about her appointment** se alegraron de su nombramiento; **to be ~ to + INF**: **I'd be ~ to help you** te ayudaría con mucho gusto; **I am ~ to inform you that ...** (frml) tengo el placer de *or* me complace comunicarle que ... (frml); **~ to meet you** encantado (de conocerlo), mucho gusto

pleasing /'pli:zɪŋ/ *adj* 1 (pleasant) agradable; **~ to the ear** agradable *or* grato al oído 2 (gratifying) ‹*news*› grato

pleasurable /'pleʒərəbəl/ *adj* placentero, agradable

pleasure /'pleʒər || 'pleʒə(r)/ *n*

A [u] 1 (happiness, satisfaction) placer *m*; **it's a ~ to listen to her** es un placer *or* da gusto escucharla; **to find** *o* **take ~ in sth** disfrutar con algo; **I get a lot of ~ out of reading** disfruto muchísimo leyendo; (*before n*) **~ seeker** hedonista *mf* 2 (in polite formulas): **with ~** con mucho gusto; **thank you — (it's) a ~** gracias — de nada *or* no hay de qué, ha sido un placer; **may I have the ~ of this dance?** ¿me concede esta pieza?; **Mr John Smith requests the ~ of your company at ...** John Smith tiene el placer de invitar a Vd a ...; **it gives me great ~ to introduce ...** es un placer para mí presentarles ...

B 1 [u] (recreation, amusement) placer *m*; **I play just for ~** toco sólo porque me gusta; (*before n*) **~ craft** embarcación *f* de recreo; **~ cruise** crucero *m* de placer 2 [c] (source of happiness) placer *m*; **the ~s of good food** los placeres de la buena mesa; **Jane is a real ~ to teach** da gusto *or* es un verdadero placer darle clases a Jane; **it was a ~** fue un placer

C [u] (choice) (frml): **at your ~** cuando (usted) guste (frml); **to be detained during Her/His Majesty's ~** (in UK) *quedar detenido indefinidamente a discreción del Ministerio del Interior*

pleasure boat *n* (steamer) barco *m* de recreo; (small craft) bote *m* de recreo

pleat¹ /pli:t/ *n* pliegue *m*; (wide) tabla *f*

pleat² *vt* plisar

pleb /pleb/ *n* (colloq & pej) ordinario, -ria *m,f*; **the ~s** la chusma (fam & pey), la plebe (hum)

plebeian /plɪ'bi:ən || plə'bi:ən/ *adj* 1 (lacking refinement) (pej) ordinario 2 (Hist) plebeyo

plebiscite /'plebəsaɪt || 'plebɪsɪt, -saɪt/ *n* plebiscito *m*

plectrum /'plektrəm/ *n* (*pl* **-trums** *or* **-tra** /-trə/) púa *f*, plectro *m*, uñeta *f* (CS), uña *f* (Méx, Ven)

pled /pled/ (AmE) *past & past p of* **plead**

pledge¹ /pledʒ/ *vt*

A 1 (promise) ‹*support/funds*› prometer; **he ~d his word** dio su palabra; **to ~ sth TO sb** prometerle algo A algn 2 (commit) **to ~ oneself to + INF** comprometerse A + INF; **she is ~d to secrecy** ha jurado que guardará el secreto

B (offer as guarantee) entregar* en garantía *or* en prenda

pledge² *n*

A 1 (promise) promesa *f*; **election ~** compromiso *m* electoral; **the P~ of Allegiance** (in US) ≈ la jura de (la) bandera; **to honor** *o* **keep a ~** cumplir una promesa, cumplir con su (*or* mi *etc*) palabra; **to make a ~ to + INF** prometer + INF; **to sign** *o* **take the ~** (Hist *or* hum) jurar no probar el alcohol 2 (of money) cantidad *f* prometida, donativo *m* prometido

B 1 (token) prenda *f* 2 (collateral) garantía *f*, aval *m*

plenary /'pli:nəri/ *adj* 1 ‹*session/meeting*› plenario 2 (unlimited): **~ powers** plenos poderes *mpl*

plenipotentiary /'plenəpə'tentʃəri || ˌplenɪpə'tenʃəri/ *adj* plenipotenciario

plenteous /'plentiəs/ *adj* (liter) copioso, abundante

plentiful /'plentɪfəl/ *adj* abundante

plentifully /'plentɪfəli/ *adv* en abundancia

plenty¹ /'plenti/ *n* [u] abundancia *f*; **in ~** en abundancia

plenty² *pron*

A 1 (large, sufficient number) muchos, -chas 2 **plenty of** muchos, -chas; **~ of books** muchos libros; **there are ~ of us** somos muchos

B 1 (large, sufficient quantity) mucho, -cha; **there was ~ to eat** había comida en abundancia, había mucha comida; **there's ~ more in here** aquí hay mucho más; **$50 is ~** 50 dólares es más que suficiente 2 **plenty of** mucho, -cha; **~ of time** tiempo de sobra; **you'll need money and ~ of it** vas a necesitar dinero, y mucho

plenty³ *adv* (AmE colloq & dial) ‹*worried/hungry/ugly*› muy; **she must love him ~** debe quererlo mucho

plethora /'pleθərə/ *n* **a ~ OF sth** una plétora DE algo

pleurisy /'plʊrəsi || 'plʊərəsi/ *n* [u] pleuresía *f*, pleuritis *f*

Plexiglas® /'pleksɪglæs || 'pleksɪglɑ:s/ *n* [u] (AmE) acrílico *m*, plexiglás® *m* (Esp)

pliable /'plaɪəbəl/ *adj* ‹*material/substance*› maleable; ‹*person/attitude*› flexible, acomodaticio (pey)

pliant /'plaɪənt/ *adj* ▸ **pliable**

pliers /'plaɪərz || 'plaɪəz/ *pl n* alicate(s) *m(pl)*, pinza(s) *f(pl)* (Méx, RPl); **a pair of ~** un(os) alicate(s), una(s) pinza(s)

plight¹ /plaɪt/ *n* (*no pl*) situación *f* difícil; **our current economic ~** las dificultades económicas que nos afligen

plight² *vt* (arch *or* frml) ‹*allegiance/loyalty*› jurar, prometer; **to ~ one's troth to sb** hacerle* promesa de matrimonio a algn (ant)

plimsoll /'plɪmsəl/ *n* (BrE) zapatilla *f* de lona, tenis *m*, playera *f* (Esp)

Plimsoll line /'plɪmsəl/ *n* (Naut) línea *f* de carga

plinth /plɪnθ/ *n* (of pillar, column) plinto *m*; (of statue) pedestal *m*

PLO *n* (= **Palestine Liberation Organization**) OLP *f*

plod /plɑ:d || plɒd/ *vi* **-dd-** 1 (walk) caminar lenta y pesadamente 2 (work): **she's still ~ding away at her thesis** sigue lidiando *or* batallando con la tesis; **how's work going? — oh, ~ding along** ¿qué tal el trabajo? — ahí va, tirando *or* (AmL exc CS) jalando

plodder /'plɑ:dər || 'plɒdə(r)/ *n*: **he's a ~** no es una lumbrera pero es de los que ponen empeño

plonk¹ /plɑ:ŋk || plɒŋk/ *vt/i* (BrE colloq) ▸ **plunk¹**

plonk² *n*

A [c] (sound) ¡pumba!, ¡plaf!

B [u] (wine) (colloq) vino *m* peleón (fam), vinacho *m* (fam)

plonk³ *adv* ¡plaf!

plop¹ /plɑ:p || plɒp/ *n* plaf *m*

plop² **-pp-** *vi* (colloq) **to ~ INTO/ONTO sth** hacer* plaf al caer en/sobre algo

■ **plop** *vt* (colloq) dejar caer

plosive /'pləʊsɪv/ *n* oclusiva *f*

plot¹ /plɑ:t || plɒt/ *n*

A (conspiracy) complot *m*, conspiración *f*

B (story) argumento *m*, trama *f*; **the ~ thickens!** (set phrase) ¡la historia se complica!

C (piece of land) terreno *m*, solar *m*, parcela *f*

plot² **-tt-** *vt*

A (mark out) ‹*curve/graph*› trazar*; ‹*position*› determinar

B (plan) ‹*rebellion/revenge*› tramar

■ **plot** *vi* **to ~ (AGAINST sb)** conspirar (CONTRA algn); **to ~ to + INF** conspirar PARA + INF

plotter /'plɑ:tər || 'plɒtə(r)/ *n* 1 (conspirator) conspirador, -dora *m,f* 2 (Comput, Tech) trazador *m* de gráficos

plotting /'plɑ:tɪŋ || 'plɒtɪŋ/ *n* [u] 1 (scheming) conspiraciones *fpl* 2 (of route, flight) trazado *m*; (of position) determinación *f*

plough /plaʊ/ *n/vt/vi* (BrE) ▸ **plow¹,²**

plough: **~man** *n* /'plaʊmən/ (*pl* **-men** /-mən/) (BrE) ▸ **plowman**; **~man's (lunch)** /'plaʊmənz/ *n* (BrE) *plato de queso, pan y encurtidos*

plover /'plʌvər || 'plʌvə(r)/ *n* (*pl* **~s** *or* **~**) chorlito *m*

plow¹, (BrE) **plough** /plaʊ/ *n* 1 (Agr) arado *m*; (*before n*) **~ horse** caballo *m* de tiro 2 (Astron) **the Plow** el Carro

plow², (BrE) **plough** *vt* ‹*land/field*› arar; ‹*waves/seas*› (liter) surcar* (liter); **to ~ a furrow** abrir* un surco con el arado; ***to ~ one's way through sth***: **she ~ed her way through the snow** se abrió camino con dificultad a través de la nieve; **he ~ed his way through a whole plate of spinach** consiguió terminarse, a duras penas, un plato entero de espinacas

■ **plow** *vi* 1 (Agr) arar la tierra 2 (proceed): **to ~ on/ahead** seguir* adelante

Phrasal verbs

• **plow back,** (BrE) **plough back** [v ▸ o ▸ adv, v ▸ adv ▸ o] ‹*profits*› reinvertir*

• **plow into,** (BrE) **plough into**

A [v ▸ prep ▸ o] (crash into) estrellarse contra

B [v ▸ o ▸ prep ▸ o] (invest) invertir* en

• **plow through,** (BrE) **plough through** [v ▸ prep ▸ o] 1 ‹*mud/snow*› abrirse* camino a través de; **I'm still ~ing through the book** todavía estoy tratanto de leer el libro, pero me cuesta 2 ‹*wall/fence*› arrasar

• **plow up,** (BrE) **plough up** [v ▸ o ▸ adv, v ▸ adv ▸ o] surcar*, arar; (causing damage) destrozar*

plowman, (BrE) **ploughman** /ˈplaʊmən/ *n* (*pl* **-men** /-mən/) labrador *m*

ploy /plɔɪ/ *n* treta *f*, ardid *m*

pluck¹ /plʌk/ *vt* 1 ‹*chicken*› desplumar; **to ~ one's eyebrows** depilarse las cejas 2 ‹*fruit/flower*› arrancar*; **to ~ sth/sb FROM sth** arrancar* algo/a algn DE algo; **to ~ up (one's) courage** armarse de valor *or* de coraje; **to ~ up courage to + INF**; armarse de valor *or* de coraje para + INF 3 (Mus) ‹*string/guitar*› puntear

■ **pluck** *vi* **to ~ AT sth** tirar DE algo, jalar DE algo (AmL exc CS)

pluck² *n* [u] valor *m*, coraje *m*

plucky /ˈplʌki/ *adj* **pluckier, pluckiest** valiente, corajudo

plug¹ /plʌg/ *n*

A (stopper) tapón *m*

B (Elec) 1 (attached to lead) enchufe *m*; (socket) toma *f* de corriente, enchufe *m*, tomacorriente *m* (AmL); ***to pull the ~ on sth*** cancelar algo 2 (*spark ~*) bujía *f*

C (publicity) (colloq): **to give sth a ~** hacerle* propaganda a algo, darle* publicidad a algo

D (*fire ~*) (AmE) boca *f* de incendio, grifo *m* (Chi)

plug² **-gg-** *vt*

A ‹*hole/gap*› tapar, rellenar

B (promote) ‹*record/book*› hacerle* propaganda a

Phrasal verbs

• **plug away** (colloq) [v ▸ adv]: **I keep ~ging away at my French** sigo dándole duro al francés (fam)

• **plug in**

A [v ▸ o ▸ adv, v ▸ adv ▸ o] enchufar

B [v ▸ adv] enchufarse

• **plug up** [v ▸ o ▸ adv, v ▸ adv ▸ o] tapar

plughole /ˈplʌghəʊl/ *n* (BrE) desagüe *m*

plum¹ /plʌm/ *n* 1 (Culin) ciruela *f*; (*before n*) **~ pudding** plum pudding *m* (*budín de pasas y especias*) 2 **~ (tree)** ciruelo *m* 3 (color) color *m* ciruela ; (*before n*) color ciruela *adj inv*

plum² *adj* (colloq) (*before n*): **it's a ~ job** es un trabajo fantástico, es un chollo (Esp fam)

plumage /ˈpluːmɪdʒ/ *n* [u] plumaje *m*

plumb¹ /plʌm/ *adv* (colloq) 1 (exactly, right) justo; **~ in the middle** justo en el centro 2 (totally) (AmE colloq & dated) **~ crazy/stupid** loco/tonto de remate (fam)

plumb² *vt*

A (fathom) ‹*mystery*› dilucidar

B (Naut) sondar, sondear

Phrasal verb

• **plumb in** [v ▸ o ▸ adv, v ▸ adv ▸ o] (BrE) instalar, conectar

plumb³ *n* 1 (Naut) plomada *f* 2 (Const) **~ (bob)** plomada *f*

plumber /ˈplʌmər || ˈplʌmə(r)/ *n* plomero, -ra *m,f* *or* (AmC, Esp) fontanero, -ra *m,f* *or* (Per) gasfitero, -ra *m,f*

plumbing /ˈplʌmɪŋ/ *n* [u] 1 (pipes) cañerías *fpl*, tuberías *fpl*; (installation) instalación *f* de agua 2 (activity) plomería *f* *or* (AmC, Esp) fontanería *f* *or* (Chi, Per) gasfitería *f*

plumbline /ˈplʌmlaɪn/ *n* (Const, Naut) plomada *f*

plume /pluːm/ *n* pluma *f*; (cluster of feathers) penacho *m*; **a ~ of smoke** una columna de humo

plumed /pluːmd/ *adj* ‹*helmet*› con penacho; ‹*hat*› con plumas; ‹*tail*› de plumas

plummet /ˈplʌmət || ˈplʌmɪt/ *vi* «*bird/aircraft*» caer* en picada *or* (Esp) en picado; «*prices/income*» caer* en picada *or* (Esp) en picado, desplomarse, irse* a pique

plump¹ /plʌmp/ *adj* **-er, -est** ‹*person/face*› (re)llenito, regordete; ‹*chicken/rabbit*› gordo

plump² *vt* 1 (put, set down) (colloq) (+ *adv compl*) plantificar* (fam), plantar (fam); **he ~ed himself down in a chair** se dejó caer pesadamente en una silla 2 (AmE Culin) ‹*raisins*› hacer* hinchar (*poniendo en remojo*)

Phrasal verbs

• **plump for** [v ▸ prep ▸ o] (colloq) decidirse *or* optar por

• **plump up** [v ▸ o ▸ adv, v ▸ adv ▸ o] ‹*pillow/cushion*› ahuecar*, sacudir

plunder¹ /ˈplʌndər || ˈplʌndə(r)/ *vt* 1 (steal from) ‹*village*› saquear; **they ~ed the pyramid of most of its treasures** despojaron la pirámide de la mayor parte de sus tesoros 2 (steal) ‹*treasure/wealth*› robar

plunder² *n* [u] 1 (objects) botín *m* 2 (action) saqueo *m*

plunge¹ /plʌndʒ/ *vt* 1 (immerse, thrust) **to ~ sth INTO sth** ‹*into liquid*› sumergir* *or* meter algo EN algo; **she ~d the knife into his heart** le hundió *or* le clavó el cuchillo en el corazón 2 (into state, condition): **the street was ~d into darkness** la calle quedó sumida en la oscuridad; **the news ~d him into the depths of depression** la noticia lo sumió en una fuerte depresión; **the nation was ~d into war** la nación se vio precipitada a una guerra

■ **plunge** *vi*

A (dive) zambullirse*; (fall) caer*; **the car ~d over the cliff** el coche se precipitó por el acantilado

B 1 (slope downward steeply) «*road/path*» descender* bruscamente 2 (drop) «*price/temperature/popularity*» caer* en picada *or* (Esp) en picado, desplomarse

plunge² *n* 1 (in water) zambullida *f*, chapuzón *m*; ***to take the ~*** (take a risk) arriesgarse*, jugarse* el todo por el todo; (get married) casarse, dar* el paso 2 (fall) caída *f* 3 (of price, value) caída *f*; (of temperature) descenso *m*; **shares took a ~** las acciones cayeron en picada *or* (Esp) en picado

plunger /ˈplʌndʒər || ˈplʌndʒə(r)/ *n* 1 (for unblocking drain) desatascador *m*, chupona *f* (Esp), destapador *m* (de caño) (Méx), sopapa *f* (RPl), sopapo *m* (Chi), chupa *f* (Col), goma *f* (Ven) 2 (in syringe) émbolo *m*

plunging /ˈplʌndʒɪŋ/ *adj* ‹*neckline*› muy profundo

plunk¹ /plʌŋk/ (AmE) *vt* poner*, plantificar* (fam); **she ~ed herself down onto the sofa** se desplomó en el sofá

■ **plunk** *vi* 1 (drop) caer* 2 (making harsh, heavy sound): **she ~ed away at the piano** aporreaba el piano (fam)

plunk² *n/adv* ▸**plonk² A, plonk³**

pluperfect /ˈpluːˈpɜːrfɪkt/ *n* pluscuamperfecto *m*

plural¹ /ˈplʊrəl/ *adj* 1 (Ling) ‹*noun/verb*› en plural; **~ form** plural *m* 2 (Pol, Sociol) ‹*society/economy*› pluralista

plural² *n* plural *m*; **in the ~** en plural

pluralism /ˈplʊrəlɪzəm || ˈplʊərəlɪzəm/ *n* pluralismo *m*

pluralistic /ˈplʊrəˈlɪstɪk || ˌplʊərəˈlɪstɪk/ *adj* pluralista

plurality /plʊˈræləti || plʊəˈræləti/ *n* (*pl* **-ties**) 1 [u] pluralidad *f* 2 [c] (AmE Pol) mayoría *f* relativa

plus¹ /plʌs/ *n* (*pl* **~es** *or* **~ses**) 1 **~** (sign) signo *m* de más, más *m* 2 (advantage, bonus) (colloq) ventaja *f*, pro *m*

plus² *adj* 1 (advantageous) (colloq) (*before n*) ‹*point*› positivo, a favor; **on the ~ side, it is very spacious** entre las ventajas *or* los pros está que es muy amplio 2 (positive) (*before noun*) ‹*ion/number*› positivo; **+2°** (*léase: plus two degrees*) +2° (*read as: dos grados sobre cero*) 3 (and more) (*pred*): **children aged 13 ~** niños de 13 años para arriba *or* de 13 años en adelante; **there must have been 100 ~ people there** debe de haber habido de cien personas para arriba 4 (Educ): **B+** (*léase: B plus*) *calificación entre A y B, más baja que A-*

plus³ *prep* más; **2 + 3 = 5** (*léase: two plus three equals five*) 2 + 3 = 5 (*read as: dos más tres es igual a cinco*); **~ the fact that ...** aparte de que ...

plus⁴ *conj* (crit) además de que

plush /plʌʃ/ *adj* lujoso

plus-size /ˈplʌsˌsaɪz/ *adj* (AmE) de talla grande

P

Pluto /ˈpluːtəʊ/ *n* Plutón *m*
plutocracy /pluːˈtɑːkrəsi/ *n* (*pl* **-cies**) plutocracia *f*
plutonium /pluːˈtəʊniəm/ *n* [u] plutonio *m*
ply[1] /plaɪ/ *n* (*pl* **plies**) 1 (of wood) chapa *f*, lámina *f* 2 (of wool, yarn) cabo *m*, hebra *f*; **three-~ wool** lana *f* de tres cabos *or* hebras
ply[2] plies, plying, plied *vt* 1 (carry out): **to ~ one's trade** ejercer* su oficio 2 ‹*oar*› mover*; ‹*tools*› manejar 3 ‹‹*ship*›› ‹*sea*› navegar* por, surcar* (liter)
■ **ply** *vi* (frml) 1 (travel a route) ‹‹*ship/plane/bus*›› hacer* el trayecto 2 (BrE): **to ~ for hire** ‹‹*taxi*›› recorrer las calles en busca de clientes
Phrasal verb
• **ply with** [v ▸ o ▸ prep ▸ o]: **he kept ~ing me with whiskey** estaba constantemente sirviéndome whisky; **to ~ sb with questions** asediar *or* acosar a algn a preguntas
plywood /ˈplaɪwʊd/ *n* [u] contrachapado *m* (*tablero en varias capas*)
pm (after midday) p.m.; **at 2 ~** a las 2 de la tarde/p.m., a las 2 p.m.
PM (BrE) *n* = **prime minister**
PMS *n* [u] = **premenstrual syndrome**
PMT *n* [u] (BrE) = **premenstrual tension**
pneumatic /nʊˈmætɪk || njuːˈmætɪk/ *adj* neumático; **~ drill** martillo *m* neumático
pneumonia /nʊˈməʊnjə/ *n* [u] pulmonía *f*, neumonía *f*
PO *n* 1 = **post office** 2 (in UK) = **postal order**
poach /pəʊtʃ/ *vt*
A (Culin) ‹*egg*› escalfar; ‹*fish*› cocer* a fuego lento; **~ed egg** huevo *m* escalfado *or* (AmL tb) poché
B (steal) ‹*game*› cazar* furtivamente; ‹*staff/ideas*› robar
■ **poach** *vi* 1 (hunt game) cazar* furtivamente 2 (encroach): **to ~ on sb's territory** meterse en terreno de algn
poacher /ˈpəʊtʃər || ˈpəʊtʃə(r)/ *n* cazador furtivo *m*
poaching /ˈpəʊtʃɪŋ/ *n* [u] caza *f* furtiva
POB *n* (= **post office box**) apdo, aptdo, C.C. (CS)
PO box *n* Apdo. postal, Apdo. de correos, C.C. (CS)
pocket[1] /ˈpɑːkət || ˈpɒkɪt/ *n*
A 1 (in garment) bolsillo *m*; ***to have sb in one's ~*** tener* a algn (metido) en el bolsillo; ***to have sth in one's ~*** tener* algo asegurado *or* (Esp tb) en el bote; ***to line one's own ~s*** forrarse (fam); ***to live/be in each other's ~s*** (BrE) estar* uno encima del otro 2 (financial resources) bolsillo *m*; **prices to suit every ~** precios para todos los bolsillos 3 (holder — in car door) portamapas *m*; (— inside, outside bag) bolsillo *m*; (— on billiard, snooker, pool table) tronera *f*
B (small area) bolsa *f*; **~s of resistance** bolsas *fpl or* focos *mpl* de resistencia
pocket[2] *vt* 1 (put in pocket) meterse *or* guardarse en el bolsillo 2 (steal, gain) (colloq) embolsarse (fam) 3 (in snooker, pool) entronerar
pocket[3] *adj* (*before n*) ‹*diary/dictionary/calculator*› de bolsillo
pocket bike *n* (esp AmE) minimoto *f*
pocketbook /ˈpɑːkətbʊk || ˈpɒkɪtbʊk/ *n* 1 (handbag) (AmE) cartera *f or* (Esp) bolso *m or* (Méx) bolsa *f* 2 (wallet) (AmE) cartera *f*, billetera *f* 3 (paperback) (AmE) libro *m* en rústica 4 (notebook) (BrE) cuaderno *m*, libreta *f*
pocketful /ˈpɑːkətfʊl || ˈpɒkɪtfʊl/ *n*: **he had a ~ of pebbles** tenía un bolsillo llenó de guijarros
pocket: **~ handkerchief** *n* pañuelo *m* (de bolsillo); **~knife** *n* navaja *f*; **~ money** *n* [u] (spending money) dinero *m* para gastos personales; (for children) (BrE) dinero *m* de bolsillo, ≈ mesada *f* (AmL), domingo *m* (Méx), propina *f* (Per); **~-size, ~-sized** *adj* de bolsillo
pockmarked /ˈpɑːkmɑːrkt || ˈpɒkmɑːkt/*adj* ‹*face/skin*› picado de viruela(s)
pod /pɑːd || pɒd/ *n* (of peas, beans) vaina *f*
POD (= **pay on delivery**) cóbrese al entregar
podcast[1] /ˈpɔːdkæst || ˈpɒd-/ *n* podcast *m* (*archivo de sonido que se distribuye a través de la tecnología RSS*
podcast[2] *vt* hacer* un podcast de
podgy /ˈpɑːdʒi || ˈpɒdʒi/ *adj* **podgier, podgiest** (BrE colloq) rechoncho, regordete, gordinflón (fam)
podiatrist /pəˈdaɪətrəst || pəˈdaɪətrɪst/ *n* (AmE) pedicuro, -ra *m,f*, podólogo, -ga, *m,f* (frml)
podiatry /pəˈdaɪətri/ *n* [u] (AmE) podología *f* (frml)
podium /ˈpəʊdiəm/ *n* estrado *m*, podio *m*
poem /ˈpəʊəm || ˈpəʊɪm/ *n* poema *m*, poesía *f*
poet /ˈpəʊət || ˈpəʊɪt/ *n* poeta *mf*, poeta, -tisa *m,f*
poetic /pəʊˈetɪk/ *adj* ‹*language*› poético; ‹*moment/beauty*› lleno de poesía; **there was ~ justice in it** fue de justicia, se hizo justicia; **~ license** licencia *f* poética
poet laureate, Poet Laureate *n* (*pl* **~s ~**) poeta laureado, poeta *or* poetisa laureada *m,f*

> **Poet Laureate**
> Un poeta designado oficialmente por la Casa Real inglesa desde 1616. Su tarea es escribir poemas para ocasiones oficiales tales como las bodas, nacimientos y defunciones reales. Conserva su título hasta su muerte. En EEUU, desde 1986, los poetas laureados son designados por la Library of Congress, pero sólo se mantienen en el cargo durante uno o dos años

poetry /ˈpəʊətri || ˈpəʊɪtri/ *n* [u] poesía *f*; (*before n*) ‹*book*› de poesía(s) *or* poemas; **~ reading** recital *m* de poesía
pogrom /ˈpəʊgrəm || ˈpɒgrəm/ *n* pogrom *m*, pogromo *m*
poignancy /ˈpɔɪnjənsi/ *n* [u] (of story, moment) lo conmovedor; (of look, plea) patetismo *m*, lo patético
poignant /ˈpɔɪnjənt/ *adj* ‹*story/moment*› conmovedor; ‹*look/plea*› patético; ‹*reminder*› doloroso, penoso
poinsettia /pɔɪnˈsetiə/ *n* poinsettia *f*, flor *f* de Pascua *or* de Navidad, Nochebuena *f* (Méx)
point[1] /pɔɪnt/ *n*
Sense **I**
A [c] 1 (dot) punto *m* 2 (*decimal ~*) ≈ coma *f*, punto *m* decimal (AmL) (*the point is used instead of the comma in some Latin American countries*); **1.5** (*léase: one point five*) 1,5 (*read as: uno coma cinco*), 1.5 (*read as: uno punto cinco*) (AmL)
B [c] 1 (in space) punto *m*; **the ~s of the compass** los puntos cardinales; **~ of departure** punto *m* de partida; **customs ~** aduana *f*; **things have reached such a ~ that ...** las cosas han llegado a tal punto *or* a tal extremo que ...; ***the ~ of no return***: **we've reached the ~ of no return** ahora ya no nos podemos echar atrás 2 (on scale) punto *m*; **freezing/boiling ~** punto de congelación/ebullición; **you're right, up to a ~** hasta cierto punto tienes razón; **she is reserved to the ~ of coldness** es tan reservada, que llega a ser fría
C [c] (in time) momento *m*; **at this ~** en ese/este momento *or* instante; **at this ~ in time** en este momento; **he was at the ~ of death** (frml) estaba agonizando; **from this ~ on** a partir de este momento; **to be on the ~ of -ING** estar* a punto de + INF
D [c] (in contest, exam) punto *m*; **to win on ~s** (in boxing) ganar por puntos; **to make ~s with sb** (AmE) hacer* méritos con algn; ▸**match point, set[1] D**
Sense **II**
A [c] 1 (item, matter) punto *m*; **the seminar will cover the following ~s** el seminario abarcará los siguientes puntos; **the main ~s of the news** un resumen de las noticias más importantes del día; **~ of honor** cuestión *f* de honor *or* pundonor; **~ of order** moción *f* de orden; **to bring up** *o* **raise a ~** plantear una cuestión; **a ~ of law** una cuestión de derecho; ***to make a ~ of -ING***: **I'll make a ~ of watching them closely** me encargaré de vigilarlos de cerca; ***to stretch a ~*** hacer* una excepción 2 (argument): **it was a ~ which had never occurred to me** era algo que nunca se me había ocurrido; **yes, that's a ~** sí, ese es un punto interesante; **to make a ~**: **that was a very interesting ~ you made** lo que señalaste *or* planteaste *or* dijiste es muy interesante; **she made the ~ that ...** observó que ...; **all right, you've made your ~!** sí, bueno, ya has dicho lo que querías decir; (conceding) sí, bueno, tienes razón; **I take your ~, but ...** te entiendo, pero ...; **~ taken** de acuerdo; **to prove one's/a ~** demostrar* que uno tiene razón *or* está en lo cierto
B (*no pl*) (central issue, meaning): **to come/get to the ~** ir* al grano; **to keep** *o* **stick to the ~** no irse* por las ramas, no salirse* del tema; **she was brief and to the ~** fue breve y concisa; **and, more to the ~ ...** y lo que es más ...; **that's beside the ~** eso no tiene nada que ver *or* no viene al caso; **the ~ is that ...** el hecho es que ...; **that's not the ~** no se trata de eso; **that's just the ~!** ¡justamente!; **to miss the ~** no entender* de qué se trata
C [u] (purpose): **what's the ~ of going on?** ¿qué sentido tiene seguir?, ¿para qué vamos a seguir?; **the whole ~ of my**

trip was to see you justamente iba a viajar (*or* he viajado *etc*) nada más que para verte, el único propósito de mi viaje era verte a ti; **there's no ~ (in) feeling sorry for yourself** no sirve de nada compadecerse

D [c] (feature, quality): **music isn't one of my strong ~s** la música no es mi fuerte; **bad ~s** defectos; **he has many good ~s** tiene muchos puntos a su favor; **the good and bad ~s of the system** los pros y los contras del sistema

(Sense III)

A [c] 1 (sharp end, tip) punta *f*; **to come to a ~** acabar en punta 2 (promontory) (Geog) punta *f*, cabo *m*

B **points** *pl* (BrE Rail) agujas *fpl*

C [c] (socket) (BrE) **(electrical** *o* **power) ~** toma *f* de corriente, tomacorriente *m* (AmL)

point² *vt* (aim, direct) señalar, indicar*; **can you ~ us in the right direction?** ¿nos puede indicar por dónde se va?, ¿nos puede señalar el camino?; **to ~ sth AT sb/sth**: **he ~ed his finger at me** me señaló con el dedo; **she ~ed the gun at him** le apuntó con la pistola; **~ the aerosol away from you** apunta para otro lado con el aerosol

■ **point** *vi* 1 (with finger, stick etc) señalar; **it's rude to ~** es de mala educación señalar con el dedo; **the gun was ~ing in my direction** la pistola apuntaba hacia mí; **to ~ AT/TO sth/sb** señalar algo/a algn; **to ~ TOWARD sth** señalar en dirección a algo 2 (call attention) **to ~ TO sth** señalar algo; **the report ~s to deficiencies in health care** el informe señala deficiencias en la asistencia sanitaria 3 (indicate, suggest) **to ~ TO sth** ‹‹*facts/symptoms*›› indicar* algo; **it all ~s to suicide** todo indica *or* hace pensar que se trata de un suicidio; **the trends ~ to an early economic recovery** los indicios apuntan a una pronta reactivación de la economía

(Phrasal verb)

• **point out** [v ▸ o ▸ adv, v ▸ adv ▸ o]

A (show) señalar; **to ~ sth/sb out TO sb**: **I'll ~ it/her out to you** te/lo la señalaré

B (make aware of) ‹*problem/advantage*› señalar; **he ~ed out to them that time was getting short** les señaló *or* les advirtió *or* les hizo notar que quedaba poco tiempo

point: **~ blank** *adv* 1 (at close range) ‹*shoot*› a quemarropa, a bocajarro 2 ‹*refuse/deny*› rotundamente, categóricamente, de plano; **~-blank** *adj* 1 (close) ‹*shot*› a quemarropa, a bocajarro; **at ~-blank range** a quemarropa, a bocajarro 2 ‹*refusal*› rotundo, categórico

pointed /'pɔɪntəd || 'pɔɪntɪd/ *adj*

A (with a point) ‹*stick/leaf*› acabado en punta, puntudo (Andes); ‹*roof/window*› apuntado; ‹*arch*› ojival; ‹*chin/nose*› puntiagudo, puntudo (Andes); ‹*shoe*› de punta, puntiagudo, puntudo (Andes); ‹*hat*› de pico

B (deliberate) ‹*remark/comment*› mordaz; **no one missed the ~ reference to her predecessor** a nadie se le escapó la clara *or* directa alusión a su antecesor

pointedly /'pɔɪntədli || 'pɔɪntɪdli/ *adv* deliberadamente; **some of us did, she said ~** —algunos sí lo hicimos —dijo lanzándole una clara indirecta

pointer /'pɔɪntər || 'pɔɪntə(r)/ *n*

A 1 (on dial, gage) aguja *f* 2 (rod) puntero *m*

B 1 (clue, signal) pista *f*; **~ TO sth** indicador *m* DE algo 2 (tip) idea *f*, sugerencia *f*

C (dog) perro, -rra *m,f* de muestra, pointer *m*

pointless /'pɔɪntləs || 'pɔɪntlɪs/ *adj* ‹*attempt*› vano, inútil; ‹*existence*› sin sentido; **it's ~ arguing with him** no tiene sentido *or* no conduce a nada discutir con él

point of view *n* (*pl* **~s ~ ~**) punto *m* de vista; **from the ~ ~ ~ of efficiency** desde el punto de vista de la eficiencia

poise¹ /pɔɪz/ *n* [u] 1 (bearing) porte *m*, elegancia *f* 2 (composure) desenvoltura *f*, aplomo *m*

poise² *vt* colocar*

poised /pɔɪzd/ *adj*

A 1 (balanced, suspended): **~ in the air** suspendido en el aire; **they were waiting with pencils ~** esperaban, lápiz en mano; **~ on the brink of disaster** al borde del desastre 2 (ready) listo, preparado; **the jaguar was ~ for attack** el jaguar estaba agazapado, listo para atacar

B (self-assured): **she is very ~** tiene mucho aplomo *or* mucha desenvoltura

poison¹ /'pɔɪzn̩/ *n* [c u] veneno *m*; **rat ~** matarratas *m*; **to take ~** envenenarse; ***what's your ~?*** (colloq & hum) ¿qué vas a tomar?; (*before n*) **~ gas** gas *m* tóxico

poison² *vt* 1 (with poison) envenenar; (make ill) intoxicar*; ‹*river/soil*› contaminar 2 (corrupt) ‹*mind/society*› corromper; ‹*relationship/atmosphere*› dañar, estropear; **to ~ sb's mind against sb** indisponer* a algn contra algn

poisoning /'pɔɪzn̩ɪŋ/ *n* [u c] envenenamiento *m*; **to die of ~** morir* envenenado; ▸**food poisoning, lead¹**

poisonous /'pɔɪzn̩əs/ *adj* 1 (containing poison) venenoso 2 (malicious, evil) ‹*remark/person*› venenoso, ponzoñoso; ‹*ideas*› pernicioso

poison-pen letter *n* anónimo *m* ponzoñoso

poke¹ /pəʊk/ *vt* 1 (jab): **to ~ the fire** atizar* el fuego; **to ~ sb's eye out** sacarle* un ojo a algn; **she ~d him in the ribs** le dio en el costado; (with elbow) le dio un codazo en el costado 2 (thrust): **she ~d her head around the door** asomó la cabeza por la puerta; **he ~d his finger through the crack** metió el dedo por la ranura; ▸**fun¹**, **nose¹ A**

■ **poke** *vi* 1 (jab) **to ~ AT sth**: **he ~d at the mouse with a stick** le dio al ratón con un palo 2 (project) asomar; **her feet were poking out of the sheets** los pies le asomaban por entre las sábanas; **a few shoots were poking up out of the soil** unos cuantos brotes asomaban en la tierra

(Phrasal verb)

• **poke about, poke around** [v ▸ adv] husmear

poke² *n* golpe *m*; (with elbow) codazo *m*; **she gave him a ~ in the ribs** le dio en el costado; (with elbow) le dio un codazo en el costado; **to give the fire a ~** atizar* el fuego

poker /'pəʊkər || 'pəʊkə(r)/ *n*

A [c] (for fire) atizador *m*; ***as stiff as a ~*** más tieso que un palo (fam)

B [u] (game) póker *m*, póquer *m*

poker-faced /'pəʊkər'feɪst || 'pəʊkə'feɪst/ *adj* (colloq) con cara de póker (fam), impasible

poky /'pəʊki/ *adj* **pokier, pokiest** (colloq) 1 (cramped) diminuto; **a ~ little room** un cuartucho diminuto (pey) 2 (slow) (AmE) lerdo

Polack /'pəʊlɑːk/ *n* (AmE sl & offensive) polaco, -ca *m,f*

Poland /'pəʊlənd/ *n* Polonia *f*

polar /'pəʊlər || 'pəʊlə(r)/ *adj* (Geog, Astron) polar

polar bear *n* oso *m* polar

polarity /pəʊ'lærəti/ *n* [c u] (*pl* **-ties**) polaridad *f*

polarization /'pəʊlərə'zeɪʃən/ *n* [u] polarización *f*

polarize /'pəʊləraɪz/ *vt* polarizar*

■ **polarize** *vi* polarizarse*

Polaroid®, polaroid /'pəʊlərɔɪd/ *adj* (*before n*) polaroid® *adj inv*

pole /pəʊl/ *n*

A 1 (fixed support) poste *m*; (*flag~*) mástil *m*; (*tent ~*) palo *m*, mástil *m* 2 (for vaulting) garrocha *f or* (Esp) pértiga *f* 3 (for barge, punt) pértiga *f*

B 1 (Geog) polo *m*; **the North/South P~** el Polo Norte/Sur; ***to be ~s apart*** ser* polos opuestos 2 (Phys) polo *m*

Pole *n* polaco, -ca *m,f*

pole: **~ax**, (BrE) **~axe** *vt* tumbar, noquear; **~cat** *n* 1 (of weasel family) turón *m* 2 (AmE) ▸**skunk**

polemic¹ /pə'lemɪk/ *n* [c u] 1 (attack) **~ (AGAINST sth/sb)** ataque *m or* invectiva *f* (CONTRA algo/algn) 2 (defense) **~ IN FAVOR OF sth/sb** defensa *f* DE algo/algn 3 (controversy) polémica *f*

polemic² /pə'lemɪk/, **-ical** /-ɪkəl/ *adj* polémico

polemics /pə'lemɪks/ *n* (+ *sing vb*) polémica *f*

pole position *n* 1 (Sport) (in motor racing) pole *f*, primera línea *f*, primera fila *f*; **to be in ~ ~** estar* en la pole, estar* en primera línea *or* fila en la parrilla de salida 2 (leading position) posición *f* de ventaja

pole: **~star**, (BrE) **P~ Star** *n* estrella *f* polar; **~-vault** *n* salto *m* con garrocha *or* (Esp) con pértiga

police¹ /pə'liːs/ *n* 1 (force) (+ *sing or pl vb*) **the ~** la policía; **to be in/join the ~** ser*/hacerse* policía; (*before n*) ‹*escort/patrol*› policial; **~ car** coche *m* patrulla *or* de policía; **~ constable** (in UK) agente *mf*; **~ custody** custodia *f* policial; **~ department** (in US) distrito *m* policial; **the ~ force** la policía; **~ officer** agente *mf*, policía *mf*; **to have a ~ record** estar* fichado *or* (CS tb) prontuariado; **~ van** (BrE) furgón *m* policial, (coche *m*) celular *m* (Esp) 2 (police officers) (*no art*, + *pl vb*) policías *mpl*

police² *vt* 1 (keep order in) ‹*streets*› patrullar; ‹*region/area*› mantener* una fuerza policial en 2 (monitor) vigilar, supervisar 3 (clean up) (AmE) limpiar

police: ~ **dog** *n* perro *m* policía; ~**man** /pə'li:smən/ *n* (*pl* **-men** /-mən/) policía *m*, agente *m*; ~ **state** *n* estado *m* policía; ~ **station** *n* comisaría *f*; ~**woman** *n* agente *f*, policía *f*, mujer *f* policía

policing /pə'li:sɪŋ/ *n* [u] 1 (keeping order) mantenimiento *m* del orden; **the ~ of the strike** la actuación policial durante la huelga 2 (monitoring) vigilancia *f*, control *m*

policy /'pɑ:ləsi || 'pɒləsi/ *n* (*pl* **-cies**)

A [u c] 1 (Pol) política *f*; ~ **ON sth**: **their ~ on education** su política en materia de educación *or* en cuanto a educación; (*before n*) ~ **document** documento *m* normativo 2 (standard practice, plan) (Busn) política *f*; **her ~ is to ignore him** su táctica es no hacerle ni caso; **it is good/bad ~** es/no es recomendable

B [c] (*insurance* ~) (contract) seguro *m*; (document) póliza *f* de seguros

policy: ~**holder** *n* asegurado, -da *m,f*; ~**maker** *n* *encargado o responsable de formular la política de un partido, comité etc*; ~**making** *n* [u] *formulación de la política a seguir por un partido, comité etc*

polio /'pəʊliəʊ/ *n* [u] polio *f*; (*before n*) ‹*vaccine*› contra la polio; ‹*epidemic*› de polio

poliomyelitis /'pəʊliəʊ'maɪə'laɪtəs/ *n* [u] poliomielitis *f*

polish¹ /'pɑ:lɪʃ || 'pɒlɪʃ/ *n* 1 [u c] (*shoe* ~) betún *m*, pomada *f* (RPl), pasta *f* (Chi); (*furniture* ~) cera *f* para muebles, lustramuebles *m* (CS); (*metal* ~) limpiametales *m*; (*floor* ~) (esp BrE) abrillantador *m* (de suelos); (*wax* ~) cera *f* (abrillantadora); (*nail* ~) esmalte *m* (de uñas) 2 [c] (sheen) brillo *m*, lustre *m* 3 (act) (*no pl*): **to give sth a ~** sacarle* brillo a algo 4 [u] (refinement): **his performance lacked ~** necesitaba refinar *or* pulir su interpretación; **he lacks ~** tiene que pulir su estilo

polish² *vt* 1 ‹*floor/table/car*› darle* *or* sacarle* brillo a; ‹*shoes*› limpiar, lustrar (esp AmL), bolear (Méx), embolar (Col); ‹*brass/chrome*› limpiar, darle* *or* sacarle* brillo a; ‹*lens/mirror*› limpiar; ‹*stone*› (by abrasion) pulir 2 (refine) pulir, perfeccionar

Phrasal verbs

- **polish off** [v ▸ o ▸ adv, v ▸ adv ▸ o] (colloq) ‹*food*› liquidarse (fam), despacharse (fam)
- **polish up** [v ▸ o ▸ adv, v ▸ adv ▸ o] ‹*skill/style*› pulir, perfeccionar

Polish¹ /'pəʊlɪʃ/ *adj* polaco

Polish² *n* [u] polaco *m*

polished /'pɑ:lɪʃt || 'pɒlɪʃt/ *adj* 1 (shiny) ‹*metal/marble*› pulido, bruñido; ‹*wood*› brillante, lustrado (esp AmL) 2 (refined) ‹*manners/accent*› refinado, elegante; ‹*performance/translation*› pulido

polisher /'pɑ:lɪʃər || 'pɒlɪʃə(r)/ *n* (machine) enceradora *f*; (person) lustrador, -dora *m,f*

polite /pə'laɪt/ *adj* **politer, politest** 1 (correct, well-bred) ‹*manner/person*› cortés, educado, correcto; **the rules of ~ behavior** las reglas de cortesía; **they were making ~ conversation** conversaban tratando de ser agradables; **I was only being ~** lo dije sólo por cortesía; **it's not ~ to shout** gritar es una falta de educación *or* es de mala educación 2 (refined): **in ~ society** en la buena sociedad; **in ~ company** entre gente educada *or* fina

politely /pə'laɪtli/ *adv* ‹*behave*› correctamente, cortésmente; ‹*ask/refuse*› con buenos modales, con educación

politeness /pə'laɪtnəs || pə'laɪtnɪs/ *n* cortesía *f*, (buena) educación *f*; **out of ~** por cortesía

politic /'pɑ:lətɪk || 'pɒlətɪk/ *adj* (frml) diplomático; **it would be ~ to go/accept** lo más diplomático sería ir/aceptar

political /pə'lɪtɪkəl/ *adj* político; ~ **asylum** asilo *m* político; **his motives are clearly ~** tiene motivaciones claramente políticas; **I'm not very ~** no me interesa mucho la política

political: ~ **correctness** *n* [u] corrección *f* política, lo políticamente correcto; ~ **economy** *n* [u] economía *f* política

politically /pə'lɪtɪkli/ *adv* políticamente; ~ **aware** con conciencia política

politically correct *adj* políticamente correcto; **a ~ ~ term** un término políticamente correcto

politician /'pɑ:lə'tɪʃən || ˌpɒlɪ'tɪʃən/ *n* político, -ca *m,f*

politicize /pə'lɪtəsaɪz || pə'lɪtɪsaɪz/ *vt* politizar*; **to become ~d** politizarse*

politics /'pɑ:lətɪks || 'pɒlətɪks/ *n*

A (+ *sing vb*) (science, activity) política *f*; **to go into** *o* **enter ~** dedicarse* a la política, meterse en política (fam)

B (+ *pl vb*) 1 (political relations) política *f*; **office ~** intrigas *or* (fam) trapicheos de oficina; **the ~ of medicine** la medicina en el contexto político 2 (political views) ideas *fpl* políticas

polka /'pəʊlkə || 'pɒlkə, 'pəʊlkə/ *n* polca *f*, polka *f*

polka dot /'pəʊkə, pəʊlkə || 'pɒlkə, 'pəʊlkə/ *n* lunar *m*, topo *m* (Esp); (*before n*) ‹*material*› de lunares *or* (Esp) topos

poll¹ /pəʊl/ *n*

A 1 (ballot) votación *f*; **to take a ~ on sth** someter algo a votación 2 (number of votes cast): **there was a 62% ~** la participación electoral fue de un 62% 3 (*opinion* ~) encuesta *f* (de opinión), sondeo *m* (de opinión)

B **polls** *pl* (polling stations) **the ~s**: **to go to the ~s** ir* *or* acudir a las urnas

poll² *vt*

A (Pol) ‹*votes*› (obtain) obtener*; (cast) emitir

B (question) ‹*electorate*› sondear, encuestar

pollen /'pɑ:lən || 'pɒlən/ *n* [u] polen *m*; (*before n*) ~ **count** índice *m* de concentración de polen en el aire

pollinate /'pɑ:ləneɪt || 'pɒləneɪt/ *vt* polinizar*

polling /'pəʊlɪŋ/ *n* [u] votación *f*; (*before n*) ~ **day** (BrE) día *m* de las elecciones; ~ **place** *o* (BrE) **station** centro *m* electoral

pollutant /pə'lu:tn̩t/ *n* [c u] (agente *m*) contaminante *m*

pollute /pə'lu:t/ *vt* 1 (Ecol) contaminar; **to become ~d** contaminarse 2 (corrupt) (frml) ‹*mind/justice*› corromper

pollution /pə'lu:ʃən/ *n* [u] contaminación *f*, polución *f*

Pollyanna /'pɑ:li'ænə/ *n* (AmE) eterna optimista *f*

polo /'pəʊləʊ/ *n* [u] polo *m*

polo: ~ **neck** *n* (BrE) 1 (style of neck) cuello *m* alto 2 ▸~ **neck sweater**; ~ **neck sweater** *n* (BrE) suéter *m* de cuello alto *or* cisne, polera *f* (RPl)

poltergeist /'pəʊltergaɪst || 'pɒltəgaɪst/ *n* poltergeist *m*

poly /'pɑ:li || 'pɒli/ *n* (*pl* ~**s**) (BrE colloq) ▸**polytechnic**

poly- /'pɑ:li || 'pɒli/ *pref* poli-

polyanthus /'pɑ:li'ænθəs/ *n* (*pl* ~**es**) prímula *f*

polyester /'pɑ:li'estər || ˌpɒli'estə(r)/ *n* [u c] poliéster *m*

polyethylene /'pɑ:li'eθəli:n/ *n* [u] (esp AmE) polietileno *m*

polygamist /pə'lɪgəməst/ *n* polígamo, -ma *m,f*

polygamous /pə'lɪgəməs/ *adj* polígamo

polygamy /pə'lɪgəmi/ *n* [u] poligamia *f*

polyglot /'pɑ:liglɑ:t/ *n* políglota *mf*, polígloto, -ta *m,f*

polygon /'pɑ:ligɑ:n || 'pɒligən/ *n* polígono *m*

polymer /'pɑ:ləmər || 'pɒlɪmə(r)/ *n* polímero *m*

Polynesia /'pɑ:lə'ni:ʒə || ˌpɒlɪ'ni:ʒə/ *n* (la) Polinesia

Polynesian /'pɑ:lə'ni:ʒən || ˌpɒlɪ'ni:ʒən/ *adj* polinesio

polyp /'pɑ:ləp || 'pɒlɪp/ *n* (Zool, Med) pólipo *m*

polystyrene /'pɑ:li'staɪri:n/ *n* [u c] poliestireno *m*

polytechnic /'pɑ:li'teknɪk || ˌpɒli'teknɪk/ *n* (formerly in UK) *institución de educación superior que otorgaba títulos de nivel universitario y distintos diplomas*

polythene /'pɑ:ləθi:n/ *n* [u] (BrE) plástico *m*, polietileno *m* (téc); (*before n*) **a ~ bag** una bolsa de plástico

polyunsaturate /'pɑ:liʌn'sætʃəreɪt || ˌpɒlɪʌn'sætʃəreɪt/ *n* poliinsaturado *m*

polyunsaturated /'pɑ:liʌn'sætʃəreɪtəd || ˌpɒlɪʌn'sætʃəreɪtɪd/ *adj* poliinsaturado

polyurethane /'pɑ:li'jʊrəθeɪn/ *n* [u c] poliuretano *m*

pom /pɑ:m || pɒm/ *n* (Austral sl & often offensive) ▸**pommy**

pomegranate /'pɑ:məgrænət/ *n* granada *f*

pommel¹ /'pʌməl/ *vt* ▸**pummel**

pommel² *n* 1 (of saddle) perilla *f* 2 (of sword) pomo *m*

pommy /'pɑ:mi || 'pɒmɪ/ *n* (*pl* **-mies**) (Austral sl & often offensive) inglés, -glesa *m,f*

pomp /pɑ:mp || pɒmp/ *n* [u] pompa *f*, fausto *m*

pompom /'pɑːmpɑːm || 'pɒmpɒm/ *n* [1] (on hat) borla *f*, pompón *m* [2] (for cheerleader) pompón *m*

pomposity /pɑːm'pɑːsəti/ *n* [u] pomposidad *f*

pompous /'pɑːmpəs/ *adj* ‹*person*› pomposo, pedante, presuntuoso; ‹*reply/word*› pomposo, ampuloso, grandilocuente; **he's a ~ ass** es un pedante y un imbécil

poncho /'pɑːntʃəʊ || 'pɒntʃəʊ/ *n* (*pl* **-chos**) poncho *m*

pond /pɑːnd || pɒnd/ *n* (man-made) estanque *m*; (natural) laguna *f*

ponder /'pɑːndər/ *vt* reflexionar *or* cavilar sobre
■ **ponder** *vi* reflexionar; **to ~ ON/OVER sth** reflexionar *or* cavilar SOBRE algo

ponderous /'pɑːndərəs || 'pɒndərəs/ *adj* ‹*movement*› lento y pesado; ‹*explanation/speech*› pesado

pong¹ /pɑːŋ || pɒŋ/ *n* [c u] (BrE colloq) peste *f* (fam), tufo *m*

pong² *vi* (BrE colloq) apestar (fam)

pontiff /'pɑːntəf || 'pɒntɪf/ *n* pontífice *m*

pontificate /pɑːn'tɪfəkeɪt || pɒn'tɪfɪkeɪt/ *vi* pontificar*

pontoon /pɑːn'tuːn || pɒn'tuːn/ *n*
A [c] (float) pontón *m*; (*before n*) **~ bridge** pontón *m*
B (BrE Games) veintiuna *f*

pony /'pəʊni/ *n* (*pl* **ponies**)
A (Zool) poni *m*
B (sl) (AmE) ▸**crib¹ C1**

pony: **~tail** *n* cola *f* de caballo, coleta *f*; **~-trekking** *n* [u] (BrE) pony-trekking *m*, viaje-aventura *m* a caballo

poodle /'puːdl/ *n* caniche *m*

poof /pʊf/, **poofter** /'pʊftər || 'pʊftə(r)/ *n* (BrE sl & pej) maricón *m* (fam & pey)

pooh¹ /puː/ *n* (BrE colloq: used to or by children) caca *f* (fam)

pooh² *interj* (expressing disgust) ¡puf!; (expressing scorn) ¡bah!

pooh-pooh /'puː'puː/ *vt* (colloq) reírse* de, desdeñar

pool¹ /puːl/ *n*
A [c] [1] (collection of water) charca *f* [2] (*swimming ~*) piscina *f*, pileta *f* (RPl), alberca *f* (esp Méx) [3] (puddle) charco *m*; **a ~ of light** un foco de luz
B [c] (common reserve) (of money) fondo *m* común; (*typing ~*) sección *f* de mecanografía; **motor** *o* (BrE) **car ~** parque *m* or (AmL tb) flota *f* de automóviles; **a ~ of talent** una reserva de talento; **~ of resources** fuente *f* de recursos
C **pools** *pl* (BrE) ▸**football pools**
D [u] (billiards) billar *m* americano, pool *m*

pool² *vt* hacer* un fondo común de

poolroom /'puːlruːm, -rʊm/ *n* sala *f* de billar

poop /puːp/ *n*
A [c] (Naut) [1] (stern) popa *f* [2] **~ (deck)** toldilla *f*, castillo *m* de popa
B [u] (information) (AmE sl) **the ~** la información, los datos
C [u] (excrement) (AmE euph) caca *f* (fam)

pooped (out) /puːpt/ *adj* (AmE sl) (*pred*) reventado (fam), hecho polvo (fam)

poor¹ /pɔːr || pɔːr, pʊə(r)/ *adj* **-er, -est**
A (not wealthy) pobre; **spiritually ~** pobre de espíritu; **sparkling wine is the ~ man's champagne** el vino espumoso es el champán de los pobres
B (unsatisfactory, bad) ‹*harvest*› pobre, escaso; ‹*diet/quality*› malo; ‹*imitation*› burdo; **she's a ~ golfer** es una jugadora de golf bastante floja *or* mala; **theory is a ~ substitute for experience** la teoría no puede reemplazar a la experiencia; **to be in very ~ health** estar* muy delicado *or* muy mal de salud
C (unfortunate) (*before n*) pobre; **~ old Charles got soaked** el pobre Charles se empapó; **you ~ thing!** ¡pobrecito!

poor² *pl n* **the ~** los pobres

poorly¹ /'pʊrli || 'pɔːli, 'pʊəli/ *adj* (*pred*) (esp BrE) mal; **to be/feel ~** estar*/sentirse* mal *or* (Esp fam) pachucho

poorly² *adv* [1] (badly) ‹*perform/play*› mal; **they were ~ paid** les pagaban muy poco; **she did very ~ in the exam** le fue muy mal en el examen; **the street was ~ lit** había poca luz en la calle [2] (showing signs of poverty) pobremente

poor White *n*: *persona de raza blanca de bajo nivel socioeconómico*

pop¹ /pɑːp || pɒp/ *n*
A (noise): **to go ~** hacer 'pum'; (burst) reventar*
B [u] (Mus) música *f* pop
C [u] (Culin) gaseosa *f*
D [c] (father) (AmE colloq) papá *m* (fam); **~** *o* **~s** (*as form of address*) papá (fam), papi (fam)

pop² **-pp-** *vi*
A «*balloon*» estallar, reventar(se)*; «*cork*» saltar; **my ears ~ped** se me destaparon los oídos; **a ~ping sound/noise** un ligero estallido
B (spring) saltar; **his eyes were ~ping (out of his head)** los ojos se le salían de las órbitas
C (go casually) (colloq): **I ~ped across the road for some milk** crucé un momento a comprar leche; **he just ~ped in to say hello** pasó un minuto a saludar; **I'm ~ping out to get some cigarettes** voy a salir un momento a comprar cigarrillos
■ **pop** *vt*
A (burst) ‹*balloon*› reventar*, hacer* estallar
B (put quickly, casually): **she ~ped her head around the door** asomó la cabeza por la puerta; **~ it into your pocket** métetelo en el bolsillo; ▸**question¹ 1**
C ‹*pill/drug*› (colloq) tragar*

Phrasal verbs

- **pop off** [v ▸ adv] (colloq) (die) estirar la pata (fam), diñarla (Esp fam), petatearse (Méx fam)
- **pop up** [v ▸ adv] (colloq) [1] (rise) «*toast*» saltar; **his head ~ped up from behind the wall** asomó la cabeza por encima del muro [2] (appear) aparecer*; **new restaurants are ~ping up all over the place** están apareciendo *or* surgiendo nuevos restaurantes por todos lados

pop³ *adj* [1] (popular) ‹*sociology/culture*› popular; ‹*music/singer*› (AmE) popular, ligero; **~ art** pop-art *m*; **~ concert** (AmE) concierto *m* popular [2] (BrE Mus) pop *adj inv*

pop. (= **population**) hab.

popcorn /'pɑːpkɔːrn || 'pɒpkɔːn/ *n* [u] palomitas *fpl* (de maíz), cabritas *fpl* (de maíz) (Chi), pororó *m* (RPl), maíz *m* pira *or* tote (Col)

pope /pəʊp/ *n* papa *m*

pop: **~eyed** /'pɑːp'aɪd || 'pɒpaɪd/ *adj*: **to be ~eyed** (naturally) tener* los ojos saltones; (in surprise) mirar con los ojos desorbitados *or* fuera de las órbitas; **~gun** *n* pistola *f* de juguete (*de aire comprimido*)

poplar /'pɑːplər || 'pɒplə(r)/ *n* [1] [c] **~ (tree)** álamo *m* (blanco); **black ~** álamo *m* negro, chopo *m* [2] [u] (wood) álamo *m*

poplin /'pɑːplən || 'pɒplɪn/ *n* [u] popelina *f*, popelín *m* (Esp)

pop: **~-out** /'pɑːpaʊt || 'pɒpaʊt/ *adj* (AmE) eyectable; **~-up** /'pɑːpʌp || 'pɒpʌp/ *adj* (*before n*) ‹*book*› móvil, con ilustraciones en relieve; ‹*toaster*› automático

poppa /'pɑːpə || 'pɒpə/ *n* (AmE) ▸**pop¹ D**

popper /'pɑːpər || 'pɒpə(r)/ *n* [1] (AmE Culin) *recipiente para hacer* **popcorn** [2] (press stud) (BrE) broche *m* or botón *m* de presión (AmL), cierre *m* automático (Esp)

poppet /'pɑːpət || 'pɒpɪt/ *n* (BrE) tesoro *m*, encanto *m*

poppy /'pɑːpi/ *n* (*pl* **-pies**) amapola *f*, adormidera *f*

poppy: **~cock** *n* [u] (colloq & dated) paparruchas *fpl* (fam), tonterías *fpl*; **~seed** *n* [u c] semilla *f* de amapola

Popsicle® /'pɑːpsɪkəl/ *n* (AmE) paleta *f* (helada) *or* (Esp) polo *m* *or* (RPl) palito *m* *or* (CS) chupete *m* helado

popsy /'pɑːpsi/ *n* (*pl* **-sies**) (BrE colloq) amiga *f*, ligue m, (Méx, Esp fam), rollete *m* (Esp fam), pinche *m* (Chi fam)

pop-top /'pɑːptɑːp || 'pɒptɒp/ *n* (AmE) anilla *f*; (*before n*) **~ can** lata *f* (*que se abre tirando de una anilla*)

populace /'pɑːpjələs || 'pɒpjʊləs/ *n* (+ *sing o pl vb*) **the ~** (common people) el pueblo; (population) la población

popular /'pɑːpjələr || 'pɒpjʊlə(r)/ *adj*
A [1] (well-liked): **he's not very ~ around here** por aquí no le tienen mucha simpatía; **he's a very ~ politician among the young** es un político muy popular entre los jóvenes; **I was never very ~ at school** nunca fui muy popular en el colegio; **to be ~ WITH sb**: **she is ~ with her students** goza de popularidad entre sus alumnos; **I'm not very ~ with her at the moment** (colloq) últimamente no soy santo de su devoción (fam) [2] ‹*resort/restaurant*› muy frecuentado; ‹*brand/product*› popular
B [1] (not highbrow, specialist) ‹*music/literature*› popular [2] (of populace) ‹*feeling*› popular; ‹*rebellion*› del pueblo, popular; **by ~ demand/request** a petición *or* (AmL tb) a pedido del público [3] (widespread) ‹*belief/notion*› generalizado

popularity /'pɑːpjə'lærəti || ˌpɒpjʊ'lærəti/ *n* [u] popularidad *f*; **the program is growing in ~** el programa goza de

P

una popularidad cada vez mayor

popularize /'pɑːpjələraɪz || 'pɒpjʊləraɪz/ *vt* 1 (make popular) popularizar*, hacer* popular 2 (make accessible) divulgar*, vulgarizar*

popularly /'pɑːpjələrli || 'pɒpjʊləli/ *adv*: **~ known as ...** vulgarmente *or* corrientemente conocido como ...

populate /'pɑːpjəleɪt || 'pɒpjʊleit/ *vt* poblar*; **sparsely ~d** con poca densidad de población

population /'pɑːpjə'leɪʃən || ˌpɒpjʊ'leɪʃən/ *n*
A [c] 1 (number) población *f*; **what is the ~ of Thailand?** ¿cuántos habitantes *or* qué población tiene Tailandia?; (*before n*) **~ explosion** explosión *f* demográfica; **~ growth** crecimiento *m* demográfico 2 (individuals) (+ *sing o pl vb*) población *f*; **the entire ~ of the town turned out to welcome them** todo el pueblo salió a darles la bienvenida
B [u] (settling) población *f*

populism /'pɑːpjəlɪzəm || 'pɒpjʊlɪzəm/ *n* [u] populismo *m*

populist /'pɑːpjələst || 'pɒpjʊlɪst/ *adj* populista

populous /'pɑːpjələs || 'pɒpjʊləs/ *adj* populoso

pop-up /'pɑːpʌp || 'pɒp-/ *n* ventana *f* emergente

porcelain /'pɔːrsələn || 'pɔːsəlɪn/ *n* [u] porcelana *f*

porch /pɔːrtʃ || pɔːtʃ/ *n* 1 (covered entrance) porche *m* 2 (veranda) (AmE) porche *m*, galería *f*

porcupine /'pɔːrkjəpaɪn || 'pɔːkjʊpaɪn/ *n* puercoespín *m*

pore /pɔːr || pɔː(r)/ *n* poro *m*

Phrasal verb

• **pore over** [v ▸ prep ▸ o] ‹*manuscript/evidence/report*› estudiar minuciosamente; **he found her poring over an atlas** la encontró enfrascada en un atlas

pork /pɔːrk || pɔːk/ *n* [u] (carne *f* de) cerdo *m*, (carne *f* de) puerco *m* (Méx), chancho *m* (Chi, Per), marrano *m* (Col); (*before n*) **~ chop** chuleta *f* de cerdo (*or* de chancho *etc*), costilla *f* de cerdo (RPl)

porn[1] /pɔːrn || pɔːn/ *n* [u] (colloq) pornografía *f*

porn[2], **porno** /'pɔːrnəʊ/ *adj* (colloq) (*before n*) porno *adj inv*

pornographic /'pɔːrnə'græfɪk/ *adj* pornográfico

pornography /pɔːr'nɑːgrəfi/ *n* [u] pornografía *f*

porous /'pɔːrəs/ *adj* poroso

porpoise /'pɔːrpəs || 'pɔːpəs/ *n* marsopa *f*

porridge /'pɔːrɪdʒ || 'pɒrɪdʒ/ *n* [u] avena *f* (*cocida*), gachas *fpl* (*de avena*) (Esp); (*before n*) **~ oats** copos *mpl* de avena

port[1] /pɔːrt || pɔːt/ *n*
A [c] (for ships) puerto *m*; **sea/inland ~** puerto marítimo/fluvial; **to enter ~** llegar* a *or* arribar a *or* tomar puerto; **to leave ~** zarpar; **~ of call** puerto *m* de escala; **our second ~ of call was the baker's** nuestra segunda parada fue en la panadería; ***any ~ in a storm*** en tiempos de guerra cualquier hoyo es trinchera; (*before n*) ‹*authority/tax/regulation*› portuario
B [u] (left side) babor *m*; **to ~** a babor
C [c] 1 (for loading) (Aviat, Naut) porta *f* 2 (Comput) puerto *m*
D [u] (Culin) oporto *m*, vino *m* de Oporto

port[2] *adj* (*before n*) ‹*lights*› de babor

portable /'pɔːrtəbəl/ *adj* portátil

portal /'pɔːrtl || 'pɔːtl/ *n* portal *m*

portcullis /pɔːrt'kʌləs || ˌpɔːt'kʌlɪs/ *n* rastrillo *m*

portend /pɔːr'tend || pɔː'tend/ *vt* (liter) augurar, presagiar

portent /'pɔːrtent || 'pɔːtent/ *n* augurio *m*, presagio *m*

portentous /pɔːr'tentəs || pɔː'tentəs/ *adj* 1 ‹*remark/tone*› solemne 2 ‹*dream*› profético

porter /'pɔːrtər || 'pɔːtə(r)/ *n*
A (at station, airport) maletero *m*, mozo *m*, changador *m* (RPl); (on expedition) porteador *m*; (in hospital) (BrE) camillero *m*
B 1 (in hotel, apartment block) portero *m* 2 (AmE Rail) (sleeping-car attendant) mozo *m*, camarero *m* (CS)

porter's lodge *n* ≈ conserjería *f*, ≈ garita *f*

portfolio /pɔːrt'fəʊliəʊ || pɔːt'fəʊliəʊ/ *n* (*pl* **-lios**)
A 1 (case) portafolio(s) *m*, cartera *f* 2 (samples of work) carpeta *f* de trabajos
B (Pol) cartera *f*; **Minister without P~** ministro, -tra *m,f* sin cartera
C (Fin) cartera *f* de acciones; (*before n*) **~ management** gestión *f* de carteras

porthole /'pɔːrthəʊl/ *n* (Naut) ojo *m* de buey, portilla *f*

portico /'pɔːrtɪkəʊ/ *n* (*pl* **-cos** *or* **-coes**) pórtico *m*

portion /'pɔːrʃən || 'pɔːʃən/ *n* 1 (of food) porción *f* (esp AmL), ración *f* (esp Esp) 2 (share, part) parte *f*

Phrasal verb

• **portion out** [v ▸ o ▸ adv, v ▸ adv ▸ o] repartir; **they ~ed out the land among themselves** se repartieron la tierra

portly /'pɔːrtli || 'pɔːtli/ *adj* **-lier, -liest** corpulento

portmanteau /pɔːrt'mæntəʊ || pɔːt'mæntəʊ/ *n* (*pl* **-teaux** *or* **-teaus** /-təʊz/) baúl *m* de viaje

portrait /'pɔːrtrət, -treɪt || 'pɔːtrɪt, -treɪt/ *n* retrato *m*; **to paint sb's ~** pintar *or* retratar a algn

portrait format *n* [u] formato *m* vertical

portray /pɔːr'treɪ || pɔː'treɪ/ *vt* 1 (depict) ‹‹*picture*›› representar 2 (describe, represent) ‹*person/scene*› describir*; **she ~s the king as weak and selfish** nos da una imagen del rey *or* nos presenta al rey como un ser débil y egoísta 3 (act) ‹*character*› interpretar

portrayal /pɔːr'treɪəl || pɔː'treɪəl/ *n* [u c] (Art) representación *f*, manera *f* de representar; (Lit) descripción *f*; (Theat) interpretación *f*

Portugal /'pɔːrtʃɪgəl || 'pɔːtjʊgl/ *n* Portugal *m*

Portuguese[1] /'pɔːrtʃə'giːz || ˌpɔːtjʊ'giːz/ *adj* portugués

Portuguese[2] *n* (*pl* ~) 1 [u] (language) portugués *m* 2 [c] (person) portugués, -guesa *m,f*

pose[1] /pəʊz/ *vt* ‹*threat*› representar; ‹*problem/question*› plantear

■ **pose** *vi* 1 (Art, Phot) posar 2 (put on an act) hacerse* el interesante 3 (pretend to be) **to ~ AS sb/sth** hacerse* pasar POR algn/algo

pose[2] *n* 1 (position of body) pose *f*, postura *f*; **to strike a ~** ponerse* en pose 2 (assumed manner) pose *f*, afectación *f*

poser /'pəʊzər || 'pəʊzə(r)/ *n* 1 (question) pregunta *f* difícil; (problem) dilema *m* 2 (person) (BrE colloq) ▸ **poseur**

poseur /pəʊ'zɜːr || pəʊ'zɜː(r)/ *n*: **he's a real ~** todo en él es pura pose *or* afectación; **the party was full of ~s** la fiesta estaba llena de gente que se las daba de interesante

posh /pɑːʃ || pɒʃ/ *adj* **-er, -est** (esp BrE colloq) elegante, pijo (Esp fam), posudo (Col fam), pituco (CS fam), cheto (RPl fam), sifrino (Ven fam), popoff (Méx fam)

position[1] /pə'zɪʃən/ *n*
A [c] 1 (location) posición *f*, ubicación *f* (esp AmL); **to take up ~(s)** ‹‹*soldier/policeman*›› apostarse*; **the castle occupies a commanding ~ above the town** el castillo domina la ciudad desde lo alto; **they changed ~** se cambiaron de lugar *or* de sitio; **to be in ~/out of ~** estar* en su sitio/fuera de lugar 2 (Sport) posición *f*
B [c] 1 (posture) posición *f*, postura *f* 2 (stance, point of view) postura *f*, posición *f*
C 1 [c] (in hierarchy) posición *f*; (in league) puesto *m*, lugar *m* 2 [c] (job, post) (frml) puesto *m* 3 [u] (social standing) posición *f*
D [c] (situation, circumstances) situación *f*; **a strong bargaining ~** una buena posición para negociar; **put yourself in my ~** ponte en mi lugar; **you're in no ~ to criticize** no eres la persona más indicada para criticar; **I'm not in a ~ to help them at the moment** en este momento no estoy en condiciones de prestarles ayuda

position[2] *vt* colocar*, poner*; **police had been ~ed at both ends of the street** habían apostado policías a ambos extremos de la calle; **he ~ed himself between the two guests of honor** se situó *or* (AmL tb) se ubicó entre los dos invitados de honor

positive /'pɑːzətɪv || 'pɒzətɪv/ *adj*
A 1 ‹*number/quantity*› positivo; ‹*electrode*› positivo; **the test was ~** (Med) el análisis dio positivo 2 (Phot) ‹*image/print*› positivo
B 1 (constructive) ‹*attitude*› positivo; ‹*criticism*› constructivo; **try ~ thinking** intenta ser más positivo; **~ discrimination** (BrE) discriminación *f* positiva 2 (for the good) ‹*influence/development*› positivo
C (definite): **there is no ~ evidence** no hay pruebas concluyentes *or* definitivas; **the group still lacks a ~ identity** al grupo todavía le falta una identidad definida
D (absolute) (*before n*) auténtico, verdadero; **it's a ~ disgrace** es una auténtica *or* verdadera vergüenza
E 1 (decisive) categórico; **she's very ~ in her likes and dislikes** es muy categórica en sus preferencias; **what we need is ~ leadership** lo que necesitamos es un liderazgo firme 2 (sure) (colloq) (*pred*): **are you sure? — positive** ¿estás seguro? — segurísimo *or* más que seguro

positively /'pɑːzətɪvli || 'pɒzətɪvli/ *adv*
A (favorably, constructively): **we view teaching experience very ~** valoramos mucho *or* muy positivamente la experiencia docente; **to think ~** no ser* negativo, ser* positivo; **they reacted ~** tuvieron una reacción/respuesta positiva
B 1 (definitely) ‹*prove*› de forma concluyente *or* fehaciente; **the body has not yet been ~ identified** todavía no se ha hecho una identificación definitiva del cadáver 2 (absolutely) ‹*delighted/furious*› verdaderamente; **the food is ~ awful** la comida es malísima

posse /'pɑːsi || 'pɒsi/ *n* 1 (in US) partida *f* (*al mando de un sheriff*) 2 (group) grupo *m* numeroso; (gang) pandilla *f*

possess /pə'zes/ *vt*
A (own, have) tener*, poseer* (frml); **to be ~ed of sth** (frml) poseer* algo (frml)
B (grip, influence) «*anger/fear*» apoderarse de; **whatever can have ~ed him to do/say such a thing?** ¿qué lo habrá llevado a hacer/decir semejante cosa?

possessed /pə'zest/ *adj* (*pred*) **to be ~ (by the devil)** estar* endemoniado, estar* poseído (por el demonio); **like/as one ~** como (un) endemoniado *or* un poseso

possession /pə'zeʃən/ *n*
A 1 [c] (sth owned) bien *m*; **all my ~s** todo lo que tengo *or* (frml) poseo 2 [c] (territory) dominio *m*, posesión *f*
B [u] (ownership) posesión *f*; (of arms) tenencia *f*; **to be in ~ of sth** estar* en posesión de algo; **she wasn't in full ~ of her faculties** no estaba en pleno uso de sus facultades mentales; **the documents are in his ~** los documentos están *or* (frml) obran en su poder; **to gain ~ of sth** apoderarse de algo; **to take ~ of sth** tomar posesión de algo; ***~ is nine parts*** *o* ***tenths of the law*** la posesión es lo que cuenta
C [u] (Occult) posesión *f*

possessive /pə'zesɪv/ *adj*
A ‹*father/mother*› posesivo; **he's very ~ about his toys** es muy egoísta con sus juguetes
B (Ling) posesivo

possessiveness /pə'zesɪvnəs/ *n* [u] actitud *f* posesiva

possessor /pə'zesər/ *n* poseedor, -dora *m,f*

possibility /'pɑːsə'bɪləti || ˌpɒsə'bɪləti/ *n* 1 [u] (likelihood) posibilidad *f*; **it's not beyond (the bounds of) ~ that it will come back** cabe la posibilidad de que vuelva, está dentro de lo posible que vuelva; **is there any ~ you could lend me the money?** ¿hay alguna posibilidad de que me prestes el dinero? 2 [c] (sth possible) posibilidad *f*; **that's always a ~** siempre queda esa posibilidad 3 **possibilities** *pl* posibilidades *fpl*, potencial *m*

possible[1] /'pɑːsəbəl || 'pɒsəbəl/ *adj* posible; **the text must be checked for any ~ mistakes** hay que revisar el texto por si hubiera algún error; **in the best ~ taste** con el mejor de los gustos; **the show was made ~ by their dedication** el espectáculo fue posible gracias a su dedicación; **it's just ~ that he may have survived** existe una remota posibilidad de que haya sobrevivido; **get here by eight if ~** llega antes de las ocho, si es posible *or* si puedes; **as far as ~ try to work on your own** en lo posible intenta trabajar sola; **as little as ~** lo menos posible; **as early as ~** lo más pronto posible

possible[2] *n* 1 [c] (person) posible candidato, -ta *m,f* 2 [u] (what can be done): **the ~** lo posible

possibly /'pɑːsəbli || 'pɒsəbli/ *adv* 1 (conceivably): **that can't ~ be true** eso no puede ser verdad; **if we ~ can** si podemos *or* si nos es posible; **as fast as they ~ could** lo más rápido que pudieron; **I couldn't ~ eat any more** me es totalmente imposible comer nada más; **I couldn't ~ allow you to pay** de ninguna manera voy a permitir que usted pague; **could you ~ give me a hand with this?** ¿sería tan amable de ayudarme con esto? 2 (perhaps) (*indep*): **will it cost more than five dollars? — possibly** ¿va a costar más de cinco dólares? — puede ser *or* posiblemente

possum /'pɑːsəm || 'pɒsəm/ *n* zarigüeya *f*, oposum *f*, comadreja *f* (CS), zorro *m* (AmC, Méx); ***to play ~*** (to pretend — to be dead) hacerse* el muerto; (— to be asleep) hacerse* el dormido

post[1] /pəʊst/ *n* [u]
A 1 [c] (pole) poste *m*; ***as deaf as a ~*** más sordo que una tapia 2 [u] (in horse racing) poste *m*; **the finishing/starting ~** el poste de llegada/salida, la meta/salida; ▸ **pip**[2]
B [u] (mail) (esp BrE) correo *m*; **to send sth by ~** *o* **through the ~** mandar *or* enviar* algo por correo; **by separate ~** en sobre aparte *or* por separado; **it's in the ~** ya ha sido enviado *or* está en camino; **was there any ~ this morning?** ¿llegó alguna carta esta mañana?; **the first/second ~** (delivery) el primer/segundo reparto; (collection) la primera/segunda recogida; **to catch/miss the ~** llegar* a/perder* la recogida
C [c] 1 (job) puesto *m*, empleo *m*; **to take up one's ~** entrar en funciones, empezar* a trabajar 2 (important position) cargo *m* 3 (place of duty) puesto *m*
D [c] (station) puesto *m*; **a frontier/customs ~** un puesto fronterizo/de aduanas

post[2] *vt*
A 1 (position) ‹*policeman/soldier*› apostar 2 (send) ‹*employee/diplomat*› destinar, mandar
B (mail) (esp BrE) ‹*letter/parcel*› echar al correo; (drop in postbox) echar al buzón; **to ~ sth to sb** mandarle *or* enviarle* algo a algn (por correo)
C 1 (announce) ‹*meeting/reward*› anunciar; ***to keep sb ~ed*** mantener* *or* tener* a algn al tanto *or* al corriente 2 **~ (up)** ‹*list/notice*› poner*, fijar

post- /pəʊst/ *pref* post-, pos-

postage /'pəʊstɪdʒ/ *n* [u] franqueo *m*; **~ and handling** (AmE), **~ and packing** (BrE) gastos *mpl* de envío

postage: **~ paid** *adv* con franqueo pagado; **~ stamp** *n* (frml) sello *m* (de correos), estampilla *f* (AmL), timbre *m* (Méx)

postal /'pəʊstl̩/ *adj* (*before n*) ‹*zone/charges*› postal; ‹*service*› postal, de correos; ‹*booking*› (BrE) por correo; **~ ballot/vote** (BrE) votación *f*/voto *m* por correo

postal order *n* (BrE) ≈ giro *m* postal

post: **~bag** *n* (BrE) (sack) bolsa *f* del correo (AmL), saca *f* del correo (Esp); (letters) correspondencia *f*; **~box** *n* (BrE) buzón *m*; **~card** *n* tarjeta *f* postal, postal *f*; **~code** *n* (BrE) código *m* postal

postdate /'pəʊst'deɪt/ *vt* 1 ‹*contract/check*› posfechar, diferir* (RPl) 2 (occur after) tener* lugar después de

poster /'pəʊstər || 'pəʊstə(r)/ *n* cartel *m*, póster *m*

poste restante /'pəʊstre'stɑːnt/ *n* (BrE) lista *f* de correos, poste *f* restante (AmL)

posterior /pɑː'stɪriər/ *n* (euph & hum) trasero *m* (fam & euf)

posterity /pɑː'sterəti || pɒ'sterəti/ *n* [u] posteridad *f*

postgraduate /pəʊst'grædʒuət/ *n* estudiante *mf* de postgrado (*before n*) ‹*student/research*› de postgrado

posthaste /'pəʊst'heɪst/ *adv* inmediatamente

posthumous /'pɑːstʃəməs || 'pɒstjʊməs/ *adj* póstumo

posthumously /'pɑːstʃəməsli || 'pɒstjʊməsli/ *adv* ‹*published*› póstumamente; ‹*awarded*› a título póstumo

posting /'pəʊstɪŋ/ *n* destino *m*

postman /'pəʊstmən/ *n* (*pl* **-men** /-mən/) (esp BrE) cartero *m*

postmark[1] /'pəʊstmɑːrk || 'pəʊstmɑːk/ *n* matasellos *m*

postmark[2] *vt* matasellar; **the envelope was ~ed York** el sobre llevaba matasellos de York

post: **~master** *n* jefe *m* de la oficina *or* sucursal de correos; **~master general** *n* (*pl* **~masters general**) director, -tora *m,f* general de correos; **~mistress** *n* jefa *f* de la oficina *or* sucursal de correos

postmortem /'pəʊst'mɔːrtəm || ˌpəʊst'mɔːtəm/ *n* 1 (esp BrE Med) **~ (examination)** autopsia *f* 2 (analysis) autopsia *f*; **they had a long ~ on their defeat** pasaron mucho tiempo haciéndole la autopsia a su derrota

postnatal /'pəʊst'neɪtl̩/ *adj* postnatal, de posparto; **~ depression** depresión *f* posparto

post: **~ office** *n* 1 [c] (place) oficina *f* de correos, correo *m* (AmL), estafeta *f* de correos (Esp) 2 [u] (institution) **the P~ Office** ≈ la Dirección General de Correos (y Telégrafos); **~ office box** *n* apartado *m* postal *or* de correos, casilla *f* postal *or* de correo(s) (CS, Per)

postoperative /'pəʊst'ɑːprətɪv || ˌpəʊst'ɒprətɪv/ *adj* (*before n*) posoperatorio

postpaid /'pəʊst'peɪd/ *adv* ▸ **postage paid**

postpone /pəʊs'pəʊn || pə'spəʊn/ *vt* aplazar*, posponer*

postponement /pəʊs'pəʊnmənt || pə'spəʊnmənt/ *n* [u c] aplazamiento *m*, postergación *f* (esp AmL)

postscript /'pəʊstskrɪpt/ *n* (to letter) postdata *f*; (to book) epílogo *m*; (to event, affair) epílogo *m*, colofón *m*

P

post-traumatic stress disorder /ˌpəʊstˌtrɔːˈmætɪk/ *n* [u] trastorno *m* por estrés postraumático

postulant /ˈpɑːstʃələnt || ˈpɒstjʊlənt/ *n* postulante *mf*

postulate /ˈpɑːstʃəleɪt || ˈpɒstjʊleɪt/ *vt* 1 (Math, Phil) postular 2 (assume) presuponer*, dar* por supuesto

posture /ˈpɑːstʃər || ˈpɒstʃə(r)/ *n* 1 [u c] (of body) postura *f* 2 [c] (attitude) (frml) postura *f*

posturing /ˈpɑːstʃərɪŋ || ˈpɒstʃərɪŋ/ *n* [u c]: **it was just ~** no eran más que poses

postwar /ˈpəʊstˈwɔːr || ˌpəʊstˈwɔː(r)/ *adj* (*before n*) ‹*society/development*› de la posguerra; **the ~ years** los años de la posguerra, la posguerra

posy /ˈpəʊzi/ *n* (*pl* **posies**) ramillete *m*

pot¹ /pɑːt || pɒt/ *n*

A [c] 1 (*cooking* ~) olla *f*; **~s and pans** cacharros *mpl* (fam), trastes *mpl* (Méx); ***it's a case of the ~ calling the kettle black*** dijo la sartén al cazo: retírate que me tiznas; ***to go to ~*** (colloq) echarse a perder, venirse* abajo; ***a watched ~ never boils*** el que espera, desespera 2 (for jam, honey etc) tarro *m*, bote *m* (Esp) 3 (*tea*~) tetera *f*; (*coffee*~) cafetera *f*; **a ~ of tea for two** té para dos 4 (in pottery) vasija *f*

B [c] (*flower*~) maceta *f*, tiesto *m* (Esp)

C (*no pl*) 1 (in card games) pozo *m*, bote *m* (esp Esp) 2 (kitty) fondo *m* común, bote *m* (esp Esp)

D [c] (large amount) (esp BrE) (*often pl*) (colloq): **he's got ~s of money** está forrado (fam)

E [u] (shot) tiro *m* al azar; **to take a ~ at sth** disparar *or* tirar al azar contra algo

F [u] (marijuana) (colloq) hierba *f* (fam), maría *f* (Esp arg), mota *f* (Méx fam)

pot² *vt* **-tt-**

A ‹*plant*› plantar (*en una maceta*)

B (in snooker, billiards) (BrE) meter, entronerar

potash /ˈpɑːtæʃ || ˈpɒtæʃ/ *n* [u] potasa *f*

potassium /pəˈtæsiəm/ *n* [u] potasio *m*; (*before n*) ‹*chloride/cyanide*› potásico

potato /pəˈteɪtəʊ/ *n* [u c] (*pl* **-toes**) papa *f* *or* (Esp) patata *f*; (*before n*) **~ chips** *o* (BrE) **crisps** papas *fpl* *or* (Esp) patatas *fpl* fritas; **~ peeler** pelapapas *m* *or* (Esp) pelapatatas *m*

pot: **~bellied** /ˈpɑːtˈbelid || ˌpɒtˈbelid/ *adj* panzudo (fam), panzón (fam), barrigón (fam), guatón (Chi fam); **~belly** *n* barriga *f* (fam), panza *f* (fam), guata *f* (Chi fam); **you're getting a bit of a ~belly** estás echando barriga

potency /ˈpəʊtn̩si/ *n* [u]

A (of drink) lo fuerte; (of symbol, spell) fuerza *f*, lo poderoso

B (*sexual* ~) potencia *f* sexual

potent /ˈpəʊtn̩t/ *adj*

A 1 ‹*drink/drug/medicine*› fuerte 2 ‹*leader/symbol*› poderoso; ‹*argument*› poderoso, convincente

B (Physiol) potente

potentate /ˈpəʊtn̩teɪt/ *n* potentado, -da *m,f*

potential¹ /pəˈtentʃəl || pəˈtenʃəl/ *n* [u] (capacity) potencial *m*; (possibilities) posibilidades *fpl*; **sales ~** potencial de ventas; **she showed great ~ as a singer** prometía mucho *or* era muy prometedora como cantante

potential² *adj* (*before n*) ‹*danger*› potencial, posible; ‹*leader*› en potencia

potentially /pəˈtentʃəli/ *adv* potencialmente

pot: **~hole** *n* 1 (cave) cueva *f* subterránea, sima *f*; (hole) sima *f* 2 (in road) bache *m*; **~holer** /ˈpɑːtˌhəʊlər || ˈpɒtˌhəʊlə(r)/ *n* (BrE) espeleólogo, -ga *m,f*; **~holing** *n* [u] (BrE) espeleología *f*

potion /ˈpəʊʃən/ *n* poción *f*, pócima *f*; **love ~** filtro *m* (de amor)

pot: **~luck** /ˈpɑːtˈlʌk || ˌpɒtˈlʌk/ *n* [u]: **to take ~luck** conformarse con lo que haya; **~ plant** *n* planta *f* (*cultivada en una maceta*), mata *f* (Col, Ven); **~pourri** /ˈpəʊpʊˈri || ˌpəʊˈpʊəri/ *n* (*pl* **~s**) popurrí *m*; **~ roast** *n* [c u] estofado *m*, carne *f* a la cacerola (AmL); **~shot** *n* (Dep) tiro *m* al azar; **to take ~shots at sb/sth** disparar *or* tirar al azar contra algn/algo

potted /ˈpɑːtəd || ˈpɒtɪd/ *adj*

A (*before n*) 1 ‹*plant*› en maceta *or* tiesto 2 (Culin): **~ meat/shrimps** *especie de paté de carne/camarones* 3 ‹*account/version*› resumido

B (drunk) (AmE colloq) borracho, cocido (fam), tomado (AmL fam)

potter¹ /ˈpɑːtər || ˈpɒtə(r)/ *n* alfarero, -ra *m,f*, ceramista *mf*; **~'s wheel** torno *m* de alfarero

potter² *vi* (BrE) (+ *adv compl*) ▸ **putter²**

pottery /ˈpɑːtəri || ˈpɒtəri/ *n* (*pl* **-ries**) 1 [u] (vessels) cerámica *f* 2 [c] (workshop) alfarería *f*, taller *m* de cerámica 3 [u] (craft) alfarería *f*, cerámica *f*

potty¹ /ˈpɑːti || ˈpɒti/ *n* (*pl* **-ties**) (colloq) orinal *m* (*para niños*) (fam), bacinica *f* (AmL exc RPl), pelela *f* (CS fam); **he's ~-trained** ya no usa pañales

potty² *adj* **-tier, -tiest** (BrE colloq) chiflado (fam), chalado (fam); **to drive sb ~** poner* a algn frenético (fam); **to be ~ ABOUT sb/sth** estar* loco POR algn /CON algo (fam)

pouch /paʊtʃ/ *n*

A 1 (small bag) bolsa *f*; **tobacco ~** petaca *f*; **hunter's ~** morral *m* de cazador 2 (for correspondence) (AmE) valija *f*

B (Anat, Zool) bolsa *f*

pouf, pouffe /puːf/ *n* (seat) (BrE) puf *m*

poulterer /ˈpəʊltərər || ˈpəʊltərə(r)/ *n* pollero, -ra *m,f*; **~'s** pollería *f*

poultice /ˈpəʊltəs || ˈpəʊltɪs/ *n* cataplasma *f*, emplasto *m*

poultry /ˈpəʊltri/ *n* [u] 1 (birds) (+ *pl vb*) aves *fpl* de corral; (*before n*) **~ farm** granja *f* avícola 2 (meat) carne *f* de ave

pounce¹ /paʊns/ *vi* saltar; **to ~ ON/UPON sb/sth** «*tiger/cat*» abalanzarse* *or* lanzarse* SOBRE algn/algo; «*person*» abalanzarse* SOBRE algn/algo

pounce² *n* salto *m*

pound¹ /paʊnd/ *n*

A (measure) libra *f* (*454 gramos*); **you've lost a few ~s** has adelgazado unos kilitos

B (Fin) libra *f*; **~ sterling** libra esterlina; (*before n*) **a ~ coin** una moneda de (una) libra

C (enclosure — for cars) depósito *m*; (— for dogs) perrera *f*

pound² *vt* 1 ‹*corn/spices*› machacar*; ‹*garlic/chili*› majar, machacar* 2 ‹*table/door*› aporrear, golpear; **the waves ~ed the wall** las olas batían contra el muro 3 (Mil) ‹*defenses*› batir, bombardear; **mortars ~ed the village to rubble** los morteros redujeron el pueblo a escombros

■ **pound** *vi* 1 (strike, beat) aporrear, golpear; **he ~ed at the door/on the table** aporreó *or* golpeó la puerta/la mesa; **waves ~ed against the cliffs** las olas batían contra el acantilado 2 «*heart*» palpitar, latir con fuerza; «*sound*» retumbar; **my head is ~ing** tengo la cabeza a punto de reventar *or* estallar, me martillea la cabeza 3 (move) (+ *adv compl*): **I could hear his feet ~ing down the corridor** oía sus pesados pasos por el pasillo

pounding /ˈpaʊndɪŋ/ *n* (*no pl*) 1 (of heart) fuertes latidos *mpl*; (of guns) martilleo *m*; **the ~ of the waves** el embate de las olas 2 (beating) (colloq) paliza *f* (fam), vapuleo *m*

pound sign *n* 1 (AmE) (key) tecla *f* (del signo) de número, tecla *f* numeral, tecla *f* de almohadilla (Esp) 2 (for currency) *signo de la libra esterlina (£)*

pour /pɔːr || pɔː(r)/ *vt* 1 (+ *adv compl*) ‹*liquid*› verter*, echar; ‹*powder*› echar; **he ~ed the tea down the sink** tiró el té por el fregadero; **money has been ~ed into the project** han invertido una gran cantidad de dinero en el proyecto; **she ~ed all her energy into her work** se volcó totalmente en su trabajo; **she ~ed scorn on his efforts** se burló de sus esfuerzos 2 **~ (out)** ‹*drink*› servir*

■ **pour** *vi* 1 (+ *adv compl*) «*blood*» manar, salir*; **people ~ed out of the stadium** grandes cantidades de personas salían del estadio; **letters came ~ing in** llegó una avalancha de cartas; **money ~ed into the country** afluyó mucho dinero al país 2 (serve tea, coffee) servir*

■ **pour** *v impers* diluviar, llover* torrencialmente *or* a cántaros; **it's ~ing (down/with rain)** está diluviando

Phrasal verb

• **pour out**

A [v ▸ o ▸ adv, v ▸ adv ▸ o] 1 ▸ **pour** *vt* 2 2 **to ~ sth out (TO sb)**: **he ~ed out his feelings (to her)** (le) reveló sus sentimientos; **she ~ed her heart out to him** se desahogó con él, le abrió su pecho (liter)

B [v ▸ adv] salir*; **people ~ed out into the streets** la gente salió en tropel a las calles; **all his troubles came ~ing out** desembuchó todos sus problemas

pouring /ˈpɔːrɪŋ/ *adj*: **he went out in the ~ rain** salió en medio de una lluvia torrencial

pout¹ /paʊt/ *vi* hacer* un mohín

pout² *n* mohín *m*

P

poverty /'pɑːvərti || 'pɒvəti/ *n* [u] pobreza *f*; (*before n*) **they live on the ~ line** tienen apenas el mínimo necesario para vivir

poverty-stricken /'pɑːvərti,strɪkən || 'pɒvəti,strɪkən/ *adj* pobrísimo, sumido en la pobreza

POW *n* = **prisoner of war**

powder[1] /'paʊdər || 'paʊdə(r)/ *n* [u]
A polvo *m*; (*before n*) **in ~ form** en polvo
B (*face* ~) polvo *m or* polvos *mpl* (de tocador); (*before n*) **~ compact** polvera *f*; **~ puff** borla *f*, cisne *m* (RPl)

powder[2] *vt*
A (cover) empolvar; **to ~ one's nose** retocarse* el maquillaje; **she's gone to ~ her nose** (euph) ha ido a lavarse las manos (euf)
B 1 (grind, pulverize) pulverizar* 2 **powdered** *past p* ‹*milk/eggs*› en polvo; **~ed sugar** (AmE) azúcar *m or f* glas, azúcar *m or f* flor (Chi), azúcar *m or f* impalpable (RPl), azúcar *m or f* en polvo (Col)

powder: **~-blue** /'paʊdər'bluː || ,paʊdə'bluː/ *adj* (*pred* **~ blue**) azul pastel *adj inv*; **~ keg** *n* barril *m* de pólvora; **~ room** *n* (euph) tocador *m* (euf); **S powder room** señoras

powdery /'paʊdəri/ *adj* como polvo, pulverulento (frml)

power[1] /'paʊər || 'paʊə(r)/ *n*
A 1 [u] (control, influence) poder *m*; (of country) poderío *m*, poder *m*; **people ~** poder popular; **~ OVER sb/sth** poder SOBRE algn/algo; **to be in ~** estar* en *or* ocupar el poder; **balance of ~** equilibrio *m* de fuerzas; **to seize ~** tomar el poder, hacerse* con el poder; **to come to ~** llegar* *or* subir al poder; (*before n*) **~ sharing** compartimiento *m* del poder; **~ struggle** lucha *f* por el poder 2 [u c] (official authority) poder *m*; **~ to + INF** poder PARA + INF; **special ~s** poderes extraordinarios; **~ of veto** derecho *m* de veto
B [c] 1 (nation) potencia *f* 2 (person, group): **the ~ behind the throne** el poder en la sombra; **the ~s that be** los que mandan, los que detentan el poder; **the ~s of darkness** las fuerzas del mal
C [u] 1 (physical strength, force) fuerza *f*; ***more ~ to your elbow*** (colloq) ¡bien hecho! 2 (of engine, loudspeaker, transmitter, telescope) potencia *f*; **processing ~** capacidad *f* de procesamiento 3 (of tradition, love) poder *m*, fuerza *f*; (of argument) fuerza *f*, lo poderoso *or* convincente
D 1 [u] (ability, capacity): **I did everything in my ~** hice todo lo que estaba en mi(s) mano(s), hice todo lo que me era posible; **that's beyond my ~** eso está fuera de mis posibilidades 2 (specific faculty) (*often pl*): **he lost the ~ of speech** perdió el habla; **~(s) of concentration** capacidad *f or* poder *m* de concentración; **mental ~s** inteligencia *f*, facultades *fpl* mentales; **he was at the height of his ~(s)** estaba en su mejor momento *or* en la plenitud de sus facultades
E [u] 1 (Eng, Phys) potencia *f*; (particular source of energy) energía *f*; **solar ~** energía solar; (*before n*) **~ brakes** servofrenos *mpl*; **~ steering** dirección *f* asistida 2 (electricity) electricidad *f*; (*before n*) **~ cable** cable *m* de energía eléctrica; **~ lines** cables *mpl* de alta tensión; **~ point** (BrE) toma *f* de corriente, enchufe *m*, tomacorriente *m* (AmL); **~ tool** herramienta *f* eléctrica
F [u] (Math) potencia *f*; **10 to the ~ of 4/of 3** 10 (elevado) a la cuarta potencia/al cubo
G (a lot): **to do sb a ~ of good** hacerle* a algn mucho bien

power[2] *vt*: **the plane is ~ed by four engines** el avión está propulsado por cuatro motores; **it's ~ed by electricity** funciona con electricidad; **steam-~ed** a *or* de vapor
■ **power** *vi* (move rapidly) (colloq) (+ *adv compl*): **we were ~ing along the highway** íbamos disparados por la carretera (fam)

power: **~-assisted** /'paʊərə'sɪstəd || 'paʊərə'sɪstɪd/ *adj*: **~-assisted steering** dirección *f* asistida; **~ base** *n* zona *f* de influencia; **~boat** *n* lancha *f* de motor, lancha *f* motora (Esp); **~ cut** *n* apagón *m*, corte *m* de luz

powerful /'paʊərfəl || 'paʊəfəl/ *adj* 1 ‹*country*› poderoso 2 ‹*serve/stroke*› potente; ‹*shoulders/arms*› fuerte 3 ‹*performance/image*› impactante; ‹*argument*› poderoso, convincente; ‹*incentive*› poderoso 4 ‹*engine/weapon*› potente; ‹*drug*› potente, fuerte; ‹*smell/current*› fuerte

powerfully /'paʊərfəli || 'paʊəfəli/ *adv* 1 ‹*hit/strike*› con fuerza; **he was ~ built** era de complexión fuerte 2 ‹*speak/argue*› convincentemente

powerhouse /'paʊərhaʊs || 'paʊəhaʊs/ *n*: **the nerve center and ~ of the corporation** el centro neurálgico y motriz de la compañía; **he's the ~ of the team** es el puntal del equipo

powerless /'paʊərləs || 'paʊəlɪs/ *adj* impotente: **they were ~ to prevent the violence** no pudieron hacer nada para impedir la violencia

power: **~ of attorney** *n* (*pl* **~s of attorney**) (Law) poder *m* (notarial); **~ plant** *n* (AmE) ▸ **~ station**; **~ station** *n* central *f* eléctrica, usina *f* eléctrica (AmS)

powwow /'paʊwaʊ/ *n* (ceremony) asamblea *f* (*de indígenas norteamericanos*); **a family ~** un consejo de familia

pp (on behalf of) (BrE Corresp) p.a., p.o., p.p.

pp. (= **pages**) págs.

PR[1] *n* [u] 1 = **public relations** 2 = **proportional representation**

PR[2] = **Puerto Rico**

practicability /'præktɪkə'bɪləti/ *n* [u] factibilidad *f*, practicabilidad *f*

practicable /'præktɪkəbəl/ *adj* factible, practicable

practical[1] /'præktɪkəl/ *adj*
A práctico; **for all ~ purposes** a efectos prácticos
B (feasible) factible, viable

practical[2] *n* (Educ) práctica *f*

practicality /'præktɪ'kæləti/ *n*
A [u] 1 (feasibility — of scheme/idea) lo práctico *or* factible 2 (usefulness — of clothes/equipment) utilidad *f*
B [u] (personal quality) sentido *m* práctico
C practicalities *pl* aspectos *mpl* prácticos

practical joke *n* broma *f*; **to play a ~ ~ on sb** hacerle* *or* gastarle una broma a algn

practically /'præktɪkli/ *adv*
A (almost, virtually) casi, prácticamente; **he ~ broke my arm!** ¡casi *or* por poco me rompe el brazo!
B (in a practical way) ‹*consider/think*› con sentido práctico

practical nurse *n* (AmE) enfermero, -ra *m,f* auxiliar (*a veces sin título*)

practice[1] /'præktəs || 'præktɪs/ *n*
A [u] (training, repetition) práctica *f*; **he's out of ~** le falta práctica; **piano ~** ejercicios *mpl* de piano; **target ~** prácticas *fpl* de tiro; **~ teaching** *o* (BrE) **teaching ~** prácticas *fpl* de magisterio; ***~ makes perfect*** la práctica hace al maestro; (*before n*) ‹*game*› de entrenamiento; **~ session** (Sport) sesión *f* de entrenamiento; (Mus) ensayo *m*
B [u] 1 (carrying out, implementing) práctica *f*; **to put sth into ~** llevar algo a la práctica, poner* algo en práctica; **in ~** en la práctica 2 (exercise of profession) ejercicio *m*; **he is in general ~** se dedica a medicina general
C [c u] (custom, procedure) costumbre *f*; **it's our ~ to take up references** solemos *or* acostumbramos pedir referencias; **it is not good commercial ~** no es una práctica comercial recomendable; **working ~s** métodos *mpl* de trabajo
D [c] 1 (Med) consultorio *m*, consulta *f* 2 (Law) bufete *m*, estudio *m* jurídico (CS)

practice[2], (BrE) **practise** *vt*
A (rehearse) practicar*; ‹*song/act*› ensayar; **I ~d my Greek on him** aproveché para practicar griego con él
B 1 ‹*belief/Christianity*› practicar*; **he doesn't ~ what he preaches** no hace lo que predica, no predica con el ejemplo 2 (carry out, perform): **he ~s black magic** practica magia negra 3 ‹‹*doctor/lawyer*›› ejercer*; **he ~s law** ejerce de *or* como abogado, ejerce la abogacía
C practicing *pres p* 1 ‹*doctor/lawyer*› en ejercicio (de su profesión) 2 ‹*Catholic*› practicante 3 ‹*homosexual*› activo
■ **practice** *vi*
A (rehearse, train) practicar*
B (professionally) ejercer*

practiced, (BrE) **practised** /'præktəst || 'præktɪst/ *adj* ‹*hand/eye*› experto; ‹*liar*› consumado

practitioner /præk'tɪʃnər || præk'tɪʃnə(r)/ *n* 1 (of an art, skill) profesional *mf* 2 (doctor) médico, -ca *m,f*; **general ~** médico, -ca *m,f* de medicina general

pragmatic /præg'mætɪk/ *adj* pragmático

pragmatism /'prægmətɪzəm/ *n* [u] pragmatismo *m*

Prague /prɑːg/ *n* Praga *f*

prairie /'preri || 'preəri/ *n* [c u] pradera *f*, llanura *f*; **the ~(s)** (in US) la Pradera

prairie: ~ **dog** *n* perro *m* de las praderas; ~ **oyster** *n*: *bebida hecha con huevo crudo y vinagre para aliviar la resaca*

praise[1] /preɪz/ *n* [u] 1 (credit, applause) elogios *mpl*, alabanzas *fpl*; **he was full of ~ for her** se deshizo en elogios *or* en alabanzas para con ella; **I've nothing but ~ for him** no tengo más que elogios para él; **she spoke in ~ of her staff** habló elogiando *or* alabando a sus empleados; ***to sing sth's/sb's ~s*** poner* algo/a algn por las nubes 2 (Relig) alabanza *f*; ~ **be to God** alabado sea Dios

praise[2] *vt* 1 (compliment) elogiar, hacer* elogio de 2 (Relig) alabar; ~ **the Lord!** (*as interj*) ¡alabado sea Dios!

praiseworthy /ˈpreɪzˌwɜːrði || ˈpreɪzˌwɜːði/ *adj* ‹*person*› digno de elogio, meritorio; ‹*performance/deed*› digno de elogio, loable, encomiable

pram /præm/ *n* (BrE) cochecito *m*

prance /præns || prɑːns/ *vi* 1 ‹‹*horse*›› brincar*, hacer* cabriolas 2 (pej) ‹‹*person*››: **she ~d into the room wearing her new dress** entró meneándose *or* pavoneándose con el vestido nuevo

(Phrasal verb)

- **prance about** 1 [v ▸ adv] brincar* 2 [v ▸ prep ▸ o] brincar* en

prank /præŋk/ *n* broma *f*; (of child) travesura *f*, diablura *f*; **to play a ~ on sb** gastarle una broma a algn

prankster /ˈpræŋkstər || ˈpræŋkstə(r)/ *n* bromista *mf*; **who's the ~ who did this?** ¿quién es el bromista *or* (iró) gracioso que hizo esto?

prat /præt/ *n* (BrE sl) imbécil *mf*

pratfall /ˈprætfɔːl/ *n* (esp AmE sl) 1 (humiliating failure) revés *m*, batacazo *m* (Esp fam) 2 (fall) porrazo *m* (fam)

prattle /ˈprætl̩/ *vi* ‹‹*adult*›› cotorrear (fam), chacharear (fam); ‹‹*child*›› balbucear; **he ~d on endlessly about his problems** estuvo horas dale que te dale hablando de sus problemas (fam)

prawn /prɔːn/ *n* (large) langostino *m*, camarón *m* (AmL); (medium) camarón *m* (AmL), gamba *f* (esp Esp), langostino *m* (CS); (small) camarón *m*, quisquilla *f* (Esp); (*before n*) ~ **cocktail** (BrE) *see* **cocktail 2**

pray[1] /preɪ/ *vi* rezar*, orar (frml); **let us ~** oremos (frml); **to ~ FOR sb/sth** rezar* *or* rogar* POR algn/algo; **to ~ for rain** rezar* para que llueva

■ **pray** *vt* (Relig): **I ~ (to) God he's all right** Dios quiera que no le haya pasado nada

pray[2] *interj* (arch): ~ **be seated** por favor tomen asiento; **and what, ~ (tell), is the point of this?** ¿y qué sentido tiene esto, si se puede saber?

prayer /prer || preə(r)/ *n* 1 [u] (praying) oración *f*; (*before n*) ~ **book** devocionario *m* 2 [c] (request, petition) oración *f*, plegaria *f*; **my ~s were answered** mis plegarias fueron atendidas *or* escuchadas; **the Lord's P~** el Padrenuestro; **to say one's ~s** rezar*, orar (frml); **to say a ~** rezar* una oración 3 (service): **Morning/Evening P~** oficio *m* de maitines/vísperas (*en la Iglesia Anglicana*)

praying mantis /ˈpreɪɪŋˈmæntəs || ˌpreɪɪŋˈmæntɪs/ *n* mantis *f* religiosa, mamboretá *m* (CS)

pre- /ˈpriː/ *pref* 1 (in advance): **~planned** planeado de antemano *or* con anticipación; *see also* **precook, prewash** *etc* 2 (before): **a ~dinner drink** una copa antes de cenar, un aperitivo

preach /priːtʃ/ *vt* 1 (Relig) predicar*; **to ~ a sermon** dar* un sermón 2 (advocate) ‹*doctrine/ideas*› preconizar*; **he's always ~ing its virtues** siempre está proclamando sus virtudes

■ **preach** *vi* 1 (deliver sermon) predicar*; ***to ~ to the converted*** gastar saliva (*convenciendo a los que ya están convencidos*) 2 (give advice) (pej) **to ~ (TO/AT sb)** dar(le)* un sermón (A algn) (pey), sermonear (a algn) (fam & pey)

preacher /ˈpriːtʃər || ˈpriːtʃə(r)/ *n* 1 (one who preaches) predicador, -dora *m,f* 2 (minister) (AmE) pastor, -tora *m,f*

preamble /ˈpriˌæmbəl, priːˈæmbəl/ *n* preámbulo *m*

prearrange /ˈpriːəˈreɪndʒ/ *vt* 1 (arrange in advance) concertar* *or* acordar* de antemano 2 **prearranged** *past p* ‹*meeting*› concertado de antemano; ‹*signal/place/time*› convenido

precarious /prɪˈkeriəs || prɪˈkeəriəs/ *adj* precario

precariously /prɪˈkeriəsli/ *adv* precariamente

precaution /prɪˈkɔːʃən/ *n* precaución *f*; **as a ~** por *or* como precaución; **to take ~s** tomar precauciones; **are you taking ~s?** (euph) ¿te estás cuidando? (euf); **to take the ~ OF -ING** tener* la precaución DE + INF

precautionary /prɪˈkɔːʃəneri/ *adj* preventivo, de precaución

precede /prɪˈsiːd/ *vt* (frml) preceder a, anteceder a; **in the months preceding the invasion** en los meses que precedieron *or* antecedieron a la invasión; **the King was ~d by his courtiers** el rey iba precedido de sus cortesanos

■ **precede** *vi* 1 (come before) preceder 2 **preceding** *pres p* ‹*day/year*› anterior; ‹*page/chapter*› anterior, precedente

precedence /ˈpresədəns/ *n* [u] precedencia *f*; **a problem which takes ~ over all others** un problema que tiene prioridad *or* precedencia sobre todos los demás

precedent /ˈpresədənt/ *n* [c u] precedente *m*; **to set a ~ (for sth)** sentar* precedente (para algo); **without ~** sin precedentes

precept /ˈpriːsept/ *n* precepto *m*

precinct /ˈpriːsɪŋkt/ *n*

A 1 (delimited zone) (BrE): **shopping ~** centro *m*/zona *f* comercial; **pedestrian ~** zona *f* peatonal 2 (AmE) (police district) distrito *m* policial; (police station) comisaría *f* 3 (voting district) (AmE) distrito *m* electoral, circunscripción *f*

B **precincts** *pl* (of city) límites *mpl*; (of cathedral, castle, hospital) recinto *m*, predio(s) *m(pl)* (esp AmL)

precious[1] /ˈpreʃəs/ *adj*

A 1 (valuable) ‹*jewel/object*› precioso, valiosísimo; ~ **metal** metal *m* precioso; ~ **stone** piedra *f* preciosa; **we lost ~ time** perdimos tiempo precioso 2 (dear) querido; **to be ~ TO sb: this necklace is very ~ to her** le tiene mucho cariño a este collar; **your friendship is very ~ to me** tengo en gran estima tu amistad 3 (iro): **her ~ son** su queridísimo hijo (iró); **you can keep your ~ ring** guárdate tu maldito anillo

B (affected) preciosista, afectado

precious[2] *adv* (colloq) (*as intensifier*): ~ **few** muy pocos, poquísimos; **she's done ~ little to help** bien poco ha hecho para ayudar

precious[3] *n* (*as form of address*) tesoro

precipice /ˈpresəpəs || ˈpresɪpɪs/ *n* precipicio *m*

precipitate[1] /prɪˈsɪpəteɪt/ *vt*

A (bring about, hasten) (frml) ‹*crisis/event/incident*› precipitar

B (hurl) (frml) precipitar, despeñar; **I was ~d into making a decision** me empujaron a tomar una decisión precipitada

■ **precipitate** *vi* 1 (Chem) precipitarse 2 (Meteo) condensarse

precipitate[2] /prɪˈsɪpətət/ *adj* (liter) ‹*exit/departure*› precipitado; **let us not be ~** no nos precipitemos

precipitation /prɪˈsɪpəˈteɪʃən || prɪˌsɪprˈteɪʃən/ *n* [u] 1 (Meteo) precipitaciones *fpl* 2 (Chem) precipitación *f* 3 (haste) (frml) precipitación *f*

precipitous /prɪˈsɪpətəs || prɪˈsɪpɪtəs/ *adj* (frml) 1 ‹*drop/slope*› cortado a pico, escarpado 2 ‹*hasty*› precipitado

precis[1], **précis** /preɪˈsiː/ *n* (*pl* ~ /-z/) resumen *m*

precis[2], **précis** *vt* sintetizar*, hacer* un resumen de

precise /prɪˈsaɪs/ *adj* 1 (accurate) ‹*calculations/measurements*› exacto; ‹*description/instructions*› preciso 2 (specific) preciso; **at that ~ moment** en ese preciso momento; **there were about 60, 59 to be ~** había unos 60, 59 para ser exacto *or* preciso 3 (meticulous) minucioso

precisely /prɪˈsaɪsli/ *adv* 1 (accurately) ‹*calculate/measure/describe*› con precisión 2 (exactly): **we have ~ one hour** tenemos exactamente una hora; **at two o'clock ~** a las dos en punto; **~ because of that** precisamente por eso; **precisely!** ¡exacto!, ¡justamente! 3 (meticulously) con minuciosidad, con sumo cuidado

precision /prɪˈsɪʒən/ *n* [u] precisión *f*; (*before n*) ‹*instrument/tool*› de precisión; ~ **timing** sincronización *f*

preclude /prɪˈkluːd/ *vt* (frml) ‹*possibility*› excluir*, descartar; **to ~ sb FROM -ING** impedirle* a algn + INF

precocious /prɪˈkəʊʃəs/ *adj* precoz

precociousness /prɪˈkəʊʃəsnəs || prɪˈkəʊʃəsnɪs/, **precocity** /prɪˈkɑːsəti || prɪˈkɒsəti/ *n* [u] precocidad *f*

preconceived /'priːkən'siːvd/ *adj* (*before n*) preconcebido

preconception /'priːkən'sepʃən/ *n* idea *f* preconcebida

precondition /'priːkən'dɪʃən/ *n* condición *f* previa

precook /'priːkʊk/ *vt* precocinar

precursor /prɪ'kɜːrsər/ *n* (frml) precursor, -sora *m,f*

predate /'priː'deɪt/ *vt* (frml) 1 (precede) ser* anterior a 2 ‹*document/letter*› antedatar (frml), poner* una fecha anterior en

predator /'predətər/ *n* depredador *m*, predador *m*

predatory /'predətɔːri ‖ 'predətri/ *adj* ‹*animal*› predador, depredador; ‹*person*› rapaz

predecessor /'predəsesər/ *n* predecesor, -sora *m,f*

predestine /'priː'destən ‖ ˌpriː'destɪn/ *vt* predestinar; **to be ~d (to + INF)** estar* predestinado (A + INF)

predetermine /ˌpriːdɪ'tɜːrmən ‖ ˌpriːdɪ'tɜːmɪn/ *vt* 1 (foreordain) predeterminar 2 (arrange in advance) determinar de antemano 3 (work out in advance) prever*

predicament /prɪ'dɪkəmənt/ *n* aprieto *m*, apuro *m*; **to be in a ~** estar* en un aprieto *or* en un apuro

predicate /'predɪkət/ *n* predicado *m*

predicative /prɪ'dɪkətɪv/ *adj* predicativo

predict /prɪ'dɪkt/ *vt* ‹*result*› predecir*, pronosticar*; **oil prices are ~ed to fall** se prevé una baja en el precio del petróleo

predictable /prɪ'dɪktəbəl/ *adj* ‹*result/outcome*› previsible; **you're so ~** siempre sales con lo mismo

predictably /prɪ'dɪktəbli/ *adv* ‹*behave/react*› de manera previsible; **he gave a ~ stupid reply** respondió con una tontería, como era de esperar

prediction /prɪ'dɪkʃən/ *n* 1 [c] (forecast) pronóstico *m*, predicción *f*; (prophecy) profecía *f*; **to make a ~ about sth** predecir* *or* pronosticar* algo 2 [u] (act) predicción *f*

predilection /'predl̩'ekʃən ‖ ˌpriːdɪ'lekʃən/ *n* (frml) predilección *f*, preferencia *f*; **to have a ~ FOR sth/sb/-ING** tener* predilección POR algo/algn/+ INF

predispose /'priːdɪs'pəʊz/ *vt* (frml) predisponer*; **to ~ sb TO sth** predisponer* a algn A algo; **to ~ sb to + INF/-ING** predisponer* a algn A + INF

predisposition /'priːdɪspə'zɪʃən/ *n* **~ TO sth** predisposición *f* *or* propensión *f* A algo

predominance /prɪ'dɑːmənəns/ *n* [u] predominio *m*

predominant /prɪ'dɑːmənənt/ *adj* predominante

predominantly /prɪ'dɑːmənəntli ‖ prɪ'dɒmɪnəntli/ *adv* predominantemente

predominate /prɪ'dɑːməneɪt/ *vi* predominar

pre-eminence /priː'emənəns/ *n* [u] (frml) preeminencia *f*

pre-eminent /priː'emənənt/ *adj* (frml) preeminente

pre-empt /priː'empt/ *vt*

A (forestall) ‹*attack/move*› adelantarse a; **she ~ed their criticism by apologizing** evitó las críticas pidiendo excusas de antemano

B (AmE) ‹*land*› *ocupar terrenos del gobierno para conseguir el derecho preferente de compra*

pre-emptive /priː'emptɪv/ *adj* 1 ‹*attack/strike*› preventivo 2 ‹*right*› preferente

preen /priːn/ *vt* ‹*feathers*› arreglar con el pico

■ *v refl* **to ~ oneself** ‹‹*bird*›› arreglarse las plumas con el pico; ‹‹*person*›› acicalarse

■ **preen** *vi* ‹‹*bird*›› arreglarse las plumas con el pico

pre-exist /'priːɪg'zɪst/ *vi* (frml) 1 preexistir 2 **pre-existing** *pres p* preexistente

pre-existent /'priːɪg'zɪstənt/ *adj* preexistente, previo

prefab /'priːfæb/ *n* (colloq) vivienda *f* prefabricada

prefabricated /'priː'fæbrɪkeɪtɪd/ *adj* prefabricado

preface¹ /'prefəs/ *n* **~ (TO sth)** ‹*to book/speech*› prefacio *m* *or* prólogo *m* (DE algo); ‹*to event*› prólogo *m* (DE algo)

preface² *vt* ‹*book*› prologar*, escribir* el prefacio de; **she ~d this by saying that ...** a modo de introducción dijo que ...

prefect /'priːfekt/ *n*

A (BrE Educ) *alumno encargado de la disciplina*, ≈ monitor, -tora *m,f*

B (official) prefecto *m*

prefer /prɪ'fɜːr ‖ prɪ'fɜː(r)/ *vt* **-rr-**

A (like better) preferir*; **to ~ sth TO sth** preferir* algo A algo; **I ~ John to Bob** me gusta más John que Bob; **to ~ to + INF** preferir* + INF; **to ~ sth/sb to + INF** preferir* QUE algo/algn (+ *subj*); **I won't go if you'd ~ me to stay** si prefieres que me quede, no iré; **to ~ THAT** preferir* QUE (+ *subj*); **I'd ~ it if you went now** preferiría que te fueras ahora

B (Law): **to ~ charges (against sb)** presentar *or* formular cargos (en contra de algn)

preferable /'prefərəbəl/ *adj* preferible; **to be ~ TO sth/-ING** ser* preferible A algo/+ INF

preferably /'prefərəbli/ *adv* (*indep*) preferentemente, de preferencia; **I'd like a size 10, ~ in red** quisiera la talla 10, de ser posible en rojo

preference /'prefərəns/ *n*

A [c u] (liking, choice) preferencia *f*; **~ FOR sth** preferencia POR algo; **in order of ~** en *or* por orden de preferencia; **in ~ to sth** antes que algo

B [u] (priority) preferencia; **they give ~ to people with experience** dan preferencia a gente con experiencia

preferential /'prefə'rentʃəl ‖ ˌprefə'renʃəl/ *adj* (*before n*) preferente, preferencial; **to give ~ treatment to sb** dar* trato preferente *or* preferencial a algn

preferment /prɪ'fɜːrmənt ‖ prɪ'fɜːmənt/ *n* [u c] (frml) promoción *f*, ascenso *m*

prefix¹ /'priːfɪks/ *n* prefijo *m*

prefix² *vt* (add at start) (frml) **to ~ sth TO sth** anteponer* algo A algo; **to ~ sth WITH sth** encabezar* algo CON algo

pregnancy /'pregnənsi/ *n* [u c] (*pl* **-cies**) (of woman) embarazo *m*, preñez *f* (frml); (of animal) preñez *f*

pregnant /'pregnənt/ *adj*

A ‹*woman*› embarazada; ‹*cow/mare*› preñada; **she's five months ~** está embarazada de cinco meses

B (liter) 1 (meaningful) ‹*pause/silence*› elocuente, cargado *or* (liter) preñado de significado 2 (full) (*pred*) **to be ~ WITH sth** estar* preñado *or* grávido DE algo (liter)

preheat /'priː'hiːt/ *vt* precalentar*

prehensile /priː'hensəl ‖ priː'hensaɪl/ *adj* prensil

prehistoric /'priːhɪ'stɔːrɪk/ *adj* ‹*animal/man*› prehistórico; ‹*machine/ideas*› antediluviano, prehistórico

prehistory /'priː'hɪstəri/ *n* [u] prehistoria *f*

prejudge /'priː'dʒʌdʒ/ *vt* prejuzgar*

prejudice¹ /'predʒədəs ‖ 'predʒʊdɪs/ *n*

A [u c] (biased opinion) prejuicio *m*; **her lack of ~** su falta de prejuicios

B [u] (injury, harm) (frml) perjuicio *m*; **without ~ to your claim** sin perjuicio de su derecho; **to the ~ of sth/sb** en perjuicio *or* en detrimento de algo/algn

prejudice² *vt*

A (influence) predisponer*; **to ~ sth/sb AGAINST/IN FAVOR OF sth/sb** predisponer* algo/a algn EN CONTRA/A FAVOR DE algo/algn

B (harm) ‹*case/claim*› perjudicar*

prejudiced /'predʒədəst ‖ 'predʒʊdɪst/ *adj* ‹*person*› lleno de prejuicios, prejuiciado (AmL); **to be ~ AGAINST/IN FAVOR OF sth/sb** estar* predispuesto EN CONTRA DE/A FAVOR DE algo/algn

prejudicial /'predʒə'dɪʃəl ‖ ˌpredʒʊ'dɪʃəl/ *adj* (frml) (*pred*) **to be ~ TO sth** ser* perjudicial PARA algo

prelate /'prelət/ *n* prelado *m*

preliminary¹ /prɪ'lɪməneri ‖ prɪ'lɪmɪnəri/ *adj* preliminar; **the ~ rounds** (Sport) la etapa de clasificación previa, las *or* los preliminares (AmL)

preliminary² *n* (*pl* **-ries**) 1 (preamble) prolegómeno *m*; **let's dispense with the preliminaries and get down to business** omitamos los prolegómenos *or* preámbulos y vayamos al grano 2 **preliminaries** *pl* (Sport) etapa *f* de clasificación previa, preliminares *mpl* *or* *fpl*

prelims /prɪ'lɪmz, 'priːlɪmz/ *pl n* 1 (Sport) ▸ **preliminaries** 2 (in UK) *primeros exámenes en algunas universidades*

preload /priː'ləʊd/ *vt* precargar*

prelude /'preljuːd/ *n* 1 (introduction) **~ (TO sth)** preludio *m* (DE algo) 2 (Mus) preludio *m*

premarital /'priː'mærətl̩/ *adj* prematrimonial

premature /'priːmə'tʊr ‖ 'prematjʊə(r)/ *adj* prematuro; ‹*senility*› precoz; **their victory celebration was ~** cantaron victoria antes de tiempo

P

prematurely /'pri:mə'tʊrli/ *adv* prematuramente, antes de tiempo; **the baby was born ~** el niño fue prematuro

premed /'pri:'med/ *n*
A (premedication) medicación *f* previa (*administrada antes de la anestesia general*)
B (Educ) *curso de preparación para la carrera de medicina*

premeditated /pri:'medəteɪtəd/ *adj* premeditado

premenstrual /'pri:'menstruəl/ *adj* premenstrual; **~ syndrome/tension** tensión *f* premenstrual

premier /prɪ'mɪr || 'premiə(r)/ *n* primer ministro, primera ministra *m,f*, premier *mf*

premiere, première /prɪ'mɪr/ *n* estreno *m*

premiership /'premjərʃɪp/ *n*
A **1** (period) mandato *m* (*de primer ministro*) **2** (office) cargo *m* de primer ministro
B **1** (Sport, in England): **the P~** la Primera División

premise /'preməs || 'premɪs/ *n*
A (Phil) premisa *f*
B **premises** *pl* (building, site) local *m*; **they've moved to new ~s** se han mudado a un nuevo local (*or* a nuevas oficinas *etc*); **meals are cooked on the ~s** las comidas se preparan en el mismo establecimiento; **they were escorted off the ~s** se los hizo salir del local; **licensed ~s** (BrE) *establecimiento autorizado para vender bebidas alcohólicas*

premium¹ /'pri:miəm/ *n* (Fin) **1** (*insurance* ~) prima *f* (de seguro) **2** (surcharge) recargo *m*; **to put a ~ on sth** hacer* hincapié en algo, darle* mucha importancia a algo; ***to be at a ~*** (in short supply) escasear; (lit: above par) estar* por encima de la par; **when time is at a ~** cuando el tiempo apremia **3** (bonus) prima *f*

premium² *adj* (*before n*) de primera, de alta calidad

Premium Bond *n* (in UK) *bono del Estado que permite ganar dinero participando en sorteos mensuales*

premonition /'pri:mə'nɪʃən/ *n* premonición *f*, presentimiento *m*; **to have a ~ of sth/that ...** tener* el presentimiento de algo/de que ..., presentir* algo/que ...

prenatal /'pri:'neɪtl/ *adj* (esp AmE) ‹*care/checkup*› prenatal; **~ clinic** *consulta médica para mujeres embarazadas*

prenuptial /pri:'nʌptʃjəl/ *adj* ‹*courtship*› prenupcial; **~ agreement** acuerdo *m* prematrimonial

preoccupation /pri:'ɑ:kjə'peɪʃən/ *n* [c u]
A (obsession) obsesión *f*; **~ WITH sth**: **his excessive ~ with hygiene** su manía *or* su obsesión con la higiene
B (concern): **my main ~ was not to offend my parents** lo que más me importaba era no ofender a mis padres

preoccupied /pri:'ɑ:kjəpaɪd || ,pri:'ɒkjʊpaɪd/ *adj* (absorbed) absorto, ensimismado; (worried) preocupado; **to be ~ WITH sth**: **I've been rather ~ with the wedding plans** me estado muy ocupado con los preparativos para la boda; **I was so ~ with my own thoughts that ...** estaba tan absorto en mis pensamientos que ...

preoccupy /pri:'ɑ:kjəpaɪ || ,pri:'ɒkjʊpaɪ/ *vt* **-pies, -pying, -pied** preocupar

preordain /'pri:ɔ:r'deɪn/ *vt* predestinar, preordinar (frml)

prep¹ /prep/ *n*
A [c] (colloq) (in US) ▸ **preparatory school 1**
B [u] (BrE) **1** (homework) deberes *mpl*, tarea *f* **2** (period) (hora *f* de) estudio *m*

prep² *vi* **-pp-** (AmE colloq) **1** (attend prep school) asistir a un **preparatory school 1** **2** (prepare) **to ~ (FOR sth)** estudiar (PARA algo)

prepackaged /'pri:'pækɪdʒd/, **prepacked** /'pri:'pækt/ *adj* empaquetado, preempaquetado

prepaid /'pri:'peɪd/ *adj* ‹*envelope*› con franqueo pagado; ‹*advertisement/insertion*› pagado por adelantado; **~ postage** franqueo *m or* porte *m* pagado

preparation /'prepə'reɪʃən/ *n*
A **1** [u] (act) preparación *f*; **in ~ for**: **they decorated the room in ~ for the party** adornaron la habitación para la fiesta; **the buildings had been cleaned in ~ for the visit** se habían limpiado los edificios como parte de los preparativos para la visita **2** [c] **preparations** *pl* (arrangements) **~ (FOR sth)** preparativos *mpl* (PARA *or* DE algo)
B [c u] (substance) preparado *m*

preparatory /prɪ'pærətɔ:ri || prɪ'pærətri/ *adj* **1** preparatorio, preliminar **2** **preparatory to** (*as prep*) antes de, como preparación para

preparatory school *n* (frml) **1** (in US) *colegio secundario privado* **2** (in UK) *colegio primario privado*

prepare /prɪ'per || prɪ'peə(r)/ *vt*
A (make ready) preparar; **~ yourself for a shock!** ¡prepárate!; **to ~ the ground for sth** preparar el terreno para algo
B (make, put together) ‹*speech/meal*› preparar; ‹*report*› redactar
■ **prepare** *vi* **to ~ (FOR sth)** prepararse (PARA algo)

prepared /prɪ'perd || prɪ'peəd/ *adj* **1** (ready in advance) ‹*speech/statement*› preparado; **I wasn't ~ for this** no contaba con esto, esto no lo había previsto; **be ~ to leave at any moment** estáte preparado para salir en cualquier momento **2** (willing) (*pred*) **to be ~ to + INF** estar* dispuesto A + INF

prepayment /'pri:'peɪmənt/ *n* [u c] pago *m* anticipado

preponderance /prɪ'pɑ:ndərəns || prɪ'pɒndərəns/ *n* [u] (frml) preponderancia *f*, predominio *m*

preposition /'prepə'zɪʃən/ *n* preposición *f*

prepossessing /'pri:pə'zesɪŋ/ *adj* (frml) (*usu neg*) atractivo, agradable

preposterous /prɪ'pɑ:stərəs/ *adj* absurdo, ridículo

preppy, preppie /'prepi/ *n* (*pl* **-pies**) (AmE) niño, -ña *m,f* bien, pijo, -ja *m,f* (Esp fam), popis *mf* (Méx fam), pituco, -ca *m,f* (CS fam), pije *mf* (Chi fam)

preprogram, (BrE also) **preprogramme** /'pri:'prəʊgræm/ *vt* preprogramar

prep school *n* ▸ **preparatory school 2**

prerecord /'pri:rɪ'kɔ:rd || ,pri:rɪ'kɔ:d/ *vt* grabar con anterioridad, pregrabar

pre-release /,pri:rɪ'li:s/ *adj* (*before n*) **1** (before official release) ‹*version/software*› pre-release (*anterior a su distribución comercial*) **2** ‹*prisoner/detainee*› en periodo de preliberación

prerequisite /'pri:'rekwəzət || ,pri:'rekwɪzɪt/ *n* requisito *m* esencial, condición *f* sine qua non

prerogative /prɪ'rɑ:gətɪv || prɪ'rɒgətɪv/ *n* **1** (right) prerrogativa *f*; **that's your ~** estás en todo tu derecho **2** (exclusive property) patrimonio *m* exclusivo

Pres (title) = **President**

presage¹ /'presɪdʒ, prɪ'seɪdʒ/ *vt* (liter) presagiar

presage² *n* (liter) presagio *m*

Presbyterian¹ /'prezbə'tɪriən/ *n* presbiteriano, -na *m,f*

Presbyterian² *adj* presbiteriano

presbytery /'prezbəteri || 'prezbɪtri/ *n* **1** (part of church) presbiterio *m* **2** (in RC church) casa *f* parroquial

preschool¹ /'pri:'sku:l/ *adj* (*before n*) ‹*child*› de edad preescolar; ‹*education*› preescolar

preschool² *n* [c u] (AmE) jardín *m* de infancia, kindergarten *m* (AmL), jardín *m* de niños (Méx), jardín *m* de infantes (RPl), jardín *m* infantil (Chi)

prescient /'preʃiənt/ *adj* (frml) profético, clarividente

prescribe /prɪ'skraɪb/ *vt* **1** ‹*drug*› recetar; ‹*rest*› recomendar* **2** (order, require) (frml) prescribir* (frml); **~d reading** libros *mpl* de lectura obligatoria

prescription /prɪ'skrɪpʃən/ *n* receta *f*; **to fill** *o* (BrE) **make up a ~** preparar una receta; **available on ~ only** en venta solamente bajo receta; (*before n*) **~ charge** (in UK) *contribución del paciente al costo de las medicinas recetadas*

prescriptive /prɪ'skrɪptɪv/ *adj* preceptivo

preseason *n* (*no pl*) pretemporada *f*

presence /'prezṇs/ *n* **1** [u] (being present) presencia *f*; **in the ~ of sb** en presencia de algn; **to make one's ~ felt** hacerse* sentir *or* notar **2** [c] (spirit) espíritu *m* **3** [u] (charisma) presencia *f*

presence of mind *n* [u] presencia *f* de ánimo

present¹ /prɪ'zent/ *vt*
A **1** (give, hand over) **to ~ sth TO sb** entregarle* algo A algn, hacerle* entrega de algo A algn (frml); **to ~ sb WITH sth** obsequiar a algn CON algo (frml), obsequiarle algo A algn (esp AmL frml) **2** (confront) **to ~ sb WITH sth**: **it ~s me with a whole host of problems** esto me plantea toda una serie de problemas; **we were ~ed with a very difficult situation** nos vimos frente a una situación muy difícil
B ‹*ticket/passport/account/motion/bill*› presentar; ‹*ideas*› presentar, exponer*; **the way it's ~ed is very important** la presentación es muy importante
C **1** (constitute) ser*, constituir*; **they ~ed an easy target**

eran un blanco fácil 2 (provide) ‹view/perspective› presentar, ofrecer*
D (Cin, Theat, Rad, TV) presentar
E (introduce) (frml) presentar; **may I ~ my husband?** permítame presentarle a mi marido; **to ~ sb TO sb** presentarle algn A algn
F (Mil): **~ arms!** ¡presenten armas!
■ *v refl* 1 (arise) «*problem/opportunity*» presentarse, surgir* 2 (appear) (frml) «*person*» presentarse 3 (display, show) presentarse; **this is how the situation ~s itself to me** así es como yo veo la situación
■ **present** *vi* (Med) «*patient/disease*» presentarse

present[2] /'preznt/ *adj*
A (at scene) (*pred*) **to be ~** estar* presente; **I wasn't ~ at the meeting** no estuve en la reunión; **all those ~** todos los presentes; **how many were ~?** ¿cuántas personas había?; **he was ~ at the scene of the accident** presenció el accidente
B (*before n*) 1 (current) actual; **at the ~ time** *o* **moment** en este momento 2 (Ling): **the ~ tense** el presente

present[3] /'preznt/ *n*
A [u] 1 (current time): **the ~** el presente; **at ~** en este momento, actualmente; **for the ~** por ahora, por el momento; **to live for the ~** vivir el momento; **there's no time like the ~** (set phrase) no dejes para mañana lo que puedas hacer hoy 2 (Ling) **the ~** el presente
B [c] (gift) regalo *m*; **to give sb a ~** regalarle algo a algn, hacerle* un regalo a algn

presentable /prɪ'zentəbəl/ *adj* presentable; **I'd better make myself ~** más vale que me arregle un poco

presentation /'pri:zen'teɪʃən/ *n*
A 1 [u c] (of gift, prize) entrega *f* 2 [c] (gift) (frml) obsequio *m* (frml), presente *m* (frml)
B 1 [u] (of document, bill, proposal) presentación *f*; **on ~ of this voucher** presentando *or* al presentar este vale 2 [c] (display) (Busn) presentación *f*, demostración *f* 3 [c] (show, production) producción *f*
C [u] (manner of presenting) presentación *f*

present-day /'prezntdeɪ/ *adj* (*before n*) actual, de hoy (en) día

presenter /prɪ'zentər/ *n* (BrE) presentador, -dora *m,f*

presently /'prezntli/ *adv* 1 (now) en este momento, actualmente 2 (soon): **I'll be with you ~** enseguida *or* en un momento estoy contigo; **~, he started to come round** pronto empezó a recobrar el conocimiento

preservation /'prezər'veɪʃən || ˌprezə'veɪʃən/ *n* [u] (of food) conservación *f*; (of specimens) conservación *f*, preservación *f*; (of building) conservación *f*

preservative /prɪ'zɜ:rvətɪv/ *n* [u c] conservante *m*

preserve[1] /prɪ'zɜ:rv || prɪ'zɜ:v/ *vt*
A 1 ‹*food*› conservar; ‹*specimen*› conservar, preservar 2 (Culin) ‹*fruit/vegetables*› hacer* conserva de 3 (maintain) ‹*building/traditions*› conservar; ‹*dignity*› conservar, mantener*
B (protect) (liter) proteger*; **heaven ~ us!** ¡Dios nos ampare!; **to ~ sb FROM sth** proteger* a algn DE algo

preserve[2] *n*
A [c] 1 (exclusive privilege, sphere): **this is the ~ of experts** esto es del dominio exclusivo de los expertos; **to be a male ~** ser* terreno *or* coto exclusivamente masculino, ser* terreno vedado a las mujeres 2 (restricted area): **game ~** coto *m or* vedado *m* de caza; **wildlife ~** (AmE) reserva *f* de animales
B (Culin) 1 [u c] (jam, jelly) confitura *f*, mermelada *f* 2 [u c] (fruit in syrup) (BrE) conserva *f*

preset /'pri:'set/ *vt* preprogramar, programar

preshrunk /'pri:'ʃrʌŋk/ *adj* preencogido

preside /prɪ'zaɪd/ *vi* presidir; **to ~ OVER sth**: **he ~d over the meeting** presidió la reunión

presidency /'prezədənsi/ *n* 1 (office) presidencia *f* 2 (period) presidencia *f*, mandato *m* (presidencial)

president /'prezədənt || 'prezɪdənt/ *n* 1 (of state) presidente, -ta *m,f* 2 (of society) presidente, -ta *m,f* 3 (of bank, corporation) (esp AmE) director, -tora *m,f*, presidente, -ta *m,f* 4 (of university) (AmE) rector, -tora *m,f*

presidential /'prezə'dentʃəl/ *adj* (*before n*) presidencial

press[1] /pres/ *n*
A [u] 1 (newspapers, journalists) prensa *f*; **the ~** la prensa; **the freedom of the ~** la libertad de prensa; (*before n*) ‹*box/gallery*› de (la) prensa; **~ agency** (BrE) agencia *f* de prensa; **~ agent** encargado, -da *m,f* de prensa; **~ clipping** *o* (BrE) **cutting** recorte *m* de prensa; **~ office** oficina *f* de prensa; **~ photographer** reportero gráfico, reportera gráfica *m,f*; **~ release** comunicado *m* de prensa; **~ run** (AmE) tirada *f* 2 (treatment by newspapers): **to get a good/bad ~** tener* buena/mala prensa, tener* buena/mala acogida por parte de la prensa
B [c] 1 (*printing ~*) prensa *f*, imprenta *f*; **to go to ~** entrar en prensa; **at the time of going to ~** al cierre de la edición 2 (publishing house) editorial *f*
C [c] (for pressing — grapes, flowers, machine parts) prensa *f*; (— trousers) prensa *f* plancha-pantalones

press[2] *vt*
A (push) ‹*button/doorbell*› apretar*, pulsar; ‹*pedal/footbrake*› pisar; **we were ~ed up against the wall by the crowd** el gentío nos apretujó contra la pared
B 1 (squeeze) apretar* 2 (in press) ‹*grapes/olives/flowers*› prensar 3 ‹*disk/album*› imprimir* 4 ‹*clothes*› planchar
C 1 (put pressure on): **when ~ed, she admitted it** cuando la presionaron, lo admitió; **to ~ sb FOR sth/to + INF**: **I ~ed him for an answer** insistí en que *or* exigí que me diera una respuesta; **they ~ed him to change his policy** ejercieron presión sobre él para que cambiara de política 2 (pursue): **they went on strike to ~ their demands** fueron a la huelga en apoyo de sus reivindicaciones; **to ~ charges against sb** presentar *or* formular cargos en contra de algn; **I didn't ~ the point** no insistí más
■ **press** *vi*
A 1 (exert pressure): **~ firmly** presione *or* apriete con fuerza; **to ~ (down) ON sth** apretar* algo, hacer* presión SOBRE algo 2 (crowd, push) «*people*» apretujarse, apiñarse
B (urge, pressurize) presionar; **to ~ FOR sth**: **they've been ~ing for an inquiry** han estado presionando para que se haga una investigación; **time ~es** *o* **is ~ing** el tiempo apremia

Phrasal verbs
- **press ahead** [v ▸ adv] **to ~ ahead (WITH sth)** seguir* adelante (CON algo)
- **press home** [v ▸ o ▸ adv, v ▸ adv ▸ o] ‹*advantage*› aprovechar
- **press on** [v ▸ adv] **to ~ on (WITH sth)** seguir* adelante (CON algo)

press conference *n* rueda *f or* conferencia *f* de prensa

pressed /prest/ *adj* (*pred*): **to be ~ for time** estar* *or* andar* escaso de tiempo; **we'll be hard ~ to replace him** nos va a resultar difícil reemplazarlo

press: ~ gang *n* (Hist) destacamento *m* de enganche; **~-gang** *vt* **to ~-gang sb INTO sth/-ING** obligar* *or* forzar* a algn A algo/+ INF

pressing /'presɪŋ/ *adj* 1 ‹*engagements/concerns*› urgente; ‹*need/desire*› apremiante 2 ‹*request/invitation*› insistente

press: ~man /'presmæn || 'presmən/ *n* (*pl* **-men** /-men || -mən/) 1 (journalist) periodista *m* 2 (printing press operator) (AmE) tipógrafo *m*; **~ stud** *n* (BrE) broche *m or* botón *m* de presión (AmL), cierre *m* automático (Esp); **~-up** *n* (BrE) flexión *f* (de brazos *or* de pecho), fondo *m*

pressure[1] /'preʃər || 'preʃə(r)/ *n*
A [u c] 1 (Phys) presión *f*; **high/low ~** (Meteo) altas/bajas presiones; (*before n*) **~ gauge** manómetro *m* 2 (press, touch) presión *f*; **to put ~ on sth** hacer* presión sobre algo
B [u] (influence, force) presión *f*; **they are under ~ to accept the offer** los están presionando para que acepten la oferta; **to bring ~ to bear on sb** ejercer* presión sobre algn; **to put ~ on sb** presionar a algn; **they put ~ on him to resign** lo presionaron para que renunciara a su puesto; **to put/pile on the ~** (colloq) apretar* los tornillos
C [u c] (demands, stress): **~ of work prevents me from coming** no puedo asistir por razones de trabajo; **the ~s of city life** las presiones *or* las tensiones a las que somete la vida urbana; **I've been under a lot of ~ recently** últimamente he estado muy agobiado

pressure[2] *vt* presionar; **to ~ sb to + INF** presionar a algn PARA QUE (+ *subj*); **to ~ sb INTO -ING**: **he was ~d into withdrawing from the competition** lo presionaron hasta que se retiró del concurso

P

pressure: ~ **cooker** *n* olla *f* a presión *or* (Esp tb) olla *f* exprés *or* (Méx) olla *f* presto; ~ **group** *n* grupo *m* de presión; ~ **pan** *n* (AmE) ▸ ~ **cooker**

pressurize /ˈpreʃəraɪz/ *vt* 1 (Aerosp, Aviat) presurizar* 2 (urge) (BrE) ▸ **pressure²**

pressurized water reactor /ˈpreʃəraɪzd/ *n* reactor *m* de agua a presión

prestige /preˈstiːʒ/ *n* [u] prestigio *m*

prestigious /preˈstɪdʒəs/ *adj* prestigioso

presto /ˈprestəʊ/ *see* **hey presto**

presumably /prɪˈzuːməbli || prɪˈzjuːməbli/ *adv* (*indep*): **you've taken the necessary steps,** ~ supongo *or* me imagino que habrás tomado las medidas pertinentes

presume /prɪˈzuːm || prɪˈzjuːm/ *vt* 1 (assume) suponer*; **I** ~ **so** supongo *or* me imagino que sí; **missing,** ~**d dead** desaparecido, dado por muerto; **a defendant is** ~**d innocent until proved guilty** un acusado es inocente hasta que se demuestre lo contrario; **Mr Vidal, I** ~**?** usted debe (de) ser el señor Vidal ¿o me equivoco? 2 (dare) **to** ~ **to + INF** atreverse A + INF

■ **presume** *vi*: **I have already** ~**d on/upon your generosity quite enough** ya he abusado bastante de su generosidad

presumption /prɪˈzʌmpʃən/ *n* 1 [u] (boldness) atrevimiento *m*, osadía *f* 2 [c u] (assumption) suposición *f*, presunción *f*; **the** ~ **is that ...** se supone que ...

presumptive /prɪˈzʌmptɪv/ *adj* presunto

presumptuous /prɪˈzʌmptʃəs/ *adj* impertinente

presuppose /ˈpriːsəˈpəʊz/ *vt* presuponer*

pretax /ˈpriːˈtæks/ *adj* ‹*profit/income*› bruto, antes de impuestos

preteen /ˈpriːˈtiːn/ *n* (AmE) preadolescente *mf*, niño, -ña *m,f* (*de 9 a 12 años*)

pretence *n* (BrE) ▸ **pretense**

pretend¹ /prɪˈtend/ *vt*

A (feign) ‹*ignorance/surprise*› fingir*, aparentar; **he** ~**ed he hadn't seen us** fingió que no nos había visto, hizo como si no nos hubiera visto; **they** ~**ed to be students** se hicieron pasar por estudiantes

B (make believe): **just** ~ **I'm not here** tú haz como si yo no estuviera; **let's** ~ **I'm the mother and you're the father** mira, yo era la mamá y tú eras el papá

C (claim) pretender; **I won't** ~ **to give you advice** no voy a pretender darte consejos

■ **pretend** *vi*

A (feign) fingir*

B (lay claim) (frml) **to** ~ **TO sth** pretender algo; **I don't** ~ **to any knowledge of ...** no pretendo saber de ...

pretend² *adj* (*used to or by children*) ‹*money/gun*› de mentira (fam)

pretender /prɪˈtendər || prɪˈtendə(r)/ *n* ~ **(TO sth)** pretendiente *mf* (A algo)

pretense, (BrE) **pretence** /ˈpriːtens, prɪˈtens || prɪˈtens/ *n*

A [c u] (simulation, display): **her air of confidence is a** ~ ese aire de seguridad suyo es fingido; **let's drop this** ~**!** ¡vamos a dejarnos de fingir!; **to make a** ~ **of sth** fingir* algo; **he made no** ~ **of impartiality** no disimuló su parcialidad; **under (the)** ~ **of wanting to help** con el pretexto de querer ayudar; **under false** ~**s** de manera fraudulenta

B (frml) 1 [c u] (claim) ~ **(TO sth)**: **he makes no** ~ **to virtue** no pretende ser virtuoso, no se las da de virtuoso 2 [u] (pretentiousness) pretensión *f*

pretension /prɪˈtentʃən/ *n* (claim) (*often pl*) pretensión *f*

pretentious /prɪˈtentʃəs || prɪˈtenʃəs/ *adj* (trying to appear — profound, sophisticated) pretencioso, con pretensiones de intelectual (*or* culto *etc*); (— elegant, luxurious) presuntuoso, pretencioso, con pretensiones de elegancia (*or* refinamiento *etc*); (if also in bad taste) cursi *or* (Chi tb) siútico

pretext /ˈpriːtekst/ *n* pretexto *m*; **on** *o* **under the** ~ **of** con el pretexto de, so pretexto de (frml)

prettily /ˈprɪtḷi || ˈprɪtɪli/ *adv* con gracia, atractivamente

pretty¹ /ˈprɪti/ *adj* **-tier, -tiest** ‹*girl/baby*› bonito, guapo, lindo (AmL); ‹*eyes/smile/name*› bonito, lindo (AmL); ‹*blouse/dress*› bonito, lindo (AmL); **it wasn't a** ~ **sight** no era nada agradable *or* (AmL tb) lindo de ver

pretty² *adv* (rather, quite) bastante; (emphatic) bien, muy; ~ **good** bastante bueno; **I** ~ **soon realized that ...** tardé bien *or* muy poco en darme cuenta de que ...; **you have to be** ~ **stupid to believe that!** ¡hay que ser bien *or* muy tonto para creerse eso!; ~ **much** más o menos; **they lost** ~ **well every game** perdieron casi *or* prácticamente todos los partidos

pretzel /ˈpretsəl/ *n* galleta *f* salada (*gen en forma de 8*)

prevail /prɪˈveɪl/ *vi*

A (triumph) «*justice/common sense*» prevalecer*, imponerse*; «*enemy*» imponerse*; **to** ~ **OVER/AGAINST sb/sth** prevalecer* SOBRE algn/algo

B (predominate) «*attitude/pessimism*» preponderar, predominar, reinar; «*situation*» reinar, imperar

Phrasal verb

• **prevail on, prevail upon** [v ▸ prep ▸ o] (frml) convencer*; **he was not to be** ~**ed upon** no se dejó convencer

prevailing /prɪˈveɪlɪŋ/ *adj* (*before n*) ‹*wind*› preponderante; ‹*trend/view*› imperante, preponderante; ‹*uncertainty*› reinante; **in the** ~ **economic climate** en el actual clima económico

prevalence /ˈprevələns/ *n* [u] 1 (widespread occurrence) preponderancia *f*; **the increasing** ~ **of divorce** el número cada vez mayor de divorcios 2 (predominance) predominio *m*; ~ **OVER sth** predominio SOBRE algo

prevalent /ˈprevələnt/ *adj* frecuente, corriente; **in areas where the disease is** ~ en zonas donde la enfermedad está extendida

prevaricate /prɪˈværəkeɪt || prɪˈværɪkeɪt/ *vi* 1 (not answer directly) andarse* con rodeos, recurrir a evasivas 2 (lie) (AmE) mentir*

prevarication /prɪˈværəˈkeɪʃən/ *n* 1 [u] (misleading answers) evasivas *fpl* 2 [c] (lie) (AmE) mentira *f*

prevent /prɪˈvent/ *vt* 1 (hinder) impedir*; **to** ~ **sb/sth (FROM) -ING, to** ~ **sb's/sth's -ING** impedir* QUE algn/algo (+ *subj*); **she was** ~**ed from attending the conference by a sudden illness** una repentina enfermedad impidió que asistiera *or* le impidió asistir al congreso 2 (forestall) ‹*crime/disease/accident*› prevenir*, evitar

preventable /prɪˈventəbəl/ *adj* evitable

preventative /prɪˈventətɪv/ *adj* ▸ **preventive**

prevention /prɪˈventʃən || prɪˈvenʃən/ *n* [u] prevención *f*; ~ ***is better than cure*** más vale prevenir que curar

preventive /prɪˈventɪv/ *adj* ‹*measure/action*› preventivo; ~ **medicine** medicina *f* preventiva

preview /ˈpriːvjuː/ *n* 1 (advance showing) preestreno *m* 2 (trailer) avance *m*, trailer *m* (Esp), sinopsis *f* (CS) 3 (foretaste) anticipo *m*, adelanto *m*

previous /ˈpriːviəs/ *adj* 1 (earlier) (*before n*) ‹*occasion/attempt/page*› anterior; ‹*experience/knowledge*› previo; **on the** ~ **day** el día anterior, la víspera; **I had a** ~ **engagement** ya tenía un compromiso, tenía un compromiso previo 2 **previous to** (*as prep*) anterior a; ~ **to this** anteriormente

previously /ˈpriːviəsli/ *adv* antes

prewar /ˈpriːˈwɔːr/ *adj* de antes de la guerra, de preguerra

prewash /ˈpriːˈwɔːʃ || ˌpriːˈwɒʃ/ *n* prelavado *m*

prey /preɪ/ *n* [u] presa *f*; **he fell** ~ **to doubts** lo asaltaron las dudas, fue presa de la duda

Phrasal verb

• **prey on, prey upon** [v ▸ prep ▸ o] 1 ‹*animal*› (hunt) cazar*; (feed on) alimentarse de 2 (exploit) explotar; **drug dealers who** ~ **on youngsters** traficantes de droga que explotan a *or* se aprovechan de los jóvenes; ▸ **mind¹ A1**

price¹ /praɪs/ *n*

A (Busn, Fin) precio *m*; (of stocks) cotización *f*, precio *m*; **house** ~**s** el precio de la vivienda; **I got a good** ~ **for the car** vendí bien el coche; **they're the same** ~ valen *or* cuestan lo mismo; **at a** ~ **of £80** por 80 libras; **at half** ~ a mitad de precio; **accommodation is available, at** *o* **for a** ~ es posible encontrar alojamiento, pero sale *or* cuesta caro; **to go up/down in** ~ subir/bajar de precio; **I couldn't put a** ~ **on it** no sabría decir cuánto vale; **I'll take the job, if the** ~ **is right** aceptaré el trabajo si (me) pagan bien; (*before n*) ~ **list** lista *f* de precios; **it's out of my** ~ **range** cuesta más de lo que puedo pagar; ~ **rise** subida *f* *or* (RPl tb) suba *f* de precios

p

B (cost, sacrifice) precio *m*; **victory was won at a terrible ~** se pagó muy cara la victoria; **they want peace at any ~** quieren la paz cueste lo que cueste *or* a toda costa; **not at any ~!** ¡de ningún modo!, ¡por nada del mundo!; **what ~ peace?** ¿va a ser posible lograr la paz?; ***to pay a/the ~ for sth*** pagar* caro algo; **that's a small ~ to pay for independence** bien vale la pena ese sacrificio para ser independiente

C (value) (liter) precio *m*; **it's beyond** *o* **without ~** no tiene precio, es invalorable; **one cannot put a ~ on freedom** la libertad no tiene precio; **she sets a high ~ on loyalty** valora mucho la lealtad

price² *vt* **1** (fix price of) (*often pass*): **their products are reasonably ~d** sus productos tienen precios razonables; **it was originally ~d at over $300** su precio original era de más de 300 dólares; **they have ~d themselves out of the market** han subido tanto los precios que se han quedado sin compradores (*or* clientes *etc*) **2** (mark price on) ponerle* el precio a; **all items must be clearly ~d** todos los artículos deben llevar el precio claramente indicado

price: **~-cutting** *n* [u] rebaja *f* de precios; **~-fixing** /ˈpraɪs,fɪksɪŋ/ *n* [u] (as commercial activity) fijación *f* de precios; (to eliminate competition) fijación *f* oligopolítica

priceless /ˈpraɪsləs || ˈpraɪslɪs/ *adj* **1** (invaluable) inestimable, invalorable (CS) **2** (very amusing) (colloq) para morirse de risa (fam)

price tag *n* etiqueta *f* (*del precio*), precio *m*; **a painting with a $2,500 ~ ~** (colloq) un cuadro de 2.500 dólares

pricey, pricy /ˈpraɪsi/ *adj* **pricier, priciest** (colloq) ‹*item*› carito (fam); ‹*store*› carero (fam)

pricing /ˈpraɪsɪŋ/ *n* [u] fijación *f* de precios; (*before n*) **~ policy** política *f* de precios

prick¹ /prɪk/ *vt*

A (pierce, wound) pinchar, picar* (Méx); **to ~ a hole in sth** hacerle* un agujero a algo; **that ~ed his conscience** eso hizo que le remordiera la conciencia

B **~ (up)** ‹*ears*› «*dog*» levantar, parar (AmL); **she ~ed up her ears at the mention of France** aguzó el oído *or* (AmL fam) paró la oreja al oír hablar de Francia

■ **prick** *vi* pinchar; «*conscience*» remorder*; **a ~ing sensation** un picor

prick² *n*

A **1** (act) pinchazo *m*, piquete *m* (Méx); **to feel the ~ of conscience** tener* remordimientos de conciencia; ***to kick against the ~s*** dar* coces contra el aguijón, tener* una actitud rebelde **2** (mark) agujero *m*

B (vulg) (penis) verga *f* (vulg), polla *f* (Esp vulg)

prickle¹ /ˈprɪkəl/ *n* **1** [c] (thorn) espina *f* **2** [c] (on hedgehog) púa *f* **3** [u] (sensation) picor *m*

prickle² *vi* «*wool*» picar*; «*beard*» pinchar, picar* (Méx); «*skin/scalp*» picar*

prickly /ˈprɪkli/ *adj* **-lier, -liest**

A **1** (with prickles) ‹*plant*› espinoso; ‹*animal*› con púas **2** (scratchy) ‹*wool*› que pica; ‹*beard*› que pincha *or* (Méx) pica; **~ feeling** picor *m*

B (colloq) **1** ‹*person*› quisquilloso, difícil, irritable **2** ‹*issue/problem*› espinoso, peliagudo (fam)

prickly: **~ heat** *n* [u] fiebre *f* miliar; **~ pear** *n* (fruit) tuna *f*, higo *m* chumbo; (plant) nopal *m*, tuna *f*, chumbera *f*

pride¹ /praɪd/ *n*

A [u] **1** (self-respect) orgullo *m*; **false ~** vanidad *f*; **to take ~ in sth**: **she takes great ~ in her work** se toma muy en serio su trabajo; **we can take ~ in our success** podemos enorgullecernos *or* estar orgullosos de nuestro éxito; ***to have*** *o* ***take ~ of place*** ocupar* el lugar de honor; ***to swallow one's ~*** tragarse* el orgullo *or* el amor propio **2** (conceit) orgullo *m*, soberbia *f*; **~ *goes before a fall*** más dura será la caída

B [c] **1** (source of pride) orgullo *m*; **the ~ of the collection** la joya *or* el orgullo de la colección; **she is her mother's ~ and joy** es el orgullo de su madre **2** (finest part) (liter) flor *f* (liter)

C [c] (of lions) manada *f*

pride² *v refl* **to ~ oneself ON sth/-ING** enorgullecerse* *or* estar* orgulloso DE algo/+ INF; **he ~s himself on his punctuality** se precia de ser puntual

priest /priːst/ *n* sacerdote *m*; (*parish* **~**) cura *m* (párroco)

priestess /ˈpriːstəs || ˈpriːstes/ *n* sacerdotisa *f*

priesthood /ˈpriːsthʊd/ *n* [u] **1** (office) sacerdocio *m*; **to enter the ~** hacerse* sacerdote, ser* ordenado sacerdote **2** (clergy) clero *m*

priestly /ˈpriːstli/ *adj* sacerdotal

prig /prɪg/ *n* mojigato, -ta *m,f*

priggish /ˈprɪgɪʃ/ *adj* mojigato

prim /prɪm/ *adj* **-mer, -mest** **1** (prudish) mojigato, gazmoño; (affected) remilgado, repipi (Esp fam); **she's so ~ and proper!** es tan correcta y formal **2** (neat) cuidado

prima ballerina /ˈpriːmə/ *n* primera bailarina *f*

primacy /ˈpraɪməsi/ *n* (frml) primacía *f*

prima donna /ˈpriːməˈdɑːnə || ˌpriːməˈdɒnə/ *n* **1** (Mus) prima donna *f*, diva *f* **2** (actor, actress, singer) (pej) divo, -va *m,f* (pey)

primaeval *adj* (BrE) ▸ **primeval**

prima facie¹ /ˈpraɪməˈfeɪʃə || ˌpraɪməˈfeɪʃiː/ *adj* (frml): **~ ~ evidence** (Law) presunciones de hecho; **to have a ~ ~ case** parecer* tener razón a primera vista

prima facie² *adv* (frml) a primera vista, prima facie (frml)

primarily /praɪˈmerəli || ˈpraɪmərɪli/ *adv* fundamentalmente, principalmente, ante todo

primary¹ /ˈpraɪmeri || ˈpraɪməri/ *adj*

A (principal) ‹*purpose/role/aim*› primordial, principal

B **1** (first, basic) ‹*source/energy*› primario; ‹*industry*› de base **2** ‹*education*› primario

primary² *n* (*pl* **-ries**)

A (in US) (Govt) primaria *f*

B **~ (color)** color *m* primario *or* fundamental

C **~ (school)** escuela *f* (de enseñanza) primaria; (*before n*) **~ (school) teacher** maestro, -tra *m,f* (de escuela)

primate *n*

A /ˈpraɪmeɪt/ (Zool) primate *m*

B /ˈpraɪmeɪt, -ət/ (Relig) primado *m*

prime¹ /praɪm/ *adj* (*no comp*) **1** (major) principal; **to be of ~ importance** ser* de primordial *or* fundamental importancia **2** (first-rate) ‹*example/location*› excelente; ‹*cut*› de primera (calidad); **in ~ condition** ‹*athlete/racehorse*› en óptimas condiciones; ‹*car/antique*› en excelente estado; **of ~ quality** de primera calidad **3** (Math) ‹*number*› primo

prime² *n* [u] (best time): **to be in one's ~** *o* **in the ~ of life** estar* en la flor de la vida *or* en la mejor edad; **he's past his ~** ya no es ningún jovencito

prime³ *vt* **1** (prepare for painting) ‹*wood/metal*› aplicar* una capa de imprimación *or* de base a; ‹*canvas*› preparar, aprestar **2** ‹*pump/gun*› cebar **3** (brief) preparar; **he'd obviously been ~d to say that** era obvio que le habían dicho que dijera eso

prime: **~ minister** *n* primer ministro, primera ministra *m,f*; **~ mover** *n* promotor, -tora *m,f*

primer /ˈpraɪmər || ˈpraɪmə(r)/ *n*

A [c u] **1** (paint) imprimación *f*, base *f* **2** (explosive) cebo *m*

B [c] (textbook) manual *m*

prime time *n* horas *fpl* de máxima *or* mayor audiencia

primeval, (BrE) **primaeval** /praɪˈmiːvəl/ *adj* primigenio

primitive /ˈprɪmətɪv || ˈprɪmɪtɪv/ *adj* **1** ‹*man/society*› primitivo; ‹*dwelling/weapon/method*› primitivo, rudimentario; ‹*urges/instincts*› primario **2** (Art) primitivo

primly /ˈprɪmli/ *adv* remilgadamente

primordial /praɪˈmɔːrdiəl || praɪˈmɔːdiəl/ *adj* primigenio

primrose /ˈprɪmrəʊz/ *n* **1** [c] primavera *f*, prímula *f* **2** **~ (yellow)** amarillo *m* pálido

primrose-yellow /ˈprɪmrəʊzˈjeləʊ/ *adj* (*pred* **primrose yellow**) amarillo pálido *adj inv*

primula /ˈprɪmjələ || ˈprɪmjʊlə/ *n* prímula *f*, primavera *f*

Primus® (stove) /ˈpraɪməs/ *n* hornillo *m* de queroseno, anafe *m*

prince /prɪns/ *n* príncipe *m*; **~ consort/regent** príncipe consorte/regente

Prince Charming *n* el príncipe azul

princely /ˈprɪnsli/ *adj* ‹*bearing*› principesco; ‹*duties*› del príncipe; ‹*gift*› magnífico, espléndido; ‹*sum*› bonito

princess /ˈprɪnsəs || ˈprɪnses/ *n* princesa *f*

principal¹ /ˈprɪnsəpəl/ *adj* (*before n*) principal

principal² *n*

A (of school) director, -tora *m,f*; (of university) rector, -tora *m,f*

P

B 1 (Theat) protagonista *mf* 2 (Mus) (leader) primer violín *mf*
C (Fin) capital *m*, principal *m*

principality /ˈprɪnsəˈpæləti/ *n* (*pl* **-ties**) principado *m*

principally /ˈprɪnsəpli/ *adv* principalmente

principle /ˈprɪnsəpəl/ *n*
A [c] (basic fact, law) principio *m*; **in ~** en principio; **on that ~** sobre esa base, partiendo de esa base
B [c u] (rule of conduct) principio *m*; **a man/woman of (high) ~** un hombre/una mujer de principios; **it was a matter of ~** era una cuestión de principios; **I never borrow money, on ~** *o* **as a matter of ~** nunca pido dinero prestado, por principio; **it's the ~ of the thing** es una cuestión de principios; **it is against my ~s** va contra mis principios

principled /ˈprɪnsəpəld/ *adj* ‹*person*› de principios

print¹ /prɪnt/ *n*
A [u] (Print) 1 (lettering) letra *f*; **in large ~** en letra grande *or* en caracteres grandes; **the fine ~** (AmE) *o* (esp BrE) **small ~** la letra menuda *or* pequeña *or* (AmL tb) chica 2 (text): **a page of ~** una página impresa; **in ~** (published) publicado; (available) a la venta; **to get into ~** publicarse*; **out of ~** agotado; **to go out of ~** agotarse; (*before n*) **~ worker** tipógrafo, -fa *m,f*
B [c] 1 (Art, Print) grabado *m* 2 (Phot) copia *f*
C [c] (of foot, finger) huella *f*, marca *f*
D [c u] (fabric) estampado *m*

print² *vt*
A 1 ‹*letter/text/design*› imprimir*; **to ~ sth ON/ONTO sth** imprimir* algo EN algo 2 ‹*fabric*› estampar 3 (publish) publicar*, editar 4 **printed** *past p* impreso; **~ed matter** (Post) impresos *mpl*; **~ed fabric** estampado *m*
B (write clearly) escribir* con letra de imprenta
C (Phot) ‹*negative*› imprimir*; **to ~ a copy from sth** sacar* una copia de algo
D (make impression) (*usu pass*): **the scene is ~ed on my memory** tengo la escena grabada en la memoria
■ **print** *vi* 1 (Print) imprimir* 2 (write without joining the letters) escribir* con letra de imprenta 3 (Phot) salir*

Phrasal verb
• **print out** [v ▸ adv ▸ o, v ▸ o ▸ adv] imprimir*

printable /ˈprɪntəbəl/ *adj* 1 (fit for publication) publicable 2 (Print) que se puede imprimir

printer /ˈprɪntər || ˈprɪntə(r)/ *n* 1 (worker) tipógrafo, -fa *m,f*, impresor, -sora *m,f*; **~'s error** error *m* de imprenta 2 (business) imprenta *f* 3 (machine) impresora *f*

printing /ˈprɪntɪŋ/ *n* 1 [u] (act, process, result) impresión *f*; **the invention of ~** la invención de la imprenta; (*before n*) ‹*ink/error*› de imprenta 2 [c] (quantity printed) edición *f*, tirada *f* 3 [u] (trade) imprenta *f*

printing press *n* imprenta *f*, prensa *f*

print: **~out** *n* [u c] listado *m*; **~ run** *n* tirada *f*; **~ shop** *n* (workshop) (Print) imprenta *f*, taller *m* de impresión; (store) *tienda especializada en grabados*

prior¹ /ˈpraɪər || ˈpraɪə(r)/ *adj* (*before n*) ‹*knowledge/warning*› previo; **I had a ~ engagement** ya tenía un compromiso, tenía un compromiso previo; **prior to** (*as prep*) antes de

prior² *n* prior *m*

prioress /ˈpraɪərəs || ˌpraɪəˈres, ˈpraɪərəs/ *n* priora *f*

prioritize /ˌpraɪˈɔːrətaɪz || ˌpraɪˈɒrətaɪz/ *vt* priorizar*

priority /praɪˈɔːrəti || praɪˈɒrɪti/ *n* (*pl* **-ties**) 1 [u] (precedence) prioridad *f*; **in order of ~** por orden de prioridad; **to give ~ to sth** dar* prioridad a algo, priorizar* algo; **top ~** prioridad absoluta; **to have/take ~ (over sth)** tener* prioridad (sobre algo); (*before n*) ‹*treatment/item*› prioritario 2 [c] (important matter, aim): **my first/number one ~ is ...** para mí lo primero *or* lo más importante es ...; **you have to get your priorities right** tienes que saber decidir qué es lo más importante 3 [u] (in traffic) (BrE) preferencia *f*

priory /ˈpraɪəri/ *n* (*pl* **-ries**) priorato *m*

prise /praɪz/ *vt* (BrE) ▸ **prize³ B**

prism /ˈprɪzəm/ *n* prisma *m*

prison /ˈprɪzn̩/ *n* prisión *f*, cárcel *f*; **he was sent to ~ for ...** lo encarcelaron *or* lo metieron preso por ...; **her accomplice went to ~ for five years** su cómplice fue condenado a cinco años de prisión; (*before n*) ‹*system/reform*› carcelario, penitenciario; **~ cell** celda *f*; **~ governor** (BrE) director, -tora *m,f* (*de una cárcel*); **~ guard** *o* (BrE) **warder** guardia *mf*, celador, -dora *m,f*; **~ officer** (BrE) funcionario, -ria *m,f* de prisiones; **~ sentence** pena *f* de prisión

prison camp *n* campo *m* de prisioneros

prisoner /ˈprɪzn̩ər || ˈprɪzn̩ə(r)/ *n* 1 (captive) prisionero, -ra *m,f*; **he was held ~** (by enemy forces) lo tuvieron prisionero; (by kidnappers) lo tuvieron secuestrado; **to take sb ~** tomar *or* (esp Esp) coger* a algn prisionero; **to take ~s** hacer* prisioneros 2 (in jail) preso, -sa *m,f*, recluso, -sa *m,f* 3 (person arrested) detenido, -da *m,f* 4 (accused) reo *mf*, acusado, -da *m,f*

prisoner of war *n* (*pl* **~s ~ ~**) prisionero, -ra *m,f* de guerra

prissy /ˈprɪsi/ *adj* **-sier, -siest** (colloq) remilgado

pristine /ˈprɪstiːn, -taɪn/ *adj* (frml & liter) inmaculado, impoluto (liter), prístino (liter); **in ~ condition** en perfecto *or* impecable estado

privacy /ˈpraɪvəsi || ˈprɪvəsi/ *n* [u] privacidad *f*; **in the ~ of one's own home** en la intimidad del hogar

private¹ /ˈpraɪvət || ˈpraɪvɪt/ *adj*
A 1 (confidential) ‹*conversation*› privado; ‹*matter*› privado, confidencial; ‹*letter*› personal 2 **in private**: **she told me in ~** me lo dijo confidencialmente *or* en confianza; **can we talk in ~?** ¿podemos hablar en privado?; **what you do in ~ is your own affair** lo que hagas en la intimidad *or* en tu vida privada es cosa tuya
B 1 (restricted): **~ view** (Art) vernissage *m*; **~ hearing** (Law) vista *f* a puerta cerrada; **they married in a ~ ceremony** celebraron la boda en la intimidad; **Ⓢ private** privado; (on envelope) personal 2 (for own use, in own possession) ‹*road/lesson/secretary*› particular; ‹*income*› personal; **~ property** propiedad *f* privada; **a gentleman of ~ means** (frml) un señor que vive de las rentas; **~ income** rentas *fpl*
C 1 (not official) ‹*visit/correspondence*› privado; **a ~ citizen** un particular; **in a ~ capacity** a título personal; **their ~ life** su vida privada 2 (unconnected to the state) ‹*school*› privado, particular, de pago (Esp); ‹*ward*› reservado; ‹*patient*› particular; **~ enterprise** la empresa privada; **to be in ~ practice** (Med) ejercer* la medicina privada; (in US) (Law) ocuparse de asuntos civiles; **~ prosecution** querella *f*
D 1 ‹*thoughts/doubts*› íntimo; **time is set aside for ~ study** se establecen ciertas horas para que cada uno estudie por su cuenta; **it's a ~ joke** es un chiste que los dos entendemos/entienden 2 ‹*person*› reservado

private² *n*
A (rank) soldado *mf* raso; **P~ Jones** el soldado Jones
B **privates** *pl* (genitals) (colloq & euph) partes *fpl* pudendas (euf & hum), intimidades *fpl* (euf & hum)

private: **~ company** *n* sociedad *f* privada (*que no cotiza en Bolsa*); **~ detective** *n* detective *mf* privado; **~ eye** *n* (colloq) sabueso *mf*

privately /ˈpraɪvətli || ˈpraɪvɪtli/ *adv*
A 1 (in private) en privado; **can I speak to you ~?** ¿puedo hablar contigo en privado *or* a solas?; **the interview was held ~** la entrevista se celebró en privado *or* a puertas cerradas 2 (not publicly): **~ held views** opiniones *fpl* personales; **they agree ~ that ...** extraoficialmente admiten que ...
B 1 (not by state or large concern): **~ educated** educado en colegio privado *or* particular; **she had the operation done ~** (BrE) la operaron en una clínica privada; **this land is ~ owned** esta tierra es de particulares 2 (by private arrangement): **to sell sth ~** vender algo personalmente *or* sin intermediarios

private: **~ member**, **~ Member** *n* (in UK) diputado, -da *m,f*, representante *mf* (*sin cargo específico en el gobierno*); **~ parts** *pl n* (euph & hum) partes *fpl* pudendas (euf & hum), intimidades *fpl* (euf & hum); **~ sector** *n* sector *m* privado

privation /praɪˈveɪʃən/ *n* [u c] (frml) privación *f*; **they endured great ~** pasaron muchas privaciones

privatization /ˈpraɪvətəˈzeɪʃən/ *n* [u] privatización *f*

privatize /ˈpraɪvətaɪz || ˈprɪvɪtaɪz/ *vt* privatizar*

privet /ˈprɪvət || ˈprɪvɪt/ *n* [u c] ligustro *m*, alheña *f*

privilege /'prɪvəlɪdʒ/ *n* [c u] 1 (special right) privilegio *m*; **parliamentary/congressional ~** [u] inmunidad *f* parlamentaria 2 (honor) (*no pl*) privilegio *m*, honor *m*; **it is my ~ to introduce ...** tengo el honor *or* el privilegio de presentarles a ...

privileged /'prɪvəlɪdʒd/ *adj* 1 (having advantages) ‹*position*› privilegiado; **for the ~ few** para una minoría privilegiada 2 (honored) (*pred*) **to be ~ to + INF** tener* el privilegio *or* el honor DE + INF

privy[1] /'prɪvi/ *adj* (frml) (*pred*) **to be ~ TO sth** tener* conocimiento DE algo

privy[2] *n* (dated) (*pl* **-vies**) retrete *m*, excusado *m*

Privy Council *n* (in UK) **the ~ ~** *comité asesor del monarca integrado por personas de reconocido prestigio*

prize[1] /praɪz/ *n* 1 (award) premio *m*; **the first ~ goes to Chris** el primer premio se lo lleva *or* lo ha ganado Chris 2 (in lottery): **first ~** el primer premio *or* el gordo; (*before n*) **~ draw** *o* (AmE) **drawing** sorteo *m*

prize[2] *adj* (*before n*) ‹*bull/essay*› premiado; **he's a ~ idiot** (colloq) es un idiota de marca mayor

prize[3] *vt*
A (value) valorar (mucho), tener* en gran estima; **a ~d possession** un bien muy preciado
B (BrE) **prise**: **to ~ information out of sb** arrancarle* información a algn; **he ~d the lid off the crate** le arrancó la tapa a la caja haciendo palanca; **he ~d the shell open with a knife** abrió la concha con un cuchillo

prize: **~fighter** *n* boxeador, -dora *m,f* profesional; **~-giving** /'praɪz,gɪvɪŋ/ *n* (BrE) entrega *f* de premios; **~ money** *n* [u] premio *m* (*en metálico*); **~winner** *n* ganador, -dora *m,f* (*de un premio*), premiado, -da *m,f*; **~winning** *adj* (*before n*) premiado, galardonado

pro[1] /prəʊ/ *n*
A (professional) (colloq) profesional *mf*; (Sport) (player) jugador, -dora *m,f* profesional; (coach) instructor, -tora *m,f*
B **pros** *pl* (advantages): **the ~s and cons** los pros y los contras

pro[2] *prep* (colloq) a favor de

pro- /'prəʊ/ *pref* pro(-)

probability /'prɑːbə'bɪləti || ,prɒbə'bɪlɪti/ *n* [u c] (*pl* **-ties**) probabilidad *f*; **in all ~ they will lose their jobs** es muy probable que pierdan su trabajo

probable /'prɑːbəbəl || 'prɒbəbəl/ *adj* ‹*outcome*› probable; ‹*reason*› posible; **it is ~ THAT** es probable QUE (+ *subj*)

probably /'prɑːbəbli || 'prɒbəbli/ *adv* (*indep*) probablemente (+ *subj*); **he'll ~ come** probablemente venga, es probable que venga; **~ not** puede que no

probate[1] /'prəʊbeɪt/ *n* [u] (process) *trámite para obtener la autenticación de un testamento*; **to grant sb ~** declarar a algn legítimo albacea

probate[2] *vt* (esp AmE) ‹*will*› autenticar*, legalizar*

probation /prəʊ'beɪʃən || prə'beɪʃən/ *n* [u]
A (Law) libertad *f* condicional; **to be on ~** estar* en libertad condicional; **to put sb on ~** dejar *or* poner* a algn en libertad condicional; (*before n*) **~ officer** *asistente social que se ocupa del seguimiento de la persona en libertad condicional*
B (trial period) período *m* de prueba; **she's on ~** está cumpliendo su período de prueba

probationary /prəʊ'beɪʃəneri/ *adj* ‹*period*› de prueba

probe[1] /prəʊb/ *vt* 1 (physically) sondar 2 (investigate) investigar*; ‹*public opinion*› sondear; ‹*mind/subconscious*› explorar
■ **probe** *vi* investigar*; **to ~ INTO sth** investigar* algo

probe[2] *n* 1 (Med, Elec) sonda *f* 2 (*space ~*) sonda *f* espacial 3 (investigation) investigación *f*

probing /'prəʊbɪŋ/ *adj* ‹*question*› sagaz, perspicaz; ‹*study*› a fondo

probity /'prəʊbəti/ *n* [u] (frml) probidad *f*

problem /'prɑːbləm || 'prɒbləm/ *n* 1 (difficulty) problema *m*; **he has a drink ~** bebe demasiado; **I'm having ~s deciding** no acabo de decidirme, me está costando decidirme; **no ~!** (colloq) ¡no hay problema!; **what's the ~?** ¿qué pasa?, ¿algún problema?; **that's their ~** es cosa suya; (*before n*) ‹*family/child*› difícil; **~ page** (BrE Journ) consultorio *m* (*de problemas sentimentales etc de los lectores*) 2 (Math) problema *m*

problematic /'prɑːblə'mætɪk/ *adj* problemático, difícil

proboscis /prə'bɑːsəs || prə'bɒsɪs/ *n* (*pl* **-cises** /-səsəs/, **-cides** /-sɪdiːz/) probóscide *f*

procedure /prə'siːdʒər || prə'siːdjə(r), prə'siːdʒə(r)/ *n* 1 [u c] (practice) procedimiento *m*; (step) trámite *m*; **the normal ~ is to ...** lo que se hace normalmente es ... 2 [c] (Comput) procedimiento *m*

proceed /prəʊ'siːd, prə- || prə'siːd, prəʊ-/ *vi*
A (move forward) (frml) ‹‹*person/vehicle*›› avanzar*; **I was ~ing along King Street when ...** circulaba por King Street cuando ...; **please ~ to gate five** les rogamos se dirijan a la puerta número cinco; **to ~ on one's way** seguir* adelante
B (continue) continuar*; **~, Mr Thomas** continúe, Sr. Thomas; **to ~ TO sth** pasar A algo; **to ~ (WITH sth)** seguir* adelante (CON algo); **to ~ to + INF**: **she ~ed to tell us why** pasó a explicarnos por qué; **he threatened to resign, then ~ed to do just that** amenazó con dimitir e ipso facto lo hizo
C (act) (frml) proceder
D (progress) marchar
E (take legal action) (frml) **to ~ AGAINST sb** demandar a algn

proceedings /prəʊ'siːdɪŋz, prə-/ *pl n* 1 (events): **~ began late** la reunión (*or* el acto *etc*) empezó tarde; **two teachers were there to keep an eye on ~** había dos profesores vigilando lo que sucedía 2 (measures) medidas *fpl*; **disciplinary ~** medidas disciplinarias; **to start** *o* (frml) **institute ~ against sb** entablarle juicio a algn 3 (minutes) actas *fpl*

proceeds /'prəʊsiːdz/ *pl n*: **the ~** (from charity sale, function) lo recaudado; **he sold the house and went to Jamaica on the ~** vendió la casa y con lo que sacó se fue a Jamaica

process[1] /'prɑːses, 'prəʊ- || 'prəʊses/ *n*
A 1 (series of actions, changes) proceso *m*; **the aging ~** el envejecimiento; **the peace ~** (journ) el proceso de paz; **the ~ of obtaining a permit** el trámite para obtener un permiso; **I am in the ~ of writing to him right now** en este preciso momento le estoy escribiendo; **we are in the ~ of buying the house** estamos con los trámites de la compra de la casa; **he lost a lot of friends in the ~** con ello perdió muchos amigos; **in ~** (AmE) en construcción 2 (method) proceso *m*, procedimiento *m*
B 1 (proceedings) (frml) acción *f* judicial 2 (writ) demanda *f*

process[2] *vt* 1 ‹*raw materials/waste*› procesar, tratar; ‹*film*› revelar 2 ‹*applications*› dar* curso a, procesar; ‹*order*› tramitar 3 ‹*data*› procesar
■ **process** *vi* /prə'ses/ (go in procession) (frml) desfilar; (Relig) ir* en procesión

process cheese (AmE), **processed cheese** (BrE) *n* [u] queso *m* fundido

processing /'prɑːsesɪŋ, 'prəʊ- || 'prəʊsesɪŋ/ *n* [u] 1 (treatment — of materials, waste) tratamiento *m*, procesamiento *m*; (— of film) revelado *m* 2 (of an order, an application) tramitación *f* 3 (Comput) procesamiento *m*; (*before n*) **~ unit** unidad *f* de proceso

procession /prə'seʃən/ *n* desfile *m*; (Relig) procesión *f*; **a funeral ~** un cortejo fúnebre; **in ~** en procesión

processor /'prɑːsesər, 'prəʊ- || 'prəʊsesə(r)/ *n*
A (*food ~*) robot *m* de cocina, multiusos *m*
B (Comput) procesador *m*, unidad *f* de proceso

proclaim /prəʊ'kleɪm, prə-|| prə'kleɪm/ *vt* 1 (announce, declare) (frml) ‹*independence*› proclamar, declarar; ‹*love*› declarar; ‹*law*› promulgar* 2 (reveal) (liter) revelar

proclamation /'prɑːklə'meɪʃən || ,prɒklə'meɪʃən/ *n* [c u] (frml) proclamación *f*, proclama *f*

proclivity /prəʊ'klɪvəti/ *n* (*pl* **-ties**) (frml) proclividad *f*, propensión *f*; **sexual proclivities** tendencias *fpl* sexuales

procrastinate /prəʊ'kræstəneɪt || prəʊ'kræstɪneɪt/ *vi* dejar las cosas para más tarde

procrastination /prəʊ'kræstə'neɪʃən || prəʊ,kræstɪ'neɪʃən/ *n* [u]: **there's no time left for ~** ya no hay tiempo para dejar las cosas para mañana

procreate /'prəʊkrieɪt/ *vi* (frml) procrear

procreation /'prəʊkri'eɪʃən/ *n* [u] (frml) procreación *f*

procure /prə'kjʊr || prə'kjʊə(r)/ *vt* 1 (obtain) (frml) procurar (frml), obtener* (frml), conseguir* 2 (bring about) (frml) conseguir*, lograr 3 (for sex): **he ~d women for his clients** les proporcionaba prostitutas a sus clientes

P

procurement /prəˈkjʊrmənt || prəˈkjʊəmənt/ *n* [u] (frml) obtención *f*; (by purchasing) adquisición *f*

prod¹ /prɑːd || prɒd/ **-dd-** *vt* 1 (poke — with elbow) darle* un codazo a; (— with sth sharp) pinchar 2 (encourage, remind): **you have to keep ~ding her or she forgets** tienes que estar constantemente recordándoselo para que no se olvide; **after some ~ding I agreed to take the job** acepté el trabajo, pero tuvieron que empujarme un poco

■ **prod** *vi* **to ~ AT sth: she ~ded at the cheese with her fork** pinchaba el queso con el tenedor

prod² *n* 1 (poke — with elbow) codazo *m*; (— with sth sharp) pinchazo *m* 2 (stimulus): **you'll have to give him a ~** vas a tener que empujarlo *or* aguijonearlo 3 (for cattle) picana *f or* (Esp) aguijada *f*

prodigal /ˈprɑːdɪgəl/ *adj* 1 (wasteful) pródigo, despilfarrador; **to be ~ WITH o** (frml) **OF sth** ser* pródigo CON algo, despilfarrar algo; **the ~ son** (Bib) el hijo pródigo 2 (lavish) (frml) pródigo; **to be ~ WITH o OF sth** ser* pródigo EN algo

prodigious /prəˈdɪdʒəs/ *adj* ‹*amount/cost*› enorme, ingente (frml); ‹*efforts/strength*› prodigioso

prodigy /ˈprɑːdədʒi || ˈprɒdɪdʒi/ *n* (*pl* **-gies**) prodigio *m*; **child ~** niño, -ña *m,f* prodigio

produce¹ /prəˈduːs || prəˈdjuːs/ *vt*

A 1 (manufacture, yield) ‹*cars/cloth*› producir*, fabricar*; ‹*coal/grain/beef*› producir*; ‹*fruit*› «*country/region*» producir*; «*tree/bush*» dar*, producir*; **these cows ~ better milk** estas vacas dan mejor leche 2 (create, give) ‹*energy/sound*› producir*; ‹*interest*› producir*, dar*, devengar*; **a university which has ~d many great scientists** una universidad que ha dado *or* de donde han salido muchos grandes científicos; **she ~s excellent work every time** su trabajo es invariablemente excelente 3 (cause) ‹*joy/reaction*› producir*, causar; ‹*effect*› surtir, producir* 4 (give birth to) ‹*young*› tener*

B (show, bring out) ‹*ticket/document*› presentar; ‹*evidence/proof*› presentar, aportar; ‹*gun/knife*› sacar*

C 1 (Cin, TV) producir*, realizar*; (Theat) ‹*play*› poner* en escena; ‹*show*› montar, poner* en escena 2 (Rad, Theat) (direct) dirigir*

produce² /ˈprɑːduːs || ˈprɒdjuːs/ *n* [u] productos *mpl* (alimenticios); Ⓢ **produce of Spain** producto de España

producer /prəˈduːsər || prəˈdjuːsə(r)/ *n*

A (manufacturer) fabricante *mf*, productor, -tora *m,f*

B 1 (Cin, TV, Theat) productor, -tora *m,f* 2 (Rad, Theat) (director) director, -tora *m,f*

-producing /prəˈduːsɪŋ || prəˈdjuːsɪŋ/ *suff*: **coal~ country** país *m* productor de carbón

product /ˈprɑːdəkt || ˈprɒdʌkt/ *n* 1 (Busn, Marketing, Math) producto *m* 2 (creation, result) producto *m*, fruto *m*; **she's a typical Harvard ~** es el típico producto de Harvard

production /prəˈdʌkʃən/ *n*

A [u] 1 (manufacture) fabricación *f*, producción *f*; **the car goes into ~ next year** el coche empezará a fabricarse el año entrante; **to take sth out of ~** dejar de fabricar algo 2 (output) producción *f*; **car/coal ~** producción automovilística/de carbón

B [u] (showing) presentación *f*; **on ~ of the correct documents** al presentar la documentación correspondiente, previa presentación de la documentación correspondiente

C [c] (staging, version) (Theat, Cin) producción *f*

D [u] 1 (act of producing) (Cin, TV) producción *f*; (Theat) puesta *f* en escena, producción *f* 2 (direction) (Rad, Theat) dirección *f*

production line *n* cadena *f* de fabricación

productive /prəˈdʌktɪv/ *adj* ‹*land/factory/mine*› productivo; ‹*meeting*› fructífero, productivo; **it's not a very ~ way to spend your time** no es una manera muy provechosa de pasar el tiempo

productively /prəˈdʌktɪvli/ *adv* productivamente; **I didn't spend my time very ~** no saqué buen partido del tiempo

productivity /ˈprəʊdʌkˈtɪvəti || ˌprɒdʌkˈtɪvəti/ *n* [u] productividad *f*; (*before n*) **~ bonus** prima *f* de *or* por productividad *or* rendimiento; **~ deal** acuerdo *m* sobre productividad

Prof /prɑːf/ (title) = **Professor**

profane¹ /prəˈfeɪn/ *adj* 1 (blasphemous) irreverente, blasfemo 2 (secular) profano

profane² *vt* (frml) profanar

profanity /prəˈfænəti/ *n* (*pl* **-ties**) 1 [u] (blasphemy) irreverencia *f*, blasfemia *f* 2 [c] (swear word) blasfemia *f*

profess /prəˈfes/ *vt* 1 (claim) (frml) ‹*desire/outrage/belief*› manifestar*, expresar; **to ~ to + INF: I don't ~ to know anything about chemistry** no presumo de saber (nada) de química; **he ~ed to be an expert** se preciaba de ser un experto, pretendía ser un experto 2 (Relig) ‹*faith/religion*› profesar

professed /prəˈfest/ *adj* 1 (declared) ‹*socialist*› declarado; ‹*Christian*› profeso 2 (purported) ‹*friend*› supuesto, pretendido

profession /prəˈfeʃən/ *n*

A 1 [c] (occupation) profesión *f*; **by ~** de profesión; **the ~s** las profesiones liberales 2 (members) (*no pl*): **the medical ~** el cuerpo médico, la clase médica; **the teaching ~** la enseñanza, la docencia

B [u c] (declaration) (frml) profesión *f*

professional¹ /prəˈfeʃn̩əl || prəˈfeʃənl̩/ *adj*

A (as opposed to amateur) (*before n*) ‹*musician/golfer*› profesional; ‹*soldier*› de carrera; **to go** *o* **turn ~** hacerse* profesional

B 1 (done, given by professionals) (*before n*): **to take ~ advice** asesorarse con un profesional (*or* un experto, técnico *etc*); **the break-in was a ~ job** los que entraron eran profesionales del robo *or* ladrones profesionales 2 (befitting a professional): **she made a very ~ job of it** lo hizo como un experto

professional² *n* profesional *mf*; (competent person) experto, -ta *m,f*

professionalism /prəˈfeʃn̩əlɪzəm || prəˈfeʃənlɪzəm/ *n* [u] 1 (qualities of professional) profesionalidad *f*, seriedad *f* 2 (Sport) profesionalismo *m*

professionally /prəˈfeʃn̩əli/ *adv* 1 (as livelihood) ‹*sing/act*› profesionalmente 2 (by qualified person): **we had the job done ~** hicimos *or* mandamos hacer el trabajo por un experto (*or* por un pintor, albañil *etc*) 3 (in a professional way) con profesionalidad; **you didn't behave very ~** no actuaste como un profesional íntegro

professor /prəˈfesər || prəˈfesə(r)/ *n* (of the highest academic rank) catedrático, -ca *m,f*; (any university teacher) (AmE) profesor universitario, profesora universitaria *m,f*

professorship /prəˈfesərʃɪp || prəˈfesəʃɪp/ *n* cátedra *f*

proffer /ˈprɑːfər || ˈprɒfə(r)/ *vt* (frml) ‹*gift/flowers/apology*› ofrecer*; ‹*advice*› brindar, dar*; ‹*condolences*› presentar

proficiency /prəˈfɪʃənsi/ *n* [u] competencia *f*

proficient /prəˈfɪʃənt/ *adj* muy competente; **she is ~ in** *o* **at swimming** es una nadadora muy competente

profile¹ /ˈprəʊfaɪl/ *n*

A 1 (side view) perfil *m*; **in ~** de perfil 2 (outline) perfil *m*, contorno *m*

B (description) perfil *m*; (written) reseña *f*

C (status): **to raise the ~ of educational matters** dar* más relieve a las cuestiones relativas a la enseñanza; **to have a high ~** tener* un papel preponderante, ocupar un lugar destacado; ***to keep a low ~*** tratar de pasar desapercibido *or* de no llamar la atención

profile² *vt* ‹*situation*› hacer* un esbozo de; **to ~ sb's life** hacer* una reseña biográfica de algn

profit¹ /ˈprɑːfət || ˈprɒfɪt/ *n* [c u] 1 (Busn, Econ) ganancias *fpl*, beneficios *mpl*, utilidades *fpl* (AmL); **we made a ~ of $2,000** obtuvimos beneficios *or* (AmL tb) utilidades de $2.000; **to sell sth at a ~** vender algo con ganancia; **this service does not operate at a ~** este servicio no es rentable; **~ and loss account** cuenta *f* de pérdidas y ganancias; (*before n*) **~ margin** margen *m* de ganancias *or* de beneficios *or* (AmL tb) de utilidades 2 (advantage) (*no pl*): **they turned the situation to their own ~** sacaron provecho de la situación

profit² *vi* **to ~ FROM sth** sacar* provecho DE algo, beneficiarse DE algo

profitability /ˈprɑːfətəˈbɪləti/ *n* [u] rentabilidad *f*

profitable /ˈprɑːfətəbəl/ *adj* 1 (Busn) ‹*company/investment/crop*› rentable, redituable (frml), lucrativo; **sportswear is very ~** la ropa de deporte deja un buen beneficio *or* margen 2 ‹*day/journey*› provechoso, fructífero

profitably /ˈprɑːfətəbli || ˈprɒfɪtəbli/ *adv* 1 (Busn) ‹*trade/operate*› de manera rentable, con rentabilidad; ‹*sell*› con ganancia *or* beneficio 2 (fruitfully) provechosamente

profiteer[1] /ˈprɑːfəˈtɪr/ *n* especulador, -dora *m,f*

profiteer[2] *vi* especular

profiteering /ˈprɑːfəˈtɪrɪŋ/ *n* [u] especulación *f*

profit: **~-making** /ˈprɑːfət,meɪkɪŋ/ *adj* (profitable) rentable, lucrativo; (which aims to make a profit) con fines lucrativos *or* de lucro; **~ sharing** *n* [u] participación *f* en las ganancias *or* los beneficios *or* (AmL tb) las utilidades; **~-taking** *n* [u] toma *f* de ganancias *or* beneficios

profligacy /ˈprɑːflɪgəsi/ *n* [u] 1 (extravagance) derroche *m*, despilfarro *m* 2 (immorality) (frml) libertinaje *m*

profligate /ˈprɑːflɪgət/ *adj* 1 (extravagant) derrochador, despilfarrador 2 (immoral) (frml) disoluto, libertino

profound /prəˈfaund/ *adj* **-er, -est** profundo

profoundly /prəˈfaʊndli/ *adv* profundamente; **he's ~ deaf** es totalmente sordo, tiene una sordera total

profundity /prəˈfʌndəti/ *n* [u] profundidad *f*

profuse /prəˈfjuːs/ *adj* abundante; ‹*bleeding*› intenso; **she offered ~ apologies** se deshizo en disculpas

profusely /prəˈfjuːsli/ *adv* ‹*bleed*› profusamente; ‹*thank*› efusivamente; **he apologized ~** se deshizo en disculpas

profusion /prəˈfjuːʒən/ *n* [u c] profusión *f*, abundancia *f*; **in ~** en abundancia, en profusión

progeny /ˈprɑːdʒəni || ˈprɒdʒəni/ *n* (*pl* **-nies**) (+ *sing o pl vb*) (frml) progenie *f* (frml)

progesterone /prəʊˈdʒestərəʊn/ *n* [u] progesterona *f*

prognosis /prɑːgˈnəʊsəs/ *n* [c u] (*pl* **-ses** /-siːz/) pronóstico *m*

prognosticate /prɑːgˈnɑːstəkeɪt/ (frml) *vt* pronosticar*
■ **prognosticate** *vi* pronosticar*, hacer* un pronóstico

program[1], (BrE) **programme** /ˈprəʊgræm/ *n*

A 1 (schedule) programa *m*; **what's your ~ for tomorrow?** ¿qué programa *or* planes tienes para mañana? 2 (for a performance, concert) programa *m* 3 (esp AmE Educ) (course) curso *m*; (syllabus) programa *m*

B (plan) programa *m*; **a research ~** un programa de investigación

C (Rad, TV) programa *m*

D (on household appliance) programa *m*

E **program** (Comput) programa *m*

program[2] **-mm-** *or* **-m-** *vt*

A (BrE also) **programme** 1 (schedule) ‹*activities*› programar, planear 2 (instruct) programar

B (Comput) programar
■ **program** *vi* (Comput) programar

programme[1] /ˈprəʊgræm/ *n* (BrE) ▸**program**[1] **A, B, C, D**

programme[2] *vt* (BrE) ▸**program**[2] *vt* **A**

programmer, (AmE also) **programer** /ˈprəʊgræmər || ˈprəʊgræmə(r)/ *n* (Comput) programador, -dora *m,f*

programming /ˈprəʊgræmɪŋ/ *n* [u] 1 (Comput) programación *f* 2 (Rad, TV) programación *f*

progress[1] /ˈprɑːgrəs || ˈprəʊgres/ *n* [u]

A (advancement) progreso *m*; (of situation, events) desarrollo *m*, evolución *f*; **the patient's ~** los progresos del paciente; **she came to check on our ~** vino a ver qué tal íbamos *or* marchábamos; **to make ~** «*pupil*» adelantar, hacer* progresos, progresar; «*patient*» mejorar; **I'm making good/slow ~ with my thesis** estoy avanzando bien/lentamente con la tesis; (*before n*) **~ report** (Adm, Busn) informe *m* sobre el avance *or* la marcha de los trabajos

B **in progress**: **talks are in ~ between the two parties** los dos partidos están manteniendo conversaciones; **while the examination is in ~** mientras dure el examen

C (forward movement) avance *m*; **to make ~** avanzar*

progress[2] /prəˈgres/ *vi* 1 (advance) «*work/science/technology*» progresar, avanzar*, adelantar; **as the vacation ~ed** a medida que pasaban las vacaciones; **I never ~ed beyond elementary calculus** nunca pasé del cálculo elemental 2 (improve) «*patient*» mejorar; **his Spanish is ~ing** va adelantando *or* haciendo progresos en español

progression /prəˈgreʃən/ *n* 1 [u c] (advance) evolución *f*; **his ~ up the scale** su ascenso en el escalafón 2 [c] (Math, Mus) progresión *f*

progressive /prəˈgresɪv/ *adj*

A ‹*attitude/thinker/measure*› progresista; **a ~ school** (Educ) una escuela activa

B ‹*deterioration/improvement*› progresivo

progressively /prəˈgresɪvli/ *adv*: **they became ~ disillusioned** se fueron desilusionando cada vez más

prohibit /prəʊˈhɪbɪt || prəˈhɪbɪt/ *vt* 1 (forbid) prohibir*; **fishing in the lake is ~ed** está prohibido *or* se prohíbe pescar en el lago; **to ~ sb FROM -ING** prohibirle* a algn + INF 2 (prevent) impedir*; **to ~ sb FROM -ING**: **the cost ~s many people from receiving treatment** el costo impide que mucha gente tenga acceso al tratamiento

prohibition /ˈprəʊəˈbɪʃən || ˌprəʊhɪˈbɪʃən/ *n* 1 [u c] prohibición *f* 2 **Prohibition** (in US history) (*no art*) la Ley seca, la Prohibición

> **Prohibition**
>
> El período, desde 1919 a 1933, durante el cual estaba prohibido en EEUU fabricar o vender alcohol o bebidas alcohólicas. La prohibición fue una medida muy impopular y resultaba demasiado oneroso hacer cumplir la ley. Por otra parte, hizo ganar una fortuna a gángsters como Al Capone que fabricaban y vendían alcohol en forma clandestina

prohibitive /prəʊˈhɪbətɪv || prəˈhɪbətɪv/ *adj* ‹*price/cost*› prohibitivo

project[1] /ˈprɑːdʒekt || ˈprɒdʒekt/ *n* 1 (scheme) proyecto *m*; (*before n*) **~ manager** director, -tora *m,f* de proyecto 2 (Educ) trabajo *m* 3 (*housing ~*) (in US) complejo *m* de viviendas subvencionadas

project[2] /prəˈdʒekt/ *vt*

A 1 ‹*beam/shadow/image*› proyectar 2 (convey) ‹*personality/image/voice*› proyectar

B (frml) ‹*missile*› lanzar*, proyectar

C 1 (extrapolate) ‹*costs/trends*› hacer* una proyección de, extrapolar 2 (forecast) pronosticar*; **the ~ed figure** la cifra prevista; **the ~ed route runs through ...** según los planes *or* según está previsto, la ruta pasaría por ...
■ **project** *vi* (jut out) sobresalir*; **the land ~s out into the sea** la tierra se adentra en el mar

projectile /prəˈdʒektl̩ || prəˈdʒektaɪl/ *n* proyectil *m*

projection /prəˈdʒekʃən/ *n*

A [u] (of image, slide) proyección *f*

B [c] (forecast) proyección *f*, pronóstico *m*, extrapolación *f*

C [c] (protuberance) saliente *f or m*

projectionist /prəˈdʒekʃənəst/ *n* proyeccionista *mf*

projector /prəˈdʒektər || prəˈdʒektə(r)/ *n* proyector *m*

prolapse /ˈprəʊlæps/ *n* [u c] prolapso *m*

proletarian /ˈprəʊləˈteriən/ *adj* proletario

proletariat /ˈprəʊləˈteriət || ˌprəʊləˈteəriət/ *n* **the ~** el proletariado

proliferate /prəˈlɪfəreɪt/ *vi* proliferar

proliferation /prəˈlɪfəˈreɪʃən/ *n* [u c] (*no pl*) proliferación *f*

prolific /prəˈlɪfɪk/ *adj* prolífico

prologue, (AmE also) **prolog** /ˈprəʊlɔːg || ˈprəʊlɒg/ *n* **~ (TO sth)** prólogo *m* (DE algo)

prolong /prəˈlɔːŋ || prəˈlɒŋ/ *vt* ‹*conversation/visit/meeting*› prolongar*, alargar*, extender*; ‹*suspense*› prolongar*; **to ~ sb's life** prolongarle* *or* alargarle* la vida a algn

prolongation /ˈprəʊlɔːŋˈgeɪʃən/ *n* [c u] prolongación *f*

prolonged /prəˈlɔːŋd || prəˈlɒŋd/ *adj* prolongado

prom /prɑːm || prɒm/ *n* 1 (ball) (in US) (colloq) baile *m* del colegio (*or* de la facultad *etc*) 2 (esplanade) (BrE colloq) ▸**promenade**[1] **A1** 3 *also* **Prom** (in UK) (Mus) *concierto en el que parte del público está de pie*

> **Proms**
>
> Una serie de conciertos de música clásica que tienen lugar en el *Albert Hall* de Londres, todos los años en el verano. Fueron iniciados en 1895 por Sir Henry Wood y su nombre es la forma abreviada de "promenade concerts", es decir conciertos durante los cuales el público permanece de pie en una zona de la sala donde se han quitado los asientos. Los *Proms* se prolongan durante ocho semanas

promenade[1] /prɑːməˈneɪd || ˈprɒmənɑːd/ *n*

A 1 (at seaside) (esp BrE) paseo *m* marítimo, malecón *m* (AmL), costanera *f* (CS) 2 (stroll) (liter) paseo *m*; (*before n*) **~ deck** cubierta *f* de paseo

B (AmE) ▸ **prom 1**

promenade² *vi* pasear(se)

promenade concert *n* (BrE fml) ▸ **prom 3**

prominence /'prɑːmənəns || 'prɒmɪnəns/ *n* **1** [u] (conspicuousness) prominencia *f*; (eminence, importance) importancia *f*, prominencia *f*; **to come to ~** adquirir* importancia; **to give ~ to sth** hacer* resaltar algo **2** [c] (small hill) (frml) loma *f*, prominencia *f*

prominent /'prɑːmənənt || 'prɒmɪnənt/ *adj* **1** ‹*position*› destacado, prominente; ‹*role/politician*› prominente, destacado, importante; **he was ~ in literary circles** era una figura destacada en el ambiente literario **2** ‹*jaw/nose*› prominente; ‹*ridge/ledge*› prominente, saliente

prominently /'prɑːmənəntli || 'prɒmɪnəntli/ *adv*: **it was ~ displayed** ocupaba un lugar prominente *or* destacado; **he figured ~ in the negotiations** desempeñó un papel prominente *or* destacado en las negociaciones

promiscuity /'prɑːməs'kjuːəti || ˌprɒmɪ'skjuːəti/ *n* [u] promiscuidad *f*

promiscuous /prə'mɪskjuəs/ *adj* promiscuo

promise¹ /'prɑːməs || 'prɒmɪs/ *n*

A [c] (pledge) promesa *f*; **I can't make any ~s** no puedo prometer nada; **to keep one's ~** cumplir (con) su (*or* mi *etc*) promesa; **you broke your ~** no cumpliste (con) tu promesa, faltaste a *or* rompiste tu promesa

B [u] (potential): **his work was full of ~** *o* **showed a lot of ~** su trabajo prometía mucho *or* era muy prometedor

promise² *vt*

A (pledge) prometer; **to ~ sb sth, to ~ sth TO sb** prometerle algo A algn; **he ~d himself a holiday** se prometió tomarse unas vacaciones; **she ~d them (that) she wouldn't tell anybody** les prometió que no se lo diría a nadie; **to ~ to + INF** prometer + INF *or* prometer QUE + INDICATIVO; **~ not to tell anybody!** prométeme que no se lo dirás a nadie

B (give indication of) prometer; **it ~s to be an exciting week** promete ser una semana emocionante

■ **promise** *vi* prometer; (swear) jurar; **I did, I ~!** ¡lo hice, te lo juro!; **I won't laugh, I ~** no me voy a reír, te lo prometo

promising /'prɑːməsɪŋ || 'prɒmɪsɪŋ/ *adj* ‹*pupil/writer/career*› prometedor; ‹*future*› halagüeño, que promete

promissory note /'prɑːməsɔːri/ *n* pagaré *m*

promontory /'prɑːməntɔːri || 'prɒməntri/ *n* (*pl* **-ries**) promontorio *m*

promote /prə'məʊt/ *vt*

A **1** (raise in rank) ‹*employee*› ascender* **2** (AmE Educ) promover* **3** (BrE Sport): **United were ~d to the Second Division** United subió *or* ascendió a segunda división

B **1** (encourage) promover*, fomentar, potenciar; ‹*growth*› estimular **2** (advocate) promover*

C **1** ‹*product/service*› promocionar, dar(le)* publicidad a **2** ‹*concert/boxing match*› organizar*

promoter /prə'məʊtər || prə'məʊtə(r)/ *n* **1** (Busn) promotor, -tora *m,f* **2** (Sport) empresario, -ria *m,f*

promotion /prə'məʊʃən/ *n*

A [u c] **1** (advancement in rank) ascenso *m*; **she got** *o* **was given (a) ~** la ascendieron, le dieron un ascenso **2** (BrE Sport) ascenso *m*, promoción *f*

B [u] **1** (of research, peace, trade) promoción *f*, fomento *m* **2** (advocacy) promoción *f*

C **1** [u] (publicity) promoción *f*, publicidad *f*, propaganda *f* **2** [c] (campaign) promoción *f*, campaña *f* publicitaria *or* de promoción

prompt¹ /prɑːmpt || prɒmpt/ *vt*

A ‹*response/outcry*› provocar*, dar* lugar a; **the decision was ~ed by ...** la decisión fue motivada por ...; **to ~ sb to + INF** mover* *or* (frml) inducir* a algn A + INF

B ‹*actor/orator*›: **she ~ed him** le apuntó *or* (fam) le sopló lo que tenía que decir

prompt² *adj* **-er, -est** ‹*delivery/reply*› rápido, pronto; **he must receive ~ treatment** se lo debe tratar inmediatamente *or* sin demora; **they are ~ in their payments** pagan puntualmente

prompt³ *adv* (BrE): **at ten o'clock ~** a las diez en punto

prompt⁴ *n* **1** (reminder) apunte *m* **2** (prompter) (colloq) apuntador, -dora *m,f* **3** (Comput) presto *m*, mensaje *m* al operador

prompter /'prɑːmptər || 'prɒmptə(r)/ *n* apuntador, -dora *m,f*; **~'s box** concha *f* del apuntador

promptly /'prɑːmptli/ *adv* **1** (on time) puntualmente **2** (speedily) ‹*pay/deliver*› sin demora, rápidamente, con prontitud **3** (instantly) de inmediato, inmediatamente

promptness /'prɑːmptnəs || 'prɒmptnɪs/ *n* [u] (speed) prontitud *f*, rapidez *f*; (punctuality) puntualidad *f*

promulgate /'prɑːmlgeɪt/ *vt* (frml) promulgar*

promulgation /'prɑːml'geɪʃən/ *n* [u] promulgación *f*

prone¹ /prəʊn/ *adj*

A (liable, disposed) (*pred*) **to be ~ TO sth** ser* propenso A algo; **to be ~ to + INF** ser* propenso a + INF, tener* tendencia a + INF

B (face downward) (tendido) boca abajo, decúbito prono *adj inv* (frml)

prone² *adv* boca abajo, decúbito prono (frml)

prong /prɔːŋ || prɒŋ/ *n* diente *m*, punta *f*

-pronged /'prɔːŋd || 'prɒŋd/ *suff*: **a three~ fork** un tenedor de tres dientes; **a two~ attack** un ataque sobre dos flancos

pronoun /'prəʊnaʊn/ *n* pronombre *m*

pronounce /prə'naʊns/ *vt* **1** ‹*sound/word/syllable*› pronunciar; **the 'e' is not ~d** la 'e' no se pronuncia *or* es muda **2** ‹*judgment/sentence*› pronunciar, dictar **3** (declare) (frml): **the doctor ~d him dead** el médico dictaminó que estaba muerto; **she tasted it and ~d it excellent** lo probó y declaró que era excelente; **he ~d himself satisfied** se manifestó satisfecho

■ **pronounce** *vi* (deliver verdict) (frml) **to ~ (ON sth)** pronunciarse (SOBRE algo)

pronounced /prə'naʊnst/ *adj* pronunciado, marcado

pronouncement /prə'naʊnsmənt/ *n* declaración *f*, dictamen *m*

pronto /'prɑːntəʊ || 'prɒntəʊ/ *adv* (colloq) volando (fam), corriendo (fam)

pronunciation /prə'nʌnsi'eɪʃən/ *n* [u] pronunciación *f*

proof¹ /pruːf/ *n*

A [u c] (conclusive evidence) prueba *f*; **~ of identity** un documento de identidad; **~ positive** prueba concluyente; **as a ~ of** como prueba de

B [c] (Print) prueba *f* (de imprenta)

C [u] (alcoholic strength) graduación *f* alcohólica; **70 ~** (American system) ≈ 35% de alcohol *or* 35° (GL); **70 degrees ~** (British system) ≈ 40% de alcohol *or* 40° (GL)

proof² *adj* (*pred*) **to be ~ AGAINST sth** ser* a prueba DE algo; **she was ~ against his flattery** era inmune *or* no era vulnerable a sus halagos

proof³ *vt* impermeabilizar*

-proof /pruːf/ *suff*: **bomb~** a prueba de bombas; *see also* **childproof, foolproof** *etc*

proof: **~read** (*past & past p* **-read** /-red/) *vt* corregir*

■ **proof** *vi* corregir* pruebas; **~reader** *n* corrector, -tora *m,f* de pruebas

prop¹ /prɑːp || prɒp/ *n*

A **1** (holding up roof etc) puntal *m* **2** (giving moral support) apoyo *m*, sostén *m*

B (Cin, Theat) accesorio *m*, objeto *m* de utilería *or* (Esp, Méx) del attrezzo; (*before n*) **~** *o* **~s department** utilería *f*, attrezzo *m* (Esp, Méx)

C (in rugby) pilar *mf*

prop² **-pp-** *vt* **to ~ sth AGAINST sth** apoyar algo EN *or* CONTRA algo; **the door was ~ped open with a brick** un ladrillo mantenía la puerta abierta

Phrasal verb

• **prop up** [v ▸ o ▸ adv, v ▸ adv ▸ o] **1** (support) ‹*wall/building*› sostener*, apuntalar **2** (lean) apoyar; **he was ~ped up in bed** estaba recostado en la cama **3** ‹*regime*› apoyar, ayudar a mantener en el poder; **the company is being ~ped up by government loans** la compañía se mantiene a flote gracias a préstamos del gobierno

propaganda /'prɑːpə'gændə || ˌprɒpə'gændə/ *n* [u] propaganda *f*; **for ~ purposes** con fines propagandísticos

propagate /'prɑːpəgeɪt/ *vt* propagar*, difundir

propagation /'prɑːpə'geɪʃən/ *n* [u] propagación *f*, difusión *f*

propane /'prəʊpeɪn/ *n* [u] propano *m*

propel /prə'pel/ *vt* **-ll-** 1 ‹*plane/ship*› propulsar, impulsar; **to ~ sb toward disaster** llevar *or* conducir* a algn hacia el desastre 2 (throw) lanzar*

propeller /prə'pelər/ *n* hélice *f*; (*before n*) **~ shaft** (Auto) árbol *m* de transmisión; (Aviat, Naut) árbol *m* de hélice

propelling pencil /prə'pelɪŋ/ *n* (BrE) portaminas *m*

propensity /prə'pensəti/ *n* (*pl* **-ties**) (frml) **~ (TO sth)** propensión *f* (A algo)

proper /'prɑːpər || 'prɒpə(r)/ *adj*

A (correct) (*before n, no comp*) ‹*treatment/procedure*› apropiado, adecuado; ‹*answer/pronunciation*› correcto; **it's not in its ~ place** no está en su sitio *or* lugar; **the ~ respect** el debido respeto

B (*before n, no comp*) 1 (genuine) verdadero; **she never has a ~ meal** nunca hace una comida como es debido *or* como Dios manda 2 (BrE colloq) (*as intensifier*) ‹*fool/mess*› verdadero, auténtico; **he's a ~ gent** es todo un caballero

C 1 ‹*behavior/person*› correcto 2 (overly decorous) recatado, remilgado

D 1 (in the strict sense) (*after n*) propiamente dicho; **the mountain ~** la montaña propiamente dicha 2 (Math): **~ fraction** fracción *f* propia 3 (belonging) (frml) (*pred*) **to be ~ TO sth** ser* propio DE algo

properly /'prɑːpərlɪ || 'prɒpəli/ *adv* 1 ‹*write/spell*› correctamente, bien; ‹*fitted/adjusted*› correctamente, debidamente, bien; ‹*work/concentrate/eat*› bien, como es debido 2 (appropriately) apropiadamente, adecuadamente; **they don't pay us ~ for the work we do** no nos pagan lo que corresponde por el trabajo que hacemos 3 (accurately, correctly): **he is more ~ known as ...** el nombre correcto de su cargo es ...; **they very ~ complained about the quality** se quejaron, con toda la razón, de la calidad; **~ speaking** hablando con propiedad *or* para ser exactos 4 (in seemly manner) correctamente, con corrección

proper name, **proper noun** *n* nombre *m* propio

property /'prɑːpərti || 'prɒpəti/ *n* (*pl* **-ties**)

A [u] (possessions) propiedad *f*; **whose ~ is it?** ¿de quién es?, ¿a quién pertenece?; **it's my personal ~** es mío *or* (frml) de mi propiedad; **public ~** bienes *mpl* públicos; **the news has become public ~** la noticia es ya del dominio público; **a man of ~** un propietario acaudalado *or* adinerado

B 1 [u] (buildings, land) propiedades *fpl*, bienes *mpl* raíces *or* inmuebles (frml); (*before n*) **~ developer** promotor inmobiliario, promotora inmobiliaria *m,f*; **~ market** mercado *m* inmobiliario; **~ owner** propietario, -ria *m,f*; **~ tax** (in US) impuesto *m* sobre la propiedad inmobiliaria 2 [c] (building) inmueble *m* (frml); (piece of land) terreno *m*, solar *m*, parcela *f*

C [c] (quality) propiedad *f*; **it has medicinal properties** posee propiedades medicinales

D [c] (Cin, Theat) **properties** *pl* (frml) utilería *f or* (Esp, Méx) attrezzo *m*

prophecy /'prɑːfəsi || 'prɒfəsi/ *n* [c u] (*pl* **-cies**) profecía *f*, vaticinio *m*

prophesy /'prɑːfəsaɪ || 'prɒfəsaɪ/ **-sies, -sying, -sied** *vt* predecir*, vaticinar; (Relig) profetizar*

■ **prophesy** *vi* profetizar*, hacer* profecías

prophet /'prɑːfət || 'prɒfɪt/ *n* profeta, -tisa *m,f*; **the ~s of doom** los catastrofistas *or* agoreros

prophetic /prə'fetɪk/ *adj* profético

prophylactic[1] /'prəʊfə'læktɪk/ *adj* profiláctico

prophylactic[2] *n* 1 (Med, Pharm) fármaco *m* profiláctico 2 (condom) profiláctico *m* (frml), preservativo *m*

propitiate /prə'pɪʃieɪt/ *vt* propiciar; **to ~ the gods** propiciarse la voluntad de los dioses

propitious /prə'pɪʃəs/ *adj* ‹*moment/time*› propicio; ‹*omen/augury*› favorable

proponent /prə'pəʊnənt/ *n* defensor, -sora *m,f*

proportion[1] /prə'pɔːrʃən || prə'pɔːʃən/ *n*

A (part) (*no pl*) parte *f*, porcentaje *m*; **a large** *o* **high ~ of the voters** gran parte de los votantes, un gran porcentaje de los votantes

B [c u] (ratio) proporción *f*; **in equal ~s** por partes iguales; **in ~ to sth** en proporción a algo; **to vary in direct/inverse ~ with sth** variar* en proporción directa/inversa a algo

C [u] (proper relation) proporción *f*; **the head isn't in ~ to the body** la cabeza no está (bien) proporcionada *or* está desproporcionada con respecto al cuerpo; **let's keep things in ~** no exageremos; **to blow sth up out of all ~** exagerar algo desmesuradamente; **his salary is out of all ~ to his talent** su sueldo no guarda proporción con su talento

D **proportions** *pl* (size) proporciones *fpl*, dimensiones *fpl*

proportion[2] *vt*: **poorly ~ed** mal proporcionado; **well-~ed** de buenas proporciones, bien proporcionado

proportional /prə'pɔːrʃnəl || prə'pɔːʃənl/ *adj* proporcional; **~ representation** representación *f* proporcional; **to be ~ TO sth** ser* proporcional A algo

proportionally /prə'pɔːrʃnəli/ *adv* proporcionalmente

proportionate /prə'pɔːrʃnət || prə'pɔːʃənət/ *adj* proporcional; **to be ~ TO sth** ser* proporcional A algo, estar* en proporción A algo

proportionately /prə'pɔːrʃnətli/ *adv* proporcionalmente

proposal /prə'pəʊzəl/ *n* 1 [c] (suggestion) propuesta *f*; **to put** *o* **make a ~ to sb** hacerle* una propuesta a algn 2 [c] (of marriage) proposición *f or* propuesta *f* matrimonial

propose /prə'pəʊz/ *vt*

A 1 (suggest) proponer*; **to ~ -ING/(THAT)** proponer* QUE (+ *subj*); **I ~d giving them more incentives** propuse darles *or* que se les dieran más incentivas; **what do you ~ we do?** ¿qué propones que hagamos? 2 **proposed** *past p*: **the ~d cuts** los recortes que se proponen implementar, los recortes que se planean 3 (in meeting) ‹*amendment*› proponer*; ‹*motion*› presentar, proponer*; **she ~d Charles as chairman** propuso *or* (AmL tb) postuló a Charles como presidente

B (intend) **to ~ to + INF, to ~ -ING** pensar* + INF; **what do you ~ to do about it?** ¿qué piensas hacer al respecto?

■ **propose** *vi* **to ~ TO sb** proponerle* matrimonio a algn; **he ~d to her** le pidió que se casara con él, le propuso matrimonio

proposer /prə'pəʊzər || prə'pəʊzə(r)/ *n* proponente *mf*

proposition[1] /'prɑːpə'zɪʃən || ,prɒpə'zɪʃən/ *n*

A (suggestion) propuesta *f*, proposición *f*; (offer) oferta *f*

B (prospect): **living alone was an inviting ~** le atraía la idea de vivir solo; **it's not a viable ~** no es viable

proposition[2] *vt* hacerle* proposiciones deshonestas a (euf), invitar a la cama

propound /prə'paʊnd/ *vt* proponer*, presentar, postular

proprietary /prə'praɪəteri || prə'praɪətri/ *adj* ‹*device/software/drug*› de marca registrada, patentado; **~ product** producto *m* de marca

proprietor /prə'praɪətər || prə'praɪətə(r)/ *n* propietario, -ria *m,f*, dueño, -ña *m,f*

propriety /prə'praɪəti/ *n* 1 [u] (correctness) corrección *f*, decoro *m* 2 **proprieties** *pl* (conventions) convenciones *fpl*, normas *fpl*

propulsion /prə'pʌlʃən/ *n* [u] propulsión *f*

pro rata[1] /'prəʊ'rɑːtə/ *adj* ‹*payment/charge*› prorrateado; **on a ~ ~ basis** a prorrata, proporcionalmente

pro rata[2] *adv* a prorrata, proporcionalmente

prorate /'prəʊ'reɪt/ *vt* (AmE) prorratear

prosaic /prəʊ'zeɪɪk/ *adj* prosaico

proscribe /prəʊ'skraɪb || prə'skraɪb/ *vt* proscribir*

proscription /prəʊ'skrɪpʃən/ *n* [u c] proscripción *f*

prose /prəʊz/ *n* 1 [u] (Lit) prosa *f*; (*before n*) **~ style** estilo *m* prosístico; **~ works** obras *fpl* en prosa 2 [c u] (Educ) ejercicio *m* de traducción inversa

prosecute /'prɑːsɪkjuːt || 'prɒsɪkjuːt/ *vt*

A (Law) **to ~ sb FOR sth** procesar *or* enjuiciar a algn POR algo

B (frml) ‹*inquiry/campaign*› llevar a cabo

■ **prosecute** *vi* 1 (bring action) iniciar procedimiento criminal, interponer* una acción judicial 2 (be prosecutor) llevar la acusación; **prosecuting attorney** (in US) fiscal *mf*; **prosecuting counsel** (in UK) ▸**prosecutor**

prosecution /'prɑːsɪ'kjuːʃən || ,prɒsɪ'kjuːʃən/ *n*

A (Law) 1 [u] (bringing to trial) interposición *f* de una acción judicial 2 [c] (court case) proceso *m*, juicio *m*; **to bring a ~ against sb** interponer* una acción judicial contra algn 3 (prosecuting side) **the ~** la acusación; (*before n*) **~ witness** testigo *mf* de cargo *or* de la acusación

B (of campaign) (frml) prosecución *f*

prosecutor /'prɑːsɪkjuːtər || 'prɒsɪkjuːtə(r)/ *n* fiscal *mf*, acusador, -dora *m,f*; (in private prosecutions) abogado, -da *m,f*

P

de *or* por la acusación *or* la parte querellante

proselytize /ˈprɑːsələtaɪz || ˈprɒsəlɪtaɪz/ *vi* hacer* proselitismo, ganar prosélitos

prospect¹ /ˈprɑːspekt || ˈprɒspekt/ *n*

A **1** [u] (possibility) posibilidad *f*; **~ OF sth** posibilidades *fpl* DE algo; **there isn't much ~ of my getting the job** no tengo *or* no hay muchas posibilidades de que me den el trabajo **2** [c] (situation envisaged) perspectiva *f*, panorama *m* **3** **prospects** *pl* (chances) perspectivas *fpl*; **a job with no ~s** un trabajo sin futuro; **a young executive with ~s** un joven ejecutivo con perspectivas de futuro *or* con porvenir

B [c] **1** (person): **he's a good ~ for the first race** tiene muchas probabilidades de ganar la primera carrera **2** (potential customer) posible cliente, -ta *m,f*, candidato, -ta *m,f*

C (view) (frml) panorama *m*, vista *f*, perspectiva *f*

prospect² /ˈprɑːspekt/ *vi* **to ~ FOR sth** buscar* algo

■ **prospect** *vt* ‹*area/river*› prospectar, explorar

prospective /prəˈspektɪv/ *adj* (*before n*) **1** (potential) ‹*customer*› posible, eventual **2** (future) ‹*husband*› futuro; **her ~ trip** el viaje que tiene en perspectiva

prospector /ˈprɑːspektər || prəˈspektə(r)/ *n* prospector, -tora *m,f*, cateador, -dora *m,f* (AmS)

prospectus /prəˈspektəs/ *n* (*pl* **~es**) **1** (Busn) prospecto *m* (*con las condiciones de emisión*) **2** (Educ) folleto *m* informativo

prosper /ˈprɑːspər || ˈprɒspə(r)/ *vi* prosperar

prosperity /prɑːˈsperəti/ *n* [u] prosperidad *f*

prosperous /ˈprɑːspərəs || ˈprɒspərəs/ *adj* próspero

prostate (gland) /ˈprɑːsteɪt || ˈprɒsteɪt/ *n* próstata *f*

prostitute¹ /ˈprɑːstətuːt || ˈprɒstɪtjuːt/ *n* prostituta *f*; **male ~** prostituto *m*

prostitute² *vt* prostituir*; **to ~ oneself** prostituirse*

prostitution /ˌprɑːstəˈtuːʃən/ *n* [u] prostitución *f*

prostrate¹ /ˈprɑːstreɪt || ˈprɒstreɪt/ *adj* postrado; **~ with grief** abatido por la pena

prostrate² /ˈprɑːstreɪt || prɒˈstreɪt/ *vt* «*illness*» postrar

■ *v refl* **to ~ oneself** postrarse

protagonist /prəʊˈtæɡənəst || prəˈtæɡənɪst/ *n* **1** (Lit) protagonista *mf* **2** (of a cause) (frml) defensor, -sora *m,f*

protect /prəˈtekt/ *vt* proteger*; ‹*rights/interests*› proteger*, salvaguardar; **to ~ sth/sb FROM/AGAINST sth/sb** proteger* algo/a algn DE/CONTRA algo/algn

■ **protect** *vi* **to ~ (AGAINST sth)** proteger* (CONTRA algo)

protection /prəˈtekʃən/ *n* [u] **~ (FROM/AGAINST sb/sth)** protección *f* (CONTRA algn/algo); **police ~** protección policial; **to be under sb's ~** estar* bajo la protección de algn; (*before n*) **~ money** *dinero que se paga al chantajista para que no cause daños en un comercio*; **~ racket** chantaje *m* (*que se practica a propietarios de comercios*)

protectionism /prəˈtekʃənɪzəm/ *n* [u] proteccionismo *m*

protectionist /prəˈtekʃənəst/ *adj* proteccionista

protective /prəˈtektɪv/ *adj* **1** ‹*headgear/covering*› protector; ‹*clothing*› de protección; **~ custody** *detención de una persona para su propia protección* **2** ‹*attitude/feelings*› protector

protector /prəˈtektər/ *n* protector, -tora *m,f*

protectorate /prəˈtektərət/ *n* protectorado *m*

protégé /ˈprəʊtəʒeɪ || ˈprɒtəˌʒeɪ/ *n* protegido, -da *m,f*

protégée /ˈprəʊtəʒeɪ || ˈprɒtəˌʒeɪ/ *n* protegida *f*

protein /ˈprəʊtiːn/ *n* [c u] proteína *f*; (*before n*) ‹*content*› proteínico

protest¹ /ˈprəʊtest/ *n* **1** [u] (expression of disagreement) protesta *f*; **without ~** sin protestar; **in ~ (at/against sth)** en señal de protesta (por/contra algo); **under ~** bajo protesta; (*before n*) **~ song** canción *f* (de) protesta **2** [c] (complaint) protesta *f* **3** [c] (demonstration) manifestación *f* de protesta

protest² /prəˈtest/ *vi* protestar; **to ~ AGAINST/ABOUT/AT sth** protestar CONTRA/ACERCA DE/POR algo; **to ~ TO sb** presentar una protesta ANTE algn

■ **protest** *vt*

A **1** (complain) **to ~ (TO sb) THAT** quejarse (A algn) DE QUE, protestar (A algn) QUE **2** (object to) (AmE) ‹*decision/action*› protestar (contra)

B (assert) ‹*love*› declarar; ‹*innocence/loyalty*› hacer* protestas de; **she ~ed that ...** afirmó enérgicamente que ...

Protestant¹ /ˈprɑːtəstənt || ˈprɒtɪstənt/ *n* protestante *mf*

Protestant² *adj* protestante

Protestantism /ˈprɑːtəstəntɪzəm/ *n* [u] protestantismo *m*

protestation /ˌprɑːtəsˈteɪʃən || ˌprɒtɪˈsteɪʃən/ *n* [u c] (of love, friendship) declaración *f*; (of loyalty, innocence) protesta *f*

protester /prəˈtestər || prəˈtestə(r)/ *n* manifestante *mf*

proto- /ˈprəʊtəʊ/ *pref* proto-

protocol /ˈprəʊtəkɔːl || ˈprəʊtəkɒl/ *n* **1** [u] (etiquette) protocolo *m* **2** [c] (of contract, treaty) protocolo *m*

proton /ˈprəʊtɑːn || ˈprəʊtɒn/ *n* protón *m*

prototype /ˈprəʊtətaɪp/ *n* prototipo *m*

protract /prəˈtrækt/ *vt* prolongar*

protracted /prəˈtræktəd || prəˈtræktɪd/ *adj* prolongado

protractor /prəˈtræktər || prəˈtræktə(r)/ *n* transportador *m*, semicírculo *m* (graduado)

protrude /prəˈtruːd/ *vi* (frml) **1** «*nail/ledge*» sobresalir* **2** **protruding** *pres p* ‹*chin*› prominente; ‹*teeth*› salido; ‹*nail*› que sobresale; **protruding eyes** ojos *mpl* saltones

protrusion /prəˈtruːʒən/ *n* [u c] (frml) protuberancia *f*, prominencia *f*

protuberance /prəʊˈtuːbərəns/ *n* [u c] protuberancia *f*

proud /praʊd/ *adj* **-er, -est** **1** (pleased) ‹*parent/winner*› orgulloso; ‹*smile/moment*› de orgullo; **to be ~ OF sb/sth** estar* orgulloso DE algn/algo; **that's nothing to be ~ of** no es como para enorgullecerse *or* estar orgulloso; **to be ~ to + INF: I am ~ to receive this award** me enorgullece *or* me llena de orgullo recibir este premio; **we are ~ to present** tenemos el honor de presentarles a; **to be ~ THAT** estar* orgulloso DE QUE; ***to do sb ~*** (colloq): **they did us ~** nos trataron a cuerpo de rey **2** (having self-respect) ‹*nation/race*› digno, altivo **3** (arrogant, haughty) orgulloso, arrogante, altanero

proudly /ˈpraʊdli/ *adv* **1** (with pleasure, satisfaction) con orgullo; **we ~ present ...** tenemos el honor de presentar ... **2** (arrogantly) orgullosamente, arrogantemente

prove /pruːv/ (*past* **proved**; *past p* **proved** *or* **proven**) *vt*

A (verify, demonstrate) ‹*theory/statement*› probar*; ‹*theorem/innocence*› probar*, demostrar*; ‹*loyalty/courage*› demostrar*; **can you ~ where you were that night?** ¿tiene pruebas de dónde estaba usted aquella noche?; **to ~ sb right/wrong** demostrar* que algn tiene razón *or* está en lo cierto/está equivocado

B **1** (test) ‹*weapon/system*› probar* **2** (Law) ‹*will*› comprobar*, verificar*

■ *v refl* **to ~ oneself**: **he was given three months to ~ himself** le dieron tres meses para que demostrara su valía

■ **prove** *vi*

A (turn out) resultar; **it ~d to be very difficult** resultó ser muy difícil

B (Culin) «*dough*» levar, leudar

proven /ˈpruːvən/ *adj* ‹*experience/ability*› probado, comprobado; **a ~ method** un método de probada eficacia

proverb /ˈprɑːvɜːrb || ˈprɒvɜːb/ *n* refrán *m*, proverbio *m*

proverbial /prəˈvɜːrbiəl || prəˈvɜːbiəl/ *adj* proverbial; **he turned up wearing his ~ red tie** apareció con la consabida corbata roja

provide /prəˈvaɪd/ *vt*

A (supply) **to ~ sb WITH sth** proveer* a algn DE algo, suministrarle *or* proporcionarle algo A algn; **to ~ sth (FOR/TO sb/sth)**: **is accommodation ~d?** ¿nos (*or* les *etc*) dan alojamiento?; **textbooks will be ~d** se proporcionarán *or* se facilitarán los libros de texto; **the garden ~s enough vegetables for the family** el huerto abastece a la familia de verduras; **the meeting ~d an opportunity to ...** la reunión ofreció *or* brindó la oportunidad de ...

B (stipulate) (frml) «*clause/contract*» estipular

■ **provide** *vi* proveer*; **the Lord will ~** Dios proveerá

Phrasal verbs

• **provide against** [v ▸ prep ▸ o] «*person*» tomar precauciones contra, precaverse *or* prevenirse* contra; «*policy*» proporcionar cobertura contra

• **provide for** [v ▸ prep ▸ o] **1** (support) ‹*family*› mantener* **2** (make arrangements for): **he left them very well ~d for** los dejó en una situación económica holgada *or* con el

P

porvenir asegurado; **I have to ~ for my old age** tengo que asegurarme el bienestar en la vejez; **every eventuality has been ~d for** se han previsto todas las eventualidades 3 (Govt, Law) prever*

provided /prə'vaɪdəd || prə'vaɪdɪd/ *conj* ~ **(that)** siempre que (+ *subj*), siempre y cuando (+ *subj*)

providence /'prɑːvədəns || 'prɒvɪdəns/ *n* [u] 1 (Relig) providencia *f*; **divine ~** la Divina Providencia 2 (fate, chance): **it was sheer ~ that ...** fue providencial que ...; ▸**tempt** 3 (foresight) (frml) previsión *f*

provident /'prɑːvədənt/ *adj* previsor, prudente

providential /'prɑːvə'dentʃəl/ *adj* (frml) providencial

provider /prə'vaɪdər || prə'vaɪdə(r)/ *n*: **the family ~** el sostén (económico) de la familia; **a major ~ of jobs in the area** una de las más importantes fuentes de trabajo de la zona

providing /prə'vaɪdɪŋ/ *conj* ▸**provided**

province /'prɑːvəns || 'prɒvɪns/ *n*
A 1 (administrative unit) provincia *f* 2 **provinces** *pl* **the ~s** las provincias; (in some Latin American countries) el interior (del país)
B 1 (area of knowledge, activity) terreno *m*, campo *m* 2 (area of responsibility) competencia *f*; **this isn't my ~** esto está fuera de mi competencia, esto no es de mi competencia

provincial /prə'vɪntʃəl || prə'vɪnʃəl/ *adj*
A (Govt) provincial
B 1 ‹*town*› de provincia(s); ‹*fashions/accent*› provinciano 2 (pej) ‹*outlook/attitude*› provinciano, pueblerino

provision[1] /prə'vɪʒən/ *n*
A [u] 1 (of funding) provisión *f*; (of food, supplies) suministro *m*, aprovisionamiento *m* 2 (what is supplied): **how can we improve existing social ~?** ¿cómo podríamos mejorar los servicios *or* las prestaciones sociales existentes?; **there is very good ~ for the elderly** las necesidades de los ancianos están muy bien atendidas
B [u] (preparatory arrangements) previsiones *fpl*; **to make ~ for the future** hacer* previsiones para el futuro; **she made no ~ for him in her will** no le dejó nada en el testamento
C [c] (stipulation) (Govt, Law) disposición *f*; **under** *o* **according to the ~s of the treaty ...** según lo que estipula el tratado ...; **with the ~ that ...** con la condición de que ..., con tal de que ...
D **provisions** *pl* provisiones *fpl*, víveres *mpl*

provision[2] *vt* abastecer*, aprovisionar

provisional /prə'vɪʒnəl || prə'vɪʒənl/ *adj* provisional, provisorio (AmS); **the P~ IRA** el IRA provisional

provisionally /prə'vɪʒnəli/ *adv* provisionalmente, provisoriamente (esp AmS), de manera provisional

proviso /prə'vaɪzəʊ/ *n* (*pl* **-sos**) (stipulation) condición *f*; (Law) condición *f*; **with the ~ that** con la condición de que (+ *subj*)

provocation /'prɑːvə'keɪʃən || ˌprɒvə'keɪʃən/ *n* [u c] provocación *f*; **at the slightest ~** a la más mínima provocación

provocative /prə'vɑːkətɪv || prə'vɒkətɪv/ *adj* 1 (causing trouble) provocador 2 (seductive) provocativo 3 (thought-provoking) (frml) que hace reflexionar

provocatively /prə'vɑːkətɪvli || prə'vɒkətɪvli/ *adv* 1 (aggressively) ‹*gesture/jeer*› de modo provocador 2 (seductively) ‹*smile/dress*› de forma provocativa

provoke /prə'vəʊk/ *vt*
A ‹*person/animal*› provocar*; **she is easily ~d** salta a la menor provocación *or* por cualquier cosa; **to ~ sb INTO -ING: I was ~d into hitting him** tanto me provocó, que le pegué; **to ~ sb to action** incitar *or* empujar a algn a actuar
B ‹*argument/revolt/criticism*› provocar*; ‹*discussion/debate*› motivar; ‹*interest/curiosity*› despertar*

provoking /prə'vəʊkɪŋ/ *adj* irritante

provost /'prəʊvəʊst || 'prɒvəst/ *n* 1 (in UK) (Educ) rector, -tora *m,f* 2 (in UK) (Relig) ≈ deán *m* 3 (in Scotland) (Govt) ≈ alcalde, -desa *m,f*

prow /praʊ/ *n* proa *f*

prowess /'praʊəs || 'praʊɪs/ *n* [u] destreza *f*, habilidad *f*; **his sexual ~** sus proezas sexuales

prowl[1] /praʊl/ *vi* merodear, rondar
■ **prowl** *vt* merodear *or* rondar por

prowl[2] *n* ronda *f*; **(to be) on the ~ (FOR sth)** (estar*) al acecho (DE algo)

prowler /'praʊlər || 'praʊlə(r)/ *n* merodeador, -dora *m,f*

proximity /prɑːk'sɪməti || prɒk'sɪməti/ *n* [u] (frml) proximidad *f*; **the two buildings are in close ~** los dos edificios están muy próximos (el uno del otro); **in the ~ of sth** en las proximidades de algo, cerca de algo

proxy /'prɑːksi || 'prɒksi/ *n* (*pl* **-xies**) 1 [c] (person) representante *mf*, apoderado, -da *m,f*; **to stand ~ for sb** representar a algn, obrar con poder de algn 2 [u] (authorization) poder *m*; **by ~** por poder *or* (Esp) por poderes; (*before n*) ‹*vote*› por poder *or* (Esp) por poderes

prude /pruːd/ *n* mojigato, -ta *m,f*, gazmoño, -ña *m,f*

prudence /'pruːdn̩s/ *n* [u] prudencia *f*

prudent /'pruːdn̩t/ *adj* prudente

prudish /'pruːdɪʃ/ *adj* mojigato, gazmoño

prune[1] /pruːn/ *n* ciruela *f* pasa *or* (CS) seca

prune[2] *vt* 1 (Hort) podar 2 ‹*essay/article*› pulir y acortar; ‹*costs/workforce*› reducir*, recortar

pruning /'pruːnɪŋ/ *n* [u c] (Hort) poda *f*; (*before n*) ~ **shears** tijeras *fpl* de podar

prurience /'prʊriəns || 'prʊəriəns/ *n* [u] (frml) lascivia *f*

prurient /'prʊriənt || 'prʊəriənt/ *adj* (frml) lascivo

pry /praɪ/ **pries, prying, pried** *vi* curiosear, husmear; **to ~ INTO sth** entrometerse EN algo; **keep it away from ~ing eyes** escóndelo de miradas indiscretas
■ **pry** *vt* (esp AmE) (+ *adv compl*): **she pried the lid off** levantó la tapa (haciendo palanca)

PS *n* (postscript) P.D.

psalm /sɑːm/ *n* salmo *m*

pseud /suːd || sjuːd/ *n* (BrE) intelectualoide *mf*

pseudo- /'suːdəʊ || 'sjuːdəʊ/ *pref* (p)seudo-

pseudonym /'suːdn̩ɪm || 'sjuːdənɪm/ *n* (p)seudónimo *m*

psoriasis /sə'raɪəsəs || sə'raɪəsɪs/ *n* [u] (p)soriasis *f*

PST (in US) = **Pacific Standard Time**

psych, psyche /saɪk/ *vt* (colloq) **to ~ sb/oneself INTO -ING** mentalizar* a algn/mentalizarse* PARA + INF

Phrasal verbs
• **psych out, psyche out** [v ▸ o ▸ adv, v ▸ adv ▸ o] (AmE sl) 1 (disconcert) poner* nervioso 2 (understand) ‹*person*› calar (fam); **I soon ~ed out the situation** pronto me di cuenta de por dónde iban los tiros (fam)
• **psych up, psyche up** [v ▸ o ▸ adv, v ▸ adv ▸ o] (sl) mentalizar*; **to ~ oneself up** mentalizarse*

psyche /'saɪki/ *n* psiquis *f*, psique *f*

psychedelic /'saɪkə'delɪk/ *adj* (p)sicodélico

psychiatric /'saɪki'ætrɪk/ *adj* (p)siquiátrico

psychiatrist /sə'kaɪətrəst/ *n* (p)siquiatra *mf*

psychiatry /sə'kaɪətri || saɪ'kaɪətri/ *n* [u] (p)siquiatría *f*

psychic[1] /'saɪkɪk/ *adj* 1 (Occult) para(p)sicológico; **you must be ~!** (colloq) ¡eres adivino! 2 (Psych) (p)síquico

psychic[2] *n* vidente *mf*, médium *mf*

psychoanalysis /'saɪkəʊə'næləsəs/ *n* [u] (p)sicoanálisis *m*

psychoanalyst /'saɪkəʊ'ænl̩əst/ *n* (p)sicoanalista *mf*

psychoanalyze /'saɪkəʊ'ænl̩aɪz/ *vt* (p)sicoanalizar*

psychobabble /'saɪkəʊbæbəl/ *n* [u] (colloq & pej) jerga *f* de la psicología popular

psychological /'saɪkə'lɑːdʒɪkəl/ *adj* (p)sicológico

psychologist /saɪ'kɑːlədʒəst/ *n* (p)sicólogo, -ga *m,f*

psychology /saɪ'kɑːlədʒi/ *n* (*pl* **-gies**) (p)sicología *f*

psychopath /'saɪkəpæθ || 'saɪkəʊpæθ/ *n* (p)sicópata *mf*

psychopathic /'saɪkə'pæθɪk || ˌsaɪkəʊ'pæθɪk/ *adj* (p)sicopático; ‹*act*› propio de un (p)sicópata

psychosis /saɪ'kəʊsəs/ *n* (*pl* **-ses** /-siːz/) (p)sicosis *f*

psychosomatic /'saɪkəsə'mætɪk/ *adj* (p)sicosomático

psychotherapist /'saɪkəʊ'θerəpəst/ *n* (p)sicoterapeuta *mf*

psychotherapy /'saɪkəʊ'θerəpi/ *n* [u] (p)sicoterapia *f*

psychotic /saɪ'kɑːtɪk || saɪ'kɒtɪk/ *adj* (p)sicótico

PTA *n* = **parent-teacher association**

PTO (= **please turn over**) sigue al dorso

PTSD *n* = **post-traumatic stress disorder** TEPT *m*

P

pub /pʌb/ *n* (BrE) ≈ bar *m*; (*before n*) **to go on a ~ crawl** ir* de bar en bar tomando copas

puberty /ˈpjuːbərti || ˈpjuːbəti/ *n* [u] pubertad *f*

pubescent /pjuːˈbesn̩t/ *adj* pubescente

pubic /ˈpjuːbɪk/ *adj* ‹hair› púbico; ‹region/bone› pubiano

public¹ /ˈpʌblɪk/ *adj* 1 (of people) público; **~ opinion** la opinión pública; **it is ~ knowledge** es de dominio público; **there is growing ~ concern** la gente está cada vez más preocupada; **it wouldn't be in the ~ interest** no beneficiaría a la ciudadanía; ▸**eye¹ A3** 2 (concerning the state) público; **at ~ expense** con fondos públicos; **~ body** organismo *m* estatal *or* público; **~ works** obras *fpl* públicas 3 ‹library/garden/footpath› público; **it's too ~ here** aquí no tenemos ninguna privacidad 4 (open, not concealed) ‹announcement/protest› público; **a well-known ~ figure** un personaje conocido, una persona muy conocida; **~ speaking** oratoria *f*; **to make sth ~** hacer* algo público; **to go ~** (journ) revelar algo a la prensa 5 **to go ~** ‹‹company›› salir* a bolsa

public² *n* (+ *sing or pl vb*) 1 [u] (people in general) **the ~** el público 2 [c] (audience) público *m* 3 **in public** en público

public-address system /ˈpʌblɪkəˈdres/ *n* (sistema *m* de) megafonía *f*, altoparlantes *mpl* (AmL)

publican /ˈpʌblɪkən/ *n* (BrE) dueño, -ña *m,f* de un bar

public assistance *n* [u] (AmE) *ayuda estatal a los sectores más necesitados de la población*; **to be on ~ ~** recibir ayuda estatal

publication /ˈpʌbləˈkeɪʃən/ *n* [c u] publicación *f*

public: **~ convenience** *n* (BrE frml) (*often pl*) aseos *mpl* públicos (frml); **~ defender** *n* (AmE) defensor, -sora *m,f* de oficio; **~ health** *n* [u] salud *f* *or* sanidad *f* pública; (*before n*) ‹authorities› sanitario; **~ holiday** *n* fiesta *f* oficial, (día *m*) feriado *m* (AmL); **~ house** *n* (BrE) ≈ bar *m*

publicist /ˈpʌbləsəst || ˈpʌblɪsɪst/ *n* publicista *mf*

publicity /pʌbˈlɪsəti/ *n* [u] publicidad *f*; (*before n*) ‹agent/manager/office› de publicidad, publicitario; **~ stunt** ardid *m* publicitario

publicize /ˈpʌbləsaɪz || ˈpʌblɪsaɪz/ *vt* 1 ‹report/agreement› hacer* público, dar* a conocer, divulgar*, publicitar 2 (Marketing) promocionar, publicitar

public limited company *n* (in UK) sociedad *f* anónima (*con cotización en la bolsa*)

publicly /ˈpʌblɪkli/ *adv* 1 públicamente, en público; **~ available** a disposición del público 2 (Govt) ‹funded/maintained› con fondos públicos

public: **~ prosecutor** *n* (esp in UK) fiscal *mf*; **~ relations** *n* relaciones *fpl* públicas; (*before n*) **~ relations officer** encargado, -da *m,f* de relaciones públicas; **~ school** *n* (in US) escuela *f* pública; (in UK) colegio *m* privado; (— boarding school) internado *m* privado; **~ sector** *n* sector *m* público; **~ servant** *n* funcionario, -ria *m,f* (del Estado); **~ service** *n* (communal provision) servicio *m* público; **cuts in ~ services** recortes *mpl* en los servicios públicos; (*before n*) **~ service corporation** (AmE) empresa *f* de servicios públicos; **~-spirited** /ˈpʌblɪkˈspɪrətəd || ˌpʌblɪkˈspɪrɪtɪd/ *adj* solidario, de espíritu cívico; **~ transportation** (AmE), **~ transport** (BrE) *n* [u] transporte *m* público; **~ utility** *n* empresa *f* de servicios públicos

publish /ˈpʌblɪʃ/ *vt* 1 ‹book/newspaper› publicar*, editar; ‹article/dissertation› publicar* 2 (make known) hacer* público, divulgar*

■ **publish** *vi* publicar*

publisher /ˈpʌblɪʃər || ˈpʌblɪʃə(r)/ *n* 1 (company) editorial *f* 2 (job title) editor, -tora *m,f*

publishing /ˈpʌblɪʃɪŋ/ *n* [u] mundo *m* *or* campo *m* editorial; (*before n*) **~ company** editorial *f*, empresa *f* *or* compañía *f* editorial; **~ house** editorial *f*, casa *f* editorial

puce /pjuːs/ *adj* morado

puck /pʌk/ *n* (in ice hockey) disco *m*, puck *m*

pucker /ˈpʌkər || ˈpʌkə(r)/ *vt* fruncir*, arrugar*; **the baby ~ed (up) its face and began to cry** el niño hizo pucheros *or* morritos y se echó a llorar

pudding /ˈpʊdɪŋ/ *n* [c u] 1 (baked, steamed) budín *m*, pudín *m* 2 (dessert) (BrE) postre *m*

pudding basin *n* (BrE) budinera *f*

puddle /ˈpʌdl̩/ *n* charco *m*

pudgy /ˈpʌdʒi/ *adj* **pudgier, pudgiest** rechoncho, regordete

puerile /ˈpjʊrəl || ˈpjʊəraɪl/ *adj* pueril, infantil

Puerto Rican¹ /ˈpwertəˈriːkən/ *adj* puertorriqueño, portorriqueño

Puerto Rican² *n* puertorriqueño, -ña *m,f*, portorriqueño, -ña *m,f*

Puerto Rico /ˈpwertəˈriːkəʊ/ *n* Puerto Rico *m*

puff¹ /pʌf/ *n*

A [c] 1 (of wind, air) ráfaga *f*; **a ~ of smoke** una nube de humo 2 (action) soplo *m*, soplido *m*; (on cigarette) chupada *f*, pitada *f* (AmL), calada *f* (Esp) 3 (sound) resoplido *m*

B [u] (breath) (BrE colloq): **out of ~** sin aliento

C [c] (Culin) pastelito *m* de hojaldre, milhojas *m*

puff² *vt* 1 (blow) soplar; **don't ~ smoke in my face** no me eches humo a la cara 2 (smoke) ‹cigarette/cigar/pipe› dar* chupadas *or* (AmL tb) pitadas *or* (Esp tb) caladas a

■ **puff** *vi*

A 1 (blow) soplar 2 (smoke) **to ~ ON** *o* **AT sth** ‹on cigarette/cigar/pipe› dar* chupadas *or* (AmL tb) pitadas *or* (Esp tb) caladas A algo

B (pant) resoplar

Phrasal verbs

• **puff out** [v ▸ o ▸ adv, v ▸ adv ▸ o] (expand) ‹cheeks› inflar, hinchar (Esp); ‹feathers› erizar*

• **puff up** [v ▸ adv] (swell) hincharse

puffed /pʌft/ *adj* 1 ‹sleeve› abombado, abullonado; **~ rice** copos *mpl* de arroz 2 **~ (out)** (out of breath) (BrE colloq) sin aliento (fam)

puffed-up /ˈpʌftˈʌp/ *adj* (*pred* **puffed up**) 1 (swollen) hinchado 2 (conceited) engreído, vanidoso

puffin /ˈpʌfən || ˈpʌfɪn/ *n* frailecillo *m*

puffiness /ˈpʌfinəs || ˈpʌfinɪs/ *n* [u] hinchazón *f*

puff paste, (BrE) **puff pastry** *n* [u] hojaldre *m*

puffy /ˈpʌfi/ *adj* **-fier, -fiest** hinchado

pug /pʌg/ *n* (dog) doguillo *m*

pugilism /ˈpjuːdʒəlɪzəm/ *n* [u] (journ) pugilismo *m* (frml)

pugilist /ˈpjuːdʒələst || ˈpjuːdʒɪlɪst/ *n* (journ) púgil *m* (frml)

pugnacious /pʌgˈneɪʃəs/ *adj* (frml) pugnaz (frml)

pug-nosed /ˈpʌgˈnəʊzd/ *adj* de nariz chata, ñato (AmS)

puke /pjuːk/ *vi* (colloq) vomitar, devolver*

■ **puke** *vt* **~ (up)** vomitar

Pulitzer Prize

Un premio de gran prestigio establecido en 1917, por Joseph Pulitzer, director de periódico y editor, que se otorga anualmente por los éxitos más destacados en el mundo del periodismo, la literatura y la música norteamericanos. Cada año se entregan trece premios

pull¹ /pʊl/ *vt*

A 1 (draw) tirar de, jalar (AmL exc CS); (drag) arrastrar 2 (in specified direction) (+ *adv compl*): **~ your chair closer to the fire** acerca *or* arrima la silla al fuego; **could you ~ the door to/the curtains, please?** por favor, cierra la puerta/corre las cortinas; **he was ~ed from the rubble alive** lo sacaron vivo de entre los escombros; **he ~ed his hat down firmly over his ears** se caló el sombrero hasta las orejas; **the current ~ed him under** la corriente lo arrastró *or* se lo llevó al fondo; ***to ~ the carpet** o **rug (out) from under sb** o **sb's feet*** fastidiarle los planes a algn, moverle* el tapete a algn (Méx fam)

B 1 (tug) tirar de, jalar (AmL exc CS); ***~ the other one!*** (BrE colloq) me estás tomando el pelo (fam); ***to ~ strings** o **wires*** (use influence) tocar* todos los resortes *or* muchas teclas, mover* hilos; ***to ~ the strings** o **wires*** (be in control) tener* la sartén por el mango 2 (tear, detach): **he ~ed the toy to bits** rompió *or* destrozó el juguete 3 (snag): **I've ~ed a thread in my sweater** me he enganchado el suéter

C 1 ‹weeds/nail› arrancar*; ‹tooth› sacar* 2 (take out) sacar*; **he ~ed a gun on them** sacó una pistola y los amenazó; *see also* **pull out**

D 1 (colloq) ‹crowd/audience› atraer*; ‹votes› conseguir* 2 ‹game/show/sale› cancelar

E (perform) (colloq): **don't you ever ~ a stunt like that on me**

p

again no me vuelvas a hacer una faena así *or* una cosa semejante; ***to ~ a fast one on sb*** hacerle* una jugarreta a algn (fam)

F (Med) ‹*muscle/tendon*› desgarrarse

■ **pull** *vi*

A 1 (drag, tug) tirar, jalar (AmL exc CS); **to ~ AT/ON sth** tirar DE *or* (AmL exc CS) jalar algo 2 (suck) **to ~ ON *o* AT sth** ‹*on pipe*› darle* una chupada *or* (AmL tb) una pitada *or* (Esp tb) una calada A algo

B 1 ‹‹*vehicle*›› (move) (+ *adv compl*): **to ~ off the road** salir* de la carretera; **to ~ into the station** entrar en la estación; *see also* **pull in, pull up** *etc* 2 (row) remar

Phrasal verbs

• **pull about** [v ▸ o ▸ adv] (mishandle) maltratar, tratar sin cuidado

• **pull ahead** [v ▸ adv] tomar la delantera; **to ~ ahead OF sb** tomarle la delantera A algn

• **pull apart**

A [v ▸ o ▸ adv] 1 (separate) separar 2 (pull to pieces) destrozar*, hacer* pedazos

B [v ▸ o ▸ adv, v ▸ adv ▸ o] (criticize) ‹*book/show*› poner* por el suelo *or* por los suelos; ‹*argument/theory*› echar por tierra, demoler*

C [v ▸ adv] (become separate) separarse

• **pull around**

A [v ▸ o ▸ adv] (turn round) ‹*boat/plane*› darle* la vuelta a, dar* vuelta (CS)

B [v ▸ adv] (recover) (BrE) recuperarse, reponerse*

• **pull away** [v ▸ adv] 1 (free oneself) soltarse*, zafarse 2 (move off) ‹‹*train/bus*›› arrancar*; **the train was ~ing away from the platform** el tren se alejaba del andén

• **pull back**

A [v ▸ adv] 1 (retreat) ‹‹*troops/enemy*›› retirarse 2 (withdraw) echarse atrás

B [v ▸ o ▸ adv, v ▸ adv ▸ o] ‹*troops*› retirar

• **pull down**

A [v ▸ o ▸ adv, v ▸ adv ▸ o] 1 (lower) ‹*blind*› bajar; *see also* **pull** *vt* **A2** 2 (demolish) ‹*building*› echar *or* tirar abajo, tumbar (Méx)

B [v ▸ o ▸ adv] (depress) deprimir, tirar abajo (fam)

C [v ▸ adv ▸ o] (earn) (AmE colloq) sacar*, ganar

• **pull in**

Sense I [v ▸ o ▸ adv, v ▸ adv ▸ o]

A 1 (draw in) ‹*nets/rope*› recoger*; ‹*claws*› retraer*; **~ your stomach in!** ¡mete *or* entra esa panza! (fam) 2 (rein in) ‹*horse*› sujetar

B 1 (attract) ‹*investments/customers*› atraer* 2 (earn) (colloq) sacar*, ganar

C (arrest) (colloq) ‹*suspect*› detener*

Sense II [v ▸ adv]

A (arrive) ‹‹*train/bus*›› llegar*

B 1 (move over) ‹‹*ship/car*›› arrimarse 2 (stop) (BrE) ‹‹*car/truck*›› parar

• **pull off** [v ▸ o ▸ adv, v ▸ adv ▸ o]

A (remove) ‹*cover/lid*› quitar, sacar*; **he ~ed his boots off** se quitó las botas

B (achieve) (colloq) conseguir*, lograr; **they ~ed off the biggest bank job of the decade** llevaron a cabo el mayor asalto a un banco de la década

• **pull on** [v ▸ o ▸ adv, v ▸ adv ▸ o] ‹*gloves/boots*› ponerse*

• **pull out**

Sense I [v ▸ adv]

A ‹‹*vehicle/driver*›› 1 (depart) arrancar*; **the train ~ed out of the station** el tren salió de la estación 2 (enter traffic): **he ~ed out right in front of me** se me metió justo delante

B (extend) ‹‹*table*›› alargarse*

C (withdraw) ‹‹*troops/partner*›› retirarse, irse*; **we're not going to ~ out of the deal** no nos vamos a echar atrás

Sense II [v ▸ o ▸ adv, v ▸ adv ▸ o]

A (extract, remove) ‹*tooth/nail/plug*› sacar*; ‹*weeds/page*› arrancar*; **he ~ed out his wallet/a $20 bill** sacó la cartera/un billete de 20 dólares

B (withdraw) ‹*team/troops*› retirar

• **pull over** 1 [v ▸ adv] ‹‹*driver/car*›› hacerse* a un lado; (to stop) acercarse* a la acera (*or* al arcén *etc*) y parar 2 [v ▸ o ▸ adv] parar

• **pull through**

A 1 [v ▸ adv] (recover) reponerse* 2 [v ▸ adv] [v ▸ prep ▸ o] (survive) salir* adelante; **to ~ through a crisis** superar una crisis

B [v ▸ o ▸ adv] [v ▸ o ▸ prep ▸ o] 1 (help recover) ayudar a recuperarse 2 (help survive) salvar, ayudar a superar

• **pull together**

A [v ▸ adv] (cooperate) trabajar *or* esforzarse* codo con codo

B [v ▸ o ▸ adv] (control oneself): **to ~ oneself together** calmarse, recobrar la compostura; **~ yourself together!** ¡vamos, cálmate!

• **pull up**

A [v ▸ o ▸ adv, v ▸ adv ▸ o] 1 (draw up) levantar, subir; **to ~ one's socks up** subirse los calcetines 2 (uproot) ‹*plant*› arrancar*

B [v ▸ o ▸ adv] 1 (halt, check): **a shout ~ed her up sharply** un grito la hizo pararse en seco 2 (reprimand) **to ~ sb up (ON sth)** regañar *or* (CS) retar a algn (POR algo)

C [v ▸ adv] (stop) ‹‹*car/driver*›› parar

pull² *n*

A [c] (tug) tirón *m*, jalón *m* (AmL exc CS); **each ~ of the oars** cada golpe de remo

B [u] 1 (pulling force) fuerza *f*; **the ~ of gravity** la fuerza de la gravedad 2 (influence) influencia *f*

C [c] (on cigarette) chupada *f*, pitada *f* (AmL), calada *f* (Esp); (on drink) sorbo *m*

D [c] (difficult journey): **it was a hard ~ up the hill** la subida de la colina fue difícil

pull: **~back** /'pʊlbæk/ *n* retirada *f*; **~-down** /'pʊldaʊn/ *adj* 1 ‹*bed*› desplegable; ‹*screen*› desenrollable 2 (Comput): **~-down menu** menú *m* desplegable

pulley /'pʊli/ *n* (*pl* **~s**) polea *f*

Pullman® /'pʊlmən/ *n*: **~ coach** *o* (AmE) **car** coche *m* pullman

pull: **~-out** *n* 1 (withdrawal) retirada *f* 2 (Journ) suplemento *m*, separata *f*; **~over**, (AmE also) **~over sweater** *n* ▸ **sweater**

pulmonary /'pʊlməneri || 'pʌlmənəri/ *adj* pulmonar

pulp¹ /pʌlp/ *n*

A [u] 1 (of fruit, vegetable) pulpa *f*, carne *f*; (of wood, paper) pasta *f* (de papel), pulpa *f* (de papel) 2 (crushed material) pasta *f*; **to beat sb to a ~** hacer* papilla a algn (fam)

B 1 [u] (worthless literature) literatura *f* barata, basura *f*; (*before n*) ‹*fiction/novel*› barato 2 [c] (magazine) (AmE) revista *f* barata

pulp² *vt* ‹*wood/paper/rags*› hacer* pasta *or* pulpa con; ‹*fruit/vegetables*› hacer* papilla *or* puré con

pulpit /'pʊlpɪt/ *n* púlpito *m*

pulsate /'pʌlseɪt || pʌl'seɪt/ *vi* ‹‹*heart*›› latir, palpitar; ‹‹*light/current*›› oscilar; **the pulsating rhythm of the music** el ritmo palpitante de la música

pulse¹ /pʌls/ *n*

A 1 (Physiol) pulso *m*; **to take sb's ~** tomarle el pulso a algn; ***to have one's finger on the ~*** estar* al tanto de lo que pasa; (*before n*) **~ rate** número *m* de pulsaciones 2 (throbbing) cadencia *f*, ritmo *m* 3 (Phys) pulsación *f*

B (Agr, Culin) legumbre *f* (*como los garbanzos, las lentejas etc*)

pulse² *vi* ‹‹*heart/blood vessel*›› latir

pulverize /'pʌlvəraɪz/ *vt* pulverizar*

puma /'pu:mə || 'pju:mə/ *n* puma *m*, león *m* (Chi, Méx)

pumice /'pʌməs/ *n* [u c] **~ (stone)** piedra *f* pómez

pummel /'pʌməl/ *vt*, (BrE) **-ll-** darle* una paliza a, aporrear

pump¹ /pʌmp/ *n*

A bomba *f*; (*gasoline o* (BrE) *petrol* **~**) surtidor *m*

B (Clothing) 1 (court shoe) (AmE) zapato *m* (de) salón 2 (gym shoe) (BrE dated) zapatilla *f*

pump² *vt*

A 1 (supply) bombear; **to ~ sth INTO sth** ‹*water/oil*› bombear algo A algo; **to ~ air into a tire** inflar *or* (Esp tb) hinchar un neumático; **they have ~ed cash into the project for years** llevan años invirtiendo dinero en el proyecto; **they ~ed him full of lead** (colloq) lo acribillaron a balazos 2 (drain) **to ~ sth OUT OF sth** sacar* algo de algo con una bomba; **to ~ sb's stomach out** hacerle* un lavado de estómago a algn; **to ~ sth dry** dejar algo seco; **to ~ sb dry** exprimir a algn 3 (ask) (colloq): **he was ~ing me for information** me estaba tratando de (son)sacar información

B ‹*handle/pedal/treadle*› mover* de arriba abajo; **he ~ed my**

P

hand me dio un fuerte apretón de manos; **to ~ iron** (colloq) hacer* pesas

■ **pump** *vi* 1 ‹‹*machine/heart*›› bombear 2 (move vigorously) moverse* con fuerza

Phrasal verb

• **pump up** [v ▸ o ▸ adv, v ▸ adv ▸ o] 1 (inflate) ‹*tire*› inflar, hinchar (Esp) 2 (psych up) (AmE) mentalizar*

pumpernickel /'pʌmpərnɪkəl || 'pʌmpənɪkəl/ *n* [u] *tipo de pan integral de centeno*

pumpkin /'pʌmpkən/ *n* [c u] calabaza *f*, zapallo *m* (CS, Per)

pun /pʌn/ *n* juego *m* de palabras, albur *m* (Méx)

punch¹ /pʌntʃ/ *n*

A 1 [c] (blow) puñetazo *m*, piña *f* (fam); ***to pack a ~*** ‹‹*speaker/play/cocktail*›› pegar* fuerte (fam); (lit) ‹‹*boxer*›› pegar* fuerte *or* duro; ***to pull (one's) ~es*** andarse* con miramientos *or* (fam) con chiquitas 2 [u] (vigor) garra *f* (fam), fuerza *f*

B [c] (for paper) perforadora *f*; (for metal, leather) sacabocados *m*

C [u] (Culin) 1 ponche *m*; (*before n*) **~ bowl** ponchera *f* 2 (in US) refresco *m* de frutas

D **Punch** (name of puppet) ≈ Polichinela; **a P~ and Judy show** *tipo de función de títeres*; ***to be as pleased as P~*** estar* más contento que unas Pascuas

punch² *vt*

A (hit) pegarle* a, darle* un puñetazo *or* (fam) una piña a

B (perforate) ‹*ticket*› picar*, perforar, ponchar (Méx); ‹*leather/metal*› perforar; **to ~ a hole in sth** hacerle* un agujero a algo; **to ~ the clock** *o* **card** fichar, marcar* *or* (Méx) checar* tarjeta; **~ed card** (BrE) ficha *f* perforada

C (AmE Agr) ‹*cattle*› aguijonear, picanear (AmL)

■ **punch** *vi* ‹‹*boxer*›› pegar*

Phrasal verbs

• **punch in** [v ▸ adv] (AmE) fichar, marcar* *or* (Méx) checar* tarjeta (*al entrar al trabajo*)

• **punch out**

A [v ▸ o ▸ adv, v ▸ adv ▸ o] (with die) troquelar; (on paper) perforar

B [v ▸ adv] (at work) (AmE) fichar, marcar* *or* (Méx) checar* tarjeta (*al salir del trabajo*)

punch: **~ bag** *n* (BrE) ▸**punching bag**; **~ card** *n* (AmE) ficha *f* perforada; **~-drunk** *adj* grogui (fam), atontado

punching bag /'pʌntʃɪŋ/ *n* (AmE) (Sport) saco *m* de arena

punch: **~ line** *n* remate *m* (*de un chiste*); **~-up** *n* (BrE colloq) pelea *f*, bronca *f* (fam)

punchy /'pʌntʃi/ *adj* **-chier, -chiest** (forceful) ‹*article*› incisivo; ‹*campaign/slogan*› con garra (fam); ‹*musical number*› brioso

punctilious /pʌŋk'tɪliəs/ *adj* puntilloso, meticuloso

punctual /'pʌŋktʃuəl || 'pʌŋktjʊəl/ *adj* puntual

punctuality /'pʌŋktʃu'æləti/ *n* puntualidad *f*

punctually /'pʌŋktʃuəli || 'pʌŋktjʊəli/ *adv* puntualmente

punctuate /'pʌŋktʃueɪt || 'pʌŋktjueɪt, 'pʌŋktʃueɪt/ *vt* 1 ‹*writing/text*› puntuar* 2 (intersperse) salpicar*; **a silence ~d only by the occasional sob** un silencio interrumpido tan sólo por algún sollozo

punctuation /'pʌŋktʃu'eɪʃən/ *n* [u] puntuación *f*; (*before n*) **~ mark** signo *m* de puntuación

puncture¹ /'pʌŋktʃər/ *n* 1 (in tire, ball) pinchazo *m*, pinchadura *f* (AmL), ponchadura *f* (Méx); **my bike has a ~** mi bicicleta tiene una rueda pinchada *or* (Méx) una llanta ponchada; **we had a ~ on the way there** pinchamos por el camino, se nos ponchó una llanta en el camino (Méx); **it has a slow ~** pierde aire 2 (Med) punción *f*

puncture² *vt* ‹*tire/ball*› pinchar, ponchar (Méx); **~d lung** pulmón *m* perforado

■ **puncture** *vi* ‹‹*tire/ball*›› pincharse

pundit /'pʌndət/ *n* experto, -ta *m,f*, entendido, -da *m,f*

pungency /'pʌndʒənsi/ *n* [u] (frml) (of taste, smell) acritud *f*; (of remark) mordacidad *f*

pungent /'pʌndʒənt/ *adj* ‹*taste/smell*› acre; ‹*remark/question*› mordaz, cáustico

punish /'pʌnɪʃ/ *vt* 1 ‹*child*› castigar*; ‹*offender/offense*› castigar*, sancionar (frml) 2 (treat harshly) ‹*error/lapse*› aprovechar; ‹*ball/opponent*› castigar*; ‹*body/engine*› castigar*, exigirle* demasiado a

punishable /'pʌnɪʃəbəl/ *adj* punible (frml); **~ BY sth** penado CON algo

punishing /'pʌnɪʃɪŋ/ *adj* ‹*schedule/treatment*› duro; ‹*pace*› agotador, extenuante

punishment /'pʌnɪʃmənt/ *n* 1 [c u] (chastisement) castigo *m*; **let the ~ fit the crime** (set phrase) que el castigo sea acorde con la gravedad del delito 2 [u] (rough treatment): **it's taken a lot of ~** ha sido muy maltratado *or* (fam) baqueteado; **he took a lot of ~ in the seventh round** se llevó una buena paliza en el séptimo asalto (fam)

punitive /'pju:nətɪv || 'pju:nɪtɪv/ *adj* (frml) 1 ‹*expedition/force*› (Mil) punitivo (frml) 2 (severe) ‹*interest rate/fine*› leonino, excesivamente gravoso

Punjabi¹ /pʌn'dʒɑ:bi/ *adj* de/del Pen(d)jab *or* Punjab

Punjabi² *n* 1 [u] (language) punjabí *m* 2 [c] (person) punjabí *mf*

punk¹ /pʌŋk/ *n*

A 1 [c] (person) **~ (rocker)** punk *mf*, punki *mf* 2 [u] **~ (rock)** punk *m*

B [c] (young hoodlum) (AmE colloq) vándalo, -la *m,f*, gamberro, -rra *m,f* (Esp)

punk² *adj*

A (*before n*) ‹*hairstyle/culture*› punk *adj inv*, punki

B (rotten) (AmE colloq) de porquería (fam)

punnet /'pʌnət || 'pʌnɪt/ *n* (BrE) cajita *f* (*para frutas*), barqueta *f* (Esp)

punt¹ *n*

A /pʌnt/ (Sport) patada *f* de despeje

B /pʌnt/ (boat) (in UK) batea *f*

C /pʊnt/ (Fin) libra *f* (irlandesa)

punt² /pʌnt/ *vi* 1 (Sport) despejar 2 (in boat): **to go ~ing** salir* de paseo en batea

■ **punt** *vt* ‹*ball*› despejar

punter /'pʌntər || 'pʌntə(r)/ *n* (BrE colloq) 1 (in betting) apostador, -dora *m,f* 2 (customer) cliente, -ta *m,f*

puny /'pju:ni/ *adj* **punier, puniest** (pej) ‹*person*› enclenque, raquítico; ‹*effort*› lastimoso, de pena (fam)

pup /pʌp/ *n* cría *f*; (of dog) cachorro, -rra *m,f*

pupa /'pju:pə/ *n* (*pl* **pupae** /-pi:/) crisálida *f*, pupa *f*

pupil /'pju:pəl || 'pju:pɪl/ *n*

A (Educ) alumno, -na *m,f*, educando, -da *m,f* (frml)

B (of eye) pupila *f*

puppet /'pʌpət || 'pʌpɪt/ *n*

A 1 (marionette) marioneta *f*, títere *m* 2 (glove puppet) títere *m*

B (stooge) títere *m*; (*before n*) ‹*regime/leader*› títere

puppeteer /'pʌpə'tɪr || ˌpʌpɪ'tɪə(r)/ *n* titiritero, -ra *m,f*

puppy /'pʌpi/ *n* (*pl* **-pies**) cachorro, -rra *m,f*

puppy: **~ fat** *n* [u] (BrE) gordura *f* de la infancia; **~ love** *n* [u] amor *m* adolescente

purchase¹ /'pɜ:rtʃəs || 'pɜ:tʃəs/ *n*

A [uc] (frml) adquisición *f* (frml), compra *f*

B (grip) (*no pl*): **to get ~** *o* **a ~ on sth** agarrarse a *or* de algo

purchase² *vt* (frml) adquirir (frml), comprar; **to ~ sth FROM sb** comprarle algo A algn

purchaser /'pɜ:rtʃəsər/ *n* (frml) comprador, -dora *m,f*

purchasing power /'pɜ:rtʃəsɪŋ || 'pɜ:tʃəsɪŋ/ *n* [u] poder *m* adquisitivo

purdah /'pɜ:rdə || 'pɜ:də/ *n* [u] reclusión *f*

pure /pjʊr || pjʊə(r)/ *adj* **purer**, **purest** 1 (unmixed) puro; **it's negligence ~ and simple** se trata de negligencia, lisa *or* simple y llanamente 2 (not applied) (*before n*) ‹*science/mathematics*› puro

purebred /'pjʊr'bred || 'pjʊəbred/ *adj* de pura raza; **a ~ horse** un purasangre

puree¹, **purée** /pjʊ'reɪ || 'pjʊəreɪ/ *n* [u c] puré *m*; **tomato ~** concentrado *m or* extracto *m or* puré *m* de tomate

puree², **purée** *vt* **-rees, -reeing, -reed** hacer* un puré con, pisar (RPl, Ven)

purely /'pjʊrli || 'pjʊəli/ *adv* ‹*decorative*› puramente, meramente; **~ by chance** por pura casualidad; **~ and simply** lisa *or* simple y llanamente

purgative¹ /'pɜ:rgətɪv || 'pɜ:gətɪv/ *n* purgante *m*

purgative² *adj* (Med) purgante, laxante; (cathartic, cleansing) catártico, depurador

purgatory /'pɜ:rgətɔ:ri || 'pɜ:gətəri/ *n* [u] purgatorio *m*

purge¹ /pɜ:rdʒ/ *vt* 1 (cleanse) purgar* 2 (Pol) ‹*party/government/committee*› hacer* una purga en, purgar*; **to ~ sth (OF sth/sb)** purgar* algo (DE algo/algn); **to ~ sb (FROM sth)** expulsar a algn (DE algo)

purge² *n* (Med, Pol) purga *f*

purification /'pjʊrəfə'keɪʃən / *n* [u] purificación *f*

purifier /'pjʊrəfaɪər/ *n* depurador *m*, purificador *m*

purify /'pjʊrəfaɪ || 'pjʊərɪfaɪ/ *vt* **-fies, -fying, -fied** purificar*; ‹*water*› depurar, purificar*, potabilizar*

purist /'pjʊrəst || 'pjʊərɪst/ *n* purista *mf*

puritan¹ /'pjʊrətn || 'pjʊərɪtən/ *n* 1 **Puritan** puritano, -na *m,f* 2 (morally) puritano, -na *m,f*

puritan² *adj* 1 **Puritan** puritano 2 (morally) puritano

puritanical /'pjʊrə'tænɪkəl || ,pjʊərɪ'tænɪkəl/ *adj* puritano

Puritanism /'pjʊrətn̩ɪzəm/ *n* [u] puritanismo *m*

purity /'pjʊrəti || 'pjʊərəti/ *n* [u] pureza *f*

purl¹ /pɜ:rl || pɜ:l/ *n* [u] punto *m* (al *or* del) revés

purl² *vt* tejer al *or* del revés

purloin /'pɜ:rlɔɪn/ *vt* (frml) hurtar (frml), sustraer* (frml)

purple¹ /'pɜ:rpəl || 'pɜ:pəl/ *adj* 1 (bluish) morado, violeta; (reddish) púrpura; **~ with rage** lívido de ira 2 (overwritten) ‹*prose/passage*› grandilocuente

purple² *n* [u] (bluish) morado *m*, violeta *m*; (reddish) púrpura *m*

purport¹ /pər'pɔ:rt || pə'pɔ:t/ *vt* (frml) **to ~ to + INF** pretender + INF; **a man ~ing to be a cousin of mine** un individuo que dice *or* afirma ser primo mío

purport² /'pɜ:rpɔ:rt/ *n* [u] (frml) sentido *m* (general)

purportedly /pɜ:r'pɔ:rtədli/ *adv* supuestamente

purpose /'pɜ:rpəs || 'pɜ:pəs/ *n*

A [c] 1 (intention, reason) propósito *m*, intención *f*; **what was your ~ in doing it?** ¿qué pretendías *or* qué te proponías con eso?; **I left the door open for a ~** por algo *or* por alguna razón dejé la puerta abierta; **for one's own ~s** por su (*or* mi *etc*) propio interés; **the machine is good enough for our ~s** la máquina sirve para lo que nos proponemos hacer con ella; **for all practical ~s** a efectos prácticos; **on ~** a propósito, adrede, ex profeso, aposta (Esp fam) 2 (use): **to serve a (useful) ~** servir* de algo; **to no ~** inútilmente

B [u] (resolution) determinación *f*; **strength of ~** determinación; **to have a/no sense of ~** tener*/no tener* una meta *or* un norte en la vida

purpose-built /'pɜ:rpəs'bɪlt || ,pɜ:pəs'bɪlt/ *adj* (BrE): **~ senior citizens' housing** viviendas *fpl* construidas especialmente para la tercera edad; **a ~ flat** *un apartamento construido como tal, que no es parte de una antigua vivienda unifamiliar*

purposeful /'pɜ:rpəsfəl || 'pɜ:pəsfəl/ *adj* ‹*person/stride*› resuelto, decidido; ‹*expression*› de determinación

purposefully /'pɜ:rpəsfəli / *adv* resueltamente

purposely /'pɜ:rpəsli/ *adv* ‹*facetious/hurtful*› deliberadamente, intencionadamente; ‹*say/do*› a propósito

purr¹ /pɜ:r || pɜ:(r)/ *vi* ronronear

▪ **purr** *vt* susurrar, decir* en un arrullo

purr² *n* ronroneo *m*

purse¹ /pɜ:rs || pɜ:s/ *n*

A 1 (for money) monedero *m*, portamonedas *m* 2 (funds) fondos *mpl*; **the public ~** el erario público

B (handbag) (AmE) cartera *f* *or* (Esp) bolso *m* *or* (Méx) bolsa *f*

purse² *vt* **to ~ one's lips** fruncir* la boca

purser /'pɜ:rsər || 'pɜ:sə(r)/ *n* sobrecargo *mf*

purse strings *pl n*: **to hold** *o* **control the ~ ~** administrar el dinero

pursuance /pər'su:əns || pə'sju:əns/ *n* [u] (frml) **in ~ of sth**: **in ~ of his duties** en el cumplimiento del deber

pursue /pər'su: || pə'sju:/ *vt*

A 1 (chase) perseguir* 2 (seek, strive for) ‹*pleasure/happiness*› buscar*; ‹*hopes/rights*› luchar por, reivindicar*

B (carry out, continue with) 1 ‹*policy/course of action*› continuar* con; ‹*research/study*› continuar* con, proseguir* (frml) 2 ‹*profession*› ejercer*, dedicarse* al ejercicio de

pursuer /pər'su:ər || pə'sju:ə(r)/ *n* perseguidor, -dora *m,f*

pursuit /pər'su:t || pə'sju:t/ *n*

A [u c] 1 (chase) persecución *f*; **she set off in ~ of the thief** salió en persecución *or* a la caza del ladrón; **with two guards in hot ~** con dos guardias pisándole los talones 2 (search, striving): **the ~ of happiness** la búsqueda de la felicidad; **in the ~ of her goals** en su lucha por alcanzar sus objetivos

B [c] (pastime, activity) actividad *f*; **her leisure ~s** sus pasatiempos

purvey /pər'veɪ || pə'veɪ/ *vt* (frml) proveer*, suministrar; **to ~ sth TO sb** proveer* *or* abastecer* a algn DE algo

purveyor /pər'veɪər / *n* (frml) proveedor, -dora *m,f*

pus /pʌs/ *n* [u] pus *m*

push¹ /pʊʃ/ *n*

A [c] 1 (gentle) empujoncito *m*; (violent) empujón *m*; **she gave the door a ~** empujó la puerta; **at the ~ of a button** con sólo apretar un botón; ***to get the ~*** (BrE colloq): **he got the ~** (from job) lo pusieron de patitas en la calle (fam); (in relationship) ella lo dejó; ***to give sb the ~*** (BrE colloq) (from job) poner* a algn de patitas en la calle (fam), echar a algn; (in relationship) dejar a algn 2 (pressure) (colloq): **she needs a bit of a ~ now and again** de vez en cuando hay que apretarle las clavijas (fam); ***at a ~***: **at a ~, I could finish it by Friday** si me apuras *or* si fuera necesario, podría terminarlo para el viernes; ***if ~ comes to shove*** *o* (BrE) ***if it comes to the ~*** en último caso; **when it came to the ~, she gave in** (BrE) a la hora de la verdad, cedió

B [c] 1 (effort) esfuerzo *m* 2 (offensive) (Mil) ofensiva *f* 3 (for sales) campaña *f*

C [u] (will to succeed) (colloq) empuje *m*, dinamismo *m*

push² *vt*

A 1 ‹*person/car/table*› empujar; **he ~ed him down the stairs** lo empujó escaleras abajo; **I ~ed the door to** *o* **shut** cerré la puerta empujándola 2 (press) ‹*button*› apretar*, pulsar; ‹*lever*› darle* a, accionar (frml) 3 (force): **to ~ prices up/down** hacer* que suban/bajen los precios; **I tried to ~ the thought to the back of my mind** traté de no pensar en ello

B (put pressure on): **you're ~ing him/yourself too hard** le/te exiges demasiado; **you can only ~ people so far** todos tenemos un límite; **to ~ sb to + INF** presionar a algn PARA QUE (+ *subj*): **to ~ sb INTO sth**: **she was ~ed into joining** la presionaron para que se hiciera socia; **to be ~ed for time/money** (colloq) andar* escaso *or* (fam) corto de tiempo/de dinero; **you'd be ~ed to find a better one** difícilmente encontrarás uno mejor

C 1 (promote) promocionar 2 (sell) (colloq) ‹*drugs*› pasar (fam), transar (CS arg), vender

D (approach) (colloq): **to be ~ing forty** rondar los cuarenta

▪ **push** *vi*

A 1 (give a push) empujar 2 (in childbirth) pujar

B (apply pressure) presionar; **to ~ FOR sth**: **we're ~ing for a decision** estamos presionando para que se decida

Phrasal verbs

- **push about** (BrE) ▸**push around**
- **push ahead** [v ▸ adv] **to ~ ahead (WITH sth)** seguir* adelante (CON algo)
- **push around** [v ▸ o ▸ adv] (colloq) mandonear (fam)
- **push back** [v ▸ o ▸ adv, v ▸ adv ▸ o] 1 (force back) ‹*person/object*› empujar hacia atrás; ‹*crowd/army*› hacer* retroceder 2 (extend) ‹*limits*› ampliar*, extender*
- **push forward**

A [v ▸ adv] avanzar*

B [v ▸ o ▸ adv, v ▸ adv ▸ o] empujar hacia adelante

- **push in** [v ▸ adv] colarse* (fam); **she ~ed in in front of me** se me coló (fam)
- **push off** [v ▸ adv] 1 (in boat) desatracar*, salir* 2 (leave, go) (colloq) largarse* (fam)
- **push on** [v ▸ adv] 1 (continue journey) seguir* el viaje 2 (continue working) seguir* adelante
- **push through** [v ▸ o ▸ adv, v ▸ adv ▸ o] ‹*legislation*› hacer* aprobar

push: **~-bike** *n* (BrE) bicicleta *f*; **~-button** *adj* (*before n*) ‹*controls/telephone*› de botones; **~chair** *n* (BrE) sillita *f* (*de paseo*), carreola *f* (Méx)

pusher /'pʊʃər || 'pʊʃə(r)/ *n* (colloq) camello *mf* (arg), jíbaro *mf* (Col, Ven arg), conecte *m,f* (Mex arg)

push: **~over** *n*: **to be a ~over** «*task/game*» ser* pan comido (fam), estar* chupado (Esp fam); «*person*» ser* un

P

incauto; ~**-start** *vt* ‹*car*› arrancar* empujando; ~**-up** *n* flexión *f* (de brazos)

pushy /'pʊʃi/ *adj* **pushier, pushiest** (colloq) prepotente, avasallador; **a ~ salesman** un vendedor agresivo

pusillanimous /'pju:sə'lænəməs || ˌpju:sɪ'lænɪməs/ *adj* (liter) pusilánime

puss /pʊs/ *n* (colloq) [1] (cat) minino, -na *m,f* (fam), gatito, -ta *m,f* (fam) [2] (face) (AmE) jeta *f* (fam)

pussy /'pʊsi/ *n* (*pl* **-sies**) [1] [c] ► **pussycat** [2] [c] (female genitals) (sl) coño *m* (vulg), concha *f* (AmS vulg)

pussy: ~**cat** *n* (colloq) minino, -na *m,f* (fam), gatito, -ta *m,f* (fam); ~**foot** *vi* (colloq): **they're just ~footing about** *o* **around** le están dando largas al asunto; ~ **willow** *n* [c u] sauce *m* blanco

pustule /'pʌstʃu:l || 'pʌstju:l/ *n* pústula *f*

put /pʊt/ (*pres p* **putting**; *past & past p* **put**) *vt*

Sense I

A [1] (place) poner*; (with care, precision etc) colocar*, poner*; (inside sth) meter, poner*; **to ~ sth in the oven** poner* *or* meter algo en el horno; **did you ~ salt in it?** ¿le pusiste *or* le echaste sal?; **he ~ it in his mouth** se lo puso en la boca; **I ~ myself on the list** me apunté *or* me puse en la lista; **~ yourself in my place** ponte en mi lugar; **she ~ the bottle to her lips** se llevó la botella a los labios; **I ~ her on the train** la acompañé hasta el tren; ***not to know where to ~ oneself*** *o* (AmE also) ***one's face*** (colloq) no saber* dónde ponerse *or* meterse; ***to ~ sth behind one*** olvidar *or* superar algo [2] (install, fit) poner*

B [1] (thrust): **he ~ his arms around her** la abrazó; **she ~ her head around the door/out of the window** asomó la cabeza por la puerta/por la ventana [2] (send, propel): **he ~ the ball into the net** lanzó la pelota a la red [3] (Sport) **to ~ the shot** lanzar* el peso

C [1] (rank) poner*; **she ~s herself first** se pone ella primero *or* en primer lugar; **to ~ sth ABOVE/BEFORE sth**: **I ~ honesty above all other virtues** para mí la honestidad está por encima de todas las demás virtudes *or* por encima de todo; **he ~s his art before everything else** antepone su arte a todo [2] (in competition): **this victory ~s them in the lead** con esta victoria pasan a ocupar la delantera [3] (estimate): **he ~s the cost somewhat higher** calcula que el costo sería algo mayor; **to ~ sth AT sth**: **I'd ~ the figure at $40,000** yo diría que la cifra es 40.000 dólares

Sense II

A (cause to be) poner*; **the doctor ~ me on a diet** el doctor me puso a régimen; **it's not easy to ~ it into English** no es fácil traducirlo al inglés; **to ~ sth to good use** ‹*time/ability/object*› hacer* buen uso de algo

B (make undergo, cause to do) **to ~ sb TO sth**: **I don't want to ~ you to any trouble** no quiero causarle ninguna molestia; **I ~ her to work** la puse a trabajar; ► **death, shame**[1] **A, test**[1] **A2** *etc*

Sense III

A [1] (attribute, assign) **to ~ sth ON sth**: **I couldn't ~ a price on it** no sabría decir cuánto vale; **I ~ a high value on our friendship** valoro mucho nuestra amistad [2] (impose) **to ~ sth ON sth/sb**: **they ~ a special duty on these goods** gravaron estos artículos con un impuesto especial; **to ~ the blame on sb** echarle la culpa a algn, culpar a algn; **it ~ a great strain on their relationship** eso sometió su relación a una gran tensión

B [1] (instill, infect) **to ~ sth IN(TO) sth**: **who ~ that idea into your head?** ¿quién te metió esa idea en la cabeza? [2] (cause to have) **to ~ sth IN(TO) sth**: **the fresh air ~ some color into his cheeks** el aire fresco le dio un poco de color a sus mejillas

C [1] (invest) **to ~ sth INTO sth** ‹*money*› invertir* algo EN algo; **I've ~ a lot of time into it** le he dedicado mucho tiempo; **she had ~ a lot of thought into it** lo había pensado mucho [2] (bet, stake) **to ~ sth ON sth** ‹*money*› apostar* *or* jugarse* algo A algo [3] (contribute) **to ~ sth TOWARD sth** contribuir* CON algo A algo, poner* algo PARA algo

D (fix, repose) **to ~ sth IN sth/sb**: **I ~ my trust in you** puse *or* (liter) deposité mi confianza en ti; **I don't ~ much faith in medicine** no le tengo mucha fe a la medicina

Sense IV

A (present) ‹*views/case*› exponer*, presentar; ‹*proposal*› presentar; **to ~ sth TO sb**: **to ~ a question to sb** hacerle* una pregunta a algn; **the employers' offer will be ~ to a mass meeting** la oferta de la patronal será sometida a votación en una asamblea; **I ~ it to you that ...** (frml) mi opinión es que ...

B (write, indicate, mark) poner*; **what shall I ~?** ¿qué pongo?; **she ~ a line through the word** tachó la palabra

C (express) decir*; **how shall I ~ it?** cómo te diría?; **(let me) ~ it this way: I wouldn't invite him again** te digo lo siguiente: no lo volvería a invitar; **to ~ sth well/badly** expresar algo bien/mal

■ **put** *vi* (Naut): **to ~ to sea** hacerse* a la mar, zarpar

Phrasal verbs

• **put about**

A [v ► o ► adv] [1] (Naut) ‹*ship*› hacer* virar en redondo [2] (spread) (colloq) ‹*story/rumor*› hacer* correr *or* circular; ***to ~ it about that ...*** hacer* correr la voz de que ...

B [v ► adv] (Naut) virar en redondo, cambiar de borda

• **put across** [v ► o ► adv, v ► adv ► o] ‹*idea/message*› comunicar*; **to ~ sth across TO sb** hacerle* entender algo A algn

• **put aside** [v ► o ► adv, v ► adv ► o] [1] (lay to one side) dejar a un lado [2] (reserve) ‹*money*› guardar, ahorrar; ‹*goods/time*› reservar [3] ‹*differences*› dejar de lado

• **put away** [v ► o ► adv, v ► adv ► o] [1] ‹*dishes/tools/clothes*› guardar [2] (save) ‹*money*› guardar, ahorrar [3] (colloq) ‹*food/drink*› zamparse (fam) [4] (colloq) ‹*criminal/lunatic*› encerrar* [5] (destroy) (AmE euph) ‹*animal*› sacrificar* (euf)

• **put back**

A [v ► o ► adv, v ► adv ► o] [1] (replace) volver* a poner; **~ that back (where you found it)!** ¡deja eso (donde estaba)! [2] (reset) ‹*clocks*› atrasar, retrasar [3] (delay, retard) ‹*project*› retrasar [4] (postpone) posponer*, aplazar*, postergar*

B [v ► o ► adv] (AmE): **he was ~ back a year** lo hicieron repetir el año

• **put by** [v ► o ► adv, v ► adv ► o] ‹*money*› ahorrar

• **put down**

Sense I [v ► o ► adv, v ► adv ► o]

A [1] (set down) ‹*bag/pen*› dejar; ‹*telephone*› colgar*; **she ~ the package down on the table** puso *or* depositó el paquete sobre la mesa; **it's one of those books you can't ~ down** es uno de esos libros que no se pueden parar de leer [2] (lay) ‹*tiles/carpet*› poner*, colocar* [3] (lower) bajar [4] ‹*passenger*› dejar

B [1] (suppress) ‹*rebellion*› sofocar* [2] (destroy) (BrE euph) ‹*animal*› sacrificar* (euf), matar

C [1] (write down) ‹*thoughts*› anotar, escribir*; ‹*name*› poner*, escribir*; **~ it down on paper** ponlo por escrito [2] (assess) **to ~ sb down AS sth** catalogar* a algn DE algo [3] (attribute) **to ~ sth down TO sth** atribuirle* algo A algo

D (in part payment) ‹*sum*› entregar*; ‹*deposit*› dejar

Sense II

A [v ► o ► adv] (belittle, humiliate) ‹*person*› rebajar; **why are you ~ting yourself down?** ¿por qué te menosprecias?

B [v ► adv] (Aviat) «*aircraft/pilot*» aterrizar*

• **put forward** [v ► o ► adv, v ► adv ► o]

A [1] ‹*theory/plan*› presentar, proponer*; ‹*suggestion*› hacer*, presentar [2] ‹*candidate*› proponer*, postular (AmL)

B [1] ‹*clocks*› adelantar [2] ‹*trip/meeting*› adelantar

• **put in**

Sense I [v ► o ► adv, v ► adv ► o]

A [1] (install) ‹*central heating/shower unit*› poner*, instalar [2] (plant) ‹*vegetables*› plantar

B (enter, submit) ‹*claim/request/tender*› presentar; **I've ~ myself in for the tournament** me he apuntado *or* inscrito en el campeonato; ► **appearance A1**

C (invest): **she ~s in a 60-hour week** trabaja *or* hace 60 horas por semana; **how much time can you put in?** ¿cuánto tiempo puedes dedicarle?

D (insert, add) ‹*word/chapter/scene*› poner*, agregar*

Sense II [v ► adv]

A (Naut) hacer* escala

B (apply) **to ~ in FOR sth** solicitar algo

• **put off**

Sense I [v ► o ► adv, v ► adv ► o]

A [1] (postpone) ‹*meeting/visit/decision*› aplazar*, posponer*, postergar* (AmL); **don't ~ it off until later** no lo dejes para más tarde; **to ~ off -ING**: **I keep ~ting off going to the dentist** siempre estoy aplazando ir al dentista [2] (stall) ‹*visitor/creditor*›: **if Saturday isn't convenient, I can ~ them off** si el sábado no es conveniente, puedo decirles que lo dejen para más adelante

B (turn off) (BrE) ‹*light*› apagar*

(Sense II) [v ▸ o ▸ adv, v ▸ adv ▸ o]

A (discourage): **the thought of the journey ~s me off going to see them** pensar en el viaje me quita las ganas de ir a visitarlos; **people get ~ off by all the technical jargon** la gente se desanima con toda esa jerga técnica; **the smell was enough to ~ anyone off** tenía un olor que daba asco; **she's not easily ~ off** no es fácil disuadirla *or* hacerla cambiar de idea

B (distract) distraer*; (disconcert) desconcertar*; **he's trying to ~ me off my serve** está tratando de que falle en el saque

C (from bus) dejar; (force to get off) hacer* bajar

• **put on**

(Sense I) [v ▸ o ▸ adv, v ▸ adv ▸ o]

A ‹*jacket/shoes*› ponerse*; **to ~ one's clothes on** vestirse*, ponerse* la ropa

B ‹*light/radio/oven*› encender*, prender (AmL); ‹*music*› poner*; **to ~ the brakes on** frenar

C (gain): **I've ~ on four kilos** he engordado cuatro kilos; **to ~ on weight** engordar

D ‹*exhibition*› organizar*; ‹*play/show*› presentar, dar*

E (assume) ‹*expression*› adoptar; **he's just ~ting it on** está haciendo teatro *or* está fingiendo; **he ~ on a foreign accent** fingió tener acento extranjero

(Sense II) [v ▸ o ▸ adv]

A (connect) (Telec): **~ him on, would you?** pásemelo, por favor

B 1 (alert) **to ~ sb on TO sb/sth**: **somebody had ~ the police on to them** alguien había puesto a la policía sobre su pista; **my neighbor ~ me on to your little game** mi vecino me alertó de lo que te traías entre manos 2 (introduce) **to ~ sb on TO sb/sth**: **I can ~ you on to someone who ...** puedo ponerte en contacto con una persona que ...; **she ~ me on to a store where ...** me dijo de *or* (CS) me dio el dato de una tienda donde ...

C (tease) (AmE colloq) tomarle el pelo a (fam)

• **put out**

(Sense I) [v ▸ o ▸ adv, v ▸ adv ▸ o]

A 1 (put outside) ‹*washing/cat*› sacar* 2 (set out) disponer*, colocar* 3 (extend) ‹*arm/tongue*› sacar*; **she ~ out her hand** tendió *or* alargó la mano 4 (dislocate) dislocarse*

B 1 (extinguish) ‹*fire/light/cigarette*› apagar* 2 (anesthetize) (colloq) dormir*, anestesiar 3 (distort): **the new prices have ~ all our estimates out** los nuevos precios significan que nuestros cálculos son ahora erróneos 4 (in baseball) ‹*hitter/runner*› sacar*, poner* 'out'

C 1 (offend, upset) molestar, ofender; **she was most ~ out** se molestó *or* se ofendió mucho 2 (inconvenience) molestar; **don't ~ yourself out!** ¡no te molestes!

D 1 (issue, publish) ‹*photograph/statement*› publicar* 2 (broadcast) transmitir

E (pass on): **they ~ the work out to contract** subcontrataron el trabajo; **the contract is being ~ out to tender** van a llamar a concurso *or* a licitación para el contrato

F (sprout) ‹*shoots/buds*› echar

(Sense II) [v ▸ o ▸ adv, v ▸ adv ▸ o] (expel) ‹*troublemaker*› echar; **you can ~ that idea out of your head** puedes sacarte esa idea de la cabeza

(Sense III) [v ▸ adv] **to ~ out to sea** hacerse* a la mar

• **put over**

A 1 ▸**put across A** 2 (AmE) ▸**put off** Sense **I A1**

B [v ▸ o ▸ adv] (trick): ***to ~ one over on sb*** (colloq) engañar a algn, pasar a algn (AmL fam)

• **put past** [v ▸ o ▸ prep ▸ o]: ***not to ~ it past sb***: **I wouldn't ~ it past her** la creo muy capaz

• **put through**

A [v ▸ o ▸ prep ▸ o] 1 (make undergo) someter a; ***to ~ sb through it*** (colloq) hacérselas* pasar (mal) a algn 2 (send to): **they ~ her through college** le costearon los estudios

B [v ▸ o ▸ adv, v ▸ adv ▸ o] (Telec): **to ~ sb through (TO sb)** pasar *or* (AmL) comunicar* *or* (Esp) poner* a algn CON algn

• **put together** [v ▸ o ▸ adv, v ▸ adv ▸ o]

A 1 (assemble) armar, montar; ‹*collection*› reunir* 2 (create) ‹*team*› formar; ‹*magazine*› producir*; ‹*meal*› preparar, hacer*; (quickly) improvisar

B (combine) juntar, reunir*; **more than everything else ~ together** más que todo lo demás junto

• **put under** [v ▸ o ▸ adv] dormir*, anestesiar

• **put up**

(Sense I) [v ▸ o ▸ adv, v ▸ adv ▸ o]

A 1 ‹*hotel*› levantar; ‹*tent*› armar 2 ‹*decorations/curtains/notice*› poner* 3 ‹*umbrella*› abrir* 4 ‹*hand*› levantar

B ‹*price/fare*› aumentar

C ‹*candidate*› proponer*, postular (AmL)

D (in accommodation) alojar; **they ~ us up for the night** nos quedamos a dormir en su casa, dormimos en su casa

(Sense II) [v ▸ adv ▸ o] 1 (present): **the team ~ up a brave performance** el equipo jugó con arrojo *or* (fam) con garra; **to ~ up resistance/a struggle/a fight** ofrecer* *or* oponer* resistencia 2 ‹*money/capital*› poner*, aportar

(Sense III) [v ▸ adv]

A (stay) (AmE colloq) quedarse, alojarse

B (pay stake) (AmE colloq) pagar* (*el dinero apostado*); ***to ~ up or shut up*** actuar* o callarse *or* quedarse callado

(Sense IV) [v ▸ o ▸ adv] (offer): **to ~ sth up for sale** poner* algo en venta

• **put up to** [v ▸ o ▸ adv ▸ prep ▸ o]: **somebody must have ~ them up to it** alguien debe haberlos empujado a ello

• **put up with** [v ▸ adv ▸ prep ▸ o] aguantar, soportar

put: **~-down** *n* (colloq) desprecio *m*, desaire *m*; **~-on** *adj* (*pred* **put on**) (colloq) ‹*accent/interest*› fingido; **his headache is all ~ on** lo del dolor de cabeza es puro cuento (fam); **~ out** *adj* (*pred*) **to be ~ out** estar* molesto

putrefaction /ˈpjuːtrəˈfækʃən/ *n* [u] putrefacción *f*

putrefy /ˈpjuːtrəfaɪ/ *vi* **-fies, -fying, -fied** pudrirse*

putrid /ˈpjuːtrəd || ˈpjuːtrɪd/ *adj* putrefacto, pútrido

putsch /pʊtʃ/ *n* golpe *m* de estado, putsch *m*

putt[1] /pʌt/ *vi* golpear la bola, potear (AmL)

■ **putt** *vt* golpear

putt[2] *n* putt *m*

putter[1] /ˈpʌtər || ˈpʌtə(r)/ *n* (club) putter *m*

putter[2] *vi* (AmE) (+ *adv compl*): **she loves ~ing around** *o* **about in the garden** le encanta entretenerse trabajando en el jardín

putting green /ˈpʌtɪŋ/ *n* putting green *m*

putty /ˈpʌti/ *n* [u] masilla *f*; ***to be (like) ~ in sb's hands***: **he's like ~ in her hands** hace con él lo que quiere

put: **~-up** *adj* (colloq) (*before n*) amañado (fam), arreglado, tamaleado (Méx fam); **a ~-up job** un montaje; **~-upon** *adj* utilizado; **I'm feeling very ~-upon** siento que están abusando de mí; **the ~-upon husband** el marido sufrido; **~-you-up** *n* (BrE colloq) cama *f* plegable

puzzle[1] /ˈpʌzəl/ *n* 1 (game) rompecabezas *m*; (toy) rompecabezas *m*, puzzle *m*; (riddle) adivinanza *f*; **crossword ~** crucigrama *m*, palabras *fpl* cruzadas; **jigsaw ~** rompecabezas *m*; puzzle *m* 2 (mystery) misterio *m*

puzzle[2] *vt*: **one thing ~s me** hay algo que no entiendo *or* que me tiene intrigado; **her reply ~d me** su respuesta me extrañó *or* me desconcertó

■ **puzzle** *vi* **to ~ OVER sth** cavilar SOBRE algo, darle* vueltas A algo

(Phrasal verb)

• **puzzle out** [v ▸ o ▸ adv, v ▸ adv ▸ o] (BrE): **I can't ~ it out** no me lo explico, no logro entenderlo

puzzled /ˈpʌzəld/ *adj* ‹*expression/tone*› de desconcierto, de perplejidad; **I'm ~ about it** me tiene perplejo; **you look ~** tienes cara de no entender *or* de estar confundido

puzzlement /ˈpʌzəlmənt/ *n* [u] perplejidad *f*

puzzling /ˈpʌzlɪŋ/ *adj* desconcertante

PVC *n* [u] PVC *m*; ‹*raincoat/sheeting*› de plástico *or* PVC

pygmy /ˈpɪgmi/ *n* (*pl* **-mies**) 1 (Anthrop) *also* **Pygmy** pigmeo, -mea *m,f* 2 (Zool) (*before n*) enano

pyjamas /pəˈdʒɑːməz/ *n* (BrE) ▸**pajamas**

pylon /ˈpaɪlɑːn/ *n* torre *f* de alta tensión

pyramid /ˈpɪrəmɪd/ *n* pirámide *f*

pyre /paɪr || ˈpaɪə(r)/ *n* pira *f*

Pyrenees /ˈpɪrəˈniːz/ *pl n* **the ~** los Pirineos, el Pirineo

Pyrex® /ˈpaɪreks/ *n* [u] pyrex® *m*, arcopal® *m*

pyromaniac /ˈpaɪrəʊˈmeɪniæk/ *n* pirómano, -na *m,f*

pyrotechnics /ˈpaɪrəˈteknɪks/ *n* 1 (science) (+ *sing vb*) pirotecnia *f* 2 (fireworks) (+ *pl vb*) fuegos *mpl* artificiales

Pyrrhic /ˈpɪrɪk/ *adj*: **~ victory** victoria pírrica

python /ˈpaɪθɑːn || ˈpaɪθən/ *n* (serpiente *f*) pitón *f*

pzazz /pəˈzæz/ *n* [u] ▸**pizazz**

Qq

Q, q /kju:/ *n* Q, q *f*
Qatar /ˈkʌtər || kæˈtɑ:(r)/ *n* Qatar
QC *n* (in UK) = **Queen's Counsel**
QED (= **quod erat demonstrandum**) Q.E.D. (frml), que es lo que había que demostrar
qty = **quantity**
quack¹ /kwæk/ *vi* «*duck*» graznar, hacer* cua cua
quack² *n* (pej)
A (charlatan) charlatán, -tana *m,f*; (professing medical skill) (~ *doctor*) curandero, -ra *m,f*; (*before n*) ‹*cure*› de curandero
B (of duck) graznido *m*
quad /kwɑ:d || kwɒd/ *n* (colloq)
A (quadruplet) cuatrillizo, -za *m,f*
B (of college) ▸**quadrangle A**
quadrangle /ˈkwɑ:dræŋgəl || ˈkwɒdræŋgəl/ *n*
A (BrE Archit) patio *m* interior
B (Math) ▸**quadrilateral**
quadrant /ˈkwɑ:drənt || ˈkwɒdrənt/ *n* cuadrante *m*
quadratic /kwɑ:ˈdrætɪk || kwɒˈdrætɪk/ *adj* cuadrático
quadrilateral /ˈkwɑ:drəˈlætərəl || ˌkwɒdrɪˈlætərəl/ *n* cuadrilátero *m*
quadruped /ˈkwɑ:drəped || ˈkwɒdrʊped/ *n* cuadrúpedo *m*
quadruple¹ /kwɑ:ˈdru:pl̩ || ˈkwɒdrʊpl̩/ *adj* cuádruple, cuádruplo
quadruple² /kwɑ:ˈdru:pl̩ || kwɒˈdru:pl̩/ *vi* cuadruplicarse*
■ **quadruple** *vt* cuadruplicar*
quadruplet /kwɑ:ˈdru:plət || ˈkwɒdrʊplət/ *n* cuatrillizo, -za *m,f*
quaff /kwɑ:f || kwɒf/ *vt* (hum) beberse, zamparse (fam)
quagmire /ˈkwægmaɪr, ˈkwɑ:g- || ˈkwɒgmaɪə(r), ˈkwæg-/ *n* 1 (bog) lodazal *m*, barrial *m* (AmL) 2 (situation) atolladero *m*
quail¹ /kweɪl/ *vi* temblar*; **she ~ed at the idea** la idea le daba pavor *or* la aterrorizaba
quail² *n* [c u] (*pl* **quails** *or* **quail**) codorniz *f*
quaint /kweɪnt/ *adj* **-er, -est** 1 (charming, picturesque) pintoresco 2 (odd) ‹*notion*› extraño, curioso
quaintly /ˈkweɪntli/ *adv* (oddly) de forma extraña *or* rara
quake¹ /kweɪk/ *vi* temblar*; **he ~d at the knees** le temblaron las piernas
quake² *n* (colloq) (earthquake) temblor *m*; (more violent) terremoto *m*
Quaker /ˈkweɪkər || ˈkweɪkə(r)/ *n* cuáquero, -ra *m,f*
qualification /ˈkwɑ:ləfəˈkeɪʃən || ˌkwɒlɪfɪˈkeɪʃən/ *n*
A [c] 1 (Educ): **she has a teaching ~** tiene título de maestra/profesora; **his ~s are very good** está muy bien calificado *or* (Esp) cualificado 2 (skill, necessary attribute) requisito *m*
B [u] 1 (eligibility) derecho *m* 2 (being accepted) clasificación *f*
C [u c] (reservation) reserva *f*; **to agree without ~** aceptar sin reservas *or* condiciones
qualified /ˈkwɑ:ləfaɪd || ˈkwɒlɪfaɪd/ *adj*
A 1 (trained) titulado; **a shortage of ~ personnel** una escasez de personal calificado *or* (Esp) cualificado; **a highly ~ candidate** un candidato muy preparado *or* con un excelente currículum; **to be ~ to + INF** tener* la titulación necesaria PARA + INF 2 (competent) (*pred*) capacitado; **to be ~ to + INF** estar* capacitado PARA + INF 3 (eligible) (*pred*) **to be ~ to + INF** reunir* los requisitos necesarios PARA + INF
B (limited) ‹*acceptance*› con reservas; **it was a ~ success** tuvo cierto éxito
qualifier /ˈkwɑ:ləfaɪər || ˈkwɒlɪfaɪə(r)/ *n*
A (Sport) 1 (competitor, team) clasificado, -da *m,f* 2 (preliminary round) eliminatoria *f*
B (Ling) calificador *m*
qualify /ˈkwɑ:ləfaɪ || ˈkwɒlɪfaɪ/ **-fies, -fying, -fied** *vt*
A (equip, entitle) **to ~ sb FOR sth/to + INF**: **his experience should ~ him for a better post** su experiencia debería permitirle acceder a un puesto mejor; **this degree qualifies you to practice anywhere in Europe** este título te habilita *or* te faculta para ejercer en cualquier parte de Europa; **their low income qualifies them for some benefits** sus bajos ingresos les dan derecho a recibir ciertas prestaciones
B 1 (limit): **I'd like to ~ the statement I made earlier** quisiera matizar lo que expresé anteriormente haciendo algunas salvedades (*or* puntualizaciones *etc*) 2 (Ling) calificar*
■ **qualify** *vi* 1 (gain professional qualification) titularse, recibirse (AmL); **to ~ AS sth** sacar* el título DE algo, recibirse DE algo (AmL) 2 (Sport) **to ~ (FOR sth)** clasificarse* (PARA algo) 3 (be entitled) **to ~ (FOR sth)** tener* derecho (A algo)
qualifying /ˈkwɑ:ləfaɪɪŋ || ˈkwɒlɪfaɪɪŋ/ *adj* (*before n*) ‹*round*› eliminatorio
qualitative /ˈkwɑ:ləteɪtɪv || ˈkwɒlɪtətɪv/ *adj* cualitativo
qualitatively /ˈkwɑ:ləteɪtɪvli || ˈkwɒlɪtətɪvli/ *adv* cualitativamente
quality¹ /ˈkwɑ:ləti || ˈkwɒləti/ *n* (*pl* **-ties**)
A [u c] (degree of excellence) calidad *f*; **of poor/excellent ~** de calidad inferior/de primera calidad; **good/poor ~ products** productos de buena calidad/de calidad inferior
B [c] (characteristic) cualidad *f*
quality² *adj* (*before n*) ‹*product*› de calidad; ‹*newspaper*› serio
quality control *n* control *m* de calidad
qualm /kwɑ:m/ *n* (*often pl*) 1 (scruple) reparo *m*, escrúpulo *m*; **to have no ~s about sth** no tener* ningún reparo *or* escrúpulo en algo 2 (misgiving) duda *f*
quandary /ˈkwɑ:ndri || ˈkwɒndri/ *n* (*pl* **-ries**) (*usu sing*) dilema *m*; **to be in a ~** estar* en un dilema
quango /ˈkwæŋgəʊ/ *n* (*pl* **-gos**) (BrE) (= **quasi-autonomous non-governmental organization**) organismo *m* *or* ente *m* semi-autónomo
quanta /ˈkwɑ:ntə || ˈkwɒntə/ *pl of* **quantum**
quantifiable /ˈkwɑ:ntəfaɪəbəl || ˈkwɒntɪfaɪəbəl/ *adj* cuantificable
quantifier /ˈkwɑ:ntəfaɪər || ˈkwɒntɪfaɪə(r)/ *n* (Ling) cuantificador *m*
quantify /ˈkwɑ:ntəfaɪ || ˈkwɒntɪfaɪ/ *vt* **-fies, -fying, -fied** cuantificar*
quantitative /ˈkwɑ:ntəteɪtɪv || ˈkwɒntɪtətɪv/ *adj* cuantitativo
quantitatively /ˈkwɑ:ntəteɪtɪvli || ˈkwɒntɪtətɪvli/ *adv* cuantitativamente

quantity /'kwɑːntəti || 'kwɒntəti/ *n* (*pl* **-ties**)
A [c u] (amount) cantidad *f*; **in ~** en grandes cantidades
B [c] (Math) cantidad *f*; ***an unknown* ~** una incógnita

quantity surveyor *n*: *ingeniero o técnico que se ocupa de mediciones y cálculo de materiales*

quantum /'kwɑːntəm || 'kwɒntəm/ *n* (*pl* **-ta**) 1 (amount) (frml) cuantía *f* 2 (Nucl Phys) cuanto *m*, quántum *m*; (*before n*) ‹*theory/mechanics*› cuántico

quantum: **~ jump** *n* 1 (Phys) salto *m* cuántico 2 ▸**quantum leap**; **~ leap** *n* salto *m* cuántico, salto *m* gigante *or* espectacular

quarantine[1] /'kwɔːrəntiːn || 'kwɒrəntiːn/ *n* [u] cuarentena *f*

quarantine[2] *vt* poner* en cuarentena

quarrel[1] /'kwɔːrəl || 'kwɒrəl/ *n* 1 (argument) pelea *f*, riña *f*; **to have a ~ with sb** pelearse con algn 2 (disagreement) discrepancia *f*; **to have no ~ with sb/sth** no tener* nada en contra de algn/algo

quarrel[2] *vi*, (BrE) **-ll-** (argue) pelearse, discutir; **they were ~ing about whose turn it was** se estaban peleando *or* estaban discutiendo sobre a quién le tocaba; **he ~ed with his family over the inheritance** riñó *or* se peleó con su familia por cuestiones de herencia

quarrelsome /'kwɔːrəlsəm || 'kwɒrəlsəm/ *adj* peleador, peleón (Esp fam)

quarry[1] /'kwɔːri || 'kwɒri/ *n* (*pl* **-ries**)
A (excavation) cantera *f*
B (prey) presa *f*

quarry[2] *vt* **-ries, -rying, -ried** ‹*stone/slate*› extraer* (*de una cantera*); ‹*land/hillside*› abrir* una cantera en

quart /kwɔːrt || kwɔːt/ *n* cuarto *m* de galón (*EEUU: 0,94 litros, RU: 1,14 litros*) ***you can't get a ~ into a pint pot*** (BrE) no se puede meter a España en Portugal

quarter[1] /'kwɔːrtər || 'kwɔːtə(r)/ *n*
A [c] 1 (fourth part) cuarta parte *f*, cuarto *m*; **a ~ of a mile/century** un cuarto de milla/siglo; **an inch and a ~** una pulgada y cuarta; **four and a** *o* **one ~ gallons** cuatro galones y cuarto 2 (*as adv*): **it's a ~ full** queda un cuarto
B [c] 1 (US, Canadian coin) moneda *f* de 25 centavos 2 (of moon) cuarto *m*
C [c] 1 (in telling time) cuarto *m*; **a ~ of an hour** un cuarto de hora; **an hour and a ~** una hora y cuarto; **it's a ~ of** *o* (BrE) **to one** es la una menos cuarto *or* (AmL exc RPl) un cuarto para la una; **a ~ after** *o* (BrE) **past one** la una y cuarto; **at (a) ~ after** *o* (BrE) **past** a las y cuarto 2 (three months) trimestre *m*; **to pay by the ~** pagar trimestralmente *or* por trimestres
D [c] 1 (district of town) barrio *m* 2 (area) parte *f*; **as is believed in some ~s** como se cree en ciertos ámbitos *or* círculos; ***at close ~s*** de cerca
E **quarters** *pl* (accommodations): **the servants' ~s** las habitaciones de la servidumbre; **married ~s** (Mil) viviendas *fpl* para familias
F [u] (mercy) (liter): **he showed** *o* **gave them no ~** no tuvo clemencia para con ellos

quarter[2] *vt* (*often pass*) (divide) ‹*carcass/body*› descuartizar*; ‹*apple*› dividir en cuatro partes; **to be hung, drawn and ~ed** ser* ahorcado, destripado y descuartizado

quarter[3] *adj* cuarto; **a ~ pound** un cuarto de libra

quarterback[1] /'kwɔːrtərbæk || 'kwɔːtəbæk/ *n* (in US football) mariscal *mf* de campo, corebac *mf* (Méx)

quarterback[2] *vt* (in US football): **he ~s the Giants** es el mariscal de campo *or* (Méx tb) el corebac de los Giants

quarter: **~final** /'kwɔːrtər'faɪnl̩ || ˌkwɔːtə'faɪnl/ *n* cuarto *m* de final; **~finalist** /'kwɔːrtər'faɪnl̩əst || ˌkwɔːtə'faɪnəlɪst/ *n* cuartofinalista *mf*; **~-hour** /ˌkwɔːrtər'aʊr || ˌkwɔːtə(r)'aʊə(r)/ *n* 1 (fifteen minutes) cuarto *m* de hora; **it lasted scarcely a ~-hour** duró apenas un cuarto de hora 2 **on the ~-hour**: **trains leave on the ~-hour** (before the hour) los trenes salen quince minutos antes de cada hora *or* (fam) salen a menos cuarto; (after the hour) los trenes salen quince minutos pasada cada hora *or* (fam) salen a y cuarto

quarterly[1] /'kwɔːrtərli || 'kwɔːtəli/ *adj* trimestral

quarterly[2] *adv* trimestralmente, cada tres meses

quarterly[3] *n* (*pl* **-lies**) publicación *f* trimestral

quarter note *n* (AmE) negra *f*

quartet /kwɔːr'tet || kwɔː'tet/ *n* cuarteto *m*

quartz /kwɔːrts || kwɔːts/ *n* [u] cuarzo *m*; (*before n*) de cuarzo

quash /'kwɑːʃ || kwɒʃ/ *vt* 1 (Law) ‹*verdict/sentence*› anular 2 (suppress) ‹*revolt*› sofocar*, aplastar; ‹*protest*› acallar

quasi- /'kweɪzaɪ, 'kwɑːzi/ *pref* cuasi

quaver[1] /'kweɪvər || 'kweɪvə(r)/ *n* 1 (in voice) temblor *m* 2 (BrE Mus) corchea *f*

quaver[2] *vi* 1 «*voice*» (in singing) vibrar; (in speech) temblar* 2 **quavering** *pres p* ‹*voice/tone*› trémulo, tembloroso

quavery /'kweɪvəri/ *adj* trémulo, tembloroso

quay /kiː/ *n* muelle *m*

quayside /'kiːsaɪd/ *n* muelle *m*

Que = **Quebec**

queasiness /'kwiːzinəs || 'kwiːzinɪs/ *n* [u] (sensación *f* de) mareo *m*, náuseas *fpl*

queasy /'kwiːzi/ *adj* **-sier, -siest** 1 (sick) mareado; **the motion made him (feel) ~** se mareó con el movimiento; **my stomach's a bit ~** tengo el estómago revuelto 2 (uneasy) intranquilo

queen /kwiːn/ *n*
A 1 (monarch) reina *f*; **Q~ Elizabeth** la reina Isabel 2 (Zool) reina *f*
B (in chess, cards) reina *f*

queen bee *n* (Zool) abeja *f* reina

queenly /'kwiːnli/ *adj* **-lier, -liest** 1 (regal) ‹*bearing*› regio, majestuoso 2 (of a queen) ‹*duties*› real, de reina

queen: **~ mother** *n* reina *f* madre; **~'s Counsel** *n* (in UK) *título conferido a ciertos abogados de prestigio*

queer[1] /kwɪr || kwɪə(r)/ *adj*
A (odd) raro, extraño
B (male homosexual) (colloq & sometimes pej) maricón (fam & pey), gay
C (unwell) (BrE colloq) (*usu pred*) mal, indispuesto

queer[2] *n* (colloq & sometimes pej) maricón *m* (fam & pey), gay *m*

queerly /'kwɪrli || 'kwɪəli/ *adv* de un modo extraño *or* raro

quell /kwel/ *vt* ‹*revolt*› sofocar*, aplastar; ‹*criticism*› acallar, acabar con; ‹*fears*› disipar, acabar con

quench /kwentʃ/ *vt* 1 ‹*thirst*› quitar, saciar (liter) 2 ‹*flames*› sofocar*, apagar*

querulous /'kwerələs || 'kwerʊləs/ *adj* ‹*voice*› quejumbroso; ‹*person*› quejumbroso, quejoso

query[1] /'kwɪri || 'kwɪəri/ *n* (*pl* **-ries**) (doubt) duda *f*; (question) pregunta *f*

query[2] *vt* **-ries, -rying, -ried** (dispute) ‹*statement/right*› cuestionar; **I'd like to ~ this bill** me parece que hay un error en esta cuenta; **she's bound to ~ these figures** seguro que pide explicaciones sobre estas cifras

quest /kwest/ *n* búsqueda *f*; **~ FOR sth** búsqueda DE algo; **to go in ~ of sth** ir* en busca *or* (liter) en pos de algo

question[1] /'kwestʃən/ *n* 1 [c] (inquiry) pregunta *f*; **to ask** *o* **put a ~** hacer* *or* (frml) formular una pregunta; ***to pop the ~*** (colloq): **he finally popped the ~** finalmente le pidió que se casara con él 2 [c] (in quiz, exam) pregunta *f*; ***the 64,000 dollar ~*** la pregunta del millón 3 [c] (issue, problem) cuestión *f*, asunto *m*, problema *m*; **the person in ~** la persona en cuestión; **if it's a ~ of money ...** si es cuestión *or* se trata de dinero ...; **that is not the ~** no se trata de eso; ***to beg the ~*** (pose the question) plantear la pregunta; (evade the issue) eludir el problema; (make unjustified assumption): **this begs the ~ whether we really want to live in this kind of society** esto da por sentado *or* tiene como premisa que éste es el tipo de sociedad en la que queremos vivir 4 [u] (doubt) duda *f*; **beyond ~** fuera de duda; **to call sth into ~** poner* algo en duda; **there's no ~ about it** no cabe duda 5 [u] (possibility) posibilidad *f*; **there was no ~ of escaping** no había ninguna posibilidad de escapar; **it is completely out of the ~** es totalmente imposible

question[2] *vt* 1 ‹*person*› hacerle* preguntas a; ‹*suspect/student*› interrogar* 2 (doubt) ‹*integrity/motives*› poner* en duda

questionable /'kwestʃənəbəl/ *adj* 1 (debatable) ‹*value/assertion*› cuestionable, discutible; **a remark in ~ taste**

un comentario de dudoso buen gusto; **it is ~ whether this is an original** es discutible que esto sea un original 2 (of dubious morality) ‹*behavior*› cuestionable

questioner /'kwestʃənər || 'kwestʃənə(r)/ *n* (interrogator) interrogador, -dora *m,f*; (in Parliament, at meeting) interpelante *mf*

questioning¹ /'kwestʃənɪŋ/ *adj* ‹*expression/voice*› inquisidor, inquisitivo; ‹*mind*› inquisitivo

questioning² *n* 1 [u] (interrogation) interrogatorio *m* 2 [u c] (doubt, challenge) cuestionamiento *m*

questioningly /'kwestʃənɪŋli/ *adv* de manera inquisidora *or* inquisitiva

question mark *n* signo *m* de interrogación

questionnaire /'kwestʃə'ner || ˌkwestʃə'neə(r)/ *n* cuestionario *m*

queue¹ /kjuː/ *n* (BrE) cola *f*; **to form a ~** hacer* cola; **join the ~** póngase en la cola; **to jump the ~** colarse* (fam), brincarse* *or* saltarse la cola (Méx fam)

queue² *vi* **queues, queueing, queued ~ (up)** (BrE) hacer* cola

queue: **~-jump** /'kjuːdʒʌmp/ *vi* (BrE) colarse, saltarse *or* (Méx) brincarse* a cola

■ **queue** *vt* ‹*waiting list/housing list*› saltarse; **~ jumping** *n* [u] (BrE): **he accused me of ~ jumping** me acusó de haberme colado *or* (Méx) de haberme saltado la cola

quibble¹ /'kwɪbəl/ *n* objeción *f* (*de poca monta*)

quibble² *vi* hacer* problemas por nimiedades; **to ~ OVER** *o* **ABOUT sth**: **who's going to ~ over** *o* **about a dollar?** ¿quién va a protestar *or* se va a quejar por un dólar?; **to ~ WITH sth**: **he ~s with everything I say** le pone peros a todo lo que digo

quiche /kiːʃ/ *n* [c u] quiche *m or f*

quick¹ /kwɪk/ *adj* **quicker, quickest** 1 (speedy) ‹*action/movement*› rápido; **it's a lot ~er by car** se va mucho más rápido en coche; **he made a ~ recovery** se repuso rápidamente; **I'll be as ~ as I can** volveré (*or* lo haré *etc*) lo más rápido que pueda; **that was ~!** ¡qué rapidez!; **OK, but make it ~** bueno, pero rápido *or* date prisa *or* (AmL tb) apúrate; **they arrived in ~ succession** llegaron muy seguidos *or* uno detrás del otro; **to be ~ on one's feet** tener* buenos reflejos 2 (brief) (*before n, no comp*) ‹*calculation/question*› rápido; ‹*nod*› breve; **to have a ~ look at sth** echarle un vistazo a algo; **he'd like a ~ word with you** quiere hablar contigo un momento 3 (easily roused): **she has a ~ temper** tiene mucho genio 4 (prompt): **he's ~ to take offense** se ofende por lo más mínimo *or* por cualquier nimiedad; **they were ~ to spot the problem** identificaron el problema rápidamente 5 (clever): **he has a ~ wit** es muy agudo; **she has a very ~ mind** es muy lista *or* rápida

quick² *adv* **quicker, quickest** rápido, rápidamente; **come ~** ven corriendo *or* rápido; **~, hide in here** rápido *or* corre, escóndete aquí; **as ~ as you can** lo más rápido *or* deprisa que puedas

quick³ *n* (flesh) (+ *sing vb*) **the ~**: **her nails were bitten to the ~** tenía las uñas en carne viva de mordérselas; ***to cut sb to the ~*** herir* a algn en lo más vivo

quick: **~-acting** /'kwɪk'æktɪŋ/ *adj* de efecto rápido; **~-and-dirty** *adj* (*pred*) rápido y sucio; **~-drying** /'kwɪk'draɪɪŋ/ *adj* de secado rápido

quicken /'kwɪkən/ *vt* ‹*rate/pulse*› acelerar; **he ~ed his pace** apretó *or* aceleró el paso

■ **quicken** *vi* «*rate/pulse*» acelerarse

quick-fire /'kwɪk'faɪr || 'kwɪkfaɪə(r)/ *adj* (*before n*): **his ~ wit** su vivo ingenio; **a series of ~ questions and answers** una ráfaga de preguntas y respuestas

quickie /'kwɪki/ *n* (colloq) uno rápido, una rápida; **let's have a ~** (drink) tomémonos una copita; (sex) echémonos un polvito (arg)

quicklime /'kwɪklaɪm/ *n* [u] cal *f* viva

quickly /'kwɪkli/ *adv* 1 (speedily) ‹*move/recover*› rápidamente, rápido 2 (promptly) ‹*understand/reply*› pronto, enseguida; **I'll do it as ~ as I can** lo haré lo más pronto que pueda, lo haré cuanto antes

quickness /'kwɪknəs || 'kwɪknɪs/ *n* [u] (of movement) rapidez *f*, velocidad *f*; (of mind, reply) rapidez *f*

quick: **~sand** *n* (*often pl*) arenas *fpl* movedizas; **~-setting** /'kwɪk'setɪŋ/ *adj* ‹*cement/glue*› rápido; **~silver** *n* [u] azogue *m*; **~-tempered** /'kwɪk'tempərd || ˌkwɪk'tempəd/ *adj* ‹*person*› de genio vivo, de mucho genio, irascible; ‹*reaction*› malhumorado; **~-witted** /'kwɪk'wɪtəd || ˌkwɪk'wɪtɪd/ *adj* agudo, ingenioso

quid /kwɪd/ *n* (*pl* ~) (pound) (BrE colloq) libra *f*

quid pro quo /'kwɪdprəʊ'kwəʊ/ *n* (*pl* ~ ~ ~s) retribución *f*

quiet¹ /'kwaɪət/ *adj*

A 1 (silent) ‹*street*› silencioso; **isn't it ~ in here!** ¡qué silencio hay aquí!; **be ~!** (to one person) ¡cállate!; (to more than one person) ¡cállense! *or* (Esp tb) ¡callaros *or* callaos!, ¡silencio!; **I couldn't keep the children ~** no logré que los niños mantuvieran silencio; **he gave them money to keep them ~** les pagó para que no hablasen *or* para que se callaran; **I kept ~ about the bill** no dije nada de lo de la factura 2 (not loud) ‹*engine*› silencioso; **he has a very ~ voice** habla muy bajo, tiene una voz muy suave; **keep it ~!** ¡no hagan *or* (Esp tb) hagáis ruido! 3 (not boisterous) ‹*manner*› tranquilo, sosegado; **you're very ~ today** hoy estás muy callada; **he's a ~ boy** es un chico muy callado

B 1 (peaceful) tranquilo; **let's just go for a ~ drink** vamos a tomarnos tranquilamente una copa; **I finally bought it for him: anything for a ~ life** al final se lo compré: ¡con tal de que me dejara en paz ...!; **they had a ~ wedding** la boda se celebró en la intimidad; **to lead a ~ life** llevar una vida tranquila 2 (not busy) ‹*day*› tranquilo 3 (private) en privado; **I'd like a ~ word with you** me gustaría hablar contigo en privado

quiet² *n* [u] 1 (silence) silencio *m*; ***on the ~*** a escondidas, con disimulo 2 (peace, tranquillity) tranquilidad *f*, calma *f*, sosiego *m*

quiet³ (AmE) *vt* 1 (silence) ‹*uproar/protests*› acallar; ‹*class*› hacer* callar 2 (calm) ‹*horse/person*› tranquilizar*; ‹*fear/suspicion*› disipar

■ **quiet** *vi* (become calmer) «*person/animal*» tranquilizarse*; «*wind/storm*» amainar, calmarse

Phrasal verb

• **quiet down** (AmE) ▸ **quieten down**

quieten /'kwaɪətn̩/ *vt* (esp BrE) ▸ **quiet³**

Phrasal verb

• **quieten down**

A [v ▸ o ▸ adv, v ▸ adv ▸ o] ‹*person*› calmar; ‹*rumors/clamor*› acallar; **he asked them to ~ down the noise** les pidió que dejaran de hacer *or* de armar ruido

B [v ▸ adv] «*person*» calmarse; «*rumors*» acallarse; **she eventually matured and ~ed down** con el tiempo maduró y sentó cabeza

quietly /'kwaɪətli/ *adv*

A (silently, not loudly) ‹*move*› silenciosamente, sin hacer ruido; ‹*say/speak*› en voz baja

B 1 (peacefully) ‹*sleep/rest*› tranquilamente 2 (unobtrusively) ‹*dress/mention/slip away*› discretamente

quietness /'kwaɪətnəs || 'kwaɪətnɪs/ *n* [u] 1 (of voice, music) suavidad *f*; (of place, engine) lo silencioso 2 (peacefulness) tranquilidad *f*, sosiego *m*

quiff /kwɪf/ *n* (BrE) copete *m*, tupé *m* (Esp), jopo *m* (CS)

quill /kwɪl/ *n* ~ **(pen)** pluma *f* (de oca *or* ganso)

quilt /kwɪlt/ *n* edredón *m*, acolchado *m* (RPl), cobija *f* (Méx); **continental ~** edredón *m* (nórdico)

quilted /'kwɪltəd || 'kwɪltɪd/ *adj* acolchado, guateado (Esp)

quin /kwɪn/ *n* (BrE colloq) ▸ **quintuplet**

quince /kwɪns/ *n* membrillo *m*; (*before n*) **~ jelly** (dulce *m* de) membrillo *m*

quinine /'kwaɪnaɪn || kwɪ'niːn/ *n* [u] quinina *f*

quint /kwɪnt/ *n* (AmE colloq) ▸ **quintuplet**

quintessence /kwɪn'tesn̩s/ *n* **the ~ OF sth** la quintaesencia DE algo

quintessential /'kwɪntə'sentʃəl || ˌkwɪntɪ'senʃəl/ *adj* (*usu before n*) por excelencia *or* antonomasia

quintessentially /'kwɪntə'sentʃəli || ˌkwɪntɪ'senʃəli/ *adv* intrínsecamente, esencialmente

quintet /kwɪn'tet/ *n* quinteto *m*

quintuplet /kwɪn'tuːplət || 'kwɪntjʊplət/ *n* quintillizo, -za *m,f*, quíntuple *mf* (Chi, Ven)

quip¹ /kwɪp/ *n* ocurrencia *f*, salida *f*

quip² *vt* **-pp-** decir* bromeando *or* haciendo un chiste

q

quirk /kwɜ:rk || kwɜ:k/ *n* 1 (of circumstance) singularidad *f*; **by a ~ of fate** por uno de esos caprichos del destino 2 (of person) rareza *f*, peculiaridad *f*

quirky /'kwɜ:rki || 'kwɜ:ki/ *adj* **-kier, -kiest** extravagante, estrafalario

quit¹ /kwɪt/ (*pres p* **quitting**; *past & past p* **quit** *or* **quitted**) *vt* 1 (give up) (esp AmE) ‹*job/habit*› dejar; ‹*contest*› abandonar; **~ it!** ¡para ya!, ¡basta ya!, ¡terminala! (RPl fam), córtala (Chi fam); **to ~ -ING** dejar DE + INF; **~ talking and listen!** ¡deja de hablar y escucha! 2 (leave) ‹*premises/town*› dejar, irse* *or* (esp Esp) marcharse de

■ **quit** *vi* 1 (stop) (esp AmE) parar; **~ while you're ahead** (set phrase) retírate ahora que vas ganando; **I ~!** ¡me voy!; (from job) ¡yo renuncio! 2 (give in) abandonar 3 (leave): **notice to ~** notificación *f* de desahucio *or* desalojo

quit² *adj* (AmE) **to be ~ OF sb/sth** haberse* librado DE algn/algo

quite /kwaɪt/ *adv*

A 1 (completely, absolutely) completamente, totalmente; **I can ~ believe it** no me cabe la menor duda; **I still can't ~ believe it** todavía no me lo creo del todo *or* no acabo de creérmelo; **I ~ agree with you** estoy totalmente *or* completamente de acuerdo contigo; **I ~ appreciate your difficulty** comprendo perfectamente tu problema; **this will only make matters worse — quite!** esto sólo va a empeorar las cosas — ¡exactamente!; **that's ~ enough!** ¡basta ya!; **is this what you wanted? — not ~** ¿es esto lo que buscaba? — no exactamente; **they're not ~ perfect** no son cien por ciento perfectos; **there isn't ~ enough** falta un poquito; **she's not ~ ten** todavía no ha cumplido los diez; **there's nothing ~ like champagne** realmente no hay como el champán; **~ the opposite** todo lo contrario 2 (*as intensifier*): **it makes ~ a difference** hace bastante diferencia; **you'll have ~ a job persuading her** te va a costar lo tuyo *or* te va a dar mucho trabajo convencerla; **~ a few of them** muchos de ellos; **that was ~ a game!** ¡fue un partidazo! (fam), ¡fue flor de partido! (CS fam); **the journey was ~ an experience** el viaje fue toda una experiencia

B (fairly) (BrE) bastante; **it's ~ warm today** hoy hace bastante calor; **there were ~ a few** había bastantes, había unos cuantos; **~ a lot of money** bastante dinero; **we see them ~ often** los vemos bastante a menudo; **it's ~ likely** es muy probable

quits /kwɪts/ *adj* **to be/get ~ (WITH sb)** estar*/quedar en paz *or* (AmL) a mano (CON algn); ***to call it ~***: **let's call it ~** (at cards) démoslo por empatado; **take the money and call it ~** toma el dinero y dejémoslo de una vez

quitter /'kwɪtər || 'kwɪtə(r)/ *n* (colloq) rajado, -da *m,f* (fam), persona *f* poco perseverante

quiver¹ /'kwɪvər || 'kwɪvə(r)/ *vi* «*person/lips*» temblar*; «*leaves*» agitarse

quiver² *n*

A (for arrows) carcaj *m*, aljaba *f*

B (movement) temblor *m*, estremecimiento *m*

quixotic /kwɪk'sɑ:tɪk || kwɪk'sɒtɪk/ *adj* quijotesco

quiz¹ /kwɪz/ *n* (*pl* **~es**) 1 (competition) concurso *m*; (*before n*) **~ show** programa *m* concurso 2 (test) (AmE) prueba *f*

quiz² *vt* **-zz-** 1 (question) ‹*suspect*› interrogar*, someter a un interrogatorio; **everyone ~zed her about her new boyfriend** todo el mundo le hacía preguntas sobre su nuevo novio 2 (test) (AmE) ‹*students*› poner* *or* hacer* una prueba a

quizmaster /'kwɪz,mæstər || 'kwɪz,mɑ:stə(r)/ *n* presentador *m* (*de un programa concurso*)

quizzical /'kwɪzɪkəl/ *adj* socarrón, burlón

quizzically /'kwɪzɪkli/ *adv* socarronamente, burlonamente

quoits /kwɔɪts, kɔɪts || kɔɪts/ *n* (+ *sing vb*): **to play ~** jugar* a los aros *or* al herrón

Quonset® (hut) /'kwɑ:nsət || 'kwɒnsɪt/ *n* (AmE) cobertizo *m* prefabricado

quorum /'kwɔ:rəm/ *n* [u] quórum *m*

quota /'kwəʊtə/ *n* (*pl* **~s**) (EC, Econ) cuota *f*, cupo *m*; **I've done my ~** yo ya he hecho mi parte; (*before n*) **~ system** sistema *m* de cuotas

quotation /kwəʊ'teɪʃən/ *n*

A (passage) cita *f*; **a dictionary of ~s** un diccionario de citas famosas

B (estimate) presupuesto *m*

quotation marks *pl n* comillas *fpl*

quote¹ /kwəʊt/ *vt*

A 1 ‹*writer/passage*› citar; ‹*reference number*› indicar*; **you've been ~d as saying that ...** se ha afirmado que usted ha dicho que ...; **but don't ~ me on that** pero no estoy absolutamente seguro, pero no lo repitas 2 ‹*example*› dar*; ‹*instance*› citar

B 1 (Busn) ‹*price*› dar*, ofrecer* 2 (Fin) cotizar*

■ **quote** *vi* (repeat, recite): **he was quoting from the Bible** citaba de la Biblia; **she can ~ from a wide range of writers** se sabe (de memoria) citas de un gran número de escritores de todo tipo; **she said, and I ~ ...** dijo, y lo repito textualmente ..., sus palabras textuales fueron ...

quote² *n* (colloq)

A (passage) cita *f*

B (estimate) presupuesto *m*; **to give sb a ~** darle* *or* hacerle* un presupuesto a algn

C **quotes** *pl* (quotation marks) comillas *fpl*; **in** *o* **between ~s** entre comillas

quote³ *interj*: **he said, ~, 'I have a gun', unquote** dijo textualmente *or* sus palabras textuales fueron: 'tengo una pistola'

quote unquote *adj* (AmE colloq) (*before n*) mal llamado

quotient /'kwəʊʃənt/ *n* (Math) cociente *m*

qv (= **quod vide**) véase

Rr

R, **r** /ɑːr || ɑː(r)/ *n* R, r *f*; **the three Rs** *lectura, escritura y aritmética*

R (in US) (Cin) (= **restricted**) menores acompañados

RA (AmE) = **Regular Army**

rabbi /ˈræbaɪ/ *n* (*pl* **-bis**) rabino, -na *m,f*; (as title) rabí *mf*

rabbit[1] /ˈræbət || ˈræbɪt/ *n* 1 [c] (Zool) conejo, -ja *m,f*; (*before n*) ~ **hutch** conejera *f*; ~ **warren** madriguera *f* de conejos 2 [u] (meat) conejo *m*

rabbit[2] *vi* (BrE colloq) darle* a la sinhueso (fam); **what's he ~ing on about?** ¿qué dice, que no para de hablar?

rabble /ˈræbəl/ *n* [u] 1 (mob) muchedumbre *f* 2 (common people) (pej) **the ~** la chusma (pey), la plebe (pey)

rabble: **~-rouser** /ˈræbəl,raʊzər || ˈræbəl,raʊzə(r)/ *n* (person) agitador, -dora *m,f*; **~-rousing** *adj* (*before n*) ‹*politician*› agitador; **a ~-rousing speech** una arenga

rabid /ˈræbəd || ˈræbɪd/ *adj* 1 ‹*dog/fox*› rabioso 2 ‹*prejudice*› virulento, feroz; ‹*socialist*› furibundo, rabioso

rabidly /ˈræbədli || ˈræbɪdli/ *adv*: **he is ~ anti-European** es un anti-europeísta furibundo *or* rabioso

rabies /ˈreɪbiːz/ *n* [u] rabia *f*

RAC *n* (in UK) = **Royal Automobile Club**

raccoon /ræˈkuːn || rəˈkuːn/ *n* [c] mapache *m*

race[1] /reɪs/ *n*

A 1 [c] (contest) carrera *f*; **boat ~** regata *f*; **to run in a ~** tomar parte en una carrera; **a ~ against the clock** una carrera contra reloj; **the ~ is on for the Republican nomination** ha empezado la contienda para la nominación republicana 2 **races** *pl* (Equ) **the ~s** las carreras (de caballos)

B [c u] (Anthrop) raza *f*; **the human ~** el género humano; (*before n*) ~ **riot** disturbio *m* racial

race[2] *vi* 1 (rush) (+ *adv compl*): **she ~d down the hill on her bike** bajó la cuesta en bicicleta a toda velocidad; **I had to ~ to the store** tuve que ir corriendo a la tienda 2 (in competition) correr, competir* 3 «*pulse/heart*» latir aceleradamente; «*engine*» acelerarse; **my mind was racing** las ideas se me agolpaban en la cabeza

■ **race** *vt* 1 (compete against) echarle *or* (RPl) jugarle* una carrera a; **come on, I'll ~ you (to that tree)!** ¡vamos, te echo *or* (RPl) juego una carrera (hasta aquel árbol)! 2 (make go too fast) ‹*engine*› acelerar

race: **~course** *n* (stadium) hipódromo *m*; (track) pista *f* (de carreras); **~goer** *n* aficionado, -da *m,f* a las carreras; **~horse** *n* caballo *m* de carrera(s)

racer /ˈreɪsər || ˈreɪsə(r)/ *n* 1 (bicycle) bicicleta *f* de carrera(s) 2 (animal) corredor, -dora *m,f*, caballo *m* (*or* perro *m* *etc*) de carrera(s)

race: **~ relations** *pl n* relaciones *fpl* raciales; **~track** *n* 1 (for cars) circuito *m*; (for runners) pista *f* de atletismo, estadio *m*; (for cycles) velódromo *m* 2 (AmE) ▶**racecourse**; **~way** /ˈreɪsweɪ/ *n* (AmE) 1 (channel — for water) canal *m*; (— for cables) tubería *f* de servicio; 2 (racecourse — for horses) pista *f* de carreras; (— for cars) autódromo *m*, circuito *m* de carreras *or* automovilístico

racial /ˈreɪʃəl/ *adj* ‹*discrimination/harmony*› racial; ~ **pride** orgullo *m* de raza

racialism /ˈreɪʃəlɪzəm/ *n* [u] (BrE) racismo *m*

racialist[1] /ˈreɪʃələst || ˈreɪʃəlɪst/ *n* (BrE) racista *mf*

racialist[2] *adj* (BrE) racista

racially /ˈreɪʃəli/ *adv* 1 ‹*mixed/prejudiced*› racialmente 2 (*indep*) desde un punto de vista racial

racing[1] /ˈreɪsɪŋ/ *n* [u] 1 (*horse ~*) carreras *fpl* de caballos; (*before n*) ‹*commentator/correspondent*› hípico 2 (sport, pastime) carreras *fpl*

racing[2] *adj* (*before n*) ‹*bicycle/car/dog*› de carrera(s); ‹*yacht*› de regata; ***to be a ~ certainty*** (BrE colloq) ser* de cajón; ***it's a ~ certainty that he'll be there*** seguro que va a estar allí, es de cajón que va a estar allí (fam)

racism /ˈreɪsɪzəm/ *n* [u] racismo *m*

racist[1] /ˈreɪsəst || ˈreɪsɪst/ *n* racista *mf*

racist[2] *adj* racista

rack[1] /ræk/ *n*

A 1 (shelf) estante *m*; (for documents) organizador *m*; (for baggage) rejilla *f*, portaequipajes *m*; (*bottle ~*) botellero *m*; (*clothes ~*) perchero *m*; (*drying ~*) tendedero *m*; *see also* **magazine A1** *etc* 2 **off the rack** (AmE) de confección

B (for torture) potro *m* (de tortura); ***to go to ~ and ruin*** venirse* abajo

rack[2] *vt* 1 (shake) (*often pass*) sacudir; **to be ~ed WITH sth**: **to be ~ed with pain** sufrir dolores atroces; **to be ~ed with doubt/guilt** estar* atormentado por la duda/el remordimiento 2 **racking** *pres p* ‹*cough*› convulsivo

Phrasal verb

• **rack up** [v ▸ o ▸ adv, v ▸ adv ▸ o] acumular

racket /ˈrækət || ˈrækɪt/ *n*

A (Sport) raqueta *f*

B (noise) (colloq) jaleo *m* (fam), bulla *f*, barullo *m*

C (business) (colloq) tinglado *m* (fam), asunto *m*

racketeer /ˈrækəˈtɪr || ˌrækəˈtɪə(r)/ *n* mafioso, -sa *m,f*

raconteur /ˈrækɑːnˈtɜːr || ˌrækɒnˈtɜː(r)/ *n* anecdotista *mf*

racquet /ˈrækət || ˈrækɪt/ *n* ▶**racket A**

racy /ˈreɪsi/ *adj* **racier, raciest** 1 (lively) animado, brioso 2 (risqué) ‹*story/joke*› subido de tono, picante

radar /ˈreɪdɑːr || ˈreɪdɑː(r)/ *n* [u] radar *m*; (*before n*) ‹*scanner/station*› de radar

radial[1] /ˈreɪdiəl/ *adj* ‹*pattern/form*› radial, radiado; ~ **engine** motor *m* en estrella

radial[2] *n* ~ **(tire)** neumático *m* radial

radiance /ˈreɪdiəns/ *n* [u] (of sun, light) resplandor *m*; (of person, smile) lo radiante

radiant /ˈreɪdiənt/ *adj* ‹*smile/eyes/look*› radiante; ‹*sun/blue*› resplandeciente, radiante

radiate /ˈreɪdieɪt/ *vt* ‹*heat/light*› irradiar, emitir; ‹*charm/enthusiasm*› irradiar, rebosar (de)

■ **radiate** *vi*: **heat ~s from the sun** el sol irradia calor

radiation /ˈreɪdiˈeɪʃən/ *n* [u] (Phys) radiación *f*; (*before n*) ~ **sickness** radiotoxemia *f*

radiator /ˈreɪdieɪtər || ˈreɪdieɪtə(r)/ *n* (for heating, in car engine) radiador *m*

radical[1] /ˈrædɪkəl/ *adj* radical; ‹*writer*› de ideas radicales, de tendencia radical

radical[2] *n* radical *mf*

radicalism /ˈrædɪkəlɪzəm/ *n* [u] radicalismo *m*

radicalize /ˈrædɪkəlaɪz/ *vt* 1 (Pol, Sociol) ‹*party/community/workers*› radicalizar* 2 (change fundamentally) cambiar radicalmente

radically /ˈrædɪkli/ *adv* radicalmente

radii /ˈreɪdiaɪ/ *pl of* **radius**

radio[1] /ˈreɪdiəʊ/ *n* (*pl* **-os**)
A [c] (receiver) radio *m* (AmL exc CS), radio *f* (CS, Esp); **I heard it on the ~** lo oí por el *or* (CS, Esp) la radio
B [u] (broadcasting, medium) radio *f*; (*before n*) ‹*show/announcer*› de radio, radiofónico; **~ operator** radiotelegrafista *mf*, radiooperador, -dora *m,f* (AmL); **~ station** emisora *f or* (AmL tb) estación *f* (de radio)

radio[2] (*3rd pers sing pres* **radios**; *pres p* **radioing**; *past & past p* **radioed**) *vt* ‹*base/person*› llamar por radio; ‹*message*› transmitir por radio
■ **radio** *vi* llamar por radio; **to ~ for help** pedir* ayuda por radio

radio: **~active** /ˈreɪdiəʊˈæktɪv/ *adj* radiactivo; **~activity** /ˈreɪdiəʊækˈtɪvəti/ *n* [u] radiactividad *f*; **~ car** *n* 1 (patrol car) radiopatrulla *m* 2 (Rad) coche *m* equipado con radiotransmisor; **~-controlled** /ˈreɪdiəʊkənˈtrəʊld/ *adj* ‹*model*› de control remoto, con radiomando, teledirigido; **~gram** *n* 1 (Telec) radiograma *m*, radiotelegrama *m* 2 ▸**~graph**; **~graph** *n* radiografía *f*

radiographer /ˈreɪdiˈɑːgrəfər ‖ ˌreɪdiˈɒgrəfə(r)/ *n* radiógrafo, -fa *m,f*

radiography /ˈreɪdiˈɑːgrəfi ‖ ˌreɪdiˈɒgrəfi/ *n* [u] radiografía *f*

radiologist /ˈreɪdiˈɑːlədʒəst ‖ ˌreɪdiˈɒlədʒɪst/ *n* radiólogo, -ga *m,f*

radio: **~ set** *n* aparato *m* de radio, radio *m* (AmL exc CS), radio *f* (CS, Esp); **~therapy** /ˈreɪdiəʊˈθerəpi/ *n* [u] radioterapia *f*

radish /ˈrædɪʃ/ *n* rabanito *m*, rábano *m*

radium /ˈreɪdiəm/ *n* [u] radio *m*

radius /ˈreɪdiəs/ *n* (*pl* **radiuses** *or* **radii**) radio *m*

RAF /ˈɑːreɪˈef/ (in UK) (= **Royal Air Force**) **the ~** la Fuerza Aérea británica

raffia /ˈræfiə/ *n* [u] rafia *f*

raffle[1] /ˈræfəl/ *n* rifa *f*, sorteo *m*; (*before n*) **~ ticket** número *m* de rifa

raffle[2] *vt* rifar, sortear

raft /ræft ‖ rɑːft/ *n*
A 1 (Naut) balsa *f*, almadía *f* 2 (anchored off beach) plataforma *f*
B (large amount) (AmE colloq) montón *m* (fam), pila *f* (AmS fam)

rafter /ˈræftər ‖ ˈrɑːftə(r)/ *n* viga *f*, par *m* (téc); **the ~s** las vigas del techo

rag /ræg/ *n*
A 1 [c] (piece of cloth) trapo *m*; ***like a red ~ to a bull*** (colloq): **mentioning that to him is like a red ~ to a bull** mencionarle eso es pincharlo para que se enfurezca; ***to lose one's ~*** (BrE colloq) explotar (fam), perder* los estribos; ▸**chew** *vt* 2 **rags** *pl* (tattered clothes) harapos *mpl*, andrajos *mpl*; **dressed in ~s** harapiento, andrajoso; ***from ~s to riches*** de la pobreza a la fortuna; **his was a classic ~s-to-riches story** el suyo fue el clásico caso del pobre que hace fortuna
B [c] (newspaper) (colloq & pej) periodicucho *m* (pey)
C [c] (BrE) (**~** *week*) *semana durante la cual los estudiantes recaudan fondos para obras benéficas*

ragamuffin /ˈrægəˌmʌfən ‖ ˈrægəˌmʌfɪn/ *n* pilluelo, -la *m,f*, golfillo, -lla *m,f*

rag: **~-and-bone man** /ˈrægənˈbəʊnmæn/ *n* (*pl* **-men** /-men/) (BrE) ▸**ragman**; **~bag** *n* batiburrillo *m*, mezcolanza *f*; **~ doll** *n* muñeca *f* de trapo

rage[1] /reɪdʒ/ *n*
A 1 [u] (violent anger) furia *f*, cólera *f* 2 [c] (fit of fury): **to be in a ~** estar* furioso
B [u] (fashion) (colloq) furor *m*, moda *f*; **to be (all) the ~** hacer* furor, ser* el último grito (de la moda)

rage[2] *vi* 1 «*storm/sea*» rugir*, bramar; «*fire*» arder furiosamente; **the battle/fire ~d for three days** la encarnizada batalla/el furioso incendio se prolongó durante tres días 2 «*person*» expresar su (*or* mi *etc*) furia, rabiar; **to ~ against sth** protestar furiosamente contra algo 3 **raging** *pres p* ‹*storm*› rugiente; ‹*sea*› embravecido; ‹*headache*› enloquecedor; ‹*argument*› enconado, airado, virulento; **he was in a raging temper** estaba furioso

ragged /ˈrægəd ‖ ˈrægɪd/ *adj* ‹*clothes/appearance*› harapiento, andrajoso; ‹*coastline*› recortado; ‹*edge*› irregular

rag: **~man** /ˈrægmæn/ *n* (*pl* **-men** /-men/) (AmE) ropavejero *m*, trapero *m*; **~top** *n* (AmE colloq) descapotable *m*, convertible *m* (AmL); **~ trade** *n* (colloq) **the ~ trade** la industria *or* el ramo de la confección

raid[1] /reɪd/ *n* 1 (Mil) asalto *m*, incursión *f* 2 (*air* **~**) bombardeo *m* aéreo, ataque *m* aéreo 3 (by thieves) atraco *m*, asalto *m* 4 (by police) redada *f*, batida *f*, allanamiento *m* (AmL)

raid[2] *vt* 1 (Mil) asaltar 2 ‹*bank*› asaltar, atracar*; **they ~ed the refrigerator** (hum) tomaron por asalto el refrigerador (hum) 3 «*police*» ‹*house/building*› hacer* una redada en, allanar (AmL) 4 (poach) (AmE) ‹*personnel*› llevarse, robar

raider /ˈreɪdər ‖ ˈreɪdə(r)/ *n* 1 (attacker) asaltante *mf* 2 (robber) asaltante *mf*, atracador, -dora *m,f*

rail[1] /reɪl/ *n*
A [c] 1 (bar) riel *m*, barra *f* 2 (*hand* **~**) pasamanos *m* 3 (barrier) baranda *f*, barandilla *f*
B 1 [c] (for trains, trams) riel *m*, raíl *m* (Esp); **the train came off the ~s** el tren descarriló; ***to go off the ~s*** (BrE colloq) (morally) descarriarse*, apartarse del buen camino; (mentally) enloquecerse* 2 [u] (railroad) ferrocarril *m*; **by ~** en *or* por ferrocarril; (*before n*) ‹*service/link*› ferroviario, de ferrocarril; **~ travel** los viajes en tren

rail[2] *vi* (frml) **to ~ AGAINST sth** clamar CONTRA algo (frml)

rail: **~car** *n* automotor *m*, autoferro *m* (Col), autovagón *m* (Per); **~card** *n* (in UK) tarjeta *f* de descuento (*para viajes en tren*)

railing /ˈreɪlɪŋ/ *n* (*often pl*) reja *f*, verja *f*

railroad[1] /ˈreɪlrəʊd/ *n* (AmE) 1 (system) ferrocarril *m*; (*before n*) ‹*station/line*› de ferrocarril, ferroviario; ‹*timetable*› de trenes 2 (track) vía *f* férrea

railroad[2] *vt*
A (push, force) ‹*bill/measures*› tramitar rápidamente (*sin la debida discusión*); **to ~ sb INTO sth**: **they were ~ed into accepting the offer** los apremiaron *or* presionaron para que aceptaran la oferta
B (convict unfairly) (AmE) condenar injustamente

rail: **~roader** /ˈreɪlrəʊdər ‖ ˈreɪlrəʊdə(r)/ *n* (AmE) ferroviario, -ria *m,f*, ferrocarrilero, -ra *m,f* (Chi, Méx); **~way** *n* (BrE) ▸**railroad**[1]; **~wayman** /ˈreɪlweɪmən/ *n* (*pl* **-men** /-mən/) (BrE) ferroviario *m*, ferrocarrilero *m* (Chi, Méx)

rain[1] /reɪn/ *n* [u c] lluvia *f*; **come in out of the ~** entra, que te estás mojando; **we were** *o* **we got caught in the ~** nos agarró *or* (esp Esp) cogió la lluvia; **(a) light ~ began to fall** empezó a lloviznar; **the ~s** (la estación de) las lluvias; ***(come) ~ or (come) shine*** (whatever the weather) llueva o truene; (whatever the situation) pase lo que pase; ***to be (as) right as ~*** estar* como nuevo *or* como si tal cosa; (*before n*) **~ cloud** nube *f* de lluvia

rain[2] *v impers* llover*; ***when it ~s, it pours*** *o* (BrE) ***it never ~s but it pours*** las desgracias nunca vienen solas

Phrasal verbs

- **rain down** [v ▸ adv] «*blows/bombs/curses*» llover*; **insults ~ed down on them** les llovieron insultos
- **rain out**, (BrE) **rain off** [v ▸ o ▸ adv, v ▸ adv ▸ o]: **to be ~ed out** *o* (BrE) **off** suspenderse *or* cancelarse a causa de la lluvia

rainbow /ˈreɪnbəʊ/ *n* arco *m* iris

rainbow trout *n* [c u] trucha *f* (arco iris)

rain: **~ check** *n* (esp AmE Sport) *vale que se recibe al suspenderse un partido por mal tiempo etc*; ***to take a ~ check on sth*** (colloq) dejar algo para otro momento; **~coat** *n* impermeable *m*, piloto *m* (Arg, Chi), pilot *m* (Ur); **~drop** *n* gota *f* de lluvia; **~fall** *n* [u] (amount) precipitaciones *fpl*; (shower) precipitación *f*, lluvia *f*; **~ forest** *n* selva *f* tropical (húmeda), bosque *m* ecuatorial *or* pluvial; **~maker** /ˈreɪnmeɪkər ‖ ˈreɪnmeɪkə(r)/ *n* 1 (creator of rain) hacedor, -dora *m,f* de lluvia; 2 (in business) (AmE colloq) triunfador, -dora *m,f* (*en los negocios*); **~proof** *adj* impermeable; **~storm** *n* temporal *m* de lluvias; **~water** *n* [u] agua *f*‡ de lluvia

rainy /ˈreɪni/ *adj* **-nier, -niest** ‹*weather/day*› lluvioso; **~ season** estación *f* de las lluvias

raise¹ /reɪz/ *vt*
(*Sense* I)
A 1 (move upwards) ‹*head/hand*› levantar, alzar*; ‹*eyebrows*› arquear; ‹*blind/window*› subir; ‹*flag*› izar*; **he ~d his eyes** levantó la vista; **he ~d his hat** se levantó el sombrero 2 (make higher) ‹*shelf/level/hem*› subir
B 1 (set upright) levantar; **Lazarus was ~d from the dead** Lázaro resucitó de entre los muertos 2 (erect) ‹*monument/building*› levantar, erigir* (frml)
C 1 ‹*pressure/temperature*› aumentar, elevar; ‹*price/salary/volume*› subir, aumentar; **she ~d her voice to me** me levantó la voz; **to ~ the school leaving age** extender* la escolaridad obligatoria 2 ‹*consciousness*› aumentar, acrecentar*; ‹*standing/reputation*› aumentar; **don't ~ his hopes** no le des demasiadas esperanzas
D (promote) **to ~ sb TO sth** ascender* *or* elevar a algn A algo
(*Sense* II)
A 1 ‹*money/funds*› recaudar; ‹*loan*› conseguir, obtener 2 ‹*army/supporters*› reclutar
B ‹*fears/doubt*› suscitar, dar* lugar a; **he managed to ~ a smile** pudo sonreír; **to ~ the alarm** dar* la alarma
C ‹*subject*› sacar*; ‹*objection/question*› formular, hacer*, plantear; **to ~ sth WITH sb** plantearle algo A algn
D 1 ‹*child/family*› criar* 2 ‹*wheat/corn*› cultivar; **they ~ cattle** se dedican a la cría de ganado

raise² *n* (AmE) aumento *m or* subida *f* de sueldo

raisin /'reɪzn/ *n* (uva *f*) pasa *f*, pasa *f* (de uva)

raison d'être /'reɪzɔːn'detrə || ˌreɪzɒn'detrə/ *n* (*pl* **~s ~**) razón *f* de ser

Raj /rɑːdʒ/ *n* **the (British) ~** el Imperio Británico en la India, el Raj

rake¹ /reɪk/ *n*
A (garden tool) rastrillo *m*; ***as thin as a ~*** (colloq) flaco como un palillo *or* palo (fam)
B (man) (dated) vividor *m*, calavera *m*

rake² *vt* ‹*leaves*› recoger* con un rastrillo, rastrillar; ‹*garden/soil*› rastrillar
(Phrasal verbs)
• **rake in** [v ▸ o ▸ adv, v ▸ adv ▸ o]: **they're raking it in** están haciendo mucho dinero, se están forrando (fam)
• **rake over** [v ▸ adv ▸ o] ‹*soil/flowerbed*› rastrillar; ‹*past events*› volver* sobre
• **rake up** [v ▸ o ▸ adv, v ▸ adv ▸ o]
A 1 ‹*leaves*› rastrillar 2 ‹*support*› conseguir*
B 1 ‹*fire*› atizar* 2 ‹*scandal/quarrel*› sacar* a relucir; **to ~ up the past** remover* *or* desenterrar* el pasado

rake-off /'reɪkɔːf || 'reɪkɒf/ *n* (colloq) tajada *f* (fam), pellizco *m* (Esp fam)

rakish /'reɪkɪʃ/ *adj* 1 (casual, jaunty) desenfadado; **she wore the hat at a ~ angle** llevaba el sombrero ladeado con gracia *or* desenfado 2 (dissolute) libertino

rally¹ /'ræli/ *n* (*pl* **-lies**)
A (mass meeting) concentración *f*; **political ~** mitin *m*, mítin *m*
B (Auto) rally *m*; (*before n*) ‹*car/driver*› de rally
C (in tennis, badminton) peloteo *m*
D (recovery) (Fin) repunte *m*; (Med) mejoría *f*

rally² **-lies, -lying, -lied** *vi*
A 1 (unite) unirse; (gather) congregarse*; **the whole country rallied to the support of the president** todo el país se unió en apoyo del presidente 2 **rallying** *pres p* ‹*call/point*› de concentración
B 1 (recover) «*person*» recuperarse, reponerse* 2 (Fin) «*currency/price*» repuntar, recuperarse
■ **rally** *vt*
A 1 ‹*support/vote*› conseguir* 2 ‹*people*› unir
B ‹*strength/spirits*› recobrar
(Phrasal verb)
• **rally round**
A [v ▸ adv]: **all the neighbors rallied round to help** todos los vecinos se juntaron para ayudar
B [v ▸ adv ▸ o]: **they all rallied round him** todos acudieron a ofrecerle apoyo

ram¹ /ræm/ *n* (Zool) carnero *m*

ram² **-mm-** *vt* 1 (force) (+ *adv compl*): **he ~med the stake into the ground** hincó *or* clavó la estaca en la tierra; **he ~med his fist through the door** atravesó la puerta de un puñetazo 2 (crash into) embestir* contra; **the ship ~med the submarine** el barco chocó con el submarino
■ **ram** *vi* **to ~ INTO sth/sb** estrellarse *or* chocar* CONTRA algo/algn
(Phrasal verb)
• **ram home** [v ▸ o ▸ adv, v ▸ adv ▸ o] ‹*point/message*› hacer* entender a la fuerza

RAM /ræm/ *n* [u] (Comput) (= **random access memory**) RAM *f*

Ramadan /'rɑːmədɑːn || ˌræmə'dæn/ *n* Ramadán *m*

ramble¹ /'ræmbəl/ *n* paseo *m*, caminata *f*; (BrE Sport) excursión *f* (*a pie*), marcha *f*; **to go for a ~** ir* a dar un paseo; (Sport) ir* de excursión *or* de marcha

ramble² *vi* 1 (walk) pasear; **to go rambling** (BrE) hacer* excursionismo, ir* de excursión *or* de marcha 2 (in speech, writing) irse* por las ramas, divagar*
(Phrasal verb)
• **ramble on** [v ▸ adv] **to ~ on (ABOUT sth)** divagar* (SOBRE algo)

rambler /'ræmblər || 'ræmblə(r)/ *n* 1 (walker) excursionista *mf* 2 (plant) rosa *f* trepadora

rambling¹ /'ræmblɪŋ/ *adj* 1 ‹*essay/lecture*› que se va por las ramas, que divaga 2 ‹*streets*› laberíntico, intrincado; **a ~ old house** una vieja casona llena de recovecos 3 ‹*rose*› trepador

rambling² *n* [u] (BrE Sport) excursionismo *m*

ramification /ˌræməfə'keɪʃən || ˌræmɪfɪ'keɪʃən/ *n* (*often pl*) ramificación *f*, repercusión *f*

ramp /ræmp/ *n* 1 (slope) rampa *f*; **entrance** *o* **on ~** (AmE) vía *f* de acceso (*a una autopista*); **exit** *o* **off ~** (AmE) vía *f* de salida (*de una autopista*) 2 (on ship, aircraft) (for passengers) escalerilla *f*; (for vehicles) rampa *f* 3 (platform) elevador *m* 4 (hump) (BrE) desnivel *m*

rampage¹ /'ræmpeɪdʒ/ *n*: **to be on the ~** arrasarlo todo; **to go on the ~** empezar* a arrasarlo todo

rampage² /ræm'peɪdʒ/ *vi* pasar arrasando

rampant /'ræmpənt/ *adj* ‹*inflation*› galopante; ‹*growth*› desenfrenado; ‹*crime*› endémico; **disease was ~** proliferaban las enfermedades

rampart /'ræmpɑːrt || 'ræmpɑːt/ *n* (bank) terraplén *m*; (wall) muralla *f*

ramrod /'ræmrɑːd || 'ræmrɒd/ *n* (rod) baqueta *f*; **her back was as straight as a ~** tenía la espalda recta *or* erguida

ramshackle /'ræmˌʃækəl/ *adj* destartalado

ran /ræn/ *past of* **run¹**

ranch¹ /ræntʃ || rɑːntʃ/ *n*: **cattle ~** finca *f* (ganadera), hacienda *f* (ganadera) (esp AmL), rancho *m* ganadero (Méx), estancia *f* (CS); **poultry ~** (AmE) granja *f* avícola; (*before n*) **~ hand** trabajador, -dora *m,f* agrícola, peón *m* (esp AmL)

ranch² *vi* (esp AmE) administrar un **ranch¹**

rancher /'ræntʃər || 'rɑːntʃə(r)/ *n* hacendado, -da *m,f*, estanciero, -ra *m,f* (CS), ranchero, -ra *m,f* (Méx); **cattle ~** ganadero, -ra *m,f*

ranch house *n* 1 (on ranch) casa *f* (*en una finca*) 2 (type of house) (AmE) chalet *m* (*de una sola planta*), bungalow *m*

rancid /'rænsəd || 'rænsɪd/ *adj* rancio; **to go ~** ponerse* rancio

rancor, (BrE) **rancour** /'ræŋkər || 'ræŋkə(r)/ *n* [u] rencor *m*

rancorous /'ræŋkərəs/ *adj* ‹*person*› rencoroso; ‹*atmosphere*› hostil, lleno de rencor

rancour *n* (BrE) ▸ **rancor**

rand /rænd/ *n* (*pl* **~**) rand *m*

R & B /'ɑːrən'biː/ *n* [u] = **rhythm and blues**

R & D /'ɑːrən'diː/ *n* [u] (= **research and development**) I & D

random /'rændəm/ *adj* 1 ‹*testing/choice*› al azar; ‹*shot*› hecho al azar; ‹*bullet*› perdido; ‹*sample*› aleatorio, seleccionado al azar 2 **at random** (*as adv*) al azar; **to hit out at ~** dar* golpes a diestra y siniestra *or* (Esp) a diestro y siniestro

random access /'rædəm'ækses/ *n* [u] acceso *m* aleatorio *or* directo; (*before n*) **random-access memory** memoria *f* de acceso aleatorio *or* directo

randomize /'rændəmaɪz/ *vt*
A (in statistics) aleatorizar*
B (Comput) *generar la implantación de números aleatorios en*

randomly /'rændəmli/ *adv* al azar

r

R & R /'ɑːrən'ɑːr || 'ɑːrən'ɑː(r)/ *n* [u] (AmE) = **rest and recreation**

randy /'rændi/ *adj* **-dier, -diest** (colloq) caliente (fam), arrecho (AmL fam), cachondo (Esp, Méx fam)

rang /ræŋ/ *past of* **ring**[2]

range[1] /reɪndʒ/ *n*

A 1 (scope) ámbito *m*, campo *m* 2 (Mus) registro *m* 3 (bracket): **if your income is within that ~** si sus ingresos están dentro de esos límites *or* son de ese orden; **within/out of our price ~** dentro de/fuera de nuestras posibilidades

B 1 (variety) gama *f*; **a wide ~ of colors/prices** una amplia gama *or* una gran variedad de colores/precios; **a wide ~ of possibilities** un amplio abanico de posibilidades; **I have a wide ~ of interests** mis intereses son múltiples y variados 2 (selection) línea *f*, gama *f*

C 1 (of gun, telescope, transmitter) alcance *m*; **at close/long ~** de cerca/lejos; **to come/be within (firing) ~** ponerse*/estar* a tiro; **it was out of ~** estaba fuera del alcance del arma 2 (of vehicle, missile) autonomía *f*; **long-~ missiles** misiles *mpl* de largo alcance 3 (sight): **it came within my ~ of vision** entró en mi campo visual *or* de visión

D (in mobile telephony) cobertura *f*; **to be out of ~** estar* fuera de cobertura; **to be in ~** tener* cobertura

E (for shooting) campo *m* de tiro

F (chain) cadena *f*; **a mountain ~** una cordillera, una cadena de montañas

G (stove) cocina *f* económica, estufa *f* (Col, Méx)

range[2] *vi* **to ~ FROM sth TO sth**: **their ages ~ from 12 to 20** tienen entre 12 y 20 años; **estimates ~ up to $20,000** hay presupuestos de hasta 20.000 dólares; **the conversation ~d over many topics** *o* **~d widely** la conversación abarcó muchos temas

■ **range** *vt*

A (line up, place) alinear

B ‹*plain/hills*› recorrer

ranger /'reɪndʒər || 'reɪndʒə(r)/ *n* 1 (in park, forest) guarda *mf* forestal, guardabosques *mf* 2 (soldier) (in US) soldado *m* de las tropas de asalto, ranger *m*

Rangoon /ræŋ'guːn/ *n* Rangún *m*

rangy /'reɪndʒi/ *adj* **-gier, -giest** (AmE) largo y delgado, larguirucho (fam)

rank[1] /ræŋk/ *n*

A [c] (line) fila *f*; **to break ~s** romper* filas; **to close ~s** cerrar* *or* estrechar filas; **General Sánchez rose from the ~s** el General Sánchez empezó como soldado raso; **to join the ~s of the unemployed** pasar a engrosar las filas del desempleo

B [c u] (status) categoría *f*; (Mil) grado *m*, rango *m*; **to be above/below sb in ~** ser* de rango superior/inferior a algn; ***to pull ~ on sb***: **she's not the type to pull ~ on anybody** no es de las que abusan de su autoridad

C [c] (*taxi ~*) (BrE) parada *f* de taxis, sitio *m* (Méx)

rank[2] *vt*

A (class): **he's ~ed fourth** está clasificado (como el) cuarto; **he ~s it among the city's best restaurants** considera que está entre los mejores restaurantes de la ciudad

B (outrank) (AmE) ser* de rango superior a

■ **rank** *vi* 1 (be classed) estar*; **it ~s among the best** está entre los mejores; **he ~s high in our esteem** lo tenemos en gran estima 2 (hold rank): **to ~ above/below sb** estar* por encima/por debajo de algn, ser* de rango superior/inferior a algn; **a high-/middle-~ing officer** un oficial de alto grado/de grado medio

rank[3] *adj*

A (*before n*) ‹*beginner*› absoluto; ‹*injustice*› flagrante

B (unpleasantly strong) ‹*smell*› fétido; ‹*taste*› repugnante; **to smell ~** oler* muy mal, apestar (fam)

rank and file *n* (Mil) (+ *pl vb*) tropa *f*; **the ~ ~ ~ of the union** las bases del sindicato

ranking[1] /'ræŋkɪŋ/ *n* ranking *m*, clasificación *f*

ranking[2] *adj* (AmE) (*before n*) de grado superior

rankle /'ræŋkəl/ *vi* doler*; **to ~ WITH sb**: **what still ~s with me is that ...** lo que no les (*or* le *etc*) puedo perdonar es que ...

■ **rankle** *vt* (AmE) irritar

ransack /'rænsæk/ *vt* ‹*room/drawer*› revolver*; ‹*house/premises*› (search) registrar (*de arriba a abajo*); (pillage) saquear

ransom[1] /'rænsəm/ *n* rescate *m*; **to hold sb to** *o* (AmE also) **for ~** exigir* un rescate por algn; **she says the army is holding the country to ~** dice que el ejército está chantajeando al país; (*before n*) **~ demand** nota *f* (*or* llamada *f etc*) exigiendo un rescate; ▸**king**

ransom[2] *vt* pagar* un rescate por

rant /rænt/ *vi* despotricar*; **my father ~ed and raved at me for half an hour** mi padre me echó un sermón *or* una perorata de media hora (fam)

rap[1] /ræp/ *n*

A [c] (blow) golpe *m*; **there was a ~ at the door** se oyó un golpe en la puerta; ▸**knuckle 1**

B (*no pl*) (AmE colloq) 1 (criticism) crítica *f*, acusación *f* 2 (conviction): **to pin a ~ on sb** endilgarle* las culpas a algn; **to take the ~ for sth** cargar* con la culpa de algo, pagar* el pato (por algo) (fam); **to beat the ~** escabullirse, quedar impune; (*before n*) **~ sheet** antecedentes *mpl* penales

C 1 [u] (chat) (colloq) charla *f*, cháchara *f* (fam) 2 [c u] (Mus) rap *m*

rap[2] **-pp-** *vi*

A (knock) dar* un golpe; **to ~ at/on the door** llamar a la puerta

B (chat) (colloq) cotorrear (fam)

■ **rap** *vt* 1 (hit): **he ~ped my knuckles** me pegó en los nudillos; ▸**knuckle 1** 2 (rebuke) (journ) amonestar

rapacious /rə'peɪʃəs/ *adj* (frml) ‹*person/character*› codicioso, avaricioso, rapaz; ‹*appetite/greed*› voraz

rape[1] /reɪp/ *n*

A 1 [u c] (sexual violation) violación *f*; (of a minor) estupro *m* 2 [u] (of the countryside, of the earth) (liter) expoliación *f* (liter)

B [u] (plant) colza *f*

rape[2] *vt* ‹*person*› violar; ‹*countryside*› (liter) expoliar (liter)

rapeseed /'reɪpsiːd/ *n* [u] semilla *f* de colza; (*before n*) **~ oil** aceite *m* de colza

rapid /'ræpəd || 'ræpɪd/ *adj* rápido, veloz

rapidity /rə'pɪdəti/ *n* [u] rapidez *f*

rapidly /'ræpədli || 'ræpɪdli/ *adv* rápidamente

rapids /'ræpədz || 'ræpɪdz/ *pl n* rápidos *mpl*

rapid transit *n* [u] línea *f* ferroviaria urbana

rapier /'reɪpiər || 'reɪpiə(r)/ *n* estoque *m*

rapist /'reɪpəst || 'reɪpɪst/ *n* violador, -dora *m,f*

rappel /rə'pel || ræ'pel/ *vi* (AmE) descender* en rappel

rapper /'ræpər || 'ræpə(r)/ *n* cantante *mf* de rap

rapping /'ræpɪŋ/ *n* [c u] (knocking) golpeteo *m*

rapport /ræ'pɔːr || ræ'pɔː(r)/ *n* [u] relación *f* de comunicación; **a close ~ exists between them** están muy compenetrados, se entienden muy bien

rapprochement /ræprəʊʃ'mɑːn || ræ'prɒʃmɒn/ *n* [u c] (frml) acercamiento *m*

rapt /ræpt/ *adj* (liter) ‹*expression/smile*› embelesado; **they listened with ~ attention** escuchaban embelesados

rapture /'ræptʃər || 'ræptʃə(r)/ *n* [u c] éxtasis *m*, arrobamiento *m* (liter), embeleso *m*; **she went into ~s over the painting** se deshizo en elogios para con el cuadro

rapturous /'ræptʃərəs/ *adj* ‹*applause/welcome*› calurosísimo

rapturously /'ræptʃərəsli/ *adv* ‹*greet*› efusivamente; ‹*applaud*› con frenesí

rare /rer || reə(r)/ *adj* **rarer** /'rerər/, **rarest** /'rerəst/

A 1 (uncommon) raro, poco común; **it is a ~ sight in this country** rara vez se ve en este país; **with a few ~ exceptions** salvo raras excepciones; **one of her ~ TV appearances** una de sus poco frecuentes apariciones en televisión 2 (liter) ‹*talent/beauty*› excepcional, singular

B (rarefied) ‹*atmosphere*› enrarecido

C (Culin) ‹*steak*› vuelta y vuelta, poco hecho (Esp), a la inglesa (Méx)

rarefied /'rerəfaɪd || 'reərɪfaɪd/ *adj* enrarecido

rarely /'rerli || 'reəli/ *adv* rara vez, pocas veces, casi nunca

rarified /'rerəfaɪd || 'reərɪfaɪd/ *adj* ▸**rarefied**

raring /'rerɪŋ || 'reərɪŋ/ *adj*: ***to be ~ to go***: **she starts tomorrow and is ~ to go** empieza mañana y está que ya no se aguanta

rarity /'rerəti || 'reərɪti/ *n* (*pl* **-ties**) 1 [c] (sth rare) algo poco común *or* fuera de lo común 2 [u] (of an occurrence) la poca frecuencia, lo raro

r

rascal /'ræskəl || 'rɑːskəl/ *n* granuja *mf*, pillo, -lla *m,f*

rash¹ /ræʃ/ *n* sarpullido *m*, erupción *f*; **he came out** *o* **broke out in a ~** le salió un sarpullido

rash² *adj* **-er, -est** ‹*person/action/decision*› precipitado; **in a ~ moment I promised her ...** en un arrebato le prometí ...

rasher /'ræʃər || 'ræʃə(r)/ *n* loncha *f*, lonja *f*

rashly /'ræʃli/ *adv* ‹*act*› precipitadamente, sin reflexionar; ‹*promise*› en un arrebato

rasp¹ /ræsp || rɑːsp/ *n* escofina *f*

rasp² *vt* 1 (scrape) ‹*wood*› raspar, escofinar 2 (say): **get out of here, he ~ed** —¡fuera de aquí! —dijo en un tono áspero

■ **rasp** *vi* hacer* un ruido áspero

raspberry /'ræz,beri || 'rɑːzbəri/ *n* (*pl* **-ries**)

A (fruit) frambuesa *f*

B (sound) (colloq) pedorreta *f* (fam); **to blow a ~ at sb** hacerle* una pedorreta a algn (fam), hacerle* una trompetilla a algn (Méx, Ven fam)

rasping /'ræspɪŋ || 'rɑːspɪŋ/ *adj* ‹*sound*› áspero; ‹*voice*› áspero, bronco; ‹*cough*› bronco, perruno (fam)

Rasta /'ræstə/ *n* (BrE colloq) rasta *mf* (fam)

Rastafarian /'ræstə'feriən || ,ræstə'feəriən/ *n* rastafari *mf*

rat /ræt/ *n* 1 (Zool) rata *f*; ***like a drowned ~*** (colloq) como un pollo mojado (fam); ***like ~s leaving a sinking ship*** como alma que lleva el diablo; ***to smell a ~*** oler(se)* algo sospechoso; (*before n*) **~ poison** raticida *m*, matarratas *m* 2 (person) (colloq) rata *f* de alcantarilla (fam), canalla *mf* (fam)

rat-a-tat-tat /'rætətæt'tæt/ *n* (*no pl*) golpeteo *m*

ratbag /'rætbæg/ *n* (BrE colloq) cascarrabias *mf* (fam)

ratchet /'rætʃət || 'rætʃɪt/ *n* trinquete *m*

rate¹ /reɪt/ *n*

A 1 (speed) velocidad; (rhythm) ritmo *m*: **their vocabulary increases at a ~ of five words a day** su vocabulario aumenta a razón de cinco palabras por día; **I'm reading at a ~ of 100 pages a day** estoy leyendo a un ritmo de 100 páginas por día; **at this ~, it'll take weeks** a este paso, nos va a llevar semanas; ***at any ~*** (at least) por lo menos; (in any case) en todo caso 2 (level, ratio): **birth ~** índice *m* de natalidad; **death ~** mortalidad *f*; **literacy ~** nivel *m* de alfabetización; **~ of inflation** tasa *f* de inflación; **~ of interest** tasa *f* *or* (esp Esp) tipo *m* de interés; **~ of exchange** tipo *m* de cambio 3 (price, charge) tarifa *f*; **peak/standard ~** tarifa *f* alta/normal; **the work is paid at a ~ of $20 per hour** el trabajo se paga a (razón de) 20 dólares por hora; **that's the going ~** eso es lo que se suele pagar

B (local tax) (formerly, in UK) (*often pl*) ≈ contribución *f* (municipal *or* inmobiliaria)

rate² *vt*

A 1 (rank, consider): **I ~ her work very highly** tengo una excelente opinión de su trabajo; **to ~ sb/sth (AS sth)**: **I ~ her as the best woman tennis player** yo la considero la mejor tenista; **how do you ~ the movie on a scale of 1 to 10?** ¿qué puntuación *or* (AmL) puntaje le darías a la película en una escala del 1 al 10? 2 (consider good) (BrE colloq) (*usu neg*): **I don't ~ her chances** no creo que tenga muchas posibilidades; **I don't ~ their new player** no me impresiona mucho su nuevo jugador

B (deserve) merecer*; (obtain): **it didn't ~ a mention** no les pareció digno de mención

■ **rate** *vi* 1 (be classed) **to ~ AS sth** estar* considerado COMO algo 2 (measure up) **to ~ WITH sb** (AmE): **Florida doesn't ~ with me** para mí Florida no vale gran cosa

rate: **~payer** /'reɪt,peɪər || 'reɪt,peɪə(r)/ *n* (formerly, in UK) contribuyente *mf*; **~ tart** *n* (BrE) (colloq) *inversor que siempre va a la caza de los mejores tipos de interés*

rather /'ræðər || 'rɑːðə(r)/ *adv*

A 1 (stating preference): **I'd ~ walk than go by bus** prefiero andar a ir en autobús; **I'd ~ you didn't smoke** preferiría que no fumaras; **I'd ~ not think about that** prefiero no pensar en eso; **I'd do anything ~ than give up dancing** haría cualquier cosa antes que dejar de bailar; **~ you than me!** ¡menos mal que eres tú y no yo! 2 (more precisely): **we're acquaintances ~ than friends** somos conocidos, más que amigos; **she has a shop, or ~ a stall** tiene una tienda, o mejor dicho un puesto

B (fairly) bastante; (somewhat) algo, un poco; **it's ~ expensive** es bastante caro; **she looks ~ like Janet** se parece algo *or* un poco a Janet; **I ~ think that ...** me da la impresión *or* tengo la sensación de que ...

ratification /'rætəfə'keɪʃən || ,rætɪfɪ'keɪʃən/ *n* [u] (frml) ratificación *f*

ratify /'rætəfaɪ || 'rætɪfaɪ/ *vt* **-fies, -fying, -fied** (frml) ratificar*

rating /'reɪtɪŋ/ *n*

A 1 [c u] (evaluation): **other polls give the party a better ~** otras encuestas dan al partido un mayor nivel de popularidad; **credit ~** clasificación *f* crediticia 2 **ratings** *pl* (Rad, TV) índice *m* de audiencia

B [c] (Tech) (class of boat, vehicle) categoría *f*, clase *f*

ratio /'reɪʃəʊ, -ʃiəʊ || 'reɪʃiəʊ/ *n* (*pl* **ratios**) proporción *f*, ratio *m* (téc); **in a ~ of two to one** en una proporción *or* relación de dos a uno; **a high pupil-teacher ~** un elevado número *or* (téc) ratio de alumnos por profesor

ration¹ /'ræʃən/ *n* 1 (allowance) ración *f*; (*before n*) **~ book** cartilla *f* de racionamiento 2 **rations** *pl* víveres *mpl*

ration² *vt* ‹*food/goods*› racionar

Phrasal verb

• **ration out** [v ▸ o ▸ adv, v ▸ adv ▸ o] distribuir* en forma racionada

rational /'ræʃn̩əl || 'ræʃənl/ *adj* 1 (able to reason) ‹*being*› racional 2 (sane, lucid): **to be ~** estar* en su (*or* mi *etc*) sano juicio, estar* cuerdo 3 (sensible) ‹*argument/suggestion*› razonable, lógico

rationale /'ræʃə'næl || ,ræʃə'nɑːl/ *n* (*no pl*) base *f*, razones *fpl*; **what's the ~ behind your decision?** ¿en qué se basa su decisión?

rationalization /'ræʃn̩ələ'zeɪʃən || ,ræʃn̩əlaɪ'zeɪʃən/ *n* 1 [u c] (Psych, Math) racionalización *f* 2 [u c] (Busn) racionalización *f*, reconversión *f*

rationalize /'ræʃn̩əlaɪz/ *vt* (Busn, Math, Psych) racionalizar*

rationally /'ræʃn̩əli/ *adv* ‹*think*› racionalmente; ‹*behave*› con sensatez, razonablemente

rationing /'ræʃənɪŋ/ *n* [u] racionamiento *m*

rat: **~ pack** *n* (colloq) periodistas *mpl* y paparazzi; **~ race** *n*: **to escape the ~ race** huir* de la febril competitividad de la vida moderna

rattle¹ /'rætl̩/ *n*

A (*no pl*) (noise) ruido *m*; (of train, carriage) traqueteo *m*

B [c] **(baby's) ~** sonajero *m*, sonaja *f* (Méx), cascabel *m* (Chi)

rattle² *vi* 1 (make noise) «*chains/bottles/keys*» repiquetear; «*door/window/engine*» vibrar; **I heard a key ~ in the lock** oí el ruido de una llave en la cerradura; **the gate ~d in the wind** la verja repiqueteaba con el viento 2 (move) (+ *adv compl*): **the carriage ~d over the cobblestones** el carruaje traqueteaba por el empedrado; **there's something rattling around in the back** hay algo suelto allí atrás

■ **rattle** *vt*

A (make rattle) ‹*keys/chain*› hacer* repiquetear; ‹*door/window*› «*wind*» hacer* vibrar; «*person*» sacudir

B (worry, scare) (colloq) poner* nervioso

Phrasal verbs

• **rattle off** [v ▸ o ▸ adv, v ▸ adv ▸ o] recitar, decir* de un tirón

• **rattle on** [v ▸ adv] hablar *or* (fam) parlotear sin parar

• **rattle through** [v ▸ prep ▸ o] ‹*speech*› decir* rápidamente, apurar (AmL)

rattler /'rætlər || 'rætlə(r)/ *n* (AmE colloq) serpiente *f* (de) cascabel, cascabel *f*

rattlesnake /'rætl̩sneɪk/ *n* serpiente *f* (de) cascabel, cascabel *f*

rattrap /'ræṭtræp/ *n* 1 (trap) ratonera *f* 2 (building) (AmE colloq) ratonera *f*; (*before n*) ‹*building/hotel*› destartalado, de mala muerte (fam)

ratty /'ræti/ *adj* **-tier, -tiest** (colloq)

A (shabby) (AmE colloq) raído, hecho pedazos (fam)

B (bad-tempered) (BrE) malhumorado; **to get ~** ponerse* de mal humor

raucous /'rɔːkəs/ *adj* (loud) estentóreo, escandaloso; (shrill) estridente

raucously /'rɔːkəsli/ *adv* (loudly) a voz en cuello, escandalosamente; (shrilly) estridentemente

raunchy /ˈrɔːntʃi/ *adj* **-chier, -chiest** (colloq)
A (earthy) ‹*humor*› picante; ‹*joke*› escabroso; ‹*voice*› aguardentoso
B (shabby) (AmE) ‹*jacket*› raído; **a ~ hotel** un hotelucho de mala muerte (fam)

ravage /ˈrævɪdʒ/ *vt* (plunder) saquear; **a country ~d by war** un país asolado *or* devastado por la guerra; **a forest ~d by fire** un bosque arrasado por el fuego; **a body ~d by disease** un cuerpo en que la enfermedad ha (*or* había *etc*) hecho estragos

ravages /ˈrævɪdʒəz || ˈrævɪdʒɪz/ *pl n* estragos *mpl*; **his face was marked by the ~ of time** el tiempo había hecho estragos en su rostro

rave[1] /reɪv/ *vi* **1** (talk deliriously) delirar **2** (talk, write enthusiastically) **to ~ ABOUT sth**: **the critics ~d about the new play** los críticos pusieron a la nueva obra por las nubes **3** (talk angrily) despotricar*

rave[2] *n* (colloq)
A (*before n*) (full of praise) **~ reviews** críticas *fpl* muy favorables
B (BrE) (party) *fiesta con música acid*

ravel /ˈrævəl/ *vt*, (BrE) **-ll-** enredar

raven /ˈreɪvən/ *n* cuervo *m*; (*before n*) **~ hair** (liter) cabello *m* negro como el azabache (liter)

ravenous /ˈrævənəs/ *adj* ‹*person/animal*› hambriento; ‹*appetite*› voraz; **I'm (absolutely) ~!** (colloq) ¡tengo un hambre devoradora *or* un hambre canina! (fam)

raver /ˈreɪvər || ˈreɪvə(r)/ *n* (BrE) **1** (swinger) (sl) juerguista *mf* **2** (Mus) (colloq) *aficionado a la música acid*

rave-up /ˈreɪvʌp/ *n* (BrE sl) juerga *f*, fiestorro *m* (Esp fam), reventón *m* (Méx fam), fiestichola *f* (RPl fam & hum), fiestoca *f* (Chi fam), bonche *m* (Ven fam)

ravine /rəˈviːn/ *n* barranco *m*, quebrada *f*

raving[1] /ˈreɪvɪŋ/ *adj* (colloq) (*before n, as intensifier*): **he's a ~ lunatic** está loco de atar (fam); (*as adv*) **he's ~ mad** está como una cabra (fam)

raving[2] *n* [uc] (*often pl*) desvarío *m*, delirio *m*

ravioli /ˌrævɪˈəʊli/ *n* [u] ravioles *mpl*

ravish /ˈrævɪʃ/ *vt* (liter) ‹*woman*› violar

ravishing /ˈrævɪʃɪŋ/ *adj* ‹*beauty*› deslumbrante

raw[1] /rɔː/ *adj*
A **1** (uncooked) ‹*meat/vegetables*› crudo **2** (unprocessed) ‹*silk*› crudo, salvaje; ‹*sugar*› sin refinar; ‹*sewage*› sin tratar; **~ milk** (AmE) leche *f* sin pasteurizar
B **1** ‹*wind*› cortante **2** (unfair): **it's a ~ deal** es una injusticia, es muy injusto
C (sore): **my fingers were ~** tenía los dedos en carne viva
D (inexperienced) verde (fam); ‹*recruit*› novato, primerizo

raw[2] *n*: ***in the ~*** (naked) en cueros (fam); (as sth really is): **nature in the ~** la naturaleza virgen

raw: **~boned** /ˈrɔːˈbəʊnd/ *adj* huesudo; **~hide** *n* [u] (leather) cuero *m* crudo *or* sin curtir; **~ material** *n* [u c] materia *f* prima

ray /reɪ/ *n*
A (beam) rayo *m*; **he's a little ~ of sunshine** es un sol
B (Mus) re *m*
C (Zool) raya *f*

rayon /ˈreɪɑːn || ˈreɪɒn/ *n* [u] rayón *m*

raze /reɪz/ *vt*: **to ~ sth (to the ground)** arrasar algo

razor /ˈreɪzər || ˈreɪzə(r)/ *n* **1** (*cutthroat ~*) navaja *f* (de afeitar *or* (esp Méx) de rasurar), barbera *f* (Col); ***to be on a ~('s) edge*** pender de un hilo **2** (*safety ~*) cuchilla *f or* máquina *f or* maquinilla *f* de afeitar, rastrillo *m* (Méx); (*before n*) **~ blade** cuchilla *f*, hoja *f* de afeitar **3** (electric) máquina *f or* maquinilla *f* de afeitar, máquina *f* de rasurar (esp Méx), afeitadora *f or* (AmC, Méx) rasuradora *f* (eléctrica)

razor: **~-sharp** /ˈreɪzərˈʃɑːrp || ˌreɪzəˈʃɑːp/ *adj* **1** ‹*blade/teeth*› muy afilado **2** ‹*wit/intellect*› muy agudo, agudísimo; **~ wire** *n* [u] alambre *m* de cuchillas

razz /ræz/ *vt* (AmE colloq) tomarle el pelo a (fam), vacilar (Méx, Esp fam)

razzle-dazzle /ˈræzəlˌdæzəl/ *n* [u] ▸ **razzmatazz**

razzmatazz /ˈræzməˈtæz/ *n* [u] (colloq) bulla *f*, alboroto *m*; (publicity) alarde *m* publicitario, bombo *m*

RC *adj* (BrE) = **Roman Catholic**

Rd = **Road**

re[1] /reɪ/ *n* (Mus) re *m*

re[2] /riː/ *prep* con relación a, con referencia a

re- /ˈriː/ *pref* re-

RE *n* (BrE) (= **religious education**) religión *f*

reach[1] /riːtʃ/ *n*
A **1** [c] (distance) alcance *m* **2** (*in phrases*) **within reach** a mi (*or* tu *etc*) alcance; **to be within easy ~** «*book*» estar* muy a mano; «*station*» quedar muy cerca; **within ~ of sth** cerca de algo; **out of** *o* **beyond reach** fuera de su (*or* mi *etc*) alcance
B [c] (of river) tramo *m*; **the upper/lower ~es of the Nile** la cuenca alta/baja del Nilo

reach[2] *vt*
A **1** (with hand) alcanzar*; **can you ~ the top shelf?** ¿alcanzas el estante de arriba? **2** (extend to) llegar* a; **my feet can hardly ~ the pedals** apenas alcanzo los pedales con los pies
B **1** ‹*destination/limit/age*› llegar* a; ‹*stage/figure*› llegar* a, alcanzar*; **applications must ~ us by ...** las solicitudes deben ser recibidas antes de ... **2** ‹*agreement/compromise*› llegar* a, alcanzar*; **I've ~ed the conclusion that ...** he llegado a la conclusión de que ...
C **1** (contact) contactar *or* ponerse* en contacto con; **where can I ~ you?** ¿cómo puedo ponerme en contacto contigo? **2** (gain access to) ‹*public/audience*› llegar* a
D (pass): **to ~ sb sth** alcanzarle* algo a algn
■ **reach** *vi* **1** (extend hand, arm): **she ~ed into her pocket** metió la mano en el bolsillo; **to ~ FOR sth**: **he ~ed for his gun** echó mano a la pistola; **she ~ed across the table for the salt** agarró *or* (esp Esp) cogió la sal, que estaba al otro lado de la mesa **2** (stretch far enough) alcanzar*; **I can't ~!** ¡no alcanzo!, ¡no llego! **3** (extend) extenderse*; **the water ~ed (up) to our knees** el agua nos llegaba hasta las rodillas; **her hair ~es down to her waist** el pelo le llega hasta la cintura

Phrasal verb
• **reach out**
A [v ▸ adv] **1** (with hand) alargar* *or* extender* la mano; **to ~out FOR sth**: **he ~ed out for the knife** alargó *or* extendió la mano para agarrar *or* (esp Esp) coger el cuchillo **2** (with thoughts, emotions) **to ~ out TO sb**: **to ~ out to the poor and oppressed** tenderles* la mano *or* tratar de llegar a los pobres y oprimidos
B [v ▸ o ▸ adv, v ▸ adv ▸ o] ‹*hand*› alargar*, extender*

react /riˈækt/ *vi* reaccionar; **to ~ WITH sth** (Phys, Chem) reaccionar CON algo; **to ~ TO sth**: **how did he ~ to the news?** ¿cómo reaccionó al oír la noticia?

reaction /riˈækʃən/ *n* [c u] reacción *f*; **what was her ~ to the news?** ¿cómo reaccionó *or* cuál fue su reacción frente a *or* ante la noticia?

reactionary[1] /riˈækʃəneri || riˈækʃənri/ *adj* (pej) reaccionario (pey)

reactionary[2] *n* (*pl* **-ries**) (pej) reaccionario, -ria *m,f* (pey)

reactor /riˈæktər || riˈæktə(r)/ *n* (*nuclear ~*) reactor *m* (nuclear)

read[1] /riːd/ (*past & past p* **read** /red/) *vt*
A ‹*book/words/map/music*› leer*; **I can't ~ your writing** no te entiendo la letra; **for '800', ~ '80'** donde dice 800 léase 80; **I ~ myself to sleep** leo hasta que me quedo dormido; ***to ~ sb's mind*** *o* ***thoughts*** adivinarle *or* leerle* el pensamiento a algn; ***to take sth as read*** /red/ dar* algo por sentado *or* por hecho
B **1** (interpret) ‹*sign/mood/situation*› interpretar; **to ~ sth INTO sth**: **I think you're ~ing too much into it** creo que le estás dando demasiada importancia **2** (hear, receive) (Telec colloq): **do you ~ me, alpha?** ¿alfa, me recibe?
C **1** «*sign/notice*» decir*; **the sign ~ /red/ 'closed for repairs'** el letrero decía *or* ponía 'cerrado por reformas' **2** (indicate) «*thermometer/gauge*» marcar* **3** (note indication) ‹*thermometer/meter*› leer*
D (BrE Educ) estudiar (*en la universidad*)
■ **read** *vi*
A «*person*» leer*; **to ~ TO sb** leerle* A algn; **to ~ ABOUT sth/sb**: **I read /red/ about it in the paper** lo leí en el diario; **to ~ THROUGH sth** leer* algo
B **1** (come across): **your article ~s well** tu artículo está bien escrito; **it ~s like a Victorian novel** tiene el estilo de una novela victoriana **2** (have as text) decir*; **his letter ~s as follows: ...** su carta dice lo siguiente ...

r

Phrasal verbs

- **read back** [v ▸ o ▸ adv, v ▸ adv ▸ o] volver* a leer
- **read off** [v ▸ o ▸ adv, v ▸ adv ▸ o] ‹*numbers/names*› leer* (*uno por uno*)
- **read out**

A [v ▸ o ▸ adv, v ▸ adv ▸ o] (read aloud) leer* (*en voz alta*); **I read** /red/ **it out to them** se lo leí

B [v ▸ o ▸ adv] (expel) (AmE) echar; **he was read** /red/ **out of the club/party** lo echaron del club/de la fiesta

- **read over, read through** [v ▸ o ▸ adv] leer* (*por entero*)
- **read up** [v ▸ adv] **to ~ up (ON sth)** estudiar (algo), investigar* (algo)

read² /ri:d/ *n* (*no pl*): **it's a good ~** es ameno, es de lectura amena; **to give sth a quick ~** hojear *or* leer* algo por encima

read³ /red/ *adj*: **to be widely** *o* **well ~** ser* muy leído, ser* de gran *or* amplia cultura

readable /'ri:dəbəl/ *adj* ‹*book/style*› ameno; ‹*writing*› legible

reader /'ri:dər || 'ri:də(r)/ *n*

A **1** (person) lector, -tora *m,f*; **she's a fast/slow ~** lee muy rápido/lento; **he's a great ~** lee mucho, le encanta leer **2** (in library) lector, -tora *m,f*, usuario, -ria *m,f*

B (Educ, Publ) (schoolbook) libro *m* de lectura; (anthology) selección *f* de textos

readership /'ri:dərʃɪp || 'ri:dəʃɪp/ *n* lectores *mpl*; **the Daily Echo has a ~ of over 10 million** el Daily Echo tiene una tirada de 10 millones

readily /'redḷi || 'redɪli/ *adv* **1** (willingly, gladly): **she ~ agreed** accedió de buena gana; **I ~ admit that ...** no tengo inconveniente *or* reparos en admitir que ... **2** (easily, quickly) ‹*understand*› fácilmente, inmediatamente; **they are ~ available** se pueden conseguir fácilmente

readiness /'redinəs || 'redinɪs/ *n* [u]

A (preparedness): **she cleaned the house in ~ for their arrival** limpió y dispuso *or* preparó la casa para su llegada

B (willingness, eagerness): **his ~ to admit his mistakes** su buena disposición para admitir sus errores

reading /'ri:dɪŋ/ *n*

A **1** [u] (activity, skill) lectura *f*; **they gathered for the ~ of the will** se reunieron para dar lectura al testamento; (*before n*) ‹*glasses*› para leer, de lectura; **she has a ~ age of 10** lee al nivel de un niño de 10 años; **~ lamp** lámpara *f* portátil; **~ list** lista *f* de lecturas recomendadas; **~ material** material *f* de lectura; **~ room** sala *f* de lectura **2** [c] (event): **poetry ~** recital *m* de poesía **3** [c] (passage) lectura *f*

B [u] **1** (material): **this book makes good/interesting ~** este libro es muy ameno/interesante **2** (study) lectura *f*; **from my ~, I developed an interest in India** a través de mis lecturas empecé a interesarme por la India

C [c] (on dial, gauge) lectura *f*; **to take a ~ of sth** leer* algo, ver* cuánto marca algo; **we took regular ~s** tomamos nota de la temperatura (*or* presión *etc*) a intervalos regulares

D [c] (interpretation) lectura *f*, interpretación *f*

readjust /'ri:ə'dʒʌst/ *vt* reajustar

■ **readjust** *vi* «*person*» **to ~ (TO sth)** readaptarse *or* volver* a adaptarse (A algo)

readjustment /'ri:ə'dʒʌstmənt/ *n* [c u] (of salaries, TV) reajuste *m*; (to circumstances) readaptación *f*

read /ri:d/: **~-only memory** /'ri:d'əʊnli/ *n* [u] memoria *f* ROM; **~out** *n* lectura *f*; **~-write** /'ri:d'raɪt/ *adj* (Comput) de lectura-escritura

ready¹ /'redi/ *adj* **-dier, -diest**

A **1** (having completed preparations) (*pred*) **to be ~** estar* listo, estar* pronto (RPl); **~ when you are!** ¡cuando quieras!; **the doctor is ~ for you now** ya puede pasar a ver al doctor; **to be ~ to + INF** estar* listo PARA + INF; **to get ~** (prepare oneself) prepararse, aprontarse (CS); (get dressed, made up etc) arreglarse, prepararse, aprontarse (CS); **(get) ~, (get) steady** *o* **set, go** preparados *or* en sus marcas *or* (Ur tb) prontos, listos ¡ya!; **to get sth/sb/oneself ~**: **I'm getting the meal ~** estoy preparando la comida; **it takes her ages to get herself/the children ~** tarda siglos en arreglarse/arreglar a los niños; **to make ~** prepararse **2** (mentally prepared) (*pred*) **to be ~ FOR sth/to + INF** estar* preparado PARA algo/PARA + INF; **phew, I'm ~ for my bed** estoy que me caigo; **I feel ~ for anything** me siento dispuesto a todo **3** (on point of) (colloq) **~ to + INF** a punto de + INF; **she looks ~ to drop** parece agotada

B (willing) dispuesto; **~ and willing** dispuesto a todo; **to be ~ to + INF** estar* dispuesto A + INF; **a ~ market** un mercado muy receptivo

C (easy, available): **there is no ~ solution to this problem** el problema no tiene fácil solución; **~ money** *o* **cash** dinero *m* (en efectivo); **~ to hand** a mano

D (quick) ‹*wit/intellect*› vivo, agudo

ready² *n* (*pl* **-dies**)

A **at the ~** listo; **the reporters waited, pens at the ~** los periodistas esperaban, bolígrafo en ristre *or* en mano

B **the readies** *pl* (cash) (BrE sl) la guita (arg), la plata (AmL fam), la lana (AmL fam), la pasta (Esp arg)

ready³ *vt* **-dies, -dying, -died** preparar

ready: **~-cooked** /'redi'kʊkt/ *adj* precocinado; **~-made** /'redi'meɪd/ *adj* ‹*suit*› de confección; ‹*soup/sauce*› preparado, precocinado; **~-made curtains** cortinas *fpl* ya hechas *or* confeccionadas; **there you have a ~-made excuse** ahí tienes la excusa, no te la tienes que inventar; **~-to-wear** /'reditə'wer || ˌreditə'weə(r)/ *adj* (*before n*) ‹*clothes*› de confección

reaffirm /'ri:ə'fɜ:rm || ˌri:ə'fɜ:m/ *vt* **1** (restate) reiterar, reafirmar **2** (strengthen) (frml) consolidar, afianzar*

reagent /ri'eɪdʒənt/ *n* [c u] reactivo *m*

real¹ /ri:l, rɪl || ri:l, rɪəl/ *adj*

A **1** (actual, not imaginary) real, verdadero; **the characters don't behave like ~ people** los personajes no se comportan como gente de verdad; **her first ~ success** su primer éxito de importancia; ***for* ~** (colloq) de verdad; **this time it's for ~** esta vez va en serio; **is he for ~?** (AmE) ¿es posible que sea tan tonto (*or* ingenuo *etc*)? **2** (actual, true) (*before n*) ‹*culprit/reason/name*› verdadero; **she's the ~ boss around here** aquí la que manda de verdad es ella **3** (genuine, not fake) ‹*fur/leather*› auténtico, genuino; ‹*gold*› de ley; **is it ~ coffee or instant?** ¿es café café o café instantáneo?; **I met a ~(, live) princess** conocí a una princesa auténtica *or* de verdad **4** (*as intensifier*) auténtico, verdadero

B (Econ) ‹*income/cost/increase*› real

real² *adv* (AmE colloq) (*as intensifier*) muy; **I'm ~ tired** estoy muy cansada, estoy cansadísima *or* (fam) super cansada; **be ~ careful, now** ojo, ten mucho cuidado

real estate *n* [u] (esp AmE) bienes *mpl* raíces *or* inmuebles, propiedad *f* inmobiliaria; (*before n*) **~ ~ agent** agente inmobiliario, -ria *m,f*, corredor, -dora *m,f* de propiedades (Chi)

realign /'ri:ə'laɪn/ *vt* ‹*currencies/positions*› realinear; ‹*salaries*› reajustar

■ **realign** *vi* (Pol) **to ~ WITH sth** formar una alianza CON algo

realism /'ri:əlɪzəm/ *n* [u] realismo *m*

realist /'ri:ələst || 'ri:əlɪst/ *n* realista *mf*

realistic /'ri:ə'lɪstɪk || ˌriə'lɪstɪk/ *adj* **1** (sensible) ‹*person/target*› realista; ‹*price*› razonable **2** (Art, Lit) realista

realistically /'ri:ə'lɪstɪkli || ˌriə'lɪstɪkli/ *adv* **1** (sensibly): **looking at it ~ ...** siendo realistas ...; **~, it couldn't be finished** (*indep*) siendo realistas, es imposible acabar antes del viernes **2** (in lifelike manner) ‹*describe/represent*› de manera realista

reality /ri'æləti/ *n* [c u] (*pl* **-ties**) realidad *f*; **the realities of life** la realidad de la vida; **to become (a) ~** hacerse* realidad; **in ~** en realidad; (*before n*) **~ check** *n* chequeo *m* de la realidad; **~ show** *n* reality show *m*; **~ TV** *n* televisión *f* basada en reality shows

realizable /'ri:əlaɪzəbəl/ *adj* (Fin) ‹*assets/property*› realizable

realization /'ri:ələ'zeɪʃən || ˌriəlaɪ'zeɪʃən/ *n* [u]

A (understanding) comprensión *f*; **I woke up to the terrible ~ that ...** al despertar comprendí horrorizado que ...

B (of plan) realización *f*

realize /'ri:əlaɪz/ *vt*

A **1** (become aware of) darse* cuenta de, comprender, caer* en la cuenta de; **she ~d (that) ...** se dio cuenta de que ..., comprendió que ... **2** (know, be aware of) saber*, darse* cuenta de; **I ~ it's expensive, but it's worth it** reconozco que es caro, pero vale la pena

B (achieve) ‹*ambition*› hacer* realidad; ‹*potential*› desarrollar; ‹*plan*› llevar a cabo
C 1 ‹*profit*› producir* 2 (turn into cash) ‹*assets*› realizar*
■ **realize** *vi* darse* cuenta

real-life /'riːl'laɪf || ˌriːəl'laɪf, ˌrɪəl-/ *adj* ‹*adventure/romance*› de la vida real; **in a ~ situation** en una situación real

really /'riːəli || 'riːəli, 'rɪəli/ *adv* 1 (in fact): **I ~ did see him!** ¡de verdad que lo vi!; **I ~ don't care** la verdad es que no me importa; **the tomato is ~ a fruit** el tomate en realidad *or* hablando con propiedad es una fruta; **do you like it? — not ~** ¿te gusta? — no mucho 2 (*as intensifier*): **it's ~ good/cheap/old** es buenísimo/baratísimo/viejísimo, es muy *or* (fam) super bueno/barato/viejo; **it was ~ hot** hacía mucho calor; **~ and truly** de verdad 3 (*as interj*): **(oh,) ~?** (expressing interest) ¿ah sí?; **really?** (expressing surprise) ¿de verdad? *or* ¡no me digas!; **well, ~!** (expressing indignation) ¡pero bueno!; **no, ~, I do want to come** no, en serio, claro que quiero ir

realm /relm/ *n* 1 (kingdom) (frml) reino *m* 2 (sphere) (*often pl*): **the ~s of the imagination** el mundo de la imaginación; **the ~ of science/politics** el mundo de la ciencia/política; **that's outside** *o* **beyond the ~s of possibility** es totalmente imposible

real: **~ property** *n* ▸**real estate**; **~ time** *n* [u] (Comput) tiempo *m* real

realtor /'riːəltər || 'rɪəltə(r)/ *n* (AmE) agente inmobiliario, -ria *m,f*, corredor, -dora *m,f* de propiedades (Chi)

realty /'riːəlti || 'rɪəlti/ *n* [u] bienes *mpl* raíces *or* inmuebles, propiedad *f* inmobiliaria

ream /riːm/ *n* 1 (measure) (Print) resma *f* 2 **reams** *pl* (great amount): **to write ~s** escribir* páginas y páginas

reamer /'riːmər || 'riːmə(r)/ *n* (AmE) exprimelimones *m*, exprimidor *m*

reap /riːp/ *vt* 1 (Agr) cosechar, recoger* 2 (gain, receive): **to ~ the benefits of sth** cosechar los beneficios de algo

reaper /'riːpər || 'riːpə(r)/ *n* 1 (person) cosechador, -dora *m,f*; **the (grim) ~** (liter) la Parca, la muerte 2 (machine) cosechadora *f*

reappear /'riə'pɪr || ˌriə'pɪə(r)/ *vi* volver* a aparecer, reaparecer*

reappearance /'riːə'pɪrəns || ˌriːə'pɪərəns/ *n* [u c] reaparición *f*

reappraisal /'riːə'preɪzəl/ *n* [u c] revaluación *f*

rear¹ /rɪr || rɪə(r)/ *n* 1 (back part) (*no pl*) parte *f* trasera *or* posterior *or* de atrás; **the courtyard at** *o* (AmE also) **in the ~ of the building** el patio de detrás del edificio; **she sat in the ~** (Auto) iba sentada atrás *or* en el asiento trasero 2 (of column, procession) (*no pl*) **the ~** la retaguardia 3 [c] (buttocks) (colloq) trasero *m* (fam)

rear² *adj* ‹*window/wheel*› de atrás, trasero; **~ lamp** *o* **light** (BrE Auto) luz *f* trasera *or* de atrás

rear³ *vt*
A (raise) ‹*child/cattle*› criar*
B (lift) ‹*head*› levantar; ▸**head¹ A**
■ **rear** *vi* **~ (up)** 1 «*horse*» empinarse, pararse en dos patas (AmL); (with anger, fear) encabritarse 2 (tower) erguirse*, alzarse*

rear: **~ end** *n* (colloq) trasero *m* (fam); **~guard** *n* retaguardia *f*

rearm /'riː'ɑːrm || ˌriː'ɑːm/ *vt* rearmar
■ **rearm** *vi* rearmarse

rearmament /'riː'ɑːrməmənt || ˌriː'ɑːməmənt/ *n* [u] rearme *m*

rearrange /'riːə'reɪndʒ/ *vt* 1 (change position of): **she had ~d the furniture** había cambiado los muebles de lugar; **~ these letters to form the name of a city** ordena estas letras de manera que formen el nombre de una ciudad 2 (change time of) ‹*appointment*› cambiar la fecha/la hora de

rear-view mirror /'rɪrvjuː || 'rɪəvjuː/ *n* (espejo *m*) retrovisor *m*

reason¹ /'riːzn̩/ *n*
A [c u] (cause) razón *f*, motivo *m*; **I'd like to know the ~ why** quisiera saber por qué *or* el porqué; **all the more ~ he should go** razón de más para que vaya; **I left it there for a ~** por algo lo dejé ahí; **for health ~s** por razones *or* motivos de salud; **with (good) ~** con razón; **for ~s best known to herself** por razones *or* motivos que sólo ella conoce, vete a saber por qué (fam); **she has good ~ to be upset** tiene razones *or* motivos para estar disgustada; **~ FOR sth** razón *or* motivo DE algo; **I have ~ to believe that ...** tengo razones *or* motivos para pensar que ...
B [u] (faculty) razón *f*
C [u] (good sense): **to listen to ~** atender* a razones; **to make sb see ~** hacer* entrar en razón a algn; **anything, within ~** cualquier cosa, dentro de lo razonable; ***it stands to ~*** es lógico

reason² *vt* pensar*
■ **reason** *vi* razonar, discurrir

Phrasal verb
• **reason out** [v ▸ o ▸ adv, v ▸ adv ▸ o] entender* (*razonando*)

reasonable /'riːzn̩əbəl/ *adj* 1 ‹*offer/request/person*› razonable; **it must be proved beyond ~ doubt** tiene que ser demostrado sin que quede lugar a duda; **you stand a ~ chance of winning** tienes bastantes posibilidades de ganar 2 ‹*price/sum*› razonable, moderado; **their shoes are very ~** sus zapatos están muy bien de precio

reasonably /'riːzn̩əbli/ *adv* 1 ‹*behave/argue*› razonablemente; **~ priced goods** artículos a precios razonables 2 (adequately, fairly): **I'm ~ certain** estoy casi seguro; **it's a ~ secure job** es un trabajo bastante seguro (, dentro de lo que cabe)

reasoned /'riːznd/ *adj* razonado

reasoning /'riːznɪŋ/ *n* [u] razonamiento *m*, lógica *f*

reassemble /'riːə'sembəl/ *vt* 1 ‹*people/group*› volver* a reunir, reunir* 2 ‹*parts/engine*› reensamblar, volver* a montar *or* armar *or* ensamblar
■ **reassemble** *vi* «*meeting/group*» volverse* a reunir, reunirse*

reassess /'riːə'ses/ *vt* ‹*chances/situation*› volver* a estudiar, reexaminar; ‹*taxes*› volver* a fijar

reassurance /'riːə'ʃʊrəns || ˌriːə'ʃʊərəns, ˌriːə'ʃɔːrəns/ *n* 1 [u] (feeling): **he drew ~ from his wife's words** lo que le dijo su mujer lo confortó *or* lo tranquilizó 2 [c u] (words, support): **he gave us countless ~s that ...** nos tranquilizó asegurándonos repetidamente que ...; **she needs constant ~ of your love** necesita que constantemente le demuestres tu amor

reassure /'riːə'ʃʊr || ˌriːə'ʃʊə(r), ˌriːə'ʃɔː(r)/ *vt* (allay anxiety) tranquilizar*; **he tried to ~ them that everything was alright** trató de tranquilizarlos asegurándoles que todo estaba bien; **she felt ~d by his presence** su presencia la tranquilizó; **to ~ sb OF sth**: **she ~d him of her affection for him** le aseguró que lo quería

reassuring /'riːə'ʃʊrɪŋ || ˌriːə'ʃʊərɪŋ, ˌriːə'ʃɔːrɪŋ/ *adj* ‹*voice/manner/answer*› tranquilizador; **he was very ~** me (*or* lo *etc*) dejó mucho más tranquilo; **it's ~ to know that ...** tranquiliza saber que ...

reassuringly /'riːə'ʃʊrɪŋli || ˌriːə'ʃʊərɪŋgli, ˌriːə'ʃɔːrɪŋli/ *adv* ‹*smile/talk*› de modo tranquilizador; **he was ~ open** su franqueza inspiraba confianza

reawaken /'riːə'weɪkən/ *vt* (liter) volver* a despertar, hacer* renacer
■ **reawaken** *vi* volver* a despertar(se), renacer*

reawakening /'riːə'weɪkənɪŋ/ *n* [u c] (liter) renacer *m* (liter), despertar *m* (liter)

rebadge /riː'bædʒ/ *vt* rebautizar*

rebase /riː'beɪs/ *vt* establecer* una nueva base para calcular

rebate /'riːbeɪt/ *n* (repayment) reembolso *m*, devolución *f*; (discount) descuento *m*; **tax ~** reembolso *or* devolución de impuestos

rebel¹ /'rebəl/ *n* rebelde *mf*; (*before n*) ‹*forces/army*› rebelde

rebel² /rɪ'bel/ *vi* **-ll- to ~ (AGAINST sth/sb)** rebelarse *or* sublevarse (CONTRA algo/algn)

rebellion /rɪ'beljən/ *n* [c u] rebelión *f*; **to rise (up) in ~** rebelarse, sublevarse

rebellious /rɪ'beljəs/ *adj* rebelde

rebirth /'riː'bɜːrθ || ˌriː'bɜːθ/ *n* [u c] renacimiento *m*

reboot /riː'buːt/ *vt* (Comput) reinicializar*, reiniciar

reborn /'riː'bɔːrn || ˌriː'bɔːn/ *adj*: **to be ~** renacer*

rebound¹ /'riːbaʊnd/ *n* (ricochet): **the ball hit him on the ~** la pelota le pegó de rebote *or* al rebotar; **she married him on the ~** se casó con él por despecho

rebound² /rɪ'baʊnd/ *vi* «*ball*» rebotar

r

rebuff[1] /rɪ'bʌf/ *n*: **to meet with/receive a ~** ser* rechazado

rebuff[2] *vt* rechazar*

rebuild /'ri:'bɪld/ *vt* (*past & past p* **rebuilt**) ‹*building/bridge/economy*› reconstruir*; **he tried to ~ his life** intentó rehacer su vida; **she rebuilt the business from scratch** levantó el negocio de cero

rebuke[1] /rɪ'bju:k/ *vt* **to ~ sb FOR sth/-ING** reprender a algn POR algo/+ INF

rebuke[2] *n* reprimenda *f*

rebut /rɪ'bʌt/ *vt* **-tt-** (frml) rebatir, refutar

rebuttal /rɪ'bʌtl̩/ *n* (frml) refutación *f*

recalcitrant /rɪ'kælsətrənt || rɪ'kælsɪtrənt/ *adj* recalcitrante, contumaz (frml)

recall[1] /rɪ'kɔ:l, 'ri:kɔ:l/ *n*

A [u] (memory) memoria *f*; **to have total ~** tener* una memoria excelente

B [u c] 1 (withdrawal of goods) retirada *f* (*del mercado*) 2 (summoning back — of an ambassador) retirada *f*; (— of Parliament) convocatoria *f* (en sesión extraordinaria) 3 (in US) (Govt) destitución *f* (*de un funcionario del gobierno mediante voto popular*)

recall[2] /rɪ'kɔ:l/ *vt*

A (remember) recordar*; **I don't ~ that we ever went there** no recuerdo que hayamos estado allí

B (call back) 1 ‹*faulty goods*› retirar (*del mercado*) 2 ‹*ambassador*› retirar; (temporarily) llamar; ‹*troops*› llamar

■ **recall** *vi* recordar*

recant /rɪ'kænt/ *vt* (frml) ‹*religion*› abjurar (de); ‹*belief/statement*› retractarse de

■ **recant** *vi* (withdraw statement) retractarse; (Relig) abjurar

recap[1] /'ri:kæp/ *n*

A (summary) (colloq) resumen *m*

B (AmE Auto) ▸**retread**[2]

recap[2] /'ri:'kæp/ **-pp-** *vt*

A (summarize) (colloq) resumir, recapitular

B (AmE Auto) ▸**retread**[1]

■ **recap** *vi* (colloq) resumir; **to ~** (*as linker*) en resumen, para resumir

recapitulate /'ri:kə'pɪtʃəleɪt || ˌri:kə'pɪtjʊleɪt/ *vt/i* (frml) recapitular, resumir

recapitulation /'ri:kə'pɪtʃə'leɪʃən || ˌri:kəpɪtjʊ'leɪʃən/ *n* [c u] (frml) recapitulación *f*, resumen *m*

recapture[1] /'ri:'kæptʃər || ˌri:'kæptʃə(r)/ *n* captura *f*

recapture[2] *vt* ‹*convict/animal*› capturar; ‹*youth/beauty*› recuperar

recast /'ri:'kæst || ˌri:'kɑ:st/ *vt* (*past & past p* **recast**) (Theat): **the play has been ~** le han cambiado el reparto a la obra, la obra tiene un nuevo reparto; **the part was ~** le dieron el papel a otro actor

recede /rɪ'si:d/ *vi* 1 (move back) «*tide*» retirarse; **the mountains ~d into the distance** las montañas se perdían en la distancia; **his hair was beginning to ~** ya tenía entradas 2 (become less likely) «*danger*» alejarse; «*prospect*» desvanecerse* 3 **receding** *pres p* ‹*chin*› hundido; **he has a receding hairline** tiene entradas

receipt /rɪ'si:t/ *n* 1 [c] (paper) recibo *m*; **to make out a ~** hacer* *or* (frml) extender* un recibo 2 [u] (act) recibo *m*, recepción *f*; **please acknowledge ~ of goods** por favor acuse recibo de la mercancía; **we are in ~ of your letter** (frml) obra en nuestro poder su carta (frml) 3 **receipts** *pl* (Fin) ingresos *mpl*, entradas *fpl*

receive /rɪ'si:v/ *vt*

A 1 ‹*letter/award/visit*› recibir; ‹*payment*› recibir, cobrar, percibir (frml); ‹*stolen goods*› comerciar con, reducir* (AmS); ‹*serve/ball*› recibir; ‹*injuries*› sufrir; ‹*blow*› recibir; **~d with thanks the sum of ...** recibí (conforme) la suma de ...; **to ~ treatment** ser* tratado 2 (react to) ‹*proposal/news/idea*› recibir, acoger* 3 **received** *past p* **R~d Pronunciation** pronunciación *f* estándar; **~d wisdom** (la) creencia popular

B (welcome, admit) (frml) recibir, acoger*; **to be ~d into the Church** ser* admitido en el seno de la Iglesia

C (Rad, TV) ‹*signal*› recibir, captar

■ **receive** *vi*: ***to be on the receiving end of sth*** ser* el blanco *or* la víctima de algo; ***it is better o more blessed to give than to ~*** más vale dar que recibir

receiver /rɪ'si:vər || rɪ'si:və(r)/ *n*

A (Telec) auricular *m*, tubo *m* (RPl), fono *m* (Chi)

B (Rad, TV) receptor *m*

C (Busn, Law) **(official) ~** síndico *m* (de quiebras); **to call in the ~s** ≈ solicitar la suspensión *or* la cesación de pagos

D (in US football) receptor, -tora *m,f*; **wide ~** receptor abierto, receptora abierta *m,f*

E (of stolen goods) comerciante *mf* de mercancía robada, reducidor, -dora *m,f* (AmS)

receivership /rɪ'si:vərʃɪp || rɪ'si:vəʃɪp/ *n* [u] sindicatura *f*; **to go into/be in ~** ≈ ser* declarado/estar* en suspensión *or* en cesación de pagos

recent /'ri:sn̩t/ *adj* reciente; **in ~ years/months/times** en los últimos años/meses/tiempos; **in the ~ past** en los últimos tiempos

recently /'ri:sn̩tli/ *adv* recientemente; **as ~ as the 1980's** todavía en los años 80; **have you seen them? — not ~** ¿los has visto? — recientemente *or* últimamente no; **until quite ~** hasta hace bien poco

receptacle /rɪ'septɪkəl/ *n* (frml) recipiente *m*, receptáculo *m*

reception /rɪ'sepʃən/ *n*

A (response, reaction) (*no pl*) recibimiento *m*, acogida *f*; **what sort of ~ did you get?** ¿qué tal te recibieron?; **the book had a favorable ~** el libro tuvo una acogida favorable *or* fue bien recibido

B [u] (admission) (frml) **~ INTO sth** admisión *f* EN algo; (*before n*) **~ center** *o* (BrE) **centre** centro *m* de acogida; **~ committee** comité *m* de bienvenida *or* recepción

C (in hotel, office) (*no art*) recepción *f*; (*before n*) **~ desk** recepción *f*

D [c] (social event) recepción *f*

E [u] (Rad, TV) recepción *f*

receptionist /rɪ'sepʃənəst || rɪ'sepʃənɪst/ *n* recepcionista *mf*

reception room *n* 1 (in hotel) salón *m* 2 (in house) (BrE) *salón, comedor o cualquier habitación donde se puede recibir*

receptive /rɪ'septɪv/ *adj* receptivo; **to be ~ TO sth** estar* abierto A algo

recess /'ri:ses/ *n*

A [u] 1 (of legislative body) receso *m* (AmL), suspensión *f* de actividades (Esp); (of committee etc) intermedio *m*, cuarto *m* intermedio (RPl) 2 (AmE Educ) recreo *m*

B [c] 1 (alcove) hueco *m*, entrada *f* 2 (secluded place) lugar *m* escondido *or* oculto

recession /rɪ'seʃn̩ || rɪ'seʃən/ *n* [c u] (Econ) recesión *f*

recharge /'ri:'tʃɑ:rdʒ || ˌri:'tʃɑ:dʒ/ *vt* volver* a cargar, recargar*

■ **recharge** *vi* volverse* a cargar, recargarse*

rechargeable /'ri:'tʃɑ:rdʒəbəl || ˌri:'tʃɑ:dʒəbəl/ *adj* recargable

recherché /rə'ʃer'ʃeɪ || rə'ʃeəʃeɪ/ *adj* (liter) rebuscado

recidivist /rɪ'sɪdəvəst || rɪ'sɪdɪvɪst/ *n* (frml) reincidente *mf*

recipe /'resəpi/ *n* 1 (Culin) receta *f*; **a ~ for cheese soufflé** una receta para hacer soufflé de queso; (*before n*) **~ book** (published) libro *m* de cocina; (personal) cuaderno *m* de recetas (de cocina) 2 (formula) **~ FOR sth** fórmula *f* PARA algo; **that's a ~ for disaster** eso es buscarse problemas

recipient /rɪ'sɪpiənt/ *n* (frml) (of letter) destinatario, -ria *m,f*; (of an organ) (Med) receptor, -tora *m,f*

reciprocal /rɪ'sɪprəkəl/ *adj* recíproco, mutuo

reciprocate /rɪ'sɪprəkeɪt/ *vt* ‹*compliment/kindness*› corresponder a, reciprocar* (AmL); **his love wasn't ~d** su amor no era correspondido

■ **reciprocate** *vi* corresponder, reciprocar* (AmL)

recital /rɪ'saɪtl̩/ *n* 1 (performance) recital *m* 2 (rendition of poem) recitado *m*, recitación *f*

recitation /'resə'teɪʃən || ˌresɪ'teɪʃən/ *n* [c u] recitado *m*, recitación *f*

recite /rɪ'saɪt/ *vt* 1 (declaim) ‹*poem*› recitar 2 (list) ‹*names*› enumerar

■ **recite** *vi* recitar

reckless /'rekləs || 'reklɪs/ *adj* ‹*plan/act*› imprudente, temerario; ‹*person*› imprudente, insensato; **~ endangerment** *o* (BrE) **driving** imprudencia *f* temeraria (al conducir)

recklessly /'rekləsli || 'reklɪsli/ *adv* imprudentemente, de modo temerario

r

recklessness /'rekləsnəs || 'reklɪsnɪs/ *n* [u] imprudencia *f*, temeridad *f*

reckon /'rekən/ *vt* [1] (calculate) calcular; **I ~ the total to be £35** calculo que en total son 35 libras [2] (consider) considerar; **he's ~ed to be one of his generation's finest writers** está considerado como uno de los mejores escritores de su generación [3] (think) (colloq) creer*; **I ~ she knew all along** yo creo que lo sabía desde el principio; **he ~s he's a good player** se cree *or* se considera buen jugador; **what do you ~?** ¿tú qué opinas?, ¿y a ti qué te parece?; **I ~ so** creo *or* me parece que sí

(Phrasal verbs)

- **reckon on, reckon upon** [v ▸ prep ▸ o]: **we didn't ~ on such a big turn-out** no contábamos con que vendría tanta gente; **to ~ on (sb/sth) -ING**: **we ~ on each customer spending about $10** calculamos que cada cliente gasta alrededor de 10 dólares; **I hadn't ~ed on that happening** no contaba con que pasara eso, no esperaba que sucediera eso
- **reckon up** [v ▸ o ▸ adv, v ▸ adv ▸ o] sumar, calcular
- **reckon with** [v ▸ prep ▸ o] [1] (face) vérselas* con; **you'll have me to ~ with** tendrás que vértelas conmigo [2] (anticipate, take into account) tener* en cuenta
- **reckon without** [v ▸ prep ▸ o] ‹*weather conditions*› no tener* en cuenta; **we'll have to ~ without his help** no podremos contar con su ayuda

reckoning /'rekənɪŋ/ *n* [u] [1] (calculation, estimate) cálculos *mpl*; **by my ~** según mis cálculos; **he was a bit out in his ~** se equivocó ligeramente en sus cálculos [2] (assessment, opinion) opinión *f* [3] (judgment) juicio *m*; **the day of ~** el día del Juicio Final

reclaim¹ /rɪ'kleɪm/ *vt* [1] ‹*rights*› reclamar, reivindicar*; **I filled in a form to ~ tax** llené un formulario para que me devolvieran parte de los impuestos; **to ~ one's luggage** (Aviat) recoger* el equipaje; (at left luggage) (pasar a) retirar el equipaje [2] (recover) recuperar; **~ed land** terreno *m* ganado al mar

reclaim² /'ri:kleɪm/ *n* [u]: **luggage ~** (BrE) recogida *f* de equipaje

reclamation /'reklə'meɪʃən/ *n* [u] (of land) rescate *m*; (of refuse, waste) recuperación *f*, reciclaje *m*

recline /rɪ'klaɪn/ *vi* [1] (lean back) recostarse*, reclinarse; (rest) apoyarse [2] ‹‹*chair/backrest*›› reclinarse [3] **reclining** *pres p* ‹*chair/seat*› reclinable, abatible; ‹*figure*› yacente (liter), recostado

■ **recline** *vt* reclinar

recliner /rɪ'klaɪnər || rɪ'klaɪnə(r)/ *n* asiento *m* (*or* sillón *m etc*) reclinable *or* abatible

recluse /rɪ'klu:s/ *n* ermitaño, -ña *m,f*

reclusive /rɪ'klu:sɪv/ *adj* dado a recluirse, que lleva una vida recluida

recognition /'rekəg'nɪʃən/ *n* [u] [1] (identification) reconocimiento *m*; **it has changed beyond** *o* **out of all ~** ha cambiado de tal manera que resulta irreconocible [2] (acknowledgment, acceptance) reconocimiento *m*; **in ~ of** (frml) en reconocimiento a *or* por (frml)

recognizable /'rekəgnaɪzəbəl/ *adj* reconocible; ‹*difference*› apreciable; **no longer ~** ya irreconocible

recognizably /'rekəgnaɪzəbli/ *adv* evidentemente

recognize /'rekəgnaɪz/ *vt* [1] (identify) ‹*face/voice/person*› reconocer* [2] (acknowledge, accept) reconocer*, admitir [3] (grant right to speak) (AmE frml) concederle *or* darle* la palabra a; **the chair ~s the gentleman from ...** tiene la palabra el representante de ...

recognized /'rekəgnaɪzd/ *adj* reconocido

recoil¹ /rɪ'kɔɪl/ *vi* [1] (shrink back) retroceder; **she ~ed in fear** retrocedió de miedo; **to ~ FROM sth** rehuir* algo [2] ‹‹*gun*›› retroceder, dar* un culatazo

recoil² /'ri:kɔɪl/ *n* [u] retroceso *m*, culatazo *m*

recollect /'rekə'lekt/ *vt*

A (remember) recordar*; **I don't ~ seeing them there** no recuerdo haberlos visto allí

B ‹*thoughts*› ordenar

■ **recollect** *vi* recordar*

recollection /'rekə'lekʃən/ *n* [u c] recuerdo *m*; **to the best of my ~** si no me falla la memoria, si mal no recuerdo; **he has no ~ of having seen you that day** no recuerda haberte visto ese día

recommence /'ri:kə'mens/ *vt* (frml) reanudar, reiniciar (frml)

■ **recommence** *vi* reanudarse, reiniciarse (frml)

recommend /'rekə'mend/ *vt* [1] (praise, declare acceptable) recomendar*; **the play has little/nothing to ~ it** la obra tiene poco/no tiene nada que se pueda recomendar [2] (advise) **to ~ sth/-ING** aconsejar *or* recomendar* algo/+ INF; **it's not to be ~ed** no es nada aconsejable *or* recomendable; **~ed dosage** dosis *f* recomendada; (on label) posología *f*; **~ed (retail) price** precio *m* de venta recomendado; **~ed reading** lecturas *fpl* recomendadas

recommendation /'rekəmen'deɪʃən/ *n* [u c] [1] (approval) recomendación *f* [2] (advice) recomendación *f*, sugerencia *f*

recompense¹ /'rekəmpens/ *n* [u] (frml) **~ (FOR sth)** ‹*for damages/loss*› indemnización *f or* compensación *f* (POR algo); ‹*for efforts*› recompensa *f* (POR algo)

recompense² *vt* (frml) **to ~ sb (FOR sth)** ‹*for damage/loss*› indemnizar* *or* compensar a algn (POR algo); ‹*for efforts*› recompensar a algn (POR algo)

reconcile /'rekənsaɪl/ *vt* [1] (make friendly) ‹*enemies/factions*› reconciliar; **they were finally ~d** finalmente se reconciliaron; **to ~ sb WITH sb**: **the tragedy helped to ~ him with his brother** la tragedia lo ayudó a reconciliarse con su hermano [2] (make consistent) **to ~ sth (WITH sth)** ‹*theories/ideals*› conciliar algo (CON algo) [3] (make resigned) **to become ~d TO sth** resignarse A algo, aceptar algo; **to ~ oneself to -ING** resignarse A + INF

reconciliation /'rekənsɪli'eɪʃən/ *n* [1] [c] (of people) **~ (WITH sb)** reconciliación *f* (CON algn) [2] [u] (of ideas, aims) **~ (WITH sth)** conciliación *f* (CON algo)

recondition /'ri:kən'dɪʃən/ *vt* reacondicionar

reconnaissance /rə'kɑ:nəzens, -səns || rɪ'kɒnɪsəns/ *n* [u c] (Mil) reconocimiento *m*

reconnoiter, (BrE) **reconnoitre** /'ri:kə'nɔɪtər, 're- || ,rekə'nɔɪtə(r)/ *vt* reconocer*

■ **reconnoiter** *vi* hacer* un reconocimiento del terreno (*or* del área *etc*)

reconquer /'ri:'kɑ:ŋkər || ,ri:'kɒŋkə(r)/ *vt* reconquistar

reconquest /'ri:'kɑ:ŋkwest || ,ri:'kɒŋkwest/ *n* [u] reconquista *f*

reconsider /'ri:kən'sɪdər || ,ri:kən'sɪdə(r)/ *vt* reconsiderar

■ **reconsider** *vi* recapacitar

reconstitute /'ri:'kɑ:nstətu:t || ,ri:'kɒnstɪtju:t/ *vt* reconstituir*

reconstruct /'ri:kən'strʌkt/ *vt* [1] ‹*town/building*› reconstruir* [2] ‹*crime/events*› reconstruir*

reconstruction /'ri:kən'strʌkʃən/ *n* [1] [u] (rebuilding) reconstrucción *f*; **R~** *período, de 1865 a 1877, durante el cual se llevó a cabo la integración de los estados Sudistas con la Unión* [2] [c] (re-creation) reconstitución *f*

record¹ /'rekərd || 'rekɔ:d/ *n*

A [1] [c] (document) documento *m*; (of attendances etc) registro *m*; (file) archivo *m*; (minutes) acta *f*‡; (note) nota *f*; **medical ~s** historial *m* médico; **keep a ~ of your expenses** anote sus gastos; **according to our ~s** según nuestros datos; **please keep this copy for your ~s** conserve esta copia para su información [2] (*in phrases*) **for the record**: **for the ~, I had no financial interest in the deal** yo no me beneficiaba con el acuerdo, que conste; **off the record**: **the minister spoke off the ~** el ministro habló extraoficialmente; **on record**: **the hottest summer on ~** el verano más caluroso del que se tienen datos; **she is on ~ as saying that ...** ha declarado públicamente que ...; **to put** *o* **place sth on ~** dejar constancia de algo, hacer* constar algo; **to set** *o* **put the ~ straight, let me point out that ...** para poner las cosas en su lugar, permítame señalar que ...

B [c] [1] (of performance, behavior): **he has a good service/academic ~** tiene una buena hoja de servicios/un buen currículum *or* historial académico; **he has a poor ~ for timekeeping** en cuanto a puntualidad, su expediente no es bueno; **our products have an excellent safety ~** nuestros productos son de probada seguridad [2] (*criminal ~*) antecedentes *mpl* (penales); **to have a ~** tener* antecedentes (penales) *or* (CS tb) prontuario

C [c] (highest, lowest, best, worst) récord *m*, marca *f*; **to break/set a ~** batir/establecer* un récord *or* una marca; **to hold the**

world ~ tener* *or* (frml) ostentar el récord *or* la marca mundial; **his latest movie has broken box-office ~s** su última película ha batido todos los récords de taquilla
D [c] (Audio, Mus) disco *m*; (*before n*) **~ company** compañía *f* discográfica; **~ store** tienda *f* de discos

record² /rɪ'kɔ:rd || rɪ'kɔ:d/ *vt*
A **1** ‹‹*person*›› (write down) anotar; (in minutes) hacer* constar; **historians ~ how Rome fell** los historiadores narran la caída de Roma **2** (register) ‹‹*instrument*›› registrar
B ‹*song/program/album*› grabar
■ **record** *vi* grabar

record³ /'rekərd || 'rekɔ:d/ *adj* (*before n, no comp*) récord *adj inv*, sin precedentes

record /'rekərd || 'rekɔ:d/: **~-breaking** /'breɪkɪŋ/ *adj* que bate todos los récords, sin precedentes; **~ card** *n* ficha *f*

recorded /rɪ'kɔ:rdəd || rɪ'kɔ:dɪd/ *adj* **1** (Rad, TV) ‹*music*› grabado; ‹*program*› grabado (*para transmitir en diferido*) **2** (known, written down) ‹*history*› escrito, documentado; ‹*fact*› del que se tiene constancia

recorded delivery *n* [u c] (in UK) *servicio de envíos postales en el cual se exige la firma del destinatario como constancia de la entrega del envío*

recorder /rɪ'kɔ:rdər || rɪ'kɔ:də(r)/ *n*
A (Mus) flauta *f* dulce
B (in UK) (Law) *abogado que actúa como juez a tiempo parcial*

recording /rɪ'kɔ:rdɪŋ || rɪ'kɔ:dɪŋ/ *n* [c u] grabación *f*; (*before n*) ‹*studio/session*› de grabación

record /'rekərd || 'rekɔ:d/: **~ library** *n* (collection) discoteca *f*; (of institution) fonoteca *f*; (lending) discoteca *f* pública; **~ player** *n* tocadiscos *m*

recount /rɪ'kaʊnt/ *vt* narrar, contar*

re-count¹ /'ri:'kaʊnt/ *vt* volver* a contar, contar* de nuevo; ‹*votes*› hacer* un segundo escrutinio de, recontar*

re-count² /'ri:kaʊnt/ *n* recuento *m*, segundo escrutinio *m*

recoup /rɪ'ku:p/ *vt* ‹*costs*› recuperar; ‹*losses*› resarcirse* de

recourse /'ri:kɔ:rs || rɪ'kɔ:s/ *n* [u] **to have ~ to sth/sb** recurrir a algo/algn

recover /rɪ'kʌvər || rɪ'kʌvə(r)/ *vt* **1** (regain) ‹*consciousness/strength*› recuperar, recobrar; ‹*investment/position/lead*› recuperar; **he was on the point of losing his temper, but ~ed himself** estuvo a punto de perder los estribos, pero se contuvo **2** (retrieve) rescatar **3** (reclaim) ‹*metal/glass/paper*› recuperar **4** (Law): **to ~ damages** obtener* indemnización por daños y perjuicios
■ **recover** *vi* **1** ‹‹*person*›› **to ~ (FROM sth)** reponerse* *or* restablecerse* *or* recuperarse (DE algo) **2** ‹‹*economy/industry*›› recuperarse, repuntar, reactivarse

re-cover /'ri:'kʌvər || ˌri:'kʌvə(r)/ *vt* ‹*chair/sofa*› retapizar*

recoverable /rɪ'kʌvərəbəl/ *adj* recuperable

recovery /rɪ'kʌvəri/ *n* (*pl* **-ries**)
A [c u] **1** (return to health) recuperación *f*, restablecimiento *m* (frml); **she made a quick ~** se recuperó *or* se mejoró rápidamente; **to be on the road to ~** estar* en vías de recuperación; (*before n*) **~ room** sala *f* de recuperación **2** (of economy, industry) recuperación *f*, reactivación *f*
B [u] (of stolen goods, missing documents) recuperación *f*; (retrieval) rescate *m*; (*before n*) **~ service** (BrE Auto) servicio *m* de grúa

re-create /'ri:kri'eɪt/ *vt* recrear

recreation /'rekri'eɪʃən/ *n* **1** [u] (leisure) esparcimiento *m*; (*before n*) **~ ground** (BrE) campo *m* de deportes; **~ room** (AmE) sala *f* de juegos **2** [c] (pastime) forma *f* de esparcimiento, pasatiempo *m* **3** [u] (in school, prison) (BrE) recreo *m*

recreational /'rekri'eɪʃn̩əl || ˌrekri'eɪʃənl̩/ *adj* recreativo

recrimination /rɪ'krɪmə'neɪʃən/ *n* [c u] (*often pl*) recriminación *f*, reproche *m*

recruit¹ /rɪ'kru:t/ *n* **1** (Mil) recluta *mf* **2** (new member): **the latest ~s to the club/staff** los nuevos socios del club/miembros del personal

recruit² *vt* (Mil) reclutar; ‹*members/volunteers*› reclutar; ‹*staff*› contratar
■ **recruit** *vi* **1** ‹‹*army*›› alistar reclutas; ‹‹*company*›› buscar* personal, reclutar gente **2** **recruiting** *pres p* ‹*agent/office*› de reclutamiento

recruitment /rɪ'kru:tmənt/ *n* [u] reclutamiento *m*

recta /'rektə/ *pl of* **rectum**

rectangle /'rektæŋgəl/ *n* rectángulo *m*

rectangular /rek'tæŋgjələr || rek'tæŋgjʊlə(r)/ *adj* rectangular

rectification /'rektəfə'keɪʃən || ˌrektɪfɪ'keɪʃən/ *n* [u c] rectificación *f*

rectify /'rektəfaɪ || 'rektɪfaɪ/ *vt* **-fies, -fying, -fied** rectificar*

rectitude /'rektətu:d || 'rektɪtju:d/ *n* [u] (frml) rectitud *f*

rector /'rektər || 'rektə(r)/ *n* **1** (Relig) rector, -tora *m,f*, ≈ párroco *m* **2** (in US) (Educ) rector, -ra *m,f*

rectory /'rektəri/ *n* (*pl* **-ries**) rectoría *f*, ≈ casa *f* del párroco

rectum /'rektəm/ *n* (*pl* **rectums** *or* **recta**) recto *m*

recumbent /rɪ'kʌmbənt/ *adj* (frml *or* hum) recostado

recuperate /rɪ'ku:pəreɪt/ *vi* **to ~ (FROM sth)** recuperarse *or* reponerse* (DE algo)

recuperation /rɪ'ku:pə'reɪʃən/ *n* [u] recuperación *f*, restablecimiento *m*

recur /rɪ'kɜ:r || rɪ'kɜ:(r)/ *vi* **-rr-** **1** ‹‹*phenomenon*›› volver* a ocurrir *or* a suceder, repetirse*; ‹‹*theme*›› repetirse*, volver* a aparecer; ‹‹*symptom*›› volver* a presentarse; **the image kept ~ring in his mind** volvía a ver la imagen una y otra vez **2** **recurring** *pres p* recurrente

recurrence /rɪ'kɜ:rəns || rɪ'kʌrəns/ *n* [c u] (of symptoms, theme) reaparición *f*; (of incident, dream) repetición *f*

recurrent /rɪ'kɜ:rənt || rɪ'kʌrənt/ *adj* recurrente

recycle /'ri:'saɪkəl/ *vt* reciclar

recycling /ri:'saɪklɪŋ/ *n* [u] reciclaje *m*, reciclado *m*

red¹ /red/ *adj* **redder, reddest**
A **1** ‹*rose/dress*› rojo, colorado; ‹*flag/signal*› rojo; **her eyes were ~** tenía los ojos enrojecidos *or* rojos; **to go ~ in the face** (with anger, heat) ponerse* colorado *or* rojo; (with embarrassment) sonrojarse, ruborizarse*, ponerse* colorado; **there'll be a few ~ faces** a unos cuantos se les va a caer la cara de vergüenza; **he has ~ hair** es pelirrojo; **the (traffic) lights were ~** el semáforo estaba (en) rojo **2** ‹*meat*› rojo; ‹*wine*› tinto
B *also* **Red** (Pol) rojo

red² *n*
A [u] (color) rojo *m*, colorado *m*; ***to see ~*** ponerse* hecho una furia *or* un basilisco; **that sort of remark makes me see ~** ese tipo de comentario me saca de quicio *or* de las casillas
B [c] *also* **Red** (Pol) (colloq & pej) rojo, -ja *m,f* (fam)
C **the red** (debt) (*no pl*): ***to be in/out of the ~*** estar*/no estar* en números rojos

red: **~ admiral** *n* vanesa *f* roja; **~-blooded** /'red 'blʌdəd || ˌred'blʌdɪd/ *adj* (colloq) (*usu before n*) (virile) (journ) ‹*male*› ardiente, fogoso; **~brick** *adj* (BrE) ‹*building*› de ladrillo (rojo); **~brick university** *universidad sin la tradición secular de las antiguas como Oxford o Cambridge*; **~cap** *n* (AmE colloq) mozo *m*, maletero *m*; **~ card** *n* (in soccer): **to show sb the ~ card** mostrarle* la tarjeta roja a algn; **~ carpet** *n*: **to roll out the ~ carpet for sb** recibir* a algn con bombos y platillos *or* (Esp) a bombo y platillo; (*before n*) **they gave us the ~-carpet treatment** nos trataron a cuerpo de rey; **~ Cross** *n* Cruz *f* Roja; **~currant** *n* grosella *f* (roja)

redden /'redn̩/ *vi* ‹‹*skin/sky*›› enrojecerse*, ponerse* rojo; (blush) ruborizarse*, ponerse* colorado, sonrojarse
■ **redden** *vt* enrojecer*

reddish /'redɪʃ/ *adj* rojizo

redecorate /'ri:'dekəreɪt/ *vt* (painting only) pintar; (painting and papering) pintar y empapelar
■ **redecorate** *vi* pintar (y empapelar)

redeem /rɪ'di:m/ *vt*
A **1** ‹*fault/error*› compensar **2** ‹*good name*› rescatar **3** ‹*sinners*› redimir **4** **redeeming** *pres p*: **they have no ~ing features** no tienen ningún punto a su favor
B **1** ‹*promise/pledge*› (frml) cumplir **2** (from pawnshop) desempeñar
■ *v refl* **to ~ oneself** reparar su (*or* mi *etc*) error

redeemable /rɪ'di:məbəl/ *adj* ‹*property*› amortizable; ‹*stocks/shares*› reembolsable; ‹*coupon/voucher*› canjeable

redeemer /rɪ'di:mər || rɪ'di:mə(r)/ *n* redentor, -tora *m,f*

redefine /'ri:dɪ'faɪn/ *vt* redefinir

redemption /rɪ'dempʃən/ *n* [u] (saving) salvación *f*; (Relig) redención *f*; **to be past** *o* **beyond** ~ no tener* arreglo *or* remedio

redeploy /'ri:dɪ'plɔɪ/ *vt* ‹*resources*› reorientar, dar* nuevo destino a; ‹*staff*› asignar un nuevo destino a, reubicar* (AmL); ‹*troops*› cambiar la disposición de

redeployment /'ri:dɪ'plɔɪmənt/ *n* [u] (of resources) reorientación *f*; (of staff) reorganización *f*, reubicación *f* (AmL)

redevelop /'ri:dɪ'veləp/ *vt* reurbanizar*

redevelopment /'ri:dɪ'veləpmənt/ *n* [u c] reurbanización *f*

red: **~-eye** /'redaɪ/ *n* 1 [u] (Photo) ojo *m* rojo 2 [c] *also* **red-eye flight** (AmE colloq) vuelo *m* matutino 3 [u] (AmE colloq) (cheap whisky) whisky *m* barato; **~-eyed** /'red'aɪd/ *adj* con los ojos enrojecidos *or* rojos; **~-faced** /'red'feɪst/ *adj*: **to be ~-faced with shame** tener* la cara colorada de vergüenza; **~-haired** /'red'herd || ˌred 'heəd/ *adj* pelirrojo; **~-handed** /'red'hændəd || ˌred 'hændɪd/ *adj*: ***to catch sb ~-handed*** agarrar *or* (esp Esp) coger* a algn con las manos en la masa; **~head** *n* pelirrojo, -ja *m,f*; **~-headed** /'red'hedəd || ˌred'hedɪd/ *adj* ▸ **~-haired**; **~ herring** *n* (in detective story) pista *f* falsa; **~-hot** /'red'hɑ:t || ˌred'hɒt/ *adj* (*pred* **~ hot**) (very hot) al rojo vivo; (colloq) (sensational) ‹*story/pictures*› al rojo vivo

redial[1] /'ri:'daɪl || ˌri:'daɪəl/ *vi/t*, (BrE) **-ll-** volver* a marcar *or* (AmS tb) a discar

redial[2] /'ri:daɪl || 'ri:daɪəl/ *n* rellamada *f*; **automatic ~** rellamada automática

Red Indian *n* (BrE) piel *mf* roja

redirect /'ri:də'rekt, -daɪ- || ˌri:daɪ'rekt, -də-/ *vt* (*often pass*) ‹*mail*› enviar* a una nueva dirección; ‹*traffic*› desviar*

rediscover /'ri:dɪ'skʌvər || ˌri:dɪ'skʌvə(r)/ *vt* redescubrir*, volver* a descubrir

rediscovery /'ri:dɪ'skʌvəri/ *n* [u c] (*pl* **-ries**) redescubrimiento *m*

redistribute /'ri:dɪ'strɪbjət || ˌri:dɪ'strɪbju:t/ *vt* redistribuir*

redistribution /ri:'dɪstrə'bju:ʃən || ˌri:dɪstrɪ'bju:ʃən/ *n* [u c] redistribución *f*

red: **~-letter** /'red'letər || ˌred'letə(r)/ *adj* (*before n*) ‹*day*› muy especial, memorable; **~ light** *n* luz *f* roja, semáforo *m* en rojo, alto *m* (Méx); **she drove through the ~ light** no respetó la luz roja, se saltó la luz roja, se pasó el alto (Méx); **~-light district** /'red'laɪt/ *n* zona *f* de tolerancia, zona *f* roja (AmL), barrio *m* chino (Esp); **~neck** *n* (in US) (pej) *sureño reaccionario de la clase baja rural*

redness /'rednəs || 'rednɪs/ *n* [u] rojez *f*

redo /'ri:'du:/ *vt* (*3rd pers sing pres* **redoes**; *past* **redid**; *past p* **redone**) 1 (do again) rehacer*, volver* a hacer 2 ▸ **redecorate** *vt*

redolent /'redḷənt || 'redələnt/ *adj* (liter) **~ OF sth** (smelling of sth) con olor A *or* (liter) con fragancia DE algo; **his style is ~ of the Impressionists** su estilo recuerda el de los impresionistas

redouble /'ri:'dʌbəl/ *vt* ‹*efforts*› redoblar, intensificar*

redoubtable /rɪ'daʊtəbəl/ *adj* imponente, temible

redound /rɪ'daʊnd/ *vi* (frml): **to ~ to sb's advantage** redundar en beneficio de algn; **it can only ~ to our credit** sólo puede aumentar nuestro prestigio

red pepper *n* 1 [u] (cayenne) pimienta *f* de cayena 2 [c u] (capsicum) *see* **pepper**[1] **B**

redraft /'ri:'dræft || ri:'drɑ:ft/ *vt* volver* a redactar

redress[1] /rɪ'dres/ *n* [u] (of a wrong) reparación *f*; (Law) compensación *f*, reparación *f*

redress[2] *vt* ‹*error/wrong*› reparar, enmendar*; ‹*imbalance*› corregir*

red: **~ Riding Hood** *n* Caperucita *f* Roja; **~ Sea** *n* **the R~ Sea** el Mar Rojo; **~shank** /'redʃæŋk/ *n* archibebe *m*; **~skin** *n* (colloq) piel *mf* roja; **~ snapper** /'snæpər || 'snæpə(r)/ *n* pargo *m*, huachinango *m* (Méx); **~ tape** *n* [u] (bureaucracy) trámites *mpl* burocráticos, papeleo *m* (fam)

reduce /rɪ'du:s || rɪ'dju:s/ *vt*

A 1 ‹*number/amount*› reducir*; ‹*tension/pressure/speed*› disminuir*, reducir*; ‹*price/taxes/rent*› reducir*, rebajar; ‹*goods*› rebajar; ‹*pain*› aliviar 2 ‹*photograph/image*› reducir*

B 1 (break down, simplify) **to ~ sth TO sth** reducir* algo A algo 2 (Math) simplificar*

C (bring to undesirable state) **to ~ sth/sb TO sth** (*often pass*): **their policies have ~d the country to poverty** sus políticas han sumido al país en la pobreza; **they ~d the city to ruins** dejaron la ciudad en ruinas; **they were ~d to begging** se vieron obligados a mendigar; **to ~ sb to tears** hacer* llorar a algn

reduced /rɪ'du:st || rɪ'dju:st/ *adj*

A (lower, lesser) ‹*number/size/prices*› reducido

B (impoverished) (frml & euph): **to live in ~ circumstances** pasar estrecheces

reduction /rɪ'dʌkʃən/ *n* [c u] (in numbers, size, spending) reducción *f*; (in prices, charges) rebaja *f*

redundancy /rɪ'dʌndənsi/ *n* [u c] (*pl* **-cies**)

A (superfluity) (frml) superfluidad *f*

B (BrE Lab Rel) (loss of job) despido *m*, cese *m*; **voluntary ~** retiro *m* voluntario *or* (Esp) baja *f* voluntaria; (with incentives) retiro *m* incentivado *or* (Esp) baja *f* incentivada; (*before n*) **~ money** *o* **pay** indemnización *f* *or* (Chi) desahucio *m* (por despido *or* cese)

redundant /rɪ'dʌndənt/ *adj*

A 1 (superfluous) superfluo 2 (Ling) redundante

B (esp BrE Lab Rel): **she was made ~** la despidieron por reducción de planilla *or* (Esp) de plantilla

redwood /'redwʊd/ *n* secoya *f*, secuoya *f*

reed /ri:d/ *n*

A (Bot) carrizo *m*, junco *m*

B (Mus) (in instrument) lengüeta *f*

reeducate /'ri:'edʒəkeɪt || ˌri:'edjʊkeɪt/ *vt* ‹*population*› reeducar*; ‹*offender*› rehabilitar

reedy /'ri:di/ *adj* **-dier, -diest** ‹*voice*› aflautado, atiplado

reef /ri:f/ *n* (Geog) arrecife *m*; (seen as hazard) escollo *m*, arrecife *m*

reefer /'ri:fər || 'ri:fə(r)/ *n* (sl & dated) ▸ **joint**[1] **E**

reef knot *n* nudo *m* de rizo, lasca *f*

reek[1] /ri:k/ *vi* 1 (stink) **to ~ (OF sth)** apestar *or* heder* (A algo) 2 (have air of) **to ~ OF sth** ‹*of corruption/fraud*› oler* A algo 3 **reeking** *pres p* maloliente, hediondo

reek[2] *n* [u] hedor *m*

reel[1] /ri:l/ *n*

A 1 (for wire, thread, tape) carrete *m* 2 (of film) rollo *m* 3 (fishing) carrete *m*, carretel *m*, reel *m* (RPl)

B (dance) *baile de origen escocés*

reel[2] *vi*

A 1 (move unsteadily) tambalearse; **he ~ed out of the room** salió de la habitación tambaleándose *or* dando tumbos 2 (feel impact): **they were still ~ing from the last price rise** todavía no se habían recuperado del impacto de la última subida de precios

B ‹‹*room/walls*›› (move in circles) dar* vueltas; **my head was ~ing** todo me daba vueltas

■ **reel** *vt* enrollar

Phrasal verbs

- **reel in** [v ▸ o ▸ adv, v ▸ adv ▸ o] ‹*line*› enrollar, recoger*; ‹*fish*› sacar* del agua enrollando el sedal
- **reel off** [v ▸ o ▸ adv, v ▸ adv ▸ o] recitar de un tirón

reelect /'ri:ə'lekt || ˌri:ɪ'lekt/ *vt* reelegir*

reemerge /'ri:ə'mɜ:rdʒ || ˌri:ɪ'mɜ:dʒ/ *vi* 1 (reappear) volver* a salir, reaparecer* 2 (regain prominence) resurgir*

reenact /'ri:ə'nækt || ˌri:ɪ'nækt/ *vt* ‹*historical event*› recrear, representar; ‹*crime*› reconstruir*, reconstituir*

reenter /'ri:'entər || ˌri:'entə(r)/ *vt* volver* a entrar en *or* (esp AmL) a

reentry /'ri:'entri/ *n* [u c] (*pl* **-tries**) reingreso *m*

reexamine /'ri:ɪg'zæmən || ˌri:ɪg'zæmɪn/ *vt* ‹*facts/evidence/student/patient*› volver* a examinar; ‹*witness*› volver* a interrogar

ref[1] /ref/ *n* (colloq) (= **referee**) árbitro, -tra *m,f*, réferi *mf* (AmL)

ref[2] /ref/ (= **reference**) ref.; **our ~: HYZ** N/ref. HYZ; **your ~: XYZ** S/ref. XYZ

refectory /rɪ'fektəri/ *n* (*pl* **-ries**) comedor *m*

r

refer /rɪ'fɜːr || rɪ'fɜː(r)/ **-rr-** *vt* 1 (direct — to source of information) remitir; (— to place) enviar*, mandar; **the reader is ~red to ...** se remite al lector a ...; **to ~ sb to a specialist** (Med) mandar *or* (AmL) derivar a algn a un especialista 2 (submit) ‹*problem/proposal*› remitir; *see also* **refer to**

Phrasal verbs

• **refer back to**

A [v ▸ adv ▸ prep ▸ o] ‹*earlier chapter*› hacer* referencia a; **I'll have to ~ back to my notes** tendré que volver a consultar mis apuntes

B [v ▸ o ▸ adv ▸ prep ▸ o]: **the matter was ~red back to the committee** el asunto se volvió a remitir a la comisión

• **refer to** [v ▸ prep ▸ o] 1 (mention) hacer* referencia a, aludir a 2 (allude to) referirse* a; **I ~ to your letter of 18th March** con relación a su carta del 18 de marzo 3 (apply to) «*regulations/orders*» atañer* a 4 (consult) ‹*dictionary/notes*› consultar; ⓢ **refer to drawer** (on check) devolver* al librador (*por falta de fondos*)

referee[1] /'refə'riː/ *n*

A 1 (Sport) árbitro, -tra *m,f*, réferi *mf* (AmL) 2 (in dispute) árbitro, -tra *m,f*

B (for job candidate) (BrE): **you need two ~s** necesitas el aval de dos personas

referee[2] *vt* arbitrar

■ **referee** *vi* arbitrar, hacer* de árbitro

reference /'refrəns, 'refərəns/ *n*

A [c u] (allusion) **~ (TO sth/sb)** alusión *f or* referencia *f* (A algo/algn); **to make ~ to sth/sb** hacer* alusión *or* referencia a algo/algn, mencionar algo/a algn; **with ~ to sth** con referencia *or* relación a algo, en relación con algo

B 1 [u] (consultation) consulta *f*; **for future ~** para futura(s) consulta(s); **for future ~, you ought to get authorization first** de aquí en adelante tenga en cuenta que primero hay que pedir autorización; (*before n*) **~ book/library** obra *f*/biblioteca *f* de consulta *or* de referencia; **for ~ use only** para consultar en sala 2 [c] (indicator) referencia *f*; (*before n*) **~ number** número *m* de referencia

C [u] (scope, remit): **point of ~** punto *m* de referencia

D [c] (for job candidate — testimonial) referencia *f*, informe *m*; (— person giving testimonial) (AmE): **you need two ~s** necesitas el aval de dos personas

referendum /'refə'rendəm/ *n* (*pl* **-dums** *or* **-da** /-də/) referéndum *m*, referendo *m*, plebiscito *m*; **to hold a ~ on sth** plebiscitar algo, someter algo a referéndum (*or* referendo *etc*)

referral /rɪ'fɜːrəl/ *n* [c u]: **I asked for (a) ~ to a specialist** pedí que me mandaran *or* (AmL) me derivaran a un especialista; **we had 600 ~s last month** el mes pasado nos enviaron 600 casos/pacientes

referred pain /rɪ'fɜːrd || rɪ'fɜːd/ *n* [u] dolor *m* reflejo

refill[1] /'riːfɪl/ *n* 1 (for pen) repuesto *m*, recambio *m*; (for lighter) carga *f*; (*before n*) ‹*pack/pad*› de repuesto, de recambio 2 (drink): **would you like a ~?** ¿te sirvo otra copa?

refill[2] /'riː'fɪl/ *vt* volver* a llenar, rellenar

refillable /'riː'fɪləbəl/ *adj* recargable

refine /rɪ'faɪn/ *vt* 1 ‹*sugar/oil*› refinar 2 (improve) ‹*design/style*› pulir, perfeccionar

refined /rɪ'faɪnd/ *adj* 1 ‹*person/manners*› refinado, fino 2 ‹*sugar/oil*› refinado

refinement /rɪ'faɪnmənt/ *n* 1 [u] (gentility, elegance) refinamiento *m*, finura *f* 2 [u c] (subtlety) refinamiento *m*, delicadeza *f* 3 [c u] (improvement) mejora *f* 4 [u] (of raw material) refinado *m*

refinery /rɪ'faɪnəri/ *n* (*pl* **-ries**) refinería *f*

refit[1] /'riːfɪt/ *n* (Naut) reparación *f*; (Const) reacondicionamiento *m*

refit[2] /'riː'fɪt/ *vt* **-tt-** ‹*ship*› reparar; ‹*building*› reacondicionar

reflect /rɪ'flekt/ *vt*

A 1 ‹*light/heat/sound*› reflejar; **her face was ~ed in the mirror** su cara se reflejaba en el espejo 2 ‹*situation/feeling/mood*› reflejar; **this is ~ed in her work** esto se refleja en su trabajo

B (think) reflexionar, meditar

■ **reflect** *vi*

A (think) **to ~ (ON sth)** reflexionar *or* meditar (SOBRE algo)

B «*light/heat*» reflejarse

Phrasal verb

• **reflect on, reflect upon** [v ▸ prep ▸ o] repercutir en; **what you say will ~ on the group as a whole** lo que digas repercutirá en la imagen de todo el grupo; **to ~ badly on sth/sb** perjudicar* algo/a algn

reflection /rɪ'flekʃən/ *n*

A 1 [u] (Opt, Phys) reflexión *f* 2 [c] (image) reflejo *m* 3 [c] (of situation, feeling) reflejo *m*

B 1 [u] (contemplation) reflexión *f*; **on** *o* **upon ~ ...** pensándolo bien ... 2 [c] (thought) reflexión *f*; (comment) observación *f*

C (disparagement) (*no pl*) **to be a ~ ON sth/sb**: **it's a sad ~ on human nature that nobody would help him** que nadie lo ayudara no dice mucho a favor de la humanidad; **this is no ~ on you, but ...** yo sé que no es culpa tuya, pero ..., no te estoy reprochando, pero ...

reflective /rɪ'flektɪv/ *adj* 1 (Phys) reflectante 2 (pensive) reflexivo, meditabundo

reflector /rɪ'flektər || rɪ'flektə(r)/ *n* (of light, heat) reflector *m*; (Auto) catafaros *m*

reflex /'riːfleks/ *n* reflejo *m*; (*before n*) ‹*response/refusal*› instintivo, automático; **~ action** acto *m* reflejo

reflexion /rɪ'flekʃən/ *n* [u c] (BrE) ▸**reflection**

reflexive /rɪ'fleksɪv/ *adj* reflexivo

reflexology /ˌriːflek'sɑːlədʒi || ˌriːflek'sɒlədʒi/ *n* [u]

A (system of massage) reflexología *f*

B (Psych) reflexología *f*

reflexotherapy /rɪˌfleksəʊ'θerəpi/ *n* [u] reflexoterapia *f*

reforestation /'riːfɔːre'steɪʃən || ˌriːˌfɒrɪ'steɪʃən/ *n* [u] reforestación *f*, repoblación *f* forestal

reform[1] /rɪ'fɔːrm || rɪ'fɔːm/ *n* [u c] reforma *f*

reform[2] *vt* reformar

■ **reform** *vi* reformarse

re-form /'riː'fɔːrm || ˌriː'fɔːm/ *vt* volver* a formar, reagrupar

■ **re-form** *vi* volver* a formarse, reagruparse

reformation /'refər'meɪʃən || ˌrefə'meɪʃən/ *n* 1 (of character) reforma *f* 2 (Relig) **the Reformation** la Reforma

reformatory /rɪ'fɔːrmətɔːri || rɪ'fɔːmətəri/ *n* (*pl* **-ries**) (in US) reformatorio *m*

reformed /rɪ'fɔːrmd || rɪ'fɔːmd/ *adj* reformado; **he's a ~ character** es otra persona

reformer /rɪ'fɔːrmər || rɪ'fɔːmə(r)/ *n* reformador, -dora *m,f*

refraction /rɪ'frækʃən/ *n* [u] refracción *f*

refrain[1] /rɪ'freɪn/ *vi* (frml) **to ~ (FROM sth/-ING)** abstenerse* (DE algo/+ INF); **kindly ~ from smoking** se ruega no fumar

refrain[2] *n* (Lit, Mus) estribillo *m*

refresh /rɪ'freʃ/ *vt* 1 refrescar*; **to ~ sb's memory** refrescarle* la memoria a algn 2 (Comput) actualizar*

refresher course /rɪ'freʃər || rɪ'freʃə(r)/ *n* (Educ) curso *m* de actualización *or* de reciclaje

refreshing /rɪ'freʃɪŋ/ *adj* ‹*drink/bath/breeze*› refrescante; ‹*sleep*› reparador; ‹*enthusiasm/honesty*› reconfortante

refreshment /rɪ'freʃmənt/ *n* 1 (food and drink): **to take some ~** (eat) tomar un tentempié; (drink) tomar algo de beber 2 **refreshments** *pl* refrigerio *m*

refried beans /'riː'fraɪd/ *pl n* frijoles *mpl* refritos

refrigerate /rɪ'frɪdʒəreɪt/ *vt* refrigerar

refrigeration /rɪ'frɪdʒə'reɪʃən/ *n* [u] refrigeración *f*

refrigerator /rɪ'frɪdʒəreɪtər || rɪ'frɪdʒəreɪtə(r)/ *n* nevera *f*, refrigerador *m*, frigorífico *m* (Esp), heladera *f* (RPl)

refuel /'riː'fjuːəl/, (BrE) **-ll-** *vt* reabastecer* de combustible

■ **refuel** *vi* repostar, reabastecerse* de combustible

refueling, (BrE) **refuelling** /'riː'fjuːəlɪŋ/ *n* [u c] repostaje *m*, reabastecimiento *m* de combustible; (*before n*) **~ stop** escala *f* técnica *or* de repostaje

refuge /'refjuːdʒ/ *n* 1 [u c] (safe place) refugio *m*; **to seek ~ from sth/sb** refugiarse de algo/algn; **to take ~** refugiarse 2 [c] (for battered women) refugio *m* (para mujeres maltratadas)

refugee /'refjʊ'dʒiː/ *n* refugiado, -da *m,f*; (*before n*) **~ camp** campamento *m* de refugiados; **to have/seek ~ status** tener*/solicitar condición de refugiado

r

refund¹ /rɪ'fʌnd/ *vt* ‹*payment*› devolver*, reintegrar (frml); ‹*expenses/postage*› reembolsar; **to ~ sb FOR sth** reembolsarle algo a algn

refund² /'riːfʌnd/ *n* reembolso *m*; **to give sb a ~** devolverle* el dinero a algn; ⊘ **no refunds** no se admiten devoluciones

refundable /rɪ'fʌndəbəl/ *adj* reembolsable

refurbish /rɪː'fɜːrbɪʃ || ˌriː'fɜːbɪʃ/ *vt* renovar*, hacer* reformas en; (restore) restaurar

refurbishment /rɪː'fɜːrbɪʃmənt || ˌriː'fɜːbɪʃmənt/ *n* [u] renovación *f*, acondicionamiento *m*

refusal /rɪ'fjuːzəl/ *n* 1 (of permission, request) denegación *f*; (of offer) rechazo *m*; (to do sth) negativa *f*; ***to give sb first ~*** darle* a algn la primera opción (de compra) 2 (Equ) plante *m*

refuse¹ /rɪ'fjuːz/ *vt* (decline) ‹*offer/gift*› rechazar*, no aceptar, rehusar*; **they ~d her request** se negaron a complacerla; **to ~ sb sth** negarle* *or* (frml) denegarle* algo a algn; **to ~ to + INF** negarse* A + INF; **she ~s to listen to reason** no quiere atender a razones

■ **refuse** *vi* 1 (decline) negarse*; **how can I ~?** ¿cómo voy a negarme?, ¿cómo voy a decir que no? 2 (Equ) rehusar*

refuse² /'refjuːs/ *n* [u] residuos *mpl*, desperdicios *mpl*; (*before n*) **~ collection** recogida *f* de basuras; **~ tip** basurero *m*, vertedero *m* (de basuras), basural *m* (AmL)

refutation /'refjʊ'teɪʃən/ *n* [u c] refutación *f*

refute /rɪ'fjuːt/ *vt* 1 (disprove) refutar, rebatir 2 (deny) (crit) negar*

regain /rɪ'geɪn, 'riː-/ *vt* recuperar, recobrar

regal /'riːgəl/ *adj* majestuoso, regio

regale /rɪ'geɪl/ *vt* **to ~ sb WITH sth** ‹*with food/drink*› agasajar *or* obsequiar a algn CON algo; **he ~d us with hilarious anecdotes** nos hizo reír con unas anécdotas divertidísimas

regalia /rɪ'geɪljə || rɪ'geɪliə/ *pl n* ropajes *mpl*, vestiduras *fpl*; **the mayor was wearing his full ~** el alcalde llevaba el traje de ceremonia

regard¹ /rɪ'gɑːrd || rɪ'gɑːd/ *vt*

A 1 (consider) considerar; **to ~ sb/sth AS sth**: **they ~ her as a genius** la consideran un genio; **I ~ it as my duty to warn you** considero (que es) mi deber advertirte; **initially, they ~ed her with suspicion** al principio recelaban de ella, al principio les inspiraba desconfianza; **a highly ~ed university** una universidad muy respetada *or* de gran reputación 2 **as regards** en lo que se refiere a, en lo que atañe a, en cuanto a

B (look at) (liter) contemplar

C (heed) (*usu neg*) considerar, tener* en cuenta

regard² *n*

A [u] 1 (esteem): **to have a high ~ for sb** tener* muy buena opinión de algn, tener* a algn en gran estima; **to hold sb/sth in high/low ~** tener* muy buena/mala opinión de algn/algo 2 (consideration) consideración *f*; **~ FOR sb/sth**: **they have no ~ for other people's feelings** no tienen ninguna consideración por los sentimientos de los demás; **she shows little ~ for convention** respeta muy poco las convenciones; **they paid no ~ to my wishes** hicieron caso omiso de mis deseos

B **regards** *pl* (greeting) saludos *mpl*, recuerdos *mpl*

C (*in phrases*) **with regard to** (con) respecto a, con relación a, en relación con; **with particular ~ to** especialmente en lo que se refiere a; **in this/that regard** en este/ese aspecto; **she is fortunate in one ~** tiene suerte en un aspecto

regarding /rɪ'gɑːrdɪŋ || rɪ'gɑːdɪŋ/ *prep* (frml) en lo que concierne *or* respecta a, en lo que se refiere a, (con) respecto a

regardless /rɪ'gɑːrdləs || rɪ'gɑːdlɪs/ *adv* 1 (in spite of everything): **I told her not to do it, but she carried on ~** le dije que no lo hiciera pero no me hizo caso *or* (fam) siguió como si tal cosa 2 **regardless of** (*prep*): **~ of the cost/consequences** cueste lo que cueste/pase lo que pase; **~ of what people say** a pesar de lo que diga la gente

regatta /rɪ'gætə/ *n* regata *f*

Regency /'riːdʒənsi/ *adj* ‹*period/house*› *de la época de la regencia del príncipe de Gales en Gran Bretaña (1811-1820)*

regenerate /rɪ'dʒenəreɪt/ *vt* (revive) revitalizar*; (Biol) regenerar

regeneration /rɪ'dʒenə'reɪʃən/ *n* 1 [u] (economic, political) regeneración *f*; **a program of urban ~** un programa de rehabilitación y revitalización urbanas 2 (Biol) regeneración *f*

regent¹ /'riːdʒənt/ *n* 1 (ruler) regente *mf* 2 (AmE Educ) *miembro del consejo rector de una institución educativa*

regent² *adj* (*after n*) regente

reggae /'regeɪ/ *n* [u] reggae *m*

regime, régime /reɪ'ʒiːm/ *n* 1 (rule) régimen *m* 2 (system) sistema *m* 3 ▸**regimen**

regimen /'redʒəmən || 'redʒɪmen/ *n* régimen *m*

regiment¹ /'redʒəmənt || 'redʒɪmənt/ *n* regimiento *m*

regiment² /'redʒəment || 'redʒɪment/ *vt* reglamentar

regimental /'redʒə'mentḷ || ˌredʒɪ'mentḷ/ *adj* (*before n*) ‹*mascot/band/tradition*› del regimiento

regimentation /'redʒəmən'teɪʃən || ˌredʒɪmen'teɪʃən/ *n* [u] reglamentación *f*, disciplina *f* (estricta)

region /'riːdʒən/ *n* 1 (Anat, Geog) (area) región *f*, zona *f*; **the London ~** Londres y sus alrededores 2 **in the region of** alrededor de; **a sum in the ~ of ...** una suma del orden de ...

regional /'riːdʒənḷ/ *adj* regional

regionalism /'riːdʒənḷɪzəm/ *n* [u c] regionalismo *m*

register¹ /'redʒəstər || 'redʒɪstə(r)/ *n*

A (record, list) registro *m*; (in school) (BrE) lista *f*; **to take** *o* **call the ~** (BrE Educ) pasar lista

B (Mus) registro *m*

C (Ling) registro *m* (idiomático)

register² *vt*

A (record) ‹*death/birth*› inscribir*, registrar; ‹*ship/car*› matricular; **are you ~ed with Dr Adams?** ¿está inscrito *or* registrado como paciente del Dr Adams?

B (Post) ‹*letter/package*› mandar certificado *or* (Méx) registrado *or* (Col, Ur) recomendado

C **registered** *past p* 1 (Fin): **~ed office** (in UK) domicilio *m* social, sede *f*; **~ed trademark** marca *f* registrada 2 (Adm): **~ed nurse** enfermero titulado, enfermera titulada *m,f*; **a Panamanian-~ed ship** un barco de matrícula panameña 3 (Post) certificado *or* (Méx) registrado *or* (Col, Ur) recomendado

D 1 (make known) ‹*protest*› hacer* constar; ‹*complaint*› presentar 2 (show): **her face ~ed no emotion** su cara no acusó *or* denotó emoción alguna; **the dial ~ed 700 volts** la aguja registraba *or* marcaba 700 voltios

E (realize) darse* cuenta de, caer* en la cuenta de; (notice): **I ~ed (the fact) that Peter was late** no se me pasó por alto el hecho de que Peter había llegado tarde

■ **register** *vi*

A (enroll) inscribirse*; (Educ) matricularse, inscribirse*; (at a hotel) registrarse; **to ~ with a doctor** (BrE) inscribirse* en la lista de pacientes de un médico; **to ~ as a Democrat/Republican** (in US) inscribirse* como votante demócrata/republicano

B 1 (show up) ser* detectado 2 (be understood, remembered): **she did tell me her name, but it didn't ~** me dijo su nombre, pero no lo retuve *or* no me quedó; **eventually it ~ed who he was** al final caí en la cuenta de quién era

Registered General Nurse *n* (in UK) *enfermero que ha cursado estudios de tres años*

register office *n* (in UK) ▸**registry office**

registrar /'redʒəstrɑːr || ˌredʒɪs'trɑː(r), 'redʒɪstrɑː(r)/ *n* 1 (Soc Adm) *funcionario encargado de llevar los registros de nacimientos, defunciones, etc* 2 (in university, college) secretario, -ria *m,f* de admisiones 3 (Med) (in UK) jefe, -fa *m,f* de admisiones

registration /'redʒə'streɪʃən || ˌredʒɪs'treɪʃən/ *n* 1 [u c] (enrollment) inscripción *f*, matrícula *f*; (Educ) inscripción *f*, matriculación *f*; (of trademark) registro *m*; (*before n*) **~ fee** cuota *f* de inscripción, matrícula *f* 2 [u] (at school) (BrE): **~ is at 9** se pasa lista a las 9 3 [u c] (BrE Auto): **a K-~ Volvo** un Volvo del 92/93; (*before n*) **~ number** (número *m* de) matrícula *f*

registry /'redʒəstri || 'redʒɪstri/ *n* (*pl* **-tries**) registro *m*; (at university) secretaría *f*; (at church) ≈ sacristía *f*

registry office *n* (in UK) ≈ juzgado *m* (de paz), notaría *f* (Col); **to get married in a ~ ~** casarse por lo civil *or* (Per, RPl, Ven) por civil *or* (Méx, Chi) por el civil

regress /rɪ'gres/ *vi* 1 (get worse) experimentar un retroceso 2 (Psych) experimentar una regresión

regression /rɪ'greʃən/ *n* 1 [u c] (decline) retroceso *m* 2 [u] (Psych) regresión *f*

regret¹ /rɪ'gret/ *vt* **-tt-** ‹*decision/mistake*› arrepentirse* de, lamentar; **we ~ any inconvenience caused** rogamos disculpen las molestias (que hayamos podido ocasionar); **to ~ -ING** arrepentirse* DE *or* lamentar + INF; **I ~ that I shall be unable to attend** lamento no poder asistir; **it is to be ~ted that ...** es lamentable que (+ *subj*); **to ~ to + INF** lamentar tener QUE + INF; **we ~ to inform you that ...** lamentamos comunicarle *or* informarle que ...

regret² *n* [u c] (sadness) pesar *m*; (remorse) arrepentimiento *m*; **it is with ~ that we announce ...** lamentamos tener que anunciar que ...; **my biggest/one ~ is that I didn't have children** lo que más lamento/lo único que lamento es no haber tenido hijos; **I've no ~s about leaving** no me arrepiento de haberme ido

regretful /rɪ'gretfəl/ *adj* ‹*expression/note*› de pesar; **she felt very ~ about it** lo lamentaba mucho

regretfully /rɪ'gretfəli/ *adv* con pesar; **~, we must say no** (*indep*) muy a nuestro pesar *or* lamentablemente, tenemos que decir que no

regrettable /rɪ'gretəbəl/ *adj* lamentable; **it is ~ that ...** es lamentable que (+ *subj*)

regrettably /rɪ'gretəbli/ *adv* lamentablemente

regroup /ri:'gru:p/ *vi* reagruparse
■ **regroup** *vt* reagrupar

regt = **regiment**

regular¹ /'regjələr || 'regjʊlə(r)/ *adj*

A 1 (evenly spaced) ‹*breathing*› acompasado; ‹*heartbeat/pulse*› regular; **at ~ intervals** (in time) con regularidad; (in space) a intervalos regulares 2 (consistent, habitual) ‹*customer/reader*› habitual, asiduo; **it's a ~ occurrence** eso es muy frecuente *or* pasa con mucha frecuencia; **to be in ~ employment** tener* empleo fijo; **a ~ income** una fuente regular de ingresos; **on a ~ basis** con regularidad, regularmente 3 (Med): **to be ~** (in bowel habits) hacer* de vientre con regularidad; (in menstrual cycles) ser* regular 4 (customary) habitual; **the ~ procedure** el procedimiento usual *or* de costumbre

B (even, symmetrical) ‹*shape*› regular; ‹*teeth*› regular, parejo (AmL); **he has ~ features** es de rasgos (bien) proporcionados

C 1 ‹*size/model*› normal; **~ grade gasoline** (AmE) gasolina *f* *or* (Andes) bencina *f* *or* (RPl) nafta *f* normal 2 (Ling) ‹*verb/plural*› regular

D (colloq) 1 (*as intensifier*) verdadero; **he's a ~ comedian** es muy gracioso 2 (straightforward) (AmE): **he's a ~ guy** es un gran tipo (fam), es un tío majo (Esp fam)

E (Mil) ‹*soldier/officer*› de carrera; **the ~ army** el ejército profesional

regular² *n*

A (customer) cliente *mf* habitual, asiduo, -dua *m,f*; **party ~** (AmE Pol) militante *mf* del partido

B (Mil) militar *mf* de carrera

regularity /'regjə'lærəti || ˌregjʊ'lærəti/ *n* [u] regularidad *f*

regularize /'regjələraɪz || 'regjʊləraɪz/ *vt* regularizar*

regularly /'regjələrli || 'regjʊləli/ *adv* con regularidad, regularmente; (frequently) a menudo, con frecuencia

regulate /'regjəleɪt || 'regjʊleɪt/ *vt* 1 ‹*speed/temperature/prices*› regular; **to ~ one's life/habits** poner* orden en su (*or* mi *etc*) vida 2 (Law) ‹*industry/profession*› regular 3 ‹*apparatus/instrument*› regular

regulation /'regjə'leɪʃən || ˌregjʊ'leɪʃən/ *n*

A [c] (rule) norma *f*, regla *f*; **it's against (the) ~s** va contra el reglamento; (*before n*) ‹*dress/haircut*› reglamentario

B [u] 1 (control, adjustment) regulación *f* 2 (policing) (Law) regulación *f*, reglamentación *f*

regulator /'regjəleɪtər || 'regjʊleɪtə(r)/ *n* 1 (mechanism) regulador *m* 2 (person, body) *persona u organismo que regula una institución*

regulatory /'regjələtɔ:ri || 'regjʊlətəri/ *adj* regulador

regurgitate /rɪ'gɜ:rdʒəteɪt || rɪ'gɜ:dʒɪteɪt/ *vt* ‹*food*› regurgitar; ‹*information*› repetir* mecánicamente *or* (fam) como un loro

rehabilitate /'ri:hə'bɪləteɪt, 'ri:ə- || ˌri:hə'bɪlɪteɪt, ˌri:ə-/ *vt* rehabilitar

rehabilitation /'ri:hə'bɪlə'teɪʃən, 'ri:ə- || ˌri:həˌbɪlɪ'teɪʃən, ˌri:ə-/ *n* [u] rehabilitación *f*

rehash¹ /'ri:hæʃ/ *n* (colloq) refrito *m*

rehash² /'ri:'hæʃ/ *vt* (colloq) hacer* un refrito de

rehearsal /rɪ'hɜ:rsəl || rɪ'hɜ:səl/ *n* [c u] ensayo *m*

rehearse /rɪ'hɜ:rs || rɪ'hɜ:s/ *vt* 1 ‹*play/concert/speech*› ensayar 2 ‹*dancers/musicians*› hacer* ensayar a
■ **rehearse** *vi* ensayar

reheat /'ri:'hi:t/ *vt* recalentar*

rehouse /'ri:'haʊz/ *vt* realojar

reign¹ /reɪn/ *n* reinado *m*

reign² *vi* 1 «*monarch*» reinar; **to ~ over sb/sth** reinar SOBRE algn/algo 2 (liter) «*chaos/peace*» reinar 3 **reigning** *pres p* ‹*monarch*› reinante; **she is the ~ing champion** es la campeona actual

reimburse /'ri:ɪm'bɜ:rs || ˌri:ɪm'bɜ:s/ *vt* ‹*expenses/cost*› reembolsar; **to ~ sb FOR sth** reembolsarle algo a algn

rein /reɪn/ *n* 1 (Equ) rienda *f*; **to hold the ~s** llevar las riendas; ***to give free ~ to sb*** darle* carta blanca a algn; ***to give free ~ to sth*** dar* rienda suelta a algo; ***to keep a tight ~ on sth*** ‹*expenses*› llevar un estricto control de algo; **his wife keeps him on a tight ~** su mujer lo tiene muy controlado 2 **reins** *pl* (for children) (BrE) arnés *m*, andadores *mpl*, andaderas *fpl* (Méx, Ven)

Phrasal verbs

- **rein back** ▸ **rein in 1**
- **rein in** [v ▸ o ▸ adv, v ▸ adv ▸ o] 1 ‹*horse*› frenar 2 (restrain, curb) frenar, refrenar

reincarnation /'ri:ɪnkɑ:r'neɪʃən || ˌri:ɪnkɑ:'neɪʃən/ *n* [u c] reencarnación *f*

reindeer /'reɪndɪr || 'reɪndɪə(r)/ *n* (*pl* ~) reno *m*

reinforce /'ri:ɪn'fɔ:rs || ˌri:ɪn'fɔ:s/ *vt* 1 ‹*material/structure*› reforzar*; **~d concrete** hormigón *m* *or* (AmL tb) concreto *m* armado 2 ‹*argument/prejudice*› reafirmar

reinforcement /'ri:ɪn'fɔ:rsmənt || ˌri:ɪn'fɔ:smənt/ *n*

A [u] (strengthening — of wall) refuerzo *m*; (— of prejudice) reafirmación *f*, consolidación *f*

B [u c] (sth that reinforces) refuerzo *m*

C **reinforcements** *pl* refuerzos *mpl*

reinsert /'ri:ɪn'sɜ:rt || ˌri:ɪn'sɜ:t/ *vt* volver* a insertar

reinstate /'ri:ɪn'steɪt/ *vt* 1 ‹*worker*› reintegrar, reincorporar; ‹*official*› restituir* *or* rehabilitar en el cargo 2 ‹*law*› reinstaurar; ‹*service*› restablecer*

reinstatement /'ri:ɪn'steɪtmənt/ *n* (of worker) reintegro *m*, reincorporación *f*; (of official) restitución *f* *or* rehabilitación *f* en el cargo

reintegration /ri:'ɪntə'greɪʃən/ *n* [u] reintegración *f*; (into society) reinserción *f* social

reissue¹ /'ri:'ɪʃu:/ *vt* ‹*stamp/coin*› volver* a emitir; ‹*book/record*› reeditar; (from library) renovar* el préstamo de; ‹*document*› volver* a expedir, reexpedir*

reissue² *n* (of stamp coin) nueva emisión *f*; (of book, record) nueva edición *f*, reedición *f*; (of document) reexpedición *f*

reiterate /ri:'ɪtəreɪt/ *vt* (frml) reiterar, repetir*

reiteration /ri:'ɪtə'reɪʃən/ *n* [u c] (frml) reiteración *f*, repetición *f*

reject¹ /rɪ'dʒekt/ *vt* rechazar*; **the machine ~ed my coin** la maquina no aceptó mi moneda

reject² /'ri:dʒekt/ *n* 1 (flawed product) artículo *m* (*or* producto *m etc*) defectuoso 2 (person): **society's ~s** los marginados sociales *or* de la sociedad; **a college/an army ~** una persona que fue rechazada por la universidad/el ejército

rejection /rɪ'dʒekʃən/ *n* [u c] rechazo *m*; (following job application) respuesta *f* negativa; **to meet with (a) ~** ser* rechazado

rejoice /rɪ'dʒɔɪs/ *vi* alegrarse mucho, regocijarse (liter); **she ~d at the news** la noticia la llenó de alegría

rejoicing /rɪ'dʒɔɪsɪŋ/ *n* [u] (festivities) celebraciones *fpl*; (emotion) júbilo *m*

rejoin /'ri:'dʒɔɪn/ *vt*

A 1 ‹*regiment/team*› reincorporarse a; ‹*firm*› reincorporarse a, reintegrarse a; **we ~ed the highway at Jackson** volvimos a tomar la autopista en Jackson 2 (reconnect) volver* a unir

B /rɪ'dʒɔɪn/ (reply) (frml) replicar* (frml)

rejoinder /rɪ'dʒɔɪndər || rɪ'dʒɔɪndə(r)/ *n* réplica *f* (frml)

rejuvenate /rɪ'dʒu:vəneɪt/ *vt* rejuvenecer*

rejuvenating /rɪ'dʒu:vəneɪtɪŋ/ *adj* rejuvenecedor

rekindle /'ri:'kɪndl̩/ *vt* ‹*flame/fire*› reavivar; ‹*desire*› reavivar, volver* a despertar; ‹*hope*› hacer* renacer

relapse¹ /'ri:læps/ *n* recaída *f*; **to have** *o* **suffer a ~** tener* *or* sufrir una recaída

relapse² /rɪ'læps/ *vi* recaer*, tener* *or* sufrir una recaída; **to ~ INTO sth**: **to ~ into unconsciousness** volver* a perder el conocimiento; **to ~ into bad habits** volver* a los malos hábitos

relate /rɪ'leɪt/ *vt*

A (link) **to ~ sth TO sth** relacionar algo CON algo; **the report ~s crime to drug abuse** el informe relaciona el crimen y el consumo de drogas

B (tell) (frml) ‹*story*› relatar, contar*, referir* (liter)

■ **relate** *vi*

A **1** (be connected with) **to ~ TO sth** estar* relacionado CON algo; **he's only interested in what ~s to himself** sólo le interesa lo que le atañe (a él) **2** **relating to** (*as prep*) relativo a, relacionado con

B (understand, sympathise with) **to ~ TO sb** sintonizar* CON algn, tener* una buena relación CON algn; **some adults can't ~ to children** algunos adultos no saben relacionarse con los niños; **to ~ TO sth** identificarse* CON algo; **I can ~ to that!** te comprendo perfectamente

related /rɪ'leɪtəd || rɪ'leɪtɪd/ *adj* **1** (of same family) (*pred*) **to be ~ (TO sb)** ser* pariente (DE algn), estar* emparentado (CON algn); **we are distantly ~** somos parientes lejanos; **she's ~ to them by marriage** es parienta política suya, es parienta suya por afinidad (frml) **2** ‹*ideas/questions/subjects*› relacionado, afín

-related /rɪ'leɪtəd || rɪ'leɪtɪd/ *suff*: **stress/drug~** relacionado con el estrés/la droga

relation /rɪ'leɪʃən/ *n*

A [c] (relative) pariente *mf*, pariente, -ta *m,f*, familiar *m*; **pictured are John Hull and James Hull (no ~)** en la fotografía aparecen John Hull y James Hull, quienes no están emparentados; **what ~ is she to you?** ¿qué parentesco tiene contigo?, ¿a ti qué te toca? (Esp fam)

B **1** [u c] (connection) relación *f*; **to bear no ~ to sth** no guardar ninguna relación con algo **2** **in relation to** (*as prep*) en relación con, con relación a

C **relations** *pl* relaciones *fpl*; **to establish/break off/restore ~s (with sb/sth)** establecer*/romper*/restablecer* relaciones (con algn/algo); **to have sexual ~s with sb** tener* relaciones sexuales con algn

relationship /rɪ'leɪʃənʃɪp/ *n*

A [c] (between people) relación *f*; **to have a good ~ with sb** llevarse bien con algn; **we have a good working ~** trabajamos bien juntos, tenemos *or* mantenemos una buena relación de trabajo

B [c u] (between things, events) relación *f*

C [u] (kinship) **~ (TO sb)** parentesco *m* (CON algn)

relative¹ /'relətɪv/ *n* pariente *mf*, pariente, -ta *m,f*, familiar *m*

relative² *adj* **1** (comparative): **the ~ merits of both systems** los pros y los contras de ambos sistemas **2** (not absolute) relativo; **it's all ~, everything's ~** (set phrase) todo es relativo (fr hecha) **3** **relative to** (in relation to) en relación con, con relación a; (compared to) en comparación con **4** (Ling) relativo

relatively /'relətɪvli/ *adv* relativamente; **~ speaking, it's not very important** tiene, relativamente, muy poca importancia

relativity /'relə'tɪvəti/ *n* [u] relatividad *f*

relaunch /ri:'lɔ:ntʃ/ *vt* **1** ‹*ship*› botar por segunda vez **2** ‹*product/publication*› relanzar*

relax /rɪ'læks/ *vi* relajarse; **~, I'll take care of everything** quédate tranquilo que yo me encargo de todo

■ **relax** *vt* relajar; **she ~ed her grip** sujetó con menos fuerza

relaxation /'ri:læk'seɪʃən/ *n* **1** [u c] (recreation) esparcimiento *m*, distracción *f*; (rest) relax *m*; **what do you do for ~?** ¿qué haces para relajarte *or* descansar? **2** [u] (of muscles, rules, vigilance) relajación *f*

relaxed /rɪ'lækst/ *adj* ‹*manner/person*› relajado, tranquilo; ‹*atmosphere/party*› informal; **they have a very ~ attitude to it all** se lo toman todo con mucha tranquilidad

relaxing /rɪ'læksɪŋ/ *adj* ‹*bath/massage*› relajante; **we spent a ~ few days in the country** pasamos unos días de descanso en el campo

relay¹ /'ri:leɪ/ *n* **1** (team — of people) relevo *m*; **to work in ~s** trabajar en *or* por relevos, ir* relevándose (*para hacer algo*); **we'll have to go in ~s** tendremos que ir por turnos *or* tandas **2** **~ (race)** (Sport) carrera *f* de relevos *or* de postas

relay² /'ri:leɪ, rɪ'leɪ/ *vt* transmitir

release¹ /rɪ'li:s/ *vt*

A **1** ‹*prisoner/hostage*› poner* en libertad, liberar; **to ~ sb FROM sth**: **she was ~d from jail** fue puesta en libertad, salió de la cárcel; **they ~d him from the contract** le condonaron las obligaciones emanadas del contrato (frml) **2** (unleash) desatar **3** ‹*funds/personnel*› ceder; **he was ~d from his normal duties** lo dispensaron de sus tareas habituales

B ‹*information/figures*› hacer* público, dar* a conocer; ‹*record/book*› sacar* (a la venta); ‹*movie*› estrenar

C (emit) ‹*gas*› despedir*

D **1** (let go) ‹*bomb*› arrojar; **he ~d his grip on her** la soltó **2** ‹*brake/clutch*› soltar*

release² *n*

A [u] **1** (from prison, captivity) puesta *f* en libertad, liberación *f* **2** (of funds, personnel) cesión *f*

B **1** [u] (of book) publicación *f*; (of record) salida *f* al mercado; (of movie) estreno *m*; **in** *o* (BrE) **on general ~** en todos los cines **2** [c] (record, movie): **new ~s** (records) novedades *fpl* discográficas; (movies) últimos estrenos *mpl*

C [u] (of gas) escape *m*

relegate /'reləgeɪt || 'relɪgeɪt/ *vt* **1** (consign, demote) **to ~ sth/sb TO sth** relegar* algo/a algn A algo **2** (BrE Sport) (*usu pass*): **the team was ~d to the third division** el equipo descendió *or* bajó a tercera división

relegation /'relə'geɪʃən || ˌrelɪ'geɪʃən/ *n* [u] **1** (demotion) relegación *f* **2** (BrE Sport) descenso *m*

relent /rɪ'lent/ *vi* ‹‹*person*›› transigir*, ceder; ‹‹*storm*›› amainar

relentless /rɪ'lentləs || rɪ'lentlɪs/ *adj* ‹*enemy/pursuer*› implacable; ‹*pursuit*› incesante; ‹*criticism*› despiadado

relentlessly /rɪ'lentləsli || rɪ'lentlɪsli/ *adv* ‹*torture/tease*› implacablemente, despiadadamente; ‹*continue*› sin cesar; **they pursued him ~** lo persiguieron sin darle tregua

relevance /'reləvəns/ *n* [u] (connection) relación *f*; (importance) relevancia *f*, significación *f*; **that has no ~ to what we were discussing** eso no guarda relación alguna con lo que estábamos tratando

relevant /'reləvənt/ *adj* ‹*document/facts*› pertinente, relevante; **applicants should have ~ experience** los candidatos deberán poseer experiencia en el sector; **a message that is still ~ today** un mensaje que todavía hoy tiene validez; **the ~ authorities** las autoridades competentes; **I don't see how that's ~** no veo qué relación tiene eso

reliability /rɪ'laɪə'bɪləti/ *n* [u] (of worker) formalidad *f*, responsabilidad *f*; (of sources, data) fiabilidad *f*; (of vehicle) fiabilidad *f*

reliable /rɪ'laɪəbəl/ *adj* **1** ‹*information/source*› fidedigno; ‹*witness*› fiable, confiable (esp AmL) **2** ‹*worker*› responsable, de confianza; ‹*vehicle*› fiable, que no falla

reliably /rɪ'laɪəbli/ *adv*: **I am ~ informed that ...** sé de fuentes fidedignas que ..., sé de buena fuente que ...

reliance /rɪ'laɪəns/ *n* [u] **1** (dependence) **~ ON sth/sb** dependencia *f* DE algo/algn **2** (trust) confianza *f*

reliant /rɪ'laɪənt/ *adj* (*pred*) **to be ~ ON sth/sb** depender DE algo/algn

relic /'relɪk/ *n* reliquia *f*; **the ceremony is a ~ from medieval times** la ceremonia es un vestigio de una tradición medieval

relief /rɪ'li:f/ *n*

A [u] (from worry, pain) alivio *m*; **much to my ~, I wasn't late** por suerte, no llegué tarde; **it's a ~ that the rain's stopped/to sit down at last** menos mal que ha parado de llover/que al fin puedo sentarme; **the news came as a great ~ to us** respiramos aliviados *or* tranquilos al oír la noticia; **I wanted some ~ from the daily routine** quería escapar un poco de la rutina diaria; **the children's antics provided some light ~** las travesuras de los niños

r

nos entretuvieron; **to give ~ from pain** calmar *or* aliviar el dolor

B [u] (aid) ayuda *f*, auxilio *m* (*de emergencia*); **to be on ~** (AmE) recibir prestaciones de la seguridad social; (*before n*) **~ agency** *organismo de ayuda a los damnificados de una catástrofe*

C [c] **1** (Mil) liberación *f* (*de una plaza sitiada*) **2** (replacement) relevo *m*; (*before n*) ‹*driver/crew*› de relevo; **~ road** vía *f* de descongestión *or* (Méx) de libramiento

D [u c] **1** (esp BrE Tax) desgravación *f* **2** (redress) (Law) desagravio *m*

E [u c] (Art, Geog) relieve *m*; **to stand out in ~** resaltar; **to bring** *o* **throw sth into ~** poner* algo de relieve; (*before n*) **~ map** mapa *m* físico; (three-dimensional) mapa *m* en relieve

relieve /rɪ'li:v/ *vt*

A ‹*pain*› calmar, aliviar, mitigar* (liter); ‹*anxiety/hardship/suffering*› mitigar*, aliviar; ‹*tension*› aliviar, relajar; ‹*monotony/uniformity*› romper*; **to ~ sb of responsibility for sth** eximir a algn de la responsabilidad de algo; **she ~d me of some of the workload** me ayudó con parte del trabajo; **to ~ sb of his/her duties** relevar a algn de su cargo

B ‹*town/fortress*› liberar

C ‹*guard/driver*› relevar

■ *v refl* **to ~ oneself** (euph) orinar

relieved /rɪ'li:vd/ *adj* aliviado; **I'm so ~ that it's all over** menos mal que ya ha pasado todo; **we were all ~ to hear that ...** a todos nos tranquilizó enterarnos de que ...

religion /rɪ'lɪdʒən/ *n* [c u] religión *f*; **to be against sb's ~** ir* contra los principios religiosos de algn

religious /rɪ'lɪdʒəs/ *adj* religioso

religiously /rɪ'lɪdʒəsli/ *adv* (scrupulously) religiosamente

relinquish /rɪ'lɪŋkwɪʃ/ *vt* **1** ‹*possession/claim/right*› renunciar a; **to ~ sth TO sb** cederle algo A algn **2** (release) (liter): **she ~ed her grip on my arm** me soltó el brazo

relish[1] /'relɪʃ/ *vt*: **I don't ~ the thought/prospect of ...** no me entusiasma *or* no me hace ninguna gracia la idea/perspectiva de ...; **she smiled, ~ing her moment of triumph** se sonrió, saboreando su momento de triunfo

relish[2] *n*

A [c u] (Culin) **1** (condiment) salsa *f* (*para condimentar*) **2** (accompaniment) (AmE) guarnición *f* (*gen a base de frutas fritas o confitadas*)

B [u] (enjoyment): **with ~** ‹*eat/drink*› con gusto, con fruición; ‹*read/listen to*› con placer, con deleite; ‹*work*› con entusiasmo, con gusto

relive /'ri:'lɪv/ *vt* revivir

reload /'ri:'ləʊd/ *vt* ‹*truck/gun*› volver* a cargar; ‹*program*› (Comput) recargar*

relocate /'ri:ləʊ'keɪt/ *vt* ‹*factory/office/employee*› (in the same labor market) trasladar; (to a cheaper labor market) deslocalizar*; ‹*refugees/slum dwellers*› reasentar*, realojar

■ **relocate** *vi* «*company*» trasladarse; «*employee*» mudarse *or* trasladarse de domicilio

relocation /'ri:ləʊ'keɪʃən/ *n* [u c] (of employees, assets) traslado *m*; (to a cheaper labor market) deslocalización *f*

reluctance /rɪ'lʌktəns/ *n* [u] renuencia *f* (frml); **they agreed, but with great ~** accedieron, pero a regañadientes; **their ~ to sign the treaty is understandable** es comprensible que se muestren reacios *or* reticentes a firmar el tratado

reluctant /rɪ'lʌktənt/ *adj* reacio, renuente; **he's a ~ teetotaler** es abstemio a su pesar *or* a regañadientes; **to be ~ to + INF**: **she seemed ~ to tell us** parecía reacia *or* renuente a decírnoslo, no parecía dispuesta a decírnoslo; **I'm ~ to sell this chair** me resisto a vender esta silla

reluctantly /rɪ'lʌktəntli/ *adv* de mala gana

rely /rɪ'laɪ/ *vi* **relies, relying, relied** **1** (have confidence) **to ~ ON** *or* **UPON sb/sth** confiar* EN algn/algo; **he can't be relied upon** no se puede confiar en él; **you can't ~ on the weather/buses** no puedes fiarte del tiempo/de los autobuses; **to ~ on sb to + INF**: **you can ~ on me not to tell anybody** puedes confiar en que no se lo contaré a nadie; **she can't be relied (up)on to help** no se puede confiar en que vaya a ayudar **2** (be dependent) **to ~ on sb/sth FOR sth** depender* DE algn/algo (PARA algo); **we ~ on the spring for our water** dependemos del manantial para el suministro de agua; **he relies on her for everything** depende de ella para todo

remain /rɪ'meɪn/ *vi*

A **1** (+ *adj or adv compl*) (continue to be) seguir*, continuar*; **he ~ed silent/standing** se mantuvo en silencio/se quedó de pie; **her condition ~s critical** su estado sigue siendo crítico, continúa en estado crítico; **these laws will ~ in force** estas leyes continuarán *or* permanecerán en vigor; **please ~ seated** por favor no se levanten, por favor permanezcan en sus asientos (frml); **I ~, yours faithfully** (Corresp frml) le saluda atentamente **2** (stay) quedarse, permanecer* (frml); **to ~ behind** quedarse

B **1** (be left) quedar; **this is all that ~s of the city** esto es todo lo que queda de la ciudad; **the fact ~s that ...** el hecho es que ..., sigue siendo cierto que ...; **to ~ to + INF**: **what still ~s to be done?** ¿qué queda por hacer?; **that ~s to be seen** eso está por verse **2** **remaining** *pres p*: **they spent the ~ing day in Paris** pasaron el día que les quedaba en París; **the ~ing ten pounds can be paid later** las diez libras restantes *or* que quedan *or* que faltan pueden pagarse más adelante

remainder[1] /rɪ'meɪndər || rɪ'meɪndə(r)/ *n* **1** (amount, number) **the ~** el resto **2** (Math) resto *m*

remainder[2] *vt*: **to ~ books** liquidar restos de edición

remains /rɪ'meɪnz/ *pl n* restos *mpl*; (of meal) sobras *fpl*, restos *mpl*

remake[1] /'ri:meɪk/ *n* nueva versión *f*

remake[2] /'ri:'meɪk/ *vt* (*past & past p* **remade**) **1** (sth done badly) volver* a hacer, rehacer* **2** (Cin) ‹*movie*› hacer* una nueva versión de

remand[1] /rɪ'mænd || rɪ'mɑ:nd/ *vt* **1** (send): **to be ~ed on bail** quedar en libertad bajo fianza; **he was ~ed in custody** se decretó su prisión preventiva **2** (to lower court) (AmE) remitir a un tribunal inferior

remand[2] *n*: **to be on ~** (in detention) estar* en prisión preventiva; **to be (out) on ~** (on bail) estar* en libertad bajo fianza

remand centre, remand home *n* (in UK) *centro para menores en prisión preventiva*

remark[1] /rɪ'mɑ:rk || rɪ'mɑ:k/ *n*

A [c] (comment) comentario *m*, observación *f*; **would you like to make a few ~s on the subject?** ¿quisiera hacer algún comentario al respecto?; **the chairwoman's opening/closing ~s** las palabras con las que la presidenta abrió/cerró la reunión; **she let it pass without ~** [u] lo dejo pasar sin comentario

B [u] (attention) (frml *or* liter): **to be worthy of ~** ser* digno de mención (frml)

remark[2] *vi* **to ~ ON** *o* **UPON sth**: **he ~ed on how young she looked** comentó lo joven que parecía; **nobody has ~ed upon the fact that ...** nadie ha mencionado el hecho de que ...

■ **remark** *vt* observar, comentar

remarkable /rɪ'mɑ:rkəbəl || rɪ'mɑ:kəbəl/ *adj* ‹*ability/event/likeness*› notable; ‹*achievement*› sorprendente; ‹*coincidence*› extraordinario; ‹*person*› excepcional; **to be ~ FOR sth** destacar(se)* POR algo

remarkably /rɪ'mɑ:rkəbli || rɪ'mɑ:kəbli/ *adv* **1** (surprisingly) sorprendentemente; **she's ~ well, considering what she's been through** está increíblemente bien para lo que acaba de pasar **2** (exceptionally) ‹*talented*› extraordinariamente; ‹*stupid*› increíblemente

remarry /'ri:'mæri/ *vi* **-ries, -rying, -ried** volver* a casarse

rematch /'ri:mætʃ/ *n* desquite *m*, revancha *f*

remedial /rɪ'mi:diəl/ *adj* **1** (Educ) ‹*teacher/classes*› de recuperación; **~ teaching/education** enseñanza *f*/educación *f* compensatoria **2** (Med) de rehabilitación

remedy[1] /'remədi/ *n* (*pl* **-dies**) remedio *m*; **~ FOR sth** remedio PARA algo; **to be beyond** *o* **past ~** [u] no tener* (ya) remedio

remedy[2] *vt* **-dies, -dying, -died** ‹*mistake/problem/situation*› remediar; ‹*injustice/evil*› reparar

remember /rɪ'membər || rɪ'membə(r)/ *vt*

A (recall) acordarse* de, recordar*; **don't you ~ me?** ¿no te acuerdas de mí?; **I can't ~ if** *o* **whether I locked the door** no recuerdo si cerré la puerta con llave; **I always ~ faces** nunca olvido una cara; **here's a little something to ~ me by** toma, un detalle para que te acuerdes

r

de mí; **he ~ed me in his will** me dejó algo en su testamento; **it was an evening to ~** fue una noche memorable; **to ~ -ING**: **she ~s leaving her watch on the table** se acuerda de *or* recuerda haber dejado el reloj encima de la mesa; **to ~ sb/sth -ING**: **I ~ him saying something about a meeting** me acuerdo de *or* recuerdo que dijo algo de una reunión; **she ~s the car coming toward her** se acuerda de *or* recuerda cuando el coche se le vino encima

B 1 (be mindful of, not forget): **I'll ~ you if anything comes up** te tendré presente *or* me acordaré de ti si surge algo; **to ~ to + INF** acordarse* DE + INF 2 (commemorate) ‹*dead*› recordar* 3 (send regards) **to ~ sb TO sb**: **~ me to your mother** dale recuerdos *or* saludos a tu madre (de mi parte); **Peter asked to be ~ed (to you)** Peter te manda recuerdos *or* saludos

■ **remember** *vi* 1 (recall) acordarse*, recordar*; **as far as I ~** que yo recuerde, por lo que recuerdo; **for as far back as I can ~** desde que tengo memoria; **if I ~ correctly** *o* **right(ly)** si mal no recuerdo; **try to ~!** ¡haz memoria! 2 (be mindful, not forget) no olvidarse; **I'll try to ~** trataré de no olvidarme

remembrance /rɪˈmembrəns/ *n* [u c] (liter *or* frml) recuerdo *m*, remembranza *f* (liter); **in ~ of sth/sb** en memoria de algo/algn; (*before n*) **R~ Sunday** (in UK) *domingo de noviembre en que se conmemora a los caídos en las dos guerras mundiales*

remind /rɪˈmaɪnd/ *vt* recordarle* a, hacerle* acordar a (RPl); **which ~s me, ...** lo que me recuerda ...; **oh, that ~s me** ¡ah! por cierto ..., y a propósito ...; **to ~ sb to + INF** recordarle* A algn QUE (+ *subj*), hacerle* acordar A algn DE QUE + INF (RPl); **to ~ sb about sth**: **~ her about the meeting** recuérdale lo de la reunión; **to ~ sb OF sth/sb**: **I am ~ed of the time when ...** eso me recuerda cuando ...; **just a few flowers to ~ you of me** unas flores para que te acuerdes de mí; **he ~s me of my grandfather** me recuerda a mi abuelo, me hace acordar a mi abuelo (RPl)

reminder /rɪˈmaɪndər || rɪˈmaɪndə(r)/ *n* 1 (note, object, action): **I'll write a ~ on my notepad** pondré una nota en el bloc para acordarme *or* no olvidarme; **a painful ~** un triste recordatorio; **the monument serves as a constant ~ of all those who died** el monumento nos recuerda constantemente a aquellos que murieron 2 (requesting payment) recordatorio *m* de pago

reminisce /ˈremәˈnɪs || ˌremɪˈnɪs/ *vi* rememorar *or* recordar* los viejos tiempos; **to ~ ABOUT sth** rememorar algo

reminiscence /ˈremәˈnɪsn̩s || ˌremɪˈnɪsn̩s/ *n* [c u] recuerdos *mpl*, memorias *fpl*; **we swapped ~s** rememoramos los viejos tiempos

reminiscent /ˈremәˈnɪsn̩t || ˌremɪˈnɪsn̩t/ *adj* 1 (similar) (*pred*) **to be ~ OF sb/sth** recordar* a algn/(a) algo 2 (nostalgic) (*before n*) ‹*sigh/smile/mood*› nostálgico, reminiscente (liter)

remiss /rɪˈmɪs/ *adj* (frml) (*pred*) negligente, descuidado; **it was ~ of me** fue negligente de mi parte

remission /rɪˈmɪʃən/ *n* [u] 1 (Relig, Law) remisión *f* 2 (Med) remisión *f*; **to be in/go into ~** estar*/entrar en remisión

remit[1] /rɪˈmɪt/ *vt* **-tt-** (frml)

A (send) ‹*payment*› remitir (frml), enviar*

B (transfer) (Law) remitir

C (cancel) (Law) ‹*sentence*› perdonar, condonar (frml); **the judge ~ted six months of his sentence** el juez le redujo la pena en seis meses

remit[2] /ˈriːmɪt/ *n* (BrE) (instructions) instrucciones *fpl*; (area of authority) competencia *f*, atribuciones *fpl*; **to fall within/outside sb's ~** estar*/no estar* dentro de las atribuciones *or* la competencia de algn

remittance /rɪˈmɪtn̩s/ *n* (frml) 1 [c] (sum) remesa *f*, envío *m* (*de dinero*) 2 [u] (act of payment) pago *m*

remnant /ˈremnənt/ *n* 1 (left-over): **a ~ of the past** una reliquia *or* un vestigio del pasado; **the ~s of a meal** los restos de una comida 2 (Tex) retazo *m*, retal *m* (Esp)

remodel /ˈriːˈmɑːdl̩ || ˌriːˈmɒdl̩/ *vt*, (BrE) **-ll-** 1 (reshape) ‹*sculpture/clay*› remodelar 2 (AmE Const) ‹*building/property*› reformar

remodeling /ˈriːˈmɑːdlɪŋ || ˌriːˈmɒdlɪŋ/ *n* [u] (AmE) reforma *f*

remonstrance /rɪˈmɑːnstrəns || rɪˈmɒnstrəns/ *n* [c u] (frml) (protest) protesta *f*; (reproach) reproche *m*, reconvención *f* (frml)

remonstrate /rɪˈmɑːnstreɪt, ˈremən- || ˈremənstreɪt/ *vi* protestar, quejarse; **to ~ WITH sb**: **she ~d with him over his selfish attitude** le reprochó su actitud egoísta, lo reconvino por su actitud egoísta (frml)

remonstration /rɪˈmɑːnˈstreɪʃən, ˈremən- || ˌremənˈstreɪʃən/ *n* [u c] (frml) protestas *fpl*

remorse /rɪˈmɔːrs || rɪˈmɔːs/ *n* [u] remordimiento *m*; **he was full of ~** sentía un gran remordimiento; **the murderer showed no ~** el asesino no sentía el menor remordimiento

remorseful /rɪˈmɔːrsfəl || rɪˈmɔːsfəl/ *adj* arrepentido, con cargo de conciencia

remorsefully /rɪˈmɔːrsfəli || rɪˈmɔːsfəli/ *adv* con gran remordimiento

remorseless /rɪˈmɔːrsləs || rɪˈmɔːslɪs/ *adj* ‹*hatred/criticism*› despiadado, implacable; ‹*cruelty*› feroz, despiadado

remorselessly /rɪˈmɔːrsləsli || rɪˈmɔːslisli/ *adv* implacablemente, sin piedad

remortgage /riːˈmɔːgɪdʒ || riːˈmɔːgɪdʒ/ *vt* 1 (with additional mortgage) constituir* una segunda (*or* tercera *etc*) hipoteca sobre 2 (with different lender) *subrogar* a la entidad crediticia en la hipoteca que grava la propiedad*

remote /rɪˈməʊt/ *adj* **-ter, -test**

A 1 (in space, time) ‹*place/part*› remoto; **~ FROM sth** apartado DE algo 2 ‹*cause/connection*› remoto 3 (aloof, abstracted) distante

B (slight) ‹*possibility/hope/resemblance*› remoto

remote: ~ control *n* [u c] mando *m* a distancia, control *m* remoto; **by ~ control** a *or* por control remoto, con mando a distancia; **~-controlled** /rɪˈməʊtkənˈtrəʊld/ *adj* (*pred* **~ controlled**) ‹*TV/hi-fi*› con mando a distancia *or* con control remoto; ‹*model/toy*› de control remoto

remotely /rɪˈməʊtli/ *adv* 1 (at all, in the least) (*usu with neg*) remotamente; **he wasn't even ~ interested** no estaba ni remotamente interesado; **it is ~ possible he'll come** existe una remota posibilidad de que venga 2 (distantly) ‹*situated*› en un lugar apartado; **the two events are not even ~ connected** no hay ni la más remota conexión entre los dos hechos

remoteness /rɪˈməʊtnəs || rɪˈməʊtnɪs/ *n* [u] (isolation, distance): **the ~ of the place** la lejanía *or* lo remoto *or* lo apartado del lugar

remould[1] /ˈriːˈməʊld/ *vt* (BrE Auto) ▸**retread**[1]

remould[2] /ˈriːməʊld/ *n* (BrE Auto) ▸**retread**[2]

removable /rɪˈmuːvəbəl/ *adj* ‹*collar/sleeve/hood/lining*› de quita y pon; ‹*handle/shelf/partition*› desmontable

removal /rɪˈmuːvəl/ *n*

A [u] 1 (extraction — of contents) extracción *f*; (— of appendix, tonsils) extirpación *f* 2 (taking off): **the ~ of the lid/cover** el quitar la tapa/cubierta

B [u] 1 (of stain, unwanted hair) eliminación *f*; **for the ~ of make-up** para desmaquillarse *or* para quitarse el maquillaje 2 (of threat, problem) eliminación *f*

C 1 [u] (moving, taking away) traslado *m* 2 [u c] (from house to house) (BrE) mudanza *f*, trasteo *m* (Col); **furniture ~(s)** transporte *m* de muebles; (*before n*) **~ man** ▸**remover B**; **~(s) van** camión *m* de mudanzas 3 (dismissal): **her ~ from office** su remoción del cargo, su destitución

remove[1] /rɪˈmuːv/ *vt*

A 1 (take off) quitar, sacar*; **she ~d her gloves** se quitó los guantes; **to ~ sth FROM sth**: **the nurse ~d the bandage from his arm** la enfermera le quitó la venda del brazo 2 (take out) ‹*contents*› sacar*; ‹*tonsils/appendix*› extirpar (frml); ‹*gallstones/bullet*› extraer* (frml)

B 1 (get rid of) ‹*stain/grease*› quitar; **to ~ unwanted hair** eliminar el vello superfluo 2 (eliminate) ‹*problem*› eliminar, acabar con; ‹*doubt*› disipar; ‹*threat/obstacle*› eliminar

C (take away, move) **to ~ sth (FROM sth)** ‹*object*› quitar algo (DE algo); **to ~ sb (FROM sth)** sacar* a algn (DE algo); **the inhabitants/valuables had been ~d to a place of safety** los habitantes/los objetos de valor habían sido trasladados a un lugar seguro

D (dismiss) **to ~ sb FROM sth** ‹*from post/position*› destituir* a algn DE algo

remove² *n*: **to be at one ~ from sth** estar* a un paso de algo

removed /rɪ'mu:vd/ *adj* (*pred*): **to be far ~ from sth** estar* muy lejos de algo

remover /rɪ'mu:vər || rɪ'mu:və(r)/ *n*
A [u] (substance): **hair ~** depilatorio *m*; **makeup ~** desmaquillador *m*; **stain ~** quitamanchas *m*
B [c] (removal man) (BrE) mozo *m* de mudanzas, empleado *m* de una compañía de mudanzas

remunerate /rɪ'mju:nəreɪt/ *vt* (frml) **to ~ sb (FOR sth)** remunerar a algn (POR algo) (frml)

remuneration /rɪ'mju:nə'reɪʃən/ *n* [u] (frml) **~ (FOR sth)** remuneración *f* (POR algo)

renaissance /'renə'sɑ:ns || rɪ'neɪsəns/ *n* 1 **Renaissance** Renacimiento *m*; (*before n*) **R~ art** arte *m* renacentista *or* del Renacimiento 2 (revival, upsurge) (liter) renacimiento *m*, nuevo despertar *m*

rename /'ri:'neɪm/ *vt* dar* un nuevo nombre a

rend /rend/ *vt* (*past & past p* **rent**) (liter *or* arch) (tear) ‹*clothes*› rasgar*, desgarrar; **a cry rent the air** un grito desgarró *or* (liter) hendió el aire

render /'rendər || 'rendə(r)/ *vt*
A (make): **to ~ sth useless/obsolete** hacer* que algo resulte inútil/obsoleto; **he was ~ed unfit for active service by ...** fue incapacitado para el servicio activo por ...
B (give, proffer) (frml) ‹*homage*› rendir*; ‹*thanks*› dar*; ‹*assistance*› prestar; **for services ~ed** por servicios prestados
C 1 (interpret) ‹*piece of music*› interpretar 2 (translate) traducir*

rendering /'rendərɪŋ/ *n* [c] 1 (performance) interpretación *f* 2 (translation) **~ (INTO sth)** traducción *f* (A algo)

rendezvous¹ /'rɑ:ndeɪvu: || 'rɒndɪvu:, -deɪvu:/ *n* (*pl* ~ /-z/) (meeting) encuentro *m*, cita *f*; (place) lugar *m* señalado para un encuentro *or* una cita

rendezvous² *vi* **-vous** /-vu:z/, **-vousing** /-vu:ɪŋ/, **-voused** /-vu:d/ **to ~ (WITH sb)** encontrarse* (CON algn)

rendition /ren'dɪʃən/ *n* interpretación *f*

renegade¹ /'renɪgeɪd/ *n* renegado, -da *m,f*

renegade² *adj* (*before n*) renegado

renege /rɪ'ni:g, rɪ'neg || rɪ'ni:g, rɪ'neɪg/ *vi* **to ~ ON sth** ‹*on commitment/agreement*› incumplir algo; **he ~d on his promise** faltó a su promesa, no cumplió su promesa

renew /rɪ'nu: || rɪ'nju:/ *vt* 1 ‹*hope/promise*› renovar*; ‹*efforts/friendship*› reanudar; ‹*library book*› renovar; **they ~ed their attack on the Romans/minister** volvieron a atacar a los Romanos/a arremeter contra el ministro 2 **renewed** *past p* renovado; **~ed outbreaks of rioting/violence** nuevos brotes de disturbios/violencia

renewable /rɪ'nu:əbəl || rɪ'nju:əbəl/ *adj* renovable

renewal /rɪ'nu:əl || rɪ'nju:əl/ *n* 1 [u] (revival) renovación *f*; **a ~ of hope** un renacimiento de la esperanza 2 [u c] (of contract, subscription) renovación *f*

renminbi /ren'mɪnbi/ *n* [u] renminbi *m*

rennet /'renət || 'renɪt/ *n* [u] cuajo *m*

renounce /rɪ'naʊns/ *vt* 1 (cede) (frml) ‹*claim/title/right*› renunciar a 2 (reject) ‹*cause/ideology/religion*› renunciar a, abjurarse de

renovate /'renəveɪt/ *vt* ‹*house/building*› renovar*; ‹*painting/furniture*› restaurar

renovation /'renə'veɪʃən/ *n* [u c] (of building) renovación *f*; (of painting, furniture) restauración *f*

renown /rɪ'naʊn/ *n* [u] renombre *m*, fama *f*

renowned /rɪ'naʊnd/ *adj* ‹*painter/poet/historian*› de renombre, conocido

rent¹ /rent/ *n*
A [u c] 1 (for accommodations, office) alquiler *m*, arrendamiento *m*, arriendo *m*, renta *f* (esp Méx); **how much is your ~?** ¿cuánto pagan de alquiler (*or* de arrendamiento *etc*)?; **it pays the ~** (set phrase) me da de comer, me da para vivir; (*before n*) **~ book** *libreta donde se anotan las cantidades satisfechas por el inquilino* 2 (for boat, suit) (esp AmE) alquiler *m*, arriendo *m* (esp Andes), renta *f* (Méx); Ⓢ **for rent** se alquila *or* (Andes tb) se arrienda *or* (Méx tb) se renta; Ⓢ **cars for rent** alquiler de coches, se alquilan *or* (Andes tb) se arriendan coches, renta de coches (Méx)
B [c] (tear, rip) (liter) rasgadura *f* (liter), rasgón *m*

rent² *vt* 1 (pay for) **to ~ sth (FROM sb)** alquilarle *or* arrendarle* *or* (Méx tb) rentarle algo (A algn) 2 **rented** *past p* ‹*accommodations*› alquilado, arrendado, rentado (Méx) 3 ▸**rent out**
■ **rent** *vi* 1 (pay for using sth) alquilar, arrendar*, rentar (Méx) 2 (cost to rent) (AmE) **this house ~s for $1200 a week** el alquiler *or* el arriendo *or* (Méx) la renta de esta casa es de 1200 dólares a la semana

Phrasal verb
• **rent out** [v ▸ o ▸ adv, v ▸ adv ▸ o] alquilar, arrendar*, rentar (Méx)

rent³ *past & past p of* **rend**

rental /'rentl/ *n* 1 [u c] (act of renting) alquiler *m*, arriendo *m* 2 [c] (charge) alquiler, renta *f* (Méx), arriendo *m* (esp Andes) 3 [c] (thing rented) (AmE): **this car is a ~** este es un coche de alquiler *or* (Méx tb) un coche rentado *or* (Andes tb) un coche arrendado

renunciation /rɪ'nʌnsi'eɪʃən/ *n* [u] (frml) 1 (of ideology) abjuración *f*, rechazo *m*; (of faith) rechazo *m*; (of claim, right, title) renuncia *f*; (of friend) repudio *m* 2 (abstinence, asceticism) renuncia *f*

reoffend /ˌri:ə'fend/ *vi* reincidir, volver* a delinquir

reopen /'ri:'əʊpən || ˌri:'əʊpən/ *vt* 1 ‹*window/book/store/road*› volver* a abrir; **to ~ lines of communication** reestablecer* las comunicaciones 2 ‹*negotiations/hostilities*› reanudar; ‹*criminal case*› volver* a abrir; ‹*trial*› reanudar
■ **reopen** *vi* 1 «*store/hospital/school*» abrir* de nuevo (sus puertas) 2 «*talks/hostilities*» reanudarse

reorganization /'ri:'ɔ:rgənə'zeɪʃən || ˌri:ˌɔ:gənaɪ'zeɪʃən/ *n* [u c] reorganización *f*

reorganize /'ri:'ɔ:rgənaɪz || ˌri:'ɔ:gənaɪz/ *vt* reorganizar*

rep /rep/ *n*
A [c] 1 (*sales* ~) representante *mf or* agente *mf* (comercial) 2 (person responsible): **safety/sports ~** responsable *mf* de seguridad/de deportes; **a union ~** un/una representante *or* (Esp) un/una enlace sindical
B [u] (BrE Theat) ▸**repertory**

Rep 1 (US title) = **Representative** 2 (AmE) = **Republican**

repair¹ /rɪ'per || rɪ'peə(r)/ *vt* 1 (mend) ‹*machinery/roof*› arreglar, reparar; ‹*shoes/clothes*› arreglar 2 (redress) ‹*error/wrong*› reparar
■ **repair** *vi* (retire, withdraw) (liter *or* hum) **to ~ TO** retirarse A

repair² *n* [u c] arreglo *m*, reparación *f*; **they do bicycle/watch/shoe ~s** arreglan bicicletas/relojes/zapatos; **~s while you wait** reparaciones al minuto; **the museum is closed for ~s** el museo está cerrado por obras; **my car is in for ~** me están arreglando el coche; **it is damaged beyond ~** no tiene arreglo; **in a good/bad state of ~, in good/bad ~** en buen/mal estado; (*before n*) **a ~ job** un arreglo; **a bicycle ~ shop** un taller de reparación de bicicletas

repairer /rɪ'perər || rɪ'peərə(r)/ *n* técnico, -ca *m,f*; **watch ~** (BrE) relojero, -ra *m,f*

repairman /rɪ'permæn || rɪ'peəmæn/ *n* (*pl* **-men** /-men/) técnico *m*

reparation /'repə'reɪʃən/ *n* 1 [u] (amends) (frml) reparación *f* (frml); **the judge ordered the tenants to make ~s to the landlord** el juez ordenó a los inquilinos que indemnizaran al propietario 2 **reparations** *pl* (Pol) indemnización *f*

repartee /'repər'teɪ || ˌrepɑ:'ti:/ *n* [u] conversación *f*, plática *f*

repast /rɪ'pæst || rɪ'pɑ:st/ *n* (liter) ágape *m* (liter *o* hum), comida *f*

repatriate /'ri:'peɪtrieɪt || ˌri:'pætrɪeɪt/ *vt* repatriar

repatriation /ri:'peɪtri'eɪʃən || ri:ˌpætrɪ'eɪʃən/ *n* [u] repatriación *f*

repay /'ri:'peɪ/ *vt* (*past & past p* **repaid**) 1 ‹*money/loan*› devolver*; ‹*debt*› pagar*, cancelar; **I have to ~ him** tengo que devolverle el dinero 2 ‹*kindness/hospitality/favor*› pagar*, corresponder a; **to ~ sb FOR sth: I'd like to ~ them for their kindness** quisiera corresponder a su amabilidad

repayable /'ri:'peɪəbəl/ *adj* (frml) (*pred*) ‹*deposit/loan*› (refundable) reintegrable, reembolsable; **the loan is ~ within three years** el préstamo es a tres años

repayment /ri:'peɪmənt/ *n* 1 [u] (act of repaying) pago *m*; (*before n*) ‹*plan/terms*› de pago; ~ **mortgage** *préstamo hipotecario en el que se va amortizando el capital al mismo tiempo que se pagan los intereses* 2 [c] (installment) plazo *m*, cuota *f* (AmL) 3 [u c] (recompense) pago *m*, recompensa *f*

repeal[1] /rɪ'pi:l/ *vt* (Govt, Law) revocar*

repeal[2] *n* [u] revocación *f*

repeat[1] /rɪ'pi:t/ *vt*

A 1 (say again) ‹*sound/word/sentence*› repetir* 2 (divulge) contar*; **don't ~ this, will you, but ...** no lo vayas a contar, pero ... 3 (recite) (AmE) ‹*lesson/poem*› repetir*, recitar

B (do again) repetir*; ‹*episode*› (Rad, TV) volver* a emitir *or* transmitir

■ *v refl* **to ~ oneself** repetirse*; **history ~s itself** la historia se repite

■ **repeat** *vi*

A (stressing instruction, statement) repetir*; ~ **after me** repitan lo que digo; **this is not, (I) ~, *not* an exercise** esto *no es* un simulacro, repito, *no es* un simulacro

B «*food*» **to ~ ON sb**: **onions ~ on me** la cebolla me repite

C **repeating** *pres p* ‹*rifle/clock/watch*› de repetición

repeat[2] *n* 1 (repetition) repetición *f*; **we want to avoid a ~ of last year's fiasco** queremos evitar que se repita el desastre del año pasado; (*before n*) ~ **performance** (Theat) repetición *f* 2 (Rad, TV) (of program) repetición *f*; (of a series) reposición *f*, retransmisión *f*

repeated /rɪ'pi:təd || rɪ'pi:tɪd/ *adj* (*before n*) ‹*warnings/attempts*› repetido, reiterado; ‹*requests*› reiterado

repeatedly /rɪ'pi:tədli || rɪ'pi:tɪdli/ *adv* repetidamente, reiteradamente

repeater /rɪ'pi:tər || rɪ'pi:tə(r)/ *n* (repeat offender) (AmE) reincidente *mf*

repel /rɪ'pel/ *vt* **-ll-** 1 (drive back) ‹*enemy/army*› repeler; ‹*advance/attack*› repeler, rechazar* 2 (ward off) ‹*insects/sharks*› repeler, ahuyentar 3 (disgust) repeler, repugnar

repellant /rɪ'pelənt/ *n* [u c]: **insect ~** repelente *m* para insectos

repellent[1] /rɪ'pelənt/ *adj* (disgusting) repelente

repellent[2] *n* ▸ **repellant**

repent /rɪ'pent/ *vi* arrepentirse*

■ **repent** *vt* arrepentirse* de

repentance /rɪ'pentṇs/ *n* [u] arrepentimiento *m*

repentant /rɪ'pentṇt/ *adj* arrepentido

repercussions /'ri:pər'kʌʃənz || ˌri:pə'kʌʃənz/ *npl* repercusiones *fpl*; **to have ~ on sth/sb** tener* repercusiones en algo/en algn, repercutir en algo/algn

repertoire /'repərtwɑ:r || 'repətwɑ:(r)/ *n* repertorio *m*

repertory /'repərtɔ:ri || 'repətəri/ *n* [u]: **to be/act/work in ~** trabajar en una compañía de repertorio; (*before n*) ‹*actor/company/theater*› de repertorio

repetition /'repə'tɪʃən/ *n* [u c] repetición *f*

repetitious /'repə'tɪʃəs/ *adj* repetitivo

repetitive /rɪ'petətɪv/ *adj* repetitivo

rephrase /'ri:'freɪz/ *vt* ‹*statement*› expresar de otra manera; ‹*request*› reformular

replace /rɪ'pleɪs/ *vt*

A 1 (take the place of) sustituir*, reemplazar*; **people are being ~d by robots on assembly lines** los robots están sustituyendo a las personas en las cadenas de montaje *or* (Méx, Chi) de ensamblaje 2 (provide replacement for) ‹*incompetent employee*› reemplazar*; ‹*damaged goods/lost item*› reponer*; ‹*broken window/battery*› cambiar; **to ~ sth WITH sth** cambiar algo POR algo

B (put back in its place) ‹*book/ornament*› volver* a poner *or* colocar; ‹*lid*› volver* a poner; ‹*receiver/handset*› colgar*

replaceable /rɪ'pleɪsəbəl/ *adj* reemplazable, sustituible; **the cups are easily ~** las tazas se pueden reponer fácilmente

replacement /rɪ'pleɪsmənt/ *n* 1 [u] (act) sustitución *f*, reemplazo *m*; (*before n*) ~ **value** (Fin) valor *m* de reposición 2 [c] (person) sustituto, -ta *m,f* 3 [c] (object): **I'll buy you a ~** te compraré uno nuevo, te compraré otro; (*before n*) ‹*doors/windows*› modular; ~ **parts** repuestos *mpl*, piezas *fpl* de recambio *or* de repuesto, refacciones *fpl* (Méx)

replay[1] /'ri:'pleɪ/ *vt*

A (Sport) ‹*game/match*› volver* a jugar, repetir*

B (Audio, Video) volver* a poner

replay[2] /'ri:pleɪ/ *n* (Sport) (*action* ~) repetición *f* (de la jugada)

replenish /rɪ'plenɪʃ/ *vt* ‹*stock*› reponer*; **we have to ~ our fuel supplies** tenemos que reabastecernos de combustible

replete /rɪ'pli:t/ *adj* (liter) ~ **WITH sth** repleto DE algo, ahíto DE algo (liter)

replica /'replɪkə/ *n* (*pl* **-cas**) réplica *f*, reproducción *f*

reply[1] /rɪ'plaɪ/ *n* (*pl* **replies**) 1 (spoken, written) respuesta *f*, contestación *f*; **I phoned her but there was no ~** la llamé pero no contestó nadie *or* (Esp) nadie cogió el teléfono; **in ~ to your letter** en respuesta a su carta; **I didn't know what to say in ~** no supe cómo responder 2 (action, response) reacción *f*, respuesta *f*

reply[2] **replies, replying, replied** *vi* 1 (answer) responder, contestar; **to ~ to sth** contestar algo, responder A algo; **to ~ to sb** responderle *or* contestarle A algn 2 (respond) responder; **he replied with a nod** respondió con un movimiento de la cabeza, asintió/se negó con la cabeza

■ **reply** *vt* responder, contestar, replicar* (liter)

repopulate /'ri:'pɑ:pjəleɪt || ˌri:'pɒpjʊleɪt/ *vt* repoblar*

report[1] /rɪ'pɔ:rt || rɪ'pɔ:t/ *n* [c]

A 1 (account) informe *m*; (piece of news) noticia *f*; (in newspaper) reportaje *m*, crónica *f*; **latest ~s indicate that ...** las últimas informaciones indican que ... 2 (evaluation) informe *m*, reporte *m* (Méx); **medical ~** parte *m* médico; **(school) ~** boletín *m* de calificaciones *or* notas, libreta *f* de calificaciones (AmL), reporte *m* (Méx); **annual ~** memoria *f* (anual); **official ~** informe *m* oficial 3 (school assignment) (AmE) redacción *f*; **a book ~** una reseña sobre un libro

B (sound) estallido *m*, detonación *f* (frml)

report[2] *vt*

A 1 (relate, announce): **several people ~ed seeing the tiger** varias personas dijeron haber visto al tigre; **he is ~ed to be very rich** se dice que es muy rico; **many companies ~ed increased profits** muchas empresas anunciaron un incremento en sus beneficios 2 (Journ) «*reporter/media*» informar sobre, reportear (Andes); **the news was widely ~ed** la noticia fue ampliamente divulgada

B 1 (notify) ‹*accident*› informar de, dar* parte de; ‹*crime*› denunciar, dar* parte de, reportar (AmL); **nothing to ~** nada que informar; **to ~ sth TO sb** dar* parte DE algo A algn; **to ~ sth stolen/sb missing** denunciar *or* (AmL tb) reportar el robo de algo/la desaparición de algn 2 (denounce) **to ~ sb (TO sb)** denunciar *or* (AmL tb) reportar a algn (A algn)

■ **report** *vi*

A (Journ) «*reporter*» informar; **Alice Jones ~ing from Kabul** Alice Jones, desde Kabul; **to ~ ON sth** informar SOBRE algo, reportear algo (Andes)

B 1 (present oneself) presentarse, reportarse (AmL); **Private Wood ~ing for duty, sir!** soldado Wood se presenta, mi teniente (*or* sargento *etc*); **to ~ sick** dar* parte de enfermo 2 (be accountable) (Busn) **to ~ TO sb** estar* bajo las órdenes de algn

Phrasal verbs

- **report back** [v ▸ adv] 1 (return): **to ~ back (to base)** regresar a la base 2 (give report) **to ~ back (TO sb)** presentar un informe (A algn)
- **report out** [v ▸ o ▸ adv, v ▸ adv ▸ o] (AmE) *devolver (un proyecto de ley) acompañado de un informe*

reportage /'repɔ:r'tɑ:ʒ || ˌrepɔ:'tɑ:ʒ/ *n* [u] reportaje *m*

report card *n* (AmE Educ) boletín *m* de calificaciones *or* notas, reporte *m* (Méx)

reportedly /rɪ'pɔ:rtədli || rɪ'pɔ:tɪdli/ *adv* (*indep*): **the minister had ~ agreed to it** según se informa, el ministro había *or* (period) habría dado su consentimiento

reported speech *n* [u] estilo *m* indirecto

reporter /rɪ'pɔ:rtər || rɪ'pɔ:tə(r)/ *n* periodista *mf*, reportero, -tera *m,f*

reporting /rɪ'pɔ:rtɪŋ || rɪ'pɔ:tɪŋ/ *n* [u] cobertura *f*

repose[1] /rɪ'pəʊz/ *n* [u] (liter) reposo *m*; **in ~** en reposo

repose[2] *vi* (liter) reposar (liter), descansar

repository /rɪ'pɑ:zətɔ:ri || rɪ'pɒzɪtəri/ *n* (*pl* **-ries**) depósito *m*, almacén *m*, bodega *f* (Andes, Méx)

repossess /'ri:pə'zes/ *vt* ‹*car/house*› recuperar la posesión de (*por falta de pago*)

repossession /ˈriːpəˈzeʃən/ *n* [u] recuperación *f* (*de un artículo o inmueble no pagado*)

repot /ˈriːˈpɑːt || ˌriːˈpɒt/ *vt* cambiar de maceta

reprehensible /ˈreprɪˈhensəbəl/ *n* reprensible

represent /ˈreprɪˈzent/ *vt*

A 1 (stand for) representar; **the dove ~s peace** la paloma representa la paz 2 (constitute) representar, constituir*; **this ~s a radical change in policy** esto representa *or* constituye un radical cambio de política

B (act as representative for) ‹*client/president*› representar; ‹*company*› (Busn) ser* representante *or* agente de

C (frml) (describe) presentar; **the press has ~ed him as an ogre** la prensa lo ha presentado como un ogro

representation /ˈreprɪzenˈteɪʃən/ *n*

A 1 [u] (in government, on board) representación *f* 2 [c] (reflection) representación *f*, reflejo *m* 3 [u c] (presence) representación *f*

B [u c] (portrayal) representación *f*

C **representations** *pl* (complaint) (frml) protesta *f* formal; **to make ~s to sb** elevar una protesta a algn (frml)

representational /ˈreprɪzenˈteɪʃn̩əl || ˌreprɪzenˈteɪʃənl̩/ *adj* figurativo

representative¹ /ˈreprɪˈzentətɪv/ *n* 1 representante *mf* 2 (in US) (Govt) representante *mf*, diputado, -da *m,f* 3 (*sales* ~) representante *mf or* agente *mf* comercial

representative² *adj* representativo; **to be ~ OF sth** ser* representativo DE algo

repress /rɪˈpres/ *vt* reprimir

repression /rɪˈpreʃən/ *n* [u] represión *f*

repressive /rɪˈpresɪv/ *adj* represivo

reprieve¹ /rɪˈpriːv/ *n* 1 (postponement) aplazamiento *m*; **he was granted a ~ of three days** se le concedieron tres días de gracia 2 (Law) (commutation) indulto *m*, conmutación *f* (*esp de la pena de muerte*)

reprieve² *vt* indultar; **the firm has been ~d for the time being** por el momento, la empresa se salva del cierre

reprimand¹ /ˈreprəmænd || ˈreprɪmɑːnd/ *n* reprimenda *f*

reprimand² *vt* reprender

reprint¹ /ˈriːprɪnt/ *n* (Publ) reimpresión *f*; (Phot) copia *f*

reprint² /ˈriːˈprɪnt/ *vt* (Publ) reimprimir*

reprisal /rɪˈpraɪzəl/ *n* represalia *f*; **to take ~s against sb/sth** tomar represalias contra algn/algo

reprise /rɪˈpriːz/ *n* repetición *f*

reproach¹ /rɪˈprəʊtʃ/ *vt* **to ~ sb FOR -ING/WITH sth**: **he ~ed her for not having written to him** le reprochó que no le hubiera escrito; **I have nothing to ~ myself with** no tengo nada que reprocharme

reproach² *n* [u c] reproche *m*; **above** *o* **beyond ~** irreprochable, intachable

reproachful /rɪˈprəʊtʃfəl/ *adj* (lleno) de reproche

reproachfully /rɪˈprəʊtʃfəli/ *adv* ‹*say*› en tono de reproche; **he looked at me ~** me miró lleno de reproche

reprobate /ˈreprəbeɪt/ *n* (frml) réprobo, -ba *m,f* (liter), depravado, -da *m,f*

reprocess /ˈriːˈprɑːses || ˌriːˈprəʊses/ *vt* reprocesar

reproduce /ˈriːprəˈduːs || ˌriːprəˈdjuːs/ *vt* reproducir*

■ **reproduce** *vi* (Biol) reproducirse*

reproduction /ˈriːprəˈdʌkʃən/ *n*

A [u] (Biol) reproducción *f*

B 1 [u] (copying) reproducción *f* 2 [c] (copy) reproducción *f*; (*before n*) **~ furniture** muebles *mpl* de reproducción

reproductive /ˈriːprəˈdʌktɪv/ *adj* reproductor

reproof /rɪˈpruːf/ *n* [u c] (frml) reprobación *f*

reprove /rɪˈpruːv/ *vt* (frml) **to ~ sb (FOR sth)** reprender *or* (frml) reconvenir* a algn (POR algo)

reproving /rɪˈpruːvɪŋ/ *adj* (frml) reprobatorio, recriminatorio

reprovingly /rɪˈpruːvɪŋli/ *adv* (frml) ‹*speak*› en tono reprobatorio; **he looked at her ~** le lanzó una mirada reprobatoria *or* recriminatoria

reptile /ˈreptl̩, -taɪl || ˈreptaɪl/ *n* reptil *m*

republic /rɪˈpʌblɪk/ *n* república *f*

republican¹ /rɪˈpʌblɪkən/ *adj* 1 (of a republic) republicano 2 **Republican** (in US) republicano

republican² *n* 1 (supporter of republic) republicano, -na *m,f* 2 **Republican** (in US) republicano, -na *m,f*

> **Republican Party**
>
> Uno de los dos principales partidos políticos de EEUU. Aunque el Partido Republicano fue fundado en 1854, por los que deseaban abolir la esclavitud, se considera más conservador que el Partido Demócrata (**Democratic Party**), el otro partido

republicanism /rɪˈpʌblɪkənɪzəm/ *n* 1 (movement) republicanismo *m* 2 **Republicanism** (in US) republicanismo *m*

repudiate /rɪˈpjuːdieɪt/ *vt* 1 (deny) ‹*accusation*› rechazar*, negar* 2 (refuse to acknowledge) ‹*liability*› negarse* a reconocer; ‹*violence/teaching*› repudiar; ‹*wife/family*› repudiar

repudiation /rɪˈpjuːdiˈeɪʃən/ *n* [u] 1 (rejection, denial) rechazo *m* 2 (refusal to acknowledge) repudio *m*, repulsa *f* (frml)

repugnance /rɪˈpʌgnəns/ *n* [u] repugnancia *f*

repugnant /rɪˈpʌgnənt/ *adj* repugnante; **to be ~ TO sb** repugnarle *or* serle* repugnante A algn

repulse /rɪˈpʌls/ *vt* repeler, rechazar*

repulsion /rɪˈpʌlʃən/ *n* [u] (frml) repulsión *f*

repulsive /rɪˈpʌlsɪv/ *adj* repulsivo, repugnante

reputable /ˈrepjətəbəl || ˈrepjʊtəbəl/ *adj* acreditado (frml), reputado (frml)

reputation /ˈrepjəˈteɪʃən || ˈrepjʊˈteɪʃən/ *n* reputación *f*, fama *f*; **~ AS sth** reputación *or* fama DE algo; **a ~ FOR sth** fama DE algo

repute /rɪˈpjuːt/ *n* [u] (frml) reputación *f*, fama *f*; **of ~** de renombre; **house of ill ~** casa *f* de mala fama

reputed /rɪˈpjuːtəd || rɪˈpjuːtɪd/ *adj* 1 (supposed): **the ~ size of her fortune** el presunto *or* supuesto tamaño de su fortuna; **to be ~ to + INF**: **she is ~ (to be) the best in the world** está considerada como la mejor del mundo 2 (highly esteemed) acreditado (frml), reputado (frml)

reputedly /rɪˈpjuːtədli || rɪˈpjʊtɪdli/ *adv* (*indep*) según se dice *or* cree

request¹ /rɪˈkwest/ *n* 1 (polite demand) petición *f*, pedido *m* (esp AmL), solicitud *f* (frml); **~ FOR sth** petición (*or* pedido *etc*) DE algo; **by popular ~** a petición *or* (esp AmL) a pedido del público; **⑤ price lists available on request** solicite nuestras listas de precios; (*before n*) **~ stop** (BrE) parada *f* discrecional 2 (for song) petición *f*, pedido *m* (esp AmL)

request² *vt* pedir*, solicitar (frml); **Mr & Mrs Tuthill ~ the pleasure of your company at ...** (frml) los señores Tuthill tienen el agrado de invitar a usted a ... (frml); **to ~ sb to + INF/THAT** pedir(le)* a algn QUE (+ *subj*)

requiem /ˈrekwiəm/ *n* 1 **~ (mass)** misa *f* de réquiem 2 (hymn for the dead) réquiem *m*

require /rɪˈkwaɪr || rɪˈkwaɪə(r)/ *vt*

A 1 (need) necesitar; (call for) ‹*patience/dedication*› requerir*, exigir*; **you can withdraw cash (as and) when ~d** puede retirar dinero según lo necesite *or* según le sea necesario; **all I ~ now is your signature** todo lo que hace falta ahora es que usted firme; **add salt as ~d** salar a gusto; **we can supply the screws if ~d** podemos suministrar los tornillos si usted así lo desea 2 (demand) **to ~ sb/sth to + INF** requerir* que algn/algo (+ *subj*); **to ~ that**: **the law ~s that you wear a helmet** la ley le obliga a llevar *or* exige que lleve casco; **to ~ sth OF sb**: **all that is ~d of you is that you observe the rules** todo lo que se te exige es que cumplas con el reglamento; **I shall do all that is ~d of me** haré todo lo que me corresponda

B **required** *past p* 1 ‹*dose/amount*› necesario; **cut the ~d number of squares** corte el número de cuadrados que haga falta *or* que sea necesario 2 (compulsory) ‹*reading/viewing*› obligado

requirement /rɪˈkwaɪrmənt || rɪˈkwaɪəmənt/ *n* 1 (*usu pl*) (need) necesidad *f*; **what are your ~s?** ¿qué necesita usted?; **to meet sb's ~s** satisfacer* las necesidades de algn 2 (demand, condition) requisito *m*

requisite¹ /ˈrekwəzət || ˈrekwɪzɪt/ *n* (frml): **toilet/smoker's ~s** (BrE) artículos *mpl* de tocador/para fumadores

requisite² *adj* (frml) necesario, requerido

requisition¹ /ˈrekwəˈzɪʃən || ˌrekwɪˈzɪʃən/ *vt* ‹*supplies*› requisar; ‹*services*› requerir*

requisition[2] *n* (demand) solicitud *f* (frml); (taking over) requisa *f*, requisición *f*

reread /ˈriːˈriːd/ *vt* (*past & past p* **reread** /ˈriːˈred/) releer*

rerelease /ˌriːrɪˈliːs/ *vt* ‹*movie*› reestrenar; ‹*record*› relanzar*

reroute /ˈriːˈruːt/ *vt* desviar*

rerun[1] /ˈriːrʌn/ *n* 1 (Cin, TV) repetición *f*, reposición *f*; **the series is in ~s** (AmE) están volviendo a dar *or* (Méx) a pasar la serie 2 (repeat) repetición *f*

rerun[2] /ˈriːˈrʌn/ *vt* (*pres p* **rerunning**; *past* **reran**; *past p* **rerun**) 1 ‹*film/series*› repetir*, reponer* 2 (Comput) ‹*program*› volver* a pasar *or* ejecutar 3 ‹*race*› repetir*

resale /ˈriːˈseɪl/ *n* reventa *f*; ⓢ **not for resale** muestra gratis

reschedule /ˈriːˈskedʒuːl || ˌriːˈʃedjuːl/ *vt* 1 (Fin) ‹*debt/repayments*› renegociar 2 ‹*project/work*› volver* a planificar; ‹*meeting*› cambiar la hora/fecha de

rescind /rɪˈsɪnd/ *vt* (frml) ‹*contract*› rescindir, anular; ‹*order/ruling*› revocar*; ‹*law*› derogar*, abolir*

rescue[1] /ˈreskjuː/ *n* [u c] rescate *m*; **to come/go to the/sb's ~**: **Mum came to the ~ and paid my phone bill** Mamá me salvó al pagar la cuenta del teléfono; **they went to his ~** acudieron a socorrerlo (liter), fueron *or* (liter) acudieron en su auxilio; (*before n*) ‹*services/team*› de rescate *or* salvamento

rescue[2] *vt* rescatar, salvar; **to ~ sb/sth FROM sth/-ING**: **he was ~d from drowning** lo salvaron de morir ahogado; **the bank ~d the company from bankruptcy** el banco salvó a la empresa de la quiebra

rescuer /ˈreskjuər || ˈreskjuːə(r)/ *n* salvador, -dora *m,f*

research[1] /rɪˈsɜːrtʃ, ˈriːsɜːrtʃ || rɪˈsɜːtʃ/ *n* [u] investigación *f*; **~ has shown that ...** las investigaciones han demostrado que ...; **~ INTO/ON sth** investigación SOBRE algo; **~ and development** investigación y desarrollo; (*before n*) **~ student** estudiante de posgrado que hace trabajos de investigación

research[2] *vi* investigar*; **to ~ INTO/ON sth** investigar* algo, hacer* una investigación SOBRE algo

■ **research** *vt* ‹*causes/problem*› investigar*, estudiar; **to ~ an article/a book** hacer* una investigación que servirá de base a un artículo/a un libro; **this article is well ~ed** este artículo está bien documentado

researcher /rɪˈsɜːrtʃər || rɪˈsɜːtʃə(r)/ *n* investigador, -dora *m,f*

resemblance /rɪˈzembləns/ *n* 1 [u] (likeness) parecido *m*, semejanza *f*; **~ TO sb/sth** parecido CON algn/algo; **his story bears little ~ to the facts** su historia tiene poco que ver con la realidad 2 [c] (point of likeness) similitud *f*

resemble /rɪˈzembəl/ *vt* parecerse* a, asemejarse a (liter)

resent /rɪˈzent/ *vt*: **he ~ed her success** le molestaba que ella tuviera éxito; **I ~ the suggestion that ...** no puedo admitir *or* me ofende que se insinúe que ...; **to ~ -ING**: **I ~ having to help him** me molesta tener que ayudarlo; **he ~s me** *o* **my telling him what to do** le sienta mal que le diga lo que tiene que hacer

resentful /rɪˈzentfəl/ *adj* ‹*person*› resentido, rencoroso; ‹*air/look*› de resentimiento; **they're ~ of her success** sienten celos de su éxito

resentment /rɪˈzentmənt/ *n* [u] resentimiento *m*, rencor *m*; **to feel ~ toward sb** guardarle rencor a algn

reservation /ˈrezərˈveɪʃən || ˌrezəˈveɪʃən/ *n*

A [c u] (booking) reserva *f*, reservación *f* (AmL)

B [c] (doubt, qualification) reserva *f*; **to have (one's) ~s about sb/sth** tener* sus (*or* mis *etc*) reservas acerca de algn/algo; **without ~** sin reservas

C [c] (land) (in US) reserva *f*, reservación *f* (AmL)

reserve[1] /rɪˈzɜːrv || rɪˈzɜːv/ *n*

A [c] (stock) reserva *f*; **I'm keeping this money in ~** este dinero lo tengo reservado

B [c] 1 **the Reserve** (Mil) la reserva 2 (Sport) (substitute player) reserva *mf*, suplente *mf*; (*before n*) ‹*goalkeeper*› de reserva; **~ team** reserva *f*

C **reserves** *pl* (Mil) reservas *fpl*; (BrE Sport) reserva *f*

D [c] (land) coto *m*, reserva *f*; (*game* **~**) coto *m* de caza; (*nature* **~**) reserva *f* natural

E [u] 1 (self-restraint) reserva *f*, cautela *f* 2 (qualification): **without ~** sin reserva

reserve[2] *vt* 1 (book) ‹*room/seat/table*› reservar 2 (keep, save) **to ~ sth (FOR sth)** reservar *or* guardar algo (PARA algo); **to ~ (one's) judgment** reservarse la opinión; **the company ~s the right to change ...** la compañía se reserva el derecho de cambiar ...

reserved /rɪˈzɜːrvd || rɪˈzɜːvd/ *adj* reservado

reservist /rɪˈzɜːrvəst || rɪˈzɜːvɪst/ *n* reservista *mf*

reservoir /ˈrezərvwɑːr || ˈrezəvwɑː(r)/ *n* 1 (of water) embalse *m*, presa *f*, represa *f* (AmS) 2 (supply, source) mina *f*

reset /ˈriːˈset/ *vt* (*pres p* **resetting**; *past & past p* **reset**)

A ‹*alarm clock*› (volver* a) poner*; ‹*counter/dial*› volver* a cero

B (Med) ‹*bone*› colocar*, componer* (AmL)

resettle /ˈriːˈsetl̩/ *vt* ‹*refugees/population*› reasentar*; ‹*area/land*› repoblar*

■ **resettle** *vi* «*refugees/population*» reestablecerse*

resettlement /ˈriːˈsetl̩mənt/ *n* [u] (of people) reasentamiento *m*; (of land) repoblación *f*, nueva colonización *f*

reshape /ˈriːˈʃeɪp/ *vt* ‹*text*› dar* nueva forma a; ‹*organization*› reestructurar; ‹*policy*› reformar

reshoot /riːˈʃuːt/ *vt* (*past & past p* **-shot**) ‹*scene/sequence*› volver* a filmar

reshuffle[1] /ˈriːˈʃʌfəl/ *vt* 1 ‹*cards*› volver* a barajar 2 ‹*cabinet*› remodelar; ‹*management*› reorganizar*

reshuffle[2] *n* reorganización *f*; **cabinet ~** remodelación *f* del gabinete

reside /rɪˈzaɪd/ *vi* (frml) 1 (live) residir (frml) 2 «*power/authority*» (be invested) **to ~ IN** *o* **WITH sb/sth** residir EN algn/algo

residence /ˈrezədəns || ˈrezɪdəns/ *n*

A 1 [u] (in a country) residencia *f*; **to take up ~** fijar su (*or* mi *etc*) residencia, establecerse*; (*before n*) **~ permit** permiso *m* de residencia 2 [u] (in building) (frml) residencia *f*; **to take up ~** instalarse 3 **~ hall** (AmE), **hall of ~** (BrE) residencia *f* universitaria *or* de estudiantes, colegio *m* mayor (Esp)

B [c] (home) residencia *f*; **his official/London ~** su residencia oficial/de Londres

residency /ˈrezədənsi || ˈrezɪdənsi/ *n* (*pl* **-cies**)

A [u] (AmE Med) internado *m*, residencia *f* (AmL)

B [c] ▸**residence B**

C [u] ▸**residence A**

resident[1] /ˈrezədənt || ˈrezɪdənt/ *n* 1 (in country) residente *mf* 2 (inhabitant — of district) vecino, -na *m,f*; (— of building) residente *mf*, vecino, -na *m,f*; (— of hotel) huésped *mf*; (— of institution) residente *mf*, interno, -na *m,f* 3 (AmE Med) médico interno, médica interna *m,f*

resident[2] *adj* 1 (in country) (*pred*) **to be ~** ser* residente 2 (living on premises) ‹*physician/chaplain*› residente

residential /ˈrezəˈdentʃəl || ˌrezɪˈdenʃəl/ *adj* ‹*area/suburb*› residencial; ‹*course*› con alojamiento para los asistentes

residual /rɪˈzɪdʒuəl || rɪˈzɪdjuəl/ *adj* residual

residue /ˈrezəduː || ˈrezɪdjuː/ *n* residuo *m*

resign /rɪˈzaɪn/ *vi* renunciar, dimitir; **to ~ FROM sth** renunciar A algo, dimitir algo; **I ~ed from the committee** renuncié a *or* dimití mi cargo en la comisión

■ **resign** *vt* ‹*position*› renunciar a, dimitir

■ *v refl* **to ~ oneself (TO sth/-ING)** resignarse (A algo/+ INF)

resignation /ˈrezɪgˈneɪʃən/ *n*

A [c u] (from job, position) renuncia *f*, dimisión *f*; **to hand in** *o* (frml) **tender one's ~** presentar su (*or* mi *etc*) dimisión *or* renuncia; **~ FROM sth**: **his ~ from the Cabinet/directorship** su dimisión de *or* su renuncia a su puesto en el gabinete/en la dirección

B [u] (acceptance, submission) resignación *f*

resigned /rɪˈzaɪnd/ *adj* ‹*expression/air*› resignado, de resignación; **to be ~ TO sth/-ING** estar* resignado A algo/+INF; **I've become ~ to that** me he resignado a eso

resilience /rɪˈzɪljəns || rɪˈzɪliəns/ *n* [u] 1 (of person) capacidad *f* de recuperación, resistencia *f* 2 (of material) elasticidad *f*

resilient /rɪˈzɪljənt || rɪˈzɪliənt/ *adj* 1 ‹*person/character*› fuerte, con capacidad de recuperación 2 ‹*material*› elástico

resin /ˈrezn̩ || ˈrezɪn/ *n* [u] resina *f*

r

resist /rɪ'zɪst/ *vt* resistir; ‹*change/plan*› oponer* resistencia a; **she found him hard to ~** le costaba resistirse a sus encantos; **I can't ~ chocolate** el chocolate me vuelve loco; **to ~ -ING** resistirse A + INF

■ **resist** *vi* [1] (fight, oppose) «*troops*» resistir, oponer* resistencia [2] (not give way) resistirse, contenerse*

resistance /rɪ'zɪstəns/ *n*

[A] [u] [1] (opposition) ~ **(TO sth/sb)** resistencia *f* (A algo/algn); **to put up ~** oponer* resistencia; ***to take o follow the line o path of least ~*** seguir* el camino más fácil [2] (movement) (+ *sing or pl vb*) **the ~** la resistencia; (*before n*) **the ~ movement** la resistencia

[B] [u] (Biol) ~ **(TO sth)** resistencia *f* (A algo)

resistant /rɪ'zɪstənt/ *adj*

[A] (opposed) (*pred*) **to be ~ TO sth/-ING** resistirse *or* oponer* resistencia A algo/+ INF

[B] (Biol) ~ **(TO sth)** resistente (A algo)

-resistant /rɪ,zɪstənt/ *suff*: **crease~** inarrugable; **stain~** que no se mancha

resit[1] /'riː'sɪt/ (*pres p* **resitting**; *past & past p* **resat** /'riː'sæt/) *vt* (BrE) ‹*examination*› volver* a presentarse a, volver* a presentar

resit[2] /'riːsɪt/ *n* (BrE): **to do a ~** volver* a presentarse a un examen, , volver* a presentar un examen, volver* a examinarse (Esp)

reskilling /riː'skɪlɪŋ/ *n* [u] reciclaje *m*, recapacitación *f*, reconversión *f*

resolute /'rezəluːt/ *adj* resuelto, decidido

resolutely /'rezəluːtli/ *adv* ‹*act*› con resolución *or* decisión, resueltamente; ‹*refuse*› con firmeza; **to be ~ opposed to sth** oponerse* firmemente a algo

resolution /'rezə'luːʃən/ *n*

[A] [c] [1] (decision) determinación *f*, propósito *m*; **New Year's ~s** buenos propósitos de Año Nuevo [2] (proposal) moción *f* [3] (in US, passed by legislature) resolución *f*

[B] [u] (resoluteness) resolución *f*, determinación *f*

[C] [u] (of problem, difficulty) solución *f*

resolve[1] /rɪ'zɑːlv || rɪ'zɒlv/ *n* [u] (resoluteness) resolución *f*, determinación *f*

resolve[2] *vt* [1] (clear up) ‹*difficulty*› resolver*; ‹*misunderstanding*› aclarar [2] (decide) resolver*; **to ~ to + INF** resolver* *or* decidir + INF

resolved /rɪ'zɑːlvd || rɪ'zɒlvd/ *adj* (*pred*) **to be ~ (to + INF)** estar* resuelto *or* decidido (A + INF)

resonance /'reznəns || 'rezənəns/ *n* resonancia *f*

resonant /'reznənt || 'rezənənt/ *adj* resonante

resonate /'rezneɪt || 'rezəneɪt/ *vi* resonar*

resort /rɪ'zɔːrt || rɪ'zɔːt/ *n*

[A] (for vacations) centro *m* turístico *or* vacacional; **a seaside ~** un centro turístico costero, un balneario (AmL); **a ski ~** una estación de esquí

[B] (recourse) recurso *m*; **as a/the last ~** como último recurso

r

Phrasal verb

• **resort to** [v ▸ prep ▸ o]: **to ~ to force/violence** recurrir a la fuerza/violencia; **they had to ~ to strike action** no les quedó más remedio que ir a la huelga

resound /rɪ'zaʊnd/ *vi* «*sound/voice*» retumbar, resonar*; **to ~ WITH sth** retumbar *or* resonar* CON algo

resounding /rɪ'zaʊndɪŋ/ *adj* (*before n*) [1] ‹*cheers/explosion*› retumbante, resonante [2] ‹*success/failure*› rotundo

resource /'riːsɔːrs || rɪ'sɔːs/ *n* [c] recurso *m*; **natural/human ~s** recursos naturales/humanos; **the new center is a valuable ~ for the community** el nuevo centro es un valioso servicio para la comunidad; **teaching ~s** material *m* didáctico; **left to their own ~s** librados a sus propios medios *or* recursos; (*before n*) **~ center** [1] *centro que suministra información, asesoramiento etc* [2] (Educ) centro *m* de material didáctico

resourceful /rɪ'sɔːrsfəl || rɪ'sɔːsfəl/ *adj* ‹*person*› de recursos, recursivo (Col)

respect[1] /rɪ'spekt/ *n*

[A] [1] [u] (esteem) respeto *m*; **to have ~ for sb** respetar algn; **with all due ~** con el debido respeto [2] [u] (consideration) consideración *f*, respeto *m*; **out of ~ for her feelings** por consideración *or* respeto hacia sus sentimientos; **she has no ~ for his wishes** no respeta sus deseos [3] **respects** *pl* respetos *mpl*; **to pay one's ~s to sb** presentarle sus (*or* mis *etc*) respetos a algn

[B] [1] [c] (way, aspect) sentido *m*, respecto *m*; **in all ~s, in every ~** desde todo punto de vista, en todo sentido; **in this ~** en cuanto a esto, en lo que a esto se refiere, en este sentido [2] (*in phrases*) **in respect of** (frml) con respecto a, en relación con, con relación a; **with respect to** (frml) (introducing subject) en lo que concierne a (frml), en cuanto a; (in relation to) con respecto a, con relación a

respect[2] *vt* [1] (hold in esteem) ‹*person/ability*› respetar [2] (have consideration for) ‹*feelings/wishes*› respetar, tener* en cuenta [3] (obey) ‹*rule/authority*› respetar, acatar

respectability /rɪ'spektə'bɪləti/ *n* [u] [1] (of conduct, clothes) decencia *f* [2] (of theory, writer) respetabilidad *f*

respectable /rɪ'spektəbəl/ *adj*

[A] [1] (socially acceptable) ‹*person/conduct*› decente, respetable; ‹*clothes*› decente [2] (unobjectionable) ‹*theory/writer*› respetable

[B] [1] (quite large) ‹*amount/salary*› respetable, considerable [2] (reasonably good) ‹*performance/score*› digno, aceptable

respectably /rɪ'spektəbli/ *adv* respetablemente; **~ dressed** decentemente vestido

respected /rɪ'spektəd || rɪ'spektɪd/ *adj* respetado

respecter /rɪ'spektər || rɪ'spektə(r)/ *n* (frml): **death is no ~ of persons** la muerte no hace distinción entre la gente

respectful /rɪ'spektfəl/ *adj* respetuoso; **~ TOWARD sb** respetuoso CON algn

respectfully /rɪ'spektfəli/ *adv* respetuosamente

respecting /rɪ'spektɪŋ/ *prep* (frml) en lo que concierne a (frml), con respecto a

respective /rɪ'spektɪv/ *adj* (*before n*) respectivo

respectively /rɪ'spektɪvli/ *adv* respectivamente

respiration /'respə'reɪʃən || ,resprɪ'reɪʃən/ *n* [u] respiración *f*

respirator /'respəreɪtər || 'respɪreɪtə(r)/ *n* [1] (Med) respirador *m* [2] (mask) máscara *f* de oxígeno

respiratory /'respərətɔːri || rɪ'spɪrətəri/ *adj* respiratorio

respite /'respət || 'respaɪt/ *n* [1] [c u] (*no pl*) (break — from work, worry) respiro *m*, descanso *m*; (— from pain) alivio *m*, tregua *f*; **without (a) ~** sin (un) respiro, sin descansar [2] [c] (reprieve) prórroga *f*

resplendent /rɪ'splendənt/ *adj* resplandeciente, resplendente (liter)

respond /rɪ'spɑːnd || rɪ'spɒnd/ *vi* [1] (reply) responder, contestar; **to ~ TO sth** responder *or* contestar A algo [2] (react) responder, reaccionar; **to ~ TO sth** responder A algo; **plants ~ to light** las plantas son sensibles a la luz

respondent /rɪ'spɑːndənt || rɪ'spɒndənt/ *n* (Law) demandado, -da *m,f*; (in an appeal) apelado, -da *m,f*

response /rɪ'spɑːns || rɪ'spɒns/ *n* [1] (reply) respuesta *f*; **in ~ to your letter** en respuesta a su carta [2] (reaction) ~ **(TO sth)**: **I asked the president for his ~ to the news** le pregunté al presidente cuál era su reacción ante la noticia; **their actions met with a violent ~** su conducta tuvo una respuesta violenta

responsibility /rɪ'spɑːnsə'bɪləti || rɪ,spɒnsə'bɪləti/ *n* (*pl* **-ties**) [1] [c] (task, duty) responsabilidad *f*; **the child is my ~** el niño está bajo mi responsabilidad; **it's his ~ to order the stationery** él es el encargado de hacer los pedidos de papelería [2] [u] (authority, accountability) responsabilidad *f*; **to take ~ for sth** responsabilizarse* *or* encargarse* *or* hacerse* cargo de algo [3] [u] (liability, blame) responsabilidad *f*; **they took full ~ for the disaster** aceptaron ser responsables del desastre; **no terrorist group has claimed ~ for the killings** los asesinatos no han sido reivindicados por ningún grupo terrorista

responsible /rɪ'spɑːnsəbəl || rɪ'spɒnsəbəl/ *adj* [1] (accountable) (*pred*) **to be ~ (FOR sth)**: **who's ~?** ¿quién es el responsable?; **a build-up of gas was ~ for the explosion** una acumulación de gas fue la causa de la explosión; **who was ~ for the flower arrangements?** ¿quién se encargó de los arreglos florales?; **to hold sb ~ for sth** responsabilizar* *or* hacer* responsable a algn de algo; **~ TO sb** responsable ANTE algn [2] (in charge) (*pred*) **to be ~ FOR sth** ser* responsable DE algo; **each nurse is ~ for five patients** cada enfermera tiene cinco pacientes a su cargo [3] (trustworthy) responsable, formal; **that's not**

a very ~ thing to do hacer eso demuestra falta de responsabilidad [4] (important) (*before n*) ‹*post*› de responsabilidad

responsibly /rɪ'spɑːnsəbli || rɪ'spɒnsɪbli/ *adv* con responsabilidad, responsablemente

responsive /rɪ'spɑːnsɪv || rɪ'spɒnsɪv/ *adj* ‹*brakes/engine*› sensible; ‹*person/nature/audience*› receptivo; **~ TO sth/sb**: **the public was not very ~ to the campaign** el público no respondió bien a la campaña; **the children were very ~ to the new teacher** los niños respondieron bien al nuevo profesor

rest¹ /rest/ *n*

Sense I

A [1] [c] (break) descanso *m*; **to have a ~** tomarse un descanso; **~ FROM sth**: **I need a ~ from cooking/work** necesito descansar de la cocina/de mi trabajo; ***to give sth a ~*** (colloq) dejar de hacer algo; **give it a ~!** ¡basta ya!, ¡cambia de disco! (fam) [2] [u] (relaxation) descanso *m*, reposo *m*; **try to get some/a good night's ~** trata de descansar un poco/de dormir bien esta noche; **to lay sb to ~** (euph) enterrar* *or* (frml) dar* sepultura a algn; ***to lay sth to ~*** enterrar* algo; (*before n*) ‹*day/period*› de descanso

B [u] (motionlessness) reposo *m*; **to come to ~** detenerse*; **his eyes came to ~ on the letter** sus ojos se posaron sobre la carta (liter)

C [c] (support) apoyo *m*

D [c] (Mus) silencio *m*

Sense II (remainder) **the ~**: **the ~ of the money** el resto del dinero, el dinero restante; **the ~ of them have finished** los demás han terminado; **the ~ of the children** los demás niños, los otros niños; **and all the ~ of it** y todo eso, etcétera, etcétera

rest² *vi*

A [1] (relax) descansar; **he could not ~ until he knew she was safe** no se tranquilizó hasta saber que estaba a salvo; **to ~ easy** estar* tranquilo [2] (lie buried) (liter) descansar (liter); **may she ~ in peace** que en paz descanse

B [1] (be supported) **to ~ ON sth**: **his head ~ed on my shoulder** tenía la cabeza recostada en *or* apoyada sobre mi hombro; **the structure ~s on eight massive pillars** la estructura descansa sobre ocho columnas gigantescas [2] (be based, depend) **to ~ ON sth** «*argument/theory*» estar* basado *or* basarse EN algo, descansar SOBRE algo [3] (stop) **to ~ ON sth/sb** «*eyes/gaze*» detenerse* *or* (liter) posarse SOBRE algo/algn

C [1] (remain): **let the matter ~** mejor no decir (*or* hacer *etc*) nada más [2] (be responsibility of) **to ~ WITH sb** «*responsibility*» recaer* SOBRE algn [3] (Law): **the prosecution/defense ~s** ha terminado el alegato del fiscal/de la defensa

■ **rest** *vt*

A (relax) descansar; **I stopped for a while to ~ my feet/eyes** paré un rato para descansar los pies/ojos; ▸**case¹ E**

B (place for support) apoyar; **she ~ed her elbows on the table** apoyó *or* puso los codos sobre la mesa

Phrasal verb

• **rest up** [v ▸ adv] (AmE) descansar

rest area *n* (AmE) ▸**rest stop 2**

restart /'riː'stɑːrt || ˌriː'stɑːt/ *vt* ‹*activity/work*› reanudar, reiniciar; ‹*engine/machine*› volver* a poner en marcha

■ **restart** *vi* «*activity/work*» reanudarse; «*engine/machine*» volver* a ponerse en marcha

restate /'riː'steɪt/ *vt* [1] (repeat) ‹*argument/opinion*› repetir* [2] (reformulate) ‹*theory/position*› replantear

restaurant /'restərɑːnt || 'restrɒnt/ *n* restaurante *m*, restorán *m*

restaurant car *n* (BrE) coche-comedor *m*, vagón *m* restaurante

restaurateur /'restərə'tɜːr || ˌrestərə'tɜː(r)/ *n*: *propietario de un restaurante*

restful /'restfəl/ *adj* ‹*place/music*› tranquilo, apacible; ‹*color*› relajante

rest home *n* hogar *m or* residencia *f* de ancianos, casa *f* de reposo (CS)

resting place /'restɪŋ/ *n* (euph): **his last** *o* **final ~ ~** su última morada (euf)

restitution /'restə'tuːʃən || ˌrestɪ'tjuːʃən/ *n* [u] [1] (return) (frml) restitución *f* (frml), devolución *f* [2] (compensation) (Law) indemnización *f*

restive /'restɪv/ *adj* [1] ‹*horse*› nervioso, intranquilo [2] (dissatisfied) ‹*unions/voters*› impaciente, descontento; **to get** *o* **become ~** impacientarse

restless /'restləs || 'restlɪs/ *adj* [1] (unsettled) ‹*person/manner*› inquieto; ‹*waves/wind*› (liter) agitado; **the patient had a ~ night** el paciente pasó mala noche *or* no descansó bien [2] (impatient) impaciente; **to get** *o* **become ~** impacientarse

restlessly /'restləsli || 'restlɪsli/ *adv* nerviosamente

restock /'riː'stɑːk || ˌriː'stɒk/ *vt* ‹*stores/larder*› reaprovisionar; ‹*lake/pond*› repoblar*

restoration /'restə'reɪʃən/ *n*

A [u] [1] (of democracy) restauración *f*, reinstauración *f*, restablecimiento *m*; (of order, peace) restablecimiento *m* [2] (to throne, power) restauración *f*, reinstauración *f* [3] (of sth lost, stolen) (frml) restitución *f* (frml), devolución *f*

B [u c] (of building, painting) restauración *f*

restore /rɪ'stɔːr || rɪ'stɔː(r)/ *vt*

A [1] (re-establish, bring back) ‹*order/peace*› restablecer*; ‹*confidence/health/energy*› devolver*; ‹*links/communications*› restablecer*; ‹*monarchy/king*› restaurar, reinstaurar; **her sight was ~d** recuperó *or* recobró la vista; **to ~ sb TO sth**: **the coup ~d him to power** el golpe lo colocó nuevamente en el poder; **to ~ sb to health** devolverle* la salud a algn; **to ~ sth to life** hacer* revivir algo [2] (give back) (frml) ‹*goods/property*› restituir* (frml); ‹*money*› restituir* (frml), reintegrar (frml); **to ~ sth TO sb** restituir(le)* algo A algn (frml)

B ‹*building/painting*› restaurar; **to ~ sth to its former glory** restituir* algo a su antigua grandeza

restorer /rɪ'stɔːrər || rɪ'stɔːrə(r)/ *n* [1] [c] (person) restaurador, -dora *m,f* [2] [u c] (*hair ~*) regenerador *m* de cabello

restrain /rɪ'streɪn/ *vt* ‹*prisoner/dog*› contener*; ‹*desire/anger*› dominar, contener*, refrenar; **to ~ sb FROM -ING**: **an order ~ing the company from building on the site** una orden judicial que prohíbe a la compañía construir en el predio

■ *v refl* **to ~ oneself** contenerse*, refrenarse

restrained /rɪ'streɪnd/ *adj* ‹*person/behavior/words*› moderado, comedido, medido (CS); ‹*colors/style*› sobrio

restraint /rɪ'streɪnt/ *n* [1] [u] (self-control) compostura *f*, circunspección *f*; **to show ~** mostrarse* comedido [2] [c] (restriction) limitación *f*, restricción *f*

restrict /rɪ'strɪkt/ *vt* ‹*numbers*› limitar; ‹*power/freedom/access*› restringir*, limitar; ‹*imports/movements*› restringir*; **to ~ sth/sb TO sth**: **discussion was ~ed to one issue** la discusión se limitó a un solo asunto; **access is ~ed to authorized personnel** sólo se permite la entrada al personal autorizado; **they were ~ed to barracks** (AmE Mil) estaban detenidos en el cuartel

restricted /rɪ'strɪktəd || rɪ'strɪktɪd/ *adj* [1] (limited) ‹*freedom*› restringido, limitado; ‹*number*› limitado; ‹*space*› limitado, reducido [2] (only for particular group) ‹*information*› confidencial; **~ area** (Mil) zona *f* restringida

restriction /rɪ'strɪkʃən/ *n* [c u] restricción *f*; **without ~** sin restricciones; **~ ON sth**: **there is no ~ on the amount you can buy** no hay ninguna restricción *or* ningún límite en cuanto a la cantidad que se puede comprar; **to place ~s on sth** imponer* restricciones a algo

restrictive /rɪ'strɪktɪv/ *adj* restrictivo; **~ practice** práctica *f* restrictiva (*que protege a los miembros de un sindicato etc*)

restring /'riː'strɪŋ/ *vt* (*past & past p* **restrung**) ‹*violin/guitar*› cambiarle las cuerdas a, volver* a encordar*; ‹*tennis racket*› volver* a encordar*; ‹*necklace/pearls*› reensartar, reenhebrar

rest room *n* (AmE) baño *m*, servicio(s) *m(pl)*

restructure /'riː'strʌktʃər || ˌriː'strʌktʃə(r)/ *vt* ‹*economy/debt*› reestructurar

rest stop *n* [1] (period) parada *f* de descanso [2] (place) (AmE) área *f*‡ de reposo

result¹ /rɪ'zʌlt/ *n*

A [c u] [1] (consequence) resultado *m*; **the end ~s** los resultados finales; **the company collapsed, with the ~ that ...** la compañía quebró, y como consecuencia ... [2] (of calculation, exam, contest) resultado *m*; **the election ~(s)** los resultados de las elecciones 3 **results** *pl* (favorable consequences): **to get ~s** obtener* resultados

B 1 **as a result** (*as linker*) por consiguiente, por ende (frml) 2 **as a result of** (*as prep*) a raíz de

result² *vi*: **a considerable saving would ~** se obtendría como resultado un ahorro considerable; **to ~ IN/FROM sth**: **it could ~ in his dismissal** podría ocasionar *or* acarrear su despido; **what could ~ from this decision?** ¿qué resultado podría tener esta decisión?

resultant /rɪ'zʌltənt/, **resulting** /rɪ'zʌltɪŋ/ *adj* (*before n*) consiguiente, resultante

resume /rɪ'zu:m || rɪ'zju:m/ *vt*

A (continue) ‹*work/journey*› reanudar

B (take again) ‹*power/post*› reasumir, volver* a asumir; **to ~ one's place** volver* a ocupar su (*or* mi *etc*) lugar

■ **resume** *vi* «*negotiations/work*» reanudarse, continuar*

resumé /'rezəmeɪ, 'rezə'meɪ || 'rezjʊmeɪ/ *n* 1 (summary) resumen *m*, reseña *f* 2 (of career) (AmE) currículum *m* (vitae), historial *m* personal, hoja *f* de vida (Col)

resumption /rɪ'zʌmpʃən/ *n* [u] reanudación *f*

resurface /'ri:'sɜ:rfəs || ˌri:'sɜ:fɪs/ *vt* repavimentar

■ **resurface** *vi* «*diver/submarine*» volver* a salir a la superficie; «*doubt/trend*» resurgir*, volver* a surgir

resurgence /rɪ'sɜ:rdʒəns || rɪ'sɜ:dʒəns/ *n* [u] resurgimiento *m*, renacer *m*

resurrect /'rezə'rekt/ *vt* desenterrar*, resucitar

resurrection /'rezə'rekʃən/ *n* [u] resurrección *f*; **the R~** la Resurrección

resuscitate /rɪ'sʌsəteɪt || rɪ'sʌsɪteɪt/ *vt* (Med) resucitar; (revive) ‹*career/marriage*› revitalizar*

resuscitation /rɪ'sʌsə'teɪʃən || rɪˌsʌsɪ'teɪʃən/ *n* [u] (Med) resucitación *f*; (revival) renacer *m*

ret (= **retired**) (R), (r)

retail¹ /'ri:teɪl/ *vt* vender al por menor *or* al detalle

■ **retail** *vi*: **it ~s at $85** su precio al público es de 85 dólares, se vende al por menor a 85 dólares

retail² *n* [u] venta *f* al por menor *or* al detalle; (*before n*) **the ~ trade** el comercio minorista; **~ price** precio *m* de venta al público, precio *m* al por menor

retail³ *adv* al por menor, al detalle

retailer /'ri:teɪlər || 'ri:teɪlə(r)/ *n* minorista *mf*, detallista *mf*

retail price index *n* (BrE) índice *m* de precios al consumo

retain /rɪ'teɪn/ *vt* ‹*property/money*› quedarse con; ‹*authority/power*› retener*; ‹*color/taste/heat*› conservar; ‹*moisture/water*› retener*; ‹*information*› retener*

retainer /rɪ'teɪnər || rɪ'teɪnə(r)/ *n* 1 (servant) (dated) criado, -da *m,f* 2 (fee) iguala *f* (*cuota fija que se paga para retener los servicios de algn*)

retake¹ /'ri:'teɪk/ *vt* (*past* **retook**; *past p* **retaken**) 1 (recapture) ‹*town/fort*› retomar, volver* a tomar 2 (Cin, TV) ‹*scene*› volver* a rodar *or* filmar 3 (Educ) ‹*exam/test*› volver* a presentarse a, volver* a presentar

retake² /'ri:teɪk/ *n* 1 (Cin, TV) nueva toma *f*; **to do a ~** repetir* una toma 2 (of exam): **to do a ~** volver* a presentar un examen, volver* a presentarse a un examen, volver* a examinarse (Esp)

retaliate /rɪ'tælieɪt/ *vi* 1 (Mil) tomar represalias, contraatacar* 2 (respond) responder; **he ~d by cutting her allowance** respondió quitándole la mesada; **to ~ AGAINST sb/sth** tomar represalias CONTRA algn/algo

retaliation /rɪ'tæli'eɪʃən/ *n* [u] represalias *fpl*; **in ~ for the bombing** en *or* como represalia por el bombardeo

retaliatory /rɪ'tæljətɔ:ri || rɪ'tæliətri/ *adj*: **~ measures** represalias *fpl*

retard¹ /rɪ'tɑ:rd || rɪ'tɑ:d/ *vt* ‹*growth*› retardar; ‹*progress*› retrasar

retard² /'ri:tɑ:rd || 'ri:tɑ:d/ *n* (AmE colloq & pej) tarado, -da *m,f* (fam)

retarded /rɪ'tɑ:rdəd || rɪ'tɑ:dɪd/ *adj* (sometimes offensive) retrasado; **he is mentally ~** es (un) débil *or* retrasado mental

retch /retʃ/ *vi* hacer* arcadas

retd (= **retired**) (R), (r)

retention /rɪ'tentʃən || rɪ'tenʃən/ *n* [u] retención *f*, conservación *f*; **water ~** retención de líquidos

retentive /rɪ'tentɪv/ *adj* ‹*memory/mind*› retentivo; **heat-~ material** material *m* que retiene *or* conserva el calor

rethink¹ /'ri:'θɪŋk/ *vt* (*past & past p* **rethought**) reconsiderar, replantearse

rethink² /'ri:θɪŋk/ *n* (*no pl*) replanteamiento *m*; **to have a ~** reconsiderar

reticence /'retəsəns || 'retɪsəns/ *n* [u] reticencia *f*

reticent /'retəsənt || 'retɪsənt/ *adj* reticente; **to be ~ ABOUT sth**: **she is rather ~ about her emotional life** es un tanto reservada en cuanto a su vida afectiva

retina /'retṇə || 'retɪnə/ *n* (*pl* **-nas** *or* **-nae** /-ni:/) retina *f*

retinue /'retṇu: || 'retɪnju:/ *n* séquito *m*, comitiva *f*

retire /rɪ'taɪr || rɪ'taɪə(r)/ *vi*

A (from job, occupation) jubilarse, retirarse; «*soldier*» retirarse (del servicio activo); «*athlete/footballer*» retirarse; **they ~d to Florida** cuando se jubilaron se fueron a vivir a Florida; **the retiring treasurer** el tesorero saliente *or* que se retira/retiraba

B 1 (retreat, withdraw) (frml) retirarse 2 (Mil) «*troops*» retirarse, replegarse* 3 (from sporting contest): **he ~d with an injured ankle** abandonó el campo de juego con un tobillo lesionado 4 (go to bed) (frml *or* hum) acostarse*, retirarse a sus (*or* mis *etc*) aposentos (frml *o* hum)

■ **retire** *vt* (from job) jubilar

retired /rɪ'taɪrd || rɪ'taɪəd/ *adj* jubilado, retirado; (Mil) retirado

retiree /rɪ'taɪ'ri: || rɪˌtaɪə'ri:/ *n* (AmE) jubilado, -da *m,f*

retirement /rɪ'taɪrmənt || rɪ'taɪəmənt/ *n* 1 [u c] (from job) jubilación *f*, retiro *m*; (from the military) retiro *m*; **early ~** jubilación anticipada; **he took early ~** se jubiló anticipadamente; **he's coming up to** *o* **for ~** le falta poco para jubilarse; (*before n*) **~ age** edad *f* para jubilarse; (Mil) edad *f* de retiro; **~ community** (AmE) *complejo habitacional para jubilados* 2 [u c] (from race, match) abandono *m*

retiring /rɪ'taɪrɪŋ || rɪ'taɪərɪŋ/ *adj* (shy) retraído

retort¹ /rɪ'tɔ:rt || rɪ'tɔ:t/ *vt* replicar* (liter), contestar

retort² *n* (reply) réplica *f* (liter), contestación *f*

retouch /'ri:'tʌtʃ/ *vt* retocar*

retrace /'ri:'treɪs/ *vt* ‹*events*› volver* sobre; **to ~ one's steps** volver* sobre sus (*or* mis *etc*) pasos

retract /rɪ'trækt/ *vt* 1 ‹*allegation/statement*› retirar 2 ‹*undercarriage*› replegar*, levantar

■ **retract** *vi* 1 (withdraw statement) retractarse, desdecirse* 2 «*undercarriage*» retraerse*, replegarse*

retractable, retractible /rɪ'træktəbəl/ *adj* ‹*wheels*› retráctil, replegable

retrain /'ri:'treɪn/ *vt* reciclar, recapacitar

■ **retrain** *vi* hacer* un curso de reciclaje *or* recapacitación

retread¹ /'ri:'tred/ *vt* (*past and past p* **~ed**) ‹*tire*› recauchutar, recauchar, reencauchar (AmC, Col, Ven), renovar* (Méx)

retread² /'ri:tred/ *n* neumático *m* recauchutado *or* recauchado, llanta *f* recauchutada *or* recauchada (AmL), llanta *f* reencauchada (AmC, Col, Ven), llanta *f* renovada (Méx)

retreat¹ /rɪ'tri:t/ *vi* «*forces/army*» retirarse, replegarse*

retreat² *n*

A (Mil) retirada *f*, repliegue *m*; **our forces are in ~** nuestras tropas se están batiendo en retirada; ***to beat a ~*** (Mil) batirse en retirada, retirarse; **when I saw him, I beat a hasty ~** en cuanto lo vi, puse pies en polvorosa (fam)

B 1 (place) refugio *m* 2 (Relig) retiro *m* espiritual

retrial /'ri:'traɪəl/ *n* nuevo juicio *m*, ≈ revisión *f* de la causa

retribution /'retrə'bju:ʃən || ˌretrɪ'bju:ʃən/ *n* [u] castigo *m*; **in ~, they executed all the prisoners** como represalia, ejecutaron a todos los prisioneros

retrieval /rɪ'tri:vəl/ *n* [u] 1 (of object, data) recuperación *f* 2 (of situation, mistake) reparación *f*, remedio *m*; **it's not beyond ~** no es irreparable *or* irremediable

retrieve /rɪ'tri:v/ *vt* 1 (recover) ‹*object/data*› recuperar 2 (salvage) ‹*furniture/jewels*› rescatar, salvar; ‹*situation*› salvar

■ **retrieve** *vi* «*gundog*» cobrar

retriever /rɪ'tri:vər || rɪ'tri:və(r)/ *n* perro *m* cobrador

retro- /'retrəʊ/ *pref* retro-

retroactive /ˈretrəʊˈæktɪv/ *adj* retroactivo

retrograde /ˈretrəgreɪd/ *adj* retrógrado

retrogressive /ˈretrəˈgresɪv/ *adj* ▸ **retrograde**

retrospect /ˈretrəspekt/ *n*: **in ~** mirando hacia atrás, en retrospectiva

retrospective¹ /ˈretrəˈspektɪv/ *adj* [1] (looking back) retrospectivo [2] (retroactive) retroactivo

retrospective² *n* (exposición *f*) retrospectiva *f*

retrospectively /ˈretrəˈspektɪvli/ *adv* en retrospectiva, mirando hacia atrás

retrovirus /ˈretrəʊ,vaɪrəs ‖ ˈretrəʊ,vaɪərəs/ *n* (*pl* **-ruses**) retrovirus *m*

return¹ /rɪˈtɜːrn ‖ rɪˈtɜːn/ *vi* [1] (go back) **to ~ (TO sth)** (to a place) volver* *or* regresar (A algo); (to former activity, state) volver* (A algo); **to ~ to what we were saying earlier, ...** volviendo a lo que decíamos anteriormente, ... [2] (reappear) ‹‹*symptom*›› volver* a aparecer, presentarse de nuevo; ‹‹*doubts/suspicions*›› resurgir*

■ **return** *vt*

A [1] (give back) devolver*, regresar (AmL exc CS), restituir* (frml); **she ~ed the letter to the file** volvió a poner la carta en el archivo [2] (reciprocate) ‹*affection*› corresponder a; ‹*blow/favor*› devolver*; ‹*greeting*› devolver*, corresponder a; **to ~ sb's call** devolverle* la llamada a algn [3] (Sport) ‹*ball*› devolver*

B (Law) ‹*verdict*› emitir

C (Govt) ‹*candidate*› (re-elect) reelegir*; (elect) (BrE) elegir*

return² *n*

A [u] [1] (to place) regreso *m*, vuelta *f*, retorno *m* (frml o liter); **on his ~** a su regreso, a su vuelta [2] (to former activity, state) vuelta *f*, retorno *m* [3] (reappearance) reaparición *f*; **many happy ~s of the day!** ¡feliz cumpleaños!, ¡que cumplas muchos más!

B [u c] (to owner) devolución *f*, regreso *m* (AmL); (of thing bought) devolución *f*

C (*in phrases*) **by return (of post)** (BrE) a vuelta de correo; **in return** a cambio, **in ~ FOR sth** a cambio DE algo

D [u c] (profit) **~ (ON sth)** rendimiento *m* (DE algo); **we haven't seen much ~ on our efforts** nuestros esfuerzos no se han visto muy recompensados

E [c] [1] (*tax ~*) declaración *f* (de la renta *or* de impuestos) [2] **returns** *pl* (data) datos *mpl*; (figures) cifras *fpl*

F [c] (Sport) devolución *f*

G [c] (ticket) (BrE) boleto *m or* (Esp) billete *m or* (Col) tiquete *m* de ida y vuelta, boleto *m* de viaje redondo (Méx)

return³ *adj* (*before n*) [1] ‹*journey/flight*› de vuelta, de regreso; ‹*ticket/fare*› (BrE) de ida y vuelta, de viaje redondo (Méx); **by ~ mail** (AmE) a vuelta de correo [2] (Sport) de vuelta

returnable /rɪˈtɜːrnəbəl ‖ rɪˈtɜːnəbəl/ *adj* ‹*deposit*› reembolsable, reintegrable; ‹*bottle*› retornable

reunification /riːˈjuːnəfəˈkeɪʃən ‖ ˌriːjuːnɪfɪˈkeɪʃən/ *n* [u] reunificación *f*

reunify /riːˈjuːnəfaɪ ‖ ˌriːˈjuːnɪfaɪ/ *vt* **-fies, -fying, -fied** reunificar*

reunion /riːˈjuːnjən/ *n* [c u] reunión *f*, reencuentro *m*; **a family ~** una reunión familiar

reunite /ˈriːjʊˈnaɪt/ *vt* ‹*family/party*› volver* a unir; **she was ~d with him after many years** se reencontró con él después de muchos años

■ **reunite** *vi* reunirse*; (reconcile) reconciliarse

reusable /ˈriːˈjuːzəbəl/ *adj* reutilizable, que puede utilizarse *or* usarse de nuevo

reuse /ˈriːˈjuːz/ *vt* reutilizar*, volver* a usar

rev¹ /rev/ *n* revolución *f*

rev² **-vv- ~ (up)** *vt* ‹*engine/car*› acelerar (*sin desplazarse*)

■ **rev** *vi*: **I could hear the car ~ving (up) outside** oía como aceleraban el coche afuera

Rev (= **Reverend**) Rvdo., Rdo.

revaluation /ˈriːˈvæljuˈeɪʃən/ *n* [u c] (of currency) revalorización *f*, revaluación *f* (esp AmL); (of property) reevaluación *f*, revaloración *f*

revalue /ˈriːˈvæljuː/, (AmE also) **revaluate** /-jueɪt/ *vt* ‹*currency*› revalorizar*, revaluar* (esp AmL); ‹*house*› reevaluar*, revalorar

revamp¹ /ˈriːˈvæmp/ *vt* ‹*kitchen/interior*› reformar; (modernize) modernizar*; ‹*image*› cambiar, poner* al día; ‹*organization*› modernizar*

revamp² *n* reforma *f*, modernización *f*; **our image needs a complete ~** necesitamos un cambio radical de imagen

reveal /rɪˈviːl/ *vt* [1] (disclose, make known) revelar, desvelar, develar (AmL); **I didn't want to ~ my ignorance** no quise poner de manifiesto mi ignorancia; **be patient and all will be ~ed** ten paciencia y ya te enterarás; **to ~ sth TO sb** revelarle algo A algn; **to ~ sth/sb AS sth: the structure was ~ed as (being) unsafe** se puso de manifiesto que la estructura no era segura; **this ~ed him to us as a coward/hero** esto nos demostró que era un cobarde/héroe [2] (bring to view) dejar ver

revealing /rɪˈviːlɪŋ/ *adj* ‹*document/statement*› revelador; ‹*neckline/garment*› atrevido, revelador

reveille /ˈrevəli ‖ rɪˈvæli/ *n* diana *f*, toque *m* de diana

revel /ˈrevəl/ *vi*, (BrE) **-ll-** (enjoy greatly) **to ~ IN sth** deleitarse CON *or* EN algo; **to ~ IN -ing** deleitarse + GER

revelation /ˈrevəˈleɪʃən/ *n* [c u] [1] (disclosure) revelación *f* [2] (Bib): **(the Book of) Revelations** el Apocalipsis

reveler, (BrE) **reveller** /ˈrevələr ‖ ˈrevələ(r)/ *n* (liter) juerguista *mf* (fam)

revelry /ˈrevəlri/ *n* (*pl* **-ries**) jolgorio *m*

revels /ˈrevəlz/ *pl n* fiestas *fpl*, festividades *fpl*

revenge¹ /rɪˈvendʒ/ *n* [u] venganza *f*; **to take (one's) ~** vengarse*, desquitarse; **in ~ for the death of his father** como venganza por la muerte de su padre, para vengar la muerte de su padre; **~ is sweet!** (set phrase) el placer de la venganza

revenge² *vt* vengar*; **to be ~d (ON sb)** vengarse* (DE algn)

■ *v refl* **to ~ oneself (ON sb)** vengarse* (DE algn)

revenue /ˈrevənuː ‖ ˈrevənjuː/ *n* [1] [u] (Tax) rentas *fpl* públicas; *see also* **Inland Revenue, Internal Revenue Service** [2] **revenues** *pl* ingresos *mpl*; **oil ~s** ingresos *mpl* provenientes del petróleo

reverberate /rɪˈvɜːrbəreɪt ‖ rɪˈvɜːbəreɪt/ *vi* ‹‹*sound*›› retumbar, resonar*; **the place ~d with the sound of their laughter** el lugar retumbaba con sus risas

reverberation /rɪvɜːrbəˈreɪʃən ‖ rɪˌvɜːbəˈreɪʃən/ *n* [c u] resonancia *f*, retumbo *m*; **the ~s of the financial crisis** las repercusiones de la crisis financiera

revere /rɪˈvɪr ‖ rɪˈvɪə(r)/ *vt* (frml) venerar, reverenciar (frml)

reverence /ˈrevrəns, ˈrevərəns/ *n* [1] [u] (veneration) veneración *f*, reverencia *f*; **to hold sb/sth in ~** tener* veneración *or* reverencia por algn/algo [2] (Relig) (*as form of address*) **Your Reverence** Reverencia

Reverend *adj* (in titles) reverendo; **the Right ~/Most ~ Paul Snow** el ilustrísimo (obispo/arzobispo) Paul Snow

reverent /ˈrevrənt, ˈrevərənt/ *adj* reverente

reverential /ˈrevəˈrentʃəl ‖ ˌrevəˈrenʃəl/ *adj* reverencial

reverie /ˈrevəri/ *n* [u c] ensueño *m*; **he was lost in (a) ~** estaba absorto

reversal /rɪˈvɜːrsəl ‖ rɪˈvɜːsəl/ *n* [c u]

A (inversion) inversión *f*

B (of trend, policy) cambio *m* completo *or* total; (of ruling, judgment) revocación *f*

C (setback) (frml) revés *m*

reverse¹ /rɪˈvɜːrs ‖ rɪˈvɜːs/ *n*

A [c] (of picture, paper) reverso *m*, dorso *m*; (of cloth, garment) revés *m*; (of coin) reverso *m*

B (*no pl*) [1] (opposite) **the ~: are you upset? — quite the ~** ¿estás disgustada? — no, al contrario *or* no, todo lo contrario; **the results are the ~ of what I expected** los resultados son todo lo contrario de lo que esperaba [2] (reverse order): **in ~** a la inversa, al revés

C **~ (gear)** (*no art*) marcha *f* atrás, reversa *f* (Col, Méx); **he came around the corner in ~ (gear)** dobló la esquina dando marcha atrás *or* (Col, Méx) en reversa

D [c u] (setback) (frml) revés *m*

E [c] (Sport) (in US football) reversible *f*

reverse² *vt*

A [1] (transpose) ‹*roles/positions*› invertir*; **to ~ the charges** (BrE Telec) llamar a cobro revertido *or* (Chi, Méx) por cobrar [2] (invert) ‹*order/process*› invertir*

B (undo, negate) ‹*policy*› cambiar radicalmente; ‹*trend*› invertir* el sentido de; ‹*verdict/decision/ruling*› revocar*

C ‹*vehicle*›: **she ~d her car around the corner** dobló la esquina dando marcha atrás *or* (Col, Méx) en reversa

▪ **reverse** *vi* ‹‹*vehicle/driver*›› dar* marcha atrás, meter reversa (Col, Méx)

reverse[3] *adj* (*before n*) **1** (back): **the ~ side** *o* **face** (of coin) el reverso; **the ~ side** (of cloth) el revés; (of paper) el reverso, el dorso **2** (backward, opposite) ‹*movement/direction/trend*› contrario, inverso; **in ~ order** en orden inverso

reverse: **~-charge call** /rɪ'vɜːrs'tʃɑːrdʒ || rɪˌvɜːs'tʃɑːdʒ/ *n* (BrE) llamada *f* a cobro revertido *or* (Chi, Méx) por cobrar; **~-engineer** /rɪˌvɜːrsendʒə'nɪr || rɪˌvɜːsendʒɪ'nɪə(r)/ *vt* aplicar la retroingeniería *or* la ingeniería invertida a

reversible /rɪ'vɜːrsəbəl || rɪ'vɜːsəbəl/ *adj* ‹*jacket/coat*› reversible

reversing lights /rɪ'vɜːrsɪŋ || rɪ'vɜːsɪŋ/ *pl n* (BrE) luces *fpl or* faros *mpl* de marcha atrás *or* (Col, Méx) de reversa

reversion /rɪ'vɜːrʒən || rɪ'vɜːʃən/ *n* **1** [u c] (to former state, practice) vuelta *f*, reversión *f* (frml) **2** [c] (Law) reversión *f*

revert /rɪ'vɜːrt || rɪ'vɜːt/ **to ~ to** **1** (to former state, actions) volver* A; **he soon ~ed to type** pronto volvió a ser el mismo de siempre **2** (to subject, topic) (frml) volver* A **3** (Law) ‹‹*land/possessions*›› revertir* A

review[1] /rɪ'vjuː/ *n*

A [c] **1** (of book, film) crítica *f*, reseña *f*; **to get good ~s** ser* ponderado por la crítica **2** (report, summary) resumen *m*, reseña *f* **3** (magazine) revista *f*

B **1** [c u] (reconsideration) revisión *f*; **salary under ~** el sueldo está en estudio **2** [c] (for exam) (AmE) repaso *m*

review[2] *vt*

A **1** (consider) ‹*situation*› examinar, estudiar **2** (reconsider) ‹*policy/case*› reconsiderar, reexaminar; ‹*salary*› reajustar

B **1** (summarize) ‹*news/events*› resumir, reseñar **2** (criticize) ‹*book/play*› hacer* (*or* escribir* *etc*) la crítica de, reseñar

C (Mil) ‹*troops*› pasar revista a, revistar

D (for exam) (AmE) repasar

▪ **review** *vi* (for exam) (AmE) repasar

reviewer /rɪ'vjuːər || rɪ'vjuːə(r)/ *n* crítico, -ca *m,f*

revile /rɪ'vaɪl/ *vt* (frml) injuriar (frml), vilipendiar (frml)

revise /rɪ'vaɪz/ *vt*

A **1** (alter) modificar*; **I had to ~ my opinion of her** tuve que cambiar de opinión respecto de ella **2** (Publ) corregir*, revisar

B (for exam) (BrE) repasar

▪ **revise** *vi* (BrE) repasar

revision /rɪ'vɪʒən/ *n*

A **1** [u c] (alteration) modificación *f* **2** [u c] (of text) corrección *f* **3** [c] (text) edición *f* corregida

B [u] (for exam) (BrE) repaso *m*

revitalize /'riː'vaɪtl̩aɪz/ *vt* vigorizar*, darle* vitalidad a; ‹*economy*› estimular, reactivar

revival /rɪ'vaɪvəl/ *n*

A [c u] **1** (renewal, upsurge): **there has been a ~ of interest in fifties music** ha habido un renovado interés por la música de los años cincuenta; **economic ~** reactivación *f* económica; **a religious ~** un renacer *or* un renacimiento religioso **2** (restoration — of old custom, practice) restablecimiento *m*, reinstauración *f* **3** (Med) reanimación *f*, resucitación *f*

B [c] (Theat) reestreno *m*, reposición *f*

revivalist /rɪ'vaɪvələst || rɪ'vaɪvəlɪst/ *adj* evangelista

revive /rɪ'vaɪv/ *vt* **1** (Med) reanimar, resucitar **2** (revitalize) ‹*economy*› reactivar, estimular; ‹*hope/interest/friendship*› hacer* renacer, reavivar; ‹*conversation*› reanimar **3** (reintroduce, restore) ‹*custom/practice*› restablecer* **4** (Theat) ‹*play*› reestrenar, reponer*

▪ **revive** *vi* ‹‹*industry/trade*›› reactivarse, repuntar; ‹‹*hope/interest/spirits*›› renacer*, resurgir*; ‹‹*patient*›› reanimarse; (come to) recobrar el sentido, volver* en sí; ‹‹*flowers/plant*›› revivir

revoke /rɪ'vəʊk/ *vt* revocar*

revolt[1] /rɪ'vəʊlt/ *n* [u c] revuelta *f*, levantamiento *m*, sublevación *f*; **to rise up in ~ against sb/sth** sublevarse *or* alzarse* contra algn/algo

revolt[2] *vi* (Pol) **to ~ (AGAINST sb/sth)** sublevarse *or* alzarse* (CONTRA algn/algo)

▪ **revolt** *vt* darle* asco a

revolting /rɪ'vəʊltɪŋ/ *adj* (nauseating) repugnante; (horrible) (colloq) asqueroso, horrible

revolution /'revə'luːʃən/ *n* [c u] revolución *f*

revolutionary[1] /'revə'luːʃəneri || ˌrevə'luːʃənəri/ *adj* revolucionario

revolutionary[2] *n* (*pl* **-ries**) revolucionario, -ria *m,f*

revolutionize /'revə'luːʃənaɪz/ *vt* revolucionar, cambiar radicalmente

revolve /rɪ'vɑːlv || rɪ'vɒlv/ *vi* **1** (rotate) girar; **to ~ AROUND sth** girar ALREDEDOR DE *or* EN TORNO A algo; **the world doesn't ~ around you, you know** no te creas que eres el centro del mundo **2** **revolving** *pres p* ‹*chair/door*› giratorio

revolver /rɪ'vɑːlvər || rɪ'vɒlvə(r)/ *n* revólver *m*

revue /rɪ'vjuː/ *n* [c u] revista *f*

revulsion /rɪ'vʌlʃən/ *n* [u] repugnancia *f*, asco *m*

reward[1] /rɪ'wɔːrd || rɪ'wɔːd/ *n* **1** [c u] (recompense) recompensa *f*; **teaching has its ~s** la enseñanza puede ser gratificante; **as a ~, they were allowed to go out** como premio los dejaron salir **2** [c] (sum of money) recompensa *f*

reward[2] *vt* (recompense) premiar, recompensar

rewarding /rɪ'wɔːrdɪŋ || rɪ'wɔːdɪŋ/ *adj* gratificante

rewind /'riː'waɪnd/ *vt* (*past & past p* **rewound**) rebobinar; **~ button** botón *m* de rebobinado

rewire /'riː'waɪr || ˌriː'waɪə(r)/ *vt* ‹*house*› renovar* la instalación eléctrica de

reword /'riː'wɜːrd || ˌriː'wɜːd/ *vt* ‹*question*› formular de otra manera; ‹*statement*› volver* a redactar

reworking /'riː'wɜːrkɪŋ || ˌriː'wɜːkɪŋ/ *n* [c u] (adaptation) adaptación *f*

rewound /'riː'waʊnd/ *past & past p of* **rewind**

rewrite[1] /'riː'raɪt/ *vt* (*past* **rewrote**; *past p* **rewritten**) **1** (alter) volver* a escribir *or* redactar; **to ~ history** enfocar* la historia desde una nueva perspectiva **2** (copy out) volver* a escribir, escribir* otra vez

rewrite[2] /'riːraɪt/ *n* nueva versión *f*; **to be in ~(s)** (AmE) estar* en proceso de revisión; (*before n*) **~ man** (AmE Journ) corrector *m* de estilo

rezone /'riː'zəʊn/ *vt* (in US) reclasificar*

RGN *n* (in UK) = **Registered General Nurse**

Rh /'ɑːr'eɪtʃ/ *n* (= **rhesus**) Rh. *m*; (*before n*) **~ factor** factor *m* Rh

rhapsody /'ræpsədi/ *n* (*pl* **-dies**) **1** (Mus) rapsodia *f* **2** (ecstasy): **to go into rhapsodies over** *o* **about sth** extasiarse hablando de algo

Rhesus /'riːsəs/ *n* [u] **~ factor** factor *m* Rhesus *or* Rh; **to be ~ positive/negative** ser* Rhesus positivo/negativo

rhetoric /'retərɪk/ *n* [u] retórica *f*

rhetorical /rɪ'tɔːrɪkəl || rɪ'tɒrɪkəl/ *adj* retórico; **~ question** *pregunta que se hace por su efecto retórico, a la que no se espera contestación*

rheumatic /ruː'mætɪk/ *adj* reumático

rheumatic fever *n* [u] fiebre *f* reumática

rheumatism /'ruːmətɪzəm/ *n* [u] reumatismo *m*

rheumatoid arthritis /'ruːmətɔɪd/ *n* [u] artritis *f* reumatoidea

rheumy /'ruːmi/ *adj* ‹*eyes*› lagañoso, legañoso

Rhine /raɪn/ *n* **the ~** el Rin

rhinestone /'raɪnstəʊn/ *n* [u c] estrás *m*

rhino /'raɪnəʊ/ *n* (*pl* **~** *or* **~s**) rinoceronte *m*

rhinoceros /raɪ'nɑːsrəs, -sərəs || raɪ'nɒsərəs, -srəs/ *n* (*pl* **-oses** *or* **~**) rinoceronte *m*

rhododendron /'rəʊdə'dendrən/ *n* rododendro *m*

rhombus /'rɑːmbəs || 'rɒmbəs/ *n* (*pl* **-buses** *or* **-bi** /-baɪ/) rombo *m*

Rhone /rəʊn/ *n* **the ~** el Ródano

rhubarb /'ruːbɑːrb || 'ruːbɑːb/ *n*

A [c u] (Bot, Culin) ruibarbo *m*

B **1** [c] (quarrel) (AmE sl) pelotera *f* (fam) **2** [u] (simulating conversation) (BrE hum) **~, ~ (,~)!** bla, bla, bla

rhyme[1] /raɪm/ *n* **1** [u c] (correspondence of sound) rima *f*; ***without ~ or reason*** sin ton ni son **2** [c] (word): **can you think of a ~ for 'mansion'?** ¿se te ocurre una palabra que rime con 'mansión'? **3** [c] (poem) rima *f*, poema *m* **4** [u] (rhymed verse) verso *m* (*en rima*)

rhyme[2] *vi/t* rimar

rhyming slang /ˈraɪmɪŋ/ *n* [u] *argot en el que se sustituye una palabra determinada por otra palabra o locución que rime con ella*

rhythm /ˈrɪðəm/ *n* [u c] ritmo *m*

rhythmic /ˈrɪðmɪk/, **-mical** /-mɪkəl/ *adj* rítmico

rhythm method *n*: *método anticonceptivo, como el de Ogino-Knaus, basado en la abstinencia sexual conforme al ciclo periódico de la mujer*

RI = Rhode Island

rib[1] /rɪb/ *n*

A [c u] (Anat, Culin) costilla *f*; (*before n*) ~ **roast** (AmE) *carne de vaca de junto a las costillas*

B (joke) (AmE) broma *f*

rib[2] *vt* **-bb-** (colloq) tomarle el pelo a (fam)

ribald /ˈrɪbəld/ *adj* ‹*comments/humor*› procaz, picaresco; ‹*person*› desfachatado, procaz

ribbed /rɪbd/ *adj* ‹*neck/sleeves*› en punto elástico, en canalé, en resorte (AmC, Col, Méx)

ribbing /ˈrɪbɪŋ/ *n* [u] (Clothing) elástico *m*, canalé *m*, resorte *m* (AmC, Col, Méx)

ribbon /ˈrɪbən/ *n* **1** [uc] (strip of fabric) cinta *f*, listón *m* (Méx) **2** [c] (as insignia, award) galón *m* **3** [c] (of typewriter, printer etc) cinta *f* **4** **ribbons** *pl* (shreds) jirones *mpl*; **her jacket hung in ~s** tenía la chaqueta hecha jirones

ribcage /ˈrɪbkeɪdʒ/ *n* caja *f* torácica, tórax *m*

rice[1] /raɪs/ *n* [u] arroz *m*; **brown/white ~** arroz integral/blanco; (*before n*) ~ **pudding** arroz con leche

rice[2] *vt* (AmE) ‹*potatoes*› pasar por el pasapurés *or* (RPl) por la puretera

rice: **~field** *n* arrozal *m*; **~ paper** *n* [u] papel *m* de arroz

ricer /ˈraɪsər || ˈraɪsə(r)/ *n* (AmE) pasapurés *m*, puretera *f* (RPl)

rich[1] /rɪtʃ/ *adj* **-er, -est**

A **1** (wealthy) rico; **to become ~** enriquecerse*, hacerse* rico **2** (opulent) ‹*banquet*› suntuoso, opulento; ‹*furnishings*› lujoso, suntuoso **3** (abundant) ‹*harvest/supply*› abundante; ‹*reward*› generoso; ‹*history/experience*› rico; ~ IN **sth**: ~ **in vitamins** rico en vitaminas

B **1** ‹*food*› *con alto contenido de grasas, huevos, azúcar etc*; **avoid ~ foods** evite las comidas pesadas *or* indigestas **2** ‹*soil*› rico, fértil; ‹*color*› cálido e intenso, brillante; ‹*voice*› sonoro

C (laughable) (colloq) cómico, gracioso; **that's ~ coming from you!** ¡tiene gracia que tú digas eso! (iró), ¡mira quién habla!

rich[2] *pl n* **the ~** los ricos

-rich /rɪtʃ/ *suff*: **protein~/vitamin~** rico en proteínas/vitaminas

riches /ˈrɪtʃəz || ˈrɪtʃɪz/ *pl n* riquezas *fpl*

richly /ˈrɪtʃli/ *adv* **1** (opulently) ‹*decorated/furnished*› lujosamente, suntuosamente **2** (abundantly): **they were ~ rewarded** recibieron una generosa recompensa; **the punishment they so ~ deserved** su bien merecido castigo

richness /ˈrɪtʃnəs || ˈrɪtʃnɪs/ *n* [u]

A **1** (opulence) riqueza *f*, lujo *m*, suntuosidad *f* **2** (of culture, experience) riqueza *f*

B **1** (of food) *alto contenido de grasas, huevos, azúcar etc* **2** (of soil) riqueza *f*, fertilidad *f*; (of color) brillantez *f*; (of voice) sonoridad *f*

rickets /ˈrɪkəts || ˈrɪkɪts/ *n* (+ *sing vb*) raquitismo *m*

rickety /ˈrɪkəti/ *adj* desvencijado, destartalado

rickshaw /ˈrɪkʃɔː/ *n*: *calesa oriental de dos ruedas tirada por un hombre*

ricochet[1] /ˈrɪkəʃeɪ/ *vi* **-chets** /-ʃeɪz/, **-cheting** /-ʃeɪɪŋ/, **-cheted** /-ʃeɪd/: **the bullet ~ed off the wall** la bala rebotó *or* (Méx tb) retachó en la pared

ricochet[2] *n*: **he was hit by a ~** una bala le dio de rebote *or* (Méx tb) de retacho

rid /rɪd/ *vt* (*pres p* **ridding**; *past & past p* **rid**): **he wants to ~ the city of beggars** quiere limpiar la ciudad de mendigos; **they finally ~ the country of corruption** al fin libraron al país de la corrupción; **he ~ them of their fears/doubts** (frml) disipó su miedo/sus dudas; **to get ~ of sth/sb** (of unwanted object) deshacerse* de; (sell) deshacerse* de, vender; (of boring person, cold) quitarse de encima; ‹*smell*› eliminar (frml), quitar; (kill) eliminar; **to be ~ of sth/sb**: **I'm glad to be ~ of the responsibility** me alegro de haberme librado de *or* quitado de encima esa responsabilidad; **you're well ~ of him** estás mejor sin él

riddance /ˈrɪdṇs/ *n* [u]: **good ~ (to bad rubbish)!** (colloq) ¡adiós y buen viaje! (fam & iró); **goodbye and good ~!** ¡adiós y hasta nunca!

ridden /ˈrɪdṇ/ *past p of* **ride**[1]

-ridden /ˌrɪdṇ/ *suff* **guilt~** atormentado por los remordimientos

riddle[1] /ˈrɪdḷ/ *n* **1** (puzzle) adivinanza *f*, acertijo *m*; **to speak in ~s** hablar en clave **2** (mystery) enigma *m*, misterio *m*

riddle[2] *vt* (perforate) (*often pass*) **to be ~d** WITH **sth**: **his body was ~d with bullets** lo habían acribillado a balazos; **she was ~d with cancer** tenía cáncer por todo el cuerpo, estaba cundida de cáncer (Méx); **the chairs are ~d with woodworm** las sillas están llenas de carcoma *or* todas carcomidas; **the organization is ~d with corruption** la corrupción ha llegado a todos los niveles de la organización

ride[1] /raɪd/ (*past* **rode**; *past p* **ridden**) *vt*

A (as means of transport) **1** **to ~ a horse** montar a caballo; **Paradise Boy, ridden by G. Moffatt** Paradise Boy, jineteado por G. Moffatt *or* con G. Moffatt en la monta **2** **to ~ a bicycle/motorbike** montar *or* (AmL tb) andar* en bicicleta/moto **3** (AmE) ‹*bus/subway/train*› ir* en

B **1** (traverse on horseback) ‹*countryside/plains*› recorrer a caballo **2** (run) ‹*race*› correr en

C (be carried upon) ‹*waves/wind*› dejarse llevar por

D (harass) (AmE colloq) tenerla* tomada con (fam)

■ **ride** *vi*

A **1** (on horse) montar *or* (AmL tb) andar* a caballo; **to go riding** ir* a montar *or* (AmL tb) a andar a caballo, ir* a hacer equitación; **we rode over to Garsville** fuimos a Garsville a caballo; **a boy riding on a donkey** un niño montado en un burro **2** (on bicycle, in vehicle) ir*; **we rode into town** fuimos al centro en bicicleta (*or* en moto *etc*); **can I ~ with you, John?** (esp AmE) ¿puedo ir contigo en el coche, John?

B (run, go) «*horse*» correr; «*vehicle*» andar*, marchar

C (be carried along, borne up) **to ~** ON **sth**: **they ~ on the backs of the working population** viven a costa de la clase trabajadora; ***to be riding high*** estar* en la cresta de la ola; ***to let sth ~***: **let it ~** déjalo correr *or* pasar; **to let things ~** dejar que las cosas sigan su curso

Phrasal verbs

- **ride on** [v ▸ prep ▸ o] depender de
- **ride out** [v ▸ o ▸ adv, v ▸ adv ▸ o] aguantar, sobrellevar
- **ride up** [v ▸ adv] subirse; **my skirt ~s up** se me sube la falda

ride[2] *n*

A (on horse, in vehicle etc): **let's go for a ~ on our bikes/in your car** vamos a dar una vuelta *or* un paseo en bicicleta/en tu coche; **will you give me a ~ on your back?** ¿me llevas a cuestas?; **it's only a short bus/taxi ~ from here** queda a poca distancia de aquí en autobús/taxi; **it was a long ~ and we were exhausted when we arrived** fue un viaje largo y llegamos agotados; **the firm has had a bumpy ~ recently** las cosas no han marchado muy bien para la empresa últimamente; **from then on, it was a smooth ~** de ahí en adelante, todo marchó sobre ruedas; **the audience gave her a rough ~** el público le hizo pasar un mal rato; **to hitch a ~** (esp AmE) hacer* dedo *or* auto-stop, pedir* aventón (Col, Méx fam); **she gave us a ~ into town** (esp AmE) nos llevó al centro en coche, nos acercó al centro, nos dio un aventón (Méx) *or* (Col fam) una palomita al centro; **I went along for the ~** aproveché el viaje, aproveché el aventón (Méx) *or* (Col fam) la palomita; ***to take sb for a ~*** (colloq) tomarle el pelo a algn (fam)

B (at amusement park): **the ~s** las atracciones, los juegos (AmL)

rider /ˈraɪdər || ˈraɪdə(r)/ *n*

A **1** (on horseback) jinete *mf*; (on bicycle) ciclista *mf*; (on motorbike) motociclista *mf*, motorista *mf* **2** (of subway, bus) (AmE) pasajero, -ra *m,f*, usuario, -ria *m,f*

B **1** (appended statement) cláusula *f* adicional; (condition) condición *f* **2** (Law) recomendación *f* (*del jurado*)

ridership /ˈraɪdərʃɪp || ˈraɪdəʃɪp/ *n* [u] (AmE) número *m* de usarios del transporte público

r

ridge /rɪdʒ/ *n* 1 (in plowed field) caballón *m* 2 (of hills) cadena *f*; (hilltop) cresta *f*; (on ocean floor) arrecife *m* 3 (Meteo): **a ~ of high pressure** un sistema de altas presiones

ridicule¹ /ˈrɪdəkju:l || ˈrɪdɪkju:l/ *n* [u] burlas *fpl*; **he's laying himself open to ~** se está exponiendo a hacer el ridículo *or* a que se burlen de él; **she became an object of ~** se convirtió en el hazmerreír de todos *or* en el centro de todas las burlas; **to hold sth/sb up to ~** ridiculizar* algo/a algn

ridicule² *vt* ridiculizar*, burlarse *or* reírse* de

ridiculous /rɪˈdɪkjələs || rɪˈdɪkjʊləs/ *adj* ridículo; **she made me look ~** me hizo quedar en ridículo; **they're asking a ~ price** es ridículo lo que piden

ridiculously /rɪˈdɪkjələsli || rɪˈdɪkjʊləsli/ *adv* ‹*behave/dress*› de forma ridícula; **it's ~ expensive** es terriblemente caro, es ridículo lo caro que es

riding /ˈraɪdɪŋ/ *n* [u] equitación *f*; (*before n*) ‹*school/lesson*› de equitación; ‹*breeches/boots*› de montar

rife /raɪf/ *adj* (*pred*) extendido; **disease is ~** cunden las enfermedades; **corruption is ~** reina la corrupción; **the village is ~ with gossip** corren innumerables rumores por el pueblo

riffle /ˈrɪfl/ *vi* **to ~ THROUGH sth**: **she ~d through the pages of the book** hojeó el libro

riffraff /ˈrɪfræf/ *n* [u] (+ *sing or pl vb*) chusma *f*, gentuza *f*

rifle¹ /ˈraɪfəl/ *n* (gun) rifle *m*, fusil *m*; (*before n*) **~ range** polígono *m* de tiro; (at fairground) tiro *m* al blanco

rifle² *vt* ‹*safe/drawers*› desvalijar; **they ~d her jewel box in search of the ring** le revolvieron el joyero en busca del anillo

■ **rifle** *vi* (search) **to ~ THROUGH sth** ‹*documents/papers*› hojear algo

rift /rɪft/ *n* 1 (in rock) fisura *f*, grieta *f* 2 (in cloud) (liter) claro *m* 3 (within party) escisión *f*, división *f*; (between people) distanciamiento *m*; (between countries) ruptura *f*

rig¹ /rɪg/ *n*

A (*oil ~*) plataforma *f* petrolífera *or* petrolera; (derrick) torre *f* de perforación

B (Naut) aparejo *m*

C 1 (uniform, outfit) (colloq) atuendo *m* 2 (equipment) (sl) equipo *m*

D (truck) (AmE sl) camión *m*

rig² **-gg-** *vt*

A (Naut) aparejar

B (fix) ‹*election/contest*› amañar, trinquetear (Méx fam); ‹*fight*› arreglar

Phrasal verbs

- **rig out** [v ▸ o ▸ adv, v ▸ adv ▸ o] (colloq) equipar
- **rig up** [v ▸ o ▸ adv, v ▸ adv ▸ o] 1 (set up) ‹*equipment*› instalar 2 (improvise) improvisar, armar

rigamarole /ˈrɪgəmərəʊl/ *n* (AmE) ▸**rigmarole**

rigging /ˈrɪgɪŋ/ *n* [u] (Naut) jarcia(s) *f(pl)*

right¹ /raɪt/ *adj*

A (correct) ‹*answer/interpretation*› correcto; **you made the ~ choice** elegiste bien; **are we going in the ~ direction?** ¿vamos bien?; **are you sure this is the ~ house?** ¿estás seguro de que ésta es la casa *or* de que es aquí?; **did you press the ~ button?** ¿apretaste el botón que debías?; **do you have the ~ change?** ¿tienes el cambio justo?; **do you have the ~ time?** ¿tienes hora (buena)?

B (not mistaken): **to be ~** «*person*» tener* razón, estar* en lo cierto; «*clock*» estar* bien; **how ~ she was!** ¡cuánta razón tenía!, ¡si habrá tenido razón!; **I hope you're ~** ojalá no te equivoques; **that can't be ~!** ¡no puede ser!; **to be ~ ABOUT sth/sb** tener* razón EN CUANTO A algo/algn; **to be ~ IN sth**: **am I ~ in thinking this has happened before?** si no me equivoco esto ya había pasado antes ¿no?; **to get sth ~**: **you got two answers ~** acertaste dos respuestas; **did I get your name ~?** ¿entendí bien tu nombre?; **I guess you're Bobby — that's ~!** tú tienes que ser Bobby — ¡el mismo! *or* ¡así es!; **two o'clock tomorrow, ~? — right!** a las dos mañana ¿de acuerdo? — ¡de acuerdo! *or* (esp Esp fam) ¡vale!

C (good, suitable) adecuado, apropiado; **the ~ temperature** la temperatura adecuada; **were the curtains the ~ length?** ¿estaban bien de largo las cortinas?; **the ~ side of the material** el derecho de la tela; **if the price is ~** si el precio es razonable, si está bien de precio; **just ~** perfecto; **I can't find the ~ key** no encuentro la llave que corresponde; **he knows all the ~ people** tiene muy buenos contactos; **you said all the ~ things** dijiste todo lo que tenías que decir; **this isn't the ~ time** éste no es el momento (apropiado); **those shoes don't look ~ with the coat** esos zapatos no quedan bien con el abrigo; **he's still on the ~ side of forty** todavía no tiene cuarenta; **that job is just ~ for him** el trabajo está hecho a su medida; **they're just ~ for each other** están hechos el uno para el otro

D (just, moral) (*pred*) **to be ~** ser* justo; **to be ~ to + INF** hacer* bien en + INF

E (*pred*) 1 (in order): **it's too quiet: something's not ~** hay demasiado silencio, algo pasa; **to put sth ~** arreglar algo 2 (fit, healthy) (colloq) bien; **she's not quite ~ in the head** no está muy bien de la cabeza

F (complete) (BrE colloq) (*before n*): **he's a ~ idiot** es un idiota redomado *or* de marca mayor; **he got himself into a ~ mess** se metió en un tremendo lío (fam)

G (Math): **~ angle** ángulo *m* recto; **~ triangle** (AmE) triángulo *m* rectángulo

H (*before n*) ‹*side/ear/shoe*› derecho

right² *adv*

A (correctly, well) bien, correctamente; **I had guessed ~** había adivinado, no me había equivocado; **nothing goes ~ for them** todo les sale mal, nada les sale bien; ***to do ~ by sb*** portarse bien con algn; ▸**serve¹** *vt* **B**

B 1 (all the way, completely): **the road goes ~ along the coast** la carretera bordea toda la costa; **~ from the start** desde el principio; **he put it ~ at the back** lo puso bien al fondo (de todo); **she filled it ~ up** lo llenó hasta el borde; **they kept hoping ~ up until the last moment** no perdieron las esperanzas hasta el último momento 2 (directly): **I live ~ next door** vivo justo al lado; **it's ~ in front of you** lo tienes allí delante *or* (fam) delante de las narices; **he was ~ here/there** estaba aquí mismo/allí mismo; **~ now** ahora mismo; **~ then** en ese preciso momento 3 (immediately): **~ after lunch** inmediatamente después de comer; **I'll be ~ back** vuelvo enseguida

C ‹*turn/look*› a la derecha

right³ *n*

A 1 [c u] (entitlement) derecho *m*; **~ to sth/+ INF** derecho A algo/+ INF; **the ~ of reply** el derecho a responder; **in her/his/its own ~**: **she is Queen in her own ~** es Reina a título propio *or* por derecho propio; **she is also a composer in her own ~** ella también es compositora; **the title is his by ~** el título le corresponde a él; **by what ~?** ¿con qué derecho? 2 **rights** *pl* derechos *mpl*; **film ~s** derechos cinematográficos; Ⓢ **all rights reserved** reservados todos los derechos; ***to be within one's ~s*** estar* en su (*or* mi *etc*) derecho

B [u c] (what is correct): **to know ~ from wrong** saber* distinguir entre el bien y el mal; **to be in the ~** tener* razón, llevar la razón, estar* en lo cierto; **by ~s you should have asked my permission** lo que correspondía era que me pidieras permiso; **to put** *o* **set sth to ~s** (esp BrE) arreglar algo

C 1 [u] (opposite the left) derecha *f*; **on the ~** a la derecha; **the one on the ~** el/la de la derecha; **to drive on the ~** manejar *or* (Esp) conducir* por la derecha; **keep (to the) ~** mantenga su derecha; **on** *o* **to my/your ~** a mi/tu derecha 2 (right turn): **take the next ~** tome *or* (esp Esp) coja la próxima a la derecha; **to make** *o* (BrE) **take a ~** girar *or* torcer* *or* doblar a la derecha 3 (Sport) (hand) derecha *f*; (blow) derechazo *m*

D [u] (Pol) **the ~** la derecha

right⁴ *vt* 1 (set upright) enderezar* 2 (redress) ‹*injustice*› reparar; **to ~ a wrong** reparar un daño

right⁵ *interj* (colloq) ¡bueno!, ¡vale! (Esp fam)

right: **~ angle** *n* ángulo *m* recto; **~-angled** /ˈraɪt ˌæŋgəld/ *adj* en ángulo recto; **~-angled triangle** (BrE) triángulo *m* rectángulo; **~ away** *adv* enseguida, altiro (Chi fam); **~-click** *n*: **do a ~-click on the icon** haz clic *or* (fam) cliquea con el botón derecho *or* secundario del ratón

righteous /ˈraɪtʃəs/ *adj* 1 (justified) ‹*indignation*› justificado 2 ‹*person*› recto, honrado

right field *n* (in baseball) 1 (area) jardín *m* derecho 2 (position): **to play ~ ~** jugar* de jardinero derecho

rightful /'raɪtfəl/ *adj* (*before n*) ‹*owner/heir*› legítimo; ‹*share/reward*› justo

rightfully /'raɪtfəli/ *adv*: **the title is ~ hers** el título le corresponde a ella (por legítimo derecho); **she is ~ acknowledged as ...** con justicia se la reconoce como ...

right: **~ half** *n* (Sport) medio *m* derecho; **~-hand** /'raɪt 'hænd/ *adj* (*before n*) ‹*column/gatepost*› de la derecha; **on the ~-hand side** a la derecha, a mano derecha; **the car has ~-hand drive** el coche tiene el volante a la derecha; **~-handed** /'raɪt'hændəd ‖ ˌraɪt'hændɪd/ *adj* ‹*person*› diestro; **he's ~-handed** escribe (*or* juega *etc*) con la derecha, es diestro; **~-hand man** /'raɪt'hænd/ *n* brazo *m* derecho

rightly /'raɪtli/ *adv* 1 (correctly, accurately): **if I remember ~** si mal no recuerdo; **I can't ~ say** (colloq) no sabría decir exactamente; **I don't ~ know** (colloq) no sé bien 2 (justly) con toda la razón; **~ or wrongly** justa o injustamente, con razón o sin ella

right: **~-minded** /'raɪt'maɪndəd ‖ ˌraɪt'maɪndɪd/ *adj* sensato; **~ of way** *n* (*pl* **~s of way**) 1 [u] (precedence in traffic) preferencia *f*; **to have (the) ~ of way** tener* preferencia; **to yield the ~ of way** (AmE) ceder el paso 2 [c] (across private land) servidumbre *f or* derecho *m* de paso; **~ on** *adj* (AmE colloq) (*pred*): **his analysis was ~ on** su análisis era muy acertado *or* (fam) daba justo en el clavo; **~-on** /'raɪt'ɑːn ‖ ˌraɪt'ɒn/ *adj* (BrE colloq & hum) progre (fam); **~-thinking** /'raɪt'θɪŋkɪŋ/ *adj* consciente; **~ wing** *n* 1 (Pol) (ala *f*‡) derecha *f* 2 (Sport) ala *f*‡ derecha; **~-wing** /'raɪt'wɪŋ/ *adj* derechista, de derecha *or* (Esp) de derechas; **~-winger** /'raɪt'wɪŋər ‖ ˌraɪt 'wɪŋə(r)/ *n* 1 (Pol) derechista *mf* 2 (Sport) ala *mf*‡ derecha, puntero *mf* derecho (AmS)

rigid /'rɪdʒəd ‖ 'rɪdʒɪd/ *adj* 1 (stiff) rígido; **~ with fear** paralizado de miedo; **I was bored ~** (BrE colloq) me aburrí como una ostra (fam) 2 (strict, rigorous) ‹*discipline*› estricto, riguroso; ‹*person/principles*› inflexible, rígido

rigidity /rɪ'dʒɪdəti/ *n* [u] 1 (stiffness) rigidez *f* 2 (strictness) rigidez *f*, falta *f* de flexibilidad

rigidly /'rɪdʒədli ‖ 'rɪdʒɪdli/ *adv* 1 (stiffly) rígidamente 2 (strictly) con rigidez, estrictamente

rigmarole /'rɪgmərəʊl/ *n* (colloq) 1 (procedure) lío *m* (fam), follón *m* (Esp fam) 2 (talk) historia *f* (fam)

rigor, (BrE) **rigour** /'rɪgər ‖ 'rɪgə(r)/ *n* [u c] rigor *m*

rigor mortis /'rɪgər'mɔːrtəs ‖ ˌrɪgə'mɔːtɪs/ *n* [u] rigidez *f* cadavérica; **~ ~ had set in** el cuerpo ya estaba rígido

rigorous /'rɪgərəs/ *adj* riguroso

rigorously /'rɪgərəsli/ *adv* rigurosamente, con rigor

rigour *n* (BrE) ▸ **rigor**

rig-out /'rɪgaʊt/ *n* (BrE colloq) atuendo *m*

rile /raɪl/ *vt* (colloq) irritar; **don't let it ~ you** no te hagas mala sangre por eso; **to get ~d** cabrearse (fam)

Riley /'raɪli/ *n*: ***to live the life of ~*** darse* la gran vida

rim /rɪm/ *n* (of cup, bowl) borde *m*; (of spectacles) montura *f*, armazón *m or f*; (of wheel) (Auto) llanta *f*, rin *m* (Col, Méx); (of bicycle wheel) aro *m*

rime /raɪm/ *n* [u] (frost) escarcha *f*

rimless /'rɪmləs ‖ 'rɪmlɪs/ *adj* ‹*spectacles*› sin montura *or* armazón

-rimmed /'rɪmd/ *suff*: **gold~/steel~** con montura *or* armazón de oro/de acero

rind /raɪnd/ *n* [u c] (of lemon, orange) cáscara *f*, corteza *f*; (of cheese) corteza *f*; (of bacon) piel *f*, borde *m*

ring[1] /rɪŋ/ *n*

A [c] 1 (on finger) anillo *m*; (woman's) anillo *m*, sortija *f*; (*before n*) **~ finger** (dedo *m*) anular *m* 2 (circular object): **the bull had a ~ through its nose** el toro tenía un aro en la nariz *or* una nariguera; **curtain ~** argolla *f*, anilla *f*; **napkin ~** servilletero *m* 3 (circular shape) círculo *m*; **to stand in a ~** hacer* un corro, formar un círculo; **the ~s of Saturn** los anillos de Saturno; **she put a ~ around the advertisement** marcó con un círculo el anuncio; **to have ~s around one's eyes** tener* ojeras; ***to run ~s around sth/sb*** darle* mil vueltas a algo/algn 4 (burner) (BrE) quemador *m*, hornilla *f* (AmL exc CS), hornillo *m* (Esp), hornalla *f* (RPl), plato *m* (Chi)

B [c] 1 (in boxing, wrestling) cuadrilátero *m*, ring *m* 2 (in circus) pista *f* 3 (*bull ~*) ruedo *m*

C [c] (of criminals) red *f*, banda *f*

D 1 [c] (sound of bell): **there was a ~ at the door** sonó el timbre de la puerta; **someone answered the phone after a couple of ~s** alguien contestó el teléfono después de un par de timbrazos 2 [u] (sound, resonance): **his voice has a harsh ~** su voz tiene un timbre áspero; **a name with a familiar ~ to it** un nombre muy conocido *or* que suena mucho; **a story with a ~ of truth** una historia verosímil 3 (telephone call) (BrE) (*no pl*): **to give sb a ~** llamar (por teléfono) a algn, telefonear a algn

ring[2] (*past* **rang**; *past p* **rung**) *vi*

A 1 (make sound) «*church bell*» sonar*, repicar*, tañer* (liter); «*doorbell/telephone/alarm/alarm clock*» sonar* 2 (operate bell) «*person*» tocar* el timbre, llamar al timbre; **to ~ FOR sb/sth**: **you have to ~ for service** tiene que llamar al timbre para que lo atiendan; **she rang for the butler** hizo sonar el timbre/la campanilla para llamar al mayordomo

B (telephone) (BrE) llamar (por teléfono), telefonear, hablar (Méx); **to ~ FOR sb/sth**: **she rang for a cab/doctor** llamó un taxi/al médico

C 1 (resound) resonar*; **the house rang with children's laughter** la casa resonaba con risas infantiles; **to ~ true** ser* *or* sonar* convincente; **her laughter rang hollow** su risa sonaba forzada 2 «*ears*» zumbar

■ **ring** *vt*

A 1 ‹*bell*› tocar* 2 (telephone) ‹*person*› (BrE) llamar (por teléfono), telefonear, hablarle a (Méx)

B (*past & past p* **ringed**) 1 (surround) cercar*, rodear 2 (with pen, pencil) marcar* con un círculo, encerrar* en un círculo

Phrasal verbs

• **ring back** (BrE)

A [v ▸ adv] volver* a llamar

B [v ▸ o ▸ adv] (ring again) volver* a llamar; (return call) llamar

• **ring in** [v ▸ adv ▸ o] ▸ **ring out B**

• **ring off** [v ▸ adv] (BrE) colgar*, cortar (CS)

• **ring out**

A [v ▸ adv] «*shot/voice*» oírse*, resonar*; «*bells*» sonar*, resonar*

B [v ▸ adv ▸ o]: ***to ~ out the old (year) and ~ in the new*** despedir* al año viejo y recibir al nuevo (al son de las campanas)

• **ring up**

A [v ▸ o ▸ adv, v ▸ adv ▸ o] (BrE) ▸ **ring**[2] *vt* **A2**

B [v ▸ adv] (BrE) ▸ **ring**[2] *vi* **B**

ring binder *n* archivador *m*, carpeta *f* de anillos *or* (Esp) de anillas

ringer /'rɪŋər ‖ 'rɪŋə(r)/ *n* 1 (double): **to be a (dead) ~ for sb** (colloq) ser* idéntico a algn, ser* un doble de algn 2 (*bell ~*) campanero, -ra *m,f*

ring-fence /'rɪŋfens/ *vt* 1 (enclose) cercar *or* vallar totalmente 2 (guard securely) ‹*jobs/company*› proteger* 3 (guarantee) ‹*budget/funds*› garantizar*

ringing[1] /'rɪŋɪŋ/ *adj* 1 (of, like bell): **she had a ~ noise in her ears** le zumbaban los oídos 2 ‹*denunciation*› categórico, rotundo; ‹*voice*› sonoro, resonante

ringing[2] *n* [u] 1 (of bell) repique *m*, toque *m*, tañido *m* (liter); (of handbell) toque *m* 2 (of doorbell, telephone) timbre *m* 3 (in ears) zumbido *m*

ringleader /'rɪŋˌliːdər ‖ 'rɪŋˌliːdə(r)/ *n* cabecilla *mf*

ringlet /'rɪŋlət/ *n* tirabuzón *m*, rizo *m*

ring: **~master** *n* maestro, -tra *m,f* de ceremonias; **~pull** *n* anilla *f*; (*before n*) **~pull can** (BrE) lata *f* (*que se abre tirando de una anilla*); **~ road** *n* (BrE) carretera *f or* ronda *f* de circunvalación, periférico *m* (AmC, Méx); **~side** *n*: **at the ~side** junto al cuadrilátero *or* ring; (*before n*) **~side seat** (at boxing match) asiento *m* junto al cuadrilátero *or* ring; (at other events) asiento *m or* butaca *f* de primera fila; **~tone** *n* tono *m* de llamada, ringtone *m*; **~worm** *n* [u] tiña *f*

rink /rɪŋk/ *n* (*ice ~*) pista *f* de hielo; (*skating ~*) pista *f* de patinaje

rinse[1] /rɪns/ *vt* 1 (wash) ‹*cutlery/hands*› enjuagar*; ‹*rice/mushrooms*› lavar 2 (to remove soap) ‹*clothes/hair*› enjuagar*, aclarar (Esp); ‹*dishes*› enjuagar*

■ **rinse** *vi* enjuagar*

r

(Phrasal verbs)

- **rinse off** [v ▸ o ▸ adv, v ▸ adv ▸ o] [1] ‹*suds/dirt*› quitar [2] ‹*plate*› enjuagar*
- **rinse out** [v ▸ o ▸ adv, v ▸ adv ▸ o] [1] ‹*clothes*› enjuagar* *or* (Esp) aclarar; ‹*cups/pans*› enjuagar*; **to ~ out one's mouth** enjuagarse* la boca [2] ‹*dirt/soap/shampoo*› quitar

rinse² *n* [1] (wash) enjuague *m*; **to give sth a ~** enjuagar* algo, darle* un enjuague a algo [2] (to remove soap — from clothes) enjuague *m*, aclarado *m* (Esp); (— from dishes) enjuague *m* [3] (tint) tintura *f* (*no permanente*); **she's had a blue ~** se ha dado reflejos azules

riot¹ /'raɪət/ *n* [1] (disorder) disturbio *m*; (mutiny) motín *m*; ***to run ~*** «*fans*» descontrolarse, desmadrarse (fam); **she let her imagination run ~** dio rienda suelta a su imaginación; (*before n*) ‹*gear/shield*› antidisturbios *adj inv*, antimotines *adj inv* (Col); **the ~ squad** la brigada antidisturbios [2] (hilarious occasion) (colloq) desmadre *m* (fam) [3] (funny person) (colloq): **she's a ~** es comiquísima, es un plato (AmS fam), es la monda (Esp fam) [4] (profusion): **a ~ of color** un derroche *or* una profusión de color

riot² *vi* causar disturbios *or* desórdenes; «*prisoners*» amotinarse

riot act *n*: ***to read the ~ ~*** leer* *or* cantar la cartilla

rioter /'raɪətər || 'raɪətə(r)/ *n* alborotador, -dora *m,f*, revoltoso, -sa *m,f*

rioting /'raɪətɪŋ/ *n* [u] disturbios *mpl*, desórdenes *mpl*

riotous /'raɪətəs/ *adj* [1] ‹*person/crowd/behavior*› descontrolado, desenfrenado; **~ assembly** (Law) alteración *f* del orden público [2] ‹*occasion/living*› desenfrenado

rip¹ /rɪp/ **-pp-** *vt* (tear) ‹*cloth*› rasgar*, romper*; **I've ~ped my skirt** me he hecho un roto *or* un rasgón en la falda; **he ~ped the photograph (in)to pieces** rompió la foto en mil pedazos; **she ~ped the letter open** abrió la carta de un rasgón; **the explosion ~ped the building apart** la explosión destrozó el edificio; **I ~ped out the page** arranqué la página

■ **rip** *vi*

[A] (tear) «*paper/cloth*» rasgarse*; **as I lifted my arm, I heard something ~** al levantar el brazo, oí un desgarrón *or* rasgón

[B] ***to let ~*** (colloq): **she really let ~ at me** me dijo de todo

(Phrasal verbs)

- **rip off** [v ▸ o ▸ adv, v ▸ adv ▸ o]

[A] (remove) arrancar*

[B] (sl) [1] (cheat) timar, estafar, tracalear (Méx, Ven fam); (exploit) explotar [2] (steal) afanar (arg), robar; ‹*song/idea*› fusilar(se) (fam) [3] (rob) (AmE) ‹*person/bank*› asaltar; ‹*writer/musician*› fusilar(se) (fam)

- **rip up** [v ▸ o ▸ adv, v ▸ adv ▸ o] romper*, hacer* pedazos

rip² *n* rasgón *m*, desgarrón *m*

RIP (= **rest in peace**) R.I.P.

rip cord *n* cordón *m* de apertura

ripe /raɪp/ *adj* [1] ‹*fruit/vegetables*› maduro; ‹*cheese*› a punto; **to live to a ~ old age** vivir muchos años [2] (ready) **to be ~ FOR sth**: **the time is ~ for change** están dadas las circunstancias para un cambio

ripen /'raɪpən/ *vi* madurar

■ **ripen** *vt* hacer* madurar

rip-off /'rɪpɔːf || 'rɪpɒf/ *n* (colloq) (con) timo *m*, estafa *f*; (theft) robo *m*; (copy) plagio *m*

riposte /rɪ'pəʊst || rɪ'pɒst/ *n* (frml) réplica *f* (frml)

ripple¹ /'rɪpəl/ *n* [1] [c] (on water) onda *f*; **a ~ of excitement** una oleada de entusiasmo; **a ~ of applause** un breve aplauso; **a ~ of laughter** una cascada de risas [2] [u c] (ice cream): **raspberry/chocolate ~** helado *m* de vainilla con vetas de frambuesa/chocolate

ripple² *vi* [1] (move) «*water*» rizarse*; «*wheat/grass*» mecerse*; «*muscles*» tensarse; **the lake/wheatfield ~d in the breeze** la brisa rizaba *or* ondulaba la superficie del lago/trigal (liter) [2] **rippling** *pres p* ‹*muscles*› tensado

■ **ripple** *vt* ‹*water*› rizar*; ‹*corn*› mecer*; ‹*muscles*› tensar

rip: **~roaring** /'rɪp'rɔːrɪŋ/ *adj* (journ) ‹*party*› animadísimo, bullicioso; ‹*success*› apoteósico, clamoroso; **~tide** *n* corriente *f* de resaca

rise¹ /raɪz/ *n*

[A] [1] (upward movement — of tide, level) subida *f*; (— in pitch) elevación *f*; ***to get a ~ out of sb*** (colloq) conseguir* que algn se fastidie; ***to take the ~ out of sb*** (colloq) tomarle el pelo a algn (fam) [2] (increase — in prices, interest rates) subida *f*, aumento *m*, alza *f*‡ (frml), suba *f* (RPl); (— in pressure, temperature) aumento *m*, subida *f*; (— in number, amount) aumento *m*; **to be on the ~** ir* en aumento, estar* aumentando [3] (in pay) (BrE) aumento *m*, incremento *m* (frml); **a pay ~** un aumento *or* (frml) un incremento salarial [4] (improvement) mejora *f*; **a ~ in living standards** una mejora en el nivel de vida

[B] (advance) ascenso *m*, ascensión *f*; **the ~ of Manchester as an industrial city** el surgimiento de Manchester como ciudad industrial; **the ~ and fall of sb/sth** la grandeza y decadencia de algn/algo, el auge y (la) caída de algn/algo; ***to give ~ to sth*** ‹*to belief*› dar* origen *or* lugar a algo; ‹*to dispute*› ocasionar *or* causar algo; ‹*to ideas*› suscitar algo

[C] (slope) subida *f*, cuesta *f*

rise² (*past* **rose**; *past p* **risen** /'rɪzn̩/) *vi*

[A] [1] (come, go up) subir; «*mist*» levantarse; «*sun/moon*» salir*; «*river*» crecer*; «*dough*» crecer*, subir; «*cake*» subir; «*fish*» picar*; **the curtain ~s at eight** la función empieza a las ocho; **a few eyebrows rose when ...** más de uno se mostró sorprendido cuando ...; **to ~ to the surface** salir* *or* subir a la superficie; **the color rose to her cheeks** se le subieron los colores, se ruborizó [2] (increase) «*price/temperature/pressure*» subir, aumentar; «*wind*» arreciar; «*wage/number/amount*» aumentar; «*tension*» crecer*, aumentar; **to ~ in price** subir *or* aumentar de precio [3] «*sound*» (become louder) aumentar de volumen; (become higher) subir de tono; **her voice never rose above a whisper** su voz no se elevó por encima de un susurro; **a few voices rose in protest** se alzaron algunas voces de protesta [4] (improve) «*standard*» mejorar; **their spirits rose** se les levantó el ánimo, se animaron

[B] [1] (slope upward) «*ground/land*» elevarse [2] (extend upwards) «*building/hill*» levantarse, alzarse*, erguirse* (liter)

[C] [1] (stand up) «*person/audience*» (frml) ponerse* de pie, levantarse, pararse (AmL); **to ~ to one's feet** ponerse* de pie, levantarse [2] (out of bed) levantarse; **~ and shine!** (colloq) ¡vamos, arriba y a espabilarse! (fam); **to ~ from the dead** resucitar de entre los muertos

[D] (in position, status): **he rose to the rank of general** ascendió al rango de general; **she has ~n in my estimation** ha ganado en mi estima

[E] (adjourn) (BrE) «*court/parliament*» levantar la sesión

[F] (revolt) **to ~ (up) (AGAINST sb/sth)** levantarse *or* alzarse* (CONTRA algn/algo)

[G] (originate) «*river*» (frml) nacer*

(Phrasal verbs)

- **rise above** [v ▸ prep ▸ o] ‹*disability*› sobreponerse* a; ‹*difficulty*› superar; ‹*prejudice*› estar* por encima de
- **rise to** [v ▸ prep ▸ o] [1] (respond to): **to ~ to the challenge** aceptar el reto; **to ~ to the occasion** estar* a la altura de las circunstancias [2] (be provoked by) ‹*taunt*› reaccionar frente a

riser /'raɪzər || 'raɪzə(r)/ *n*: **to be an early/late ~** ser* madrugador/dormilón

risible /'rɪzəbəl/ *adj* (frml) risible, hilarante (frml)

rising¹ /'raɪzɪŋ/ *n* [1] (rebellion) levantamiento *m* [2] (movement) subida *f*

rising² *adj* (*before n*) [1] (moving upwards) ‹*tide/level*› creciente; **the ~ sun** el sol naciente [2] (increasing) ‹*number*› creciente; ‹*temperature*› creciente, en aumento; ‹*fears/tension*› creciente, cada vez mayor; ‹*prices/interest rates*› en alza *or* en aumento; **the country is faced with ~ unemployment** el país se ve enfrentado a cifras de desempleo cada vez más altas [3] (sloping) ‹*ground*› en pendiente

rising³ *adv* (BrE Educ): **the ~ fives** los niños que están por cumplir los cinco años

rising damp *n* [u] humedad *f* (*que sube de los cimientos por las paredes*)

risk¹ /rɪsk/ *n* [1] [c u] (danger) riesgo *m*; **is there any ~ of the bomb exploding?** ¿hay algún peligro de que estalle la bomba?; **there's no ~ of anyone knowing you here** no hay riesgo *or* peligro de que alguien te conozca aquí; **at the ~ of -ING** a riesgo de + INF; **those most at ~ from the disease** los que corren mayor riesgo *or* peligro de contraer la enfermedad; **our jobs are at ~** nuestros trabajos están en *or* corren peligro; **at one's own ~** por su (*or* mi *etc*) cuenta y riesgo, bajo su (*or* mi *etc*) propia responsabilidad; **to take a ~** correr un riesgo; **to take**

~s arriesgarse, correr riesgos; **he runs the ~ of being arrested** corre el riesgo *or* peligro de que lo detengan; **it isn't worth the ~** no vale la pena arriesgarse *or* correr el riesgo; **a health ~** un peligro para la salud 2 (Fin) riesgo *m*; **to be a good/bad ~** constituir* un riesgo aceptable/inaceptable

risk[2] *vt* 1 (put in danger) arriesgar*, poner* en peligro 2 (expose oneself to) arriesgarse* a, correr el riesgo de; **he ~s failure** se arriesga a fracasar; **are you going to take your umbrella? — no, I think I'll ~ it** ¿vas a llevar el paraguas? — no, creo que me voy a arriesgar; **to ~ -ING** arriesgarse* A *or* correr el riesgo DE + INF

risky /'rɪski/ *adj* **-kier, -kiest** arriesgado, riesgoso (AmL)

risotto /rɪ'zɔːtəʊ || rɪ'zɒtəʊ/ *n* [c u] (*pl* **-tos**) risotto *m*, ≈ arroz *m* a la cazuela

risqué /rɪ'skeɪ, 'rɪskeɪ/ *adj* atrevido, subido de tono

rissole /'rɪsəʊl/ *n* ≈ croqueta *f*

rite /raɪt/ *n* rito *m*

rite of passage *n* (*pl* **~s ~ ~**) rito *m* iniciático *or* de iniciación; (*before n*) **rite(s)-of-passage** ‹*film/book/drama*› iniciático

ritual[1] /'rɪtʃuəl/ *n* [u c] ritual *m*

ritual[2] *adj* ‹*slaughter/dance*› ritual; **the ~ greetings** los saludos formularios *or* de rigor

ritualistic /'rɪtʃuə'lɪstɪk/ *adj* ritualista

ritzy /'rɪtsi/ *adj* **-zier, -ziest** lujoso

rival[1] /'raɪvəl/ *n* rival *mf*; **they were ~s for her affection** competían por su cariño; **~ TO sb/sth** rival DE algn/algo; **the product has several ~s** el producto tiene mucha competencia

rival[2] *adj* (*before n*) ‹*company*› rival, competidor; **they brought out a ~ product** sacaron un producto que les (*or* nos *etc*) va a hacer la competencia

rival[3] *vt*, (BrE) **-ll-**: **his voice ~s that of the lead singer** su voz no tiene nada que envidiarle a la del cantante principal; **I can't ~ that** con eso no puedo competir

rivalry /'raɪvəlri/ *n* [u c] (*pl* **-ries**) rivalidad *f*, competencia *f*

river /'rɪvər || 'rɪvə(r)/ *n* río *m*; **by the ~** a la orilla del río; **up/down ~** río arriba/abajo; ***to sell sb down the ~*** traicionar a algn; (*before n*) ‹*traffic/port*› fluvial; ‹*mouth/basin*› del río; ‹*fish*› de río *or* de agua dulce

river: **~bank** *n* ribera *f*, margen *f* (*de un río*); **~bed** *n* lecho *m* (*de un río*); **~ blindness** *n* [u] ceguera *f* de los ríos, oncocerosis *f* (téc); **~ Plate** *n* Río *m* de la Plata; **~side** *n* ribera *f*, margen *f* (*de un río*); (*before n*) ‹*café*› a orillas del río

rivet[1] /'rɪvət || 'rɪvɪt/ *n* remache *m*, roblón *m*

rivet[2] *vt* 1 (attach) remachar; **to ~ sth TO sth** unir algo a algo con remaches 2 (fix) (*usu pass*) **to be ~ed TO/ON sth/sb**: **my eyes were ~ed to the screen** estaba absorto, con los ojos clavados en la pantalla; **their eyes were ~ed on her** no le quitaban los ojos de encima 3 (fascinate) (*usu pass*) fascinar; **the audience was ~ed** el público estaba fascinado

riveting /'rɪvətɪŋ/ *adj* fascinante

Riviera /'rɪvi'erə || ˌrɪvi'eərə/ *n*: **the (French) ~** la Costa Azul; **the Italian ~** la Riviera

rivulet /'rɪvjələt || 'rɪvjʊlɪt/ *n* (liter) arroyo *m*, riachuelo *m*

Riyadh /riː'ɑːd || ri'jɑːd/ *n* Riad *m*, Riyad *m*

RMT *n* (in UK) = **National Union of Rail, Maritime and Transport Workers**

RN *n* 1 (in US) = **Registered Nurse** 2 (in UK) = **Royal Navy**

RNA *n* [u] (= **ribonucleic acid**) RNA *m*, ARN *m*

roach /rəʊtʃ/ *n*

A (fish) (*pl* **~** *or* **~es**) 1 (American) carpa *f* 2 (European) rubio *m*

B (*cock~*) (AmE) cucaracha *f*

road /rəʊd/ *n*

A (for vehicles — in town) calle *f*; (— out of town) carretera *f*; (— minor) camino *m*; **five miles down the ~** a cinco millas siguiendo la carretera/el camino; **there's a baker's over** *o* **across the ~** enfrente *or* al otro lado de la calle hay una panadería; **by ~** por carretera, por tierra; **my car's off the ~** (BrE) tengo el coche fuera de circulación *or* averiado; **to take to the ~** empezar* a vagar por los caminos; ***to have one for the ~*** (colloq) tomarse la del estribo, tomarse la penúltima; (*before n*) ‹*accident*› de tráfico *or* (AmL tb) de tránsito; **~ racing** (in car) carreras *fpl* automovilísticas (*en carretera*); (on foot) carrera *f* a pie por carretera; **~ safety** seguridad *f* en la carretera; **~ sense** instinto *m* de conductor; **~ sign** señal *f* vial *or* de tráfico *or* (AmL tb) de tránsito; **~ tax** impuesto *m* de rodaje, patente *f* (CS), tenencia *f* (Méx); **~ transport** transporte *m* por carretera

B (route, way) camino *m*; **we're on the right ~** vamos por buen camino *or* bien encaminados; **this could mean the end of the ~ for the company** esto podría acabar con la compañía; **the economy is on the ~ to recovery** la economía está en vías de recuperación

C **on the road**: **that car shouldn't be on the ~** ese coche no debería estar en circulación; **we've been on the ~ for four days** llevamos cuatro días viajando; **they were on the ~ before six** se pusieron en camino antes de las seis, antes de las seis ya estaban en camino; **to take a circus/band on the ~** llevar un circo/un grupo de gira; **let's get this show on the ~** (colloq) pongamos manos a la obra

road: **~block** *n* control *m* (de carretera); **~ hog** *n* (colloq) loco, -ca *m,f* del volante; **~house** *n*: *restaurante o bar al lado de la carretera*

roadie /'rəʊdi/ *n*: *persona encargada de transportar y montar el equipo de un grupo musical en gira*

road: **~map** *n* (Geog) mapa *m* de carreteras; (peace plan) hoja *f* de ruta; **~roller** /'rəʊdrəʊlər || 'rəʊdrəʊlə(r)/ *n* apisonadora *f*, aplanadora *f* (AmL); **~ show** *n* (Rad) *programa de emisiones del equipo móvil desde distintas localidades*; (Theat) *gira de una compañía de teatro*; **~side** *n* borde *m* de la carretera/del camino; (*before n*) **~side repairs** auxilio *m* en carretera; **~ sweeper** *n* (person) barrendero, -ra *m,f*; (machine) barredera *f*, barredora *f*; **~-test** *vt* someter a una prueba de carretera; **~way** *n* calzada *f*; **~works** *pl n* (BrE) obras *fpl* (de vialidad); **~worthy** *adj* **-thier, -thiest** apto para circular

roam /rəʊm/ *vt* vagar* *or* deambular por

■ **roam** *vi* vagar*, errar* (liter); **tigers ~ freely in the jungle** tigres deambulan en libertad por la selva; **to ~ AROUND** *o* (BrE also) **ABOUT sth**: **she spent the week ~ing around Paris** pasó la semana dando vueltas por París; **I'm not having you ~ing around the streets** no quiero que andes deambulando *or* vagando por las calles

roaming /'rəʊmɪŋ/ *n* [u] itinerancia *f*

roan /rəʊn/ *adj* ruano

roar[1] /rɔːr || rɔː(r)/ *vi* ‹‹*lion/tiger/engine*›› rugir*; ‹‹*sea/wind/fire*›› bramar, rugir*; ‹‹*cannon*›› tronar*; **to ~ with laughter** reírse* a carcajadas; **the trucks ~ed past** los camiones pasaron con un estruendo; **he ~ed off on his motorbike** se alejó en la moto haciendo un ruido infernal

■ **roar** *vt*: **how dare you! he ~ed** —¡cómo se atreve! —rugió *or* bramó; **the fans ~ed their appreciation** los hinchas manifestaron su aprobación a voz en cuello

roar[2] *n* [c u] (of lion, tiger) rugido *m*; (of person) rugido *m*, bramido *m*; (of thunder) fragor *m*, estruendo *m*; (of traffic, engine, guns) estruendo *m*; (of crowd) clamor *m*

roaring /'rɔːrɪŋ/ *adj* (*before n*) ‹*waves*› rugiente; ‹*traffic*› estruendoso; **we soon had a ~ fire going** a los pocos minutos el fuego ardía que daba gusto; **the fruitsellers were doing a ~ trade** los vendedores de frutas estaban haciendo su agosto

roast[1] /rəʊst/ *adj* ‹*meat/potatoes*› asado (*al horno*); ‹*coffee*› tostado, torrefacto; ‹*corn/chestnuts*› asado, a la(s) brasa(s); **~ beef** rosbif *m*, rosbeef *m*

roast[2] *n* asado *m* (*al horno*)

roast[3] *vt* 1 ‹*meat/potatoes*› asar; ‹*coffee beans*› tostar*, torrefaccionar; ‹*peanuts*› tostar* 2 (reprimand): **they were ~ed for arriving late** les dieron un buen sermón por llegar tarde 3 (ridicule) (AmE) ‹*person*› ridiculizar*

■ **roast** *vi* 1 ‹‹*meat*›› asarse 2 (be hot) (colloq) asarse (de calor) (fam)

roaster /'rəʊstər || 'rəʊstə(r)/ *n* (pan) (AmE) fuente *f* de horno (*para asados*), asadera *f* (RPl)

roasting[1] /'rəʊstɪŋ/ *n* 1 [u] (Culin) (*before n*) ‹*chicken/meat*› para asar; **~ pan** *o* (BrE) **dish** *o* **tin** fuente *f* de horno (*para asados*), asadera *f* (RPl) 2 (*no pl*) (colloq) (scolding) sermón *m*, bronca *f* (fam)

roasting[2] *adj* (colloq): **it's absolutely ~** hace un calor que te asas (fam)

r

rob /rɑ:b || rɒb/ *vt* **-bb-** [1] (steal from) ‹*bank*› asaltar, atracar*, robar; ‹*person*› robarle a; **I've been ~bed!** ¡me han robado!; **to ~ sb OF sth** robarle algo A algn [2] (deprive) **to ~ sb/sth OF sth** privar a algn/algo DE algo; **the last-minute goal ~bed them of the championship** el gol de último momento les birló el campeonato

robber /'rɑ:bər || 'rɒbə(r)/ *n* ladrón, -drona *m,f*; **bank ~** atracador, -dora *m,f or* asaltante *mf* de bancos

robbery /'rɑ:bəri || 'rɒbəri/ *n* [u c] (*pl* **-ries**) robo *m*, asalto *m*; **armed ~** asalto *m or* atraco *m* a mano armada; **bank ~** asalto *m or* atraco *m* a un banco; **it's sheer** *o* **daylight ~!** (colloq) es un auténtico robo

robe¹ /rəʊb/ *n*
A [1] (worn by magistrates, academics) (*often pl*) toga *f*; **ceremonial ~s** vestiduras *fpl* ceremoniales [2] (worn by students) (AmE) toga *f*
B (worn in house) bata *f*, salto *m* de cama (CS)

robe² *vt* (frml *or* liter) **to ~ sb (IN sth)** vestir* a algn (DE algo)

robin /'rɑ:bən || 'rɒbɪn/ *n* (European) petirrojo *m*; (N. American) ceón *m*, tordo *m* norteamericano

robot /'rəʊbɑ:t || 'rəʊbɒt/ *n* robot *m*

robust /rəʊ'bʌst/ *adj* ‹*person/animal*› robusto, fuerte; ‹*health*› de hierro; ‹*appetite*› bueno; ‹*material/construction*› resistente, sólido

rock¹ /rɑ:k || rɒk/ *n*
A [u] (substance) roca *f*
B [c] [1] (crag, cliff) peñasco *m*, peñón *m*; ***as solid as a ~*** firme *or* sólido como una roca [2] (in sea) roca *f*, escollo *m*; **the ship ran onto the ~s** el barco encalló en las rocas; ***on the ~s***: **Scotch on the ~s** whisky con hielo; **their marriage is on the ~s** su matrimonio anda muy mal [3] (boulder) roca *f* [4] (stone) piedra *f*; ***to get one's ~s off*** (AmE sl) tirar (arg), coger* (Méx, RPl, Ven vulg), follar (Esp vulg); ***to have ~s in one's head*** (AmE sl): **he has ~s in his head** le falta un tornillo
C [c] (jewel) (sl) piedra *f*
D [u] (BrE Culin) *barra de caramelo de colores*
E [u] (music) rock *m*; (*before n*) ‹*band/concert*› de rock; ‹*music*› rock *adj inv*

rock² *vt* [1] (gently) ‹*cradle*› mecer*; ‹*child*› acunar; **he ~ed Rosie to sleep** acunó a Rosie hasta que se durmió [2] (violently) sacudir, estremecer*; **the scandal ~ed New York** el escándalo convulsionó *or* conmocionó a Nueva York
■ **rock** *vi*
A [1] (gently) mecerse*, balancearse [2] (violently) ‹‹*building*›› sacudirse, estremecerse*; **to ~ with laughter** desternillarse de risa
B (Mus) rocanrolear, bailar rock

rock and roll *n* [u] ▸**rock'n'roll**

rockbottom¹ /'rɑ:k'bɑ:təm || ˌrɒk'bɒtəm/ *adj*: **~ prices** precios *mpl* bajísimos *or* de saldo

rockbottom² *n*: **to hit/reach ~** tocar* fondo

rock: **~ cake** *n* (in UK) *bollo con frutos secos*; **~ candy** *n* [u] (AmE) *dulce de azúcar cristalizado*; **~ climbing** *n* [u] escalada *f* en roca

rocker /'rɑ:kər || 'rɒkə(r)/ *n*
A [1] (under chair, cradle) balancín *m*; ***to be off one's ~*** (colloq) estar* chiflado *or* chalado (fam); ***to go off one's ~*** (colloq) perder* la chaveta (fam) [2] (rocking chair) mecedora *f*
B (rock performer, fan) rockero, -ra *m,f*

rockery /'rɑ:kəri || 'rɒkəri/ *n* (*pl* **-ries**) *jardín o parte de un jardín con rocas y plantas alpestres*

rocket¹ /'rɑ:kət || 'rɒkɪt/ *n* [1] (spacecraft) cohete *m* espacial [2] (missile) cohete *m*, misil *m*; (*before n*) **~ launcher** lanzacohetes *m*, lanzamisiles *m* [3] (firework) cohete *m*, volador *m*, cuete *m* (AmL)

rocket² *vi* [1] (rise) ‹‹*price*›› dispararse, ponerse* por las nubes; **she ~ed to stardom** se convirtió en una estrella *or* llegó al estrellato de la noche a la mañana [2] **rocketing** *pres p* ‹*inflation*› galopante; **~ing prices** precios que se disparan *or* que suben vertiginosamente
■ **rocket** *vt*: **the movie ~ed him to stardom** la película lo lanzó al estrellato

rock: **~face** *n* pared *f* rocosa; **~ garden** *n* ▸**rockery**; **~-hard** /'rɑ:k'hɑ:rd || ˌrɒk'hɑ:d/ *adj* (duro) como una piedra

Rockies /'rɑ:kiz || 'rɒki:z/ *pl n* **the ~** las (Montañas) Rocallosas *or* Rocosas

rocking /'rɑ:kɪŋ || 'rɒkɪŋ/: **~ chair** *n* mecedora *f*; **~ horse** *n* caballito *m* mecedor *or* de balancín

rock: **~'n'roll** /'rɑ:kən'rəʊl || ˌrɒkən'rəʊl/ *n* [u] rocanrol *m*, rock and roll *m*; **~ plant** *n* planta *f* rupestre; **~ salt** *n* [u] sal *f* gema *or* de grano; **~-solid** /'rɑ:k'sɑ:ləd || ˌrɒk'sɒlɪd/ *adj* (*pred* **~ solid**) sólido como una piedra; **the other states are ~-solid Republican** los otros distritos son sólidamente republicanos

rocky /'rɑ:ki || 'rɒki/ *adj* **rockier, rockiest**
A ‹*ground*› rocoso; ‹*path*› pedregoso
B (unsteady) [1] ‹*start*› incierto; ‹*period*› de incertidumbre; ‹*base*› nada sólido, tambaleante [2] ‹*furniture*› inestable, poco firme

Rocky Mountains *pl n* **the ~ ~** las Montañas Rocallosas *or* Rocosas

rococo¹ /rə'kəʊkəʊ/ *n* [u] rococó *m*

rococo² *adj* rococó *adj inv*

rod /rɑ:d || rɒd/ *n* [1] (bar) varilla *f*, barra *f*; (in engine) vástago *m* [2] (*fishing ~*) caña *f* (de pescar) [3] (for punishment) vara *f*, férula *f*; ***to make a ~ for one's own back*** crearse problemas; ***to rule with a ~ of iron*** *o* ***an iron ~*** gobernar* con mano de hierro; ***spare the ~ and spoil the child*** la letra con sangre entra

rode /rəʊd/ *past of* **ride¹**

rodent /'rəʊdn̩t/ *n* roedor *m*

rodeo /'rəʊdiəʊ, rə'deɪəʊ/ *n* (*pl* **-os**) rodeo *m*

roe /rəʊ/ *n*
A [u c] (of fish) hueva *f*
B [c] **~ (deer)** corzo, -za *m,f*

roger /'rɑ:dʒər || 'rɒdʒə(r)/ *interj* (Telec) ¡comprendido!, ¡roger!

rogue¹ /rəʊg/ *n* pícaro, -ra *m,f*, pillo, -lla *m,f*

rogue² *adj* (*before n*) [1] ‹*elephant/male*› solitario [2] ‹*trader/company*› deshonesto

roguish /'rəʊgɪʃ/ *adj* ‹*wink/grin*› pícaro, lleno de picardía; ‹*child*› pícaro, pillo

role, rôle /rəʊl/ *n* [1] (Cin, Theat) papel *m* [2] (function) papel *m*, rol *m*; **what ~ does she play in the company?** ¿qué papel desempeña *or* cuál es su rol en la compañía?; (*before n*) **~ model** modelo *m* de conducta

role-play /'rəʊlpleɪ/ *n* [c u] teatro *m* improvisado; (Psych) psicodrama *m*; (in language teaching) role-play *m*

roll¹ /rəʊl/ *n*
A (Culin) **(bread) ~** pancito *m or* (Esp) panecillo *m or* (Méx) bolillo *m*
B (of paper, wire, fabric) rollo *m*; (of banknotes) fajo *m*; **a ~ of film** un rollo *or* un carrete (de fotos), una película; **~s of fat** rollos *mpl*; (around waist) rollos *mpl*, michelines *mpl* (fam), llantas *fpl* (AmL fam)
C [1] (rocking) balanceo *m*, bamboleo *m* [2] (turning over) voltereta *f*
D (sound — of drum) redoble *m*; (— of thunder) retumbo *m*
E (list) lista *f*; **to call the ~** pasar lista; **honor ~** *o* (BrE) **~ of honour** (Mil) lista *f* de honor; (Educ) cuadro *m* de honor
F (of dice) tirada *f*; ***to be on a ~*** (AmE colloq) estar* de buena racha

roll² *vi*
A [1] (rotate) ‹‹*ball/barrel*›› rodar*; **the bottle was ~ing around inside the crate** la botella rodaba dentro del cajón; **the children were ~ing around on the ground** los niños estaban revolcándose en el suelo [2] (turn over): **the car ~ed over three times** el coche dio tres vueltas de campana; **~ (over) onto your stomach/back** ponte boca abajo/boca arriba, date la vuelta *or* (CS) date vuelta; **they all ~ed around laughing** todos se revolcaron de risa; ***to be ~ing in money*** *o* ***in it*** (colloq) estar* forrado (de oro) (fam) [3] (sway) ‹‹*ship/car/plane*›› balancearse, bambolearse
B (move) (+ *adv compl*): **the column of trucks ~ed by** los camiones pasaban uno detrás del otro; **the car began to ~ down the hill** el coche empezó a deslizarse cuesta abajo; **tanks ~ed into the capital at dawn** los tanques entraron en la capital al amanecer; **tears ~ed down his cheeks** las lágrimas le corrían por las mejillas
C (begin operating) ‹‹*camera*›› empezar* a rodar; ‹‹*press*›› ponerse* en funcionamiento; **let the good times ~!** ¡que vengan los buenos tiempos!
D (make noise) ‹‹*drum*›› redoblar; ‹‹*thunder*›› retumbar

E **rolling** *pres p* ‹*countryside/hills*› ondulado; ‹*strikes/power cuts*› escalonado
■ **roll** *vt*
A 1 ‹*ball/barrel*› hacer* rodar; ‹*dice*› tirar; **I'll ~ you for it** (AmE) vamos a echarlo a los dados 2 (turn over): **the nurse ~ed me over onto my side** la enfermera me puso de costado *or* de lado 3 **to ~ one's eyes** poner* los ojos en blanco
B ‹*cigarette*› liar*; **the hedgehog ~ed itself into a ball** el erizo se hizo un ovillo *or* una bola; **a circus, museum and craft fair all ~ed into one** un circo, un museo y una feria de artesanía, todo en uno; **she ~ed up her sleeves** se arremangó
C (flatten) ‹*lawn*› pasarle el rodillo a; ‹*dough/pastry*› estirar
D (Ling): **to ~ one's 'r's** hacer* vibrar las erres
E (sl) (rob) (AmE) asaltar; **they ~ed him for everything he had** le robaron todo lo que tenía

Phrasal verbs
- **roll back** [v ▸ o ▸ adv, v ▸ adv ▸ o] (reduce) (AmE) ‹*prices/salaries*› bajar, reducir*
- **roll by** ▸**roll on 1**
- **roll in** [v ▸ adv] 1 (arrive in large quantities) llegar* en grandes cantidades, llover* 2 (arrive late): **he ~ed in at eleven** apareció a las once
- **roll on** [v ▸ adv] 1 (pass) «*time/months*» pasar 2 (arrive) (colloq): **~ on vacation time!** ¡que lleguen pronto las vacaciones!
- **roll out**
A [v ▸ o ▸ adv, v ▸ adv ▸ o] ‹*dough/pastry*› estirar
B [v ▸ adv] (AmE colloq) levantarse (de la cama)
- **roll over** [v ▸ o ▸ adv, v ▸ adv ▸ o] ‹*loan/repayments*› refinanciar
- **roll up** [v ▸ adv] (arrive) (colloq) aparecer*; **they finally ~ed up at ten** finalmente aparecieron a las diez; **~ up, ~ up!** (BrE) ¡acérquense y miren!; *see also* **roll²** *vt* **B**

roll: ~back *n* (AmE) reducción *f* (*a un nivel anterior*); **~ call** *n* 1 (calling of roll): **~ call is 9 a.m.** pasan lista a las nueve de la mañana 2 (list) lista *f*
rolled /rəʊld/ *adj*: **~ gold** metal *m* (en)chapado en oro; **~ oats** copos *mpl* de avena
rolled-up /'rəʊld'ʌp/ *adj* ‹*newspaper*› enrollado; ‹*umbrella*› cerrado
roller /'rəʊlər || 'rəʊlə(r)/ *n*
A (for lawn, in machine, for applying paint) rodillo *m*
B (for hair) rulo *m*, rulero *m* (Per, RPl), marrón *m* (Col), tubo *m* (Méx, Chi); **to put one's hair in ~s** ponerse* rulos (*or* ruleros *etc*)
C (for moving sth) 1 (cylinder) rodillo *m* 2 (caster) ruedecita *f*, ruedita *f* (esp AmL)
D (wave) ola *f* grande
roller: ~ blind *n* persiana *f or* cortina *f* de enrollar; **~ coaster** *n* montaña *f* rusa; **~ derby** *n* (AmE) carrera *f* de patinaje (sobre ruedas); **~ skate** *n* patín *m* (de ruedas); **~-skate** /'rəʊlərskeɪt || 'rəʊləskeɪt/ *vi* patinar (*sobre ruedas*); **to go ~-skating** ir* a patinar; **~ skating** *n* [u] patinaje *m* (*sobre ruedas*)
rolling /'rəʊlɪŋ/: **~ pin** *n* rodillo *m*, palo *m or* palote *m* de amasar (RPl), rollo *m* pastelero (Esp), uslero *m* (Chi); **~ stock** *n* [u] material *m* rodante *or* móvil
roll: ~neck *n* (BrE) **~neck (collar)** cuello *m* vuelto *or* alto *or* (RPl) volcado; **~neck (sweater)** suéter *m* de cuello vuelto *or* alto *or* (RPl) volcado; **~-on** *adj* (*before n*) ‹*deodorant*› de bola; **~out** /'rəʊlaʊt/ *n* [u] 1 (launch) lanzamiento *m*, presentación *m* 2 (of aircraft) rodaje *m* por la pista de aterrizaje; **~-top** /'rəʊl'tɑːp || 'rəʊltɒp/ *adj* (*before n*) ‹*desk/breadbin*› de tapa corrediza
roly-poly /'rəʊli'pəʊli/ *adj* (colloq) gordinflón (fam), regordete
ROM /rɑːm || rɒm/ *n* [u] (= **read-only memory**) ROM *f*
Roman¹ /'rəʊmən/ *adj* 1 (of, from Rome) romano; **a ~ nose** un perfil romano 2 **roman** ‹*numeral*› romano; ‹*alphabet*› latino; **~ type** letra *f* redonda
Roman² *n* romano, -na *m,f*
Roman Catholic¹ *n* católico, -ca *m,f*
Roman Catholic² *adj* católico
romance¹ /rə'mæns, 'rəʊmæns || rəʊ'mæns/ *n*
A 1 [c] (affair) romance *m*, idilio *m* 2 [u] (feeling) romanticismo *m* 3 [u] (attractive quality) lo romántico, lo poético
B [c u] (Lit) 1 (love story) novela *f* romántica *or* de amor, novela *f* rosa (fam) 2 (tale of chivalry) novela *f* de caballerías, romance *m*
C [u] **Romance** (Ling) romance *m*
romance² *vi* (have love affair) tener* amores; (fantasize) fantasear, soñar*
Romance /rə'mæns, 'rəʊmæns || rəʊ'mæns/ *adj* ‹*languages*› romance, románico
Romania /rəʊ'meɪniə/ *n* Rumania *f*, Rumanía *f*
Romanian¹ /rəʊ'meɪniən/ *adj* rumano
Romanian² *n* 1 [u] (language) rumano *m* 2 [c] (person) rumano, -na *m,f*
Romansch, Romansh /rəʊ'mɑːntʃ || rəʊ'mænʃ/ *n* [u] romanche *m*, rético *m*
romantic¹ /rəʊ'mæntɪk, rə-/ *adj* romántico
romantic² *n* romántico, -ca *m,f*
romantically /rəʊ'mæntɪkli, rə-/ *adv* de manera romántica; **to be ~ involved with sb** estar* involucrado sentimentalmente con algn
romanticism /rəʊ'mæntəsɪzəm, rə- || rəʊ'mæntɪsɪzəm/ *n* [u] romanticismo *m*
romanticize /rəʊ'mæntəsaɪz, rə- || rəʊ'mæntɪsaɪz/ *vt* idealizar*
Romany¹ /'rɑːməni, 'rəʊ- || 'rɒməni, 'rəʊ-/ *adj* gitano
Romany² *n* (*pl* **-nies**) 1 [c] (person) gitano, -na *m,f* 2 [u] (language) romaní *m*
Rome /rəʊm/ *n* Roma *f*; ***~ wasn't built in a day*** no se ganó Zamora en una hora; ***when in ~, do as the Romans (do)*** donde fueres haz lo que vieres
romp¹ /rɑːmp || rɒmp/ *n* 1 (frolic) retozo *m* 2 (sexual) revolcón *m* (fam) 3 (play, film, novel) (journ) *obra divertida y sin pretensiones* 4 (easy race to win) carrera *f* fácil
romp² *vi* 1 (frolic) retozar* 2 (move boisterously) correr alegremente 3 (move with ease) (+ *adv compl*): **she ~ed through the exam** no tuvo problemas para hacer el examen; **he ~ed home** ganó sin dificultades, barrió (fam)
rompers /'rɑːmpərz || 'rɒmpəz/ *pl n*, (also BrE) **romper suit** /'rɑːmpər || 'rɒmpə(r)/ *n* mameluco *m* (AmL), pelele *m* (Esp), enterito *m* (RPl), osito *m* (Chi)
roof¹ /ruːf/ *n* (*pl* **~s** /ruːfs, ruːvz/) 1 (of building) tejado *m*, techo *m* (AmL); **she found herself without a ~ over her head** se quedó sin techo; **to live under the same ~** vivir bajo el mismo techo; ***to go through/hit the ~*** «*prices*» dispararse, ponerse* por las nubes; «*person*» ponerse* furioso, explotar (fam); ***to raise the ~*** poner* el grito en el cielo; (*before n*) **~ garden** terraza *f or* azotea *f* ajardinada; **~ restaurant** restaurante *m* panorámico (*en lo alto de un edificio*) 2 (of car) techo *m*; (*before n*) **~ rack** baca *f*, portaequipajes *m*, parrilla *f* (AmL) 3 **the ~ of the mouth** el paladar
roof² *vt* techar
roofing /'ruːfɪŋ/ *n* [u] materiales *mpl* para techar
rooftop /ruːftɑːp || 'ruːftɒp/ *n* tejado *m*, techo *m* (AmL); ***to shout sth from the ~s*** proclamar algo a los cuatro vientos
rook /rʊk/ *n* 1 (Zool) grajo *m* 2 (in chess) torre *f*
rookery /'rʊkəri/ *n* (*pl* **-ries**) 1 (colony of rooks) colonia *f* de grajos 2 (breeding place) lugar *m* de cría, colonia *f*
rookie /'rʊki/ *n* (colloq) 1 (novice) novato, -ta *m,f*, principiante *mf*, bisoño, -ña *m,f* 2 (military recruit) recluta *m*
room¹ /ruːm, rʊm/ *n*
A [c] (in house, building) habitación *f*, pieza *f* (esp AmL); (bedroom) habitación *f*, dormitorio *m*, cuarto *m*, pieza *f* (esp AmL), recámara *f* (Méx); (for meeting) sala *f*; (for wedding reception) sala *f*, salón *m*; Ⓢ **rooms to hire** *o* **for rent** *o* (BrE also) **to let** se alquilan habitaciones; (*before n*) **~ temperature** temperatura *f* ambiente
B [u] (space) espacio *m*, lugar *m*, sitio *m*; **there's ~ for one more** cabe uno más, hay espacio *or* sitio *or* lugar para uno más; **there's ~ for improvement** se puede mejorar; **there is no ~ for delay/error** no hay ningún margen para retrasos/errores; ▸**cat**
room² *vi*: **I'm ~ing with another student** vivo con *or* comparto una habitación (*or* un apartamento *etc*) con otro estudiante
room clerk *n* (AmE) recepcionista *mf*
roomer /'ruːmər, 'rʊ- || 'ruːmə(r)/ *n* (AmE) inquilino, -na *m,f*

r

roomful /'ru:mfʊl, 'rʊm-/ *n*: **a ~ of people** una habitación llena de gente

rooming house /'ru:mɪŋ, 'rʊmɪŋ/ *n* (AmE) pensión *f*

room: **~mate** *n* (sharing room) compañero, -ra *m,f* de habitación *or* de cuarto; (sharing apartment) compañero, -ra *m,f* de apartamento *or* (Esp) de piso; **~ service** *n* [u] servicio *m* a las habitaciones

roomy /'ru:mi, 'rʊmi/ *adj* **-mier, -miest** amplio

roost¹ /ru:st/ *n* percha *f*, palo *m*; ***to rule the ~*** llevar la batuta

roost² *vi* posarse (*para pasar la noche*); ***to come home to ~***: **they've neglected the problem for years and now the** *o* **their chickens are coming home to ~** llevan años sin ocuparse del problema y ahora están pagando las consecuencias

rooster /'ru:stər || 'ru:stə(r)/ *n* (esp AmE) gallo *m*

root¹ /ru:t/ *n*

A (of plant, hair, tooth) raíz *f*; **to pull a plant up by the** *o* **its ~s** arrancar* una planta de raíz; **to take ~** ‹‹*plant*›› echar raíces, arraigar*; ‹‹*idea*›› arraigarse*; **to put down ~s** ‹‹*person*›› echar raíces, afincarse*; (*before n*) **~ vegetable** *raíz o tubérculo comestible como la zanahoria, el boniato etc*

B **1** (origin) raíz *f*; **to get to the ~ of a problem** llegar* a la raíz de un problema; (*before n*) **~ cause** causa *f* fundamental **2** **roots** *pl* (family, background) raíces *fpl*

C (Ling) raíz *f*

D (Math) raíz *f*

root² *vi*

A (search, forage) ‹‹*pig*›› hozar*; **she was ~ing around in the attic for her racket** estaba hurgando entre las cosas del desván buscando su raqueta

B (Bot) echar raíces, arraigar*

Phrasal verbs

- **root for** [v ▸ prep ▸ o] (support) ‹*team*› animar, alentar; ‹*candidate/party*› hacer* campaña por
- **root out** [v ▸ o ▸ adv, v ▸ adv ▸ o] **1** (remove) ‹*corruption*› arrancar* de raíz, erradicar* **2** (find) ‹*cause/truth*› averiguar*

root beer *n* [u c] (in US) *refresco hecho con distintas raíces*

rooted /'ru:təd || 'ru:tɪd/ *adj* arraigado; **he stood there, ~ to the spot** se quedó como clavado *or* paralizado donde estaba; **a deeply ~ prejudice** un prejuicio profundamente arraigado; **to be ~ IN sth** originarse *or* tener* sus orígenes EN algo

rooter /'ru:tər || 'ru:tə(r)/ *n* (AmE colloq) hincha *mf* (fam)

rootless /'ru:tləs || 'ru:tlɪs/ *adj* desarraigado

rope¹ /rəʊp/ *n* [c u] cuerda *f*, soga *f*; (Naut) cabo *m*; ***give them enough ~ and they'll hang themselves*** déjalos hacer lo que quieran y ya verás cómo se cavan su propia fosa; ***to show sb/know the ~s***: **Mike will show you the ~s** Mike te enseñará cómo funciona todo; **ask Helen, she knows the ~s** pregúntale a Helen, que está muy al tanto de todo

r

rope² *vt* **1** (tie) atar, amarrar (AmL exc RPl) (*con una cuerda*) **2** (lasso) (AmE) ‹*steer/cattle*› enlazar* *or* (Méx) lazar* *or* (CS) lacear

Phrasal verbs

- **rope in** [v ▸ o ▸ adv, v ▸ adv ▸ o] (recruit) (colloq) (*usu pass*) agarrar (fam)
- **rope off** [v ▸ o ▸ adv, v ▸ adv ▸ o] ‹*area*› acordonar

rope ladder *n* escala *f* *or* escalera *f* de cuerda *or* de soga

ropey, ropy /'rəʊpi/ *adj* **ropier, ropiest** (BrE colloq) ‹*wine*› malo, chungo (Esp arg); **I feel a bit ~** me siento bastante mal, estoy bastante pachucho (Esp fam)

rosary /'rəʊzəri/ *n* (*pl* **-ries**) rosario *m*; **to say the ~** rezar* el rosario

rose¹ /rəʊz/ *past of* **rise²**

rose² *n*

A (Bot) (flower) rosa *f*; (plant) rosal *m*; **life's not all ~s** la vida no es un lecho de rosas; **she's an English ~** es la típica belleza inglesa con cutis de porcelana; ***everything's coming up ~s*** todo está saliendo a pedir de boca; (*before n*) **~ bush** rosal *m*

B (on watering can, shower) roseta *f*, alcachofa *f*, flor *f* (RPl), regadera *f* (Col, Méx, Ven)

rosé /rəʊ'zeɪ || 'rəʊzeɪ/ *n* [u c] (vino *m*) rosado *m*

rose: **~bud** *n* capullo *m* *or* pimpollo *m* de rosa; **~-colored** /'rəʊz'kʌlərd || 'rəʊzkʌləd/ *adj* ▸ **rose-tinted**; **~hip** *n* escaramujo *m*

rosemary /'rəʊz,meri || 'rəʊzməri/ *n* [u] romero *m*

rose-tinted /'rəʊz'tɪntəd || ,rəʊz'tɪntɪd/ *adj*: ***to see things through ~ glasses*** *o* ***spectacles*** ver* las cosas de color de rosa

rosette /rəʊ'zet/ *n* escarapela *f*

rose: **~water** *n* [u] agua *f*‡ de rosas; **~wood** *n* [u] palo *m* de rosa, palisandro *m*

Rosh Hashana(h) /'rəʊʃhə'ʃɑ:nə || ,rɒʃ,hə'ʃɑ:nə,rɒʃ,hɑ:'ʃɑ:nɑ:/ *n* el Año Nuevo judío

roster /'rɑ:stər || 'rɒstə(r)/ *n* **1** (*duty ~*) lista *f* de turnos **2** (list) lista *f*

rostrum /'rɑ:strəm || 'rɒstrəm/ *n* (*pl* **-trums** *or* **-tra** /-trə/) (for public speaking) tribuna *f*, estrado *m*; (for orchestra conductor) podio *m*

rosy /'rəʊzi/ *adj* **rosier, rosiest** ‹*cheeks*› sonrosado; ‹*outlook*› halagüeño, optimista

rot¹ /rɑ:t || rɒt/ *n* [u] **1** (Biol) podredumbre *f*, putrefacción *f*; **the ~ set in** las cosas empezaron a decaer *or* a venirse abajo; **to stop the ~** tomar medidas para cortar por lo sano **2** (nonsense) (esp BrE colloq) tonterías *fpl*

rot² **-tt-** *vi* ‹‹*plant/flesh*›› pudrirse*; **to ~ away** pudrirse*

■ **rot** *vt* ‹*wood/tree*› pudrir*; **sugar ~s the teeth** el azúcar pica *or* caria los dientes

rota /'rəʊtə/ *n* (BrE) lista *f* (de turnos)

rotary /'rəʊtəri/ *adj* ‹*motion/movement*› rotatorio, rotativo; ‹*mower*› rotatorio

rotate /'rəʊteɪt || rəʊ'teɪt/ *vi* **1** (turn about axis) girar, dar* vueltas, rotar **2** (take turns) turnarse, rotarse

■ **rotate** *vt* **1** (turn, spin) (hacer*) girar, dar* vueltas a **2** (alternate) ‹*crops*› alternar, rotar

rotation /rəʊ'teɪʃən/ *n* [u c] rotación *f*; **we deal with the calls in strict ~** atendemos las llamadas por estricto orden de llegada

rote /rəʊt/ *n*: **by ~** de memoria; (*before n*) **~ learning** memorización *f*

rotisserie /rəʊ'tɪsəri/ *n* **1** (restaurant) asador *m*, grill *m* (CS), asadero *m* (Col) **2** (spit) asador *m*, spiedo *m* (CS)

rotor /'rəʊtər || 'rəʊtə(r)/ *n* rotor *m*

rotten /'rɑ:tn || 'rɒtn/ *adj* **1** (decayed) ‹*wood/fruit*› podrido; ‹*tooth*› picado, cariado; **to spoil sb ~** mimar demasiado, malcriar* a algn **2** (bad) (colloq) ‹*weather*› horrible, asqueroso; ‹*food/film/novel*› pésimo; **that's a ~ thing to do** eso es una maldad; **he's a ~ singer** canta pésimo; **to feel ~** (ill) sentirse* mal *or* pésimo *or* (Esp fam) fatal; **I felt ~ about leaving her alone** me sentí mal por haberla dejado sola

rotund /rəʊ'tʌnd/ *adj* (corpulent) (hum & euph) voluminoso, rechoncho

rouble /'ru:bəl/ *n* (BrE) rublo *m*

rouge /ru:ʒ/ *n* [u] colorete *m*

rough¹ /rʌf/ *adj* **-er, -est**

A **1** (not smooth) ‹*surface/texture/skin*› áspero, rugoso; ‹*cloth*› basto; ‹*hands*› áspero, basto; ***to take the ~ with the smooth*** estar* a las duras y a las maduras **2** (uneven) ‹*ground/road*› desigual, lleno de baches; ‹*terrain*› agreste, escabroso **3** ‹*sea*› agitado, picado, encrespado; ‹*weather*› tempestuoso, tormentoso; **we had a ~ crossing** el barco se movió mucho durante la travesía **4** ‹*sound/voice*› áspero, ronco

B (colloq) **1** (unpleasant, hard) ‹*life*› duro; **she had a ~ time of it** lo pasó muy mal; **to be ~ ON sb** ser* duro CON algn **2** (ill): **I feel a bit ~** no estoy muy bien, me siento bastante mal

C (not gentle) ‹*child/game*› brusco; ‹*neighborhood*› peligroso; **you'll break the doll if you're too ~ with it** vas a romper la muñeca si no la tratas con más cuidado; **~ stuff** (colloq) violencia *f*

D **1** (crude, unpolished) tosco, rudo; **a ~ draft** un borrador; **it was ~ justice** el castigo fue duro pero justo *or* merecido **2** (approximate) aproximado; **can you give me a ~ idea how much it'll cost?** ¿me puede dar más o menos una idea de lo que costará?; **it would take six months, at a ~ guess** calculo que llevaría unos seis meses más o menos *or* aproximadamente

rough² *adv* **1** ‹*sleep/live*› *a la intemperie o sin las comodidades más básicas* **2** (violently): **if he won't agree, they'll play**

it ~ si no acepta, se van a poner duros; **to cut up ~** (colloq) ponerse* hecho una fiera (fam)

rough³ *n*
A (in golf) **the ~** el rough
B (draft) borrador *m*; **in (the) ~** en borrador

rough⁴ *vt*: **to ~ it** (colloq) pasar sin comodidades

Phrasal verbs

- **rough out** [v ▸ o ▸ adv, v ▸ adv ▸ o] ‹*drawing*› bosquejar, esbozar*; ‹*speech*› preparar en borrador
- **rough up** [v ▸ o ▸ adv, v ▸ adv ▸ o] (colloq) darle* una paliza a

roughage /ˈrʌfɪdʒ/ *n* [u] fibra *f* (*de los alimentos*)

rough: **~-and-ready** /ˈrʌfənˈredi/ *adj* improvisado; **~-and-tumble** /ˈrʌfənˈtʌmbəl/ *n* [u]: **kids enjoy a bit of ~-and-tumble** a los niños les gustan los juegos bruscos

roughen /ˈrʌfən/ *vt* poner* áspero

roughly /ˈrʌfli/ *adv* 1 (approximately) aproximadamente; **~ speaking, the organ acts as a filter** el órgano se comporta como un filtro, por así decirlo 2 (not gently) ‹*play*› bruscamente, de manera violenta; **to treat sb ~** maltratar *or* tratar mal a algn 3 (crudely) toscamente

roughneck /ˈrʌfnek/ *n* (colloq & pej) matón *m*

roughness /ˈrʌfnəs ‖ ˈrʌfnɪs/ *n* [u]
A 1 (of texture) aspereza *f* 2 (of terrain) lo agreste *or* escabroso 3 (of sea) lo agitado
B (violence) brusquedad *f*, violencia *f*

roughshod /ˈrʌfˈʃɑːd ‖ ˈrʌfʃɒd/ *adv*: **to ride ~ over sth/sb**: **he rides ~ over other people's feelings** no tiene la menor consideración para con los sentimientos de los demás; **she will ride ~ over anyone who stands in her way** se llevará por delante a quien se interponga en su camino

roulette /ruːˈlet/ *n* [u] ruleta *f*; (*before n*) **~ wheel** ruleta *f*

Roumania /ruːˈmeɪniə/ *etc* ▸**Romania** *etc*

round¹ /raʊnd/ *adj*
A 1 (circular, spherical) redondo 2 (not angular) ‹*corner*› curvo; **she has very ~ shoulders** es muy cargada de espaldas, es muy encorvada
B ‹*number*› redondo

round² *n*
A [c] (circle) círculo *m*, redondel *m*, redondela *f* (Andes); **theater in the ~** teatro *m* circular
B [c] 1 (series) serie *f*; **~ of talks** ronda *f* de conversaciones; **the daily ~** la rutina diaria; **his life is one long ~ of meetings** su vida es una continua sucesión de reuniones 2 (burst): **let's have a ~ of applause for ...** un aplauso para ...
C [c] (Sport, Games) (of tournament, quiz) vuelta *f*; (in boxing, wrestling) round *m*, asalto *m*; (in golf) vuelta *f*, recorrido *m*; (in showjumping) recorrido *m*; (in card games) partida *f*
D 1 (of visits) (*often pl*): **the doctor is off making his ~s** *o* (BrE) **is on his ~s** el doctor está haciendo visitas a domicilio *or* visitando pacientes; **the nurse does her ~ of the wards at midday** la enfermera hace la ronda de las salas a mediodía; **we had to make** *o* (BrE) **do** *o* **go the ~s of all the relatives** tuvimos que ir de visita a casa de todos los parientes 2 [c] (of watchman) ronda *f*; (of postman, milkman) (BrE) recorrido *m*; **he does a paper ~** hace un reparto de periódicos
E [c] (of drinks) ronda *f*, vuelta *f*, tanda *f* (Col, Méx); **this is my ~** esta ronda *or* vuelta *or* (Col, Méx tb) tanda la pago yo
F [c] (shot) disparo *m*; (bullet) bala *f*
G [c] (of bread) (BrE): **a ~ of toast** una tostada *or* (Méx) un pan tostado; **a ~ of sandwiches** un sándwich
H [c] (Mus) canon *m*

round³ *vt* 1 (go around) ‹*corner*› doblar, dar* la vuelta a 2 (make round) ‹*edge*› redondear

Phrasal verbs

- **round down** [v ▸ o ▸ adv, v ▸ adv ▸ o] ‹*price/total*› redondear (*por defecto*)
- **round off**
A [v ▸ o ▸ adv, v ▸ adv ▸ o] 1 ‹*sharp edge*› redondear, alisar 2 (end suitably) ‹*day/meal*› terminar, rematar 3 ‹*number*› redondear
B [v ▸ adv] concluir*, terminar
- **round on** [v ▸ prep ▸ o] volverse* contra
- **round up** [v ▸ o ▸ adv, v ▸ adv ▸ o] 1 ‹*price/total*› redondear (*por exceso*) 2 ‹*sheep/cattle*› rodear, reunir*; ‹*criminals*› hacer* una redada de; ‹*people*› reunir*

round⁴ *adv* (esp BrE)
A 1 (in a circle): **we walked all the way ~** dimos toda la vuelta; **they ran ~ and ~** dieron vueltas y vueltas corriendo; **all year ~** durante todo el año 2 (so as to face in different direction): **to spin ~** dar media vuelta; *see* **turn round** 3 (on all sides) alrededor; **everyone crowded ~** todo el mundo se apiñó alrededor
B 1 (from one place, person to another): **to have a look ~** echar un vistazo; **the curator took us ~** el conservador nos mostró *or* nos enseñó el museo (*or* la colección *etc*); **a list was handed ~** se hizo circular una lista 2 (at, to different place): **she's ~ at Ed's** está en casa de Ed; **we're having friends ~ for a meal** hemos invitado a unos amigos a comer; *see also* **call round** 3 **all round** (in every respect) en todos los sentidos; (for everybody) a todos; **he bought drinks all ~** compró bebidas para todos

round⁵ *prep* (esp BrE)
A (encircling) alrededor de; **the wall ~ the garden** el muro que rodea el jardín; **~ the corner** a la vuelta (de la esquina)
B 1 (in the vicinity of) cerca de, en los alrededores de; **she lives ~ here** vive por aquí; **~ about 5 o'clock** alrededor de las cinco 2 (within, through): **he does odd jobs ~ the house** hace arreglitos en la casa; **we had a look ~ the cathedral** (le) echamos un vistazo a la catedral

round- /raʊnd/ *pref*: **~faced** de cara redonda; **~shouldered** cargado de espaldas, encorvado

roundabout¹ /ˈraʊndəbaʊt/ *n* (BrE) 1 ▸**merry-go-round** 2 (in park) tiovivo *m* 3 (Transp) rotonda *f*, glorieta *f*, óvalo *m* (Per)

roundabout² *adj* ‹*route*› indirecto; **he said it in a very ~ way** lo dijo con muchos rodeos *or* circunloquios

rounded /ˈraʊndəd ‖ ˈraʊndɪd/ *adj*
A 1 (curved) redondeado 2 (plump) relleno, rellenito (fam) 3 (Culin) ‹*teaspoon/tablespoon*› colmado
B ‹*view/report*› equilibrado

rounders /ˈraʊndərz/ *n sing* (UK) *juego parecido al béisbol*

roundly /ˈraʊndli/ *adv* 1 ‹*assert/condemn/deny*› rotundamente, categóricamente; ‹*criticize*› duramente 2 ‹*defeat*› completamente, de manera aplastante

roundness /ˈraʊndnəs ‖ ˈraʊndnɪs/ *n* [u] redondez *f*

round: **~ robin** *n* 1 (petition, protest) *petición o protesta colectiva en la cual los nombres de los firmantes forman un círculo* 2 (circular, memo) circular *f* 3 (tournament) (esp AmE) torneo *m* (*en el que cada participante se enfrenta con cada uno de los demás*); **~ table** *n* mesa *f* redonda; (*before n*) **~-table discussion** mesa *f* redonda; **~ the clock** *adv* las 24 horas, día y noche; **~ trip** *n* 1 (there and back) (viaje *m* de) ida *f* y vuelta, viaje *m* redondo (Méx) 2 (return fare) (AmE) tarifa *f* de ida y vuelta *or* (Méx) de viaje redondo; (*before n*) **~-trip ticket** pasaje *m or* (Esp) billete *m* de ida y vuelta, boleto *m* redondo (Méx) 3 (circular route) (BrE) circuito *m*; **~-up** *n* 1 (of livestock) rodeo *m* 2 (by police, army) redada *f* 3 (summary) resumen *m*, síntesis *f*

rouse /raʊz/ *vt* 1 (wake, stir) **to ~ sb (FROM** *o* **OUT OF sth)** despertar* a algn (DE algo) 2 (arouse) provocar*; **to ~ sb TO sth**: **his criticism ~d me to action** sus críticas me movieron a hacer algo

rousing /ˈraʊzɪŋ/ *adj* ‹*speech*› vehemente, enardecedor; ‹*cheers/applause*› caluroso, entusiasta

rout¹ /raʊt/ *n* derrota *f* aplastante

rout² *vt* derrotar *or* vencer* de forma aplastante

Phrasal verb

- **rout out** [v ▸ o ▸ adv, v ▸ adv ▸ o] 1 (chase) hacer* salir 2 (find) encontrar*; (look for) buscar*

route¹ /ruːt, raʊt ‖ ruːt/ *n* 1 (way) camino *m*, ruta *f*; (of bus) ruta *f*, recorrido *m*; **air/sea ~** ruta aérea/marítima; **if you want to go that ~** (AmE colloq) si quieres hacerlo de esa manera 2 (highway) (AmE) carretera *f*, ruta *f* (RPl) 3 (delivery round) (AmE) recorrido *m*

route² *vt* (*pres p* **routing** *or* (BrE also) **routeing**) enviar*; **the plane was ~d through Frankfurt to avoid the fog** desviaron el avión a Francfort debido a la niebla

router *n* /ˈraʊtər‖ ˈruːtə/ 1 (in carpentry) acanalador *m* 2 (Comput) router *m*, enrutador *m*, encaminador *m*

routine[1] /ruː'tiːn/ *n*
A [c u] (regular pattern) rutina *f*; **as a matter of ~** como rutina
B [c] (of gymnast, skater, comedian) número *m*
routine[2] *adj* **1** (usual) ‹*procedure/inquiries/investigation*› de rutina **2** (ordinary, dull) rutinario
routinely /ruː'tiːnli/ *adv* como rutina, rutinariamente
routing number /'ruːtɪŋ/ *n* (in US) código *m* de sucursal y banco
rove /rəʊv/ *vt* recorrer, vagar* *or* (liter) errar* por
■ **rove** *vi* «*eyes/gaze*» recorrer; **to ~ OVER sth** recorrer algo
rover /'rəʊvər || 'rəʊvə(r)/ *n* trotamundos *mf*
roving /'rəʊvɪŋ/ *adj* (*before n*) errante; **~ reporter** periodista *mf* sin destino fijo
row[1] *n*
(Sense I) /rəʊ/
A **1** (straight line) hilera *f*; (of people, seats) fila *f*; **they lined up in ~s** hicieron filas *or* se formaron en fila; **a seat in the front/fifth ~** un asiento en primera fila/en la quinta fila **2** (in knitting) vuelta *f*, corrida *f* (Chi)
B (succession) serie *f*; **four times in a ~** cuatro veces seguidas
C (Leisure, Sport): **we went for a ~** fuimos a remar
(Sense II) /raʊ/ **1** (noisy argument) pelea *f*, riña *f*; **to have a ~ with sb** pelearse *or* reñir* con algn **2** (about a public matter) disputa *f* **3** (noise) (*no pl*) ruido *m*, bulla *f* (fam)
row[2] *vt* /rəʊ/: **he ~ed the boat towards the shore** remó hacia la orilla; **we ~ed them across the river** los llevamos hasta la otra orilla a remo
■ **row** *vi*
(Sense I) /rəʊ/ remar; **to go ~ing** salir* *or* ir* a remar; **to ~ across a river** cruzar* un río a remo
(Sense II) /raʊ/ pelearse, reñir*
rowan /'rəʊən/ *n* **~ (tree)** serbal *m*
rowboat /'rəʊbəʊt/, (BrE) **rowing boat** /'rəʊɪŋ/ *n* bote *m* a remo *or* de remos
rowdy /'raʊdi/ *adj* **-dier, -diest** ‹*person*› escandaloso, alborotador; (quarrelsome) pendenciero; ‹*place*› bullicioso; ‹*meeting*› tumultuoso
rower /'rəʊər || 'rəʊə(r)/ *n* remero, -ra *m,f*
row house /'rəʊ/ *n* (AmE) *casa adosada en una hilera de casas idénticas*
rowing /'rəʊɪŋ/ *n* [u]
A /'rəʊɪŋ/ (Sport) remo *m*
B /'raʊɪŋ/ (quarrelling) peleas *fpl*, riñas *fpl*
rowing boat *n* (BrE) ▸**rowboat**
royal[1] /'rɔɪəl/ *adj* **1** (monarchic) real; **princess ~** *título conferido a veces a la hija mayor de un monarca británico* **2** (magnificent) espléndido, regio **3** (AmE colloq) (*as intensifier*) ‹*nuisance*› soberano (fam)
royal[2] *n* (journ) miembro *mf* de la familia real
royal: **~-blue** /'rɔɪəl'bluː/ *adj* (*pred* **~ blue**) azul real *adj inv*; **~ Highness** *n*: **Her/Your R~ Highness** Su/Vuestra Alteza Real
royalist[1] /'rɔɪəlɪst/ *n* monárquico, -ca *m,f*
royalist[2] *adj* monárquico
royal jelly *n* [u] jalea *f* real
royally /'rɔɪəli/ *adv* **1** ‹*entertain/welcome*› espléndidamente, con mucha pompa **2** (AmE colloq) (*as intensifier*) ‹*annoy*› soberanamente
royalty /'rɔɪəlti/ *n* (*pl* **-ties**)
A [u] **1** (people) (+ *sing or pl vb, no art*): **when ~ is** *o* **are in residence** cuando algún miembro de la familia real está en palacio; **we were treated like ~** nos trataron a cuerpo de rey **2** (status) realeza *f*
B [c] (payment) (*often pl*) derechos *mpl* de autor, regalías *fpl*, royalties *mpl*
rpm (= revolutions per minute) r.p.m.
RSPCA *n* (in UK) **= Royal Society for the Prevention of Cruelty to Animals**
RSVP (please reply) s.r.c., se ruega contestación, R.S.V.P.
Rt Hon (UK title) **= Right Honourable**
rub[1] /rʌb/ **-bb-** *vt* **1** (with hand, finger) frotar; (firmly) restregar*, refregar*; (massage) masajear, friccionar; **to ~ one's eye/eyes** restregarse* *or* refregarse* *or* (Méx) tallarse el ojo/los ojos; **~ the cream on your skin** aplíquese frotando la crema en la piel; **to ~ one's hands together** frotarse las manos; **~ the fat into the flour** mezclar la grasa y la harina con los dedos; ***not to have two farthings** o **halfpennies** o **pennies to ~ together*** (BrE) no tener* donde caerse muerto (fam); ***to ~ sb the wrong way*** (AmE) caerle* mal a algn **2** (with a cloth) frotar; **she ~bed the glass clean** frotó el cristal hasta que quedó limpio
■ **rub** *vi* **to ~ AGAINST/ON sth**: **these shoes ~ against** *o* **on my heels** estos zapatos me rozan los talones; **the cat ~bed against my legs** el gato se me restregó contra las piernas
(Phrasal verbs)
• **rub down** [v ▸ o ▸ adv, v ▸ adv ▸ o] **1** ‹*horse*› almohazar*; **~ yourself down well with a towel** séquese bien frotándose *or* dándose fricciones con una toalla **2** (using sandpaper) lijar
• **rub in** [v ▸ o ▸ adv, v ▸ adv ▸ o] ‹*cream/lotion*› aplicar* frotando; **~ in the butter** mezcle la mantequilla deshaciéndola con los dedos; ***to ~ it in***: **there's no need to ~ it in!** no hace falta que me (*or* se *etc*) lo refriegues por la nariz *or* las narices
• **rub off**
A [v ▸ o ▸ adv, v ▸ adv ▸ o] ‹*dirt/marks*› quitar frotando *or* restregando *or* refregando; (from blackboard) (BrE) borrar
B [v ▸ adv] (come off) «*dirt/stain*» salir* (*al frotar*)
• **rub off on** [v ▸ adv ▸ prep ▸ o]: **I hope his luck will ~ off on me** espero que se me contagie *or* (fam) se me pegue su suerte
• **rub out** [v ▸ o ▸ adv, v ▸ adv ▸ o] **1** ‹*writing*› borrar **2** (kill) (AmE sl) pasaportar (arg), liquidar (fam)
• **rub up** [v ▸ o ▸ adv, v ▸ adv ▸ o] ‹*metal*› pulir, sacarle* brillo a; ‹*wood*› lustrar, sacarle* brillo a; ***to ~ sb up the wrong way*** caerle* mal a algn
• **rub up against** [v ▸ adv ▸ prep ▸ o] «*cat*» frotarse *or* restregarse* contra
rub[2] *n*
A **1** (act): **give my feet a ~** masajéame los pies **2** (polish): **to give sth a ~** frotar algo (con un paño)
B (difficulty) **the ~** el problema
rubber /'rʌbər || 'rʌbə(r)/ *n*
A **1** [u] (substance) goma *f*, caucho *m*, hule *m* (Méx); (*before n*) **~ ring** flotador *m* **2** [c] (eraser) (BrE) goma *f* (de borrar), borrador *m* (Col) **3** **rubbers** *pl* (AmE) chanclos *mpl or* (CS) galochas *fpl* **4** [c] (condom) (esp AmE sl) globo *m* (Esp fam), paracaídas *m* (fam), goma *f* (fam), forro *m* (RPl fam)
B [c] (in bridge, whist) rubber *m*, serie *f* de partidos
rubber: **~ band** *n* goma *f* (elástica), gomita *f* (RPl), banda *f* elástica (Ven), elástico *m* (Chi), caucho *m* (Col), liga *f* (Méx); **~ bullet** *n* bala *f* de goma *or* caucho *or* (Méx) hule; **~neck** *vi* (AmE sl) (snoop) (pej) curiosear, fisgonear (fam); (sightsee) hacer* turismo; **~necker** /'rʌbər,nekər || 'rʌbə,nekə(r)/ *n* (AmE sl) (staring, gaping person) (pej) mirón, -rona *m,f* (fam); (sightseer, tourist) turista *mf*; **~ plant** *n* ficus *m*, gomero *m* (CS), caucho *m* (Col); **~ stamp** *n* (device) sello *m*, tampón *m*; (approval) visto *m* bueno; **~-stamp** /'rʌbər'stæmp || ,rʌbə'stæmp/ *vt* ‹*paper/invoice*› sellar; (approve) ‹*decision/proposal/application*› autorizar*; **~ tree** *n* árbol *m* del caucho, caucho *m* (Col), hule *m* (Méx)
rubbery /'rʌbəri/ *adj* ‹*texture*› gomoso; ‹*material*› parecido a la goma *or* al caucho *or* (Méx) al hule; ‹*meat/cheese*› correoso
rubbing /'rʌbɪŋ/ *n* **1** [u] (action) frotamiento *m*, fricción *f* **2** [c] (Art) *calco obtenido pasando carboncillo sobre imágenes grabadas en metal, monedas etc*
rubbish[1] /'rʌbɪʃ/ *n* [u] **1** (refuse) basura *f*; **household ~** residuos *mpl* domésticos; (*before n*) ‹*bag*› de *or* para la basura; **~ bin** (BrE) cubo *m or* (CS) tacho *m or* (Méx) bote *m or* (Col) caneca *f or* (Ven) tobo *m* de la basura; **~ dump** *o* **tip** (BrE) vertedero *m* (de basuras), basurero *m*, basural *m* (AmL) **2** (junk) (colloq) porquerías *fpl* (fam) **3** (nonsense) (colloq) tonterías *fpl*, estupideces *fpl*, chorradas *fpl* (Esp fam), pavadas *fpl* (RPl fam); **to talk ~** decir* estupideces (*or* tonterías *etc*)
rubbish[2] *vt* (BrE) poner* por los suelos
rubbishy /'rʌbɪʃi/ *adj* (worthless) ‹*novel/movie*› pésimo, de porquería (AmS fam); ‹*souvenirs*› de pacotilla
rubble /'rʌbəl/ *n* [u] escombros *mpl*

r

rub-down /ˈrʌbdaʊn/ *n* fricción *f*, friega *f*; **to give a horse a ~** almohazar* un caballo

rube /ruːb/ *n* (AmE sl) pueblerino, -na *m,f*, paleto, -ta *m,f* (Esp fam & pey), pajuerano, -na *m,f* (RPl fam & pey), indio, -dia *m,f* (Méx fam)

rubella /ruːˈbelə/ *n* [u] rubeola *f*, rubéola *f*

ruble, (BrE) **rouble** /ˈruːbəl/ *n* rublo *m*

rubric /ˈruːbrɪk/ *n* 1 (heading) título *m*, epígrafe *m*, rúbrica *f* 2 (introduction, explanation) *instrucciones impresas en un examen*

ruby /ˈruːbi/ *n* [c] (*pl* **rubies**) (gem) rubí *m*; (*before n*) **~ wedding (anniversary)** bodas *fpl* de rubí

ruby-red /ˈruːbiˈred/ *adj* (*pred* **ruby red**) rojo rubí *adj inv*

RUC *n* = **Royal Ulster Constabulary**

ruche[1] /ruːʃ/ *n*: *tira de tela plisada o fruncida*

ruche[2] *vt* (gather) fruncir*; (pleat) plisar

ruck /rʌk/ *n* (pucker) pliegue *m*; (wrinkle) arruga *f*

Phrasal verb

- **ruck up** [v ▸ adv] arrugarse*

rucksack /ˈrʌksæk, ˈrʊk-/ *n* mochila *f*, morral *m*

ruckus /ˈrʌkəs/ *n* (*pl* **-uses**) (colloq) jaleo *m* (fam), follón *m* (Esp fam)

ructions /ˈrʌkʃənz/ *pl n* (colloq) jaleo *m* (fam), follón *m* (Esp fam)

rudder /ˈrʌdər || ˈrʌdə(r)/ *n* timón *m*

ruddy /ˈrʌdi/ *adj* **-dier, -diest**
A (reddish) ‹*complexion*› rubicundo; ‹*glow/sky*› rojizo
B (BrE colloq & dated) maldito (fam), condenado (fam)

rude /ruːd/ *adj*
A 1 (bad-mannered) ‹*person*› maleducado, grosero; ‹*remark*› grosero, descortés; **they were very ~ about my cooking** hicieron comentarios muy poco amables sobre la comida que había preparado; **to be ~ TO sb** ser* grosero CON algn; **it's ~ to speak with your mouth full** es (de) mala educación hablar con la boca llena 2 (vulgar) (esp BrE) grosero; **he said a ~ word** dijo una grosería *or* una palabrota *or* una mala palabra
B (liter) 1 ‹*tools*› rudimentario 2 ‹*person*› tosco, basto
C (harsh) brusco; ▸**awakening**
D (robust) (liter): **to be in ~ health** gozar* de muy buena salud

rudely /ˈruːdli/ *adv* (impolitely) groseramente

rudeness /ˈruːdnəs || ˈruːdnɪs/ *n* [u] 1 (impoliteness) grosería *f*, mala educación *f* 2 (vulgarity) (BrE) ordinariez *f*

rudimentary /ˈruːdəˈmentri || ˌruːdɪˈmentri/ *adj* rudimentario

rudiments /ruːdəmənts || ˈruːdɪmənts/ *pl n* rudimentos *mpl*, nociones *fpl* elementales

rue /ruː/ *vt* lamentar, arrepentirse* de

rueful /ˈruːfəl/ *adj* atribulado, compungido

ruefully /ˈruːfəli/ *adv* con arrepentimiento

ruff /rʌf/ *n* (collar) gorguera *f*; (on animal, bird) collar *m*

ruffian /ˈrʌfiən/ *n* rufián *m*, villano *m*

ruffle[1] /ˈrʌfəl/ *n* (frill) volante *m or* (RPl) volado *m or* (Chi) vuelo *m*

ruffle[2] *vt* 1 (disturb, mess) ‹*hair*› alborotar, despeinar; ‹*feathers*› erizar*; ‹*clothes*› arrugar* 2 (irritate, upset) ‹*person*› alterar, contrariar

ruffled /ˈrʌfəld/ *adj*
A 1 (crumpled, messed) ‹*hair*› alborotado, despeinado; ‹*feathers*› erizado; ‹*clothes/fabric*› arrugado 2 (irritated, discomposed) alterado; **to get ~** alterarse
B (with ruffles) ‹*dress/shirt/hem*› con volantes *or* (RPl) volados *or* (Chi) vuelos

rug /rʌg/ *n* 1 (small carpet) alfombra *f*, alfombrilla *f*, tapete *m* (Col, Méx); ▸**pull**[1] **A2** 2 (blanket) manta *f* de viaje 3 (toupee) (AmE colloq) peluquín *m*, tupé *m*

rugby /ˈrʌgbi/ *n* [u] rugby *m*; (*before n*) **~ league/union** *rugby que se juega con trece/quince jugadores en cada equipo*

> **rugby**
>
> En el rugby, los equipos tratan de llevar la pelota, de forma ovalada, o darle con el pie hacia la línea de gol del equipo contrario a fin de marcar un ensayo (*try*). Pueden obtener más puntos con una conversión (*conversion*), es decir, lanzando la pelota con el pie por entre los postes de la portería contraria. También se pueden ganar más puntos con los *penalty goals* y los *drop goals* o puntos marcados tirando a la portería con el pie, durante el juego. Existen dos sistemas, el de la *Rugby League* y el de la *Rugby Union*, que difieren ligeramente en cuanto a las normas y al tanteo. Los equipos de la primera, están compuestos por trece jugadores, los de la segunda por quince. Los jugadores de la *Rugby League* siempre han sido profesionales, mientras que en la *Rugby Union* el profesionalismo fue aceptado sólo en 1995

rugged /ˈrʌgəd || ˈrʌgɪd/ *adj* 1 ‹*rocks/coast*› escarpado; ‹*terrain*› accidentado, escabroso 2 (tough) ‹*construction/engine*› fuerte, resistente; ‹*conditions/existence*› duro 3 (strong-featured) ‹*face*› de facciones duras 4 (unrefined) ‹*manners/style*› tosco, basto

rugger /ˈrʌgər || ˈrʌgə(r)/ *n* [u] (BrE) rugby *m*

ruin[1] /ˈruːən || ˈruːɪn/ *n* 1 (sth ruined) (*often pl*) ruina *f*; **the town lay in ~s** la ciudad estaba en ruinas; **his life/career was in ~s** su vida/carrera estaba arruinada 2 (cause) (*no pl*) ruina *f*, perdición *f*; **drink will be the ~ of her** la bebida será su ruina *or* perdición 3 [u] (state) ruina *f*; **he's heading for financial ~** va derecho a la ruina *or* a la bancarrota

ruin[2] *vt*
A (destroy) ‹*city/building*› destruir*; ‹*career/life*› arruinar, acabar con; ‹*hopes*› destruir*, echar por tierra; ‹*plans*› arruinar, echar por tierra; **if they open a supermarket next to my store, I'll be ~ed** si abren un supermercado al lado de mi tienda me van a hacer quebrar *or* me van a arruinar
B (spoil) ‹*dress/carpet/toy*› estropear; ‹*party/surprise*› echar a perder, estropear, arruinar

ruination /ˈruːəˈneɪʃən || ˌruːɪˈneɪʃən/ *n* [u] destrucción *f*

ruined /ˈruːənd || ˈruːɪnd/ *adj* ‹*building/city*› en ruinas; ‹*reputation/career*› arruinado

ruinous /ˈruːənəs || ˈruːɪnəs/ *adj* ruinoso

rule[1] /ruːl/ *n*
A [c] (regulation, principle) regla *f*, norma *f*; **a set of ~s** un reglamento; **it's against the ~s** está prohibido; **~s and regulations** reglamento *m*; **to bend** *o* **stretch the ~s** apartarse un poco de las reglas; **to work to ~** (Lab Rel) hacer* huelga de celo, trabajar a reglamento (CS); **~ of thumb** regla general
B (general practice, habit) (*no pl*): **as a ~** por lo general, generalmente; **I make it a ~ to reply promptly to letters** tengo por norma contestar las cartas enseguida
C [u] (government) gobierno *m*; (of monarch) reinado *m*; **to be under foreign ~** estar* bajo dominio extranjero; **the ~ of law** el imperio de la ley; ▸**majority A1**
D [c] (measure) regla *f*

rule[2] *vt*
A (govern, control) ‹*country*› gobernar*, administrar; ‹*person*› dominar; ‹*emotion*› controlar
B (pronounce) dictaminar
C (draw) ‹*line*› trazar* con una regla; **~d paper** papel *m* con renglones

■ **rule** *vi*
A 1 (govern) gobernar*; «*monarch*» reinar; **to ~ OVER sb** gobernar* a algn, reinar SOBRE algn 2 (predominate, be current) imperar
B (pronounce) **to ~ (ON sth)** fallar *or* resolver* (EN algo); **to ~ against/in favor of sb/sth** fallar *or* resolver* en contra/a favor de algn/algo

Phrasal verbs

- **rule off** [v ▸ o ▸ adv, v ▸ adv ▸ o] separar con una línea
- **rule out** [v ▸ o ▸ adv, v ▸ adv ▸ o] ‹*possibility*› descartar; ‹*course of action*› hacer* imposible; **his injury ~s him out for tomorrow's game** su lesión lo excluye del partido de mañana

rulebook /ˈruːlbʊk/ *n* reglamento *m*; **to do sth by the ~** hacer* algo de acuerdo a las normas (establecidas)

ruler /'ruːlər || 'ruːlə(r)/ *n*
A (leader) gobernante *mf*; (sovereign) soberano, -na *m,f*
B (measure) regla *f*

ruling¹ /'ruːlɪŋ/ *n* fallo *m*, resolución *f*; **to give** *o* **make a ~ that ...** fallar *or* resolver* que ...

ruling² *adj* (*before n*) **1** (in power) ‹*monarch*› reinante; **the ~ Party** el partido en el poder; **the ~ classes** las clases dirigentes **2** (dominant) ‹*principle/factor*› dominante

rum /rʌm/ *n* [c u] ron *m*

Rumania /ruː'meɪniə/ *etc* ▸**Romania** *etc*

rumba /'rʌmbə/ *n* rumba *f*; **to do** *o* **dance the ~** bailar la rumba

rumble¹ /'rʌmbəl/ *n*
A (sound) ruido *m* sordo; (of thunder) estruendo *m*; (of stomach) ruido *m* de tripas (fam)
B (fight) (AmE sl) pelea *f*

rumble² *vi* «*guns/drums*» hacer* un ruido sordo; «*thunder*» retumbar; **my stomach's rumbling** me suenan las tripas (fam)
■ **rumble** *vt* (BrE colloq) ‹*person*› calar (fam)

ruminant /'ruːmənənt || 'ruːmɪnənt/ *n* rumiante *m*

ruminate /'ruːməneɪt || 'ruːmɪmeɪt/ *vi* **1** (Zool) rumiar **2** (ponder) **to ~ ON/ABOUT sth** cavilar SOBRE algo, rumiar algo

rumination /'ruːmə'neɪʃən || ˌruːmɪ'neɪʃən/ *n* **1** [u] (Zool) rumia *f* **2** (thought) (*often pl*) cavilación *f*, reflexión *f*

rummage¹ /'rʌmɪdʒ/ *vi* hurgar*; **she ~d about** *o* **around in the drawer** revolvió (en) *or* hurgó en el cajón

rummage² *n* **1** (action) (*no pl*): **I had a ~ through my old things** rebusqué entre mis cosas viejas **2** [u] (odds and ends) (AmE) cosas *fpl* viejas; (*before n*) **~ sale** *mercadillo de beneficencia donde se venden artículos de segunda mano*

rummy /'rʌmi/ *n* [u] rummy *m*

rumor¹, (BrE) **rumour** /'ruːmər || 'ruːmə(r)/ *n* rumor *m*; **~ has it (that) ...** se rumorea que ..., corre el rumor de que ...

rumor², (BrE) **rumour** *vt* (*usu pass*) rumorear; **it is ~ed that ...** se rumorea que ..., corre el rumor de que ...; **she is ~ed to be very beautiful** se dice que es muy bonita

rump /rʌmp/ *n* **1** [c] (of horse) grupa *f*, ancas *fpl* **2** [u] (Culin) cadera *f*, cuadril *m* (RPl); (*before n*) **~ steak** filete *m* de cadera, churrasco *m* de cuadril (RPl) **3** [c] (bottom) (colloq & hum) trasero *m* (fam), culo *m* (Esp fam), traste *m* (fam)

rumple /'rʌmpəl/ *vt* **~ (up)** arrugar*

rumpus /'rʌmpəs/ *n* (*pl* **~es**) lío *m*, escándalo *m*, jaleo *m* (fam); **to kick up** *o* **make a ~ (about sth)** armar un lío *or* un escándalo (sobre algo); (*before n*) **~ room** (AmE) cuarto *m* de juegos

run¹ /rʌn/ (*pres p* **running**; *past* **ran**; *past p* **run**) *vi*

Sense I

A correr; **I had to ~ for the train** tuve que correr para no perder el tren; **he ran downstairs/indoors** bajó/entró corriendo; **~ for your lives!** ¡sálvese quien pueda!
B (colloq) (drive) ir* (*en coche*); **I ~ down/over/up to Birmingham most weekends** la mayoría de los fines de semana voy a Birmingham
C **1** (go): **the truck ran into the ditch/over the cliff** el camión cayó en la cuneta/se despeñó por el acantilado; **the wagons ~ on tracks** los vagones corren sobre rieles **2** (Transp): **the trains ~ every half hour** hay trenes cada media hora; **this service ~s only on Saturdays** este servicio funciona solamente los sábados
D **1** (flow) «*water/oil*» correr; (drip) gotear; **the water ran hot/cold** empezó a salir agua caliente/fría; **the river ~s through the town/into the sea** el río pasa por la ciudad/desemboca en el mar; **she left the water/faucet** (AmE) *o* (BrE) **tap ~ning** dejó la llave abierta (AmL) *or* (Esp) el grifo abierto *or* (RPl) la canilla abierta *or* (Per) el caño abierto; **my nose is ~ning** me gotea la nariz **2** (pass) pasar; **the rope ~s over this pulley** la cuerda pasa por esta polea
E (travel): **our thoughts were ~ning along** *o* **on the same lines** nuestros pensamientos iban por el mismo camino; **a shiver ran down my spine** me dio un escalofrío
F (Pol) «*candidate*» presentarse, postularse (AmL); **he is ~ning for Governor again** se va a volver a presentar *or* (AmL tb) a postular como candidato a Gobernador; **she'll be ~ning against two other candidates** se enfrentará a otros dos candidatos

Sense II (operate, function): **with the engine ~ning** con el motor encendido *or* en marcha *or* (AmL tb) prendido; **it ~s off batteries/on gas** funciona con pilas *or* a pila(s)/a gas; **the talks have been ~ning smoothly** las conversaciones han marchado sobre ruedas; **the work is ~ning six months behind schedule** el trabajo lleva seis meses de retraso

Sense III

A (extend) **1** (in space): **the streets ~ parallel to each other** las calles corren paralelas; **the path ~s across the field/around the lake** el sendero atraviesa el campo/bordea el lago; **this idea ~s through the whole book** esta idea se repite *or* está presente a lo largo del libro **2** (in time): **the film ~s for 95 minutes** la película dura 95 minutos; **the show will ~ for 10 weeks** el espectáculo estará en cartel 10 semanas; **the contract ~s for a year** el contrato es válido por un año *or* vence al cabo de un año
B **1** (be, stand): **feelings are ~ning high** los ánimos están caldeados; **inflation is ~ning at 4%** la tasa de inflación es del 4%; **it ~s in the family** es de familia, le (*or* me *etc*) viene de familia; ▸**water¹ C1** **2** (become): **stocks are ~ning low** se están agotando las existencias; *see also* **dry¹ A3, short² B**; **to ~ TO sth**: **to ~ to fat** echar carnes (fam); *see also* **seed¹ A2**
C (of stories, sequences) decir*; **how did that line ~?** ¿cómo decía *or* era esa línea?; **the argument ~s as follows** el argumento es el siguiente
D (melt, merge) «*butter/cheese/icing*» derretirse*; «*paint/makeup*» correrse; «*color*» desteñir*, despintarse (Méx)
E «*stockings*» hacerse* carreras, correrse (AmL)

■ **run** *vt*

Sense I

A **1** ‹*race/marathon*› correr, tomar parte en **2** (chase): **the Green candidate ran them a close third** el candidato de los verdes quedó en tercer lugar a muy poca distancia de ellos; **they were ~ out of town** los hicieron salir del pueblo, los corrieron del pueblo (AmL fam)
B **1** (push, move) pasar; **he ran his fingers through his beard** se mesaba la barba; **she ran her finger down the list** recorrió la lista con el dedo; **~ a comb through your hair** pásate un peine (por el pelo) **2** (drive) ‹*person*› (colloq) llevar (*en coche*); **he ran the truck into the ditch** se metió con el camión en la cuneta
C (cause to flow): **to ~ a bath** preparar un baño; **to ~ sth under the tap** (BrE) hacer* correr agua sobre algo
D **1** (extend) ‹*cable/wire*› tender* **2** (pass) (hacer*) pasar
E **1** (smuggle) ‹*guns*› contrabandear, pasar (de contrabando) **2** (get past) ‹*blockade*› burlar; **to ~ a (red) light** (AmE) saltarse un semáforo (en rojo), pasarse un alto (Méx)

Sense II

A (operate) ‹*engine*› hacer* funcionar; ‹*program*› (Comput) pasar, ejecutar
B (manage) ‹*business/organization/department*› dirigir*, llevar; **the state-~ television network** la cadena de televisión estatal *or* del Estado; **who's ~ning this business?** ¿aquí quién es el que manda?; **he ~s the financial side of the business** se encarga *or* se ocupa del aspecto financiero del negocio
C **1** (Transp) ‹*flight*› tener*; **we ~ regular buses to the airport** tenemos un servicio regular de autobuses al aeropuerto; **they ~ extra trains on Saturdays** los sábados ponen más trenes **2** (maintain) tener*; **she ~s her own car** ella tiene su propio coche; **I can't afford to ~ a car** no puedo mantener un coche; **it's very cheap to ~** es muy económico
D ‹*tests*› realizar*, llevar a cabo; ‹*classes/concerts*› organizar*; «*newspaper*» ‹*article*› publicar*; ▸**fever A1, risk¹ 1, temperature 2**

Phrasal verbs

- **run about** ▸**run around 1**
- **run across** [v ▸ prep ▸ o] **1** (meet) ‹*person*› encontrarse* *or* toparse con **2** (find) ‹*object*› encontrar*
- **run after** [v ▸ prep ▸ o] (pursue) correr detrás de *or* tras; (romantically) andar* detrás de, perseguir*
- **run along** [v ▸ adv] irse*; **~ along now, it's late** bueno, vete, que es tarde
- **run around** [v ▸ adv] **1** (play) «*children*» corretear; (busy oneself) andar * de un lado para otro; **why should I ~ around after you?** ¿por qué tengo que estar haciéndote de sirvienta?, ¿por qué tengo que estar yo atendiéndote a ti? **2** (keep company) (colloq) salir*; **who's she ~ning**

around with now? ¿ahora con quién sale?

- **run at** [v ▸ prep ▸ o] **1** (attack) abalanzarse* sobre **2** (in order to jump): **you can clear the ditch if you ~ at it** puedes saltar la zanja si tomas carrera *or* (Esp) carrerilla
- **run away** [v ▸ adv]

A (escape) huir*, escaparse, fugarse*; (run off) salir* corriendo, huir*; **she ran away from home** se escapó de casa; **you can't ~ away from reality** no puedes evadirte de la realidad

B ‹‹*liquid*›› irse*

- **run away with** [v ▸ adv ▸ prep ▸ o]

A **1** ‹*race/contest*› ganar fácilmente, alzarse* con **2** (take over): **she lets her imagination ~ away with her** se deja llevar por la imaginación

B **1** (steal) robarse, alzarse* con **2** (elope with) escaparse *or* fugarse* *or* irse* con, huirse* con (Méx)

- **run down**

Sense **I** [v ▸ o ▸ adv, v ▸ adv ▸ o]

A **1** ‹*battery*› (Auto) descargar*; (in radio, shaver etc) gastar **2** (reduce) ‹*staff/services*› ir* recortando *or* reduciendo; ‹*production*› ir* restringiendo **3** ‹*stocks/supplies*› agotar

B (disparage) (colloq) criticar*, hablar mal de

C ‹*pedestrian*› atropellar

Sense **II** [v ▸ adv] **1** ‹‹*battery*›› (Auto) descargarse*; (in radio, shaver etc) gastarse, agotarse **2** ‹‹*business/factory*›› venirse* abajo **3** ‹‹*stocks/supplies*›› agotarse

- **run in** [v ▸ o ▸ adv] **1** (BrE Auto) ‹*car/engine*› hacer* el rodaje de **2** (arrest) (colloq) llevar preso
- **run into** [v ▸ prep ▸ o] **1** (collide with) ‹*vehicle*› chocar* con; ‹*wall/tree*› chocar* *or* darse* contra **2** (meet by chance) encontrarse* *or* toparse con **3** (encounter) ‹*opposition/problem*› toparse *or* tropezar* con, encontrar* **4** (amount to): **the cost ~s into millions of dollars** el costo asciende a millones de dólares
- **run off**

A [v ▸ o ▸ adv, v ▸ adv ▸ o] **1** (produce) ‹*copies*› tirar; ‹*photocopies*› sacar* **2** ‹*liquid*› sacar*

B [v ▸ adv] **1** (depart) salir* corriendo **2** ‹‹*liquid*›› correr

- **run off with** [v ▸ adv ▸ prep ▸ o] ▸**run away with B1, 2**
- **run on** [v ▸ adv] **1** (continue running) seguir* corriendo; (run ahead): **you ~ on, I'll catch up with you** tú ve delante, que ya te alcanzaré **2** (continue, last): **the meeting ran on till nine o'clock** la reunión siguió *or* se alargó hasta las nueve
- **run out** [v ▸ adv] **1** (exhaust supplies): **I was going to make some tea, but we've ~ out** iba a hacer té, pero se nos ha acabado; **to ~ out OF sth** quedarse SIN algo **2** (become exhausted) ‹‹*money*›› acabarse; ‹‹*supplies/stock*›› acabarse, agotarse; ‹‹*lease/policy*›› vencer*, caducar*; **her luck ran out** la abandonó la suerte, se le acabó la suerte; **time is ~ning out for them** les queda poco tiempo, se les está acabando el tiempo
- **run out on** [v ▸ adv ▸ prep ▸ o] abandonar, dejar plantado (fam)
- **run over**

A [v ▸ o ▸ adv, v ▸ adv ▸ o] ‹*pedestrian*› atropellar

B [v ▸ adv] **1** (overflow) ‹‹*liquid*›› derramarse; ‹‹*container*›› desbordarse, rebosar **2** (exceed time limit) excederse *or* pasarse del tiempo previsto

C [v ▸ prep ▸ o] (review) ‹*details/plan*› repasar, volver* sobre; (rehearse) ‹*scene*› ensayar, volver* sobre

- **run through** [v ▸ prep ▸ o] **1** (rehearse) ensayar **2** ▸**run over C**
- **run to** [v ▸ prep ▸ o] **1** (amount to): **the report ~s to 614 pages** el informe ocupa 614 páginas; **the film ~s to over four hours** la película dura más de cuatro horas **2** (extend to): **if your taste ~s to something a little more exotic …** si sus gustos son algo más exóticos … **3** (suffice for) (BrE) ‹‹*income/resources*›› alcanzar* para, dar* para (fam) **4** (afford) (BrE) permitirse
- **run up**

A [v ▸ adv ▸ o] **1** ‹*total/debts*› ir* acumulando; **she'd ~ up quite a bill in the restaurant** debía bastante dinero en el restaurante **2** ‹*flag*› izar*

B [v ▸ o ▸ adv, v ▸ adv ▸ o] ‹*dress*› hacer* (*rápidamente*)

- **run up against** [v ▸ adv ▸ prep ▸ o] ‹*difficulty/obstacle*› toparse *or* tropezar* con

run² *n*

A (on foot): **she goes for a short ~ every day** todos los días sale a correr un poco; **he does everything at a ~** todo lo hace (deprisa y) corriendo *or* a la(s) carrera(s); **to break into a ~** echar a correr; ***on the ~***: **the children keep her on the ~ all day** los niños la tienen todo el día en danza; **after seven years on the ~ (from the law)** después de estar siete años huyendo de la justicia; ***to give sb a (good) ~ for her/his money*** hacerle* sudar tinta a algn; ***to have a good ~ for one's money***: **he was champion for six years, he had a good ~ for his money** fue campeón durante seis años, no se puede quejar; ***to have the ~ of sth*** tener* libre acceso a algo, tener* algo a su (*or* mi etc) entera disposición; ***to make a ~ for it*** escaparse

B **1** (trip, outing) vuelta *f*, paseo *m* (*en coche*) **2** (journey): **the outward ~** el trayecto *or* viaje de ida; **it's only a short/10-mile ~** está muy cerca/sólo a 10 millas

C **1** (sequence): **a ~ of good/bad luck** una racha de buena/mala suerte, una buena/mala racha **2** (period of time): **in the long ~** a la larga; **in the short ~** a corto plazo

D (tendency) corriente *f*; **in the normal ~ of events** normalmente, en el curso normal de los acontecimientos

E (heavy demand) **~ ON sth**: **there's been a ~ on these watches** estos relojes han estado muy solicitados *or* han tenido mucha demanda; **a ~ on sterling** una fuerte presión sobre la libra; **a ~ on the banks** una corrida bancaria, un pánico bancario

F (Cin, Theat) temporada *f*

G (Publ) (*print* ~) tirada *f*

H **1** (track) pista *f*; **ski ~** pista de esquí **2** (for animals) corral *m*

I (in stocking, knitted garment) carrera *f*

J (in baseball, cricket) carrera *f*

K **the runs** *pl* (diarrhea) (colloq) diarrea *f*, churrias *fpl* (Col fam)

runaround /'rʌnəraʊnd/ *n*: ***to give sb the ~*** (colloq) jugar* con algn, tomarle el pelo a algn (fam)

runaway¹ /'rʌnəweɪ/ *n* fugitivo, -va *m,f*

runaway² *adj* (*before n*) **1** ‹*slave/prisoner*› fugitivo **2** ‹*train/truck*› fuera de control; ‹*horse*› desbocado **3** ‹*inflation*› galopante, desenfrenado; ‹*spending*› desmedido; ‹*success*› clamoroso, arrollador

run: **~down** *n* **1** (summary) resumen *m*; **give me a ~down on the situation** ponme al corriente de la situación **2** (reduction) reducción *f*; **~-down** /'rʌn'daʊn/ *adj* (*pred* **~ down**) **1** (tired, sickly) (*usu pred*) **to be/feel ~down** estar*/sentirse* cansado *or* débil **2** (dilapidated) ‹*district/hotel*› venido a menos, en decadencia

rung¹ /rʌŋ/ *past p of* **ring²**

rung² *n* **1** (of ladder, chair) travesaño *m* **2** (in career, organization) peldaño *m*

run-in /'rʌnɪn/ *n*

A (confrontation) (colloq) **~ WITH sb/sth** roce *m* CON algn/algo

B (trial run) prueba *f*, ensayo *m*

runner /'rʌnər || 'rʌnə(r)/ *n*

A **1** (in race) corredor, -dora *m,f*; (taking messages) mensajero, -ra *m,f*; **I'm not a fast ~** no corro rápido **2** (in baseball) corredor, -dora *m,f*

B **1** (on sled) patín *m* **2** (for drawer) riel *m*, guía *f*

C (escape): ***to do a ~*** (BrE colloq) salir* corriendo, largarse* (fam)

runner: **~ bean** *n* (esp BrE) habichuela *f* (Col) *or* (Esp) judía *f* verde *or* (Chi) poroto *m* verde *or* (RPl) chaucha *f or* (Ven) vainita *f or* (Méx) ejote *m*; **~-up** /'rʌnər'ʌp/ *n* (*pl* **~s-up**): **to be ~-up** quedar en segundo lugar *or* puesto

running¹ /'rʌnɪŋ/ *n* [u] **1** (exercise): **~ is a good form of exercise** correr es muy buen ejercicio; ***to be in/out of the ~ (for sth)***: **there are five candidates in the ~ for the post** hay cinco candidatos compitiendo *or* en liza por el puesto; **this has put him out of the ~ for the nomination** esto descarta la posibilidad de que sea nominado; ***to make (all) the ~*** (Sport) ir* en cabeza; **you can't expect him to make** *o* **do all the ~** no puedes pretender que él lo haga todo *or* tome todas las iniciativas; (*before n*) ‹*shorts*› de deporte; **~ shoes** zapatillas *fpl* de deporte; **~ track** pista *f* de atletismo **2** (of machine) funcionamiento *m*, marcha *f* **3** (management) gestión *f*, dirección *f*

running² *adj* (*before n, no comp*)

A **1** (done on the run): **protestors were involved in a ~ battle with the police** hubo escaramuzas *or* refriegas entre la policía y los manifestantes; **~ game** (in US football) ofensiva *f* terrestre; **to take a ~ jump** saltar tomando carrera *or* (Esp) carrerilla; **go take a ~ jump!** (colloq) ¡anda

r

y vete por ahí! (fam), ¡vete por un tubo! (Méx fam) 2 (continuous) ‹*joke*› continuo; **I don't need a ~ commentary on each news item!** ¡no necesito que me comentes todas las noticias a medida que las dan!; **~ water** agua *f*‡ corriente

B (discharging) ‹*sore*› supurante

running³ *adv*: **the third day ~** el tercer día consecutivo *or* seguido

running: **~ costs** *pl n* (of machine, car) gastos *mpl* de mantenimiento; (of company) costos *mpl or* (Esp) costes *mpl* corrientes *or* de operación; **~ mate** *n* compañero, -ra *m,f* de candidatura; (of presidential candidate) candidato, -ta *m,f* a la vicepresidencia

runny /'rʌni/ *adj* **-nier, -niest** 1 ‹*eyes*› lloroso; **I've got a ~ nose** me gotea la nariz, no hago más que moquear 2 ‹*sauce*› líquido, chirle (RPl); **the omelette was ~ in the middle** la tortilla no estaba cuajada en el centro

run: **~-off** *n* [c] (Pol) segunda votación *f*; (Sport) eliminatoria *f*; **~-of-the-mill** /'rʌnəvðə'mɪl/ *adj* (*pred* **~ of the mill**) ‹*job/car*› común *or* normal y corriente; ‹*acting/singing*› mediocre, nada destacado

runt /rʌnt/ *n* 1 (Agr) *animal más pequeño de una camada* 2 (puny person) alfeñique *m*, mequetrefe *m*

run: **~-through** *n* ensayo *m*, práctica *f*; **~-up** *n* 1 (preparatory period) **~-up TO sth** período *m* previo A algo 2 (Sport) carrera *f*, carrerilla *f* (Esp) (*antes de saltar, lanzar la jabalina etc*); **~way** *n* (Aviat) pista *f or* (Chi tb) cancha *f* de aterrizaje; (for fashion models) (AmE) pasarela *f*

rupee /ru:pi:, ru:'pi:/ *n* rupia *f*

rupture¹ /'rʌptʃər || 'rʌptʃə(r)/ *n* 1 [u c] (break) ruptura *f* 2 [c] (hernia) hernia *f*

rupture² *vt* ‹*casing/container*› romper*; ‹*blood vessel/membrane*› romper*, reventar*

■ **rupture** *vi* «*organ*» desgarrarse; «*appendix*» reventarse*

rural /'rʊrəl || 'rʊərəl/ *adj* rural

ruse /ru:s, ru:z || ru:z/ *n* artimaña *f*, treta *f*

rush¹ /rʌʃ/ *n*

A 1 (haste) (*no pl*) prisa *f*, apuro *m* (AmL); **in all the ~, I forgot my umbrella** con la prisa *or* (AmL) con el apuro, se me olvidó el paraguas; **what's (all) the ~?** ¿qué prisa *or* (AmL tb) qué apuro hay?; **I'm in a ~** tengo prisa, ando *or* estoy apurado (AmL); **everything happened in a ~** todo pasó de repente 2 [c] (movement): **a ~ of air** una ráfaga de aire; **a ~ of water** un torrente de agua; **there was a ~ for the exit** todo el mundo se precipitó hacia la salida 3 [c] (Sport) ataque *m*; (in US football) carga *f* 4 [c] (burst of activity): **there's a mad ~ on to meet the deadline** estamos trabajando como locos tratando de terminar a tiempo (fam); **the Christmas ~** el gran movimiento del período de las fiestas de fin de año en los comercios

B [c u] (Bot) junco *m*

rush² *vi* 1 (hurry) darse* prisa, apurarse (AmL); **there's no need to ~** no hay prisa, no hay apuro (AmL); **don't ~!** ¡con calma!, ¡despacio!; **she ~ed through the first course** se comió el primer plato a todo correr *or* a la(s) carrera(s) 2 (run) (+ *adv compl*): **she ~ed after him** corrió tras él; **she ~ed in/out** entró/salió corriendo; **to ~ around** *o* (BrE also) **about** ir* de acá para allá, correr de un lado para otro; **just a minute: don't ~ off!** espera un minuto, no salgas corriendo 3 (surge, flow): **blood ~ed to his face** (from embarrassment) se puso colorado; (from anger) se le subió la sangre a la cabeza

■ **rush** *vt* 1 ‹*job/preparation*› hacer* a todo correr *or* a la(s) carrera(s), hacer* deprisa y corriendo; ‹*person*› meterle prisa a, apurar (AmL); **to ~ sb INTO sth/-ING**: **I don't want to be ~ed into (making) a decision** no quiero que me hagan tomar una decisión precipitada; **I'm a bit ~ed at the moment** en este momento estoy muy ocupado 2 (send, take hastily): **supplies were ~ed out to the area** se enviaron suministros urgentemente a la zona; **she was ~ed to hospital** la trasladaron (frml) *or* llevaron rápidamente al hospital

(Phrasal verb)

• **rush into** [v ▸ prep ▸ o]: **don't ~ into anything** no te precipites, no tomes ninguna decisión precipitada

rush: **~ hour** *n* hora *f* pico (AmL), hora *f* punta (Esp); **~ job** *n* (colloq) (urgent) trabajo *m* urgente; (hastily done): **it was a ~ job** se hizo a todo correr *or* deprisa y corriendo *or* a la(s) carrera(s)

rusk /rʌsk/ *n* galleta *f* (*dura, para bebés*)

russet /'rʌsət || 'rʌsɪt/ *n* [u] color *m* rojizo; (*before n*) ‹*leaves/hair*› rojizo

Russia /'rʌʃə/ *n* Rusia *f*

Russian¹ /'rʌʃən/ *adj* ruso

Russian² *n* 1 [u] (language) ruso *m* 2 [c] (person) ruso, -sa *m,f*

Russian: **~ Federation** *n* Federación *f* Rusa; **~ roulette** *n* [u] ruleta *f* rusa

rust¹ /rʌst/ *n* [u] 1 (on metal) óxido *m*, herrumbre *f*, orín *m* 2 (color) color *m* ladrillo *or* teja

rust² *vi* oxidarse, herrumbrarse

■ **rust** *vt* oxidar, herrumbrar

(Phrasal verb)

• **rust up** [v ▸ adv] oxidarse, herrumbrarse

rustic¹ /'rʌstɪk/ *adj* rústico

rustic² *n* pueblerino, -na *m,f*

rustle¹ /rʌsəl/ *vi* «*leaves*» susurrar; «*paper*» crujir; «*silk*» hacer* frufrú

■ **rustle** *vt*

A (make sound) «*wind*» ‹*leaves*› hacer* susurrar; **he ~d the sheets of paper impatiently** movió impaciente los papeles

B (steal) ‹*cattle/horses*› robar

rustle² *n* (of leaves) susurro *m*; (of paper) crujido *m*; (of silk) frufrú *m*

(Phrasal verb)

• **rustle up** [v ▸ o ▸ adv, v ▸ adv ▸ o] preparar, improvisar

rustler /'rʌslər || 'rʌslə(r)/ *n* ladrón, -drona *m,f* de ganado, cuatrero, -ra *m,f*

rustling /'rʌslɪŋ/ *n* [u] robo *m* (*de ganado*), cuatrerismo *m*

rustproof /'rʌstpru:f/ *adj* ‹*surface/metal*› inoxidable; ‹*coating*› anticorrosivo, antioxidante

rusty /'rʌsti/ *adj* **-tier, -tiest** 1 ‹*nail/lock*› oxidado, herrumbrado; **to get** *o* (BrE also) **go ~** oxidarse, herrumbrarse; **my German is a bit ~** tengo muy olvidado el alemán 2 (in color) ladrillo *adj inv*

rut /rʌt/ *n*

A [c] (groove) surco *m*, rodada *f*; ***to be in a ~*** estar* anquilosado; ***to get into a ~*** anquilosarse

B [u] (Zool) celo *m*

rutabaga /'ru:tə'beɪgə || ˌru:tə'beɪgə/ *n* [u] (AmE) colinabo *m*, nabo *m* sueco

ruthless /'ru:θləs || 'ru:θlɪs/ *adj* ‹*enemy*› despiadado, implacable; ‹*persecution*› implacable, inexorable; ‹*determination*› firme, inflexible

ruthlessly /'ru:θləsli || 'ru:θlɪsli/ *adv* ‹*oppress/exterminate*› sin piedad *or* misericordia; ‹*criticize*› despiadadamente

ruthlessness /'ru:θləsnəs || 'ru:θlɪsnɪs/ *n* [u] falta *f* de piedad *or* misericordia, crueldad *f*

Rwanda /rʊ'ændə/ *n* Ruanda *f*

Rwandan /rʊ'ændən/ *adj* ruandés

rye /raɪ/ *n* [u] 1 (plant, grain) centeno *m* 2 **~ (bread)** pan *m* de centeno 3 **~ (whiskey)** whisky *m* de centeno

r

Ss

S, s /es/ *n* S, s *f*

S 1 (Geog) (= **south**) S 2 (Clothing) (= **small**) P

SA 1 = **South Africa** 2 (AmE) = **South America**

Sabbath /'sæbəθ/ *n* (Jewish) sábado *m*; (Christian) domingo *m*

sabbatical[1] /sə'bætɪkəl/ *n* (year) año *m* sabático; (period) período *m* sabático; **to go on ~, to take a ~** tomarse un año/un período sabático

sabbatical[2] *adj* (Educ) ‹*year*› sabático

saber, (BrE) **sabre** /'seɪbər || 'seɪbə(r)/ *n* sable *m*

saber rattling, (BrE) **sabre-rattling** /'seɪbər,rætlɪŋ || 'seɪbə,rætlɪŋ/ *n* [u] belicosidad *f*, bravuconería *f*

sable /'seɪbəl/ *n* (*pl* **~s** *or* **~**) marta *f* cibelina *or* cebellina; (*before n*) ‹*coat/fur*› de marta

sabotage[1] /'sæbətɑːʒ/ *n* [u] sabotaje *m*

sabotage[2] *vt* sabotear

saboteur /'sæbə'tɜːr || ,sæbə'tɜː(r)/ *n* saboteador, -dora *m,f*

sabre *n* (BrE) ▸**saber**

sac /sæk/ *n* saco *m*

saccharin /'sækərən || 'sækərɪn/ *n* [u] sacarina *f*

saccharine /'sækərən || 'sækərɪn, -riːn/ *adj* (sickly sweet) ‹*smile/charm/tones*› empalagoso, almibarado

sachet /sæ'ʃeɪ || 'sæʃeɪ/ *n* (of shampoo, cream, perfume) sachet *m*; (of powder, sugar) (BrE) sobrecito *m*, bolsita *f*

sack[1] /sæk/ *n*

A [c] 1 (large bag) saco *m*, costal *m* 2 (paper bag) (AmE) bolsa *f* (de papel)

B (dismissal) (BrE colloq): **to give sb the ~** echar a algn (del trabajo), botar a algn (del trabajo) (AmL fam)

C (bed) (colloq) **the ~** la cama, el sobre (fam); ▸**hit[1] A1**

D (Sport) (in baseball) almohadilla *f*, base *f*

sack[2] *vt*

A (dismiss) (BrE colloq) ‹*person/employee*› echar (del trabajo), botar (del trabajo) (AmL fam)

B (destroy) ‹*town/city*› saquear

sackcloth /'sækklɔːθ || 'sækklɒθ/ *n* [u] arpillera *f*; ***to wear ~ and ashes*** darse* golpes de pecho

sackful /'sækfʊl/ *n* saco *m*, costal *m*; **letters were arriving by the ~** llegaban cartas a montones

sacrament /'sækrəmənt/ *n* 1 (ceremony) sacramento *m* 2 **Sacrament** (Eucharist): **the (Blessed** *o* **Holy) S~** el Santísimo Sacramento

sacred /'seɪkrəd || 'seɪkrɪd/ *adj* 1 (blessed, holy) ‹*ground/animal*› sagrado; **~ TO sb/sth** consagrado A algn/algo; **is nothing ~ any more?** ¿ya no se respeta nada? 2 (with religious subject) ‹*text*› sagrado; ‹*music*› sacro

sacred cow *n* vaca *f* sagrada

sacrifice[1] /'sækrəfaɪs || 'sækrɪfaɪs/ *n*

A (Occult, Relig) 1 [u] (practice, act) sacrificio *m* 2 [c] (offering) ofrenda *f*, víctima *f* (propiciatoria)

B [u c] (giving up) sacrificio *m*; **to make ~s** sacrificarse*

C [c] (in baseball) sacrificio *m*

sacrifice[2] *vt* sacrificar*

■ **sacrifice** *vi* (in baseball) sacrificarse*

sacrificial /'sækrə'fɪʃəl || ,sækrɪ'fɪʃəl/ *adj* expiatorio

sacrilege /'sækrəlɪdʒ || 'sækrɪlɪdʒ/ *n* [u] sacrilegio *m*

sacrilegious /'sækrə'lɪdʒəs || ,sækrɪ'lɪdʒəs/ *adj* sacrílego

sacristan /'sækrəstən || 'sækrɪstən/ *n* sacristán, -tana *m,f*

sacristy /'sækrəsti || 'sækrɪsti/ *n* (*pl* **-ties**) sacristía *f*

sacrosanct /'sækrəʊsæŋkt/ *adj* sacrosanto

sad /sæd/ *adj* **-dd-** 1 (unhappy) ‹*person/face*› triste; ‹*expression*› triste, de tristeza; **to feel ~** estar* *or* sentirse* triste; **I was very ~ at the news of his death** la noticia de su muerte me entristeció *or* me apenó mucho 2 (causing grief) ‹*news/loss*› triste; **how ~!** ¡qué pena! 3 (regrettable, deplorable) (*before n*): **the ~ fact is that ...** la triste realidad es que ...; **~ to say** lamentablemente

SAD *n* [u] (= **seasonal affective disorder**) TAE *m*

sadden /'sædn̩/ *vt* entristecer*, apenar

saddle[1] /'sædl̩/ *n* (on horse) silla *f* (de montar), montura *f*; (on bicycle) sillín *m*, asiento *m*; **she's back in the ~ now** ha vuelto a tomar *or* (esp Esp) coger las riendas

saddle[2] *vt* 1 **~ (up)** ‹*horse/camel*› ensillar 2 (burden) (colloq) cargar*; **to ~ sb WITH sth** ‹*job/task*› endilgarle* *or* (esp AmL) encajarle algo A algn; **we're ~d with him** tenemos que cargar con él

Phrasal verb

• **saddle up**

A [v ▸ adv] ensillar

B [v ▸ o ▸ adv, v ▸ adv ▸ o] ensillar

saddle: **~-bag** /'sædl̩bæg/ *n* (on horse) alforja *f*; (on bicycle) maletero *m*; **~ sore** *adj*: **to be ~ ~** estar* dolorido de tanto montar

sadism /'seɪdɪzəm/ *n* [u] sadismo *m*

sadist /'seɪdəst || 'seɪdɪst/ *n* sádico, -ca *m,f*

sadistic /sə'dɪstɪk/ *adj* sádico

sadly /'sædli/ *adv* 1 (sorrowfully) ‹*smile/speak*› tristemente, con tristeza 2 (regrettably): **he is ~ lacking in tact** lamentablemente no tiene nada de tacto; **you are ~ mistaken** estás totalmente equivocado 3 (unfortunately) (*indep*) lamentablemente, desgraciadamente

sadness /'sædnəs || 'sædnɪs/ *n* [u] tristeza *f*

sadomasochism /'seɪdəʊ'mæsəkɪzəm/ *n* [u] sadomasoquismo *m*

sadomasochist /'seɪdəʊ'mæsəkəst || ,seɪdəʊ'mæsəkɪst/ *n* sadomasoquista *mf*

sad sack *n* (AmE colloq) inútil *mf*

sae, SAE *n* (BrE) (= **stamped, addressed envelope**) ▸**SASE**

safari /sə'fɑːri/ *n* [c u] safari *m*; **to be/go on ~** estar*/ir* de safari; (*before n*) **~ jacket** sahariana *f*; **~ park** safari-park *m*, reserva *f*

safe[1] /seɪf/ *adj* **safer, safest**

A 1 (secure from danger) (*pred*) seguro; **his reputation is ~** su reputación está a salvo; **you are not ~ here** corres peligro aquí; **keep these documents ~** guarda estos documentos en un lugar seguro; **your secret is ~ with me** puedes confiar en que guardaré tu secreto; **to be ~ FROM sb/sth**: **we'll be ~ from prying eyes/from him here** aquí estaremos a salvo de curiosos/de él 2 (unharmed) (*pred*): **they were found ~ and well** *o* **~ and sound** los encontraron sanos y salvos 3 (offering protection) ‹*haven/refuge*› seguro

B (not dangerous) seguro; **that ladder isn't very ~** esa escalera no es muy segura; **is the water ~ to drink?** ¿se puede beber el agua sin peligro?; **have a ~ journey** (que tengas) buen viaje

C (not risky) ‹*investment*› seguro, sin riesgo; ‹*method/contraceptive*› seguro, fiable; **he's a very ~ driver** conduce con prudencia; **it's ~ to say that ...** se puede decir sin temor a equivocarse que ...; **~ sex** sexo *m* seguro *or* sin riesgo; **we'd better leave at four o'clock to be on the ~ side** mejor salgamos a las cuatro por si acaso; ***better (to be) ~ than sorry*** más vale prevenir que curar; ▸**play²** *vt Sense* **II A2**

safe² *n* (for valuables) caja *f* fuerte, caja *f* de caudales; (*before n*) **~ cracker** *o* (BrE) **breaker** ladrón, -drona *m,f* de cajas fuertes

safe: **~-conduct** /'seɪf'kɑːndʌkt || ˌseɪf'kɒndʌkt/ *n* [u] protección *f*; **~-deposit** /'seɪfdɪ'pɑːzət || 'seɪfdɪ'pɒzɪt/ *n* (vaults) cámara *f* acorazada; **~-deposit (box)** caja *f* de seguridad

safeguard¹ /'seɪfgɑːrd || 'seɪfgɑːd/ *n* salvaguarda *f*, garantía *f*; **as a ~** como medida preventiva

safeguard² *vt* salvaguardar, defender*, proteger*

■ **safeguard** *vi* **to ~ AGAINST sth** proteger* CONTRA algo

safe: **~ harbour** *n* (AmE) horario *m* de protección; **~ house** *n* piso *m* franco, enterradero *m* (RPl); **~keeping** *n* [u]: **he gave her the watch for ~keeping** le dio el reloj para que lo guardara en lugar seguro *or* (esp Esp frml) para que lo pusiera a buen recaudo

safely /'seɪfli/ *adv*

A **1** (without mishap, unharmed): **we got home ~** llegamos a casa sin novedad *or* sin ningún percance **2** (without danger) sin peligro; **drive ~** conduzca con prudencia

B (in a safe place, securely): **he's ~ behind bars** está entre rejas, donde no puede hacer daño; **my savings are ~ invested** tengo mis ahorros en inversiones seguras *or* sin riesgos

C (with certainty) ‹*say/assume*› sin temor a equivocarse (*or* equivocarnos) *etc*

safety /'seɪfti/ *n* (*pl* **-ties**)

A [u] (security, freedom from risk) seguridad *f*; **there's ~ in numbers** se está más seguro en un grupo grande; **~ first** la seguridad ante todo; (*before n*) ‹*device/fuse/precautions*› de seguridad; **~ measures** precauciones *fpl*, medidas *fpl* de seguridad; **~ rail** barandilla *f*; **~ regulations** normas *f* de seguridad

B [u] (certainty) seguridad *f*; **I think we can say with complete ~ that ...** creo que podemos decir con total *or* absoluta seguridad que ...

C [c] **~ (catch)** (on gun) seguro *m*

D [c] (in US football) (AmE) (player) safety *m*

safety: **~ belt** *n* cinturón *m* de seguridad; **~ curtain** *n* telón *m* anti-incendios *or* de seguridad; **~-deposit box** /'seɪftidɪ'pɑːzət || ˌseɪftidɪ'pɒzɪt/ *n* (AmE) caja *f* de seguridad; **~ harness** *n* arnés *m* de seguridad; **~ match** *n* fósforo *m or* (Esp) cerilla *f or* (AmC, Méx tb) cerillo *m* de seguridad; **~ net** *n* (for acrobats) red *f* de seguridad; (protection) protección *f*; **~ pin** *n* imperdible *m*, gancho *m* (Andes), alfiler *m* de gancho (CS, Ven), gancho *m* de nodriza (Col), seguro *m* (Méx); **~ razor** *n* maquinilla *f or* (AmL) maquinita *f* de afeitar; **~ valve** *n* (Mech Eng) válvula *f* de seguridad; (outlet) válvula *f* de escape

S

saffron /'sæfrən/ *n* [u] (Bot, Culin) azafrán *m*

sag /sæg/ *vi* **-gg-**

A **1** «*beams/ceiling*» combarse; **the bed ~ged in the middle** la cama se hundía en el medio **2** (hang down, droop): **~ging breasts** pechos *mpl* caídos

B **1** «*spirits/courage/resolution*» flaquear, decaer* **2** **sagging** *pres p* ‹*prices/values*› que no repuntan

saga /'sɑːgə/ *n* saga *f*; (long story) historia *f*, saga *f*

sage /seɪdʒ/ *n*

A [u] (Bot, Culin) salvia *f*

B [c] (wise man) sabio *m*

Sagittarius /'sædʒə'teriəs || ˌsædʒɪ'teəriəs/ *n* **1** (sign) (*no art*) Sagitario **2** [c] (person) Sagitario *or* sagitario *mf*, sagitariano, -na *m,f*; *see also* **Aquarius**

sago /'seɪgəʊ/ *n* [u] sagú *m*

Sahara /sə'hærə || sə'hɑːrə/ *n* **the ~** el Sahara *or* (Esp) el Sáhara

said¹ /sed/ *past & past p of* **say¹**

said² *adj* (frml) (*before n*): **the ~ property/lady** dicha propiedad/señora (frml)

sail¹ /seɪl/ *n*

A (Naut) **1** [c u] (of ship, boat) vela *f*; **to set ~** (start journey) zarpar, hacerse* a la mar; «*yacht/galleon*» hacerse* a la vela **2** (trip) (*no pl*) viaje *m* en barco (*or* en velero *etc*); **to go for a ~** salir* a navegar

B [c] (of windmill) aspa *f*‡

sail² *vt* **1** (control) ‹*boat/ship*› gobernar*, manejar **2** (travel, cross): **to ~ the Atlantic single-handed** cruzar* el Atlántico en solitario

■ **sail** *vi*

A **1** (travel) «*ship/boat*» navegar*; «*person/passenger*» ir* en barco, navegar*; **to ~ around the world** dar* la vuelta al mundo en barco; **to ~ east/west** navegar* hacia el *or* en dirección este/oeste; **to go ~ing** salir a navegar **2** (depart) «*person/ship*» zarpar, salir*

B (move effortlessly): **to ~ into/out of a room** entrar en/salir* de una habitación con aire majestuoso; **the weeks just seem to ~ past** las semanas van pasando sin que uno se dé cuenta

Phrasal verb

• **sail through** [v ▸ prep ▸ o]: **you'll ~ through the exam** aprobarás el examen con los ojos cerrados *or* sin ningún problema; **he ~ed through the interview** la entrevista le resultó muy fácil

sail: **~board** *n* tabla *f* a vela *or* de windsurf; **~boarding** /'seɪlˌbɔːrdɪŋ || 'seɪlˌbɔːdɪŋ/ *n* [u] windsurf *m*, windsurfing *m*; **~boat** *n* (AmE) velero *m*, barco *m* de vela; **~cloth** *n* [u] lona *f*

sailing /'seɪlɪŋ/ *n* **1** [u] (skill) navegación *f*; ***to be (all) plain ~*** ser* muy fácil *or* sencillo, ser* coser y cantar **2** [u] (Sport) vela *f*, yachting *m*, navegación *f* a vela **3** [c] (departure) salida *f*; (*before n*) ‹*time/date*› de salida

sailing: **~ boat** *n* (BrE) ▸**sailboat**; **~ ship** *n* velero *m*, barco *m or* buque *m* de vela

sailor /'seɪlər || 'seɪlə(r)/ *n* **1** (seaman) marinero *m*; **to be a bad/good ~** marearse/no marearse con facilidad **2** (Sport) navegante *mf*

saint /seɪnt/ *n* **1** (canonized person) santo, -ta *m,f*; **she was made a ~ in 1912** la canonizaron en 1912 **2** **Saint** /seɪnt || sənt/ (*before name*) san, santa [**santo** *is used before Domingo, Tomás, Tomé and Toribio*]; **S~ Patrick's Day** el día *or* la fiesta de San Patricio **3** (unselfish person) santo, -ta *m,f*; **he's no ~** no es ningún santito (fam)

sainthood /'seɪnthʊd/ *n* [u] santidad *f*

saintly /'seɪntli/ *adj* **-lier, -liest** ‹*person*› santo; ‹*life*› piadoso; ‹*expression/smile*› angelical

saint: **~ Petersburg** /seɪnt'piːtərzbɜːrg || ˌsənt'piːtəzbɜːg/ *n* San Petersburgo; **~'s day** *n* (*pl* **~s' days**) día *m or* fiesta *f* de un santo; (name day) día *m* del santo

sake /seɪk/ *n* **1** (benefit, account): **don't do it just for my ~** no lo hagas sólo por mí; **for your own ~** por tu propio bien; **for the ~ of the children** por los niños; **for old times' ~** por nuestra vieja amistad *or* por los viejos tiempos **2** (purpose, end): **art for art's ~** el arte por el arte; **for the ~ of argument** *o* **for argument's ~** pongamos por caso **3** (*in interj phrases*): **for goodness'** *o* **heaven's ~!** ¡por Dios! *or* ¡por favor!; **for God's ~!** ¡por el amor de Dios!; **but why, for Pete's ~?** (colloq) ¿pero por qué, caramba? (fam)

salacious /sə'leɪʃəs/ *adj* (frml) ‹*mind/grin*› salaz (frml), lascivo; ‹*book/joke*› obsceno

salad /'sæləd/ *n* [u c] ensalada *f*; (*before n*) **~ bowl** ensaladera *f*; **~ dressing** aliño *m* para ensalada

salad cream *n* [u] (BrE) *aliño para ensalada parecido a la mayonesa*

salamander /'sæləmændər || 'sæləmændə(r)/ *n* (Myth, Zool) salamandra *f*

salami /sə'lɑːmi/ *n* [u c] (*pl* **-mis**) salami *or* (CS) salame *m*

salary /'sæləri/ *n* (*pl* **-ries**) sueldo *m*; (*before n*) ‹*increase/review*› salarial; **~ earner** empleado, -da *m,f*

sale /seɪl/ *n*

A **1** [u] (act of selling) venta *f* **2** [c] (individual transaction) venta *f*; **to make a ~** vender algo; Ⓢ **all sales final** (AmE) no se aceptan devoluciones **3** [c] (auction) subasta *f*, remate *m* (AmL)

B (*in phrases*) **for sale**: Ⓢ **for sale** se vende; **to put sth up for ~** poner* algo en venta *or* a la venta; **on sale** (at reduced price) (AmE): **toys are on ~ this week** esta semana los juguetes están rebajados *or* en liquidación; (offered for sale) (BrE): **on ~ now at leading stores** ya está a la venta en los principales comercios; **the new model goes on**

~ this week el nuevo modelo sale a la venta esta semana; **(on) sale or return** (BrE) en depósito, en consignación

C (clearance) liquidación *f*; (seasonal reductions) rebajas *fpl*; (*before n*) ‹*price*› de liquidación

D sales 1 *pl* (volume sold) (*sometimes sing*) (volumen *m* de) ventas *fpl*; (*before n*) ‹*figures/promotion/campaign*› de ventas 2 (department) (+ *sing o pl vb*) ventas (+ *sing vb*); **she works in ~s** trabaja en ventas; (*before n*) ‹*department/manager/executive*› de ventas; **the ~s force** el personal de ventas, los vendedores

saleroom /'seɪlru:m, -rʊm/ *n* (BrE) ▸**salesroom 1**

sales /seɪlz/: **~ account** *n* (cuenta *f*) ventas *fpl*; **~clerk** *n* (AmE) vendedor, -dora *m,f*, dependiente, -ta *m,f*; **~ conference** *n* conferencia *f* de ventas; **~girl** *n* vendedora *f*, dependienta *f*; **~lady** *n* vendedora *f*, dependienta *f*; **~man** /'seɪlzmən/ *n* (*pl* **-men** /-mən/) (in shop) vendedor *m*, dependiente *m*; (representative) representante *m*, viajante *m*, corredor *m* (RPl); **~person** *n* (in shop) vendedor, -dora *m,f*, dependiente, -ta *m,f*; (representative) representante *mf*, corredor, -dora *m,f* (RPl); **~ pitch** *n* [u c] discurso *m*, argumentos *mpl* (*de un vendedor*); **~ rep** *n* representante *mf or* agente *mf* comercial; **~ representative** *n* representante *mf or* agente *mf* comercial; **~room** *n* (AmE) 1 (for auctions) sala *f* de subastas, sala *f* de remates (AmL) 2 (showroom) salón *m* de exposición (y ventas); **~ slip** *n* (AmE) recibo *m*, comprobante *m* (de compra *or* venta), boleta *f* (CS); **~ talk** *n* [u] palabrería *f* de vendedor; **~ tax** *n* [u] impuesto *m* sobre las ventas; **~woman** *n* (in shop) vendedora *f*, dependienta *f*; (representative) representante *f*, corredora *f* (RPl)

salient /'seɪliənt/ *adj* (striking) (frml) (*before n*) destacado

saline /'seɪli:n || 'seɪlaɪn/ *adj* salino

saliva /sə'laɪvə/ *n* [u] saliva *f*

salivate /'sæləveɪt || 'sælɪveɪt/ *vi* salivar

sallow /'sæləʊ/ *adj* **-er, -est** cetrino, amarillento

sally /'sæli/ *n* (*pl* **-lies**) (Mil) misión *f*; **to make a ~ into enemy territory** hacer* una incursión en territorio enemigo

(Phrasal verb)

- **sally forth**: **-lies, -lying, -lied** [v ▸ adv] (arch *or* hum) salir*, hacer* una salida

salmon /'sæmən/ *n* [c u] (*pl* ~) (Culin, Zool) salmón *m*; (*before n*) ‹*river/industry*› salmonero

salmonella /'sælmə'nelə/ *n* (*pl* ~ *or* **-llae** /-li:/) salmonella *f*; (*before n*) **~ poisoning** intoxicación *f* por salmonella, salmonelosis *f*

salon /sə'lɑ:n || 'sælɒn/ *n* (business): **hairdressing ~** peluquería *f*; **beauty ~** salón *m* de belleza

saloon /sə'lu:n/ *n*

A 1 (bar) (AmE) bar *m*, taberna *f* (*del Lejano Oeste*) 2 **~ (bar)** (lounge bar) (BrE) bar *m* (*de mayor categoría*)

B ~ (car) (BrE) sedán *m*, turismo *m*

C (on ship) salón *m*

salt¹ /sɔ:lt/ *n* 1 [u] (Culin) sal *f*; ***to be the ~ of the earth*** ser* la sal de la tierra; ***(to be) worth one's ~***: **any teacher worth her ~** toda maestra que se precie de tal, toda maestra digna de ese nombre; ***to rub ~ into the wound(s)*** hurgar* en la herida; ***to take sth with a pinch o grain of ~*** no creerse* algo al pie de la letra, tomar algo con pinzas (CS) 2 [c] (Chem) sal *f*

salt² *vt* 1 (put salt on) ‹*vegetables/meat*› salar, ponerle* *or* echarle sal a; ‹*road*› echar sal en 2 **salted** *past p* salado

(Phrasal verb)

- **salt away** [v ▸ o ▸ adv, v ▸ adv ▸ o] (colloq) ‹*money/profits*› guardar

salt³ *adj* 1 (salted) (*before n*) ‹*meat/cod*› salado, en salazón 2 (saline) (*before n*) ‹*pond/lake*› salobre, de agua salada 3 ‹*air*› salobre; ‹*taste*› salado, a sal

salt: **~ beef** *n* [u]: *carne de vaca curada en salmuera*; **~ cellar** *n* salero *m*; **~ flats** *pl n* salinas *fpl*; **~mine** *n* mina *f* de sal, salina *f*; **~ pork** *n* [u] tocino *m*; **~water** *adj* ‹*lake*› de agua salada, salobre; ‹*fish*› de mar, de agua salada

salty /'sɔ:lti/ *adj* **-tier, -tiest** 1 (full of salt) ‹*food/taste*› salado 2 (earthy) ‹*language*› salado, picante; ‹*wit*› mordaz

salubrious /sə'lu:briəs/ *adj* 1 (healthy) (frml) saludable, salubre 2 (wholesome) (*usu neg*): **not a very ~ district** un barrio muy poco recomendable

salutary /'sæljəteri || 'sæljʊtri/ *adj* saludable, beneficioso

salutation /'sæljə'teɪʃən || ˌsælju:'teɪʃən/ *n* [u c] (frml) 1 (greeting) saludo *m*, salutación *f* (liter) 2 (in letter) fórmula *f* de encabezamiento

salute¹ /sə'lu:t/ *n* 1 [c] (gesture) saludo *m*, venia *f* (RPl) 2 [c] (firing of guns) salva *f*; **a 21-gun ~** una salva de 21 cañonazos 3 (tribute) homenaje *m*, reconocimiento *m*

salute² *vt* 1 (Mil) ‹*officer*› saludar 2 (acknowledge, pay tribute) (frml) ‹*courage/achievement*› rendir* homenaje a

■ **salute** *vi* (Mil) **to ~ (TO sb)** hacerle* el saludo *or* (RPl) la venia (A algn)

Salvadoran¹ /'sælvə'dɔ:rən/ *adj* ▸**Salvadorean¹**

Salvadoran² *n* ▸**Salvadorean²**

Salvadorean¹, **Salvadorian** /'sælvə'dɔ:riən/ *adj* salvadoreño

Salvadorean², **Salvadorian** *n* salvadoreño, -ña *m,f*

salvage¹ /'sælvɪdʒ/ *vt* rescatar

salvage² *n* [u] (rescue) rescate *m*

salvage operation *n* operación *f* de rescate

salvation /sæl'veɪʃən/ *n* [u] salvación *f*

Salvation Army *n* Ejército *m* de Salvación

salve¹ /sæv || sælv/ *n* 1 [u c] (ointment) bálsamo *m*, ungüento *m* 2 [c] (comfort) (*no pl*) **a ~ TO sth** un bálsamo PARA algo

salve² *vt*: **to ~ one's conscience** acallar la voz de su (*or* mi *etc*) conciencia

salvo /'sælvəʊ/ *n* (*pl* **-vos** *or* **-voes**) salva *f*

Samaritan /sə'mærətn̩ || sə'mærɪtən/ *n* (Bib) samaritano, -na *m,f*; **the good ~** el buen samaritano; **the ~s** (charitable organization) los samaritanos

samba /'sæmbə/ *n* (*pl* **-bas**) samba *f or m*

same¹ /seɪm/ *adj* (*before n*) mismo, misma; **the two boxes are exactly the ~** las dos cajas son exactamente iguales; **you men are all the ~** todos los hombres son *or* (Esp) sois iguales; **it's always the ~** siempre pasa lo mismo; **the ~ AS sth**: **we're in the ~ position as before/as you** estamos igual que antes/en tu misma situación; **that dress is the ~ as mine** ese vestido es igual al mío; **the ~ thing happened to me** a mí me pasó lo mismo; **~ time, ~ place** a la misma hora en el mismo sitio; **I'm glad you see things the ~ way (as) I do** me alegro de que veas las cosas como yo; **they are one and the ~ (person/thing)** son la mismísima persona/cosa; **on that very ~ day** ese mismísimo día

same² *pron* 1 : **the ~** lo mismo; **I wish I could say the ~** ¡ojalá pudiera decir lo mismo!; **I'll have the ~** para mí lo mismo; **the ~ goes for you** también va por ti; **I've had enough — ~ here!** (colloq) ya estoy harto — ya somos dos (fam); **have a nice vacation!— ~ to you!** ¡felices vacaciones! — ¡igualmente! *or* ¡lo mismo digo! 2 **all the same, just the same** igual; (*as linker*) de todas formas *or* maneras, así y todo, sin embargo, no obstante (frml); ***it's all the ~ to me/you/them*** me/te/les da lo mismo, me/te/les da igual

same³ *adv*: **the ~** igual; **they're written differently but pronounced the ~** se escriben distinto, pero se pronuncian igual; **how do you feel? — about the ~** ¿qué tal estás? — más o menos igual

same-day /'seɪm'deɪ/ *adj* ‹*service/delivery*› en el día

sameness /'seɪmnəs || 'seɪmnɪs/ *n* [u] (monotony) monotonía *f*, uniformidad *f*

same-sex /'seɪm'seks/ *adj* ‹*partner/couple*› del mismo sexo; ‹*marriage/relationship*› entre personas del mismo sexo; ‹*school*› sólo para niños/niñas

sample¹ /'sæmpəl || 'sɑ:mpəl/ *n* 1 (specimen) muestra *f*; **a blood ~** (Med) una muestra de sangre; (*before n*) **~ question/paper** pregunta *f*/examen *m* tipo 2 (Busn) muestra *f* 3 (for statistics) muestra *f*

sample² *vt* ‹*food*› degustar, probar*

sampler /'sæmplər || 'sɑ:mplə(r)/ *n* 1 (embroidery) dechado *m* 2 (collection) (AmE) muestra *f* (representativa)

sanatorium /'sænə'tɔ:riəm/ *n* (*pl* **-riums** *or* **-ria** /-riə/) sanatorio *m* (*para convalecientes*)

S

sanctify /'sæŋktəfaɪ || 'sæŋktɪfaɪ/ *vt* **-fies, -fying, -fied** santificar*

sanctimonious /'sæŋktə'məʊniəs || ˌsæŋktɪ'məʊniəs/ *adj* (frml) ‹*attitude/comment*› moralista, gazmoño, mojigato

sanction[1] /'sæŋkʃən/ *n*
A [u] (authorization) autorización *f*, sanción *f*
B [c] **1** **sanctions** *pl* (coercive measures) sanciones *fpl*; **economic ~s** sanciones económicas **2** (penalty) sanción *f* **3** (restraint) freno *m*

sanction[2] *vt* ‹*act/initiative*› sancionar (frml), dar* su (*or* mi *etc*) sanción a (frml), aprobar*; ‹*injustice*› consentir*

sanctity /'sæŋktəti/ *n* [u] **1** (inviolability) inviolabilidad *f* **2** (holiness) santidad *f*

sanctuary /'sæŋktʃueri || 'sæŋktjʊəri/ *n* (*pl* **-ries**) **1** [u] (protection, safety) asilo *m*, refugio *m*; **to take ~** refugiarse; (claiming protection of a church) acogerse* a sagrado **2** [c] (place of refuge) santuario *m*, refugio *m* **3** [c] (for animals) reserva *f*

sanctum /'sæŋktəm/ *n* (*pl* **-tums** *or* **-ta** /-tə/) (frml) sagrario *m*; **the inner ~** el sanctasanctórum

sand[1] /sænd/ *n* **1** [u] arena *f*; **~-colored** color arena *adj inv*; ***to build on ~*** hacer* castillos de naipes **2** [c] (expanse of sand) (*often pl*) arena *f*; **the desert ~s** las arenas del desierto

sand[2] *vt* **~ (down)** (make smooth) ‹*wood/furniture*› lijar; ‹*floor*› pulir

sandal /'sændl/ *n* sandalia *f*

sandbag[1] /'sændbæg/ *n* saco *m* de arena, saco *m* terrero

sandbag[2] **-gg-** *vt*
A (barricade) proteger* con sacos de arena *or* sacos terreros
B (bully) (AmE colloq) forzar*, obligar* con *or* por medio de amenazas
C (deceive) (AmE sl): **he was ~ging me** no estaba jugando a tope, para engañarme
■ **sandbag** *vi* (AmE sl) dejarse ganar

sand: **~bank** *n* banco *m* de arena; **~bar** *n* barra *f* (de arena); **~blast** *vt* ‹*stonework/building*› pulir (*con un chorro de arena*); **~box** *n* (AmE) cajón *m* de arena (*en parques y jardines*); **~boy** *n* (BrE): ***to be as happy as a ~boy*** estar* como unas Pascuas, estar* de lo más contento; **~castle** *n* castillo *m* de arena; **~ dune** *n* duna *f*

sander /'sændər || 'sændə(r)/ *n* (machine) lijadora *f*

sand: **~ fly** *n* jején *m*, mosquito *m*; **~lot** *n* (AmE) *solar utilizado para deportes*; (*before n*) ‹*baseball/team*› de barrio, amateur; **~man** /'sændmæn/ *n* **the ~man** *personaje del folclor que hace dormir a los niños poniéndoles arena en los ojos*

sandpaper[1] /'sænd,peɪpər || 'sænd,peɪpə(r)/ *n* [u] papel *m* de lija

sandpaper[2] *vt* lijar

sand: **~piper** *n* lavandera *f*, andarríos *m*; **~pit** *n* (BrE) ▸**sandbox**; **~stone** *n* [u] arenisca *f*; **~storm** *n* tormenta *f* de arena; **~ trap** *n* (in golf) (AmE) búnker *m*

sandwich[1] /'sænwɪtʃ || 'sændwɪdʒ/ *n* (*pl* **-wiches**) sándwich *m*, emparedado *m*, ≈ bocadillo *m* (Esp); **a ham ~** un sándwich de jamón; (*before n*) **~ bar** sandwichería *f*; **~ box** (BrE) fiambrera *f*, lonchera *f* (AmL); **~ loaf** (BrE) pan *m* de molde; **~ toaster** sandwichera *f*

sandwich[2] *vt* (*usu pass*): **a small house ~ed between the church and the library** una casita metida *or* encajonada entre la iglesia y la biblioteca; **I was ~ed between two fat women** estaba apretujado entre dos gordas

sandwich: **~ board** *n* cartelones *mpl* (*que lleva un hombre-anuncio*); **~ course** *n* (BrE) *curso durante el cual se alterna el aprendizaje con el trabajo práctico*; **~ man** /mæn/ *n* (*pl* **men** /men/) hombre-anuncio *m*

sandy /'sændi/ *adj* **-dier, -diest** **1** ‹*beach/path*› de arena; ‹*soil*› arenoso; **the towels were all ~** las toallas estaban llenas de arena **2** (in color) ‹*hair*› rubio rojizo *adj inv*

sand-yachting /'sænd,jɑːtɪŋ || 'sænd,jɒtɪŋ/ *n* [u] navegación *f* a vela sobre arena

sane /seɪn/ *adj* **saner, sanest** **1** (not mad) cuerdo; **it's the only thing that keeps me ~** es lo que impide que me vuelva loco **2** (sensible) sensato

sang /sæŋ/ *past of* **sing**

sangfroid /'sɑːŋ'frwɑː || 'sɒŋfrwɑː/ *n* [u] sangre *f* fría

sanguine /'sæŋgwən || 'sæŋgwɪn/ *adj* (frml) (optimistic) confiado, optimista

sanitarium /'sænə'teriəm || ˌsænɪ'teəriəm/ *n* **1** (AmE) ▸**sanatorium** **2** (health resort) clínica *f*

sanitary /'sænəteri || 'sænɪtri/ *adj* **1** (concerning health) (*before n*) ‹*conditions/regulations*› sanitario, de salubridad; ‹*engineer/engineering*› de saneamiento, sanitario; ‹*inspector*› de sanidad **2** (hygienic) higiénico, salubre

sanitary napkin, (BrE) **sanitary towel** *n* compresa *f*, paño *m* higiénico

sanitation /'sænə'teɪʃən || ˌsænɪ'teɪʃən/ *n* [u] **1** (hygiene) condiciones *fpl* de salubridad **2** (waste disposal system) servicios *mpl* sanitarios

sanitation worker *n* (AmE) empleado, -da *m,f* del servicio de recogida de basuras, basurero, -ra *m,f*, recolector, -tora *m,f* de residuos (RPl frml)

sanitize /'sænətaɪz || 'sænɪtaɪz/ *vt* **1** (disinfect) desinfectar **2** (make inoffensive) (pej) hacer* potable; **a ~d version** una versión aséptica

sanity /'sænəti/ *n* [u] **1** (mental health) razón *f*, cordura *f*; **to lose one's ~** perder* la razón **2** (good sense) sensatez *f*

sank /sæŋk/ *past of* **sink**[1]

Sanskrit /'sænskrɪt/ *n* [u] sánscrito *m*

Santa Claus /'sæntəklɔːz/ *n* Papá Noel, San Nicolás, Santa Claus, Viejo *m* Pascuero (Chi)

sap[1] /sæp/ *n*
A [u] savia *f*
B [c] (fool) (colloq & dated) infeliz *mf*, inocentón, -tona *m,f* (fam)

sap[2] *vt* **-pp-** ‹*strength/energy/enthusiasm*› minar, socavar; ‹*confidence/health*› minar

sapling /'sæplɪŋ/ *n* árbol *m* joven

sapphire /'sæfaɪr || 'sæfaɪə(r)/ *n* **1** [c] (gem) zafiro *m* **2** [u] (color) azul *m* zafiro; (*before n*) ‹*eyes/sea/dress*› azul zafiro *adj inv*

Saragossa /'særə'gɑːsə || ˌsærə'gɒsə/ *n* Zaragoza *f*

sarcasm /'sɑːrkæzəm || 'sɑːkæzəm/ *n* [u] sarcasmo *m*

sarcastic /sɑːr'kæstɪk/ *adj* sarcástico, mordaz

sarcastically /sɑːr'kæstɪkli || sɑː'kæstɪkli/ *adv* sarcásticamente, con sarcasmo *or* sorna

sarcophagus /sɑːr'kɑːfəgəs || sɑː'kɒfəgəs/ *n* (*pl* **-guses** *or* **-gi** /-gaɪ/) sarcófago *m*

sardine /sɑːr'diːn || sɑː'diːn/ *n* (Culin, Zool) sardina *f*; ***to be packed like ~s*** ir*/estar* como sardinas en lata

Sardinia /sɑːr'dɪniə || sɑː'dɪniə/ *n* Cerdeña *f*

sardonic /sɑːr'dɑːnɪk || sɑː'dɒnɪk/ *adj* sardónico

Sargasso Sea /sɑːr'gæsəʊ || sɑː'gæsəʊ/ *n* **the ~ ~** el Mar de los Sargazos

sari /'sɑːri/ *n* (*pl* **~s**) sari *m*

sarnie /'sɑːrni || 'sɑːni/ *n* (BrE colloq) sándwich *m*, bocata *f* (Esp fam)

sarong /sə'rɑːŋ || sə'rɒŋ/ *n* sarong *m*

SARS /sɑːrz/ *n* (**= severe acute respiratory syndrome**) SRAS *m*, SARS *m*

sarsaparilla /'sæspə'rɪlə || ˌsɑːsəpə'rɪlə/ *n* zarzaparrilla *f*

sartorial /sɑːr'tɔːriəl || sɑː'tɔːriəl/ *adj* (liter *or* hum): **renowned for his ~ elegance** famoso por su elegancia en el vestir

SAS (in UK) (**= Special Air Service**) *regimiento especializado en operaciones clandestinas*, ≈ GEO *mpl* (*en Esp*)

SASE *n* (AmE) (**= self-addressed stamped envelope**): **I enclose an ~** adjunto sobre franqueado (a mi nombre)

sash /sæʃ/ *n*
A (on dress) faja *f*; (on uniform — around waist) fajín *m*; (— over shoulder) banda *f*
B (of window) marco *m*; (*before n*) **~ window** ventana *f* de guillotina; **~ cord** cuerda *f* de ventana de guillotina

sashay /sæ'ʃeɪ || 'sæʃeɪ/ *vi* (AmE colloq) andar* pavoneándose *or* (fam) dándose aires

Sask = **Saskatchewan**

sass[1] /sæs/ *n* [u] (AmE colloq) frescura *f* (fam), descaro *m*

sass[2] *vt* (AmE colloq) hablarle descaradamente a

sassafras /'sæsəfræs/ *n* sasafrás *m*

Sassenach /'sæsənæk/ *n* (Scot often pej) inglés, -glesa *m,f*

S

sassy /'sæsi/ *adj* **-sier, -siest** (AmE colloq) 1 (impertinent) caradura (fam), fresco (fam) 2 (brash, jazzy) ‹*hat/style*› llamativo y atrevido

sat /sæt/ *past & past p of* **sit**

Sat (= **Saturday**) sáb.

SAT *n* 1 (in US) = **Scholastic Aptitude Test** 2 (in UK) = **Standard Assessment Task** *o* **Test**

> **SAT**
>
> En EEUU corresponde a las siglas de *Scholastic Aptitude Test*. Una prueba de aptitud que se hace normalmente en el último año del **high school**. Hay que aprobarla para entrar a la mayor parte de las universidades. En Inglaterra y Gales significa *Standard Assessment Test* o *Task*, prueba que se hace a los alumnos de todos los colegios, a los 7, 11, y 14 años, a fin de evaluar su progreso

Satan /'seɪtn̩/ *n* Satanás, Satán

satanic /sə'tænɪk/ *adj* satánico

Satanism /'seɪtn̩ɪzəm || 'seɪtənɪzəm/ *n* [u] satanismo *m*

satchel /'sætʃəl/ *n* cartera *f* (*de colegial*)

sate /seɪt/ *vt* (liter) (*usu pass*) ‹*appetite/lust*› saciar (liter); **to be ~d WITH sth** estar* ahíto DE algo (liter)

satellite /'sætl̩aɪt || 'sætəlaɪt/ *n*
A 1 (Aerosp) satélite *m* (artificial); (*before n*) ‹*communications*› vía satélite; **~ TV** televisión *f* por *or* vía satélite; **~ dish** antena *f* parabólica 2 (Astron) satélite *m*
B 1 (dependent body, state) satélite *m*; (*before n*) **a ~ country/state** un país/estado satélite 2 **~ (town)** ciudad *f* satélite

satiate /'seɪʃieɪt/ *vt* (liter) ‹*person*› llenar hasta el hastío; ‹*desire/appetite/lust*› saciar (liter); **to be ~d with food/pleasure** estar* ahíto de comida/hastiado de placer (liter)

satin /'sætn̩ || 'sætɪn/ *n* [u c] satén *m*, raso *m*, satín *m* (AmL); (*before n*) satinado; **a ~ finish** un acabado satinado

satire /'sætaɪr || 'sætaɪə(r)/ *n* 1 [c] (composition) **a ~ (ON sth)** una sátira (DE *or* A algo) 2 [u] (genre, mode) sátira *f*

satirical /sə'tɪrɪkəl/ *adj* satírico

satirist /'sætərəst || 'sætərɪst/ *n* escritor satírico, escritora satírica *m,f*

satirize /'sætəraɪz/ *vt* satirizar*

satisfaction /'sætəs'fækʃən || ˌsætɪs'fækʃən/ *n* [u]
A (contentment) satisfacción *f*; **~ AT sth/-ING** satisfacción POR algo/+ INF; **~ WITH sth** satisfacción CON algo; **~ guaranteed or your money back** si no queda satisfecho, le devolvemos el dinero; **the matter was settled to everybody's ~** el asunto quedó solucionado a plena satisfacción de todos
B (frml) 1 (fulfillment — of desire, needs) satisfacción *f*; (— of terms, conditions, claim) cumplimiento *m* 2 (reparation) satisfacción *f*, reparación *f*

satisfactorily /'sætəs'fæktrəli || ˌsætɪs'fæktərɪli/ *adv* satisfactoriamente, de manera satisfactoria

satisfactory /'sætəs'fæktri || ˌsætɪs'fæktəri/ *adj* satisfactorio

satisfied /'sætəsfaɪd || 'sætɪsfaɪd/ *adj* ‹*expression/customer*› satisfecho; ‹*smile*› de satisfacción; **(to be) ~ WITH sb/sth** (estar*) satisfecho CON algn/algo

satisfy /'sætəsfaɪ || 'sætɪsfaɪ/ **-fies, -fying, -fied** *vt*
A 1 (please, gratify) satisfacer* 2 (meet, comply with) ‹*requirements*› llenar, reunir*; ‹*demand*› satisfacer*
B (convince) (*often pass*) **to ~ sb OF sth** convencer* a algn DE algo; **I had to ~ myself that he was right** tuve que asegurarme de que tenía razón
■ **satisfy** *vi* 1 (please) satisfacer* 2 (suffice) bastar, ser* suficiente

satisfying /'sætəsfaɪɪŋ || 'sætɪsfaɪɪŋ/ *adj* 1 (pleasing) ‹*result/job*› satisfactorio 2 (filling) ‹*meal*› que llena

satsuma /sæt'suːmə/ *n* satsuma *f* (*tipo de mandarina*)

saturate /'sætʃəreɪt/ *vt*
A (drench) ‹*cloth*› empapar; ‹*person*› (colloq) empapar; **we were ~d** nos empapamos
B (fill) ‹*market/mind/place*› saturar
C (Chem, Phys) saturar

saturation /'sætʃə'reɪʃən/ *n* [u]
A (Busn, Marketing) saturación *f*; (*before n*) ‹*coverage/publicity*› (Journ, Marketing) exhaustivo; **~ point** punto *m* de saturación; **the children have reached ~ point** los niños ya están saturados
B (Chem, Phys) saturación *f*

Saturday /'sætərdeɪ, -di || 'sætədeɪ, -di/ *n* sábado *m*; *see also* **Monday**

Saturn /'sætərn || 'sætən/ *n* Saturno *m*

satyr /'seɪtər || 'sætə(r)/ *n* (Myth) sátiro *m*

sauce /sɔːs/ *n*
A [c u] (Culin) salsa *f*; **white ~** salsa blanca, bechamel *f*; **apple ~** compota *f or* (esp AmL) puré *m* de manzana; ***what's ~ for the goose is ~ for the gander*** si está bien que uno lo haga, está bien que lo haga cualquiera
B [u] (impudence) cara *f* (fam), frescura *f* (fam)

sauce: **~boat** *n* salsera *f*; **~pan** *n* cacerola *f*, cazo *m* (Esp); (large) olla *f*

saucer /'sɔːsər || 'sɔːsə(r)/ *n* platillo *m*

saucy /'sæsi, 'sɔːsi || 'sɔːsi/ *adj* **-cier, -ciest** insolente, fresco (fam)

Saudi[1] /'saʊdi/ *adj* saudita, saudí

Saudi[2] *n* saudita *mf*, saudí *mf*

Saudi: **~ Arabia** *n* Arabia *f* Saudita, Arabia *f* Saudí; **~ Arabian** *adj* saudita, saudí

sauna /'sɔːnə/ *n* sauna *f*, sauna *m* (AmL)

saunter[1] /'sɔːntər || 'sɔːntə(r)/ *vi* pasear; **she ~ed in/out** entró/salió andando despacio; **he ~ed up to the counter** se acercó al mostrador con paso despreocupado

saunter[2] *n* paseo *m*, vuelta *f*

sausage /'sɔːsɪdʒ || 'sɒsɪdʒ/ *n* [c u] (for cooking) salchicha *f*; (cold, cured) embutido *m*; ***not a ~*** (BrE colloq) nada de nada (fam); (*before n*) **~ meat** carne *f* de salchicha

sausage roll *n* (BrE) *salchicha envuelta en hojaldre*

sauté /sɔː'teɪ || 'səʊteɪ/ *vt* **-tés, -téeing** *or* **-téing, -téed** *or* **-téd** saltear, sofreír*

savage[1] /'sævɪdʒ/ *adj* 1 (fierce, wild) ‹*beast/attack*› salvaje, feroz; ‹*blow*› violento; ‹*persecution/criticism*› feroz, despiadado; ‹*cuts/reductions*› salvaje 2 (uncivilized) ‹*tribe/people*› salvaje

savage[2] *n* salvaje *mf*

savage[3] *vt* atacar* salvajemente *or* con fiereza a; **the movie was ~d by the critics** los críticos pusieron la película por los suelos

savagely /'sævɪdʒli/ *adv* ‹*attack/fight*› salvajemente, ferozmente; ‹*criticize*› despiadadamente, ferozmente

savagery /'sævɪdʒri/ *n* [u] (ferocity — of attack, blow) ferocidad *f*, violencia *f*; (— of criticism) ferocidad *f*, fiereza *f*; (— of cuts, reductions) severidad *f*, lo salvaje

savanna, savannah /sə'vænə/ *n* [c u] sabana *f*

save[1] /seɪv/ *vt*
A 1 (rescue, preserve) ‹*job/reputation/marriage*› salvar; **rescue workers ~d 20 people** los trabajadores del servicio de salvamento rescataron a 20 personas; **to ~ sth/sb FROM sth/-ING** salvar algo/a algn DE algo/ + INF; **to ~ sb from herself/himself** impedir* que algn siga haciéndose daño; **God ~ the King/Queen!** ¡Dios salve *or* guarde al Rey/a la Reina!; ***to ~ one's bacon*** *o* ***neck*** *o* ***skin*** (colloq) salvar el pellejo (fam) 2 (redeem) ‹*soul/sinner*› salvar, redimir
B 1 (be economical with) ‹*money/fuel/space/time*› ahorrar 2 (spare, avoid) ‹*trouble/expense/embarrassment*› ahorrar, evitar; **to ~ (sb) sth/-ING**: **drip-drying the shirts ~s ironing them** si dejas escurrir las camisas, te evitas *or* te ahorras tener que plancharlas; **it will ~ you a journey** te ahorrarás un viaje
C 1 (keep, put aside) guardar; ‹*money*› ahorrar; **don't eat it now; ~ it for later** no te lo comas ahora; déjalo para luego; **to ~ oneself for sb/sth** reservarse para algn/algo; **to ~ one's energy/strength** guardarse las energías/las fuerzas; ***to ~ one's breath*** (colloq) no gastar saliva (fam) 2 (Comput) guardar, almacenar
D (Sport) ‹*shot/penalty*› detener*, salvar
■ **save** *vi* ahorrar; **to ~ ON sth** ahorrar algo

Phrasal verb

• **save up**
A [v ▸ adv] ahorrar; **I'm saving up for a car/to buy a car** estoy ahorrando para (comprarme) un coche
B [v ▸ o ▸ adv, v ▸ adv ▸ o] ahorrar

save[2] *n* parada *f*

S

save³ *prep* (frml) [1] (apart from) ~ **(for)** salvo, excepto, con excepción de [2] ~ **for** (if it weren't for): **he would have died, ~ for the fact that ...** se habría muerto, si no hubiera sido porque ... *or* de no haber sido porque ...

saver /'seɪvər || 'seɪvə(r)/ *n* ahorrador, -dora *m,f*, ahorrista *mf* (RPl), ahorrante *mf* (Chi)

saving¹ /'seɪvɪŋ/ *n*

A [1] [u] (accumulation) ahorro *m* [2] **savings** *pl* ahorros *mpl*; **life ~s** los ahorros de toda una vida; (*before n*) **~s account** cuenta *f* de ahorros

B [c] (economy) ahorro *m*; **~s** *o* **a ~ of $1,000 a week** un ahorro de 1.000 dólares por semana; **to make ~s** hacer* economías, economizar*

saving² *adj* (*before n*) *see* **grace¹ B3**

-saving /,seɪvɪŋ/ *suff*: **money~/time~** que ahorra dinero/tiempo

savings /'seɪvɪŋz/: **~ and loan** *n* **~ and loan (association/company)** (AmE) sociedad *f* de ahorro y préstamos; **~ bank** *n* caja *f* de ahorros

savior, (BrE) **saviour** /'seɪvjər || 'seɪvjə(r)/ *n* [1] (rescuer) salvador, -dora *m,f* [2] **Savior** (Relig) **the/our S~** el/nuestro Salvador

savor¹, (BrE) **savour** /'seɪvər || 'seɪvə(r)/ *vt* ‹*food/wine*› saborear, paladear; ‹*experience/feeling*› saborear; ‹*sight/memory*› recrearse en

savor², (BrE) **savour** *n* (taste) sabor *m*; (hint, trace) dejo *m*

savory¹ /'seɪvəri/ *n* [u c] (*pl* **-ries**) (Bot, Culin) ajedrea *f*

savory², (BrE) **savoury** /'seɪvəri/ *adj* (tasty) sabroso; (wholesome) (*usu with neg*) limpio; **it doesn't make very ~ reading** no es una lectura muy sana

savour *vt/n* (BrE) ▸ **savor¹,²**

savoury¹ /'seɪvəri/ *n* (*pl* **-ries**) (BrE) *platillo salado que se sirve al final de una comida*

savoury² *adj* (BrE) [1] ▸ **savory²** [2] (not sweet) salado

savvy /'sævi/ *adj* **-vier, -viest** (AmE colloq) espabilado (fam), despabilado (fam)

saw¹ /sɔː/ *past of* **see¹**

saw² *n*

A (tool — manual) sierra *f*; (— with one handle) serrucho *m*; (power-driven) sierra *f* mecánica

B (saying) dicho *m*

saw³ (*past p* **sawed** *or* (esp BrE) **sawn**) *vt* (with handsaw) cortar (*con serrucho*), serruchar (AmL); (with a larger saw) cortar (*con sierra*), serrar*, aserrar*; **to ~ sth up** cortar algo en trozos con una sierra/un serrucho

■ **saw** *vi* (with handsaw) cortar (*con serrucho*), serruchar (AmL); (with a larger saw) cortar (*con sierra*), serrar*

saw: **~buck** *n* (AmE) [1] ▸ **sawhorse** [2] (ten-dollar bill) (sl) (billete *m* de) diez dólares *mpl*; **~dust** *n* [u] serrín *m*, aserrín *m* (esp AmL)

sawed-off /'sɔːd'ɔːf || 'sɔːdɒf/, (BrE) **sawn-off** /'sɔːnɔːf || 'sɔːnɒf/ *adj*: **~ shotgun** escopeta *f* recortada, escopeta *f* de cañón recortado *or* de cañones recortados

saw: **~fish** /'sɔːfɪʃ/ *n* (*pl* ~ *or* **~es**) pez *m* sierra; **~horse** *n* caballete *m*, burro *m* (*para serrar*); **~mill** *n* (factory) aserradero *m*; (machine) aserrador *m*

sawn /sɔːn/ *past p of* **saw³**

sawn-off *adj* (BrE) ▸ **sawed-off**

sax /sæks/ *n* (colloq) saxo *m* (fam)

saxophone /'sæksəfəʊn/ *n* saxofón *m*, saxófono *m*; (*before n*) **~ player** saxofonista *mf*

saxophonist /'sæksəfəʊnəst || sæk'sɒfənɪst/ *n* saxofonista *mf*

say¹ /seɪ/ (*pres* **says** /sez/; *past & past p* **said** /sed/) *vt*

A (utter, express in speech) ‹*word/sentence/mass*› decir*; ‹*prayer*› rezar*; **to ~ good morning to sb** darle* los buenos días a algn; **I said yes/no** dije que sí/no; **he said yes/no to my proposal** aceptó/rechazó mi propuesta; **go away, she said** —vete— dijo; **he didn't ~ a word** no dijo ni una palabra *or* (fam) ni pío; **well said!** ¡bien dicho!; **to ~ sth TO sb** decirle* algo A algn; **don't ~ you forgot!** ¡no me digas que se te olvidó!; **I can't ~ when they'll be back** no sé cuándo volverán; **who shall I ~ is calling?** ¿de parte de quién?; **well, what can I ~?** ¿y qué quieres que te diga?; **it was, how** *o* **what shall I ~, a tricky situation** fue, cómo te (lo) diría, una situación delicada; **if you disagree, ~ so** si no está de acuerdo, dígalo; **why didn't you ~ so before?** haberlo dicho antes; **I should ~ so** (emphatic agreement) eso digo yo; (probability) yo diría que sí; **that's to ~** es decir; **it doesn't ~ much for ...** no dice mucho de ...; **there's a lot to be said for waiting** hay muchas razones por las que bien vale la pena esperar; **there's nothing more to be said!** ¡no hay más que decir!; **to ~ the least** como mínimo; **what have you got to ~ for yourself?** a ver, explícate; **the less said about it, the better** cuanto menos se hable del asunto, mejor; **~ no more** no me digas más; **you can ~ that again!** ¡y que lo digas!; **it goes without ~ing that ...** huelga decir que ..., ni que decir tiene que ..., por supuesto que ...; **though I ~ it myself** modestia aparte, no es por decirlo; **that's easier said than done** del dicho al hecho hay mucho trecho; **no sooner said than done** dicho y hecho; **when all's said and done** al fin y al cabo; ***before you could ~ knife*** *o* ***Jack Robinson*** en un santiamén, en un abrir y cerrar de ojos

B [1] (state) decir*; **it said in the paper that ...** el periódico decía *or* ponía que ... [2] «*watch/dial*» marcar*

C [1] (suppose) (colloq) suponer*, poner*; **(let's) ~ that ...** supongamos *or* pongamos que ...; **shall we ~ tomorrow?** ¿qué tal mañana? (fam) [2] (estimate) decir*

D [1] (allege) decir*; **he's been ill, or so he ~s** ha estado enfermo, al menos eso es lo que dice; **to be said to + INF**: **she's said to be very mean/strict** dicen que es muy tacaña/severa [2] (decide, pronounce) decir*; **that's really not for me to ~** eso no me corresponde a mí decirlo

E (respond to suggestion) (colloq): **what do** *o* **would you ~ to a cup of tea** ¿quieres *or* (esp Esp) te apetece una taza de té?, ¿qué te parece si nos tomamos un té?; **I wouldn't ~ no to a drink** no rechazaría una copa

■ **say** *vi* decir*; **I'd rather not ~** prefiero no decirlo; **it's hard to ~** es difícil decirlo; **you were ~ing?** ¿(qué) decías?; **who ~s** *o* **~s who?** (colloq) ¿quién lo dice?; **you don't ~!** (colloq) ¡no me digas!; **I ~!** (BrE colloq): **I ~! what a lovely dress!** ¡pero qué vestido más bonito!

say² *interj* (AmE colloq) ¡oye! (fam); **~, that's a great idea!** ¡oye, qué buena idea! (fam); **~, buddy** ¡eh, amigo!

say³ *n* (*no pl*) [1] (statement of view): **to have one's ~** dar* su (*or* mi *etc*) opinión [2] (power) **~ (IN sth)**: **I have no ~ in the matter** yo no tengo ni voz ni voto en el asunto; **to have the final ~ (in sth)** tener* la última palabra (en algo)

saying /'seɪɪŋ/ *n* refrán *m*, dicho *m*; **as the ~ goes** como dice el refrán *or* dicho

say-so /'seɪsəʊ/ *n* (*no pl*) (colloq) visto bueno *m*; **I'm not going to do it just on your ~** no voy a hacerlo sólo porque tú lo digas

S-bend /'esbend/ *n* (BrE) sifón *m*

SC = **South Carolina**

scab /skæb/ *n*

A (on wound) costra *f*, postilla *f*

B (strike breaker) (pej) esquirol *mf* (pey), rompehuelgas *mf* (pey), carnero, -ra *m,f* (RPl fam & pey)

scabbard /'skæbərd || 'skæbəd/ *n* vaina *f* (*de una espada*), funda *f*

scads /skædz/ *pl n* (AmE colloq): **~ of money/food/people** montones *mpl* de dinero/comida/gente (fam)

scaffold /'skæfəld, -fəʊld/ *n* (Const) andamio *m*; (for execution) patíbulo *m*, cadalso *m*

scaffolding /'skæfəldɪŋ, '-fəʊldɪŋ/ *n* [u] (structure) andamiaje *m*, andamios *mpl*; (materials) andamiaje *m*

scalawag /skæləwæg/, (esp BrE) **scallywag** *n* (colloq) pillo, -lla *m,f* (fam)

scald¹ /skɔːld/ *vt* [1] (burn) ‹*person/skin*› escaldar [2] (treat with hot water) ‹*instrument*› esterilizar* (*con agua hirviendo*); ‹*vegetables/meat*› escaldar [3] (heat) ‹*milk*› calentar* (*sin que llegue al punto de ebullición*)

scald² *n* escaldadura *f*

scalding /'skɔːldɪŋ/ *adj* ‹*liquid/tea*› hirviendo

scale¹ /skeɪl/ *n*

Sense I

A (*no pl*) [1] (extent, size) escala *f*; **on a large/small ~** en gran/pequeña escala [2] (of map, diagram) escala *f*; **to draw/make sth to ~** dibujar/hacer* algo a escala; ⊗ **not to scale** no está a escala; (*before n*) ‹*model/drawing*› a escala

B [c] (on measuring instrument) escala *f*; **on a ~ of 1 to 10** en una escala del 1 al 10; **wage ~** escala salarial; **~ of charges** tarifa *f* de precios (*or* honorarios *etc*)

S

C [c] (Mus) escala *f*
D [c] [1] (for weighing) (*usu pl*) balanza *f*, pesa *f*; **bathroom ~s** una báscula *or* pesa (de baño); **a kitchen ~** una balanza *or* una pesa de cocina, un peso; ▸**tip² B1** [2] (pan) platillo *m*

Sense II

A [c] (on fish, snake) escama *f*; ***the ~s fell from my/her/their eyes*** se me/le/les cayó la venda de los ojos
B [u] (deposit — in kettle, pipes) sarro *m*

scale² *vt* ‹*mountain/wall/rock face*› escalar; ‹*ladder*› subir

Phrasal verbs

- **scale down** [v ▸ o ▸ adv, v ▸ adv ▸ o] ‹*model/drawing*› reducir* (a escala); ‹*operation/investment*› recortar, disminuir*; **a ~d-down model/version** una maqueta/versión a escala (reducida)
- **scale up** [v ▸ o ▸ adv, v ▸ adv ▸ o] ‹*drawing/model*› agrandar (a escala); ‹*operation/investment*› ampliar*

scallion /'skæljən/ *n* (AmE) [1] (young onion) cebolleta *f*, cebollino *m*, cebolla *f* de verdeo (RPl), cebollín *m* (Chi) [2] (shallot) chalote *m*, chalota *f*

scallop /'skæləp/ *n* (shellfish) vieira *f*, ostión *m* (CS); (shell) concha *f* de vieira *or* (CS) de ostión, venera *f*

scalloped /'skæləpt/ *adj*
A (wavy) festoneado
B (Culin): **~ potatoes** papas *fpl or* (Esp) patatas *fpl* gratinadas *or* al gratén

scallywag /'skæliwæg/ *n* (BrE) ▸**scalawag**

scalp¹ /skælp/ *n* (Anat) cuero *m* cabelludo; (as trophy) cabellera *f*

scalp² *vt*: **to ~ sb** arrancarle* la cabellera a algn

scalpel /'skælpəl/ *n* bisturí *m*, escalpelo *m*

scaly /'skeɪli/ *adj* **-lier, -liest** ‹*fish/skin*› escamoso

scam /skæm/ *n* (colloq) chanchullo *m* (fam)

scamp /skæmp/ *n* (colloq) bribón, -bona *m,f* (fam), granuja *mf*

scamper /'skæmpər || 'skæmpə(r)/ *vi* corretear; **she ~ed off** se fue correteando

scampi /'skæmpi/ *pl n* langostinos *mpl* (*gen rebozados*)

scan¹ /skæn/ **-nn-** *vt*
A «*person*» [1] ‹*horizon*› escudriñar, otear, escrutar (liter) [2] ‹*noticeboard/newspaper*› recorrer con la vista; ‹*report/paper*› echarle un vistazo a
B [1] (Med) ‹*body/brain*› hacer* un escáner *or* scanner de; (with ultrasound scanner) hacer* una ecografía de [2] «*radar/sonar*» explorar
C (Lit) medir*, escandir
■ **scan** *vi* (Lit): **how does this line ~?** ¿cómo se mide este verso?; **his poetry doesn't ~** su poesía no se atiene a las reglas de la métrica

scan² *n* [1] (Med) escáner *m*, scanner *m*, escanograma *m*; (ultrasound) ecografía *f* [2] (Astron, Comput, Mil) exploración *f*

scandal /'skændl̩/ *n* [1] [c] (outrage) escándalo *m*; **to cause a ~** provocar* un escándalo; **it's a ~ that ...** es un escándalo *or* una vergüenza que ... (+ *subj*) [2] [u] (gossip) chismorreo *m*; **a juicy bit of ~** un chisme jugoso

scandalize /'skændl̩aɪz/ *vt* escandalizar*; **they were ~d** se escandalizaron

scandalmonger /'skændl̩,mɑːŋgər || 'skændl̩,mʌŋgə(r)/ *n* chismoso, -sa *m,f*

scandalous /'skændl̩əs/ *adj* escandaloso; **it's ~ the way she's been treated** es un escándalo *or* es vergonzoso cómo la han tratado

scandalously /'skændl̩əsli/ *adv* ‹*treat*› de forma escandalosa; ‹*expensive*› escandalosamente

Scandinavia /'skændə'neɪviə || ,skændɪ'neɪviə/ *n* Escandinavia *f*

Scandinavian¹ /'skændə'neɪviən || ,skændɪ'neɪviən/ *adj* escandinavo

Scandinavian² *n* escandinavo, -va *m,f*

scanner /'skænər || 'skænə(r)/ *n* [1] (Med) escáner *m*, scanner *m*, escanógrafo *m*; (ultrasound) ecógrafo *m* [2] (Comput) analizador *m* de léxico, explorador *m*

scant /skænt/ *adj* (inadequate) (*usu before n*) escaso

scantily /'skæntl̩i || 'skæntɪli/ *adv* ‹*furnished*› escasamente; **~ clad** ligero de ropa

scanty /'skænti/ *adj* **-tier, -tiest** ‹*information*› insuficiente, escaso; ‹*evidence*› insuficiente; ‹*meal*› poco abundante, frugal; ‹*costume/lingerie*› breve

scapegoat /'skeɪpgəʊt/ *n* chivo *m* expiatorio, chivo *m* emisario, cabeza *f* de turco

scar¹ /skɑːr || skɑː(r)/ *n* [1] (on skin — from cut, burn, operation) cicatriz *f*; (— from smallpox, vaccination) marca *f*, señal *f* [2] (on plant, tree) marca *f*

scar² *vt* **-rr-** ‹*tree/stem*› dejar una marca en; **his face was badly ~red** tenía una enorme cicatriz en el rostro; **she'll be ~red for life** (physically) le va a quedar (la) cicatriz; (emotionally) va a quedar marcada

scarce /skers || skeəs/ *adj* escaso; **to be ~** escasear; ***to make oneself ~*** esfumarse (fam)

scarcely /'skersli || 'skeəsli/ *adv* apenas; **I could ~ understand what he was saying** apenas podía entender lo que decía

scarcity /'skersəti || 'skeəsəti/ *n* [c u] (*pl* **-ties**) (shortage) escasez *f*, carestía *f*; (infrequency) lo poco común; (*before n*): **it has ~ value** es valioso por lo escaso

scare¹ /sker || skeə(r)/ *vt* ‹*person/animal*› asustar; **you ~d me!** ¡qué susto me diste!
■ **scare** *vi* asustarse

Phrasal verbs

- **scare away, scare off** [v ▸ o ▸ adv, v ▸ adv ▸ o] ‹*animal*› espantar, ahuyentar
- **scare up** [v ▸ o ▸ adv, v ▸ adv ▸ o] (AmE colloq) (improvise) improvisar; (get) conseguir*, agenciarse (fam)

scare² *n* [1] (fright, shock) susto *m*; **to give sb a ~** darle* un susto a algn [2] (panic) (Journ): **bomb ~** amenaza *f* de bomba; **the AIDS ~** el pánico del sida; (*before n*) **~ story** historia *f* alarmista

scarecrow /'skerkrəʊ || 'skeəkrəʊ/ *n* espantapájaros *m*; (person) (colloq) espantajo *m* (fam)

scared /skerd || skeəd/ *adj* asustado; **I'm ~** tengo miedo, estoy asustada; **she's ~ to death** está que se muere de miedo, está con un miedo *or* un susto que se muere; **to be ~ OF sth/sb** tenerle* miedo A algo/algn; **to be ~ OF -ING** tener* miedo DE + INF; **to be ~ to + INF**: **she's ~ to go out at night** le da miedo salir de noche

scaredy-cat /'skerdikæt || 'skeədikæt/ *n* (colloq) miedoso, -sa *m,f*, miedica *mf* (Esp fam)

scaremongering /'sker,mɑːŋgərɪŋ || 'skeəmʌŋgərɪŋ/ *n* [u] alarmismo *m*

scarf /skɑːrf || skɑːf/ *n* (*pl* **~s** *or* **scarves**) [1] (muffler) bufanda *f* [2] (square) pañuelo *m*

scarlet¹ /'skɑːrlət || 'skɑːlət/ *adj* (rojo) escarlata *adj inv*; **to turn ~** ponerse* colorado

scarlet² *n* [u] rojo *m* escarlata

scarlet fever *n* [u] escarlatina *f*

scarper /'skɑːrpər || 'skɑːpə(r)/ *vi* (BrE sl) largarse* (fam), rajar (Bol, CS fam)

scarves /skɑːrvz || skɑːvz/ *pl of* **scarf**

scary /'skeri || 'skeəri/ *adj* **-rier, -riest** (colloq) ‹*film*› de miedo, de terror; **it was a ~ experience for us** pasamos mucho miedo

scathing /'skeɪðɪŋ/ *adj* ‹*criticism/condemnation*› mordaz, feroz; ‹*irony/wit/sarcasm*› mordaz, cáustico

scatological /'skætl̩'ɑːdʒɪkəl || ,skætə'lɒdʒɪkəl/ *adj* escatológico

scatter /'skætər || 'skætə(r)/ *vt*
A ‹*salt/grit*› esparcir*; ‹*seeds*› sembrar* (a voleo); **to ~ sth OVER/ON sth**: **clothes lay ~ed all over the room** había ropa desparramada *or* tirada por toda la habitación; **we ~ed the ashes on the garden** esparcimos las cenizas por el jardín
B (disperse) ‹*crowd/group*› dispersar; **the gunfire ~ed the birds** el tiro desperdigó a los pájaros; **they are now ~ed all over the country** ahora están desperdigados *or* diseminados por todo el país
■ **scatter** *vi* «*crowd/light*» dispersarse

scatter: **~brained** /'skætər'breɪnd || 'skætəbreɪnd/ *adj* ‹*person*› atolondrado, despistado; **~ cushion** *n* cojín *m*, almohadón *m*

scattered /'skætərd || 'skætəd/ *adj* (*before n*) ‹*fighting*› aislado, disperso; ‹*applause/outbreak*› aislado; ‹*community*› diseminado; **~ showers** chubascos *mpl* aislados

scattershot /'skætərʃɑːt || 'skætəʃɒt/ *adj* (AmE) (*before n*) ‹*approach/effect*› amplio y disperso

S

scatty /ˈskæti/ *adj* **-tier, -tiest** (BrE colloq) (scatterbrained) atolondrado, despistado; (crazy) chiflado (fam), chalado (fam)

scavenge /ˈskævəndʒ || ˈskævɪndʒ/ *vi* **to ~ FOR sth** escarbar *or* hurgar* en busca de algo

scavenger /ˈskævəndʒər || ˈskævɪndʒə(r)/ *n* 1 (animal, bird) carroñero, -ra *m,f* 2 (person) *persona que busca comida etc hurgando en los desperdicios*

scenario /səˈneriəʊ, -ˈnæ- || sɪˈnɑːriəʊ/ *n* (*pl* **-os**) 1 (Cin, TV) guión *m* 2 (of future) perspectiva *f*, panorama *m*, escenario *m* (period); **the best-/worst-case ~** el mejor/peor de los panoramas

scene /siːn/ *n*

A 1 (place): **Golden Square, the ~ of violent demonstrations** Golden Square, escenario de violentas manifestaciones; **the ~ of the crime** la escena *or* el lugar del crimen; **the police were on the ~ within minutes** la policía llegó al lugar de los hechos en pocos minutos; **to appear on the ~** aparecer*, llegar*; **to set the ~ (for sth)** situar* la escena (de algo) 2 (view, situation) escena *f*; **~s from everyday life** escenas de la vida cotidiana

B (in play, book etc) escena *f*; **Act One, S~ Three** acto primero, escena tercera

C (stage setting) decorado *m*; ***behind the ~s*** entre bastidores; (*before n*) **~ change** cambio *m* de decorado

D (fuss, row) escena *f*; **to make** *o* **create a ~** hacer* una escena, armar un escándalo, montar un número (Esp fam)

E (sphere) ámbito *m*; **the political ~** el ámbito político; **the (gay) scene** el ambiente (gay); **the drug ~** el mundo de la droga; **it's not my ~** (colloq) no es lo mío

scenery /ˈsiːnəri/ *n* [u]

A (surroundings) paisaje *m*

B (Theat) escenografía *f*, decorado *m*

scenic /ˈsiːnɪk/ *adj* 1 (picturesque) ‹*drive/road/view*› pintoresco 2 (Cin, Theat) ‹*shot/backdrop*› panorámico

scent¹ /sent/ *n* 1 [c u] (fragrance) perfume *m*, fragancia *f*, aroma *m* 2 [c u] (perfume) (BrE) perfume *m* 3 (trail) rastro *m*; **to put** *o* **throw sb off the ~** despistar a algn

scent² *vt* 1 (smell) «*animal*» olfatear, oler*; «*person*» oler* 2 (sense) ‹*danger/victory*› intuir*, presentir* 3 (perfume) ‹*air/room/skin*› perfumar 4 **scented** *past p* ‹*writing paper*› perfumado; ‹*rose*› fragante

scepter, (BrE) **sceptre** /ˈseptər || ˈseptə(r)/ *n* cetro *m*

sceptic *etc* (BrE) ▸**skeptic** *etc*

sceptre *n* (BrE) ▸**scepter**

schedule¹ /ˈskedʒuːl || ˈʃedjuːl/ *n*

A (plan) programa *m*, calendario *m*; **the flight is due to arrive on ~** el vuelo llegará a la hora prevista; **we are falling behind ~** nos estamos atrasando con respecto al programa *or* al calendario; **the work is on/ahead of ~** llevamos el trabajo al día/adelantado

B [c] 1 (list) (frml) lista *f*; **~ of charges** (Law) pliego *m* de cargos 2 (appendix) anexo *m*, apéndice *m* 3 (AmE) (timetable — for transport) horario *m*; (— for classes) horario *m* (de clases)

schedule² *vt* (timetable, plan) (*usu pass*) programar; **additional meetings have been ~d** se han fijado *or* programado más reuniones; **to be ~d to + INF**: **the conference is ~d to take place in August** la conferencia está planeada para el mes de agosto; **to be ~d FOR sth**: **the building is ~d for demolition** está prevista la demolición del edificio

scheduled /ˈskedʒuːld || ˈʃedjuːld/ *adj* (*before n*) 1 (planned) ‹*meeting/visit*› previsto, programado; **the ~ time of arrival/departure** la hora de llegada/salida 2 (not chartered) ‹*flight/service*› regular

schematic /skɪˈmætɪk/ *adj* esquemático

scheme¹ /skiːm/ *n* 1 (design): **rhyme ~** rima *f*; **man's place in the ~ of things** el lugar del hombre en el (orden del) universo 2 (plan) plan *m*; (underhand) ardid *m*; (plot) confabulación *f*, conspiración *f* 3 (project) (BrE) plan *m*; **a pension ~** un plan de pensiones

scheme² *vi* intrigar*; (plot) conspirar

scheming¹ /ˈskiːmɪŋ/ *adj* intrigante, maquinador

scheming² *n* [u] maquinaciones *fpl*, intrigas *fpl*

schism /ˈsɪzəm, ˈskɪzəm/ *n* [u c] cisma *m*; **it produced ~s within the group** creó escisiones en el grupo

schizophrenia /ˈskɪtsəˈfriːniə/ *n* [u] esquizofrenia *f*

schizophrenic¹ /ˈskɪtsəˈfrenɪk, -ˈfriːnɪk || ˌskɪtsəʊˈfrenɪk, -friːnɪk/ *n* esquizofrénico, -ca *m,f*

schizophrenic² *adj* esquizofrénico

schlemiel /ʃləˈmiːl/ *n* (AmE sl & pej) pobre infeliz *mf*

schlep, schlepp /ʃlep/ **-pp-** *vi* (AmE colloq): **I ~ped all the way there** me pegué la paliza de ir hasta allí (fam)

■ **schlep** *vt* ‹*shopping/furniture*› arrastrar

schmaltz, schmalz /ʃmɔːlts/ *n* [u] (colloq) sensiblería *f*

schmaltzy, schmalzy /ˈʃmɔːltsi/ *adj* **-zier, -ziest** (colloq) sensiblero, sentimentaloide

schmooze /ʃmuːz/ *vi* (AmE) (colloq) chismear (fam), chismorrear (fam), cotillear (Esp fam), chismosear (Col, CS fam)

schmoozer /ˈʃmuːzə(r)/ *n persona que usa la labia para crear contactos*

schmuck /ʃmʌk/ *n* (esp AmE) pendejo *m* (AmL exc CS) *or* (Esp) gilipollas *m or* (AmS) pelotudo *m or* (Andes, Ven) huevón *m* (vulg)

schnitzel /ˈʃnɪtsəl/ *n* [c u] escalope *m or* (Chi) escalopa *f*

scholar /ˈskɑːlər || ˈskɒlə(r)/ *n* 1 (learned person) erudito, -ta *m,f*, estudioso, -sa *m,f*; **Arabic/Latin ~** arabista *mf*/latinista *mf* 2 (holder of scholarship) becario, -ria *m,f*

scholarly /ˈskɑːlərli || ˈskɒləli/ *adj* ‹*person*› erudito, docto; ‹*attainments*› en el campo académico; ‹*appearance*› de intelectual

scholarship /ˈskɑːlərʃɪp || ˈskɒləʃɪp/ *n*

A [c] (grant) beca *f*; **athletic ~** (AmE) beca *f* deportiva

B [u] (scholarliness) erudición *f*

scholastic /skəˈlæstɪk/ *adj* (*before n*) (Educ frml) ‹*achievement/profession/opinion*› académico

school¹ /skuːl/ *n*

A [c u] 1 (in primary, secondary education) colegio *m*, escuela *f*; **to go to ~** ir* al colegio *or* a la escuela; **are you still at** *o* (AmE) **in school?** ¿todavía vas al colegio?; **to leave ~** terminar la escuela; **when do the children go back to ~?** ¿cuándo empiezan las clases?, ¿cuándo vuelven los niños al colegio?; **he teaches ~** (AmE) es maestro; **I'll see you after ~** te veo después de clase; **I missed ~ yesterday** ayer falté a clase *or* al colegio; (*before n*) ‹*uniform/rules*› del colegio; ‹*bus/inspector*› escolar; **children of ~ age** niños *mpl* en edad escolar; **~ fees** *cuotas que se pagan en un colegio particular*, colegiatura *f* (Méx); **~ report** (BrE) boletín *m or* (Méx) boleta *f* de calificaciones *or* notas; **~ year** año *m* escolar *or* lectivo 2 (college, university) (AmE) universidad *f* 3 (department) facultad *f*; **he graduated from law/medical ~** se licenció en derecho/medicina, se recibió de abogado/médico (AmL); **the S~ of Law** la Facultad *or* (Chi tb) la Escuela de Derecho

B [c u] (other training establishment) academia *f*, escuela *f*; **language ~** academia *f or* escuela *f* de idiomas

C [c] (tendency, group) escuela *f*; **there are several ~s of thought on this issue** sobre este tema hay varias corrientes de opinión

D [c] (of fish) cardumen *m*; (of dolphins, whales) grupo *m*

school² *vt* ‹*animal*› adiestrar; ‹*person*› instruir*; (train) capacitar

school: **~boy** *n* colegial *m*, escolar *m*; (*before n*) ‹*slang/humor*› de niños (de colegio); **~child** *n* colegial, -giala *m,f*, escolar *mf*; **~days** *pl n* tiempos *mpl or* años *mpl* de colegio; **~friend** *n* amigo, -ga *m,f* del colegio; **~girl** *n* colegiala *f*, escolar *f*; **~house** *n* escuela *f*

schooling /ˈskuːlɪŋ/ *n* [u] educación *f*, estudios *mpl*

school: **~kid** *n* (colloq) niño, -ña *m,f* (*que va al colegio*); **~-leaver** /ˈskuːlˌliːvər || ˈskuːlˌliːvə(r)/ *n* (BrE) joven *mf* que termina el colegio; **~-leaving age** *n* (BrE) *edad hasta la cual es obligatoria la escolaridad*; **~marm** /ˈskuːl mɑːrm || ˈskuːlmɑːm/, **~ma'am** /ˈskuːlmæm || ˈskuːlmɑːm/ *n* (colloq) maestra *f*; **~master** *n* (BrE frml) (in primary school) maestro *m*; (in secondary school) profesor *m*; **~mate** *n* compañero, -ra *m,f* de colegio; **~mistress** *n* (BrE frml) (in primary school) maestra; (in secondary school) profesora *f*; **~room** *n* aula *f*‡, clase *f*; **~teacher** *n* (in primary school) maestro, -tra *m,f*; (in secondary school) profesor, -sora *m,f*; **~teaching** *n* [u] enseñanza *f*, docencia *f*; **~work** *n* [u] trabajo *m* escolar

schooner /ˈskuːnər || ˈskuːnə(r)/ *n*

A (Naut) goleta *f*

B 1 (glass for beer) (AmE) jarra *f or* bock *m or* (Méx) tarro *m* de cerveza 2 (glass for sherry) (BrE) copa *f* de jerez

sciatica /saɪ'ætɪkə/ *n* [u] ciática *f*

science /'saɪəns/ *n* 1 [u] (in general) ciencia *f*; ***to blind sb with*** ~ (hum) deslumbrar a algn con sus (*or* tus *etc*) conocimientos 2 [u c] (academic subject) ciencia *f*; **the ~s** las ciencias

science: ~ **fiction** *n* [u] ciencia ficción *f*; ~ **park** *n*: *polígono de desarrollo tecnológico vinculado a una universidad*

scientific /'saɪən'tɪfɪk/ *adj* científico

scientifically /'saɪən'tɪfɪkli/ *adv* científicamente

scientist /'saɪəntəst || 'saɪəntɪst/ *n* científico, -ca *m,f*

Scientologist /'saɪən'tɑːlədʒəst || ˌsaɪən'tɒlədʒɪst/ *n* cientólogo, -ga *m,f*

Scientology /'saɪən'tɑːlədʒi/ *n* [u] Cientología *f*

sci-fi /'saɪ'faɪ/ *n* [u] (colloq) ciencia *f* ficción

Scilly Isles /'sɪli/, **Scillies** /'sɪliz/ *pl n* **the** ~ ~ las islas Scilly *or* Sorlingas

scintillating /'sɪntḷeɪtɪŋ || 'sɪntɪleɪtɪŋ/ *adj* ‹*wit/conversation*› chispeante

scissors /'sɪzərz || 'sɪzəz/ *n* (+ *pl vb*) tijeras *fpl*, tijera *f*; **a pair of ~** unas tijeras, una tijera

sclerosis /sklə'rəʊsəs || sklɪə'rəʊsɪs/ *n* [u c] (*pl* **-ses** /-siːz/) esclerosis *f*

scoff[1] /skɑːf || skɒf/ *vi* **to ~** (**AT sb/sth**) burlarse *or* mofarse (DE algn/algo)

■ **scoff** *vt* (eat greedily) (BrE colloq) ‹*food*› engullirse*, zamparse, morfarse (RPl arg)

scoff[2] *n* burla *f*, mofa *f*

scold /skəʊld/ *vt* reprender, regañar, retar (CS)

scolding /'skəʊldɪŋ/ *n* reprimenda *f*, regaño *m* (AmL fam), reto *m* (CS), regañina *f* (Esp fam)

scollop /'skɑːləp || 'skɒləp/ *n* ▸ **scallop**

scone /skəʊn, skɑːn || skɒn, skəʊn/ *n* (in UK) *bollito que se come untado de mantequilla, mermelada etc*, scone *m* (CS), bisquet *m* (Méx)

scoop[1] /skuːp/ *n*

A 1 (for grain, flour) pala *f*, poruña *f* (Chi); (for ice-cream) pala *f*, cuchara *f* 2 (measure) (of ice-cream) bola *f*; (of mashed potatoes) cucharada *f*

B 1 (Journ) primicia *f* 2 (AmE colloq) (information): **the ~** la información; **what's the ~**? ¿qué hay?

scoop[2] *vt*

A (pick up): **he ~ed some rice from the bag** (with a scoop) sacó un poco de arroz de la bolsa con una pala *or* (Chi) con una poruña; (with hand) sacó un puñado de arroz de la bolsa; **they ~ed the water out of the boat** achicaron el agua del bote

B (gain) (colloq) ganar; **he ~ed the major awards** acaparó *or* se llevó los premios más importantes

Phrasal verbs

• **scoop out**

A [v ▸ o ▸ adv, v ▸ adv ▸ o] ‹*flour/rice/soil*› sacar* (*con pala, cuchara etc*)

B [v ▸ adv ▸ o] (hollow) ‹*hole/tunnel*› excavar

• **scoop up** [v ▸ o ▸ adv, v ▸ adv ▸ o] recoger* (*con pala, cuchara etc*)

scoot /skuːt/ *vi* (colloq) salir* pitando (fam), irse* a toda prisa; **go on, ~!** ¡anda, lárgate! (fam)

scooter /'skuːtər || 'skuːtə(r)/ *n* 1 (*motor ~*) escúter *m*, Vespa® *f* 2 (toy) patinete *m*, patín *m* del diablo (Méx), monopatín *m* (CS, Ven)

scope /skəʊp/ *n* [u] 1 (of law, regulations, reform) alcance *m*; (of influence) ámbito *m*, esfera *f*; (of investigation, activities) campo *m* 2 (opportunity, room) posibilidades *fpl*; **there is still ~ for improvement** aún se pueden mejorar las cosas

scorch[1] /skɔːrtʃ || skɔːtʃ/ *vt* ‹*fabric*› chamuscar*, quemar; ‹‹*sun*›› ‹*plant*› quemar, agostar, abrasar; **~ed-earth policy** *estrategia militar que consiste en arrasar todo lo que puede serle útil al enemigo*

■ **scorch** *vi* (become scorched) ‹‹*fabric*›› chamuscarse*

scorch[2] *n* quemadura *f* superficial; (*before n*) ~ **mark** marca *f* de quemadura superficial

scorcher /'skɔːrtʃər || 'skɔːtʃə(r)/ *n* (colloq) día *m* abrasador *or* de mucho calor

scorching /'skɔːrtʃɪŋ || 'skɔːtʃɪŋ/ *adj* ‹*sun*› abrasador; ‹*heat/day*› infernal, abrasador; (*as adv*) **it was ~ hot** hacía un calor achicharrante

score[1] /skɔːr || skɔː(r)/ *n*

A 1 (in game): **the final ~** el resultado final; **there was no ~** no hubo goles (*or* tantos *etc*); **what's the ~?** ¿cómo van?, ¿cómo va el marcador?; **what was the ~?** ¿cómo terminó el partido (*or* encuentro *etc*)?; **to keep (the) ~** llevar la cuenta de los tantos (*or* goles *etc*); (*before n*) **~ draw** (BrE) empate *m*; **no-~ draw** (BrE) empate *m* a cero 2 (in competition, test etc) puntuación *f*, puntaje *m* (AmL)

B 1 (account): **I have no worries on that ~** en lo que a eso se refiere, no me preocupo; ***to have a ~ to settle*** tener* una cuenta pendiente; **to have a ~ to settle with sb** tener* que arreglar cuentas con algn, tener* que ajustarle las cuentas a algn; ***to settle old ~s*** ajustar *or* saldar (las) cuentas pendientes 2 (situation) (colloq): **I told him about my past, so he knows the ~** le hablé de mi pasado, así que está al tanto de la situación; **what's the ~? are we going out or not?** ¿qué pasa? *or* ¿en qué quedamos? ¿salimos o no salimos?

C (Mus) 1 (notation) partitura *f* 2 (music for show, movie) música *f*

D (twenty) veintena *f*; **she lived to be four ~ years and ten** (liter) vivió hasta los 90 años; **there were ~s of people there** había muchísima gente, había montones de gente (fam)

score[2] *vt*

A 1 (Sport) ‹*goal*› marcar*, meter, hacer*, anotar(se) (AmL); **to ~ a basket** encestar; **you ~ 20 points for that** eso te da *or* (AmL tb) con eso te anotas 20 puntos 2 (in competition, test) ‹‹*person*›› sacar*; **I ~d 70%** saqué 70 sobre 100 3 (win) ‹*success*› lograr, conseguir*

B (cut, mark) ‹*surface/paper*› marcar*

C (criticize) (AmE journ) criticar*

D (Mus) ‹*piece*› (write) escribir*, componer*; (arrange) hacer* un arreglo de

■ **score** *vi*

A 1 (Sport) marcar*, anotar(se) (AmL) un tanto 2 (in competition, test): **he ~d well in the exam** obtuvo *or* sacó una buena puntuación *or* (AmL tb) un puntaje alto en el examen

B (do well) destacar(se)*; **to ~ OVER sth/sb** aventajar *or* superar A algo/algn

C (obtain drugs) (sl) conseguir* droga, conectar (Méx arg)

Phrasal verb

• **score out, score through** [v ▸ o ▸ adv, v ▸ adv ▸ o] (BrE) tachar

score: **~board** *n* marcador *m*; **~card** *n* tarjeta *f* (*en que se anota la puntuación en deportes como el boxeo y el golf*); **~keeper** *n*: *persona encargada del marcador*

scorer /'skɔːrər || 'skɔːrə(r)/ *n* 1 (player) *jugador que marca uno o más tantos*; **who were the ~s?** ¿quiénes marcaron (*or* hicieron los goles *etc*)?, ¿quiénes fueron los anotadores? (AmL) 2 (scorekeeper): **who's going to be ~?** ¿quién se va a encargar del marcador?

scorn[1] /skɔːrn || 'skɔːn/ *n* [u] (contempt) desdén *m*, desprecio *m*; **to pour ~ on sth** desdeñar *or* menospreciar algo

scorn[2] *vt* 1 (reject) ‹*offer/advice*› desdeñar 2 (despise) ‹*person/efforts*› desdeñar, despreciar, menospreciar

scornful /'skɔːrnfəl || 'skɔːnfəl/ *adj* desdeñoso; **to be ~ of sth** desdeñar algo; **the children were ~ of her** los niños la trataban con desdén

scornfully /'skɔːrnfəli || 'skɔːnfəli/ *adv* con desdén, desdeñosamente

Scorpio /'skɔːrpiəʊ || 'skɔːpiəʊ/ *n* (*pl* **-os**) 1 (sign) (*no art*) Escorpio, Escorpión 2 [c] (person) Escorpio *mf or* escorpio *mf*, Escorpión *mf or* escorpión *mf*, escorpiano, -na *m,f*; *see also* **Aquarius**

scorpion /'skɔːrpiən || 'skɔːpiən/ *n* escorpión *m*, alacrán *m*

Scot /skɑːt || skɒt/ *n* escocés, -cesa *m,f*

scotch[1] /skɑːtʃ || skɒtʃ/ *vt* ‹*plan/efforts*› echar por tierra, frustrar; ‹*rumors*› acallar, poner* fin a

scotch[2], **Scotch** *n* [u c] whisky *m or* güisqui *m* (escocés)

Scotch /skɑːtʃ || skɒtʃ/ *adj* ‹*person/tune/town*› (crit) escocés; **~ whisky** whisky *m or* güisqui *m* escocés

Scotch: ~ **broth** *n* [u] *sopa de cordero, papas y cebada*; ~ **egg** *n*: *huevo duro envuelto en carne de salchicha y rebozado*; **~tape** *vt* (AmE) pegar* con cinta Scotch® (*or* cel(l)o *etc*); ~ **tape**® *n* [u] (AmE) cinta *f* Scotch®, cel(l)o® *m*

S

(Esp), (cinta *f*) durex® *m* (AmL)

scot-free /ˈskɑːtˈfriː ‖ ˌskɒtˈfriː/ *adj* (*pred*): **to get away ~** (without punishment) quedar impune *or* sin castigo

Scotland /ˈskɑːtlənd ‖ ˈskɒtlənd/ *n* Escocia *f*

Scots[1] /skɑːts ‖ skɒts/ *adj* (*before n*) escocés

Scots[2] *n* [u] *inglés que se habla en Escocia*

Scots: **~man** /ˈskɑːtsmən ‖ ˈskɒtsmən/ *n* (*pl* **-men** /-mən/) escocés *m*; **~woman** *n* escocesa *f*

Scottish /ˈskɑːtɪʃ ‖ ˈskɒtɪʃ/ *adj* escocés

> **Scottish Parliament**
>
> El Parlamento escocés, establecido en 1999, se reúne en Edimburgo, capital de Escocia. Tiene competencia legislativa y ejecutiva respecto a los asuntos internos de Escocia y, a diferencia de la Asamblea Nacional de Gales (**Welsh Assembly**), posee limitados poderes para variar el tipo básico del impuesto sobre la renta. De los 129 diputados (*Members of the Scottish Parliament* o *MSPs*), 73 son elegidos directamente por mayoría relativa y los 56 (*Additional Members*) restantes de acuerdo con el sistema de representación proporcional

scoundrel /ˈskaʊndrəl/ *n* (dated) sinvergüenza *mf*, bribón, -bona *m,f*, pillo, -lla *m,f*

scour /skaʊr ‖ ˈskaʊə(r)/ *vt*
A 1 (rub hard) ‹*surface/pan*› fregar*, restregar* 2 **~ away** *o* **off** (remove) ‹*dirt/grease*› quitar
B (search thoroughly) ‹*area/building*› registrar, dar* una batida en

scourer /ˈskaʊrər ‖ ˈskaʊərə(r)/ *n* (BrE) ▸ **scouring pad**

scourge /skɜːrdʒ ‖ skɜːdʒ/ *n* 1 (cause of suffering) azote *m*; **the ~ of war/famine** el azote *or* el flagelo de la guerra/del hambre 2 (whip) (liter) azote *m*

scouring /ˈskaʊrɪŋ ‖ ˈskaʊərɪŋ/: **~ pad** *n* estropajo *m*, esponja *f*, esponjilla *f* (*metálica o plástica para fregar las cacerolas*); **~ powder** *n* [c u] polvo *m* limpiador, limpiador *m* en polvo, pulidor *m* (RPl)

scouse /skaʊs/ *adj* (BrE colloq) de Liverpool

scout[1] /skaʊt/ *n*
A 1 (person) explorador, -dora *m,f*, escucha *mf* 2 (look, search) (*no pl*): **to have a ~ around (the area)** explorar *or* recorrer la zona, hacer* un reconocimiento de la zona
B *also* **Scout** (*boy* **~**) explorador *m*, (boy) scout *m*; (*girl* **~**) exploradora *f*, (girl) scout *f*; (*before n*) **the ~ movement** el escutismo, el movimiento de los scouts
C (*talent* **~**) cazatalentos *mf*

scout[2] *vi* 1 (Mil) reconocer* el terreno 2 (search) **to ~ FOR sth** andar* en busca de algo

(Phrasal verb)

- **scout around** [v ▸ adv] **to ~ around (FOR sth)** buscar* (algo)

scoutmaster /ˈskaʊtˌmæstər ‖ ˈskaʊtˌmɑːstə(r)/ *n*: *jefe de un grupo de scouts*

scowl[1] /skaʊl/ *n* ceño *m* fruncido

scowl[2] *vi* fruncir* el ceño, poner* mala cara; **to ~ AT sb** mirar a algn con el ceño fruncido

scrabble /ˈskræbəl/ *vi* «*dog/chicken*» escarbar; **I was scrabbling frantically for a foothold** buscaba desesperadamente un lugar donde apoyar el pie; **I was scrabbling about in the dark looking for my key** estaba buscando la llave a tientas en la oscuridad

scraggy /ˈskrægi/ *adj* **-gier, -giest** 1 (scrawny) esmirriado, flaco, escuálido 2 (tough) ‹*meat*› duro, malo

scram /skræm/ *vi* **-mm-** (colloq): **go on, ~!** ¡fuera *or* largo de aquí! (fam)

scramble[1] /ˈskræmbəl/ *n*
A (*no pl*) 1 (chaotic rush): **several people were hurt in the ~** varias personas salieron lastimadas del barullo *or* de la confusión *or* de la rebatiña; **~ FOR sth**: **there was a last-minute ~ for tickets** a último momento hubo una rebatiña para conseguir entradas 2 (difficult climb) subida *f or* escalada *f* difícil
B [c] (BrE Sport) carrera *f* de motocross

scramble[2] *vi*
A 1 (clamber) (+ *adv compl*): **to ~ to one's feet** levantarse, ponerse* de pie (*apresuradamente o con dificultad*); **we ~d through the bushes** nos abrimos paso con dificultad a través de los arbustos; **he ~d up the rocks** subió las rocas gateando 2 (struggle, compete) **to ~ FOR sth** pelearse POR algo, andar* a la rebatiña POR algo
B (Aviat, Mil) despegar* (*con urgencia*)
■ **scramble** *vt* 1 (mix) mezclar; **to ~ eggs** hacer* huevos revueltos 2 ‹*message*› codificar*, cifrar

scrambled egg /ˈskræmbəld/ *n* [c u] (Culin) huevos *mpl* revueltos

scrap[1] /skræp/ *n*
A 1 [c] (of paper, cloth, leather) pedacito *m*, trocito *m*; **she ate every last ~** se comió hasta el último bocado 2 (single bit) (*with neg, no pl*): **she hasn't done a ~ of work** no ha movido un dedo, no ha hecho absolutamente nada, no ha dado golpe (Esp fam); **it doesn't make a ~ of difference what you think** lo que tú pienses no importa en lo más mínimo
B **scraps** *pl* sobras *fpl*, sobros *mpl* (AmC)
C [u] (reusable waste): **we sold our car for ~** vendimos el coche como chatarra; (*before n*) **~ dealer** chatarrero, -ra *m,f*; **~ iron** chatarra *f*; **~ merchant** chatarrero, -ra *m,f*; **~ paper** papel *m* para borrador
D [c] (fight) (colloq) agarrada *f* (fam), pelea *f*

scrap[2] **-pp-** *vt* 1 (abandon, cancel) ‹*idea*› desechar, descartar; ‹*plan*› abandonar; ‹*regulation*› abolir* 2 (convert to scrap) ‹*car/ship/machinery*› desguazar* *or* (Méx) deshuesar *or* (Chi) desarmar 3 (throw away) tirar a la basura, botar (AmL exc RPl)
■ **scrap** *vi* (colloq) pelearse

scrapbook /ˈskræpbʊk/ *n* álbum *m* de recortes

scrape[1] /skreɪp/ *n*
A 1 (act): **to give sth a ~** raspar algo 2 (sound) chirrido *m*
B (predicament) (colloq) lío *m* (fam), apuro *m*; **to get into a ~** meterse en un lío (fam)

scrape[2] *vt*
A 1 (rub against) rozar*; (grate against) rascar* 2 (damage, graze) ‹*paintwork*› rayar; ‹*knee/elbow*› rasparse, rasguñarse
B 1 (clean) ‹*toast*› raspar; ‹*carrot/potato*› pelar; ‹*woodwork*› raspar, rascar*, rasquetear; **to ~ sth OFF** *o* **FROM sth**: **~ the mud off your boots** quítales el barro a las botas (*con un cuchillo, contra una piedra etc*) 2 **~ (out)** ‹*bowl/pan*› fregar*, restregar*
C (narrowly achieve): **to ~ a majority** apenas alcanzar* una escasa mayoría
■ **scrape** *vi* (rub, grate) rozar*; (make a noise) chirriar

(Phrasal verbs)

- **scrape along**, **scrape by** [v ▸ adv] arreglárselas, apañárselas (Esp fam)
- **scrape through** [v ▸ adv] [v ▸ prep ▸ o] ‹*exam*› aprobar* raspando *or* arañando *or* (fam) por los pelos
- **scrape together**, **scrape up** [v ▸ o ▸ adv, v ▸ adv ▸ o] ‹*money*› juntar *or* reunir* a duras penas; ‹*support*› conseguir* (*con dificultad*)

scraper /ˈskreɪpər ‖ ˈskreɪpə(r)/ *n* (tool) rasqueta *f*, espátula *f*; (for shoes) limpiabarros *m*

scrapheap /ˈskræphiːp/ *n*: **to throw sth on the ~** desechar algo; **at 50 he found himself on the ~** a los 50 años se vio sin trabajo y sin perspectivas de futuro

scrappy /ˈskræpi/ *adj* **-pier, -piest**
A ‹*report/presentation*› deshilvanado
B (full of fight) (AmE journ) luchador

scrapyard /ˈskræpjɑːrd ‖ ˈskræpjɑːd/ *n* chatarrería *f*; (for cars) cementerio *m* de automóviles, desguace *m or* (Méx) deshuesadero *m or* (Chi) desarmaduría *f*

scratch[1] /skrætʃ/ *n* [c]
A 1 (injury) rasguño *m*, arañazo *m*; **he escaped without a ~** resultó ileso, salió sin un rasguño 2 (on paint, record, furniture) rayón *m* 3 (sound) chirrido *m* 4 (act) (*no pl*): **can you give my back a ~?** ¿me rascas la espalda?
B (*in phrases*) **from scratch**: **he learned German from ~** aprendió alemán empezando desde cero; **I had to start from ~** tuvo que empezar desde cero; **to be up to ~** (colloq) dar* la talla

scratch[2] *vt* 1 (damage) ‹*paint/record/furniture*› rayar 2 (with claws, nails) arañar 3 ‹*name/initials*› marcar*, grabar 4 (to relieve itch) ‹*bite/rash*› rascarse*; **could you ~ my back for me?** ¿me rascas la espalda?; ***you ~ my back and I'll ~ yours*** favor con favor se paga, hoy por ti, mañana por mí
■ **scratch** *vi*
A 1 (damage, wound) arañar 2 (rub) «*wool/sweater*» raspar,

picar* [3] (to relieve itching) rascarse* [4] (make scratching sound) rascar*

[B] (withdraw) (Sport) retirarse

Phrasal verb

• **scratch out** [v ▸ o ▸ adv, v ▸ adv ▸ o] [1] (gouge): **to ~ sb's eyes out** sacarle* los ojos a algn [2] (strike out) ‹*name/sentence*› tachar; (on ticket) rascar*, raspar

scratch³ *adj* (*before n*) [1] (haphazard, motley) ‹*team/meal*› improvisado [2] (Sport) ‹*player/runner*› de primera

scratch: **~ line** *n* (AmE Sport) línea *f* de salida; **~ pad** *n* [1] (notepad) (AmE) bloc *m* de notas; [2] (Comput) scratch pad *m*, bloc *m* de notas de rápido acceso

scratchy /ˈskrætʃi/ *adj* **scratchier, scratchiest** [1] ‹*wool/sweater*› áspero, que raspa *or* pica [2] ‹*record*› rayado; ‹*pen/nib*› que raspa [3] ‹*writing/drawing*› garabateado

scrawl¹ /skrɔːl/ *n* [1] [c] (mark) garabato *m* [2] [u] (handwriting) garabatos *mpl*

scrawl² *vt* garabatear

■ **scrawl** *vi* garabatear, hacer* garabatos

scrawny /ˈskrɔːni/ *adj* **-nier, -niest** ‹*person*› esquelético, escuálido, canijo; ‹*arms/legs*› esquelético, descarnado

scream¹ /skriːm/ *n* [1] (loud cry) grito *m*, chillido *m*; (louder) alarido *m* [2] (sb funny) (colloq) (*no pl*): **she's a real ~** ¡es graciosísima!, ¡es un caso!, ¡es un plato! (AmS fam)

scream² *vi* «*person*» gritar, chillar; «*baby*» llorar a gritos, berrear; **she ~ed with laughter** soltó una risotada; **to ~ AT sb** gritarle A algn; **to ~ FOR sth: he ~ed for help** gritó pidiendo ayuda

■ **scream** *vt* ‹*insult*› gritar, soltar*; ‹*command*› dar* a voces *or* a gritos; **they ~ed abuse at him** lo insultaron a voz en cuello; **to ~ sth AT sb** gritarle algo A algn

screech¹ /skriːtʃ/ *n* (of terror, pain) alarido *m*, grito *m*; (of joy) chillido *m*, grito *m*; (of brakes) chirrido *m*, rechinón *m* (Méx); (of siren) pitido *m*, aullido *m*

screech² *vi* «*person/animal*» chillar; «*brakes/tires*» chirriar*; «*siren*» aullar*; **she ~ed with laughter** soltó una carcajada estridente; **the car ~ed to a halt** el coche paró en seco con un chirrido *or* (Méx) con un rechinón

■ **screech** *vt* chillar

screen¹ /skriːn/ *n*

[A] [1] (movable device) pantalla *f*; (folding) biombo *m*; (as partition) mampara *f* [2] (protective, defensive) cortina *f*; (at window) mosquitero *m*

[B] (Cin, Comput, Phot, TV) pantalla *f*; **the silver ~** el cine, el celuloide (period); **the big ~** la pantalla grande; **the small ~** la pequeña pantalla, la pantalla chica (AmL); (*before n*) ‹*adaptation*› al cine, a la pantalla grande; **~ rights** derechos *mpl* de adaptación al cine

screen² *vt*

[A] [1] (conceal) ocultar, tapar; **to ~ sth/sb FROM sth: the trees ~ the house from the road** los árboles no dejan ver la casa desde la carretera; **we were ~ed from view by the wall** la pared nos tapaba [2] (protect) proteger*; **to ~ sth/sb FROM sth** proteger* algo/a algn DE algo

[B] ‹*TV program*› emitir; ‹*film*› proyectar

[C] (check, examine) ‹*blood donor*› someter a una revisión (médica) *or* a un chequeo; ‹*applicants/candidates*› someter a una investigación de antecedentes; **to ~ sb/sth FOR sth: the cans are ~ed for possible contamination** las latas se examinan por si estuvieran contaminadas; **to ~ sb for cancer** someter a algn a un chequeo para el diagnóstico precoz del cáncer

Phrasal verbs

• **screen off** [v ▸ o ▸ adv, v ▸ adv ▸ o] ‹*area/bed/patient*› aislar*, separar (*con un biombo o una mampara*)

• **screen out** [v ▸ o ▸ adv, v ▸ adv ▸ o] eliminar (*habiendo hecho una investigación*)

screen: **~ door** *n* puerta *f* mosquitera; **~ dump** *n* volcado *m* de pantalla

screening /ˈskriːnɪŋ/ *n*

[A] [c u] (Cin) proyección *f*; (TV) emisión *f*

[B] [c u] (examination) (Med) revisión *f* (médica), chequeo *m* (*esp para detección precoz*); (of candidates) investigación *f* de antecedentes

screen: **~play** *n* guión *m*; **~ print** *n* serigrafía *f*; **~-printing** *n* serigrafiado *m*; **~ test** *n* prueba *f* (cinematográfica); **~writer** *n* guionista *mf*

screw¹ /skruː/ *n*

[A] [1] (Const, Tech) tornillo *m*; ***to have a ~ loose*** (colloq & hum): **he's/you've got a ~ loose** le/te falta un tornillo (fam & hum); ***to put the ~s on sb*** apretarle* las tuercas a algn [2] (action) (*no pl*) vuelta *f*; (*before n*) ‹*lid/top*› de rosca [3] (Aviat, Naut) hélice *f*

[B] (sexual intercourse) (vulg) (*no pl*): **to have a ~** echar(se) un polvo (fam), coger* (Méx, RPl, Ven vulg), follar (Esp vulg), culear (Andes vulg)

[C] (prison guard) (sl) guardia *m*, madero *m* (Esp arg)

screw² *vt*

[A] [1] (Const, Tech) atornillar; **~ the lid on tight** enrosca bien la tapa; **to ~ sth down (securely)** atornillar (bien) algo; **to ~ sth in** atornillar algo; **~ the two pieces together** una las dos piezas con un tornillo/con tornillos [2] (crumple): **he ~ed the letter into a ball** hizo una bola con la carta

[B] [1] (vulg) (have sex with): **to ~ sb** tirarse a algn (vulg), coger* a algn (Méx, RPl, Ven vulg), follar a algn (Esp vulg), culearse a algn (Andes vulg) [2] (*in interj phrases*) **~ you!** ¡vete a la mierda *or* (Méx) a la chingada! (vulg), ¡andá a cagar! (RPl vulg); **~ what she says!** ¡me cago en lo que diga ella! (vulg)

[C] (sl) [1] (exploit, cheat) esquilmar, hacer* guaje (Méx fam); **she's ~ing him for everything she can get** lo está exprimiendo al máximo, le está chupando la sangre [2] (extort) **to ~ sth OUT OF sb/sth** sacarle* algo A algn/algo

■ **screw** *vi*

[A] (Const): **to ~ in/on** atornillarse

[B] (have sex) (vulg) echar(se) un polvo (fam), coger* (Méx, RPl, Ven vulg), follar (Esp vulg), culear (Andes vulg)

Phrasal verb

• **screw up**

Sense I [v ▸ o ▸ adv, v ▸ adv ▸ o]

[A] (tighten) ‹*bolt*› apretar*

[B] (crumple) ‹*letter/paper*› arrugar*, estrujar; **he ~ed the envelope up into a ball** hizo una bola con el sobre

[C] (make nervous, confused) (colloq) (*usu pass*) poner* neurótico (fam); **he's very ~ed up** (permanent characteristic) tiene muchos traumas

[D] (spoil, botch) (sl) fastidiar (fam); **I really ~ed up the exam** de verdad que metí la pata en el examen (fam)

Sense II [v ▸ adv] (bungle a situation) (sl) cagarla* (vulg)

screw: **~ball** *n* [1] (eccentric person) (AmE colloq) excéntrico, -ca *mf*, chiflado, -da *m,f* (fam); [2] (in baseball) torniquete *m*, tirabuzón *m*; **~driver** *n* destornillador *m*, desarmador *m* (Méx), desatornillador *m* (AmC, Chi); **~-top** *adj* ‹*bottle*› con tapón de rosca; ‹*jar*› con tapa de rosca; **~-up** *n* (AmE sl) (blunder, mess) lío *m* (fam), metedura *f or* (AmL) metida *f* de pata (fam); (person) inútil *mf*, nulo, -la *m,f*

screwy /ˈskruːi/ *adj* **screwier, screwiest** (colloq) ‹*idea/plan*› descabellado; ‹*person*› chiflado (fam)

scribble¹ /ˈskrɪbəl/ *n* [c u] garabato *m*

scribble² *vt* garabatear; **I ~d (down) a few ideas on a scrap of paper** anoté rápidamente algunas ideas en un papel

■ **scribble** *vi* garabatear, hacer* garabatos

scribe /skraɪb/ *n* [1] (Hist) (copyist) escriba *m* [2] *also* **Scribe** (Bib) escriba *m* [3] (clerk) escribiente *mf*

scrimmage¹ /ˈskrɪmɪdʒ/ *n* [1] (struggle) refriega *f* [2] (in US football) escaramuza *f*

scrimmage² *vi* hacer* la línea de golpeo *or* de contacto

scrimp /skrɪmp/ *vi* **to ~ ON sth** escatimar EN algo; **to ~ and save** cuidar mucho el dinero

script /skrɪpt/ *n*

[A] [1] [u] (handwriting) letra *f* [2] [c] (style of writing) caligrafía *f* [3] [c] (alphabet) escritura *f*

[B] [1] [c] (text — of film, broadcast) guión *m*; (— of speech) texto *m* [2] (computer program, instructions) script *m*, secuencia *f* de comandos

scripture /ˈskrɪptʃər || ˈskrɪptʃə(r)/ *n* [u c] [1] (Relig) **the (Holy) S~s** las (Sagradas) Escrituras; **Buddhist ~s** escritos *mpl* sagrados budistas [2] (Educ) religión *f*

scriptwriter /ˈskrɪptˌraɪtər/ *n* guionista *mf*

scroll¹ /skrəʊl/ *n* [1] (of paper, parchment) rollo *m*; (award) pergamino *m* [2] (Archit) voluta *f*

scroll² *vi*: **to ~ up/down** hacer* avanzar/retroceder el texto que aparece en pantalla

scrooge /skruːdʒ/ *n* (colloq) tacaño, -ña *m,f*

S

scrotum /'skrəʊtəm/ *n* (*pl* **-tums** *or* **-ta** /-tə/) escroto *m*

scrounge¹ /skraʊndʒ/ (colloq) *vt* **to ~ sth FROM/OFF sb** ‹*food/cigarette/money*› gorronearle *or* gorrearle *or* (RPl) garronearle *or* (Chi) bolsearle algo A algn (fam)

■ **scrounge** *vi* gorronear *or* gorrear *or* (RPl) garronear *or* (Chi) bolsear (fam)

scrounge² *n* (BrE colloq) (*no pl*): **to be always on the ~** vivir gorroneando *or* gorreando *or* (RPl) garroneando *or* (Chi) bolseando (fam)

scrounger /'skraʊndʒər || 'skraʊndʒə(r)/ *n* (colloq) gorrón, -rrona *m,f* *or* (RPl) garronero, -ra *m,f* *or* (Chi) bolsero, -ra *m,f* (fam); (from welfare state) parásito, -ta *m,f* (fam)

scrub¹ /skrʌb/ *n*

A [u] (vegetation) matorrales *mpl*

B (act) (*no pl*): **he gave the floor a good ~** fregó bien el piso (*con cepillo*); (*before n*) **~ brush** (AmE) cepillo *m* de fregar

scrub² **-bb-** *vt*

A (scour) ‹*floor/table*› fregar*; ‹*knees/hands*› restregar*, refregar*

B (BrE colloq) (cancel) ‹*event/game/meeting*› cancelar

Phrasal verb

• **scrub up** [v ▸ adv] «*doctor/nurse*» lavarse (*antes de una operación*)

scrubber /'skrʌbər || 'skrʌbə(r)/ *n* **1** (scourer) estropajo *m* **2** (promiscuous woman) (BrE sl) putona *f* (fam)

scrubbing brush /'skrʌbɪŋ/ *n* cepillo *m* de fregar

scruff /skrʌf/ *n*

A (person) (BrE colloq) *persona desaliñada*; **he's such a ~!** anda siempre con una(s) facha(s) ... (fam)

B : **by the ~ of the neck** por el pescuezo, por el cogote

scruffy /'skrʌfi/ *adj* **-fier, -fiest** (colloq) ‹*person*› dejado, desaliñado; **I'm too ~ to go in there** no puedo entrar ahí en esta(s) facha(s) *or* con esta(s) pinta(s) (fam); **a ~-looking building** un edificio de aspecto destartalado

scrum /skrʌm/ *n* (in rugby) melé *f* (ordenada), scrum *m*

scrum half *n* medio melé *mf*

scrummage /'skrʌmɪdʒ/ *n* ▸**scrum**

scrumptious /'skrʌmpʃəs/ *adj* (colloq) ‹*meal*› para chuparse los dedos (fam), de rechupete (fam)

scrunch /skrʌntʃ/ *vt* (colloq) **1** (crunch) ‹*snow/gravel*› hacer* crujir **2** (crush) **~ (up)**: **she ~ed the paper (up) into a ball** estrujó el papel y lo hizo una pelota

scrunchie, scrunchy /'skrʌntʃi/ *n* (*pl* **-chies**) *banda elástica circular para sujetar el pelo*

scruple /'skru:pəl/ *n* (*usu pl*) escrúpulo *m*; **she'd have no ~s about firing you** te echaría sin ningún miramiento

scrupulous /'skru:pjələs || 'skru:pjʊləs/ *adj* escrupuloso; **she pays ~ attention to detail** es muy detallista

scrupulously /'skru:pjələsli || 'skru:pjʊləsli/ *adv* escrupulosamente; **~ clean** impecable

scrutinize /'skru:tṇaɪz || 'skru:tɪnaɪz/ *vt* ‹*document*› inspeccionar, examinar; ‹*face*› escudriñar

scrutiny /'skru:tṇi || 'skru:tɪni/ *n* [c u] (*pl* **-nies**) (close examination) examen *m*; **his methods will not bear close ~** sus métodos no resistirán un examen riguroso

scuba /'sku:bə/: **~-dive** /'sku:bədaɪv/ *vi* hacer* submarinismo; **~ diver** *n* buzo *m*, submarinista *mf*; **~ diving** *n* [u] buceo *m*, submarinismo *m*; **to go ~ diving** (ir* a) bucear, hacer* submarinismo

scuff¹ /skʌf/ *n*: **a ~-resistant floor** un suelo que no se marca; (*before n*) **~ mark** marca *f*, rozadura *f*

scuff² *vt* ‹*floor*› dejar marcas en; ‹*leather*› raspar

scuffle /'skʌfəl/ *n* refriega *f*, escaramuza *f*

scull¹ /skʌl/ *n* espadilla *f*

scull² *vi* remar (*con espadilla*)

scullery /'skʌləri/ *n* (*pl* **-ries**) *habitación anexa a la cocina donde se fregaba, se preparaban las verduras etc*

sculpt /skʌlpt/ *vt/i* esculpir

sculptor /'skʌlptər || 'skʌlptə(r)/ *n* escultor, -tora *m,f*

sculptress /'skʌlptrəs || 'skʌlptrɪs/ *n* escultora *f*

sculpture¹ /'skʌlptʃər || 'skʌlptʃə(r)/ *n* [c u] escultura *f*

sculpture² *vt* **1** (form, shape) esculpir **2** **sculptured** *past p* ‹*features*› bien cincelado

scum /skʌm/ *n*

A [u] (on liquid) capa *f* de suciedad

B (colloq) **1** (people) escoria *f*; **the ~ of the earth** la escoria de la sociedad **2** (individual): **you ~!** ¡cerdo! (fam), ¡canalla!

scumbag /'skʌmbæg/ *n* (sl) cerdo, -da *m,f* (fam)

scupper /'skʌpər || 'skʌpə(r)/ *vt* (BrE) ‹*ship*› hundir; ‹*plan/talks*› echar por tierra; **now we're ~ed** (colloq) estamos acabados (fam)

scurrilous /'skɜ:rələs || 'skʌrɪləs/ *adj* difamatorio, insidioso

scurry /'skɜ:ri || 'skʌri/ *vi*: **he scurried away** *o* **off** salió disparado; **they could hear mice ~ing around in the attic** oían corretear ratones en el desván

scurvy /'skɜ:rvi || 'skɜ:vi/ *n* [u] (Med) escorbuto *m*

scuttle¹ /'skʌtḷ/ *n* (*coal ~*) cubo *m* para el carbón

scuttle² *vt* (Naut) ‹*ship*› hundir; ‹*plans, talks*› echar por tierra

■ **scuttle** *vi*: **the children ~d away** *o* **off** los niños se escabulleron rápidamente

scuttlebutt /'skʌtḷbʌt/ *n* [u] (AmE colloq) rumores *mpl*

scythe /saɪð/ *n* guadaña *f*

SD, S Dak = South Dakota

SE (= **southeast**) SE

sea /si:/ *n*

A [c] **1** (*often pl*) (ocean) mar *m* [*The noun* **mar** *is feminine in literary language and in some set idiomatic expressions*]; **a house by the ~** una casa a orillas del mar, una casa junto al mar; **to go/travel by ~** ir*/viajar en barco; **on the high ~s** en alta mar; **to put (out) to ~** hacerse* a la mar; **we've been at ~ for a month** hace un mes que estamos embarcados *or* que zarpamos; **to dump waste at ~** verter* desechos en el mar; ***to feel/be at ~***: **this left him feeling completely at ~** esto lo confundió totalmente; **at first I was all at ~** al principio me sentí totalmente perdido *or* confundido; (*before n*) ‹*route/transport*› marítimo; ‹*battle*› naval; ‹*god*› del mar; ‹*nymph*› marino; **the ~ air/breeze** el aire/la brisa del mar; **~ crossing** travesía *f* **2** (inland) mar *m*

B (swell, turbulence) (*usu pl*): **heavy** *o* **rough ~s** mar *f* gruesa, mar *m* agitado *or* encrespado *or* picado

C (large mass, quantity) (*no pl*): **a ~ of faces** una multitud de rostros; **a ~ of people** una riada de gente

sea: **~ anemone** *n* anémona *f* *or* ortiga *f* de mar; **~bed** *n* **the ~bed** el lecho marino, el fondo del mar; **~ bird** *n* ave *f*‡ marina; **~board** *n* costa *f*, litoral *m*; **~borne** *adj* ‹*goods*› transportado por vía marítima; ‹*invasion/attack*› naval; **~ change** *n* cambio *m* radical; **~coast** *n* costa *f*, litoral *m*; **~ cow** *n* vaca *f* marina, manatí *m*; **~ dog** *n* (liter & hum) lobo *m* de mar (liter); **~ elephant** *n* elefante *m* marino; **~farer** /'si:ˌferər || 'si:ˌfeərə(r)/ *n* marino *m*, navegante *m*; **~faring** /'si:ˌferɪŋ || 'si:ˌfeərɪŋ/ *adj* (liter) ‹*people*› marinero; ‹*man*› de mar; **~food** *n* [u] mariscos *mpl*, marisco *m* (Esp); (*before n*) ‹*cocktail*› de mariscos *or* (Esp) de marisco; **~food restaurant** marisquería *f*; **~front** *n* paseo *m* marítimo, malecón *m* (AmL), costanera *f* (CS); (*before n*) ‹*hotel/restaurant*› frente al mar; **~going** *adj* ‹*vessel*› de altura; **~gull** *n* gaviota *f*; **~horse** *n* caballito *m* de mar

seal¹ /si:l/ *n*

A [c] (implement, impression) sello *m*; **he gave the plan his ~ of approval** dio su aprobación al plan; ***to set the ~ on sth*** ratificar* algo

B [c] **1** (security device) precinto *m* **2** (airtight closure) cierre *m* hermético; (on glass jar) aro *m* de goma

C (Zool) **1** [c] (animal) foca *f* **2** [u] (skin) (piel *f* de) foca *f*

seal² *vt*

A **1** ‹*envelope/parcel*› cerrar*; (with tape) precintar; (with wax) lacrar; **a ~ed envelope** un sobre cerrado *or* sellado; **~ed with a kiss** sellado con un beso; **my lips are ~ed** (set phrase) soy una tumba, prometo no decir nada **2** ‹*jar/container*› cerrar* herméticamente; ‹*tomb/door*› precintar; ‹*wood*› sellar

B (affix seal to) ‹*document/treaty*› sellar; **signed, ~ed and delivered** firmado y sellado

C (decide, determine) ‹*victory/outcome*› decidir; **their fate was ~ed** su destino estaba escrito

Phrasal verbs

• **seal in** [v ▸ o ▸ adv, v ▸ adv ▸ o] conservar

• **seal off** [v ▸ o ▸ adv, v ▸ adv ▸ o] ‹*area/road/building*› acordonar; ‹*exit*› cerrar*

• **seal up** [v ▸ o ▸ adv, v ▸ adv ▸ o] ‹*letter/parcel*› cerrar*; (with

S

wax) sellar; (with tape) precintar

sea-lane /'siːleɪn/ *n* ruta *f* marítima

sealant /'siːlənt/ *n* sellador *m*

sea: **~ legs** *pl n*: **to find** *o* **get one's ~ legs** (colloq) acostumbrarse al movimiento de un barco; **~ level** *n* nivel *m* del mar; **above/below ~ level** sobre/bajo el nivel del mar

sealing wax /'siːlɪŋ/ *n* [u] lacre *m*

sea lion *n* león *m* marino

sealskin /'siːlskɪn/ *n* [u] piel *f* de foca

seam /siːm/ *n*

A 1 (stitching) costura *f*; ***to be bursting at the ~s*** ⟨⟨*building/suitcase*⟩⟩ estar* hasta el tope *or* hasta los topes; **to come apart at the ~s** ⟨⟨*organization/setup*⟩⟩ venirse* abajo; (lit: split) **her skirt was coming apart at the ~s** se le estaba descosiendo la falda 2 (join) juntura *f*

B 1 (of coal, gold) veta *f*, filón *m* 2 (Geol) grieta *f*

seaman /'siːmən/ *n* (*pl* **-men** /-mən/) (sailor) marinero *m*; (officer) marino *m*

seamanship /'siːmənʃɪp/ *n* [u] arte *m* de navegar *or* de la navegación

sea mile *n* milla *f* marina

seamless /'siːmləs || 'siːmlɪs/ *adj* ⟨*stockings/knitting*⟩ sin costuras; ⟨*blend/performance*⟩ perfecto

seamstress /'siːmstrəs || 'semstrɪs/ *n* costurera *f*

seamy /'siːmi/ *adj* **-mier, -miest** sórdido

seance, séance /'seɪɑːns/ *n* sesión *f* de espiritismo

sea: **~plane** *n* hidroavión *m*; **~port** *n* puerto *m* marítimo

sear /sɪr || sɪə(r)/ *vt* 1 ⟨*flesh/arm*⟩ quemar, chamuscar*; ⟨*meat*⟩ (Culin) dorar rápidamente a fuego muy vivo 2 (wither) ⟨⟨*heat*⟩⟩ secar*, achicharrar, abrasar; ⟨⟨*frost/wind*⟩⟩ secar*

search¹ /sɜːrtʃ || sɜːtʃ/ *vt* ⟨*building*⟩ registrar, catear (Méx), esculcar* (Col, Méx); ⟨*person*⟩ cachear, registrar, catear (Méx), requisar (Col); ⟨*luggage*⟩ registrar, revisar (AmL), esculcar* (Col, Méx); ⟨*records/files*⟩ buscar* en, examinar; **to ~ sth/sb FOR sth**: **she ~ed the attic for the letters** revolvió el ático buscando las cartas; **they ~ed him for drugs** lo cachearon (*or* registraron etc) para ver si tenía drogas; **~ *me!*** (colloq) ¡yo qué sé! (fam)

■ **search** *vi* buscar*; **to ~ FOR sth/sb** buscar* algo/a algn; **to ~ THROUGH sth**: **she ~ed through his papers for his will** buscó su testamento entre sus papeles

Phrasal verb

• **search out** [v ▸ o ▸ adv, v ▸ adv ▸ o] ⟨*reason*⟩ averiguar*, tratar de descubrir

search² *n* 1 (hunt, quest) **~ (FOR sth/sb)** búsqueda *f* (DE algo/algn); **we went in ~ of a policeman** fuimos a buscar un policía 2 (examination, scrutiny — of building, pockets) registro *m*, esculque *m* (Col, Méx); (— of records, documents) inspección *f*, examen *m*; **body ~** cacheo *m*, requisa *f* (AmL), cateo *m* (Méx) 3 (Comput) búsqueda *f*

searcher /'sɜːrtʃər || 'sɜːtʃə(r)/ *n*: *miembro de una partida de rescate*; **~s are looking for the injured climber** una partida de rescate busca al montañista accidentado

searching /'sɜːrtʃɪŋ || 'sɜːtʃɪŋ/ *adj* ⟨*look*⟩ inquisitivo, escrutador; ⟨*question*⟩ perspicaz

search: **~light** *n* reflector *m*; **~ party** *n* partida *f* de rescate; **~ warrant** *n* orden *f* de registro *or* (AmL) de allanamiento *or* (Chi, Méx) de cateo

searing /'sɪrɪŋ || 'sɪərɪŋ/ *adj* ⟨*pain*⟩ punzante, agudo; ⟨*heat*⟩ abrasador

sea: **~scape** /'siːskeɪp/ *n* marina *f*; **~shell** *n* concha *f* (de mar); **~shore** *n* [u] orilla *f* del mar; **~sick** *adj* mareado; **do you get ~sick?** ¿te mareas (en los viajes por mar)?; **~sickness** *n* [u] mareo *m* (*en los viajes por mar*); **~side** *n* [u] costa *f*; (*before n*) ⟨*hotel*⟩ de la costa; ⟨*town*⟩ de la costa, costero; **a ~side resort** un centro de veraneo costero, un balneario (AmL); **~ snake** *n* serpiente *f* marina

season¹ /'siːzn̩/ *n*

A (division of year) estación *f*

B (for specific activity, event, crop) temporada *f*; **the mating ~** el celo; **S~'s greetings!** ¡Felices fiestas!; **high/low ~** temporada alta/baja; **a ~ of Buñuel films** un ciclo de películas de Buñuel

C (*in phrases*) **in season** (of female animal) en celo; (of fresh food, game): **cherries are in ~** es época *or* temporada de cerezas, las cerezas están en temporada; **fruits in ~** fruta del tiempo; **off season** (Tourism) fuera de temporada, en temporada baja; **out of season** (of fresh food) fuera de temporada; (Tourism) fuera de temporada

season² *vt*

A (Culin) condimentar, sazonar; (with salt and pepper) salpimentar*

B ⟨*wood*⟩ secar*, curar

seasonable /'siːznəbəl/ *adj* ⟨*weather/temperatures*⟩ propio de la época del año *or* de la estación

seasonal /'siːznəl || 'siːzənl̩/ *adj* ⟨*variations/fluctuations*⟩ estacional; ⟨*vegetables*⟩ del tiempo, de temporada; ⟨*demand*⟩ de estación *or* temporada, estacional; **~ employment** trabajo *m* temporal

seasonal affective disorder *n* [u] trastorno *m* afectivo estacional, TAE *m*

seasoned /'siːznd/ *adj*

A (experienced) ⟨*troops/traveler*⟩ avezado, experimentado, baquiano (RPl)

B ⟨*food*⟩ condimentado, sazonado; **highly ~** muy condimentado

C ⟨*wood*⟩ seco, curado

seasoning /'siːznɪŋ/ *n* [u c] (Culin) condimento *m*, sazón *f*

season ticket *n* abono *m* (de temporada); (*before n*) **~ ~ holders** las personas en posesión de un abono

seat¹ /siːt/ *n*

A (place to sit) asiento *m*; (on bicycle) asiento *m*, sillín *m*; (in theater) asiento *m*, butaca *f*; **please have** *o* **take a ~** tome asiento, por favor (frml), siéntese, por favor; **I took a ~ at the back** me senté en el fondo; **I've got two ~s for tonight's performance** tengo dos entradas para la función de esta noche; **there aren't any ~s left** (in cinema) no quedan localidades; **can you keep my ~ for me?** ¿me guardas el lugar *or* el asiento?

B 1 (of chair) asiento *m* 2 (of garment) fondillos *mpl*, fundillos *mpl* (AmS)

C 1 (Govt) escaño *m*, banca *f* (RPl), curul *m* (Col, Méx); **to have a ~ on a committee** ser* miembro de una comisión 2 (constituency) (BrE) distrito *m* electoral

D 1 (center) sede *f*; **the ~ of government** la sede del gobierno 2 (of family) residencia *f*, casa *f* solariega

seat² *vt* 1 ⟨*child*⟩ sentar*; **please be ~ed** (frml) tomen asiento, por favor (frml); **to remain ~ed** permanecer* sentado 2 (have room for) ⟨⟨*auditorium*⟩⟩ tener* cabida *or* capacidad para; **how many does the bus ~?** ¿cuántas plazas *or* cuántos asientos tiene el autobús?; **this table ~s 6** en esta mesa caben seis personas

seat belt *n* cinturón *m* de seguridad

seating /'siːtɪŋ/ *n* [u] número *m* de asientos; (*before n*) **~ capacity** aforo *m*

sea: **~ urchin** *n* erizo *m* de mar; **~ wall** *n* malecón *m*, espigón *m*, tajamar *m* (CS); **~water** *n* [u] agua *f*‡ de mar, agua *f*‡ salada; **~way** *n* ruta *f* marítima; **~weed** *n* [u] alga *f*‡ marina; **~worthy** *adj* ⟨*ship*⟩ en condiciones de navegar, marinero

sec /sek/ (*pl* **secs**) (= **second**) seg.

secateurs /ˌsekə'tɜːrz || ˌsekə'tɜːz/ *pl n* (BrE) tijeras *fpl* de podar (*de tipo yunque*)

secede /sɪ'siːd/ *vi* **to ~ (FROM sth)** ⟨⟨*province*⟩⟩ separarse (DE algo)

secluded /sɪ'kluːdəd || sɪ'kluːdɪd/ *adj* ⟨*house/area*⟩ apartado, aislado; ⟨*life/existence*⟩ solitario

seclusion /sɪ'kluːʒən/ *n* [u] 1 (state) aislamiento *m*; **to live in ~** vivir recluido *or* aislado 2 (act) reclusión *f*

second¹ /'sekənd/ *adj*

A 1 segundo; **he had a ~ cup of tea** se tomó otra taza de té; **he's already had a ~ helping** ya ha repetido *or* (Chi) se ha repetido; **he won't do that a ~ time** no lo volverá a hacer; **to give sb a ~ chance** darle* a algn otra oportunidad; **every ~ Tuesday/week** cada dos martes/semanas, martes/semana por medio (CS, Per); **~ generation** segunda generación *f*; **~ home** segunda vivienda *f*; **~ language** segundo idioma *m* 2 (in seniority, standing) segundo; **our service is ~ to none** nuestro servicio es insuperable

B (elliptical use): **I leave on the ~ (of the month)** me voy el (día) dos

S

second² *adv* 1 (in position, time, order) en segundo lugar; **work comes ~, family first** la familia está antes que el trabajo 2 (secondly) en segundo lugar 3 (with superl): **the ~ tallest boy in the class** el chico que le sigue al más alto de la clase; **the ~ highest building** el segundo edificio en altura

second³ *n*
A 1 (of time) segundo *m*; (*before n*) **~ hand** segundero *m* 2 (moment) segundo *m*; **it doesn't take a ~** no lleva ni un segundo, es cosa de un segundo
B 1 **~ (gear)** (Auto) (*no art*) segunda *f* 2 (in competition): **he finished a good/poor ~** quedó en un honroso/deslucido segundo lugar 3 (BrE Educ): **upper/lower ~** *segunda y tercera nota de la escala de calificaciones de un título universitario*
C (in boxing, wrestling) segundo *m*; (in dueling) padrino *m*
D (substandard product) artículo *m* con defectos de fábrica
E **seconds** *pl* (second helping) (colloq): **to have ~s** repetir*, repetirse* (Chi)

second⁴ *vt*
A (support) ‹*motion/candidate*› secundar
B /sɪ'kɒnd/ (attach) (BrE) **to ~ sb (TO sth)** trasladar a algn temporalmente (A algo)

secondary /'sekənderi || 'sekəndri/ *adj*
A 1 (subordinate) ‹*matter*› de interés secundario; ‹*road*› secundario; **to be ~ TO sth** ser* de menor importancia QUE algo 2 (not primary, original) ‹*source*› de segunda mano; ‹*industry*› derivado; ‹*infection*› secundario; ‹*strike/action/picketing*› de solidaridad
B (Educ) ‹*teacher/pupils*› de enseñanza secundaria; **~ education** enseñanza *f* secundaria

secondary school *n* instituto *m or* colegio *m* de enseñanza secundaria, liceo *m* (CS, Ven)

second best¹ *n* [u]: **he won't accept ~ ~** sólo se conforma con lo mejor

second best² *adv*: **to come off ~ ~ (to sb)** quedar en segundo puesto (después de algn)

second: **~ class** *adv* 1 (Transp) ‹*travel/go*› en segunda (clase) 2 (of mail — in US) con tarifa para impresos; (— in UK) por correo regular; **~-class** /'sekənd'klæs || ˌsekənd'klɑːs/ *adj* (*pred* **~ class**) 1 (inferior) ‹*goods/service*› de segunda (clase *or* categoría), de calidad inferior 2 (Post): **~-class matter** (in US) impresos *mpl*; **~-class mail** (in UK) *servicio regular de correos, que tarda más en llegar a destino que el de primera clase* 3 (in UK) (Transp) ‹*travel/ticket/compartment*› de segunda (clase) 4 (BrE Educ): **~-class degree** *título calificado con la segunda o tercera nota que es posible obtener*; **~ cousin** *n* primo segundo, prima segunda *m,f*

seconder /'sekəndər || 'sekəndə(r)/ *n*: *persona que secunda or apoya una moción o propuesta*; **is there a ~ for the proposal?** ¿alguién secunda *or* apoya la propuesta?

second half *n* (Sport) segundo tiempo *m*

second-hand¹ /'sekənd'hænd/ *adj* (*pred* **second hand**) 1 (not new) ‹*car/clothes*› de segunda mano, usado; ‹*bookstore*› de viejo; ‹*shop*› de artículos de segunda mano 2 (not original) ‹*account/information*› de segunda mano

second-hand² *adv*: **to buy sth ~** comprar algo de segunda mano; **to learn sth ~** enterarse de algo por terceros

second-in-command /'sekəndɪnkə'mænd || ˌsekəndɪnkə'mɑːnd/ *n* (*pl* **seconds-in-command**) número dos *mf* (*persona directamente por debajo de la autoridad máxima de una organización, departamento etc*)

secondly /'sekəndli/ *adv* (*indep*) en segundo lugar

secondment /sɪ'kɑːndmənt || sɪ'kɒndmənt/ *n* (BrE): **she's on ~ to the research institute** ha sido enviada *or* trasladada en comisión al instituto de investigación

second: **~-rate** /'sekənd'reɪt/ *adj* mediocre; **~ sight** *n* [u] clarividencia *f*; **~-string** /'sekənd'strɪŋ/ *adj* de reserva, suplente

secrecy /'siːkrəsi/ *n* [u] secreto *m*; **the meeting was held in ~** la reunión se llevó a cabo en secreto; **I was told in (the) strictest ~** me lo dijeron muy confidencialmente

secret¹ /'siːkrət || 'siːkrɪt/ *n* secreto *m*; **in ~** en secreto; **can you keep a ~?** ¿sabes guardar un secreto?; **is she in on the ~?** ¿lo sabe?, ¿está al corriente?; **an open ~** un secreto a voces; **he kept it a ~ from her for years** se lo ocultó durante años; **to make no ~ of sth** no esconder *or* ocultar algo

secret² *adj* secreto; **to keep sth ~ from sb** ocultarle algo a algn

secret agent *n* agente *mf* secreto

secretarial /ˌsekrə'teriəl || ˌsekrə'teəriəl/ *adj* ‹*job*› de oficina, de secretaria/secretario; **~ course** curso *m* de secretariado

secretariat /ˌsekrə'teriæt || ˌsekrə'teəriət/ *n* secretaría *f*

secretary /'sekrəteri || 'sekrətri/ *n* (*pl* **-ries**)
A (in office, of committee, of society) secretario, -ria *m,f*
B (Govt) ministro, -tra *m,f*, secretario, -ria *m,f* (Méx); **S~ of the Treasury** Ministro, -tra *m,f* de Hacienda

secretary: **~-general** /'sekrəteri'dʒenrəl || ˌsekrətri 'dʒenrəl/ *n* (*pl* **secretaries-general**) secretario, -ria *m,f* general; **~ of State** *n* (*pl* **Secretaries of State**) (Govt) (in US) secretario, -ria *m,f* de Estado (de los Estados Unidos); (in UK) ministro, -tra *m,f*, secretario, -ria *m,f* (Méx)

secrete /sɪ'kriːt/ *vt*
A (Biol, Physiol) segregar*, secretar
B (hide) (frml) ocultar

secretion /sɪ'kriːʃən/ *n* [u c] secreción *f*

secretive /'siːkrətɪv/ *adj* ‹*person/behavior*› reservado, hermético; **to be ~ ABOUT sth/sb** ser* reservado en lo que respecta a algo/algn

secretly /'siːkrətli || 'siːkrɪtli/ *adv* ‹*meet/plan*› secretamente, en secreto, a escondidas

secret: **~ police** *n* [u] policía *f* secreta; **~ service** *n* 1 (intelligence service) servicio *m* secreto, servicio(s) *m(pl)* de inteligencia 2 **the Secret Service** (in US) *organización cuyas funciones incluyen la protección del Presidente y evitar la falsificación de moneda*

sect /sekt/ *n* secta *f*

sectarian /sek'teriən || sek'teəriən/ *adj* ‹*views/violence*› sectario; ‹*schooling/school*› confesional

section¹ /'sekʃən/ *n*
A 1 (of object, newspaper, orchestra) sección *f*; (of machine, piece of furniture) parte *f*; (of road) tramo *m*; (of city, population, public opinion) sector *m*; **the first ~ of the book** la primera parte del libro; **~ two, subsection one** (of document) artículo dos, punto *or* inciso primero 2 (unit of land) (AmE) *640 acres o 2,59km²*
B (department) sección *f*; (*before n*) ‹*manager/supervisor*› de sección
C (in geometry, drawing) sección *f*, corte *m*
D 1 (thin slice) sección *f* 2 (in surgery) sección *f*

section² *vt* ‹*map/area*› dividir; ‹*line*› segmentar; **they ~ed off part of the office** separaron parte de la oficina con una mampara (*or* tabique *etc*)

sector /'sektər || 'sektə(r)/ *n* sector *m*; **the private/public ~** el sector privado/público

secular /'sekjələr || 'sekjʊlə(r)/ *adj* ‹*education*› laico, secular; ‹*society/art*› secular

secure¹ /sɪ'kjʊr || sɪ'kjʊə(r)/ *adj*
A 1 (safe) ‹*fortress/hideaway*› seguro; **his future is ~** tiene el futuro asegurado; **to make sth ~ against sth** proteger* algo contra algo 2 (emotionally) ‹*childhood/home/relationship*› estable 3 (assured, guaranteed) ‹*job/income/investment*› seguro; **to be financially ~** tener* seguridad económica
B (firm, firmly fastened) ‹*foothold/shelf*› firme; ‹*foundation*› sólido; **is the rope ~?** ¿está bien sujeta la cuerda?; **to make sth ~** asegurar algo

secure² *vt*
A (obtain) ‹*ticket/job/votes/support*› conseguir*, obtener* (frml); **to ~ sb's release** conseguir* la libertad de algn
B (fasten, fix firmly) ‹*door/gate/shelf*› asegurar
C (Fin) ‹*loan*› garantizar*; **a ~d loan** un préstamo con garantía
D (make safe) **to ~ sth (AGAINST sth)** ‹*area/building*› proteger* *or* fortificar* algo (CONTRA algo)
■ **secure** *vi* **to ~ AGAINST sth** protegerse* CONTRA algo

securely /sɪ'kjʊrli || sɪ'kjʊəli/ *adv* bien; **~ tied/fastened** bien atado/bien sujeto

security /sɪ'kjʊrəti || sɪ'kjʊərəti/ *n* (*pl* **-ties**)
A [u] 1 (against crime, espionage etc) seguridad *f*; **national ~** la seguridad nacional; (*before n*) **~ forces** fuerzas *fpl* de seguridad; **~ guard** guarda jurado, guarda jurada *m,f*; **a**

~ **risk** un peligro para la seguridad; ~ **system** sistema *m* de seguridad [2] (department) (+ *sing o pl vb*) departamento *m* de seguridad
B [u] [1] (safety, certainty) seguridad *f*; **emotional** ~ seguridad en el plano afectivo [2] (protection) seguro *m*
C (Fin) [1] [u] (guarantee) garantía *f*; **to stand** ~ **for sb** salir* garante *or* fiador de algn, servirle* *or* (RPl) salirle* de garantía a algn [2] **securities** *pl* (Fin) valores *mpl*, títulos *mpl*; (*before n*) **the securities market** el mercado de valores

Security Council *n* **the (United Nations)** ~ ~ el Consejo de Seguridad (de las Naciones Unidas)

sedan /sɪ'dæn/ *n*
A (car) (AmE) sedán *m*
B ~ **(chair)** palanquín *m*, silla *f* de manos

sedate¹ /sɪ'deɪt/ *adj* ‹*person/lifestyle/pace*› reposado, tranquilo; ‹*color/decor*› sobrio

sedate² *vt* (Med) ‹*patient/animal*› sedar, administrar sedantes a; **she was heavily ~d** le habían administrado un fuerte sedante

sedately /sɪ'deɪtli/ *adv* ‹*walk/move*› reposadamente

sedation /sɪ'deɪʃən/ *n* [u] sedación *f*; **to be under** ~ estar* bajo el efecto de los sedantes

sedative /'sedətɪv/ *n* sedante *m*

sedentary /'sedn̩teri || 'sedn̩tri/ *adj* sedentario

sedge /sedʒ/ *n* [u] juncia *f*

sediment /'sedəmənt || 'sedɪmənt/ *n* [u] [1] (in wine, coffee) poso *m*, asiento *m* [2] (Geol) sedimento *m*

sedimentary /'sedə'mentəri, -tri || ˌsedɪ'mentəri, -tri/ *adj* sedimentario

sedition /sɪ'dɪʃən/ *n* [u] sedición *f*

seditious /sɪ'dɪʃəs/ *adj* sedicioso

seduce /sɪ'du:s || sɪ'dju:s/ *vt* [1] (sexually) seducir* [2] (tempt) seducir*, tentar*; **to ~ sb INTO -ING** tentar* a algn A/+ INF

seducer /sɪ'du:sər || sɪ'dju:sə(r)/ *n* seductor, -tora *m,f*

seduction /sɪ'dʌkʃən/ *n* [u c] (sexual) seducción *f*

seductive /sɪ'dʌktɪv/ *adj* ‹*manner/clothing/person*› seductor; ‹*offer*› tentador, atrayente

seductively /sɪ'dʌktɪvli/ *adv* seductoramente

seductress /sɪ'dʌktrəs || sɪ'dʌktrɪs/ *n* seductora *f*

see¹ /si:/ (*past* **saw**; *past p* **seen**) *vt*

(Sense I)

A [1] ver*; **I can't see a thing!** ¡no veo nada!; **we haven't ~n her for a while** hace un tiempo que no la vemos; **there wasn't a policeman to be ~n** no había ningún policía; **to ~ sb/sth + INF**: **I didn't ~ her arrive** no la vi llegar; **we'll be sorry to ~ her go** nos va a dar pena que se vaya; **to ~ sb/sth -ING**: **I can ~ somebody coming this way** veo venir a alguien; **I thought I was ~ing things** pensé que estaba viendo visiones; **I'll believe it when I ~ it** hasta que no lo vea no lo creo; ***to be glad to ~ the back of sb*** alegrarse de que algn se vaya [2] ‹*film/play*› ver* [3] (look at, inspect) ver*; ~ **page 20** ver página 20; **may I ~ your ticket?** ¿me permite su entrada (*or* boleto *etc*)?
B [1] (perceive, notice) ver*; **I don't know what she ~s in him** no sé qué es lo que le ve *or* qué es lo que ve en él; **anyone can ~ she's upset** cualquiera se da cuenta de que está disgustada [2] (learn from reading, hearing): **I ~ Mrs Baker's retiring** así que se jubila la señora Baker; **I ~ from your application form that ...** he leído en su solicitud que …
C (understand) ver*; **he didn't ~ the joke** no le vio la gracia (al chiste); **do you ~ what I mean?** ¿entiendes?, ¿te das cuenta?; **I can ~ (that) you're in a difficult position, but ...** me doy cuenta de *or* comprendo que estás en una situación difícil, pero …
D (consider, regard) ver*; **the way I ~ it, as I ~ it** a mi modo de ver, tal como yo lo veo; **I ~ nothing wrong in it** yo no le encuentro nada de malo
E [1] (visualize): **can you ~ him as a teacher?** ¿te lo imaginas de profesor? [2] (envisage, foresee): **I can ~ there'll be problems** veo que va a haber problemas; **to ~ sth/sb -ING**: **I can't ~ it working** no creo que vaya a funcionar; **I can ~ her working abroad** la imagino trabajando en el extranjero [3] (accept) (AmE colloq): **we could move Johnson over to Sales — OK, I can ~ that** podríamos pasar a Johnson a Ventas — bueno, eso me parece bien
F [1] (find out, determine) ver*; **I'll have to ~ what I can do** tendré que ver qué puedo hacer; **we'll have to (wait and) ~** habrá que esperar y ver; **that remains to be ~n** eso está por verse [2] (ensure) **to ~ THAT**: ~ **that it doesn't happen again** que no vuelva a suceder
G [1] (experience, undergo): **I doubt if I'll live to ~ it** no creo que yo llegue a verlo *or* que yo llegue a ver el día; **I want to travel and ~ (a bit of) life** quiero viajar y ver mundo [2] (be the occasion of) (journ): **in a week which has ~n the start of ...** en una semana que ha visto el inicio de …; **next Thursday ~s the launch of the new model** el próximo jueves es la fecha señalada para el lanzamiento del nuevo modelo

(Sense II)

A [1] (meet) ver*; **I'm ~ing him on Tuesday** lo voy a ver el martes; **when can I ~ you again?** ¿cuándo nos podemos volver a ver? [2] (go out with) (colloq) salir* con; **they've been ~ing each other for two months** hace dos meses que salen juntos [3] (saying goodbye) (colloq): ~ **you!** ¡hasta luego!, ¡hasta la vista!; ~ **you around!** ¡nos vemos!; ~ **you later/tonight/soon/on Saturday!** ¡hasta luego/esta noche/pronto/el sábado!; **(I'll) be ~ing you!** ¡hasta pronto!
B (visit) [1] (socially) ver* [2] (for consultation) ver*; **you should ~ a specialist** deberías ver a *or* ir a un especialista; **I want to ~ the manager** quisiera ver al gerente *or* hablar con el gerente; **to ~ sb ABOUT sth**: **can I ~ you about something privately?** ¿podría hablar con usted de un asunto privado?
C (receive) ver*, atender*; **the doctor will ~ you now** el doctor lo verá *or* lo atenderá ahora
D (escort, accompany) acompañar; **to ~ sb to the door** acompañar a algn a la puerta

■ **see** *vi*
A [1] ver*; **I can ~ better from here** desde aquí veo mejor; ***~ing is believing*** ver para creer [2] (look, inspect) ver*; **let me ~!** ¡déjame ver!; ~ **for yourself!** ¡compruébalo tú mismo!
B (understand, realize) ver*; **can't you ~ he loves you?** ¿no te das cuenta de *or* no ves que te quiere?; **as far as I can ~** por lo que yo veo; **I ~** (expressing realization) ya veo; (accepting explanation) entiendo
C (consider, think) ver*; **let's ~** vamos a ver, veamos; **I'll ~, but I can't promise anything** voy a ver, pero no te puedo prometer nada
D (find out) ver*; **will it work? — try it and ~** ¿funcionará? — prueba a ver; **what's going on? — you'll soon ~** ¿qué pasa? — ya lo verás

(Phrasal verbs)

- **see about** [v ▸ prep ▸ o] (colloq) [1] (deal with): **a man came to ~ about the leaking roof** vino un hombre por lo de la gotera; **we'll soon ~ about that!** ya lo veremos … [2] (consider, decide): **may I borrow the car? — I'll have to ~ about that** ¿me prestas el coche? — tendré que pensarlo
- **see in** [v ▸ o ▸ adv, v ▸ adv ▸] ‹*New Year*› recibir, esperar
- **see off** [v ▸ o ▸ adv, v ▸ adv ▸ o]
A (say goodbye to) despedir*, despedirse* de
B (get rid of) deshacerse* de; **the dog saw them off** el perro los ahuyentó
- **see out** [v ▸ o ▸ adv, v ▸ adv ▸ o]
A (show out) ‹*person*› acompañar (hasta la puerta); **I'll ~ you out** te acompaño hasta la puerta; **I can ~ myself out** no hace falta que me acompañes
B ‹*old year*› despedir*
- **see over** [v ▸ prep ▸ o] ‹*property/house*› visitar, recorrer
- **see through**
A [v ▸ prep ▸ o] (not be deceived by) calar; **I saw through him from the start** lo calé desde el primer momento (fam)
B [v ▸ o ▸ adv] [v ▸ o ▸ prep ▸ o] (last): **make sure this ~s you through**con esto te tienes que alcanzar; **$20 won't ~ me through the week** 20 dólares no me van a alcanzar hasta el fin de semana
C [v ▸ o ▸ adv] (carry to completion) terminar; **I'll ~ this thing through if it kills me!** ¡voy a llevar esto a buen a término aunque me mate!
- **see to** [v ▸ prep ▸ o] (attend to) ocuparse de; **to ~ to it (that)**: **you must ~ to it that the doors are locked** debes asegurarte de que cierren las puertas con llave

see² *n* (diocese) sede *f*; **the Holy S~** la Santa Sede

S

seed¹ /siːd/ *n*
A 1 [c] (of plant) semilla *f*, simiente *f* (liter); (of orange, grape) (AmE) pepita *f*, semilla *f*; ▸ **sow¹** *vt* 2 [u] (collectively) semillas *fpl*, simiente *f*; **I grew these tomatoes from ~** estos tomates los planté en almácigo; **to go** *o* **run to ~** (lit) «*plant*» granar; (deteriorate): **a great actor gone to ~** un gran actor en decadencia
B [c] (origins) (*often pl*) germen *m*, semilla *f*; **to sow the ~s of doubt** sembrar* (el germen de) la duda
C [c] (Sport) cabeza *mf* de serie, sembrado, -da *m,f* (Méx)

seed² *vt* (Sport) (*usu pass*): **a ~ed player** un jugador cabeza de serie, un sembrado (Méx)

seed: **~bed** *n* (Agr, Hort) semillero *m*, almácigo *m*; **~cake** *n* [u c] (Culin) *torta de semillas de alcaravea*

seedless /'siːdləs || 'siːdlɪs/ *adj* sin pepitas *or* semillas

seedling /'siːdlɪŋ/ *n* planta *f* de semillero *or* almácigo

seed pod *n* vaina *f*

seedy /'siːdi/ *adj* **-dier, -diest** ‹*nightclub/bar*› sórdido, de mala muerte (fam), cutre (Esp fam); ‹*appearance*› desastrado, abandonado; ‹*apartment/resort*› sórdido; **some ~ characters** unos individuos con mala pinta

seeing /'siːɪŋ/ *conj* (colloq) **~ (that)** *o* **~ as** *o* (crit) **~ as how**: **~ (that) you're here, you may as well help** ya que estás aquí, nos puedes ayudar

seek /siːk/ (*past & past p* **sought**) *vt* 1 (search for) (frml) ‹*person/object*› buscar* 2 (try to obtain) ‹*work/shelter/companionship*› buscar*; ‹*solution/explanation*› tratar de encontrar, buscar*; **to ~ one's fortune** probar* fortuna 3 (request) ‹*approval/help*› pedir*; **we had to ~ the advice of a specialist** tuvimos que asesorarnos con un especialista, tuvimos que consultar a un especialista 4 (try to bring about) (frml) ‹*reconciliation*› buscar*, tratar de lograr; **to ~ to + INF** tratar DE + INF, intentar + INF
■ **seek** *vi* (frml) buscar*; **to ~ FOR/AFTER sth** ir* en pos de algo (liter), ir* en busca de algo

Phrasal verb
• **seek out** [v ▸ o ▸ adv, v ▸ adv ▸ o] ‹*person*› buscar*; ‹*opinion*› pedir*

seeker /'siːkər || 'siːkə(r)/ *n*: **treasure ~s** buscadores *mpl* de tesoros; **a ~ after truth** una persona en busca de *or* (liter) en pos de la verdad

seem /siːm/ *vi*
A (give impression) parecer*; **things aren't always what they ~** las apariencias engañan; **it certainly ~s that way** eso parece *or* así parece, por cierto; **strange as it may ~** por raro que parezca, aunque no lo parezca; **to ~ to + INF**: **she ~s to like you** parece que le caes bien; **she ~s not** *o* **doesn't ~ to have noticed** no parece haberse dado cuenta; **so it ~s, so it would ~** eso parece, así parece; **that ~s like a good idea** ésa me parece una buena idea; **it ~s like years since I saw you** parece que han pasado años que no te veo
B 1 (get impression) **to ~ to + INF**: **I ~ to remember that you ...** creo recordar que tú ... 2 (in sb's opinion) parecer*; **it ~s to me/him/them that ...** me/le/les parece que ...; **it doesn't ~ right to me** a mí no me parece bien 3 (toning down statement) parecer*; **I can't ~ to remember where I put it** no logro acordarme de dónde lo puse; **it ~s to be closed** parece que está cerrado; **what ~s to be the trouble?** veamos ¿de qué se trata?

seeming /'siːmɪŋ/ *adj* (*before n*) aparente

seemingly /'siːmɪŋli/ *adv* ‹*honest/complicated*› aparentemente

seemly /'siːmli/ *adj* **-lier, -liest** (frml) ‹*behavior/dress*› correcto, apropiado

seen /siːn/ *past p of* **see¹**

seep /siːp/ *vi* «*liquid/moisture*» filtrarse; **water was ~ing into her shoes** el agua le estaba calando los zapatos

seer /sɪr || sɪə(r)/ *n* (liter) profeta *mf*, vidente *mf*

seesaw /'siːsɔː/ *n* (in playground) balancín *m*, subibaja *m*

seethe /siːð/ *vi* 1 (be agitated) bullir*; **to ~ WITH sth**: **her mind was seething with images** las imágenes bullían en su cerebro; **the town was seething with tourists** la ciudad estaba plagada de turistas 2 (be angry) estar* furioso; **I was absolutely seething** me hervía la sangre, estaba furioso, estaba que ardía

see-through /'siːθruː/ *adj* transparente

segment /'segmənt/ *n* 1 (Math) (of circle, sphere, line) segmento *m* 2 (of citrus fruit) gajo *m*; 3 (section) sector *m*

segregate /'segrɪgeɪt/ *vt* ‹*races/sexes*› segregar*; ‹*rival groups*› mantener* aparte; **~d school** *escuela en la que se practica la segregación racial*

segregation /'segrɪ'geɪʃən/ *n* [u] segregación *f*

Seine /sem/ *n* **the ~** el Sena

seismic /'saɪzmɪk/ *adj* (Geol) sísmico

seize /siːz/ *vt*
A (grab, snatch) ‹*hand/object*› agarrar; ‹*opportunity*› aprovechar; ‹*power*› tomar, hacerse* con
B 1 (capture) ‹*town/fortress*› tomar, apoderarse de; ‹*person*› detener* 2 ‹*assets/property*› (confiscate) confiscar*; (impound) embargar*; ‹*cargo/contraband*› confiscar*, decomisar; ‹*drugs/arms*› incautar, incautarse de; ‹*copies of book*› secuestrar
C (overcome) (*usu pass*): **she was ~d with panic** fue presa del pánico; **he was ~d with the desire to ...** lo acometió el deseo de ..., sintió ganas de ...

Phrasal verbs
• **seize on, seize upon** [v ▸ prep ▸ o] ‹*chance*› aprovechar; **her remarks were ~d on by the opposition** la oposición se apresuró a sacar partido de sus declaraciones
• **seize up** [v ▸ adv] «*engine*» agarrotarse, fundirse (AmL); «*muscles*» agarrotarse; «*traffic*» paralizarse*

seizure /'siːʒər || 'siːʒə(r)/ *n*
A 1 [u] (of power) toma *f* 2 [u] (capture) toma *f* 3 [u c] (of property) confiscación *f*; (impoundment) embargo *m*; (of cargo, contraband) confiscación *f*, decomiso *m*; (of arms, drugs) incautación *f*
B [c] (Med) ataque *m*

seldom /'seldəm/ *adv* rara vez, pocas veces, casi nunca

select¹ /sɪ'lekt/ *vt* ‹*gift/book/wine*› elegir*, escoger*, seleccionar; ‹*candidate/team member*› seleccionar

select² *adj* 1 (exclusive) ‹*school*› de élite, exclusivo; ‹*district*› distinguido, exclusivo 2 (choice) ‹*fruit/wine*› selecto, de primera (calidad) 3 (especially chosen) ‹*group*› selecto; **only the ~ few** sólo los escogidos

select committee, **Select Committee** *n* (in UK) *comisión investigadora compuesta por diputados del gobierno y la oposición*

selection /sɪ'lekʃən/ *n*
A [u c] (act, thing chosen) selección *f*, elección *f*; **to make a ~** hacer* una selección
B [u c] (Busn) (of chocolates, buttons, yarns) surtido *m*; **a wide ~ of new and used cars** una amplia gama de coches nuevos y usados

selective /sɪ'lektɪv/ *adj* 1 ‹*control/recruitment*› selectivo; ‹*reporting*› parcial; **~ education** *sistema que emplea un procedimiento selectivo para la admisión de alumnos en determinadas escuelas*; **~ service** (AmE) servicio *m* militar obligatorio, conscripción *f* (AmL) 2 (discriminating) **to be ~**: **he's fairly ~ about who he mixes with** elige *or* escoge mucho sus amistades

selector /sɪ'lektər || sɪ'lektə(r)/ *n* (Sport) seleccionador, -dora *m,f*

self /self/ *n* [c] (*pl* **selves**): **she's her old ~ again** vuelve a ser la de antes; **you're not your usual cheerful ~** no estás tan alegre como de costumbre

self- /'self/ *pref* 1 (concerning the self): **~disgust/~doubt** asco *m*/duda *f* de sí mismo 2 (with no outside agency) auto; **~financing** autofinanciado

self: **~-addressed** /'selfə'drest/ *adj*: *con el nombre y la dirección del remitente*; **send a ~-addressed envelope to ...** envíe un sobre con su nombre y dirección a ...; **~-adhesive** /'selfəd'hiːsɪv/ *adj* autoadhesivo; **~-aggrandizement** /ˌselfə'grændəzmənt || ˌselfə'grændɪzmənt/ *n* [u] propio engrandecimiento *m*, autobombo *m* (fam); **~-appointed** /'selfə'pɔɪntəd || ˌselfə'pɔɪntɪd/ *adj* ‹*spokesperson/chief*› autoproclamado; **~-assertiveness** /ˌselfə'sɜːrtɪvnəs || ˌselfə'sɜːtɪvnɪs/ *n* [u] autoasertividad *f*; **~-assured** /'selfə'ʃʊrd || ˌselfə'ʃʊəd, ˌselfə'ʃɔːd/ *adj* seguro de sí mismo; **~-catering** /'self'keɪtərɪŋ/ *adj* (BrE) ‹*accommodation*› equipado con cocina; **~ holiday** vacaciones *fpl* en apartamentos (*or* estudios *etc*); **~-centered**, (BrE) **~-centred** /'self'sentərd || ˌself'sentəd/ *adj* egocéntrico; **~-confessed** /'selfkən'fest/ *adj* (*before n*) confeso; **~-confidence** /'self'kɑːnfədəns || ˌself'kɒnfɪdəns/ *n* [u] confianza *f* en sí mismo; **~-confident** /'self'kɑ:nfədənt || ,self 'kɒnfɪdənt/ *adj* seguro de sí mismo; **~-conscious** /'self'kɑ:ntʃəs || ,self'kɒnʃəs/ *adj* 1 (shy, embarrassed) ‹*person/manner*› tímido; **she's very ~-conscious about her nose** tiene complejo *or* está muy acomplejada por su nariz; **she felt very ~-conscious** se sintió muy cohibida; 2 (unspontaneous, unnatural) (pej) afectado; ‹*acting/delivery*› afectado, acartonado; **~-consciously** /'self'kɑ:ntʃəsli || ,self'kɒnʃəsli/ *adv* 1 (shyly) ‹*behave/speak*› con timidez; 2 (unspontaneously) (pej) ‹*behave/speak*› de manera afectada; **~-contained** /selfkən'teɪnd/ *adj* 1 ‹*flat*› (BrE) *con cocina y cuarto de baño propios* 2 ‹*person*› (independent) independiente; (reserved) reservado; **~-control** /'selfkən'trəʊl/ *n* [u] dominio *m* de sí mismo, autocontrol *m*; **~-defeating** /'selfdɪ'fi:tɪŋ/ *adj* contraproducente; **~-defense**, (BrE) **~-defence** /'selfdɪ'fens/ *n* [u] 1 (Law): **to act in ~-defense** actuar* en defensa propia 2 (fighting technique) defensa *f* personal; **~-denial** /'selfdɪ'naɪəl/ *n* [u] abnegación *f*, sacrificio *m*; **~-destruct** /'selfdɪ'strʌkt/ *vi* autodestruirse*; **~-destructive** /,selfdɪ'strʌktɪv/ *adj* autodestructivo; **~-determination** /'selfdɪ'tɜ:rmə'neɪʃən || ,selfdɪ,tɜ:mɪ'neɪʃən/ *n* [u] autodeterminación *f*; **~-discipline** /'self'dɪsəplɪn || ,self'dɪsɪplɪn/ *n* [u] autodisciplina *f*; **~-drive** /'self'draɪv/ *adj* (BrE) ‹*car/hire*› sin chofer *or* (Esp) sin chófer; ‹*holiday*› con transporte en coche propio *or* (AmL) en auto propio; **~-employed** /'selfɪm'plɔɪd/ *adj* autónomo, por cuenta propia; **~-esteem** /'selfɪ'sti:m/ *n* [u] autoestima *f*, amor *m* propio; **~-evident** /'self'evədənt || ,self'evɪdənt/ *adj* ‹*truth*› manifiesto; ‹*conclusion*› evidente, obvio; **~-explanatory** /'selfɪk'splænətɔ:ri || ,selfɪk'splænətri/ *adj*: **the instructions are ~-explanatory** las instrucciones son muy claras *or* muy fáciles de entender; **~-expression** /'selfɪk'spreʃən/ *n* [u] expresión *f* personal; **~-fulfilling** /'selffʊl'fɪlɪŋ/ *adj* ‹*prophecy/prediction*› que acarrea su propio cumplimiento; **~-government** /'self'gʌvərnmənt || ,self'gʌvənmənt/ *n* [u] autogobierno *m*, autonomía *f*; **~-help** /'self'help/ *n* [u] autoayuda *f*; (Econ) autofinanciación *f*, autofinanciamiento *m*; (*before n*) **~-help group** grupo *m* de apoyo mutuo; **~-image** /'self'ɪmɪdʒ/ *n* imagen *f* de sí mismo; **~-importance** /'selfɪm'pɔ:rtn̩s || ,selfɪm'pɔ:tn̩s/ *n* [u] engreimiento *m*, presunción *f*; **~-important** /'selfɪm'pɔ:rtn̩t || ,selfɪm'pɔ:tn̩t/ *adj* engreído, presumido; **~-imposed** /'selfɪm'pəʊzd/ *adj* ‹*exile/task*› voluntario, autoimpuesto; ‹*rules/punishment*› autoimpuesto; **~-improvement** /,selfɪm'pru:vmənt/ *n* [u] autosuperación *f*; **~-indulgent** /'selfɪn'dʌldʒənt/ *adj* demasiado indulgente consigo mismo, que se permite excesos; **~-inflicted** /'selfɪn'flɪktəd || ,selfɪn'flɪktɪd/ *adj* autoinfligido; **~-interest** /'self'ɪntrəst || ,self'ɪntrɪst/ *n* [u] interés *m* (personal)

selfish /'selfɪʃ/ *adj* egoísta

selfishly /'selfɪʃli/ *adv* egoístamente

selfishness /'selfɪʃnəs || 'selfɪʃnɪs/ *n* [u] egoísmo *m*

selfless /'selfləs || 'selflɪs/ *adj* desinteresado

selflessly /'selfləsli || 'selflɪsli/ *adv* desinteresadamente

selflessness /'selfləsnəs || 'selflɪsnɪs/ *n* [u] desinterés *m*

self: **~-made** /'self'meɪd/ *adj* (*before n*) ‹*man/woman*› que ha alcanzado su posición gracias a sus propios esfuerzos; **~-perpetuating** /'selfpər'petʃueɪtɪŋ || ,selfpə'petjʊeɪtɪŋ/ *adj* ‹*situation/activity/problem*› que se autoperpetúa; **~-pity** /'self'pɪti/ *n* [u] autocompasión *f*; **~-pitying** /'self'pɪtiɪŋ/ *adj* autocompasivo; **~-portrait** /'self'pɔ:rtrət || ,self'pɔ:trɪt/ *n* autorretrato *m*; **~-possessed** /'selfpə'zest/ *adj* dueño de sí (mismo), sereno; **~-preservation** /'self'prezər'veɪʃən || ,selfprezə'veɪʃən/ *n* [u]: **the instinct of ~-preservation** el instinto de conservación *or* supervivencia; **~-proclaimed** /'selfprə'kleɪmd/ *adj* (frml) ‹*leader/anarchists*› autoproclamado, sedicente; **~-raising** /'self'reɪzɪŋ/ *adj* (BrE) ▸ **~-rising**; **~-regarding** /,selfrɪ'gɑ:rdɪŋ || ,selfrɪ'gɑ:dɪŋ/ *adj* 1 (self-respecting) de consideración por sí mismo 2 (vain) (pej) engreído; **~-regulation** /'selfregjə'leɪʃən || ,selfregjʊ'leɪʃən/ *n* autorregulación *f*; **~-reliant** /'selfrɪ'laɪənt/ *adj* independiente; **~-respect** /'selfrɪ'spekt/ *n* [u] dignidad *f*, amor *m* propio; **~-respecting** /'selfrɪ'spektɪŋ/ *adj* (*before n*): **no ~-respecting editor would work for them** ningún editor que se precie trabajaría para ellos; **~-righteous** /'self'raɪtʃəs/ *adj* ‹*person*› con pretensiones de superioridad moral; ‹*tone*› de superioridad moral; **~-rising** /'self'raɪzɪŋ/ *adj* (AmE) ‹*flour*› con polvos de hornear (AmL), con levadura (Esp), leudante (RPl); **~-sacrifice** /'self'sækrəfaɪs || ,self'sækrɪfaɪs/ *n* [u] sacrificio *m*; **~same** *adj* (*before n*) ‹*person/day/place*› mismísimo; **~-satisfied** /'self'sætəsfaɪd || ,self'sætɪsfaɪd/ *adj* ufano, satisfecho de sí mismo, (auto)suficiente; ‹*expression/grin*› de (auto)suficiencia; **~-seeking** /'self'si:kɪŋ/ *adj* egoísta, interesado

self-service[1] /'self'sɜ:rvəs || ,self'sɜ:vɪs/, (esp AmE) **self-serve** /-'sɜ:rv/ *adj*: **~ restaurant** autoservicio *m*, self-service *m*

self-service[2] *n* [u] autoservicio *m*

self: **~-study** /'self'stʌdi/ *n* autoestudio *m*; (*before n*) **~-study skills** técnicas *fpl* de autoestudio; **~-styled** /'self'staɪld/ *adj* (*before n*) sedicente, autollamado; **~-sufficiency** /'selfsə'fɪʃənsi/ *n* [u] independencia *f*; (Econ) autosuficiencia *f*, autarquía *f*; **~-sufficient** /'selfsə'fɪʃənt/ *adj* ‹*person*› independiente; ‹*country*› autosuficiente, autárquico; **to be ~-sufficient IN sth** autoabastecerse* DE algo; **~-supporting** /'selfsə'pɔ:rtɪŋ || ,selfsə'pɔ:tɪŋ/ *adj* ‹*student*› económicamente independiente; ‹*organization*› autofinanciado; **~-taught** /'self'tɔ:t/ *adj* autodidacta, autodidacto; **~-worth** /'self'wɜ:rθ || 'self'wɜ:θ/ *n* [u] autoestima *f*

sell /sel/ (*past & past p* **sold**) *vt*

A 1 ‹*goods/house/shares/player/insurance*› vender; Ⓢ **sell by 11.4.96** fecha límite de venta: 11-4-96; **to ~ sth TO sb, to ~ sb sth** venderle algo A algn; **to ~ sth FOR sth** vender algo EN *or* POR algo; **to ~ sth AT sth**: **they are ~ing it at half price** lo están vendiendo a mitad de precio; **to ~ sth at a loss** vender algo perdiendo dinero; ***to ~ sb short***: **he's been sold short** (unfairly treated) no lo han tratado como merece; (ripped off) lo han timado; **don't ~ yourself short** tienes que hacerte valer, no te subestimes 2 (achieve sales figure of): **her novel sold a million in a year** se vendieron un millón de ejemplares de su novela en un año

B (colloq) (make acceptable) **to ~ sth TO sb, to ~ sb sth** convencer* a algn DE algo; ***to be sold on sth***: **he's completely sold on the idea** está convencido de que es una magnífica idea; ▸ **river**

■ **sell** *vi* 1 ‹‹*person/company*›› vender 2 (be sold) ‹‹*product*›› venderse; **to ~ AT/FOR sth** venderse A/POR algo

Phrasal verbs

• **sell off** [v ▸ o ▸ adv, v ▸ adv ▸ o] vender; (cheaply) liquidar

• **sell out**

A [v ▸ adv ▸ o] 1 (sell all of) ‹*stock*› agotar; ‹*article*› agotar las existencias de 2 (dispose of) ‹*shares/holding*› vender, deshacerse* de

B [v ▸ adv] 1 (sell all stock) ‹‹*shop*›› **to ~ out (OF sth)**: **we've** *o* **we're sold out of bread** no nos queda pan, se nos ha agotado el pan 2 (be sold) ‹‹*stock/tickets*›› agotarse; Ⓢ **sold out** (Cin, Theat) agotadas las localidades 3 (dispose of holding) vender *or* liquidar el negocio 4 (be traitor) ‹‹*leader/artist*›› venderse

• **sell up** (esp BrE)

A [v ▸ adv ▸ o] ‹*business*› liquidar, vender

B [v ▸ adv] vender el negocio (*or* la casa *etc*)

sell-by date /'selbaɪ/ *n* (BrE) fecha *f* límite de venta; **this food is past its ~-by date** esta comida ya se pasó de la fecha límite

seller /'selər || 'selə(r)/ *n* (person, company) vendedor, -dora *m,f*

selling /'selɪŋ/ *n* [u] ventas *fpl*; (*before n*) **~ price** precio *m* de venta

sellotape /'seləteɪp/ *vt* (BrE) ▸ **scotchtape**

Sellotape® /'seləteɪp/ *n* [u] (BrE) ▸ **Scotch tape**

sell-out /'selaʊt/ *n*

A (performance) éxito *m* de taquilla

B (betrayal) capitulación *f*

selvage, selvedge /'selvɪdʒ/ *n* orillo *m*

selves /selvz/ *pl of* **self**

semantic /sɪ'mæntɪk/ *adj* semántico

semantics /sɪ'mæntɪks/ *n* (+ *sing vb*) semántica *f*

semaphore /'seməfɔ:r || 'seməfɔ:(r)/ *n* [u] código *m* de señales

S

semblance /ˈsembləns/ *n* [u] (frml) **~ OF sth** apariencia *f* DE algo; **they managed to maintain some ~ of order** lograron mantener cierta apariencia de orden

semen /ˈsiːmən/ *n* [u] semen *m*

semester /səˈmestər ‖ sɪˈmestə(r)/ *n* (in US) semestre *m* (*lectivo*)

semi /ˈsemi/ *n* (colloq) [1] (truck) (AmE) ▸**semitrailer 1** [2] (house) (BrE) casa *f* pareada *or* adosada

semi- /ˈsemi, ˈsemaɪ ‖ ˈsemi/ *pref* semi-

semibreve /ˈsemibriːv/ *n* (BrE) redonda *f*, semibreve *f*

semicircle /ˈsemiˌsɜːrkəl ‖ ˈsemiˌsɜːkəl/ *n* semicírculo *m*

semicircular /ˈsemiˈsɜːrkjələr ‖ ˌsemiˈsɜːkjʊlə(r)/ *adj* semicircular

semicolon /ˈsemiˈkəʊlən/ *n* punto y coma *m*

semiconscious /ˈsemiˈkɑːntʃəs ‖ ˌsemiˈkɒnʃəs/ *adj* semiconsciente

semidetached /ˈsemidɪˈtætʃt/ *adj*: **a ~ house** una casa pareada *or* adosada

semifinal /ˈsemiˈfaɪnl̩/ *n* semifinal *f*

semifinalist /ˈsemiˈfaɪnl̩əst ‖ ˌsemiˈfaɪnl̩ɪst/ *n* semifinalista *mf*

seminal /ˈsemənl̩ ‖ ˈsemɪnl̩/ *adj* (frml) ‹*book/idea*› fundamental, de gran influencia

seminar /ˈsemənɑːr ‖ ˈsemɪnɑː(r)/ *n* seminario *m*

seminary /ˈsemənerі ‖ ˈsemɪnəri/ *n* (*pl* **-ries**) seminario *m*

semiprecious /ˈsemiˈpreʃəs/ *adj* semiprecioso

semiquaver /ˈsemiˌkweɪvər ‖ ˈsemiˌkweɪvə(r)/ *n* (BrE) semicorchea *f*

semiskilled /ˈsemiˈskɪld/ *adj* semicalificado *or* (Esp) semicualificado

semiskimmed /ˈsemiˈskɪmd/ *adj*: **~ milk** leche *f* semidescremada *or* (Esp tb) semidesnatada

semitone /ˈsemitəʊn/ *n* semitono *m*

semitrailer /ˈsemiˌtreɪlər ‖ ˈsemiˌtreɪlə(r)/ *n* (AmE) [1] (truck) camión *m* articulado, trailer *m* (Méx) [2] (trailer) remolque *m*, acoplado *m* (CS)

semolina /ˈseməˈliːnə/ *n* [u] [1] (wheat flour) (AmE) sémola *f* [2] (for dessert) (BrE) crema *f* de sémola

Sen (US title) = **Senator**

senate /ˈsenət ‖ ˈsenɪt/ *n* [1] (Govt) **the Senate** el senado *or* Senado [2] (of university) ≈ rectorado *m*, junta *f* de gobierno (Méx) (*junta integrada por el rector y algunos profesores*)

> **Senate**
>
> El Senado es la cámara alta del Congreso (**Congress**) de Estados Unidos. Está formado por 100 senadores (*senators*), dos por cada estado, que son elegidos por períodos de seis años. Toda nueva ley debe ser aprobada por el Senado y la Cámara de Representantes (**House of Representatives**), pero el Senado tiene responsabilidad especial en asuntos relacionados con la política exterior

S

senator /ˈsenətər ‖ ˈsenətə(r)/ *n* senador, -dora *m,f*

senatorial /ˈsenəˈtɔːriəl/ *adj* ‹*office/rank*› de senador, senatorial

send /send/ (*past & past p* **sent**) *vt*

A (dispatch) ‹*letter/parcel/flowers/greetings*› mandar, enviar*; **~ her my love** mándale saludos *or* recuerdos de mi parte

B (direct, cause to go) ‹*messenger/envoy/reinforcements*› mandar, enviar*; **to ~ sb on an errand/a course** mandar a algn a hacer un recado *or* mandado/un curso; **to ~ sb FOR sth**: **he sent me for some beer** me mandó a comprar cerveza, me mandó a por cerveza (Esp fam); **to ~ sb to prison** mandar a algn a la cárcel; ***to ~ sb packing*** mandar a algn a freír espárragos (fam)

C [1] (propel, cause to move): **the assassination sent shock waves around the world** el asesinato conmocionó al mundo; **the thought of it sent a shiver down my spine** me dio un escalofrío de sólo pensarlo; **the blow sent him reeling** el golpe lo dejó tambaleándose; **she sent everything flying** lo hizo saltar todo por los aires [2] (transmit) ‹*signal/current*› enviar*, mandar

D ‹*person*› (+ *compl*): **her remark sent him into fits of laughter** su comentario lo hizo morir de risa; **to ~ sb to sleep** dormir* a algn

■ **send** *vi*: **we'll have to ~ to the States for spares** tendremos que encargar repuestos de Estados Unidos, tendremos que mandar (a) pedir repuestos a Estados Unidos (AmL)

Phrasal verbs

• **send away**

A [v ▸ o ▸ adv, v ▸ adv ▸ o] [1] (dismiss): **don't ~ me away** no me digas que me vaya; **she sent the beggar away empty-handed** despachó al mendigo con las manos vacías [2] (send elsewhere) mandar, enviar*; **the film has to be sent away for processing** hay que mandar *or* enviar la película a revelar

B [v ▸ adv] ▸**send off C**

• **send back** [v ▸ o ▸ adv, v ▸ adv ▸ o] ‹*purchase*› devolver*, mandar de vuelta; ‹*person*› hacer* volver

• **send down** [v ▸ o ▸ adv, v ▸ adv ▸ o] (BrE) [1] (from university) (*usu pass*) expulsar [2] (to prison) (colloq) meter preso

• **send for** [v ▸ prep ▸ o] [1] (ask to come) ‹*priest/doctor/ambulance*› mandar a buscar, mandar llamar (AmL); **they sent for reinforcements** pidieron que enviaran refuerzos [2] (order) ‹*catalog/application form*› pedir*; ‹*books/tapes/clothes*› encargar*, pedir*

• **send in** [v ▸ o ▸ adv, v ▸ adv ▸ o] [1] ‹*troops*› enviar*, mandar [2] (by post) ‹*entry/coupon/application*› mandar, enviar* [3] (into room) ‹*person*› hacer* pasar; **~ him in** hágalo pasar

• **send off**

A [v ▸ o ▸ adv, v ▸ adv ▸ o] (dispatch) ‹*letter/parcel/goods*› despachar, mandar; ‹*person*› mandar

B [v ▸ o ▸ adv, v ▸ adv ▸ o] (BrE Sport) expulsar, echar

C [v ▸ adv] **to ~ off FOR sth**: **I sent off for a brochure** escribí pidiendo un folleto, mandé pedir un folleto (AmL)

• **send on** [v ▸ o ▸ adv, v ▸ adv ▸ o] [1] (in advance) ‹*luggage*› enviar* *or* mandar por adelantado; **they sent him on (ahead) with the message** lo mandaron adelante con el mensaje [2] (forward) ‹*mail*› hacer* seguir

• **send out**

A [v ▸ o ▸ adv, v ▸ adv ▸ o] [1] (emit) ‹*heat*› despedir*, irradiar; ‹*signal/radio waves*› emitir [2] (on errand) mandar; ‹*scouts/emissaries*› mandar, enviar* [3] ‹*invitations*› mandar, enviar*

B [v ▸ o ▸ adv (▸ prep ▸ o)] (ask to leave) echar (de una clase); **they sent me out of the room while they discussed it** me hicieron salir de la habitación *or* me mandaron afuera mientras lo discutían

C [v ▸ adv] **to ~ out FOR sth**: **we sent out for coffee** mandamos traer (un) café

• **send up** [v ▸ o ▸ adv, v ▸ adv ▸ o]

A (to prison) (AmE) meter preso

B (satirize) (BrE colloq) parodiar, burlarse de

sender /ˈsendər ‖ ˈsendə(r)/ *n* remitente *mf*

send: **~-off** *n* (colloq) despedida *f*; **~-up** *n* (esp BrE colloq) parodia *f*

Senegal /ˈsenɪˈgɔːl/ *n* (el) Senegal

Senegalese /ˈsenɪgəˈliːz/ *adj* senegalés

senile /ˈsiːnaɪl/ *adj* senil, chocho (fam); **to go ~** quedarse senil, chochear (fam)

senile dementia *n* [u] demencia *f* senil

senility /sɪˈnɪləti/ *n* [u] senilidad *f*

senior[1] /ˈsiːnjər ‖ ˈsiːniə(r)/ *adj*

A [1] (superior in rank): **a ~ colleague** un superior; **a ~ officer in the Army** un oficial de alto rango del Ejército; **~ editor** editor, -tora *m,f*, redactor, -tora *m,f* sénior; **~ lecturer** (BrE) ≈ profesor adjunto, profesora adjunta *m,f*, ≈ agregado, -da *m,f* a cátedra; **~ partner** socio mayoritario, socia mayoritaria *m,f*; **~ TO sb**: **she's ~ to him** es su superior [2] (older): **the ~ members of a club** los socios más antiguos de un club; **Robert King, S~** (esp AmE) Robert King, padre *or* sénior

B (Educ) **~ school** (in UK) colegio *m* secundario; **the ~ boys** los chicos mayores *or* de los últimos cursos; **~ year** (in US) último año *or* curso

senior[2] *n*

A [1] (older person): **he's five years my ~** me lleva cinco años, es cinco años mayor que yo [2] (person of higher rank) superior *m* [3] (AmE) ▸**senior citizen**

B (Educ) estudiante *mf* del último año *or* curso

senior: **~ citizen** *n* persona *f* de la tercera edad; **~ high (school)** *n* (in US) *colegio donde se imparten los tres últimos años de la enseñanza secundaria*

seniority /siːn'jɔːrəti || ˌsiːni'ɒrəti/ *n* [u] 1 (in rank) jerarquía *f* 2 (in length of service) antigüedad *f*

sensation /sen'seɪʃən/ *n*

A [c u] (feeling, impression) sensación *f*

B [c] 1 (furor) sensación *f*; **to cause** *o* **create a ~** causar sensación, hacer* furor 2 (success): **the play was a ~ on Broadway** la obra fue todo un éxito *or* (fam) un exitazo en Broadway

sensational /sen'seɪʃn̩əl || sen'seɪʃənl̩/ *adj* 1 (causing furor) que causa sensación 2 (sensationalist) sensacionalista 3 (very good) (colloq) sensacional (fam)

sensationalism /sen'seɪʃn̩əlɪzəm || sen'seɪʃənəlɪzəm/ *n* [u] sensacionalismo *m*

sensationalist /sen'seɪʃn̩ələst || sen'seɪʃənl̩ɪst/ *adj* sensacionalista

sensationalize /sen'seɪʃn̩əlaɪz || sen'seɪʃənl̩aɪz/ *vt* sensacionalizar*

sense[1] /sens/ *n*

A 1 [c] (physical faculty) sentido *m*; **the ~ of hearing/smell/taste/touch** el (sentido del) oído/olfato/gusto/tacto 2 **senses** *pl* (rational state): **no one in his (right) ~s would do something like that** una persona en su (sano) juicio *or* en sus cabales no haría una cosa así; **to come to one's ~s** entrar en razón; ***to take leave of one's ~s*** perder* el juicio, volverse* loco

B 1 (impression) (*no pl*) sensación *f*; **I felt a ~ of belonging/betrayal** me sentí aceptado/traicionado; **she has an exaggerated ~ of her own importance** se cree más importante de lo que es 2 [c u] (awareness) sentido *m*; **~ of direction/rhythm** sentido de la orientación/del ritmo; **she has no ~ of decency** no tiene vergüenza; **I lost all ~ of time** perdí completamente la noción del tiempo; **~ of humor** sentido *m* del humor

C [u] 1 (*common ~*) sentido *m* común; **she had the (good) ~ to leave her phone number** tuvo la sensatez *or* el tino de dejar su número de teléfono; **I have more ~ than to contradict my boss** no soy tan tonto como para contradecir a mi jefe; **I'm going to knock** *o* **beat some ~ into him!** voy a hacerlo entrar en razón; **I can't make him see ~** no puedo hacerlo entrar en razón 2 (point, value) sentido *m*; **there's not much ~ in doing it again** no tiene mucho sentido volver a hacerlo

D [c] 1 (meaning) sentido *m*, significado *m*; **in every ~ of the word** en todo sentido; **the different ~s of the word** las distintas acepciones *or* los distintos significados de la palabra; **he is a professional in the full ~ (of the term)** es un profesional en toda la extensión de la palabra 2 (aspect, way): **in a ~ they're both correct** en cierto modo *or* sentido ambos tienen razón; **it must in no ~ be taken as the final offer** no debe de ningún modo *or* de ninguna manera interpretarse como la oferta final

E **to make ~** 1 (be comprehensible) tener* sentido; **this sentence doesn't make much ~** esta frase no tiene mucho sentido 2 (be sensible): **what he said made a lot of ~** lo que dijo era muy razonable *or* sensato; **it doesn't make economic ~** no es recomendable desde el punto de vista económico; ***to make ~ of sth*** entender* algo; **I can't make ~ of this letter** no logro entender esta carta

sense[2] *vt* 1 (be aware of) sentir*, notar; **I ~d that they weren't very happy** sentí *or* intuí que no estaban muy contentos 2 (detect) (Tech) detectar

senseless /'sensləs || 'senslɪs/ *adj*

A (pointless) ‹*act/destruction/murder*› sin sentido

B (unconscious) inconsciente, sin sentido; **they beat him ~** lo golpearon hasta dejarlo inconsciente *or* sin sentido

sensibilities /ˌsensə'bɪlətiz/ *pl n* sensibilidad *f*; **to offend sb's ~** herir* la sensibilidad de algn

sensible /'sensəbəl/ *adj* 1 ‹*person/approach/attitude*› sensato; ‹*decision*› prudente; **be ~, you can't do it all on your own** sé razonable, no lo puedes hacer todo tú solo 2 ‹*clothes/shoes*› cómodo y práctico

sensibly /'sensəbli/ *adv* ‹*act*› con sensatez, con tino

sensitive /'sensətɪv/ *adj*

A 1 (emotionally responsive) ‹*person*› sensible; ‹*performance/account*› lleno de sensibilidad; **to be ~ TO sth**: **to be ~ to music** tener* sensibilidad para la música; **to be ~ to sb's needs** ser* *or* (Chi, Méx tb) estar* muy consciente de las necesidades de algn 2 (touchy) ‹*person*› susceptible; **he's very ~ to criticism** es muy susceptible a la crítica

B (physically responsive) ‹*skin*› sensible, delicado; ‹*teeth/instrument/film*› sensible; **~ TO sth** sensible A algo

C 1 (secret) ‹*document/information*› confidencial 2 (requiring tact) ‹*topic/issue*› delicado

sensitively /'sensətɪvli/ *adv* con sensibilidad

sensitivity /ˌsensə'tɪvəti/ *n* [u]

A 1 (emotional responsiveness) **~ (TO sth)** sensibilidad *f* (FRENTE A algo) 2 (touchiness) **~ (TO sth)** susceptibilidad *f* (A algo)

B (physical responsiveness) **~ (TO sth)** sensibilidad *f* (A algo)

C (of information) confidencialidad *f*; (of issue) lo delicado

sensitize /'sensətaɪz || 'sensɪtaɪz/ *vt* sensibilizar*; (to a social problem) concientizar* *or* (Esp) concienciar

sensor /'sensər || 'sensə(r)/ *n* sensor *m*

sensory /'sensəri/ *adj* sensorial

sensual /'sentʃuəl || 'senʃʊəl/ *adj* sensual

sensuality /'sentʃu'æləti || ˌsenʃʊ'æləti/ *n* [u] sensualidad *f*

sensuous /'sentʃuəs || 'sensjʊəs/ *adj* sensual

sent /sent/ *past & past p of* **send**

sentence[1] /'sentn̩s || 'sentəns/ *n*

A (Ling) oración *f*

B (Law) sentencia *f*; **he's serving a life ~** está cumpliendo una condena a cadena perpetua; **the death ~** la pena de muerte; **the court gave her a two-year ~** el tribunal la sentenció *or* la condenó a dos años de prisión; **to pass ~ (on sb)** dictar *or* pronunciar sentencia (contra algn), sentenciar (a algn); **she is under ~ of death** la han condenado a (la pena de) muerte

sentence[2] *vt* **to ~ sb (TO sth)** condenar *or* sentenciar a algn (A algo); **he was ~d to death** lo condenaron a (la pena de) muerte, lo sentenciaron a muerte

sentiment /'sentɪmənt/ *n*

A 1 [u] (feeling) sentir *m*, sentimiento *m* 2 [c] (view) opinión *f*, parecer *m*; **my ~s exactly** *o* **entirely** estoy totalmente de acuerdo

B [u] (sentimentality) sensiblería *f*, sentimentalismo *m*

sentimental /'sentɪ'mentl̩/ *adj* 1 (emotional) ‹*person/movie/song*› sentimental 2 (concerning emotions) (*usu before n*): **it had ~ value** tenía (un) valor sentimental; **a ~ journey** un viaje nostálgico

sentimentality /'sentɪmen'tæləti/ *n* [u] sentimentalismo *m*

sentimentalize /'sentɪ'mentl̩aɪz/ *vt* dar* una visión sentimental de

sentry /'sentri/ *n* (*pl* **-tries**) centinela *m*; (*before n*) **to be on ~ duty** estar* de guardia

sentry box *n* garita *f*, puesto *m* de guardia

Seoul /səʊl/ *n* Seúl *m*

Sep (= **September**) sept.

separable /'seprəbəl, 'sepərəbəl/ *adj* separable

separate[1] /'sepərət/ *adj* 1 (individual) ‹*beds/rooms/bank accounts*› separado; **they lead ~ lives** hacen vida aparte; ***to go our/their ~ ways*** irse* cada uno por su lado 2 (physically apart) aparte *adj inv*; **the gym is in a ~ building** el gimnasio está en un edificio aparte *or* en otro edificio; **~ FROM sth** separado DE algo; **keep your passport ~ from your wallet** no guarde juntos el pasaporte y la billetera 3 (distinct, different): **this word has three ~ meanings** esta palabra tiene tres significados distintos; **answer each question on a ~ sheet of paper** conteste cada pregunta en una hoja aparte

separate[2] /'sepəreɪt/ *vt* 1 (set apart) separar; **to ~ sth/sb FROM sth/sb** separar algo/a algn DE algo/algn 2 (keep apart) separar; **to be ~d FROM sb** estar* separado DE algn 3 (distinguish) distinguir*, diferenciar; **to ~ sth FROM sth** distinguir* *or* diferenciar algo DE algo 4 (Tech) extraer*

■ **separate** *vi* 1 (move apart) separarse 2 «*couple*» separarse

Phrasal verbs

• **separate off** [v ▸ o ▸ adv, v ▸ adv ▸ o] ‹*area/section/group*› separar

• **separate out**

A [v ▸ adv] «*elements/ingredients*» separarse; «*mixture/emulsion*» disgregarse*

B [v ▸ o ▸ adv, v ▸ adv ▸ o] ‹*elements/ingredients*› separar; ‹*considerations/factors*› distinguir*

separated /'sepəreɪtəd || 'sepəreɪtɪd/ *adj* separado

S

separately /'seprətli, 'sepərətli/ *adv* 1 (apart) por separado 2 (individually) separadamente, por separado

separation /'sepə'reɪʃən/ *n* [c u] separación *f*

separatism /'seprətɪzəm, 'sepərətɪzəm/ *n* [u] separatismo *m*

separatist /'seprətəst, 'sepə- || 'sepərətɪst, 'seprə-/ *n* separatista *mf*; (*before n*) ‹*group/movement*› separatista

sepia /'siːpiə/ *n* [u] sepia *m*; (*before n*) ‹*print/photograph*› en sepia

Sept (= **September**) sept.

September /sep'tembər || sep'tembə(r)/ *n* septiembre *m*, setiembre *m*; *see also* **January**

septet /sep'tet/ *n* septeto *m*

septic /'septɪk/ *adj* séptico; **the wound turned** *o* **went** ~ la herida se infectó

septicemia, (BrE) **septicaemia** /'septə'siːmiə || ˌseptɪ'siːmiə/ *n* [u] septicemia *f*

septic tank *n* pozo *m* séptico, fosa *f* séptica, cámara *f* séptica (CS)

sepulcher, (BrE) **sepulchre** /'sepəlkər || 'sepəlkə(r)/ *n* (liter) sepulcro *m*; ***a whited*** ~ un sepulcro blanqueado

sequel /'siːkwəl/ *n* 1 (Cin, Lit, TV) ~ **(TO sth)** continuación *f* (DE algo) 2 (later events) ~ **(TO sth)** secuela *f or* consecuencia *f* (DE algo)

sequence /'siːkwəns/ *n*

A (order): **a logical** ~ un orden lógico, una secuencia lógica; **the police established the** ~ **of events** la policía estableció cómo se sucedieron los hechos; **it's better to look at the pictures in** ~ es mejor ver las fotos en *or* por orden

B 1 (series) serie *f* 2 (Math, Mus) secuencia *f*

C (Cin, TV) secuencia *f*

sequential /sɪ'kwentʃəl || sɪ'kwenʃəl/ *adj* (frml) ‹*processes*› consecutivo, secuencial

sequin /'siːkwən || 'siːkwɪn/ *n* lentejuela *f*

Serb /sɜːrb || sɜːb/ *adj/n* ▸ **Serbian**[1,2]

Serbia /'sɜːrbiə || 'sɜːbiə/ *n* Serbia *f*, Servia *f*

Serbian[1] /'sɜːrbiən || 'sɜːbiən/ *adj* serbio, servio

Serbian[2] *n* serbio, -bia *m,f*, servio, -via *m,f*

Serbo-Croat /'sɜːrbəʊ'krəʊæt || ˌsɜːbəʊ'krəʊæt/, **Serbo-Croatian** /-krəʊ'eɪʃən/ *n* [u] serbocroata *m*

serenade[1] /'serə'neɪd/ *n* serenata *f*

serenade[2] *vt* darle* (una) serenata a

serendipity /'serən'dɪpəti/ *n* [u] serendipia *f* (*don de descubrir cosas sin proponérselo*)

serene /sə'riːn || sɪ'riːn/ *adj* 1 (calm) sereno 2 (in title) **His/Her S~ Highness** Su Alteza Serenísima

serenely /sə'riːnli || sɪ'riːnli/ *adv* ‹*smile*› serenamente, con serenidad; **he remained** ~ **indifferent** ni se inmutó

serenity /sə'renəti || sɪ'renəti/ *n* [u] serenidad *f*

serf /sɜːrf || sɜːf/ *n* siervo, -va *m,f*

serfdom /'sɜːrfdəm || 'sɜːfdəm/ *n* [u] servidumbre *f*

S

serge /sɜːrdʒ || sɜːdʒ/ *n* [u] sarga *f*

sergeant /'sɑːrdʒənt || 'sɑːdʒənt/ *n* sargento *mf*; **first** ~ (in US Army, marines) sargento *mf* primero

sergeant major *n* ≈ brigada *mf*

serial[1] /'sɪriəl || 'sɪəriəl/ *adj* 1 (in series) consecutivo; ~ **killer** asesino, -na *m,f* en serie, asesino, -na *m,f* múltiple 2 (in episodes) ‹*thriller*› seriado, en capítulos 3 (Comput) ‹*input/access/interface*› en serie

serial[2] *n* 1 (Rad, TV) serie *f*, serial *m or* (CS) serial *f* 2 (Publ): **it was published as a** ~ se publicó por entregas

serialization /'sɪriələ'zeɪʃən || ˌsɪəriəlaɪ'zeɪʃən/ *n* [c u] serialización *f*

serialize /'sɪriəlaɪz || 'sɪəriəlaɪz/ *vt* serializar*, seriar; **the book was** ~**d in a national newspaper** el libro apareció por entregas/capítulos en un periódico nacional

serial number *n* número *m* de serie

series /'sɪriːz || 'sɪəriːz/ *n* (*pl* ~) 1 (succession) serie *f*, sucesión *f*; **she made a** ~ **of mistakes** cometió una serie *or* una sucesión de errores 2 (set, group): **a TV/radio** ~ una serie *or* un serial *or* (CS) una serial de televisión/radio; **a** ~ **of concerts/lectures** un ciclo *or* un programa de conciertos/conferencias 3 (in baseball, cricket) serie *f* 4 (Elec): **in** ~ en serie

serious /'sɪriəs || 'sɪəriəs/ *adj*

A 1 (in earnest, sincere) serio; **I'm** ~ lo digo en serio *or* de veras; **you can't be** ~**!** ¡estás loco!, ¡me estás tomando el pelo! (fam); **come on now, be** ~**!** vamos, vamos, más formalidad; **to be** ~ **ABOUT sth/-ING**: **I'm** ~ **about this** lo digo en serio; **are you** ~ **about wanting to change your job?** ¿en serio quieres cambiar de trabajo? 2 (committed) (*before n*) ‹*student/worker*› dedicado 3 (not lightweight) (*before n*) ‹*newspaper/play/music*› serio

B 1 (grave, severe) ‹*injury/illness*› grave; **things are getting** ~ las cosas se están poniendo serias 2 (of importance, major): **I have** ~ **doubts about him** tengo mis serias dudas acerca de él; **we're talking** ~ **money here** (colloq) no estamos hablando de dos centavos

seriously /'sɪriəsli || 'sɪəriəsli/ *adv*

A 1 (not frivolously) seriamente, con seriedad; **don't take it** ~ no te lo tomes en serio; **she takes herself so** ~ se da mucha importancia; ~ **though** (*indep*) hablando en serio, fuera de broma 2 (genuinely, sincerely): **you can't** ~ **mean that** no lo puedes estar diciendo en serio

B (gravely) ‹*ill/injured*› gravemente

seriousness /'sɪriəsnəs || 'sɪəriəsnɪs/ *n* [u] seriedad *f*; **he said it in all** ~ lo dijo muy en serio

sermon /'sɜːrmən || 'sɜːmən/ *n* sermón *m*; **the S~ on the Mount** el Sermón de la Montaña

serpent /'sɜːrpənt || 'sɜːpənt/ *n* (snake) (liter) sierpe *f* (liter), serpiente *f*

serrated /'serəɪtəd || sə'reɪtɪd/ *adj* ‹*edge/blade/knife*› serrado, dentado; ‹*leaf*› dentado

serried /'serid/ *adj* (*before n*) (frml) apretado

serum /'sɪrəm || 'sɪərəm/ *n* 1 [u] (*blood* ~) suero *m* (sanguíneo) 2 [u c] (antitoxin) suero *m*

servant /'sɜːrvənt || 'sɜːvənt/ *n* 1 (domestic employee) criado, -da *m,f*, sirviente, -ta *m,f* 2 (sb, sth that serves) servidor, -dora *m,f*; **a faithful** ~ **of the cause** un leal servidor de la causa

serve[1] /sɜːrv || sɜːv/ *vt*

A (work for) ‹*God/monarch/party*› servir* a

B (help, be useful to) servir*; **if (my) memory** ~**s me correctly** si la memoria me es fiel, si la memoria no me falla; **it** ~**s no useful purpose** no sirve para nada (útil); ***to*** ~ ***sb right*** (colloq): **it** ~**s her right!** ¡se lo merece!, ¡lo tiene bien merecido!, ¡le está bien empleado! (Esp)

C 1 (Culin) ‹*food/drink*› servir*; **S serves four** (in recipe) para cuatro personas; (on packet) cuatro raciones *or* porciones; **dinner is** ~**d** (frml) la cena está servida 2 (in shop) (BrE) atender*; **are you being** ~**d?** ¿lo atienden?

D (Transp): **the bus route serving Newtown** el servicio *or* la línea de autobuses que va a Newtown; **Riem airport** ~**s Munich** Riem es el aeropuerto de Munich

E (Law) ‹*summons/notice/order*› entregar*, hacer* entrega de; **to** ~ **sth ON sb**, **to** ~ **sb WITH sth**: **they** ~**d a summons on all the directors** todos los directivos recibieron una citación judicial; **she was** ~**d with divorce papers** recibió notificación de la demanda de divorcio

F (complete) ‹*apprenticeship*› hacer*; ‹*sentence*› cumplir

■ **serve** *vi*

A 1 (be servant) (liter) servir* 2 (in shop) (BrE) atender* 3 (distribute food) servir*

B (spend time, do duty): **to** ~ **in the army** servir* en el ejército; **to** ~ **on a committee** integrar una comisión, ser* miembro de una comisión

C (have effect, function) **to** ~ **to + INF** servir* PARA + INF; **it only** ~**d to heighten tension** sólo sirvió para aumentar la tensión; **let this** ~ **as a warning** que esto te (*or* les *etc*) sirva de advertencia

D (Sport) sacar*, servir*

Phrasal verbs

• **serve out** [v ▸ o ▸ adv, v ▸ adv ▸ o]

A (distribute) ‹*portion/course*› servir*

B (complete) ‹*apprenticeship/sentence*› cumplir

• **serve up** [v ▸ o ▸ adv, v ▸ adv ▸ o] ‹*food*› servir*

serve[2] *n* servicio *m*, saque *m*

server /'sɜːrvər || 'sɜːvə(r)/ *n*

A 1 (utensil) cubierto *m* de servir 2 (dish) fuente *f*, (tray) bandeja *f*

B (Sport) *jugador que tiene el saque*

C (Comput) servidor *m*

service[1] /'sɜːrvəs || 'sɜːvɪs/ *n*

A [u] [1] (duty, work) servicio *m*; **five years' (length of) ~** cinco años de antigüedad *or* de trabajo [2] (as domestic servant): **he went into ~ in 1932** se puso a trabajar como criado en 1932 [3] (given by a tool, machine): **you'll get years of ~ from this iron** esta plancha le durará años; **to come into ~** entrar en servicio *or* en funcionamiento

B [u c] (of professional, tradesman, company) servicio *m*; **24-hour emergency ~** servicio de emergencia (durante) las 24 horas del día; **we no longer require your ~s** ya no precisamos sus servicios; ⓢ **services 1 mile** (BrE) área de servicio a 1 milla

C [c u] (assistance) servicio *m*; **she has done us all a ~** nos ha hecho a todos un favor *or* servicio; **my staff are at your ~** mis empleados están a sus órdenes *or* a su entera disposición *or* a su servicio; **how can I be of ~ to you?** ¿en qué puedo ayudarlo *or* servirlo?

D [c] (organization, system) servicio *m*; **telephone/postal ~** servicio telefónico/postal; **the bus/rail ~** el servicio de autobuses/trenes; **there's a daily/an hourly ~ to Boston** hay un servicio diario/un tren (*or* autobús *etc*) cada hora a Boston

E (Mil): **the (armed) ~s** las fuerzas armadas

F [u] (in shop, restaurant) servicio *m*; ⓢ **service not included** servicio no incluido

G [c u] (overhaul, maintenance) revisión *f*, servicio *m* (AmL), service *m* (RPl); (*before n*) ‹*contract/package*› de mantenimiento; **~ engineer** técnico, -ca *m,f* de mantenimiento

H [c] (Relig) oficio *m* religioso; **funeral ~** funeral *m*; **wedding ~** ceremonia *f* de boda

I [c] (in tennis) servicio *m*, saque *m*; **first/second ~!** ¡primer/segundo saque *or* servicio!; **to break sb's ~** romper* el servicio de algn, romperle* el servicio a algn

J [c] (*dinner ~*) vajilla *f*

service[2] *vt*

A (overhaul, maintain) ‹*car*› hacerle* una revisión *or* (AmL) un servicio *or* (RPl) un service a; ‹*machine/appliance*› hacerle* el mantenimiento a

B (Fin) ‹*debt/loan*› atender* el servicio de (frml)

serviceable /'sɜːrvəsəbəl || 'sɜːvɪsəbəl/ *adj* [1] (usable): **it's old, but still perfectly ~** está viejo pero todavía sirve *or* se puede usar perfectamente [2] (durable) resistente, duradero [3] (practical) práctico

service: **~ area** *n* área *f* de servicio; **~ charge** *n* [1] (in restaurant) servicio *m*; **there is a ~ charge of 10%** se cobra un 10% de servicio [2] (in banking) comisión *f* [3] (for maintenance — of apartment) gastos *mpl* comunes *or* (Esp) de comunidad; (— of office) gastos *mpl* de mantenimiento; **~ elevator** *n* (AmE) montacargas *m*; **~ entrance** *n* entrada *f* de servicio; **~ industry** *n* sector *m* (de) servicios; **~ lift** *n* (BrE) montacargas *m*; **~man** /'sɜːrvəsmən || 'sɜːvɪsmən/ *n* (*pl* **-men** /-mən/) militar *m*, soldado *m*; **~ provider** *n* (Comput) proveedor *m* de servicios de Internet; **~ road** *n* vía *f* de acceso; **~ sector** *n* sector *m* de servicios, sector *m* terciario; **~ station** *n* estación *f* de servicio; **~woman** *n* militar *f*, soldado *f*

serviette /'sɜːrvi'et || ˌsɜːvi'et/ *n* (BrE) servilleta *f*; (*before n*) **~ ring** servilletero *m*

servile /'sɜːrvəl || 'sɜːvaɪl/ *adj* servil

serving /'sɜːrvɪŋ || 'sɜːvɪŋ/ *n* porción *f*, ración *f*; (*before n*) **~ dish** fuente *f*; **~ spoon** cuchara *f* de servir

servitude /'sɜːvətuːd || 'sɜːvɪtjuːd/ *n* [u] servidumbre *f*

sesame /'sesəmi/ *n* [u] [1] ajonjolí *m*, sésamo *m*; (*before n*) ‹*oil/seed*› de ajonjolí *or* sésamo [2] (Lit): **open ~!** ¡ábrete sésamo!

session /'seʃən/ *n*

A (Adm, Govt, Law) [1] (single meeting) sesión *f*; **to be in ~** estar* en sesión, estar* reunido, estar* sesionando (esp AmL) [2] (series of meetings — of Congress, Parliament) sesión *f*; (— of negotiations, talks) ronda *f*

B (period of time) sesión *f*; **a photo/recording ~** una sesión fotográfica/de grabación

C (Educ) [1] (academic year) curso *m*, año *m* académico [2] (term) trimestre *m*; (semester) semestre *m* [3] (lesson) hora *f* de clase

set[1] /set/ *n*

A [1] (of tools, golf clubs, bowls, pens, keys) juego *m*; (of books, records) colección *f*; (of stamps) serie *f*; **a ~ of cutlery** un juego de cubiertos, una cubertería; **a ~ of saucepans** una batería de cocina; **a matching ~ of sheets and pillowcases** un juego de cama; **a ~ of dentures** una dentadura postiza; **a boxed ~** un juego en estuche [2] (Math) conjunto *m*

B (+ *sing o pl vb*) (BrE Educ) *grupo de estudiantes seleccionados de acuerdo a sus aptitudes*

C (TV) aparato *m*, televisor *m*; (Rad) aparato *m*, receptor *m*

D (in tennis, squash) set *m*; (*before n*) **~ point** bola *f* de set, punto *m* para set (Méx), set point *m* (CS)

E [1] (Theat) (stage) escenario *m*; (scenery) decorado *m* [2] (Cin) plató *m*

F (in hairdressing) marcado *m*; **shampoo and ~** lavado *m* y marcado

set[2] *adj*

A (established, prescribed) ‹*wage/price*› fijo; **meals are at ~ times** las comidas son a determinadas horas; **there are no ~ times for visiting** no hay horas de visita establecidas; **~ book** (Educ) obra *f* prescrita *or* del programa; **a ~ phrase** una frase hecha; **we ordered the ~ menu** (BrE) pedimos el menú del día

B (*pred*) [1] (ready, prepared): **to be ~** estar* listo, estar* pronto (RPl); **is everything ~ for the meeting?** ¿está todo preparado *or* listo *or* (RPl) pronto para la reunión?; **all ~ (to go)?** ¿listos? [2] (likely, about to) (journ) **to be ~ to + INF** llevar camino de + INF [3] (determined, resolute): **he was all ~ to walk out** estaba totalmente decidido *or* resuelto a irse; **she's absolutely ~ on that bicycle** está empeñada en que tiene que ser esa bicicleta; **he's dead ~ on going to college** está resuelto *or* decidido a ir a la universidad sea como sea

C [1] (rigid, inflexible): **to be ~ in one's ways** tener* costumbres muy arraigadas [2] (solid) ‹*yoghurt/custard/jelly*› cuajado

set[3] (*pres p* **setting**; *past & past p* **set**) *vt*

A (put, place) poner*, colocar*; **he ~ a pitcher of cider before us** nos puso una jarra de sidra delante

B [1] (cause to be, become): **to ~ sb free** poner* en libertad *or* liberar a algn; **to ~ sb loose** soltar* a algn; **to ~ fire to sth, to ~ sth on fire** prenderle fuego a algo [2] (make solid, rigid) ‹*jelly/cheese*› cuajar; ‹*cement*› hacer* fraguar

C [1] (prepare) ‹*trap*› tender*; ‹*table*› poner*; **~ three places for dinner** pon cubiertos para tres para la cena [2] (Med) ‹*bone*› encajar, componer* (AmL) [3] ‹*hair*› marcar* [4] (Print) ‹*type*› componer*

D (adjust) ‹*oven/alarm clock/watch*› poner*

E [1] (arrange, agree on) ‹*date/time*› fijar, acordar*; ‹*agenda*› establecer*, acordar* [2] (impose, prescribe) ‹*target*› establecer* [3] (allot) ‹*task*› asignar; ‹*homework*› mandar, poner*; ‹*exam/test/problem*› poner*; ‹*text*› prescribir* [4] (establish) ‹*precedent*› sentar*; ‹*record/standard*› establecer*; ‹*fashion*› dictar, imponer*; **to ~ a good example** dar* buen ejemplo [5] (fix, assign) ‹*price/bail*› fijar

F (cause to do, start): **she ~ them to work in the garden** los puso a trabajar en el jardín; **the news ~ my pulse racing** la noticia hizo que se me disparara el pulso; **to ~ sth going** poner* algo en marcha

G (*usu pass*) [1] ‹*book/film*› ambientar; **the novel is ~ in Japan** la novela está ambientada en el Japón [2] (locate) ‹*building*› situar*

H [1] (mount, insert) ‹*gem*› engarzar*, engastar; ‹*stake*› hincar*, clavar; **the posts are ~ in concrete** los postes están puestos en hormigón; **the crown is ~ with rubies** la corona tiene incrustaciones de rubíes [2] **to ~ a poem to music** ponerle* música a un poema

I (turn, direct): **we ~ our course for the nearest island** pusimos rumbo a la isla más cercana; ▸**sail**[1] **A1**

■ **set** *vi*

A (go down) «*sun/moon*» ponerse*

B [1] (become solid, rigid) «*jelly*» cuajar(se); «*cement*» fraguar* [2] «*bone*» soldarse*

Phrasal verbs

- **set about** [v ▸ prep ▸ o] [1] (begin, tackle): **he ~ about his task energetically** emprendió su tarea con energía; **I spent a long time deciding how to ~ about the task** me llevó mucho tiempo decidir cómo acometer la tarea; **we ~ about cleaning the room** nos pusimos a limpiar la habitación [2] (attack) atacar*, agredir; **they ~ about him with sticks** empezaron a darle *or* a golpearlo con palos
- **set against** [v ▸ o ▸ prep ▸ o]

A (cause to quarrel) poner* en contra de, enemistar con

B (balance, compare): **the advantages must be ~ against the**

disadvantages hay que contraponer *or* sopesar los pros y los contras; **these costs can be ~ against your total income** (Tax) estos gastos pueden deducirse de sus ingresos

• **set apart** [v ▸ o ▸ adv] (make different) distinguir*, hacer* distinto *or* diferente; **her extraordinary talent ~s her apart from the other children** su extraordinario talento la hace distinta *or* diferente de los otros niños

• **set aside** [v ▸ o ▸ adv, v ▸ adv ▸ o] [1] (save, reserve) ‹*food/goods*› guardar, apartar, reservar; ‹*time*› dejar; ‹*money*› guardar, ahorrar [2] (put to one side, shelve) ‹*book/project*› dejar (de lado) [3] (disregard) ‹*hostility/bitterness*› dejar de lado; ‹*rules/formality*› prescindir de

• **set back**

A [v ▸ o ▸ adv, v ▸ adv ▸ o] [1] (delay) ‹*progress*› retrasar, atrasar; ‹*clock*› atrasar [2] (place at a distance) (*usu pass*): **the house is ~ well back from the road** la casa está bastante apartada de la carretera

B [v ▸ o ▸ adv] (cost) (colloq): **the trip ~ me back £100** el viaje me costó 100 libras *or* me salió en 100 libras

• **set by** [v ▸ o ▸ adv, v ▸ adv ▸ o] ‹*supplies*› guardar, reservar, apartar; ‹*money*› guardar, ahorrar

• **set down** [v ▸ o ▸ adv, v ▸ adv ▸ o] [1] (put down) ‹*object*› poner*, colocar*; (emphatically) depositar [2] ‹*passenger*› dejar [3] (record in writing): **she ~ down her experiences in her autobiography** escribió *or* relató sus experiencias en su autobiografía; **all the facts you need are ~ down in this book** todos los datos que necesitas están en este libro [4] (prescribe) ‹*rule/condition*› establecer*, fijar

• **set forth**

A [v ▸ adv] (depart) (liter) partir (liter), salir*

B [v ▸ o ▸ adv, v ▸ adv ▸ o] (outline, present) (frml) ‹*argument/theory*› exponer*; ‹*aims/policies/proposition*› presentar

• **set in** [v ▸ adv] (gain hold) «*infection*» declararse; **if rust/decay ~s in** una vez que empieza a oxidarse/deteriorarse; **after the operation complications ~ in** después de la operación surgieron complicaciones

• **set off**

A [v ▸ adv] (begin journey) salir*; **when do you ~ off on your trip?** ¿cuándo sales *or* te vas de viaje?

B [v ▸ o ▸ adv, v ▸ adv ▸ o] [1] (activate) ‹*bomb/mine*› hacer* explotar *or* estallar; ‹*alarm*› hacer* sonar; ‹*firework*› lanzar*, tirar [2] (start) ‹*speculation*› dar* lugar a; **the photographs ~ us off reminiscing** las fotos nos hicieron empezar a rememorar [3] (enhance) hacer* resaltar, darle* realce a [4] (offset) **to ~ sth off AGAINST sth** deducir* algo DE algo; **these expenses can be ~ off against income** (Tax) estos gastos se pueden deducir de los ingresos

• **set on**

A [v ▸ prep ▸ o] (attack) atacar*, agredir*; **he was ~ on by thieves** fue atacado por ladrones

B [v ▸ o ▸ prep ▸ o]: **we ~ the dogs on him** le echamos *or* le lanzamos los perros; **she ~ a private detective on him** contrató a un detective privado para que lo siguiera

• **set out**

A [v ▸ adv] [1] (begin journey) salir*, partir (liter *or* frml) [2] (begin, intend): **I didn't ~ out with that intention** no empecé con esa intención; **to ~ out to + INF**: **I didn't ~ out to offend him** no era mi intención ofenderlo; **she had failed in what she had ~ out to achieve** no había logrado lo que se había propuesto

B [v ▸ o ▸ adv, v ▸ adv ▸ o] [1] (expound) ‹*argument/theory*› exponer* [2] (display, arrange) ‹*goods*› exponer*; ‹*chess pieces*› colocar*; **the children's work was ~ out on the tables** el trabajo de los niños estaba expuesto *or* dispuesto sobre las mesas

• **set to** [v ▸ adv] (begin) empezar*; **we ~ to with a will** empezamos *or* nos pusimos a trabajar con ganas

• **set up**

(*Sense I*) [v ▸ o ▸ adv, v ▸ adv ▸ o]

A [1] (erect, assemble) ‹*monument*› levantar, erigir* (frml); ‹*machine/tent*› montar, armar; ‹*type*› (Print) componer*; **they ~ up (their) camp near the river** acamparon cerca del río [2] (arrange, plan) ‹*meeting*› convocar* a, llamar a; **we hope to ~ up a deal with them** esperamos llegar a un trato con ellos

B [1] (institute, found) ‹*committee/commission*› crear; ‹*inquiry*› abrir*; ‹*business*› montar [2] (establish) ‹*record*› establecer*

C (establish): **he ~ her up in an apartment** le puso un apartamento; **she ~ herself up as a photographer** se estableció como fotógrafa; **she's ~ up for life now** ahora tiene todos los problemas resueltos, ahora tiene el porvenir asegurado

D (colloq) [1] (frame) tenderle* una trampa a [2] (rig) arreglar; **the fight was ~ up** la pelea estaba arreglada

(*Sense II*) [v ▸ o ▸ adv] (invigorate, restore health of) reanimar

(*Sense III*) [v ▸ adv] (establish in business) **to ~ up AS sth** establecerse* COMO algo

• **set upon** ▸ **set on A**

set: **~-aside** *n* [u] [1] (AmE) *política de repartir determinada cantidad de trabajo a compañías administradas por minorías (étnicas)* [2] (BrE) *also* **~-aside policy** *política de retirar tierras de la producción para reducir excedentes de cosechas*; **~back** *n* revés *m*, contratiempo *m*; **~ piece** *n* [1] (Mus) *pieza que se suele tocar en determinadas ocasiones*; (for music exam) pieza *f* obligatoria [2] (Sport) jugada *f* preparada, jugada *f* prefabricada *or* de laboratorio; **~ square** *n* escuadra *f*; (with two equal sides) cartabón *m*

settee /se'tiː/ *n* sofá *m*

setter /'setər || 'setə(r)/ *n* (dog) setter *mf*

setting /'setɪŋ/ *n*

A (of dial, switch) posición *f*; **leave the heater on its highest/lowest ~** deja el calentador en el máximo/mínimo

B [1] (of novel, movie) escenario *m* [2] (surroundings) marco *m*, entorno *m* [3] (for gem) engarce *m*, engaste *m*, montura *f*

C (*place* ~) cubierto *m*

D (Mus) arreglo *m*, versión *f*

setting lotion *n* [u c] fijador *m*

settle /'setl̩/ *vt*

A [1] ‹*price/terms/time*› acordar*, fijar; **it's all been ~d, we're going to Miami** ya está (todo) decidido *or* arreglado, nos vamos a Miami; **that's ~d then, we'll meet at seven** bueno, pues entonces ya está, nos vemos a las siete; **that ~s it: I never want to see him again** ya no me cabe duda: no lo quiero volver a ver [2] (resolve) ‹*dispute/problem*› resolver*, solucionar; **they ~d their differences** resolvieron sus diferencias [3] (put an end to) ‹*foolishness/nonsense*› (colloq) acabar con; **that should ~ him!** ¡así aprenderá!

B ‹*bill/account*› pagar*; ‹*debt*› saldar, liquidar

C ‹*country/region*› colonizar*, poblar*

D (make comfortable) ‹*patient/child*› poner* cómodo; **she ~d herself deep in the sofa** se arrellanó en el sofá

E (make calm) ‹*child*› calmar; ‹*doubts*› disipar; ‹*stomach*› asentar*

■ **settle** *vi*

A (come to live) establecerse*, afincarse*; **they ~d in Iowa** se establecieron *or* se afincaron en Iowa

B (become calm) «*person*» tranquilizarse*, calmarse

C [1] (make oneself comfortable) ponerse* cómodo; **I ~d deeper into the armchair** me arrellané *or* me puse cómodo en el sillón [2] «*bird*» posarse

D [1] «*dust*» asentarse*; «*snow*» cuajar [2] (sink) «*soil/foundations*» asentarse*; «*sediment*» depositarse, precipitarse

E [1] (pay) saldar la cuenta (*or* la deuda *etc*), pagar*; **you can ~ with me tomorrow** podemos arreglar las cuentas mañana [2] (Law): **to ~ out of court** resolver* una disputa extrajudicialmente, transar extrajudicialmente (AmL)

(Phrasal verbs)

• **settle back** [v ▸ adv] (recline) recostarse*; (relax): **just ~ back and enjoy yourselves** pónganse cómodos y diviértanse

• **settle down**

A [v ▸ adv] [1] (become calm): **things seem to have ~d down after the riots** parece que las cosas se han apaciguado *or* calmado después de las revueltas; **~ down please, children** niños, por favor, tranquilos [2] (get comfortable): **they ~d down for a long wait** se prepararon para una larga espera; **we ~d down for the night** nos acomodamos para pasar la noche [3] (apply oneself): **~ down to your work** pónganse a trabajar [4] (in place, activity): **she's settling down well in her new school** se está adaptando bien a su nueva escuela; **you should get a job and ~ down** deberías conseguirte un trabajo y establecerte *or* echar raíces en algún sitio [5] (become more responsible) sentar* (la) cabeza

B [v ▸ o ▸ adv] (make calm) calmar, tranquilizar*

• **settle for** [v ▸ prep ▸ o] conformarse con; **why ~ for less?** ¿por qué conformarse con menos?

• **settle in** [v ▸ adv]: **I'll come and see you when you've**

~d in te vendré a ver cuando estés instalado; **she's settling in well in her new job** se está adaptando bien a su nuevo trabajo
- **settle into** [v ▸ prep ▸ o] ‹*school/job*› adaptarse a; ‹*routine*› acostumbrarse *or* hacerse* a
- **settle on** [v ▸ prep ▸ o] ‹*date/place*› decidirse por
- **settle up** [v ▸ adv] (colloq) arreglar (las) cuentas

settled /'setld/ *adj* 1 (established, unchanging) ‹*habits/life*› ordenado; ‹*order*› estable 2 ‹*weather*› estable 3 (colonized) ‹*area/region*› colonizado, poblado

settlement /'setlmənt/ *n*
A [c] (agreement) acuerdo *m*, convenio *m*; **to reach/achieve a ~** llegar* a/lograr un acuerdo *or* convenio; **wage ~** (agreement) convenio *m* (laboral), acuerdo *m* salarial; (increase) aumento *m* (salarial)
B 1 [u] (of account, bill) pago *m*; (of debt) liquidación *f*, satisfacción *f* 2 [c] (payment) pago *m*; **they offered her an out-of-court ~ of £20,000** extrajudicialmente le ofrecieron 20.000 libras para que se desistiera de su demanda
C [u] (of dispute) resolución *f*, solución *f*; **~ out of court** (re)solución *f* extrajudicial, transacción *f* extrajudicial
D [c] (village) asentamiento *m*, poblado *m*
E [u] (of country, region) colonización *f*, población *f*

settler /'setlər || 'setlə(r)/ *n* colono, -na *m,f*, poblador, -dora *m,f*

set-to /'set,tu:/ *n* (colloq) bronca *f* (fam), agarrada *f* (fam)

set-up /'setʌp/ *n* (colloq) (situation, arrangement) sistema *f*, organización *f*; (pej) tinglado *m* (fam & pey)

seven[1] /'sevən/ *n* siete *m*; *see also* **four**[1]

seven[2] *adj* siete *adj inv*; **we're open ~ days a week** abrimos todos los días (de la semana); *see also* **four**[2]

sevenfold /'sevənfəʊld/ *adj/adv see* **-fold**

seventeen /'sevən'ti:n/ *adj/n* diecisiete *adj inv/m*

seventeenth[1] /'sevən'ti:nθ/ *adj* decimoséptimo; *see also* **fifth**[1]

seventeenth[2] *adv* en decimoséptimo lugar; *see also* **fifth**[2]

seventeenth[3] *n* 1 (Math) diecisieteavo *m* 2 (part) diecisieteava parte *f*

seventh[1] /'sevənθ/ *adj* séptimo; *see also* **fifth**[1]

seventh[2] *adv* en séptimo lugar; *see also* **fifth**[2]

seventh[3] *n* 1 (Math) séptimo *m* 2 (part) séptima parte *f*

seventieth[1] /'sevəntiəθ/ *adj* septuagésimo; *see also* **fifth**[1]

seventieth[2] *adv* en septuagésimo lugar; *see also* **fifth**[2]

seventieth[3] *n* 1 (Math) setentavo *m* 2 (part) setentava *or* septuagésima parte *f*

seventy /'sevənti/ *adj/n* setenta *adj inv/m*; **there were ~ people** había setenta personas; **there were ~ of us** éramos setenta; **during the seventies** en la década de los setenta, en los (años) setenta; **he's in his seventies** tiene unos setenta y tantos años, tiene setenta y pico de años (fam); **temperatures in the lower/upper seventies** temperaturas de entre setenta y setenta y cinco/de entre setenta y cinco y ochenta grados Fahrenheit; (*before n*) **seventies fashions/music** modas *fpl*/música *f* de los (años) setenta

sever /'sevər || 'sevə(r)/ *vt* 1 (cut) ‹*rope/chain*› cortar; **the saw ~ed his finger** la sierra le cortó *or* le amputó *or* (frml) le cercenó el dedo 2 (break off) ‹*communications*› cortar; ‹*relations*› romper*, cortar
■ **sever** *vi* romperse*, cortarse

several[1] /'sevrəl/ *adj* varios, -rias

several[2] *pron* varios, varias

severance /'sevərəns/ *n* [u] 1 (of relations, links) ruptura *f* 2 (Lab Rel) cese *m*; (*before n*) **~ pay** indemnización *f* por cese

severe /sə'vɪr || sɪ'vɪə(r)/ *adj* **severer, severest**
A 1 (strict, harsh) ‹*punishment/judge*› severo; ‹*discipline*› riguroso, estricto 2 (austere) ‹*style/colors*› austero
B 1 (serious, bad) ‹*illness/injury*› grave; ‹*pain*› fuerte, grande; ‹*problem*› serio, grave; ‹*winter*› severo, duro; ‹*weather*› inclemente 2 (difficult, rigorous) ‹*test*› duro, difícil; ‹*conditions*› estricto, riguroso

severely /sə'vɪrli || sɪ'vɪəli/ *adv*
A (strictly, harshly) ‹*punish/criticize*› con severidad, severamente
B 1 (seriously) ‹*ill*› gravemente 2 (rigorously): **it ~ tested the contestants** fue *or* supuso una dura prueba para los participantes

severity /sə'verəti || sɪ'verəti/, **severeness** /sə'vɪrnəs || sɪ'vɪənɪs/ *n* [u]
A (strictness, harshness) severidad *f*; **the ~ of the winter** el rigor *or* la severidad del invierno
B 1 (of illness, injury) gravedad *f*; (of pain) intensidad *f* 2 (of test, examination) lo difícil

Seville /sə'vɪl/ *n* Sevilla *f*

Seville orange *n* naranja *f* amarga

sew /səʊ/ (*past* **sewed**; *past p* **sewn** *or* **sewed**) *vt* coser; ‹*seam/hem*› hacer*; **to ~ sth on** coser *or* pegar* algo
■ **sew** *vi* coser

Phrasal verb
- **sew up** [v ▸ o ▸ adv, v ▸ adv ▸ o] 1 (close) ‹*tear/opening*› coser; ‹*cut/wound*› coser, suturar 2 (clinch) (colloq) (*usu pass*): **I thought the deal was already ~n up** yo creía que el trato ya era un hecho *or* ya estaba arreglado

sewage /'su:ɪdʒ || 'su:ɪdʒ, 'sju:ɪdʒ/ *n* [u] aguas *fpl* negras *or* residuales, aguas *fpl* servidas (CS); (*before n*) **~ system** sistema *m* de alcantarillado; **~ farm** *o* **plant** *o* **works** planta *f* de tratamiento de aguas residuales (*or* negras *etc*); **~ treatment** tratamiento *m* de aguas residuales (*or* negras *etc*)

sewer /'su:ər || 'su:ə(r), 'sju:ə(r)/ *n* 1 (underground) alcantarilla *f*, cloaca *f* 2 (drain) (AmE) boca *f* de (la) alcantarilla, sumidero *m*, coladera *f* (Méx)

sewerage /'su:ərɪdʒ || 'su:ərɪdʒ, 'sju:ərɪdʒ/ *n* [u] 1 (system) alcantarillado *m* 2 ▸ **sewage**

sewing /'səʊɪŋ/ *n* [u] 1 (activity) costura *f*; (*before n*) **~ basket** costurero *m* 2 (sth sewn) labor *f*, costura *f*

sewing machine *n* máquina *f* de coser

sewn /səʊn/ *past p of* **sew**

sex[1] /seks/ *n*
A [u] 1 (sexual matters) sexo *m*; (*before n*) ‹*film/magazine*› de sexo; **~ appeal** sex-appeal *m*; **~ drive** libido *f*, líbido *f*; **~ education** educación *f* sexual; **~ life** vida *f* sexual; **~ maniac** maníaco, -ca *m,f* sexual; **~ object** objeto *m* sexual; **~ offender** delincuente *m,f* sexual; **~ symbol** sex symbol *mf* 2 (intercourse) relaciones *fpl* sexuales; **to have ~ with sb** tener* relaciones sexuales con algn, acostarse* con algn
B 1 [c u] (gender) sexo *m*; (*before n*) ‹*chromosome/hormone/organs*› sexual; **~ change operation** operación *f* de cambio de sexo 2 [c] (men, women collectively) sexo *m*; **the opposite ~** el sexo opuesto; **the fair/weaker ~** (dated) el bello sexo/sexo débil (ant); (*before n*) **~ discrimination** discriminación *f* sexual

sex[2] *vt* sexar

sexism /'seksɪzəm/ *n* [u] sexismo *m*; (toward women) machismo *m*, sexismo *m*

sexist[1] /'seksəst || 'seksɪst/ *n* sexista *mf*; (toward women) machista *mf*, sexista *mf*

sexist[2] *adj* ‹*attitude/joke*› sexista; (toward women) machista, sexista

sextant /'sekstənt/ *n* sextante *m*

sextet /seks'tet/ *n* 1 (players) sexteto *m* 2 (music) sexteto *m*

sexton /'sekstən/ *n* sacristán *m*

sexual /'sekʃuəl/ *adj* sexual; **~ abuse** abusos *mpl* deshonestos; (rape) violación *f*; **~ harassment** acoso *m or* hostigamiento *m* sexual; **~ intercourse** relaciones *fpl* sexuales; **~ orientation** orientación *f* sexual

sexuality /'sekʃu'æləti/ *n* [u] sexualidad *f*

sexually /'sekʃuəli/ *adv* sexualmente; **a ~ transmitted disease** una enfermedad de transmisión sexual

sexy /'seksi/ *adj* **sexier, sexiest** 1 (sexually attractive) sexy 2 (erotic) ‹*book/film/talk*› erótico

SF *n* [u] = **science fiction**

Sgt (title) (= **Sergeant**) Sgto.

sh /ʃ/ *interj* ¡sh!, ¡chitón!

shabbily /'ʃæbəli || 'ʃæbɪli/ *adv* 1 (poorly): **they were ~ dressed** iban mal *or* pobremente vestidos; **a ~ furnished room** una habitación con muebles muy viejos 2 (badly, unfairly) ‹*treat/behave*› mal

shabby /'ʃæbi/ *adj* **-bier, -biest** 1 ‹*carpet/sofa/jacket*› gastado, muy usado; (threadbare) raído 2 (bad, unfair): **a**

S

~ trick una mala pasada; **what a ~ way to treat him** qué manera más fea de tratarlo

shack /ʃæk/ *n* choza *f*, casucha *f*, rancho *m* (AmL), jacal *m* (Méx), bohío *m* (AmC, Col)

(Phrasal verb)

• **shack up** [v ▸ adv] (colloq) **to ~ up WITH sb** irse* a vivir *or* (fam) arrejuntarse CON algn

shackle /ˈʃækəl/ *vt* 1 ‹*prisoner*› ponerle* grilletes a, encadenar 2 (hamper, restrict) coartar, constreñir*

shackles /ˈʃækəlz/ *pl n* 1 (fetters) grilletes *mpl* 2 (constraints) ataduras *fpl*, trabas *fpl*

shade¹ /ʃeɪd/ *n*

A [u] (dark place) sombra *f*; **we sat in the ~** nos sentamos a la sombra; **25°C in the ~** 25°C a la sombra; ***to put sth/sb in the ~*** hacerle* sombra a algo/algn, eclipsar algo/a algn

B [c] 1 (*lamp~*) pantalla *f* 2 (over window) (AmE) persiana *f*, estor *m* (Esp)

C 1 [c] (of color) tono *m* 2 [c] (degree of difference, nuance) matiz *m*; **varying ~s of meaning** diferentes matices de significado; **every ~ of opinion** toda clase de opiniones, opiniones de todas clases 3 (slight amount) (colloq) (*no pl*) poquitín *m* (fam), pizca *f* (fam)

D **shades** *pl* (sl) ▸**sunglasses**

shade² *vt*

A (protect from sun, light) ‹*eyes/face*› proteger* del sol/de la luz; **her seat was ~d from the sun** su asiento estaba resguardado del sol

B (Art) ~ **(in)** ‹*background/area*› sombrear

C (defeat narrowly) (AmE colloq) ganarle por muy poco a, ganarle por un pelo *or* por los pelos a (fam)

shadow¹ /ˈʃædəʊ/ *n*

A [cu] (unlit area) sombra *f*; **the ~ of war** la sombra de la guerra; **to have ~s under one's eyes** tener* ojeras; ***to cast a ~ over sth*** ensombrecer* *or* empañar algo

B 1 [c] (remnant, vestige) sombra *f*; **she was a ~ of her former self** no era ni sombra de lo que había sido 2 (trace) (*no pl*): **without the slightest ~ of (a) doubt** sin la más mínima (sombra de) duda

C [c] (BrE Pol) (*before n*): **the ~ cabinet** el gabinete fantasma *or* en la sombra; **he was ~ Education Secretary** era el portavoz de la oposición para asuntos de educación

shadow² *vt* (follow) ‹*suspect*› seguir* de cerca a

shadow-boxing /ˈʃædəʊˌbɑːksɪŋ ‖ ˈʃædəʊˌbɒksɪŋ/ *n* [u] *práctica de boxeo con un adversario imaginario*

shadowy /ˈʃædəʊi/ *adj* 1 (indistinct) ‹*form/outline/figure*› impreciso, vago 2 (elusive, little known) ‹*character*› misterioso, enigmático 3 (full of shadows) ‹*place/forest*› oscuro

shady /ˈʃeɪdi/ *adj* **-dier, -diest** 1 (giving shade) ‹*place/garden*› sombreado, donde hay sombra; ‹*tree*› que da mucha sombra 2 (disreputable) (colloq) ‹*deal/business*› turbio; ‹*character*› sospechoso

shaft¹ /ʃæft ‖ ʃɑːft/ *n*

A 1 (of arrow, spear) asta *f*‡, astil *m*; (of hammer, ax) mango *m*; (of cart) vara *f* 2 (of light) rayo *m*

B (Mech Eng) eje *m*

C (of elevator) hueco *m*; (of mine) pozo *m*, tiro *m*

S

shaft² *vt* (AmE sl) 1 (betray) ‹*person*› joder (vulg) 2 (fire) echar, darle* la patada a (arg)

shag¹ /ʃæg/ *n*

A (bird) cormorán *m*

B [c] (act of sexual intercourse) (BrE vulg): **to have a ~** echar(se) un polvo (fam), tirar (vulg), follar (Esp vulg), coger* (Méx, RPl, Ven vulg), culear (Andes vulg)

shag² **-gg-** *vt*

A (Sport AmE colloq) ‹*ball*› fildear; **to ~ flies** fildear elevados

B (have sex with) (BrE vulg) tirarse a (vulg), follar (Esp vulg), coger* (Méx, RPl, Ven vulg), culearse a (Andes vulg)

■ **shag** *vi*

A (Sport AmE colloq) recoger* pelotas/bolas

B (BrE vulg) tirar (vulg), follar (Esp vulg), coger* (Méx, RPl, Ven vulg), culear (Andes vulg)

shagged out /ʃægd/ *adj* (BrE sl) (*pred*) **to be ~ ~** estar* reventado *or* hecho polvo (fam)

shaggy /ˈʃægi/ *adj* **-gier, -giest** ‹*dog*› lanudo, peludo; ‹*beard/hair*› enmarañado, greñudo

shaggy dog story *n* (colloq) chiste *m* malo (*largo*)

shake¹ /ʃeɪk/ (*past* **shook**; *past p* **shaken**) *vt*

A 1 (cause to move, agitate) ‹*bottle/cocktail*› agitar; ‹*person*› sacudir, zarandear; ‹*building/foundations*› sacudir, hacer* temblar; ‹*dice*› agitar, revolver* (AmL); **she shook herself free of him** se liberó de él de una sacudida; **to ~ sth OFF/FROM sth**: **I shook the dust off** *o* **from my coat** me sacudí el polvo del abrigo; **to ~ sth OUT OF sth**: **she shook the sand out of the towel** sacudió la toalla para quitarle la arena; **to ~ hands** darse* la mano, darse* un apretón de manos; **to ~ hands with sb** darle* *or* estrecharle la mano a algn; **to ~ sb's hand, to ~ sb by the hand** darle* *or* estrecharle la mano a algn, darle* un apretón de manos a algn; **to ~ hands on a deal** cerrar* un trato con un apretón de manos; **to ~ one's head** negar* con la cabeza; (meaning yes) (AmE) asentir* con la cabeza 2 (brandish) ‹*sword/stick*› agitar, blandir; **to ~ one's fist at sb** amenazar* a algn con el puño

B 1 (undermine, impair) ‹*courage/nerve*› hacer* flaquear; ‹*faith*› debilitar; **the scandal has ~n the financial world** el escándalo ha conmocionado al mundo de las finanzas 2 (shock, surprise) ‹*person*› impresionar, afectar; **he needs to be ~n out of his apathy** necesita un revulsivo que lo saque de su apatía

■ **shake** *vi*

A (move, tremble) «*earth*» temblar*; «*hand/voice*» temblar*; **the branches shook in the wind** las ramas se agitaban con el viento; **he was shaking with fear/cold/rage** estaba temblando de miedo/frío/rabia

B (shake hands) (colloq): **let's ~ on it** ¡choca esos cinco! (fam), ¡chócala(s)! (fam); **they shook on it** sellaron el acuerdo con un apretón de manos

(Phrasal verbs)

• **shake down** (colloq) [v ▸ o ▸ adv] (AmE) 1 (extort money): **they shook me down for a couple of hundred dollars** me sacaron *or* (fam) me hicieron largar doscientos dólares 2 (search) ‹*person*› cachear, registrar

• **shake off** [v ▸ o ▸ adv, v ▸ adv ▸ o] ‹*pursuer/reporter*› deshacerse* *or* zafarse de; ‹*habit*› quitarse; ‹*cold*› quitarse de encima; **she couldn't ~ off her depression** no podía salir de su depresión

• **shake out** [v ▸ o ▸ adv, v ▸ adv ▸ o] ‹*cloth/mat/bag*› sacudir

• **shake up** [v ▸ o ▸ adv, v ▸ adv ▸ o]

A ‹*liquid*› agitar

B (colloq) ‹*industry/personnel*› reorganizar* totalmente

C (disturb, shock) (colloq): **is he hurt? — no, just a bit ~n up** ¿se ha hecho daño? — no, se ha llevado un susto (y está un poco alterado)

shake² *n*

A (act) sacudida *f*; (violent) sacudida *m* violenta, sacudón *m* (AmL); **he gave my hand a firm ~** me dio un fuerte apretón de manos; **he replied with a ~ of the head** contestó negando con la cabeza; ***in two ~s (of a lamb's tail)*** (colloq) en un periquete *or* en un santiamén *or* en una patada (fam); ***to be no great ~s*** (colloq) no ser* gran cosa (fam)

B (*milk ~*) (AmE) batido *m*, (leche *f*) malteada *f* (AmL), licuado *m* con leche (AmL), merengada *f* (Ven)

C **shakes** *pl* (trembling) (colloq): **he got the ~s** le dio *or* le entró la tembladera *or* (Méx) la temblorina (fam)

D (deal, treatment) (AmE colloq) (*no pl*): **a fair ~** un trato justo

shakedown /ˈʃeɪkdaʊn/ *n* (AmE colloq) 1 (extortion) timo *m* (fam), estafa *f*; **$100 a ticket? that's a ~!** ¿$100 la entrada? ¡qué robo! (fam) 2 (search): **let's give this place one hell of a ~** vamos a revisar bien esto

shaken /ˈʃeɪkən/ *past p of* **shake¹**

shaker /ˈʃeɪkər ‖ ˈʃeɪkə(r)/ *n* 1 (for cocktails) coctelera *f* 2 (for salt) salero *m*; (for pepper) pimentero *m*; (for sugar) azucarero *m* 3 (for dice) cubilete *m*, cacho *m* (Andes)

Shakespearean, Shakespearian /ʃeɪkˈspɪriən ‖ ʃeɪkˈspɪəriən/ *adj* shakesperiano

shake-up /ˈʃeɪkʌp/ *n* (colloq) gran reorganización *f*

shaky /ˈʃeɪki/ *adj* **-kier, -kiest** 1 (trembling) ‹*hands/voice*› tembloroso, tembleque (fam); ‹*writing*› de trazo poco firme 2 (unsteady) ‹*table*› poco firme; ‹*structure*› tambaleante, poco firme *or* sólido; ‹*health*› delicado; ‹*currency/government*› débil; ‹*theory/start*› flojo; **I still feel a bit ~** todavía no me siento del todo bien

shale /ʃeɪl/ *n* [u] esquisto *m*, pizarra *f*

shall /ʃæl, *weak forms* ʃl, ʃəl/ *v mod* (*past* **should**)

A (*with 1st person*) 1 (in statements about the future): **I/we ~ be very interested to see what happens** tendré/tendremos mucho interés en ver qué sucede; **we shan't be able to come** (BrE) no podremos *or* no vamos a poder venir

2 (making suggestions, asking for assent) [*The present tense is used in this type of question in Spanish*] ~ **I open/close the window?** ¿abro/cierro la ventana?, ¿quieres (*or* quiere *etc*) que abra/cierre la ventana?; ~ **we go out tonight?** ¿qué te (*or* le *etc*) parece si salimos esta noche?; ~ **we dance?** ¿bailamos?; **I'll ask him, ~ I?** le pregunto ¿sí? *or* ¿te (*or* le *etc*) parece?; **whatever ~ we do?** (BrE) ¿qué podemos hacer?

B (*with 2nd and 3rd persons*) (in commands, promises etc): **they ~ not pass** no pasarán; **thou shalt not steal** (Bib) no robarás

shallot /ʃəˈlɑːt || ʃəˈlɒt/ *n* chalote *m*, chalota *f*

shallow /ˈʃæləʊ/ *adj* **-er, -est** 1 (not deep) ‹*water/pond/river*› poco profundo; ‹*dish*› llano, plano, bajo (Chi); **~ breathing** respiración *f* superficial 2 (superficial) ‹*person*› superficial

shallows /ˈʃæləʊz/ *pl n* bajío *m*, bajo *m*

shalt /ʃælt/ (arch) *2nd pers sing pres indic of* **shall B**

sham¹ /ʃæm/ *n* 1 [c u] (pretense) farsa *f* 2 [c] (impostor) farsante *mf*

sham² *adj* (pej) (*no comp*) ‹*emotion/interest/sympathy*› fingido, falso; ‹*antiques/diamonds*› falso, de imitación; **it was a ~ trial** el juicio fue una farsa

sham³ **-mm-** *vt* ‹*enthusiasm/grief/illness*› fingir*, simular

■ **sham** *vi* «*person*» fingir*

shamble /ˈʃæmbəl/ *vi* 1 «*person*» caminar arrastrando los pies; **he ~d off** se fue arrastrando los pies 2 **shambling** *pres p* ‹*figure/gait*› desgarbado, desgalichado

shambles /ˈʃæmbəlz/ *n* (+ *sing vb*) caos *m*, desquicio *m* (RPl); **they left the place a ~** lo dejaron todo patas arriba (fam)

shambolic /ʃæmˈbɑːlɪk || ʃæmˈbɒlɪk/ *adj* (BrE colloq) caótico

shame¹ /ʃeɪm/ *n*

A [u] (feeling) vergüenza *f*, pena *f* (AmL exc CS); **have you no (sense of) ~?** ¿es que has perdido la vergüenza?, ¿es que no tienes vergüenza?; **her actions brought ~ on the family** lo que hizo fue la vergüenza de la familia; **~ on you!** ¡qué vergüenza!, ¡debería darte vergüenza!; ***to put sb to ~***: **she's such a good hostess, she puts me to ~** es tan buena anfitriona que me hace sentir culpable

B (pity) (*no pl*) lástima *f*, pena *f*; **what a ~!** ¡qué lástima!; **it's a ~ you can't go** es una pena que no puedas ir

shame² *vt* avergonzar*, apenar (AmL exc CS); **to ~ sb INTO -ING**: **they ~d us into paying** nos hicieron avergonzarnos de tal manera que al final pagamos

shamefaced /ˈʃeɪmˈfeɪst/ *adj* avergonzado, abochornado, apenado (AmL exc CS)

shameful /ˈʃeɪmfəl/ *adj* vergonzoso

shamefully /ˈʃeɪmfəli/ *adv* vergonzosamente

shameless /ˈʃeɪmləs || ˈʃeɪmlɪs/ *adj* ‹*lie/exploitation*› descarado; ‹*liar/cheat*› desvergonzado, sinvergüenza

shampoo¹ /ʃæmˈpuː/ *n* (*pl* **-poos**) 1 (product) champú *m* 2 (act) lavado *m*; **~ and set** lavado *m* y marcado

shampoo² *vt* **-poos, -pooing, -pooed** ‹*hair*› lavar; ‹*carpet/upholstery*› limpiar

shamrock /ˈʃæmrɑːk || ˈʃæmrɒk/ *n* [u c] trébol *m*

shandy /ˈʃændi/ *n* [u c] (*pl* **-dies**) (BrE) cerveza *f* con limonada, ≈ clara *f* (en Esp)

Shangri-la /ˈʃæŋgriˈlɑː/ *n* paraíso *m* (terrenal)

shank /ʃæŋk/ *n*

A (shin) espinilla *f*, canilla *f*

B (Tech) (of tool) mango *m*; (of key, anchor) tija *f*; (of screw) vástago *m*, tallo *m*, varilla *f*

shan't /ʃænt || ʃɑːnt/ **= shall not**

shanty /ˈʃænti/ *n* (*pl* **-ties**)

A (hut) casucha *f*, rancho *m* (AmL), chabola *f* (Esp)

B (*sea ~*) (BrE) canción *f* de marineros

shantytown /ˈʃænti͵taʊn/ *n* barriada *f* (AmL), chabolas *fpl* (Esp), población *f* callampa (Chi), villa *f* miseria (Arg), ciudad *f* perdida (Méx), cantegril *m* (Ur), ranchos *mpl* (Ven)

shape¹ /ʃeɪp/ *n*

A 1 [c] (visible form) forma *f*; **it is triangular in ~** tiene forma triangular; **in the ~ of a cross** en forma de cruz; **they come in all ~s and sizes** los hay de muy diversos tipos; **to be out of ~** estar* deformado; **to take ~** tomar forma 2 [u] (general nature, outline) conformación *f*, configuración *f*; **the ~ of things to come** lo que nos espera

3 [c] (unidentified person, thing) figura *f*, bulto *m*

B [u] (guise): **assistance in the ~ of food stamps** ayuda consistente en vales canjeables por comida; **I won't tolerate bribery in any ~ or form** no pienso tolerar sobornos de ningún tipo

C [u] (condition, order): **she's in pretty good/bad ~** está bastante bien/mal (de salud); **to keep** *o* **stay in ~** mantenerse* en forma; ***to knock*** *o* ***lick sth/sb into ~*** ‹*team/new recruits*› poner* algo/a algn a punto *or* en forma

D [c] (mold, pattern) molde *m*

shape² *vt*

A ‹*object/material*› darle* forma a; **to ~ sth INTO sth**: **she ~d the dough into a ring** formó un anillo con la masa

B (influence) ‹*events*› determinar; ‹*character/ideas*› formar

■ **shape** *vi* **~ (up)** «*project*» tomar forma; «*plan*» desarrollarse; **how's the team shaping (up)?** ¿qué tal marcha *or* va el equipo?

Phrasal verb

• **shape up** [v ▸ adv] 1 ▸**shape²** *vi* 2 (improve, pull oneself together) entrar en vereda (fam)

shaped /ʃeɪpt/ *adj*: **an oddly ~ object** un objeto de forma extraña; **to be ~ like sth** tener* forma de algo

-shaped /ʃeɪpt/ *suff*: **L~/heart~** con *or* en forma de L/corazón

shapeless /ˈʃeɪpləs || ˈʃeɪplɪs/ *adj* informe, sin forma

shapely /ˈʃeɪpli/ *adj* **-lier, -liest** ‹*figure*› bien modulado, hermoso; ‹*legs*› torneado, bien proporcionado; **a ~ blonde** una rubia curvilínea

shard /ʃɑːrd || ʃɑːd/ *n* casco *m*, fragmento *m*

share¹ /ʃer || ʃeə(r)/ *n*

A [c] (portion) parte *f*; **how much is my ~ of the bill?** ¿cuánto me toca pagar a mí?; **she must take her ~ of the blame** debe aceptar que tiene parte de la culpa; **he's had his ~ of bad luck** ha tenido bastante mala suerte *or* su buena cuota de mala suerte; **I only want my fair ~** sólo quiero lo que en justicia me corresponde; ***to work on ~s*** (AmE) trabajar como socios

B (Busn, Fin) 1 (held by partner) (*no pl*) participación *f*; **I own a half ~ in a fishing boat** soy copropietario de un pesquero 2 [c] (held by shareholder) acción *f*; **to hold ~s in a company** tener* acciones en una compañía; (*before n*) **~ capital** capital *m* social; **~ certificate** (título *m or* certificado *m* de) acción *f*; **~ index** índice *m* de cotización en bolsa; **~ prices** cotización *f* de las acciones

share² *vt*

A 1 (use jointly) **to ~ sth (WITH sb)** compartir algo (CON algn) 2 (have in common) ‹*interest/opinion*› compartir; ‹*characteristics*› tener* en común

B 1 (divide) dividir; **we agreed to ~ all expenses** decidimos compartir todos los gastos 2 (communicate) ‹*experience/knowledge*› intercambiar; **I'd like to ~ my feelings with you** me gustaría expresarles mis sentimientos

■ **share** *vi* 1 (use jointly) compartir; **you may have to ~ with somebody** puede ser que tengas que compartir la habitación (*or* el despacho *etc*) con algn; **to ~ and ~ alike** compartir las cosas 2 (have a part) **to ~ IN sth** compartir algo, participar DE algo

Phrasal verb

• **share out** [v ▸ o ▸ adv, v ▸ adv ▸ o] ‹*profits/food*› repartir, distribuir*

share: **~cropper** *n* aparcero, -ra *m,f*; **~holder** *n* accionista *mf*; **~holding** /ˈʃer͵həʊldɪŋ || ˈʃeə͵həʊldɪŋ/ *n* 1 [u] (ownership) accionariado *m* 2 [c] (stake) participación *f*; **~-out** *n* reparto *m*, distribución *f*; **~ware** /ˈʃerwer || ˈʃeəweə(r)/ *n* [u] shareware *m*, *programa cuyo autor solicita una retribución después de un período de evaluación*

shark /ʃɑːrk || ʃɑːk/ *n* 1 (Zool) tiburón *m* 2 (person) (colloq) explotador, -dora *m,f*

sharp¹ /ʃɑːrp || ʃɑːp/ *adj* **-er, -est**

A 1 ‹*knife/edge/scissors*› afilado, filoso (AmL), filudo (Chi, Per); ‹*features*› anguloso, muy marcado; **it has a ~ point** es muy puntiagudo; **have you got a ~er pencil?** ¿tienes un lápiz con más punta? 2 ‹*pain*› agudo, fuerte 3 ‹*wind*› cortante; ‹*frost*› crudo, fuerte 4 ‹*noise/cry*› agudo; ‹*crack*› seco 5 ‹*taste*› ácido

B 1 (abrupt, steep) ‹*bend/angle*› cerrado; ‹*turn*› brusco; ‹*rise/fall/descent*› brusco 2 (sudden) repentino, súbito

C 1 (keen) ‹*eyesight*› agudo, bueno; ‹*hearing*› fino, agudo, bueno; **keep a ~ lookout** mantén los ojos bien abiertos; **keep a ~ eye on those two over there** no les quites el

S

ojo de encima a esos dos de ahí 2 (acute) ‹*wit/mind*› agudo
D (clear, unblurred) ‹*photo/TV picture*› nítido; ‹*outline*› definido; ‹*impression*› claro; ‹*contrast*› marcado
E (harsh, severe) ‹*rebuke/criticism*› duro, severo; ‹*retort*› cortante, áspero; **to have a ~ tongue** ser* muy mordaz, tener* una lengua muy afilada
F 1 (clever, shrewd) ‹*person*› listo, astuto, vivo (fam); ‹*move*› astuto 2 (elegant) (colloq): **he's a ~ dresser** tiene mucho estilo para vestirse
G (Mus) 1 (referring to key) sostenido 2 (too high): **you're ~** estás desafinando (*por cantar o tocar demasiado alto*)

sharp² *adv*
A (exactly): **at six o'clock ~** a las seis en punto
B (abruptly): **turn ~ right** gire a la derecha en curva cerrada; **to pull up ~** pararse en seco; **look ~** (BrE colloq) ¡acelera! (fam), ¡date prisa!, ¡apúrate! (AmL)
C (Mus): **to sing/play ~** cantar/tocar* demasiado alto

sharp³ *n* (Mus) sostenido *m*

sharpen /ˈʃɑːrpən || ˈʃɑːpən/ *vt* 1 ‹*knife/blade/claws*› afilar; ‹*pencil*› sacarle* punta a 2 ‹*appetite*› abrir*

sharpener /ˈʃɑːrpṇər || ˈʃɑːpṇə(r)/ *n* (*knife* ~) afilador *m*; (*pencil* ~) sacapuntas *m*

sharp-eyed /ˈʃɑːrpˈaɪd || ˌʃɑːpˈaɪd/ *adj* con ojo de lince

sharpish /ˈʃɑːrpɪʃ || ˈʃɑːpɪʃ/ *adv* (BrE colloq) prontito (fam)

sharply /ˈʃɑːrpli || ˈʃɑːpli/ *adv*
A 1 (steeply, abruptly) ‹*drop/fall/increase*› bruscamente; ‹*bend*› repentinamente, de pronto 2 (suddenly, swiftly) de repente, repentinamente
B 1 (acutely) ‹*aware/conscious*› tremendamente 2 ‹*outlined/defined*› claramente, nítidamente; **two ~ contrasting styles** dos estilos en marcado contraste
C (harshly) ‹*answer/speak/criticize*› con dureza *or* severidad

sharpness /ˈʃɑːrpnəs || ˈʃɑːpnɪs/ *n* [u]
A (of knife) lo afilado *or* (AmL tb) lo filoso *or* (Chi, Per tb) lo filudo; (of point) lo puntiagudo; (of pain) agudeza *f*, lo agudo; (of cry, sound) lo agudo; (of features) lo anguloso
B (abruptness) brusquedad *f*; **the ~ of the bend** lo cerrado de la curva
C (acuteness) agudeza *f*; **the ~ of his intellect/mind** su perspicacia; **the ~ of his reflexes/reactions** su rapidez de reflejos/para reaccionar
D (clarity) nitidez *f*

sharp: **~ practice** *n* [u c] artimañas *fpl*, triquiñuelas *fpl*; **~shooter** *n* tirador, -dora *m,f* de primera; **~-tongued** /ˈʃɑːrpˈtʌŋd || ˌʃɑːpˈtʌŋd/ *adj* ‹*criticism*› mordaz; ‹*person*› de lengua mordaz; **~-witted** /ˈʃɑːrpˈwɪtəd || ˌʃɑːpˈwɪtɪd/ *adj* listo, agudo

shat /ʃæt/ *past and past p of* **shit²**

shatter /ˈʃætər || ˈʃætə(r)/ *vt*
A 1 (break) ‹*window/plate*› hacer* añicos *or* pedazos 2 ‹*health/nerves*› destrozar*; ‹*confidence/hopes*› destruir*, echar por tierra; ‹*silence/calm*› romper*
B (*usu pass*) 1 (shock): **she was ~ed by the news** la noticia la dejó destrozada 2 (exhaust) (BrE colloq): **I arrived home feeling completely ~ed** llegué a casa hecho polvo *or* muerto de cansancio (fam)
■ **shatter** *vi* «*window/glass*» hacerse* añicos *or* pedazos

shattering /ˈʃætərɪŋ/ *adj* (devastating) ‹*blow/loss*› tremendo, terrible; ‹*defeat*› aplastante; ‹*experience*› demoledor, terrible

shatterproof /ˈʃætərpruːf || ˈʃætəpruːf/ *adj* inastillable

shave¹ /ʃeɪv/ *vt*
A ‹*person*› afeitar *or* (esp Méx) rasurar; **she ~s her legs** se afeita *or* (esp Méx) se rasura las piernas; **to ~** *o* (BrE also) **to ~ off one's beard/mustache** afeitarse *or* (esp Méx) rasurarse la barba/el bigote
B (touch in passing) rozar*
■ **shave** *vi* «*person*» afeitarse *or* (esp Méx) rasurarse; «*razor*» afeitar

shave² *n* afeitada *f or* (esp Méx) rasurada *f*; **to have a ~** afeitarse *or* (esp Méx) rasurarse; ***a close*** *o* ***narrow ~*** (colloq): **we won in the end, but it was a pretty close ~** al final ganamos, pero por los pelos *or* por un pelo (fam)

shaven /ˈʃeɪvən/ *adj* ‹*chin/face*› afeitado *or* (esp Méx) rasurado; ‹*head*› rapado

shaver /ˈʃeɪvər || ˈʃeɪvə(r)/ *n* (*electric* ~) máquina *f* de afeitar, afeitadora *f or* (esp Méx) rasuradora *f*

shaving /ˈʃeɪvɪŋ/ *n* 1 (*before n*) ‹*cream/soap*› de afeitar *or* (esp Méx) de rasurar; **~ brush** brocha *f* (de afeitar) 2 [c] **shavings** *pl* (pieces) virutas *fpl*; **wood/metal ~s** virutas de madera/metal

shawl /ʃɔːl/ *n* chal *m*, mantón *m*

she /ʃiː, *weak form* ʃi/ *pron* ella; **~'s a writer/my sister** es escritora/mi hermana; **~ didn't say it, I did** no fue ella quien lo dijo, sino yo; **Lisa Swenson? who's ~?** ¿Lisa Swenson? ¿quién es Lisa Swenson?; **could I speak to Mary, please? — this is ~** (AmE) ¿podría hablar con Mary, por favor? — al aparato *or* habla con ella

she- /ˈʃiː/ *pref*: **~bear** osa *f*, hembra *f* de oso; **~wolf** loba *f*, hembra *f* de lobo

s/he (= **he or she**) él/ella

sheaf /ʃiːf/ *n* (*pl* **sheaves**) 1 (Agr) gavilla *f* 2 (of notes) fajo *m*; (of arrows) haz *m*

shear /ʃɪr || ʃɪə(r)/ *vt*
A (*past* **sheared**; *past p* **shorn**) ‹*sheep*› esquilar, trasquilar; ‹*hair/curls*› cortar; **to be shorn OF sth** (frml) ser* despojado DE algo (frml)
B (*past p* **sheared**) (break) ‹*bolt/shaft*› romper*
■ **shear** *vi* (*past p* **sheared**) 1 (cut) **to ~ THROUGH sth** atravesar* algo 2 (break) romperse*; **to ~ off** romperse*

shears /ʃɪrz || ʃɪəz/ *pl n* (for grass, hedge) podaderas *fpl*, tijeras *fpl* de podar; (for metal) cizallas *fpl*; (for shearing sheep) tijeras *fpl* de esquilar

sheath /ʃiːθ/ *n* (*pl* **~s** /ʃiːðz/)
A 1 (for sword, knife) funda *f*, vaina *f*; (for wiring) cubierta *f* 2 (Bot) vaina *f*
B (contraceptive) (BrE) preservativo *m*, condón *m*

sheathe /ʃiːð/ *vt* 1 (put into sheath) ‹*sword*› envainar, enfundar 2 (cover) ‹*cable/wire/pipes*› revestir*

sheath knife *n* cuchillo *m* de monte

sheaves /ʃiːvz/ *pl of* **sheaf**

shed¹ /ʃed/ (*pres p* **shedding**; *past & past p* **shed**) *vt*
A 1 ‹*tears/blood*› derramar 2 ‹*leaves/horns/skin*› mudar; ‹*clothing*› quitarse, despojarse de (frml) 3 ‹*cares/inhibitions*› liberarse de; ‹*workers/jobs*› deshacerse* de; **he's ~ 33 lbs** ha adelgazado 33 libras
B (send out) ‹*light*› emitir
■ **shed** *vi* «*dog/cat*» pelechar, mudar de pelo

shed² *n* 1 (hut) cabaña *f*; (*garden* ~) cobertizo *m*, galpón *m* (RPl) 2 (larger building) nave *f*, galpón *m* (CS)

she'd /ʃiːd/ 1 = **she would** 2 = **she had**

sheen /ʃiːn/ *n* [u] brillo *m*, lustre *m*

sheep /ʃiːp/ *n* (*pl* ~) oveja *f*; ***to count ~*** contar* ovejas *or* corderitos; ***to separate the ~ from the goats*** separar el grano de la paja; (*before n*) **~ farming** cría *f* de ganado ovino *or* lanar

sheepdog /ˈʃiːpdɔːg || ˈʃiːpdɒg/ *n* perro *m* pastor *or* ovejero

sheepish /ˈʃiːpɪʃ/ *adj* avergonzado

sheepishly /ˈʃiːpɪʃli/ *adv* con vergüenza, tímidamente

sheepskin /ˈʃiːpskɪn/ *n* 1 [c u] (skin) piel *f* de borrego *or* de cordero, corderito *m* (RPl) 2 [c] (garment) abrigo *m* de piel de borrego *or* de cordero, gamulán® *m* (RPl)

sheer¹ /ʃɪr || ʃɪə(r)/ *adj* **sheerer, sheerest**
A (pure, absolute) (*as intensifier*) puro; **by ~ coincidence** por pura casualidad; **it's ~ nonsense to suggest that ...** es un verdadero disparate decir que ...; **the ~ size of the problem** la mera magnitud del problema
B (vertical) ‹*drop*› a pique, vertical; ‹*cliff*› escarpado, cortado a pico *or* a pique
C (fine) ‹*stockings/nylon/fabric*› muy fino, transparente

sheer² *adv* (vertically): **the cliffs rise ~ out of the sea** los acantilados se yerguen verticalmente sobre el mar

Phrasal verbs
• **sheer away** [v ▸ adv] «*ship/plane*» desviarse*
• **sheer off** [v ▸ adv] desviarse*, cambiar de rumbo

sheet /ʃiːt/ *n*
A (on bed) sábana *f*; ***as white as a ~*** blanco como el papel
B (of paper) hoja *f*; (of wrapping paper) pliego *m*, hoja *f*; (of stamps) pliego *m*; **information** *o* **fact ~** folleto *m*
C 1 (of metal) chapa *f*, plancha *f*, lámina *f*; **a ~ of glass** un vidrio, una placa de vidrio 2 (of ice) capa *f*; **a ~ of flame** una cortina de llamas; **the rain was coming down in ~s** llovía a cántaros; (*before n*) **~ lightning** relámpagos *mpl* difusos

S

sheeting /ˈʃiːtɪŋ/ *n* [u] (Tex) tela *f* (*para hacer sábanas*); **steel/plastic ~** acero *m*/plástico *m* en planchas *or* chapas

sheet: **~ metal** *n* [u] metal *m* en planchas *or* chapas; **~ music** *n* [u] partituras *fpl*

sheik, sheikh /ʃiːk || ʃeɪk/ *n* jeque *m*

shekel /ˈʃekəl/ *n* shekel *m*, siclo *m*

shelf /ʃelf/ *n* (*pl* **shelves**)

A 1 (in cupboard, bookcase) estante *m*, balda *f* (Esp); (on wall) estante *m*, anaquel *m*, repisa *f*, balda *f* (Esp); (in oven) parrilla *f*; **a set of shelves** unos estantes, una estantería; ***to be left on the ~*** quedarse para vestir santos 2 **off the shelf**: **you can buy it off the ~** se puede comprar hecho

B (Geol): **continental ~** plataforma *f* continental

shelf life *n* [u] *tiempo que puede conservarse un producto perecedero sin que se deteriore*

shell[1] /ʃel/ *n*

A 1 (of egg, nut) cáscara *f*; (of sea mollusk) concha *f*; (of tortoise, turtle, snail, crustacean) caparazón *m or f*, carapacho *m*; **pastry ~** (Culin) base *f* (*de masa*); ***to come out of one's ~*** salir* del cascarón; ***to go back*** *o* ***retreat into one's ~*** retraerse* 2 (of building) estructura *f*, armazón *m or f*, esqueleto *m*; (of vehicle) armazón *m or f*

B (Mil) 1 (for artillery) proyectil *m*, obús *m* 2 (for small arms) cartucho *m*

shell[2] *vt*

A (Culin) ‹*peas*› pelar, desvainar; ‹*nuts/eggs/prawns*› pelar; ‹*mussel/clam*› quitarle la concha a, desconchar

B (Mil) ‹*position/troops/city*› bombardear

■ **shell** *vi* (Mil) bombardear

Phrasal verb

• **shell out** (colloq)

A [v ▸ o ▸ adv, v ▸ adv ▸ o] ‹*money*› aflojar (fam), soltar* (fam)

B [v ▸ adv] soltar* *or* aflojar (la mosca) (fam)

she'll /ʃiːl, *weak form* ʃɪl/ **= she will**

shell: **~fire** *n* [u] fuego *m* de artillería; **~fish** *n* (*pl* **~fish**) 1 [c] (creature) marisco *m* 2 [u] (collectively) mariscos *mpl*, marisco *m* (Esp); **~shock** *n* [u] neurosis *f* de guerra; **~shocked** *adj* traumatizado por la guerra; **~ suit** *n* equipo *m or* (Esp) chándal *m or* (Chi, Per) buzo *m or* (Méx) pants *mpl or* (Col) sudadera *f* de nylon

shelter[1] /ˈʃeltər || ˈʃeltə(r)/ *n*

A [c] (building) refugio *m*; **bomb** *o* **air-raid ~** refugio antiaéreo

B [u] 1 (protection): **to take ~** refugiarse, guarecerse*; **to run for ~** correr a refugiarse 2 (accommodations): **to give ~ to sb** acoger* a algn, darle* alojamiento a algn; **to seek ~ for the night** buscar* donde pasar la noche; **they need food, ~, and clothing** necesitan alimentos, albergue y ropa

shelter[2] *vt* 1 (protect from weather) **to ~ sth/sb (FROM sth)** resguardar algo/a algn (DE algo) 2 **to ~ sb (FROM sb)** ‹*criminal/fugitive*› darle* cobijo A algn (para protegerlo DE algn)

■ **shelter** *vi* **to ~ (FROM sth)** refugiarse *or* guarecerse* *or* resguardarse (DE algo)

sheltered /ˈʃeltərd || ˈʃeltəd/ *adj* ‹*valley/harbor*› abrigado; ‹*life*› protegido; **she had a ~ upbringing** creció muy protegida de la realidad de la vida, fue criada entre algodones (pey); **~ housing** (BrE) *viviendas vigiladas para ancianos y minusválidos*

shelve /ʃelv/ *vt* (postpone) ‹*plan/project*› archivar, aparcar*, darle* carpetazo a

■ **shelve** *vi* bajar, descender*

shelves /ʃelvz/ *pl of* **shelf**

shelving /ˈʃelvɪŋ/ *n* [u] (sets of shelves) estantería *f*

shenanigans /ʃəˈnænɪgənz/ *pl n* (colloq) 1 (trickery) chanchullos *mpl* (fam) 2 (mischief) travesuras *fpl*

shepherd[1] /ˈʃepərd || ˈʃepəd/ *n* pastor *m*

shepherd[2] *vt* conducir*, guiar*

shepherdess /ˈʃepərˈdəs || ˌʃepəˈdes/ *n* pastora *f*

shepherd's pie *n* [u c] *plato de carne picada cubierta con puré de papas*, pastel *m* de papas *or* de carne (CS)

sherbet /ˈʃɜːrbət || ˈʃɜːbət/ *n* 1 (sorbet) (AmE) sorbete *m*, helado *m* de agua (CS), nieve *f* (Méx) 2 (powder) (BrE) *polvos efervescentes con sabor a frutas*, sidral® *m* (Esp)

sherd /ʃɜːrd || ʃɜːd/ *n* ▸ **shard**

sheriff /ˈʃerəf || ˈʃerɪf/ *n* 1 (in US) sheriff *mf* 2 (in England and Wales) *representante de la corona* 3 (in Scotland) *juez principal de un distrito*

sherry /ˈʃeri/ *n* [u c] (*pl* **-ries**) jerez *m*

she's /ʃiːz, *weak form* ʃɪz/ 1 **= she is** 2 **= she has**

shield[1] /ʃiːld/ *n*

A (Hist, Mil) escudo *m*; **riot ~** escudo *m* antidisturbios

B (protective cover on machine) revestimiento *m*; **eye ~** visera *f* protectora; (*before n*) **~ law** (in US) *ley que establece que los periodistas no están obligados a revelar fuentes de información*

shield[2] *vt* **to ~ sth/sb (FROM sb/sth)** proteger* algo/a algn (DE algn/algo); **the bushes ~ed them from view** los matorrales los ocultaban

shift[1] /ʃɪft/ *vt*

A 1 (change position of) ‹*object/furniture*› correr, mover*; **to ~ the scenery** (Theat) cambiar el decorado 2 (transfer, switch): **they tried to ~ the responsibility onto us** trataron de cargarnos la responsabilidad

B (BrE colloq) 1 (move, remove): **~ yourself, will you!** ¡quítate de ahí!; **I can't ~ this nail** este clavo no hay quien lo saque 2 (get rid of) ‹*stain*› quitar, sacar* (esp AmL); ‹*cold/allergy*› quitarse de encima

C (sell) ‹*stock*› vender

■ **shift** *vi*

A 1 (change position, direction) «*cargo*» correrse; «*wind*» cambiar; **he ~ed uneasily in his chair** se movía intranquilo en la silla 2 (switch, change over): **the focus of attention has ~ed to Europe** el foco de atención ha pasado a Europa 3 **shifting** *pres p* ‹*opinion/moods*› cambiante; **~ing sands** arenas *fpl* movedizas

B (BrE) 1 (move) (colloq): **~ up/along a bit** córrete un poco 2 (budge) ceder, transigir*

C (manage): **to ~ for oneself** arreglárselas solo

D (change gear) (AmE) cambiar de marcha *or* de velocidad

shift[2] *n*

A (change in position) cambio *m*; **there was a ~ in public opinion** hubo un cambio *or* un viraje en la opinión pública; **a major population ~** un desplazamiento masivo de población

B (work period) turno *m*; **to work the day/night ~** hacer* el turno de día/de noche; **to work (in) ~s** trabajar por turnos; (*before n*) **~ work/worker** trabajo *m*/trabajador, -dora *m,f* por turnos

C 1 (undergarment) enagua *f* 2 (dress) vestido *m* suelto

D (AmE Auto) palanca *m* de cambio *or* (Méx) de velocidades

shift key *n* tecla *f* de las mayúsculas

shiftless /ˈʃɪftləs || ˈʃɪftlɪs/ *adj* holgazán, haragán

shift: **~ lever** *n* (AmE) palanca *f* de cambios; **~ lock** *n* tecla *f* fijamayúsculas

shifty /ˈʃɪfti/ *adj* **-tier, -tiest** ‹*expression/eyes*› furtivo; ‹*appearance*› sospechoso

Shiite[1] /ˈʃiːaɪt/ *n* chiíta *mf*, shií *mf*

Shiite[2] *adj* chiíta, shií

shilling /ˈʃɪlɪŋ/ *n* chelín *m*

shilly-shally /ˈʃɪliˌʃæli/ *vi* **-lies, -lying, -lied** titubear, vacilar; **stop ~ing!** ¡déjate de titubeos!

shilly-shallying *n* [u] titubeos *mpl*, dudas *fpl*

shimmer[1] /ˈʃɪmər || ˈʃɪmə(r)/ *n* brillo *m*, resplandor *m*

shimmer[2] *vi* «*water/silk*» brillar; «*lights*» titilar; (in water) rielar (liter)

shin[1] /ʃɪn/ *n* 1 (Anat) espinilla *f*, canilla *f*; (*before n*) **~ guard/pad** espinillera *f* 2 (of beef) (BrE) jarrete *m*

shin[2] *vi* **-nn-**: **he ~ned up the tree** se trepó al árbol

shinbone /ˈʃɪnbəʊn/ *n* tibia *f*

shindig /ˈʃɪndɪg/ *n* (colloq) fiesta *f*, juerga *f* (fam)

shindy /ˈʃɪndi/ *n* (*pl* **-dies**) (colloq) lío *m* (fam), escándalo *m*

shine[1] /ʃaɪn/ *n* [u] brillo *m*; **to give one's shoes a ~** limpiarse *or* (esp AmL) lustrarse *or* (Col) embolarse *or* (Méx) bolearse los zapatos; ***to take a ~ to sb*** (colloq): **they really took a ~ to each other** quedaron prendados el uno del otro; ***to take the ~ off sth*** deslucir* *or* empañar algo

shine[2] *vi* (*past & past p* **shone**) 1 (gleam, glow) «*star/sun/eyes*» brillar; «*metal/glass/shoes*» relucir*, brillar 2 (excel) **to ~ (AT sth)** destacar(se*) (EN algo)

■ **shine** *vt*

A (*past & past p* **shone**) (point) (+ *adv compl*): **to ~ a light on sth** alumbrar algo con una luz

B (*past & past p* **shined**) (polish) ‹*brass/furniture*› sacarle*

S

brillo a, lustrar (esp AmL); ‹*shoes*› limpiar *or* (esp AmL) lustrar *or* (Col) embolar *or* (Méx) bolear

Phrasal verb

- **shine out** [v ▸ adv] «*light/sun/integrity*» brillar

shingle /ˈʃɪŋgəl/ *n*

A [u] (stones) guijarros *mpl*; (*before n*) ~ **beach** playa *f* de guijarros

B [c] (signboard) (AmE) placa *f*; ***to put*** *o* ***hang up one's*** ~ (colloq) abrir* una consulta (*or* bufete *etc*)

shingles /ˈʃɪŋgəlz/ *n* (Med) (+ *sing vb*) herpes *m*, culebrilla *f*

shining /ˈʃamɪŋ/ *adj* ‹*eyes*› brillante, luminoso; ‹*hair/metal*› brillante, reluciente, lustroso

shinny[1] /ˈʃɪni/ *vi* **-nies, -nying, -nied** (AmE) ▸**shin**[2]

shinny[2] *n* [u] (AmE Sport) *deporte parecido al hockey sobre hierba*

Shintoism /ˈʃɪntəʊɪzm/ *n* [u] sintoismo *m*

shinty /ˈʃɪnti/ *n* [u] (BrE Sport) ▸**shinny**[2]

shiny /ˈʃami/ *adj* **-nier, -niest** ‹*hair/fabric/plastic*› brillante; ‹*shoe*› brillante, lustroso; **a ~ new coin** una moneda nueva y reluciente

ship[1] /ʃɪp/ *n* barco *m*, buque *m*, embarcación *f* (frml); **a sailing ~** un velero; **a passenger ~** un barco *or* un buque de pasajeros; **on board ~** a bordo; **to abandon ~** abandonar el barco; ***like ~s that pass in the night*** como extraños; ***to run a tight ~*** ser* muy eficiente

ship[2] **-pp-** *vt* 1 (send by sea) enviar* *or* mandar por barco 2 (send) enviar*, despachar

Phrasal verbs

- **ship off** [v ▸ o ▸ adv, v ▸ adv ▸ o] 1 ‹*goods/freight*› despachar, expedir* 2 (send away) ‹*son/daughter*› despachar (fam)
- **ship out** [v ▸ o ▸ adv, v ▸ adv ▸ o] enviar* *or* mandar por barco

ship: **~builder** *n* constructor, -tora *m,f* naval; **~building** *n* [u] construcción *f* naval; **~load** *n* cargamento *m*; **by the ~load, in ~loads** a montones (fam); **~mate** *n* camarada *mf* de a bordo

shipment /ˈʃɪpmənt/ *n* (goods) envío *m*, remesa *f*

shipowner /ˈʃɪpˌəʊnər || ˈʃɪpəʊnə(r)/ *n* (person) armador, -dora *m,f*; (company) naviera *f*

shipper /ˈʃɪpər || ˈʃɪpə(r)/ *n* 1 (sender) consignador, -dora *m,f* 2 (exporter) exportador, -dora *m,f*

shipping /ˈʃɪpɪŋ/ *n* [u] 1 (ships) barcos *mpl*, embarcaciones *fpl* (frml); (*before n*) ‹*lane/route*› de navegación; **~ agent** consignatario, -ria *m,f* 2 (transportation of freight) transporte *m*; **~ by air/rail/road/sea** transporte aéreo/por ferrocarril/por carretera/marítimo; (*before n*) **~ charge** gastos *mpl* de envío *or* de expedición

ship: **~shape** *adj* (*pred*) limpio y ordenado; **~-to-shore** /ˈʃɪptəˈʃɔːr || ˌʃɪptəˈʃɔː(r)/ *adj* ‹*radio/telephone/link*› de barco a tierra

shipwreck[1] /ˈʃɪprek/ *n* naufragio *m*

shipwreck[2] *vt* (*usu pass*): **~ed sailors** marineros *mpl* náufragos; **to be ~ed** naufragar*

shipyard /ˈʃɪpjɑːrd || ˈʃɪpjɑːd/ *n* (*often pl*) astillero *m*

shire /ʃaɪr || ˈʃaɪə(r)/ *n* (in UK) condado; **the Shires** *los condados rurales de la región central de Inglaterra*

shire horse *n*: *caballo de tiro parecido al percherón*

shirk /ʃɜːrk/ *vt* ‹*task/duty/responsibility*› eludir, rehuir*

■ **shirk** *vi* haraganear

shirker /ˈʃɜːrkər || ˈʃɜːkə(r)/ *n* haragán, -gana *m,f*

shirt /ʃɜːrt || ʃɜːt/ *n* (man's) camisa *f*; (woman's) camisa *f*, blusa *f* (camisera); ***to give sb the ~ off one's back*** darle* hasta la camiseta a algn; ***keep your ~ on!*** (colloq) ¡no te sulfures! (fam); ***to lose one's ~*** perder* hasta la camisa *or* la camiseta (fam)

shirt: **~dress** *n* (vestido *m*) camisero *m*, chemisier *m* (RPl); **~front** *n* pechera *f*; **~sleeve** *n* manga *f* de camisa; **in (one's) ~sleeves** en mangas de camisa; **~tail** *n* faldón *m* (*de camisa*); **~waist**, (BrE) **~waister** /-ˈweɪstər/ *n* ▸**~dress**

shirty /ˈʃɜːrti || ˈʃɜːti/ *adj* **-tier, -tiest** (colloq) agresivo, borde (Esp fam); **to get ~** sulfurarse (fam), cabrearse (fam)

shit[1] /ʃɪt/ *n* (vulg)

A 1 [u] (feces) mierda *f* (vulg); ***in the ~*** (esp BrE): **now we really are in the ~** ahora sí que estamos jodidos (vulg); ***to beat the ~ out of sb*** moler* a algn a palos (fam), sacarle* la mugre a algn (AmL fam), hacer* mierda a algn (Méx vulg), cagar* a algn a golpes (RPl vulg); ***to scare the ~ out of sb*** hacer* que algn se cague de miedo (vulg), acojonar a algn (Esp vulg); ***when the ~ hits the fan*** cuando la mierda empiece a salpicar (vulg); ▸**creek 1** 2 (act) (*no pl*): **to take** *o* (BrE) **have a ~** cagar* (vulg) 3 **shits** *pl* (diarrhea) **the ~s** cagalera *f or* (CS tb) cagadera *f* (vulg); **he/I got the ~s** le/me dio cagalera *or* (CS tb) cagadera (vulg)

B 1 [u] (nonsense) imbecilidades *fpl*, gilipolleces *fpl* (Esp vulg), pendejadas *fpl* (AmL exc CS vulg), huevadas (Andes, Ven vulg), boludeces *fpl* (Col, RPl vulg) 2 [u] (lies, exaggeration): **he's full of ~** es un mentiroso de mierda (vulg)

C 1 [u c] (sth worthless) mierda *f* (vulg); ***not to give a ~***: **she doesn't give a ~ what anyone thinks** le importa un carajo *or* (Méx) una chingada lo que piensen los demás (vulg) 2 [c] (person) mierda *mf* (vulg)

shit[2] (*pres p* **shitting**; *past & past p* **shit** *or* **shat**) (vulg) *vi* cagar* (vulg)

■ *v refl* **to ~ oneself** (involuntarily) cagarse* (encima) (vulg); (be very scared) cagarse* de miedo (vulg)

shit[3] *interj* (vulg) ¡carajo! (vulg), ¡mierda! (vulg)

shit[4] *adv* (vulg) (*as intensifier*): **she's ~ scared** está cagada de miedo (vulg); **he's ~ hot at his job** es un fenómeno *or* un as en su trabajo

shitless /ˈʃɪtləs || ˈʃɪtlɪs/ *adv* (vulg): **to be scared ~** estar* cagado de miedo (vulg)

shitty /ˈʃɪti/ *adj* **-tier, -tiest** (vulg) ‹*weather/work*› de mierda (vulg); **I'm feeling really ~ today** hoy estoy muy jodido (vulg); **it was a ~ thing to do** fue una putada (vulg)

shiver[1] /ˈʃɪvər || ˈʃɪvə(r)/ *n* 1 (tremor) escalofrío *m*, estremecimiento *m*; **the scream sent ~s** *o* **a ~ down my spine** el grito me produjo escalofríos 2 **shivers** *pl*: **to have the ~s** tener* escalofríos, tener* chuchos (de frío) (RPl fam)

shiver[2] *vi* (with cold) temblar*, tiritar; (with fear) temblar*; (with anticipation) estremecerse*

shivery /ˈʃɪvəri/ *adj*: **to feel ~** tener* escalofríos

shlemiel *n* ▸**schlemiel**

shlep, shlepp *vi* ▸**schlep**

shlock *n* (colloq) porquerías *fpl* (fam)

shmaltz, shmalz *etc* ▸**schmaltz**

shmuck *n* ▸**schmuck**

shoal /ʃəʊl/ *n*

A 1 (of fish) cardumen *m*, banco *m* 2 (of people) montón *m* (fam)

B (sandbank) bajío *m*, banco *m* de arena

shock[1] /ʃɑːk || ʃɒk/ *n*

A [c] 1 (of impact) choque *m*, impacto *m*; (of earthquake, explosion) sacudida *f* 2 (*electric* ~) descarga *f* (eléctrica), golpe *m* de corriente; **I got a ~** me dio una descarga *or* un golpe de corriente, me dio corriente

B 1 [u] (Med) shock *m*; **to be in (a state of) ~** estar* en estado de shock; **he was suffering from ~** estaba en estado de shock 2 [u c] (distress, surprise) shock *m*, impresión *f*; **to get a ~** llevarse un shock *or* una impresión; **I nearly died of ~** por poco me muero del shock *or* de la impresión; **the news came as a great ~ to us** la noticia nos conmocionó; **he's in for a ~ when he finds out** se va a llevar un shock cuando se entere; (*before n*) (journ) **a ~ announcement** un anuncio sorprendente, un bombazo (fam) 3 (scare) susto *m*; **to get a ~** llevarse un susto; **what a ~ you gave me!** ¡qué susto me diste *or* me pegaste!

C [c] (bushy mass): **a ~ of hair** una mata de pelo

shock[2] *vt* (stun, appal) horrorizar*; (scandalize) escandalizar*, horrorizar*; (scare) asustar; **my mother is easily ~ed** mi madre se escandaliza *or* se horroriza por cualquier cosa

■ **shock** *vi* impactar, impresionar

shock absorber /əbˈsɔːrbər || əbˈzɔːbə(r)/ *n* amortiguador *m*

shocked /ʃɑːkt || ʃɒkt/ *adj* 1 (appalled) horrorizado; **a ~ silence greeted the announcement** la gente quedó muda de asombro al oír el anuncio; **we were ~ at their callousness** nos horrorizó su crueldad 2 (scandalized): **I was ~ to hear that ...** me indigné cuando me enteré de que ...

shocking /ˈʃɑːkɪŋ || ˈʃɒkɪŋ/ *adj* 1 ‹*news/report*› espeluznante, horrible, horroroso 2 ‹*weather/cough*› espantoso, horrible 3 ‹*behavior/language*› escandaloso, vergonzoso

shockingly /ˈʃɑːkɪŋli || ˈʃɒkɪŋli/ *adv* 1 (badly) de una manera espantosa, terriblemente mal 2 (*as intensifier*) ‹*bad/expensive*› terriblemente, increíblemente

shocking-pink /ˈʃɑːkɪŋˈpɪŋk || ˌʃɒkɪŋˈpɪŋk/ *adj* (*pred* ~ **pink**) rosa fosforito *or* shocking *adj inv*

shock: ~**proof**, ~**-resistant** *adj* ‹*watch/mechanism*› a prueba de golpes; ~ **tactics** *pl n* tácticas *fpl* de choque; ~ **troops** *pl n* tropas *fpl* de asalto *or* de choque; ~ **wave** *n* (Phys) onda *f* expansiva

shod /ʃɑːd || ʃɒd/ *past & past p of* **shoe**[2]

shoddily /ˈʃɑːdəli || ˈʃɒdɪli/ *adv* 1 (poorly) ‹*made/furnished*› muy mal 2 (meanly) ‹*behave*› de manera despreciable

shoddy /ˈʃɑːdi || ˈʃɒdi/ *adj* **-dier, -diest** 1 (of inferior quality) ‹*goods/workmanship*› de muy mala calidad; ~ **work** chapuza *f* 2 (mean) ‹*behavior/treatment*› bajo, mezquino

shoe[1] /ʃuː/ *n* 1 (Clothing) zapato *m*; **put your ~s on** ponte los zapatos, cálzate; **they sell ~s** venden zapatos *or* (frml) calzado; ***to be in sb's ~s***: **I wouldn't like to be in her ~s** no me gustaría estar en su lugar *or* (fam) en su pellejo; ***to fit like an old ~*** (AmE) sentar* como un guante; ***to step into sb's ~s*** pasar a ocupar el puesto de algn; (*before n*) ~ **polish** betún *m*, pomada *f* (RPl) *or* (Chi) pasta *f* de zapatos; ~ **repairer** zapatero, -ra *m,f* 2 (for horse) herradura *f* 3 (*brake* ~) zapata *f*

shoe[2] *vt* (*pres* **shoes**; *pres p* **shoeing**; *past & past p* **shod**) ‹*horse*› herrar*

shoe: ~**brush** *n* cepillo *m* de los zapatos; ~**horn** *n* calzador *m*; ~**lace** *n* cordón *m* (de zapato), agujeta *f* (Méx), pasador *m* (Per); **to tie one's ~laces** atarse *or* (AmL exc RPl) amarrarse los cordones de los zapatos (*or* las agujetas *etc*); ~**shine (boy)** *n* (esp AmE) limpiabotas *m*, lustrabotas *m* (AmS), bolero *m* (Méx), embolador *m* (Col); ~**string** *n* (Clothing) 1 ▸ ~**lace** 2 ***on a ~string*** con poquísimo dinero; ~**tree** *n* horma *f*

shone /ʃəʊn, ʃɑːn || ʃɒn/ *past & past p of* **shine**[2]

shoo[1] /ʃuː/ *interj* ¡fuera!, ¡zape!, ¡úscale! (Méx)

shoo[2] *vt* **shoos, shooing, shooed**: **I ~ed the birds off** *o* **away** espanté *or* ahuyenté a los pájaros; **she ~ed the cats off the sofa** echó a los gatos del sofá

shook /ʃʊk/ *past of* **shake**[1]

shoot[1] /ʃuːt/ *n*

A (Bot) (bud, young leaf) brote *m*, retoño *m*, renuevo *m*; (from seed, potato) brote *m*

B (shooting expedition) cacería *f*

C (Cin) rodaje *m*, filmación *f*

shoot[2] (*past & past p* **shot**) *vt*

A 1 ‹*person/animal*› pegarle* un tiro *or* un balazo a; **they shot him three times in the legs** le pegaron tres tiros en las piernas; **she was shot in the arm** recibió un balazo en el brazo; **they shot him dead, they shot him to death** (AmE) lo mataron a tiros/de un tiro; **to ~ oneself** pegarse* un tiro; **you'll get me shot!** (colloq) ¡me van a matar por tu culpa! (fam); ***to ~ the breeze*** *o* ***bull*** (AmE) darle* a la lengua *or* a la sinhueso (fam) 2 (hunt) ‹*duck/rabbit/deer*› cazar*

B 1 (fire) ‹*bullet*› disparar, tirar; ‹*arrow/missile*› lanzar*, arrojar; ‹*glance*› lanzar*; **to ~ questions at sb** acribillar a algn a preguntas 2 (eject, propel) lanzar*, despedir*

C (pass swiftly): **to ~ the rapids** salvar los rápidos; **to ~ the lights** (BrE colloq) saltarse la luz roja *or* (Méx tb) pasarse los altos

D 1 (Sport) ‹*ball/puck*› lanzar*; ‹*goal*› marcar*, anotar(se) (AmL); **he shot four baskets** encestó cuatro veces 2 (play) (AmE) jugar* a; **to ~ craps/billiards** jugar* a los dados/al billar

E (Cin) rodar*, filmar

F (inject) (sl) ‹*heroin/cocaine*› chutarse (arg), picarse* (arg)

■ **shoot** *vi*

A 1 (fire weapon) disparar; **don't move or I'll ~!** ¡no se mueva o disparo!; **to ~ to kill** disparar *or* tirar a matar; **to ~ AT sb/sth** dispararle A algn/A algo 2 (hunt) cazar*; **to go ~ing** ir* de caza 3 (proceed) (colloq): **can I ask you something? — sure, ~!** ¿te puedo preguntar algo? — claro ¡dispara! *or* (AmL) ¡pregunta nomás!

B (move swiftly): **their record shot straight to number one** su disco subió directamente al número uno; **she ~ past** pasó como una bala *or* como un bólido (fam); **he shot out of his seat** saltó del asiento

C (Sport) tirar, disparar, chutar, chutear (CS); **to ~ at goal** tirar al arco *or* (Esp) a puerta

(Phrasal verbs)

- **shoot down** [v ▸ o ▸ adv, v ▸ adv ▸ o] 1 ‹*plane*› derribar, abatir 2 ‹*argument*› rebatir
- **shoot for** [v ▸ prep ▸ o] (AmE) aspirar a
- **shoot off** [v ▸ adv] (leave quickly) irse* *or* salir* disparado *or* (fam) como un bólido
- **shoot out**

A [v ▸ adv] (emerge quickly) salir* disparado *or* (fam) como un bólido

B [v ▸ o ▸ adv, v ▸ adv ▸ o] ***to ~ it out (with sb)***: **the terrorists shot it out with the police** los terroristas y la policía la emprendieron a tiros

- **shoot up** [v ▸ adv] 1 (grow tall) crecer* mucho 2 (go up quickly) «*prices/temperature*» dispararse; «*flames*» alzarse*; «*buildings*» aparecer* (de la nada) 3 (inject drugs) (sl) chutarse (arg), picarse* (arg)

shoot[3] *interj* (AmE colloq) ¡miércoles! (fam & euf), ¡mecachis! (fam & euf)

shooter /ˈʃuːtər || ˈʃuːtə(r)/ *n* (sl) pistola *f*, chata *f* (Esp arg), hierro *m* (Ven arg)

shooting /ˈʃuːtɪŋ/ *n*

A 1 [u] (exchange of fire) tiroteo *m*, balacera *f* (AmL), baleo *m* (Chi); (shots) tiros *mpl*, disparos *mpl* 2 [u c] (killing) asesinato *m*; (execution) fusilamiento *m*

B [u] (hunting) caza *f*

C [u] (Cin) rodaje *m*, filmación *f*

shooting: ~ **gallery** *n* barraca *f or* puesto *m* de tiro al blanco; ~ **match** *n*: **the whole ~ match** (colloq) todo el tinglado (fam); ~ **star** *n* estrella *f* fugaz

shoot-out /ˈʃuːtaʊt/ *n* tiroteo *m*, balacera *f* (AmL), baleo *m* (Chi)

shop[1] /ʃɑːp || ʃɒp/ *n*

A 1 [c] (retail outlet) tienda *f*, negocio *m* (CS), comercio *m* (frml); **to go to the ~s** ir* de compras; **what time do the ~s close?** ¿a qué hora cierran las tiendas?; ***all over the ~*** (BrE colloq) por todas partes 2 (business) (colloq): **to set up ~ as a doctor** abrir* una consulta, establecerse* como médico; **to shut up ~** cerrar*; ***to talk ~*** hablar del trabajo

B [u] (AmE Educ) taller *m*, manualidades *fpl*

shop[2] **-pp-** *vi* hacer* compras, comprar; **to go ~ping** ir* de compras *or* de tiendas; **to ~ FOR sth**: **we were ~ping for Christmas presents** estábamos comprando los regalos de Navidad; **she went ~ping for a winter coat** salió a buscar un abrigo de invierno

■ **shop** *vt*

A (inform on) (BrE sl) vender

B (visit store) (AmE) recorrer

(Phrasal verb)

- **shop around** [v ▸ adv] (colloq) comparar precios

shop: ~ **assistant** *n* (BrE) dependiente, -ta *m,f*, empleado, -da *m,f* (de tienda) (AmL), vendedor, -dora *m,f* (CS); ~ **floor** *n* (part of factory) taller *m*; (workers) obreros *mpl*, trabajadores *mpl*; (as union members) bases *fpl* sindicales; ~ **front** *n* (BrE) fachada *f* (*de una tienda*); ~**keeper** *n* comerciante *mf*, tendero, -ra *m,f*; ~**lifter** /ˈʃɑːpˌlɪftər || ˈʃɒpˌlɪftə(r)/ *n* ladrón, -drona *m,f* (*que roba en las tiendas*), mechero, -ra *m,f* (arg); ~**lifting** /ˈʃɑːpˌlɪftɪŋ || ˈʃɒpˌlɪftɪŋ/ *n* [u] hurto *m* (*en las tiendas*)

shopper /ˈʃɑːpər || ˈʃɒpə(r)/ *n* comprador, -dora *m,f*

shopping /ˈʃɑːpɪŋ || ˈʃɒpɪŋ/ *n* [u] 1 (act): **to do the ~** hacer* la compra *or* (AmS) las compras, hacer* el mercado (Col, Ven), hacer* el mandado (Méx); (*before n*) ‹*basket*› de la compra *or* (AmS) de las compras 2 (purchases) compras *fpl*

shopping: ~ **bag** *n* 1 (given by store) (AmE) bolsa *f* (*de plástico, papel etc*) 2 (owned by customer) (BrE) bolsa *f* (de la compra *or* (AmS) de las compras); ~ **cart** *n* (AmE) carrito *m* (de la compra *or* (AmS) de las compras); ~ **center**, (BrE) ~ **centre** ▸ ~ **mall**; ~ **list** *n* lista *f* de la compra *or* (Col, Ven) del mercado *or* (Méx) del mandado *or* (AmS) de las compras; ~ **mall** *n* (esp AmE) centro *m* comercial; ~ **trolley** *n* (BrE) 1 ▸ ~ **cart** 2 (bag on wheels) carrito *m*, changuito *m* (RPl)

S

shop: **~-soiled** *adj* deteriorado; **~ steward** *n* representante *mf or* (Esp) enlace *mf* sindical; **~ window** *n* escaparate *m*, vitrina *f* (AmL), aparador *m* (AmC, Col, Méx); **~worn** *adj* (AmE) ‹*goods*› deteriorado; ‹*clichés*› gastado

shore¹ /ʃɔːr || ʃɔː(r)/ *n*

A [c] **1** (of sea, lake) orilla *f*; **they have a house by the ~** tienen una casa a la orilla del mar/lago **2** (coast) costa *f*, ribera *f*; **a mile off ~** a una milla de la costa

B **1** [u] (land): **to go on ~** bajar a tierra (firme) **2** **shores** *pl* (country) (liter) tierras *fpl*; **on these ~s** en estas tierras

shore² *vt* ▸ **shore up**

(Phrasal verb)

• **shore up** [v ▸ o ▸ adv, v ▸ adv ▸ o] ‹*building/wall*› apuntalar; ‹*share price*› sostener*, apuntalar

shoreline /ˈʃɔːrlaɪn || ˈʃɔːlaɪn/ *n* costa *f*, ribera *f*

shorn /ʃɔːrn || ʃɔːn/ *past p of* **shear** *vt* **A**

short¹ /ʃɔːrt || ʃɔːt/ *adj* **-er, -est**

A (of length, height, distance) ‹*hair/skirt/grass*› corto; ‹*person*› bajo; **they only live a ~ way off** *o* **away** viven muy cerca; **we've only got a ~ way to go** ya nos falta poco (para llegar)

B **1** (brief) ‹*visit/vacation/trip*› corto; **the days are getting ~er** los días van acortándose; **a ~ time ago** hace poco (tiempo); **a ~ while ago** hace poco rato, hace un ratito (fam); **in just a few ~ years** en pocos años; **to have a ~ memory** tener* mala memoria; **the ~ answer to that is no** en una palabra: no; **Liz is ~ for Elizabeth** Liz es el diminutivo de Elizabeth; **we call him Rob for ~** lo llamamos Rob para abreviar; **~ and sweet** (set phrase): **her visit was ~ and sweet** su visita fue corta: lo bueno si breve dos veces bueno **2** (Ling) ‹*vowel/syllable*› breve **3** **in short** (briefly) (*as linker*) en resumen, resumiendo

C (brusque, impatient) ‹*manner*› brusco, cortante; **she has a ~ temper** tiene muy mal genio

D (inadequate, deficient) escaso; **to be in ~ supply** escasear; **time is getting ~** queda poco tiempo, se está acabando el tiempo; **we're/they're still ~ six people** (AmE) *o* (BrE) **six people ~** todavía nos/les faltan seis personas; **(to be) ~ OF sth/sb**: **we're very ~ of time** estamos muy cortos *or* escasos de tiempo; **they were ~ of staff** no tenían suficiente personal; **do you get ~ of breath?** ¿se queda sin aliento?; **we're still a long way ~ of our target** estamos todavía muy lejos de nuestro objetivo; **he's just ~ of six feet tall** mide poco menos de seis pies; **nothing ~ of a miracle can save us now** sólo un milagro nos puede salvar

short² *adv*

A (suddenly, abruptly): **he cut ~ his vacation** interrumpió sus vacaciones; **he stopped ~ when he saw me** se paró en seco cuando me vio; **they stopped ~ of firing him** les faltó poco para echarlo; **he was brought up ~ by what she said** lo que ella dijo lo dejó helado; ***to be caught ~*** (need toilet) (colloq): **I was caught ~ at the station** me entraron unas ganas terribles de ir al baño *or* al servicio en la estación

B (below target, requirement): **to fall ~** «*shell/arrow*» quedarse corto; **to fall ~ OF sth**: **we fell ~ of our target** no alcanzamos nuestro objetivo; **to fall ... ~ OF sth**: **the arrow fell several meters ~ of its target** la flecha cayó a varios metros del blanco; **to go ~ (OF sth)**: **we never went ~ of food** nunca nos faltó la comida; **my patience is running ~** se me está acabando *or* agotando la paciencia

short³ *n*

A (Elec) cortocircuito *m*, corto *m*

B (Cin) cortometraje *m*, corto *m*

C (drink) (BrE) *copa de bebida alcohólica de las que se sirven en pequeñas cantidades, como el whisky o el coñac*

D **shorts** *pl* **1** (short trousers) shorts *mpl*, pantalones *mpl* cortos; **a pair of ~s** unos shorts; **bathing ~s** traje *m* de baño, bañador *m* (Esp) **2** (men's underwear) (AmE) calzoncillos *mpl*

short⁴ *vi* (Elec) hacer* un cortocircuito

■ **short** *vt* provocar* un cortocircuito en

(Phrasal verb)

• **short out** (AmE Elec)

A [v ▸ adv] «*fuse*» fundirse; «*iron/hairdryer*» hacer* (un) cortocircuito

B [v ▸ o ▸ adv, v ▸ adv ▸ o] ‹*fuse*› fundir

shortage /ˈʃɔːrtɪdʒ || ˈʃɔːtɪdʒ/ *n* [c u] **~ (OF sth/sb)** falta *f or* escasez *f* (DE algo/algn); **there is no ~ of ideas/helpers** no faltan ideas/colaboradores

short: **~bread** *n* [u] *galleta dulce de mantequilla*; **~cake** *n* **1** [u c] *tarta de fruta* **2** [u] (BrE) *tipo de* **~bread**; **~-change** /ˈʃɔːrtˈtʃeɪndʒ || ˌʃɔːtˈtʃeɪndʒ/ *vt* **1** (in shop): **he ~-changed me** me dio mal el cambio *or* (AmL tb) el vuelto, me dio de menos **2** (deprive of due) (colloq) no ser* justo con; **~ circuit** *n* (Elec) cortocircuito *m*; **~-circuit** /ˈʃɔːrtˈsɜːrkət || ˌʃɔːtˈsɜːkɪt/ *vt* provocar* un cortocircuito en. *vi* hacer* (un) cortocircuito; **~coming** *n* defecto *m*, deficiencia *f*, punto *m* flaco (fam); **~crust (pastry)** *n* [u] (BrE) pasta *f* quebradiza (*tipo de masa para empanadas, tartas etc*); **~ cut** *n* **1** (route) atajo *m*; **to take a ~ cut** tomar un atajo, (a)cortar camino **2** (time-saving method): **there are no ~ cuts to success** no hay fórmulas mágicas para el éxito; (*before n*) **~-cut key** atajo *m* de teclado, tecla *f* de acceso directo

shorten /ˈʃɔːrtn̩ || ˈʃɔːtn̩/ *vt* ‹*skirt/sleeves*› acortar; ‹*text/report*› acortar, abreviar; **plans to ~ the working week** planes para reducir la jornada laboral; **to ~ the odds** aumentar las probabilidades

■ **shorten** *vi* «*days/nights*» acortarse

short: **~fall** *n* **~fall (IN sth)**: **a ~fall of 7% in revenues** un déficit de 7% en los ingresos; **this year there's been a ~fall in science graduates** este año el número de licenciados en ciencias ha estado por debajo de lo esperado; **~-haired** /ˈʃɔːrtherd || ˌʃɔːtˈheəd/ *adj* de pelo corto; **~hand** *n* [u] taquigrafía *f*; **~-handed** /ˈʃɔːrtˈhændəd || ˌʃɔːtˈhændɪd/ *adj*: **we are ~-handed** no tenemos mano de obra/personal suficiente; **~hand typist** *n* (BrE) taquimecanógrafo, -fa *m,f*; **~-haul** /ˈʃɔːrtˈhɔːl || ˌʃɔːtˈhɔːl/ *adj* (*before n*) ‹*flight*› corto, de corto recorrido; ‹*route*› de vuelos cortos; **~ list** *n* lista *f* de candidatos preseleccionados; **~-list** *vt* preseleccionar; **~-lived** /ˈʃɔːrtˈlɪvd/ *adj* ‹*success/enthusiasm*› efímero, fugaz; ‹*recovery*› pasajero; **her happiness was ~-lived** la felicidad le duró poco

shorthand typing *n* [u] taquimecanografía *f*

shortly /ˈʃɔːrtli || ˈʃɔːtli/ *adv* **1** (soon) dentro de poco; **he'll be leaving ~ for Paris** saldrá dentro de poco *or* (frml) en breve para París; **I'll be with you ~** enseguida estoy con usted, no tardaré en atenderlo; **~ before/after midnight** poco antes/después de la medianoche **2** (briefly) en una palabra **3** (curtly) bruscamente

shortness /ˈʃɔːrtnəs || ˈʃɔːtnɪs/ *n* [u]

A **1** (of hair, skirt) lo corto; (of person) baja estatura *f*; (of distance) lo corto; (of message) brevedad *f* **2** (of visit, trip) brevedad *f*, lo breve **3** (brusqueness) brusquedad *f*

B (deficiency) **~ OF sth** ‹*of time/money/staff*› falta *f* DE algo; **~ of breath** falta *f* de aliento

short: **~-range** /ˈʃɔːrtˈreɪndʒ || ˌʃɔːtˈreɪndʒ/ *adj* ‹*missile/weapon*› de corto alcance; ‹*aircraft*› de autonomía limitada, de corto radio de acción; ‹*forecast/prediction*› a corto plazo; **~sighted** /ˈʃɔːrtˈsaɪtəd || ˌʃɔːtˈsaɪtɪd/ *adj* **1** (esp BrE Med) miope, corto de vista **2** ‹*attitude/policy*› corto de miras, miope, con poca visión de futuro; **~sightedness** /ˈʃɔːrtˈsaɪtədnəs || ˌʃɔːtˈsaɪtɪdnɪs/ *n* [u] **1** (Med) miopía *f* **2** (of action, policy) falta *f* de visión (de futuro), miopía *f*; **~-sleeved** /ˈʃɔːrtˈsliːvd || ˌʃɔːtˈsliːvd/ *adj* de manga corta; **~-staffed** /ˈʃɔːrtˈstæft || ˌʃɔːtˈstɑːft/ *adj*: **they/we were ~-staffed** les/nos faltaba personal, no tenían/no teníamos personal suficiente; **~-stay** /ˈʃɔːrtˈsteɪ || ˌʃɔːtˈsteɪ/ *adj* (*before n*) (BrE): **~-stay car park** estacionamiento *m or* (Esp) aparcamiento *m* para períodos cortos; **~stop** *n* (in baseball — position) short stop *m*, paracorto *m* (Col, Ven), paradas *fpl* cortas (Méx); (— player) torpedero, -ra *m,f*, parador, -dora *m,f* en corto (Méx); **~ story** *n* cuento *m*, narración *f* corta, relato *m* breve; (*before n*) **~-story writer** cuentista *mf*; **~-tempered** /ˈʃɔːrtˈtempərd || ˌʃɔːtˈtempəd/ *adj* de mal genio, irascible; **~-term** /ˈʃɔːrtˈtɜːrm || ˌʃɔːtˈtɜːm/ *adj* ‹*planning/benefits/memory*› a corto plazo; **~ time** *n* [u] (BrE) jornada *f* reducida *or* de horario reducido; **~wave** /ˈʃɔːrtˈweɪv || ˌʃɔːtˈweɪv/ *n* [u] onda *f* corta

shot¹ /ʃɑːt || ʃɒt/ *past & past p of* **shoot²**

shot² *n*

A [c] **1** (from gun, rifle) disparo *m*, tiro *m*, balazo *m*; (from cannon) cañonazo *m*; **she fired three ~s** disparó tres veces; ***a ~ in the dark*** un palo de ciego; ***like a ~***: **if they offered it to me, I'd take it like a ~** si me lo ofrecieran, no dudaría un minuto en aceptarlo (fam); **she was off like**

a ~ salió disparada *or* (fam) como un bólido; ***parting ~*** palabras *fpl* de despedida; ***to call the ~s*** mandar 2 (marksman): **a good/poor ~** un buen/mal tirador

B (colloq) 1 [c] (attempt, try): **it costs $50 a ~** son 50 dólares por vez; **~ AT sth/-ING**: **I'd like another ~ at it** me gustaría volver a intentarlo *or* volver a hacer la tentativa; **have a ~ at it** ¿por qué no lo intentas?, haz la prueba; **she had another ~ at convincing them** nuevamente trató de convencerlos; **he gave it his best ~** lo hizo lo mejor que pudo 2 (chance) (*no pl*): **an 8 to 1 ~** una probabilidad entre 8; ***a long ~***: **it's a very long ~, but it might just work** es una posibilidad muy remota pero quizás resulte; ***not by a long ~*** ni por asomo, ni mucho menos

C [c] 1 (Phot) foto *f* 2 (Cin) toma *f*; **location ~s** exteriores *mpl*

D [u] (pellets): **(lead) ~** perdigones *mpl*

E [c] (used in shotput) bala *f*, peso *m* (Esp); **to put the ~** lanzar* la bala *or* (Esp) el peso

F [c] (in soccer) disparo *m*, tiro *m*, chut *m*, chute *m*; (in basketball) tiro *m*, tirada *f*; (in golf, tennis) tiro *m*

G [c] 1 (injection) inyección *f*; ***a ~ in the arm*** una ayuda, un estímulo 2 (of drink) poquito *m*

shot³ *adj*

A 1 (variegated): **~ silk** seda *f* tornasolada 2 (pervaded, permeated): **to be ~ through with sth** tener* un dejo *or* un matiz de algo

B (worn-out) (esp AmE colloq) deshecho, hecho polvo (fam)

C (rid) (BrE colloq): **to get ~ of sth/sb** sacarse* *or* quitarse algo/a algn de encima, deshacerse* de algo/algn

shot: **~gun** *n* escopeta *f*; (*before n*) **they had a ~gun wedding** se tuvieron que casar, se casaron de penalty (Esp) *or* (Méx) de emergencia *or* (RPl) de apuro *or* (Chi) apurados (fam); **~put** /ˈʃɑːtpʊt || ˈʃɒtpʊt/ *n* (event) lanzamiento *m* de bala *or* (Esp) de peso; **~-putter** /ˈʃɑːtˌpʊtər || ˈʃɒtˌpʊtə(r)/ *n* lanzador, -dora *m,f* de bala *or* (Esp) de peso

should¹ /ʃʊd/ *past of* **shall**

should² *v mod*

A (expressing desirability) debería (*or* deberías *etc*), debiera (*or* debieras *etc*); **you ~ be studying** deberías *or* debieras estar estudiando, tendrías que estar estudiando; **you ~ have thought of that before** deberías *or* debieras haber pensado en eso antes, tendrías *or* tenías que haber pensado en eso antes; **I've brought you some flowers — oh, you ~n't have** te he traído unas flores — ¡no te deberías *or* debieras haber molestado! *or* ¡no te tenías *or* tendrías que haber molestado!; **you ~'ve seen the look on her face!** ¡tenías *or* tendrías que haber visto la cara que puso!

B (indicating probability, logical expectation) debería (*or* deberías *etc*) (de), debiera (*or* debieras *etc*) (de); **it ~ add up to 100** tendría que *or* debería (de) *or* debiera (de) dar *or* sumar 100; **how ~ I know?** ¿cómo quieres que sepa?, ¿cómo voy a saber (yo)?; **why ~ they want to come here?** ¿por qué han *or* habrían de querer venir aquí?

C (*with first person only*) 1 (conditional use) (BrE frml): **I ~ like to see her** me gustaría verla; **I ~n't be surprised if they didn't turn up** no me sorprendería que no aparecieran 2 (venturing a guess) (BrE): **I ~n't think it's very old** no creo que sea muy antiguo; **I ~ think she must be over 80** yo diría que debe tener más de 80 3 (expressing indignation): **he said he was sorry — I ~ think so too!** pidió perdón — ¡faltaría más! *or* ¡era lo menos que podía hacer!; **she won't be asking us for any money — I ~ think not!** no nos va a pedir dinero — ¡faltaría más! *or* ¡sería el colmo!

D (subjunctive use) (*with all persons*): **it's natural that he ~ want to go with her** es natural *or* lógico que quiera ir con ella; **if you ~ happen to pass a bookshop ...** si pasaras *or* si llegaras a pasar por una librería ...

E (expressing amused surprise): **and who ~ turn up but her ex-husband!** ¿y quién te parece que apareció? ¡su ex-marido!

shoulder¹ /ˈʃəʊldər || ˈʃəʊldə(r)/ *n*

A 1 (Anat) hombro *m*; **to look over one's ~** mirar por encima del hombro; **to stand ~ to ~** estar* hombro con hombro; **to cry** *o* **weep on sb's ~** desahogarse* con algn; **a ~ to cry on** un paño de lágrimas; ***straight from the ~*** sin rodeos; ***to give sb the cold ~*** hacerle* el vacío a algn; ***to rub ~s with sb*** codearse con algn 2 (Clothing) hombro *m* 3 (Culin) paletilla *f*, paleta *f*

B (of road) arcén *m*, berma *f* (Andes), acotamiento *m* (Méx), banquina *f* (RPl), hombrillo *m* (Ven)

shoulder² *vt* 1 (place on shoulder) ‹*knapsack*› ponerse* *or* echarse al hombro; ‹*blame/responsibility*› cargar* con 2 (push) empujar con el hombro; **I was ~ed aside** me hicieron a un lado a empujones; ***to ~ one's way*** abrirse* paso a empujones

shoulder: **~ bag** *n* bolso *m* *or* (CS) cartera *f* *or* (Méx) bolsa *f* (*con correa larga para colgar del hombro*); **~ blade** *n* omóplato *m*; **~-length** /ˈʃəʊldərˈleŋθ || ˌʃəʊldəˈleŋθ/ *adj*: **~-length hair** pelo *m* *or* melena *f* hasta los hombros; **~ pad** *n* hombrera *f*; **~ strap** *n* (of garment) tirante *m* *or* (CS) bretel *m*; (of bag) correa *f*

shouldn't /ˈʃʊdn̩t/ = **should not**

shout¹ /ʃaʊt/ *n* grito *m*; **give me a ~ when you're ready** (colloq) avísame cuando estés listo, pégame un grito cuando estés listo (fam)

shout² *vi* gritar; **to ~ AT sb** gritarle A algn; **don't ~ at me** ¡no me grites!; **to ~ TO sb** gritarle A algn; **to ~ FOR sb** llamar a algn a gritos; **to ~ FOR sth** pedir* algo a gritos; **to ~ for help** pedir* auxilio a gritos; **to ~ for joy** gritar de alegría

■ **shout** *vt* gritar; **I ~ed (out) a warning** les (*or* le *etc*) grité advirtiéndoles (*or* advirtiéndole *etc*)

■ *v refl*: **to ~ oneself hoarse** gritar hasta quedarse ronco *or* afónico

Phrasal verbs

- **shout down** [v ▸ o ▸ adv, v ▸ adv ▸ o] hacer* callar a gritos
- **shout out**

A [v ▸ o ▸ adv, v ▸ adv ▸ o] ‹*answer*› gritar, dar* a gritos

B [v ▸ adv] dar* *or* pegar* un grito

shouting /ˈʃaʊtɪŋ/ *n* [u] griterío *m*, vocerío *m*; ***it's all over but*** *o* (BrE) ***bar the ~*** esto ya es cosa hecha *or* asunto concluido; (*before n*) **to have a ~ match** (colloq) pelearse a gritos *or* a voces

shove¹ /ʃʌv/ *vt* 1 (push roughly) empujar; **she ~d him away** lo apartó de un empujón; **they ~d her out of the way** la quitaron de en medio a empellones *or* a empujones 2 (put) (colloq) poner*, meter

■ **shove** *vi* empujar; **everyone was pushing and shoving** todo el mundo andaba a (los) empujones *or* a (los) empellones; **~ over/up!** (colloq) córrete, hazte a un lado

Phrasal verb

- **shove off** [v ▸ adv] 1 (Naut) desatracar* 2 (leave) (colloq) largarse* (fam)

shove² *n* empujón *m*, empellón *m*

shovel¹ /ˈʃʌvəl/ *n*

A (spade) pala *f*

B (*power ~*) excavadora *f*

shovel² *vt*, (BrE) **-ll-** ‹*coal*› palear; ‹*snow*› espalar; **he ~ed his food down** (colloq) engulló *or* se zampó la comida

shovelful /ˈʃʌvəlfʊl/ *n* palada *f*

show¹ /ʃəʊ/ (*past* **showed**; *past p* **shown** *or* **showed**) *vt*

A 1 ‹*photograph/passport*› mostrar*, enseñar; **to ~ sb sth, to ~ sth TO sb** mostrarle* algo A algn; **he won't ~ his face around here again** ése no vuelve a aparecer por aquí; ***to have nothing/something to ~ for sth***: **they had little/nothing to ~ for their years of work** vieron poco/no vieron recompensados sus años de trabajo; **she has something to ~ for her efforts** sus esfuerzos han dado fruto *or* le han reportado algo 2 ‹*feelings*› demostrar*, exteriorizar*; ‹*interest/enthusiasm/taste*› demostrar*, mostrar*; ‹*courage*› demostrar* (tener); **he ~s her no respect** no le tiene ningún respeto, le falta al respeto; **could you ~ me the way?** ¿me podría indicar el camino? 3 (allow to be seen): **this carpet ~s every mark** en esta alfombra se notan todas las marcas; **he's started to ~ his age** se le han empezado a notar los años

B 1 (depict, present): **this photo ~s her working in her garden** en esta foto está trabajando en el jardín; **does the map ~ places of interest?** ¿están señalados *or* marcados en el mapa los lugares de interés?; **as ~n in fig. 2** como se indica *or* se muestra en la figura 2 2 (record, register) ‹‹*barometer/dial/indicator*›› marcar*, señalar, indicar*; ‹*profit/loss*› arrojar; **the fuel light's ~ing red** la luz del combustible está en rojo

C 1 (demonstrate) ‹*truth/importance*› demostrar*; **it just goes to ~ how wrong you can be about people** eso te demuestra cómo te puedes equivocar con la gente 2 (teach) enseñar; **I ~ed her how to do it** le enseñé

cómo se hacía; **I'll ~ them!** (colloq) ¡ya van a ver!
D (by accompanying) (+ *adv compl*): **he ~ed us to our seats** nos llevó *or* nos acompañó hasta nuestros asientos; **to ~ sb in** hacer* pasar a algn; **to ~ sb out** acompañar a algn a la puerta; **I'll ~ myself out** no hace falta que me acompañes; **to ~ sb over a building** mostrarle* *or* enseñarle a algn un edificio; **they ~ed us around the church** nos mostraron el interior de la iglesia
E 1 (screen) ‹*movie*› dar*, pasar, proyectar (frml), poner* (Esp); ‹*program*› dar*, poner* (Esp), emitir (frml); ‹*slides*› pasar, proyectar (frml); **they ~ed the game on TV** dieron el partido por televisión 2 (exhibit) ‹*paintings/sculpture*› exponer*, exhibir; ‹*horse/dog*› presentar, exponer*
■ **show** *vi*
A (be visible) «*dirt/stain*» verse*, notarse; «*emotion/scar*» notarse; **your petticoat is ~ing** se te ve la enagua; **I did it in a hurry — yes, it ~s!** lo hice deprisa y corriendo — ¡sí, se nota! *or* ¡sí, y así quedó!; **to ~ through** verse*; **you mustn't let your feelings ~** no dejes transparentar lo que sientes
B 1 (be screened) (Cin): **it's ~ing at the Trocadero** la están dando en el Trocadero, la ponen en el Trocadero (Esp) 2 (exhibit) «*artist*» exponer*, exhibir
C (turn up) (colloq) aparecer*
■ *v refl* **to ~ oneself** 1 (become visible) «*person*» asomarse, dejarse ver 2 (prove to be) demostrar* ser; (turn out to be) resultar ser; **he ~ed himself to be a great player** demostró ser un gran jugador

Phrasal verbs

• **show off**
A [v ▸ adv] lucirse*; **stop ~ing off** déjate de hacer tonterías *or* gracias
B [v ▸ o ▸ adv, v ▸ adv ▸ o] 1 (display for admiration) ‹*wealth/knowledge*› presumir de, hacer* alarde de; **he wanted to ~ off his new car** quería lucir el coche nuevo; **to ~ sth off TO sb** mostrarle* *or* enseñarle orgullosamente algo A algn 2 (display to advantage) ‹*beauty/complexion*› hacer* resaltar, realzar*

• **show up**
A [v ▸ o ▸ adv, v ▸ adv ▸ o] 1 (reveal) ‹*mistake/deception*› poner* de manifiesto (frml) 2 (embarrass) ‹*parents/friends*› hacer* quedar mal 3 (lead upstairs) ‹*visitor/guest*› hacer* subir
B [v ▸ adv] 1 (be visible) «*imperfection*» notarse 2 (be revealed) «*trend/fact*» revelarse, ponerse* de manifiesto 3 (arrive) (colloq) aparecer* (fam)

show² *n*
A [c] (exhibition) (Art) exposición *f*; **agricultural ~** feria *f* agrícola y ganadera, exposición *f* rural (RPl); **boat ~** salón *m* náutico; **to be on ~** estar* expuesto *or* en exhibición; **to put sth on ~** exponer* algo; (*before n*) **~ house** (BrE) casa *f* piloto
B [c] 1 (stage production) espectáculo *m*; **to put on a ~** montar un espectáculo; ***the ~ must go on*** hay que seguir adelante; ***to get the ~ on the road*** (colloq) poner* manos a la obra; **let's get this ~ on the road** ¡manos a la obra!; ***to steal the ~*** «*actor*» robarse el espectáculo, llevarse todos los aplausos 2 (on television, radio) programa *m*; **the Olga Winters S~** el show de Olga Winters
C (*no pl*) 1 (display) muestra *f*, demostración *f*; **a ~ of force** un despliegue de fuerza; **to vote by a ~ of hands** votar a mano alzada 2 (outward appearance): **I made a ~ of enthusiasm** fingí estar entusiasmado; **their plush office is simply for ~** su elegante oficina es sólo para darse tono; **with a great ~ of indignation** con grandes muestras de indignación
D (colloq) (*no pl*) 1 (activity, organization) asunto *m*; **to run the ~** llevar la voz cantante, llevar la batuta (fam), ser* el amo del cotarro (fam) 2 (performance) (BrE): **to put up a good/poor ~** hacer* un buen/mal papel, defenderse* bien/mal; **good ~!** ¡espléndido!, ¡bravo!; **poor ~!** ¡qué mal!

show: **~biz** /ˈʃəʊbɪz/ *n* [u] (colloq) mundo *m* del espectáculo, farándula *f* (period); (*before n*) ‹*personality/news*› del mundo del espectáculo; **~boat** *n* 1 (Theat) *barco donde se dan representaciones teatrales* 2 (AmE) ▸ **show-off**; **~ business** *n* [u] mundo *m* del espectáculo, farándula *f* (period)

showcase¹ /ˈʃəʊkeɪs/ *n*
A (advantageous setting): **the series is simply a ~ for its stars** la serie no es más que un vehículo para el lucimiento de sus estrellas
B (cabinet) vitrina *f*

showcase² *vt* (AmE) exhibir

showdown /ˈʃəʊdaʊn/ *n* enfrentamiento *m*, confrontación *f*; **to have a ~ with sb** enfrentarse con algn, tener* una agarrada *or* (AmL tb) un agarrón con algn (fam)

shower¹ /ˈʃaʊər || ˈʃaʊə(r)/ *n*
A (in bathroom) ducha *f*, regadera *f* (Méx); **he's in the ~** se está duchando *or* bañando; **to take** *o* (BrE) **have a ~** ducharse, darse* una ducha, bañarse; (*before n*) **~ cap** gorro *m* de ducha; **~ curtain** cortina *f* de ducha; **~ gel** gel *m* de baño
B (Meteo) chaparrón *m*, chubasco *m*; (heavier) aguacero *m*; **a ~ of sparks** una lluvia de chispas
C (people) (BrE colloq) (*no pl*) panda *f* *or* (CS) manga *f* de inútiles (*or* pesados *etc*) (fam)
D (party) (AmE) *fiesta en la que los invitados obsequian a la homenajeada con motivo de su próxima boda, el nacimiento de su niño etc*

shower² *vt* 1 (spray) regar*; **to ~ sb WITH sth** tirarle algo A algn 2 (bestow lavishly) **to ~ sth ON sb**: **congratulations were ~ed (up)on the winner** le llovieron felicitaciones al ganador; **to ~ sb WITH sth**: **the country ~ed him with honors** el país lo colmó de honores
■ **shower** *vi* 1 (wash) ducharse, darse* una ducha, bañarse 2 (be sprayed) «*water/leaves/stones*» caer*; «*letters/congratulations/protests*» llover*

showerproof /ˈʃaʊərpruːf || ˈʃaʊəpruːf/ *adj* semi-impermeable

showery /ˈʃaʊəri/ *adj* ‹*weather/day*› lluvioso, de lluvia

show: **~girl** *n* corista *f*; **~ground** *n* recinto *m* ferial, real *m* de la feria

showing /ˈʃəʊɪŋ/ *n*
A (performance) actuación *f*; **their poor ~ in the last elections** el pobre resultado que obtuvieron en las últimas elecciones; **to make a good/poor ~** hacer* (un) buen/mal papel; **on her present ~** tal como está ahora
B (Cin, TV) proyección *f*, pase *m*

show: **~ jumper** *n* 1 (male) jinete *m*; (female) amazona *f*, jinete *f* 2 (horse) caballo *m* de salto; **~ jumping** *n* [u] concursos *mpl* hípicos; **~man** /ˈʃəʊmən/ *n* (*pl* **-men** /-mən/) (entertainer) artista *m*, showman *m*; (producer) empresario *m*, hombre *m* del espectáculo

showmanship /ˈʃəʊmənʃɪp/ *n* [u] sentido *m* de la teatralidad

shown /ʃəʊn/ *past p of* **show¹**

show: **~-off** *n* (colloq) fanfarrón, -rrona *m,f*, fantasma *mf* (Esp fam), fardón, -dona *m,f* (Esp fam); **~room** *n* (*often pl*) salón *m* de exposición (y ventas); **~-stopper** /ˈʃəʊˌstɑːpər || ˈʃəʊˌstɒpə(r)/ *n* (colloq): **to be a (real) ~-stopper** causar sensación; **~ trial** *n*: *juicio llevado a cabo como demostración de poderío*

showy /ˈʃəʊi/ *adj* **showier, showiest** 1 (gaudy) ‹*clothes*› llamativo; ‹*behavior*› extravagante 2 (attractive) ‹*clothes/plumage/flowers*› vistoso, llamativo

shrank /ʃræŋk/ *past of* **shrink¹**

shrapnel /ˈʃræpnl/ *n* [u] metralla *f*

shred¹ /ʃred/ *n* (of paper, fabric) tira *f*, trozo *m*; (of tobacco) brizna *f*, hebra *f*; **not a (single) ~ of evidence** ni una (sola) prueba; **not a ~ of truth** ni pizca de verdad; **to be in ~s** «*clothes/fabric*» estar* hecho jirones *or* tiras; «*argument/reputation*» estar* destrozado *or* hecho trizas; **to tear sth to ~s** ‹*paper/material*› hacer* trizas algo; ‹*argument/reputation*› destrozar* algo, hacer* trizas algo; **to tear sb to ~s** hacer* trizas a algn

shred² *vt* **-dd-** ‹*cabbage/lettuce*› cortar en tiras; ‹*documents*› destruir*, triturar

shredder /ˈʃredər || ˈʃredə(r)/ *n* (for paper) trituradora *f*; (for vegetables) cortadora *f*

shrew /ʃruː/ *n* 1 (Zool) musaraña *f* 2 (woman) arpía *f*, bruja *f*, fiera *f*

shrewd /ʃruːd/ *adj* **-er, -est** ‹*person*› astuto, sagaz, vivo (fam); ‹*move/investment*› hábil, inteligente; ‹*argument/assessment*› hábil, perspicaz, sagaz; ‹*remark*› perspicaz; **he's a ~ businessman** es un astuto hombre de negocios

shriek¹ /ʃriːk/ *n* (of delight, terror) grito *m*, chillido *m*; (of pain) grito *m*, alarido *m*; **we could hear ~s of laughter** oíamos risotadas

shriek² *vi* gritar, chillar; **to ~ with laughter** reírse* histéricamente; **to ~ AT sb** gritarle *or* chillarle A algn

S

■ **shriek** *vt* gritar, chillar

shrift /ʃrɪft/ *n* [u]: **to give sth short ~** ‹*idea/suggestion*› desestimar *or* desechar algo de plano; **to give sb short ~** echar a algn con cajas destempladas; **the idea got short ~** la idea fue desestimada *or* desechada de plano

shrill /ʃrɪl/ *adj* **-er, -est** ‹*whistle/cry/laugh*› agudo, estridente; ‹*voice*› agudo, chillón

shrimp /ʃrɪmp/ *n*
A (*pl* **~** *or* (BrE also) **~s**) (large) (AmE) langostino *m*, camarón *m* (AmL); (medium) camarón *m* (AmL), gamba *f* (esp Esp), langostino *m* (CS); (small) (BrE) camarón *m*, quisquilla *f* (Esp); (*before n*) **~ cocktail** *see* **cocktail 2**
B (*pl* **~s**) (small person) (colloq & pej) renacuajo, -ja *m,f* (fam & pey), enano, -na *m,f* (fam & pey)

shrine /ʃraɪn/ *n* (holy place) santuario *m*, santo lugar *m*; (chapel) capilla *f*; (in out-of-the-way place) ermita *f*

shrink¹ /ʃrɪŋk/ (*past* **shrank** *or* **shrunk**; *past p* **shrunk** *or* **shrunken**) *vi*
A (diminish in size) «*clothes/fabric*» encoger(se)*; «*meat*» achicarse*; «*wood/metal*» contraerse*; «*area*» reducirse*, verse* reducido (frml); «*amount/number*» reducirse*, disminuir*; «*person*» achicarse*
B (recoil) retroceder, recular (fam); **to ~ back** *o* **away from sth/sb** echarse atrás *or* retroceder ante algo/algn; **to ~ FROM sth/-ING**: **I will not ~ from the truth** no me voy a acobardar ante la verdad; **he will not ~ from doing his duty** no rehuirá cumplir con su obligación
■ **shrink** *vt* ‹*clothes/fabric*› encoger*; ‹*costs*› reducir*, recortar

shrink² *n* (colloq) loquero, -ra *m,f* (fam), psiquiatra *mf*

shrinkage /'ʃrɪŋkɪdʒ/ *n* [u] (of clothes, fabric) encogimiento *m*; (of wood, metal) contracción *f*

shrink: **~-resistant** /'ʃrɪŋkrɪˌzɪstənt/ *adj* que no encoge, inencogible; **~-wrap** /'ʃrɪŋk'ræp/ *vt* **-pp-** retractilar; **~-wrapped** /'ʃrɪŋkræpt/ *adj* **1** (in shrink-wrapping) ‹*goods*› retractilado **2** (Comput) de paquetes

shrivel /'ʃrɪvəl/, (BrE) **-ll-** **~ (up)** *vi* «*leaf/plant*» marchitarse, secarse*; «*fruit/vegetables*» resecarse* y arrugarse*, perder* frescura; «*skin*» ajarse, arrugarse
■ **shrivel** *vt* ‹*leaf/plant*› secar*, resecar*, marchitar

shroud¹ /ʃraʊd/ *n* (for corpse) mortaja *f*, sudario *m*; **a ~ of secrecy** (journ) un velo de silencio

shroud² *vt* envolver*; **to be ~ed IN sth**: **the town was ~ed in fog** (liter) un velo de niebla envolvía la ciudad (liter); **a case ~ed in mystery** (journ) un caso envuelto en un velo de misterio, un caso rodeado de misterio

Shrove Tuesday /ʃrəʊv/ *n* martes *m* de Carnaval

shrub /ʃrʌb/ *n* arbusto *m*, mata *f*

shrubbery /'ʃrʌbəri/ *n* (*pl* **-beries**) **1** [u] (mass of shrubs) arbustos *mpl*, matas *fpl* **2** [c] (part of garden) (esp BrE) macizo *m* de arbustos

shrug¹ /ʃrʌg/ *n*: **with a ~ (of her shoulders)** encogiéndose de hombros

shrug² **-gg-** *vi* encogerse* de hombros
■ **shrug** *vt*: **to ~ one's shoulders** encogerse* de hombros

Phrasal verb

• **shrug off** [v ▸ o ▸ adv, v ▸ adv ▸ o] ‹*misfortune/disappointment*› superar, sobreponerse* a; ‹*criticism*› hacer* caso omiso de, no dejarse afectar por

shrunk /ʃrʌŋk/ *past & past p of* **shrink¹**

shrunken¹ /ʃrʌnkən/ *past p of* **shrink¹**

shrunken² *adj* ‹*body*› consumido, empequeñecido; **a ~ head** una cabeza reducida

shuck /ʃʌk/ *vt* **1** ‹*pea*› pelar, desenvainar; ‹*clam*› abrir*, desbullar **2** **~ (off)** (AmE colloq) ‹*coat*› quitarse; ‹*boyfriend*› plantar (fam), botar (AmL exc RPl fam); ‹*career*› abandonar, plantar (fam), dejar botado (AmL exc RPl fam)

shucks /ʃʌks/ *interj* (AmE colloq) ¡caray! (fam), ¡caramba! (fam)

shudder¹ /'ʃʌdər ‖ 'ʃʌdə(r)/ *vi* **1** «*person*» estremecerse*; **I ~ to think what she might be doing** tiemblo de *or* con sólo pensar qué estará haciendo; **I ~ to think!** ¡no quiero ni pensar!, ¡me dan escalofríos de sólo pensarlo! **2** «*bus/train/plane*» dar* sacudidas *or* bandazos, zarandearse (de un lado al otro); «*building*» temblar*; «*machine*» vibrar; **to ~ to a halt** pararse abruptamente

shudder² *n* **1** (of person) estremecimiento *m*, escalofrío *m* **2** (of vehicle, engine) sacudida *f*

shuffle¹ /'ʃʌfəl/ *vt*
A **to ~ one's feet** arrastrar los pies
B ‹*cards*› barajar; ‹*papers*› barajar, revolver*
■ **shuffle** *vi* caminar *or* andar* arrastrando los pies; **his shuffling gait** su andar pesado

shuffle² *n*
A (gait) (*no pl*): **he walks with a ~** camina *or* anda arrastrando los pies
B **1** (of cards): **to give the cards a ~** barajar las cartas; ***to be*** *o* ***get lost in the ~*** (AmE) «*object*» perderse* en la confusión **2** (of personnel) reestructuración *f*

shun /ʃʌn/ *vt* **-nn-** ‹*person/society*› rechazar*, rehuir*; ‹*publicity/limelight*› evitar, rehuir*

shunt /ʃʌnt/ *vt* **1** (Rail) cambiar de vía **2** (move, divert) (+ *adv compl*): **they ~ed us from one window to another** nos mandaban de una ventanilla a la otra

shush /ʃʊʃ/ *vt* acallar, hacer* callar
■ **shush** *vi* (*usu in imperative*) callarse; **~!** ¡chitón!, ¡silencio!

shut¹ /ʃʌt/ (*pres p* **shutting**; *past & past p* **shut**) *vt*
A **1** ‹*window/book/eyes*› cerrar*; **she ~ her finger in the door** se agarró *or* se pilló el dedo en la puerta; **they ~ the door in my face** me dieron con la puerta en las narices; **~ your mouth!** (colloq) ¡cállate la boca! (fam), ¡cierra el pico! (fam) **2** ‹*store/business*› cerrar*
B (confine) encerrar*; **he ~ himself in his room** se encerró en su cuarto
■ **shut** *vi*
A «*door/window*» cerrar(se)*
B (esp BrE) (cease business — for day) cerrar*; (— permanently) cerrar* (sus puertas)

Phrasal verbs

• **shut away** [v ▸ o ▸ adv, v ▸ adv ▸ o] ‹*papers/valuables*› guardar bajo llave; ‹*person*› encerrar*; **to ~ oneself away** encerrarse*

• **shut down**
A [v ▸ adv] «*factory/business*» cerrar*; «*machinery*» apagarse*, desconectarse
B [v ▸ o ▸ adv, v ▸ adv ▸ o] ‹*factory/business*› cerrar*; ‹*machinery*› apagar*, desconectar; **the strike has ~ down all rail services** la huelga ha paralizado totalmente el ferrocarril

• **shut in** [v ▸ o ▸ adv, v ▸ adv ▸ o] (confine, enclose) encerrar*

• **shut off**
A [v ▸ o ▸ adv, v ▸ adv ▸ o] **1** ‹*water/electricity*› cortar; ‹*engine*› apagar*, desconectar **2** (isolate) (*often pass*) ‹*place/person*› aislar*
B [v ▸ adv] «*water/electricity*» cortarse; «*engine*» apagarse*, desconectarse

• **shut out** [v ▸ o ▸ adv, v ▸ adv ▸ o] **1** ‹*person/animal*› dejar (a)fuera; ‹*light/heat*› no dejar entrar; **to ~ oneself out** quedarse (a)fuera **2** (AmE Sport) ‹*team/pitcher*› ganarle a (*sin conceder ni un gol o carrera etc*)

• **shut up**
A [v ▸ o ▸ adv, v ▸ adv ▸ o] **1** (close) ‹*house/office*› cerrar* **2** (confine) ‹*dog/person*› encerrar*
B [v ▸ o ▸ adv] (silence) (colloq) ‹*person*› hacer* callar, cerrarle* la boca a
C [v ▸ adv] **1** (close business) cerrar* **2** (stop talking) (colloq) callarse; **~ up!** ¡cállate (la boca)!, ¡cierra el pico! (fam)

shut² *adj* (*pred*) **to be ~** «*box/window/book*» estar* cerrado; **the door slammed ~** la puerta se cerró de un portazo

shut: **~down** *n* (of hospital, college) cierre *m*; (of power) corte *m*; (of services) paralización *f*; **~-eye** *n* [u] (colloq): **to get a bit of ~-eye** echarse un sueñecito *or* (esp AmL) un sueñito (fam); **~-in** *adj* (confined) enclaustrado, encerrado; **~out** *n* (AmE) *partido ganado sin que marque el contrario*; **a 4-0 ~out** un partido ganado cuatro a cero

shutter /'ʃʌtər ‖ 'ʃʌtə(r)/ *n*
A (on window) postigo *m*, contraventana *f*; ***to put up the ~s*** bajar la cortina
B (Phot) obturador *m*; (*before n*) **~ speed** tiempo *m* de exposición

shuttle¹ /'ʃʌtl̩/ *n*
A (in loom, sewing machine) lanzadera *f*
B **1** (Aviat) puente *m* aéreo; (bus, train service) servicio *m* (regular) de enlace; (*before n*) **~ diplomacy** diplomacia *f* al estilo Kissinger; **~ service** servicio *m* de enlace; (Aviat) puente *m* aéreo **2** (*space* **~**) transbordador *m* *or* lanzadera *f* espacial

shuttle² *vi* (by plane) volar* (regularmente); (by bus, train) viajar (regularmente); **to ~ back and forth** ir* y venir*
■ **shuttle** *vt* ‹*passengers*› transportar, llevar

shuttlecock /ˈʃʌtl̩kɑːk || ˈʃʌtl̩kɒk/ *n* volante *m*, plumilla *f*, rehilete *m*, gallito *m* (Col, Méx)

shy¹ /ʃaɪ/ *adj* **shyer, shyest**
A ‹*person*› tímido, vergonzoso; ‹*smile*› tímido; ‹*animal*› huraño, asustadizo; **I felt very ~ in front of all those people** me sentía cohibido delante de toda esa gente; **don't be ~** no seas tímido, que no te dé vergüenza
B (lacking) (AmE colloq) (*pred, no comp*) **to be ~ of sth**: **we were ~ of funds** andábamos escasos *or* (fam) cortos de fondos; **he was four years ~ of being eligible to retire** le faltaban cuatro años para poder jubilarse

shy² **shies, shying, shied** *vi* «*horse*» respingar*

shyly /ˈʃaɪli/ *adv* tímidamente, con timidez

shyness /ˈʃaɪnəs || ˈʃaɪnɪs/ *n* [u] (of person) timidez *f*; (of animal) lo asustadizo

shyster /ˈʃaɪstər || ˈʃaɪstə(r)/ *n* (colloq) sinvergüenza *mf*, granuja *mf*; (lawyer) picapleitos *mf* (fam)

SI *adj* (*before n*) ‹*nomenclature*› del sistema S.I.

Siam /ˈsaɪˈæm/ *n* Siam *m*

Siamese /ˈsaɪəˈmiːz/ *n* (*pl* ~) ~ **(cat)** gato *m* siamés

Siamese twins *pl n* (hermanos) siameses *mpl*, (hermanas) siamesas *fpl*

Siberia /saɪˈbɪriə || saɪˈbɪəriə/ *n* Siberia *f*

sibilant /ˈsɪbələnt || ˈsɪbɪlənt/ *adj* sibilante

sibling /ˈsɪblɪŋ/ *n* (frml) (brother) hermano *m*; (sister) hermana *f*

sic /sɪk/ *adv* (frml) sic

Sicily /ˈsɪsəli || ˈsɪsɪli/ *n* Sicilia *f*

sick¹ /sɪk/ *adj* **-er, -est**
A (ill) enfermo; **to get ~** (AmE) caer* enfermo, enfermar, enfermarse (AmL); **to be off ~** estar* ausente por enfermedad; **~ building syndrome** síndrome *m* del edificio enfermo
B (nauseated) (*pred*): **to feel ~** (dizzy, unwell) estar* mareado; (about to vomit) tener* ganas de vomitar *or* de devolver, tener* náuseas; **to be ~** vomitar, devolver*; **you make me ~!** ¡me das asco!; **it makes me ~ the way she gets away with it** me da rabia *or* (AmL tb) me enferma cómo se sale con la suya
C **1** (disturbed, sickened) (*pred*): **to be ~ with fear/worry** estar* muerto de miedo/preocupación; **to be ~ at heart** (liter) estar* muy angustiado **2** (weary, fed up) **to be ~ OF sth/-ING** estar* harto DE algo/+ INF; **I'm ~ and tired** o **~ to death of hearing that** estoy absolutamente harto *or* (fam) hasta la coronilla de oír eso; **I'm ~ of the sight of that woman** esa mujer me tiene harto
D (gruesome) ‹*person/mind*› morboso; ‹*humor/joke*› de muy mal gusto

sick² *n*
A **the ~** (+ *pl vb*) los enfermos
B [u] (vomit) (BrE colloq) vómito *m*

sick: **~ bag** *n* (BrE) bolsa *f* para el mareo; **~ bay** *n* enfermería *f*; **~bed** *n* (liter) lecho *m* de enfermo (liter); **~ call** *n* (AmE) *llamado para presentarse a dar parte de enfermo a enfermería*; **~ day** *n* (AmE) día *m* de permiso *or* (Esp) de baja *or* (RPl) de licencia por enfermedad

sicken /ˈsɪkən/ *vt* dar* rabia, enfermar (AmL); (stronger) asquear
■ **sicken** *vi* **1** (become sick) (liter) caer* enfermo, enfermar **2** (BrE) **to be ~ing FOR sth** estar* incubando algo

sickening /ˈsɪkənɪŋ/ *adj* **1** (disgusting, discouraging): **it's ~, isn't it?** da mucha rabia ¿no?; (stronger) da asco ¿no?, es asqueante ¿no? **2** (nauseating, shocking) ‹*smell/sight*› nauseabundo; ‹*thud/crash/crunch*› escalofriante, horrible

sickeningly /ˈsɪkənɪŋli/ *adv* ‹*obsequious/condescending*› asquerosamente; **she's ~ clever/efficient** es tan inteligente/eficiente que da rabia

sick headache *n* jaqueca *f*, migraña *f*

sickle /ˈsɪkəl/ *n* hoz *f*

sick leave *n* [u] permiso *m* *or* (Esp) baja *f* *or* (RPl) licencia *f* por enfermedad

sickly¹ /ˈsɪkli/ *adj* **-lier, -liest** **1** (unhealthy) ‹*complexion/child*› enfermizo **2** (cloying) ‹*taste/smell*› empalagoso; ‹*color/green*› horrible, asqueroso

sickly² *adv*: **~ sweet** demasiado empalagoso *or* (Andes tb) hostigoso

sickness /ˈsɪknəs || ˈsɪknɪs/ *n* **1** [c] (disease) (liter) enfermedad *f* **2** [u] (nausea) náuseas *fpl*; (vomiting) vómitos *mpl*;

sick: **~ note** *n* (BrE) certificado *m* de enfermedad, baja *f* (Esp); **~ pay** *n* [u] *salario que se percibe mientras se está con permiso por enfermedad*; **~room** *n* (in school, factory) (BrE) enfermería *f*; (in house) *habitación de un enfermo*

side¹ /saɪd/ *n*
A (surface — of cube, record, coin, piece of paper) lado *m*, cara *f*; (— of building, cupboard) lado *m*, costado *m*; (— of mountain, hill) ladera *f*, falda *f*; **we laid the wardrobe on its ~** colocamos el armario de costado *or* de lado; Ⓢ **this side up** este lado hacia arriba; **they threw him over the ~** lo arrojaron por la borda; **1,000 words is about three ~s** 1.000 palabras son más o menos tres carillas; **the right/wrong ~ of the fabric** el derecho/revés de la tela; ▸ **coin¹**
B (boundary, edge): **he left it on the ~ of his plate** lo dejó en el plato, a un lado *or* (RPl) a un costado; **they were playing by the ~ of the pool** estaban jugando junto a *or* al lado de la piscina; **the house is by the ~ of a lake** la casa está a orillas de un lago
C (of person) costado *m*; (of animal) ijada *f*, ijar *m*; **a ~ of beef** media res *f*; **Roy stood at her ~** Roy estaba a su lado; **he flew in from Washington to be at her ~** voló desde Washington para estar con ella *or* para acompañarla; **they sat ~ by ~** estaban sentados uno junto al otro *or* uno al lado del otro; **to work ~ by ~ with sb** trabajar codo con codo con algn; ***to get on the wrong ~ of sb*** ganarse la antipatía de algn; ***to stay* o *keep on the right ~ of sb*** no predisponer* a algn en contra de uno
D (contrasted area, part, half) lado *m*; **the driver's/passenger's ~** el lado del conductor/pasajero; **they drive on the left-hand ~ of the road** conducen por la izquierda; **the church is on the left-hand ~** la iglesia está a mano izquierda; **from ~ to ~** de un lado al otro; **on both ~s/either ~ of sth** a ambos lados/a cada lado de algo; **to move to one ~** hacerse* a un lado; **to take sb to one ~** llamar a algn aparte; **to put sth on** o **to one ~**: **I'll put it to one ~ until I have more time** lo voy a dejar hasta que tenga más tiempo; **he swam to the other ~ of the river** nadó hasta la otra orilla *or* hasta el otro lado del río; **she walked past on the other ~ of the street** pasó por la acera de enfrente; **he's the right/wrong ~ of 40** tiene menos/más de 40 años; **she received support from all ~s** recibió apoyo de todos los sectores; ***on the ~***: **he repairs cars on the ~** arregla coches como trabajo extra; ▸ **track¹ F1**
E **1** (faction): **to change ~s** cambiarse de bando; **to take ~s** tomar partido; **to take sb's ~** ponerse* de parte *or* del lado de algn; **whose ~ are you on?** ¿tú de parte de quién estás?; **she worked for the other ~** trabajó para el enemigo; **he came down on the ~ of the union** falló a favor del sindicato **2** (Sport) equipo *m*
F (area, aspect) lado *m*, aspecto *m*; **you must listen to both ~s of the story** hay que oír las dos versiones *or* las dos campanas; **we've kept our ~ of the bargain** nosotros hemos cumplido con nuestra parte del trato; **it's a little on the short/expensive ~** es un poco corto/caro
G (line of descent): **on her father's ~** por parte de su padre *or* por el lado paterno

Phrasal verb

- **side with** [v ▸ prep ▸ o] ponerse* de parte *or* del lado de, tomar partido por

side² *adj* (*before n, no comp*) **1** ‹*door/entrance/wall*› lateral; **a ~ street** una calle lateral, una lateral **2** (incidental, secondary) ‹*issue*› secundario **3** (Culin): **~ dish** acompañamiento *m*, guarnición *f*; **a ~ order of vegetables** una porción de verduras como acompañamiento *or* guarnición; **a ~ salad** una ensalada (*como acompañamiento*)

side: **~ arm** *n*: *arma que se lleva en el costado o colgada del cinturón*; **~board** *n* **1** (piece of furniture) aparador *m*, seibó *m* (Ven); **2** **~boards** *pl* (BrE) ▸ **~burns**; **~burns** *pl n* (*sometimes sing*) patillas *fpl*; **~-by-~** /ˈsaɪdbaɪˈsaɪd/ *adj* (*pred* **side by side**) ‹*comparison/bench test*› uno al lado del otro; **~car** *n* sidecar *m*; **~ effect** *n* (Pharm) efecto *m* secundario; (incidental result) consecuencia *f* indirecta; **~kick** *n* (colloq) adlátere *mf*; **~light** *n* (BrE Auto) luz *f* de posición, piloto *m* (Esp), cocuyo *m* (Col, Ven)

sideline¹ /ˈsaɪdlaɪn/ *n*
A (Sport) **1** (line) línea *f* de banda **2** **sidelines** *pl* (area) *zona que rodea el campo de juego*; **to remain on the ~s** mantenerse* al margen
B (subsidiary activity) actividad *f* suplementaria

sideline² *vt* (AmE) (*often pass*) ‹*player*› dejar fuera del equipo; ‹*politician*› marginar

side: **~long** *adj* (*before n*) ‹*glance*› de reojo, de soslayo, de refilón; **~saddle** *adv* ‹*ride/sit*› a mujeriegas (*con las dos piernas hacia el mismo lado*); **~show** *n* (at fair) puesto *m*, barraca *f*; **~splitting** /ˈsaɪdˌsplɪtɪŋ/ *adj* divertidísimo, para morirse de risa; **~step -pp-** *vt* ‹*blow/opponent*› esquivar; ‹*problem/issue/question*› eludir, esquivar
■ **side** *vi* hacerse* a un lado; **~swipe** *n* **1** (remark) crítica *f*, ataque *m* (*hecho al pasar*) **2** (glancing blow) roce *m*; **~track¹** *vt* **1** (from subject) hacer* desviar del tema **2** (from purpose): **sorry, I got ~tracked** perdón, me entretuve *or* me distraje haciendo otra cosa; **~track²** *n* **1** (path, road) camino *m* secundario **2** (Rail) (AmE) apartadero *m*, vía *f* muerta; **~walk** *n* (AmE) acera *f*, banqueta *f* (Méx), andén *m* (AmC, Col), vereda *f* (CS, Per)

sideward¹ /ˈsaɪdwərd || ˈsaɪdwəd/, (BrE esp) **sidewards** /-z/ *adv* ▸**sideways¹ 1**

sideward² *adj* ▸**sideways²**

sideways¹ /ˈsaɪdweɪz/ *adv* **1** ‹*glance*› de reojo, de soslayo, de refilón; ‹*walk*› de lado/de costado **2** (with side part forward) de lado; **it will only go through ~ on** sólo va a pasar de lado *or* de costado

sideways² *adj* ‹*look*› de reojo, de soslayo, de refilón; ‹*movement*› lateral, de lado

siding /ˈsaɪdɪŋ/ *n* (Rail) apartadero *m*, vía *f* muerta

sidle /ˈsaɪdl̩/ *vi* **to ~ in/out** entrar/salir* sigilosamente; **to ~ up to sb** acercársele* sigilosamente a algn

SIDS *n* (= **sudden infant death syndrome**) SMIS *m*

siege /siːdʒ/ *n* sitio *m*; **the city was under ~** la ciudad estaba sitiada; **state of ~** estado *m* de sitio; **to lay ~ to a castle** sitiar un castillo

sienna /siˈenə/ *n* [u] (color) siena *m*

Sierra Leone /siˈerəliˈəʊn/ *n* Sierra Leona *f*

siesta /siˈestə/ *n* siesta *f*; **to have a ~** dormir* *or* echarse una siesta

sieve¹ /sɪv/ *n* (Culin) (for flour etc) tamiz *m*, cedazo *m*, cernidor *m*; (for liquids) colador *m*; (Hort, Min) criba *f*, harnero *m*; ▸**memory A1**

sieve² *vt* ‹*flour*› (BrE) tamizar*, cernir*, cerner*; ‹*earth*› cribar, harnear (Andes, Méx)

sift /sɪft/ *vt* **1** ‹*sugar/flour*› tamizar*, cernir*, cerner*; (sprinkle) espolvorear **2** ‹*facts/evidence*› pasar por el tamiz

sigh¹ /saɪ/ *vi* suspirar; **to ~ FOR sth/sb** (liter) suspirar POR algo/algn; **to ~ WITH sth**: **he ~ed with relief/contentment** suspiró aliviado/satisfecho

sigh² *n* suspiro *m*; **to heave a ~** dar* un suspiro, suspirar

sight¹ /saɪt/ *n*
A [u] (*eye~*) vista *f*; **to lose one's ~** perder* la vista *or* la visión; **to have poor ~** tener* mala vista, ver* mal
B [u] (range of vision): **to come into ~** aparecer*; **to lose ~ of sth/sb** perder* algo/a algn de vista; **the finishing line was now in ~** ya se veía la meta; **we were in ~ of victory, victory was within ~** la victoria estaba cercana; **she watched until they were out of ~** los siguió con la mirada hasta que los perdió de vista; **(get) out of my ~!** ¡fuera de aquí!; **I daren't let him out of my ~ for a second** no me atrevo a dejarlo solo ni un minuto; ***out of ~, out of mind*** ojos que no ven, corazón que no siente
C (act of seeing, view) (*no pl*): **at first ~** a primera vista; **it was love at first ~** fue amor a primera vista, fue un flechazo; **to catch ~ of sth/sb**: **we caught ~ of them going up the mountain** los vimos *or* los avistamos subiendo la montaña; **as he opened the drawer, I caught ~ of the gun** cuando abrió el cajón, pude ver el revólver; **to know sb by ~** conocer* a algn de vista; **to play at** *o* **by ~** (Mus) tocar* a primera vista; **deserters will be shot on ~** los desertores serán fusilados en el acto; **I can't stand the ~ of him** (colloq) no lo puedo ver (fam);
D [c] **1** (thing seen): **the sparrow is a familiar ~ in our gardens** el gorrión se ve con frecuencia en nuestros jardines; **it's not a pretty ~** (colloq) no es muy agradable de ver; ***it is/it was a ~ for sore eyes*** da/daba gusto verlo **2** (of untidy or absurd appearance) **a ~** (colloq): **I look a ~!** ¡estoy horrorosa!, ¡qué parezco!; **she looks a ~ in that dress** ese vestido le queda espantoso **3** **sights** *pl* (famous places): **to see the ~s** visitar los lugares de interés
E **1** [c] (of gun) mira *f* **2** **sights** *pl* (ambition): **to have sth in one's ~s, to have one's ~s on sth** tener* la mira puesta en algo
F (lot) (colloq): **a (far** *o* **damn) ~ happier/richer** muchísimo más feliz/rico; **it's a (far** *o* **damn) ~ better** es muchísimo mejor; **he's a ~ too clever** se pasa de listo

sight² *vt* ‹*land/ship*› divisar, avistar; ‹*person/animal*› ver*

sighted /ˈsaɪtəd || ˈsaɪtɪd/ *adj* vidente; **he's partially ~** tiene visión parcial

sight: **~-read** *vt/i* (*past & past p* **-read** /-red/) repentizar*; **~seeing** /ˈsaɪtˌsiːɪŋ/ *n* [u]: **to go ~seeing** ir* a visitar los lugares de interés; (*before n*) **a ~seeing tour** una excursión por los lugares de interés; **~seer** /ˈsaɪtˌsiːər/ *n* turista *mf*, visitante *mf*

sign¹ /saɪn/ *n*
A **1** [c u] (indication) señal *f*, indicio *m*; **all the ~s are that ...** todo parece indicar que ...; **he showed ~s of wanting to leave** dio muestras de querer irse; **he showed little ~ of enthusiasm at the news** demostró muy poco entusiasmo por la noticia; **there's no ~ of them yet** todavía no han llegado; **there was no ~ of him anywhere** no estaba por ninguna parte; **it's a ~ of the times** es un indicio de los tiempos que corren; **that's a good ~** eso es (una) buena señal **2** [c] (omen) presagio *m*
B [c] (gesture) seña *f*, señal *f*; **to make a ~ to sb** hacerle* una seña *or* una señal a algn; **to make the ~ of the cross** hacerse* la señal de la cruz, santiguarse*
C [c] **1** (notice, board) letrero *m*, cartel *m*; (in demonstration) pancarta *f* **2** (*road ~*) señal *f* (vial)
D [c] **1** (symbol) símbolo *m*; (Math) signo *m*; **plus/minus ~** signo (de) más/menos **2** (Astrol) signo *m*

sign² *vt* **1** (write signature on) firmar; **to ~ one's name** firmar **2** (hire) ‹*actor*› contratar; ‹*player*› fichar
■ **sign** *vi*
A **1** (write name) firmar **2** (Busn) **to ~ (WITH sb)** firmar un contrato (CON algn)
B **1** (gesture) **to ~ TO sb to + INF**: **she ~ed to me to sit down** me hizo una seña *or* una señal para que me sentara **2** (use sign language) comunicarse* por señas
■ *v refl* **to ~ oneself** firmarse; **he ~ed himself (as) J. Bell** se firmaba J. Bell, firmaba con el nombre de J. Bell

Phrasal verbs

- **sign away** [v ▸ o ▸ adv, v ▸ adv ▸ o] ‹*rights/property*› ceder, firmar la renuncia a
- **sign for** [v ▸ prep ▸ o] ‹*goods/parcel*› firmar el recibo de
- **sign in**

A [v ▸ adv] ‹‹*resident/visitor*›› firmar el registro (*al llegar*)
B [v ▸ o ▸ adv, v ▸ adv ▸ o] ‹*guest*› firmar por

- **sign off** [v ▸ adv] **1** (Rad, TV) despedirse*, cerrar* la transmisión **2** (in letter) despedirse*
- **sign off (on) sth** [v ▸ prep ▸ o] ‹*accounts/proposal*› aprobar*
- **sign on**

A [v ▸ adv] **1** (enlist) ‹‹*recruit*›› alistarse, enrolarse, enlistarse (AmC, Col, Ven) **2** (in UK) (Soc Adm) *anotarse para recibir el seguro de desempleo*, apuntarse al paro (Esp)
B [v ▸ o ▸ adv, v ▸ adv ▸ o] (hire) ‹*workers*› contratar; ‹*soldiers*› reclutar

- **sign out**

A [v ▸ adv] ‹‹*resident/visitor*›› firmar el registro (*al salir*)
B [v ▸ o ▸ adv, v ▸ adv ▸ o]: **~ the book out** firme el registro al retirar el libro

- **sign over** [v ▸ o ▸ adv, v ▸ adv ▸ o] ‹*rights*› firmar cediendo; **he ~ed everything over to her** lo puso todo a nombre de ella
- **sign up**

A [v ▸ adv] (for a course) inscribirse*, matricularse, anotarse (RPl); (to join the army) alistarse, enrolarse, enlistarse (AmC, Col, Ven)
B [v ▸ o ▸ adv, v ▸ adv ▸ o] ‹*soldiers*› reclutar; ‹*player*› fichar, contratar; ‹*worker*› contratar

signal¹ /ˈsɪgnl̩/ *n*
A (agreed sign, indication) señal *f*; **the busy ~** (AmE Telec) el tono *or* la señal de ocupado *or* (Esp) de comunicando; **to call the ~s** (AmE Sport) llamar las señales, decir* la jugada; **I call the ~s around here** (AmE) aquí quien manda soy yo, aquí

S

yo soy quien llevo la voz cantante; (*before n*) ~ **flag** bandera *f* de señales
B (Rail) señal *f*
C (Electron) señal *f*

signal², (BrE) **-ll-** *vt* 1 (indicate) señalar 2 (Auto): **she ~ed a left turn** señalizó *or* indicó que iba a doblar a la izquierda 3 (gesture) (AmE) hacerle* señas/una seña a
■ **signal** *vi* 1 (gesture) **to ~ (TO sb)** hacer(le)* señas/una seña (a algn); **she ~ed to us to leave** nos hizo señas/una seña para que nos fuéramos 2 (Auto) señalizar*, poner* el intermitente *or* (Col, Méx) la direccional *or* (Chi) el señalizador

signal box *n* (BrE) garita *f* de señales

signally /'sɪgnəli/ *adv* (frml) ‹*improve/worsen*› notablemente; **he has ~ failed to prove it** ha fracasado rotundamente al tratar de demostrarlo

signalman /'sɪgnl̩mən/ *n* (*pl* **-men** /-mən/) (Rail) guardavía *m*

signatory /'sɪgnətɔːri || 'sɪgnətəri/ *n* (*pl* **-ries**) firmante *mf*, signatario, -ria *m,f* (frml)

signature /'sɪgnətʃʊr || 'sɪgnətʃə(r)/ *n*
A (written name) firma *f*, rúbrica *f* (frml); **to put one's ~ to a petition** firmar una petición
B (Mus): **time ~** compás *m*, tiempo *m*
C (on prescription) (AmE) indicaciones *fpl* para el paciente
D (Print) 1 (binding guide) signatura *f* 2 (section) pliego *m*

signature tune *n* (BrE) sintonía *f*, cortina *f* musical (CS)

signet ring /'sɪgnət/ *n* (anillo *m* *or* sortija *f* de) sello *m*

significance /sɪg'nɪfɪkəns/ *n* [u] importancia *f*, trascendencia *f*, relevancia *f*

significant /sig'nɪfɪkənt/ *adj* 1 (important, considerable) importante 2 (meaningful) ‹*look/smile*› expresivo, elocuente; ‹*fact/remark*› significativo

significantly /sɪg'nɪfɪkəntli/ *adv* ‹*improve/change/increase*› considerablemente, apreciablemente; **they're ~ different** hay una diferencia apreciable entre ellos

signify /'sɪgnəfaɪ || 'sɪgnɪfaɪ/ *vt* **-fies, -fying, -fied** 1 (denote, mean) significar*, querer* decir 2 (indicate) ‹*approval/consent*› expresar

signing /'saɪnɪŋ/ *n* 1 (act of signing) firma *f*, rúbrica *f* (frml) 2 (Sport) fichaje *m*

sign: ~ **language** *n* [u c] lenguaje *m* gestual *or* de gestos; **to talk in ~ language** hablar por señas; **~-off** *n* (AmE) (end of day's broadcasting) cierre *m* de emisión; (speech, music) *pieza musical o palabras de despedida*

signpost¹ /'saɪnpəʊst/ *n* señal *f*, poste *m* indicador

signpost² *vt* 1 (point to) señalar; (draw attention to) destacar* 2 (BrE Auto) ‹*way/route*› señalizar*

signwriter /'saɪn,raɪtər || 'saɪn,raɪtə(r)/ *n* rotulista *mf*

Sikh¹ /siːk/ *n* sij *mf*

Sikh² *adj* sij *adj inv*

silage /'saɪlɪdʒ/ *n* [u] ensilaje *m*, ensilado *m* (*forraje fermentado en silos*)

silence¹ /'saɪləns/ *n* silencio *m*; **in ~** en silencio; **~!** ¡silencio!, ¡hagan silencio!; **to break the ~** romper* el silencio; **to pass over sth in ~** silenciar algo; **to reduce sb to ~** dejar a algn sin habla; **~ *is golden*** el silencio es oro

silence² *vt* 1 ‹*cries/voice*› acallar; ‹*child/animal*› hacer* callar, acallar 2 ‹*opposition/criticism*› silenciar, amordazar*; ‹*conscience*› (liter) acallar

silencer /'saɪlənsər || 'saɪlənsə(r)/ *n* 1 (on gun) silenciador *m* 2 (on car) (BrE) silenciador *m*, mofle *m* (AmC, Méx)

silent /'saɪlənt/ *adj* 1 (noiseless, still) ‹*night/forest*› silencioso 2 (not speaking) ‹*gesture/protest*› mudo; **she was ~ for a moment** se quedó callada un momento; **the hall fell ~** se hizo silencio en la sala; **the 'h' is ~** la hache es muda; **a ~ movie** una película muda

silently /'saɪləntli/ *adv* 1 (noiselessly) ‹*creep/glide/enter*› silenciosamente 2 (without speaking) ‹*pray/stand/listen*› en silencio, calladamente

silent partner *n* socio, -cia *m,f* capitalista

silhouette¹ /'sɪlu'et/ *n* silueta *f*

silhouette² *vt* (*usu pass*) **to be ~d AGAINST sth** perfilarse *or* recortarse CONTRA *or* SOBRE algo (liter)

silicon /'sɪləkən || 'sɪlɪkən/ *n* [u] silicio *m*; (*before n*) ‹*chip/wafer*› (Comput) de silicio, silíceo

silicone /'sɪləkəʊn || 'sɪlɪkəʊn/ *n* [u] silicona *f*, silicón *m* (Méx); (*before n*) de siliconas *or* (Méx) silicones

silk /sɪlk/ *n* [u] seda *f*; **artificial/pure ~** seda artificial/natural

silken /'sɪlkən/ *adj* (liter) 1 (of silk) ‹*gown/shirt*› de seda 2 (like silk) ‹*hair/skin*› sedoso, como la seda 3 (suave) ‹*tones/voice*› suave, aterciopelado

silk: **~moth** /'sɪlkmɔːθ || 'sɪlkmɒθ/ *n* mariposa *f* de la seda; **~ screen** *n* [u] serigrafía *f*; (*before n*) ‹*printing/technique*› serigráfico; **~ screen print** serigrafía *f*; **~-stocking** /'sɪlk'stɑːkɪŋ || ,sɪlk'stɒkɪŋ/ *adj* (AmE) (*before n*) aristocrático, de clase alta; **~worm** *n* gusano *m* de seda

silky /'sɪlki/ **-kier, -kiest** *adj* 1 ‹*fabric/fur*› sedoso, como de seda; **~ smooth** (*as adv*) suave como la seda 2 ▸ **silken 3**

sill /sɪl/ *n* 1 (*window~*) alféizar *m*, antepecho *m* 2 (in window) pieza *f* de apoyo; (in door) umbral *m*

silliness /'sɪlinəs || 'sɪlinɪs/ *n* [u] tontería *f*; **stop this ~** déjate de tonterías

silly /'sɪli/ *adj* **-lier, -liest** (foolish) ‹*person*› tonto, bobo (fam); ‹*remark/idea/mistake*› tonto; ‹*name/hat*› ridículo; ‹*grin/laugh*› tonto, estúpido; **you ~ fool!** ¡imbécil!; **you ~ girl!** ¡tonta!; **that was a very ~ thing to say/do** lo que dijiste/hiciste fue una tontería; **to scare sb ~** darle* un susto de muerte a algn; **to make sb look ~** dejar en ridículo a algn; **the ~ season** (BrE) *período del verano en que los periódicos, al no haber actividad política, llenan sus páginas de noticias triviales*

silo /'saɪləʊ/ *n* (*pl* **-los**) silo *m*

silt /sɪlt/ *n* [u] cieno *m*, limo *m*, légamo *m*

(Phrasal verb)
• **silt up** [v ▸ adv] encenagarse*

silver¹ /'sɪlvər || 'sɪlvə(r)/ *n* [u]
A (metal) plata *f*
B 1 (household items) platería *f*, plata *f* 2 (coins) monedas *fpl* (*de plata, aluminio etc*)
C (color) (color *m*) plata *m*

silver² *adj* 1 (made of silver) de plata 2 (in color) plateado; ‹*hair*› canoso, cano (liter), de plata (liter) 3 (representing 25 years) (*before n*): **~ anniversary/jubilee** el vigésimo quinto aniversario; **~ wedding** (BrE) bodas *fpl* de plata

silver: **~ birch** *n* abedul *m*; **~fish** *n* (*pl* **~fish**) lepisma *f*; **~ foil** *n* [u] 1 (BrE Culin) papel *m* de aluminio *or* de plata 2 (Metall) hoja *f* de plata; **~ gilt** *n* plata *f* dorada; **~ paper** *n* (colloq) 1 (wrapping) papel *m* de plata *or* plateado *or* de estaño 2 (BrE) papel *m* metalizado; **~-plate** /'sɪlvər'pleɪt || ,sɪlvə'pleɪt/ *vt* dar*(le) un baño de plata a, platear; **~side** /'sɪlvərsaɪd || 'sɪlvəsaɪd/ *n* 1 (fish) [c] pejerrey *m* (*americano*) 2 [u] (BrE Culin) *corte de carne vacuna del cuarto trasero*; **~smith** *n* platero, -ra *m,f*, orfebre *mf*; **~ware** /'sɪlvərwer || 'sɪlvəweə(r)/ *n* [u] platería *f*, plata *f*

silvery /'sɪlvəri/ *adj* 1 ‹*voice/laugh*› argentino (liter) 2 ‹*sheen*› plateado; ‹*hair*› canoso, cano (liter), plateado (liter)

SIM card /sɪm/ *n* tarjeta *f* SIM

similar /'sɪmələr || 'sɪmɪlə(r)/ *adj* similar, parecido, semejante; **to be ~ TO sth** parecerse* A algo, ser* parecido *or* similar A algo; **it's ~ in size to a sparrow** es de tamaño parecido al de un gorrión

similarity /'sɪmə'lærəti || ,sɪmɪ'lærəti/ *n* (*pl* **-ties**) 1 [u] (likeness — between things) similitud *f*, parecido *m*, semejanza *f*; (— between persons) parecido *m* 2 [c] (common feature) semejanza *f*, similitud *f*, elemento *m* en común

similarly /'sɪmələrli || 'sɪmɪləli/ *adv* 1 (in a similar way) de modo parecido *or* similar 2 (equally) igualmente 3 (*as linker*) asimismo, del mismo modo

simile /'sɪməli || 'sɪmɪli/ *n* [c u] símil *m*

simmer /'sɪmər || 'sɪmə(r)/ *vi* «*liquid*» hervir* a fuego lento; «*controversy/dispute*» fermentar; **she was ~ing with anger** estaba a punto de estallar de ira
■ **simmer** *vt* ‹*liquid/food*› hervir* a fuego lento

(Phrasal verb)
• **simmer down** [v ▸ adv] (colloq) tranquilizarse*

simper¹ /'sɪmpər || 'sɪmpə(r)/ *vi* sonreír(se)* como un tonto/una tonta

■ **simper** *vt* decir* con una sonrisa tonta

simper² *n* sonrisa *f* tonta

simple /'sɪmpəl/ *adj* **simpler** /-plər/, **simplest** /-pləst/
A (uncomplicated) ‹*task/problem*› sencillo, simple; **the machine is very ~ to use** la máquina es de fácil manejo *or* es fácil de manejar; **keep it ~** no lo compliques
B (straightforward): **the ~ truth is (that) ...** la pura verdad es que ...; **it's a ~ statement of fact** es simplemente *or* meramente la constatación de un hecho; **for the ~ reason that ...** por la sencilla razón de que ...
C (plain, unpretentious) ‹*dress/food*› sencillo, simple
D 1 (unsophisticated, humble) simple 2 (backward) simple, corto de alcances
E ‹*interest*› simple

simple-minded /'sɪmpəl'maɪndəd || ˌsɪmpəl'maɪndɪd/ *adj* simple, corto de alcances

simpleton /'sɪmpəltən/ *n* (unintelligent person) (pej) simplón, -plona *m,f*; (foolish person) bobo, -ba *m,f* (fam), bobalicón, -cona *m,f* (fam)

simplicity /sɪm'plɪsəti/ *n* [u] simplicidad *f*, sencillez *f*

simplify /'sɪmpləfaɪ || 'sɪmplɪfaɪ/ *vt* **-fies, -fying, -fied** simplificar*

simplistic /sɪm'plɪstɪk/ *adj* simplista

simply /'sɪmpli/ *adv*
A 1 (only, merely) simplemente, sencillamente; **to receive a free sample, ~ fill in the form** para recibir una muestra gratis no tiene más que llenar el cupón; **they were not chosen ~ on merit** no se los eligió sólo por sus méritos; **I ~ wanted to help** simplemente *or* solamente quería ayudar 2 (absolutely) ‹*wonderful/awful*› sencillamente; **I was ~ furious!** estaba realmente *or* francamente furioso
B 1 (plainly) con sencillez *or* simplicidad, sencillamente 2 (in simple language) simplemente, sencillamente

simulate /'sɪmjəleɪt || 'sɪmjʊleɪt/ *vt* 1 (reproduce) simular; **a ~d attack** un simulacro de ataque 2 (feign) simular, aparentar, fingir* 3 **simulated** *past p* simulado

simulation /ˌsɪmjə'leɪʃən || ˌsɪmjʊ'leɪʃən/ *n* [u c] simulacro *m*, simulación *f*

simultaneous /'saɪməl'teɪniəs || ˌsɪməl'teɪniəs/ *adj* simultáneo

simultaneously /'saɪməl'teɪniəsli || ˌsɪməl'teɪniəsli/ *adv* simultáneamente, a la vez, al mismo tiempo

sin¹ /sɪn/ *n* [c u] pecado *m*; **the seven deadly ~s** los siete pecados capitales; **for my ~s** (hum) para mi castigo (hum); ***to be as miserable as ~*** ser* un/una cascarrabias; ***to be as ugly as ~*** ser* más feo que pegarle a Dios *or* que Picio (fam)

sin² *vi* **-nn-** pecar*

since¹ /sɪns/ *conj*
A (in time) desde que; **~ coming to London** desde que vino (*or* vine *etc*) a Londres; **it's years ~ I've been to France** hace años que no voy a Francia
B (introducing a reason): **~ you can't go, can I have your ticket?** ya que no puedes ir ¿me das tu entrada?; **~ that is not the case ...** como no es así, puesto que no es ése el caso ... (frml)

since² *prep* desde; **they've worked there (ever) ~ 1970** han trabajado allí desde 1970; **~ the party he's only seen her twice** desde la fiesta sólo la ha visto dos veces; **how long is it ~ your operation?** ¿cuánto (tiempo) hace de tu operación?

since³ *adv* (from then till now) desde entonces; **she has lived here ever ~** desde entonces que vive aquí; **... but she had ~ remarried** ... pero (en el ínterin) ella se había vuelto a casar; **long ~** (colloq) hace mucho

sincere /sɪn'sɪr || sɪn'sɪə(r)/, **sincerer, sincerest** *adj* sincero

sincerely /sɪn'sɪrli || sɪn'sɪəli/ *adv* sinceramente; **I ~ hope so!** ¡eso espero!; **~ (yours)** *o* (BrE) **yours ~** (saluda) a usted atentamente, atentamente

sincerity /sɪn'serəti/ *n* [u] sinceridad *f*

sinecure /'saɪnɪkjʊr, 'sɪn- || 'saɪnɪkjʊə(r), 'sɪn-/ *n* sinecura *f*

sinew /'sɪnju:/ *n* (tendon) tendón *m*; (in meat) nervio *m*

sinewy /'sɪnju:i/ *adj* ‹*arms*› nervudo

sinful /'sɪnfəl/ *adj* ‹*person*› pecador; ‹*act*› pecaminoso

sing /sɪŋ/ (*past* **sang**; *past p* **sung**) *vi* 1 «*person/bird*» cantar; **to ~ alto/bass** tener* voz de tenor/de bajo 2 «*wind/kettle*» silbar

■ **sing** *vt* ‹*song/chorus*› cantar, entonar; **to ~ sb to sleep** cantarle a algn para que se duerma

Phrasal verbs

- **sing along** [v ▸ adv] **to ~ along (WITH sb)** cantar (CON algn)
- **sing out** [v ▸ adv] «*person/choir*» cantar (*fuerte y claramente*)

Singapore /'sɪŋgəpɔ:r || ˌsɪŋə'pɔ:(r)/ *n* Singapur *m*

singe /sɪndʒ/ *vt* **singes, singeing, singed** ‹*garment/cloth*› chamuscar*, quemar; **to ~ one's beard/eyebrows** chamuscarse* *or* quemarse la barba/las cejas

singer /'sɪŋər || 'sɪŋə(r)/ *n* cantante *mf*; **he's not a bad ~** no canta mal

singing /'sɪŋɪŋ/ *n* [u] 1 (of person, bird) canto *m*; **she teaches ~** enseña canto; **I can hear ~** oigo cantar; (*before n*) **a good ~ voice** una buena voz (para el canto) 2 (noise — of kettle) silbido *m*; (— in ears) zumbido *m*

single¹ /'sɪŋgəl/ *adj*
A (just one) (*before n*) solo; **a ~ issue dominated the talks** un solo *or* único tema dominó las conversaciones; **it's the ~ most important issue** es el tema más importante *or* de mayor importancia; **the largest ~ shareholder** el mayor accionista individual; **every ~ day** todos los días sin excepción, todos los santos días (fam); (*with neg*) **not a ~ house was left standing** no quedó ni una sola casa en pie
B (*before n*) 1 (for one person) ‹*room*› individual; ‹*bed/sheet*› individual, de una plaza (AmL) 2 (not double) ‹*lens/engine/line*› solo; ‹*flower*› simple; **~ figures** cifras *fpl* de un solo dígito; **in ~ file** en fila india 3 (BrE Transp) ‹*fare/ticket*› de ida, sencillo
C (unmarried) soltero; **I'm ~** soy *or* (Esp tb) estoy soltero

Phrasal verb

- **single out** [v ▸ o ▸ adv, v ▸ adv ▸ o]: **I can't ~ out any individual** no puedo señalar a nadie en particular; **she was ~d out for criticism** se la criticó a ella en particular

single² *n*
A (Audio, Mus) single *m*, (disco *m*) sencillo *m*; **a 12-inch ~** un maxi-single
B 1 (ticket) (BrE) boleto *m* *or* (Esp) billete *m* de ida 2 (room) (habitación *f*) individual *f* *or* sencilla *f*
C **singles** *pl* (*before n*) **~s bar** *bar para personas en busca de pareja*
D (Sport) 1 (in baseball) sencillo *m* 2 (in cricket) tanto *m*; *see also* **singles**

single: **~-breasted** /'sɪŋgəl'brestəd || ˌsɪŋgəl'brestɪd/ *adj* de una fila de botones, derecho (AmL); **~ cream** *n* (BrE) crema *f* líquida, nata *f* líquida (Esp); **~-decker** /'sɪŋgəl'dekər || ˌsɪŋgəl'dekə(r)/ *n* autobús *m* de un piso; **~-figure** /'sɪŋgəl'fɪgjər || ˌsɪŋgəl'fɪgə(r)/ *adj* (*before n*): **~-figure inflation** inflación *f* de menos del 10%; **~-handed** /'sɪŋgəl'hændəd || ˌsɪŋgəl'hændɪd/ *adv* sin (la) ayuda de nadie; **~ market** *n* mercado *m* único; **~-minded** /'sɪŋgəl'maɪndəd || ˌsɪŋgəl'maɪndɪd/ *adj* decidido, resuelto; **her ~-minded pursuit of fame** la determinación con que buscaba la fama; **~ parent** *n*: **he's/she's a ~ parent** es un padre/una madre que cría a su(s) hijo(s) sin pareja; (*before n*) **~-parent family** familia *f* monoparental

singles /'sɪŋgəlz/ *pl n* (Sport) individuales *mpl*, singles *mpl* (AmL); **the men's/ladies' ~** los individuales masculinos/femeninos, los singles de caballeros/de damas (AmL)

singles bar *n* (AmE) bar *m* de solteros, bar *m* de ligue (fam)

single-sex /'sɪŋgəl'seks/ *adj*: **~ school** escuela *f* sólo para niños/niñas

singlet /'sɪŋglət || 'sɪŋglɪt/ *n* (BrE) camiseta *f*

single-track /'sɪŋgəl'træk/ *adj* 1 (Rail) de vía única; **a ~ railroad** una vía única 2 (BrE) ‹*road*› de un solo carril

singly /'sɪŋgli/ *adv* por separado, uno por uno

singsong¹ /'sɪŋsɔ:ŋ || 'sɪŋsɒŋ/ *n* 1 (tone) (*no pl*) sonsonete *m* 2 (singing session) (BrE): **they had a ~ on the train** se pusieron a cantar en el tren

S

singsong[2] *adj* ‹*accent/tones/voice*› cantarín

singular[1] /ˈsɪŋgjələr || ˈsɪŋgjʊlə(r)/ *adj*
A (Ling) singular; **the second person ~** la segunda persona del singular
B (frml) (*usu before n*) ‹*beauty/achievement*› singular (frml); ‹*adventure/occurrence*› raro, extraño, singular

singular[2] *n* [u c] singular *m*; **in the ~** en singular

singularly /ˈsɪŋgjələrli || ˈsɪŋgjʊləli/ *adv* (*as intensifier*) ‹*attractive/inept*› particularmente, singularmente; **~ gifted** excepcionalmente dotado

sinister /ˈsɪnɪstər || ˈsɪnɪstə(r)/ *adj* siniestro

sink[1] /sɪŋk/ (*past* **sank**; *past p* **sunk**) *vi*
A 1 «*ship/stone*» hundirse; **the sediment ~s to the bottom of the jar** el sedimento se deposita en el fondo del frasco; ***to leave sb to ~ or swim*** abandonar a algn a su suerte 2 (subside) **to ~ (INTO sth)** «*building/foundations*» hundirse (EN algo); **he sank back into the chair** se arrellanó en el sillón; **she sank to the floor** se desplomó en el suelo
B (fall, drop) «*water/level*» descender*, bajar; «*price/value*» caer* a pique; «*attendance/output*» decaer*, bajar; **the pound has sunk to an all-time low** la libra ha alcanzado el nivel más bajo en la historia
C 1 (decline) declinar; **she's ~ing fast** se está apagando rápidamente 2 (degenerate) degradarse; **I'd never ~ so low** nunca caería tan bajo 3 (be discouraged): **my heart sank** se me cayó el alma a los pies; **that ~ing feeling** (BrE) esa desazón, ese desaliento

■ **sink** *vt*
A 1 ‹*ship*› hundir; ‹*object/body*› hundir, sumergir* 2 (ruin) ‹*plan/business/person*› hundir, acabar con
B (bury, hide) ‹*pipe/cable*› enterrar*, esconder
C 1 (drive in) **to ~ sth IN/INTO sth**: **the dog sank its teeth into my thigh** el perro me clavó *or* me hincó los dientes en el muslo 2 (excavate) ‹*shaft*› abrir*, excavar; ‹*well*› perforar, abrir*
D (invest) **to ~ sth IN/INTO sth** invertir* algo EN algo
E (Sport) ‹*ball/putt*› meter (*en el hoyo*); **he sank two baskets** encestó dos veces
F (forget) olvidar, dejar a un lado; **to ~ one's differences** olvidar *or* dejar a un lado sus (*or* nuestras *etc*) diferencias

Phrasal verb

- **sink in** [v ▸ adv] (colloq): **it finally sank in that we weren't going to get paid** finalmente nos dimos cuenta *or* caímos en la cuenta de que no nos iban a pagar; **it still hasn't sunk in that he's dead** todavía no ha (*or* han *etc*) asumido el hecho de que ha muerto

sink[2] *n* 1 (in kitchen) fregadero *m*, lavaplatos *m* (Andes), pileta *f* (RPl) 2 (washbasin) (AmE) lavabo *m*, lavamanos *m*, lavatorio *m* (CS), pileta *f* (RPl)

sinkhole /ˈsɪŋkhəʊl/ *n* 1 (Geol) dolina *f* 2 (AmE) (in city) antro *m*; **it's a ~ of corruption** es un antro de corrupción 3 (AmE) (loss maker) elefante *m* blanco

sinking /ˈsɪŋkɪŋ/ *n* [c u] hundimiento *m*

sinner /ˈsɪnər || ˈsɪnə(r)/ *n* pecador, -dora *m,f*

sinuous /ˈsɪnjuəs/ *adj* (frml) sinuoso, serpenteante

sinus /ˈsaɪnəs/ *n* (*pl* **-nuses**) seno *m* (nasal)

Sioux /suː/ *n* (*pl* ~) siux *mf*, sioux *mf*

sip[1] /sɪp/ *vt* **-pp-** sorber, beber *or* tomar a sorbos

sip[2] *n* sorbo *m*; **in ~s** a sorbos; **to have/take a ~ of sth** tomar un sorbo de algo; **give me a ~** dame un sorbito

siphon /ˈsaɪfən/ *n* sifón *m*

Phrasal verb

- **siphon off** [v ▸ o ▸ adv, v ▸ adv ▸ o] 1 ‹*liquid/fuel*› sacar* con sifón, trasvasar 2 ‹*money*› desviar*

sir /sɜːr || sɜː/ *n*
A 1 (as form of address — to male customer) señor, caballero; (— to male teacher) (BrE) profesor, señor; **have they arrived, sergeant? — yes, ~** ¿ya han llegado, sargento? — sí, mi teniente (*or* mi capitán *etc*) 2 (Corresp): **Dear Sir/S~s,** De mi mayor consideración:, Muy señor mío/señores míos:; **S~,** (to editor of paper) Señor Director: 3 (*as intensifier*) (colloq): **yes/no ~!** ¡sí,/no, señor! (fam)
B **Sir** (as title) sir *m*; **S~ George Payne** sir George Payne

sire[1] /saɪr/ *n* (Zool) padre *m*; (Equ) padre *m*, padrón *m* (AmL)

sire[2] *vt* «*animal*» ser* el padre de, padrear

siren /ˈsaɪrən/ *n*
A (device) sirena *f*
B (Myth) sirena *f*

sirloin /ˈsɜːrlɔɪn || ˈsɜːlɔɪn/ *n* [u c] *preciado corte de carne vacuna del cuarto trasero*

sirree /səˈriː/ *n* (AmE colloq) (*as intensifier*): **yes/no ~!** ¡sí,/no, señor!

sirup *n* (AmE) ▸ **syrup**

sirupy *adj* (AmE) ▸ **syrupy**

sissy /ˈsɪsi/ *n* (*pl* **-sies**) (colloq & pej) mariquita *mf* (fam)

sister /ˈsɪstər || ˈsɪstə(r)/ *n*
A 1 (sibling) hermana *f*; (*before n*) ‹*company*› afiliado, asociado; **~ ship** buque *m* gemelo 2 (woman comrade) compañera *f*, camarada *f*; (in feminism) hermana *f*, compañera *f*
B 1 (nun) hermana *f*, monja *f*; (before name) hermana, Sor; **S~ Petra** la hermana Petra, Sor Petra 2 (nurse) (BrE) enfermera *f* jefe *or* jefa (*a cargo de una o más salas*)

sisterhood /ˈsɪstərhʊd || ˈsɪstəhʊd/ *n* 1 [c] (association of women) asociación *f* de mujeres 2 [c] (Relig) congregación *f* 3 [u] (sisterly relationship) solidaridad *f* (*entre mujeres*)

sister-in-law /ˈsɪstərənlɔː || ˈsɪstərɪnlɔː/ *n* (*pl* **sisters-in-law**) cuñada *f*

sisterly /ˈsɪstərli || ˈsɪstəli/ *adj* (propio) de hermana

sit /sɪt/ (*pres p* **sitting**; *past & past p* **sat**) *vi*
A 1 (sit down) sentarse*; **he sat on my knee** se me sentó en las rodillas 2 (be seated) estar* sentado; **don't just ~ there: do something!** ¡no te quedes ahí sentado: haz algo!; **~ still!** ¡quédate quieto!; ***to be ~ting pretty*** (colloq) estar* bien situado *or* (fam) colocado
B 1 (Art) **to ~ (FOR sb/sth)** ‹*for artist/photograph*› posar (PARA algn/algo) 2 (Adm, Govt): **to ~ in Congress** tener* un escaño en el Congreso, ser* diputado/senador; *see also* **sit on A** 3 (be in session) «*committee/court*» reunirse* en sesión, sesionar (esp AmL)
C (weigh): **his crime sat heavy on his conscience** el crimen le pesaba en la conciencia
D (brood) «*hen/bird*» empollar; **to ~ on the eggs** empollar (los huevos)
E **sitting** *pres p* ‹*figure*› sentado; **in a ~ting position** sentado; **~ting tenant** (BrE) inquilino, -na *m,f* (*a quien no se puede desalojar*)

■ **sit** *vt*
A (cause to be seated) ‹*person*› sentar*; ‹*object*› poner*, colocar* (*en posición vertical*); **~ yourself beside me** siéntate a mi lado *or* junto a mí
B (BrE Educ): **to ~ an exam** hacer* *or* dar* *or* (CS) rendir* *or* (Méx) tomar un examen, examinarse (Esp); **she did not ~ the exam** no se presentó al examen

Phrasal verbs

- **sit around** [v ▸ adv]: **he ~s around all day doing nothing** se pasa el día sentado sin hacer nada
- **sit back** [v ▸ adv] (colloq) 1 (lean back) recostarse*; (relax): **just ~ back and listen** ponte cómodo y escucha 2 (fail to act) cruzarse* de brazos
- **sit down**
A [v ▸ adv] (take a seat) sentarse*; **please ~ down** siéntese *or* (frml) tome asiento, por favor
B [v ▸ o ▸ adv] (cause to be seated) sentar*
- **sit in** [v ▸ adv] 1 (attend) **to ~ in (ON sth)**: **he used to ~ in on my classes** asistía a mis clases como oyente (*or* observador *etc*) 2 (as protest) hacer* una sentada *or* (Méx) un sitin
- **sit on** [v ▸ prep ▸ o]
A ‹*committee/jury*› formar parte de, ser* miembro de
B (colloq) 1 (withhold) ‹*information*› mantener* oculto 2 (fail to deal with) ‹*application/claim*› no dar* trámite a, retener*
- **sit out** [v ▸ o ▸ adv, v ▸ adv ▸ o] 1 (wait until end of) ‹*siege*› aguantar; ***to ~ it out*** aguantarse 2 (not participate in) ‹*dance*› no bailar; ‹*game*› no tomar parte en
- **sit through** [v ▸ prep ▸ o]: **I sat through two boring lectures** me escuché dos conferencias aburridas (de cabo a rabo); **one of the worst plays I've ever had to ~ through** una de las peores obras que jamás haya tenido que soportar *or* aguantar
- **sit up**
A [v ▸ adv] 1 (in upright position) «*person/patient*» incorporarse; «*dog*» sentarse* sobre las patas traseras; **that should make them ~ up and take notice** eso debería alertarlos 2 (with straight back) ponerse* derecho, enderezarse* 3 (not go to bed): **we sat up talking till one o'clock** nos quedamos (levantados) conversando hasta la una

B [v ▸ o ▸ adv] ‹*child/doll*› sentar*

sitcom /ˈsɪtkɑːm || ˈsɪtkɒm/ *n* (colloq) ▸**situation comedy**

sit-down¹ /ˈsɪtdaʊn/ *n* **1** (Lab Rel, Pol) sentada *f*, sitin *m* (Méx) **2** (rest) (BrE) (*no pl*): **I must just have a ~, I'm exhausted** tengo que sentarme un rato, estoy agotado

sit-down² *adj* (*before n*): **~ dinner** cena *f* servida en la mesa; **~ strike** huelga *f* de brazos caídos

site /saɪt/ *n* **1** (location) emplazamiento *m* (frml); (piece of land) terreno *m*, solar *m*; **built on the ~ of a Roman temple** construido en el lugar que ocupaba un templo romano **2** (*building ~*) obra *f* **3** (*archeological ~*) yacimiento *m* (arqueológico) **4** (*camp~*) camping *m*

sit-in /ˈsɪtɪn/ *n* (demonstration) sentada *f*, sitin *m* (Méx); (strike) encierro *m*, ocupación *f* or toma *f* (*del lugar de trabajo*)

sitter /ˈsɪtər || ˈsɪtə(r)/ *n* **1** (Art) modelo *mf* **2** (*baby~*) baby sitter *mf*, canguro *mf* (Esp)

sitting /ˈsɪtɪŋ/ *n* **1** (for meal etc) turno *m*; **I watched three movies at** *o* **in a single ~** vi tres películas de una sentada *or* de un tirón (fam) **2** (of committee, parliament) sesión *f* **3** (for painter, photographer) sesión *f*

sitting: **~ duck** *n* (colloq) presa *f* fácil, blanco *m* seguro; **~ room** *n* (BrE) sala *f* de estar, living *m* (esp AmL), salón *m* (esp Esp); **~ target** *n* ▸**~ duck**

situate /ˈsɪtʃueɪt || ˈsɪtjʊeɪt/ *vt* (locate) (*often pass*) ‹*building/town*› situar*, ubicar* (esp AmL), emplazar* (frml)

situation /ˌsɪtʃuˈeɪʃən || ˌsɪtjʊˈeɪʃən/ *n*

A (circumstances, position) situación *f*; **in the classroom ~, children ...** en el ámbito de la clase, los niños ...

B (job) (frml) empleo *m*; **S situations vacant/wanted** ofertas/demandas de empleo

C (setting) situación *f*, ubicación *f*, emplazamiento *m* (frml)

situation comedy *n* [c u] comedia *f* (*acerca de situaciones de la vida diaria*)

sit-up /ˈsɪtʌp/ *n* (ejercicio *m*) abdominal *m* (*levantando el torso del suelo*)

six¹ /sɪks/ *n* seis *m*; (in ice hockey) equipo *m*; ***it's ~ of one and half a dozen of the other*** (colloq) (it makes no difference) da lo mismo; (both parties are to blame) los dos tienen parte de la culpa; ***to be (all) at ~es and sevens*** (colloq) estar* hecho un lío (fam)); ***to give sb ~ of the best*** darle* unos buenos azotes a algn; ***to knock sb for ~*** (BrE) tumbar a algn; **the news really knocked him for ~** la noticia lo dejó pasmado; *see also* **four¹**

six² *adj* seis *adj inv*; *see also* **four²**

six: **~-pack** *n* paquete *m* de seis unidades; **~pence** /ˈsɪkspəns/ *n*: *moneda de seis peniques antiguos*; **~-shooter** /ˈsɪksˌʃuːtər || ˌsɪksˈʃuːtə(r)/ *n* (AmE colloq) revólver *m* (*con seis cámaras*)

sixteen /sɪksˈtiːn/ *adj/n* dieciséis *adj inv/m*

sixteenth¹ /ˈsɪksˈtiːnθ/ *adj* decimosexto; *see also* **fifth¹**

sixteenth² *adv* en decimosexto lugar; *see also* **fifth²**

sixteenth³ *n* **1** (Math) dieciseisavo *m* **2** (part) dieciseisava parte *f*

sixteenth note *n* (AmE) semicorchea *f*

sixth¹ /sɪksθ/ *adj* **1** sexto **2** (elliptical use): **the upper/lower ~** (in UK) el último/penúltimo año de la enseñanza secundaria; *see also* **fifth¹**

sixth² *adv* en sexto lugar; *see also* **fifth²**

sixth³ *n* **1** (Math) sexto *m* **2** (part) sexta parte *f*, sexto *m*

sixth: **~ form** *n* (in UK) *los dos últimos años de la enseñanza secundaria*; **~ sense** *n* sexto sentido *m*

sixtieth¹ /ˈsɪkstiəθ/ *adj* sexagésimo; *see also* **fifth¹**

sixtieth² *adv* en sexagésimo lugar; *see also* **fifth²**

sixtieth³ *n* **1** (Math) sesentavo *m* **2** (part) sesentava *or* sexagésima parte *f*

sixty /ˈsɪksti/ *adj/n* sesenta *adj inv/m*; **the Swinging Sixties** los movidos años sesenta; *see also* **seventy**

sizable /ˈsaɪzəbəl/ *adj* ‹*fortune*› considerable; ‹*property*› de proporciones considerables

size /saɪz/ *n*

A (dimensions) tamaño *m*; (of problem, task) magnitud *f*, envergadura *f*; **what ~ is it?** ¿de qué tamaño es?, ¿qué tamaño tiene?, ¿cómo es de grande?; **their house is half/twice the ~ of ours** su casa es la mitad/el doble de grande que la nuestra; ***that's about the ~ of it*** (colloq) de eso se trata; (as answer) tú lo has dicho, así es; ***to cut sb down to ~*** poner* a algn en su sitio, bajarle los humos a algn (fam)

B (of clothes) talla *f* or (RPl) talle *m*; (of shoes, gloves) número *m*; **what ~ do you take?** ¿qué talla *or* (RPl) talle tiene *or* usa?; **I take (a) ~ 10 in shoes** calzo *or* (Esp tb) gasto el número 10; **try this one on for ~** pruébese éste a ver cómo le queda la talla *or* (RPl) el talle

Phrasal verb

• **size up** [v ▸ o ▸ adv, v ▸ adv ▸ o] (colloq) ‹*problem*› evaluar*; **she ~d him up straightaway** enseguida lo caló; **they ~d each other up warily** se miraron recelosamente, como midiéndose

-size /saɪz/, **-sized** /saɪzd/ *suff*: **medium~** de tamaño mediano

sizeable *adj* ▸**sizable**

-sized /saɪzd/ *suff* ▸**-size**

sizzle /ˈsɪzəl/ *vi* chisporrotear, crepitar

sizzling /ˈsɪzlɪŋ/ *adj* ‹*fat/sausages*› muy caliente; (*as adv*): **a ~ hot day** un día de calor abrasador

skanky /ˈskæŋki/ *adj* **-kier, -kiest** (colloq) ‹*clothes/shirt*› asqueroso, guarro (Esp fam); ‹*girl/bride*› con pinta de putilla (fam); ‹*bar/motel*› de mala muerte, cutre (Esp fam)

skate¹ /skeɪt/ *n*

A [c] (*ice ~*) patín *m* (*para patinaje sobre hielo*); (*roller ~*) patín *m* (*de ruedas*); ***to get*** *o* ***put one's ~s on*** (BrE) darse* prisa, apurarse (AmL)

B [u c] (*pl ~ or ~s*) (Culin, Zool) raya *f*

skate² *vi* patinar; **to go skating** ir* a patinar

Phrasal verbs

• **skate around**, (BrE also) **skate round** [v ▸ prep ▸ o] (colloq) ‹*problem/difficulty*› esquivar

• **skate over** [v ▸ prep ▸ o] ‹*problem/issue*› tratar muy por encima

skateboard /ˈskeɪtbɔːrd || ˈskeɪtbɔːd/ *n* monopatín *m or* (CS, Méx, Ven) patineta *f*

skateboarder /ˈskeɪtbɔːrdər || ˈskeɪtbɔːdə(r)/ *n* monopatinador, -dora *m,f*, patinador, -dora *m,f* de patineta (AmL)

skater /ˈskeɪtər || ˈskeɪtə(r)/ *n* patinador, -dora *m,f*

skating /ˈskeɪtɪŋ/ *n* [u] (*ice ~*) patinaje *m* sobre hielo; (*roller ~*) patinaje *m* sobre ruedas; (*before n*) **~ rink** pista *f* de patinaje

skein /skeɪn/ *n* (of yarn) madeja *f*

skeleton¹ /ˈskelətn || ˈskelɪtn/ *n* **1** (Anat) esqueleto *m*; ***a ~ in sb's closet*** *o* (BrE) ***cupboard*** *un secreto vergonzoso que se intenta mantener oculto* **2** (of building, vehicle) armazón *m or f*, estructura *f*

skeleton² *adj* (*before n*) ‹*service*› mínimo, básico; ‹*crew/staff*› reducido

skeleton key *n* llave *f* maestra

skeptic, (BrE) **sceptic** /ˈskeptɪk/ *n* escéptico, -ca *m,f*

skeptical, (BrE) **sceptical** /ˈskeptɪkəl/ *adj* ‹*person/attitude*› escéptico; **to be ~ OF** *o* **ABOUT sb/sth** tener* dudas ACERCA DE *or* CON RESPECTO A algn/algo

skeptically, (BrE) **sceptically** /ˈskeptɪkli/ *adv* con escepticismo

skepticism, (BrE) **scepticism** /ˈskeptɪsɪzəm/ *n* [u] escepticismo *m*

sketch¹ /sketʃ/ *n*

A (drawing) bosquejo *m*, esbozo *m*; (for painting, sculpture etc) boceto *m*, bosquejo *m*, esbozo *m*; (*before n*) **~ map** croquis *m*

B **1** (Theat, TV) sketch *m*, apunte *m* **2** (Lit) *breve ensayo o composición literaria*

sketch² *vt* **1** (draw) hacer* un bosquejo de, bosquejar **2** ‹*idea/plot*› esbozar*, bosquejar

■ **sketch** *vi* hacer* bosquejos *or* bocetos

sketch: **~book** *n* cuaderno *m* de bocetos; **~pad** *n* bloc *m* de dibujo

sketchy /ˈsketʃi/ *adj* **-chier, -chiest** ‹*account/treatment*› muy superficial; ‹*knowledge*› muy básico

skewbald /ˈskjuːbɔːld/ *adj* pío

skewer /ˈskjuːər || ˈskjuːə(r)/ *n* pincho *m*, brocheta *f*, brochette *f* (RPl)

skew-whiff /ˈskjuːˈhwɪf || ˌskjuːˈwɪf/ *adj* (BrE colloq) (*pred*) **to be ~** estar* torcido, estar* chueco (AmL)

S

ski[1] /skiː/ *n* esquí *m*; (*before n*) ~ **boots** botas *fpl* de esquiar; ~ **mask** verdugo *m*, pasamontañas *m*; ~ **pants** pantalones *mpl* de esquí; ~ **pole** *o* (BrE) **stick** bastón *m* (de esquí); ~ **run** pista *f* de esquí

ski[2] *vi* **skis, skiing, skied** esquiar*; **to go ~ing** ir* a esquiar; **we ~ed down the mountain** bajamos la montaña esquiando

skid[1] /skɪd/ *n*

A (slide) (Auto) patinazo *m*, derrape *m*, derrapaje *m*, patinada *f* (AmL); **to go into a ~** patinar, derrapar; (*before n*) ~ **marks** marcas *fpl* de un patinazo

B (for moving goods) rastra *f*; ***to be on the ~s*** (colloq) ir* cuesta abajo; ***to put the ~s under sb*** hacerle* *or* (Esp) ponerle* la zancadilla a algn, (a)serrucharle el piso a algn (CS)

C (support) (AmE) larguero *m*

skid[2] *vi* **-dd-** «*car/plane/wheels*» patinar, derrapar; «*person*» resbalarse; «*object*» deslizarse*; **we ~ded off the road** patinamos *or* derrapamos y nos salimos de la carretera; **the vehicle ~ded to a halt** el vehículo se detuvo tras dar un patinazo

skid row /rəʊ/ *n* [u] (AmE colloq) barrios *mpl* bajos; **he's heading for ~ ~** va a terminar mal

skier /ˈskiːər || ˈskiə(r)/ *n* esquiador, -dora *m,f*

skiing /ˈskiːɪŋ/ *n* [u] esquí *m*

skijump /ˈskiːdʒʌmp/ *n* 1▸ (ramp) trampolín *m*, pista *f* de salto 2▸ (action) salto *m* con esquís

skilful *etc* (BrE) ▸**skillful** *etc*

skilift /ˈskiːlɪft/ *n* telesquí *m*

skill /skɪl/ *n* 1▸ [u] (ability) habilidad *f*; **technical ~** destreza *f*; **her ~ as a negotiator** su habilidad para negociar; **game of ~** juego *m* de ingenio; ~ IN/AT **sth**: **her ~ at (doing) crosswords** su habilidad para hacer crucigramas *or* para los crucigramas; **the post requires ~ in administration** el puesto requiere dotes *or* aptitudes administrativas 2▸ [c] (technique): **typing is a very useful ~ to have** saber escribir a máquina es muy útil; **the course develops your analytical ~s** el curso desarrolla su capacidad analítica; **she has no secretarial ~s** no sabe taquigrafía ni mecanografía (*or* procesamiento de textos *etc*); **social ~s** don *m* de gentes

skilled /skɪld/ *adj* ‹*negotiator*› hábil, experto; ‹*pilot*› diestro, experto; ‹*worker/labor*› calificado *or* (Esp) cualificado; ‹*work*› de especialista, especializado

skillet /ˈskɪlət || ˈskɪlɪt/ *n* 1▸ (frying pan) sartén *f or* (AmL tb) sartén *m* 2▸ (saucepan) (BrE) *cacerola pequeña con mango largo*

skillful, (BrE) **skilful** /ˈskɪlfəl/ *adj* ‹*liar/play*› hábil; ‹*surgeon/mechanic*› diestro; (at sewing, craftwork) habilidoso, diestro, hábil

skillfully, (BrE) **skilfully** /ˈskɪlfəli/ *adv* hábilmente, con habilidad

skim /skɪm/ **-mm-** *vt*

A (Culin) ‹*milk*› descremar, desnatar (Esp); ‹*soup*› espumar; ~ **the fat off the stock** quítele la grasa al caldo

B 1▸ (glide over) ‹*water/treetops*› pasar casi rozando 2▸ (throw): **to ~ stones** hacer* cabrillas, hacer* patitos (CS, Méx), hacer* pan y quesito (Col)

C (read quickly) leer* por encima, echarle una ojeada a

■ **skim** *vi*

A (glide): **the speedboat ~med over the sea** la lancha apenas rozaba la superficie del mar

B (read quickly) leer* por encima; **my eye ~med down the page** le eché una ojeada *or* un vistazo a la página; **to ~ THROUGH sth** leer* algo por encima

skim milk, (BrE) **skimmed milk** /skɪmd/ *n* [u] leche *f* descremada *or* (Esp tb) desnatada

skimobile /ˈskiːməbiːl/ *n* (AmE) motoesquí *m* (*de nieve*), esquimóvil *m*

skimp /skɪmp/ *vi* (colloq) **to ~ (ON sth)** escatimar (algo), cicatear (algo) (fam), mezquinar (algo) (esp AmL)

skimpy /ˈskɪmpi/ *adj* **-pier, -piest** ‹*meal/portion*› mezquino, pobre; ‹*funds*› escaso; **a ~ nightdress** un brevísimo camisón

skin[1] /skɪn/ *n* 1▸ [u] (of person) piel *f*; (esp of face; in terms of quality, condition) cutis *m*, piel *f*; (in terms of color) tez *f*, piel *f*; ***by the ~ of one's teeth*** por un pelo (fam), por los pelos (fam); ***it's no ~ off my nose*** a mí me trae sin cuidado, ¿a mí qué me importa?; ***to be all ~ and bones*** estar* hecho un esqueleto, estar* en los huesos; ***to get under sb's ~*** (colloq) crisparle los nervios a algn, sacar* a algn de quicio; ***to have a thick/thin ~*** ser* insensible/muy sensible a las críticas; ***to have sb under one's ~*** (colloq) estar* loco por algn (fam); ***to jump*** *o* ***leap out of one's ~***: **I nearly jumped out of my ~ when ...** casi me muero del susto cuando ... (fam); (*before n*) ‹*disease*› de la piel, cutáneo; ~ **graft** injerto *m* (cutáneo); ▸**save**[1] *vt* **A1** 2▸ [u c] (of animal, bird, fish) piel *f* 3▸ [u c] (of tomatoes, plums, sausage) piel *f*; (of potatoes, bananas) piel *f*, cáscara *f* 4▸ [u] (on milk, custard) nata *f*; (on paint) capa *f* dura

skin[2] *vt* **-nn-** 1▸ ‹*animal*› despellejar, desollar*; **to ~ sb alive** desollar* vivo a algn, arrancarle* la piel a tiras a algn; **~ the tomatoes** quíteles la piel a los tomates, pele los tomates 2▸ (scrape) ‹*knee/elbow*› despellejar, pelar

skin: **~deep** /ˈskɪnˈdiːp/ *adj* (*pred*) **to be ~deep** ser* superficial; **~diver** *n* buzo *m*, submarinista *mf*; **~diving** *n* [u] submarinismo *m*, buceo *m*; **~flint** *n* (colloq) roñoso, -sa *m,f* (fam), tacaño, -ña *m,f*, amarrete, -ta *m,f* (AmS fam), pichirre *mf* (Ven fam)

skinful /ˈskɪnfʊl/ *n*: ***to have had a ~*** (colloq) estar* como una cuba (fam)

skinhead /ˈskɪnhed/ *n* cabeza *mf* rapada

-skinned /skɪnd/ *suff*: **smooth~/red~** de piel suave/roja

skinny /ˈskɪni/ *adj* **-nier, -niest** ‹*person*› flacucho (fam); ‹*coffee/latte/mocha*› (colloq) con leche descremada *or* (Esp) desnatada

skint /skɪnt/ *adj* (BrE colloq) (*pred*): **to be ~** estar* pelado (fam), estar* pato (CS fam), estar* pelando gajos (Ven fam)

skintight /ˈskɪnˈtaɪt/ *adj* muy ceñido, muy ajustado

skip[1] /skɪp/ *n*

A (jump) brinco *m*, saltito *m*

B (BrE) (container) contenedor *m* (*para escombros, basura etc*)

skip[2] **-pp-** *vi*

A 1▸ (move lightly and quickly): **he ~ped along the path** iba brincando *or* dando saltitos por el camino 2▸ (with rope) (BrE) ▸*vt* **B**

B (in writing, speaking, reading) saltar; **to ~ over sth** saltarse *or* (RPl) saltearse algo

■ **skip** *vt*

A 1▸ (omit) ‹*page/chapter*› saltarse, saltearse (RPl); **I think I'll ~ dinner today** creo que hoy no voy a cenar *or* (fam) voy a pasar de cenar; **his heart ~ped a beat** le dio un vuelco el corazón; **~ it!** (colloq) ¡déjalo!, ¡olvídalo! 2▸ (not attend) ‹*class/meeting*› faltar a, fumarse (fam)

B (jump) (AmE): **to ~ rope** saltar a la cuerda *or* (Esp tb) a la comba, saltar (al) lazo (Col), saltar al cordel (Chi)

C **to ~ town** (leave) (AmE) desaparecer* del mapa (fam)

skipper[1] /ˈskɪpər || ˈskɪpə(r)/ *n* (colloq) 1▸ (of boat) patrón, -trona *m,f*, capitán, -tana *m,f*; (of plane) capitán, -tana *m,f* 2▸ (Sport) (coach) entrenador, -dora *m,f*; (captain) capitán, -tana *m,f*; (*as form of address*) jefe, -fa (fam)

skipper[2] *vt* (colloq) ‹*boat/plane*› capitanear

skip rope, (BrE) **skipping rope** /ˈskɪpɪŋ/ *n* ▸**jump rope**

skirmish /ˈskɜːrmɪʃ/ *n* (Mil) escaramuza *f*, refriega *f*

skirt[1] /skɜːrt || skɜːt/ *n* falda *f*, pollera *f* (CS)

skirt[2] *vt* 1▸ (run alongside) bordear 2▸ ▸**skirt around**

Phrasal verb

• **skirt around**, (BrE also) **skirt round** [v ▸ prep ▸ o] 1▸ ‹*mountain/lake*› bordear 2▸ ‹*issue/problem*› eludir

skirting (board) /ˈskɜːrtɪŋ || ˈskɜːtɪŋ/ *n* [c u] (BrE) zócalo *m*, rodapié *m*, guardapolvo *m* (Chi)

skit /skɪt/ *n* (Theat) sketch *m* satírico

skittish /ˈskɪtɪʃ/ *adj* 1▸ (capricious) ‹*person*› voluble, veleidoso 2▸ (nervous) ‹*horse*› asustadizo

skittle /ˈskɪtl̩/ *n* bolo *m*

skittles /ˈskɪtl̩z/ *n* (+ *sing vb*) bolos *mpl*; **to have a game of ~** jugar* a los bolos

skive /skaɪv/ *vi* (BrE colloq) 1▸ (not work) holgazanear, gandulear (fam), sacar* la vuelta (Chi fam), hacer* sebo (RPl fam) 2▸ ▸**skive off 2**

Phrasal verb

• **skive off** (BrE colloq) [v ▸ adv] 1▸ (disappear) escurrir el bulto (fam), escaparse, pirarse (Esp fam) 2▸ (stay away — from school) hacer* novillos (fam), hacerse* la rata *or* la rabona (RPl fam), irse* de pinta (Méx fam), hacer* la cimarra *or* capear (clases) (Chi fam), capar clase (Col fam); (— from work) no ir* a trabajar, capear (Chi) *or* (Col) capar trabajo (fam)

skiver /'skaɪvər || 'skaɪvə(r)/ *n* (BrE colloq) vago, -ga *m,f* (fam), haragán, -gana *m,f*, capeador, -dora *m,f* (Chi fam)

skivvy /'skɪvi/ *n* (*pl* **-vies**)
A (servant) (BrE colloq) fregona *f* (pey), sirvienta *f*
B **skivvies**® *pl* (underwear) (AmE colloq) ropa *f* interior; **in his skivvies** en paños menores (fam & hum)

skulduggery, skullduggery /skʌl'dʌgəri/ *n* [u] trapicheo *m* (fam), tejemanejes *mpl*

skulk /skʌlk/ *vi*: **I saw him ~ing in the background** lo vi al fondo, tratando de pasar desapercibido; **what are you doing ~ing around in here?** ¿qué haces merodeando por aquí?

skull /skʌl/ *n* cráneo *m*; **the ~ and crossbones** la bandera pirata con la calavera

skullcap /'skʌlkæp/ *n* casquete *m*; (Relig) solideo *m*

skullduggery *n* [u] ▸**skulduggery**

skunk /skʌŋk/ *n* (Zool) mofeta *f*, zorrillo *m* (AmL), zorrino *m* (CS), mapurite *m* (AmC, Ven); ***to be as drunk as a ~*** (AmE colloq & hum) estar* como una cuba (fam)

sky /skaɪ/ *n* [u c] (*pl* **skies**) cielo *m*, firmamento *m* (liter); ***the ~'s the limit*** todo es posible; ***to praise sth/sb to the skies*** poner* algo/a algn por las nubes

sky: **~-blue** /'skaɪ'blu:/ *adj* (*pred* **~ blue**) (dark) azul cielo *adj inv*; (light) azul celeste *adj inv*, celeste (AmL); **~dive** /'skaɪdaɪv/ *vi* hacer* paracaidismo acrobático; **~diving** *n* [u] paracaidismo *m* (*en la modalidad de caída libre*); **~high** /'skaɪ'haɪ/ *adj*: **prices are ~high** los precios están por las nubes *or* son astronómicos; **~jack** *vt* secuestrar (*un avión*); **~lark** *n* alondra *f*; **~light** *n* tragaluz *m*, claraboya *f*; **~line** *n* **1** (horizon) (línea *f* del) horizonte *m* **2** (of city): **the Manhattan ~line** los edificios de Manhattan recortados contra el horizonte; **~scraper** *n* rascacielos *m*

slab /slæb/ *n* **1** (of stone) losa *f*; (of concrete) bloque *m*; (of wood) tabla *f*; (of cake, bread) pedazo *m*, trozo *m* (*grueso*); (of chocolate) tableta *f* **2** (in mortuary) (colloq) **the ~** la mesa de autopsias

slack¹ /slæk/ *adj* **-er, -est**
A (loose) ‹*rope/cable*› flojo; **the rope went ~** la cuerda se aflojó
B (lax, negligent) ‹*student*› poco aplicado; ‹*piece of work*› flojo; **they're very ~ about paying on time** son muy negligentes en cuanto a pagar puntualmente
C (not busy) ‹*period*› de poca actividad, de poco movimiento

slack² *n*
A [u] (rope, wire): **there's too much ~ in the rope** la cuerda está demasiado floja; ***to take up the ~ in sth*** tensar algo
B **slacks** *pl* pantalones *mpl* (de sport)

slack³ *vi* (colloq) haraganear, flojear (fam), hacer* el vago (Esp fam)

slacken /'slækən/ *vi* **1** (become looser) «*rope/wire*» aflojarse **2** (diminish) ▸**slacken off A**
■ **slacken** *vt* **1** (loosen) ▸**slacken off B** **2** (reduce) ‹*speed*› reducir*; ‹*pace*› aflojar

Phrasal verb
• **slacken off**
A [v ▸ adv] «*wind*» amainar, aflojar; «*student*» aflojar el ritmo de trabajo; «*speed/rate*» disminuir*; «*trade/demand*» decaer*, disminuir*
B [v ▸ o ▸ adv, v ▸ adv ▸ o] (loosen) ‹*rope/wire*› aflojar

slacker /'slækər || 'slækə(r)/ *n* (colloq) vago, -ga *m,f* (fam), flojo, -ja *m,f* (fam)

slag /slæg/ *n*
A [u] (Metall) escoria *f*; (Min) escombro *m*, escoria *f*; (*before n*) **~ heap** escorial *m*, escombrera *f*
B [c] (promiscuous woman) (BrE sl & pej) putilla *f* (fam & pey), fulana *f* (fam & pey)

Phrasal verb
• **slag off**: **-gg-** [v ▸ o ▸ adv, v ▸ adv ▸ o] (BrE sl) ‹*person*› hablar pestes de (fam); ‹*record/film*› poner* por los suelos

slain /sleɪn/ *past p of* **slay**

slake /sleɪk/ *vt* (liter) ‹*thirst*› saciar, aplacar*

slalom /'slɑ:ləm/ *n* slalom *m*

slam¹ /slæm/ **-mm-** *vt*
A **1** (close violently): **to ~ the door** dar* un portazo; **to ~ the door shut** cerrar* la puerta de un portazo; **she ~med the door in my face** me dio con la puerta en las narices **2** (put with force): **he ~med the book down on the table** tiró el libro sobre la mesa; **to ~ on the brakes** pegar* un frenazo
B (criticize) (journ) atacar* violentamente
■ **slam** *vi* «*door*» cerrarse* de un portazo *or* de golpe

slam² *n* (*no pl*): **the door shut with a ~** la puerta se cerró de un portazo; **she closed the book with a ~** cerró el libro de un golpe

slander¹ /'slændər || 'slɑ:ndə(r)/ *n* [u c] calumnia *f*, difamación *f*

slander² *vt* ‹*person*› calumniar, difamar

slanderous /'slændərəs || 'slɑ:ndərəs/ *adj* calumnioso, difamatorio

slang /slæŋ/ *n* [u] argot *m*; **army/student ~** argot *m or* jerga *f* militar/estudiantil

slanging match /'slæŋɪŋ/ *n* (BrE colloq) bronca *f* (fam), intercambio *m* de insultos

slant¹ /slænt || slɑ:nt/ *n*
A [u] (slope) inclinación *f*; (of roof, floor) pendiente *f*; **on a** *o* **the ~** inclinado
B [c] (point of view) enfoque *m*; (bias) sesgo *m*

slant² *vi* **1** «*handwriting*» inclinarse **2** **slanting** *pres p* ‹*roof/handwriting*› inclinado; ‹*eyes*› rasgado
■ **slant** *vt* ‹*account/report*› darle* un sesgo a; (give bias to) presentar tendenciosamente

slap¹ /slæp/ *vt* **-pp-**
A (hit): **to ~ sb** (on face) pegarle* *or* darle* una bofetada *or* (AmL tb) una cachetada a algn, abofetear a algn, cachetear a algn (AmL); (on arm, leg) pegarle* *or* darle* una palmada a algn
B **1** (put with force) tirar; **she ~ped the contract down on the desk** tiró *or* (fam) plantó el contrato en el escritorio **2** (put, apply carelessly): **he ~ped some paint on it** le dio una mano de pintura rápidamente; **she ~ped on some makeup** se maquilló de cualquier manera **3** (impose) (colloq) **to ~ sth ON sth**: **they ~ped another 5% on the price** le encajaron un 5% de aumento al precio (fam); **to ~ sb WITH sth** (AmE): **we've been ~ped with a large fine** nos han encajado *or* metido un multazo (fam)

slap² *n* (on face) bofetada *f*, cachetada *f* (AmL); (on back, leg) palmada *f*; **he gave me a ~ on the back** me dio una palmada *or* una palmadita en la espalda; ***a ~ in the face*** (rebuff, insult) una bofetada; ***a ~ on the wrist*** un tirón de orejas (fam), un palmetazo

slap³ *adv* (colloq): **she walked ~ into the tree** se dio de narices contra el árbol; **I arrived ~ in the middle of the meeting** llegué justo en plena reunión

slap: **~-bang** /'slæp'bæŋ/ *adv* (colloq) **1** (directly) justo; **it's ~-bang in the center of town** está justo en el centro *or* (Méx tb) en el mero centro de la ciudad **2** (violently): **he went ~-bang into the door** se dio de narices contra la puerta ¡paf! (fam); **~dash** *adj* ‹*work*› chapucero (fam); **~happy** /'slæp'hæpi/ *adj* (colloq) **1** (foolish) (AmE) tocado (fam) **2** (careless) (BrE) ‹*person*› despreocupado; ‹*work*› descuidado; **~stick** *n* [u] bufonadas *fpl*, payasadas *fpl*; (*before n*) **~stick comedy** astracanada *f*; **~-up** *adj* (BrE colloq): **a ~-up meal** una comilona (fam), un banquetazo (fam)

slash¹ /slæʃ/ *n*
A (cut — on body) cuchillada *f*, tajo *m*; (— in tire, cloth) raja *f*, corte *m*
B (oblique) barra *f* (oblicua)

slash² *vt*
A ‹*person/face*› acuchillar, tajear (AmL); ‹*tires/coat*› rajar; **he ~ed his wrists** se cortó las venas
B (reduce) ‹*prices/taxes*› rebajar drásticamente; Ⓢ **prices slashed** espectaculares rebajas

slash-and-burn /'slæʃən(d)'bɜ:rn || 'slæʃən(d)'bɜ:n/ *adj* (*before n*)
A (Agr) de talar y quemar
B (ruthless) implacable, despiadado

slat /slæt/ *n* (of wood) listón *m*, tablilla *f*; (of other material) tira *f*

slate¹ /sleɪt/ *n*
A **1** [u] (rock) pizarra *f* **2** [c] (roof tile) pizarra *f*
B [c] (for writing on) pizarra *f*; ***to have a clean ~*** no tener* borrones en la hoja de servicios; **to wipe the ~ clean** hacer* borrón y cuenta nueva; ***to put sth on the ~*** (BrE) apuntar algo en la cuenta

S

C [c] (list of candidates) (AmE) lista *f* de candidatos

slate² *vt*

A ‹*roof*› empizarrar

B (criticize) ‹*book/film/writer*› poner* por los suelos

C (AmE) **to be ~d** 1 (scheduled): **the convention is ~d for March** la convención está programada para marzo 2 (chosen, destined): **he's ~d to replace the director** es el candidato para sustituir al director

slaughter¹ /'slɔːtər || 'slɔːtə(r)/ *n* [u] 1 (of animals) matanza *f* 2 (massacre) masacre *f*, matanza *f*, carnicería *f*

slaughter² *vt* 1 (kill) ‹*pig/cattle*› matar, carnear (CS); ‹*civilians/troops*› matar salvajemente, masacrar 2 (defeat) (colloq) ‹*opponent/team*› darle* una paliza a (fam)

slaughterhouse /'slɔːtərhaʊs || 'slɔːtəhaʊs/ *n* matadero *m*

Slav /slɑːv/ *n* eslavo, -va *m,f*

slave¹ /sleɪv/ *n* esclavo, -va *m,f*; **to be a ~ TO sth** ser* esclavo DE algo; (*before n*) **~ trade** comercio *m* *or* trata *f* de esclavos; **~ trader** negrero, -ra *m,f*

slave² *vi* (colloq): **I've been slaving away all day** he estado trabajando como un negro *or* como un burro todo el día (fam); **to ~ AT *o* OVER sth**: **he's been slaving (away) at *o* over the report for days** lleva días trabajando como un negro *or* como un burro con el informe

slave: **~ driver** *n* (colloq) negrero, -ra *m,f* (fam); **~ labor**, (BrE) **~ labour** *n* [u] 1 (ill-paid work): **this job is just ~ labor** en este trabajo te explotan, aquí son unos negreros (fam) 2 (Hist): **roads built by ~ labor** carreteras *fpl* construidas con el trabajo de los esclavos

slaver /'slævər || 'slævə(r)/ *vi* babear

slavery /'sleɪvəri/ *n* [u] esclavitud *f*; **he was sold into ~** lo vendieron como esclavo

Slavic /'slɑːvɪk/ *adj* eslavo

slavish /'sleɪvɪʃ/ *adj*

A (unoriginal) falto de originalidad

B (servile) ‹*attitude*› servil; ‹*devotion*› ciego, incondicional

slavishly /'sleɪvɪʃli/ *adv*

A ‹*follow/copy*› ciegamente

B (subserviently) servilmente

Slavonic /slə'vɑːnɪk || slə'vɒnɪk/ *adj* eslavo

slaw /slɔː/ *n* [u] (AmE) *ensalada de repollo, zanahoria y cebolla con mayonesa*

slay /sleɪ/ *vt* (*past* **slew**; *past p* **slain**) (liter *or* journ) asesinar, dar* muerte a

sleaze /sliːz/ *n* sordidez *f*; (*before n*) **the ~ factor was decisive in his defeat** su pasado turbio (*or* su affaire *etc*) fue un factor decisivo en su derrota

sleazebag /'sliːzbæg/, **sleazeball** /'sliːzbɔːl/ *n* (AmE colloq) canalla *mf*

sleazy /'sliːzi/ *adj* **-zier, -ziest** ‹*district/bar*› sórdido; ‹*character/type*› de mala pinta

sled¹ /sled/ *n* (AmE) trineo *m*

sled² *vi* **-dd-** (AmE) ir* en trineo

S

sledge /sledʒ/ *n/vi* ▸ **sled**[1,2]

sledgehammer /'sledʒˌhæmər || 'sledʒˌhæmə(r)/ *n* mazo *m*, almádena *f*

sleek /sliːk/ *adj* **-er, -est** 1 (glossy) ‹*hair/fur*› lacio y brillante 2 (well-groomed) acicalado, pulcro 3 (stylish, elegant) de líneas elegantes

sleep¹ /sliːp/ *n*

A [u c] sueño *m*; **I need eight hours' ~** yo necesito ocho horas de sueño; **to go to ~** dormirse*; **she went to ~ almost immediately** se durmió *or* se quedó dormida casi inmediatamente; **my foot has gone to ~** se me ha dormido el pie; **I can't get to ~** no puedo dormirme, no puedo conciliar el sueño; **try and get some ~** trata de dormir un poco; **I haven't had a decent night's ~ in weeks** hace semanas que no duermo una noche entera; **the cat had to be put to ~** (euph) hubo que sacrificar al gato (euf); **to walk in one's ~** ser* sonámbulo; **to talk in one's ~** hablar dormido; ***not to lose any ~ over sb/sth*** no perder* el sueño *or* no preocuparse por algn/algo

B [u] (in eyes) lagañas *fpl*, legañas *fpl*

sleep² (*past & past p* **slept**) *vi* dormir*; **to ~ late** dormir* hasta tarde; **goodnight, ~ tight!** hasta mañana, que duermas bien *or* que descanses; **his bed had not been slept in** no había dormido en su cama; ***to ~ like a log*** *o* (BrE) ***top*** (colloq) dormir* como un tronco *or* como un lirón *or* como un bendito (fam)

■ **sleep** *vt*: **the hotel ~s 200 guests** el hotel tiene 200 camas *or* puede alojar a 200 personas

Phrasal verbs

- **sleep around** [v ▸ adv] (colloq & pej) acostarse* con cualquiera
- **sleep in** [v ▸ adv] 1 (sleep late) dormir* hasta tarde 2 «*servant/nurse*» vivir en (la) casa (*or* hospital *etc*)
- **sleep off** [v ▸ o ▸ adv, v ▸ adv ▸ o]: **he's still ~ing it off** (colloq) todavía está durmiendo la mona (fam); **they had a huge meal and went to bed to ~ it off** se atiborraron de comida y se fueron a dormir para reponerse
- **sleep on** [v ▸ prep ▸ o] ‹*decision/problem*› consultar con la almohada
- **sleep through** [v ▸ prep ▸ o]: **he slept through the alarm clock** no oyó el despertador y siguió durmiendo; **he slept through the whole film** durmió durante toda la película; **she'll ~ through anything** es capaz de seguir durmiendo aunque haya mucho ruido
- **sleep together** [v ▸ adv] (euph) tener* relaciones (sexuales)
- **sleep with** [v ▸ prep ▸ o] (euph) acostarse* con (euf)

sleeper /'sliːpər || 'sliːpə(r)/ *n*

A (person): **to be a heavy/light ~** tener* el sueño pesado/ligero

B (Rail) 1 (berth) litera *f*, cama *f* 2 (sleeping car) coche *m* cama, coche *m* dormitorio (CS) 3 (train) tren *m* con coches camas *or* (CS) coches dormitorio

C (on track) (Rail) durmiente *m* *or* (Esp) traviesa *f*

sleeping /'sliːpɪŋ/ *n* [u] (*before n*) **what are the ~ arrangements for tonight?** ¿dónde *or* cómo vamos a dormir esta noche?

sleeping: **~ bag** *n* saco *m* *or* (RPl) bolsa *f* de dormir; **~ Beauty** *n* la Bella Durmiente (del Bosque); **~ car** *n* (Rail) coche *m* cama, coche *m* dormitorio (CS); **~ partner** *n* (BrE Busn) socio, -cia *m,f* capitalista; **~ pill** *n* somnífero *m*, pastilla *f* para dormir; **~ policeman** *n* (BrE) ▸ **speed bump**; **~ sickness** *n* [u] enfermedad *f* del sueño; **~ tablet** *n* (BrE) ▸ **~ pill**

sleepless /'sliːpləs || 'sliːplɪs/ *adj*: **I had another ~ night** pasé otra noche en blanco *or* sin poder dormir

sleep: **~over** /'sliːpəʊvər || 'sliːpəʊvə(r)/ *n* (AmE) 1 (by employee — at place of work) permanencia *f* nocturna en el lugar de trabajo; (— on business trip) viaje *m* de negocios con estancia nocturna 2 (of guest) estancia *f* nocturna; **~walk** *vi* caminar dormido; **~walker** *n* sonámbulo, -la *m,f*

sleepy /'sliːpi/ *adj* **-pier, -piest** 1 (drowsy) ‹*expression*› adormilado, somnoliento, soñoliento; ‹*eyes*› de dormido; **to be/feel ~** tener* sueño; **to look ~** tener* cara de sueño; **I always get ~ in the afternoons** siempre me entra *or* me da sueño por la tarde 2 ‹*town/atmosphere*› aletargado

sleepyhead /'sliːpihed/ *n* (colloq) dormilón, -lona *m,f* (fam)

sleet¹ /sliːt/ *n* [u] aguanieve *f*

sleet² *v impers*: **it was ~ing** caía aguanieve

sleeve /sliːv/ *n* 1 (of garment) manga *f*; **to roll up one's ~s** arremangarse*; ***to have sth up one's ~*** (colloq) tener* algo planeado; ***to keep sth up one's ~*** reservarse un recurso; ***to laugh up one's ~*** reírse* disimuladamente de algn 2 (of record) (BrE) funda *f*, carátula *f*

sleeveless /'sliːvləs || 'sliːvlɪs/ *adj* sin mangas

sleigh /sleɪ/ *n* trineo *m*

sleight of hand /slaɪt/ *n* [u] prestidigitación *f*, juegos *mpl* de manos

slender /'slendər || 'slendə(r)/ *adj* **-derer, -derest** 1 ‹*person/figure*› delgado, esbelto; ‹*waist/neck*› fino, delgado 2 ‹*means/resources*› escaso, exiguo; ‹*majority*› estrecho; ‹*hope*› remoto; **by a ~ margin** por un estrecho margen

slenderize /'slendəraɪz/ *vt* (AmE) adelgazar*

slenderness /'slendərnəs || 'slendənɪs/ *n* delgadez *f*, esbeltez *f*

slept /slept/ *past & past p of* **sleep²**

sleuth /sluːθ/ *n* sabueso *mf*, detective *mf*

slew¹ /sluː/ *past of* **slay**

slew², (AmE also) **slue** /sluː/ *vt* (+ *adv compl*): **to ∼ the car/boat around** *o* **round** dar* la vuelta

■ **slew** *vi*: **the car ∼ed to the left** el coche dio un giro brusco a la izquierda

slice¹ /slaɪs/ *n*

A [c] (piece — of bread) rebanada *f*; (— of cake) trozo *m*, pedazo *m*; (— of cheese) rebanada *f*; (— of lemon, cucumber) rodaja *f*; (— of meat) tajada *f*; (— of ham) loncha *f*, lonja *f*, feta *f* (RPl); (— of melon) raja *f*

B [c] (implement) (BrE) pala *f*; **fish ∼** pala *f* para servir

C (Sport) **1** (spin on ball) (*no pl*) efecto *m* **2** [c] (shot — in tennis) tiro *m* cortado *or* con efecto; (— in golf) slice *m*

slice² *vt*

A (cut into slices) ‹*bread*› cortar (en rebanadas); ‹*meat*› cortar (en tajadas); ‹*cake*› cortar (en trozos); ‹*lemon/cucumber*› cortar (en rodajas); ‹*ham*› cortar (en lonchas); **to ∼ sth in two** *o* **in half** cortar algo en dos *or* por la mitad; ***any way you ∼ it*** (AmE colloq) lo mires por donde lo mires, sea como sea

B ‹*ball*› (in tennis) cortar, darle* con efecto a; (in golf) darle* oblicuamente a

■ **slice** *vi* **1** (cut): **the spade ∼d into the soft clay** la pala se hundió en la tierra blanda **2** (be cut): **this bread/ham doesn't ∼ very well** este pan/jamón es muy difícil de cortar *or* no se puede cortar bien

slicer /ˈslaɪsər || ˈslaɪsə(r)/ *n*: **bread ∼** (máquina *f*) rebanadora *f* de pan; **cheese ∼** pala *f* para cortar queso; **meat ∼** máquina *f* de cortar fiambre

slick¹ /slɪk/ *adj* **-er, -est**

A **1** (superficial) ‹*book/program*› ingenioso pero insustancial **2** ‹*person*› (glib) de mucha labia; (clever) hábil; ‹*reply*› fácil **3** (professional, smart) ‹*performance/production*› muy logrado *or* pulido

B (slippery) (AmE) ‹*surface*› resbaladizo, resbaloso (AmL)

slick² *n* (*oil* ∼) marea *f* negra

slick³ *vt*: **to ∼ one's hair down** alisarse el pelo; **his sleek, ∼ed-back hair** su pelo lacio y brillante peinado hacia atrás

slicker /ˈslɪkər || ˈslɪkə(r)/ *n* (AmE)

A ▸ **raincoat**

B ▸ **city slicker**

slide¹ /slaɪd/ (*past & past p* **slid** /slɪd/) *vi*

A (slip) (deliberately) deslizarse*; (accidentally) deslizarse*, resbalar(se); **the plate slid (off) onto the floor** el plato (se) resbaló y cayó al suelo; ***to let things ∼*** dejar que las cosas se vengan abajo

B **1** (move smoothly, glide) (+ *adv compl*): **the door ∼s open** la puerta se abre corriéndola; **she slid quietly out of the room** salió sigilosamente de la habitación **2** **sliding** *pres p*: **sliding door** puerta *f* corrediza

■ **slide** *vt* (+ *adv compl*): **she slid the book across the table toward him** le pasó el libro deslizándolo por la mesa; **to ∼ the bolt back** correr el cerrojo

slide² *n*

A (in playground, pool) tobogán *m*, resbaladilla *f* (Méx), rodadero *m* (Col), resbalín *m* (Chi)

B **1** (action — accidental) resbalón *m*, resbalada *f*; (— deliberate) deslizamiento *m* **2** (decline in prices) bajón *m*

C **1** (Phot) diapositiva *f*, transparencia *f*, filmina *f*; (*before n*) **∼ projector** proyector *m* de diapositivas; **∼ show** proyección *f* de diapositivas **2** (for microscope — glass plate) portaobjetos *m*; (— specimen) muestra *f*

D (for hair) (BrE) ▸ **barrette**

slide rule *n* regla *f* de cálculo

sliding scale /ˈslaɪdɪŋ/ *n* escala *f* móvil

slight¹ /slaɪt/ *adj* **-er, -est**

A **1** ‹*improvement/accent*› ligero, leve; **she has a ∼ temperature** tiene un poco de fiebre; **she walks with a ∼ limp** cojea ligeramente; **he gets upset at the ∼est thing** se molesta por la menor tontería *or* por cualquier nimiedad; **I haven't the ∼est idea** no tengo (ni) la menor *or* (ni) la más remota idea; **do you mind? — not in the ∼est** ¿te importa? — en absoluto *or* para nada; **he's not the ∼est bit interested** no le interesa en lo más mínimo *or* en absoluto **2** (minimal) escaso; **their chances are ∼** tienen muy pocas posibilidades

B (slim) delgado, menudo

slight² *vt* (frml) **1** (offend, ignore) desairar, hacerle* un desaire *or* un desprecio a **2** (belittle) ‹*work/contribution*› hablar con desdén de

slight³ *n* (frml) desaire *m*, desprecio *m*

slightly /ˈslaɪtli/ *adv*

A (a little) ‹*improve/change*› ligeramente, levemente, un poco; ‹*rain/snow*› ligeramente; ‹*different*› ligeramente; **it will sting ∼** te va a escocer un poco; **I know him only ∼** apenas si lo conozco

B (slimly): **∼ built** de complexión delgada *or* menuda

slim¹ /slɪm/ *adj* **-mm-** **1** (thin) ‹*person/figure*› esbelto, delgado; ‹*waist*› fino; ‹*volume/column*› fino **2** (scant) ‹*chance/hope*› escaso; ‹*majority*› estrecho

slim² *vi* **-mm-** **1** **∼ (down)** (become slimmer) ‹‹*person*›› adelgazar*, bajar de peso **2** (BrE) (diet) hacer* régimen *or* dieta; **I'm ∼ming** estoy a régimen *or* a dieta

slime /slaɪm/ *n* [u] **1** (thin mud) limo *m*, cieno *m* **2** (of snail, slug etc) baba *f*

slimeball /ˈslaɪmbɔːl/ *n* (esp AmE colloq) canalla *mf*

slimline /ˈslɪmlaɪn/ *adj* **1** ‹*briefcase/calculator*› plano, delgado **2** (low-calorie) (BrE) ‹*lemonade/margarine*› light *adj inv*, bajo en calorías, dietético

slimmer /ˈslɪmər || ˈslɪmə(r)/ *n* (BrE) *persona que está a régimen*

slimming /ˈslɪmɪŋ/ *n* [u] (BrE) adelgazamiento *m*

slimy /ˈslaɪmi/ *adj* **-mier, -miest** **1** (slippery) ‹*substance*› viscoso; ‹*surface*› viscoso **2** ‹*person/manner*› excesivamente obsequioso, falso, falluto (RPl fam)

sling¹ /slɪŋ/ *n* **1** (Med) cabestrillo *m*; **to have one's arm in a ∼** llevar el brazo en un cabestrillo **2** (for carrying a baby) canguro *m* **3** (for lifting) eslinga *f*

sling² (*past & past p* **slung**) *vt* (colloq) **1** (throw) tirar, lanzar*, arrojar, aventar* (Col, Méx, Per) **2** (hang) ‹*line/hammock*› colgar*, guindar (Col, Ven); **he wore his coat slung over his shoulders** llevaba el abrigo echado por encima de los hombros

Phrasal verb

• **sling out** [v ▸ o ▸ adv, v ▸ adv ▸ o] (BrE colloq)

A (got rid of) tirar (a la basura), botar (a la basura) (AmL exc RPl)

B (expel) ‹*person*› echar

sling: **∼back** *n* sandalia *f*/zapato *m* de tacón (*con el talón descubierto*); **∼shot** *n* (AmE) tirachinas *m*, honda *f* (CS, Per), cauchera *f* (Col), resortera *f* (Méx), china *f* (Ven)

slink /slɪŋk/ *vi* (*past & past p* **slunk**) (+ *adv compl*): **he slunk upstairs to his room** subió a su habitación sigilosamente *or* a hurtadillas; (with shame, embarrassment) subió avergonzado a su habitación; **to ∼ off** *o* **away** escabullirse*, escaparse

slinky /ˈslɪŋki/ *adj* **-kier, -kiest** ‹*dress*› ceñido, ajustado

slip¹ /slɪp/ *n*

A slide) resbalón *m*, resbalada *f* (AmL); ***to give sb the ∼*** (colloq) lograr zafarse de algn

B (mistake) error *m*, equivocación *f*; **a ∼ of the tongue/pen** un lapsus (linguae/cálami); ***there's many a ∼ twixt cup and lip*** del dicho al hecho hay mucho trecho

C (of paper): **a ∼ of paper** un papelito, un papel; ▸ **deposit² A1**

D (undergarment) combinación *f*, enagua *f*, viso *m*, fondo *m* (Méx)

E (of person): **a ∼ of a girl** una chiquilla, una chiquilina (AmL)

slip² **-pp-** *vi*

A **1** (slide, shift position) ‹‹*person*›› resbalar(se); ‹‹*clutch*›› patinar; **the knife ∼ped and he cut himself** se le fue el cuchillo y se cortó; **it just ∼ped out of my hands** se me resbaló de las manos **2** ‹‹*standards/service*›› decaer*, empeorar; **you're ∼ping** tu trabajo (*or* aplicación *etc*) ya no es lo que era

B **1** (move unobtrusively) (+ *adv compl*): **he ∼ped into the room without being observed** entró en la habitación sin que lo vieran; **we managed to ∼ past the guards** logramos pasar sin que nos vieran los guardias **2** (escape, be lost): **to let ∼ an opportunity, to let an opportunity ∼** dejar escapar una oportunidad; **they let the contract ∼ through their fingers** se dejaron quitar el contrato de las manos; **I didn't mean to say that: it just ∼ped out** no quería decirlo, pero se me escapó *or* salió; **I let (it) ∼ that ...** se me escapó que ... **3** (go quickly): **he's just ∼ped out to the bank** ha salido un momento al banco **4** (change): **I'll just ∼ into something more comfortable** me voy a poner algo más cómodo

S

■ **slip** *vt*
A 1 (put unobtrusively) (+ *adv compl*) poner*, meter, deslizar*; **she ~ped a coin into his hand** le pasó disimuladamente una moneda; **he ~ped his arm around her waist** le pasó el brazo por la cintura 2 (pass) **to ~ sth TO sb** pasarle algo A algn con disimulo
B 1 (break loose from): **don't let the dog ~ its leash** no dejes que se suelte el perro; ***to ~ sb's mind*** *o* ***memory***: **it completely ~ped my mind** me olvidé *or* se me olvidó por completo 2 (in knitting) ‹*stitch*› pasar sin tejer

Phrasal verbs

- **slip away** «*person/opportunity*» escabullirse*; «*hours/time*» pasar
- **slip by** [v ▸ adv] «*time*» pasar, transcurrir
- **slip in** [v ▸ o ▸ adv, v ▸ adv ▸ o] ‹*comment/reference*› incluir*, agregar*
- **slip off**

A [v ▸ o ▸ adv, v ▸ adv ▸ o] ‹*clothes/shoes*› quitarse
B [v ▸ adv] escabullirse*

- **slip on** [v ▸ o ▸ adv, v ▸ adv ▸ o] ‹*clothes/shoes*› ponerse*
- **slip past** ▸**slip by**
- **slip up** [v ▸ adv] equivocarse*, cometer un error

slip: **~knot** *n* nudo *m* corredizo; **~-on** *adj* ‹*shoes*› sin cordones

slipped disc /slɪpt/ *n* hernia *f* de disco

slipper /'slɪpər || 'slɪpə(r)/ *n* zapatilla *f*, pantufla *f* (esp AmL), chancla *f* (Col)

slippery /'slɪpəri/ *adj* 1 ‹*surface/ground/soap*› resbaladizo, resbaloso (AmL) 2 ‹*person*› (elusive) escurridizo, evasivo; (untrustworthy) que no es de fiar

slippy /'slɪpi/ *adj* ▸**slippery 1**

slip: **~-road** *n* (BrE) vía *f* de acceso (*a una autopista*)/vía *f* de salida (*de una autopista*); **~shod** *adj* chapucero (fam), descuidado; **~stream** *n* estela *f*; **~-up** *n* error *m*, descuido *m*, metedura *f* de pata (fam); **~way** *n* grada *f*

slit[1] /slɪt/ *n* (opening) rendija *f*, hendidura *f*; (cut) raja *f*

slit[2] *vt* (*pres p* **slitting**; *past & past p* **slit**) cortar, rajar (Méx); **to ~ sb's throat** degollar a algn, cortarle el pescuezo a algn (fam)

slither /'slɪðər || 'slɪðə(r)/ *vi* «*snake*» deslizarse*

sliver /'slɪvər || 'slɪvə(r)/ *n* 1 (of glass, wood) astilla *f* 2 (thin slice) tajada *f* (*or* rodaja *f etc*) fina; *see also* **slice[1] A**

slob /slɑːb || slɒb/ *n* (colloq) vago, -ga *m,f* (fam), dejado, -da *m,f*, atorrante *mf* (CS fam); **you fat ~!** ¡cerdo! (fam)

slobber /'slɑːbər || 'slɒbə(r)/ *vi* babear, babosear

sloe /sləʊ/ *n* 1 (fruit) endrina *f* 2 (bush) endrino *m*

slog[1] /slɑːg || slɒg/ *n* (colloq) (*no pl*): **we've got a long ~ ahead of us** tenemos un largo y arduo camino por delante

slog[2] **-gg-** *vi* caminar trabajosamente; **we ~ged up the hill** subimos la colina con dificultad *or* con gran esfuerzo

Phrasal verb

- **slog away** [v ▸ adv] (BrE colloq) sudar tinta (fam), trabajar duro (esp AmL)

slogan /'sləʊgən/ *n* (Busn) slogan *m*, eslogan *m*; (Pol) lema *m*, consigna *f*

sloop /sluːp/ *n* balandro *m*

slop /slɑːp || slɒp/ **-pp-** *vi* (colloq) 1 (spill) derramarse, volcarse* 2 (splash): **to ~ around** *o* **about** «*person*» chapotear; «*water*» agitarse haciendo ruido

slope[1] /sləʊp/ *n* 1 (sloping ground) cuesta *f*, pendiente *f*, barranca *f* (RPl); ***the slippery ~***: **they are on the slippery ~ to bankruptcy** van camino de la bancarrota 2 (of mountain) ladera *f*, falda *f* 3 (for skiing) pista *f* de esquí, cancha *f* de esquí (CS)

slope[2] *vi*: **her handwriting ~s backward/forward** tiene la letra inclinada hacia atrás/adelante; **the road begins to ~ downward** el camino empieza a descender

Phrasal verb

- **slope off** [v ▸ adv] (esp BrE colloq) escabullirse*, darse* el bote (Esp arg), tomárselas (RPl arg)

sloping /'sləʊpɪŋ/ *adj* ‹*field/floor*› en declive; ‹*roof/handwriting*› inclinado

sloppy /'slɑːpi || 'slɒpi/ *adj* **-pier, -piest**
A (careless) ‹*manners/work*› descuidado; ‹*presentation*› descuidado, desprolijo (CS); **he's such a ~ dresser** viste tan mal, anda tan desaliñado *or* desarreglado

B ‹*kiss*› baboso

slosh /slɑːʃ || slɒʃ/ *vt* (splash) echar
■ **slosh** *vi* **to ~ around** *o* **about** «*person*» chapotear; «*liquid*» agitarse haciendo ruido

sloshed /slɑːʃt || slɒʃt/ *adj* (colloq) (*pred*) **to be ~** estar* borracho, estar* como una cuba (fam); **to get ~** emborracharse, agarrarse *or* (Esp) cogerse* un pedo (fam)

slot[1] /slɑːt || slɒt/ *n*
A 1 (opening) ranura *f* 2 (groove) ranura *f*, muesca *f*
B (Rad, TV) espacio *m*

slot[2] **-tt-** *vt* (insert) **to ~ sth INTO sth** encajar algo EN algo
■ **slot** *vi* **to ~ INTO sth** encajar EN algo

Phrasal verbs

- **slot in**

A [v ▸ adv] «*shelf/part*» encajar
B [v ▸ o ▸ adv, v ▸ adv ▸ o] ‹*component*› hacer* encajar

- **slot together** [v ▸ adv] «*parts/items*» encajar (*unos con otros*)

sloth /sləʊθ/ *n* 1 [c] (Zool) perezoso *m* 2 [u] (laziness) (frml) pereza *f*

slothful /'sləʊθfəl/ *adj* (frml) perezoso, indolente

slot machine *n* 1 (vending machine) distribuidor *m* automático, máquina *f* expendedora 2 (for gambling) máquina *f* tragamonedas *or* (Esp tb) tragaperras

slouch[1] /slaʊtʃ/ *vi* 1 (droop shoulders): **don't ~!** ¡ponte derecho!; **I found her ~ed in an armchair** la encontré repatingada *or* (Esp) repantigada en un sillón 2 (walk) (+ *adv compl*): **he ~ed into/out of the room** entró en/salió de la habitación arrastrando los pies

slouch[2] *n*
A (of posture): **he walks with a ~** camina con los hombros caídos
B (of person) (colloq): **to be no ~** no ser* manco (fam); **she's no ~ when it comes to ...** no se queda atrás *or* (fam) no es manca cuando se trata de ...

slough off [v ▸ adv ▸ o] *vt* 1 (Zool) ‹*skin*› mudar de 2 ‹*responsibility*› librarse de; **to ~ ~ a habit** abandonar una costumbre

Slovak /'sləʊvæk/ *n* 1 [c] (person) eslovaco, -ca *m,f* 2 [u] (language) eslovaco *m*

Slovakia /sləʊ'vɑːkiːə || sləʊ'vækiə/ *n* Eslovaquia *f*

Slovene /'sləʊviːn/ *n* 1 [c] (person) esloveno, -na *m,f* 2 [u] (language) esloveno *m*

Slovenia /sləʊ'viːnjə/ *n* Eslovenia *f*

slovenly /'slʌvənli/ *adj* **-lier, -liest** ‹*work*› descuidado; ‹*person*› desaliñado, desaseado

slow[1] /sləʊ/ *adj* **-er, -est**
A ‹*speed/rate/reactions*› lento; **she's a ~ learner** tiene problemas de aprendizaje, le cuesta aprender; **I'm a ~ reader** leo despacio; **in a ~ oven** en horno tibio; **it has a ~ leak** *o* (BrE) **puncture** pierde aire; **to be ~ to + INF** tardar EN + INF; **he was ~ to anger** tenía mucha paciencia; ▸**mark[1] C2**
B 1 (not lively) ‹*novel/plot*› lento; **business is ~** no hay mucho movimiento (en el negocio) 2 (stupid) (euph) poco despierto (euf), corto (de entendederas) (fam)
C (of clock, watch): **the kitchen clock is ~** el reloj de la cocina (se) atrasa *or* está atrasado; **my watch is five minutes ~** mi reloj está cinco minutos atrasado

slow[2] *vi*: **growth has ~ed considerably** el ritmo de crecimiento ha disminuido considerablemente; **the train ~ed to a stop** el tren fue disminuyendo la velocidad hasta detenerse
■ **slow** *vt*: **we ~ed our pace** aflojamos el paso *or* aminoramos la marcha; **bad weather ~ed their progress** el mal tiempo los retrasó

Phrasal verbs

- **slow down**

A [v ▸ adv] 1 (go more slowly) «*runner*» aflojar el paso, aminorar la marcha; «*vehicle/driver*» reducir* la velocidad; «*speaker*» hablar más despacio 2 (be less active) (colloq) tomarse las cosas con más calma
B [v ▸ o ▸ adv, v ▸ adv ▸ o] 1 ‹*process*› hacer* más lento, ralentizar*, enlentecer* 2 ‹*vehicle/engine*› reducir* la velocidad de

- **slow up** ▸**slow down**

slow[3] *adv* lentamente, despacio; **my watch runs ~** mi reloj (se) atrasa; Ⓢ **slow!** despacio; **to go ~** «*driver/*

S

walker›› avanzar* lentamente, ir* despacio; ‹‹workers›› (BrE) trabajar a reglamento, hacer* huelga de celo (Esp), hacer* una operación tortuga (Col)

slow- *pref* **~acting** ‹*poison/drug*› de efecto retardado; **~burning** de combustión lenta

slow: **~coach** *n* (BrE colloq) tortuga *f* (fam); **~ cooker** *n*: *olla eléctrica para guisos de cocimiento lento*

slowly /'sləʊli/ *adv* lentamente, despacio; **~ but surely** sin prisa pero sin pausa

slow: **~ motion** *n* [u] cámara *f* lenta; **in ~ motion** en *or* (Esp) a cámara lenta; **~-moving** /'sləʊ'mu:vɪŋ/ *adj* lento; **~poke** *n* (AmE colloq) tortuga *f* (fam); **~-witted** /'sləʊ'wɪtəd || ,sləʊ'wɪtɪd/ *adj* corto de entendederas (fam), torpe; **~worm** *n* lución *m*

sludge /slʌdʒ/ *n* 1 (mud) lodo *m*, fango *m*, barro *m* 2 (waste oil) (Auto) sedimento(s) *m(pl)* 3 (sewage) *sedimentos de las aguas residuales*

slue /slu:/ *vt/i* (AmE) ▸**slew²**

slug¹ /slʌg/ *n*

A (Zool) babosa *f*

B (bullet) bala *f*, posta *f*

C 1 (drink) (colloq) trago *m* 2 (blow) (colloq) tortazo *m* (fam)

slug² *vt* **-gg-** (colloq) pegarle* un tortazo a (fam), darle* un mamporro a (fam); ***to ~ it out*** agarrarse a tortazos (fam)

sluggish /'slʌgɪʃ/ *adj* 1 (slow-moving) lento; ‹*stream/river*› de aguas mansas; **the car's very ~** el coche no está respondiendo bien; **the drug makes you feel ~** el fármaco te aletarga 2 ‹*growth*› lento; ‹*market*› inactivo

sluggishly /'slʌgɪʃli/ *adv* lentamente, con lentitud

sluice¹ /slu:s/ *n* 1 (barrier) presa *f*, represa *f* (AmS) 2 (sluicegate) compuerta *f*

sluice² *vt*: **to ~ sth down/out** lavar *or* enjuagar* algo con abundante agua

sluicegate /'slu:sgeɪt/ *n* compuerta *f*

slum¹ /slʌm/ *n* 1 (poor urban area) (*often pl*) barrio *m* bajo, barriada *f* (AmL exc CS), barrio *m* de conventillos (CS); (*before n*) **~ clearance** demolición *f* de viviendas insalubres; **~ dwelling** tugurio *m* 2 (filthy place) (colloq & pej) pocilga *f*, chiquero *m* (AmL)

slum² *vt* **-mm-**: ***to ~ it*** vivir a lo pobre

slumber¹ /'slʌmbər || 'slʌmbə(r)/ *n* (liter) (*often pl*) sueño *m*

slumber² *vi* (liter) dormir*

slummy /'slʌmi/ *adj* **-mier, -miest** (colloq) miserable, sórdido

slump¹ /slʌmp/ *n* 1 (economic depression) depresión *f* 2 (in prices, sales) caída *f or* baja *f* repentina, bajón *m*; (in attendance, interest) disminución *f*, bajón *m*

slump² *vi*

A (collapse) (+ *adv compl*) desplomarse; **they found her ~ed over her desk** la encontraron desplomada sobre su escritorio; **he ~ed into a chair** se dejó caer en un sillón

B 1 ‹‹*prices/output/sales*›› caer* *or* bajar repentinamente 2 ‹‹*morale*›› sufrir un bajón

slung /slʌŋ/ *past & past p of* **sling²**

slunk /slʌŋk/ *past & past p of* **slink**

slur¹ /slɜ:r || slɜ:(r)/ *n*

A (insult, stigma): **a racist/cowardly ~** un comentario racista/infamante; **to cast a ~ on sb** injuriar *or* difamar a algn

B (Mus) ligado *m*; (mark) ligadura *f*

slur² *vt* **-rr-**

A (pronounce unclearly): **he tends to ~ his words (together)** tiende a arrastrar las palabras

B (Mus) ligar*

slurp¹ /slɜ:rp || slɜ:p/ *vt* sorber (*haciendo ruido*)

slurp² *n* sorbetón *m*

slurred /slɜ:rd || slɜ:d/ *adj*: **her speech was ~** arrastraba las palabras

slurry /'slɜ:ri || 'slʌri/ *n* [u] 1 (of mud, cement) *compuesto acuoso de lodo, cemento etc* 2 (Agr) estiércol *m* líquido

slush /slʌʃ/ *n* [u]

A (melted snow) nieve *f* fangosa *or* medio derretida

B (sentimental trash) sensiblería *f*

slush fund *n* fondo *m* de reptiles, fondo *m* para sobornos

slushy /'slʌʃi/ *adj* **-shier, -shiest**

A (wet) ‹*street*› cubierto de nieve medio derretida; ‹*snow*› fangoso, medio derretido

B (sentimental) sentimentaloide, sensiblero

slut /slʌt/ *n* 1 (slovenly woman) puerca *f* (fam), guarra *f* (Esp fam) 2 (immoral woman) putilla *f* (fam), fulana *f* (fam)

sly /slaɪ/ *adj* **-er, -est** 1 (cunning) ‹*person*› astuto, ladino, taimado; **you're a ~ one** ¡qué pillo eres!, ¡eres un zorro!; ***on the ~*** a escondidas, a hurtadillas 2 (roguish) ‹*look/grin*› malicioso, travieso, pícaro

smack¹ /smæk/ *n*

A [c] 1 (slap, blow) manotazo *m*, manotada *f*, palmada *f* (AmL); **a ~ in the face** (colloq) una bofetada, una cachetada (AmL); **a ~ on the bottom** un azote; **she gave the little boy a ~** le pegó al niño 2 (sound) chasquido *m* 3 (kiss) besote *m* (fam), beso *m* sonoro *or* (Méx) tronado

B [u] (heroin) (sl) caballo *m* (arg), heroína *f*

smack² *vt* 1 (slap) ‹*child*› pegarle* a (*con la mano*); **you'll get your bottom ~ed** te voy a dar una paliza *or* (AmL) unas palmadas *or* (Méx) una nalgada 2 (punch) (colloq) darle* un puñetazo *or* una piña a (fam) 3 **to ~ one's lips** relamerse

■ **smack** *vi* **to ~ OF sth** oler* A algo

smack³, (AmE also) **smack dab** *adv* (colloq): **~ in the middle** justo en el medio; **he went ~ into a tree** se dio contra un árbol

smacker /'smækər || 'smækə(r)/ *n* (colloq & dated)

A (kiss) besote *m* (fam)

B 1 (dollar) (AmE) dólar *m*, verde *m* (fam) 2 (pound) (BrE) libra *f*

small¹ /smɔ:l/ *adj* **-er, -est**

A 1 (in size) pequeño, chico (esp AmL); **to cut sth up ~** cortar algo en trocitos (pequeños); **a ~ waist** una cintura muy estrecha; **~ letters** letras *fpl* minúsculas; **he's a conservative with a ~ 'c'** es de ideas conservadoras en el sentido amplio de la palabra; **the ~ screen** la pequeña pantalla, la pantalla chica (AmL); ***to be ~ beer*** *o* (AmE also) ***~ potatoes***: **for him $2,000 is ~ beer** para él 2.000 dólares no son nada *or* son poca cosa 2 (in number, amount, value) ‹*family*› pequeño, chico (esp AmL); ‹*sum/price*› módico, reducido 3 (not much): **they have ~ chance of succeeding** tienen pocas probabilidades de lograrlo; **~ wonder!** no es de extrañar, no me extraña

B 1 (unimportant, trivial) ‹*mistake/problem*› pequeño, de poca importancia 2 (humble, modest): **to start in a ~ way** empezar* de forma muy modesta; **to feel ~** sentirse* insignificante *or* (fam) poca cosa; **I'm sorry, he said in a ~ voice** —lo siento —dijo en un hilo de voz

small² *n*

A **the ~ of the back** *región baja de la espalda, que corresponde al segmento dorsal de la columna vertebral*

B **smalls** *pl* (BrE colloq & dated) ropa *f* interior, paños *mpl* menores (hum)

small: **~ ad** *n* (BrE) anuncio *m* (clasificado), aviso *m* (clasificado) (AmL); **~ arms** *pl n*: *armas de bajo calibre*; **~ change** *n* [u] cambio *m*, (dinero *m*) suelto *m*, sencillo *m* (AmL), feria *f* (Méx fam); **~ claims court** *n* (in UK) *tribunal que conoce de causas de mínima cuantía*; **~holder** *n* (BrE) pequeño agricultor, pequeña agricultora *m,f*; (Econ, Pol) minifundista *mf*; **~holding** *n* (BrE) granja *f* pequeña, parcela *f*, chacra *f* (CS, Per); (Econ, Pol) minifundio *m*; **~ hours** *pl n* **the (wee) ~ hours (of the morning)** la madrugada; **~ intestine** *n* intestino *m* delgado

smallish /'smɔ:lɪʃ/ *adj* (*no comp*) ‹*person*› más bien menudo; ‹*room/town*› tirando a pequeño *or* (esp AmL) a chico

small-minded /'smɔ:l'maɪndəd || ,smɔ:l'maɪndɪd/ *adj* cerrado, de miras estrechas

smallness /'smɔ:lnəs || 'smɔ:lnɪs/ *n* [u] lo pequeño, lo chico (esp AmL)

small: **~pox** /'smɔ:lpɑ:ks || 'smɔ:lpɒks/ *n* [u] viruela *f*; **~ print** *n* [u] (BrE) **the ~ print** la letra pequeña *or* menuda, la letra chica (AmL); **~-scale** /'smɔ:l'skeɪl/ *adj* 1 ‹*map/model*› a *or* en pequeña escala 2 ‹*operation/project*› de poca monta *or* envergadura; **~ talk** *n* [u]: **I'm hopeless at making ~ talk** no sirvo para la charla *or* la conversación sobre temas triviales; **~-time** /'smɔ:l'taɪm/ *adj* de poca monta *or* importancia; **~-town** /'smɔ:l'taʊn/ *adj* pueblerino

S

smarmy /'smɑːrmi || 'smɑːmi/ *adj* **-mier, -miest** (colloq) ‹*voice*› meloso; **he's a ~ individual** es un adulón *or* (Esp tb) un pelota *or* (Méx tb) un barbero *or* (CS, Ven tb) un chupamedias *or* (Chi tb) un patero (fam)

smart¹ /smɑːrt || smɑːt/ *adj* **-er, -est**
A (esp BrE) **1** (neat, stylish) ‹*appearance/dress*› elegante; **you're looking very ~ today** hoy estás muy elegante **2** (chic) ‹*hotel/neighborhood*› elegante, fino; **the ~ set** la gente bien
B (clever, shrewd) ‹*child*› listo, vivo; ‹*answer*› inteligente, agudo; **she's made some very ~ business moves** ha hecho algunas operaciones muy inteligentes *or* acertadas; **don't get ~ with me!** ¡no te hagas el vivo *or* el listo conmigo!
C **1** (brisk, prompt) ‹*pace*› rápido **2** (forceful) ‹*blow/rap/tap*› seco, fuerte
D (automated) ‹*machine/terminal*› inteligente

smart² *vi* **1** (sting) «*eyes*» escocer*, picar*, arder; «*wound*» escocer*, arder (CS) **2** (suffer) **to ~ FROM sth** resentirse* DE algo
Phrasal verb
• **smart off** [v ▸ adv] (AmE colloq) ser* insolente

smart: **~ alec**, (BrE also) **~ aleck** /'ælɪk/ *n* (colloq) sabihondo, -da *m,f* (fam), sabelotodo *mf* (fam); **~-ass**, (BrE) **~-arse** *n* (sl) ▸ **~ alec**; **~ bomb** *n* bomba *f* inteligente; **~ card** *n* tarjeta *f* electrónica

smarten up
A [v ▸ o ▸ adv, v ▸ adv ▸ o] ‹*house/town*› arreglar
B [v ▸ adv] «*person*» mejorar su (*or* mi *etc*) aspecto

smartly /'smɑːrtli || 'smɑːtli/ *adv*
A (stylishly) elegantemente; **she dresses so ~** se viste muy elegante
B **1** (briskly, promptly) ‹*walk/march*› a paso rápido **2** (forcefully) ‹*hit/knock*› con fuerza

smartness /'smɑːrtnəs || 'smɑːtnɪs/ *n* [u]
A **1** (neatness): **~ is essential in this job** en este trabajo es imprescindible la buena presencia **2** (chic) elegancia *f*
B (cleverness, shrewdness) agudeza *f*, viveza *f*

smarts /smɑːrts || smɑːts/ *n* [u] (AmE colloq) cacumen *m* (fam), coco *m* (fam); **to have the ~ to do sth** tener* cacumen para hacer algo

smartypants /'smɑːrtipænts || 'smɑːtipænts/ *n* (*pl* **~**) (colloq) ▸ **smart alec**

smash¹ /smæʃ/ *n*
A **1** (sound) estrépito *m*, estruendo *m*; **there was a loud ~ as he dropped the plates** los platos se le cayeron con gran estrépito **2** (collision) (BrE) choque *m*
B **1** (blow) golpe *m* **2** (in tennis, badminton, squash) smash *m*, remate *m*, remache *m*
C (success) (colloq) exitazo *m* (fam)

smash² *vt*
A (break) ‹*furniture*› romper*, destrozar*; ‹*car*› destrozar*; ‹*glass*› romper*; (into small pieces) hacer* añicos
B (destroy) ‹*rebellion*› aplastar, sofocar*; ‹*drug racket/spy ring*› acabar con, desarticular; ‹*hopes*› echar por tierra, destruir*; **he ~ed the world record** batió *or* rompió el record mundial
C **1** (hit, drive forcefully): **I ~ed my fist through the window** rompí la ventana de un puñetazo **2** (in tennis, badminton, squash) rematar, remachar
■ **smash** *vi*
A (shatter) hacerse* pedazos; **it ~ed into a thousand pieces** se hizo añicos, se rompió en mil pedazos
B (crash) **to ~ AGAINST/INTO sth** estrellarse *or* chocar* CONTRA algo
Phrasal verbs
• **smash in** [v ▸ o ▸ adv, v ▸ adv ▸ o] ‹*door*› tirar abajo; ‹*window/glass*› romper*; **he threatened to ~ my face in** (colloq) me amenazó con partirme *or* romperme la cara (fam)
• **smash up** [v ▸ o ▸ adv] (colloq) destrozar*

smash-and-grab /'smæʃən'græb/ *n* (BrE) robo *m* (*en el que se rompe el escaparate de una tienda*)

smashed /smæʃt/ *adj* (*after n*) (sl): **to be ~** estar* borracho, estar* pedo *or* (RPl) en pedo (arg), estar* cuete (Méx fam), estar* pedado (Col fam), estar* curado (CS fam); **to get ~** emborracharse, agarrarse un pedo (arg), encuetarse (Méx fam), pegarse* una peda (Col fam), curarse (CS fam)

smash hit *n* (colloq) exitazo *m* (fam); (*before n*) **a smash-hit movie** una película supertaquillera

smashing /'smæʃɪŋ/ *adj* (BrE colloq) ‹*place/party*› fantástico, super bueno (fam), chévere (AmL exc CS fam), macanudo (CS, Per fam)

smashup /'smæʃʌp/ *n* (colloq) choque *m* violento, colisión *f*; **he was in a ~** tuvo un accidente

smattering /'smætərɪŋ/ *n* (*no pl*) nociones *fpl*, conocimientos *mpl* rudimentarios; **I have a ~ of German** tengo nociones *or* conocimientos rudimentarios del alemán, chapurreo el alemán (fam)

smear¹ /smɪr || smɪə(r)/ *n*
A (stain) mancha *f*
B (slander, slur) calumnia *f*; (*before n*) **~ campaign** campaña *f* difamatoria *or* de desprestigio
C (Med) **1** (sample) frotis *m* **2** **~ (test)** citología *f*, frotis *m* cervical, Papanicolau *m* (AmL)

smear² *vt*
A **1** (spread, daub) **to ~ sth ON(TO)/OVER sth** ‹*paint/grease*› embadurnar algo de algo; ‹*butter*› untar algo con algo; **to ~ sth WITH sth**: **the walls were ~ed with filth** las paredes estaban cubiertas de mugre **2** (smudge) ‹*make-up/paint*› correr
B (slander, libel) difamar, desprestigiar
■ **smear** *vi* «*paint/ink/lipstick*» correrse

smell¹ /smel/ *n* **1** [c] (odor) olor *m*; **these roses have no ~** estas rosas no tienen perfume; **there's a strong ~ of garlic in here** huele mucho a ajo; **the sweet ~ of success** la seducción del éxito **2** (sniff) (colloq) (*no pl*): **to have** *o* **take a ~ at** *o* **of sth** oler* algo, tomarle el olor a algo (AmL) **3** [u] (sense of smell) olfato *m*

smell² (*past & past p* **smelled** *or* (BrE also) **smelt**) *vt* **1** (sense) oler*; **I can ~ freshly baked bread** hay olor a pan recién hecho, siento olor a pan recién hecho (esp AmL); **we could ~ gas/burning** olía a gas/quemado, había olor a gas/quemado **2** (sniff at) «*person*» oler*; «*animal*» olfatear **3** (recognize): **to ~ danger** olfatear el peligro
■ **smell** *vi* (give off odor) oler*; **that ~s good!** ¡qué bien huele!, ¡qué rico olor! (AmL); **it ~s off** huele a podrido, tiene olor a podrido; **it ~s in here** ¡qué mal huele aquí!, ¡qué mal olor hay aquí! (CS); **he ~s** huele mal; **his breath ~s** tiene mal aliento; **to ~ OF sth** oler* A algo

smelling salts /'smelɪŋ/ *pl n* sales *fpl* (aromáticas)

smelly /'smeli/ *adj* **-lier, -liest** (odorous) que huele mal; (stronger) apestoso, hediondo; **that ~ French cheese** ese queso francés que huele tan fuerte

smelt¹ /smelt/ (BrE) *past & past p of* **smell²**

smelt² *vt* fundir

smidge(o)n, smidgin /'smɪdʒən/ *n* (colloq) pizca *f*

smile¹ /smaɪl/ *n* sonrisa *f*; **to give sb a ~** sonreírle* a algn; **he had a big ~ on his face** sonreía de oreja a oreja; **the good news certainly put a ~ on her face** por cierto que la buena noticia la alegró mucho

smile² *vi* **1** sonreír*; **what are you smiling about?** ¿de qué te ríes?, ¿a qué viene esa sonrisa?; **keep smiling!** ¡que no decaiga el ánimo!; **to ~ with pleasure** sonreír* de placer; **to ~ AT sb** sonreírle* A algn; **to ~ ON sb** sonreírle A algn; ***to come up smiling*** salir* bien parado **2** **smiling** *pres p* ‹*face/eyes*› sonriente
■ **smile** *vt*: **she ~d her thanks** dio las gracias sonriendo *or* con una sonrisa

smirk¹ /smɜːrk || smɜːk/ *n* sonrisita *f* (*de suficiencia, de complicidad, etc*)

smirk² *vi* sonreírse* (*con suficiencia, complicidad etc*)

smite /smaɪt/ *vt* (*past* **smote**; *past p* **smitten**) (liter *or* arch) golpear; **her conscience smote her** le remordía la conciencia, su conciencia la atormentaba

smith /smɪθ/ *n* herrero, -ra *m,f*

smithereens /'smɪðə'riːnz/ *pl n*: **to smash sth to ~** hacer* algo pedazos *or* añicos *or* trizas

Smithsonian Institution /smɪθ'səʊniən/ *n* (in US): **the ~ ~** el Instituto Smithsoniano

Smithsonian Institution

Una institución nacional en EEUU que está compuesta de varios museos y centros de investigación en Washington DC. Comúnmente se la suele llamar "*the nation's attic*" ("el desván de la nación")

S

smithy /'smɪθi || 'smɪði/ *n* (*pl* **-thies**) herrería *f*, forja *f*

smitten¹ /'smɪtn̩/ *past p of* **smite**

smitten² *adj* (*pred*) 1 (afflicted) (liter *or* hum): **to be ~ with the plague** sufrir el azote de la peste; **to be ~ with remorse** estar* afligido por el remordimiento 2 (keen): **we are quite ~ with the idea** estamos muy entusiasmados con la idea; **she's really ~ with him** está verdaderamente loca por él

smock /smɑːk || smɒk/ *n* 1 (of fisherman, artist) blusón *m*, bata *f* 2 (dress) vestido *m* amplio; (for pregnancy) vestido *m* premamá *or* de futura mamá *or* (Chi) maternal

smog /smɑːg || smɒg/ *n* [u] smog *m*, niebla *f* tóxica

smoke¹ /sməʊk/ *n*

A [u] (from fire) humo *m*; **to go up in ~** «*books/papers*» quemarse; «*hopes*» esfumarse, desvanecerse*; «*ambitions/plans*» quedar en agua de borrajas; ***there's no ~ without fire*** cuando el río suena ... (piedras lleva *or* agua lleva)

B 1 [c] (cigarette) (colloq) cigarrillo *m*, pitillo *m*, pucho *m* (AmL fam) 2 (act) (*no pl*): **to have a ~** fumarse un cigarrillo

smoke² *vi*

A «*person*» fumar; **do you mind if I ~?** ¿te molesta que fume *or* si fumo?

B (give off smoke) echar humo, humear

■ **smoke** *vt*

A ‹*cigarettes/tobacco*› fumar; **I ~ ten a day** (me) fumo diez al día; **he ~s a pipe** fuma en pipa

B (cure) ‹*fish/cheese*› ahumar*

Phrasal verbs

- **smoke out** [v ▸ o ▸ adv, v ▸ adv ▸ o] 1 (flush out) hacer* salir (*ahumando su guarida etc*) 2 (fill with smoke) (BrE) ▸ **smoke up**
- **smoke up** [v ▸ adv ▸ o, v ▸ o ▸ adv] (AmE) ‹*room/house*› llenar de humo, ahumar*

smoke-bomb /'sməʊkbɑːm || 'sməʊkbɒm/ *n* bomba *f* de humo

smoked /sməʊkt/ *adj* 1 ‹*cheese/fish*› ahumado 2 ‹*glass/lens*› ahumado

smoke: **~ detector** *n* detector *m* de humo; **~-free** /'sməʊk'friː/ *adj* ‹*policy*› contra la emisión de humos; ‹*office/zone*› donde no se puede fumar

smokeless /'sməʊkləs || 'sməʊklɪs/ *adj* ‹*fuel*› que arde sin humo; **~ zone** (in UK) *zona donde está prohibido usar combustibles que produzcan humo*

smoker /'sməʊkər || 'sməʊkə(r)/ *n* fumador, -dora *m,f*; **he's a heavy ~** fuma mucho; **~'s cough** tos *f* de fumador

smoke: **~screen** *n* cortina *f* de humo; **~ signal** *n* señal *f* de humo; **~stack** *n* chimenea *f*; (*before n*) ‹*industry*› pesado

smoking /'sməʊkɪŋ/ *n* [u] ⓢ **no smoking** prohibido fumar; **~ is harmful to your health** fumar es perjudicial para la salud; **to give up** *o* **stop ~** dejar de fumar

smoking: **~ car** *n* (AmE) vagón *m or* (Chi, Méx) carro *m* de fumadores; **~ compartment** *n* compartimento *m* de fumadores; **~ jacket** *n* batín *m*

smoky /'sməʊki/ *adj* **-kier, -kiest** 1 (emitting smoke) ‹*fire/chimney*› que echa humo, humeante 2 (like smoke) ‹*taste/flavor*› a humo, como a ahumado 3 (full of smoke) ‹*room*› lleno de humo; ‹*atmosphere*› cargado de humo

smolder, (BrE) **smoulder** /'sməʊldər || 'sməʊldə(r)/ *vi* «*fire*» arder (*sin llama*); «*eyes*» arder

smooch /smuːtʃ/ *vi* (colloq) besuquearse

smooth¹ /smuːð/ *adj* **-er, -est**

A 1 ‹*texture/stone*› liso, suave; ‹*skin*› suave, terso; ‹*sea/lake*› tranquilo, en calma; **this razor gives a ~ shave** esta navaja afeita muy al ras *or* (Esp tb) da un afeitado muy apurado; **the steps are worn ~** los peldaños están lisos por el uso; ***as ~ as a baby's bottom*** suave como la piel de un bebé; ▸ **millpond, rough¹ A1** 2 (of consistency) ‹*batter/sauce*› sin grumos, homogéneo 3 (of taste) ‹*wine/whiskey*› suave

B 1 (of movement) ‹*acceleration/take-off*› suave; ‹*flight*› cómodo, bueno; **it was a ~ crossing** el mar estaba en calma, fue una buena travesía 2 (trouble-free) ‹*journey*› sin complicaciones *or* problemas

C 1 (easy, polished) ‹*style/performance*› fluido 2 (glib, suave) (pej) poco sincero; **he's a ~ talker** tiene mucha labia, tiene un pico de oro; ▸ **operator B2**

smooth² *vt* 1 ‹*dress/sheets/hair*› alisar, arreglar 2 (polish) pulir 3 (ease): **to ~ sb's path** *o* **way** allanarle el camino *or* el terreno a algn

Phrasal verbs

- **smooth away** [v ▸ o ▸ adv, v ▸ adv ▸ o] ‹*wrinkles*› hacer* desaparecer; ‹*difficulties*› allanar
- **smooth down** [v ▸ o ▸ adv, v ▸ adv ▸ o] ‹*hair/clothes*› alisar
- **smooth out** [v ▸ o ▸ adv, v ▸ adv ▸ o] 1 ‹*sheets/creases*› alisar 2 ‹*difficulties/problems*› resolver*, allanar
- **smooth over** [v ▸ o ▸ adv, v ▸ adv ▸ o] ‹*differences*› dejar de lado

smoothie /'smuːði/ *n* 1 (colloq & pej) *individuo de mucha labia, de modales muy pulidos y/o muy atildado en el vestir* 2 (fruit drink) smoothie *m*

smoothly /'smuːðli/ *adv*

A 1 (of movement) ‹*take off/drive*› suavemente 2 (without problems) sin problemas, sin complicaciones; **the business is running very ~** el negocio marcha sobre ruedas

B (glibly, suavely) (pej) ‹*talk*› con mucha labia

smooth: **~-talk** /'smuːðtɔːk/ *vt* (colloq) ‹*person*› hacerle* el artículo a (fam), darle* jabón a (Esp fam), hacerle* la barba a (Méx fam), hacerle* la pata a (Chi fam); **he ~-talked his way out of the fine** con labia y zalamerías logró que no le aplicaran la multa; **~-talking** /'smuːð'tɔːkɪŋ/ *adj* (pej) persuasivo

smoothy *n* (*pl* **-thies**) ▸ **smoothie**

smote /sməʊt/ *past of* **smite**

smother /'smʌðər || 'smʌðə(r)/ *vt* 1 (stifle) ‹*person*› asfixiar, ahogar*; ‹*flames*› sofocar*, extinguir*, apagar* 2 (suppress) ‹*report*› silenciar, echar tierra sobre; ‹*yawn/giggle*› reprimir, contener* 3 (cover profusely) **to ~ sb/sth WITH/IN sth**: **she ~ed him with kisses** lo cubrió de besos; **he ~s everything in tomato sauce** todo lo come bañado en salsa de tomate

smoulder *vi* (BrE) ▸ **smolder**

smudge¹ /smʌdʒ/ *n* mancha *f*, manchón *m*

smudge² *vt* ‹*ink/outline*› correr, emborronar; (deliberately) difuminar

■ **smudge** *vi* «*paint/ink*» correrse

smudgy /'smʌdʒi/ *adj* **smudgier, smudgiest** ‹*page/writing*› emborronado, sucio; ‹*outline*› borroso

smug /smʌg/ *adj* **-gg-** ‹*expression/smile*› de suficiencia, petulante; ‹*person*› pagado de sí mismo, petulante

smuggle /'smʌgəl/ *vt* ‹*tobacco/drugs*› contrabandear, pasar de contrabando, hacer* contrabando de; **he ~d the watches past** *o* **through customs** pasó los relojes de contrabando (por la aduana); **I ~d her into my room** la hice entrar a mi habitación a escondidas

smuggler /'smʌglər || 'smʌglə(r)/ *n* contrabandista *mf*

smuggling /'smʌglɪŋ/ *n* [u] contrabando *m*; (*before n*) ‹*ring/racket*› de contrabandistas

smugly /'smʌgli/ *adv* con aire de suficiencia

smut /smʌt/ *n* 1 [u] (offensive material) inmundicia *f*, indecencia *f* 2 [c] (dirt, soot) mancha *f* de tizne, tiznajo *m*

smutty /'smʌti/ *adj* **-tier, -tiest** 1 ‹*film/joke*› indecente, inmundo, obsceno 2 ‹*face/clothes*› tiznado

snack¹ /snæk/ *n* tentempié *m*, refrigerio *m* (frml); **to have a ~** comer algo ligero *or* (esp AmL) liviano, tomar(se) un tentempié *or* (frml) un refrigerio

snack² *vi* comer algo ligero *or* (esp AmL) liviano, tomar(se) un tentempié *or* (frml) un refrigerio; **to ~ ON sth**: **we ~ed on apples** nos comimos unas manzanas

snack bar *n* bar *m*, cafetería *f*

snag¹ /snæg/ *n* 1 (difficulty) inconveniente *m*, problema *m*, pega *f* (Esp fam) 2 (in fabric, stocking) enganchón *m*, enganche *m* (CS), jalón *m* (Méx)

snag² *vt* **-gg-** enganchar

snail /sneɪl/ *n* caracol *m*; **at a ~'s pace** a paso de tortuga

snake¹ /sneɪk/ *n* culebra *f*, serpiente *f*; (poisonous) víbora *f*; ***a ~ in the grass*** un traidor, un judas

snake² *vi* «*river/road*» serpentear

snake: **~bite** *n* [c u] mordedura *f* de serpiente; **~ charmer** *n* encantador, -dora *m,f* de serpientes; **~s and ladders** *n* (BrE) (+ *sing vb*) ≈ juego *m* de la oca;

~**skin** *n* [u] piel *f* de serpiente, cuero *m* de víbora (RPl), cuero *m* de culebra (Chi)

snap¹ /snæp/ *n*
A [c] (sound) chasquido *m*, ruido *m* seco
B ~ **(fastener)** (AmE) 1 (on clothes) broche *m or* botón *m* de presión (AmL), (cierre *m*) automático *m* (Esp) 2 (on handbag, necklace) broche *m*
C [c] (photo) (colloq) foto *f*, instantánea *f*
D [c] (Meteo): **a cold** ~ una ola de frío
E [u] (BrE) 1 (card game) *juego de baraja en el que se canta 'snap' cada vez que aparecen dos cartas iguales* 2 (*as interj*) (colloq): **I got 83% — ~! (so did I)** yo saqué un 83% — ¡chócate ésa *or* chócatela *or* chócala (, yo también)!
F (easy task) (AmE colloq) (*no pl*): **it's a** ~ es facilísimo; está tirado (fam), es una papa *or* un bollo (RPl fam), es chancaca (Chi fam)

snap² -pp- *vt*
A 1 (break) partir 2 (cause to make sharp sound): **she ~ped the lid/book shut** cerró la tapa/el libro de un golpe; ▸**finger¹**
B (utter sharply) decir* bruscamente; **shut up, he ~ped** —cállate —dijo bruscamente
C (photograph) ‹*person/thing*› sacarle* una foto a
■ **snap** *vi*
A (bite): **the dog ~ped at my ankles** el perro me quiso morder los tobillos
B 1 (break) «*twigs/branch*» romperse*, quebrarse* (esp AmL); «*elastic*» romperse*; **it just ~ped off in my hand** se me partió *or* (esp AmL) se me quebró en la mano; **the plank ~ped in two** la tabla se partió en dos; **my patience ~ped** se me acabó la paciencia 2 (click): **to ~ shut** cerrarse* (con un clic)
C (speak sharply) hablar con brusquedad; **sorry, I didn't mean to ~** perdona, no quise saltar así
D (move quickly): ***to ~ out of it*** (of depression) animarse, reaccionar; (of lethargy, inertia) espabilarse; **~ out of it!** ¡anímate!, ¡reacciona!

Phrasal verbs
• **snap back** [v ▸ adv] (AmE colloq) recuperarse
• **snap up** [v ▸ o ▸ adv, v ▸ adv ▸ o] ‹*offer*› no dejar escapar; **by the time we got there, all the bargains had been ~ped up** cuando llegamos ya se habían agotado todas las gangas

snap³ *adj* ‹*decision/judgment*› precipitado, repentino

snapdragon /ˈsnæp,drægən/ *n* dragón *m*, boca *f* de dragón, perrito *m* (AmL), conejito *m* (Arg), boca *f* de sapo (Ur)

snappy /ˈsnæpi/ *adj* **-pier, -piest** 1 ‹*dog*› que muerde; ‹*person*› irascible, irritable; ‹*retort*› brusco, cortante 2 (brisk, lively) (colloq) ‹*pace*› ágil, brioso; ‹*conversation*› animado, vivaz; **put your uniform on and make it ~!** ponte el uniforme ¡y rápido! 3 (stylish) (colloq) elegante

snapshot /ˈsnæpʃɑːt || ˈsnæpʃɒt/ *n* foto *f*, instantánea *f*

snare¹ /sner || sneə(r)/ *n*
A (to catch animals) trampa *f*, cepo *m*
B ~ **(drum)** tambor *m* (*con bordón*)

snare² *vt* atrapar

snarl¹ /snɑːrl || snɑːl/ *n* gruñido *m*

snarl² *vi* gruñir*; **to ~ AT sb** gruñirle* A algn
■ **snarl** *vt*
A (say) gruñir*
B ▸**snarl up**

Phrasal verb
• **snarl up** [v ▸ adv ▸ o] (*usu pass*) ‹*ball of wool*› enmarañar, enredar; ‹*traffic*› atascar*; **the city center was ~ed up** el tráfico estaba paralizado en el centro de la ciudad

snarl-up /ˈsnɑːrlʌp || ˈsnɑːlʌp/ *n* (BrE colloq) lío *m* (fam), embrollo *m*; (in traffic) atasco *m*, embotellamiento *m*

snatch¹ /snætʃ/ *vt*
A 1 (grab): **she ~ed the letter out of my hand** me arrancó la carta de las manos; **to ~ sth FROM sb** arrebatarle algo A algn 2 (steal) (colloq & journ) robar (*arrebatando*) 3 (kidnap) (journ) secuestrar, raptar
B 1 (take hurriedly) ‹*opportunity*› no dejar pasar; **he ~ed forty winks during the sermon** se echó una cabezadita durante el sermón 2 ‹*victory*› hacerse* con; ‹*goal*› meter
■ **snatch** *vi* arrebatar; **to ~ AT sth: he ~ed at the keys** trató de agarrar *or* (esp Esp) de coger las llaves

snatch² *n*
A 1 (robbery) (BrE journ) robo *m* 2 (kidnapping) (journ) secuestro *m*, rapto *m*
B 1 (fragment) fragmento *m* 2 (brief spell) rato *m*; **to sleep in ~es** dormir* (de) a ratos

sneak¹ /sniːk/ (*past & past p* **sneaked** *or* (AmE also) **snuck**) *vt* 1 (smuggle) (+ *adv compl*): **he ~ed the files out of the office** sacó los archivos de la oficina a escondidas *or* a hurtadillas; **she tried to ~ him in without paying** trató de colarlo sin pagar 2 (take furtively): **to ~ a look at sth/sb** mirar algo/a algn con disimulo *or* subrepticiamente
■ **sneak** *vi*
A (go furtively) (+ *adv compl*): **to ~ in** entrar a hurtadillas *or* con disimulo *or* (fam) de extranjis; **to ~ away** escabullirse*; **he managed to ~ past the guard** logró pasar sin que el guardia se diera cuenta
B (tell tales) (BrE colloq) ir* con cuentos (fam), chivarse (Esp fam); **to ~ ON sb** acusar a algn, chivarse DE algn (Esp fam)

Phrasal verb
• **sneak up** [v ▸ adv] **to ~ up (ON sb)**: **don't ~ up on me like that!** ¡no te me aparezcas así, de repente!

sneak² *n* (BrE colloq) soplón, -plona *m,f* (fam), acusete *mf* (fam), acusón, -sona *m,f* (AmL fam), chivato, -ta *m,f* (Esp fam)

sneak³ *adj* (*before n*) ~ **preview** (Cin, TV) preestreno *m*

sneakers /ˈsniːkərz || ˈsniːkəz/ *pl n* zapatillas *fpl* (de deporte), tenis *mpl*, playeras *fpl* (Esp), championes *mpl* (Ur)

sneaking /ˈsniːkɪŋ/ *adj* (*before n, no comp*) ‹*wish*› secreto; **she had a ~ feeling that ...** tenía la sensación *or* impresión de que ...

sneak thief *n* ratero, -ra *m,f*

sneaky /ˈsniːki/ *adj* **-kier, -kiest** (colloq) ‹*person*› artero, taimado; ‹*behavior*› solapado

sneer¹ /snɪr || snɪə(r)/ *vi* adoptar un aire despectivo; **to ~ AT sb/sth: he ~ed at his challengers** miró desdeñosamente a sus contrincantes; **she ~ed at my attempts** se burló de mis intentos

sneer² *n* 1 (expression) expresión *f* desdeñosa 2 (remark) comentario *m* desdeñoso *or* despectivo, burla *f*

sneering /ˈsnɪrɪŋ || ˈsnɪərɪŋ/ *adj* ‹*remark*› desdeñoso

sneeze¹ /sniːz/ *vi* estornudar; ***it's not to be ~d at*** (colloq) no es de despreciar *or* desdeñar, no es para hacerle ascos (fam)

sneeze² *n* estornudo *m*

snide /snaɪd/ *adj* ‹*remark/comment*› insidioso, malicioso

sniff¹ /snɪf/ *vt* (smell) «*person*» oler*; «*animal*» olfatear
■ **sniff** *vi* 1 «*animal*» husmear, olfatear, olisquear; «*person*»: **stop ~ing!** ¡no hagas ese ruido con la nariz!, ¡no te sorbas la nariz!; **to ~ AT sth** «*person*» oler* algo; «*animal*» olfatear *or* olisquear algo 2 (be dismissive) **to ~ AT sth/sb** despreciar *or* desdeñar algo/a algn

Phrasal verb
• **sniff out** [v ▸ adv ▸ o] 1 «*dog*» ‹*drugs*› descubrir* husmeando *or* olfateando 2 ‹*crime/danger*› olerse*

sniff² *n* (act, sound): **I heard sobs and ~s coming from her bedroom** oí sollozos y resuellos que venían de su habitación; **have a ~ of this** huele esto

sniffer dog /ˈsnɪfər || ˈsnɪfə(r)/ *n* (BrE) perro *m* rastreador

sniffle¹ /ˈsnɪfəl/ *vi* (due to cold) sorberse la nariz *or* (fam) los mocos; (when crying) gimotear

sniffle² *n* (cold) (colloq): **to have a ~** *o* **the ~s** estar* resfriado, tener* moquera (AmL fam)

snifter /ˈsnɪftər || ˈsnɪftə(r)/ *n* 1 (colloq) copita *f* (fam), traguito *m* (fam) 2 (brandy glass) (AmE) copa *f* de coñac

snigger¹ /ˈsnɪgər || ˈsnɪgə(r)/ *n* risilla *f*, risita *f*

snigger² *vi* reírse* (*por lo bajo*); **to ~ AT** *o* **ABOUT sth** reírse* *or* burlarse DE algo

snip¹ /snɪp/ *n*
A 1 (act) tijeretazo *m*, corte *m* 2 (sound) tijereteo *m* 3 (piece) recorte *m*, pedazo *m*
B (bargain) (BrE colloq) ganga *f* (fam), chollo *m* (Esp fam), pichincha *f* (RPl fam)

snip² *vt* **-pp-** cortar (*con tijera*); **to ~ sth off** cortar algo

snipe /snaɪp/ *vi* 1 (Mil) **to ~ (AT sb)** disparar (SOBRE algn), dispararle A algn (*desde un escondite*) 2 (criticize) **to ~ (AT sth/sb)** criticar* (algo/a algn)

sniper /ˈsnaɪpər || ˈsnaɪpə(r)/ *n* francotirador, -dora *m,f*

snippet /ˈsnɪpət || ˈsnɪpɪt/ *n* (of conversation) trozo *m*, fragmento *m*; **we have only been able to get ~s of information** sólo hemos podido conseguir algunos datos aislados

snippy /ˈsnɪpi/ *adj* **-pier, -piest** (AmE colloq) atrevido, insolente; **to get ~ with sb** insolentarse con algn

snitch /snɪtʃ/ *vt* (colloq) birlar, afanar (arg), mangar* (Esp arg)

■ **snitch** *vi* (colloq) ir* con el cuento (fam), chivarse (Esp fam); **to ~ ON sb** acusar a algn, chivarse DE algn (Esp fam)

snivel /ˈsnɪvəl/ *vi*, (BrE) **-ll-** lloriquear, gimotear

snob /snɑːb || snɒb/ *n* (e)snob *mf*; **she's a music ~** se las da de entendida en música

snobbery /ˈsnɑːbəri || ˈsnɒbəri/ *n* [u] (e)snobismo *m*

snobbish /ˈsnɑːbɪʃ || ˈsnɒbɪʃ/ *adj* (e)snob

snog[1] /snɑːg || snɒg/ *vi* **-gg-** (BrE colloq) besuquearse, darse* *or* pegarse* el lote (Esp fam), chapar (RPl fam), fajar (Méx fam), atracar* (Chi fam)

snog[2] *n* (BrE colloq): **to have a ~** ▸**snog**[1]

snook /snuːk/ *n*: ***to cock a ~ at sb/sth*** (BrE) burlarse de algn/algo

snooker[1] /ˈsnʊkər || ˈsnuːkə(r)/ *n* snooker *m* (*modalidad de billar que se juega con 15 bolas rojas y 6 de otro color*)

snooker[2] *vt* (BrE colloq) poner* en un jaque *or* en un brete *or* en un apuro

snoop[1] /snuːp/ *vi* (colloq) husmear, fisgonear

snoop[2] *n* (colloq) (*no pl*): **he had a good ~ around while you were out** estuvo husmeando *or* curioseando *or* fisgoneando por ahí mientras no estabas

snooper /ˈsnuːpər || ˈsnuːpə(r)/ *n* (colloq) fisgón, -gona *m,f*

snooty /ˈsnuːti/ *adj* **-tier, -tiest** (colloq) ‹*person*› estirado (fam), altanero; ‹*attitude*› altanero, de superioridad

snooze[1] /snuːz/ *vi* (colloq) dormitar, echar una cabezada (fam), echarse un sueñecito *or* (esp AmL) un sueñito (fam), echarse una siestecita *or* (esp AmL) siestita (fam)

snooze[2] *n* (colloq) sueñecito *m* (fam), sueñito *m* (esp AmL fam), siestecita *f* (fam), siestita *f* (esp AmL fam); **to have a ~** echar una cabezada (fam), echarse un sueñecito (*or* sueñito *etc*) (fam)

snore[1] /snɔːr || snɔː(r)/ *vi* roncar*

snore[2] *n* ronquido *m*

snoring /ˈsnɔːrɪŋ/ *n* [u] ronquidos *mpl*

snorkel /ˈsnɔːrkəl || ˈsnɔːkəl/ *n* esnórkel *m*

snort[1] /snɔːrt || snɔːt/ *vi* bufar, resoplar; **she ~ed with laughter** soltó una risotada

■ **snort** *vt* [1] (utter) bramar, gruñir* [2] (inhale) (sl) ‹*cocaine*› esnifar (arg)

snort[2] *n* bufido *m*, resoplido *m*

snot /snɑːt || snɒt/ *n* (vulg) mocos *mpl*

snot-nosed /ˈsnɑːtnəʊzd || ˈsnɒtnəʊzd/ *adj* (colloq) [1] ‹*child*› mocoso [2] (uppity) (BrE) ‹*person*› estirado (fam); ‹*attitude*› de superioridad, altanero

snotty /ˈsnɑːti || ˈsnɒti/ *adj* **-tier, -tiest** (colloq) [1] ‹*handkerchief*› lleno de mocos; ‹*child*› mocoso [2] (snooty) ‹*person*› estirado (fam); ‹*attitude*› de superioridad, altanero

snotty-nosed /ˈsnɑːtiˌnəʊzd || ˈsnɒtiˌnəʊzd/ *adj* (BrE) ▸**snot-nosed**

snout /snaʊt/ *n* (of animal) hocico *m*, morro *m*

snow[1] /snəʊ/ *n*

A [1] [u] nieve *f*; ***as pure as the driven ~*** puro y virginal; ***as white as ~*** blanco como la nieve, níveo (liter); (*before n*) **~ shower** nevada *f*, precipitación *f* de nieve (period) [2] [c] (snowfall) nevada *f*

B [u] (cocaine) (sl) nieve *f* (arg)

snow[2] *v impers* nevar*

■ **snow** *vt* (AmE) (overwhelm) (sl) apabullar; (persuade) convencer*, camelar (Esp fam)

Phrasal verbs

- **snow in** [v ▸ o ▸ adv]: **to be ~ed in** estar* aislado por la nieve
- **snow under** [v ▸ o ▸ adv]: **I'm ~ed under with work** estoy agobiada *or* desbordada de trabajo

snowball[1] /ˈsnəʊbɔːl/ *n*

A (Meteo) bola *f* de nieve; ***not to have o stand a ~'s chance in hell*** no tener* ni la más mínima posibilidad

B (Culin) (dessert) (AmE) granizado *m*, raspado *m* (Col, Méx)

snowball[2] *vi* «*problems*» agravarse, aumentar

snow: **~ blindness** *n* [u] *ceguera pasajera causada por el resplandor de la nieve*; **~blower** /ˈsnəʊbləʊər || ˈsnəʊbləʊə(r)/ *n* soplanieves *m*; **~boarding** /ˈsnəʊbɔːrdɪŋ || ˈsnəʊbɔːdɪŋ/ *n* [u] snowboard *m*; **~bound** *adj* bloqueado *or* aislado por la nieve; **~-capped** /ˈsnəʊˈkæpt/ *adj* nevado, coronado de nieve (liter); **~drift** *n*: *nieve acumulada durante una ventisca*; **~drop** *n* campanilla *f* de invierno; **~fall** *n* [c u] nevada *f*; **~flake** *n* copo *m* de nieve; **~ line** *n* límite *m* de las nieves perpetuas; **~man** /ˈsnəʊmæn/ *n* (*pl* **-men** /-men/) muñeco *m* *or* (Chi) mono *m* de nieve; **~mobile** /ˈsnəʊməbiːl/ *n* (sleigh) trineo *m* a motor; (motor vehicle) moto *f* de nieve, motonieve *f*; **~ pea** *n* (AmE) tirabeque *m*, arveja *f* *or* (Esp) guisante *m* *or* (esp Méx) chícharo *m* mollar; **~plow**, (BrE) **~plough** *n* quitanieves *m*; **~shoe** *n* raqueta *f*; **~storm** *n* tormenta *f* de nieve, ventisca *f*, nevazón *m* (CS); **~-white** /ˈsnəʊˈhwaɪt || ˌsnəʊˈwaɪt/ *adj* blanco como la nieve, níveo (liter); **~ White** *n* Blancanieves

snowy /ˈsnəʊi/ *adj* **snowier, snowiest** [1] ‹*day*› nevoso, de nieve; ‹*weather*› nevoso; ‹*landscape/path*› nevado [2] (liter) (white) blanco como la nieve, níveo (liter)

SNP *n* (in UK) **the ~** (= **Scottish National Party**)

snub[1] /snʌb/ *vt* **-bb-** [1] ‹*person*› desairar; (by looking the other way) voltearle *or* (Esp) volverle* la cara a, darle* vuelta la cara a (CS) [2] (reject) ‹*offer*› desdeñar, rechazar*

snub[2] *n* desaire *m*

snub[3] *adj* ‹*nose*› respingón, respingado (AmL)

snub-nosed /ˈsnʌbˈnəʊzd/ *adj* ‹*person*› de nariz respingona *or* (AmL tb) respingada, ñato (AmS)

snuck /snək/ (AmE colloq) *past and past p of* **sneak**[1]

snuff[1] /snʌf/ *n* [u] rapé *m*

snuff[2] *vt* [1] ‹*wick*› cortar; ***to ~ it*** (BrE colloq) estirar la pata (fam), diñarla (Esp fam), petatearla (Méx fam), cantar para el carnero (RPl arg) [2] ‹*candle*› apagar*

Phrasal verb

- **snuff out** [v ▸ o ▸ adv, v ▸ adv ▸ o] [1] ‹*candle*› apagar* [2] ‹*rebellion*› sofocar*

snuffbox /ˈsnʌfbɑːks || ˈsnʌfbɒks/ *n* caja *f* de rapé

snuffle[1] /ˈsnʌfəl/ *vi* [1] (person) ▸**sniffle**[1] [2] «*dog/badger*» resoplar

snuffle[2] *n* ▸**sniffle**[2]

snug /snʌg/ *adj* [1] (cozy) ‹*room/cottage*› cómodo y acogedor; **he was ~ and warm in bed** estaba cómodo y calentito en la cama; ▸**bug**[1] **A1** [2] (close-fitting) ceñido, ajustado; **the jacket was a ~ fit** la chaqueta le (*or* me *etc*) ceñía muy bien

snuggle /ˈsnʌgəl/ *vi* acurrucarse*; **I found them ~d (up) on the settee** los encontré acurrucados en el sofá; **he ~d up against her** se le arrimó

snugly /ˈsnʌgli/ *adv* [1] (cosily): **~ tucked up in bed** cómodo y abrigado en la cama [2] (tightly): **the trousers fit ~** los pantalones ciñen *or* ajustan muy bien

so[1] /səʊ/ *adv*

A [1] (very) (*before adj and adv*) tan; (*with verb*) tanto; **he did it ~ quickly** lo hizo tan rápido; **you're ~ right** tienes tanta razón; **I'm ~ glad to meet you** me alegro tanto de conocerte; **there's ~ much work to do** hay tanto (trabajo) que hacer; **thank you ~ much** muchísimas gracias [2] (as much as that) (*before adj and adv*) tan; (*with verb*) tanto; **why are you ~ stubborn?** ¿por qué eres tan terco? [3] (*in comparisons*) **not ~ ... as**: **we've never been ~ busy as we are now** nunca hemos estado tan ocupados como ahora; **it's not ~ much a hobby as an obsession** no es tanto un hobby como una obsesión

B [1] (up to a certain point, limit): **I can only eat ~ fast** no puedo comer más rápido; **we can admit just ~ many and no more** sólo podemos dejar entrar a equis cantidad de gente y no más [2] (unspecified amount): **they charge us ~ much a day** nos cobran tanto por día [3] (the amount indicated): **the fish was ~ long** el pescado era así de largo [4] **or so** más o menos; **we'll need 20 or ~ chairs** nos harán falta unas 20 sillas (más o menos)

C (with clauses of result or purpose) **~ ... (that)** tan ... que; **he was ~ rude (that) she slapped him** fue tan grosero, que le dio una bofetada; **he ~ hated the job, he left** odiaba tanto el trabajo, que lo dejó; **~ ... as to + INF**: **I'm not**

S

~ **stupid as to believe him** no soy tan tonta como para creerle; **would you be ~ kind as to explain this to me?** (frml) ¿tendría la gentileza de explicarme esto?

D [1] (thus, in this way): **the street was ~ named because ...** se le puso ese nombre a la calle porque ...; **if you feel ~ inclined** si tienes ganas, si te apetece (esp Esp); **hold the bat like ~** agarra el bate así *or* de esta manera [2] (as stated) así; **that is ~** (frml) así es; **I know quite a bit about that — is that ~?** yo sé bastante de eso — ¡no me digas!; **not ~** no es cierto, no es así; **if ~, they're lying** si es así *or* de ser así, están mintiendo [3] (as desired): **everything has to be just ~** todo tiene que estar justamente como ella (*or* él *etc*) quiere [4] **and so on** *o* **and so forth** etcétera

E [1] (*replacing clause, phrase, word*): **he thinks she's gifted and I think ~ too** él cree que tiene talento y yo también *or* y yo opino lo mismo; **is he coming tomorrow? — it seems ~** ¿viene mañana? — así *or* eso parece; **will he be pleased? — I expect ~** ¿estará contento? — me imagino que sí; **I got a bit dirty — ~ I see** me ensucié un poco — sí, ya veo; **I told you ~** ¿no te lo dije?; **is she interested? — very much ~** ¿le interesa? — sí, y mucho [2] (contradicting) (used esp by children): **she wasn't there — she was ~!** no estaba allí — ¡sí que estaba!

F (*with v aux*) [1] (also, equally): **Peter agrees and ~ does Bill** Peter está de acuerdo y Bill también [2] (indeed): **you promised — ~ I did!** lo prometiste — ¡es verdad! *or* ¡tienes razón!

G [1] (indicating pause or transition) bueno; **~ here we are again** bueno, aquí estamos otra vez [2] (introducing new topic): **~ what's new with you?** y ¿qué hay *or* qué cuentas de nuevo? [3] (querying, eliciting information): **~ now what do we do?** ¿y ahora qué hacemos? [4] (summarizing, concluding) así que; **~ now you know** así que ya sabes [5] (expressing surprised reaction) así que, conque; **~ that's what he's after!** ¡así que *or* conque eso es lo que quiere! [6] (challenging): **but she's not a Catholic — so?** pero no es católica — ¿y qué (hay)?; **~ what?** ¿y qué?

so² *conj*

A (*in clauses of purpose or result*) [1] **so (that)**: **she said it slowly, ~ (that) we'd all understand** lo dijo despacio, para que *or* de manera que todos entendiéramos; **she said it slowly, ~ (that) we all understood** lo dijo despacio, así que *or* de manera que todos entendimos; ***not ~ (as) you'd notice*** (colloq): **has he cleaned in here? — not ~ as you'd notice** ¿ha limpiado aquí? — pues si ha limpiado, no lo parece [2] **so as to + INF** para + INF; **they set off early ~ as to get good seats** salieron temprano para conseguir buenas localidades

B (therefore, consequently) así que, de manera que; **he wasn't at home, ~ I called again** no estaba en casa, así que *or* de manera que volví a llamar más tarde; **~ *there!*** ¡para que sepas!

so³ *n* (Mus) sol *m*

soak¹ /səʊk/ *vt* [1] ‹*lentils/clothes*› (immerse) poner* en *or* a remojo, dejar remojando; (leave immersed) dejar en *or* a remojo [2] (drench) empapar; **to be ~ed (to the skin)** estar* empapado, estar* calado hasta los huesos

■ **soak** *vi* [1] (lie in liquid): **to leave sth to ~** dejar algo en *or* a remojo, dejar algo remojando [2] (penetrate) (+ *adv compl*): **to ~ into/through sth** calar algo; **wipe it up before it ~s in** límpialo antes de que se absorba

Phrasal verb

• **soak up** [v ▸ o ▸ adv, v ▸ adv ▸ o] [1] ‹*water/blood/ink*› absorber, embeber [2] ‹*sun/atmosphere*› empaparse de; ‹*knowledge/information*› absorber

soak² *n*: **to give sth a ~** poner* algo en *or* a remojo

soaking¹ /'səʊkɪŋ/ *n*: **to get a ~** empaparse; **he gave me a ~** me empapó

soaking² *adj* empapado; **you're ~** estás empapada, estás calada hasta los huesos; (*as adv*) **it's ~ wet** está empapado *or* chorreando

so-and-so /'səʊənsəʊ/ *n* (colloq)

A [u] (unspecified person) (*no art*) fulano, -na *m,f*; **Mr S~** don *or* señor Fulano (de Tal)

B [c] (unpleasant person) (euph): **some ~ has used up all the hot water** algún hijo de su (santa) madre me dejó sin agua caliente (euf)

soap¹ /səʊp/ *n*

A [u c] jabón *m*; **toilet ~** jabón de tocador; ***no ~*** (AmE): **we tried to persuade her, but it was no ~** tratamos de convencerla, pero no hubo forma *or* (AmL tb) no hubo caso; (*before n*) **~ dish** jabonera *f*

B ▸**soap opera**

soap² *vt* enjabonar, jabonar; **to ~ one's hands** enjabonarse *or* jabonarse las manos

soap: **~box** *n*: *cajón que sirve de tarima a un orador callejero*; **~flakes** *pl n* jabón *m* en escamas; **~ opera** *n* [c u] (TV) telenovela *f*, culebrón *m*; (Rad) radionovela *f*, comedia *f* (AmL); **~ powder** *n* [u c] (BrE) jabón *m* en polvo, detergente *m* (*en polvo*); **~suds** *pl n* espuma *f* (*de jabón*)

> **soap opera**
>
> Nombre humorístico del culebrón o telenovela. Su nombre se debe al hecho de que las primeras *soap operas* (óperas de jabón) emitidas por radio en EEUU eran financiadas por compañías de jabón

soapy /'səʊpi/ *adj* **-pier, -piest** [1] (lathery) ‹*water*› jabonoso; ‹*cloth/hands*› enjabonado [2] (like soap) ‹*smell/taste*› a jabón

soar /sɔːr || sɔː(r)/ *vi*

A [1] (fly) «*bird/glider*» planear [2] (rise) «*bird/kite*» elevarse, remontarse, remontar el vuelo; «*prices/costs*» dispararse; «*hopes*» aumentar, renacer*; «*popularity*» aumentar; **their spirits ~ed** se les levantó el ánimo [3] (tower) «*skyscraper/mountain*» alzarse*, elevarse, erguirse* (liter)

B **soaring** *pres p* ‹*inflation*› galopante, de ritmo vertiginoso; ‹*popularity*› en alza; **a ~ing dollar** un dólar en alza; **caused by ~ temperatures** causado por una subida vertiginosa de las temperaturas

sob¹ /sɑːb || sɒb/ **-bb-** *vi* sollozar*

■ **sob** *vt* decir* sollozando *or* entre sollozos; **to ~ oneself to sleep** sollozar* hasta quedarse dormido; **to ~ one's heart out** llorar a lágrima viva

sob² *n* sollozo *m*

sober /'səʊbər || 'səʊbə(r)/ *adj*

A (not drunk) sobrio; **I am perfectly ~** estoy perfectamente sobrio *or* despejado

B [1] (serious, grave) ‹*expression*› grave; ‹*young man*› serio, formal; ‹*occasion*› formal [2] (subdued) ‹*dress/colors*› sobrio

Phrasal verb

• **sober up**

A [v ▸ adv]: **he's ~ed up now** ya está sobrio, ya se le ha pasado la borrachera

B [v ▸ o ▸ adv, v ▸ adv ▸ o] despejar

sobering /'səʊbərɪŋ/ *adj* ‹*experience*› aleccionador; **it's a ~ thought** te hace pensar

soberly /'səʊbərli || 'səʊbəli/ *adv* [1] (seriously, gravely) con seriedad [2] (in a subdued manner) ‹*dress/decorate*› sobriamente, con sobriedad

sobersides /'səʊbərsaɪdz/ *n* (AmE colloq) soso, -sa *m,f* (fam)

sobriety /səʊ'braɪəti, sə- || sə'braɪəti/ *n* [u] [1] (seriousness, gravity) seriedad *f*, sensatez *f* [2] (not being drunk) (*before n*) **~ test** (AmE) prueba *f* del alcohol *or* de alcoholemia

sob story *n* (colloq) dramón *m* (fam), tragedia *f*

so-called /'səʊ'kɔːld/ *adj* (*usu before n*) [1] (commonly named) (así) llamado *or* denominado [2] (indicating skeptical attitude) ‹*expert/do-gooder*› supuesto, presunto

soccer /'sɑːkər/ *n* [u] fútbol *m or* (AmC, Méx) futbol *m*

sociable /'səʊʃəbəl/ *adj* ‹*person*› sociable; **come on, have a drink, just to be ~** vamos, tómate algo, para acompañarnos

social¹ /'səʊʃəl/ *adj* social; **a ~ climber** un arribista, un trepador; **he has no ~ graces** no sabe cómo comportarse; **~ life** vida *f* social; **I'm only a ~ drinker** sólo bebo cuando estoy con gente

social² *n* (colloq) reunión *f* (social)

social: **~ democracy**, **S~ Democracy** *n* [u] socialdemocracia *f*, democracia *f* social; **~ democrat**, **S~ Democrat** *n* socialdemócrata *mf*; **~ history** *n* [1] [u] (subject) historia *f* social [2] [c] (account) historia *f* social, sociohistoria *f* [3] [c] (of individual) (Soc Adm) historial *m* social; **~ housing** *n* [u] viviendas *fpl* subvencionadas, viviendas *fpl* de protección oficial (*en Esp*); ≈ vivien-

S

das *fpl* de interés social (*en Méx, Per*); ≈ viviendas *fpl* económicas (*en RPl*)

socialism /'səʊʃəlɪzəm/ *n* [u] socialismo *m*

socialist¹, **Socialist** /'səʊʃələst/ *adj* socialista

socialist², **Socialist** *n* socialista *mf*

socialite /'səʊʃəlaɪt/ *n*: *persona que figura mucho en sociedad*

socialize /'səʊʃəlaɪz/ *vt*

A (Psych) socializar*

B (AmE Pol) ‹*industry/production*› nacionalizar*

■ **socialize** *vi* alternar; (at party) circular; **they don't ~ much** no alternan *or* no salen mucho, no hacen mucha vida social

socially /'səʊʃəli/ *adv* **1** (relating to the community) ‹*divisive/useful*› socialmente; (*indep*) desde el punto de vista social **2** (in social situations): **we don't meet ~** no tenemos trato social, no alternamos en los mismos círculos; **it's not ~ acceptable** está mal visto, no se considera correcto

social: **~ science** *n* [u c] ciencia *f* social; **~ security** *n* [u] (BrE) seguridad *f* social; **~ service** *n* **1** [u] (welfare work) (AmE) asistencia *f or* trabajo *m* social **2** [c] (in UK) servicio *m* social; **~ studies** *pl n*: *historia, geografía y otras asignaturas afines*; **~ work** *n* [u] asistencia *f* social; **~ worker** *n* (Soc Adm) asistente, -ta *m,f* social, trabajador, -dora *m,f* social (Méx), visitador, -dora *m,f* social (Chi)

society /sə'saɪəti/ *n* (*pl* **-ties**)

A **1** [u c] (community) sociedad *f*; **in polite ~** entre la gente educada **2** [u] (fashionable elite) (alta) sociedad *f*; **to enter ~** entrar *or* ser* presentado en sociedad

B [c] (association, club) sociedad *f*; **a literary ~** una sociedad literaria, un círculo literario

socio- /'səʊsiəʊ, 'səʊʃiəʊ/ *pref* socio-

sociologist /'səʊsi'ɑːlədʒəst, -ʃi-/ *n* sociólogo, -ga *m,f*

sociology /'səʊsi'ɑːlədʒi, -ʃi-/ *n* [u] sociología *f*

sock¹ /sɑːk || sɒk/ *n* calcetín *m*, media *f* (AmL); **ankle ~s** calcetines cortos, soquetes *mpl* (CS); ***to pull one's ~s up*** (BrE) esforzarse*, poner* empeño; ***to put a ~ in it*** (esp BrE colloq) cerrar* el pico (fam)

sock² *vt* (colloq) pegarle* un puñetazo *or* (fam) una piña a, pegarle* una trompada a (AmS fam), pegarle* un combo a (Chi, Per fam); **to ~ sb one** darle* una a algn (fam); ***to ~ it to sb*** (colloq): **go out there on stage and ~ it to 'em!** ¡sube al escenario y demuéstrales quién eres!

socket /'sɑːkət || 'sɒkɪt/ *n* **1** (Anat) (of eye) cuenca *f*, órbita *f*; (of joint) fosa *f*, hueco *m*; **you nearly pulled my arm out of its ~** casi me desencajas *or* me sacas el brazo **2** (Elec) (for plug) enchufe *m*, toma *f* de corriente, tomacorriente *m* (AmL); (for light bulb) portalámparas *m* **3** (Tech) encaje *m*; (*before n*) **~ wrench** llave *f* de tubo

sod¹ /sɑːd || sɒd/ *n*

A **1** [c] (piece of turf) tepe *m*, champa *f* (Andes) **2** [u] (ground) (liter) tierra *f*, suelo *m*

B [c] (BrE) **1** (obnoxious person) (vulg) cabrón, -brona *m,f* (vulg); **he's a selfish ~** es un egoísta de mierda (vulg) **2** (fellow) (sl): **I feel sorry for the poor ~** me da lástima el pobre tipo *or* el pobre diablo (fam); **you lucky ~!** ¡qué potra tienes! (fam), ¡qué suertudo eres! (AmL fam), ¡qué culo tenés! (RPl arg) **3** (sth difficult, unpleasant) (vulg) joda *f* (AmL vulg), coñazo *m* (Esp vulg); ***~ all*** (BrE vulg): **he's done ~ all** no ha hecho un carajo (vulg)

sod² *vt* (BrE vulg): **oh ~ it! I forgot to go to the bank!** ¡mierda! *or* ¡carajo! ¡me olvidé de ir al banco!; **~ them!** ¡que se vayan a la mierda! (vulg)

Phrasal verb

- **sod off** [v ▸ adv] (BrE vulg) (*usu in imperative*): **~ off!** ¡déjate de joder! (vulg), ¡vete *or* (RPl) andáte a la mierda! (vulg), ¡vete a tomar por culo! (Esp vulg)

soda /'səʊdə/ *n*

A **1** [u] (soda water) soda *f*, agua *f*‡ de seltz; **scotch and ~** whisky *m* con soda *or* sifón **2** [c u] (flavored) (AmE) refresco *m*, fresco *m* (AmL); **orange ~** naranjada *f* **3** [c] (ice-cream soda) (AmE) ice-cream soda *m* (AmL) (*refresco con helado*)

B [u] (Chem) soda *f*, sosa *f*

soda: **~ bread** *n*: *pan hecho con levadura química o polvo de hornear*; **~ cracker** *n* (AmE) galletita *f* salada; **~ fountain** *n* (AmE) fuente *f* de sodas, ≈ heladería *f*; **~ pop** *n* (AmE) refresco *m*; **~ water** *n* [u] soda *f*, agua *f*‡ de seltz

sodden /'sɑːdn̩ || 'sɒdn̩/ *adj* empapado

sodding /'sɑːdɪŋ || 'sɒdɪŋ/ *adj* (BrE sl) (*as intensifier*) puñetero (fam), maldito (fam)

sodium /'səʊdiəm/ *n* [u] sodio *m*

sodium: **~ bicarbonate** *n* [u] bicarbonato *m* sódico *or* de sodio; **~ chloride** /'klɔːraɪd/ *n* [u] cloruro *m* sódico *or* de sodio

sodomy /'sɑːdəmi || 'sɒdəmi/ *n* [u] sodomía *f*

sofa /'səʊfə/ *n* sofá *m*; (*before n*) **~ bed** sofá-cama *m*

soft /sɔːft || sɒft/ *adj* **-er, -est**

A **1** (not hard) blando; ‹*cushion/mattress*› blando, mullido; ‹*dough/clay/pencil*› blando; ‹*metal*› maleable, dúctil; **to go ~** ablandarse **2** (smooth) ‹*fur/fabric*› suave; ‹*skin*› suave, terso

B **1** (mild, subdued) ‹*breeze*› suave; ‹*light/color*› suave, tenue **2** (quiet) ‹*music*› suave; **in a ~ voice** en voz baja

C **1** (lenient) blando, indulgente; **to be ~ ON *o* WITH sb** ser* blando *or* indulgente CON algn; **to take a ~er line on sth** adoptar una actitud menos intransigente sobre algo **2** (feeble-minded) (colloq): **to be ~ (in the head)** ser* estúpido

D (easy) (colloq) ‹*life*› fácil; **the ~ option** el camino fácil; **a ~ target** un blanco fácil; **~ sell** venta *f* blanda (*venta sin técnicas agresivas*)

E (emotionally attached): **to be ~ on sb** tener* debilidad por algn

F ‹*drugs*› blando; ‹*pornography*› blando

G (Chem) ‹*water*› blando

H ‹*consonant*› débil

soft: **~ball** *n* [u] softball *m* (*especie de béisbol que se juega con pelota blanda*); **~-boiled** /'sɔːft'bɔɪld || ˌsɒft'bɔɪld/ *adj* ‹*egg*› pasado por agua; **~cover** /'sɔːft'kʌvər || 'sɒftˌkʌvə(r)/ *n* libro *m* en rústica *or* en pasta blanda; (*before n*) ‹*edition*› en rústica, en pasta blanda; **~ drink** *n* [c u] refresco *m* (*bebida no alcohólica*)

soften /'sɔːfən || 'sɒfən/ *vt*

A ‹*clay/butter/leather*› ablandar; ‹*skin*› suavizar*; ‹*light/color*› suavizar*, ‹*contours/edges*› difuminar

B (mitigate) ‹*effect*› atenuar*, mitigar*; **to ~ the blow** suavizar* *or* amortiguar* el golpe; **to ~ one's position** adoptar una postura menos intransigente

C (Chem) ‹*water*› ablandar, descalcificar*

■ **soften** *vi*

A «*clay/butter/leather*» ablandarse; «*skin*» suavizarse*; «*light/color*» suavizarse*

B **1** (become gentler) «*person/heart*» ablandarse; «*voice*» suavizarse*, dulcificarse* **2** (become more moderate) volverse* menos intransigente

Phrasal verb

- **soften up** [v ▸ o ▸ adv, v ▸ adv ▸ o] **1** (make soft) ablandar **2** ‹*person*› ablandar

softener /'sɔːfn̩ər || 'sɒfn̩ə(r)/ *n* **1** (for water) descalcificador *m* **2** (for fabric) suavizante *m*

soft: **~ fruit** *n* [u] (esp BrE) *frutas como las frambuesas, moras, fresas etc*; **~ furnishings** *pl n* (BrE) *artículos como almohadones, cortinas, alfombras etc*; **~hearted** *adj* bueno

softie *n* ▸ **softy**

softly /'sɔːftli || 'sɒftli/ *adv* **1** (gently) ‹*touch*› suavemente; **~ lit** iluminado con luz tenue **2** (quietly) ‹*speak*› bajito; ‹*creep/move*› sin hacer ruido **3** (tenderly) dulcemente

softly-softly /'sɔːftli'sɔːftli || ˌsɒftli'sɒftli/ *adj* (colloq) ‹*approach*› cauteloso; **~ tactics** mano *f* blanda

softness /'sɔːftnəs || 'sɒftnɪs/ *n* [u]

A **1** (of mattress, cushion) lo blando *or* mullido, blandura *f*; (of clay, butter) lo blando **2** (of fabric, hair) suavidad *f*; (of skin) suavidad *f*, tersura *f*

B **1** (of breeze) suavidad *f*, lo suave; (of color) lo tenue **2** (of music, voice) lo bajo

C (leniency) blandura *f*; (moral weakness) debilidad *f*

soft: **~ pedal** *n* pedal *m* suave; **~-pedal** /'sɔːft'pedl̩ || ˌsɒft'pedl̩/, (BrE) **-ll-** *vt* (journ) ‹*subject/issue*› restarle importancia a, minimizar* **~-pedal** *vi* (journ) tratar de no llamar la atención; **~ shoulder** *n* (AmE) arcén *m* blando *or* de tierra, berma *f* de tierra (Andes), banquina *f* de tierra (RPl), acotación *f* de tierra (Méx), hombrillo *m* de tierra (Ven); **~-soap** /'sɔːft'səʊp || ˌsɒft'səʊp/ *vt* (colloq) halagar*, hacerle* el artículo a (fam), darle* jabón a (Esp fam); **~-spoken** /'sɔːft'spəʊkən || ˌsɒft'spəʊkən/ *adj* de voz suave; **~ top** *n* (AmE) (car) descapotable *m*, convertible *m* (AmL); (roof) capota *f*; **~ toy** *n* (BrE) *muñeco de peluche*

S

o *trapo*; ~**ware** /'sɔːftwer || 'sɒftweə(r)/ *n* software *m*; ~**wood** *n* 1 [u] (wood) madera *f* de coníferas 2 [c] (tree) conífera *f*

softy /'sɔːfti/ *n* (*pl* **-ties**) (colloq) blandengue *mf* (fam)

soggy /'sɑːgi || 'sɒgi/ *adj* **-gier, -giest** ‹*ground/grass*› empapado, saturado; ‹*vegetables*› pasado

soh /səʊ/ *n* (Mus) sol *m*

soil¹ /sɔɪl/ *n* 1 [u c] (earth) tierra *f* 2 (country, homeland) (liter) tierra *f*; **on British** ~ en suelo británico 3 [u] (filth, dirt) (AmE) suciedad *f*

soil² *vt* ‹*sheet/collar*› ensuciar, manchar

soiled /sɔɪld/ *adj* ‹*linen*› sucio; ‹*goods*› dañado

soiree, soirée /swɑː'reɪ/ *n* (frml) soirée *f*, velada *f*

sojourn /'səʊdʒɜːrn || 'sɒdʒən/ *n* (liter) estadía *f* (AmL), estancia *f* (Esp, Méx)

sol /səʊl || sɒl/ *n* (Mus) sol *m*

solace /'sɑːləs || 'sɒlɪs/ *n* (liter) 1 [u] (comfort) solaz *m* (liter), consuelo *m* 2 [c] (source of comfort) consuelo *m*

solar /'səʊlər || 'səʊlə(r)/ *adj* solar

solarium /səʊ'leriəm || sə'leəriəm/ *n* (*pl* **-riums** *or* **-ria** /-riə/) 1 (sun terrace) solárium *m*, solario *m*, solana *f* 2 (sun bed) cama *f* solar

solar: ~ **plexus** /'pleksəs/ *n* **the** ~ **plexus** el plexo solar; ~ **system** *n* **the** ~ **system** el sistema solar

sold /səʊld/ *past & past p of* **sell**

solder /'sɑːdər || 'səʊldə(r)/ *vt* soldar*

solder gun, **soldering gun** /'sɑːdərɪŋ || 'səʊldərɪŋ/ *n* (AmE) pistola *f* de soldar

soldering iron /'sɑːdərɪŋ || 'səʊldərɪŋ/ *n* soldador *m*

soldier /'səʊldʒər || 'səʊldʒə(r)/ *n* soldado *mf*; (officer) militar *mf*; **an old** ~ un ex-combatiente; **to play (at)** ~**s** jugar* a la guerra; **tin** ~ soldadito *m* de plomo

(Phrasal verb)

• **soldier on** [v ▸ adv] (BrE colloq) seguir* al pie del cañon *or* en la brecha

sole¹ /səʊl/ *n*

A 1 (of foot) planta *f* 2 (of shoe) suela *f*

B (fish) (*pl* ~ *or* ~**s**) lenguado *m*

sole² *adj* (*before n*) 1 (only) único 2 (exclusive) ‹*rights*› exclusivo; **they are** ~ **agents for ...** tienen la representación exclusiva de ...

sole³ *vt* (*usu pass*): **to have one's shoes** ~**d and heeled** hacerles* poner suelas y tacones *or* (CS, Per) tacos a los zapatos

solely /'səʊlli/ *adv* 1 (wholly) únicamente, exclusivamente; **he's** ~ **responsible** es el único responsable 2 (only, simply) sólo, solamente, únicamente

solemn /'sɑːləm || 'sɒləm/ *adj* 1 (serious, formal) ‹*occasion/silence*› solemne 2 (grave) ‹*person*› serio; ‹*face*› solemne

solemnity /sə'lemnəti/ *n* solemnidad *f*

solemnize /'sɑːləmnaɪz/ *vt* (frml) solemnizar* (frml)

solemnly /'sɑːləmli || 'sɒləmli/ *adv* 1 (formally) ‹*swear/warn*› solemnemente 2 (gravely) ‹*say/look*› con aire de gravedad

solenoid /'səʊlənɔɪd/ *n* solenoide *m*

solicit /sə'lɪsət || sə'lɪsɪt/ *vt* 1 ‹‹*prostitute*›› abordar (*buscando clientes*) 2 (request, ask for) (frml) ‹*information/help*› solicitar (frml), pedir*

■ **solicit** *vi* ‹‹*prostitute*›› ejercer la prostitución callejera (*abordando a posibles clientes*)

soliciting /sə'lɪsətɪŋ || sə'lɪsɪtɪŋ/ *n* [u] ejercicio *m* de la prostitución callejera (*abordando a posibles clientes*)

solicitor /sə'lɪsətər || sə'lɪsɪtə(r)/ *n* 1 (in US and in UK) *abogado responsable de los asuntos legales de un municipio o de un departamento gubernamental* 2 (in UK) abogado, -da *m,f* (*que prepara causas legales y desempeña también funciones de notario*)

Solicitor General *n* (*pl* ~**s** ~) (in US) ≈ Subsecretario de Justicia; (in UK) *adjunto del Procurador General de la Nación*

solid¹ /'sɑːləd || 'sɒlɪd/ *adj* **-er, -est**

A 1 (not liquid or gaseous) sólido; ~ **food** alimentos *mpl* sólidos; **to become** ~ solidificarse*; **it's frozen** ~ se congeló 2 (not hollow) ‹*rubber ball/tire*› macizo 3 (Math) tridimensional

B 1 (unbroken) ‹*line/row*› continuo, ininterrumpido; **a** ~ **mass** una masa compacta 2 (continuous) (colloq) ‹*month/year*› seguido

C 1 (physically sturdy) ‹*furniture/house*› sólido; ‹*meal*› consistente 2 (substantial, valuable) ‹*knowledge/reason*› sólido; **a good** ~ **worker** un trabajador serio y responsable 3 (firm, definite) ‹*offer*› en firme

D 1 (pure) ‹*metal/wood*› macizo, puro; ‹*rock*› vivo 2 (unanimous) ‹*support/agreement*› unánime

solid² *n*

A 1 (Chem, Phys) sólido *m* 2 (Math) sólido *m*

B **solids** *pl* 1 (in, from liquid) sólidos *mpl*, sustancias *fpl* sólidas 2 (food) alimentos *mpl* sólidos

solid³ *adv* (colloq): **to be packed/jammed** ~ estar* lleno hasta el tope *or* hasta los topes

solidarity /'sɑːlə'dærəti || ˌsɒlɪ'dærəti/ *n* [u] ~ (WITH **sb/sth**) solidaridad *f* (CON algn/algo)

solid fuel *n* [u c] 1 (coal) carbón *m* 2 (rocket fuel) combustible *m* sólido

solidify /sə'lɪdəfaɪ/ **-fies, -fying, -fied** *vi* solidificarse*

■ **solidify** *vt* solidificar*

solidity /sə'lɪdəti/ *n* [u] solidez *f*

solidly /'sɑːlədli || 'sɒlɪdli/ *adv* 1 (sturdily) ‹*fixed/grounded*› firmemente; ‹*made*› sólidamente; **a** ~ **built house** una casa de construcción sólida; **he's** ~ **built** es de complexión robusta 2 (thoroughly) ‹*reasoned/argued*› concienzudamente 3 (unanimously) unánimemente 4 (continuously) (BrE) ‹*walk/argue/rain*› sin parar

solid-state /'sɑːləd'steɪt || ˌsɒlɪd'steɪt/ *adj* (*before n*) 1 (Phys): ~ **physics** física *f* del estado sólido 2 (Electron) de estado sólido

soliloquy /sə'lɪləkwi/ *n* (*pl* **-quies**) soliloquio *m*

solitaire /'sɑːləˌter || 'sɒlɪˌteə(r)/ *n*

A [c] ~ **(diamond)** solitario *m*

B [u] (Games) solitario *m*; **to play** ~ hacer* solitarios

solitary /'sɑːləteri || 'sɒlɪtəri/ *adj* 1 (alone) ‹*person/life/journey*› solitario; **a** ~ **place** un lugar solitario *or* apartado 2 (single) (*before n*) solo

solitary confinement *n* [u] incomunicación *f*; **he's been put in/he's in** ~ ~ lo han incomunicado

solitude /'sɑːlətuːd || 'sɒlɪtjuːd/ *n* [u] soledad *f*

solo¹ /'səʊləʊ/ *n* (*pl* **-los**) solo *m*; **a violin** ~ un solo de violín

solo² *adj* 1 (Mus) ‹*violin/voices*› solista; ‹*album*› en solitario; ‹*piece*› para voz/instrumento solista; **to go** ~ lanzarse* como solista 2 (Aviat) ‹*attempt/flight*› en solitario

solo³ *adv* en solitario

soloist /'səʊləʊəst || 'səʊləʊɪst/ *n* solista *mf*

so long *interj* (colloq) hasta luego, hasta la vista

solstice /'sɑːlstəs || 'sɒlstɪs/ *n* solsticio *m*

soluble /'sɑːljəbəl || 'sɒljʊbəl/ *adj*

A ‹*substance*› soluble

B ‹*problem/mystery*› soluble

solution /sə'luːʃən/ *n*

A [c] (to problem) ~ (TO **sth**) solución *f* (A algo)

B [c u] (Chem) solución *f*

solvable /'sɑːlvəbəl || 'sɒlvəbl/ *adj* ‹*crime/puzzle*› soluble, que tiene solución

solve /sɑːlv || sɒlv/ *vt* ‹*mystery/equation*› resolver*; ‹*conflict*› solucionar; ‹*crossword puzzle*› sacar*; **to** ~ **a crime** esclarecer* un crimen; **to** ~ **a riddle** encontrar* la solución a una adivinanza/un enigma

solvent¹ /'sɑːlvənt/ *adj* ‹*company/person*› solvente

solvent² *n* disolvente *m*, solvente *m*; (*before n*) ~ **abuse** (frml) inhalación *f* de disolventes

Somali¹ /sə'mɑːli/ *adj* somalí

Somali² *n* 1 [c] (person) somalí *mf* 2 [u] (language) somalí *m*

Somalia /sə'mɑːliə/ *n* Somalia *f*

somber, (BrE) **sombre** /'sɑːmbər || 'sɒmbə(r)/ *adj* 1 (dark) sombrío, oscuro y apagado, triste 2 (melancholy) ‹*mood/thought*› sombrío; ‹*music*› lúgubre

some¹ /sʌm, *weak form* səm/ *adj*

A 1 (unstated number or type) (+ *pl n*) unos, unas; **there were** ~ **boys/girls in the park** había unos *or* algunos niños/unas *or* algunas niñas en el parque; **I need** ~ **new shoes/scissors** necesito (unos) zapatos nuevos/una tijera nueva; **would you like ~ cherries?** ¿quieres (unas) cerezas?; **there are ~ good restaurants around here** por aquí hay buenos restaurantes 2 (unstated quantity or type) (+ *uncount n*): **~ paint fell on my head** me cayó (un poco de) pintura en la cabeza; **you'll need ~ French currency** vas a necesitar algo de dinero francés; **I can give you ~ information** te puedo dar (alguna) información; **let's go home and have ~ dinner** vayamos a casa a cenar; **would you like ~ coffee?** ¿quieres café?

B (a, one) (+ *sing count noun*) algún, -guna; **they owe us ~ sort of explanation** nos deben algún tipo de explicación; **~ compromise may still be found** todavía puede llegarse a un acuerdo; **~ day I'll get my revenge** ya me vengaré algún día; **~ day soon** un día de éstos

C 1 (particular, not all) (+ *pl n*) algunos, -nas; **I like ~ modern artists** algunos artistas modernos me gustan; **in ~ ways** en cierto modo; **~ people never learn** hay gente que no aprende nunca 2 (part of, not whole) (+ *uncount n*): **~ German wine is red, but most is white** Alemania produce algunos vinos tintos pero la mayoría son blancos; **~ Shakespeare is very rarely performed** algunas obras de Shakespeare no se representan casi nunca

D 1 (not many, a few) algunos, -nas 2 (not much, a little) un poco de

E 1 (several, many): **she's been bed-ridden for ~ years now** hace años que está postrada en cama 2 (large amount of): **we've known each other for quite ~ time now** ya hace mucho (tiempo) que nos conocemos; **there'll be ~ celebrating in Wales tonight** esta noche sí que habrá fiesta en Gales

F (colloq) 1 (expressing appreciation): **that's ~ car you've got!** ¡vaya coche que tienes!, ¡qué cochazo tienes! 2 (stressing remarkable, ridiculous nature): **that was ~ exam!** ¡vaya examen!; **you do ask ~ questions!** ¡haces cada pregunta! 3 (expressing irony): **~ present! I had to pay for it!** ¡qué regalo ni qué regalo! ¡lo tuve que pagar yo!; **~ friend you are!** ¡qué buen amigo eres! (iró)

some² *pron*

A 1 (a number of things or people) algunos, -nas 2 (an amount): **there's no salt left; we'll have to buy ~** no queda sal; vamos a tener que comprar

B 1 (a number of a group) algunos, -nas; **~ are mine and the others belong to Peter** algunos son míos y los otros son de Peter 2 (part of an amount): **~ of what I've written** algo *or* parte de lo que he escrito; **the coffee's ready: would you like ~?** el café está listo: ¿quieres?

C (certain people) algunos, -nas; **~ say that ...** algunos dicen que ...

some³ *adv* (approximately) unos, unas; alrededor de; **there were ~ fifty people there** había unas cincuenta personas, había alrededor de cincuenta personas

somebody¹ /'sʌm,bɑːdi || 'sʌmbədi/ *pron* alguien; **~'s coming** viene alguien; **shut the door, ~!** ¡que alguien cierre la puerta!; **~ else got the job** le dieron el trabajo a otro *or* a otra persona; **there's ~ I'd like you to meet** quiero presentarte a un amigo (*or* compañero *etc*); **~ or other must have dropped it** se le debe de haber caído a alguien; **who was it? — John ~** ¿quién era? — John algo *or* John no sé cuánto (fam)

somebody² *n* (*no pl*): **to be (a) ~** ser* alguien

somehow /'sʌmhaʊ/ *adv* 1 (by some means) de algún modo, de alguna manera *or* de alguna forma; **~ or other he managed to repay his debts** de algún modo u otro, pudo pagar sus deudas 2 (in some way, for some reason): **it isn't the same, ~** no sé por qué, pero no es lo mismo

someone /'sʌmwʌn/ *pron* ▸**somebody¹**

someplace /'sʌmpleɪs/ *adv* (AmE) ▸**somewhere¹ A**

somersault¹ /'sʌmərsɔːlt || 'sʌməsɒlt, -sɔːlt/ *n* (on ground) voltereta *f*, vuelta *f* (de) carnero (CS); (from height) (salto *m*) mortal *m*; (of car) vuelta *f* de campana; **to turn ~s** hacer* volteretas, dar* vueltas (de) carnero (CS)

somersault² *vi* (on ground) hacer* volteretas, dar* vueltas (de) carnero (CS); (from height) dar* un (salto) mortal

something¹ /'sʌmθɪŋ/ *pron*

A algo; **~ has happened to her** algo le ha pasado; **have ~ to eat/drink** come/bebe algo; **do you know ~? I think we're lost** ¿sabes una cosa *or* sabes qué? creo que nos hemos perdido; **or ~ of the kind** o algo por el estilo; **it's not ~ to be proud of** no es como para estar orgulloso; **that was ~ I hadn't expected** eso no me lo esperaba; **is it ~ I said?** ¿qué pasa? ¿qué he dicho?; **it's not much, but it's ~** no es mucho, pero algo es

B 1 (in vague statements or approximations): **she's 30 ~** tiene treinta y pico años (fam); **he said it was because of the traffic or ~** dijo que era por el tráfico o qué se yo; **have you gone mad or ~?** ¿te has vuelto loco o qué?, ¿es que te has vuelto loco? 2 **something like**: **~ like 200 spectators** unos 200 espectadores; **he looks ~ like his brother** se parece algo a su hermano 3 **something of** (rather): **she's ~ of an eccentric** es algo excéntrica; **it came as ~ of a surprise** me (*or* nos *etc*) sorprendió un poco

C (sth special): **it was quite ~ for a woman to reach that position** era todo un logro *or* (fam) no era moco de pavo que una mujer alcanzara esa posición; **that party was ~ else!** (colloq) ¡la fiesta estuvo genial *or* fue demasiado! (fam); **she's quite ~, isn't she?** (in looks) está bien ¿eh?; (in general) ¡qué mujer (*or* chica *etc*)! ¿no?; ***to have (got) ~*** (be talented) tener* algo; (perceive sth significant): **I think you might have ~ there** puede que tengas razón

something² *n* (*no pl*): **won't you have a little ~ (to eat/drink)?** ¿no quieres comer/beber algo?; **she has that certain ~** tiene ese no sé qué

something³ *adv* (colloq): **my back's playing me up ~ chronic** ¡la espalda me tiene ... !

sometime¹ /'sʌmtaɪm/ *adv* (at unspecified time): **I'll get around to it ~** ya lo haré en algún momento; **we'll have to finish it ~ or another** algún día habrá que terminarlo, tarde *or* temprano habrá que terminarlo; **~ next week** un día de la semana que viene; **let's do it ~ soon** hagámoslo pronto; **we met ~ last summer** nos conocimos el verano pasado(, no recuerdo cuándo)

sometime² *adj* (*before n*) (frml) ex, antiguo

sometimes /'sʌmtaɪmz/ *adv* a veces, algunas veces

someway /'sʌmweɪ/ *adv* (AmE) ▸**somehow**

somewhat /'sʌmhwɑːt || 'sʌmwɒt/ *adv* algo, un tanto

somewhere¹ /'sʌmhwer || 'sʌmweə(r)/ *adv*

A (in, at, to a place): **it must be ~ in your office** tiene que estar en tu despacho, en algún lado *or* sitio *or* lugar; **shall we go ~ else?** ¿vamos a otro sitio *or* lugar *or* lado?; ***to get ~*** avanzar*, adelantar

B (in approximations): **it happened ~ around Easter** sucedió alrededor de Semana Santa; **we spent ~ around $10,000** gastamos cerca de *or* alrededor de 10.000 dólares; **he's ~ in his sixties** tiene unos sesenta y tantos años *or* (fam) unos sesenta años y pico

somewhere² *pron*: **will there be ~ open?** ¿habrá algo (*or* algún sitio *etc*) abierto?; **she's found ~ to live** ha encontrado casa (*or* habitación *etc*); **she comes from ~ near Boston** es de cerca de Boston

somnolent /'sɑːmnələnt || 'sɒmnələnt/ *adj* (liter) ‹*eyes*› somnoliento; ‹*heat*› que adormece; ‹*mood*› aletargado

son /sʌn/ *n* 1 (male child) hijo *m*; **her youngest/eldest ~** su hijo menor/mayor; **God, the S~** Dios Hijo 2 (*as form of address*) hijo

sonar /'səʊnɑːr || 'səʊnɑː(r)/ *n* sónar *m*

sonata /sə'nɑːtə/ *n* (*pl* **-tas**) (Mus) sonata *f*

song /sɔːŋ || sɒŋ/ *n* 1 [c] (piece) canción *f*; **to burst into ~**[u] ponerse* a cantar; ***to buy/sell sth for a ~*** (colloq) comprar/vender algo por una bicoca (fam) 2 [u] (of bird) canto *m*

song: **~ and dance** *n*: ***to make a ~ and dance about sth*** (colloq) hacer* muchos aspavientos por algo; **~bird** *n* pájaro *m* cantor; **~book** *n* cancionero *m*; **~ thrush** *n* tordo músico *m*, zorzal *m*; **~writer** *n* compositor, -tora *m,f* (*de canciones*)

sonic /'sɑːnɪk || 'sɒnɪk/ *adj* sónico

sonic boom *n* estruendo *m* (*que se produce al romper la barrera del sonido*)

son-in-law /'sʌnɪnlɔː/ *n* (*pl* **sons-in-law**) yerno *m*, hijo *m* político

sonnet /'sɑːnət || 'sɒnɪt/ *n* soneto *m*

sonny /'sʌni/ *n* (colloq) (*as form of address*) hijito (fam), nene (fam), mijito (AmL fam)

son: **~ of a bitch** *n* (*pl* **sons of bitches**) (esp AmE sl) 1 (person) hijo *m* de puta, hijo *m* (Méx) de la chingada (vulg) 2 (object) condenado, -da *m,f* (fam); **I can't get the ~ of a bitch to start!** ¡el condenado no quiere arrancar!

(fam); ~ **of a gun** *n* (colloq & dated) sinvergüenza *m*, granuja *m*; **that lucky ~ of a gun** el suertudo ése (AmL), la suerte que tiene el tío (Esp fam)

soon /su:n/ *adv* **-er, -est**
A (shortly, after a while) pronto, dentro de poco; **I left ~ afterward** yo me fui poco después; **it'll ~ be spring** ya falta poco para (que empiece) la primavera; **they're coming ~ after eight** vienen poco después de las ocho; **see you ~** hasta pronto; **~er or later** tarde o temprano
B 1 (early, quickly) pronto; **how ~ can you be here?** ¿cuándo puedes llegar?, ¿qué tan pronto puedes llegar? (AmL); **I finished ~er than I expected** terminé antes de lo que esperaba; **all too ~ the vacation was over** las vacaciones pasaron volando; **none too ~, not a minute** *o* **moment too ~** no antes de tiempo; **to speak too ~** hablar antes de tiempo; **thank God she's gone — don't speak too ~** gracias a Dios que se ha ido — no cantes victoria; **it'll be here tonight — as ~ as that?** estará aquí esta noche — ¿tan pronto?; **as ~ as possible** lo antes posible, cuanto antes; **the ~er the better** cuanto antes mejor; **she'd steal your purse as ~ as look at you** no tendría ningún escrúpulo en robarte el monedero 2 (*as conj*): **as ~ as** en cuanto, tan pronto como; **as ~ as you've finished, you can go** en cuanto hayas terminado *or* tan pronto como hayas terminado, te puedes ir; **no ~er had we set out than it began to rain** apenas nos habíamos puesto en camino cuando empezó a llover; **no ~er said than done** dicho y hecho
C (*in phrases*) **as soon ... (as)**: **I'd just as ~ stay at home (as go out)** no me importaría quedarme en casa, tanto me da quedarme en casa (como salir); **sooner ... (than)**: **I'd ~er not go, to be honest** a decir verdad, preferiría no ir; **~er you than me!** mejor tú que yo, me alegro de no ser yo el que tiene que hacerlo

soot /sʊt/ *n* [u] hollín *m*

soothe /su:ð/ *vt* 1 (calm) ‹*person*› calmar, tranquilizar*; ‹*nerves*› calmar 2 (relieve) ‹*pain/cough*› aliviar, calmar

soothing /'su:ðɪŋ/ *adj* 1 (calming) ‹*voice/words*› tranquilizador; ‹*music/bath*› relajante 2 (pain-relieving) ‹*ointment/syrup*› balsámico; ‹*medicine*› calmante

soothsayer /'su:θ,seɪər || 'su:θ,seɪə(r)/ *n* (arch) adivino, -na *m,f*

sooty /'sʊti/ *adj* cubierto de hollín

sop /sɑ:p || sɒp/ *n* concesión *f*; **~ TO sth/sb**: **as a ~ to sb's feelings** para no herir los sentimientos de algn; **she gave him the job as a ~ to her conscience** le dio el empleo para acallar su conciencia

sophisticated /sə'fɪstəkeɪtəd || sə'fɪstɪkeɪtɪd/ *adj* 1 (urbane, worldly-wise) ‹*appearance/clothes/person*› sofisticado 2 (complex) ‹*machine/technique*› complejo, altamente desarrollado *or* perfeccionado

sophistication /sə'fɪstə'keɪʃən || sə,fɪstɪ'keɪʃən/ *n* [u] 1 (urbanity) sofisticación *f* 2 (complexity) complejidad *f*

sophistry /'sɑ:fəstri/ *n* [u c] (*pl* **-ries**) sofistería *f*

sophomore /'sɑ:fəmɔ:r/ *n* (AmE) estudiante *mf* de segundo curso (*en una universidad o colegio secundario*)

soporific /'sɑ:pə'rɪfɪk / *adj* ‹*speech/drug*› soporífero

sopping[1] /'sɑ:pɪŋ || 'sɒpɪŋ/ *adj* empapado, calado

sopping[2] *adv* (*as intensifier*) ~ **wet** (of people) calado hasta los huesos, hecho una sopa; (of clothes) chorreando

soppy /'sɑ:pi || 'sɒpi/ *adj* **-pier, -piest** (BrE colloq) ‹*lovesong/novel*› sentimentaloide, sensiblero; **he's completely ~ about her** se le cae la baba por ella (fam)

soprano[1] /sə'prænəʊ/ *n* (*pl* **-nos**) soprano *mf*

soprano[2] *adj* ‹*voice/recorder*› soprano; ‹*part/role*› de soprano

sorbet /sɔ:r'beɪ, 'sɔ:rbət || 'sɔ:beɪ/ *n* [u c] sorbete *m*, helado *m* de agua (CS), nieve *f* (Méx)

sorcerer /'sɔ:rsərər/ *n* (liter) hechicero *m*, brujo *m*

sorceress /'sɔ:rsərəs/ *n* (liter) hechicera *f*, bruja *f*

sorcery /'sɔ:rsəri/ *n* [u] (liter) hechicería *f*, brujería *f*

sordid /'sɔ:rdəd || 'sɔ:dɪd/ *adj* 1 (base) ‹*method/deal*› vergonzoso, infame; **do you want all the ~ details?** (colloq) ¿te interesan los detalles escabrosos? 2 (squalid, dirty) ‹*hotel/conditions*› sórdido, miserable

sore[1] /sɔ:r || sɔ:(r)/ *adj* **sorer** /'sɔ:rər || 'sɔ:rə(r)/, **sorest** /'sɔ:rəst || 'sɔ:rɪst/ 1 (painful) ‹*finger/foot*› dolorido, adolorido; ‹*eye*› irritado; ‹*lips*› reseco; **she has a ~ throat** le duele la garganta; **a ~ *point/subject*** un punto/tema delicado 2 (angry) (AmE colloq) **to be ~ AT** *o* **WITH sb** estar* picado CON algn (fam) 3 (great) (liter) enorme; **to be in ~ need of sth** tener* necesidad acuciante de algo

sore[2] *n* llaga *f*, úlcera *f*

sorehead /'sɔ:rhed || 'sɔ:hed/ *n* (AmE colloq) amargado, -da *m,f*, cascarrabias *mf* (fam)

sorely /'sɔ:rli || 'sɔ:li/ *adv* 1 (*as intensifier*): **he'll be ~ missed** lo echaremos (*or* echarán *etc*) muchísimo de menos; **to be ~ in need of sth** necesitar algo urgentemente, tener* necesidad acuciante de algo 2 (severely) (liter) ‹*afflicted/offended*› profundamente

sorority /sə'rɔ:rəti || sə'rɒrəti/ *n* (*pl* **-ties**) (in US) hermandad *f* femenina (*en universidades norteamericanas*)

> **sorority**
>
> Una hermandad de mujeres en muchos establecimientos de la enseñanza superior en EEUU. Sus miembros comparten una *sorority house*. El nombre de cada sorority está compuesto de dos o tres letras griegas, tales como *Chi Omega* o *Kappa Kappa Gamma*. Suelen hacer obras de caridad y trabajos comunitarios. Algunas *sororities* también son organizaciones académicas o profesionales. *Ver tb* **fraternity**

sorrel /'sɔ:rəl/ *n* [u] (Bot, Culin) acedera *f*, hierba *f* salada

sorrow /'sɑ:rəʊ || 'sɒrəʊ/ *n* 1 [u c] (sadness, grief) ~ **(AT** *o* **OVER sth)** pesar *m* *or* pena *f* *or* dolor *m* (POR algo); ~ **(FOR/AT sth)** pesar (POR algo); ***to drown one's ~s*** (colloq) ahogar* las penas 2 [c] (cause of sadness) disgusto *m*

sorrowful /'sɑ:rəʊfəl/ *adj* afligido, apesadumbrado

sorrowfully /'sɑ:rəʊfəli/ *adv* 1 ‹*say/gaze*› con tristeza 2 (unfortunately) (AmE) (*indep*) lamentablemente

sorry /'sɑ:ri || 'sɒri/ *adj* **-rier, -riest**
A (*pred*) 1 (grieved, sad): **I'm ~** lo siento; **oh, I *am* ~; when did it happen?** ¡cuánto lo siento!; ¿cuándo ocurrió?; **to feel** *o* **be ~ FOR sb**: **I feel so ~ for you/him** te/lo compadezco; **I felt** *o* **was so ~ for him when he got turned down** me dio mucha pena *or* lástima cuando lo rechazaron; **to feel ~ for oneself** lamentarse de su (*or* tu *etc*) suerte; **to be ~ ABOUT sb/sth**: **I'm very ~ about what happened** siento *or* lamento mucho lo que ocurrió; **to be ~ to + INF**: **I wasn't ~ to see the back of him** no me apenó *or* no lamenté que se fuera; **I'm ~ to have to tell you that ...** siento tener que decirte que ...; **to be ~ (THAT)** sentir* QUE (+ *subj*) 2 (apologetic, repentant): **to say ~** pedir* perdón, disculparse; **I'm ~, I didn't mean to offend you** perdóname *or* lo siento *or* disculpa, no fue mi intención ofenderte; **~ to bother you, but ...** perdone *or* disculpe que lo moleste, pero ...; **to be ~ FOR/ABOUT sth** arrepentirse* DE algo; **I'm very/terribly/awfully ~ about last night** siento muchísimo lo de anoche, mil perdones por lo de anoche; **to be ~ (THAT)**: **I'm ~ I didn't make it to your party** siento no haber podido ir a tu fiesta
B (*as interj*) 1 (expressing apology) perdón, lo siento; **(awfully/so) ~!** (BrE) ¡perdone!, ¡disculpe!; **~, I didn't realize it was you** perdona *or* perdóname *or* disculpa *or* discúlpame, no me había dado cuenta de que eras tú 2 (asking speaker to repeat) (BrE) ¿cómo (dice)?
C (pitiful, miserable) (*before n*) ‹*tale*› lamentable, lastimoso; **he was a ~ sight** tenía un aspecto lamentable

sort[1] /sɔ:rt || sɔ:t/ *n*
A (kind, type) 1 (of things) tipo *m*, clase *f*; **all ~s of adventures** todo tipo *or* toda clase de aventuras, aventuras de todo tipo *or* de toda clase, todo género *or* toda suerte de aventuras (liter); **what ~ of car is it?** ¿qué tipo *or* clase de coche es?; **you know the ~ of thing I mean** ya sabes a lo que me refiero; **I believe he's a musician or something of the ~** creo que es músico o algo por el estilo; **don't tell lies: I didn't say anything of the ~** no digas mentiras: no dije nada semejante; **you'll do nothing of the ~!** ¡ni se te ocurra! 2 (of people): **she's not the ~ to let you down** no es de las que te fallan; **I'm not that ~ of girl** yo no soy de ésas; **I know your ~** (BrE) ya sé de qué pie cojeas; **a bad/good ~** (BrE) una mala/buena persona; ***it takes all ~s (to make a world)*** hay de todo en la viña del Señor 3 (approximating to): **a ~ of** *o* **~ of a** una especie de; **it's ~ of a bluish-green color** es una especie de verde azulado
B (*in phrases*) **of sorts, of a sort**: **he gave us a meal of ~s** nos dio una comida, si se le puede llamar comida; **sort of**

(colloq): **it's ~ of sad to think of him all alone** da como pena pensar que está solo (fam); **do you want to go? — well, ~ of** ¿quieres ir? — bueno, en cierto modo sí; **out of sorts** mal, pachucho (Esp fam); **I'm feeling a bit out of ~s** no me encuentro muy bien

sort² *vt* 1 (classify) ‹*papers/letters*› clasificar* 2 (mend) arreglar

Phrasal verbs

• **sort out** [v ▸ o ▸ adv, v ▸ adv ▸ o]

A 1 (put in order) ‹*books/photos*› ordenar, poner* en orden; ‹*desk/room*› ordenar; ‹*finances*› organizar*; **I needed the break to ~ myself out** necesitaba el respiro para poner mis pensamientos en orden 2 (separate out) separar

B 1 (arrange) (BrE) ‹*date*› fijar; ‹*deal/compromise*› llegar* a; **have you ~ed out your holiday yet?** ¿ya tienes las vacaciones organizadas?, ¿ya has arreglado tus vacaciones? 2 (resolve) ‹*problem/dispute*› solucionar; ‹*misunderstanding*› aclarar; **things will ~ themselves out** ya se arreglará todo; **I haven't yet ~ed out what I'm going to do** todavía no he decidido qué voy a hacer

C (deal with) (BrE colloq): **leave him to me, I'll ~ him out!** déjame a mí, que yo ya lo voy a arreglar (fam)

• **sort through** [v ▸ prep ▸ o] ‹*papers/files*› revisar

sort code *n* (BrE) (of bank branch) número *m* de sucursal

sortie /'sɔːrti || 'sɔːti/ *n* 1 (Aviat, Mil) misión *f* de combate 2 (excursion) salida *f*, escapada *f* (fam)

sorting office /'sɔːrtɪŋ/ *n* oficina *f* de clasificación del correo

SOS *n* S.O.S. *m*

so-so¹ /'səʊsəʊ/ *adj* (colloq) así así (fam), así asá (fam), mediocre; **what's that novel like? — oh, ~** ¿qué tal es esa novela? — ni fu ni fa (fam)

so-so² *adv* (colloq) así así (fam), así asá (fam), regular

soufflé /suː'fleɪ || 'suːfleɪ/ *n* [u c] suflé *m*

sought /sɔːt/ *past & past p of* **seek**

sought-after /'sɔːt'æftər || 'sɔːt,ɑːftə(r)/ *adj* (*pred* **sought after**) ‹*product*› solicitado, en demanda; ‹*prize*› codiciado; ‹*area*› en demanda

soul /səʊl/ *n*

A [c] (Relig) alma *f*‡; **my mother, God rest her ~, loved this house** mi madre, que en paz descanse *or* que en gloria esté, le tenía mucho cariño a esta casa; **she put her heart and ~ into the task** se entregó a la tarea en cuerpo y alma

B [c] (person): **I won't tell a (living) ~** no se lo diré a nadie; **there wasn't a ~ about** no había ni un alma; **poor old ~! she can hardly walk** ¡pobrecilla! *or* ¡pobrecita! casi no puede caminar

C (personification): **the ~ of discretion/kindness** la discreción/la amabilidad personificada

D [u] **~ (music)** soul *m*

soul: ~ brother *n* (AmE sl) hermano *m*; **~-destroying** /'səʊldɪ'strɔɪɪŋ/ *adj* desmoralizador; **~ food** *n* (AmE) *comida tradicional de los negros del Sur de los Estados Unidos*

soulful /'səʊlfəl/ *adj* enternecedor, conmovedor

soulless /'səʊlləs || 'səʊllɪs/ *adj* ‹*building*› frío e impersonal, falto de carácter; ‹*routine/job*› tedioso

soul: ~mate *n* alma *f*‡ gemela; **~-searching** *n* [u] introspección *f*; **~ sister** *n* (AmE sl) hermana *f*

sound¹ /saʊnd/ *n*

Sense I

A [u c] 1 (noise) sonido *m*; (unpleasant, disturbing) ruido *m*; **we heard the ~ of footsteps** oímos (unos) pasos; **don't make a ~!** ¡no hagas ni el menor ruido!; **there wasn't a ~ to be heard** no se oía absolutamente nada; **he woke up to the ~ of birds singing** se despertó con el canto de los pájaros 2 (of music, instrument) sonido *m* 3 (Ling) sonido *m*; **a vowel ~** un sonido vocálico

B [u] 1 (Phys) sonido *m*; (*before n*) **the ~ barrier** la barrera del sonido; **a ~ wave** una onda sonora 2 (Audio, Rad, TV) sonido *m*; **turn the ~ up/down** sube/baja el volumen; (*before n*) **~ effects** efectos *mpl* sonoros

C (impression conveyed) (colloq) (*no pl*): **I don't like the ~ of that at all** eso no me huele nada bien; **by** *o* **from the ~ of it, everything's going very well** parece que *or* por lo visto todo marcha muy bien

Sense II [c] 1 (channel) paso *m*, estrecho *m* 2 (inlet) brazo *m*

sound² *vi*

A 1 (give impression) sonar*; **your voice ~s** *o* **you ~ different on the phone** tu voz suena distinta por teléfono; **you ~ as if** *o* **as though you could do with a rest** me da la impresión de que no te vendría mal un descanso; **it ~s as if** *o* **as though they're here now** (por el ruido) parece que ya están aquí; **that ~s like Susan now** ésa debe (de) ser Susan 2 (seem) parecer*; **we'll leave at ten; how does that ~ to you?** saldremos a las diez ¿qué te parece?; **it ~s as if** *o* **as though you had a great time** parece que lo pasaste fenomenal; **~s like fun!** (colloq) ¡qué divertido!

B (make noise, resound) «*bell/alarm*» sonar*

■ **sound** *vt*

A 1 ‹*trumpet/horn*› tocar*, hacer* sonar; **the chairman ~ed a note of warning in his speech** en su discurso, el presidente llamó a la cautela 2 (articulate) ‹*letter/consonant*› pronunciar

B ▸ **sound out**

Phrasal verbs

• **sound off** [v ▸ adv] 1 (give opinions) (colloq) **to ~ off (ABOUT sth)** pontificar* *or* sentar* cátedra (SOBRE algo) 2 (speak loudly) (AmE) hablar fuerte

• **sound out** [v ▸ o ▸ adv, v ▸ adv ▸ o] tantear, sondear

sound³ *adj* **-er, -est**

A 1 (healthy) sano; **safe and ~** sano y salvo; **I, Peter Smith, being of ~ mind ...** (frml) yo, Peter Smith, (estando) en pleno uso de mis facultades ... (frml) 2 (in good condition) ‹*basis/foundation*› sólido, firme; ‹*timber*› en buenas condiciones

B 1 (valid) ‹*reasoning/knowledge*› sólido; ‹*advice/decision*› sensato 2 (reliable) ‹*colleague/staff*› responsable, formal

C 1 (deep) ‹*sleep*› profundo 2 (hard, thorough) **a ~ spanking** una buena paliza

sound⁴ *adv* **-er, -est**: **~ asleep** profundamente dormido

soundboard /'saʊndbɔːrd/ *n* ▸ **sounding board 3**

-sounding /,saʊndɪŋ/ *suff*: **pleasant~** de sonido agradable; **a foreign~ name** un nombre que suena (*or* sonó *etc*) extranjero

sounding board *n* 1 (for ideas) caja *f* de resonancia 2 (over platform, stage) tornavoz *m* 3 (on instrument) tabla *f* armónica resonante, secreto *m*

soundly /'saʊndli/ *adv*

A 1 (deeply) ‹*sleep*› profundamente 2 (thoroughly): **she was ~ spanked** se llevó una buena paliza

B (solidly, validly) sólidamente

soundproof¹ /'saʊndpruːf/ *adj* insonorizado

soundproof² *vt* insonorizar*

sound: ~ system *n* equipo *m* de sonido; **~track** *n* banda *f* sonora

soup /suːp/ *n* sopa *f*; **clear ~** caldo *m*, consomé *m*; ***in the ~*** (colloq) en un brete (fam), en la olla (Méx fam); (*before n*) **~ plate** plato *m* sopero; **~ spoon** cuchara *f* sopera

souped-up /'suːpd'ʌp/ *adj* (colloq) (Auto) trucado (fam)

soup kitchen *n* comedor *m* de beneficencia

sour¹ /saʊər || 'saʊə(r)/ *adj* **sourer, sourest** 1 (sharp, acid) ‹*fruit/wine*› ácido, agrio 2 (spoiled) ‹*milk*› agrio, cortado; **to go** *o* **turn ~** «*milk*» cortarse, agriarse; «*relationship/plan*» estropearse, echarse a perder 3 (bad-tempered, disagreeable) agrio, avinagrado

sour² *vt* 1 ‹*milk*› agriar 2 ‹*relationship/occasion*› amargar*

■ **sour** *vi* «*milk/cream*» agriarse, cortarse

source /sɔːrs || sɔːs/ *n*

A 1 (origin, supply) fuente *f*; **my only ~ of income** mi única fuente de ingresos; **the ~ of infection** el foco de la infección; **to trace a problem to its ~** encontrar* el origen *or* la raíz de un problema; **tax will be deducted at ~** los impuestos se descontarán directamente del sueldo 2 (of river) nacimiento *m*

B (providing information) 1 (person) (journ) fuente *f*; **police/government/reliable ~s** fuentes policiales/gubernamentales/fidedignas 2 (text, document) fuente *f*

sour: ~ cream, (BrE also) **~ed cream** /saʊrd/ *n* [u] crema *f or* (Esp tb) nata *f* agria; **~dough** *n* [u] (AmE) masa *f* fermentada (*para hacer pan*)

sourly /'saʊərli || 'saʊəli/ *adv* agriamente

sourpuss /'saʊərpʊs/ *n* (colloq) amargado, -da *m,f*

S

souse /saʊs/ *vt* marinar, macerar; **~d herrings** ≈ arenques en escabeche

south¹ /saʊθ/ *n* [u]

A 1 (point of the compass, direction) sur *m*; **the ~, the S~** el sur, el Sur; **to the ~ of the city** al sur de la ciudad; **~-~east** sursudeste; **~-~west** sursudoeste 2 (region): **the ~, the S~** el sur; **a town in the ~ of Texas** una ciudad del sur *or* en el sur de Texas

B **the South** (in US history) el Sur, los estados sudistas

C **South** (in bridge) Sur *m*

south² *adj* (*before n*) ‹*wall/face*› sur *adj inv*, meridional; ‹*wind*› del sur

south³ *adv* al sur; **the house faces ~** la casa da *or* mira al sur; **he headed ~** se dirigió hacia el sur; **~ OF sth** al sur DE algo; **down ~**: **they live down ~** viven en el sur; **let's go down ~** vayamos al sur

South Africa *n* Sudáfrica *f*, Suráfrica *f*

South African¹ *adj* sudafricano, surafricano

South African² *n* sudafricano, -na *m,f*, surafricano, -na *m,f*

South America *n* América *f* del Sur *or* del Sud, Sudamérica *f*, Suramérica *f*

South American¹ *adj* sudamericano, suramericano

South American² *n* sudamericano, -na *m,f*, suramericano, -na *m,f*

southbound /'saʊθbaʊnd/ *adj* ‹*traffic/train*› que va (*or* iba *etc*) hacia el sur *or* en dirección sur

southeast¹, **Southeast** /'saʊθ'iːst/ *n* [u] **the ~** 1 (direction) el sudeste *or* Sudeste, el sureste *or* Sureste 2 (region) el sudeste *or* sureste

southeast² *adj* sudeste *adj inv*, sureste *adj inv*, del sudeste *or* sureste, sudoriental

southeast³ *adv* hacia el sudeste *or* sureste, en dirección sudeste *or* sureste

south: **~easterly** /'saʊθ'iːstərli/ *adj* ‹*wind*› del sudeste *or* sureste; **~eastern** /'saʊθ'iːstərn / *adj* sudeste *adj inv*, sureste *adj inv*, del sudeste *or* sureste, sudoriental

southerly /'sʌðərli/ *adj* ‹*wind*› del sur; ‹*latitude*› sur *adj inv*; **in a ~ direction** hacia el sur, en dirección sur

southern /'sʌðərn || 'sʌðən/ *adj* ‹*region*› del sur, meridional, sur *adj inv*; ‹*country*› del sur, meridional; **~ Italy/Poland** el sur de Italia/Polonia; **the ~ states** (in US) los estados del sur; **~ Europe** Europa *f* meridional, el Sur de Europa; **the S~ Hemisphere** el hemisferio austral *or* sur; **the ~ lights** la aurora austral

Southern Cross *n* **the ~ ~** la Cruz del Sur

Southerner, southerner /'sʌðərnər || 'sʌðənə(r)/ *n* sureño, -ña *m,f*

southern-fried /ˌsʌðərn'fraɪd || ˌsʌðən'fraɪd/ *adj* (AmE) frito, (rebozado) con harina, huevo y pan rallado

southernmost /'sʌðərnməʊst || 'sʌðənməʊst/ *adj* (*before n*) ‹*town/island*› más meridional; **the ~ point of the country** el extremo sur del país; **the ~ city in the world** la ciudad más austral del mundo

south: **~ Sea Islands** *pl n* **the S~ Sea Islands** las islas del Pacífico Sur; **~ Seas** *pl n* **the S~ Seas** los mares del (hemisferio) Sur

southward¹ /'saʊθwərd/, **southwardly** /-li/ *adj* (*before n*): **in a ~ direction** hacia el sur, en dirección sur

southward², (BrE also) **southwards** /-z/ *adv* hacia el sur; **~ OF sth** al sur DE algo

southwest¹, **Southwest** /'saʊθ'west/ *n* [u] **the ~** 1 (direction) el sudoeste *or* Sudoeste, el suroeste *or* Suroeste 2 (region) el sudoeste *or* suroeste

southwest² *adj* sudoeste *adj inv*, suroeste *adj inv*, del sudoeste *or* suroeste

southwest³ *adv* hacia el sudoeste *or* suroeste, en dirección sudoeste *or* suroeste

south: **~westerly** /'saʊθ'westərli/ *adj* ‹*wind*› del sudoeste *or* suroeste; **~western** /'saʊθ'westərn/ *adj* sudoccidental, sudoeste *adj inv*, suroeste *adj inv*

souvenir /'suːvənɪr || ˌsuːvə'nɪə(r)/ *n* **~ (OF sth)** recuerdo *m or* souvenir *m* (DE algo)

sou'wester /saʊ'westər || saʊ'westə(r)/ *n* 1 (Clothing) sueste *m* 2 (Meteo) garbino *m*

sovereign¹ /'sɑːvrən || 'sɒvrɪn/ *n*

A (monarch) soberano, -na *m,f*

B (coin) soberano *m*, libra *f* (de oro)

sovereign² *adj* soberano; **~ debt** deuda *f* soberana

sovereignty /'sɑːvrənti || 'sɒvrənti/ *n* [u] 1 (control, rule) dominio *m*, soberanía *f* 2 (autonomy) soberanía *f*

Soviet /'səʊviet, 'sɑːviət 'səʊviət/ *adj* (Hist) soviético

Soviet Union *n* (Hist) **the ~ ~** la Unión Soviética

sow¹ /səʊ/ (*past* **sowed**; *past p* **sowed** *or* **sown**) *vt* ‹*seeds/field*› sembrar*; **to ~ (the seeds of) doubt in sb's mind** sembrar* (la semilla de) la duda en algn

■ **sow** *vi* sembrar*

sow² /saʊ/ *n* cerda *f*, puerca *f*

sown /səʊn/ *past p of* **sow¹**

sox /sɑːks || sɒks/ (AmE colloq) *pl of* **sock¹**

soy /sɔɪ/, (BrE) **soya** /'sɔɪə/ *n* [u] soya *f* (AmL), soja *f* (Esp)

soy: **~ bean**, (BrE) **soya bean** *n* soya *f* (AmL), soja *f* (Esp); **~ sauce** *n* [u] salsa *f* de soya (AmL) *or* (Esp) soja

sozzled /'sɑːzəld || 'sɒzəld/ *adj* (BrE colloq) (*pred*) **to be ~** estar* como una cuba *or* (AmL) tomado (fam); **to get ~** mamarse (fam)

spa /spɑː/ *n* 1 (resort) balneario *m*; (with hot springs) termas *fpl*, balneario *m* 2 (spring) manantial *m* (*de agua mineral*) 3 (health club) (AmE) gimnasio *m*

space¹ /speɪs/ *n*

A [u] 1 (Phys) espacio *m*; **to stare into ~** mirar al vacío 2 (Aerosp) espacio *m*; (*before n*) ‹*station/program*› espacial; **~ invaders** (Games) marcianitos *mpl*

B 1 [u] (room) espacio *m*, sitio *m*, lugar *m*; **leave some ~ for dessert** deja un lugarcito para el postre; **to take up ~** ocupar espacio; **advertising ~** espacio publicitario 2 [c] (empty area) espacio *m*; **wide open ~s** amplios espacios abiertos; **is there a ~ for this in the case?** ¿cabe esto en la maleta?; **a parking ~** un sitio *or* lugar para estacionar *or* (Esp) aparcar; **let's clear a ~ for it first** hagámosle (un) sitio primero

C (of time) (*no pl*) espacio *m*; **in the ~ of one hour** en el espacio *or* lapso de una hora

D [c] (Print) espacio *m*; (*before n*) **~ bar** espaciador *m*

space² *vt* **~ (out)** espaciar

space: **~ age** *n* **the ~ age** la era espacial; **~-age** *adj* ‹*technology*› futurista, espacial; **~ capsule** *n* cápsula *f* espacial; **~craft** *n* (*pl* **~craft**) nave *f* espacial

spaced-out /'speɪsd'aʊt/ *adj* (colloq) (on drugs) drogado, pacheco (Méx arg), colocado (Esp fam)

space: **~ heater** *n* (AmE) calentador *m*; **~man** /'speɪsmæn/ *n* (*pl* **-men** /-men/) astronauta *m*, cosmonauta *m*; **~-saving** /'speɪs'seɪvɪŋ/ *adj* que ocupa poco espacio, que economiza espacio; **~ship** *n* nave *f* espacial, astronave *f*; **~ shuttle** *n* lanzadera *f or* transbordador *m* espacial; **~ travel** *n* viajes *mpl* por el espacio; **~ walk** *n* paseo *m* espacial; **~-walk** *vi* pasear por el espacio

spacing /'speɪsɪŋ/ *n* [u] (Print) espaciado *m*; **in double ~** a doble espacio

spacious /'speɪʃəs/ *adj* ‹*house/room*› amplio, espacioso; ‹*park*› grande, extenso

spade /speɪd/ *n*

A (tool) pala *f*; ***to call a ~ a ~*** llamar al pan, pan y al vino, vino, llamar a las cosas por su nombre

B **spades** *pl* (suit) (+ *sing or pl vb*) picas *fpl*; ***in ~s*** (AmE colloq): **you have our support, in ~s** te apoyamos cien por ciento

spadework /'speɪdwɜːrk/ *n* [u] trabajo *m* preparatorio

spaghetti /spə'geti/ *n* [u] espaguetis *mpl*, spaghetti *mpl*

Spain /speɪn/ *n* España *f*

spake /speɪk/ (arch) *past of* **speak**

spam¹ /spæm/ *n* [u]

A (Comput) (colloq) spam *m*, correo *m* basura, correo *m* masivo no solicitado

B (meat product) ▸ **Spam**®

spam² *vt* (colloq) enviarle spam *or* correo basura a

Spam®, **spam** /spæm/ *n* [u] *fiambre enlatado hecho con carne de cerdo*

span¹ /spæn/ *n* 1 (full extent — of hand) palmo *m*; (— of wing) envergadura *f*; (— of bridge, arch) luz *f* 2 (part of bridge) arco *m* 3 (of time) lapso *m*, espacio *m*, período *m* 4 (range): **at**

S

this age children have a short attention ~ a esta edad los niños no pueden mantener la atención por períodos prolongados; **the whole ~ of American history** la historia americana en toda su extensión; ▸**life span**

span² *vt* **-nn-** 1 (extend over) abarcar*; **a career that ~ned 60 years** una carrera que abarcó 60 años *or* que se extendió a lo largo de 60 años 2 (cross) «*bridge*» ‹*river*› extenderse* sobre, cruzar*

span³ (arch) *past of* **spin²**

spangle /'spæŋgəl/ *n* (Clothing) lentejuela *f*

Spaniard /'spænjərd || 'spænjəd/ *n* español, -ñola *m,f*

spaniel /'spænjəl/ *n* spaniel *m*

Spanish¹ /'spænɪʃ/ *adj* español; ‹*language*› castellano, español

Spanish² *n* 1 [u] (language) castellano *m*, español *m* 2 (people) (+ *pl vb*) **the ~** los españoles; (Hispanics) los hispanos

Spanish: **~ America** *n* Hispanoamérica *f*; **~ omelet**, (BrE) **~ omelette** *n* tortilla *f* de papas *or* (Esp) patatas, tortilla *f* española

spank /'spæŋk/ *vt* darle* unas palmadas a (*en las nalgas*)

spanking¹ /'spæŋkɪŋ / *n* paliza *f*, zurra *f* (*en las nalgas*)

spanking² *adv* (dated) (*as intensifier*) **~ new** flamante, nuevísimo; **~ clean** limpísimo

spanner /'spænər || 'spænə(r)/ *n* (BrE) (*adjustable* **~**) llave *f* inglesa; (*box* **~**) llave *f* de tubo; (*plug* **~**) llave *f* de bujías; ***to throw a ~ in the works*** fastidiarlo todo

spar¹ /spɑːr || spɑː(r)/ *n* (Naut) palo *m*

spar² *vi* **-rr-** 1 (in boxing) entrenarse 2 (argue) discutir

spare¹ /sper || speə(r)/ *adj* 1 (not in use) de más; **have you got a ~ umbrella you could lend me?** ¿tienes un paraguas de más que me puedas prestar?; **have you got any ~ paper** *o* (BrE also) **any paper ~?** ¿tienes un poco de papel que no te haga falta?; ***to go ~*** (BrE colloq) (become distraught) enloquecerse*, volverse* loco; (lit: be available) sobrar 2 (in case of need) (*before n*) ‹*key/cartridge*› de repuesto 3 (free) libre; **if you've got a ~ minute** si tienes un minuto (libre)

spare² *n* 1 (reserve): **I'll take a ~ just in case** llevaré uno de repuesto por si acaso 2 **spares** *pl* (spare parts) (BrE) repuestos *mpl or* (Méx) refacciones *fpl*

spare³ *vt*

A 1 (do without): **can you ~ your dictionary for a moment?** ¿me permites el diccionario un momento, si no lo necesitas?; **if you can ~ the time** si tienes *or* dispones de tiempo 2 (give) **to ~ (sb) sth**: **can you ~ me a pound?** ¿tienes una libra que me prestes/des?; **can you ~ me a few minutes?** ¿tienes unos minutos?; **to ~ a thought for sb** pensar* un momento en algn 3 **to spare** (*as adj*): **there's food to ~** hay comida de sobra; **have you got a few minutes to ~?** ¿tienes unos minutos?; **we arrived at the station with half an hour to ~** llegamos a la estación con media hora de anticipación

B 1 (keep from using, stint) (*usu neg*): **to ~ no effort** no escatimar esfuerzos; **to ~ no expense** no reparar en gastos 2 (save, relieve) **to ~ sb sth** ‹*trouble/embarrassment*› ahorrarle algo A algn; **~ me the details** ahórrate los detalles 3 (show mercy, consideration toward) perdonar; **to ~ sb's life** perdonarle la vida a algn; **to ~ sb's feelings** no herir* los sentimientos de algn

spare: **~ part** *n* repuesto *m or* (Méx) refacción *f*; **~rib** *n* costilla *f* (*con poca carne*); **~ room** *n* cuarto *m* de huéspedes *or* (Esp) de los invitados *or* (Chi) de los alojados, recámara *f* de visitas (Méx); **~ time** *n* [u] tiempo *m* libre; **~ tire**, (BrE) **~ tyre** *n* 1 (Auto) rueda *f* de repuesto *or* (Esp tb) de recambio, llanta *f* de refacción (Méx), auxiliar *f* (RPl) 2 (fat around waist) (colloq) michelines *mpl* (fam), llanta *f* (AmL fam); **~ wheel** *n* (BrE) ▸**~ tire 1**

sparing /'sperɪŋ || 'speərɪŋ/ *adj* moderado; **be a bit ~ with the sugar** no derroches azúcar *or* trata de economizar azúcar

sparingly /'sperɪŋli/ *adv* ‹*use*› con moderación

spark¹ /spɑːrk || spɑːk/ *n*

A [c] (from fire, flint) chispa *f*; ***to make ~s fly*** armar una bronca (fam)

B 1 [u] (liveliness) chispa *f*; **she's lost some of her ~** ya no tiene la chispa de antes 2 [c] (trace) pizca *f*

spark² *vt*, (BrE also) **spark off** ‹*rioting/revolution*› hacer* estallar, desencadenar, desatar; ‹*interest*› suscitar, despertar*; ‹*criticism*› provocar*

sparking plug /'spɑːrkɪŋ/ *n* (BrE) ▸**spark plug**

sparkle¹ /'spɑːrkəl || 'spɑːkəl/ *vi* «*gem/glass*» centellear, destellar, brillar; «*eyes*» brillar

sparkle² *n* 1 (*no pl*) (of gem, glass) destello *m*, brillo *m*; (of eyes) brillo *m* 2 [u] (animation) chispa *f*, brillo *m*

sparkler /'spɑːrklər/ *n* (firework) luz *f* de Bengala

sparkling /'spɑːrklɪŋ || 'spɑːklɪŋ/ *adj* 1 (shining) ‹*gems/stars*› centelleante, brillante; ‹*eyes*› chispeante, brillante 2 ‹*wit/conversation*› chispeante 3 (effervescent) ‹*wine*› espumoso, espumante

spark plug *n* bujía *f*, chispero *m* (AmC)

sparring partner /'spɑːrɪŋ/ *n* 1 (Sport) sparring *m* 2 (in argument) antagonista *mf*, contrincante *mf*

sparrow /'spærəʊ/ *n* gorrión *m*

sparrowhawk /'spærəʊhɔːk/ *n* gavilán *m*

sparse /spɑːrs || spɑːs/ *adj* ‹*population/vegetation*› escaso, poco denso; ‹*furniture*› escaso; ‹*beard/hair*› ralo

sparsely /'spɑːrsli || 'spɑːsli/ *adv*: **the area was ~ populated** la zona estaba escasamente *or* muy poco poblada, la zona tenía baja densidad de población; **the room is ~ furnished** la habitación tiene pocos *or* escasos muebles

spartan /'spɑːrtn̩ || 'spɑːtn̩/ *adj* ‹*conditions*› espartano

spasm /'spæzəm/ *n* (Med) espasmo *m*; **to go into ~** contraerse* espasmódicamente

spasmodic /spæz'mɑːdɪk || spæz'mɒdɪk/ *adj* 1 ‹*growth/activity*› irregular 2 (Med) ‹*pain/cough*› espasmódico

spasmodically /spæz'mɑːdɪkli || spæz'mɒdɪkli/ *adv* de manera irregular *or* discontinua, a rachas

spastic /'spæstɪk/ *n* espástico, -ca *m,f*

spat¹ /spæt/ *n*

A (quarrel) (colloq) rencilla *f*, discusión *f*

B **spats** *pl* (Clothing) polainas *fpl*

spat² *past & past p of* **spit²**

spate /speɪt/ *n* (of orders, letters) avalancha *f*, aluvión *m*, torrente *m*; (of robberies, accidents) racha *f*, serie *f*; ***to be in (full) ~*** (BrE) «*river*» estar* crecido

spatial /'speɪʃəl/ *adj* (*before n*) espacial, del espacio

spatter /'spætər || 'spætə(r)/ *vt* ‹*mud/blood*› salpicar*; **to ~ sth/sb WITH sth** salpicar* algo/a algn DE algo

■ **spatter** *vi* «*paint/blood*» salpicar*

spatula /'spætʃələ || 'spætjʊlə/ *n* 1 (Culin) (for turning, serving) pala *f* (de servir); (for scraping out bowls) espátula *f* 2 (Pharm, Med) espátula *f*

spawn¹ /spɔːn/ *n* [u] 1 (of fish) hueva(s) *f(pl)*; (of frogs) huevas *fpl* 2 (Bot) micelio *m*

spawn² *vi* «*frogs/fish*» desovar

spay /speɪ/ *vt* ‹*cat/bitch*› esterilizar* (*extirpando los ovarios*)

SPCA *n* (in US) (= **Society for the Prevention of Cruelty to Animals**) ≈ Asociación *f* protectora de animales

SPCC *n* (in US) (= **Society for the Prevention of Cruelty to Children**) ≈ Asociación *f* de proteccíon a la infancia

speak /spiːk/ (*past* **spoke** *or* (arch) **spake**; *past p* **spoken**) *vi*

A 1 (say sth) hablar; **sorry, did you ~?** perdón ¿dijiste algo? *or* ¿me hablaste?; **to ~ TO** *o* (esp AmE) **WITH sb** hablar CON algn, hablarle A algn; **wake up Mark, ~ to me!** ¡Mark despierta, di algo!; **they are not ~ing (to each other)** no se hablan, no se dirigen la palabra; **I don't know her to ~ to** sólo la conozco de vista; **I've often heard her ~ about it** a menudo la he oído hablar de eso; **to ~ OF sth/sb/-ING** hablar DE algo/algn/+ INF; **you never spoke of this to anyone?** ¿nunca hablaste de esto con nadie?; **they don't have much money to ~ of** no tienen mucho dinero, que digamos; **~ing personally, I think ...** personalmente, creo que ...; **roughly/generally ~ing** en términos generales; **legally/morally ~ing** desde el punto de vista legal/moral; **so to ~** por así decirlo 2 (on telephone): **hello, Barbara Mason ~ing ...** buenas tardes, habla *or* (Esp tb) soy Barbara Mason; **could I ~ to Mrs Hodges, please? — ~ing!** ¿podría hablar con la Sra. Hodges, por favor? — con ella (habla); **who's ~ing,**

S

please? (to caller) ¿de parte de quien?; (to person answering a call) ¿con quién hablo?

B (make speech) hablar; **the delegate rose to ~** el delegado se levantó para hacer uso de la palabra (frml); **to ~ ON** *o* **ABOUT sth** hablar ACERCA DE *or* SOBRE algo

■ **speak** *vt* **1** (say, declare): **nobody spoke a word** nadie dijo nada, nadie abrió la boca (fam); **to ~ one's mind** *o* **thoughts** hablar claro *or* con franqueza; **to ~ the truth** decir* la verdad **2** ‹*language*› hablar; **do you ~ English?** ¿habla inglés?; **S English spoken** se habla inglés

Phrasal verbs

• **speak for**

A [v ▸ prep ▸ o] hablar por; **I think I ~ for all of us when I say that ...** creo que hablo por todos al decir que ...; **we'd love to meet him — ~ for yourself!** nos encantaría conocerlo — ¡eso lo dirás por ti!; **the facts ~ for themselves** los hechos son elocuentes

B **to be spoken for** (engaged) (dated *or* hum) estar* comprometido; (reserved) estar* reservado

• **speak out** [v ▸ adv]: **to ~ out FOR/AGAINST sth**: **he spoke out against corruption** denunció la corrupción existente; **she spoke out for the strikers** defendió a los huelguistas

• **speak up** [v ▸ adv] **1** (speak loudly, clearly) hablar más fuerte *or* más alto **2** (speak boldly) decir* lo que se piensa; **to ~ up FOR sb** defender* a algn

speakeasy /'spi:k,i:zi/ *n* (*pl* **-easies**) (in US) bar *m* clandestino

speaker /'spi:kər || 'spi:kə(r)/ *n*

A **1** (person who speaks): **all eyes turned to the ~** todas las miradas se volvieron hacia quien hablaba **2** (in public) orador, -dora *m,f* **3** (of language) hablante *mf*; **a native ~ of Spanish, a Spanish native ~** un hablante nativo de español **4** (Govt) presidente, -ta *m,f*; **Madam S~** Señora Presidente

B (Audio) **1** (loudspeaker) altavoz *m*, (alto)parlante *m* (AmS) **2** (of hi-fi) baf(f)le *m*, parlante *m* (AmS)

speakerphone /'spi:kərfəʊn || 'spi:kəfəʊn/ *n* (AmE) teléfono *m* de manos libres

speaking /'spi:kɪŋ/ *adj* (*before n*): **a good ~ voice** una voz muy clara (*or* potente *etc*); **a ~ part** (Cin, Theat) un papel hablado; **to be on ~ terms with sb** estar* en buenas relaciones con algn

-speaking /,spi:kɪŋ/ *suff* -hablante, -parlante; **Spanish~** hispanohablante, hispanoparlante; **French~** francófono; **English~** de habla inglesa

speaking clock *n* (BrE) servicio *m* grabado de información horaria, hora *f* oficial

spear[1] /spɪr || 'spɪə(r)/ *n*

A **1** (weapon) lanza *f* **2** (for fishing) arpón *m*

B (of grass) brizna *f*; **asparagus ~s** espárragos *mpl*

spear[2] *vt* ‹*fish*› arponear; **he ~ed the meat with his fork** pinchó la carne con el tenedor

spearhead[1] /'spɪrhed || 'spɪəhed/ *n* **1** (of spear) punta *f* de lanza **2** (leading troops) vanguardia *f* **3** (of attack, campaign etc) punta *f* de lanza

spearhead[2] *vt* **1** (Mil) encabezar* **2** (take leading role in) (journ) encabezar*, ser* la punta de lanza de

spearmint /'spɪrmɪnt || 'spɪəmɪnt/ *n* [u] menta *f* verde

spec /spek/ *n*: **on ~** (colloq) por si las moscas (fam)

special[1] /'speʃəl/ *adj* **1** (exceptional) (*before n*) ‹*favor/request*› especial; **a ~ price** un precio especial *or* de ocasión; **he makes me feel ~** me hace sentir muy apreciada; **what's so ~ about Steve?** ¿qué tiene Steve de especial? **2** (for specific purpose) (*before n*) ‹*arrangements/fund*› especial; **~ powers** (Govt) poderes *mpl* extraordinarios **3** (particular, individual) especial, particular; **my ~ interest is medieval poetry** me interesa especialmente *or* en especial *or* en particular la poesía medieval; **children with ~ needs** (Educ) niños que requieren una atención diferenciada; **what are you doing tonight? — nothing ~** ¿qué haces esta noche? — nada en especial

special[2] *n*

A (train) tren *m* especial

B **~ (constable)** (in UK) *civil que en determinadas situaciones cumple tareas de policía*

C **1** (Culin) plato *m* especial; **the chef's ~** especialidad *f* del día **2** (special offer) oferta *f* especial; **on ~** (AmE) de *or* en oferta

special: **~ Branch** *n* (in UK) *departamento policial encargado de velar por la seguridad del Estado*; **~ delivery** *n* [u] correo *m* exprés *or* expreso; **~ education** *n* [u] educación *f or* pedagogía *f* especial *or* diferencial; **~ effects** *pl n* efectos *mpl* especiales

specialist /'speʃələst || 'speʃəlɪst/ *n* **1** (expert) especialista *mf*; (*before n*) ‹*knowledge/dictionary/shop*› especializado **2** (Med) especialista *mf*

speciality /'speʃi'æləti/ *n* (*pl* **-ties**) (BrE) ▸**specialty**[1]

specialization /'speʃələ'zeɪʃən || ,speʃəlar'zeɪʃən/ *n* **1** [u] (specializing) **~ (IN sth)** especialización *f* (EN algo) **2** [c] (special subject) especialidad *f*, especialización *f*

specialize /'speʃəlaɪz/ *vi* **to ~ (IN sth)** especializarse* (EN algo)

specialized /'speʃəlaɪzd/ *adj* especializado

specially /'speʃəli/ *adv* **1** (specifically) especialmente, expresamente **2** (especially) ‹*long/difficult*› particularmente; **why did you choose that one ~?** ¿por qué escogió ése precisamente *or* en particular?

special school *n* escuela *f or* colegio *m* de educación especial *or* diferencial

specialty[1] /'speʃəlti/ *n* (*pl* **-ties**) (AmE) **1** (special interest, skill) especialidad *f* **2** (product) especialidad *f*; **chef's ~** especialidad *f* del día; **lace is a ~ of the region** el encaje es una de las artesanías típicas de la región

specialty[2] *adj* (AmE) (*before n: no comp*) ‹*merchandise/store*› especializado

species /'spi:ʃi:z/ *n* (*pl* ~) (Biol) especie *f*

specific /spɪ'sɪfɪk || spə'sɪfɪk/ *adj* **1** (particular, individual) específico; **give ~ examples** dé ejemplos concretos; **have you a ~ reason for asking?** ¿me preguntas por algún motivo en particular *or* en especial?; **~ TO sth/sb** específico *or* propio DE algo/algn **2** (explicit, unambiguous) explícito, preciso **3** (exact, precise) preciso

specifically /spɪ'sɪfɪkli || spə'sɪfɪkli/ *adv* **1** (explicitly) ‹*state/mention*› explícitamente **2** (specially, particularly) específicamente **3** (more precisely) en concreto

specification /'spesəfə'keɪʃn || ,spesɪfɪ'keɪʃən/ *n*

A [u] (act of specifying) especificación *f*

B [c] (*often pl*) **1** (detailed plan) especificación *f* **2** (requirement) especificación *f* **3** (condition) requisito *m*

specific gravity *n* peso *m* específico

specify /'spesəfaɪ || 'spesɪfaɪ/ *vt* **-fies, -fying, -fied** **1** (state exactly) especificar*; **he didn't ~ a particular time** no especificó *or* no precisó la hora **2** (stipulate, lay down) especificar*

specimen /'spesəmən || 'spesɪmən/ *n* **1** (sample — of rock, plant, tissue) muestra *f*, espécimen *m*; (— of blood, urine) muestra *f*; (— of work, handwriting) muestra *f*; (*before n*) de muestra; **~ signature** espécimen *m* de firma **2** (individual item, example) ejemplar *m*, espécimen *m*

specious /'spi:ʃəs/ *adj* (frml) especioso (frml), engañoso

speck[1] /spek/ *n* **1** (spot, stain) manchita *f* **2** (particle, tiny bit) mota *f*; **the wool has ~s of red and blue in it** la lana tiene motitas *or* pintitas rojas y azules **3** (trace) pizca *f*

speck[2] *vt* (*usu pass*): **the blanket was ~ed with blood** la manta estaba salpicada de sangre

speckle[1] /'spekəl/ *n* motita *f*, pintita *f*

speckle[2] *vt* (*usu pass*) motear; **it's gray ~d with green** es gris moteado de verde; **a ~d hen** una gallina pinta *or* (RPl) bataraza

specs /speks/ *pl n*

A (specifications) (colloq) especificaciones *fpl*

B (spectacles) (colloq & dated) ▸**spectacle B**

spectacle /'spektɪkəl || 'spektəkəl/ *n*

A (show, sight) espectáculo *m*; ***to make a ~ of oneself*** dar* un *or* el espectáculo (fam)

B **spectacles** *pl* gafas *fpl*, anteojos *mpl* (esp AmL), lentes *mpl* (esp AmL); **a pair of ~s** un par de gafas (*or* anteojos *etc*), unas gafas (*or* unos anteojos *etc*)

spectacle case *n* (BrE) estuche *m* de gafas *or* anteojos

spectacular[1] /spek'tækjələr || spek'tækjʊlə(r)/ *adj* espectacular

spectacular[2] *n* programa *m* especial

spectacularly /spek'tækjələrli/ *adv* ‹*increase/improve*› de modo espectacular, espectacularmente; **the coast is**

S

~ beautiful la costa es de una belleza espectacular

spectator /'spekteɪtər || spek'teɪtə(r)/ *n* espectador, -dora *m,f*; (*before n*) **~ sport** deporte *m* espectáculo

specter, (BrE) **spectre** /'spektər || 'spektə(r)/ *n* 1 (ghost) (liter) espectro *m* 2 (disturbing prospect) fantasma *m*, espectro *m*

spectra /'spektrə/ *pl of* **spectrum**

spectral /'spektrəl/ *adj* (liter) espectral

spectre /'spektər/ *n* (BrE) ▸ **specter**

spectrum /'spektrəm/ *n* (*pl* **-tra**)
A (Opt, Phys) espectro *m*
B (range) espectro *m*, gama *f*; **the political ~** el espectro político; **a broad ~ of views** una amplia gama de opiniones; **at the other end of the ~** en el extremo opuesto

speculate /'spekjəleɪt || 'spekjʊleɪt/ *vi*
A (Fin) especular; **to ~ on the stock market** jugar* a la bolsa
B (guess, conjecture) **to ~ (ON** *o* **ABOUT sth)** hacer* conjeturas *or* especular (SOBRE algo)

speculation /'spekjə'leɪʃən || ˌspekjʊ'leɪʃən/ *n* [u c]
A (Fin) especulación *f*; **property ~** especulación en *or* con bienes raíces
B (reflection, conjecture) especulación *f*; **there is mounting ~ about it** se intensifican las especulaciones al respecto

speculative /'spekjələtɪv || 'spekjʊlətɪv/ *adj*
A (Fin) ‹*venture/purchase/sale*› especulativo
B (theoretical) ‹*ideas/conclusions*› especulativo; **all this is purely ~** todo esto es meramente especulativo

speculator /'spekjəleɪtər/ *n* (Fin) especulador, -dora *m,f*; **a property ~** un especulador en bienes raíces

sped /sped/ *past & past p of* **speed²**

speech /spiːtʃ/ *n*
A 1 [u] (act, faculty) habla *f*‡; **freedom of ~** libertad *f* de expresión *or* de palabra; (*before n*) **~ defect** defecto *m* del habla *or* de pronunciación; **~ impediment** impedimento *m* del habla 2 [u] (manner of speaking) forma *f* de hablar 3 [u c] (language, dialect) habla *f*‡; **in casual ~** en el habla coloquial
B [c] 1 (oration) discurso *m*, alocución *f* (frml); **~! ~!** (hum) ¡que hable! ¡que hable!; **to make** *o* (frml) **deliver a ~ (on** *o* **about sth)** dar* *or* (frml) pronunciar un discurso (sobre *or* acerca de algo) 2 (Theat) parlamento *m*
C [u] (Ling): **direct/indirect** *o* **reported ~** estilo *m or* discurso *m* directo/indirecto

speech day *n* (BrE) día *m* de entrega de premios

speechless /'spiːtʃləs || 'spiːtʃlɪs/ *adj*: **she was ~ with rage** enmudeció de rabia; **I'm ~!** no sé qué decir

speech: **~ therapist** *n* foniatra *mf*, logopeda *mf*; **~ therapy** *n* [u] foniatría *f*, logopedia *f*

speed¹ /spiːd/ *n*
A 1 [c u] (rate of movement, progress) velocidad *f*; **what ~ were you doing?** ¿a qué velocidad ibas?; **what is its top ~?** ¿cuál es la velocidad máxima (que da)?; **they set off at top/high ~** salieron a toda/alta velocidad, salieron a todo lo que da; **to pick up** *o* **gather ~** cobrar *or* ganar *or* (esp Esp) coger* velocidad 2 (relative quickness) rapidez *f*; **the ~ with which the matter was resolved** la rápidez con la que se resolvió el asunto
B [c] (Phot): **film ~** sensibilidad *f* de la película; **shutter ~** tiempo *m* de exposición
C [c] (gear) velocidad *f*, marcha *f*
D [u] (amphetamine) (sl) anfetas *fpl* (fam)

speed² *vi* 1 (*past & past p* **sped**) (go, pass quickly) (+ *adv compl*): **the car sped off** *o* **away around the corner** el coche se alejó doblando la esquina a toda velocidad; **he sped by** *o* **past in his new sports car** nos pasó a toda velocidad con su nuevo coche deportivo; **the hours sped by** las horas pasaron volando 2 (*past & past p* **speeded**) (drive too fast) «*car/motorist*» ir* a velocidad excesiva; **he was fined for ~ing** lo multaron por exceso de velocidad

■ **speed** *vt* (*past & past p* **speeded**) (hasten) acelerar; **helicopters are being used to ~ supplies to the area** están usando helicópteros para hacer llegar los suministros rápidamente a la zona

Phrasal verb

• **speed up** (*past & past p* **speeded**)
A [v ▸ adv] 1 (move faster) «*vehicle/driver*» acelerar; «*walker*» apretar* el paso 2 «*process/production*» acelerarse; **we'll have to ~ up** tendremos que darnos prisa, tendremos que apurarnos (AmL)
B [v ▸ o ▸ adv, v ▸ adv ▸ o] 1 ‹*vehicle*› acelerar 2 ‹*work/production*› acelerar

speed: **~boat** *n* (lancha *f*) motora *f*; **~ bump** *n* badén *m*, guardia *m* tumbado (Esp), tope *m* (Méx), policía *m* acostado (Col), lomo *m* de burro (RPl), baden *m* (Chi); **~ camera** *n* radar *m* (fijo), fotorradar *m* (Chi); **~ dating** *n* [u] citas *fpl* rápidas, multicitas *fpl*

speedily /'spiːdḷi/ *adv* con toda prontitud

speed limit *n* velocidad *f* máxima, límite *m* de velocidad; **to exceed** *o* **break the ~ ~** sobrepasar la velocidad permitida *or* el límite de velocidad

speedometer /spɪ'dɑːmətər || spiː'dɒmɪtə(r)/ *n* velocímetro *m*, indicador *m* de velocidad

speed: **~ restriction** *n* límite *m* de velocidad; **~ skating** *n* [u] patinaje *m* de velocidad; **~ trap** *n* control *m* de velocidad (*por radar*); **~way** *n* 1 [u] (sport) carreras *fpl* de motocicletas 2 [c] **~way (track)** pista *f*, circuito *m* 3 [c] (AmE Transp) autopista *f*

speedy /'spiːdi/ *adj* **-dier, -diest** ‹*reply/delivery*› rápido; ‹*solution*› pronto, rápido; **to wish sb a ~ recovery** desearle una pronta mejoría a algn

spell¹ /spel/ *n*
A (*magic* ~) encanto *m*, hechizo *m*, encantamiento *m*; **evil ~** maleficio *m*; **to cast a ~ over** *o* **to put a ~ on sth/sb** hechizar* *or* embrujar algo/a algn; **she is completely under his ~** la tiene totalmente embelesada
B 1 (of weather) período *m* 2 (period of time) período *m*, temporada *f*; **I was going through a bad ~** estaba pasando por una mala racha

spell² (*past & past p* **spelled** *or* (BrE also) **spelt**) *vt*
A (write) escribir*; (orally) deletrear; **how do you ~ Zimbabwe?** ¿cómo se escribe Zimbabwe?; **could you ~ it for me?** ¿me lo deletrea?
B (mean) significar*; (foretell) anunciar, augurar

■ **spell** *vi*: **he can't ~** tiene mala ortografía, no sabe escribir correctamente; (orally) no sabe deletrear

Phrasal verb

• **spell out** [v ▸ o ▸ adv, v ▸ adv ▸ o] 1 ‹*word*› deletrear 2 (explain) explicar* en detalle; **don't you understand? do I have to ~ it out?** ¿no entiendes? ¿te lo tengo que decir letra por letra?

spell: **~binding** *adj* ‹*speech/film*› fascinante; **as an orator he was absolutely ~binding** como orador cautivaba al público; **~bound** *adj* embelesado, maravillado; **~ check** *n* corrector *m* ortográfico; **~-check** *vt* corregir* las faltas de ortografía de

speller /'spelər || 'spelə(r)/ *n* (person): **she/he is a good/poor ~** tiene buena/mala ortografía

spelling /'spelɪŋ/ *n* 1 [u] (system, ability) ortografía *f*; **to be good/bad at ~** tener* buena/mala ortografía; (*before n*) **~ checker** corrector *m* ortográfico; **~ mistake** falta *f* de ortografía 2 [c] (of a word) grafía *f*, ortografía *f*

spelt /spelt/ (BrE) *past & past p of* **spell²**

spelunker /spɪ'lʌŋkər/ *n* (AmE) espeleólogo, -ga *m,f*

spelunking /spɪ'lʌŋkɪŋ/ *n* (AmE) espeleología *f*

spend /spend/ *vt* (*past & past p* **spent**)
A 1 ‹*money*› gastar; **to ~ sth ON sb/sth** gastar algo EN algn/algo 2 (expend) **to ~ sth (ON sth)** dedicarle* algo A algo, invertir* algo EN algo; **she spent two months on that painting** (se) pasó dos meses con ese cuadro, le dedicó dos meses a ese cuadro; **don't ~ too long on each question** no le dediquen mucho tiempo a cada pregunta; **~ your time wisely** emplea bien el tiempo
B (pass) ‹*period of time*› pasar; **where did you ~ Christmas?** ¿dónde pasaste la Navidad?; **I spent five years as a salesman** (me) pasé cinco años trabajando como vendedor
C (exhaust) agotar; **the hurricane had spent its force** el huracán había agotado *or* perdido su fuerza

spending /'spendɪŋ/ *n* [u] gastos *mpl*; **I've had to cut back on my ~** he tenido que reducir mis gastos; **public ~ has increased since last year** el gasto público ha aumentado desde el año pasado; **~ ON sth**: **~ on defense** los gastos de defensa; (*before n*) **~ cut** recorte *m* presupuestario; **~ power** poder *m* adquisitivo *or* de compra

S

spending money *n* [u] dinero *m* para gastos personales

spendthrift /'spendθrɪft/ *n* despilfarrador, -dora *m,f*, derrochador, -dora *m,f*, gastador, -dora *m,f*, botarate *mf*

spent[1] /spent/ *past & past p of* **spend**

spent[2] *adj* 1 (used) ‹*match/ammunition*› usado 2 (exhausted): **the storm was ~** la tormenta había perdido *or* agotado su fuerza

sperm /spɜːrm/ *n* (*pl* ~ *or* **~s**) 1 [u] (seminal liquid) semen *m*, esperma *m or f* 2 [c] (gamete) espermatozoide *m*, espermio *m*; (*before n*) **~ count** cuenta *f* espermática

spermicide /'spɜːrməsaɪd || 'spɜːmɪsaɪd/ *n* [c u] espermicida *m*, espermaticida *m*

sperm whale *n* cachalote *m*

spew /spjuː/ *vi* 1 ‹‹*water*›› salir* a borbotones; **lava ~ed forth from the volcano** el volcán arrojaba *or* vomitaba lava 2 (vomit) (BrE sl) vomitar, arrojar, lanzar* (fam)

■ **spew** *vt* ‹*lava*› arrojar, vomitar; ‹*flames*› arrojar

sphere /sfɪr || sfɪə(r)/ *n*

A 1 (globe) esfera *f* 2 (Astron, Hist) esfera *f*; **the celestial ~** la bóveda *or* esfera celeste

B (field, circle) esfera *f*, ámbito *m*; **~ of influence** esfera de influencia

spherical /'sfɪrɪkəl || 'sferɪkəl/ *adj* esférico

Sphinx /sfɪŋks/ *n* **the ~** la Esfinge

spice[1] /spaɪs/ *n* 1 [c u] (seasoning) especia *f*; (*before n*) **~ rack** especiero *m* 2 [u] (zest, interest) sabor *m*; **to add ~ to a story** hacer* un relato más sabroso; ▸**variety 1**

spice[2] *vt* 1 (Culin) (*often pass*) condimentar, sazonar* 2 (add excitement to) darle* sabor a; **to ~ up a story** darle* más sabor a un relato

spick-and-span /'spɪkən'spæn/ *adj* (colloq) (*pred*): **she likes to keep her room ~** le gusta tener la habitación limpia y ordenada

spicy /'spaɪsi/ *adj* **-cier, -ciest** 1 ‹*sauce/food*› (highly seasoned) muy condimentado; (with spices) con muchas especias; (hot, peppery) picante 2 (racy) ‹*story/account*› sabroso; (with sexual connotations) picante

spider /'spaɪdər || 'spaɪdə(r)/ *n* (Zool) araña *f*; **~** *o* (BrE) **~'s web** telaraña *f*, tela *f* de araña

spidery /'spaɪdəri/ *adj*: **~ handwriting** letra *f* de trazos delgados e inseguros

spiel /spiːl || ʃpiːl/ *n* (colloq) perorata *f* (fam), rollo *m* (fam)

spigot /'spɪgət/ *n* 1 (faucet) (AmE) llave *f or* (Esp) grifo *m or* (RPl) canilla *f or* (Per) caño *m or* (AmC) paja *f* 2 (bung) tapón *m* (*de barril*) 3 (tap on cask) espita *f*

spike[1] /spaɪk/ *n*

A 1 (pointed object) punta *f*, púa *f*, pincho *m or* (Arg) pinche *m*; (on track shoes) clavo *m or* (Chi, Ven) púa *f or* (Col) carramplón *m* 2 (Elec Eng, Phys) pico *m* 3 **~ (heel)** (AmE) ▸**stiletto B**

B **spikes** *pl* (running shoes) zapatillas *fpl* de clavos *or* (Chi, Ven) de púas *or* (Col) con carramplones, picos *mpl* (Méx)

spike[2] *vt*

A (pierce) pinchar, clavar

B (add sth to) (colloq): **they ~d his lemonade with vodka** le echaron vodka en la limonada

spiky /'spaɪki/ *adj* **-kier, -kiest** 1 (having spikes) con puntas *or* púas *or* pinchos 2 (sharp, pointed) puntiagudo, picudo, puntudo (Col, CS) 3 ‹*hair*› de punta

spill[1] /spɪl/ (*past & past p* **spilled** *or* **spilt**) *vt* ‹*liquid*› derramar, verter*; (knock over) volcar*; **I spilt my coffee on the sofa** se me cayó el café en el sofá

■ **spill** *vi* ‹‹*liquid*›› derramarse; **the coins ~ed onto the floor** las monedas cayeron al suelo; **people ~ed (out) into the streets** la gente se volcó *or* se echó a las calles

Phrasal verb

• **spill over** [v ▸ adv] ‹‹*container*›› desbordarse; ‹‹*liquid*›› rebosar; ‹‹*fighting/conflict*›› extenderse*

spill[2] *n*

A (for lighting fires — of wood) astilla *f*; (— of paper) papel *m* enrollado

B ▸**spillage**

spillage /'spɪlɪdʒ/ *n* [u c] vertido *m*, derrame *m*

spilt /spɪlt/ *past & past p of* **spill**[1]

spin[1] /spɪn/ *n*

A 1 (act): **to give sth a ~** hacer* girar algo 2 [c] (in washing machine): **give the sheets a ~** centrifuga las sábanas; (*before n*) ‹*speed/program*› de centrifugado 3 [u] (on ball) (Sport) efecto *m*, chanfle *m* (AmL); **to put ~ on the ball** lanzar* la pelota con efecto, darle* chanfle a la pelota (AmL)

B [c] 1 (of aircraft) barrena *f*, caída *f* en espiral; ***to be in a (flat)*** **~** estar* muy confuso *or* confundido, estar* sin saber qué hacer *or* qué pensar 2 (Auto) trompo *m*

C [c] (ride) (colloq): **to go for a ~** ir* a dar un paseo en coche (*or* en moto *etc*), ir* a dar un garbeo (Esp fam)

D [u] (bias) interpretación *f* favorable (*no imparcial*)

spin[2] (*pres p* **spinning**; *past* **spun** *or* (arch) **span**; *past p* **spun**) *vt*

A 1 (turn) ‹*wheel*› hacer* girar; ‹*top*› hacer* girar *or* bailar 2 ‹*washing*› centrifugar* 3 ‹*ball*› darle* efecto a, darle* chanfle a (AmL)

B 1 ‹*wool/cotton*› hilar 2 ‹*web*› tejer

C (interpret with bias) ‹*news/event*› darle* una sesgo positivo a, sesgar* favorablemente

■ **spin** *vi*

A 1 (rotate) ‹‹*wheel*›› girar; ‹‹*top*›› girar, bailar; **my head is ~ning** la cabeza me da vueltas 2 ‹‹*washing machine*›› centrifugar* 3 (move rapidly) (+ *adv compl*): dar* vueltas; **the glass spun across the table** el vaso fue rodando por la mesa; **the car spun out of control** el coche sufrió un trompo 4 (Aviat) caer* en barrena

B (Tex) hilar

Phrasal verb

• **spin out** [v ▸ o ▸ adv, v ▸ adv ▸ o] ‹*money/salary*› estirar; ‹*vacation/story*› alargar*, prolongar*

spina bifida /'spaɪnə'bɪfədə/ *n* [u] espina *f* bífida

spinach /'spɪnɪtʃ || 'spɪnɪdʒ, -ɪtʃ/ *n* [u] (Bot) espinaca *f*; (Culin) espinaca(s) *f(pl)*

spinal /'spaɪnl/ *adj* de la columna vertebral; **~ nerve** nervio *m* raquídeo *or* espinal; **~ tap** punción *f* lumbar

spinal: **~ column** *n* columna *f* vertebral, espina *f* dorsal; **~ cord** *n* médula *f* espinal

spindle /'spɪndl/ *n* 1 (Mech Eng) eje *m* 2 (Tex) huso *m*

spindly /'spɪndli/ *adj* **-dlier, -dliest** ‹*legs*› largo y flaco; ‹*plant*› alto y débil

spin: **~ drier** *n* centrifugadora *f* (*de ropa*); **~-dry** /'spɪn 'draɪ/ *vt* **-dries, -drying, -dried** centrifugar*; **~ dryer** *n* ▸**~ drier**

spine /spaɪn/ *n*

A 1 (Anat) columna *f* (vertebral), espina *f* dorsal; ***to send a chill up*** *o* ***shivers down sb's*** **~** producirle* escalofríos a algn; **a shiver ran down my ~** un escalofrío me recorrió la espalda 2 (of book) lomo *m*

B (on animal) púa *f*; (on plant) espina *f*

spine-chilling /'spaɪn,tʃɪlɪŋ/ *adj* espeluznante

spineless /'spaɪnləs || 'spaɪnlɪs/ *adj* 1 (cowardly, weak) débil, sin carácter 2 (Zool) invertebrado

spinner /'spɪnər || 'spɪnə(r)/ *n* 1 (Tex) hilandero, -ra *m,f* 2 (drier) centrifugadora *f*

spinney /'spɪni/ *n* (*pl* **-neys**) (BrE) bosquecillo *m*, soto *m*

spinning /'spɪnɪŋ/ *n* [u] (Tex) hilado *m*

spinning: **~ top** *n* trompo *m*, peonza *f*; **~ wheel** *n* rueca *f*

spin-off /'spɪnɔːf || 'spɪnɒf/ *n* (product) producto *m* derivado; (result) resultado *m* indirecto

spinster /'spɪnstər || 'spɪnstə(r)/ *n* soltera *f*

spiral[1] /'spaɪrəl || 'spaɪərəl/ *n* 1 (shape, movement) espiral *f* 2 (of smoke) voluta *f*, espiral *f*

spiral[2] *adj* ‹*shape*› de espiral, acaracolado; **~ staircase** escalera *f* de caracol

spiral[3] *vi*, (BrE) **-ll-** 1 (increase) ‹‹*unemployment*›› escalar; ‹‹*prices*›› dispararse 2 (move) (+ *adv compl*): **to ~ up/down** subir/bajar en espiral

spire /spaɪr || 'spaɪə(r)/ *n* aguja *f*, chapitel *m*

spirit[1] /'spɪrət || 'spɪrɪt/ *n*

A 1 [u] (life force, soul) espíritu *m*; **the ~ is willing but the flesh is weak** a pesar de las buenas intenciones, la carne es débil 2 [c] (Occult) espíritu *m*

B [c] (person) persona *f*; **a free ~** una persona a quien no preocupan los convencionalismos

C [u] (vigor, courage) espíritu *m*, temple *m*; **this horse/child has plenty of ~** este caballo/esta niña tiene mucho brío; **to break sb's ~** quebrantarle el espíritu a algn

D (mental attitude, mood) (*no pl*) espíritu *m*; **the party/Christmas ~** el espíritu festivo/navideño; **that's the ~!** ¡así se hace!, ¡así me gusta!; **in a ~ of great self-sacrifice** con gran espíritu de sacrificio; **she entered into the ~ of things** entró en ambiente

E **spirits** *pl* (emotional state): **to be in good ~s** estar* animado, tener* la moral alta; **to be in high ~s** estar* muy animado *or* de muy buen humor; **keep your ~s up** ¡arriba ese ánimo *or* esos ánimos!; **his ~s fell** se desanimó *or* se desmoralizó

F **spirits** *pl* (alcohol) bebidas *fpl* alcohólicas (*de alta graduación*), licores *mpl*

spirit² *vt*: **to ~ sth away** hacer* desaparecer algo como por arte de magia; **the prisoner was ~ed away during the night** el prisionero desapareció *or* se esfumó durante la noche como por arte de magia

spirited /'spɪrətəd || 'spɪrɪtɪd/ *adj* ‹*horse/child*› brioso, lleno de vida; ‹*reply*› enérgico; ‹*defense*› ardiente, vehemente; **the team gave a ~ performance** el equipo jugó con garra *or* brío

spirit level *n* nivel *m* (de burbuja *or* de aire)

spiritual¹ /'spɪrɪtʃuəl || 'spɪrɪtjʊəl/ *adj* espiritual

spiritual² *n* (*negro* ~) espiritual *m* (negro)

spiritualism /'spɪrɪtʃuəlɪzəm || 'spɪrɪtjʊəlɪzəm/ *n* [u] [1] (Occult) espiritismo *m* [2] (Phil) espiritualismo *m*

spirituality /'spɪrɪtʃu'æləti/ *n* [u] espiritualidad *f*

spit¹ /spɪt/ *n*

A [u] (saliva) saliva *f*; **~ *and polish*** (attention to neatness, appearance) pulcritud *f*: **all that table needs is a bit of ~ and polish** lo que le hace falta a esa mesa es una buena limpieza; ***to be the (dead) ~ of sb*** ser* el vivo retrato de algn; ▸**image C1**

B [c] (for roasting) asador *m* (*en forma de varilla*), espetón *m*, spiedo *m* (CS)

C [c] (of land) punta *f*, lengua *f*

spit² *vi* (*pres p* **spitting**; *past & past p* **spat** *or* (AmE esp) **spit**) [1] «*person/animal*» escupir; **to ~ IN/ON sth** escupir EN algo; **to ~ AT sb** escupirle A algn; **it's within ~ting distance of here** está a un paso de aquí; ▸**image C1** [2] «*fire/fat*» chisporrotear [3] «*cat*» bufar

■ **spit** *vt* (*past & past p* **spat**) ‹*food/blood*› escupir; **she spat obscenities at the guards** les soltó una sarta de obscenidades a los guardias

■ **spit** *v impers* (colloq): **it's ~ting (with rain)** caen algunas gotas (de lluvia), está chispeando (fam)

Phrasal verb

- **spit out** [v ▸ o ▸ adv, v ▸ adv ▸ o] ‹*food/drink*› escupir; **~ *it out!*** (colloq) ¡desembucha! (fam)

spite¹ /spaɪt/ *n* [u]

A (malice) maldad *f*; (resentment) rencor *m*, resentimiento *m*

B **in spite of** (*as prep*) a pesar de; **in ~ of everything** a pesar de todo, pese a todo; **she did it in ~ of herself** lo hizo a pesar de que no era ésa su intención

spite² *vt* molestar, fastidiar

spiteful /'spaɪtfəl/ *adj* ‹*remark*› malicioso; ‹*person*› malo; (resentful) rencoroso; **it was ~ of you to blame her** fue una maldad echarle la culpa a ella

spittle /'spɪtl̩/ *n* [u] baba *f*

spittoon /spɪ'tu:n/ *n* escupidera *f*

spiv /spɪv/ *n* (BrE sl) vivales *m* (fam), avivado *m* (CS fam)

splash¹ /splæʃ/ *n*

A [1] [c u] (spray) salpicadura *f*; ***to make a ~*** (make an impression) producir* *or* causar un revuelo; (lit: in liquid) salpicar* [2] [c] (sound): **we heard a ~** oímos el ruido de algo al caer al agua; **~! he fell in** ¡plaf! *or* ¡zas! se cayó al agua [3] (paddle, swim) (*no pl*) chapuzón *m*

B [1] (small quantity) (*no pl*) **a ~** un poco [2] [c] (mark, patch) salpicadura *f*, mancha *f*, manchón *m*

C [c] (Journ): **they've done a front-page ~ on it** lo han puesto a toda plana en la primera página

splash² *vt*

A (with liquid) salpicar*; **to ~ sth ON/OVER sth/sb** salpicar* algo/a algn DE algo; **to ~ sth/sb WITH sth** salpicar* algo/a algn DE algo

B (in newspaper): **the scandal was ~ed all over the front page** el escándalo venía a toda plana en la primera página

■ **splash** *vi* [1] «*water/paint*» salpicar* [2] «*person/animal*» chapotear

Phrasal verbs

- **splash down** [v ▸ adv] amarizar*, amerizar*
- **splash out** (BrE colloq)

A [v ▸ adv] darse* un lujo; **to ~ out ON sth** gastar(se) un dineral EN algo (fam)

B [v ▸ o ▸ adv, v ▸ adv ▸ o] (buying a treat) gastarse

splash: **~down** *n* (Aerosp) amarizaje *m*, amerizaje *m*; **~guard** *n* (AmE) guardabarros *m*, guardafangos *m*, salpicadera *f* (Méx), tapabarros *m* (Chi, Per)

splatter /'splætər || 'splætə(r)/ *vt/i* ▸**spatter**

splay /spleɪ/ *vt* **~ (out)** (spread apart) ‹*fingers*› abrir*, separar; **to ~ one's legs** abrirse* de piernas

spleen /spli:n/ *n* [c u] [1] (Anat) bazo *m* [2] (anger) (liter) ira *f*, cólera *f*; **to vent one's ~ (on sb)** desahogar* su (*or* mi *etc*) ira *or* cólera (contra algn)

splendid /'splendəd || 'splendɪd/ *adj* [1] (very good) ‹*idea/opportunity/meal*› espléndido, magnífico, maravilloso; **that's (absolutely) ~, congratulations to you both** ¡cuánto me alegro! los felicito [2] (grand, imposing) ‹*clothes/building*› magnífico; ‹*ceremony*› lleno de esplendor

splendor, (BrE) **splendour** /'splendər || 'splendə(r)/ *n* [1] [u] (magnificence) esplendor *m*, magnificencia *f* [2] **splendors** *pl* (liter) maravillas *fpl*

splice /splaɪs/ *vt* **~ (together)** ‹*ropes*› (Naut) coser, ayustar; ‹*tape/film*› unir, empalmar; ‹*wood*› ensamblar

splint /splɪnt/ *n* tablilla *f*; **to put a ~ on sth/sb** entablillar algo/a algn

splinter¹ /'splɪntər/ *n* (of wood) astilla *f*; (of glass, bone, metal) esquirla *f*; (*before n*) **~ group** grupo *m* escindido

splinter² *vi* [1] (break into pieces) «*wood/bone*» astillarse; **some bits of metal ~ed off** se desprendieron algunos trocitos de metal [2] «*political party/society*» escindirse

■ **splinter** *vt* ‹*wood/bone*› astillar

split¹ /splɪt/ *n*

A [1] (in garment, cloth — in seam) descosido *m*; (— part of design) abertura *f*, raja *f*, tajo *m* (CS) [2] (in wood, glass) rajadura *f*, grieta *f*

B [1] (Pol) escisión *f*; (Relig) cisma *m*, escisión *f* [2] (break up) ruptura *f*, separación *f* [3] (share-out, distribution): **a six-way ~ would give everyone $1,500** si se dividiera la suma en seis partes, cada uno se llevaría $1.500

C **splits** *pl*: **to do the ~s** abrirse* completamente de piernas, hacer* el spagat (Esp)

D (bottle) (AmE) *botella individual de vino o champán*

split² *adj*

A [1] (damaged) ‹*wood*› rajado, partido; ‹*lip*› partido; **her trousers were ~ at the seams** tenía las costuras de los pantalones descosidas [2] (cleft) ‹*logs*› partido

B [1] (divided): **~ decision** decisión *f* no unánime; **~ personality** doble personalidad *f*; **~ shift** horario *m* (de trabajo) partido *or* no corrido [2] (in factions) dividido

split³ (*pres p* **splitting**; *past & past p* **split**) *vt*

A [1] (break) ‹*wood/stone*› partir; **to ~ the atom** fisionar *or* desintegrar el átomo; **to ~ sth in two/in half** partir algo en dos/por la mitad [2] (burst): **he bent down and ~ his pants** se agachó y reventó los pantalones; **she ~ her head open** se partió *or* se abrió la cabeza; ***to ~ one's sides (laughing)*** partirse *or* troncharse *or* desternillarse de risa [3] (divide into factions) ‹*nation/church*› dividir, escindir

B (divide, share) ‹*cost/food*› dividir; **do you want to ~ a bottle?** ¿nos tomamos una botella a medias?

■ **split** *vi*

A (crack, burst) «*wood/rock*» partirse, rajarse; «*leather/seam*» abrirse*, romperse*; **his bag ~ (open)** se le rompió *or* rajó la bolsa; **I've got a ~ting headache** tengo un dolor de cabeza espantoso

B «*political party/church*» dividirse, escindirse

C (leave) (sl) abrirse* (arg), largarse* (fam)

D (denounce) (BrE colloq) **to ~ ON sb** acusar *or* (Méx fam) rajar a algn, chivarse DE algn (Esp fam)

Phrasal verbs

- **split away**, **split off** [v ▸ adv] «*faction/group*» **to ~ away** *o* **off FROM sth** escindirse *or* separarse DE algo
- **split up**

A [v ▸ adv] «*couple/band*» separarse; «*crowd*» dispersarse; **to ~ up INTO sth**: **let's ~ up into groups** dividámonos en grupos

B [v ▸ o ▸ adv, v ▸ adv ▸ o] ‹*wrestlers/boxers*› separar; ‹*lovers*›

S

hacer* que se separen; ~ **them up into groups** divídelos en grupos

split: ~ **end** *n* 1 (of hair): **I've got ~ ends** tengo las puntas abiertas *or* (CS) florecidas, tengo horquillas (Col) *or* (Méx) orzuela *or* (Ven) horquetillas 2 (in US football) ala *f‡* abierta; **~-level** /ˈsplɪtˈlevəl/ *adj* 1 ‹*apartment*› en dos niveles 2 ‹*cooker*› (BrE) *con grill en la parte superior*; ~ **pea** *n* arveja *f* seca *or* (Esp) guisante *m* seco *or* (esp Méx) chícharo *m* seco; ~ **second** *n* fracción *f* de segundo; (*before n*) **~-second timing** sincronización *f* perfecta

splodge /splɑːdʒ || splɒdʒ/ *n* (BrE colloq) manchón *m*

splurge /splɜːrdʒ || splɜːdʒ/ *n* (colloq) derroche *m*; **to go on a ~** salir* a gastar a lo loco (fam)

splutter¹ /ˈsplʌtər || ˈsplʌtə(r)/ *n* (of flames, fat) chisporroteo *m*; (of engine) resoplido *m*

splutter² *vi* 1 «*fire/fat*» chisporrotear, crepitar; «*engine*» resoplar 2 «*person*» resoplar; (in anger, embarrassment etc) farfullar, barbotar

spoil¹ /spɔɪl/ (*past & past p* **spoiled** *or* (BrE also) **spoilt**) *vt*
A 1 ‹*party/surprise*› echar a perder, estropear, arruinar; **these buildings have ~ed the coastline** estos edificios han afeado la costa; **I don't want to ~ your fun but ...** no les quiero aguar la fiesta pero ...; **it will ~ your appetite** te quitará el apetito 2 (invalidate) anular; **~ed** *o* (BrE also) **~t papers** papeletas *fpl* nulas
B (overindulge) ‹*child*› consentir*, malcriar*, mimar demasiado; **go on, ~ yourself** vamos, date un gusto; **to be ~ed for choice** tener* mucho de donde elegir
■ **spoil** *vi*
A «*food/meal*» echarse a perder, estropearse
B (be eager) (colloq) **to be ~ing FOR sth** estar* *or* andar* buscando algo

spoil² *n* (*usu pl*) botín *m*; **the division of the ~(s)** el reparto del botín

spoiled /spɔɪld/, (BrE also) **spoilt** /spɔɪlt/ *adj* mimado, malcriado, consentido

spoiler /ˈspɔɪlər || ˈspɔɪlə(r)/ *n*
A (Auto, Aviat) spoiler *m*
B (AmE Pol) *candidato o equipo que no tiene posibilidades de ganar pero puede impedir que otro gane*

spoilsport /ˈspɔɪlspɔːrt/ *n* (colloq) aguafiestas *mf* (fam)

spoils system /spɔɪlz/ *n* (AmE) tráfico *m* de influencias, amiguismo *m*, clientelismo *m* (AmL)

spoilt¹ /spɔɪlt/ (BrE) *past & past p of* **spoil¹**

spoilt² *adj* (BrE) ▸ **spoiled**

spoke¹ /spəʊk/ *n* rayo *m* (*de una rueda*); ***to put a ~ in sb's wheel*** (BrE colloq) fastidiarle los planes a algn (fam)

spoke² *past of* **speak**

spoken¹ /ˈspəʊkən/ *past p of* **speak**

spoken² *adj* (*before n*) hablado, oral

spokesman /ˈspəʊksmən/ *n* (*pl* **-men** /-mən/) portavoz *m*, vocero *m* (esp AmL); ~ **FOR sth** portavoz *m* *or* vocero *m* DE algo

spokesperson /ˈspəʊksˌpɜːrsn̩ || ˈspəʊksˌpɜːsn̩/ *n* portavoz *mf*, vocero, -ra *m,f* (esp AmL)

spokeswoman /ˈspəʊksˌwʊmən/ (*pl* **-women**) *n* portavoz *f*, vocera *f* (esp AmL)

sponge¹ /spʌndʒ/ *n*
A 1 [c] (Zool) esponja *f* 2 [c] (for bath) esponja *f*; ▸ **throw in 2**
B [c u] (Culin) ~ **(cake)** bizcocho *m*, bizcochuelo *m* (CS)

sponge² *vt* (clean) pasar una esponja (*or* una toalla húmeda *etc*) por; **to ~ the dirt off sth** limpiar algo con una esponja/con un trapo
■ **sponge** *vi* gorronear (fam), gorrear (fam), garronear (RPl fam), bolsear (Chi fam); **he lives by sponging on** *o* **off his relatives** vive a costillas de sus parientes

sponge: ~ **bag** *n* (BrE) neceser *m*, bolsa *f* del aseo; ~ **finger** *n* (BrE) plantilla *f* *or* (Esp) soletilla *f* *or* (Arg) vainilla *f* *or* (Chi) galleta *f* de champaña

sponger /ˈspʌndʒər || ˈspʌndʒə(r)/ *n* (colloq & pej) gorrón, -rrona *m,f* (fam), gorrero, -ra *m,f* (fam), garronero, -ra *m,f* (RPl fam), bolsero, -ra *m,f* (Chi fam)

sponsor¹ /ˈspɑːnsər || ˈspɒnsə(r)/ *n* 1 (of program, show) patrocinador, -dora *m,f*; (of sporting event) patrocinador, -dora *m,f*, espónsor *mf*, sponsor *mf*; (for the arts) mecenas *mf* 2 (for membership): **you need two members to act as ~s** te tienen que presentar dos socios 3 (of bill, motion) proponente *mf*

sponsor² *vt* 1 (promote) ‹*program/event/festival*› patrocinar, auspiciar; ‹*research/expedition*› subvencionar, financiar; **~ed swim/walk** (BrE) *evento en el cual los participantes reciben donativos para una obra benéfica de acuerdo a la distancia recorrida* 2 ‹*applicant/application*› apoyar, respaldar 3 ‹*bill/motion*› (present) presentar; (support) apoyar

sponsorship /ˈspɑːnsərʃɪp || ˈspɒnsəʃɪp/ *n* 1 (financing) patrocinio *m*, auspicio *m*; (of the arts) mecenazgo *m*; (of sports) patrocinio *m*, esponsorización *f* 2 (of application) respaldo *m* 3 (of bill, motion) respaldo *m*, apoyo *m*

spontaneous /spɑːnˈteɪniəs/ *adj* espontáneo

spontaneously /spɑːnˈteɪniəsli/ *adv* espontáneamente

spoof /spuːf/ *n* (colloq) 1 (parody) parodia *f*, burla *f* 2 (hoax) broma *f*

spook /spuːk/ *n* (colloq)
A (ghost) fantasma *m*, espectro *m*
B (secret policeman, policewoman) (AmE colloq & pej) agente *mf* de la policía secreta, tira *mf* (AmL arg & pey), secreta *mf* (Esp fam)
C (spy) espía *mf*

spooky /ˈspuːki/ *adj* **-kier, -kiest** (colloq) espeluznante

spool /spuːl/ *n* carrete *m*, carretel *m* (AmL)

spoon¹ /spuːn/ *n* 1 (piece of cutlery) cuchara *f*; (small) cucharita *f*, cucharilla *f*; ***to be born with a silver ~ in one's mouth*** nacer* en cuna de oro 2 (spoonful) (colloq) cucharada *f*; (small) cucharadita *f*

spoon² *vt*: ~ **the juices over the meat** rocíe la carne con su jugo; ~ **the filling into the tomatoes** rellene los tomates con una cuchara

spoonerism /ˈspuːnərɪzəm/ *n*: *transposición, de efecto cómico, de los sonidos iniciales de dos palabras*

spoonfeed /ˈspuːnfiːd/ *vt* (*past & past p* **-fed**) 1 ‹*baby/invalid*› darle* de comer en la boca a 2 (Educ): **she ~s her students** se lo da todo mascado *or* todo digerido a sus alumnos

spoonful /ˈspuːnfʊl/ *n* (*pl* **~s** *or* **spoonsful**) cucharada *f*; (small) cucharadita *f*

sporadic /spəˈrædɪk/ *adj* esporádico

sporadically /spəˈrædɪkli/ *adv* ‹*occur/visit*› esporádicamente; ‹*effective/sparkling*› por momentos

spore /spɔːr || spɔː(r)/ *n* espora *f*

sporran /ˈspɔːrən || ˈspɒrən/ *n* escarcela *f* (*bolsa que se lleva sobre la falda escocesa*)

sport¹ /spɔːrt || spɔːt/ *n*
A [c u] deporte *m*; **he enjoys ~s** *o* (BrE) **~** le gustan los deportes, le gusta el deporte
B (person): **to be a good ~** (to be sporting) tener* espíritu deportivo; (to be understanding) ser* comprensivo

sport² *vt* ‹*clothes/hairstyle*› lucir*

sport³ *adj* (AmE) 1 (Sport) ‹*equipment*› de deportes 2 (casual) ‹*clothes*› sport *adj inv*, de sport

sportcoat /ˈspɔːrtkəʊt || ˈspɔːtkəʊt/ *n* (AmE) chaqueta *f* *or* (AmL tb) saco *m* sport, americana *f*

sporting /ˈspɔːrtɪŋ || ˈspɔːtɪŋ/ *adj*
A (fair, sportsmanlike) ‹*spirit*› deportivo; **it's very ~ of you to offer to help** es muy amable de su parte ofrecerse a ayudar; **you have a ~ chance of winning** tienes bastantes posibilidades *or* (AmL tb) una buena chance de ganar
B (*no comp*) (relating to sport) ‹*press/interests*› deportivo

sports /spɔːrts || spɔːts/ *adj* 1 (Sport) (page/program) de deportes; ~ **complex** polideportivo *m* 2 (casual) ‹*clothes/shirt*› sport *adj inv*, de sport

sports: ~ **car** *n* coche *m* deportivo, carro *m* sport (AmL exc CS), auto *m* sport *or* deportivo (CS); ~ **center**, (BrE) **sports centre** polideportivo *m*, centro *m* deportivo *or* de deportes; ~ **coat** *n* ▸ **sportcoat**; ~ **jacket** *n* (BrE) ▸ **sportcoat**; **~man** /ˈspɔːrtsmən || ˈspɔːtsmən/ *n* (*pl* **-men** /-mən/) deportista *m*; **~manlike** /ˈspɔːrtsmənlaɪk/ *adj* deportivo; **~manship** /ˈspɔːrtsmənʃɪp/ *n* [u] espíritu *m* deportivo, deportividad *f*; **~wear** *n* [u] (Sport) ropa *f* de deporte; (casual) ropa *f* (de) sport; **~woman** *n* deportista *f*

sporty /ˈspɔːrti || ˈspɔːti/ *adj* **-tier, -tiest** 1 ‹*person*› deportista, aficionado a los deportes 2 (Auto) deportivo

spot¹ /spɑːt || spɒt/ *n*
A 1 (dot — on material) lunar *m*, mota *f*, pepa *f* (Col, Ven fam);

(— on animal's skin) mancha *f*; ***to knock ~s off sth/sb*** (colloq) darle* cien *or* cien mil vueltas a algo/algn (fam), darle* sopas con honda(s) a algo/algn (Esp fam) [2] (blemish, stain) mancha *f* [3] (pimple) (BrE) grano *m*, espinilla *f* (AmL); **she broke out** *o* **came out in ~s** le salieron granos
[B] [1] (location, place) lugar *m*, sitio *m*; **don't move from that ~ until I get back** no te muevas de ahí hasta que vuelva; ***on the ~***: **firemen were quickly on the ~** los bomberos se presentaron sin demora en el lugar del siniestro; **he had to decide on the ~** tuvo que decidir en ese mismo momento; **they were killed on the ~** los mataron allí mismo; **on-the-~ fine** *multa que se paga en el acto*; ***to be rooted to the ~*** quedarse clavado en el sitio *or* paralizado [2] (difficult situation): **to be in a (tight) ~** estar* en apuros *or* en un lío *or* en un aprieto; ***to put sb on the ~*** poner* a algn en un apuro *or* aprieto
[C] (of character, personality) punto *m*; **science is my weak ~** las ciencias son mi punto débil; **you've touched a rather sore ~ there** has puesto el dedo en la llaga; ***to have a soft ~ for sb/sth*** (colloq) tener* debilidad por algn/algo; ***to hit the ~*** (esp AmE) caer* muy bien
[D] [1] (drop) gota *f* [2] (small amount) (BrE colloq) (*no pl*): **do you fancy a ~ of supper?** ¿quieres cenar algo?; **the garden could do with a ~ of rain** al jardín le vendría bien que lloviera un poco
[E] (Rad, TV) (time) espacio *m*; **a commercial ~** un spot publicitario, una cuña publicitaria, un anuncio
[F] (position, job) (AmE) puesto *m*
[G] ▸**spotlight**

spot² *vt* **-tt-**
[A] ‹*error*› descubrir*; ‹*bargain*› encontrar*; **he finally ~ted her in the crowd** al final la vio *or* la divisó *or* (AmL tb) la ubicó entre el gentío; **he's good at ~ting talent** sabe reconocer talento donde lo hay; **see if you can ~ the difference** a ver si te das cuenta de cuál es la diferencia
[B] (mark) (*usu pass*) manchar

spot check *n*: control *o* inspección realizada al azar

spotless /ˈspɑːtləs || ˈspɒtlɪs/ *adj* [1] ‹*clothes*› impecable; ‹*house*› limpísimo [2] ‹*reputation/record*› intachable

spotlight /ˈspɑːtlaɪt || ˈspɒtlaɪt/ *n* (in theater) foco *m*; (on building) reflector *m*; (in house) spot *m*, luz *f* direccional

spot-on /ˈspɑːtˈɑːn || ˌspɒtˈɒn/ *adj* (BrE colloq) exacto; **what Martha said was absolutely ~** Martha dio en el clavo con lo que dijo (fam)

spotted /ˈspɑːtəd || ˈspɒtɪd/ *adj* ‹*tie/material*› de *or* a lunares *or* motas; **a ~ dog** un perro con manchas; **a ~ cow** una vaca pintada

spotty /ˈspɑːti || ˈspɒti/ *adj* **-tier, -tiest** (BrE) ‹*skin/complexion*› lleno de granos; ‹*youth/teenager*› con la cara llena de granos; **he's very ~** tiene muchos granos

spouse /spaʊs/ *n* (frml *or* hum) cónyuge *mf* (frml), consorte *mf* (frml *o* hum)

spout¹ /spaʊt/ *n* [1] (of teapot, kettle) pico *m*, pitorro *m* (Esp) [2] (pipe — on gutter) canalón *m*; (— on fountain, gargoyle) caño *m*; ***up the ~*** (BrE colloq): **our plans are up the ~** los planes se nos han ido al garete (fam); **he's really up the ~ now** ahora sí que se ha metido en un lío (fam) [3] (jet) chorro *m*

spout² *vt* ‹*oil/liquid*› arrojar *or* expulsar chorros de
■ **spout** *vi* [1] «*liquid*» salir* a chorros; «*whale*» expulsar chorros de agua [2] «*person*» perorar, soltar* peroratas

sprain¹ /spreɪn/ *n* esguince *m*, distensión *f*

sprain² *vt* hacerse* un esguince en, distenderse*

sprang /spræŋ/ *past of* **spring¹**

sprat /spræt/ *n* espadín *m* (*pez de la familia de los arenques*)

sprawl¹ /sprɔːl/ *vi* [1] «*person*» sentarse* (*or* tumbarse *etc*) de forma poco elegante; **he sent him ~ing with one punch** lo tumbó de un golpe [2] «*city/town*» **to ~ ACROSS/OVER sth** extenderse* POR algo

sprawl² *n* (of built-up area) expansión *f*; **urban ~** expansión urbana descontrolada

spray¹ /spreɪ/ *vt* [1] ‹*liquid*› pulverizar*, aplicar* con atomizador; ‹*paint*› aplicar* con pistola pulverizadora; **she ~ed a little perfume on her wrists** se puso *or* se echó un poco de perfume en las muñecas [2] ‹*plants*› rociar* (*con atomizador*); **~ the affected area twice daily** pulverizar* sobre la zona afectada dos veces al día; **to ~ the fruit trees with insecticide** fumigar* los árboles frutales con insecticida

spray² *n*
[A] [1] [u c] (fine drops) rocío *m* [2] [c] (liquid in spray form) espray *m*; (*before n*) ‹*deodorant/polish*› en aerosol, en espray, en atomizador [3] (implement) rociador *m*
[B] [c] (bunch) ramillete *m*

sprayer /ˈspreɪər || ˈspreɪə(r)/ *n* [1] ▸**spray²** **A3** [2] ▸**spray gun**

spray gun *n* pistola *f* pulverizadora

spread¹ /spred/ (*past & past p* **spread**) *vt*
[A] (extend) [1] (in space) ‹*arms/legs*› extender*; ‹*map/sails*› desplegar*; ‹*wings*› desplegar*, extender [2] (in time): **the plan allows you to ~ the cost over five years** el plan le permite pagar el costo a lo largo de cinco años
[B] [1] ‹*paint/glue*› extender*; ‹*seeds/sand*› esparcir*; **to ~ butter on a piece of toast** untar una tostada con mantequilla; **our resources are thinly ~** hemos tenido que estirar nuestros recursos al máximo [2] ‹*knowledge/news*› difundir, propagar*; ‹*influence*› extender*; ‹*rumor*› hacer* correr, difundir; ‹*disease*› propagar*; ‹*fear*› sembrar*; ‹*ideas/culture*› diseminar, divulgar*
[C] (cover): **~ the surface thickly with adhesive** unte *or* embadurne la superficie con abundante pegamento
■ **spread** *vi*
[A] «*disease*» propagarse*; «*liquid*» extenderse*; «*fire*» extenderse*, propagarse; «*ideas/culture*» diseminarse, divulgarse*; «*panic/fear*» cundir; «*influence/revolt*» extenderse*; **the plague ~ to Europe** la plaga se extendió a Europa
[B] (extend in space, time) extenderse*
[C] «*paint*» extenderse*; «*butter*» untarse, extenderse*

Phrasal verb

• **spread out** [v ▸ adv] [1] (move apart) «*troops*» desplegarse* [2] (extend) extenderse*

spread² *n*
[A] [u] (diffusion — of disease) propagación *f*; (— of ideas) difusión *f*, divulgación *f*, diseminación *f*; (— of fire) propagación *f*; (— of nuclear weapons) proliferación *f*
[B] [u] [1] (of wings, sails) envergadura *f* [2] (range, extent): **a broad ~ of opinion** un amplio abanico de opiniones
[C] [c] (Culin) [1] (meal) (colloq) festín *m*, banquete *m* [2] (paste) *pasta para extender sobre pan, tostadas etc*; **cheese ~** queso *m* cremoso para untar
[D] [c] (Journ, Print): **it was advertised in a full-page ~** venía anunciado a plana entera
[E] [c] (ranch) (AmE & Austral colloq & dial) finca *f*, hacienda *f* (AmL), estancia *f* (RPl), fundo *m* (Chi)

spread: ~ betting *n* [u]: *modalidad de apuesta en que lo que se gana o pierde depende de la cantidad en que difiere lo apostado de los resultados en algún acontecimiento deportivo*; **~-eagled** /ˈspredˈiːgəld/ *adj* con los brazos y piernas abiertos; **~sheet** *n* hoja *f* de cálculo

spree /spriː/ *n*: **out on a drinking ~** de juerga (fam), de parranda (fam); **to go on a shopping ~** ir* de expedición a las tiendas; **he went on a spending ~** salió a gastar dinero a lo loco (fam)

sprig /sprɪg/ *n* ramito *m*

sprightly /ˈspraɪtli/ *adj* **-lier, -liest** ‹*person*› lleno de brío, vivaz; ‹*walk/step*› ágil

spring¹ /sprɪŋ/ (*past* **sprang** *or* (esp AmE) **sprung**; *past p* **sprung**) *vi*
[A] [1] (leap) saltar; **I sprang out of bed** salté de la cama; **to ~ to one's feet** levantarse *or* ponerse* de pie de un salto *or* como movido por un resorte; **to ~ to attention** ponerse* firme; **to ~ into action** entrar en acción; **the engine sprang into life** de pronto el motor se puso en marcha [2] (pounce): **the tiger was poised to ~** el tigre estaba agazapado, listo para atacar; **to ~ AT sb/sth**: **the dog sprang at his throat** el perro se le tiró al cuello
[B] [1] (liter) «*stream*» surgir*, nacer*; «*shoots*» brotar; **where did you ~ from?** (colloq) ¿y tú de dónde has salido? [2] **to ~ FROM sth** «*ideas/doubts*» surgir* DE algo; «*problem*» provenir* DE algo
■ **spring** *vt* [1] (produce suddenly) **to ~ sth ON sb**: **he sprang a surprise on them** les dio una sorpresa [2] : **to ~ a leak** empezar* a hacer agua

Phrasal verb

• **spring up** [v ▸ adv] «*stores/housing estates*» surgir*; «*plant*» brotar; «*wind*» levantarse; **she sprang up from her seat** se levantó del asiento de un salto

S

spring² *n*
A [u c] (season) primavera *f*; **in (the) ~** en primavera; (*before n*) ‹*weather/showers*› primaveral
B [c] (Geog) manantial *m*, fuente *f*
C [c] (jump) salto *m*, brinco *m*
D **1** [c] (in watch, toy) resorte *m*; (in mattress) muelle *m*, resorte *m* (AmL) **2** (elasticity) (*no pl*) elasticidad *f*; **to walk with a ~ in one's step** caminar con brío *or* energía

spring: **~board** *n* **1** (Sport) trampolín *m* **2** (point of departure) trampolín *m*; **~ chicken** *n* pollo *m* pequeño y tierno; ***she's no ~ chicken*** ya no es ninguna niña; **~clean** /'sprɪŋ'kli:n/ *vt* (BrE) ‹*house*› hacer* una limpieza general en *vi* hacer* limpieza general; **~cleaning** /'sprɪŋ'kli:nɪŋ/ *n* (*no pl*) limpieza *f* general; **~ onion** *n* (BrE) cebolleta *f*, cebollino *m*, cebolla *f* de verdeo, cebollín *m* (Chi); **~ roll** *n* rollito *m* (de) primavera (*plato de la cocina china*); **~time** *n* primavera *f*; **in ~time** en primavera

springy /'sprɪŋi/ *adj* **-gier, -giest** ‹*mattress/grass*› mullido; ‹*floor*› elástico

sprinkle /'sprɪŋkəl/ *vt* **1** (scatter) **to ~ sth ON sth**: **to ~ water on the plants** rociar* las plantas con agua; **to ~ sugar on sth** espolvorear algo con azúcar; **~ the almonds on top** esparza las almendras por encima **2** (cover) **to ~ sth/sb WITH sth**: **~ the board with flour** espolvoree la tabla con harina; **he ~d the congregation with holy water** roció a los fieles con agua bendita

sprinkler /'sprɪŋklər || 'sprɪŋklə(r)/ *n* **1** (on hose) aspersor *m*, válvula *f*; (for sugar, flour) espolvoreador *m*; (on watering can) (BrE) roseta *f*, alcachofa *f*, regadera *f* (Col, Méx, Ven), flor *f* (RPl) **2** (*garden ~*) aspersor *m* **3** (for firefighting) (*usu pl*) rociador *m*; (*before n*) **~ system** sistema *m* de rociadores

sprinkling /'sprɪŋklɪŋ/ *n*: **a ~ of vinegar** unas gotas de vinagre; **add a ~ of sugar** espolvoree con un poco de azúcar; **there was a ~ of children in the audience** había algunos niños entre el público

sprint¹ /sprɪnt/ *n* **1** (fast run) (e)sprint *m*; **to make a ~ for the bus** pegarse* *or* echarse una carrera para alcanzar el autobús **2** (short race) (Sport) carrera *f* corta; **the 200m ~** los 200 metros planos *or* (Esp) lisos *or* (RPl) llanos

sprint² *vi* **1** (Sport) (e)sprintar **2** (run fast): **I ~ed after him** salí corriendo tras él a toda velocidad

sprinter /'sprɪntər || 'sprɪntə(r)/ *n* (e)sprínter *mf*, velocista *mf*

sprite /spraɪt/ *n* duendecillo *m*

sprocket /'sprɑ:kət || 'sprɒkɪt/ *n* **1** (tooth) diente *m* **2** **~ (wheel)** rueda *f* dentada, piñón *m* **3** (for film) carrete *m* receptor, tambor *m* dentado

sprout¹ /spraʊt/ *vt* ‹*leaves/shoots*› echar
■ **sprout** *vi* «*plant*» echar retoños, retoñar; «*leaf*» brotar, salir*; «*seeds*» germinar

sprout² *n*
A (new growth) brote *m*, retoño *m*
B **1** (*Brussels ~*) col *f* *or* (AmS) repollito *m* de Bruselas **2** (shoot) brote *m* **3** ▸**beanshoot**

spruce¹ /spru:s/ *n* **1** [c] (tree) picea *f*, abeto *m* falso **2** [u] (wood) picea *f*

Phrasal verb
• **spruce up** [v ▸ o ▸ adv, v ▸ adv ▸ o] ‹*garden/room*› arreglar

spruce² *adj* **sprucer, sprucest** ‹*appearance*› cuidado, acicalado; ‹*garden*› cuidado, arreglado

sprung¹ /sprʌŋ/ *past p & (esp AmE) past of* **spring¹**

sprung² *adj* ‹*mattress*› de muelles, de resortes (AmL)

spry /spraɪ/ *adj* **-er, -est** lleno de vida, dinámico

spud /spʌd/ *n* (colloq) papa *f* *or* (Esp) patata *f*

spun¹ /spʌn/ *past & past p of* **spin²**

spun² *adj* ‹*silk/cotton*› hilado

spunk /spʌŋk/ *n* [u] **1** (courage) (colloq) agallas *fpl* (fam) **2** (semen) (BrE vulg) leche *f* (vulg)

spur¹ /spɜ:r || spɜ:(r)/ *n* **1** espuela *f*; ***on the ~ of the moment*** sin pensarlo; ***to win o gain one's ~s*** demostrar* su (*or* mi *etc*) valía **2** (stimulus) acicate *m*, aguijón *m*

spur² *vt* **-rr-** **1** (Equ) ‹*horse*› espolear **2** **~ (on)** (urge on) ‹*person/team*› estimular, alentar*

spurious /'spjʊriəs/ *adj* **1** (not genuine) ‹*document*› falso **2** (dubious) ‹*argument/conclusion*› falaz, espurio

spurn /spɜ:rn || spɜ:n/ *vt* desdeñar, rechazar*

spurt¹ /spɜ:rt || spɜ:t/ *n* **1** (of speed, activity): **she works in ~s** trabaja por rachas; **a final ~ won him the race** con un esfuerzo final, ganó la carrera **2** (jet) chorro *m*

spurt² *vi* **1** «*runner*» acelerar **2** «*liquid/steam*» salir* a chorros

sputter /'spʌtər || 'spʌtə(r)/ *vi* «*engine*» petardear; «*candle/fat*» chisporrotear

spy¹ /spaɪ/ *n* (*pl* **spies**) espía *mf*; (*before n*) ‹*satellite/ship*› espía *adj inv*; ‹*story*› de espías, de espionaje; **~ ring** red *f* de espionaje

spy² **spies, spying, spied** *vi* **1** (watch secretly) espiar*; **to ~ ON sb** espiar* a algn **2** (work as spy) espiar*; **to ~ ON sth/sb** espiar* algo/a algn
■ **spy** *vt* descubrir*, ver*; **to play 'I ~'** (BrE) jugar* al veo-veo

spy: **~glass** *n* catalejo *m*; **~hole** *n* mirilla *f*, ojo *m* mágico (AmL)

sq *adj* (= **square**): **220 ~ m** 220 m²

Sq (= **Square**) Pza.

squabble¹ /'skwɑ:bəl || 'skwɒbəl/ *vi* pelear(se), reñir*

squabble² *n* pelea *f*, riña *f*

squad /skwɑ:d || skwɒd/ *n* **1** (Mil) pelotón *m*; (of workmen) cuadrilla *f*, brigada *f* **2** (of policemen) brigada *f*; **death ~** escuadrón *m* de la muerte; **drug** *o* **narcotics ~** brigada *f* antidroga *or* de estupefacientes **3** (Sport) equipo *m*

squad car *n* (AmE) coche *m* *or* (AmL tb) auto *m* patrulla, patrullero *m* (CS, Per)

squadron /'skwɑ:drən || 'skwɒdrən/ *n* (Mil, Aviat) escuadrón *m*; (Naut) escuadra *f*

squadron leader *n* (BrE) mayor *m* *or* (Esp) comandante *m* (*en la fuerza aérea*)

squalid /'skwɑ:ləd || 'skwɒlɪd/ *adj* **1** (dirty) ‹*existence/house*› miserable **2** (sordid) ‹*story/business*› sórdido

squall¹ /skwɔ:l/ *n* borrasca *f*, turbión *m*; **~s of rain** chubascos *mpl*, aguaceros *mpl*

squall² *vi* chillar, berrear

squally /'skwɔ:li/ *adj* **1** (weather) borrascoso **2** ‹*cry/voice*› chillón **3** ‹*meeting*› borrascoso, turbulento

squalor /'skwɑ:lər || 'skwɒlə(r)/ *n* [u] miseria *f*

squander /'skwɑ:ndər || 'skwɒndə(r)/ *vt* ‹*money*› despilfarrar, derrochar; ‹*fortune*› dilapidar; ‹*opportunity/time*› desaprovechar, desperdiciar

square¹ /skwer || skweə(r)/ *n*
A **1** (shape) cuadrado *m*; (in fabric design) cuadro *m* **2** (of cloth, paper) (trozo *m*) cuadrado *m*; **a silk (head) ~** un pañuelo de seda cuadrado **3** (on chessboard) casilla *f*, escaque *m*; (in crossword) casilla *f*; ***to go back to ~ one*** volver* a empezar desde cero
B (in town, city) plaza *f*
C (Math) cuadrado *m*
D (instrument) escuadra *f*
E (conventional person) (colloq) soso, -sa *m,f* (fam), carroza *mf* (Esp fam), zanahorio, -ria *m,f* (Col, Ven fam)

square² *adj* **squarer, squarest**
A **1** ‹*box/table/block*› cuadrado; **the room is 15 feet ~** la habitación mide 15 (pies) por 15 (pies) **2** (having right angles) ‹*corner/edges*› en ángulo recto, a escuadra **3** ‹*face*› cuadrado; ‹*jaw*› angular, cuadrado
B (Math) (*before n*) ‹*yard/mile*› cuadrado
C **1** (fair, honest): **he'll give you a ~ deal** no te va a engañar; **to be ~ WITH sb** ser* franco CON algn **2** (large and wholesome) (*before n*) ‹*meal*› decente **3** (even) (*pred*): **the teams were (all) ~** los equipos iban empatados *or* iguales; **to get ~ with sb** ajustarle las cuentas a algn
D (conventional) (colloq) soso (fam), rígidamente convencional, carroza (Esp fam), zanahorio (Col, Ven fam)

square³ *adv*: **he hit me ~ on the mouth** me dio de lleno en la boca, me dio en plena boca; **to look sb ~ in the eye** mirar a algn (directamente) a los ojos

square⁴ *vt*
A (make square) ‹*angle/side*› cuadrar; **he ~d his shoulders** se puso derecho
B (Math) elevar al cuadrado
C **1** (settle, make even) ‹*debts/accounts*› pagar*, saldar; **to ~ sth WITH sb** arreglar algo CON algn **2** (Sport) ‹*match/game*› igualar **3** (reconcile) ‹*facts/principles*› conciliar; **I couldn't ~ it with my conscience** mi conciencia no me lo permitía
■ **square** *vi* «*ideas/arguments*» concordar*; **to ~ WITH sth** concordar* *or* cuadrar CON algo

(Phrasal verbs)

- **square up** [v ▸ adv] (settle debts) (colloq) **to ~ up (WITH sb)** arreglar cuentas (CON algn)
- **square up to** [v ▸ adv ▸ prep ▸ o] hacer* frente a

squared /skwerd || skweəd/ *adj* [1] ‹*paper*› cuadriculado [2] (Math) (*after n*) (elevado) al cuadrado

square dance *n* cuadrilla *f*

squarely /'skwerli || 'skweəli/ *adv* [1] (directly): **the blow hit him ~ on the nose** el golpe le dio de lleno en la nariz, el golpe le dio en plena nariz; **blame was placed ~ on the police** se culpó directamente a la policía [2] (honestly) ‹*deal/treat*› como es debido

square: **S~ Mile** *n*: **the S~ Mile** la City (*zona donde está situado el centro financiero de Londres*); **~ root** *n* raíz *f* cuadrada

squash¹ /skwɑːʃ || skwɒʃ/ *n*

A (crush) (*no pl*): **it was a terrible ~ on the train** íbamos (*or* iban *etc*) terriblemente apretados *or* apretujados en el tren

B [u] (Sport) squash *m*

C [u] (drink) (BrE) *refresco a base de extractos*; **orange ~** naranjada *f*

D [c u] (Bot, Culin) *nombre genérico de varios tipos de calabaza y zapallo*

squash² *vt*

A [1] (crush) ‹*fruit/insect*› aplastar, espachurrar (fam), apachurrar (AmC, Andes fam), espichar (Col) [2] (squeeze) meter (*apretando*); **we were all ~ed (up) against the wall** estábamos todos apiñados contra la pared

B (suppress, silence) (colloq) ‹*protests/rumors*› acallar; **he needs to be ~ed now and then** de vez en cuando hay que bajarle los humos; **she ~ed Tom's arguments flat** echó por tierra los argumentos de Tom

■ **squash** *vi* (+ *adv compl*): **we all ~ed into his study** nos metimos todos en su despacho; **could I ~ in?** ¿quepo yo también?; **to ~ up** apretarse*

squashy /'skwɑːʃi || 'skwɒʃi/ *adj* **-shier, -shiest** ‹*fruit*› blando; ‹*ground*› húmedo y mullido

squat¹ /skwɑːt || skwɒt/ *vi* **-tt-**

A (crouch) agacharse, ponerse* en cuclillas

B (in building, on land) *ocupar un inmueble ajeno sin autorización*

squat² *n* (BrE) *vivienda o tierra ocupada sin autorización*

squat³ *adj* **-tt-** ‹*person*› rechoncho y bajo, retacón (RPl); ‹*building/church*› achaparrado

squatter /'skwɑːtər || 'skwɒtə(r)/ *n* (in building) ocupante *mf* ilegal, ocupa *or* okupa *mf* (Esp), paracaidista *mf* (Méx)

squaw /skwɔː/ *n* india *f* (*de tribu norteamericana*)

squawk¹ /skwɔːk/ *n* (of bird) graznido *m*; **she gave** *o* **let out a ~** pegó un chillido

squawk² *vi* «*bird*» graznar; «*person*» chillar

squeak¹ /skwiːk/ *n*

A (of animal, person) chillido *m*; (of hinge) chirrido *m*; (of shoes) crujido *m*; **to give** *o* **let out a ~** pegar* un chillido; **I don't want to hear a ~ out of anyone** (colloq & hum) no quiero que se oiga ni el vuelo de una mosca

B (escape) (colloq): **a narrow** *o* (AmE also) **close ~**: **we got there in time, but it was a narrow ~** llegamos a tiempo, pero por un pelo *or* por los pelos (fam)

squeak² *vi* [1] «*animal/person*» chillar; «*hinge*» chirriar*; «*shoes*» crujir [2] (pass by a narrow margin): **to ~ past/through** pasar raspando (fam)

■ **squeak** *vt* chillar, gritar

squeaky /'skwiːki/ *adj* **-kier, kiest** ‹*hinge/pen*› chirriante; ‹*voice*› chillón, de pito; **~ clean** limpísimo, super limpio (fam)

squeal¹ /skwiːl/ *vi* [1] (make noise) «*person/animal*» chillar; «*brakes/tires*» chirriar*, rechinar [2] (inform) (colloq) cantar (fam), chivarse (Esp fam), sapear (Ven fam); **to ~ ON sb** delatar a algn, sapear a algn (Ven fam)

■ **squeal** *vt* chillar, gritar

squeal² *n* (of animal) chillido *m*; (of person) grito *m*, chillido *m*; (of brakes, tires) chirrido *m*; **the children's ~s of laughter** las risas de los niños

squeamish /'skwiːmɪʃ/ *adj* (affected by the sight of blood etc) impresionable, aprensivo; (fastidious) delicado, remilgado; **I'm not ~** a mí no me da asco *or* yo no soy delicado

squeeze¹ /skwiːz/ *n*

A [c] [1] (application of pressure) apretón *m*; **he gave her hand a ~** le dio un apretón de manos; **to put the ~ on sb** (colloq) apretar* a algn [2] (restrictions): **a credit ~** una restricción crediticia; **they are planning a ~ on health and education spending** piensan recortar el presupuesto destinado a salud y educación [3] (hug) apretón *m* [4] (small amount — of toothpaste, glue) poquito *m*, pizca *f*; (— of lemon) gota *f*, chorrito *m*

B (confined, restricted condition) (colloq) (*no pl*): **it will be a (tight) ~** vamos (*or* van *etc*) a estar apretados

squeeze² *vt* [1] (press) ‹*tube/pimple*› apretar*, espichar (Col); ‹*lemon*› exprimir; **he ~d her arm** le apretó el brazo; **to ~ a cloth (out)** retorcer* *or* escurrir un trapo; ***to ~ sb dry*** exprimir a algn, dejar seco a algn (fam) [2] (extract) ‹*liquid/juice*› extraer*, sacar*; **he tried to ~ more money out of them** trató de sacarles más dinero [3] (apply constraints to): **profit margins have been ~d** los márgenes de ganancia se han visto reducidos considerablemente [4] (force, fit) meter; **I can ~ you in tomorrow morning** le puedo hacer un huequito mañana por la mañana

■ **squeeze** *vi*: **they ~d in through the hole** se metieron por el agujero

squeezer /'skwiːzər || 'skwiːzə(r)/ *n* (esp BrE) exprimidor *m*

squelch¹ /skweltʃ/ *vi* «*shoes/hooves*» *hacer* un ruido como de succión*; **they went ~ing through the mud** iban chapoteando por el barro

squelch² *n*: *ruido como de succión*

squib /skwɪb/ *n* (firework) (esp BrE) petardo *m*, buscapiés *m*, vieja *f* (Chi); ***a damp ~*** (BrE colloq) un fiasco

squid /skwɪd/ *n* (*pl* ~) calamar *m*; (small) chipirón *m*; **fried ~** calamares a la romana

squiggle /'skwɪgəl/ *n* [1] (line) garabato *m* [2] (movement) culebreo *m*

squiggly /'skwɪgli/ *adj* **-glier, -gliest** ‹*writing*› garabateado, garrapatoso; ‹*line*› serpenteante

squint¹ /skwɪnt/ *n* (condition) bizquera *f*, estrabismo *m*; **to have a slight ~** ser* un poco bizco

squint² *vi* [1] (attempting to see) entrecerrar* los ojos; **to ~ AT sth/sb** mirar algo/a algn entrecerrando los ojos [2] (be cross-eyed) bizquear, torcer* la vista

squire /skwaɪr || 'skwaɪə(r)/ *n* [1] (Hist, Mil) escudero *m* [2] (in UK: landowner) señor *m*

squirm /skwɜːrm || skwɜːm/ *vi* [1] (move) retorcerse*; **he'll try to ~ out of doing it** va a tratar de librarse de hacerlo, va a tratar de hurtarle *or* (AmL tb) de sacarle el cuerpo [2] (feel embarrassed): **she ~ed with embarrassment** no sabía dónde meterse de la vergüenza

squirrel /skwɜːrl || 'skwɪrəl/ *n* ardilla *f*

squirt¹ /skwɜːrt || skwɜːt/ *n*

A (stream) chorrito *m*

B (person) (colloq) mequetrefe *m* (fam)

squirt² *vt* ‹*liquid*› echar un chorro de; **they ~ed him with water** lo rociaron con agua

■ **squirt** *vi* «*liquid*» salir* a chorros

Sr (= **Senior**) Sr.

Sri Lanka /sriː'lɑːŋkə, ʃriː-/ *n* Sri Lanka *m*

Sri Lankan /sriː'lɑːŋkən, ʃriː/ *adj* esrilanqués

SS (Naut) = **steamship**

SSE (= **south-southeast**) SSE

SSW (= **south-southwest**) SSO

St [1] (= **Saint**) S(an), Sta. **~ Thomas** Sto. Tomás [2] (= **Street**) c/; **21 Baker ~** c/ Baker 21

stab¹ /stæb/ *n* [1] (with knife) puñalada *f*, cuchillada *f*, navajazo *m*; ***a ~ in the back*** una puñalada trapera *or* por la espalda; ***to have** o **make** o **take a ~ at sth*** intentar algo; (*before n*) **~ wound** herida *f* de arma blanca, puñalada *f*, cuchillada *f* [2] (sudden sensation): **a ~ of pain** una punzada de dolor, un dolor punzante *or* agudo; **she felt a sudden ~ of guilt** la acometió un sentimiento de culpabilidad

stab² **-bb-** *vt* (with knife) apuñalar, acuchillar; **he had been ~bed to death** había muerto apuñalado *or* acuchillado; **he ~bed the needle into my arm** me clavó la aguja en el brazo; ***to ~ sb in the back*** darle* una puñalada trapera *or* por la espalda a algn

■ **stab** *vi* [1] **to ~ AT sth/sb**: **he ~bed at the letter/at her with his finger** señalaba la carta/la señalaba golpeándola

S

con el dedo 2 **stabbing** *pres p* ‹*pain/sensation*› punzante

stabbing /'stæbɪŋ/ *n* apuñalamiento *m*

stability /stə'bɪləti/ *n* [u] estabilidad *f*; ~ **pact** (in EU) pacto *m* de estabilidad

stabilize /'steɪbəlaɪz/ *vt* estabilizar*

■ **stabilize** *vi* estabilizarse*

stabilizer /'steɪbəlaɪzər || 'steɪbəlaɪzə(r)/ *n* estabilizador *m*; (Culin) estabilizante *m*

stable[1] /'steɪbəl/ *adj* **-bler, -blest** 1 (firm, steady) ‹*structure/platform*› estable, sólido; ‹*relationship/government*› estable; ‹*economy/currency*› estable; **the patient's condition is** ~ el estado del paciente es estacionario 2 (Psych) equilibrado 3 (Chem, Phys) estable

stable[2] *n* (*often pl*) (for horses) caballeriza *f*, cuadra *f*; (for other livestock) establo *m*; (*before n*) ~ **boy** *o* **lad/girl** mozo *m*/moza *f* de cuadra; ▸ **door 1**

stable[3] *vt* poner* *or* guardar en la cuadra

staccato /stə'kɑːtəʊ/ *adj* (Mus) staccato; ‹*voice/delivery*› entrecortado

stack[1] /stæk/ *n*

A 1 (pile) montón *m*, pila *f* 2 (many, much) (colloq) (*often pl*) montón *m* (fam), pila *f* (AmS fam); **I've got ~s** *o* **a ~ of homework** tengo montones *or* un montón de deberes

B (*chimney* ~) (cañón *m* de) chimenea *f*

stack[2] *vt*

A ~ **(up)** (pile up) amontonar, apilar; **the table was ~ed high with crockery** sobre la mesa había un montón de loza

B (prearrange): **the cards** *o* **odds are ~ed against them** las circunstancias les son desfavorables, llevan las de perder

stadium /'steɪdiəm/ *n* (*pl* **-diums** *or* **-dia**) estadio *m*

staff[1] /stæf || stɑːf/ *n*

A 1 (as group) (+ *sing o pl vb*) personal *m*; **the teaching** ~ el personal docente, el profesorado; **the editorial** ~ los redactores, la redacción; **a member of** ~ un empleado; (*before n*) ~ **meeting** (Educ) reunión *f* de profesores 2 (as individuals) (BrE) (*pl* ~) (+ *pl vb*) empleados *mpl*

B 1 (*pl* **staffs** *or* **staves** /steɪvz/) (stick) bastón *m*; (of bishop) báculo *m*, cayado *m*; ~ **of office** bastón *m* de mando 2 (*flag* ~) asta *f*‡

C (Mus) ▸ **stave B**

staff[2] *vt* proveer* *or* dotar de personal

staff: ~ **nurse** *n* (BrE) enfermero, -ra *m,f* jefe; ~**room** *n* (BrE) sala *f* de profesores

stag /stæg/ *n* ciervo *m*, venado *m*

stage[1] /steɪdʒ/ *n*

A 1 (platform) tablado *m*; (in theater) escenario *m*; **to go on** ~ salir* a escena *or* al escenario; ***to set the ~ for sth*** crear el marco para algo; (*before n*) ~ **designer** escenógrafo, -fa *m,f*; ~ **door** entrada *f* de artistas 2 (medium) **the** ~ el teatro 3 (profession) **the** ~ el teatro, las tablas (period); **to go on the** ~ hacerse* actor/actriz; (*before n*) ‹*actress*› de teatro; ~ **name** nombre *m* artístico

B (in development, activity) fase *f*, etapa *f*; **the early ~s of pregnancy** los primeros meses del embarazo; **at a later** ~ más adelante; **at some** ~ en algún momento; **I'd reached the ~ where I didn't care any more** había llegado a un punto en que ya no me importaba; **by this** ~ a esas alturas; **to do sth in ~s** hacer* algo por etapas

C (of rocket) fase *f*

stage[2] *vt*

A 1 ‹*event*› organizar*, montar; ‹*strike/demonstration*› hacer*; ‹*attack*› llevar a cabo, perpetrar; ‹*coup*› dar*; **she ~d a comeback five years later** hizo su reaparición cinco años más tarde 2 (engineer, arrange) arreglar, orquestar

B (Theat) ‹*play*› poner* en escena, representar

stage: ~**coach** *n* diligencia *f*; ~ **fright** *n* [u] miedo *m* a salir a escena; ~**hand** *n* tramoyista *mf*; ~**manage** *vt* ‹*event*› orquestar, arreglar; ‹*play*› dirigir*; ~ **manager** *n* director, -tora *m,f* de escena; ~**struck** *adj*: **to be ~struck** sentirse* fascinado por el mundo del teatro; ~ **whisper** *n* aparte *m*

stagger /'stægər || 'stægə(r)/ *vi* tambalearse; **she ~ed into the room** entró en la habitación tambaleándose

■ **stagger** *vt*

A (amaze) dejar estupefacto *or* helado *or* pasmado

B ‹*shifts/payments*› escalonar

staggered /'stægərd || 'stægəd/ *adj*

A (amazed) estupefacto, helado, pasmado; **I was absolutely** ~ me quedé estupefacto *or* helado *or* pasmado

B (alternating): ~ **junction** empalmes *mpl* contrarios sucesivos; ~ **working hours** horario *m* escalonado

staggering /'stægərɪŋ/ *adj* asombroso, sorprendente

staging /'steɪdʒɪŋ/ *n* (Theat) puesta *f* en escena, montaje *m*

stagnant /'stægnənt/ *adj* 1 ‹*water*› estancado; ‹*pool*› de agua estancada 2 ‹*economy/industry*› estancado

stagnate /'stægneɪt || stæg'neɪt/ *vi* «*water*» estancarse*; «*economy/industry*» estancarse*; «*person*» anquilosarse

stagnation /stæg'neɪʃən/ *n* estancamiento *m*

stag: ~ **night** *n* 1 (for men only): **Thursday is ~ night at Harry's Bar** los jueves abren sólo para hombres en Harry's Bar 2 ▸ ~ **party 1**; ~ **party** *n* 1 (before wedding) despedida *f* de soltero 2 (all-male celebration) fiesta *f* para hombres, noche *f* de cuates (Méx)

staid /steɪd/ *adj* **-er, -est** serio, formal; ‹*clothes*› serio, sobrio; (pej) aburrido

stain[1] /steɪn/ *n* 1 (dirty mark) mancha *f* 2 (dye) tintura *f*, tinte *m* 3 (on character) mancha *f*, mácula *f* (liter)

stain[2] *vt* 1 (mark) ‹*clothes/skin*› manchar; **to be ~ed WITH sth** estar* manchado DE algo 2 (dye) ‹*wood*› teñir*

■ **stain** *vi* 1 «*wine/tea*» manchar 2 «*fabric*» mancharse

stained glass /steɪnd/ *n* [u] vidrio *m* *or* cristal *m* de colores; (*before n*) ~ ~ **window** vitral *m*, vidriera *f* (de colores)

stainless /'steɪnləs || 'steɪnlɪs/ *n* [u] (AmE colloq) acero *m* inoxidable

stainless steel *n* [u] acero *m* inoxidable; (*before n*) ‹*blade/cutlery*› de acero inoxidable

stain remover *n* [c u] quitamanchas *m*

stair /ster || steə(r)/ *n* 1 **stairs** *pl* (flight of stairs, stairway) escalera(s) *f(pl)*; **life below ~s** (BrE) la vida de la servidumbre 2 (single step) escalón *m*, peldaño *m*

stair: ~**case** *n* escalera(s) *f(pl)*; ~**lift** /'sterlɪft || 'steəlɪft/ *n* salvaescaleras *m*, subescaleras *m*; ~**way** *n* escalera(s) *f(pl)*; ~**well** *n* caja *f* *or* hueco *m* de la escalera

stake[1] /steɪk/ *n*

A (pole) estaca *f*; **to be burned at the** ~ ser* quemado en la hoguera; ***to pull up ~s*** (AmE colloq) levantar campamento

B 1 (bet) apuesta *f*; **the ~s are high** es mucho lo que está en juego; **to be at** ~ estar* en juego; **she has too much at** ~ se juega demasiado en ello 2 (interest): **to have a ~ in a company** tener* participación *or* intereses en una compañía; **we parents naturally have a ~ in our children's future** como padres es natural que nos incumba el futuro de nuestros hijos

C **stakes** *pl*: **she's second in the popularity ~s** ocupa el segundo lugar en el índice de popularidad

stake[2] *vt*

A (risk) ‹*money/reputation/life*› jugarse*; **to ~ sth ON sth**: **I'd ~ my last dime on it** me jugaría hasta el último centavo a que es así

B 1 (mark with stakes) marcar* con estacas, estacar*; **the government was quick to ~ its claim** el gobierno se apresuró a reclamar su parte 2 ‹*tree/plant*› arrodrigar*

Phrasal verb

• **stake out** [v ▸ o ▸ adv, v ▸ adv ▸ o] (colloq) mantener* vigilado

stakeholder /'steɪk,həʊldər || 'steɪk,həʊldə(r)/ *n* 1 (in gambling) depositario, -ria *m,f* de una apuesta; (in purchases) depositario, -ria *m,f* de una entrega *or* (AmL) cuota inicial, depositario, -ria *m,f* de una entrada (Esp), depositario, -ria *m,f* de un pie (Chi) 2 (interested party) interesado, -da *m,f*

stakeout /'steɪkaʊt/ *n* (sl) operación *f* de vigilancia

stalactite /stə'læktaɪt || 'stæləktaɪt/ *n* estalactita *f*

stalagmite /stə'lægmaɪt || 'stæləgmaɪt/ *n* estalagmita *f*

stale /steɪl/ *adj* **staler, stalest** 1 ‹*bread*› no fresco, añejo (fam); (hard) duro; ‹*butter/cheese*› rancio; ‹*beer*› pasado; ‹*air*› viciado 2 (hackneyed) ‹*joke/news*› añejo, viejo; ‹*ideas*› trasnochado

stalemate /'steɪlmeɪt/ *n* [u c] (in chess) tablas *fpl* (*por ahogar al rey*); **to be at/to reach a ~** estar* en/llegar a un punto muerto *or* un impasse

stalk¹ /stɔːk/ *n* (of plant) tallo *m*; (of leaf, flower) pedúnculo *m*, tallo *m*; (of fruit) rabillo *m*, cabito *m* (RPl)

stalk² *vt* ‹*prey/game*› acechar; **famine ~s the land** (liter) la hambruna asola la región (*or* el país *etc*)

■ **stalk** *vi*: **she ~ed off without a word** se fue muy ofendida (*or* indignada *etc*) sin decir palabra

stalker /'stɔːkər || 'stɔːkə(r)/ *n* 1 (of animals) acechador, -dora *m,f* 2 (of person) asediador, -dora *m,f*, acosador, -dora *m,f*, acechador, -dora *m,f*

stalking horse /'stɔːkɪŋ/ *n* (Pol) *candidato presentado para favorecer a otro, dividir a la oposición etc*

stall¹ /stɔːl/ *n*

A (in market) puesto *m*, tenderete *m*

B 1 **stalls** *pl* (in theater, movie house) (BrE) platea *f*, patio *m* de butacas, luneta *f* (Col, Méx) 2 (in church): **the choir ~s** la sillería del coro

C (in stable) compartimiento *m*

stall² *vi*

A «*engine/car*» pararse, ahogarse, calarse (Esp), atascarse* (Méx); «*plane*» entrar en pérdida

B (come to standstill) «*talks*» estancarse*, llegar* a un punto muerto *or* a un impasse

C (play for time) (colloq): **quit ~ing** no andes con rodeos *or* con evasivas; **~ing tactics** maniobras *fpl* dilatorias

■ **stall** *vt*

A ‹*engine/car*› parar, ahogar*, calar (Esp), atascar* (Méx); ‹*plane*› hacer* entrar en pérdida

B ‹*negotiations/growth*› paralizar*

C (delay) (colloq) entretener*; **try and ~ her** trata de entretenerla

stallholder /'stɔːlˌhəʊldər/ *n* (esp BrE) puestero, -ra *m,f* (AmL) (*persona que tiene un puesto en un mercado*)

stallion /'stæljən/ *n* semental *m*

stalwart¹ /'stɔːlwərt || 'stɔːlwət/ *adj* ‹*supporter*› incondicional, fiel; ‹*faith*› inquebrantable

stalwart² *n* incondicional *mf*

stamen /'steɪmən/ *n* estambre *m*

stamina /'stæmənə || 'stæmɪnə/ *n* [u] resistencia *f*

stammer¹ /'stæmər || 'stæmə(r)/ *n* tartamudeo *m*; **to speak with a ~** tartamudear

stammer² *vi* tartamudear

■ **stammer** *vt* ‹*reply/apology*› balbucear, farfullar

stamp¹ /stæmp/ *n*

A 1 (*postage ~*) sello *m*, estampilla *f* (AmL), timbre *m* (Méx); (*before n*) **~ collecting** filatelia *f*; **~ collector** coleccionista *mf* de sellos (*or* estampillas *etc*), filatelista *mf* 2 (*trading ~*) cupón *m*, vale *m*

B 1 (instrument) sello *m*, timbre *m* (Chi); (*rubber ~*) sello *m or* (Chi tb) timbre *m* (de goma); **metal ~** cuño *m*, sello *m* 2 (printed mark) sello *m*

C (character) impronta *f*; **the ~ of genius** la impronta *or* el sello (distintivo) de la genialidad; **she left her ~ on the institute** dejó su impronta *or* huella en el instituto

stamp² *vt*

A (with foot) ‹*ground*› dar* una patada en; **to ~ one's foot** dar* una patada en el suelo; **to ~ sth down** apisonar algo

B ‹*letter/parcel*› franquear, ponerle* sellos (*or* estampillas *etc*) a, estampillar (AmL), timbrar (Méx); **a ~ed addressed envelope** un sobre franqueado *or* (AmL tb) estampillado *or* (Méx) timbrado con su dirección

C 1 ‹*passport/ticket*› sellar 2 ‹*coin*› acuñar, troquelar; **the words were ~ed on her memory** tenía las palabras grabadas en la memoria; **she ~ed her personal style on the company** le imprimió su sello personal a la compañía

■ **stamp** *vi* 1 (with foot) «*person*» dar* patadas en el suelo; «*horse*» piafar; **he ~ed on the spider** le dio un pisotón a la araña 2 (walk): **she ~ed upstairs** subió la escalera pisando fuerte

Phrasal verbs

• **stamp on** [v ▸ prep ▸ o] ‹*proposal*› rechazar* de plano; ‹*attempt*› sofocar*, aplastar

• **stamp out** [v ▸ o ▸ adv, v ▸ adv ▸ o] 1 ‹*fire*› apagar* (con los pies) 2 (suppress) ‹*resistance*› aplastar; ‹*rebellion*› sofocar*; ‹*crime*› erradicar*, acabar con 3 (punch out) ‹*shape*› troquelar

stamp duty *n* [u c] (BrE) timbrado *m or* sellado *m* fiscal

stampede¹ /stæm'piːd/ *n* estampida *f*, desbandada *f*; **there was a ~ toward the exit/to buy shares** la gente se precipitó hacia la salida/se lanzó a comprar acciones

stampede² *vt* 1 ‹*cattle/horses*› hacer* salir en estampida *or* desbandada 2 (force, push) empujar; **they were ~d into a hasty decision** los empujaron a tomar una decisión precipitada

■ **stampede** *vi* «*herd/crowd*» salir* en estampida

stamping ground /'stæmpɪŋ/ *n* (colloq) territorio *m*

stamp tax *n* [u c] (AmE) timbrado *m or* sellado *m* fiscal

stance /stæns || stɑːns/ *n* 1 (attitude, viewpoint) postura *f*, posición *f*; **to take a tough ~ on sth** adoptar una postura firme (con) respecto a algo 2 (physical) postura *f*

stanch /stɔːntʃ/ *vt* ‹*bleeding*› contener*; ‹*cut*› restañar

stand¹ /stænd/ *n*

A 1 (position) lugar *m*, sitio *m* 2 (attitude) postura *f*, posición *f*; **to take a ~ on sth** adoptar una postura *or* posición (con) respecto a algo 3 (resistance) resistencia *f*; **to make a ~ against sth** oponer* resistencia a algo; **Custer's Last S~** la última batalla de Custer

B 1 (pedestal, base) pie *m*, base *f* 2 (for sheet music) atril *m* 3 (for coats, hats) perchero *m*

C (at fair, exhibition) stand *m*, caseta *f*; (larger) pabellón *m*; **newspaper ~** puesto *m* de periódicos; **a hot-dog ~** (esp AmE) un puesto de perritos calientes

D (for spectators) (*often pl*) tribuna *f*

E (witness box) (AmE) estrado *m*; **to take the ~** subir al estrado

stand² (*past & past p* **stood**) *vi*

A 1 (be, remain upright) «*person*» estar* de pie, estar* parado (AmL): **I was so tired I could hardly ~** estaba tan cansado que apenas podía tenerme en pie; **I've been ~ing here for hours** llevo horas aquí de pie *or* (AmL) aquí parado; **she was ~ing at the window** estaba junto a la ventana 2 (rise) levantarse, ponerse* de pie, pararse (AmL); **her hair stood on end** se le pusieron los pelos de punta, se le pararon los pelos (AmL); *see also* **stand up** 3 (in height): **the tower ~s 30 meters high** la torre tiene *or* mide 30 metros de altura

B (move, take up position) ponerse*, pararse (AmL); **~ over there** ponte *or* (AmL tb) párate allí; **~ clear!** ¡apártense!; **he stood on a chair** se subió a *or* (AmL tb) se paró en una silla; **to ~ aside** hacerse* a un lado, apartarse; **can you ~ on your head?** ¿sabes pararte de cabeza *or* (Esp) hacer el pino?; **you stood on my toe!** ¡me pisaste!

C 1 (be situated, located): **the chapel ~s on the site of a pagan temple** la capilla ocupa el lugar de un antiguo templo pagano; **a church stood here long ago** hace mucho tiempo aquí había una iglesia; **I won't ~ in your way** no seré yo quien te lo impida 2 (hold position): **where do you ~ on this issue?** ¿cuál es tu posición en cuanto a este problema?; **he ~s high in their esteem** lo tienen en mucha estima; **you never know where you ~ with him** con él uno nunca sabe a qué atenerse 3 (be mounted, fixed): **a hut ~ing on wooden piles** una choza construida *or* que descansa sobre pilotes de madera

D 1 (stop, remain still) «*person*»: **they stood and stared** se quedaron mirando; **don't just ~ there!** ¡no te quedes ahí parado!; **I was left ~ing there looking like a fool** me dejaron allí plantado como un tonto; **can't you ~ still for two minutes?** ¿no puedes estarte quieto un minuto?; **time stood still** el tiempo se detuvo; **the train ~ing at platform five** el tren que está en el andén número cinco; Ⓢ **no standing** (AmE) estacionamiento prohibido, prohibido estacionarse; **to ~ firm** *o* **fast** mantenerse* firme; ***to leave sb ~ing*** dejar muy atrás a algn 2 (remain undisturbed) «*batter/water*»: **leave to ~** dejar reposar; **water stood in puddles on the floor** había charcos de agua en el suelo 3 (survive, last): **these walls have stood for centuries** estas paredes tienen cientos de años; **the tower is still ~ing** la torre sigue en pie

E (remain unchanged, valid) «*law/agreement*» seguir* vigente *or* en vigor; **the offer still ~s** la oferta sigue en pie; **what I said still ~s** lo que dije sigue siendo válido; **his argument ~s or falls on this point** todo su argumento depende de este punto

S

F 1 (be): **the house ~s empty** la casa está vacía; **he ~s accused of treason** se lo acusa de traición; **I ~ corrected** tienes razón 2 (be currently): **as things ~** tal (y) como están las cosas; **to ~ AT sth: unemployment ~s at 17%** el desempleo alcanza el 17%; **receipts ~ at $150,000** el total recaudado asciende a 150.000 dólares 3 (be likely to) **to ~ to + INF: he ~s to lose a fortune** puede llegar a perder una fortuna; **what does she ~ to gain out of this?** ¿qué es lo que puede ganar con esto ?
G (for office, election) (BrE) presentarse (como candidato); **to ~ FOR sth: she is ~ing for the presidency** se va a presentar como candidata a la presidencia
■ **stand** *vt*
A (place) poner*; (carefully, precisely) colocar*; **he stood the ladder against the wall** puso *or* colocó *or* apoyó la escalera contra la pared; **he stood himself near the door** se puso cerca de la puerta
B 1 (tolerate, bear) (*with* **can, can't, won't**) ‹*pain/noise*› aguantar, soportar; **I can't ~ him** no lo aguanto *or* soporto, no lo trago (fam); **I can't ~ the sight of him** no lo puedo ni ver; **I can't ~ it any longer!** ¡no puedo más!, ¡no aguanto más!; **to ~ -ING: she can't ~ being interrupted** no soporta *or* no tolera que la interrumpan 2 (withstand) ‹*heat/strain*› soportar, resistir; **the chair won't ~ his weight** la silla no le va a aguantar su peso; **to ~ the test of time** resistir el paso del tiempo
C (pay for) ‹*drink/dinner*› invitar a

Phrasal verbs

- **stand apart** [v ▸ adv] **to ~ apart (FROM sth)** 1 (be distinguished) distinguirse* (DE algo) 2 (hold aloof) distanciarse (DE algo)
- **stand back** [v ▸ adv] 1 (move away) **to ~ back (FROM sth)** apartarse *or* alejarse (DE algo) 2 (become detached) **to ~ back (FROM sth)** distanciarse (DE algo)
- **stand by**

A [v ▸ adv] 1 (remain uninvolved) mantenerse* al margen; **people just stood by and did nothing** la gente estaba allí mirando sin hacer nada 2 (be at readiness) «*army/troops*» estar* en estado de alerta; **we'll be ~ing by in case you need us** allí estaremos por si nos necesitan; **~ by for take-off!** ¡listos para despegar!
B [v ▸ prep ▸ o] 1 ‹*promise*› mantener*; ‹*decision*› atenerse* a; **I ~ by what I said earlier** me atengo a lo que dije antes; **I ~ by my offer** mi oferta sigue en pie 2 (support) ‹*friend*› apoyar, no abandonar

- **stand down** [v ▸ adv] 1 (relinquish position) retirarse; (resign) renunciar, dimitir 2 (Law) «*witness*» abandonar el estrado
- **stand for** [v ▸ prep ▸ o] 1 (represent) «*initials/symbol*» significar*; **what does PS ~ for?** ¿qué significa PS?; **CTI ~s for ...** CTI son las siglas de ...; **he has betrayed everything he once stood for** ha traicionado todo aquello con lo que se lo solía identificar 2 (put up with) (*usu with neg*) consentir*, tolerar
- **stand in** [v ▸ adv] **to ~ in FOR sb** sustituir* a algn
- **stand out** [v ▸ adv]

A 1 (project) **to ~ out (FROM sth)** sobresalir* (DE algo) 2 (be conspicuous, contrast) sobresalir*, destacar(se)*; **the phrase is underlined to make it ~ out** la frase está subrayada para que resalte
B (be firm, hold out) **to ~ out AGAINST sth/sb** oponerse* firmemente A algo/algn; **to ~ out FOR sth** luchar POR algo

- **stand over** [v ▸ prep ▸ o] (supervise, watch closely) vigilar; **I can't work with somebody ~ing over me** no puedo trabajar con alguien mirándome
- **stand up**

A [v ▸ adv] 1 (get up) ponerse* de pie, levantarse, pararse (AmL); ***to ~ up and be counted*** dar* la cara por sus (*or* mis *etc*) principios (*or* creencias *etc*) 2 (be, remain standing): **~ up straight** ponte derecho; **the tripod won't ~ up properly** el trípode no se sostiene bien 3 (endure, withstand wear) resistir; **this evidence wouldn't ~ up in court** cualquier tribunal desestimaría estas pruebas; **to ~ up TO sth** ‹*to cold/pressure*› resistir *or* soportar algo; **the argument doesn't ~ up to close examination** el argumento no resiste un análisis minucioso; *see also* **stand up to**
B [v ▸ o ▸ adv] 1 (set upright) poner* de pie, levantar 2 (not keep appointment with) (colloq) dejar plantado a (fam)

- **stand up for** [v ▸ adv ▸ prep ▸ o] defender*; **I can ~ up for myself** me puedo defender solo
- **stand up to** [v ▸ adv ▸ prep ▸ o] ‹*person/threats*› hacerle* frente a; *see also* **stand up A3**

standalone /ˈstændəˈləʊn/ *adj* (*before n*) autónomo

standard¹ /ˈstændərd || ˈstændəd/ *n*
A 1 (level) nivel *m*; (quality) calidad *f*; **your typing is not of the required ~** tu mecanografía no está al nivel de lo que se exige; **the ~ of education leaves much to be desired** la calidad de la educación deja mucho que desear; **~ of living** nivel *m or* estándar *m* de vida 2 (norm): **she sets very high ~s** exige un estándar *or* nivel muy alto; **the product was below ~** el producto no era de la calidad requerida; **up to ~** del nivel requerido *or* de la calidad requerida 3 (official measure) estándar *m*
B 1 (yardstick) criterio *m*, parámetro *m*; **even by Mafia ~s** incluso para la mafia; **by any** *o* **anybody's ~s** se mire por donde se mire *or* desde cualquier punto de vista 2 **standards** *pl* (moral principles) principios *mpl*; **declining ~s in society** decadencia moral en la sociedad
C (flag, emblem) estandarte *m*

standard² *adj*
A (normal) ‹*size*› estándar *adj inv*, normal; ‹*model*› (Auto) estándar *adj inv*, de serie; ‹*procedure*› habitual; ‹*reaction*› típico, normal; **it's ~ (practice) to ask for security** pedir garantías es la norma, se suele pedir garantías
B (officially established) ‹*weight/measure*› estándar *adj inv*, oficial; **~ time** hora *f* oficial
C 1 ‹*work/reference*› clásico 2 ‹*English/French/pronunciation*› estándar *adj inv*

standard: **~-bearer** *n* abanderado, -da *m,f*, portaestandarte *mf*; (leader) adalid *mf*, abanderado, -da *m,f*; **~-class** *adj* (in UK) (Rail) ‹*ticket/carriage*› de segunda (clase); **~-issue** /ˌstændərdˈɪʃuː || ˌstændədˈɪsjuː/ *adj* 1 (in armed forces) ‹*rations/uniform*› reglamentario 2 (unexceptional) normal y corriente, común y corriente (AmL)

standardization /ˈstændərdəˈzeɪʃən/ *n* [u] estandarización *f*

standardize /ˈstændərdaɪz/ *vt* estandarizar*

standard lamp *n* (BrE) lámpara *f* de pie

standby¹ /ˈstændbaɪ/ *n* (*pl* **-bys**) 1 (thing, person one can turn to): **frozen meals are a useful ~** las comidas congeladas son muy socorridas; **you should always carry a spare fan belt as a ~** siempre se debe llevar una correa de ventilador de repuesto por lo que pudiera pasar 2 (state of readiness): **to be on ~** «*police/squadron*» estar* en estado de alerta; «*engineer*» estar* de guardia; «*appliance*» estar* en posición de espera *or* en standby; (*before n*) **~ time** tiempo *m* de autonomía 3 **~ (ticket)** (Aviat) pasaje *m or* (Esp) billete *m* stand-by

standby² *adj* (*before n*) 1 (ready for emergency) de emergencia, de reserva; **to be on ~ duty** estar* de guardia 2 (Aviat) ‹*passenger/ticket/fare*› stand-by *adj inv*

standby³ *adv* ‹*fly/go*› stand-by

standee /ˈstænˈdiː/ *n* (AmE) *espectador o pasajero de pie*

stand-in /ˈstændɪn/ *n* suplente *mf*; (Cin) doble *mf*

standing¹ /ˈstændɪŋ/ *n* [u] 1 (position) posición *f*; (prestige) prestigio *m*; **his ~ in the community** la posición que tiene en la comunidad; **she's in very good ~ with the party chiefs** los jefes del partido la tienen en gran estima 2 (duration): **an agreement of long ~** un acuerdo vigente desde hace tiempo; **friends of more than 20 years' ~** amigos desde hace más de 20 años

standing² *adj* (*before n, no comp*) 1 (permanent) permanente; **~ charge** cuota *f* fija; (for utilities) cuota *f* abono; **~ committee** comisión *f* permanente; **we have a ~ invitation to stay with them** estamos invitados a ir a quedarnos en su casa cuando queramos; **it's a ~ joke that he never pays for a single drink** tiene fama de no invitar nunca a una copa 2 (upright, not seated) ‹*passenger*› de pie, parado (AmL); **~ room only!** ¡no quedan asientos!

standing order *n* 1 (with bank) (BrE) orden *f* permanente de pago 2 (with supplier) pedido *m* fijo

standoff /ˈstændɔːf || ˈstændɒf/ *n* (AmE) 1 (tie, draw) empate *m* 2 (deadlock) callejón *m* sin salida

standoffish /ˈstændˈɔːfɪʃ/ *adj* distante, estirado (fam)

stand: **~pipe** *n* (BrE) *grifo que se instala provisionalmente en la calle*; **~point** *n* punto *m* de vista; **~still** *n* (*no pl*): **to bring sth to a ~still** ‹*activity/production*› paralizar* algo; ‹*vehicle/machine*› parar algo; **the whole town came to a ~still** la ciudad quedó totalmente paralizada; **the traffic**

was at a ~still el tráfico estaba paralizado; **~up** *adj* (*before n*): **a ~up comic** un cómico de micrófono; **a ~up argument** una discusión violenta; **it turned into a ~up fight** se fueron a las manos

stank /stæŋk/ *past of* **stink**[2]

stanza /'stænzə/ *n* (*pl* **-zas**) estrofa *f*

staple[1] /'steɪpəl/ *n*

A (for fastening paper, cloth etc) grapa *f*, ganchito *m*, corchete *m* (Chi); (*before n*) **~ gun** grapadora *f*, engrapadora *f* (AmL)

B **1** (basic food) alimento *m* básico **2** (principal product) producto *m* principal **3** (raw material) materia *f* prima

staple[2] *adj* ‹*food/ingredient*› básico; ‹*industry*› principal; **rice is their ~ diet** se alimentan principalmente a base de arroz

staple[3] *vt* grapar, engrapar (AmL), corchetear (Chi); **to ~ sth together** grapar *or* (AmL tb) engrapar *or* (Chi) corchetear algo

stapler /'steɪplər/ *n* grapadora *f*, engrapadora *f* (AmL)

star[1] /stɑːr || stɑː(r)/ *n*

A (Astrol, Astron) (astral body) astro *m*; (visible in the sky at night) estrella *f*; **to be born under a lucky ~** nacer* con buena estrella; ***to see ~s*** ver* las estrellas; ***to thank one's lucky ~s*** (colloq) dar* gracias al cielo; (*before n*) **~ sign** signo *m* del zodíaco

B (symbol) estrella *f*; (asterisk) asterisco *m*; **a four-~ hotel** un hotel de cuatro estrellas; **two-/four-~ petrol** (BrE) gasolina *f or* (RPl) nafta *f* normal/súper, bencina *f* corriente/especial (Andes)

C (celebrity) estrella *f*; (*before n*) **~ attraction** atracción *f* estelar *or* especial; **~ quality** madera de estrella; **~ witness** testigo *mf* principal

star[2] **-rr-** *vt*

A (Cin, Theat, TV): **the famous film which ~red Bogart and Bergman** la famosa película que tuvo como protagonistas a Bogart y Bergman; **'2005', ~ring Mike Kirnon** '2005', con (la actuación estelar de) Mike Kirnon

B (mark) ‹*passage/items*› marcar* con un asterisco

■ **star** *vi*: **she has ~red in several films** ha protagonizado varias películas

starboard[1] /'stɑːrbərd/ *n* [u] estribor *m*; **to ~** a estribor

starboard[2] *adj* (*before n*) de estribor

starch[1] /stɑːrtʃ || stɑːtʃ/ *n* **1** [u] almidón *m* **2** (starchy food) fécula *f*, almidón *m*

starch[2] *vt* almidonar

starchy /'stɑːrtʃi || 'stɑːtʃi/ *adj* **-chier, -chiest** **1** ‹*diet*› a base de féculas *or* de almidones **2** ‹*person/attitude*› almidonado, ceremonioso, acartonado

stardom /'stɑːrdəm || 'stɑːdəm/ *n* [u] estrellato *m*; **to rise to ~** alcanzar* el estrellato

stardust /'stɑːrdʌst || 'stɑːdʌst/ *n* [u] polvo *m* de estrellas; ***to have ~ in one's eyes*** estar* lleno de ilusiones

stare[1] /ster || steə(r)/ *vi* mirar (*fijamente*); **it's rude to ~** es de mala educación quedarse mirando a la gente *or* clavarle los ojos a la gente; **to ~ AT sb/sth**: **we ~d at each other** nos quedamos mirando; **what are you staring at?** ¿qué miras?; **he ~d at her** le clavó los ojos, se la quedó mirando de hito en hito (liter); **he was staring at the portrait** tenía los ojos clavados en el retrato; **I ~d back at her** le sostuve la mirada; **she sat staring into space** estaba sentada mirando al vacío

stare[2] *n* mirada *f* (*fija*); **she gave him a defiant ~** lo miró desafiante *or* le lanzó una mirada desafiante

star: **~fish** *n* (*pl* **-fish**) estrella *f* de mar; **~gazing** /'stɑːr'geɪzɪŋ/ *n* [u] observación *f* de los astros

stark[1] /stɑːrk || stɑːk/ *adj* **-er, -est** ‹*landscape*› agreste, inhóspito; ‹*truth*› escueto, desnudo; ‹*realism*› descarnado, crudo; **in ~ contrast** en marcado contraste

stark[2] *adv*: **~ naked** completamente desnudo, en cueros (vivos) (fam), encuerado (Méx fam), calato (Per fam); **to be ~ raving mad** (colloq) estar* loco de atar (fam)

starkers /'stɑːrkərz || 'stɑːkəz/ *adj* (BrE colloq & hum) (*pred*) completamente desnudo, en cueros (vivos) (fam), encuerado (Méx fam), calato (Per fam)

starkly /'stɑːrkli || 'stɑːkli/ *adv* ‹*portrayed/revealed*› de forma descarnada, crudamente

starlet /'stɑːrlət || 'stɑːlɪt/ *n* starlet(te) *f* (*joven actriz que aspira al estrellato*)

starlight /'stɑːrlaɪt || 'stɑːlaɪt/ *n* [u] luz *f* de las estrellas

starling /'stɑːrlɪŋ || 'stɑːlɪŋ/ *n* estornino *m*

starlit /'stɑːrlɪt / *adj* iluminado por la luz de las estrellas

starry /'stɑːri/ *adj* **-rier, -riest** estrellado

starry-eyed /'stɑːri'aɪd/ *adj* **1** (full of illusions) ‹*person*› iluso, soñador **2** (dreamy): **she gazed at him all ~** lo miraba arrobada

star: **~s and Stripes** *n* **the S~s and Stripes** la bandera de los EEUU, la bandera de las barras y las estrellas; **~-spangled** /'stɑːr,spæŋgəld || 'stɑː,spæŋgəld/ *adj* (liter) ‹*sky/heavens*› tachonado de estrellas (liter); **~-Spangled Banner** *n* **the S~ Spangled Banner** **1** (Mus) el himno de las barras y las estrellas (*himno nacional de EEUU*) **2** ▸**S~s and Stripes**; **~-studded** /'stɑːr,stʌdəd || 'stɑː,stʌdɪd/ *adj* ‹*sky*› (liter) tachonado de estrellas (liter); **a ~-studded cast** un reparto estelar

> **Stars and Stripes**
>
> La bandera de EEUU. Sus cincuenta estrellas (*stars*) representan los cincuenta estados y las trece franjas horizontales representan las primeras colonias que constituyeron Estados Unidos en la época de la independencia. También recibe el nombre de *Old Glory* o *Star-spangled banner*

start[1] /stɑːrt || stɑːt/ *n*

A **1** (beginning) principio *m*, comienzo *m*; **at the ~** al principio, al comienzo; **from the ~** desde el principio *or* comienzo; **from ~ to finish** del principio al fin, desde el principio hasta el fin; **to make a ~ (ON sth)** empezar* algo; **to make an early ~** empezar* temprano; (on a journey) salir* temprano, ponerse* en camino a primera hora; **to make a fresh** *o* **new ~** empezar* *or* comenzar* de nuevo; **to get (sth) off to a good/bad ~** empezar* (algo) bien *or* con el pie derecho/mal *or* con el pie izquierdo **2** **for a ~** (*as linker*) para empezar

B (Sport) **1** (of race) salida *f* **2** (lead, advantage) ventaja *f*

C (jump): **to give a ~** «*person/horse*» dar* un respingo; **to give sb a ~** darle* *or* pegarle* un susto a algn, asustar a algn; **I woke up with a ~** me desperté sobresaltado

start[2] *vt*

A (begin) ‹*conversation/journey/negotiations*› empezar*, comenzar*, iniciar; ‹*job/course*› empezar*, comenzar*; **I ~ work at eight** empiezo *or* entro a trabajar a las ocho; **don't ~ that again!** ¡no vuelvas con eso!; **to ~ -ING, to ~ to + INF** empezar* A + INF

B (cause to begin) ‹*race*› dar* comienzo a, largar* (CS, Méx); ‹*fire/epidemic*› provocar*; ‹*argument/fight*› empezar*; ‹*war*› «*incident*» desencadenar; **we want to ~ a family** queremos empezar a tener hijos; **her words ~ed me thinking** sus palabras me dieron que pensar; ***to get sb ~ed*** (colloq) darle* cuerda a algn (fam)

C (establish) ‹*business*› abrir*, montar; ‹*organization*› fundar

D (cause to operate) ‹*engine/dishwasher*› encender*, prender (AmL); ‹*car*› arrancar*, hacer* partir (Chi)

■ **start** *vi*

(Sense I)

A **1** (begin) «*school/term/meeting*» empezar*, comenzar*, iniciarse (frml); «*noise/pain/journey/race*» empezar*, comenzar*; **prices ~ at $30** cuestan a partir de 30 dólares; **to get ~ed** empezar*, comenzar*; **to ~ again** *o* (AmE also) **over** volver* a empezar, empezar* *or* comenzar* de nuevo; **to ~ BY -ING** empezar* POR + INF; **the tour ~s from the station** la excursión sale de la estación; **~ing (from) next January** a partir del próximo mes de enero **2** **to ~ with** (*as linker*): primero *or* para empezar; **I was optimistic to ~ with** al principio estaba llena de optimismo

B **1** (originate) empezar*, originarse; **it all ~ed from an idea I had as a student** todo surgió de una idea que tuve cuando era estudiante **2** (be founded) ser* fundado

C (set out) (+ *adv compl*): **to ~ back** emprender el regreso; **it's time we ~ed (for) home** es hora de volver a casa, es hora de que nos pongamos en camino a casa; **we ~ from the hotel at six** salimos del hotel a las seis

D (begin to operate) «*car*» arrancar*, partir (Chi); «*dishwasher*» empezar* a funcionar, ponerse* en marcha

(Sense II) (move suddenly) dar* un respingo; (be frightened) asustarse, sobresaltarse; **I ~ed (up) from my chair** me levanté de la silla de un salto; **she ~ed at the noise** el ruido la sobresaltó *or* la asustó

S

Phrasal verbs

- **start off**

A [v ▸ adv] 1 ▸**start out 1** 2 (begin moving) arrancar* 3 (begin) empezar*; **to ~ off ON sth: she ~ed off on a lengthy explanation** se embarcó en una larga explicación, empezó a dar una larga explicación

B [v ▸ o ▸ adv, v ▸ adv ▸ o] (begin) ‹*discussion/concert*› empezar*

C [v ▸ o ▸ adv] (get sb started): **I'll do the first one, just to ~ you off** yo haré el primero, para ayudarte a empezar; **to ~ sb off ON sth: I ~ed them off on some scales** para empezar, los puse a hacer unas escalas; **don't ~ him off on politics!** (colloq) ¡no le des cuerda para que empiece a hablar de política! (fam)

- **start on** [v ▸ prep ▸ o]

A (begin) ‹*cleaning/book*› empezar* (con)

B (criticize) (colloq) meterse con (fam)

- **start out** [v ▸ adv] 1 (set out) salir*, partir (frml) 2 (in life, career) empezar* 3 (begin) **to ~ out (BY) -ING: I ~ed out liking him** al principio me gustaba; **we ~ed out (by) thinking it would be easy** empezamos pensando que sería fácil

- **start over** (AmE) [v ▸ adv] [v ▸ o ▸ adv] volver* a empezar, empezar* *or* comenzar* de nuevo

- **start up**

A [v ▸ adv] 1 ▸**start** *vi Sense* I D 2 (begin business) empezar* 3 (begin activity) «*music/siren*» empezar* a sonar; «*band*» empezar* a tocar

B [v ▸ o ▸ adv, v ▸ adv ▸ o] 1 ‹*engine/car/machinery*› arrancar*, poner* en marcha, hacer* partir (Chi) 2 ‹*business*› montar, poner* en marcha 3 ‹*conversation*› entablar; ‹*discussion*› empezar*

starter /'stɑːrtər || 'stɑːtə(r)/ *n*

A (Culin) entrada *f*, primer plato *m*, entrante *m* (Esp); ***for ~s*** (colloq) para empezar

B (Sport) 1 (official) juez *mf* de salida 2 (competitor) participante *mf*, competidor, -dora *m,f*

C (Auto) motor *m* de arranque

starting /'stɑːrtɪŋ || 'stɑːtɪŋ/: **~ block** *n* (*usu pl*) bloque *m* de salida; **~ gate** *n* cajones *mpl* de salida, arrancadero *m* automático (Méx), partidor *m* automático (Col); **~ grid** *n* parrilla *f* de salida, parrilla *f* de largada (CS); **~ line** *n* línea *f* de salida; **~ point** *n* **~ point (FOR sth)** punto *m* de partida (DE/PARA algo); **~ price** *n* (Sport) cotización *f* inicial; **~ salary** *n* sueldo *m* inicial

startle /'stɑːrtl̩ || 'stɑːtl̩/ *vt* sobresaltar, asustar

startling /'stɑːrtlɪŋ || 'stɑːtlɪŋ/ *adj* 1 (surprising) asombroso, sorprendente; ‹*similarity/coincidence*› extraordinario 2 (alarming) ‹*report/increase*› alarmante

start-up /'stɑːrtʌp || 'stɑːtʌp/ *adj* ‹*capital/costs*› inicial

starvation /stɑːr'veɪʃən || stɑː'veɪʃən/ *n* [u] hambre *f*‡, inanición *f*; (*before n*) **~ diet** dieta *f* de hambre; **~ wages** salario *m* de hambre

starve /stɑːrv || stɑːv/ *vt* 1 (deny food) privar de comida a, hacer* pasar hambre a; **I'm ~d** (AmE colloq) me muero de hambre, tengo un hambre canina (fam); **to ~ oneself** pasar hambre 2 (deprive) **to ~ sth/sb OF sth** privar algo/A algn DE algo

■ **starve** *vi* (die) morirse* de hambre *or* de inanición; (feel hungry) pasar hambre; **I'm starving** (BrE colloq) me muero de hambre, tengo un hambre canina (fam)

starving /'stɑːrvɪŋ || 'stɑːvɪŋ/ *adj* hambriento, famélico

stash¹ /stæʃ/ *vt* **~ (away)** (colloq) (hide) esconder; (save) ir* ahorrando *or* acumulando; **she's got millions ~ed away** tiene millones guardaditos (fam)

stash² *n* (colloq) alijo *m*

state¹ /steɪt/ *n*

Sense I

A 1 [c] (nation) estado *m*; (*before n*) **~ visit** visita *f* oficial, visita *f* de estado 2 [c] (division of country) estado *m*; **the S~s** los Estados Unidos; (*before n*) ‹*law/taxes/police*› (in US) del estado, estatal

B [u c] (Govt) estado *m*; **affairs of ~** asuntos *mpl* de estado; **Church and S~** la Iglesia y el Estado; (*before n*) (esp BrE) ‹*control/funding*› estatal; **~ education** enseñanza *f* pública; **~ pension** pensión *f* del estado; **~ school** escuela *f* pública *or* estatal *or* del estado

C [u] (pomp): **to lie in ~** yacer* en capilla ardiente; (*before n*) **~ occasion** ocasión *f* solemne

Sense II [c] 1 (condition) estado *m*; **~ of war/emergency** estado de guerra/emergencia; **S~ of the Union message** (in US) mensaje *m or* informe *m* presidencial sobre el estado de la Nación; **in a poor ~ of repair** en bastante mal estado; **~ of health** (estado *m* de) salud *f*; **~ of mind** estado de ánimo; **I was in no (fit) ~ to make a decision** no estaba en condiciones de tomar una decisión; **what a ~ of affairs!** ¡qué situación tan lamentable! 2 (poor condition) (colloq): **just look at the ~ of your fingernails!** ¡mira cómo tienes esas uñas!; **she always leaves the kitchen in a ~** siempre deja la cocina hecha un asco (fam) 3 (anxious condition) (colloq): **to be in/get (oneself) into a ~ about sth** estar*/ponerse* nervioso por algo

state² *vt* «*person*» ‹*facts/case*› exponer*; ‹*problem*› plantear, exponer*; ‹*name/address*› (in writing) escribir*, consignar (frml); (orally) decir*; «*law/document*» establecer*, estipular; **he ~d that he had seen her there earlier** afirmó haberla visto antes allí; **to ~ one's views** dar* su (*or* mi *etc*) opinión, exponer* su (*or* mi *etc*) punto de vista; **he clearly ~d that ...** dijo *or* manifestó claramente que ...; **as ~d above** como se indica más arriba

stated /'steɪtəd || 'steɪtɪd/ *adj* 1 (specified, fixed) ‹*amount/sum*› indicado, establecido; ‹*date/time*› señalado, indicado 2 (declared): **their ~ intention** la intención que han expresado

State Department *n* (in US) **the ~ ~** el Departamento de Estado de los EEUU, ≈ el Ministerio de Asuntos Exteriores *or* de Relaciones Exteriores

stateless /'steɪtləs || 'steɪtlɪs/ *adj* apátrida, sin patria

stately /'steɪtli/ *adj* **-lier, -liest** ‹*air/deportment*› majestuoso

stately home *n* (in UK) casa *f* solariega

statement /'steɪtmənt/ *n*

A 1 [c] (declaration) declaración *f*, afirmación *f*; **official ~** comunicado *m* oficial; **the poem was seen as a political/feminist ~** se interpretó el poema como una proclama política/feminista 2 [c] (to police, in court) declaración *f*; **to make a ~** (Law) prestar declaración 3 [c u] (exposition) exposición *f*

B [c] (of accounts) informe *m* anual; (*bank ~*) estado *m or* extracto *m* de cuenta

state: **~-of-the-art** /'steɪtəvðiˈɑːrt || ˌsteɪtəvðiˈɑːt/ *adj* ‹*computer/turntable*› último modelo *adj inv*; **~-of-the-art technology** tecnología *f* (de) punta *or* de vanguardia; **~room** *n* 1 (on ship, train) camarote *m* 2 (in palace) salón *m* (*para grandes recepciones*); **~side**, **~side** *adv* (AmE colloq) en/a/hacia los Estados Unidos

statesman /'steɪtsmən/ *n* (*pl* **-men** /-mən/) estadista *m*, hombre *m* de estado

statesmanlike /'steɪtsmənlaɪk/ *adj* ‹*conduct/approach*› propio de un estadista

state: **~ trooper** *n* (AmE) policía *m,f* estatal; **~wide** /'steɪt'waɪd/ *adj* de un extremo al otro del estado

static¹ /'stætɪk/ *adj*

A ‹*situation*› estacionario

B ‹*electricity*› estático

static² *n* [u] 1 (electricity) electricidad *f* estática 2 (interference) estática *f*, interferencia *f*, parásitos *mpl*

station¹ /'steɪʃən/ *n*

A 1 (Rail) estación *f* 2 (*bus ~*) estación *f or* terminal *f* de autobuses

B (place of operations) **research ~** centro *m* de investigación; **weather ~** estación *f* meteorológica; *see also* **fire station, gas station, police station** *etc*

C (TV) canal *m*; (Rad) emisora *f*, estación *f*, radio *f*

D 1 (Mil) puesto *m*; **action ~s!** ¡zafarrancho de combate!, ¡a sus puestos de combate! 2 (Relig): **the S~s of the Cross** el Vía Crucis, las Estaciones de la Cruz

E (social rank) condición *f*, clase *f* social; **to have ideas above one's ~** tener* delirios de grandeza

station² *vt* 1 (position) ‹*sentries*› apostar*, emplazar*; **she ~ed herself behind the wall** se colocó detrás de la pared 2 (post) (*usu pass*) ‹*personnel*› destinar, destacar*; ‹*fleet/troops*› emplazar*, estacionar

stationary /'steɪʃəneri || 'steɪʃənri/ *adj* 1 (not moving) ‹*object/vehicle*› estacionario, detenido, que no está en movimiento; **he remained ~** no se movió, permaneció inmóvil (frml) 2 (fixed in place) ‹*engine/gun*› fijo

stationer /'steɪʃənər/ *n*: **~'s (shop)** papelería *f*

stationery /'steɪʃəneri || 'steɪʃənəri/ *n* [u] 1 (writing materials) artículos *mpl* de papelería *or* de escritorio 2 (writing paper) papel *m* y sobres *mpl* de carta

station: ~ **house** *n* (AmE) 1 (police station) comisaría *f* 2 ▸**fire station**; ~**master** *n* jefe, -fa *m,f* de estación; ~ **wagon** *n* (AmE) ranchera *f*, (coche *m*) familiar *m*, camioneta *f* (AmL), rural *f* (RPl), station (wagon) *m* (Chi)

statistic /stə'tɪstɪk/ *n* estadística *f*

statistical /stə'tɪstɪkəl/ *adj* estadístico

statistically /stə'tɪstɪkli/ *adv* ‹*prove/show*› por medio de estadísticas; ‹*valid/significant*› estadísticamente

statistician /'stætə'stɪʃən/ *n* estadístico, -ca *m,f*

statistics /stə'tɪstɪks/ *n* (+ *sing vb*) estadística *f*

statue /'stætʃu: || 'stætju:, 'stætʃu:/ *n* estatua *f*

Statue of Liberty – the Statue of Liberty

La famosa estatua situada en la *Liberty Island* en la bahía de Nueva York, representa a una mujer que lleva la antorcha de la libertad. Fue un obsequio de Francia al pueblo de EEUU

statuesque /'stætʃu'esk/ *adj* (frml) escultural

statuette /'stætʃu'et || ˌstætjʊ'et, ˌstætʃʊ'et/ *n* estatuilla *f*

stature /'stætʃər || 'stætʃə(r)/ *n* 1 (status) talla *f*; **a person of ~** una persona importante *or* destacada 2 (height) (frml) estatura *f*, talla *f*

status /'stætəs || 'steɪtəs/ *n* (*pl* **-tuses**)

A 1 [u c] (category, situation): **member ~** categoría *f* de socio; **the ~ of women** la condición jurídica y social de las mujeres; **what's his legal ~?** ¿cuál es su situación legal?; **it has no legal ~** no tiene validez; **marital ~** estado *m* civil; **the group has no official ~** el grupo no está oficialmente reconocido como tal; **financial ~** situación *f* or posición *f* económica 2 [u] (*social* ~) posición *f* social, estatus *m* 3 [u] (kudos) estatus *m*, prestigio *m*, standing *m*; (*before n*) **~ symbol** símbolo *m* de estatus *or* de prestigio

B [u] (state, condition) situación *f*; (*before n*) **~ report** informe *m* de progreso

status quo /kwəʊ/ *n* statu quo *m*

statute /'stætʃu:t || 'stætju:t, 'stætʃu:t/ *n* ley *f*; **by ~** por ley; **the university ~s** el estatuto *or* los estatutos de la universidad; (*before n*) **~ book** código *m*; **~ law** derecho *m* escrito

statutory /'stætʃutɔ:ri || 'stætjʊtəri, 'stætʃu:təri/ *adj* ‹*right/obligation*› legal, establecido por la ley; ‹*penalty*› establecido por la ley; ‹*authority/body*› creado por la ley; **~ rape** (AmE) *relaciones sexuales con un menor*

staunch[1] /stɔ:ntʃ/ *adj* **-er, -est** ‹*supporter*› incondicional, acérrimo; ‹*Protestant*› acérrimo, devoto

staunch[2] *vt* ▸**stanch**

stave /steɪv/ *n*

A (of barrel, hull) duela *f*

B (Mus) pentagrama *m*

Phrasal verbs

- **stave in** (*past & past p* **staved** *or* **stove**) [v ▸ o ▸ adv, v ▸ adv ▸ o] ‹*door/hull*› romper*
- **stave off** (*past & past p* **staved**) [v ▸ o ▸ adv, v ▸ adv ▸ o] ‹*defeat/disaster*› evitar; ‹*danger/threat*› conjurar

staves 1 *pl of* **staff**[1] **B1** 2 *pl of* **stave**

stay[1] /steɪ/ *vi*

A 1 (in specified place, position) quedarse, permanecer* (frml); **~ there** quédate ahí, no te muevas de ahí; **~ close to us** no te alejes de nosotros; **~!** (to dog) ¡quieto!; **to ~ ahead** mantenerse a la cabeza; **unemployment is here to ~** el desempleo se ha convertido en un problema permanente; ***to ~ put*** quedarse 2 (in specified state): **~ still/single** quédate quieto/soltero; **try and ~ sober** trata de no emborracharte; **we ~ed friends** seguimos siendo amigos; **to ~ awake** mantenerse* despierto

B 1 (remain, not leave) quedarse; **can you ~ to *o* for dinner?** ¿te puedes quedar a cenar? 2 (reside temporarily) quedarse; (in a hotel etc) hospedarse, alojarse, quedarse; **I'm ~ing with friends** me estoy quedando en casa de unos amigos; **we ~ed at the Hilton** nos hospedamos *or* nos alojamos *or* nos quedamos en el Hilton; **he's ~ing with us over Easter** va a pasar la Semana Santa con nosotros; **can Matthew ~ the night?** ¿Matthew se puede quedar a dormir *or* a pasar la noche?

■ **stay** *vt*

A (survive) ‹*distance/pace*› aguantar, resistir

B (suspend) ‹*execution/sentence*› suspender

Phrasal verbs

- **stay away** [v ▸ adv] 1 (not go near) **to ~ away FROM sth/sb** no acercarse* A algo/algn 2 (not go to) ‹‹*public*›› no acudir
- **stay behind** [v ▸ adv] (after meeting, party etc) quedarse; **to ~ behind after school** (esp BrE) quedarse después de clases
- **stay down** [v ▸ adv] (in lowered position) no levantarse; **I glued it but it won't ~ down** lo pegué pero se sigue levantando
- **stay in** [v ▸ adv] 1 (remain in position) quedarse en su sitio; **this nail won't ~ in** este clavo se sale 2 (remain indoors) quedarse en casa
- **stay off** [v ▸ prep ▸ o]: **I ~ed off work today** hoy no fui a trabajar
- **stay on** [v ▸ adv] 1 (remain in position) quedarse en su sitio; **my hat won't ~ on** se me cae el sombrero 2 (at school, in job) quedarse
- **stay out** [v ▸ adv] 1 (not come home): **to ~ out all night** pasar toda la noche fuera; **he usually ~s out late** normalmente no vuelve hasta tarde 2 (out of doors) quedarse fuera 3 (remain on strike) seguir* en huelga
- **stay out of** [v ▸ adv ▸ prep ▸ o] 1 (avoid): **try to ~ out of trouble/his way** procura no meterte en líos/no cruzarte en su camino; **~ out of the sun** quédate a la sombra 2 (not get involved in) no meterse en
- **stay over** [v ▸ adv] quedarse (a dormir)
- **stay up** [v ▸ adv] 1 (not fall or sink) ‹‹*tent/pole*›› sostenerse*; **his trousers won't ~ up** se le caen los pantalones 2 (not go to bed) quedarse levantado

stay[2] *n*

A (time) estadía *f* (AmL), estancia *f* (Esp, Méx); **I'd like to go for a longer ~** me gustaría ir a quedarme más tiempo; **after an overnight ~ in Paris** después de hacer noche *or* después de pernoctar en París, **during her ~ in hospital** mientras estuvo en el hospital

B (Law): **~ of execution** suspensión *f* del cumplimiento de la sentencia

C 1 (rope, wire) estay *m* 2 (Clothing, Hist) **~s** (*pl*) corsé *m*

stay-at-home /'steɪəthəʊm/ *n* persona *f* casera

staying power /'steɪɪŋ/ *n* [u] resistencia *f*, aguante *m*

STD *n* [c] (Med) = **sexually transmitted disease**

stead /sted/ *n*: **in sb's ~** (liter) en lugar de algn; ***to stand sb in good ~*** resultarle *or* serle* muy útil a algn

steadfast /'stedfæst || 'stedfɑ:st/ *adj* (liter) ‹*refusal*› firme, categórico, rotundo; ‹*resolve*› inquebrantable, férreo; ‹*gaze*› fijo; ‹*loyalty*› a toda prueba

steadfastly /'stedfæstli/ *adv* (liter) ‹*refuse*› categóricamente; ‹*uphold*› tenazmente; ‹*gaze*› fijamente

steadily /'stedḷi || 'stedɪli/ *adv* 1 (constantly, gradually) ‹*breathe/beat/work*› regularmente, a un ritmo constante; **her condition is ~ deteriorating** continúa *or* sigue empeorando; **a ~ increasing number** un número cada vez mayor 2 (incessantly) ‹*rain/work*› sin cesar, sin parar, continuamente 3 (not shaking) ‹*gaze*› fijamente, sin apartar la vista; ‹*walk*› con paso seguro

steady[1] /'stedi/ *adj* **-dier, -diest**

A (not shaky) ‹*gaze*› fijo; ‹*chair/table/ladder*› firme, seguro; **with a ~ hand** con pulso firme; **you need a ~ hand** hay que tener mucho pulso; **hold the camera ~** no muevas la cámara; **she isn't very ~ on her feet** le flaquean las piernas

B 1 (constant) ‹*breeze/rain/speed*› constante; ‹*rhythm/pace*› constante, regular; ‹*flow/stream*› continuo; ‹*improvement/decline/increase*› constante; ‹*prices/currency*› estable; **the patient is making ~ progress** el paciente sigue mejorando 2 (regular) (*before n*) ‹*job*› fijo, estable; ‹*income*› regular, fijo; **~ boyfriend** novio *m*; **~ girlfriend** novia *f* 3 (dependable) ‹*person/worker*› serio, formal

C (*as interj*) ¡cuidado!, ¡ojo! (fam)

steady[2] **-dies, -dying, -died** *vt* 1 (make stable) ‹*table/ladder*› (by holding) sujetar (para que no se mueva); **to ~ oneself** recobrar el equilibrio 2 (make calm) calmar, tranquilizar*; **she had a drink to ~ her nerves** se tomó una copa para calmarse

■ **steady** *vi* estabilizarse*

S

steady[3] *adv*: **to go ~ (with sb)** (colloq & dated) ser* novio/novia (de algn), noviar (con algn) (AmL)

steak /steɪk/ *n*
A (for grilling, frying) **1** [c] bistec *m*, filete *m*, churrasco *m* (CS), bife *m* (RPl, Bol) **2** [u] (cut) carne *f* para filete (*or* bistec *etc*)
B [u] (cut for braising, stewing) (BrE) carne *f* para guisar *or* estofar; (*before n*) **~ and kidney pie** pastel *m* de carne y riñones
C [c] (of ham) rodaja *f*; (of fish) filete *m*

steak house *n*: *restaurante especializado en bistecs*, ≈ churrasquería *f* (AmS)

steal /stiːl/ (*past* **stole**; *past p* **stolen**) *vt*
A **1** ‹*object/idea*› robar, hurtar (frml); **to ~ sth FROM sb** robarle algo A algn; **he stole some money from the till** robó dinero de la caja **2** (sneak) (liter): **to ~ a glance at sth/sb** echar una mirada furtiva a algo/algn
B **stolen** *past p* **1** ‹*money/property*› robado **2** (liter) ‹*moments/pleasures*› robado, escamoteado
■ **steal** *vi*
A robar, hurtar (frml); **he was convicted of ~ing** lo condenaron por robo
B (go stealthily) (+ *adv compl*): **to ~ away** *o* **off** escabullirse; **they stole into the room** entraron en la habitación a hurtadillas, entraron sigilosamente en la habitación; **to ~ up on sb** acercarse* sigilosamente a algn

stealth /stelθ/ *n* [u] sigilo *m*; **by ~** furtivamente

stealthily /ˈstelθəli/ *adv* a hurtadillas, furtivamente

stealth tax *n* (BrE): *impuesto diseñado para que sus efectos quedan desapercibidos por los contribuyentes*

stealthy /ˈstelθi/ *adj* **-thier, -thiest** ‹*movement/departure*› furtivo; ‹*footsteps*› sigiloso

steam[1] /stiːm/ *n* [u] vapor *m*; **full ~ ahead!** ¡a todo vapor!; **we're going full ~ ahead with the project** vamos a ponernos a toda marcha con el proyecto; ***to get up ~*** (lit) «*engine/driver*» dar* presión; ***to let off ~*** desahogarse*, dar* rienda suelta a su (*or* mi *etc*) indignación (*or* energía *etc*); ***to run out of ~*** «*person/project*» perder* ímpetu; ***under one's own ~*** por sus (*or* mis *etc*) propios medios; (*before n*) **~ iron** plancha *f* de vapor

steam[2] *vt* **1** (Culin) ‹*vegetables/rice*› cocinar *or* cocer* al vapor; ‹*pudding*› cocinar *or* cocer* al baño (de) María **2** **to ~ a letter open** abrir* una carta con vapor
■ **steam** *vi*
A (give off steam) echar vapor; «*hot food*» humear
B (+ *adv compl*): **the train ~ed into the station** el tren entró en la estación echando vapor

Phrasal verbs
• **steam over** ▸**steam up A**
• **steam up**
A [v ▸ adv] «*window/glass*» empañarse
B [v ▸ o ▸ adv, v ▸ adv ▸ o] ‹*window/glass*› empañar; ***to be/get ~ed up about sth***: **people are getting ~ed up about the issue** se están caldeando los ánimos al respecto

steam: **~boat** *n* vapor *m*, barco *m* de *or* a vapor; **~ engine** *n* **1** (Mech Eng) motor *m* de *or* a vapor **2** (esp BrE Rail) locomotora *f or* máquina *f* de *or* a vapor

steamer /ˈstiːmər || ˈstiːmə(r)/ *n*
A (Naut) vapor *m*, buque *m or* barco *m* de *or* a vapor
B (cooking vessel) vaporera *f*

steamroller[1] /ˈstiːmˌrəʊlər || ˈstɪːmˌrəʊlə(r)/ *n* apisonadora *f*, aplanadora *f* (AmL)

steamroller[2] *vt* **1** ‹*road/tarmac*› apisonar, aplanar **2** ‹*opposition*› aplastar **3** (force): **they ~ed the plan through the committee** aplastando a la oposición, hicieron que la comisión aprobara el plan

steamship /ˈstiːmʃɪp/ *n* vapor *m*, barco *m or* buque *m* de *or* a vapor

steamy /ˈstiːmi/ *adj* **-mier, -miest** ‹*room/atmosphere*› lleno de vapor; ‹*heat*› húmedo; ‹*window/glass*› empañado

steed /stiːd/ *n* (liter) corcel *m* (liter)

steel[1] /stiːl/ *n* [u] (Metall) acero *m*; (*before n*) ‹*girder/helmet*› de acero; **the ~ industry** la industria siderúrgica

steel[2] *v refl* **to ~ oneself FOR sth/to + INF** armarse de valor PARA algo/PARA + INF; **she had ~ed herself against his entreaties** se había hecho fuerte para no ceder a sus súplicas

steel: **~ band** *n*: *banda de percusión típica del Caribe*; **~ mill** *n* planta *f* de laminación del acero; **~ wool** *n* [u] lana *f* de acero, virulana® *f* (Arg), fibra *f* metálica (Méx); **~worker** *n* obrero siderúrgico, obrera siderúrgica *m,f*; **~works** *n* (*pl* **-works**) (+ *sing or pl vb*) planta *f* siderúrgica, acería *f*, acerería *f*

steely /ˈstiːli/ *adj* **-lier, -liest** ‹*gaze/expression*› duro; ‹*determination*› férreo; **~-eyed** de mirada dura

steep[1] /stiːp/ *adj* **-er, -est**
A **1** ‹*slope*› empinado; ‹*drop*› brusco, abrupto; ‹*descent*› en picada *or* (Esp) en picado **2** (large) ‹*increase/decline*› considerable, pronunciado
B (excessive) (colloq) **1** (of prices) alto, excesivo; **that's a bit ~!** ¡qué caro! **2** (unreasonable): **it's a bit ~ to expect them to work without a break** no es muy razonable que digamos, esperar que trabajen sin un descanso

steep[2] *vt* (to soften, clean) remojar, dejar en *or* a remojo; (to flavor) macerar; **a city ~ed in history** una ciudad de gran riqueza histórica
■ **steep** *vi* «*fruit*» macerarse

steeple /ˈstiːpəl/ *n* torre *f*, campanario *m*, aguja *f*

steeple: **~chase** *n* carrera *f* de obstáculos; **~jack** *n*: *persona que repara chimeneas, torres etc*

steeply /ˈstiːpli/ *adv* **1** ‹*slope/rise*› abruptamente; ‹*fall/drop*› vertiginosamente **2** ‹*increase/decline*› considerablemente; **prices rose ~** los precios se dispararon

steer[1] /stɪr || stɪə(r)/ *n*
A **1** (young bull) novillo *m* **2** (castrated bull) buey *m*
B (tip, advice) (AmE sl) dato *m*; **a bum ~** un pésimo dato

steer[2] *vt* **1** ‹*vehicle/plane*› dirigir*, conducir*; ‹*ship*› gobernar*; **the captain ~ed (a course) for home** el capitán puso rumbo a casa; **we must ~ a moderate course** tenemos que adoptar una línea moderada; **to ~ one's way through the crowd** abrirse* paso entre la multitud **2** (guide) llevar, conducir*; **she ~ed the conversation around to the subject of money** llevó la conversación hacia el tema del dinero
■ **steer** *vi* **1** (Naut) estar* *or* ir* al timón; (Auto) ir* al volante; **to ~ by a compass/the stars** guiarse* por la brújula/las estrellas; **he ~ed for the harbor** navegó con rumbo al puerto; ***to ~ clear of sth/sb*** evitar algo/a algn; **~ well clear of them** no tengas nada que ver con ellos, evítalos a toda costa **2** (handle) «*vehicle*»: **the new model ~s effortlessly** el nuevo modelo tiene muy buena dirección

steerage /ˈstɪrɪdʒ || ˈstɪərɪdʒ/ *n* [u]: **to travel ~** viajar en tercera clase *or* en la bodega (del barco)

steering /ˈstɪrɪŋ || ˈstɪərɪŋ/ *n* [u] dirección *f*

steering: **~ column** *n* árbol *m or* columna *f* de dirección; **~ committee** *n* comité *m* directivo; **~ wheel** *n* (Auto) volante *m*, timón *m* (Col, Per); (Naut) timón *m*

stellar /ˈstelər || ˈstelə(r)/ *adj* estelar

stem[1] /stem/ *n*
A (of plant) tallo *m*; (of leaf) peciolo *m*, pecíolo *m*; (of fruit) pedúnculo *m*
B **1** (of glass) pie *m* **2** (of pipe) boquilla *f*, caña *f*
C (Ling) raíz *f*
D (Naut): **from ~ to stern** de proa a popa

stem[2] **-mm-** *vt* ‹*flow/bleeding*› contener*, parar; ‹*outbreak/decline*› detener*, poner* freno a
■ **stem** *vi* **to ~ FROM sth** provenir* DE algo

stem cell *n* célula *f* madre, célula *f* primordial, célula *f* troncal; (*before n*) **~ ~ research** investigación *f* de las células madres *or* troncales *or* primordiales

stench /stentʃ/ *n* fetidez *f*, hedor *m* (liter); **there's a terrible ~ in here** aquí huele muy mal, aquí apesta (fam)

stencil[1] /ˈstensəl || ˈstensɪl/ *n* **1** (for lettering, decoration) plantilla *f*, troquel *m* **2** (for duplicating) stencil *m*, cliché *m* (Esp)

stencil[2] *vt*, (BrE) **-ll-** **1** ‹*design/pattern*› *escribir, dibujar o pintar utilizando una plantilla* **2** (duplicate) mimeografiar*, multicopiar, multigrafiar* (Ven)

steno /ˈstenəʊ/ *n* (AmE colloq) **1** ▸**stenographer** **2** ▸**stenography**

stenographer /stəˈnɑːgrəfər || steˈnɒgrəfə(r)/ *n* (esp AmE) taquígrafo, -fa *m,f*, estenógrafo, -fa *m,f*

stenography /stəˈnɑːgrəfi/ *n* [u] (AmE) taquigrafía *f*

step[1] /step/ *n*
A [c] (footstep, pace) paso *m*; **to take a ~ forward** dar* un paso adelante; **to follow in sb's ~s** seguir* los pasos de algn;

to be/keep one ~ ahead: **they're one ~ ahead of us** nos llevan cierta ventaja; **he tries to keep one ~ ahead of his students** trata de que sus alumnos no lo aventajen; ***to watch one's ~*** (be cautious, behave well) andarse* con cuidado *or* con pie de plomo; **watch your ~** (when walking) mira por dónde caminas

B 1 [c] (of dance) paso *m* 2 [u] (in marching, walking) paso *m*; **to be in/out of ~** llevar/no llevar el paso; (in dancing) llevar/no llevar el compás *or* el ritmo; **to break ~** romper* el paso; ***in/out of ~ with sb/sth***: **the leaders are out of ~ with the wishes of the majority** los líderes no sintonizan con los deseos de la mayoría

C (distance) (*no pl*): **it's only a ~ away** está a un paso; **it's a fair ~ from here to the station** hay un buen trecho hasta la estación

D [c] (move) paso *m*; (measure) medida *f*; **a ~ in the right direction** un paso hacia adelante; **to take ~s (to + INF)** tomar medidas (PARA + INF)

E 1 [c] (on stair) escalón *m*, peldaño *m*; (on ladder) travesaño *m*, escalón *m*; **S mind the step** cuidado con el escalón; **the museum ~s** la escalinata *or* las escaleras del museo; **a flight of ~s** un tramo *m* de escalera 2 **steps** *pl* (stepladder) (BrE) escalera *f* (*de mano or de tijera*)

F [c] 1 (degree in scale) peldaño *m*, escalón *m*; **that would be a ~ up in her career** eso significaría un ascenso para ella 2 (AmE Mus): **whole ~** tono *m*; **half ~** semitono *m*

step² *vi* **-pp-**: **would you ~ inside/outside for a moment?** ¿quiere pasar/salir un momento?; **to ~ off a plane** bajarse de un avión; **she ~ped over the threshold** atravesó el umbral; **to ~ IN/ON sth** pisar algo; **sorry, I ~ped on your toe** perdón, te pisé; ***to ~ on it*** *o* ***on the gas*** (colloq) darse* prisa, apurarse (AmL), meterle (AmL fam)

Phrasal verbs

- **step aside** [v ▸ adv] (move aside) hacerse* a un lado, apartarse; (resign, go) renunciar, dimitir
- **step back** [v ▸ adv] (move back) dar* un paso atrás, retroceder; (become detached) **to ~ back (FROM sth)** distanciarse (DE algo)
- **step down** [v ▸ adv] 1 (get down) bajar 2 (resign) renunciar, dimitir, dejar su (*or* mi *etc*) puesto
- **step forward** [v ▸ adv] (move forward) dar* un paso adelante; (present oneself) ofrecerse*
- **step in** [v ▸ adv] (intervene) intervenir*, tomar cartas en el asunto
- **step out** [v ▸ adv] (walk quickly) apretar* el paso
- **step up** [v ▸ o ▸ adv, v ▸ adv ▸ o] (increase) ‹*production/campaign*› intensificar*; ‹*efforts/security*› redoblar; ‹*attacks*› redoblar, aumentar la frecuencia de

step: **~brother** *n* hermanastro *m*; **~ by step** *adv* (one stage at a time) paso a paso; (gradually) poco a poco; **~-by-step** /'stepbaɪ'step/ *adj* ‹*instructions*› detallado, paso a paso; ‹*approach*› paso a paso; **~child** *n* (son) hijastro *m*; (daughter) hijastra *f*; **~daughter** *n* hijastra *f*; **~father** *n* padrastro *m*; **~ladder** *n* escalera *f* de mano *or* de tijera; **~mother** *n* madrastra *f*

steppe /step/ *n* [u] (*often pl*) estepa *f*

stepping-stone /'stepɪŋstəʊn/ *n*: *cada una de las piedras que se colocan para cruzar un arroyo, un pantano etc*; **a ~ to success** un peldaño en el camino del éxito

step: **~sister** *n* hermanastra *f*; **~son** *n* hijastro *m*; **~-up** *n* (*no pl*) (in expenditure, investment) aumento *m*; (in terrorist activity) escalada *f*; (in campaign) intensificación *f*

stereo¹ /'steriəʊ/ *n* (*pl* **-os**) 1 [c] (player) estéreo *m*, equipo *m* (estereofónico *or* estéreo) 2 [u] (sound) estéreo *m*; **in ~** en estéreo, en sonido estereofónico

stereo² *adj* estéreo *adj inv*, estereofónico

stereophonic /'steriə'fɑːnɪk/ *adj* (frml) estereofónico

stereotype¹ /'steriətaɪp/ *n* estereotipo *m*

stereotype² *vt* (brand) ‹*person*› catalogar*, estereotipar

stereotyped /'steriətaɪpt/ *adj* estereotipado

sterile /'sterəl || 'steraɪl/ *adj* estéril

sterility /stə'rɪləti/ *n* [u] esterilidad *f*

sterilization /'sterələ'zeɪʃən/ *n* [cu] esterilización *f*

sterilize /'sterəlaɪz/ *vt* esterilizar*

sterilizer /'sterəlaɪzər || 'sterəlaɪzə(r)/ *n* esterilizador *m*

sterling¹ /'stɜːrlɪŋ || 'stɜːlɪŋ/ *n* [u] (Fin) la libra (esterlina); **in ~** en libras (esterlinas)

sterling² *adj*

A (*no comp*) 1 (Fin): **the pound ~** la libra esterlina 2 (silver) de plata de ley; **~ silver** plata *f* de ley

B (excellent) invaluable, invalorable (CS); **he did some ~ work for us** efectuó un excelente trabajo para nosotros

stern¹ /stɜːrn || stɜːn/ *n* popa *f*

stern² *adj* **-er, -est** severo; **I thought you were made of ~er stuff** te creía más fuerte

sternly /'stɜːrnli || 'stɜːnli/ *adv* severamente

steroid /'stɪrɔɪd, 'ste- || 'stɪərɔɪd, 'ste-/ *n* esteroide *m*

stethoscope /'steθəskəʊp/ *n* estetoscopio *m*

stevedore /'stiːvədɔːr/ *n* estibador, -dora *m,f*

stew¹ /stuː || stjuː/ *n* estofado *m*, guiso *m*; ***to be/get in a ~*** (colloq) estar*/ponerse* nervioso

stew² *vt* ‹*meat*› estofar, guisar; ‹*fruit*› hacer* compota de

■ **stew** *vi* «*meat/fruit*» cocer*; ***to let sb ~ in her/his own juice*** dejar sufrir a algn

steward /'stuːərd || 'stjuːəd/ *n*

A (on ship) camarero *m*; (on plane) auxiliar *m* de vuelo, sobrecargo *m*, aeromozo *m* (AmL)

B 1 (manager — of estate) administrador, -dora *m,f*; (— of club) director administrativo, directora administrativa *m,f* 2 (BrE) (in horse-racing) comisario, -ria *m,f* (de carreras); (in athletics) juez *mf* 3 (at public gatherings) (BrE) *persona encargada de supervisar al público en eventos deportivos etc*

stewardess /'stuːərdəs || 'stjuːədes/ *n* 1 (on ship) camarera *f* 2 (on plane) auxiliar *f* de vuelo, azafata *f*, sobrecargo *f*, aeromoza *f* (AmL), cabinera *f* (Col), hostess *f* (Chi)

stewed /stuːd || stjuːd/ *adj* 1 (Culin) (*usu before n*) ‹*beef/lamb*› (BrE) estofado, guisado; ‹*fruit*› en compota; **~ apple** compota *f* de manzana 2 (BrE) ‹*tea*› *demasiado cargado por haberlo dejado reposar demasiado tiempo*

stewing steak /'stuːɪŋ || 'stjuːɪŋ/ *n* [u] *carne para estofar*

stick¹ /stɪk/ *n*

A [c] (of wood) palo *m*, vara *f*; (twig) ramita *f*; (for fire) astilla *f*; ***more than you can shake a ~ at*** (esp AmE colloq): **they get more tourists than you can shake a ~ at** reciben turistas a montones (fam); ***to be in a cleft ~*** estar* metido en un aprieto *or* un apuro; ***to get (hold of) the wrong end of the ~*** (colloq) entenderlo* todo al revés, tomar el rábano por las hojas

B [c] 1 (*walking ~*) bastón *m* 2 (*drum~*) palillo *m*, baqueta *f* (Méx) 3 (*hockey ~*) palo *m*

C [c] (of celery, rhubarb) rama *f*, penca *f*; (of dynamite) cartucho *m*; (of rock, candy) palo *m*; (of sealing wax) barra *f*; **a ~ of cinnamon** un pedazo de canela en rama; **a ~ of chalk** una tiza; **a ~ of chewing gum** un chicle

D [u] (BrE) (criticism, punishment) (colloq): **to get/take ~ from sb** recibir/aguantar (los) palos de algn (fam); **to give sb/sth ~** darle* palos *or* un palo a algn/algo (fam)

E **sticks** *pl* **the ~s** (colloq): **to live out in the ~s** vivir en la Cochinchina *or* (Esp tb) en las Batuecas

stick² (*past & past p* **stuck**) *vt*

A (attach, glue) pegar*; **I stuck a patch over the hole** puse un parche encima del agujero; **I stuck the handle (back) on with glue** pegué el asa con cola; **I'll ~ the pieces together** voy a pegar los pedazos

B 1 (thrust) ‹*needle/knife/sword*› clavar; **I stuck the needle in my finger** me clavé la aguja en el dedo 2 (impale) **to ~ sth ON sth** clavar algo EN algo

C (put, place) (colloq) poner*; **~ it in the oven** ponlo *or* mételo en el horno; **~ your head out of the window** asoma *or* saca la cabeza por la ventana; **I stuck it back in my pocket** me lo metí de nuevo en el bolsillo; **~ it there!** (AmE) ¡choca esa mano!, ¡chócala! (fam); **she knows where she can ~ her offer!** (colloq) ¡ella sabe muy bien dónde se puede meter esa oferta! (fam); ***to ~ it to sb*** (AmE colloq) (castigate) darle* duro *or* con todo a algn; (swindle) aprovecharse de algn

D (tolerate) (esp BrE colloq) aguantar, soportar; **I don't know how you ~ him** no sé cómo lo aguantas *or* soportas

■ **stick** *vi*

A (adhere) «*glue*» pegar*; «*food*» pegarse*; **these labels won't ~ (on)** estas etiquetas no (se) pegan; **to ~ TO sth** pegarse* *or* (frml) adherirse* A algo; **the two pages have stuck together** las dos páginas se han pegado; **they'll never make the charge ~** nunca van a poder probar que es culpable; **the song stuck in my mind** la canción se me quedó grabada

B (become jammed) atascarse*; **the car stuck in the mud** el coche se atascó en el barro; **the words stuck in my**

S

throat no me salían las palabras; ***to ~ in sb's gullet*** *o* ***throat***: **what ~s in my gullet** *o* **throat is that ...** lo que me indigna *or* (fam) lo que tengo atravesado es que ...
C (in card games) plantarse; *see also* **stuck**

Phrasal verbs

- **stick around** [v ▸ adv] (colloq) quedarse
- **stick at** [v ▸ prep ▸ o] (colloq) ‹*exercises/work*› seguir* con; **~ at it** sigue así
- **stick by** [v ▸ prep ▸ o] ‹*opinion*› mantener*; ‹*friend*› no abandonar; ‹*promise*› mantener* en pie
- **stick out**

A [v ▸ adv] 1 (protrude) sobresalir*; **I saw a gun ~ing out of his pocket** vi que le asomaba un revólver del bolsillo 2 (be obvious) resaltar; **he really ~s out in a crowd** uno enseguida lo nota en un grupo de gente; ▸**mile, thumb**[1]
B [v ▸ o ▸ adv, v ▸ adv ▸ o] (stretch out) (colloq) ‹*hand*› extender*, alargar*, sacar*; **to ~ one's chest/tongue out** sacar* (el) pecho/la lengua
C 1 [v ▸ o ▸ adv] (endure) (colloq) ‹*job*› aguantar en; **you'll have to ~ it out** vas a tener que aguantarte *or* (Esp tb) aguantar mecha (fam) 2 [v ▸ adv] (hold out): **they are ~ing out for 8%** no van a ceder por menos del 8%

- **stick to** [v ▸ prep ▸ o] 1 (hold to) ‹*road/path*› seguir* por; ‹*principles*› mantener*, no apartarse de; ‹*rules*› ceñirse* a, atenerse* a; **they didn't ~ to the agreement** no cumplieron con *or* no respetaron el acuerdo; **I'll ~ to my original plan** seguiré con mi plan original 2 (not digress from) ‹*subject/facts*› ceñirse* a; **~ to the point** no te vayas por las ramas (fam), no te apartes del tema 3 (restrict oneself to) limitarse a 4 (continue at, persevere in) seguir* con, perseverar con 5 (follow closely): **~ close to me** no te separes de mí, pégate a mí (fam)
- **stick together** [v ▸ adv] no separarse, quedarse juntos; (support each other) mantenerse* unidos
- **stick up**

A [v ▸ o ▸ adv, v ▸ adv ▸ o] 1 (on wall) ‹*notice*› colocar*, poner* 2 (raise) ‹*hand*› levantar; **~ 'em up!** ¡manos arriba!, ¡arriba las manos! 3 (rob) asaltar
B [v ▸ adv] (project): **something was ~ing up out of the ground** algo sobresalía del suelo; **the tower ~s up above the housetops** la torre se alza por encima de los tejados; **her hair was ~ing up** tenía el pelo de punta, tenía el pelo parado (AmL)

- **stick up for** [v ▸ adv ▸ prep ▸ o] ‹*person*› sacar* la cara por, defender*; ‹*principle/idea*› defender*; **to ~ up for oneself** hacerse* valer
- **stick with** [v ▸ prep ▸ o] 1 (stay close to) no separarse de 2 (remain faithful to) ‹*husband/friend*› no abandonar, mantenerse* fiel a; **I'll ~ with my old brand** me quedo con mi marca de antes 3 (continue, persevere with) perseverar con, seguir* adelante con

sticker /'stɪkər || 'stɪkə(r)/ *n* (label) etiqueta *f*; (with slogan etc) pegatina *f*, adhesivo *m*

sticking /'stɪkɪŋ/: **~ plaster** *n* (BrE) 1 [c] (individual strip) curita® *f* (AmL), tirita® *f* (Esp) 2 [u] (tape) esparadrapo *m*, cinta *f* adhesiva, tela *f* emplástica (CS); **~ point** *n* escollo *m*

stick: **~ insect** *n* insecto *m* palo; **~-in-the-mud** *n* (colloq): **don't be such a ~-in-the-mud** no seas tan rutinario e inflexible *or* rutinario y rígido

stickleback /'stɪkəlbæk/ *n* espinoso *m*

stickler /'stɪklər || 'stɪklə(r)/ *n*: **he's a ~ for discipline** insiste mucho en la disciplina

stick: **~-on** *adj* adhesivo; **~ shift** *n* (AmE) 1 (lever) palanca *f* de cambio(s) *or* (Méx) de velocidades 2 (car) coche *m* (de transmisión) estándar *or* manual; **~up** *n* (colloq) atraco *m*, asalto *m*

sticky /'stɪki/ *adj* **stickier, stickiest**
A 1 ‹*label*› autoadhesivo; ‹*surface*› pegajoso 2 ‹*climate*› húmedo y caluroso; ‹*day/weather*› bochornoso
B (difficult) (colloq) ‹*problem/issue*› peliagudo; ‹*situation*› violento, difícil
C (esp AmE colloq) ‹*music/sentiments*› empalagoso (fam)

stiff[1] /stɪf/ *adj* **-er, -est**
A 1 ‹*collar/bristles*› duro; ‹*fabric*› tieso, duro; ‹*corpse*› rígido; ‹*muscles*› entumecido, agarrotado; **to have a ~ neck** tener* tortícolis; **I'm ~ after that walk** estoy dolorido *or* (esp AmL) adolorido despues de la caminata 2 ‹*paste/dough*› consistente; **beat the egg whites until they are ~** bata las claras hasta que estén firmes
B ‹*test/climb*› difícil, duro; ‹*resistance*› férreo, tenaz; ‹*penalty*› fuerte, severo; ‹*terms/conditions*› duro; ‹*breeze/drink*› fuerte
C ‹*person/manner*› almidonado, acartonado, estirado; ‹*bow/smile*› forzado, poco espontáneo

stiff[2] *adv* (colloq): **I'm frozen ~** estoy helado hasta los huesos (fam); **we were bored ~** nos aburrimos como ostras (fam); **scared ~** muerto de miedo

stiff[3] *n* (sl) fiambre *m* (fam), cuerpo *m*

stiffen /'stɪfən/ *vt* 1 (with starch) almidonar; (with fabric underneath) armar 2 **~ (up)** ‹*resolve*› fortalecer*
■ **stiffen** *vi*
A 1 **~ (up)** (become rigid) «*person/muscles/joint*» agarrotarse, anquilosarse 2 (become firm) endurecerse* 3 (in manner, reaction) ponerse* tenso
B (become stronger) «*competition*» hacerse* más duro; «*breeze*» aumentar

stiffening /'stɪfənɪŋ/ *n* [u]
A (Tex) entretela *f*
B (of muscles, joints) entumecimiento *m*

stiffly /'stɪfli/ *adv* 1 ‹*walk/move*› rígidamente, con rigidez 2 ‹*greet*› fríamente; ‹*bow*› con fría formalidad

stiffness /'stɪfnəs || 'stɪfnɪs/ *n* [u] 1 (of collar) rigidez *f*, dureza *f*; (of muscles) rigidez *f*, agarrotamiento *m*; (of joints) anquilosamiento *m*, dureza *f* 2 (of penalty, fine, terms) dureza *f*; (of competition) dureza *f* 3 (formality) frialdad *f*

stifle /'staɪfəl/ *vt*
A (suffocate) (*often pass*) ‹*person*› sofocar*
B (suppress) ‹*flames*› sofocar*; ‹*yawn*› contener*, reprimir; ‹*noise*› ahogar*; ‹*anger*› contener*, dominar; ‹*freedom of expression*› reprimir, ahogar*

stifling /'staɪflɪŋ/ *adj* ‹*heat*› sofocante, agobiante; (*as adv*) **a ~ hot day** un día (de calor) sofocante

stigma /'stɪgmə/ *n*
A (*pl* **-mas**) (disgrace) estigma *m*
B **stigmata** /stɪg'mɑːtə/ *pl* (Relig) estigmas *mpl*

stigmatize /'stɪgmətaɪz/ *vt* marcar*, estigmatizar*

stile /staɪl/ *n*: *escalones que permiten pasar por encima de una cerca*

stiletto /stɪ'letəʊ/ *n* (*pl* **-tos** *or* **-toes**)
A (knife) estilete *m*
B **~ (heel)** tacón *m* de aguja, taco *m* aguja *or* alfiler (CS); **she was wearing ~s** llevaba zapatos (de tacón) de aguja *or* (CS) de taco aguja *or* alfiler

still[1] /stɪl/ *adv*
A (even now, even then) todavía, aún; **there's ~ plenty left** todavía *or* aún queda mucho; **they were ~ dancing** todavía *or* aún estaban bailando, seguían bailando; **I ~ can't understand it** sigo sin entender; **are we ~ friends?** ¿seguimos siendo amigos?
B (*as intensifier*) aún, todavía; **more serious ~, they haven't replied** y lo que es más grave aún *or* y lo que es todavía más grave, no han contestado
C (*as linker*) 1 (even so, despite that) aun así; **they say it's safe, but I'm ~ scared** dicen que no hay peligro pero igual *or* aun así tengo miedo 2 (however) de todos modos; **I don't think it will work; ~, we can always try** no creo que funcione; pero bueno, igual podemos intentarlo

still[2] *adj* 1 (motionless) ‹*lake/air*› en calma, quieto, tranquilo; **sit/stand ~** quédate quieto; **he lay ~** estaba tendido sin moverse; **hold the camera ~** no muevas la cámara; **her heart stood ~ for a moment** el corazón se le paró un momento 2 ‹*orange drink/mineral water*› sin gas, no efervescente

still[3] *n*
A [c] (Cin, Phot) fotograma *m*
B [c] 1 (distillery) destilería *f* 2 (distilling apparatus) alambique *m*
C [u] (quiet) (poet): **in the ~ of the night** en la quietud de la noche (liter)

still[4] *vt* ‹*wind/waves*› apaciguar*; ‹*fears/cries*› acallar

still: **~birth** *n*: *parto en el que el niño nace muerto*; **~born** /'stɪl'bɔːrn || 'stɪlbɔːn/ *adj* nacido muerto, mortinato (frml); **the child was ~born** el niño nació muerto; **~ life** *n* (*pl* **~ lifes**) naturaleza *f* muerta, bodegón *m*

stillness /'stɪlnəs || 'stɪlnɪs/ *n* [u] quietud *f*, calma *f*

stilt /stɪlt/ *n* 1 (for walking) zanco *m* 2 (Archit) pilote *m*

S

stilted /'stɪltəd || 'stɪltɪd/ *adj* 1 ‹*conversation/manner*› forzado, poco natural 2 ‹*language/writing*› rebuscado; ‹*acting*› acartonado

Stilton (cheese)® /'stɪltn̩/ *n* [u] *queso azul de origen inglés*

stimulant /'stɪmjələnt || 'stɪmjʊlənt/ *n* 1 (Pharm) estimulante *m* 2 (stimulus) estímulo *m*, acicate *m*

stimulate /'stɪmjəleɪt || 'stɪmjʊleɪt/ *vt* 1 ‹*nerves/circulation*› estimular 2 ‹*interest/curiosity*› despertar*, estimular; ‹*debate*› fomentar, estimular; **to ~ sb to + INF** estimular *or* alentar* a algn PARA QUE (+ *subj*)

stimulating /'stɪmjəleɪtɪŋ/ *adj* estimulante

stimulation /'stɪmjə'leɪʃən || ˌstɪmjʊ'leɪʃən/ *n* [u] estímulo *m*; (of economy) estimulación *f*

stimulus /'stɪmjələs/ *n* [c u] (*pl* **-li** /-laɪ/) estímulo *m*

sting¹ /stɪŋ/ *n*

A [c] 1 (organ of bee, wasp) aguijón *m*; ***a ~ in the tail*** (BrE): **their offer had a ~ in the tail** su oferta tenía un gran pero 2 (action, wound) picadura *f*

B (*no pl*) 1 (pain) escozor *m*, ardor *m* (CS) 2 (hurtfulness): **there was a ~ in her words** sus palabras fueron hirientes

C [c] (confidence game) (AmE sl) timo *m* (fam), golpe *m* (fam)

sting² (*past & past p* **stung**) *vt*

A «*bee/scorpion/nettle*» picar*

B 1 (cause pain) hacer* escocer, hacer* arder (CS) 2 (mentally, emotionally) herir* profundamente 3 (goad, incite) **to ~ sb INTO sth** incitar a algn A + INF

C (cheat, overcharge) (sl): **I was stung for $65** me clavaron 65 dólares (fam)

■ **sting** *vi*

A «*insect/nettle*» picar*

B 1 (hurt physically) «*iodine/ointment*» hacer* escocer, hacer* arder (CS); «*cut*» escocer*, arder (CS); «*rain*» azotar; **her eyes were ~ing** le escocían *or* le ardían los ojos 2 (mentally, emotionally) herir* (profundamente) 3 **stinging** *pres p* ‹*rebuke/criticism*› punzante, hiriente, **~ing pain** escozor *m*, ardor *m* (CS)

stinging nettle /'stɪŋɪŋ/ *n* ortiga *f*

stingray /'stɪŋreɪ/ *n* raya *f* venenosa

stingy /'stɪndʒi/ *adj* **-gier -giest** ‹*person*› tacaño, roñoso (fam), agarrado (fam); ‹*portion/contribution*› mezquino

stink¹ /stɪŋk/ *n* [u] 1 (bad smell) hediondez *f*, hedor *m* (liter), mal olor *m*, peste *f* (fam) 2 (fuss) (colloq) escándalo *m*, lío *m* (fam), follón *m* (Esp fam); **to make** *o* **kick up a ~** armar un lío (*or* un escándalo *etc*)

stink² (*past* **stank** *or* **stunk**; *past p* **stunk**) *vi* 1 (smell badly) «*person/place/breath*» apestar; **to ~ OF sth** apestar A algo 2 (be very bad) (colloq): **the whole business ~s** todo el asunto da asco; **the idea ~s** es una pésima idea

Phrasal verbs

- **stink out** [v ▸ o ▸ adv, v ▸ adv ▸ o] 1 (drive out) hacer* salir (*usando bombas fétidas etc*) 2 (BrE) ▸ **stink up**
- **stink up** (AmE) [v ▸ o ▸ adv, v ▸ adv ▸ o] ‹*house/room*› (hacer*) apestar, dejar hediondo

stink bomb *n* bomba *f* fétida

stinker /'stɪŋkər || 'stɪŋkə(r)/ *n* (colloq): **the exam was a (real) ~** el examen fue endiabladamente difícil

stinking¹ /'stɪŋkɪŋ/ *adj* (*before n*) 1 (smelly) hediondo, fétido, apestoso 2 (very bad) (colloq): **I've got a ~ cold** tengo un resfriado espantoso; **keep your ~ job!** ¡quédate con tu maldito *or* asqueroso trabajo! (fam)

stinking² *adv* (colloq) (*as intensifier*): **they're ~ rich** están podridos de dinero (fam), están podridos en plata (AmL fam)

stint¹ /stɪnt/ *n*

A [c] 1 (fixed amount, share): **I've done my ~ for today** hoy ya he hecho mi parte *or* lo que me tocaba *or* lo que me correspondía 2 (period) período *m*; **he did a five-year ~ in the army** pasó (un período de) cinco años en el ejército; **her brief ~ as a guide** la breve temporada en que trabajó de guía

B [u] **without ~** generosamente, sin restricciones

stint² *vt* ‹*food*› escatimar; **to ~ sb OF sth** escatimarle algo A algn; **she ~ed herself of food for our sake** se privó de comer por nosotros

■ **stint** *vi* **to ~ ON sth** escatimar algo

stipend /'staɪpend/ *n* estipendio *m*

stipple /'stɪpəl/ *vt* ‹*surface/pattern*› puntear; **~d WITH sth** salpicado DE algo

stipulate /'stɪpjəleɪt || 'stɪpjʊleɪt/ *vt* ‹*amount/condition/time*› estipular

■ **stipulate** *vi* (AmE) **to ~ FOR sth** estipular algo

stipulation /'stɪpjə'leɪʃən || ˌstɪpjʊ'leɪʃən/ *n* condición *f*, estipulación *f*

stir¹ /stɜːr || stɜː(r)/ *n* 1 [c] (action) **to give sth a ~** revolver* *or* (Esp) remover* algo 2 [u] (movement) movimiento *m*, agitación *f* 3 [u] (excitement) revuelo *m*, conmoción *f*; **to cause** *o* **create** *o* **make a ~** causar revuelo

stir² **-rr-** *vt*

A (mix) ‹*liquid/mixture*› revolver*, remover* (Esp); **to ~ sth INTO sth**: **~ the cream into the soup** añada la crema a la sopa y revuelva *or* (Esp) remueva

B 1 (move slightly) agitar, mover* 2 (get moving) (colloq) mover*; **come on, ~ yourself!** ¡vamos, muévete! (fam) 3 (waken) despertar*

C 1 (arouse) ‹*sympathies*› despertar*; ‹*imagination*› estimular 2 (move, affect) conmover* 3 (provoke, incite) **to ~ sb into action** empujar *or* incitar a algn a la acción

■ **stir** *vi*

A 1 (change position) moverse*, agitarse 2 (venture out) moverse*, salir* 3 (wake up) despertarse*; (get up) levantarse; **it was midday before anyone ~red** nadie se levantó hasta el mediodía; **nobody is ~ring yet** no hay nadie despierto todavía, nadie se ha despertado todavía

B (cause trouble) (BrE colloq) armar lío (fam), meter cizaña

Phrasal verb

- **stir up** [v ▸ o ▸ adv, v ▸ adv ▸ o] ‹*mud/waters*› revolver*, remover* (Esp); ‹*memories*› despertar*, traer* a la memoria; ‹*hatred/unrest/revolt*› provocar*; ‹*opposition/discontent*› promover*, suscitar; **to ~ up trouble** armar lío (fam); **she's ~ring things up again** ya está otra vez revolviendo las cosas *or* (fam) tratando de armar lío

stir: **~-crazy** /'stɜːr'kreɪzi || ˌstɜː'kreɪzi/ *adj* (AmE sl) loco de atar (fam); **to go ~-crazy** perder* la chaveta (fam), **~-fry** /'stɜːr'fraɪ || 'stɜːfraɪ/ *vt* **-fries, -frying, -fried** *freír en poco aceite y removiendo constantemente*

stirring¹ /'stɜːrɪŋ/ *adj* ‹*words/music/speech*› conmovedor

stirring² *n* movimiento *m*; **the first ~s of spring/unrest** los primeros indicios de la primavera/de descontento

stirrup /'stərəp || 'stɪrəp/ *n* estribo *m*

stitch¹ /stɪtʃ/ *n*

A 1 (in sewing) puntada *f*; **I put a couple of ~es in it** le di unas puntadas; ***a ~ in time (saves nine)*** una puntada a tiempo ahorra ciento 2 (in knitting) punto *m* 3 (Med) punto *m*

B (piece of clothing): **he didn't have a ~ on** estaba en cueros (fam)

C (pain) (*no pl*) punzada *f* *or* (CS) puntada *f* (en el costado), flato *m* (Esp); **I got a ~** me dio una punzada *or* (CS) puntada (en el costado), me dio flato (Esp); ***to be in ~es*** (colloq) morirse* *or* troncharse *or* desternillarse de risa; **he had us all in ~es** nos tenía muertos de risa

stitch² *vt* 1 (sew) coser 2 (embroider) bordar 3 (Med) suturar

■ **stitch** *vi* 1 (sew) coser 2 (embroider) bordar

stitching /'stɪtʃɪŋ/ *n* [u] 1 (stitches) puntadas *fpl*; (as ornament) pespuntes *mpl* 2 (embroidery) bordado *m*

stoat /stəʊt/ *n* armiño *m*

stock¹ /stɑːk || stɒk/ *n*

A 1 (supply) (*often pl*) reserva *f*; **we need to get some ~s in** necesitamos abastecernos *or* aprovisionarnos 2 [u] (of shop, business) existencias *fpl*, estoc *m*, stock *m*; **to have sth in ~** tener* algo en estoc *or* en existencias; **we're out of ~ of green ones** no nos quedan verdes, las verdes se han agotado *or* están agotadas; **to take ~ of sth** hacer* un balance de algo, evaluar* algo

B (Fin) 1 [u] (shares) acciones *fpl*, valores *mpl*; (government securities) bonos *mpl* *or* papel *m* del Estado; **I have some ~ in that company** tengo algunas acciones en esa compañía 2 **~s and bonds** *o* (BrE) **~s and shares** acciones *fpl*; (including government securities) acciones *fpl* y bonos *mpl* del Estado

C [u] (livestock) ganado *m*; (*before n*) **~ farmer** ganadero, -ra *m,f*; **~ farming** ganadería *f*, cría *f* de ganado

D [u] (descent) linaje *m*, estirpe *f*; **I'm of pioneer ~** soy des-

cendiente de pioneros; **to come of good ~** ser* de buena familia
E [c] (of gun) culata *f*
F [u] (Culin) caldo *m*
G [c] (plant, flower) alhelí *m*
H **stocks** *pl* (Hist) **the ~s** el cepo
I [u] (AmE Theat) (*no art*) repertorio *m*; (*before n*) ‹*play/company*› de repertorio

stock² *vt*
A (Busn) vender
B (fill) ‹*store*› surtir, abastecer*; ‹*larder*› llenar; **to ~ (up) the freezer** llenar el congelador; **to ~ a lake with fish** poblar* un lago de peces

Phrasal verb

- **stock up** [v ▸ adv] abastecerse*, aprovisionarse; (Busn) hacer* un estoc, proveerse* de existencias; **to ~ up ON/WITH sth**: **we'd better ~ up on coffee before it goes up** más vale que compremos bastante café *or* hagamos una buena provisión de café antes de que suba

stock³ *adj* (*before n*) **1** ‹*size*› estándar *adj inv*; ‹*model*› de serie, estándar *adj inv* **2** ‹*response*› típico; ‹*character*› típico; **a ~ phrase** un cliché, una frase hecha

stockade /stɑːˈkeɪd || stɒˈkeɪd/ *n* **1** (fence) empalizada *f*, estacada *f* **2** (area) cercado *m*, recinto *m* cercado **3** (AmE Mil) prisión *f* militar

stock: **~breeder** *n* ganadero, -ra *m,f*; **~breeding** *n* [u] ganadería *f*; **~broker** *n* corredor, -dora *m,f* de valores *or* de Bolsa, agente *mf* de Bolsa; **~ car** *n* **1** (Auto, Sport) stock car *m* (*automóvil reforzado que se emplea en carreras con colisiones*) **2** (for livestock) vagón *m* de ganado; **~-car racing** /ˈstɑːkˌkɑːr || ˈstɒkˌkɑː(r)/ *n* [u] carreras *fpl* de stock-car; **~ company** *n* (AmE) **1** (Fin) sociedad *f* anónima **2** (Theat) compañía *f* de repertorio; **~ control** *n* [u] control *m* de existencias; **~ cube** *n* cubito *m* de caldo; **~ exchange** *n* bolsa *f* (de valores), Bolsa *f*; **~holder** *n* accionista *mf*

Stockholm /ˈstɑːkhəʊlm || ˈstɒkhəʊm/ *n* Estocolmo

stockily /ˈstɑːkəli/ *adv*: **~ built** de complexión robusta

stocking /ˈstɑːkɪŋ || ˈstɒkɪŋ/ *n* media *f*; **a pair of ~s** un par de medias, unas medias

stockinged /ˈstɑːkɪŋd || ˈstɒkɪŋd/ *adj*: **in ~ feet** sin zapatos, con sólo calcetines

stocking: **~ filler** *n* (BrE) ▸ **~ stuffer**; **~ stitch** *n* [u] punto *m* jersey *or* de media; **~ stuffer** /ˈstʌfər || ˈstʌfə(r)/, (BrE) **~ filler** *n* regalito *m* de Navidad (*que tradicionalmente se deja en un calcetín colgado en la chimenea*)

stock-in-trade /ˈstɑːkɪnˈtreɪd / *n* (speciality) especialidad *f*

stockist /ˈstɑːkəst || ˈstɒkɪst/ *n* (BrE) proveedor, -dora *m,f*, distribuidor, -dora *m,f*

stock: **~jobber** /ˈstɑːkˌdʒɑːbər || ˈstɒkˌdʒɒbə(r)/ *n* (AmE) ▸ **stockbroker**; **~man** /ˈstɑːkmən || ˈstɒkmən/ *n* (*pl* **-men** /-mən/) (owner) ganadero *m*; **~ market** *n* mercado *m* de valores, mercado *m* (bursátil); (*before n*) **~ market crash** crac *m or* descalabro *m* bursátil

stockpile¹ /ˈstɑːkpaɪl || ˈstɒkpaɪl/ *n* (of oil, coal) reservas *fpl*; **the world's nuclear ~** el arsenal nuclear del mundo

stockpile² *vt* almacenar, hacer* acopio de

stock: **~room** *n* almacén *m*, depósito *m*, bodega *f* (Méx); **~-still** /ˈstɑːkˈstɪl || ˌstɒkˈstɪl/ *adj* inmóvil; **~taking** *n* [u] (esp BrE) **1** (Busn): **~taking took three weeks** hacer el inventario nos llevó tres semanas; **closed for stocktaking** cerrado por inventario **2** (review) balance *m*

stocky /ˈstɑːki/ *adj* **stockier, stockiest** bajo y fornido

stockyard /ˈstɑːkjɑːrd || ˈstɒkjɑːd/ *n* (AmE) corral *m*

stodgy /ˈstɑːdʒi || ˈstɒdʒi/ *adj* **-dgier, -dgiest** **1** ‹*person/performance*› aburrido, pesado **2** (BrE) ‹*food*› feculento, pesado

stoic /ˈstəʊɪk/ *n* estoico, -ca *m,f*

stoical /ˈstəʊɪkəl/ *adj* estoico

stoically /ˈstəʊɪkli/ *adv* con estoicismo, estoicamente

stoicism /ˈstəʊəsɪzəm || ˈstəʊɪsɪzəm/ *n* [u] estoicismo *m*

stoke /stəʊk/ *vt* **~ (up)** **1** ‹*fire/furnace*› echarle carbón (*or* leña *etc*) a **2** ‹*hatred*› avivar, alimentar; ‹*tensions*› agudizar*

Phrasal verb

- **stoke up** [v ▸ o ▸ adv, v ▸ adv ▸ o] ▸ **stoke**

stoker /ˈstəʊkər || ˈstəʊkə(r)/ *n* fogonero, -ra *m,f*

stole¹ /stəʊl/ *past of* **steal¹**

stole² *n* estola *f*

stolen /ˈstəʊlən/ *past p of* **steal¹**

stolid /ˈstɑːləd || ˈstɒlɪd/ *adj* impasible, imperturbable

stomach¹ /ˈstʌmək/ *n* **1** (organ) estómago *m*; **I have an upset ~** ando mal del estómago; **on an empty ~** con el estómago vacío, en ayunas; ***to have no ~ for sth***: **they had no ~ for an all-out strike** no tenían ganas de ir a una huelga general; (*before n*) **~ pains** dolor *m* de estómago; **~ upset** problema *m* estomacal, trastorno *m* gástrico (frml) **2** (belly) barriga *f* (fam), panza *f* (fam), guata *f* (Chi fam); **she lay on her ~** estaba tendida boca abajo

stomach² *vt* (*usu neg*) **1** ‹*food/drink*› tolerar **2** ‹*insults/insolence/person*› soportar, aguantar

stomach: **~ache** *n* [c u] dolor *m* de estómago; (in lower abdomen) dolor *m* de barriga *or* (frml) de vientre; **~ pump** *n* bomba *f* estomacal

stomp /stɑːmp || stɒmp/ *vi* (+ *adv compl*): **to ~ in/out** entrar/salir* pisando fuerte

stone¹ /stəʊn/ *n*
A **1** [u] (material) piedra *f* **2** [c] (small piece) piedra *f*; ***(only o no more than) a ~'s throw away*** a un paso, a tiro de piedra (fam); ***to leave no ~ unturned*** no dejar piedra sin mover **3** [c] (block) (Const) piedra *f* **4** [c] (of grave) lápida *f*
B [c] **1** (gem) piedra *f* **2** (in kidney) cálculo *m*, piedra *f* **3** (of fruit) hueso *m*, cuesco *m*, carozo *m* (CS), pepa *f* (Col)
C [c] (*pl* **~** *or* **~s**) (in UK) *unidad de peso = 14 libras o 6,35kg*

stone² *vt*
A (throw stones at) ‹*person*› apedrear, lapidar; **she was ~d to death** murió lapidada *or* apedreada; ***~ me o the crows!*** (BrE colloq) ¡caray! (fam)
B (BrE) ‹*fruit*› quitarle el hueso *or* el cuesco *or* (CS) el carozo *or* (Col) la pepa a, deshuesar, descarozar (CS)

stone: **~ Age** *n* Edad *f* de Piedra; **~-broke** /ˈstəʊn ˈbrəʊk/ *adj* (AmE colloq) pelado (fam)

stone-cold¹ /ˈstəʊnˈkəʊld/ *adj* (colloq) helado

stone-cold² *adv* (colloq): **he was ~ sober** no había bebido ni una gota

stoned /stəʊnd/ *adj* (colloq) (*usu pred*) **1** (from drugs) volado, pacheco (Méx), colocado (Esp fam); **to get ~** volarse*, ponerse* pacheco (Méx), colocarse* (Esp fam) **2** (from alcohol) como una cuba (fam), tomado (AmL fam)

stone: **~-dead** /ˈstəʊnˈded/ *adj* (colloq): **the blow killed him ~-dead** el golpe lo mató en el acto; **that killed the business ~-dead** eso dio al traste con el negocio (fam); **~-deaf** /ˈstəʊnˈdef/ *adj* (colloq) sordo como una tapia (fam); **~ground** *adj* molido tradicionalmente; **~mason** *n* picapedrero *m*, cantero *m*; **~wall** /ˈstəʊn ˈwɔːl/ *vi* (be evasive) andarse* con evasivas; (be obstructive) utilizar* tácticas obstruccionistas; **~walling** /ˈstəʊn ˌwɔːlɪŋ/ *n* [u] **1** (in answering) evasivas *fpl* **2** (in procedures) obstrucción *f*, bloqueo *m* **3** (BrE Sport) (táctica *f* del) cerrojo *m*; **~ware** /ˈstəʊnwer || ˈstəʊnweə(r)/ *n* [u] cerámica *f* de gres; **~washed** /ˈstəʊnwɔːʃt / *adj* lavado a la piedra; **~work** *n* [u] cantería *f*, mampostería *f*

stony¹ /ˈstəʊni/ *adj* **-nier, -niest**
A ‹*soil/ground/path*› pedregoso
B ‹*look/stare/person*› frío, glacial; ‹*silence*› sepulcral; **a ~ heart** un corazón de piedra

stony² *adv* (BrE colloq): **to be ~ broke** estar* en la ruina, estar* pelado (fam), estar* sin un duro (Esp fam), estar* en la olla (Col fam)

stood /stʊd/ *past & past p of* **stand²**

stooge /stuːdʒ/ *n* **1** (in comedy) *personaje del cual se burlan otros en una comedia* **2** (lackey, puppet) títere *m*

stool /stuːl/ *n*
A [c] (seat) taburete *m*, banco *m*; ***to fall between two ~s*** nadar entre dos aguas
B [c u] (feces) (Med) deposición *f* (frml)

stool pigeon *n* (colloq) **1** (informer) soplón, -plona *m,f* (fam) **2** (decoy) señuelo *m*

stoop¹ /stuːp/ *vi*
A **1** (have a stoop): **he ~s a little** es un poco cargado de espaldas *or* encorvado **2** **stooping** *pres p* ‹*posture*› encorvado; ‹*shoulders*› caído
B (bend over) agacharse

S

C (demean oneself): **how could she ~ so low?** ¿cómo pudo llegar tan bajo?; **to ~ TO sth/-ING** rebajarse A algo/+ INF

stoop² *n*

A (of shoulders) (*no pl*): **she walks with a ~** camina encorvada

B (of house) (AmE) entrada *f* (*a la que se accede por una escalinata*)

stop¹ /stɑːp || stɒp/ *n*

A (halt): **to work without a ~** trabajar sin parar; **to bring sth to a ~** ‹*train/car*› detener* *or* parar algo; ‹*conversation/proceedings*› poner* fin a *or* interrumpir algo; **to come to a ~** «*vehicle/aircraft*» detenerse*; «*production/conversation*» interrumpirse; **to put a ~ to sth** ‹*to mischief/malpractice*› poner* fin a algo

B 1 (break on journey) parada *f*; **we made a ~ at a service station** paramos en una estación de servicio; **after an overnight ~ in Madrid** después de hacer noche *or* de pasar la noche en Madrid 2 (stopping place) parada *f*, paradero *m* (AmL exc RPl)

C (punctuation mark) (esp BrE) punto *m*; (in telegrams) stop *m*; *see also* **full stop**

D (Mus) (on organ) registro *m*; ***to pull out all the ~s*** tocar* todos los registros

stop² **-pp-** *vt*

A 1 (halt) ‹*taxi/bus*› parar; ‹*person*› parar, detener*; **we were ~ped by the police** nos paró la policía; **I ~ped the car and got out** paré *or* detuve el coche y me bajé 2 (switch off) ‹*machine/engine*› parar

B 1 (bring to an end, interrupt) ‹*decline/inflation*› detener*, parar; ‹*discussion/abuse*› poner* fin a, acabar con; **~ that noise!** ¡deja de hacer ruido!; **the trial was ~ped** se suspendió el juicio; **rain ~ped play** la lluvia interrumpió el partido 2 (cease): **~ what you're doing and listen to me** deja lo que estás haciendo y escúchame; **~ it!** ¡basta ya!; **~ that nonsense!** ¡déjate de tonterías!; **to ~ -ING** dejar DE + INF; **~ arguing!** ¡dejen de discutir!; **I couldn't ~ laughing** no podía parar de reírme; **he never ~s talking** habla sin parar

C (prevent): **what's ~ping you?** ¿qué te lo impide?; **I had to tell him, I couldn't ~ myself** tuve que decírselo, no pude contenerme; **to ~ sb (FROM) -ING** (esp BrE) impedirle* a algn + INF, impedir* QUE algn (+ *subj*); **they locked him up to ~ him (from) escaping** lo encerraron para impedir que se escapara; **to ~ sth -ING** impedir* QUE algo (+ *subj*); **to ~ sth happening** impedir* que ocurra algo

D 1 (cancel, withhold) ‹*subscription*› cancelar; ‹*payment*› suspender; **to ~ (payment of) a check** dar* orden de no pagar un cheque 2 (deduct) (BrE) descontar*, retener*; **the boss ~ped £30 out of my wages** el jefe me descontó *or* me retuvo 30 libras del sueldo

E (block) ‹*hole*› tapar; ‹*gap*› rellenar; ‹*tooth*› empastar

F (parry) ‹*blow/punch*› parar, detener*

■ **stop** *vi*

A 1 (halt) «*vehicle/driver*» parar, detenerse*; **~, thief!** ¡al ladrón!; **~ or I'll shoot!** ¡alto o disparo!; ***to ~ at nothing*** estar* dispuesto a hacer cualquier cosa, no pararse en barras 2 (interrupt journey) «*train/bus*» parar; **let's ~ here and have a rest** hagamos un alto *or* paremos aquí para descansar 3 (cease operating) «*watch/clock/machine*» pararse

B 1 (cease): **the rain has ~ped** ha dejado *or* parado de llover, ya no llueve; **the pain/bleeding has ~ped** ya no le (*or* me *etc*) duele/sale sangre; **the noise ~ped** dejó de oírse el ruido; **this squandering of funds must ~** este derroche de fondos tiene que terminar 2 (interrupt activity) parar; **she never ~s** no para un minuto; **I didn't ~ to think** no me detuve a pensar

C (colloq) (stay) quedarse; **I can't ~** no me puedo quedar

Phrasal verbs

- **stop by** [v ▸ adv] [v ▸ prep ▸ o]: **why don't you ~ by tonight?** ¿por qué no (te) pasas por aquí (*or* por casa *etc*) esta noche?; **I ~ped by (at) the store for some milk** pasé por la tienda para comprar leche
- **stop in** [v ▸ adv] (colloq) 1 (call in): **Bill ~ped in for a chat** Bill pasó por aquí para charlar 2 (stay inside) (BrE) quedarse adentro, no salir*; (stay at home) quedarse en casa, no salir*
- **stop off** [v ▸ adv]: **I ~ped off at home to change** pasé por casa para cambiarme; **we ~ped off in San Juan for a few hours** paramos unas horas en San Juan
- **stop out** [v ▸ adv] (BrE) 1 (not come home) (colloq) no volver* a casa, quedarse por ahí (fam) 2 (on strike) (colloq) hacer* huelga, parar (AmL)
- **stop over** [v ▸ adv] 1 (break journey) parar; (overnight) hacer* noche, pasar la noche 2 (Aviat) «*plane*» hacer* escala
- **stop up**

A [v ▸ o ▸ adv, v ▸ adv ▸ o] 1 (block) (*usu pass*) atascar* 2 (fill) ‹*hole/crack*› tapar, rellenar

B [v ▸ adv] (BrE) ▸ **stay up 2**

stop: **~cock** *n* llave *f* de paso; **~gap** *n* recurso *m* provisional *or* (AmS tb) provisorio, medida *f* provisional *or* (AmS tb) provisoria; (*before n*) ‹*measure/arrangement*› provisional, provisorio (AmS); **~light** *n* (traffic light) semáforo *m*; (brake light) luz *f* de freno *or* de frenado; **~-off** *n* (colloq) parada *f*; **~over** *n* (break in journey) parada *f*; (stay) estadía *f* (AmL), estancia *f* (Esp, Méx); (Aviat) escala *f*

stoppage /ˈstɑːpɪdʒ || ˈstɒpɪdʒ/ *n*

A 1 (in play, production) interrupción *f*; **the time added on for ~s** (in soccer) el tiempo de descuento, los descuentos (CS) 2 (strike) huelga *f*, paro *m* (AmL) 3 (cancellation) suspensión *f* 4 (deduction) (BrE) retención *f*

B (blockage) obstrucción *f*

stopper /ˈstɑːpər || ˈstɒpə(r)/ *n* tapón *m*

stopping train /ˈstɑːpɪŋ || ˈstɒpɪŋ/ *n* (BrE) *tren con parada en todas las estaciones*

stop: **~ press** *n* noticias *fpl* de última hora; **~ sign** *n* stop *m*, señal *f* de pare, (señal *f* de) alto *m* (Méx), disco *m* pare (Chi); **~watch** *n* cronómetro *m*

storage /ˈstɔːrɪdʒ/ *n* [u] 1 (of goods) depósito *m*, almacenamiento *m*, almacenaje *m*; **to put one's furniture into ~** mandar los muebles a un depósito; (*before n*) **~ room** trastero *m*; **we have plenty of ~ space** tenemos mucho lugar *or* espacio para guardar cosas; **~ tank** tanque *m* de almacenamiento 2 (Comput) almacenamiento *m* 3 (cost) (gastos *mpl* de) almacenaje *m*

storage heater *n* (BrE) acumulador *m*, radiador *m* de acumulación

store¹ /stɔːr || stɔː(r)/ *n*

A 1 [c u] (stock, supply) reserva *f*, provisión *f*; **a ~ of witty anecdotes** una colección de anécdotas graciosas; ***in ~***: **we always keep some drink in ~** siempre tenemos bebida de reserva; **there's a surprise in ~ for her** la espera una sorpresa, se va a llevar una sorpresa; **we have a surprise in ~ for you** te tenemos (preparada) una sorpresa; **who knows what the future has in ~?** ¿quién sabe lo que nos deparará el futuro?; ***to set great/little ~ by sth*** dar* mucho/poco valor a algo 2 **stores** *pl* (Mil, Naut) pertrechos *mpl*

B 1 (warehouse, storage place) (*often pl*) almacén *m*, depósito *m*, bodega *f* (Méx) 2 [u] (storage) (BrE): **all our furniture is in ~** tenemos todos los muebles en depósito

C [c] 1 (shop) (esp AmE) tienda *f*; **a shoe/hardware ~** una zapatería/ferretería 2 (*department ~*) grandes almacenes *mpl*, tienda *f*; (*before n*) **~ card** tarjeta *f* de crédito (*expedida por una tienda*); **~ detective** guarda *mf* *or* vigilante *mf* no uniformado (*en una tienda*)

store² *vt* 1 (keep) ‹*food/drink/supplies*› guardar; (Busn) almacenar; ‹*information*› almacenar; ‹*electricity*› acumular; **~ in a cool, dry place** consérvese en un lugar fresco y seco; **the children's old toys are ~d (away) in the attic** los juguetes viejos de los niños están guardados en el desván 2 (Comput) ‹*data/program*› almacenar

■ **store** *vi* «*fruit/vegetables*» conservarse

Phrasal verb

- **store up** [v ▸ o ▸ adv, v ▸ adv ▸ o] 1 ‹*supplies*› almacenar 2 ‹*resentment*› ir* acumulando

store³, **store-bought** /ˈstɔːrbɔːt || ˈstɔːbɔːt/ *adj* (AmE) ‹*clothes*› de confección; ‹*cake*› comprado

store: **~front** *n* (AmE) frente *m*, fachada *f* (*de una tienda*); **~house** *n* 1 (warehouse) almacén *m*, depósito *m*, bodega *f* (Méx) 2 (source) mina *f*; **a veritable ~house of information** una verdadera mina de información; **~keeper** *n* tendero, -ra *m,f*; **~room** *n* almacén *m*, depósito *m*, bodega *f* (Méx); (for food) despensa *f*

storey /ˈstɔːri/ *n* (BrE) ▸ **story** *Sense* **II**

-storied, (BrE) **-storeyed** /ˈstɔːrid/ *suff*: **three~/five~** de tres/cinco pisos

stork /stɔːrk || stɔːk/ *n* cigüeña *f*

storm¹ /stɔːrm || stɔːm/ *n*

A (Meteo) tormenta *f*; **a ~ at sea** una tempestad, un tempo-

S

ral; ***a ~ in a teacup*** (BrE) una tormenta en un vaso de agua; ***to take sth by ~*** ‹*city/fortress*› tomar algo por asalto, asaltar algo; **she took New York's audiences by ~** cautivó al público neoyorquino, tuvo un éxito clamoroso en Nueva York; ***to weather*** *o* ***ride (out) the ~*** capear el temporal
B (of abuse) torrente *m*; (of protest) ola *f*, tempestad *f*; (uproar) escándalo *m*, revuelo *m*

storm² *vi*
A (move violently) (+ *adv compl*): **she ~ed into the office** irrumpió en la oficina, entró en la oficina como un vendaval; **furious, he ~ed out of the meeting** abandonó la reunión furioso
B (express anger) despotricar*, vociferar; **he ~ed at the manager** le dijo de todo al gerente
■ **storm** *vt*
A (attack, capture) ‹*city/fortress*› tomar por asalto, asaltar; ‹*house*› irrumpir en
B (say angrily) bramar

storm: **~-bound** *adj* ‹*airport*› cerrado por el mal tiempo; ‹*city*› paralizado por el mal tiempo; **~ cloud** *n* nube *f* *or* nubarrón *m* de tormenta; **~ door** *n* contrapuerta *f*, antepuerta *f*

storming /ˈstɔːrmɪŋ/ *n* **~ OF sth** asalto *m* A algo

storm: **~ lantern** *n* farol *m*; **~ trooper** *n* soldado *m* de las tropas de asalto

stormy /ˈstɔːrmi || ˈstɔːmi/ *adj* **-mier, -miest** 1 (Meteo) tormentoso; ‹*sea*› tempestuoso 2 (turbulent) ‹*relationship*› tempestuoso

story /ˈstɔːri/ *n* (*pl* **-ries**)
Sense **I**
A 1 (account) historia *f*, relato *m*; (tale) cuento *m*; (genre) (Lit) cuento *m*; **tell me a ~** cuéntame un cuento; **the book tells the ~ of the expedition** el libro relata la expedición; **that's a long ~** eso es largo de contar; **to cut a long ~ short** en pocas palabras; **but that's not the end of the ~** pero ahí no termina; **it's the ~ of my life!** (set phrase) siempre me pasa lo mismo; **according to his/your ~** según él/tú; **what's the ~?** (AmE) bueno ¿qué pasa?; **he gave me the ~ on the new models** (AmE) me dio información sobre los nuevos modelos; ***that's (quite) another*** *o* ***a different ~*** eso es otro cantar, eso es harina de otro costal; ***the same old ~*** la (misma) historia de siempre 2 (anecdote) anécdota *f*; (joke) chiste *m*; **the ~ goes that ...** cuenta la leyenda que ...
B (plot) argumento *m*, trama *f*
C (Journ) artículo *m*; **he has a nose for a good ~** tiene buen olfato para lo que es noticia
D (lie) (colloq) cuento *m* (fam), mentira *f*; **don't tell stories** no me vengas con cuentos (fam), no digas mentiras
Sense **II** (BrE) **storey** (of building) piso *m*, planta *f*; **on the first ~** (in US) en la planta baja; (in UK) en el primer piso; **a four-~ building** un edificio de cuatro pisos

story: **~book** *n* libro *m* de cuentos; (*before n*) **a ~book romance** un romance de cuento de hadas; **~ line** *n* (plot) argumento *m*; (script) guión *m*; **~teller** /ˈstɔːriˌtelər || ˈstɔːriˌtelə(r)/ *n* 1 (narrator) narrador, -dora *m,f* 2 (writer) escritor, -tora *m,f* 3 (liar) (colloq) mentiroso, -sa *m,f*, cuentista *mf* (fam), cuentero, -ra *m,f* (RPl fam)

stout¹ /staʊt/ *adj* **-er, -est** 1 ‹*person/figure*› robusto, corpulento 2 ‹*rope*› resistente, fuerte; ‹*door*› sólido; **a pair of ~ shoes** un par de zapatos fuertes 3 (staunch) ‹*resistance*› firme, tenaz

stout² *n* [u] cerveza *f* negra

stoutly /ˈstaʊtli/ *adv* 1 ‹*made/built*› sólidamente 2 (staunchly) ‹*resist*› con firmeza; ‹*deny/refuse*› rotundamente

stove /stəʊv/ *n* 1 (for cooking) cocina *f*, estufa *f* (Col, Méx); (ring) calentador *m*, hornillo *m*; **electric/gas ~** cocina *or* (Col, Méx) estufa eléctrica/de *or* a gas 2 (for warmth) estufa *f*, calentador *m*

stove in *past & past p of* **stave in**

stow /stəʊ/ *vt* (put away) guardar, poner*; (hide) esconder; (Naut) estibar; **she ~ed the glasses (away) carefully** guardó los vasos cuidadosamente
Phrasal verb
• **stow away** [v ▸ adv] viajar de polizón

stowage /ˈstəʊɪdʒ/ *n* [u] (Naut) 1 (storage capacity) bodega *f* 2 (stowing) estiba *f*

stowaway /ˈstəʊəˌweɪ/ *n* polizón *mf*

straddle /ˈstrædl/ *vt* 1 (sit, stand astride) ‹*horse*› sentarse* a horcajadas sobre; **the town ~s the river** la ciudad se extiende a ambas orillas del río 2 (be noncommittal about) (AmE) ‹*issue/question*› eludir

strafe /streɪf, strɑːf/ *vt* (Mil) ‹*troops/airfield*› bombardear

straggle /ˈstrægəl/ *vi*
A (spread untidily) «*plant*» crecer* desordenadamente; **the village ~d along the valley** el pueblo se extendía por el valle sin orden ni concierto
B 1 (wander): **the procession ~d along the road** la procesión avanzaba desordenadamente por la carretera 2 (lag behind, fall away) rezagarse*, quedarse rezagado

straggler /ˈstræglər || ˈstræglə(r)/ *n* rezagado, -da *m,f*

straggly /ˈstrægli/ *adj* **-glier, -gliest** ‹*hair*› desordenado, desgreñado; ‹*beard*› descuidado

straight¹ /streɪt/ *adj* **-er, -est**
A 1 (not curved or wavy) recto; ‹*hair*› lacio, liso; **to walk in a ~ line** caminar en línea recta; **keep your knees ~** no dobles las rodillas; **he walks with a ~ back** camina muy erguido 2 (level, upright, vertical) (*pred*) **to be ~** estar* derecho; **is my tie ~?** ¿tengo la corbata derecha *or* bien puesta?; **your tie isn't ~** llevas *or* tienes la corbata torcida
B (in order) (*pred*): **is my hair ~?** ¿tengo bien el pelo?; **I have to get** *o* **put my room ~** tengo que ordenar mi cuarto; **if I pay for the coffees, we'll be ~** si pago los cafés quedamos *or* estamos en paz *or* (CS) a mano; **to get sth ~**: **let's get this ~** a ver si nos entendemos; **you have to make sure you've got your facts ~** tienes que asegurarte de que la información que tienes es correcta; **to set the record ~** dejar las cosas en claro; ***to put*** *o* ***set sb ~ about sth*** aclararle algo a algn
C 1 (direct, clear) ‹*denial/refusal*› rotundo, categórico; **it's a ~ choice between buying a car or going on holiday** la alternativa es clara: o se compra un coche o se va de vacaciones; **I made $20,000 ~ profit** saqué 20.000 dólares limpios de beneficio; **she got ~ A's** ≈ sacó sobresaliente en todo 2 (unmixed) ‹*gin/vodka*› solo
D (honest, frank) ‹*question*› directo; ‹*answer*› claro; **all I want is a ~ yes or no** lo único que quiero es que me digas que sí o que no, sin más; **I've been absolutely ~ with you about the whole business** no te he ocultado nada del asunto
E (successive): **he won in ~ sets** (Sport) ganó sin conceder *or* sin perder ningún set; **she's had five ~ wins** ha ganado cinco veces seguidas; **this is the fifth ~ day it's happened** (AmE) éste es el quinto día seguido que pasa
F 1 (serious) ‹*play/actor*› dramático, serio 2 (conventional) (colloq) convencional 3 (heterosexual) (colloq) heterosexual

straight² *adv*
A 1 (in a straight line) ‹*walk*› en línea recta; **they live ~ across from us** viven justo enfrente de nosotros; **she looked ~ ahead** miró al frente; **the truck was coming ~ at me** el camión venía derecho *or* justo hacia mí; **I aimed ~ for his heart** le apunté justo al corazón; **he made ~ for the bar** se fue derecho al bar; **look me ~ in the eye** mírame a la cara; **keep ~ on until you come to the lights** sigue derecho hasta llegar al semáforo; **the bullet went ~ through his arm** la bala le atravesó el brazo 2 (erect) ‹*sit/stand*› derecho; **sit up ~** ponte derecho
B 1 (directly) directamente; **I came ~ home from work** vine directamente *or* derecho a casa después del trabajo; **she drank it ~ from the bottle** se lo bebió directamente de la botella; **I joined the army ~ from school** me alisté en el ejército en cuanto terminé el colegio 2 (immediately): **~ after dinner** inmediatamente después de cenar, en cuanto terminé de cenar; **I'll bring it ~ back** enseguida lo devuelvo; **she said ~ off she wasn't paying** (colloq) dijo de entrada que ella no pagaba; **I'll come ~ to the point** iré derecho *or* directamente al grano; **~ away** ▸ **straightaway**
C (colloq) 1 (frankly) con franqueza; **she told him ~ out** se lo dijo sin rodeos 2 (honestly): **are you playing ~ with me?** ¿estás jugando limpio conmigo?; ***to go ~***: **he swore he'd go ~** prometió que se reformaría
D (clearly) ‹*see/think*› con claridad; **I can't think ~** no puedo pensar claro *or* con claridad
E (Theat) ‹*play*› de manera clásica

straight³ *n* (on race track): **the ~** la recta

S

straight: **~ and narrow** *n* [u] **the ~ and narrow** el buen camino, el camino recto; **his mother kept him on the ~ and narrow** su madre lo mantuvo sobre buen camino; **~away** /ˈstreɪtəˈweɪ/, **~ away** *adv* enseguida, inmediatamente

straighten /ˈstreɪtn̩/ *vt* [1] (make straight) ‹*nail/wire*› enderezar*; ‹*hair*› alisar, estirar; ‹*bedclothes/tablecloth*› estirar; ‹*picture*› enderezar*, poner* derecho; **he ~ed his tie** se enderezó la corbata; **~ your back** ponte derecho [2] (tidy) ‹*room/papers*› arreglar, ordenar; ‹*bed*› estirar

■ **straighten** *vi* ▸**straighten out B**

Phrasal verbs

• **straighten out**

A [v ▸ o ▸ adv, v ▸ adv ▸ o] [1] (make straight) ‹*nail/wire*› enderezar*, poner* derecho; ‹*bedclothes/tablecloth*› estirar [2] ‹*confusion/misunderstanding*› aclarar; ‹*problem*› resolver*, arreglar

B [v ▸ adv] «*road/river*» hacerse* recto

• **straighten up**

A [v ▸ o ▸ adv, v ▸ adv ▸ o] [1] (make straight) ‹*picture*› enderezar*, poner* derecho; **~ up your shoulders!** ¡ponte derecho! [2] (tidy) ‹*room/papers*› ordenar, arreglar; ‹*bed*› arreglar, estirar; **I'd better ~ myself up a bit** más vale que me arregle un poco

B [v ▸ adv] (stand up straight) ponerse* derecho, enderezarse*

straight: **~faced** /ˈstreɪtˈfeɪst/ *adj*: **he said it completely ~faced** lo dijo muy serio *or* sin reírse; **~forward** *adj* [1] (honest, frank) ‹*person*› franco, sin dobleces; ‹*answer*› franco [2] (uncomplicated) ‹*problem/question/answer*› sencillo; **~jacket** *n* ▸**straitjacket**; **~ man** *n*: *personaje serio de una pareja de cómicos*; **~ ticket** *n* (in US) (*no pl*): **to vote the/a ~ ticket** votar a *or* por candidatos de un mismo partido para todos los cargos

straight-up /ˈstreɪtˈʌp/ *adj* (AmE colloq) llano, campechano

strain¹ /streɪn/ *n*

A [u c] (tension) tensión *f*; (pressure) presión *f*; **the rope snapped under the ~** la cuerda se rompió debido a la tensión a la que estaba sometida; **it puts a ~ on your spine** ejerce presión sobre la columna vertebral; **the incident put a ~ on Franco-German relations** las relaciones franco-alemanas se volvieron tirantes a raíz del incidente; **she's been under great** *o* **a lot of ~** ha estado pasando una época de mucha tensión *or* de mucho estrés

B [c u] (Med) (resulting from wrench, twist) torcedura *f*; (on a muscle) esguince *m*

C **strains** *pl* (tune): **the ~s of a flute could be heard in the distance** se oía una flauta a lo lejos

D [1] [c] (type — of plant) variedad *f*; (— of virus) cepa *f*; (— of animal) raza *f* [2] (streak) (*no pl*) veta *f*

strain² *vt*

A (exert): **to ~ one's eyes/voice** forzar* la vista/voz; **to ~ one's ears** aguzar* el oído; **he ~ed every muscle to lift the weight** usó todas sus fuerzas para levantar el peso

B [1] (overburden) ‹*beam/support*› ejercer* demasiada presión sobre [2] (injure): **to ~ one's back** hacerse* daño en la espalda; **to ~ a muscle** hacerse* un esguince [3] (overtax, stretch) ‹*relations*› someter a demasiada tensión, volver* tenso *or* tirante; ‹*credulity/patience*› poner* a prueba

C (filter) filtrar; (Culin) colar*; ‹*vegetables/rice*› escurrir; **~ the lumps from the sauce with a sieve** pase la salsa por un tamiz para eliminar los grumos

■ *v refl* **to ~ oneself** hacerse* daño; **don't ~ yourself** (iro) no te vayas a herniar (iró)

■ **strain** *vi*: **the porters ~ed under the load** los mozos iban agobiados por la carga; **to ~ AT sth** tirar DE algo; **to ~ to + INF** hacer* un gran esfuerzo PARA + INF

strained /streɪnd/ *adj*

A [1] (tense) ‹*relations/atmosphere*› tenso, tirante; ‹*face/expression*› tenso, crispado; ‹*voice*› forzado [2] (unnatural, forced) ‹*manner/humor*› forzado

B (Med) ‹*eyes*› cansado; **a ~ muscle** un esguince

strainer /ˈstreɪnər || ˈstreɪnə(r)/ *n* (Culin) colador *m*

strait /streɪt/ *n*

A (Geog) (*often pl*) estrecho *m*; **the S~ of Magellan, the Magellan S~(s)** el estrecho de Magallanes

B **straits** *pl* (difficulties, difficult position): **to be in dire/desperate ~s** estar* en grandes apuros/en una situación desesperada; **to be in financial ~s** pasar estrecheces, pasar apuros económicos

strait: **~jacket** *n* camisa *f* de fuerza, chaleco *m* de fuerza (CS); **~laced** /ˈstreɪtˈleɪst/ *adj* puritano, mojigato

strand¹ /strænd/ *n*

A (of rope, string) ramal *m*; (of thread, wool) hebra *f*; (of wire) filamento *m*; **a ~ of hair** un pelo

B (of opinion) corriente *f*; (in group, movement) tendencia *f*

C (beach) (liter) playa *f*

strand² *vt* (*usu pass*) [1] (Naut): **the ship was ~ed on a sandbank** el barco quedó encallado *or* varado en un banco de arena; **a whale was ~ed by the tide** la marea dejó una ballena varada en la playa [2] (leave helpless): **they left me ~ed** me abandonaron a mi suerte, me dejaron tirado *or* (AmL exc RPl) botado (fam); **~ed tourists** turistas con problemas para volver a casa

strange /streɪndʒ/ *adj* **stranger, strangest**

A (odd) raro, extraño; **what a ~ thing to say!** ¡qué cosa más rara de decir!; **truth is ~r than fiction** la realidad supera a la ficción; **you're/she's a ~ one** (colloq) mira que eres raro/es rara (fam); **I feel ~ wearing a suit** me siento raro *or* incómodo con traje; **it is ~ (THAT)** es raro QUE (+ *subj*); **I find it ~ (that) they haven't replied** me extraña que no hayan contestado; **~ as it may seem** por extraño que parezca

B [1] (unfamiliar, unaccustomed) ‹*faces/handwriting*› desconocido; **to taste/smell ~** saber*/oler* raro [2] (alien) (liter): **in a ~ land** en tierras extrañas; **a ~ language** una lengua foránea

strangely /ˈstreɪndʒli/ *adv* ‹*behave/act*› de una manera rara *or* extraña; **he was ~ quiet** era raro *or* extraño lo callado que estaba; **~ (enough)** (*indep*) aunque parezca mentira, aunque parezca raro *or* extraño

strangeness /ˈstreɪndʒnəs || ˈstreɪndʒnɪs/ *n* [u] [1] (oddness) rareza *f*, lo extraño [2] (unfamiliarity) novedad *f*

stranger /ˈstreɪndʒər || ˈstreɪndʒə(r)/ *n* desconocido, -da *m,f*; (from another place) forastero, -ra *m,f*; **don't speak to ~s** no hables con extraños *or* desconocidos; **hello, ~!** (colloq) ¡dichosos los ojos que te ven!; **I'm a ~ here myself** yo tampoco soy de aquí; **to be no ~ to sth**: **she's no ~ to New York** conoce Nueva York bastante bien; **he's no ~ to violence** la violencia no le es desconocida

strangle /ˈstræŋgəl/ *vt* [1] ‹*person*› estrangular [2] ‹*originality*› coartar; ‹*protests*› sofocar*, ahogar* [3] **strangled** *past p* ahogado; **a ~d cry** un grito ahogado; **in a ~d voice** con voz ahogada *or* estrangulada

stranglehold /ˈstræŋgəlhəʊld/ *n* [1] (Sport) llave *f* al cuello [2] (absolute control) poder *m*, dominio *m*; **they have a ~ over the supply of copper** tienen el monopolio del suministro de cobre

strangler /ˈstræŋglər/ *n* estrangulador, -dora *m,f*

strangling /ˈstræŋglɪŋ/ *n* [c u] estrangulación *f*

strangulation /ˈstræŋgjəˈleɪʃən/ *n* [u] estrangulación *f*

strap¹ /stræp/ *n* [1] (of leather) correa *f*; (of canvas) asa *f*‡; **watch ~** (BrE) correa *f* de reloj [2] (on bus, train) agarradera *f* [3] (*shoulder ~*) tirante *m*, bretel *m* (CS) [4] (punishment) (BrE): **to give sb the ~** darle* a algn con la correa

strap² *vt* **-pp-** [1] (tie) atar *or* sujetar con una correa, amarrar con una correa (AmL exc RPl); **to ~ oneself in** ponerse* *or* abrocharse el cinturón de seguridad [2] **~ (up)** (BrE Med) ‹*ankle/wrist*› vendar

strapless /ˈstræpləs || ˈstræplɪs/ *adj* sin tirantes, sin breteles (CS), strapless *adj inv* (Méx, Ven)

strapline /ˈstræplaɪn/ *n* (heading) titular *m*

strapped /stræpt/ *adj* (colloq) (*pred*): **to be ~ for cash** andar* corto de dinero

strapping /ˈstræpɪŋ/ *adj* robusto, fornido

Strasbourg /ˈstrɑːsbɜrg || ˈstræzbɜːg/ *n* Estrasburgo *m*

strata /ˈstreɪtə, ˈstrætə || ˈstrɑːtə, ˈstreɪtə/ *pl of* **stratum**

stratagem /ˈstrætədʒəm/ *n* [c u] estratagema *f*

strategic /strəˈtiːdʒɪk/ *adj* estratégico

strategist /ˈstrætədʒəst || ˈstrætədʒɪst/ *n* estratega *mf*

strategy /ˈstrætədʒi/ *n* [c u] (*pl* **-gies**) estrategia *f*

stratification /ˈstrætəfəˈkeɪʃən/ *n* [u] estratificación *f*

stratify /ˈstrætəfaɪ || ˈstrætɪfaɪ/ **-fies, -fying, -fied** *vt* (*usu pass*) estratificar*

stratosphere /ˈstrætəsfɪr/ *n* estratosfera *f*

stratum /ˈstreɪtəm, ˈstræ-/ *n* (*pl* **-ta**) estrato *m*

stratus /ˈstreɪtəs, ˈstrɑː-/ *n* (*pl* **-ti**/-taɪ/) estrato *m*

straw /strɔː/ *n* 1 [u c] paja *f*; **we'll draw ~s for it** el que saque la paja *or* pajita más corta lo hace; **I always draw the short ~** siempre me toca a mí bailar con la más fea (fam & hum); ***to be the last*** *o* ***final ~*** ser* el colmo, ser* lo último; ***to clutch*** *o* ***grasp at ~s*** aferrarse desesperadamente a una esperanza; ***the ~ which broke the camel's back*** la gota que colmó el vaso *or* (Méx) que derramó el vino; (*before n*) **~ hat** sombrero *m* de paja; **~ mat** estera *f* 2 [c] (for drinking) pajita *f*, paja *f*, caña *f* (Esp), pitillo *m* (Col), popote *m* (Méx); **to drink sth through a ~** beber algo con una pajita (*or* paja *etc*)

strawberry /ˈstrɔːˌberi || ˈstrɔːbəri/ *n* (*pl* **-ries**) (fruit) fresa *f*, frutilla *f* (Bol, CS); (large) fresón *m*

straw poll, straw vote *n* sondeo *m* informal de opinión

stray¹ /streɪ/ *vi* 1 (wander away) apartarse, alejarse; (get lost) extraviarse*, perderse*; **to ~ FROM sb/sth**: **we ~ed from the rest of the group** nos apartamos *or* nos alejamos del resto del grupo; **several sheep ~ed from the flock** varias ovejas se separaron del resto del rebaño *or* se descarriaron; **we ~ed off the path** nos apartamos del camino; **I ~ed into a military zone** me metí sin querer en una zona militar 2 (digress): **he kept ~ing from the issue** se apartaba *or* se desviaba una y otra vez del tema; **he let his thoughts ~** se puso a pensar en otra cosa

stray² *adj* 1 ‹*dog*› (ownerless) callejero, vago; (lost) perdido; ‹*sheep*› descarriado 2 (random, scattered): **a ~ bullet** una bala perdida; **a few ~ hairs** algunos pelos sueltos

stray³ *n* (ownerless animal) perro *m*/gato *m* callejero *or* vago; (lost animal) perro *m*/gato *m* perdido

streak¹ /striːk/ *n*

A 1 (line, band) lista *f*, raya *f*; (in hair) reflejo *m*, mechón *m*; (in meat, marble) veta *f*; (of ore) veta *f*, filón *m*; **a ~ of lightning** un relámpago 2 (in personality) veta *f*; **she has a mean ~** tiene una veta mezquina

B (spell) racha *f*; **to have** *o* **be on a winning/losing ~** tener* una buena/mala racha

streak² *vi*

A (move rapidly) (+ *adv compl*): **she ~ed into the lead** rápida como un rayo, se colocó a la cabeza; **it ~ed past the window** pasó como una centella por delante de la ventana

B (run naked) (colloq) hacer* streaking (*correr desnudo en un lugar público*)

■ **streak** *vt*: **tears ~ed her face** tenía el rostro surcado de lágrimas; **she's had her hair ~ed** se ha hecho mechones *or* reflejos *or* (RPl) claritos *or* (Méx) luces *or* (Chi) visos (en el pelo); **to be ~ed WITH sth**: **his clothes were ~ed with paint** llevaba la ropa manchada *or* (AmL tb) chorreada de pintura; **her hair is ~ed with gray** tiene el cabello entrecano

streaker /ˈstriːkər || ˈstriːkə(r)/ *n* (colloq) streaker *mf* (*persona que corre desnuda en un lugar público*)

streaky /ˈstriːki/ *adj* **-kier, -kiest** 1 (uneven): **the paint's dried ~** el color no ha quedado uniforme al secarse la pintura, el color ha quedado disparejo al secarse la pintura (AmL) 2 (BrE Culin): **~ bacon** tocino *m* *or* (Esp) bacon *m* *or* (RPl) panceta *f*

stream¹ /striːm/ *n*

A 1 (small river) arroyo *m*, riachuelo *m* 2 (current) corriente *f*

B (flow): **a thin ~ of water** un chorrito de agua; **a ~ of lava** un río de lava; **a ~ of abuse** una sarta de insultos; **there is a continuous ~ of traffic** pasan vehículos continuamente, el tráfico es ininterrumpido; **~s of people** un torrente de personas

C (BrE Educ) *conjunto de alumnos agrupados según su nivel de aptitud para una asignatura*

stream² *vi*

A 1 (flow) (+ *adv compl*): **blood ~ed from the wound** salía *or* manaba mucha sangre de la herida; **water ~ed from the burst pipe** el agua salía a chorros *or* a torrentes de la tubería rota; **tears were ~ing down her cheeks** lloraba a lágrima viva; **the sunlight was ~ing in through the window** el sol entraba a raudales por la ventana; **the children ~ed in from the yard** los niños entraron en tropel del patio 2 (run with liquid): **the walls ~ed with water** corría agua por las paredes; **I've got a ~ing cold** tengo un resfriado muy fuerte, me gotea constantemente la nariz

B (wave) ‹‹*flag/hair*›› ondear

■ **stream** *vt*

A (emit): **my nose ~ed blood** me salía mucha sangre de la nariz; **his eyes ~ed tears** se le saltaban las lágrimas

B (BrE Educ) *dividir (a los alumnos) en grupos según su aptitud para una asignatura*

streamer /ˈstriːmər || ˈstriːmə(r)/ *n*

A 1 (banner) banderín *m* 2 (of paper) serpentina *f*

B (AmE Journ) titular *m* a toda página

stream: **~line** *vt* ‹*car/plane*› hacer* más aerodinámico el diseño de, aerodinamizar*; ‹*organization/production*› racionalizar*, hacer* más eficiente; **~lined** *adj* ‹*car/plane*› aerodinámico; ‹*methods/production*› racionalizado; **~ of consciousness** *n* (*no pl*) monólogo *m* interior

street /striːt/ *n* calle *f*; **it's on** *o* (BrE) **in Elm S~** queda en la calle Elm; **to walk the ~s** andar* *or* deambular por las calles; ‹‹*prostitute*›› hacer* la calle *or* (Esp tb) la carrera; **the whole ~ turned out to welcome them** todos los vecinos salieron a recibirlos; **the S~** (AmE colloq) Wall Street; ***to be on easy ~*** (colloq) estar* forrado (fam); ***to be on the ~s*** hacer* la calle *or* (Esp tb) la carrera; **to go on the ~s** prostituirse*; ***to be right up one's ~*** (colloq): **the job would be right up her ~** sería un trabajo ideal para ella; **the movie is right up your ~** es justo el tipo de película que a ti te encanta; ***to be ~s ahead of sb/sth***: **the company is ~s ahead of its competitors** la compañía está muy por encima de la competencia; **she's ~s ahead of her classmates** les da mil vueltas a sus compañeros de clase (fam); ***to be ~s apart***: **the two sides are still ~s apart** todavía hay un abismo entre las dos partes; (*before n*) ‹*musician/theater*› callejero; **~ corner** esquina *f*; **~ crime** delincuencia *f* callejera; **~ map** *o* **plan** plano *m* de la ciudad, callejero *m* (Esp); **~ market** mercado *m* al aire libre, feria *f* (CS); **~ people** (AmE) gente *f* de la calle

street: **~car** *n* (AmE) tranvía *m*, carro *m* (Chi); **~ cleaner** *n* (AmE) barrendero, -ra *m,f*; **~ credibility, ~ cred** /kred/ *n* [u] (esp BrE) *imagen de persona moderna, familiarizada con la cultura urbana*; **~ door** *n* puerta *f* de (la) calle; (of apartment block) puerta *f* de (la) calle, portal *m*; **~ fighting** *n* [u] riñas *fpl* *or* refriegas *fpl* callejeras; **~ lamp** *n* farol *m*, farola *f* (Esp); **~ level** *n*: **at ~ level** a nivel de la calle; **~ light** *n* ▸ **~ lamp**; **~ lighting** *n* [u] alumbrado *m* (público); **~ sweeper** *n* (person) barrendero, -ra *m,f*; (machine) (máquina *f*) barredora *f*, barredera *f*; **~ value** *n* valor *m* de reventa; **~walker** *n* prostituta *f* callejera; **~wise** *adj* (colloq) espabilado, avispado (fam)

strength /streŋθ/ *n*

A [u] (of persons) 1 (physical energy) fuerza(s) *f(pl)*; (health) fortaleza *f* física; **he doesn't know his own ~!** ¡no sabe la fuerza que tiene!; **to get one's ~ back** recobrar las fuerzas; **to save one's ~** ahorrar (las) energías 2 (emotional, mental) fortaleza *f*; (in adversity) fortaleza *f*, entereza *f*; **~ of will** fuerza *f* de voluntad; **~ of character** firmeza *f* *or* fortaleza *f* de carácter; **~ of purpose** resolución *f*, determinación *f*; **give me ~!** (colloq) ¡Dios me dé paciencia!

B [u] (of economy, currency) solidez *f*; **political/military ~** poderío *m* político/militar

C [u] 1 (of materials) resistencia *f*; (of wind, current) fuerza *f*; (of drug, solution) concentración *f*; (of alcoholic drink) graduación *f*; **full-~** sin diluir; **half-~** diluido al 50% 2 (of sound, light) potencia *f*; (of emotions) intensidad *f* 3 (of argument, evidence) lo convincente; (of protests) lo enérgico; **we employed her on the ~ of his recommendation** la contratamos basándonos en su recomendación; **on the ~ of that performance she was offered a part** en virtud de esa actuación le ofrecieron un papel

D [c] (strong point) virtud *f*, punto *m* fuerte; ***from ~ to ~***: **the firm has gone from ~ to ~ since she took over** la empresa ha tenido un éxito tras otro desde que ella está al frente; **his career seems to be going from ~ to ~** su carrera marcha viento en popa

E [u c] (force in numbers) número *m*; **we're below** *o* **under ~ at the moment** en este momento estamos cortos de personal; **their fans were there in ~** sus hinchas estaban allí en bloque *or* en masa

S

strengthen /ˈstreŋθən/ *vt* ‹*muscle/limb/teeth*› fortalecer*; ‹*wall/furniture/glass*› reforzar*; ‹*support*› aumentar, acrecentar*; **this has ~ed my conviction that ...** esto me ha convencido aún más de que ...

■ **strengthen** *vi* «*limb/muscle*» fortalecerse*; «*opposition/support*» aumentar, acrecentarse*

strenuous /ˈstrenjuəs/ *adj* 1 ‹*activity*› agotador, extenuante 2 ‹*denial*› vigoroso, enérgico; ‹*opposition*› tenaz; **despite our ~ efforts to locate them** a pesar de nuestros denodados esfuerzos por localizarlos

strep throat /strep/ *n* [u] (AmE colloq): **to have ~ ~** tener* una inflamación de garganta

stress¹ /stres/ *n*

A 1 [u c] (tension) tensión *f*; (Med) estrés *m*, tensión, f; **she's under a lot of ~** está sometida a muchas presiones; **the ~es and strains of modern living** las tensiones y presiones de la vida moderna 2 [u] (Phys, Tech) tensión *f*

B 1 [u] (emphasis) énfasis *m*, hincapié *m*; **to lay ~ on sth** poner* énfasis *or* hacer* hincapié en algo, enfatizar* algo 2 [c u] (Ling, Lit) acento *m* (tónico); **the ~ is** *o* **falls on the second syllable** se acentúa (en) la segunda sílaba

stress² *vt* 1 (emphasize) poner* énfasis *or* hacer* hincapié en, enfatizar*, recalcar*; **I must ~ once again that ...** vuelvo a insistir en que ..., vuelvo a recalcar que ... 2 (Ling) ‹*word/syllable/vowel*› acentuar*

stressed-out /ˈstrestˈaʊt/ *adj* (colloq) estresado, tenso

stressful /ˈstresfəl/ *adj* ‹*life/job*› estresante

stretch¹ /stretʃ/ *vt*

A ‹*arm/leg*› estirar, extender*; ‹*wing*› extender*, desplegar*; **I'm just going out to ~ my legs** voy a salir a estirar las piernas

B 1 (widen) ensanchar 2 ‹*sheet/canvas*› extender*

C (eke out) ‹*money/resources*› estirar

D 1 (make demands on) exigirle* a: **my job doesn't ~ me** mi trabajo no me exige lo suficiente; **she's not being ~ed at school** en el colegio no le exigen de acuerdo a su capacidad 2 (strain): **our resources are ~ed to the limit** nuestros recursos están empleados al máximo, nuestros recursos no dan más de sí; **my nerves are ~ed to breaking point** tengo los nervios a punto de estallar

E ‹*truth/meaning*› forzar*, distorsionar; ‹*rules*› apartarse un poco de; **that's ~ing it a bit** (colloq) eso es exagerar un poco

■ **stretch** *vi*

A «*person*» estirarse; (when sleepy) desperezarse*

B 1 (reach, extend) «*forest/sea/influence/power*» extenderse* 2 (in time): **to ~ back** remontarse; **to ~ over a period** alargarse* *or* prolongarse* durante un período; **a miserable future ~ed before her** tenía un sombrío futuro por delante

C 1 (be elastic) «*elastic/rope*» estirarse 2 (become loose, longer) «*garment*» estirarse, dar* de sí

D (be enough) «*money/resources/supply*» alcanzar*, llegar*; **our money won't ~ that far** no nos va a alcanzar el dinero; **I can't ~ to a new car** no me alcanza el dinero para un coche nuevo

■ *v refl* **to ~ oneself** (physically) estirarse; (when sleepy) desperezarse*

(Phrasal verb)

• **stretch out**

A [v ▸ o ▸ adv, v ▸ adv ▸ o] 1 (extend) ‹*legs/arms*› estirar; **he ~ed himself out on the sand** se tendió sobre la arena 2 (make last longer) ‹*money/speech*› estirar

B [v ▸ adv] 1 (reach out): **he ~ed out to turn off the alarm clock** alargó la mano para apagar el despertador 2 (lie full length) tenderse* 3 (extend — in space) extenderse*; (— in time) alargarse*; **the days ~ed out ahead of her** le parecía tener una eternidad por delante

stretch² *n*

A (act of stretching) (*no pl*): **to have a ~** estirarse; (when sleepy) desperezarse*; **to give sth a ~** estirar algo; **at full ~** (fully extended) estirado al máximo; **~ *of the imagination***: **by no ~ of the imagination could he be described as an expert** de ningún modo se lo podría calificar de experto; **that can't be true, not by any ~ of the imagination** eso ni por asomo puede ser verdad

B [c] 1 (expanse — of road, river) tramo *m*, trecho *m*; **the final** *o* **home ~** la recta final; ***not by a long ~*** (ni) con mucho, ni mucho menos 2 (period) período *m*; **he did a ten-year ~ in the army** estuvo *or* pasó (un período de) diez años en el ejército; **he did a three-year ~** (colloq) estuvo tres años a la sombra (fam); ***at a ~*** (without a break) sin parar; (in an extremity) como máximo

C [u] (elasticity) elasticidad *f*

stretch³ *adj* (*before n, no comp*) ‹*fabric/pants*› elástico; **~ limo** (colloq) limusina *f* (*grande*)

stretcher /ˈstretʃər || ˈstretʃə(r)/ *n* (Med) camilla *f*

stretcher: **~-bearer** *n* camillero, -ra *m,f*; **~ case** *n*: *enfermo o herido que tiene que ser transportado en camilla*

stretch marks *pl n* estrías *fpl*

stretchy /ˈstretʃi/ *adj* **-chier, -chiest** elástico

strew /stru:/ *vt* (*past* **strewn** /stru:n/ *past p* **strewn** *or* **strewed** /-d/) ‹*gravel/seeds*› esparcir*; ‹*objects*› (untidily) desparramar; **to ~ sth WITH sth**: **they ~ed the street with petals** esparcieron pétalos por toda la calle; **the floor was ~n with toys** había juguetes desparramados por toda la habitación

stricken /ˈstrɪkən/ *adj* 1 (afflicted) **~ WITH sth**: **~ with terrible arthritis** aquejado de terrible artritis; **a country ~ with famine** un país asolado por el hambre; **I was suddenly ~ with remorse** de pronto me empezó a remorder la conciencia 2 (damaged) ‹*vessel*› siniestrado (frml), dañado; (devastated) ‹*area/valley*› damnificado, afectado 3 (sorrowful) ‹*community/families*› afligido, acongojado 4 (wounded) (liter *or* arch) ‹*soldier/deer*› herido

-stricken /ˌstrɪkən/ *suff*: **doubt~** acosado por la duda; **drought~** asolado por la sequía

strict /strɪkt/ *adj* **-er, -est**

A 1 (severe) estricto, severo; **to be ~ WITH sb** ser* estricto *or* severo CON algn 2 (rigorous) ‹*vegetarian*› estricto, riguroso

B 1 (exact, precise) (*before n*) estricto, riguroso; **in the ~ sense of the word** en el sentido estricto *or* riguroso de la palabra 2 (complete) (*before n*) absoluto; **in ~est secrecy** en el más absoluto secreto

strictly /ˈstrɪktli/ *adv* 1 (severely) con severidad, severamente, rigurosamente 2 (rigorously) estrictamente; **smoking is ~ prohibited** fumar está terminantemente prohibido; **~ (speaking)** (*indep*) en rigor, en sentido estricto, hablando con propiedad 3 (exactly) totalmente; **that's not ~ true** eso no es totalmente *or* del todo cierto 4 (exclusively) exclusivamente; **this is ~ between ourselves** que quede entre nosotros, que no salga de aquí

strictness /ˈstrɪktnəs || ˈstrɪktnɪs/ *n* [u] 1 (severity) severidad *f*, rigurosidad *f* 2 (rigorousness) lo estricto

stricture /ˈstrɪktʃər/ *n* (frml) (censure) crítica *f*

stride¹ /straɪd/ *vi* (*past* **strode**; *past p* **stridden** /ˈstrɪdn̩/) (+ *adv compl*): **he strode up and down the platform** iba y venía por el andén dando grandes zancadas; **he strode away/off angrily** se fue furioso, dando grandes zancadas; **she strode purposefully into the room** entró con aire resuelto en la habitación

stride² *n* 1 (long step) zancada *f*, tranco *m*; **in one** *o* **a single ~** de una zancada; ***to make (great) ~s*** hacer* (grandes) progresos 2 (gait) paso *m*; ***to get into one's ~*** agarrar *or* (esp Esp) coger* el ritmo; ***to put*** *o* ***throw sb off her/his ~*** hacerle* perder el ritmo a algn; ***to take sth in one's ~*** tomarse algo con calma

strident /ˈstraɪdn̩t/ *adj* estridente

strife /straɪf/ *n* [u] (journ *or* frml) conflictos *mpl*; (armed) luchas *fpl*; **family/industrial ~** conflictos familiares/laborales; **a country torn by civil ~** un país destrozado por las luchas intestinas *or* internas

strike¹ /straɪk/ (*past & past p* **struck**) *vt*

A 1 (hit) ‹*person*› pegarle* a, golpear; ‹*blow*› dar*, pegar*; ‹*key*› pulsar; **to ~ sb a blow** darle* un golpe a algn, golpear a algn 2 (collide with, fall on) «*vehicle*» chocar* *or* dar* contra; «*stone/ball*» pegar* *or* dar* contra; «*lightning/bullet*» alcanzar*; **I struck my head on the beam** me di (un golpe) en la cabeza contra la viga; **the tree was struck by lightning** el árbol fue alcanzado por un rayo

B 1 (cause to become): **to ~ sb blind/dumb** dejar ciego/mudo a algn; **I was struck dumb when I saw what she'd done** me quedé muda *or* sin habla cuando vi lo que había hecho; **to ~ sb dead** matar a algn 2 (introduce): **to ~ fear/terror into sb** infundirle miedo/terror a algn

C 1 (occur to) ocurrirse (+ *me/te/le etc*); **an awful thought struck me** se me ocurrió algo terrible; **it ~s me (that) ...** me da la impresión de que ..., se me ocurre que ...

S

2 (impress) parecerle* a; **how did she ~ you?** ¿qué impresión te causó?; **it ~s me as odd** me parece raro; **I was struck by his changed appearance** me llamó la atención lo cambiado que estaba

D ‹*oil/gold*› encontrar*, dar* con; ***to ~ it lucky*** tener* un golpe de suerte; ***to ~ it rich*** hacer* fortuna

E 1 ‹*match/light*› encender* 2 ‹*coin/medal*› acuñar

F 1 (Mus) ‹*note*› dar*; ‹*chord*› tocar* 2 ‹‹*clock*›› dar*; **the clock struck the hour/five (o'clock)** el reloj dio la hora/las cinco

G (enter into, arrive at): **to ~ a deal** llegar* a un acuerdo, cerrar* un trato; **to ~ a balance between ...** encontrar* el justo equilibrio entre ...

H (adopt) ‹*pose/attitude*› adoptar

I (take down) ‹*sail/flag*› arriar*; ‹*tent*› desmontar; **to ~ camp** levantar el campamento

J (delete) suprimir; **his name was struck off the register** se borró su nombre del registro; *see also* **strike off**

■ **strike** *vi*

A (hit) ‹‹*person*›› golpear, asestar un golpe; ‹‹*lightning*›› caer*; **lightning never ~s in the same place twice** los rayos nunca caen dos veces en el mismo sitio; ***(to be) within striking distance (of sth)*** (estar*) a un paso (de algo); ***to ~ lucky*** (BrE) tener* un golpe de suerte

B 1 (attack) ‹‹*bombers/commandos*›› atacar*; ‹‹*snake/tiger*›› atacar*, caer* sobre su presa; **to ~ AT sth/sb** atacar* algo/a algn 2 (happen suddenly) ‹‹*illness/misfortune*›› sobrevenir*; ‹‹*disaster*›› ocurrir

C (withdraw labor) hacer* huelga, declararse en huelga *or* (esp AmL) en paro; **to ~ for higher pay** hacer* huelga *or* (esp AmL) hacer* un paro por reivindicaciones salariales

D ‹‹*clock*›› dar* la hora

Phrasal verbs

- **strike back** [v ▸ adv] **to ~ back (AT sb)** (Mil) contraatacar* (a algn); **he struck back at his critics** devolvió el golpe a sus detractores
- **strike down** [v ▸ o ▸ adv, v ▸ adv ▸ o] 1 ‹‹*illness*›› (liter): **she was struck down with cholera** fue abatida por el cólera (liter); **she was struck down in her prime** su vida fue segada en flor (liter) 2 (AmE Law) revocar*
- **strike home** [v ▸ adv] 1 ‹‹*blow/bullet/shell*›› dar* en el blanco 2 ‹‹*criticism/remark*›› dar* en el blanco
- **strike off** [v ▸ o ▸ adv, v ▸ adv ▸ o] 1 (delete) tachar 2 (disqualify) (BrE) ‹*doctor/lawyer*› prohibirle* el ejercicio de la profesión a
- **strike on** [v ▸ prep ▸ o] ‹*solution*› dar* con; **I/he struck on a plan** se me/le ocurrió un plan
- **strike out**

Sense I [v ▸ adv]

A (physically, verbally) **to ~ out (AT sb/sth)** arremeter (CONTRA algn/algo)

B (set out, proceed) emprender el camino *or* la marcha; **to ~ out FOR sth**: **they struck out for the summit** emprendieron el camino hacia la cumbre; **to ~ out on one's own** ponerse* a trabajar por cuenta propia

C 1 (in baseball) poncharse 2 (fail) (AmE) fracasar

Sense II [v ▸ o ▸ adv, v ▸ adv ▸ o]

A (remove from list) tachar

B (in baseball) ponchar

- **strike through** [v ▸ adv ▸ o] ‹*name*› tachar
- **strike up**

A [v ▸ adv ▸ o] 1 (begin) entablar; **to ~ up a friendship with sb** entablar *or* trabar amistad con algn 2 (start to play) ‹*tune*› empezar* a tocar

B [v ▸ adv] ‹‹*band*›› empezar* a tocar

- **strike upon** ▸**strike on**

strike² *n*

A (stoppage) huelga *f*, paro *m* (esp AmL); **to be on ~** estar* en *or* de huelga, estar* en *or* de paro (esp AmL); **to come out** *o* **go (out) on ~** ir* a la huelga, declararse en huelga, ir* al paro (esp AmL), declararse en paro (esp AmL); **hunger ~** huelga de hambre; (*before n*) **to take ~ action** ir* a la huelga; **~ fund** fondo *m* de resistencia; **~ pay** subsidio *m* de huelga *or* (esp AmL) de paro

B (find) descubrimiento *m*; **a lucky ~** (colloq) un golpe de suerte

C (attack) ataque *m*

D (Sport) 1 (in bowling) pleno *m*, chuza *f* (Méx) 2 (in baseball) strike *m*

strike: **~bound** *adj* ‹*factory/port*› paralizado por la huelga; **~breaker** *n* rompehuelgas *mf*, esquirol *mf* (pey), carnero, -ra *m,f* (RPl fam & pey)

striker /'straɪkər || 'straɪkə(r)/ *n*

A (Lab Rel) huelguista *mf*

B (in soccer) delantero, -ra *m,f*, artillero, -ra *m,f*, ariete *mf*

striking /'straɪkɪŋ/ *adj*

A (eye-catching) ‹*resemblance/similarity*› sorprendente, asombroso; ‹*color*› llamativo; **a ~ woman** una mujer muy atractiva; **a ~ beauty** una belleza que llama la atención; **the most ~ feature of the report is ...** el aspecto más destacado del informe es ...

B (Lab Rel) (*before n*) ‹*worker/nurse/miner*› en huelga

strikingly /'straɪkɪŋli/ *adv* ‹*similar*› sorprendentemente; **she is ~ beautiful** es de una belleza despampanante *or* que llama la atención

strimmer /'strɪmə(r)/ *n* motoguadaña *f*

string¹ /strɪŋ/ *n*

A 1 [u c] (cord, length of cord) cordel *m*, bramante *m* (Esp), mecate *m* (AmC, Méx, Ven), pita *f* (Andes), cáñamo *m* (Andes), piolín *m* (RPl); **a piece of ~** un (trozo de) cordel (*or* bramante *etc*) 2 [c] (on parka) cordón *m*; (on apron) cinta *f*; (on puppet) hilo *m*; ***no ~s attached*** sin compromisos, sin condiciones; ***to be tied to sb's apron ~s*** estar* pegado a las faldas de algn: ***to have sb on a ~*** tener* a algn en un puño; ▸**pull¹** *vt* **B1**

B [c] 1 (on instrument) cuerda *f*; (*before n*) **~ quartet** cuarteto *m* de cuerdas 2 (on racket) cuerda *f* 3 (in archery) cuerda *f*; ***to have several ~s*** *o* ***more than one ~ to one's bow*** tener* varios recursos 4 **strings** *pl* (Mus) cuerdas *fpl*

C [c] 1 (set — of pearls, beads) sarta *f*, hilo *m*; (— of onions, garlic) ristra *f* 2 (series — of people) sucesión *f*; (— of vehicles) fila *f*, hilera *f*; (— of events) serie *f*, cadena *f*; (— of curses, complaints, lies) sarta *f*, retahíla *f*

string² (*past & past p* **strung**) *vt*

A (suspend) colgar*

B 1 ‹*guitar/racket/bow*› encordar*, ponerle* (las) cuerdas a 2 ‹*beads/pearls*› ensartar, enhebrar

Phrasal verbs

- **string along** (colloq) [v ▸ o ▸ adv] (mislead) tomarle el pelo a (fam) (*dando esperanzas falsas*)
- **string out**

A [v ▸ adv] ‹‹*troops*›› desplegarse*

B [v ▸ o ▸ adv, v ▸ adv ▸ o] 1 ‹*essay/act*› alargar*, estirar 2 (*usu pass*): **sentries were strung out along the road** había vigías apostados a intervalos a lo largo de la carretera

- **string together** [v ▸ o ▸ adv, v ▸ adv ▸ o] ‹*thoughts*› coordinar, hilar; **she could barely ~ two sentences together in German** apenas podía hilar un par de frases en alemán
- **string up** [v ▸ o ▸ adv, v ▸ adv ▸ o] 1 ‹*banner/lights*› colgar* 2 (hang) (colloq) colgar* (fam), linchar

string: **~ bag** *n* bolsa *f* de red; **~ bean** *n* ▸**runner bean**

stringed /strɪŋd/ *adj* (Mus) ‹*instrument*› de cuerda; **twelve-~** de doce cuerdas

stringency /'strɪndʒənsi/ *n* [u] 1 (rigorousness, strictness) rigor *m* 2 (austerity) estrechez *f*

stringent /'strɪndʒənt/ *adj* ‹*measures/control/testing*› riguroso, estricto; ‹*budget*› reducido

string-pulling /'strɪŋ,pʊlɪŋ/ *n* [u] amiguismo *m*, palanca *f* (AmL fam), enchufismo *m* (Esp fam)

string vest *n* (BrE) camiseta *f* de malla

stringy /'strɪŋi/ *adj* **-gier, -giest** ‹*plant/root*› fibroso, con hebras; ‹*meat*› fibroso; ‹*hair*› grasiento, grasoso (esp AmL)

strip¹ /strɪp/ **-pp-** *vt*

A 1 (remove covering from) ‹*bed*› deshacer*, quitar la ropa de; ‹*wood/furniture*› quitarle la pintura (*or* el barniz *etc*) a, decapar; **we ~ped the walls** quitamos el papel de la pared; **to ~ sth away** quitar *or* sacar* algo; **to ~ sb (naked)** desnudar a algn 2 (remove contents from) ‹*room/house*› vaciar* 3 **stripped** *past p* (without extras) (AmE) (*after n*) sin accesorios, sin extras 4 (deprive) **to ~ sb OF sth** despojar a algn DE algo

B (Auto, Tech) 1 (damage) ‹*gears*› estropear 2 **~ (down)** (dismantle) desmontar

■ **strip** *vi* 1 (undress) desnudarse, desvestirse*; **to ~ naked** desnudarse; **to ~ to the waist** desnudarse de la cintura para arriba 2 (do striptease) hacer* striptease

S

Phrasal verb

• **strip off**

A [v ▸ o ▸ adv, v ▸ adv ▸ o] ‹*wallpaper/paint*› quitar; ‹*leaves*› arrancar*; **to ~ off one's clothes** quitarse la ropa, desvestirse*

B [v ▸ adv] (undress) (BrE) desnudarse, calatearse (Per fam)

strip² *n*

A [c] 1 (of leather, cloth, paper) tira *f*; (— of metal) tira *f*, cinta *f*; ***to tear sb off a ~*** *o* ***to tear a ~ off sb*** (BrE colloq) poner* a algn de vuelta y media (fam) 2 (of land, sea, forest, light) franja *f*

B [c] (BrE Sport) (colores *mpl* del) equipo *m*

C (striptease) (*no pl*) striptease *m*

strip: **~ cartoon** *n* (BrE) historieta *f*, tira *f* cómica; **~ club** *n* club *m* de striptease

stripe /straɪp/ *n* raya *f*, lista *f*

striped /straɪpt/ *adj* a *or* de rayas, rayado, listado

strip: **~ joint** *n* club *m* de striptease; **~light** *n* (BrE) tubo *m* fluorescente, tubolux® *m* (RPl); **~lighting** *n* [u] (BrE) luz *f* fluorescente

stripling /'strɪplɪŋ/ *n* mozuelo *m*, mozalbete *m*

stripped pine /strɪpt/ *n* [u] madera *f* de pino lavada

stripper /'strɪpər || 'strɪpə(r)/ *n* (performer — male) striptisero *m*; (— female) striptisera *f*, encueratriz *f* (Méx fam)

strip: **~ poker** *n* [u] *tipo de póquer en que se pagan las deudas quitándose prendas de vestir*; **~ search** *n*: *registro al que se somete a una persona y en el que se le exige desnudarse*; **~-search** /'strɪp'sɜːrtʃ || 'strɪp,sɜːtʃ/ *vt* hacer* desnudar y registrar; **~tease** *n* striptease *m*

stripy /'straɪpi/ *adj* **-pier, -piest** a rayas *or* listas, rayado

strive /straɪv/ *vi* (*past* **strove** *or* **strived**; *past p* **striven** /'strɪvən/) **to ~ FOR** *o* **AFTER sth** luchar *or* esforzarse* por alcanzar algo; **to ~ to + INF** esforzarse* POR + INF

strobe (light) /strəʊb/ *n* luz *f* estroboscópica

strode /strəʊd/ *past of* **stride¹**

stroke¹ /strəʊk/ *n*

A (Sport) 1 (in ball games) golpe *m* 2 (in swimming — movement) brazada *f*; (— style) estilo *m* 3 (in rowing — movement) palada *f*, remada *f*; ***to put sb off her/his ~*** hacerle* perder el ritmo (a algn)

B 1 (blow) golpe *m*; **six ~s of the whip** seis latigazos 2 (of piston — motion) tiempo *m*; (— distance) carrera *f* 3 (of clock) campanada *f*; **on the ~ of eleven** al dar las once

C 1 (of thin brush) pincelada *f*; (of thick brush) brochazo *m*; (of pen, pencil) trazo *m*; **apply using light, quick ~s** aplicar dando ligeros toques 2 (oblique, slash) barra *f*, diagonal *f*

D 1 (action, feat) golpe *m*; **a ~ of genius** una genialidad; ***at a ~*** de (un) golpe; ***not to do a ~ of work*** no hacer* absolutamente nada, no dar* *or* pegar* golpe (fam) 2 (instance): **a ~ of luck** un golpe de suerte

E (Med) ataque *m* de apoplejía, derrame *m* cerebral

F (caress) caricia *f*

stroke² *vt* (caress) acariciar

stroll¹ /strəʊl/ *vi* pasear(se), dar* un paseo; **they ~ed in three hours late** entraron tan tranquilos con tres horas de retraso

stroll² *n* paseo *m*; **to have** *o* **take** *o* **go for a ~** dar* un paseo *or* una vuelta, ir* de paseo

stroller /'strəʊlər || 'strəʊlə(r)/ *n*

A (person) paseante *mf*

B (pushchair) (esp AmE) sillita *f* (de paseo), cochecito *m*, carreola *f* (Méx)

strong¹ /strɔːŋ || strɒŋ/ *adj* **stronger** /'strɔːŋgər || 'strɒŋgə(r)/, **strongest** /'strɔːŋgəst || 'strɒŋgɪst/

A 1 (physically powerful) ‹*person/arm*› fuerte; **to have ~ nerves** tener* (los) nervios de acero; **to be ~** «*person*» ser* fuerte *or* fornido; (for lifting things etc) tener* fuerza; ***to have a ~ stomach*** tener* mucho estómago; (lit) poder* comer de todo 2 (healthy, sound) ‹*heart/lungs*› fuerte, sano; ‹*constitution*› robusto 3 (firm) ‹*character/leader*› fuerte; ‹*leadership*› firme

B 1 (solid) ‹*material/construction*› fuerte, resistente 2 (powerful) ‹*country/army*› fuerte, poderoso; ‹*currency/economy*› fuerte 3 ‹*current/wind*› fuerte

C 1 (deeply held) ‹*views/beliefs*› firme; ‹*faith*› firme, sólido; ‹*support*› firme; **I'm a ~ believer in discipline** creo firmemente en la disciplina 2 (forceful) ‹*protest*› enérgico; ‹*argument/evidence*› de peso, contundente, convincente; **he protested in the ~est possible terms** protestó de la manera más enérgica

D (definite) 1 ‹*tendency/resemblance*› marcado; ‹*candidate*› con muchas *or* buenas posibilidades; **she has a ~ foreign accent** tiene un fuerte *or* marcado acento extranjero 2 ‹*features*› marcado, pronunciado; ‹*chin*› pronunciado

E (good) ‹*team*› fuerte; ‹*cast*› sólido; **tact is not one of her ~ points** el tacto no es su punto fuerte; **she's a ~ swimmer** es una buena nadadora; ***to be ~ on sth***: **she's ~ on French history** su fuerte es la historia francesa

F 1 (concentrated) ‹*color/light*› fuerte, intenso; ‹*tea/coffee*› cargado; ‹*beer/painkiller*› fuerte; ‹*solution*› concentrado 2 (pungent) ‹*smell/flavor*› fuerte 3 (unacceptable) ‹*language*› fuerte, subido de tono

G (in number) (*no comp*): **an army ten thousand ~** un ejército de diez mil hombres

strong² *adv*: **to be going ~** «*car/machine*» marchar bien; «*organization*» ir* *or* marchar viento en popa; **he's 85 and still going ~** tiene 85 años y sigue (estando) en plena forma

strong: **~-arm** *adj* (*before n*): **~-arm tactics** mano *f* dura; **~box** *n* caja *f* fuerte *or* de caudales; **~hold** *n* (Mil) (fortress) fortaleza *f*, bastión *m*; (town) plaza *f* fuerte; (center of support) bastión *m*, baluarte *m*

strongly /'strɔːŋli || 'strɒŋli/ *adv*

A 1 (powerfully) fuerte, con fuerza 2 (sturdily) ‹*made/welded*› sólidamente

B 1 (deeply, ardently) totalmente; **I ~ disagree** estoy totalmente en desacuerdo; **he feels ~ that ...** está totalmente convencido de que ...; **I ~ believe that ...** tengo la certeza *or* la plena convicción de que ...; **it's something I feel very ~ about** es algo que me parece sumamente importante 2 (forcefully) ‹*protest/criticize*› enérgicamente; **a ~-worded letter** una carta bastante dura; **I ~ advise you not to sell** te recomiendo con insistencia que no vendas 3 (cogently) ‹*argue/reason*› convincentemente

C 1 (intensely, greatly) ‹*identify*› totalmente, plenamente; **she felt ~ drawn to him** sentía una fuerte atracción hacia él; **it smelled ~ of garlic** despedía un fuerte olor a ajo, olía mucho a ajo 2 (to a large extent) ‹*decrease/contrast*› considerablemente; **she's ~ tipped to succeed him** se perfila como firme candidata a sucederlo

strong: **~man** /'strɔːŋmæn || 'strɒŋmæn/ *n* (*pl* **-men** /-men/) 1 (in circus) forzudo *m*, hombre *m* fuerte (AmL) 2 (Pol) hombre *m* fuerte; **~-minded** /'strɔːŋ'maɪndəd || ,strɒŋ'maɪndɪd/ *adj* resuelto, decidido; **~ room** *n* cámara *f* acorazada; **~-willed** /'strɔːŋ'wɪld || ,strɒŋ 'wɪld/ *adj* (determined) tenaz; (obstinate) terco, tozudo

strontium /'strɑːntʃəm || 'strɒntiəm/ *n* [u] estroncio *m*

stroppy /'strɑːpi || 'strɒpi/ *adj* **-pier, -piest** (BrE colloq) ‹*person/answer*› insolente, borde (Esp fam); **don't get ~ with me** no te insolentes conmigo, no te pongas borde conmigo (Esp fam)

strove /strəʊv/ *past of* **strive**

struck¹ /strʌk/ *past & past p of* **strike¹**

struck² *adj* (impressed) (*pred*) **to be ~ WITH/BY sb/sth**: **you certainly seem very ~ with her** parece que te ha caído muy bien *or* que te ha causado muy buena impresión; **I was quite ~ by their professionalism** me llamó la atención *or* me admiró su profesionalismo; **to be ~ ON sb/sth**: **I'm not very ~ on the idea** la idea no me entusiasma *or* (fam) no me vuelve loco; **she's really ~ on him** está loca por él (fam)

structural /'strʌktʃərəl/ *adj* estructural

structurally /'strʌktʃərəli/ *adv* estructuralmente; (*indep*) desde el punto de vista estructural; **the house is ~ sound** la casa tiene una estructura muy sólida

structure¹ /'strʌktʃər || 'strʌktʃə(r)/ *n*

A [u c] (composition, organization) estructura *f*

B [c] (thing constructed) construcción *f*

structure² *vt* ‹*argument/novel/speech*› estructurar

struggle¹ /'strʌgəl/ *n* 1 (against opponent) lucha *f*; (physical) refriega *f*; **to put up a ~** luchar, oponer* resistencia; **to give up without a ~** rendirse* sin luchar 2 (against difficulties) lucha *f*; **to give up the ~** abandonar la lucha; **his ~ for survival** su lucha por la supervivencia; **it's a ~ to make ends meet** cuesta mucho llegar a fin de mes; **we had quite a ~ to convince him** nos costó bastante convencerlo

S

struggle² *vi*
A 1 (thrash around) forcejear; **I tried to ~ free** forcejeé tratando de liberarme 2 (contend, strive) luchar; **she had to ~ to support her family** tuvo que luchar para mantener a su familia; **to ~ (AGAINST/WITH sth)** luchar (CONTRA algo); **to ~ FOR sth** luchar POR algo 3 (be in difficulties) pasar apuros
B (move with difficulty) (+ *adv compl*): **he ~d up the hill** subió penosamente la cuesta; **he ~d to his feet** se levantó con gran dificultad; **they ~d on through the storm** siguieron adelante con gran esfuerzo en medio de la tormenta

strum /strʌm/ **-mm-** *vt* ‹*guitar/banjo/tune*› rasguear
■ **strum** *vi* **to ~ ON sth** rasguear algo

strung /strʌŋ/ *past & past p of* **string** ²

strung-out /ˈstrʌŋˈaʊt/ *adj* (*pred* **strung out**) (AmE sl) 1 (disturbed) nervioso, tenso 2 (addicted) (*pred*) **to be ~ ~ ON sth/sb** estar* enganchado A algo/algn (arg)

strut¹ /strʌt/ *vi* **-tt-** (+ *adv compl*): **to ~ around** *o* **about** pavonearse; **he ~ted into/out of the room** entró en/salió de la habitación pavoneándose *or* dándose aires; **the cock ~ted up and down the yard** el gallo se paseaba ufano por el patio

strut² *n* (Const) tornapunta *f*, puntal *m*; (Aviat) riostra *f*

strychnine /ˈstrɪknaɪn, -niːn/ *n* [u] estricnina *f*

Stuart /ˈstuːərt/ *n* Estuardo; **the ~s** los Estuardo

stub¹ /stʌb/ *n* 1 (of candle, pencil) cabo *m*; (of cigarette) colilla *f*, pucho *m* (AmL fam) 2 (of receipt) resguardo *m*, talón *m*; (of check) talón *m* (AmL), matriz *f* (Esp)

stub² **-bb-** *vt*: **to ~ one's toe** darse* en el dedo (*del pie*); **he ~bed his toe on the chair** se dio con el dedo contra la silla

Phrasal verb
• **stub out** [v ▸ o ▸ adv, v ▸ adv ▸ o] ‹*cigarette*› apagar*

stubble /ˈstʌbəl/ *n* [u] 1 (Agr) rastrojo *m* 2 (of beard): **he had three days' ~ on his chin** tenía una barba de tres días

stubbly /ˈstʌbli/ *adj* ‹*beard/growth*› de varios días; ‹*chin/cheeks*› sin afeitar

stubborn /ˈstʌbərn || ˈstʌbən/ *adj* 1 ‹*person/nature*› (obstinate) terco, testarudo, tozudo; (resolute) tenaz, tesonero, perseverante; ‹*refusal/resistance/insistence*› pertinaz 2 ‹*cold/weeds*› pertinaz, persistente; ‹*stain*› rebelde

stubbornly /ˈstʌbərnli || ˈstʌbənli/ *adv* (obstinately) tercamente; (resolutely) tenazmente, con tesón; ‹*independent/conservative*› porfiadamente

stubbornness /ˈstʌbərnnəs/ *n* [u] terquedad *f*

stubby /ˈstʌbi/ *adj* **-bier, -biest**: **she had ~ little legs** era retacona; **~ little fingers** deditos *mpl* regordetes

stuck¹ /stʌk/ *past & past p of* **stick²**

stuck² *adj* (*pred*) 1 (unable to move): **the drawer is ~** el cajón se ha atascado; **the door is ~** la puerta se ha atrancado; **she's ~ at home with the kids all day** está todo el día metida en la casa con los niños; ***to get ~ in*** (BrE colloq): **come on, get ~ in before it gets cold** vamos, ataquen *or* (Esp) atacar, que se enfría (fam); **he sat down and got ~ into the task** se sentó y se metió de lleno en la tarea 2 (at a loss) atascado; **I got ~ on the second question** me quedé atascado en la segunda pregunta; **to be ~ FOR sth** (colloq): **he's never ~ for something to do/say** siempre tiene algo que hacer/decir; **I'm rather ~ for cash** ando corto de dinero 3 (burdened) (colloq) **to be/get ~ WITH sth/sb**: **I was ~ with the bill** me tocó pagar la cuenta, me cargaron el muerto (fam); **I got ~ with Bob all evening** tuve que aguantar a Bob toda la noche

stuck-up /ˈstʌkˈʌp/ *adj* (colloq) estirado (fam), creído (fam)

stud¹ /stʌd/ *n*
A 1 (nail, knob) tachuela *f*; (on shield) tachón *m* 2 (on sports boot) (BrE) taco *m*, toperol *m* (Chi) 3 (on road) tachón *m*; (reflective) catafaros *m*, estoperol *m* (Andes), ojo *m* de gato (CS) 4 (earring) arete *m* or (Esp) pendiente *m* (*en forma de bolita*), tornillo *m* (Ur) 5 (for collar, shirtfront) gemelo *m* (*para cuello o pechera de camisa*)
B 1 (male animal) semental *m* 2 **~ (farm)** criadero *m* de caballos, haras *m* (CS, Per) 3 (man) (colloq) semental *m* (fam)

stud² *vt* **-dd-** (*usu pass*) (with studs) tachonar; **the sky was ~ded with stars** el cielo estaba tachonado de estrellas (liter); **a diamond-~ded tiara** una tiara con incrustaciones de brillantes

student /ˈstuːdn̩t || ˈstjuːdn̩t/ *n* (at university) estudiante *mf*; (at school) (esp AmE) alumno, -na *m,f*; **university ~s** (estudiantes) universitarios *mpl*; **a medical ~** un/una estudiante de medicina; **~s of Sartre** los estudiosos de Sartre; **an English ~, a ~ of English** un/una estudiante de inglés; **an English ~** (by nationality) un estudiante inglés/una estudiante inglesa; (*before n*) ‹*newspaper/protest*› estudiantil; **in my ~ days** cuando yo estudiaba; **~ driver** (AmE) aprendiz *mf* de conductor; **~ nurse** estudiante *mf* de enfermería; **~ teacher** estudiante *mf* de profesorado/magisterio

student union *n* 1 (association) asociación *f* de estudiantes 2 (building) *centro estudiantil en el campus*

studied /ˈstʌdid/ *adj* ‹*pose/manner/nonchalance*› estudiado, afectado, fingido; ‹*insult*› intencionado, deliberado

studio /ˈstuːdiəʊ || ˈstjuːdiəʊ/ *n* 1 (Art, Mus, Phot) estudio *m* 2 (Cin, Rad, TV) estudio *m*; (*before n*) **the ~ audience** el público presente en el estudio 3 (company) estudios *mpl* 4 **~ (apartment** *o* (BrE also) **flat)** estudio *m*

studious /ˈstuːdiəs || ˈstjuːdiəs/ *adj* 1 (hard-working) estudioso, aplicado 2 (careful, deliberate) deliberado

studiously /ˈstuːdiəsli || ˈstjuːdiəsli/ *adv* 1 (industriously) con aplicación 2 (carefully, deliberately): **he's always ~ polite to her** siempre se esfuerza en ser cortés con ella; **he ~ avoided giving any reply** se guardó muy bien de dar una respuesta

study¹ /ˈstʌdi/ *n* (*pl* **-dies**)
A [u] (act, process of learning) estudio *m*; (*before n*) **~ group** grupo *m* de trabajo; **~ guide** manual *m* de estudio; **~ hall** (AmE) sala *f* de estudio
B **studies** *pl* 1 (work of student) estudios *mpl* 2 (academic discipline) **Spanish studies** lengua *f* y civilización *f* españolas; **business studies** empresariado *m* *or* (Esp) empresariales *fpl*
C [c] (room) estudio *m*
D [c] 1 (investigation, examination) estudio *m*, investigación *f*; **to make a ~ of sth** estudiar *or* investigar* algo 2 (published report, thesis) trabajo *m*
E [c] (Art, Liter, Mus) estudio *m*; **her face was a ~** su cara era un poema

study² **-dies, -dying, -died** *vt* 1 (at school, university) estudiar 2 (investigate, research into) estudiar, investigar* 3 (examine, scrutinize) estudiar
■ **study** *vi* estudiar; **she's ~ing to be a doctor/lawyer** estudia medicina/derecho; **to ~ UNDER** *o* **WITH sb** «*painter/musician*» ser* discípulo DE algn, estudiar CON algn; «*postgraduate student*» realizar* su (*or* mi *etc*) investigación bajo la dirección de algn

stuff¹ /stʌf/ *n* [u]
A (colloq) 1 (substance, matter): **what's this ~ called?** ¿cómo se llama esto *or* (fam) esta cosa?; **I can't eat this ~** esto yo no lo trago (fam); **this wine is good ~** este vino es del bueno *or* está muy bien; **what sort of ~ does he write?** ¿qué tipo de cosa(s) escribe?; ***that's the ~!*** ¡así se hace!, ¡así me gusta!; ***to do one's ~***: **she went out on stage and did her ~** salió al escenario e hizo lo suyo; ***to know one's ~*** ser* un experto en la materia 2 (miscellaneous items) cosas *fpl*; **and ~ like that** y cosas de ésas, y cosas por el estilo; **I left all my ~ at her house** dejé todas mis cosas en su casa
B (nonsense, excuse) (colloq): **surely you don't believe all that ~ he tells you?** tú no te creerás todo lo que te cuenta ¿no?; **~ and nonsense!** (dated) ¡puro cuento! (fam)
C (basic element): **their expedition has become the ~ of legend** su expedición se ha convertido en una leyenda; **that's the ~ of politics** en eso consiste la política

stuff² *vt*
A 1 (fill) ‹*quilt/mattress/toy*› rellenar; ‹*hole/leak*› tapar; **to ~ sth WITH sth**: **we ~ed our pockets with apples** nos llenamos los bolsillos de manzanas; ***to ~ oneself/one's face*** (colloq) darse* un atracón (fam), ponerse* morado *or* ciego (Esp fam) 2 (Culin) rellenar 3 (in taxidermy) disecar* 4 (AmE Pol) ‹*ballot box*› adulterar
B 1 (thrust) **to ~ sth INTO sth** meter algo EN algo; **she ~ed the books into the bag** metió los libros en la bolsa 2 (put) (colloq) poner* 3 (esp BrE sl): **I told him where he could ~ his advice** le dije qué podía hacer con sus consejos; **~ her!** ¡que se joda! (vulg)

stuffed /stʌft/ *adj* 1 (in taxidermy) disecado; (toy) de peluche 2 ‹*pepper/tomatoes*› relleno; **tomatoes ~ with tuna fish** tomates *mpl* rellenos de atún 3 (full) (colloq) lleno; **I'm ~** estoy lleno, estoy que no puedo más; ***get ~!*** (esp BrE vulg) ¡vete a cagar! (vulg), ¡vete a tomar por culo! (Esp vulg)

stuffed: **~ shirt** *n* (colloq) estirado, -da *m,f* (fam); **~ up** *adj* (*pred*) (colloq): **to be ~ up** estar* congestionado; **my nose is all ~ up** tengo la nariz tapada

stuffiness /ˈstʌfinəs || ˈstʌfinɪs/ *n* [u]
A 1 (of room) aire *m* viciado, ambiente *m* cargado 2 (of nose) congestión *f*
B (of person, opinions, organization) rigidez *f*

stuffing /ˈstʌfɪŋ/ *n* [u] 1 (in pillow, mattress, toy) relleno *m*; ***to knock the ~ out of sb*** (colloq) dejar a algn para el arrastre (fam) 2 (Culin) relleno *m*

stuffy /ˈstʌfi/ *adj* **-fier, -fiest**
A 1 ‹*air*› viciado; **it's ~ in here** aquí falta el aire 2 ‹*nose*› tapado
B (staid) colloq) ‹*person*› acartonado, estirado (fam); ‹*club/organization*› convencional

stultifying /ˈstʌltəfaɪɪŋ/ *adj* (frml) ‹*inactivity/routine*› sofocante; ‹*boredom*› que embota *or* atrofia la sensibilidad

stumble /ˈstʌmbəl/ *vi* 1 (trip) tropezar*, dar* un traspié; **to ~ OVER/AGAINST sth** tropezar* CON algo 2 (move unsteadily) (+ *adv compl*): **to ~ along/in/out** ir*/entrar/salir* a tropezones *or* a trompicones 3 (in speech) atrancarse*; **he ~d over the long words** se atrancaba la lengua con las palabras largas

Phrasal verbs
- **stumble across** ▸**stumble on**
- **stumble on, stumble upon** [v ▸ prep ▸ o] dar* con, encontrar*

stumbling block /ˈstʌmblɪŋ/ *n* escollo *m*; **~ ~ TO sth** traba *f or* impedimento *m* PARA algo

stump[1] /stʌmp/ *n*
A 1 (of tree) tocón *m*, cepa *f*; (of limb) muñón *m*; (of pencil, candle) cabo *m*; (of cigar) colilla *f*, pucho *m* (AmL fam); **the blackened ~s of his teeth** los renegridos trozos de dientes que le quedaban 2 (in cricket) palo *m*
B (AmE Pol) tribuna *f*; **he spent the year on the ~** ha estado todo el año haciendo campaña

stump[2] *vt*
A (baffle) (colloq) (*often pass*): **the problem has me ~ed** el problema me tiene perplejo; **I'm completely ~ed for an answer** no sé qué contestar
B (canvass) (AmE): **to ~ the country** hacer* campaña por el país
■ **stump** *vi*
A (walk heavily) (+ *adv compl*): **he ~ed up the stairs** subió ruidosamente las escaleras
B (campaign) (AmE) hacer* campaña

Phrasal verb
- **stump up** (BrE colloq)
A [v ▸ adv] aflojar (fam), apoquinar (Esp fam)
B [v ▸ adv ▸ o] soltar* (fam), aflojar (fam)

stumpy /ˈstʌmpi/ *adj* **-pier, -piest** ‹*person*› achaparrado, retacón; ‹*legs*› corto

stun /stʌn/ *vt* **-nn-**
A (make unconscious) dejar sin sentido; (daze) aturdir
B 1 (amaze) dejar atónito *or* (fam) helado *or* pasmado 2 (shock) dejar anonadado

stung /stʌŋ/ *past & past p of* **sting**[2]

stun grenade *n* granada *f* de aturdimiento *or* estruendo, granada *f* aturdidora

stunk /stʌŋk/ *past p of* **stink**[2]

stunned /stʌnd/ *adj*
A (unconscious) sin sentido; (dazed) aturdido
B (shocked, amazed) ‹*expression*› de asombro; **he was ~ when they told him** se quedó atónito *or* (fam) helado *or* pasmado cuando se lo dijeron

stunning /ˈstʌnɪŋ/ *adj* ‹*success/performance*› sensacional; ‹*person/dress*› despampanante

stunningly /ˈstʌnɪŋli/ *adv*: **she dresses quite ~** se viste de maravilla; **she is ~ beautiful** es de una belleza despampanante

stunt[1] /stʌnt/ *n*
A (feat of daring) proeza *f*; **she does all her own ~s** (Cin, TV) hace todas las escenas peligrosas ella misma; (*before n*) **~man/woman** especialista *mf*
B (hoax, trick) truco *m*, maniobra *f*; (*publicity ~*) ardid *m* publicitario; **to pull a ~ on sb** (colloq) hacerle* *or* gastarle una broma pesada a algn

stunt[2] *vt* detener*, atrofiar

stunted /ˈstʌntəd || ˈstʌntɪd/ *adj* ‹*growth/development*› atrofiado; ‹*tree/body*› raquítico

stupefy /ˈstuːpəfaɪ || ˈstjuːpɪfaɪ/ *vt* **-fies, -fying, -fied** (*usu pass*) (astonish) dejar estupefacto, causar estupor a

stupefying /ˈstuːpəfaɪɪŋ || ˈstjuːpɪˈfaɪɪŋ/ *adj* pasmoso

stupendous /stuːˈpendəs/ *adj* (colloq) ‹*effort/strength*› tremendo; ‹*success*› formidable; ‹*failure*› mayúsculo

stupid /ˈstuːpəd || ˈstjuːpɪd/ *adj*
A 1 ‹*person/idea*› tonto (fam); **don't be ~** ¡no seas tonto!; **what a ~ thing to do/say!** ¡qué tontería *or* estupidez!; **it was ~ of me to accept** fue una estupidez aceptar; **I did something ~** hice una tontería *or* una estupidez; **he made me look really ~** me dejó en ridículo; **you ~ idiot!** ¡imbécil! 2 (expressing irritation) (colloq) maldito (fam), pinche (Méx fam); **the ~ machine kept my card** el maldito *or* (Méx) pinche cajero me tragó la tarjeta (fam)
B (unconscious): **to drink oneself ~** beber hasta perder el sentido

stupidity /stuːˈpɪdəti / *n* [u] estupidez *f*, tontería *f*

stupidly /ˈstuːpədli || ˈstjuːpɪdli/ *adv* tontamente

stupor /ˈstuːpər/ *n* [u] (Med) estupor *m*; (lethargy) aletargamiento *m*; **in a drunken ~** en un sopor etílico (frml o hum)

sturdily /ˈstɜːrdḷi || ˈstɜːdɪli/ *adv* ‹*built/made*› sólidamente

sturdiness /ˈstɜːrdinəs || ˈstɜːdinɪs/ *n* [u] 1 (robustness) solidez *f* 2 (determination) tenacidad *f*

sturdy /ˈstɜːrdi || ˈstɜːdi/ *adj* **-dier, -diest** 1 ‹*build/legs/figure*› robusto, macizo; ‹*furniture/bicycle*› sólido y resistente 2 ‹*resistance/opposition*› férreo, tenaz

sturgeon /ˈstɜːrdʒən || ˈstɜːdʒən/ *n* [c u] (*pl ~*) esturión *m*

stutter[1] /ˈstʌtər || ˈstʌtə(r)/ *n* tartamudeo *m*; **to have a slight ~** tartamudear un poco

stutter[2] *vi* tartamudear
■ **stutter** *vt* balbucear, decir* tartamudeando; **he ~ed (out) an excuse** balbuceó una excusa

stutterer /ˈstʌtərər || ˈstʌtərə(r)/ *n* tartamudo, -da *m,f*

St Valentine's Day ▸**Valentine's Day**

sty /staɪ/ *n* (*pl* **sties**) 1 (*pig~*) pocilga *f*, chiquero *m* (AmL) 2 ▸**stye**

stye /staɪ/ *n* (*pl* **sties** *or* **styes**) orzuelo *m*

style[1] /staɪl/ *n*
A [c u] 1 (manner of acting) estilo *m*; **his ~ of living** su estilo de vida; **telling lies is not my ~** decir mentiras no va conmigo; ***to cramp sb's ~*** inhibir *or* cohibir* a algn, limitar a algn en su libertad de acción 2 (Art, Lit, Mus) estilo *m*; **interiors in the Baroque ~** interiores de estilo barroco; **in the ~ of William Morris** al estilo *or* a la manera de William Morris
B [u] (elegance) estilo *m*; **to live/travel in ~** vivir/viajar a lo grande
C 1 [c] (type, model) diseño *m*, modelo *m* 2 [u c] (fashion) moda *f*; **long skirts are back in ~** las faldas largas vuelven a estar de moda; **to go out of ~** pasar de moda 3 [c] (*hair ~*) peinado *m*

style[2] *vt*
A (design, shape) ‹*car/furniture/clothes*› diseñar; **to ~ hair** peinar
B (name, designate) (frml) llamar; **he ~s himself Count** se hace llamar conde

-style /staɪl/ *suff*: **American~** al estilo americano, a la americana

styli /ˈstaɪlaɪ/ *pl of* **stylus**

styling /ˈstaɪlɪŋ/ *n* [u] (of car, suit) diseño *m*

stylish /ˈstaɪlɪʃ/ *adj* ‹*furniture/clothes/decor*› con mucho estilo, elegante; ‹*person*› con clase *or* estilo, estiloso (AmL fam); ‹*resort/restaurant*› elegante

stylishly /ˈstaɪlɪʃli/ *adv* ‹*furnished/dressed/decorated*› con estilo; ‹*live/entertain*› a lo grande, por todo lo alto

stylist /ˈstaɪləst/ *n* 1 (*hair ~*) estilista *mf*, peluquero, -ra *m,f*, peinador, -dora *m,f* (Méx) 2 (Lit) estilista *mf*

stylistic /staɪˈlɪstɪk/ *adj* estilístico

stylized /ˈstaɪlaɪzd/ *adj* estilizado

stylus /'staɪləs/ *n* (*pl* **-li** *or* **-luses**) 1 (on record player) aguja *f*, púa *f* (RPl) 2 (for writing) estilo *m*

stymie /'staɪmi/ *vt* **-mies, -mying, -mied** ‹*attempt*› obstaculizar*, frustrar; **that problem's really ~d them** están estancados con ese problema; **we're well and truly ~d now** (colloq) ahora sí que estamos arreglados *or* (AmL tb) embromados *or* (CS tb) fritos (fam)

styptic /'stɪptɪk/ *adj* astringente, estíptico; **~ pencil** barrita *f* astringente

Styrofoam® /'staɪrəfəʊm/ *n* [u] (AmE) espuma *f* de poliestireno

suave /swɑːv/ *adj* **suaver, suavest** ‹*voice*› engolado, meloso, untuoso; **he's too ~ for my liking** lo encuentro demasiado fino y sofisticado

sub[1] /sʌb/ *n* (colloq) 1 (substitute) suplente *mf*, sustituto, -ta *m,f* 2 (subeditor) redactor, -tora *m,f* 3 (submarine) submarino *m* 4 (advance payment) (BrE) anticipo *m* 5 **subs** *pl* (subscription) cuota *f*

sub[2] **-bb-** *vi* (colloq)
■ **sub** *vt* ▸**subedit** (substitute) **to ~ FOR sb** sustituir* a algn

sub- /'sʌb/ *pref* sub-

subaltern /sə'bɔːltərn || 'sʌbəltn̩/ *n* (BrE) *oficial de rango inferior al de capitán*

subaqua /sʌb'ækwə/ *adj* ‹*equipment/club*› de submarinismo; **~ diving** submarinismo *m*, natación *f* subacuática

subclause /'sʌbklɔːz/ *n* 1 (of contract) cláusula *f* subsidiaria 2 (of sentence) (Ling) cláusula *f* subordinada

subcommittee /'sʌbkə,mɪti/ *n* subcomité *m*

subconscious[1] /'sʌb'kɑːntʃəs || sʌb'kɒnʃəs/ *adj* ‹*thoughts/motive/desire*› subconsciente; **the ~ mind** el subconsciente

subconscious[2] *n* **the ~** el subconsciente

subconsciously /'sʌb'kɑːntʃəsli || sʌb'kɒnʃəsli/ *adv* subconscientemente

subcontinent /'sʌb'kɑːntn̩ənt || sʌb'kɒntɪnənt/ *n* subcontinente *m*; **the S~** el subcontinente indio

subcontract /,sʌb'kɑːntrækt/ *vt* subcontratar

subcontractor /sʌb'kɑːntræktər/ *n* subcontratista *mf*

subculture /'sʌbkʌltʃər || 'sʌbkʌltʃə(r)/ *n* subcultura *f*

subdirectory /'sʌbdə,rektəri, 'sʌbdaɪ- || 'sʌbdaɪ,rektəri, 'sʌbdɪ-/ *n* (*pl* **-ries**) subdirectorio *m*

subdivide /'sʌbdə'vaɪd || ,sʌbdɪ'vaɪd/ *vt* 1 (divide again) subdividir 2 (divide into lots) (AmE) ‹*land*› parcelar

subdivision /'sʌbdə'vɪʒən || ,sʌbdɪ'vɪʒən/ *n*
A [u] 1 (act) subdivisión *f* 2 (of land) (AmE) parcelación *f*
B [c] 1 (part) subdivisión *f* 2 (of land) (AmE) parcela *f*

subdue /səb'duː || səb'djuː/ *vt* 1 (bring under control) ‹*person*› someter, dominar; ‹*passion/anger*› contener*, domeñar (liter) 2 (vanquish) (liter) sojuzgar* (liter)

subdued /səb'duːd || səb'djuːd/ *adj* 1 (restrained) ‹*lighting/color*› tenue, apagado 2 (unusually quiet) ‹*person/atmosphere*› apagado; ‹*reaction*› contenido

subedit /'sʌb'edət || ,sʌb'edɪt/ *vt* (BrE) ‹*book/proofs*› corregir*, revisar; ‹*newspaper*› revisar y compaginar

subeditor /'sʌb'edətər/ *n* (BrE) redactor, -tora *m,f*

subhead /'sʌbhed/, **subheading** /'sʌb,hedɪŋ/ *n* subtítulo *m*

subhuman /'sʌb'hjuːmən/ *adj* infrahumano

subject[1] /'sʌbdʒɪkt/ *n*
A (topic) tema *m*; **to change the ~** cambiar de tema; **to drop the ~** dejar el tema; **to get off the ~** salirse* *or* desviarse* del tema, irse* por las ramas; **to keep off a ~** evitar un tema; **while we're on the ~, who ...?** a propósito del tema *or* ya que estamos hablando de esto ¿quién ...?; **to be the ~ of controversy** ser* objeto de polémica; **I'd like to raise the ~ of finance** quisiera plantear el problema de la financiación
B (discipline) asignatura *f*, materia *f* (esp AmL), ramo *m* (Chi)
C (Pol) súbdito, -ta *m,f*
D (Ling) sujeto *m*

subject[2] /'sʌbdʒɪkt/ *adj*
A (owing obedience) ‹*people/nation/province*› sometido; **~ to French laws** bajo jurisdicción francesa
B 1 (liable, prone) **to be ~ TO sth** ‹*to change/delay*› estar* sujeto A algo, ser* susceptible DE algo; ‹*to flooding/subsidence/temptation*› estar* expuesto A algo; ‹*to ill health/depression*› ser* propenso A algo 2 (conditional upon) **to be ~ TO sth** estar* sujeto A algo; **~ to contract** sujeto a confirmación por contrato

subject[3] /səb'dʒekt/ *vt*
A (force to undergo) **to ~ sth/sb TO sth** someter algo/a algn A algo
B (make submissive) ‹*nation/people*› someter, sojuzgar*

subject index *n* índice *m* de materias

subjection /səb'dʒekʃən/ *n* [u] 1 (subjugation) **~ (TO sb/sth)** sometimiento *m* *or* sujeción *f* (A algn/algo) 2 (making subject) sometimiento *m* 3 (exposure) (frml) **~ TO sth** exposición *f* A algo

subjective /səb'dʒektɪv/ *adj* subjetivo

subjectively /səb'dʒektɪvli/ *adv* subjetivamente

subject matter *n* [u] (theme) tema *m*; (content) contenido *m*

subjugate /'sʌbdʒəgeɪt || 'sʌbdʒʊgeɪt/ *vt* 1 (conquer) ‹*people/country*› subyugar*, sojuzgar*, someter 2 (subordinate) **to ~ sth TO sth** supeditar algo A algo

subjugation /'sʌbdʒə'geɪʃən || ,sʌbdʒʊ'geɪʃən/ *n* [u] subyugación *f* (frml); (of needs) supeditación *f*

subjunctive[1] /səb'dʒʌŋktɪv/ *n* subjuntivo *m*; **in the ~** en subjuntivo

subjunctive[2] *adj* subjuntivo

sublet[1] /'sʌb'let/ *vt/i* (*pres p* **-letting**; *past & past p* **-let**) subarrendar*

sublet[2] *n* (AmE) subarriendo *m*; **the apartment is a ~** el apartamento es subarrendado

sub-lieutenant /'sʌbluː'tenənt || ,sʌblef'tenənt/ *n* (BrE) alférez *mf* de navío, subteniente *mf*

sublime /sə'blaɪm/ *adj*
A 1 (noble, pure) sublime; **from the ~ to the ridiculous** (set phrase) de lo sublime a lo ridículo, de un extremo al otro 2 (excellent, wonderful) sensacional, magnífico
B (utter) (*as intensifier*) ‹*contempt/indifference*› supremo, absoluto; **~ ignorance** ignorancia *f* supina

submachine gun /'sʌbmə'ʃiːn/ *n* metralleta *f*

submarine /'sʌbmə'riːn/ *n* submarino *m*

submariner /'sʌbmərɪːnər/ *n* submarinista *mf*

submerge /səb'mɜːrdʒ || səb'mɜːdʒ/ *vt* 1 (cover, flood) sumergir* 2 (plunge) **to ~ sth IN sth** sumergir* algo EN algo; **I ~d myself in work** me sumergí en el trabajo
■ **submerge** *vi* ‹‹*submarine/diver*›› sumergirse*

submersion /səb'mɜːrʒən || səb'mɜːʃən/ *n* [u] inmersión *f*, sumersión *f*

submission /səb'mɪʃən/ *n*
A 1 [u] (surrender) sumisión *f*; **to beat sb into ~** someter a algn a base de golpes 2 [c] (in wrestling) rendición *f*
B [c] 1 (plan, proposal) propuesta *f*; **to make a ~ to sb** presentarle una propuesta a algn 2 (report) informe *m* 3 (Law) alegato *m*
C [u] (presentation) presentación *f*

submissive /səb'mɪsɪv/ *adj* sumiso, dócil

submissively /səb'mɪsɪvli/ *adv* sumisamente

submissiveness /səb'mɪsɪvnəs || səb'mɪsɪvnɪs/ *n* [u] sumisión *f*

submit /səb'mɪt/ **-tt-** *vt*
A (refer for consideration) ‹*claim/report/application*› presentar
B (subject) **to ~ sth/sb TO sth** someter algo/a algn A algo; **to ~ oneself to sth/sb** someterse a algo/algn
C (contend) sostener*
■ **submit** *vi* rendirse*; **do you ~?** ¿te rindes?; **to ~ TO sth/sb**: **he finally ~ted to their demands/threats** finalmente accedió a lo que pedían/cedió ante sus amenazas; **they were forced to ~ to military discipline** los obligaron a someterse a la disciplina militar

subnormal /'sʌb'nɔːrməl || sʌb'nɔːməl/ *adj* por debajo de lo normal; ‹*person*› retrasado, subnormal

subordinate[1] /sə'bɔːrdn̩ət || sə'bɔːdɪnət/ *adj* 1 (inferior, secondary) ‹*rank/position/officer*› subordinado 2 (Ling) subordinado; **~ clause** oración *f* subordinada

subordinate[2] *n* subordinado, -da *m,f*, subalterno, -na *m,f*

subordinate[3] /sə'bɔːrdn̩eɪt || sə'bɔːdɪneɪt/ *vt* **to ~ sth TO sth/sb** subordinar algo A algo/algn

S

subplot /'sʌbplɑːt || 'sʌbplɒt/ *n* argumento *m* secundario

sub-prime /sʌb'praɪm/ *adj* ‹*loans/market*› sub prime (*dirigido a clientes de bajos recursos o con un historial de crédito deficiente*)

subscribe /səb'skraɪb/ *vi*
A (buy) **to ~ (TO sth)** (*to magazine/newspaper*) suscribirse* (A algo)
B (support, agree with) **to ~ TO sth** suscribir* algo (frml); **I ~ to the view that ...** yo soy de la opinión de que ...
■ **subscribe** *vt*
A (contribute) donar, contribuir* con
B (reserve, apply for): **most courses are already fully ~d** la mayoría de los cursos están ya completos

subscriber /səb'skraɪbər || səb'skraɪbə(r)/*n*
A (to paper, magazine) suscriptor, -tora *m,f*; (to telephone service) (BrE) abonado, -da *m,f*
B (to theory, idea) **~ (TO sth)** partidario, -ria *m,f* (DE algo)

subscription /səb'skrɪpʃən/ *n* 1 (to magazine) suscripción *f*; (for theatrical events) abono *m*; **to take out a ~ (to sth)** suscribirse*/abonarse a algo; (*before n*) **~ rate** tarifa *f* de suscriptores 2 (membership fees) (BrE) cuota *f*

subsection /'sʌbsekʃən/ *n* 1 (of document) artículo *m* 2 (of organization) (Busn) subdivisión *f*

subsequent /'sʌbsɪkwənt/ *adj* (*before n*) ‹*events/developments*› posterior, subsiguiente, ulterior (frml); **on a ~ visit** en una visita posterior (frml); **~ TO sth** (frml): **~ to our discussions** tras nuestras conversaciones

subsequently /'sʌbsɪkwəntli/ *adv* posteriormente

subservience /səb'sɜːrviəns || səb'sɜːviəns/ *n* [u] **~ (TO sth/sb)** sumisión *f* ciega (A algo/algn)

subservient /səb'sɜːrviənt/ *adj* (obsequious) servil

subside /səb'saɪd/ *vi*
A «*land/road/foundations*» hundirse
B (abate) «*storm/wind*» amainar; «*floods/swelling*» decrecer*, bajar; «*excitement*» decaer*; «*anger*» calmarse, pasarse; «*laughter*» apagarse*; «*pain/noise*» remitir

subsidence /'sʌbsədn̩s / *n* [u] hundimiento *m*

subsidiarity /'səbsɪdi'ærəti/ *n* (EC) subsidiariedad *f*

subsidiary[1] /səb'sɪdieri || səb'sɪdiəri/ *adj* 1 (secondary) ‹*role/interest*› secundario; **~ company** empresa *f* filial; **~ subject** materia *f* complementaria 2 (supplementary) ‹*income*› adicional, extra; ‹*payment/loan*› subsidiario

subsidiary[2] *n* (*pl* **-ries**) 1 (Busn) filial *f* 2 (BrE Educ) *asignatura complementaria (de un programa universitario)*

subsidize /'sʌbsədaɪz || 'sʌbsɪdaɪz/ *vt* (support with money) subvencionar, subsidiar (AmL)

subsidy /'sʌbsədi/ *n* (*pl* **-dies**) subvención *f*, subsidio *m*

subsist /səb'sɪst/ *vi* subsistir; **to ~ ON sth**: **we ~ed on bread and rice** subsistimos a base de pan y arroz

subsistence /səb'sɪstəns/ *n* [u] subsistencia *f*; (*before n*) ‹*agriculture/crop/farming*› de subsistencia; **~ wage** sueldo *m* de hambre; **to live at ~ level** vivir con lo justo para subsistir

subsoil /'sʌbsɔɪl/ *n* [u] subsuelo *m*

substance /'sʌbstəns/ *n*
A [c] (type of matter) sustancia *f*
B [u] 1 (solid quality, content) sustancia *f*; (of book) enjundia *f*, sustancia *f*; **the two main issues of ~** los dos puntos fundamentales *or* esenciales 2 (foundation) fundamento *m* 3 (main points): **the ~** la sustancia, lo esencial; **in ~** en lo esencial

substandard /'sʌb'stændərd || ˌsʌb'stændəd/ *adj* (inferior) ‹*goods/clothes*› de calidad inferior; **~ housing** viviendas *fpl* que no cumplen con los requisitos de habitabilidad

substantial /səb'stæntʃəl || səb'stænʃəl/ *adj*
A 1 ‹*amount/income/loan*› considerable, importante 2 ‹*changes/difference*› sustancial; ‹*contribution*› importante
B 1 (sturdy, solid) ‹*furniture/building*› sólido; **of ~ build** de complexión robusta 2 (nourishing, filling) ‹*meal*› sustancioso 3 (wealthy) (frml *or* liter) acaudalado

substantially /səb'stæntʃəli/ *adv* 1 (considerably) ‹*change/progress/decrease*› de manera sustancial *or* considerable 2 (essentially) sustancialmente; **what he says is ~ true** lo que dice es fundamentalmente cierto

substantiate /səb'stæntʃieɪt || səb'stænʃieɪt/ *vt* ‹*rumors/story/statement*› confirmar, corroborar; **can you ~ these accusations?** ¿puede probar estas acusaciones?

substantive[1] /'sʌbstəntɪv/ *adj* (frml) ‹*evidence/proof*› sustantivo (frml), de peso; ‹*change*› sustancial; ‹*issue*› fundamental

substantive[2] *n* (Ling) sustantivo *m*

substation /'sʌbsteɪʃən/ *n* 1 (post office) (AmE) estafeta *f* de correos 2 (Elec) subestación *f*

substitute[1] /'sʌbstətuːt || 'sʌbstɪtjuːt/ *n* 1 (thing) **~ (FOR sth)** sucedáneo *m* (DE algo); **sugar ~** sucedáneo *m* del azúcar; **there's no ~ for experience** nada puede sustituir a la experiencia 2 (person) sustituto, -ta *m,f*, reemplazo *m*, suplente *mf*; **to be a ~ FOR sb** sustituir* a algn

substitute[2] *vt* sustituir*, reemplazar*; **to ~ sth FOR sth**: **~ honey for sugar** sustituya el azúcar por miel
■ **substitute** *vi* **to ~ FOR sth/sb**: **can you ~ for me (on) Friday?** ¿me puedes sustituir *or* reemplazar el viernes?

substitute teacher *n* (AmE) (profesor, -sora *m,f*) suplente *mf*

substitution /ˌsʌbstə'tuːʃən || ˌsʌbstɪ'tjuːʃən/ *n* [u c] sustitución *f*; **the ~ of wholewheat bread for white** la sustitución del pan blanco por pan integral

subteen /'sʌb'tiːn/ *n* (AmE colloq) preadolescente *mf*

subtenant /'sʌb'tenənt/ *n* subarrendador, -dora *m,f*

subterfuge /'sʌbtərfjuːdʒ || 'sʌbtəfjuːdʒ/ *n* [c u] subterfugio *m*; **she resorted to ~** recurrió a subterfugios

subterranean /'sʌbtə'reɪniən/ *adj* subterráneo

subtitle[1] /'sʌbˌtaɪtl̩/ *n* subtítulo *m*

subtitle[2] *vt* (*usu pass*) subtitular

subtle /'sʌtl̩/ *adj* **subtler** /'sʌtl̩ər /, **subtlest** /'sʌtl̩əst/
A 1 (delicate, elusive) ‹*fragrance*› sutil; **a ~ shade of pink** un rosa muy tenue; **a ~ hint of basil** un ligerísimo gusto a albahaca 2 (not obvious) ‹*difference/distinction/hint*› sutil; ‹*change*› imperceptible 3 (tactful) (colloq) delicado, discreto
B 1 ‹*mind/intellect/remark*› perspicaz, agudo 2 ‹*argument/device*› ingenioso, sutil; ‹*irony*› fino

subtlety /'sʌtl̩ti/ *n* (*pl* **-ties**)
A 1 [u c] (delicacy, elusiveness) sutileza *f* 2 [u] (tact, finesse) delicadeza *f*; **to lack ~** ser* poco delicado
B 1 [u] (perceptiveness) sutileza *f*, perspicacia *f* 2 [u c] (ingenuity) sutileza *f*

subtly /'sʌtli/ *adv*
A 1 (delicately, elusively) sutilmente 2 (tactfully) con delicadeza *or* discreción
B 1 (perceptively) ‹*remark/observe*› perspicazmente, con agudeza 2 (ingeniously, cleverly) ‹*argue/design*› ingeniosamente, hábilmente

subtotal /'sʌbtəʊtl̩/ *n* subtotal *m*, total *m* parcial

subtract /səb'trækt/ *vt* **to ~ sth (FROM sth)** restar algo (DE algo)

subtraction /səb'trækʃən/ *n* [u c] resta *f*, sustracción *f*

subtropical /'sʌb'trɑːpɪkəl/ *adj* subtropical

suburb /'sʌbɜːrb || 'sʌbɜːb/ *n* barrio *m* *or* (Méx) colonia *f* residencial de las afueras; **the ~s** los barrios periféricos *or* de las afueras (de la ciudad)

suburban /sə'bɜːrbən || sə'bɜːbən/ *adj* ‹*area*› suburbano; ‹*shopping mall*› de las afueras; ‹*life/attitude*› aburguesado

suburbia /sə'bɜːrbiə || sə'bɜːbiə/ *n* [u] *zonas residenciales de las afueras de una ciudad*

subversion /səb'vɜːrʒən || səb'vɜːʃən/ *n* [u] subversión *f*

subversive[1] /səb'vɜːrsɪv || səb'vɜːsɪv/ *adj* subversivo

subversive[2] *n* elemento *m* subversivo

subvert /səb'vɜːrt || səb'vɜːt/ *vt* (frml)
A (undermine) ‹*government/system*› socavar las bases de; ‹*authority*› minar
B (corrupt) subvertir*

subway /'sʌbweɪ/ *n*
A [c u] (AmE Rail) metro *m*, subterráneo *m* (RPl); (*before n*) **~ station** estación *f* de metro *or* (RPl) de subterráneo
B [c] (BrE) (for pedestrians) paso *or* pasaje *m* subterráneo

subzero /'sʌb'ziːrəʊ/ *adj* ‹*temperatures*› bajo cero

succeed /sək'siːd/ *vi*
A (have success) «*plan*» dar* resultado, surtir efecto; «*person*»: **she tried to persuade him, but did not ~** intentó convencerlo pero no lo consiguió *or* no lo logró; **to ~ IN sth/-ING**: **he's ~ed in all that he's done** ha tenido éxito en todo lo que ha hecho; **to ~ in life** triunfar en la vida; **he finally ~ed in passing the exam** al final logró

S

aprobar el examen; **you'll only ~ in making matters worse** sólo conseguirás empeorar las cosas; ***if at first you don't ~, try, try again*** el que la sigue la consigue
B **to ~ (TO sth)**: **he ~ed to the throne** subió al trono; **to ~ to a title** heredar un título
■ **succeed** *vt* suceder; **who ~ed him?** ¿quién lo sucedió?, ¿quién fue su sucesor?

succeeding /sək'si:dɪŋ/ *adj (before n)* subsiguiente; **in the ~ weeks** en las semanas subsiguientes; **~ generations** las generaciones futuras *or* venideras; **each ~ year was worse** cada año que pasaba las cosas iban peor

success /sək'ses/ *n* [c u] éxito *m*; **to be a ~** ser* un éxito; **he's a ~ with the girls** tiene éxito con las chicas; **did you have any ~ (in) finding a job?** ¿pudiste conseguir trabajo?; **he always makes a ~ of any venture he is involved in** siempre saca adelante sus proyectos con éxito; **to meet with ~** tener* éxito; **without ~** sin (ningún) éxito *or* resultado; *(before n)* **the police's ~ rate in solving crimes** el porcentaje de casos que la policía logra resolver; **we're proud of our high ~ rate in these exams** estamos orgullosos de nuestro alto porcentaje de aprobados en estos exámenes

successful /sək'sesfəl/ *adj* ‹*person*› de éxito, exitoso (AmL); **he's a ~ businessman** es un próspero hombre de negocios; **the ~ applicant for the job** el candidato que obtenga el puesto; **he was ~ at last** finalmente lo logró *or* lo consiguió; **to be ~ in life** triunfar en la vida; **to be ~ IN -ING**: **they were ~ in persuading their colleagues** lograron convencer a sus colegas

successfully /sək'sesfəli/ *adv* satisfactoriamente

succession /sək'seʃən/ *n*
A 1 [u] (act of following) sucesión *f*; **for 6 years in ~** durante seis años consecutivos *or* seguidos; **in rapid ~** uno tras otro 2 [c] (series) sucesión *f*, serie *f*
B [u] (to office, rank) sucesión *f*; **to be first in ~ to the throne** ser* el primero en la línea de sucesión al trono; **in ~ to sb** como sucesor de algn

successive /sək'sesɪv/ *adj (before n)* consecutivo; **three ~ days** tres días consecutivos *or* seguidos; **~ governments have tackled the problem** sucesivos gobiernos han intentado resolver el problema

successively /sək'sesɪvli/ *adv* sucesivamente

successor /sək'sesər || sək'sesə(r)/ *n* sucesor, -sora *m,f*

success story *n* éxito *m*

succinct /sək'sɪŋkt/ *adj* sucinto, conciso

succinctly /sək'sɪŋktli/ *adv* sucinta, sucintamente

succor¹, (BrE) **succour** /'sʌkər || 'sʌkə(r)/ *n* [u] (liter) socorro *m*; **to give ~ to the weak and helpless** socorrer al débil y al indefenso

succor², (BrE) **succour** *vt* (liter) socorrer

succulent¹ /'sʌkjələnt || 'sʌkjʊlənt/ *adj*
A (juicy) ‹*fruit/meat*› suculento
B (Bot) ‹*leaves/stems*› carnoso; **~ plant** suculenta *f*

succulent² *n* (Bot) suculenta *f*

succumb /sə'kʌm/ *vi* (yield) **to ~ (TO sth)** sucumbir (A algo)

such¹ /sʌtʃ/ *adj*
A 1 (emphasizing degree, extent) tal (+ *noun*); tan (+ *adj*); **I woke up with ~ a headache** me levanté con tal dolor de cabeza ...; **~ a charming girl!** ¡qué chica más *or* tan encantadora!; **she gave me ~ a look!** ¡me miró de una manera ... !; **I've got ~ a lot of work to do** tengo tanto (trabajo) que hacer; **I've never heard ~ nonsense** nunca he oído semejante *or* tamaña estupidez 2 *(with clauses of result or purpose)* **such ... (that)** tal/tan ... que; **I was in ~ pain (that) I couldn't sleep** tenía tanto *or* tal dolor que no pude dormir 3 *(in comparisons)* **such ... as** tan ... como; **~ a patient teacher as you** un maestro tan paciente como tú
B 1 (of this, that kind) tal; **~ children are known as ...** a dichos *or* a tales niños se los conoce como ...; **~ a journey would take weeks** un viaje así *or* como ése llevaría semanas; **there's no ~ thing as the perfect crime** el crimen perfecto no existe; **I said no ~ thing!** ¡yo no dije tal cosa!; **you'll do no ~ thing!** ¡de ninguna manera! 2 (unspecified) tal; **the letter tells you to go to ~ a house on ~ a date** la carta te dice que vayas a tal casa en tal fecha; **until ~ time as we are notified** (frml) hasta (el momento en) que se nos notifique

such² *pron*
A 1 (of the indicated kind) tal; **~ were her last words** tales fueron sus últimas palabras; **~ is life** (set phrase) así es la vida (fr hecha); **snakes, lizards and ~** serpientes, lagartijas y cosas por el estilo 2 **such as** como; **many modern inventions, ~ as radar ...** muchos inventos modernos, (tales) como el radar ...; **I've read many of his books — ~ as?** he leído muchos de sus libros — ¿(como) por ejemplo? 3 **as such** como tal/tales; **he was a great leader and will be remembered as ~** fue un gran líder y será recordado como tal
B 1 **such as, such ... as** (frml): **~ (people) as were dissatisfied** quienes estaban descontentos 2 (indicating lack of quantity, quality): **the evidence, ~ as it is, seems to ...** las pocas pruebas que hay parecen ...
C (of such a kind, extent, degree) **such that** tal ... que; **the pain was ~ that I screamed** fue tal el dolor *or* fue tan grande el dolor, que grité

such-and-such /'sʌtʃənsʌtʃ/ *adj* tal (o cual); **we were told to get ~ a book** nos dijeron que compráramos tal (o cual) libro

suchlike¹ /'sʌtʃlaɪk/ *adj* (colloq) *(before n)*: **George, Mabel and ~ bores** George, Mabel y otros pelmas por el estilo (fam)

suchlike² *pron* (colloq) (of things) cosas por el estilo, cosas de ésas, esas cosas; (of people) gente por el estilo

suck¹ /sʌk/ *vt* 1 «*person*» ‹*finger/candy*› chupar; ‹*liquid*› (through a straw) sorber; «*vacuum cleaner*» aspirar; «*pump*» succionar, aspirar; «*insect*» ‹*blood/nectar*› chupar; **to ~ one's thumb** chuparse el dedo; **to ~ sth up** ‹*dust*› aspirar algo; ‹*liquid*› (through a straw) sorber algo; **the roots ~ (up) moisture out of** *o* **from the soil** las raíces absorben la humedad de la tierra 2 (pull, draw) (+ *adv compl*) arrastrar; **she was ~ed down** *o* **under by the current** la corriente se la tragó
■ **suck** *vi*
A «*person*» chupar; **to ~ AT sth** chupar algo; **the baby was ~ing at his mother's breast** el bebé estaba mamando; **to ~ ON sth** ‹*on pipe/pen*› chupar algo
B (be objectionable) (AmE sl): **the movie really ~s** la película es una mierda (vulg)

Phrasal verbs

- **suck in** [v ▸ o ▸ adv, v ▸ adv ▸ o] (draw in) ‹*air/breath*› tomar; ‹*cheeks/stomach*› meter
- **suck up to** [v ▸ adv ▸ prep ▸ o] (colloq) lamerle el culo a (vulg), hacerle* la pelota a (Esp fam), chuparle las medias a (RPl fam), hacerle* la barba (Méx) *or* (Chi) la pata a (fam), lambonear (Col fam)

suck² *n (no pl)* chupada *f*; **to give ~** (arch) dar* el pecho, amamantar

sucker¹ /'sʌkər || 'sʌkə(r)/ *n*
A (colloq) (fool) (pej) imbécil *mf*; **to play sb for a ~** (AmE) engañar a algn como a un chino (fam); ***to be a ~ for sth***: **I'm a ~ for musicals** las comedias musicales son mi debilidad; **he's a ~ for punishment** es un masoquista; *(before n)* **~ bet** (AmE) apuesta *f* de bobos; **~ punch** (AmE) golpe *m* a traición
B (suction device — on animal, plant) ventosa *f*; (— made of rubber) (BrE) ventosa *f*
C (Bot) (shoot) chupón *m*, mamón *m*

sucker² *vt* (AmE colloq) **to ~ sb INTO -ING** embaucar* a algn PARA QUE (+ *subj*)

suckle /'sʌkəl/ *vt* amamantar, darle* de mamar a
■ **suckle** *vi* mamar

sucrose /'su:krəʊs, -krəʊz/ *n* [u] sacarosa *f*

suction /'sʌkʃən/ *n* [u] succión *f*; (of water, air etc) aspiración *f*

Sudan /su:'dɑ:n/ *n* **(the) ~** (el) Sudán

Sudanese¹ /'su:dn̩'i:z || ˌsu:də'ni:z/ *adj* sudanés

Sudanese² *n (pl ~)* sudanés, -nesa *m,f*

sudden /'sʌdn̩/ *adj* 1 (rushed) repentino, súbito; (unexpected) imprevisto, inesperado; **isn't this all rather ~?** ¿esto no es un poco apresurado *or* precipitado?; ***all of a ~*** de repente, de pronto, repentinamente 2 (abrupt) ‹*movement*› brusco

sudden death *n* (in tennis) muerte *f* súbita; *(before n)* ‹*play-off/round*› de desempate

S

sudden infant death syndrome *n* [u] síndrome *m* de muerte infantil súbita

suddenly /'sʌdn̩li/ *adv* 1 (unexpectedly) de repente, de pronto 2 (abruptly) bruscamente

suddenness /'sʌdn̩nəs || 'sʌdn̩nɪs/ *n* [u] 1 (unexpectedness) lo imprevisto, lo inesperado; (of decision, change) lo repentino 2 (abruptness) brusquedad *f*, lo brusco

suds /sʌdz/ *pl n* 1 (froth) espuma *f* de jabón 2 (soapy water) agua *f* jabonosa

sue /su:/ *vt* **to ~ sb (FOR sth)** demandar a algn (POR algo); **they ~d her for libel** le entablaron juicio por difamación

■ **sue** *vi* (Law) entablar una demanda, poner* pleito (Esp); **to ~ FOR sth** demandar POR algo

suede /sweɪd/ *n* [u] ante *m*, gamuza *f*

suet /'su:ət || 'su:ɪt, 'sju:ɪt/ *n* [u] sebo *m*, grasa *f* de pella

suffer /'sʌfər || 'sʌfə(r)/ *vt* 1 (undergo) ‹*injury/damage/loss*› sufrir; ‹*pain*› padecer*, sufrir; **to ~ hardship** pasar necesidades 2 (endure) aguantar, tolerar 3 (permit) (liter) **to ~ sb to + INF** dejar QUE algn (+ *subj*)

■ **suffer** *vi* 1 (experience pain, difficulty) sufrir; **to ~ FOR sth** sufrir las consecuencias DE algo 2 (be affected, deteriorate) «*health/eyesight*» resentirse*; «*business/performance/relationship*» verse* afectado, resentirse* 3 (be afflicted) **to ~ FROM sth** sufrir *or* (frml) padecer* DE algo; **he ~s from asthma** sufre *or* (frml) padece de asma

sufferance /'sʌfərəns/ *n* [u]: **on ~** de mala gana

sufferer /'sʌfərər || 'sʌfərə(r)/ *n* **~ (FROM sth)**: **~s from arthritis** quienes sufren de artritis, los artríticos

suffering /'sʌfərɪŋ/ *n* [u] sufrimiento *m*, dolor *m*

suffice /sə'faɪs/ *vi* (frml) bastar, ser* suficiente; **~ it to say that ...** basta con decir que ...

■ **suffice** *vt* ser* suficiente para

sufficiency /sə'fɪʃənsi/ *n* [u] (frml) cantidad *f* suficiente

sufficient /sə'fɪʃənt/ *adj* suficiente, bastante; **two are ~ for my purposes** con dos me basta, con dos tengo suficiente; **my income is hardly ~ to live on** mis ingresos apenas (si) me alcanzan para vivir

sufficiently /sə'fɪʃəntli/ *adv* lo suficientemente; **it's not ~ clear** no queda (lo) suficientemente claro

suffix /'sʌfɪks/ *n* sufijo *m*

suffocate /'sʌfəkeɪt/ *vt* asfixiar, ahogar*

■ **suffocate** *vi* asfixiarse, ahogarse*

suffocating /'sʌfəkeɪtɪŋ/ *adj* ‹*smoke/environment/routine*› asfixiante; ‹*heat*› sofocante, agobiante

suffocation /'sʌfə'keɪʃən/ *n* [u] asfixia *f*

suffrage /'sʌfrɪdʒ/ *n* sufragio *m*

suffragette /'sʌfrə'dʒet/ *n* sufragista *f*

suffuse /sə'fju:z/ *vt* (liter) «*color*» teñir*; «*emotion*» invadir, envolver*; «*light*» bañar; **the sky was ~d with red** el cielo estaba teñido de arrebol (liter)

sugar[1] /'ʃʊgər || 'ʃʊgə(r)/ *n*

A [u c] azúcar *m or f*; **how many ~s do you take?** ¿cuánto azúcar quieres?; (*before n*) **~ bowl** *o* (BrE also) **basin** azucarero *m*, azucarera *f* (esp AmL); **~ cube** *o* **lump** terrón *m* de azúcar; **~ mill** *o* **refinery** refinería *f* de azúcar, azucarera *f*, ingenio *m* azucarero, central *f* azucarera (Per)

B (AmE colloq) (*as form of address*) cariño (fam), cielo (fam)

sugar[2] *vt* echarle *or* ponerle* azúcar a, azucarar; **~ed almonds** peladillas *fpl*; ▸**pill 1**

sugar: **~ beet** *n* [c u] remolacha *f* azucarera *or* (Méx) betabel *m* blanco; **~ cane** *n* [c u] caña *f* de azúcar; **~-coated** /'ʃʊgər'kəʊtəd || ˌʃʊgə'kəʊtɪd/ *adj* cubierto de azúcar; **~ daddy** *n* (colloq) *viejo rico amante de una mujer joven*

sugary /'ʃʊgəri/ *adj* 1 ‹*syrup/drink/taste*› dulce, azucarado 2 ‹*tones/smile*› meloso, almibarado; ‹*romance/movie*› sensiblero, empalagoso

suggest /səg'dʒest || sə'dʒest/ *vt*

A 1 (propose) sugerir*, proponer*; **to ~ sth TO sb** sugerirle* algo A algn; **to ~ -ING** sugerir* + INF, sugerir* QUE (+ *subj*); **she ~ed leaving them a note** sugirió dejarles *or* que les dejáramos una nota; **to ~ TO sb THAT** sugerirle* a algn QUE (+ *subj*); **he ~ed to me that I (should) look for another job** me sugirió que buscara otro trabajo 2 (offer for consideration): **can you ~ a possible source for this rumor?** ¿se le ocurre quién puede haber empezado este rumor?; **no one is ~ing you stole the money** nadie está diciendo que se robó el dinero 3 (imply, insinuate) insinuar*; **are you ~ing (that) my son is a thief?** ¿insinúa usted que mi hijo es un ladrón? 4 **to ~ itself**: **an idea ~ed itself to him** se le ocurrió una idea

B (indicate, point to) indicar*; **his reaction ~ed a guilty conscience** su reacción indicaba que se sentía culpable

C (evoke, bring to mind) sugerir*

suggestible /səg'dʒestəbəl/ *adj* sugestionable

suggestion /səg'dʒestʃən || sə'dʒestʃən/ *n*

A 1 [c u] (proposal) sugerencia *f*; **to make a ~** hacer* una sugerencia; **to make improper ~s** hacer* proposiciones deshonestas *or* indecorosas; **I'm open to ~s** acepto sugerencias; **have you any ~s for speeding up the process?** ¿se le ocurre algo para acelerar el proceso?; **it was your ~ to have a picnic** fuiste tú quien propuso *or* sugirió ir de picnic; **I bought it at my wife's ~** lo compré porque mi mujer me lo sugirió, lo compré a instancias de mi mujer (frml) 2 [c] (explanation, theory) teoría *f* 3 [c] (insinuation) insinuación *f*

B [c u] 1 (indication, hint) indicio *m*; **there was no ~ of foul play** no había indicios de que se hubiese cometido un crimen 2 (slight trace) (*no pl*): **a (slight) ~ of saffron** un ligerísimo sabor a azafrán

C [u] (Psych) sugestión *f*

suggestive /səg'dʒestɪv || sə'dʒestɪv/ *adj*

A ‹*gesture/laugh*› insinuante, provocativo

B (*pred*) **to be ~ OF sth** 1 (indicative) parecer* indicar algo 2 (reminiscent) hacer* pensar EN algo, evocar* algo

suggestively /səg'dʒestɪvli/ *adv* de modo insinuante

suicidal /'su:ə'saɪdl̩ || ˌsu:ɪ'saɪdl, ˌsju:-/ *adj* suicida; **I came out of the interview feeling absolutely ~** salí de la entrevista con el ánimo por los suelos; **it would be ~** sería una verdadera locura

suicide /'su:əsaɪd || 'su:ɪsaɪd, 'sju:-/ *n* 1 [u c] (act) suicidio *m*; **to commit ~** suicidarse; (*before n*) ‹*attempt/pact*› de suicidio; ‹*mission/bombing*› suicida; **~ bomber** terrorista *mf* suicida, kamikaze *m*; **~ note** carta *f* de despedida de un suicida; **~ pilot** (in Pacific War) kamikaze *m* 2 [c] (person) (liter) suicida *mf*

suit[1] /su:t || su:t, sju:t/ *n*

A (Clothing) (male) traje *m*, terno (AmS); (female) traje *m* (de chaqueta), traje *m* sastre

B (Law) juicio *m*, pleito *m*; **to file ~** *o* **bring a ~ against sb** demandar a algn, llevar a algn a juicio

C (in cards) palo *m*; ***to follow ~*** (do likewise) seguir* su (*or* nuestro *etc*) ejemplo, hacer* lo mismo; (lit: in cards) jugar* una carta del mismo palo, seguir* el palo

suit[2] *vt*

A (be convenient to, please) venirle* bien a, convenirle* a; **Tuesday would ~ me better** me vendría mejor el martes, me convendría más el martes; **whenever it ~s you** cuando te venga bien, cuando te convenga; ***to ~ oneself*** hacer* lo que uno quiere; **~ yourself!** ¡haz lo que quieras!, ¡haz lo que te dé la gana! (fam)

B 1 (be appropriate, good for): **the job doesn't ~ him** el trabajo no es para él *or* no le va; **they ~ each other very well** son de caracteres muy compatibles; **the furniture doesn't ~ the house** los muebles no van con la casa 2 (look good on) «*hairstyle/dress*» quedarle *or* (esp Esp) irle* bien a; **that color really ~s you** ese color te queda muy bien *or* te favorece; *see also* **suited**

C (adapt) **to ~ sth TO sth/sb** adaptar algo A algo/algn

suitability /'su:tə'bɪləti/ *n* [u] 1 (practical) lo apropiado *or* adecuado; **her ~ for the job** su idoneidad para el puesto 2 (social, moral) lo apropiado

suitable /'su:təbəl || 'su:təbəl, 'sju:-/ *adj* 1 (appropriate) apropiado, adecuado; **(to be) ~ FOR sb/sth/-ING** (ser*) apropiado *or* adecuado PARA algn/algo/+ INF 2 (acceptable, proper) apropiado; **the program is not ~ for children** el programa no es apropiado *or* apto para niños 3 (convenient) conveniente; **is nine o'clock ~ for you?** ¿le viene bien a las nueve?, ¿le resulta conveniente a las nueve?

suitably /'su:təbli/ *adv* ‹*qualified*› adecuadamente; ‹*dressed/equipped*› apropiadamente, como es debido; **he was ~ apologetic** pidió disculpas como correspondía

suitcase /'su:tkeɪs/ *n* maleta *f*, petaca *f*, valija *f* (RPl)

suite /swi:t/ *n*

A 1 (of rooms) suite *f*; **the bridal** *o* **honeymoon ~** la suite nupcial 2 (of furniture) juego *m*; **three-piece ~** juego de

S

sofá y dos sillones, juego de sala de tres piezas, tresillo *m* (Esp); **bedroom/dining-room ~** (juego de) dormitorio *m*/comedor *m* 3▸ (Mus) suite *f*

B (retinue) séquito *m*, comitiva *f*

suited /'su:təd || 'su:tɪd, 'sju:/ *adj* (*pred*) **to be ~ TO sth** ‹‹*thing*›› ser* apropiado *or* adecuado PARA algo; **I'm not ~ to this type of work** no sirvo para este tipo de trabajo; **they are very well ~ (to each other)** están hechos el uno para el otro

suitor /'su:tər || 'su:tə(r), 'sju:-/ *n* (dated) pretendiente *m*

sulfate, (BrE) **sulphate** /'sʌlfeɪt/ *n* [c u] sulfato *m*

sulfide, (BrE) **sulphide** /'sʌlfaɪd/ *n* [c u] sulfuro *m*

sulfur, (BrE) **sulphur** /'sʌlfər || 'sʌlfə(r)/ *n* [u] azufre *m*; (*before n*) **~ dioxide** dióxido *m* *or* bióxido *m* de azufre, anhídrido *m* sulfuroso

sulfuric acid, (BrE) **sulphuric acid** /sʌl'fjʊrɪk || sʌl 'fjʊərɪk/ *n* [u] ácido *m* sulfúrico

sulk¹ /sʌlk/ *vi* enfurruñarse, alunarse (RPl fam), amurrarse (Chi fam); **he's ~ing** está enfurruñado, está alunado (RPl fam) *or* (Chi fam) amurrado

sulk² *n*: **she's in a ~** *o* (fam) **she's got the ~s** está enfurruñada, está alunada (RPl) *or* (Chi) amurrada (fam)

sulky /'sʌlki/ *adj* **-kier, -kiest** ‹*child*› con tendencia a enfurruñarse; ‹*look/reply*› malhumorado

sullen /'sʌlən/ *adj* ‹*person/nature/mood*› hosco, huraño

sully /'sʌli/ *vt* **-lies, -lying, -lied** (liter) ‹*name/record/reputation*› mancillar (liter), manchar

sultan /'sʌltn̩/ *n* sultán *m*

sultana /sʌl'tænə/ *n* (Culin) pasa *f* sultana *or* de Esmirna

sultry /'sʌltri/ *adj* **-trier, -triest**

A ‹*climate/day*› sofocante, bochornoso

B ‹*voice/smile/person*› sensual, seductor

sum /sʌm/ *n*

A (calculation — in general) cuenta *f*; (— addition) suma *f*, adición *f* (frml); **she's very good at ~s** es muy buena para hacer cuentas

B (total, aggregate) suma *f*, total *m*; **that's the ~ (total) of my knowledge** eso es todo lo que sé

C (of money) suma *f* *or* cantidad *f* (de dinero)

Phrasal verb

• **sum up**: **-mm-**

A [v ▸ o ▸ adv, v ▸ adv ▸ o] 1▸ (summarize) ‹*discussion/report*› resumir, sintetizar* 2▸ (assess) ‹*person*› catalogar*; **she quickly ~med up the situation** enseguida se hizo una composición de lugar

B [v ▸ adv] 1▸ (summarize) recapitular; **to ~ up, our analysis shows that ...** resumiendo *or* en resumen, nuestro análisis demuestra que ... 2▸ (Law) recapitular

summarily /sʌ'merəli || 'sʌmərɪli/ *adv* sumariamente

summarize /'sʌməraɪz/ *vt* ‹*speech/book/plot*› resumir, hacer* un resumen de

■ **summarize** *vi* resumir; **to ~** (as linker) resumiendo, en resumen

summary¹ /'sʌməri/ *n* (*pl* **-ries**) resumen *m*

summary² *adj* 1▸ ‹*dismissal*› inmediato 2▸ ‹*trial/judgment*› sumario

summation /sʌ'meɪʃən/ *n* (frml)

A 1▸ [u] (adding) suma *f* 2▸ [c] (sum, total) suma *f*, total *m*

B [c] 1▸ (summary) resumen *m*, recapitulación *f* 2▸ (AmE Law) recapitulación *f*

summer¹ /'sʌmər || 'sʌmə(r)/ *n* verano *m*, estío *m* (liter); **in (the) ~** en (el) verano; **we spent the ~ in France** pasamos el verano *or* veraneamos en Francia; **it was high ~** era pleno verano; **a ~'s day** un día de verano; (*before n*) ‹*weather/clothes/vacation*› de verano; **~ camp** (in US) colonia *f* de vacaciones; **the ~ season** la estación veraniega *or* estival

summer² *vi* ‹‹*people*›› pasar el verano, veranear; ‹‹*cattle/birds*›› pasar el verano

> **summer camp**
>
> En EEUU, una de las miles de colonias de vacaciones en el campo, donde los padres envían a sus hijos durante las vacaciones de verano a participar en actividades recreativas y deportivas, tales como la natación, el senderismo o técnicas de supervivencia a la intemperie

summer: **~house** *n* cenador *m*; **~ school** *n* (in US) clases *fpl* de verano (*gen de repaso*); (in UK) curso *m* de verano; **~time** *n* verano *m*, estío *m* (liter); **in (the) ~time** en (el) verano; **~ time** *n* [u] (BrE) horario *m* de verano

summery /'sʌməri/ *adj* veraniego, de verano

summing-up /'sʌmɪŋ'ʌp/ *n* (*pl* **summings-up**) recapitulación *f*

summit /'sʌmət || 'sʌmɪt/ *n*

A (of mountain) cumbre *f*, cima *f*; **at the ~ of his career** en la cumbre *or* cima de su carrera; **the ~ of her ambition** el súmmum de su ambición, su máxima ambición

B **~ (conference)** (conferencia *f*) cumbre *f*

summon /'sʌmən/ *vt* 1▸ (send for) ‹*servant/waiter*› llamar, mandar llamar (AmL); ‹*police/doctor*› llamar; ‹*help/reinforcements*› pedir*; ‹*meeting/parliament*› convocar* 2▸ (Law) ‹*witness/defendant*› citar, emplazar* 3▸ ▸**summon up**

Phrasal verb

• **summon up** [v ▸ adv ▸ o] 1▸ (gather): **he ~ed up the courage to ask her** se armó de valor para preguntárselo; **I couldn't even ~ up the strength to get up the stairs** ni siquiera pude reunir fuerzas para subir la escalera 2▸ (call up) ‹*thoughts/memories*› evocar*

summons¹ /'sʌmənz/ *n* (*pl* **-monses**) 1▸ (Law) citación *f*, citatorio *m* (Méx); **to issue a ~** despachar una citación *or* (Méx) un citatorio; **to serve a ~ on sb** entregarle* una citación *or* (Méx) un citatorio a algn 2▸ (for help etc) llamamiento *m*, llamado *m* (AmL)

summons² *vt* (Law) citar, emplazar*

Sumo /'su:məʊ/ *n* [u] (sport) sumo *m*; (*before n*) **~ wrestler** (luchador *m* de) sumo *m*

sump /sʌmp/ *n* 1▸ (for oil) (esp BrE) cárter *m* 2▸ (Min) sumidero *m* 3▸ (cesspit) pozo *m* negro *or* séptico

sumptuous /'sʌmptʃuəs || 'sʌmptjʊəs/ *adj* ‹*fabric/color*› suntuoso; ‹*mansion/decor*› lujoso, suntuoso

sumptuously /'sʌmptʃuəsli/ *adv* ‹*dine/entertain*› a cuerpo de rey; ‹*decorated/furnished*› suntuosamente

sun¹ /sʌn/ *n* [c u] sol *m*; **the ~ is shining** hace sol, brilla el sol; **the ~'s in my eyes** me da el sol en los ojos; **let's sit out of/in the ~** sentémonos a la sombra/al sol; ***under the ~***: **I've tried everything under the ~** he probado de todo; **she called him every name under the ~** le dijo de todo; **there's nothing new under the ~** no hay nada nuevo bajo el sol; (*before n*) ‹*hat*› para el sol; **~ blind** (BrE) toldo *m*; **~ block** (BrE) filtro *m* solar; **~ parlor** *o* (BrE) **lounge** jardín *m* de invierno

sun² *v refl* **-nn-**: **to ~ oneself** tomar el sol *or* (CS tb) tomar sol, asolearse (AmL)

Sun (= **Sunday**) dom.

sun: **~-baked** *adj* ‹*bricks*› secado al sol; ‹*road/desert*› calcinado; **~bathe** *vi* tomar el sol *or* (CS tb) tomar sol, asolearse (AmL); **~bathing** *n* [u] baños *mpl* de sol; **~beam** *n* rayo *m* de sol; **~bed** *n* cama *f* solar; **~burn** *n* [u] quemadura *f* de sol; **~burned**, (BrE also) **~burnt** *adj* 1▸ (painfully) quemado por el sol 2▸ (brown) bronceado, tostado, quemado (AmL), moreno (Esp), asoleado (Méx)

sundae /'sʌndeɪ/ *n* sundae *m* (*helado con fruta, crema, jarabe etc*)

Sunday /'sʌndeɪ, '-di/ *n* (day) domingo *m*; (*before n*) ‹*mass*› dominical; **in one's ~ best** vestido de domingo, endomingado; **~ driver** (pej) dominguero, -ra *m,f* (pey) (*conductor lento y extremadamente precavido*); **~ opening** apertura *f* de las tiendas los domingos; **~ school** *sesiones dominicales de catequesis para niños*; *see also* **Monday**

sun: **~ deck** *n* 1▸ (Naut) cubierta *f* superior 2▸ (AmE Archit) solario *m*; **~dial** *n* reloj *m* de sol; **~down** *n* (*no art*) puesta *f* de(l) sol; **at ~down** al atardecer, a la caída de la tarde; **~-drenched** /'sʌn'drentʃt/ *adj* (*before n*) bañado por el sol; **~dress** *n* vestido *m* de tirantes, solera *f* (CS); **~-dried** /'sʌn'draɪd/ *adj* secado al sol

sundries /'sʌndriz/ *pl n* 1▸ (goods) artículos *mpl* diversos 2▸ (expenses) gastos *mpl* varios

sundry¹ /'sʌndri/ *adj* varios, diversos

sundry² *pron*: **all and ~** todos sin excepción, todo el mundo

sunflower /'sʌnflaʊr/ *n* girasol *m*; (*before n*) **~ oil** aceite *m* de girasol; **~ seed** semilla *f* de girasol, pipa *f* (Esp)

sung /sʌŋ/ *past p of* **sing**

S

sunglasses /ˈsʌnˌglæsəz || ˈsʌnˌglɑːsɪz/ *pl n* gafas *fpl or* (esp AmL) lentes *mpl or* anteojos *mpl* de sol

sunk¹ /sʌŋk/ *past p of* **sink¹**

sunk² *adj (pred)* 1 (in trouble) (colloq) **to be ~** estar* perdido 2 (immersed) **to be ~ IN sth** ‹*in depression*› estar* sumido EN algo (liter)

sunken /ˈsʌŋkən/ *adj* 1 *(before n)* ‹*ship/treasure*› hundido, sumergido 2 *(before n)* ‹*garden/patio*› a nivel más bajo 3 (hollow) ‹*eyes/cheeks*› hundido

sun: **~ lamp** *n* lámpara *f* de rayos ultravioletas; **~light** *n* [u] sol *m*, luz *f* del sol; **place out of direct ~light** evitar la luz del sol directa; **~lit** *adj* soleado; **~lounger** /ˈsʌnˌlaʊndʒər/ *n* sillón *m* de jardín, tumbona *f* (Esp)

Sunni¹ /ˈsʊni || ˈsʊni, ˈsʌni/ *n* 1 (individual) suní *mf*, sunita *mf* 2 (sect) (+ *pl vb*) **the ~** los suní, los sunitas

Sunni² *adj* suní, sunita

sunny /ˈsʌni/ *adj* **-nier, -niest** 1 ‹*day*› de sol; ‹*room/garden*› soleado; **in ~ weather** cuando hace sol; **it's ~ today** hoy hace sol; **I like my eggs ~ side up** (esp AmE Culin) me gustan los huevos fritos sólo por un lado 2 (good-humored) ‹*disposition*› alegre, risueño; ‹*smile*› alegre

sun: **~rise** *n* salida *f* del sol; **at ~rise** al amanecer, al alba (liter); **~roof** *n* techo *m* corredizo; **~screen** *n* filtro *m* solar; **~set** *n* puesta *f* de(l) sol, crepúsculo *m* (liter); **at ~set** al atardecer, a la caída de la tarde; **~shade** *n* (BrE) (awning) toldo *m*; (parasol) sombrilla *f*; **~shine** *n* 1 [u] sol *m* 2 (colloq) (*as form of address*) (*no pl*) nene, -na (fam), mijito, -ta (AmL fam), majo, -ja (Esp fam); **~spot** *n* 1 (Astron) mancha *f* solar 2 (resort) (colloq) *lugar de veraneo con mucho sol*; **~stroke** *n* [u] insolación *f*; **to get ~stroke** insolarse, agarrar *or* (esp Esp) coger* una insolación; **~tan** *n* [u c] bronceado *m*, moreno *m* (Esp); **to get a ~tan** broncearse, tostarse*, quemarse (AmL); (*before n*) ‹*oil/lotion*› bronceador; **~tanned** *adj* bronceado, tostado, quemado (AmL), moreno (Esp), asoleado (Méx); **~trap** *n*: *lugar muy soleado y resguardado*; **~-up** *n* (*no art*) amanecer *m*, salida *f* del sol; **at ~-up** al amanecer; **~worshipper** *n* (sunbather) (hum) fanático, -ca *m,f* del sol

super /ˈsuːpər || ˈsuːpə(r)/ *adj* (colloq) ‹*party/film/meal*› genial (fam), súper *adj inv* (fam); **that dress looks ~ on you** ese vestido te queda genial; **what a ~ idea!** ¡qué idea más genial! (fam); (*as interj*) **oh, ~!** ¡genial! (fam), ¡bárbaro! (fam)

superannuated /ˈsuːpərˈænjueɪtəd || ˌsuːpərˈænjʊeɪtɪd/ *adj* (pej) ‹*person/ideas*› caduco, anticuado

superannuation /ˈsuːpərˈænjuˈeɪʃən/ *n* [u] (BrE frml) 1 (pension) (pensión *f* de) jubilación *f*; (*before n*) **~ contributions** cotizaciones *fpl* al fondo de pensión; **~ scheme** plan *m* de jubilación 2 (retirement) jubilación *f*

superb /sʊˈpɜːrb || suːˈpɜːb/ *adj* magnífico, espléndido

superbly /sʊˈpɜːrbli || suːˈpɜːbli/ *adv* ‹*work/function*› a la perfección; ‹*written/furnished*› soberbiamente

supercharged /ˈsuːpərtʃɑːrdʒd || ˈsuːpətʃɑːdʒd/ *adj* ‹*engine/vehicle*› sobrealimentado

supercharger /ˈsuːpərˌtʃɑːrdʒər || ˈsuːpəˌtʃɑːdʒə(r)/ *n* sobrealimentador *m*

supercilious /ˈsuːpərˈsɪliəs/ *adj* desdeñoso, altanero

superciliously /ˈsuːpərˈsɪliəsli || ˌsuːpəˈsɪliəsli/ *adv* con desdén *or* altanería, desdeñosamente

super-duper /ˈsuːpərˈduːpər || ˌsuːpəˈduːpə(r)/ *adj* (colloq & dated) ‹*occasion/car*› fabuloso (fam); ‹*meal*› espléndido

superficial /ˈsuːpərˈfɪʃəl || ˌsuːpəˈfɪʃəl/ *adj*
A ‹*wound/resemblance/person*› superficial
B ‹*area/measurements*› de superficie

superficiality /ˈsuːpərˌfɪʃiˈæləti || ˌsuːpəˌfɪʃiˈælɪti/ *n* [u c] (*pl* **-ties**) superficialidad *f*

superficially /ˈsuːpərˈfɪʃəli || ˌsuːpəˈfɪʃəli/ *adv* superficialmente; (*indep*) en apariencia, a primera vista

superfluous /suːˈpɜːrfluəs || suːˈpɜːflʊəs/ *adj* superfluo; **it is ~ to say ...** está de más decir ...

superfluously /suːˈpɜːrfluəsli || suːˈpɜːflʊəsli/ *adv* ‹*add/comment*› innecesariamente, sin necesidad

supergrass /ˈsuːpərgræs || ˈsuːpəgrɑːs/ *n* (BrE colloq) supersoplón, -plona *m,f* (fam)

superhighway /ˈsuːpərˈhaɪweɪ || ˈsuːpəˌhaɪweɪ/ *n* 1 (AmE Auto) autopista *f* 2 (Comput): **the information ~** la autopista de la comunicación

superhuman /ˈsuːpərˈhjuːmən || ˌsuːpəˈhjuːmən/ *adj* ‹*efforts/courage*› sobrehumano

superimpose /ˈsuːpərɪmˈpəʊz/ *vt* superponer*

superintend /ˈsuːpərɪnˈtend/ *vt* supervisar

superintendent /ˈsuːpərɪnˈtendənt/ *n* 1 (person in charge — of maintenance, hostel, swimming pool) encargado, -da *m,f*; (— of building) (AmE) portero, -ra *m,f*; (— of institution) director, -tora *m,f* 2 (police officer) (in US) superintendente *mf* (*jefe de un departamento de policía*); (in UK) comisario, -ria *m,f* de policía

superior¹ /sʊˈpɪriər || suːˈpɪəriə(r)/ *adj*
A 1 (better) **to be ~ (TO sth/sb)** ser* superior (A algo/algn), ser* mejor (QUE algo/algn); **our cars are ~ in design to theirs** nuestros coches superan a los suyos en el diseño 2 (above average) ‹*workmanship/writer*› de gran calidad; **~ quality goods** productos *mpl* de primera calidad
B (arrogant) ‹*tone/smile*› de superioridad *or* suficiencia; **he's so ~** se da unos aires de superioridad
C (higher in rank, status): **his ~ officer** su superior
D (in amount, number): **given their ~ numbers, we cannot win** dada su superioridad numérica, no podemos ganar
E (above) (frml) **to be ~ TO sth** estar* por encima DE algo
F (higher, upper) superior

superior² *n* 1 (in rank, position) superior *m* 2 (in ability): **she has few ~s** pocos la superan 3 (Relig): **Mother S~** Madre *f* Superiora

superiority /sʊˈpɪriˈɔːrəti/ *n* [u] superioridad *f*

superlative¹ /sʊˈpɜːrlətɪv/ *adj* (excellent) inigualable, excepcional; **silk of ~ quality** seda de primerísima calidad

superlative² *n* superlativo *m*; **in the ~** en superlativo

superlatively /sʊˈpɜːrlətɪvli/ *adv* excepcionalmente

superman /ˈsuːpərmæn || ˈsuːpəmæn/ *n* (*pl* **-men** /-men/) superhombre *m*; **S~** Supermán

supermarket /ˈsuːpərˌmɑːrkət/ *n* supermercado *m*

supermodel /ˈsuːpərˈmɑːdl || ˈsuːpəˌmɒdl/ *n* supermodelo *f*

supernatural¹ /ˈsuːpərˈnætʃərəl/ *adj* sobrenatural

supernatural² *n* **the ~** lo sobrenatural

superpower /ˈsuːpərpaʊər/ *n* superpotencia *f*

superscript¹ /ˈsuːpərskrɪpt || ˈsuːpəskrɪpt/ *adj* (*before n*) volado, superíndice

superscript² *n* superíndice *m*

supersede /ˈsuːpərˈsiːd || ˌsuːpəˈsiːd/ *vt* (*often pass*) ‹*idea/method*› reemplazar*, sustituir*; **~d technology** tecnología *f* superada *or* desbancada

supersonic /ˈsuːpərˈsɑːnɪk/ *adj* supersónico

superstar /ˈsuːpərstɑːr/ *n* superestrella *f*, gran estrella *f*

superstate /ˈsuːpərsteɪt || ˈsuːpəsteɪt/ *n* superestado *m*

superstition /ˈsuːpərˈstɪʃən/ *n* [u c] superstición *f*

superstitious /ˈsuːpərˈstɪʃəs/ *adj* supersticioso

superstore /ˈsuːpərstɔːr/ *n* (BrE) hipermercado *m*

superstructure /ˈsuːpərˌstrʌktʃər/ *n* superestructura *f*

supertanker /ˈsuːpərˌtæŋkər/ *n* superpetrolero *m*

supervise /ˈsuːpərvaɪz || ˈsuːpəvaɪz/ *vt* 1 ‹*project/staff*› supervisar; ‹*thesis*› dirigir* 2 (watch over) vigilar

supervision /ˈsuːpərˈvɪʒən/ *n* [u] supervisión *f*

supervisor /ˈsuːpərvaɪzər || ˈsuːpəvaɪzə(r)/ *n* 1 (overseer) supervisor, -sora *m,f* 2 (official) (in US) alcalde, -desa *m,f* (*elegido anualmente o cada dos años*) 3 (in UK university) director, -tora *m,f* de tesis

supervisory /ˈsuːpərˈvaɪzəri || ˈsuːpəvaɪzəri/ *adj* ‹*duties/post/capacity*› de supervisor

supine /sʊˈpaɪn || ˈsuːpaɪn/ *adj* 1 (lying on back) (frml): **to be/lie ~** estar*/estar* tendido en decúbito supino *or* dorsal (frml) 2 (passive) (pej) lánguido, abúlico

supper /ˈsʌpər || ˈsʌpə(r)/ *n* [u c] (evening meal) cena *f*, comida *f* (esp AmL); **to have ~** cenar, comer (esp AmL); **what's for ~?** ¿qué hay de cena?

suppertime /ˈsʌpərtaɪm || ˈsʌpətaɪm/ *n* [u c] hora *f* de cenar *or* (esp AmL) de comer

supplant /səˈplænt/ *vt* sustituir*, reemplazar*

supple /ˈsʌpəl/ *adj* **-pler** /-plər || -plə(r)/, **-plest** /-pləst || -plɪst/ ‹*body/fingers*› ágil; ‹*leather*› fino y flexible, suave

supplement¹ /ˈsʌpləmənt || ˈsʌplɪmənt/ *n*
A (addition to diet, income) complemento *m*

S

B 1 (additional part — at end of book) apéndice *m*; (— published separately) suplemento *m* 2 (section of newspaper — separate) suplemento *m*; (— inserted) separata *f*

supplement² /'sʌpləment || 'sʌplɪment/ *vt* ‹*diet/income*› complementar; ‹*report*› completar

supplementary /'sʌplə'mentəri/ *adj* suplementario

suppleness /'sʌpəlnəs || 'sʌpəlnɪs/ *n* [u] (of body, mind) agilidad *f*; (of leather) flexibilidad *f*, suavidad *f*

supplicant /'sʌpləkənt || 'sʌplɪkənt/ *n* suplicante *mf*

supplication /'sʌplə'keɪʃən/ *n* [u c] súplica *f*

supplier /sə'plaɪər || sə'plaɪə(r)/ *n* (Busn) proveedor, -dora *m,f*, abastecedor, -dora *m,f*

supply¹ /sə'plaɪ/ *n* (*pl* **-plies**)

A [u] (provision) suministro *m*; **the law of ~ and demand** la ley de la oferta y la demanda; **the water/electricity ~** el suministro de agua/electricidad; (*before n*) ‹*route/ship*› de abastecimiento

B (stock, store): **food supplies are running low** se están agotando las provisiones *or* los víveres *or* (Mil) los pertrechos; **we need fresh supplies of paper** tenemos que pedir una nueva remesa de papel; **we only have a month's ~ of coal left** sólo nos queda carbón para un mes; (Busn) las existencias de carbón sólo van a durar un mes; **office supplies** material *m or* artículos *mpl* de oficina; **she has an endless ~ of patience/jokes** tiene una paciencia inagotable/un repertorio interminable de chistes; **to be in short ~** escasear

supply² *vt* **-plies, -plying, -plied**

A 1 (provide, furnish) ‹*electricity/gas*› suministrar; ‹*goods*› suministrar, abastecer* *or* proveer* de; ‹*evidence/information*› proporcionar, facilitar 2 ‹*retailer/manufacturer*› abastecer*; **to ~ sb WITH sth** ‹*with equipment*› proveer* a algn DE algo; (Busn) abastecer* a algn DE algo, suministrarle algo A algn; ‹*with information*› facilitarle *or* proporcionarle algo A algn

B (meet) (frml) ‹*demand/need*› satisfacer*; ‹*deficiency*› suplir

supply: **~ chain** *n* canal *m* de producción y distribución, cadena *f* de producción y distribución; **~ teacher** *n* (BrE) (profesor, -sora *m,f*) suplente *mf*

support¹ /sə'pɔːrt || sə'pɔːt/ *vt*

A (hold up) ‹*bridge/structure*› sostener*; **the roof is ~ed by six columns** el tejado descansa sobre *or* se apoya en seis columnas; **the chair couldn't ~ his weight** la silla no pudo aguantar *or* resistir su peso

B 1 (maintain, sustain) ‹*family/children*› mantener*, sostener*, sustentar; **to ~ oneself** ganarse la vida *or* (liter) el sustento; **the hospital is ~ed entirely by private donations** el hospital está enteramente financiado por donaciones de particulares 2 (Comput) admitir

C 1 (back) ‹*cause/motion*› apoyar; **which team do you ~?** ¿de qué equipo eres (hincha)?; **I ~ the Greens** estoy con los verdes 2 (back up) apoyar

D (corroborate) ‹*theory*› respaldar, confirmar, sustentar

support² *n*

A 1 [c] (of structure) soporte *m* 2 [u] (physical): **the pillars provide the ~ for the arches** los pilares sirven de apoyo a los arcos; **to lean on sb for ~** apoyarse en algn (para sostenerse)

B 1 [u] (financial) ayuda *f* (económica), apoyo *m* (económico); **he has no means of ~** no tiene ninguna fuente de ingresos 2 [c] (person) sostén *m*

C [u] (backing, encouragement) apoyo *m*, respaldo *m*; **I've had absolutely no ~ from you** no me has apoyado en absoluto; **I went with her to give her (moral) ~** la acompañé para que se sintiera apoyada *or* respaldada

D [u] 1 (Mil) apoyo *m*, refuerzo *m* 2 (backup) servicio *m* al cliente; **technical/dealer ~** servicio técnico/de ventas; (*before n*) ‹*package/material*› adicional, suplementario

E **in support of** (*as prep*): **he spoke in ~ of the motion** habló a favor de *or* en apoyo de la moción; **a demonstration in ~ of the President** una manifestación de apoyo al presidente; **she could produce no evidence in ~ of her claim** no pudo presentar pruebas en apoyo de su demanda

supportable /sə'pɔːrtəbəl || sə'pɔːtəbəl/ *adj* (liter) soportable, tolerable; **barely ~** casi insoportable *or* intolerable

support band *n* grupo *m* telonero

supporter /sə'pɔːrtər || sə'pɔːtə(r)/ *n* 1 (adherent) partidario, -ria *m,f* 2 (Sport) hincha *mf*, seguidor, -dora *m,f*

supporting /sə'pɔːrtɪŋ/ *adj* (*before n*) ‹*role*› secundario; ‹*actor*› secundario, de reparto; **~ act** número *m* telonero

supportive /sə'pɔːrtɪv || sə'pɔːtɪv/ *adj*: **she's been very ~** me (*or* lo *etc*) ha apoyado mucho, me (*or* le *etc*) ha dado todo su apoyo

suppose /sə'pəʊz/ *vt*

A 1 (assume, imagine) suponer*, imaginarse; **I ~ you want more money** supongo *or* (me) imagino que querrás más dinero; **~ it doesn't turn up** suponte que no aparece; **I don't ~ you could take me there?** tú no podrías llevarme hasta allí ¿no?; **~ he phones and you're not in** ¿y si llama y tú no estás?, suponte que llama y tú no estás; **I ~ so** supongo *or* me imagino que sí; **can Peter come too? — oh, I ~ so** ¿Peter puede ir con nosotros? — bueno, si no hay más remedio …; **I ~ not** *o* **I don't ~ so** supongo que no *or* no creo 2 (making suggestions): **~ we take this with us** ¿y si nos lleváramos esto?, ¿qué tal si nos llevamos esto? 3 (believe, think) creer*; **what do you ~ he'll do?** ¿tú qué crees que hará? 4 (postulate) suponer*; **let us ~ that x = a + b** supongamos que x = a + b

B **to be supposed to + INF** 1 (indicating obligation, expectation): **I'm ~d to start work at nine** se supone que tengo que empezar a trabajar a las nueve; **aren't you ~d to be at home?** ¿tú no tendrías que estar en casa?; **you're not ~d to tell anyone** no se lo tienes que decir a nadie 2 (indicating intention): **what's that ~d to be?** ¿y eso qué se supone que es?; **what's that ~d to mean?** ¿y qué quieres (*or* quieren *etc*) decir con eso, (si se puede saber)? 3 (indicating general opinion): **it's ~d to be a very interesting book** dicen que es un libro muy interesante; **you're ~d to be the expert, not me** el experto se supone que eres tú, no yo

C (presuppose) (frml) suponer*

supposed /sə'pəʊzəd || sə'pəʊzd/ *adj* (*before n*) ‹*date/time/author*› supuesto

supposedly /sə'pəʊzədli/ *adv* supuestamente

supposing /sə'pəʊzɪŋ/ *conj* 1 (expressing hypothesis) suponiendo que; **~ she agrees, will they let us go?** suponiendo que ella esté de acuerdo ¿nos dejarán ir?; **~ you win? — I won't — but just ~** ¿y si ganas? — no voy a ganar —bueno, pero suponte que sí ganas; **always ~ we have the money to buy it** siempre y cuando tengamos el dinero para comprarlo 2 (introducing suggestion) ¿y si … ?, ¿qué tal si … ?

supposition /'sʌpə'zɪʃən/ *n* [u c] suposición *f*; **it's pure ~** no son más que suposiciones

suppository /sə'pɑːzətɔːri || sə'pɒzɪtri/ *n* (*pl* **-ries**) supositorio *m*

suppress /sə'pres/ *vt* 1 ‹*anger/laughter*› contener*, reprimir; ‹*feelings*› reprimir 2 ‹*text*› suprimir; ‹*facts/evidence/truth*› ocultar; ‹*newspaper*› retirar de la circulación 3 ‹*revolt/rebellion*› sofocar*, reprimir; ‹*political party/organization*› suprimir

suppression /sə'preʃən/ *n* [u] 1 (of feelings) represión *f*, inhibición *f* 2 (of text) supresión *f*; (of evidence) ocultación *f*; (of book) prohibición *f* 3 (of revolt) represión *f*

suppressor /sə'presər || sə'presə(r)/ *n* (Auto, Elec, Rad, TV) resistencia *f* supresora, supresor *m*

supra- /'suːprə/ *pref* supra-

supremacy /sə'preməsi || suː'preməsi, sjuː-/ *n* [u] supremacía *f*; **air/naval ~** supremacía aérea/naval

supreme /suː'priːm || suː'priːm, sjuː-/ *adj*

A (of highest authority) ‹*power*› supremo; ‹*authority*› supremo, sumo; **S~ Commander** Comandante *m* Supremo *or* en jefe

B (extreme) ‹*effort*› supremo; **with ~ indifference** con la mayor *or* con suprema indiferencia; **the ~ irony would be if …** el colmo de la ironía sería que …

Supreme Court *n* **the ~ ~** el Tribunal Supremo *or* (esp AmL) la Corte Suprema *or* (Ur) la Suprema Corte (de Justicia)

supremely /suː'priːmli/ *adv* (*as intensifier*) sumamente

surcharge¹ /'sɜːrtʃɑːrdʒ || 'sɜːtʃɑːdʒ/ *n* recargo *m*; **import ~** sobretasa *f* de importación

surcharge² *vt* (*usu pass*) ‹*person*› aplicar* un recargo a; **the parcel was ~d** hubo que pagar un recargo por el paquete

S

sure¹ /ʃʊr || ʃʊə(r), ʃɔː(r)/ *adj* **surer, surest**

A (convinced) (*pred*) seguro; **to be ~ ABOUT sth** estar* seguro DE algo; **I like it but I'm not too ~ about the color** me gusta, pero el color no me convence del todo; **I'm not ~ I agree with you** no sé si estoy de acuerdo contigo; **I'm not ~ who/why/what ...** no sé muy bien quién/por qué/qué ...; **he's not ~ if he can come** no sabe si va a poder venir; **fascinating, I'm ~** (iro) ¡interesantísimo, no cabe duda! (iró); **to be ~ OF sth/sb** estar* seguro DE algo/algn; **are you ~ of your facts?** ¿estás seguro de lo que dices?; **I want to be ~ of getting there on time** quiero asegurarme de que voy a llegar a tiempo; **to be ~ of oneself** (convinced one is right) estar* seguro; (self-confident) ser* seguro de sí mismo

B (certain): **one thing is ~: he's lying** lo que está claro *or* lo que es seguro es que está mintiendo; **it's ~ to rain** seguro que llueve; **she's ~ to be there** seguro que va a estar allí; **be ~ to let me know** no dejes de avisarme; **be ~ not to touch it** no lo vayas a tocar; **to make ~ of sth** asegurarse de algo; **make ~ (that) you're not late** no vayas a llegar tarde; **~ thing!** (*as interj*) (colloq) ¡claro (que sí)!, ¡por supuesto!

C (accurate, reliable) ‹*remedy/method*› seguro; ‹*judgment/aim*› certero; ‹*indication*› claro; ‹*ground*› seguro

D (*in phrases*) **for sure**: **we don't know anything for ~** no sabemos nada seguro *or* con seguridad; **we'll win for ~** seguro que ganamos; **to be sure** (admittedly) (*indep*) por cierto; **it could be improved on, to be ~, but ...** se podría mejorar, por cierto, pero ...

sure² *adv*

A (colloq) (*as intensifier*): **she ~ is clever, she's ~ clever** ¡qué lista es!, ¡si será lista!; **he ~ likes to talk** ¡cómo le gusta hablar!, ¡si le gustará hablar!; **he ~ could use a bath!** no le vendría mal darse un baño; **do you like it? — I ~ do!** ¿te gusta? — ¡ya lo creo!

B (of course) por supuesto, claro; **may I join you? — ~, sit down!** ¿me permites? — ¡claro que sí *or* no faltaría más *or* por supuesto, siéntate!

C **sure enough** efectivamente, en efecto

sure: **~fire** *adj* (*before n*) ‹*method*› segurísimo, infalible; **he's a ~fire winner** tiene la victoria asegurada; **~footed** /ˈʃʊrˈfʊtəd/ *adj* ‹*goat/cat*› de pie firme

surely /ˈʃʊrli || ˈʃʊəli, ˈʃɔːli/ *adv*

A **1** (expressing conviction): **~ the real problem is ...** el verdadero problema, digo yo *or* me parece a mí, es ...; **~ she doesn't mean that!** ¡no puede ser que lo diga en serio! **2** (expressing uncertainty): **he must be mistaken, ~?** tiene que estar equivocado ¿no? **3** (expressing disbelief): **~ you don't believe that!** ¡no te creerás eso!; **you're not going to tell her, ~?** no me digas que se lo vas a decir, no se lo irás a decir ¿verdad?; **~ not!** ¡no es posible! *or* ¡no puede ser!; **it was 3,000 — 1,000, ~?** fueron 3.000 — ¿no eran 1.000?

B (undoubtedly, certainly) seguramente, sin duda

C (gladly, willingly) por supuesto, desde luego

surety /ˈʃʊrəti || ˈʃʊərɪti, ˈʃɔːrɪti/ *n* [c u] (*pl* **-ties**) **1** (security) fianza *f*, garantía *f* **2** (person) fiador, -dora *m,f*, garante *mf*; **to stand ~ for sb** servirle* de fiador a algn

surf¹ /sɜːrf || sɜːf/ *n* [u] **1** (waves) olas *fpl* (*rompientes*); (swell) oleaje *m* **2** (foam) espuma *f*

surf² *vi* hacer* surf *or* surfing

■ **surf** *vt* (Comput) explorar, navegar* en; **to ~ the Internet/Web** navegar* *or* surfear en *or* por Internet/la web

surface¹ /ˈsɜːrfəs || ˈsɜːfəs/ *n*

A **1** (of solid, land) superficie *f*; **(road) ~** (Auto) pavimento *m*, firme *m* (Esp); **he just scratched the ~ of the problem** trató el problema muy superficialmente *or* muy por encima; (*before n*) ‹*wound/mark*› superficial; ‹*resemblance/charm*› superficial **2** (of liquid, sea) superficie *f*; **to come/rise to the ~** «*diver/submarine*» salir*/subir a la superficie; «*feelings*» aflorar, salir* a la superficie **3** **on the surface** (superficially) en apariencia, a primera vista

B (Math) **~ (area)** superficie *f*, área *f*‡

surface² *vi* «*diver/submarine/fish*» salir* a la superficie; «*problems/difficulties*» aflorar, aparecer*, surgir*; **he ~d ten years later in Brazil** reapareció en el Brasil diez años después; **he hasn't ~d yet** (hum) todavía no ha dado señales de vida (hum)

■ **surface** *vt* ‹*road*› revestir*, recubrir*; (with asphalt) asfaltar

surface: **~ mail** *n* [u] correo *m* de superficie; **by ~ mail** por vía terrestre/marítima; **~ tension** *n* [u] tensión *f* superficial; **~-to-air missile** *n* /ˈsɜːrfəstəˈer || ˌsɜːfɪstəˈeə(r)/ misil *m* tierra-aire

surf: **~board** /ˈsɜːrfbɔːrd || ˈsɜːfbɔːd/ *n* tabla *f* de surf *or* de surfing; **~boarder** /ˈsɜːrfˌbɔːrdər || ˈsɜːfˌbɔːdə(r)/ *n* surfista *mf*, surfeador, -dora *m,f* (AmL), surfer *mf*; **~boarding** /ˈsɜːrfˌbɔːrdɪŋ || ˈsɜːfˌbɔːdɪŋ/ *n* [u] surf *m*, surfing *m*

surfeit /ˈsɜːrfət || ˈsɜːfɪt/ *n* (liter) **a ~ OF sth** un exceso *or* (liter) una plétora DE algo

surfer /ˈsɜːrfər || ˈsɜːfə(r)/ *n*

A (Sport) surfista *mf*

B (Comput) internauta *mf*, surfeador, -dora *m,f* (AmL)

surfing /ˈsɜːrfɪŋ || ˈsɜːfɪŋ/ *n* [u] surf *m*, surfing *m*

surge¹ /sɜːrdʒ || sɜːdʒ/ *n*: **a ~ of people** una oleada de gente; **we felt a new ~ of hope** sentimos renacer nuestras esperanzas; **a ~ in demand/sales** un repentino aumento de la demanda/las ventas; **a power ~** (Elec) una subida de tensión *or* de voltaje

surge² *vi* **1** «*wave*» levantarse; «*sea*» hincharse; **the crowd ~d out through the gates** la gente salió en tropel por las puertas; **anger/hatred ~d up inside her** la ira/el odio la invadió; **to ~ ahead** tomar la delantera; **to ~ ahead of sb** adelantársele a algn **2** «*demand/sales/popularity*» aumentar vertiginosamente

surgeon /ˈsɜːrdʒən || ˈsɜːdʒən/ *n* cirujano, -na *m,f*

surgeon general *n* (*pl* **~s ~**) (in US) **the S~ G~** ≈ La Dirección General de Salud Pública

surgery /ˈsɜːrdʒəri || ˈsɜːdʒəri/ *n* (*pl* **-ries**)

A [u] (science) cirugía *f*; **he underwent ~** fue intervenido quirúrgicamente (frml), fue operado

B (BrE) **1** [c] (room) consultorio *m*, consulta *f* **2** [c u] (consultation period of doctor) consulta *f*; (*before n*) ‹*times/hours*› de consulta

surgical /ˈsɜːrdʒɪkəl || ˈsɜːdʒɪkəl/ *adj* **1** ‹*instruments/treatment*› quirúrgico; **~ mask** mascarilla *f* **2** ‹*boot/stocking*› ortopédico; **~ appliance** aparato *m* ortopédico

surgical spirit *n* [u] (BrE) alcohol *m* (*de 90°*)

surly /ˈsɜːrli || ˈsɜːli/ *adj* **-lier, -liest** hosco

surmise¹ /sərˈmaɪz/ *n* (frml) conjetura *f*, suposición *f*

surmise² *vt* (frml) conjeturar (frml), suponer*

surmount /sərˈmaʊnt || səˈmaʊnt/ *vt* (overcome) ‹*difficulty/obstacle*› superar, vencer*

surmountable /sərˈmaʊntəbəl/ *adj* superable

surname /ˈsɜːrneɪm || ˈsɜːneɪm/ *n* apellido *m*

surpass /sərˈpæs || səˈpɑːs/ *vt* **1** (better) superar; **she's really ~ed herself this time** (iro) esta vez sí que se ha lucido (iró) **2** (exceed, go beyond) ‹*expectations*› superar, sobrepasar, rebasar; **it ~es all belief** es increíble

surplice /ˈsɜːrplɪs || ˈsɜːplɪs/ *n* sobrepelliz *f*

surplus¹ /ˈsɜːrpləs || ˈsɜːpləs/ *n* (*pl* **~es**) (of produce, stock) excedente *m*; (of funds) superávit *m*

surplus² *adj* ‹*goods/stocks*› excedente; **they need to use up their ~ energy** necesitan gastar la energía que les sobra; **~ value** plusvalía *f*; **to be ~ to requirements** sobrar, estar* de más, no ser* necesario

surprise¹ /səˈpraɪz/ *n* **1** [u] (astonishment) sorpresa *f*; **a look of ~** una mirada sorprendida *or* de sorpresa; **oh!, he said, in some ~** ¡oh! —dijo, algo sorprendido; **to my ~** para mi sorpresa **2** [c] (thing, event) sorpresa *f*; **the result was** *o* **came as something of a ~** el resultado fue en cierto modo una sorpresa; **it's no ~ to me that she won** no me sorprende que haya ganado; **to give sb a ~** darle* una sorpresa a algn; (*before n*) ‹*gift/packet*› sorpresa *adj inv*; **after their ~ defeat in Wednesday's game ...** después de la inesperada derrota del miércoles pasado ... **3** [u] (catching sb unprepared): **to take sb by ~** sorprender a algn, pillar *or* (esp Esp) coger* a algn desprevenido; (*before n*) ‹*visit/attack*› sorpresa *adj inv*

surprise² *vt* **1** (astonish) sorprender; **I was ~d by his vehemence** su vehemencia me sorprendió **2** (catch unawares) sorprender, pillar *or* agarrar *or* (esp Esp) coger* desprevenido

surprised /səˈpraɪzd/ *adj* ‹*look*› sorprendido, de sorpresa; **to be ~: I've never been so ~ in my life!** nunca en la vida me había llevado una sorpresa así; **don't be ~ if he doesn't like it** no te sorprenda si no le gusta; **to be ~ AT sth/sb: I'm ~ at John missing a meeting** me extraña *or* me sorprende que John haya faltado a la reunión; **well, I'm ~ at you, Laura** bueno, Laura, me sorprendes; **she was ~ at how easy it was** le sorprendió lo fácil que era; **I'm ~ (THAT) ...** me sorprende *or* me extraña QUE ... (+ *subj*); **to be ~ to + INF: I was very ~ to hear of your engagement** me sorprendió mucho enterarme de tu compromiso

surprising /sə'praɪzɪŋ/ *adj* ‹*achievement/success*› sorprendente, asombroso; ‹*disclosure*› sorprendente; **it's hardly ~ he's upset** no es de extrañarse que esté disgustado

surprisingly /sə'praɪzɪŋli/ *adv* **1** ‹*quiet/near/good*› sorprendentemente; **~ little research has been done on the subject** es sorprendente lo poco que se ha investigado en el tema **2** (*indep*): **~, she feels no resentment** no está resentida, lo cual es sorprendente; **they were, not ~, very worried** como es lógico, estaban muy preocupados

surreal /sə'ri:əl/ *adj* surrealista

surrealism, Surrealism /sə'ri:əlɪzəm/ *n* [u] surrealismo *m*

surrealist, Surrealist /sə'ri:ələst || sə'ri:əlɪst/ *n* surrealista *mf*; (*before n*) ‹*painter/poem*› surrealista

surrender¹ /sə'rendər || sə'rendə(r)/ *vt* **1** (Mil) ‹*arms/town*› rendir*, entregar* **2** (hand over) (frml) ‹*document/ticket*› entregar* **3** (relinquish) ‹*right/claim*› renunciar a

■ **surrender** *vi* «*soldier/army*» rendirse*; **to ~ TO sb** entregarse* A algn

■ *v refl* **to ~ oneself TO sth** ‹*to indulgence/idleness*› dejarse vencer POR algo

surrender² *n* **1** [u c] (capitulation) rendición *f*, capitulación *f* **2** (submission) (*no pl*) claudicación *f* **3** (frml) (*no pl*) (handing over — of passport, document) entrega *f*; (— of rights) renuncia *f*

surreptitious /'sʌrəp'tɪʃəs/ *adj* ‹*glance/wink*› furtivo, subrepticio

surreptitiously /'sʌrəp'tɪʃəsli/ *adv* a escondidas, subrepticiamente; **he glanced ~ at his watch** le echó una mirada furtiva a su reloj

surrogate¹ /'sʌrəgət/ *n* (frml) sustituto *m*

surrogate² *adj* ‹*material*› sucedáneo; **~ mother** (in childbearing) madre *f* suplente *or* de alquiler

surround¹ /sə'raʊnd/ *vt* **1** (encircle) ‹*place/person*› rodear; **the house is ~ed by trees** la casa está rodeada de árboles; **the garden was ~ed by a fence** el jardín estaba cercado por una valla; **mystery ~s the events leading up to his death** los acontecimientos que llevaron a su muerte están rodeados de *or* envueltos en misterio **2** (Mil) ‹*enemy/position*› rodear, cercar*

surround² *n* marco *m*

surrounding /sə'raʊndɪŋ/ *adj* (*before n*) ‹*countryside/area*› de alrededor; **the ~ villages** los pueblos de alrededor, los pueblos vecinos

surroundings /sə'raʊndɪŋz/ *pl n* **1** (of town, village) alrededores *mpl*, aledaños *mpl* **2** (environment) ambiente *m*, entorno *m*; **a house in beautiful ~** una casa en el marco de un hermoso paisaje

surtax /'sɜ:rtæks || 'sɜ:tæks/ *n* [c u] recargo *m*, sobretasa *f*

surveil /sər'veɪl || sə'veɪl/ *vt* (AmE) vigilar

surveillance /sər'veɪləns || 'sə'veɪləns/ *n* [u] vigilancia *f*; **to be under strict ~** estar* bajo una estrecha vigilancia

survey¹ /'sɜ:rveɪ || 'sɜ:veɪ/ *n*

A **1** (of land) inspección *f*, reconocimiento *m*; (for mapping) medición *f* **2** (of building) inspección *f*, peritaje *m*, peritación *f*; (written report) informe *m* del perito, peritaje *m*, peritación *f*

B (overall view) visión *f* general *or* de conjunto

C (investigation) estudio *m*; (poll) encuesta *f*, sondeo *m*

survey² /sər'veɪ || sə'veɪ/ *vt*

A **1** ‹*land/region*› (measure) medir*; (inspect) inspeccionar, reconocer* **2** ‹*building*› inspeccionar, llevar a cabo un peritaje de

B **1** (look at) contemplar, mirar **2** (view, consider) ‹*situation/plan/prospects*› examinar, analizar*

C (question) ‹*group*› encuestar, hacer* un sondeo de

surveying /sər'veɪɪŋ/ *n* [u] agrimensura *f*, topografía *f*

surveyor /sər'veɪər || sə'veɪə(r)/ *n* **1** (of land) agrimensor, -sora *m,f*, topógrafo, -fa *m,f* **2** (of building) perito, -ta *m,f*

survival /sər'vaɪvəl/ *n* **1** [u] (continued existence) sobrevivencia *f*, supervivencia *f*; **the ~ of the fittest** la ley del más fuerte; (*before n*) ‹*kit/pack*› de sobrevivencia *or* supervivencia **2** [c] (custom, belief) **~ (FROM sth)** vestigio *m* (DE algo)

survive /sər'vaɪv || sə'vaɪv/ *vi* **1** (continue in existence) «*person/animal/plant*» sobrevivir; «*custom/tradition/belief*» sobrevivir, perdurar; «*book/relic*» conservarse; **of the original expedition few ~d** de los integrantes de la expedición inicial quedaban pocos vivos; **her last surviving descendant** su último descendiente vivo; **one of the few surviving examples** uno de los pocos ejemplos que quedan **2** (cope, get by) (colloq): **how are you doing? — oh, surviving!** ¿qué tal andas? — ya lo ves, tirando (fam); **is it serious? — you'll ~** ¿es grave? — mira, de ésta no te mueres; **to ~ ON sth: he ~s on black coffee and fruit** vive *or* se alimenta a base de café y fruta; **I can just ~ on $100 a week** con 100 dólares semanales apenas me alcanza para vivir

■ **survive** *vt*

A ‹*accident/crash*› salir* con vida de; ‹*war/earthquake*› sobrevivir a; ‹*experience*› superar

B (outlive) ‹*person*› sobrevivir; **he is ~d by his wife and two children** lo sobreviven su esposa y dos hijos

survivor /sər'vaɪvər || sə'vaɪvə(r)/ *n* superviviente *mf*, sobreviviente *mf*; **don't worry about him: he's a ~** (colloq) no te preocupes por él, es de los que salen a flote

susceptibility /sə'septə'bɪləti/ *n* [u] **~ (TO sth)** ‹*to attack*› vulnerabilidad *f* (FRENTE A algo); ‹*to colds/infection*› propensión *f* (A algo)

susceptible /sə'septəbəl/ *adj*

A **1** (open, vulnerable) **~ TO sth** ‹*to colds/infection*› propenso A algo; **he's ~ to a bit of flattery** se le puede persuadir halagándolo **2** (touchy) susceptible, sensible

B (capable) (frml) **~ OF sth** (of change, improvement) susceptible DE algo

suspect¹ /sə'spekt/ *vt*

A **1** (believe guilty) ‹*person*› sospechar de; **to ~ sb OF sth/-ING: I ~ him of the murder** sospecho que es el asesino; **we ~ him of lying** sospechamos que miente **2** (doubt, mistrust) ‹*sincerity/probity*› dudar de, tener* dudas acerca de

B **1** (believe to exist): **they ~ nothing** no sospechan nada; **arson is not ~ed** no existen sospechas de que el incendio haya sido provocado **2** **suspected** *past p*: **a ~ed fracture** una posible fractura; **the ~ed murderer** el presunto asesino

C (think probable) imaginarse; **I ~ed as much** ya me lo imaginaba *or* figuraba; **to ~ (THAT)** imaginarse QUE; **I ~ed I'd find you here** me imaginaba que te iba a encontrar aquí; **I ~ (that) it may be more serious than that** me temo que pueda ser más grave

■ **suspect** *vi*: **just as I ~ed** tal como lo imaginaba

suspect² /'sʌspekt/ *n* (person) sospechoso, -sa *m,f*

suspect³ /'sʌspekt/ *adj* ‹*package/behavior*› sospechoso; ‹*document/evidence*› de dudosa autenticidad

suspend /sə'spend/ *vt*

A **1** ‹*payment/work*› suspender **2** ‹*judgment*› posponer*, postergar* (esp AmL)

B (debar, ban) suspender; ‹*student*› expulsar temporariamente, suspender (AmL); **he was ~ed from office** fue separado de su cargo

C (hang) (*often pass*) suspender; **it seemed to hang ~ed in mid air** parecía estar suspendido en el aire

suspended /sə'spendəd/: **~ animation** *n* [u] muerte *f* aparente; **in a state of ~ animation** con las constantes vitales reducidas al mínimo; **~ sentence** *n*: *pena de prisión que no se cumple a menos que el delincuente reincida*

suspender belt /sə'spendər || sə'spendə(r)/ *n* (BrE) portaligas *m*, liguero *m*

suspenders /sə'spendərz/ *pl n* (*sometimes sing*)

A (braces) (AmE) tirantes *mpl or* (RPl) tiradores *mpl or* (Chi) suspensores *mpl or* (Col) cargaderas *fpl*

B (for stockings, socks) (BrE) ligas *fpl*

suspense /sə'spens/ *n* [u] (in literary work, movie) suspenso *m or* (Esp) suspense *m*; **the ~ is killing me!** ¡la intriga *or* la incertidumbre me está matando!; **to keep sb in ~** mantener* a algn sobre ascuas *or* en vilo

suspension /sə'spenʃən/ *n*

A [u c] **1** (cessation) suspensión *f* **2** (deferment) aplazamiento *m*, postergación *f* (esp AmL)

B [c u] (banning, withdrawal) suspensión *f*; (of student) expulsión *f*

temporaria, suspensión *f* (AmL); ~ **from duty** separación *f* del cargo
C [u] (hanging, being hung) suspensión *f*
D [u] (Auto) suspensión *f*
suspension: ~ **bridge** *n* puente *m* colgante; ~ **points** *pl n* (AmE) puntos *mpl* suspensivos
suspicion /sə'spɪʃən/ *n*
A [c u] (belief) sospecha *f*; (mistrust) desconfianza *f*, recelo *m*; **I have my ~s** tengo mis sospechas; **he's under/above ~** está bajo sospecha/por encima de toda sospecha; **they're being held on ~** los han detenido como sospechosos
B (trace, hint) (*no pl*) atisbo *m*
suspicious /sə'spɪʃəs/ *adj* **1** (mistrustful) ‹*mind/person*› desconfiado, suspicaz; **to be ~ OF/ABOUT sb/sth** desconfiar* DE algn/algo **2** (arousing suspicion) ‹*actions/movements*› sospechoso
suspiciously /sə'spɪʃəsli/ *adv* **1** (mistrustfully) ‹*regard/watch*› con desconfianza, con recelo **2** (arousing suspicion) ‹*act*› sospechosamente; **it looked ~ like a trap** tenía todo el aspecto *or* (fam) toda la pinta de ser una trampa
suss /sʌs/ *vt* ~ **(out)** (BrE sl) **1** (realize) darse* cuenta de; **I soon ~ed what he was up to** pronto me di cuenta de lo que andaba tramando **2** (work out) calar (fam); **I've got her ~ed** la tengo calada (fam); **I've got it ~ed** le he agarrado *or* (Esp) cogido la onda (fam)
sustain /sə'steɪn/ *vt*
A (support) ‹*life*› preservar, sustentar; ‹*hope/interest*› mantener*; **they were ~ed by their faith** su fe los sostenía
B (keep up, prolong) ‹*pretense/conversation*› mantener*; ‹*effort*› sostener*
C (suffer) ‹*injury/loss/defeat*› sufrir
D (confirm, uphold) ‹*objection*› admitir; ‹*claim*› apoyar
sustainability /sʌsteɪnə'bɪləti/ *n* [u] sostenibilidad *f*
sustainable /sə'steɪnəbəl/ *adj* sostenible
sustained /sə'steɪnd/ *adj* ‹*efforts*› sostenido, continuo; **her appearance was greeted by ~ applause** su aparición fue largamente ovacionada
sustaining /sə'steɪnɪŋ/ *adj* ‹*food/diet*› nutritivo
sustenance /'sʌstənəns/ *n* [u] alimento *m*, sustento *m*
suture /'su:tʃər || 'su:tʃə(r)/ *n* (Med) sutura *f*
SUV *n* (= **Sports Utility Vehicle**) SUV *m*
svelte /sfelt, sv-/ *adj* (slim) esbelto
SW **1** (= **southwest**) SO **2** = **shortwave**
swab¹ /swɑ:b || swɒb/ *n* **1** (of cotton, gauze) hisopo *m* húmedo **2** (specimen) muestra *f*, frotis *m*
swab² *vt* **-bb-** **1** ‹*wound*› limpiar (*con algodón, gasa etc*) **2** **to ~ (down)** ‹*deck*› lavar, limpiar
swaddle /'swɑ:dl̩ || 'swɒdl̩/ *vt* envolver*
swag /swæg/ *n* [u] (sl & dated) botín *m*
swagger¹ /'swægər || 'swægə(r)/ *n* **1** (gait): **they walked with a ~** caminaban erguidos, con aire arrogante **2** (conduct) fanfarronería *f*, fantochada *f*
swagger² *vi* caminar *or* andar* con aire arrogante; **he ~ed up to the bar** se acercó al bar con aire arrogante
Swahili /swɑ:'hi:li || swə'hi:li/ *n* [u] swahili *m*, suajili *m*
swallow¹ /'swɑ:ləʊ || 'swɒləʊ/ *n*
A (Zool) golondrina *f*
B (gulp) trago *m*; **in one ~** de un trago
swallow² *vt*
A ‹*food/drink*› tragar*; **she ~ed it in one gulp** lo pasó de un trago
B ‹*lies/insult/taunts*› tragarse* (fam); **that's a bit hard to ~** eso no hay quien se lo trague (fam); **to ~ one's pride** tragarse* el orgullo
C ▸ **swallow up**
■ **swallow** *vi* tragar*; **to ~ hard** tragar saliva
Phrasal verb
• **swallow up** [v ▸ o ▸ adv, v ▸ adv ▸ o] **1** (use up) ‹*money/time*› consumir, tragarse* (fam), comerse (fam) **2** (cause to disappear) tragarse*; **they were ~ed up by the darkness** se los tragó *or* los envolvió la oscuridad
swam /swæm/ *past of* **swim¹**
swamp¹ /swɑ:mp || swɒmp/ *n* pantano *m*, ciénaga *f*; (of sea water) marisma *f*, ciénaga *f*
swamp² *vt* **1** (with water) ‹*land*› anegar*, inundar; **a huge wave ~ed the frail craft** una enorme ola se tragó la frágil embarcación **2** (overwhelm) (*often pass*): **they were ~ed by offers of help** recibieron una avalancha de ofertas de ayuda; **I'm absolutely ~ed with work** estoy inundada de trabajo
swampland /'swɑ:mplænd || 'swɒmplænd/ *n* [u c] (*often pl*) pantano *m*, ciénaga *f*; (of sea water) marisma *f*
swampy /'swɑ:mpi/ *adj* **-pier, -piest** pantanoso
swan¹ /swɑ:n || swɒn/ *n* cisne *m*
swan² *vi* **-nn-** (esp BrE colloq): **to ~ about** *o* **around** andar* pavoneándose por ahí; **we have so much work to do and she goes ~ning off to the theatre!** ¡con todo el trabajo que tenemos, ella se va al teatro olímpicamente!
swank¹ /swæŋk/ *n* (BrE colloq) **1** [u] (boasting) fanfarronada *f* (fam) **2** [u] (show): **just for ~** sólo para lucirse *or* para darse tono **3** [c] (person) fanfarrón, -rrona *m,f* (fam)
swank² *vi* (BrE colloq) fanfarronear (fam)
swanky /'swæŋki/ *adj* **-kier, -kiest** (colloq) **1** (boastful) (pej) ‹*person*› fanfarrón (fam) **2** (classy) chic *adj inv*, pijo (Esp fam), pituco (CS fam), popoff *adj inv* (Méx fam)
swan song *n* canto *m* de cisne
swap¹ /swɑ:p || swɒp/ *n* (colloq) (exchange) cambio *m*, trueque *m*; **we can do a ~** podemos cambiárnoslos
swap² **-pp-** *vt* ‹*possessions/ideas*› intercambiar; **to ~ sth FOR sth** cambiar algo POR algo; **I'll ~ (you) my stamp album for your bike** te cambio el álbum de sellos por la bici; **to ~ sth WITH sb** cambiarle algo A algn; **I ~ped places with Helen** le cambié el sitio a Helen
■ **swap** *vi*: **try to ~ with a friend** trata de cambiárselo (*or* cambiárselos *etc*) a un amigo
Phrasal verb
• **swap around,** (BrE also) **swap round** **1** [v ▸ o ▸ adv] cambiar de sitio; **I ~ped the glasses around** cambié las copas de sitio **2** [v ▸ adv] cambiar
SWAPO /'swɑ:pəʊ || 'swɒpəʊ/ *n* (*no art*) (= **South-West Africa People's Organization**) el SWAPO
swarm¹ /swɔ:rm || swɔ:m/ *n* enjambre *m*; **~s of reporters** una multitud de periodistas
swarm² *vi* ‹‹*bees*›› enjambrar; **people ~ed around the stalls** la gente se aglomeraba *or* se apiñaba alrededor de los puestos; **the flies ~ed around the meat** las moscas revoloteaban alrededor de la carne; **the crowd ~ed into the square** la multitud irrumpió en la plaza; **to ~ WITH sb/sth**: **the beaches were ~ing with tourists** las playas eran un hormiguero de turistas
swarthy /'swɔ:rði || 'swɔ:ði/ *adj* **-thier, -thiest** moreno
swashbuckling /'swɑ:ʃ,bʌklɪŋ || 'swɒʃ,bʌklɪŋ/ *adj* ‹*tale/film/hero*› de capa y espada; ‹*role*› de aventurero
swastika /'swɑ:stɪkə/ *n* svástica *f*, esvástica *f*
swat /swɑ:t || swɒt/ **-tt-** *vt* ‹*insect*› matar (*con matamoscas, periódico etc*)
■ **swat** *vi* **to ~ AT sth** intentar darle A algo; **he was ~ting at the wasps** estaba tratando de matar las avispas
swath /swɑ:θ, swɔ:θ || swɔ:θ, swɒθ/, **swathe** /sweɪð/ *n* (of grass, land) franja *f*; ***to cut a ~*** (AmE dated) causar sensación; ***to cut a ~ through sth*** abrirse* camino a través de algo
swathe /sweɪð/ *vt* (*often pass*) envolver*; **his foot was ~d in bandages** tenía el pie vendado
sway¹ /sweɪ/ *n* [u]
A (movement) balanceo *m*, oscilación *f*
B (influence) influjo *m*; (domination) dominio *m*; **to hold ~** ‹‹*ideas*›› prevalecer*; ‹‹*leader*›› ejercer* dominio; **to hold ~ OVER sb** ejercer* dominio SOBRE algn
sway² *vi*
A (swing) ‹‹*branch/tree*›› balancearse; ‹‹*building/tower*›› bambolearse, balancearse, oscilar; **the wheat was ~ing in the breeze** el trigo se mecía con la brisa
B (veer) ‹‹*public opinion*›› cambiar, dar* un viraje
■ **sway** *vt*
A (influence) ‹*person/crowd*› influir* en, influenciar
B (move) ‹*hips*› menear, bambolear
Swaziland /'swɑ:zilænd/ *n* Swazilandia *f*, Suazilandia *f*
swear /swer || sweə(r)/ (*past* **swore**; *past p* **sworn**) *vt* ‹*allegiance/fidelity/revenge*› jurar; **they swore an oath of obedience** juraron obediencia; **she ~s blind she didn't know** (colloq) jura y perjura que no lo sabía (fam); **I could have sworn I left it there** hubiera jurado que lo dejé ahí; **we've all been sworn to secrecy** nos han hecho prometer que no diremos nada
■ **swear** *vi* **1** (vow) jurar **2** (curse) decir* palabrotas,

S

soltar* tacos (Esp fam), mentar* madres (Méx fam); **to ~ AT sb** insultar a algn (*usando palabrotas*)

Phrasal verbs

- **swear by** [v ▸ prep ▸ o] (value highly) ‹*gadget*› ser* un entusiasta de; ‹*remedy*› tenerle* una fe ciega a
- **swear in** [v ▸ o ▸ adv, v ▸ adv ▸ o] ‹*jury/witness/president*› tomarle juramento a, juramentar; **she will be sworn in on Monday** prestará juramento el lunes
- **swear to** [v ▸ prep ▸ o]: **I ~ to God I never touched it** te juro por Dios que no lo toqué; **but I couldn't ~ to it** pero no podría jurarlo

swearing /'swerɪŋ || 'sweərɪŋ/ *n* [u]: **there's a lot of ~ in the film** dicen muchas palabrotas en la película; **she hates all that ~** odia ese vocabulario soez

swearing-in /'swerɪŋ'ɪn/ *n* [u] toma *f* de juramento

swearword /'swerwɜːrd || 'sweəwɜːd/ *n* palabrota *f*, mala palabra *f*, taco *m* (Esp), garabato *m* (Chi)

sweat¹ /swet/ *n*

A [u c] (perspiration) sudor *m*, transpiración *f*; **by the ~ of his brow** con el sudor de su frente; **I woke up in a ~** me desperté empapado en sudor; **I broke out in a cold ~** me vino un sudor frío; ***to get into a ~ about sth*** preocuparse por algo

B [u] (hard work) (esp BrE colloq) paliza *f* (fam), esfuerzo *m*; ***no ~*** (colloq) ningún problema

sweat² (*past & past p* **sweated** *or* (AmE also) **sweat**) *vi*

A (perspire) sudar, transpirar; **to ~ with fear** sudar de miedo

B (work hard) sudar la gota gorda (fam), deslomarse trabajando

Phrasal verbs

- **sweat off** [v ▸ adv ▸ o] ‹*pounds/kilos*› adelgazar* sudando
- **sweat out** [v ▸ o ▸ adv, v ▸ adv ▸ o]: **to ~ out a cold** quitarse un resfriado sudando; ***to ~ it out*** (colloq): **they'll have to ~ it out until they're relieved** van a tener que aguantar hasta que los releven

sweatband /'swetbænd/ *n* (around wrist) muñequera *f*; (around head) cinta *f*, vincha *f* (AmS), huincha *f* (Bol, Chi, Per)

sweater /'swetər || 'swetə(r)/ *n* suéter *m*, pulóver *m*, jersey *m* (Esp), buzo *m* (Ur), chompa *f* (Per), chomba *f* (Chi)

sweat: **~shirt** *n* sudadera *f*, camiseta *f* gruesa, buzo *m* (Arg), polerón *m* (Chi); **~shop** *n*: *fábrica donde se explota a los trabajadores*; **~suit** *n* (AmE) equipo *m* (de deportes), chándal *m* (Esp), pants *mpl* (Méx), buzo *m* (Chi, Per), sudadera *f* (Col), jogging *m* (RPl)

sweaty /'sweti/ *adj* **-tier, -tiest** sudado, transpirado

swede /swiːd/ *n* (esp BrE) colinabo *m*, nabo *m* sueco

Swede /swiːd/ *n* sueco, -ca *m,f*

Sweden /'swiːdn̩/ *n* Suecia *f*

Swedish¹ /'swiːdɪʃ/ *adj* sueco

Swedish² *n* [u] **1** (language) sueco *m* **2** (people) (+ *pl vb*) **the ~** (people) los suecos

sweep¹ /swiːp/ *n*

A (act) (*no pl*) barrido *m*, barrida *f*; **give it a ~** dale un barrido *or* una barrida, bárrelo

B **1** [c] (movement): **with a ~ of his arm** con un amplio movimiento del brazo; **with a ~ of his scythe** con un golpe de la guadaña; **the broad ~s of his brush strokes** el ancho trazo de sus pinceladas **2** [c] (curve — of road, river) curva *f* **3** (range) (*no pl*) alcance *m*, extensión *f*

C [c] (search) peinado *m*, rastreo *m*

D [c] (*chimney ~*) deshollinador, -dora *m,f*

sweep² (*past & pp* **swept**) *vt*

A **1** (clean) ‹*floor/path*› barrer; ‹*chimney*› deshollinar **2** (remove) ‹*leaves/dirt*› barrer; ‹*mines*› barrer; **he swept the crumbs off the table** limpió la mesa de migas; **she swept the leaves into a pile** barrió la terraza (*or* el patio *etc*) y amontonó las hojas; **he swept the coins into a box** con la mano reunió las monedas y las deslizó en una caja; ***to ~ sth under the rug*** *o* (BrE) ***carpet*** correr un velo sobre algo

B (touch lightly, brush) ‹*surface*› rozar*

C **1** (pass over, across): **severe storms swept the coast** grandes tormentas azotaron *or* barrieron la costa; **the epidemic is ~ing the country** la epidemia se extiende como un reguero de pólvora por el país **2** (remove by force) arrastrar; **we were being swept out to sea by the tide** la marea nos arrastraba mar adentro

D **1** (scan) recorrer **2** (search) ‹*area*› peinar, rastrear

■ **sweep** *vi*

A (+ *adv compl*) **1** (move rapidly): **the car swept by** *o* **past** el coche pasó rápidamente **2** (move proudly): **she swept into the room** entró majestuosamente en la habitación; **he swept past as if I wasn't there** pasó por mi lado con la cabeza en alto, como si yo no existiera

B (+ *adv compl*) **1** (spread): **fire swept through the hotel** el fuego se propagó *or* se extendió por todo el hotel; **panic swept through the ranks** cundió el pánico en las filas **2** (extend): **the path ~s down to the road** el sendero baja describiendo una curva hasta la carretera

Phrasal verbs

- **sweep aside** [v ▸ o ▸ adv, v ▸ adv ▸ o] **1** ‹*object*› apartar **2** ‹*opposition/objection/doubts*› desechar
- **sweep away** [v ▸ o ▸ adv, v ▸ adv ▸ o] **1** (carry away) ‹‹*flood/storm*›› arrastrar **2** (abolish) erradicar*
- **sweep up**

A [v ▸ adv] (clear up) barrer, limpiar

B [v ▸ o ▸ adv, v ▸ adv ▸ o] **1** (clear up) ‹*dust/leaves*› barrer y recoger* **2** (gather up) ‹*belongings/bags*› recoger*; **he swept her up in his arms** la levantó en brazos

sweeper /'swiːpər || 'swiːpə(r)/ *n*

A **1** (*road~*) barrendero, -ra *m,f*, barredor, -dora *m,f* (Per) **2** (*carpet ~*) cepillo *m* mecánico

B (in soccer) líbero *mf*, barredor, -dora *m,f* (Chi)

sweeping /'swiːpɪŋ/ *adj* **1** ‹*movement*› amplio; ‹*gesture*› dramático, histriónico **2** (indiscriminate) (pej): **that's rather a ~ statement, isn't it?** ¿no estás generalizando demasiado? **3** (far-reaching) ‹*reforms/changes*› radical; ‹*powers*› amplio

sweepings /'swiːpɪŋz/ *pl n* (dirt) basura *f*

sweepstakes /'swiːpsteɪks/, (BrE) **sweepstake** /'swiːpsteɪk/ *n* **1** (race) *carrera en la que el ganador se lleva todas las apuestas* **2** (lottery) lotería *f*

sweet¹ /swiːt/ *adj* **-er, -est**

A ‹*taste*› dulce; (with sugar) dulce, azucarado; **avoid ~ things** evite los dulces

B **1** (fresh, wholesome) ‹*smell*› agradable **2** ‹*water*› dulce

C **1** (pleasant, gratifying) ‹*sounds/voice/music*› dulce, melodioso; **for him victory was ~** la victoria le supo a gloria; **good night, ~ dreams** buenas noches y que sueñes con los angelitos; **she always goes her own ~ way** siempre hace lo que (se) le da la real gana **2** (kind, lovable) ‹*nature/temper/smile*› dulce; **she's a very ~ person** es un encanto (de persona); **it was very ~ of her to offer** fue un detalle que se ofreciese **3** (attractive) ‹*baby/puppy*› rico (fam), mono (fam), amoroso (AmL fam)

sweet² *n*

A [c] (item of confectionery) (BrE) caramelo *m* *or* (AmL exc RPl) dulce *m*

B [u c] (dessert) (BrE) postre *m*

C **sweets** *pl* (sugary food) (AmE) dulces *mpl*

D (*as form of address*): **my ~** mi vida, mi cielo

sweet: **~-and-sour** *adj* (*before n*) ‹*pork/sauce*› agridulce; **~breads** *pl n* mollejas *fpl*, lechecillas *fpl* (Esp); **~ chestnut** *n* **1** (fruit) castaña *f* (dulce) **2** (tree) castaño *m* (dulce); **~corn** *n* [u] maíz *m* tierno, elote *m* (Méx), choclo *m* (AmS), jojoto *m* (Ven)

sweeten /'swiːtn̩/ *vt*

A **1** ‹*drink/dish*› endulzar*, azucarar **2** ‹*air/breath*› refrescar*

B **1** (with extra money, benefits) ‹*offer/deal/sale*› hacer* más atractivo *or* apetecible **2** (colloq) (soften the attitude of) ablandar

sweetener /'swiːtn̩ər || 'swiːtn̩ə(r)/ *n* **1** (Culin) endulzante *m*; (artificial) edulcorante *m* **2** (bribe) (colloq) soborno *m*, coima *f* (CS, Per fam), mordida *f* (Méx fam)

sweetheart /'swiːthɑːrt || 'swiːthɑːt/ *n* **1** (lover, darling) novio, -via *m,f*, enamorado, -da *m,f*; **my childhood ~** el novio/la novia de mi infancia **2** (colloq) (*as form of address*) (mi) amor, mi vida, cariño

sweetie /'swiːti/ *n* (colloq)

A **~ (pie)** **1** (person) encanto *m*, cielo *m* **2** (*as form of address*) mi vida, tesoro

B (sweet, candy) (BrE) caramelo *m* *or* (AmL exc RPl) dulce *m*

sweetly /'swiːtli/ *adv* ‹*smile/sing*› dulcemente, con dulzura; **~ scented** de agradable fragancia; **she very ~ offered to do it** muy amablemente se ofreció a hacerlo

sweet-natured /'swi:t'neɪtʃərd/ *adj* dulce

sweetness /'swi:tnəs/ *n* [u] 1 (sugary taste) dulzor *m* 2 (of smell) lo agradable 3 (of person, character) dulzura *f*; ***to be (all) ~ and light*** estar* hecho un encanto

sweet: **~ pea** *n* alverjilla *f or* (RPl) arvejilla *f or* (Esp) guisante *m* de olor *or* (Méx) chícharo *m* de olor *or* (Chi) clarín *m*; **~ potato** *n* boniato *m*, batata *f*, camote *m* (Andes, Méx); **~shop** *n* (BrE) tienda *f* de golosinas; **~-talk** *vt* (colloq) engatusar (fam), camelar (Esp fam); **to ~-talk sb INTO -ING** engatusar *or* (Esp) camelar a algn PARA QUE (+ *subj*) (fam); **~-talking** *adj* (colloq) zalamero; **~-tempered** /'swi:t'tempərd || ˌswi:t'tempəd/ *adj* de carácter dulce; **~ william** /'wɪljəm/ *n* minutisa *f*

swell[1] /swel/ (*past p* **swollen** *or* (AmE esp) **swelled**) *vi*
A «*wood/sails/face/ankles*» hincharse; «*river/stream*» crecer*, subir
B (increase) «*population/crowd*» crecer*, aumentar; **the applause ~ed to a crescendo** los aplausos se fueron haciendo cada vez más fuertes
■ **swell** *vt*
A (increase in size) ‹*body/joint/features*› hinchar; ‹*sails*› hinchar; ‹*river*› hacer* crecer *or* subir
B (increase in number, volume) ‹*population/total/funds*› aumentar; **to ~ the ranks of the unemployed** engrosar las filas del desempleo

Phrasal verb
• **swell up** [v ▸ adv] hincharse; **my/her finger ~ed up** se me/le hinchó el dedo

swell[2] *n* 1 (of sea) oleaje *m*; **a heavy ~** un fuerte oleaje, una marejada 2 (surge, movement) oleada *f*

swell[3] *adj* (fine, excellent) (AmE colloq) fenomenal (fam), bárbaro (fam)

swelling /'swelɪŋ/ *n* [c u] hinchazón *f*

swelter /'sweltər || 'sweltə(r)/ *vi* sofocarse* de calor

sweltering /'sweltərɪŋ/ *adj* sofocante, bochornoso; **it was ~** hacía un calor sofocante

swept /swept/ *past & past p of* **sweep**[2]

swept-back /'swept'bæk/ *adj* ‹*hair*› peinado hacia atrás

swerve[1] /swɜ:rv || swɜ:v/ *vi* «*vehicle/driver/horse*» virar bruscamente, dar* un viraje brusco; «*ball*» ir* con efecto; **he ~d in and out of the traffic** zigzagueó por entre el tráfico
■ **swerve** *vt* ‹*vehicle*› hacer* virar bruscamente

swerve[2] *n* 1 [c] (movement — of vehicle) viraje *m* brusco, volantazo *m* (Méx); (— of boxer, footballer) finta *f*, regate *m* (Esp) 2 [u] (of ball) efecto *m*

swift[1] /swɪft/ *adj* **-er, -est** 1 ‹*runner/movement/animal*› veloz, rápido; **a ~-flowing river** un río de corriente rápida 2 ‹*reply/reaction/denial*› rápido; **he was ~ to reply** no tardó en contestar; **he was ~ to anger** (liter) era propenso a arrebatos de ira

swift[2] *n* vencejo *m*

swiftly /'swɪftli/ *adv* (rapidly) rápidamente, con rapidez, velozmente; (promptly) con prontitud *or* rapidez

swiftness /'swɪftnəs || 'swɪftnɪs/ *n* [u] (speed) rapidez *f*, velocidad *f*; (of reply, reaction) rapidez *f*, prontitud *f*

swig[1] /swɪg/ *n* (colloq) trago *m*; **to take** *o* **have a ~ of sth** tomarse un trago de algo

swig[2] *vt/i* **-gg-** (colloq) tomar, beber

swill[1] /swɪl/ *n*
A [u] 1 (for pigs) comida *f* para cerdos 2 (colloq) (disgusting food, drink) bazofia *f* (fam), porquería *f* (fam)
B (with water) (*no pl*): **a ~ (out/down)** (wash) una lavada; (rinse) un enjuague

swill[2] *vt*
A (wash, rinse) **to ~ sth (out)** ‹*cups/pans*› lavar/enjuagar* algo
B (drink) (colloq & pej) ‹*beer*› tomar *or* beber (*a grandes tragos*)

swim[1] /swɪm/ (*pres p* **swimming**; *past* **swam**; *past p* **swum**) *vi*
A «*person/animal/fish*» nadar; **can you ~?** ¿sabes nadar?; **are you going ~ming?** ¿vas a ir a nadar?; **he swam across the river** cruzó el río nadando *or* a nado; **we had to ~ for it** tuvimos que nadar para salvarnos
B 1 (float) flotar 2 (be immersed, overflowing) (*usu in -ing form*) **to ~ IN sth** nadar *or* flotar EN algo; **the tomatoes were ~ming in oil** los tomates nadaban *or* flotaban en aceite; **to ~ WITH sth**: **the bathroom floor was ~ming with water** el suelo del baño estaba cubierto de agua
C (of blurred, confused perceptions) dar* vueltas; **my head was ~ming** la cabeza me daba vueltas
■ **swim** *vt* ‹*length*› nadar, hacer*; ‹*river*› cruzar* a nado; **to ~ breaststroke** nadar pecho *or* (Esp) a braza

swim[2] *n*: **to go for a ~** ir* a nadar; **to have a ~** nadar, bañarse, darse* un baño; **it's a long ~ to the island** hay que nadar un buen trecho para llegar a la isla; ***to be in the ~*** estar* al tanto de lo que pasa, estar* en la onda (fam)

swimmer /'swɪmər || 'swɪmə(r)/ *n* nadador, -dora *m,f*

swimming /'swɪmɪŋ/ *n* [u] natación *f*; **~ is fun** nadar es divertido; (*before n*) **~ cap** gorro *m or* gorra *f* (de baño)

swimming: **~ bath** *n*, **~ baths** *pl n* (BrE) piscina *f* cubierta, alberca *f* techada (Méx), pileta *f* cubierta (RPl); **~ costume** *n* (BrE) ▸**swimsuit**; **~ pool** *n* piscina *f*, alberca *f* (Méx), pileta *f* (RPl); **~ trunks** *pl n* traje *m* de baño, bañador *m* (Esp), vestido *m* de baño (Col) (*de caballero*)

swim: **~suit** *n* traje *m* de baño, bañador *m* (Esp), vestido *m* de baño (Col), malla *f* (de baño) (RPl); **~wear** *n* [u] trajes *mpl* de baño, bañadores *mpl* (Esp), mallas *fpl* (de baño) (RPl), vestidos *mpl* de baño (Col)

swindle[1] /'swɪndl/ *n* estafa *f*, timo *m* (fam)

swindle[2] *vt* estafar, timar; **I've been ~d** me han estafado *or* timado; **to ~ sb OUT OF sth**: **they ~d her out of her savings** la estafaron y le quitaron sus ahorros

swindler /'swɪndlər || 'swɪndlə(r)/ *n* estafador, -dora *m,f*

swine /swaɪn/ *n* 1 (*pl* ~) (pig, hog) cerdo *m* 2 (*pl* **~s**) (contemptible person) (colloq) cerdo, -da *m,f* (fam), canalla *mf*, cabrón, -brona *m,f* (Esp fam)

swing[1] /swɪŋ/ (*past & past p* **swung**) *vi*
A 1 (hang, dangle) balancearse; (on a swing) columpiarse *or* (RPl) hamacarse*; «*pendulum*» oscilar 2 (convey oneself): **the monkeys swung from tree to tree** los monos saltaban de árbol en árbol colgados *or* (Col, Méx, Ven) guindados de las ramas (*or* de las lianas *etc*)
B 1 (move on pivot): **the door swung open/shut** *o* **to** la puerta se abrió/se cerró; **the door was ~ing in the wind** la puerta se mecía con el viento 2 (turn) girar *or* doblar (*describiendo una curva*); **the ball swung away** la pelota salió desviada
C (shift, change) «*opinion/mood*» cambiar, oscilar; **his views ~ from one extreme to another** sus ideas pasan de un extremo a otro; **the country is ~ing to the left** el país está virando *or* dando un viraje hacia la izquierda
D 1 **to ~ INTO sth** ‹*into action/operation*›: **the emergency plans swung into operation/action** se pusieron en marcha los planes de emergencia 2 (attempt to hit) **to ~ AT sb/sth** intentar pegarle *or* darle A algn/algo
E (be lively, up to date) (colloq) «*party*» estar* muy animado
■ **swing** *vt*
A (move to and fro) ‹*arms/legs*› balancear; ‹*object on rope*› hacer* oscilar; **to ~ one's hips** contonearse, contonear *or* menear las caderas
B 1 (convey): **he swung himself into the saddle** se montó en la silla de un salto; **he swung his suitcase up onto the rack** subió la maleta al portaequipaje de un envión 2 (wave, brandish) ‹*club/hammer*› blandir
C 1 (colloq) (manage) arreglar; **if you want that job, I think I can ~ it** si quieres ese puesto, creo que puedo arreglarlo 2 (shift): **this could ~ the vote our way** esto podría inclinar la votación a nuestro favor; **he managed to ~ public opinion behind him** logró poner a la opinión pública de su lado

Phrasal verb
• **swing around**, (BrE also) **swing round**
A [v ▸ adv] 1 (change direction, turn) «*vehicle*» dar* un viraje, girar *or* virar (en redondo); **she swung around to face me** giró sobre sus talones para darme la cara; **the wind has swung around to the east** el viento ha cambiado hacia el este 2 (change views) **to ~ around TO sth** dar* un giro *or* un viraje HACIA algo
B [v ▸ o ▸ adv] 1 ‹*car/boat*› hacer* girar en redondo 2 (change): **we hope to ~ them around to our point of view** esperamos poder convencerlos de que tenemos razón

swing[2] *n*
A 1 [c u] (movement) oscilación *f*, vaivén *m* 2 [c] (distance) *arco que describe un objeto que oscila* 3 [c] (blow, stroke) golpe

S

m; (in golf, boxing) swing *m*; **to take a ~ at sb/sth** intentar darle a algn/algo (*con un palo, una raqueta etc*)
B [c] **1** (shift) cambio *m*; **a ~ in public opinion** un cambio *or* un viraje en la opinión pública; **a ~ back to traditional values** una vuelta a los valores tradicionales; **the ~s of the market** (Fin) las fluctuaciones del mercado **2** (Pol) viraje *m*; **a ~ to the Democrats of 4%** un viraje del 4% en favor de los demócratas
C **1** [u c] (rhythm, vitality): **there was a ~ in her step** andaba con brío; ***to be in full ~*** estar* en pleno desarrollo; **the party was in full ~** la fiesta estaba ya muy animada; **exams are in full ~** estamos (*or* están *etc*) en plena época de exámenes; ***to get into the ~ of sth*** agarrarle el ritmo *or* (Esp) cogerle* el tranquillo a algo; ***to go with a ~*** ‹‹*business/conference*›› marchar sobre ruedas; ‹‹*party*›› estar* muy animado **2** [u] (Mus) swing *m*
D [c] (Leisure) columpio *m or* (RPl) hamaca *f*; **to have a ~** columpiarse *or* (RPl) hamacarse*; ***it's a question of ~s and roundabouts*** (BrE) lo que se pierde en una cosa se gana en la otra

swing: **~ bin** *n* cubo *m or* (CS) tacho *m or* (Méx) bote *m or* (Col) caneca *f or* (Ven) tobo *m* de la basura (*con tapa de vaivén*); **~ bridge** *n* puente *m* giratorio; **~ door** *n* puerta *f* (de) vaivén

swingeing /ˈswɪndʒɪŋ/ *adj* (BrE) ‹*criticism*› durísimo, feroz; ‹*increases/cuts*› salvaje

swinging /ˈswɪŋɪŋ/ *adj* **1** (lively, fashionable) (colloq) con mucha marcha (fam), con mucho swing (fam); **the ~ sixties** los acelerados años 60 **2** (bouncing, rhythmic) (*before n*) ‹*step/gait*› cadencioso

swinging door *n* (AmE) ▸**swing door**

swing shift *n* (AmE) turno *m* de tarde

swipe¹ /swaɪp/ *n* (colloq) (blow) golpe *m*; (verbal attack) ataque *m*; **to take a ~ at sb/sth** (physically) intentar darle *or* pegarle a algn/algo

swipe² *vt* (colloq)
A (hit) darle* (un golpe) a
B (steal) afanarse (arg), volarse* (Méx fam)
■ **swipe** *vi* **to ~ AT sth/sb** intentar darle a algo/algn

swipe card *n* tarjeta *f* de banda magnética

swirl¹ /swɜːrl || swɜːl/ *n* (of water, dust, people) remolino *m*; (of smoke) voluta *f*, espiral *f*; **the ~ of the dancers' skirts** el movimiento de las faldas de las bailarinas; **a ~ of whipped cream** un copo de crema *or* (Esp) de nata batida

swirl² *vi* ‹‹*water/dust/paper*›› arremolinarse; ‹‹*dancers/skirts*›› girar

swish¹ /swɪʃ/ *n* **1** (of cane) silbido *m* **2** (of water) rumor *m*, susurro *m* **3** (of skirt) frufrú *m*; **the ~ of the curtains** el ruido de las cortinas al correrlas

swish² *vt* ‹*cane/whip*› agitar en el aire (*produciendo un silbido*); **the horse was ~ing its tail** el caballo sacudía la cola; **she ~ed the water around the bowl** agitó el agua en el bol
■ **swish** *vi* ‹‹*cane*›› producir* un silbido; ‹‹*water*›› borbotear; ‹‹*skirts*›› hacer* frufrú

swish³ *adj* **-er, -est** (BrE colloq) elegante, pijo (Esp fam), pituco (CS fam), popoff *adj inv* (Méx fam)

Swiss¹ /swɪs/ *adj* suizo

Swiss² *n* (*pl* ~) suizo, -za *m,f*

swiss roll, **Swiss roll** *n* [u c] (BrE) brazo *m* de gitano *or* (Andes) de reina, arrollado *m* (*dulce*) (RPl)

switch¹ /swɪtʃ/ *vt*
A **1** (change) cambiar de; **I ~ jobs** *o* **my job every six months** cada seis meses cambio de trabajo; **she ~ed the topic of conversation** desvió la conversación hacia otro tema, cambió de tema de conversación; **to ~ sth (FROM sth) TO sth**: **my appointment has been ~ed to Tuesday** me cambiaron la cita al martes **2** (exchange) ‹*suitcases/roles*› intercambiar; **can we ~ seats, please?** ¿no me cambiaría el asiento, por favor?
B (Elec, Rad, TV): **to ~ channels** cambiar de canal; **~ the heater to the lowest setting** ponga la estufa en 'mínimo'
C (shunt) (AmE Rail) desviar*, cambiar de vía
■ **switch** *vi* cambiar; **there's no direct train, you'll have to ~** (AmE) no hay un tren directo, vas a tener que cambiar *or* hacer trasbordo; **I ~ed to Channel Four** cambié al Canal Cuatro; **the scene ~es from New York to the French Riviera** la escena pasa de Nueva York a la Riviera francesa; **we've ~ed from electricity to gas** hemos empezado a usar gas en lugar de electricidad; **I ~ed back to my old brand** volví a mi marca de antes

Phrasal verbs
• **switch around,** (BrE also) **switch round**
A [v ▸ adv] (exchange positions, roles) cambiar
B [v ▸ o ▸ adv, v ▸ adv ▸ o] **1** ‹*wires/cables*› intercambiar **2** (rearrange) ‹*furniture*› cambiar de sitio
• **switch off**
A [v ▸ o ▸ adv, v ▸ adv ▸ o] ‹*light/TV/heating*› apagar*; ‹*gas/electricity/water*› cortar, desconectar; **the machine ~es itself off automatically** la máquina se apaga automáticamente
B [v ▸ adv] **1** ‹‹*light/machine/heating*›› apagarse* **2** (lose interest, relax) (colloq) desconectar (fam)
• **switch on**
A [v ▸ o ▸ adv, v ▸ adv ▸ o] (esp BrE) ‹*light/heating/machine*› encender*, prender (AmL); **the power was ~ed on again two hours later** la electricidad volvió dos horas más tarde; **he can ~ on the charm when he wants to** es un encanto cuando quiere
B [v ▸ adv] ‹‹*light/heating/machine*›› encenderse*, prenderse
• **switch over**
A [v ▸ adv] **1** (change) **to ~ over TO sth** cambiar A algo **2** (change channels) cambiar de canal **3** (exchange positions, roles) cambiar
B [v ▸ o ▸ adv, v ▸ adv ▸ o] ‹*wires/cables*› intercambiar
• **switch round** (BrE) ▸**switch around**

switch² *n*
A **1** (Elec) interruptor *m*, llave *f* (de encendido/de la luz) **2** (points) (AmE Rail) agujas *fpl*
B **1** (shift, change): **a ~ of emphasis** un cambio de énfasis; **his ~ from drama to fiction** su paso del teatro a la novela **2** (exchange) intercambio *m*, trueque *m*; **to make a ~** hacer* un intercambio
C (stick, cane) vara *f*

switch: **~back** *n* **1** (road) *carretera con cambios de rasante y/o curvas muy pronunciadas* **2** (roller coaster) (BrE) montaña *f* rusa; **~blade (knife)** *n* (AmE) navaja *f* automática *or* (Méx) de resorte; **~board** *n* centralita *f*, conmutador *m* (AmL); (*before n*) **~board operator** telefonista *mf*; **~ hitter** *n* (AmE) bateador ambidiestro, bateadora ambidiestra *m,f*; **~over** *n* **~over (FROM sth TO sth)** cambio *m* (DE algo A algo)

Switzerland /ˈswɪtsərlənd || ˈswɪtsələnd/ *n* Suiza *f*

swivel¹ /ˈswɪvəl/, (BrE) **-ll-** *vi* girar; **she ~ed around to look at me** se volvió para mirarme
■ **swivel** *vt* hacer* girar

swivel² *n* plataforma *f* giratoria; (*before n*) **~ chair** silla *f* giratoria

swollen¹ /ˈswəʊlən/ *past p of* **swell¹**

swollen² *adj* ‹*ankle/knee/joints*› hinchado; **~ glands** ganglios *mpl* inflamados; **~ with pride** henchido de orgullo; **the river was ~** el río iba crecido

swoon¹ /swuːn/ *vi* **1** (show rapture) **to ~ (OVER sb)** derretirse* (POR algn) **2** (faint) (arch *or* liter) desvanecerse*

swoon² *n* (arch *or* liter) desvanecimiento *m*; **to fall into** *o* **in a ~** desvanecerse*, sufrir un desvanecimiento

swoop¹ /swuːp/ *vi* ‹‹*aircraft*›› descender* *or* bajar en picada *or* (Esp) en picado; ‹‹*bird of prey*›› abatirse; ‹‹*police*›› llevar a cabo una redada

swoop² *n* (of bird, aircraft) descenso *m* en picada *or* (Esp) en picado; (by police) redada *f*; ***in*** *o* ***at one fell ~*** de una sola vez, de un tirón (fam)

swop /swɑːp || swɒp/ *vt/vi/n* ▸**swap¹,²**

sword /sɔːrd || sɔːd/ *n* espada *f*; **by fire and the ~** a sangre y fuego; ***a double-edged ~*** un arma de doble filo *or* dos filos; ***to cross ~s with sb*** pelearse con algn

sword: **~fish** *n* (*pl* **~fish** *or* **~fishes**) pez *m* espada; **~sman** *n* (*pl* **-men**) espadachín *m*, espada *m*

swore /swɔːr || swɔː(r)/ *past of* **swear**

sworn¹ /swɔːrn || swɔːn/ *past p of* **swear**

sworn² *adj* (*before n*)
A ‹*enemy*› declarado, acérrimo
B ‹*statement*› jurado

swot¹ /swɑːt/ *n* (BrE colloq & pej) matado, -da *m,f or* (Col) pilo, -la *m,f or* (Chi) mateo, -tea *m,f or* (Per) chancón, -cona *m,f or* (RPl) traga *mf or* (Esp) empollón, -llona *m,f* (fam & pey)

S

swot[2] **-tt-** *vi* (BrE colloq) estudiar como loco (fam), empollar (Esp fam), matearse (Chi fam), tragar* (RPl fam)

(Phrasal verb)

• **swot up** (BrE colloq)

A [v ▸ o ▸ adv, v ▸ adv ▸ o] estudiar como loco (fam)

B [v ▸ adv] ▸**swot**[2]; **to ~ up ON sth** ▸**swot up A**

SWOT /swɑ:t || swɒt/ *n* (= **strengths, weaknesses, opportunities, threats**) DAFO *f*; **~ analysis** análisis *m* DAFO

swum /swʌm/ *past p of* **swim**[1]

swung /swʌŋ/ *past & past p of* **swing**[1]

sycamore /'sɪkəmɔ:r || 'sɪkəmɔ:(r)/ *n* [1] (plane tree) (AmE) plátano *m* (de sombra) [2] **~ (maple)** plátano *m* (falso), sicómoro *m*, sicomoro *m*

sycophant /'sɪkəfænt/ *n* adulador, -dora *m,f*

sycophantic /'sɪkə'fæntɪk/ *adj* adulador, lisonjero

syllable /'sɪləbəl/ *n* sílaba *f*; **I explained it to him in words of one ~** se lo expliqué en forma más que clara

syllabub /'sɪləbʌb/ *n*: *dulce hecho con leche o crema con azúcar, licor y jugo de limón*

syllabus /'sɪləbəs/ *n* (*pl* **-buses**) plan *m* de estudios; (of a particular subject) programa *m*

sylph /sɪlf/ *n* sílfide *f*

sylphlike /'sɪlflaɪk/ *adj* ‹*figure*› de sílfide

symbiosis /'sɪmbaɪ'əʊsəs/ *n* (*pl* **-oses**) simbiosis *f*

symbiotic /'sɪmbaɪ'ɑ:tɪk/ *adj* simbiótico

symbol /'sɪmbəl/ *n* símbolo *m*

symbolic /sɪm'bɑ:lɪk || sɪm'bɒlɪk/ **-ical** /-ɪkəl/ *adj* simbólico; **to be ~ OF sth** simbolizar* algo

symbolically /sɪm'bɑ:lɪkli/ *adv* simbólicamente

symbolism /'sɪmbəlɪzəm/ *n* [u] simbolismo *m*

symbolize /'sɪmbəlaɪz/ *vt* [1] (be a symbol of) simbolizar* [2] (represent) representar simbólicamente

symmetrical /sə'metrɪkəl || sɪ'metrɪkəl/ *adj* simétrico

symmetrically /sə'metrɪkli / *adv* simétricamente

symmetry /'sɪmətri/ *n* [u] simetría *f*

sympathetic /'sɪmpə'θetɪk/ *adj*

A (understanding) comprensivo; **they offered a ~ ear** me escucharon con amabilidad; **they weren't in the least ~** no demostraron ninguna comprensión; **to be ~ TO/TOWARD sb/sth**: **he was most ~ to me when my wife died** me dio todo su apoyo y comprensión cuando murió mi mujer

B (approving) ‹*response/view*› favorable; ‹*audience*› bien dispuesto, receptivo; **to be ~ TO sth** ‹*to a cause/regime*› simpatizar* CON algo; ‹*to a request/demand*› mostrarse* favorable A algo

sympathetically /'sɪmpə'θetɪkli/ *adv* [1] (with understanding) ‹*listen/consider/respond*› con comprensión [2] (showing pity) con compasión

sympathize /'sɪmpəθaɪz/ *vi* [1] (commiserate): **I ~ with him** lo compadezco [2] (understand) **to ~ (WITH sth/sb)** comprender *or* entender* (algo/a algn) [3] (support, approve) **to ~ WITH sth** ‹*with cause/aims*› simpatizar* CON algo; ‹*with request/demand*› mostrarse* favorable A algo

sympathizer /'sɪmpəθaɪzər/ *n* simpatizante *m,f*

sympathy /'sɪmpəθi/ *n* (*pl* **-thies**)

A [1] [u] (pity) compasión *f*, lástima *f* [2] (condolences) (*often pl*): **please accept this expression of our deepest ~** *o* **sympathies** le rogamos acepte nuestro más sentido pésame *or* nuestras más sinceras condolencias (frml); **you have my deepest ~** lo acompaño en el sentimiento (fr hecha)

B [1] [u] (support, approval): **I was in/out of ~ with the majority** estaba/no estaba de acuerdo con la mayoría; **to come out in ~ with sb** (Lab Rel) declararse en huelga en solidaridad con algn; (*before n*) ‹*strike/action*› solidario, de solidaridad [2] **sympathies** *pl* (loyalty, leanings) (*often pl*) simpatías *fpl*; **Republican sympathies** tendencias *fpl* republicanas

symphony /'sɪmfəni/ *n* (*pl* **-nies**) sinfonía *f*; (*before n*) **~ orchestra** orquesta *f* sinfónica

symposium /sɪm'pəʊziəm/ *n* (*pl* **-siums** *or* **-sia** /-ziə/) **~ (ON sth)** simposio *m* (SOBRE algo)

symptom /'sɪmptəm/ *n* síntoma *m*

symptomatic /'sɪmptə'mætɪk/ *adj* **~ (OF sth)** sintomático (DE algo)

synagogue /'sɪnəgɑ:g || 'sɪnəgɒg/ *n* sinagoga *f*

sync /sɪŋk/ *n* [u] (colloq) sincronización *f*; **to be in/out of ~ (with sth)** estar*/no estar* sincronizado (con algo)

synchromesh /'sɪŋkrəʊmeʃ/ *n* [u] sincronizador *m* (*del cambio de marchas*)

synchronization /'sɪŋkrənə'zeɪʃən/ *n* [u] sincronización *f*

synchronize /'sɪŋkrənaɪz/ *vt* [1] **to ~ sth (WITH sth)** sincronizar* algo (CON algo); **~d swimming** natación *f* sincronizada, nado *m* sincronizado (Méx) [2] (set to same time) ‹*clocks/watches*› sincronizar*

■ **synchronize** *vi* **to ~ (WITH sth)** ‹‹*movements/soundtrack*›› estar* sincronizado (CON algo)

syncopated /'sɪŋkəpeɪtəd || 'sɪŋkəpeɪtɪd/ *adj* sincopado

syncopation /'sɪŋkə'peɪʃən/ *n* [u] síncopa *f*

syndicate[1] /'sɪndəkət || 'sɪndɪkət/ *n* [1] (group, cartel) agrupación *f*; **a crime ~** una organización mafiosa [2] (in US) (Journ, TV) agencia *f* de distribución periodística

syndicate[2] /'sɪndəkeɪt || 'sɪndɪkeɪt/ *vt* (in US) ‹*column/article/interview*› distribuir* (*a diferentes medios de comunicación*); **his column is ~d all over the country** su columna se publica en periódicos de todo el país

syndication /'sɪndə'keɪʃən || ˌsɪndɪ'keɪʃən/ *n* [u] (in US) distribución *f* (*a diferentes medios de comunicación*)

syndrome /'sɪndrəʊm/ *n* síndrome *m*

synergy /'sɪnərdʒi || 'sɪnədʒi/ *n* [u] (*pl* **-gies**) sinergia *f*

synod /'sɪnəd/ *n* sínodo *m*

synonym /'sɪnənɪm/ *n* **~ (FOR sth)** sinónimo *m* (DE algo)

synonymous /sə'nɑ:nəməs || sɪ'nɒnɪməs/ *adj* ‹*terms/phrases*› sinónimo; ‹*ideas*› análogo; **to be ~ WITH sth** ser* sinónimo DE algo

synopsis /sə'nɑ:psəs/ *n* (*pl* **-opses** /-si:z/) sinopsis *f*

syntax /'sɪntæks/ *n* [u] sintaxis *f*

synthesis /'sɪnθəsəs/ *n* (*pl* **-theses**) síntesis *f*

synthesize /'sɪnθəsaɪz/ *vt* sintetizar*

synthesizer /'sɪnθəsaɪzər/ *n* sintetizador *m*

synthetic[1] /sɪn'θetɪk/ *adj* sintético

synthetic[2] *n* fibra *f* sintética, tejido *m* sintético

syphilis /'sɪfələs || 'sɪfɪlɪs/ *n* [u] sífilis *f*

syphon *n/vt* /'saɪfən/ ▸**siphon**

Syria /'sɪriə/ *n* Siria *f*

Syrian /'sɪriən/ *adj* sirio

syringe[1] /sə'rɪndʒ/ *n* (Med) jeringa *f*, jeringuilla *f*

syringe[2] *vt* **~ (out)** ‹*ear/sinuses*› hacer* un lavado de

syrup /'sɜ:rəp, 'sɪ- || 'sɪrəp/ *n* [u] [1] (Culin) (sugar solution) almíbar *m*; (with other ingredients) jarabe *m*, sirope *m* [2] (medicine) jarabe *m*; **cough ~** jarabe para la tos

syrupy /'sɜ:rəpi, 'sɪ- || 'sɪrəpi/ *adj* [1] ‹*mixture/consistency*› espeso como jarabe [2] (cloying) ‹*voice/smile*› almibarado

system /'sɪstəm/ *n*

A [1] [u c] (ordered structure) sistema *m*, método *m* [2] [c] (procedure) sistema *m*; **filing/classification ~** sistema de archivo/clasificación [3] [c] (organizational whole) sistema *m*; **the prison ~** el sistema penitenciario

B [c] [1] (technical, mechanical) sistema *m*; **all ~s go!** ¡todo bien! [2] (Comput) sistema *m* [3] (Audio) equipo *m* (de sonido *or* audio)

C [c] [1] (Anat, Physiol): **the digestive ~** el aparato digestivo; **the nervous ~** el sistema nervioso [2] (body) cuerpo *m*, organismo *m*; **my ~ can't cope with so much food** mi cuerpo *or* mi organismo no puede con tanta comida; ***to get sb/sth out of one's ~***: **it took me years to get her out of my ~** me llevó años olvidarla *or* sacármela de la cabeza; **I had to say it; I needed to get it out of my ~** se lo tuve que decir; me tenía que desahogar

D [c] [1] (form of government) sistema *m* [2] (establishment, status quo): **the ~** el sistema; **he tried to beat the ~** intentó burlar el sistema

E [c] (for gambling) fórmula *f*, martingala *f* (CS)

systematic /'sɪstə'mætɪk/ *adj* sistemático

systematically /'sɪstə'mætɪkli/ *adv* sistemáticamente

systematize /'sɪstəmətaɪz/ *vt* sistematizar*

systems /'sɪstəmz/ *adj* (*before n*) ‹*development/design/programming*› de sistemas

systems: **~ analysis** *n* [u] análisis *m* de sistemas; **~ analyst** *n* analista *mf* de sistemas

S

Tt

T, **t** /tiː/ *n* T, t *f*; ***to a T*** (colloq): ***to fit sb to a T*** *o* (AmE also) ***down to a T*** sentarle* a algn como un guante; ***to suit sb to a T*** «*arrangement*» venirle* a algn de maravilla; «*dress/outfit*» sentarle* a algn de maravilla

ta /tɑː/ *interj* (BrE colloq) ¡gracias!

tab /tæb/ *n*

A 1 (flap) lengüeta *f* 2 (label — for indexing) ceja *f*; (— on clothing) etiqueta *f*

B (account, bill) (colloq) cuenta *f*; ***to keep ~s on sth/sb*** tener* algo/a algn controlado; ***to pick up the ~*** (colloq): **the company will pick up the ~** la empresa corre con los gastos; **they left early and I had to pick up the ~** se fueron pronto y acabé pagando yo la cuenta

C (on typewriter, word processor) tabulador *m*; (*before n*) ‹*character/key/stop*› de tabulación; (setting): **to set ~s** definir tabuladores

D (ring pull) (AmE) anilla *f*

Tabasco® **(sauce)** /tə'bæskəʊ/ *n* [u] tabasco® *m*

tabby[1] /'tæbi/ *n* (*pl* **-bies**) gato atigrado, gata atigrada *m,f*

tabby[2] *adj* atigrado

table[1] /'teɪbəl/ *n*

A (piece of furniture) mesa *f*; **dinner's on the ~!** ¡la cena está servida!; **don't do that at the ~** no hagas eso en la mesa; **come and sit at** *o* (BrE also) **on our ~** siéntate con nosotros; **to lay** *o* **set the ~** poner* la mesa; **to clear the ~** levantar *or* (Esp) quitar la mesa; **the negotiating ~** la mesa de negociaciones; ***on the ~***: **to put sth on the ~** (present sth for discussion) (esp BrE) poner* algo sobre el tapete; (postpone discussion on sth) (AmE) posponer* *or* (esp AmL) postergar* algo; ***to do sth under the ~*** hacer* algo bajo cuerda *or* mano; ***to drink sb under the ~***: **she can drink me under the ~** me da cien mil vueltas bebiendo; ***to turn the ~s***: **the ~s are turned** se ha vuelto *or* (CS) se dio vuelta la tortilla (fam), se han cambiado las tornas; **to turn the ~s on one's adversaries** volverles* las tornas a sus (*or* mis *etc*) adversarios; (*before n*) ‹*knife/lamp/wine*› de mesa; **~ football** (BrE) futbolín *m*, taca-taca *m* (Chi), metegol *m* (Arg), futbolito *m* (Ur); **~ linen** mantelería *f*, ropa *f* de mesa (Esp); **~ mat** (mantelito *m*) individual *m*; **~ manners** modales *mpl* en la mesa

B 1 (list) tabla *f*; **multiplication** *o* (used by children) **times ~s** tablas de multiplicar; **the four-times ~** la tabla del cuatro 2 (*league* ~) (BrE) liga *f*, clasificación *f*

table[2] *vt* 1 (postpone) (AmE) ‹*debate/bill*› posponer*, postergar* (esp AmL) 2 (submit) (BrE) ‹*proposal/motion*› presentar

tableau /'tæbləʊ/ *n* (*pl* **-leaux** *or* **-leaus** /-ləʊz/) (Art) retablo *m*; (Theat) cuadro *m* vivo

table: **~cloth** *n* mantel *m*; **~ d'hôte** /'tɑːbəl'dəʊt/ *adj*: **~ d'hôte menu** menú *m* del día (*a precio fijo*); **~-hop** *vi* **-pp-** (AmE colloq) ir* de mesa en mesa; **~land** *n* meseta *f*, altiplanicie *f*; **~spoon** *n* (utensil) cuchara *f* grande *or* de servir; (measure) cucharada *f* (grande); **~spoonful** /'teɪbəl'spuːnfʊl || 'teɪbəlspuːnfəl/ *n* (*pl* **-spoonfuls** *or* **-spoonsful**) cucharada *f* (grande)

tablet /'tæblət || 'tæblɪt/ *n* 1 (pill) pastilla *f*, comprimido *m* 2 (of soap) (BrE) pastilla *f* 3 (plaque) placa *f*; (commemorative, of stone) lápida *f*

table: **~ tennis** *n* [u] ping-pong *m*, tenis *m* de mesa; (*before n*) **~-tennis bat** *o* (AmE also) **paddle** raqueta *f* *or* pala *f* de ping-pong; **~top** *n*: *tablero de una mesa*; **~ware** /'teɪbəlwer || 'teɪbəlweə(r)/ *n* [u] *vajilla, cubertería, cristalería etc*

tabloid /'tæblɔɪd/ *n* tabloide *m* (*formato de periódicos utilizado por la prensa popular*); (*before n*) ‹*journalism*› popular, dirigido a las masas; (sensationalist) sensacionalista

taboo[1] /tə'buː/ *adj* tabú *adj inv*

taboo[2] *n* (*pl* **taboos**) tabú *m*

tabulate /'tæbjəleɪt || 'tæbjʊleɪt/ *vt* ‹*results/data*› tabular, presentar en forma de tabla

tabulator /'tæbjə'leɪtər || 'tæbjʊˌleɪtə(r)/ *n* tabulador *m*

tacit /'tæsət || 'tæsɪt/ *adj* tácito

tacitly /'tæsətli || 'tæsɪtli/ *adv* tácitamente

taciturn /'tæsətɜːrn || 'tæsɪtɜːn/ *adj* taciturno

tack[1] /tæk/ *n*

A [c] 1 (nail) tachuela *f*; ***to get down to brass ~s*** (colloq) ir* al grano 2 (*thumb~*) (AmE) tachuela *f*, chincheta *f* (Esp), chinche *f* (AmC, Méx, RPl), chinche *m* (Andes)

B [c] 1 (Naut) bordada *f* 2 (direction): **to change ~** cambiar de enfoque *or* táctica *or* política

C [c] (stitch) (BrE) puntada *f*; (seam) hilván *m*

D [u] (Equ) arreos *mpl*, aperos *mpl* (AmL)

tack[2] *vt*

A 1 (nail) ‹*carpet*› clavar con tachuelas 2 (pin, fasten) ‹*notice/list*› clavar con tachuelas (*or* chinchetas *etc*)

B (stitch) (BrE) hilvanar

■ **tack** *vi* (Naut) dar* bordadas

Phrasal verbs

• **tack down** [v ▸ o ▸ adv, v ▸ adv ▸ o] ‹*carpet*› clavar con tachuelas

• **tack on** [v ▸ o ▸ adv, v ▸ adv ▸ o] agregar*, añadir

tacking /'tækɪŋ/ *n* [u] 1 (Naut) virada *f* 2 (stitching) (BrE) hilván *m*, hilvanes *mpl*

tackle[1] /'tækəl/ *n*

A [u] (equipment): **sports ~** equipo *m* de deporte; **fishing ~** aparejo *m* *or* avíos *mpl* de pesca

B [c] (Sport) (in rugby, US football) placaje *m*, tacle *m* (AmL); (in soccer) entrada *f* fuerte

C [u] (Naut) aparejo *m*, polea *f*

tackle[2] *vt*

A 1 (come to grips with) ‹*problem*› enfrentar, abordar, tratar de resolver; ‹*subject*› tratar; ‹*task*› abordar, emprender; **are you ready to ~ the garden now?** ¿estás listo para emprenderla con *or* atacar el jardín? 2 (confront) ‹*intruder/colleague*› enfrentar, enfrentarse con; **it's high time you ~d him about the rent** ya es hora de que le plantees cara a cara lo del alquiler

B (Sport) (in rugby, US football) placar*, taclear (AmL); (in soccer) entrarle a

■ **tackle** *vi* (Sport) placar*, taclear (AmL)

tacky /'tæki/ *adj* **tackier, tackiest**

A (cheap, tawdry) ‹*jewelry/decorations*› chabacano, hortera (Esp fam), naco (Méx fam), lobo (Col fam), rasca (Chi fam), mersa (RPl fam)

B (sticky) pegajoso

tact /tækt/ *n* [u] tacto *m*

tactful /'tæktfəl/ *adj* ‹*person*› de mucho tacto, diplomático; ‹*question/reply*› diplomático; **that wasn't very ~ of you** en eso demostraste tener muy poco tacto

tactfully /'tæktfəli/ *adv* ‹*inquire/mention*› discretamente, con mucho tacto, con mucha diplomacia; **the letter was very ~ worded** era una carta escrita con mucho tacto

tactic /'tæktɪk/ *n* táctica *f*

tactical /'tæktɪkəl/ *adj* táctico; **~ voting** votación *f* táctica

tactician /tæk'tɪʃən/ *n* estratega *mf*

tactics /'tæktɪks/ *n* (Mil) (+ *sing or pl vb*) táctica *f*

tactile /'tæktḷ || 'tæktaɪl/ *adj* táctil

tactless /'tæktləs || 'tæktlɪs/ *adj* ‹*person*› poco diplomático, falto de tacto; ‹*remark/question*› poco diplomático, indiscreto

tactlessly /'tæktləsli || 'tæktlɪsli/ *adv* con poco tacto

tad /tæd/ *n*: **a tad** (colloq) un poco

Tadjikistan /tɑː,dʒiːkɪ'stɑːn/ ▸ **Tadzhikistan**

tadpole /'tædpəʊl/ *n* renacuajo *m*

Tadzhikistan /tɑː,dʒiːkɪ'stɑːn// *n* Tayiquistán *m*, Tadzhikistán *m*

taffeta /'tæfətə || 'tæfɪtə/ *n* [u c] tafetán *m*, tafeta *f* (Méx, RPl)

taffy /'tæfi/ *n* [c u] (AmE Culin) caramelo *m* masticable

tag[1] /tæg/ *n*

A [c] (label) etiqueta *f* (*atada*)

B [u] (Games): **to play ~** jugar* al corre que te pillo *or* (Méx) a la roña *or* (Col) a la lleva *or* (RPl) a la mancha *or* (Chi) a la pinta

C [c] (Ling) coletilla *f*; (*before n*) **~ question** coletilla interrogativa

tag[2] **-gg-** *vt*

A (label) ‹*article/item*› etiquetar, ponerle* una etiqueta a; (Comput) codificar*; **she was ~ged the Iron Lady** se le puso el apodo de Dama de Hierro

B (in baseball) agarrar fuera de base

Phrasal verbs

- **tag along** [v ▸ adv]: **do you mind if I ~ along?** ¿les importa si los acompaño *or* (fam) si me les pego?; **her little sister always ~s along after us** su hermanita nos sigue a todas partes
- **tag on** [v ▸ o ▸ adv, v ▸ adv ▸ o] agregar*, añadir
- **tag out** [v ▸ o ▸ adv, v ▸ adv ▸ o] (in baseball) agarrar fuera de base

tag: **~ end** *n* (AmE colloq) (of program, debate) final *m*, última parte *f*; (of era) final *m*, últimos años *mpl*; **~ line** *n* (AmE) (punch line) remate *m* de un chiste; (repeated phrase) eslogan *m*

Tagus /'teɪgəs/ *n* **the ~** el Tajo

Tahiti /tə'hiːti/ *n* Tahití *m*

tail[1] /teɪl/ *n*

A 1 (of horse, fish, bird) cola *f*; (of dog, pig) rabo *m*, cola *f*; ***to be on sb's ~*** pisarle los talones a algn, seguir* a algn de cerca; ***to turn ~*** poner* pies en polvorosa; ***with one's ~ between one's legs*** con el rabo entre las piernas, con la cola entre las patas (Méx) 2 (buttocks) (colloq) trasero *m* (fam), cola *f* (AmL fam), pompis *m* (Esp fam)

B (of plane, comet, kite) cola *f*; (of shirt, coat) faldón *m*; *see also* **tails A**

C (pursuer) (colloq): **to put a ~ on sb** hacer* seguir a algn

tail[2] *vt* (follow) ‹*suspect*› seguir*

Phrasal verb

- **tail off** [v ▸ adv] 1 (diminish) «*demand*» disminuir*, mermar 2 (fade) «*sound/words*» apagarse*

tail: **~back** *n* 1 (BrE) caravana *f*, cola *f* (*debida a un embotellamiento*) 2 (in US football) defensa ofensivo, defensa ofensiva *m,f*; **~board** *n* ▸ **tailgate**[1] **1**; **~coat** *n* frac *m*

-tailed /teɪld/ *suff*: **long~/thin~** de cola larga/delgada

tail end *n*: **the ~ ~** (of film, concert) el final, los últimos minutos, la última parte; (of procession) la cola

tailgate[1] /'teɪlgeɪt/ *n* 1 (Auto) puerta *f* trasera *or* de atrás (*de un coche de cinco o tres puertas*) 2 **~ (party)** (AmE colloq) *picnic al lado del coche*

tailgate[2] *vt* (esp AmE) manejar *or* (Esp) conducir* pegado a ■ **tailgate** *vi* manejar *or* (Esp) conducir* pegado al vehículo de delante

taillight /'teɪllaɪt/ *n* luz *f* trasera, calavera *f* (Méx)

tailor[1] /'teɪlər || 'teɪlə(r)/ *n* sastre *m*; **he went to the ~'s** fue al sastre *or* a la sastrería

tailor[2] *vt*

A (Clothing) 1 (make) confeccionar 2 **tailored** *past p* (*before n*) ‹*jacket/skirt*› (fitted) entallado; (lined, structured etc) armado, tipo sastre

B (adapt) adaptar

tailor-made /'teɪlər'meɪd || ,teɪlə'meɪd/ *adj* 1 ‹*suit/dress*› hecho a (la) medida 2 (perfectly suited) ‹*product/plan*› a la medida de sus (*or* nuestras *etc*) necesidades; **the job is ~ for her** es un trabajo a su medida

tail: **~piece** *n* (appendage — written) apéndice *m*, apostilla *f*, coletilla *f*; (— spoken) coletilla *f*; **~pipe** *n* (AmE Auto) tubo *m or* (RPl) caño *m* de escape, exhosto *m* (Col)

tails /teɪlz/ *n*

A (tailcoat) (+ *pl vb*) frac *m*

B (on coin) (+ *sing vb*) cruz *f*, sello *m* (Andes, Ven), sol *m* (Méx), ceca *f* (Arg)

tail: **~spin** *n*: ***to go into a ~spin*** «*economy/business*» caer* en picada *or* (Esp) en picado; «*lit: aircraft*» entrar en barrena; **~wind** *n* viento *m* de cola

taint[1] /teɪnt/ *vt* 1 (contaminate) ‹*meat/water*› contaminar 2 (dishonor) ‹*name/reputation*› mancillar (liter), deshonrar; **his writings are ~ed with racism** su obra está contaminada de racismo

taint[2] *n* 1 [c] (trace) dejo *m* 2 [u] (stain) mancha *f*, mácula *f* (liter); **to be free of ~** estar* limpio de toda mancha *or* mácula

Taiwan /'taɪ'wɑːn/ *n* Taiwan *m*

Taiwanese[1] /'taɪwə'niːz/ *adj* taiwanés

Taiwanese[2] *n* (*pl* ~) taiwanés, -nesa *m,f*

take[1] /teɪk/ (*past* **took**; *past p* **taken**) *vt*

Sense I (carry, lead, drive) llevar; **~ an umbrella** lleva un paraguas; **shall I ~ the chairs inside/upstairs?** ¿llevo las sillas adentro/arriba?, ¿meto/subo las sillas?; **to ~ the garbage out** sacar la basura; **we took him home** lo llevamos a (su) casa; **she took us into her office** nos hizo pasar a su oficina; **I'll ~ you up/down to the third floor** subo/bajo contigo al tercer piso, te llevo al tercer piso; **to ~ the dog (out) for a walk** sacar* el perro a pasear; **this path ~s you to the main road** este camino lleva *or* por este camino se llega a la carretera; **her job often ~s her to Paris** va con frecuencia a París por motivos de trabajo; **if you decide to ~ the matter further** si decide proseguir con el asunto

Sense II

A 1 ‹*train/plane/bus/taxi*› tomar, coger* (esp Esp); **are you taking the car?** ¿vas a ir en coche?; **I had to ~ the bus back** tuve que volver en autobús; **we took the elevator** (AmE) *o* (BrE) **lift to the restaurant** tomamos *or* (esp Esp) cogimos el ascensor para subir/bajar al restaurante 2 ‹*road/turning*› tomar, agarrar (esp AmL), coger* (esp Esp); **I took the wrong road** me equivoqué de camino 3 ‹*bend*› tomar, coger* (esp Esp); ‹*fence*› saltar

B 1 (grasp, seize) tomar, agarrar (esp AmL), coger* (esp Esp); **he took her by the hand** la tomó *or* (esp AmL) la agarró *or* (esp Esp) la cogió de la mano; **he took the opportunity** aprovechó la oportunidad; **he took control of the situation** se hizo dueño de la situación; **she took the knife from him** le quitó el cuchillo 2 (take charge of): **may I ~ your coat?** ¿me permite el abrigo?; **would you mind taking the baby for a moment?** ¿me tienes al niño un momento? 3 (occupy): **~ a seat** siéntese, tome asiento (frml); **this chair is ~n** esta silla está ocupada

C (remove, steal) llevarse; **somebody's ~n my purse!** ¡alguien se me ha llevado el monedero!

D (catch): **it took us by surprise** nos sorprendió; **he was ~n completely unawares** lo agarró *or* (esp Esp) lo cogió completamente desprevenido; **to be ~n ill** caer* enfermo

E 1 (capture) ‹*town/fortress/position*› tomar; ‹*pawn/piece*› comer 2 (win) ‹*prize/title*› llevarse, hacerse* con; ‹*game/set*› ganar 3 (receive as profit) hacer*, sacar*

F ‹*medicine/drugs*› tomar; **have you ~n your tablets?** ¿te has tomado las pastillas?; **I don't ~ sugar in my coffee** no le pongo azúcar al café

G 1 (buy, order) llevar(se); **I'll ~ this pair** (me) llevo este par; **I'll ~ 12 ounces** déme *or* (Esp tb) póngame 12 onzas 2 (buy regularly) comprar; **we ~ The Globe** nosotros compramos *or* leemos The Globe 3 (rent) ‹*cottage/apartment*› alquilar, coger* (Esp)

H 1 (acquire) ‹*lover*› buscarse*; **to ~ a wife/husband** casar-

t

se [2] (sexually) (liter) ‹*woman*› poseer*

(Sense III)

A (of time) «*job/task*» llevar; «*process*» tardar; «*person*» tardar, demorar(se) (AmL); **it took longer than expected** llevó *or* tomó más tiempo de lo que se creía; **the flight ~s two hours** el vuelo dura dos horas; **it took weeks for him to recover** tardó semanas en recuperarse; **the letter took a week to arrive** la carta tardó *or* (AmL tb) se demoró una semana en llegar; **it took me a long time to do it** me llevó mucho tiempo hacerlo

B (need): **it ~s courage to do a thing like that** hay que tener *or* hace falta *or* se necesita valor para hacer algo así; **it took four men to lift it** se necesitaron cuatro hombres para levantarlo; ***to have (got) what it ~s*** (colloq) tener* lo que hay que tener *or* lo que hace falta

C [1] (wear): **what size shoes do you ~?** ¿qué número calzas?; **she ~s a 14** usa la talla *or* (RPl) el talle 14 [2] (Auto): **this car ~s diesel** este coche consume diesel [3] (Ling) construirse* con, regir*

(Sense IV)

A (accept) ‹*money/bribes/job*› aceptar; **do you ~ checks?** ¿aceptan cheques?; **~ it or leave it** (set phrase) lo tomas o lo dejas; **you'll have to ~ my word for it** vas a tener que fiarte de mi palabra; **~ it from me** hazme caso; **I won't ~ no for an answer** no me voy a dar por vencido así como así; **~ that, you scoundrel!** (dated) ¡toma, canalla!

B [1] (hold, accommodate): **the tank ~s/will ~ 42 liters** el tanque tiene una capacidad de 42 litros; **we can ~ up to 50 passengers** tenemos cabida para un máximo de 50 pasajeros [2] (admit, receive) ‹*patients/pupils*› admitir, tomar, coger* (Esp); **they ~ lodgers** alquilan habitaciones; **we don't ~ telephone reservations** *o* (BrE) **bookings** no aceptamos reservas por teléfono

C [1] (withstand, suffer) ‹*strain/weight*› aguantar; ‹*beating/blow*› recibir [2] (tolerate, endure) aguantar; **I can't ~ it any longer!** ¡no puedo más!, ¡ya no aguanto más!; **he can't ~ a joke** no sabe aceptar *or* no se le puede hacer una broma [3] (bear): **how is he taking it?** ¿qué tal lo lleva?; **she's ~n it very badly/well** lo lleva muy mal/bien; *see also* **heart B, C**

D [1] (understand, interpret) tomarse; **she took it the wrong way** se lo tomó a mal, lo interpretó mal; **don't ~ it personally** no te lo tomes como algo personal; **to ~ sth as read/understood** dar* algo por hecho/entendido; **I ~ it that you didn't like him much** por lo que veo no te cayó muy bien; *see also* **take for** [2] (consider) (*in imperative*) mirar; **~ Japan, for example** mira el caso del Japón, por ejemplo

(Sense V)

A [1] ‹*steps/measures*› tomar; ‹*exercise*› hacer*; **to ~ a walk/a step forward** dar* un paseo/un paso adelante; **~ a look at this!** ¡mira esto! [2] (supervise, deal with): **would you ~ that call, please?** ¿puede atender esa llamada por favor?

B (Educ) [1] (teach) (BrE) darle* clase a; **she ~s us for Chemistry** nos da clase de química [2] (learn) ‹*subject*› estudiar, hacer*; ‹*course*› hacer*; **to ~ an exam** hacer* *or* dar* *or* (CS) rendir* *or* (Méx) tomar un examen, examinarse (Esp)

C [1] (record) tomar; **we took regular readings** tomamos nota de la temperatura (*or* presión *etc*) a intervalos regulares [2] (write down) ‹*notes*› tomar; **he took my name and address** me tomó el nombre y la dirección

D (adopt): **he ~s the view that ...** opina que ..., es de la opinión de que ...; **she took an instant dislike to him** le tomó antipatía inmediatamente; *see also* **liking 1, offense B2, shape¹ A1** *etc*

■ **take** *vi*

A [1] «*seed*» germinar; «*cutting*» prender [2] «*dye*» agarrar (esp AmL), coger* (esp Esp)

B (receive) recibir; **all you do is ~, ~, ~** no piensas más que en ti

(Phrasal verbs)

- **take aback** [v ▸ o ▸ adv] (*usu pass*) sorprender, desconcertar*; **I was ~n aback by his attitude** su actitud me sorprendió *or* me desconcertó
- **take after** [v ▸ prep ▸ o] salir* a, parecerse* a; **he ~s after his father** salió a su padre, se parece a su padre
- **take along** [v ▸ o ▸ adv, v ▸ adv ▸ o] llevar
- **take apart** [v ▸ o ▸ adv] [1] (dismantle) desmontar [2] (search thoroughly) (colloq): **the police took the place apart** la policía lo dejó todo patas arriba (fam) [3] (show weakness of) ‹*argument*› desbaratar, echar por tierra
- **take around**, (BrE) **take round** [1] [v ▸ o ▸ prep ▸ o] (show) ‹*house/estate*› mostrar*, enseñar (esp Esp) [2] [v ▸ o ▸ adv] (guide, accompany) llevar; **I took them around and introduced them to everyone** los llevé por la oficina (*or* el colegio *etc*) y se los presenté a todo el mundo
- **take aside** [v ▸ o ▸ adv] llevar aparte *or* a un lado
- **take away**

(Sense I) [v ▸ o ▸ adv, v ▸ adv ▸ o]

A [1] (carry, lead away) ‹*person/object*› llevarse [2] (remove, confiscate) ‹*possession*› quitar, sacar* (RPl); **to ~ sth away FROM sb** quitarle *or* (RPl tb) sacarle* algo A algn; **her children were ~n away from her** le quitaron a los niños [3] (erase, obliterate): **this will ~ the pain away** con esto se te pasará el dolor; **this will ~ the taste away** esto te quitará el sabor de la boca

B (Math): **34 ~ away 13 equals 21** 34 menos 13 es igual a 21; **if you ~ away 13 from 34 ...** si a 34 le restas 13 ...

(Sense II) [v ▸ o ▸ adv]: **~ *it away!*** (colloq) ¡adelante!

(Sense III) [v ▸ adv ▸ o] (BrE) ‹*food*› llevar; **to eat here or ~ away?** ¿para comer aquí o para llevar?

- **take away from** [v ▸ adv ▸ prep ▸ o]: **it ~s away from one's enjoyment of the music** hace que uno disfrute menos de la música
- **take back**

A [v ▸ o ▸ adv, v ▸ adv ▸ o] [1] (return) devolver* [2] (repossess) llevarse [3] (accept back): **she wouldn't ~ back the money she'd lent me** no quiso que le devolviera el dinero que me había prestado; **I wonder if she'll ~ him back** me pregunto si aceptará que vuelva [4] (withdraw, retract) ‹*statement*› retirar

B [v ▸ o ▸ adv] (in time): **this song ~s me back!** ¡qué recuerdos me trae esta canción!; **it ~s me back to my childhood** me transporta a mi niñez

- **take down** [v ▸ o ▸ adv, v ▸ adv ▸ o] [1] ‹*curtains/decorations/notice*› quitar [2] (dismantle) ‹*tent/market stall*› desmontar [3] (lower): **to ~ down one's pants** (AmE) bajarse los pantalones [4] (write down) ‹*name/address*› apuntar, anotar
- **take for** [v ▸ o ▸ prep ▸ o] tomar por; **what do you ~ me for?** ¿pero tú qué te crees (que soy)?; **sorry, I took you for somebody else** perdone, lo confundí con otra persona
- **take from** [v ▸ o ▸ prep ▸ o] [1] (derive): **the town ~s its name from ...** la ciudad debe su nombre a ... [2] (subtract) restar de
- **take home** [v ▸ adv ▸ o]: **she ~s home less than £600** su sueldo neto *or* líquido es de menos de 600 libras
- **take in**

(Sense I) [v ▸ o ▸ adv, v ▸ adv ▸ o]

A (move indoors) ‹*chairs/toys*› meter (dentro), llevar para dentro, entrar (esp AmS)

B [1] (give home to) ‹*orphan*› recoger*; ‹*lodger*› alojar [2] (do): **she ~s in washing/ironing** es lavandera, lava para afuera (CS)/es planchadora, plancha para afuera (CS)

C (grasp, register) ‹*impressions/information/news*› asimilar; **he didn't ~ in what was happening** no se dio cuenta de lo que estaba pasando

D (make narrower) ‹*dress/waist*› meterle *or* tomarle a

E «*plant/roots*» ‹*water/nutrients*› asimilar

(Sense II) [v ▸ o ▸ adv] (deceive) engañar

(Sense III) [v ▸ adv ▸ o] [1] (include) ‹*areas/topics*› incluir*, abarcar* [2] (visit) visitar, incluir* (*en el recorrido*)

- **take off**

(Sense I) [v ▸ o ▸ adv, v ▸ adv ▸ o] [v ▸ o ▸ prep ▸ o]

A (detach, remove) quitar, sacar*; **the hurricane took the roof off the house** el huracán le arrancó el tejado a la casa; **she took her make-up off** se quitó *or* (esp AmL) se sacó el maquillaje; **to ~ off one's dress/shoes** quitarse *or* (esp AmL) sacarse* el vestido/los zapatos

B [1] (cut off) ‹*branch/shoot*› cortar; ‹*limb*› amputar; **the hairdresser took too much off the back** el peluquero me cortó mucho atrás [2] (deduct) descontar*; **that haircut ~s years off him** ese corte de pelo le quita años de encima

C (have free): **she's ~n the morning off (from) work** se ha tomado la mañana libre

D (imitate) (colloq) imitar, remedar

(Sense II) [v ▸ adv] [1] «*aircraft/pilot*» despegar*, decolar (AmL); «*flight*» salir* [2] (succeed) «*career*» tomar vuelo [3] (depart) largarse* (fam), irse*

t

Sense III [v ▸ o ▸ adv] (convey) llevar(se); **to ~ oneself off** irse*

Sense IV [v ▸ o ▸ adv] [v ▸ o ▸ prep ▸ o]

A (remove) quitar, sacar* (esp AmL); **~ your foot off the clutch** levanta el pie del embrague; **~ your hands off me!** ¡quítame las manos de encima!, ¡no me toques!; **the soup has been ~n off the menu** han quitado la sopa del menú

B (take away from) (colloq) quitar, sacar* (CS); **I took the gun off him** le quité *or* (CS tb) le saqué la pistola

- **take on**

A [v ▸ o ▸ adv, v ▸ adv ▸ o] 1 (employ) ‹*staff*› contratar, tomar (esp AmL) 2 (undertake) ‹*work*› encargarse* de, hacerse* cargo de; ‹*responsibility/role*› asumir; ‹*client/patient*› aceptar, tomar; **she ~s on too much** se echa demasiado encima, se carga de responsabilidades 3 (tackle) ‹*opponent*› enfrentarse a, aceptar el reto de; ‹*problem/issue*› abordar; **I took him on at tennis** me le enfrenté en tenis

B [v ▸ adv ▸ o] (assume) ‹*expression*› adoptar; ‹*appearance*› adquirir*, asumir; **the town took on an air of festivity** el pueblo asumió un aire festivo

- **take out**

Sense I [v ▸ o ▸ adv, v ▸ adv ▸ o]

A 1 (remove physically) sacar*; **she took the book out of the suitcase** sacó el libro de la maleta; **it takes all the fun out of it** le quita toda la gracia; ***to ~ sb out of herself/himself*** hacer* que algn se olvide de sus problemas; ***to ~ it out of sb*** «*fight/race*» dejar a algn rendido; **this weather certainly ~s it out of you** este tiempo lo deja a uno sin ganas de nada 2 (exclude) eliminar, excluir*, sacar* 3 (transport) sacar* 4 (AmE) ‹*food*› llevar; **food to ~ out** comida para llevar

B 1 (withdraw) ‹*money*› sacar*, retirar 2 (deduct) deducir*

C (produce) sacar*; **he took out a gun** sacó una pistola

Sense II

A [v ▸ o ▸ adv, v ▸ adv ▸ o] 1 (extract) ‹*tooth*› sacar*, extraer* (frml); ‹*appendix*› sacar*, extirpar (frml) 2 (obtain) ‹*insurance/permit*› sacar*

B (eliminate) ‹*enemy/opposition*› eliminar

Sense III [v ▸ o ▸ adv] (accompany, conduct): **he'd like to ~ her out** le gustaría invitarla a salir; **she took me out to dinner** me invitó a cenar; **to ~ the dog out for a walk** sacar* el perro a pasear; **you never ~ me out** nunca me llevas *or* me sacas a ningún lado

- **take out on** [v ▸ o ▸ adv ▸ prep ▸ o]: **she ~s her frustration out on her children** descarga su frustración en los niños; **there's no need to ~ it out on me** no tienes por qué desquitarte *or* (AmL tb) agarrártela conmigo
- **take over**

A [v ▸ adv] 1 (assume control): **when the Democrats took over** cuando los demócratas asumieron el poder; **he will ~ over as managing director** asumirá el cargo de director ejecutivo; **you've been driving for hours, shall I ~ over?** llevas horas manejando *or* (Esp) conduciendo ¿tomo yo el volante?; **to ~ over FROM sb** sustituir* a algn; (in shift work) relevar a algn 2 (seize control, overrun) «*army*» hacerse* con el poder; **whenever she comes she ~s over completely** siempre que viene toma el mando por su cuenta *or* se hace cargo de todo; **a world in which computers have ~n over** un mundo en el que las computadoras han llegado a dominarlo *or* controlarlo todo

B [v ▸ o ▸ adv, v ▸ adv ▸ o] (take charge of) ‹*responsibility/role*› asumir; ‹*job*› hacerse* cargo de; ‹*company*› absorber; **(on his death) his daughter took over the business** (cuando él murió,) su hija tomó las riendas de la compañía

- **take round** (BrE) ▸ **take around**
- **take through** [v ▸ o ▸ prep ▸ o] explicar* paso por paso; **I'll ~ you through the different steps again** repasemos otra vez *or* volvamos sobre los distintos pasos
- **take to** [v ▸ prep ▸ o] 1 (respond well to, develop liking for): **he didn't ~ to life in the country** no se adaptó a la vida en el campo; **she took to teaching immediately** enseguida le tomó gusto a la enseñanza, la enseñanza se le dio bien desde el principio; **they took to each other at once** se gustaron inmediatamente 2 (form habit of): **to ~ to drink** darse* a la bebida; **to ~ to -ING** darle* a algn POR + INF; **she's ~n to calling us at all hours** le ha dado por llamarnos a todas horas 3 (go to): **to ~ to the hills** «*rebels*» huir* al monte; **to ~ to one's bed** meterse en cama
- **take up**

Sense I [v ▸ o ▸ adv, v ▸ adv ▸ o]

A 1 (pick up) ‹*bag/book*› tomar, agarrar (esp AmL), coger* (esp Esp) 2 (accept) ‹*offer/challenge*› aceptar 3 (adopt) ‹*cause*› hacer* suyo (*or* mío *etc*) 4 (begin): **he's ~n up pottery/badminton** ha empezado a hacer cerámica/a jugar al badminton; **when she took up her new role as director** cuando empezó a desempeñar *or* cuando asumió sus funciones de directora

B (lift) ‹*carpet/floorboards*› levantar

C 1 (continue) ‹*story*› seguir*, continuar*; ‹*thread*› retomar; ‹*conversation*› reanudar 2 (pursue) ‹*issue/point*› volver* a

D (shorten) ‹*skirt*› acortar; ‹*hem*› subir

Sense II [v ▸ adv ▸ o]

A (use up, absorb) 1 ‹*time*› llevar; **most of my time is ~n up with ...** se me va casi todo el tiempo en ... 2 ‹*space*› ocupar

B (move into) ‹*position*› tomar

- **take upon** [v ▸ o ▸ prep ▸ o] **to ~ sth upon oneself**: **he took the responsibility upon himself** asumió la responsabilidad; ***to ~ it upon oneself to*** **+ INF**: **I took it upon myself to cancel the flight** me arriesgué y cancelé el vuelo; **he took it upon himself to invite her to my party** se creyó con derecho a invitarla a mi fiesta
- **take up on** [v ▸ o ▸ adv ▸ prep ▸ o] 1 (take person at word): **I may well ~ you up on that** a lo mejor te tomo la palabra *or* te acepto el ofrecimiento; **can I still ~ you up on that drink?** ¿aquella invitación a tomar algo sigue en pie? 2 (challenge): **I must ~ you up on that** sobre eso discrepo con usted
- **take up with**

A [v ▸ adv ▸ prep ▸ o] (form relationship with) (pej) empezar* a juntarse con

B [v ▸ o ▸ adv ▸ prep ▸ o] (raise with): **I shall be taking the matter up with the manager** le voy a plantear el asunto al director

take² *n*

A (Cin) toma *f*

B 1 (earnings) ingresos *mpl*, recaudación *f* 2 (share) parte *f*; (commission) comisión *f*

takeaway¹ /ˈteɪkəweɪ/ *adj* (BrE) ‹*meal/pizza*› para llevar; ‹*restaurant*› de comida para llevar

takeaway² *n* (BrE) 1 (restaurant) restaurante *m* de comida para llevar 2 (meal) comida *f* preparada; **we had a ~** compramos comida para llevar

take-home pay /ˈteɪkhəʊm/ *n* [u] sueldo *m* neto

taken¹ /ˈteɪkən/ *past p of* **take¹**

taken² *adj* (*pred*) **to be ~ WITH sth/sb**: **I was quite ~ with him** me cayó muy bien, me gustó mucho; **they were very ~ with the house** les encantó la casa, quedaron prendados de la casa

takeoff /ˈteɪkɔːf || ˈteɪkɒf/ *n*

A (Aviat) despegue *m*, decolaje *m* (AmL); **the plane is ready for ~** el avión está listo para despegar *or* (AmL tb) decolar

B (caricature, imitation) (colloq) parodia *f*

takeout¹ /ˈteɪkaʊt/ *adj* (AmE) ‹*meal/pizza*› para llevar; ‹*restaurant*› de comida para llevar

takeout² *n* [u] comida *f* preparada; **what do you say we have ~ tonight?** ¿qué te parece si compramos algo hecho para cenar?

takeover /ˈteɪkəʊvər/ *n* 1 (Govt) toma *f* del poder; **military ~** golpe *m* militar, toma *f* del poder por parte de los militares 2 (Busn) absorción *f*, adquisición *f* (*de una empresa por otra*); (*before n*) **~ bid** oferta *f* pública de adquisición, OPA *f*; **to make a ~ bid FOR a company** lanzar* una oferta pública de adquisición *or* una opa SOBRE una empresa

taker /ˈteɪkər || ˈteɪkə(r)/ *n* interesado, -da *m,f*; **there's plenty of soup left: any ~s?** queda mucha sopa ¿alguien quiere más *or* tiene interés?

taking /ˈteɪkɪŋ/ *n* 1 : **it's yours for the ~** es tuyo si lo quieres; **there are plenty of apples there for the ~** hay muchas manzanas para el que quiera 2 **takings** *pl* (BrE Busn) recaudación *f*; (at box office) taquilla *f*, entrada *f*; **to count the day's ~s** hacer* (la) caja

talc /tælk/ *n* [u] polvos *mpl* de talco, talco *m* (AmL)

talcum powder /ˈtælkəm/ *n* [u] polvos *mpl* de talco, talco *m* (AmL)

tale /teɪl/ *n* cuento *m*, relato *m*; **ah now, thereby hangs a ~** (set phrase) ah, eso es toda una historia; ***to tell ~s*** (*used by or to children*) contar* chismes *or* cuentos; **that's not**

t

true: you're telling ~s! ¡mentira! ¡eso es un cuento chino! (fam)

talent /'tælənt/ *n* 1 [u c] (aptitude, skill) talento *m*; **she has a ~ for languages** tiene mucha facilidad para los idiomas 2 [u] (talented people) gente *f* con talento 3 [u] (attractive women or men) (BrE colloq): **they were eyeing up the ~** estaban pasando revista al personal presente (hum)

talented /'tæləntəd || 'tæləntɪd/ *adj* talentoso, de talento

talent scout, (BrE also) **talent spotter** *n* cazatalentos *mf*

talisman /'tæləsmən || 'tælɪzmən/ *n* (*pl* **~s**) talismán *m*

talk[1] /tɔːk/ *vi*

A 1 (speak) hablar; (converse) hablar, platicar* (esp AmC, Méx); **everyone stopped ~ing** todo el mundo se calló; **stop ~ing!** ¡silencio!; **he never stops ~ing** no para de hablar, habla hasta por los codos (fam); **they ~ed and ~ed** hablaron largo y tendido; **to ~ ABOUT sb/sth** hablar DE algn/algo; **he doesn't know what he's ~ing about** no tiene idea de lo que está hablando; **the year's most ~ed-about event** el acontecimiento más comentado del año; **you ate it all? ~ about greedy!** (colloq) ¿te lo comiste todo? ¡hay que ser glotón!; **for a basic kit you're ~ing about $900** (colloq) para un equipo básico hay que pensar en unos 900 dólares; **to ~ OF sth/-ING** hablar DE algo/DE + INF; **~ing of which, how was your exam?** a propósito, ¿cómo te fue el examen?; **to ~ TO sb**: **are you ~ing to me ?** ¿me hablas a mí?; **I wasn't ~ing to you** yo no estaba hablando contigo *or* no te estaba hablando a ti; **we're not ~ing to each other** no nos hablamos; **to ~ to oneself** hablar solo; **to ~ WITH sb** hablar *or* (AmC, Méx tb) platicar* CON algn; **you can ~!** *o* **you can't ~!** *o* **look who's ~ing!** (colloq) ¡mira quién habla!; **now you're ~ing!** (colloq) ¡así se habla! 2 **talking** *pres p* ‹*doll*› que habla; ‹*book*› grabado

B 1 (have discussion) hablar; **is there somewhere we can ~?** ¿podemos hablar en privado?; **the two sides are ready to ~** las dos partes están dispuestas a negociar; **to ~ ABOUT sth** (discuss sth) discutir algo; (hold talks about sth) entrar en negociaciones SOBRE algo 2 (give talk) **to ~ (ABOUT/ON sth)** hablar (DE/SOBRE algo), dar* una charla (SOBRE algo) 3 (gossip) hablar; **you can't stop people ~ing** no se puede evitar que la gente haga comentarios

■ **talk** *vt*

A (speak) (colloq): **they were ~ing Italian** hablaban (en) italiano; **to ~ golf/economics** hablar de golf/economía; **don't ~ nonsense!** ¡no digas tonterías!

B (argue, persuade) **to ~ sb INTO/OUT OF sth/-ING** convencer* a algn DE QUE/DE QUE NO (+ *subj*); **he ~ed me into doing it** me convenció de que lo hiciera; **see if you can ~ her out of it!** a ver si puedes convencerla de que no lo haga; ***to ~ one's way*** *o* ***oneself out of/into sth***: **she tried to ~ her way out of it** ‹*of a difficult situation*› intentó salir del embrollo contando una historia; ‹*of an arrangement*› intentó librarse del compromiso contando una historia; **she ~ed herself into the job** habló tan bien que le dieron el trabajo

Phrasal verbs

- **talk around**, (BrE also) **talk round** [v ▸ o ▸ adv] (persuade) convencer*; **to ~ sb around TO sth/-ING**: **he ~ed them around to his point of view/to accepting the offer** los convenció de que tenía razón/de que aceptaran la oferta
- **talk back** [v ▸ adv] (be disrespectful) contestar *or* responder (mal)
- **talk down** 1 [v ▸ o ▸ adv, v ▸ adv ▸ o] ‹*pilot*› dirigir* por radio (*en un aterrizaje*) 2 [v ▸ o ▸ adv] (persuade to come down): **we managed to ~ him down from the roof** hablando conseguimos que se bajara del techo
- **talk down to** [v ▸ adv ▸ prep ▸ o] hablarle en tono condescendiente a
- **talk over** [v ▸ o ▸ adv, v ▸ adv ▸ o] ‹*problem/issue*› discutir, hablar de
- **talk round** (BrE) ▸**talk around**
- **talk through** [v ▸ o ▸ adv, v ▸ adv ▸ o]: **to ~ sb through sth** (discuss) hablar con algn de algo; (explain) explicarle* algo a algn

talk[2] *n*

A [c] 1 (conversation) conversación *f*; **it's time we had a little ~** ya es hora de que hablemos seriamente; **I had a long ~ with him** estuve hablando *or* (AmC, Méx tb) platicando un rato largo con él 2 (lecture) charla *f*; **to give a ~ about** *o* **on sth** dar* una charla sobre algo 3 **talks** *pl* (negotiations) conversaciones *fpl*, negociaciones *fpl*; **to have** *o* **hold ~s** mantener* *or* sostener* conversaciones; **the two leaders met for ~s** los dos líderes se reunieron para dialogar

B [u] 1 (suggestion, rumor): **there is ~ of his retiring** se habla de que *or* corre la voz de que se va a jubilar; **it was the ~ of the town** (set phrase) era la comidilla del lugar 2 (words) (colloq & pej) palabrería *f* (fam & pey), palabras *fpl*; **it's just ~!** es pura palabrería (fam & pey), no son más que palabras; ***to be all ~ (and no action)*** hablar mucho y no hacer* nada

talkative /'tɔːkətɪv/ *adj* ‹*person*› conversador, hablador

talker /'tɔːkər || 'tɔːkə(r)/ *n* hablador, -dora *m,f*, conversador, -dora *m,f*; **he's a smooth ~** tiene mucha labia (fam)

talking /'tɔːkɪŋ/ *n* [u]: **no ~, please!** ¡silencio, por favor!; **I could hear ~ in the next room** oí que alguien hablaba en la habitación de al lado; **let me do the ~** déjame hablar a mí

talking: **~ point** *n* tema *m* de conversación; **~-to** *n* (*pl* **-tos**) (colloq): **to give sb a good ~-to** leerle* la cartilla a algn (fam), echarle un buen sermón a algn

talk show *n* programa *m* de entrevistas

tall /tɔːl/ *adj* **-er, -est** alto; **he's ~ for his age** es alto para su edad; **how ~ are you?** ¿cuánto mides?; **he's nearly 6 feet ~** mide casi 6 pies; **that tree is almost 50 feet ~** ese árbol tiene casi 50 pies de altura; ***that's a ~ order*** eso es mucho pedir

tallboy /'tɔːlbɔɪ/ *n* (BrE) cómoda *f* (alta)

tallow /'tæləʊ/ *n* [u] sebo *m*

tall story, **tall tale** *n* cuento *m* chino (fam)

tally[1] /'tæli/ *n* (*pl* **-lies**) cuenta *f*; **keep (a) ~ of how much I owe you** ve anotando lo que te debo, lleva la cuenta de lo que te debo

tally[2] *vi* **-lies, -lying, -lied** «*versions*» coincidir, concordar*; «*amounts/totals*» coincidir, cuadrar

Talmud /'tælmʊd/ *n* **the ~** el Talmud

talon /'tælən/ *n* garra *f*

tamarind /'tæmərɪnd/ *n* tamarindo *m*

tambourine /'tæmbə'riːn/ *n* pandereta *f*

tame[1] /teɪm/ *adj* **tamer, tamest** 1 ‹*animal*› (by nature) manso, dócil; (tamed) domado, domesticado 2 (unexciting) ‹*show/story*› insulso, insípido

tame[2] *vt* ‹*wild animal*› domar; ‹*stray*› domesticar*; ‹*passion*› dominar, domar

Tamil[1] /'tæməl || 'tæmɪl/ *adj* tamil, tamul

Tamil[2] *n* 1 [c] (person) tamil *mf*, tamul *mf* 2 [u] (language) tamul *m*

tamp /tæmp/ *vt* **~ (down)** ‹*earth*› apisonar; ‹*tobacco*› apretar*, tacar* (Col)

tamper with /'tæmpər || 'tæmpə(r)/ [v ▸ prep ▸ o] ‹*engine/controls*› tocar*, andar* con (fam); ‹*lock*› tratar de forzar; ‹*document/figures*› alterar

tampon /'tæmpɑːn || 'tæmpɒn/ *n* tampón *m*

tan[1] /tæn/ **-nn-** *vt* 1 ‹*leather/hide*› curtir 2 «*sun*» ‹*body/skin*› broncear, tostar*, poner* moreno

■ **tan** *vi* (become suntanned) broncearse, quemarse (AmL), ponerse* moreno; **to ~ easily** broncearse *or* ponerse* moreno con facilidad

tan[2] *n* 1 (on skin) bronceado *m*, moreno *m* (esp Esp) 2 (color) habano *m*

tan[3] *adj* ‹*shoes/sweater*› habano

tandem /'tændəm/ *n* (bicycle) tándem *m*; ***in ~*** ‹*drive/ride*› uno detrás del otro; ‹*operate/work*› conjuntamente

tang /tæŋ/ *n* [c u] (strong taste) sabor *m* fuerte; (sharp taste) acidez *f*; (smell) olor *m* penetrante

tangent /'tændʒənt/ *n* tangente *f*; ***to go*** *o* ***fly off at*** *o* ***on a ~*** irse* por las ramas

tangerine /'tændʒə'riːn/ *n* 1 (Bot, Culin) (fruit) mandarina *f*, tangerina *f*; (tree) mandarino *m*, tangerino *m* 2 (color) naranja *m*; (*before n*) naranja *adj inv*

tangible /'tændʒəbəl/ *adj* tangible

tangibly /'tændʒəbli/ *adv* perceptiblemente

tangle[1] /'tæŋgəl/ *vt* ‹*threads/wool*› enredar, enmarañar; **to get ~d (up)** enredarse

■ **tangle** *vi* «*threads/rope*» enredarse

t

(Phrasal verbs)

- **tangle up** [v ▸ o ▸ adv, v ▸ adv ▸ o] 1 ‹*threads/wool*› enredar, enmarañar 2 (confuse): **he got terribly ~d up trying to explain himself** se hizo un enredo *or* (fam) lío tratando de explicarse 3 (embroil) (*usu pass*): **to get ~d up in sth** verse* implicado en algo
- **tangle with** [v ▸ prep ▸ o] (colloq) ‹*bully*› meterse con

tangle[2] *n* 1 (of threads, hair) enredo *m*, maraña *f*, embrollo *m*; (of weeds, undergrowth) maraña *f*; **the ropes lay in a ~ on the floor** las cuerdas estaban hechas una maraña *or* un enredo en el suelo 2 (muddle, confusion) lío *m*, enredo *m*; **to get into a ~** armarse un lío

tangled /'tæŋgəld/ *adj* ‹*threads*› enredado; ‹*situation*› complicado

tango[1] /'tæŋgəʊ/ *n* (*pl* **-gos**) tango *m*

tango[2] *vi* **-goes, -going, -goed** bailar el tango, tanguear; ***it takes two to ~*** (colloq) esas cosas no se hacen sin cooperación

tangy /'tæŋi/ *adj* **-gier, -giest** ‹*aroma*› penetrante; ‹*taste*› ácido

tank[1] /tæŋk/ *n*

A (for liquid, gas) depósito *m*, tanque *m*; (on trucks, rail wagons etc) cisterna *f*; **fuel ~** depósito *m* del combustible; (Auto) tanque *m*, depósito *m*

B (Mil) tanque *m*, carro *m* de combate

C (jail) (AmE sl) cárcel *f*, cana *f* (AmS arg), bote *m* (Méx, Ven arg), trullo *m* (Esp arg)

tank[2] *vi* (AmE colloq) ‹‹*stock market*›› venirse* abajo; ‹‹*movie/show*›› fracasar estrepitosamente

(Phrasal verb)

- **tank up** [v ▸ adv] 1 (with fuel) llenar el tanque, repostar 2 (with alcohol) (colloq) tomarse unas cuantas (fam)

tankard /'tæŋkərd || 'tæŋkəd/ *n* jarra *f*, pichel *m* (ant)

tanked up /tæŋkt/ *adj* (colloq) borracho, como una cuba (fam)

tanker /'tæŋkər || 'tæŋkə(r)/ *n* 1 (ship) buque *m* cisterna *or* tanque; **(oil) ~** petrolero *m* 2 (truck) camión *m* cisterna, pipa *f* (Méx)

tankful /'tæŋkfʊl/ *n* tanque *m*

tank top *n* (sleeveless T-shirt) (AmE) camiseta *f* sin mangas; (sleeveless sweater) (BrE) chaleco *m* de punto

tanned /tænd/ *adj* bronceado, moreno

tanner /'tænər || 'tænə(r)/ *n* curtidor, -dora *m,f*

tannery /'tænəri/ *n* (*pl* **-ries**) curtiduría *f*, tenería *f*, curtiembre *f* (AmL)

tannin /'tænən || 'tænɪn/ *n* [u] tanino *m*

tanning /'tænɪŋ/ *n* [u]

A (of hides) curtido *m*

B (of skin) bronceado *m*; (*before n*) **~ lotion** bronceador *m*

Tannoy® /'tænɔɪ/ *n* (BrE) sistema *m* de megafonía; **to announce sth over** *o* **on the ~** anunciar algo por los altavoces *or* (AmL tb) parlantes

tantalize /'tæntḷaɪz || 'tæntəlaɪz/ *vt* 1 (arouse curiosity, desire in) tentar*, atraer* 2 (torment) atormentar, martirizar*

tantalizing /'tæntḷaɪzɪŋ || 'tæntəlaɪzɪŋ/ *adj* tentador

tantamount /'tæntəmaʊnt/ *adj* **to be ~ TO sth** equivaler* A algo

tantrum /'tæntrəm/ *n* berrinche *m*, rabieta *f*, pataleta *f* (fam); **Jack had** *o* **threw a (temper) ~** a Jack le dio un berrinche *or* (fam) una pataleta, Jack hizo un berrinche (Méx)

Tanzania /'tænzə'ni:ə/ *n* Tanzania *f*, Tanzanía *f*

Tanzanian /'tænzə'ni:ən/ *adj* tanzano

tap[1] /tæp/ *n*

A [c] 1 (for water) (BrE) llave *f* *or* (Esp) grifo *m* *or* (RPl) canilla *f* *or* (Per) caño *m* *or* (AmC) paja *f*, chorro *m* (AmC, Ven) 2 (*gas ~*) llave *f* del gas 3 (on barrel) espita *f*; ***on ~*** (lit) ‹*beer*› de barril; (ready for use): **we have all that information on ~** tenemos toda esa información al alcance de la mano

B [c] (listening device) micrófono *m* de escucha; **they put a ~ on his phone** le intervinieron *or* (fam) pincharon el teléfono

C [c] (light blow) toque *m*, golpecito *m*; **there was a gentle ~ at the door** tocaron suavemente a la puerta

D [u] ▸**tap dancing**

tap[2] **-pp-** *vt*

A (strike lightly) ‹*window/door*› dar* un toque *or* golpecito en; **he was ~ping his fingers on the table** tamborileaba con los dedos sobre la mesa; **to ~ in a command** (Comput) teclear una orden

B 1 ‹*tree*› sangrar 2 **~ (off)** ‹*liquid*› sacar* 3 ‹*resources/reserves*› explotar, aprovechar 4 (colloq) **to ~ sb FOR sth** ‹*for money/information*› intentar sacarle algo a algn

C ‹*telephone*› intervenir*, pinchar (fam); ‹*conversation*› interceptar, escuchar

D (designate) (AmE) **to ~ sb FOR sth** nombrar a algn PARA algo

■ **tap** *vi* 1 (strike lightly) **to ~ AT/ON sth** dar* toques *or* golpecitos EN algo 2 (make tapping sound) dar* golpecitos, tamborilear, repiquetear

(Phrasal verb)

- **tap out** [v ▸ o ▸ adv, v ▸ adv ▸ o] ‹*rhythm*› pulsar

tap: **~ dance** *vi* bailar claqué *or* (Méx) tap, hacer* zapateo americano (CS); **~ dancing** *n* [u] claqué *m*, tap *m* (Méx), zapateo *m* americano (CS)

tape[1] /teɪp/ *n*

A [u c] 1 (of paper, cloth) cinta *f* 2 (adhesive) cinta *f* adhesiva; (Med) esparadrapo *m*, cinta *f* adhesiva; *see also* **masking tape, Scotch tape**® *etc* 3 (Sport) cinta *f* de llegada 4 ▸**tape measure**

B 1 [u] (*magnetic ~*) (Audio, Comput, Video) cinta *f* (magnética); **I have it on ~** lo tengo grabado *or* en cinta 2 [c] (Audio, Video) cinta *f*; **I made a ~ of the performance** grabé la actuación (en una cinta)

tape[2] *vt*

A (record) (Audio, Video) ‹*music/film/interview*› grabar; ***to have (got) sb ~d*** (esp BrE colloq) tener* calado a algn (fam); **I've got the system ~d** le he agarrado la onda *or* (Esp) cogido el tranquillo al sistema (fam)

B (stick) pegar* con cinta adhesiva (*or* cinta Scotch® *etc*); (fasten) sujetar con cinta adhesiva (*or* cinta Scotch® *etc*)

C **~ (up)** 1 ‹*parcel*› sujetar con cinta adhesiva (*or* cinta Scotch® *etc*) 2 (AmE Med) ‹*limb*› vendar

■ **tape** *vi* (Audio, Video) grabar

tape: **~ deck** *n* platina *f*, pletina *f*; **~ measure** *n* cinta *f* métrica, metro *m*

taper[1] /'teɪpər || 'teɪpə(r)/ *n* (candle) vela *f* (*larga y delgada*), candela *f*

taper[2] *vi* afilarse, estrecharse; **the stick ~s to a point** el palo termina *or* remata en punta

■ **taper** *vt* afilar, estrechar

(Phrasal verb)

- **taper off**

A [v ▸ adv] 1 (diminish) ‹‹*enthusiasm/efforts*›› decaer*, disminuir*; ‹‹*demand/sales*›› disminuir*, bajar; **I haven't stopped smoking, but I'm trying to ~ off** (AmE) no he dejado el cigarrillo, pero estoy tratando de fumar menos 2 ▸**taper**[2] *vi*

B [v ▸ o ▸ adv, v ▸ adv ▸ o] 1 ‹*expenditure*› reducir* 2 ▸**taper**[2] *vt*

tape: **~-record** /'teɪprɪ'kɔ:rd || 'teɪprɪkɔ:d/ *vt* grabar; **~ recorder** *n* grabador *m*, grabadora *f*; (for cassette format) grabador *m*, grabadora *f*, casete *m* (Esp); **~ recording** *n* [c u] grabación *f* (magnetofónica)

tapered /'teɪpərd || 'teɪpəd/ *adj* ‹*stick*› afilado; ‹*trousers*› estrecho

tapestry /'tæpəstri/ *n* (*pl* **-tries**)

A 1 [c u] (wall hanging) tapiz *m*; **it's all part of life's rich ~** (set phrase) ¡son cosas de la vida! (fr hecha) 2 [u] (art form) tapicería *f*

B [u] (needlepoint) bordado *m* en cañamazo

tapeworm /'teɪpwɜ:rm || 'teɪpwɜ:m/ *n* (lombriz *f*) solitaria *f*, tenia *f*

tapioca /'tæpi'əʊkə/ *n* [u] tapioca *f*

tap root *n* raíz *f* principal

taps /tæps/ *n* (AmE) toque *m* de silencio

tapwater /'tæp,wɔ:tər || 'tæp,wɔ:tə(r)/ *n* [u] agua *f*‡ de la llave *or* (Esp) del grifo *or* (RPl) de la canilla *or* (Per) del caño *or* (AmC) de la paja *or* (AmC, Ven) del chorro

tar[1] /tɑ:r || tɑ:(r)/ *n* [u] 1 (for roads) alquitrán *m*, chapopote *m* (Méx); (in cosmetics) brea *f* 2 (in cigarettes) alquitrán *m*; **low ~ cigarettes** cigarrillos *mpl* de bajo contenido en alquitrán

tar[2] *vt* **-rr-** ‹*road/fence*› alquitranar; ‹*roof*› impermeabilizar* (*con alquitrán*); **to ~ and feather sb** emplumar a algn

tarantula /tə'ræntʃələ || tə'ræntjʊlə/ *n* tarántula *f*

tardy /ˈtɑːrdi || ˈtɑːdi/ *adj* **-dier, -diest** (frml *or* liter) **1** (belated) ‹*departure/reply*› tardío **2** (slow) ‹*progress*› lento **3** (late) (AmE): **I am/was ~** voy a llegar/llegué tarde

tare /ter || teə(r)/ *n*
A (weight) tara *f*
B **tares** *pl* (Bib) cizaña *f*

target¹ /ˈtɑːrgət || ˈtɑːgɪt/ *n*
A **1** (thing aimed at) blanco *m*, objetivo *m*; (Mil) objetivo *m*; (board) (Sport) diana *f*; **the shot was right on/way off ~** el tiro dio de lleno en el blanco/se desvió mucho; **dead on ~!** ¡diana! **2** (of criticism, protest) blanco *m*; **his criticisms were right on/way off ~** sus críticas dieron en el blanco/iban totalmente desencaminadas; **~ FOR/OF sth** blanco DE algo
B (objective, goal) objetivo *m*; **to set oneself a ~** fijarse un objetivo *or* una meta; **above/below ~** por encima/debajo del objetivo previsto; **to be on ~** ir* de acuerdo a lo previsto (*or* al plan de trabajo *etc*); (*before n*) ‹*date/figure*› fijado; ‹*area/zone*› (Mil) objetivo *adj inv*; ‹*audience/market*› (Marketing) objetivo *adj inv*

target² *vt* **1** (select as target): **the company is ~ing the small investor** la empresa está intentando captar al pequeño inversor; **ten mines have been ~ed for closure** diez minas han sido identificadas como candidatas al cierre **2** (direct, aim) ‹*publicity/advertising*› dirigir*; **to ~ benefits at those most in need** concentrar la ayuda en los más necesitados

target practice *n* [u] ejercicios *mpl or* prácticas *fpl* del tiro

tariff /ˈtærəf || ˈtærɪf/ *n*
A (price list) (BrE) tarifa *f*
B (Tax) arancel *m* (aduanero); (*before n*) **~ barrier** *o* **wall** barrera *f* arancelaria

tarmac¹ /ˈtɑːrmæk || ˈtɑːmæk/ *n* [u] **1** **tarmac**® (AmE) (tar mixture) asfalto *m*, chapopote *m* (Méx); (*before n*) ‹*road/surface*› asfaltado **2** (surface — in airport, racetrack) pista *f*; (— on road) asfalto *m*

tarmac² *vt* **-ck-** (BrE) asfaltar

Tarmac® *n* (BrE) ▸**tarmac¹ 1**

tarnish¹ /ˈtɑːrnɪʃ || ˈtɑːnɪʃ/ *vt* **1** (make dull) ‹*silver*› deslustrar, poner* negro **2** (spoil) ‹*reputation/name*› empañar, manchar
■ **tarnish** *vi* **1** «*silver*» deslustrarse, ponerse* negro **2** «*fame*» empañarse, mancharse

tarnish² *n* [u] falta *f* de lustre *or* brillo

tarnished /ˈtɑːrnɪʃt || ˈtɑːnɪʃt/ *adj* **1** ‹*metal/cutlery*› falto de lustre *or* brillo **2** ‹*reputation*› empañado, manchado

tarot /ˈtærəʊ/ *n*: **the ~** el tarot; (*before n*) **~ card** carta *f* de tarot

tarpaulin /tɑːrˈpɔːlən || tɑːˈpɔːlɪn/ *n* **1** [c] (sheet) lona *f* **2** [u] (material) lona *f* impermeabilizada

tarragon /ˈtærəgən/ *n* [u] estragón *m*

tarry /ˈtæri/ *vi* **-ries, -rying, -ried** (arch *or* liter) **1** (remain) permanecer* **2** (delay) detenerse*, demorarse (AmL)

tart¹ /tɑːrt || tɑːt/ *n*
A (Culin) (large) tarta *f*, kuchen *m* (Chi); (individual) tartaleta *f*, tarteleta *f* (RPl)
B (promiscuous woman) (colloq) fulana *f* (fam), puta *f* (vulg), piruja *f* (Col, Méx fam), loca *f* (RPl fam), chusca *f* (Chi fam)

Phrasal verb
• **tart up** (BrE colloq) **1** [v ▸ o ▸ adv] **to ~ oneself up** *o* **get ~ed up** acicalarse (fam), emperifollarse (fam) **2** [v ▸ o ▸ adv, v ▸ adv ▸ o] ‹*building/room*› remodelar

tart² *adj* **1** (acid) ‹*taste/apple*› ácido, agrio **2** (cutting) ‹*rejoinder/remark*› cortante, áspero

tartan /ˈtɑːrtn̩ || ˈtɑːtn̩/ *n* **1** [u] (cloth) tela *f* escocesa *or* de cuadros escoceses; (*before n*) ‹*skirt/scarf*› escocés, de tela escocesa **2** [c] (pattern) tartán *m*

tartar /ˈtɑːrtər || ˈtɑːtə(r)/ *n*
A [u] (Dent) sarro *m*
B [c] *also* **Tartar** (fearsome person) (colloq & dated) fiera *f* (fam)

Tartar /ˈtɑːrtər || ˈtɑːtə(r)/ *n* tártaro, -ra *m,f*

tartar(e) sauce /ˈtɑːrtər || ˈtɑːtə(r)/ *n* [u] salsa *f* tártara

tartly /ˈtɑːrtli/ *adv* de manera cortante, con aspereza

task¹ /tæsk/ *n* tarea *f*; **I had to persuade her, no easy ~** tuve que convencerla, lo cual no fue nada fácil; **to give** *o* **set sb a ~** asignarle una tarea a algn; ***to take sb to ~*** llamarle la atención *or* leerle* la cartilla a algn

task² *vt*: **to ~ sb to do sth/with doing sth** asignarle *or* encomendarle* a algn la tarea de hacer algo

task: **~ force** *n* equipo *m* operativo, grupo *m* de trabajo; (Mil) destacamento *m* (especial), fuerza *f* de tareas; **~master** *n*: **to be a hard ~master** ser* muy estricto y exigente

tassel /ˈtæsəl/ *n* borla *f*

taste¹ /teɪst/ *n*
A [u] **1** (flavor) sabor *m*, gusto *m*; **a strong ~ of garlic** un fuerte sabor *or* gusto a ajo; **it has no ~** no sabe a nada; **the sweet ~ of freedom/success** el dulce sabor de la libertad/del éxito; ***to leave a bad ~ in the mouth*** dejarle a algn (un) mal sabor de boca **2** (sense) gusto *m*
B (*no pl*) **1** (sample, small amount): **can I have a ~ of your ice cream?** ¿me dejas probar tu helado? **2** (experience): **we got a ~ of what was to come** fue un anticipo de lo que nos esperaba; **it was their first ~ of democracy** era su primera experiencia de la democracia; ***a ~ of one's own medicine***: **I'll give her a ~ of her own medicine** la voy a tratar como ella trata a los demás, le voy a dar una sopa de su propio chocolate (Méx)
C [c u] (liking) gusto *m*; **a ~ (FOR sth)**: **if you have a ~ for adventure ...** si te gusta la aventura ...; **to be to one's ~** ser* de su (*or* mi *etc*) gusto; **it's not to everyone's ~** no le gusta a todo el mundo, no es del gusto de todo el mundo; **add salt to ~** añadir sal a voluntad *or* al gusto; ***there's no accounting for ~*** sobre gustos no hay nada escrito
D [u] (judgment) gusto *m*; **she has excellent ~ in clothes** tiene un gusto excelente para vestirse, se viste con muy buen gusto; **in bad ~** de mal gusto; **in extremely poor ~** de pésimo gusto

taste² *vt* **1** (test flavor of) ‹*food/wine*› probar* **2** (test quality of) ‹*food*› degustar; ‹*wine*› catar **3** (perceive flavor): **I can't ~ the sherry in the soup** la sopa no me sabe a jerez, no le siento gusto a jerez a la sopa (AmL) **4** (eat) comer, probar*; **he hadn't ~d food for six days** llevaba seis días sin probar bocado *or* sin comer nada **5** (experience) ‹*happiness/freedom*› conocer*, disfrutar de
■ **taste** *vi* saber*; **it ~s bitter** tiene (un) sabor *or* gusto amargo, sabe amargo; **this ~s delicious** esto está delicioso *or* riquísimo; **to ~ OF sth** saber* A algo

taste bud *n* papila *f* gustativa

tasteful /ˈteɪstfəl/ *adj* ‹*decor/display*› de buen gusto

tastefully /ˈteɪstfəli/ *adv* ‹*decorated/furnished*› con (buen) gusto; **the subject is ~ treated** el tema está tratado con delicadeza

tasteless /ˈteɪstləs/ *adj* **1** (flavorless) ‹*food*› insípido, soso, desabrido **2** (in bad taste) ‹*decor/remark*› de mal gusto

taster /ˈteɪstər || ˈteɪstə(r)/ *n* **1** (person) degustador, -dora *m,f*; **wine ~** catador, -dora *m,f* (de vinos), catavinos *mf* **2** (sample) muestra *f* (*de degustación*)

tasty /ˈteɪsti/ *adj* **-tier, -tiest** **1** ‹*dish/meal*› sabroso, apetitoso, rico **2** (interesting, attractive) ‹*man/woman*› (BrE colloq) buenísimo

tat /tæt/ *n* [u] (BrE colloq) porquerías *fpl* (fam)

ta-ta /tæˈtɑː/ *interj* (BrE colloq) adiós, chau (fam)

tattered /ˈtætərd || ˈtætəd/ *adj* ‹*clothes*› hecho jirones; ‹*pride/image*› destrozado

tatters /ˈtætərz || ˈtætəz/ *pl n*: **to be in ~** «*clothes*» estar* hecho jirones; **her reputation is in ~** su reputación está destrozada

tattle /ˈtætl̩/ *vi* **1** (chatter) cotorrear (fam), darle* a la sinhueso (fam & hum) **2** (tell tales) (AmE) acusar, chivarse (Esp fam), alcahuetear (fam fam), rajarse (Méx fam)

tattler /ˈtætlər || ˈtætlə(r)/, **tattletale** /ˈtætl̩teɪl/ *n* **1** (gossip) chismoso, -sa *m,f*, cotilla *mf* (Esp fam) **2** (telltale) (esp AmE) soplón, -plona *m,f* (fam), acusete *mf* (fam), acusica *mf* (Esp fam), rajón, -na *m,f* (Méx fam), alcahuete, -ta *m,f* (CS fam)

tattoo¹ /tæˈtuː/ *n* (*pl* **-toos**)
A (picture) tatuaje *m*
B (display) *espectáculo militar con música*

tattoo² *vt* **-toos, -tooing, -tooed** tatuar*

tattooist /tæˈtuːəst || tæˈtuːɪst/ *n* tatuador, -dora *m,f*

tatty /ˈtæti/ *adj* **-tier, -tiest** (BrE colloq) ‹*clothes/shoes*› gastado, estropeado; ‹*furniture*› estropeado

taught /tɔːt/ *past & past p of* **teach**

taunt[1] /tɔːnt/ *vt* provocar* mediante burlas; **to ~ sb FOR sth** burlarse *or* mofarse DE algn POR algo

taunt[2] *n* (insult) insulto *m*; (jibe) pulla *f*

Taurus /'tɔːrəs/ *n* [1] (sign) (*no art*) Tauro [2] [c] (person) Tauro *or* tauro *mf*, taurino, -na *m,f*; *see also* **Aquarius**

taut /tɔːt/ *adj* [1] (tight) ‹*rope/wire/sail*› tenso, tirante; ‹*skin*› tirante [2] (tense) ‹*expression/nerves*› tenso, tirante [3] (firm, trim) ‹*body/thighs*› de carnes prietas *or* apretadas

tauten /'tɔːtn̩/ *vi* «*rope/muscles*» tensarse

▪ **tauten** *vt* ‹*rope/wire*› tensar

tautological /'tɔːtə'lɑːdʒɪkəl || ˌtɔːtə'lɒdʒɪkəl/, **tautologous** /tɔː'tɑːləgəs || tɔː'tɒləgəs/ *adj* tautológico

tautology /tɔː'tɑːlədʒi || tɔː'tɒlədʒi/ *n* [c u] (*pl* **-gies**) tautología *f*

tavern /'tævərn || 'tævən/ *n* taberna *f*

tawdry /'tɔːdri/ *adj* **-drier, -driest** ‹*jewelry/decorations*› de oropel, de relumbrón; ‹*outfit/decor*› de mal gusto, charro (AmL), hortera (Esp); ‹*affair*› escabroso

tawny /'tɔːni/ *adj* **-nier, -niest** leonado, pardo rojizo *adj inv*

tawny owl *n* cárabo *m*, antillo *m*

tax[1] /tæks/ *n* [u c] (Fin) (individual charge) impuesto *m*, tributo *m* (frml); (in general) impuestos *mpl*; **how much ~ do you pay** ¿cuánto paga de impuestos?; **I paid $1,500 in ~(es)** pagué 1.500 dólares de *or* en impuestos; **to put** *o* **place a ~ on sth** gravar algo con un impuesto; **~ on goods/services** impuesto sobre mercancías/servicios; **before/after ~es** *o* (BrE) **~: I earn £17,000 before/after ~(es)** gano 17.000 libras sin descontar/descontados los impuestos, gano 17.000 libras brutas/netas; **$20 including ~** 20 dólares impuestos incluidos; (*before n*) **~ abatement** *o* (BrE) **relief** desgravación *f* fiscal; **~ bracket** ≈ banda *f* impositiva; **for ~ purposes** a efectos fiscales *or* impositivos; **~ rebate** *o* **refund** devolución *f* de impuestos; **the ~ year** (in UK) el año *or* ejercicio fiscal

tax[2] *vt*

[A] ‹*company/goods/earnings*› gravar; **we're being ~ed too highly** nos están cobrando demasiado en impuestos

[B] (strain) ‹*resources/health/strength*› poner* a prueba

taxable /'tæksəbəl/ *adj* ‹*goods*› sujeto a impuestos; **~ income** ingresos *mpl* gravables, ≈ base *f* imponible

tax allowance *n* (BrE) ▸ **tax exemption**

taxation /tæk'seɪʃən/ *n* [u] (taxes) impuestos *mpl*, cargas *fpl* fiscales; (system) sistema *m* *or* régimen *m* tributario *or* fiscal

tax: **~ code** *n* (in UK) código *m* impositivo *or* fiscal; **~ collector** *n* recaudador, -dora *m,f* de impuestos; **~-deductible** /'tæksdɪ'dʌktəbəl/ *adj* ‹*expenses/loss*› desgravable; **~ disc** *n* (BrE Auto) *adhesivo que indica que se ha pagado el impuesto de circulación*; **~ evasion** *n* [u] evasión *f* fiscal *or* de impuestos; (large scale) fraude *m* fiscal; **~ exemption** *n* (AmE) desgravación *f* fiscal, deducción *f* impositiva; **~ exile** *n* (esp BrE) *exiliado por motivos fiscales*; **~-free** /'tæks'friː/ *adj* ‹*income/investment*› libre de impuestos; **~ haven** *n* paraíso *m* fiscal

taxi[1] /'tæksi/ *n* (*pl* **~s**) taxi *m*; **to go by ~** ir* en taxi; (*before n*) **~ driver** taxista *mf*

taxi[2] *vi* **taxies, taxiing** *or* **taxying, taxied** (Aviat) rodar* por la pista de despegue/de aterrizaje, carretear (AmL)

taxicab /'tæksikæb/ *n* ▸ **taxi**[1]

taxidermist /'tæksədɜːrməst || 'tæksɪˌdɜːmɪst/ *n* taxidermista *mf*

taxidermy /'tæksə'dɜːrmi || 'tæksɪˌdɜːmi/ *n* [u] taxidermia *f*

taxing /'tæksɪŋ/ *adj* ‹*question/problem*› difícil, complicado; ‹*job*› (physically) agotador; (mentally) difícil, que exige mucho

taxi stand, (BrE) **taxi rank** *n* parada *f* *or* (Chi, Col) paradero *m* *or* (Méx) sitio *m* de taxis

tax: **~man** /'tæksmæn/ (*pl* **-men** /-men/) *n* (colloq) **the ~man** Hacienda *f*, el fisco, la impositiva (RPl); **~payer** *n* contribuyente *mf*; **~ return** *n* declaración *f* de la renta *or* (esp AmL) de impuestos

TB *n* [u] = **tuberculosis**

T-bar /'tiːˌbɑːr || 'tiːˌbɑː(r)/ *n* [1] (T-shaped bar, beam) barra *f* en forma de T [2] (ski lift) *also* **T-bar lift** telesquí *m*

tbs, tbsp = **tablespoon(s)**

te /tiː/ *n* (BrE Mus) si *m*

tea /tiː/ *n*

[A] [1] [u] (drink, leaves, plant) té *m*; **a pot of ~** una tetera de té; **lemon ~** (BrE) té con limón; ***not for all the ~ in China*** (dated) ni por todo el oro del mundo [2] [c] (cup of tea) (BrE): **two ~s, please** dos tés, por favor

[B] [c u] (meal) [1] (in the afternoon) té *m*, merienda *f*, onces *fpl* (Andes); **to have ~** tomar el té, merendar*, tomar onces (Andes) [2] (evening) (BrE) cena *f*, comida *f* (AmL); **to have ~** cenar, comer (AmL)

[C] [u c] (infusion) (*herb* ~) infusión *f*, agua *f*‡ (AmC, Andes), té *m* de yuyos (Per, RPl)

tea: **~ bag** *n* bolsita *f* de té; **~ break** *n* (in UK) descanso *m*; **to have a ~ break** hacer* *or* tomarse un descanso (*para tomar un té*); **~ caddy** *n* caja *f* (*para guardar el té*)

teach /tiːtʃ/ (*past & past p* **taught**) *vt* ‹*subject*› dar* clases de, enseñar; ‹*pupils/students*›: **who ~es you?** ¿quien te da clase?; **the course is taught by Dr Green** el curso lo da *or* (frml) lo imparte el profesor Green; **to ~ school** (AmE) dar* clase(s) en un colegio; **to ~ sth TO sb** dar* clase(s) DE algo A algn, enseñar algo A algn; **he taught himself Greek** aprendió griego él solo *or* por su cuenta; **to ~ sb to + INF** enseñarle A algn A + INF; **she taught him to swim** le enseñó a nadar; **will you ~ me how to do that trick?** ¿me enseñas (a hacer) ese truco?; **that'll ~ her** eso le servirá de lección *or* de escarmiento; **I'll ~ you to tell lies!** ¡ya te voy a enseñar yo a ti a decir mentiras!

▪ **teach** *vi* dar* clase(s); **I'd like to ~** me gustaría ser profesor *or* dedicarme a la enseñanza

teacher /'tiːtʃər || 'tiːtʃə(r)/ *n* profesor, -sora *m,f*, docente *mf* (frml), enseñante *mf* (period); **primary school ~** maestro, -tra *m,f*; **he is an English ~** *o* **a ~ of English** es profesor de inglés

teacher: **~s college** *n* (AmE) (for primary education) escuela *f* normal *or* (Esp) de profesorado de EGB; (for secondary education) instituto *m* de profesorado *or* (Esp) de ciencias de la educación *or* (Chi) pedagógico; **~ training** *n* [u] formación *f* pedagógica *or* de profesorado; (*before n*) **~ training college** (BrE) ▸ **~s college**

tea chest *n* caja *f* de embalaje (*utilizada en mudanzas*)

teaching /'tiːtʃɪŋ/ *n*

[A] [u] (profession) enseñanza *f*, docencia *f*; (*before n*) ‹*post/position*› docente, de profesor/profesora; **the ~ profession** la enseñanza, la docencia; **the ~ staff** el profesorado

[B] (doctrine) (*often pl*) enseñanza *f*; **the ~(s) of Christ** las enseñanzas de Cristo

teaching: **~ assistant** *n* [1] (in US university) ayudante *mf* de cátedra; [2] (in UK school) maestro, -tra *m,f* auxiliar, pasante *mf*; **~ hospital** *n* hospital *m* clínico *or* (RPl) de clínicas; **~ practice** *n* (BrE) práctica *f* docente

tea: **~ cloth** *n* (BrE) ▸ **tea towel**; **~ cozy**, (BrE) **~ cosy** *n* cubretetera *m*; **~cup** *n* taza *f* de té

teak /tiːk/ *n* [u] (madera *f* de) teca *f*

tealeaf /'tiːliːf/ *n* (*pl* **-leaves**) hoja *f* de té

team[1] /tiːm/ *n* [1] (of players, workers) equipo *m*; **the players on** *o* (BrE) **in my team** los jugadores de mi equipo; (*before n*) ‹*captain/leader*› del equipo; ‹*game*› de equipo; **it was a ~ effort** fue un trabajo de equipo [2] (of horses) tiro *m*; (of oxen) yunta *f*

team[2] *vi* **to ~ (WITH sth)** combinar (CON algo)

(Phrasal verb)

• **team up** [v ▸ adv] asociarse, unirse; **to ~ up WITH sb** asociarse CON algn

team: **~mate** *n* compañero, -ra *m,f* de equipo; **~ player** *n* trabajador, -dora *m,f* en equipo; **must be a good ~ player** se valora capacidad de trabajo en equipo; **~ spirit** *n* [u] espíritu *m* de equipo, compañerismo *m*

teamster /'tiːmstər/ *n* (AmE) camionero, -ra *m,f*

Teamsters (Union) /'tiːmstərz || 'tiːmstəz/ *n* (AmE) sindicato *m* del transporte

teamwork /'tiːmwɜːrk || 'tiːmwɜːk/ *n* [u] trabajo *m* *or* labor *f* de equipo

tea: **~ party** *n* té *m*; **to give** *o* **hold a ~ party** dar* un té; **~pot** *n* tetera *f*

tear[1] *n*

[A] /tɪr || tɪə(r)/ lágrima *f*; **to burst into ~s** echarse *or* ponerse* a llorar; **to end in ~s** acabar mal; **his eyes filled with ~s** se le llenaron los ojos de lágrimas; **to be in**

t

~s estar* llorando; **I was moved to ~s** lloré de la emoción; **it brought ~s to my eyes** hizo que se me saltaran las lágrimas, me hizo llorar; **I was bored to ~s** me aburrí como una ostra (fam)

B /ter || teə(r)/ rotura *f*, roto *m* (Esp); (rip, slash) desgarrón *m*, rasgón *m*; *see also* **wear¹ A2**

tear² /ter || teə(r)/ (*past* **tore**; *past p* **torn**) *vt* **1** ‹*cloth/paper*› romper*, rasgar*; **I tore my shirt climbing the fence** me hice un desgarrón en *or* me rompí la camisa subiendo la valla; **a torn T-shirt** una camiseta rota; **to ~ a muscle** desgarrarse un músculo; **I tore the letter in half** rompí la carta por la mitad; **to ~ a hole in sth** hacer* un agujero en algo; **I tore open the letter** abrí la carta, abrí *or* rasgué el sobre; **to ~ sth to pieces** *o* **bits** *o* **shreds** ‹*cloth/paper*› hacer* algo pedazos; ‹*play/essay*› hacer* algo pedazos *or* trizas *or* (fam) polvo; ‹*argument*› echar algo por tierra; **to ~ sb to pieces** *o* **bits** *o* **shreds** (lit: dismember) descuartizar* a algn; «*critic*» hacer* a algn pedazos *or* trizas *or* (fam) polvo; ***that's torn it!*** (BrE colloq & dated) ¡se ha ido todo al traste *or* al garete! (fam) **2** (divide) (*usu pass*) dividir; **a nation torn by civil war** una nación dividida *or* desgarrada por la guerra civil; **he was torn between his sense of duty and his love for her** se debatía entre el sentido del deber y su amor por ella **3** (remove forcibly) **to ~ sth FROM sth** arrancar* algo DE algo

■ **tear** *vi*

A «*cloth/paper*» romperse*, rasgarse*; **~ along the dotted line** arrancar* *or* rasgar* por la línea de puntos

B **1** (rush) (+ *adv compl*): **to ~ along** ir* a toda velocidad; **to ~ after sb** salir* corriendo *or* lanzarse* tras algn; **she went ~ing (off) down the road** salió como un bólido por la carretera (fam) **2** **tearing** *pres p*: **he was in a ~ing hurry** iba con muchísima prisa *or* (AmL tb) apuradísimo

Phrasal verbs

- **tear apart** [v ▸ o ▸ adv]: **they tore the place apart looking for the money** lo destrozaron todo buscando el dinero; **the country is being torn apart by civil war** la guerra civil está desgarrando el país; **the critics tore his last novel apart** los críticos se ensañaron con su última novela; **it ~s me apart to see him like that** me desgarra verlo así
- **tear at** [v ▸ prep ▸ o] **1** (scratch) arañar; (tear) rasgar* **2** (pull) ‹*wrapping/bandages*› tirar de, jalar de (AmL exc CS)
- **tear away** [v ▸ o ▸ adv, v ▸ adv ▸ o] ‹*paper/covering*› arrancar*; **you can't ~ him away from his computer** no hay manera de arrancarlo *or* sacarlo de delante de la computadora; **can you ~ yourself away from the TV for one minute?** ¿puedes hacer un gran esfuerzo y dejar de mirar televisión un momento?
- **tear down** [v ▸ o ▸ adv, v ▸ adv ▸ o] ‹*wall/fence/building*› derribar, tirar abajo
- **tear into** [v ▸ prep ▸ o] **1** (attack physically) emprenderla a golpes con, arremeter contra **2** (attack verbally) arremeter contra
- **tear off** [v ▸ o ▸ adv, v ▸ adv ▸ o] ‹*branch/sheet/wrapping*› arrancar*; **he tore his jacket off** se quitó la chaqueta de un tirón; **~ off the lower part of the form** recorte la parte inferior del formulario
- **tear out** [v ▸ o ▸ adv, v ▸ adv ▸ o] ‹*grass/piece of paper*› arrancar*; **I was practically ~ing my hair out** estaba desesperado, estaba que me subía por las paredes
- **tear up** [v ▸ o ▸ adv, v ▸ adv ▸ o] **1** ‹*paper/letter*› romper* **2** (pull up) ‹*stake/tree-stump*› arrancar*

tearaway /'terəweɪ || 'teərəweɪ/ *n* (BrE colloq) granuja *mf*, gamberro, -rra *m,f* (Esp)

teardrop /'tɪrdrɑ:p || 'tɪədrɒp/ *n* lágrima *f*

tearful /'tɪrfəl || 'tɪəfəl/ *adj* ‹*look/expression*› lloroso; ‹*farewell/story*› triste, emotivo; **she got a bit ~** se le saltaron las lágrimas, se emocionó un poco

tearfully /'tɪrfəli || 'tɪəfəli/ *adv* llorando, con lágrimas en los ojos

tear /tɪr || tɪə(r)/: **~ gas** *n* [u] gas *m* lacrimógeno; **~jerker** /'tɪr,dʒɜ:rkər || 'tɪə,dʒɜ:kə(r)/ *n* (colloq): **the movie is a real ~jerker** la película es un verdadero dramón (fam), la película es de lo más lacrimógena (hum)

tearoff /'terɔ:f || 'teərɒf/ *adj* ‹*calendar*› de taco; **a ~ notepad** un bloc de notas

tearoom /'ti:ru:m, -rʊm/ *n* salón *m* de té, confitería *f* (RPl)

tearstained /'tɪrsteɪnd || 'tɪəsteɪnd/ *adj* manchado de lágrimas

tease¹ /ti:z/ *vt*

A **1** (make fun of) tomarle el pelo a (fam); (cruelly) burlarse *or* reírse de **2** (annoy) hacer* rabiar, fastidiar, jorobar (fam); **stop teasing the cat!** ¡deja de jorobar al gato! **3** (tantalize sexually) provocar*, incitar

B ‹*hair/wool*› cardar

■ **tease** *vi*: **don't take any notice, he's only teasing** no le hagas caso, te está tomando el pelo (fam)

Phrasal verb

- **tease out** [v ▸ o ▸ adv] **to ~ sth out OF sth** sacar* algo DE algo con cuidado

tease² *n* (colloq) **1** (joker) bromista *mf* **2** (flirt): **she's a terrible ~** es muy coqueta *or* provocativa

tea: **~ service**, **~ set** *n* juego *m* de té; **~shop** *n* (esp BrE) ▸ **tearoom**

teasing /'ti:zɪŋ/ *n* [u] tomaduras *fpl* de pelo (fam); (cruel) burlas *fpl*

tea: **~spoon** *n* **1** (spoon) cucharita *f*, cucharilla *f* **2** (quantity) cucharadita *f*; **~spoonful** *n* (*pl* **-spoonfuls** *or* **-spoonsful**) cucharadita *f*; **~ strainer** *n* colador *m* (*pequeño*)

teat /ti:t/ *n* **1** (Zool) tetilla *f* **2** (of feeding bottle) (BrE) ▸ **nipple 2**

tea: **~time** *n* (time — of afternoon snack) la hora del té, ≈ la hora de merendar, la hora de onces (Andes); (— of evening meal) (BrE) la hora de cenar *or* (AmL tb) de comer; **~ towel** *n* (BrE) paño *m* *or* trapo *m* de cocina, repasador *m* (RPl); **~ trolley** *n* (BrE) carrito *m*

tech /tek/ *n* (BrE colloq) ▸ **technical college**

technical /'teknɪkəl/ *adj*

A **1** (of technology, technique) ‹*education/equipment/skill*› técnico **2** (specialized) ‹*language/translator*› técnico; ‹*dictionary*› técnico, especializado; **~ term** tecnicismo *m*, término *m* técnico

B (in strict terms): **it was a ~ victory** en teoría fue una victoria

technical college *n* (in UK) escuela *f* politécnica, ≈ instituto *m* de formación profesional (*en Esp*), ≈ universidad *f* del trabajo (*en Ur*)

technicality /'teknɪ'kæləti/ *n* (*pl* **-ties**) (detail) detalle *m* técnico

technically /'teknɪkli/ *adv* **1** (of technology) técnicamente; (*indep*) desde el punto de vista técnico **2** (of technique) técnicamente; (*indep*) técnicamente, desde el punto de vista técnico **3** (strictly speaking) estrictamente hablando

technical support *n* [u] asistencia *f* técnica

technician /tek'nɪʃən/ *n* (skilled worker) técnico *mf*, técnico, -ca *m,f*; **dental ~** mecánico, -ca *m,f* dentista *or* dental

Technicolor® /'teknɪkʌlər || 'teknɪkʌlə(r)/ *n* [u] tecnicolor® *m*

technique /tek'ni:k/ *n* [c u] técnica *f*

technocrat /'teknəkræt/ *n* tecnócrata *mf*

technocratic /,teknə'krætɪk/ *adj* tecnocrático

technological /'teknə'lɑ:dʒɪkəl || ,teknə'lɒdʒɪkəl/ *adj* tecnológico

technologically /'teknə'lɑ:dʒɪkli || ,teknə'lɒdʒɪkli/ *adv* tecnológicamente

technology /tek'nɑ:lədʒi || tek'nɒlədʒi/ *n* [u c] (*pl* **-gies**) tecnología *f*

technology: **~ park** *n* parque *m* tecnológico; **~ transfer** *n* [u] transferencia *f* de tecnología

technophobe /'teknəfəʊb/ *n* tecnófobo, -ba *m,f*

teddy /'tedi/ (*pl* **-dies**), **teddy bear** *n* osito *m* de peluche

tedious /'ti:diəs/ *adj* ‹*speaker*› aburrido, pesado; ‹*work/task*› tedioso, aburrido, fastidioso

tedium /'ti:diəm/ *n* [u] tedio *m*, aburrimiento *m*

tee¹ /ti:/ *n*

A (in golf) **1** (peg) tee *m* (*soporte para la pelota de golf*) **2** (area) punto *m* de salida

B ▸ **T**

tee² *vt* ‹*ball*› colocar* (en el tee)

Phrasal verbs

- **tee off**

A [v ▸ adv] (golf) dar* el primer golpe

B [v ▸ o ▸ adv, v ▸ adv ▸ o] (make angry) (AmE sl) cabrear (fam)
• **tee up** (golf)
A [v ▸ adv] colocar* la pelota (en el tee)
B [v ▸ o ▸ adv] ‹*ball*› colocar* (en el tee)

teem /ti:m/ *vi* **1** (abound) **to ~ WITH sth: the forest is ~ing with birds** el bosque está repleto de pájaros; **the streets were ~ing with people** las calles hervían *or* estaban abarrotadas de gente **2** (pour): **it's ~ing (with rain)** está diluviando

teenage /'ti:neɪdʒ/, (BrE also) **teenaged** /-d/ *adj* ‹*girl/boy*› adolescente; ‹*fashions*› juvenil, para adolescentes; **in their ~ years many people ...** durante la adolescencia mucha gente ...

teenager /'ti:neɪdʒər || 'ti:neɪdʒə(r)/ *n* adolescente *mf*

teens /ti:nz/ *pl n* adolescencia *f*; **the boy was in his early/late ~** el chico tendría unos trece o catorce/dieciocho o diecinueve años

teeny /'ti:ni/ *adj* **-nier, -niest** chiquitito, chiquitín, pequeñito; **a ~ bit** un poquitín, un poquitito

tee shirt *n* ▸**T-shirt**

teeter /'ti:tər || 'ti:tə(r)/ *vi* «*drunk/invalid*» tambalearse; **they are ~ing on the edge of war** están al borde de la guerra

teeter-totter /'ti:tər,tɑ:tər || 'ti:tə,tɒtə(r)/ *n* (AmE) ▸**seesaw**

teeth /ti:θ/ *pl of* **tooth**

teethe /ti:ð/ *vi*: **she's teething** le están saliendo los dientes, está cortando los dientes (RPl)

teething /'ti:ðɪŋ/ : **~ ring** anillo *m* de dentición; **~ troubles** /'ti:ðɪŋ/*pl n* problemas *mpl* iniciales

teetotal /'ti:'təʊtl̩/ *adj* ‹*person*› abstemio

teetotaler, (BrE) **teetotaller** /'ti:'təʊtl̩ər || ti:'təʊtl̩ə(r)/ *n* abstemio, -mia *m,f*

TEFL /'tefəl/ *n* [u] (BrE) (= **teaching English as a foreign language**) *enseñanza del inglés como lengua extranjera*

Teflon® /'teflɑ:n || 'teflɒn/ *n* [u] Teflon® *m*, Teflón® *m*, Tefal® *m*

Tehran, Teheran /'teɪ'ræn, 'teə'rɑ:n/ *n* Teherán *m*

tel (= **telephone number**) Tel., fono (CS)

tele- /'teli/ *pref* tele-

telebanking /'teli,bæŋkɪŋ/ *n* [u] telebanca *f*

telecast¹ /'telikæst || 'telikɑ:st/ *n* (AmE) transmisión *f or* emisión *f* (por televisión)

telecast² *vt* (*past & past p* **telecast**) (AmE) ‹*program*› transmitir, emitir, televisar

telecommunications /'telikə'mju:nə'keɪʃənz || ,telikə,mju:nɪ'keɪʃənz/ *n* **1** (methods) (+ *pl vb*) telecomunicaciones *fpl* **2** (science) (+ *sing vb*) telecomunicaciones *fpl*

telecommuting /'telikə'mju:tɪŋ/ *n* [u] trabajo *m* a distancia (*utilizando fax, teléfono etc*)

telegram /'teləgræm || 'telɪgræm/ *n* telegrama *m*

telegraph¹ /'teləgræf || 'telɪgrɑ:f/ *n* **1** [u] (method) telégrafo *m*; (*before n*) ‹*wire/cable*› telegráfico; **~ pole** poste *m* telegráfico **2** [c] (message) telegrama *m*, despacho *m* telegráfico

telegraph² *vt* **1** ‹*message/congratulations*› telegrafiar* **2** (signal) (esp AmE) avisar, anunciar
■ **telegraph** *vi* telegrafiar*, mandar un telegrama

telepathic /'telə'pæθɪk || ,telɪ'pæθɪk/ *adj* ‹*message*› telepático; ‹*person*› con telepatía, telépata; **I must be ~** debo tener telepatía

telepathy /tə'lepəθi/ *n* [u] telepatía *f*

telephone¹ /'teləfəʊn || 'telɪfəʊn/ *n* teléfono *m*; **over the ~** por teléfono; (*before n*) ‹*message/line*› telefónico; ‹*company*› de teléfonos, telefónico; **~ number** (número *m* de) teléfono, fono *m* (Chi); **~ operator** operador, -dora *m,f*, telefonista *mf*; *see also* **phone¹**

telephone² *vt* telefonear, llamar por teléfono a, hablarle a (Méx)
■ **telephone** *vi* telefonear, hablar (Méx); **I'll ~ for a taxi/an ambulance** telefonearé *or* llamaré para pedir un taxi/para que venga una ambulancia, llamaré a un taxi/a una ambulancia; *see also* **phone²**

telephone: **~ book** *n* ▸**~ directory**; **~ booth**, (BrE) **~ box** *n* cabina *f* telefónica *or* de teléfonos; **~ directory** *n* guía *f* telefónica *or* de teléfonos, directorio *m* telefónico (AmL exc CS); **~ exchange** *n* central *f* telefónica *or* de teléfonos

telephonist /tə'lefənəst || tə'lefənɪst/ *n* (BrE) telefonista *mf*

telephoto lens /'telə'fəʊtəʊ || ,telɪ'fəʊtəʊ/ *n* teleobjetivo *m*

teleprinter /'telə,prɪntər || 'telɪprɪntə(r)/ *n* (BrE) teletipo *m*

TelePrompter®, **teleprompter** /'telə,prɑ:mptər || 'telɪprɒmptə(r)/ *n* (AmE) autocue® *m*, teleprompter *m*

telesales /'teliseɪlz/ *pl n* televentas *fpl*

telescope¹ /'teləskəʊp || 'telɪskəʊp/ *n* telescopio *m*

telescope² *vt* ‹*book/report/events*› resumir, abreviar
■ **telescope** *vi* plegarse* (*como un telescopio*)

telescopic /'telə'skɑ:pɪk || ,telɪs'kɒpɪk/ *adj* telescópico; **~ umbrella** paraguas *m* plegable automático

teletext /'telitekst/ *n* teletex(to) *m*, videotex(to) *m*

telethon /'teləθɑ:n || 'telɪθɒn/ *n* (TV) *programa de larga duración para recaudar fondos con fines benéficos*

Teletype®, **teletype** /'telətaɪp || 'telɪtaɪp/, **teletypewriter** /'telə'taɪpraɪtər || ,telɪ'taɪpraɪtə(r)/ *n* (AmE) teletipo *m*

televangelist /,telə'vændʒələst || ,telɪ'vændʒəlɪst/ *n* telepredicador, -dora *m,f*

televise /'teləvaɪz || 'telɪvaɪz/ *vt* ‹*event/game*› televisar, transmitir, retransmitir (Esp)

television /'teləvɪʒən || 'telɪvɪʒən/ *n* **1** [u] (medium, industry) televisión *f*; **on ~** en *or* por (la) televisión; (*before n*) ‹*studio/screen*› de televisión; ‹*program/broadcast*› de televisión, televisivo; **~ licence** (in UK) *impuesto que se paga por tener un receptor de televisión* **2** [c] **~ (set)** televisor *m*, (aparato *m* de) televisión *f*

teleworking /'teləwɜ:rk || 'telɪwɜ:k/ *n* [u] teletrabajo *m*, trabajo *m* a distancia

telex¹ /'teleks/ *n* [c u] télex *m*

telex² *vt* ‹*message/news*› enviar* por télex; **he ~ed her immediately** le puso un télex inmediatamente

tell /tel/ (*past & past p* **told**) *vt*
A (inform, reveal) decir*; **as I was ~ing you** como te estaba *or* iba diciendo; **he was told that ...** le dijeron que ...; **could you ~ me the way to the station?** ¿me podría decir *or* indicar cómo se llega a la estación?; **~ me when you've finished** dime *or* avísame cuando hayas terminado; **I am pleased to be able to ~ you that ...** (Corresp) me complace comunicarle *or* informarle que ...; **it's not easy, I can ~ you** no es fácil, te lo aseguro *or* garantizo; **you're ~ing me!** (colloq) ¡me lo vas a decir a mí!; **I told you so!** ¿no te lo dije?; **I can't ~ you how relieved I am!** ¡no te imaginas el alivio que siento!
B (recount, relate) ‹*joke/tale*› contar*; **~ me a story** cuéntame un cuento; **the poem ~s how ...** el poema cuenta *or* (frml) narra *or* relata cómo ...; **to ~ sb ABOUT sb/sth: she's told me all about you** me ha hablado mucho de ti; **~ us about Lima** cuéntanos cómo es Lima (*or* qué tal te fue en Lima *etc*)
C (instruct, warn) decir*; **do as** *o* **what you're told** haz lo que se te dice; **to ~ sb to + INF** decirle* a algn QUE (+ *subj*); **she told me to be quiet** me dijo que me callara
D **1** (ascertain, know): **I could ~ from her voice that she was upset** por la voz me di cuenta de que estaba disgustada; **there's no ~ing what might happen** no se sabe lo que podría ocurrir; **to be able to ~ the time** saber* decir la hora **2** (distinguish) **to ~ sth/sb (FROM sth/sb)** distinguir* algo/a algn (DE algo/algn); **to ~ right from wrong** discriminar entre lo que está bien y lo que está mal; **I can't ~ the difference** yo no veo *or* no noto ninguna diferencia
E (count): **all told** en total
■ **tell** *vi*
A **1** (reveal): **promise you won't ~?** ¿prometes que no se lo vas a contar *or* decir a nadie?; **ah, that would be ~ing** ah, eso es un secreto; **to ~ ON sb (TO sb)** (colloq) acusar a algn (A *or* CON algn) **2** (relate) (liter): **more than words can ~** más de lo que pueden expresar las palabras; **it ~s of great suffering** habla de grandes sufrimientos
B (know) saber*; **you never can ~** nunca se sabe
C (count, have an effect): **her age is beginning to ~** se le está empezando a notar la edad; **he made every punch ~** hizo contar cada golpe; **his influence told** su influencia

t

fue decisiva; **to ~ AGAINST sb/sth** obrar EN CONTRA DE algn/algo; **to ~ ON sb**: **the strain is beginning to ~ on him** la tensión lo está empezando a afectar

Phrasal verbs

- **tell apart** [v ▸ o ▸ adv] distinguir*
- **tell off** [v ▸ o ▸ adv, v ▸ adv ▸ o] (colloq) regañar, reñir* (esp Esp), retar (CS), resondrar (Per), rezongar* (AmC, Ur)

teller /ˈtelər || ˈtelə(r)/ *n* [1] (in bank) cajero, -ra *m,f* [2] (of votes) escrutador, -dora *m,f*

telling /ˈtelɪŋ/ *adj* [1] (effective) ‹*criticism/argument*› contundente [2] (revealing) ‹*sign/remark*› revelador, elocuente

tellingly /ˈtelɪŋli/ *adv* [1] (effectively) eficazmente [2] (revealingly) de forma reveladora

telling-off /ˈtelɪŋˈɔːf || ˌtelɪŋˈɒf/ *n* (esp BrE colloq) (*no pl*) reprimenda *f*, regaño *m* (esp AmL), regañina *f* (esp Esp), reto *m* (CS); **to give sb a ~** regañar a algn, retar a algn (CS), rezongar* a algn (AmC, Ur)

telltale[1] /ˈtelteɪl/ *adj* (*before n*) ‹*sign/smell*› revelador

telltale[2] *n* (person) (colloq) soplón, -plona *m,f* (fam), acusete *mf* (fam), acusica *mf* (Esp fam), rajón, -jona *m,f* (Méx fam), alcahuete, -ta *m,f* (CS fam)

telly /ˈteli/ *n* [u c] (*pl* **-lies**) (BrE colloq) tele *f* (fam)

temerity /təˈmerəti || tɪˈmerɪti, tə-/ *n* [u] (boldness) temeridad *f*, audacia *f*; (effrontery) audacia *f*, osadía *f*

temp[1] /temp/ *n* empleado, -da *m,f* eventual *or* temporal

temp[2] *vi* hacer* trabajo eventual *or* temporal

temper[1] /ˈtempər || ˈtempə(r)/ *n* [1] (*no pl*) (mood) humor *m*; (temperament, disposition) carácter *m*, genio *m*; **to have a bad ~** tener* mal genio; **to be in a good/bad ~** estar* de buen/mal humor *or* genio; **my ~ got the better of me** perdí los estribos; **~, ~!** ¡qué geniecito! (fam) [2] [c u] (rage): **to be in a ~** estar* furioso *or* hecho una furia; (*before n*) **~ tantrum** pataleta *f* (fam) [3] [c u] (composure): **to lose one's ~** perder* los estribos

temper[2] *vt*

A (moderate) ‹*criticism*› atenuar*, suavizar*; ‹*enjoyment*› empañar

B (Metall) templar

tempera /ˈtempərə/ *n* [u] témpera *f*, pintura *f* al temple

temperament /ˈtemprəmənt/ *n* [1] [c] (character) temperamento *m* [2] [u] (moodiness) mal genio *m*

temperamental /ˈtemprəˈmentl/ *adj* [1] (volatile, difficult) ‹*person*› temperamental; **the car's been a bit ~ lately** el coche me está dando problemas últimamente [2] (innate) ‹*aversion/inability*› innato

temperance /ˈtempərəns/ *n* [u] [1] (moderation) (frml) templanza *f* (frml), moderación *f*, temperancia *f* (frml) [2] (abstinence from alcohol) abstinencia *f* de bebidas alcohólicas; (*before n*) ‹*movement*› antialcohólico

temperate /ˈtempərət/ *adj* ‹*climate/zone*› templado

temperature /ˈtemprətʃər || ˈtemprətʃə(r)/ *n* [c u] [1] (Phys) temperatura *f*; **air/body/water ~** la temperatura del aire/cuerpo/agua [2] (Med) (reading on thermometer) temperatura *f*; (abnormally high reading) temperatura *f*, fiebre *f*; **to take sb's ~** tomarle la temperatura a algn; **to have** *o* **run a ~** tener* fiebre *or* calentura *or* (CS) temperatura; **he has a ~ of 102°** ≈ tiene casi 39° de fiebre

tempest /ˈtempəst || ˈtempɪst/ *n* (liter) tempestad *f* (liter); ***a ~ in a teapot*** (AmE) una tormenta en un vaso de agua

tempestuous /temˈpestʃuəs || temˈpestjʊəs/ *adj* [1] ‹*relationship*› tempestuoso; ‹*person*› apasionado [2] ‹*winds/sea*› (liter) tempestuoso (liter)

template /ˈtempleɪt, -plet || ˈtempleɪt/ *n* plantilla *f*

temple /ˈtempəl/ *n*

A (Relig) templo *m*

B (Anat) sien *f*

tempo /ˈtempəʊ/ *n* (*pl* **-pos** *or* **-pi** /-pi/) ritmo *m*; (Mus) tempo *m*

temporal /ˈtempərəl/ *adj* [1] (not eternal) ‹*pleasure*› temporal [2] (secular) (Relig) temporal, secular

temporarily /ˈtempəˈrerəli || ˈtempərərɪli/ *adj* temporalmente, temporariamente (AmL)

temporary /ˈtempəreri || ˈtemprəri/ *adj* ‹*accommodation/arrangement*› temporal, provisional, provisorio (AmS); ‹*improvement*› pasajero; ‹*job/work/worker*› eventual, temporal, temporario (AmL); **as a ~ measure** como medida provisional *or* (AmS tb) provisoria

tempt /tempt/ *vt* (*often pass*) tentar*; **to ~ fate** *o* **providence** tentar* a la suerte; **to be ~ed to + INF** estar* tentado DE + INF; **to ~ sb INTO sth/-ING**: **they ~ed me into staying another week** me convencieron de que me quedara otra semana; **may I ~ you to a little more?** ¿le sirvo un poco más?

temptation /tempˈteɪʃən/ *n* [u c] tentación *f*; **I couldn't resist the ~ to take revenge** no pude resistir la tentación de vengarme

tempter /ˈtemptər || ˈtemptə(r)/ *n* tentador *m*; **the T~** (Relig) el Tentador, el demonio

tempting /ˈtemptɪŋ/ *adj* ‹*offer*› tentador, atractivo; ‹*dish/cake*› tentador, apetecible; **it is ~ to speculate on what might have happened** la idea de especular sobre lo que podría haber pasado es tentadora

temptress /ˈtemptrəs || ˈtemptrɪs/ *n* tentadora *f*

ten[1] /ten/ *n* diez *m*; **hundreds, ~s and units** centenas, decenas y unidades; **~s of thousands** decenas de miles; **it's ~ to** *o* (AmE also) **of three** son las tres menos diez, son diez para las tres (AmL exc RPl); **it's ~ past** *o* (AmE also) **after three** son las tres y diez; **~ to one it'll rain** (te) apuesto a que llueve; *see also* **four**[1]

ten[2] *adj* diez *adj inv*; *see also* **four**[2]

tenable /ˈtenəbəl/ *adj* [1] ‹*theory/argument*› defendible, sostenible [2] ‹*position*› defendible

tenacious /təˈneɪʃəs || tɪˈneɪʃəs/ *adj* ‹*fighter/hold*› tenaz; ‹*belief*› firme

tenaciously /təˈneɪʃəsli || tɪˈneɪʃəsli/ *adv* tenazmente, con tenacidad

tenacity /təˈnæsəti || tɪˈnæsəti/ *n* [u] tenacidad *f*

tenancy /ˈtenənsi/ *n* [c u] (*pl* **-cies**) (holding, possession) tenencia *f*; (period): **during their ~** mientras ellos fueron (*or* sean *etc*) los inquilinos *or* arrendatarios; (*before n*) **~ agreement** contrato *m* de alquiler *or* arriendo

tenant /ˈtenənt/ *n* inquilino, -na *m,f*, arrendatario, -ria *m,f*

tenant farmer *n* arrendatario, -ria *m,f*

tench /tentʃ/ *n* [u c] tenca *f*

tend /tend/ *vi*

A (have tendency, be inclined) tender*; **to ~ to + INF** tender* A + INF; **women ~ to live longer than men** las mujeres tienden a *or* suelen vivir más que los hombres; **I ~ to agree with you** me inclino a pensar como usted; **he ~s to catch colds easily** tiene tendencia *or* propensión a resfriarse

B (attend) **to ~ TO sth/sb** ocuparse DE algo/algn

■ **tend** *vt* ‹*sheep/flock*› cuidar (de), ocuparse de; ‹*invalids/victims*› cuidar (de), atender*; ‹*garden/grave*› ocuparse de

tendency /ˈtendənsi/ *n* (*pl* **-cies**) [1] (inclination, direction) tendencia *f*; (Med) propensión *f*, tendencia *f*; **~ to + INF** tendencia A + INF; **he has a ~ to put on weight** tiene tendencia *or* propensión a engordar; **~ TOWARD sth** tendencia HACIA algo [2] **tendencies** *pl* (proclivities): **criminal tendencies** tendencias *fpl* delictivas

tendentious /tenˈdentʃəs || tenˈdenʃəs/ *adj* tendencioso

tender[1] /ˈtendər || ˈtendə(r)/ *adj* [1] (sensitive) ‹*spot*› sensible; ‹*issue*› delicado, espinoso; **it still feels a bit ~** todavía me duele/me molesta un poco; **at the ~ age of 12** a la tierna edad de 12 años [2] (not tough) ‹*meat*› tierno [3] (affectionate, loving) ‹*gesture/smile*› tierno

tender[2] *n* [1] [c u] (Busn) (offer) propuesta *f*, oferta *f*, plica *f* (Esp); **to put sth out to ~** sacar* algo a concurso *or* a licitación, licitar algo (esp AmS); **to put up** *o* **submit a ~ for sth** presentarse a concurso *or* a una licitación para algo [2] [u] (*legal* ~) moneda *f* de curso legal

tender[3] *vi* «*company*» presentarse a concurso *or* a una licitación

■ **tender** *vt* (frml) ‹*resignation/apologies*› presentar, ofrecer*

tender: **~foot** *n* (*pl* **-feet** *or* **-foots**) (AmE) novato, -ta *m,f*, principiante *mf*; **~hearted** /ˈtendərˈhɑːrtəd || ˌtendəˈhɑːtɪd/ *adj* bondadoso, de buen corazón

tenderize /ˈtendəraɪz/ *vt* ‹*meat*› ablandar

tenderizer /ˈtendəraɪzər || ˈtendəraɪzə(r)/ *n* maza *f* (*para ablandar la carne*)

tenderloin /ˈtendərlɔɪn || ˈtendəlɔɪn/ *n* [u c] (of pork) lomo *m*; (of beef) lomo *m*, filete *m*, solomillo *m* (Esp)

tenderly /ˈtendərli || ˈtendəli/ *adv* tiernamente, con ternura

t

tenderness /ˈtendərnəs || ˈtendənɪs/ *n* [u] 1 (of meat) lo tierno 2 (affection) ternura *f*, cariño *m*

tendon /ˈtendən/ *n* tendón *m*

tendril /ˈtendrəl || ˈtendrɪl/ *n* zarcillo *m*

tenement /ˈtenəmənt/ *n* casa *f* de vecinos *or* de vecindad, vecindad *f* (Méx), conventillo *m* (CS)

tenet /ˈtenət || ˈtenɪt/ *n* principio *m*

tenfold /ˈtenfəʊld/ *adj/adv see* **-fold**

Tenn = Tennessee

tenner /ˈtenər || ˈtenə(r)/ *n* 1 ($10) (AmE sl) (billete *m* de) diez dólares *mpl* 2 (£10) (BrE colloq) (billete *m* de) diez libras *fpl*

tennis /ˈtenəs || ˈtenɪs/ *n* [u] tenis *m*; (*before n*) ~ **court** cancha *f or* (Esp) pista *f* de tenis; ~ **elbow** sinovitis *f* del codo, codo *m* de tenista; ~ **match** partido *m* de tenis; ~ **player** tenista *mf*; ~ **raquet** raqueta *f* de tenis; ~ **shoes** zapatillas *fpl* (de tenis), tenis *mpl*, championes *mpl* (Ur)

tenor[1] /ˈtenər || ˈtenə(r)/ *n*
A [c u] (Mus) tenor *m*; **he is a** ~ tiene voz de tenor
B (frml) (sense) tenor *m*

tenor[2] *adj* (*before n*) ‹*voice/part/range*› de tenor; ‹*recorder/saxophone*› tenor

ten: ~**pin bowling** *n* [u] (BrE) ▸ ~**pins**; ~**pins** *n* (+ *sing vb*) (AmE) bolos *mpl*, bowling *m*

tense[1] /tens/ *adj* 1 (strained) ‹*atmosphere/situation*› tenso; **it was a very** ~ **finish** fue una final muy emocionante 2 (nervous) nervioso, tenso 3 (taut) ‹*wire*› tenso, tirante; ‹*body/muscles*› en tensión, tenso

tense[2] *vt* ‹*muscles*› poner* tenso, tensar

Phrasal verb
• **tense up** [v ▸ adv] (colloq) ponerse* tenso

tense[3] *n* (Ling) tiempo *m*

tensely /ˈtensli/ *adv* con tensión, tensamente

tension /ˈtentʃən || ˈtenʃən/ *n*
A [c u] 1 (of situation) tensión *f*, tirantez *f* 2 (felt by person) tensión *f* 3 (between two parties) conflicto *m*
B [u] (tautness) tensión *f*; (in sewing, knitting) tensión *f*
C [u] (Elec) tensión *f*; **high/low** ~ alta/baja tensión

tent /tent/ *n* tienda *f* (de campaña), carpa *f* (AmL), tolda *f* (Col); (*before n*) ~ **peg** estaca *f*

tentacle /ˈtentɪkəl || ˈtentəkəl/ *n* tentáculo *m*

tentative /ˈtentətɪv/ *adj* 1 (provisional) ‹*plan/arrangement*› provisional, provisorio (AmS); ‹*offer*› tentativo 2 (hesitant) ‹*person*› indeciso; **may I make a** ~ **suggestion?** ¿podría, si me permiten, hacer una sugerencia?

tentatively /ˈtentətɪvli/ *adv* 1 (provisionally) ‹*conclude/propose*› provisionalmente, provisoriamente (esp AmL) 2 (hesitantly): **they have begun, very** ~**, to diversify their operations** han empezado muy cautelosamente a diversificar sus operaciones

tenterhooks /ˈtentərhʊks || ˈtentəhʊks/ *pl n*: ***to be/keep sb on*** ~ estar*/tener* a algn en *or* sobre ascuas

tenth[1] /tenθ/ *adj* décimo; *see also* **fifth**[1]

tenth[2] *adv* (in position, time, order) en décimo lugar; *see also* **fifth**[2]

tenth[3] *n* 1 (Math) décimo *m* 2 (part) décima parte *f*; **nine** ~**s of the population** el 90% de la población

tenuous /ˈtenjuəs/ *adj* ‹*claim/argument*› poco fundado, endeble; ‹*link/connection*› indirecto

tenure /ˈtenjər || ˈtenjə(r)/ *n* 1 [u] (of property, land) tenencia *f*, ocupación *f* 2 [u c] (period of office) ejercicio *m*, ocupación *f* 3 [u] (Educ) (job security) puesto *m* permanente, titularidad *f* (*en una universidad*)

tepee /ˈtiːpiː/ *n* tipi *m*

tepid /ˈtepəd || ˈtepɪd/ *adj* ‹*drink/water*› tibio; ‹*welcome*› poco cálido; ‹*reaction*› poco entusiasta

tequila /təˈkiːlə/ *n* tequila *m*

term[1] /tɜːrm || tɜːm/ *n*

Sense I
A (word) término *m*; **in general/simple** ~**s** en términos generales/lenguaje sencillo; **a** ~ **of abuse** un insulto; **they protested in the strongest possible** ~**s** protestaron en forma sumamente enérgica
B 1 (period) período *m*, periodo *m*; **the President's first** ~ **in office** el primer mandato del presidente; **in the short/long** ~ a corto/largo plazo 2 (in school, university) trimestre *m*; **the fall** *o* (BrE) **autumn/spring/summer** ~ el primer/segundo/tercer trimestre 3 (to due date) plazo *m*; **the** ~ **of the loan expired** venció el plazo del préstamo; **the baby was born at (full)** ~ fue un embarazo a término

Sense II **terms** *pl*
A (conditions) condiciones *fpl*; **on equal** ~**s** en igualdad de condiciones, en pie de igualdad; **we offer easy** ~**s** ofrecemos facilidades de pago; ~**s of reference** (of an inquiry) competencia *f*, atribuciones *fpl* y responsabilidades *fpl*; ***to come to*** ~***s with sth*** aceptar algo
B (relations) relaciones *fpl*; **to be on good/bad** ~**s with sb** estar* en buenas/malas relaciones con algn, llevarse bien/mal con algn; **we are not on speaking** ~**s** no nos hablamos; **they were on first name** ~**s** se llamaban por el nombre de pila, ≈ se tuteaban
C 1 (sense): **in financial/social** ~**s** desde el punto de vista financiero/social; **in real** ~**s** en términos reales 2 **in terms of**: **I was thinking more in** ~**s of ...** yo estaba pensando más bien en ...; **in** ~**s of efficiency, our system is superior** en cuanto a eficiencia, nuestro sistema es superior

term[2] *vt* calificar* de

terminal[1] /ˈtɜːrmənl || ˈtɜːmɪnl/ *adj* 1 (of, relating to death) ‹*cancer/illness*› terminal; ‹*patient*› (en fase) terminal, desahuciado; **in a state of** ~ **decline** en un estado de irreversible decadencia 2 (at end) (*before n*) ‹*point/stage*› terminal; ~ **station** estación *f* terminal

terminal[2] *n* 1 (Transp) (at airport) terminal *f* , terminal *m* (Chi); **train** ~ estación *f* terminal; **bus** ~ terminal *f or* (Chi) *m* de autobuses 2 (Comput) terminal *m* 3 (Elec) terminal *m*, polo *m*

terminally /ˈtɜːrmənəli || ˈtɜːmɪnəli/ *adv*: **he's** ~ **ill** está en fase terminal, está desahuciado

terminate /ˈtɜːrməneɪt || ˈtɜːmɪneɪt/ *vt* (frml) ‹*discussion/relationship*› poner* fin a; ‹*contract*› poner* término a; ‹*employee*› (AmE) despedir*, cesar (frml *or* period); **to** ~ **a pregnancy** interrumpir un embarazo

■ **terminate** *vi* «*lease/relationship*» terminarse; **your employment will** ~ **on January 31st** causará baja *or* quedará cesante el 31 de enero; **this train** ~**s here** éste es el final del recorrido de este tren, hemos llegado a destino

termination /ˈtɜːrməˈneɪʃən || ˌtɜːmɪˈneɪʃən/ *n* 1 [u] (of contract) (frml) terminación *f*; ~ **of employment** baja *f*, cese *m* 2 [u c] (Med): ~ **of pregnancy** interrupción *f* del embarazo; **she had to have a** ~ tuvieron que hacerle un aborto

terminology /ˈtɜːrməˈnɑːlədʒi || ˌtɜːmɪˈnɒlədʒi/ *n* [u c] (*pl* **-gies**) terminología *f*

terminus /ˈtɜːrmənəs || ˈtɜːmɪnəs/ *n* (*pl* **-nuses** *or* **-ni** /-niː, -naɪ || -naɪ/) (of buses) terminal *f or* (Chi) *m*; (of trains) estación *f* terminal

termite /ˈtɜːrmaɪt || ˈtɜːmaɪt/ *n* termita *f*

term: ~ **paper** *n* (in US) *trabajo escrito exigido al finalizar el trimestre*; ~**time** *n* (BrE) época *f* de clases

terrace /ˈterəs || ˈterəs, ˈterɪs/ *n* 1 (patio) terraza *f* 2 (balcony) (AmE) terraza *f* 3 (on hillside) terraza *f* 4 (row of houses) (BrE) *hilera de casas adosadas* 5 **terraces** *pl* (BrE Sport) gradas *fpl*, tribunas *fpl* (CS)

terraced /ˈterəst || ˈterəst, ˈterɪst/ *adj* 1 (Agr, Geog) ‹*hillside/slope*› en terrazas *or* bancales 2 ‹*house*› (BrE) adosado (*en una hilera de casas uniformes*)

terra-cotta /ˈterəˈkɑːtə || ˌterəˈkɒtə/ *n* [u] terracota *f*

terrain /teˈreɪn/ *n* [u c] terreno *m*

terrapin /ˈterəpən || ˈterəpɪn/ *n* galápago *m*, tortuga *f* de agua dulce *or* de río

terrestrial /təˈrestriəl/ *adj* terrestre

terrible /ˈterəbəl/ *adj* 1 (very bad) ‹*movie/singer/weather*› espantoso, atroz, malísimo, fatal (Esp fam); **to feel** ~ (ill) sentirse* *or* encontrarse* pésimo *or* muy mal; (guilty, ashamed) sentirse* muy mal; **that's** ~**!** ¡qué terrible!, ¡qué horror!; **you're** ~**!** ¡qué malo eres! 2 (*as intensifier*): **what a** ~ **shame!** ¡qué lástima más grande!; **it's a** ~ **waste of time** es una pérdida lamentable de tiempo

terribly /ˈterəbli/ *adv* 1 (very badly) ‹*suffer*› terriblemente; ‹*sing/act*› terriblemente mal, fatal (Esp fam); **I miss you** ~ te echo muchísimo de menos 2 (colloq) (*as intensifier*): **I**

t

was ~ worried/nervous estaba preocupadísima/nerviosísima; **I'm not feeling ~ well** no me siento muy bien que digamos

terrier /'teriər || 'teriə(r)/ *n* terrier *mf*

terrific /tə'rɪfɪk/ *adj* 1 (enormous) (colloq) ‹*crash/speed*› tremendo, increíble; ‹*argument*› espantoso 2 (very good) (colloq) ‹*party/cook*› estupendo, genial (fam), de miedo (fam); ‹*idea/news/car*› estupendo, bárbaro (fam), fantástico (fam); **they had a ~ time** lo pasaron fenomenal *or* (Esp tb) pipa (fam); **(that's) ~!** ¡genial! (fam), ¡fenomenal! (fam), ¡chévere! (AmL exc CS fam); **(oh) ~!** (iro) ¡(pues) qué bien! (iró)

terrified /'terəfaɪd || 'terɪfaɪd/ *adj* ‹*crowd*› aterrorizado, aterrado; ‹*shout*› de terror; **to be ~ OF sth/sb** tenerle* terror *or* pánico A algo/algn; **to be ~ OF -ING: he's ~ of failing** le aterra *or* le da terror la idea de fracasar; **to be ~ THAT** tener* terror DE QUE (+ *subj*); **they were ~ they might be too late** estaban aterrados pensando que no iban a llegar a tiempo

terrify /'terəfaɪ || 'terɪfaɪ/ *vt* **-fies, -fying, -fied** aterrorizar*; **spiders ~ me** les tengo pánico *or* terror *or* horror a las arañas; **the explosion terrified us out of our wits** la explosión nos dio un susto de muerte

terrifying /'terəfaɪɪŋ || 'terɪfaɪɪŋ/ *adj* ‹*experience/story/sound*› aterrador, espantoso, espeluznante; **I found him ~ when I was a child** de pequeño le tenía verdadero terror

territorial /'terə'tɔːriəl || ,terɪ'tɔːriəl/ *adj* 1 (Pol) ‹*rights/dispute*› territorial 2 (Zool) ‹*animal/bird*› que tiene un sentido muy desarrollado de su territorio

territory /'terətɔːri || 'terɪtəri, -tri/ *n* [u c] (*pl* **-ries**) territorio *m*

terror /'terər || 'terə(r)/ *n*

A 1 [u] (fear) terror *m*; **they fled in ~** huyeron aterrorizados *or* despavoridos; **he lives in ~ of being found out** vive aterrorizado ante la posibilidad de que lo descubran 2 [u c] (frightening person, thing): **the ~s of war** los horrores de la guerra; **she was the ~ of her subordinates** tenía aterrorizados a sus subalternos

B [c] (difficult person) (colloq): **that kid is a little ~** ese niño es un diablillo (fam)

terrorism /'terərɪzəm/ *n* [u] terrorismo *m*

terrorist /'terərəst || 'terərɪst/ *n* terrorista *mf*; (*before n*) ‹*group/bomb*› terrorista

terrorize /'terəraɪz/ *vt* ‹*person/neighborhood*› aterrorizar*, tener* atemorizado; **he ~d her into lying to the police** la atemorizó para que mintiera a la policía

terror-stricken /'terər,strɪkən || 'terə,strɪkən/, **terror-struck** /-strʌk/ *adj* aterrorizado

terry /'teri/ *n* [u] **~ (cloth** *o* (BrE also) **towelling)** (fabric) (tela *f* de) toalla *f*, felpa *f*

terse /tɜːrs || tɜːs/ *adj* ‹*answer/person*› seco, lacónico

tersely /'tɜːrsli || tɜːsli/ *adv* lacónicamente

tertiary /'tɜːrʃieri || 'tɜːʃəri/ *adj* 1 (Econ) terciario 2 (Educ): **~ education** (BrE) educación *f* superior *or* de nivel terciario

Terylene® /'terəliːn || 'terɪliːn/ *n* [u] (BrE) Terylene® *m*

TESL /'tesəl/ *n* (= **teaching English as a second language**) *enseñanza del inglés como segunda lengua*

test¹ /test/ *n*

A 1 (Educ) prueba *f*; (multiple-choice type) test *m*; **to do** *o* **take a ~** hacer* una prueba/un test; **to give** *o* **set sb a ~** hacerle* *or* ponerle* a algn una prueba/un test 2 (of machine, drug) prueba *f*; **to put sth to the ~** poner* algo a prueba; ***to stand the ~ of time*** resistir el paso del tiempo; (*before n*) ‹*run/flight*› experimental, de prueba 3 (analysis, investigation): **blood/urine ~** análisis *m* de sangre/orina; **to have an eye/a hearing ~** hacerse* un examen de la vista/del oído; **he had an AIDS ~** se le hizo la prueba del sida

B (Sport) partido *m* internacional

test² *vt* 1 ‹*student/class*› examinar, hacerle* una prueba a; ‹*knowledge/skill*› evaluar*; **to ~ sb ON sth** examinar a algn SOBRE algo 2 **~ (out)** ‹*product/vehicle/weapon*› probar*, poner* a prueba; **these cosmetics have not been ~ed on animals** no se han utilizado animales en las pruebas de laboratorio de estos cosméticos 3 ‹*friendship/endurance*› poner* a prueba 4 ‹*blood/urine*› analizar*; ‹*sight/hearing/reflexes*› examinar; ‹*hypothesis*› comprobar*; **you need your eyes ~ed** tienes que hacerte examinar la vista; **to ~ sb FOR sth: she was ~ed for AIDS** se le hizo un análisis para determinar si tenía el sida; **to ~ sth FOR sth: the eggs were ~ed for salmonella** los huevos fueron analizados para determinar si estaban infectados de salmonela

■ **test** *vi* (carry out a test) hacer* pruebas; (Med) hacer* análisis; **just ~ing!** (hum) era sólo para ver qué decías; **she ~ed positive** su análisis dio positivo

testament /'testəmənt/ *n*

A (will) testamento *m*; **the last will and ~ of ...** el testamento y última voluntad de ...

B **Testament** (Bib): **the Old/New T~** el Antiguo/Nuevo Testamento

test: **~ ban** *n* (Mil, Pol) suspensión *f or* prohibición *f* de pruebas nucleares; **~ card** *n* (BrE) ▸**test pattern**; **~ case** *n*: *caso que sienta jurisprudencia*; **~ drive** *n* (Auto) prueba *f* de circulación en carretera; **~-drive** *vt* (*past* **-drove**; *past p* **-driven**) (Auto) probar* (*en carretera*)

tester /'testər || 'testə(r)/ *n* (sample) frasco *m* (*or* aerosol *m etc*) de muestra

testicle /'testɪkəl/ *n* testículo *m*

testify /'testəfaɪ || 'testɪfaɪ/ **-fies, -fying, -fied** *vi* 1 (Law frml) prestar declaración, testificar*; **to ~ TO sth** declarar *or* testificar* algo 2 (demonstrate) (frml) **to ~ TO sth** atestiguar* algo, ser* testimonio DE algo

■ **testify** *vt* (Law) declarar, testificar*

testily /'testəli || 'testɪli/ *adv* con irritación

testimonial /'testə'məʊniəl || ,testɪ'məʊniəl/ *n* 1 (reference, recommendation) recomendación *f* 2 (tribute, gift) tributo *m*, homenaje *m*

testimony /'testəməʊni || 'testɪməni/ *n* (*pl* **-nies**) 1 [u c] (Law) declaración *f*, testimonio *m* 2 (demonstration) (frml) (*no pl*) **to be (a) ~** *o* **to bear ~ TO sth** ser* *or* dar* testimonio DE algo, atestiguar* algo

testing¹ /'testɪŋ/ *n* [u] pruebas *fpl*

testing² *adj* duro, arduo; **this has been a ~ time for us** éstos han sido tiempos difíciles para nosotros

testing ground *n* (journ) terreno *m* de pruebas

test match *n* (Sport) partido *m* internacional

testosterone /te'stɑːstərəʊn || te'stɒstərəʊn/ *n* [u] testosterona *f*

test: **~ paper** *n* (Educ) examen *m*, prueba *f*; **~ pattern** *n* (AmE) carta *f* de ajuste; **~ pilot** *n* piloto *mf* de pruebas; **~ tube** *n* probeta *f*, tubo *m* de ensayo; (*before n*) **~-tube baby** niño, -ña *m,f* probeta

testy /'testi/ *adj* **-tier, -tiest** irritable, de mal genio

tetanus /'tetṇəs || 'tetṇəs/ *n* [u] tétano(s) *m*; (*before n*) ‹*vaccine*› antitetánico, del *or* contra el tétano(s)

tetchy /'tetʃi/ *adj* **tetchier, tetchiest** irritable

tête-à-tête /'tetə'tet || ,teɪtɑː'teɪt/ *n* tête-à-tête *m*

tether¹ /'teðər || 'teðə(r)/ *n* (rope) soga *f*; (chain) cadena *f*; ▸**end¹ A1**

tether² *vt* ‹*animal*› atar, amarrar

Tex = **Texas**

text¹ /tekst/ *n*

A [u c] texto *m*

B [c] (textbook) (AmE) libro *m* de texto

text² *vi* mandar un mensaje de texto

■ **text** *vt* mandar un mensaje de texto a

textbook /'tekstbʊk/ *n* libro *m* de texto; (*before n*) ‹*case/approach*› clásico

text-editor *n* editor *m* de texto

textile /'tekstaɪl/ *n* [c u] textil *m*; (*before n*) ‹*factory/industry*› textil; ‹*worker*› (del sector) textil

text: **~ message** *n* mensaje *m* de texto, SMS *m*; **~phone** *n* teléfono *m* de texto

textual /'tekstʃuəl || 'tekstjuəl/ *adj* ‹*error/differences*› textual

texture /'tekstʃər || 'tekstʃə(r)/ *n* [u c] textura *f*

textured /'tekstʃərd || 'tekstʃəd/ *adj* ‹*wallpaper*› con textura, con relieve

TGWU *n* (in UK) = **Transport and General Workers' Union**

Thai¹ /taɪ/ *adj* tailandés

Thai² *n* 1 [c] (person) tailandés, -desa *m,f* 2 [u] (language) tailandés *m*

t

Thailand /'taɪlænd/ *n* Tailandia *f*

thalidomide /θə'lɪdəmaɪd/ *n* [u] talidomida *f*

Thames /temz/ *n* **the ~** el Támesis

than¹ /ðæn, *weak form* ðən/ *conj* **1** (in comparisons) que; (with quantity) de; **I'm feeling better ~ I was** me siento mejor que antes; **more/less ~ we had asked for** más/menos de lo que habíamos pedido; **the situation is even worse ~ we thought** la situación es aún peor de lo que pensábamos **2** (with alternatives): **I'd rather walk ~ go by bus** prefiero ir a pie a tomar el autobús; **I'd sooner die ~ marry you** prefiero morirme antes que casarme contigo **3** (except, besides) que; **I had no alternative ~ to resign** no tenía otra alternativa que dimitir **4** (when) cuando; **no sooner had I sat down ~ the bell rang** apenas me había sentado cuando sonó el timbre, en cuanto me senté sonó el timbre

than² *prep* (in comparisons) que; (with quantity) de; **his house is bigger ~ mine** su casa es más grande que la mía; **more ~ £200/20 days** más de 200 libras/20 días

thank /θæŋk/ *vt* **1** (demonstrate gratitude to) **to ~ sb (FOR sth)** darle* las gracias a algn (POR algo), agradecerle* (algo) a algn; **I can't ~ you enough for what you did** nunca podré agradecerte bastante lo que hiciste **2** (hold responsible): **she's got her father to ~ for her hang-ups** los complejos que tiene se los debe a su padre; **you've only yourself to ~** la culpa sólo la tienes tú **3** (*in interj phrases*): **~ God/heaven(s)** menos mal, gracias a Dios; **~ goodness you came** menos mal que viniste; *see also* **thank you**

thankful /'θæŋkfəl/ *adj* ‹*look/smile*› de agradecimiento, agradecido; **you should be ~ you're fit and well** deberías dar gracias a Dios por tu salud; **let's be ~ we got there in time** menos mal *or* gracias a Dios que llegamos a tiempo

thankfully /'θæŋkfəli/ *adv* **1** (gratefully): **she smiled ~ up at me** me sonrió agradecida **2** (*indep*) menos mal, gracias a Dios

thankless /'θæŋkləs || 'θæŋklɪs/ *adj* ‹*task/job*› ingrato

thanks /θæŋks/ *pl n* **1** (expression of gratitude) agradecimiento *m*; **a letter/speech of ~** una carta/unas palabras de agradecimiento; **Ⓢ received with thanks** pagado; **is that all the ~ I get?** ¿es así cómo se me lo agradece?; **to give ~ for sth** dar* gracias por algo **2** (*as interj*) **~!** ¡gracias!; **~ very much** *o* **a lot!** ¡muchas gracias!; **~ a million!** ¡mil gracias!, ¡un millón de gracias!; **~ a lot** *o* **a bundle!** (iro) ¡hombre, muchas gracias! *or* ¡mira qué bien! (iró); **~ for nothing!** ¡muchas gracias! (iró); **many ~ (for sth/-ING)** muchas gracias (por algo/+ INF) **3** **thanks to** gracias a; **it's no ~** *o* **it's small ~ to you that we got the contract** no fue gracias a ti que conseguimos el contrato

thanksgiving /'θæŋks'gɪvɪŋ/ *n* **1** acción *f* de gracias **2** **Thanksgiving (Day)** (in US) el día de Acción de Gracias (*que conmemora la primera cosecha de los* **Pilgrim Fathers**)

thank: ~ you *interj* ¡gracias!; **~ you very much** muchas gracias; **to say ~ you** dar* las gracias; **~ you for coming/your help** gracias por venir/tu ayuda; **~-you** *n*: **without so much as a ~-you** sin siquiera dar las gracias; **a special ~-you to ...** doy/damos las gracias muy especialmente a ...; (*before n*) ‹*letter/gift*› de agradecimiento

that¹ /ðæt/ *pron*

A (*pl* **those**) (demonstrative) ése, ésa; (*neuter*) eso; **those** ésos, ésas; (*to refer to something more distant, to the remote past*) aquél, aquélla; (*neuter*) aquello; **those** aquéllos, aquéllas [*According to the Real Academia Española the accent can be omitted when there is no ambiguity*] **what's ~?** ¿qué es eso?; **who's ~ over there?** quién es ése/ésa?; **those are $20 and those over there $21.50** ésos cuestan 20 dólares y aquéllos de allá 21,50; **~'s why she never went back** por eso nunca volvió; **who's ~, please?** (on telephone) ¿con quién hablo, por favor?; **~'s impossible/wonderful!** ¡es imposible/maravilloso!; **those who have been less fortunate** los que no han tenido tanta suerte; **is ~ so?** ¡no me digas!, ¿ah, sí?; **don't talk like ~!** ¡no hables así!, ¡no digas eso!; **eat it up now, ~'s a good girl!** vamos, cómetelo todo ¡así me gusta!; **come on, it's not as bad as all ~** vamos, que no es para tanto

B (*in phrases*) **at that** (moreover) además; (thereupon): **at ~ they all burst out laughing** al oír (*or* ver *etc*) eso, todos se echaron a reír; **for all that** por eso; **he has enormous power and wealth, but is still unhappy for all ~** tiene mucho poder y muchas riquezas, pero aún así es infeliz; **that is: we're all going, all the adults, ~ is** vamos todos, es decir, todos los adultos; **you're welcome to come along, ~ is, if you'd like to** encantados de que vengas, siempre que quieras venir, claro; **that's it!: ~'s it for today** eso es todo por hoy; **is ~ it? — no, there's another bag to come** ¿ya está? — no, todavía falta otra bolsa; **now lift your left arm: ~'s it!** ahora levanta el brazo izquierdo ¡eso es! *or* ¡ahí está!; **~'s it: I've had enough!** ¡se acabó! ¡ya no aguanto más!; **that's that: you're not going and ~'s ~!** no vas y no hay más que hablar *or* y se acabó

C /ðət, *strong form* ðæt/ (relative) que; **a voice ~ reminded him of somebody** una voz que le recordaba a alguien; **it wasn't Helen (~) you saw** no fue a Helen a quien viste, no fue a Helen que viste (AmL); **the reason (~) she resigned** el motivo por el que dimitió; **the way (~) he spoke** la forma en que habló

that² /ðæt/ *adj* (*pl* **those**) ese, esa; **those** esos, esas; (*to refer to sth more distant, to the remote past*) aquel, aquella; **those** aquellos, aquellas; **do you know ~ boy/girl?** ¿conoces a ese chico/esa chica?; **those two records** esos dos discos; **I prefer ~ one** prefiero ése/ésa; **I like those yellow ones** me gustan ésos amarillos; **in those days** en aquellos tiempos; **it's been one of those days** ha sido uno de esos días en que todo sale mal

that³ /ðət, *strong form* ðæt/ *conj* que; **she said (~) ...** dijo que ...; **the news ~ our team had won** la noticia de que nuestro equipo había ganado; **I'm glad (~) you're here** me alegro de que estés aquí; **she talks so fast ~ I can't understand** habla tan rápido que no le entiendo; **it's not ~ I mind what he does but ...** no es que me importe lo que hace, pero ...; **they died ~ others might live** (liter) murieron para que otros pudieran vivir

that⁴ /ðæt/ *adv* tan; **ten thirty? ~ late already?** ¿las diez y media? ¿ya es tan tarde?; **I'm not ~ interested, really** la verdad es que no me interesa tanto; **she can't be all ~ stupid** no es posible que sea tan tonta

thatch¹ /θætʃ/ *n* **1** [u] (roofing) *paja, juncos etc utilizados como techumbre*, quincha *f* (AmS) **2** [c] (roof) tejado *m* de paja (*or* de juncos *etc*), techo *m* de quincha (AmS)

thatch² *vt* ‹*roof*› cubrir* *or* techar con paja (*or* juncos *etc*), empajar, quinchar (AmS)

thatched /θætʃt/ *adj* ‹*roof*› de paja (*or* de juncos *etc*) *or* (AmS) de quincha; ‹*cottage*› con el tejado de paja (*or* de juncos *etc*), quinchado (AmS)

thaw¹ /θɔː/ *vi* ‹‹*snow/ice*›› derretirse*, fundirse; ‹‹*frozen food*›› descongelarse; ‹‹*atmosphere/relations*›› hacerse* más cordial

■ **thaw** *vt* ‹*snow/ice*› derretir*, fundir, deshacer*; ‹*frozen food*› descongelar

■ **thaw** *v impers* (Meteo) deshelar*

Phrasal verb

• **thaw out**

A [v ▸ o ▸ adv, v ▸ adv ▸ o] descongelar

B [v ▸ adv] descongelarse

thaw² *n* (Meteo, Pol) deshielo *m*

the¹ */before vowel* ði, ðɪ; *before consonant* ðə, *strong form* ðiː/ *def art*

A (*sing*) el, la; (*pl*) los, las

B (*emphatic use*): **do you mean *the* Dr Black?** ¿te refieres al famoso Dr Black?; **it's *the* novel to read just now** en este momento, es la novela que hay que leer

C **1** (with names): **Henry ~ First** Enrique primero; **~ Smiths** los Smith **2** (in abstractions, generalizations) (+ *sing vb*): **~ possible/sublime** lo posible/sublime; **~ young/old** los jóvenes/viejos

D (per) por; **three dollars ~ yard** tres dólares la yarda; **they sell it by ~ square foot** lo venden por pie cuadrado; **I get paid by ~ hour** me pagan por hora

E (used instead of possessive pron) (colloq) (*sing*) el, la; (*pl*) los, las; **how's ~ family?** ¿qué tal la familia? (fam)

the² */before vowel* ði; *before consonant* ðə/ *adv* (+ *comp*) **1** (*as conj*) cuanto; **~ more you have, ~ more you want** cuanto más tienes, más quieres; **~ sooner, ~ better** cuanto antes, mejor **2** (*in comparisons*): **I'm ~ richer for this experience** me he enriquecido con esta experiencia; **that's all ~ more reason not to give in** mayor razón para no ceder

t

theater, (BrE) **theatre** /ˈθiːətər || ˈθɪətə(r)/ *n*
A 1 [c] (building) teatro *m*; (*before n*) **I've got two ~ tickets** tengo dos entradas para el teatro 2 [u] (theatrical world) **the ~** el teatro, la escena 3 [u] (drama) teatro *m*; (*before n*) ‹*company/critic*› teatral, de teatro
B [c] (*movie ~*) (AmE) cine *m*
C [c] (*operating ~*) (BrE) quirófano *m*, sala *f* de operaciones

theatergoer, (BrE) **theatregoer** /ˈθiːətərˌgəʊər || ˈθɪətəˌgəʊə(r)/ *n* 1 (Theat): **he's a keen ~** es muy aficionado al teatro, va mucho al teatro 2 (AmE) ▸ **moviegoer**

theatrical /θiˈætrɪkəl/ *adj* 1 ‹*debut/event/circles*› teatral 2 (exaggerated) ‹*gesture/person*› teatral, histriónico

thee /ðiː/ *pron* (arch *or* dial *or* poet) te; (after prepositions) ti

theft /θeft/ *n* [u c] robo *m*; **there have been several cases of ~** ha habido varios robos

their /ðer || ðeə(r)/ *adj* 1 (*sing*) su; (*pl*) sus; **they washed ~ hands** se lavaron las manos 2 (belonging to indefinite person) (*sing*) su; (*pl*) sus; **whoever called didn't leave ~ number** la persona que ha llamado no dejó su teléfono

theirs /ðerz || ðeəz/ *pron* (*sing*) suyo, -ya; (*pl*) suyos, -yas; **~ is blue** el suyo/la suya *or* el/la de ellos es azul; **a friend of ~** un amigo suyo *or* de ellos

them /ðem, *weak form* ðəm/ *pron*
A 1 (as direct object) los, las; (referring to people) los *or* (Esp tb) les, las; **where did you buy ~?** ¿dónde los/las compraste?; **he has two sons, do you know ~?** tiene dos hijos ¿los *or* (Esp tb) les conoces? 2 (as indirect object) les; (with direct object pronoun present) se; **I lent ~ some money** les presté dinero; **I lent it to ~** se lo presté 3 (after preposition) ellos, ellas; **for/with ~** para/con ellos/ellas; **there were four of ~** eran cuatro
B (emphatic use) ellos, ellas; **that'll be ~** deben de ser ellos
C (indefinite person): **there's someone at the door, shall I show ~ in?** hay alguien en la puerta ¿lo hago pasar?; **if anyone calls, tell ~ that ...** si llama alguien, dile que ...
D (for themselves) (AmE colloq *or* dial) se; **they ought to get ~ a car** deberían comprarse un coche

theme /θiːm/ *n*
A (subject, principal idea) tema *m*; (*before n*) **~ park** parque *m* temático
B (Cin, Rad, TV) tema *m*; (*before n*) **~ song** (repeated melody) tema *m* musical; (of TV program) (AmE) música *f* de un programa (*or* una serie *etc*); **~ tune** (BrE) música *f* del programa (*or* de la serie *etc*)
C (essay) (AmE Educ) trabajo *m*

themselves /ðəmˈselvz/ *pron* 1 (reflexive): **they behaved ~** se portaron bien; **they bought ~ a new car** se compraron otro coche; **they only think of ~** sólo piensan en sí mismos; **they were by ~** estaban solos/solas 2 (emphatic) ellos mismos, ellas mismas 3 (normal selves): **the children aren't ~** los niños no son los de siempre 4 (indefinite person or persons): **if anyone's interested, they can find out for ~** si a alguien le interesa, puede averiguarlo por sí mismo

then¹ /ðen/ *adv*
A 1 (at that time) entonces; **it was ~ that I remembered** fue entonces *or* en ese momento cuando *or* (AmL tb) que me acordé; **they repaired the shoes for me ~ and there** me arreglaron los zapatos en el acto *or* en el mismo momento 2 (in those days) en aquel entonces, en aquella época, a la sazón (liter)
B (*after prep*): **between ~ and now** desde entonces hasta ahora; **by ~** para entonces; **from ~ on(ward)** a partir de ese momento, desde entonces; **(up) until** *o* **till ~, up to ~** hasta entonces
C 1 (next, afterward) después, luego 2 (in those circumstances) entonces; **you might lose your job: what would you do ~?** podrías perder el trabajo ¿y entonces qué harías?; **what ~?** ¿entonces qué? 3 (besides, in addition) además; **(and) ~ there's a third argument** además hay un tercer argumento
D 1 (as a consequence): **hold on tight and ~ you won't fall** agárrate fuerte que así no te caes *or* y entonces no te caerás 2 (in that case) entonces; ***you* try doing it, ~!** ¡inténtalo tú, entonces!
E **then again** (*as linker*) también; **he might get it and ~ again he might not** puede que lo consiga y (también) puede que no

then² *adj* (*before n*) entonces; **the ~ leader** el entonces líder

thence /ðens/ *adv* 1 (from that) (frml) (*as linker*) de ahí 2 (from there) (liter) desde allí

thenceforth /ˈðensˈfɔːrθ || ðensˈfɔːθ/, **thenceforward** /ˈðensˈfɔːrwərd || ˌðensˈfɔːwəd/ *adv* (liter) desde entonces, a partir de entonces

theologian /ˈθiəˈləʊdʒən/ *n* teólogo, -ga *m,f*

theological /ˈθiəˈlɑːdʒɪkəl || ˌθiəˈlɒdʒɪkəl/ *adj* teológico

theology /θiˈɑːlədʒi || θiˈɒlədʒi/ *n* [u c] (*pl* **-gies**) teología *f*

theorem /ˈθiərəm / *n* teorema *m*

theoretical /ˈθiəˈretɪkəl/ *adj* teórico

theoretically /ˈθiəˈretɪkli/ *adv* teóricamente, en teoría

theorize /ˈθiəraɪz/ *vi* especular, teorizar*

theory /ˈθiəri/ *n* [c u] (*pl* **-ries**) teoría *f*; **in ~** en teoría, teóricamente

therapeutic /ˈθerəˈpjuːtɪk/ *adj* terapéutico

therapist /ˈθerəpəst || ˈθerəpɪst/ *n* terapeuta *mf*

therapy /ˈθerəpi/ *n* [c u] (*pl* **-pies**) terapia *f*

there¹ /ðer || ðeə(r)/ *adv*
A 1 (close to person being addressed) ahí; (further away) allí, ahí (esp AmL); (less precise, further) allá; **what have you got ~?** ¿qué tienes ahí?; **up/down ~** ahí arriba/abajo; **you ~!** (colloq) ¡oye, tú! (fam), ¡che(, vos)! (RPl fam); **~'s the train!** ¡ahí viene el tren!; ***to have been ~ (before)*** (colloq): **I know what it's like, I've been ~ before** ya sé lo que es, a mí también me ha tocado pasar por eso 2 (*in phrases*) **there and then**: **they solved it for me ~ and then** me lo resolvieron en el acto *or* en el momento; **I made up my mind ~ and then to ask her** en ese mismo momento me decidí a pedírselo; **so there!** (colloq) ¡para que sepas! (fam)
B (calling attention to sth, pointing sth out etc): **~'s the bell, it must be her!** ¡el timbre! debe de ser ella; **~ you are** (giving sth) aquí tiene; **~ we are: that's that done!** ¡ya está! ¡listo!; **it's a pity, but ~ we** *o* **you are** es una lástima pero así son las cosas; **~ he goes: politics again!** ¡ya está otra vez con la política!; **~ go my chances of promotion!** ¡adiós ascenso!; **eat it all up, ~'s a good boy** vamos, cométělo todo ¡así me gusta!
C 1 (present): **lots of his friends were ~** estaban muchos de sus amigos; **who's ~?** (at the door) ¿quién es?; (in the dark) ¿quién anda ahí?; **is Tony ~?** ¿está Tony?; ***not to be all ~*** (colloq): **he's not all ~** le falta un tornillo (fam), no está bien de la cabeza (fam) 2 (at destination): **they should be ~ by now** ya deben de haber llegado
D 1 (at that point): **he went on from ~ to become a director** de ahí pasó a ser director 2 (at that point): **you're right ~** ahí *or* en eso tienes razón
E (*as interj*) 1 (when action is complete): **~! that's the last of the boxes** ¡listo! ésa es la última caja 2 (coaxing, soothing): **~, ~, don't cry!** vamos *or* (Esp tb) venga *or* (Méx tb) ándale, no llores; **~ now! see how easy it is?** ahí está ¿ves qué fácil es?

there² /ðer *weak form* ðər || ðeə(r) *weak form* ðə(r)/ *pron*: **there is/are** hay; **there was** había/hubo; **there will be** habrá; **~ was nobody there** no había nadie; **once upon a time ~ was a princess** érase una vez una princesa; **~ were two demonstrations last week** hubo dos manifestaciones la semana pasada; **~'s no sugar left** no queda azúcar, se ha acabado el azúcar; **~ comes a time when ...** llega un momento en el que ...

there: **~about** /ˈðerəbaʊt || ˈðeərəbaʊt/ *adv* (AmE) ▸ **~abouts**; **~abouts** *adv* 1 (near that figure, time): **he was 25 or ~abouts** tenía unos 25 años, tenía alrededor de 25 años; **she'll get here on Sunday at 12 o'clock or ~abouts** llegará alrededor de las 12 el domingo o por ahí 2 (in that vicinity) por allí, en los alrededores; **~after** /ðerˈæftər || ðeərˈɑːftə(r)/ *adv* (frml) a partir de entonces; **~by** /ˈðerˈbaɪ || ðeəˈbaɪ, ˈðeəbaɪ/ *adv* (frml) de ese modo, así; **~fore** /ˈðerfɔːr || ˈðeəfɔː(r)/ *adv* por lo tanto, por consiguiente, luego (liter); **~in** /ðeˈrɪn || ðeərˈɪn/ *adv* allí; **and ~in lies the problem/its great attraction** y allí está el problema/en eso reside su gran atractivo

there's /ðerz *weak form* ðərz || ðeəz *weak form* ðəz/ 1 **= there is** 2 **= there has**

thermal¹ /'θɜːrməl || 'θɜːməl/ *adj* 1 ‹*stream/bath*› termal 2 ‹*underwear/glove*› térmico

thermal² *n* (Meteo) *corriente ascendiente de aire caliente*

thermal imaging /'ɪmɪdʒɪŋ/ *n* [u] captación *f* de imágenes térmicas

thermometer /θər'mɑːmətər || θə'mɒmɪtə(r)/ *n* termómetro *m*

thermonuclear /'θɜːrməʊ'nuːkliər || ,θɜːməʊ'njuːkliə(r)/ *adj* termonuclear

Thermos® (flask) /'θɜːrməs || 'θɜːməs/, (AmE also) **thermos (bottle)** *n* termo *m*

thermostat /'θɜːrməstæt || 'θɜːməstæt/ *n* termostato *m*

thesaurus /θɪ'sɔːrəs/ *n* (*pl* **-ruses** *or* **-ri** /-raɪ/) diccionario *m* ideológico *or* de ideas afines, tesauro *m*

these /ðiːz/ *pl of* **this**[1,2]

thesis /'θiːsəs || 'θiːsɪs/ *n* (*pl* **-ses** /-siːz/) (dissertation) tesis *f*; (shorter) tesina *f*

thespian /'θespiən/ *n* (liter *or* hum) actor, actriz *m,f*

they /ðeɪ/ *pron* 1 (pl of he, she, it) ellos, ellas; **who are ~?** ¿quiénes son?; **~ didn't come** no vinieron; **~'re the ones who should apologize** son ellos los que *or* quienes deberían disculparse 2 (indefinite person or persons): **someone called, but ~ didn't leave a message** llamó una persona, pero no dejó recado; **~'ve dug up the road** han levantado la calle 3 (people): **~ say he's a millionaire** dicen *or* se dice que es millonario

they'd /ðeɪd/ 1 **= they would** 2 **= they had**

they'd've /ðeɪdəv/ **= they would have**

they'll /ðeɪl/ **= they will**

they're /ðer *weak form* ðər || ðeə(r) *weak form* ðeə(r)/ **= they are**

they've /ðeɪv/ **= they have**

thick¹ /θɪk/ *adj* **-er, -est**
A 1 ‹*layer/book/fabric*› grueso, gordo (fam); ‹*line/brush stroke*› grueso; **it's 5cm ~** tiene 5cm de espesor *or* de grosor 2 (in consistency) ‹*soup/sauce/paint*› espeso 3 (dense) ‹*vegetation/fog/smoke*› espeso, denso; ‹*fur*› tupido; ‹*beard/eyebrows*› poblado; **she has ~ hair** tiene mucho pelo
B (covered, filled) (*pred*) **to be ~ WITH sth** estar* lleno DE algo
C (heavy) ‹*accent*› fuerte, marcado
D (colloq) 1 (stupid) burro (fam), corto (fam) 2 (close) (*pred*) **to be ~ (WITH sb)** estar* a partir (de) un piñón *or* (CS) un confite (con algn)

thick² *adv* 1 (thickly): **he slices the bread too ~** corta el pan demasiado grueso *or* (fam) gordo 2 **thick and fast**: **the snow was falling ~ and fast** estaba nevando copiosamente; **ideas came ~ and fast** llovían las ideas

thick³ *n*: **she likes to be in the ~ of things** le gusta estar donde está la acción; **in the ~ of night** (AmE) en plena noche; ***through ~ and thin*** tanto en las duras como en las maduras, tanto en las buenas como en las malas

thicken /'θɪkən/ *vt* ‹*sauce/paint*› espesar
■ **thicken** *vi* «*sauce/paint*» espesar(se); «*fog*» hacerse* más espeso *or* denso; **the plot ~s** (set phrase) esto se pone cada vez más interesante

thicket /'θɪkət || 'θɪkɪt/ *n* matorral *m*

thickhead /'θɪkhed/ *n* (colloq) burro, -rra *m,f* (fam)

thickly /'θɪkli/ *adv* 1 (in a thick layer): **spread the jam ~** pon una capa gruesa de mermelada 2 (densely) ‹*populated*› densamente

thickness /'θɪknəs || 'θɪknɪs/ *n* [u c] (of fabric, wire) grosor *m*; (of paper, wood, wall) espesor *m*, grosor *m*; **it comes in two ~es** viene en dos grosores

thick: **~set** /'θɪk'set/ *adj* ‹*man*› fornido, macizo; **~-skinned** /'θɪk'skɪnd/ *adj* insensible

thief /θiːf/ *n* (*pl* **thieves** /θiːvz/) ladrón, -drona *m,f*; ***to be as thick as thieves*** ser* uña y carne *or* (hum) uña y mugre *or* (RPl) carne y uña; ***to set a ~ to catch a ~*** nada mejor que un ladrón para atrapar a otro ladrón

thieve /θiːv/ *vi/t* robar

thieving /'θiːvɪŋ/ *adj* (colloq) (*before n*) ladrón

thigh /θaɪ/ *n* muslo *m*

thimble /'θɪmbəl/ *n* dedal *m*

thin¹ /θɪn/ *adj* **-nn-**
A 1 ‹*layer/slice/wall/ice*› delgado, fino; **my patience was wearing ~** se me estaba acabando la paciencia 2 (not fat) ‹*person/body/arm*› delgado, flaco; ‹*waist*› delgado, fino
B 1 (in consistency) ‹*soup/sauce*› claro, poco espeso, chirle (RPl) 2 (not dense) ‹*hair*› ralo, fino y poco abundante
C (weak, poor) ‹*voice*› débil; ‹*excuse/argument/disguise*› pobre, poco convincente

thin² *adv*: **to cut sth ~** cortar algo en rebanadas (*or* capas *etc*) delgadas; **spread the jam ~** ponga poca mermelada

thin³ -nn- *vt* ‹*paint*› diluir*, rebajar; ‹*sauce*› aclarar, hacer* menos espeso
■ **thin** *vi*: **his hair is ~ning** está perdiendo pelo

Phrasal verbs

• **thin down**
A [v ▸ adv] (become slimmer) adelgazar*
B [v ▸ o ▸ adv, v ▸ adv ▸ o] ‹*sauce/soup*› hacer* menos espeso, aclarar; ‹*paint*› diluir*

• **thin out**
A [v ▸ adv] «*traffic*» disminuir; «*forest*» hacerse* ralo *or* menos denso; «*audience*» mermar
B [v ▸ o ▸ adv, v ▸ adv ▸ o] ‹*plants*› entresacar*

thine /ðaɪn/ *pron* (arch *or* dial *or* poet) (*sing*) tuyo, -ya; (*pl*) tuyos, -yas

thing /θɪŋ/ *n*
A (physical object) cosa *f*; **what's that ~?** ¿qué es eso?; **a ~ of great beauty** un objeto de gran belleza; **the damn ~ refuses to start** (colloq) el maldito no quiere arrancar (fam); **I love your dress — what, this old ~?** me encanta tu vestido — ¿este trapo viejo?; **she's got one of those bottle-warmer ~s** (colloq) tiene uno de esos cacharros *or* (Esp, Méx) chismes para calentar biberones (fam)
B (non-material) cosa *f*; **a very funny ~ happened** pasó algo muy cómico *or* una cosa muy cómica; **one ~ that bothers me is ...** algo que me molesta es ...; **the only ~ to do is ...** lo único que se puede hacer es ...; **or some such ~** o algo parecido; **you know the sort of ~** tú sabes a qué me refiero; **I'm too old for this kind of ~** yo soy muy viejo para estos trotes; **these ~s happen** son cosas que pasan; **the same ~ happened to me** a mí me pasó lo mismo; **its a good ~ (that) ...** menos mal que ...; **all good ~s (must) come to an end** (set phrase) lo bueno se acaba pronto *or* dura poco; **first ~s first** hay que empezar por el principio; **the last ~ I expected** lo que menos me imaginaba; **what with one ~ and another** *o* **the other** entre una cosa y otra; **for one ~** en primer lugar, para empezar; **there's only one ~ for it: we'll have to walk** no hay más remedio que ir a pie; **he hadn't done a ~** no había hecho absolutamente nada; **all ~s being equal, we should arrive by 10** si no ocurre ningún imprevisto, deberíamos llegar antes de las 10; **you did the right ~ by saying no** hiciste bien en decir que no; **to expect great ~s of sb/sth** esperar mucho de algn/algo; **we had champagne, the real ~!** tomamos champán ¡del auténtico!; ***it's just one of those ~s*** son cosas que pasan, son cosas de la vida; ***to be a close/near ~***: **they won, but it was a close ~** ganaron, pero raspando *or* por un pelo *or* por los pelos
C (affair, matter) asunto *m*; **I'm fed up with the whole ~** estoy harto del asunto; ***to be on to*** *o* ***onto a good ~*** (colloq) tenérselo* bien montado (fam), tener* un chollo (Esp fam); ***to make a big ~ of sth*** (colloq) (of problem, mistake) armar un escándalo por algo
D **the thing** 1 (that which, what) lo que; **the ~ I liked best** lo que más me gustó 2 (what is appropriate, needed): **this necklace is just the ~ for Helen** este collar es ideal para Helen; **I've got just the ~ for you** tengo exactamente lo que necesitas *or* lo que te hace falta 3 (crucial point, factor): **the ~ is to be there early** lo importante es llegar temprano; **the ~ is, I've forgotten where I put it** resulta que *or* el caso es que *or* lo que pasa es que me he olvidado de dónde lo puse
E **things** *pl* 1 (belongings, equipment) cosas *fpl*; **he washed the breakfast ~s** lavó las cosas del desayuno; **we packed our ~s and left** hicimos las maletas *or* (RPl) las valijas *or* (Méx) las petacas y nos fuimos; **bring your swimming ~s** traigan traje de baño y toalla, etcétera 2 (matters, the situation) cosas *fpl*; **if ~s don't improve** si las cosas no mejoran; **I need time to think ~s over** necesito tiempo para pensarlo; **by the look of ~s** según parece; **how are ~s at home?** ¿qué tal andan las cosas en casa?; **how's ~s?** (colloq) ¿qué tal? (fam); **how are ~s with you?** ¿y tú qué tal andas? (fam) 3 (matters): **a taste for all ~s**

t

Greek un gusto por todo lo griego

F (person, creature): **he didn't know what to do, poor ~!** el pobre no sabía qué hacer; **you poor ~!** ¡pobrecito!; **you lucky ~!** ¡qué suerte tienes!

G (preference, fad) (colloq): **opera isn't really my ~** en realidad la ópera no es lo mío; **I want to be able to do my own ~** yo quiero estar a mi aire; ***to have a ~ about sb/sth*** (colloq): **he has a ~ about cleanliness** es un maniático de la limpieza, tiene manía con la limpieza; **he seems to have quite a ~ about her** parece que le ha dado fuerte con ella (fam)

H (in expressions of time): **first ~ (in the morning)** a primera hora (de la mañana); **that's what I always do last ~ (at night)** eso es lo último que hago todas las noches antes de acostarme; **the next ~ I knew, it was midnight** cuando me di cuenta, era medianoche

thingamabob /'θɪŋəməbɑːb || 'θɪŋəməbɒb/, **thingamajig** /-dʒɪg/ *n* (colloq) [1] (thing) cosa *f*, chisme *m* (Esp, Méx fam), coso *m* (AmS fam), vaina *f* (Col, Per, Ven fam) [2] (person): **~, what's her name?** (BrE) fulana *or* aquélla ¿cómo se llama?

thingamy, thingummy /'θɪŋəmi/ *n* (*pl* **-mies**) ▸**thingamabob**

think[1] /θɪŋk/ (*past & past p* **thought**) *vi*

A (use one's mind) pensar*; **~ hard/carefully** piénsalo mucho/bien; **it makes you ~, doesn't it?** da qué pensar *or* te hace pensar ¿no?; **to ~ for oneself** pensar* por sí mismo; **to ~ ABOUT sth** pensar* EN algo; (consider) pensar* algo; **I'll have to ~ about it** tendré que pensarlo, (me) lo tendré que pensar; **it doesn't bear ~ing about** mejor ni pensarlo; **to ~ OF sth/sb** pensar* EN algo/algn; **~ of the expense** piensa en el gasto; **I hadn't thought of that** no se me había ocurrido eso; **come to ~ of it ...** ahora que lo pienso ...; **just ~ of it!** ¡imagínate!; ***to ~ better of sth***: **I was going to ask her but thought better of it** se lo iba a preguntar pero recapacité y cambié de idea; ***to ~ twice*** pensarlo* dos veces

B (intend, plan) **to ~ OF -ING** pensar* + INF; **what are you ~ing of doing tonight?** ¿qué piensas hacer esta noche?, ¿qué tienes planeado hacer esta noche?

C [1] (find, come up with) **to ~ OF sth**: **can you ~ of anything better?** ¿se te ocurre algo mejor?; **I couldn't ~ of anything to say** no se me ocurrió qué decir [2] (remember) **to ~ OF sth** acordarse* DE algo; **I can't ~ of his name** no me puedo acordar de su nombre

D (have opinion): **to ~ highly of sb** tener* muy buena opinión de algn, tener* a algn en muy buen concepto; **he ~s a lot of you** te aprecia mucho; **I don't ~ much of her boyfriend** no tengo muy buena impresión de su novio; **she ~s nothing of spending $500 in a restaurant** ella gasta 500 dólares en un restaurante como si tal cosa; **~ nothing of it** no tiene ninguna importancia

■ **think** *vt*

A [1] (reflect, ponder) pensar*; **what are you ~ing?** ¿qué estás pensando?; **(just) ~ what that would cost** piensa (en) lo que costaría [2] (remember): **I can't ~ where it was** no me puedo acordar de dónde estaba; **I didn't ~ to look there** no se me ocurrió mirar allí

B [1] (suppose, imagine, expect) pensar*; **I thought you knew** pensé que lo sabías; **that's what *you* ~** eso es lo que tú crees *or* piensas; **what do you ~ you're doing?** ¿pero tú qué te crees?; **who would have thought it?** ¿quién lo hubiera dicho *or* imaginado?, ¿quién lo iba a decir?; **who do you ~ you are?** ¿quién te crees que eres?, ¿qué te crees?; **I can't ~ why he refused** no me explico *or* no entiendo por qué se negó; **I thought you'd be there** pensé *or* creí que estarías allí; **I'll help as well — I should ~ so (too)!** yo también ayudo — ¡me imagino que sí! *or* ¡pues faltaría más!; **she wouldn't accept the money — I should ~ not!** no quiso aceptar el dinero — ¡pues bueno fuera! *or* ¡no faltaba más! [2] (indicating intention): **we thought we'd eat out tonight** esta noche tenemos pensado salir a cenar

C (believe) creer*; **who do you ~ did it?** ¿quién crees que lo hizo?, ¿quién te parece que lo hizo?; **I ~ you'll find it's the only way** ya verá usted que es la única manera; **I thought as much** ya me parecía *or* ya me lo imaginaba; **I thought him rude/pleasant** me pareció *or* lo encontré grosero/agradable; **I ~ so/I don't ~ so** creo que sí *or* me parece que sí/creo que no *or* me parece que no

Phrasal verbs

• **think ahead** [v ▸ adv]: **you have to ~ ahead** tienes que ser previsor; **they are already ~ing ahead to the next elections** ya están pensando en *or* planeando de cara a las próximas elecciones

• **think back** [v ▸ adv] recordar*; **~ back** haz memoria; **to ~ back TO sth** recordar* algo, acordarse* DE algo

• **think out** [v ▸ o ▸ adv, v ▸ adv ▸ o]: **she had thought out very carefully what she was going to say** había pensado muy bien *or* planeado cuidadosamente lo que iba a decir; **a well thought-out proposal** una propuesta bien elaborada

• **think over** [v ▸ o ▸ adv] pensar*; **~ things** *o* **it over carefully first** primero piénsatelo bien, reflexiona antes de decidir

• **think through** [v ▸ o ▸ adv, v ▸ adv ▸ o] ‹*project*› planear detenidamente; ‹*idea*› considerar *or* estudiar detenidamente

• **think up** [v ▸ o ▸ adv, v ▸ adv ▸ o] ‹*excuse*› inventar; ‹*slogan*› crear, idear

think[2] *n* (*no pl*): **I'll have to have a ~ about it** tendré que pensarlo *or* pensármelo; **if you think that, you've got another ~ coming** si te crees eso estás muy equivocado *or* (Esp fam) lo llevas claro

thinker /'θɪŋkər || 'θɪŋkə(r)/ *n* pensador, -dora *m,f*

thinking[1] /'θɪŋkɪŋ/ *n* [u] ideas *fpl*, pensamiento *m*; **to my (way of) ~** a mi modo de ver, en mi opinión; **to do some serious ~** reflexionar seriamente; **good ~!** ¡buena idea!; **that was quick ~ on her part** con eso demostró gran rapidez mental

thinking[2] *adj* (*before n, no comp*) pensante, inteligente

think tank *n* gabinete *m* estratégico, comité *m* asesor

thinly /'θɪnli/ *adv* [1] ‹*slice*› en rebanadas finas [2] (sparsely): **~ populated** con poca densidad de población, poco poblado [3] (scarcely) apenas; **a ~ veiled threat** una amenaza apenas velada

thinner /'θɪnər || 'θɪnə(r)/ *n* [u c] disolvente *m*, diluyente *m*, tíner *m* (AmL)

thinness /'θɪnnəs || 'θɪnnɪs/ *n* [u] [1] (fineness — of slice, layer) lo delgado *or* fino; (— of fabric) ligereza *f*, lo delgado *or* fino [2] (of person) delgadez *f*, flacura *f*

thin-skinned /'θɪn'skɪnd/ *adj* susceptible

third[1] /θɜːrd || θɜːd/ *adj* tercero [**tercero** *becomes* **tercer** *when it precedes a masculine singular noun*]; **the Third Age** la tercera edad; ***~ time lucky*** a la tercera va la vencida, la tercera es la vencida; *see also* **fifth[1]**

third[2] *adv* [1] (in position, time, order) en tercer lugar [2] (with superl): **the ~ highest mountain** la montaña que ocupa el tercer lugar en altura, la tercera montaña en altura; *see also* **fifth[2]**

third[3] *n*

A [1] (Math) tercio *m* [2] (part) tercera parte *f*, tercio *m* [3] (Mus) tercera *f*

B **~ (gear)** (Auto) (*no art*) tercera *f*

C (BrE Educ) *cuarta nota de la escala de calificaciones de un título universitario*

third: ~ class *adv* ‹*mail*› (in US) con tarifa económica; **~-class** /'θɜːrd'klæs || ˌθɜːd'klɑːs/ *adj* (*pred* **~ class**) [1] ‹*mail*› (in US) (Post) de franqueo económico; **~-class degree** (in UK) ▸**third[3] C** [2] (inferior) de tercera, de baja categoría; **~ degree** *n*: **to give sb the ~ degree** (colloq) hacerle* un interrogatorio a algn

thirdly /'θɜːrdli || 'θɜːdli/ *adv* (*indep*) en tercer lugar

third: ~ party *n* tercero *m*, tercera persona *f*; (*before n*) **~-party insurance** seguro *m* contra terceros; **~-rate** /'θɜːrd'reɪt || ˌθɜːd'reɪt/ *adj* de tercera, bastante malo; **~ World** *n* **the T~ World** el Tercer Mundo; (*before n*) ‹*nation/politics/leaders*› tercermundista

thirst[1] /θɜːrst || θɜːst/ *n* [u] sed *f*; **~ for vengeance/excitement** sed *or* ansia(s) *f(pl)* de venganza/emociones

thirst[2] *vi* **to ~ FOR** *o* (liter) **AFTER sth** tener* sed *or* ansias DE algo, estar* sediento DE algo (liter)

thirsty /'θɜːrsti || 'θɜːsti/ *adj* **-tier, -tiest** [1] ‹*person/animal*› que tiene sed, sediento (liter); **to be ~** tener* sed [2] (causing thirst) ‹*work*› que da sed

thirteen /'θɜːr'tiːn || ˌθɜː'tiːn/ *adj/n* trece *adj inv/m*

thirteenth[1] /'θɜːr'tiːnθ || ˌθɜː'tiːnθ/ *adj* decimotercero; (before masculine singular nouns) decimotercer; *see also* **fifth[1]**

thirteenth[2] *adv* en decimotercer lugar; *see also* **fifth[2]**

thirteenth³ *n* 1 (Math) treceavo *m* 2 (part) treceava parte *f*

thirtieth¹ /ˈθɜːrtiəθ || ˈθɜːtiəθ/ *adj* trigésimo; *see also* **fifth¹**

thirtieth² *adv* en trigésimo lugar; *see also* **fifth²**

thirtieth³ *n* 1 (Math) treintavo *m* 2 (part) treintava *or* trigésima parte *f*

thirty /ˈθɜːrti || ˈθɜːti/ *adj/n* treinta *adj inv/m*; *see also* **seventy**

this¹ /ðɪs/ *pron* (*pl* **these**)

A éste, -ta; (*neuter*) esto; **these** éstos, -tas [*According to the Real Academia Española the accent can be omitted when there is no ambiguity*]; **~ is the dining room and ~ is the kitchen** éste es el dormitorio y ésta es la cocina; **what is ~?** ¿qué es esto?; **~ is mine and that is yours** esto es mío y eso es tuyo; **~ is John's father** (on photo) éste es el padre de John; (introducing) te presento al padre de John; **~ is where you work?** ¿aquí es donde trabajas?; **~ is Jack Smith (speaking)** (on telephone) habla Jack Smith, soy Jack Smith; **what's all ~ I hear about you getting married?** ¿qué es eso de que te casas?

B (*in phrases*) **at this**: **at ~, he flew into a rage** al oír (*or* ver *etc*) esto, se puso furioso; **with this**: **with ~, she left** habiendo dicho (*or* hecho *etc*) esto, se fue; **this is it**: **~ is it, the big moment has arrived!** bueno, llegó la hora; **~ *and that***: **what have you been up to lately? — oh, ~ and that** ¿qué has hecho últimamente? — nada en particular

this² *adj* (*pl* **these**)

A este, -ta; (*pl*) estos, -tas; **look at ~ tree/house** mira este árbol/esta casa; **whose are these books/coins?** ¿de quién son estos libros/estas monedas?; **I like these yellow ones** me gustan éstos amarillos/éstas amarillas; **~ time next year** el año que viene por estas fechas

B (in narration) (colloq): **suddenly these three guys came up to me and ...** de repente se me acercan tres tipos y ... (fam)

this³ *adv*. **my desk is ~ big** mi escritorio es así de grande; **now we've come ~ far ...** ya que hemos venido hasta aquí ...; **I never thought it would be ~ expensive** nunca pensé que fuera a ser tan caro

thistle /ˈθɪsəl/ *n* cardo *m*

tho' /ðəʊ/ *contr of* ▸**though¹**

thong /θɔːŋ || θɒŋ/ *n* 1 (leather strip) correa *f* 2 (sandal) (AmE) chancla *f*, chancleta *f*, ojota *f* (CS)

thorax /ˈθɔːræks/ *n* (*pl* **-raxes** *or* **-races** /-ræsiːs/) tórax *m*

thorn /θɔːrn || θɔːn/ *n* 1 (spine) espina *f*; ***to be a ~ in sb's flesh*** *o* ***side*** ser* una espina que algn tiene clavada 2 (shrub) espino *m*

thorny /ˈθɔːrni || ˈθɔːni/ *adj* **-nier, -niest** ‹*plant*› espinoso; ‹*problem/issue*› espinoso, peliagudo

thorough /ˈθɜːrəʊ || ˈθʌrə/ *adj* 1 (conscientious) ‹*person*› concienzudo, cuidadoso; ‹*search/investigation*› meticuloso, riguroso; ‹*wash/clean*› a fondo; ‹*knowledge*› sólido 2 (complete) (*before n*) ‹*idiot*› perfecto; **a ~ waste of time** una total *or* absoluta pérdida de tiempo

thoroughbred¹ /ˈθɜːrəbred || ˈθʌrəbred/ *n* 1 **Thoroughbred** (horse) pura sangre *mf* 2 (pure-bred animal) animal *m* de raza

thoroughbred² *adj* ‹*horse*› de pura sangre, de raza

thorough: **~fare** /ˈθərəˈfer || ˈθʌrəfeə(r)/ *n* 1 (street) (liter) calle *f*, vía *f* 2 (public road) vía *f* pública, carretera *f*; ⊗ **no thoroughfare** (in cul-de-sac) calle cortada; (in private road) prohibido el paso; **~going** *adj* ‹*reform/revision*› concienzudo, profundo; ‹*analysis*› minucioso, riguroso

thoroughly /ˈθɜːrəʊli || ˈθʌrəli/ *adv* 1 ‹*wash/clean*› a fondo, a conciencia; ‹*research*› rigurosamente, meticulosamente; ‹*examine*› minuciosamente, meticulosamente; ‹*work*› concienzudamente 2 (completely) ‹*understand*› perfectamente; **we ~ enjoyed ourselves** nos divertimos muchísimo *or* (fam) de lo lindo; **she's ~ unpleasant** es de lo más desagradable

thoroughness /ˈθɜːrəʊnəs || ˈθʌrənɪs/ *n* [u] (of worker) meticulosidad *f*, esmero *m*; (of research) meticulosidad *f*, rigurosidad *f*

those /ðəʊz/ *pl of* **that** *adj*, *pron* **A**

thou /ðaʊ/ *pron* (arch *or* poet) tú; (Relig) vos (arc)

though¹ /ðəʊ/ *conj* 1 (despite the fact that) aunque; **the house, ~ small, is very comfortable** la casa, aunque *or* si bien (es) pequeña, es muy cómoda 2 (but) aunque

though² *adv* (nevertheless, however): **it's easy, ~, to understand their feelings** sin embargo, es fácil comprender sus sentimientos; **the course is difficult; it's interesting, ~** el curso es difícil, pero es interesante

thought¹ /θɔːt/ *past & past p of* **think¹**

thought² *n*

A 1 [u] (intellectual activity) pensamiento *m* 2 [u] (deliberation): **after much ~** tras mucho pensarlo *or* tras reflexionar mucho sobre el asunto; **a lot of ~ went into this decision** se pensó *or* se reflexionó mucho antes de tomar esta decisión; **I'll give it some ~** lo pensaré; **I've never given it much ~** no me he detenido a pensarlo; **to be deep in ~** estar* absorto en sus (*or* mis *etc*) pensamientos; **to be lost in ~** estar* ido

B [c] 1 (reflection) pensamiento *m*; **to read sb's ~s** adivinarle el pensamiento a algn; **what are your ~s on the matter?** ¿tú qué opinas al respecto?; ***not to give sth a second*** *o* ***another ~***: **at the time I didn't give it another ~** en ese momento no le di mayor importancia; **I mailed it and never gave it a second ~** la eché al correo y no volví a pensar en ello; ***to have second ~s (about sth)***: **I'm having second ~s about accepting their offer** me están entrando dudas sobre si aceptar o no su oferta; **on second ~(s)** pensándolo bien 2 (idea) idea *f*; **I've just had a ~** se me acaba de ocurrir una idea; **it was a kind ~ to send her flowers** fue todo un detalle mandarle flores; **the ~ never even entered my head** *o* **crossed my mind** ni se me pasó por la cabeza; **~ OF sth**: **the mere ~ of food made her feel sick** le daban náuseas de sólo pensar en comida; **he couldn't bear the ~ of leaving them** la idea de abandonarlos se le hacía intolerable; **the ~ THAT** la idea DE QUE 3 (concern, consideration) (*no pl*) **~ (FOR sb/sth)**: **my first ~ was for the baby** en lo primero que pensé fue en el bebé; **with no ~** *o* **without a ~ for her own safety** sin pensar para nada en su propia seguridad; **it's the ~ that counts** (set phrase) lo que importa es la atención *or* el detalle

thoughtful /ˈθɔːtfəl/ *adj* 1 ‹*person/conduct*› (kind) atento, amable; (considerate) considerado; **a present? how ~ of you!** ¿un regalo? ¡qué detalle! *or* ¡qué amabilidad! 2 (pensive) pensativo, meditabundo

thoughtfully /ˈθɔːtfəli/ *adv* 1 (considerately): **he had ~ left some food for us** había tenido la amabilidad de dejarnos algo de comer 2 (pensively) pensativamente

thoughtless /ˈθɔːtləs || ˈθɔːtlɪs/ *adj* 1 (inconsiderate) ‹*person/remark*› desconsiderado; **it was ~ of me to say that** fue una falta de consideración por mi parte decir eso 2 (unthinking) irreflexivo, descuidado

thoughtlessly /ˈθɔːtləsli || ˈθɔːtlɪsli/ *adv* 1 (without consideration) desconsideradamente 2 (without thinking) sin pensar

thoughtlessness /ˈθɔːtləsnəs || ˈθɔːtlɪsnɪs/ *n* [u] 1 (lack of consideration) desconsideración *f*, falta *f* de consideración 2 (lack of reflection) irreflexión *f*, descuido *m*

thought-provoking /ˈθɔːtprəˌvəʊkɪŋ/ *adj* que hace pensar *or* reflexionar

thousand /ˈθaʊznd/ *n* mil *m*; **a ~ thanks** mil gracias, un millón de gracias; *see also* **hundred**

thousandth¹ /ˈθaʊzəndθ/ *adj* milésimo; *see also* **fifth¹**

thousandth² *adv* en milésimo lugar; *see also* **fifth²**

thousandth³ *n* 1 (Math) milésimo *m* 2 (part) milésima parte *f*

thrall /θrɔːl/ *n* [u] (liter): **to be in ~ to sb** ser* esclavo de algn; **to have** *o* **hold sb in ~** tener* a algn subyugado

thrash /θræʃ/ *vt* 1 (beat) golpear; (as punishment) azotar, darle* una paliza a 2 (defeat) (colloq) ‹*opponent*› darle* una paliza a (fam)

■ **thrash** *vi*: **~ (around** *o* **about)** revolverse*, retorcerse*; (in mud, water) revolcarse*

Phrasal verb

• **thrash out** [v ▸ o ▸ adv, v ▸ adv ▸ o] 1 (try to resolve) ‹*problem*› discutir, tratar de resolver 2 (agree on) ‹*policy*› llegar* a un acuerdo sobre

thrashing /ˈθræʃɪŋ/ *n* 1 (beating) paliza *f*, zurra *f*; **to give sb a ~** darle* una paliza a algn 2 (heavy defeat) (colloq)

t

paliza *f* (fam); **to give sb/get a ~** llevarse una paliza/darle* una paliza a algn (fam)

thread¹ /θred/ *n* [1] [c u] (filament) hilo *m*; **to follow/lose/pick up the ~ of a plot/conversation** seguir*/perder*/retomar el hilo de una trama/conversación; ***to hang by a ~*** pender de un hilo [2] [c] (of screw) rosca *f*, filete *m*

thread² *vt* ‹*needle/sewing machine*› enhebrar; ‹*bead*› ensartar; **to ~ sth ONTO sth** ensartar algo EN algo; **to ~ sth THROUGH sth** pasar algo POR algo; ***to ~ one's way*** abrirse* paso; **she ~ed her way through the crowd** se abrió paso entre la multitud

threadbare /ˈθredber || ˈθredbeə(r)/ *adj* gastado, raído

threat /θret/ *n* amenaza *f*; **to make a ~ against sb** amenazar* a algn; **to obtain money with ~s** (AmE Law) obtener* dinero mediante intimidación *or* amenazas; **death ~** amenaza de muerte; **to be under ~** «*way of life*» verse* amenazado; «*factory*» estar* bajo amenaza de cierre

threaten /ˈθretn/ *vt* [1] (menace) ‹*person/life/stability/peace*› amenazar*; **to ~ sb WITH sth** amenazar* a algn CON algo; **they were ~ed with dismissal** los amenazaron con despedirlos *or* con el despido; **the hospital is ~ed with closure** la amenaza de cierre se cierne sobre el hospital, el hospital corre peligro de que lo cierren; **species ~ed with extinction** especies *fpl* amenazadas de extinción [2] (give warning of) ‹*action/violence*› amenazar* con; **to ~ to + INF** «*person*» amenazar* CON + INF; «*problem/unrest*» amenazar* + INF

■ **threaten** *vi* «*danger/storm*» amenazar*

threatening /ˈθretn̩ɪŋ/ *adj* amenazador

threateningly /ˈθretn̩ɪŋli/ *adv* ‹*loiter/gesture*› de modo amenazador, amenazadoramente; ‹*speak*› en tono amenazador

three¹ /θriː/ *n* tres *m*; *see also* **four¹**

three² *adj* tres *adj inv*; *see also* **four²**

three: **~-D** *n* 3D *f*; **the movie's in ~-D** la película es en 3D; **~-day eventing** /ˈθriːˈdeɪ/ *n* [u] certámenes *mpl or* pruebas *fpl* de tres días (*en hípica*); **~-dimensional** /ˈθriːdəˈmentʃnəl, -daɪ- || ˌθriːdaɪˈmenʃənl, -daɪ-/ *adj* tridimensional; **~fold** *adj/adv see* **-fold**; **~-legged** *adj* (*before n*) de tres patas; **~-legged race** *n*: *carrera en que una persona lleva atada una pierna a la del compañero*, carrera *f* de tres pies (Chi); **~pence** /ˈθrepəns, ˈθrə- / *n* tres peniques *mpl*; **~-piece** /ˈθriːˈpiːs/ *adj* (*before n*): **~-piece suit** traje *m* con chaleco, terno *m*; **~-piece suite** juego *m* de living (*de sofá y dos sillones*) (AmL), tresillo *m* (Esp); **~-ply** /ˈθriːˈplaɪ/ *adj* (*before n*) ‹*yarn*› de tres hebras; ‹*wood/tissue*› de tres capas; **~-point turn** *n* (BrE) *maniobra de cambio de sentido de un vehículo en tres movimientos*; **~-quarter** /ˈθriːˈkwɔːrtər || ˌθriːˈkwɔːtə(r)/ *adj* (*before n*): **~-quarter(-length) sleeve** manga *f* tres cuartos

three-quarters¹ /ˈθriːˈkwɔːrtərz || ˌθriːˈkwɔːtəz/ *pron* las tres cuartas partes

three-quarters² *adv*: **it's ~ full** contiene el 75% *or* las tres cuartas partes de su capacidad

threesome /ˈθriːsəm/ *n*: *grupo de tres personas*

three: **~-way** /ˈθriːˈweɪ/ *adj* (*before n*) ‹*junction/valve*› triple; **a ~-way discussion** una discusión entre tres personas (*or* grupos *etc*); **~-wheeler** /ˈθriːˈhwiːlər || ˌθriːˈwiːlə(r)/ *n* (car) coche *m* de tres ruedas; (tricycle) triciclo *m*

threshold /ˈθreʃhəʊld/ *n* [1] (doorway) umbral *m*; ***to be on the ~ of sth*** estar* en el umbral *or* a las puertas de algo [2] (limit) umbral *m*, límite *m*; **pain ~** umbral de dolor; **he has a low boredom ~** aguanta poco sin aburrirse

threw /θruː/ *past of* **throw¹**

thrice /θraɪs/ *adv* (arch & liter) tres veces

thrift /θrɪft/ *n*

A [u] (frugality) economía *f*, ahorro *m*; (*before n*) **~ account** (AmE) cuenta *f* de ahorro(s); **~ shop** (esp AmE) *tienda que vende artículos de segunda mano con fines benéficos*

B [c] (savings bank) (AmE) caja *f* de ahorro(s)

thriftiness /ˈθrɪftinəs || ˈθrɪftɪnɪs/ *n* [u] ▸ **thrift A**

thrifty /ˈθrɪfti/ *adj* **-tier, -tiest** económico, ahorrativo

thrill¹ /θrɪl/ *n* [1] (tremor, wave): **he felt a ~ of fear** se estremeció de miedo [2] (excitement): **meeting her was a real ~** fue verdaderamente emocionante conocerla, me hizo mucha ilusión conocerla (Esp); **he gets a ~ out of the kids' enjoyment** él goza con que los niños disfruten

thrill² *vt* emocionar; **it ~ed me to think that ...** me emocionaba *or* (Esp tb) hacía mucha ilusión pensar que ...; **the prospect doesn't exactly ~ me** la verdad es que la perspectiva no me entusiasma

■ **thrill** *vi* **to ~ TO sth** estremecerse* CON algo

thrilled /θrɪld/ *adj* (*pred*) **to be ~ (ABOUT/WITH sth)** estar* encantado *or* contentísimo *or* (fam) chocho (CON algo); **she was ~ (to bits) with the present** quedó encantada *or* contentísima *or* (fam) chocha con el regalo; **to be ~ to + INF**: **she was ~ to meet him** le encantó *or* (Esp tb) le hizo mucha ilusión conocerlo

thriller /ˈθrɪlər || ˈθrɪlə(r)/ *n* (Cin, Lit) novela *f* (*or* película *f etc*) de misterio *or* de suspenso *or* (Esp) de suspense

thrilling /ˈθrɪlɪŋ/ *adj* emocionante

thrive /θraɪv/ *vi* (*past* **thrived** *or* (liter) **throve**; *past p* **thrived**) «*business/town*» prosperar; «*plant*» crecer* con fuerza; **how is she? — she's thriving!** ¿cómo está? — estupendamente *or* cada día mejor; **to ~ ON sth**: **he ~s on hard work** cuando está mejor es cuando tiene mucho trabajo

thriving /ˈθraɪvɪŋ/ *adj* (*before n*) ‹*business/town*› próspero; **a ~ black market** un floreciente mercado negro

thro' /θruː/ (poet) ▸ **through¹,²**

throat /θrəʊt/ *n* garganta *f*; (neck) cuello *m*; **to clear one's ~** aclararse la voz, carraspear; ***to be at one another's ~s*** estar* como (el) perro y (el) gato; ***to jump down sb's ~*** echársele encima a algn, arremeter contra algn; ***to ram** o **thrust** o **force sth down sb's ~***: **she's always trying to ram** *o* **thrust** *o* **force her ideas down other people's ~s** siempre está tratando de imponerles sus ideas a los demás; ▸ **stick²** *vi* **B**

throaty /ˈθrəʊti/ *adj* **-tier, -tiest** ‹*voice*› ronco; ‹*cough*› de garganta; ‹*laugh/chuckle*› gutural

throb¹ /θrɑːb || θrɒb/ *vi* **-bb-** [1] (pulsate, vibrate) «*heart/pulse*» latir con fuerza; «*engine*» vibrar; **the city ~s with life** la ciudad vibra de actividad [2] (with pain): **his leg was ~bing** tenía un dolor punzante en la pierna; **his wound was ~bing** sentía la sangre latirle en la herida; **my head is ~bing** me va a estallar la cabeza

throb² *n* [1] (of engine) vibración *f*; (of heart) latido *m* [2] (of wound, headache) dolor *m* punzante

throbbing¹ /ˈθrɑːbɪŋ || ˈθrɒbɪŋ/ *adj* (*before n*) ‹*sound/rhythm*› vibrante, palpitante; ‹*pain/ache*› punzante

throbbing² *n* ▸ **throb²**

throes /θrəʊz/ *pl n* [1] (*death ~*) agonía *f*; **to be in one's (death) ~** *o* **in the ~ of death** agonizar*, estar agonizando [2] **in the ~ of**: **the country was in the ~ of civil war** el país estaba sumido en una guerra civil; **we were in the ~ of moving house** estábamos en plena mudanza, estábamos en tren de mudarnos de casa (RPl)

thrombosis /θrɑːmˈbəʊsəs || θrɒmˈbəʊsɪs/ *n* [u c] (*pl* **-ses** /-siːz/) trombosis *f*

throne /θrəʊn/ *n* trono *m*; **to be on/to ascend the ~** ocupar el trono/subir *or* ascender* al trono; **the Swedish ~** la corona sueca; **he remains the power behind the ~** sigue siendo quien detenta realmente el poder

throng¹ /θrɔːŋ || θrɒŋ/ *n* muchedumbre *f*, multitud *f*

throng² *vi*: **fans ~ed into the stadium** los hinchas entraron en tropel al estadio; **people ~ed to see her pass** la gente acudió en masa a verla pasar

■ **throng** *vt* ‹*street/square*› atestar, abarrotar

throttle¹ /ˈθrɑːtl̩ || ˈθrɒtl/ *vt* [1] (strangle) ahogar*, estrangular [2] (gag, silence) ‹*press*› acallar, silenciar

throttle² *n* [1] **~ (valve)** (Mech) regulador *m*, estrangulador *m*; (Auto) acelerador *m* (*que se acciona con la mano*); **at full ~** a toda marcha, a toda máquina [2] (pedal) acelerador *m*

through¹ /θruː/ *prep*

A [1] (from one side to the other) por; **it went right ~ the wall** atravesó la pared de lado a lado; **to hear/feel sth ~ sth** oír*/sentir* algo a través de algo; **he was shot ~ the head** le pegaron un balazo en la cabeza; **the truck crashed ~ the barrier** el camión se llevó la barrera por delante; **they struggled on ~ the crowd** siguieron abriéndose paso entre la multitud; **he spoke ~ clenched teeth** habló entre dientes; **we drove ~ Munich** atravesamos Munich (*en coche*); **she glanced ~ the magazine** hojeó la revista; **I worked my way ~ the textbook** me leí el texto de punta a punta [2] (past, beyond) **to be ~ sth**

t

haber* pasado algo; **we're ~ the preliminary stages already** ya hemos pasado las fases iniciales
B 1 (in time): **we worked ~ the night** trabajamos durante toda la noche; **half-way ~ his speech** en medio de su discurso, cuando iba (*or* vaya *etc*) por la mitad del discurso; **after everything we've been ~ together** después de todo lo que hemos pasado juntos; **~ the centuries** a través de los siglos 2 (until and including) (AmE): **Tuesday ~ Thursday** de martes a jueves; **offer good ~ May 31** oferta válida hasta el 31 de mayo; **October ~ December** desde octubre hasta diciembre inclusive
C (by): **she spoke ~ an interpreter** habló a través de un intérprete; **I heard about it ~ a friend** me enteré a través de *or* por un amigo; **~ his help** gracias a su ayuda *or* mediante su ayuda; **~ no fault of her own** sin tener culpa alguna

through² *adv*
A (from one side to the other): **the train sped ~ without stopping** el tren pasó a toda velocidad sin parar; **he barged ~** pasó dando empujones; **the red paint shows ~** se nota la pintura roja que hay debajo; *see also* **get, pull, put** *etc* **through**
B (in time): **all night ~** durante toda la noche; **we worked ~ without a break** trabajamos sin parar para descansar
C 1 (completely): **wet/soaked ~** mojado/calado hasta los huesos 2 **through and through**: **he's a soldier ~ and ~** es militar hasta la médula

through³ *adj*
A (Transp) (*before n*) ‹*train/route*› directo; **~ traffic** tráfico *m* de paso; **no through road** calle sin salida
B (finished) (colloq) (*pred*): **aren't you ~ yet?** ¿no has terminado aún?; **as a journalist, you're ~** como periodista, estás acabado; **to be ~ WITH sb/sth** haber* terminado CON algn/algo; **to be ~ (WITH) -ING: I'm ~ trying to be nice to you** no pienso seguir tratando de ser amable contigo
C (BrE Telec): **you're ~!** ¡hable!; **we're ~ to Madrid** nos han conectado con Madrid

throughout¹ /θruːˈaʊt/ *prep*
A (all over): **~ Europe/the world** en toda Europa/en todo el mundo *or* en el mundo entero; **there were notices ~ the building** había avisos por todo el edificio
B (in time): **~ the afternoon/the weekend** (durante) toda la tarde/todo el fin de semana; **~ his career** a lo largo de toda su carrera

throughout² *adv* 1 (all over) totalmente; **the house is carpeted/beautifully decorated ~** la casa está totalmente alfombrada/toda la casa tiene una decoración preciosa 2 (in time) desde el principio hasta el fin; **his behavior ~ was irreproachable** su conducta nunca dejó de ser intachable

throughway /ˈθruːweɪ/ *n* (AmE) autopista *f*

throve /θrəʊv/ *past of* **thrive**

throw¹ /θrəʊ/ (*past* **threw**; *past p* **thrown**) *vt*
A 1 ‹*ball/stone*› tirar, aventar* (Col, Méx, Per); ‹*grenade/javelin*› lanzar*; **she threw her beer in his face** le tiró la cerveza a la cara; **she threw the ball back** devolvió la pelota; **to ~ sth AT sth/sb** tirarle algo A algo/algn; **to ~ sth TO sb, to ~ sb sth** tirarle *or* (Col, Méx, Per) aventarle* algo A algn; **he threw her a rope** le echó una cuerda 2 ‹*dice*› echar, tirar; **to ~ a six** sacar* un seis
B (send, propel) (+ *adv compl*): **he threw himself at his opponent** se le echó encima a su adversario, se abalanzó sobre su adversario; **to ~ sb into jail** meter a algn preso *or* en la cárcel; **to ~ sb out of work** echar a algn del trabajo; **to ~ oneself into a task** meterse de lleno en una tarea; ***to ~ sb to the lions* o *wolves*** arrojar a algn a las fieras
C 1 (direct, aim): **a remark ~n into the conversation** un comentario que se deja caer en la conversación 2 (project): **to ~ one's voice** proyectar la voz
D (put, cast): **she threw a blanket over him** le puso *or* le echó una manta encima; **to ~ suspicion on(to) sb** hacer* recaer las sospechas sobre algn
E (unseat) «*horse*» ‹*rider*› desmontar, tirar
F (disconcert) desconcertar*
G (have, hold) ‹*party*› hacer*, dar*; **he threw a fit/tantrum** le dio un ataque/una pataleta
H (operate) ‹*switch/lever*› darle* a
I ‹*pot*› tornear, modelar en un torno
■ **throw** *vi* 1 (project — ball, stone) tirar 2 (— dice) tirar

Phrasal verbs
- **throw around,** (BrE also) **throw about** [v ▸ o ▸ adv, v ▸ adv ▸ o]: **they were in the garden ~ing a ball around** estaban en el jardín jugando con *or* pasándose una pelota; **we were ~n around in the back of the van** nos íbamos sacudiendo en la parte de atrás de la camioneta; **to ~ one's money around** despilfarrar *or* derrochar el dinero
- **throw aside** [v ▸ o ▸ adv, v ▸ adv ▸ o] 1 (to one side) ‹*logs/stones/person*› echar a un lado 2 (push back) ‹*sheets/blankets*› echar hacia atrás
- **throw away** [v ▸ o ▸ adv, v ▸ adv ▸ o] 1 (discard) ‹*can/paper*› tirar (a la basura), botar (a la basura) (AmL exc RPl) 2 (waste) ‹*opportunity*› desaprovechar, desperdiciar; ‹*money*› malgastar, despilfarrar, tirar, botar (AmL exc RPl)
- **throw back** [v ▸ o ▸ adv, v ▸ adv ▸ o] 1 ‹*ball*› devolver*; **she threw back at me everything I'd said** me echó en cara todo lo que había dicho 2 (pull back) ‹*curtains*› (des)correr; ‹*bedclothes*› echar atrás
- **throw back on** [v ▸ adv ▸ prep ▸ o] (*usu pass*): **we were ~n back on our wits/our own resources** tuvimos que valernos de nuestro ingenio/nuestros recursos
- **throw down** [v ▸ adv ▸ o] ‹*object*› tirar, lanzar* (*hacia abajo*); ‹*challenge*› lanzar*
- **throw in** [v ▸ o ▸ adv, v ▸ adv ▸ o] 1 (contribute) ‹*remark*› hacer* 2 (include): **take them all and I'll ~ this radio in free!** si los lleva todos, le doy esta radio de regalo *or* (AmL) de ñapa *or* (CS, Per tb) de yapa; ***to ~ in the sponge* o *towel*** tirar la esponja *or* la toalla
- **throw off** [v ▸ o ▸ adv, v ▸ adv ▸ o] 1 ‹*jacket/hat*› quitarse (*rápidamente*) 2 (rid oneself of) ‹*illness/habit*› quitarse; ‹*pursuer*› despistar, zafarse de; ‹*doubts/burden*› librarse de, deshacerse* de
- **throw on** [v ▸ o ▸ adv, v ▸ adv ▸ o] 1 ‹*coat/shirt*› echarse encima, ponerse* (*rápidamente*) 2 ‹*wood/coal*› echar
- **throw out**

A [v ▸ o ▸ adv, v ▸ adv ▸ o] 1 (discard) tirar (a la basura), botar (a la basura) (AmL exc RPl) 2 (reject) ‹*bill/proposal*› rechazar 3 (in baseball) ‹*runner*› sacar*, poner* en out
B [v ▸ o ▸ adv, v ▸ adv ▸ o] (expel, eject) echar; (out of college, country) expulsar, echar
C [v ▸ o ▸ adv] (make wrong) ‹*calculations/arrangements*› desbaratar
- **throw together** [v ▸ o ▸ adv, v ▸ adv ▸ o] 1 (assemble) improvisar; **I just threw a few things together and we left** metí un par de cosas en una bolsa y nos fuimos 2 (bring into contact): **fate had ~n us together** había querido el destino que nuestros caminos se cruzaran
- **throw up**

Sense I [v ▸ adv ▸ o]
A (raise) ‹*hands*› levantar, alzar*
B 1 (produce) ‹*results*› arrojar, dar*; ‹*difficulty*› presentar 2 (bring to light) ‹*facts/discrepancies*› revelar (la existencia de), poner* en evidencia
C (abandon) (colloq) ‹*job/studies*› dejar

Sense II [v ▸ adv] (vomit) (colloq) devolver*, arrojar, vomitar

throw² *n*
A 1 (of ball) tiro *m*; (of javelin, discus) lanzamiento *m* 2 (of dice) tirada *f*, lance *m*; **it's your ~** te toca tirar
B (AmE) 1 (bedspread) cubrecama *m* 2 (shawl) chal *m*, echarpe *m*
C (sl) **a ~** cada uno; **they cost *o* are $17 a ~** cuestan 17 dólares cada uno

throw: **~away** *adj* (*before n*) 1 (disposable) ‹*cup/container*› desechable, de usar y tirar 2 (casual) ‹*remark*› hecho como de pasada; **~back** *n* 1 **~back (TO sth)**: **this year's styles are a ~back to the twenties** los estilos de este año son una vuelta a la moda de los años veinte 2 (Biol) atavismo *m*; **~-in** *n* (in soccer, basketball) saque *m* de banda; (in baseball) lanzamiento *m*

thrown /θrəʊn/ *past p of* **throw¹**

thru /θruː/ *adv/prep* (AmE) ▸ **through¹,²**

thrush /θrʌʃ/ *n*
A [c] (bird) tordo *m*, zorzal *m*
B [u] (Med) aftas *fpl*

thrust¹ /θrʌst/ (*past & past p* **thrust**) *vt* (push) empujar; (push out) sacar*; (insert) clavar; **she ~ her head out of the window** sacó la cabeza por la ventana; **to ~ sth AT sb**: **she ~ the book at me** me tendió el libro bruscamente *or* con agresividad; **to ~ sth INTO sth**: **he ~ his knife into**

t

the bundle/his hands into his pockets clavó su cuchillo en el fardo/se metió las manos en los bolsillos

(Phrasal verbs)

- **thrust aside** [v ▸ o ▸ adv, v ▸ adv ▸ o] ‹*object/person*› hacer* a un lado, apartar (*bruscamente*)
- **thrust on, thrust upon** [v ▸ o ▸ prep ▸ o]: **the role of mediator was ~ on her by circumstances** las circunstancias le impusieron el papel de mediadora; **he ~ himself on us** nos impuso su presencia, se nos pegó (fam)

thrust² *n*
A [c] 1 (with sword) estocada *f* 2 (push) empujón *m* 3 (attack, advance) ofensiva *f*
B [c] (general direction): **the (main) ~ of the report is that ...** la idea central del informe es que ...
C [u] (impetus) empuje *m*, fuerza *f*

thrusting /'θrʌstɪŋ/ *adj* (BrE) (*before n*) ambicioso

thruway /'θru:weɪ/ *n* (AmE) autopista *f*

thud¹ /θʌd/ *n* ruido *m* sordo

thud² *vi* **-dd-** caer* (*or* chocar* *etc*) con un golpe *or* ruido sordo

thug /θʌg/ *n* matón *m*

thumb¹ /θʌm/ *n* pulgar *m*, dedo *m* gordo (fam); **to suck one's ~** chuparse el dedo; ***to be all ~s*** *o* (BrE also) ***all fingers and ~s***: **I'm all ~s today** hoy estoy muy torpe con las manos; ***to be under sb's ~*** estar* dominado por algn; ***to get the ~s down/up from sb*** ser* rechazado por algn/recibir la aprobación de algn; ***to give the ~s up/down to sth*** aprobar*/rechazar* algo; ***to stick out like a sore ~*** «*building/person/object*» desentonar terriblemente, no pegar* ni con cola (fam); ***to twiddle one's ~s*** estar* sin hacer nada, estar* perdiendo el tiempo; ▸**green¹ A**

thumb² *vt* 1 : **I ~ed a lift** *o* (AmE also) **a ride home** me fui a casa a dedo (fam), me fui a casa de aventón (Col, Méx) 2 ‹*book*› hojear; **a well ~ed book** un libro muy usado

(Phrasal verb)

- **thumb through** [v ▸ prep ▸ o] hojear

thumb: ~ index *n* índice *m* recortado; **~nail** *n* uña *f* del pulgar; (*before n*) **~nail sketch** pequeña reseña *f*; **~print** *n* huella *f* *or* impresión *f* digital (*del pulgar*); **~screw** *n* empulgueras *fpl*; **~tack** *n* (AmE) tachuela *f*, chinche *m* (Andes), chinche *f* (AmC, Méx, RPl), chincheta *f* (Esp)

thump¹ /θʌmp/ *n* 1 (sound) golpazo *m* 2 (blow) golpazo *m*, mamporro *m* (fam)

thump² *vt* golpear; **he ~ed the table with his fist** pegó un puñetazo en la mesa; **I ~ed him one** (colloq) le pegué un puñetazo
■ **thump** *vi*: **to ~ on a wall/door** dar* unos golpes en una pared/puerta; **her heart was ~ing** el corazón le latía con fuerza

thumping /'θʌmpɪŋ/ *adj* (colloq) (*before n*) ‹*victory/majority*› aplastante; **I've got a ~ headache** me va a estallar la cabeza; **a ~ great suitcase/pay rise** (*as adv*) (BrE) una maleta/un aumento descomunal

thunder¹ /'θʌndər || 'θʌndə(r)/ *n* 1 [u] (Meteo) truenos *mpl*; **a clap of ~** un trueno; ***to look like ~*** *o* ***as black as ~*** tener* cara de pocos amigos, estar* echando chispas; ***to steal sb's ~*** quitarle la primicia a algn 2 [c] (sound): **the ~ of the traffic** el estruendo del tráfico

thunder² *v impers* tronar*
■ **thunder** *vi* (move loudly): **they ~ed up the stairs** subieron las escaleras ruidosamente; **the train ~ed through the station** el tren pasó por la estación con gran estruendo
■ **thunder** *vt* (shout): **get out! he ~ed** —¡fuera de aquí! —bramó *or* rugió

thunder: ~bolt *n* rayo *m*; **her appointment came as a ~bolt** su nombramiento cayó como una bomba; **~clap** *n* trueno *m*; **~cloud** *n* nubarrón *m*

thunderous /'θʌndərəs/ *adj* atronador, estruendoso

thunder: ~storm *n* tormenta *f* eléctrica; **~struck** *adj* (*pred*) atónito, estupefacto

thundery /'θʌndəri/ *adj* tormentoso

Thurs, Thur (= **Thursday**) juev.

Thursday /'θɜ:rzdeɪ, -di || 'θɜ:zdeɪ, -di/ *n* jueves *m*; *see also* **Monday**

thus /ðʌs/ *adv*
A 1 (in this way) (frml) así, de este modo 2 (by this means) (*as linker*): **she refused, ~ provoking a storm of protest** se negó, provocando con ello una lluvia de protestas
B (consequently) (*as linker*) por lo tanto, por consiguiente (frml)
C thus far (frml) (up to here) hasta aquí; (up to there) hasta allí; (up to now) hasta ahora; (up to then) hasta entonces

thwack /θwæk/ *n* 1 (blow) golpe *m*, porrazo *m* (fam) 2 (sound) zurriagazo *m*

thwart /θwɔ:rt || θwɔ:t/ *vt* ‹*plan/attempt*› frustrar; **the police managed to ~ the robbers** la policía logró burlar a los ladrones

thy /ðaɪ/ *adj* (arch *or* dial *or* liter) tu

thyme /taɪm/ *n* [u] tomillo *m*

thyroid (gland) /'θaɪrɔɪd/ *n* tiroides *f*, glándula *f* tiroidea

thyself /ðaɪ'self/ *pron* (arch *or* dial *or* liter): **know ~** conócete a ti mismo

ti /ti:/ *n* (Mus) si *m*

tiara /ti'ɑ:rə/ *n* diadema *f*

Tibet /tɪ'bet/ *n* el Tíbet

Tibetan¹ /tɪ'betn̩/ *adj* tibetano

Tibetan² *n* 1 [c] (person) tibetano, -na *m,f* 2 [u] (language) tibetano *m*

tic /tɪk/ *n* tic *m*

tick¹ /tɪk/ *n*
A [c] 1 (sound) tic *m*; **~, tock** tic, tac 2 (moment) (BrE colloq) segundito *m*; **I'll be back in half a ~** *o* **in a ~** *o* **in two ~s** enseguida vuelvo
B [c] (Zool) garrapata *f*
C [c] (mark) (BrE) marca *f*, visto *m*, tic *m*, palomita *f* (Méx)
D [u] (credit) (BrE colloq): **to buy sth on ~** comprar algo (de) fiado (fam)

tick² *vi* «*clock/watch*» hacer* tictac; **the seconds ~ed away** pasaban los segundos; ***what makes sb ~***: **I'd like to know what makes him ~** me gustaría saber qué es lo que lo mueve
■ **tick** *vt* (BrE) ‹*name/answer*› marcar* (*con un visto or una palomita etc*)

(Phrasal verbs)

- **tick off** [v ▸ o ▸ adv, v ▸ adv ▸ o] 1 (annoy) (AmE colloq) fastidiar; **to be ~ed off WITH sb** estar* enojado *or* (esp Esp) enfadado CON algn; **to be ~ed off WITH sth** estar* harto DE algo 2 (mark with tick) (esp BrE) marcar*, ponerle* visto a (Esp) 3 (scold) (BrE colloq) regañar, reñir* (esp Esp), retar (CS), rezongar* (AmC, Ur), resondrar (Per)
- **tick over** [v ▸ adv] «*engine*» estar* en marcha, marchar al ralentí; **the business is just ~ing over** (esp BrE) el negocio va tirando (fam)

ticker /'tɪkər || 'tɪkə(r)/ *n*
A (tape machine) (AmE) teleimpresora *f*
B (heart) (colloq) corazón *m*

ticker tape *n* [u] cinta *f* de teleimpresora; (*before n*) **a ticker-tape parade** (in US) un desfile triunfal

ticket /'tɪkət || 'tɪkɪt/ *n*
A (for bus, train) boleto *m* *or* (Esp) billete *m*; (for plane) pasaje *m* *or* (Esp) billete *m*; (for theater, museum etc) entrada *f*; (for baggage, coat etc) ticket *m*; (from cleaner's, repair shop etc) ticket *m*, resguardo *m*; (for lottery) billete *m*, número *m*; (for parking) ticket *m*; **that role was his ~ to fame** ese papel fue su pasaporte a la fama; ***to be (just) the ~*** (colloq): **this screwdriver is just the ~** este destornillador es justo lo que se necesita; (*before n*) **~ collector** revisor, -sora *m,f*; **~ office** (Transp) mostrador *m* (*or* ventanilla *f* *etc*) de venta de pasajes (*or* billetes *etc*); (Theat) taquilla *f*, boletería *f* (AmL); **~ taker** (AmE Sport, Theat) portero, -ra *m,f*
B 1 (label) etiqueta *f* 2 (for traffic violation) multa *f*
C (Pol) 1 (list of candidates) lista *f* 2 (policy) programa *m* (político *or* electoral)

ticket: ~holder /'tɪkət,həʊldər || 'tɪkɪt,həʊldə(r)/ *n*: *persona en posesión de una entrada, boleto, billete etc*; **~-machine** *n* máquina *f* expendedora de boletos *or* (Esp) billetes

ticking /'tɪkɪŋ/ *n* [u] 1 (of clock) tictac *m* 2 (Tex) cutí *m* (*tela de colchones*)

ticking-off /'tɪkɪŋ'ɔ:f || ,tɪkɪŋ'ɒf/ *n* (*pl* **tickings-off** /-ɪŋz-/) (BrE colloq) regaño *m* *or* (Esp fam) rapapolvo *m* *or* (CS fam) café *m*; **to give sb a ~** pegarle* a algn un regaño, echarle a algn un rapapolvo (Esp fam), darle* a algn un café (CS fam)

tickle[1] /ˈtɪkəl/ *vt* **1** ‹*person*› hacerle* cosquillas a **2** (amuse, please) hacerle* gracia a; ***to be ~d pink*** (colloq) estar* chocho (fam), estar* contentísimo

■ **tickle** *vi* «*wool/beard*» picar*; **stop it: that ~s!** ¡basta, que me hace cosquillas!

tickle[2] *n* cosquilleo *m*; **I have a ~ in my throat** tengo un picor en la garganta, me pica la garganta

tickler /ˈtɪklər || ˈtɪklə(r)/ *n* (AmE) recordatorio *m*, ayuda memoria *m*

ticklish /ˈtɪklɪʃ/ *adj* **1** ‹*person*›: **to be ~** tener* cosquillas, ser* cosquilloso *or* (Méx) cosquilludo **2** ‹*problem/situation*› peliagudo, delicado

tick: **~tacktoe** /ˈtɪktækˈtəʊ/ *n* [u] ▸**tic-tac-toe**; **~tock** /ˈtɪkˈtɑːk || ˈtɪk,tɒk/ *n* tictac *m*

ticky-tacky /ˈtɪkiˈtæki/ *adj* (AmE colloq) ‹*houses/furniture*› hecho de cartón

tic-tac-toe /ˈtɪktækˈtəʊ/ *n* [u] (AmE) tres en raya *m*, tres en línea *m* (Col), ta-te-ti *m* (RPl), gato *m* (Chi, Méx)

tidal /ˈtaɪdl̩/ *adj* ‹*river/estuary*› con régimen de marea

tidal wave *n* maremoto *m*

tidbit /ˈtɪdbɪt/ *n* (AmE) ▸**titbit**

tiddler /ˈtɪdlər || ˈtɪdlə(r)/ *n* (BrE colloq) pececito *m*

tiddly /ˈtɪdli/ *adj* **-lier, -liest** (colloq) (tipsy) alegre, achispado

tiddlywinks /ˈtɪdliwɪŋks/ *n* [u] juego *m* de las pulgas

tide /taɪd/ *n*

A (Geog) marea *f*; **the ~ is in/out** la marea está alta/baja; **high/low ~** marea alta/baja; **at high/low ~** en pleamar/bajamar

B (current, movement) corriente *f*; **the rising ~ of violence** la creciente oleada de violencia; ***the ~ is turning/has turned*** (lit: at high or low water) está cambiando/ha cambiado la marea; **the ~ has turned in his favor** las cosas se están poniendo a su favor; ***to swim against the ~*** ir* *or* navegar* contra la corriente; ▸**time**[1] *Sense* **IA**

Phrasal verb

- **tide over** [v ▸ o ▸ adv]: **this should ~ us over until next month** nos arreglaremos con esto hasta el próximo mes

tide: **~land** *n* (AmE) *tierra que queda cubierta cuando la marea está alta*; **~mark** *n* (Geog) *marca que deja la marea*; (around bath, on neck) (BrE colloq) marca *f or* cerco *m* de mugre

tidily /ˈtaɪdl̩i || ˈtaɪdɪli/ *adv* ordenadamente, prolijamente (RPl)

tidiness /ˈtaɪdinəs || ˈtaɪdɪnɪs/ *n* [u] orden *m*, prolijidad *f* (RPl)

tidy[1] /ˈtaɪdi/ *adj* **tidier, tidiest**

A ‹*room/cupboard/person*› ordenado, prolijo (RPl); ‹*garden/lawn*› bien cuidado; ‹*appearance*› arreglado, pulcro

B (considerable) (colloq) (*before n*) ‹*sum/profit*› bonito (fam), considerable

tidy[2] **tidies, tidying, tidied** *vt* arreglar, ordenar

Phrasal verbs

- **tidy away** [v ▸ o ▸ adv, v ▸ adv ▸ o] (esp BrE) ‹*toys/papers*› recoger*, ordenar, poner* en su sitio
- **tidy out** [v ▸ o ▸ adv, v ▸ adv ▸ o] ‹*room/cupboard*› (vaciar* y) ordenar
- **tidy up**

A [v ▸ o ▸ adv, v ▸ adv ▸ o] ‹*room/desk*› ordenar, arreglar; ‹*toys*› ordenar, recoger*; **to ~ oneself up** arreglarse

B [v ▸ adv] ordenar

tie[1] /taɪ/ *n*

A (Clothing) **1** (*neck~*) corbata *f*; **to tie one's ~** hacerse* el nudo de la corbata; (*before n*) **~ rack** corbatero *m* **2** (on clothing) lazo *m*

B **1** (bond) lazo *m*, vínculo *m*; **blood ~s** lazos *mpl* de parentesco; **diplomatic ~s** relaciones *fpl* diplomáticas; **I have no ~s here** no hay nada que me retenga aquí **2** (obligation, constraint) atadura *f*; **family ~s** obligaciones *fpl* familiares

C (Sport) **1** (equal score) empate *m*; (*before n*) **~ game/match** (AmE) empate *m* **2** (*cup ~*) (BrE) partido *m* de copa

tie[2] **ties, tying, tied** *vt*

A **1** (make) ‹*knot/bow*› hacer* **2** (fasten) ‹*shoelaces/parcel*› atar, amarrar (AmL exc RPl); **she ~d the dog to the tree** ató *or* (AmL exc RPl) amarró el perro al árbol; **she ~d her hair back** se recogió el pelo; **his hands were ~d together** tenía las manos atados; ***to be fit to be ~d*** (AmE colloq) estar* hecho una furia; ***with one arm*** *o* ***hand ~d behind one's back*** (easily) (colloq) con los ojos cerrados

B **1** (link) **to ~ sth TO/WITH sth** relacionar *or* ligar* algo CON algo **2** (restrict) ‹*person*› atar; **she's tied to a strict timetable** está obligada a cumplir un horario estricto

C (Games, Sport) ‹*game*› empatar

■ **tie** *vi*

A (fasten) «*dress/apron*» atarse

B (draw) «*teams/contestants*» empatar; **they ~d for second place** ambos consiguieron el segundo puesto

Phrasal verbs

- **tie down**

A [v ▸ o ▸ adv, v ▸ adv ▸ o] ‹*load/prisoner*› atar, amarrar (AmL exc RPl)

B [v ▸ o ▸ adv] **1** (restrict, limit) atar **2** (oblige, commit): **the minister refused to be ~d down** el ministro no quiso comprometerse

- **tie in** [v ▸ adv] (agree, coincide) **to ~ in (WITH sth)** concordar* *or* cuadrar (CON algo)
- **tie up**

Sense **I** [v ▸ o ▸ adv, v ▸ adv ▸ o]

A ‹*parcel/animal*› atar, amarrar (AmL exc RPl); ***to ~ up loose ends*** atar cabos sueltos

B **1** (keep busy) **to be ~d up** estar* ocupado **2** (make unavailable) ‹*capital/assets*› inmovilizar*; **all our money is ~d up in property** todo nuestro dinero está invertido *or* metido en bienes raíces **3** (impede) (AmE) ‹*traffic/project*› paralizar*, parar

C (finalize) (BrE) ‹*deal*› cerrar*; ‹*arrangements*› finalizar*

D (connect) **to be ~d up WITH sth** estar* ligado A *or* relacionado CON algo

Sense **II** [v ▸ adv] (Naut) atracar*

tie: **~break** *n* ▸**~breaker 1**; **~breaker** *n* **1** (in tennis) muerte *f* súbita **2** (in quiz game) pregunta *f* de desempate **3** (casting vote) (AmE) voto *m* de calidad

tied /taɪd/ *adj* (drawn) empatado

tie: **~-in** *n* (connection) conexión *f*, relación *f*; **~pin** *n* alfiler *m* de corbata, fistol *m* (Méx)

tier /tɪr || tɪə(r)/ *n* **1** (row, layer) hilera *f* superpuesta; **the seats are arranged in ~s** los asientos son en gradas **2** (of cake) piso *m* **3** (in hierarchy) escalón *m*, nivel *m*

tiered /tɪrd || tɪəd/ *adj* ‹*seats*› en gradas; **a three-~ cake** un pastel de tres pisos

tie: **~ tack** *n* (AmE) alfiler *m* de corbata, fistol *m* (Méx); **~-up** *n* **1** (connection) conexión *f*; **2** (stoppage, jam) (AmE) embotellamiento *m*

tiff /tɪf/ *n* pelea *f*, riña *f*

tiger /ˈtaɪgər || ˈtaɪgə(r)/ *n* (*pl* **~s** *or* **~**) tigre *m*

tiger economy *n* economía *f* emergente, economía *f* tigre

tight[1] /taɪt/ *adj* **-er, -est**

A **1** (fitting closely) ‹*dress/skirt*› ajustado, ceñido; (if uncomfortable, unsightly) apretado **2** (stiff, hard to move) ‹*screw/bolt*› apretado, duro **3** (with nothing to spare) ‹*margin*› estrecho; ‹*schedule*› apretado; **there's room for four, but it's a ~ squeeze** caben cuatro, pero bastante apretados; **to be on a ~ budget** tener* un presupuesto muy limitado; **money's ~** están (*or* estamos *etc*) apretados *or* escasos de dinero **4** (close) ‹*game/finish*› reñido **5** (restricted): **I can't breathe; my chest feels ~** no puedo respirar, siento una opresión en el pecho

B **1** (firm) ‹*embrace*› estrecho, apretado, fuerte **2** (strict) ‹*security/control*› estricto; **he keeps a ~ hold on expenditure** mantiene estricto control sobre los gastos

C **1** (sharp) ‹*bend*› cerrado **2** (closely formed) ‹*knot/knitting*› apretado

D **1** (taut) ‹*cord/thread*› tirante, tenso **2** (not leaky) ‹*seal*› hermético

E (difficult, problematic) ‹*situation*› difícil

F (colloq) **1** (mean) ▸**tightfisted** **2** (drunk) (*pred*) borracho, como una cuba (fam); **to get ~** emborracharse

tight[2] *adv*: **hold (on) ~!** ¡agárrate bien *or* fuerte!; **screw the lid on ~** aprieta bien el tapón; **sleep ~!** ¡que duermas bien!; **we'll have to sit ~ and see what happens** vamos a tener que esperar a ver qué pasa

t

tightassed /'taɪt'æst || ,taɪt'ɑːst/ *adj* (AmE sl) 1 (unwilling to relax) reprimido 2 (mean) ▸ **tightfisted**

tighten /'taɪtn̩/ *vt* 1 ‹nut/bolt/knot› apretar*; ‹rope› tensar; **to ~ one's belt** apretarse* el cinturón; **he ~ed his hold on my arm** me apretó más el brazo, me agarró el brazo más fuerte 2 (make stricter) ‹regulations› hacer* más estricto *or* rígido; **security has been ~ed** se han tomado medidas de seguridad más estrictas

■ **tighten** *vi* «muscles» tensarse; «knot» apretarse*

Phrasal verb

• **tighten up**

A [v ▸ o ▸ adv, v ▸ adv ▸ o] ‹laws/rules› hacer* más estricto; **to ~ up security** reforzar* las medidas de seguridad

B [v ▸ adv] 1 (become stricter) ponerse* más severo *or* estricto; **to ~ up on sth**: **they've ~ed up on expenses** están controlando más los gastos 2 «muscles» ponerse* tenso, tensarse

tight: **~fisted** /'taɪt'fɪstəd || ,taɪt'fɪstɪd/ *adj* (colloq) agarrado (fam), amarrete (AmS fam), pinche (AmC fam), pichirre (Ven fam); **~fitting** /'taɪt'fɪtɪŋ/ *adj* ‹jeans› ajustado, ceñido; **~-knit** /'taɪt'nɪt/ *adj* muy unido; **~-lipped** /taɪt'lɪpt/ *adj* ‹silence› hermético; ‹anger/disapproval› mudo; **they sat ~-lipped throughout the skit** vieron todo el número sin abrir la boca *or* sin decir palabra

tightly /'taɪtli/ *adv*: **it must be ~ tied/fastened** hay que atarlo fuerte/asegurarlo bien; **he was holding her hand ~** la tenía agarrada fuerte de la mano; **a ~ controlled process** un proceso estrictamente *or* rigurosamente controlado

tightness /'taɪtnəs || 'taɪtnɪs/ *n* [u]

A (of clothes, shoes) lo ajustado *or* ceñido; (if uncomfortable) lo apretado

B 1 (of hold, grip) lo fuerte 2 (of control, security) rigurosidad *f*, lo estricto

C (in one's chest) opresión *f*; **he felt (a) ~ in his chest** sentía una opresión en el pecho

tightrope /'taɪtrəʊp/ *n* cuerda *f* floja; **to walk a ~** caminar por la cuerda floja, maromear (Col, Méx, Ven); (*before n*) **~ walker** funámbulo, -la *m,f*, equilibrista *mf*

tights /taɪts/ *pl n* 1 (for ballet etc) malla(s) *f(pl)*, leotardo(s) *m(pl)* 2 (BrE) ▸ **pantyhose**

tightwad /'taɪtwɑːd || 'taɪtwɒd/ *n* (AmE colloq) apretado, -da *m,f* (fam), agarrado, -da *m,f* (fam), amarrete, -ta *m,f* (AmS fam)

tigress /'taɪgrəs || 'taɪgrɪs/ *n* tigresa *f*

tile[1] /taɪl/ *n* 1 (for floor) baldosa *f*, losa *f*; (for wall) azulejo *m* 2 (for roof) (BrE) teja *f*; ***on the ~s*** (BrE) de juerga *or* parranda (fam)

tile[2] *vt* ‹roof› tejar; ‹floor› embaldosar; ‹wall› revestir* de azulejos, azulejar, alicatar (Esp)

tiling /'taɪlɪŋ/ *n* [u] (on roof) tejado *m*; (on floor) embaldosado *m*; (on wall) azulejos *mpl*, alicatado *m* (Esp)

till[1] /tɪl/ *conj/prep* ▸ **until**[1,2]

till[2] *n* (cash register) caja *f* (registradora); (drawer) caja *f*; ***to have one's fingers/hand in the ~*** (colloq) estar* robando dinero de la caja

till[3] *vt* cultivar, labrar

tiller /'tɪlər || 'tɪlə(r)/ *n* (Naut) caña *f or* barra *f* del timón; **at the ~** al timón

tilt[1] /tɪlt/ *vt* inclinar; **he ~ed his head to one side** ladeó la cabeza; **to ~ sth back/forward** inclinar algo hacia atrás/adelante

■ **tilt** *vi* (slope) inclinarse; **the chair nearly ~ed over** la silla casi se cae para atrás

tilt[2] *n* [u c] (slope) inclinación *f*; **sideways ~** ladeo *m*; ***(at) full ~*** a toda velocidad, a toda máquina, a todo trapo

timber /'tɪmbər || 'tɪmbə(r)/ *n* 1 [u] (material) madera *f* (*para construcción*); ***to be managerial ~*** (esp AmE) tener* madera de directivo; (*before n*) ‹house› de madera; **the ~ trade** la industria maderera; **~ yard** (BrE) almacén *m* de maderas 2 [u] (trees) árboles *mpl* (madereros); **~!** (*as interj*) ¡cuidado(, que cae)! 3 [c] (beam) viga *f*, madero *m*

timberland /'tɪmbərlænd || 'tɪmbəlænd/ *n* [u] (AmE) terreno *m* maderero

time[1] /taɪm/ *n*

Sense I

A [u] (past, present, future) tiempo *m*; **~ and space** el tiempo y el espacio; **as ~ goes by** *o* **passes** a medida que pasa el tiempo, con el paso *or* el correr del tiempo; **at this point** *o* **moment in ~** en este momento, en el momento presente; **(only) ~ will tell** el tiempo (lo) dirá; **how ~ flies!** ¡qué rápido pasa el tiempo!; ***(from) ~ out of mind*** desde tiempos inmemoriales; ***~ and tide wait for no man*** el tiempo pasa inexorablemente; (*before n*) ‹travel› en el tiempo; **~ machine** máquina *f* del tiempo

B [u] (time available, necessary for sth) tiempo *m*; **we have all the ~ in the world** tenemos tiempo de sobra; **could I have five minutes of your ~?** ¿podría concederme cinco minutos?; **there's no ~ to lose** no hay tiempo que perder; **to make ~ for sth** hacer(se)* *or* encontrar* tiempo para algo; **to make ~** (hurry) (AmE colloq) darse* prisa, apurarse (AmL); **he does it to pass the ~** lo hace para pasar el tiempo; **I spend all my ~ reading/thinking** me paso todo el tiempo leyendo/pensando; **it takes ~ to get used to the climate** lleva *or* toma tiempo acostumbrarse al clima; **it's worth taking a little extra ~ over the job** vale la pena dedicarle un poco más de tiempo al trabajo; **to take one's ~**: **just take your ~** tómate todo el tiempo que necesites *or* quieras; **you took your ~!** ¡cómo has tardado!; ***to buy ~*** ganar tiempo; ***to have a lot of/no ~ for sb/sth***: **I have no ~ for people like her** no soporto a la gente como ella; **I've got a lot of ~ for him** me cae muy bien; ***to have ~ on one's hands***: **I had ~ on my hands** me sobraba el tiempo; ***to play for ~*** tratar de ganar tiempo

C (*no pl*) (period — of days, months, years) tiempo *m*; (— of hours) rato *m*; **that was a long ~ ago** eso fue hace mucho (tiempo); **they lived in Paris for a ~/for a long ~** vivieron un tiempo/mucho tiempo *or* muchos años en París; **long ~ no see!** (colloq) ¡tanto tiempo (sin verte)!; **some ~ later I saw them leave** al rato los vi salir; **some ~ later they moved to Brussels** (un) tiempo después se mudaron a Bruselas, tras cierto tiempo se mudaron a Bruselas; **for some considerable ~** *o* **for quite some ~ now there have been rumors that ...** hace ya bastante tiempo que se rumorea que ...; **in an hour's/three months'/ten years' ~** dentro de una hora/tres meses/diez años; **cooking ~** tiempo *m* de cocción; **your ~'s up** se te (*or* les *etc*) ha acabado el tiempo; ***for the ~ being*** por el momento, de momento; ***to serve*** *o* (colloq) ***do ~*** cumplir una condena, estar* a la sombra (fam)

D (*in phrases*) **against time** contra reloj; **all the time** (constantly) constantemente; (the whole period) todo el tiempo; **I knew it all the ~** lo supe desde el principio; **in time** (early enough) a tiempo; (eventually) con el tiempo; **you arrived just in ~** llegaste justo a tiempo; **we got back in ~ to watch the film** volvimos a tiempo para ver la película; **you'll get used to it in ~** con el tiempo te acostumbrarás; **in good time** con tiempo; **all in good ~** cada cosa a su tiempo, todo a su debido tiempo; **in no time (at all)** rapidísimo, en un abrir y cerrar de ojos, en un santiamén

E [u] (*air~*) (Rad, TV) espacio *m*

F [u c] (for journey, race, task) tiempo *m*; **what's your fastest ~ over 400m?** ¿cuál es tu mejor tiempo *or* marca en los 400 metros?

G [u] (with respect to work): **to take** *o* (BrE also) **have ~ off** tomarse tiempo libre; **we get ~ and a half** nos pagan hora y media de sueldo por cada hora trabajada

H 1 [c] (epoch, age) (*often pl*) época *f*, tiempo *m*; **at one ~** en una época *or* un tiempo, en otros tiempos; **in ~s of crisis** en épocas *or* tiempos de crisis; **in former ~s** antiguamente; **in Tudor ~s** en la época de los Tudor, en tiempos de los Tudor; **there was a ~ when** *o* **~ was when ...** hubo un tiempo cuando ...; **it's a sign of the ~s** es un indicio de los tiempos en que vivimos; **in ~s to come** en el futuro, en tiempos venideros; ***to be ahead of one's ~***: **he's ahead/he was ahead of his ~** se ha adelantado/se adelantó a su época; ***to be behind the ~s*** «ideas» ser* anticuado, estar* desfasado; «person» estar* atrasado de noticias (fam); ***to keep up with*** *o* ***abreast of the ~s*** mantenerse* al día 2 [u] (with respect to a person's life): **that was before your ~** eso fue antes de que tú nacieras (*or* empezaras a trabajar aquí *etc*); **it won't happen in our ~** no viviremos para verlo; **I've seen some funny things in my ~ but ...** he visto cosas raras en mi vida pero ...; **she**

was a great athlete in her ~ fue una gran atleta en su época

(Sense II)

A 1 [u] (by clock) hora *f*; **what's the ~?, what ~ is it?** ¿qué hora es?; **do you have the ~?** ¿tienes hora?; **the ~ is ten minutes to ten** son las diez menos diez minutos, son diez para las diez (AmL exc RPl); **to be able to tell the ~** *o* (AmE also) **tell ~** saber* (decir) la hora; **British Summer T~** horario *m* de verano; **Eastern Standard T~** (in US) hora *f* de la costa atlántica; **this clock keeps good ~** este reloj está siempre en hora; ***not to give sb the ~ of day*** no darle* a algn ni la hora; ***to pass the ~ of day (with sb)***: **now she never even passes the ~ of day with me** ahora ni siquiera me saluda; **we passed the ~ of day** charlamos un ratito; (*before n*) **~ switch** temporizador *m*; **~ zone** huso *m* horario 2 [c u] (of event) hora *f*; **do you know the ~s of the trains?** ¿sabes el horario de los trenes?; **~ FOR sth/to + INF**: **we have to arrange a ~ for the next meeting** tenemos que fijar una fecha y hora para la próxima reunión; **is it ~ to go yet?** ¿ya es hora de irse?; **it's ~ you left** *o* **you were leaving** es hora de que te vayas; **at breakfast ~** a la hora del desayuno

B [c] (point in time): **at this ~ of (the) year** en esta época del año; **at this ~ of night** a estas horas de la noche; **at the present/this particular ~** en este momento/este preciso momento; **at no ~ was that my intention** en ningún momento fue ésa mi intención; **it should be kept closed at all ~s** debe mantenerse siempre cerrado; **at the best of ~s** en el mejor de los casos; **this ~ next year** el año que viene para estas fechas; **it'll be dark by the ~ we get there** (para) cuando lleguemos ya estará oscuro; **by that** *o* **this ~ we were really worried** para entonces ya estábamos preocupadísimos; **from that ~ on** a partir de entonces, desde entonces; **it's high ~ somebody did something** ya es hora *or* ya va siendo hora de que alguien haga algo; **she's resigned, and not before ~** ha renunciado, y ya era hora; **the ~ has come for us to make a decision** ha llegado el momento de que tomemos una decisión; **there's a ~ and a place for everything** hay un momento y un lugar para todo; ***my/her ~ has come*** me/le ha llegado el momento; ***to bide one's ~*** esperar el momento oportuno; ***to die before one's ~*** morir* tempranamente *or* prematuramente

C [c] (instance, occasion) vez *f*; **three ~s a day** tres veces por día; **I've been there many a ~** *o* **many ~s** he estado allí en numerosas ocasiones *or* muchas veces; **nine ~s out of ten** en el noventa por ciento de los casos, la gran mayoría de las veces; **third ~ lucky!** ¡la tercera es la vencida!; **let's leave it for another** *o* **some other ~** dejémoslo para otro momento; **you paid (the) last ~** la última vez *or* la otra vez pagaste tú; **for the last ~: no!** por última vez ¡no!; **let's try one more ~** probemos otra vez *or* una vez más

D (*in phrases*) **about time**: **it's about ~ someone told him** ya es hora *or* ya va siendo hora de que alguien se lo diga; **I've finished — and about ~ too!** he terminado — ¡ya era hora!; **ahead of time**: **the first stage was completed ahead of ~** la primera fase se terminó antes de tiempo; **any time**: **come any ~** ven cuando quieras *or* en cualquier momento; **call me any ~ between nine and eleven** llámame a cualquier hora entre las nueve y las once; **I'd rather work for Mary any ~** yo prefiero trabajar para Mary, toda la vida (y cien años más); **they should be here any ~ (now)** en cualquier momento llegan, deben de estar por llegar de un momento al otro; **at a time**: **four at a ~** de cuatro en cuatro *or* (AmL tb) de a cuatro; **one at a ~!** ¡de a uno!, ¡uno por uno! *or* ¡uno por vez!; **I can only do one thing at a ~** sólo puedo hacer una cosa a la *or* por vez; **for months at a ~** durante meses enteros; **at the same time** (simultaneously) al mismo tiempo; (however) (*as linker*) al mismo tiempo, de todas formas; **at times** a veces; **at this time** (AmE) ahora, en este momento; **every time**: **I make the same mistake every ~!** ¡siempre cometo el mismo error!; **gin or whisky? — give me whisky every ~!** ¿ginebra *or* whisky? — para mí whisky, toda la vida; **every** *o* **each time** (*as conj*) (whenever) cada vez; **from time to time** de vez en cuando; **on time** (on schedule): **the buses hardly ever run on ~** los autobuses casi nunca pasan a su hora *or* puntualmente; **she's never on ~** nunca llega temprano, siempre llega tarde; **time after time** *o* **time and (time) again** una y otra vez

E [c] (experience): **to have a good/bad/hard ~** pasarlo bien/mal/muy mal; **have a good ~!** ¡que te diviertas (*or* que se diviertan *etc*)!, ¡que lo pases (*or* pasen *etc*) bien!; **don't give me a hard ~** (esp AmE) no me mortifiques; **thank you for a lovely ~** gracias por todo, lo hemos pasado estupendamente

F [u] (Mus) compás *m*; **in ~ to the music** al compás de la música; **out of ~** descompasado, fuera de compás; **to beat/keep ~** marcar*/seguir* el compás; ***to mark ~*** (march on the spot) marcar* el paso; (make no progress) hacer* tiempo; (*before n*) **~ signature** llave *f* de tiempo

G **times** *pl* (Math): **it's four ~s bigger** es cuatro veces más grande; (*before n*) **~s table** tabla *f* de multiplicar

time² *vt* 1 (Sport) cronometrar; **I've ~d how long it takes me** he calculado cuánto tiempo me lleva 2 (choose time of): **the bomb was ~d to go off at ten o'clock** la bomba estaba programada para explotar a las diez; **the demonstration was ~ed to coincide with his arrival** la hora de la manifestación estaba calculada para coincidir con su llegada; **you ~d your entrance perfectly** no podrías haber elegido un mejor momento para entrar; **his comment was well ~d** su comentario fue muy oportuno; **his shot was badly ~d** no calculó bien el momento en que debía chutar/disparar

time: **~-and-motion** /'taɪmən'məʊʃən/ *adj* (*before n*): **~-and-motion study** estudio *m* de racionalización del trabajo *or* de tiempo(s) y movimiento(s) *or* de productividad; **~ bomb** *n* bomba *f* de tiempo *or* de relojería; **~ capsule** *n* cápsula *f* del tiempo; **~ clock** *n* reloj *m* registrador, reloj *m* checador (Méx); **~-consuming** *adj* que lleva mucho tiempo; **that would be too ~-consuming** eso llevaría demasiado tiempo; **~ deposit** *n* (AmE) depósito *m* a plazo fijo; **~-honored**, (BrE) **~-honoured** *adj* ‹*method*› consagrado (por la tradición); ‹*ritual*› de larga tradición; **~keeper** *n* 1 (Sport) cronometrador, -dora *m,f* 2 (worker) (BrE): **to be a good/bad ~keeper** ser* puntual/impuntual; **~keeping** *n* [u] (BrE) puntualidad *f*; **bad ~keeping** impuntualidad *f*

timeless /'taɪmləs || 'taɪmlɪs/ *adj* (liter) eterno

time: **~ limit** *n* plazo *m*; **~ line** línea *f* de tiempo, cronología *m*

timely /'taɪmli/ *adj* **-lier, -liest** oportuno

time: **~ out** *n* [c u] 1 (Sport) tiempo *m* (muerto); **to take (a) ~ out (from sth)** (AmE) tomarse un descanso (de algo) 2 (*as interj*) (AmE) ¡un momento!; **~piece** *n* (frml) reloj *m*

timer /'taɪmər || 'taɪmə(r)/ *n* temporizador *m*; (of oven, video etc) reloj *m* (automático)

times /taɪmz/ *prep*: **3 ~ 4 is 12** 3 (multiplicado) por 4 son 12

time: **~saving** *adj* que ahorra tiempo; **~scale** *n* escala *f* de tiempo; **~share** *n* 1 [u] (system) multipropiedad *f*, tiempo *m* compartido; (*before n*) ‹*apartment/property*› en multipropiedad, en tiempo compartido 2 [c] (property) multipropiedad *f*; **~sharing** *n* [u] (Comput) trabajo *m* en tiempo compartido; **~sheet** *n* hoja *f* de asistencia, planilla *f* de control de horas; **~-stamp** *vt* timbrar con el sello de tiempo

timetable¹ /'taɪm,teɪbəl/ *n* 1 (Transp) horario *m* 2 (esp BrE Educ) horario *m* 3 (schedule, programme) agenda *f*

timetable² *vt* (esp BrE) programar

time: **~ warp** *n* salto *m* en el tiempo; **the region is stuck in a ~ warp** la región se ha detenido en el tiempo; **~worn** *adj* ‹*buildings/furniture*› desgastado; ‹*procedures/traditions*› añejo; ‹*joke/saying*› gastado

timid /'tɪməd || 'tɪmɪd/ *adj* ‹*person/approach*› tímido; ‹*animal*› huraño

timidity /tə'mɪdəti || tɪ'mɪdəti/ *n* [u] timidez *f*

timidly /'tɪmədli || 'tɪmɪdli/ *adv* tímidamente, con timidez

timing /'taɪmɪŋ/ *n* [u] 1 (choice of time): **the ~ of the election** la fecha escogida para las elecciones; **the ~ of the action was disastrous** la acción fue de lo más inoportuna; **that was good ~: we've just arrived** calculaste muy bien el tiempo: acabamos de llegar 2 (Mus, Sport) ritmo *m*; **a comedian with brilliant ~** un cómico con un genial sentido de la oportunidad 3 (Auto): **check/adjust the ~** revise/ajuste la chispa *or* el encendido

timorous /'tɪmərəs/ *adj* (liter) medroso (liter), timorato

timpani /'tɪmpəni/ *pl n* timbales *mpl*

tin¹ /tɪn/ *n*
A **1** (metal) estaño *m* **2** (tinplate) (hoja)lata *f*; (*before n*) ‹*soldier*› de plomo; **~ can** lata *f or* (Esp tb) bote *m or* (Chi tb) tarro *m* (*de conservas, bebidas etc*)
B **1** (can) (esp BrE) lata *f or* (Esp tb) bote *m or* (Chi tb) tarro *m* (*de conservas, bebidas etc*) **2** (for storage) lata *f*, bote *m* (Esp) **3** (for baking) molde *m*

tin² *vt* **-nn-** (put in tins) (BrE) ‹*food*› enlatar

tinderbox /ˈtɪndərbɑːks || ˈtɪndəbɒks/ *n* caja *f* de la yesca

tinfoil /ˈtɪnfɔɪl/ *n* [u] (made of tin) papel *m* de estaño; (made of aluminium) papel *m* de aluminio, papel *m* albal® (Esp)

tinge¹ /tɪndʒ/ *n* **1** (of color) tinte *m*, matiz *m* **2** (hint) dejo *m*, matiz *m*

tinge² *vt* (*usu pass*) **1** (color) **to be ~d WITH sth** estar* matizado DE algo **2** (temper) **to be ~d WITH sth**: **words ~d with bitterness** palabras con un dejo *or* matiz de amargura

tingle¹ /ˈtɪŋgəl/ *vi*: **it makes your skin ~** te hace sentir un cosquilleo *or* hormigueo en la piel; **my cheeks were tingling after being outside** me ardían las mejillas después de haber estado fuera; **to ~ WITH sth**: **I was tingling with excitement** me estremecía de la emoción

tingle² *n* cosquilleo *m*, hormigueo *m*

tingling /ˈtɪŋglɪŋ/ *n* [u] cosquilleo *m*, hormigueo *m*

tinhorn¹ /ˈtɪnhɔːrn || ˈtɪnhɔːn/ *n* (AmE colloq) fanfarrón, -rrona *m,f*

tinhorn² *adj* fanfarrón

tinker¹ /ˈtɪŋkər || ˈtɪŋkə(r)/ *n* hojalatero, -ra *m,f*, calderero, -ra *m,f*

tinker² *vi* **to ~ WITH sth** ‹*with car/television*› hacerle* pequeños ajustes A algo; (pej) juguetear CON algo

tinkle¹ /ˈtɪŋkəl/ *n* tintineo *m*, tilín *m*; **to give sb a ~** (call on telephone) (BrE colloq) pegarle* un telefonazo *or* darle* un toque a algn (fam)

tinkle² *vi* «*bell/glass*» tintinear; **a tinkling laugh** una risa cristalina

tinned /tɪnd/ *adj* (BrE) enlatado, en *or* de lata, en *or* de tarro (Chi)

tinny /ˈtɪni/ *adj* **-nier, -niest** **1** (metallic) ‹*sound*› metálico; ‹*taste*› a lata, metálico **2** (of cheap metal) ‹*car/stove*› de lata

tin: **~ opener** *n* (BrE) abrelatas *m*; **~plate** *n* [u] hojalata *f*; **~pot** *adj* (pej) ‹*town/dictator*› de pacotilla

tinsel /ˈtɪnsəl/ *n* [u] espumillón *m* (*guirnalda dorada o plateada para decoraciones navideñas*)

tint¹ /tɪnt/ *n* **1** [c] (of color) tinte *m*, matiz *m*; (color) tono *m* **2** [u] (for hair) tintura *f*, tinte *m*

tint² *vt* teñir*

tinted /ˈtɪntəd || ˈtɪntɪd/ *adj* ‹*glass*› coloreado; ‹*lenses*› con un tinte; ‹*hair*› teñido

tiny /ˈtaɪni/ *adj* **tinier, tiniest** minúsculo, diminuto

tip¹ /tɪp/ *n*
A (end, extremity) punta *f*; (of stick, umbrella) contera *f*, regatón *m*; (*filter ~*) filtro *m*; **the westernmost ~ of Britain** el extremo occidental de Gran Bretaña; **he was standing on the ~s of his toes** estaba de puntillas *or* (CS) en puntas de pie; ***the ~ of the iceberg*** la punta del iceberg; ***to have sth on the ~ of one's tongue*** tener* algo en la punta de la lengua
B **1** (helpful hint) consejo *m* (práctico) **2** (in betting) pronóstico *m*, fija *f* (CS, Per)
C (gratuity) propina *f*
D (BrE) (rubbish dump) vertedero *m* (de basuras), basurero *m*, basural *m* (AmL); **your room is a ~** (colloq) tienes el cuarto hecho una pocilga

tip² **-pp-** *vt*
A (give gratuity to) darle* (una) propina a
B **1** (tilt) inclinar; **the child ~ped the glass upside down** el niño le dio la vuelta al vaso *or* (CS) dio vuelta el vaso; ***to ~ the balance*** *o* ***the scales*** inclinar la balanza a su (*or* mi *etc*) favor; **he ~ped the scales at 72kg** (colloq) pesó 72 kilos **2** (pour, throw) tirar, botar (AmL exc RPl); **she ~ped the contents of her bag on the floor** volcó el contenido de su bolso en el suelo; **it's ~ping it down outside** (BrE colloq) está lloviendo a cántaros
C **1** (predict, forecast) (BrE): **to ~ the winner** pronosticar* quién va a ser el ganador; **he is widely ~ped as the next party leader** todos los pronósticos coinciden en que será el próximo líder del partido **2** (warn, inform) (AmE) avisar(le a), pasarle el dato a (CS), darle* un chivatazo a (Esp fam)

■ **tip** *vi*
A (give gratuity) dar* propina
B (tilt) inclinarse, ladearse
C (dump rubbish) (BrE): ⊘ **no tipping** prohibido arrojar basura/escombros

Phrasal verbs

• **tip off** [v ▸ o ▸ adv, v ▸ adv ▸ o] ‹*police/criminal*› avisar(le a), pasarle el dato a (CS), darle* un chivatazo a (Esp fam)

• **tip over**
A [v ▸ o ▸ adv, v ▸ adv ▸ o] (knock over, upend) volcar*
B [v ▸ adv] (fall over, topple) caerse*

• **tip up**
A [v ▸ o ▸ adv, v ▸ adv ▸ o] (overturn) ‹*container*› voltear *or* (Esp) darle* la vuelta a *or* (CS) dar* vuelta
B [v ▸ adv] (tilt upward) levantarse

tip-off /ˈtɪpɔːf || ˈtɪpɒf/ *n* **1** (inside information) dato *m*, soplo *m* (fam), chivatazo *m* (Esp fam) **2** (telltale sign) (AmE) claro indicio *m*

tipped /tɪpt/ *adj* (*filter-~*) con filtro

-tipped /ˈtɪpt/ *suff*: **poison~/steel~** con punta envenenada/de acero

tipple /ˈtɪpəl/ *n* (colloq): **what's your (favorite) ~?** ¿cuál es tu bebida preferida?

tippler /ˈtɪplər || ˈtɪplə(r)/ *n* (colloq) borrachín, -china *m,f* (fam)

tipster /ˈtɪpstər || ˈtɪpstə(r)/ *n* pronosticador, -dora *m,f*

tipsy /ˈtɪpsi/ *adj* **-sier, -siest** entonado (fam), achispado (fam); **to get ~** entonarse (fam)

tiptoe¹ /ˈtɪptəʊ/ *vi* **-toes, -toeing, -toed** caminar *or* (esp Esp) andar* de puntillas, caminar en puntas de pie (CS)

tiptoe² *n*: **on ~** de puntillas, en puntas de pie (CS)

tiptop /ˈtɪpˈtɑːp || ˌtɪpˈtɒp/ *adj* de primera, excelente; **in ~top condition** en excelente estado, como nuevo

tip-truck /ˈtɪpˌtrʌk/ *n* (AmE) volquete *m*, volqueta *f*

tirade /taɪˈreɪd/ *n* diatriba *f*

tire¹ /taɪr || ˈtaɪə(r)/ *vt* cansar

■ **tire** *vi* **1** (become weary) cansarse **2** (become bored) **to ~ OF sth/sb/-ING** cansarse *or* aburrirse DE algo/algn/+ INF

Phrasal verb

• **tire out** [v ▸ o ▸ adv, v ▸ adv ▸ o] agotar, dejar exhausto; **to be ~d out** estar* agotado *or* rendido

tire², (BrE) **tyre** /taɪr || ˈtaɪə(r)/ *n* neumático *m*, llanta *f* (AmL), goma *f* (RPl); (*before n*) **~ pressure/valve** presión *f*/válvula *f* del neumático *or* (AmL) de la llanta *or* (RPl) de la goma

tired /taɪrd || ˈtaɪəd/ *adj* **1** (weary) cansado; **to get ~** cansarse; **you look ~** tienes cara de cansado **2** (fed up) **to be ~ OF sth/sb/-ING** estar* cansado *or* harto DE algo/algn /+ INF; **to get/grow ~ of sth/sb/-ING** cansarse *or* hartarse DE algo/algn /+ INF **3** (hackneyed) ‹*joke*› trasnochado, trillado, manido **4** (old, faded) ‹*lettuce/salad*› mustio; ‹*sofa/chair*› (viejo y) gastado

tiredness /ˈtaɪrdnəs || ˈtaɪədnɪs/ *n* [u] cansancio *m*

tireless /ˈtaɪrləs || ˈtaɪəlɪs/ *adj* ‹*person*› infatigable, incansable; ‹*patience/efforts*› inagotable

tirelessly /ˈtaɪrləsli || ˈtaɪəlɪsli/ *adv* incansablemente, infatigablemente

tiresome /ˈtaɪrsəm || ˈtaɪəsəm/ *adj* ‹*person*› pesado; ‹*task*› tedioso

tiring /ˈtaɪrɪŋ || ˈtaɪərɪŋ/ *adj* cansador (AmS), cansado (AmC, Esp, Méx)

'tis /tɪz/ (poet *or* dial) **= it is**

tissue /ˈtɪʃuː || ˈtɪʃuː, ˈtɪsjuː/ *n*
A [u c] (Anat, Bot) tejido *m*
B **1** [c] (paper handkerchief) pañuelo *m* de papel, Kleenex® *m* **2** [u] **~ (paper)** papel *m* de seda
C [c] (web) (liter) trama *f*; **a ~ of lies** una trama de mentiras

tit /tɪt/ *n*
A (Zool) paro *m*
B (sl) (breast) teta *f* (fam)

titanium /taɪˈteɪniəm, ˈtɪ- || tɪˈteɪniəm/ *n* [u] titanio *m*

titbit /ˈtɪtbɪt/ *n* **1** (of food) exquisitez *f* **2** (of gossip) chisme *m*

titchy /ˈtɪtʃi/ *adj* **titchier, titchiest** (BrE colloq) ‹*person*› enano (fam), petiso (AmS fam)

t

tit for tat *n*: **it was ~ ~ ~** fue ojo por ojo, diente por diente

tit-for-tat /ˈtɪtfərˈtæt || ˌtɪtfəˈtæt/ *adj (before n)*: **a ~ killing** un asesinato en represalia

titillate /ˈtɪtḷeɪt || ˈtɪtɪleɪt/ *vt* [1] (excite sexually) excitar [2] (stimulate) (liter) despertar*

titillating /ˈtɪtḷeɪtɪŋ || ˈtɪtɪleɪtɪŋ/ *adj* [1] (sexually exciting) excitante [2] (stimulating) (liter) estimulante

title[1] /ˈtaɪtḷ/ *n*

A [c] (of creative work) título *m*; *(before n)* **~ role** papel *m* protagónico *(de la obra del mismo nombre)*

B [c] [1] (designation, label) título *m* [2] (status) tratamiento *m* *(como Sr, Sra, Dr etc)* [3] (noble rank) título *m* (nobiliario *or* de nobleza) [4] (Sport) título *m*; *(before n)* **~ fight** combate *m* por el título

C (Law) [1] [u] (right of ownership) **~ (TO sth)** derecho *m* (A algo) [2] [c] (document) título *m* de propiedad

D titles *pl* (Cin, TV) créditos *mpl*, títulos *mpl* (de crédito)

title[2] *vt* ‹*book/painting/song*› titular, intitular (frml)

titled /ˈtaɪtḷd/ *adj* con título (nobiliario *or* de nobleza)

title: **~ deed** *n (usu pl)* título *m* de propiedad; **~holder** *n* campeón, -peona *m,f*; **~ page** *n* portada *f*, carátula *f*

titter[1] /ˈtɪtər || ˈtɪtə(r)/ *vi* reírse* disimuladamente

titter[2] *n* risita *f* ahogada

tittle-tattle /ˈtɪtḷˌtætḷ/ *n* (colloq) [1] (items of gossip) chismes *mpl* [2] (informer) (AmE) soplón, -plona *m,f*

titular /ˈtɪtʃələr || ˈtɪtjʊlə(r)/ *adj* ‹*head/leader*› nominal

tizz /tɪz/, **tizzy** /ˈtɪzi/ *n* (colloq): **to be in/get in(to) a ~** estar*/ponerse* nervioso

T-junction /ˈtiːˌdʒʌŋkʃən/ *n* (BrE) cruce *m* *(en forma de T)*

TLC (colloq hum) = **tender loving care**

TN = **Tennessee**

to[1] /tuː; *weak form* tə/ *prep*

A [1] (indicating destination) a; **we're going ~ Paris** vamos a París; **I'll drive you ~ the station** te llevo a la estación; **we went ~ John's** fuimos a casa de John, fuimos a lo de John (RPl), fuimos donde John (esp AmL); **you can wear it ~ a party/the wedding** puedes ponértelo para una fiesta/la boda [2] (indicating direction) hacia; **move a little ~ the right** córrete un poco hacia la derecha; **he turned ~ me** se volvió hacia mí; **it's pointing ~ the east** señala al Este [3] (indicating position) a; **~ the left/right of sth** a la izquierda/derecha de algo; **a mile ~ the south of Milton** una milla al sur de Milton

B (against, onto): **she clasped him ~ her** lo estrechó contra ella; **they stuck the poster ~ the wall** pegaron el cartel en la pared

C [1] (as far as) hasta; **she can count (up) ~ 100 now** ya sabe contar hasta 100; **~ a certain extent** hasta cierto punto; **a year ago ~ the day** hace exactamente un año [2] (until) hasta; **I can't stay ~ the end** no puedo quedarme hasta el final [3] (indicating range): **there will be 30 ~ 35 guests** habrá entre 30 y 35 invitados; *see also* **from D**

D [1] (showing indirect object): **who did you send/give it ~?** ¿a quién se lo mandaste/diste?; **give it ~ me** dámelo; **what did you say ~ him/them?** ¿qué le/les dijiste?; **I'll hand you over ~ Jane** te paso *or* (Esp tb) te pongo con Jane; **I was singing/talking ~ myself** estaba cantando/hablando solo; **~ me, he will always be a hero** para mí, siempre será un héroe; **he was very kind/rude ~ me** fue muy amable/grosero conmigo [2] (in toasts, dedications): **here's ~ Toby** brindemos por Toby; **here's ~ a Happy New Year** ¡Feliz Año Nuevo!; **best wishes ~ you both** los mejores deseos para ambos; **~ Paul with love from Jane** para Paul, con cariño de Jane

E (indicating proportion, relation): **how many ounces are there ~ the pound?** ¿cuántas onzas hay en una libra?; **600 pesos ~ the US dollar** 600 pesos por dólar; **it does 30 miles ~ the gallon** da *or* rinde 30 millas por galón, ≈ consume 6.75 litros a los *or* por cada cien kilómetros; **Barcelona won by two goals ~ one** Barcelona ganó por dos (goles) a uno; **there's a 10 ~ 1 chance of ...** hay una probabilidad de uno en 10 de ...; **that's nothing ~ what followed** eso no es nada comparado *or* en comparación con lo que vino después

F (concerning): **what do you say ~ that?** ¿qué dices a eso?, ¿qué te parece (eso)?; ***that's all there is ~ it*** eso es todo; ***there's nothing ~ it*** es muy simple *or* sencillo

G [1] (in accordance with): **~ all appearances** según parece; **they are not ~ my taste** no son de mi gusto [2] (producing): **~ my horror/delight ...** para mi horror/alegría ... [3] (indicating purpose): **~ this end** con este fin

H (indicating belonging) de; **the key ~ the front door** la llave de la puerta principal; **the solution ~ the problem** la solución al *or* del problema; **it has a nice ring/sound ~ it** suena bien

I (telling time) (BrE): **ten ~ three** las tres menos diez, diez para las tres (AmL exc RPl)

J (accompanied by): **we danced ~ the music** bailamos al compás de la música; **they sang it ~ the tune of 'Clementine'** lo cantaron con la melodía de 'Clementine'

to[2] /tə/ *(in infinitives)*

A [1] **~ sing/fear/leave** cantar/temer/partir; **I want ~ dance** quiero bailar; **I want them ~ dance** quiero que bailen [2] (in order to) para; **I do it ~ save money** lo hago para ahorrar dinero [3] (indicating result): **he awoke ~ find her gone** cuando despertó, ella ya se había ido; **I walked 5 miles only ~ be told they weren't home** caminé 5 millas para que me dijeran que no estaban en casa [4] (without vb): **I'd love ~!** ¡me encantaría!; **he doesn't want ~** no quiere

B *(after adj or n)*: **it's easy/difficult ~ do** es fácil/difícil de hacer; **you're too young ~ drink wine** eres demasiado joven para beber vino; **she was the first ~ arrive** fue la primera en llegar; **it's nothing ~ worry about** no hay por qué preocuparse; **she has a lot ~ do** tiene mucho que hacer

to[3] /tuː/ *adv* (shut): **I pulled the door ~** cerré la puerta

toad /təʊd/ *n* [1] (Zool) sapo *m* [2] (obnoxious person) (colloq): **you lying ~!** ¡mentiroso de porquería! (fam)

toad: **~-in-the-hole** /ˈtəʊdɪnðəˈhəʊl/ *n* [u] (BrE Culin) *salchichas horneadas en una masa de leche, huevo y harina*; **~stool** *n* hongo *m* *(no comestible)*

toady[1] /ˈtəʊdi/ *n* (*pl* **dies**) adulador, -dora *m,f*, pelota *mf* (Esp fam), chupamedias *mf* (CS, Ven fam), lambiscón, -cona *m,f* (Méx fam), lambón, -bona *m,f* (Col fam)

toady[2] *vi* **-dies, -dying, -died to ~ TO sb** adular a algn, darle* coba a algn

to and fro[1] /frəʊ/ *adv* de un lado a otro

to and fro[2] *vi* (*pres p* **to-ing and fro-ing**) (BrE) *(only in -ing form)*: **we spent all day to-ing and fro-ing between home and the hospital** nos pasamos todo el día yendo y viniendo *or* en idas y venidas de casa al hospital

to-and-fro /ˈtuːənˈfrəʊ/ *n* (BrE) *(no pl)* ir y venir *m*

toast[1] /təʊst/ *n*

A [u] tostadas *fpl*, pan *m* tostado; **a piece** *o* **slice of ~** una tostada *or* (Chi, Méx) un pan tostado; ***as warm as ~*** muy calentito; *(before n)* **~ rack** portatostadas *m*

B [c] [1] (tribute) **~ (TO sb)** brindis *m* (POR algn); **we drank a ~ to him** brindamos por él; **I'd like to propose a ~ to absent friends** brindemos por nuestros amigos ausentes [2] (person): **she is the ~ of Broadway tonight** todo el mundo la aclama esta noche en Broadway

toast[2] *vt*

A (Culin) ‹*bread/muffin*› tostar*; **I'm just ~ing myself in front of the fire** me estoy calentando junto al fuego; **~ed sandwich** sándwich *m* tostado *or* (CS) caliente

B (drink tribute to) ‹*person/success*› brindar por

■ **toast** *vi* «*bread/muffin*» tostarse*

toaster /ˈtəʊstər || ˈtəʊstə(r)/ *n* tostadora *f* (eléctrica), tostador *m*

tobacco /təˈbækəʊ/ *n* [u c] (*pl* **-cos** *or* **-coes**) tabaco *m*; **rolling/pipe ~** tabaco *or* picadura *f* para liar cigarrillos/de pipa; *(before n)* **the ~ industry** la industria tabacalera

tobacconist /təˈbækənəst || təˈbækənɪst/ *n*: *expendedor de tabaco, cigarrillos y artículos para el fumador*, ≈ estanquero, -ra *m,f (en Esp)*; **~'s (shop)** tabaquería *f*, tienda *f* de artículos para fumador, ≈ estanco *m (en Esp)*

-to-be /təˈbiː/ *suff*: **father~/husband~** futuro padre/esposo

toboggan[1] /təˈbɑːgən || təˈbɒgən/ *n* trineo *m*, tobogán *m*

toboggan[2] *vi* deslizarse* en trineo *or* tobogán

tod /tɑːd || tɒd/ *n*: ***on one's ~*** (BrE colloq) solo

today[1] /təˈdeɪ/ *adv* [1] (this day) hoy; **a week from ~** *o* (BrE also) **~ week** dentro de una semana, de aquí a una semana; **I last saw her a year ago ~** hoy hace un año que la vi por última vez; ~ **of all days** justo *or* precisamente hoy; **here ~, gone tomorrow** (set phrase) hoy aquí, mañana quién sabe dónde [2] (nowadays) hoy (en) día, actualmente, en la actualidad

today² *n* (*no art*) [1] (this day): **~'s papers** los periódicos de hoy; **(as) from ~** a partir de hoy *or* del día de hoy [2] (present age) hoy, hoy (en) día

toddle /'tɑːdl̩ || 'tɒdl̩/ *vi* [1] «*child*» empezar a caminar *or* (esp Esp) a andar, dar* los primeros pasos; **she ~d into the room** entró en la habitación (con paso inseguro) [2] (go) (colloq & hum) (+ *adv compl*): **it's time I was toddling off** *o* **along** ya es hora de que me vaya

toddler /'tɑːdlər || 'tɒdlə(r)/ *n* niño pequeño, niña pequeña *m,f* (*entre un año y dos años y medio de edad*)

toddy /'tɑːdi || 'tɒdi/ *n* (*pl* **-dies**) *bebida hecha con whisky, coñac o ron, agua hirviendo, azúcar y limón*

to-do /tə'duː/ *n* (colloq) (*no pl*) lío *m*, jaleo *m*, follón *m* (Esp fam); **to make a ~ about sth** armar un lío *or* jaleo por algo

toe¹ /təʊ/ *n* [1] (of foot) dedo *m* (*del pie*); **big ~** dedo *m* gordo (del pie); **from head** *o* **tip** *o* **top to ~** de pies a cabeza, de arriba a abajo; ***to be on one's ~s*** estar* *or* mantenerse* alerta; ***to step*** *o* ***tread on sb's ~s*** (colloq) (offend) ofender a algn; (lit) pisar a algn [2] (of sock) puntera *f*; (of shoe) puntera *f*, punta *f*

toe² *vt*: ***to ~ the line*** *o* (AmE also) ***mark*** acatar la disciplina; **to ~ the party line** acatar la línea del partido

toe: **~cap** *n* puntera *f*; **~hold** *n* punto *m* de apoyo (*para el pie*); ***to get*** *o* ***gain a ~hold in sth*** ‹*in market/organization*› conseguir* una posición favorable *or* ventajosa en algo; **~nail** *n* uña *f* (*del pie*)

TOEFL *n* = **Test of English as a Foreign Language**

> **TOEFL – Test of English as a Foreign Language**
>
> Un examen que, a la hora de solicitar el ingreso a una universidad americana, evalúa el dominio del inglés de aquellos estudiantes cuya lengua materna no es este idioma

toff /tɑːf || tɒf/ *n* (BrE colloq) encopetado, -da *m,f*, pituco, -ca *m,f* (CS, Per fam)

toffee /'tɑːfi || 'tɒfi/ *n* [u c] toffee *m* (*golosina hecha con azúcar y mantequilla*), caluga *f* (Chi); ***he can't sing for ~*** (BrE colloq) es un pésimo cantante

toffee: **~ apple** *n* (BrE) manzana *f* acaramelada; **~-nosed** /'tɑːfi'nəʊzd || 'tɒfi,nəʊzd/ *adj* (BrE colloq) estirado (fam)

tofu /'təʊfuː/ *n* [u] tofu *m*, queso *m* de soya (esp AmL) *or* soja (Esp)

toga /'təʊgə/ *n* toga *f*

together¹ /tə'geðər || tə'geðə(r)/ *adv*

A (in each other's company): **they walked ~ for part of the way** caminaron juntos/juntas un trecho; **we sat ~ in silence** estuvimos (todos/los dos) sentados en silencio; **we left them alone ~** los dejamos solos a los dos; **they were separated for a while, but they're ~ again now** estuvieron separados un tiempo, pero ahora han vuelto a juntarse; **these knives and forks don't all belong ~** estos cuchillos y tenedores no son del mismo juego; *see also* **come, get, keep together**

B [1] (in combination, collaboration): **let's write the letter ~** escribamos juntos/juntas la carta; **we must face this crisis ~** debemos hacer frente a esta crisis unidos; **pink and orange don't go ~ very well** el rosa no va *or* no pega muy bien con el naranja [2] (at the same time) juntos; **all ~ now!** ¡todos (juntos *or* a la vez)!; **we were at school ~** fuimos compañeros de colegio; **you have to push both buttons ~** hay que pulsar los dos botones simultáneamente *or* a la vez

C (in, into contact): **we stuck the broken cup ~ again** pegamos la taza que se había roto; **the pieces slot ~** las piezas encajan unas en otras; **they were brought ~ by chance** el destino los unió; *see also* **put together** *etc*

D (one with the other): **add the two figures ~** suma las dos cantidades

E **together with** junto con

together² *adj* (colloq) centrado, equilibrado

togetherness /tə'geðərnəs || tə'geðənɪs/ *n* [u] unión *f*

toggle /'tɑːgəl || 'tɒgəl/ *n* [1] (button) muletilla *f*, botón *m* de trenca *or* (CS) de montgomery [2] (Comput) flip-flop *m*

toggle switch *n* flip-flop *m* de conmutación

tog out, tog up: **-gg-** /tɑːg || tɒg/ [v ▸ o ▸ adv, v ▸ o ▸ adv] (BrE colloq) vestir*; **to get ~ged out** *o* **up** vestirse*, emperifollarse (fam & hum)

togs /tɑːgz || tɒgz/ *pl n* (colloq) ropa *f*

toil¹ /tɔɪl/ *n* [u] (liter) trabajo *m* duro, gran esfuerzo *m*

toil² *vi* (liter) [1] (work) trabajar duro [2] (move slowly): **to ~ up a hill** subir penosamente una cuesta

toilet /'tɔɪlət || 'tɔɪlɪt/ *n*

A [c] (room) baño *m* (esp AmL), servicio *m* (esp Esp), váter *m* (Esp); (bowl) water *m* *or* (Esp) váter *m*, taza *f*, inodoro *m*; **public ~s** baños *mpl* públicos (esp AmL), servicios *mpl* (esp Esp); (*before n*) **~ paper** papel *m* higiénico, papel *m* confort (Chi); **~ roll** rollo *m* de papel higiénico

B [u] (washing and dressing) (liter & dated) arreglo *m* personal; (*before n*) **~ bag** neceser *m*, bolsa *f* de aseo; **~ soap** jabón *m* de tocador; **~ water** agua *f*‡ de colonia

toiletries /'tɔɪlətriz || 'tɔɪlɪtriz/ *pl n* artículos *mpl* de tocador *or* de perfumería

toilet-train /'tɔɪləttreɪn || 'tɔɪlɪttreɪn/ *vt* ‹*child*› enseñar a pedir para ir al baño *or* (Esp) al váter; **he's (been) ~ed** ya no usa pañales

to-ing and fro-ing /'tuːɪŋən'frəʊɪŋ/ *n* [u c] (*pl* **~s ~ ~s**) (BrE colloq) idas *fpl* y venidas *fpl*, ir y venir *m*

token¹ /'təʊkən/ *n*

A (expression, indication): **a small ~ of gratitude** un pequeño obsequio como muestra *or* prueba de agradecimiento; **as a ~ of respect** en señal de respeto; ***by the same ~*** de igual modo

B [1] (coin) ficha *f*, cospel *m* (Arg) [2] (voucher) (BrE) vale *m*; (given as present) vale *m*, cheque-regalo *m*

token² *adj* (*before n, no comp*) ‹*fine/gesture*› simbólico; **the panel is made up of four men plus a ~ woman** el panel está integrado por cuatro hombres y la mujer que hay que incluir por pura fórmula

tokenism /'təʊkənɪzəm/ *n* [u] formulismo *m*

Tokyo /'təʊkiəʊ/ *n* Tokio *m*

told /təʊld/ *past & past p of* **tell**

tolerable /'tɑːlərəbəl || 'tɒlərəbəl/ *adj* [1] (endurable) ‹*pain/noise*› tolerable, soportable [2] (passable) pasable

tolerably /'tɑːlərəbli || 'tɒlərəbli/ *adv*: **she sings ~ well** canta razonablemente bien, canta pasablemente

tolerance /'tɑːlərəns/ *n* [u] [1] (forbearance) tolerancia *f*; (*before n*) **~ zone** zona *f* de tolerancia [2] (Med) tolerancia *f*

tolerant /'tɑːlərənt || 'tɒlərənt/ *adj* ‹*person/society*› tolerante; **to be ~ OF sb/sth** ser* tolerante CON algn/algo

tolerantly /'tɑːlərəntli || 'tɒlərəntli/ *adv* con tolerancia

tolerate /'tɑːləreɪt || 'tɒləreɪt/ *vt* [1] (be tolerant of) ‹*view/attitude/behavior*› tolerar [2] (stand, endure) ‹*person/pain/noise*› soportar, aguantar [3] (Med) tolerar

toleration /'tɑːlə'reɪʃən || ,tɒlə'reɪʃən/ *n* [u] tolerancia *f*

toll¹ /təʊl/ *n* [c] [1] (Transp) peaje *m*, cuota *f* (Méx); (*before n*) **~ call** (AmE) llamada *f* interurbana, conferencia *f* (Esp); **~ road/tunnel** carretera *f*/túnel *m* de peaje *or* (Méx) de cuota [2] (cost, damage): **the traffic ~** (AmE) el número de accidentes de tráfico; **the climate took a ~ on his health** el clima le afectó la salud

toll² *vt* (liter) ‹*bell*› tañer*, tocar*
■ **toll** *vi* «*bell*» tocar*, doblar

toll: **~booth** *n* cabina *f* de peaje; **~bridge** *n* puente *m* de peaje *or* (Méx) de cuota

toll-free¹ /'təʊl'friː/ *adj* (AmE) ‹*number/call*› gratuito

toll-free² *adv* (AmE) gratuitamente

tollway /'təʊlweɪ/ *n* (AmE) carretera *f* de peaje *or* (Méx) cuota

tom /tɑːm || tɒm/ *n* gato *m* (macho)

Tom /tɑːm || tɒm/ *n*: ***every ~, Dick and/or Harry*** cualquier hijo de vecino

tomato /tə'meɪtəʊ || tə'mɑːtəʊ/ *n* (*pl* **-toes**) [1] (fruit) tomate *m* *or* (Méx) jitomate *m*; (*before n*) **~ sauce/soup** salsa *f*/sopa *f* de tomate *or* (Méx) de jitomate [2] **~ (plant)** tomatera *f*, tomate *m*, jitomate *m* (Méx)

tomb /tuːm/ *n* tumba *f*, sepulcro *m*

tombola /tɑːm'bəʊlə || tɒm'bəʊlə/ *n* tómbola *f*

tomboy /'tɑːmbɔɪ || 'tɒmbɔɪ/ *n* niña *f* poco femenina, machona *f* (RPl), machetona *f* (Méx), varonera *f* (Arg)

tombstone /'tuːmstəʊn/ *n* lápida *f*

tomcat /'tɑːmkæt || 'tɒmkæt/ *n* gato *m* (macho)

tome /təʊm/ *n* (hum) libro *m*, librote *m*

tomfoolery /'tɑːm'fuːləri || ˌtɒm'fuːləri/ *n* [u] payasadas *fpl*

Tommy gun /'tɑːmi || 'tɒmi/ *n* (colloq) metralleta *f*

tomorrow[1] /tə'mɔːrəʊ, tə'mɑːrəʊ || tə'mɒrəʊ/ *adv* **1** (on the day after today) mañana; **~ morning/afternoon** mañana por la mañana/tarde, mañana en la mañana/tarde (AmL), mañana a la *or* de mañana/tarde (RPl); **we'll see you a week from ~** *o* (BrE also) **~ week** *o* **a week ~** te vemos de mañana en ocho días; **the day after ~** pasado mañana; **we got married a year ago ~** mañana hará un año que nos casamos **2** (in the future) mañana, el día de mañana

tomorrow[2] *n* (*no art*) **1** (day after today) mañana *adv*; **~ is Monday/my birthday** mañana es lunes/mi cumpleaños; ***never put off till ~ what you can do today*** no dejes para mañana lo que puedas hacer hoy **2** (future) mañana *m*; **the doctors of ~** los médicos del mañana *or* del futuro; **I wonder what ~ will bring** me pregunto qué nos depara el futuro; **they were spending money like there was no ~** (colloq) estaban gastando dinero a troche y moche *or* a diestra y siniestra *or* (Esp) a diestro y siniestro

tom-tom /'tɑːmtɑːm || 'tɒmtɒm/ *n* tam-tam *m*

ton /tʌn/ *n*

A **1** (unit of weight) tonelada *f* (*EEUU: 907kg., RU: 1.016kg.*); **this suitcase weighs a ~** (colloq) esta maleta pesa una tonelada (fam); ***to come down on sb like a ~ of bricks*** darle* duro a algn; *see also* **metric ton** **2** (unit of capacity) (Naut) tonelada *f* (cúbica)

B (large amount) (colloq) (*usually pl*): **~s of people/money/work** montones *mpl* de gente/dinero/trabajo (fam)

tone[1] /təʊn/ *n*

A **1** [u c] (quality of sound, voice) tono *m*; **don't speak to me in that ~ of voice!** ¡no me hables en ese tono! **2** **tones** *pl* (sound) sonido *m*; (voice) voz *f* **3** [c] (Telec) señal *f* (sonora); **engaged ~** (BrE) señal *f or* tono *m* de ocupado *or* (Esp) de comunicando

B [c] (shade) tono *m*, tonalidad *f*

C [u] **1** (mood, style) tono *m*; **to set the ~** marcar* la pauta **2** (standard, level) nivel *m*; **to raise/lower the ~ of sth** levantar/bajar el nivel de algo

D [u] (of muscle) tono *m* (muscular)

E [c] (Mus) **1** (interval) tono *m* **2** (note) (AmE) nota *f*

tone[2] *vi* **to ~ (in) (WITH sth)** combinar *or* armonizar* (CON algo)

■ **tone** *vt* (revitalize) ‹*muscles/skin*› tonificar*

(Phrasal verbs)

• **tone down** [v ▸ o ▸ adv, v ▸ adv ▸ o] ‹*language*› moderar; ‹*color*› atenuar*

• **tone up** [v ▸ o ▸ adv, v ▸ adv ▸ o] ‹*muscles/body*› tonificar*, dar* tono a

tone-deaf /'təʊn'def/ *adj*: **to be ~** no tener* oído (musical)

toner /'təʊnər || 'təʊnə(r)/ *n* [u c] **1** (for skin) tónico *m*, loción *f* tonificante **2** (for photocopier) toner *m*

tongs /tɑːŋz, tɔːŋz || tɒŋz/ *pl n* tenacillas *fpl*, pinza(s) *f(pl)*; **a pair of ~** unas tenacillas, una(s) pinza(s)

tongue /tʌŋ/ *n*

A [c] **1** (Anat) lengua *f*; **to set ~s wagging** dar* que hablar; ***to bite one's ~*** (colloq) morderse* la lengua; ***to get one's ~ around sth*** (colloq) pronunciar algo; ***to have a cruel*** *o* ***sharp*** *o* ***wicked ~*** tener* lengua viperina *or* de víbora; ***to have a loose ~*** hablar más de la cuenta; ***to hold one's ~*** callarse, contenerse*; ***to keep a civil ~ in one's head*** expresarse en lenguaje respetuoso; ***to say sth (with) ~ in cheek*** decir* algo medio burlándose *or* medio en broma **2** [u c] (Culin) lengua *f*

B [c] (of flame) lengua *f*; (on shoe) lengüeta *f*

C [c] (language) lengua *f*, idioma *m*

tongue: **~-tied** *adj* ‹*youth/suitor*› tímido, cohibido; **he gets ~-tied when she's around** se cohíbe *or* se corta cuando está ella; **~ twister** *n* trabalenguas *m*

tonic /'tɑːnɪk || 'tɒnɪk/ *n*

A **1** [c] (pick-me-up) tónico *m*; **his visits are a real ~ for her** sus visitas le suben mucho la moral **2** [u] **~ (water)** (agua *f*‡) tónica *f*

B [c] (Mus) tónica *f*

tonight[1] /tə'naɪt/ *adv* esta noche

tonight[2] *n* (*no art*) esta noche *f*

tonnage /'tʌnɪdʒ/ *n* [u c] (Naut) tonelaje *m*

tonne /tʌn/ *n* tonelada *f* (*métrica*)

tonsil /'tɑːnsəl || 'tɒnsəl/ *n* (Anat) amígdala *f*; **he had his ~s out** lo operaron de las amígdalas

tonsillitis /'tɑːnsə'laɪtəs || ˌtɒnsɪ'laɪtɪs/ *n* [u] amigdalitis *f*

tony /təʊni/ *adj* **-nier, -niest** (AmE colloq) fino, elegante

too /tuː/ *adv*

A **1** (excessively) demasiado; **there were ~ many people/cars** había demasiada gente/demasiados coches; **four mistakes? that's four ~ many** ¿cuatro faltas? son cuatro faltas de más; **these shoes are too big/small for me** estos zapatos me quedan grandes/pequeños; **that's ~ difficult for her to understand** es demasiado difícil para que lo entienda **2** (*in phrases*) **I know that all** *o* **only ~ well** eso bien que lo sé; **all** *o* **only ~ often** muy a menudo, con mucha frecuencia

B **1** (as well) también **2** (emphatic): **he apologized — I should think so ~!** se disculpó — ¡era lo menos que podía hacer!; **quite right ~!** ¡bien hecho!

C (very) muy; **I'm not ~ sure** no estoy muy seguro; **he didn't seem ~ keen on the idea** no parecía gustarle mucho la idea

took /tʊk/ *past of* **take**[1]

tool /tuːl/ *n* (instrument) instrumento *m*; (workman's etc) herramienta *f*; **garden ~s** herramientas *fpl or* utensilios *mpl* de jardinería; **they are the ~s of his trade** son sus herramientas de trabajo; ***to down ~s*** (BrE) declararse en huelga

tool: **~bag** *n* bolsa *f* de herramientas; **~box** *n* caja *f* de herramientas; **~kit** *n* juego *m* de herramientas; **~shed** *n* cobertizo *m* (*para herramientas*)

toot[1] /tuːt/ *n*

A (sound — of car horn) bocinazo *m*

B (drunken binge) (AmE colloq): **to go on a ~** irse* de farra *or* juerga

toot[2] *vi* ‹‹*driver*›› tocar* la bocina *or* el claxon, pitar; ‹‹*car horn*›› sonar*

■ **toot** *vt* ‹*car horn*› tocar*

tooth /tuːθ/ *n* (*pl* **teeth**) **1** (of person, animal) diente *m*; (molar) muela *f*; **front teeth** dientes *mpl* de adelante; **back teeth** muelas *fpl*; ***to be armed to the teeth*** estar* armado hasta los dientes; ***to be fed up to the back teeth with sth*** (colloq) estar* hasta la coronilla *or* hasta las narices de algo (fam); ***to be long in the ~*** ser* entrado en años; ***to fight ~ and nail*** luchar a brazo partido; ***to get one's teeth into sth*** (colloq) hincarle* el diente a algo; ***to grit one's teeth*** aguantarse; (lit) apretar* los dientes; ***to have a sweet ~*** ser* goloso; ***to kick sb in the teeth, to give sb a kick in the teeth*** humillar a algn; **it was a real kick in the teeth for him** fue una gran humillación para él; ***to lie through one's teeth*** mentir* descaradamente, mentir* con toda la barba *or* (Méx) con todos los dientes; ***to put*** *o* ***set sb's teeth on edge*** darle* dentera a algn, destemplarle los dientes a algn (AmL); ***to show one's teeth*** ‹‹*dog*›› mostrar* *or* enseñar los dientes; ‹‹*person/government*›› mostrar* *or* enseñar los dientes *or* las uñas; (*before n*) **~ decay** caries *f* dental **2** (of zip, saw, gear) diente *m*; (of comb) púa *f*, diente *m*

tooth: **~ache** *n* [u c] dolor *m* de muelas; **~brush** *n* cepillo *m* de dientes; **~ fairy** *n* ≈ ratoncito *m or* ratón *m* Pérez, ≈ los ratones (RPl)

toothless /'tuːθləs || 'tuːθlɪs/ *adj* desdentado

tooth: **~paste** *n* [u c] dentífrico *m*, pasta *f* dentífrica *or* de dientes; **~pick** *n* palillo *m* (de dientes), escarbadientes *m*, mondadientes *m*

toothy /'tuːθi/ *adj* **-thier, -thiest** dentudo, dientudo; **she gave me a ~ smile** me sonrió mostrando los dientes

top[1] /tɑːp || tɒp/ *n*

A **1** (highest part) parte *f* superior *or* de arriba; (of mountain) cima *f*, cumbre *f*, cúspide *f*; (of tree) copa *f*; (of page) parte *f* superior; (of head) coronilla *f*; **from ~ to bottom** de arriba abajo; **he stood at the ~ of the stairs** estaba en lo alto de la escalera; **his name is at the ~ of the list** su nombre es el primero de la lista *or* encabeza la lista; ***at the ~ of***

t

one's voice a voz en cuello *or* en grito, a grito pelado (fam); ***off the ~ of one's head***: **I can't think of any of them off the ~ of my head** no se me ocurre ninguno en este momento **2** (BrE) (of road) final *m*

B (of hierarchy) (highest rank, position): **she came ~ of the class in English** sacó la mejor nota de la clase en inglés; **our team reached the ~ of the league** nuestro equipo se colocó a la cabeza de la liga; **he worked his way to the ~** se abrió camino hasta la cima de su profesión

C **1** (upper part): **the table has a marble ~** el tablero de la mesa es de mármol; **the ~ of the milk** (BrE) *crema que se acumula en el cuello de la botella de leche*; **to float/rise to the ~** salir* a la superficie **2** (rim, edge) borde *m*; **fill it to the ~** llénalo hasta el borde

D (Clothing): **a blue ~** una blusa (*or* un suéter *or* un top *etc*) azul

E **on top** (*as adv*) encima, arriba; **he can't stay on ~ for ever** no puede ser siempre el primero; **he's getting a bit thin on ~** (colloq) se está quedando calvo *or* (AmC, Méx fam) pelón *or* (CS fam) pelado; ***to come out on ~*** salir* ganando

F **on top of** (*as prep*) ‹*cupboard/piano*› encima de; **the tent collapsed on ~ of us** la tienda se nos cayó encima; **it's just been one thing on ~ of another** ha sido una cosa detrás de otra *or* una cosa tras otra; **they managed to get on ~ of the situation** consiguieron controlar la situación; **don't let things get on ~ of you** no dejes que las preocupaciones te abrumen; ***to feel on ~ of the world*** estar* contentísimo; **and on ~ of it all** *o* **on ~ of all that, she lost her job** y encima *or* para colmo *or* como si esto fuera poco, se quedó sin trabajo

G **over the top** (exaggerated) (esp BrE colloq): **the costumes were way over the ~** los trajes eran una exageración; **I feel she went rather over the ~** creo que se pasó un poco (fam)

H (cover, cap — of jar, box) tapa *f*, tapón *m* (Esp); (— of pen) capuchón *m*, capucha *f*; (cork) tapón *m*; ***to blow one's ~*** (colloq) explotar (fam)

I **~ (gear)** (BrE Auto) directa *f*

A (*spinning ~*) trompo *m*, peonza *f*; ▸**sleep²** *vi*

top² *adj* (*before n*)

A **1** (uppermost) ‹*layer/shelf*› de arriba, superior; ‹*step/coat of paint*› último; ‹*note*› más alto; **on the ~ floor** en el último piso; **the ~ left-hand corner of the page** la esquina superior izquierda de la página **2** (maximum) ‹*speed/temperature*› máximo, tope; **people pay ~ prices for these wines** la gente paga los precios más altos por estos vinos

B **1** (best): **to be ~ quality** ser* de primera calidad; **the service is ~ class** el servicio es de primera **2** (in ranked order): **our ~ priority is ...** nuestra prioridad absoluta es ...; **the T~ 40** (Mus) *los 40 discos más vendidos*, ≈ los 40 principales (*en Esp*) **3** (leading, senior) ‹*scientists/chefs*› más destacado; **the ~ jobs** los mejores puestos; **a ~ official** un alto funcionario; **she has a ~ post at the embassy** tiene un cargo importante en la embajada

top³ **-pp-** *vt*

A (exceed, surpass) ‹*offer/achievement*› superar; **unemployment ~ped the 3 million mark** el índice de desempleo superó *or* rebasó los 3 millones; ***to ~ it all*** para coronarlo, para colmo, (más) encima

B (beat) (AmE): **the Tigers ~ped the Mariners 6-2** (AmE) los Tigers se impusieron a los Mariners por 6 a 2

C (head) ‹*list/league*› encabezar*

D (cover) ‹*column/building*› rematar, coronar; **~ped with chocolate/cheese** con chocolate/queso por encima

■ *v refl* **to ~ oneself**

A (surpass oneself) (AmE colloq) superarse

B (commit suicide) (BrE sl) matarse, suicidarse

Phrasal verbs

- **top off** [v ▸ o ▸ adv, v ▸ adv ▸ o] ‹*meal/session*› terminar
- **top out**

A [v ▸ adv ▸ o] ‹*building*› terminar la fase de edificación de

B [v ▸ adv] (AmE) ‹‹*demand/consumption*›› tocar* techo

- **top up** [v ▸ o ▸ adv, v ▸ adv ▸ o] ‹*glass/container*› llenar; ‹*battery*› (Auto) cargar*; ‹*cell phone/mobile phone*› recargar*; ‹*income/capital*› suplementar; **let me ~ you up!** déjame servirte un poco más

top and tail *vt* (BrE) ‹*gooseberries/green beans*› limpiar (*cortándoles las puntas, los rabillos etc*)

topaz /'təʊpæz/ *n* [u c] topacio *m*

top: **~ banana** *n* (AmE colloq) (boss) mandamás *mf* (fam), mero mero *m* (Méx fam), capo *m* (CS fam); **~coat** *n* (Clothing) abrigo *m*; **~ dog** *n* (colloq): **to be ~ dog** ir* a la cabeza; **~ dollar** *n* [u] (AmE colloq): **to pay ~ dollar FOR sth** pagar* un precio alto POR algo; **~ drawer** *n* **the ~ drawer** la alta sociedad, la flor y nata (de la sociedad); **~flight** /'tɑ:p'flaɪt || ˌtɒp'flaɪt/ *adj* (*before n*) de primera (clase); **~ hat** *n* sombrero *m* de copa, chistera *f* (Esp), galera *f* (RPl); **~-heavy** /'tɑ:p'hevi || ˌtɒp'hevi/ *adj* ‹*structure*› inestable (*por ser muy pesado en su parte superior*)

topic /'tɑ:pɪk || 'tɒpɪk/ *n* tema *m*

topical /'tɑ:pɪkəl || 'tɒpɪkəl/ *adj* de interés actual, de actualidad

topless /'tɑ:pləs/ *adj* topless; **to go ~** andar* topless

top: **~-level** /'tɑ:p'levəl || ˌtɒp'levəl/ *adj* (*before n*): **~-level talks** conversaciones *fpl* de alto nivel; **a ~-level official** un alto funcionario; **~most** *adj* (*before n*) ‹*branch/shelf*› más alto, de más arriba; ‹*layer*› superior; **~notch** /'tɑ:p'nɑ:tʃ || ˌtɒp'nɒtʃ/ *adj* de primera; **~-of-the-line** /'tɑ:pəvðə'laɪn || ˌtɒpəvðə'laɪn/, (BrE also) **~-of-the-range** /'tɑ:pəvðə'reɪndʒ || ˌtɒpəvðə'reɪndʒ/ *adj* ‹*design*› de primerísima calidad

topography /tə'pɑ:grəfi || tə'pɒgrəfi/ *n* [u c] topografía *f*

topper /'tɑ:pər || 'tɒpə(r)/ *n* **1** (colloq) ▸**top hat** **2** (action, remark) (AmE): **we'll never find a ~ for it** no vamos a encontrar nada que lo supere

topping /'tɑ:pɪŋ || 'tɒpɪŋ/ *n* [c u]: **an ice-cream with chocolate ~** un helado con (salsa de) chocolate por encima; **choose your own pizza ~** elija los ingredientes para cubrir su pizza

topple /'tɑ:pəl || 'tɒpəl/ *vi* (fall) caerse*; **she ~d over** perdió el equilibrio y se cayó

■ **topple** *vt* **1** (overthrow) ‹*government/dictator*› derrocar*, derribar **2** (overturn) volcar*

top: **~-ranking** /'tɑ:p'ræŋkɪŋ || ˌtɒp'ræŋkɪŋ/ *adj* (*before n*) de alto nivel, importante; **~-secret** /'tɑ:p'si:krət || ˌtɒp'si:krɪt/ *adj* (*pred* **~ secret**) secreto, reservado; **~-security** /'tɑ:psɪ'kjʊrəti || ˌtɒpsɪ'kjʊərəti/ *adj* (BrE) (*before n*) ‹*prison/wing/prisoner*› de máxima seguridad

topsy-turvy /'tɑ:psi'tɜ:rvi || ˌtɒpsi'tɜ:vi/ *adj* (colloq) ‹*room*› desordenado, patas (para) arriba (fam); **what a ~ world we live in!** ¡el mundo está loco!

top-up /'tɑ:pʌp || 'tɒpʌp/ *n* (BrE): **who's ready for a ~?** ¿quién quiere más vino (*or* cerveza *etc*)?

Torah /'tɔ:rə/ *n* **the ~** la *or* el Torá

torch /tɔ:rtʃ || tɔ:tʃ/ *n*

A **1** (flame) antorcha *f*, tea *f*; ***to carry a ~ for sb*** estar* perdidamente enamorado de algn; ***to put sth to the ~, to set a ~ to sth*** prenderle fuego a algo **2** (electric) (BrE) linterna *f*

B (arsonist) (AmE sl) incendiario, -ria *m,f*

torchlight /'tɔ:rtʃlaɪt || 'tɔ:tʃlaɪt/ *n* [u]: **by ~** a la luz de la(s) antorcha(s); (*before n*) ‹*procession*› con antorchas

tore /tɔ:r || tɔ:(r)/ *past of* **tear²**

torment¹ /'tɔ:rment || 'tɔ:ment/ *n* [u c] tormento *m*; **to be in ~** sufrir mucho, sufrir lo indecible

torment² /tɔ:r'ment || tɔ:'ment/ *vt* atormentar, torturar; (tease) martirizar*

tormentor /tɔ:r'mentər || tɔ:'mentə(r)/ *n* torturador, -dora *m,f*

torn /tɔ:rn || tɔ:n/ *past p of* **tear²**

tornado /tɔ:r'neɪdəʊ || tɔ:'neɪdəʊ/ *n* (*pl* **-does** *or* **-dos**) tornado *m*

torpedo¹ /tɔ:r'pi:dəʊ || tɔ:'pi:dəʊ/ *n* (*pl* **-does**)

A (Mil) torpedo *m*; (*before n*) **~ boat** torpedero *m*

B (sandwich) (AmE) *sándwich hecho con una barra entera de pan*

torpedo² *vt* **-does, -doing, -doed** torpedear

torpid /'tɔ:rpəd || 'tɔ:pɪd/ *adj* (frml) ‹*mind*› aletargado

torpor /'tɔ:rpər || 'tɔ:pə(r)/ *n* [u] (frml) letargo *m*, sopor *m*

torrent /'tɔ:rənt || 'tɒrənt/ *n* torrente *m*; **a ~ of abuse** un torrente de insultos

torrential /tɔ:'rentʃəl || tə'renʃəl/ *adj* torrencial

torrid /'tɔ:rəd || 'tɒrɪd/ *adj* ‹*climate/heat*› tórrido; ‹*affair/relationship*› apasionado, tempestuoso

torso /'tɔ:rsəʊ || 'tɔ:səʊ/ *n* (*pl* **-sos**) torso *m*

tortoise /'tɔ:rtəs || 'tɔ:təs/ *n* tortuga *f*

tortoiseshell¹ /'tɔːrtəʃel, -təsʃəl || 'tɔːtəsʃel, 'tɔːtəʃəl/ *n* **1** [u] (material) carey *m*, concha *f* **2** [c] (~ *cat*) gato *m* pardo

tortoiseshell² *adj* **1** (made of tortoiseshell) ‹*ornament/earrings*› de carey *or* concha **2** (color) de color carey; ‹*cat*› pardo

tortuous /'tɔːrtʃuəs || 'tɔːtjʊəs/ *adj* tortuoso, sinuoso

torture¹ /'tɔːrtʃər || 'tɔːtʃə(r)/ *n* [u c] tortura *f*; **under ~ he gave their names** dio sus nombres porque lo torturaron; **these exercises are ~!** ¡estos ejercicios son una tortura *or* un suplicio!

torture² *vt* **1** ‹*person/animal*› torturar; **she was ~d by doubts/jealousy** las dudas/los celos la atormentaban **2** **tortured** *past p* ‹*person/mind/soul*› atormentado

torturer /'tɔːrtʃərər || 'tɔːtʃərə(r)/ *n* torturador, -dora *m,f*

Tory¹ /'tɔːri/ *n* (*pl* **Tories**) **1** (in UK) tory *mf* **2** (in US history) realista *mf*

Tory² *adj* ‹*party/voter*› (in UK) conservador, tory

toss¹ /tɔːs || tɒs/ *n* **1** (throw) lanzamiento *m*; **with a ~ of his head** con un movimiento brusco de la cabeza **2** (of coin): **to decide sth on** *o* **by the ~ of a coin** decidir *or* sortear algo a cara o cruz (*or* a cara o sello *etc*); *see also* **toss²** *vt* **1**; **to win/lose the ~** ganar/perder* jugándoselo a cara o cruz (*or* sello *etc*); ***not to give a ~*** (BrE sl): **I don't give a ~ what you think** a mí me importa un pito (fam) *or* (vulg) carajo lo que pienses; ***to argue the ~*** (BrE) seguir* discutiendo

toss² *vt* **1** (throw) ‹*ball*› tirar, lanzar*, aventar* (Col, Méx, Per); ‹*pancake*› darle* la vuelta a, dar* vuelta (CS) (*lanzándolo al aire*); **let's ~ a coin** echémoslo a cara o cruz *or* (Andes, Ven) a cara o sello *or* (Arg) a cara o ceca *or* (Méx) a águila o sol **2** (agitate) ‹*boat/passengers/cargo*› sacudir, zarandear; **she ~ed her head/hair back** sacudió la cabeza hacia atrás/se echó el pelo para atrás con un movimiento de cabeza **3** (Culin) ‹*salad*› mezclar **4** (AmE colloq) ‹*party*› dar*

■ **toss** *vi* **1** (be flung about) agitarse, sacudirse; ‹‹*boat*›› bambolearse, dar* bandazos; **to ~ and turn** dar* vueltas (*en la cama*) **2** (flip coin) **to ~ FOR sth**: **we ~ed for the last apple** nos jugamos la última manzana a cara o cruz (*or* a cara o sello *etc*)

(Phrasal verbs)

• **toss away** [v ▸ o ▸ adv, v ▸ adv ▸ o] (colloq) ‹*wrapping/envelope*› tirar, botar (AmL exc RPl)

• **toss off**

A [v ▸ o ▸ adv, v ▸ adv ▸ o] (produce quickly, easily) ‹*essay/letter*› escribir*, mandarse (AmS fam)

B [v ▸ adv] (BrE vulg) hacerse* *or* (Chi, Per) correrse la *or* una paja (vulg)

• **toss up**

A [v ▸ adv] **1** (vomit) (AmE colloq) devolver*, arrojar, vomitar **2** (BrE) ▸**toss²** *vi* **2**

B [v ▸ o ▸ adv, v ▸ adv ▸ o] (vomit) (AmE colloq) devolver*, arrojar, vomitar

toss-up /'tɔːsʌp || 'tɒsʌp/ *n* (colloq): **who do you think will win? — it's a ~ between Johnson and Smith** ¿quién crees que va a ganar? — está entre Johnson y Smith; **it's a ~ whether he'll get the job** no hay ninguna seguridad de que le vayan a dar el trabajo

tot /tɑːt || tɒt/ *n* **1** (young child) pequeño, -ña *m,f*, chiquito, -ta *m,f* (esp AmL) **2** (of alcohol) copita *f*

(Phrasal verb)

• **tot up**: **-tt-** [v ▸ o ▸ adv, v ▸ adv ▸ o] (colloq) sumar

total¹ /'təʊtl̩/ *adj* **1** (whole, overall) (*before n*) ‹*amount/number/output*› total **2** (complete) ‹*destruction*› total; ‹*failure*› rotundo, absoluto; **a ~ stranger** una persona totalmente desconocida; **the place was in ~ chaos** reinaba allí el caos más absoluto

total² *n* total *m*

total³ *vt*, (BrE) **-ll-**

A **1** (amount to) ascender* *or* elevarse a un total de **2** (add up) ‹*figures*› sumar, totalizar*

B (wreck) (AmE colloq): **the car was ~ed** el coche quedó totalmente destrozado

totalitarian /təʊ'tælə'teriən || ˌtəʊtælɪ'teəriən/ *adj* totalitario

totalitarianism /təʊ'tælə'teriənɪzəm || ˌtəʊtælɪ'teəriənɪzəm/ *n* [u] totalitarismo *m*

totality /təʊ'tæləti/ *n* [c] (*pl* **-ties**) (frml) totalidad *f*

totally /'təʊtl̩i || 'təʊtəli/ *adv* ‹*destroyed/unjustified*› totalmente, completamente; **they are ~ without scruples** no tienen el más mínimo escrúpulo

tote /təʊt/ *vt* (esp AmE colloq) ‹*weapons*› llevar; ‹*bag*› cargar* con, acarrear

(Phrasal verb)

• **tote up** (AmE) ▸**tot up**

tote bag *n* bolsa *f or* bolso *m* grande, bolsón *m* (RPl)

totem /'təʊtəm/ *n* tótem *m*; (*before n*) **~ pole** tótem *m*

totter /'tɑːtər || 'tɒtə(r)/ *vi* ‹‹*person/object/government*›› tambalearse; **the regime is ~ing on the brink of collapse** el régimen está a punto de caer

tottering /'tɑːtərɪŋ || 'tɒtərɪŋ/ *adj* ‹*steps*› inseguro, vacilante

toucan /'tuːkæn || 'tuːkən, 'tuːkæn/ *n* tucán *m*

touch¹ /tʌtʃ/ *n*

A **1** [u] (sense) tacto *m*; **smooth to the ~** suave al tacto **2** [c] (physical contact): **the cold ~ of marble** el tacto frío del mármol; **at the ~ of a button** con sólo tocar un botón; ***to be a soft ~*** (colloq) (be generous) ser* un buenazo

B [c] (small amount, degree — of humor, irony) dejo *m*, toque *m*; (— of paint) toque *m*; **add a ~ of salt** agregue una pizca de sal; **a ~ of fever** un poco de fiebre, unos quintos de fiebre (AmL); **a ~** (*as adv*) algo, un poquito

C **1** [c] (detail) detalle *m*; **to add** *o* **put the final** *o* **finishing ~es/~ to sth** darle* los últimos toques/el último toque a algo **2** (effect) (*no pl*) toque *m*; **the personal ~** el toque personal

D (skill) (*no pl*) habilidad *f*; **a politician with the common ~** un político que está en sintonía con el pueblo

E [u] (communication): **to get/keep** *o* **stay in ~ with sb** ponerse*/mantenerse* en contacto con algn; **I'll be in ~** ya te escribiré (*or* llamaré *etc*); **I lost ~ with her** perdí el contacto con ella; **how can I get in ~ with you?** ¿cómo me puedo poner en contacto con usted?, ¿cómo lo puedo contactar?; **I'm a bit out of ~ with what's happening** no estoy muy al corriente *or* al tanto de lo que está pasando; **they're completely out of ~** no tienen ni idea

F [u] (in rugby): **to kick for ~** intentar mandar la pelota fuera del campo de juego; **the ball went into ~** la pelota salió por la banda

touch² *vt*

A **1** (be in physical contact with) tocar*; **he ~ed her hand** le tocó la mano; **the bed was ~ing the wall** la cama estaba pegada a *or* tocaba la pared; **Ⓢ please do not touch the exhibits** se ruega no tocar **2** (brush, graze) rozar*, tocar* **3** (approach) (colloq) **to ~ sb FOR sth**: **he ~ed me for $50** me pidió 50 dólares

B **1** (reach): **I can't ~ my toes** no llego *or* no alcanzo a tocarme los pies; **my feet don't ~ the bottom** (of pool) no hago pie, no toco fondo **2** (equal) (*usu neg*): **nobody can ~ her in this type of role** es inigualable *or* no tiene rival en este tipo de papel

C (*usu neg*) **1** (interfere with) tocar*; **don't ~ anything** no toques nada **2** (deal with): **they won't ~ foreign cars** no quieren saber nada de coches extranjeros **3** (eat, drink) probar*; **he didn't ~ his lunch** no tocó la comida, no probó bocado

D **1** (affect, concern) afectar **2** (move emotionally): **he was ~ed by her kindness** su amabilidad lo enterneció *or* le llegó al alma; **I was deeply ~ed** me emocioné

■ **touch** *vi* **1** (with finger, hand) tocar* **2** (come into physical contact) ‹‹*hands*›› rozarse*; ‹‹*wires*›› tocarse*

(Phrasal verbs)

• **touch down** [v ▸ adv] **1** (Aerosp, Aviat) (on land) aterrizar*, tomar tierra; (on sea) acuatizar*, amarizar*, amerizar*; (on moon) alunizar* **2** (in rugby) marcar* un ensayo *or* try (*al poner el balón en el suelo*)

• **touch off** [v ▸ o ▸ adv, v ▸ adv ▸ o] ‹*riot/argument*› provocar*, hacer* estallar, desencadenar

• **touch on** [v ▸ prep ▸ o] ‹*subject*› tocar*, mencionar

• **touch up** [v ▸ o ▸ adv, v ▸ adv ▸ o] **1** (alter, enhance) ‹*photograph/painting*› retocar*; ‹*article/essay*› arreglar **2** (touch sexually) (BrE colloq) manosear, toquetear, magrear (Esp fam)

• **touch upon** [v ▸ prep ▸ o] ▸**touch on**

touch: **~-and-go** /'tʌtʃən'gəʊ/ *adj*: **I passed the exam, but it was ~-and-go** aprobé el examen, pero por poco; **how is the patient? — it's ~-and-go at the moment** ¿cómo está el paciente? — en situación crítica; **~down**

n [1] (Aerosp, Aviat) (on land) aterrizaje *m*; (on sea) amerizaje *m*, amarizaje *m*, amaraje *m*; (on moon) alunizaje *m*; [2] (in US football) touchdown *m*, anotación *f*, ensayo *m*; (in rugby) ensayo *m*

touché /tu:'ʃeɪ/ *interj* (deferring to a witty reply) apúntate un tanto

touched /tʌtʃt/ *adj* (colloq) (*after n*) tocado (fam); *see also* **touch**[2] *vt* **D2**

touching /'tʌtʃɪŋ/ *adj* enternecedor, conmovedor

touch: ~ **judge** *n* juez *mf* de banda, juez *mf* de línea; ~**line** *n* línea *f* de banda; ~ **pad** *n* touch pad *m*, almohadilla *f* táctil *or* de contacto; ~**-sensitive** /'tʌtʃ 'sensətɪv/ *adj* sensible al tacto; ~**stone** *n* (criterion) piedra *f* de toque; ~**-Tone**® *n*: *sistema de telefonía electrónica*; ~**-type** *vi* escribir* a máquina *or* mecanografiar* al tacto

touchy /'tʌtʃi/ *adj* **-chier, -chiest** ‹*person*› susceptible; ‹*subject/situation*› delicado; **she's a bit ~ about her accent** no le gusta que hagan comentarios sobre su acento

touchy-feely /'tʌtʃi'fi:li/ *adj* (colloq) [1] ‹*person*› tocón (fam), toquetón (CS fam); ‹*course/program/approach*› que recalca el aspecto humano [2] (corny) ‹*politician*› (pej) sensiblero; ‹*management style*› que te toca la fibra sensible

tough[1] /tʌf/ *adj* **-er, -est**

A [1] (strong, hard-wearing) ‹*fabric/clothing*› resistente, fuerte [2] (not tender) ‹*meat*› duro; (leathery) correoso

B ‹*person*› [1] (physically, emotionally resilient) fuerte [2] (aggressive, violent) bravucón

C [1] (strict, uncompromising) ‹*boss/teacher*› severo, exigente, estricto; ‹*policy/discipline*› duro, de mano dura; **to be ~ ON sb** (strict) ser* duro *or* severo CON algn; (unfair) ser* injusto PARA CON algn; **to get ~ WITH sb** ponerse* duro CON algn [2] (difficult) ‹*exam/decision/question*› difícil, peliagudo; **the job was ~ going** el trabajo se me hizo muy cuesta arriba; **they had a ~ time** las pasaron muy mal, pasaron las de Caín [3] (unfortunate): **it was ~ for the losers** fue una verdadera lástima para el equipo que perdió; **~ (luck)!** (colloq) ¡mala suerte!

tough[2] *adv* (colloq) (aggressively): **stop acting ~** no te hagas el gallito *or* el machito (fam)

tough[3] *n* (colloq) matón *m* (fam)

toughen /'tʌfən/ ~ **(up)** *vt* [1] (strengthen) ‹*muscles*› endurecer*; ‹*material*› hacer* más fuerte *or* resistente [2] ‹*person*› hacer* más fuerte [3] (make stricter) ‹*stance/approach*› volver* más firme

toughie /'tʌfi/ *n* (colloq) [1] (difficult question): **the exam was a real ~** el examen fue dificilísimo; **will he win? — hmm, that's a ~** ¿ganará? — ¡vaya preguntita! [2] (person) matoncito *m*

toughness /'tʌfnəs || 'tʌfnɪs/ *n* [u]

A (of material) dureza *f*, resistencia *f*

B (aggressiveness) actitud *f* agresiva

toupee /tu:'peɪ || 'tu:peɪ/ *n* peluquín *m*, tupé *m*

tour[1] /tʊr || tʊə(r), tɔ:(r)/ *n* [1] (Leisure) (by bus, car) viaje *m*, gira *f*; (of castle, museum) visita *f*; (of town) visita *f* turística, recorrido *m* turístico; **they went on a ~ of** *o* **around Europe** se fueron de gira *or* de viaje por Europa; **he gave us a ~ of the house** nos mostró *or* (esp Esp) nos enseñó la casa; **guided ~** (of castle, museum) visita *f* guiada *or* con guía; (of area, country) excursión *f* (organizada), tour *m*, viaje *m* organizado; (*before n*) **~ guide** guía *mf* de turismo *or* (Méx) de turistas; **~ operator** (travel agency) tour operador *m*, operador *m* turístico [2] (official visit) (to country, region) gira *f*, viaje *m*; (of factory, hospital) visita *f* [3] (Mus, Sport, Theat) gira *f*, tournée *f*; **to be/go on ~** ‹‹*play/orchestra/team*›› estar*/ir* de gira [4] (Mil): **~ of duty** período *m* de servicio

tour[2] *vt* [1] (Leisure) ‹*country/area*› recorrer, viajar por [2] (visit officially) ‹*factory/hospital*› visitar [3] (Mus, Sport, Theat) ‹‹*team/group*›› ‹*country/Europe*› ir* de gira *or* hacer* una gira por

■ **tour** *vi*

A (Leisure) (by bus, car) viajar

B (Mus, Sport, Theat) ‹‹*company/team*›› hacer* una gira

tour de force /'tʊrdə'fɔ:s || ˌtʊədə'fɔ:s/ *n* (*pl* **~s ~ ~**) (frml) hazaña *f*, tour *m* de force

tourer /'tʊrər || 'tʊərə(r)/ *n* [1] (vehicle) turismo *m* [2] (bicycle) bicicleta *f* de paseo *or* turismo [3] (caravan) caravana *f*, tráiler *m* (AmL), rulot *f* (Esp), casa *f* rodante (CS), cámper *m* (Chi, Méx)

touring /'tʊrɪŋ || 'tʊərɪŋ, 'tɔ:r-/ *adj* ‹*exhibition*› ambulante; ‹*team*› que está de gira

tourism /'tʊrɪzəm || 'tʊərɪzəm, 'tɔ:r-/ *n* [u] turismo *m*

tourist /'tʊrəst || 'tʊərɪst, 'tɔ:r-/ *n* turista *mf*; (*before n*) **~ bureau** *o* **office** oficina *f* de (información y) turismo; **~ class** clase *f* turista; **~ guide** (book) guía *f* turística; (person) guía *mf* de turismo *or* (Méx) de turistas; **the ~ industry** el turismo, la industria del turismo; Ⓢ **tourist information** información y turismo, oficina de turismo; **the ~ season** la temporada turística; **it's a real ~ trap** atrae a muchos turistas

touristy /'tʊrəsti || 'tʊərɪsti, 'tɔ:r-/ *adj* (colloq) ‹*town*› demasiado turístico, comercializado

tournament /'tʊrnəmənt || 'tɔ:nəmənt/ *n* (Games, Sport) torneo *m*

tourniquet /'tʊrnɪkət || 'tʊənɪkeɪ/ *n* torniquete *m*

tousled /'taʊzəld/ *adj* ‹*hair*› despeinado, alborotado

tout[1] /taʊt/ *vi* (solicit): **to ~ for customers** andar* a la caza de clientes

■ **tout** *vt* [1] (offer, sell) ‹*wares*› ofrecer*; ‹*tickets*› (BrE) revender [2] (promote) ‹*idea/product*› promocionar

tout[2] *n* (*ticket* ~) (BrE) revendedor, -dora *m,f* (de entradas)

tow[1] /təʊ/ *n* [u] (Auto, Naut) remolque *m*; **to give sth/sb a ~** remolcar* algo/a algn; Ⓢ **on tow** (BrE) vehículo remolcado; ***in* ~** (lit) a remolque; (following behind) a la zaga

tow[2] *vt* ‹*car/boat/trailer*› remolcar*, llevar a remolque; **they ~ed the car away** se llevaron el coche a remolque

toward /tɔ:rd || tə'wɔ:d/, (esp BrE) **towards** /tɔ:rdz || tə'wɔ:dz/ *prep*

A [1] (in the direction of) hacia; **further south, ~ the Mexican border** más al sur, más cerca de la frontera con México [2] (facing): **she sat with her back ~ me/~ the fire** estaba sentada de espaldas a mí/a la chimenea

B (of time) hacia, alrededor de

C (as contribution): **she gave us $100 ~ it** nos dio 100 dólares como contribución, contribuyó con 100 dólares

D (regarding) para con, hacia; **your attitude ~ them** tu actitud para con *or* hacia ellos

towaway /'təʊəˌweɪ/ *n* (AmE): **~s average 200 cars a week** la grúa se lleva un promedio de 200 coches por semana; (*before n*) **~ zone** *zona donde opera la grúa*

towel[1] /'taʊəl/ *n* toalla *f*; (*before n*) **~ bar** *o* (BrE) **rail** toallero *m* (*de barra*); ▸**throw in**

towel[2] *vt*, (BrE) **-ll-** secar* con toalla; **to ~ sb/oneself down** *o* **off** *o* **dry** secar* a algn/secarse* con una toalla

toweling, (BrE) **towelling** /'taʊəlɪŋ/ *n* [u] (tela *f* de) toalla *f*, felpa *f*

tower /'taʊər || 'taʊə(r)/ *n* torre *f*; ***to be a ~ of strength*** ser* un gran apoyo

(Phrasal verb)

• **tower above, tower over** [v ▸ prep ▸ o] [1] (be taller than) ‹*landscape*› dominar; ‹*building*› descollar* sobre; ‹*person*› destacar* sobre [2] (greatly exceed in quality, ability etc) estar* muy por encima de, descollar* sobre

tower block *n* (BrE) (residential) edificio *m or* bloque *m* de apartamentos *or* (AmL tb) de departamentos *or* (Esp tb) de pisos, torre *f*; (of offices) edificio *m or* bloque *m* de oficinas, torre *f*

towering /'taʊərɪŋ/ *adj* (*before n*) [1] ‹*building/tree*› altísimo [2] ‹*achievement/genius*› destacado, sobresaliente

tow: **~head** *n* (AmE) ▸**blond**[2]; **~headed** *adj* (AmE) ▸**blond**[1]; **~line** *n* ▸**towrope**

town /taʊn/ *n* [c u] (in general) ciudad *f*; (smaller) pueblo *m*, población *f*; **to go into ~** (from outside) ir* a la ciudad; (from suburb) ir* al centro; **in ~** (not outside) en la ciudad; (in center) en el centro; **the best hotel in ~** el mejor hotel de la ciudad; **they live out of ~** viven en las afueras; **she's out of ~ at the moment** está de viaje en este momento; ***to go out on the ~, to have a night on the ~*** ir* *or* salir* de juerga; ***to go to ~ on sth*** (by spending a lot) tirar la casa por la ventana, no reparar en gastos; **the press went to ~ on the story** la prensa se ha despachado a su gusto con la historia; ***to paint the ~ red*** irse* de juerga; (*before n*) ‹*dweller/life*› de la ciudad, urbano; **~ center** *o* (BrE) **centre** centro *m* de la ciudad

town: **~ clerk** *n* (in US) *funcionario encargado de llevar los registros de nacimientos, defunciones etc*; **~ council** *n* (in UK) ayuntamiento *m*, municipio *m*, municipalidad *f*, concejo *m* municipal; **~ councillor** *n* (esp BrE) concejal,

-jala *m,f*, edil, edila *m,f*; ~ **crier** /ˈkraɪər || ˈkraɪə(r)/ *n* pregonero *m*; ~ **hall** *n* ayuntamiento *m*, municipalidad *f*, municipio *m*, alcaldía *f*, presidencia *f* municipal (Méx), intendencia *f* (RPl); ~ **house** *n* [1] (Archit) *casa unifamiliar moderna construida en una hilera de casas similares* [2] (house in town) casa *f* de la ciudad; ~ **meeting** *n* (in US) concejo *m* municipal de vecinos; ~ **planner** *n* urbanista *mf*; ~ **planning** *n* [u] urbanismo *m*; ~**sfolk** *pl n* ▸**townspeople**

township /ˈtaʊnʃɪp/ *n* [1] (in US) (Govt) municipio *m*, municipalidad *m*, ayuntamiento *m* [2] (in South Africa) distrito *m* segregado

townspeople /ˈtaʊnzˌpiːpəl/ *pl n* [1] (in particular place) **the** ~ los vecinos (del lugar) [2] (urban dwellers) gente *f* de (la) ciudad

tow: ~**path** *n* camino *m* de sirga; ~**rope** *n* (Naut) sirga *f*; (Auto) cuerda *f or* cable *m* de remolque; ~ **truck** *n* grúa *f*

toxic /ˈtɑːksɪk || ˈtɒksɪk/ *adj* tóxico

toxicology /ˈtɑːksɪˈkɑːlədʒi || ˌtɒksɪˈkɒlədʒi/ *n* [u] toxicología *f*

toxic shock syndrome *n* [u] síndrome *m* del shock tóxico

toxin /ˈtɑːksən || ˈtɒksɪn/ *n* toxina *f*

toy¹ /tɔɪ/ *n* juguete *m*

(Phrasal verb)

• **toy with** [v ▸ prep ▸ o] ‹*pen/earring/food*› juguetear con; ‹*idea/possibility*› darle* vueltas a; ‹*person/affections*› jugar* con

toy² *adj* [1] ‹*car/gun*› de juguete; ~ **soldier** soldadito *m* (de juguete) [2] (miniature) ‹*dog/poodle*› enano

toy: ~ **boy** *n* (BrE colloq) *amante joven de una mujer mayor*; ~**shop** *n* juguetería *f*

trace¹ /treɪs/ *n*

A [1] [c u] (indication) señal *f*, indicio *m*, rastro *m*; **there was no** ~ *o* **there were no** ~**s of a struggle** no había señales *or* indicios *or* rastros de que hubiera habido una pelea; **they can't find any** ~ **of my letter** no encuentran mi carta por ninguna parte; **to disappear** *o* **vanish without (a)** ~ desaparecer* sin dejar rastro [2] [c] (small amount): ~**s of poison** rastros de veneno; **there was a** ~ **of sadness in his voice** había un dejo de tristeza en su voz; **without a** ~ **of resentment** sin un asomo de resentimiento

B [c] (harness strap) tirante *m*; ***to kick over the*** ~***s*** rebelarse

trace² *vt*

A [1] (chart): **the documentary** ~**s the history of the organization** el documental examina *or* analiza paso a paso la historia de la organización [2] (find) ‹*criminal/witness*› localizar*, ubicar* (AmL); **they can't** ~ **my application form** no encuentran mi solicitud [3] (follow) seguirle* la pista *or* el rastro a, rastrear [4] (find origin of) ‹*fault/malfunction*› descubrir*; **I can** ~ **my family back to the 17th century** los orígenes de mi familia se remontan al siglo XVII; **to** ~ **a call** averiguar* de dónde proviene una llamada

B [1] (on tracing paper) calcar* [2] (draw) ‹*line/outline*› trazar*

trace element *n* oligoelemento *m*

trachea /ˈtreɪkiːə || trəˈkiːə/ *n* (*pl* **-as** *or* **-ae** /-kiːiː/) tráquea *f*

tracing paper /ˈtreɪsɪŋ/ *n* [u] papel *m* de calco *or* de calcar

track¹ /træk/ *n*

A (mark) pista *f*, huellas *fpl*; **to be on sb's** ~**(s)** seguirle* la pista *or* el rastro a algn; **to put** *o* **throw sb off one's/the** ~ despistar a algn; ***to cover one's*** ~***s*** no dejar rastros; ***to keep/lose*** ~ ***of sth/sb***: **the police have been keeping** ~ **of his movements** la policía le ha estado siguiendo la pista; **make sure you keep** ~ **of the time** ten cuidado de que no se te pase la hora; **to keep/lose** ~ **of the conversation/argument** seguir*/perder* el hilo de la conversación/la discusión; **I've lost** ~ **of a lot of old friends** he perdido contacto con muchos de mis viejos amigos; **I lost all** ~ **of the time** perdí por completo la noción del tiempo, no me di cuenta de la hora; ***to make*** ~***s*** (colloq) irse*, ponerse* en camino; ***to stop (dead) in one's*** ~***s*** pararse en seco

B [1] (road, path) camino *m*, sendero *m*; ***off the beaten*** ~ (away from the crowds, tourists) fuera de los caminos trillados; (in an isolated place) en un sitio muy retirado *or* aislado [2] (course of thought, action): **to be on the right/wrong** ~ estar* bien/mal encaminado, ir* por buen/mal camino

C [1] (*race* ~) pista *f*; ***to have the inside*** ~ ***(on sth)*** (AmE) (have the advantage) estar* en una situación de ventaja; (be informed about) estar* al tanto *or* al corriente (de algo); (*before n*) ~ **events** atletismo *m* en pista [2] (horse-racing) (AmE): **to go to the** ~ ir* al hipódromo *or* a las carreras (de caballos)

D [u] (track events) (AmE) atletismo *m* en pista

E (AmE Educ) *grupo de alumnos seleccionados de acuerdo a sus aptitudes*

F (Rail) [1] [c] (way) vía *f* (férrea); **to jump/leave the** ~**(s)** descarrilar(se); ***the wrong side of the*** ~***s*** los barrios bajos (fam); **to be from the wrong side of the** ~**s** ser* de origen humilde [2] [u] (rails etc) vías *fpl*

G (song, piece of music) tema *m*, pieza *f*

H (on tank) oruga *f*

I (for curtains) riel *m*

track² *vt*

A (follow) ‹*animal*› seguirle* la pista a, rastrear; ‹*person*› seguirle* la pista a

B (deposit with feet) (AmE): **they** ~**ed mud all over the floor** dejaron el suelo cubierto de barro

(Phrasal verb)

• **track down** [v ▸ o ▸ adv, v ▸ adv ▸ o] (trace) ‹*criminal/lost object*› localizar*, encontrar*; ‹*missing person*› averiguar* el paradero de, dar* con; **to try to** ~ **down the cause of the problem** tratar de averiguar la causa del problema

track and field *n* [u] atletismo *m*; (*before n*) ~ ~ ~ **events** pruebas *fpl* de atletismo

tracker /ˈtrækər || ˈtrækə(r)/ *n* rastreador, -dora *m,f*; (*before n*) ~ **dog** perro *m* rastreador

tracker fund *n* fondo *m* referenciado (*a un índice*)

tracking /ˈtrækɪŋ/ *n* [u] (AmE Educ) *división del alumnado en grupos de acuerdo al nivel académico*

track: ~ **record** *n* historial *m*, antecedentes *mpl*; ~ **shoe** *n* zapatilla *f* de atletismo; ~**suit** *n* equipo *m* (de deportes), chándal *m* (Esp), pants *mpl* (Méx), buzo *m* (Chi, Per), sudadera *f* (Col), jogging *m* (RPl)

tract /trækt/ *n*

A (of land, sea) extensión *f*

B (Anat) tracto *m*

C (short treatise) tratado *m* breve; (pamphlet) folleto *m*

tractable /ˈtræktəbəl/ *adj* (frml) ‹*person/animal*› dócil, manejable

traction /ˈtrækʃən/ *n* [u] [1] (Mech Eng, Med) tracción *f* [2] (grip) agarre *m*, adherencia *f*

traction engine *n* locomóvil *f*, máquina *f* de vapor locomóvil

tractor /ˈtræktər || ˈtræktə(r)/ *n* [1] (Agr) tractor *m* [2] (truck) cabeza *f*

tractor-trailer /ˈtræktərˈtreɪlər || ˌtræktəˈtreɪlə(r)/ *n* (AmE) camión *m* con remolque *or* (CS tb) con acoplado, tráiler *m* (Esp, Méx)

trade¹ /treɪd/ *n*

A [1] [u] (buying, selling) comercio *m*; **domestic/foreign** ~ comercio interior/exterior; **they were doing a roaring** *o* **brisk** ~ **in umbrellas** estaban haciendo un gran negocio con los paraguas; (*before n*) ~ **agreement** acuerdo *m* comercial; ~ **barrier** barrera *f* arancelaria; ~ **deficit** *o* **gap** déficit *m* en la balanza comercial [2] [u] (business, industry) industria *f*; **the hotel** ~ la hotelería, la industria hotelera [3] [c] (skilled occupation) oficio *m*; **he's a carpenter by** ~ es carpintero de oficio [4] (people in particular trade): **the** ~ el gremio; **as they say in the** ~ como dicen los del gremio *or* los entendidos [5] [u] (customers): **it's designed to attract the tourist** ~ está pensado para atraer a los turistas

B [1] (exchange): **I'll make** *o* **do a** ~ **with you** te lo/la cambio [2] (of players) (AmE Sport) traspaso *m* [3] (player) (AmE Sport) jugador traspasado, jugadora traspasada *m,f*

trade² *vi* [1] (buy, sell) comerciar; **the company has ceased trading** la compañía ha dejado de operar, la compañía ha cerrado; **to** ~ **under the name of ...** operar bajo el nombre de ...; **to** ~ **IN sth** comerciar EN algo [2] (exchange) hacer* un cambio *or* un canje

■ **trade** *vt* [1] ‹*blows/insults/secrets*› intercambiar; **to** ~ **sth FOR sth** cambiar *or* canjear algo POR algo; **to** ~ **sth WITH sb** (AmE) cambiarle algo A algn; **I wouldn't mind trading places with him** ya quisiera yo estar en su lugar *or* en su

t

pellejo 2 (AmE Sport) ‹*player*› traspasar

Phrasal verbs

- **trade in** [v ▸ o ▸ adv, v ▸ adv ▸ o] ‹*car/refrigerator*› entregar* como parte del pago
- **trade on** [v ▸ prep ▸ o] ‹*beauty/disability*› explotar, capitalizar*

trade: **~-in** *n* 1 (article): **they took my old car as a ~-in** aceptaron mi coche usado como parte del pago 2 (transaction) *transacción por la cual se da un artículo usado como parte del pago*, venpermuta *f* (Col); **~mark** *n* 1 (symbol, name) marca *f* (de fábrica); **registered ~mark** marca registrada 2 (distinctive characteristic) sello *m* característico; **~ name** *n* (of article) nombre *m* comercial; (of company) razón *f* social; **~-off** *n*: **it's a ~-off between price and quality** hay que sacrificar un poco la calidad para conseguir un buen precio

trader /ˈtreɪdər || ˈtreɪdə(r)/ *n* (merchant) comerciante *mf*; **market ~** puestero, -ra *m,f*, feriante *mf* (CS), marchante, -ta *m,f* (Méx)

trade: **~ secret** *n* secreto *m* comercial; **~sman** /ˈtreɪdzmən/ *n* (*pl* **-men** /-mən/) 1 (shopkeeper) (dated) comerciante *m*, tendero *m* 2 (deliveryman) proveedor *m*; ⓢ **tradesman's entrance** (BrE) entrada de servicio, puerta de servicio; **~s union** *etc* (BrE) ▸ **~ union** *etc*; **~ union** *n* sindicato *m*, gremio *m* (CS, Per); **to form a ~ union** sindicarse*, sindicalizarse* (AmL), agremiarse (CS, Per); (*before n*) ‹*leader*› sindical, sindicalista, gremial; **the ~ union movement** el movimiento sindical; **~ unionism** /ˈjuːnjənɪzəm/ *n* [u] sindicalismo *m*, gremialismo *m* (CS, Per); **~ unionist** *n* sindicalista *mf*, miembro *m,f* de un sindicato, gremialista *mf* (CS, Per)

trading /ˈtreɪdɪŋ/ *n* [u] 1 (in goods) comercio *m*, actividad *f* *or* movimiento *m* comercial; (*before n*) ‹*profit/loss*› de explotación 2 (on stock exchange) contratación *f*, operaciones *fpl* (bursátiles)

trading: **~ estate** *n* (BrE) zona *f* industrial, polígono *m* industrial (Esp); **~ post** *n*: *establecimiento comercial en un lugar poco poblado*; **~ stamp** *n* cupón *m*

tradition /trəˈdɪʃən/ *n* [u c] tradición *f*; **in the best Irish ~** a la mejor usanza irlandesa; **by ~** por tradición

traditional /trəˈdɪʃn̩əl || trəˈdɪʃənl̩/ *adj* tradicional

traditionally /trəˈdɪʃn̩əli/ *adv* 1 (in a traditional manner) a la manera tradicional 2 (customarily) (*indep*) tradicionalmente

traffic /ˈtræfɪk/ *n* [u]

A 1 (vehicles) tráfico *m*, circulación *f*, tránsito *m* (esp AmL); (*before n*) **~ policeman** agente *m* *or* policía *m* de tráfico *or* de tránsito 2 (of ships) tráfico *m* 3 (of aircraft) tráfico *m* aéreo

B 1 (goods, people transported) tránsito *m*, movimiento *m* 2 (pedestrians) (AmE) tránsito *m* de peatones 3 (paying customers) (AmE) clientela *f*

C (trafficking) tráfico *m*; **drug ~** tráfico de drogas, narcotráfico *m*

Phrasal verb

- **traffic in**: **-ck-** [v ▸ prep ▸ o] ‹*drugs/pornography*› traficar* en

t

traffic: **~ circle** *n* (AmE) rotonda *f*, glorieta *f*, óvalo *m* (Per); **~ island** *n* isla *f* peatonal, refugio *m*; **~ jam** *n* embotellamiento *m*, atasco *m*

trafficker /ˈtræfɪkər || ˈtræfɪkə(r)/ *n* traficante *mf*

trafficking /ˈtræfɪkɪŋ/ *n* [u] tráfico *m*

traffic: **~ light** *n* (*often pl*) semáforo *m*; **~ sign** *n* señal *f* vial *or* de tráfico *or* de tránsito; **~ warden** *n* (in UK) *persona que controla el estacionamiento de vehículos en las ciudades*

tragedy /ˈtrædʒədi/ *n* [c u] (*pl* **-dies**) tragedia *f*

tragic /ˈtrædʒɪk/ *adj* trágico

tragically /ˈtrædʒɪkli/ *adv* trágicamente

tragicomedy /ˈtrædʒɪˈkɑːmədi || ˌtrædʒɪˈkɒmədi/ *n* [u c] tragicomedia *f*

trail¹ /treɪl/ *n* 1 (left by animal, person) huellas *fpl*, rastro *m*; (of dust) estela *f*; **the storms left a ~ of destruction** las tormentas destruyeron *or* arrasaron todo a su paso; **to be on the ~ of sb/sth** seguir* la pista de algn/algo, seguirle* la pista a algn/algo 2 (path) sendero *m*, senda *f*

trail² *vt*

A 1 (drag) ‹*towel/rope*› arrastrar 2 (deposit): **they ~ed mud all over the house** dejaron toda la casa llena de barro a su paso

B 1 (follow) ‹*person/animal/vehicle*› seguir* la pista de, seguirle* la pista a, rastrear 2 (lag behind) ‹*opponent/leader*› ir* a la zaga de; **we ~ed them by six points** nos llevaban seis puntos de ventaja

■ **trail** *vi*

A (drag) arrastrar; **her skirt was ~ing on the floor** iba arrastrando la falda por el suelo

B 1 (lag behind) «*team/contender*» ir* a la zaga 2 (walk wearily) andar con paso cansino; **we ~ed back home again** nos volvimos a casa desanimados

C «*plant*» trepar; «*branches*» colgar*

Phrasal verb

- **trail away, trail off** [v ▸ adv] «*voice/sound*» irse* apagando

trail: **~blazer** *n* pionero, -ra *m,f*; **~breaker** *n* (AmE) ▸ **~blazer**

trailer /ˈtreɪlər || ˈtreɪlə(r)/ *n*

A 1 (for boats, equipment) remolque *m* 2 (*house ~*) (AmE) caravana *f*, tráiler *m*, (AmL), casa *f* rodante (CS, Ven), cámper *f* (Chi, Méx), rulot *f* (Esp) 3 (on truck) tráiler *m*, remolque *m*, acoplado *m* (CS)

B (Cin, TV) **~** (**FOR sth**) avance(s) *m(pl)* *or* (Esp tb) tráiler *m* *or* (CS) sinopsis *f*

trailer: **~ park** *n* (AmE) 1 (site) camping *m* para caravanas (*or* tráilers *etc*) 2 (*before n*) (colloq) ‹*friend*› chabacano, hortera (Esp fam), naco (Méx fam), rasca (CS fam); ‹*manners*› de chabacano, de hortera (Esp fam), de naco (Méx fam), de rasca (CS fam); ‹*hair style*› de mal gusto, hortera (Esp fam), de naco (Méx fam), rasca (CS fam); **~ truck** *n* (AmE) camión *m* articulado

train¹ /treɪn/ *n*

A (Rail) tren *m*; **fast ~** tren expreso *or* rápido; **local** *o* (BrE) **slow ~** *tren que para en todas las estaciones*; **to take the ~** tomar *or* (esp Esp) coger* el tren; **to travel/go by ~** viajar/ir* en tren; (*before n*) **~ driver** (BrE) maquinista *mf*; **~ timetable** (esp BrE) horario *m* de trenes; **the ~ journey** el viaje en tren; **~ set** ferrocarril *m* de juguete

B 1 (of servants, followers) séquito *m*, cortejo *m* 2 (of events, disasters) serie *f*; **~ of thought**: **to lose one's ~ of thought** perder* el hilo (de las ideas)

C (of dress, robe) cola *f*

train² *vt*

A 1 (instruct) ‹*athlete*› entrenar; ‹*soldier*› adiestrar; ‹*child*› enseñar; (accustom) acostumbrar, habituar*; ‹*animal*› enseñar; (to perform tricks etc) amaestrar, adiestrar; ‹*employee/worker*› (in new skill etc) capacitar; ‹*teacher*› formar; **they are being ~ed to use the machine** los están capacitando en el uso de la máquina, les están enseñando a usar la máquina 2 ‹*voice/ear*› educar* 3 ‹*plant*› guiar*

B (aim) **to ~ sth ON sth/sb** ‹*camera/telescope*› enfocar* algo/a algn con algo; ‹*gun*› apuntarle A algo/algn con algo

■ **train** *vi* 1 (receive instruction) «*nurse/singer/musician*» estudiar; **she's ~ing to be a nurse/teacher** estudia enfermería/magisterio, estudia para enfermera/maestra 2 (Sport) entrenar(se)

trained /treɪnd/ *adj* 1 ‹*worker/personnel*› calificado (esp AmL), cualificado (Esp); **a ~ teacher** un profesor titulado *or* diplomado *or* (AmL tb) recibido; **a highly ~ army** un ejército muy bien adiestrado 2 ‹*seal/elephant*› amaestrado, adiestrado; ‹*dog*› entrenado 3 ‹*ear/voice*› educado

trainee /treɪˈniː/ *n* 1 (Busn, Ind) (in a trade) aprendiz, -diza *m,f*; (*before n*) **a ~ hairdresser** un aprendiz de peluquero; **~ manager** *empleado que está haciendo prácticas de gerencia* 2 (recruit) (AmE Mil) recluta *mf*

trainer /ˈtreɪnər || ˈtreɪnə(r)/ *n*

A (of athletes) entrenador, -dora *m,f*; (of racehorse) preparador, -dora *m,f*; (of performing animals) amaestrador, -dora *m,f*, adiestrador, -dora *m,f*

B (training shoe) (BrE colloq) zapatilla *f* de deporte, tenis *m*; **~s** deportivas (Esp)

training /ˈtreɪnɪŋ/ *n* [u] 1 (instruction) capacitación *f*; (*before n*) ‹*course/period*› de capacitación 2 (Sport) entrenamiento *m*; **to be in ~ for sth** estar* entrenando *or* entrenándose para algo; (*before n*) **~ shoe** (BrE) zapatilla *f* de deporte, tenis *m*; **~s** deportivas (Esp)

train: **~man** /ˈtreɪnmən, -mæn/ *n* (*pl* **-men** /-mən, -men/) (AmE) *empleado del ferrocarril*; **~ spotter** /ˈspɑːtər

|| 'spɒtə(r)/n: *persona que tiene como hobby anotar y coleccionar números de locomotoras y vagones*

traipse /treɪps/ *vi* (colloq) (+ *adv compl*): **I ~d all over town** me pateé (fam) *or* me recorrí (a pie) toda la ciudad

trait /treɪt/ *n* rasgo *m*, característica *f*

traitor /'treɪtər || 'treɪtə(r)/ *n* traidor, -dora *m,f*

trajectory /trə'dʒektəri/ *n* (*pl* **-ries**) trayectoria *f*

tram /træm/ *n* (BrE Transp) tranvía *m*

tram: **~car** *n* (BrE) ▸**tram**; **~line** *n* 1 (esp BrE Transp) (track) (*often pl*) vía *f or* carril *m* de tranvía; 2 **~lines** *pl* (in tennis) (BrE) líneas *fpl* laterales

tramp[1] /træmp/ *vi* (+ *adv compl*) (walk heavily): **the prisoners ~ed along in the rain** los prisioneros marchaban pesadamente bajo la lluvia; **they ~ed to the nearest village** fueron a pie *or* caminaron hasta el pueblo más cercano

■ **tramp** *vt* 1 (walk around) ‹*town/city*› recorrerse (a pie), patearse (fam) 2 (tread) (+ *adv compl*) ‹*dirt/snow*›: **she ~ed mud all over the kitchen floor** ensució *or* llenó de barro todo el suelo de la cocina

tramp[2] *n*

A [c] 1 (vagrant) vagabundo, -da *m,f* 2 (loose woman) (AmE colloq) mujerzuela *f*, golfa *f* (Esp fam)

B (*no pl*) 1 (walk) caminata *f* 2 (sound) ruido *m* de pasos

trample /'træmpəl/ *vt* (stamp on, crush) pisotear; **they were ~d to death** murieron aplastados

■ **trample** *vi* 1 **to ~ ON sth** ‹*on coat/newspaper*› pisotear algo; **police horses ~d on demonstrators** los caballos de la policía arrollaron *or* atropellaron a los manifestantes 2 (ignore) **to ~ ON sth** ‹*on rights*› pisotear *or* atropellar algo; **to ~ OVER sb** pisotear a algn

trampoline /'træmpəli:n/ *n* trampolín *m*, cama *f* elástica

tramway /'træmweɪ/ *n* 1 (for trams) ▸**tramline A** 2 (cable railway) (AmE) funicular *m*, teleférico *m*

trance /træns || trɑ:ns/ *n* [c u] trance *m*; **to be in a ~** estar* en trance; **to fall** *o* **go into a ~** entrar en trance

tranquil /'træŋkwəl || 'træŋkwɪl/ *adj* ‹*place*› tranquilo; ‹*person/atmosphere*› tranquilo, sereno; ‹*existence*› tranquilo, apacible (liter)

tranquility, (BrE) **tranquillity** /træŋ'kwɪləti/ *n* [u] (of place, atmosphere) paz *f*, tranquilidad *f*; (of person) calma *f*, serenidad *f*

tranquilize, (BrE) **tranquillize** /'træŋkwəlaɪz || 'træŋkwɪlaɪz/ *vt* sedar, dar* un sedante a

tranquilizer, (BrE) **tranquillizer** /'træŋkwəlaɪzər || 'træŋkwɪlaɪzə(r)/ *n* sedante *m*, tranquilizante *m*; **to be on ~s** estar* tomando sedantes *or* tranquilizantes

transact /trænz'ækt/ *vt*: **to ~ business (with sb)** negociar (con algn), hacer* negocios (con algn)

transaction /trænz'ækʃən/ *n* 1 [c] (deal) transacción *f*, operación *f* 2 [u] (act of transacting) (frml) negociación *f*

transatlantic /'trænzət'læntɪk/ *adj* transatlántico

transcend /træn'send/ *vt* (frml) 1 (go beyond) ‹*boundaries*› ir* más allá de, trascender* 2 (overcome) ‹*limitation/differences*› superar

transcendent /træn'sendənt/ *adj* ‹*joy/hope*› (liter) sin límites

transcendental /'trænsen'dentl̩/ *adj* trascendental; **~ meditation** meditación *f* trascendental

transcribe /træn'skraɪb/ *vt* transcribir*

transcript /'trænskrɪpt/ *n*

A (written copy) transcripción *f*

B (AmE Educ) expediente *m* académico

transcription /træn'skrɪpʃən/ *n* [u c] transcripción *f*

transfer[1] /træns'fɜ:r || træns'fɜ:(r)/ **-rr-** *vt*

A 1 ‹*funds/account*› transferir* 2 ‹*property/right*› transferir*, traspasar, transmitir 3 ‹*call*› pasar; **can you ~ me to Sales?** ¿me puede comunicar *or* (Esp tb) poner con Ventas? 4 ‹*employee/prisoner*› trasladar; ‹*player*› (esp BrE) traspasar; ‹*object*› pasar

B (change): **she ~red schools when she was 12** se cambió de colegio a los 12 años

■ **transfer** *vi* (Transp) hacer* transbordo, transbordar; **to ~ TO sth**: **John ~red to another course/department** John se cambió a otro curso/se trasladó a otro departamento

transfer[2] /'trænsfɜ:r || 'trænsfɜ:(r)/ *n*

A 1 [u c] (Fin, Law) (of funds, accounts) transferencia *f*; (of property) transferencia *f*, traspaso *m*, transmisión *f*; (of power) transferencia *f* 2 [u c] (of employee) traslado *m*; (of player) (esp BrE) traspaso *m*; (*before n*) **~ fee** traspaso *m* 3 [u c] (of passengers) transbordo *m* 4 [c] (person): **the club's latest ~** (esp BrE) el último fichaje del club

B [c] (Transp) 1 (journey) traslado *m* 2 (permit) (AmE) *billete mediante el cual se puede cambiar de tren o autobús sin pago adicional*

C [c] (design) calcomanía *f*

transferable /træns'fɜ:rəbəl/ *adj* transferible; **not ~** intransferible

transferal /træns'fɜ:rəl/ *n* [u c] (AmE) ▸**transfer**[2] **A 1, 2**

transference /'trænsfərəns, træns'fɜ:rəns/ *n* [u] 1 (of energy, authority) (frml) transferencia *f*; **thought ~** transmisión *f* del pensamiento 2 (Psych) transferencia *f*

transfiguration /'trænsˈfɪgjə'reɪʃən || trænsˌfɪgə'reɪʃən/ *n* [u] 1 (transformation) (liter) transformación *f*, transfiguración *f* 2 (Relig) **the T~** la Transfiguración

transfigure /træns'fɪgjər || træns'fɪgə(r)/ *vt* (liter) transformar, transfigurar

transfix /træns'fɪks/ *vt* (make motionless) (*usu pass*) paralizar*; **she was ~ed with terror** se quedó paralizada de terror *or* petrificada

transform /træns'fɔ:rm || træns'fɔ:m/ *vt* transformar

transformation /'trænsfər'meɪʃən || ˌtrænsfə'meɪʃən/ *n* transformación *f*

transformer /træns'fɔ:rmər || træns'fɔ:mə(r)/ *n* transformador *m*

transfusion /træns'fju:ʒən/ *n* [u c] transfusión *f*; **she was given a (blood) ~** le hicieron una transfusión (de sangre)

transgenic /ˌtrænz'dʒenɪk || ˌtrænz'dʒenɪk, ˌtrɑ:nz-/ *adj* transgénico

transgress /træns'gres || trænz'gres/ *vt* (frml) 1 ‹*law/commandment*› transgredir (frml), infringir* 2 (go beyond) exceder, sobrepasar

■ **transgress** *vi* **to ~ (AGAINST sth/sb)** pecar* (CONTRA algo/algn)

transgression /træns'greʃən || trænz'greʃən/ *n* [u c] (frml) transgresión *f* (frml), infracción *f*; (Relig) pecado *m*, falta *f*

transient[1] /'trænziənt, 'trænʃənt || 'trænziənt/ *adj* ‹*joy/pain*› pasajero, fugaz, efímero

transient[2] *n* (vagrant) (AmE) vagabundo, -da *m,f*

transistor /træn'zɪstər, -'sɪstər || træn'zɪstə(r), -'sɪstə(r)/ *n* 1 transistor *m* 2 **~ (radio)** (esp BrE) transistor *m*, radio *f or* (AmL exc CS) radio *m* transistor *or* a transistores

transit /'trænsət, -zət || 'trænzɪt, -sɪt/ *n* 1 [u] (passage) tránsito *m*; **passengers in ~** pasajeros *mpl* en *or* de tránsito; **it was damaged/lost in ~** se dañó/se perdió en el viaje; (*before n*) **~ camp** *campamento temporal para soldados, prisioneros, refugiados etc* 2 [u] (AmE Transp) transporte *m*; (*before n*) **~ police** policía *f* de tráfico *or* tránsito; **~ system** sistema *m* de transporte(s)

transition /træn'zɪʃən/ *n* [u c] (change) transición *f*; **~ FROM sth TO sth** transición *f* DE algo A algo; (*before n*) ‹*period/stage*› de transición

transitional /træn'zɪʃn̩əl || træn'zɪʃənl/ *adj* ‹*stage/period*› de transición

transitive /'trænsətɪv/ *adj* transitivo

transitory /'trænsətɔ:ri || 'trænsɪtri/ *adj* transitorio, pasajero

translatable /træns'leɪtəbəl/ *adj* (*pred*) traducible

translate /træns'leɪt/ *vt* 1 ‹*word/sentence/book*› traducir*; **to ~ sth (FROM sth) INTO sth**: **~ the text from Spanish into French** traduzca el texto del español al francés 2 (convert) **to ~ sth INTO sth**: **~d into centigrade this is 42 degrees** (expresado) en grados centígrados son 42 grados; **to ~ ideas into action** llevar ideas a la práctica

■ **translate** *vi* (Ling) «*person*» traducir*; «*word*» traducirse*; **the word ~s as 'love' in English** esta palabra se traduce por 'love' en inglés; **the poem doesn't ~ well into French** el poema pierde mucho al ser traducido al francés

translation /træns'leɪʃən/ *n* [c u] traducción *f*; **I've only read it in ~** sólo lo he leído traducido *or* en traducción

translator /træns'leɪtər || træns'leɪtə(r)/ *n* traductor, -tora *m,f*

t

translucent /træns'lu:sn̩t || træns'lu:sn̩t/ *adj* traslúcido, translúcido

transmission /trænz'mɪʃən/ *n* 1 [u] (conveyance) transmisión *f* 2 [u c] (broadcasting) transmisión *f*, emisión *f* 3 [u] (of disease) transmisión *f* 4 [u c] (Auto) transmisión *f*

transmit /trænz'mɪt/ **-tt-** *vt* 1 (convey) ‹*light/sound/heat*› transmitir 2 (broadcast) transmitir, emitir 3 ‹*disease/infection*› transmitir, contagiar
■ **transmit** *vi* transmitir, emitir

transmitter /'trænzmɪtər || trænz'mɪtə(r)/ *n* 1 (Rad, TV) transmisor *m* 2 (Telec) micrófono *m*

transmute /trænz'mju:t/ *vt* **to ~ sth (INTO sth)** transmutar *or* convertir* algo (EN algo)

transparency /træns'pærənsi/ *n* (*pl* **-cies**)
A [u] (of material) transparencia *f*
B [c] (Phot) (slide) transparencia *f*, diapositiva *f*

transparent /træns'pærənt/ *adj* ‹*material/glass/paper*› transparente; ‹*meaning*› claro, transparente

transpire /træn'spaɪr || træn'spaɪə(r)/ *vi*
A 1 (become apparent): **it ~s that ...** resulta (ser) que ...; **it finally ~d that ...** finalmente resultó que ... 2 (happen) ocurrir, pasar, suceder
B (Biol, Bot) transpirar

transplant[1] /træns'plænt || træns'plɑ:nt/ *vt* (Hort, Med) trasplantar

transplant[2] /'trænsplænt || 'trænsplɑ:nt/ *n* (Med) trasplante *m*; **he's had a heart/kidney ~** le han hecho un trasplante de corazón/riñón; **hair ~** implante *m* capilar *or* de cabello

transport[1] /'trænspɔ:rt || 'trænspɔ:t/ *n*
A 1 [u] (movement) (esp BrE) transporte *m*; (*before n*) ‹*network/costs*› de transporte; **~ system** sistema *m* de transporte(s) 2 [u] (vehicle) (esp BrE): **salesperson required: own ~ essential** se necesita vendedor: vehículo propio imprescindible 3 [c] (shipment) (AmE) remesa *f*
B [c] (of emotion) (liter) (*often pl*): **she was in ~s of delight at the news** estaba extática con la noticia

transport[2] /træns'pɔ:rt || træns'pɔ:t/ *vt*
A 1 ‹*goods/animals/people*› transportar; **as you enter the palace you are ~ed to another age** al entrar al palacio uno se transporta a otra época 2 (Hist) ‹*convict*› deportar
B (affect) (liter) (*usu pass*): **to be ~ed with joy/delight** estar* extasiado/embelesado

transportation /'trænspər'teɪʃən || ,trænspɔ:'teɪʃən/ *n* [u] 1 (of objects, people) transporte *m* 2 (vehicle) ▸**transport**[1] **A2** 3 (Hist) (of convicts) deportación *f*

transport café *n* (BrE) *restaurante en la carretera usado esp por camioneros*

transporter /træns'pɔ:rtər || træns'pɔ:tə(r)/ *n* transportador *m*

transpose /træns'pəʊz/ *vt* 1 (change order of) ‹*words/letters*› trasponer*, transponer* 2 (Mus) ‹*piece/chord*› transportar

transsexual /træns'sekʃuəl || træns'sekʃʊəl/ *n* transexual *mf*

transverse /trænz'vɜ:rs || 'trænzvɜ:s/ *adj* (frml) ‹*section/beam/engine*› transversal

transvestite /trænz'vestaɪt/ *n* travestido *m*, travesti *m*, travestí *m*

trap[1] /træp/ *n*
A 1 (for animals, people) trampa *f*; **to lay** *o* **set a ~ for sb** tenderle* una trampa *or* una celada a algn; **to fall/walk into a ~** caer* en una trampa 2 ▸**trapdoor**
B (mouth) (sl): **to keep one's ~ shut** no abrir* la boca (fam), no decir* nada; **shut your ~!** ¡cierra el pico! (fam), ¡cállate (la boca)!

trap[2] *vt* **-pp** 1 (snare) ‹*animal*› cazar* (*con trampa*) 2 (cut off, catch) (*often pass*) atrapar; **the driver was ~ped in the wreckage** el conductor quedó atrapado en el vehículo siniestrado; **she ~ped her finger in the door** se agarró *or* se pilló *or* (Esp tb) se cogió el dedo en la puerta 3 (trick, deceive): **he ~ped me into a confession/into admitting that ...** me tendió una trampa y confesé/reconocí que ... 4 ‹*liquid/gas/light/heat*› retener*

trapdoor, **trap door** /træp'dɔ:r || 'træpdɔ:(r)/ trampilla *f*

trapeze /træ'pi:z, trə- || trə'pi:z/ *n* trapecio *m*; (*before n*) **~ artist** trapecista *mf*

trapper /'træpər || 'træpə(r)/ *n* trampero, -ra *m,f*, cazador, -dora *m,f*

trappings /'træpɪŋz/ *pl n* 1 (paraphernalia): **she was seduced by the ~ of office** se dejó seducir por toda la ceremonia que conlleva el cargo; **all the ~ of success** los símbolos del éxito, todo lo que acompaña el éxito 2 (of horse) arreos *mpl*, jaeces *mpl*

Trappist /'træpəst || 'træpɪst/ *adj* trapense, de la Trapa

trapshooting /'træp,ʃu:tɪŋ/ *n* [u] (AmE) tiro *m* al plato

trash[1] /træʃ/ *n* [u] 1 (refuse) (AmE) basura *f*; (*before n*) **~ bag** bolsa *f* de la basura; **~ can** cubo *m or* (CS, Per) tacho *m or* (Méx) bote *m or* (Col) caneca *f or* (Ven) tobo *m* de la basura 2 (worthless stuff) basura *f*; **stop talking ~!** ¡deja de decir estupideces! 3 (worthless people) (AmE colloq) escoria *f*

trash[2] *vt* (AmE) 1 (dispose of) botar (a la basura) (AmL exc RPl), tirar (a la basura) (Esp, RPl) 2 (criticize) (colloq) ‹*movie/book*› poner* por los suelos *or* por el suelo; ‹*person*› despellejar (fam), poner* verde (Esp fam) 3 (vandalize) (sl) destrozar*

trashman /'træʃmæn/ *n* (*pl* **-men** /-men/) (AmE) basurero *m*

trashy /'træʃi/ *adj* **-shier, -shiest** ‹*souvenir*› barato, de porquería (fam), rasca (CS fam); ‹*movie/magazine*› malo; **a ~ novel** una novelucha

trauma /'trɔ:mə/ *n* 1 [c u] (*pl* **-mas**) (shock, painful experience) trauma *m* 2 [c] (*pl* **-mas** *or* **-mata**) (Psych) trauma *m*; (Med) traumatismo *m*, trauma *m*

traumatic /trɔ:'mætɪk/ *adj* traumático, traumatizante

traumatize /'trɔ:mətaɪz/ *vt* traumatizar*

travel[1] /'trævəl/, (BrE) **-ll-** *vi*
A (make journey) viajar; **to ~ by air** *o* **by plane** viajar en avión, volar*; **to ~ by rail** *o* **train** viajar en tren; **to ~ overland/by road** viajar por tierra/por carretera; **passengers ~ing to Budapest** los pasajeros con destino a Budapest; **I spent a month ~ing around France** estuve un mes viajando por *or* recorriendo Francia
B 1 (move, go) «*vehicle*» desplazarse*, ir*; «*light/waves*» propagarse*; **we were ~ing at more than 80mph** íbamos a más de 80 millas por hora; **news ~s fast** las noticias vuelan; **the liquid ~s along this pipe** el líquido corre *or* va por esta tubería 2 (go fast) (colloq): **he was really ~ing!** ¡iba/venía a toda velocidad *or* (fam) como una bala!
C (react to being transported): **this wine ~s very well** la calidad de este vino no se ve afectada por el transporte
D (Busn) ser* viajante *or* representante *or* (RPl tb) corredor
■ **travel** *vt* ‹*country/world*› viajar por, recorrer; ‹*road/distance*› recorrer

travel[2] *n* 1 [u] (activity) viajes *mpl*; **his job involves a lot of ~** tiene que viajar mucho por su trabajo; **Acme T~** Viajes *mpl* Acme; (*before n*) ‹*company/brochure*› de viajes; ‹*industry*› turístico; ‹*book*› de *or* sobre viajes; **~ expenses** gastos *mpl* de viaje *or* desplazamiento; **~ insurance** seguro *m* de viaje 2 **travels** *pl* viajes *mpl*; **he's off on his ~s again** está de viaje otra vez; **if you see Pete in your ~s** (colloq) si ves a Pete por ahí

travel: **~ agency** *n* agencia *f* de viajes; **~ agent** *n* agente *mf* de viajes; **~ agent's** agencia *f* de viajes; **~ bureau** *n* agencia *f* de viajes

traveled, (BrE) **-ll-** /'trævəld/ *adj*: **he is widely ~** *o* **very well-~** ha viajado mucho, es muy viajado (AmS)

traveler, (BrE) **-ll-** /'trævlər || 'trævlə(r)/ *n* 1 viajero, -ra *m,f*; **she's a seasoned ~** ha viajado mucho, es una persona muy viajada (AmS) 2 (Busn) representante *mf*, viajante *mf*, corredor, -dora *m,f* (RPl) 3 (itinerant person) (BrE) *persona que ha adoptado el estilo de vida errante de los gitanos*

traveler's check, (BrE) **traveller's cheque** *n* cheque *m* de viaje *or* de viajero

traveling[1], (BrE) **-ll-** /'trævlɪŋ/ *n* [u] (for pleasure, business): **do you like ~?** ¿te gusta viajar?; (*before n*) **~ expenses** gastos *mpl* de viaje *or* de desplazamiento

traveling[2], (BrE) **-ll-** *adj* 1 (for journeys) ‹*clothes/rug/companion*› de viaje 2 (itinerant) ‹*circus/exhibition*› ambulante, itinerante; **~ salesman** viajante *m*, representante *m*, corredor *m* (RPl)

travelog, (BrE) **travelogue** /'trævəlɔ:g || 'trævəlɒg/ *n* documental *m* sobre viajes

t

travel: ~-sick *adj* (BrE) mareado; **to be** *o* **feel ~-sick** estar* mareado; **to get ~-sick** marearse; **~ sickness** *n* [u] (BrE) mareo *m*

traverse /trəˈvɜːrs/ *vt* (cross) (frml) atravesar*, cruzar*

travesty /ˈtrævəsti/ *n* (*pl* **-ties**) (pej) parodia *f*, farsa *f*; **this trial is a ~ of justice** este juicio es una farsa

trawl¹ /trɔːl/ *vi* hacer* pesca de arrastre, pescar* con red de arrastre

■ **trawl** *vt* 1 (Naut) ‹*waters/seabed*› pescar* en (*con red de arrastre*) 2 (search) **to ~ sth FOR sth** buscar* algo EN algo; **he was ~ing the newspapers for jobs** estaba buscando ofertas de empleo en los periódicos

trawl² *n* **~ (net)** red *f* de (pesca de) arrastre

trawler /ˈtrɔːlər || ˈtrɔːlə(r)/ *n* barca *f* pesquera (*utilizada para hacer pesca de arrastre*), bou *m*

tray /treɪ/ *n* bandeja *f*; (for ice cubes) cubetera *f*; (*baking* ~) bandeja *f or* placa *f* (de horno)

treacherous /ˈtretʃərəs/ *adj* 1 ‹*person*› traicionero, traidor; **a ~ act** una traición 2 (dangerous, unpredictable) ‹*bend*› peligroso; ‹*sea/current*› traicionero; **~ weather conditions** condiciones climáticas adversas

treacherously /ˈtretʃərəsli/ *adv* (disloyally) traidoramente, a traición

treachery /ˈtretʃəri/ *n* [u c] (*pl* **-ries**) traición *f*; **an act of ~** una traición

treacle /ˈtriːkəl/ *n* [u] (esp BrE) melaza *f*

treacly /ˈtriːkli/ *adj* **-lier, -liest** ‹*substance*› meloso; ‹*manner/voice*› meloso, empalagoso

tread¹ /tred/ (*past* **trod**; *past p* **trodden** *or* **trod**) *vi* pisar; **to ~ in sth** pisar algo; **to ~ carefully** *o* **warily** andarse* con cuidado *or* con cautela *or* con pie(s) de plomo; **a journalist who ventures where others fear to ~** un periodista que se aventura a entrar donde otros no se atreven; **to ~ softly** intentar no hacer ruido; *see also* **tread on**

■ **tread** *vt* 1 (crush): **she trod the earth down** apisonó la tierra; **you're ~ing mud into the carpet** estás embarrando la alfombra con los zapatos; **to ~ grapes** pisar uvas; **to ~ water** flotar (*en posición vertical*) 2 (make): **they've trodden a hole in the carpet** han hecho un agujero en la alfombra; **she followed the well-trodden path into marriage** siguió el trillado camino del matrimonio

Phrasal verb

• **tread on** [v ▸ prep ▸ o] (esp BrE) pisar; **someone trod on my foot** alguien me pisó

tread² *n*

A [c u] (step, footfall) paso *m*; (steps) pasos *mpl*; **to walk with a heavy ~** andar* con paso cansino

B [c u] (molding — on tire) banda *f* de rodamiento; (— on sole of shoe) dibujo *m*

C [c] (of stair) escalón *m*, peldaño *m*

treadle /ˈtredl̩/ *n* pedal *m*

treadmill /ˈtredmɪl/ *n* 1 (unrewarding situation) rutina *f* 2 (Hist, Med) rueda *f* de andar 3 (in gym) cinta *f* de andar *or* correr, trotadora *f* (Chi)

treason /ˈtriːzn̩/ *n* [u] traición *f*; **an act of ~** una traición

treasonable /ˈtriːzn̩əbəl || ˈtriːzn̩əbəl/, **treasonous** /ˈtriːzn̩əs/ *adj*: **~ offense** delito *m* de traición

treasure¹ /ˈtreʒər || ˈtreʒə(r)/ *n* 1 [u] (hoard of wealth) tesoros *mpl* 2 [c] (sth valuable, prized) tesoro *m*; (*before n*) **~ hunt** (Games) búsqueda *f* del tesoro; **a ~ house of information** una mina de información 3 (term of endearment) tesoro *m*

treasure² *vt* 1 (value greatly): **thank you for the book, I shall always ~ it** gracias por el libro, lo guardaré como algo muy especial; **I ~ the moments we spent together** el recuerdo de los momentos que pasamos juntos es muy preciado para mí 2 **treasured** *past p* ‹*possession*› preciado

treasurer /ˈtreʒərər || ˈtreʒərə(r)/ *n* tesorero, -ra *m,f*

treasure trove *n* [u] tesoro *m* (oculto)

treasury /ˈtreʒəri/ *n* (*pl* **-ries**)

A 1 (public, communal funds) erario *m*, tesoro *m* 2 **the Treasury** *o* **the treasury** el fisco, la hacienda pública, el tesoro (público); **Department of the T~** (in US) Departamento *m* del Tesoro, (*de los Estados Unidos*) ≈ ministerio *m* de Hacienda; (*before n*) **T~ Secretary** (in US) Secretario *m* del Tesoro (*de los Estados Unidos*), ≈ ministro *m* de Hacienda

B (anthology) antología *f*

treat¹ /triːt/ *vt*

A (+ *adv compl*) 1 (behave toward) ‹*person/animal*› tratar; **to ~ sb like a child** tratar a algn como a un niño; **how's life been ~ing you?** (colloq) ¿cómo te trata la vida? (fam) 2 (use, handle) ‹*tool/vehicle*› tratar 3 (regard, consider): **to ~ sth with suspicion** ver* algo con sospecha; **you seem to ~ this whole thing as a joke** pareces tomarte a broma todo esto

B (process) ‹*wood/fabric/sewage*› tratar

C (deal with) (frml) ‹*subject*› tratar

D (Med) ‹*patient/disease*› tratar; **she's being ~ed for an ulcer** está en tratamiento por una úlcera

E (entertain): **I'm ~ing you** te invito yo; **to ~ sb TO sth**: **may I ~ you to lunch?** ¿te puedo invitar a comer?; **why don't you ~ yourself to a new dress?** ¿por qué no te das un gusto y te compras un vestido nuevo?; **we were ~ed to a performance of traditional dancing** nos ofrecieron un espectáculo de bailes folklóricos

treat² *n* gusto *m*; **I bought myself an ice cream as** *o* **for a ~** me compré un helado para darme (un) gusto; **as a special ~** como algo muy especial; **there's a ~ in store for you** te espera una bonita sorpresa; **this is *my* ~** invito *or* pago yo; ***to come on/go down a ~*** (BrE colloq): **the project is coming on a ~** el proyecto marcha sobre ruedas; **this champagne goes down a ~** este champán es una delicia; ***to work a ~*** salir* a las mil maravillas

treatise /ˈtriːtəs || ˈtriːtɪs, -ɪz/ *n* **~ (ON sth)** tratado *m* (SOBRE algo)

treatment /ˈtriːtmənt/ *n* [u c]

A (handling — of person, animal, object) trato *m*; (— of subject, idea) tratamiento *m*; **her ~ of her children** la manera como trata a sus hijos; **the furniture has had some rough ~** se les ha dado un muy mal trato a los muebles

B (of metal, fabric, waste) tratamiento *m*; ***to get/give sb the (full) ~***: **those thugs certainly gave him the ~** esos matones le dieron una buena paliza; **we got the full ~: luxury accommodation, champagne ...** nos trataron a cuerpo de rey: alojamiento de lujo, champán ...

C (Med) tratamiento *m*; **I'm having ~ for my back** estoy recibiendo tratamiento por mi problema de espalda

treaty /ˈtriːti/ *n* (*pl* **-ties**) (Pol) tratado *m*

treble¹ /ˈtrebəl/ *n* 1 [c] (singer) tiple *mf*, soprano *mf*; (voice) voz *f* de tiple *or* soprano 2 [u] (Audio) agudos *mpl*

treble² *vt* triplicar*

■ **treble** *vi* triplicarse*

treble³ *adj*

A (threefold) triple; **three nine ~ five** (BrE) tres nueve cinco cinco cinco

B (*before n*) (Mus) ‹*voice/part*› de tiple *or* soprano

treble clef *n* clave *f* de sol

tree /triː/ *n* árbol *m*; **apple/palm/walnut ~** manzano *m*/palmera *f*/nogal *m*; ***money doesn't grow on ~s*** el dinero no crece en los árboles, el dinero cuesta ganarlo; ***to be barking up the wrong ~*** errar* el tiro; ***you/one can't see the forest*** *o* (BrE) ***the wood for the ~s*** los árboles no dejan ver el bosque; (*before n*) **~ house** *cabaña construida en un árbol para juegos infantiles*; **~ line** *límite a partir del cual no crece vegetación boscosa*; **~ surgeon** arboricultor, -tora *m,f*; **~ trunk** tronco *m*

treeless /ˈtriːləs || ˈtriːlɪs/ *adj* sin árboles

tree: ~-lined *adj* (*before n*) bordeado de árboles, arbolado; **~top** *n* copa *f* de árbol

trek¹ /trek/ *n* (hike) caminata *f*; **it's quite a ~ to the shops** hay un buen paseo hasta llegar a las tiendas

trek² *vi* **-kk-** caminar; **to go ~king** hacer* senderismo; **I had to ~ all over London looking for the book** (colloq) tuve que patearme todo Londres buscando el libro (fam)

trekking /ˈtrekɪŋ/ *n* senderismo *m*, trekking *m*

trellis /ˈtreləs || ˈtrelɪs/ *n* enrejado *m*, espaldar *m*, espaldera *f*

tremble¹ /ˈtrembəl/ *vi* temblar*; **I was trembling with fear** temblaba de miedo; **my legs/hands were trembling** me temblaban las piernas/las manos; **her voice ~d with emotion** la voz le temblaba de emoción

tremble² *n* temblor *m*; **to be all of a ~** (BrE colloq) estar* *or* temblar* como un flan (fam)

tremendous /trɪˈmendəs/ *adj* 1 (great, huge) ‹*difference/disappointment*› tremendo, enorme; ‹*speed/success*› tremendo; ‹*explosion/blow*› terrible, tremendo; **she was a**

t

~ **help** me (*or* nos *etc*) ayudó muchísimo 2 (very good) formidable; **we had a ~ time** lo pasamos estupendo *or* fantástico

tremendously /trɪ'mendəsli/ *adv* tremendamente, enormemente

tremor /'tremər || 'tremə(r)/ *n* 1 (quiver) temblor *m*; **with a ~ in her voice** con voz temblorosa 2 (*earth* ~) temblor *m* (de tierra), seísmo *m*, sismo *m* (AmL)

tremulous /'tremjələs || 'tremjʊləs/ *adj* (liter) (trembling) ‹*voice/hand*› trémulo (liter), tembloroso

trench /trentʃ/ *n* 1 (ditch) zanja *f* 2 (Mil) trinchera *f*; (*before n*) ~ **warfare** guerra *f* de trincheras

trenchant /'trentʃənt/ *adj* incisivo, mordaz

trench coat *n* trinchera *f*, gabardina *f*, impermeable *m*

trend /trend/ *n* 1 (pattern, tendency) tendencia *f*; **a ~ TOWARD sth** una tendencia A *or* HACIA algo; **that's the general ~ among young people** ésa es la tónica general entre los jóvenes; **to set the ~** marcar* la pauta; **upward/downward ~** tendencia alcista *or* al alza/bajista *or* a la baja 2 (fashion) moda *f*

trendsetter /'trend,setər || 'trend,setə(r)/ *n*: *persona que inicia una moda*

trendy /'trendi/ *adj* **-dier, -diest** moderno, modernoso (fam); **she was wearing a very ~ outfit** iba vestida muy moderna *or* a la última moda; **this part of town is getting very ~** este barrio se está poniendo de moda

trepidation /'trepə'deɪʃən || ,trepɪ'deɪʃən/ *n* [u] (frml) (fear) temor *m* (frml), miedo *m*; (worry, anxiety) inquietud *f*; **I entered his office, in** *o* **with ~** entré atemorizado en su oficina

trespass[1] /'trespəs/ *vi*

A (Law) *entrar sin autorización en propiedad ajena*; **they were ~ing on my land** habían entrado en mi propiedad sin autorización; ⊗ **no trespassing** prohibido el paso, propiedad privada

B (offend) (arch): **as we forgive them that ~ against us** así como nosotros perdonamos a nuestros deudores

trespass[2] *n*

A [u c] (Law) *entrada sin autorización en propiedad ajena*

B [c] (offense) (arch): **forgive us our ~es** perdónanos nuestras deudas

trespasser /'trespəsər || 'trespəsə(r)/ *n* intruso, -sa *m,f*; ⊗ **trespassers will be prosecuted** ≈ prohibido el paso, propiedad privada

tress /tres/ *n* (liter) 1 (lock of hair) mechón *m* 2 **tresses** *pl* (hair) cabellera *f* (liter), cabellos *mpl*

trestle /'tresəl/ *n* caballete *m*

trews /'tru:z/ *pl n* (BrE) *pantalones de tela escocesa*

tri- /'traɪ/ *pref* tri-

trial[1] /'traɪəl/ *n*

A (Law) 1 [c] (court hearing) proceso *m*, juicio *m*; **murder/rape ~** proceso *or* juicio por asesinato/violación 2 [u] (judgment) juicio *m*; **if the case goes to ~** si el caso va a juicio; **she was brought to ~** fue procesada; **to be on ~ for murder** estar* siendo procesado por asesinato; **to stand ~** ser* procesado *or* juzgado; **to give sb a fair ~** juzgar* a algn con imparcialidad

B [u c] (test) prueba *f*; **clinical ~** ensayo *m* clínico; **on ~** a prueba; **you learn by ~ and error** uno aprende equivocándose *or* por ensayo y error

C [c] (trouble) padecimiento *m*, sufrimiento *m*; **~s and tribulations** tribulaciones *fpl*

D (Sport) (*usu pl*) prueba *f* de selección

trial[2] *adj* ‹*period/flight*› de prueba; **to employ sb on a ~ basis** contratar a algn a prueba; **~ offer** oferta *f* especial (*para promover un producto nuevo*); **~ run** prueba *f*

triangle /'traɪ,æŋgəl/ *n* (Math, Mus) triángulo *m*

triangular /traɪ'æŋgjələr || traɪ'æŋgjʊlə(r)/ *adj* triangular

triathlete /,traɪ'æθli:t/ *n* triatleta *mf*

triathlon /,traɪ'æθlɑ:n, -lən || ,traɪ'æθlɒn, -lən/ *n* triatlón *m*

tribal /'traɪbəl/ *adj* tribal

tribe /traɪb/ *n* tribu *f*

tribesman /'traɪbzmən/ *n* (*pl* **-men** /-mən/) miembro *m* de una tribu

tribulation /'trɪbjə'leɪʃən || ,trɪbjʊ'leɪʃən/ *n* [u c] (liter) tribulación *f*

tribunal /traɪ'bju:nl/ *n* 1 (court) tribunal *m* 2 (committee of inquiry) (BrE) comisión *f* investigadora

tributary /'trɪbjəteri || 'trɪbjʊtəri/ *n* (*pl* **-ries**) (river) afluente *m*, río *m* tributario

tribute /'trɪbju:t/ *n*

A [c u] (acknowledgment) homenaje *m*, tributo *m* (AmL); **to pay ~ to sb/sth** rendir* homenaje *or* (AmL tb) tributo a algn/algo; **the movie is a ~ to the courage of these men** la película rinde homenaje *or* (AmL tb) tributo a la valentía de estos hombres

B [u] (payment) tributo *m*

trice /traɪs/ *n*: **in a ~** en un periquete (fam), en un santiamén (fam)

triceps /'traɪseps/ *n* (*pl* ~) tríceps *m*

trick[1] /trɪk/ *n*

A 1 (ruse) trampa *f*, ardid *m*; (*before n*) **~ photography** trucaje *m*; **a ~ question** una pregunta con trampa; *see also* **dirty tricks** 2 (prank, joke) broma *f*, jugarreta *f*; **my eyes/memory must be playing ~s on me** debo de estar viendo visiones/me debe estar engañando la memoria; **she's up to her old ~s again** ya está otra vez haciendo de las suyas; **how's ~s?** (sl) ¿qué onda? (AmL arg), ¿qué tal? (fam)

B (feat, skilful act) truco *m*; **to do card ~s** hacer* trucos con las cartas; **magic ~** truco de magia; **the ~ is to add the oil slowly** el truco *or* el secreto está en añadir el aceite poco a poco; **we've tried every ~ in the book** hemos intentado todo lo habido y por haber; **the ~s of the trade** los trucos del oficio; **give it a good thump, that should do the ~** dale un buen golpe y verás como funciona; ▸**dog[1]**

C (in card games) baza *f*; **to take/win** *o* **make a ~** hacerse*/ganar una baza; ***he/she doesn't miss*** *o* ***never misses a ~*** no se le escapa ni una

trick[2] *vt* engañar; **to ~ sb INTO -ING** engañar a algn PARA QUE (+ *subj*); **to ~ sb OUT OF sth** birlarle algo a algn

trick[3] *adj* (*before n*) 1 ‹*cigar/spider*› de juguete, de mentira, de pega (Esp fam) 2 (AmE) ‹*knee/elbow*› con problemas

trickery /'trɪkəri/ *n* [u] artimañas *fpl*

trickle[1] /'trɪkəl/ *vi* (+ *adv compl*) 1 «*liquid*»: **perspiration ~d down his forehead** le corrían gotas de sudor por la frente; **the water was trickling away** el agua se iba escurriendo poco a poco 2 (arrive, go): **letters are still trickling in** todavía se está recibiendo alguna que otra carta; **the audience began to ~ back into the hall** poco a poco el público fue volviendo a la sala

■ **trickle** *vt*: **he ~d water over the leaves** dejó caer un hilito de agua sobre las hojas

trickle[2] *n* hilo *m*; **the river is now no more than a ~** el río ya no es más que un hilito (de agua); **applications have slowed to a ~** ya sólo se recibe alguna que otra solicitud

trickle charger *n* cargador *m* de batería (*para carga de entretenimiento*)

trick or treat[1] *n*: *frase con la cual en la noche de Halloween los niños amenazan con una jugarreta si no reciben un regalo*

trick or treat[2], **trick-or-treat** *vi*: **to go ~ ~ ~ing** *salir a recorrer casas amenazando con una jugarreta si no se recibe un regalo*

trickster /'trɪkstər || 'trɪkstə(r)/ *n* embaucador, -dora *m,f*

tricky /'trɪki/ *adj* **trickier, trickiest** 1 (difficult) ‹*task/problem*› difícil, peliagudo, que tiene sus bemoles 2 (sensitive, delicate) ‹*matter/problem*› delicado 3 (devious) ‹*person/scheme*› taimado, astuto

tricolor, (BrE) **tricolour** /'traɪ,kʌlər || 'trɪkələ(r)/ *n* bandera *f* tricolor

tricycle /'traɪsɪkəl/ *n* triciclo *m*

trident /'traɪdnt/ *n* tridente *m*

tried /traɪd/ *adj* ‹*method/procedure*› probado; **~ and tested products** productos *mpl* de probada calidad

triennial /traɪ'eniəl/ *adj* (frml) trienal

trifle /'traɪfəl/ *n*

A 1 [c] (trivial thing) nimiedad *f* 2 (small amount) (*no pl*) insignificancia *f*; **it's a ~ too salty** (*as adv*) está un poquitín *or* un pelín salado (fam)

B [u c] (Culin) *postre de bizcocho, jerez, crema y frutas*, sopa *f* inglesa (RPl)

(Phrasal verb)

- **trifle with** [v ▸ prep ▸ o] ‹*person/emotions*› jugar* con

trifling /'traɪflɪŋ/ *adj* insignificante, sin importancia

trigger¹ /'trɪgər || 'trɪgə(r)/ *n*

A **1** (of gun) gatillo *m*; **to pull the ~** apretar* el gatillo; (*before n*) **~ finger** índice *m* **2** (of camera, machine) disparador *m*

B (catalyst) **~ (FOR sth)**: **it can be a ~ for an asthmatic reaction** puede provocar reacciones asmáticas

trigger² *vt* **~ (off)** ‹*reaction/response*› provocar*; ‹*revolt*› desencadenar, hacer* estallar

trigger-happy /'trɪgər'hæpi || 'trɪgəhæpi/ *adj* (colloq) que dispara a la menor provocación

trigonometry /'trɪgə'nɑːmətri || ˌtrɪgə'nɒmətri/ *n* [u] trigonometría *f*

trilby /'trɪlbi/ *n* (*pl* **-bies**) (BrE) sombrero *m* (*de fieltro*)

trill¹ /trɪl/ *n* **1** (in music, of birdsong) trino *m* **2** (Ling) vibración *f*

trill² *vi* «*bird*» trinar, gorjear

trillion /'trɪljən/ *n* **1** (esp in US: 10^{12}) billón *m* **2** (esp in UK: 10^{18}) trillón *m*; *see also* **hundred**

trilogy /'trɪlədʒi/ *n* (*pl* **-gies**) trilogía *f*

trim¹ /trɪm/ *adj* **-mm-** **1** (slim) ‹*figure/person*› esbelto, estilizado **2** (neat) ‹*uniform/suit*› elegante, de buen corte

trim² *n*

A [u] (good condition): ***to be in (good)* ~** estar* en buen estado *or* en buenas condiciones; **swimming keeps me in ~** la natación me mantiene en forma *or* en buen estado físico

B [c] (cut) recorte *m*; **just a ~, please** córteme sólo las puntas, por favor; **to give the hedge a ~** recortar el seto

C [u] (on clothes) adornos *mpl*; (along edges) ribete *m*

D (on bodywork of car) banda *f* lateral; (inside car) tapicería *f*

trim³ *vt* **-mm-**

A **1** (cut) ‹*hair/beard/edges*› recortar; ‹*bush/branches*› recortar, podar; **~ the fat off the meat** quítele la grasa a la carne **2** (reduce) ‹*staff*› reducir*, recortar; ‹*budget/spending*› recortar

B **1** (decorate) ‹*dress/hat*› adornar; **~med with velvet** con adornos de terciopelo; (round edge) con ribetes de terciopelo, ribeteado de terciopelo **2** (upholster) (Auto) tapizar*

C (Naut) ‹*sail*› orientar

D (defeat decisively) (AmE colloq) darle* una paliza a (fam)

trimester /traɪ'mestər || traɪ'mestə(r)/ *n* (AmE) trimestre *m*

trimming /'trɪmɪŋ/ *n*

A [u c] (on clothes) adorno *m*; (along edges) ribete *m*

B **trimmings** *pl* **1** (accompaniments): **turkey with all the ~s** pavo con la guarnición tradicional **2** (offcuts) recortes *mpl*

Trinidad /'trɪnədæd || 'trɪnɪdæd/ *n* Trinidad *f*; **~ and Tobago** Trinidad y Tobago

Trinity /'trɪnəti/ *n* **the (Holy) ~** la (Santísima) Trinidad

trinket /'trɪŋkət || 'trɪŋkɪt/ *n* chuchería *f*, baratija *f*

trio /'triːəʊ/ *n* trío *m*

trip¹ /trɪp/ *n*

A (journey) viaje *m*; (excursion) excursión *f*; (outing) salida *f*; **she's going on a ~ to Japan** se va de viaje al Japón; **a ~ to the zoo/dentist** una visita al zoológico/dentista

B **1** (stumble, fall) tropezón *m*, traspié *m* **2** (attempt to make sb fall) zancadilla *f*

C (sl) **1** (drug-induced) viaje *m* (arg), colocón *m* (arg), pasón *m* (Méx arg) **2** (obsession): **she's been on a real guilt ~ lately** le ha dado por sentirse culpable últimamente; *see also* **ego trip**

trip² **-pp-** *vi*

A (stumble) tropezar*; **to ~ ON/OVER sth** tropezar* CON algo; **they were ~ping over themselves to help him** se deshacían por ayudarlo

B (move lightly and easily) (+ *adv compl*): **she ~ped along beside him** caminaba a su lado con paso airoso *or* ligero; **her surname doesn't exactly ~ off the tongue** su apellido no es muy fácil de pronunciar, que digamos

■ **trip** *vt* **1** **~ (up)** (make stumble — intentionally) hacerle* una zancadilla a, ponerle* *or* echarle una *or* la zancadilla a (Esp) **2** (set off) ‹*alarm*› activar, hacer* que se dispare

(Phrasal verbs)

- **trip over** [v ▸ adv] tropezar* y caerse*
- **trip up**

A [v ▸ adv] (make mistake) equivocarse*, meter la pata (fam)

B [v ▸ o ▸ adv, v ▸ adv ▸ o] **1** (cause to make mistake) hacer* equivocar **2** ▸ **trip²** *vt* **1**

tripe /traɪp/ *n* [u] **1** (Culin) mondongo *m* (AmS) *or* (Esp) callos *mpl or* (Méx) pancita *f or* (Chi) guatitas *fpl* **2** (nonsense) (colloq) paparruchas *fpl* (fm), chorradas *fpl* (Esp fam), mamadas *fpl* (Méx fam), babosadas *fpl* (AmC, Col, Méx fam), leseras *fpl* (Chi fam)

triple¹ /'trɪpəl/ *adj* triple

triple² *adv*: **~ the amount** el triple

triple³ *vt* triplicar*

■ **triple** *vi* **1** (increase threefold) triplicarse* **2** (in baseball) (AmE) hacer* un triple *or* un triplete

triple⁴ *n* (in baseball) (AmE) triple *m*, triplete *m*

triple: **~ jump** *n* triple salto *m* (de longitud); **~ jumper** *n* saltador, -dora *m,f* de triple salto

triplet /'trɪplət || 'trɪplɪt/ *n* trillizo, -za *m,f*

triplicate /'trɪpləkət || 'trɪplɪkət/ *n*: **in ~** por triplicado

tripod /'traɪpɑːd || 'traɪpɒd/ *n* trípode *m*

Tripoli /'trɪpəli/ *n* Trípoli *m*

tripper /'trɪpər || 'trɪpə(r)/ *n* (BrE) excursionista *mf*

triptych /'trɪptɪk/ *n* tríptico *m*

trite /traɪt/ *adj* **triter, tritest** trillado

triumph¹ /'traɪəmf || 'traɪʌmf/ *n* [c u] (victory) triunfo *m*; **they returned in ~** regresaron triunfalmente; **~ OVER sb/sth** triunfo SOBRE algn/algo

triumph² *vi* triunfar; **to ~ OVER sb/sth** triunfar SOBRE algn/algo

triumphal /traɪ'ʌmfəl/ *adj* ‹*procession/march*› triunfal; **~ arch** arco *m* de triunfo

triumphant /traɪ'ʌmfənt/ *adj* ‹*troops/team*› triunfador; ‹*moment/entry*› triunfal; ‹*smile*› de triunfo, triunfal

triumphantly /traɪ'ʌmfəntli/ *adv* triunfalmente

trivia /'trɪviə/ *pl n* trivialidades *fpl*, banalidades *fpl*, nimiedades *fpl*

trivial /'trɪviəl/ *adj* ‹*events/concerns*› trivial, banal; ‹*sum/details*› insignificante, nimio

triviality /'trɪvi'æləti/ *n* (*pl* **-ties**)

A [c] **1** (matter) trivialidad *f*, banalidad *f*, nimiedad *f* **2** (remark, idea): **we exchanged trivialities** hablamos de cosas intrascendentes

B [u] (of event, conversation, book) trivialidad *f*, banalidad *f*

trivialize /'trɪviəlaɪz/ *vt* trivializar*, quitarle importancia a

trod /trɑːd || trɒd/ *past and past p of* **tread¹**

trodden /'trɑːdn̩ || 'trɒdn̩/ *past p of* **tread¹**

Trojan¹ /'trəʊdʒən/ *adj* troyano; **the ~ Horse/War** el caballo/la guerra de Troya

Trojan² *n* (Hist) troyano, -na *m,f*; ***to work like a* ~** trabajar como un burro (fam)

troll /trəʊl/ *n* gnomo *m* (*de la mitología escandinava*)

trolley /'trɑːli || 'trɒli/ *n*

A **1** **~ (bus)** trolebús *m* **2** **~ (car)** (AmE) tranvía *m*

B (BrE) (for food, drink) carrito *m*, mesa *f* rodante; (at station, airport, in supermarket) carro *m*, carrito *m*; (in hospital) carrito *m*; (for going shopping) carrito *m*; (in mine) vagoneta *f*; ***to be off one's* ~** (BrE colloq) estar* chiflado (fam), estar* mal de la cabeza

trollop /'trɑːləp || 'trɒləp/ *n* (dated) mujerzuela *f*, mujer *f* de la calle

trombone /trɑːm'bəʊn || trɒm'bəʊn/ *n* trombón *m*

trombonist /trɑːm'bəʊnəst || trɒm'bəʊnɪst/ *n* trombón *mf*

tromp /trɑːmp || trɒmp/ *vi* (AmE colloq): **to ~ on/over sth** pisotear algo

■ **tromp** *vt* pisotear, pisar

troop¹ /truːp/ *n*

A **1** (unit) compañía *f*, (of cavalry) escuadrón *m* **2** (of Scouts) tropa *f* **3** (of people) (colloq) tropel *m*

B **troops** *pl* (soldiers): **our ~s** nuestras tropas; **500 ~s** 500 soldados

troop² *vi* (+ *adv compl*): **they ~ed past the coffin** desfilaron ante el féretro (frml); **to ~ in/out** entrar/salir* en tropel *or* en masa

■ **troop** *vt*: **to ~ the colour** (BrE) desfilar con la bandera

troop carrier *n* transporte *m* de tropas

t

trooper /ˈtruːpər || ˈtruːpə(r)/ *n* 1 (cavalryman) soldado *m* de caballería; ***to swear like a*** ~ hablar como un carretero *or* una verdulera 2 (state police officer) (AmE) agente *mf*

troopship *n: barca para el transporte de tropas*

trophy /ˈtrəʊfi/ *n* (*pl* **-phies**) trofeo *m*

tropic /ˈtrɑːpɪk || ˈtrɒpɪk/ *n* 1 (line) trópico *m*; **the T~ of Cancer/Capricorn** el trópico de Cáncer/Capricornio 2 **tropics** *pl* (area) **the ~s** el trópico

tropical /ˈtrɑːpɪkəl || ˈtrɒpɪkəl/ *adj* tropical

trot[1] /trɑːt || trɒt/ *n* (*no pl*) trote *m*; **to go at a ~** ir* al trote, trotar; **to break into a ~** empezar* a trotar; ***on the*** ~ (BrE colloq): **four times/nights on the ~** cuatro veces/noches seguidas; ***to have the ~s*** (colloq) tener* diarrea, estar* churriento (Col) *or* (Chi) churrete (fam), tener* cagalera (Esp) *or* (Méx) chorrillo (fam)

trot[2] **-tt-** *vi* 1 (Equ) ⟨⟨*horse/rider*⟩⟩ trotar 2 (go) (+ *adv compl*): **I'm just ~ting across** *o* **over to the library** voy un momento hasta la biblioteca

■ **trot** *vt* hacer* trotar

Phrasal verb

• **trot out** [v ▸ o ▸ adv, v ▸ adv ▸ o] ⟨*excuses/clichés*⟩ salir* con; ⟨*facts*⟩ recitar de memoria *or* (fam) como un loro

troth /trɑːθ, trəʊθ || trəʊθ/ *n* (arch) ▸ **plight[2]**

trotter /ˈtrɑːtər || ˈtrɒtə(r)/ *n*: **pig's ~s** (Culin) manitas *fpl* de cerdo

trouble[1] /ˈtrʌbəl/ *n*

A [u c] 1 (problems, difficulties) problemas *mpl*; (particular problem) problema *m*; **family/financial ~** problemas familiares/económicos; **here comes ~!** ¡mira quién viene! (fam); **this could mean ~** puede que esto traiga cola; **it's just asking for ~** es buscarse problemas; **the company's in ~** la empresa está pasando unas dificultades; **if you're ever in ~ ...** si alguna vez estás en apuros ...; **to get into ~** meterse en problemas *or* en líos; **to get sb into ~** meter a algn en problemas; (make pregnant) dejar embarazada a algn, dejar a algn con encargo (AmL fam & euf); **to get sb out of ~** sacar* a algn de apuros *or* aprietos; **to have ~ with sb/sth** tener* problemas con algn/algo; **to have ~ -ING: he has ~ walking** le cuesta caminar; **we had no ~ finding it** lo encontramos sin problemas; **to make ~ for oneself** crearse problemas; **what's the ~?** ¿qué pasa?; **the ~ is ...** lo que pasa es que ..., el problema es que ... 2 (illness): **stomach/heart ~** problemas *mpl or* trastornos *mpl* estomacales *or* de estómago/cardíacos *or* de corazón; **what seems to be the ~?** ¿qué síntomas tiene?

B [u] (effort) molestia *f*; **I don't want to put you to any ~** no quiero ocasionarle ninguna molestia; **it's not worth the ~** no vale *or* no merece la pena; **thanks very much — it's no ~!** muchas gracias — ¡no hay de qué!; **to go to the ~ of doing sth, to take the ~ to do sth** molestarse en hacer algo; **don't go to any ~** no te compliques demasiado; **to take ~ over sth** esmerarse *or* poner* cuidado en algo

C [u] (strife, unrest) (*often pl*): **industrial/racial ~s** conflictos *mpl* laborales/raciales; **the ~s in Northern Ireland** los disturbios de Irlanda del Norte; **to cause ~** causar problemas, armar líos (fam); **to look for ~** buscar* camorra; (*before n*) **~ spot** punto *m* conflictivo

trouble[2] *vt* 1 (worry) preocupar; **don't let it ~ you** no te preocupes (por eso) 2 (bother) molestar; **don't ~ yourself** no se moleste; **I'm sorry to ~ you** perdone *or* disculpe la molestia; **to ~ to + INF** molestarse EN + INF, tomarse el trabajo DE + INF 3 (cause discomfort) ⟨⟨*sore back/injury*⟩⟩ molestar

troubled /ˈtrʌbəld/ *adj* 1 (disturbed) ⟨*person*⟩ preocupado, atribulado; ⟨*look*⟩ de preocupación; ⟨*sleep*⟩ inquieto, agitado 2 (strife-torn) (journ) ⟨*region/industry*⟩ aquejado de problemas

trouble: **~maker** *n* alborotador, -dora *m,f*; **~shooter** *n* (within company) *persona que se envía a resolver problemas, crisis etc*; (mediator) mediador, -dora *m,f*, conciliador, -dora *m,f*

troublesome /ˈtrʌbəlsəm/ *adj* ⟨*child*⟩ problemático; ⟨*task*⟩ difícil, pesado; ⟨*situation*⟩ problemático, conflictivo; ⟨*cough*⟩ molesto, molestoso (AmL)

trough /trɔːf || trɒf/ *n*

A (container — for water) abrevadero *m*, bebedero *m*; (— for feed) comedero *m*

B 1 (on land, seabed) hoya *f*, depresión *f* 2 (Meteo): **a ~ of low pressure** una depresión, una zona de bajas presiones

trounce /traʊns/ *vt* derrotar de forma aplastante, darle* una paliza a (fam)

troupe /truːp/ *n* (Theat) compañía *f* teatral; (in circus) troupe *f*

trouper /ˈtruːpər || ˈtruːpə(r)/ *n*: **she's a real ~** (colloq) siempre está dispuesta a echar una mano

trouser /ˈtraʊzər || ˈtraʊzə(r)/ *adj* ⟨*leg/pocket*⟩ del pantalón

trousers /ˈtraʊzərz || ˈtraʊzəz/ *pl n* pantalón *m*, pantalones *mpl*; **a pair of ~** un pantalón, unos pantalones, un par de pantalones; ▸ **wear[2]** *vt* **A2**

trouser suit *n* (BrE) traje *m* pantalón, traje *m* de chaqueta y pantalón

trousseau /ˈtruːsəʊ/ *n* (*pl* **-x** *or* **-s** /-z/) ajuar *m*

trout /traʊt/ *n* [u c] (*pl* **trout** *or* Zool **trouts**) trucha *f*

trove /trəʊv/ *n see* **treasure trove**

trowel /ˈtraʊəl/ *n* 1 (Const) paleta *f*, llana *f*; ***to lay it on with a ~*** recargar* las tintas 2 (for gardening) desplantador *m*, palita *f*

Troy /trɔɪ/ *n* Troya *f*

truant /ˈtruːənt/ *n*: *alumno que falta a clase sin autorización*; **to play ~** faltar a clase, hacer* novillos *or* (Méx) irse* de pinta *or* (RPl) hacerse* la rata *or* la rabona *or* (Per) la vaca *or* (Chi) hacer* la cimarra *or* (Col) capar clase (fam), jubilarse (Ven)

truce /truːs/ *n* tregua *f*; **to call a ~** suspender las hostilidades

truck[1] /trʌk/ *n*

A [c] 1 (vehicle) camión *m*; (*before n*) **~ driver** camionero, -ra *m,f*; **~ stop** (AmE) bar *m* de carretera 2 (BrE Rail) furgón *m*, vagón *m*

B [u] (vegetables, fruit) (AmE) productos *mpl* de la huerta; (*before n*) **~ farmer** horticultor, -tora *m,f*; **~ farming** horticultura *f*; **~ garden** huerta *f*

C [u] (dealings): **to have no ~ with sb** no tener trato con algn; **he'll have no ~ with it/them** no quiere saber nada del asunto/de ellos

truck[2] *vt* (AmE) ⟨*goods*⟩ transportar en camión

■ **truck** *vi* trabajar de camionero/camionera

trucker /ˈtrʌkər || ˈtrʌkə(r)/ *n* (AmE) (driver) camionero, -ra *m,f*, transportista *mf*

trucking /ˈtrʌkɪŋ/ *n* [u] (AmE) transporte *m* por carretera; (*before n*) ⟨*company*⟩ de transportes por carretera

truculent /ˈtrʌkjələnt || ˈtrʌkjʊlənt/ *adj* malhumorado y agresivo

trudge /trʌdʒ/ *vi* caminar con dificultad

■ **trudge** *vt* ⟨*streets/hills*⟩ recorrer (*con cansancio, dificultad etc*)

true[1] /truː/ *adj* **truer, truest**

A 1 (consistent with fact, reality): **to be ~** ser* cierto, ser* verdad; **it can't be ~!** ¡no puede ser!; **a ~ story** una historia verídica; **to come ~** hacerse* realidad; **to hold ~** ser* válido; **~, inflation has fallen, but ...** cierto, la inflación ha disminuido, pero ...; **how ~!** *o* **too ~!** ¡si será cierto!; **you never said** *o* **spoke a ~r word!** ¡tú lo has dicho!; **they're so stupid it's not ~** (esp BrE) parece mentira que sean tan tontos, son increíblemente tontos 2 (accurate, exact) (*before n*) ⟨*account*⟩ verídico; ⟨*copy*⟩ fiel; **in the ~st sense of the word** en el sentido estricto de la palabra

B (real, actual, genuine) (*before n*) ⟨*purpose/courage*⟩ verdadero; ⟨*friend*⟩ auténtico, de verdad; **a ~ Frenchman** un francés auténtico; **~ north** el norte geográfico; **it's ~ love** es amor de verdad

C (faithful) fiel; **~ TO sth/sb** fiel A algo/algn; **to be ~ to one's word** ser* fiel a *or* mantener* su (*or* mi *etc*) palabra; **~ to form**: **~ to form, he arrived late** como era de esperar, llegó tarde; **she was acting ~ to form, telling everyone what to do** como siempre, estaba dándole órdenes a todo el mundo

D (Tech) (*pred*): **to be ~** ⟨⟨*wall/upright*⟩⟩ estar* a plomo; ⟨⟨*beam*⟩⟩ estar* a nivel; ⟨⟨*wheel/axle*⟩⟩ estar* alineado *or* centrado; ⟨⟨*instrument*⟩⟩ estar* bien calibrado; **his aim is ~** tiene buena puntería

true[2] *n*: **to be out of ~** ⟨⟨*wall/upright*⟩⟩ no estar* a plomo

t

true: **~-blue** /'truː'bluː/ *adj* (Pol) ‹*conservative*› hasta la médula; **~-life** /'truː'laɪf/ *adj* (journ) (*before n*) ‹*story*› verídico; ‹*experience*› real, auténtico; **~-to-life** /'truːtə'laɪf/ *adj* (*pred* **~ to life**) ‹*novel/film*› realista; ‹*situation*› verosímil

truffle /'trʌfəl/ *n* trufa *f*

truism /'truːɪzəm/ *n* (obvious truth) hecho *m* que salta a la vista, perogrullada *f* (fam)

truly /'truːli/ *adv* 1 (in reality) verdaderamente, realmente 2 (*as intensifier*) ‹*amazing/fantastic*› verdaderamente, realmente 3 (accurately, exactly): **it may ~ be called a masterpiece** puede, con toda justicia, calificarse de obra maestra 4 (sincerely) ‹*grateful*› sinceramente, verdaderamente; ‹*concerned*› francamente, verdaderamente; **I'm ~ sorry** lo siento de verdad *or* de veras; **yours ~** (Corresp) cordiales saludos; **who ended up doing it? yours ~!** (hum) ¿quién terminó haciéndolo? un servidor *or* (Esp tb) aquí, menda (fam)

trump[1] /trʌmp/ *n* 1 **~ (card)** (Games) triunfo *m* 2 **~ (card)** (resource, weapon) baza *f* 3 **trumps** *pl* (suit) triunfo *m*; **hearts are ~s** triunfan corazones, los corazones son triunfo; ***to come up*** *o* (BrE also) ***turn up ~s***: **her father always came up ~s** su padre nunca le fallaba; **Al turned up ~s, scoring in the last minute** Al salvó la situación al meter un gol en el último minuto

trump[2] *vt* ‹*card*› matar (*con un triunfo*)

trumped-up /'trʌmpt'ʌp/ *adj* (*before n*) ‹*charge/evidence*› falso, fabricado

trumpet[1] /'trʌmpət || 'trʌmpɪt/ *n* trompeta *f*; ▸**blow**[2] *vt* **B**

trumpet[2] *vi* «*elephant*» barritar

■ **trumpet** *vt* pregonar a los cuatro vientos, anunciar con bombos y platillos *or* (Esp) a bombo y platillo

trumpeter /'trʌmpətər || 'trʌmpɪtə(r)/ *n* trompetista *mf*, trompeta *mf*

truncate /'trʌŋkeɪt || trʌŋ'keɪt/ *vt* (frml) truncar*

truncheon /'trʌntʃən/ *n* (esp BrE) porra *f*, cachiporra *f*

trundle /'trʌndl̩/ *vi* (+ *adv compl*): **the cart ~d along/down the lane** el carro avanzaba lentamente por el camino

■ **trundle** *vt* ‹*barrow*› tirar de

trunk /trʌŋk/ *n*

A 1 (of tree) tronco *m* 2 (torso) tronco *m*

B (of elephant) trompa *f*

C 1 (box) baúl *m* 2 (of car) (AmE) maletero *m*, cajuela *m* (Méx), baúl *m* (Col, Ven, RPl), maleta *f* (Chi), maletera *f* (Per)

D **trunks** *pl* (Clothing) (for swimming) traje *m* de baño *or* (Esp tb) bañador *m* (*de hombre*), vestido *m* de baño (Col) (*de caballero*);

trunk: **~ call** *n* (BrE) llamada *f* de larga distancia *or* interurbana, conferencia *f* (Esp); **~ road** *n* (BrE) carretera *f* principal

truss /trʌs/ *vt* ‹*chicken/duck*› atar

(Phrasal verb)

• **truss up** [v ▸ o ▸ adv, v ▸ adv ▸ o] atar

trust[1] /trʌst/ *n*

A 1 [u] (confidence, faith) confianza *f*; **to have ~ IN sb/sth** tener* confianza EN algn/algo; **on ~** (without verification) bajo palabra; (on credit) a crédito; **to put** *o* **place one's ~ in sb/sth** depositar su (*or* mi *etc*) confianza en algn/algo; **to take sb on ~** fiarse* de algn; **take it on ~ that ...** ten por seguro que ... 2 [u c] (responsibility): **a position of ~** un puesto de confianza *or* responsabilidad

B (Fin) 1 [c] (money, property) fondo *m* de inversiones 2 [c] (institution) fundación *f* 3 [u] (custody) (Law) fideicomiso *m*; **to hold sth in ~ for sb** mantener* algo en fideicomiso para algn

trust[2] *vt*

A (have confidence in) ‹*person*› confiar* en, tener* confianza en; (in negative sentences) fiarse* de; **he can't be ~ed** no es de fiar; **I wouldn't ~ him as far as I could throw him** no me fío un pelo de él (fam); **to ~ sb to + INF: can they be ~ed to be there on time?** ¿podemos confiar en que van a llegar a tiempo?; **I don't ~ them to do as they're told** no me fío de que vayan a obedecer; **I've broken it — ~ you!** (iro) se me ha roto — ¡típico!; **to ~ sb WITH sth** confiarle* algo A algn

B (hope, assume) (frml) esperar; **we ~ you enjoyed yourselves** esperamos que se hayan divertido

■ **trust** *vi* **to ~ IN sb/sth** confiar* *or* tener* confianza EN algn/algo; **to ~ TO sth** confiar* EN algo; **to ~ to luck** dejar algo librado al azar

trusted /'trʌstəd || 'trʌstɪd/ *adj* (*before n*) leal, de confianza

trustee /'trʌs'tiː/ *n* 1 (of money, property) fideicomisario, -ria *m,f*, fiduciario, -ria *m,f* 2 (of institution) miembro *m* del consejo de administración

trustful /'trʌstfəl/ *adj* ▸**trusting**

trust fund *n* fondo *m* fiduciario *or* de fideicomiso

trusting /'trʌstɪŋ/ *adj* confiado

trustworthy /'trʌstˌwɜːrði || 'trʌstˌwɜːði/ *adj* ‹*colleague/child*› digno de confianza; ‹*account/witness*› fidedigno

trusty /'trʌsti/ *adj* (*before n*) (liter) fiel, leal

truth /truːθ/ *n* (*pl* **~s** /truːðz/) 1 [u] (quality, condition) verdad *f*; (of account, story) veracidad *f*; **tell me the ~** dime la verdad; **if (the) ~ be known/told, he just isn't interested** la verdad es que no le interesa; ***(the) ~ will out*** las mentiras tienen las patas cortas, se pilla antes al mentiroso que al cojo 2 [c] (fact) verdad *f*; *see also* **home truth**

truthful /'truːθfəl/ *adj* ‹*person*› que dice la verdad, veraz, sincero; ‹*testimony*› veraz, verídico; ‹*answer*› veraz; ‹*depiction*› fiel

truthfully /'truːθfəli/ *adv* sinceramente

try[1] /traɪ/ *n* (*pl* **tries**)

A 1 [c] (attempt) intento *m*, tentativa *f*; **it's worth a ~** vale la pena intentarlo *or* hacer la tentativa *or* hacer la prueba; **that's not the right answer, but it was a good ~** ésa no es la respuesta, pero no estabas tan desencaminado 2 (trial) (*no pl*): **we'll give him a ~** le daremos una oportunidad; **this wine should be worth a ~** merece la pena probar este vino

B [c] (in rugby) ensayo *m*

try[2] **tries, trying, tried** *vt*

A 1 (attempt) intentar; **to ~ to + INF** tratar DE + INF, intentar + INF, **~ to** *o* (colloq) **~ and concentrate** trata de *or* intenta concentrarte; **~ not to forget** procura no olvidarte; **just you ~ it!** ¡atrévete!, ¡haz la prueba!; **it's ~ing to rain** (colloq) parece que quiere llover (fam) 2 (attempt to operate): **he tried all the windows** probó a abrir todas las ventanas; **she tried the switch, but nothing happened** le dio al interruptor, pero nada de nada

B 1 (experiment with) ‹*product/technique/food*› probar*; **~ some** pruébalo, prueba un poquito; **to ~ -ING: have you tried frying it?** ¿has probado a freírlo?; **~ looking at the problem from another angle** prueba con un enfoque distinto del problema 2 (have recourse to): **I'll ~ his work number** voy a probar a llamarlo al trabajo; **I tried several bookshops before I found a copy** busqué en *or* recorrí varias librerías antes de encontrar un ejemplar

C 1 (put to the test) ‹*person/courage*› poner* a prueba; **to ~ one's luck at sth** probar* suerte con algo 2 (put strain on) ‹*patience*› poner* a prueba

D (Law) ‹*person*› procesar, juzgar*; ‹*case*› ver*; **to ~ sb FOR sth** juzgar* a algn POR algo

■ **try** *vi*: **you must ~ harder** tienes que esforzarte más; **the team just isn't ~ing** el equipo no está haciendo ningún esfuerzo; **I can't do it: you ~** no puedo, prueba *or* inténtalo tú; **to ~ one's best** *o* **hardest** hacer* todo lo posible; **she couldn't be hurtful if she tried** es incapaz de herir a nadie

(Phrasal verbs)

• **try for** [v ▸ prep ▸ o] ‹*prize/place*› tratar de conseguir

• **try on** [v ▸ o ▸ adv, v ▸ adv ▸ o] ‹*skirt/shoes/hat*› probarse*, medirse* (Col, Méx); ***to ~ it on (with sb)*** (BrE colloq): **don't ~ it on with me!** ¡cuidadito con pasarte de la raya conmigo! (fam)

• **try out**

A [v ▸ o ▸ adv, v ▸ adv ▸ o] (test) ‹*product/method*› probar*; ‹*employee/player*› probar*, poner* a prueba; **to ~ sth out ON sb** probar* algo CON algn

B [v ▸ adv] (be tested) **to ~ out (FOR sth)** presentarse a una prueba (PARA algo)

trying /'traɪɪŋ/ *adj* ‹*day/experience*› duro; **I find him quite ~** es una persona que pone a prueba mi paciencia

try: **~-on** *n* 1 (of clothes) (AmE) prueba *f* 2 (trick, pretense) (BrE colloq) triquiñuela *f* (fam); **~out** *n* prueba *f*

tryst /trɪst/ *n* (liter) (appointment) cita *f*; (place) lugar *m* de encuentro

t

tsar /zɑːr || zɑː(r)/ *n* zar *m*

tsetse fly /'tsetsi, 'te-/ *n* mosca *f* tsetsé

T-shirt /'tiːʃɜːrt || 'tiːʃɜːt/ *n* 1 (outer garment) camiseta *f* 2 (undershirt) (AmE) camiseta *f*

tsp = teaspoon(s)

tub /tʌb/ *n* 1 (large vessel — for holding liquids) cuba *f*; (— for washing clothes) tina *f* 2 (*bath*~) bañera *f*, tina *f* (AmL), bañadera *f* (Arg) 3 (for ice cream, margarine) envase *m* (*gen de plástico*), tarrina *f* (Esp) 4 (boat, ship) (colloq & hum) chalana *f*; (small) cascarón *m* de nuez

tuba /'tuːbə || 'tjuːbə/ *n* tuba *f*

tubby /'tʌbi/ *adj* **-bier, -biest** (colloq) rechoncho (fam), regordete (fam)

tube /tuːb || tjuːb/ *n*

A (pipe, container) tubo *m*; ***to go down the ~(s)*** (colloq) venirse* abajo, irse* al traste (fam)

B (television) (esp AmE colloq): **the ~** la tele (fam)

C (London underground railway) (BrE colloq): **the ~** el metro, el subte (Arg); **let's go by ~** vamos en metro *or* (Arg) en subte

tuber /'tuːbər || 'tjuːbə(r)/ *n* (Bot) tubérculo *m*

tuberculosis /tʊ'bɜːrkjə'ləʊsəs || tjʊ,bɜːkjʊ'ləʊsɪs/ *n* [u] tuberculosis *f*

tube top *n* (AmE) bustier *m* elástico

tubing /'tuːbɪŋ || 'tjuːbɪŋ/ *n* [u] tubería *f*

tubular /'tuːbjələr || 'tjuːbjʊlə(r)/ *adj* tubular

TUC *n* (in UK) **= Trades Union Congress**

tuck¹ /tʌk/ *n* [c] (fold, pleat) jareta *f*, alforza *f* (CS), pliegue *m*

tuck² *vt* meter; **he ~ed the blanket firmly under the mattress** metió bien la manta debajo del colchón; **it looks better ~ed into your skirt** queda mejor por dentro (de la falda); **she ~ed the magazine under her arm** se colocó la revista debajo del brazo

■ **tuck** *vi*: **the blouse ~s into the skirt** la blusa va *or* se lleva por dentro (de la falda)

(Phrasal verbs)

• **tuck away**

A [v ▸ o ▸ adv, v ▸ adv ▸ o] (eat) (colloq) zamparse (fam), pulirse (fam), mandarse (AmL fam)

B [v ▸ o ▸ adv] (put away) guardar; **the house is ~ed away at the foot of the hill** la casa está enclavada en un rincón al pie de la colina

• **tuck in**

A [v ▸ adv] (eat) (colloq) ponerse* a comer, atacar* (fam)

B [v ▸ o ▸ adv, v ▸ adv ▸ o] 1 (in trousers, under mattress) meter; **~ your shirt in** métete la camisa por dentro (de los pantalones) 2 ‹*child/invalid*› arropar

• **tuck into** [v ▸ prep ▸ o] (colloq) ponerse* a comer, atacar* (fam)

• **tuck up** [v ▸ o ▸ adv] **to ~ sb up (in bed)** arropar a algn (en la cama)

tuckered out /'tʌkərd || 'tʌkəd/ *adj* (AmE colloq) (*pred*) molido (fam), hecho polvo (fam), de cama (AmL fam)

tuck shop *n* (BrE) tienda *f* de golosinas (*en una escuela*)

Tudor /'tuːdər || 'tjuːdə(r)/ *n* Tudor *mf*; **the ~s** los Tudor; (*before n*) ‹*king/architecture*› tudor *adj inv*

Tues, Tue (**= Tuesday**) mart.

Tuesday /'tuːzdeɪ, -di || 'tjuːzdeɪ, -di/ *n* martes *m*; *see also* **Monday**

tuft /tʌft/ *n* 1 (of hair) mechón *m*; (on top of head) copete *m* 2 (of grass) mata *f*

tug¹ /tʌg/ **-gg-** *vt* 1 (pull) ‹*sleeve/cord*› tirar de, jalar (de) (AmL exc CS) 2 (drag) arrastrar

■ **tug** *vi* **to ~ AT sth** tirar DE algo, jalar (DE) algo (AmL exc CS); **to ~ ON sth** darle* *or* pegarle* un tirón A algo, jalar algo (AmL exc CS)

tug² *n*

A (pull) tirón *m*, jalón *m* (AmL exc CS); **to give sth a ~** tirar de algo, jalar (de) algo (AmL exc CS), darle* *or* pegarle* un tirón a algo, darle* *or* pegarle* un jalón a algo (AmL exc CS)

B **~ (boat)** (Naut) remolcador *m*

tug of war *n: juego de tira y afloja con una cuerda*

tuition /tʊ'ɪʃən || tjuː'ɪʃən/ *n* [u] 1 (instruction) (frml) **~ (IN sth)** clases *fpl* (DE algo); **she's having private ~** está tomando *or* le están dando clases particulares; (*before n*) **~ fees** ≈ matrícula *f* 2 (fees) matrícula *f*

tulip /'tuːləp || 'tjuːlɪp/ *n* tulipán *m*

tulle /tuːl || tjuːl/ *n* [u] tul *m*

tumble¹ /'tʌmbəl/ *n* 1 (of acrobat) voltereta *f* 2 (fall) caída *f*; **to take a ~** caerse*

tumble² *vi*

A (fall) caerse*; **he ~d off his horse** se cayó del caballo; **the pile of cans came tumbling down** el montón de latas se vino abajo; **I ~d into bed** me dejé caer en la cama

B (roll, turn) «*acrobat*» dar* volteretas; «*kitten/children*» revolcarse*, retozar*

(Phrasal verb)

• **tumble to** [v ▸ prep ▸ o] ‹*scheme*› darse* cuenta de

tumble: **~down** *adj* (*before n*) en ruinas; **~ dryer** /'tʌmbəl'draɪər || 'tʌmbəl,draɪə(r)/ *n* secadora *f*

tumbler /'tʌmblər || 'tʌmblə(r)/ *n* (glass) vaso *m* (*de lados rectos*)

tumbleweed /'tʌmbəlwiːd/ *n* [u] planta *f* rodadora

tummy /'tʌmi/ *n* (*pl* **-mies**) (used to or by children) barriga *f* (fam), pancita *f* (fam), tripita *f* (fam), guatita *f* (Chi fam)

tumor, (BrE) **tumour** /'tuːmər || 'tjuːmə(r)/ *n* tumor *m*

tumult /'tuːmʌlt || 'tjuːmʌlt/ *n* [u c] tumulto *m*; **her thoughts were in (a) ~** se sentía totalmente confundido

tumultuous /tʊ'mʌltʃuəs || tjʊ'mʌltjʊəs/ *adj* ‹*applause/welcome*› apoteósico

tuna /'tuːnə || 'tjuːnə/ *n* (*pl* **~** *or* **~s**) atún *m*; (*before n*) **a ~ (fish) sandwich** un sándwich de atún

tundra /'tʌndrə/ *n* [u] tundra *f*

tune¹ /tuːn || tjuːn/ *n* 1 [c] (melody) melodía *f*; (piece) canción *f*, tonada *f*; **that's a nice ~** qué música más bonita!; ***to call the ~*** llevar la batuta *or* la voz cantante; ***to change one's ~*** cambiar de parecer; ***to the ~ of sth***: **expenses to the ~ of $500 a day** 500 dólares al día en concepto de gastos 2 [u] (correct pitch): **to sing out of ~** desafinar, desentonar; **to sing in ~** cantar bien; **this string is in/out of ~** esta cuerda está afinada/desafinada; ***to be in/out of ~ with sth/sb***: **a leader in ~ with the people** un líder en sintonía con el pueblo; **the building is quite out of ~ with its surroundings** el edificio desentona *or* no está en armonía con su entorno

tune² *vt* 1 (Mus) ‹*instrument*› afinar 2 (Auto) ‹*engine*› poner* a punto, afinar 3 (Rad, TV) sintonizar*

■ **tune** *vi* (Rad, TV) **to ~ TO sth** ‹*to station/wavelength*› sintonizar* algo

(Phrasal verb)

• **tune in** [v ▸ adv] **to ~ in TO sth** sintonizar* (CON) algo

tuneful /'tuːnfəl || 'tjuːnfəl/ *adj* melódico

tuneless /'tuːnləs || 'tjuːnlɪs/ *adj* poco melodioso

tuner /'tuːnər || 'tjuːnə(r)/ *n* 1 (*piano ~*) (Mus) afinador, -dora *m,f* de pianos 2 (Rad) sintonizador *m*

tungsten /'tʌŋstən/ *n* [u] tungsteno *m*

tunic /'tuːnɪk || 'tjuːnɪk/ *n* 1 (of military uniform) guerrera *f* 2 (in ancient Rome) túnica *f* 3 (women's blouse, jacket) casaca *f*

tuning /'tuːnɪŋ || 'tjuːnɪŋ/ *n* [u] 1 (on string instrument) afinación *f* 2 (for frequency selection) sintonía *f* 3 (Auto) puesta *f* a punto

tuning fork *n* diapasón *m*

Tunisia /tuː'niːʒə || tjuː'nɪziə/ *n* Túnez *m*

Tunisian¹ /tuː'niːʒən || tjuː'nɪziən/ *adj* tunecino

Tunisian² *n* tunecino, -na *m,f*

tunnel¹ /'tʌnl/ *n* (for road, railway, canal) túnel *m*; (in mine) galería *f*, socavón *m*

tunnel², (BrE) **-ll-** *vi* abrir* *or* hacer* un túnel

■ **tunnel** *vt* ‹*passage*› abrir*; **they ~ed their way out of prison** escaparon de la cárcel abriendo *or* haciendo un túnel

tunnel vision *n* [u] (Opt) visión *f* de túnel; (narrow-mindedness) estrechez *f* de miras

tunny /'tʌni/ *n* [c u] (*pl* **-nies** *or* **-ny**) atún *m*

tuppence /'tʌpəns/ *n* (BrE) ▸ **twopence**

tuppenny /'tʌpəni/ *adj* (BrE) ▸ **twopenny**

turban /'tɜːrbən || 'tɜːbən/ *n* turbante *m*

turbid /'tɜːrbəd || 'tɜːbɪd/ *adj* turbio

turbine /'tɜːrbən, -baɪn || 'tɜːbaɪn/ *n* turbina *f*

turbo /ˈtɜːrbəʊ || ˈtɜːbəʊ/ *n* (compressor) turbocompresor *m*, turbo *m*

turbo: **~-charge** /ˈtɜːrbəʊtʃɑːrdʒ || ˈtɜːbəʊtʃɑːdʒ/ *vt* equipar con turbocompresor a; **~-charged** *adj* turbo; **~jet** *n* 1 (aircraft) turborreactor *m* 2 **~jet (engine)** turborreactor *m*

turbot /ˈtɜːrbət || ˈtɜːbət/ *n* (*pl* ~ *or* ~**s**) rodaballo *m*

turbulence /ˈtɜːrbjələns || ˈtɜːbjʊləns/ *n* [u] turbulencia *f*

turbulent /ˈtɜːrbjələnt || ˈtɜːbjʊlənt/ *adj* turbulento

turd /tɜːrd || tɜːd/ *n* (vulg) (excrement) zurullo *m* (fam), sorete *m* (RPl vulg), cerote *m* (AmC, Méx vulg)

tureen /tjʊˈriːn, tə- || tjʊəˈriːn/ *n* sopera *f*

turf¹ /tɜːrf || tɜːf/ *n* (*pl* ~**s** *or* **turves**)

A 1 [u] (grass) césped *m* 2 [c] (square of grass) (esp BrE) tepe *m*

B (horseracing): **the** ~ el turf, la hípica

turf² *vt* (Hort) ‹*garden*› encespedar, colocar* tepes en

Phrasal verb

• **turf out** [v ▸ o ▸ adv, v ▸ adv ▸ o] (BrE colloq) ‹*person*› echar, poner* de patitas en la calle (fam), correr (fam), botar (AmL exc RPl); ‹*rubbish/clothes*› tirar, botar (AmL exc RPl)

turf: ~ **accountant** *n* (BrE frml) corredor, -dora *m,f* de apuestas; ~ **war** *n* (colloq) lucha *f* interna por el control

turgid /ˈtɜːrdʒəd || ˈtɜːdʒɪd/ *adj* ‹*waters*› crecido; ‹*style/prose*› ampuloso

Turin /ˈtʊrən || tjʊəˈrɪn/ *n* Turín

Turk /tɜːrk || tɜːk/ *n* turco, -ca *m,f*

turkey /ˈtɜːrki || ˈtɜːki/ *n* (*pl* ~**s**)

A 1 [c] (bird) pavo *m*, guajolote *m* (Méx), chompipe *m* (AmC); ***to talk*** ~ (esp AmE colloq) hablar a las claras (fam) 2 [u] (meat) pavo *m*

B [c] (failure) (AmE Theat sl) bodrio *m* (fam)

Turkey /ˈtɜːrki || ˈtɜːki/ *n* Turquía *f*

Turkish¹ /ˈtɜːrkɪʃ || ˈtɜːkɪʃ/ *adj* turco

Turkish² *n* [u] turco *m*

Turkish: ~ **bath** *n* baño *m* turco; ~ **delight** *n* [u] delicia *f* turca (*dulce gelatinoso recubierto de azúcar*)

Turkmenistan /ˌtɜːrkmenɪˈstɑːn || ˌtɜːkmenɪˈstɑːn/ *n* Turkmenistán *m*

turmeric /ˈtɜːrmərɪk || ˈtɜːmərɪk/ *n* [u] cúrcuma *f*, azafrán *m* de las Indias

turmoil /ˈtɜːrmɔɪl || ˈtɜːmɔɪl/ *n* [u] confusión *f*, agitación *f*; **her mind was in (a)** ~ estaba totalmente confundida *or* desconcertada

turn¹ /tɜːrn || tɜːn/ *n*

A 1 (rotation) vuelta *f*; **give it another** ~ dale otra vuelta; **a half** ~ media vuelta; ***to a*** ~: **the meat was done to a** ~ la carne estaba hecha a la perfección, la carne estaba en su punto justo 2 (change of direction) vuelta *f*, giro *m*; ⊖ **no left turn** prohibido girar *or* doblar *or* torcer a la izquierda 3 (bend) curva *f*; (turning): **take the next left/right** ~ tome *or* (esp Esp) coja *or* (esp AmL) agarre la próxima a la izquierda/derecha; ***at every*** ~ a cada paso, a cada momento 4 (change, alteration): **a** ~ **in the weather** un cambio en el tiempo; **this dramatic** ~ **of events** este dramático giro de los acontecimientos; **events took an unexpected** ~ los acontecimientos dieron un giro inesperado; **to take a** ~ **for the better** empezar* a mejorar; **to take a** ~ **for the worse** empeorar, ponerse* peor; **the** ~ **of the century** el final del siglo (*y el principio del siguiente*); ***to be on the*** ~ «*events/tide*» estar* cambiando; «*leaves*» estar* cambiando de color; «*milk/food*» (BrE) estar* echándose a perder

B 1 (place in sequence): **whose** ~ **is it?** ¿a quién le toca?; **I think it's my** ~ creo que me toca (el turno) a mí; **you'll have to wait your** ~ vas a tener que esperar que te toque (el turno); ***to take*** ~***s*** *o* ***to take it in*** ~***(s)*** turnarse; **we'll take** ~**s** *o* **we'll take it in** ~**(s) to do the cooking** nos vamos a turnar para cocinar, vamos a cocinar por turnos 2 (*in phrases*) **by turns** sucesivamente; **in turn**: **each in** ~ **was asked the same question** a cada uno de ellos se le hizo la misma pregunta; **out of turn**: **she realized she'd spoken out of** ~ se dio cuenta de que su comentario (*or* interrupción *etc*) había estado fuera de lugar

C (service): **to do sb a good** ~ hacerle* un favor a algn; ***one good*** ~ ***deserves another*** favor con favor se paga

D (form, style): **she has a logical/practical** ~ **of mind** es muy lógica/práctica; **she has a witty** ~ **of phrase** tiene una manera ingeniosa de expresarse

E 1 (bout of illness, disability): **he had a funny** ~ le dio un ataque (*or* un mareo *etc*) 2 (nervous shock) susto *m*; **you gave me quite a** ~ me diste un buen susto

F (act) (esp BrE) número *m*

turn² *vt*

A 1 (rotate) ‹*knob/handle/wheel*› (hacer*) girar; **he** ~**ed the key in the lock** hizo girar la llave en la cerradura 2 (set, regulate) **to** ~ **sth TO sth**: ~ **the knob to 'hot'** ponga el indicador en 'caliente'; **he** ~**ed the oven to a lower temperature** bajó la temperatura del horno

B 1 (change position, direction of) ‹*head*› volver*, voltear (AmL exc RPl); ~ **your head a little to the side** gira la cabeza un poco hacia un lado; **she** ~**ed her back on them** les volvió *or* les dio la espalda, les volteó la espalda (AmL exc RPl); **he slipped out while my back was** ~**ed** salió disimuladamente mientras yo estaba de espaldas; **the nurse** ~**ed her onto her side** la enfermera la puso de lado; **can you** ~ **the TV this way a bit?** ¿puedes poner el televisor más para este lado? 2 (direct, apply) **to** ~ **sth TO sth**: **I** ~**ed my mind to more pleasant thoughts** me puse a pensar en cosas más agradables; **the administration has** ~**ed its efforts to ...** la administración ha dirigido sus esfuerzos a ...; **they** ~**ed the situation to their own profit** utilizaron la situación para su propio provecho; ▸**advantage 2**

C 1 (reverse) ‹*mattress/omelette*› darle* la vuelta a, voltear (AmL exc CS), dar* vuelta (CS); ‹*page*› pasar, volver*, dar* vuelta (CS); ‹*soil*› remover*, voltear (AmL exc CS), dar* vuelta (CS); **he** ~**ed the card face down** puso *or* volvió la carta boca abajo; **she sat** ~**ing the pages of a magazine** estaba sentada hojeando una revista 2 (upset): **it** ~**s my stomach** me revuelve el estómago

D 1 (go around) ‹*corner*› dar* la vuelta a, dar* vuelta (CS) 2 (pass): **she's just** ~**ed 30** acaba de cumplir (los) 30

E (send): **I couldn't simply** ~ **him from my door** no le podía negar ayuda, no le podía volver la espalda, ▸ **loose¹ B**

F 1 (change, transform) volver*; **to** ~ **sth TO/INTO sth** transformar *or* convertir* algo EN algo; **they've** ~**ed the place into a pigsty!** ¡han puesto la casa (*or* la habitación *etc*) como una pocilga!; **she** ~**ed him into a frog** lo convirtió en un sapo; **the experience** ~**ed him into a cynic** se volvió cínico con la experiencia 2 (make sour) ‹*milk*› agriar 3 (confuse) ‹*mind*› trastornar

G 1 (shape — on lathe) tornear; (— on potter's wheel) hacer* 2 (formulate): **a well-**~**ed phrase** una frase elegante *or* pulida

H (make) ‹*profit*› sacar*

■ **turn** *vi*

A (rotate) «*handle/wheel*» girar, dar* vuelta(s); **the key** ~**ed easily in the lock** la llave giró fácilmente en la cerradura; **it made my stomach** ~ me revolvió el estómago; **the earth** ~**s on its axis every 24 hours** la Tierra gira sobre su eje cada 24 horas; **the outcome of the election** ~**s on one crucial factor** el resultado de las elecciones depende de un factor decisivo; **my head was** ~**ing** todo me daba vueltas

B 1 (to face in different direction) «*person*» volverse*, darse* la vuelta, voltearse (AmL exc CS), darse* vuelta (CS); «*car*» dar* la vuelta, dar* vuelta (CS); **she** ~**ed to me with a smile** me miró sonriéndome, se volvió hacia mí con una sonrisa; **he** ~**ed onto his side** se volvió *or* se puso de lado; **left/right** ~**!** (BrE Mil) ¡media vuelta a la izquierda/derecha! 2 (change course, direction): **the army then** ~**ed north** entonces el ejército cambió de rumbo, dirigiéndose al norte; **to turn into a side street** meterse en una calle lateral; **to** ~ **left/right** girar *or* doblar *or* torcer* a la izquierda/derecha 3 (curve) «*road/river*» torcer*

C 1 (focus on): **to** ~ **to another subject** pasar a otro tema, cambiar de tema; **his mind** ~**ed to thoughts of escape** se puso a pensar en escaparse 2 (resort, have recourse to): **to** ~ **to violence/a friend** recurrir a la violencia/un amigo; **she had no one to** ~ **to** no tenía a quien recurrir; **to** ~ **to drink** darse* a la bebida; **to** ~ **to sb/sth FOR sth**: **she** ~**ed to her parents for support** recurrió *or* acudió a sus padres en busca de apoyo; **he** ~**ed to nature for inspiration** buscó inspiración en la naturaleza

D 1 (become): **his face** ~**ed red** se le puso la cara colorada; **things were** ~**ing nasty** las cosas se estaban poniendo feas; **her hair had** ~**ed gray** había encanecido; **he** ~**ed professional** se hizo profesional; **Ed Wright, naturalist**

t

~ed politician Ed Wright, naturalista convertido en *or* vuelto político 2 (be transformed) **to ~ INTO sth** convertirse* EN algo; **water ~s into steam** el agua se convierte *or* se transforma en vapor; **to ~ TO sth** (liter) convertirse* EN algo; **everything he touched ~ed to gold** todo lo que tocaba se convertía en oro 3 (change) «*luck/weather/tide*» cambiar 4 (change color) «*leaves*» cambiar de color 5 (go sour) «*milk*» agriarse

E (when reading): **~ to page 19** abran el libro en la página 19, vayan a la página 19; **~ back a couple of pages** vuelvan atrás un par de páginas

F (AmE Busn) «*merchandise*» venderse

Phrasal verbs

• **turn against**

A [v ▸ prep ▸ o] ponerse* *or* volverse* en contra de

B [v ▸ o ▸ prep ▸ o]: **she ~ed them against me/each other** los puso en mi contra/puso a uno en contra del otro

• **turn around,** (BrE also) **turn round**

A [v ▸ adv] 1 (to face different direction) darse* la vuelta, volverse*, voltearse (AmL exc CS), darse* vuelta (CS) 2 (react) (colloq): **I can't ~ around and tell her she isn't needed any more** no puedo salir ahora con que no la necesitamos más 3 (reverse) «*weather/luck/economy*» cambiar completamente, dar* *or* pegar* un vuelco

B [v ▸ o ▸ adv] ‹*book/picture*› darle* la vuelta a, voltear (AmL exc CS), dar* vuelta (CS); **could you ~ the TV around this way a little?** ¿podrías poner el televisor un poco más para este lado?

C [v ▸ o ▸ adv] 1 (set on new course) ‹*company/economy*› sanear 2 (get ready) ‹*order*› despachar

• **turn aside** [v ▸ adv] darse* la vuelta, voltearse (AmL exc CS), darse* vuelta (CS)

• **turn away**

A [v ▸ adv] apartarse

B [v ▸ o ▸ adv, v ▸ adv ▸ o] 1 ‹*head/face*› volver*, voltear (AmL exc RPl), dar* vuelta (CS); **he ~ed his eyes away** apartó la mirada 2 (send away) ‹*business*› no aceptar; **the doorman ~ed them away** el portero no los dejó entrar; **the stadium was already full and many people had to be ~ed away** el estadio ya estaba lleno y mucha gente se tuvo que volver a casa

• **turn back**

A [v ▸ adv] 1 (go back) volver*, regresar, devolverse* (AmL exc RPl) 2 (change plan) echarse *or* volverse* atrás

B [v ▸ o ▸ adv, v ▸ adv ▸ o] 1 (send back): **he was ~ed back at the border** en la frontera lo hicieron regresar *or* lo mandaron de vuelta 2 (fold) ‹*bedclothes*› doblar 3 (reset) ‹*clock*› retrasar, atrasar; *see also* **clock¹ 1**

• **turn down** [v ▸ o ▸ adv, v ▸ adv ▸ o] 1 (fold back) ‹*collar/brim/sheets*› doblar 2 (diminish) ‹*heating/volume/temperature*› bajar 3 (reject) ‹*offer/application*› rechazar*; ‹*job/candidate*› rechazar*, no aceptar; **her request for a loan was ~ed down** le negaron el préstamo, no le concedieron el préstamo

• **turn in**

A [v ▸ adv] (go to bed) (colloq) acostarse*

B [v ▸ o ▸ adv, v ▸ adv ▸ o] (hand in, over) ‹*work/report*› entregar*; ‹*criminal*› (colloq) entregar*

• **turn off**

A [v ▸ o ▸ adv, v ▸ adv ▸ o] ‹*light/radio/heating*› apagar*; ‹*faucet/tap*› cerrar*; ‹*water*› cortar; ‹*electricity*› desconectar

B [v ▸ o ▸ adv, v ▸ adv ▸ o] (repel) (colloq): **to ~ sb off** darle* asco a algn, repugnar a algn; **it ~s me right off when people start talking about money** pierdo totalmente el interés cuando la gente se pone a hablar de dinero; (stronger) me revienta que la gente se ponga a hablar de dinero (fam)

C [v ▸ adv] 1 (from road) doblar; **we ~ed off into a side street** nos metimos en una calle lateral 2 (switch off) apagarse*

• **turn on**

A [v ▸ o ▸ adv, v ▸ adv ▸ o] 1 ‹*light/television/oven*› encender*, prender (AmL); ‹*faucet/tap*› abrir*; ‹*water*› dejar correr; ‹*electricity*› conectar 2 (stimulate, excite) (colloq) gustar; (sexually) excitar; **oh well, whatever ~s you on!** (hum) bueno, sobre gustos …

B [v ▸ adv] (switch on) encenderse*, prenderse (AmL)

C [v ▸ prep ▸ o] (attack) atacar*

D [v ▸ o ▸ prep ▸ o] (aim at): **she ~ed the spotlight on them** los enfocó con el reflector; **I'll ~ the hose on you!** ¡mira que te mojo con la manguera!

• **turn out**

A [v ▸ o ▸ adv, v ▸ adv ▸ o] 1 (switch off) ‹*light*› apagar* 2 (empty) ‹*pockets/cupboard*› vaciar* 3 (dress) (*usu pass*): **to be well ~ed out** ir* *or* estar* bien vestido

B [v ▸ adv ▸ o] (produce) ‹*goods/films*› sacar*, producir*

C [v ▸ o ▸ adv, v ▸ adv ▸ o] 1 (force to leave) echar; **to ~ sb out of his/her home** echar *or* sacar* a algn de su casa 2 (tip out) ‹*cake/loaf*› desmoldar

D [v ▸ adv] 1 (attend): **several thousand ~ed out to welcome the Pope** varios miles de personas acudieron *or* fueron/vinieron a recibir al Papa 2 (result, prove): **everything ~ed out well** todo salió *or* resultó bien; **as it o things ~ed out, nobody called** al final no llamó nadie; **he ~ed out to have been there before** resulta que había estado allí antes

• **turn over**

A [v ▸ o ▸ adv] 1 (flip, reverse) ‹*mattress/omelet*› darle* la vuelta a, voltear (AmL exc CS), dar* vuelta (CS); ‹*soil*› remover*, voltear (AmL exc CS), dar* vuelta (CS); **she ~ed the idea over in her mind** le dio vueltas a la idea en la cabeza 2 (Auto) ‹*engine*› hacer* funcionar

B [v ▸ o ▸ adv, v ▸ adv ▸ o] (hand over) ‹*prisoner/document*› entregar*

C [v ▸ adv ▸ o] 1 (Busn): **we ~ed over $8 million last year** facturamos 8 millones de dólares el año pasado, tuvimos un volumen de ventas (*or* transacciones *etc*) de 8 millones de dólares el año pasado 2 ‹*page*› pasar, volver*, dar* vuelta (CS)

D [v ▸ adv] 1 (onto other side) darse* la vuelta, darse* vuelta (CS); **~ over onto your stomach** póngase boca abajo; **the car ~ed over** el coche volcó *or* dio una vuelta de campana 2 (Auto) «*engine*» funcionar 3 (turn page) pasar *or* volver* la página, dar* vuelta la página (CS)

• **turn round** (esp BrE) ▸ **turn around**

• **turn up**

A [v ▸ o ▸ adv, v ▸ adv ▸ o] 1 ‹*collar*› levantarse, subirse; **she ~ed up the brim of her hat** se dobló el ala del sombrero hacia arriba 2 (shorten) ‹*trousers*› acortar; ‹*hem*› subir 3 (increase) ‹*heater/oven/volume*› subir; ‹*radio*› subir el volumen de

B [v ▸ adv] (colloq) 1 (be found) «*sth lost*» aparecer*; **something better will ~ up** algo mejor saldrá *or* surgirá 2 (arrive) (BrE) llegar*; **he ~ed up late for work** llegó tarde a trabajar; **we waited half an hour, but she didn't ~ up** esperamos media hora, pero no apareció

C [v ▸ adv ▸ o] (reveal, find) ‹*evidence/clues*› revelar, descubrir*

• **turn upon** ▸ **turn on C**

turn: **~about**, **~around** *n* giro *m*, cambio *m*; **~coat** *n* renegado, -da *m,f*, chaquetero, -ra *m,f* (Esp fam)

turndown¹ /'tɜ:rndaʊn || 'tɜ:ndaʊn/ *adj* ‹*collar*› vuelto

turndown² *n* (AmE colloq) rechazo *m*

turned-up /'tɜ:rnd'ʌp || ,tɜ:nd'ʌp/ *adj* ‹*nose*› respingón, respingado (AmL)

turning /'tɜ:rnɪŋ || 'tɜ:nɪŋ/ *n* (in town) bocacalle *f*; **we've missed the ~** nos hemos pasado la calle

turning point *n* momento *m* decisivo *or* crucial

turnip /'tɜ:rnəp || 'tɜ:nɪp/ *n* [c u] nabo *m*

turn: **~-off** *n* 1 (sth offputting) (colloq): **it's a real ~-off** te quita las ganas (fam); (it's repellent) te repugna; 2 (road) salida *f*; **~-on** *n* (colloq): **it's a big ~-on for him** lo excita, lo vuelve loco (fam); **~out** *n* 1 (at election) número *m* de votantes; (at public spectacle) número *m* de asistentes; **there was a high/low ~out** votó/asistió mucha/poca gente; 2 (clearout) (BrE) (*no pl*) limpieza *f* general; **~over** *n* [u] 1 (volume — of business) facturación *f*; (— of sales) facturación *f*, volumen *m* de ventas 2 (of stock) rotación *f* 3 (of staff) movimiento *m*, renovación *f*; 4 [c] (Culin) empanada *f* (esp AmL), empanadilla *f* (esp Esp); **~pike** *n* 1 (highway) (AmE) autopista *f* de peaje *or* (Méx) de cuota 2 (Hist) (tollgate) barrera *f* de peaje; (road) camino *m* de peaje; **~ signal** *n* (AmE) intermitente *m*, direccional *f* (Col, Méx), señalizador *m* (*de viraje*) (Chi); **~stile** *n* torniquete *m*, molinete *m* (RPl); **~table** *n* 1 (Audio) (platter) plato *m*; (deck) platina *f*, tornamesa *f or m* (AmL) 2 (in microwave oven) plato *m* giratorio 3 (Rail) plataforma *f* giratoria

turnup *n*

A (Clothing) 1 (hem) dobladillo *m* 2 (on trousers) (BrE) vuelta *f or* (RPl) botamanga *f or* (Chi) bastilla *f or* (Méx) valenciana *f*;

B (surprise) (BrE colloq): ***now there's a ~up for the books!*** ¡qué sorpresa!, ¡no lo puedo creer!

turpentine /ˈtɜːrpəntaɪn || ˈtɜːpəntaɪn/ *n* [u] aguarrás *m*, trementina *f*

turps /tɜːrps || tɜːps/ *n* [u] (colloq) ▸ **turpentine**

turquoise[1] /ˈtɜːrkwɔɪz || ˈtɜːkwɔɪz/ *n* 1 [u c] turquesa *f* 2 [u] **~ (blue)** (color) (azul *m*) turquesa *f*

turquoise[2] *adj*: **~ (blue)** (azul) turquesa *adj inv*

turret /ˈtɜːrət || ˈtʌrɪt/ *n* (Archit) torrecilla *f*

turtle /ˈtɜːrtl̩ || ˈtɜːtl̩/ *n* 1 (marine reptile) tortuga *f* marina *or* de mar; ***to turn ~*** zozobrar 2 (AmE) (tortoise) tortuga *f*

turtle: **~dove** *n* tórtola *f*; **like two ~doves** como dos tortolitos; **~neck** *n* 1 **~neck (collar)** cuello *m* alto; (turning over) cuello *m* vuelto, cuello *m* de cisne (Esp), cuello *m* volcado (RPl) 2 **~neck (sweater)** suéter *m* de cuello vuelto (*or* de cisne *etc*), polera *f* (RPl)

turves /tɜːrvz || tɜːvz/ *pl of* **turf**[1]

tush /tʊʃ/ *n* (AmE sl) culo *m* (fam: en algunas regiones vulg), trasero *m* (fam), pandero *m* (fam)

tusk /tʌsk/ *n* colmillo *m*

tussle[1] /ˈtʌsəl/ *n* pelea *f*, lucha *f*

tussle[2] *vi* **to ~ (WITH sb) (FOR/OVER sth)** pelearse (CON algn) (POR algo)

tussock /ˈtʌsək/ *n* mata *f* de hierba

tut[1] /tʌt/ *interj* 1 (expressing disapproval) ¡vamos! 2 (expressing impatience, annoyance) ¡qué cosa!, ¡pucha! (AmS fam & euf)

tut[2] *vi* **-tt-** (make noise) chasquear la lengua (*en señal de desaprobación*)

tutelage /ˈtuːtl̩ɪdʒ || ˈtjuːtɪlɪdʒ/ *n* [u] (frml) tutela *f*

tutor[1] /ˈtuːtər || ˈtjuːtə(r)/ *n* 1 (private teacher) profesor, -sora *m,f* particular 2 (at university) (BrE) tutor, -tora *m,f* (*profesor que supervisa el trabajo de un estudiante*) 3 (book) método *m*

tutor[2] *vt* (teach — privately) darle* clases particulares a; (— at university) (BrE) darle* clases a

■ **tutor** *vi* dar* clases, dictar clases (AmL frml)

tutorial /tuːˈtɔːriəl || tjuːˈtɔːriəl/ *n*: *clase individual o con un pequeño número de estudiantes*

tutti-frutti /ˈtuːtiˈfruːti/ *n* [u] (ice cream) helado *m* de tutti-frutti; (flavor) tutti-frutti *m*

tut-tut /ˈtʌtˈtʌt/ *vi* **-tt-** criticar*

tutu /ˈtuːtuː/ *n* (*pl* **~s**) tutú *m*

tux /tʌks/ *n* (AmE colloq) ▸ **tuxedo**

tuxedo /tʌkˈsiːdəʊ/ *n* (*pl* **-dos** *or* **-does**) (AmE) esmoquin *m*, smoking *m*

TV *n* [c u] (= **television**) televisión *f*, tele *f* (fam), TV *f*; (*before n*) **~ set** televisor *m*, televisión *f*

twaddle /ˈtwɑːdl̩ || ˈtwɒdl̩/ *n* [u] (colloq) estupideces *fpl*, bobadas *fpl* (fam)

twang[1] /twæŋ/ *n* (of guitar) tañido *m*; (of voice, accent): **his voice has a nasal ~** tiene la voz gangosa; **she speaks with a Westerner's ~** habla con el acento nasal del Oeste de los Estados Unidos

twang[2] *vt* ‹*string/wire*› hacer* vibrar (*tensando y soltando*); ‹*guitar*› pulsar las cuerdas de

'twas /twɑːz, *weak form* twəz || twɒz, *weak form* twəz/ (poet) **= it was**

tweak[1] /twiːk/ *vt* pellizcar* (*retorciendo*)

tweak[2] *n* pellizco *m*

twee /twiː/ *adj* (BrE) cursi

tweed /twiːd/ *n* 1 [u] (Tex) tweed *m*; (*before n*) ‹*jacket/suit*› de tweed 2 **tweeds** *pl* (Clothing) *prendas de tweed*

'tween /twiːn/ *prep* (poet) **= between**

tweet /twiːt/ *vi* piar*, gorjear

tweezers /ˈtwiːzərz || ˈtwiːzəz/ *pl n* pinza(s) *f(pl)*; **a pair of ~** una(s) pinza(s)

twelfth[1] /twelfθ/ *adj* duodécimo; *see also* **fifth**[1]

twelfth[2] *adv* en duodécimo lugar; *see also* **fifth**[2]

twelfth[3] *n* 1 (Math) doceavo *m* 2 (part) doceava parte *f*

Twelfth Night *n* Noche *f* de Reyes

twelve /twelv/ *adj/n* doce *adj inv/m*; **~ (o'clock) midnight/noon** las doce de la noche/del mediodía

twentieth[1] /ˈtwentiəθ/ *adj* vigésimo; **today is my ~ birthday** hoy cumplo veinte años; *see also* **fifth**[1]

twentieth[2] *adv* en vigésimo lugar; *see also* **fifth**[2]

twentieth[3] *n* 1 (Math) veinteavo *m* 2 (part) veinteava *or* vigésima parte *f*

twenty /ˈtwenti/ *adj/n* veinte *adj inv/m*; *see also* **seventy**

twenty-first[1] /ˈtwentiˈfɜːrst || ˌtwentiˈfɜːst/ *adj* vigesimoprimero; **~ (birthday) party** fiesta *f* de los 21 años; *see also* **fifth**[1]

twenty-first[2] *adv* en vigesimoprimer lugar; *see also* **fifth**[2]

twenty-first[3] *n*: **it's his ~ on Saturday** el sábado cumple veintiún años

twenty-four-seven /ˈtwentiˌfɔːrˈsevən || ˈtwentiˌfɔːˈsevən/ *adv* (esp AmE colloq) durante las veinticuatro horas, siete días a la semana, de día y de noche, toda la semana (fam)

twerp *n* (BrE) ▸ **twirp**

twice /twaɪs/ *adv* 1 (two times) dos veces; **~ a week/year** dos veces por semana/año; **I'd think ~ before doing it** (me) lo pensaría dos veces *or* muy bien antes de hacerlo; **the ~-weekly meetings** las reuniones, que tienen lugar dos veces por semana 2 (double): **~ three is six** dos por tres es (igual a) seis; **I've got ~ as many as you** yo tengo el doble que tú; **he's ~ your age/height** te dobla en edad/altura

twiddle /ˈtwɪdl̩/ *vt* (hacer*) girar

■ **twiddle** *vi* **to ~ WITH sth** juguetear CON algo

twig[1] /twɪg/ *n* ramita *f*

twig[2] **-gg-** (BrE colloq) *vi* caer* (fam), darse* cuenta

■ **twig** *vt* darse* cuenta de

twilight /ˈtwaɪlaɪt/ *n* [u] 1 (dusk) crepúsculo *m*; **at ~** al ponerse el sol 2 (half-light) penumbra *f*; **the room was in ~** la habitación estaba en penumbra *or* a media luz 3 (period of decline) (liter) crepúsculo *m* (liter), ocaso *m* (liter)

twill /twɪl/ *n* [u] sarga *f*

twin[1] /twɪn/ *n* mellizo, -za *m,f*, gemelo, -la *m,f* (esp Esp); [*in Latin America* **gemelo** *tends to be used to refer to an identical twin*] cuate *mf* (Méx); **identical ~s** gemelos idénticos *or* (téc) univitelinos, gemelos (AmL)

twin[2] *adj* 1 ‹*brother/sister*› mellizo, gemelo (esp Esp); *see* **twin**[1] 2 (paired): **the ~ evils of poverty and violence** la pobreza y la violencia, dos males que siempre van de la mano; **~ beds** camas *fpl* gemelas; **~ town** ciudad *f* hermana

twin[3] *vt* **-nn-** (BrE) (*usu pass*) **to be ~ned WITH sth** estar* hermanado CON algo

twine[1] /twaɪn/ *n* [u] cordel *m*, bramante *m* (Esp), cáñamo *m* (Andes), piolín *m* (RPl), mecate *m* (AmC, Méx, Ven), lienza *f* (Chi)

twine[2] *vt* entretejer; **the ivy has ~d itself around the tree** la hiedra se ha enroscado alrededor del árbol; **he ~d his arms around her waist** le rodeó la cintura con los brazos

■ **twine** *vi* **to ~ AROUND sth** enroscarse* ALREDEDOR DE algo

twin-engined /twɪnˈendʒənd || ˌtwɪnˈendʒɪnd/ *adj* bimotor, -tora

twinge /twɪndʒ/ *n* (of pain) punzada *f*, puntada *f* (CS); **she felt a ~ of remorse** sintió una punzada de remordimiento

twinkle[1] /ˈtwɪŋkəl/ *n* 1 (of lights, stars) centelleo *m*, titilar *m* 2 (in eye) brillo *m*; **when you were just a ~ in your father's eye** (hum) cuando no eras más que un proyecto (hum)

twinkle[2] *vi* 1 «*light/star*» titilar, centellear 2 «*eyes*» brillar

twinkling /ˈtwɪŋklɪŋ/ *n*: ***in the ~ of an eye*** en un abrir y cerrar de ojos, en un santiamén (fam)

twin: **~set** *n* conjunto *m* (*de suéter y chaqueta de punto*); **~tub** *n* (BrE) *lavadora de dos tambores, uno para lavar y el otro para centrifugar la ropa*

twirl[1] /twɜːrl || twɜːl/ *vt* ‹*cane/baton*› (hacer*) girar, revolear (CS); **he was ~ing his mustache** se estaba retorciendo el bigote

■ **twirl** *vi* «*baton*» girar, revolear (CS)

twirl[2] *n*: **with a ~ of his cane** haciendo girar *or* (CS) revolear el bastón por el aire

twirp, (BrE) **twerp** /twɜːrp || twɜːp/ *n* (colloq) imbécil *mf*, papanatas *mf* (fam), pendejo, -ja *m,f* (AmL exc CS fam),

t

huevón, -vona *m,f* (Andes, Ven fam), gilipollas *mf* (Esp fam *o* vulg)

twist[1] /twɪst/ *vt*

A 1 (screw, coil) retorcer*; **to ~ sth AROUND sth** enrollar *or* enroscar* algo ALREDEDOR DE algo 2 (turn) ‹*handle/knob*› girar; **to ~ the top off a bottle** desenroscar* la tapa de una botella; **he ~ed her arm** le retorció el brazo; **to be ~ed (up)** estar* enredado; ▸ **little finger**

B 1 (distort) retorcer*; **his face was ~ed with pain** tenía el rostro crispado por el dolor 2 (sprain) torcer*; **I ~ed my ankle** me torcí el tobillo 3 (alter, pervert) ‹*words*› tergiversar; ‹*meaning*› torcer*

■ **twist** *vi* 1 (wind, coil) «*rope/wire*» enrollarse, enroscarse*; «*road/river*» serpentear 2 (turn, rotate) girar; **the cap ~s off** el tapón se desenrosca 3 (dance) bailar el twist

twist[2] *n*

A 1 (bend — in wire, rope) vuelta *f*, onda *f*; (— in road, river) recodo *m*, vuelta *f*; ***round the ~*** (BrE colloq) loco, chiflado (fam) 2 (turning movement) giro *m*; **to give sth a ~** hacer* girar algo 3 (sth twisted): **a ~ of paper** un cucurucho de papel; **a ~ of thread** un torzal de hilo; **a ~ of lemon** una rodajita de limón (*retorcida*)

B (in story, events) giro *m* inesperado, vuelta *f* de tuerca; **by a (strange) ~ of fate** por una de esas (extrañas) vueltas que da la vida

C (dance) twist *m*; **to do the ~** bailar el twist

twisted /'twɪstəd || 'twɪstɪd/ *adj* ‹*grin*› contrahecho, retorcido; ‹*mind/sense of humor*› retorcido; **a ~ version of events** una versión distorsionada de los hechos

twister /'twɪstər || 'twɪstə(r)/ *n* (AmE colloq) (tornado) (AmE) tornado *m*

twistoff /'twɪstɔːf || 'twɪstɒf/ *adj* (*before n*) ‹*lid/cap*› de media rosca

twit /twɪt/ *n* (BrE colloq) imbécil *mf*

twitch[1] /twɪtʃ/ *vi* «*tail/nose*» moverse*

■ **twitch** *vt* ‹*tail/ears*› mover*; **she ~ed back the curtain** abrió la cortina de un tirón *or* (AmL exc CS) de un jalón

twitch[2] *n* 1 (tic) tic *m* 2 (pull) tirón *m*, jalón *m* (AmL exc CS)

twitchy /'twɪtʃi/ *adj* **twitchier, twitchiest** nervioso, agitado

twitter[1] /'twɪtər || 'twɪtə(r)/ *vi* 1 «*birds*» gorjear 2 «*person*» parlotear, cotorrear (fam)

twitter[2] *n* [u] 1 (of bird) gorjeo *m* 2 (of person) parloteo *m*, cotorreo *m* (fam); ***to be in a ~*** *o* (BrE also) ***all of a ~*** (colloq) estar* muy excitado

two[1] /tuː/ *n* dos *m*; **~ by ~** (liter) de dos en dos, de a dos (AmL); **to cut sth in ~** cortar algo en dos *or* por la mitad; **they are ~ of a kind** son tal para cual; ***that makes ~ of us*** (colloq) ya somos dos (fam); ***to put ~ and ~ together*** atar cabos; **he put ~ and ~ together and made five** llegó a una conclusión errada; ***~ can play at that game*** donde las dan las toman; ***~'s company, three's a crowd*** el tercero está de más; *see also* **four**[1]

two[2] *adj* dos *adj inv*; *see also* **four**[2]

two: **~-bit** *adj* (AmE) (*before n*) (insignificant) (colloq) de tres al cuarto (fam), de medio pelo (fam); **~-cycle** *adj* (AmE) de dos tiempos; **~-dimensional** /'tuːdə'mentʃnəl, -daɪ- || ˌtuːdɪ'menʃənl̩, -daɪ-/ *adj* bidimensional; **~-edged** /'tuː'edʒd/ *adj* de doble filo; **~-faced** /'tuː'feɪst/ *adj* (colloq) falso, doble (Andes, Ven fam); **~fisted** /'tuː'fɪstəd || ˌtuː'fɪstɪd/ *adj* (AmE colloq) vehemente; **~fold** *adj/adv see* **-fold**; **~pence** /'tʌpəns/ *n* dos peniques *mpl*; **~-piece** *adj* ‹*swimsuit*› de dos piezas; **~-piece suit** traje *m or* (Col) vestido *m* de dos piezas, ambo *m* (CS); **~-ply** *adj* (*before n*) ‹*yarn*› de dos hebras; ‹*wood/tissue*› de dos capas

two-seater[1] /'tuː'siːtər || ˌtuː'siːtə(r)/ *adj* (*before n*) ‹*car/plane*› biplaza, de dos plazas

two-seater[2] *n* biplaza *m*

twosome /'tuːsəm/ *n* 1 (pair) pareja *f* 2 (game) partida *f or* juego *m* para dos personas

two: **~-stroke** *adj* (BrE) de dos tiempos; **~-time** *vt* (colloq) (be unfaithful to) ponerle* *or* meterle los cuernos a (fam), engañar, ponerle* el gorro a (Chi fam); (double-cross) engañar; **~-tone** *adj* de dos tonos

'twould /twʊd/ (poet) = **it would**

two: **~-up two-down** /'tuːʌp'tuːdaʊn/ *n* (BrE) *casa pequeña de dos plantas con dos habitaciones en cada una*; **~-way** /'tuː'weɪ/ *adj* ‹*traffic/street*› de doble sentido *or* dirección, de doble vía (Col), de doble mano (RPl); ‹*agreement*› bilateral; ‹*race/contest*› (AmE) de dos (participantes); **~-way mirror** *cristal que funciona como espejo por un lado y como ventana por el otro*; **~-way radio** aparato *m* emisor y receptor; **they have to make concessions too: it's a ~-way process** tiene que haber concesiones mutuas *or* de ambas partes; **~-wheeler** /'tuː'hwiːlər || ˌtuː'wiːlə(r)/ *n* bicicleta *f*

TX = **Texas**

tycoon /taɪ'kuːn/ *n* magnate *mf*

tympani /'tɪmpəni/ *pl n* timbales *mpl*

type[1] /taɪp/ *n*

A [c] 1 (sort, kind) tipo *m*; **it's a ~ of ...** (in descriptions, definitions) es una especie de ...; **he's not my ~** no es mi tipo (de hombre); **I know his ~** conozco a los de su calaña; **he's the jealous ~** es del tipo de hombre celoso 2 (typical example) tipo *m*, ejemplo *m* típico; (stereotype) estereotipo *m*

B [u] (Print) (characters) tipo *m* (de imprenta); **in large/small ~** en caracteres grandes/pequeños, en letra grande/pequeña

type[2] *vt* escribir* a máquina, tipear (AmS); **could you ~ this for me?** ¿me puedes pasar *or* escribir esto a máquina?

■ **type** *vi* escribir* a máquina, tipear (AmS)

Phrasal verbs

• **type out** [v ▸ o ▸ adv, v ▸ adv ▸ o] escribir* a máquina, tipear (AmS)

• **type up** [v ▸ o ▸ adv, v ▸ adv ▸ o] pasar a máquina, tipear (AmS)

type: **~cast** *vt* (*past & past p* **-cast**) ‹*actor*› encasillar (*en cierto tipo de papel*); **~face** *n* tipo *m* (de imprenta), (tipo *m* de) caracteres *mpl*, (tipo *m* de) letra *f*; **~script** *n* [c u] texto *m* mecanografiado, manuscrito *m* (*de una obra, novela etc*); **~set** (*pres p* **-setting**; *past & past p* **-set**) *vt* componer*; **~setter** *n* 1 (person) cajista *mf*, componedor, -dora *m,f* 2 (machine) monotipo *m*; **~write** (*past* **-wrote**; *past p* **-written**) *vt* (*usu pass*) escribir* a máquina, mecanografiar*; **~writer** *n* máquina *f* de escribir

typhoid (fever) /'taɪfɔɪd/ *n* [u] (fiebre *f*) tifoidea *f*

typhoon /'taɪ'fuːn/ *n* tifón *m*

typhus /'taɪfəs/ *n* [u] tifus *m*, tifo *m*

typical /'tɪpɪkəl/ *adj* típico; **with ~ lack of tact** con su típica *or* característica falta de tacto; **that's just ~ of her** eso es típico de ella; **he arrived late — (how) ~!** llegó tarde — ¡típico! *or* ¡cuándo no!; **isn't that ~: it's starting to rain!** (colloq) ¡no podía fallar: está empezando a llover!

typically /'tɪpɪkli/ *adv* típicamente; **~, she arrived late** (*indep*) como de costumbre *or* para variar, llegó tarde

typify /'tɪpəfaɪ || 'tɪpɪfaɪ/ *vt* **-fies, -fying, -fied** tipificar*, ser* representativo de

typing /'taɪpɪŋ/ *n* [u] mecanografía *f*; **I offered to do some ~ for him** me ofrecí a pasarle algunas cosas a máquina; (*before n*) ‹*error*› de máquina; ‹*lesson*› de mecanografía, de dactilografía; ‹*paper*› para escribir a máquina

typing pool *n* (typists) mecanógrafos *mpl*, dactilógrafos *mpl*; (department) servicio *m* de mecanografía *or* dactilografía

typist /'taɪpəst || 'taɪpɪst/ *n* mecanógrafo, -fa *m,f*, dactilógrafo, -fa *m,f*

typographic /'taɪpə'græfɪk/, **-ical** /-ɪkəl/ *adj* tipográfico

typography /taɪ'pɑːgrəfi || taɪ'pɒgrəfi/ *n* [u] tipografía *f*

tyrannical /tə'rænɪkəl || tɪ'rænɪkəl/ *adj* tiránico

tyrannize /'tɪrənaɪz/ *vt* tiranizar*

tyranny /'tɪrəni/ *n* [u] tiranía *f*

tyrant /'taɪrənt/ *n* tirano, -na *m,f*

tyre /taɪr || 'taɪə(r)/ *n* (BrE) ▸ **tire**[2]

tzetze fly /'tsetsi, 'te-/ *n* ▸ **tsetse fly**

t

Uu

U, u /juː/ *n* U, u *f*

U (in UK) (Cin) (= **universal**) apta para todo público (AmL), todos los públicos (Esp)

UAE *pl n* (= **United Arab Emirates**) EAU *mpl*

ubiquitous /juːˈbɪkwətəs || juːˈbɪkwɪtəs/ *adj* omnipresente (frml), ubicuo (frml)

U-boat /ˈjuːbəʊt/ *n* submarino *m* (*alemán*)

UCAS /ˈjuːkæs/ *n* (in UK) = **Universities and Colleges Admissions Service**

udder /ˈʌdər || ˈʌdə(r)/ *n* ubre *f*

UEFA /juːˈeɪfə/ *n* (*no art*) (= **Union of European Football Associations**) la UEFA

UFO *n* (= **unidentified flying object**) ovni *m*, OVNI *m*

Uganda /juːˈgændə/ *n* Uganda *f*

Ugandan /juːˈgændən/ *adj* ugandés

ugh /ɜːh, ɪʌx/ *interj* ¡puf! (fam), ¡puaj! (fam)

ugliness /ˈʌglinəs || ˈʌglɪnɪs/ *n* [u] (of person, face) fealdad *f*

ugly /ˈʌgli/ *adj* **uglier, ugliest** [1] (not pretty) ‹*person/clothes*› feo [2] (unpleasant) ‹*rumor*› inquietante, alarmante; ‹*wound*› feo; ‹*crime*› horrible; **he's in an ~ mood** tiene un humor de perros

ugly duckling *n* patito *m* feo

uh /ʌh, ɜːr || ʌh, ɜː(r)/ *interj* (expressing hesitation) este ..., esto ... (Esp)

UHF *n* (= **ultra-high frequency**) UHF *f*

uh-huh /ˈʌˈhʌ/ *interj* (affirming, agreeing) ajá (fam)

UHT *adj* (BrE) (= **ultra high temperature**) UHT, UAT (AmL), uperizado (Esp)

uh-uh /ˈʌhʌh/ *interj* (disagreeing, negating) ah, no

UK *n* (= **United Kingdom**) RU *m*

Ukraine /juːˈkreɪn/ *n* Ucrania *f*

Ukrainian[1] /juːˈkreɪniən/ *adj* ucraniano, ucranio

Ukrainian[2] *n* [1] [c] (person) ucraniano, -na *m,f*, ucranio, -nia *m,f* [2] [u] (language) ucraniano *m*, ucranio *m*

ulcer /ˈʌlsər || ˈʌlsə(r)/ *n* (internal) úlcera *f*; (external) llaga *f*; **a stomach ~** una úlcera de estómago; **a mouth ~** una llaga en la boca

ulcerated /ˈʌlsəreɪtəd || ˈʌlsəreɪtɪd/ *adj* ulcerado

ulcerous /ˈʌlsərəs/ *adj* ulceroso

U-lock /ˈjuː,lɑːk || ˈjuː,lɒk/ *n* candado *m* en forma de U, candado *m* de horquilla (*para bicicletas*), (candado *m*) U-lock *m* (AmL)

Ulster /ˈʌlstər || ˈʌlstə(r)/ *n* el Ulster

ulterior /ʌlˈtɪriər || ʌlˈtɪəriə(r)/ *adj* oculto; **~ motive** segunda intención *f*, motivo *m* oculto

ultimata /ˈʌltəˈmeɪtə || ˌʌltɪˈmeɪtə/ *pl of* **ultimatum**

ultimate[1] /ˈʌltəmət || ˈʌltɪmət/ *adj*

A [1] (eventual, final) ‹*aim/destination*› final; **who has ~ responsibility?** ¿quién es el responsable en última instancia? [2] (fundamental, original) primordial, fundamental; **the ~ cause of the problem** la raíz del problema

B [1] (utmost, supreme) ‹*sacrifice*› máximo, supremo; **he's the ~ authority on the subject** es la máxima autoridad en el tema [2] (most sophisticated) (journ): **the ~ sound system** lo último en sistemas de sonido, el no va más en sistemas de sonido (fam)

ultimate[2] *n*: **the ~ (in sth)** lo último en algo, el no va más en algo (fam); **the ~ in bad taste** el colmo del mal gusto

ultimately /ˈʌltəmətli || ˈʌltɪmətli/ *adv* [1] (finally) en última instancia [2] (in the long run) a la larga

ultimatum /ˈʌltəˈmeɪtəm || ˌʌltɪˈmeɪtəm/ *n* (*pl* **-tums** *or* **-ta**) ultimátum *m*

ultra- /ˈʌltrə/ *pref* ultra-, super- (fam)

ultrahigh /ˈʌltrəˈhaɪ/ *adj*: **~ frequency** frecuencia *f* ultraelevada, UHF *f*

ultramarine[1] /ˈʌltrəməˈriːn/ *adj* azul ultramarino *or* (de) ultramar *adj inv*

ultramarine[2] *n* [u] azul *m* ultramarino *or* (de) ultramar

ultrasonic /ˈʌltrəˈsɑːnɪk || ˌʌltrəˈsɒnɪk/ *adj* ultrasónico

ultrasound /ˈʌltrəsaʊnd/ *n* [1] [u] (Phys) ultrasonido *m* [2] [c u] (Med) ecografía *f*

ultraviolet /ˈʌltrəˈvaɪələt/ *adj* ‹*light/rays*› ultravioleta *adj inv*

um /ʌm/ *interj* este ..., esto ... (Esp)

umber /ˈʌmbər || ˈʌmbə(r)/ *n* [u] sombra *f*

umbilical cord /əmˈbɪlɪkəl || ʌmˈbɪlɪkəl/ *n* (Anat) cordón *m* umbilical

umbrage /ˈʌmbrɪdʒ/ *n*: **to take ~ (AT sth)** ofenderse *or* sentirse* agraviado (POR algo)

umbrella /ʌmˈbrelə/ *n* (*pl* **-las**) (against rain) paraguas *m*; (against sun) sombrilla *f*; (*before n*) **~ stand** paragüero *m*; **~ organization** *organización que aglutina a varios grupos*

umlaut /ˈʊmlaʊt/ *n* diéresis *f*, crema *f*

umpire[1] /ˈʌmpaɪr || ˈʌmpaɪə(r)/ *n* árbitro, -tra *m,f*; (in baseball) umpire *mf*, ampáyar *mf* (Col)

umpire[2] *vt* arbitrar

umpteen /ˈʌmpˈtiːn/ *adj* (colloq) tropecientos (fam), miles *or* un millón de

umpteenth /ˈʌmpˈtiːnθ/ *adj* (colloq) enésimo; **for the ~ time** por enésima vez

un- /ʌn/ *pref* in-, des-, no, sin, poco; *see individual words*

'un /ən/ **= one** (colloq): **that's a good ~!** ¡esa sí que es buena! (fam)

UN *n* (= **United Nations**) ONU *f*

unabashed /ˈʌnəˈbæʃt/ *adj*: **she continued her speech ~** continuó con su discurso impertérrita *or* sin inmutarse; **she displayed an attitude of ~ greed** mostró su codicia con total desenfado *or* sin ningún reparo

unabated /ˈʌnəˈbeɪtəd || ˌʌnəˈbeɪtɪd/ *adj* (liter): **with ~ enthusiasm** con un entusiasmo que no ha disminuido (*or* disminuyó *etc*) en lo más mínimo *or* (liter) sigue (*or* siguió *etc*) incólume; **the storm continued ~** el temporal continuaba con toda su furia

unable /ʌnˈeɪbəl/ *adj* (*pred*) **to be ~ to + INF** no poder* + INF; **she was ~ to attend** no pudo *or* le fue imposible asistir; **he was ~ to beat his opponent** fue incapaz de vencer a su contrincante

unabridged /ˈʌnəˈbrɪdʒd/ *adj* íntegro

unacceptable /ˈʌnəkˈseptəbəl/ *adj* ‹*conduct/standard*› inaceptable, inadmisible; ‹*terms/conditions*› inadmisible

unaccompanied /ˈʌnəˈkʌmpənid/ *adj* [1] ‹*luggage*› no acompañado; ‹*person*› solo [2] (Mus) ‹*singing*› sin acompañamiento; ‹*instrument*› solo

unaccountable /ˈʌnəˈkaʊntəbəl/ *adj* [1] (inexplicable) incomprensible, inexplicable [2] (not responsible) (frml) (*pred*) **to be ~ FOR sth**: **he was held to be ~ for his actions** se consideró que no era responsable de sus actos

unaccounted for /ˈʌnəˈkaʊntəd|| ˌʌnəˈkaʊntɪd/ *adj* (*pred*): **the rest of the money is ~ ~** no se han dado explicaciones sobre qué sucedió con el resto del dinero; **three members of the crew are still ~ ~** siguen sin aparecer tres miembros de la tripulación

unaccustomed /ˈʌnəˈkʌstəmd/ *adj* 1 (unusual) desacostumbrado, poco habitual 2 (unused) **to be ~ TO sth/-ING** no estar* acostumbrado A algo/+ INF

unacknowledged /ˈʌnəkˈnɑːlɪdʒd || ˌʌnəkˈnɒlɪdʒd/ *adj* ‹*authority/champion/heir*› no reconocido; **my letter went ~** no acusaron recibo de mi carta

unacquainted /ˈʌnəˈkweɪntəd || ˌʌnəˈkweɪntɪd/ *adj* (frml) **to be ~ WITH sth** desconocer* algo

unadorned /ˈʌnəˈdɔːrnd || ˌʌnəˈdɔːnd/ *adj* (liter) ‹*beauty*› puro, sin adornos; **the plain, ~ facts** la verdad pura y simple *or* lisa y llana

unadulterated /ˈʌnəˈdʌltəreɪtəd || ˌʌnəˈdʌltəreɪtɪd/ *adj* 1 ‹*wine/substance*› no adulterado 2 ‹*nonsense/bliss*› auténtico, verdadero

unadventurous /ˈʌnədˈventʃərəs/ *adj* ‹*choice/design*› poco atrevido *or* audaz

unaffected /ˈʌnəˈfektəd || ˌʌnəˈfektɪd/ *adj* 1 (sincere, natural) ‹*person*› natural, sencillo; ‹*manners*› natural, nada estudiado *or* afectado 2 (not damaged, hurt) no afectado

unafraid /ˈʌnəˈfreɪd/ *adj*: **to be ~ OF sth** no temerle A algo

unaided /ˈʌnˈeɪdəd || ʌnˈeɪdɪd/ *adj* sin ayuda

unalterable /ˈʌnˈɔːltərəbəl/ *adj* ‹*decision/law*› irrevocable, definitivo; ‹*belief/conviction*› inalterable, profundo

unaltered /ˈʌnˈɔːltərd || ʌnˈɔːltəd/ *adj*: **my opinion remains ~** mi opinión sigue siendo la misma, no he cambiado de opinión

unambiguous /ˈʌnæmˈbɪgjuəs/ *adj* inequívoco, que no deja lugar a dudas

unambitious /ˈʌnæmˈbɪʃəs/ *adj* poco ambicioso

un-American /ˈʌnəˈmerəkən || ʌnəˈmerɪkən/ *adj* 1 (anti-American) antiamericano 2 (untypical) poco americano

unanimous /juːˈnænəməs || juːˈnænɪməs/ *adj* unánime

unanimously /juːˈnænəməsli || juːˈnænɪməsli/ *adv* ‹*vote/declare/state*› unánimemente; ‹*elect*› por unanimidad

unannounced /ˈʌnəˈnaʊnst/ *adj* ‹*arrival/guest*› inesperado, imprevisto; **to arrive ~** llegar* sin previo aviso

unanswerable /ˈʌnˈænsərəbəl || ʌnˈɑːnsərəbəl/ *adj* ‹*proof*› irrefutable, incontestable; **an ~ question** una pregunta a la que no se puede responder

unanswered /ˈʌnˈænsərd || ʌnˈɑːnsəd/ *adj* ‹*question/letter*› sin contestar; **to go ~** no obtener* respuesta

unappetizing /ˈʌnˈæpətaɪzɪŋ/ *adj* ‹*dish/smell*› poco apetitoso; ‹*idea/prospect*› poco apetecible

unappreciative /ˈʌnəˈpriːʃətɪv/ *adj* ‹*person*› ingrato, desagradecido; ‹*audience*› que no sabe apreciar lo que se le ofrece; **to be ~ OF sth** no apreciar *or* valorar algo

unapproachable /ˈʌnəˈprəʊtʃəbəl/ *adj* ‹*person*› inabordable, poco accesible *or* asequible

unapt /ˈʌnˈæpt/ *adj* 1 (unsuitable) ‹*remark/comment*› inapropiado, inconveniente, inoportuno; ‹*person*› no apto 2 (unlikely) (AmE) (*pred*) **to be ~ to + INF: she's ~ to believe what she's told** es poco probable que se crea lo que le digan

unarmed /ˈʌnˈɑːrmd || ʌnˈɑːmd/ *adj* ‹*person*› desarmado; **~ combat** combate *m* sin armas

unashamed /ˈʌnəˈʃeɪmd/ *adj*: **I'm an ~ admirer of his work** no tengo ningún reparo en reconocer que admiro su obra; **he was quite ~ about it** no le dio vergüenza ninguna, no se avergonzó para nada

unashamedly /ˈʌnəˈʃeɪmədli || ˌʌnəˈʃeɪmɪdli/ *adv* sin vergüenza

unasked /ˈʌnˈæskt || ʌnˈɑːskt/ *adj* (*pred*) 1 ‹*question*› sin formular 2 (uninvited): **he did it ~** lo hizo sin que nadie se lo pidiera, lo hizo (de) motu proprio

unassailable /ˈʌnəˈseɪləbəl/ *adj* (frml) ‹*fortress*› inexpugnable; ‹*reputation*› incuestionable; **his position is ~** su posición es invulnerable

unassisted /ˈʌnəˈsɪstəd || ˌʌnəˈsɪstɪd/ *adj* sin ayuda

unassuming /ˈʌnəˈsuːmɪŋ || ˌʌnəˈsjuːmɪŋ/ *adj* sencillo, sin pretensiones

unattached /ˈʌnəˈtætʃt/ *adj* 1 (not affiliated) independiente 2 (not married) sin ataduras, libre

unattainable /ˈʌnəˈteɪnəbəl/ *adj* inalcanzable

unattended /ˈʌnəˈtendəd || ˌʌnəˈtendɪd/ *adj* (*usu pred*) 1 (unwatched, unsupervised): **to leave sb ~** dejar a algn solo; **don't leave your luggage ~** vigile su equipaje en todo momento 2 (not dealt with) desatendido, descuidado

unattractive /ˈʌnəˈtræktɪv/ *adj* poco atractivo

unauthorized /ˈʌnˈɔːθəraɪzd/ *adj* no autorizado

unavailable /ˈʌnəˈveɪləbəl/ *adj*: **that number is ~** ese número está desconectado (*or* averiado *etc*); **the minister is ~ for comment** el ministro no desea hacer ningún comentario

unavoidable /ˈʌnəˈvɔɪdəbəl/ *adj* inevitable

unavoidably /ˈʌnəˈvɔɪdəbli/ *adv*: **the train was ~ delayed** el tren sufrió un retraso inevitable

unaware /ˈʌnəˈwer || ˌʌnəˈweə(r)/ *adj* 1 (not conscious) (*pred*) **to be ~ OF sth** ignorar algo, no ser* consciente DE algo; **they were ~ of my presence** no sabían que yo estaba allí 2 (naive): **politically/socially ~** sin conciencia política/social

unawares /ˈʌnəˈwerz || ˌʌnəˈweəz/ *adv*: **to catch** *o* **take sb ~** agarrar *or* (esp Esp) coger* a algn desprevenido *or* por sorpresa

unbalanced /ˈʌnˈbælənst/ *adj* 1 (not in equilibrium) ‹*diet/composition*› desequilibrado; ‹*view/report*› tendencioso, partidista 2 (deranged): **mentally ~** desequilibrado, trastornado

unbearable /ˈʌnˈberəbəl || ʌnˈbeərəbəl/ *adj* insoportable, inaguantable, insufrible

unbearably /ˈʌnˈberəbli || ʌnˈbeərəbli/ *adv* insoportablemente; **it's ~ hot** hace un calor insoportable

unbeatable /ˈʌnˈbiːtəbəl/ *adj* ‹*team*› invencible; ‹*quality/value*› insuperable, inmejorable; ‹*price*› imbatible

unbeaten /ˈʌnˈbiːtn/ *adj* ‹*champion/army*› invicto, que nunca ha sido vencido; ‹*record*› insuperado

unbecoming /ˈʌnbɪˈkʌmɪŋ/ *adj* (frml) 1 (unseemly) ‹*behavior/language*› indecoroso; **~ TO sb** impropio DE algn 2 (unflattering) ‹*clothes/hairstyle*› poco favorecedor

unbeknown /ˈʌnbɪˈnəʊn/, **unbeknownst** /-ˈnəʊnst/ *adv* (liter) **~ TO sb**: **~ to me** sin yo saberlo; **~ to the family** sin el conocimiento de la familia

unbelievable /ˈʌnbəˈliːvəbəl || ˌʌnbɪˈliːvəbəl/ *adj* increíble

unbelievably /ˈʌnbəˈliːvəbli || ˌʌnbɪˈliːvəbli/ *adv* increíblemente

unbeliever /ˈʌnbəˈliːvər || ˌʌnbɪˈliːvə(r)/ *n* (Relig liter) no creyente *mf*, infiel *mf*

unbelieving /ˈʌnbəˈliːvɪŋ || ˌʌnbɪˈliːvɪŋ/ *adj* (incredulous) ‹*smile/look*› de incredulidad

unbending /ˈʌnˈbendɪŋ/ *adj* ‹*person/attitude*› inflexible; ‹*determination*› firme

unbiased /ˈʌnˈbaɪəst/ *adj* ‹*opinion/report/person*› imparcial, objetivo

unblemished /ˈʌnˈblemɪʃt/ *adj* ‹*reputation/character*› intachable, sin mancha, sin tacha

unblock /ˈʌnˈblɑːk || ʌnˈblɒk/ *vt* ‹*drain/sink*› desatascar*, destapar (AmL)

unbolt /ˈʌnˈbəʊlt/ *vt* ‹*gate/door*› descorrer el pestillo *or* cerrojo de

unborn /ˈʌnˈbɔːrn || ʌnˈbɔːn/ *adj* ‹*child*› que todavía no ha nacido, nonato; **generations as yet ~** (liter) las generaciones venideras (liter)

unbounded /ˈʌnˈbaʊndəd || ʌnˈbaʊndɪd/ *adj* (liter) ‹*optimism/courage*› sin límites; ‹*hope*› infinito

unbowed /ˈʌnˈbaʊd/ *adj* (liter) ‹*spirit*› incólume

unbranded /ʌnˈbrændəd || ʌnˈbrændɪd/ *adj*
A ‹*product*› sin marca
B ‹*livestock*› sin marcar

unbreakable /ˈʌnˈbreɪkəbəl/ *adj* irrompible

unbridled /ˈʌnˈbraɪdl̩d/ *adj* desenfrenado

unbroken /ˈʌnˈbrəʊkən/ *adj* 1 (intact) ‹*crockery/glass/seal*› intacto, en perfecto estado 2 (continuous) ‹*silence/descent/run*› ininterrumpido 3 (unbeaten, unsubdued) ‹*spirit/pride*› indómito

unbuckle /ˈʌnˈbʌkəl/ *vt* desabrochar

U

unburden /ˈʌnˈbɜːrdn̩ || ʌnˈbɜːdn̩/ *vt* (liter) (relieve) ‹*conscience*› descargar*; **to ~ oneself to sb** desahogarse* con algn, abrirle* el pecho *or* el corazón a algn

unbusinesslike /ˈʌnˈbɪznəslaɪk || ʌnˈbɪznɪslaɪk/ *adj* poco profesional

unbutton /ˈʌnˈbʌtn̩/ *vt* desabotonar, desabrochar

uncalled-for /ˈʌnˈkɔːldfɔːr || ʌnˈkɔːlfɔː(r)/ *adj* ‹*criticism/remark*› fuera de lugar; **his rudeness was quite ~** su grosería fue totalmente gratuita

uncanny /ˈʌnˈkæni/ *adj* raro, extraño, asombroso

uncaring /ˈʌnˈkerɪŋ || ʌnˈkeərɪŋ/ *adj* ‹*society/attitude*› indiferente

unceasing /ˈʌnˈsiːsɪŋ/ *adj* (liter) incesante

unceasingly /ˈʌnˈsiːsɪŋli/ *adv* (liter) incesantemente, sin cesar

uncensored /ˈʌnˈsensərd || ʌnˈsensəd/ *adj* no censurado; **the ~ version** la versión íntegra

unceremonious /ˈʌnˈserəˈməʊniəs || ˌʌnˌserɪˈməʊniəs/ *adj* brusco, poco ceremonioso

unceremoniously /ˈʌnˈserəˈməʊniəsli || ˌʌnˌserɪˈməʊniəsli/ *adv* bruscamente, sin ceremonias

uncertain /ˈʌnˈsɜːrtn̩ || ʌnˈsɜːtn̩/ *adj*

A **1** (unsure) (*pred*) **to be ~ ABOUT/OF sth** no estar* seguro DE algo; **we're ~ (as to) whether we should go** no estamos seguros de si debemos ir (o no) **2** (hesitant) ‹*voice/movement*› vacilante

B **1** (doubtful) ‹*prospects/future*› incierto; **it is ~ who will win** no está claro quién va a ganar **2** (changeable, unreliable) ‹*weather/situation*› inestable

C (vague): **in no ~ terms** muy claramente, inequívocamente

uncertainty /ˈʌnˈsɜːrtn̩ti || ʌnˈsɜːtn̩ti/ *n* [u] **1** (doubt) incertidumbre *f*, duda *f*; **~ ABOUT sth**: **there is some ~ about** *o* **as to his whereabouts** no se conoce con seguridad su paradero **2** (of outcome, future) incertidumbre *f*, lo incierto

unchallenged /ˈʌnˈtʃæləndʒd || ˌʌnˈtʃælɪndʒd/ *adj* ‹*doctrine/assumption*› incontestado; **his remarks cannot go ~** sus comentarios no pueden quedar sin respuesta

unchanged /ˈʌnˈtʃeɪndʒd/ *adj* (*usu pred*): **she was quite ~** no había cambiado para nada; **the ceremony has remained ~ for centuries** la ceremonia se ha celebrado de la misma forma durante siglos

unchanging /ˈʌnˈtʃeɪndʒɪŋ/ *adj* (*before n*) inalterable, inmutable

uncharacteristic /ˈʌnˈkærəktəˈrɪstɪk/ *adj* desacostumbrado, inusitado; **~ OF sb/sth** desacostumbrado *or* raro EN algn/algo

uncharacteristically /ˈʌnˈkærəktəˈrɪstɪkli/ *adv*: **an ~ frank answer** una respuesta de una franqueza inusitada

uncharitable /ˈʌnˈtʃærətəbəl || ʌnˈtʃærɪtəbəl/ *adj* ‹*act/remark*› poco caritativo

uncharted /ˈʌnˈtʃɑːrtəd || ʌnˈtʃɑːtɪd/ *adj* inexplorado, desconocido, ignoto (liter)

unchecked /ˈʌnˈtʃekt/ *adj* (uncurbed) libre, sin obstáculos; **they allowed corruption to go ~** no pusieron freno a la corrupción

uncivilized /ˈʌnˈsɪvəlaɪzd || ʌnˈsɪvɪlaɪzd/ *adj* **1** ‹*country/people*› incivilizado, primitivo **2** (unacceptable) ‹*behavior*› poco civilizado, incivilizado; **at this ~ hour** a estas horas intempestivas

unclaimed /ˈʌnˈkleɪmd/ *adj* sin reclamar

unclassified /ˈʌnˈklæsəfaɪd || ʌnˈklæsɪfaɪd/ *adj* **1** (not classed) sin clasificar **2** (not secret) ‹*information*› no confidencial

uncle /ˈʌŋkəl/ *n* tío *m*; **U~ Bob/John** tío Bob/John; ***to say*** *o* ***cry ~*** (AmE colloq) rendirse*, darse* por vencido

unclean /ˈʌnˈkliːn/ *adj* **1** (ritually prohibited) ‹*food/animal*› impuro **2** (dirty) sucio **3** (impure) ‹*mind/thought*› impuro

unclear /ˈʌnˈklɪr || ʌnˈklɪə(r)/ *adj* **1** (uncertain) (*pred*): **he explained it twice, but I'm still rather ~** lo explicó dos veces, pero todavía no lo tengo muy claro; **to be ~ ABOUT sth**: **he was ~ about his reasons for doing it** no dio una explicación muy clara de sus motivos **2** (obscure) poco claro, confuso; **the meaning is ~** el significado no está claro

uncleared /ʌnˈklɪrd || ʌnˈklɪəd/ *adj*

A (Fin) ‹*check*› no compensado

B ‹*land/forest*› cubierto de vegetación

Uncle Sam /sæm/ *n* (colloq) (el) Tío Sam (fam)

> **Uncle Sam**
>
> Personaje imaginario que representa a EEUU, a su gobierno y ciudadanos. Tiene barba blanca y su vestimenta es roja, blanca y azul. Lleva un sombrero alto con estrellas. Se utiliza para apelar al patriotismo norteamericano

unclouded /ˈʌnˈklaʊdəd || ʌnˈklaʊdɪd/ *adj* ‹*sky*› despejado, sin nubes

uncoil /ˈʌnˈkɔɪl/ *vi* desenroscarse*

■ **uncoil** *vt* ‹*rope*› desenroscar*

uncomfortable /ˈʌnˈkʌmfərtəbəl || ʌnˈkʌmftəbəl/ *adj* **1** (physically) ‹*bed/position*› incómodo; **this chair's very ~** esta silla es muy incómoda; **are you ~ in that jacket?** ¿estás incómodo en ese sillón/con esa chaqueta? **2** (uneasy) incómodo, violento; **I felt ~ there** no me sentía a gusto allí; **to make things ~ for sb** crearle dificultades *or* problemas a algn **3** (disconcerting) ‹*reminder*› molesto, desagradable

uncommitted /ˈʌnkəˈmɪtəd || ˌʌnkəˈmɪtɪd/ *adj* no comprometido

uncommon /ʌnˈkɑːmən || ʌnˈkɒmən/ *adj* **1** (rare) raro, poco corriente *or* común *or* frecuente **2** (remarkable) (*before n*) singular, poco común *or* frecuente

uncommonly /ʌnˈkɑːmənli || ʌnˈkɒmənli/ *adv* extraordinariamente, singularmente; **not ~** con cierta *or* relativa frecuencia

uncommunicative /ˈʌnkəˈmjuːnəkeɪtɪv || ˌʌnkəˈmjuːnɪkətɪv/ *adj* poco comunicativo, reservado

uncomplaining /ˈʌnkəmˈpleɪnɪŋ/ *adj* resignado

uncomplainingly /ˈʌnkəmˈpleɪnɪŋli/ *adv* con resignación, sin quejarse

uncomplicated /ˈʌnˈkɑːmpləkeɪtəd || ʌnˈkɒmplɪkeɪtɪd/ *adj* ‹*lifestyle/relationship*› sin complicaciones; ‹*character/style*› poco complicado, sencillo

uncomplimentary /ˈʌnˈkɑːmpləˈmentəri || ˌʌnkɒmplɪˈmentri/ *adj* ‹*remarks*› poco halagador; ‹*report*› desfavorable

uncomprehending /ˈʌnkɑːmprɪˈhendɪŋ || ˌʌnkɒmprɪˈhendɪŋ/ *adj* (frml) atónito, perplejo

uncompromising /ʌnˈkɑːmprəmaɪzɪŋ || ʌnˈkɒmprəmaɪzɪŋ/ *adj* inflexible, intransigente

unconcealed /ˈʌnkənˈsiːld/ *adj* (*usu before n*) ‹*amusement/contempt*› no disimulado

unconcerned /ˈʌnkənˈsɜːrnd || ˌʌnkənˈsɜːnd/ *adj* indiferente; **they were ~ about the outcome** no les preocupaba el resultado, el resultado les era indiferente

unconditional /ˈʌnkənˈdɪʃn̩əl || ˌʌnkənˈdɪʃənl/ *adj* incondicional; **~ surrender** rendición *f* incondicional

unconditionally /ˈʌnkənˈdɪʃn̩əli/ *adv* sin condiciones, incondicionalmente

unconfirmed /ˈʌnkənˈfɜːrmd || ˌʌnkənˈfɜːmd/ *adj* no confirmado

unconnected /ˈʌnkəˈnektəd || ˌʌnkəˈnektɪd/ *adj* **1** (unrelated) sin conexión; **these incidents are completely ~** estos incidentes no guardan ninguna relación (entre sí); **to be ~ WITH sth** no guardar relación *or* no estar* relacionado CON algo **2** (incoherent) inconexo, sin hilación

unconscious[1] /ˈʌnˈkɑːntʃəs || ʌnˈkɒnʃəs/ *adj*

A (Med) inconsciente; **to become ~** perder* el conocimiento *or* el sentido; **she lay ~ on the floor** estaba (tendida) en el suelo sin sentido

B **1** (involuntary) ‹*habit/act*› involuntario, inconsciente **2** (unaware) (*pred*) **to be ~ OF sth** no ser* consciente DE algo

C (Psych) ‹*thoughts/desire*› inconsciente; **the ~ mind** el inconsciente

unconscious[2] *n* **the ~** el inconsciente

unconsciously /ˈʌnˈkɑːntʃəsli || ʌnˈkɒnʃəsli/ *adv* inconscientemente

unconsciousness /ˈʌnˈkɑːntʃəsnəs || ʌnˈkɒnʃəsnɪs/ *n* [u] (Med) inconsciencia *f*

U

unconstitutional /ˈʌnˈkɑːnstəˈtuːʃn̩əl || ˌʌnkɒnstɪˈtjuːʃənl̩/ *adj* inconstitucional
uncontested /ˈʌnkənˈtestəd || ˌʌnkənˈtestɪd/ *adj* ‹*will*› no impugnado; ‹*leader*› indiscutible; **his election was ~** fue el único candidato al cargo
uncontrollable /ˈʌnkənˈtrəʊləbəl/ *adj* ‹*trembling*› incontrolable; ‹*urge*› irresistible, irrefrenable; ‹*laughter*› incontenible; **that child is ~** a ese niño no hay quien lo controle
uncontrollably /ˈʌnkənˈtrəʊləbli/ *adv* de modo incontrolable
uncontrolled /ˈʌnkənˈtrəʊld/ *adj* incontrolado
unconventional /ˈʌnkənˈventʃn̩əl || ˌʌnkənˈvenʃənl̩/ *adj* poco convencional, original
unconvinced /ˈʌnkənˈvɪnst/ *adj*: **I'm still ~** aún no estoy muy convencida; **to be ~ OF sth/THAT** no estar* convencido DE algo/DE QUE
unconvincing /ˈʌnkənˈvɪnsɪŋ/ *adj* poco convincente
uncool /ˈʌnˈkuːl/ *adj* (sl): **he's so ~** (conservative) es muy conservador; (unfashionable) no está en la onda
uncooperative /ˈʌnkəʊˈɑːpərətɪv || ˌʌnkəʊˈɒpərətɪv/ *adj* poco dispuesto a colaborar *or* cooperar
uncoordinated /ˈʌnkəʊˈɔːrdn̩eɪtəd || ˌʌnkəʊˈɔːdɪneɪtɪd/ *adj* ‹*person*› falto de coordinación; ‹*movements*› no coordinado
uncork /ˈʌnˈkɔːrk || ʌnˈkɔːk/ *vt* descorchar, abrir*
uncorroborated /ˈʌnkəˈrɑːbəreɪtəd || ˌʌnkəˈrɒbəreɪtɪd/ *adj* no confirmado, no corroborado
uncountable /ˈʌnˈkaʊntəbəl/ *adj* (Ling) no numerable
uncountable noun *n* sustantivo *m* incontable *or* no contable, nombre *m* incontable *or* no contable
uncount noun *n* ▸**uncountable noun**
uncouple /ˈʌnˈkʌpəl/ *vt* **to ~ sth (FROM sth)** desenganchar algo (DE algo)
uncouth /ʌnˈkuːθ/ *adj* zafio, burdo, ordinario
uncover /ˈʌnˈkʌvər || ʌnˈkʌvə(r)/ *vt* 1 (remove covering of) destapar 2 (reveal, lay bare) ‹*treasure*› dejar al descubierto 3 (expose) ‹*scandal/plot*› revelar, sacar* a la luz
uncritical /ˈʌnˈkrɪtɪkəl/ *adj* ‹*acceptance/admiration*› ciego, que no cuestiona nada; ‹*audience*› falto de sentido crítico
uncrossed /ˈʌnˈkrɔːst || ʌnˈkrɒst/ *adj* (in UK) ‹*check*› al portador (*sin cruzar o barrar*)
uncrowned /ˈʌnˈkraʊnd/ *adj* no coronado; **he's the ~ king of jazz** se le reconoce como el rey del jazz
unction /ˈʌŋkʃən/ *n* [u] (Relig) unción *f*; **extreme ~** extremaunción *f*
unctuous /ˈʌŋktʃuəs || ˈʌŋktjʊəs/ *adj* empalagoso
uncultivated /ˈʌnˈkʌltəveɪtəd || ʌnˈkʌltɪveɪtɪd/ *adj* 1 ‹*land*› sin cultivar, inculto (frml) 2 ‹*mind/talent*› sin cultivar, no cultivado
uncultured /ˈʌnˈkʌltʃərd || ʌnˈkʌltʃəd/ *adj* inculto, sin cultura
uncurl /ˈʌnˈkɜːrl || ʌnˈkɜːl/ *vt* desenrollar, estirar*
■ **uncurl** *vi* «*snake*» desenroscarse*
uncut /ˈʌnˈkʌt/ *adj*
A 1 ‹*grass/hedge*› sin cortar 2 ‹*diamond/gem*› sin tallar, en bruto; ‹*stone/marble*› sin labrar
B (unabridged) íntegro, completo
undamaged /ˈʌnˈdæmɪdʒd/ *adj* intacto, que no ha sufrido desperfectos
undated /ˈʌnˈdeɪtəd || ʌnˈdeɪtɪd/ *adj* sin fecha, sin fechar
undaunted /ˈʌnˈdɔːntəd || ʌnˈdɔːntɪd/ *adj* impertérrito; **she was ~ by their threats** no se dejó intimidar por sus amenazas
undecided /ˈʌndɪˈsaɪdəd || ˌʌndɪˈsaɪdɪd/ *adj* 1 (wavering) (*usu pred*) indeciso; **we are ~ whether or not to go** aún no sabemos si ir o no 2 (not solved) ‹*question/issue*› pendiente, no resuelto
undeclared /ˈʌndɪˈklerd || ˌʌndɪˈkleəd/ *adj* ‹*love/admiration*› secreto; **~ income** ingresos *mpl* no declarados
undefeated /ˈʌndɪˈfiːtəd || ˌʌndɪˈfiːtɪd/ *adj* invicto
undefended /ˈʌndɪˈfendəd || ˌʌndɪˈfendɪd/ *adj* ‹*frontier/city*› desguarnecido; ‹*goal*› (Sport) vacío
undefined /ˈʌndɪˈfaɪnd/ *adj* no definido
undelete /ˌʌndɪˈliːt/ *vt* (Comput) recuperar
undemanding /ˈʌndɪˈmændɪŋ || ˌʌndɪˈmɑːndɪŋ/ *adj* ‹*job*› cómodo, que exige poco; ‹*person*› poco exigente
undemocratic /ˈʌnˈdeməˈkrætɪk/ *adj* no democrático
undemonstrative /ˈʌndɪˈmɑːnstrətɪv / *adj* poco expresivo
undeniable /ˈʌndɪˈnaɪəbəl/ *adj* innegable
undeniably /ˈʌndɪˈnaɪəbli/ *adv* sin lugar a dudas; **it is ~ true that ...** es innegable *or* no puede negarse que ...
under[1] /ˈʌndər || ˈʌndə(r)/ *prep*
A (beneath) debajo de, abajo de (AmL); **~ the starry sky** bajo el cielo estrellado (liter); **~ a magnifying glass** a través de una lupa
B (less than) menos de; **if you're ~ 18** si tienes menos de 18 años; **a number ~ 20** un número inferior a 20
C ‹*name/heading*› bajo; **look ~ 'textiles'** mira en *or* bajo 'textiles'
D 1 ‹*government/authority*› bajo; **he served ~ General Baldwin** estuvo a las órdenes del general Baldwin; **he has 20 people ~ him** tiene 20 personas a su mando 2 (subject to): **to be ~ discussion** estarse* discutiendo; **I'm ~ instructions not to reveal anything** tengo instrucciones de no revelar nada; **he was ~ the impression that ...** tenía la impresión de que ...
E (according to) según; **~ the terms of the contract** según los términos del contrato
under[2] *adv*
A 1 (under water): **they pushed him ~** lo empujaron debajo del agua 2 (anesthetized): **she's still ~** todavía está bajo los efectos de la anestesia; *see also* **keep, knuckle, put** *etc* **under**
B (less) menos; **it will cost $10 or ~** costará 10 dólares como mucho
under- /ˈʌndər/ *pref* 1 (below, lower): **the ~mentioned** los abajo mencionados 2 (less than proper): **they are ~represented on the committee** no tienen la representación que les corresponde en la comisión; *see also* **underdone, underestimate** *etc* 3 (of lesser rank) sub-; **~manager** subgerente *m*
under: **~achiever** /ˈʌndərəˈtʃiːvər || ˌʌndərəˈtʃiːvə(r)/ *n: persona que no rinde al nivel de su capacidad o al nivel exigido*; **~age** /ˈʌndərˈeɪdʒ/ *adj* (*before n*) ‹*person*› menor de edad; **~age drinking** consumo *m* de bebidas alcohólicas por menores de edad; **~arm** *adj* (*before n*) 1 **~arm deodorant** desodorante *m* (para las axilas) 2 (Sport) ‹*service/bowling*› sin levantar el brazo por encima del hombro; **~belly** *n* (Zool) vientre *m*; **the (soft) ~belly of Europe** (journ) el punto vulnerable *or* débil de Europa; **~carriage** *n* tren *m* de aterrizaje; **~charge** /ˈʌndərˈtʃɑːrdʒ || ˌʌndəˈtʃɑːdʒ/ *vt* cobrarle de menos a; **~class** *n* clase *f* marginada; **~clothes** *pl n* ropa *f* interior; **~clothing** *n* [u] ropa *f* interior; **~coat**, (AmE also) **~coating** *n* 1 [u] (paint) pintura *f* base 2 [c] (coating) primera mano *f or* capa *f* de pintura; 3 [u c] (AmE Auto) tratamiento *m* anticorrosivo del chasis; **~cook** /ˈʌndərˈkʊk || ˌʌndəˈkʊk/ *vt* no cocinar del todo; **the meat was ~cooked** la carne estaba poco cocida *or* (esp Esp) poco hecha; **~cover** /ˈʌndərˈkʌvər || ˌʌndəˈkʌvə(r)/ *adj* secreto; **~current** *n* 1 (of discontent, unrest) trasfondo *m*, corriente *f* subyacente 2 (of water) contracorriente *f*; **~cut** /ˈʌndərˈkʌt || ˌʌndəˈkʌt/ *vt* (*pres p* **-cutting**; *past & past p* **-cut**) ‹*competitor*› vender más barato *or* a un precio más bajo que; **~developed** /ˈʌndərdɪˈveləpt || ˌʌndədɪˈveləpt/ *adj* ‹*muscles/potential*› poco desarrollado; ‹*nation*› subdesarrollado; **~development** *n* 1 (Econ, Pol) subdesarrollo *m* 2 (physical) falta *f* de desarrollo **~dog** *n* 1 (in game, contest) **the ~dog** el que tiene menos posibilidades 2 (disadvantaged person) desamparado, -da *m,f*, desvalido, -da *m,f*; **~done** /ˈʌndərˈdʌn || ˌʌndəˈdʌn/ *adj* ‹*meat*› poco cocido, poco hecho (Esp); **~employed** /ˈʌndərɪmˈplɔɪd/ *adj* ‹*person*› subempleado; ‹*resources/space*› infrautilizado; **~estimate** /ˈʌndərˈestəmeɪt || ˌʌndərˈestɪmeɪt/ *vt* 1 (guess too low): **they ~estimated the cost by $500** calcularon el costo en 500 dólares menos de lo que correspondía, al calcular el costo se quedaron cortos en 500 dólares 2 (underrate) subestimar; **~fed** /ˈʌndərˈfed || ˌʌndəˈfed/ *adj* subalimentado, desnutrido; **~felt** *n* [u] (BrE) *fieltro que se pone debajo de las alfombras*; **~foot** /ˈʌndərˈfʊt || ˌʌndəˈfʊt/ *adv* debajo de los pies; **it's slippery ~foot** el suelo está resbaladizo; **to trample sth ~foot**

pisotear algo; **~fund** /ˈʌndərˈfʌnd || ˌʌndəˈfʌnd/ *vt* infradotar, no dotar *or* no proveer* de suficientes fondos a; **~garment** *n* (frml *or* dated) prenda *f* interior *or* íntima; **~go** /ˈʌndərˈgəʊ || ˌʌndəˈgəʊ/ *vt* (*3rd pers sing pres* **-goes**; *pres p* **-going**; *past* **-went**; *past p* **-gone**) ‹*change/hardship*› sufrir; **she'll have to ~go major surgery** la van a tener que operar, va a tener que ser sometida a una intervención quirúrgica (frml); **he is ~going treatment** está en tratamiento; **~graduate** /ˈʌndərˈgrædʒuət || ˌʌndəˈgrædʒʊət/ *n* estudiante universitario, -ria *m,f* (*de licenciatura*); (*before n*) ‹*course/student*› universitario

underground[1] /ˈʌndərgraʊnd || ˈʌndəgraʊnd/ *adj* (*before n*) 1 ‹*cave/stream/parking*› subterráneo 2 ‹*organization*› clandestino 3 (avant-garde) ‹*music/film*› underground *adj inv*

underground[2] /ˈʌndərˈgraʊnd || ˌʌndəˈgraʊnd/ *adv* 1 (under the earth) bajo tierra 2 (into hiding): **to go ~** pasar a la clandestinidad

underground[3] /ˈʌndərgraʊnd || ˈʌndəgraʊnd/ *n* [u c]
A *also* **Underground** (BrE Transp) metro *m*, subterráneo *m* (RPl); **to go on the ~** *o* **by ~** viajar *or* ir* en metro *or* (RPl) subterráneo
B 1 (secret organization) movimiento *m* clandestino 2 (subculture) underground *m*

under: **~growth** *n* [u] maleza *f*, monte *m* bajo, sotobosque *m*; **~hand** /ˈʌndərˈhænd || ˌʌndəˈhænd/, **~handed** /ˈʌndərˈhændəd || ˌʌndəˈhændɪd/ *adj* ‹*person*› solapado; ‹*method/means/dealings*› poco limpio; **~investment** *n* [u] infrainversión *f*, inversión insuficiente; **~lain** /ˈʌndərˈleɪn || ˌʌndəˈleɪn/ *past p of* **underlie**

underlay[1] /ˈʌndərˈleɪ || ˌʌndeˈleɪ/ *past of* **underlie**

underlay[2] /ˈʌndərleɪ || ˈʌndəleɪ/ *n* (BrE) ▸ **underfelt**

under: **~lie** /ˈʌndərˈlaɪ || ˌʌndəˈlaɪ/ *vt* (*3rd pers sing pres* **-lies**; *pres p* **-lying**; *past* **-lay**; *past p* **-lain**) subyacer* a; **~line** *vt* ‹*word/mistake*› subrayar; ‹*difference/importance*› subrayar, destacar*, hacer* hincapié en

underling /ˈʌndərlɪŋ || ˈʌndəlɪŋ/ *n* subordinado, -da *m,f*, subalterno, -na *m,f*

under: **~lying** /ˈʌndərˈlaɪɪŋ || ˌʌndəˈlaɪɪŋ/ *adj* (*before n*) subyacente; **~manned** /ˈʌndərˈmænd || ˌʌndəˈmænd/ *adj* ‹*factory*› con personal *or* con mano de obra insuficiente; **~manning** /ˈʌndərˈmænɪŋ || ˌʌndəˈmænɪŋ/ *n* [u] falta *f* de personal (*or* de mano de obra *etc*); **~mine** /ˈʌndərˈmaɪn || ˌʌndəˈmaɪn/ *vt* ‹*health/strength*› minar, debilitar; **it ~mined her self-confidence** le hizo perder confianza en sí misma; **you're ~mining my authority** me estás desautorizando *or* quitando autoridad

underneath[1] /ˈʌndərˈniːθ || ˌʌndəˈniːθ/ *prep* debajo de, abajo de (AmL)

underneath[2] *adv* debajo, abajo; **they dug a tunnel ~** excavaron un túnel por debajo *or* por abajo; **~, she's very insecure** en el fondo es muy insegura

underneath[3] *n* parte *f* inferior *or* de abajo

under: **~nourished** /ˈʌndərˈnɜːrɪʃt || ˌʌndəˈnʌrɪʃt/ *adj* desnutrido; **~paid** /ˈʌndərˈpeɪd || ˌʌndəˈpeɪd/ *adj* mal pagado, mal pago (RPl); **~pants** *pl n* calzoncillos *mpl*, calzones *mpl* (Méx), interiores *mpl* (Col, Ven); **~pass** *n* (for traffic) paso *m* inferior; **pedestrian ~pass** pasaje *m* subterráneo; **~pin** /ˈʌndərˈpɪn || ˌʌndəˈpɪn/ *vt* **-nn-** 1 (Const) apuntalar 2 ‹*argument/claim*› respaldar, sustentar; **~play** /ˈʌndərˈpleɪ || ˌʌndəˈpleɪ/ *vt* (play down) ‹*importance*› minimizar*; ‹*danger/issue*› quitarle *or* restarle importancia a; **~privileged** /ˈʌndərˈprɪvəlɪdʒd || ˌʌndəˈprɪvəlɪdʒd/ *adj* desfavorecido; **~rate** /ˈʌndərˈreɪt || ˌʌndəˈreɪt/ *vt* 1 ‹*ability/opponent*› subestimar 2 **~rated** *past p* ‹*writer/play*› no debidamente apreciado *or* valorado; **~score** /ˈʌndərˈskɔːr || ˌʌndəˈskɔː(r)/ *vt* ‹*word/line*› subrayar; ‹*fact/need*› subrayar, poner* de relieve, recalcar*; **~sea** /ˈʌndərˈsiː || ˌʌndəˈsiː/ *adj* (*before n*) submarino; **~secretary** /ˈʌndərˈsekrəteri || ˌʌndəˈsekrətri/ *n* subsecretario, -ria *m,f*; **~sell** *vt* (*past & past p* **-sold**) ‹*competitor*› vender más barato que; **~shirt** *n* (AmE) camiseta *f* (interior); **~shorts** *pl n* (AmE) calzoncillos *mpl* (*en forma de pantalón corto*); **~side** *n* parte *f* inferior *or* de abajo; **~signed** /ˈʌndərˈsaɪnd || ˌʌndəˈsaɪnd/ *n* (*pl* ~) (frml) **the ~signed** el abajo firmante, la abajo firmante, (*pl*) los abajo firmantes, las abajo firmantes; el suscrito, la suscrita, (*pl*) los suscritos, las suscritas (frml); **~sized** /ˈʌndərˈsaɪzd || ˌʌndəˈsaɪzd/ *adj* más pequeño de lo normal; **~skirt** *n* enagua(s) *f(pl)*, viso *m*, fondo *m* (Méx); **~sold** /ˈʌndərˈsəʊld || ˌʌndəˈsəʊld/ *past and past p of* **undersell**; **~staffed** /ˈʌndərˈstæft || ˌʌndəˈstɑːft/ *adj*: **to be ~staffed** estar* muy escaso *or* falto de personal

understand /ˈʌndərˈstænd || ˌʌndəˈstænd/ (*past & past p* **-stood**) *vt*
A 1 (grasp meaning of) entender*; **I can make myself understood** me puedo hacer entender; **I can't ~ why he did it** no logro entender *or* comprender por qué lo hizo; **I don't want it to happen again; have I made myself understood?** no quiero que vuelva a suceder ¿está claro? 2 (interpret) entender*, interpretar; **as I ~ it, ...** según tengo entendido, ..., por lo que entiendo, ..., según creo, ...; **what do you ~ by the term 'deprivation'?** ¿qué entiendes tú por 'privaciones'? 3 (sympathize, empathize with) comprender, entender*
B (believe, infer): **the president is understood to favor the second option** se cree que el presidente prefiere la segunda opción; **I ~ you play tennis** tengo entendido que juega al tenis; **am I to ~ that you won't help?** ¿entonces quiere decir que no me van a ayudar?; **I was given to ~ I'd get my money back** me dieron a entender que me devolverían el dinero; *see also* **understood**[2]
■ **understand** *vi* entender*, comprender

understandable /ˈʌndərˈstændəbəl || ˌʌndəˈstændəbəl/ *adj* comprensible; **it is ~ THAT** es comprensible *or* es normal QUE (+ *subj*)

understandably /ˈʌndərˈstændəbli || ˌʌndəˈstændəbli/ *adv*: **he's ~ upset** está disgustado, lo cual es comprensible

understanding[1] /ˈʌndərˈstændɪŋ || ˌʌndəˈstændɪŋ/ *n*
A [u] 1 (grasp) entendimiento *m*; **we now have a better** *o* **greater ~ of it** ahora lo entendemos *or* lo comprendemos mejor 2 (interpretation) interpretación *f*; **that's not my ~ of what he meant** no es así como yo interpreto sus palabras 3 (sympathy) comprensión *f*; **these exchanges promote international ~** estos intercambios fomentan el entendimiento *or* la concordia entre las naciones
B [c] (agreement, arrangement) acuerdo *m*; **to come to** *o* **reach an ~ (with sb)** llegar* a un acuerdo (con algn); **to have an ~ (with sb)**: **we had an ~ that we'd share the work** habíamos convenido que compartiríamos el trabajo
C [u] (belief): **it was my ~ that I would get the job** tenía entendido *or* creía que me darían el trabajo; **on the ~ that** bien entendido que, con la condición de que

understanding[2] *adj* comprensivo

under: **~state** /ˈʌndərˈsteɪt || ˌʌndəˈsteɪt/ *vt* (underestimate) subestimar; (play down) quitarle *or* restarle importancia a, minimizar; **~stated** /ˈʌndərˈsteɪtəd || ˌʌndəˈsteɪtɪd/ *adj* ‹*decor/style*› sobrio, sencillo; **an ~stated performance** una actuación moderada y comedida; **~statement** /ˈʌndərˈsteɪtmənt || ˈʌndəsteɪtmənt/ *n* [c u]: **to say it wasn't well attended is an ~statement** decir que no estuvo muy concurrido es quedarse corto; **that's the ~statement of the year!** (colloq) ése es el eufemismo del año; **a master of ~statement** un experto en la descripción mesurada y comedida

understood[1] /ˈʌndərˈstʊd || ˌʌndəˈstʊd/ *past & past p of* **understand**

understood[2] *adj* (assumed): **they didn't say so, but it was ~** no lo dijeron pero quedó sobreentendido; **expenses will be paid, that's ~** se sobreentiende que nos (*or* les *etc*) pagarán los gastos

under: **~study** *n* suplente *mf*, sobresaliente *mf*; **~take** /ˈʌndərˈteɪk || ˌʌndəˈteɪk/ *vt* (*past* **-took**; *past p* **-taken**) 1 (take upon oneself) ‹*responsibility*› asumir; ‹*obligation*› contraer*; ‹*task*› emprender 2 (promise, guarantee) **to ~take to + INF** comprometerse A + INF; **~taker** *n* ▸ **mortician**; **~taking** /ˈʌndərˈteɪkɪŋ || ˌʌndəˈteɪkɪŋ/ *n* 1 (task) empresa *f*, tarea *f* 2 (promise) promesa *f*; **~tone** *n* 1 (low voice): **to speak in an ~tone** hablar en voz baja 2 (hint) trasfondo *m*; **~took** /ˈʌndərˈtʊk || ˌʌndəˈtʊk/ *past of* **~take**; **~tow** *n* resaca *f*; **~used** /ˈʌndərˈjuːzd || ˌʌndəˈjuːzd/ *adj* infrautilizado, subutilizado; **~value** /ˈʌndərˈvæljuː || ˌʌndəˈvæljuː/ *vt* ‹*goods*› subvalorar; ‹*person/skill*› subvalorar, subestimar

underwater[1] /ˈʌndərˈwɔːtər || ˌʌndəˈwɔːtə(r)/ *adj* submarino

U

underwater² *adv* debajo del agua

under: **~wear** *n* [u] ropa *f* interior; **~weight** /ˈʌndər ˈweɪt || ˌʌndəˈweɪt/ *adj* ‹*person/baby*› de peso más bajo que el normal; **she's 20lb ~weight** pesa 20 libras menos de lo que debería; **~went** /ˈʌndərˈwent || ˌʌndəˈwent/ *past of* **undergo**; **~world** *n* 1 (Myth) **the U~world** el infierno, el averno (liter) 2 (criminals): **the ~world** el hampa, los bajos fondos; **~write** /ˈʌndərˈraɪt/ *vt* (*past* **-wrote**; *past p* **-written**) 1 (in insurance) asegurar 2 (guarantee financially) ‹*project/venture*› financiar; **~writer** *n* (in insurance) asegurador, -dora *m,f*; (on second insurance) reasegurador, -dora *m,f*; **~written** /ˈʌndər ˈrɪtn̩/ *past p of* **~write**; **~wrote** /ˈʌndərˈrəʊt/ *past of* **~write**

undeserved /ˈʌndɪˈzɜːrvd || ˌʌndɪˈzɜːvd/ *adj* inmerecido

undeserving /ˈʌndɪˈzɜːrvɪŋ || ˌʌndɪˈzɜːvɪŋ/ *adj* ‹*person*› de poco mérito; ‹*cause*› poco meritorio; **to be ~ OF sth** (frml) ser* indigno DE algo, no merecer* algo

undesirable¹ /ˈʌndɪˈzaɪrəbəl || ˌʌndɪˈzaɪərəbəl/ *adj* 1 (unwanted) ‹*consequence/side effect*› no deseado 2 (objectionable) ‹*person*› indeseable

undesirable² *n* indeseable *mf*

undetected /ˈʌndɪˈtektəd/ *adj* ‹*crime*› que no se ha descubierto; ‹*error*› que ha pasado inadvertido; **many crimes go ~** hay muchos delitos que no se descubren

undeterred /ˈʌndɪˈtɜːrd || ˌʌndɪˈtɜːd/ *adj* (*pred*): **she carried on ~** siguió impertérrita *or* sin inmutarse; **~ by the weather** sin amilanarse ante el mal tiempo

undeveloped /ˈʌndɪˈveləpt/ *adj*
A ‹*resources/region*› sin explotar
B (Phot) ‹*film*› sin revelar

undid /ˈʌnˈdɪd/ *past of* **undo**

undies /ˈʌndiz/ *pl n* (colloq) ropa *f* interior

undignified /ˈʌnˈdɪgnəfaɪd || ʌnˈdɪgnɪfaɪd/ *adj* 1 (lacking modesty) indecoroso 2 (inappropriate to status) poco digno

undiluted /ˈʌndaɪˈluːtəd || ˌʌndaɪˈljuːtɪd/ *adj* ‹*juice*› sin diluir; **the ~ truth** la verdad lisa y llana; **it is ~ pleasure** es puro placer

undiminished /ˈʌndəˈmɪnɪʃt/ *adj* no disminuido

undiplomatic /ˈʌnˈdɪpləˈmætɪk/ *adj* poco diplomático, indiscreto

undischarged /ˈʌndɪsˈtʃɑːrdʒ || ˌʌndɪsˈtʃɑːdʒd/ *adj* ‹*bankrupt*› no rehabilitado; ‹*debt*› no liquidado, sin pagar

undisciplined /ˈʌnˈdɪsəplənd/ *adj* indisciplinado

undisclosed /ˈʌndɪsˈkləʊzd/ *adj* no revelado

undiscovered /ˈʌndɪsˈkʌvərd || ˌʌndɪsˈkʌvəd/ *adj* (not found) no descubierto; (unknown) desconocido

undiscriminating /ˌʌndɪsˈkrɪməneɪtɪŋ || ˌʌndɪ ˈskrɪmɪneɪtɪŋ/ *adj* ‹*mind/audience/taste*› que no discrimina, sin sentido crítico, fácil de complacer; ‹*choice*› sin sentido crítico

undisguised /ˈʌndɪsˈgaɪzd/ *adj* manifiesto, abierto

undismayed /ˈʌndɪsˈmeɪd/ *adj* (*pred*) impertérrito, impasible; **~ by successive failures** sin dejarse desanimar por los sucesivos fracasos

undisputed /ˈʌndɪˈspjuːtəd || ˌʌndɪˈspjuːtɪd/ *adj* ‹*champion/leader*› indiscutido, indiscutible, incontestable; ‹*facts*› innegable

undistinguished /ˈʌndɪˈstɪŋgwɪʃt/ *adj* mediocre

undisturbed /ˈʌndɪˈstɜːrbd || ˌʌndɪˈstɜːbd/ *adj* 1 (untouched): **everything was left ~** todo se dejó tal cual estaba 2 (uninterrupted) ‹*sleep*› tranquilo 3 (unworried) tranquilo; **he seemed ~ by the rumors** los rumores parecían no perturbarlo *or* preocuparlo

undivided /ˈʌndɪˈvaɪdəd || ˌʌndɪˈvaɪdɪd/ *adj*: **you have my ~ attention** tienes toda mi atención

undo /ˈʌnˈduː/ *vt* (*3rd pers sing pres* **-does**; *pres p* **-doing**; *past* **-did**; *past p* **-done**)
A (unfasten) ‹*button/jacket/buckle*› desabrochar; ‹*zipper*› abrir*; ‹*knot/parcel*› desatar, deshacer*; ‹*shoelaces*› desatar, desamarrar (AmL exc RPl)
B (put right) ‹*wrong*› reparar, enmendar*

undocumented /ˌʌnˈdɔːkjuːməntəd/ *adj* 1 (unrecorded) ‹*event/report/species*› no documentado 2 (without legal documents) ‹*alien/immigrant*› indocumentado 3 (Comput) sin documentar

undoing /ˈʌnˈduːɪŋ/ *n* [u] perdición *f*, ruina *f*

undone¹ /ˈʌnˈdʌn/ *past p of* **undo**

undone² *adj* (*pred*) 1 (unfastened): **your shoelaces are ~** llevas los cordones de los zapatos desatados *or* (AmL exc RPl) desamarrados; **to come ~** «*knot*» deshacerse*, desatarse; «*button*» desabrocharse 2 (not started) sin empezar; (unfinished) sin terminar; **the job was left ~** el trabajo se dejó *or* se quedó a medias

undoubted /ʌnˈdaʊtəd || ʌnˈdaʊtɪd/ *adj* indudable

undoubtedly /ʌnˈdaʊtədli || ʌnˈdaʊtɪdli/ *adv* indudablemente, sin duda

undreamed-of /ˈʌnˈdremtɑːv, ˈʌnˈdriːmdɑːv || ʌnˈdriː mdɒv/, (BrE also) **undreamt-of** /ˈʌnˈdremtɑːv || ʌn ˈdremtɒv/ *adj* inimaginable, nunca soñado

undress¹ /ˈʌnˈdres/ *vt* desvestir*, desnudar; **to get ~ed** desvestirse*, desnudarse
■ **undress** *vi* desvestirse*, desnudarse

undress² *n* [u] (frml) **in a state of ~** desnudo

undressed /ˈʌnˈdrest/ *adj* desnudo, desvestido

undrinkable /ˈʌnˈdrɪŋkəbəl/ *adj* (poisonous) no potable; (unpalatable) imbebible

undue /ˈʌnˈduː || ʌnˈdjuː/ *adj* (*before n*) excesivo, demasiado

undulate /ˈʌndʒəleɪt || ˈʌndjʊleɪt/ *vi* ondular

undulating /ˈʌndʒəleɪtɪŋ || ˈʌndjʊleɪtɪŋ/ *adj* (*before n*) ondulante

undulation /ˈʌndʒəˈleɪʃən || ˌʌndjʊˈleɪʃən/ *n* [c u] ondulación *f*

unduly /ˈʌnˈduːli || ʌnˈdjuːli/ *adv* excesivamente, demasiado

undying /ˈʌnˈdaɪɪŋ/ *adj* (liter) imperecedero (liter), eterno

unearned /ˈʌnˈɜːrnd || ʌnˈɜːnd/ *adj* (Fin): **~ income** rendimientos *mpl* del capital

unearth /ˈʌnˈɜːrθ || ʌnˈɜːθ/ *vt* 1 ‹*remains*› desenterrar* 2 ‹*fact/document*› descubrir*, sacar* a la luz

unearthly /ˈʌnˈɜːrθli || ʌnˈɜːθli/ *adj* **-lier, -liest** sobrenatural; **at this ~ hour** a estas horas (intempestivas)

unease /ˈʌnˈiːz/ *n* [u] (nervousness) inquietud *f*, desasosiego *m*, desazón *f*; (tension, discontent) malestar *m*, descontento *m*

uneasily /ˈʌnˈiːzəli || ʌnˈiːzɪli/ *adv* inquietamente, con inquietud

uneasy /ˈʌnˈiːzi/ *adj* **-sier, -siest** 1 (anxious, troubled) inquieto, preocupado; **she had an ~ conscience** no tenía la conciencia tranquila 2 (awkward, constrained) ‹*laugh/silence*› incómodo, molesto 3 (insecure, precarious) ‹*peace/alliance*› precario

uneatable /ˈʌnˈiːtəbəl/ *adj* incomible

uneaten /ˈʌnˈiːtn̩/ *adj*: **to leave sth ~** dejar algo sin comer

uneconomic /ˈʌnˈekəˈnɑːmɪk, -ˈiːkə- || ˌʌnˌiːkəˈnɒmɪk, -ˌek-/ *adj* poco rentable, antieconómico

uneconomical /ˈʌnˈekəˈnɑːmɪkl̩, -ˈiːkə- || ˌʌnˌiːkə ˈnɒmɪkəl, -ˌek-/ *adj* poco económico

uneducated /ˈʌnˈedʒəkeɪtəd || ˌʌnˈedjʊkeɪtɪd/ *adj* sin educación, inculto

unemotional /ˈʌnɪˈməʊʃn̩əl || ˌʌnɪˈməʊʃənl̩/ *adj* 1 (feeling no emotion) ‹*person*› indiferente 2 (showing no emotion) ‹*account/report*› objetivo

unemployable /ˈʌnɪmˈplɔɪəbəl/ *adj* inempleable

unemployed¹ /ˈʌnɪmˈplɔɪd/ *adj* 1 ‹*person*› desempleado, desocupado, parado (Esp), en paro (Esp), cesante (Chi) 2 (unused) ‹*resource*› ocioso, sin utilizar

unemployed² *pl n* **the ~** los desempleados, los desocupados, los parados (Esp), los cesantes (Chi)

unemployment /ˈʌnɪmˈplɔɪmənt/ *n* [u] 1 (being out of work) desempleo *m*, desocupación *f*, paro *m* (Esp), cesantía *f* (Chi); (*before n*) **~ benefit** *o* (AmE also) **compensation** subsidio *m* de desempleo, paro *m* (Esp), subsidio *m* de cesantía (Chi) 2 (number of unemployed) desempleo *m*, número *m* de desempleados, paro *m* (Esp), cesantía *f* (Chi)

unencumbered /ˌʌnɪnˈkʌmbərd || ˌʌnɪnˈkʌmbəd/ *adj* 1 (unburdened) libre de peso 2 (Law) libre de gravamen *or* gravámanes

unending /ˈʌnˈendɪŋ/ *adj* interminable, sin fin

unendurable /ˈʌnɪnˈdʊrəbəl || ˌʌnɪnˈdjʊərəbəl/ *adj* inaguantable, insoportable

unenterprising /ˈʌnˈentərpraɪzɪŋ || ʌnˈentəpraɪzɪŋ/ *adj* poco emprendedor, falto de iniciativa

unenthusiastic /ˈʌnɪnˈθuːziˈæstɪk || ˌʌnɪnθjuːziˈæstɪk/ *adj* poco entusiasta

unenthusiastically /ˈʌnɪnˈθuːziˈæstɪkli || ˌʌnɪnˌθjuːzɪˈæstɪkli/ *adv* con poco entusiasmo

unenviable /ˈʌnˈenviəbəl/ *adj* nada envidiable

unequal /ˈʌnˈiːkwəl/ *adj* 1 ‹*contest/amounts*› desigual 2 (inadequate) (frml) **to be ~ TO sth**: **he proved ~ to the demands of the task** no estuvo a la altura de lo que se esperaba

unequaled, (BrE) **unequalled** /ˈʌnˈiːkwəld/ *adj* sin igual, sin par, sin parangón

unequivocal /ˈʌnɪˈkwɪvəkəl/ *adj* (frml) ‹*reply/refusal*› inequívoco, claro; ‹*support/victory*› rotundo

unequivocally /ˈʌnɪˈkwɪvəkli/ *adv* (frml) sin lugar a dudas, claramente

unerring /ˈʌnˈerɪŋ || ʌnˈɜːrɪŋ/ *adj* certero, infalible

UNESCO /juːˈneskəʊ/ *n* (*no art*) (= **United Nations Educational, Scientific and Cultural Organization**) la UNESCO

unethical /ʌnˈeθɪkəl/ *adj* inmoral, poco ético

uneven /ˈʌnˈiːvən/ *adj*

A 1 (not straight) torcido 2 (not level) ‹*surface*› desigual, irregular, disparejo (AmL); ‹*ground*› desnivelado, desigual, disparejo (AmL)

B 1 (irregular) ‹*breathing/pulse*› irregular 2 (not uniform, inconsistent) ‹*color/paint*› poco uniforme, disparejo (AmL); ‹*performance/quality*› desigual, dispar, disparejo (AmL)

C (unequal) ‹*widths/lengths/contest*› desigual

unevenly /ˈʌnˈiːvənli/ *adv* 1 (not uniformly) de modo poco uniforme 2 (unequally): **they are ~ matched** son muy dispares *or* de niveles muy desiguales

uneventful /ˈʌnɪˈventfəl/ *adj* ‹*journey*› sin incidentes; ‹*day*› tranquilo; ‹*life/past*› sin acontecimientos de nota

uneventfully /ˈʌnɪˈventfəli/ *adv*: **the day passed ~** no sucedió nada de particular en todo el día

unexceptional /ˈʌnɪkˈsepʃn̩əl || ˌʌnɪkˈsepʃənl/ *adj* normal, corriente, sin nada de extraordinario

unexciting /ˈʌnɪkˈsaɪtɪŋ/ *adj* ‹*prospect/job*› poco estimulante; ‹*food*› insulso, poco apetitoso

unexpected /ˈʌnɪkˈspektəd || ˌʌnɪkˈspektɪd/ *adj* ‹*reaction/visitor*› inesperado; ‹*result/delay*› imprevisto; **this is an ~ pleasure** ¡qué sorpresa tan agradable!

unexpectedly /ˈʌnɪkˈspektədli || ˌʌnɪkˈspektɪdli/ *adv* ‹*arrive*› de improviso, sin previo aviso; ‹*happen*› de forma imprevista, cuando nadie lo esperaba

unexplained /ˈʌnɪkˈspleɪnd/ *adj*: **his disappearance remains ~** su desaparición sigue siendo un misterio

unexploded /ˈʌnɪkˈspləʊdəd/ *adj* sin detonar

unexploited /ˈʌnɪkˈsplɔɪtəd || ˌʌnɪkˈsplɔɪtɪd/ *adj* sin explotar, inexplotado

unexplored /ˈʌnɪkˈsplɔːrd || ˌʌnɪksˈplɔːd/ *adj* ‹*territory*› inexplorado

unexpressed /ˈʌnɪkˈsprest/ *adj* tácito

unexpurgated /ˈʌnˈekspərgeɪtəd || ʌnˈekspəgeɪtɪd/ *adj* (frml) sin expurgar, íntegro

unfailing /ʌnˈfeɪlɪŋ/ *adj* ‹*optimism/courtesy*› indefectible, a toda prueba; ‹*interest/support*› constante; ‹*source/supply*› inagotable

unfailingly /ʌnˈfeɪlɪŋli/ *adv*: **he was ~ polite** era de una cortesía a toda prueba, era indefectiblemente cortés

unfair /ˈʌnˈfer || ʌnˈfeə(r)/ *adj* ‹*treatment/criticism/decision*› injusto; ‹*competition*› desleal; **it was ~ of him to blame you** fue injusto que te echara la culpa a ti; **it's so ~!** ¡es una injusticia!, ¡no hay derecho!; **~ dismissal** despido *m* improcedente *or* injustificado; **~ TO/ON sb**: **it's ~ to** *o* **on the others** es injusto para los demás

unfairly /ˈʌnˈferli || ʌnˈfeəli/ *adj* injustamente

unfaithful /ˈʌnˈfeɪθfəl/ *adj* ‹*spouse/lover*› infiel; ‹*follower*› desleal; **to be ~ TO sb** serle* infiel/desleal A algn

unfamiliar /ˈʌnfəˈmɪljər || ˌʌnfəˈmɪliə(r)/ *adj* 1 (unknown) ‹*face/surroundings*› desconocido, nuevo 2 (unacquainted): **I'm ~ with his work** no estoy muy familiarizado con su obra; **we're not ~ with this type of situation** tenemos experiencia de este tipo de situación

unfamiliarity /ˈʌnfəˈmɪliˈærəti/ *n* [u] 1 (strangeness) lo desconocido 2 (lack of knowledge) **~ WITH sth** falta *f* de familiaridad CON algo

unfashionable /ˈʌnˈfæʃn̩əbəl/ *adj* ‹*clothes/ideas*› fuera de moda, pasado de moda; ‹*district*› poco elegante

unfasten /ˈʌnˈfæsn̩ || ʌnˈfɑːsn̩/ *vt* ‹*seat belt/button/jacket*› desabrochar; ‹*door*› abrir*; ‹*knot*› (loosen) soltar*, aflojar; (undo) deshacer*, desatar

unfathomable /ˈʌnˈfæðəməbəl/ *adj* ‹*depths*› insondable, inconmensurable; ‹*mystery*› incomprensible

unfavorable, (BrE) **unfavourable** /ˈʌnˈfeɪvrəbəl/ *adj* 1 (adverse) ‹*conditions*› desfavorable, poco propicio; ‹*wind*› en contra 2 (negative) ‹*report/comparison*› desfavorable, negativo

unfavorably, (BrE) **unfavourably** /ˈʌnˈfeɪvrəbli/ *adv* ‹*regard/react*› desfavorablemente; **the critics reviewed the show ~** la crítica fue muy negativa con el espectáculo

unfazed /ʌnˈfeɪzd/ *adj* (*pred*) (colloq): **they were totally ~** ni siquiera se inmutaron, estaban como si nada hubiera pasado (fam); **she was ~ by the heckling** ni se inmutó *or* (fam) hizo como si nada cuando la interrumpieron

unfeeling /ʌnˈfiːlɪŋ/ *adj* ‹*person*› insensible; ‹*remark/attitude*› poco compasivo, duro

unfinished /ˈʌnˈfɪnɪʃt/ *adj* (incomplete) sin terminar, inacabado; **we have some ~ business to deal with** tenemos unos asuntos pendientes que tratar

unfit /ˈʌnˈfɪt/ *adj* 1 (unsuitable): **he was ~ for the job** no estaba capacitado para el trabajo; **~ for human consumption** no apto para el consumo; **he's ~ to hold public office** es indigno de desempeñar un cargo público 2 (physically): **I'm ~** no estoy en forma, estoy fuera de forma; **the doctor declared him ~ for work** el médico dictaminó que estaba incapacitado para trabajar

unflagging /ˈʌnˈflægɪŋ/ *adj* ‹*energy/enthusiasm*› inagotable; ‹*interest*› sostenido

unflappable /ˈʌnˈflæpəbəl/ *adj* imperturbable

unflattering /ˈʌnˈflætərɪŋ/ *adj* ‹*remark/description*› poco halagüeño; ‹*dress*› poco favorecedor

unflinching /ʌnˈflɪntʃɪŋ/ *adj* ‹*courage/stoicism*› a toda prueba; ‹*expression*› inmutable; ‹*resolve*› inquebrantable

unfold /ˈʌnˈfəʊld/ *vt* ‹*tablecloth/map*› desdoblar, extender*; ‹*newspaper*› abrir*; ‹*wings*› desplegar*; ‹*arms*› descruzar*

■ **unfold** *vi* 1 ‹‹*flower/leaf*›› abrirse*; ‹‹*wings*›› desplegarse* 2 (be revealed) ‹‹*story/events*›› desarrollarse; ‹‹*scene/landscape*›› extenderse*, desplegarse*

unforeseeable /ˈʌnfɔːrˈsiːəbəl || ˌʌnfɔːˈsiːəbəl/ *adj* imprevisible

unforeseen /ˈʌnfɔːrˈsiːn || ˌʌnfɔːˈsiːn/ *adj* imprevisto

unforgettable /ˈʌnfərˈgetəbəl || ˌʌnfəˈgetəbəl/ *adj* inolvidable

unforgivable /ˈʌnfərˈgɪvəbəl || ˌʌnfəˈgɪvəbəl/ *adj* imperdonable

unforgiving /ˈʌnfərˈgɪvɪŋ || ˌʌnfəˈgɪvɪŋ/ *adj* implacable

unformed /ˈʌnˈfɔːrmd || ʌnˈfɔːmd/ *adj* ‹*mass*› informe, amorfo; ‹*plan*› no madurado; ‹*personality*› no formado

unforthcoming /ˈʌnfɔːrθˈkʌmɪŋ || ˌʌnfɔːθˈkʌmɪŋ/ *adj* 1 (reserved) poco comunicativo, reservado; **when asked about his plans, he was very ~** se mostró muy reticente cuando le preguntaron acerca de sus planes 2 (unhelpful) poco dispuesto a ayudar

unfortunate¹ /ʌnˈfɔːrtʃn̩ət || ʌnˈfɔːtʃənət/ *adj* 1 (unlucky) ‹*coincidence*› desafortunado, desventurado (liter); **he has been very ~** ha tenido muy mala suerte; **it was ~ that the weather was so bad** fue una pena que hiciera tan mal tiempo 2 (unsuitable) ‹*remark*› desafortunado, inoportuno, poco feliz; ‹*choice of words*› desacertado, desafortunado, poco feliz; ‹*habit*› lamentable

unfortunate² *n* desgraciado, -da *m,f*

unfortunately /ʌnˈfɔːrtʃn̩ətli || ʌnˈfɔːtʃənətli/ *adv* (*indep*) lamentablemente, desafortunadamente; (stronger) desgraciadamente, por desgracia

unfounded /ˈʌnˈfaʊndəd || ʌnˈfaʊndɪd/ *adj* infundado

unfreeze /ˈʌnˈfriːz/ (*past* **unfroze**; *past p* **unfrozen**) *vt* descongelar

■ **unfreeze** *vi* descongelarse

unfriendly /ˈʌnˈfrendli/ *adj* **-lier, -liest** 1 ‹*person*› poco amistoso; (stronger) antipático; ‹*attitude*› desagradable,

U

poco amistoso; ~ TO *o* TOWARD **sb**: **she was very ~ to** *o* **toward them** estuvo muy antipática *or* desagradable con ellos 2 ‹*terrain/climate*› hostil

unfrock /'ʌn'frɑːk || ʌn'frɒk/ *vt* retirar del sacerdocio

unfroze /'ʌn:frəʊz/ *past of* **unfreeze**

unfrozen /'ʌn'frəʊzn̩/ *past p of* **unfreeze**

unfulfilled /'ʌnfʊl'fɪld/ *adj* 1 (unsatisfied): **to feel ~** no sentirse* realizado 2 (unrealized) ‹*ambition/hope*› frustrado; ‹*prophecy*› no cumplido

unfunny /'ʌn'fʌni/ *adj* sin nada de gracia

unfurl /'ʌn'fɜːrl || ʌn'fɜːl/ *vt* desplegar*
■ **unfurl** *vi* desplegarse*

unfurnished /'ʌn'fɜːrnɪʃt || ʌn'fɜːnɪʃt/ *adj* sin amueblar

ungainly /ʌn'geɪnli/ *adj* ‹*person*› desgarbado; ‹*movement*› torpe, desgarbado

ungenerous /'ʌn'dʒenərəs/ *adj* ‹*reward/tip*› poco generoso; ‹*remark/attitude*› mezquino

unglazed /'ʌn'gleɪzd/ *adj* 1 ‹*pottery*› sin esmaltar 2 ‹*window/door*› sin vidrios *or* (esp Esp) cristales

ungodly /'ʌn'gɑːdli || ʌn'gɒdli/ *adj* impío; **at some ~ hour** (hum) a una hora infame (fam)

ungovernable /'ʌn'gʌvərnəbəl || ʌn'gʌvənəbəl/ *adj* 1 ‹*country/people*› ingobernable 2 (liter) ‹*rage/passion*› incontrolable, irreprimible, incontenible

ungracious /'ʌn'greɪʃəs/ *adj* descortés

ungraciously /'ʌn'greɪʃəsli/ *adv* ‹*agree*› de mala gana

ungrammatical /'ʌngrə'mætɪkəl/ *adj* gramaticalmente incorrecto

ungrateful /'ʌn'greɪtfəl/ *adj* desagradecido, ingrato, malagradecido

ungrudging /'ʌn'grʌdʒɪŋ/ *adj* ‹*support/assistance*› generoso, desinteresado; ‹*admiration*› sin resquemores; ‹*praise*› sincero

unguarded /'ʌn'gɑːrdəd || ʌn'gɑːdɪd/ *adj* 1 (incautious): **in an ~ moment** en un momento de descuido 2 ‹*entrance/building*› sin vigilancia; ‹*goal*› desprotegido

unhappily /'ʌn'hæpəli || ʌn'hæpɪli/ *adv* 1 (sadly) ‹*sigh*› tristemente, con tristeza 2 (unfortunately) (*indep*) lamentablemente

unhappiness /'ʌn'hæpinəs || ʌn'hæpinɪs/ *n* [u] 1 (lack of happiness) infelicidad *f*; (stronger) desdicha *f*; (sadness) tristeza *f* 2 (dissatisfaction) descontento *m*

unhappy /'ʌn'hæpi/ *adj* **-pier, -piest**
A 1 (sad) ‹*childhood*› infeliz; (stronger) desgraciado, desdichado; **it has an ~ ending** termina mal, tiene un final triste 2 (worried) (*pred*) **to be ~ ABOUT sth/-ING**: **I was ~ about the children being left alone** me preocupaba *or* inquietaba que los niños se quedaran solos; **I'm ~ about sneaking away like this** no me gusta esto de escabullirme así 3 (discontented) (*pred*) descontento; **to be ~ ABOUT sth** no estar* contento CON algo; **to be ~ WITH sth/sb** no estar* contento CON algo/algn
B 1 (inopportune) ‹*remark*› desafortunado, poco feliz, inoportuno 2 (unfortunate) ‹*coincidence/day*› desafortunado, desventurado (liter)

unharmed /'ʌn'hɑːrmd || ʌn'hɑːmd/ *adj*: **the vase was ~** el florero quedó intacto; **he escaped ~** salió *or* resultó ileso

UNHCR *n* (= **United Nations High Commission for Refugees**) ACNUR *m*

unhealthy /'ʌn'helθi/ *adj* **-thier, -thiest** 1 ‹*person*› de mala salud; ‹*complexion*› enfermizo; ‹*climate/conditions*› poco saludable, insalubre, malsano; ‹*food*› malo para la salud 2 (morbid) ‹*interest/obsession*› malsano, morboso

unheard /'ʌn'hɜːrd || ʌn'hɜːd/ *adj*: **her remark went ~** no oyeron su observación

unheard of /'ʌn'hɜːrdɑːv || ʌn'hɜːdɒv/ *adj* insólito; **it's ~ ~ for anyone to win three years running** es insólito *or* es algo sin precedentes que alguien gane tres años seguidos

unheeded /'ʌn'hiːdəd || ʌn'hiːdɪd/ *adj*: **her advice went ~** hicieron caso omiso de sus consejos, desatendieron *or* desoyeron sus consejos

unhelpful /'ʌn'helpfəl/ *adj* ‹*assistant/secretary*› poco servicial; **he was most ~** no se mostró nada dispuesto a ayudar; **her comments were ~** sus comentarios no sirvieron de nada

unhesitating /'ʌn'hezəteɪtɪŋ || ʌn'hezɪteɪtɪŋ/ *adj* ‹*reply*› resuelto, decidido; **his acceptance was ~** aceptó sin vacilar

unhinge /'ʌn'hɪndʒ/ *vt* ‹*person/mind*› trastornar

unhitch /'ʌn'hɪtʃ/ *vt* ‹*horse/trailer*› desenganchar

unholy /'ʌn'həʊli/ *adj* **-lier, -liest** 1 (wicked) (liter) ‹*desire/thought*› impuro, pecaminoso; ‹*alliance/union*› nefasto 2 (dreadful) (colloq) ‹*noise/row*› de mil demonios (fam)

unhook /'ʌn'hʊk/ *vt* 1 ‹*curtains/picture*› descolgar* 2 (unfasten) ‹*dress*› desabrochar

unhurried /'ʌn'hɜːrid || ʌn'hʌrid/ *adj* ‹*steps/movement*› pausado, lento; ‹*existence*› apacible, tranquilo

unhurt /'ʌn'hɜːrt || ʌn'hɜːt/ *adj* ileso; **to escape ~** salir* *or* resultar ileso

unhygienic /'ʌnhaɪ'dʒiːnɪk/ *adj* antihigiénico

uni- /'juːni/ *pref* uni-

UNICEF /'juːnɪsef/ *n* (*no art*) (= **United Nations International Children's Emergency Fund**) UNICEF *m or f*

unicorn /'juːnəkɔːrn || 'juːnɪkɔːn/ *n* unicornio *m*

unicycle /'juːnəˌsaɪkəl || 'juːnɪˌsaɪkəl/ *n* monociclo *m*

unidentified /'ʌnaɪ'dentəfaɪd || ˌʌnaɪ'dentɪfaɪd/ *adj* no identificado; **~ flying object** objeto *m* volador *or* (Esp) volante no identificado, ovni *m*

unification /'juːnəfə'keɪʃən || ˌjuːnɪfɪ'keɪʃən/ *n* [u] unificación *f*

uniform¹ /'juːnəfɔːrm || 'juːnɪfɔːm/ *n* uniforme *m*; **(full) dress ~** uniforme de gala; **to be in ~** ir* de uniforme, estar* uniformado; (to be in the army) vestir* uniforme

uniform² *adj* ‹*shape/color/length*› uniforme; ‹*temperature/speed*› constante

uniformed /'juːnəfɔːrmd || 'juːnɪfɔːmd/ *adj* uniformado

uniformity /'juːnə'fɔːrməti || ˌjuːnɪ'fɔːməti/ *n* [u] uniformidad *f*

uniformly /'juːnəfɔːrmli || 'juːnɪfɔːmli/ *adv* de modo uniforme, uniformemente

unify /'juːnəfaɪ || 'juːnɪfaɪ/ *vt* **-fies, -fying, -fied** (unite) ‹*country/people*› unir

unilateral /'juːnɪ'lætərəl/ *adj* unilateral

unimaginable /'ʌnə'mædʒənəbəl || ˌʌnɪ'mædʒɪnəbəl/ *adj* inimaginable

unimaginative /'ʌnə'mædʒənətɪv || ˌʌnɪ'mædʒɪnətɪv/ *adj* ‹*person*› poco imaginativo, sin imaginación; ‹*story/design*› falto de imaginación

unimpaired /'ʌnɪm'perd || ˌʌnɪm'peəd/ *adj*: **his sight is ~** tiene una vista perfecta; **the quality is ~** la calidad no se ve afectada

unimpeachable /'ʌnɪm'piːtʃəbəl/ *adj* ‹*conduct/character*› intachable, impecable, irreprochable

unimpeded /'ʌnɪm'piːdəd || ˌʌnɪm'piːdɪd/ *adj* libre de obstáculos *or* trabas

unimportant /'ʌnɪm'pɔːrtn̩t || ˌʌnɪm'pɔːtn̩t/ *adj* ‹*matter/detail*› sin importancia; **it seemed ~** no parecía importante, no parecía tener importancia

unimpressed /'ʌnɪm'prest/ *adj*: **I was ~ by her performance** su actuación no me convenció mucho

uninformed /'ʌnɪn'fɔːrmd || ˌʌnɪn'fɔːmd/ *adj* ‹*opinion/guess*› sin fundamento; **~ ABOUT sth**: **she was ~ about what was going on in the country** no estaba al tanto *or* al corriente de lo que estaba pasando en el país

uninhabitable /'ʌnɪn'hæbətəbəl || ˌʌnɪn'hæbɪtəbəl/ *adj* inhabitable

uninhabited /'ʌnɪn'hæbətəd || ˌʌnɪn'hæbɪtɪd/ *adj* ‹*house*› deshabitado; ‹*region/island*› despoblado

uninhibited /'ʌnɪn'hɪbətəd || ˌʌnɪn'hɪbɪtɪd/ *adj* desinhibido, sin inhibiciones, desenfadado

uninitiated /'ʌnɪ'nɪʃieɪtəd || ˌʌnɪ'nɪʃieɪtɪd/ *pl n* **the ~** los no iniciados

uninspired /'ʌnɪn'spaɪrd || ˌʌnɪn'spaɪəd/ *adj* poco inspirado

uninspiring /'ʌnɪn'spaɪrɪŋ || ˌʌnɪn'spaɪərɪŋ/ *adj* ‹*company*› poco estimulante; ‹*menu/subject*› aburrido; ‹*scenery*› monótono

uninstal, (BrE) **uninstall** /ˌʌnɪn'stɔːl/ *n* desinstalación *f*

unintelligent /ʌnɪn'telədʒənt || ,ʌnɪn'telɪdʒənt/ *adj* poco inteligente

unintelligible /'ʌnɪn'telədʒəbəl || ,ʌnɪn'telɪdʒəbəl/ *adj* ininteligible, incomprensible

unintended /'ʌnɪn'tendəd || ,ʌnɪn'tendɪd/ *adj* ‹*consequences*› no buscado, no planeado; ‹*pun*› no deliberado

unintentional /'ʌnɪn'tentʃṇəl || ,ʌnɪn'tenʃənḷ/ *adj* involuntario, no deliberado

unintentionally /'ʌnɪn'tentʃṇəli || ,ʌnɪn'tenʃṇəli/ *adv* ‹*hurt/hear*› involuntariamente, sin querer; **the dialogue is ~ funny** el diálogo resulta cómico sin que ellos se lo propongan

uninterested /'ʌn'ɪntrəstəd || ʌn'ɪntrestɪd/ *adj* indiferente; **~ IN sth**: **she was totally ~ in my work** no demostró ningún interés en mi trabajo

uninteresting /'ʌn'ɪntrəstɪŋ/ *adj* ‹*topic*› sin interés; ‹*person/outcome*› poco interesante

uninterrupted /'ʌn'ɪntə'rʌptəd || ,ʌnɪntə'rʌptɪd/ *adj* **1** (undisturbed) ininterrumpido, sin interrupción **2** (continuous) constante, incesante

uninvited /'ʌnɪn'vaɪtəd || ,ʌnɪn'vaɪtɪd/ *adj*: **they came ~** vinieron sin que nadie los invitara

uninviting /'ʌnɪn'vaɪtɪŋ/ *adj* ‹*appearance*› poco atractivo; ‹*prospect*› poco halagüeño; ‹*food*› poco apetitoso

union /'juːnjən/ *n*

A [u c] (act, state) unión *f*

B **the Union** (the United States) los Estados Unidos; (in Civil War) la Unión

C [c] (Lab Rel) sindicato *m*, gremio *m* (CS, Per); (*before n*) ‹*official/movement*› sindical, gremial (CS, Per); **~ card** carné *m* de afiliado

D [c] (at college, university) asociación *f or* federación *f* de estudiantes

unionist /'juːnjənəst || 'juːnjənɪst/ *n*

A **Unionist** (Pol) (in UK, US) unionista *mf*

B (Lab Rel) sindicalista *mf*

unionize /'juːnjənaɪz || 'juːnjənaɪz/ *vt* sindicalizar* (esp AmL), sindicar* (esp Esp)

■ **unionize** *vi* sindicalizarse* (esp AmL), sindicarse* (esp Esp)

union: **~ Jack** *n* bandera *f* del Reino Unido; **~ of Soviet Socialist Republics** *n* (Hist) **the ~ of Soviet Socialist Republics** la Unión de Repúblicas Socialistas Soviéticas

> **Union Jack** *o* **Union Flag**
>
> El nombre que recibe la bandera del Reino Unido. Está formada por las cruces de San Jorge (*St George*), patrono de Inglaterra, de San Andrés (*St Andrew*), patrono de Escocia, y de San Patricio (*St Patrick*), patrono de Irlanda. Gales y su patrono San David no están representados en ella

unique /jʊ'niːk/ *adj* **1** (sole) (*no comp*) ‹*specimen/collection*› único; **~ TO sth**: **plants ~ to this region** plantas que sólo se dan *or* que se dan exclusivamente en esta región **2** (unparalleled) (*no comp*) ‹*opportunity*› único, excepcional

uniquely /jʊ'niːkli/ *adv* ‹*gifted/suited*› excepcionalmente

uniqueness /jʊ'niːknəs || juː'niːknɪs/ *n* [u] singularidad *f*

unisex /'juːnəseks || 'juːnɪseks/ *adj* unisex *adj inv*

unison /'juːnəsən || 'juːnɪsən/ *n* [u]: **to play/sing in ~** tocar*/cantar al unísono; **to act in ~** obrar de forma conjunta *or* al unísono

UNISON *n* (in UK) (*no art*) *sindicato general de empleados*

unit /'juːnət || 'juːnɪt/ *n*

A **1** (item) (Busn) unidad *f*; (*before n*) ‹*cost/price*› por unidad, unitario **2** (part, machine) (Elec, Mech Eng) unidad *f* **3** (of furniture) módulo *m* **4** (building): **office ~s to rent** se alquilan oficinas

B (group) unidad *f*; **tank/cavalry ~** unidad blindada/de caballería *f*; **the family ~** el núcleo *or* grupo familiar, la familia

C (of measurement) unidad *f*

D (Educ) (in course) módulo *m*, unidad *f*

Unitarian /'juːnə'terian || ,juːnɪ'teəriən/ *adj* unitario

unite /jʊ'naɪt || juː'naɪt/ *vt* unir

■ **unite** *vi* unirse

united /jʊ'naɪtəd || juː'naɪtɪd/ *adj* unido; **they are ~ in their grief/joy** los une el dolor/la alegría; **~ we stand, divided we fall** (set phrase) unidos venceremos (fr hecha)

united: **~ Arab Emirates** *pl n* **the U~ Arab Emirates** los Emiratos Árabes Unidos; **~ Kingdom** *n* **the U~ Kingdom** el Reino Unido (*Gran Bretaña e Irlanda del Norte*); **~ Nations (Organization)** *n* (+ *sing o pl vb*) (la Organización de) las Naciones Unidas; **~ States** *n* (*usu* + *sing vb*) **the U~ States** los Estados Unidos; (*before n*) ‹*citizen/forces*› estadounidense, (norte)americano, de los Estados Unidos; **~ States of America** *n* (frml) (*usu* + *sing vb*) **the U~ States of America** los Estados Unidos de América (frml)

> **United Kingdom**
>
> El Reino Unido de Gran Bretaña e Irlanda del Norte (*United Kingdom of Great Britain and Northern Ireland*) comprende Inglaterra, Escocia, Gales e Irlanda del Norte. Es miembro de la **Commonwealth** y de la Unión Europea

unit trust *n* (BrE Fin) fondo *m* de inversión mobiliaria

unity /'juːnəti/ *n* [u c] (*pl* **-ties**) unidad *f*; **~ is strength** la unión hace la fuerza

universal /'juːnə'vɜːrsəl || ,juːnɪ'vɜːsəl/ *adj* **1** (general) general; **this practice is becoming ~** esta práctica se está generalizando **2** (worldwide) ‹*peace/law*› universal **3** (all-purpose, versatile) ‹*adaptor*› universal; **~ joint** *o* **coupling** junta *f* universal *or* cardán

universally /'juːnə'vɜːrsəli || ,juːnɪ'vɜːsəli/ *adv* ‹*known/admired*› mundialmente, universalmente; ‹*applicable*› para todo

universe /'juːnəvɜːrs || 'juːnɪvɜːs/ *n* universo *m*

university /'juːnə'vɜːrsəti || ,juːnɪ'vɜːsəti/ *n* [c u] (*pl* **-ties**) universidad *f*; **she is at the ~** (AmE) *o* (BrE) **at ~** está en la universidad; **she left (the) ~ in 1980** terminó la carrera en 1980; (*before n*) ‹*town/life/education*› universitario; **~ student** (estudiante *mf*) universitario, -ria *m,f*

unjust /'ʌn'dʒʌst/ *adj* injusto

unjustifiable /'ʌn'dʒʌstəfaɪəbəl || ʌn'dʒʌstɪfaɪəbəl/ *adj* injustificable

unjustified /'ʌn'dʒʌstəfaɪd || ʌn'dʒʌstɪfaɪd/ *adj* injustificado

unjustly /'ʌn'dʒʌstli/ *adv* injustamente

unkempt /'ʌn'kempt/ *adj* (frml) ‹*appearance*› descuidado, desarreglado; ‹*hair*› despeinado

unkind /'ʌn'kaɪnd/ *adj* **-er, -est** **1** (unpleasant) poco amable; (cruel) cruel, malo; **that was very ~ of you** eso fue muy poco amable de tu parte; **~ remarks** comentarios *mpl* hirientes; **to be ~ TO sb** tratar mal a algn **2** ‹*climate/weather*› inclemente

unkindly /'ʌn'kaɪndli/ *adv* ‹*treat*› mal, con poca amabilidad; (cruelly) cruelmente; **I didn't mean it ~** no lo dije con mala intención

unknowing /'ʌn'nəʊɪŋ/ *adj*: **he was an ~ accomplice** era cómplice sin saberlo

unknowingly /'ʌn'nəʊɪŋli/ *adv*: **I ~ let the secret out** sin darme cuenta revelé el secreto; **I ~ insulted/hurt her** sin saberlo la insulté/le hice daño

unknown[1] /'ʌn'nəʊn/ *adj* desconocido; **her whereabouts are ~** se desconoce su paradero; **it is virtually ~ for anyone to refuse** prácticamente nunca se niega nadie

unknown[2] *n* **1** [u] (phenomenon, experience) **the ~** lo desconocido **2** [c] (Math) incógnita *f* **3** [c] (person) desconocido, -da *m,f*

unknown[3] *adv*: **~ to her** sin ella saberlo, sin que ella lo supiera

unlace /'ʌn'leɪs/ *vt* desatar, desamarrar (AmL exc RPl)

unlatch /'ʌn'lætʃ/ *vt* descorrer el pestillo de

unlawful /'ʌn'lɔːfəl/ *adj* ‹*conduct/activity*› ilegal; ‹*possession/association*› ilícito; **~ entry** allanamiento *m* de morada, violación *f* de domicilio (CS, Ven)

unlawfully /'ʌn'lɔːfəli/ *adv* ‹*behave/act*› ilegalmente; ‹*possess/associate*› ilícitamente

unleaded /'ʌn'ledəd || ʌn'ledɪd/ *adj* sin plomo

unleash /'ʌn'liːʃ/ *vt* ‹*dog*› soltar*, desatar; ‹*anger/imagination*› dar(le)* rienda suelta a; ‹*war*› desencadenar

unleavened /'ʌn'levənd/ *adj* ‹*bread*› ázimo, sin levadura

unless /ʌn'les, ən-/ *conj* a no ser que (+ *subj*), a menos que (+ *subj*); **~ I'm very much mistaken** si no estoy muy equivocado, a menos que *or* a no ser que esté muy equivocada

unlicensed /'ʌn'laɪsn̩st/ *adj* ‹*dog*› sin patente; ‹*casino*› no autorizado, ilegal; ‹*trade/pilot*› sin licencia

unlike¹ /'ʌn'laɪk/ *prep* 1 (not similar to) diferente *or* distinto de; **it's ~ any other food I have eaten** no se parece a nada que haya comido antes 2 (untypical of): **it's ~ you to be so optimistic** tú no sueles ser tan optimista, es raro en ti ser tan optimista 3 (in contrast to) a diferencia de; **~ the rest of the family** a diferencia del resto de la familia

unlike² *adj* (dissimilar) diferente, distinto

unlikely /'ʌn'laɪkli/ *adj* **-lier, liest** 1 (improbable) ‹*outcome/victory*› improbable, poco probable; **that is highly** *o* **most ~** eso es muy poco probable; **they're ~ to agree** es poco probable que acepten 2 (far-fetched) ‹*story/explanation*› inverosímil, increíble 3 (odd, unexpected) insólito; **an ~ couple** una extraña pareja, una pareja dispareja (AmL)

unlimited /'ʌn'lɪmətəd || ʌn'lɪmɪtɪd/ *adj* 1 (not restricted) ‹*money/supply/powers*› ilimitado 2 (Busn) ‹*partnership/liability*› ilimitado

unlined /'ʌn'laɪnd/ *adj* 1 ‹*paper*› sin pautar; ‹*skin/forehead*› sin arrugas 2 ‹*dress/jacket*› sin forro

unlisted /'ʌn'lɪstəd || ʌn'lɪstɪd/ *adj* 1 ‹*securities/company*› (Fin) no cotizado en bolsa 2 ‹*number*› (AmE Telec) que no figura en la guía telefónica, privado (Méx)

unlit /'ʌn'lɪt/ *adj* ‹*road*› sin luz, sin alumbrado; ‹*room*› sin luz, sin iluminación

unload /'ʌn'ləʊd/ *vt* 1 ‹*ship/cargo*› descargar* 2 (get rid of) (colloq) ‹*goods/stolen goods*› deshacerse* de; **to ~ sth ON sb** endosarle *or* encajarle algo A algn (fam)

■ **unload** *vi* «*ship/truck*» descargar*

unlock /'ʌn'lɑːk || ʌn'lɒk/ *vt* abrir* (*algo que está cerrado con llave*); **she left the door ~ed** no cerró la puerta con llave

■ **unlock** *vi*: **this door won't ~** esta puerta no se puede abrir

unlovable /'ʌn'lʌvəbəl/ *adj* antipático, que no se hace querer

unloved /'ʌn'lʌvd/ *adj*: **he feels ~** siente que nadie lo quiere

unloving /'ʌn'lʌvɪŋ/ *adj* poco cariñoso *or* afectuoso

unluckily /'ʌn'lʌkəli || ʌn'lʌkɪli/ *adv* 1 (unfortunately) (*indep*) desgraciadamente, lamentablemente 2 (without luck) sin suerte

unlucky /'ʌn'lʌki/ *adj* **unluckier, unluckiest** 1 (unfortunate) ‹*person*› sin suerte, desafortunado; ‹*day*› funesto, de mala suerte; **to be ~** tener* mala suerte 2 (bringing bad luck) ‹*omen*› funesto, nefasto; ‹*object*› que trae mala suerte; **it's ~ to walk under ladders** es de mala suerte pasar por debajo de una escalera

unmade /'ʌn'meɪd/ *adj* ‹*bed*› sin hacer, destendido (AmL)

unmanageable /'ʌn'mænɪdʒəbəl/ *adj* ‹*child/horse*› rebelde, difícil de controlar; ‹*hair*› rebelde

unmanly /'ʌn'mænli/ *adj* ‹*conduct/attitude*› impropio de un hombre, poco viril

unmanned /'ʌn'mænd/ *adj* (needing no crew) ‹*vehicle/rocket*› sin tripulación; ‹*space flight*› no tripulado

unmannerly /'ʌn'mænərli || ʌn'mænəli/ *adj* (frml) descortés

unmarked /'ʌn'mɑːrkt || ʌn'mɑːkt/ *adj*
A 1 (without identification) ‹*banknotes*› sin marcar; ‹*grave*› sin nombre; **~ car** coche *m* particular (*utilizado por la policía*), coche *m* K *or* camuflado (Esp) 2 (without stains, marks) sin marcas
B (BrE Sport) ‹*player*› desmarcado

unmarried /'ʌn'mærid/ *adj* soltero

unmask /'ʌn'mæsk || ʌn'mɑːsk/ *vt* desenmascarar, descubrir*

unmatched /'ʌn'mætʃt/ *adj* inigualable, incomparable, sin par (liter)

unmentionable /'ʌn'mentʃn̩əbəl || ʌn'menʃənəbəl/ *adj* inmencionable, innombrable, tabú *adj inv*

unmercifully /'ʌn'mɜːrsɪfəli || ʌn'mɜːsɪfəli/ *adv* despiadadamente, sin piedad

unmistakable /'ʌnmə'steɪkəbəl || ˌʌnmɪ'steɪkəbəl/ *adj* ‹*voice/smell/style*› inconfundible; ‹*proof*› inequívoco

unmistakably /'ʌnmə'steɪkəbli || ˌʌnmɪ'steɪkəbli/ *adv* ‹*show/demonstrate*› inequívocamente, sin dejar lugar a dudas; **his accent was ~ German** tenía un acento alemán inconfundible

unmitigated /'ʌn'mɪtəgeɪtəd || ʌn'mɪtɪgeɪtɪd/ *adj* ‹*tedium/failure*› absoluto; **the book was ~ rubbish** el libro era pura bazofia

unmotivated /'ʌn'məʊtəveɪtəd || ʌn'məʊtɪveɪtɪd/ *adj* 1 ‹*attack/murder*› sin motivo 2 (lacking drive) sin motivación, falto de entusiasmo *or* interés

unmoved /'ʌn'muːvd/ *adj*: **his playing left them ~** su interpretación los dejó fríos; **how can you be** *o* **remain ~ by such a tragedy?** ¿cómo puede dejarte indiferente una tragedia así?

unnamed /'ʌn'neɪmd/ *adj* no identificado

unnatural /'ʌn'nætʃərəl/ *adj* 1 (not normal, unusual) poco natural *or* normal 2 (awkward, affected) ‹*acting/smile*› poco natural, forzado 3 (depraved, against nature) (frml) ‹*lust/perversion/love*› antinatural

unnaturally /'ʌn'nætʃrəli/ *adv* ‹*behave/speak*› de manera poco natural; ‹*swollen*› anormalmente

unnecessarily /'ʌnnesə'serəli || ˌʌnnesə'serɪli, ˌʌn'nesəserɪli/ *adv* ‹*rude/cruel*› innecesariamente; **they died ~** murieron innecesariamente *or* inútilmente *or* en vano

unnecessary /ʌn'nesəseri || ʌn'nesəsəri/ *adj* innecesario; **~ details** detalles *mpl* superfluos; **don't put yourself to ~ trouble** no te molestes demasiado

unneighborly, (BrE) **unneighbourly** /ʌn'neɪbərli || ʌn'neɪbəli/ *adj* ‹*behavior/attitude/act*› poco sociable, impropio de un buen vecino; ‹*person*› poco sociable, insociable

unnerve /'ʌn'nɜːrv || ʌn'nɜːv/ *vt* poner* nervioso, hacer* sentir incómodo, turbar (liter)

unnerving /'ʌn'nɜːrvɪŋ || ʌn'nɜːvɪŋ/ *adj* desconcertante, que pone nervioso

unnoticed /'ʌn'nəʊtəst || ʌn'nəʊtɪst/ *adj* (*pred*): **to go ~** pasar desapercibido *or* inadvertido

UNO *n* = **United Nations Organization** ONU *f*

unobservant /'ʌnəb'zɜːrvənt || ˌʌnəb'zɜːvənt/ *adj* poco observador

unobserved /'ʌnəb'zɜːrvd || ˌʌnəb'zɜːvd/ *adj* (*usu pred*): **to pass ~** pasar desapercibido *or* inadvertido

unobstructed /'ʌnəb'strʌktəd || ˌʌnəb'strʌktɪd/ *adj* ‹*access/passage*› libre, despejado; **we had an ~ view of the sea** teníamos una vista panorámica del mar

unobtainable /'ʌnəb'teɪnəbəl/ *adj* imposible de conseguir; **the number is ~** (BrE Telec) el número está desconectado

unobtrusive /'ʌnəb'truːsɪv/ *adj* discreto

unoccupied /'ʌn'ɑːkjəpaɪd || ʌn'ɒkjʊpaɪd/ *adj* 1 ‹*seat/room/toilet*› desocupado, libre; ‹*house*› deshabitado, desocupado 2 (Mil) ‹*territory/zone*› no ocupado

unofficial /'ʌnə'fɪʃəl/ *adj* ‹*meeting/strike/report*› no oficial; **speaking in an ~ capacity** hablando extraoficialmente *or* con carácter no oficial

unofficially /'ʌnə'fɪʃəli/ *adv* extraoficialmente

unopened /'ʌn'əʊpənd/ *adj* sin abrir

unopposed /'ʌnə'pəʊzd/ *adj* sin oposición

unorganized /'ʌn'ɔːrgənaɪzd || ʌn'ɔːgənaɪzd/ *adj* 1 (disorganized) desorganizado 2 ‹*labor/workers*› no sindicalizado (esp AmL) *or* (esp Esp) no sindicado

unoriginal /'ʌnə'rɪdʒənl/ *adj* poco original, sin originalidad

unorthodox /ʌn'ɔːrθədɑːks || ʌn'ɔːθədɒks/ *adj* poco ortodoxo

unpack /'ʌn'pæk/ *vt* ‹*bags/briefcase*› sacar* las cosas de, desempacar* (AmL); ‹*suitcase*› deshacer*, desempacar* (AmL)

■ **unpack** *vi* deshacer* las maletas, desempacar* (AmL)

unpaid /'ʌn'peɪd/ *adj* ‹*work/volunteer*› no retribuido, no remunerado; ‹*leave*› sin sueldo; ‹*debt*› pendiente, no liquidado; **the invoice is still ~** la factura todavía está por cobrar/por pagar

U

unpalatable /ˈʌnˈpæləṭəbəl/ *adj* 1 ‹*food/drink*› de sabor desagradable 2 ‹*fact/truth*› desagradable, difícil de digerir *or* aceptar

unparalleled /ˈʌnˈpærəleld/ *adj* ‹*success/achievement*› sin paralelo, sin precedentes, sin parangón; ‹*failure/disaster*› sin precedentes; ‹*beauty*› incomparable, sin igual, sin par (liter)

unpardonable /ˈʌnˈpɑːrdn̩əbəl || ʌnˈpɑːdn̩əbəl/ *adj* inexcusable, imperdonable

unpatriotic /ˈʌnpeitriˈɑːtɪk || ˌʌnpætriˈɒtɪk, -peɪtri-/ *adj* ‹*act*› antipatriótico; ‹*person*› poco patriota

unpaved /ˈʌnˈpeɪvd/ *adj* sin pavimentar

unperturbed /ˈʌnpərˈtɜːrbd || ˌʌnpəˈtɜːbd/ *adj* impasible, impertérrito; **she carried on** ~ siguió sin inmutarse

unpick /ˈʌnˈpɪk/ *vt* ‹*hem/dress*› descoser; ‹*seam*› deshacer*

unpin /ˈʌnˈpɪn/ *vt* **-nn-** ‹*dress*› quitarle los alfileres a; ‹*hair*› quitarse las horquillas de

unpleasant /ˈʌnˈpleznt/ *adj* ‹*remark/surprise/taste*› desagradable; ‹*person*› desagradable, antipático; (rude) grosero

unpleasantly /ˈʌnˈplezntli/ *adv* ‹*speak/grin/stare*› de manera desagradable; **it was** ~ **hot** hacía un calor desagradable

unpleasantness /ˈʌnˈplezntnəs || ʌnˈplezntnɪs/ *n* [u] (of person) carácter *m* desagradable; (on a particular occasion) actitud *f* desagradable; **there was no need for all that** ~ no había ninguna necesidad de crear una situación tan desagradable *or* violenta

unplug /ˈʌnˈplʌg/ *vt* **-gg-** desenchufar, desconectar

unpolished /ˈʌnˈpɑːlɪʃt || ʌnˈpɒlɪʃt/ *adj* 1 ‹*floor*› sin encerar; ‹*shoes*› sin abrillantar, sin lustrar (esp AmL); ‹*gem*› sin pulir 2 (not perfected) ‹*performance*› poco pulido; ‹*person/manners*› poco pulido *or* refinado

unpolluted /ˈʌnpəˈluːtəd || ˌʌnpəˈluːtɪd/ *adj* no contaminado

unpopular /ˈʌnˈpɑːpjələr || ʌnˈpɒpjʊlə(r)/ *adj* impopular; **as a child I was always** ~ de pequeño nunca tuve muchos amigos; **to make oneself** ~ «*politician*» hacerse* impopular; **she's made herself very** ~ **among her staff** se ha granjeado la antipatía del personal; **to be** ~ **WITH sb**: **he is** ~ **with everybody** le cae muy mal a todo el mundo

unpopularity /ˈʌnˈpɑːpjəˈlærəti || ˌʌnˌpɒpjʊˈlærəti/ *n* [u] impopularidad *f*

unprecedented /ˈʌnˈpresədentəd || ʌnˈpresɪdentɪd/ *adj* ‹*success/hostility*› sin precedentes; ‹*decision*› inaudito

unpredictable /ˈʌnprɪˈdɪktəbəl/ *adj* ‹*result/weather*› imprevisible; **she's very** ~ nunca se sabe cómo va a reaccionar

unprejudiced /ˈʌnˈpredʒədəst || ʌnˈpredʒʊdɪst/ *adj* 1 (impartial) objetivo, imparcial 2 (not bigoted) sin prejuicios

unprepared /ˈʌnprɪˈperd || ˌʌnprɪˈpeəd/ *adj* 1 (not ready) (*pred*) **to be** ~ **(FOR sth)** no estar* preparado (PARA algo) 2 (not expecting) (*pred*) **to be** ~ **FOR sth** no esperar algo; **he was** ~ **for her reaction** no esperaba que fuera a reaccionar así, su reacción lo agarró *or* (esp Esp) cogió desprevenido 3 ‹*speech*› improvisado

unprepossessing /ˈʌnpriːpəˈzesɪŋ/ *adj* ‹*appearance*› poco atractivo

unpretentious /ˈʌnprɪˈtentʃəs || ˌʌnprɪˈtenʃəs/ *adj* sin pretensiones

unprincipled /ˈʌnˈprɪnsəpəld/ *adj* sin escrúpulos *or* principios, carente de escrúpulos *or* principios (frml)

unprintable /ˈʌnˈprɪntəbəl/ *adj* ‹*reply/letter*› impublicable; ‹*comment*› irrepetible

unproductive /ˈʌnprəˈdʌktɪv/ *adj* ‹*capital/business*› improductivo; ‹*meeting*› infructuoso, que no conduce a nada

unprofessional /ˈʌnprəˈfeʃn̩əl || ˌʌnprəˈfeʃənl̩/ *adj* poco profesional, contrario a la ética profesional

unprofitable /ˈʌnˈprɑːfətəbəl || ʌnˈprɒfɪtəbəl/ *adj* no rentable, que no produce (beneficios)

unprompted /ˈʌnˈprɑːmptəd || ʌnˈprɒmptɪd/ *adj* ‹*gesture*› espontáneo; **he did it** ~ lo hizo (de) motu proprio

unpronounceable /ˈʌnprəˈnaʊnsəbəl/ *adj* impronunciable

unprotected /ˈʌnprəˈtektəd || ˌʌnprəˈtektɪd/ *adj* sin protección; ~ **sex** relaciones *fpl* sexuales sin el uso de preservativos (frml)

unproven /ˈʌnˈpruːvən/ *adj* ‹*theory*› (que está) por demostrar *or* probar; ‹*ability*› aún no demostrado; **the case against him remains** ~ los cargos en su contra aún no han sido probados

unprovoked /ˈʌnprəˈvəʊkt/ *adj* no provocado

unpublished /ˈʌnˈpʌblɪʃt/ *adj* ‹*diary/manuscript*› inédito, no publicado

unpunctual /ˈʌnˈpʌŋktʃuəl || ʌnˈpʌŋktjʊəl, -tʃʊəl/ *adj* impuntual, poco puntual

unpunished /ˈʌnˈpʌnɪʃt/ *adj*: **to go** ~ «*person*» quedar sin castigo; «*crime*» quedar impune *or* sin castigo

unqualified /ˈʌnˈkwɑːləfaɪd || ʌnˈkwɒlɪfaɪd/ *adj*
A (complete, total) ‹*approval/agreement*› incondicional, sin restricciones; ‹*disaster*› absoluto; **the campaign was an** ~ **success/failure** la campaña fue un éxito/fracaso rotundo
B (without qualifications) ‹*teacher/nurse*› sin titulación *or* título, no titulado; ‹*staff*› no calificado *or* (Esp) cualificado

unquestionable /ˈʌnˈkwestʃənəbəl/ *adj* 1 (beyond doubt) ‹*sincerity/loyalty*› incuestionable, innegable 2 (incontestable) ‹*ruling/judgment*› inapelable; ‹*authority*› indiscutible

unquestionably /ˈʌnˈkwestʃənəbli/ *adv* incuestionablemente, indudablemente, sin lugar a dudas; (*indep*) sin lugar a dudas

unquestioning /ˈʌnˈkwestʃənɪŋ/ *adj* ‹*obedience/faith*› ciego; ‹*loyalty*› incondicional, ciego

unquote /ˈʌnkwəʊt/ *interj*: *see* **quote**³

unquoted /ˈʌnˈkwəʊtəd || ʌnˈkwəʊtɪd/ *adj* (Fin) que no cotiza en Bolsa

unravel /ˈʌnˈrævəl/, (BrE) **-ll-** *vt* 1 ‹*threads/string*› desenredar, desenmarañar 2 ‹*mystery*› desentrañar, aclarar
■ **unravel** *vi* «*wool/sweater*» deshacerse*

unreadable /ˈʌnˈriːdəbəl/ *adj* 1 ‹*handwriting/manuscript*› ilegible 2 ‹*novel/prose/author*› muy difícil de leer

unreal /ˈʌnˈriːl || ʌnˈriːl, ʌnˈrɪəl/ *adj* irreal; **what a party!** ~**!** (AmE colloq) ¡qué fiesta! ¡fue algo increíble!

unrealistic /ˈʌnriːəˈlɪstɪk || ˌʌnrɪəˈlɪstɪk/ *adj* ‹*expectations*› poco realista; **it's** ~ **to expect that** no es realista esperar eso

unrealistically /ˈʌnriːəˈlɪstɪkli || ˌʌnrɪəˈlɪstɪkli/ *adv*: **their expectations are** ~ **high** tienen unas expectativas muy poco realistas

unreality /ˈʌnriˈæləti/ *n* [u] irrealidad *f*

unrealized /ˈʌnˈriːəlaɪzd || ʌnˈrɪəlaɪzd/ *adj* ‹*potential/talent*› sin explotar; ‹*ambition/dream*› que no se ha realizado *or* cumplido

unreasonable /ˈʌnˈriːzn̩əbəl/ *adj* ‹*person/attitude*› poco razonable, irrazonable; ‹*demand/price*› excesivo, poco razonable; **you're being totally** ~ tu actitud es muy poco razonable

unreasonably /ʌnˈriːzn̩əbli/ *adv* 1 (excessively) ‹*expensive/strict*› excesivamente, injustificadamente 2 (wrongly, irrationally) ‹*behave/react*› de manera poco razonable

unreceptive /ˈʌnrɪˈseptɪv/ *adj* poco receptivo

unrecognizable /ˈʌnˈrekəgnaɪzəbəl/ *adj* irreconocible

unrecognized /ˈʌnˈrekəgnaɪzd/ *adj* 1 (not identified) ‹*signature/danger*› no identificado 2 (unacknowledged) ‹*achievement/talent/claim*› no reconocido

unredeemed /ˈʌnrɪˈdiːmd/ *adj* 1 (unmitigated) ‹*ugliness/squalor*› absoluto 2 (not paid, cashed) ‹*pledge/bond*› no redimido

unrefined /ˈʌnrɪˈfaɪnd/ *adj* ‹*flour/sugar*› sin refinar, no refinado; ‹*gold/ore*› en estado bruto; ‹*person/manners*› poco refinado *or* pulido; ~ **oil** crudo *m*

unrehearsed /ˈʌnrɪˈhɜːrst || ˌʌnrɪˈhɜːst/ *adj* 1 (unprepared) no ensayado 2 (spontaneous) improvisado

unrelated /ˈʌnrɪˈleɪtəd || ˌʌnrɪˈleɪtɪd/ *adj* ‹*facts/events*› no relacionados (entre sí)

unrelenting /ˈʌnrɪˈlentɪŋ/ *adj* ‹*pursuit/opposition*› implacable; **the wind/pain was** ~ el viento/dolor era constante

unreliable /ˈʌnrɪˈlaɪəbəl/ *adj* ‹*person*› informal; ‹*information*› poco fidedigno; ‹*weather*› variable, inestable; **my**

car/watch is ~ de mi coche/reloj no te puedes fiar

unrelieved /ˈʌnrɪˈliːvd/ *adj* ‹*boredom/gloom*› total, absoluto; ‹*suffering*› continuo, sin tregua

unremarkable /ˈʌnrɪˈmɑːrkəbəl || ˌʌnrɪˈmɑːkəbəl/ *adj* ‹*appearance*› común y corriente, que no llama la atención; ‹*life/book*› poco interesante

unremitting /ˈʌnrɪˈmɪtɪŋ/ *adj* (frml) ‹*hostility/struggle*› sin tregua; ‹*effort*› infatigable; ‹*devotion*› absoluto, total

unrepeatable /ˈʌnrɪˈpiːtəbəl/ *adj*
A (verbally shocking) irrepetible, que no puede repetirse
B (occurring only once) ‹*offer/success*› irrepetible

unrepentant /ˈʌnrɪˈpentn̩t/ *adj* impenitente; **to be ~ (ABOUT sth)** no arrepentirse* (DE algo)

unreported /ˈʌnrɪˈpɔːrtəd || ˌʌnrɪˈpɔːtɪd/ *adj* ‹*crime*› no denunciado; **many cases go ~** muchos casos no se ponen en conocimiento de las autoridades *or* no se denuncian

unrepresentative /ˈʌnreprəˈzentətɪv/ *adj* poco representativo; **to be ~ OF sth** no ser* representativo DE algo

unrepresented /ˈʌnreprɪˈzentəd || ˌʌnreprɪˈzentɪd/ *adj* ‹*minority/party*› sin representación

unrequited /ˈʌnrɪˈkwaɪtəd || ˌʌnrɪˈkwaɪtɪd/ *adj* ‹*love*› no correspondido

unreserved /ˈʌnrɪˈzɜːrvd || ˌʌnrɪˈzɜːvd/ *adj* 1 (unstinted) ‹*admiration/support*› incondicional, sin reservas 2 (frank) ‹*opinion*› abierto, franco 3 (not allocated) sin reservar

unreservedly /ˈʌnrɪˈzɜːrvədli || ˌʌnrɪˈzɜːvɪdli/ *adv* ‹*praise/approve/recommend*› sin reservas; ‹*apologize*› profusamente

unresolved /ˈʌnrɪˈzɑːlvd || ˌʌnrɪˈzɒlvd/ *adj* ‹*dispute/mystery*› no resuelto

unresponsive /ˈʌnrɪˈspɑːnsɪv || ˌʌnrɪˈspɒnsɪv/ *adj* 1 (unmoved) ‹*audience/attitude/expression*› indiferente, frío; ‹*pupil*› que no responde 2 (physically) insensible

unrest /ˈʌnˈrest/ *n* [u] (Pol) descontento *m*, malestar *m*; (active) disturbios *mpl*; **civil ~** descontento *or* malestar social

unrestrained /ˈʌnrɪˈstreɪnd/ *adj* ‹*violence/exploitation*› incontrolado; ‹*greed*› desmedido; ‹*joy/anger*› desenfrenado, sin freno

unrestricted /ˈʌnrɪˈstrɪktəd || ˌʌnrɪˈstrɪktɪd/ *adj* ‹*power/growth*› ilimitado; ‹*area*› de libre acceso

unrewarded /ˈʌnrɪˈwɔːrdəd || ˌʌnrɪˈwɔːdɪd/ *adj* no recompensado; **to go ~** no ser* recompensado, no recibir recompensa

unrewarding /ˈʌnrɪˈwɔːrdɪŋ || ˌʌnrɪˈwɔːdɪŋ/ *adj* ‹*task*› ingrato, poco gratificante; ‹*experience/discussion*› infructuoso, poco fructífero

unripe /ˈʌnˈraɪp/ *adj* verde, que no está maduro

unrivaled, (BrE) **unrivalled** /ˈʌnˈraɪvəld/ *adj* incomparable, inigualable; **for sheer tactlessness she is ~** en cuanto a falta de tacto, no tiene rival *or* igual

unroadworthy /ˈʌnˈrəʊdˌwɜːrði || ʌnˈrəʊdˌwɜːði/ *adj* ‹*vehicle/condition*› no apto para circular

unroll /ˈʌnˈrəʊl/ *vt* desenrollar
■ **unroll** *vi* desenrollarse

unruffled /ˈʌnˈrʌfəld/ *adj* 1 (undisturbed) ‹*manner*› sereno 2 (smooth) liso

unruly /ˈʌnˈruːli/ *adj* **-lier, -liest** ‹*class*› indisciplinado, difícil de controlar; ‹*conduct*› rebelde; ‹*child*› revoltoso; ‹*hair*› rebelde

unsafe /ˈʌnˈseɪf/ *adj* ‹*vehicle/street/area*› inseguro, peligroso; **that car is ~ to drive** es un peligro manejar *or* (Esp) conducir ese coche; **we feel ~ at night** por la noche nos sentimos inseguros

unsaid /ˈʌnˈsed/ *adj*: **to leave sth ~** callar(se) algo, no decir* algo; **some things are better left ~** algunas cosas es mejor callarlas *or* no decirlas

unsalable, unsaleable /ˈʌnˈseɪləbəl/ *adj* invendible

unsalted /ˈʌnˈsɔːltəd || ʌnˈsɔːltɪd/ *adj* sin sal

unsatisfactory /ˈʌnˈsætəsˈfæktri || ˌʌnsætɪsˈfæktəri/ *adj* ‹*performance/work/outcome*› insatisfactorio, poco satisfactorio; ‹*explanation*› poco convincente; **the result is most ~** el resultado deja mucho que desear

unsatisfied /ˈʌnˈsætəsfaɪd || ʌnˈsætɪsfaɪd/ *adj* ‹*curiosity/demand*› insatisfecho; **she was ~ with their answer** no quedó satisfecha con su respuesta, su respuesta no la satisfizo

unsatisfying /ˈʌnˈsætəsfaɪɪŋ || ʌnˈsætɪsfaɪɪŋ/ *adj* ‹*meal*› que no llena *or* satisface; ‹*job*› poco gratificante, que no satisface; ‹*ending*› decepcionante

unsavory, (BrE) **unsavoury** /ˈʌnˈseɪvəri/ *adj* ‹*topic/character*› desagradable; ‹*deal*› sucio

unscathed /ˈʌnˈskeɪðd/ *adj* (*pred*) (unhurt) ileso; (of reputation etc) indemne; **the village survived the bombing ~** el pueblo no sufrió daños en el bombardeo

unscented /ˈʌnˈsentəd || ʌnˈsentɪd/ *adj* sin perfume

unscheduled /ˈʌnˈskedʒuːld || ʌnˈʃedjuːld/ *adj* no programado, no previsto

unschooled /ˈʌnˈskuːld/ *adj* (untrained, unversed) ‹*person*› no instruido; ‹*ear/taste*› no cultivado

unscientific /ˈʌnˈsaɪənˈtɪfɪk/ *adj* falto de rigor científico

unscramble /ˈʌnˈskræmbəl/ *vt* 1 (decipher) ‹*code/signal*› descifrar; (TV) descodificar* 2 (sort out) ‹*affairs/ideas*› poner* en orden

unscrew /ˈʌnˈskruː/ *vt* ‹*screw/panel*› destornillar, desatornillar; ‹*lid*› desenroscar*
■ **unscrew** *vi* «*screw/panel*» destornillarse, desatornillarse; «*lid*» desenroscarse*

unscrupulous /ˈʌnˈskruːpjələs || ʌnˈskruːpjʊləs/ *adj* ‹*person*› inescrupuloso, sin escrúpulos; ‹*conduct*› poco honesto, inescrupuloso

unseasonable /ˈʌnˈsiːzn̩əbəl/ *adj* ‹*weather/frost*› impropio de la estación

unseasonably /ˈʌnˈsiːzn̩əbli/ *adv*: **it's ~ cold/warm** hace un frío/calor anormal para esta época

unseasonal /ʌnˈsiːzn̩əl/ *adj* poco habitual para la estación del año

unseat /ˈʌnˈsiːt/ *vt* 1 ‹*rider*› desmontar, derribar 2 ‹*government*› derribar, derrocar*; **she was ~ed at the last election** perdió su escaño en las últimas elecciones

unsecured /ˈʌnsɪˈkjʊrd || ˌʌnsɪˈkjʊəd/ *adj* (Fin) ‹*stock*› no garantizado, sin garantía; **~ loan** préstamo *m* *or* crédito *m* sin garantía *or* caución, crédito *m* a sola firma

unseeded /ˈʌnˈsiːdəd || ʌnˈsiːdɪd/ *adj* ‹*team/player*› que no es cabeza de serie

unseeing /ˈʌnˈsiːɪŋ/ *adj* (liter): **she stared with ~ gaze** *o* **eyes at him** lo miraba sin verlo *or* con la mirada perdida; **his poor ~ eyes** sus pobres ojos ciegos

unseemly /ˈʌnˈsiːmli/ *adj* ‹*conduct/language*› impropio, indecoroso; ‹*dress*› indecoroso

unseen /ˈʌnˈsiːn/ *adj* 1 (invisible) ‹*danger/obstacle*› oculto 2 (unnoticed) sin ser visto; **they crept out ~** salieron sigilosamente sin que nadie lo advirtiera 3 (not previously seen): **to buy sth (sight) ~** comprar algo sin haberlo visto antes 4 (BrE) ‹*translation*› a primera vista

unselfconscious /ˈʌnselfˈkɑːntʃəs || ˌʌnselfˈkɒnʃəs/ *adj* natural, no cohibido; **he was quite ~ about his weight** no le preocupaba su peso

unselfish /ˈʌnˈselfɪʃ/ *adj* ‹*person*› nada egoísta, generoso; ‹*act*› desinteresado, generoso

unselfishly /ˈʌnˈselfɪʃli/ *adv* desinteresadamente, generosamente

unsentimental /ˈʌnˈsentəˈmentl̩ || ˌʌnsentɪˈmentl̩/ *adj* ‹*person/outlook*› poco sentimental

unserviceable /ˈʌnˈsɜːrvəsəbəl || ʌnˈsɜːvɪsəbəl/ *adj* ‹*machine/vehicle*› inservible, inutilizable

unsettle /ˈʌnˈsetl/ *vt* ‹*plans*› alterar; ‹*situation*› desestabilizar*; **the question clearly ~d him** la pregunta lo desconcertó visiblemente

unsettled /ˈʌnˈsetl̩d/ *adj*
A 1 (troubled) ‹*period*› agitado; ‹*childhood*› poco estable; **she's ~ and nervous** está inquieta y nerviosa 2 (changeable) ‹*weather*› inestable
B 1 (undecided) ‹*issue/question/dispute*› pendiente (de resolución), sin resolver; ‹*future*› incierto 2 (unpaid) ‹*debt/account*› pendiente, sin saldar

unsettling /ˈʌnˈsetlɪŋ/ *adj* ‹*news/prospect/doubt*› inquietante; ‹*effect*› desestabilizador, perturbador; **she found the situation very ~** la situación le producía un gran desasosiego

unshakable, unshakeable /ˈʌnˈʃeɪkəbəl/ *adj* inquebrantable

U

unshaven /ˈʌnˈʃeɪvən/ *adj* sin afeitar, sin rasurar (esp Méx)

unsheathe /ˈʌnˈʃiːð/ *vt* desenvainar, desenfundar

unshockable /ˈʌnˈʃɑːkəbəl ‖ ʌnˈʃɒkəbəl/ *adj*: **she's totally ~** no se escandaliza por nada

unsightly /ʌnˈsaɪtli/ *adj* **-lier, -liest** feo, antiestético

unsigned /ˈʌnˈsaɪnd/ *adj* sin firmar; **the contract is still ~** el contrato todavía no se ha firmado

unsinkable /ˈʌnˈsɪŋkəbəl/ *adj* ‹*ship*› que no se puede hundir; **she's ~** nada puede con ella

unskilled /ˈʌnˈskɪld/ *adj* (Lab Rel) ‹*worker*› no calificado *or* (Esp) cualificado; ‹*work*› no especializado

unskimmed /ʌnˈskɪmd/ *adj* entero, sin descremar *or* (Esp) desnatar, no descremada *or* (Esp) desnatada

unsmiling /ˈʌnˈsmaɪlɪŋ/ *adj* adusto

unsociable /ˈʌnˈsəʊʃəbəl/ *adj* ‹*person/disposition*› insociable, poco sociable, huraño; **at an ~ hour** a una hora intempestiva

unsocial hours /ˈʌnˈsəʊʃəl/ *pl n* (BrE): **to work ~ ~** trabajar a horas fuera de lo normal

unsold /ˈʌnˈsəʊld/ *adj* no vendido; **the house remained ~ for several months** la casa estuvo sin venderse varios meses

unsolicited /ˈʌnsəˈlɪsətəd ‖ ˌʌnsəˈlɪsɪtɪd/ *adj* que no se ha pedido *or* solicitado; **~ mail** *propaganda que se recibe por correo*; **~ manuscript** original *m* no solicitado

unsolved /ˈʌnˈsɑːlvd ‖ ʌnˈsɒlvd/ *adj* no resuelto; **the murder is still ~** el asesinato continúa sin esclarecerse *or* resolverse

unsophisticated /ˈʌnsəˈfɪstəkeɪtəd ‖ ˌʌnsəˈfɪstɪkeɪtɪd/ *adj* ‹*person*› sencillo; (naïve) ingenuo; ‹*tastes/technology*› simple, poco sofisticado

unsound /ˈʌnˈsaʊnd/ *adj* ‹*floorboards/foundations*› poco sólido *or* seguro; ‹*argument*› poco sólido; ‹*health*› precario; **to be of ~ mind** (Law) tener* perturbadas las facultades mentales; **the building is structurally ~** los cimientos y las paredes del edificio no son sólidos

unsparing /ˈʌnˈsperɪŋ ‖ ʌnˈspeərɪŋ/ *adj* ‹*criticism/severity/judgment*› implacable, despiadado; **he was ~ in his efforts** no regateó *or* escatimó esfuerzos

unspeakable /ˈʌnˈspiːkəbəl/ *adj* ‹*evil/cruelty*› incalificable, atroz; ‹*joy/ecstasy*› indescriptible, inefable

unspeakably /ˈʌnˈspiːkəbli/ *adv* ‹*arrogant/tedious*› insoportablemente

unspecified /ˈʌnˈspesəfaɪd ‖ ʌnˈspesɪfaɪd/ *adj* no especificado, indeterminado

unspectacular /ˈʌnspekˈtækjələr ‖ ˌʌnspekˈtækjʊlə(r)/ *adj* ‹*progress/career*› nada espectacular

unspoiled /ˈʌnˈspɔɪld/, (BrE also) **unspoilt** /ˈʌnˈspɔɪlt/ *adj* ‹*countryside*› que conserva su belleza natural

unspoken /ˈʌnˈspəʊkən/ *adj* ‹*agreement/approval*› tácito; ‹*wish*› no expresado, íntimo

unsporting /ˈʌnˈspɔːrtɪŋ ‖ ʌnˈspɔːtɪŋ/ *adj* (esp BrE) antideportivo, poco deportivo

unsportsmanlike /ˈʌnˈspɔːrtsmənlaɪk ‖ ʌnˈspɔːtsmənlaɪk/ *adj* antideportivo, poco deportivo

unstable /ˈʌnˈsteɪbəl/ *adj* **1** (unsteady) ‹*structure/foundation*› inestable, poco firme *or* sólido **2** (not secure) ‹*government/weather/person*› inestable; **economically ~** sin estabilidad económica **3** (changeable) ‹*prices*› variable **4** (Chem, Nucl Phys) ‹*compound/atom*› inestable

unsteadily /ˈʌnˈstedḷi/ *adv* de modo inseguro *or* vacilante

unsteady /ˈʌnˈstedi/ *adj* ‹*chair/ladder*› inestable, poco firme; ‹*walk/step*› vacilante, inseguro; ‹*hand*› tembloroso; ‹*voice*› tembloroso, entrecortado; **he was ~ on his feet** *o* **legs** caminaba con paso vacilante *or* inseguro

unstick /ˈʌnˈstɪk/ *vt* (*past & past p* **unstuck**) despegar*, quitar

unstinting /ˈʌnˈstɪntɪŋ/ *adj*: **his ~ generosity** su generosidad sin límites; **to be ~ IN sth**: **they were ~ in their efforts** no escatimaron esfuerzos; **he was ~ in his praise** fue pródigo en sus alabanzas

unstintingly /ˈʌnˈstɪntɪŋli/ *adv* ‹*work*› infatigablemente, incansablemente; ‹*praise/give*› con prodigalidad

unstop /ˈʌnˈstɑːp ‖ ʌnˈstɒp/ *vt* **-pp-** ‹*drain/pipe*› desatascar*, destapar (AmL)

unstoppable /ˈʌnˈstɑːpəbəl ‖ ʌnˈstɒpəbəl/ *adj* incontenible, imparable

unstuck¹ /ˈʌnˈstʌk/ *past & past p of* **unstick**

unstuck² *adj* despegado; ***to come ~*** «*label/stamp*» despegarse*; (fail, founder): **that's where your theory comes ~** ahí es donde tu teoría hace agua *or* se viene abajo; **he came ~ when he tried to use the card again** el plan le falló cuando quiso volver a usar la tarjeta

unsubscribe /ˌʌnsʌbsˈkraɪb/ *vi* (on a website) darse* de baja, cancelar la suscripción

unsubstantiated /ˈʌnsəbˈstæntʃieɪtəd ‖ ˌʌnsəbˈstænʃieɪtɪd/ *adj* no corroborado, no fundamentado

unsubtle /ˈʌnˈsʌtḷ/ *adj* poco sutil

unsuccessful /ˈʌnsəkˈsesfəl/ *adj* ‹*attempt*› infructuoso, fallido, vano; **the ~ outcome of the talks** el fracaso de las negociaciones; **to be ~ with men/women** no tener* éxito con los hombres/las mujeres; **we regret to inform you that your application has been ~** lamentamos informarle que no ha sido seleccionado; **they were ~ in their attempt to find the treasure** fracasaron en su intento de encontrar el tesoro

unsuccessfully /ˈʌnsəkˈsesfəli/ *adv* en vano, sin éxito, sin resultado alguno

unsuitable /ˈʌnˈsuːtəbəl/ *adj* ‹*clothing*› poco apropiado *or* adecuado; ‹*candidate*› poco idóneo; ‹*moment/time*› inconveniente; **the weather is ~ for sailing** el tiempo no es indicado para salir a navegar; **this program is ~ for children** este programa no es apropiado *or* es inconveniente para niños

unsuitably /ˈʌnˈsuːtəbli/ *adv* inadecuadamente, inapropiadamente

unsuited /ˈʌnˈsuːtəd ‖ ʌnˈsuːtɪd/ *adj* (*pred*) **to be ~ TO**: **her clothes are ~ to the climate/occasion** su ropa no es la apropiada *or* la adecuada *or* la indicada para el clima/la ocasión; **she is ~ to this work** no sirve para este trabajo; **they are completely ~ (to each other)** son totalmente incompatibles

unsullied /ˈʌnˈsʌlid/ *adj* (liter) impoluto (liter), inmaculado, sin mancha; **~ by sth** no ensuciado por algo

unsung /ˈʌnˈsʌŋ/ *adj*: **the ~ heroes of the revolution** los héroes olvidados de la revolución

unsupported /ˈʌnsəˈpɔːrtəd ‖ ˌʌnsəˈpɔːtɪd/ *adj* **1** ‹*structure*› sin base *or* apoyo; **he's unable to walk ~** no puede caminar sin ayuda **2** ‹*claim/statement*› sin pruebas que lo corroboren *or* respalden

unsure /ˈʌnˈʃʊr ‖ ʌnˈʃʊə(r), ʌnˈʃɔː(r)/ *adj* (uncertain) inseguro, indeciso; **to be ~ ABOUT sth**: **I'm ~ about that** no estoy seguro de eso; **I'm ~ about asking her** no sé si pedírselo o no; **to be ~ OF sth**: **I'm ~ of my own feelings** me siento inseguro de mis sentimientos; **to be ~ of oneself** estar* *or* sentirse* inseguro de sí mismo

unsurpassed /ˈʌnsərˈpæst ‖ ˌʌnsəˈpɑːst/ *adj* ‹*beauty/mastery*› sin igual, sin par (liter); **he is ~ in his knowledge of the subject** nadie lo supera en conocimiento del tema

unsuspecting /ˈʌnsəˈspektɪŋ/ *adj* desprevenido, confiado; **to be ~** no sospechar nada

unsweetened /ˈʌnˈswiːtṇd/ *adj* (without sugar) sin azúcar; (without sweeteners) sin edulcorantes

unswerving /ʌnˈswɜːrvɪŋ ‖ ʌnˈswɜːvɪŋ/ *adj* ‹*loyalty*› inquebrantable, a toda prueba; ‹*determination*› férreo, a toda prueba

unsympathetic /ˈʌnˈsɪmpəˈθetɪk/ *adj* **1** (showing no sympathy) ‹*person/attitude*› indiferente, poco comprensivo **2** (unfavorable) ‹*account*› adverso, desfavorable; **she was ~ to our cause** no veía nuestra causa con simpatía **3** (unlikable) ‹*character*› antipático, poco agradable

unsystematic /ˈʌnˈsɪstəˈmætɪk/ *adj* poco sistemático, sin método

untainted /ˈʌnˈteɪntəd ‖ ʌnˈteɪntɪd/ *adj* ‹*food/water*› no contaminado; ‹*reputation*› sin mancha *or* tacha, intachable, intacto

untamed /ˈʌnˈteɪmd/ *adj* ‹*animal*› sin domar; ‹*wilderness/forests*› virgen, agreste; ‹*passion/forces of nature*› indómito

untangle /ˈʌnˈtæŋgəl/ *vt* ‹*hair/threads*› desenredar, desenmarañar; ‹*mystery*› esclarecer*, dilucidar, desentrañar

untapped /ˈʌnˈtæpt/ *adj* sin explotar

untarnished /ˈʌnˈtɑːrnɪʃt ‖ ʌnˈtɑːnɪʃt/ *adj* sin tacha, sin mancha

U

untaught /ˈʌnˈtɔːt/ *adj* (liter) (uneducated) (pej) sin instrucción, ignorante

untaxed /ˈʌnˈtækst/ *adj* libre de impuestos

untenable /ˈʌnˈtenəbəl/ *adj* (frml) insostenible, indefendible

untended /ˈʌnˈtendəd || ʌnˈtendɪd/ *adj* [1] ‹*garden*› descuidado, abandonado [2] ‹*wound*› descuidado; ‹*patient*› desatendido

untested /ˈʌnˈtestəd || ʌnˈtestɪd/ *adj* ‹*theory*› no verificado *or* probado; ‹*product/device*› no probado, no puesto a prueba

unthinkable¹ /ˈʌnˈθɪŋkəbəl/ *adj* inconcebible, inimaginable

unthinkable² *n* **the ~** lo inconcebible, lo inimaginable

unthinking /ˈʌnˈθɪŋkɪŋ/ *adj* [1] (not thinking) ‹*rage*› irreflexivo; ‹*moment*› de irreflexión [2] (uncritical) ‹*acceptance*› precipitado

untidily /ˈʌnˈtaɪdli || ʌnˈtaɪdɪli/ *adv* descuidadamente, sin cuidado, desprolijamente (RPl)

untidiness /ˈʌnˈtaɪdinəs || ʌnˈtaɪdinɪs/ *n* [u] (of person's appearance) desaliño *m*, lo descuidado, desprolijidad *f* (RPl); (of room, desk) desorden *m*, desprolijidad *f* (RPl); (of handwriting, schoolwork) lo descuidado, lo desprolijo (RPl)

untidy /ˈʌnˈtaɪdi/ *adj* **-dier, -diest** ‹*room/desk*› desordenado; ‹*appearance*› desaliñado, descuidado, desprolijo (RPl); ‹*writing/schoolwork*› descuidado, desprolijo (RPl); ‹*person*› desordenado, desprolijo (RPl)

untie /ˈʌnˈtaɪ/ *vt* **unties, untying, untied** ‹*knot*› deshacer*, desatar; ‹*shoelaces*› desatar, desamarrar (AmL exc RPl); ‹*dog/horse*› soltar*, desatar, desamarrar (AmL exc RPl)

until¹ /ʌnˈtɪl, ənˈtɪl/ *conj* hasta que; **please wait ~ I arrive** por favor espera hasta que yo llegue; **she didn't go to bed ~ Tom got back** no se acostó hasta que Tom (no) volvió; **I knew she wouldn't go to bed ~ Tom got back** yo sabía que no se iba a acostar hasta que Tom (no) volviera

until² *prep* hasta; **~ now/then** hasta ahora/entonces

untimely /ˈʌnˈtaɪmli/ *adj* [1] ‹*death/end*› prematuro [2] ‹*announcement*› inoportuno; ‹*arrival*› inoportuno, intempestivo

untiring /ˈʌnˈtaɪrɪŋ || ʌnˈtaɪərɪŋ/ *adj* infatigable, incansable

untiringly /ˈʌnˈtaɪrɪŋli || ʌnˈtaɪərɪŋli/ *adv* ‹*work*› infatigablemente, incansablemente

untold /ˈʌnˈtəʊld/ *adj* [1] (incalculable) (*before n*) ‹*wealth/sums*› incalculable, fabuloso; ‹*misery/pleasures*› indecible, inenarrable, inefable [2] (not told) ‹*secret*› sin desvelar, sin revelar

untouchable /ˈʌnˈtʌtʃəbəl/ *adj* intocable

Untouchable *n* intocable *mf*

untouched /ˈʌnˈtʌtʃt/ *adj* [1] (not handled) intacto, sin tocar; **it is ~ by human hand(s)** no ha sido tocado por la mano del hombre; **he left his food ~** no probó la comida [2] (safe, unharmed): **miraculously the church was ~** milagrosamente la iglesia quedó intacta

untoward /ˈʌnˈtɔːrd , ˌʌntəˈwɔːrd || ˈʌntəˈwɔːd/ *adj* (frml) [1] (adverse) perjudicial, adverso; **I hope nothing ~ has happened** espero que no haya pasado nada (que haya que lamentar) [2] (unseemly, improper) indecoroso, indigno

U

untrained /ˈʌnˈtreɪnd/ *adj* falto de formación *or* capacitación; ‹*teacher*› sin título; **to the ~ eye/ear ...** para (el ojo/oído de) quien no es experto ...

untrammeled, (BrE) **untrammelled** /ˈʌnˈtræməld/ *adj* (liter) **~ BY sth** libre DE algo

untranslatable /ˈʌntrænsˈleɪtəbəl/ *adj* intraducible

untreated /ˈʌnˈtriːtəd || ʌnˈtriːtɪd/ *adj* ‹*sewage/waste*› sin tratar *or* procesar; **~, the disease can be fatal** si no se trata, la enfermedad puede ser mortal

untried /ˈʌnˈtraɪd/ *adj* [1] (not tested) ‹*method*› no probado; ‹*person*› no puesto a prueba [2] (Law) ‹*person*› no procesado; ‹*case*› no sometido a juicio

untroubled /ˈʌnˈtrʌbəld/ *adj* ‹*expression/conscience*› tranquilo; ‹*period/life*› tranquilo, apacible; **she seemed ~ by the prospect** no parecía que la perspectiva la inquietase *or* preocupase

untrue /ˈʌnˈtruː/ *adj* [1] (false) ‹*statement*› falso; **it is ~ (to say) that ...** es falso *or* no es cierto que ... [2] (unfaithful) (liter) (*pred*) **to be ~ TO sb/sth**: **to be ~ to one's principles** no ser* fiel a sus (*or* mis *etc*) principios; **my only love was ~ to me** mi único amor me fue infiel

untrustworthy /ˈʌnˈtrʌstˌwɜːrði || ʌnˈtrʌstˌwɜːði/ *adj* ‹*person*› de poca confianza; ‹*source*› no fidedigno; **she's totally ~** no es de fiar en absoluto

untruth /ˈʌnˈtruːθ/ *n* (*pl* **untruths** /ʌnˈtruːðz/) (frml) falsedad *f*

untruthful /ˈʌnˈtruːθfəl/ *adj* ‹*account/answer*› falso; ‹*person*› falso, mentiroso

untypical /ˈʌnˈtɪpɪkəl/ *adj* atípico, poco representativo

unused *adj*

A /ˈʌnˈjuːzd/ [1] (new) sin estrenar, nuevo [2] (not made use of) ‹*land*› no utilizado *or* aprovechado, ocioso

B /ˈʌnˈjuːst/ (*pred*) **to be ~ TO sth/-ING** no estar* acostumbrado A algo/+ INF

unusual /ˈʌnˈjuːʒuəl/ *adj* ‹*illness/opinion/sight*› poco corriente *or* común, fuera de lo corriente *or* común, inusual; **he spoke with ~ frankness** habló con inusitada *or* insólita franqueza; **that's ~ for her** eso es raro en ella; **did you notice anything ~ about him?** ¿le notaste algo raro *or* fuera de lo normal?; **it's ~ for him to be still in bed** es raro que todavía no se haya levantado

unusually /ˈʌnˈjuːʒuəli/ *adv* ‹*tall/windy/complicated*› excepcionalmente, inusitadamente; **he was in an ~ happy mood** estaba de muy buen humor, lo cual es raro *or* insólito en él; **she was ~ talkative** estaba más conversadora que de costumbre

unvarnished /ˈʌnˈvɑːrnɪʃt || ʌnˈvɑːnɪʃt/ *adj* [1] (not varnished) sin barnizar [2] (plain): **the ~ truth** la verdad sin adornos, la pura verdad

unveil /ˈʌnˈveɪl/ *vt* ‹*plaque/statue*› descubrir*, develar (AmL)

unversed /ˈʌnˈvɜːrst || ʌnˈvɜːst/ *adj* (*pred*) **to be ~ IN sth** no ser* versado EN algo

unvoiced /ˈʌnˈvɔɪst/ *adj* no expresado *or* manifestado

unwaged /ˈʌnˈweɪdʒd/ *pl n* (BrE) no asalariados *mpl*, personas *fpl* sin trabajo remunerado

unwanted /ˈʌnˈwɔːntəd || ʌnˈwɒntɪd/ *adj* ‹*pregnancy/child*› no deseado; ‹*object*› superfluo, que no se necesita; **I feel ~ here** siento que estoy de más aquí

unwarranted /ˈʌnˈwɔːrəntəd || ʌnˈwɒrəntɪd/ *adj* injustificado, sin justificación alguna

unwary /ˈʌnˈweri || ʌnˈweəri/ *adj* **-rier, -riest** incauto, desprevenido, confiado

unwashed¹ /ˈʌnˈwɔːʃt || ʌnˈwɒʃt/ *adj* sucio, sin lavar

unwashed² *pl n* **the great ~** (hum & pej) el populacho (pey), la plebe (pey)

unwavering /ˈʌnˈweɪvərɪŋ/ *adj* ‹*loyalty/belief*› inquebrantable; ‹*determination*› férreo, a toda prueba; ‹*gaze/stare*› fijo

unwelcome /ˈʌnˈwelkəm/ *adj* ‹*visit*› inoportuno; ‹*guest*› inoportuno, poco grato; ‹*news*› desagradable, poco grato; ‹*suggestion*› inoportuno, fuera de lugar; **we were made to feel ~** nos hicieron sentir que estábamos de más

unwelcoming /ˈʌnˈwelkəmɪŋ/ *adj* ‹*landscape*› inhóspito; ‹*person*› frío, antipático; ‹*house*› poco acogedor

unwell /ˈʌnˈwel/ *adj* mal; **to be** *o* **feel ~** sentirse* mal, no sentirse* bien; **he looks ~** tiene mala cara

unwholesome /ˈʌnˈhəʊlsəm/ *adj* [1] (unhealthy) ‹*diet/climate*› poco sano *or* saludable, malsano [2] (unpleasant) ‹*smell/appearance/person*› desagradable

unwieldy /ʌnˈwiːldi/ *adj* **-dier, -diest** [1] ‹*tool/weapon/tome*› pesado y difícil de manejar [2] ‹*system/procedure*› rígido, poco flexible

unwilling /ˈʌnˈwɪlɪŋ/ *adj* mal dispuesto; **to be ~ to + INF** no querer* + INF, no estar* dispuesto a + INF

unwillingly /ˈʌnˈwɪlɪŋli/ *adv* de mala gana, a regañadientes

unwind /ˈʌnˈwaɪnd/ (*past & past p* **unwound**) *vt* desenrollar; **to come unwound** desenrollarse

■ **unwind** *vi*

A ‹‹*rope/tape*›› desenrollarse; ‹‹*plot*›› irse* desarrollando

B (relax) (colloq) relajarse

unwise /ˈʌnˈwaɪz/ *adj* ‹*action/decision*› poco prudente *or* sensato, desaconsejable; **anyone ~ enough to try will be punished** se castigará al insensato que lo intente; **it**

would be ~ of you to do that hacer eso no sería sensato

unwitting /ˈʌnˈwɪtɪŋ/ *adj* involuntario

unwittingly /ˈʌnˈwɪtɪŋli/ *adv* sin ser consciente (de ello), sin darse* cuenta

unwonted /ˈʌnˈwɔːntəd || ʌnˈwəʊntɪd/ *adj* (frml) inusitado, insólito, desacostumbrado

unworkable /ˈʌnˈwɜːrkəbəl || ʌnˈwɜːkəbəl/ *adj* impracticable, no viable

unworldly /ˈʌnˈwɜːrldli || ʌnˈwɜːldli/ *adj* [1] (unconcerned with material things) poco materialista, idealista [2] (unsophisticated) con poco mundo

unworthy /ˈʌnˈwɜːrði || ʌnˈwɜːði/ *adj* **-thier, -thiest** indigno; **to be ~ OF sb/sth** no ser* digno DE algn/algo; **a subject ~ of our attention** un tema que no merece nuestra atención *or* que no es digno de nuestra atención; **to be ~ to + INF** no ser* digno DE + INF

unwound /ˈʌnˈwaʊnd/ *past & past p of* **unwind**

unwrap /ˈʌnˈræp/ *vt* **-pp-** desenvolver*, abrir*

unwritten /ˈʌnˈrɪtn/ *adj* ‹*rule*› no escrito, sobreentendido; ‹*agreement*› verbal, de palabra; ‹*constitution/law*› basado en el derecho consuetudinario

unyielding /ˈʌnˈjiːldɪŋ/ *adj* ‹*person*› inflexible; ‹*opposition*› implacable, rígido

unzip /ˈʌnˈzɪp/ **-pp-** *vt* [1] (Clothing): **could you ~ me/my dress?** ¿me bajas la cremallera *or* (AmL) el cierre *or* (Méx, Ven) el zíper? [2] (Comput) descomprimir

up¹ /ʌp/ *adv*

Sense I

A [1] (in upward direction): **~ a bit ... left a bit** un poco más arriba ... un poco a la izquierda; **we went all the way ~ to the top** subimos hasta la cima; **we saw them on the way ~** los vimos cuando subíamos; **from the waist ~** desde la cintura para arriba; **~ United!** (BrE) ¡arriba el United! [2] (upstairs): **I dashed back ~ to fetch my jacket** volví a subir corriendo a buscar mi chaqueta

B [1] (of position) arriba; **~ here/there** aquí/allí arriba; **300ft ~** a una altura de 300 pies [2] (upstairs, on upper floor): **your book is ~ in my room** tu libro está arriba en mi habitación [3] (raised, pointing upward): **with the lid/blinds ~** con la tapa levantada/las persianas levantadas *or* subidas; **face ~** boca arriba [4] (removed): **I had the floorboards ~** había quitado *or* levantado las tablas del suelo

C [1] (upright): **the nurse helped him ~** la enfermera lo ayudó a sentarse [2] (out of bed): **they're not ~ yet** todavía no se han levantado; **we were ~ all night** pasamos la noche en vela; **she's ~ and about again** (colloq) está dando guerra otra vez (fam)

D [1] (of numbers, volume, intensity): **she had the volume ~ high** tenía el volumen muy alto; **prices are 5% ~** *o* **~ (by) 5% on last month** los precios han aumentado un 5% con respecto al mes pasado; **from $25/the age of 11 ~** a partir de 25 dólares/de los 11 años [2] (in league, table, hierarchy): **~ ten places from last year** diez puestos más arriba que el año pasado; **it's a step ~ for me** para mí es un paso adelante; **from the rank of lieutenant ~** desde el rango de teniente para arriba

E [1] (in or toward north): **~ north** en el norte; **the journey ~ from Munich** el viaje desde Munich hacia el norte [2] (at or to another place): **the path ~ to the house** el sendero hasta la casa; **I'm going ~ to John's for the weekend** voy a casa de John a pasar el fin de semana; **to go ~ to town** (esp BrE) ir* a la ciudad (*or* a Londres *etc*)

F (in position, erected): **is the tent ~?** ¿ya han armado la tienda *or* (AmL) la carpa?; **the pictures/shelves are ~** los cuadros/estantes están colocados *or* puestos

G (going on) (colloq): **what's ~ with you?** ¿a ti qué te pasa?; **what's ~?** (what's the matter?) ¿qué pasa?; (as greeting) (AmE) ¿qué hay? (colloq), ¿qué onda? (AmL arg), ¿qué hubo *or* quiubo? (Chi, Col, Méx, Ven fam)

H (finished): **your time is ~** se te ha acabado el tiempo

I (Sport) [1] (ahead in competition): **they're three goals ~ on the home team** le van ganando por tres goles al equipo local; ***to be one ~ on sb*** tener* una ventaja sobre algn [2] (for each side) (AmE): **the game was tied 15 ~** empataron 15 a 15

J (under consideration): **she will be ~ before the board/judge** comparecerá ante la junta/el juez

Sense II (*in phrases*)

A **up against** [1] (next to) contra [2] (confronted by): **you don't know what you're ~ against** no sabes a lo que te enfrentas; ***to be ~ against it*** estar* contra las cuerdas

B **up and down** [1] (vertically): **to jump ~ and down** dar* saltos; **to look sb ~ and down** mirar a algn de arriba abajo [2] (back and forth) de arriba abajo [3] (of mood): **she's been rather ~ and down** ha tenido bastantes altibajos de humor

C **up for** (subject to): **the motion ~ for debate today** la moción que sale hoy a debate *or* se debate hoy; **there are five nominees ~ for treasurer** hay cinco candidatos a tesorero

D **up on** (knowledgeable) (*pred*): **how well ~ are you on what's been happening?** ¿cuánto sabes *or* qué tan enterado estás de lo que ha estado sucediendo?

E **up till** *o* **until** hasta

Sense III **up to**

A (as far as, as much as) hasta; **~ to here/now/a certain point** hasta aquí/ahora/cierto punto; **~ to twice as big** hasta el doble de grande

B [1] (equal to): **it isn't ~ to the usual standard** no es del alto nivel al que estamos acostumbrados; ▸**come up to 2** [2] (capable of): **she's not ~ to the job** no tiene las condiciones necesarias para el trabajo, no puede con el trabajo (fam); **do you feel ~ to going out?** ¿te sientes con fuerzas/ánimos (como) para salir?; **my spelling is not ~ to much** (BrE) mi ortografía deja bastante que desear

C (depending on): **that's entirely ~ to you** eso, como tú quieras; **it's not ~ to me to decide** no me corresponde a mí decidir, no soy yo quien tiene que decidir

D **to be ~ to sth** (colloq): **they're ~ to their usual tricks** están haciendo de las suyas; **I'm sure they're ~ to something** (planning) estoy segura de que algo están tramando *or* algo se traen entre manos; (doing) estoy segura de que algo (*or* alguna travesura *etc*) están haciendo; **she's ~ to no good** no anda en nada bueno; **what have you been ~ to lately?** ¿en qué has andado últimamente?

up² *prep*

A [1] (in upward direction): **to go ~ the stairs/hill** subir la escalera/colina; **he hid the money ~ the chimney** escondió el dinero en la chimenea [2] (at higher level): **80ft ~ the cliff** a 80 pies del pie del acantilado; **further ~ the salary scale** más arriba en el escalafón

B [1] (along): **to go/come ~ the river** ir*/venir* por el río; **the journey ~ the coast** el viaje a lo largo de la costa; **he travels ~ and down the country** viaja por todo el país; **she walked ~ and down the room** iba de un lado a otro de la habitación [2] (further along): **it's just ~ the road** está un poco más allá *or* adelante

up³ *adj*

A (*before n*) (going upward): **the ~ escalator** la escalera mecánica para subir

B (elated) (AmE colloq) (*pred*): **I feel really ~ at the moment** me siento como en las nubes

up⁴ **-pp-** *vt* (colloq) ‹*price/costs*› aumentar, subir; ‹*bid/offer*› aumentar, superar

■ **up** *vi*: **to ~ and go** agarrar *or* (esp Esp) coger* e irse*

up⁵ *n*: ***to be on the ~ and ~*** (colloq) (honest) (AmE) «*businessman/salesperson*» ser* de buena ley, ser* de fiar; (succeeding) (BrE) «*business/company*» marchar *or* ir* cada vez mejor, estar* en alza; **life's little ~s and downs** las vicisitudes de la vida; **their marriage has had its ~s and downs** su matrimonio ha tenido sus altibajos

up: **~-and-coming** /ˈʌpənˈkʌmɪŋ/ *adj* (*before n*): **an ~-and-coming artist/actor** un artista/actor que promete *or* que llegará lejos *or* con mucho futuro; **~beat** *adj* (colloq) optimista; **~braid** /ʌpˈbreɪd/ *vt* (frml) reprender, reconvenir* (frml); **~bringing** /ˈʌpˌbrɪŋɪŋ/ *n* (*no pl*) educación *f*; **~coming** /ˈʌpˈkʌmɪŋ/ *adj* (*before n*) ‹*election/meeting*› próximo, que se acerca; **~country** /ʌpˈkʌntri/ *adv* tierra adentro, hacia el interior

update¹ /ʌpˈdeɪt/ *vt* [1] ‹*manual/report/information*› poner* al día, actualizar*; ‹*machinery/technology*› poner* al día, modernizar*; ‹*file*› (Comput) poner* al día [2] (give latest information to) mantener* al tanto *or* al corriente

update² /ˈʌpdeɪt/ *n* [1] (information): **to give sb an ~ on sth** poner* a algn al día *or* al tanto de algo; **now for the latest ~ on the situation** ahora las últimas novedades sobre la situación 2 (sth updated) puesta *f* al día, actualización *f*

upend /ʌp'end/ *vt* poner* vertical, parar (AmL)

upfront¹ /'ʌp'frʌnt/ *adj*
A (Busn) (*before n*) ‹*costs/commitment*› inicial
B (open, honest) (colloq) ‹*person/statement*› franco, abierto

upfront² *adv* por adelantado

upgrade /ʌp'greɪd/ *vt* 1 (raise status of) ‹*employee*› ascender*, elevar de categoría; ‹*job*› elevar la categoría de; ‹*salaries*› aumentar, mejorar; **they ~d it to a three-star hotel** lo subieron a la categoría de hotel de tres estrellas 2 (improve) ‹*facilities*› mejorar; ‹*service/computer*› elevar el nivel de prestaciones de

upheaval /ʌp'hi:vəl/ *n* [u c] **a period of great social/political ~** una época de gran agitación social/política; **all the ~ of moving house** todo el trastorno que implica una mudanza; **it was a terrible emotional ~ for her** fue muy traumático para ella

upheld /ʌp'held/ *past & past p of* **uphold**

uphill¹ /'ʌp'hɪl/ *adv* cuesta arriba, en subida

uphill² *adj* ‹*path*› en cuesta, en subida; ‹*battle/task*› arduo; **it was an ~ struggle** fue muy difícil, nos (*or* les *etc*) costó mucho

up: **~hold** /ʌp'həʊld/ *vt* (*past & past p* **~held**) 1 ‹*tradition*› conservar; ‹*faith/principle*› mantener*; **to ~hold the Constitution** respetar y defender la constitución 2 (Law) ‹*decision/verdict*› confirmar; **~holder** /ʌp'həʊldər || ˌʌp'həʊldə(r)/ *n* defensor, -sora *m,f*

upholster /ʌp'həʊlstər || ʌp'həʊlstə(r)/ *vt* tapizar*

upholstery /ʌp'həʊlstəri/ *n* [u] 1 (stuffing, springs) relleno *m* 2 (covers) tapizado *m* 3 (craft, trade) tapicería *f*

up: **~keep** *n* [u] 1 (running, maintenance) mantenimiento *m* 2 (costs) gastos *mpl* de mantenimiento; **~land** /'vplənd/ *adj* (*before n*) **~land regions** tierras *fpl* altas; **~lift** /'ʌplɪft/ *vt* ‹*spirit/mind*› elevar; **I felt ~lifted** se me elevó el espíritu; **~lifting** /ʌp'lɪftɪŋ/ *adj* (spiritually) que eleva el espíritu; (emotionally) que anima, que levanta el ánimo

upload *vt* (Comput) cargar*, subir

upmarket¹ /'ʌp'mɑ:rkət || ˌʌp'mɑ:kɪt/ *adj* ‹*store/hotel/car*› de categoría, para gente pudiente

upmarket² *adv*: **to go/move ~** subir de categoría

upon /ə'pɑ:n || ə'pɒn/ *prep* (frml) 1 (on): **she placed the cards ~ the table** puso las cartas sobre la mesa; **~ their arrival, they were shown to their room** a su llegada, se los condujo a su habitación; **there are trains ~ the hour, every hour** hay un tren por hora, a la hora en punto; **~ -ING** al + INF; **~ entering the room** al entrar a la habitación 2 (indicating imminent or unexpected arrival) **to be ~ sb**: **the enemy was ~ us** teníamos al enemigo encima; **winter is already ~ us** ya estamos prácticamente en invierno 3 (indicating large numbers): **thousands ~ thousands** miles y miles

upper¹ /'ʌpər || 'ʌpə(r)/ *adj* (*before n*)
A 1 (spatially, numerically) superior; ‹*lip*› superior, de arriba; **~ age limit** límite *m* (máximo) de edad 2 (in rank, importance) ‹*ranks/echelons*› superior, más elevado; **the ~ chamber** *o* **~ house** (Pol) la cámara alta
B (Geog) alto; **the U~ Danube** el alto Danubio; **~ Manhattan** el norte de Manhattan

upper² *n*
A 1 (of shoe) *parte superior del calzado* 2 ***to be on one's ~s*** (colloq) estar* más pobre que las ratas
B (drug) (sl) anfeta *f* (arg)

upper: **~ case** *n* [u] caja *f* alta; (*before n*) **an ~-case letter** una letra mayúscula; **~ class** *n* clase *f* alta; **~-class** /'ʌpər'klæs || ˌʌpə'klɑ:s/ *adj* de clase alta; **~-crust** /'ʌpər'krʌst || ˌʌpə'krʌst/ *adj* (colloq & hum) de la flor y nata; **~most** *adj* ‹*branches/floor/part*› más alto; **what was ~most in my mind** lo que más me preocupaba, lo que tenía presente por encima de todo

uppity /'ʌpəti/ *adj* (colloq): **to be ~** darse* aires de superioridad; **she got ~** se le subieron los humos

upright¹ /'ʌpraɪt/ *adj* 1 (vertical) ‹*post/position*› vertical; ‹*posture*› derecho, erguido; **to place/stand sth ~** colocar*/poner* algo de pie *or* vertical 2 (honest) ‹*character/citizen*› recto

upright² *n*
A (Archit, Const) montante *m*
B **~ (piano)** piano *m* vertical

up: **~rising** *n* levantamiento *m*, alzamiento *m*; **~river** /'ʌp'rɪvər || ˌʌp'rɪvə(r)/ *adv* río arriba; **~roar** *n* [u] (noise, chaos) tumulto *m*, alboroto *m*, barahúnda *f*; (outcry) protesta *f* airada

uproarious /ʌp'rɔ:riəs/ *adj* 1 (noisy) ‹*debate*› tumultuoso; ‹*applause/welcome/success*› clamoroso, estrepitoso 2 (hilarious) ‹*jokes*› divertidísimo; **~ laughter** carcajadas *fpl*

uproariously /ʌp'rɔ:riəsli/ *adv* ‹*laugh*› a carcajadas, a mandíbula batiente

uproot /ʌp'ru:t/ *vt* 1 (Hort) ‹*plant*› arrancar* de raíz, desarraigar* (téc) 2 (displace) ‹*person*› desarraigar*

upset¹ /'ʌp'set/ *adj*
A (unhappy, hurt) disgustado; (distressed) alterado; (offended) ofendido; (disappointed) desilusionado; **he would be most ~ to hear you talk like that** se disgustaría mucho si te oyera hablar así
B (Med): **I have an ~ stomach** estoy *or* ando mal del estómago, estoy descompuesto (del estómago) (esp AmL)

upset² /'ʌp'set/ *vt* (*pres p* **upsetting**; *past & past p* **upset**)
A (hurt) disgustar; (distress) alterar, afectar; (offend) ofender; **his thoughtlessness ~ her** le molestó su desconsideración
B (make ill): **it ~s my stomach** me cae mal, me sienta mal (al estómago)
C 1 (throw into disorder) ‹*plans/calculations*› desbaratar, trastornar; **to ~ the balance of sth** desequilibrar algo 2 (knock over) ‹*jug/boat*› volcar*; ‹*milk/contents*› derramar

upset³ /'ʌpset/ *n*
A [c u] 1 (disturbance, upheaval) trastorno *m*; **a big ~ to their plans** un gran revés *or* contratiempo para sus planes 2 (emotional trouble) disgusto *m*
B [c] (surprise result) (Pol, Sport) sorpresa *f*
C [c] (Med): **to have a stomach ~** estar* mal del estómago, estar* descompuesto del estómago (esp AmL)

upsetting /'ʌp'setɪŋ/ *adj* ‹*news*› (distressing) triste; (shocking) terrible; ‹*behavior*› ofensivo; **the separation was very ~ for the child** la separación afectó *or* perturbó mucho al niño

upshot /'ʌpʃɑ:t || 'ʌpʃɒt/ *n*: **the ~ of it all is that ...** lo que resulta de todo esto es que ...; **what was the ~ of the discussion?** ¿en qué quedó *or* acabó la discusión?

upside down /'ʌpsaɪd/ *adj* al revés (*con la parte de arriba abajo*); **to turn sth ~ ~** ‹*object*› poner* algo boca abajo, darle* la vuelta a algo, dar* vuelta algo (CS); ‹*theory/world*› revolucionar; **the burglars turned the house ~ ~** los ladrones no dejaron cosa sin revolver en la casa, los ladrones dejaron la casa patas arriba (fam)

upstage¹ /'ʌp'steɪdʒ/ *vt* eclipsar

upstage² *adv*: **to enter/exit/stand ~** entrar por/salir* por/estar* en el fondo del escenario

upstairs¹ /'ʌp'sterz || ˌʌp'steəz/ *adv* arriba; **to be ~** estar* arriba; **to go ~** subir

upstairs² *n* (+ *sing vb*) piso *m or* planta *f* de arriba; (*before n*) ‹*window/rooms*› del piso de arriba, de arriba

up: **~standing** /ʌp'stændɪŋ/ *adj* 1 (honest, responsible) cabal, íntegro; 2 (on one's feet) (frml) (*pred*) de pie, en pie (frml); **the court will be ~standing** la sala se pondrá en pie; **~start** *n* arribista *mf*, advenedizo, -za *m,f*

upstate¹ /'ʌp'steɪt/ *adv* (AmE): **he lives ~** vive en el norte del estado (*fuera de la capital*); **to go ~** ir* hacia el norte

upstate² *adj* (AmE) ‹*voters*› de fuera de la capital; **~ New York** el norte del estado de Nueva York

up: **~stream** /'ʌp'stri:m/ *adv* río *or* corriente arriba; **~surge** *n* **~surge OF/IN sth** ‹*of/in violence*› recrudecimiento *m* DE algo; ‹*in demand/production*› aumento *m* DE *or* EN algo; **~swing** *n* **~swing (IN sth)** ‹*in production/demand*› alza *f* (EN algo)

upsydaisy /'ʌpsə'deɪzi || 'ʌpsiˌdeɪzi/ *interj* ¡upa lelé *or* lalá!

up: **~take** *n* [u] ***to be quick on the ~take*** agarrar *or* (esp Esp) coger* las cosas al vuelo; ***to be slow on the ~take*** ser* duro de mollera; **~tight** /'ʌp'taɪt/ *adj* (colloq) nervioso, tenso; **don't get so ~tight (about it)!** no te pongas

U

tan neura (por una cosa así) (fam); **~-to-date** /'ʌptə 'deɪt/ *adj* (*pred* ~ **to date**) ‹*figures/information/report*› al día, actualizado; **to be ~ to date (with sth)** estar* al día *or* al corriente (de algo); **~-to-the-minute** /'ʌptəðə 'mɪnət || ˌʌptəðə'mɪnɪt/ *adj* (*pred* ~ **to the minute**) (journ) ‹*report*› de último momento, de última hora; ‹*news*› de máxima actualidad; ‹*coverage*› completo y actualizado

uptown¹ /'ʌp'taʊn/ *adj* (AmE) ‹*bus/traffic*› que va hacia el norte/hacia el distrito residencial (de la ciudad)

uptown² *adv* (AmE): **they live/went ~** viven en/fueron hacia el norte/hacia el distrito residencial de la ciudad

up: **~turn** *n* (in demand, production) repunte *m*, mejora *f*; **~turned** /'ʌp'tɜːrnd || 'ʌptɜːnd/ *adj* ‹*end*› vuelto hacia arriba; ‹*nose*› respingón, respingado (AmL); ‹*table*› boca abajo, patas arriba

upward¹ /'ʌpwərd || 'ʌpwəd/ *adj* (*before n*) ‹*pressure/direction*› hacia arriba; ‹*movement/spiral*› ascendente; ‹*tendency*› al alza

upward², (esp BrE) **upwards** /-z/ *adv* ‹*climb/look*› hacia arriba; **face ~** boca arriba; **everyone from 60 ~** todas las personas de 60 años para arriba *or* de 60 años o más; **~ of 50 people/$100** más de 50 personas/100 dólares

upwardly mobile /'ʌpwərdli || 'ʌpwədli/ *adj* de movilidad social ascendente

Urals /'jʊrəlz || 'jʊərəlz/ *pl n* **the ~** los Urales

uranium /jʊ'reɪniəm/ *n* [u] uranio *m*

Uranus /'jʊərənəs, jʊə'reɪnəs/ *n* Urano *m*

urban /'ɜːrbən || 'ɜːbən/ *adj* ‹*area/community*› urbano; ‹*life*› urbano, en las urbes; **the ~ poor** los pobres de las ciudades; **~ renewal** remodelación *f* urbana

urbane /ɜːr'beɪn/ *adj* (frml) fino y cortés, urbano (frml)

urbanization /'ɜːrbənə'zeɪʃən/ *n* [u] urbanización *f*

urbanize /'ɜːrbənaɪz || 'ɜːbənaɪz/ *vt* urbanizar*

urchin /'ɜːrtʃən || 'ɜːtʃɪn/ *n* golfillo, -lla *m,f*, pilluelo, -la *m,f*, palomilla *mf* (Chi, Per), gamín, -mina *m,f* (Col)

Urdu /'ʊrduː || 'ʊəduː/ *n* [u] urdu *m*

ureter /jʊ'rətər || jʊə'riːtə(r)/ *n* uréter *m*

urethra /jʊ'riːθrə || jʊə'riːθrə/ *n* (*pl* **urethras** *or* **urethrae** /-θriː/) uretra *f*

urge¹ /ɜːrdʒ || ɜːdʒ/ *n* ganas *fpl*, impulso *m*; **the creative ~** el impulso creativo *or* creador; **sexual ~s** impulsos *mpl* sexuales; **he had a strong ~ to punch him** le entraron unas ganas enormes de darle un puñetazo

urge² *vt* (exhort) instar (frml), exhortar (frml); (entreat) pedir* con insistencia, rogar*; **to ~ sb to + INF** instar a algn A QUE (+ *subj*) (frml), pedirle* A algn con insistencia QUE (+ *subj*); **I ~ you to reconsider** le pido encarecidamente que lo reconsidere

Phrasal verb

- **urge on** [v ▸ o ▸ adv] ‹*person/team*› animar, alentar*; ‹*horse*› espolear; **to ~ sb on TO sth**: **their fans ~d them on to victory** los hinchas los animaron *or* alentaron a conseguir la victoria

urgency /'ɜːrdʒənsi || 'ɜːdʒənsi/ *n* [u] 1▸ (of situation, problem) urgencia *f*; **he treated it as a matter of ~** se ocupó de ello con la mayor urgencia 2▸ (of tone, plea) apremio *m*, urgencia *f*

urgent /'ɜːrdʒənt || 'ɜːdʒənt/ *adj* 1▸ (pressing) ‹*matter/case/letter*› urgente; **it's in ~ need of repair** hay que repararlo urgentemente 2▸ (insistent) ‹*tone/plea*› apremiante; ‹*knock*› insistente

urgently /'ɜːrdʒəntli/ *adv* urgentemente, con urgencia

urinal /'jʊrənl̩ || jʊə'raɪnl̩/ *n* 1▸ (place) urinario *m* 2▸ (receptacle) orinal *m*

urinary /'jʊrəneri/ *adj*: **~ tract** tracto *m* urinario

urinate /'jʊrəneɪt || 'jʊərɪneɪt/ *vi* (frml) orinar

urine /'jʊrən || 'juərɪn/ *n* [u] orina *f*

urn /ɜːrn || ɜːn/ *n* 1▸ (vase) urna *f* 2▸ (for ashes) urna *f* funeraria 3▸ (for tea, coffee) *recipiente grande para hacer o mantener caliente té, café etc*

urology /jʊ'rɑːlədʒi || jʊə'rɒlədʒi/ *n* [u] urología *f*

Uruguay /'jʊrəgwaɪ || 'jʊərəgwaɪ/ *n* Uruguay *m*

Uruguayan¹ /'jʊrə'gwaɪən || ˌjʊərə'gwaɪən/ *adj* uruguayo

Uruguayan² *n* uruguayo, -ya *m,f*

us /ʌs, *weak form* əs/ *pron*

A 1▸ (as direct object) nos; **they helped ~** nos ayudaron 2▸ (as indirect object) nos; **he gave ~ the book** nos dio el libro; **he gave it to ~** nos lo dio 3▸ (after preposition) nosotros, -tras; **for/with ~** para/con nosotros/nosotras; **there were four of ~** éramos cuatro; **he's one of ~** es de los nuestros

B (emphatic use) nosotros, -tras; **it was ~** fuimos nosotros

C 1▸ (for ourselves) (AmE colloq *or* dial) nos; **let's go and get ~ some beer** vamos a comprarnos unas cervezas 2▸ (me) (esp BrE colloq) me; **do ~ a favor, will you?** ¿me quieres hacer un favor?

US *n* (+ *sing vb*) EEUU, EE UU, EE.UU.; **she studied in the ~** estudió en los Estados Unidos

USA *n* 1▸ (= **United States of America**) EEUU, EE UU, EE.UU. 2▸ (= **United States Army**) ejército *m* estadounidense *or* de los EEUU

usable, useable /'juːzəbəl/ *adj* utilizable

USAF *n* (= **United States Air Force**) la Fuerza Aérea de los EEUU

usage /'juːsɪdʒ/ *n* 1▸ [u c] (Ling) uso *m* 2▸ [u c] (custom, practice) costumbre *f*, uso *m*; **common ~** práctica *f* común 3▸ [u] (use) uso *m*, utilización *f*

USB *n* (= **universal serial bus**) USB *m*; (*before n*) **~ key** llave *f or* lápiz *m* de memoria USB; **~ port** puerto *m* USB

use¹ /juːs/ *n*

A [u] (of machine, substance, method, word) uso *m*, empleo *m*, utilización *f*; ⓢ **instructions for use** instrucciones, modo de empleo; **drug ~** el consumo de drogas; **the ~ of force** el empleo *or* uso de la fuerza; **to lose the ~ of an arm** perder* el uso de un brazo; **to be in ~** «*machine*» estar* funcionando *or* en funcionamiento; «*word/method*» emplearse, usarse; **the elevator is in constant ~** el ascensor se usa constantemente; **the machine was out of ~ all last week** la máquina no funcionó durante toda la semana pasada; **to make ~ of sth** usar algo, hacer* uso de algo; **I must make better ~ of my time** debo emplear *or* aprovechar mejor el tiempo; **to put sth to good ~** hacer* buen uso de algo

B [c] (application, function) uso *m*; **she has her ~s** para algo sirve, a veces nos (*or* les *etc*) es útil; **I have no further ~ for these tools** ya no necesito estas herramientas

C [u] (usefulness): **to be (of) ~ to sb** serle* útil *or* de utilidad a algn, servirle* a algn; **these scissors aren't much ~** estas tijeras no sirven para nada; **I'm not much ~ at cooking** no se me da muy bien la cocina, no sirvo para cocinar; **is this (of) any ~ to you?** ¿te sirve de algo esto?; **it's no ~** es inútil, no hay manera, no hay caso (AmL); **it's no ~ complaining** de nada sirve quejarse, no se consigue nada quejándose *or* con quejarse; **what's the ~ (of -ING)?** ¿de qué sirve (+ INF)?, ¿qué sentido tiene (+ INF)?

D (right to use): **to have the ~ of sb's car/office** poder* usar el coche/la oficina de algn

use² /juːz/ *vt*

A 1▸ (for task, purpose) usar; **this camera is easy to ~** esta cámara es muy fácil de usar *or* es de fácil manejo; **don't ~ bad language** no digas palabrotas; **to ~ drugs** consumir drogas; **a technique ~d in this treatment** una técnica que se emplea *or* se utiliza *or* se usa en este tratamiento; **~ your head/imagination** usa la cabeza/la imaginación; **she could ~ her free time to better purpose** podría aprovechar mejor su tiempo libre; **to ~ sth to + INF** usar *or* utilizar* algo PARA + INF; **~ a knife to open it** usa *or* utiliza un cuchillo para abrirla, ábrela con un cuchillo; **what's this ~d for?** ¿y esto para qué sirve *or* para qué se usa?; **to ~ sth AS sth** usar algo DE *or* COMO algo 2▸ (avail oneself of) ‹*service/facilities*› utilizar*, usar, hacer* uso de; **may I ~ your phone?** ¿puedo hacer una llamada *or* llamar por teléfono?; **may I ~ your toilet?** ¿puedo pasar *or* ir al baño?

B (do with) (colloq): **I could ~ a drink/the money** no me vendría mal un trago/el dinero

C (consume) ‹*food/fuel*› consumir, usar; ‹*money*› gastar; ⓢ **use by 3 Feb 97** fecha de caducidad: 3 feb 97, consumir antes del 3 feb 97

D (manipulate, exploit) (pej) utilizar*, usar (esp AmL); **I felt I'd been ~d** me sentí utilizado *or* (esp AmL) usado

■ **use** *v mod* /juːs/ (*in neg, interrog sentences*): **I didn't ~ to visit them very often** no solía visitarlos muy a menudo;

U

where did you ~ to live? ¿dónde vivías?; *see also* **used²**

Phrasal verb

- **use up** [v ▸ o ▸ adv, v ▸ adv ▸ o] ‹*supplies/strength*› agotar, consumir; ‹*leftovers*› usar, aprovechar; ‹*allowance*› gastarse; **they'd ~d up all the hot water** habían usado toda el agua caliente

useable *adj* ▸**usable**

use-by date /'ju:z,baɪ/ *n* (BrE) fecha *f* de caducidad

used¹ *adj*

A /ju:zd/ 1 ‹*needle/stamp*› usado 2 (secondhand) ‹*car/clothing*› usado, de segunda mano

B /ju:st/ (accustomed) (*pred*) **to be ~ TO sth/-ING** estar* acostumbrado A algo/+ INF; **I'm not ~ to this heat/getting up early** no estoy acostumbrado a tanto calor/a madrugar; **to get ~ TO sth/-ING** acostumbrarse A algo/+ INF; **I got ~ to him** me acostumbré a él; **I got ~ to the idea** me hice a la idea

used² /ju:st/ *v mod* (indicating former state, habit) (*only in past*) **~ to (+ INF)**: **there ~ to be a shop next door** antes había una tienda al lado; **things aren't what they ~ to be** (set phrase) las cosas ya no son lo que eran; **I ~ to work in that shop** (antes) trabajaba en esa tienda; **do you play chess? — I ~ to** ¿juegas al ajedrez? — antes solía jugar *or* ya no; *see also* **use²** *v mod*

useful /'ju:sfəl/ *adj* ‹*invention/tool/information*› útil; ‹*experience*› útil, provechoso; **that's a ~ thing to know** viene bien *or* es útil saberlo; **to come in ~** (BrE) ser* útil, venir* bien; **to make oneself ~** ayudar, echar una mano; **come on, make yourself ~** venga, ayuda en algo

usefully /'ju:sfəli/ *adv* útilmente; **I spent my time very ~ at the library** aproveché muy bien el tiempo en la biblioteca

usefulness /'ju:sfəlnəs || 'ju:sfəlnɪs/ *n* [u] utilidad *f*; **this law/machine has outlived its ~** esta ley/máquina ha quedado desfasada *or* ha dejado de prestar utilidad

useless /'ju:sləs || 'ju:slɪs/ *adj* 1 (ineffective) ‹*object/tool/person*› inútil; **these scissors are ~** estas tijeras no sirven para nada 2 (futile) inútil; **it would be ~** sería inútil, no serviría de nada 3 (not capable) (colloq) ‹*person*› inútil, negado (fam); **to be ~ AT sth/-ING** ser* negado PARA algo/ + INF (fam)

uselessly /'ju:sləsli || 'ju:slɪsli/ *adv* inútilmente, en vano

user /'ju:zər || 'ju:zə(r)/ *n* usuario, -ria *m,f*; **drug ~** consumidor, -dora *m,f* de drogas; (addict) drogadicto, -ta *m,f*, toxicómano, -na *m,f*

user-friendly /'ju:zər'frendli || ,ju:zə'frendli/ *adj* fácil de usar *or* de utilizar

usher¹ /'ʌʃər || 'ʌʃə(r)/ *n* 1 (Cin, Theat) acomodador, -dora *m,f* 2 (at wedding) *persona allegada a los novios que se encarga de recibir y sentar a los invitados en la iglesia* 3 (in UK) (Law) ujier *mf*

usher² *vt*: **to ~ sb to her/his seat** conducir* a algn hasta su asiento; **he ~ed her into the room** la hizo pasar a la habitación

Phrasal verb

- **usher in** [v ▸ o ▸ adv, v ▸ adv ▸ o] ‹*person*› hacer* pasar; ‹*new era*› marcar* el comienzo de, ser* el preludio de

usherette /'ʌʃə'ret/ *n* acomodadora *f*

USMC *n* = **United States Marine Corps**

USN *n* = **United States Navy**

USS = **United States ship**

USSR *n* (Hist) (= **Union of Soviet Socialist Republics**) URSS *f*

usual¹ /'ju:ʒuəl/ *adj* ‹*method/response/comment*› acostumbrado, habitual, usual; ‹*time/place/route*› de siempre, de costumbre; ‹*clothes/appearance*› de costumbre; **she wasn't her ~ self** no era la de siempre; **as ~** como de costumbre, como siempre; **as is ~ at these events** como suele ocurrir *or* pasar en estas ocasiones; **it is ~ for candidates to apply in writing** lo normal *or* habitual es que los candidatos hagan su solicitud por escrito

usual² *n* (colloq) (*no pl*) (drink, order): **my** *o* **the ~, please** lo de siempre, por favor

usually /'ju:ʒuəli/ *adv* normalmente, por lo general, usualmente; **what do you ~ do in the evenings?** ¿qué sueles hacer por las noches?

usurer /'ju:ʒərər || 'ju:ʒərə(r)/ *n* usurero, -ra *m,f*

usurp /jʊ'sɜ:rp || ju:'zɜ:p/ *vt* (frml) usurpar

usurper /jʊ'sɜ:rpər || ju:'zɜ:pə(r)/ *n* (frml) usurpador, -dora *m,f* (frml)

usury /'ju:ʒəri/ *n* [u] usura *f*

UT = **Utah**

utensil /ju:'tensəl || ju:'tensɪl/ *n* utensilio *m*; **kitchen ~s** utensilios de cocina

uterus /'ju:tərəs/ *n* (*pl* **-teri** /-təraɪ/ *or* **-teruses**) útero *m*, matriz *f*

utilitarian /ju:'tɪlə'teriən || ,ju:tɪlɪ'teəriən/ *adj* utilitario

utility /ju:'tɪləti/ *n* (*pl* **-ties**) 1 [u] (usefulness) (frml) utilidad *f* 2 [c] (*public service ~*) empresa *f* de servicio público

utility room *n*: *cuarto para lavar y planchar*

utilize /'ju:tḷaɪz || 'ju:tɪlaɪz/ *vt* (frml) utilizar*, hacer* uso de

utmost¹ /'ʌtməʊst/ *adj* (*before n*) 1 (greatest) mayor, sumo; **with the ~ care** con el mayor cuidado, con sumo cuidado; **of the ~ importance** de suma importancia, sumamente importante, importantísimo 2 (farthest) ‹*edge/limit*› extremo

utmost² *n*: **to do one's ~ (to + INF)** esforzarse* al máximo *or* hacer* todo lo posible (PARA + INF)

utopia, Utopia /ju:'təʊpiə/ *n* (*pl* **-as**) utopía *f*

utopian, Utopian /ju:'təʊpiən/ *adj* utópico

utter¹ /'ʌtər || 'ʌtə(r)/ *adj* (*as intensifier*) completo, total, absoluto; **what ~ nonsense!** ¡qué disparate!

utter² *vt* ‹*word*› decir*, pronunciar; ‹*cry*› dar*, proferir* (frml); **he didn't ~ a sound** no dijo nada *or* ni una palabra, no dijo ni pío (fam)

utterly /'ʌtərli || 'ʌtəli/ *adv* (*as intensifier*) completamente, totalmente; **I ~ despise him** siento el más absoluto desprecio por él

uttermost /'ʌtərməʊst || 'ʌtəməʊst/ *adj/n* ▸**utmost¹·²**

U-turn /'ju:tɜ:rn || 'ju:tɜ:n/ *n* (Auto) cambio *m* de sentido, giro *m* *or* vuelta *f* en U (CS); **to make** (AmE) *o* (BrE) **do a ~** cambiar de sentido, dar* vuelta *or* girar en U (CS); **they made** *o* **did a ~ on taxation** dieron un giro de 180° en materia de impuestos

UV *adj* (= **ultraviolet**) UV *adj inv*, ultravioleta

Uzbekistan /'ʊzbekɪ'stɑ:n/ *n* Uzbekistán *m*

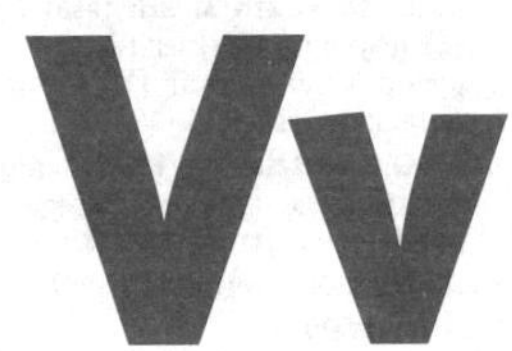

V, v /viː/ *n* V, v *f*

v

A ▶**vs**

B (see) (frml) véase

C (*pl* **vv**) (Bib, Lit) (= **verse**): **Exodus ch. 4, v. 18** Éxodo 4,18

D (colloq) (= **very**) muy

V (Elec) (= **volt(s)**) V *(read as: voltio(s))*

VA *n* = **Virginia**

vacancy /ˈveɪkənsi/ *n* [c] (*pl* **-cies**) [1] (job) vacante *f*; **to fill a ~** cubrir* *or* proveer* una vacante; Ⓢ **vacancies** ofertas de trabajo [2] (in hotel) habitación *f* libre; Ⓢ **no vacancies** completo, cupo agotado (Méx)

vacant /ˈveɪkənt/ *adj*

A [1] ‹*building/premises*› desocupado, vacío; **~ lot** terreno *m* sin construir, terreno *m* baldío (AmL) [2] ‹*post*› vacante; Ⓢ **situations vacant** ofertas de trabajo [3] ‹*room*› disponible, libre; ‹*seat/space*› libre

B (blank) ‹*look/expression*› ausente, distraído

vacantly /ˈveɪkəntli/ *adv* con expresión ausente

vacate /ˈveɪkeɪt ‖ veɪˈkeɪt, və-/ *vt* (frml) ‹*building*› desocupar, desalojar; ‹*seat/hotel room*› dejar libre; ‹*job/post*› abandonar, dejar

vacation¹ /veɪˈkeɪʃən/ *n* [u c] (esp AmE) (from work) vacaciones *fpl*, licencia *f* (Col, Méx, RPl); (from studies) vacaciones *fpl*; **to be on ~** estar* de vacaciones; **to go on ~** ir* *or* irse* de vacaciones; (*before n*) **~ home** casa *f* de veraneo *or* de campo; **~ resort** centro *m* turístico

vacation² *vi* (AmE) pasar las vacaciones, vacacionar (Méx)

vacationer /veɪˈkeɪʃn̩ər ‖ vəˈkeɪʃənə(r)/, **vacationist** /-ʃənəst ‖ -ʃənɪst/ *n* (AmE) turista *mf*; (in summer) veraneante *mf*

vaccinate /ˈvæksəneɪt ‖ ˈvæksɪneɪt/ *vt* vacunar

vaccination /ˈvæksəˈneɪʃən ‖ ˌvæksɪˈneɪʃən/ *n* [c u] vacunación *f*

vaccine /vækˈsiːn ‖ ˈvæksiːn/ *n* [c u] vacuna *f*

vacillate /ˈvæsəleɪt/ *vi* (hesitate) vacilar; (sway) oscilar

vacuous /ˈvækjuəs/ *adj* ‹*smile*› vacuo; ‹*expression*› de vacuidad; ‹*remark*› insustancial

vacuum¹ /ˈvækjuəm, -juːm/ *n* vacío *m*; (*before n*) **~ pump** bomba *f* neumática

vacuum² *vi* pasar la aspiradora, aspirar (AmL)

■ **vacuum** *vt* pasar la aspiradora por, aspirar (AmL)

vacuum: **~ bottle** *n* (AmE) termo *m*; **~ cleaner** *n* aspiradora *f*; **~ flask** *n* termo *m*; **~-packed** /ˈvækjuəmˈpækt, -juːm-/ *adj* envasado al vacío

vagabond /ˈvægəbɑːnd ‖ ˈvægəbɒnd/ *n*, vagabundo, -da *m,f*

vagaries /ˈveɪgəriz/ *pl n* (*sometimes sing*) (whims) caprichos *mpl* (frml); (eccentricities) rarezas *fpl*, manías *fpl*

vagina /vəˈdʒaɪnə/ *n* vagina *f*

vaginal /ˈvædʒənl̩, vəˈdʒaɪnl̩ ‖ vəˈdʒaɪnl̩/ *adj* vaginal

vagrancy /ˈveɪgrənsi/ *n* [u] vagabundeo *m*, vagancia *f*

vagrant /ˈveɪgrənt/ *n* vagabundo, -da *m,f*

vague /veɪg/ *adj* **vaguer, vaguest** [1] (imprecise, unclear) ‹*term/wording/concept*› impreciso, vago; **there was ~ talk of a move** se habló vagamente de una posible mudanza; **to be ~ ABOUT sth: she was ~ about her involvement** fue poco explícita acerca de su participación [2] (indistinct) ‹*outline*› borroso [3] (absentminded) ‹*expression*› distraído; ‹*person*› distraído, despistado

vaguely /ˈveɪgli/ *adv* [1] (in imprecise, unclear way) ‹*explain*› vagamente, con imprecisión, de manera imprecisa; ‹*answer/define*› con vaguedad *or* imprecisión; ‹*recognize/remember*› vagamente; ‹*suspicious/ridiculous*› ligeramente, un tanto; **he looks ~ like his father** tiene un ligero parecido con *or* a su padre [2] (absentmindedly) distraídamente

vain /veɪn/ *adj* **-er, -est**

A (self-admiring) vanidoso, presumido, vano (frml)

B (*before n, no comp*) [1] (futile) ‹*attempt*› vano, inútil; ‹*hope/belief*› vano [2] (empty, worthless) ‹*promise/words*› vano [3] **in vain** en vano, vanamente, inútilmente

vainly /ˈveɪnli/ *adv*

A (uselessly) en vano, vanamente, inútilmente

B (conceitedly) con vanidad, vanidosamente

valance /ˈvæləns/ *n* [1] (frill) cenefa *f* [2] (on curtain rail) galería *f*, bastidor *m*

vale /veɪl/ *n* (poet) valle *m*

valedictory /ˈvæləˈdɪktəri ‖ ˌvælɪˈdɪktəri/ *adj* (frml) de adiós, de despedida

valency /ˈveɪlənsi/ *n* (*pl* **-cies**) (Chem) valencia *f*

valentine /ˈvæləntaɪn/ *n* [1] (card) *tarjeta de tono humorístico y/o amoroso que se envía anónimamente el día de San Valentín* [2] *also* **Valentine** (person) enamorado, -da *m,f*

Valentine's Day /ˈvæləntaɪnz/ *n* el día de San Valentín, el día de los enamorados

valet¹ /ˈvælət/ *n* [1] (servant) ayuda *m* de cámara, valet *m* [2] (in hotel) mozo *m* de hotel; (*before n*) **~ service** servicio *m* de planchado [3] (AmE) (for cars) estacionador, -dora *m,f* de coches (esp AmL), parqueador, -dora *m,f* (AmL), aparcacoches *mf* (Esp)

valet² /ˈvælət ‖ ˈvælɪt/ *vt* ‹*car*› limpiar el interior de

valiant /ˈvæljənt/ *adj* ‹*hero/deed*› valiente, valeroso; ‹*attempt/effort*› valeroso

valiantly /ˈvæljəntli/ *adv* valientemente, con valor

valid /ˈvæləd ‖ ˈvælɪd/ *adj* [1] ‹*contract/passport*› válido [2] ‹*argument*› válido; ‹*excuse/criticism*› legítimo, válido; **that's a ~ point** en eso tienes (*or* tienen *etc*) razón

validate /ˈvælədeɪt ‖ ˈvælɪdeɪt/ *vt* [1] (frml) ‹*theory*› dar* validez a, validar (frml) [2] (Law) ‹*contract/document*› validar [3] ‹*parking ticket*› (AmE) sellar [4] (Comput) validar

validation /ˈvæləˈdeɪʃən/ *n* [c u] validación *f* (frml)

validity /vəˈlɪdəti/ *n* [u] validez *f*

valley /ˈvæli/ *n* (*pl* **-leys**) valle *m*

valor, (BrE) **valour** /ˈvælər ‖ ˈvælə(r)/ *n* [u] (liter) bravura *f* (liter), valor *m*, valentía *f*

valuable /ˈvæljuəbəl/ *adj* [1] (financially) valioso [2] (precious, useful) ‹*resource/advice/ally*› valioso; ‹*time*› precioso

valuables /ˈvæljuəbəlz/ *pl n* objetos *mpl* de valor

valuation /ˈvæljuˈeɪʃən/ *n* [1] [c] (act) valoración *f*, tasación *f* [2] [u] (value given) tasación *f*, valoración *f*

value¹ /ˈvæljuː/ *n*

A [u c] (worth) valor *m*; **to gain** *o* **increase (in) ~** aumentar de valor, revalorizarse*; **to lose (in) ~** depreciarse; **books to the ~ of $500** libros por valor de 500 dólares; **have you anything of ~ in your bag?** ¿lleva algo de valor en el bolso?; **~ for money** una buena relación calidad-precio; **that's good ~ (for money)** está muy bien de precio; **they place a very high ~ on loyalty** valoran mucho la lealtad; **nutritional ~** valor nutritivo

B **values** *pl* (standards) valores *mpl*

value² *vt* **1** (Fin) ‹*assets/property*› tasar, valorar, avaluar* (AmL); **to ~ sth AT sth** tasar (*or* valorar *etc*) algo EN algo **2** (regard highly) ‹*friendship/advice*› valorar, apreciar; ‹*freedom/privacy*› valorar **3** **valued** *past p* ‹*friend/colleague*› apreciado, estimado

value: **~-added tax** /'vælju:'ædəd || ˌvælju:'ædɪd/ *n* impuesto *m* al valor agregado *or* (Esp) sobre el valor añadido; **~ judgment** *n* juicio *m* de valor

valueless /'vælju:ləs || 'vælju:lɪs/ *adj* sin valor

valve /vælv/ *n*

A **1** (Mech Eng) válvula *f*; **inlet/outlet ~** válvula *f* de entrada/salida **2** (on tire) válvula *f* **3** (on musical instrument) pistón *m* **4** (Anat) válvula *f*

B (esp BrE Electron) válvula *f*, lámpara *f*

vampire /'væmpaɪr || 'væmpaɪə(r)/ *n*

A (Myth) vampiro *m*

B ~ **(bat)** vampiro *m*

van /væn/ *n* **1** (Auto) furgoneta *f*, camioneta *f*, vagoneta *f* (Méx) **2** (BrE Rail) furgón *m*

vandal /'vændl/ *n* vándalo *m*, gamberro, -rra *m,f* (Esp)

vandalism /'vændlɪzəm/ *n* [u] vandalismo *m*

vandalize /'vændlaɪz/ *vt* destrozar*, estropear (*adrede*)

vane /veɪn/ *n* **1** (*weather* ~) veleta *f* **2** (shaft, blade — of propeller) paleta *f*; (— of windmill) aspa *f*

vanguard /'vængɑ:rd || 'vængɑ:d/ *n* vanguardia *f*; **to be in the ~ (of sth)** estar* en *or* a la vanguardia (de algo)

vanilla /və'nɪlə/ *n* [u] vainilla *f*; (*before n*) ‹*ice cream*› de vainilla

vanish /'vænɪʃ/ *vi* desaparecer*; ‹‹*doubts/fears*›› desaparecer*, disiparse

vanishing /'vænɪʃɪŋ/: **~ cream** *n* [uc] crema *f* evanescente; **~ point** *n* punto *m* de fuga

vanity /'vænəti/ *n* (*pl* **-ties**)

A [u c] **1** (about appearance) vanidad *f* **2** (pride) orgullo *m*, vanidad *f* **3** (emptiness, frivolity) (liter) vanidad *f* (liter)

B [c] (dressing table) (AmE) tocador *m*

vanity case *n* neceser *m*

vanquish /'væŋkwɪʃ/ *vt* (liter) vencer*, derrotar

vantage point /'væntɪdʒ || 'vɑ:ntɪdʒ/ *n* posición *f* estratégica *or* ventajosa; (for view) mirador *m*

vapid /'væpəd || 'væpɪd/ *adj* ‹*smile/person*› insulso, insípido; ‹*remark*› sin interés, insulso

vapor, (BrE) **vapour** /'veɪpər || 'veɪpə(r)/ *n* [c u] (on glass) vaho *m*; (steam) vapor *m*

vaporize /'veɪpəraɪz/ *vi* evaporarse, vaporizarse*

■ **vaporize** *vt* vaporizar*

vapour *n* (BrE) ▸**vapor**

variable¹ /'veriəbəl || 'veəriəbəl/ *adj* variable

variable² *n* **1** (Math) variable *f* **2** (factor) factor *m*, variable *f*

variable-geometry /ˌveriəbəldʒi'ɑ:mətri || ˌveəriəbəldʒi'ɒmətri/ *adj* (*before n*) de geometría variable

variance /'veriəns || 'veəriəns/ *n* [u c]: **to be at ~ with sth** no estar* de acuerdo con algo, discrepar de algo; **to be at ~ with sb** estar* en desacuerdo con algn, discrepar con *or* de algn

variant¹ /'veriənt || 'veəriənt/ *n* variante *f*

variant² *adj* (*before n, no comp*) ‹*interpretation/opinion*› divergente; ‹*pronunciation/form*› alternativa

variation /'veri'eɪʃən || ˌveəri'eɪʃən/ *n* **1** [u c] (fluctuation, change) variación *f*; **~ IN sth**: **~s in temperature** variaciones de temperatura **2** [u] (difference) diferencias *fpl*; **there was little ~ in opinion** hubo pocas diferencias de opinión **3** [c] (permutation) **~ ON sth** variación *f* DE *or* SOBRE algo; **his stories are all ~s on the same theme** todos sus cuentos son variaciones sobre el mismo tema **4** [c] (Mus) variación *f*

varicose veins /'værəkəʊs || 'værɪkəʊs/ *pl n* (*sometimes sing*) varices *fpl*, várices *fpl* (esp AmL)

varied /'verid || 'veərid/ *adj* variado

variegated /'verɪgeɪtəd || 'veərɪgeɪtɪd/ *adj* abigarrado, multicolor

variety /və'raɪəti/ *n* (*pl* **-ties**) **1** [u] (diversity) variedad *f*, diversidad *f*; **~ *is the spice of life*** en la variedad está el gusto **2** [c] (assortment) **~ OF sth**: **the fabric comes in a ~ of shades** la tela viene en varios colores; **for a ~ of reasons** por varias *or* distintas *or* diversas razones **3** [c] (sort) clase *f*

variety show *n* (Theat) espectáculo *m* de variedades

varifocals /ˌverɪ'fəʊkəlz || ˌveərɪ'fəʊkəlz/ *pl n* gafas *fpl* progresivas, lentes *mpl* progresivos (AmL), lentes *fpl* progresivas (Esp)

various /'veriəs || 'veəriəs/ *adj* **1** (several) (*before n, no comp*) varios **2** (different, diverse) diferentes, diversos

variously /'veriəsli || 'veəriəsli/ *adv*: **she has been ~ considered as a heroine and a traitor** se la ha considerado de forma muy diversa: a veces como heroína y a veces como traidora

varmint /'vɑ:rmənt || 'vɑ:mɪnt/ *n* (AmE dial) (person) canalla *mf*; (animal) alimaña *f*

varnish¹ /'vɑ:rnɪʃ/ *n* barniz *m*; (for nails) (BrE) esmalte *m*

varnish² *vt* barnizar*; **to ~ one's nails** (BrE) pintarse las uñas

vary /'veri || 'veəri/, **varies, varying, varied** *vi* **1** (change, fluctuate) variar*; **the temperature varies between 50° and 57°** la temperatura oscila entre 50° y 57°; **the routine never varies** la rutina nunca cambia; **when do you finish work? — it varies** ¿cuándo sales del trabajo? — depende **2** (differ) ‹‹*accounts/standards/prices*›› variar*; **opinions on the subject ~** hay diversas opiniones al respecto **3** (diverge) **to ~ FROM sth** desviarse* *or* apartarse DE algo **4** **varying** *pres p* ‹*amounts/conditions*› variable; **with ~ing degrees of success** con mayor o menor éxito

■ **vary** *vt* ‹*routine*› variar*, cambiar; ‹*diet*› dar* variedad a

vase /veɪs || vɑ:z/ *n* (for flowers) florero *m*; (ornament) jarrón *m*

vasectomy /və'sektəmi/ *n* [c u] (*pl* **-mies**) vasectomía *f*

Vaseline®, vaseline /'væsəli:n/ *n* [u] vaselina *f*

vassal /'væsəl/ *n* vasallo, -lla *m,f*

vast /væst || vɑ:st/ *adj* ‹*size/wealth*› inmenso, enorme; ‹*area*› vasto, extenso; ‹*range/repertoire*› muy extenso, amplísimo; ‹*experience/knowledge*› vasto; **the ~ majority of people** la inmensa mayoría de la gente; **~ sums of money** sumas *fpl* astronómicas de dinero

vastly /'væstli || 'vɑ:stli/ *adv* ‹*superior/improved*› infinitamente; **~ in excess of legal limits** muy por encima de los límites permitidos

vat /væt/ *n* cuba *f*, tanque *m*

VAT *n* [u] (= **value-added tax**) IVA *m*

Vatican /'vætɪkən/ *n* **the ~** el Vaticano

Vatican City *n* Ciudad *f* del Vaticano

vaudeville /'vɔ:dəvɪl/ *n* [u] vodevil *m*

vault¹ /vɔ:lt/ *n*

A **1** (basement) sótano *m*; **wine ~** bodega *f*, cava *f* **2** (strongroom): **bank ~** cámara *f* acorazada, bóveda *f* de seguridad (AmL) **3** (crypt) cripta *f*; **the family ~** el panteón familiar

B (Archit) bóveda *f*

vault² *vi* saltar (*apoyándose en algo*); **he ~ed over the fence** saltó (por encima de) la cerca

■ **vault** *vt* saltar

vaulted /'vɔ:ltəd || 'vɔ:ltɪd/ *adj* ‹*ceiling/roof*› abovedado

vaulting horse /'vɔ:ltɪŋ/ *n* potro *m*

vaunted /'vɔ:ntəd || 'vɔ:ntɪd/ *adj* (journ): **the much ~ new model** el tan pregonado modelo nuevo

vblog /vblɔ:g || vblɒg/ *n* (= **video blog**) videoblog *m*, vblog *m*

VC *n* (in UK) = **Victoria Cross**

VCR *n* = **videocassette recorder**

VD *n* [u] = **venereal disease**

VDT *n* (esp AmE) = **visual display terminal**

VDU *n* = **visual display unit**

've /əv/ = **have**

veal /vi:l/ *n* [u] ternera *f* (*de animal muy joven y de carne pálida*)

vector /'vektər || 'vektə(r)/ *n*

A (Aviat, Math) vector *m*

B (Biol) vector *m*, portador, -dora *m,f*

VE-Day /'vi:'i:deɪ/ *n*: *día de la victoria aliada en Europa en la segunda guerra mundial*

veep /vi:p/ *n*(Am journ) vicepresidente, -ta *m,f*

V

veer /vɪr || vɪə(r)/ *vi* «*vehicle/horse*» dar* un viraje, virar; «*wind*» cambiar de dirección; **the road ∼s to the left** el camino tuerce *or* se desvía hacia la izquierda; **they ∼ed from one extreme to the other** se pasaron de un extremo al otro

veg /vedʒ/ *n* [u c] (*pl* ∼) (BrE colloq) verdura *f*

vegan /'viːgən/ *n* vegetariano estricto, vegetariana estricta *m,f*

veganism /'viːgənɪzəm/ *n* [u] veganismo *m*, vegetarianismo *m* estricto

vegetable /'vedʒtəbəl/ *n*

A 1 (Culin) verdura *f*; (*before n*) ‹*soup*› de verduras; **∼ garden/patch** huerto *m*, huerta *f* 2 (plant) vegetal *m*; (*before n*) ‹*oil/fats*› vegetal; ‹*dyes/colors*› (de origen) vegetal

B (person) vegetal *m*

vegetarian¹ /'vedʒə'teriən || ˌvedʒɪ'teəriən/ *n* vegetariano, -na *m,f*

vegetarian² *adj* vegetariano

vegetarianism /'vedʒə'teriənɪzəm || ˌvedʒɪ'teəriənɪzəm/ *n* [u] vegetarianismo *m*

vegetate /'vedʒəteɪt || 'vedʒɪteɪt/ *vi* vegetar

vegetation /'vedʒə'teɪʃən || ˌvedʒɪ'teɪʃən/ *n* [u] vegetación *f*

veggie /'vedʒi/ *n* (colloq) vegetariano, -na *m,f*; (*before n*) **∼ burger** hamburguesa *f* vegetariana

vehemence /'viːəməns/ *n* [u] (of criticism, denial) vehemencia *f*; (of feelings) intensidad *f*, vehemencia *f*

vehement /'viːəmənt/ *adj* ‹*criticism/denial*› vehemente; ‹*feelings*› intenso, vehemente

vehemently /'viːəməntli/ *adv* con vehemencia, vehementemente

vehicle /'viːəkəl/ *n* vehículo *m*; **the column was a ∼ for his prejudices** la columna del periódico servía de vehículo para expresar sus prejuicios

veil¹ /veɪl/ *n* velo *m*; **to take the ∼** (Relig) tomar el hábito *or* el velo; (cover) velo *m*; **to draw a ∼ over sth** correr *or* echar un (tupido) velo sobre algo

veil² *vt* 1 (cover with a veil) : **to ∼ one's face/head** taparse *or* cubrirse* con un velo, velarse (liter); **the hills were ∼ed in mist** (liter) un velo *or* un halo de bruma envolvía las montañas 2 ‹*facts/truth*› velar, ocultar; ‹*feelings*› disimular, ocultar

veiled /veɪld/ *adj* ‹*face/woman*› tapado *or* cubierto con un velo; ‹*threat/insult*› velado

vein /veɪn/ *n*

A (Anat, Bot, Zool) vena *f*

B 1 (of ore, mineral) veta *f*, filón *m*, vena *f* 2 (in marble, cheese) veta *f*

C (*no pl*) (mood, style) vena *f*; **in a lighter ∼, did you know ... ?** pasando a algo menos serio ¿sabías que ... ?

Velcro® /'velkrəʊ/ *n* [u] velcro® *m*

vellum /'veləm/ *n* [u] 1 (parchment) vitela *f* 2 (writing paper) papel *m* de vitela

velocity /və'lɑːsəti || və'lɒsəti/ *n* [u c] (*pl* **-ties**) velocidad *f*

velour /və'lʊr || və'lʊə(r)/ *n* [u] velour *m*, velvetón *m*

velvet /'velvət || 'velvɪt/ *n* [u] terciopelo *m*

velvety /'velvəti/ aterciopelado

venal /'viːnl̩/ *adj* (frml) ‹*judge*› venal (frml), sobornable; ‹*activities*› corrupto

vendetta /ven'detə/ *n* vendetta *f*; **to carry on a ∼ against sb** hacer* una campaña en contra de algn

vending machine /'vendɪŋ/ *n* máquina *f* expendedora, distribuidor *m* automático

vendor /'vendər || 'vendə(r)/ *n* 1 (Busn, Law) vendedor, -dora *m,f* 2 (*street* ∼) vendedor, -dora *m,f* ambulante 3 ▸**vending machine**

veneer /və'nɪr || vɪ'nɪə(r)/ *n* 1 [u c] (of wood, gold) enchapado *m*, chapa *f* 2 [u] (outer appearance) **∼ OF sth** capa *f* *or* barniz *m* DE algo

venerable /'venərəbəl/ *adj* venerable

venerate /'venəreɪt/ *vt* venerar, reverenciar

veneration /'venə'reɪʃən/ *n* [u] veneración *f*

venereal /və'nɪriəl || və'nɪəriəl/ *adj* venéreo; **∼ disease** enfermedad *f* venérea

Venetian blind /və'niːʃən/ *n* persiana *f* veneciana *or* de lamas, persiana *f* americana (Arg), cortina *f* veneciana (Ur)

Venezuela /'venə'zweɪlə || ˌvenɪ'zweɪlə/ *n* Venezuela *f*

Venezuelan¹ /'venə'zweɪlən || ˌvenɪ'zweɪlən/ *adj* venezolano

Venezuelan² *n* venezolano, -na *m,f*

vengeance /'vendʒəns/ *n* [u] venganza *f*; **to take ∼ ON sb** vengarse* DE algn; **with a ∼** (colloq) de verdad *or* con ganas

vengeful /'vendʒfəl/ *adj* vengativo

venial /'viːniəl/ *adj* ‹*sin*› venial; ‹*fault*› sin importancia; ‹*offense*› leve, venial

Venice /'venəs || 'venɪs/ *n* Venecia *f*

venison /'venəsən || 'venɪsən/ *n* [u] (carne *f* de) venado *m*

venom /'venəm/ *n* [u] 1 (Zool) veneno *m* 2 (malice) ponzoña *f*, veneno *m*, malevolencia *f*

venomous /'venəməs/ *adj* ‹*snake/spider*› venenoso; ‹*look/words*› ponzoñoso, lleno *or* cargado de veneno

vent¹ /vent/ *n* 1 (in building, tunnel) (conducto *m* de) ventilación *f*; (in chimney, furnace) tiro *m* 2 (*air* ∼) (shaft) respiradero *m*; (grille) rejilla *f* de ventilación; ***to give ∼ to sth*** dar* rienda suelta a algo

vent² *vt* ‹*feelings/rage/frustration*› dar* rienda suelta a, dar* salida a; **she ∼ed her anger on the children** descargó su ira sobre los niños

ventilate /'ventl̩eɪt || 'ventɪleɪt/ *vt*

A ‹*room/blood*› ventilar

B ‹*subject/argument*› ventilar, airear

ventilation /'ventl̩'eɪʃən || ˌventɪ'leɪʃən/ *n* [u] 1 (in room, building) ventilación *f* 2 (system) sistema *m* de ventilación; (*before n*) **∼ shaft** pozo *m* de ventilación

ventilator /'ventl̩eɪtər || 'ventɪleɪtə(r)/ *n* (Med) respirador *m* (artificial), ventilador *m*

ventricle /'ventrɪkəl/ *n* ventrículo *m*

ventriloquist /ven'trɪləkwəst || ven'trɪləkwɪst/ *n* ventrílocuo, -cua *m,f*

venture¹ /'ventʃər || 'ventʃə(r)/ *n* 1 (Busn) operación *f*, empresa *f*; **a new business ∼** una nueva empresa 2 **∼ INTO sth** incursión *f* EN algo

venture² *vi* atreverse, aventurarse; **they rarely ∼ out after dark** rara vez salen después del anochecer

■ **venture** *vt* 1 ‹*opinion/guess*› aventurar; **if I may ∼ to suggest** (frml) si se me permite aventurar una sugerencia; **to ∼ to + INF** atreverse A + INF, osar + INF (liter) 2 (frml) ‹*life/money*› arriesgar*; ***nothing ∼d, nothing gained*** quien nada arriesga, nada gana

Phrasal verb

• **venture forth** [v ▸ adv] (frml) arriesgarse* *or* aventurarse a salir

venture: ∼ capital *n* [u] capital *m* (de) riesgo; **∼ capitalism** *n* [u] capitalismo *m* de riesgo, inversiones *fpl* de capital de riesgo

venue /'venjuː/ *n* (for event): **∼s: Boston, NY City** lugares de actuación (*or* presentación *etc*): Boston, Nueva York; **the match will be played at a neutral ∼** el partido se jugará en campo neutral

Venus /'viːnəs/ *n* Venus *m*

veracity /və'ræsəti/ *n* [u] (frml) veracidad *f*

veranda, verandah /və'rændə/ *n* galería *f*, veranda *f*

verb /vɜːrb || vɜːb/ *n* verbo *m*

verbal /'vɜːrbəl || 'vɜːbəl/ *adj* verbal

verbalize /'vɜːrbəlaɪz || 'vɜːbəlaɪz/ *vt* expresar verbalmente *or* con palabras, verbalizar*

verbally /'vɜːrbəli || 'vɜːbəli/ *adv* 1 (in words) verbalmente 2 (in speech) ‹*agree/state*› verbalmente, de palabra

verbatim /vər'beɪtəm || vɜː'beɪtɪm/ *adv* al pie de la letra, palabra por palabra

verbiage /'vɜːrbiɪdʒ || 'vɜːbiɪdʒ/ *n* [u] verborrea *f*, verborragia *f*

verbose /vər'bəʊs || vɜː'bəʊs/ *adj* ampuloso, bombástico, verboso

verdant /'vɜːrdn̩t || 'vɜːdn̩t/ *adj* (liter) verdeante (liter), verde

verdict /'vɜːrdɪkt || 'vɜːdɪkt/ *n* 1 (Law) veredicto *m*; **a ∼ of guilty/not guilty** un veredicto de culpabilidad/inocencia; **to bring in** *o* **return a ∼** «*jury*» dar* *or* emitir un veredicto; **to deliver a ~** ⟨⟨*magistrate*⟩⟩ pronunciar sentencia, fallar; **to reach a ~** llegar* a un acuerdo sobre el veredicto [2] (opinion) juicio *m*; **to give one's ~ on sb/sth** dar* su (*or* mi *etc*) opinión sobre algn/algo; **well then, what's your ~?** bueno ¿qué te parece?

verdure /ˈvɜːrdʒər || ˈvɜːdjə(r)/ *n* [u] (liter) verdor *m*

verge /vɜːrdʒ || vɜːdʒ/ *n*

A [1] (border) (BrE) borde *m* [2] **to be on the ~ of sth**: **a species on the ~ of extinction** una especie en grave peligro de extinción; **she was on the ~ of tears** estaba al borde de las lágrimas, estaba a punto de ponerse a llorar; **to be on the ~ of -ING** estar* a punto de + INF

B (of road) (BrE) arcén *m*

(Phrasal verb)

• **verge on** [v ▸ prep ▸ o] rayar en, ser* rayano en

verger /ˈvɜːrdʒər || ˈvɜːdʒə(r)/ *n* sacristán *m*

verifiable /ˈverəfaɪəbəl || ˈverɪfaɪəbəl/ *n* verificable, comprobable

verification /ˈverəfəˈkeɪʃən || ˌverɪfɪˈkeɪʃən/ *n* [u] [1] (confirmation) confirmación *f*, corroboración *f* [2] (checking) verificación *f*, comprobación *f*

verify /ˈverəfaɪ || ˈverɪfaɪ/ *vt* **-fies, -fying, -fied** [1] (confirm) ⟨*doubts/fears/theory*⟩ confirmar, corroborar [2] (check) ⟨*fact/statement*⟩ verificar*, comprobar*

veritable /ˈverətəbəl || ˈverɪtəbəl/ *adj* (frml *or* hum) auténtico, verdadero

vermilion /vərˈmɪljən || vəˈmɪljən/ *adj* bermellón *adj inv*

vermin /ˈvɜːrmən || ˈvɜːmɪn/ *n* (*pl* ~) [1] (animals) alimañas *fpl* [2] (insects) bichos *mpl* [3] (people) indeseables *mpl*

vermouth /vərˈmuːθ || ˈvɜːməθ/ *n* [u c] vermut *m*, vermú *m*

vernacular¹ /vərˈnækjələr || vəˈnækjʊlə(r)/ *n* (native language) lengua *f* vernácula; (local speech) habla *f* local

vernacular² *adj* (*usu before n*) ⟨*language*⟩ vernáculo

verruca /vəˈruːkə/ *n* verruga *f*

versatile /ˈvɜːrsətl̩ || ˈvɜːsətaɪl/ *adj* ⟨*person*⟩ polifacético, versátil; ⟨*mind*⟩ flexible; ⟨*tool/material*⟩ versátil, de múltiples usos

versatility /ˈvɜːrsəˈtɪləti || ˌvɜːsəˈtɪləti/ *n* [u] versatilidad *f*

verse /vɜːrs || vɜːs/ *n*

A [u] (poetry) verso *m*, poesía *f*; **blank/free ~** verso *m* blanco/libre

B [c] [1] (short poem) verso *m*, rima *f* [2] (stanza) estrofa *f* [3] [c] (in Bible) versículo *m*

versed /vɜːrst || vɜːst/ *adj* (*pred*): **to be well ~ in sth** ser* muy versado en algo

version /ˈvɜːrʒən || ˈvɜːʃən/ *n* [1] (variant form) versión *f*; **an updated ~ of the opera** una versión actualizada de la ópera [2] (account) versión *f*; **what's your ~ of the events?** ¿cuál es tu versión de los hechos? [3] (model) versión *f*, modelo *m*

versus /ˈvɜːrsəs || ˈvɜːsəs/ *prep* (Law) contra; (Sport) contra, versus; **city life ~ country life** la vida de ciudad frente a *or* en oposición a la vida del campo

vertebra /ˈvɜːrtəbrə || ˈvɜːtəbrə/ *n* (*pl* **-bras** *or* **-brae** /-breɪ/) vértebra *f*

vertebrate /ˈvɜːrtəbrət || ˈvɜːtɪbrət/ *n* vertebrado *m*

vertical /ˈvɜːrtɪkəl || ˈvɜːtɪkəl/ *adj* vertical; **there is a ~ drop to the sea below** hay una caída a pique *or* (Méx) en pique hasta el mar

vertically /ˈvɜːrtɪkli || ˈvɜːtɪkli/ *adv* verticalmente

vertiginous /vɜːrˈtɪdʒənəs || vɜːˈtɪdʒɪnəs/ *adj* (liter) vertiginoso, que produce vértigo

vertigo /ˈvɜːrtɪgəʊ || ˈvɜːtɪgəʊ/ *n* [u] vértigo *m*

verve /vɜːrv || vɜːv/ *n* [u] brío *m*

very¹ /ˈveri/ *adv* [1] (extremely) muy; **she's ~ tall/clever/fat** es muy alta/inteligente/gorda; (more emphatic) es altísima/inteligentísima/gordísima; **was he upset? — very** ¿estaba disgustado? — mucho; **it was ~ hot/cold** hacía mucho calor/frío [2] (*in phrases*) **very much**: **thank you ~ much** muchas gracias; **did you enjoy it? — yes, ~ much indeed** ¿te gustó? — sí, mucho; **very well** muy bien; **I couldn't ~ well refuse** ¡cómo me iba a negar! [3] (emphatic): **the ~ next day** precisamente al día siguiente; **at the ~ most/least** como máximo/mínimo; **nothing but the ~ best** sólo lo mejor de lo mejor

very² *adj* (*before n*) [1] (exact, precise) mismo; **for that ~ reason** por esa misma razón, por eso mismo; **ah! the ~ person I wanted to see!** ¡ah, justo la persona a quien quería ver! [2] (absolute, extreme): **let's start from the ~ beginning** empecemos desde el principio [3] (actual) mismo; **its ~ existence is threatened** su misma existencia se halla amenazada [4] (mere, sheer) solo, mero; **the ~ mention of her name** la sola *or* mera mención de su nombre; **walk out without paying? the ~ idea!** ¿irnos sin pagar? ¡cómo se te ocurre!

vespers /ˈvespərz || ˈvespəz/ *pl n* vísperas *fpl*

vessel /ˈvesəl/ *n*

A (Naut frml) navío *m* (frml), nave *f* (liter); **passenger ~** buque *m or* barco *m* de pasajeros

B (receptacle) (frml) recipiente *m*; (*drinking* ~) vasija *f*; ***empty ~s make most noise*** mucho ruido y pocas nueces

C (Anat, Bot) vaso *m*; **blood ~** vaso sanguíneo

vest¹ /vest/ *n* [1] (waistcoat) (AmE) chaleco *m* [2] (undergarment) (BrE) camiseta *f*

vest² *vt* (frml): **he was ~ed with special powers** fue investido de *or* con poderes especiales (frml); **the authority ~ed in a judge** la autoridad conferida a un juez

vested interest /ˈvestəd || ˈvestɪd/ *n* [1] [u] (personal stake) **to have a ~ ~ in -ING/sth** tener* gran interés en + INF/algo [2] **vested interests** *pl* intereses *mpl* creados

vestibule /ˈvestəbjuːl || ˈvestɪbjuːl/ *n* vestíbulo *m*

vestige /ˈvestɪdʒ/ *n* (trace) vestigio *m*; **there's not a ~ of truth in his story** no hay ni un ápice de verdad *or* ni rastros de verdad en lo que dice

vestments /ˈvestmənts/ *pl n* (Relig) (*sometimes sing*) vestiduras *fpl*

vestry /ˈvestri/ *n* (*pl* **-tries**) sacristía *f*

vet¹ /vet/ *n*

A (Vet Sci) veterinario, -ria *m,f*

B (veteran) (AmE colloq) veterano, -na *m,f*

vet² *vt* **-tt-** ⟨*applicant*⟩ someter a investigación; ⟨*application/proposal*⟩ examinar, investigar*

veteran /ˈvetərən/ *n* [1] (of war) veterano, -na *m,f* de guerra [2] (of military service) (AmE) licenciado *m* del servicio militar [3] (experienced person) veterano, -na *m,f*

veteran: **~ car** *n* (BrE) coche *m* antiguo (*fabricado antes de 1919*); **~s Day** /ˈvetərənz/ *n* (in US) día *m* del Armisticio

veterinarian /ˈvetərəˈneriən || ˌvetərɪˈneəriən/ *n* (AmE) médico veterinario, médica veterinaria *m,f*

veterinary /ˈvetərəneri || ˈvetrɪnəri/ *adj* veterinario; **~ science** veterinaria *f*; **~ surgeon** (BrE frml) médico veterinario, médica veterinaria *m,f*

veto¹ /ˈviːtəʊ/ *n* (*pl* **vetoes**) [1] [u] (power to ban) veto *m*; **the right of ~** el derecho de *or* al veto [2] [c] (ban) veto *m*, prohibición *f*; **to put a ~ on sth** vetar algo

veto² *vt* **vetoes, vetoing, vetoed** vetar

vetting /ˈvetɪŋ/ *n* (of application, proposal) examen *m*, investigación *f*; **positive ~** investigación *f* de antecedentes

vex /veks/ *vt* [1] (annoy) irritar, sacar* de quicio [2] (worry, puzzle) desconcertar*

vexation /vekˈseɪʃən/ *n* [u c] irritación *f*

vexatious /vekˈseɪʃəs/ *adj* (frml) irritante, enojoso

vexed /vekst/ *adj*

A (contentious) (*before n*): **the ~ question of ...** el polémico *or* controvertido tema de ...

B [1] (annoyed) ⟨*expression/tone*⟩ irritado; **to be ~** estar* enojado (esp AmL), estar* enfadado (esp Esp) [2] (worried, puzzled) desconcertado

VHF (**= very high frequency**) VHF

via /ˈvaɪə, ˈviːə || ˈvaɪə/ *prep* [1] (by way of) vía [2] (by means of) a través de, por medio de

viability /ˈvaɪəˈbɪləti/ *n* [u] viabilidad *f*

viable /ˈvaɪəbəl/ *adj* viable

viaduct /ˈvaɪədʌkt/ *n* viaducto *m*

vibes /vaɪbz/ *pl n* (atmosphere) (sl) vibraciones *fpl* (fam)

vibrant /ˈvaɪbrənt/ *adj* [1] (lively, exuberant) ⟨*color*⟩ vibrante; ⟨*emotion*⟩ a flor de piel, vehemente; ⟨*atmosphere*⟩ efervescente [2] (resonant) ⟨*voice*⟩ vibrante, sonoro

vibrate /ˈvaɪbreɪt || vaɪˈbreɪt/ *vi* [1] ⟨⟨*engine/floor/string*⟩⟩ vibrar [2] (pulse, thrill) **to ~ WITH sth** bullir* DE algo

vibration /vaɪˈbreɪʃən/ *n* [u c] vibración *f*

vibrato /vɪ'brɑːtəʊ/ *n* [u] vibrato *m*; **with ~** en vibrato

vibrator /'vaɪbreɪtər || vaɪ'breɪtə(r)/ *n* vibrador *m*

vicar /'vɪkər || 'vɪkə(r)/ *n* (Anglican) (esp in UK) párroco *m*

vicarage /'vɪkərɪdʒ/ *n* vicaría *f*, casa *f* del párroco

vicarious /vɪ'keriəs || vɪ'keəriəs/ *adj* indirecto; **he gets a ~ pleasure from it** indirectamente le proporciona placer

vicariously /vɪ'keriəsli || vɪ'keəriəsli/ *adv* indirectamente; **to experience sth ~** experimentar algo a través de otra persona

vice /vaɪs/ *n*

A [u c] (wickedness) vicio *m*; (*before n*) **the ~ squad** la brigada *f* anti-vicio

B [c] (BrE) ▸**vise**

vice- /'vaɪs/ *pref* vice-

vice: **~-chancellor** /'vaɪs'tʃænsḷər || ˌvaɪs'tʃɑːnsələ(r)/ *n* (in UK) (Educ) ≈ rector, -tora *m,f*; **~ president** *n* vicepresidente, -ta *m,f*; **~-principal** /'vaɪs'prɪnsəpəl/ *n* (AmE) subdirector, -tora *m,f*

viceroy /'vaɪsrɔɪ/ *n* virrey *m*

vice versa /'vaɪsi'vɜːrsə, 'vaɪs'vɜːrsə || ˌvaɪsi'vɜːsə, ˌvaɪs 'vɜːsə/ *adv* viceversa

vicinity /vɪ'sɪnəti/ *n* [u] (frml) inmediaciones *fpl*, alrededores *mpl*; **there are few shops in this ~** hay pocas tiendas en esta zona; **in the ~ of $100** alrededor de los 100 dólares, unos 100 dólares

vicious /'vɪʃəs/ *adj* **1** (savage, violent) ‹*dog*› fiero, malo; ‹*thug/criminal*› despiadado, sanguinario; ‹*attack*› feroz, salvaje; ‹*crime*› atroz, sanguinario; **he has a ~ temper** tiene muy mal genio; **there's a ~ streak in him** tiene una veta violenta **2** (malicious) ‹*gossip/rumor*› malicioso **3** (depraved) (liter) ‹*habit*› depravado

vicious circle *n* círculo *m* vicioso

viciously /'vɪʃəsli/ *adv* brutalmente, ferozmente

vicissitudes /vɪ'sɪsətuːdz || -tjuːdz || vɪ'sɪsɪtjuːdz/ *pl n* (frml) (*sometimes sing*) vicisitudes *fpl*, avatares *mpl*

victim /'vɪktəm || 'vɪktɪm/ *n* víctima *f*; **cancer ~s** víctimas del cáncer; **the flood ~s** los damnificados por las inundaciones; **to fall ~ to sth** ser* víctima de algo

victimization /'vɪktəmə'zeɪʃən || ˌvɪktɪmaɪ'zeɪʃən/ *n* [u] trato *m* injusto *or* discriminatorio

victimize /'vɪktəmaɪz || 'vɪktɪmaɪz/ *vt* victimizar*, tratar injustamente, discriminar

victor /'vɪktər || 'vɪktə(r)/ *n* vencedor, -dora *m,f*

Victoria Cross /vɪk'tɔːriə/ *n* (in UK) *la más alta condecoración militar británica*

Victorian /vɪk'tɔːriən/ *adj* victoriano

victorious /vɪk'tɔːriəs/ *adj* ‹*army*› victorioso; ‹*team*› vencedor, ganador

victory /'vɪktəri/ *n* [u c] (*pl* **-ries**) victoria *f*, triunfo *m*; (Mil) victoria *f*; **to win a ~ (over sb/sth)** obtener* una victoria (sobre algn/algo)

victualler /'vɪtḷər || 'vɪtḷə(r)/ *n*: **licensed ~** (BrE frml) *persona encargada de un establecimiento que expende bebidas alcohólicas*

victuals /'vɪtḷz/ *pl n* (arch) vituallas *fpl*, víveres *mpl*

video¹ /'vɪdiəʊ/ *n* (*pl* **videos**) **1** [u] (medium) video *m* *or* (Esp) vídeo *m*; **on ~** en video *or* (Esp) vídeo; (*before n*) ‹*channel/signal*› de video *or* (Esp) vídeo; **~ camera** videocámara *f*; **~ recorder** aparato *m* de video *or* (Esp) vídeo; **~ recording** grabación *f* en video *or* (Esp) vídeo **2** [c] (recording) video *m* *or* (Esp) vídeo *m*; **a home ~** un video *or* (Esp) vídeo casero; **a pop ~** un videoclip; (*before n*) **~ film** videofilm *m*; **~ nasty** *videofilm pornográfico y/o de violencia* **3** [c] (recorder) video *m* *or* (Esp) vídeo *m*

video² *vt* **videoes, videoing, videoed** grabar

video: **~cassette** /'vɪdiəʊkə'set/ *n* videocasete *m*; (*before n*) **~cassette recorder** magnetoscopio *m*, video *m* *or* (Esp) vídeo *m*; **~ display unit** *n* pantalla *f* (de visualización), monitor *m*; **~ game** *n* videojuego *m*

videotape¹ /'vɪdiəʊteɪp/ *n* [u c] (magnetic tape) cinta *f* de video *or* (Esp) vídeo

videotape² *vt* grabar en video *or* (Esp) vídeo, videograbar

vie /vaɪ/ *vi* **vies, vying, vied to ~ (WITH sb) (FOR sth)**: **they ~ed with each other for their mother's affection** se rivalizaban por conseguir el cariño de su madre; **various factions are vying for control of the party** varias facciones se disputan el control del partido *or* pugnan por hacerse con el control del partido

Vienna /vi'enə/ *n* Viena *f*

Viennese /'viə'niːz/ *adj* vienés

Vietnam /'viːet'nɑːm, -næm || vjet'næm/ *n* Vietnam *m*; (*before n*) **the ~ War** la guerra de(l) Vietnam

Vietnamese¹ /vi'etnə'miːz || ˌvɪetnə'miːz/ *adj* vietnamita

Vietnamese² *n* (*pl* **~**) **1** [c] (person) vietnamita *mf* **2** [u] (language) vietnamita *m*

view¹ /vjuː/ *n*

A [u] **1** (sight) vista *f*; **as we turned right, the hotel came into ~** al torcer a la derecha pudimos ver el hotel *or* el hotel apareció ante nuestra vista; **to be hidden from ~** estar* oculto; **in full ~ of sb/sth** a la vista de algn/algo **2** (range of vision): **we had a good ~ of the stage** veíamos muy bien el escenario; **you're blocking my ~** me estás tapando, no me dejas ver

B [c] (scene, vista) vista *f*; **an apartment with an ocean ~** un apartamento con vista al mar

C [c] (opinion, attitude) opinión *f*, parecer *m*; **you have a peculiar ~ of things** tienes una visión extraña de las cosas; **to have *o* hold ~s on/about sth** tener* ideas *or* opiniones sobre algo; **she takes the ~ that ...** ella opina que ...; ***to take a dim ~ of sth*** (colloq): **she took a dim ~ of his arriving so late** no le pareció nada bien que llegara tan tarde; ***to take the long/short ~*** adoptar una perspectiva amplia/limitada

D (plan, intention): **with a ~ to -ING, with the ~ of -ING** con la idea DE + INF, con vistas A + INF

E (*in phrases*) **in view**: **always keep your ultimate goal in ~** nunca pierdas de vista el objetivo que persigues; **with this in ~** con este fin; **in view of** en vista de; **in ~ of the fact that ...** en vista de que ..., dado que ... (frml); **on view**: **the winning entries will go on ~ to the public on Saturday** las obras premiadas podrán verse *or* se expondrán al público a partir del sábado

view² *vt*

A (look at) ‹*sights/scene/television*› ver*, mirar; **~ed from the side, he resembles his brother** (visto) de perfil, se parece a su hermano

B (inspect) **1** ‹*property*› ver* **2** ‹*accounts*› examinar

C (regard) ver*, considerar; **we ~ the matter with concern** el asunto nos preocupa

■ **view** *vi* (TV) ver* la televisión; **the ~ing public** los televidentes

viewer /'vjuːər || 'vjuːə(r)/ *n* **1** (person) telespectador, -dora *m,f*, televidente *mf* **2** (for slides) visionadora *f*

viewfinder /'vjuː'faɪndər || 'vjuˌfaɪndə(r)/ *n* visor *m*

viewing /'vjuːɪŋ/ *n* **1** [u c] (of house) visita *f*; (of items to be auctioned) exposición *f*; **Ⓢ viewing by appointment** se ruega concertar cita para visitar (la propiedad) **2** [c] (at an art gallery) vernissage *m*

viewpoint /'vjuːpɔɪnt/ *n* punto *m* de vista; **from his ~** desde su punto de vista

vigil /'vɪdʒəl || 'vɪdʒɪl/ *n* **1** (watch) (liter *or* journ) vela *f*; **to keep (a) ~ over sth** velar sobre algo **2** (Relig) vigilia *f*

vigilance /'vɪdʒələns || 'vɪdʒɪləns/ *n* [u] vigilancia *f*

vigilant /'vɪdʒələnt || 'vɪdʒɪlənt/ *adj* alerta, vigilante, atento

vigilante /'vɪdʒə'lænti || ˌvɪdʒɪ'lænti/ *n* vigilante, -ta *m,f* (*miembro de un grupo parapolicial*); (*before n*) **~ group** grupo *m* *or* escuadra *f* de vigilancia

vignette /vɪn'jet/ *n* **1** (literary sketch) estampa *f* **2** (Art, Phot, Publ) viñeta *f*

vigor, (BrE) **vigour** /'vɪgər || 'vɪgə(r)/ *n* [u] vigor *m*, energía *f*

vigorous /'vɪgərəs/ *adj* ‹*exercise/defense*› enérgico; ‹*denial*› rotundo; ‹*growth*› vigoroso; ‹*economy*› pujante

vigorously /'vɪgərəsli/ *adv* ‹*exercise/protest*› enérgicamente; ‹*deny*› rotundamente

vigour *n* [u] (BrE) ▸**vigor**

Viking /'vaɪkɪŋ/ *n* vikingo, -ga *m,f*

vile /vaɪl/ *adj* **viler, vilest** **1** (evil, despicable) (liter) vil (liter) **2** (colloq) ‹*taste/food*› vomitivo (fam), asqueroso, repugnante; ‹*color/weather*› horrible, inmundo; **to have a**

V

~ **temper** tener* muy mal genio

vilification /ˌvɪləfəˈkeɪʃən || ˌvɪlɪfrˈkeɪʃən/ *n* [u] (frml) vilipendio *m* (frml)

vilify /ˈvɪləfaɪ || ˈvɪlɪfaɪ/ *vt* **-fies, -fying, -fied** (frml) vilipendiar (frml)

villa /ˈvɪlə/ *n* 1 (Hist) villa *f* 2 (holiday house) chalet *m*; (in the country) chalet *m*, casa *f* de campo

village /ˈvɪlɪdʒ/ *n* (large) pueblo *m*; (small) aldea *f*; (*before n*) ~ **hall** *sala comunal de un pueblo*

villager /ˈvɪlədʒər || ˈvɪlɪdʒə(r)/ *n* (of large village) vecino, -na *m,f or* habitante *mf* del pueblo; (of small village) aldeano, -na *m,f*

villain /ˈvɪlən/ *n* 1 (rascal) (hum) granuja (hum), pillo (hum) 2 (in fiction) villano, -na *m,f*; **the ~ of the piece** el malo de la obra (fam) 3 (criminal) (BrE sl) maleante *mf*

villainous /ˈvɪlənəs/ *adj* infame, espantoso

villainy /ˈvɪləni/ *n* [u c] (*pl* **-nies**) (liter) vileza *f*, infamia *f* (liter)

vim /vɪm/ *n* [u] (colloq) empuje *m*, brío *m*; **with ~ and vigor** con gran brío

vinaigrette /ˌvɪnɪˈgret/ *n* [u c] vinagreta *f*

vindicate /ˈvɪndəkeɪt || ˈvɪndɪkeɪt/ *vt* (frml) 1 (justify) ‹*action*› justificar*; ‹*assertion*› confirmar; ‹*right*› reivindicar* 2 (free from blame) ‹*person*› vindicar* (frml)

vindication /ˌvɪndəˈkeɪʃən || ˌvɪndɪˈkeɪʃən/ *n* [u] 1 (of warnings) confirmación *f*; (of claim, methods) reivindicación *f* 2 (exoneration) vindicación *f* (frml)

vindictive /vɪnˈdɪktɪv/ *adj* vengativo

vine /vaɪn/ *n* 1 (*grape*~) (on ground) vid *f*; (climbing) parra *f*; (*before n*) ~ **grower** viticultor, -tora *m,f* 2 (climbing plant) enredadera *f*; **hanging ~s** lianas *fpl*

vinegar /ˈvɪnɪgər || ˈvɪnɪgə(r)/ *n* [u] vinagre *m*

vineyard /ˈvɪnjərd, -jɑːrd || ˈvɪnjəd, -jɑːd/ *n* viñedo *m*, viña *f*

vintage¹ /ˈvɪntɪdʒ/ *n* 1 (wine, year) cosecha *f*; **the 1963 ~** la cosecha de 1963 2 (harvest, season) vendimia *f*

vintage² *adj* (*before n, no comp*) 1 ‹*wine*› añejo 2 (outstanding, classic) excelente; **1966 was a ~ year for British football** 1966 fue un año excelente para el fútbol británico 3 (typical) típico; **the speech was ~ Churchill** fue un típico discurso a lo Churchill

vintage car *n* (esp BrE) coche *m* antiguo (*fabricado entre 1919 y 1930*)

vintner /ˈvɪntnər || ˈvɪntnə(r)/ *n* vinicultor, -tora *m,f*, vitivinicultor, -tora *m,f*, viñatero, -ra *m,f*

vinyl /ˈvaɪnḷ/ *n* [u c] vinilo *m*

viola /viˈəʊlə/ *n* (Mus) viola *f*

violate /ˈvaɪəleɪt/ *vt*

A ‹*agreement/rights*› violar; ‹*ban*› desobedecer*; **to ~ sb's privacy** no respetar la privacidad de algn

B ‹*shrine/grave*› profanar

violation /ˌvaɪəˈleɪʃən/ *n* [u c] (of agreement, law, right) violación *f*; (of promise) incumplimiento *m*; **human rights ~s** violaciones de los derechos humanos; **a traffic ~** una infracción de tráfico; **to be in ~ of sth** contravenir* algo (frml)

violence /ˈvaɪələns/ *n* [u] violencia *f*; **to use ~** hacer* uso de la fuerza *or* de la violencia; **to do ~ to sth** distorsionar algo

violent /ˈvaɪələnt/ *adj* 1 (involving physical force) ‹*person/behavior*› violento; **he met a ~ death** tuvo una muerte violenta 2 (strong, forceful) ‹*storm/explosion/kick*› violento, fuerte; ‹*grief*› intenso; ‹*pain*› violento, intenso; **he has a ~ temper** tiene muy mal genio; **she took a ~ dislike to him** le tomó una manía terrible

violently /ˈvaɪələntli/ *adv* violentamente; **he is ~ opposed to the proposal** se opone terminantemente a la propuesta; **she was ~ sick** vomitó mucho

violet /ˈvaɪələt/ *n* 1 [c] (Bot) violeta *f*; ***a shrinking ~*** una persona tímida y modesta 2 [u] (color) violeta *m*; (*before n*) violeta *adj inv*

violin /ˌvaɪəˈlɪn/ *n* violín *m*; **first ~** (leader) primer violín *mf*, concertino *m*; **first/second ~s** primeros/segundos violines; (*before n*) ~ **case** estuche *m* de violín

violinist /ˌvaɪəˈlɪnəst || ˌvaɪəˈlɪnɪst/ *n* violinista *mf*

violoncello /ˌvaɪələnˈtʃeləʊ/ *n* (*pl* **-los**) (frml) violoncelo *m*, violonchelo *m*

VIP *n* (colloq) (= **very important person**) VIP *mf*; (*before n*) ~ **lounge** sala *f* de VIPS; **they gave him (the) ~ treatment** lo trataron como a un VIP

viper /ˈvaɪpər || ˈvaɪpə(r)/ *n* víbora *f*

viral /ˈvaɪrəl || ˈvaɪərəl/ *adj* viral, vírico

virgin¹ /ˈvɜːrdʒən || ˈvɜːdʒɪn/ *n* virgen *f*; **the (Blessed) V~ Mary** la (Santísima) Virgen María

virgin² *adj* 1 ‹*innocence/modesty*› virginal; **the ~ birth** el alumbramiento virginal (*de la Virgen María*) 2 ‹*forest*› virgen; ‹*snow*› intacto 3 (unprocessed): ~ **wool** lana *f* virgen; ~ **olive oil** aceite *m* de oliva virgen

virginal /ˈvɜːrdʒənl || ˈvɜːdʒɪnl/ *adj* virginal

Virgin Islands *pl n* Islas *fpl* Vírgenes

virginity /vərˈdʒɪnəti || vəˈdʒɪnɪti/ *n* [u] virginidad *f*; **to lose one's ~** perder* la virginidad

Virgo /ˈvɜːrgəʊ || ˈvɜːgəʊ/ *n* (*pl* **-gos**) 1 (sign) (*no art*) Virgo 2 [c] (person) Virgo *or* virgo *mf*; *see also* **Aquarius**

virile /ˈvɪrəl || ˈvɪraɪl/ *adj* viril, varonil

virility /vəˈrɪləti/ *n* [u] virilidad *f*

virtual /ˈvɜːrtʃuəl || ˈvɜːtjʊəl, ˈvɜːtʃʊəl/ *adj* (*before n*)

A (near total): **traffic is at a ~ standstill** el tráfico está prácticamente paralizado

B (Comput, Opt) virtual

virtually /ˈvɜːrtʃuəli || ˈvɜːtjʊəli, ˈvɜːtʃʊəli/ *adv* prácticamente, casi

virtual reality *n* realidad *f* virtual

virtue /ˈvɜːrtʃuː || ˈvɜːtjuː, ˈvɜːtʃuː/ *n*

A [u c] (moral excellence) virtud *f*; ***to make a ~ of necessity*** hacer* de la necesidad virtud

B [c] (advantage) ventaja *f*; **there's no ~ in speed at the expense of accuracy** no tiene mérito trabajar rápido si se cometen errores

C **by** *o* (frml) **in virtue of** (*as prep*) en virtud de

D [u] (chastity, fidelity) virtud *f*

virtuosity /ˌvɜːrtʃuˈɑːsəti || ˌvɜːtjʊˈɒsəti, ˌvɜːtʃʊˈɒsəti/ *n* [u] virtuosismo *m*

virtuoso /ˌvɜːrtʃuˈəʊsəʊ || ˌvɜːtjʊˈəʊsəʊ, ˌvɜːtʃʊˈəʊsəʊ/ *n* (*pl* **-sos** *or* **-si** /-si/) virtuoso, -sa *m,f*, artista *mf*; (*before n*) ‹*performance*› propio de un virtuoso

virtuous /ˈvɜːrtʃuəs || ˈvɜːtjʊəs, ˈvɜːtʃʊəs/ *adj* virtuoso

virulent /ˈvɪrələnt, ˈvɪrjə- || ˈvɪrʊlənt, ˈvɪrjʊ-/ *adj* ‹*infection*› virulento; ‹*attack/opposition*› violento, virulento

virus /ˈvaɪrəs || ˈvaɪərəs/ *n* (*pl* **~es**) virus *m*

visa /ˈviːzə/ *n* (*pl* **-s**) visado *m*, visa *f* (AmL)

vis-à-vis /ˈviːzəˈviː || ˌviːzɑːˈviː/ *prep* con respecto a, respecto de, con relación a, en relación con

visceral /ˈvɪsərəl/ *adj* (liter) visceral

viscose /ˈvɪskəʊs/ *n* [u] (Tex) viscosilla *f*

viscount /ˈvaɪkaʊnt/ *n* vizconde *m*

viscous /ˈvɪskəs/ *adj* viscoso

vise, (BrE) **vice** /vaɪs/ *n* torno *m or* tornillo *m* de banco

visibility /ˌvɪzəˈbɪləti/ *n* [u] visibilidad *f*

visible /ˈvɪzəbəl/ *adj*

A 1 (able to be seen) visible 2 (noticeable) ‹*sign/improvement*› evidente, palpable; **with no ~ means of support** aparentemente sin recursos

B (Econ) ‹*earnings/exports*› visible

visibly /ˈvɪzəbli/ *adv* visiblemente; **he was ~ thinner** estaba visiblemente más delgado; **she was ~ moved** su emoción era manifiesta

vision /ˈvɪʒən/ *n*

A 1 [u] (faculty of sight) visión *f*, vista *f*; **perfect ~** visión perfecta; **good/poor ~** buena/mala vista 2 (visibility) visibilidad *f*; **field of ~** campo *m* visual

B [u] (imagination, foresight) visión *f* (de futuro)

C [c] 1 (dreamlike revelation) visión *f* 2 (mental image, concept) imagen *f*, visión *f*; **I had ~s of you being rushed to hospital** ya me imaginaba que te habrían llevado de urgencia al hospital

visionary¹ /ˈvɪʒəneri || ˈvɪʒənri/ *adj* 1 (farsighted) ‹*leader/plan*› con visión de futuro 2 (unrealistic) utópico

visionary² *n* (*pl* **-ries**) 1 (dreamer) visionario, -ria *m,f* 2 (seer) iluminado, -da *m,f*, visionario, -ria *m,f*

visit¹ /ˈvɪzət || ˈvɪzɪt/ *n* visita *f*; **to pay a ~ to sb** hacerle* una visita a algn, ir* a ver a algn; **this is my first ~ to Rome** esta es la primera vez que visito Roma, esta es la primera visita que hago a Roma

visit² *vt*

A ‹*museum/town*› visitar; ‹*friend*› visitar, ir*/venir* a ver

B (liter) (*usu pass*) (inflict) **to ~ sth ON sb** infligirle* algo A algn

■ **visit** *vi* **1** (pay a call) hacer* una visita; (stay) estar* de visita; **to go ~ing** ir* de visita **2** **visiting** *pres p* ‹*team*› visitante; ‹*lecturer*› invitado **3** (chat) (AmE colloq) **to ~ WITH sb** charlar (CON algn) (fam)

visitation /ˈvɪzəˈteɪʃən || ˌvɪzɪˈteɪʃən/ *n*

A **1** (Occult) aparición *f* **2** (act of God) azote *m*

B (Relig) (official call) visita *f* (pastoral)

visiting /ˈvɪzətɪŋ || ˈvɪzɪtɪŋ/ *n* [u] (*before n*) **~ hours** horario *m* de visitas

visiting card *n* tarjeta *f* de visita

visitor /ˈvɪzətər || ˈvɪzɪtə(r)/ *n* (to museum, town etc) visitante *mf*; (to person's home) visita *f*; **only two ~s per patient** visitas de dos personas como máximo por paciente; **~s' book** libro *m* de visitas

visitor center *n* (AmE) centro *m* de informaciones

visor /ˈvaɪzər || ˈvaɪzə(r)/ *n* visera *f*

vista /ˈvɪstə/ *n* vista *f*; (panoramic) panorama *m*

visual /ˈvɪʒuəl/ *adj* visual; **the ~ arts** las artes plásticas *or* visuales; **~ display unit** pantalla *f*, monitor *m*

visualize /ˈvɪʒuəlaɪz/ *vt* **1** (picture mentally) imaginar, imaginarse, visualizar* **2** (expect) prever*

visually /ˈvɪʒuəli/ *adv* visualmente

vital /ˈvaɪtl̩/ *adj*

A **1** (essential) ‹*equipment/supplies*› esencial, fundamental; **to be ~ TO sb/sth** ser* de vital *or* fundamental importancia PARA algn/algo **2** (crucial, decisive) ‹*factor/issue*› decisivo, de vital importancia; **a matter of ~ importance** un asunto de vital importancia **3** (necessary for life) ‹*organ/function*› vital

B (vigorous) ‹*person*› vital, lleno de vitalidad *or* de vida

vitality /vaɪˈtæləti/ *n* [u] vitalidad *f*

vitally /ˈvaɪtli || ˈvaɪtəli/ *adv*: **it is ~ important** es de vital *or* fundamental importancia

vital statistics *pl n* **1** (in demography) estadísticas *fpl* demográficas **2** (of a woman) (hum) medidas *fpl*

vitamin /ˈvaɪtəmən || ˈvɪtəmɪn, ˈvaɪt-/ *n* vitamina *f*; (*before n*) **~ content/complex** contenido *m*/complejo *m* vitamínico; **~ pill** *o* **tablet** vitamina *f*

vitiate /ˈvɪʃieɪt/ *vt* (frml) **1** (spoil) menoscabar, desmerecer* **2** ‹*contract/agreement*› viciar

vitreous /ˈvɪtriəs/ *adj* ‹*substance/sheen*› vítreo; ‹*china/enamel*› vidriado

vitriol /ˈvɪtriəl/ *n* [u] (rancor) virulencia *f*, vitriolo *m*

vitriolic /ˈvɪtriˈɑːlɪk || ˌvɪtriˈɒlɪk/ *adj* virulento, vitriólico

vituperation /vaɪˈtuːpəˈreɪʃən, vɪ- || vɪˈtjuːpəˈreɪʃən/ *n* [u] (frml) vituperio *m* (frml)

viva /ˈvaɪvə/ *n* (BrE Educ) (for MA, PhD) defensa *f* de la tesis; (for BA) *examen oral que decide la nota global de la licenciatura*

vivacious /vəˈveɪʃəs || vɪˈveɪʃəs/ *adj* vivaz, lleno de vida

viva voce¹ /ˈvaɪvəˈvəʊtʃi/ *adj* (frml): **~ ~ examination** ▸**viva**

viva voce² *adv* (frml) oralmente

vivid /ˈvɪvəd || ˈvɪvɪd/ *adj* **1** ‹*color*› vivo, intenso **2** ‹*memory/dream*› vívido; ‹*account/description*› gráfico, vívido **3** ‹*imagination*› rico, fértil

vividly /ˈvɪvədli || ˈvɪvɪdli/ *adv* **1** ‹*colored/painted*› vistosamente **2** ‹*describe*› vívidamente, gráficamente

vividness /ˈvɪvədnəs || ˈvɪvɪdnɪs/ *n* [u] **1** (of colors) intensidad *f*, lo vivo **2** (of description) lo gráfico *or* vívido

vivisection /ˈvɪvəˈsekʃən || ˌvɪvɪˈsekʃən/ *n* [u c] vivisección *f*

vixen /ˈvɪksən/ *n* (Zool) zorra *f*, raposa *f*

viz /vɪz/ *adv* a saber

VJ-Day /ˈviːˈdʒeɪdeɪ/ *n*: *día de la victoria aliada sobre el Japón*

V-neck /ˈviːnek/, (BrE also) **V-necked** /ˈviːnekt/ *adj* de escote *or* cuello en pico, de escote en V

vocabulary /vəʊˈkæbjəleri || vəʊˈkæbjʊləri/ *n* (*pl* **-ries**) vocabulario *m*

vocal /ˈvəʊkəl/ *adj* **1** (Mus) vocal **2** (vociferous): **a very ~ minority** una minoría que se hace oír

vocal cords *pl n* cuerdas *fpl* vocales

vocalist /ˈvəʊkələst || ˈvəʊkəlɪst/ *n* cantante *mf*; **backing ~** integrante *mf* del coro

vocation /vəʊˈkeɪʃən/ *n* vocación *f*

vocational /vəʊˈkeɪʃn̩əl || vəʊˈkeɪʃənl̩/ *adj*: **~ guidance** orientación *f* profesional; **~ training** ≈ formación *f* profesional

vocative /ˈvɑːkətɪv || ˈvɒkətɪv/ *n* vocativo *m*

vociferate /vəʊˈsɪfəreɪt || vəˈsɪfəreɪt/ *vi* (frml) vociferar

vociferous /vəʊˈsɪfərəs || vəˈsɪfərəs/ *adj* ‹*crowd/assembly*› vociferante; ‹*protest*› ruidoso

vociferously /vəʊˈsɪfərəsli || vəˈsɪfərəsli/ *adv* ruidosamente

vodka /ˈvɑːdkə || ˈvɒdkə/ *n* [u c] vodka *m*

vogue /vəʊg/ *n* [c u] (fashion) moda *f*; **to be in ~** estar* de moda *or* en boga; **to come into ~** ponerse* de moda

voice¹ /vɔɪs/ *n*

A [c u] **1** (sound, faculty) voz *f*; **to hear ~s** oír* voces; **in a low/loud ~** en voz baja/alta; **to lose one's ~** quedarse afónico *or* sin voz; **to raise/lower one's ~** levantar/bajar la voz; **the ~ of experience** la voz de la experiencia; ***to give ~ to sth*** expresar algo; ***with one ~*** unánimemente **2** (Mus) voz *f*; **she's in good ~ tonight** esta noche está cantando muy bien

B **1** (opinion) (*no pl*) voz *f*; **to have no ~ in sth** no tener* voz en algo; ***to be of one ~*** ser* de la misma opinión **2** [u] (instrument, agency) portavoz *m*, voz *f*

C (Ling) [c] (verb form) voz *f*; **active/passive ~** voz activa/pasiva

voice² *vt* ‹*opinion/concern/anger*› expresar

voice: **~-activated** /ˌvɔɪsˈæktəveɪtəd || ˌvɔɪsˈæktɪveɪtɪd/ *adj* (*before n*) accionado con la voz; **~ box** *n* laringe *f*

voiced /vɔɪst/ *adj* (Ling) sonoro

voiceless /ˈvɔɪsləs || ˈvɔɪslɪs/ *adj* (Ling) sordo

voice mail *n* **1** [u] (facility) buzón *f* de voz, correo *m* de voz **2** [c] (message) mensaje *m* de voz

voice-over /ˈvɔɪsˌəʊvər || ˈvɔɪsˌəʊvə(r)/ *n* voz *f* en off, voz *f* superpuesta

void¹ /vɔɪd/ *n* vacío *m*

void² *adj*

A (empty) (liter) (*pred*) **to be ~ OF sth** estar* desprovisto *or* falto de algo

B (invalid) (Law) nulo, inválido; **to make sth ~** anular *or* invalidar algo

voile /vɔɪl || vɔɪl, vwɑːl/ *n* [u] voile *m*

vol (*pl* **vols**) (**= volume**) **1** (book) vol., t. **2** (Phys) vol.

volatile /ˈvɑːlətl̩ || ˈvɒlətaɪl/ *adj* **1** (Chem) volátil **2** ‹*person/personality*› imprevisible, voluble **3** ‹*situation/market*› inestable, volátil

volcanic /vɑːlˈkænɪk /vɒlˈkænɪk/ *adj* volcánico

volcano /vɑːlˈkeɪnəʊ /vɒlˈkeɪnəʊ/ *n* (*pl* **-noes** *or* **-nos**) volcán *m*

vole /vəʊl/ *n* ratón *m* de campo

volition /vəʊˈlɪʃən || vəˈlɪʃən/ *n* [u] (frml) volición *f* (frml); **of one's own ~** por voluntad propia, voluntariamente, (de) motu proprio

volley¹ /ˈvɑːli || ˈvɒli/ *n*

A (of shots) descarga *f* (cerrada); (of protests, blows) lluvia *f*

B (Sport) volea *f*

volley² *vt/i* volear

volleyball /ˈvɑːlibɔːl || ˈvɒlibɔːl/ *n* [u] vóleibol *m*, balonvolea *m*

volt /vəʊlt/ *n* voltio *m*

voltage /ˈvəʊltɪdʒ/ *n* [c u] voltaje *m*

volte-face /ˈvɔːltˈfɑːs || ˌvɒltˈfɑːs/ *n* (*pl* ~) (frml) cambio *m* radical de opinión (*or* de política *etc*)

voluble /ˈvɑːljəbəl || ˈvɒljʊbəl/ *adj* ‹*speaker/supporter*› locuaz; ‹*speech/remarks*› prolijo, extenso

volubly /ˈvɑːljəbli || ˈvɒljʊbli/ *adv* con locuacidad

volume /ˈvɑːljuːm || ˈvɒljuːm/ *n*

A [u c] (Phys) (of a body) volumen *m*; (of container) capacidad *f*

B [u] (amount) cantidad *f*, volumen *m*; (of business, trade) volumen *m*

C [u] (of sound) volumen *m*

D [c] **1** (book) tomo *m*, volumen *m* **2** **volumes** *pl* (a great deal) montones *mpl* (fam); ***to speak ~s for sb/sth*** decir* mucho de algn/algo

voluminous /və'lu:mənəs || və'lu:mɪnəs/ *adj* **1** ‹*blouse/skirt*› amplísimo **2** ‹*correspondence*› voluminoso; ‹*file*› abultado

voluntarily /'vɑ:lən'terəli || 'vɒləntrɪli/ *adv* voluntariamente, por voluntad propia

voluntary /'vɑ:lənteri || 'vɒləntri/ *adj*

A (unforced) voluntario; **~ redundancy** (BrE) baja *f* incentivada

B (unpaid) ‹*work*› voluntario; ‹*organization*› de beneficencia; **~ worker** voluntario, -ria *m,f*

volunteer¹ /'vɑ:lən'tɪr || ,vɒlən'tɪər/ *n* voluntario, -ria *m,f*; (*before n*) ‹*organization*› de voluntarios

volunteer² *vt* ofrecer*; **to ~ one's services** ofrecer* sus (*or* mis *etc*) servicios; **he's not going to ~ the information** no nos dará la información (de) motu proprio; **Harry's gone, she ~ed** —Harry se ha ido —dijo sin que nadie se lo hubiera preguntado

■ **volunteer** *vi* ofrecerse*; **to ~ to + INF** ofrecerse* A + INF; **he ~ed for the navy** (Mil) se alistó como voluntario en la marina

voluptuous /və'lʌptʃuəs/ *adj* voluptuoso

vomit¹ /'vɑ:mət || 'vɒmɪt/ *vi/t* vomitar

vomit² *n* [u] vómito *m*

voodoo /'vu:du:/ *n* vudú *m*

voracious /vɔ:'reɪʃəs || və'reɪʃəs/ *adj* voraz

voraciously /vɔ:'reɪʃəsli || və'reɪʃəsli/ *adv* con voracidad, vorazmente

voracity /vɔ:'ræsəti || və'ræsəti/, *n* [u] voracidad *f*

vortex /'vɔ:rteks /'vɔ:teks/ *n* (*pl* **-texes** *or* **-tices** /-tɪsi:z/) **1** (of whirlpool, whirlwind) vórtice *m* **2** (of events) (frml) torbellino *m*

vote¹ /vəʊt/ *n*

A **1** [c] (ballot cast) voto *m*, sufragio *m* (frml); **to cast one's ~** (frml) emitir su (*or* mi *etc*) voto (frml) **2** [u] (right to vote) **the ~** el sufragio, el derecho de *or* al voto; **to give sb/gain the ~** conceder a algn/conseguir* el sufragio *or* el derecho de *or* al voto

B **1** [c] (act) votación *f*; **to put sth to the ~, to take a ~ on sth** someter algo a votación **2** [u c] (collective decision): **to pass a ~ of confidence/no confidence** aprobar* un voto de confianza/de censura; **she proposed a ~ of thanks to the Chairman** pidió que constara el agradecimiento de todos al presidente

vote² *vi* votar; **to ~ FOR sb** votar POR *or* A algn; **to ~ ON sth** someter algo a votación; **to ~ FOR/AGAINST sth** votar A FAVOR DE/EN CONTRA DE algo

■ **vote** *vt*

A **1** (support, choose) votar por, votar; **I've ~d Democrat all my life** toda la vida he votado por *or* a los demócratas **2** (elect) elegir* por votación; **she was ~d onto the board** fue elegida por votación para integrar la junta; **to ~ sb into office** votar por *or* a algn para un cargo; **to ~ sb out of office** votar para reemplazar a algn en su cargo **3** (declare, judge) considerar

B **1** (approve) aprobar*; **they ~ed themselves a pay increase** se aprobaron un aumento de sueldo **2** (decide) **to ~ to + INF** votar POR + INF **3** (propose) (colloq) **to ~ (THAT)** votar por QUE (+ *subj*) (fam); **I ~ (that) we go by taxi** yo voto por que vayamos en taxi

(Phrasal verbs)

• **vote down** [v ▸ o ▸ adv, v ▸ adv ▸ o] rechazar* (*por votación*)

• **vote in** [v ▸ o ▸ adv, v ▸ adv ▸ o] elegir* (*por votación*)

• **vote out** [v ▸ o ▸ adv, v ▸ adv ▸ o] no reelegir*

vote-catching /'vəʊt,kætʃɪŋ/ *adj* electoralista

voter /'vəʊtər || 'vəʊtə(r)/ *n* votante *mf*; **swing** *o* (BrE) **floating ~** votante indeciso

voting /'vəʊtɪŋ/ *n* [u] votación *f*; (*before n*) **~ paper** (BrE) papeleta *f or* (AmL tb) boleta *f* (de voto)

votive /'vəʊtɪv/ *adj* votivo; **~ offering** exvoto *m*

vouch /vaʊtʃ/ *vi* **to ~ FOR sb** responder POR algn; **to ~ FOR sth** responder DE algo, dar* fe DE algo

■ **vouch** *vt* **to ~ THAT** dar* fe DE QUE

voucher /'vaʊtʃər || 'vaʊtʃə(r)/ *n* **1** (cash substitute) vale *m* **2** (receipt) justificante *m*, comprobante *m*

vouchsafe /'vaʊtʃ'seɪf/ *vt* (liter) conceder (liter); **to ~ an explanation** ofrecer una explicación

vow¹ /vaʊ/ *n* voto *m*, promesa *f*; **he made a ~ never to see her again** juró que no la volvería a ver **to take (one's) ~s** (Relig) hacer* los votos, profesar

vow² *vt* jurar, hacer* voto de (frml); **to ~ to + INF**: **I ~ed to avenge my brother** juré que vengaría a mi hermano

vowel /'vaʊəl/ *n* vocal *f*; (*before n*) ‹*sound/system*› vocálico

voyage¹ /'vɔɪɪdʒ/ *n* viaje *m*; **(sea) ~** travesía *f*

voyage² *vi* (liter) viajar

voyager /'vɔɪədʒər || 'vɔɪɪdʒə(r)/ *n* (liter) viajero, -ra *m,f*; (by sea) navegante *mf*

voyeur /vwɑ:'jɜ:r, 'vɔɪ- || vwɑ:'jɜ:(r), 'vɔɪ-/ *n* voyeur *mf*, mirón, -rona *m,f*

voyeuristic /'vwɑ:jɜ:r'ɪstɪk/ *adj* voyeurista

VP = Vice President

vs = versus

V-shaped /'vi:ʃeɪpt/ *adj* en forma de V

V-sign /'vi:saɪn/ *n* **1** (for victory) signo *m* de la victoria **2** (vulgar gesture) (in UK): **to give sb the ~** ≈ hacerle* un corte de mangas a algn

VSO *n* (in UK) **= Voluntary Service Overseas**

VT, Vt = Vermont

vulcanize /'vʌlkənaɪz/ *vt* vulcanizar*

vulgar /'vʌlgər || 'vʌlgə(r)/ *adj*

A **1** (ill-mannered, coarse) ‹*person/remark*› grosero, ordinario, vulgar **2** (tasteless) ‹*taste/furniture/suit*› de mal gusto, ordinario, chabacano

B (of the people) (frml) ‹*belief/opinion*› del vulgo; **V~ Latin** latín *m* vulgar

C (Math): **~ fraction** fracción *f* común *or* ordinaria

vulgarity /vʌl'gærəti/ *n* (*pl* **-ties**) **1** [u] (coarseness) ordinariez *f*, grosería *f*, vulgaridad *f* **2** [u] (tastelessness) mal gusto *m*, chabacanería *f* **3** [c] (*usu pl*) (action, expression) grosería *f*, vulgaridad *f*

vulnerability /'vʌlnərə'bɪləti/ *n* [u] vulnerabilidad *f*

vulnerable /'vʌlnərəbəl/ *adj* vulnerable; **to be ~ TO sth** ser* vulnerable A algo

vulture /'vʌltʃər || 'vʌltʃə(r)/ *n* **1** (Zool) buitre *m*; (*turkey* **~**) gallinazo *m*, zopilote *m* (AmC, Méx), zamuro *m* (Ven) **2** (greedy opportunist) buitre *m*

vulva /'vʌlvə/ *n* (*pl* **-vas** *or* **-vae** /-vi:/) vulva *f*

vv = verses

Ww

W, w /'dʌbəljuː/ *n* W, w *f*

W 1 (Elec) (= **watt(s)**) W 2 (Geog) (= **west**) O

WA = **Washington**

wacky /'wæki/ *adj* **wackier, wackiest** (colloq) ‹*person*› chiflado (fam), chalado (fam); ‹*clothes/hairstyle*› estrambótico, extravagante; ‹*idea*› descabellado

wad /wɑːd || wɒd/ *n*
A (roll, bundle — of bills, notes) fajo *m*; (— of papers) montón *m*, tambache *m* (Méx); (— tied together) lío *m*
B (of paper, cloth) taco *m*; **a ~ of (absorbent) cotton** *o* (BrE) **cotton wool** un pedazo de algodón

wadding /'wɑːdɪŋ || 'wɒdɪŋ/ *n* [u] 1 (for packing) relleno *m* 2 (Med) *gasa o algodón formando una compresa o apósito*

waddle /'wɑːdl̩ || 'wɒdl̩/ *vi* «*person*» caminar *or* andar* como un pato; «*duck*» caminar balanceándose

wade /weɪd/ *vi* caminar (*por el agua, barro etc*); **they ~d across the stream** vadearon el arroyo

Phrasal verbs
- **wade in** [v ▸ adv] (colloq) meterse
- **wade through** [v ▸ prep ▸ o] (colloq) leerse* (*algo difícil, largo, aburrido etc*)

wader /'weɪdər || 'weɪdə(r)/ *n* 1 (Zool) ave *f*‡ zancuda 2 **waders** *pl* (Clothing) botas *fpl* de pescador

wading pool /'weɪdɪŋ/ *n* (AmE) *piscina portátil para niños*

wafer /'weɪfər || 'weɪfə(r)/ *n*
A 1 (Culin) galleta *f* de barquillo, oblea *f* 2 (Relig) hostia *f*
B 1 (thin piece) lámina *f* 2 (Comput, Electron) lámina *f or* oblea *f* (de silicio)

wafer-thin /'weɪfər'θɪn || ˌweɪfə'θɪn/ *adj* finísimo, delgadísimo

waffle¹ /'wɑːfəl || 'wɒfəl/ *n*
A [c] (Culin) wafle *m* (AmL), gofre *m* (Esp)
B [u] (nonsense) (BrE pej) palabrería *f*, palabrerío *m*; (in essay, exam) paja *f* (fam)

waffle² *vi* (esp BrE) hablar sin decir nada, cantinflear (fam); (in essay, exam) meter paja (fam), payar (RPl)

waft /wɑːft || 'wɒft/ *vi* (+ *adv compl*): **the smell of coffee that ~ed from the kitchen** el olor a café que venía de la cocina; **a feather ~ed in on the breeze** una pluma entró flotando con la brisa

wag¹ /wæg/ **-gg-** *vt* ‹*tail*› menear, mover*; **he ~ged his finger at her** le hizo un gesto admonitorio con el dedo
■ **wag** *vi* «*tail*» menearse, moverse*

wag² *n* 1 (of tail): **the dog greeted us with a ~ of its tail** el perro nos recibió meneando *or* moviendo el rabo 2 (wit, joker) bromista *mf*

wage¹ /weɪdʒ/ *n* (rate of pay) sueldo *m*, salario *m* (frml); **wages** (actual money) sueldo *m*, paga *f*; **minimum ~** salario mínimo; **a day's ~s** un jornal; **I'll pay you when I get my ~s** te pagaré cuando cobre; (*before n*) **~ claim** reivindicación *f* salarial; **~ increase** aumento *m or* incremento *m or* mejora *f* salarial *or* de sueldo

wage² *vt*: **to ~ war** hacer* la guerra; **to ~ war on** *o* **against sb** hacerle* la guerra a algn; **to ~ a campaign against sth** hacer* (una) campaña contra algo

wage earner *n* 1 (wage-paid worker) asalariado, -da *m,f* 2 (in paid employment): **they are all ~ ~s** todos trabajan

wager¹ /'weɪdʒər || 'weɪdʒə(r)/ *n* apuesta *f*; **to lay** *o* **make a ~** hacer* una apuesta, apostar*

wager² *vt* apostar*; **to ~ (THAT)** apostar* (A) QUE

wage worker *n* (AmE) ▸**wage earner**

waggish /'wægɪʃ/ *adj* ‹*person*› bromista, burlón; ‹*remark*› jocoso, burlón

waggle /'wægəl/ *vt* (colloq) mover*
■ **waggle** *vi* moverse*

waggon *n* (BrE) ▸**wagon**

wagon /'wægən/ *n*
A (drawn by animals) carro *m*; (covered) carromato *m*; ***on the ~***: **to go on the ~** dejar de beber; **he's been on the ~ since May** desde mayo que no bebe *or* que no prueba el alcohol; ***to fix sb's ~*** (AmE colloq): **I'll fix his ~!** ¡ya me las pagará!; (*before n*) **~ train** caravana *f* de carromatos
B 1 (delivery truck) (AmE) furgoneta *f or* camioneta *f* de reparto 2 (BrE Rail) vagón *m* de mercancías

wagtail /'wægteɪl/ *n* motacila *f*, aguzanieves *f*, lavandera *f*

waif /weɪf/ *n* (liter) *persona o animal sin hogar*; **~s and strays** niños *mpl* abandonados, gamines *mpl* (Col), palomillas *mpl* (Andes fam)

wail¹ /weɪl/ *vi* «*person*» llorar, gemir*; «*siren/bagpipes*» gemir*; «*wind*» aullar*, gemir*, ulular

wail² *n* (expressing grief) gemido *m*, lamento *m*; (of siren, wind) gemido *m*; (of new-born baby) vagido *m*; **a ~ of protest** un grito de protesta

wailing /'weɪlɪŋ/ *n* [u] llanto *m*, gemidos *mpl*; **the ~ of the wind/sirens** el gemir del viento/de las sirenas

waist /weɪst/ *n* 1 (Anat) (waistline) cintura *f*, talle *m*; **it's too tight around the ~** le (*or* me *etc*) queda muy apretado de cintura *or* talle; **stripped to the ~** desnudo de la cintura para arriba; **she has a short ~** es corta de talle 2 (of garment) talle *m*

waist: **~band** *n* pretina *f*, cinturilla *f*; **~coat** *n* (esp BrE) chaleco *m*; **~-deep** /'weɪst'diːp/ *adj* (*pred* **~ deep**): **we waded ~ deep through the river** vadeamos el río con el agua hasta la cintura

-waisted /'weɪstəd || 'weɪstɪd/ *suff*: **high~/drop~** de talle alto/bajo

waist: **~-high** /'weɪst'haɪ/ *adj* (*pred* **~ high**) que llega a la altura de la cintura; **~line** *n* (of garment) talle *m*; (of body) cintura *f*, talle *m*; **I'm watching my ~line** estoy guardando la línea

wait¹ /weɪt/ *vi*
A 1 esperar; **I ~ed (for) hours** estuve horas esperando, esperé horas; **~ until he asks you** espera (a) que él te pregunte; **sorry to keep you ~ing** perdón por hacerlo esperar; **just you ~!** ¡ya vas a ver!; **we'll have to ~ and see** habrá que esperar a ver qué pasa; **I can't ~ to see his face** me muero de ganas de ver la cara que pone; Ⓢ **shoe repairs while you wait** se arregla calzado en el acto; **to ~ FOR sth/sb** esperar algo/a algn; **well, what are you ~ing for?** ¿(a) qué esperas?, ¿(a) qué estás esperando?; **to ~ FOR sb/sth to + INF** esperar (A) QUE algn/algo (+ *subj*) 2 (be postponed) «*business/repairs*» esperar; **that will have to ~** eso tendrá que esperar
B (serve) **to ~ ON sb** atender* a algn; **to ~ at table** (BrE) servir* a la mesa; ▸**hand¹ B**
■ **wait** *vt*
A (await): **to ~ one's chance** esperar la oportunidad; **you have to ~ your turn** tienes que esperar (a) que te toque
B (serve): **to ~ table** (AmE) servir* a la mesa

(Phrasal verb)

- **wait up** [v ▸ adv] 1 (not go to bed) **to ~ up (FOR sb)** esperar (A algn) levantado 2 (pause) (AmE colloq) (*usu in imperative*): **~ up!** ¡(espera) un momento!

wait² *n* (*no pl*) espera *f*; **we're in for a long ~** vamos a tener que esperar un buen rato, tenemos para rato (fam); ***to lie in ~ for sb/sth*** estar* al acecho de algn/algo

waiter /'weɪtər || 'weɪtə(r)/ *n* camarero *m*, mesero *m* (AmL), mozo *m* (Col, CS), mesonero *m* (Ven)

waiting /'weɪtɪŋ/ *n* [u]

A (for something to happen) espera *f*; ⊘ **no waiting** prohibido estacionar

B (serving) trabajar de camarero (*or* mesero *etc*)

waiting: **~ list** *n* lista *f* de espera; **~ room** *n* sala *f* de espera

wait list *n* (AmE) ▸**waiting list**

waitperson /'weɪt,pɜːrsn || 'weɪt,pɜːsn/ *n* (*pl* **~s**) (AmE) camarero, -ra *m,f*, mesero, -ra *m,f* (AmL), mozo, -za *m,f* (Col, CS), mesonero, -ra *m,f* (Ven)

waitress /'weɪtrəs || 'weɪtrɪs/ *n* camarera *f*, mesera *f* (AmL), moza *f* (Col, CS), mesonera *f* (Ven)

waive /weɪv/ *vt* (frml) 1 (not apply) ‹*rule*› no aplicar*; ‹*condition*› no exigir* 2 (renounce) ‹*right/privilege*› renunciar a

wake¹ /weɪk/ (*past* **woke**; *past p* **woken**) *vt* despertar*; *see also* **wake up A**

■ **wake** *vi* 1 (become awake) despertar*, despertarse* 2 (be awake) (*only in -ing form*): **my waking hours** las horas que paso despierta

(Phrasal verb)

- **wake up**

A [v ▸ o ▸ adv, v ▸ adv ▸ o] despertar*; **to ~ sb's ideas up** (BrE) espabilar *or* despabilar a algn

B [v ▸ adv] (become awake) despertarse*; **he woke up to find himself in hospital** al despertar se dio cuenta de que estaba en el hospital; **~ up!** ¡despiértate!; (pay attention) ¡espabílate!, ¡despabílate!; **to ~ up TO sth** ‹*to danger/fact*› darse* cuenta *or* tomar conciencia DE algo

wake² *n*

A (of ship) estela *f*; **in the ~ of sth**: **the hurricane left a trail of destruction in its ~** el huracán dejó una estela de destrucción a su paso; **in the ~ of the revolution** tras la revolución

B (for dead person) velatorio *m*, velorio *m*

wakeful /'weɪkfəl/ *adj* 1 (unable to sleep) desvelado 2 (sleepless) (liter): **to have a ~ night** pasar la noche en vela 3 (alert) (liter) alerta

waken /'weɪkən/ (liter) *vt/i* despertar*

wake-up call /'weɪkʌp/ *n* 1 (telephone call) servicio *m* de despertador 2 (warning) llamada *f* de aviso

wakey-wakey /'weɪki'weɪki/ *interj* (BrE colloq): **~!** ¡vamos, despierta!

Wales /weɪlz/ *n* (el país de) Gales

walk¹ /wɔːk/ *vi*

A (go by foot) caminar, andar* (esp Esp); (in a leisurely way) pasear; **~, don't run!** ¡camina, no corras!; **I'll ~ with you as far as the library** te acompaño hasta la biblioteca; **to ~ BY** *o* **PAST sth** pasar POR algo; **you can't just ~ by without helping** no puedes seguir de largo sin pararte a ayudar; **he ~ed down/up the steps** bajó/subió los peldaños; **to ~ in/out** entrar/salir*; **to ~ up to sb** acercarse* a algn; ***to ~ tall*** ir* *or* andar* con la cabeza en alto

B (not use bus, car, etc) ir* a pie, ir* caminando *or* (esp Esp) andando; **there was no elevator so we had to ~ up** no había ascensor, así que tuvimos que subir por la escalera

C (Sport) (in baseball) dar* una base por bolas, pasar por bolas

■ **walk** *vt*

A (go along) ‹*hills/path*› recorrer, caminar por

B 1 (take for walk) ‹*dog*› pasear, sacar* a pasear; **she ~ed us off our feet** nos dejó agotados de tanto que nos hizo caminar 2 (accompany) acompañar; **I'll ~ you home** te acompaño hasta tu casa

(Phrasal verbs)

- **walk away** [v ▸ adv] (from a place) alejarse; **the driver ~ed away unhurt/with a few scratches** el conductor salió ileso/se escapó con sólo unos rasguños
- **walk away with** ▸**walk off with 2**
- **walk into** [v ▸ prep ▸ o] 1 (enter) ‹*room/building*› entrar en, entrar a (AmL) 2 (fall into) ‹*trap*› caer* en 3 (obtain easily) ‹*job*› conseguir* sin ningún problema 4 (collide with) darse* contra, llevarse por delante
- **walk off**

A 1 [v ▸ adv] (go away) irse*, marcharse (esp Esp) 2 [v ▸ adv, v ▸ prep ▸ o] (Sport) retirarse, salir*

B [v ▸ o ▸ adv, v ▸ adv ▸ o]: **we went out to ~ off our lunch** salimos a dar un paseo para bajar la comida

- **walk off with** [v ▸ adv ▸ prep ▸ o] 1 (take) llevarse 2 (win) ‹*prize*› llevarse
- **walk on** [v ▸ adv] seguir* su (*or* mi *etc*) camino
- **walk out** [v ▸ adv] 1 (Lab Rel) abandonar el trabajo (*como media reivindicatoria*) 2 (quit): **they have threatened to ~ out of the conference** han amenazado con retirarse de *or* abandonar el congreso (en señal de protesta)
- **walk out on** [v ▸ adv ▸ prep ▸ o] ‹*lover/family*› dejar, abandonar, dejar plantado (fam)
- **walk over** [v ▸ prep ▸ o] (colloq): **the Bears will ~ all over them** los Bears les van a dar una paliza (fam); **don't let him ~ all over you** no te dejes pisotear *or* atropellar (por él)

walk² *n*

A 1 (leisurely) paseo *m*; (long) caminata *f*; **to go for** *o* **take a ~** ir* a pasear *or* a dar un paseo, ir* a caminar (esp AmL); **she took the dog for a ~** sacó a pasear el perro; **it's five minutes'** *o* **a five-minute ~ from here** está *or* queda a cinco minutos de aquí a pie 2 (Sport) marcha *f*

B 1 (route): **there's a beautiful ~ through the woods** se puede hacer un paseo precioso por el bosque 2 (path) (esp AmE) camino *m*

C 1 (gait) andar *m*, manera *f* de caminar *or* andar 2 (speed) (*no pl*): **at a ~** al paso; *see also* **walk of life**

walk: **~about** *n* (BrE) *paseo que un político, miembro de la realeza etc da entre el público*; **~away** *n* (AmE colloq) paseo *m* (fam)

walker /'wɔːkər || 'wɔːkə(r)/ *n* 1 (sb that walks): **to be a fast/slow ~** caminar *or* andar* rápido/despacio; **I'm a great ~** me encanta caminar *or* andar 2 (hiker) excursionista *mf* 3 (Sport) marchador, -dora *m,f*, marchista *mf*

walkie-talkie /'wɔːki'tɔːki/ *n* walkie-talkie *m*

walk-in /'wɔːkɪn/ *adj*: **~ closet** vestidor *m*

walking¹ /'wɔːkɪŋ/ *n* [u]: **I do a lot of ~** yo camino *or* ando mucho; (*before n*) ‹*tour*› a pie; **is it within ~ distance?** ¿se puede ir a pie *or* caminando *or* andando?; **at a ~ pace** a paso de peatón

walking² *adj*: **she's a ~ encyclopedia** (hum) es una enciclopedia ambulante (hum); **he's a ~ miracle** vive de milagro

walking: **~ papers** *pl n* (AmE colloq) despido *m*; **to give sb her/his ~ papers** echar a algn, poner* a algn de patitas en la calle (fam); **~ stick** *n* bastón *m*

Walkman® /'wɔːkmən/ *n* (*pl* **-mans** /-mənz/) walkman® *m*

walk: **~ of life** *n*: **people from all ~s of life** gente de todas las profesiones y condiciones sociales; **~-on** *n* (*before n*) **~-on part** (Theat) papel *m* de figurante *or* comparsa; (Cin) papel *m* de extra; **~out** *n* (from talks, meeting) *retirada en señal de protesta*; (strike) *abandono del trabajo como medida reivindicatoria*; **~over** *n* (victory by default) walkover *m* (*victoria por la no comparecencia del contrincante*); (easy victory) (colloq) paseo *m* (fam); **~-up** *n* (AmE) (building) edificio *m* sin ascensor; (apartment, office) *apartamento u oficina en un edificio sin ascensor*; **~way** *n* (bridge) puente *m*, pasarela *f*; (passageway) pasillo *m*; (path) sendero *m*; **a covered ~way connects the two buildings** un pasaje cubierto conecta los dos edificios

wall /wɔːl/ *n*

A 1 (freestanding) muro *m*; (of castle, city) muralla *f*; **garden ~** tapia *f*, muro *m*; ***it's like talking to a brick ~*** es como hablarle a la pared; ***to go/be driven to the ~*** «*company/business*» irse* a pique; ***up the ~***: **she drives me up the ~** me saca de quicio, me enerva; **she'll go up the ~ when she finds out** se va a poner furiosa cuando se entere 2 (barrier) barrera *f*; **a ~ of fire** una barrera de fuego; ***to come up against a brick ~*** darse* de narices contra una pared

B (of building, room) pared *f*, muralla *f* (Chi); **this must not go** *o* **pass beyond these (four) ~s** esto que no salga de aquí; ***to have one's back to the ~*** estar* en un apuro *or* en un aprieto; ***~s have ears*** las paredes oyen; (*before n*) **~ bars**

W

(BrE Sport) espalderas *fpl*; **~ chart** gráfico *m* mural; **~ hanging** tapiz *m*; **~ painting** mural *m*
C (of stomach, artery) pared *f*

(Phrasal verbs)

- **wall in** [v ▸ o ▸ adv, v ▸ adv ▸ o] ‹*garden/playground*› tapiar, cercar* con un muro *or* una pared *or* una tapia
- **wall off** [v ▸ o ▸ adv, v ▸ adv ▸ o] separar con un muro *or* una pared *or* una tapia
- **wall up** [v ▸ o ▸ adv, v ▸ adv ▸ o] ‹*doorway/window*› tapiar, condenar; ‹*person/body*› emparedar

wallaby /'wɑːləbi || 'wɒləbi/ *n* (*pl* **-bies**) ualabí *m*

walled /wɔːld/ *adj* ‹*city*› amurallado; ‹*garden*› tapiado, cercado por una tapia *or* un muro

wallet /'wɑːlət || 'wɒlɪt/ *n* **1** (for money) cartera *f*, billetera *f* **2** (folder) carpeta *f*

wall: **~-eyed** /'wɔːl'aɪd/ *adj* (with opaque cornea) con leucoma; **~flower** *n* **1** (Bot) alhelí *m* **2** (person) (colloq): **she was always a ~flower** nunca la sacaban a bailar, siempre planchaba (Bol, CS fam), siempre comía pavo (Col fam)

wallop¹ /'wɑːləp || 'wɒləp/ *vt* (colloq) darle* una paliza a

wallop² *n* (colloq) golpazo *m* (fam)

wallow /'wɑːləʊ || 'wɒləʊ/ *vi* **1** (bathe) «*animal*» revolcarse*; **I love to ~ in a hot bath** me encanta estarme horas disfrutando de un baño caliente **2** (delight): **to ~ in self-pity** regodearse *or* deleitarse en la autocompasión

wallpaper¹ /'wɔːl,peɪpər/ *n* [u c] **1** (on a wall) papel *m* pintado *or* tapiz *or* de empapelar **2** (for a computer screen) fondo *m* de pantalla *or* de escritorio

wallpaper² *vt* empapelar

Wall Street /wɔːl/ *n* Wall Street (*centro financiero de los EEUU*)

> **Wall Street**
>
> Una calle en Manhattan, Nueva York, donde se encuentran la Bolsa neoyorquina y las sedes de muchas instituciones financieras. Cuando se habla de *Wall Street*, a menudo se está refiriendo a esas instituciones

wall-to-wall /'wɔːltə'wɔːl/ *adj* (*before n*): **~ carpet/carpeting** alfombra *f* de pared a pared, moqueta *f* (Esp), moquette *f* (RPl)

wally /'wɑːli || 'wɒli/ *n* (*pl* **-lies**) (BrE colloq) imbécil *mf*

walnut /'wɔːlnʌt/ *n* **1** [c] (nut) nuez *f*, nuez *f* de Castilla (Méx) **2** [c] **~ (tree)** nogal *m* **3** [u] (wood) nogal *m*

walrus /'wɔːlrəs/ *n* (*pl* **~es** *or* **~**) morsa *f*

Walter Mitty /,wɔːltər 'mɪti || ,wɔːltə 'mɪti/ *n*: **a ~ ~ character** un soñador *m*, una soñadora *f*

waltz¹ /wɔːls, wɔːlts/ *n* vals *m*

waltz² *vi*
A (dance) valsar, valsear; **can you ~?** ¿sabes bailar el vals?, ¿sabes valsar *or* valsear?
B (walk) (colloq): **she ~ed into the office and asked for a raise** entró tan campante *or* con gran desenfado en la oficina y pidió un aumento de sueldo

(Phrasal verb)

- **waltz through** [v ▸ prep ▸ o] (colloq) ‹*interview/test*› pasar con los ojos cerrados

wan /wɑːn || wɒn/ *adj* **1** (pallid) ‹*face/complexion*› pálido **2** ‹*smile*› lánguido

wand /wɑːnd || wɒnd/ *n* **1** (of sorcerer, conjuror) varita *f* mágica **2** (of office) bastón *m* de mando

wander¹ /'wɑːndər || 'wɒndə(r)/ *vi* **1** (+ *adv compl*) (walk — in a leisurely way) pasear; (— aimlessly) deambular, vagar*; **she ~ed around the room in a daze** daba vueltas por la habitación como aturdida; **we're going to ~ back now** vamos a volver sin prisas; **he ~ed in at ten** llegó a las diez tan campante *or* como si tal cosa; **his fingers ~ed over the keyboard** sus dedos recorrieron el teclado **2** (stray): **don't let the children ~ away from the car** no dejes que los niños se alejen del coche; **don't ~ off! we're leaving in five minutes** no te vayas por ahí, que dentro de cinco minutos nos vamos; **don't let your mind ~!** ¡no te distraigas!; **don't ~ off the point** no divagues, no te vayas por las ramas **3** **wandering** *pres p* ‹*actors*› itinerante; ‹*tribe*› nómada; ‹*salesman*› ambulante; **to have ~ing hands** tener* las manos largas
■ **wander** *vt* (for recreation) pasear por; (lost) dar* vueltas por; **to ~ the streets** deambular *or* vagar* por las calles, caminar sin rumbo fijo

wander² *n* (esp BrE) (*no pl*) vuelta *f*, paseo *m*; **we're going to have a ~ around the shops** vamos a dar una vuelta *or* un paseo por las tiendas

wanderer /'wɑːndərər || 'wɒndərə(r)/ *n* trotamundos *mf*

wanderings /'wɑːndərɪŋz || 'wɒndərɪŋz/ *pl n* correrías *fpl*, andanzas *fpl*

wanderlust /'wɑːndərlʌst || 'wɒndəlʌst/ *n* [u] ansias *fpl* de conocer mundo

wane¹ /weɪn/ *vi* **1** «*moon*» menguar* **2** «*interest/popularity*» decaer*, disminuir*, declinar; **her strength was waning** estaba perdiendo las fuerzas **3** **waning** *pres p* ‹*moon*› menguante; ‹*interest/popularity/influence*› decreciente

wane² *n*: **to be on the ~** «*moon*» estar* menguando; «*popularity*» estar* decayendo *or* disminuyendo

wangle /'wæŋgəl/ *vt* (colloq) ‹*job/ticket*› agenciarse (fam); **I managed to ~ some money out of my dad** conseguí sacarle dinero a mi padre

wank /wæŋk/ *vi* (BrE vulg) hacerse* la *or* una paja (vulg), correrse la *or* una paja (Chi, Per vulg), hacerse* una chaqueta (Méx vulg), hacerse* la manuela (Ven vulg)

wanker /'wæŋkər || 'wæŋkə(r)/ *n* (BrE vulg) (idiot) pendejo *m or* (Esp) gilipollas *m or* (AmS) pelotudo, -da *m,f or* (Andes, Ven) huevón *m* (vulg)

wanna /'wɑːnə || 'wɒnə/ (colloq) **= want to**

wannabe /'wɑːnəbiː || 'wɒnəbiː/ *n* (colloq & pej) aspirante *mf*; **all the showbiz ~s will be there** todos los que quieren pertenecer al mundo del espectáculo estarán allí

want¹ /wɔːnt || wɒnt/ *vt*
A **1** (require, desire) querer*; **(it's) just what I('ve) always ~ed!** (set phrase) ¡(es) justo lo que quería!; **the boss ~s you** el jefe te quiere ver *or* quiere hablar contigo; **he's ~ed on the phone** hay una llamada para él, lo llaman por teléfono; **I know when I'm not ~ed!** sé muy bien cuando estoy de más; **she ~s it ready today** quiere que esté listo hoy; **does he ~ the book back?** ¿quiere que le devuelvan (*or* le devolvamos *etc*) el libro?; **everything you could ~ from a car** todo lo que se le puede pedir a un coche; **to ~ to + INF** querer* + INF; **she can be charming when she ~s to (be)** es un encanto cuando quiere *or* cuando se lo propone; **to ~ sb/sth to + INF** querer* QUE algn/algo (+ *subj*); **what do you ~ me to do?** ¿qué quieres que haga?; **to ~ sb/sth -ING** querer* QUE algn/algo (+ *subj*); **he doesn't ~ them snooping around** no quiere que anden husmeando por allí **2** «*police*» buscar*; **Ⓢ wanted** se busca; **he is ~ed for murder/for questioning** lo buscan por asesinato/para interrogarlo **3** (as price for sth) pedir*; **how much does she ~ for the picture?** ¿cuánto pide por el cuadro? **4** ‹*person*› (sexually) desear
B (need) necesitar; **that child ~s a good thrashing** a ese niño le hace falta una buena paliza; **Ⓢ gardener wanted** se necesita *or* se precisa jardinero; **we all like to feel ~ed** a todos nos gusta sentir que nos necesitan; **the last thing I ~ is a cold** maldita la falta que me hace resfriarme ahora; **you ~ to see a doctor** tienes que ver a un médico; **the house ~s cleaning** hay que limpiar la casa
■ **want** *vi* (lack) (frml) (*usu with neg*): **you/they will ~ for nothing** no te/les faltará nada

want² *n*
A [c u] (requirement, need) necesidad *f*; **to be in ~ of sth** tener* necesidad de algo
B [u] (lack, absence) falta *f*, carencia *f* (frml); **for ~ of sth** a falta de algo; **if she doesn't become champion, it won't be for ~ of trying** si no llega a ser campeona, no será porque no lo haya intentado
C [u] (destitution, penury) miseria *f*, indigencia *f*

wanted /'wɔːntəd || 'wɒntɪd/ *adj* ‹*criminal/terrorist*› buscado (por la policía); *see also* **want¹ A2**

wanting /'wɔːntɪŋ || 'wɒntɪŋ/ *adj* (frml) (*pred*) **1** (missing): **a strong story line is ~ from all his works** todas sus obras carecen de un argumento sólido (frml) **2** (inadequate): **he was found ~** se demostró que no estaba capacitado

wanton /'wɔːntn̩ || 'wɒntən/ *adj* **1** (willful) sin sentido, gratuito **2** (licentious) ‹*lifestyle*› licencioso, disipado

war /wɔːr || wɔː(r)/ *n* [c u] guerra *f*; **First/Second World W~, World W~ I/II** Primera/Segunda Guerra Mundial; **to**

W

be at ~ with sb/sth estar* en guerra con algn/algo; **to declare ~ on sb/sth** declararle la guerra a algn/algo; **to go to ~ (with sb) (over sth)** entrar en guerra (con algn) (por algo); **an act of ~** un acto bélico *or* de guerra; **the ~ on crime** la lucha contra la delincuencia; **a ~ of words** una discusión; **the class ~** la lucha de clases; ***to be in the ~s***: **you look as if you've been in the ~s!** ¡parece que vienes de la guerra!; (*before n*) **~ baby** *niño nacido durante la guerra*; **~ memorial** monumento *m* a los caídos

warble /'wɔːrbəl || 'wɔːbəl/ *vi* trinar, gorjear

warbler /'wɔːrblər || 'wɔːblə(r)/ *n* curruca *f*, sílvido *m*

war cry *n* grito *m* de guerra

ward /wɔːrd || wɔːd/ *n*

A (in hospital) sala *f*

B (Govt) *subdivisión de un municipio a efectos electorales y administrativos*

C (person) pupilo, -la *m,f*; **~ of court** pupilo, -la *m,f* bajo tutela judicial

Phrasal verb

- **ward off** [v ▸ adv ▸ o] ‹*attack*› rechazar*; ‹*blow*› desviar*; ‹*danger*› conjurar; ‹*illness*› protegerse* *or* prevenirse* contra

warden /'wɔːrdn̩ || 'wɔːdn̩/ *n* (of castle, museum) guardián, -diana *m,f*; (of hostel, home) encargado, -da *m,f*; (of university, college) rector, -tora *m,f*; (*church~*) coadjutor *m*; (*fire ~*) (AmE) encargado, -da *m,f* de la lucha contra incendios; (*game ~*) guardabosque(s) *mf*; (of prison) (AmE) director, -tora *m,f* (*de una cárcel*)

warder /'wɔːrdər || 'wɔːdə(r)/ *n* (BrE) celador, -dora *m,f* (*de una cárcel*)

wardrobe /'wɔːrdrəʊb || 'wɔːdrəʊb/ *n* **1** (clothes cupboard) armario *m*, ropero *m* (esp AmL); **fitted** *o* **built-in ~** (BrE) armario *m* empotrado, clóset *m* (AmL exc RPl), placar(d) *m* (RPl) **2** (set of clothes) guardarropa *m*, vestuario *m*

warehouse /'werhaʊs || 'weəhaʊs/ *n* depósito *m*, almacén *m*, bodega *f* (Chi, Col, Méx)

wares /werz || weəz/ *pl n* mercancía(s) *f(pl)*, mercadería(s) *f(pl)* (AmS)

warfare /'wɔːrfer || 'wɔːfeə(r)/ *n* [u] guerra *f*, enfrentamiento *m* bélico (period)

warfarin /'wɔːrfərɪn || 'wɔːfərɪn/ *n* [u] warfarina *f*

war: **~ game** *n* (Mil) simulacro *m* de combate; (Games) juego *m* de guerra; **~head** *n* cabeza *f*, ojiva *f*; **~horse** *n* veterano, -na *m,f*

warily /'werəli || 'weərɪli/ *adv* ‹*drive/speak*› con cautela, cautelosamente; **they eyed each other ~** se miraron con recelo; ***to tread ~*** andarse* con pie(s) de plomo

war: **~like** *adj* guerrero, belicoso; **~lord** *n* caudillo *m*

warm¹ /wɔːrm || wɔːm/ *adj* **-er, -est**

A ‹*water/day*› tibio, templado; ‹*climate/wind*› cálido; **eat it while it's ~** cómetelo antes de que se enfríe; **the ~est room in the house** la habitación más caliente de la casa; **it's ~er in June** en junio hace más calor; **it's nice and ~ in here** aquí (se) está calentito; **it's not very ~ in here** hace un poco de frío aquí; **I'm lovely and ~ now** estoy muy calentito ahora; **~ clothes** ropa *f* de abrigo *or* (RPl, Ven tb) abrigada *or* (Andes, Méx tb) abrigadora; **to get ~** «*person*» entrar en calor, calentarse*; «*room*» calentarse*

B **1** (affectionate, cordial) ‹*person*› cariñoso, afectuoso; ‹*welcome*› caluroso, cálido **2** ‹*color/atmosphere*› cálido

C **1** (in riddles) (*pred*) caliente; **France? — no! — Poland? — you're getting ~er!** ¿Francia? — ¡no! — ¿Polonia? — ¡caliente, caliente!; **am I getting ~er?** ¿me estoy acercando a la respuesta? **2** (fresh) ‹*scent/trail*› reciente, fresco

warm² *vt* calentar*; **to ~ oneself** calentarse*

■ **warm** *vi* **1** (become hotter) calentarse* **2** (become affectionate) **to ~ TO** *o* **TOWARD sb**: **we soon ~ed to** *o* **toward her** pronto se ganó nuestra simpatía; **I didn't ~ to him** no me resultó muy simpático

Phrasal verbs

- **warm over** [v ▸ o ▸ adv, v ▸ adv ▸ o] (AmE Culin) calentar*
- **warm up**

A [v ▸ adv] **1** (become warmer) «*place/food*» calentarse*; «*person*» entrar en calor, calentarse* **2** «*engine/apparatus*» calentarse* **3** (become lively) «*party/match*» animarse, ponerse* animado **4** (for action) «*athlete*» hacer* ejercicios de calentamiento

B [v ▸ o ▸ adv, v ▸ adv ▸ o] **1** (heat) ‹*food/place*› calentar*; **have a hot drink to ~ you up** tómate algo caliente para entrar en calor **2** ‹*engine/apparatus*› calentar* **3** (make lively) animar **4** (for action) ‹*muscles/voice*› calentar*

warm³ *n*: **come into the ~** entra, que aquí está calentito (fam)

warm-blooded /'wɔːrm'blʌdəd || ˌwɔːm'blʌdɪd/ *adj* (Zool) de sangre caliente

warmed-over /'wɔːrmd'əʊvər || ˌwɔːmd'əʊvə(r)/ *adj* (AmE) ‹*food*› recalentado; ‹*ideas/policies*› (pej) trillado, manido

warm-hearted /'wɔːrm'hɑːrtəd || ˌwɔːm'hɑːtɪd/ *adj* afectuoso, cariñoso

warmly /'wɔːrmli || 'wɔːmli/ *adv* **1** (referring to temperature): **wrap up ~!** ¡abrígate bien!; **~ dressed** bien abrigado **2** ‹*congratulate/welcome*› calurosamente; ‹*smile*› afectuosamente; **I can ~ recommend her** la recomiendo con toda confianza

warmongering /'wɔːrˌmɑːŋgərɪŋ || 'wɔːˌmʌŋgərɪŋ/ *n* [u] belicismo *m*

warmth /wɔːrmθ || wɔːmθ/ *n* [u] **1** (heat) calor *m*; **we huddled together for ~** nos acurrucamos juntos para darnos calor **2** (of welcome) lo caluroso **3** (of color, atmosphere) calidez *f*

warm-up /'wɔːrmʌp || 'wɔːmʌp/ *n* (exercise) ejercicio *m* de calentamiento; (practice) (pre)calentamiento *m*; **today's game is a ~ for the final** el partido de hoy es un entrenamiento para la final

warn /wɔːrn || wɔːn/ *vt* **1** (admonish) advertir*; **I'm ~ing you!** ¡te lo advierto!; **be ~ed!** ¡cuidado!; **to ~ sb not to + INF**: **we had been ~ed not to go** nos habían advertido que no fuéramos **2** (inform, advise) avisar, advertir*; **they were ~ed about the rats** les advirtieron que había ratas; **to ~ sb AGAINST sth/sb** prevenir* a algn CONTRA algo/algn; **we were ~ed against swimming in the river** nos advirtieron que era peligroso nadar en el río

Phrasal verb

- **warn off** [v ▸ o ▸ adv, v ▸ adv ▸ o] (frighten away): **I began making inquiries, but I was ~ed off in no uncertain terms** empecé a hacer averiguaciones, pero me advirtieron claramente que no continuara

warning /'wɔːrnɪŋ || 'wɔːnɪŋ/ *n* **1** [c u] (advice, threat) advertencia *f*; **a word of ~: don't be late!** una advertencia *or* te lo advierto: no llegues tarde; **the flags are a ~ that it's unsafe to bathe** las banderas advierten *or* indican que es peligroso bañarse; **the player was given an official ~** el jugador recibió una amonestación; (*before n*) **~ light** señal *f* luminosa, luz *f* indicadora; **~ shot** disparo *m* de advertencia; **~ sign** señal *f* de aviso *or* de alerta **2** [u] (prior notice) aviso *m*; **they arrived without ~** llegaron sin avisar *or* sin previo aviso; **I gave you plenty of ~** te avisé con tiempo de sobra; **we need three days' ~** tienen que avisarnos con tres días de antelación

warp¹ /wɔːrp || wɔːp/ *n*

A (Tex) urdimbre *f*

B (twist) (*no pl*) alabeo *m*, pandeo *m*

warp² *vt* ‹*wood/metal*› alabear, combar, pandear

■ **warp** *vi* «*wood/metal*» alabearse, combarse, pandearse

war: **~paint** *n* [u] pintura *f* de guerra; **she's putting on her ~paint** (colloq & hum) se está poniendo el revoque (fam & hum); **~path** *n*: ***to be on the ~path*** (colloq & hum) estar* con ganas de pelear, estar* buscando camorra

warped /wɔːrpt || wɔːpt/ *adj* **1** ‹*timber/metal*› alabeado, combado, pandeado; ‹*record*› combado **2** ‹*mind/sense of humor*› retorcido

warplane /'wɔːrpleɪn || 'wɔːpleɪn/ *n* avión *m* de combate

warrant¹ /'wɔːrənt || 'wɒrənt/ *n* **1** [c] (written authorization) (Law) orden *f* judicial; (*search ~*) orden *f* de registro *or* (AmL tb) de allanamiento; **to have a ~ for sb's arrest** tener* una orden de arresto contra algn **2** [c] (voucher) vale *m* **3** [u] (justification) (frml) justificación *f*

warrant² *vt*

A (justify) justificar*; **the case does not ~ further investigation** el caso no merece que se continúe con la investigación

B (guarantee) (*often pass*) garantizar*

warrant officer *n* ≈ suboficial *mf*

W

warranty /'wɔːrənti || 'wɒrənti/ *n* [c u] (*pl* **-ties**) garantía *f*; **to be in** *o* **under ~** estar* bajo *or* en garantía; **extended ~** garantía ampliada

warren /'wɔːrən || 'wɒrən/ *n* (Zool) madriguera *f* (*de conejos*), conejera *f*

warring /'wɔːrɪŋ/ *adj* (*before n*) ‹*countries/tribes*› en guerra; ‹*factions*› enfrentado

warrior /'wɔːrjər || 'wɒriə(r)/ *n* guerrero, -ra *m,f*

Warsaw /'wɔːrsɔː || 'wɔːsɔː/ *n* Varsovia *f*

warship /'wɔːrʃɪp || 'wɔːʃɪp/ *n* buque *m* *or* barco *m* de guerra

wart /wɔːrt || wɔːt/ *n* verruga *f*; **~s *and all*** con todos sus defectos *or* todas sus imperfecciones

warthog /'wɔːrthɔːg || 'wɔːthɒg/ *n* jabalí *m* verrugoso

war: **~time** *n* [u]: **during** *o* **in ~time** durante la guerra, en tiempo de guerra; **~torn** *adj* devastado *or* arrasado por la guerra; **~-weary** *adj* cansado de la guerra

wary /'weri || 'weəri/ *adj* **warier, wariest** cauteloso, precavido; **to be ~ OF sb/sth** no fiarse* DE algn/algo, recelar DE algn/algo

was /wɑːz, *weak form* wəz || wɒz, *weak form* wəz/ *past of* **be**

wash¹ /wɔːʃ || wɒʃ/ *n*

A [c] [1] (act): **to have a ~** lavarse; **I'll give the car a ~** voy a lavar el coche, voy a darle una lavada al coche (AmL); **he/it needs a (good) ~** le hace falta un (buen) baño/lavado [2] (in washing machine) lavado *m* [3] (laundry): **I do a ~ every Monday** los lunes lavo la ropa *or* (Esp tb) hago la colada; **your shirt is in the ~** tu camisa está lavándose; ***it will all come out in the ~*** (colloq) (things will sort themselves out) todo se va a arreglar; (all will be revealed) ya se revelará todo

B [u] (left by boat, plane) estela *f*

C [u c] [1] (of paint) capa *f*, mano *f* [2] (Art) aguada *f*

wash² *vt*

A (clean) ‹*shirt/car/fruit*› lavar; ‹*floor*› fregar*, lavar (esp AmL); **to ~ one's face/hair** lavarse la cara/la cabeza *or* el pelo; **to ~ the dishes** fregar* *or* lavar los platos

B (carry away) (+ *adv compl*): **the body had been ~ed ashore by the tide** la corriente había arrastrado el cuerpo hasta la orilla; **the wave nearly ~ed him overboard** la ola casi lo arrojó por la borda; *see also* **wash away, wash up**

■ **wash** *vi*

A [1] (clean oneself) lavarse [2] (do dishes) lavar, fregar* [3] (do laundry) «*washing machine/person*» lavar (la ropa), hacer* la colada (Esp)

B (come clean): **this shirt ~es well** esta camisa se lava bien; ***it won't*** **~** (colloq) no va a colar (fam)

Phrasal verbs

- **wash away** [v ▸ o ▸ adv, v ▸ adv ▸ o] [1] (carry away) ‹*hut/bridge/pier*› llevarse, arrasar con [2] (cleanse) ‹*dirt*› quitar (*lavando*)
- **wash down** [v ▸ o ▸ adv, v ▸ adv ▸ o] [1] (clean) ‹*paintwork/wall*› lavar [2] (accompany) (colloq): **a plate of pasta ~ed down with the local wine** un plato de pasta acompañado del vino de la región *or* rociado con el vino de la región
- **wash out**

A [v ▸ o ▸ adv, v ▸ adv ▸ o] [1] ‹*sink/cloth*› (clean) lavar; (rinse) enjuagar* [2] (prevent, spoil) (colloq): **heavy rain ~ed out most of the games** fuertes lluvias hicieron que se cancelara la mayoría de los partidos

B [v ▸ adv] (disappear): **the stain will ~ out** la mancha saldrá *or* se quitará al lavarlo

- **wash over** [v ▸ prep ▸ o] «*waves/water*» bañar; **to let sth ~ over one**: **she lets their criticism ~ over her** sus críticas le resbalan; **I let the music ~ over me** dejé que la música me envolviera, me dejé llevar por la música
- **wash up**

A [v ▸ adv] [1] (wash oneself) (AmE) lavarse [2] (wash dishes) (BrE) lavar los platos, fregar* (los platos)

B [v ▸ o ▸ adv, v ▸ adv ▸ o] [1] (deposit) (*usu pass*) **to be ~ed up** «*body/wreckage*» ser* traído por la corriente [2] ‹*dishes*› (BrE) lavar, fregar*

Wash = **Washington**

washable /'wɔːʃəbəl || 'wɒʃəbəl/ *adj* lavable

wash: **~basin** *n* (BrE) ▸**~bowl**; **~bowl** *n* (AmE) [1] (in modern bathroom) lavabo *m*, lavamanos *m*, lavatorio *m* (CS), pileta *f* (RPl) [2] (bowl) palangana *f*, jofaina *f*, lavatorio *m* (Chi, Per); **~cloth** *n* (AmE) toallita *f* (*para lavarse*), ≈ manopla *f*

washed /wɔːʃt || wɒʃt/: **~-out** *adj* (*pred* **~ out**) [1] (faded) ‹*fabric*› descolorido; ‹*color*› pálido, lavado (RPl fam) [2] (exhausted) rendido, agotado; **~-up** /'wɔːʃt'ʌp/ *adj* (*pred* **~ up**) (AmE colloq) acabado

washer /'wɔːʃər || 'wɒʃə(r)/ *n*

A (Tech) (ring) arandela *f*; (— on faucet) arandela *f*, junta *f*, suela *f*, cuerito *m* (CS fam), empaque *m* (Col, Ven)

B ▸**washing machine**

washing /'wɔːʃɪŋ || 'wɒʃɪŋ/ *n* [1] [u] (laundry — dirty) ropa *f* para lavar; (— clean) ropa *f* lavada; **to do the ~** lavar la ropa, hacer* la colada (Esp) [2] [u c] (act) lavado *m*

washing: **~ line** *n* (BrE) cuerda *f* para tender la ropa; **~ machine** *n* máquina *f* de lavar, lavadora *f*, lavarropas *m* (RPl); **~ powder** *n* [u c] (esp BrE) jabón *m* en polvo, detergente *m*; **~-up** /'wɔːʃɪŋ'ʌp || ˌwɒʃɪŋ'ʌp/ *n* [u] (BrE): **to do the ~-up** lavar los platos, fregar* (los platos); (*before n*) **~-up liquid** lavavajillas *m*

wash: **~out** *n* (failure) (colloq) desastre *m* (fam); **~room** *n* baño(s) *m(pl)*, servicios *mpl* (esp Esp); **~stand** *n* lavabo *m*, lavatorio *m* (AmL); **~tub** *n* tina *f* de lavar

wasn't /'wɑːznt || 'wɒznt/ = **was not**

wasp /wɑːsp || wɒsp/ *n* avispa *f*; **~s' nest** avispero *m*

WASP /wɑːsp || wɒsp/ *n* (esp AmE) (= **white Anglo-Saxon Protestant**) *persona de la clase privilegiada de los EEUU, blanca, anglosajona y protestante*

> **WASP, Wasp – White Anglo-Saxon Protestant**
>
> En EEUU el término se emplea para referirse a una persona blanca cuya familia es originaria del Reino Unido y de religión protestante. Los *Wasps* están considerados como las personas con mejor posición social y con mayor poder político

waspish /'wɑːspɪʃ || 'wɒspɪʃ/ *adj* ‹*comment*› sardónico, punzante, mordaz; ‹*character*› sardónico, cáustico

wastage /'weɪstɪdʒ/ *n* [u]: **there is too much ~ of raw material** se desperdicia demasiada materia prima; **we are trying to reduce ~** tratamos de aprovechar mejor el material; **natural ~** (of workforce) bajas *fpl* vegetativas

waste¹ /weɪst/ *n*

A [u] (of fuel, materials) desperdicio *m*, derroche *m*; **a ~ of time** una pérdida de tiempo; **it's a ~ of money** es tirar el dinero; **a ~ of effort** un esfuerzo inútil; **there is no ~ in this ham** este jamón no tiene desperdicio; **we can save money by avoiding ~** podemos economizar evitando los despilfarros; **she's working as a waitress: it's such a ~!** trabaja de camarera: ¡qué desperdicio!; **to go to ~** «*talent*» desperdiciarse; «*food*» echarse a perder

B [u] [1] (refuse) residuos *mpl*, desechos *mpl*; **human ~** excrementos *mpl* [2] (surplus matter) material *m* sobrante *or* de desecho

C **wastes** (*pl*): **the deserted ~s of Antarctica** las desiertas inmensidades *or* extensiones de la Antártica

waste² *vt*

A ‹*talents/efforts*› desperdiciar, malgastar; ‹*money/electricity*› despilfarrar, derrochar; ‹*food*› tirar, desperdiciar; ‹*time*› perder*; ‹*space*› desaprovechar, desperdiciar; **you're wasting my time** me estás haciendo perder el tiempo; **you're wasting your breath!** estás gastando saliva inútilmente; **your work won't be ~d** tu trabajo no ha sido en vano; **to ~ sth ON sb/sth**: **you've ~d your money on that car** has tirado *or* mal gastado el dinero comprando ese coche; **the irony was ~d on her** no captó la ironía

B **wasted** *past p* [1] (misused, futile) ‹*time/money*› perdido; ‹*opportunity/space*› desperdiciado, desaprovechado; ‹*effort*› inútil; **it was a ~d journey** fue un viaje en balde [2] (shrunken) ‹*body*› debilitado, consumido; ‹*limb*› atrofiado

C (kill) (AmE sl) liquidar (fam), cargarse* (fam)

■ **waste** *vi* [1] (squander) **~ *not, want not*** quien no malgasta no pasa necesidades [2] ▸**waste away**

Phrasal verb

- **waste away** [v ▸ adv] «*person/body*» consumirse; «*muscle*» atrofiarse

waste³ *adj*

A ‹*ground*› (barren) yermo; (not cultivated) baldío, sin cultivar; ***to lay* ~** arrasar

B ‹*material/matter*› de desecho

waste: **~basket** *n* (esp AmE) ▸**waste-paper basket**; **~ disposal** *n* [u] eliminación *f* de residuos *or* desechos;

W

(*before n*) ~ **disposal unit** triturador *m or* trituradora *f* de desperdicios *or* de basura

wasteful /'weɪstfəl/ *adj* ‹*person*› despilfarrador, derrochador; ‹*method*› poco económico

waste: ~**land** *n* [c u] (*often pl*) (barren land) páramo *m*, tierra *f* yerma *or* baldía; (uncultivated land) erial *m*; ~ **paper** *n* [u] papel *m* sobrante; ~**-paper basket**, ~**-paper bin** /'weɪst'peɪpər || ˌweɪst'peɪpə(r)/ *n* papelera *f*, cesto *m or* canasto *m* de los papeles, papelero *m* (CS); ~ **pipe** *n* tubo *m or* tubería *f* de desagüe

waster /'weɪstər || 'weɪstə(r)/ *n* vago, -ga *m,f*

wasting /'weɪstɪŋ/ *adj* (*before n*): ~ **disease** enfermedad *f* que consume

wastrel /'weɪstrəl/ *n* (liter) gandul, -dula *m,f*

watch¹ /wɑːtʃ || wɒtʃ/ *n*

A [c] (timepiece) reloj *m* (*de pulsera/de bolsillo*); (*before n*) ~ **band** *o* (BrE) **strap** correa *f* de reloj

B [u] (observation) vigilancia *f*; **to be on the ~ for sb/sth**: **she was on the ~ for the postman** estaba esperando a ver si veía al cartero; **the mother is constantly on the ~ for possible danger** la madre está constantemente alerta por si hay algún peligro; **to keep** ~ hacer* guardia; **to keep ~ over sth/sb** vigilar algo/a algn; **to keep a ~ on sth/sb** vigilar algo/a algn

C 1 [c] (period of time) guardia *f*; **I took the first** ~ yo hice la primera guardia 2 [c] (individual) guardia *mf*, vigía *mf*; (group) guardia *f* 3 [u] (duty): **to be on** ~ estar* de guardia, hacer* guardia

watch² *vt*

A ‹*person/expression*› observar, mirar; ‹*movie/game*› mirar, ver*; **to ~ television** ver* *or* mirar televisión; **now, ~ this carefully** ahora, miren *or* observen con atención; **to ~ sb/sth + INF**: **we ~ed the children open their presents** miramos como los niños abrían sus regalos; **we ~ed the sun go down** miramos la puesta de sol

B 1 (keep under observation) ‹*suspect/house*› vigilar; **we're being ~ed** nos están vigilando; ***a ~ed kettle*** *o* ***pot never boils*** el que espera desespera 2 (look after) ‹*luggage/children*› cuidar, vigilar 3 (pay attention to) mirar (con atención); ~ **what you're doing!** ¡mira lo que haces!; **I've got to ~ the time** tengo que estar atenta a la hora; **the staff are always ~ing the clock** los empleados están siempre pendientes del reloj; **investors are ~ing the situation with interest** los inversores están siguiendo la situación muy de cerca

C (be careful of) ‹*diet/weight*› vigilar, tener* cuidado con; **we'll have to ~ what we spend** tendremos que mirar (mucho) lo que gastamos; ~ **what you say** ten cuidado con lo que dices; ~ **your head!** ¡cuidado con la cabeza!; ~ ***it!*** (colloq) ¡cuidado!, ¡ojo! (fam), ¡abusado! (Méx fam)

■ **watch** *vi*

A 1 (look on) mirar; **we ~ed carefully as she did it** miramos con atención mientras lo hacía; **the whole country ~ed as the events unfolded** la nación entera siguió el desarrollo de los acontecimientos 2 (pay attention) prestar atención 3 (wait for) **to ~ FOR sth/sb** esperar algo/a algn; **to ~ for sb/sth to + INF** esperar A QUE algn/algo (+ *subj*)

B (keep vigil) (liter) velar

Phrasal verbs

- **watch out** [v ▸ adv] 1 (be careful) tener* cuidado; ~ **out!** ¡(ten) cuidado!, ¡ojo! (fam), ¡abusado! (Méx fam); **to ~ out FOR sth/sb** tener* cuidado *or* (fam) ojo CON algo/algn 2 (look carefully) estarse* atento; **to ~ out FOR sth/sb**: ~ **out for spelling mistakes** estáte atento por si hay faltas de ortografía; ~ **out for Mary** mira a ver si ves a Mary
- **watch over** [v ▸ prep ▸ o] ‹*patient/child*› cuidar (de); ‹*safety/interests*› velar por

watchdog /'wɑːtʃdɔːg || 'wɒtʃdɒg/ *n* 1 (dog) perro *m* guardián 2 (person) guardián, -diana *m,f*; (for utilities) regulador *m*

watchful /'wɑːtʃfəl || 'wɒtʃfəl/ *adj* vigilante, atento; **to keep a ~ eye on sth/sb** vigilar algo/a algn muy de cerca

watch: ~**maker** *n* relojero, -ra *m,f*; ~**man** /'wɑːtʃmən || 'wɒtʃmən/ *n* (*pl* **-men** /mən/) vigilante *m*; ~**tower** *n* atalaya *f*, torre *f* de vigilancia; ~**word** *n* (motto) lema *m*, consigna *f*; (password) contraseña *f*

water¹ /'wɔːtər || 'wɔːtə(r)/ *n* [u]

A agua *f*‡; **drinking/running** ~ agua potable/corriente; **to be/lie under** ~ estar*/quedar inundado; **the kitchen was 2 ft under** ~ la cocina tenía 2 pies de agua; **high/low** ~ marea *f* alta/baja; **to go across** *o* **over the** ~ cruzar* a la otra orilla, cruzar* el charco (fam); **to spend money like** ~ gastar a manos llenas; ***like ~ off a duck's back*** como quien oye llover; ***to be in/get into hot*** ~ estar*/meterse en una buena (fam); ***to hold*** ~ tenerse* en pie; **that theory just doesn't hold** ~ esa teoría hace agua por todos lados; ***to pour*** *o* ***throw cold ~ over sth*** ponerle* trabas a algo; ***to test the*** ~ tantear el terreno; ~ ***under the bridge***: **that's all ~ under the bridge** eso ya es agua pasada; (*before n*) ‹*bird/plant*› acuático; ~ **heater** calentador *m* (de agua); ~ **power** energía *f* hidráulica; ~ **pump** bomba *f* hidráulica; ~ **sports** deportes *mpl* acuáticos

B 1 (urine) (frml & euph): **to pass** *o* **make** ~ orinar, hacer* aguas (menores) (euf), hacer* de las aguas (Méx euf) 2 (Med): ~ **on the brain** hidrocefalia *f*; ~ **on the knee** derrame *m* sinovial

C **waters** *pl* 1 (of sea, river) aguas *fpl*; ***to muddy the ~s*** enmarañar *or* enredar las cosas; ***still ~s run deep*** del agua mansa líbreme Dios, que de la brava me libro yo 2 (at spa): **to take the ~s** tomar las aguas 3 (amniotic fluid) aguas *fpl*; **the/her ~s broke** rompió aguas, rompió la bolsa de aguas

water² *vi*: **her eyes began to** ~ empezaron a llorarle los ojos *or* a saltársele las lágrimas; **his mouth ~ed** se le hizo agua la boca *or* (Esp) la boca agua

■ **water** *vt* 1 ‹*plant/garden/land*› regar* 2 ‹*horse/cattle*› dar* de beber a, abrevar

Phrasal verb

- **water down** [v ▸ o ▸ adv, v ▸ adv ▸ o] 1 (dilute) ‹*liquid/mixture*› diluir*; ‹*wine/beer*› aguar, bautizar* (hum) 2 ‹*policy/criticism*› suavizar*, atenuar*

water: ~ **bed** *n* cama *f* de agua; ~ **biscuit** *n* (esp BrE) galleta *f* de agua; ~ **bottle** *n* cantimplora *f*; ~ **butt** *n* barril *m* (*para recoger el agua de la lluvia*); ~ **cannon** *n* (*pl* **cannon** *or* **cannons**) camión *m* cisterna antidisturbios, carro *m* neptuno (RPl), guanaco *m* (Chi fam); ~ **closet** *n* (BrE frml) inodoro *m* (frml), wáter *m*, váter *m* (Esp fam); ~**color**, (BrE) ~**colour** *n* [u c] acuarela *f*; **in ~colors** a la acuarela; ~**-cooled** *adj* refrigerado por agua; ~**course** *n* (river, canal) curso *m* de agua; (channel, route) curso *m* del agua; ~**cress** *n* [u] berro *m*; ~ **diviner** /də'vaɪnər || dɪ'vaɪnə(r)/ *n* (BrE) zahorí *mf*; ~**fall** *n* cascada *f*, salto *m* de agua; (large) catarata *f*; ~**fowl** *n* (*pl* **-fowls** *or* **-fowl**) ave *f*‡ acuática; ~**front** *n* (beside lake, river) *zona de una ciudad que bordea un lago o río*; (docks) (esp AmE) muelles *mpl*; ~ **hole** *n* ▸ **watering hole 1**

watering /'wɔːtərɪŋ/: ~ **can** *n* regadera *f*; ~ **hole** *n* 1 (for animals) abrevadero *m* 2 (pub, bar) (hum) bar *m*, abrevadero *m* (hum)

water: ~ **jump** *n* foso *m* (de agua); ~ **lily** *n* nenúfar *m*

waterlogged /'wɔːtərlɔːgd || 'wɔːtəlɒgd/ *adj* ‹*land/soil*› anegado, inundado; ‹*shoes*› empapado, lleno de agua

Waterloo /'wɔːtər'luː || ˌwɔːtə'luː/ *n*: ***that's where he met his*** ~ ahí fue donde le llegó su San Martín

water: ~**mark** *n* filigrana *f*; ~**melon** *n* [c u] sandía *f*; ~ **mill** *n* molino *m* de agua; ~ **parting** *n* (AmE) ▸ **watershed 1**; ~ **pistol** *n* pistola *f* de agua; ~ **polo** *n* [u] waterpolo *m*

waterproof¹ /'wɔːtərpruːf/ *adj* ‹*fabric*› impermeable; ‹*mascara*› a prueba de agua; ‹*watch*› sumergible

waterproof² *n* (esp BrE) prenda *f* impermeable

waterproof³ *vt* impermeabilizar*

water: ~ **rat** *n* rata *f* de agua; ~**-repellent**, ~**-resistant** *adj* impermeabilizado, hidrófugo; ~**shed** *n* 1 (divide) (línea *f*) divisoria *f* de aguas; ***to mark a ~shed*** marcar* un hito; (in TV programming) horario *m* de protección 2 (drainage basin) (AmE) cuenca *f*; ~**side** *n* **the ~side** la ribera, la orilla; (*before n*) ‹*restaurant/hotel*› ribereño; ~**-ski** *vi* **-skis, -skiing, -skied** hacer* esquí acuático; ~**-skiing** *n* [u] esquí *m* acuático; ~ **slide** *n* tobogán *m* acuático; ~ **softener** *n* (substance) ablandador *m* de agua, descalcificador *m*; (apparatus) descalcificadora *f*; ~ **table** *n* nivel *m* freático; ~**tight** *adj* 1 ‹*seal/container*› hermético; ‹*boat*› estanco 2 ‹*argument*› irrebatible, sin fisuras; ‹*alibi*› a toda prueba; ‹*contract/law*› sin lagunas *or* vacíos; ~**way** *n* (river) vía *f* fluvial; (canal) vía *f or* canal *m* navegable; ~ **wheel** *n* (for driving machinery) rueda *f* hidráulica; (for raising water) noria *f*; ~ **wings** *pl n* flotadores *mpl* (*que se colocan en los brazos*); **~works** *n* (*pl* **~works**) [1] (for water supply) (+ *sing or pl vb*) planta *f* de tratamiento y depuración de agua, purificadora *f*; ***to turn on the ~works*** echarse a llorar como una magdalena [2] (urinary system) (BrE colloq & euph) (+ *pl vb*) vías *fpl* urinarias

watery /ˈwɔːtəri/ *adj* [1] (of, like water) acuoso; **he went to a ~ grave** (liter) el mar fue su tumba (liter) [2] ‹*beer/gravy*› aguado [3] ‹*eyes*› lloroso

watt /wɑːt || wɒt/ *n* vatio *m*

wattage /ˈwɑːtɪdʒ || ˈwɒtɪdʒ/ *n* vataje *m*

wattle /ˈwɑːtl̩ || wɒtl̩/ *n* [u] zarzo *m*; **~ and daub fence** valla *f* de adobe y cañas

wave¹ /weɪv/ *n*

A [1] (of water) ola *f*; ***to make ~s*** hacer* olas, causar problemas; (*before n*) **~ power** (Ecol) energía *f* mareomotriz [2] (in hair) onda *f* [3] (Phys) onda *f*

B (surge, movement) oleada *f*; **a ~ of nausea came over him** le vinieron náuseas

C (gesture): **she gave them a ~** les hizo adiós/los saludó con la mano

wave² *vt*

A [1] (shake, swing) ‹*handkerchief/flag*› agitar; **she ~d her hand sadly** hizo adiós con la mano, llena de tristeza; **to ~ sth around** agitar algo; **she ~d her stick at them** los amenazó agitando su bastón en el aire; **she ~d goodbye to him** le hizo adiós con la mano [2] (direct) (+ *adv compl*): **the policeman ~d us on** el policía nos hizo señas para *or* de que siguiéramos adelante

B (curl) ‹*hair*› marcar*, ondular

■ **wave** *vi*

A (signal): **he ~d when he saw us** nos saludó con la mano al vernos; **to ~ AT** *o* **TO sb** (to say goodbye) hacerle* adiós A algn con la mano; (in greeting) saludar a algn con la mano; (to attract attention): **he ~d at** *o* **to me to come over** me hizo señas para que me acercara

B (sway, flutter) «*corn/trees*» agitarse, mecerse* con el viento; «*flag*» ondear, flamear

Phrasal verbs

- **wave aside** [v ▸ o ▸ adv, v ▸ adv ▸ o] [1] (with hand): **he ~d me aside** me hizo señas para que me hiciera a un lado [2] ‹*arguments/attempts*› rechazar*, desechar
- **wave away** [v ▸ o ▸ adv, v ▸ adv ▸ o]: **she ~d him away** le hizo señas para *or* de que se fuera
- **wave down** [v ▸ o ▸ adv, v ▸ adv ▸ o]: **we were ~d down by a policeman** un policía nos hizo señas para que paráramos

wave: **~band** *n* banda *f* de frecuencia; **short/medium ~band** onda *f* corta/media; **~length** *n* longitud *f* de onda; ***to be on the same ~length*** estar* en la misma onda, sintonizar*; **~ machine** *n* generador *m* de olas

waver /ˈweɪvər || ˈweɪvə(r)/ *vi*

A (falter) «*person*» flaquear; «*faith*» tambalearse

B (be indecisive) titubear, vacilar

waverer /ˈweɪvərər || ˈweɪvərə(r)/ *n* indeciso, -sa *m,f*

wavy /ˈweɪvi/ *adj* **wavier, waviest** ondulado

wax¹ /wæks/ *n* [u] [1] cera *f* [2] (*ear~*) cera *f* (de los oídos), cerumen *m* [3] (*sealing ~*) lacre *m*

wax² *vt* [1] (treat with wax) ‹*floor/table/skis*› encerar [2] (to remove hair) depilar con cera

■ **wax** *vi*

A (increase) «*moon*» crecer*; **his popularity ~ed and waned** su popularidad sufrió muchos altibajos

B (become): **she ~ed lyrical about the painting** se deshizo en elogios hablando del cuadro

waxed paper /wækst/ *n* (BrE) papel *m* encerado *or* de cera *or* (Esp tb) parafinado *or* (RPl) (de) manteca *or* (Chi) (de) mantequilla

waxen /ˈwæksn̩/ *adj* (liter) [1] (pale) ‹*face/complexion*› céreo (liter), pálido [2] (made of wax) ‹*figure/image*› de cera

wax: **~work** *n* figura *f* de cera; **~works** *n* (*pl* **~works**) (+ *sing or pl vb*) museo *m* de cera

waxy /ˈwæksi/ *adj* **waxier, waxiest** ‹*substance*› parecido a la cera, ceroso

way¹ /weɪ/ *n*

Sense I

A [c] [1] (route) camino *m*; **the ~ back** el camino de vuelta *or* de regreso; **we had to go the long ~ (around)** tuvimos que dar toda la vuelta; **let's go a different ~** vayamos por otro lado *or* camino; **the ~ in/out** la entrada/salida; **I saw her on the ~ out** la vi a la salida; **this style is on the ~ in/out** este estilo se está poniendo/pasando de moda; **it's difficult to find one's ~ around this town** es difícil orientarse *or* no perderse en esta ciudad; **you'll soon find your ~ around the office/system** en poco tiempo te familiarizarás con la oficina/el sistema; **can you find your ~ there by yourself?** ¿sabes ir solo?; **I'll find my own ~ out** no te molestes en acompañarme; **I can drop the package off on my ~** de paso puedo dejar el paquete; **we're going the wrong ~** nos hemos equivocado de camino, vamos mal; **which ~ did you come?** ¿por dónde viniste?; **which ~ did he go?** ¿por dónde fue?; (following sb) ¿por dónde se fue?; **could you tell me the ~ to the city center?** ¿me podría decir por dónde se va *or* cómo se llega al centro (de la ciudad)?; **I'll make my own ~ there** iré por mi cuenta; **on my ~ to work** de camino al trabajo; **I'm on my ~!** ahora mismo salgo *or* voy, ¡voy para allí!; **the doctor is on her ~** la doctora ya va para allí/viene para aquí; **the goods are on their ~** la mercancía está en camino *or* ya ha salido; **I'll tell you on the ~** te lo cuento por el camino; **winter's on the ~** ya falta poco para que empiece el invierno; **did you find the ~ to Trier all right?** ¿llegaste bien a Trier?; **I don't know the ~ up/down** no sé por dónde se sube/se baja; **she's well on her ~ to recovery** ya está casi recuperada del todo; **to lead the ~** ir* delante; **to lose one's ~** perderse*; **there is no ~ around it** no hay otra solución *or* salida; ***there are no two ~s about it*** no tiene *or* no hay vuelta de hoja; ***to go one's own ~***: **she'll go her own ~** hará lo que le parezca; ***to go out of one's ~*** (make a detour) desviarse* del camino; (make special effort): **they went out of their ~ to be helpful** se desvivieron *or* hicieron lo indecible por ayudar; ***to go the ~ of sth/sb*** acabar como algo/algn, correr la misma suerte de algo/algn [2] (road, path) camino *m*, senda *f*; **the Appian W~** la vía Apia; **the people over the ~** (BrE) los vecinos de enfrente

B [c u] (passage, space): **we hacked a ~ through the undergrowth** nos abrimos camino entre la maleza; **to be/get in the ~** estorbar; **she doesn't let her work get in the ~ of her social life** no deja que el trabajo sea un obstáculo para su vida social; **to stand in the ~**: **they stood in our ~** nos impidieron el paso; **I couldn't see it, she was standing in my ~** no podía verlo, ella me tapaba (la vista); **I won't stand in your ~** no seré yo quien te lo impida; **to stand in the ~ of progress** obstaculizar* *or* entorpecer* el progreso; **(get) out of the ~!** ¡hazte a un lado!, ¡quítate de en medio!; **to move sth out of the ~** quitar algo de en medio; **I'd like to get this work out of the ~** quisiera quitar este trabajo de en medio; **to keep out of sb's ~** rehuir* a algn, evitar encontrarse con algn; **make ~!** ¡abran paso!

C [c] (direction): **it's that ~** es en esa dirección, es por ahí; **this ~!** ¡por aquí!; **we didn't know which ~ to go** no sabíamos por dónde ir *or* qué dirección tomar; **which ~ did they go?** ¿por dónde (se) fueron?; **this ~ and that** de un lado a otro, aquí y allá; **which ~ does the house face?** ¿hacia dónde mira *or* está orientada la casa?; **we're both going the same ~** vamos para el mismo lado *or* en la misma dirección; **look the other ~!** ¡mira para otro lado!; **the hurricane is heading this ~** el huracán viene hacia aquí *or* en esta dirección; **if you're ever down our ~, call in** (colloq) si algún día andas por nuestra zona, ven a vernos; **whichever ~ you look at it, it's a disaster** es un desastre, lo mires por donde lo mires; **you've got your T-shirt on the wrong ~ around** llevas la camiseta al *or* del revés; **the other ~ around** al revés; **which ~ up should it be?** ¿cuál es la parte de arriba?; **to split sth three/five ~s** dividir algo en tres/cinco partes; **every which ~** (AmE) para todos lados; ***to come sb's ~*** (lit) «*person/animal*» venir* hacia algn; **none of the money ever came our ~** no nos tocó ni un céntimo del dinero; **then bad luck began to come my ~** entonces empecé a tener una mala racha; ***to go sb's ~***: **are you going my ~?** ¿vas en mi misma dirección?; **the decision went our ~** se decidió en nuestro favor; ***to put work/business sb's ~*** conseguirle* trabajo/clientes a algn; **~ *to go!*** (AmE colloq) ¡así se hace!, ¡bien hecho!

D (distance) (*no pl*): **there's only a short ~ to go now** ya falta *or* queda poco para llegar; **he came all this ~ just to see me** (colloq) se dió el viaje hasta aquí sólo para verme; **we're still some ~ from home** todavía nos queda un

W

trecho para llegar a casa; **it's a long ~ from here to Rio** Río queda muy lejos de aquí; **we passed a church some ~ back** hace ya un rato que pasamos una iglesia; **you have to go back a long ~, to the Middle Ages** hay que remontarse a la Edad Media; **it's a very long ~ down/up** hay una buena bajada/subida; **the exam is still some ~ off** todavía falta bastante para el examen; **he's come a long ~** ha venido de muy lejos; **we've come a long ~ since those days** hemos evolucionado *or* avanzado mucho desde entonces; **my salary has to go a long ~** tengo que estirar mucho el sueldo; **a little goes a long ~** un poco cunde *or* (AmL tb) rinde mucho; **Springfield? that's quite a ~s from here** (AmE colloq) ¿Springfield? eso está requetelejos de aquí (fam); **we had to walk all the ~ up** tuvimos que subir a pie hasta arriba; ***to go all the ~*: do you think he might go all the ~ and fire them?** ¿te parece que puede llegar a echarlos?; **they went all the ~** (had sex) tuvieron relaciones, hicieron el amor; ***to go some/a long ~ toward sth*** contribuir* en cierta/gran medida a algo; *see also* **way¹** *Sense* **III**

(*Sense* **II**)

A [c] (method, means) forma *f*, manera *f*, modo *m*; **we must try every possible ~ to convince them** tenemos que tratar de convencerlos por todos los medios; **there's no ~ of crossing the border without a passport** es imposible cruzar la frontera sin pasaporte; **it doesn't matter to me one ~ or the other** me da igual una cosa u otra; **it doesn't matter either ~** de cualquier forma *or* manera, no importa; **there are many ~s in which it will be useful** será útil en muchos sentidos; **all right, we'll do it your ~** muy bien, lo haremos a tu manera *or* como tú quieras; **to learn sth the hard ~** aprender algo a fuerza de palos *or* golpes; **to do sth the hard/easy ~** hacer* algo de manera difícil/fácil; **that's not the ~ to do it!** ¡así no se hace!; **that's the ~!** ¡así se hace!; ***he wants to have it both ~s*** lo quiere todo, lo quiere la chancha y los cinco reales *or* los veinte (RPl fam); ***you can't have it both ~s*** tienes que elegir entre una cosa u otra

B [c] (manner) manera *f*, modo *m*, forma *f*; **in a subtle ~** de manera *or* modo *or* forma sutil; **the ~ you behaved was disgraceful** te comportaste de (una) manera *or* forma vergonzosa; **is this the ~ you treat all your friends?** ¿así (es como) tratas a todos tus amigos?; **that's one ~ of looking at it** es una manera *or* un modo *or* una forma de verlo; **that's no ~ to talk to your mother!** ¡así no se le habla a la madre!; **what a ~ to go!** (set phrase) ¡mira que acabar *or* terminar así!; **he's in a bad ~** está muy mal; **that's just his ~** así es él; **that's the ~ it goes** así son las cosas, así es la vida; **it looks that ~** así *or* eso parece; **this ~ it's better for everyone** así es mejor para todos; **the ~ I see it** tal y como yo lo veo, a mi modo *or* manera de ver; **the ~ things are** *o* **stand at the moment** tal y como están las cosas en este momento; ***in a big ~*: they let us down in a big ~** nos fallaron de mala manera; **he fell for her in a big ~** quedó prendado de ella; ***to have a ~ with ...*: to have a ~ with children/people** saber* cómo tratar a los niños/saber* cómo tratar a la gente, tener* don de gentes; **to have a ~ with animals** tener* mucha mano con los animales; **to have a ~ with words** tener* mucha labia *or* facilidad de palabra

C [c] **1▸** (custom, characteristic): **the ~s of our people** las costumbres de nuestro pueblo; **you'll get used to our ~s** ya te irás haciendo a nuestra manera de hacer las cosas; **he has a ~ of making people feel at ease** sabe hacer que la gente se sienta cómoda; **she has a ~ of popping up unexpectedly** tiene la costumbre de aparecer donde menos te la esperas; **to get into/out of the ~ of sth** (BrE) acostumbrarse a/perder* la costumbre de algo; ***to be set in one's ~s*** estar* muy acostumbrado a hacer las cosas de cierta manera; ***to mend one's ~s*** dejar las malas costumbres, enmendarse* **2▸** (wish, will): **to get/have one's (own) ~** salirse* con la suya (*or* mía *etc*); **have it your own ~ then!** ¡lo que tú quieras!, ¡como tú digas!; ***to have it all one's own ~*** salirse* con la suya (*or* mía *etc*); ***to have one's (evil*** *o* ***wicked) ~ with sb*** llevarse a algn al huerto (fam), pasar a algn por las armas (fam)

D [c] (feature, respect) sentido *m*, aspecto *m*; **in a ~, it's like losing an old friend** de alguna manera *or* en cierta forma *or* en cierto sentido es como perder a un viejo amigo; **our product is in no ~ inferior to theirs** nuestro producto no es de ninguna manera *or* en ningún sentido inferior al suyo; **you were in no ~ to blame** tú no tuviste ninguna culpa; *see also* **way¹** *Sense* **III**

(*Sense* **III**) (*in phrases*)

A **by the way** (*indep*) a propósito, por cierto; **but that's all by the ~: what I really wanted to say was ...** pero eso no es a lo que iba: lo que quería decir es que ...

B **by way of** (*as prep*) **1▸** (via) vía, pasando por **2▸** (to serve as) a modo *or* manera de; **by ~ of introduction/an apology** a modo *or* manera de introducción/disculpa

C **in the way of** (as regards) (*as prep*): **don't expect too much in the ~ of help** en cuanto a ayuda, no esperes mucho; **there wasn't much in the ~ of opposition** no hubo gran oposición

D **no way** (colloq): **no ~ will I lend it to you** ni loco te lo presto (fam); **no ~ is he/she going to do it** de ninguna manera lo va a hacer (fam); **no ~!** ¡ni hablar! (fam)

E **to give way** **1▸** (break, collapse) «*ice/rope/cable*» romperse*; «*floor*» hundirse, ceder; **the table gave ~ under the weight** la mesa no aguantó el peso **2▸** (succumb, give in) **to give ~ TO sth** ‹*to threats/blackmail*› ceder A *or* ANTE algo; **she gave ~ to tears** no pudo contener las lágrimas y se echó a llorar; **don't give ~ to pessimism** no te dejes vencer por el pesimismo **3▸** (BrE Transp) **to give ~ (TO sb/sth)** ceder el paso (A algn/algo); Ⓢ **give way** ceda el paso **4▸** (be replaced, superseded by) **to give ~ TO sth** dejar *or* dar* paso A algo

F **under way**: **to get under ~** ponerse* en marcha, comenzar*; **to get a meeting under ~** dar* comienzo a una reunión; **an investigation is under ~** se está llevando a cabo *or* se ha abierto una investigación

way² *adv* (colloq): **~ back in February** allá por febrero; **~ behind** muy por detrás; **~ down south** allá por el sur; **they were ~ out in their calculations** se equivocaron en mucho en los cálculos; **~ past midnight** mucho después de la medianoche; **profits are ~ up on last year** los beneficios están muy por encima de los del año pasado; **~ and away** (*as intensifier*) (AmE) con mucho, lejos (AmL fam)

wayfarer /ˈweɪˌferər || ˈweɪˌfeərə(r)/ *n* (liter) caminante *mf*

way: ~lay /ˈweɪˈleɪ/ *vt* (*past & past p* **~laid**) abordar, detener*; **~-out** /ˈweɪˈaʊt/ *adj* (*pred* **~ out**) (colloq) ultramoderno, estrambótico (fam); **~s and means** *pl n* **~s and means (OF -ING)** métodos *mpl* (DE + INF); **~side** *n* **the ~side** el borde del camino; ***to fall by the ~side*** quedarse por el *or* a mitad de camino

wayward /ˈweɪwərd || ˈweɪwəd/ *adj* díscolo, caprichoso

WC *n* (BrE) WC *m*

we /wiː, *weak form* wi/ *pron* nosotros, -tras; **~ English** nosotros los ingleses; **the Royal ~** el plural mayestático, el Nos real; **it's ~ who should be grateful** (frml) somos nosotros quienes deberíamos estar agradecidos; **they're more advanced than ~ are** están más adelantados que nosotros

weak /wiːk/ *adj* **-er, -est**

A **1▸** ‹*person/muscles*› débil; ‹*structure*› poco sólido, endeble; ‹*economy/currency*› débil; ‹*handshake*› flojo; **I was too ~ to lift it** no me daban las fuerzas para levantarlo; **to have a ~ heart** sufrir del corazón; **he was ~ with hunger** se sentía débil del hambre que tenía; **to grow ~** debilitarse **2▸** (ineffectual) ‹*character/leader*› débil

B **1▸** (not competent) ‹*student/performance*› flojo, pobre **2▸** (not convincing) ‹*argument/excuse*› poco convincente, pobre

C (diluted) ‹*coffee/tea*› poco cargado; ‹*beer*› suave, aguado (pey); ‹*solution*› diluido

weaken /ˈwiːkən/ *vt* ‹*body/limb*› debilitar; ‹*structure/power/currency/economy*› debilitar; ‹*determination*› menoscabar

■ **weaken** *vi* «*person/animal*» (physically) debilitarse; «*resolve*» flaquear; «*power*» debilitarse; (relent) ceder, aflojar; **don't ~ in your resolve** no cedas en tu propósito

weak-kneed /ˈwiːkˈniːd/ *adj* pusilánime

weakling /ˈwiːklɪŋ/ *n* alfeñique *m*

weakly /ˈwiːkli/ *adv* ‹*say*› con voz débil, débilmente; **he struggled ~ and then gave in** se rindió sin apenas oponer resistencia

weak-minded /ˈwiːkˈmaɪndəd || ˌwiːkˈmaɪndɪd/ *adj* sin carácter

weakness /ˈwiːknəs || ˈwiːknɪs/ *n*

A [u] **1▸** (of body, defenses) debilidad *f*; (of structure, material) falta

W

f de solidez, endeblez *f*; (of argument) pobreza *f* **2** (ineffectualness) falta *f* de carácter, flaqueza *f*

B [c] **1** (weak point — in structure, policy) punto *m* débil; (— in person's character) flaqueza *f*, punto *m* débil *or* (fam) flaco; **we all have our ~es** todos tenemos nuestras debilidades **2** (liking) debilidad *f*, flaqueza *f*; **chocolate is one of my ~es** el chocolate es una de mis flaquezas, tengo debilidad por el chocolate; **to have a ~ for sth** tener* debilidad por algo

weak-willed /ˈwiːkˈwɪld/ *adj* ‹*person*› de poca (fuerza de) voluntad; **to be ~** tener* poca fuerza de voluntad

weal /wiːl/ *n* verdugón *m* (*de un golpe dado con una cuerda, correa etc*)

wealth /welθ/ *n* [u]

A **1** (money, possessions) riqueza *f*, riquezas *fpl* (liter) **2** (Econ) riqueza *f*

B (large quantity): **a ~ of sth** abundancia *f* de algo

wealthy¹ /ˈwelθi/ *adj* **-thier, -thiest** ‹*person/family*› adinerado, acaudalado, rico; ‹*nation/area*› rico

wealthy² *n* **the ~** los ricos, la gente adinerada

wean /wiːn/ *vt* ‹*baby/young*› destetar; **to ~ sb OFF sth**: **we ~ed him off drugs** conseguimos que dejara las drogas, conseguimos desengancharle de las drogas (Esp)

weapon /ˈwepən/ *n* arma *f*‡; **~s of mass destruction** armas de destrucción masiva

weaponry /ˈwepənri/ *n* [u] armamento *m*, armas *fpl*

wear¹ /wer || weə(r)/ *n* [u]

A **1** (use): **you should get a good ten years' ~ out of that coat** ese abrigo te debería durar por lo menos diez años; **I've had a lot of ~ out of these shoes** les he dado mucho uso *or* (fam) trote a estos zapatos; **carpets that stand hard ~** alfombras que resisten el uso constante **2** (damage) desgaste *m*; **the sofa's showing signs of ~** el sofá está un poco gastado; **~ and tear** uso *m or* desgaste natural; ***to look the worse for ~***: **she looked very much the worse for ~ after the sleepless night** se le notaban los efectos de la noche en vela

B **1** (wearing of clothes): **clothes for evening/everyday ~** ropa para la noche/para diario *or* para todos los días **2** (clothing) ropa *f*; **children's ~** ropa de niños

wear² (*past* **wore**; *past p* **worn**) *vt*

A **1** (at specific moment) ‹*clothes/jewelry/watch*› llevar; **she was ~ing a black dress** llevaba un vestido negro; **what perfume are you ~ing?** ¿qué perfume llevas *or* te has puesto?; **she wasn't ~ing any makeup** no llevaba maquillaje; **he's ~ing his glasses** lleva puestas las gafas; **I've got nothing to ~** no tengo qué ponerme; **she was ~ing green** vestía de verde **2** (usually) ‹*glasses*› llevar, usar; ‹*makeup/perfume/earrings*› usar; **she doesn't ~ skirts** no usa *or* no se pone faldas; **he ~s size 44 shoes** calza (el) 44; **she ~s green a lot** se viste mucho de verde; **she ~s her hair in a ponytail** se peina con cola de caballo; ***to ~ the trousers*** *o* (AmE also) ***pants*** llevar los pantalones

B (through use): **he had worn the collar threadbare** había gastado el cuello hasta dejarlo raído de tanto uso; **the step had been worn smooth** el peldaño se había alisado con el uso; **she's worn holes in the soles** se le han agujereado las suelas

■ **wear** *vi*

A (through use) «*collar/carpet/brakes*» gastarse; **to ~ smooth** alisarse; ***to ~ thin*** (lit: through use) «*cloth/metal*» gastarse; «*joke*» perder* la gracia; **her patience began to ~ thin** empezó a perder la paciencia

B (last) (+ *adv compl*) durar; **to ~ well** «*cloth/clothes*» durar mucho; «*person*» conservarse bien

(Phrasal verbs)

• **wear away**

A [v ▸ o ▸ adv, v ▸ adv ▸ o] (erode) ‹*rock*› desgastar, erosionar; ‹*pattern/inscription*› borrar

B [v ▸ adv] (become eroded) «*rock*» desgastarse, erosionarse; «*inscription*» borrarse

• **wear down**

A [v ▸ o ▸ adv, v ▸ adv ▸ o] **1** (by friction) ‹*heel/pencil*› gastar **2** (weaken) ‹*resistance*› menoscabar; ‹*person*› agotar, acabar con

B [v ▸ adv] «*heel/tread*» gastarse

• **wear off** [v ▸ adv] **1** (be removed) «*paint*» quitarse, salirse* **2** (disappear) «*distress/numbness*» pasarse, quitarse; **the novelty was beginning to ~ off** ya estaba dejando de ser una novedad

• **wear on** [v ▸ adv] «*winter/years*» pasar, transcurrir (*lentamente*); «*meeting/drought*» continuar*; **as the day wore on** a medida que iban pasando las horas

• **wear out**

A [v ▸ o ▸ adv, v ▸ adv ▸ o] **1** (through use) ‹*shoes/carpet/batteries*› gastar **2** (exhaust) ‹*person*› agotar, dejar rendido, dejar de cama (AmL fam); **to ~ oneself out** agotarse

B [v ▸ adv] (through use) «*shoes/towel/batteries*» gastarse

• **wear through** [v ▸ adv] (get hole in) «*soles/cloth*» agujerearse; **the jacket had worn through at the elbows** la chaqueta tenía los codos raídos *or* tenía agujeros en los codos

wearily /ˈwɪrəli || ˈwɪərɪli/ *adv* ‹*walk/move*› cansinamente; **he sighed ~** suspiró cansado

weariness /ˈwɪrinəs || ˈwɪərinɪs/ *n* [u] cansancio *m*, fatiga *f*; (mental) hastío *m*

wearing /ˈwerɪŋ || ˈweərɪŋ/ *adj* **1** (tiring, tiresome) cansado *or* (AmS) cansador *or* (Col, Ven) cansón **2** (damaging): **it's very ~ on the nerves** te saca de quicio

wearisome /ˈwɪrisəm || ˈwɪərisəm/ *adj* pesado, aburrido

weary¹ /ˈwɪri || ˈwɪəri/ *adj* **-rier, -riest** ‹*person/legs*› cansado; ‹*sigh*› de cansancio; **to be ~ OF sth/-ING** estar* cansado *or* harto *or* aburrido DE algo/+ INF; **to grow ~ OF sth** cansarse *or* hartarse *or* aburrirse DE algo

weary² **-ries, -rying, -ried** *vt* **1** (tire) cansar **2** (annoy) hartar, cansar, aburrir

■ **weary** *vi* (frml *or* liter) (tire) **to ~ OF sth/sb** cansarse *or* hartarse *or* aburrirse DE algo/algn

weasel /ˈwiːzəl/ *n* **1** (Zool) comadreja *f* **2** (person) (colloq & pej) rata *f* (fam & pey)

weather¹ /ˈweðər || ˈweðə(r)/ *n* [u] tiempo *m*; **good/bad ~** buen/mal tiempo; **in hot ~** cuando hace calor, en tiempo caluroso; **what's the ~ like?** ¿cómo está el tiempo?, ¿qué tiempo hace?; **what's the ~ like in Mexico?** ¿qué clima tiene México?; **you can't go out in this ~** no puedes salir con este tiempo; **they work outdoors in all ~s**[c] trabajan a la intemperie haga el tiempo que haga; ***to be under the ~*** no estar* *or* (fam) no andar* muy bien; ***to make heavy ~ of sth*** complicarse* la vida con algo (colloq); **you're making very heavy ~ of sewing that button on!** ¡qué manera de complicarse la vida para coser un simple botón!; (*before n*) **~ forecaster** meteorólogo, -ga *m,f*; ‹*map/chart*› meteorológico; **~ forecast** pronóstico *m* del tiempo

weather² *vt*

A **1** (wear) ‹*rocks*› erosionar; ‹*surface*› desgastar; ‹*skin/face*› curtir **2** ‹*wood*› secar*, curar

B (survive): *see* **storm¹ A**

■ **weather** *vi* «*rock*» erosionarse; «*surface*» desgastarse

weather: **~beaten** *adj* ‹*face/sailor*› curtido; ‹*walls/rocks*› azotado por los elementos; **~cock** *n* veleta *f*

weathered /ˈweðərd || ˈweðəd/ *adj* ‹*rocks/brick/stone*› erosionado (*por la acción de los elementos*); ‹*wood*› curado

weather: **~man** /ˈweðərmæn || ˈweðəmæn/ *n* (*pl* **-men** /-men/) *hombre que transmite el pronóstico del tiempo por radio o televisión*; **~proof** *adj* impermeable; **~ vane** *n* veleta *f*

weave¹ /wiːv/ *vt*

A (*past* **wove**; *past p* **woven**) **1** ‹*cloth/mat*› tejer (*en telar*); ‹*basket/web*› tejer; ‹*story/plot*› tejer; **they wove a roof out of branches** hicieron un techo entretejiendo ramas **2** (thread together) ‹*threads*› entretejer, entrelazar*; ‹*branches/straw*› entretejer; **she ~s these anecdotes into her lectures** entreteje *or* intercala estas anécdotas en sus conferencias

B (*past* **wove** *or* **weaved**; *past p* **woven** *or* **weaved**): **he ~d his way through the crowd** se abrió camino (en zigzag) entre la multitud

■ **weave** *vi*

A (*past* **wove**; *past p* **woven**) (make cloth, baskets) tejer; ***to get weaving*** (BrE colloq) poner* manos a la obra

B **1** (*past* **wove** *or* **weaved**; *past p* **woven** *or* **weaved**) «*road*» serpentear, zigzaguear; «*person*» zigzaguear; **the cyclist was weaving in and out of the traffic** el ciclista iba zigzagueando por entre el tráfico **2** (*past & past p* **weaved**) (sway) tambalearse, bambolearse

weave² *n* [u c] trama *f*, tejido *m*

weaver /ˈwiːvər || ˈwiːvə(r)/ *n* tejedor, -dora *m,f*

weaving /ˈwiːvɪŋ/ *n* [u] (of cloth) tejido *m*
web /web/ *n*
A (*spider's* ~) telaraña *f*; **a ~ of intrigue** una red de intriga; **a ~ of lies** una maraña de mentiras
B (on bird's, frog's foot) membrana *f* interdigital
C (Comput): **the W~** *o* **~** la *or* el web; **World Wide Web** telaraña *f* mundial; (*before n*) **~ design** diseño *m* de páginas web; **~ designer** diseñador, -dora *m,f* de páginas web
webbed /webd/ *adj* palmeado
web: ~ browser *n* navegador *m* de Internet; **~cam** /ˈwebkæm/ *n* webcam *f*, cámara *f* web
web-footed /ˈwebˈfʊtəd/ *adj* palmípedo
webinar /ˈwebɪnɑː(r)/ *n* webinario *m*, seminario *m* web
web: ~link *n* enlace *m* web; **~log** *n* weblog *m*, bitácora *f*
wed /wed/ (*past & past p* **wedded** *or* **wed**) *vt* **1** (marry) (dated *or* journ) ‹*man/woman*› casarse con; **with this ring I thee ~** recibe este anillo *or* esta alianza como símbolo de nuestra unión **2** **wedded** *past p* ‹*bliss/life*› conyugal; **lawful ~ded wife** legítima esposa; **lawful ~ded husband** legítimo esposo **3** (attach, commit) (frml) **to be ~ded (TO sth)** estar* empeñado en algo
■ **wed** *vi* casarse
we'd /wiːd/ **1** = **we had** **2** = **we would**
Wed (= **Wednesday**) miérc.
wedding /ˈwedɪŋ/ *n* **1** (ceremony) boda *f*, casamiento *m*, matrimonio *m* (AmS exc RPl); **to have a church/civil** (AmE) *o* (BrE) **registry-office ~** casarse por la iglesia *or* (RPl) por iglesia/por lo civil *or* (Per, RPl, Ven) por civil *or* (Chi, Méx) por el civil; (*before n*) **~ breakfast** banquete *m* nupcial; **~ cake** tarta *f or* pastel *m* de boda, torta *f* de matrimonio *or* de novios (AmS exc CS), torta *f* de casamiento (RPl) *or* (Chi) de novia; **~ dress** vestido *m or* traje *m* de novia; **~ march** marcha *f* nupcial; **~ night** noche *f* de bodas; **~ reception** banquete *m* de bodas, fiesta *f* de matrimonio (Chi); **~ ring** alianza *f*, anillo *m* de boda, argolla *f* (de matrimonio) (Chi) **2** (anniversary): **silver/golden ~** bodas *fpl* de plata/oro
wedge¹ /wedʒ/ *n* **1** (for securing) cuña *f*, calce *m*, calzo *m* **2** (for splitting) cuña *f*; ***the thin end of the ~*** el principio de algo peor; ***to drive a ~ between two people/groups*** abrir* una brecha entre dos personas/grupos **3** (shape): **a ~ of cheese/cake** un trozo grande de queso/pastel
wedge² *vt* **1** (secure): **to ~ a door open** ponerle* una cuña a una puerta para que no se cierre **2** (squeeze) meter (*a presión*); **she was ~d between two fat men** estaba apretujada entre dos gordos
wedlock /ˈwedlɑːk ‖ ˈwedlɒk/ *n* [u] (frml) matrimonio *m*
Wednesday /ˈwenzdeɪ, -di/ *n* miércoles *m*; *see also* **Monday**
wee¹ /wiː/ *adj* **1** (small) (esp Scot, IrE) pequeño, chico (esp AmL); **a ~ drink** una copita, un tragito; **in the ~ small hours** *o* **the ~ hours** a las altas horas de la madrugada **2** **a ~ bit**: **a ~ bit late/less** un poco tarde/un poquito menos
wee² *n* (BrE colloq) (*no pl*): **to have** *o* **do a ~** hacer* pis *or* pipí (fam), hacer* del uno (Méx, Per fam)
wee³ *vi* (BrE colloq) hacer* pis *or* pipí (fam)
weed¹ /wiːd/ *n*
A (Hort) **1** [c] hierbajo *m*, mala hierba *f*, yuyo *m* (RPl), maleza *f* (AmL) **2** [u] (aquatic growth) algas *fpl*
B [u] (marijuana) (sl) hierba *f* (arg), monte *m* (AmC, Col, Ven fam)
C [c] (feeble person) (BrE colloq) alfeñique *m*
weed² *vt* deshierbar, desherbar*, desmalezar* (AmL), sacar* los yuyos de (RPl)
■ **weed** *vi* deshierbar, desherbar*, desmalezar* (AmL), sacar* los yuyos (RPl)
Phrasal verb
• **weed out** [v ▸ o ▸ adv, v ▸ adv ▸ o] **1** (Hort) quitar, arrancar* **2** ‹*errors/items*› eliminar; ‹*applicants*› eliminar
weedkiller /ˈwiːdˌkɪlər ‖ ˈwiːdˌkɪlə(r)/ *n* herbicida *m*
weedy /ˈwiːdi/ *adj* **-dier, -diest** **1** (lanky) (AmE) larguirucho (fam) **2** (feeble, puny) (BrE colloq) enclenque
week /wiːk/ *n* **1** (7 days) semana *f*; **in a ~** dentro de una semana; **once a ~** una vez por semana *or* a la semana; **$100 a ~** 100 dólares semanales *or* por semana; **we get paid by the ~** nos pagan semanalmente; **(on) Tuesday ~** *o* (BrE also) **a ~ on Tuesday** el martes que viene no, el otro *or* del martes en ocho días; **she arrived a ~ (ago) yesterday** ayer hizo una semana que llegó; **~ in, ~ out** semana tras semana; **Holy W~** Semana Santa **2** (working days): **I never go out in** *o* **during the ~** nunca salgo los días de semana *or* entre semana; **a four-day/35 hour ~** una semana (laboral) de cuatro días/35 horas
week: ~day *n* día *m* de semana; **he gets up early (on) ~days** se levanta temprano los días de semana *or* entre semana; **~end** /ˈwiːkend ‖ wiːkˈend/ *n* fin *m* de semana; **long ~end** fin *m* de semana largo, puente *m*
weekly¹ /ˈwiːkli/ *adj* semanal
weekly² *adv* semanalmente; **we get paid ~** nos pagan por semana
weekly³ *n* (*pl* **weeklies**) semanario *m*
weenie /ˈwiːni/ *n* (AmE colloq) pitito *m* (fam), pichulín *m* (AmL fam), pipí *f* (Bol, Col, Méx fam), colita *f* (Esp fam)
weeny /ˈwiːni/ *adj* **-nier, -niest** (colloq) pequeñito, chiquito (esp AmL)
weep¹ /wiːp/ *vi* (*past & past p* **wept**)
A (cry) llorar; **I could have wept** era como para llorar; **to ~ FOR sb** llorar POR algn; (for dead person) llorar A algn; **to ~ OVER sth** llorar POR algo; **to ~ with joy** llorar de alegría
B (exude liquid) «*wound/eye*» supurar
weep² *n* (esp BrE) (*no pl*): **I had a good ~** me desahogué llorando un rato
weeping /ˈwiːpɪŋ/ *n* [u] llanto *m*
weeping willow *n* sauce *m* llorón
weepy¹ /ˈwiːpi/ *adj* **-pier, -piest** (colloq)
A **1** ‹*person*›: **to feel ~** tener* ganas de llorar; **she's very ~ these days** de un tiempo a esta parte llora por nada *or* está muy llorona **2** ‹*film/play*› que hace llorar, lacrimógeno (hum), cebollento (Chi fam)
B ‹*eye*› lloroso
weepy² *n* (*pl* **-pies**) (BrE colloq & journ) dramón *m* (fam & pey), melodrama *m*
weevil /ˈwiːvəl/ *n* gorgojo *m*
weft /weft/ *n* [u] trama *f*
weigh /weɪ/ *vt*
A ‹*person/load/food*› pesar; **to ~ oneself** pesarse
B (consider) ‹*factors/arguments/evidence*› sopesar; **to ~ sth AGAINST sth** comparar algo CON algo, contraponer* algo A algo
C (Naut): **to ~ anchor** levar anclas
■ **weigh** *vi*
A (measure in weight) «*person/load/food*» pesar; **how much** *o* **what do you ~?** ¿cuánto pesas?; **this bag ~s a ton!** (colloq) ¡esta bolsa pesa un quintal *or* una tonelada!
B (count): **your inexperience will ~ against you** tu falta de experiencia será un factor en tu contra; **this ~ed heavily in her favor** esto la favoreció enormemente
Phrasal verbs
• **weigh down** [v ▸ o ▸ adv, v ▸ adv ▸ o] **1** (impose weight on): **the bag was ~ing me down** la bolsa me pesaba mucho; **trees ~ed down with fruit** árboles cargados de fruta **2** (depress) abrumar **3** ▸**weight down**
• **weigh in** [v ▸ adv]
A «*boxer/runner*»: **the champion ~ed in at 160 lbs** el campeón pesó 160 libras; **they haven't ~ed in yet** aún no los han pesado
B (in discussion, conversation) intervenir*; **to ~ in WITH sth**: **she ~ed in with harsh criticism of our methods** intervino criticando duramente nuestros métodos
• **weigh on** [v ▸ prep ▸ o]: **it still ~ed heavily on her conscience** todavía sentía un gran cargo de conciencia; **it ~s heavily on my mind** me preocupa mucho
• **weigh out** [v ▸ o ▸ adv, v ▸ adv ▸ o] pesar
• **weigh up** [v ▸ o ▸ adv, v ▸ adv ▸ o] ‹*situation*› considerar, ponderar; ‹*pros and cons*› sopesar, considerar, ponderar; ‹*person*› evaluar*, formarse una opinión de
weighbridge /ˈweɪbrɪdʒ/ *n* báscula *f* de puente
weight¹ /weɪt/ *n*
A [u c] (mass, heaviness) peso *m*; **it's sold by ~** se vende al peso *or* por peso; **the bag is 5kg in ~** la bolsa pesa 5kg; **what ~ are you?** ¿cuánto pesas?; **to gain** *o* **put on ~** engordar, subir de peso; **to lose ~** adelgazar*, perder* peso; **you mustn't lift heavy ~s** no debe levantar cosas

pesadas; **sit down, take the ~ off your feet** siéntate y descansa un poco; **that has taken a ~ off my mind** eso me ha sacado un peso de encima; ***to be worth one's ~ in gold*** valer* su peso en oro; ***to pull one's ~*****: John isn't pulling his ~** John no trabaja como debería; ***to throw one's ~ around*** mandonear (fam); ***to throw one's ~ behind sth*** apoyar algo con dedicación
B [u] (importance, value) peso *m*; **to lend/add ~ to sth** darle* más peso a algo; **his views don't carry much ~ with her** ella no respeta mucho sus opiniones, para ella sus opiniones no cuentan mucho
C **1** (unit) peso *m*; **~s and measures** pesos y medidas **2** (for scales, clocks) pesa *f* **3** (Sport) pesa *f*; (*before n*) **~ training** entrenamiento *m* con pesas

weight² *vt* **1** (make heavier) darle* peso a; ‹*fishing net*› lastrar **2** (bias): **to be ~ed against/in favor of sb** perjudicar*/favorecer* a algn

Phrasal verb
- **weight down** [v ▸ o ▸ adv, v ▸ adv ▸ o] **1** ‹*tarpaulin/papers*› sujetar con algo pesado **2** ‹*body*› (to make it sink) ponerle* un lastre a

weighting /'weɪtɪŋ/ *n* (BrE Busn) suplemento *m* *or* prima *f* *or* plus *m* (salarial); **London ~** suplemento salarial por trabajar en Londres

weightless /'weɪtləs || 'weɪtlɪs/ *adj* ingrávido

weightlessness /'weɪtləsnəs || 'weɪtlɪsnɪs/ *n* [u] ingravidez *f*

weight: ~lifter /'weɪt,lɪftər || 'weɪt,lɪftə(r)/ *n* levantador, -dora *m,f* de pesas, pesista *mf* (Andes), halterófilo, -la *m,f*; **~lifting** /'weɪt,lɪftɪŋ/ *n* [u] levantamiento *m* de pesas, halterofilia *f*; **~-watching** /'weɪt,wɑːtʃɪŋ || 'weɪt,wɒtʃɪŋ/ *n* [u] cuidado *m* del peso *or* de la línea

weighty /'weɪti/ *adj* **-tier, -tiest** ‹*argument*› de peso, importante; ‹*matter*› importante

weir /wɪr || wɪə(r)/ *n* presa *f*

weird /wɪrd || wɪəd/ *adj* **-er, -est** **1** (strange) (colloq) raro, extraño; **all sorts of ~ and wonderful things** las cosas más increíbles **2** (unearthly) ‹*apparition/figure*› misterioso

weirdo /'wɪrdəʊ || 'wɪədəʊ/ *n* (*pl* **-os**) (colloq) bicho *m* raro (fam)

welcome¹ /'welkəm/ *interj* bienvenido; **~ home/to Chicago!** ¡bienvenido a casa/a Chicago!; **~ back!** me alegro de que hayas vuelto

welcome² *adj* **1** (gladly received) ‹*guest*› bienvenido; ‹*change/news*› grato; **he knows how to make people feel ~** sabe acoger a la gente; **an extra pair of hands is always ~** siempre se agradece la ayuda de alguien más; **it was a ~ relief** fue un gran alivio **2** (freely permitted) **to be ~ to + INF: you're ~ to use the phone** el teléfono está a tu disposición; **to be ~ TO sth: you're ~ to these books** puedes llevarte estos libros, si quieres; **she's ~ to try** que pruebe, si quiere **3** (responding to thanks): **you're ~!** ¡de nada!, ¡no hay de qué!

welcome³ *vt* (greet) darle* la bienvenida a; (receive): **he was warmly ~d by her family** su familia le dio una calurosa acogida; **they ~d me with open arms** me recibieron con los brazos abiertos; **this news is to be ~d** es para alegrarse de esta noticia; **we would ~ any advice you can give us** le agradeceríamos cualquier consejo que pudiera darnos

welcome⁴ *n* bienvenida *f*, recibimiento *m*, acogida *f*; **to give sb a warm ~** acoger* a algn calurosamente, darle* a algn una calurosa bienvenida *or* acogida *or* un caluroso recibimiento

welcoming /'welkəmɪŋ/ *adj* **1** ‹*ceremony/delegation*› de bienvenida *or* recibimiento **2** ‹*smile/hug*› acogedor, cordial; **the little bar looked very ~** el barcito parecía muy acogedor

weld /weld/ *vt* soldar*; **you have to ~ the plates (together)** hay que soldar las placas
■ **weld** *vi* soldar*

welder /'weldər || 'weldə(r)/ *n* (person) soldador, -dora *m,f*; (device) soldadora *f*

welding /'weldɪŋ/ *n* [u] soldadura *f*

welfare /'welfer || 'welfeə(r)/ *n* [u]
A (well-being) bienestar *m*
B (Soc Adm) **1** (assistance) asistencia *f* social; **child ~** protección *f* a la infancia **2** (payment) (AmE) prestaciones *fpl* sociales

welfare state *n* estado *m* de bienestar, estado *m* benefactor

well¹ /wel/ *adv* (*comp* **better**; *superl* **best**)
A (to high standard, satisfactorily) ‹*sing/write/work*› bien; **I explained it as ~ as I could** lo expliqué lo mejor que pude; **to do ~: you did very ~** lo hiciste muy bien; **he's doing very ~** le van muy bien las cosas; **he's done ~ for himself** ha sabido abrirse camino; **mother and baby are doing ~** madre e hijo se encuentran muy bien; **~ done!** ¡así se hace!, ¡muy bien!; **to go ~** «*performance/operation*» salir* bien; ▸**worth¹ 2**
B (thoroughly) ‹*wash/dry/know*› bien; **I can ~ understand your concern** entiendo perfectamente su preocupación; **it was ~ worth the effort** realmente valió la pena; **he knows only too ~ that ...** bien sabe *or* sabe de sobra que ...; **~ and truly** (colloq): **I'm ~ and truly fed up** estoy requete harto (fam); **he was ~ and truly drunk** estaba pero bien borracho *or* completamente borracho; ***to be ~ away*** (BrE colloq): **two beers and he's ~ away** con dos cervezas le alcanza para ponerse alegre
C **1** (considerably) (*no comp*) bastante; **until ~ into the next century** hasta bien entrado el siglo que viene **2** (with justification): **you may ~ ask!** ¡muy buena pregunta!; **she was horrified, as ~ she might be** se horrorizó, y con razón; **she couldn't very ~ deny it** ¿cómo iba a negarlo?
D (advantageously) ‹*marry*› bien; **to do ~ to + INF** hacer* bien en + INF, deber + INF; **she'd be ~ advised to see a lawyer** sería aconsejable que consultara a un abogado; **to come off ~** *o* **do ~ out of sth** salir* bien parado de algo
E (*in phrases*) **1** **as well** (in addition) también; **are they coming as ~?** ¿ellos también vienen?; **and she lied to me as ~!** ¡y además me mintió! **2** **as well as** (in addition to) además de; **at night as ~ as during the day** tanto de noche como durante el día **3** **may/might as well: I might as ~ not bother, for all the notice they take** para el caso que me hacen, no sé por qué me molesto *or* no vale la pena que me moleste; **now you've told him, you may as ~ give it to him!** ahora que se lo has dicho dáselo ¿total?

well² *adj* (*comp* **better**; *superl* **best**)
A (healthy) bien; **you look ~** tienes buena cara *or* buen aspecto; **how are you? — I'm very ~, thank you** ¿cómo estás? — muy bien, gracias; **get ~ soon!** ¡que te mejores!
B (pleasing, satisfactory) bien; **all is not ~** algo va mal; **that's all ~ and good, but ...** todo eso está muy bien, pero ...; **it's all very ~ for him to talk, but ...** él podrá decir todo lo que quiera pero ..., es muy fácil hablar, pero ...; ***all's ~ that ends well*** bien está lo que bien acaba; ▸**alone¹ 2**
C **as well: it would be as ~ to keep this quiet** mejor no decir nada de esto; **it's just as ~ I've got some money with me** menos mal que llevo dinero encima

well³ *interj*
A **1** (introducing/continuing topic, sentence) bueno, bien; **~, shall we get started?** bueno *or* bien ¿empezamos?; **~ now** *o* **then, what's the problem?** a ver ¿qué es lo que pasa? **2** (expressing hesitation): **do you like it? — well ...** ¿te gusta? — pues *or* (esp AmL) este ...
B **1** (expressing surprise): **~, ~, ~! look who's here!** ¡vaya, vaya! *or* ¡anda! ¡mira quién está aquí!; **~, I never!** ¡qué increíble! **2** (expressing indignation) bueno; **~, if that's how you feel ...!** bueno, si eso es lo que piensas ... **3** (dismissively) ¡bah! **4** (expressing resignation) bueno; **(oh) ~, that's the way it goes** bueno ... ¡qué se le va a hacer!
C **1** (expressing expectation): **~? I'm listening** bien, tú dirás, ¿sí? te escucho; **~? who won?** bueno ¿y quién ganó? **2** (expressing skepticism) bueno; **(yes,) ~, that remains to be seen** (sí,) bueno, eso está por verse

well⁴ *n*
A **1** (for water) pozo *m*, aljibe *m* **2** (for oil, gas) pozo *m*
B **1** (for stairs) caja *f* *or* hueco *m* de la escalera **2** (for ventilation) (BrE) patio *m* (de luces *or* de luz), pozo *m* de aire

Phrasal verb
- **well up** [v ▸ adv] «*water*» brotar, manar; **tears ~ed up in his eyes** los ojos se le llenaron de lágrimas

well- /'wel/ *pref* bien; **~made** bien hecho; **~paid** bien remunerado

we'll /wiːl/ **= we will**

well: **~-adjusted** /ˈweləˈdʒʌstəd ‖ ˌweləˈdʒʌstɪd/ *adj* (*pred* ~ **adjusted**) (Psych) equilibrado; **~-attended** /ˈweləˈtendəd ‖ ˌweləˈtendɪd/ *adj* (*pred* ~ **attended**) ‹*concert/exhibition*› muy concurrido, con mucho público; **the meeting was very ~ attended** asistió mucha gente a la reunión; **~-balanced** /ˈwelˈbælənst/ *adj* (*pred* ~ **balanced**) ‹*person*› equilibrado; ‹*diet*› equilibrado, balanceado; **~-behaved** /ˈwelbɪˈheɪvd/ *adj* (*pred* ~ **behaved**) ‹*child*› que se porta bien, bueno; ‹*dog*› obediente; **~-being** /ˈwelˈbiːɪŋ/ *n* [u] bienestar *m*; **~-bred** /ˈwelˈbred/ *adj* (*pred* ~ **bred**) distinguido, fino; **~-built** /ˈwelˈbɪlt/ *adj* (*pred* ~ **built**) 1 ‹*house/ship*› bien construido 2 ‹*person*› fornido; **~-chosen** /ˈwelˈtʃəʊzn̩/ *adj* (*pred* ~ **chosen**) ‹*gift*› bien elegido *or* escogido; **I gave him a few ~-chosen words!** ¡le dije cuatro cosas bien dichas!; **~-developed** /ˈweldɪˈveləpt/ *adj* (*pred* ~ **developed**) (muy) desarrollado; **~-disposed** /ˈweldɪˈspəʊzd/ *adj* (*pred* ~ **disposed**) dispuesto a colaborar (*or* ayudar *etc*); **~-done** /ˈwelˈdʌn/ *adj* (*pred* ~ **done**) (Culin) bien cocido *or* (Esp) muy hecho; **~-dressed** /ˈwelˈdrest/ *adj* (*pred* ~ **dressed**) bien vestido; **~-educated** /ˈwelˈedʒəkeɪtəd ‖ ˌwelˈedjʊkeɪtɪd/ *adj* (*pred* ~ **educated**) culto, instruido; **~-fed** /ˈwelˈfed/ *adj* (*pred* ~ **fed**) bien alimentado; **~-founded** /ˈwelˈfaʊndəd ‖ ˌwelˈfaʊndɪd/ *adj* (*pred* ~ **founded**) bien fundado, justificado; **~-groomed** /ˈwelˈgruːmd/ *adj* (*pred* ~ **groomed**) 1 ‹*person*› bien arreglado; ‹*hair*› bien peinado 2 ‹*horse/garden*› bien cuidado; **~-heeled** /ˈwelˈhiːld/ *adj* (*pred* ~ **heeled**) (colloq) platudo (AmL fam), de pelas (Esp fam); **they're ~ heeled** tienen plata (AmS fam) *or* (Esp) pelas *or* (Méx) lana (fam)

wellies *pl of* **welly**

well-informed /ˈwelɪnˈfɔːrmd ‖ ˌwelɪnˈfɔːmd/ *adj* bien informado; **to be ~ about sth** estar* muy informado sobre algo, estar* muy al corriente *or* (CS tb) muy interiorizado de algo

wellington (boot) /ˈwelɪŋtən/ *n* 1 (short boot) (AmE) botín *m*, bota *f* (*corta*) 2 (gumboot) (BrE) bota *f* de goma *or* de agua *or* de lluvia, catiusca *f* (Esp)

well: **~-intentioned** /ˈwelɪnˈtentʃənd ‖ ˌwelɪnˈtenʃənd/ *adj* (*pred* ~ **intentioned**) bienintencionado; **to be ~ intentioned** tener* buenas intenciones; **~-kept** /ˈwelˈkept/ *adj* (*before n* ~ **kept**) 1 ‹*house/lawns*› bien cuidado 2 ‹*secret*› bien guardado; **~-known** /ˈwelˈnəʊn/ *adj* (*pred* ~ **known**) ‹*person*› conocido, famoso; **it is ~ known that ...** es bien sabido que ...; **~-mannered** /ˈwelˈmænərd ‖ ˌwelˈmænəd/ *adj* (*pred* ~ **mannered**) de buenos modales, educado; **~-meaning** /ˈwelˈmiːnɪŋ/ *adj* (*pred* ~ **meaning**) ‹*person*› bienintencionado; **he's ~ meaning, but ...** lo hace con la mejor intención, pero ...; **~-nigh** /ˈwelˈnaɪ/ *adv* ‹*impossible/destitute*› prácticamente; **~-off** /ˈwelˈɔːf ‖ ˌwelˈɒf/ *adj* (*pred* ~ **off**) adinerado, acomodado; **to be ~ off FOR sth** tener* cantidad DE algo; **~-placed** /ˈwelˈpleɪst/ *adj* (*pred* ~ **placed**) ‹*shot/throw*› certero; **~-preserved** /ˈwelprɪˈzɜːrvd ‖ ˌwelprɪˈzɜːvd/ *adj* (*pred* ~ **preserved**) ‹*artefact/find*› en buen estado, bien conservado; **he is ~ preserved** se conserva bien; **~-read** /ˈwelˈred/ *adj* (*pred* ~ **read**) culto, instruido; **~-spoken** /ˈwelˈspəʊkən/ *adj* (*pred* ~ **spoken**) ‹*person*› de habla educada; **he's very ~ spoken** es muy bien hablado; **~-stocked** /ˈwelˈstɑːkt ‖ ˌwelˈstɒkt/ *adj* (*pred* ~ **stocked**) ‹*store/fridge*› bien surtido; ‹*lake/stream*› lleno de peces; ‹*library*› muy completo; **~-thought-of** /ˈwelˈθɔːtɑːv ‖ ˌwelˈθɔːtɒv/ *adj* (*pred* ~ **thought of**) ‹*company*› de prestigio, de buen nombre; **he is ~ thought of** está muy bien considerado *or* conceptuado; **~-timed** /ˈwelˈtaɪmd/ *adj* (*pred* ~ **timed**) oportuno; **~-to-do** /ˈweltəˈduː/ *adj* ‹*businessman/family*› adinerado, acaudalado; ‹*neighborhood*› de gente adinerada; **~-tried** /ˈwelˈtraɪd/ *adj* (*pred* **well tried**) ‹*method/tactic*› muy comprobado; ‹*recipe*› muy probado; **~-wisher** /ˈwelˌwɪʃər ‖ ˈwelˌwɪʃə(r)/ *n*: **she received lots of cards from ~-wishers** recibió muchas tarjetas en que le deseaban una pronta recuperación (*or* mucha felicidad *etc*); **~-worn** /ˈwelˈwɔːrn ‖ ˌwelˈwɔːn/ *adj* (*pred* ~ **worn**) ‹*coat/carpet*› muy gastado; ‹*phrase*› muy trillado *or* manido

welly /ˈweli/ *n* (*pl* **-lies**) (BrE Clothing colloq) ▸ **wellington (boot) 2**

welsh /welʃ/ *vi* (colloq) **to ~ ON sth/sb**: **she ~ed on the debt** se hizo la sueca y no pagó la deuda (fam); **he'll ~ on you** te va a fallar, no va a cumplir lo que te prometió

Welsh¹ /welʃ/ *adj* galés

Welsh² *n* 1 [u] (language) galés *m* 2 (people) (+ *pl vb*) **the ~** los galeses

> **Welsh**
>
> El idioma galés (*Cymraeg*) hoy comparte con el inglés cierta oficialidad administrativa en Gales. De origen céltico, como el bretón y el córnico, sigue siendo la lengua materna de más del 20% de la población galesa y ha experimentado un resurgimiento durante los últimos cuarenta años. Se estudia como materia obligatoria en la mayor parte de los colegios de Gales. Los letreros y otras señales de las ciudades aparecen normalmente en inglés y galés, al menos en teoría y según lo decida cada ayuntamiento

> **Welsh Assembly – National Assembly for Wales (NAfW)**
>
> La Asamblea Nacional de Gales, que empezó a funcionar en 1999 en la capital galesa, Cardiff, posee poderes legislativos secundarios limitados. A diferencia del Parlamento Escocés no se le ha otorgado el derecho a variar el tipo básico del impuesto sobre la renta. De sus 60 diputados (*Assembly Members* o *AMs*), 40 son elegidos directamente y 20 a través de listas regionales por medio del sistema de representación proporcional

Welsh: **~man** /ˈwelʃmən/ *n* (*pl* **-men** /-mən/) galés *m*; **~ rabbit**, **~ rarebit** /ˈrerbət ‖ ˈreəbɪt/ *n* [u c] *tostada con queso derretido*

welt /welt/ *n* (weal) verdugón *m*

welter /ˈweltər ‖ ˈweltə(r)/ *n* (*no pl*) (of facts, details) fárrago *m*, maremágnum *m*

welterweight /ˈweltərweɪt ‖ ˈweltəweɪt/ *n* peso *m* welter, peso *m* medio-mediano

wench /wentʃ/ *n* (arch *or* hum) moza *f* (ant), muchacha *f*; **a serving ~** una criada *or* una sirvienta

wend /wend/ *vt*: ***to ~ one's way***: **they ~ed their way home** se pusieron en camino a casa

went /went/ *past of* **go¹**

wept /wept/ *past & past p of* **weep¹**

were /wɜːr ‖ wɜː(r), *weak form* wər ‖ wə(r)/ 1 *2nd pers sing past ind of* **be** 2 *1st, 2nd & 3rd pers pl past ind of* **be** 3 *subjunctive of* **be**

we're /wɪr ‖ wɪə(r)/ **= we are**

weren't /wɜːrnt ‖ wɜːnt/ **= were not**

werewolf /ˈwɪrwʊlf ‖ ˈwɪəwʊlf/ *n* (*pl* **-wolves**) hombre *m* lobo, lobizón *m* (Per, RPl)

west¹ /west/ *n* [u]

A 1 (point of the compass, direction) oeste *m*; **the ~, the W~** el oeste, el Oeste; **to the ~ of the city** al oeste de la ciudad; **~-north~** oesnoroeste 2 (region) **the ~, the W~** el oeste; **a town in the ~ of Wales** una ciudad del *or* en el oeste de Gales

B **the West** 1 (the Occident) (el) Occidente *m* 2 (Pol, Hist) el Oeste 3 (in US) el Oeste (americano)

C **West** (in bridge) Oeste *m*

west² *adj* (*before n*) oeste *adj inv*, occidental; ‹*wind*› del oeste

west³ *adv* al oeste; **the house faces ~** la casa da *or* está orientada al oeste; **~ OF sth** al oeste DE algo; **it is ~ of Atlanta** está al oeste de Atlanta; **out ~** (in US) en el oeste; ***to go ~*** (BrE colloq) «*thing/chance*» irse* al garete (fam)

west: **~ Bank** *n* **the W~ Bank** Cisjordania *f*; **~bound** *adj* que va (*or* iba *etc*) hacia el *or* en dirección oeste; **~ Country** *n* (in UK) **the W~ Country** el West Country (*el sudoeste de Inglaterra, esp los condados de Cornualles, Devon y Somerset*)

westerly /ˈwestərli ‖ ˈwestəli/ *adj* ‹*wind*› del oeste; **in a ~ direction** hacia el oeste, en dirección oeste

western¹ /ˈwestərn ‖ ˈwestən/ *adj* 1 (Geog) oeste *adj inv*, del oeste, occidental; **the ~ areas of the country** las zonas oeste *or* occidentales del país 2 (occidental) (Geog, Pol) occidental 3 (of US West) del oeste, de los estados del oeste

western² *n* western *m*, película *f* (*or* novela *f etc*) del Oeste *or* de vaqueros

W

Westerner, westerner /ˈwestərnər || ˈwestənə(r)/ *n* **1** (person from west): *nativo o habitante del oeste del país o de la región* **2** (occidental) occidental *mf*

westernized /ˈwestərnaɪzd || ˈwestənaɪzd/ *adj* occidentalizado

westernmost /ˈwestərnməʊst || ˈwestənməʊst/ *adj* (*before n*) ‹*town/island*› más al oeste; **the ~ point of the country** el extremo occidental *or* oeste del país

West Germany *n* (Hist) Alemania *f* Federal *or* Occidental

West Indian[1] *adj* antillano; (in UK) afroantillano

West Indian[2] *n* antillano, -na *m,f*; (in UK) afroantillano, -na *m,f*

West Indies /ˈɪndiz/ *pl n* **the ~ ~** las Antillas

westward[1] /ˈwestwərd || ˈwestwəd/, **westwardly** /-li/ *adj* (*before n*): **in a ~ direction** hacia el oeste, en dirección oeste

westward[2], (BrE) **westwards** /-z/ *adv* ‹*travel/turn*› hacia el oeste; **~ OF sth** al oeste DE algo

wet[1] /wet/ *adj* **-tt-**

A **1** (moist) ‹*floor/grass/clothes*› mojado; (damp) húmedo; ‹*concrete/plaster*› blando; **you are ~ through** estás calado hasta los huesos, estás empapado; **S wet paint** pintura fresca *or* recién pintado *or* (Esp tb) ojo, pinta; **~ WITH sth** mojado DE algo; **her eyes were ~ with tears** tenía los ojos llenos de lágrimas; **to get ~** mojarse; **he got his feet ~** se mojó los pies **2** (rainy) ‹*weather/day*› lluvioso; **it's too ~ to go out** llueve demasiado como para salir; **it's been very ~** ha llovido mucho

B (ineffectual, foolish) (BrE colloq) ‹*person*› apocado, timorato

wet[2] *vt* (*pres p* **wetting**; *past & past p* **wet** *or* **wetted**) mojar; (dampen) humedecer*; **to ~ one's lips** mojarse/humedecerse* los labios; **to ~ the bed** mojar la cama, hacerse* pipí *or* pis en la cama; **to ~ oneself** orinarse, hacerse* pipí *or* pis (encima) (fam), mearse (fam *o* vulg)

wet[3] *n*

A [u] (rain) (colloq): **come in out of the ~** entra, no te quedes ahí bajo la lluvia

B [c] (ineffectual person) (BrE colloq) timorato, -ta *m,f*; **a Tory ~** (in UK) un conservador moderado

wet: **~back** *n* (AmE colloq & pej) espalda *mf* mojada, mojado, -da *m,f*; **~ blanket** *n* (colloq) aguafiestas *mf* (fam); **~ dream** *n* (colloq) sueño *m* húmedo; **~land** /ˈwetlænd || ˈwetlənd/ *n* [u] (*often pl*) humedal *m*; (*before n*) ‹*area*› pantanoso; ‹*wildlife/plant*› de pantano

wetness /ˈwetnəs || ˈwetnɪs/ *n* [u] **1** (of surface, material) lo mojado **2** (of weather) lo lluvioso

wet: **~ nurse** *n* ama *f*‡ de cría *or* de leche, nodriza *f*; **~ suit** *n* traje *m* de neoprene *or* de neopreno

we've /wiːv/ **= we have**

whack[1] /hwæk || wæk/ *n* (blow) golpe *m*, porrazo *m*; (sound) ¡zas!

whack[2] *vt* golpear, aporrear; ‹*person*› pegarle* a

whacking /ˈhwækɪŋ || ˈwækɪŋ/ *adv* (esp BrE colloq): **~ great/big** bestial (fam), colosal (fam); **a ~ big salary** un sueldazo (fam)

whacky /ˈhwæki || ˈwæki/ ▸**wacky**

whale /hweɪl || weɪl/ *n*

A (*pl* **~s** *or* **~**) (Zool) ballena *f*

B (colloq) (*as intensifier*): **we had a ~ of a time** lo pasamos bomba *or* genial (fam); **it's a ~ of a pay increase** (esp AmE) es un tremendo aumento de sueldo (fam)

whalebone /ˈhweɪlbəʊn || ˈweɪlbəʊn/ *n* **1** [u] (Zool) barba *f* de ballena **2** [c] (in corsets etc) ballena *f*

whaler /ˈhweɪlər || ˈweɪlə(r)/ *n* (person) ballenero, -ra *m,f*; (ship) ballenero *m*

whaling /ˈhweɪlɪŋ || ˈweɪlɪŋ/ *n* [u] caza *f* *or* pesca *f* de ballenas; (*before n*) ‹*vessel/industry*› ballenero

whammy /ˈhwæmi || ˈwæmi/ *n* (*pl* **-mies**) (colloq) palo *m* (fam), revés *m*

wharf /hwɔːrf || wɔːf/ *n* (*pl* **wharves** /hwɔːrvz/) muelle *m*, embarcadero *m*

what[1] /hwɑːt || wɒt/ *pron*

A (in questions) qué; **~'s that?** ¿qué es eso?; **~'s the problem?** ¿cuál es el problema?; **~ is 28 divided by 12?** ¿cuánto es 28 dividido (por) 12?; **~'s 'I don't understand' in Russian?** ¿cómo se dice 'no entiendo' en ruso?; **~ do you mean?** ¿qué quieres decir?; **~ did you pay?** ¿cuánto pagaste?; **~'s the jacket made (out) of?** ¿de qué es la chaqueta?; **I threw it away — you did *what*?** lo tiré a la basura — *¿qué?*; **what?** (say that again) ¿cómo?, ¿qué?; (expressing disbelief) ¿qué?, ¿que qué?

B (*in phrases*) **or what?** (colloq) ¿o qué?; **are you stupid, or ~?** ¿eres tonto o qué?; **so what?** ¿y qué?; **what about**: **but ~ about the children?** y los niños ¿qué?; **~ about my work? — ~ about it?** ¿y mi trabajo? — ¿y qué?; **you know Julie's boyfriend? — yes, ~ about him?** ¿conoces al novio de Julie? — sí ¿por qué?; **what ... for**: **~'s this button for?** ¿para qué es este botón?; **~ are you complaining for?** ¿por qué te quejas?; ***to give sb ~ for*** (colloq) darle* una buena a algn (fam); **what have you** (colloq): **she sells postcards and souvenirs and ~ have you** vende postales, recuerdos y esas cosas *or* y demás; **what if**: **~ if she finds out?** ¿y si se entera?; **what ... like**: **~'s she like?** ¿cómo es?; **~ does he look like?** ¿cómo es físicamente?, ¿qué aspecto tiene?; **~'s his new film like?** ¿qué tal es su nueva película?; **what of**: **so we're not married: ~ of it?** no estamos casados ¿y qué?; **what's-her/-his/-its-name** (colloq): **go and ask ~'s-her-name next door** ve y pregúntale a la de al lado ¿cómo se llama?; **the ~'s-its-name** *o* **~-d' you call it is broken** la cosa ésa está rota (fam), el chisme ése está roto (Esp, Méx fam); **what with** entre; **~ with one thing and another, I haven't had time** entre una cosa y otra, no he tenido tiempo

C **1** (in indirect speech) qué; **she knows ~ to do** ella sabe qué hacer; **Mike will tell you ~'s ~** Mike te pondrá al tanto de todo; **I still don't know ~'s ~ in the office** aún no sé cómo funcionan las cosas en la oficina; **(do) you know ~? I'll ask him for a raise!** ¿sabes qué? *or* ¿sabes qué te digo? ¡le voy a pedir aumento!; **(I'll) tell you ~, ...** mira, ... **2** (relative use) lo que; **they did ~ they could** hicieron lo que pudieron; **I don't know and, ~'s more, I don't care** no lo sé y lo que es más, no me importa

what[2] *adj*

A **1** (in questions) qué; **what book are you reading?** ¿qué libro estás leyendo?; **~ color are the walls?** ¿de qué color son las paredes?; **~ more does he want?** ¿qué más quiere? **2** (in indirect speech) qué; **she didn't know ~ color to choose/~ language they were speaking** no sabía qué color elegir/en qué idioma estaban hablando **3** (all of the, any): **~ few hotels there were were full** los pocos hoteles que había, estaban llenos; **~ little she owned she left to her son** lo poco que tenía, se lo dejó a su hijo

B (in exclamations) qué; **~ a surprise!** ¡qué sorpresa!; **~ a friend you've turned out to be!** (iro) ¡valiente *or* vaya amigo has resultado ser tú!; **~ a lot of people!** ¡cuánta gente!, ¡qué cantidad de gente!

whatever[1] /hwɑːtˈevər || wɒtˈevə(r)/ *pron*

A (in questions, exclamations) qué; **~ is she doing?** ¿qué (es lo que) está haciendo?, ¿qué diablos está haciendo? (fam); **she resigned — ~ for?** renunció — ¿a santo de qué?; **~ next!** ¡ya es el colmo!, ¡lo que nos faltaba!

B **1** (no matter what): **~ you do, don't laugh!** hagas lo que hagas ¡no te vayas a reír!; **~ the weather** haga el tiempo que haga; **he talked about percentiles, ~ they are** habló de percentiles, que no tengo ni idea de qué son *or* (fam) de lo que son **2** (all that): **they let him do ~ he likes** lo dejan hacer todo lo que quiere; **here's $5: buy yourself a sandwich or ~** aquí tienes $5: cómprate un bocadillo o algo; **~ you say** lo que tú digas, como quieras

whatever[2] *adj* **1** (no matter what): **don't give up, ~ doubts you may have** no renuncies, tengas las dudas que tengas; **if, for ~ reason, you decide not to go** si por cualquier motivo decides no ir; **all people, of ~ race or creed** todos, cualquiera sea su raza o credo **2** (any): **~ changes are necessary** los cambios que sean necesarios, cualquier cambio que sea necesario

whatever[3] *adv* (*as intensifier*): **none/nothing ~** ninguno/nada en absoluto; **I don't think there's any chance ~ of persuading them** creo que no hay absolutamente ninguna posibilidad de persuadirlos

whatnot /ˈhwɑːtnɑːt || ˈwɒtnɒt/ *n*: **they brought coats and blankets and ~** trajeron abrigos y mantas y qué sé yo qué más (fam)

whatsit /ˈhwɑːtsət || ˈwɒtsɪt/ *n* (colloq) cosa *f*, chisme *m* (Esp, Méx fam), coso *m* (AmS fam), vaina *f* (Col, Per, Ven fam)

whatsoever[1] /ˈhwɑːtsəʊˈevər || ˌwɒtsəʊˈevə(r)/ *pron* (liter): **~ your heart desires** todo lo que desees, fuere lo que fuere (liter)

whatsoever[2] *adv*: **is there any truth in these rumors? — none ~** ¿hay algo de cierto en estos rumores? — nada en absoluto *or* absolutamente nada

wheat /hwiːt || wiːt/ *n* [u] trigo *m*; **a field of ~** un trigal; ***to separate the ~ from the chaff*** separar *or* apartar el grano de la paja; (*before n*) **~ field** trigal *m*

wheatgerm /ˈhwiːtdʒɜːrm || ˈwiːtdʒɜːm/ *n* [u] germen *m* de trigo

wheedle /ˈhwiːdḷ || ˈwiːdḷ/ *vt* 1 (coax, flatter) **to ~ sth OUT OF sb** sonsacarle* algo a algn; ***to ~ one's way into sb's confidence*** ganarse la confianza de algn a base de halagos 2 **wheedling** *pres p* ‹tone/voice› adulador

wheel[1] /hwiːl || wiːl/ *n*

A 1 (of vehicle) rueda *f*; ***to oil the ~s*** allanar el camino; ***to set o put (the) ~s in motion*** poner* las cosas en marcha; ***~s within ~s*** entresijos *mpl* 2 (*potter's ~*) torno *m*

B (*steering ~ — of car*) volante *m*; (— of ship) timón *m*; **at the ~** (of car) al volante; (of ship) al timón

C **wheels** *pl* (car) (colloq) coche *m*

wheel[2] *vt* ‹*bicycle/wheelchair*› empujar; ‹*person*› llevar (*en silla de ruedas etc*)

■ **wheel** *vi* 1 (turn suddenly) **~ (around** *o* (BrE) **round)** «*person*» girar sobre sus (*or* mis *etc*) talones, darse* media vuelta, volverse*; ***to ~ and deal*** (colloq) andar* en tejemanejes (fam) 2 (BrE Mil) hacer* conversión, cambiar de frente 3 (circle) dar* vueltas; «*birds*» revolotear

Phrasal verb

• **wheel out** [v ▸ o ▸ adv, v ▸ adv ▸ o] ‹*argument*› sacar* a relucir; ‹*expert*› traer*, presentar

wheel: **~barrow** *n* carretilla *f*; **~chair** *n* silla *f* de ruedas; **~ clamp** *n* cepo *m*

wheeled /hwiːld || wiːld/ *adj* ‹*vehicle*› con ruedas; ‹*transport*› rodado

-wheeled /hwiːld || wiːld/ *suff*: **four~** de cuatro ruedas

wheelhouse /ˈhwiːlhaʊs || ˈwiːlhaʊs/ *n* timonera *f*

wheelie bin, wheely bin *n* (BrE colloq) contenedor *m* de basura con ruedas

wheeling and dealing /ˈhwiːlɪŋənˈdiːlɪŋ || ˌwiːlɪŋən ˈdiːlɪŋ/ *n* (colloq) tejemanejes *mpl* (fam)

wheeze[1] /hwiːz || wiːz/ *vi* «*person*» respirar con dificultad, resollar* (*produciendo un sonido sibilante como los asmáticos*); «*machine*» resollar*

wheeze[2] *n* resuello *m* (*sonido sibilante producido al respirar*)

whelk /hwelk || welk/ *n* buccino *m* (*especie de caracol marino*)

when[1] /hwen || wen/ *adv*

A (in questions, indirect questions) cuándo; **~ did you arrive?** ¿cuándo llegaste?; **I asked him ~ the next train was** le pregunté cuándo salía el próximo tren; **that was ~ I realized that ...** fue entonces cuando *or* (esp AmL tb) que me di cuenta de que ...; **say ~!** di cuándo

B (as relative): **the year ~ we got married** el año en que nos casamos; **in December, ~ we were on holiday** en diciembre, cuando estábamos de vacaciones

when[2] *conj*

A 1 (temporal sense) cuando; **I'll ask him ~ I see him** se lo preguntaré cuando lo vea; **reduce speed ~ approaching a junction** reduzca la velocidad al acercarse a un cruce 2 (if) si, cuando; **these results aren't bad ~ you compare them with ...** estos resultados no son malos si *or* cuando se los compara con ...

B 1 (since, considering that) si, cuando; **why go to a hotel ~ you can stay here?** ¿por qué ir a un hotel si *or* cuando te puedes quedar aquí? 2 (although) cuando; **he said he was 18 ~ in fact he's only 15** dijo que tenía 18 años cuando en realidad sólo tiene 15

when[3] *pron* cuándo; **~ do you have to be in London by?** ¿para cuándo tienes que estar en Londres?; **since ~ have they had the farm?** ¿desde cuándo tienen la granja?, ¿cuánto hace que tienen la granja?

whence /hwens || wens/ *adv* 1 (in questions) (arch) de dónde 2 (as relative) (liter) de donde 3 (frml) (*as linker*): **the book was written in New England, ~ the title** el libro se escribió en Nueva Inglaterra, de ahí el título

whenever[1] /hwenˈevər || wenˈevə(r)/ *conj* 1 (every time that) siempre que; **~ I hear that song I think of Spain** siempre que *or* cada vez que escucho esa canción, me acuerdo de España; **~ you need help, just ask** siempre que necesites ayuda, no tienes más que pedir 2 (at whatever time): **we'll go ~ you're ready** saldremos cuando estés listo; **~ it is, I won't be going** sea cuando sea, yo no pienso ir

whenever[2] *adv* 1 (no matter when): **next Monday or ~** el lunes o cuando sea 2 (in questions) cuándo

where[1] /hwer || weə(r)/ *adv*

A dónde; (indicating direction) adónde, dónde; **~'s Lewes?** ¿dónde está *or* queda Lewes?; **~ are you taking me?** ¿(a)dónde me llevan?; **~ are you from?** ¿de dónde eres?; **put the scissors back ~ they belong** vuelve a poner la tijera en su sitio; **that's ~ you're mistaken** en eso estás equivocado; ***~ it's at*** (colloq): **Aspen's OK for skiing, but Hartlepool is really ~ it's at** Aspen no está mal para esquiar, pero adonde hay que ir es a Hartlepool

B (as relative) donde; **the house ~ she was born** la casa donde nació

where[2] *conj* 1 donde; (indicating direction) adonde, donde; **you won't be needing any money ~ you're going** adonde vas no te hará falta dinero 2 (in cases where) cuando; **~ her private life is concerned ...** cuando se trata de su vida privada ...; **~ appropriate** cuando *or* allí donde sea apropiado 3 (contrasting) cuando; **~ others would lose heart, she remains optimistic** cuando otros perderían el ánimo, ella permanece optimista

whereabouts[1] /ˈhwerəˈbaʊts || ˌweərəˈbaʊts/ *adv*: **~ in Austria do you live?** ¿en qué parte de Austria vives?

whereabouts[2] /ˈhwerəbaʊts || ˈweərəbaʊts/*n* (+ *sing or pl vb*) paradero *m*; **nobody knows his ~** se desconoce su paradero

whereas /hwerˈæz || ˌweərˈæz/ *conj* mientras que, en tanto que (frml)

whereby /hwerˈbaɪ || weəˈbaɪ/ *pron* (frml): **there are other means ~ agreement may be reached** hay otros medios por los cuales se puede llegar a un acuerdo; **a system ~ payments are made automatically** un sistema por *or* según el cual los pagos se efectúan automáticamente

wherefore[1] /ˈhwerfɔːr || ˈweəfɔː(r)/ *adv* (arch) por qué

wherefore[2] *n see* **why**[3]

wherein /hwerˈɪn || weərˈɪn/ *adv* (frml): **an ancient tome, ~ it is recorded that ...** un antiguo tomo, en el que *or* cual consta que ...

whereupon /ˈhwerəpɑːn || ˌweərəˈpɒn/ *conj*

A (*as linker*) con lo cual

B (on which) (frml) sobre el/la cual

wherever[1] /hwerˈevər || weərˈevə(r)/ *adv* 1 (in questions) dónde; **~ can they be?** ¿dónde pueden estar?, ¿dónde diablos pueden estar? (fam) 2 (no matter where) (colloq) en cualquier parte *or* lado

wherever[2] *conj*: **you can use your card ~ you see this sign** puede usar su tarjeta (en cualquier establecimiento) donde vea este símbolo; **~ he goes, I'll go too** vaya donde vaya *or* dondequiera que vaya, yo iré tambien; **she said it was in Pando, ~ that is** dijo que quedaba en Pando, que no tengo ni idea de dónde está; **you can sit ~ you like** puedes sentarte donde quieras

wherewithal /ˈhwerwɪðɔːl || ˈweəwɪðɔːl/ *n* **the ~** los medios; **we don't have the ~ to do this** no tenemos los recursos *or* no contamos con los medios para hacer esto

whet /hwet || wet/ *vt* **-tt-** ‹*interest/curiosity*› estimular, avivar; **the walk ~ted our appetites** la caminata nos abrió el apetito

whether /ˈhweðər || ˈweðə(r)/ *conj*: **she hasn't decided ~ to apply** no ha decidido si solicitarlo (o no); **tell me ~ you need us or not** *o* **~ or not you need us** dime si nos necesitas o no; **I doubt ~ he knew** dudo que lo supiera; **~ you like it or not** te guste o no te guste; **~ by chance or by design** ya sea por casualidad o a propósito

whew /hwjuː/ *interj* ¡uf!

whey /hweɪ || weɪ/ *n* [u] suero *m* (*de la leche*)

which[1] /hwɪtʃ || wɪtʃ/ *pron*

A 1 (*in questions*) (*sing*) cuál; (*pl*) cuáles; **~ of you wrote this?** ¿cuál *or* quién de ustedes escribió esto? 2 (in indirect use) cuál; **do you know ~ she chose?** ¿sabes cuál eligió?;

W

I can never remember ~ is ~ nunca recuerdo cuál es cuál

B (as relative): **the parcel ~ arrived this morning** el paquete que llegó esta mañana; **the newspaper in ~ the article appeared** el diario en el que *or* en el cual apareció el artículo; **he said it was an accident, ~ I know is not true** dijo que había sido un accidente, lo cual sé que no es cierto

which² *adj*

A **1** (in questions) (*sing*) qué, cuál; (*pl*) qué, cuáles; **in ~ European city is it?** ¿en qué *or* cuál ciudad europea está? **2** (in indirect questions) (*sing*) qué, cuál; (*pl*) qué, cuáles; **ask her ~ chapters we have to read** pregúntale qué *or* cuales capítulos hay que leer

B (as relative): **we arrived at two, by ~ time they had gone** llegamos a las dos y para entonces ya se habían ido; **in ~ case** en cuyo caso

whichever¹ /hwɪtʃ'evər || wɪtʃ'evə(r)/ *pron* **1** (no matter which): **there are several options, but ~ you choose ...** hay varias opciones, pero elijas la que elijas *or* cualquiera que elijas ... **2** (the one, ones that): **buy ~ is cheaper** compra el que sea más barato **3** (in questions) (*sing*) cuál; (*pl*) cuáles

whichever² *adj* **1** (no matter which): **~ party is in power** sea cual sea *or* cualquiera que sea el partido que esté en el poder; **~ date you decide on, let me know in advance** elija la fecha que elija, hágamelo saber con anticipación **2** (any that): **you can write about ~ subject you know best** puedes escribir sobre el tema que mejor conozcas, sea cual sea *or* fuere **3** (in questions) (*sing*) cuál; (*pl*) cuáles

whiff /hwɪf || wɪf/ *n* **1** (smell) olorcillo *m*; (unpleasant) tufillo *m*, olorcillo *m* **2** (sniff) (colloq): **have a ~ of this milk** huele esta leche, tómale el olor a esta leche (AmL)

while¹ /hwaɪl || waɪl/ *conj*

A (in time) mientras; **S keys cut while you wait** se hacen llaves al momento; **they don't drink ~ on duty** no beben cuando *or* mientras están de guardia

B (though) aunque; **the situation, ~ tense, seems unlikely to lead to war** la situación aunque tensa, no es probable que lleve a una guerra

C (whereas) mientras que, en tanto que (frml)

Phrasal verb

- **while away** [v ▸ adv ▸ o, v ▸ o ▸ adv]: **we had a game of chess to ~ away the time** jugamos una partida de ajedrez para pasar el rato

while² *n* **1** (period of time): **wait a ~** (a few days, weeks) espera un tiempo; (a few minutes, hours) espera un rato; (a very short period) espera un ratito *or* un momentito; **it's a ~ since we had any news** hace tiempo que no tenemos noticias; **it's been a good ~ since we had any rain** hace bastante (tiempo) que no llueve; **he was here a little ~ ago** hace un ratito estaba aquí; **after a ~ she realized** después de *or* al cabo de un rato se dio cuenta; **she knew all the ~ that he was dead** supo desde el principio que estaba muerto; **I'll be back in a little ~** enseguida vuelvo; **she'll be here in a short ~** llegará dentro de un ratito **2** **(every) once in a while** de vez en cuando; *see also* **worth¹ 2**

whilst /hwaɪlst || waɪlst/ *conj* (BrE) ▸**while¹**

whim /hwɪm || wɪm/ *n* [c u] capricho *m*, antojo *m*; **they left for Rio on a ~** se les antojó irse a Río y se fueron

whimper¹ /'hwɪmpər || 'wɪmpə(r)/ *vi* gimotear, lloriquear

whimper² *n* quejido *m*

whimsical /'hwɪmzɪkəl || 'wɪmzɪkəl/ *adj* ‹*person*› caprichoso, antojadizo; ‹*smile*› (enigmatic) enigmático; (playful) juguetón; ‹*mood*› voluble

whine¹ /hwaɪn || waɪn/ *vi* **1** «*dog*» aullar*, gañir; «*person*» gemir*; «*child*» lloriquear; **a bullet ~d past me** una bala me pasó silbando por al lado; **in a whining voice** con voz quejumbrosa *or* plañidera **2** (complain) (pej) **to ~ (ABOUT sth)** quejarse (DE algo)

whine² *n* **1** (of dog) aullido *m*, gañido *m*; (of person) quejido *m*, gemido *m*; (of engine) chirrido *m*; (of bullet) silbido *m* **2** (complaint) (pej) queja *f*

whinge /hwɪndʒ || wɪndʒ/ *vi* **whinges, whingeing, whinged** (BrE colloq & pej) **to ~ (ABOUT sth)** quejarse (DE algo)

whinny /'hwɪni || 'wɪni/ *vi* (*3rd pers sing pres* **whinnies**; *pres p* **whinnying**; *past & past p* **whinnied**) «*horse*» relinchar

whip¹ /hwɪp || wɪp/ *n*

A (in horse riding) fusta *f*, fuete *m* (AmL exc CS); (of tamer) látigo *m*; (for punishment) azote *m*; ***to crack the ~*** hacer* restallar el látigo

B (Pol) (person) *diputado responsable de la disciplina de su grupo parlamentario*

C (Culin) batido *m*

whip² **-pp-** *vt*

A **1** (lash) ‹*horse*› pegarle* a (*con la fusta*), fustigar*; ‹*person*› azotar; ‹*child*› darle* una paliza *or* un azote a **2** (defeat) (colloq) darle* una paliza a (fam) **3** (beat) ‹*egg whites*› batir; ‹*cream*› batir *or* (Esp) montar; **~ped cream** crema *f* batida *or* (Esp) nata *f* montada **4** (incite) ▸**whip up A2**

B **1** (take quickly) (+ *adv compl*): **they ~ped him to the airport** lo llevaron a toda prisa al aeropuerto; **she ~ped out her notebook** sacó rápidamente la libreta **2** (steal) (BrE colloq) birlar (fam), volar* (Méx, Ven fam)

C (bind) ‹*rope*› reforzar*

Phrasal verb

- **whip up** [v ▸ o ▸ adv, v ▸ adv ▸ o]

A **1** (arouse) ‹*trouble/unrest*› provocar*, crear; ‹*hatred*› fomentar; ‹*support*› conseguir* **2** (incite) ‹*crowd*› incitar, agitar **3** «*wind*» ‹*sea/waves*› agitar; ‹*dust*› levantar

B **1** (beat, whisk) ‹*egg whites*› batir; ‹*cream*› batir, montar (Esp) **2** (prepare hurriedly) (colloq) ‹*meal*› improvisar

whiplash /'hwɪplæʃ || 'wɪplæʃ/ *n* **1** (blow) latigazo *m*, trallazo *m* **2** **~ (injury)** (Med) traumatismo *m* cervical

whippersnapper /'hwɪpər,snæpər || 'wɪpə,snæpə(r)/ *n* (dated) mocoso, -sa *m,f* (fam)

whippet /'hwɪpət || 'wɪpɪt/ *n* galgo *m* inglés

whipping /'hwɪpɪŋ || 'wɪpɪŋ/ *n* **1** (punishment) paliza *f*, azotaina *f*; **to give sb a ~** darle* una paliza *or* azotaina a algn **2** (defeat) paliza *f* (fam)

whipping: **~ boy** *n* (colloq) chivo *m* expiatorio, cabeza *mf* de turco; **~ cream** *n* [u] crema *f* para batir *or* (Esp) nata *f* líquida para montar

whip-round /'hwɪpraʊnd || 'wɪpraʊnd/ *n* (BrE colloq) colecta *f*, vaca *f* (AmL fam); **to have a ~** hacer* una colecta, hacer* una vaca (AmL fam)

whir¹, (BrE) **whirr** /hwɜːr || wɜː(r)/ *vi* «*machine/propellers*» runrunear, zumbar; «*wings*» hacer* ruido (*al batirse*)

whir², (BrE) **whirr** *n* (of machine, propellers) runrún *m*, zumbido *m*; (of bird's wings) aleteo *m*; (of insect's wings) zumbido *m*

whirl¹ /hwɜːrl || wɜːl/ *vi* **1** (spin) «*person*» girar, dar* vueltas; «*leaves/dust*» arremolinarse; **my mind** *o* **head was ~ing** la cabeza me daba vueltas **2** (move fast) (+ *adv compl*): **he ~ed around** se dio media vuelta rápidamente

■ **whirl** *vt* (+ *adv compl*) hacer* girar

whirl² *n* (turn) giro *m*, vuelta *f*; (of dust) remolino *m*, torbellino *m*; **the social ~** el ajetreo de la vida social; **my head was in a ~** la cabeza me daba vueltas; ***to give sth a ~*** (colloq): **let's give it a ~** hagamos la prueba, intentémoslo

whirl: **~pool** *n* vorágine *f*, remolino *m*; **~wind** *n* torbellino *m*; **a ~wind of meetings, parties and interviews** un torbellino *or* una vorágine de reuniones, fiestas y entrevistas; (*before n*) **a ~wind romance** un idilio arrollador

whirr /hwɜːr || wɜː(r)/ *vi/n* (BrE) ▸**whir¹,²**

whisk¹ /hwɪsk || wɪsk/ *vt*

A **1** (Culin) ‹*eggs/mixture*› batir **2** (swish) ‹*tail*› sacudir, agitar; **he ~ed the breadcrumbs off the table with his napkin** sacudió las migas de la mesa con su servilleta

B (convey quickly) (+ *adv compl*): **she was ~ed off to a meeting** se la llevaron a una reunión a toda prisa; **he ~ed away the plates** retiró los platos rápidamente

whisk² *n*

A (Culin) batidor *m*; **electric ~** batidora *f* eléctrica, batidor *m* eléctrico

B (movement) sacudida *f*

whisker /'hwɪskər || 'wɪskə(r)/ *n*

A **1** [c] (single hair) pelo *m* (*de la barba*) **2** (narrow margin) (*no pl*) pelo *m*; **they came within a ~ of losing** faltó un pelo

W

or faltó muy poco para que perdieran

B **whiskers** *pl* **1** (of animal) bigotes *mpl* **2** (dated) (mustache) bigote(s) *m(pl)*; (sideburns) patillas *fpl*

whiskey /'hwɪski || 'wɪski/ *n* [u c] (*pl* **-keys**) whisky *m*, güisqui *m* (*esp americano o irlandés*)

whisky /'hwɪski || 'wɪski/ *n* [u c] (*pl* **-kies**) whisky *m*, güisqui *m* (*esp escocés*)

whisper¹ /'hwɪspər || 'wɪspə(r)/ *vi* **1** ‹‹*person*›› cuchichear; **stop ~ing!** ¡basta de cuchicheos! **2** (liter) ‹‹*wind/leaves*›› susurrar (liter)

■ **whisper** *vt* ‹*remark/words*› susurrar; **to ~ sth TO sb** susurrarle algo *or* decirle* algo al oído a algn

whisper² *n* **1** (soft voice) susurro *m*; **yes, he said in a ~** —sí —susurró *or* dijo en voz baja; **they spoke in ~s** hablaban cuchicheando *or* en susurros **2** (rumor) rumor *m*; **there's a ~ going around that ...** se rumorea que ...

whist /hwɪst || wɪst/ *n* [u] whist *m* (*juego de naipes*)

whistle¹ /'hwɪsəl || 'wɪsəl/ *vi* **1** (make sound) ‹‹*person*›› silbar; (loudly) chiflar; ‹‹*referee*›› pitar; ‹‹*kettle*›› silbar, pitar; ‹‹*train*›› pitar; ‹‹*wind*›› silbar, aullar*; ***to ~ for sth*** (colloq): **if they want more money, they can ~ for it** si quieren más dinero, van a tener que esperar sentados (fam) **2** (speed, rush) (+ *adv compl*): **to ~ by** ‹‹*bullet/arrow*›› pasar silbando

■ **whistle** *vt* ‹*tune*› silbar

whistle² *n* **1** (instrument) silbato *m*, pito *m*; **to blow a ~** tocar* un silbato *or* pito, pitar; **a factory ~** la sirena de una fábrica; ***as clean as a ~***: **your lungs are as clean as a ~** no tiene absolutamente nada en los pulmones; **his record is as clean as a ~** tiene un historial sin mancha; ***to blow the ~ on sb*** (inform on) delatar a algn; (reprimand) llamar a algn al orden; ***to blow the ~ on sth*** (put a stop to) tomar medidas para acabar con algo; ***to wet one's ~*** (hum) echarse un trago **2** (sound — made with mouth) silbido *m*; (loud) chiflido *m*; (— made by referee's whistle) silbato *m*, pitido *m*; (— of kettle) silbido *m*, pitido *m*; (— of train) pitido *m*; (— of wind, bullet) silbido *m*

whistle-stop /'hwɪsəlstɑ:p || 'wɪsəlstɒp/ *n* **1** (brief appearance): (*before n*) **~ tour** gira *f* relámpago **2** (station, town) (AmE) apeadero *m*

whit /hwɪt || wɪt/ *n* (frml): **not a ~** ni un ápice, ni pizca

white¹ /hwaɪt || waɪt/ *adj* **-er, -est** **1** ‹*paint/cat/bread/wine/chocolate*› blanco; ‹*grapes*› blanco; ‹*coffee/tea*› con leche; **she had a ~ wedding** se casó de blanco; **he went ~ (with fear/anger)** se puso blanco *or* pálido (de miedo/rabia) **2** (Caucasian) blanco

white² *n*

A [u] (color) blanco *m*; **dressed in ~** vestido de blanco

B [c] *also* **White** (person) blanco, -ca *m,f*

C [c] **1** (of egg) clara *f* **2** (of eye) blanco *m*

D **whites** *pl* **1** (laundry) ropa *f* blanca **2** (esp BrE Sport): **he was in tennis/cricket ~s** llevaba el equipo blanco de tenis/cricket

white: **~bait** *n* [u] morralla *f*, chanquetes *mpl* (Esp), cornalitos *mpl* (Arg), majuga *f* (Ur); **~-blood cell**, **white-blood corpuscle** *n* glóbulo *m* blanco; **~-collar** /'waɪt'kɑ:lər || ˌwaɪt'kɒlə(r)/ *adj* ‹*worker/job*› no manual; (clerical) de oficina, administrativo; **~ elephant** *n* (building, project) elefante *m* blanco; (object) *objeto superfluo*; (*before n*) **~ elephant stall** *puesto de venta de artículos de segunda mano con fines benéficos*; **~-faced** /'hwaɪt'feɪst || ˌwaɪt'feɪst/ *adj* pálido; (with rage, fear) lívido, pálido; **~ gasoline**, **~ gas** *n* (AmE) gasolina *f or* (Andes) bencina *f or* (RPl) nafta *f* sin plomo; **~ goods** *pl n* (linen) ropa *f* blanca (*mantelería, ropa de cama etc*); (appliances) electrodomésticos *mpl* de línea blanca; **~ heat** *n* [u] rojo *m* blanco; **~ horses** *pl n* cabrillas *fpl*, olas *fpl* encrespadas; **~-hot** /'hwaɪt'hɑ:t || ˌwaɪt'hɒt/ *adj* ‹*metal*› al rojo blanco; ‹*performance/intensity*› candente; **~ House** *n* **the W~ House** la Casa Blanca; **~ lie** *n* mentira *f* piadosa

> **Whitehall**
>
> Una calle del centro de Londres donde están situadas una gran parte de las oficinas del gobierno. Los periodistas utilizan a menudo el término para referirse al gobierno y la administración

> **White House – The White House**
>
> La residencia y el despacho oficial del presidente de Estados Unidos, situada en Washington. Los periodistas utilizan a menudo el término "the White House" para referirse al Presidente y a sus consejeros

whiten /'hwaɪtn̩ || 'waɪtn̩/ *vt* blanquear

■ **whiten** *vi* ‹‹*hair*›› encanecer*, ponerse* blanco; ‹‹*face*›› palidecer*, ponerse* pálido

white: **~ paper** *n* (in UK) libro *m* blanco (*documento oficial en el que se consigna la política gubernamental sobre determinado asunto*); **~ sauce** *n* [u] salsa *f* blanca *or* bechamel, bechamel *f*; **~ slave** *n*: *mujer vendida como prostituta*; (*before n*) **~ slave trade** trata *f* de blancas; **~ spirit** *n* [u] (BrE) espíritu *m* de petróleo (*usado como sustituto del aguarrás*); **~ tie** *n* **1** [c] (bow tie) corbata *f* de lazo *or* (Esp) pajarita *f or* (Chi) corbata *f* de humita *or* (Ur) moñita *f* blanca **2** [u] (formal dress) traje *m* de etiqueta con corbata de moño (*or* pajarita *etc*) blanca

whitewash¹ /'hwaɪtwɔ:ʃ || 'waɪtwɒʃ/ *n*

A **1** [u] (Const) cal *f*, lechada *f*, aguacal *f*‡ **2** [c u] (cover-up) (colloq) tapadera *f* (fam), encubrimiento *m*

B [c] (defeat) (colloq) paliza *f* (fam)

whitewash² *vt* ‹*wall/building*› blanquear, encalar, enjalbegar*

white water *n* aguas *fpl* rápidas

whiting /'hwaɪtɪŋ || 'waɪtɪŋ/ *n* (*pl* **~s** *or* **~**) pescadilla *f*

whitish /'hwaɪtɪʃ || 'waɪtɪʃ/ *adj* blanquecino, blancuzco

whitlow /'hwɪtləʊ || 'wɪtləʊ/ *n* panadizo *m*

Whitsun /'hwɪtsən || 'wɪtsən/ *n* (esp BrE) Pentecostés *f*

Whit Sunday *n* (esp BrE) (el domingo de) Pentecostés *f*

whittle /'hwɪtl̩ || 'wɪtl̩/ *vt* tallar

(Phrasal verbs)

• **whittle away**

A [v ▸ o ▸ adv, v ▸ adv ▸ o] ‹*funds/resources*› ir* mermando; ‹*influence*› ir* reduciendo *or* disminuyendo; ‹*rights*› ir* menoscabando

B [v ▸ adv] **to ~ away AT sth** ir* minando *or* socavando algo

• **whittle down** [v ▸ o ▸ adv, v ▸ adv ▸ o] ‹*expenses*› recortar, reducir*; ‹*applicants*› reducir* el numero de

whiz, whizz /hwɪz || wɪz/ *vi* **-zz-** (+ *adv compl*): **to ~ by** ‹‹*bullet/arrow*›› pasar zumbando; ‹‹*car*›› pasar zumbando *or* como una bala *or* un bólido; **I ~zed down the hill on my bike** bajé la colina en bicicleta como un bólido *or* como una bala; **I ~zed through my homework** hice los deberes zumbando *or* a toda velocidad

whiz kid, whizz kid *n* (colloq) lince *m* (fam), prodigio *m*

who /hu:/ *pron*

A **1** (in questions) (*sing*) quién; (*pl*) quiénes; **~ is that?** ¿quién es ése?; **~ are they?** ¿quiénes son?; **~ are you writing to?** ¿a quién le estás escribiendo?; **Bridget ~?** ¿Bridget qué *or* cuánto?; **~ do you think you are?** ¿tú qué te crees? **2** (in indirect questions) quién; **I don't know ~ you're talking about** no sé de quién estás hablando; **a letter from you know ~** una carta de ya sabes quién *or* (fam) del/de la que te dije

B **1** (as relative): **the boy ~ won the prize** el chico que ganó el premio; **there are blankets for those ~ want them** hay mantas para quienes quieran **2** (the one, ones that): **you can tell ~ you like** se lo puedes decir a quien/quienes quieras

WHO *n* (= **World Health Organization**) OMS *f*

whoa /wəʊ/ *interj* ¡so!; **~, that's plenty!** ¡basta! *or* ¡ya! *or* (Esp fam) ¡vale! eso es mucho

who'd /hu:d/ **1** = **who had** **2** = **who would**

whodunit, whodunnit /'hu:'dʌnət || ˌhu:'dʌnɪt/ *n* (colloq) novela *f* policíaca

whoever /hu:'evər || hu:'evə(r)/ *pron* **1** (no matter who): **she's not coming in here, ~ she is** aquí no entra, quien quiera que sea *or* sea quien sea; **~ you ask** se lo preguntes a quien se lo preguntes, a quienquiera que se lo preguntes **2** (the one, ones who): **~ did this must be insane** quienquiera que *or* quien haya hecho esto debe (de) estar loco; **I'll invite ~ I like** voy a invitar a quien (se) me dé la gana **3** (in questions) quién

whole¹ /həʊl/ *adj*

A **1** (entire) (*before n, no comp*): **there's a ~ bottle left** queda

W

una botella entera; **he drank the ~ bottle** se tomó toda la botella, se tomó la botella entera *or* íntegra; **they've eaten the ~ lot!** ¡se lo han comido todo!; **the ~ truth** toda la verdad; **~ milk** leche *f* entera *or* sin descremar *or* (Esp) sin desnatar; **~ number** (Math) (número *m*) entero *m* **2** (emphatic use): **I'm fed up with the ~ affair** estoy harto del asunto

B (*pred*) (in one piece) entero; **she swallowed it ~** se lo tragó entero

whole[2] *n* **1** (integral unit) todo *m*; **the ~ of sth**: **the ~ of the morning** toda la mañana; **a threat to the ~ of mankind** una amenaza para toda la humanidad *or* para la humanidad entera **2** (*in phrases*) **as a whole**: **this will affect Europe as a ~** esto va a afectar a Europa en su totalidad; **on the whole** (*indep*) en general

whole: **~food** *n* [u c] (BrE) alimentos *mpl* integrales; **~-grain** *adj* integral; **~hearted** /ˈhəʊlˈhɑːrtəd || ˌhəʊlˈhɑːtɪd/ *adj* ‹*approval*› sin reservas; ‹*support*› incondicional

wholeheartedly /ˈhəʊlˈhɑːrtədli || ˌhəʊlˈhɑːtɪdli/ *adv* ‹*approve*› sin reservas; ‹*support*› sin reservas, incondicionalmente; **to agree ~** estar* totalmente de acuerdo

whole: **~meal** *adj* (BrE) integral; **~ note** *n* (AmE) semibreve *f*, redonda *f*

wholesale[1] /ˈhəʊlseɪl/ *adj* **1** (Busn) (*before n*) al por mayor **2** ‹*destruction*› sistemático, total; ‹*slaughter*› sistemático; ‹*condemnation*› absoluto; ‹*rejection*› en bloque

wholesale[2] *adv* **1** (Busn) ‹*buy/sell*› al por mayor **2** (on a large scale) de modo general; **they rejected the proposals ~** rechazaron las propuestas en bloque

wholesaler /ˈhəʊlseɪlər || ˈhəʊlseɪlə(r)/ *n* mayorista *mf*

wholesome /ˈhəʊlsəm/ *adj* **1** (healthy) ‹*food/climate*› sano, saludable **2** (morally good) ‹*image*› de persona sana

wholewheat /ˈhəʊlhwiːt || ˈhəʊlwiːt/ *adj* integral

who'll /huːl/ = **who will**

wholly /ˈhəʊlli/ *adv* totalmente, completamente

whom /huːm/ *pron* (frml) **1** (in questions, indirect questions): **~ did you visit?** ¿a quién visitaste?; **a letter from ~?** ¿una carta de quién? **2** (as relative): **the cousin ~ I mentioned earlier** el primo que *or* a quien mencioné antes; **the girls, both of ~ could dance** las chicas, que ambas sabían bailar

whoop[1] /huːp, hwuːp || huːp, wuːp/ *vi* gritar, chillar

■ **whoop** *vt*: ***to ~ it up*** (colloq) (make merry) armar jolgorio (fam)

whoop[2] *n* grito *m*, chillido *m*

whoopee /ˈhwʊpiː || ˈwʊpiː/ *interj* (colloq) ¡yupi! (fam), ¡viva!

whooping cough /ˈhuːpɪŋ/ *n* [u] tos *f* ferina *or* convulsa *or* convulsiva

whoops /hwʊps || wʊps/ *interj* ¡ay!, ¡epa! (AmS fam), ¡híjole! (Méx fam)

whoosh /hwuːʃ || wuːʃ/ *vi*: **the car ~ed past** el coche pasó haciendo 'zuum'; **the water came ~ing out** el agua salió en un chorro

whop /hwɑːp || wɒp/ *vt* **-pp-** (AmE colloq) pegarle* a

whopper /ˈhwɑːpər || ˈwɒpə(r)/ *n* (colloq) **1** (sth big): **it's a ~!** ¡es enorme! *or* (fam) ¡qué grandote! **2** (lie): **he told me a ~** me dijo tremenda mentira *or* (Esp tb) tremenda trola *or* (CS tb) flor de mentira (fam)

whopping /ˈhwɑːpɪŋ || ˈwɒpɪŋ/ *adj* (colloq) enorme; **a ~ great house/dog** una casa/un perro enorme

whore /hɔːr || hɔː(r)/ *n* (pej) puta *f* (vulg & pey)

who's /huːz/ **1** = **who is** **2** = **who has**

whose[1] /huːz/ *pron* (*sing*) de quién; (*pl*) de quiénes; **~ is this?** ¿de quién es esto?; **~ are these?** ¿de quién/de quiénes son éstos?

whose[2] *adj* **1** (in questions, indirect questions) (*sing*) de quién; (*pl*) de quiénes; **~ book is this?** ¿de quién es este libro?; **~ keys are these?** ¿de quién son estas llaves?; **~ coats are those?** ¿de quiénes son esos abrigos?; **do you know ~ house that is?** ¿sabes de quién es esa casa? **2** (as relative) (*sing*) cuyo; (*pl*) cuyos; **the man ~ job I took over** el hombre cuyo puesto ocupé; **a colleague ~ children go to that school** un colega cuyos hijos van a ese colegio

who've /huːv/ = **who have**

why[1] /hwaɪ || waɪ/ *adv* por qué; **~ are you laughing?** ¿por qué te ríes?; **~ not?** ¿por qué no?; **~ don't you apply for the post?** ¿por qué no solicitas el puesto?; **there's no reason ~ you shouldn't do it** no hay ningún motivo para que no lo hagas; **this is ~ the attempt failed** fue por esto *or* por esta razón que el intento fracasó; **because he lied to me, that's ~!** ¡porque me mintió! ¡por eso!; **the reason ~ he couldn't attend** la razón por la cual no pudo asistir

why[2] *interj* ¡vaya!, ¡anda!; **~, of course!** ¡por supuesto que sí!

why[3] *n* porqué *m*; **she has to know the ~s and wherefores** tiene que saber todas las razones *or* todos los detalles

WI **1** = **Wisconsin** **2** (in UK) = **Women's Institute**

wick /wɪk/ *n* mecha *f*; ***to get on sb's ~*** (BrE colloq) sacar* de quicio a algn

wicked[1] /ˈwɪkəd || ˈwɪkɪd/ *adj* **-er, -est** **1** (evil) ‹*person*› malvado, perverso, malo; ‹*thought*› malo; ‹*lie*› infame, vil; **that was a ~ thing to do** eso fue una maldad **2** (vicious) ‹*blow*› malintencionado; **a ~-looking knife** un cuchillo siniestro; **a ~ temper** un carácter terrible *or* (fam) de todos los diablos **3** (mischievous) ‹*grin/laugh*› travieso, pícaro **4** (scandalous) (colloq) ‹*price/waste*› escandaloso

wicked[2] *pl n*: **(there's) no peace** *o* **rest for the ~** (set phrase) no hay paz *or* descanso para los malvados

wickedness /ˈwɪkədnəs || ˈwɪkɪdnɪs/ *n* [u] maldad *f*, perversidad *f*

wicker /ˈwɪkər || ˈwɪkə(r)/ *n* [u] mimbre *m*

wickerwork /ˈwɪkərwɜːrk || ˈwɪkəwɜːk/ *n* [u] **1** (articles) artículos *mpl* de mimbre **2** (activity) cestería *f* **3** ▸ **wicker**

wicket /ˈwɪkət || ˈwɪkɪt/ *n*

A (in cricket) **1** (area of pitch) *área central del terreno de juego* **2** (stumps and bails) palos *mpl* **3** (batsman's turn): **to take a ~** eliminar a un bateador

B **1** **~ (door** *o* **gate)** portezuela *f*, portillo *m* **2** (window) (AmE) ventanilla *f*

wide[1] /waɪd/ *adj* **wider, widest**

A (in dimension) ‹*river/feet/trousers*› ancho; ‹*gap*› grande; ‹*desert/ocean*› vasto; **it's two meters ~** tiene *or* mide dos metros de ancho; **to get ~r** ensancharse; **she looked at me with ~ eyes** me miró con los ojos muy abiertos

B (in extent, range) ‹*experience/powers*› amplio; ‹*area*› amplio, extenso; **a ~ variety of things** una gran variedad de cosas; **the newspaper with the ~st circulation** el diario de mayor circulación; **the ~ world** el ancho mundo

C (off target) ‹*ball/shot*› desviado; **~ OF sth** lejos DE algo; ▸ **mark**[1] **D**

wide[2] *adv* **wider, widest**

A (completely, fully): **her mouth gaped ~** se quedó boquiabierta *or* con la boca abierta; **~ apart**: **with your feet ~ apart** con los pies bien *or* muy separados; **~ awake**: **to be ~ awake** estar* completamente espabilado *or* despierto; **open ~!** abra bien la boca, abre grande (fam); **~ open**: **you left the door ~ open** dejaste la puerta abierta de par en par; **I'm going into this with my eyes ~ open** sé muy bien en qué me estoy metiendo; **he's laid himself ~ open to criticism** él mismo se ha expuesto a que lo critiquen; **the game is ~ open** el partido no está definido

B (off target): **the ball went ~** la pelota se desvió; **~ OF sth** lejos DE algo

-wide /waɪd/ *suff*: **area~** en toda la zona

wide: **~-angle lens** /ˈwaɪdˈæŋgəl/ *n* granangular *m*; **~-eyed** /ˈwaɪdˈaɪd/ *adj*: **he stared at her in ~-eyed amazement** se quedó mirándola con ojos como platos

widely /ˈwaɪdli/ *adv* **1** (extensively): **she is very ~ traveled** ha viajado mucho; **a ~ read young man** un joven de extensa cultura; **it was ~ publicized** se le dio mucha publicidad **2** (commonly): **a ~ held view** una opinión muy extendida; **a ~ read newspaper** un diario muy leído **3** (to a large degree) ‹*vary*› mucho

widen /ˈwaɪdn̩/ *vt* ‹*road/entrance*› ensanchar; ‹*range/debate/scope*› ampliar*

■ **widen** *vi* «*road/tunnel*» ensancharse; **the gap between us has ~ed** las diferencias entre nosotros se han acentuado

(Phrasal verb)

• **widen out** [v ▸ adv] «*road/river/tunnel*» ensancharse

W

wide: **~-open** /'waɪd'əʊpən/ *adj* (*before n*) ‹*door*› abierto de par en par; **with ~-open eyes** con los ojos muy abiertos; **the ~-open spaces** los espacios abiertos; *see also* **wide²** A; **~-ranging** /'waɪd'reɪndʒɪŋ/ *adj* ‹*powers/curriculum*› amplio; ‹*interests*› variado, diverso; ‹*effects*› de gran alcance; **~spread** *adj* ‹*custom/belief*› extendido, generalizado; **to become ~spread** ‹‹*custom/belief*›› extenderse*, generalizarse*

widow¹ /'wɪdəʊ/ *n* viuda *f*; **war ~** viuda de guerra

widow² *vt*: **to be ~ed** enviudar, quedar viudo; **his ~ed sister** su hermana viuda

widower /'wɪdəʊər || 'wɪdəʊə(r)/ *n* viudo *m*

width /wɪdθ/ *n* 1 [u c] (measurement) ancho *m*, anchura *f*; **what ~ is the cloth?** ¿qué ancho tiene la tela?, ¿cuánto mide *or* tiene la tela de ancho? 2 [c] (in swimming pool) ancho *m*

widthwise /'wɪdθwaɪz/, **widthways** /-weɪz/ *adv* a lo ancho

wield /wiːld/ *vt* ‹*sword*› blandir, empuñar; ‹*power/authority*› ejercer*

wiener /'wiːnər || 'wiːnə(r)/ *n* (AmE) salchicha *f* de Frankfurt

wife /waɪf/ *n* (*pl* **wives**) esposa *f*, mujer *f*

wig /wɪg/ *n* peluca *f*

wiggle¹ /'wɪgəl/ *vt* ‹*toes*› mover*; ‹*hips*› contonear, menear

■ **wiggle** *vi* 1 ‹‹*hips*›› contonearse 2 ‹‹*road*›› serpentear

wiggle² *n* 1 (of hips) contoneo *m*, meneo *m* 2 (in road) curva *f*

wiggly /'wɪgli/ *adj* **wigglier, wiggliest** ‹*line*› ondulado; ‹*road*› serpenteante

wigwam /'wɪgwɑːm || 'wɪgwæm/ *n* wigwam *m*

wild¹ /waɪld/ *adj* **-er, -est**

A 1 ‹*animal*› salvaje; (in woodland) salvaje, montaraz; ‹*plant/flower*› silvestre; ‹*vegetation*› agreste; **a ~ beast** una fiera, una bestia salvaje 2 (uncivilized) ‹*tribe*› salvaje 3 (desolate) ‹*country*› agreste, salvaje

B 1 (unruly) ‹*party/lifestyle*› desenfrenado, alocado; **we've had some ~ times together!** ¡hemos hecho cada locura juntos! 2 (random, uncontrolled) ‹*attempt*› desesperado; **a ~ guess** una conjetura hecha totalmente al azar 3 ‹*allegation/exaggeration*› absurdo, disparatado; **it never occurred to me in my ~est dreams that ...** ni en mis sueños más descabellados se me ocurrió nunca que …

C 1 (violent) (liter) ‹*sea/waters*› embravecido, proceloso (liter); ‹*wind*› fuertísimo, furioso (liter) 2 (frantic) ‹*excitement/dancing*› desenfrenado; ‹*shouting*› desaforado; ‹*appearance/stare*› de loco; **they were ~ with excitement** estaban locos de entusiasmo; **her perfume was driving him ~** su perfume lo estaba enloqueciendo *or* volviendo loco 3 (enthusiastic) (colloq) (*pred*) **to be ~ ABOUT sb/sth**: **he's ~ about her** está loco por ella (fam); **I'm not ~ about the idea** la idea no me enloquece 4 (angry) (colloq) (*pred*): **it makes me ~** me saca de quicio, me da mucha rabia (fam)

wild² *adv*: **these flowers grow ~** estas flores son silvestres; **to live ~** vivir en estado salvaje; ***to run ~***: **these kids have been allowed to run ~** a estos niños los han criado como salvajes; **the garden has run ~** la maleza ha invadido el jardín; **I let my imagination run ~** di rienda suelta a mi imaginación

wild³ *n* [u] **the ~**: **how to survive in the ~** cómo sobrevivir lejos de la civilización; **an opportunity to observe these animals in the ~** una oportunidad de observar estos animales en libertad *or* en su hábitat natural; **out in the ~s** (hum) donde el diablo perdió el poncho *or* (Esp) en el quinto pino (fam)

wild: **~ boar** *n* jabalí *m*; **~ card** *n* (Comput) comodín *m*

wildcat¹ /'waɪldkæt/ *n* (*pl* **~s** *or* **~**) 1 (European) gato *m* montés 2 (bobcat) (esp AmE) lince *m*

wildcat² *adj* (*before n, no comp*) 1 (risky) ‹*project/speculation*› arriesgado, riesgoso (esp AmL) 2 ‹*strike*› salvaje

wildebeest /'wɪldəbiːst || 'wɪldɪbiːst/ *n* (*pl* **-beests** *or* **-beest**) ñu *m*

wilderness /'wɪldərnəs || 'wɪldənɪs/ *n* 1 [c u] (wasteland) páramo *m*; (jungle) jungla *f* 2 [u] (undeveloped land) (AmE) parque *m* natural

wild: **~fire** *n* [u] (AmE) fuego *m* arrasador; ***to spread like ~fire*** (also BrE) extenderse* como un reguero de pólvora; **~fowl** *n* (*pl* **-fowls** *or* **-fowl**) ave *f*‡ de caza; **~-goose chase** /'waɪld'guːs/ *n*: **I'm not going into town again on another ~-goose chase** no pienso ir otra vez al centro a perder el tiempo para nada; **they sent him off on a ~-goose chase** lo mandaron a no sé qué tontería *or* (hum) a ver si llovía; **~life** *n* [u] fauna *f* y flora *f*; (*before n*) ‹*sanctuary/reserve*› natural

wildly /'waɪldli/ *adv*

A 1 (frantically) ‹*kick/struggle/rush*› como (un) loco; **he looked at them ~** los miró con los ojos desorbitados 2 (violently) ‹*rage/blow*› con furia

B 1 (in undisciplined fashion) ‹*live*› desordenadamente, desenfrenadamente; **they behaved ~** se portaron como salvajes 2 (haphazardly, randomly) ‹*shoot/guess*› a lo loco, a tontas y a locas (fam)

C (extremely): **~ funny** comiquísimo, para morirse de risa (fam); **~ inaccurate estimates** cálculos absolutamente errados

wildness /'waɪldnəs || 'waɪldnɪs/ *n* [u] 1 (of landscape) lo agreste; (of tribe, people) lo salvaje 2 (of storm, sea) furia *f*

Wild West *n* **the ~ ~** el Lejano Oeste; (*before n*) ‹*adventure/story*› del oeste

wiles /waɪlz/ *pl n* artimañas *fpl*, tretas *fpl*

wilful *etc* (BrE) ► **willful** *etc*

will¹ /wɪl/ *v mod* (*past* **would**) [**'ll** *es la contracción de* **will**, **won't** *de* **will not** *y* **'ll've** *de* **will have**]

A 1 (talking about the future): **he'll come on Friday** vendrá el viernes, va a venir el viernes; **he said he would come on Friday** dijo que vendría *or* iba a venir el viernes; **he won't ever change his ways** no cambiará nunca, no va a cambiar nunca; **~ you be staying at Jack's?** ¿te vas a quedar en casa de Jack?; **at the end of this month, he'll have been working here for a year** este fin de mes hará *or* va a hacer un año que trabaja aquí; **you won't leave without me, ~ you?** no te irás sin mí ¿no? 2 (expressing resolution) (*with first person*): **I won't let you down** no te fallaré, no te voy a fallar

B 1 (expressing willingness): **~** *o* **would you do me a favor?** ¿quieres hacerme un favor?, ¿me haces un favor?; **she won't tell us what happened** no nos quiere decir qué pasó; **I won't stand for this** no pienso tolerar esto 2 (in orders): **be quiet, ~ you!** cállate, ¿quieres?, ¡quieres callarte! 3 (in invitations): **~ you have a drink?** ¿quieres tomar algo?; **you'll stay for dinner, won't you?** te quedas a cenar ¿no?

C (expressing conjecture): **won't they be having lunch now?** ¿no estarán comiendo ahora?; **you ~ have gathered that ...** te habrás dado cuenta de que …; **that would have been in 1947** eso debe (de) haber sido en 1947

D 1 (indicating habit, characteristic): **I'll watch anything on television** yo soy capaz de mirar cualquier cosa en la televisión; **he'd get drunk every Saturday** se emborrachaba *or* solía emborracharse todos los sábados; **he *will* jump to conclusions** él siempre tiene que precipitarse a sacar conclusiones; **you won't be told, ~ you?** ¡qué cosa! ¿por qué no haces caso? 2 (indicating capability): **it ~ do 40 miles per gallon** hace 40 millas por galón; **this door won't shut** esta puerta no cierra *or* no quiere cerrar

■ **will** *vt* (*past & past p* **willed**)

A 1 (urge, try to cause): **I was ~ing her to get the answer right** estaba deseando con todas mis fuerzas *or* con toda mi voluntad que diera la respuesta correcta 2 (desire, ordain) (frml) ‹‹*God*›› disponer*, querer*

B (bequeath) legar*, dejar en testamento

will² *n*

A [u] 1 (faculty) voluntad *f*; **this machine has a ~ of its own** esta máquina está endiablada 2 (determination, willpower) voluntad *f*; **to break sb's ~** doblegar* a algn; **to lose the ~ to live** perder* las ansias *or* las ganas de vivir; **they set about their tasks with a ~** se pusieron a trabajar con empeño; ***where there's a ~, there's a way*** querer es poder 3 (desire, intention) voluntad *f*; **it was God's ~** Dios así lo quiso, fue la voluntad divina; **patients may come and go at ~** los pacientes pueden entrar y salir a voluntad *or* cuando quieren *or* (frml) cuando les place

B [c] (testament) testamento *m*; **last ~ and testament** última voluntad y testamento

W

willful, (BrE) **wilful** /ˈwɪlfəl/ *adj*
A (deliberate) ‹*misconduct/neglect*› intencionado, deliberado; ‹*damage*› causado con premeditación
B (obstinate) ‹*person*› terco, testarudo, obstinado

willfully, (BrE) **wilfully** /ˈwɪlfəli/ *adv*
A (deliberately) intencionadamente, deliberadamente
B (obstinately) ‹*refuse*› con terquedad *or* tozudez

willies /ˈwɪliz/ *pl n* (colloq): **it gives me/I get the ~** me pone los pelos de punta (fam)

willing /ˈwɪlɪŋ/ *adj* **1** (eager, compliant) (*before n*) ‹*servant/worker*› servicial; **to lend a ~ hand** dar* una mano espontáneamente; ***to show ~*** (BrE) dar* muestras de buena voluntad **2** (inclined) (*pred*) **to be ~ to + INF** estar* dispuesto A + INF

willingly /ˈwɪlɪŋli/ *adv* (gladly) con gusto, de buen grado; (readily, freely) por voluntad propia; **can you help out? — yes, ~** ¿nos podría dar una mano? — claro, encantado

willingness /ˈwɪlɪŋnəs || ˈwɪlɪŋnɪs/ *n* [u] buena voluntad *f*, buena disposición *f*; **~ to + INF**: **they have indicated their ~ to make concessions** han señalado que están dispuestos a hacer concesiones

will-o'-the-wisp /ˈwɪləðəˈwɪsp/ *n* **1** (light) fuego *m* fatuo **2** (sth elusive) quimera *f*

willow /ˈwɪləʊ/ *n* sauce *m*

willowy /ˈwɪləʊi/ *adj* esbelto

willpower /ˈwɪlpaʊər || ˈwɪlpaʊə(r)/ *n* [u] fuerza *f* de voluntad, voluntad *f*

willy /ˈwɪli/ *n* (BrE colloq) ▸**weenie**

willy-nilly /ˈwɪliˈnɪli/ *adv* **1** (haphazardly) de cualquier manera **2** (like it or not) sea como sea

wilt¹ /wɪlt/ (arch) *2nd pers sing pres of* **will¹**

wilt² *vi* «*plant/flower*» ponerse* mustio, marchitarse; **we were ~ing in the heat** el calor nos estaba haciendo languidecer

wily /ˈwaɪli/ *adj* **wilier, wiliest** astuto, artero

wimp /wɪmp/ *n* (colloq) pelele *m* (fam)

win¹ /wɪn/ (*pres p* **winning**; *past & past p* **won**) *vt*
A (gain) ‹*prize/title*› ganar; ‹*support*› conseguir*, ganarse; ‹*fame/recognition*› ganarse; ‹*affection*› ganarse, granjearse; ‹*scholarship/promotion*› conseguir*, obtener* (frml); ‹*contract*› conseguir*; **their perseverance won them universal admiration** su perseverancia les granjeó *or* les valió la admiración de todos; **to ~ sb's heart** conquistar el corazón de algn; **to ~ sth back** recuperar algo
B (be victorious in) ‹*war/race/bet/election*› ganar; **you can't ~ them all** (colloq) no se puede pretender ganarlas todas
■ **win** *vi* ganar; **they're ~ning 3-1** van ganando 3 a 1; **to ~ AT sth** ‹*at cards/billiards/golf*› ganar A algo; **to ~ BY sth** ganar POR algo; **OK, you ~!** (colloq) está bien, como tú digas; **you can't ~!** (colloq) ¡no hay caso!

Phrasal verbs
• **win over**, (BrE also) **win round** [v ▸ o ▸ adv, v ▸ adv ▸ o] conquistarse *or* ganarse a; **to ~ sb over** *o* **round TO sth**: **she succeeded in ~ning them over to the cause/her side** logró conquistarlos para la causa/ponerlos de su lado
• **win through** [v ▸ adv] salir* adelante

win² *n* victoria *f*, triunfo *m*; **the Dolphins have had no ~s so far** los Dolphins no han ganado hasta ahora; **he had a ~ on the horses** ganó en las carreras

wince¹ /wɪns/ *vi* hacer* un gesto de dolor; (shudder) estremecerse*; **some of the things he said made me ~** algunas de las cosas que dijo me dieron vergüenza ajena; **to ~ AT sth**: **she ~d at the pain** hizo un gesto *or* una mueca de dolor

wince² *n* gesto *m or* mueca *f* (de dolor)

winch¹ /wɪntʃ/ *n* cabrestante *m*, torno *m*

winch² *vt*: *levantar con un torno o cabrestante*

Winchester /ˈwɪntʃestər || ˈwɪntʃɪstə(r)/ *n* **~ (disk)** (Comput) disco *m* Winchester

wind¹ /wɪnd/ *n*
A [c u] (Meteo) viento *m*; **to run before the ~** (Naut) ir* con el viento en popa *or* a favor; **a ~ of change was blowing** soplaban vientos nuevos; ***in the ~***: **a change is in the ~** se viene un cambio; ***like the ~*** como un bólido (fam); ***to get the ~ up*** (BrE colloq) asustarse, pegarse* un susto (fam); ***to get ~ of sth*** enterarse de algo, olerse* algo (fam); ***to know/find out which way*** *o* ***how the ~ is blowing*** saber*/averiguar* por dónde van los tiros (fam); ***to put the ~ up sb*** (BrE colloq) asustar a algn, meterle miedo a algn (fam); ***to sail close to the ~***: **be careful what you say, you're sailing very close to the ~** cuidado con lo que dices, te estás por pasar de la raya; ***to scatter sth to the four ~s*** desperdigar* algo; ***to take the ~ out of sb's sails*** desinflar a algn; ***to throw caution to the ~(s)*** echar la precaución por la borda, abandonar toda precaución; ***it's an ill ~ that blows nobody any good*** no hay mal que por bien no venga; (*before n*) **~ power** energía *f* eólica; **~ tunnel** (Auto, Aviat) túnel *m* aerodinámico; **~ turbine** turbina *f* eólica
B [u] (in bowels) gases *mpl*, ventosidad *f*; **to have ~** tener* gases; **to break ~** eliminar gases (euf), tirarse un pedo (fam)
C [u] (breath) aliento *m*, resuello *m*; ***to get one's second ~*** recobrar las energías
D [u] (Mus) instrumentos *mpl* de viento; (*before n*) **~ instrument** instrumento *m* de viento

wind² *vt*
Sense I /wɪnd/ **1** «*exertion*» dejar sin aliento *or* resuello; «*blow*» cortarle la respiración a **2** ‹*baby*› sacarle* el aire a (fam)
Sense II /waɪnd/ (*past & past p* **wound** /waʊnd/)
A (coil) ‹*yarn/wool*› ovillar, devanar; **the bandage had been wound too tightly** tenía la venda muy apretada; **to ~ sth AROUND** *o* (esp BrE) **ROUND sth** enroscar* *or* enrollar algo ALREDEDOR DE algo; **to ~ sth ON(TO) sth** enroscar* *or* enrollar algo EN algo; **to ~ sth into a ball** hacer* un ovillo con algo; **the fisherman wound in the line** el pescador fue cobrando sedal; **to ~ the film on** (hacer*) correr la película; **to ~ the tape back** rebobinar la cinta
B **1** (turn) ‹*handle*› hacer* girar, darle* vueltas a; ‹*clock/watch*› darle* cuerda a **2** (hoist, pull) levantar
■ **wind** *vi* /waɪnd/ (*past & past p* **wound** /waʊnd/) **1** «*river/road*» serpentear **2** **winding** *pres p* ‹*river/road*› sinuoso, serpenteante; **the ~ing streets** el laberinto de calles

Phrasal verbs
• **wind down**
A [v ▸ o ▸ adv, v ▸ adv ▸ o] ‹*window*› (Auto) bajar; ‹*production/trade*› reducir* paulatinamente
B [v ▸ adv] (colloq) relajarse
• **wind up**
A [v ▸ o ▸ adv, v ▸ adv ▸ o] **1** (tighten spring) ‹*watch/toy*› darle* cuerda a **2** (bring to conclusion) ‹*meeting/speech*› cerrar*, poner* fin a **3** (close down) ‹*company*› cerrar*, liquidar
B [v ▸ o ▸ adv] **1** (make excited) animar **2** (colloq) (make angry) torear, darle* manija a (RPl fam); (tease) tomarle el pelo a (fam)
C [v ▸ adv] **1** (end up, find oneself) (colloq) terminar, acabar; **he'll ~ up in jail** va a terminar *or* acabar en la cárcel, va a ir a parar a la cárcel; **I wound up in Boston** fui a parar *or* a dar a Boston **2** (conclude) «*speaker*» concluir*, terminar **3** (come to end) «*project/campaign*» concluir*, terminar **4** «*toy/doll*»: **it ~s up at the back** se le da cuerda por detrás

wind /wɪnd/: **~bag** *n* (colloq) cotorra *f* (fam), charlatán, -tana *m,f*; **~break** *n* barrera *f* contra el viento; **~-chill factor** *n* sensación *f* térmica; **~fall** *n* **1** (fruit) *fruta caída del árbol* **2** (unexpected benefit): **the $100 prize was a nice little ~fall** el premio de 100 dólares le (*or* me *etc*) cayó como llovido del cielo; **~ farm** parque *m* eólico; **~lass** /ˈwɪndləs/ *n* cabrestante *m*, torno *m*; **~mill** *n* molino *m* de viento

window /ˈwɪndəʊ/ *n*
A **1** (of building) ventana *f*; (of car) ventanilla *f*, luna *f*; (of shop) escaparate *m* (esp Esp), vitrina *f* (AmL), vidriera *f* (AmL); **to clean the ~s** limpiar los vidrios *or* (Esp) cristales; ***to fly/go out (of) the ~*** «*plans*» venirse* abajo, desbaratarse; «*hopes*» desvanecerse*; ***to throw sth out (of) the ~*** (colloq) echar algo por la borda; (*before n*) **~ box** jardinera *f*; **~ cleaner** (product) limpiacristales *m*, limpiavidrios *m* (esp AmL); (person) limpiacristales *mf*, limpiavidrios *mf* (esp AmL); **~ ledge** alféizar *m or* repisa *f* de la ventana **2** (sales counter) ventanilla *f*
B (Comput) ventana *f*, recuadro *m*

window: **~ dresser** *n* escaparatista *mf* (esp Esp), vitrinista *mf* (AmL), vidrierista *mf* (AmL); **~ dressing** *n* [u] **1** (in shop) escaparatismo *m* (esp Esp), vitrinismo *m* (AmL),

W

vidrierismo *m* (AmL) [2] (pretense, mask): **don't be taken in by the ~ dressing** no te dejes engañar por las apariencias *or* la imagen que quieren presentar; **~pane** *n* vidrio *m or* (Esp) cristal *m* (*de una ventana*); **~ seat** *n* (in train, plane) asiento *m* junto a la ventanilla; **~-shop** *vi* **-pp-**: **to go ~-shopping** ir* a mirar vitrinas *or* vidrieras *or* (esp Esp) escaparates; **~-shopping** /ˈwɪndəʊˌʃɑːpɪŋ || ˈwɪndəʊˌʃɒpɪŋ/ *n* [u]: **the only thing to do was ~-shopping** lo único que había para hacer era ir a mirar escaparates *or* (AmL fam) ir a vitrinear; **~sill** *n* alféizar *m or* repisa *f* de la ventana

wind /wɪnd/: **~pipe** *n* tráquea *f*; **~proof** *adj* a prueba de viento; **~screen** *n* (BrE) ▸ **~shield**; **~shield** *n* (AmE) parabrisas *m*; (*before n*) **~shield wiper** limpiaparabrisas *m*, limpiador *m* (Méx); **~sock** *n* manga *f* de viento; **~surf** *vi* hacer* windsurf *or* windsurfing, hacer* surf a vela; **~surfer** *n* (person) tablista *mf*, surfista *mf*; (board) tabla *f* de windsurf; **~surfing** *n* [u] windsurf *m*, windsurfing *m*, surf *m* a vela; **~swept** *adj* ‹*beach/plain*› azotado por el viento; ‹*person*› despeinado; ‹*hair*› alborotado

wind-up /ˈwaɪndʌp/ *n* (BrE colloq) broma *f*, chiste *m*

windward /ˈwɪndwərd || ˈwɪndwəd/ *adj* de barlovento

windy /ˈwɪndi/ *adj* **-dier, -diest** ‹*day/weather*› ventoso, de viento; **it's ~** hace viento, está ventoso

wine /waɪn/ *n* [u c] [1] (beverage) vino *m*; (*before n*) **~ cellar** bodega *f*; **~ list** carta *f* de vinos; **~ merchant** (BrE) vinatero, -ra *m,f*; **~ rack** botellero *m*; **~ waiter** sommelier *m*, sumiller *m* [2] (color) rojo *m* granate; (*before n*) rojo granate *adj inv*

wine: **~ and dine** *vt* agasajar (*con una comida*); **~ bar** *n* bar *m* (*especializado en vinos*); **~ glass** *n* copa *f* de vino; **~growing** *n* [u] viticultura *f*; (*before n*) ‹*area/region*› vinícola; ‹*country*› productor de vino; **~ gum** *n* (BrE) gominola *f*; **~ taster** catador, -dora *m,f* (*de vinos*), catavinos *mf*; **~tasting** /ˈwaɪnˌteɪstɪŋ/ *n* [1] [u] (act, skill) cata *f or* catadura *f* de vinos [2] [c] (event) degustación *f* de vinos

wing¹ /wɪŋ/ *n*

[A] [c u] (Zool) ala *f*‡; **a bird on the ~** un pájaro volando *or* en vuelo; **to take ~** (liter) levantar *or* alzar* el vuelo; ***to clip sb's ~s*** cortarle las alas a algn; ***to spread*** *o* ***stretch one's ~s***: **he wants to spread his ~s** quiere alzar *or* levantar el vuelo; ***under sb's/sth's ~***: **she took the new girl under her ~** se hizo cargo de la chica nueva

[B] (Aviat) ala *f*‡

[C] (BrE Auto) guardabarros *m or* (Méx) salpicadera *f or* (Chi, Per) tapabarros *m*; (*before n*) **~ mirror** espejo *m* retrovisor exterior

[D] (Sport) [1] (part of field) ala *f*‡ [2] (player, position) ala *mf*‡, alero *mf*, extremo *mf*

[E] (Pol) ala *f*‡; *see also* **left wing 1, right wing 1**

[F] (of building) ala *f*‡

[G] **wings** *pl* [1] (Theat) **the ~s** los bastidores; ***to wait in the ~s***: **if he doesn't play well, there are others waiting in the ~s** si no juega bien, hay quienes están listos para sustituirlo [2] (insignia) (Aviat, Mil) insignia *f*

wing² *vt*: ***to ~ one's way***: **we were soon ~ing our way to Italy** poco tiempo después estábamos camino a Italia; ***to ~ it*** (improvise) (AmE colloq) arreglárselas sobre la marcha

wing: **~ collar** *n*: *cuello de camisa de esmoquin o frac*; **~ commander** *n* (in UK) ≈ teniente *m* coronel (*de la Fuerza Aérea*), ≈ vicecomodoro *m* (*en Arg*)

-winged /wɪŋd/ *suff*: **four~** de cuatro alas

winger /ˈwɪŋər || ˈwɪŋə(r)/ *n* (Sport) (in soccer) ala *mf*‡, alero *mf*; (in rugby) ala *f*‡; *see also* **left-winger, right-winger**

wing: **~ nut** *n* palomilla *f*, tuerca *f* (de) mariposa; **~span** *n* envergadura *f*

wink¹ /wɪŋk/ *n* guiño *m*, guiñada *f*; **to give sb a ~** guiñarle el ojo a algn; ***not to get a ~ of sleep*** no pegar* (el *or* un) ojo; ***to get*** *o* ***grab forty ~s*** dar* una cabezadita, hacerse* *or* echarse una siestecita

wink² *vi* [1] «*person*» guiñar el ojo, hacer* un guiño *or* una guiñada [2] (flash) «*light*» parpadear, titilar

winkle /ˈwɪŋkəl/ *n* bígaro *m*

(Phrasal verb)

- **winkle out** [v ▸ o ▸ adv, v ▸ adv ▸ o]: **I've still not ~d the truth out of them** todavía no he logrado sonsacarles *or* arrancarles la verdad

winner /ˈwɪnər || ˈwɪnə(r)/ *n* [1] (of prize, lottery) ganador, -dora *m,f*; (of competition, contest) ganador, -dora *m,f*, vencedor, -dora *m,f* [2] (goal) gol *m* (*or* tanto *m etc*) decisivo *or* de la victoria [3] (success): ***to be onto a ~*** (colloq): **they're onto a ~ with their latest idea** su última idea va a ser un exitazo (fam)

winning /ˈwɪnɪŋ/ *adj* [1] (victorious) (*before n*) ‹*candidate/team*› ganador; ‹*goal/shot*› de la victoria, decisivo; **to hold the ~ hand** llevar las de ganar [2] (appealing) ‹*smile/personality*› encantador

winning post *n* (poste *m* de) llegada *f*, meta *f*

winnings /ˈwɪnɪŋz/ *pl n* ganancias *fpl* (*obtenidas en el juego*)

winnow /ˈwɪnəʊ/ *vt* aventar*

wino /ˈwaɪnəʊ/ *n* (*pl* **~s**) (colloq) borrachín, -china *m,f* (fam)

winsome /ˈwɪnsəm/ *adj* (liter) encantador

winter¹ /ˈwɪntər || ˈwɪntə(r)/ *n* [u c] invierno *m*; **in (the) ~** en invierno; **last ~** el invierno pasado; **a ~'s day** un día de invierno; (*before n*) ‹*weather/temperatures*› invernal; **~ Olympics** (*pl*) Juegos *mpl* (Olímpicos) de Invierno; **~ sports** deportes *mpl* de invierno

winter² *vi* «*animal/bird*» invernar, hibernar; «*person/army*» pasar el invierno, invernar

wintertime /ˈwɪntərtaɪm || ˈwɪntətaɪm/ *n* [u] invierno *m*; **in (the) ~** en invierno

wintry /ˈwɪntri/ *adj* **-trier, -triest** invernal, de invierno

wipe¹ /waɪp/ *n* [1] (action): **give the table a ~ with a damp cloth** pásale un trapo húmedo a la mesa; **give your nose a ~** límpiate la nariz [2] (cloth) toallita *f*; **baby ~** toallita *f* húmeda (*para bebé*)

wipe² *vt* [1] (clean) ‹*floor/table*› limpiar, pasarle un trapo a; ‹*dishes*› secar*; **she ~d the mirror clean** limpió el espejo (con un trapo); **~ your nose** límpiate la nariz [2] (remove) (+ *adv compl*): **she ~d the mud off her hands** se limpió el barro de las manos; **he ~d the tears from his eyes** se secó *or* (liter) se enjugó las lágrimas; **you can ~ that grin off your face!** ¡más vale que no te rías! [3] (rub) (+ *adv compl*) ‹*cloth/rag*› pasar

■ **wipe** *vi* (dry dishes) secar*

(Phrasal verbs)

- **wipe away** [v ▸ o ▸ adv, v ▸ adv ▸ o] ‹*tears*› secar*, enjugar* (liter); ‹*blood*› limpiar; ‹*memory*› borrar
- **wipe off**

[A] [v ▸ o ▸ adv, v ▸ adv ▸ o] [1] (remove) ‹*mud/oil*› limpiar; **she ~d off what was on the blackboard** borró la pizarra [2] (erase) ‹*recording*› borrar

[B] [v ▸ adv] «*mud/mark*» salir*

- **wipe out** [v ▸ o ▸ adv, v ▸ adv ▸ o] [1] (clean) limpiar, pasarle un trapo a [2] (cancel) ‹*deficit*› cancelar; ‹*lead/advantage*› eliminar [3] (destroy, eradicate) ‹*species/population*› exterminar; ‹*resistance*› acabar con; ‹*disease*› erradicar*; ‹*army*› aniquilar [4] (erase) ‹*writing*› borrar; ‹*memory*› borrar [5] (exhaust) (colloq) dejar hecho polvo (fam)
- **wipe up** [v ▸ o ▸ adv, v ▸ adv ▸ o] (clean up) limpiar

wiper /ˈwaɪpər || ˈwaɪpə(r)/ *n* (*windshield o* (BrE) *windscreen* ~) limpiaparabrisas *m*, limpiador *m* (Méx)

wire¹ /waɪr || ˈwaɪə(r)/ *n*

[A] [1] [c u] (metal strand) alambre *m*; (*before n*) **~ fence** alambrada *f*, alambrado *m* (AmL); **~ netting** red *f* de alambre [2] [u] (fencing, mesh) alambrada *f*, alambrado *m* (AmL) [3] [c] (finishing line) (AmE): **the ~** la línea de llegada, la meta; ***down to the ~*** hasta el último momento; ***under the ~*** por un pelo *or* (Esp) por los pelos (fam)

[B] [c] [1] (Elec, Telec) cable *m*; ▸ **cross²** *vt* **B** [2] (telegram) (colloq) telegrama *m* [3] (teletype machine) (AmE colloq) teletipo *m*; **hot off the ~** de última hora

wire² *vt*

[A] [1] (Elec): **to be ~d to sth** estar* conectado a algo; **the plug has been wrongly ~d** han conectado mal los cables del enchufe [2] (telegraph) (colloq): **~ me when you get there** mándame un telegrama cuando llegues; **they ~d me some money** me mandaron un giro telegráfico

[B] (fasten): **the parts are ~d in place** las piezas van sujetas con alambre; **she had her jaws ~d (together)** le inmovilizaron las mandíbulas

wire cutters *pl n* cortaalambres *m*, pinzas *fpl* de corte (Méx); (large) cizallas *fpl*, cizalla *f*

wireless /ˈwaɪrlɪs || ˈwaɪələs/ *adj* ‹*device/technology*› inalámbrico, sin cables *or* hilos; ~ **telephony** telefonía *f* inalámbrica *or* sin hilos

wire: ~**tapping** /ˈwaɪr,tæpɪŋ || ˈwaɪə,tæpɪŋ/ *n* [u] (AmE) escuchas *fpl* telefónicas; ~**walker** *n* (AmE) equilibrista *mf*, funámbulo, -la *m,f*; ~ **wool** *n* ▸**steel wool**

wiring /ˈwaɪrɪŋ || ˈwaɪərɪŋ/ *n* [u] (Elec) cableado *m*, instalación *f* eléctrica

wiry /ˈwaɪri || ˈwaɪəri/ *adj* **wirier, wiriest** 1 ‹*person*› enjuto y nervudo 2 ‹*hair*› áspero, hirsuto

Wis = **Wisconsin**

wisdom /ˈwɪzdəm/ *n* [u] sabiduría *f*; **the government, in their ~, had ignored these reports** (iro) el gobierno, en su infinita sabiduría, había hecho caso omiso de estos informes (iró)

wisdom tooth *n* muela *f* del juicio

wise /waɪz/ *adj* **wiser, wisest** 1 (prudent) ‹*person*› prudente, sensato; ‹*choice/decision*› acertado, prudente; **it would be ~ to call first** sería prudente *or* aconsejable llamar antes 2 (learned, experienced) sabio; **the three W~ Men** los Reyes Magos; **it's easy to be ~ after the event** es muy fácil criticar a posteriori; ***to be none the ~r***: **I'm none the ~r** sigo sin entender *or* sin enterarme; **eat one: no-one will be any the ~r** cómete una, nadie se va a dar cuenta; ***to get ~ with sb*** (AmE colloq) insolentarse con algn 3 (aware) (colloq) **to be ~ TO sth/sb**: **don't worry, I'm ~ to him/his tricks** no te preocupes que lo conozco muy bien *or* (fam) ya lo tengo calado/le conozco las mañas

Phrasal verb

- **wise up** (colloq) [v ▸ adv] (d)espabilarse, avivarse (AmL fam), apiolarse (RPl fam); **to ~ up TO sth** darse* cuenta DE algo

-wise /waɪz/ *suff* 1 (with reference to): **price~/weather~** en lo que respecta al precio/tiempo 2 (in particular way): **length~** a lo largo

wise: ~**crack** *n* broma *f*, chiste *m*; ~ **guy** *n* (colloq): **OK, who's the ~ guy?** a ver ¿quién ha sido el gracioso?; **OK, ~ guy, what's the answer?** ¿y, sabelotodo, cuál es la respuesta? (fam)

wisely /ˈwaɪzli/ *adv* sabiamente, prudentemente

wish¹ /wɪʃ/ *n* 1 (desire) deseo *m*; **to make a ~** pedir* un deseo; **her ~ came true** su deseo se hizo realidad, se le cumplió el deseo; **his last** *o* **dying ~** su última voluntad; **they got married against my ~es** se casaron en contra de mi voluntad; **your ~ is my command** (set phrase) tus deseos son órdenes (fr hecha); **~ to + INF: I've no ~ to upset you, but ...** no quisiera disgustarte, pero ...; **I've no great ~ to see the play** no tengo muchas ganas de ver la obra 2 **wishes** *pl* (greetings): **give your mother my best ~es** dale a tu madre muchos recuerdos de mi parte, cariños a tu madre (AmL); **with our best ~es for a speedy recovery** deseándole una pronta mejoría; **best ~es, Jack** saludos *or* un abrazo de Jack

wish² *vt* 1 (desire fervently) desear; **to ~ sth ON sb** desearle algo A algn; **to ~ (THAT)**: **I ~ I hadn't come** ¡ojalá no hubiera venido!; **I ~ I were rich** ¡ojalá fuera rico!; **she ~ed she hadn't told him** lamentó habérselo dicho; **I ~ you wouldn't say things like that** me disgusta mucho que digas esas cosas; **I do ~ you'd told me before!** ¡me lo podrías haber dicho antes! 2 (want) (frml) desear (frml), querer*; **should you ~ to do so ...** si así lo deseara ... (frml); **to ~ sb/sth to + INF** desear que algn/algo (+ *subj*) (frml) 3 (want for sb) desear; **we ~ you every happiness** te deseamos lo mejor; **~ me luck!** ¡deséame suerte!; **he called to ~ me (a) happy birthday** me llamó para desearme feliz cumpleaños; **to ~ sb good night** darle* las buenas noches a algn; **to ~ sb well** desearle suerte *or* lo mejor a algn; **I ~ you well** espero que te vaya bien

■ **wish** *vi* 1 (make magic wish) pedir* un deseo 2 (want, desire): **as you ~, sir** como usted mande *or* diga, señor; **if you ~** como quieras

Phrasal verbs

- **wish away** [v ▸ o ▸ adv, v ▸ adv ▸ o]: **you can't just ~ the problem away** no puedes hacer como el avestruz; **to ~ one's life away** desperdiciar la vida
- **wish for** [v ▸ prep ▸ o]: **what more could one ~ for?** ¿qué más se puede pedir?; **you couldn't ~ for a better husband** es el marido ideal

wishbone /ˈwɪʃbəʊn/ *n* espoleta *f*, hueso *m* de la suerte, apostador *m* (Col)

wishful thinking /ˈwɪʃfəl/ *n* [u]: **do you know for sure that they're leaving or is it just ~ ~?** ¿sabes a ciencia cierta que se van o es simplemente lo que tú querrías?

wishing well /ˈwɪʃɪŋ/ *n* pozo *m* de los deseos

wish list *n* lista *f* de deseos

wishy-washy /ˈwɪʃi,wɔːʃi || ˈwɪʃi,wɒʃi/ *adj* (colloq) ‹*color*› sin gracia; ‹*coffee*› aguado, insípido; ‹*argument*› flojo, endeble

wisp /wɪsp/ *n* (of smoke) voluta *f*; (of hair) mechón *m*; **a ~ of a girl** una niña menudita

wispy /ˈwɪspi/ *adj* **-pier, -piest** ‹*cloud*› tenue; ‹*hair*› ralo

wistful /ˈwɪstfəl/ *adj* ‹*smile/thought*› nostálgico

wistfully /ˈwɪstfəli/ *adv* con añoranza *or* nostalgia

wit¹ /wɪt/ *n*

A (*often pl*) (intelligence) inteligencia *f*; (ingenuity) ingenio *m*; ***to be at one's ~s' end*** estar* desesperado, no saber* más qué hacer; ***to frighten*** *o* ***scare sb out of her/his ~s*** (colloq) darle* a algn un susto de muerte (fam); ***to have/keep one's ~s about one*** estar* alerta *or* atento, andar* con mucho ojo; ***to live by one's ~s*** vivir de su (*or* mi *etc*) ingenio

B 1 [u] (humor) ingenio *m*, agudeza *f*; **she has a dry ~** es muy aguda *or* mordaz 2 [c] (person) persona *f* ingeniosa *or* ocurrente, ingenio *m*

wit² *vi*: **to ~** a saber

witch /wɪtʃ/ *n* bruja *f*

witch: ~**craft** *n* [u] brujería *f*, hechicería *f*; ~ **doctor** *n* hechicero *m*, brujo *m*; ~**-hunt** *n* caza *f* de brujas

witching hour /ˈwɪtʃɪŋ/ *n* **the ~ ~** la medianoche

with /wɪð, wɪθ/ *prep*

A 1 (in the company of) con; **she went ~ him/them/me/you** fue con él/con ellos/conmigo/contigo; **go ~ your sister** ve con tu hermana, acompaña a tu hermana; **I'm staying ~ a friend** estoy en casa de un amigo; **I'll be ~ you in a moment** enseguida estoy contigo (*or* te atiendo *etc*); **she had brought it ~ her** lo había traído (consigo); **the bad weather is still ~ us** seguimos con mal tiempo; ***are you ~ me?*** (colloq) ¿entiendes (*or* entienden *etc*)?, ¿me sigues (*or* siguen *etc*)? 2 (member, employee, client etc of) en; **are you still ~ Davis Tools?** ¿sigues en Davis Tools?; **I've been banking ~ them for years** hace años que tengo cuenta en ese banco 3 (in agreement, supporting) con; **I'm ~ you on that** en eso estoy contigo

B (in descriptions): **the shirt is black ~ white stripes** la camisa es negra a *or* con rayas blancas; **the man ~ the beard/the red tie** el hombre de barba/corbata roja; **a tall woman ~ long hair** una mujer alta con el pelo largo *or* de pelo largo; **he is married, ~ three children** está casado y tiene tres hijos

C 1 (indicating manner) con; **the proposal was greeted ~ derision** la propuesta fue recibida con burlas; **it was done ~ no fuss** se hizo sin aspavientos 2 (by means of, using) con; **she ate it ~ her fingers** lo comió con la mano 3 (as a result of): **trembling ~ fright** temblando de miedo; **this wine improves ~ age** este vino mejora con el tiempo; **~ luck** con suerte

D (where sb, sth is concerned) con; **you can never tell ~ her** con ella nunca se sabe; **the trouble ~ Roy is that ...** lo que pasa con Roy es que ...; **what's up ~ you/him today?** (colloq) ¿qué te/le pasa hoy?

E 1 (in the same direction as): **~ the tide/flow** con la marea/corriente 2 (in accordance with) según

F (*after adv, adv phrase*): **come on, out ~ it!** ¡vamos, suéltalo!; **away ~ him!** ¡llévenselo!; **off ~ her head!** ¡que le corten la cabeza!

withdraw /wɪðˈdrɔː/ (*past* **-drew**; *past p* **-drawn**) *vt*

A 1 (recall, remove) ‹*troops/representative*› retirar; ‹*hand/arm*› retirar, apartar; ‹*coin/note*› retirar de la circulación; ‹*product*› retirar de la venta; **they withdrew their children from the school** sacaron a sus niños del colegio 2 ‹*money/cash*› retirar, sacar*

B 1 (cancel, discontinue) ‹*support/funding*› retirar; ‹*permission*› cancelar; **they threatened to ~ their labor** amenazaron con ir a la huelga 2 (rescind) ‹*application/charges*› retirar; ‹*demand*› renunciar a 3 (retract) ‹*statement/allegation*› retirar, retractarse de

■ **withdraw** *vi* 1 «*troops/competitor/candidate*» retirarse 2 (socially) recluirse*; (psychologically) retraerse*

W

withdrawal /wɪð'drɔːəl/ *n*
A **1** [u c] (of troops, team, representative) retirada *f*; (of coinage) retirada *f* de la circulación; (of product) retirada *f* de la venta **2** [u] (method of contraception) coitus *m* interruptus, marcha *f* atrás (fam)
B [u] (of support, funding) retirada *f*, retiro *m* (AmL); (of application, nomination, competitor) retirada *f*
C (Psych) retraimiento *m*
D [c u] (of cash) retirada *f*, retiro *m* (AmL)
E [u] (from drugs) abandono *m*; (*before n*) ~ **symptoms** síndrome *m* de abstinencia

withdrawn¹ /wɪð'drɔːn/ *past p of* **withdraw**

withdrawn² *adj* retraído, encerrado en sí mismo

withdrew /wɪð'druː/ *past of* **withdraw**

wither /'wɪðər || 'wɪðə(r)/ *vi* ⟨⟨*plant/flower*⟩⟩ marchitarse; ⟨⟨*limb*⟩⟩ atrofiarse

withered /'wɪðərd || 'wɪðəd/ *adj* ⟨*plant/flower*⟩ marchito, mustio; ⟨*limb*⟩ atrofiado

withering /'wɪðərɪŋ/ *adj* **1** ⟨*heat*⟩ abrasador, agostador **2** ⟨*look*⟩ fulminante

withers /'wɪðərz || 'wɪðəz/ *pl n* cruz *f*

withhold /wɪθ'həʊld || wɪð'həʊld/ *vt* (*past & past p* **-held**) ⟨*payment/funds*⟩ retener*; ⟨*truth*⟩ ocultar; ⟨*consent/assistance*⟩ negar*; ⟨*information*⟩ no revelar, no dar* a conocer

withholding (tax) /wɪθ'həʊldɪŋ || wɪð'həʊldɪŋ/ *n* [u] (in US) *parte de los impuestos de un empleado que su empleador paga directamente al gobierno*

within¹ /wɪð'ɪn/ *prep*
A **1** (inside) dentro de; **from ~ the house** desde dentro de *or* desde el interior de la casa; **~ these four walls** entre estas cuatro paredes **2** (inside limits of): **~ a radius of 20 miles** en un radio de 20 millas; **it is ~ our reach** está a nuestro alcance; **~ the bounds of possibility** dentro de lo posible; **it is not ~ my power to help you** no está en mi poder ayudarte; **~ the law** dentro de la ley
B (indicating nearness) a; **we were ~ 150m of the summit** estábamos a 150m de la cumbre; **the measurements are correct to ~ 1mm** las medidas tienen un margen de error de 1mm
C (in less than): **~ the time allotted** dentro del tiempo establecido; **they'll be here ~ the hour** *o* **~ an hour** estarán aquí en menos de una hora; **the paint dries ~ minutes of being applied** la pintura se seca a los pocos minutos de ser aplicada

within² *adv* (arch *or* liter) dentro; **Ⓢ apply within** infórmese aquí

with-it /'wɪðət || 'wɪðɪt/ *adj* (*pred* **with it**) (colloq)
A (trendy) ⟨*hairdo/clothes*⟩ a la última moda; **he's always been really ~ ~** ha estado siempre muy en la onda (fam)
B (alert) (*pred*) (d)espabilado

without /wɪð'aʊt/ *prep* sin; **he left ~ them/me/you** se fue sin ellos/mí/ti; **I wouldn't be ~ a car** no podría prescindir del coche por nada del mundo; **~ anyone to talk to/anything to do** sin nadie con quien hablar/nada que hacer; **do it ~ cheating** hazlo sin hacer trampas; **he noticed it ~ my saying anything** se dio cuenta sin que yo dijera nada; *see also* **do, go without**

withstand /wɪð'stænd/ *vt* (*past & past p* **-stood**) ⟨*attack*⟩ resistir; ⟨*heat/pain*⟩ soportar, aguantar, resistir

witless /'wɪtləs || 'wɪtlɪs/ *adj* tonto, estúpido; ***to scare sb* ~**: **the thought of it scared him ~** pensar en ello le daba pavor

witness¹ /'wɪtnəs || 'wɪtnɪs/ *n*
A [c] **1** (Law) testigo *mf*; **to call sb as a ~** citar a algn como testigo; **~ for the prosecution/defense** testigo de cargo/de la defensa *or* de descargo; (*before n*) **~ stand** *o* (BrE) **box** estrado *m* **2** (to event) **to be ~/a ~ TO sth** ser* testigo DE algo **3** (to contract, signature) testigo *mf*; **to stand ~** atestiguar*, testificar*
B [u] (testimony, evidence) **to be ~ TO sth** ser* testimonio *or* prueba DE algo, atestiguar* algo; **to bear ~** (in a court of law) atestiguar*, testificar*; **to bear false ~** (Bib) levantar falsos testimonios

witness² *vt* **1** (observe, see) ⟨*change/event*⟩ ser* testigo de; ⟨*crime/accident*⟩ presenciar, ser* testigo de, ver*; **this region is ~ing an unprecedented economic upturn** esta región está viviendo una reactivación económica sin precedentes **2** (authenticate) (Law) ⟨*signature*⟩ atestiguar*; ⟨*will*⟩ atestiguar* la firma de

witter /'wɪtər || 'wɪtə(r)/ *vi* (BrE colloq) **~ (on) (ABOUT sth)** parlotear (DE algo) (fam)

witticism /'wɪtəsɪzəm || 'wɪtɪsɪzəm/ *n* agudeza *f*; (in conversation) salida *f*, ocurrencia *f*

wittily /'wɪtəli || 'wɪtɪli/ *adv* ingeniosamente; (funnily) con gracia *or* chispa

witty /'wɪti/ *adj* **-tier, -tiest** ⟨*person*⟩ ingenioso, ocurrente, agudo; (funny) gracioso, con chispa; ⟨*answer/remark*⟩ ingenioso, agudo

wives /waɪvz/ *pl of* **wife**

wizard /'wɪzərd || 'wɪzəd/ *n* **1** (Occult) mago *m*, brujo *m* **2** (genius) (colloq) genio *m* (fam)

wizened /'wɪzn̩d/ *adj* (wrinkled) arrugado; (withered) marchito

wk = week

WNW (= west-northwest) ONO

woad /wəʊd/ *n* [u] *tintura azul, parecida al añil*

wobble /'wɑːbəl || 'wɒbəl/ *vi* **1** (tremble) ⟨⟨*jelly*⟩⟩ temblar*; **his voice ~s on the high notes** le tiembla la voz en los agudos **2** (sway, waver) ⟨⟨*cyclist*⟩⟩ bambolearse; ⟨⟨*wheel*⟩⟩ bailar; ⟨⟨*chair*⟩⟩ tambalearse
■ **wobble** *vt* mover*, bambolear

wobbly /'wɑːbli || 'wɒbli/ *adj* **-blier, -bliest** **1** ⟨*voice*⟩ tembloroso **2** ⟨*wheel/tooth*⟩ flojo; ⟨*table/chair*⟩ poco firme, que se tambalea; **my legs are ~** me tiemblan las piernas

woe /wəʊ/ *n* **1** [u] (sorrow) congoja *f* (liter), aflicción *f*; **a tale of ~** un drama, una historia trágica; **~ betide you if you lose it!** ¡pobre de ti *or* ay de ti si lo pierdes!; **~ is me!** (arch & liter) ¡pobre de mí! **2** **woes** *pl* (afflictions, troubles) males *mpl*, tribulaciones *fpl*

woebegone /'wəʊbɪgɔːn || 'wəʊbɪgɒn/ *adj* angustiado, cariacontecido

woeful /'wəʊfəl/ *adj* **1** (deplorable) ⟨*neglect/ignorance*⟩ lamentable, deplorable **2** (sorrowful) (liter) ⟨*person*⟩ acongojado (liter), afligido; ⟨*expression*⟩ desconsolado, de angustia *or* de congoja

wog /wɑːg || wɒg/ *n* (BrE sl & offensive) extranjero, -ra *m,f*

woke /wəʊk/ *past of* **wake¹**

woken /wəʊkən/ *past p of* **wake¹**

wolf¹ /wʊlf/ *n* (*pl* **wolves**) **1** (Zool) lobo *m*; ***a ~ in sheep's clothing*** un lobo disfrazado de cordero; ***to cry ~***: **he's cried ~ once too often** ya ha venido demasiadas veces con el mismo cuento; ***to keep the ~ from the door*** mantenerse* a flote, no pasar miseria, parar la olla (CS, Per fam) **2** (womanizer) (colloq) donjuán *m*, tenorio *m*

wolf² *vt* **~ (down)** devorar(se), engullir(se)*; **don't ~ your food** no engullas la comida de esa forma

wolf: **~ cub** *n* lobezno *m*, lobato *m*; **~hound** *n* perro *m* lobo; **~ whistle** *n* silbido *m or* chiflido *m* (*de admiración*)

wolves /wʊlvz/ *pl of* **wolf¹**

woman /'wʊmən/ *n* (*pl* **women**) mujer *f*; (*as form of address*) mujer; **an old ~** una señora *or* mujer mayor *or* de edad; (less respectful) una vieja; **a young ~** una chica, una joven (frml); **he ran off with another ~** se fue con otra; **you're a lucky ~** tienes suerte; **she's a sick ~** está muy enferma; **a ~'s work is never done** (set phrase) el trabajo de la casa no se acaba nunca; **the women's movement** el movimiento de liberación de la mujer; ***a ~'s touch*** el toque femenino; ***to be one's own ~*** ser* una mujer independiente; (*before n*) **a ~ lawyer/dentist** una abogada/dentista; **a ~ friend of mine** una amiga mía

womanhood /'wʊmənhʊd/ *n* [u] **1** (being a woman) condición *f* de mujer; **she's reached ~** ya se ha hecho mujer, ya es una mujer **2** (women) (liter) mujeres *fpl*

womanize /'wʊmənaɪz/ *vi* andar* detrás de las mujeres *or* (fam) de las faldas

womanizer /'wʊmənaɪzər || 'wʊmənaɪzə(r)/ *n* mujeriego *m*, donjuán *m*

womankind /'wʊmənkaɪnd/ *n* [u] las mujeres

womanly /'wʊmənli/ *adj* femenino

womb /wuːm/ *n* útero *m*, matriz *f*

women /'wɪmɪn/ *pl of* **woman**

women: **~folk** *pl n* mujeres *fpl*; **~'s liberation**, **~'s lib** /lɪb/ liberación *f* de la mujer; **~'s room** *n* (AmE) baño *m or* (Esp) servicios *mpl* de damas *or* señoras

won¹ /wʌn/ *past & past p of* **win¹**

won² *n* [u] won *m*

wonder¹ /ˈwʌndər || ˈwʌndə(r)/ *n*

A [u] (awe, curiosity) asombro *m*; **we gazed in ~ at the scene** contemplamos la escena maravillados

B [c] (marvel, miracle) maravilla *f*; **it's a ~ (that) he didn't break his neck** es asombroso *or* es un milagro que no se matara; **no ~ you feel tired!** no me extraña que estés cansado *or* ¡con razón estás cansado!; **~s will never cease!** (hum) ¡eso sí que es increíble!; ***to work*** *o* ***do ~s***: **he's worked ~s with this room** verdaderamente, ha transformado esta habitación; **that hairstyle does ~s for him** ese corte de pelo lo favorece muchísimo

wonder² *vi* **1** (ponder, speculate): **why do you ask? — oh, I was just ~ing** ¿por qué preguntas? — por nada *or* por saber; **who can that be, I ~?** ¿quién será?, ¿quién podrá ser?; **he said it was an accident — I ~** dijo que fue un accidente — tengo mis dudas; **I ~ about you sometimes** a veces de veras me preocupas **2** (marvel, be surprised) maravillarse; **to ~ AT sth**: **I ~ at your patience** me maravilla *or* me asombra la paciencia que tienes; **gone off with his secretary, I shouldn't ~** no me extrañaría que se hubiera ido con la secretaria

■ **wonder** *vt* **1** (ask oneself) preguntarse; **I ~ why I bother** no sé por qué me molesto; **I ~ if** *o* **whether he'll be there** me pregunto si estará; **we were ~ing if you'd like to come around to dinner** estábamos pensando si te gustaría venir a casa a cenar **2** (be amazed): **I ~ (that) she didn't fire you on the spot** me sorprende que no te haya echado inmediatamente

wonder³ *adj* (*before n*) ‹*drug/cure*› milagroso

wonderful /ˈwʌndərfəl || ˈwʌndəfəl/ *adj* maravilloso; **we had a ~ time** lo pasamos maravillosamente *or* fenomenal *or* de maravilla; **you did it? that's ~!** ¿lo lograste? ¡estupendo! *or* ¡qué maravilla!

wonderfully /ˈwʌndərfli || ˈwʌndəfəli/ *adv* maravillosamente, de maravilla; **they get on ~ together** se llevan a las mil maravillas, se llevan de maravilla

wonderland /ˈwʌndərlænd || ˈwʌndəlænd/ *n* país *m* de las maravillas; **Alice in W~** Alicia en el país de las maravillas

wondrous /ˈwʌndrəs/ *adj* (liter) maravilloso

wonky /ˈwɑːŋki/ *adj* **-kier, -kiest** (BrE colloq) **1** (unsteady) ‹*chair/table*› poco firme **2** (askew) torcido

wont¹ /wɑːnt || wəʊnt/ *adj* (liter *or* hum) (*pred, no comp*) **to be ~ to + INF** soler* *or* acostumbrar + INF

wont² *n* (liter *or* hum) costumbre *f*; **as is her ~** como tiene por costumbre, como suele hacer

won't /wəʊnt/ **= will not**

woo /wuː/ *vt* ‹*woman*› cortejar; ‹*customers/investors*› atraer*; ‹*voters*› buscar* el apoyo de; **her task is to ~ back lost voters** su tarea consiste en volver a captar los votos perdidos

wood /wʊd/ *n*

A [u] (material) madera *f*; (firewood) leña *f*; ***to touch ~*** *o* (AmE) ***knock on ~*** tocar* madera

B (wooded area) (*often pl*) bosque *m*; ***to be out of the ~(s)*** estar* fuera de peligro *or* a salvo

C (Sport) **1** [c] (in golf) palo *m* de madera **2** [c] (in bowls) bola *f*

D (cask, barrel): **matured** *o* **aged in the ~** añejado en barril

wood: **~ carving** *n* **1** [u] (technique) tallado *m* en madera **2** [c] (object) talla *f* (de madera); **~cock** *n* (*pl* **-cocks** *or* **-cock**) becada *f*, chocha *f*; **~cut** *n* grabado *m*; **~cutter** *n* leñador, -dora *m,f*

wooded /ˈwʊdəd || ˈwʊdɪd/ *adj* boscoso

wooden /ˈwʊdn̩/ *adj* **1** (made of wood) de madera; **~ leg** pata *f* de palo (fam) **2** (stiff) ‹*expression*› rígido; ‹*performance*› acartonado

wood: **~land** /ˈwʊdlənd/ *n* [u] (*often pl*) bosque *m*; (*before n*) ‹*birds/plants*› de los bosques; **~louse** *n* (*pl* **-lice** /-laɪs/) cochinilla *f*, chanchito *m* (Andes, CS fam); **~pecker** /ˈwʊdˌpekər || ˈwʊdˌpekə(r)/ *n* pájaro *m* carpintero, pico *m* (barreno *or* carpintero); **~ pigeon** *n* paloma *f* torcaz; **~pile** *n* (AmE) montón *m* de leña; **~ pulp** *n* [u] (ground wood) pulpa *f* de madera; (with added chemicals) pasta *f* de papel; **~shed** *n* leñera *f*; **~wind** /ˈwʊdwɪnd/ *n* (*pl* **~wind** *or* **~winds**) **the ~wind(s)** los instrumentos de viento de madera; **~work** *n* [u] **1** (wooden fittings) carpintería *f*; ***to come*** *o* ***crawl out of the ~work*** (colloq) salir* de quién sabe dónde (fam) **2** (BrE) ▸ **~working**; **~working** *n* [u] (AmE) (carpentry) carpintería *f*; (cabinet making) ebanistería *f*; (craftwork) artesanía *f* en madera; **~worm** *n* (*pl* **~worm**) **1** [c] (larva) carcoma *f*, polilla *f* de la madera **2** [u] (infestation): **the table's full of ~worm** la mesa está llena de carcoma *or* está toda carcomida

woody /ˈwʊdi/ *adj* **-dier, -diest** leñoso

woof *n*

A [c] /wʊf/ (of dog) (colloq) ladrido *m*; **~ ~!** ¡guau guau!

B [u] /wuːf/ (Tex) trama *f*

wool /wʊl/ *n* [u] lana *f*; **pure new ~** pura lana virgen; ***to pull the ~ over sb's eyes*** engañar a algn, taparle el cielo con un harnero a algn (RPl)

woolen, (BrE) **woollen** /ˈwʊlən/ *adj* de lana

woolens, (BrE) **woollens** /ˈwʊlənz/ *pl n* (Clothes) prendas *fpl* de lana

wooly¹, (BrE) **woolly** /ˈwʊli/ *adj* **-lier, -liest** **1** ‹*hat/sweater*› de lana **2** (unclear) ‹*thinking/argument*› vago, impreciso

wooly², (BrE) **woolly** *n* (*pl* **-lies**) (colloq) prenda *f* de lana

woozy /ˈwuːzi/ *adj* **-zier, -ziest** (colloq) atontado, grogui (fam)

wop /wɑːp || wɒp/ *n* (sl & offensive) italiano, -na *m,f*, bachicha *mf* (CS fam, a veces pey), tano, -na *m,f* (RPl fam & pey)

word¹ /wɜːrd || wɜːd/ *n*

A [c] (term, expression) palabra *f*, vocablo *m* (frml), voz *f* (frml); **'greenhouse' is written as one ~** 'greenhouse' se escribe todo junto; **it's a long** *o* **big ~** es una palabra difícil; **bad** *o* **naughty** *o* **rude ~** palabrota *f*, mala palabra *f* (esp AmL), garabato *m* (Chi); **what's the German ~ for 'dog'?** ¿cómo se dice 'perro' en alemán?, **what's another ~ for 'holiday'?** dame un sinónimo de 'holiday'; **he was ... what's the ~? ... excommunicated** lo ... ¿cómo se dice? ... lo excomulgaron; **she was lucky — lucky isn't the ~!** tuvo suerte — ¡suerte es poco decir!; **for want of a better ~** por así decirlo; **he didn't say so in so many ~s, but that's what he meant** no lo dijo así *or* con esas palabras, pero eso es lo que quiso decir; **in other ~s** (introducing a reformulation) es decir, o sea; **I have serious doubts about it — in other ~s you don't trust me** tengo mis serias dudas al respecto — lo que me estás diciendo es que no me tienes confianza; **she's been promoted again — ~s fail me!** la han vuelto a ascender — ¡no me lo puedo creer!; **to have a way with ~s** tener* mucha labia *or* facilidad de palabra; **it was too funny for ~s** fue graciosísimo; ***to be lost for ~s*** no encontrar* palabras, no saber* qué decir

B [c] (thing said) palabra *f*; **a ~ of warning** una advertencia; **a ~ of advice** un consejo; **I didn't say a ~!** ¡yo no dije nada!; **she left without a ~** se fue sin decir nada; **I can't hear a ~ you're saying** no te oigo nada; **I don't believe a ~ of it** no me lo creo; **she doesn't speak a ~ of English** no habla ni una palabra de inglés; **you're twisting my ~s!** ¡estás tergiversando lo que dije!; **he always has a kind ~ for everybody** es amable con todo el mundo; **famous last ~s!** (set phrase): **nothing can possibly go wrong —famous last ~s!** nada puede salir mal —¡sí, créetelo! (iró); **without a ~ of a lie** (BrE) ¡palabra (de honor)!; ***by ~ of mouth***: **the news spread by ~ of mouth** la noticia se fue transmitiendo *or* propagando de boca en boca; **people got to know about it by ~ of mouth** la gente se enteró porque se corrió la voz; ***from the ~ go*** desde el primer momento *or* desde el principio, desde el vamos (CS); ***the last ~***: **to have the last ~** tener* *or* decir* la última palabra; **the last ~ in computers** la última palabra en computadoras; ***to eat one's ~s***: **I was forced to eat my ~s** me tuve que tragar lo que había dicho; ***to get a ~ in edgewise*** *o* (BrE) ***edgeways*** meter baza, meter la cuchara (fam); ***to hang on sb's every ~*** sorber las palabras de algn; ***to have a ~ with sb about sth*** hablar con algn de *or* sobre algo; ***to have a ~ in sb's ear about sth*** (BrE) hablar en privado con algn de *or* sobre algo; ***to have ~s with sb*** tener* unas palabras con algn; ***to put in a (good) ~ for sb*** recomendar* a algn; (for sb in trouble) interceder por algn; ***to put ~s into sb's mouth***

W

atribuirle* a algn algo que no dijo; ***to take the ~s out of sb's mouth*** quitarle la(s) palabra(s) de la boca a algn; ***to waste ~s*** gastar saliva; ***to weigh one's ~s*** medir* sus (*or* mis *etc*) palabras; ***there's many a true ~ spoken in jest!*** lo dices en broma, pero ...; ▸**mince**[1]

C (assurance) (*no pl*) palabra *f*; **to keep/give one's ~** cumplir/dar* su (*or* mi *etc*) palabra; **to break one's ~, to go back on one's ~** faltar a su (*or* mi *etc*) palabra; **we only have his ~ for it** no tenemos pruebas de ello, solo su palabra; **you can take my ~ for it** te lo aseguro; **a man of his ~** un hombre de palabra; ***to be as good as one's ~***: **he was there all right, as good as his ~** allí estaba, tal como lo había prometido; ***to take sb at her/his ~*** tomarle la palabra a algn

D 1 [u] (news, message): **there is still no ~ of survivors** todavía no se sabe si hay supervivientes; **she left ~ with her secretary that ...** dejó recado con la secretaria de que ..., le dejó dicho a la secretaria que ... (CS); **~ has it that ...** corre la noticia *or* el rumor *or* la voz de que ..., dicen que ..., se dice que ...; **to put the ~ out** *o* **about that ...** hacer* correr la voz de que ... 2 (instruction): **if you need a hand just say the ~** si quieres que te ayude no tienes más que pedirlo; **to give the ~ (to + INF)** dar* la orden (de + INF)

E **words** *pl* 1 (lyrics) letra *f* 2 (Theat): **he forgot his ~s** se le olvidó lo que tenía que decir

F [c] (Comput) palabra *f*

G 1 (Bib) **the W~** el Verbo 2 (Relig) **the ~** el evangelio, la palabra de Dios

word[2] *vt* ‹*document/letter*› redactar; ‹*question*› formular

word for word *adv* ‹*repeat/copy*› palabra por palabra, textualmente; ‹*translate*› literalmente, palabra por palabra

wording /ˈwɜːrdɪŋ || ˈwɜːdɪŋ/ *n* (of paragraph, letter) redacción *f*; (of question) formulación *f*

word: **~ of mouth** *n* 1 [u] (speech): **they rely on ~ of mouth for publicity** su publicidad depende de la recomendación verbal *or* de palabra 2 (*before n*): **a ~-of-mouth recommendation** una recomendación verbal *or* de palabra; **~-perfect** /ˈwɜːrdˈpɜːrfɪkt || ˌwɜːdˈpɜːfɪkt/ *adj*: **he studied the part until he was ~-perfect** se estudió el papel hasta que se lo supo perfectamente *or* al dedillo; **~play** *n* [u] juegos *mpl* de palabras; **~ processing** *n* [u] tratamiento *m* de textos, procesamiento *m* de textos *or* de palabras; **~ processor** *n* procesador *m* de textos *or* de palabras

wordy /ˈwɜːrdi || ˈwɜːdi/ *adj* **-dier, -diest** verboso, farragoso

wore /wɔːr || wɔː(r)/ *past of* **wear**[2]

work[1] /wɜːrk || wɜːk/ *n*

A [u] (labor, tasks) trabajo *m*; **it was a lot of ~** dio mucho trabajo; **the building ~ is still going on** todavía están en obras; **~ has already started on the film** ya han empezado a filmar *or* rodar; **she's got a lot of ~ to do to catch up** va a tener que trabajar mucho para ponerse al día; **the house needs a lot of ~ done** *o* (BrE) **doing to it** la casa necesita muchos arreglos; **she put a lot of ~ into it** puso mucho esfuerzo *or* empeño en ello; **to set to ~** ponerse* a trabajar, poner* manos a la obra; **keep up the good ~** ¡sigue (*or* sigan *etc*) así!; **it's hard ~ digging** cavar es muy duro; **that was quick ~!** ¡qué rapidez!; **I've done a good day's ~** he aprovechado bien el día; ***it's all in a day's ~*** es el pan nuestro de cada día; ***to have one's ~ cut out***: **she's going to have her ~ cut out to get the job done in time** le va a costar terminar el trabajo a tiempo; ***to make short ~ of sth***: **Pete made short ~ of the ironing** Pete planchó todo rapidísimo; **you made short ~ of that pizza!** ¡te has despachado pronto la pizza!; ***all ~ and no play makes Jack a dull boy*** hay que dejar tiempo para el esparcimiento

B [u] (employment) trabajo *m*; **she does a lot of ~ for the government** trabaja mucho para el gobierno; **to look for/find ~** buscar*/encontrar* trabajo; **to go to ~** ir* a trabajar *or* al trabajo; **they both go out to ~** (BrE) los dos trabajan (afuera); **I start/finish ~ at seven** entro a trabajar *or* al trabajo/salgo del trabajo a las siete

C (*in phrases*) **at work**: **he's at ~** está en el trabajo, está en la oficina (*or* la fábrica *etc*); **they were hard at ~** estaban muy ocupados trabajando; **other forces were at ~** intervenían otros factores, había otros factores en juego; Ⓢ **men at work** obras, hombres trabajando; **in work** (BrE): **those in ~** quienes tienen trabajo; **off work**: **she was off ~ for a month after the accident** después del accidente estuvo un mes sin trabajar; **he took a day off ~** se tomó un día libre; **out of work**: **the closures will put 1,200 people out of ~** los cierres dejarán en la calle a 1.200 personas; **to be out of ~** estar* sin trabajo *or* desocupado *or* desempleado *or* (Chi tb) cesante, estar* parado *or* en el paro (Esp); (*before n*) **out-of-work** desocupado, desempleado, parado (Esp), cesante (Chi)

D 1 [c] (product, single item) obra *f*; **a ~ of art** una obra de arte 2 [u] (output) trabajo *m*; **a piece of ~** un trabajo; **an exhibition of recent ~ by Sam Pym** una exposición de obras recientes de Sam Pym; **it was the ~ of a professional** era obra de un profesional; *see also* **works**

work[2] *vi*

A «*person*» trabajar; **I ~ as a receptionist** trabajo de recepcionista; **he ~s nights** trabaja de noche; **to get ~ing** ponerse* a trabajar, poner* manos a la obra; **to ~ hard** trabajar mucho *or* duro; **we ~ a 40-hour week** nuestra semana laboral es de 40 horas; **to ~ AT sth**: **you have to ~ at your service** tiene que practicar el servicio; **a relationship is something you have to ~ at** una relación de pareja requiere cierto esfuerzo; **she was ~ing away at her accounts** estaba ocupada con su contabilidad; **to ~ FOR sb** trabajar PARA algn; **to ~ for oneself** trabajar por cuenta propia; **to ~ FOR sth**: **fame didn't just come to me: I had to ~ for it** la fama no me llegó del cielo, tuve que trabajar para conseguirla; **he's ~ing for his finals** está estudiando *or* está preparándose para los exámenes finales; **to ~ IN sth**: **to ~ in marble** trabajar el mármol *or* con mármol; **to ~ in oils** pintar al óleo, trabajar con óleos; **to ~ ON sth**: **he's ~ing on his car** está arreglando el coche; **scientists are ~ing on a cure** los científicos están intentando encontrar una cura; **she hasn't been fired yet, but she's ~ing on it** (hum) todavía no la han echado, pero parece empeñada en que lo hagan; **we're ~ing on the assumption that ...** partimos del supuesto de que ...; **the police had very little to ~ on** la policía tenía muy pocas pistas; **to ~ UNDER sb** trabajar bajo la dirección de algn

B 1 (operate, function) «*machine/system*» funcionar; «*drug/person*» actuar*; **to ~ against/in favor of sb/sth** obrar en contra/a favor de algn/algo; ***it ~s both ways***: **you have to make an effort too, you know: it ~s both ways** tú también tienes que hacer el esfuerzo, ¿sabes? funciona igual *or* (esp AmL) parejo para los dos 2 (have required effect) «*drug/plan/method*» surtir efecto; **her idea didn't ~** su idea no resultó; **try it, it might ~** pruébalo, quizás resulte; **the play doesn't ~ on TV** la obra no se presta para televisión; **these colors just don't ~ together** estos colores no pegan *or* no combinan

C (slip, travel) (+ *adv compl*): **the oil has to ~ through the engine** el aceite tiene que circular por el motor; **his socks had ~ed down to his ankles** se le habían caído los calcetines; *see also* **free**[1] **A3**, **loose**[1] **A2**

■ **work** *vt*

A 1 (force to work) hacer* trabajar; **to ~ oneself to death** matarse trabajando 2 (exploit) ‹*land/soil*› trabajar, labrar; ‹*mine*› explotar 3 ‹*nightclubs/casinos*› trabajar en 4 (pay for by working): **he ~ed his passage to Australia** se costeó el pasaje a Australia trabajando en el barco

B (cause to operate): **do you know how to ~ the machine?** ¿sabes manejar la máquina?; **this lever ~s the sprinkler system** esta palanca acciona el sistema de riego; **the pump is ~ed by hand** la bomba funciona manualmente

C 1 (move gradually, manipulate) (+ *adv compl*): **~ the brush into the corners** mete bien el cepillo en los rincones; **I'll try to ~ that quote into the article** trataré de meter esa cita en el artículo; ***to ~ one's way***: **we ~ed our way toward the exit** nos abrimos camino hacia la salida; **I ~ed my way through volume three** logré terminar el tercer volumen; **she ~ed her way to the top of her profession** trabajó hasta llegar a la cima de su profesión 2 (shape, fashion) ‹*clay/metal*› trabajar; ‹*dough*› sobar, amasar; **~ the flour into the mixture** vaya añadiendo la harina a la mezcla

D 1 (*past & past p* **worked** *or* **wrought**) (bring about) ‹*miracle*› hacer*; *see also* **wrought**[1] 2 (manage, arrange) (colloq) arreglar; **she ~ed it so that I didn't have to pay** se las arregló *or* se las ingenió para que yo no tuviera que pagar

(Phrasal verbs)

- **work off** [v ▸ o ▸ adv, v ▸ adv ▸ o] (get rid of): **you can ~ off a few kilos in the gym** puede rebajar algunos kilos en el gimnasio
- **work out**

(Sense I) [v ▸ adv]

A **1** (turn out) salir*, resultar; **to ~ out well/badly** salir* *or* resultar bien/mal; **to ~ out AT sth: it ~s out at $75 a head** sale (a) 75 dólares por cabeza **2** (be successful) «*plan*» salir* bien

B (train, exercise) (Sport) hacer* ejercicio

(Sense II) [v ▸ o ▸ adv, v ▸ adv ▸ o]

A **1** (solve) ‹*sum*› hacer*; ‹*riddle/puzzle*› resolver*; **things will ~ themselves out** las cosas se arreglarán solas; **they've got to ~ things out for themselves** tienen que resolver las cosas por sí mismos **2** (find, calculate) ‹*percentage/probability*› calcular; **have you ~ed out the answer?** ¿lo has resuelto? **3** (understand) entender*; **I couldn't ~ out what he meant** no lograba entender qué quería decir

B (devise, determine) ‹*solution*› idear, encontrar*; ‹*plan*› elaborar, idear; ‹*procedure*› idear, desarrollar; **we've ~ed out a deal with the unions** hemos llegado a un acuerdo con los sindicatos; **the details still have to be ~ed out** todavía falta finalizar los detalles; **I've got to ~ out what to do with the money** tengo que decidir qué hacer con el dinero; **to have it all ~ed out** tenerlo* todo resuelto *or* planeado

C (complete) ‹*prison sentence*› cumplir; **to ~ out one's notice** trabajar hasta el final del período de preaviso

- **work over** [v ▸ o ▸ adv] (sl) darle* una paliza a, sacarle* la mugre a (AmL fam)
- **work up** [v ▸ o ▸ adv, v ▸ adv ▸ o] **1** (stimulate): **they had ~ed up an appetite** se les había abierto el apetito; **I couldn't ~ up much enthusiasm** no me entusiasmaba demasiado; **to ~ up a sweat** empezar* a sudar **2** (excite, arouse): **she gets very ~ed up about it** se pone como loca; **to ~ sb/oneself up INTO sth: she ~s herself up into a state** se pone como loca; **they had been ~ed up into a frenzy** los habían puesto frenéticos, los habían exaltado
- **work up to** [v ▸ adv ▸ prep ▸ o]: **the action ~s up to a climax** la trama se desarrolla hasta llegar a un clímax; **I wonder what he's ~ing up to** me pregunto qué se propone

workable /ˈwɜːrkəbəl || ˈwɜːkəbəl/ *adj* **1** ‹*arrangement/solution*› factible, viable **2** ‹*mine/deposits*› explotable

workaday /ˈwɜːrkədeɪ || ˈwɜːkədeɪ/ *adj* (everyday) ‹*event/clothes*› de todos los días; (prosaic) prosaico, banal

workaholic /ˈwɜːrkəˈhɔːlɪk || ˌwɜːkəˈhɒlɪk/ *n* (colloq) trabajoadicto, -ta *m,f*, fanático, -ca *m,f* del trabajo

work: **~basket** *n* costurero *m*; **~bench** *n* banco *m or* mesa *f* de trabajo; **~book** *n* cuaderno *m* de ejercicios; **~day** *n* **1** (part of day) jornada *f* laboral; **a seven-hour ~day** una jornada laboral de siete horas **2** (weekday) día *m* hábil *or* laborable *or* laboral *or* de trabajo

worker /ˈwɜːrkər || ˈwɜːkə(r)/ *n* **1** trabajador, -dora *m,f*; **he's a good/slow ~** trabaja bien/lentamente; **office ~** oficinista *mf*, empleado, -da *m,f* de oficina, administrativo, -va *m,f*; **building ~s** obreros *mpl* de la construcción **2** (ant, bee) obrera *f*

work: **~ force** *n* [u] (of nation) población *f* activa; (of company) personal *m*, planta *f* laboral, plantilla *f* (Esp); **~house** *n* (BrE Hist) asilo *m* de pobres (*que debían trabajar a cambio de comida y alojamiento*)

working /ˈwɜːrkɪŋ || ˈwɜːkɪŋ/ *adj* (*before n*)

A **1** ‹*mother/parent*› que trabaja; **~ population** población *f* activa; **of ~ age** en edad de trabajar; **it's still a ~ farm** sigue funcionando como granja **2** ‹*hours/conditions*› de trabajo; **all my ~ life** toda mi vida activa *or* laboral; **we have a good ~ relationship** trabajamos muy bien juntos

B **1** (capable of operating): **it's in perfect ~ order** funciona perfectamente **2** (suitable for working with) ‹*hypothesis*› de trabajo; **I have a ~ knowledge of Russian** tengo conocimientos básicos de ruso; **a ~ majority** una mayoría suficiente

working: **~ class** *n* (*sometimes pl*) **the ~ class(es)** la clase obrera *or* trabajadora; **~-class** /ˈwɜːrkɪŋˈklæs || ˌwɜːkɪŋˈklɑːs/ *adj* ‹*person*› de clase obrera *or* trabajadora; ‹*area*› obrero; **~ day** *n* **1** (weekday) día *m* hábil *or* laborable *or* laboral *or* de trabajo; **allow 3 ~ days for the order to arrive** el pedido tardará tres días hábiles en llegar **2** ▸ **workday 1**; **~ party** *n* equipo *m or* grupo *m* de trabajo

workings /ˈwɜːrkɪŋz || ˈwɜːkɪŋz/ *pl n* (of machine) funcionamiento *m*

work: **~load** *n* (volumen *m* de) trabajo *m*; **~man** /ˈwɜːrkmən || ˈwɜːkmən/ *n* (*pl* **-men** /-mən/) obrero *m*; ***a bad ~man always blames his tools*** el cojo siempre le echa la culpa al empedrado

workmanlike /ˈwɜːrkmənlaɪk || ˈwɜːkmənlaɪk/ *adj* eficiente, profesional

workmanship /ˈwɜːrkmənʃɪp || ˈwɜːkmənʃɪp/ *n* [u] (of craftsman) trabajo *m*; (of object) factura *f*; **a fine piece of ~** un trabajo esmerado; **it's just poor ~** no es más que falta de habilidad profesional; **a piece of fine ~** una pieza de excelente factura

work: **~mate** *n* (BrE) compañero, -ra *m,f* de trabajo; **~out** *n* sesión *f* de ejercicios *or* gimnasia; **~ permit** *n* permiso *m* de trabajo, trabajo *m*; **~place** *n* lugar *m* de trabajo, trabajo *m*; **~-related** /ˈwɜːrkrɪˌleɪtəd || ˈwɜːkrɪˌleɪtɪd/ *adj* ‹*illness*› laboral, relacionado con el trabajo; ‹*stress/issue*› relacionado con el trabajo; **is it ~-related?** ¿está relacionado con el trabajo?; **~room** *n* taller *m*

works /wɜːrks || wɜːks/ *n*

A (actions) (liter) (+ *pl vb*) obras *fpl*

B (engineering operations) (+ *pl vb*) obras *fpl*; **road ~** obras viales

C (factory) (+ *sing or pl vb*) fábrica *f*

D (mechanism) (+ *pl vb*) mecanismo *m*

E (all) (colloq): **there were candles, soft music, the ~!** había velas, música ambiental y toda la historia (fam); ***to give sb the ~*** (give lavish treatment) tratar a algn a cuerpo de rey; (beat up) pegarle* la paliza del siglo a algn (fam), sacarle* la mugre a algn (AmL fam)

work: **~ shadowing** *n* [u] *observación directa de una persona en su puesto de trabajo*; **~sheet** *n* **1** (record of work) hoja *f* de trabajo **2** (exercise sheet) (BrE) hoja *f* de ejercicios; **~shop** *n* taller *m*; **~shy** *adj* haragán, vago (fam), flojo (fam); **~station** *n* (Comput) terminal *m* de trabajo; **~surface** *n* **1** (area) superficie *f* de trabajo **2** ▸ **~top**; **~top** *n* encimera *f*, mesada *f* (RPl); **~-to-rule** /ˈwɜːrktəˈruːl || ˌwɜːktəˈruːl/ *n* huelga *f* pasiva *or* (Esp) de celo, trabajo *m* a reglamento (CS)

world /wɜːrld || wɜːld/ *n*

A (earth) mundo *m*; **the longest bridge in the ~** el puente más largo del mundo; **he proved that the ~ was round** demostró que la tierra era redonda; **to see the ~** ver* mundo; **politicians from all over the ~** políticos de todo el mundo; **to travel all over the ~** viajar por todo el mundo; **there were celebrations all over the ~** *o* **the ~ over** hubo festejos en todo el mundo *or* en el mundo entero; **it's a strange ~!** ¡qué mundo éste!; **the best of all possible ~s** el mejor de los mundos; **~'s** (AmE) *o* (BrE) **~ record time** récord *m or* marca *f* mundial; ***(it's a) small ~!*** el mundo es un pañuelo, ¡qué pequeño *or* (AmL) chico es el mundo!; ***the ~ is his/her oyster*** tiene el mundo a sus pies; ***to be dead*** *o* ***lost to the ~*** estar* profundamente dormido; ***to be out of this ~*** «*food/music*» ser* increíble *or* fantástico; ***to bring sb into the ~*** traer* a algn al mundo; ***to come into the ~*** venir* al mundo; ***to have the best of both ~s*** tener* todas las ventajas; ***money makes the ~ go around*** poderoso caballero es don dinero; (*before n*) ‹*economy/peace*› mundial; ‹*politics/trade*› internacional

B **1** (people generally) mundo *m*; **what is the ~ coming to?** ¿adónde vamos a ir a parar?; **he thinks the ~ owes him a living** piensa que tiene derecho a vivir sin trabajar; ***to watch the ~ go by*** ver* pasar a la gente **2** (society): **they've gone up in the ~** han prosperado mucho (*or* hecho fortuna *etc*); **a woman/man of the ~** una mujer/un hombre de mundo; **that's the way of the ~** ¡así es la vida!

C (specific period, group) mundo *m*; **the art ~** el mundo del arte; **to live in a ~ of one's own** vivir en su (*or* mi *etc*) propio mundo

D (*as intensifier*): **there's a ~ of difference between ...** hay una diferencia enorme entre ..., hay un abismo entre ...; **we are ~s apart** no tenemos nada que ver, somos como el día y la noche; **it did her a ~ of good** le hizo la mar de bien; **he thinks the ~ of her** tiene un altísimo concepto de ella; **for all the ~ as if nothing had happened** tal como si no hubiera pasado nada; **to have all the time in the ~** tener* todo el tiempo del mundo; **without a care in the ~** sin ninguna preocupación; **nothing in the ~ will make me change my mind** nada en el mundo me hará cambiar de opinión; **who in the ~ is going to believe that?** ¿quién diablos *or* demonios se va a creer eso? (fam)

E (Relig): **this/the other ~** este/el otro mundo; **the ~ to come** el más allá

world: ~ **Bank** *n* **the W~ Bank** el Banco Mundial; ~ **champion** *n* campeón, -peona *m,f* mundial; ~ **championship** *n* campeonato *m* mundial; **~-class** *adj* de talla mundial; ~ **Cup** *n* **the W~ Cup** el Mundial, la Copa del Mundo; **~-famous** /ˈwɜːrld ˈfeɪməs || ˌwɜːldfˈfeɪməs/ *adj* mundialmente famoso, de fama mundial; ~ **leader** *n* (Pol) *jefe de estado de una gran potencia*

World Series

Las series de encuentros de béisbol que tienen lugar cada año para elegir al mejor equipo profesional de béisbol de EEUU

worldly /ˈwɜːrldli || ˈwɜːldli/ *adj* **1** ‹*goods*› material; ‹*desires*› mundano **2** ‹*person*› de mucho mundo; ‹*manner/charm*› sofisticado

worldly-wise /ˈwɜːrldliˈwaɪz || ˌwɜːldliˈwaɪz/ *adj* de mucho mundo

world: ~ **record** *n* récord *m or* marca *f* mundial; (*before n*) **~-record holder** plusmarquista *mf* mundial; ~ **Series** *n* (in US baseball) **the W~ Series** la Serie Mundial, el campeonato mundial de béisbol; ~ **War** *n* guerra *f* mundial; **W~ War One/Two** la primera/segunda Guerra Mundial; **~-weary** *adj* **-rier, -riest** ‹*person*› cansado de la vida, hastiado; ‹*attitude*› de hastío

worldwide[1] /ˈwɜːrldˈwaɪd || ˌwɜːldˈwaɪd/ *adj* mundial

worldwide[2] *adv* ‹*travel*› por todo el mundo; **they are famous ~** son mundialmente famosos

worm[1] /wɜːrm || wɜːm/ *n* **1** (*earth~*) gusano *m*, lombriz *f* (de tierra); (as term of abuse) gusano *m*; ***the ~ turns*** la paciencia se agota *or* tiene un límite **2** (maggot) gusano *m* **3** **worms** *pl* (Med) lombrices *fpl*; **he never stops eating: he must have ~s** no para de comer, debe tener la (lombriz) solitaria

worm[2] *vt*

A **1** (wriggle): ***to ~ one's way*** (+ *adv compl*): **she ~ed her way** *o* **herself into their confidence** se ganó su confianza con astucia **2** **to ~ sth OUT OF sb** ‹*secret/information*› sonsacarle* algo A algn

B (Vet Sci) ‹*dog/cat*› desparasitar

worm-eaten /ˈwɜːrmˌiːtn̩ || ˈwɜːmˌiːtn̩/ *adj* ‹*fruit*› agusanado; ‹*wood*› carcomido

worn[1] /wɔːrn || wɔːn/ *past p of* **wear**[2]

worn[2] *adj* ‹*tire/clothes*› gastado; ‹*carpet*› raído, desgastado; ‹*flagstones/steps*› desgastado, gastado

worn-out /ˈwɔːrnˈaʊt || ˌwɔːnˈaʊt/ *adj* (*pred* **worn out**) **1** ‹*shoes/clothes*› muy gastado **2** (exhausted) rendido, agotado

worried /ˈwɜːrid || ˈwʌrid/ *adj* ‹*look/voice*› de preocupación; ‹*person*› preocupado; **to get ~** preocuparse, inquietarse; **to be ~ ABOUT sb/sth** estar* preocupado POR algn/algo; **she's ~ that she'll lose her job** tiene miedo de perder el trabajo; **to be ~ sick** estar* preocupadísimo *or* muy preocupado

worrier /ˈwɜːriər || ˈwʌriə(r)/ *n*: **she's such a ~** se preocupa *or* se angustia tanto por todo

worry[1] /ˈwɜːri || ˈwʌri/ *n* (*pl* **-ries**) **1** [c] (trouble, problem) preocupación *f*; **that's the least of our worries** eso es lo que menos nos preocupa; **financial worries** problemas *mpl* económicos; **our eldest son is a great ~ to us** nuestro hijo mayor nos da *or* nos causa muchas preocupaciones **2** [u] (distress, anxiety) preocupación *f*, inquietud *f*; **this has been a great source of ~ to her** esto la ha tenido muy preocupada *or* inquieta

worry[2] **-ries, -rying, -ried** *vt*

A (trouble) preocupar, inquietar; **I don't want to ~ him** no quiero preocuparlo *or* inquietarlo; **what's ~ing you?** ¿qué es lo que te preocupa?; **I don't want to ~ you with my problems** no te quiero molestar con mis problemas

B **1** (harass, attack) ‹‹*dog*›› ‹*sheep*› acosar **2** (work on) ‹‹*dog*›› ‹*bone*› juguetear con

■ **worry** *vi* preocuparse, inquietarse; **there's no need to ~** no hay por qué preocuparse; **not to ~** (BrE) no te preocupes; **shall I wash the dishes? — no, don't ~** ¿quieres que lave los platos? — no, no te molestes; **to ~ ABOUT sth/sb** preocuparse POR algo/algn; **I ~ about her living on her own** me preocupa que viva sola; **I still owe you some money — no, don't ~ about it** aún te debo dinero — no, déjalo

worrying /ˈwɜːriŋ || ˈwʌriŋ/ *adj* inquietante, preocupante

worse[1] /wɜːrs || wɜːs/ *adj* (*comp of* **bad**[1]) peor; **cheer up! it could be ~** ¡anímate! podría ser peor; **these scissors are ~ than useless** estas tijeras no sirven para nada; **the play wasn't very good, but I've seen ~** la obra no era muy buena, pero las he visto peores; **he couldn't have phoned at a ~ time** no podía haber llamado en peor momento *or* en un momento menos oportuno; **he could've been hurt or ~** podría haber resultado herido, o podría haberle pasado algo peor; **to get ~** empeorar; **Grandad has got ~ since he's been in hospital** el abuelo se ha puesto peor desde que está en el hospital; **his hearing is getting ~ and ~** oye cada vez menos; **things are getting ~ and ~** las cosas van de mal en peor, las cosas están cada vez peor; **if you scratch it, it'll only make it ~** si te rascas, es peor; **to make things ~, it started snowing** por si fuera poco, empezó a nevar; **what was ~ was that ...** peor aún fue que ...; **they looked none the ~ for their misadventure** no tenían mal aspecto a pesar de su desventura

worse[2] *adv* (*comp of* **badly**) peor; **you could do ~ than take that job** harías bien en aceptar ese trabajo

worse[3] *n* **the ~** el (*or* la *etc*) peor; **a change for the ~** un cambio para mal; **he's taken a turn for the ~** se ha puesto peor, ha empeorado

worsen /ˈwɜːrsn̩ || ˈwɜːsn̩/ *vi/t* empeorar

worse-off /ˈwɜːrsɔːf || ˌwɜːsˈɒf/ *adj* (*pred* **worse off**) **1** (financially) en peor posición económica; **I ended up $50 ~ ~** *o* **~ ~ by $50** salí perdiendo 50 dólares **2** (emotionally, physically) (*pred*) **to be ~ ~** estar* peor

worship[1] /ˈwɜːrʃəp || ˈwɜːʃɪp/ *n*

A [u] culto *m*, adoración *f*; **sun ~** el culto al sol, la adoración del sol; **freedom of ~** libertad *f* de cultos; **an object of ~** un objeto de veneración; **act of ~** ceremonia *f* religiosa

B [c] **Worship** (as title): **Your/His W~** (of magistrate) Su Señoría; (of mayor) el señor alcalde

worship[2], (BrE) **-pp-** *vt* ‹*God*› adorar, venerar, rendir* culto a; ‹*success/wealth*› rendir* culto a; ‹*hero*› idolatrar; **he ~s her** la adora

■ **worship** *vi* (Relig): **the church where we ~** nuestra iglesia

worshipper /ˈwɜːrʃəpər || ˈwɜːʃɪpə(r)/ *n* (Relig) fiel *m*; **~s of Baal** los adoradores de Baal

worst[1] /wɜːrst || wɜːst/ *adj* (*superl of* **bad**[1]) peor; **he's the ~ student in the class** es el peor alumno de la clase; **he ran his ~ ever race** corrió peor que nunca; **~ of all** lo peor de todo; **the ~ thing about her is her selfishness** lo peor que tiene es lo egoísta que es

worst[2] *adv* (*superl of* **badly**): **she did (the) ~ (of all) in both exams** le fue peor que a nadie en los dos exámenes

worst[3] *n*

A **the ~** **1** (+ *sing vb*) lo peor; **his sister brings out the ~ in him** cuando está con su hermana está peor que nunca; ***if (the) ~ comes to (the) ~*** en el peor de los casos; ***to get*** *o* ***have the ~ of it*** salir* perdiendo, llevarse la peor parte **2** (+ *pl vb*) los peores

B **1** **at worst** en el peor de los casos **2** **at her/his/its worst**: **I'm at my ~ in the morning** la mañana es mi peor momento del día; **this is racism at its ~** esto es racismo de la peor especie

worsted /ˈwʊrstəd || ˈwʊstɪd/ *n* [u] estambre *m*

worth[1] /wɜːrθ || wɜːθ/ *adj* (*pred*) **1** (equal in value to) **to be ~** valer*; **it's ~ $200/a lot of money** vale $200/mucho dinero; **it's a nice coat, but it isn't ~ the money** el abrigo es bonito, pero no como para pagar ese precio; **goods ~ £5,000 were stolen** robaron mercancías por valor de 5.000 libras; **she must be ~ millions** debe ser

W

millonaria; **how much is it ~?** ¿cuánto vale?; **how much is it ~ for me to keep quiet about it?** ¿cuánto me dan por no decir nada?; **it's more than my job's ~ to let you in** estoy arriesgando el puesto si te dejo entrar; **they ran for all they were ~** corrieron con todas sus fuerzas *or* a más no poder; **this is my opinion, for what it's ~** ésta es mi opinión, si es que a alguien le interesa 2 (worthy of): **the museum is ~ a visit** vale *or* merece la pena visitar el museo; **it's ~ a try** vale *or* merece la pena intentarlo; **it might be ~ checking whether they've received it** convendría comprobar si lo han recibido; **that's ~ knowing** es bueno saberlo; **don't argue with them, it isn't ~ it** no discutas con ellos, no vale *or* no merece la pena; **you keep an eye on him, and I'll make it ~ your while** tú vigílalo, que yo ya te compensaré; **if a job's ~ doing, it's ~ doing well** (set phrase) si se hace un trabajo, hay que hacerlo bien

worth² *n* [u] 1 (equivalent): **$2,000 dollars' ~ of furniture** muebles por valor de 2.000 dólares 2 (of thing) valor *m*; (of person) valía *f*; **to prove one's ~** demostrar* su (*or* mi *etc*) valía

worthless /ˈwɜːrθləs || ˈwɜːθlɪs/ *adj* ‹*object*› sin ningún valor; ‹*person*› despreciable; **to be ~** no tener* ningún valor, no valer* nada

worthwhile /ˈwɜːrθˈhwaɪl || wɜːθˈwaɪl/ *adj* ‹*enterprise/project*› que vale la pena; **the look on their faces made it all ~** valió *or* mereció la pena sólo por ver la cara que pusieron

worthy¹ /ˈwɜːrði || ˈwɜːði/ *adj* **-thier, -thiest**

A 1 (appropriate, equal) ‹*opponent/successor*› digno; **to be ~ OF sth/sb** ser* digno DE algo/algn; **this work isn't ~ of you** este trabajo te desmerece *or* no está a tu altura 2 (deserving) **~ OF sth** digno DE algo; **a point ~ of mention** algo digno de mención, algo que vale *or* merece la pena mencionar; **to be ~ OF sth** ser* digno *or* merecedor DE algo

B (good, estimable) ‹*person*› respetable, honorable; ‹*attempt*› encomiable, meritorio; **a ~ cause** una buena causa

worthy² *n* (*pl* **-thies**) personaje *m* importante *or* ilustre

would /wʊd/ *v mod* [**'d** *es la contracción de* **would**, **wouldn't** *de* **would not** *y* **'d've** *de* **would have**]

A *past of* **will¹**

B 1 (in conditional sentences): **I ~ if I could** lo haría si pudiera; **if I had known, I ~n't have come** si lo hubiera sabido no habría *or* no hubiera venido; **who ~ have thought it?** ¿quién lo hubiera *or* habría pensado? 2 (giving advice): **I ~ have a word with her about it (if I were you)** yo (que tú) lo hablaba *or* hablaría con ella 3 (tentatively expressing opinions): **I ~ agree with Roy** yo estoy de acuerdo con Roy, yo diría que Roy tiene razón

C (expressing wishes): **I wish you'd stop pestering me!** ¡deja de fastidiarme por Dios!; **if only she'd take your advice** ¡si siguiera tus consejos ... !, ¡ojalá siguiera tus consejos!

D 1 (in requests): **~ you type this for me please?** ¿me haría el favor de pasar esto a máquina?; **go and call him, ~ you?** ve a llamarlo ¿sí? *or* ¿me haces el favor? 2 (in invitations): **~ you like a cup of coffee?** ¿quieres una taza de café?; **~ you like to come with us? — I'd love to** ¿quieres *or* te gustaría venir con nosotros? — me encantaría

E 1 (expressing criticism): **she *would* (have to) spoil the surprise** tenía que estropear la sorpresa, ¡típico! *or* ¡no podía fallar! 2 (indicating sth is natural): **he said no — well, he ~, ~n't he?** dijo que no — bueno ¿qué otra cosa iba a decir? *or* era de esperar ¿no? *or* es lógico ¿no?

would-be /ˈwʊdbiː/ *adj* (*before n*): **a ~ star/poet** un aspirante a estrella/poeta

wouldn't /ˈwʊdn̩t/ = **would not**

would've /ˈwʊdəv/ = **would have**

wound¹ /wuːnd/ *n* herida *f*; **to reopen old ~s** abrir* viejas heridas; ***to lick one's ~s*** lamerse las heridas

wound² /wuːnd/ *vt/i* herir*

wound³ /waʊnd/ *past & past p of* **wind²** *vt Sense* **II**, *vi*

wounded¹ /ˈwuːndəd || ˈwuːndɪd/ *adj* ‹*soldier/animal/pride*› herido; ‹*look/tone*› dolido

wounded² *pl n* **the ~** los heridos

wounding /ˈwuːndɪŋ/ *adj* hiriente

wound up /ˈwaʊndˈʌp/ *adj*: **to get ~ ~** ponerse* nervioso

wove /wəʊv/ *past of* **weave¹**

woven /ˈwəʊvən/ *past p of* **weave¹**

wow¹ /waʊ/ *interj* (colloq) ¡ah!, ¡pa! (RPl fam)

wow² *vt* (sl) ‹*audience*› enloquecer* (fam), volver* loco a (fam)

WP *n* 1 [c] = **word processor** 2 [u] = **word processing**

WPC *n* (in UK) = **woman police constable**

wpm (= **words per minute**) palabras por minuto

WRAC *n* (formerly in UK) = **Women's Royal Army Corps**

WRAF *n* (formerly in UK) = **Women's Royal Air Force**

wraith /reɪθ/ *n* espectro *m*, aparición *f*

wrangle¹ /ˈræŋgəl/ *vi* 1 (argue) discutir, reñir* 2 (herd cattle) (AmE) arrear *or* (Méx) rejuntar ganado

wrangle² *n* altercado *m*, disputa *f*, riña *f*

wrangler /ˈræŋglər || ˈræŋglə(r)/ *n* (AmE) vaquero *m*, cowboy *m*

wrap¹ /ræp/ **-pp-** *vt* 1 (cover) ‹*parcel/gift*› envolver*; **to ~ sth/sb IN/WITH sth** envolver* algo/a algn EN/CON algo 2 (wind, entwine): **she ~ped a shawl about her** se envolvió en un chal; **he ~ped his arms around her** la estrechó entre sus brazos

Phrasal verb

• **wrap up**

A [v ▸ o ▸ adv, v ▸ adv ▸ o] 1 ▸**wrap¹** *vt* **1** 2 (complete) (colloq) ‹*order/sale*› conseguir*; **to ~ up a deal** cerrar* un trato 3 (conclude) (colloq) ‹*meeting*› dar* fin a; **that ~s it up for today** eso es todo por hoy 4 (engross) (colloq) **to be ~ped up IN sth**: **she's totally ~ped up in her work** no piensa más que en su trabajo, vive para su trabajo; **they're completely ~ped up in each other** no tienen ojos más que el uno para el otro

B [v ▸ adv] 1 (dress warmly) abrigarse*; **~ up well** *o* **warmly** abrígate bien 2 (shut up) (BrE colloq) cerrar* el pico (fam)

wrap² *n*

A 1 (shawl) chal *m*, pañoleta *f* 2 (robe) (AmE) bata *f*, salto *m* de cama (CS)

B (wrapper, wrapping) envoltorio *m*; ***to keep sth under ~s*** (colloq) mantener* algo en secreto; ***to take the ~s off sth*** (colloq) sacar* algo a la luz

wraparound /ˈræpəˌraʊnd/ *adj* ‹*skirt/dress*› cruzado

wrapper /ˈræpər || ˈræpə(r)/ *n* envoltorio *m*, envoltura *f*

wrapping /ˈræpɪŋ/ *n* [c u] envoltorio *m*, envoltura *f*

wrapping paper *n* [u] (plain) papel *m* de envolver; (decorative) papel *m* de regalo

wrap-up /ˈræpʌp/ *n* (AmE journ) resumen *m*

wrath /ræθ || rɒθ/ *n* [u] (liter) cólera *f*, ira *f*

wreak /riːk/ *vt* (liter) ‹*destruction/chaos*› sembrar* (liter); **they ~ed vengeance on the villagers** descargaron su venganza contra los pobladores; **to ~ havoc** causar estragos

wreath /riːθ/ *n* corona *f*

wreathe /riːð/ *vt* (liter) adornar; **the mountains were ~d in mist** las montañas estaban envueltas en bruma; **she/her face was ~d in smiles** era toda sonrisas

wreck¹ /rek/ *n*

A (ship) restos *mpl* del naufragio; (vehicle) restos *mpl* del avión (*or* tren *etc*) siniestrado

B (sth, sb ruined): **are you still driving that old ~?** (colloq) ¿todavía andas en ese cacharro? (fam); **the attack left him a physical ~** el ataque lo dejó hecho una ruina; **he's a nervous ~** tiene los nervios destrozados

C (destruction): **the ~ of the Titanic** el naufragio del Titanic

wreck² *vt* 1 ‹*ship*› provocar* el naufragio de, hacer* naufragar; ‹*train*› hacer* descarrilar; ‹*car*› destrozar*; **the ship was ~ed on the rocks** el barco naufragó al chocar contra las rocas 2 (damage) destrozar* 3 (demolish) (AmE) ‹*house/building*› demoler*, tirar abajo, derribar 4 (spoil, ruin) ‹*plans/chances*› echar por tierra; ‹*marriage/happiness*› destrozar*; **drinking ~ed her health** la bebida le arruinó la salud

wreckage /ˈrekɪdʒ/ *n* [u] (of plane, car, ship) restos *mpl*; (of house) ruinas *fpl*, escombros *mpl*

wrecked /rekt/ *adj* (sl) (*pred*) **to be/feel ~** estar*/sentirse* hecho polvo (fam)

wrecker /'rekər || 'rekə(r)/ *n* (AmE) 1 (demolition worker) obrero *m* de demolición *or* derribo 2 (car dismantler) desguazador *m or* (Méx) deshuesador *m*

wrecking /'rekɪŋ/ *n* [u] (AmE) 1 (demolition) demolición *f*, derribo *m* 2 (car recovery) grúa *f*, auxilio *m*

wren /ren/ *n*
A (Zool) carrizo *m*
B **Wren** *mujer miembro de la marina británica*

wrench¹ /rentʃ/ *vt* 1 (pull) arrancar*; **he ~ed the door off its hinges** desgoznó *or* desquició la puerta; **you nearly ~ed my arm out of its socket!** ¡casi me dislocas el brazo!; **to ~ oneself away** soltarse* *or* zafarse de un tirón *or* (AmL exc CS) de un jalón 2 (sprain) ‹*muscle*› desgarrarse; ‹*joint*› dislocarse*

wrench² *n*
A 1 (twist, pull) tirón *m*, jalón *m* (AmL exc CS) 2 (emotional pain) dolor *m* (*causado por una separación*); **it was a terrible ~ leaving my family** fue muy doloroso tener que separarme de mi familia
B (tool) llave *f* inglesa; *see also* **monkey wrench**

wrest /rest/ *vt* **to ~ sth FROM sb** arrancarle* algo A algn

wrestle /'resəl/ *vi* 1 (Sport) luchar 2 (grapple) **to ~ WITH sb/sth**: **she ~d with her attacker** forcejeó con *or* luchó contra *or* con su agresor; **all night he ~d with his conscience** pasó toda la noche batallando con su conciencia

wrestler /'reslər || 'reslə(r)/ *n* luchador, -dora *m,f*

wrestling /'reslɪŋ/ *n* [u] lucha *f*

wretch /retʃ/ *n* (liter) 1 (unfortunate person) desdichado, -da *m,f*, infeliz *mf*; **the (poor) ~** el pobre desdichado *or* infeliz, el pobre diablo (fam) 2 (despicable person) desgraciado, -da *m,f*

wretched /'retʃəd || 'retʃɪd/ *adj* 1 (abject, pitiable) ‹*existence/creature*› desdichado, desgraciado 2 (very bad) (colloq) ‹*weather*› horrible, espantoso; **to feel ~** sentirse* muy mal; **I can't untie this ~ knot** no puedo desatar este condenado *or* maldito nudo (fam)

wriggle /'rɪgəl/ *vi* 1 (move) retorcerse*; **to ~ along** ‹‹*worm*›› avanzar* serpenteando *or* culebreando; **the children ~d in their seats** los niños se movían inquietos en sus asientos; **I ~d through the gap** me metí por el agujero 2 (with embarrassment): **to make sb ~** hacerle* pasar vergüenza a algn

■ **wriggle** *vt* ‹*body/toes*› mover*

Phrasal verb

• **wriggle out of** [v ▸ adv ▸ prep ▸ o] ‹*dress/jeans*› quitarse (*con dificultad*); **to ~ out of a chore** ingeniárselas para librarse de un trabajo; **don't try to ~ out of it!** ¡no trates de escabullirte!

wriggly /'rɪgli/ *adj* **-glier, -gliest** (esp BrE) ‹*fish*› movedizo, escurridizo; ‹*worm*› que serpentea

wring /rɪŋ/ (*past & past p* **wrung**) *vt*
A 1 ‹*cloth/garment*› escurrir, retorcer*, estrujar 2 **to ~ sth FROM/OUT OF sb** ‹*confession/information*› arrancarle* algo A algn
B ‹*neck*› retorcer*; **to ~ one's hands** retorcerse* las manos

Phrasal verb

• **wring out** [v ▸ o ▸ adv, v ▸ adv ▸ o]
A ‹*cloth/swimsuit*› retorcer*, escurrir, estrujar
B ‹*water*› escurrir; ‹*truth/money*› sacar*

wringer /'rɪŋər || 'rɪŋə(r)/ *n* rodillo *m* (*para escurrir la ropa*)

wringing /'rɪŋɪŋ/ *adv*: **to be ~ wet** estar* empapado *or* hecho una sopa

wrinkle¹ /'rɪŋkəl/ *n*
A 1 (in skin) arruga *f* 2 (in cloth, paper) arruga *f*; ***to iron out the ~s*** limar las asperezas
B (AmE) 1 (tip, shortcut) (colloq) truco *m*, tip *m* (Méx) 2 (angle, aspect) enfoque *m*

wrinkle² *vi* ‹‹*skin/garment*›› arrugarse*

wrinkled /'rɪŋkəld/ *adj* arrugado; **to get ~** arrugarse*

wrinkly /'rɪŋkli/ *adj* **-klier, -kliest** (colloq) arrugado

wrist /rɪst/ *n* (Anat) muñeca *f*; **to slash one's ~s** cortarse las venas; ***to slap sb on the ~, to slap sb's ~*** darle* un tirón de orejas a algn

wrist: **~band** *n* (bracelet) pulsera *f*; (strap) correa *f*; (sweatband) muñequera *f*; **~watch** *n* reloj *m* (de) pulsera

W

writ /rɪt/ *n* (Law) (issued by a court) orden *f or* mandato *m* judicial; **to issue a ~ (against sb)** expedir* una orden *or* un mandato (contra algn); **to serve a ~ on sb** notificarle* una orden *or* un mandato a algn; **a ~ of habeas corpus** un recurso de hábeas corpus

write /raɪt/ (*past* **wrote**; *past p* **written**) *vt* 1 (put in writing) escribir*; **how do you ~ that?** ¿cómo se escribe?; **I wrote him a letter** le escribí una carta; **to ~ sb a check** *o* (BrE) **cheque** extenderle* *or* hacerle* un cheque a algn; ***(to have sth) written all over one/one's face***: **jealousy was written all over him/his face** se le notaba a la legua/en la cara que estaba celoso 2 (write letter to) (AmE) escribirle* a 3 (Comput) escribir*; **to ~ sth to disk** *o* (BrE also) **disc** traspasar algo a un disco

■ **write** *vi* escribir*; **this pencil doesn't ~ very well** este lápiz no escribe muy bien; **she ~s for a newspaper/for television** escribe en un periódico/para la televisión; **to ~ ABOUT/ON sth** escribir* ACERCA DE *or* SOBRE algo; **to ~ TO sb** escribirle* A algn; **I am writing in response to the advertisement which ...** me dirijo a ustedes con relación al anuncio que ...; **I ~ home once a week** escribo a casa una vez por semana; ***to be nothing to ~ home about*** no ser* nada del otro mundo *or* (fam) nada del otro jueves

Phrasal verbs

• **write away** [v ▸ adv] **to ~ away FOR sth**: **she wrote away for a form** escribió pidiendo que le mandaran un formulario

• **write back** [v ▸ adv] **to ~ back (TO sb)** contestar(le A algn)

• **write down** [v ▸ o ▸ adv, v ▸ adv ▸ o] anotar, apuntar

• **write in**
A [v ▸ o ▸ adv, v ▸ adv ▸ o] 1 (insert) ‹*name/word*› escribir*, incluir* 2 (include) ‹*safeguard/condition*› incluir*
B [v ▸ adv] ‹‹*viewer/reader*›› escribir*

• **write off**
A [v ▸ adv] ▸**write away**
B [v ▸ o ▸ adv, v ▸ adv ▸ o] 1 (consider beyond repair) ‹*vehicle*› declarar siniestro total 2 (damage beyond repair) (BrE) destrozar*, hacer* polvo (fam) 3 (consider a failure, disregard) ‹*marriage/project*› dar* por perdido 4 ‹*debt*› cancelar

• **write out** [v ▸ o ▸ adv, v ▸ adv ▸ o]
A 1 (write fully, copy) escribir*; **to ~ sth out neatly** *o* (colloq) **in neat** pasar algo en *or* (Esp) a limpio 2 (complete, fill out) ‹*prescription*› escribir*; ‹*check/receipt*› hacer*, extender* (frml)
B ‹*character/part*› eliminar (*del libreto*)

• **write up** [v ▸ o ▸ adv, v ▸ adv ▸ o] 1 (rewrite fully) ‹*report/notes*› pasar en *or* (Esp) a limpio 2 (describe) ‹*experiment/visit*› redactar un informe sobre

write: **~ head** *n* cabeza *f* de escritura; **~-off** /'raɪtɔːf || 'raɪtɒf/ *n* (sth beyond repair): **the car was a ~** el coche fue declarado un siniestro total *or* (fam) quedó hecho chatarra; **their marriage is a ~** su matrimonio es un fracaso; **~-protect** /ˌraɪtprə'tekt/ *vt* proteger* contra escritura

writer /'raɪtər || 'raɪtə(r)/ *n* (author) escritor, -tora *m,f*; **the ~ of the letter** el autor de la carta; **~'s cramp** calambre *m* (*que da por escribir mucho*)

write-up /'raɪtʌp/ *n* (colloq) (review) crítica *f*, reseña *f*; (report) artículo *m*, reportaje *m*

writhe /raɪð/ *vi* ‹‹*snake*›› retorcerse*; **to ~ in agony** *o* **in pain** retorcerse* de dolor; **to ~ with embarrassment/shame** no saber* dónde meterse de la vergüenza

writing /'raɪtɪŋ/ *n* 1 [u] (script) escritura *f* 2 [u] (written material): **the wall was covered in ~** la pared estaba llena de pintadas *or* de graffiti; **the ~'s rather blurred** la letra está algo borrosa; **in ~** por escrito; ***the ~ is on the wall***: **the ~ was on the wall for the company** la compañía tenía los días contados; (*before n*) **~ desk** escritorio *m*; **~ materials** artículos *mpl* de escritorio; **~ pad** bloc *m*; **~ paper** papel *m* de carta 3 [u] (BrE) (handwriting) letra *f*; **I can't read your ~** no entiendo tu letra 4 [u] (act of composing): **~ takes up a lot of my time** paso mucho tiempo escribiendo; **at the time of ~** en el momento de escribir estas líneas 5 [u] (written composition) literatura *f*; **an excellent piece of ~** un trabajo excelente 6 **writings** *pl*: **the ~s of Swift** la obra de Swift; **her philosophical ~s** sus escritos filosóficos

written¹ /'rɪtn̩/ *past p of* **write**

written² *adj* ‹*examination/language*› escrito; **~ permission** permiso *m* por escrito

WRNS /renz/ *n* (formerly in UK) = **Women's Royal Naval Service**

wrong¹ /rɔːŋ || rɒŋ/ *adj*

A **1** (incorrect, inappropriate)‹*answer*› equivocado; **the answer is ~** la respuesta está mal *or* equivocada, la respuesta es incorrecta *or* (frml) errónea; **the time given in the newspaper was ~** la hora que salió en el periódico estaba mal; **you've given me the ~ change** se ha equivocado al darme el cambio; **we've taken the ~ bus** nos hemos equivocado de autobús; **he went in the ~ direction** tomó *or* (esp Esp) cogió para dónde no debía; **my food went down the ~ way** la comida se me fue por el otro lado (fam); **I did it the ~ way** lo hice mal; **you're in the ~ job, you should be a painter** te has equivocado de oficio, deberías ser pintor; **this is the ~ time to mention the subject** éste no es (el) momento oportuno para mencionar el tema; **it's the ~ time of year for cherries** no es época de cerezas; **she always says the ~ thing** siempre dice lo que no debe; **the picture is the ~ way up** el cuadro está al revés; **I'm the ~ person to ask** no soy la persona indicada para contestar esa pregunta **2** (mistaken) (*pred*) **to be ~** estar* equivocado; **he was ~ about the date** estaba equivocado respecto de la fecha; **I was ~ about her** la había juzgado mal

B (morally): **stealing is ~** robar está mal; **I was ~ to abandon him** hice mal en dejarlo; **you were ~ to shout at her like that** no debiste haberle gritado así, estuviste mal en gritarle así; **I haven't done anything ~** no he hecho nada malo; **there's nothing ~ with a drink now and then** tomarse una copa de vez en cuando no tiene nada de malo; **what's ~ with that?** ¿qué hay de malo en eso?

C (amiss) (*pred*): **what's ~?** ¿qué pasa?; **what's ~ with you?** ¿qué te pasa?, ¿qué tienes?; **there's something ~ with her** algo le pasa; **something's ~ with the lock** la cerradura no anda bien, algo le pasa a la cerradura; **there's nothing ~ with your heart** su corazón está perfectamente bien

D (reverse): **the ~ side** el revés

wrong² *adv* ‹*answer*› mal, incorrectamente; **I assume you're paying — well, you assume ~** imagino que pagas tú — pues estás en un error *or* te equivocas; **I did it all ~** lo hice todo mal; **to get sth ~: you've got your facts ~** estás mal informado; **you've got it all ~: we're trying to help you** no has entendido nada: estamos tratando de ayudarte; **to get sb ~** (colloq): **I got him all ~** me equivoqué totalmente con él; **don't get me ~** no me malinterpretes; **to go ~** «*machinery*» estropearse, descomponerse* (AmL); «*plans*» salir* mal, fallar; **it's straight ahead, you can't go ~** siga derecho, no se puede perder *or* (Esp tb) no tiene pérdida; **he began to go ~ at college** en la universidad empezó a ir por mal camino

wrong³ *n* **1** [u c] (immoral action) mal *m*; (injustice) injusticia *f*; **to know right from ~** saber* distinguir entre el bien y el mal; **in her eyes he can do no ~** para ella, es incapaz de hacer nada malo; **to be in the ~** estar* equivocado; ***two ~s don't make a right*** con un error no se subsana otro **2** [c] (Law) agravio *m*

wrong⁴ *vt* (frml): **she had been ~ed by her family** su familia había sido muy injusta con ella

wrong: **~doing** *n* [u c]: **his sense of ~doing oppressed him** lo agobiaba la conciencia de haber obrado mal; **she was punished for her ~doings** la castigaron por sus fechorías; **~foot** /ˈrɔːŋˈfʊt || ˌrɒŋˈfʊt/ *vt* (Sport) ‹*opponent*› hacer(le)* un amago *or* amague a, desubicar* (AmL)

wrongful /ˈrɔːŋfəl || ˈrɒŋfəl/ *adj* ‹*accusation/punishment*› injusto; **~ arrest** (Law) arresto *m* ilegal; **~ dismissal** (Law) despido *m* improcedente *or* injustificado

wrongly /ˈrɔːŋli || ˈrɒŋli/ *adv* ‹*spell/pronounce*› mal, incorrectamente; ‹*believe/assume*› equivocadamente; ‹*accuse*› injustamente

wrote /rəʊt/ *past of* **write**

wrought¹ /rɔːt/ (*past & past p of* **work²** *vt* **D1**) (frml *or* liter): **the devastation ~ by the war** los estragos causados por la guerra; **a miraculous change had been ~ in him** un cambio milagroso se había operado en él

wrought² *adj*: **~ iron** hierro *m* forjado; **finely ~ features** (liter) rasgos finamente cincelados (liter)

wrung /rʌŋ/ *past & past p of* **wring**

WRVS *n* (in UK) = **Women's Royal Voluntary Service**

wry /raɪ/ *adj* **wrier, wriest** ‹*smile/laugh/joke*› irónico, sardónico; **to make a ~ face** torcer* el gesto, poner* mala cara

wryly /ˈraɪli/ *adv* irónicamente

WSW (= **west-southwest**) OSO

WV, W Va = West Virginia

WWI *n* = **World War One**

WWII *n* = **World War Two**

WY, Wyo = Wyoming

W

X, **x** /eks/ *n* 1▸ (letter) X, x *f*; **if you can't write, just make an X** si no sabe escribir, haga *or* ponga una cruz 2▸ (sb, sth unknown) X; **Mr X** el señor X 3▸ (symbolizing kiss): **Love, Helen XXX** besos *or* un beso, Helen 4▸ (Cin) (in US) prohibida para menores de 18 años

xenophobia /ˈzenəˈfəʊbiə/ *n* [u] xenofobia *f*

xenophobic /ˈzenəˈfəʊbɪk/ *adj* xenófobo

xerox /ˈzɪrɑːks, ˈze- || ˈzɪərɒks/ *vt* fotocopiar, xerografiar*

XL = extra large

Xmas /ˈkrɪsməs, ˈeksməs/ *n* Navidad *f*

X-rated /ˈeksˈreɪtəd || ˌeksˈreɪtɪd/ *adj* (BrE) ‹*film*› sólo para adultos, clasificado X (Esp)

X-ray[1], **x-ray** /ˈeksreɪ/ *n* 1▸ (ray) rayo *m* X; **to have ~ eyes** *o* **vision** (colloq & hum) tener* una vista que traspasa las paredes, tener* vista de rayos X 2▸ (photograph) radiografía *f*; **I had a chest ~** me hicieron *or* me sacaron una radiografía de tórax

X-ray[2], **x-ray** *vt* hacer* *or* sacar* una radiografía de, radiografiar*

xylophone /ˈzaɪləfəʊn/ *n* xilofón *m*, xilófono *m*

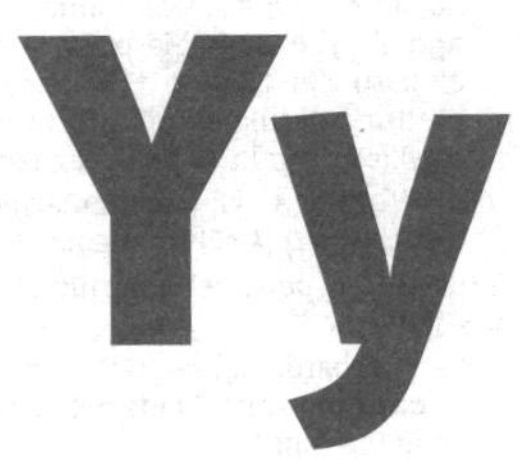

Y, y /waɪ/ *n* Y, y *f*

yacht¹ /jɑːt || jɒt/ *n* 1 (sailing boat — large) velero *m*, yate *m*; (— small) balandro *m*; (*before n*) **~ club** club *m* náutico; **~ race** regata *f* 2 (pleasure cruiser) yate *m*

yacht² *vi* (*only in -ing form*) navegar* (a vela); **she went ~ing** se fue a navegar

yachting /ˈjɑːtɪŋ || ˈjɒtɪŋ/ *n* [u] navegación *f* a vela

yachtsman /ˈjɑːtsmən || ˈjɒtsmən/ *n* (*pl* **-men** /-mən/) aficionado *m* a la vela; (in competitions) regatista *m*

yachtswoman /ˈjɑːtsˌwʊmən || ˈjɒtsˌwʊmən/ *n* (*pl* **-women**) aficionada *f* a la vela; (in competitions) regatista *f*

yack /jæk/ *vi* (colloq) cotorrear (fam)

yah /jɑː/ *interj* (colloq) ¡ja, ja!

yak¹ /jæk/ *vi* **-kk-** ▸**yack**

yak² *n* yac *m*, yak *m*

yam /jæm/ *n* 1 (plant, vegetable) ñame *m* 2 (AmE) ▸**sweet potato**

yank¹ /jæŋk/ *vt* (tug) ‹*rope*› tirar de, jalar de (AmL exc CS); **he ~ed the drawer right out** sacó el cajón de un tirón

■ **yank** *vi* **to ~ AT/ON sth** tirar *or* (AmL exc CS) jalar DE algo

yank² *n* tirón *m*, jalón *m* (AmL exc CS)

Yank /jæŋk/ *n* (BrE colloq & often pej) ▸**Yankee¹ 3**

Yankee¹ /ˈjæŋki/ *n* 1 (Hist) yanqui *mf* 2 (sb from Northern US) (AmE colloq) norteño, -ña *m,f* 3 (US citizen) (colloq: in BrE often pej) yanqui *mf* (fam & pey), gringo, -ga *m,f* (fam & pey)

Yankee² *adj* (*before n*) 1 (Hist) yanqui 2 (of Northern US) (AmE colloq) norteño 3 (of US) (colloq: in BrE often pej) yanqui (fam & pey), gringo (fam & pey)

yap¹ /jæp/ *vi* **-pp-** 1 (bark) ladrar (*con ladridos agudos*) 2 (gossip) (colloq & pej) darle* a la sinhueso (fam)

yap² *n* (bark) ladrido *m* (*agudo*)

yard /jɑːrd || jɑːd/ *n*

A 1 (of school, prison) patio *m* 2 (of house) (BrE) patio *m*; (garden) (AmE) jardín *m* 3 (*stock~*) corral *m*

B (*boat~, ship~*) astillero *m*; (*goods ~, freight ~*) almacén *m*, depósito *m*

C (measure) yarda *f* (*0,91m*); **it's 100 ~s down the road** ≈ está a unos 100 metros de aquí

yardage /ˈjɑːrdɪdʒ || ˈjɑːdɪdʒ/ *n* [u] medida *f* (*en yardas*)

yard: **~arm** *n* (Naut) penol *m*; **~ sale** *n* (AmE) ▸**garage sale**; **~stick** *n* criterio *m*, patrón *m*

yarn /jɑːrn || jɑːn/ *n*

A [u c] (Tex) hilo *m*

B [c] (tale) (colloq) historia *f*; ***to spin a ~*** inventar una historia

yashmak /ˈjæʃmæk/ *n* velo *m* (*que llevan algunas musulmanas*)

yawn¹ /jɔːn/ *vi* 1 «*person/animal*» bostezar* 2 «*pit/chasm*» (liter) abrirse*

yawn² *n* 1 (action) bostezo *m* 2 (bore) (colloq) plomo *m* (fam), aburrimiento *m*, rollazo *m* (Esp fam)

yawning /ˈjɔːnɪŋ/ *adj* (*before n*) enorme; **there's a ~ gap** *o* **chasm between his words and his actions** entre lo que dice y lo que hace hay un abismo

yd (*pl* **yd** *or* **yds**) = **yard**

ye¹ /jiː/ *pron* (arch *or* dial) vosotros, -tras

ye² *def art* (mock archaic) (*sing*) el, la; (*pl*) los, las; **~ olde Tudor Tavern** la vieja taberna Tudor

yea¹ /jeɪ/ *n* (AmE) voto *m* a favor

yea² *interj* (arch) sí

yea³ *adv* (indeed, truly) (arch) sí, ¡sin duda!

yeah /jeə/ *interj* (colloq) sí

year /jɪr || jɪə(r)/ *n*

A (period of time) año *m*; **last ~** el año pasado; **next ~** el año que viene, el próximo año; **this time last ~ ...** el año pasado por estas fechas ...; **every ~** todos los años, cada año; **every other** *o* **every second ~** cada dos años, un año sí y otro no; **once or twice a ~** una o dos veces al *or* por año; **it costs $500 a ~** cuesta 500 dólares al año; **all (the) ~ round** todo el año; **it'll be a ~ next Monday/August** el lunes que viene/en agosto hará un año; **by the ~ 2000** para el año 2000; **in all my ~s as a teacher ...** en todos mis años que ha trabajado de profesor, ...; **I'll return in a ~** *o* **in a ~'s time** volveré dentro de un año; **over the ~s I've grown accustomed to it** con el tiempo *or* con los años me he ido acostumbrando; **~ after ~/~ in, ~ out** año tras año; **from ~ to ~** de un año a otro; **I'm 12 ~s old** tengo doce años; **she got five ~s** (colloq) le cayeron cinco años (fam); ***the ~ one*** *o* (BrE) ***the ~ dot*** (colloq) el año de Maricastaña *or* de la pera (fam)

B **years** *pl* 1 (a long time): **it's ~s since I saw him, I haven't seen him for ~s** hace años que no lo veo; **that was ~s ago** de eso hace mucho tiempo *or* muchos años; **~s ago, there was a church here** años atrás, aquí había una iglesia; **that dress takes ~s off you** ese vestido te quita años (de encima); **he looks ~s older** parece mucho mayor; **it put ~s on me** me avejentó *or* me envejeció, me echó años encima 2 (age): **he's very mature for his ~s** es muy maduro para su edad; **he must be well on in ~s** debe ser bastante entrado en años

C 1 (Educ) curso *m*, año *m*; **she was in my ~ at school** estaba en el mismo curso que yo en el colegio; **I'm still in (the) first ~** todavía estoy en primer año *or* en primero 2 (of wine) cosecha *f*

-year /jɪr || jɪe(r)/ *suff*: **a third~ student** un estudiante de tercer año *or* de tercero

year: **~book** *n* anuario *m*; **~-end** /ˈjɪrˈend || jɪərˈend/ *n* (AmE) (*no pl*): **by ~-end** hacia fin de año; (*before n*) **~-end report** (also BrE) informe *m* de fin de año; **~-end sale** ≈ rebajas *fpl* de fin de temporada

yearly¹ /ˈjɪrli || ˈjɪəli/ *adj* anual; **on a ~ basis** cada año, anualmente

yearly² *adv* cada año, anualmente; **twice ~** dos veces al *or* por año

yearn /jɜːrn || jɜːn/ *vi* **to ~ to + INF** anhelar *or* ansiar* + INF; **to ~ FOR sth** añorar algo

yearning /ˈjɜːrnɪŋ || ˈjɜːnɪŋ/ *n* [u c] **~ FOR sth/to + INF** anhelo *m* *or* ansia *f*‡ DE algo/+ INF

year-old /ˈjɪrˈəʊld || ˈjɪərˈəʊld/ *adj* (*before n*) de un año de edad

-year-old /jərˈəʊld || jɪərˈəʊld/ *suff*: **a thirty-two~woman** una mujer de treinta y dos años; **a six~** un niño/una niña de seis años

year-on-year /ˈjɪrɑːnˈjɪr || ˈjɪərɒnˈjɪə(r)/ *adj* (*before n*) interanual

yeast /jiːst/ *n* [u c] levadura *f*

yell¹ /jel/ *vi* gritar, chillar; **to ~ AT sb** gritarle A algn

■ **yell** *vt* ‹*order/reply*› gritar

yell² *n* (shout) grito *m*, chillido *m*; **to let out/give a ~** soltar/dar* *or* pegar* un grito

yellow[1] /ˈjeləʊ/ *adj* 1 amarillo; ‹*hair*› muy rubio *or* (Méx) güero *or* (Col) mono *or* (Ven) catire; ‹*traffic light*› (AmE) amarillo, ámbar *adj inv*; ‹*skin*› amarillo; **the paper was ~ with age** el papel se había puesto amarillo *or* amarillento con el paso del tiempo 2 (sensationalist): **the ~ press** la prensa amarilla *or* amarillista *or* sensacionalista 3 (cowardly) (colloq) gallina (fam), cagueta(s) (fam), cobarde

yellow[2] *n* 1 [u] (color) amarillo *m* 2 [u c] (yolk) yema *f* 3 [c] (signal) (AmE) luz *f* amarilla

yellow[3] *vi* ponerse* amarillo *or* amarillento

yellow: **~belly** *n* (colloq) gallina *mf* (fam), cagueta(s) *mf* (fam), cobarde *mf*; **~ card** *n* (in soccer): **to show sb the ~ card** mostrarle* la tarjeta amarilla a algn; **~ fever** *n* [u] fiebre *f* amarilla

yellowish /ˈjeləʊɪʃ/, **yellowy** /ˈjeləʊi/ *adj* amarillento

yellow: **~ pages**, (BrE) **~ Pages**® *pl n* (Telec) páginas *fpl* amarillas; **~ Sea** *n* **the Y~ Sea** el Mar Amarillo

yelp[1] /jelp/ *vi* dar* un gañido *or* aullido

yelp[2] *n* gañido *m*, aullido *m*

Yemen /ˈjemən/ *n* Yemen *m*; **South ~** Yemen *m* del Sur

Yemeni /ˈjeməni/ *adj* yemenita

yen /jen/ *n*

A (longing) (colloq) (*no pl*) **to have a ~ to + INF** morirse* de ganas DE + INF (fam), tener* unas ganas locas DE + INF (fam)

B (*pl* ~) (Fin) yen *m*

yeoman /ˈjəʊmən/ *n* (*pl* **-men** /-mən/) 1 (Hist) (freeholder) *vasallo propietario de la tierra que cultivaba* 2 **Yeoman of the Guard** (in UK) alabardero *m* de la Casa Real

yes[1] /jes/ *interj*

A 1 (affirmative reply) sí; **please say ~** por favor di que sí; **are you ready? — ~, I am** ¿estás listo? — sí; **you didn't tell me — ~, I did!** no me lo dijiste — ¡sí que te lo dije! 2 (obeying order, request) sí; **be there by nine o'clock — ~, OK** estáte allí antes de las nueve — bueno *or* (Esp tb) vale 3 (answering call, inquiry) sí; **Fred — yes?** Fred — ¿sí? *or* ¿qué?

B 1 (expressing pleasure, satisfaction) sí; **~! what a good idea!** ¡sí! ¡qué buena idea! 2 (emphasizing) sí; **you could win $5,000, ~, $5,000!** ¡puede ganar 5.000 dólares, sí, 5.000 dólares!

yes[2] *n* (*pl* **~es**) 1 (affirmative reply) sí *m* 2 (vote) voto *m* a favor

yes-man /ˈjesmæn/ *n* (*pl* **-men** /-men/) (pej): **he's a ~** es de los que dicen amén a todo

yesterday[1] /ˈjestərdeɪ, -di || ˈjestədeɪ, -di/ *adv* ayer; **~ morning** ayer por la mañana, ayer en la mañana (AmL), ayer a la mañana *or* de mañana (RPl); **they left a week ~** ayer hizo una semana que se fueron

yesterday[2] *n*: **~ was a busy day** ayer fue un día de mucha actividad; **the day before ~** anteayer

yesteryear /ˈjestərjɪr || ˈjestəjɪə(r)/ *n* (liter) (*no art*): **the songs of ~** las canciones de antaño (liter)

yet[1] /jet/ *adv*

A 1 (up to this or that time, till now) (*with neg*) todavía, aún; **I haven't eaten** *o* (AmE also) **I didn't eat ~** todavía *or* aún no he comido, todavía no comí (RPl); **as ~** aún, todavía 2 (now, so soon) (*with neg*) todavía; **shall I call him? — not (just) ~** ¿lo llamo? — (no,) todavía no 3 (thus far) (*after superl*): **it's his best book ~** es el mejor libro que ha escrito hasta ahora

B (by now, already) (*with interrog*) ya; **has she decided** *o* (AmE also) **did she decide ~?** ¿ya se ha decidido?, ¿ya se decidió? (AmL)

C (still) todavía, aún; **there's half an hour ~ before they arrive** todavía *or* aún falta media hora para que lleguen

D (eventually, in spite of everything): **I'll get even with you ~** ya me las pagarás (algún día); **we may win ~** todavía podemos ganar

E (*as intensifier*) 1 (even) (*with comp*) aún, todavía; **the story becomes ~ more complicated** el cuento se complica aún *or* todavía más 2 (in addition, besides): **~ more problems** más problemas aún; **~ another mistake** otro error más; **we had to go back ~ again** tuvimos que volver otra vez más (aún)

F (but, nevertheless) (*as linker*) sin embargo

yet[2] *conj* pero

yeti /ˈjeti/ *n* (*pl* ~) yeti *m*

yew /juː/ *n* [c u] tejo *m*

YHA *n* (= **Youth Hostels Association**) Asociación *f* de Albergues Juveniles *or* de la Juventud

Yiddish /ˈjɪdɪʃ/ *n* [u] yídish *m*, yiddish *m*

yield[1] /jiːld/ *vt*

A (surrender) ‹*position/territory*› ceder; **to ~ one's right of way** (AmE Transp) ceder el paso; **to ~ sth TO sb** cederle algo A algn

B ‹*crop/fruit/mineral/oil*› producir*; ‹*results*› dar*, arrojar; **these bonds ~ 9.2%** estos bonos rinden *or* dan un (interés del) 9,2%; **the inquiry ~ed no new evidence** la investigación no aportó nuevas pruebas

■ **yield** *vi*

A 1 (give way) ceder; **she ~ed to their threats** cedió a *or* ante sus amenazas 2 (give priority) **to ~ TO sth/sb** dar* prioridad A algo/algn; **yield** (AmE) ceda el paso

B ‹‹*ground/ice*›› ceder

Phrasal verb

- **yield up** [v ▸ o ▸ adv, v ▸ adv ▸ o] (liter) ‹*secret*› revelar

yield[2] *n* [u c] rendimiento *m*; **to give a good/poor ~** dar* un buen/mal rendimiento, producir* *or* rendir* mucho/poco

yippee /ˈjɪpi/ *interj* (colloq) ¡yupi! (fam)

YMCA *n* 1 (= **Young Men's Christian Association**) YMCA *f*, Asociación *f* Cristiana de Jóvenes 2 [c] **~ (hostel)** albergue *m* de la YMCA *or* de la Asociación Cristiana de Jóvenes

yo /jəʊ/ *interj* (sl) hola

yob /jɑːb || jɒb/ *n* (BrE) vándalo *m*, gamberro *m* (Esp), patotero *m* (CS fam)

yobbo /ˈjɑːbəʊ || ˈjɒbəʊ/ *n* (*pl* **-bos** *or* **-boes**) (BrE) ▸ **yob**

yodel /ˈjəʊdl̩/ *vi*, (BrE) **-ll-** cantar al estilo tirolés

yoga /ˈjəʊgə/ *n* [u] yoga *m*

yoghurt, yoghourt, yogurt /ˈjəʊgərt || ˈjɒgət/ *n* [u c] yogur *m*, yoghourt *m*

yoke[1] /jəʊk/ *n*

A 1 (for oxen, horses) yugo *m* 2 (burden, bondage) yugo *m*

B (*pl* ~) (pair of oxen) yunta *f*

C (of dress, shirt) canesú *m*

yoke[2] *vt* ‹*oxen*› uncir*, enyuntar

yokel /ˈjəʊkəl/ *n* (pej *or* hum) pueblerino, -na *m,f* *or* (Méx) indio, -dia *m,f* *or* (Col) montañero, -ra *m,f* *or* (RPl) pajuerano, -na *m,f* *or* (Chi) huaso, -sa *m,f* (pey *o* hum)

yolk /jəʊk/ *n* [c u] yema *f* (de huevo)

yon /jɑːn || jɒn/ *adj* (poet *or* dial) aquel, aquella; (*pl*) aquellos, aquellas

yonder[1] /ˈjɑːndər || ˈjɒndə(r)/ *adj* (poet *or* dial) ▸ **yon**

yonder[2] *adv* (poet *or* dial) allá; **over/up/down ~** allá lejos/arriba/abajo

yonks /jɑːŋks || jɒŋks/ *n* [u] (BrE colloq): **I haven't been there for ~** hace siglos *or* (Esp tb) la tira que no voy por allí (fam)

yoo-hoo /ˈjuːhuː/ *interj* ¡yuju!, ¡eh!

yore /jɔːr || jɔː(r)/ *n* [u] (liter): **in days of ~** antaño (liter), en otros tiempos

Yorkshire pudding /ˈjɔːrkʃɪr || ˈjɔːkʃə, ˈjɔːksɪə(r)/ *n* [c u] *masa horneada a base de leche, huevos y harina que se sirve tradicionalmente con el rosbif*

you /juː/ *pron*

A (sing) 1 (as subject — familiar) tú, vos (AmC, RPl); (— formal) usted; **now ~ try** ahora prueba tú/pruebe usted, ahora probá vos (AmC, RPl); **that hat's not ~** ese sombrero no te favorece; **if I were ~** yo que tú/que usted, yo en tu/en su lugar, yo que vos (AmC, RPl); **poor ~!** ¡pobrecito!; **~ liar!** ¡mentiroso! 2 (as direct object — familiar) te; (— formal, masculine) lo, le (Esp); (— formal, feminine) la; **I saw ~, Pete** te vi, Pete; **I saw ~, Mr Russell** lo vi, señor Russell, le vi, señor Russell (Esp) 3 (as indirect object — familiar) te; (— formal) le; (— with direct object pronoun present) se; **I told ~** te dije/le dije; **I gave it to ~** te lo di/se lo di 4 (after prep — familiar) ti, vos (AmC, RPl); (— formal) usted; **for ~** para ti/usted, para vos (AmC, RPl); **with ~** contigo/con usted; **she's taller than ~** es más alta que tú

B (pl) 1 (as subject, after preposition — familiar) ustedes (AmL), vosotros, -tras (Esp); (— formal) ustedes; **be quiet, ~ two** ustedes dos: ¡cállense!, vosotros dos: ¡callaos! (Esp); **come on, ~ guys!** vamos, chicos 2 (as direct object — familiar) los, las (AmL), os (Esp); (— formal, masculine) los, les (Esp); (— formal,

y

feminine) las; **I heard ~, gentlemen** los *or* (Esp tb) les oí, caballeros; **I heard ~, boys/girls** los/las oí, chicos/chicas (AmL), os oí, chicos/chicas (Esp) 3 (as indirect object — familiar) les (AmL), os (Esp); (— formal) les; (— with direct object pronoun present) se; **I gave ~ the book** les *or* (Esp tb) os di el libro; **I gave it to ~** se *or* (Esp tb) os lo di

C (one) 1 (as subject) uno, una; **~ can't do that here** aquí uno no puede *or* no se puede *or* no puedes hacer eso 2 (as direct object) te; **people stop ~ in the street and ask for money** la gente te para en la calle y te pide dinero, la gente lo para a uno en la calle y le pide dinero 3 (as indirect object) te; **they never tell ~ the truth** nunca te dicen la verdad, nunca le dicen la verdad a uno

you'd /ju:d/ 1 **= you had** 2 **= you would**

you-know-who /ˌju:nəʊ'hu:/ *n* (colloq) ya sabes quién (fam)

you'll /ju:l/ **= you will**

young¹ /jʌŋ/ *adj* **younger** /'jʌŋgər || 'jʌŋgə(r)/, **youngest** /'jʌŋgəst || 'jʌŋgɪst/ 1 ‹*animal/person*› joven; **I have a ~er brother** tengo un hermano menor; **she is four years ~er than me** tiene cuatro años menos que yo, es cuatro años menor que yo; **this is Patricia, our ~est** ésta es Patricia, la (más) pequeña *or* la menor; **a ~ man/woman** un/una joven; **a ~ lady** una señorita, una chica joven; **her ~ man** su novio; **now listen to me, ~ man/lady** escúcheme jovencito/jovencita; **~ people** la gente joven, los jóvenes, la juventud; **the ~er generation** la nueva generación, la gente joven; **to die/marry ~** morir*/casarse joven; **to be ~ at heart** ser* joven de espíritu; **you're only ~ once** (set phrase) sólo se es joven una vez (en la vida); **the night is ~** (set phrase) la noche es joven (fr hecha) 2 ‹*appearance/manner/complexion*› juvenil; **she's very ~ for her age** *o* **years** parece más joven de lo que es; **you're as ~ as you feel** (set phrase) la juventud se lleva dentro (fr hecha) 3 ‹*rhubarb/spinach*› tierno; ‹*wine*› joven

young² *pl n* 1 (humans) **the ~** los jóvenes, la juventud 2 (animals) crías *fpl*

youngster /'jʌŋstər || 'jʌŋstə(r)/ *n* chico, -ca *m,f*

your *adj* /jʊr, *weak form* jər || jɔ:(r), *weak form* jʊə(r)/ 1 (belonging to one person) (*sing, familiar*) tu; (*pl, familiar*) tus; (*sing, formal*) su; (*pl formal*) sus; **wash ~ hands** lávate/lávese las manos 2 (belonging to more than one person) (*sing, familiar*) su (AmL), vuestro, -tra (Esp); (*pl, familiar*) sus (AmL), vuestros, -tras (Esp); (*sing, formal*) su; (*pl, formal*) sus; **put ~ shoes on** pónganse *or* (Esp) pone(r)os los zapatos 3 (one's): **if ~ name begins with A ...** si tu/su nombre empieza con A ...; **you have to take ~ shoes off in a mosque** hay que quitarse los zapatos en una mezquita

you're /jʊər || jʊə(r), jɔ:(r)/ **= you are**

yours /jʊrz || jɔ:z/ *pron* 1 (belonging to one person) (*sing, familiar*) tuyo, -ya; (*pl, familiar*) tuyos, -yas; (*sing, formal*) suyo, -ya; (*pl formal*) suyos, -yas; **is this ~?** ¿esto es tuyo/suyo?; **~ is here** el tuyo/la tuya/el suyo/la suya está aquí; **a friend of ~** un amigo tuyo/suyo 2 (belonging to more than one person) (*sing, formal*) suyo, -ya; (*pl, formal*) suyos, -yas; (*sing, familiar*) suyo, -ya (AmL), vuestro, -tra (Esp); (*pl, familiar*) suyos, -yas (AmL), vuestros, -tras (Esp); **~ are here, children** los suyos *or* los de ustedes están aquí, niños (AmL), los vuestros están aquí, niños (Esp); **is he a friend of ~?** ¿es amigo de ustedes *or* suyo *or* (Esp) vuestro? 3 (Corresp): **~, Daniel** un abrazo, Daniel; **~ sincerely** le saluda atentamente

yourself /jər'self || jɔ:'self/ *pron* 1 (reflexive): **describe ~** (formal) descríbase; (familiar) descríbete; **stop thinking about ~** (formal) deje de pensar en sí mismo; (familiar) deja de pensar en ti mismo; **by ~** solo/sola 2 (emphatic use) (formal) usted mismo, usted misma; (familiar) tú mismo, tú misma; **did you make it ~?** (formal) ¿lo hizo usted mismo/misma?; (familiar) ¿lo hiciste tú mismo/misma?; **suit ~** (formal) haga lo que quiera; (familiar) haz lo que quieras; **you're a musician ~, I hear** usted también es *or* (*familiar*) tú también eres músico, tengo entendido 3 (normal self): **just relax and be ~** relájate y compórtate con naturalidad; **you're not ~ today** hoy no eres el/la de siempre 4 (oneself) uno mismo, una misma

yourselves /jər'selvz || jɔ:'selvz/ *pron* 1 (reflexive): **behave ~!** ¡pórtense bien! (AmL), ¡porta(r)os bien! (Esp); **by ~** solos/solas 2 (emphatic use) (formal) ustedes mismos/mismas; (familiar) ustedes mismos/mismas *or* (Esp) vosotros mismos/vosotras mismas; **you've probably noticed it ~** probablemente lo habrán observado ustedes mismos 3 (normal selves): **just be ~** compórtense *or* (Esp) comporta(r)os con naturalidad

youth /ju:θ/ *n* [u] (*pl* **youths** /ju:ðz/)

A (early life) juventud *f*; **in my ~** cuando era joven, en mi juventud

B [u] (young people) (+ *sing or pl vb*) juventud *f*; **today's ~** la juventud *or* los jóvenes de hoy; (*before n*) ‹*movement/orchestra*› juvenil; **~ club** club *m* de jóvenes

C [c] (young man) (frml) joven *m*

youthful /'ju:θfəl/ *adj* ‹*enthusiasm/manner*› juvenil; ‹*folly/ignorance*› de juventud

youthfulness /'ju:θfəlnəs || 'ju:θfəlnɪs/ *n* [u] juventud *f*

youth hostel *n* albergue *m* juvenil *or* de la juventud

you've /ju:v/ **= you have**

yowl¹ /jaʊl/ *vi* «*person*» dar* alaridos; «*dog*» aullar*; «*cat*» maullar*

yowl² *n* (of person) alarido *m*, grito *m* (*de dolor*); (of dog) aullido *m*; (of cat) maullido *m*

yo-yo /'jəʊjəʊ/ *n* (toy) yo-yo *m*; ***to go up and down like a ~*** (colloq) subir y bajar a lo loco; **I was up and down like a ~ all afternoon** me pasé toda la tarde de arriba para abajo

yr (*pl* **yrs**) **= year**

yuck /jʌk, jək || jʌk/ *interj* (colloq) ¡puaj! (fam)

yucky /'jʌki, 'jəki || 'jʌki/ *adj* **yuckier, yuckiest** (colloq) asqueroso

Yugoslav /'ju:gəʊslɑ:v || 'ju:gəslɑ:v/ *adj/n* ▸**Yugoslavian¹,²**

Yugoslavia /ˌju:gəʊ'slɑ:viə || ˌjʊgə'slɑ:viə/ *n* (Hist) Yugoslavia *f*

Yugoslavian¹ /ˌju:gəʊ'slɑ:viən || ˌjʊgə'slɑ:viən/ *adj* (Hist) yugoslavo

Yugoslavian² *n* (Hist) yugoslavo, -va *m,f*

yuk /jʌk, jək || jʌk/ *interj* (colloq) ¡puaj! (fam)

yukky /'jʌki, 'jəki || 'jʌki/ *adj* **-kier, -kiest** (colloq) asqueroso

yule /ju:l/: **~ log**, **~ log** *n* (Culin) tronco *m* de Navidad; **~tide**, **~tide** *n* (liter) la(s) Navidad(es)

yummy /'jʌmi/ *adj* **-mier, -miest** (colloq) riquísimo; (*as interj*) **~!** ¡hmm!, ¡qué rico!

yum yum /'jʌm'jʌm/ *interj* (colloq) ñam ñam (fam)

yuppie, yuppy /'jʌpi/ *n* (*pl* **-pies**) (colloq) yuppy *mf* (fam)

YWCA *n* (**= Young Women's Christian Association**) YWCA *f*, Asociación *f* de Jóvenes Cristianas

Zz

Z, z /ziː || zed/ *n* Z, z *f*
zaftig /ˈzɑːftɪg/ *adj* (AmE) ‹*woman*› rellenita y curvilínea
Zambia /ˈzæmbiə/ *n* Zambia *f*
Zambian /ˈzæmbiən || ˈzæmbiən/ *adj* zambiano
zany /ˈzeɪni/ *adj* **zanier, zaniest** (colloq) ‹*person*› chiflado (fam), alocado; ‹*adventure*› loco; ‹*clothes*› estrafalario
Zanzibar /ˈzænzəbɑːr || ˈzænzɪbɑː(r)/ *n* Zanzíbar *m*
zap /zæp/ *vt* **-pp-** 1 (defeat, blast) (colloq) liquidar (fam) 2 (Comput) eliminar, borrar

Phrasal verb

- **zap through** [v ▸ prep ▸ o]
A (finish) (colloq): **he ~ped through the work in a morning** despachó el trabajo en una mañana
B [v ▸ adv] (TV) hacer• zapping

zeal /ziːl/ *n* [u] (Pol, Relig) fervor *m*, celo *m*; **in her ~ for reform ...** en su afán reformista ...
zealot /ˈzelət/ *n* (fanatic) fanático, -ca *m,f*
zealous /ˈzeləs/ *adj* ‹*follower*› ferviente, entusiasta; ‹*worker*› que pone gran celo en su trabajo, entusiasta
zebra /ˈziːbrə || ˈzebrə, ziː-/ *n* (*pl* **-bras** *or* **-bra**) cebra *f*
zebra crossing *n* (BrE) paso *m* de cebra *or* de peatones
zee /ziː/, (BrE) **zed** /zed/ *n* zeta *f*
zelig /ˈzelɪg/ *n* camaleón *m*
Zen /zen/ *n* [u] (Relig) zen *m*
zenith /ˈziːnəθ || ˈzenɪθ/ *n* (Astron) cenit *m*, zenit *m*; **at the ~ of her popularity** en el cenit de su popularidad
zephyr /ˈzefər || ˈzefə(r)/ *n* (poet) céfiro *m* (liter)
zeppelin /ˈzepələn || ˈzepəlɪn/ *n* zepelín *m*
zero[1] /ˈzɪrəʊ, ˈziː- || ˈzɪərəʊ/ *n* (*pl* **zeros** *or* **zeroes**) 1 (number) cero *m*; **the temperature fell below ~** la temperatura bajó de los cero grados; **your chances of winning are ~** no tienes ninguna posibilidad de ganar, tus posibilidades de ganar son nulas; (*before n*) **~ hour** hora *f* cero 2 (person) (AmE colloq): **he's a total ~** es un inútil
zero[2] *adj* 1 cero *adj inv*; **~ degrees centigrade** cero grados centígrados; **~ gravity/visibility** gravedad *f*/visibilidad *f* nula 2 (colloq): **her understanding of the subject is ~** no tiene ni la más remota idea del tema

Phrasal verb

- **zero in on** [v ▸ adv ▸ prep ▸ o] ‹*target*› apuntarle directamente a; ‹*issue/problem*› centrarse en

zero-rated /ˈzɪrəʊˈreɪtɪd, ziː- || ˌzɪərəʊˈreɪtɪd/ *adj* (Tax) ‹*goods/item*› no sujeto a IVA
zest /zest/ *n* [u] 1 (gusto, relish) entusiasmo *m*, brío *m*; **his performance lacked ~** le faltó garra a su actuación (fam); **he lost his ~ for life** perdió las ganas de vivir 2 (piquancy, flavor) sabor *m*, sazón *f* 3 (Culin) cáscara *f*, peladura *f*; **add the grated ~ of one lemon** agregue la ralladura de un limón
zester /ˈzestər || ˈzestə(r)/ *n*: *utensilio concebido para obtener tiras finas de las cáscaras de los cítricos*
zigzag[1] /ˈzɪgzæg/ *n* zigzag *m*
zigzag[2] *adj* (*before n*) en zigzag, zigzagueante
zigzag[3] *vi* **-gg-** zigzaguear
zilch /zɪltʃ/ *n* [u] (sl) nada de nada; **how much did you get? — zilch** ¿cuánto te dieron? — ni cinco (fam)
zillion /ˈzɪljən/ *n* (colloq): **I have ~s of things to do** tengo tropecientas cosas que hacer (fam)
Zimbabwe /zɪmˈbɑːbwi/ *n* Zimbabwe *m*
Zimbabwean /zɪmˈbɑːbwiən/ *adj* zimbabuense
zinc /zɪŋk/ *n* [u] cinc *m*, zinc *m*
zing[1] /zɪŋ/ *vi* (colloq) ‹‹*bullet*›› silbar; **to ~ past** pasar silbando
zing[2] *n* (colloq) 1 (hiss) (*no pl*) silbido *m* 2 [u] (pep) chispa *f* (fam)
Zionism /ˈzaɪənɪzəm/ *n* [u] sionismo *m*
Zionist /ˈzaɪənəst || ˈzaɪənɪst/ *adj* sionista
zip[1] /zɪp/ *n*
A [u] (vigor) (colloq) garra *f* (fam), brío *m*
B [c] (fastener) (BrE) ▸ **zipper**[1]
zip[2] **-pp-** *vt* ‹*pocket/bag*› cerrar• la cremallera *or* (AmL tb) el cierre *or* (AmC, Méx, Ven tb) el zíper de
■ **zip** *vi*
A (with zipper): **the suitcase ~s open/shut** la maleta se abre/cierra con cremallera (*or* cierre *etc*); **the hood ~s on** la capucha se pone con cremallera (*or* cierre *etc*)
B (move fast) (colloq): **the morning ~ped by** la mañana (se) pasó volando (fam); **we ~ped through the work** (nos) despachamos el trabajo en un santiamén (fam); **we ~ped along** íbamos a toda mecha *or* a todo trapo (fam)

Phrasal verb

- **zip up** [v ▸ o ▸ adv, v ▸ adv ▸ o] ‹*bag*› cerrar•; **will you ~ me up, please?** ¿me subes la cremallera *or* (AmL tb) el cierre?

zip: **~ code** *n* (AmE) código *m* postal; **~ disk** *n* disco *m* zip; **~ fastener** *n* (BrE) ▸ **zipper**[1]; **~-on** *adj* (*before n*) ‹*hood/lining*› que se puede quitar, desmontable
zipper[1] /ˈzɪpər || ˈzɪpə(r)/ *n* (AmE) cremallera *f*, cierre *m* (AmL); **to do up/undo the ~** cerrar•/abrir• la cremallera (*or* el cierre)
zipper[2] *vt* (AmE) ▸ **zip**[2] *vt*
zippy /ˈzɪpi/ *adj* **-pier, -piest** (colloq) brioso
zit /zɪt/ *n* (colloq) grano *m*
zither /ˈzɪðər || ˈzɪðə(r)/ *n* cítara *f*
zodiac /ˈzəʊdiæk/ *n* **the ~** el zodíaco *or* zodiaco
zombie /ˈzɑːmbi/ *n* zombie *mf*, zombi *mf*
zone /zəʊn/ *n* 1 (area) zona *f*; **time ~** huso *m* horario 2 (AmE) distrito *m*
zonked (out) /zɑːŋkt || zɒŋkt/ *adj* (sl) 1 (high — on drugs) colgado (arg), colocado (arg); (— on drink) curda (arg), borracho 2 (exhausted): **to be ~** estar• hecho polvo
zoo /zuː/ *n* (*pl* **zoos**) zoológico *m*, zoo *m* (esp Esp)
zoological /ˈzəʊəˈlɑːdʒɪkəl/ *adj* (*before n*) zoológico
zoologist /zəʊˈɑːlədʒəst/ *n* zoólogo, -ga *m,f*
zoology /zəʊˈɑːlədʒi || zəʊˈɒlədʒi, zuː-/ *n* [u] zoología *f*
zoom[1] /zuːm/ *n*
A (sound) (*no pl*) zumbido *m*
B **~ (lens)** (Cin, Phot, TV) teleobjetivo *m*, zoom *m*
zoom[2] *vi* (move fast) (colloq) (+ *adv compl*): **to ~ along/past/off** ir•/pasar/salir• zumbando *or* como un bólido (fam); **she ~ed through her work** hizo el trabajo volando (fam)

Phrasal verb

- **zoom in** [v ▸ adv] **to ~ in (ON sth/sb)** hacer• un zoom in (SOBRE algo/algn)

zucchini /zʊˈkiːni/ *n* (*pl* **~** *or* **~s**) (AmE) calabacín *m*, calabacita *f* (Méx), zapallito *m* (largo *or* italiano) (CS)
Zulu[1] /ˈzuːluː/ *adj* zulú
Zulu[2] *n* 1 [c] (person) zulú *mf* 2 [u] (language) zulú *m*
zygote /ˈzaɪgəʊt/ *n* cigoto *m*, zigoto *m*

Appendices

Apéndices

Spanish verb tables

1 Guide to Verb Tables

Every Spanish verb entry in the dictionary is cross-referred to one of the conjugation models shown in the following tables. The reference is given in square brackets immediately after the headword.

All the simple tenses are shown for **hablar** [A1], **meter** [E1], and **partir** [I1], the conjugation models for regular -ar, -er, and -ir verbs. For other verbs only the irregular tenses are given.

Compound tenses are not listed in the tables. The perfect tenses are formed with the relevant tense of the auxiliary **haber** and the past participle:

Le *he hablado* de ti
Lamento que se *haya ofendido*
El profesor nos *había visto*
Cuando *hubo terminado* de hablar, ...
Para entonces ya *habremos terminado*
Si lo *hubiera sabido, habría llamado*

The continuous tenses are formed with the relevant tense of the auxiliary **estar** and the present participle:

Estoy estudiando el problema
Cuando llegó, *estábamos cerrando*
Estuvieron esperando mucho tiempo
¿*Han estado hablando* de mí?

Other verbs such as **andar**, **ir**, and **venir** can also be used as auxiliaries to express different nuances of meaning:

Andaba diciendo que ...
A medida que lo *fui conociendo*...
¿Por qué no te *vas vistiendo*?
Hace mucho tiempo que te lo *vengo diciendo*

2 Voseo

In parts of Latin America the pronoun 'vos' replaces 'tú' in the spoken language. This has different degrees of acceptability depending on the region. Whereas in some countries it is considered substandard and characteristic of uneducated speech, in others—notably in the River Plate area and in some Central American countries—it is the standard form of the second person singular.

'Vos' has its corresponding verb forms in the present tense and the imperative. These vary slightly from area to area. The following are the standard forms in Central America and the River Plate area:

Present indicative

hablar	vos hablás
meter	vos metés
partir	vos partís

Imperative

hablar	hablá
meter	meté
partir	partí
sentarse	sentate
moverse	movete
vestirse	vestite

There are also special forms for the present subjunctive and the negative imperative, although these are less widely used (many speakers use the forms corresponding to 'tú' in these cases, given in brackets here):

Present subjunctive

hablar	que vos hablés (que vos hables)
meter	que vos metás (que vos metas)
partir	que vos partás (que vos partas)

Negative imperative

hablar	no hablés (no hables)
meter	no metás (no metas)
partir	no partás (no partas)

Note that in Uruguay the verb forms corresponding to 'vos' are often used with the pronoun 'tú':

tú sabés que ...
tú no te imaginás cómo ...

3 Verbs ending in -ar

A1 hablar

gerundio (gerund)	participio pasado (past participle)	indicativo (indicative) presente (present)	imperfecto (imperfect)	pretérito indefinido (past simple)	futuro (future)
habl**ando**	habl**ado**	habl**o**	habl**aba**	habl**é**	habl**aré**
		habl**as**	habl**abas**	habl**aste**	habl**arás**
		habl**a**	habl**aba**	habl**ó**	habl**ará**
		habl**amos**	habl**ábamos**	habl**amos**	habl**aremos**
		habl**áis**	habl**abais**	habl**asteis**	habl**aréis**
		habl**an**	habl**aban**	habl**aron**	habl**arán**

condicional (conditional)	subjuntivo (subjunctive) presente (present)	imperfecto (imperfect)	futuro (future)	imperativo (imperative)
habl**aría**	habl**e**	habl**ara***	habl**are**	
habl**arías**	habl**es**	habl**aras**	habl**ares**	habl**a**
habl**aría**	habl**e**	habl**ara**	habl**are**	habl**e**
habl**aríamos**	habl**emos**	habl**áramos**	habl**áremos**	habl**emos**
habl**aríais**	habl**éis**	habl**arais**	habl**areis**	habl**ad**
habl**arían**	habl**en**	habl**aran**	habl**aren**	habl**en**

* all **-ar** verbs have an alternative form in which **-ara** is replaced by **-ase**, e.g. habl**ase**, habl**ases**, habl**ase**, habl**ásemos**, habl**aseis**, habl**asen**

A2 sacar

indicativo pretérito indefinido	subjuntivo presente	imperativo
saqué	saque	
sacaste	saques	saca
sacó	saque	saque
sacamos	saquemos	saquemos
sacasteis	saquéis	sacad
sacaron	saquen	saquen

A3 pagar

indicativo pretérito indefinido	subjuntivo presente	imperativo
pagué	pague	
pagaste	pagues	paga
pagó	pague	pague
pagamos	paguemos	paguemos
pagasteis	paguéis	pagad
pagaron	paguen	paguen

A4 cazar

indicativo pretérito indefinido	subjuntivo presente	imperativo
cacé	cace	
cazaste	caces	caza
cazó	cace	cace
cazamos	cacemos	cacemos
cazasteis	cacéis	cazad
cazaron	cacen	cacen

A5 pensar

indicativo presente	pretérito indefinido	subjuntivo presente	imperativo
pienso	pensé, etc	piense	
piensas		pienses	piensa
piensa		piense	piense
pensamos		pensemos	pensemos
pensáis		penséis	pensad
piensan		piensen	piensen

A6 empezar

indicativo presente	pretérito indefinido	subjuntivo presente	imperativo
empiezo	empecé	empiece	
empiezas	empezaste	empieces	empieza
empieza	empezó	empiece	empiece
empezamos	empezamos	empecemos	empecemos
empezáis	empezasteis	empecéis	empezad
empiezan	empezaron	empiecen	empiecen

A7 regar

indicativo presente	pretérito indefinido	subjuntivo presente	imperativo
riego	regué	riegue	
riegas	regaste	riegues	riega
riega	regó	riegue	riegue
regamos	regamos	reguemos	reguemos
regáis	regasteis	reguéis	regad
riegan	regaron	rieguen	rieguen

A8 rogar

indicativo presente	pretérito indefinido	subjuntivo presente	imperativo
ruego	rogué	ruegue	
ruegas	rogaste	ruegues	ruega
ruega	rogó	ruegue	ruegue
rogamos	rogamos	roguemos	roguemos
rogáis	rogasteis	roguéis	rogad
ruegan	rogaron	rueguen	rueguen

A9 trocar

indicativo presente	pretérito indefinido	subjuntivo presente	imperativo
trueco	troqué	trueque	
truecas	trocaste	trueques	trueca
trueca	trocó	trueque	trueque
trocamos	trocamos	troquemos	troquemos
trocáis	trocasteis	troquéis	trocad
truecan	trocaron	truequen	truequen

A10 contar

indicativo presente	pretérito indefinido	subjuntivo presente	imperativo
cuento	conté, etc	cuente	
cuentas		cuentes	cuenta
cuenta		cuente	cuente
contamos		contemos	contemos
contáis		contéis	contad
cuentan		cuenten	cuenten

A11 forzar

indicativo presente	pretérito indefinido	subjuntivo presente	imperativo
fuerzo	forcé	fuerce	
fuerzas	forzaste	fuerces	fuerza
fuerza	forzó	fuerce	fuerce
forzamos	forzamos	forcemos	forcemos
forzáis	forzasteis	forcéis	forzad
fuerzan	forzaron	fuercen	fuercen

A12 agorar

indicativo presente	pretérito indefinido	subjuntivo presente	imperativo
agüero	agoré, etc	agüere	
agüeras		agüeres	agüera
agüera		agüere	agüere
agoramos		agoremos	agoremos
agoráis		agoréis	agorad
agüeran		agüeren	agüeren

A13 avergonzar

indicativo presente	pretérito indefinido	subjuntivo presente	imperativo
avergüenzo	avergoncé	avergüence	
avergüenzas	avergonzaste	avergüences	avergüenza
avergüenza	avergonzó	avergüence	avergüence
avergonzamos	avergonzamos	avergoncemos	avergoncemos
avergonzáis	avergonzasteis	avergoncéis	avergonzad
avergüenzan	avergonzaron	avergüencen	avergüencen

A14 desosar

indicativo presente	pretérito indefinido	subjuntivo presente	imperativo
deshueso	desosé, etc	deshuese	
deshuesas		deshueses	deshuesa
deshuesa		deshuese	deshuese
desosamos		desosemos	desosemos
desosáis		desoséis	desosad
deshuesan		deshuesen	deshuesen

A15 jugar

indicativo presente	pretérito indefinido	subjuntivo presente	imperativo
juego	jugué	juegue	
juegas	jugaste	juegues	juega
juega	jugó	juegue	juegue
jugamos	jugamos	juguemos	juguemos
jugáis	jugasteis	juguéis	jugad
juegan	jugaron	jueguen	jueguen

A16 desaguar

indicativo pretérito indefinido	subjuntivo presente	imperativo
desagüé	desagüe	
desaguaste	desagües	desagua
desaguó	desagüe	desagüe
desaguamos	desagüemos	desagüemos
desaguasteis	desagüéis	desaguad
desaguaron	desagüen	desagüen

A17 vaciar

indicativo presente	pretérito indefinido	subjuntivo presente	imperativo
vacío	vacié, etc	vacíe	
vacías		vacíes	vacía
vacía		vacíe	vacíe
vaciamos		vaciemos	vaciemos
vaciáis		vaciéis	vaciad
vacían		vacíen	vacíen

A18 actuar

indicativo presente	pretérito indefinido	subjuntivo presente	imperativo
actúo	actué, etc	actúe	
actúas		actúes	actúa
actúa		actúe	actúe
actuamos		actuemos	actuemos
actuáis		actuéis	actuad
actúan		actúen	actúen

A19 aislar

indicativo presente	pretérito indefinido	subjuntivo presente	imperativo
aíslo	aislé, etc	aísle	
aíslas		aísles	aísla
aísla		aísle	aísle
aislamos		aislemos	aislemos
aisláis		aisléis	aislad
aíslan		aíslen	aíslen

A20 ahincar

indicativo presente	pretérito indefinido	subjuntivo presente	imperativo
ahínco	ahinqué	ahínque	
ahíncas	ahincaste	ahínques	ahínca
ahínca	ahincó	ahínque	ahínque
ahincamos	ahincamos	ahinquemos	ahinquemos
ahincáis	ahincasteis	ahinquéis	ahincad
ahíncan	ahincaron	ahínquen	ahínquen

A21 arcaizar

indicativo presente	pretérito indefinido	subjuntivo presente	imperativo
arcaízo	arcaicé	arcaíce	
arcaízas	arcaizaste	arcaíces	arcaíza
arcaíza	arcaizó	arcaíce	arcaíce
arcaizamos	arcaizamos	arcaicemos	arcaicemos
arcaizáis	arcaizasteis	arcaicéis	arcaizad
arcaízan	arcaizaron	arcaícen	arcaícen

A22 cabrahigar

indicativo presente	pretérito indefinido	subjuntivo presente	imperativo
cabrahígo	cabrahigué	cabrahígue	
cabrahígas	cabrahigaste	cabrahígues	cabrahíga
cabrahíga	cabrahigó	cabrahígue	cabrahígue
cabrahigamos	cabrahigamos	cabrahiguemos	cabrahiguemos
cabrahigáis	cabrahigasteis	cabrahiguéis	cabrahigad
cabrahígan	cabrahigaron	cabrahíguen	cabrahíguen

A23 aunar

indicativo		subjuntivo	imperativo
presente	pretérito indefinido	presente	
aúno	auné, etc	aúne	
aúnas		aúnes	aúna
aúna		aúne	aúne
aunamos		aunemos	aunemos
aunáis		aunéis	aunad
aúnan		aúnen	aúnen

A24 andar

indicativo	subjuntivo
pretérito indefinido	imperfecto
anduve	anduviera
anduviste	anduvieras
anduvo	anduviera
anduvimos	anduviéramos
anduvisteis	anduvierais
anduvieron	anduvieran

A25 dar

indicativo		subjuntivo	
presente	pretérito indefinido	presente	imperfecto
doy	di	dé	diera
das	diste	des	dieras
da	dio	dé	diera
damos	dimos	demos	diéramos
dais	disteis	deis	dierais
dan	dieron	den	dieran

A26 errar

indicativo	subjuntivo	imperativo
presente	presente	
yerro	yerre	
yerras	yerres	yerra
yerra	yerre	yerre
erramos	erremos	erremos
erráis	erréis	errad
yerran	yerren	yerren

A27 estar

gerundio	participio pasado	indicativo			
		presente	imperfecto	pretérito indefinido	futuro
estando	estado	estoy	estaba	estuve	estaré
		estás	estabas	estuviste	estarás
		está	estaba	estuvo	estará
		estamos	estábamos	estuvimos	estaremos
		estáis	estabais	estuvisteis	estaréis
		están	estaban	estuvieron	estarán

condicional	subjuntivo		imperativo
	presente	imperfecto	
estaría	esté	estuviera	
estarías	estés	estuvieras	está
estaría	esté	estuviera	esté
estaríamos	estemos	estuviéramos	estemos
estaríais	estéis	estuvierais	estad
estarían	estén	estuvieran	estén

4 Verbs ending in -er

E1 meter

gerundio (gerund)	participio pasado (past participle)	indicativo (indicative) presente (present)	imperfecto (imperfect)	pretérito indefinido (past simple)	futuro (future)
met**iendo**	met**ido**	met**o**	met**ía**	met**í**	met**eré**
		met**es**	met**ías**	met**iste**	met**erás**
		met**e**	met**ía**	met**ió**	met**erá**
		met**emos**	met**íamos**	met**imos**	met**eremos**
		met**éis**	met**íais**	met**isteis**	met**eréis**
		met**en**	met**ían**	met**ieron**	met**erán**

condicional (conditional)	subjuntivo (subjunctive) presente (present)	imperfecto (imperfect)	futuro (future)	imperativo (imperative)
met**ería**	met**a**	met**iera***	met**iere**	
met**erías**	met**as**	met**ieras**	met**ieres**	met**e**
met**ería**	met**a**	met**iera**	met**iere**	met**a**
met**eríamos**	met**amos**	met**iéramos**	met**iéremos**	met**amos**
met**eríais**	met**áis**	met**ierais**	met**iereis**	met**ed**
met**erían**	met**an**	met**ieran**	met**ieren**	met**an**

* all **-er** verbs have an alternative form in which **-era** is replaced by **-ese**, e.g. met**iese**, met**ieses**, met**iese**, met**iésemos**, met**ieseis**, met**iesen**

E2 vencer

indicativo presente	pretérito indefinido	subjuntivo presente	imperativo
venzo	vencí, etc	venza	
vences		venzas	vence
vence		venza	venza
vencemos		venzamos	venzamos
vencéis		venzáis	venced
vencen		venzan	venzan

E3 conocer

indicativo presente	pretérito indefinido	subjuntivo presente	imperativo
conozco	conocí, etc	conozca	
conoces		conozcas	conoce
conoce		conozca	conozca
conocemos		conozcamos	conozcamos
conocéis		conozcáis	conoced
conocen		conozcan	conozcan

E4 placer

indicativo presente	pretérito indefinido	subjuntivo presente	imperfecto	futuro	imperativo
plazco	plací	plazca	placiera	placiere	
places	placiste	plazcas	placieras	placieres	place
place	plació[1]	plazca[3]	placiera[4]	placiere[5]	plazca
placemos	placimos	plazcamos	placiéramos	placiéremos	plazcamos
placéis	placisteis	plazcáis	placierais	placiereis	placed
placen	placieron[2]	plazcan	placieran	placieren	plazcan

alternative forms, applicable only to the verb 'placer':
[1]plugo; [2]pluguieron; [3]plega or plegue; [4]pluguiera or pluguiese; [5]pluguiere.

E5 yacer

indicativo presente	pretérito indefinido	subjuntivo presente	imperativo
yazco[1]	yací, etc	yazca[2]	
yaces		yazcas	yace[3]
yace		yazca	yazca
yacemos		yazcamos	yazcamos
yacéis		yazcáis	yaced
yacen		yazcan	yazcan

[1]alternative forms: yazgo or yago; [2]alternative conjugations: yazga, yazgas, etc or yaga, yagas, etc.
[3]alternative conjugations: yaz, yazga or yaga, yazgamos or yagamos, yaced, yazgan or yagan.

E6 coger

indicativo presente	pretérito indefinido	subjuntivo presente	imperativo
cojo	cogí, etc	coja	
coges		cojas	coge
coge		coja	coja
cogemos		cojamos	cojamos
cogéis		cojáis	coged
cogen		cojan	cojan

E7 tañer

gerundio	indicativo pretérito indefinido	subjuntivo imperfecto
tañendo	tañí	tañera
	tañiste	tañeras
	tañó	tañera
	tañimos	tañéramos
	tañisteis	tañerais
	tañeron	tañeran

E8 entender

indicativo presente	pretérito indefinido	subjuntivo presente	imperativo
entiendo	entendí	entienda	
entiendes	entendiste	entiendas	entiende
entiende	entendió	entienda	entienda
entendemos	entendimos	entendamos	entendamos
entendéis	entendisteis	entendáis	entended
entienden	entendieron	entiendan	entiendan

E9 mover

indicativo presente	pretérito indefinido	subjuntivo presente	imperativo
muevo	moví, etc	mueva	
mueves		muevas	mueve
mueve		mueva	mueva
movemos		movamos	movamos
movéis		mováis	moved
mueven		muevan	muevan

E10 torcer

indicativo		subjuntivo	imperativo
presente	pretérito indefinido	presente	
tuerzo	torcí, etc	tuerza	
tuerces		tuerzas	tuerce
tuerce		tuerza	tuerza
torcemos		torzamos	torzamos
torcéis		torzáis	torced
tuercen		tuerzan	tuerzan

E11 volver

participio pasado	indicativo		subjuntivo	imperativo
	presente	pretérito indefinido	presente	
vuelto	vuelvo	volví, etc	vuelva	
	vuelves		vuelvas	vuelve
	vuelve		vuelva	vuelva
	volvemos		volvamos	volvamos
	volvéis		volváis	volved
	vuelven		vuelvan	vuelvan

E12 oler

indicativo		subjuntivo	imperativo
presente	pretérito indefinido	presente	
huelo	olí, etc	huela	
hueles		huelas	huele
huele		huela	huela
olemos		olamos	olamos
oléis		oláis	oled
huelen		huelan	huelan

E13 leer

gerundio	indicativo	subjuntivo
	pretérito indefinido	imperfecto
leyendo	leí	leyera
	leíste	leyeras
	leyó	leyera
	leímos	leyéramos
	leísteis	leyerais
	leyeron	leyeran

E14 proveer

participio pasado	indicativo	subjuntivo
	pretérito indefinido	imperfecto
provisto	proveí	proveyera
	proveíste	proveyeras
	proveyó	proveyera
	proveímos	proveyéramos
	proveísteis	proveyerais
	proveyeron	proveyeran

E15 caber

indicativo				condicional	subjuntivo		imperativo
presente	imperfecto	pretérito indefinido	futuro		presente	imperfecto	
quepo	cabía	cupe	cabré	cabría	quepa	cupiera	
cabes	cabías	cupiste	cabrás	cabrías	quepas	cupieras	cabe
cabe	cabía	cupo	cabrá	cabría	quepa	cupiera	quepa
cabemos	cabíamos	cupimos	cabremos	cabríamos	quepamos	cupiéramos	quepamos
cabéis	cabíais	cupisteis	cabréis	cabríais	quepáis	cupierais	cabed
caben	cabían	cupieron	cabrán	cabrían	quepan	cupieran	quepan

E16 caer

gerundio	participio pasado	indicativo			subjuntivo		imperativo
		presente	imperfecto	pretérito indefinido	presente	imperfecto	
cayendo	caído	caigo	caía	caí	caiga	cayera	
		caes	caías	caíste	caigas	cayeras	cae
		cae	caía	cayó	caiga	cayera	caiga
		caemos	caíamos	caímos	caigamos	cayéramos	caigamos
		caéis	caíais	caísteis	caigáis	cayerais	caed
		caen	caían	cayeron	caigan	cayeran	caigan

E17 haber

indicativo				condicional	subjuntivo		imperativo
presente	imperfecto	pretérito indefinido	futuro		presente	imperfecto	
he	había	hube	habré	habría	haya	hubiera	
has	habías	hubiste	habrás	habrías	hayas	hubieras	he
ha	había	hubo	habrá	habría	haya	hubiera	haya
hemos	habíamos	hubimos	habremos	habríamos	hayamos	hubiéramos	hayamos
habéis	habíais	hubisteis	habréis	habríais	hayáis	hubierais	habed
han	habían	hubieron	habrán	habrían	hayan	hubieran	hayan

E18 hacer

participio pasado	indicativo			condicional	subjuntivo		imperativo
	presente	pretérito indefinido	futuro		presente	imperfecto	
hecho	hago	hice	haré	haría	haga	hiciera	
	haces	hiciste	harás	harías	hagas	hicieras	haz
	hace	hizo	hará	haría	haga	hiciera	haga
	hacemos	hicimos	haremos	haríamos	hagamos	hiciéramos	hagamos
	hacéis	hicisteis	haréis	haríais	hagáis	hicierais	haced
	hacen	hicieron	harán	harían	hagan	hicieran	hagan

E19 rehacer

participio pasado	indicativo presente	pretérito indefinido	futuro	condicional	subjuntivo presente	imperfecto	imperativo
rehecho	rehago	rehíce	reharé	reharía	rehaga	rehiciera	
	rehaces	rehiciste	reharás	reharías	rehagas	rehicieras	rehaz
	rehace	rehízo	rehará	reharía	rehaga	rehiciera	rehaga
	rehacemos	rehicimos	reharemos	reharíamos	rehagamos	rehiciéramos	rehagamos
	rehacéis	rehicisteis	reharéis	reharíais	rehagáis	rehicierais	rehaced
	rehacen	rehicieron	reharán	reharían	rehagan	rehicieran	rehagan

E20 satisfacer

indicativo presente	pretérito indefinido	futuro	condicional	subjuntivo presente	imperfecto	imperativo
satisfago	satisfice	satisfaré	satisfaría	satisfaga	satisficiera	
satisfaces	satisficiste	satisfarás	satisfarías	satisfagas	satisficieras	satisfaz[1]
satisface	satisfizo	satisfará	satisfaría	satisfaga	satisficiera	satisfaga
satisfacemos	satisficimos	satisfaremos	satisfaríamos	satisfagamos	satisficiéramos	satisfagamos
satisfacéis	satisficisteis	satisfaréis	satisfaríais	satisfagáis	satisficierais	satisfaced
satisfacen	satisficieron	satisfarán	satisfarían	satisfagan	satisficieran	satisfagan

[1] alternative form: satisface

E21 poder

gerundio	participio pasado
pudiendo	podido

indicativo presente	pretérito indefinido	futuro	condicional	subjuntivo presente	imperfecto	imperativo
puedo	pude	podré	podría	pueda	pudiera	
puedes	pudiste	podrás	podrías	puedas	pudieras	puede
puede	pudo	podrá	podría	pueda	pudiera	pueda
podemos	pudimos	podremos	podríamos	podamos	pudiéramos	podamos
podéis	pudisteis	podréis	podríais	podáis	pudierais	poded
pueden	pudieron	podrán	podrían	puedan	pudieran	puedan

E22 poner

participio pasado	indicativo presente	pretérito indefinido	futuro	condicional	subjuntivo presente	imperfecto	imperativo
puesto	pongo	puse	pondré	pondría	ponga	pusiera	
	pones	pusiste	pondrás	pondrías	pongas	pusieras	pon
	pone	puso	pondrá	pondría	ponga	pusiera	ponga
	ponemos	pusimos	pondremos	pondríamos	pongamos	pusiéramos	pongamos
	ponéis	pusisteis	pondréis	pondríais	pongáis	pusierais	poned
	ponen	pusieron	pondrán	pondrían	pongan	pusieran	pongan

E23 traer

gerundio	participio pasado	indicativo presente	indicativo pretérito indefinido	subjuntivo presente	subjuntivo imperfecto	imperativo
trayendo	traído	traigo	traje	traiga	trajera	
		traes	trajiste	traigas	trajeras	trae
		trae	trajo	traiga	trajera	traiga
		traemos	trajimos	traigamos	trajéramos	traigamos
		traéis	trajisteis	traigáis	trajerais	traed
		traen	trajeron	traigan	trajeran	traigan

E24 querer

indicativo presente	indicativo imperfecto	indicativo pretérito indefinido	indicativo futuro	condicional	subjuntivo presente	subjuntivo imperfecto	imperativo
quiero	quería	quise	querré	querría	quiera	quisiera	
quieres	querías	quisiste	querrás	querrías	quieras	quisieras	quiere
quiere	quería	quiso	querrá	querría	quiera	quisiera	quiera
queremos	queríamos	quisimos	querremos	querríamos	queramos	quisiéramos	queramos
queréis	queríais	quisisteis	querréis	querríais	queráis	quisierais	quered
quieren	querían	quisieron	querrán	querrían	quieran	quisieran	quieran

E25 saber

indicativo presente	indicativo pretérito indefinido	indicativo futuro	condicional	subjuntivo presente	subjuntivo imperfecto	imperativo
sé	supe	sabré	sabría	sepa	supiera	
sabes	supiste	sabrás	sabrías	sepas	supieras	sabe
sabe	supo	sabrá	sabría	sepa	supiera	sepa
sabemos	supimos	sabremos	sabríamos	sepamos	supiéramos	sepamos
sabéis	supisteis	sabréis	sabríais	sepáis	supierais	sabed
saben	supieron	sabrán	sabrían	sepan	supieran	sepan

E26 ser

gerundio	participio pasado	indicativo presente	indicativo imperfecto	indicativo pretérito indefinido	indicativo futuro
siendo	sido	soy	era	fui	seré
		eres	eras	fuiste	serás
		es	era	fue	será
		somos	éramos	fuimos	seremos
		sois	erais	fuisteis	seréis
		son	eran	fueron	serán

condicional	subjuntivo presente	subjuntivo imperfecto	subjuntivo futuro	imperativo
sería	sea	fuera	fuere	
serías	seas	fueras	fueres	sé
sería	sea	fuera	fuere	sea
seríamos	seamos	fuéramos	fuéremos	seamos
seríais	seáis	fuerais	fuereis	sed
serían	sean	fueran	fueren	sean

E27 tener

indicativo			condicional	subjuntivo		imperativo
presente	pretérito indefinido	futuro		presente	imperfecto	
tengo	tuve	tendré	tendría	tenga	tuviera	
tienes	tuviste	tendrás	tendrías	tengas	tuvieras	ten
tiene	tuvo	tendrá	tendría	tenga	tuviera	tenga
tenemos	tuvimos	tendremos	tendríamos	tengamos	tuviéramos	tengamos
tenéis	tuvisteis	tendréis	tendríais	tengáis	tuvierais	tened
tienen	tuvieron	tendrán	tendrían	tengan	tuvieran	tengan

E28 valer

indicativo			condicional	subjuntivo		imperativo
presente	pretérito indefinido	futuro		presente	imperfecto	
valgo	valí	valdré	valdría	valga	valiera	
vales	valiste	valdrás	valdrías	valgas	valieras	vale
vale	valió	valdrá	valdría	valga	valiera	valga
valemos	valimos	valdremos	valdríamos	valgamos	valiéramos	valgamos
valéis	valisteis	valdréis	valdríais	valgáis	valierais	valed
valen	valieron	valdrán	valdrían	valgan	valieran	valgan

E29 ver

participio pasado	indicativo			subjuntivo	imperativo
	presente	imperfecto	pretérito indefinido	presente	
visto	veo	veía	vi	vea	
	ves	veías	viste	veas	ve
	ve	veía	vio	vea	vea
	vemos	veíamos	vimos	veamos	veamos
	veis	veíais	visteis	veáis	ved
	ven	veían	vieron	vean	vean

E30 romper

participio pasado
roto

E31 verter

gerundio	indicativo		subjuntivo	imperativo
	presente	pretérito indefinido	imperfecto	
vertiendo[1]	vierto	vertí	vertiera[4]	
	viertes	vertiste	vertieras	vierte
	vierte	vertió[2]	vertiera	vierta
	vertemos	vertimos	vertiéramos	vertamos
	vertéis	vertisteis	vertierais	verted
	vierten	vertieron[3]	vertieran	viertan

alternative forms: [1]virtiendo; [2]virtió; [3]virtieron; [4]virtiera, virtieras, etc.

5 Verbs ending in -ir

I1 partir

gerundio (gerund)	participio pasado (past participle)	indicativo (indicative) presente (present)	imperfecto (imperfect)	pretérito indefinido (past simple)	futuro (future)
part**iendo**	part**ido**	part**o**	part**ía**	part**í**	part**iré**
		part**es**	part**ías**	part**iste**	part**irás**
		part**e**	part**ía**	part**ió**	part**irá**
		part**imos**	part**íamos**	part**imos**	part**iremos**
		part**ís**	part**íais**	part**isteis**	part**iréis**
		part**en**	part**ían**	part**ieron**	part**irán**

condicional (conditional)	subjuntivo (subjunctive) presente (present)	imperfecto (imperfect)	futuro (future)	imperativo (imperative)
part**iría**	part**a**	part**iera***	part**iere**	
part**irías**	part**as**	part**ieras**	part**ieres**	part**e**
part**iría**	part**a**	part**iera**	part**iere**	part**a**
part**iríamos**	part**amos**	part**iéramos**	part**iéremos**	part**amos**
part**iríais**	part**áis**	part**ierais**	part**iereis**	part**id**
part**irían**	part**an**	part**ieran**	part**ieren**	part**an**

* all **-ir** verbs have an alternative form in which **-era** is replaced by **-ese**, e.g. part**iese**, part**ieses**, part**iese**, part**iésemos**, part**ieseis**, part**iesen**

I2 distinguir

indicativo presente	pretérito indefinido	subjuntivo presente	imperativo
distingo	distinguí, etc	distinga	
distingues		distingas	distingue
distingue		distinga	distinga
distinguimos		distingamos	distingamos
distinguís		distingáis	distinguid
distinguen		distingan	distingan

I3 delinquir

indicativo presente	pretérito indefinido	subjuntivo presente	imperativo
delinco	delinquí, etc	delinca	
delinques		delincas	delinque
delinque		delinca	delinca
delinquimos		delincamos	delincamos
delinquís		delincáis	delinquid
delinquen		delincan	delincan

I4 zurcir

indicativo presente	pretérito indefinido	subjuntivo presente	imperativo
zurzo	zurcí, etc	zurza	
zurces		zurzas	zurce
zurce		zurza	zurza
zurcimos		zurzamos	zurzamos
zurcís		zurzáis	zurcid
zurcen		zurzan	zurzan

I5 lucir

indicativo presente	pretérito indefinido	subjuntivo presente	imperativo
luzco	lucí, etc	luzca	
luces		luzcas	luce
luce		luzca	luzca
lucimos		luzcamos	luzcamos
lucís		luzcáis	lucid
lucen		luzcan	luzcan

I6 reducir

indicativo		subjuntivo		imperativo
presente	pretérito indefinido	presente	imperfecto	
reduzco	reduje	reduzca	redujera	
reduces	redujiste	reduzcas	redujeras	reduce
reduce	redujo	reduzca	redujera	reduzca
reducimos	redujimos	reduzcamos	redujéramos	reduzcamos
reducís	redujisteis	reduzcáis	redujerais	reducid
reducen	redujeron	reduzcan	redujeran	reduzcan

I7 dirigir

indicativo		subjuntivo	imperativo
presente	pretérito indefinido	presente	
dirijo	dirigí, etc	dirija	
diriges		dirijas	dirige
dirige		dirija	dirija
dirigimos		dirijamos	dirijamos
dirigís		dirijáis	dirigid
dirigen		dirijan	dirijan

I8 regir

indicativo		subjuntivo	imperativo
presente	pretérito indefinido	presente	
rijo	regí, etc	rija	
riges		rijas	rige
rige		rija	rija
regimos		rijamos	rijamos
regís		rijáis	regid
rigen		rijan	rijan

I9 gruñir

gerundio	indicativo	subjuntivo
	pretérito indefinido	imperfecto
gruñendo	gruñí	gruñera
	gruñiste	gruñeras
	gruñó	gruñera
	gruñimos	gruñéramos
	gruñisteis	gruñerais
	gruñeron	gruñeran

I10 asir

indicativo		subjuntivo	imperativo
presente	pretérito indefinido	presente	
asgo	así, etc	asga	
ases		asgas	ase
ase		asga	asga
asimos		asgamos	asgamos
asís		asgáis	asid
asen		asgan	asgan

I11 sentir

gerundio	participio pasado	indicativo		subjuntivo		imperativo
		presente	pretérito indefinido	presente	imperfecto	
sintiendo	sentido	siento	sentí	sienta	sintiera	
		sientes	sentiste	sientas	sintieras	siente
		siente	sintió	sienta	sintiera	sienta
		sentimos	sentimos	sintamos	sintiéramos	sintamos
		sentís	sentisteis	sintáis	sintierais	sentid
		sienten	sintieron	sientan	sintieran	sientan

I12 discernir

indicativo		subjuntivo	imperativo
presente	pretérito indefinido	presente	
discierno	discerní, etc	discierna	
disciernes		disciernas	discierne
discierne		discierna	discierna
discernimos		discernamos	discernamos
discernís		discernáis	discernid
disciernen		disciernan	disciernan

I13 adquirir

indicativo		subjuntivo	imperativo
presente	pretérito indefinido	presente	
adquiero	adquirí, etc	adquiera	
adquieres		adquieras	adquiere
adquiere		adquiera	adquiera
adquirimos		adquiramos	adquiramos
adquirís		adquiráis	adquirid
adquieren		adquieran	adquieran

I14 pedir

gerundio	participio pasado	indicativo		subjuntivo		imperativo
		presente	**pretérito indefinido**	**presente**	**imperfecto**	
pidiendo	pedido	pido	pedí	pida	pidiera	
		pides	pediste	pidas	pidieras	pide
		pide	pidió	pida	pidiera	pida
		pedimos	pedimos	pidamos	pidiéramos	pidamos
		pedís	pedisteis	pidáis	pidierais	pedid
		piden	pidieron	pidan	pidieran	pidan

I15 ceñir

gerundio	participio pasado	indicativo			subjuntivo		imperativo
		presente	**imperfecto**	**pretérito indefinido**	**presente**	**imperfecto**	
ciñendo	ceñido	ciño	ceñía	ceñí	ciña	ciñera	
		ciñes	ceñías	ceñiste	ciñas	ciñeras	ciñe
		ciñe	ceñía	ciñó	ciña	ciñera	ciña
		ceñimos	ceñíamos	ceñimos	ciñamos	ciñéramos	ciñamos
		ceñís	ceñíais	ceñisteis	ciñáis	ciñerais	ceñid
		ciñen	ceñían	ciñeron	ciñan	ciñeran	ciñan

I16 dormir

gerundio	participio pasado	indicativo		subjuntivo		imperativo
		presente	**pretérito indefinido**	**presente**	**imperfecto**	**futuro**
durmiendo	dormido	duermo	dormí	duerma	durmiera	
		duermes	dormiste	duermas	durmieras	duerme
		duerme	durmió	duerma	durmiera	duerma
		dormimos	dormimos	durmamos	durmiéramos	durmamos
		dormís	dormisteis	durmáis	durmierais	dormid
		duermen	durmieron	duerman	durmieran	duerman

I17 embaír

gerundio	indicativo	subjuntivo
	pretérito indefinido	**imperfecto**
embayendo	embaí	embayera
	embaíste	embayeras
	embayó	embayera
	embaímos	embayéramos
	embaísteis	embayerais
	embayeron	embayeran

I18 reír

gerundio	participio pasado
riendo	reído

indicativo presente	imperfecto	pretérito indefinido	futuro	condicional	subjuntivo presente	imperfecto	imperativo
río	reía	reí	reiré	reiría	ría	riera	
ríes	reías	reíste	reirás	reirías	rías	rieras	ríe
ríe	reía	rió	reirá	reiría	ría	riera	ría
reímos	reíamos	reímos	reiremos	reiríamos	riamos	riéramos	riamos
reís	reíais	reísteis	reiréis	reiríais	riáis	rierais	reíd
ríen	reían	rieron	reirán	reirían	rían	rieran	rían

I19 argüir

gerundio	participio pasado	indicativo presente	imperfecto	pretérito indefinido	subjuntivo presente	imperfecto	imperativo
arguyendo	argüido	arguyo	argüía, etc	argüí	arguya	arguyera	
		arguyes		argüiste	arguyas	arguyeras	arguye
		arguye		arguyó	arguya	arguyera	arguya
		argüimos		argüimos	arguyamos	arguyéramos	arguyamos
		argüís		argüisteis	arguyáis	arguyerais	argüid
		arguyen		arguyeron	arguyan	arguyeran	arguyan

I20 huir

gerundio	participio pasado	indicativo presente	imperfecto	pretérito indefinido	subjuntivo presente	imperfecto	imperativo
huyendo	huido	huyo	huía, etc	huí	huya	huyera	
		huyes		huiste	huyas	huyeras	huye
		huye		huyó	huya	huyera	huya
		huimos		huimos	huyamos	huyéramos	huyamos
		huís		huisteis	huyáis	huyerais	huid
		huyen		huyeron	huyan	huyeran	huyan

I21 rehuir

indicativo presente	pretérito indefinido	subjuntivo presente	imperativo
rehúyo	rehuí, etc	rehúya	
rehúyes		rehúyas	rehúye
rehúye		rehúya	rehúya
rehuimos		rehuyamos	rehuyamos
rehuís		rehuyáis	rehuid
rehúyen		rehúyan	rehúyan

I22 prohibir

indicativo presente	pretérito indefinido	subjuntivo presente	imperativo
prohíbo	prohibí, etc	prohíba	
prohíbes		prohíbas	prohíbe
prohíbe		prohíba	prohíba
prohibimos		prohibamos	prohibamos
prohibís		prohibáis	prohibid
prohíben		prohíban	prohíban

I23 reunir

indicativo		subjuntivo	imperativo
presente	pretérito indefinido	presente	
reúno	reuní, etc	reúna	
reúnes		reúnas	reúne
reúne		reúna	reúna
reunimos		reunamos	reunamos
reunís		reunáis	reunid
reúnen		reúnan	reúnan

I24 decir

gerundio	participio pasado
diciendo	dicho

indicativo				condicional	subjuntivo		imperativo
presente	imperfecto	pretérito indefinido	futuro		presente	imperfecto	
digo	decía	dije	diré	diría	diga	dijera	
dices	decías	dijiste	dirás	dirías	digas	dijeras	di
dice	decía	dijo	dirá	diría	diga	dijera	diga
decimos	decíamos	dijimos	diremos	diríamos	digamos	dijéramos	digamos
decís	decíais	dijisteis	diréis	diríais	digáis	dijerais	decid
dicen	decían	dijeron	dirán	dirían	digan	dijeran	digan

I25 bendecir

participio pasado	indicativo			condicional	imperativo
	presente	pretérito indefinido	futuro		
bendecido	bendigo	bendije	bendeciré	bendeciría	
	bendices	bendijiste	bendecirás	bendecirías	bendice
	bendice	bendijo	bendecirá	bendeciría	bendiga
	bendecimos	bendijimos	bendeciremos	bendeciríamos	bendigamos
	bendecís	bendijisteis	bendeciréis	bendeciríais	bendecid
	bendicen	bendijeron	bendecirán	bendecirían	bendigan

I26 erguir

gerundio	indicativo		subjuntivo		imperativo
	presente	pretérito indefinido	presente	imperfecto	
irguiendo	yergo[1]	erguí	yerga[2]	irguiera	
	yergues	erguiste	yergas	irguieras	yergue[3]
	yergue	irguió	yerga	irguiera	yerga
	erguimos	erguimos	yergamos	irguiéramos	yergamos
	erguís	erguisteis	yergáis	irguierais	erguid
	yerguen	irguieron	yergan	irguieran	yergan

[1]alternative conjugation: irgo, irgues, irgue, erguimos, erguís, irguen; [2]alternative conjugation: irga, irgas, irga, irgamos, irgáis, irgan;
[3]alternative conjugation: irgue, irga, irgamos, erguid, irgan.

I27 ir

gerundio	participio pasado	indicativo presente	imperfecto	pretérito indefinido	futuro
yendo	ido	voy	iba	fui	iré
		vas	ibas	fuiste	irás
		va	iba	fue	irá
		vamos	íbamos	fuimos	iremos
		vais	ibais	fuisteis	iréis
		van	iban	fueron	irán

condicional	subjuntivo presente	imperfecto	futuro	imperativo
iría	vaya	fuera	fuere	
irías	vayas	fueras	fueres	ve
iría	vaya	fuera	fuere	vaya
iríamos	vayamos	fuéramos	fuéremos	vayamos
iríais	vayáis	fuerais	fuereis	id
irían	vayan	fueran	fueren	vayan

I28 oír

gerundio	participio pasado
oyendo	oído

indicativo presente	imperfecto	pretérito	futuro indefinido	condicional	subjuntivo presente	imperfecto	imperativo
oigo	oía	oí	oiré	oiría	oiga	oyera	
oyes	oías	oíste	oirás	oirías	oigas	oyeras	oye
oye	oía	oyó	oirá	oiría	oiga	oyera	oiga
oímos	oíamos	oímos	oiremos	oiríamos	oigamos	oyéramos	oigamos
oís	oíais	oísteis	oiréis	oiríais	oigáis	oyerais	oíd
oyen	oían	oyeron	oirán	oirían	oigan	oyeran	oigan

I29 salir

indicativo presente	pretérito indefinido	futuro	condicional	subjuntivo presente	imperfecto	imperativo
salgo	salí, etc	saldré	saldría	salga	saliera	
sales		saldrás	saldrías	salgas	salieras	sal
sale		saldrá	saldría	salga	saliera	salga
salimos		saldremos	saldríamos	salgamos	saliéramos	salgamos
salís		saldréis	saldríais	salgáis	salierais	salid
salen		saldrán	saldrían	salgan	salieran	salgan

I30 seguir

indicativo presente	pretérito indefinido	subjuntivo presente	imperfecto	imperativo
sigo	seguí	siga	siguiera	
sigues	seguiste	sigas	siguieras	sigue
sigue	siguió	siga	siguiera	siga
seguimos	seguimos	sigamos	siguiéramos	sigamos
seguís	seguisteis	sigáis	siguierais	seguid
siguen	siguieron	sigan	siguieran	sigan

I31 venir

gerundio	indicativo			condicional	subjuntivo		imperativo
	presente	pretérito indefinido	futuro		presente	imperfecto	
viniendo	vengo	vine	vendré	vendría	venga	viniera	
	vienes	viniste	vendrás	vendrías	vengas	vinieras	ven
	viene	vino	vendrá	vendría	venga	viniera	venga
	venimos	vinimos	vendremos	vendríamos	vengamos	viniéramos	vengamos
	venís	vinisteis	vendréis	vendríais	vengáis	vinierais	venid
	vienen	vinieron	vendrán	vendrían	vengan	vinieran	vengan

I32 abolir

This is a regular verb but in the present indicative it is only used in the first and second person plural.

I33 abrir

participio pasado
abierto

I34 escribir

participio pasado
escrito

I35 freír

gerundio	participio pasado	indicativo		subjuntivo		imperativo
		presente	pretérito indefinido	presente	imperfecto	
friendo	frito	frío	freí	fría	friera	
		fríes	freíste	frías	frieras	fríe
		fríe	frió	fría	friera	fría
		freímos	freímos	friamos	friéramos	friamos
		freís	freísteis	friáis	frierais	freíd
		fríen	frieron	frían	frieran	frían

I36 imprimir

participio pasado
impreso

I37 morir

gerundio	participio pasado	indicativo		subjuntivo	
		presente	pretérito indefinido	presente	imperfecto
muriendo	muerto	muero	morí	muera	muriera
		mueres	moriste	mueras	murieras
		muere	murió	muera	muriera
		morimos	morimos	muramos	muriéramos
		morís	moristeis	muráis	murierais
		mueren	murieron	mueran	murieran

I38 pudrir

infinitivo	participio pasado
pudrir, podrir	podrido

All other forms are regular and are derived from the infinitive pudrir e.g. pudro, pudres, etc.

Los verbos irregulares ingleses

La siguiente tabla comprende todos los verbos irregulares que se incluyen en el diccionario excepto los verbos modales (e.g. *can, must*) y aquéllos formados por un verbo base precedido por un prefijo con guión (e.g. *re-lay*). Éstos conservan la irregularidad del verbo del cual derivan.

Las formas irregulares que sólo se usan en algunas acepciones se indican con un asterisco (e.g. **abode*).

La información completa acerca del uso, la pronunciación, etc de cada verbo se encontrará en el artículo correspondiente.

infinitive/ infinitivo	past tense/ pretérito	past participle/ participio pasado
abide	abided, *abode	abided, *abode
arise	arose	arisen
awake	awoke	awoken
be	was/were	been
bear	bore	borne
beat	beat	beaten
become	became	become
befall	befell	befallen
beget	begot, (arch) begat	begotten
begin	began	begun
behold	beheld	beheld
bend	bent	bent
beseech	beseeched, besought	beseeched, besought
beset	beset	beset
bespeak	bespoke	bespoken, bespoke
bestride	bestrode	bestridden
bet	bet	bet
bid	*bade, bid	*bidden, bid
bind	bound	bound
bite	bit	bitten
bleed	bled	bled
bless	blessed	blessed, (arch) blest
blow	blew	blown, *blowed
break	broke	broken
breed	bred	bred
bring	brought	brought
broadcast	broadcast	broadcast
browbeat	browbeat	browbeaten
build	built	built
burn	burned, burnt	burned, burnt
bust	busted, (BrE also) bust	busted, (BrE also) bust
buy	bought	bought
cast	cast	cast
catch	caught	caught
chide	chided, chid	chided, chid, chidden
choose	chose	chosen
cleave	cleaved, *cleft, (arch) *clove	cleaved, *cleft, (arch) *cloven
cling	clung	clung
come	came	come
cost	*cost, *costed	*cost, *costed
countersink	countersank	countersunk
creep	crept	crept
crow	crowed, (arch) crew	crowed
cut	cut	cut
deal	dealt	dealt
dig	dug	dug
dive	dived, (AmE also) dove	dived
do	did	done
draw	drew	drawn
dream	dreamed, (BrE also) dreamt	dreamed, (BrE also) dreamt
drink	drank	drunk
drive	drove	driven
dwell	dwelt, dwelled	dwelt, dwelled
eat	ate	eaten
fall	fell	fallen
feed	fed	fed
feel	felt	felt
fight	fought	fought
find	found	found
flee	fled	fled
fling	flung	flung
floodlight	floodlit	floodlit
fly	flew	flown
forbear	forbore	forborne
forbid	forbade, forbad	forbidden
forecast	forecast, forecasted	forecast, forecasted
foresee	foresaw	foreseen
foretell	foretold	foretold
forget	forgot	forgotten
forgive	forgave	forgiven
forsake	forsook	forsaken
forswear	forswore	forsworn
freeze	froze	frozen
gainsay	gainsaid	gainsaid
get	got	got, (AmE also) gotten
gird	girded, girt	girded, girt
give	gave	given
go	went	gone
grind	ground	ground
grow	grew	grown
hamstring	hamstrung	hamstrung
hang	*hung, *hanged	*hung, *hanged
have	had	had

infinitive/ infinitivo	past tense/ pretérito	past participle/ participio pasado
hear	heard	heard
heave	*heaved, *hove	*heaved, *hove
hew	hewed	hewn, hewed
hide	hid	hidden, (arch) hid
hit	hit	hit
hold	held	held
hurt	hurt	hurt
inlay	inlaid	inlaid
input	input, inputted	input, inputted
inset	inset, (AmE also) insetted	inset, (AmE also) insetted
interweave	interwove, interweaved	interwoven, interweaved
keep	kept	kept
kneel	kneeled, knelt	kneeled, knelt
knit	knitted, *knit	knitted, *knit
know	knew	known
lay	laid	laid
lead	led	led
lean	leaned, (BrE also) leant	leaned, (BrE also) leant
leap	leaped, (BrE also) leapt	leaped, (BrE also) leapt
learn	learned, (BrE also) learnt	learned, (BrE also) learnt
leave	left	left
lend	lent	lent
let	let	let
lie (*yacer etc*)	lay	lain
light	lighted, lit	lighted, lit
lose	lost	lost
make	made	made
mean	meant	meant
meet	met	met
miscast	miscast	miscast
misdeal	misdealt	misdealt
mishear	misheard	misheard
mishit	mishit	mishit
mislay	mislaid	mislaid
mislead	misled	misled
misread /ˈmɪsˈriːd/	misread /ˈmɪsˈred/	misread /ˈmɪsˈred/
misspell	misspelled, (BrE also) misspelt	misspelled, (BrE also) misspelt
misspend	misspent	misspent
mistake	mistook	mistaken
misunderstand	misunderstood	misunderstood
mow	mowed	mown, mowed
outbid	outbid	outbid, (AmE also) outbidden
outdo	outdid	outdone
outfight	outfought	outfought
outgrow	outgrew	outgrown
outlay	outlaid	outlaid
output	output, outputted	output, outputted
outrun	outran	outrun
outsell	outsold	outsold
outshine	outshone	outshone
overbid	overbid	overbid
overcome	overcame	overcome
overdo	overdid	overdone
overdraw	overdrew	overdrawn
overeat	overate	overeaten
overfly	overflew	overflown
overhang	overhung	overhung
overhear	overheard	overheard
overlay	overlaid	overlaid
overlie	overlay	overlain
overpay	overpaid	overpaid
override	overrode	overridden
overrun	overran	overrun
oversee	oversaw	overseen
overshoot	overshot	overshot
oversleep	overslept	overslept
overtake	overtook	overtaken
overthrow	overthrew	overthrown
partake	partook	partaken
pay	paid	paid
plead	pleaded, (AmE also) pled	pleaded, (AmE also) pled
prove	proved	proved, proven
put	put	put
quit	quit, quitted	quit, quitted
read /riːd/	read /red/	read /red/
rebuild	rebuilt	rebuilt
recast	recast	recast
redo	redid	redone
remake	remade	remade
rend	rent	rent
repay	repaid	repaid
reread /ˈriːˈriːd/	reread /ˈriːˈred/	reread /ˈriːˈred/
rerun	reran	rerun
resell	resold	resold
reset	reset	reset
resit	resat	resat
retake	retook	retaken
retell	retold	retold
rethink	rethought	rethought
rewrite	rewrote	rewritten
rid	rid	rid
ride	rode	ridden
ring	rang	rung
rise	rose	risen
run	ran	run
saw	sawed	sawed, (esp BrE) sawn
say	said	said
see	saw	seen
seek	sought	sought
sell	sold	sold

Los verbos irregulares ingleses

infinitive/ infinitivo	past tense/ pretérito	past participle/ participio pasado
send	sent	sent
set	set	set
sew	sewed	sewn, sewed
shake	shook	shaken
shear	sheared	*shorn, *sheared
shed	shed	shed
shine	*shone, *shined	*shone, *shined
shit	shit, shat	shit, shat
shoe	shod	shod
shoot	shot	shot
show	showed	shown, showed
shrink	shrank, shrunk	shrunk, shrunken
shrive	shrove, shrived	shriven, shrived
shut	shut	shut
sing	sang	sung
sink	sank	sunk
sit	sat	sat
slay	slew	slain
sleep	slept	slept
slide	slid	slid
sling	slung	slung
slink	slunk	slunk
slit	slit	slit
smell	smelled, (BrE also) smelt	smelled, (BrE also) smelt
smite	smote	smitten
sow	sowed	sowed, sown
speak	spoke	spoken
speed	*sped, *speeded	*sped, *speeded
spell	spelled, (BrE also) spelt	spelled, (BrE also) spelt
spend	spent	spent
spill	spilled, spilt	spilled, spilt
spin	spun, (arch) span	spun
spit	spat, (esp AmE) spit	spat, (esp AmE) spit
split	split	split
spoil	spoiled, (BrE also) spoilt	spoiled, (BrE also) spoilt
spotlight	*spotlit, *spotlighted	*spotlit, *spotlighted
spread	spread	spread
spring	sprang, (AmE also) sprung	sprung
stand	stood	stood
stave	staved, *stove	staved, *stove
steal	stole	stolen
stick	stuck	stuck
sting	stung	stung
stink	stank, stunk	stunk
strew	strewed	strewn, strewed
stride	strode	stridden
strike	struck	struck
string	strung	strung
strive	strove	striven
sublet	sublet	sublet
swear	swore	sworn
sweat	sweated, (AmE also) sweat	sweated, (AmE also) sweat

infinitive/ infinitivo	past tense/ pretérito	past participle/ participio pasado
sweep	swept	swept
swell	swelled	swollen, (AmE esp) swelled
swim	swam	swum
swing	swung	swung
take	took	taken
teach	taught	taught
tear	tore	torn
tell	told	told
think	thought	thought
thrive	thrived, (liter) throve	thrived, (arch) thriven
throw	threw	thrown
thrust	thrust	thrust
tread	trod	trodden, trod
typecast	typecast	typecast
typeset	typeset	typeset
typewrite	typewrote	typewritten
unbend	unbent	unbent
underbid	underbid	underbid
undercut	undercut	undercut
undergo	underwent	undergone
underlie	underlay	underlain
underpay	underpaid	underpaid
undersell	undersold	undersold
understand	understood	understood
undertake	undertook	undertaken
underwrite	underwrote	underwritten
undo	undid	undone
unfreeze	unfroze	unfrozen
unlearn	unlearned, (BrE also) unlearnt	unlearned, (BrE also) unlearnt
unstick	unstuck	unstuck
unwind	unwound	unwound
uphold	upheld	upheld
upset	upset	upset
wake	woke	woken
waylay	waylaid	waylaid
wear	wore	worn
weave	wove, *weaved	woven, *weaved
wed	wedded, wed	wedded, wed
weep	wept	wept
wet	wet, wetted	wet, wetted
win	won	won
wind *(dar cuerda etc)*	wound	wound
withdraw	withdrew	withdrawn
withhold	withheld	withheld
withstand	withstood	withstood
work	worked, *wrought	worked, *wrought
wring	wrung	wrung
write	wrote	written

Index to Spanish–English culture notes
Índice de las notas culturales Español–Inglés

Índice de las notas culturales Inglés–Español
Index to English–Spanish culture notes

adjetivo	**adj**	adjective
adjetivo invariable	**adj inv**	invariable adjective
Administración	**Adm**	Administration
adverbio	**adv**	adverb
Espacio	**Aerosp**	Aerospace
Agricultura	**Agr**	Agriculture
alguien	**algn**	somebody
América Central	**AmC**	Central America
inglés norteamericano	**AmE**	American English
América Latina	**AmL**	Latin America
América del Sur	**AmS**	South America
Anatomía	**Anat**	Anatomy
Andes	**Andes**	Andes
anticuado	**ant**	dated
Antropología	**Anthrop**	Anthropology
arcaico	**arc, arch**	archaic
Arqueología	**Archeol**	Archeology
Arquitectura	**Archit**	Architecture
argot	**arg**	slang
Argentina	**Arg**	Argentina
Armas	**Arm**	Arms
Arqueología	**Arqueol**	Archeology
Arquitectura	**Arquit**	Architecture
artículo	**art**	article
Arte	**Arte, Art**	Art
Astrología	**Astrol**	Astrology
Astronomía	**Astron**	Astronomy
Audio	**Audio**	Audio
inglés australiano	**Austral**	Australian English
Automovilismo	**Auto**	Cars
Aviación	**Aviac, Aviat**	Aviation
Biblia	**Bib**	Bible
Biología	**Biol**	Biology
Bolivia	**Bol**	Bolivia
Botánica	**Bot**	Botany
inglés británico	**BrE**	British English
Comercio	**Busn**	Business
numerable	**C**	countable
causativo	**caus**	causative
Química	**Chem**	Chemistry
Ingeniería química	**Chem Eng**	Chemical Engineering
Chile	**Chi**	Chile
Cine	**Cin**	Cinema
Ingeniería civil	**Civil Eng**	Civil Engineering
Indumentaria	**Clothing**	Clothing
Cocina	**Coc**	Cookery
Colombia	**Col**	Colombia
familiar	**colloq**	colloquial
Comercio	**Com**	Business
Informática	**Comput**	Computing
conjunción	**conj**	conjunction
Construcción	**Const**	Building
Correspondencia	**Corresp**	Correspondence
numerable	**count**	countable
Costa Rica	**CR**	Costa Rica
uso criticado	**crit**	criticized usage
Cono Sur	**CS**	Southern Cone
Cuba	**Cu**	Cuba
Cocina	**Culin**	Cookery
anticuado	**dated**	dated
artículo definido	**def art**	definite article
Odontología	**Dent**	Dentistry
Deporte	**Dep**	Sport
Derecho	**Der**	Law
dialecto	**dial**	dialect
Ecuador	**Ec**	Ecuador
Ecología	**Ecol**	Ecology
Economía	**Econ**	Economics

Educación	**Educ**	Education
Electricidad	**Elec**	Electricity
Ingeniería eléctrica	**Elec Eng**	Electrical Engineering
Electrónica	**Electrón, Electron**	Electronics
enfático	**enf**	emphatic
Ingeniería	**Eng**	Engineering
Equitación	**Equ**	Equestrianism
especialmente	**esp**	especially
España	**Esp**	Spain
Espacio	**Espac**	Aerospace
Espectáculos	**Espec**	Entertainment
Unión Europea	**EU**	European Union
eufemismo	**euf, euph**	euphemism
excepto	**exc**	excluding
femenino	**f**	feminine
véase página ix	**f‡**	*see page ix*
familiar	**fam**	colloquial
Farmacología	**Farm**	Pharmacology
Ferrocarriles	**Ferr**	Railways
Filosofía	**Fil**	Philosophy
Finanzas	**Fin**	Finance
Física	**Fís**	Physics
Fisco	**Fisco**	Tax
Fisiología	**Fisiol**	Physiology
Fotografía	**Fot**	Photography
femenino plural	**fpl**	feminine plural
frase hecha	**fr hecha**	set phrase
formal	**frml**	formal
Juegos	**Games**	Games
generalmente	**gen**	generally
Geografía	**Geog**	Geography
Geología	**Geol**	Geology
gerundio	**ger**	gerund
Gobierno	**Gob, Govt**	Government
Guatemala	**Gua**	Guatemala
Historia	**Hist**	History
Honduras	**Hon**	Honduras
Horticultura	**Hort**	Horticulture
humorístico	**hum**	humorous
Imprenta e Industria editorial	**Impr**	Printing and Publishing
inglés de la India	**Ind**	Indian English
artículo indefinido	**indef art**	indefinite article
Indumentaria	**Indum**	Clothing
Informática	**Inf**	Computing
Ingeniería	**Ing**	Engineering
interjección	**interj**	exclamation
inglés de Irlanda	**IrE**	Irish English
irónico	**iró, iro**	ironical
lenguaje periodístico	**journ**	journalese
Periodismo	**Journ**	Journalism
Juegos	**Jueg**	Games
Relaciones Laborales	**Lab Rel**	Labor Relations
Derecho	**Law**	Law
Ocio	**Leisure**	Leisure
lenguaje infantil	**leng infantil**	used to or by children
Lingüística	**Ling**	Linguistics
Literatura	**Lit**	Literature
literario	**liter**	literary
locución	**loc**	phrase
locución adjetiva	**loc adj**	adjectival phrase
locución adverbial	**loc adv**	adverbial phrase
locución conjuntiva	**loc conj**	conjunctive phrase
locución preposicional	**loc prep**	prepositional phrase